The College Music Society

Directory of Music Faculties in Colleges and Universities, U.S. and Canada

2012 - 2013

Directory of Music Faculties in Colleges and Universities, U.S. and Canada, 2012-2013

34TH EDITION

Original title for Editions 1, 2, 3:

Directory of Music Faculties in American Colleges and Universities

1st ed. 1967-1968 (copyright 1967)
2nd ed. 1968-1970 (copyright 1968)
3rd ed. 1970-1972 (copyright 1970)

Revised title for the fourth and following editions:

Directory of Music Faculties in Colleges and Universities, U.S. and Canada

4th ed. 1972-1974 (copyright 1972)	19th ed. 1997-1998 (copyright 1997)
5th ed. 1974-1976 (copyright 1974)	20th ed. 1998-1999 (copyright 1998)
6th ed. 1976-1978 (copyright 1976)	21st ed. 1999-2000 (copyright 1999)
7th ed. 1978-1980 (copyright 1979)	22nd ed. 2000-2001 (copyright 2000)
8th ed. 1980-1982 (copyright 1980)	23rd ed. 2001-2002 (copyright 2001)
9th ed. 1982-1984 (copyright 1983)	24th ed. 2002-2003 (copyright 2002)
10th ed. 1984-1986 (copyright 1985)	25th ed. 2003-2004 (copyright 2003)
11th ed. 1986-1988 (copyright 1987)	26th ed. 2004-2005 (copyright 2004)
12th ed. 1988-1990 (copyright 1989)	27th ed. 2005-2006 (copyright 2005)
13th ed. 1990-1992 (copyright 1990)	28th ed. 2006-2007 (copyright 2006)
14th ed. 1992-1994 (copyright 1992)	29th ed. 2007-2008 (copyright 2007)
15th ed. 1993-1994 (copyright 1993)	30th ed. 2008-2009 (copyright 2008)
16th ed. 1994-1995 (copyright 1994)	31st ed. 2009-2010 (copyright 2009)
17th ed. 1995-1996 (copyright 1995)	32nd ed. 2010-2011 (copyright 2010)
18th ed. 1996-1997 (copyright 1996)	33rd ed. 2011-2012 (copyright 2011)

Commencing with the 4th edition, the *Directory* includes material in Part IV which was originally published in 1971 as a separate publication entitled *Index to Graduate Degrees in Music, U.S. and Canada*.

Beginning with the 15th edition, the *Directory* was published annually.

Published by:
The College Music Society, 312 East Pine Street, Missoula, MT 59802
ISBN: 978-1-881913-31-3
© 2012 by The College Music Society

Contents

The College Music Society. iv

Preface. vi

The Mailing Label Service. vi

Description of the Directory. vii

Statistical Compendium. viii

U.S. and Canada Abbreviations. ix

The Directory

    Part I.   Directory of Institutions. 1

    Part II.   Index by Area of Teaching Interest. 413
                 Alphabetical Listing of Faculty. 765

    Part III. Index by Area of Administration. 915
                 Alphabetical Listing of Administrators. 937

    Part IV. Index of Graduate Degrees. 953

    Part V.   Alphabetical Listing of Institutions. 969

THE COLLEGE MUSIC SOCIETY

The Mission of CMS – The College Music Society promotes music teaching and learning, musical creativity and expression, research and dialogue, and diversity and interdisciplinary interaction. A consortium of college, conservatory, university, and independent musicians and scholars interested in all disciplines of music, the Society provides leadership and serves as an agent of change by addressing concerns facing music in higher education.

Membership – Membership in The College Music Society is an important component of your professional life. CMS helps develop a broad network of both human and information resources. The Society provides services that will not be found elsewhere, supporting your professional work daily, weekly, and long-term. CMS enhances your work in music as your professional life evolves from student days through retirement. CMS services and activities optimize your valuable time by gathering the professional information you need and presenting it in ways that make it useful to you.

Likewise, the Society's members make the critical difference to music in higher education. The dialogue among CMS members expands horizons and is a means of effective change and growth, not just in your professional life but also for the entire field of music. Your membership enhances networking possibilities for everyone in the music profession and increases your communications opportunities with others. Your participation makes this critical difference possible.

Membership in The College Music Society provides access to the full array of CMS benefits and services described below. To join, visit the CMS Web site at http://www.music.org or call the Society's Executive Office at (406) 721-9616.

Engagement and Outreach – CMS represents to a variety of constituents in both creative and practical ways the issues and concerns of the music in higher education community. CMS sponsors opportunities for engagement and outreach both on-campus and with the community. Members are welcome to participate in all initiatives including:

- *Community Engagement*–creating more environments and improving communication skills with the general public.

- *Higher Education*–providing liaison between music associations and higher education organizations, articulating the essential need for and changing roles of music units in higher education, and advocating for artistic and educational integrity of music programs.

- *International Initiatives*–liaison with music faculty and institutions outside the United States and overseeing opportunities for dialogue and exchange through international conferences.

- *Music Business-Industry*–liaison with the music business and industry and identifying goals in common between the music business and music in higher education communities.

Career Development – CMS brings focus to the professional lives and interests of its members, from student days through retirement. CMS assists with employment seeking skills, mentoring, leadership initiatives, financial planning, thriving in your career.

- *Academic Careers*–addressing professional careers of music faculty.

- *Academic Leadership and Administration*–focusing on leadership, developmental, and career issues of administrative work in music.

- *Academic Citizenship*–consideration of our responsibility as members of the broader higher education community.

- *Careers Outside the Academy*–addressing professional opportunities for independent musicians and scholars in the music business and industry field.

Professional Activities – Through its professional activities, CMS gathers, considers, and disseminates ideas on the philosophy and practice of music. CMS creates forums in which individuals working in the various areas of music can interact and communicate. Recognizing the richness of musical diversity and the challenge of balancing the traditions of the past with the possibilities of the future, members are united by a dedication to the science of learning and the art of teaching and are engaged in a dialogue that will shape the field of music in the years ahead. Through its professional activities, CMS fosters the continuing education and renewal of college and university music faculty, shares the fruits of music research, develops and enhances music instruction, and celebrates the importance of teaching. Members are welcome to participate in all professional activities including:

- *Conferences*–Nine conferences held each spring throughout the United States; an annual fall conference held in the United States or Canada; a biennial summer international conference held outside North America.

- *Professional Development*–Institutes, workshops, symposia, and other events providing opportunities to hone teaching skills and consider issues of concern to the music and higher education community.

- *Publications*–The interdisciplinary journal, *College Music Symposium, Monographs and Bibliographies in American Music, Sourcebooks in American Music,* and *Cultural Expressions in Music*.

- *Forums and Dialogues*–Identification and analysis of professional concerns, and development of projects, programs, publications, and professional development initiatives designed to address issues within them.

Information Services – CMS makes available a wealth of information concerning the field of music, as well as the music and higher education community. The following on-line data resources will help meet your needs for current information:

- *Employment Opportunities* through the *Music Vacancy List*, the most comprehensive job listings available to musicians in higher education.

- *Faculties and Institutions*–over 40,000 music faculty at 1,800 institutions in the United States and Canada.

- *International Music Organizations*–over 350 organizations that offer support to the music field.

- *Support for Work in Music*–companies in the music business and industry sector.

- *Calendar of Music Conferences*–upcoming conferences and program deadlines.

- *News of the Profession*–upcoming events in the music field.

- Enjoy *Personal Email Forwarding* through music.org.

The College Music Society • 312 East Pine Street • Missoula MT 59802 • USA
(406) 721-9616 • cms@music.org • http://www.music.org

PREFACE

Since 1967, the *Directory of Music Faculties in Colleges and Universities, U.S. and Canada* has proven to be an invaluable source of information. In addition to names, addresses, and phone numbers, it serves as a guide to disciplines, curricula and degree programs, and research specialties, spanning the length and breadth of the United States and Canada.

This volume reflects the hard work, at both the research and editorial levels, of a dedicated, highly capable staff. The College Music Society extends appreciation especially to Julie Johnson who directs CMS data services.

We hope you enjoy browsing through this volume and using its information, and not only for reasons of sheer practicality. In fact, we hope you will find the *Directory* provocative, and perhaps even innovative in its updated features. In all of the forgoing, it reflects the ever-changing, ever-stimulating nature of our profession, and of The College Music Society which represents that profession so broadly.

THE MAILING LABEL SERVICE

The information contained in the *Directory* is also available in the form of mailing labels. Lists may be selected by area of teaching specialization, and may be ordered by single specialization or by combining various specializations with duplications eliminated. In addition, labels may be requested for specific states, provinces, zip codes, or institutions.

Labels are available in the traditional laser pressure-sensitive format, as well as in electronic format when working with a professional mailing house. We encourage you to take advantage of this useful service. For information, please get in touch with The College Music Society by calling (406) 721-9616, sending e-mail to cms@music.org, visiting the CMS Website at http://www.music.org, or writing to CMS at 312 East Pine Street, Missoula, MT 59802.

DESCRIPTION OF THE *DIRECTORY*

Part I. Directory of Institutions
Institutions are listed in alphabetical order within each state or province. Each institution is identified by a code consisting of the letter abbreviation of the state or province and a four digit number. The following information is listed for each institution.

    A. Address, office telephone, fax number, Web site and e-mail address.

    B. Description of the institution and the graduate degrees offered.

    C. Names and titles of up to five administrators.

    D. Alphabetical listing of faculty with the following information for each faculty member:

        1. Rank - If no rank is given, none was furnished or the institution does not rank its faculty. The Chair, Dean, or Director is designated as such.

        2. Name

        3. Highest Degree Earned - The following abbreviations are used:

B	Baccalaureate Degree
M	Master's Degree
MFA	Master of Fine Arts Degree
D	Doctoral Degree
Dipl	Diploma
Cert	Certificate

        4. Areas of Teaching Specialization - Up to five areas are listed. For easy reference, the key to these codes is found inside both the front and back covers.

Part IIa. Index by Area of Teaching Interest
This section provides lists of teachers in all 169 teaching areas. Each faculty member is cross-referenced by institutional code. All additional specialization codes provided for each individual are also listed. Kindly note the table of contents for this section on page 400.

Part IIb. Alphabetical Listing of Faculty
This section provides an alphabetical listing of all faculty and includes the code for the institution at which they work.

Part IIIa. Index by Area of Administration
This section provides lists of persons working in eight major areas of music administration. Each administrator is cross-referenced by institutional code. All additional administrative codes provided for each individual are also listed. Kindly note the table of contents for this section on page 878.

Part IIIb. Alphabetical Listing of Administrators
This section provides an alphabetical listing of all administrators and includes the code for the institution at which they work.

Part IV. Index of Graduate Degrees
Each of the various graduate degrees is given, followed by a listing of those schools which offer that degree.

Part V. Alphabetical Listing of Institutions
Each institution appearing in Part I is listed followed by the institutional code number.

STATISTICAL COMPENDIUM FROM THE 2012 - 2013 *DIRECTORY*

INSTITUTIONAL STATISTICS

- This edition of the *Directory* includes 1,793 institutions. The 2011-2012 edition included 1,793 institutions.

- Of the 1,793 institutions:

    894 are listed as 4 year colleges
    404 have graduate programs
    502 are listed as 2 year colleges
    11 operate only as graduate schools
      7 institutions list no description

FACULTY STATISTICS

- This edition of the *Directory* includes 43,982 faculty. The 2011-2012 edition included 43,283 faculty.

- Of the 43,283 faculty:

    5,576 are professors
    4,795 are associate professors
    4,339 are assistant professors
    11,178 are full-time instructors/lecturers
    5,647 are part-time faculty
    411 are visiting faculty
    6,614 are adjunct faculty
    412 are artist-in-residence
    1,333 are emeritus
    3,625 faculty are not ranked

    15,195 have a doctoral degree
    19,835 have a master's degree
    4,905 have a bachelor's degree
    21 have a professional certificate
    405 have a professional diploma
    4,295 have no degree listed

- Of the 43,982 faculty, 27,324 (62%) are male, 16,154 (37%) are female. The gender of 504 persons (1%) has not been identified in the CMS database.

United States and Canada Abbreviations

Listings in Part I are alphabetized by U.S. postal abbreviation codes. Canadian institutions appear at the beginning of Part I; the U.S. follows thereafter. The table below provides an alphabetical list of the provinces and states, and includes the beginning page number in Part I for each state or province.

Canada

Province	Abbreviation	Page
Alberta	AA	3
British Columbia	AB	6
Manitoba	AC	9
Newfoundland	AD	10
New Brunswick	AE	10
Nova Scotia	AF	10
Ontario	AG	11
Quebec	AI	18
Saskatchewan	AJ	22

United States

State	Abbreviation	Page	State	Abbreviation	Page
Alabama	AL	23	Montana	MT	229
Alaska	AK	23	Nebraska	NE	245
Arizona	AZ	34	Nevada	NV	259
Arkansas	AR	30	New Hampshire	NH	248
California	CA	38	New Jersey	NJ	250
Colorado	CO	77	New Mexico	NM	257
Connecticut	CT	83	New York	NY	260
Delaware	DE	90	North Carolina	NC	231
District of Columbia	DC	87	North Dakota	ND	243
Florida	FL	91	Ohio	OH	291
Georgia	GA	103	Oklahoma	OK	307
Guam	GU	113	Oregon	OR	313
Hawaii	HI	113	Pennsylvania	PA	318
Idaho	ID	123	Puerto Rico	PR	337
Illinois	IL	125	Rhode Island	RI	338
Indiana	IN	145	South Carolina	SC	340
Iowa	IA	115	South Dakota	SD	345
Kansas	KS	154	Tennessee	TN	347
Kentucky	KY	160	Texas	TX	356
Louisiana	LA	167	Utah	UT	378
Maine	ME	194	Vermont	VT	390
Maryland	MD	187	Virgin Islands	VI	389
Massachusetts	MA	172	Virginia	VA	381
Michigan	MI	196	Washington	WA	391
Minnesota	MN	207	West Virginia	WV	407
Mississippi	MS	225	Wisconsin	WI	398
Missouri	MO	216	Wyoming	WY	410

Directory of Institutions

Directory of Institutions

AA0010 Ambrose University College
Department of Music
150 Ambrose Circle SW
Calgary, AB T3H 0L5 Canada
(403) 410-2000   Fax: (403) 571-2556
www.ambrose.edu
E-mail: icharter@ambrose.edu

4 Year Institution, CAQC, ABHE

Program Head: Don E. Quantz, 80A

Assoc Prof	Charter, Ian R.	M	12A,13A,31A,32E,60
Assoc Prof	Gnandt, Edwin E.	M	13A,66A,42,13B,66D
Assoc Prof	Quantz, Don E.	PhD	12A,32D,36,40,41

AA0015 Concordia Univ College of Alberta
School of Music
7128 Ada Blvd
Edmonton, AB T5B 4E4 Canada
(780) 479-9313   Fax: (780) 491-6895
music.concordia.ab.ca
E-mail: music@concordia.ab.ca

4 and 3 Year Institution

Coordinator, Music: John Hooper, 80A
Dir., Undergraduate Studies: Jonathan Strand, 80B
Events and Services Coordinator: Wendy Fraser, 80F

Assoc Prof	Berg, Joy L.	M	60A,66A
Prof	Hooper, John	D	60A,13,10

AA0020 MacEwan University
Alberta College Campus
Conservatory of Music
10050 MacDonald Dr Rm 622
Edmonton, AB T5J 2B7 Canada
(780) 633-3725   Fax: (780) 633-3755
www.macewan.ca/conservatory
E-mail: conservatory@macewan.ca

Manager: Brenda Philp, 80A

	Aldridge, Robert		62D
	Baciu, Bianca	D	66A,66B,66C
	Benson, Lary	B	61
	Berg, Reinhard	M	13,10,12A,66A,66G
	Boddez, Karla		66A
	Bryant, Jeff	B	63A
	Bumanis, Nora	AD	62E
	Cameron, Tristan	B	10A,10C,10D,70
	Casgrain, Robert	M	66A
	Creaghan, Andrew		70
	Damur, Bill	M	64A,70
	Davidson, Ryan	M	70
	Davis, Dan	M	64E
	De Freitas, Simon Marc	M	66A
Emerita	DeMarco, Sherrill	DIPL	61
	Dundjerski, Petar	M	60B,64A
	Ehret, Don		70
	Elossias, Hannah		62E
	Fearon, Mary	M	63B
	Forestier, Marie	M	62A
	Forestier, Michel	M	70
Emerita	Gale, Marie	M	62A
	Gayler, Liane	B	64A
	Goodchild, Melissa	M	64C
	Hagel, Clint	B	31A,36,61,66C
	Haythorne, Geraldine	A	66A,66B
	Hiebert, Shannon		61,66A
	Ho, Frank	M	62A
	Ho, Sarah	M	66A
	Jarillo Alvarado, Lyanne		62A
	Kim, Eileen	M	66A
	Kim, Yona		66A
	King, Margaret		66A,64A
	Klakowich, Robert		13A,13B,13C,13D,13E
	Lam, Sze-Sze		66A
	Langor, Suzanne		63B
	Loewen, Judy	B	66A,66H
	Long, Ron		61,54
	Lou, Dorothy		66A
	Lowrey, Alden	B	63C
	Lowrey, Ariane	M	66A
	Luzanac, Inna		66A
	McCormick, John	B	65,50
	McNaughton, Karen	B	66A
	Mellors, Carol		66A
	Meyers, Heather		61
	Milenkovic, Michelle		32A,61
	Miller, Cory		61
	Munn, Alexandra	DIPL	66A,66C
	Murphy, Glenda		66A
	Noton, Donna	M	66A
	Pawlowski, Lauressa		61
	Raycroft, Elizabeth		61
	Rosen, Robert		66A
	Ross, Don		64C
	Sanders, Trevor		70
	Sawchuk, Judy-Lynn		61
	Sech, Svetlana		61
	Sharkey-Pryma, Maura		61
	Silveira, Mathias		62A
	Smith, Caitlin Maura		62C
	Stolte, Charles		64E
	Stolyar, Marina	M	66A
	Sutherland, Daniel	M	64C
	Tetel, Ioan		62D
	Towill, John		70
	Tutt, David	B	66A
	Watson, Cameron		66A
	Weber, Marliss	M	54
	Woodman, Ian		63C
	Woodman, Sarah		62B
	Yu, Joanne	M	62C
	Zwicker, Keri		62E

AA0025 Grande Prairie Regional College
Department of Fine Arts-Music
10726 106 Ave
Grande Prairie, AB T8V 4C4 Canada
(780) 539-2909   Fax: (780) 539-2446
www.finearts.gprc.ab.ca/
E-mail: finearts@gprc.ab.ca

2 Year Institution

Chair: Geoffrey Whittall, 80A

Inst	Gorgichuk, Carmen	M	11,13,66
Inst	Howey, Robert J.	D	12A,13B,37,46,64
Inst	McIntyre, Chris	B	70,34
Inst	Murray, John	M	61,36,13A,13C
Inst	Whittall, Geoffrey	M	14,65,20,13,11

AA0032 Keyano College
Department of Visual & Perf Art
8115 Franklin Ave
Ft. McMurray, AB T9H 2H7 Canada
(780) 791-8979   Fax: (780) 791-4963
www.keyano.ca
E-mail: vpa@keyano.ca

2 Year Institution

Chair: Peter Ellis, 80A
Dir., Institute/Festival/Workshop: William Prouten, 80F

Inst	Durocher, Michael	DIPL	72
Inst	Ellis, Peter	M	38,62,51,36
Vstng Prof	Gray, Joel	DIPL	63A
Inst	Lipman, Agnes	DIPL	70
Inst	Parr, Kimerica	M	61
Inst	Prouten, William	M	13,47,64,53,29A
Inst	Sabine, David	M	35,13A,13C,37,65

AA0035 The King's University College
Department of Music
9125 50 St
Edmonton, AB T6B 2H3 Canada
(780) 465-3500 x 8025   Fax: (780) 465-3534
www.kingsu.ca
E-mail: cara-joy.roeseler@kingsu.ca

Christian 4 Year Liberal Arts Institution

Chair: Joachim Segger, 80A
Dir., Cultural Events: Charles Stolte, 80F

Inst PT	Abele, Catherine	M	61
Inst PT	Aikman, Merla	DIPL	61
Inst PT	Cheung, Alissa	M	66C

Inst PT	Eeles, Mark	M	62C
Inst PT	Elossais, Hannah	DIPL	62E
Inst PT	Faulkner, Elizabeth	B	64A
Inst PT	Forestier, Michel	DIPL	70
Inst PT	Giesbrecht, Marnie	D	66G
Inst PT	Grieger, Evelyn	D	60A
Inst PT	Jean, Rachel	B	67C
Prof Emeritus	Kloppers, Jacobus	D	11,12A,12,66G,31A
Inst PT	Koch, Elizabeth	B	64A,48
Inst PT	Lee, Kyung-A		66C
Inst PT	Lowrey, Alvin	B	63A
Inst PT	Lowrey, Ariane	M	66C
Inst PT	Mast, Ivan	B	63C
Inst PT	McCormick, John	B	65
Inst PT	McIntosh, Catherine	B	63C
Inst PT	Olson, Janna	M	66A,66B
Inst PT	Onciul, Gerald	B	63B
Inst PT	Persson, Diane	M	64D
Inst PT	Pilon, Charles	B	62A
Inst PT	Raycroft, Elizabeth	M	61
Inst PT	Regehr, Leanne	M	66A,66C
Inst PT	Ross, Don	M	64C
Prof	Segger, Joachim	D	13,13J,66A,66B,43
Assoc Prof	Stolte, Charles	M	64E,13A,13,10,43
Inst PT	Takahashi, Hiromi	B	64B
Asst Prof	Turgeon, Melanie E.	D	60,36,42,13C,32D
Inst PT	Urke, Jan	DIPL	62D
Inst PT	Whetham, Scott	DIPL	63D
Inst PT	Zuidhof, Jessica	B	66A

AA0040 Medicine Hat College

Conservatory of Music & Dance
299 College Dr SE
Medicine Hat, AB T1A 3Y6 Canada
(403) 529-3880   Fax: (403) 504-3554
www.mhc.ab.ca
E-mail: dnielsen@mhc.ab.ca

Transfer Courses

Artistic Manager: Lyle Rebbeck, 80A
Dean: Len Vandervaart, 80A

Inst	Atwood, Jodi		52
Inst	Bardston, Robert	M	66H,66B,38,41,62C
Inst	Bootland, Christine	M	62C
Inst	Cleland, George	M	38,41,62A,62B
Inst	Collier, Joanne	M	36,61
Inst	Dobek-Shandro, Elaine	M	66A,66C
Inst	Harder, Glen	M	36,61,47
Inst	Helm, Jon E.	M	13A,13,12A,63,49
Inst	Kohls, Shauna	M	66A
Inst	Lefever, Todd	D	70
Inst	Lyon, Taylene	B	61,47,53
Inst	Massini, Ryan		50,65
Inst	Rebbeck, Lyle	M	47,48,64,53
Inst	Schneider, Eugene	B	66A,66C
Inst	Shandro, Constantine	B	66A,66C
Inst	Supeene, Susan	B	32A,61,36
Inst	Terrance, Christine	B	52
Inst	Tzigalanis, Voula	B	52
Inst	Van Der Sloot, Michael	B	62A,62B,38,41
Inst	Welling, Jennifer	M	61

AA0050 Mount Royal University

The Conservatory
4825 Mount Royal Gate SW
Calgary, AB T3E 6K6 Canada
(403) 440-6821   Fax: (403) 440-6594
www.mtroyal.ca/conservatory
E-mail: pdornian@mtroyal.ca

2 Year Institution

Chair: Jim Brenan, 80A
Director: Paul Dornian, 80A
Manager, Choral, Cred & Academy Prg.: William Van der Sloot, 80E

	Agopian, Edmond	M	62A,41,38
	Albright, Robyn		66C
	Andrievsky, Alexandra	B	66A
	Arnold, Scott		70
	Athparia, Colleen		66A
	Baril, Gianetta		62E
	Bennie, Ron		66C
	Bergmann, Elizabeth		66A,66C,41
	Bergmann, Marcel		66A,66C,41
	Bertsch, Rolf		66A
	Bingham, Roxanne Laycock	M	66A,66D
	Brenan, Jim	M	64E
	Buschmeyer, Corrinne		61
	Buschmeyer, Ralf		70
	Campbell, Tim	DIPL	
	Carruthers, Ian	M	10,13
	Case, Elaine	D	61
	Climie, Stanley	B	12A,48,64C
	Cockburn, Neil	M	66G,67F,12A
	Colquhoun, Jocelyn	M	64C
	De Boeck, Garry		47,65,29,35B
	De Toledo, Rubim		47,53
	Denis, Kimberley		61,35A,36
	Dornian, Kathy	M	66A,66C,32A
	Dornian, Paul	M	64C
	Drayson, Susan		32A
	Eastep, Michael	M	63D
	Edmonton-Boehm, Nigel	M	62C
	Engstrom, Howard	B	63A
	Eselson, Lauren	M	41,64A
	Ferguson, David	M	36
	Feria, Marissa	M	32A,66A
	Forer, Colette		66A
	Frizzell, Patricia		32A
	Gardner, Mike	M	13,47,64E
	Garrett, Sheila	B	62D
	Gonzalez, Ariel		36
	Grigoriu, Katrina	DIPL	32A,62A,62B
	Haager, Julia	M	32A,66C
	Henschell, Lana		66C
	Herbst-Walker, Nikki		66C
	Hlasny, Susan		66A,13
	Hornby, Tyler	M	65
	Huck, Patricia		32A,66A
	Hyde, John		10,13,62D
	Jablonski, Krzysztof		66A
	Jalilian, Zeinab	B	32A
	Jancewicz, Peter	D	66A
	Janz, Tim	M	13
	Johnson, Dawn	M	61
	Jones, Lucie	M	64C
	Jurchuk, Tobi	DIPL	32A,62A
	Kadz, John	M	41,62C
	Kilchyk, Olena	M	32A,62C
	Landa, Jean	M	64B
	Lane, Diane		62A
	Lee, Kum-Sing	M	66A
	Light, Susan	B	62A
	Lim, Malcolm	B	65
	Longhi, Ami		66C
	Louie, Bonnie	M	62A
	Lubiarz, Stephen		62A
	Mahon, Brad	B	70
	Maier, Ralph	B	70
	Matiation, Laurie	M	63B
	Mauthe, Holger	B	32A
	McCosh, Ruth	M	13A,66A
	McGillivray, Angie	B	36
	Mcleod Metz, Caroline		66C
	Mirhady, Tom		62C
	Montgomery, Glen		66A,32A
	Morin, Carmen	DIPL	32A,66A
	Moroz, David	DIPL	66A
	Murdoch, Kenneth	B	66A
	Naumchyk, Alena		66C
	Nesterov, Dmitry	M	66C
	Neumann, Ben	B	32B,38,51,62A
	Newman, Margaret		66G
	Ng, Elsie		66A
	Obrecht, Guy	D	12A,13,47
	O'Brien, Dean		62A,62B
	Page, Sandra	B	13A,13,66A
	Perlau, Anita	B	36,32A
	Plotnick, Jeff	B	38,41
	Popowich, Jamie	DIPL	32A,36
	Pulos, Nick	M	38,62B,41
	Rae, Wendy	B	13,32A,66A
	Rebozo, Elizabeth		66A
	Reside, Judy	B	64A
	Richardson, Dustyn		64E
	Rodriguez, Ariana		66A
	Ruberg-Gordon, Susanne	M	66C
	Rudzik, Sarina Rommedahl	B	32I
	Rumpel, Greg		70
	Sandvoss, Beth Root		62C
	Schlessinger, Laura	M	62C
	Schuett, Mike	M	65
	Scriggins, Elizabeth		32A,62A
	Serpas, Roberto		70
	Spencer, Reid		54,61
	Stoll, Derek		66A
	Sullivan, Mary		64A
	Sussman, David	M	64B
	Szanto, Judit	B	32A
	Szojka, Elisabeth	DIPL	62A
	Tapia-Carreto, Veronica	D	10,13
	Taylor-Bilenki, Jan	B	32A
	Thompson, John	DIPL	38,62B,41
	Tominaga, Akiko	M	66A,66C
	Van der Sloot, Alexsandra		62A
	Van der Sloot, William	M	62A,41
	VanDieman, Jeremy	M	38,62A

AA0080 Red Deer College

Department of Music
PO Box 5005
Red Deer, AB T4N 5H5 Canada
(403) 342-3516   Fax: (403) 347-0399
www.rdc.ab.ca/performing_arts
E-mail: jacy.morissette@rdc.ab.ca

2 Year Institution

Chair: Dale J. Wheeler, 80A
Curriculum Coordinator: Steve Sherman, 80D
Dir, Institute/Festival/Workshop: Joyce Howdle, 80F

Rank	Name	Degree	Codes
Prof	Bell, Malcolm E.	D	10,13,47,65
PT	Bradley, Annette	B	66A,32B,13C,66D,42
PT	Braun, Sharon	DIPL	61
PT	Corlett, Neil		63A
PT	Doody, Jeremy	B	70
PT	Farion, Rob	DIPL	65
PT	Frizzell, Shannon	DIPL	70
Prof	Hoffart, Danica	M	36,61,54,13C
PT	Howdle, Joyce	B	64C
PT	Isenor, Ted	D	12A
PT	McMurray, Louise	B	63B
PT	Phagoo, Curtis	DIPL	70
Prof	Sherman, Steve	B	32E,37,63A,46,35
PT	Vuori, Ruston	M	66D,13
PT	Ward, Doug	M	64A,64C,64E
Prof	Wheeler, Dale J.	D	66A,66B,66D,66C,42
Prof	Wong, Sui-Fan	DIPL	35C,35G

AA0100 Univ of Alberta

Department of Music
3-82 Fine Arts Bldg
Edmonton, AB T6G 2C9 Canada
(780) 492-3263   Fax: (780) 492-9246
www.music.ualberta.ca
E-mail: music@ualberta.ca

4 Year Institution, Graduate School

Master of Arts in Music, Master of Music in Composition, Master of Music in Performance, Doctor of Music in Composition, PhD in Music, Master of Music in Choral Conducting, Doctor of Music in Performance, Doctor of Music in Choral Conducting

Chair: David Gramit, 80A
Dir., Undergraduate Studies: Janet Scott Hoyt, 80B
Dir., Graduate Studies: Jacques C. Despres, 80C

Rank	Name	Degree	Codes
Inst	Abele, Catherine	M	61
Inst	Adamek, Magdalena	D	66A,66C
Inst	Admiral, Roger	D	41,43
Inst	Au, Aaron		62A,62B,51
Inst	Balcetis, Allison	M	64E
Inst	Baril, Ray	M	46
Prof	Bashaw, Howard	D	10,13
Prof Emeritus	Berg, Wesley P.	D	12A,20G
Lect	Bor, Mustafa	M	13
Inst	Bostrand, Eva	M	42
Inst	Brenan, Craig	D	63
Inst	Bumanis, N.	B	62E
Prof	Cairns, Debra	D	60,36
Inst	Campbell, Jeff	M	64C
Inst	Dalen, Brenda	M	12A
Prof	Despres, Jacques C.	DMA	66A,42
Inst	Dubyk, Jerrold	M	64
Inst	Dundjerski, Petar	M	60B
Prof	Dust, Tom	D	46
Prof Emeritus	Forsyth, Malcolm	D	13,10F,10,38
Assoc Prof	Frishkopf, Michael	D	20A,20F,14,31C
Asst Prof	Gier, Christina B.	D	12A,12D,12B,12,15
Prof	Giesbrecht-Segger, Marnie		66G
Prof	Gramit, David	D	12
Inst	Grieger, Evelyn	D	36,60A
Inst	Hackleman, Allene	B	63B
Asst Prof	Hannesson, Mark	M	10B,10A
	Hettinger, Bruce A.		66F
Inst	Howe, Stuart	DIPL	39,61

Rank	Name	Degree	Codes
	Visscher, Murray		70
	Vrba, Cenek		62A,41
	Waite, Janice	M	66A,66C,41
	Woo, Claudia		66A
	Zandboer, Sheldon		66A
	Zanjani, Azadeh	B	32A,66A
	Zavzavadjian, Sylvia	B	32A,66A,66C
	Zayarny, Iryna		66A

Inst	Hudelson, Charles	B	64C
Assoc Prof	Ingraham, Mary	D	12
Inst	Jones, Brian	B	65
Inst	Kaur, Kamaljeet	D	61,20E
Prof Emeritus	Kenneson, Claude E.	M	13A,11
Inst	Kerley, Jolaine	M	61,55
Prof	Klumpenhouwer, Henry	D	13,12
Inst	Kpogo, Robert	M	20B
Inst	Levia, Beth		64B
Inst	Lotsberg, Carl		70
Inst	Lowrey, Alvin	M	63A
Inst	MacDonald, Michael	M	12,14
Inst	Mathur, Sharmila	M	20E,62
Inst	McCormick, John	B	65
Inst	McPherson, John		63C
Asst Prof	Moshaver, Maryam A.	M	13J
Prof Emeritus	Munn, Alexandra M.	DIPL	66A,66B,66C
Inst	Persson, Diane	M	64D
Prof Emeritus	Pier, Fordyce C.	D	37,49,63A
Prof Emerita	Prochazka, Tanya	DIPL	62C,41
Prof Emerita	Qureshi, Regula	D	14
Inst	Rao, Nikhail	M	20E,65
Prof	Ratzlaff, Leonard	DMA	60,36
Inst	Regehr, Leanne	D	39
Asst Prof	Schroeder, Angela	D	37,48,60B
Assoc Prof	Scott Hoyt, Janet	M	66A,66B,42
Asst Prof	Smallwood, Scott	D	10A,10B
Inst	Smith, Murray	D	65
Librarian	Snyder, Laura	M	16
Asst Prof	Spinetti, Frederico	D	14,20B
Prof Emeritus	Stangeland, Robert A.	D	66A
Prof	Street, William H.	D	60,37,64E
Inst	Talpash, Andriy	D	10,13
Assoc Prof	Tao, Patricia	D	66A,41
Assoc Prof	Tardif, Guillaume	D	62B,41
Inst	Taylor, J. Chris	M	63C
Inst	Turnhull, Elizabeth	DIPL	39,61
Inst	Urke, Jan	DIPL	62D
Inst	Vallee, Mickey	M	14C
Inst	Whetham, S.	B	63D
Inst	Whitehead, Russell		63A
Prof Emeritus	Wiens, Harold H.	DIPL	61,42
Inst	Younge, Shelley	B	64A

AA0110 Univ of Alberta-Augustana Campus

Department of Fine Arts
4901-46 Ave
Camrose, AB T4V 2R3 Canada
(780) 679-1100   Fax: (780) 679-1129
www.augustana.ualberta.ca/
E-mail: music@augustana.ca

4 Year Liberal Arts University

Chair: Anne-Marie Link, 80A
Conservatory Administrator, Preparatory Division: Charlene Brown, 80E

Rank	Name	Degree	Codes
Inst	Admiral, Roger	D	13B,13C,10A,42
Inst	Avdeeff, Melissa	D	11,12,14C
Inst	Brown, Charlene	B	61,32A
Assoc Prof	Carpenter, Alexander	D	12,13C,13B,11,13E
Assoc Prof	Corcoran, Kathleen	M	12A,61,39
Inst	Hawkins, Michelle Kennedy	M	32A,61,66A
Inst	Khaner, Lidia	M	64B
Inst	Luzanac, Inna	M	66A,42
Inst	Massey, Michael	B	38
Inst	Murphy, Joy-Anne	M	61
Assoc Prof	Ries, Ardelle	D	13C,36,60A
Inst	Rusinak, Dennis	M	64E,64C
Inst	Sanders, Trevor		13A,70,13B,13C
Prof	Schlosser, Milton	D	66A,66B
Inst	Schoen, Kathleen	B	64A,67C
Inst	Schoen, Thomas		62A,41
Inst	Spila, Tom	B	37
Inst	Traa, Olav		63
Inst	Ward, Susan	M	66A
Inst	Wiebe, John	D	36,60A
Inst	Willcox, Carolyn	B	32A,66A
Inst	Yin, Jei	M	64C,64E

AA0150 Univ of Calgary

Department of Music
2500 University Dr NW
Calgary, AB T2N 1N4 Canada
(403) 220-5376   Fax: (403) 284-0973
music.ucalgary.ca
E-mail: music@ucalgary.ca

4 Year Institution, Graduate School

Master of Music in Composition, Master of Music in Performance, Master of Music in Conducting, Master of Music in Music Education, PhD in Composition, PhD in Music Education, PhD in Musicology, Master of Arts in Musicology

Head of Music: William S. Jordan, 80A
Dir., Undergraduate Studies: Joelle Welling, 80B
Dir., Graduate Studies: Friedemann Sallis, 80C
Dir., Artist/Performance Series: Kathy Race, 80F

Prof	Agopian, Edmond	M	38,41,51,62A,42
Inst PT	Amsel, Stephen	M	64C
Inst PT	Baril, Gianetta	M	62E
Prof	Bell, Allan	M	13,10,20G,10F
Prof	Bell, Donald M.		61
Prof	Brown, Jeremy S.	D	37,64E,29,12G,48
Prof Emeritus	Brown, Malcolm	D	
Prof Emeritus	Buehning, Walter P.	D	
Prof Emeritus	Choksy, Lois	M	
Inst PT	Christianson, Donald G.	M	36
Inst PT	Climie, Stan	B	64C
Prof Emeritus	Cramer, Eugene	D	
Inst PT	Davenport, Francesca	M	64D
Prof	DeLong, Kenneth	D	12,13J
Prof Emeritus	Doolittle, Quenten D.	D	
Assoc Prof	Eagle, David	D	13,10F,10,34,43
Inst PT	Eastep, Michael	M	63D,49
Prof	Edwards, Malcolm V.	M	32,36,60A
Prof	Engle, Marilyn	M	41,66A,66B,66C,12B
Inst PT	Engstrom, Howard	B	63A,49
Inst PT	Eselson, Lauren	M	64A
Assoc Prof	Fields, Kenneth	D	10B,34
Prof	Foreman, Charles	M	66A,66B,66C,20G,41
Inst PT	Garrett, Charles	M	62D
Inst PT	Guha-Thakurta, Sonya	M	13A
Inst PT	Harris, Julie	M	55
Prof Emeritus	Hertz, Talmon	M	
Assoc Prof	Horvath, Janos	M	32B,32D,36,42,13C
Inst	Hrynkiw, Patricia	D	61
Inst PT	Jones, Gareth	B	37,49
Inst PT	Jones, Lucie	M	64A
Prof	Jordan, William S.	D	13,10,10F
Inst PT	Klassen, Gwen	M	64A
Assoc Prof	Levtov, Vladimir	D	41,66A,66C,66D,42
Inst PT	Mahon, Brad	D	12,14
Inst PT	Maier, Ralph	D	70,41,12,14
Inst PT	Matiation, Laurie	M	63B
Prof Emeritus	Nielsen, Kenneth L.	M	
Inst PT	O'Brien, Dean		62D
Inst FT	Radford, Laurie	D	10,10F,13,43
Inst PT	Reid, John	B	29A
Prof Emeritus	Roberts, John P.L.	M	
Prof Emeritus	Roman, Zoltan	D	
Assoc Prof	Sallis, Friedemann	D	12,13
Inst PT	Sandvoss, Beth Root	M	62C
Assoc Prof Emeritus	Schultz, Willard	M	
Inst PT	Scott, James	M	63C
Prof Emeritus	Searchfield, John W.	M	
Inst PT	Squance, Rod Thomas	D	20,50,65
Inst PT	Sussman, David	B	64B
Asst Prof	Welling, Joelle	D	13,61
Inst PT	Whidden, Collen	D	40
Inst PT	Yu, Hongmei		14

AA0200 Univ of Lethbridge
Department of Music
4401 University Dr
Lethbridge, AB T1K 3M4 Canada
(403) 329-2495   Fax: (403) 382-7127
www.uleth.ca/finearts/music
E-mail: deanna.oye@uleth.ca

4 Year Institution, 2 Year Graduate Program

Chair: Deanna Oye, 80A
Dean: Desmond Rochfort, 80A
Dir., Music Conservatory: Margaret Mezei, 80E

PT	Barron, Jason	M	13A
Assoc Prof	Black, Brian	D	12,66C,13E
Prof Emeritus	Blair, Dean G.	M	
Adj	Boehm, Norbert		62A
Assoc Prof	Boon, Rolf J.	D	13,34,10,35
Adj	Boutin, Lise	M	62A
Asst Prof	Burleigh, Ian G.		13L,34
Adj	Cable, Howard	D	10,11,35,47,60
Adj	Davenport, Francesca	M	64D
Lect	Davies, Josh	D	63A,47,29A,13C
Prof Emeritus	Evelyn, George E.	D	
PT	Freeman, Wendy	M	37,13C
PT	Gieck, Sarah	M	64A
Lect	Hansen, Bente	M	66A,13
Assoc Prof	Hendsbee, Blaine	M	61,39
PT	Herrington, Carolyn	D	66C,11
Prof Emeritus	Hicken, Ken	D	
PT	Ichikawa, Andrew		33
Prof Emeritus	Jackson, J.P. Christopher	D	
Prof	Jurkowski, Edward	D	13,12A,34
PT	Ketcheson, Dale		70
PT	Klassen, Glenn	D	36,38,40,60
PT	Knight, Gregory	B	66C
Lect	Mason, Adam	M	13A,11,65
Other	Mezei, Margaret	M	13A,64C,64E
Lect	Montgomery, Glen	DIPL	66A
Other	Morris, Christopher	B	
Assoc Prof	Oye, Deanna	D	66A,66C,66,13C,66B
Lect	Richards, Mark C.	D	13,12A
Adj	Rodgers, Mark	M	62C
Lect	Sanden, Paul	M	12,12A
Asst Prof	Schaller, Thilo	M	34,35
Asst Prof	Schultz, Arlan N.	PhD	10,34,13,12B
Prof	Staples, Thomas	D	60,11,49,63
Lect	Stewart, D. Andrew	D	34D,10B,45,35A
Other	Streibel, Bruce	B	72
Lect	Stringer, Sandra	D	61,36,11
PT	Sullivan, Nick A.	M	63D,63C,13C
PT	Sussman, David	M	64B
Adj	Tagg, Graham		62B
Prof	Visentin, Peter	M	12A,62A,67B,11
Assoc Prof	Wasiak, Ed	D	32,37,63A
Asst Prof	Youngdahl, Janet Ann	D	36,12A,61

AB0040 Art Institute of Vancouver-Burnaby
Department of Recording Arts
3264 Beta Ave
Burnaby, BC V5G 4K4 Canada
(604) 298-5400   Fax: (604) 298-5403
www.artinstitutes.edu/vancouver

1-3 year certificates in Recording Arts

CEO/President: Niels Hartvig-Nielson, 80A
Director of Corporate Relations: Cliff Jones
Director of Education: Don Ramos

PT	Coulas, Ben		34,35D,35G,34D
Inst FT	Czink, Andrew		35D,35G,34D
Inst FT	Feindell, S.		35D,35G,34D
Inst PT	Fuschetto, W.		13A,13B
FT	Gorrie, Gregg		34D
Inst FT	Hamann, Wolfgang		35A,35D,35E,35F
	Miles, Dean		35G,35H
PT	Vermeulen, Ron		35A,35D,35G
PT	Wade, Brett		35D,35G
PT	Woodyard, Jim		35D,35G
PT	Young, Jeff		34D,35D,35E,35F,35G

AB0050 Douglas College
Department of Music
PO Box 2503
New Westminster, BC V3L 5B2 Canada
(604) 527-5495   Fax: (604) 527-5528
www.douglas.bc.ca/programs/music.html
E-mail: ollenj@douglascollege.ca

2 Year Institution
Member of CUMS

Coordinator: Joy Ollen, 80A

Inst	Barrington, Barrie	D	66A,66D
Inst PT	Brady, Angus	B	63D
Inst	Caldwell, Robert	B	45,65,34,46,41
Inst PT	Cavadas, Angela		62A
Inst PT	Chernoff, Marea	M	64B
Inst PT	Fedoruk, Brenda	B	64A
Inst	Fisher, Blair	M	37,47,63A,63,46
Inst	Glofcheskie, John	M	13A,13,12A
Inst	Hannan, Eric	M	36,61
Inst PT	Hutter, Patricia	B	62D
Inst PT	MacDonald, Colin		64E
Inst PT	Nikolova, Iliana	M	66D
Inst	Northcott, Erica	B	61
Inst	Ollen, Joy	D	13
Inst PT	Ramsbottom, Gene		64C
Inst PT	Round, Sue		62C
Inst PT	Shier, Robin	M	37,63A,63,46
Inst	Silverman, Ellen	M	66A
Inst	Smith, Douglas	M	13A,13,10,13C,12
Inst PT	Sparkes, Doug	B	63C
Inst	Strutt, Michael	M	70
Inst PT	Walker, Heather		63B

AB0060 Kwantlen Polytech University
Department of Music
12666 72nd Ave
Surrey, BC V3W 2M8 Canada
(604) 599-3315   Fax: (604) 599-3277
www.kwantlen.ca/music
E-mail: music@kwantlen.ca

4 Year Institution

Chair: Don Hlus, 80A

PT	Bortolussi, Paolo	D	64A,48,13
PT	Caldwell, Robert	B	50,65
PT	Chernoff, Marea	M	64B,48
PT	Cox, Gregory	B	63C,49
PT	Dyck, Calvin	D	51,62A
PT	Greene, Ted	B	13A,34
PT	Hampton, Ian		51,62C
Inst	Hayes, Jane	M	66A,66D,13B,42,66B
Inst	Hlus, Don	M	35A,70
Inst	Jeffrey, Wayne	D	35A,37,49,48,63B
Inst	Lamberton, Elizabeth	D	12A
PT	Light, Chris	B	62D
PT	Nystrom, Alison	M	61
PT	Peng, Bo	M	62C,51
PT	Pogrebnoy, Nikita	M	62B,51
PT	Proznick, Jodi	M	29
Inst	Quong, Meijane	D	66A,66D,13C
PT	Ryga, Campbell		29,46,47,64E
PT	Sheffield, Robert	M	64C,48
PT	Shih, Patricia	B	62A,51
PT	Shorthouse, Tom	B	63A,47,49,42
Inst	Skoumal, Zdenek	D	10A,13
PT	Stiles, Allen	M	13B,66A,66D
Inst	Suderman, Gail	M	36,61,40,39
PT	Thorpe, Allan	D	64D
PT	Throness, Dale	M	61,39
PT	Tones, Daniel	D	20,50,65
PT	van Deursen, John	D	47,38,63C,63D

AB0070 Selkirk College
Contemporary Music & Tech Prog
820 Tenth St
Nelson, BC V1L 3C7 Canada
(250) 505-1357   Fax: (250) 352-5716
www.selkirk.bc.ca
E-mail: donmacd@shaw.ca

2 Year Diploma Program

Head: Don MacDonald, 80A
Coordinator, Studio: Steven Parish

	Hodge, Cheryl	B	10,36,61,53,35H
	Landsberg, Paul	M	13A,70,53,47,29
	MacDonald, Don		10,61,62A,64E,35A
	Mahe, Darren	B	13,47,70,53,12A
	Parenteau, Gilles		10F,45,66,35H
	Parish, Steven	B	65,20G,34,35C
	Spielman, Mark	B	13A,47,62D,20G

AB0080 Simon Fraser University
School for the Contemp Arts-Music
8888 University Dr
Burnaby, BC V5A 1S6 Canada
(604) 291-3363   Fax: (604) 291-5907
www.sfu.ca/sca
E-mail: ca@sfu.ca

4 Year Institution, Contemporary Music Program

MFA

Director: Martin Gotfrit, 80A
Dir., Graduate Studies: David K. MacIntyre, 80C
Advisor: Dean Lastoria, 80D
Associate Director: Colin Browne, 80H

Asst Prof	Eigenfeldt, Arne	D	10,45,34,35,12F
Assoc Prof	Gotfrit, Martin	M	10,45,34,35,12F
Prof	MacIntyre, David K.	M	13,10,39,43
Prof	Truax, Barry D.	M	10,45,34,35C,13L
Prof	Underhill, Owen	M	13,60,10,12,43

AB0090 Trinity Western University
Department of Music
7600 Glover Rd
Langley, BC V2Y 1Y1 Canada
(604) 888-7511   Fax: (604) 513-2066
www.twu.ca
E-mail: thorpe@twu.ca

4 Year, Private, Christian, Liberal Arts University

Chair: Allan Thorpe, 80A

Adj	Bortolussi, Paolo	D	64A
Adj	Caldwell, Bob	B	65
Adj	Chernoff, Marea	M	64B
Adj	Christian, Henry	B	63A
Adj	Farrugia, Greg	B	63C
Adj	Gallo, Tony	D	64E,14
Adj	Gibbson, Jef	B	34
Adj	Hampton, Ian		62C
Adj	Harder, Caroline	D	61
Adj	Harris, Ray	M	61
Prof	Janzen, Wesley	D	60,12A,36,31A
Adj	Klukas, Suzanne	M	66A,66C
Adj	Ledressay, Joanne	M	64C,32B
Adj	Light, Chris	B	62D
Adj	Mingus, Richard	M	63B
Adj	Norman, Edward	B	66G
Adj	Nystrom, Alison	M	61
Adj	Olsen, Tim		70
Prof	Rushton, David	D	13,60,32C,31A
Assoc Prof	Squires, David	D	10,12A
Adj	Suderman, Betty	D	66A
Asst Prof	Thompson, Jonathan	D	11,36,12A,60,38
Assoc Prof	Thorpe, Allan	D	13,48,64D,13A,37
Adj	Volpe Bligh, Elizabeth	B	62E
Adj	Von Koenigsloew, Heilwig	M	61
Assoc Prof	Warren, Jeff	D	12B,13F,47,62D

AB0100 Univ of British Columbia
School of Music
6361 Memorial Rd
Vancouver, BC V6T 1Z2 Canada
(604) 822-3113   Fax: (604) 822-4884
www.music.ubc.ca
E-mail: musicsec@ubc.ca

4 Year Institution, Graduate School

Master of Arts in Music Theory, Master of Arts in Ethnomusicology, Master of Music in Composition, Master of Music in Performance, Master of Music in Opera, PhD in Ethnomusicology, PhD in Music Theory, DMA in Composition, DMA in Performance, PhD in Musicology, Master of Arts in Musicology

Dean: Gage Averill, 80A
Director: Richard Kurth, 80A
Coord., Communication & Concert Management: Laurie Townsend, 80F
Dir., Summer Music Institute: Martin C. Berinbaum, 80G

Prof	Averill, Gage	D	12,14
Lect PT	Barcza, Peter		61
Lect PT	Beckett, Hal	B	10C
Prof	Benjamin, William E.	D	13,10
Asst Prof	Bennett, Dwight	M	38,60B
Prof Emeritus	Berinbaum, Martin C.	M	60B,37,49,63A
Lect PT	Berkman, Jeremy	M	63C
Lect PT	Boothroyd, David	M	61
Lect PT	Bortolussi, Paolo	D	43
Prof Emeritus	Brown, Donald G.	DIPL	61
Assoc Prof	Buechner, Sara Davis	D	66A,42
Prof	Butler, Gregory G.	D	13,10,12A,12
Lect PT	Chai, Susan	M	66D
Lect PT	Chan, Amanda	M	42,66A
Assoc Prof	Chang, Dorothy	D	10A,10F,10
Prof	Chatman, Stephen G.	D	13,10,43
Asst Prof	Choi, Eugenia	M	62A,51
Lect PT	Cole, Roger	B	64B
Prof	Coop, Jane A.	M	41,66A
Lect PT	Cox, Gregory	B	63C
Prof Emeritus	Dawes, Andrew		41,51,62A,42
Inst	Dawson, Terence	D	66A
Lect PT	Di Novo, Nancy	M	62A
Asst Prof	Dodson, Alan	D	13
Lect PT	Enns, Alice	B	66A
Lect PT	Epp, Richard	M	39,66C
Lect PT	Esson, Dennis	M	46
Prof Emeritus	Fankhauser, James L.	M	13,36,55,61
Lect PT	Fedoruk, Brenda	B	64A
Assoc Prof	Fisher, Alexander	D	12,55,67D
Lect PT	Friedman, Kenneth J.	M	62D

Rank	Name	Deg	Codes
Lect PT	Fullerton, J. Graeme	D	12C
Lect PT	Gaetanne, Marisa	M	61
Lect PT	Gal, Peter	B	64B
Lect PT	Griffiths, Vern	M	65
Prof	Hamel, Keith A.	D	13,10,34
Asst Prof	Hamm, Corey D.	D	66A
Assoc Prof	Harding, David	B	51,62A,62B,41,42
Prof	Hermiston, Nancy	B	12A,39,61
Assoc Prof	Hesselink, Nathan	D	14
Lect PT	Holzschuh, Craig	M	39
Lect PT	Hoy, Patricia A.	DMA	66A
Lect PT	Inguanti, Cris	M	64C
Lect PT	Kinsman, Benjamin	B	63B
Lect PT	Knopp, Larry	M	63A
Lect	Konoval, Brandon	D	11
Prof Emeritus	Kreider, J. Evan	D	12
Lect PT	Krutzen, Heidi	M	62E
Prof	Kurth, Richard	D	13
Asst Prof	Langager, Graeme	D	36,60A
Lect PT	Lee, Helen		61
Lect PT	Littleford, James	B	63A
Prof Emeritus	Loban, John A.	M	41,51,62A
Lect PT	Maloff, Nikolai	D	13
Lect PT	Matheson, Alan	B	63A
Lect PT	McCoy, David	M	66A
Lect PT	McDonald, Aaron	M	65
Lect PT	McGhee, Lorna		64A,41
Prof	Metzer, David	D	13,29A,15
Assoc Prof	Micznik, Vera G.	D	12,12B,12A
Lect PT	Mingus, Richard	M	63B
Prof Emeritus	Morris, Robert B.	D	61
Lect PT	Morrison, Kenneth	D	13
Lect PT	Murray, Michael		66G
Lect PT	Nolan, Julia	M	64E,32E,42
Lect PT	Nurse, Ray		55
Lect PT	Oke, Doreen	B	66H
Asst Prof	Oostwoud, Roelof		61
Lect PT	Orson, Beth		64B
Lect PT	Paslawski, Gordon	M	13
Prof Emeritus	Piltz, Hans-Karl	M	11,62
Inst	Pritchard, Bob	D	13,10,34
Assoc Prof Emeritus	Pullan, Bruce	M	36
Lect PT	Ramsbottom, Gene		64C
Prof	Read, Jesse	M	38,41,64D,67E
Prof Emeritus	Reubart, G. Dale	D	66A
Prof	Roeder, John B.	D	13
Prof Emeritus	Sawyer, John E.	D	55,67A,12A
Prof	Sharon, Rena	M	66C
Prof Emeritus	Silverman, Robert	D	42,66A
Lect PT	Skovorodnikov, Eugene	M	66A
Lect PT	Sparkes, Douglas	M	63C
Lect PT	Stride, Frederick	B	47,29
Lect PT	Strutt, Michael	DIPL	70
Asst Prof	Taylor, Robert C.	D	37,49,60B,63A
Prof	Tenzer, Michael	D	20D,14
Lect PT	Thomson-Price, Heather		61
Prof Emeritus	Thrasher, Alan R.	D	20D,14
Prof Emeritus	Throness, Dale	M	61
Prof Emeritus	Tickner, French A.	M	12A,39,61
Lect PT	Tsabar, David	M	20E
Lect PT	Van Deursen, John	D	49,63C,37
Lect PT	Volpe Bligh, Elizabeth		62E
Lect PT	Wean, Ellis		63D
Lect PT	Wilkins Wong, Miranda	M	66A
Assoc Prof	Wilson, Eric J.	M	41,62C
Prof Emeritus	Wilson, Eugene N.	D	10A,13
Assoc Prof	Wood, Jasper	M	62A,51

AB0150 Univ of Victoria

School of Music
Box 1700 Station CSC
Victoria, BC V8W 2Y2 Canada
(250) 721-7903   Fax: (250) 721-6597
www.finearts.uvic.ca/music
E-mail: musi@finearts.uvic.ca

4 Year Institution, Graduate School

Master of Arts in Historical Musicology, Master of Music in Composition, Master of Music in Performance, PhD in Historical Musicology, Master of Arts in Musicology, Master of Arts in Musicology with Performance

Acting Director: Susan Lewis-Hammond, 80A
Graduate Advisor: Eugene Dowling, 80C
Graduate Advisor: Jonathan Goldman, 80C

Rank	Name	Deg	Codes
Asst Prof	Biro, Daniel Peter	D	13B,13C,13E,13F,10A
Lect PT	Bonkowski, Anita	M	29A,29B,13A,13B,13D
Lect PT	Booker, Anthony	M	66C
Asst Prof	Boyle, Patrick	D	20A,29B,47,53
Asst Prof	Butterfield, Benjamin		61,39
Assoc Prof	Butterfield, Christopher	M	13,10,43
Prof	Celona, John	D	13,10,43
Lect PT	Clanton, Wendell	M	64E,47
Lect PT	Clenman, David	DIPL	13,12A,13A,13B,13C
Asst Prof	Csaba, Ajtony	M	38,60B
Senior Lect	Dowling, Eugene	M	42,13C,63C,63D
Adj	Driessen, Peter	D	10B,35C,35D
Lect PT	Dunn, Alexander	D	70,13A
Lect PT	Eccleston, Colleen	B	14C
Artist in Res	Elliott-Goldschmid, Ann	B	62A,42
Assoc Prof	Fillion, Michelle	D	12
Lect PT	Froese, Garry W.	D	40
Asst Prof	Goldman, Jonathan	D	12,13
Lect PT	Grimm, Anne	DIPL	61
Lect PT	Gunter, Jenny	M	64D
Lect PT	Hale, Charlotte	DIPL	66C
Lect PT	Hanson, Jordan	B	20A,20B
Artist in Res	Highbaugh Aloni, Pamela	M	62C,42
Artist in Res	Hood, Joanna	M	62B,42
Lect PT	Keddy, Michael	M	60B
Assoc Prof	Kellan, Kurt	B	41,63B
Assoc Prof	King, Gerald	D	32,37,60B
Prof	Kostek, Patricia	M	48,64C
Prof	Krebs, Harald M.	D	13,66C
Lect PT	Kwok, May Ling	M	66A
Assoc Prof	Lewis-Hammond, Susan	D	12
Lect PT	Linwood, William	B	65
Lect PT	MacInnes, Scott	B	63C
Lect PT	Mares, Michelle	B	66A
Other	McNally, Kirk	M	10B,34D,34E,35C,35D
Lect PT	Olsen, Alex	B	62D
Assoc Prof	Pohran Dawkins, Alexandra	B	42,64B
Lect PT	Poole, Elissa	D	11
Prof	Ranger, Louis	B	49,63A,41
Assoc Prof	Rowe, Arthur	M	66A
Prof	Schloss, Andrew	D	10B,34,14,20H,13L
Vstng Asst Prof	Snizek, Suzanne	D	64A,42
Lect PT	Solar-Kinderman, Eva	DIPL	66A,66C
Artist in Res	Stanis, Sharon	M	42,62A
Adj	Tilney, Colin	B	12A,66E
Prof	Vogt, Bruce	M	66A,66C
Senior Lect	Young, Susan	M	61,36,13C,39

AB0200 Vancouver Academy of Music

1270 Chestnut St
Vancouver, BC V6J 4R9 Canada
(604) 734-2301   Fax: (604) 731-1920
www.vam.bc.ca
E-mail: collegeregistrar@vam.bc.ca

4 & 2 Year Institution

Executive Director: Joseph Elworthy, 80A
College Registrar: Ruth Enns, 80D,80H

Rank	Name	Deg	Codes
Asst Prof	Ambrose, Lorraine	B	66A
PT	Barnes, Ariel	B	62C
PT	Brickman, Martha	M	66A
PT	Cannon, Alexander	DMA	63A
PT	Chan, Amanda	DMA	66A,66C
PT	Chernoff, Marea	B	64B
Lect PT	Cole, Roger	B	64B
PT	Coope, Ann-Katherine	B	64C
Lect PT	Cox, Gregory	B	63C,38
PT	D'Angelo, Mark	M	63A
PT	Dansereau, Sophie	M	64D
PT	Dawes, Andrew	B	41
PT	Driedger-Klassen, Robyn	B	61
PT	Duckles, Lee	B	62C
Assoc Prof	Elworthy, Joseph	M	62C,42,38
Lect	Enns, Ruth	D	12A
PT	Fedoruk, Brenda	B	64A
PT	Fisk, Martin	B	65
PT	Fraser, Judith	DIPL	62C
PT	G'froerer, Brian	B	63B
PT	Haskins, David	M	63B
PT	Hill, Lawrie	B	62A
PT	Hurst, Chloe	M	13A,13B,13C
PT	Inguanti, Cris	M	64C
PT	Kelly, Rebecca	B	66A,66D
PT	Kyne, Nadia	M	64A
PT	Lebeda, Wiktor	M	62D
Assoc Prof	Lee, Kum Sing	M	66A
PT	Leggatt, Jacqueline	DMA	13,10A
PT	Marks, Erin	M	64B
PT	Marple, Ellen	B	63C
PT	Matyukov, Saida	M	66A
PT	Meek, David	B	61
PT	Nguyen, Hanh	B	70
PT	Otake, Miya	B	62E
PT	Perriment, Andrew	FLCM	13D,13C
PT	Roland, Isabelle	M	62A,62B
Assoc Prof	Rozek, Robert	M	62A,62B,38
PT	Rozsnyal, Zoltan	B	62C
Lect	Smith, Douglas	M	13,10F,10A
PT	Stieda, Nicki	B	62A
PT	Takizawa, Marcus	M	62B
PT	Wright, Nicholas	B	62A

AB0210 Victoria Conservatory of Music
School of Music
900 Johnson St
Victoria, BC V8V 3N4 Canada
(250) 386-5311   Fax: (250) 386-6602
www.vcm.bc.ca
E-mail: post-secondaryregistrar@vcm.bc.ca

1 and 2 Year Institution, Diploma Programs offered through Camosun College

Chair, Post Secondary School: Mary Byrne, 80A
Executive Director: Jane Butler McGregor, 80A
Registrar, Post-Secondary Programs: Fuchsia Shier, 80D
Dir., Summer Programs: Emily Nagelbach, 80G

	Argenta, Nancy		61
	Attrot, Ingrid		61
	Beauchesne, Paul	M	63D
	Braaten, Brenda		13C
	Brett, Kathleen		61
	Brown, Stephen	ARCT	10,13A,13B,13C,13D
	Byrne, Mary	D	64A
	Cal, Anna	M	66A
	Cheramy, Rob		70
	Clements, Gordon	M	46,47,29B,64E,64C
	De Burgh, Susan	ARCT	66A
	Dunn, Alexander	D	70
	Elliott, Marsha	M	64A
	Graham, Damian	B	65
	Holliston, Robert	AVCM	66C,12A,11,39,66A
	Kiffner, Paula	M	62C,42
	Kwok, May Ling	M	66A
	LeBlanc, Eric		29A
	Low, Linda	B	66A,66D,66B
	McFetridge, George		66A
	Roessingh, Karel		66D
	Smith, Joey	M	29B,29C,47
	Stobbe, Linda	FTCL	66A
	Syer, Jamie	D	66A,66B
	Velinova, Gergana	M	61
	Volet, Richard	M	64A
	Wiksyk, Crystal	AVCM	13A,13B,13C,13H
	Wood, Winifred	AMM	66A,66B
	Wraggett, Wes		10A,10B,13B,13L

AC0050 Brandon University
School of Music
270-18th St
Brandon, MB R7A 6A9 Canada
(204) 727-9631   Fax: (204) 728-6839
www.brandonu.ca/music
E-mail: music@brandonu.ca

4 Year Institution, Graduate School

Master of Music in Music Education, Master of Music in Performance & Literature, Master of Music in Collaborative Piano, Master of Music in Composition, Master of Music in Conducting, Master of Music in Performance

Dean: Michael I. Kim, 80A
Dir., Undergraduate Studies: Sheelagh Chadwick, 80B
Dir., Undergraduate Studies: Gregory Gatien, 80B
Dir., Undergraduate Studies: Sheila Scott, 80B
Dir., Graduate Studies: T. Patrick Carrabre, 80C

Assoc Prof	Bach, Edward	D	63A
Assoc Prof	Cain, Michael	M	29,47,66A
Prof	Carrabre, T. Patrick	D	13,10,43,20G,35
Asst Prof	Chadwick, Sheelagh	D	32,32C
Assoc Prof	Dagenais, Andree		36,40,42,60A
Inst	Dixon, Kara	M	13A,13C
Asst Prof	DuWors, Kerry	M	62A,62B,51
	Forman, Naomi	M	61
	Fournier, Gilles		62D,29
Assoc Prof	Gatien, Gregory	M	64E,29A,47
Assoc Prof	Ginader, Gerhard	D	13,10,45,62A
Assoc Prof	Gordon, William	DIPL	10F,12A,63B
	Hall, Sarah	M	13J,61
	Hasselfield, Bart	B	63D
	Helmer, John	M	63D,63C
	Hennen, Nancy	M	64A
Prof Emeritus	Jones, Lawrence	D	66A,12A
	Kim, Kyung	D	66A
Prof	Kim, Michael I.	D	66A
	Letkemann, David	M	70
	Madrya, Paul	M	70
Assoc Prof	Masaki, Megumi	D	13,66A,66C,43,66B
Asst Prof	McCallum, Wendy M.	D	64E,32E,37,60B,32
Prof Emeritus	Nichols, Kenneth	D	66A,13
	Normandeau, Dale	B	29,70
Asst Prof	Platz, Eric	M	46,47,29
Asst Prof	Playfair, David M.	M	61,39
Prof Emeritus	Richardson, Robert	M	66A
Prof Emerita	Richardson, Sylvia	M	61
	Rogers, Sharon		13A,13C
Assoc Prof	Scott, Sheila	D	32,32B
Asst Prof	Simonot, Colette	D	12A
	Sparks, Victoria	D	65,50
	Star, Allison	D	13A,13C
Assoc Prof	Tselyakov, Alexander	DIPL	66A,42,66B
Asst Prof	Wood, Catherine M.	D	64C,13
Asst Prof	Zacharius, Leanne	D	38,62C,51
	Zimmerman, Brian	M	29,70

AC0100 Univ of Manitoba
Marcel A. Desautels Faculty of Music
65 Dafoe Rd
Winnipeg, MB R3T 2N2 Canada
(204) 474-9310   Fax: (204) 474-7546
www.umanitoba.ca/music
E-mail: music@umanitoba.ca

4 & 5 Year Institution, Graduate School

Master of Music in Composition, Master of Music in Performance, Master of Music in Conducting

Dean: Edmund N. Dawe, 80A
Dir., Graduate Studies: Karen Jensen, 80C
Registrar: Susan Leeson, 80D
Admissions Coordinator: Shelley O'Leary, 80D
Dir., Preparatory Division: Mary Hawn, 80E
Facilites and Events: Sue Stone Scott, 80F
Associate Dean: Joan Linklater, 80H

PT	Anderson, Valdine	DIPL	61
PT	Bailey, Craig		47,64E
Asst Prof	Bonness, Will	B	29B,47,66A
Assoc Prof	Braun, Mel	M	39,61
Assoc Prof	Burleson, Richard F.	M	14,55,67G
PT	Byrne, David	M	13,12A
Asst Prof	Chung, Minna Rose	D	62C,42,51
PT	Dahl, Tracy	B	61
Asst Prof	Davis, Quincy	B	29,65,47
Inst FT	Dawe, Karla	M	13A,13J,13C
PT	Denby, Steven	B	36
PT	Dyer, Steve	M	63C
PT	Epp, Jeremy		65
PT	Evans, Patty		63B
PT	Fast, Bobbi	B	63D
Assoc Prof	Fitzell, Gordon D.	D	10,34,43
PT	Fletcher, Donna	M	61,54
PT	Friesen, Darryl	M	66A
Asst Prof	Friesen, Elroy	M	36,60A,32D
Asst Prof	Gardner, Derrick	M	63A,29A,46,47
Assoc Prof	Gillis, Richard	D	63A,49
PT	Gomon, Naoum	DIPL	64C
PT	Hanley, Bede	B	64B
Asst Prof	Harrington, Allen	M	64D,64E,42,48
FT	Hawn, Mary		
PT	Heilbrunn, Micah		64C
PT	Helmer, John	M	63C
PT	Hildebrand, Ed	M	36
PT	Hildebrand, Millie		36
Assoc Prof	Horton, Charles T.	M	66A,13D,13E,13F
PT	Huisman, Monica	DIPL	61
PT	Husband, Julie	B	64
Prof	Jensen, Karen	D	61,11
Assoc Prof	Kehler Siebert, Judith	D	66A,66C,66D,42
FT	Kirby, Anna-Lisa		47,61
Assoc Prof	Kirby, Steve	M	29,47,62D
PT	Klassen, David	M	61
PT	Kristjanson, William	B	32C
PT	Kula, Jeff	B	32C
PT	Lee, Chris	M	63D
PT	Lee, Richard		38
Assoc Prof	Linklater, Fraser	D	63A,32E,37,48,60B
Asst Prof	Linklater, Joan	M	32A
Assoc Prof	Loewen, Laura		66A,39,66C
PT	MacDonald, Ken		63B
Inst FT	MacLaren, Robert	DIPL	61,40
PT	MacMillan, Robin	D	64B
Assoc Prof	Mahrenholz, Simone	PhD	
Assoc Prof	Markstrom, Kurt	D	12
Prof	Matthews, Michael	D	10
Assoc Prof	Moroz, David	D	66A,66B
PT	Oberheu, Stephen		63D
Assoc Prof	Pokhanovski, Oleg	D	62A,51,42
PT	Ridd, Laurel		64A
PT	Robbins, Catherine	M	32D,32C,60A

PT	Roberts, Layla		64A
PT	Robertson, James		63B
Inst FT	Roy, Larry	M	70,47,53
Assoc Prof	Sandred, Orjan	D	10,13,34
PT	Scholz, Dan		62B
PT	Smith, Stewart	M	63D,34C
PT	Sparks, Victoria	B	65,50
PT	Turner, Connie	M	32C
FT	Twaddle, Katherine	B	39
PT	Tyborowski, Richard	DIPL	70
PT	Van der Hooft, Rose	M	61
PT	Watson Lyons, Lois	DIPL	61

AD0050 Memorial Univ of Newfoundland
School of Music
St John's, NL A1C 5S7 Canada
(709) 864-7486   Fax: (709) 864-2666
www.mun.ca/music/home
E-mail: ellenw@mun.ca

4 Year Institution, Graduate School
Member of CUMS

Master of Arts in Ethnomusicology, Master of Music in Performance, Master of Music in Conducting, PhD in Ethnomusicology

Dean: Ellen F. Waterman, 80A
Associate Dean: Maureen Volk, 80H

Assoc Prof	Bendzsa, Paul	M	60,47,64C,64E
Inst PT	Brennan, Bill	M	46
Asst Prof	Bulmer, Karen	D	63C,63D
Asst Prof	Caslor, Jason	D	37,38,60B
Assoc Prof	Cheramy, Michelle	D	64A,13B
Inst PT	Collins, Darryl	B	70
Asst Prof	Cook, Nathan J.	DMA	42,62C
Prof	Dahn, Nancy	D	41,62A,62B
Adj Prof	David, Marc	D	38
Prof	Diamond, Beverley	D	14
Inst PT	Duff, Jim	M	14C
Prof	Dunsmore, Douglas	D	36,60A
Prof	Gordon, Thomas	D	12A
Assoc Prof	Gosine, C. Jane	D	12A
Adj Prof	Harris Walsh, Kristen	D	14
Inst PT	Holden, Valerie	M	64B
Adj Prof	Kearney Guigne, Anna	D	14
Lect	Klaus, Alan S.	M	63A,63B
Assoc Prof	Leibel, Jane	D	61
Inst PT	Neville, Shelley	M	61
Asst Prof	Power, Rob	M	65
Asst Prof	Proulx, Sylvie	M	70
Assoc Prof	Regehr, Vernon	D	62C,38,42
Prof	Rice, Paul	D	12A
Assoc Prof	Ross, Clark	D	13,10
Assoc Prof	Schiller, Caroline	D	39,61
Inst PT	Smith, Christina	M	14
Asst Prof	Staniland, Andrew	D	34,10
Prof	Steeves, Timothy	D	66A
Assoc Prof	Szego, Kati	D	12A,14,20
Prof	Szutor, Kristina	D	66A,66C,66B
Asst Prof	Tonelli, Chris	D	14
Prof	Volk, Maureen	D	66A,66B
Prof	Waterman, Ellen F.	D	64A,14

AE0050 Mount Allison University
Department of Music
134 Main St
Sackville, NB E4L 1A6 Canada
(506) 364-2374   Fax: (506) 364-2376
www.mta.ca/music
E-mail: musdept@mta.ca

4 Year Institution

Head & Dir., Summer Programs: Elizabeth A. Wells, 80A,80G

Assoc Prof	Code, Belinda B.	M	41,64A,64B,64D
PT	Deschenes, Michel		65
Assoc Prof	Ferguson, Danise J.	M	13,41,62C
PT	Gould, Monette		61
PT	Groom, Peter	M	61
PT	Higham, Peter	M	70
PT	Johnson, Lynn	M	66A
Asst Prof	MacLean, Alasdair	D	10A,34,13
Assoc Prof	Martin, Gayle H.	D	60A,66G,36,12A,55D
Asst Prof	Martin, Jeffrey A.		32,35
Assoc Prof	Pridmore, Helen	D	61,39,41
Assoc Prof	Rogosin, David	D	66A,12A,66C
Asst Prof	Runge, Stephen M.	D	66A,66B,66C
Assoc Prof	Tucker, Gary	D	13A,13,12
Prof	Vogan, Nancy F.	D	11,32
Assoc Prof	Wells, Elizabeth A.	D	12A,12,14,20G

AE0100 Univ de Moncton
Departement de Musique
Faculte Des Arts
Et Des Sciences Sociales
Moncton, NB E1A 3E9 Canada
(506) 858-4041   Fax: (506) 858-4166
www.umoncton.ca
E-mail: richard.boulanger@umoncton.ca

4 & 5 Year Institution

Chair: Richard Boulanger, 80A

Prof	Boisvert, Jean-Guy	D	41,64C,64E
Prof	Boulanger, Richard	D	12A,12,66A
Prof	Cardin, Michel	D	41,67G,70
PT	Castonguay, Roger	M	12A,10A,13A
PT	Deschenes, Michel	B	50,65
Prof	Gibson, Richard L.	D	13,10F,10,37,63
Prof	Lord, Roger	D	13,66A,66D
Prof	Richard, Monique M.	D	32,36,40,60A
Prof	Roy, Lisa	D	39,61

AE0120 Univ of New Brunswick (UNB)
Centre for Musical Arts
Memorial Hall, UNB Campus
9 Bailey Dr, PO Box 4400
Fredericton, NB E3B 5A3 Canada
(506) 453-4697   Fax: (506) 453-4697
cel.unb.ca/music
E-mail: rhornsby@unb.ca

4 Year Liberal Arts Institution

Director: Richard Hornsby, 80A,80F,80G,80B

Inst PT	Francavilla, Nadia	B	10C,62A
	Hornsby, Richard	M	64C,12A,29A,34,60
Inst PT	Kershaw, Yvonne	M	64A,64D,10A,11,13A
Inst PT	Pinnock, Rob	B	10D
Inst PT	Runefors, Bjorn	M	36,37,13,11,64A

AF0050 Acadia University
School of Music
Denton Hall 231
Wolfville, NS B4P 2R6 Canada
(902) 585-1512   Fax: (902) 585-1037
music.acadiau.ca
E-mail: barbara.jordan@acadiau.ca

4 Year Institution

Director: Jeff Hennessy, 80A
Dir., Artist Series: Ardith Haley, 80F

Lect PT	Adam, Mark	M	11,13C,46,47,65
Prof	Both, Christoph	D	13F,62,34
Lect PT	Britten, Sandra	B	48,64A
Lect PT	Brownell, Jack	D	49,63D,63C
Lect PT	Bruce, Cynthia	M	13C,33,66D,12A
Assoc Prof	Callon, Gordon J.	D	12A,13D
Lect PT	Chapman, Don		35G,35D
Asst Prof	Charke, Derek	D	13D,13E,10,13
Lect PT	Cormier, Eugene	B	13A,34,70
Lect PT	Dietz, Curtis	B	63A
Lect PT	Earl, Nicole	B	66A
Prof	Fisher, Stan F.	D	32E,12A
Lect PT	Haley, Ardith	B	35E,37
Lect PT	Hansen, Jessica	B	66A
Assoc Prof	Hansen, John	M	66A
Lect PT	Harwood, Elizabeth		36,66G
Lect PT	Heikalo, Daniel		70
Lect PT	Hennessy, Jeff	M	13D,13E
Asst Prof	Hopkins, Mark E.	D	37,32E,32C,60,60B
Lect PT	King, Jennifer	M	66C
Asst Prof	Lauzon, Paul	M	33,12F
Lect PT	Lee, Mary	B	63B
Lect PT	Mallin, Claire	M	13C,40,61,60A
Lect PT	Martin, Mary Lou		52
Lect PT	McPhee, Rosemary	B	33,40
Lect PT	Naylor, Stephen		34,10B

Lect PT	Oore, Danny	B	64E
Lect PT	Plaskett, Anna	B	33
Lect PT	Rockwell, Paula	M	61,39
Lect	Rushton, Christianne		12A,15,32D,61
Lect PT	Scott, Tara	M	66C
Lect PT	Shorley, Ken	B	20
Lect PT	St. Clair, Lisa	B	54
Lect	Tomarelli, Ron	B	66A,66B
Lect PT	Wilkinson, Chris		62

AF0100 Dalhousie University

Department of Music
DAC Room 514
6101 University Ave
Halifax, NS B3H 4R2 Canada
(902) 494-2418   Fax: (902) 494-2801
music.dal.ca
E-mail: music@dal.ca

4 Year Institution, Graduate Institution

Master of Arts in Musicology

Chair: Jennifer Bain, 80A
Acting Chair: Jacqueline Warwick, 80A
Administrative Officer: Lesley Brechin, 80B,80D,80F
Dir., Undergraduate Studies: Lynn Stodola, 80B
Dir., Graduate Studies: Estelle Joubert, 80C

PT	Adams, Gary	M	37,48
Assoc Prof	Allen, Peter	M	66A,66C,66B,41,42
Assoc Prof	Bain, Jennifer	D	13E,13F,13B,13J,13
Assoc Prof	Baur, Steven	D	11,12A,12D,12E,14C
Assoc Prof	Blais, Jerome	D	10,13
PT	Bradshaw, Dean	M	66C,66D
PT	Brownell, Jack	M	63D
PT	Cowger, Kelsey	M	12
PT	Creighton, Patricia	B	64A
PT	Crofts, Tim	M	29A
PT	Daley, Caron	M	13A,13C,36
Assoc Prof	Djokic, Philippe	M	62B,38,41,51,62A
PT	Feierabend, Christine		64A
PT	Gray, D'Arcy	M	50,65
PT	Hayes-Davis, Lucy	M	39,61
PT	Hoffman, Adrian	M	11
Asst Prof	Joubert, Estelle	D	12
PT	Kasper, Max		62D
PT	Lemieux, Suzanne	M	64B
PT	Macmillan, Scott	B	70
PT	Mathis, Eric	M	63C
PT	McCarthy, Elizabeth	M	64A
PT	Parker, David	M	63B
PT	Rapson, John	B	64C
PT	Reach, Douglas	B	70
Prof Emeritus	Schroeder, David	D	13,12A,12,12E,12C
Prof	Servant, Gregory W.	D	39,61
PT	Sheppard, Craig	B	45,35C
PT	Stern, Jeffrey	M	63A,49
Assoc Prof	Stodola, Lynn	M	42,66A,66C,41
Assoc Prof	Swanston, Marcia	B	39,61,40
PT	Torbert, Jeffrey	B	70
PT	Wahlstrom, Lynette	B	66A
PT	Walt, Shimon		62C
Assoc Prof	Warwick, Jacqueline	D	12A,12D,14C,15,29A

AF0120 Maritime Conserv of Perform Arts

6199 Chebucto Rd
Halifax, NS B3L 1K7 Canada
(902) 423-6995   Fax: (902) 423-6029
www.maritimeconservatory.com
E-mail: admin@maritimeconservatory.com

Non-Profit, Diploma Granting Institution

Dir., Administration: Cynthia Creaser, 80A
Chair, Board of Governors: Ann Smith, LLB, 80A
Dir., Development: Janet Hull, 80D

	Adams, Norman	M	62C
	Bates, Alexandra	B	62A,62B
	Bergstrom, Anne	M	64A
	Billington, Ryan	M	61,29,36
	Bird, Carolyn	B	66A
	Bjornsen, Lawrence	M	62D
	Blackie, Ruth	M	64C,13
	Boddie, Susan	M	61
	Boucher, Gillian		62A
	Boyko, Megan	B	62C
	Bradshaw, Dean	M	13,66A
	Britten, Sandra		64A
	Brown, Susanne	B	62A,62B
	Burgess, Gina	B	62A
	Danson, Joan	M	62C
	Davis, Jason	DIPL	61
	Diepeveen, Susan	M	66A,32A
	Dietz, Curtis	DIPL	63A
	Docking, Simon	D	66A
	Durnford, Jacqueline	M	66A
	Eager, Jim	M	63C
	Haley, Geordie		70
	Hearn, Carmelita	B	13A,66A,66D
	Hodder, Christy	B	62
	Jackson, Janice	B	61,54
	Jeffrey, Andrea	M	61
	Kemp, Sean	DIPL	62A
	Kirson-Jones, Chloe	M	66A
	Kristof, Rosemary		66A
	MacDonald, Pamela	D	61,39
	MacDonald, Scott	B	64E
	MacGillivary, Rod	M	60,63C,63D
	Mark, Amanda	B	64A
	Matheson, Jennifer	B	10,66D,66A
	McCarthy, Cheryl		66A,61
	McMurray, Mary	B	61
	Miles, Debbie	M	62A
	O'Hagan, Cheryl Reid	B	62E
	Oliver, Kristen	B	62
	O'Neill, Adrian	B	70
	Palmer, Christopher		64D
	Pavlovskaia, Natalia	M	66A
	Pearse, Lukas	M	62D
	Phillips, Paula	B	61,32A
	Reiner, Craig	B	65
	Ro, Betty	M	66A
	Royle, Frances	B	13A,66A
	Schabloski, Lana	B	64B
	Schroeder, Linda	M	64A
	Scott, Tara	M	66A
	Shaw, Olive	B	62C
	Shaw, Patricia	M	64C
	Simons, Paul		66A
	Smith, Gillian	M	62A
	Von Syberg, Carol		66A
	Walsh, Eileen	D	64C,13
	Whalen, Marc	D	70
	Williams, Ifan		62C
	Wyman, Pat		62A,62B,38

AF0150 St Francis Xavier University

Department of Music
PO Box 5000
Antigonish, NS B2G 2W5 Canada
(902) 867-2106   Fax: (902) 867-3654
www.stfx.ca/academic/music
E-mail: music@stfx.ca

4 Year Institution

Chair: Gene Smith, 80A
Dir., Artist/Performance Series: Michael Steinitz, 80F

Asst Prof	Billington, Ryan	M	36,40,29,61
Assoc Prof	Brunkhorst, Kevin	M	70,34,29
Assoc Prof	Carter, Greg	M	64E,29,10
Prof	Genge, Anthony	D	13,66A,20G,29
Adj	Gray, D'Arcy	M	12A
Lect	Hanlon, Jake	M	29,70
Assoc Prof	O'Mahoney, Terrence	M	50,65,29,10D,66A
Prof	Smith, Gene	M	13,47,49,63C,29
Lect	Sutherland, Dan		62D,53
Assoc Prof	Tynan, Paul	M	37,63A,29

AG0050 Brock University

Department of Music
500 Glenridge Ave
St Catharines, ON L2S 3A1 Canada
(905) 688-5550 x 3817   Fax: (905) 688-4861
www.brocku.ca/music
E-mail: music@brocku.ca

4 Year Institution
Member of CUMS

Chair: Brian E. Power, 80A
Assistant Chair: Karin Di Bella, 80H

Inst PT	Adams, Brent	M	63D
Inst PT	Ball, Terry	B	62A,62B

Inst PT	Cleland, George	M	62A
Inst PT	Cleland, Gordon	M	62C
Inst PT	Cox, Terrance	M	20G,29A
Assoc Prof	Debly, Patricia	D	12A,12C
Asst Prof	Di Bella, Karin	D	66A,66B,66C
Inst PT	Dydnansky, Patricia	M	64A
Inst PT	Earp, Jonathan		70
Inst PT	Fornelli, Devon	M	65,50
Inst PT	Fralick, Janice	B	63B
Inst PT	Fralick, Steve	B	63C
Inst PT	Kalman, Zoltan	B	64C,48,64E,37
Inst PT	Kingham, Lesley	M	66G,66C,66A
Assoc Prof	Landey, Peter	D	12B,13J,10A,10B,10F
Inst PT	Linton, Deborah	M	61,13C
Assoc Prof	Loewen, Harris	D	60,36
Assoc Prof	Power, Brian E.	D	62A,67,12A,12C,13G
Inst PT	Reiman, Erika	D	66A
Inst PT	Robinson, Greg		63A
Asst Prof	Royal, Matthew	D	13,11,12B
Inst PT	Thomas, Laura	B	65
Inst PT	Thomas, Suzanne	B	62E
Inst PT	White, Tim	M	63A,49
Inst PT	Wolanski, Rob	M	62D

AG0070 Cambrian College of Applied Arts

School of Bus., Media & Creative Arts
1400 Barrydowne Rd
Sudbury, ON P3A 3V8 Canada
(705) 566-8101   Fax: (705) 560-1449
www.cambrianc.on.ca
E-mail: jamie.arrowsmith@cambrianc.on.ca

3 Year Institution

Prof Emerita	Arrowsmith, Brenda	B	48,64,10F,13A,13B
Prof	Arrowsmith, Jamie	M	38,60B,62,13A,13B
Prof	Biggs, Charlene	D	11,66A,66B,66C
Prof Emeritus	Candelaria, Philip	M	70,41
Inst PT	Churchill, Rachel	M	64
Inst PT	Comartin, Keenan	M	70
Adj Prof	Gibson, Ian	M	65,50
Prof	Gould, Matt	D	70,41
Inst PT	Laframboise, Damien	M	66A
Inst PT	Large, Mike	M	35
Inst PT	Lee, Alexandra	B	62C
Inst PT	Leonard, Charlotte	D	63D
Inst PT	McNally, Blair	B	32F,34D,63D
Inst PT	Millar, Tania	DIPL	66A,66D,13C
Inst PT	Ng-Au, Marie	B	66A,66D
Inst PT	Pandolfo, Susan	B	61
Inst PT	Schneider-Gould, Beth Ilana	M	62A
Prof	Teed, Pamela	M	13A,61
Inst PT	Walsh, Allan	B	64E,72
Inst PT	Wells, Deanne	B	61
Inst PT	Ysereef, Alan	M	70

AG0100 Carleton University

SSAC-Music/911A Loeb Bldg
1125 Colonel By Dr
Ottawa, ON K1S 5B6 Canada
(613) 520-5770   Fax: (613) 520-3905
www.carleton.ca
E-mail: tasneem_ujjainwala@carleton.ca

4 Year Institution, Graduate School

Master of Arts

Director SSAC: Brian Foss, 80A
Assistant Dir., Music: Anna Hoefnagels, 80H

PT	Allaire, Jean-Sebastien	M	12,13,36,60A
PT	Armstrong, Kathy	M	13,20A
Inst	Bussiere, Michael	M	13A,13,45,34
	Coghill, Jack		
Assoc Prof	Deaville, James	D	12,29,35
Assoc Prof	Echard, William	D	12,20,29,34,35
Prof	Finn, Geraldine	D	12E,12C
Adj Research Prof	Gardner, David	D	12A,12
Inst	Giles, Jennifer	M	13,12B,14A
Prof Emeritus	Gillingham, Bryan	D	12A,12,36
PT	Higney, John	M	12A
Asst Prof	Hoefnagels, Anna	D	12,20
Adj Research Prof	Kallmann, Helmut	D	20G
Prof Emerita	Keillor, Elaine	D	12A,12,14,66A,20G
Asst Prof	Luko, Alexis	D	12
PT	McKinley, Kathy	D	14
Prof Emerita	Piper, Deirdre	D	13,10,12A
Prof	Shepherd, John	D	12B,35B,12E,12C
Asst Prof	Stewart, Jesse		12
Prof	Theberge, Paul		35,35H
Adj Research Prof	Wicke, Peter	D	12,35,12F
Assoc Prof	Wright, James	D	13,10

AG0130 Harris Institute

118 Sherbourne St
Toronto, ON M5A 2R2 Canada
(416) 367-0178   Fax: (416) 367-5534
www.harrisinstitute.com
E-mail: info@harrisinstitute.com

Programs in Recording Arts Management & Producing/Engineering Program

President: John Harris, 80A
Technical Director: Chris Munro, 80A
General Manager: Juliet Suddaby, 80A
Director: Lance Reckzin, 80H
Dir., Producing/Engineer Program: Doug McClement
Dir., Recording Arts Management: Bob Roper

PT	Armstrong, Stephen		34A
PT	Balogh, Mike		35A
PT	Baxter, David		10
PT	Betts, David		35A
PT	Booth, Todd		10A,10D,10F,11,13
	Botly, George		10
PT	Broome, Dan		35
PT	Cairo, Bo		35C
PT	Champniss, Kim Clarke		35A
PT	Cornblum, Marcy		35A
PT	Devonish, Jay		35
PT	Di Gioia, Robert		35
PT	Duffy, Patrick		35
PT	Eldridge, Scott		35A
PT	Flohil, Richard		35
PT	France, Chris T.		35A
PT	Frayne, Bryant		35A
PT	Fried, Joe		35
PT	Gagnon, Paul		35
PT	Garbutt, Don		34,10
PT	Gorbachow, Yuri		34
PT	Hamilton, Peter		35
	Harris, John		35
PT	Henderson, Kate		35
PT	Hubbard, Gary		35
PT	Hussain, Azra		35
PT	Hyland, Greg		34A
PT	Janik, Liz		35
PT	Lecuyer, Stephane		35
PT	Lewis, Colin		35
PT	Mather, Bill		35
PT	McClement, Doug		34
PT	McLay, Mark		34
PT	McLuhan, Eric		35
PT	Moran, Kenny		34
PT	Nixon, Janis		34H
PT	Notter, Tim		35
PT	Parliament, Roland		35
PT	Pilchner, Martin		34
PT	Pollock, Heather		35
PT	Proulx, Ron		35
PT	Quilico, David		35
PT	Richardson, Jack		34
PT	Roche, Deryck		34
	Rogers, Tom		34
PT	Roper, Bob		35
PT	Ruoso-Loughlin, Alana		35
PT	Saxberg, Catherine		35
PT	Sernyk, Glenn		35
PT	Smith, Anne-Marie		35
PT	Somerton, Clinton		35
	Suddaby, Juliet		
PT	Vanderwoude, Matt		10A,11,13,29,34
PT	Zimbel, Ike		35

AG0150 Laurentian University

Department of Music
935 Ramsey Lake Rd
Sudbury, ON P3E 2C6 Canada
(705) 675-1151 x2520   Fax: (705) 671-3875
www.laurentian.ca
E-mail: yhirota@laurentian.ca

4 & 3 Year Institution

Chair: Yoko Hirota, 80A

Inst PT	Biggs, Charlene	D	66A
Inst PT	Churchill, Rachel	B	64A
Inst PT	Gibson, Ian	M	65
Assoc Prof	Hall, Robert	D	13,60,36,61,10F

Directory of Institutions

Assoc Prof	Hirota, Yoko	D	66,13B,12A,66A,12B
Inst PT	Jones, Thomas	M	62D
Inst PT	Laframboise, Damian	M	66A,66D
Inst PT	Lemay, Robert	D	13,10,12A
Assoc Prof	Leonard, Charlotte	D	12A,63D,63C,15,63B
Inst PT	Lesk, Sally	B	37
Inst PT	Macdonald, David	M	11,13A
Inst PT	Quebec, Brian	DIPL	62D
Inst PT	Rinaldo, Ben	DIPL	70
Inst PT	Scherzinger, Peter	B	63A
Inst PT	Teed, Pamela	M	61
Inst PT	Thibodeau, Gilles	B	63B
Inst PT	Valley, Myriam	DIPL	64A
Inst PT	Walsh, Allan	B	64E,47,46,29A,29B
Inst PT	Wells-Hunt, Deanne	DIPL	61
Inst PT	Wiseman, Jeff	B	61
Inst PT	Yzereef, Allan	M	70

AG0170 Lakehead University

Department of Music
955 Oliver Rd
Thunder Bay, ON P7B 5E1 Canada
(807) 343-8787   Fax: (807) 345-2394
music.lakeheadu.ca
E-mail: djobinbe@lakeheadu.ca

4 Year Undergraduate Institution

Chair & Dir., Artist/Performance Series: Glenn Colton, 80A,80F

PT	Bacon, Anthony	M	62C
PT	Blanchet, Martin	M	62D
PT	Breton, Jean-Francois	M	65,13C,50
Prof	Carastathis, Aris	D	13,10,43
PT	Clarke, Penelope	B	13A,64A
Assoc Prof	Colton, Glenn	D	12,20G,14C,14D
PT	Cotton, Patricia	M	61
PT	Douglas, Madonna	B	62A
PT	Dungan, Doris	M	64A
PT	Erickson, Kim	B	13,36,20,39
PT	Gibson, Colleen	B	64B
PT	Gibson, Jeff		63B
PT	Holborn, George	B	61
PT	Hongisto, Erik	M	63C
PT	Hsu, E-Chen	M	64C
PT	Jillings, Cathy	B	62B
Assoc Prof	Jobin-Bevans, Dean	D	60,36,40,39
PT	Klazek, Merrie	M	63A,48,49
PT	Marrier, Susan	M	66G
PT	McGhee, Mary	B	61
PT	Morrison, Heather	B	41,66A
PT	Pepe, Dino	B	64E
PT	Reid, Darlene Chepil	D	13F,13I,10
PT	Roy, Joseph	M	70,13E
PT	Tchougounov, Evgueni	D	66,66A,13C
PT	Wevers, Harold	B	64D

AG0200 McMaster University

School of the Arts
1280 Main St W
Hamilton, ON L8S 4M2 Canada
(905) 525-9140 x 27671   Fax: (905) 527-6793
sota.humanities.mcmaster.ca
E-mail: sota@mcmaster.ca

4 Year Institution, Graduate School

Master of Arts in Music Criticism

Director: Hayden Maginnis, 80A

Inst PT	Bedard, Elise	M	61
Inst PT	Brownwell, John		32C,65
Inst PT	Classen, Lita		61
Inst PT	Colenbrander, Caroline		61
Inst PT	Cunningham, Richard		40,61
Assoc Prof	Deaville, James A.	D	11,12A,12,41,12C
Inst PT	Dempsey, Kevin		65
Inst PT	Desrosiers, Cecile		66
Inst PT	Elbeck, Lance		66A
Inst PT	Elliott, Paula	B	64A
Inst PT	Englert, Don		64E
Assoc Prof	Fast, Susan	D	13A,11,12A,12,55
Inst PT	Feket, Robert		66A
Inst PT	Gerry, David		64A
Inst PT	Grimwood, Paul		66G,66H,66D
Assoc Prof	Hall, Frederick A.	D	11,12A,12,20G
Assoc Prof	Hartwell, Hugh	D	13,10,11,29
Inst PT	Holinaty, William		53
Inst PT	Holler, David		36

Inst PT	Hunter, Judy		66A
Inst PT	Jarvis, Willie		62D,47
Inst PT	Kalman, Zoltan		64C
Inst PT	Kanovich, Leokadia		66
Inst PT	Karan, Leon		66
Assoc Prof	Kinder, Keith	D	37,41,49,63
Inst PT	Lorcini, Marie		62E
Inst PT	McFadden, Jeff		70
Asst Prof	McGowan, James		10,11
Inst PT	Milleker, Troy		62D
Asst Prof	Mitchell, Andrew	D	11
Inst PT	Moolenbeek, William J.		64E
Inst PT	Morton, Rebecca		62C
Inst PT	Nelson, Nancy		64B
	Peterson, Jon		64B
Inst PT	Pierre, Stephen		64C
Inst PT	Polci, Mike		63C
Prof Emeritus	Rapoport, Paul	D	13,11,12A,12
Assoc Prof	Renwick, William J. M.	D	13,60,13J
Inst PT	Shields, Bob		47,70
Inst PT	Shulman, Suzanne	B	64A
Assoc Prof PT	Tryon, Valerie		66A
Inst PT	Van Weelden, Pam		66
Inst PT	Vizante, Sonia		62A
Prof Emeritus	Walker, Alan	D	13,12A,12
Prof Emeritus	Wallace, William	D	13,10F,10
Inst PT	White, Timothy		63A
Inst PT	Zacarelli, Alla		66A

AG0250 Queens University

School of Music
Harrison-LeCaine Hall
Room 204
Kingston, ON K7L 3N6 Canada
(613) 533-2066   Fax: (613) 533-6808
queensu.ca/music
E-mail: music@queensu.ca

4 Year Institution

Director: Margaret Edith Walker, 80A
Chair, Undergraduate Studies: Clara Marvin, 80B
Dir., Conservatory: Karma Tomm, 80E
Dir., Artist Series: John Burge, 80F
Associate Director: Ireneus Zuk, 80H

Assoc Prof	Allik, Kristi A.	D	10,45,34,32F
Prof Emeritus	Anhalt, Istvan	D	13,10
Adj Lect	Baird, Dianne	M	61
Adj Lect	Beaudette, Eileen	B	62B
Adj Lect	Bolte, Barbara	B	64B
Adj Lect	Brunette, Chantal	B	63C,63D
Prof	Burge, John	D	13,10,10F,13I
Adj Lect	Cameron, David	M	66G
Adj Asst Prof	Craig, Gordon	M	37,64C,48,38,41
Adj Lect	Dalbec-Szczesniak, Gisele	M	62A,62B
Adj Asst Prof	Davidson, Tom	M	13B,66A,66D
Prof Emeritus	Fisher, Alfred	D	13,10
Assoc Prof	Frederickson, Karen	D	32,36,60A
Adj Asst Prof	Freeman, Peter	M	64E
Adj Lect	Gagnon, Sylvain	B	63D
Adj Asst Prof	Gartshore, Donelda	B	64A,48,67C
Adj Lect	Hanlon, Jeff	D	70,41
Prof Emeritus	Keane, David R.	M	13,10
Adj Lect	Kelly, Bruce	M	61,36
Adj Lect	Kwasniewska, Ewelina	M	61
Assoc Prof	Lamb, Roberta	D	32,15,67C
Adj Lect	Lee, Eric	B	62D
Adj Lect	Legere, Katie	B	64D
Adj Asst Prof	Lind, Stephanie	D	13B,13D,13E,13F
Asst Prof	Malyshko, Olga	D	12A,12,71,55
Assoc Prof	Marvin, Clara	D	12A,12,12E
Adj Lect	McDonald, Elizabeth	M	61
Adj Lect	Mozetich, Marjan	B	10
Adj Lect	Namer, Dina	M	66A,66C,66H
Assoc Prof	Pegley, Kip	D	14C,15,32E
Adj Lect	Ranganathan, Lakshmi	B	20E
Assoc Prof	Ravenscroft, Brenda	D	13,13F,13A
Adj Asst Prof	Reifel, Carol-Lynn	B	61
Asst Prof	Rogalsky, Matt	D	10,45,34,32F
Adj Assoc Prof	Runions, Greg	M	47,50,32,65
Adj Asst Prof	Shannon, Adrienne	D	66A,66C
Adj Lect	Shipp, Daniel	B	41
Adj Asst Prof	Sirett, Mark G.	D	36,60
Prof	Smith, Gordon E.	D	12,14,20G,12C
Adj Lect	Spaulding, Neil	B	63B
Adj Lect	Szczesniak, Michel	M	66A,66C
Adj Assoc Prof	Tormann, Cynthia	D	66A,13C,66D
Adj Lect	Tormann, Wolf	M	62C,51
Adj Lect	Tremblay, Dan	M	63A
Adj Asst Prof	Walker, Margaret Edith	D	14,12G,13K,20E,12A
Prof	Zuk, Ireneus	D	66A,66B

Page 13

AG0300 The Glenn Gould School of
The Royal Conservatory of Music
273 Bloor Street West
Toronto, ON M5S 1W2 Canada
(416) 408-2824 x 452   Fax: (416) 408-5025
www.rcmusic.ca/ggs
E-mail: glenngouldschool@rcmusic.ca

Post Secondary Music School offering professional programs; 2 and 4 Year programs

Artist Diploma, Performance Diploma

Dean: James Anagnoson, 80A
Managing Director: Cathy Blewett, 80A
President: Peter C. Simon, 80A
Registrar: Robin Lockert, 80D
Associate Dean: Barry Shiffman, 80H

Faculty	Abberger, John	M	67D
Faculty	Anagnoson, James	M	66A
Faculty	Atkinson, Keith	M	64B,42
Faculty	Bankas, Atis	M	62A
Faculty	Beach, David	PhD	13I
Faculty	Beecher, Jeffrey	B	62D
Faculty	Berard, Marie	DIPL	62A
Faculty	Bogle, Stephanie	B	61
Faculty	Burry, Dean	M	10
Faculty	Carletti, Marina		
Faculty	Chong, John	PhD	33
Faculty	Cullen, Burke	PhD	
Faculty	Current, Brian	D	43
Faculty	Dann, Steven	B	42,62B
Faculty	Deland, Neil	B	63B
Faculty	Diamond, Tom		
Faculty	Dorsey, Richard	M	64B
Faculty	Durand, Marc	M	66A
Faculty	Edison, Noel	B	36,60A
Faculty	Epperson, Bryan	DIPL	62C,42
Faculty	Esch, Michael	D	66A,12A
	Foley, Christopher	D	12A
	Galieva-Szokolay, Julia	D	13B,13C
Faculty	Goldhamer, Brahm	B	66C,39
Faculty	Gongos, Chris	B	63B,42
Faculty	Hall, Jeffrey	B	63D
Faculty	Hetherington, David	B	62C
Faculty	Howard, Markus	B	61
Faculty	Jackson, Fraser	M	64D
Faculty	Jackson, Nadina Mackie	DIPL	64D
Faculty	Jeffrey, Sarah	M	64B,42
Faculty	Johnson, Sasha	B	63D
Faculty	Jordan, Patrick	B	12A
Faculty	Kantor, Paul	M	62A
Faculty	Katz, Joel	B	61,12A
Faculty	Kent, David	M	65A,65B,42
Faculty	Kinton, Leslie	PhD	66A
Faculty	Kwan, Andrew	B	35F
Faculty	Lamon, Jeanne	M	67B
Faculty	Littler, William	B	11
Faculty	Loman, Judy	DIPL	62E
Faculty	Longworth, Peter	DIPL	42,66C
Faculty	Lopinski, Janet	D	12A
Faculty	Louie, David	M	66A
Faculty	MacPhail, Jean	B	61
Faculty	Markow, Andrew	DIPL	12A,66B
Faculty	Mayer, Uri	DIPL	60B,38
Faculty	McCandless, Andrew		63A,42
Faculty	McLean, Kathleen	DIPL	64D
Faculty	Mehringer, Richard	M	
Faculty	Monoyios, Ann	M	67H
Faculty	Nedecky, Jason	M	40
Faculty	Nediger, Charlotte	M	67F
Faculty	Newman, Leslie	M	64A,42
Faculty	Orlov, Marietta	M	66A
Faculty	Perry, John	M	66A
Faculty	Petrenko, Jurgen	M	40
Faculty	Philcox, Stephen	M	66C
Faculty	Rappoport, Katharine	M	12A
Faculty	Raum, Erika	B	62A,42
Faculty	Roslak, Roxolana	DIPL	61
Faculty	Rudolph, John	M	65B
Faculty	Rudolph, Kathleen	D	64A,42
Faculty	Seiler, Mayumi	M	62A
Faculty	Sherman, Donna	B	61
Faculty	Shiffman, Barry	B	42
Faculty	Silva-Marin, Guillermo		
Faculty	Skazinetsky, Mark		62A
Faculty	Smiley, Jayne	B	
Faculty	Sweeney, Michael	M	64D
Faculty	Tarver, Jennifer		
Faculty	Tchoubar, Katerina	B	
Faculty	Thurgood, George	M	13,29
Faculty	Tiefenbach, Peter	M	12A,66C
Faculty	Tung, Jennifer		66C
Faculty	Valdepenas, Joaquin	M	64C
Faculty	Wang, Li	DIPL	66A
Faculty	Weckstrom, Virginia	B	42,66C
Faculty	Werner, Dianne	B	66A
Faculty	Whicher, Monica	DIPL	61
Faculty	White, Michael	B	34
Faculty	Widner, Paul	B	62C,42
Faculty	Wolfe, Gordon	M	63C,42

AG0350 Univ of Guelph
School of Fine Art & Music
Zavitz Hall Room 201
Guelph, ON N1G 2W1 Canada
(519) 824-4120 x 53988   Fax: (519) 821-5482
www.uoguelph.ca/sofam
E-mail: rmcginni@uoguelph.ca

4 Year Institution

Director: John Kissick, 80A

PT	Aldcroft, Ken		70
FT	Carter, Shannon	M	11,12,13A
PT	Collins, Rosemary		66A
PT	Davidson, Dave		63C
PT	Evans, Glyn		61
Asst Prof	Francis, Kimberly	D	15,13,12
PT	French, Bruce	B	70
PT	Goddard, John		48,65
Assoc Prof	Harley, James I.	D	10B,10A,34
PT	Janzen, Henry	M	42,62B,62A
PT	Klaehn, Andrew		64C,64E
PT	Knelman, Jennifer		13A,11
PT	Maher, Betty		66C
PT	Maness, Jane	B	63D
Assoc Prof	McCarthy, Marta	D	60A,36,13C
PT	McGillvray, Bruce		70
FT	McKittrick, Cam	M	34
PT	Orlando, Joe		70
PT	Sorbara, Joe		43,65
Asst Prof	Spring, Howard	D	14,70,29,12A,13D
PT	Swinden, Laurel		64A
PT	Thibodeau, Theresa		61
PT	Warren, Ted		47

AG0400 Univ of Ottawa
School of Music
50 University
Ottawa, ON K1N 6N5 Canada
(613) 562-5733   Fax: (613) 562-5140
www.music.uottawa.ca
E-mail: music@uottawa.ca

4 Year Institution, Graduate School

Master of Arts in Music Theory, Master of Arts in Musicology, Master of Music

Director: Lori Burns, 80A
Chair: Stephane Lemelin, 80A
Coord., Cultural Activities: Hali Krawchuk, 80F

Adj Prof	Armstrong, John	D	13,10F,10
PT	Brown, Donna		61
PT	Burden, Douglas	B	63C,37,41
Prof	Burns, Lori	D	13,14C
PT	Candelaria, Philip	B	70
PT	Casagrande, Angela		64B
PT	Churchfield, Camille		64A
Assoc Prof	Comeau, Gilles	D	32,13
Prof	Currie, David	B	60,38,41,62D
Prof	Dineen, P. Murray	D	13,12
PT	Donegani, Denis	B	70
PT	Donnelly, Karen		63A
Assoc Prof	Ewashko, Laurence J.	DIPL	32,36
Emeritus	Gellman, Steven	DIPL	13,10F,10
PT	Godin, Jon-Thomas		13
PT	Graham, Sandra		61,39
Other	Gress, Daniel	M	63B
PT	Hamann, Charles	M	64B
PT	Herbiet, Victor	M	64E
PT	Hodgins, Glenn		35
PT	Holmes, Karen	M	55,66G,66H
Asst Prof	Jalbert, David	M	
Vstng Prof	Korjus, Ingemar	DIPL	39,61
PT	Labrosse, Martin		63D
PT	Lacroix, Frederic	D	66A
PT	Laroche, Yves	B	46,47
Prof	Lemelin, Stephane	D	66,41
Assoc Prof	Marleyn, Paul	DIPL	62C
Prof	Merkley, Paul	D	12
PT	Millard, Christopher		64D

Asst Prof	Moore, Christopher	D	12A,12B,12D
Assoc Prof	Parmer, Dillon	M	11,12,12B,12C
Asst Prof	Pedneault-Deslauriers, Julie	D	13,10
PT	Prefontaine, Paule	B	62A
Assoc Prof	Prevost, Roxane	D	13
Vstng Prof	Regehr, Rennie	M	62B,42
PT	Renshaw, Don		63C
PT	Roux, Patrick	DIPL	70
PT	Rupp, Eric	M	63A
PT	Rupp, Susan		
Prof Emeritus	Sevilla, Jean-Paul		66A,42
PT	Simpson, Ken		65
Assoc Prof	Stewart, David		62A,41
PT	Sykes, Kimball	B	64C
PT	Tanno-Kimmons, Yoriko		61
PT	Trepanier, Louis		70
Prof	Tunis, Andrew	M	41,66A
PT	Wade, Jonathan	B	65
PT	Woods, Alyssa	M	13

AG0450 Univ of Toronto
Faculty of Music
Edward Johnson Bldg
Toronto, ON M5S 2C5 Canada
(416) 978-3750   Fax: (416) 946-3353
www.music.utoronto.ca
E-mail: undergrad.music@utoronto.ca

4 Year Institution, Graduate School

Graduate Certificate in Performance, Master of Music in Composition, Master of Music in Performance, Master of Music in Music Education, PhD in Music Education, Doctor of Music in Composition, PhD in Musicology, Master of Arts in Musicology, Diploma in Operatic Performance

Dean: Russell Hartenberger, 80A
Associate Dean, Undergraduate Education: Robin W. Elliott, 80B,80H
Associate Dean, Graduate Education: Gillian MacKay, 80C,80H

Prof	Aide, William	B	66A,66B,41,66C
Inst PT	Aitken, Dianne		64A
Senior Lect	Albano, Michael	B	39
Inst PT	Albrecht, Peg	M	64A
Prof	Apfelstadt, Hilary		32D
Adj Prof	Armenian, Raffi		60,38
Inst PT	Atkinson, Keith		64B
Inst PT	Bach, Mia		66C
Inst PT	Bambrick, Heather		61,29
Inst PT	Barnes, Peter		61
Assoc Prof	Bartel, Lee R.	D	32
Prof	Beach, David	D	13E,13I,13J
Prof Emeritus	Beckwith, John	M	10,20G
	Beecher, Jeffrey		62D
Inst PT	Bentley, JoAnne	M	61
Inst PT	Berard, Marie		62A
Inst PT	Bergs, Roger		10
Prof Emeritus	Berman, Melvin		
Inst PT	Blackman, Daniel		62B
Inst PT	Blaser, Lynn	B	61
Inst PT	Borys, Roman		62C
Inst PT	Bourque, David	M	48,37,38,64C,60B
Assoc Prof	Bowen, William	D	12A
Inst PT	Bradley, Deborah	D	32,66
Inst PT	Braid, David		29,66A
Asst Prof	Briskin, David		60B
Inst PT	Brownell, John	B	32,65
Inst PT	Bryce, Pandora E.	M	64A
Prof Emeritus	Buczynski, Walter		13,10F,10,66A
Asst Prof	Cain, M. Celia		12,20G
Inst PT	Carli, Rob		64E
Inst PT	Carver, Kate		39
Prof Emeritus	Chenette, Stephen	M	37,41,63A
Inst PT	Christie, Max		64C
Prof Emeritus	Ciamaga, Gustav	M	13,10,45,34
Assoc Prof	Clark, Caryl L.	D	12A,12
Inst PT	Clarke, Terry		65,29
Prof Emeritus	Craig, James		39
Inst PT	Cullen, John		60B
Inst PT	Dahlen, Sienna		61
Inst PT	Dawes, Christopher		66A
Inst PT	Dawson, Tim		62D
Inst PT	Dean, Alex		64E
Assoc Prof	Dolloff, Lori-Anne	D	32A,32B,60,36,66C
Inst PT	Donnelly, Chris		66A
Inst PT	Dorsey, Richard		64B
Inst PT	Dowling, Thomas		32,64C
Inst PT	Downing, Andrew		29
Inst PT	Duncan, Christine		29
Inst PT	Dunyo, Fred		20A
Inst PT	Duplessis, Ginette		61
Assoc Prof	Edwards, Darryl		61
Prof	Elliott, Robin W.	D	12,12A,20G
Inst PT	Englert, Don		64E

Prof	Falck, Robert A.	D	11,12A,12
Inst PT	Fallis, David		12A
Inst PT	Finch, Mary-Katherine		62C
Inst PT	Fratia, Salvatore		63D
Inst PT	Freeman, Graham		12A
Inst PT	Geringas, Marina	M	66A
Inst PT	Gongos, Chris		63B
Assoc Prof	Gould, Elizabeth	D	32
Inst PT	Grant, Allison		39
Inst PT	Grant, Andrea		39
Prof	Haines, John D.	D	12A,12,20F
Inst PT	Haines, Mary Enid		67
Prof Emeritus	Hall, Doreen		32
Inst PT	Hall, Jeffrey		63D
Inst PT	Halladay, Wallace	D	64E
Prof	Harmantas, Frank	M	41,49
Prof	Hartenberger, Russell	D	50,65,53
Prof	Hatzis, Christos	D	10,35H,34,35C,13L
Inst PT	Helmer, Terence		41,62B
Inst PT	Hennigar, Harcus	B	63B
Inst PT	Hoeppner, Susan	B	64A
Prof Emeritus	Holman, Derek	D	13,10
Senior Lect	Horst, Sandra	M	39
Prof	Hughes, Andrew	D	11,12,13J,12G
Senior Lect	Im, Miah		39
Inst PT	Israelievitch, Jacques		62A
Inst PT	Jackson, Fraser	M	64D
Inst PT	Jasavala, John	M	63C
Inst PT	John, Bina	D	32
Inst PT	Johnson, John		64C
Inst PT	Johnston, Beverley	B	65
Assoc Prof	Johnston, Gregory	D	11,12A,12,31A
Inst PT	Kassner, Eli		70
Inst PT	Katz, Brian	B	32
Prof Emeritus	Kenins, Talivaldis	B	10
Inst PT	Kimura, Etsuko		62A
Assoc Prof	Kippen, James R.	D	12A,14
Assoc Prof	Koga, Midori	D	66A,66D
Asst Prof	Komisaruk, Kevin M.	D	66
Senior Lect	Kruspe, John	B	13
Lect	Kulesha, Gary		10,63C,29
Inst PT	Kuzmenko, Larysa	B	13A,13,66A
Inst PT	Kwan, Andrew		35B
Inst PT	Lewis, Jim		29,47
Inst PT	Li, Teng		62B
Inst PT	Loewen, Che Anne	M	61,66A
Inst PT	Loman, Judy		62E
Inst PT	Lukiwski, Terry		29,63C
Inst PT	Lysenko, Boris	D	66A
Inst PT	MacDonald, Kirk		29
Prof	MacDonald, Lorna E.	M	61
Inst PT	Macerollo, Joseph	M	68
Prof	MacKay, Gillian	D	37,42,63A,60B,60
Inst PT	Mackie-Jackson, Nadina		64D
Inst PT	MacPhail, Jean		61
Prof Emeritus	Maniates, Maria R.	D	11,12A,12,12B
Inst PT	Markow, Andrew		66A
Inst PT	Martinelli, Lisa	M	29,61,47
Inst PT	Martins, Sandra Lau	D	61
Assoc Prof	Mayo, John	D	12A,12
Asst Prof	McClelland, Ryan	D	13
Inst PT	McDonagh, Brian	M	66A
Inst PT	McEvenue, Kelly		39
Inst PT	McFadden, Jeffrey	M	70
Prof Emeritus	McGee, Timothy J.	D	12A,12,55
Inst PT	McLaren, Robert	B	65,29
Inst PT	McLean, Kathleen	DIPL	64D
	McMorrow, Kathleen	B	16
Inst PT	Melville, Alison	M	32,67B
Inst PT	Metcalf, Curtis	M	63
Inst PT	Metelsky, Lynda	M	66A
	Meyers Sawa, Suzanne	M	16
Inst PT	Miller, Rob		
Prof Emeritus	Morawetz, Oskar	M	10
Prof Emeritus	Morey, Carl	D	11,12A,12,20G
Inst PT	Morrison, Mary		61
Inst PT	Morton, Joelle		67
Inst PT	Murley, Michael		64E,29
Inst PT	Nagata, Gary		20D,65
Inst PT	Nediger, Charlotte		66H
Inst PT	Neill, Dave	M	29
Inst PT	Nelsen, Jeff		63B
Inst PT	Newman, Leslie		64A
Inst PT	Nimmons, Phil	B	32,47,29
Prof	Nin, Chan Ka	D	13A,13,10,10F
Inst PT	Occhipinti, David		70,29
Inst PT	Oh, Gregory		66A
Inst PT	Orlov, Marietta	M	66A
Inst PT	Orlowski, Joseph		64C
Lect	Packman, Jeffrey L.		13J
Asst Prof	Palej, Norbert	D	10,13
Assoc Prof	Parker, James	D	66A,66C
Assoc Prof	Parker, Mary Ann	D	11,12A,12
Inst PT	Parr, Patricia		66A
Inst PT	Patipatanakoon, Annalee	DIPL	62A
Senior Lect	Patrick, Dennis M.	M	13,45,13L,34,35C
Inst PT	Patterson, Roy		29
Inst PT	Pellegrino, Francesco		
Inst PT	Petchersky, Alma		66A
Asst Prof	Philcox, Steven		66A

Inst PT	Pierre, Stephen		64C
Asst Prof	Pilzer, Joshua	D	14
Inst PT	Poloz, Zimfira		32
Asst Prof	Promane, Terry	DIPL	29,47
Inst PT	Radford, Gabe		63B
Inst PT	Raferty, Patrick		61
Assoc Prof	Ralls, Stephen	M	39
Assoc Prof	Rao, Doreen	D	32,36,60,61
Lect	Rapoport, Alexander	M	13
Inst PT	Rapoport, Katharine	M	62A,62B
Inst PT	Raum, Erika		62A
Assoc Prof	Read, Paul	M	47,29
Inst PT	Relyea, Gary		61
Inst PT	Restivo, Dave		66A,29
Senior Lect	Reynolds, Jeffrey L.	D	49,63A,37,29A
Inst PT	Richardson, Abby		13
Asst Prof	Ries, Tim		29
Inst PT	Robertson, Eric		10,13
Inst PT	Robinson, Gerald	B	64D
Inst PT	Rogers, Paul		62
Inst PT	Rolfe, James		10,13
Assoc Prof	Rolston, Shauna	M	62C
Inst PT	Rudolph, John	M	50
Inst PT	Sanborn, Chase		63A,29
Inst PT	Sanger, Annette	D	20D
Prof Emeritus	Schabas, Ezra	M	32
Inst PT	Scholtz, Clare	M	64B
Inst PT	Schwing-Braun, Eraine		61
Prof	Shand, Patricia	D	32C,51,62A,62B
Inst PT	Shields, Larry		32,63C
Inst PT	Shulman, Nora	B	64A
Asst Prof	Sicsic, Henri-Paul	D	66A
Inst PT	Sicsic, Nancy		66A
Inst PT	Simonelli, John		63B
Inst PT	Skazinetsky, Mark		62A
Inst PT	Spragg, James		63A
Asst Prof	Stanbridge, Alan	D	12
Inst PT	Stewart, Douglas		64A
Inst PT	Stoll, Peter	M	64C
Asst Prof	Stowe, Cameron	D	66A,66C
Inst PT	Sweeney, Gordon	DIPL	63C
Inst PT	Sweeney, Michael	M	64D
Inst PT	Tait, Edward		62D
Inst PT	Taurins, Ivars		67A
Inst PT	Tetreault, Mark		63D
Inst PT	Thomson, Richard		64C
Inst PT	Tkachenko, Tanya		66A
Inst PT	Toyich, Boyanna	B	66A
Inst PT	Turcotte, Kevin	B	63A
Inst PT	Tuttle, John	B	36,31A
Inst PT	Upchurch, Elizabeth		39
Inst PT	Valdepenas, Joaquin		64C
Inst PT	Vivian, Jim	B	62D,29
Assoc Prof	Walter, Cameron	D	32,63C,63D,37,44
Inst PT	Watson, Joan		63B
Inst PT	Watts, Camille	B	64C
Prof Emeritus	Weinzweig, John	M	10
Inst PT	Whale, Mark		32
Inst PT	Whicker, Monica		
Inst PT	Widner, Paul		62,38
Inst PT	Williamson, Gary		66A
Inst PT	Wolfe, Gordon		63C
Inst PT	Wong, Lydia		66A
Inst PT	Woomert, Barton R.		63A
Inst PT	Wright, Patricia	D	66
Senior Lect	Wright, William	B	13,66G
Inst PT	Young, David		62D
Inst PT	Young, Geoff		70
Inst PT	Yu, Helen		61

AG0470 Univ of Waterloo

Department of Music
Conrad Grebel University
140 Westmount Rd N
Waterloo, ON N2L 3G6 Canada
(519) 885-0220 x 24226   Fax: (519) 885-0014
uwaterloo.ca/music
E-mail: music@uwaterloo.ca

4 Year Institution

Chair: Laura J. Gray, 80A
Undergraduate Officer: Kenneth Hull, 80B

Prof	Enns, Leonard J.	D	13,60,10,36
Assoc Prof	Gray, Laura J.	D	11,12A,12,14,20
Assoc Prof	Hull, Kenneth	D	11,12A,31A,36
Assoc Prof	Weaver, Carol Ann	D	13,10,12,20A,29A

AG0500 Univ of Western Ontario

Don Wright Faculty of Music
Talbot College
1151 Richmond St
London, ON N6A 3K7 Canada
(519) 661-2043   Fax: (519) 661-3531
www.music.uwo.ca
E-mail: music@uwo.ca

4 Year Institution, Graduate School

Artist Diploma, Master of Arts in Music Theory, Master of Music in Composition, Master of Music in Music Education, PhD in Music, Master of Arts in Musicology, Master of Music in Performance & Literature, Master of Arts in Popular Music & Culture

Dean: Robert Wood, 80A
Dean: Betty Anne Younker, 80A
Associate Dean, Undergraduate: Victoria Meredith, 80B
Associate Dean, Graduate: Richard S. Parks, 80C

Lect PT	Abbott, Norman	M	62C
Lect PT	Adams, Brent		63D
Emeritus	Aldrich, Ralph E.	B	41,51,62A,62B
	Ansari, Emily	M	12
Lect PT	Audet, Peter	M	63A
Assoc Prof	Baerg, Theodore	B	39,61
Prof Emerita	Bailey, Kathryn	M	13
Prof Emeritus	Bailey, Terence	D	12,12C
Lect PT	Bakan, Jonathon E.		12
Adj PT	Ball, Jill	D	65
Lect PT	Barron, Virginia		62B
Lect PT	Bartley, Peter	B	32A,62A
Lect PT	Beamish, Gwen	M	66A,66B
Prof Emeritus	Behrens, Jack	D	13,10,20G
Prof	Bracey, John-Paul	M	66A,66B
Prof Emerita	Bratuz, Damjana	D	66A,66B
Lect PT	Brubacher, Scott		13
Lect PT	Chiles, Torin W.	M	61
Prof Emeritus	Clements, Peter J.	M	13,10,45
Assoc Prof	Coates, Norma	D	12A,12D,15,35A
	Collins, Peter		63C
Lect PT	Conrod, Derek	B	63B
Asst Prof	Cuciurean, John D.	D	13
Asst Prof	Daniel, Omar	D	13,10,10F,34,35C
Lect PT	Davidson, Sarah		62E
Prof Emerita	Dixon, Gail S.	D	13
Prof Emeritus	Downs, Philip	D	12,13J
Lect PT	Dunn-Prosser, Barbara	M	61
Lect PT	Emond, Paul		
Prof	Fiske, Harold	D	32,12F
Lect PT	Fleet, Ken	M	32D
	Franck, Peter	D	13
Lect PT	Franklin, Ian	B	64B
Asst Prof	Frehner, Paul	D	13,10
Lect PT	Gassi, Gloria	M	36,32
Lect PT	George, Ron	B	63B
Prof Emeritus	Giron, Arsenio	M	13,10
Asst Prof	Goehring, Edmund J.	D	12A,12E
Lect PT	Gorbasew, A. 'Sasha'	B	63B
Prof Emeritus	Green, J. Paul	D	60,12B,32,12C
Asst Prof	Green, Patricia D.	M	61
Prof	Grier, James	D	12,13J
Prof Emeritus	Heard, Alan	M	13,10F,10
Lect PT	Helsen, Katherine E.	D	12C
	Herrington, Carolyn A.		66A
Asst Prof	Hess, John	D	66A,66C,41,39
Lect PT	Hibbard, James		66A
Asst Prof	Hodgson, Aaron	M	63A
Asst Prof	Hodgson, Jay	D	14,29,35C,35D,12
Prof Emeritus	Hughes, Robert	M	32,50,65
Lect PT	Jasavala, John	M	63C
Prof Emeritus	Johnson, Deral J.	M	60,36
	Johnson, Marie		64C
Lect PT	Kalman, Zoltan		64C
	Kinton, Leslie	ABD	66A
Prof	Koprowski, Peter P.	D	13,10
Lect PT	Krause Wiebe, Anita		61
Lect PT	Kubica, Robert	M	70
Lect PT	Laidlaw, George	M	64E
Lect PT	Laing, Laurence 'Corky'	B	12
Lect PT	Lanza, Joseph	B	38,41,51,62A
Lect PT	Little, Gwenlynn		61
	Loo, Janet	M	61,32D
Lect PT	Lundberg, Kim	M	13,10F
Lect PT	Mallon, Rachel	M	61
Assoc Prof	Mangsen, Sandra	D	12,66H
Lect PT	Martin, Melvin		62A
Lect PT	McCumber, Gary	B	37,41
Prof Emeritus	McIntosh, John S.	D	13,66G,66C,31A
Prof	McKay, James R.	M	37,38,41,64D,12F
Prof Emeritus	McKellar, Donald A.	M	60,32
Prof Emeritus	McLean, Hugh J.	M	12,14A,66G,31A
Lect PT	Menard, Aileen		12A

Adj Prof PT	Meredith, Henry M.	D	32,63A,63B,67E
Assoc Prof	Meredith, Victoria	D	60,32,36,41
Lect PT	Moir, Jennifer	M	36,61
Asst Prof	Mooney, Kevin	D	13,13J,12C
Assoc Prof	Myska, David	D	13,10,45,34,35C
Assoc Prof	Neufeld, Gerald	D	36,55D,60,32
Assoc Prof	Neville, Donald	D	12A,12,12B
Assoc Prof	Nolan, Catherine	D	13,13J
Lect PT	O'Neill, Amy	B	64A
	O'Neill, Susan	D	32
Prof	Parks, Richard S.	D	13
	Payne, Mark	M	66C
Lect PT	Piche, Rick	B	70
Prof Emeritus	Reimer, Alvin H.	B	61
Asst Prof	Richardson, Colleen	D	60B,37,32E,41,42
Emeritus	Riseling, Robert A.	D	13,37,38,41,64C
Asst Prof	Roland-Wieczorek, Sophie	D	61
Adj PT	Rudolph, Kathleen	D	64A
Lect PT	Sarma, Barbara		
Lect PT	Schultz, Kirsten M.		20
Assoc Prof	Semmens, Richard	D	12,13J,55,67B,13L
Lect PT	Shackleton, Peter	B	64C
Lect PT	Short, Jackalyn	B	61
Prof Emeritus	Skelton, Robert A.	D	60,38,41,51,62
Lect PT	Smith, Bruce	B	47
Lect PT	Spicer, Shawn	M	63A
Lect PT	Steele, Sherry		61
Assoc Prof	Stokes, Jeffrey	D	12,62D
Prof Emeritus	Summers, Jerome	M	60,38,64C,67B,43
Asst Prof	Sylvestre, Stephan	M	66A
Prof Emeritus	Tait, Malcolm		62C
	Tandberg, Irene		62A
Lect PT	Thompson, Anne	M	64A
Lect PT	Thompson, Bobbi Amanda		64E
Prof	Toft, Robert	D	10D,12A,12C,13J
Emeritus	Turini, Ronald		41,66A
Lect PT	Usher, Barry	B	64C
Lect PT	Van Berkel, Wilma		70
Asst Prof	Veblen, Kari	D	32A,32B
Asst Prof	Vogel, Annette-Barbara	DIPL	62A
Lect PT	Whalen, Laura	B	61
Lect PT	Wiebe, Allison	M	66A
Asst Prof	Wiebe, Thomas	D	62C,41
Lect PT	Wieczorek, Todd	D	61
Assoc Prof	Wilkinson, Fiona	M	48,64A
Lect PT	Wood, Rachel	M	61
Assoc Prof	Wood, Robert	D	32C,34,12F,12,12C
Asst Prof	Woodford, Paul	M	60,12B,32,37,63
Assoc Prof	Wright, Ruth	D	32
Lect PT	Yanchus, Tina	M	66A
Prof	Younker, Betty Anne	D	32

AG0550 Univ of Windsor
School of Music
401 Sunset Ave
Windsor, ON N9B 3P4 Canada
(519) 253-3000 x 2780   Fax: (519) 971-3614
www.uwindsor.ca/music
E-mail: music@uwindsor.ca

4 Year Institution

Music Contact: Philip I. Adamson, 80A
Dir., Admissions: Dorothy McMahon, 80D

Assoc Prof	Adamson, Philip I.	D	66A,66B,66C,13C,66C
Inst PT	Andrew, Lesley	M	61
Inst PT	Benton, Robert	M	63D
Assoc Prof	Bick, Sally M.	D	12
Inst PT	Bloom, Bradley	D	36
Prof Emeritus	Butler, E. Gregory	D	66A,66B
Asst Prof	Clements-Cortes, Amy	D	33
Inst PT	Cox, Gregory	B	32E
Emeritus PT	Dearing, Steven	M	70
Inst PT	Dwyer, Peggy	M	61
Inst PT	Fazecash, Robert	B	46,47,63A,29
Prof Emeritus	Henrikson, Steven	M	61
Inst PT	Inselman, Elsie	M	61
Inst PT	Karloff, Michael		29,46,66A
Inst PT	Klugh, Vaughn	M	70,29,46,61
Assoc Prof	Lee, Brent	D	13,10,45,43,53
Inst PT	Ley, Amy	M	62E
Inst PT	Litke, David	D	13
Inst PT	Lockwood, Timothy		63B
Inst PT	McIntosh, Andrew	M	62C
Inst PT	Moor, Ric	M	37
Inst PT	Nurullah, Shahida	B	29,46,61
Prof Emeritus	Palmer, David	M	66A,66G,31A,13C,66H
Asst Prof	Papador, Nicholas G.	D	13A,13B,13D,65,32E
Inst PT	Penny, Nicholas		62B
Inst PT	Price, Jeffrey	M	64E,29,46
Inst PT	Robilliard, David	M	65
Inst PT	Scheirich, Lillian	B	62A
Inst PT	Scholfield, Faith	M	64B
Inst PT	Sheldon, Gregory	B	62D
Inst PT	Stone, Michael	B	63C
Inst PT	Sun, Liyan	M	61
Inst PT	Turner, Ross		63A
Inst PT	Varner, Eric Van der Veer	D	64D
Inst PT	Wagner, Jaimie	M	64A
Asst Prof	Waldron, Janice Lynn	D	32

AG0600 Wilfrid Laurier University
Faculty of Music
75 University Ave W
Waterloo, ON N2L 3C5 Canada
(519) 884-0710 x 2956   Fax: (519) 747-9129
www.wlu.ca
E-mail: jdobbin@wlu.ca

4 Year Institution

Master of Music in Music Therapy

Dean: Charles D. Morrison, 80A

Assoc Prof	Ahonen-Eerikainen, Heidi	D	33
Artist in Res	Alexeyev, Anya	DIPL	66A
Assoc Prof	Arnason, Carolyn	D	33
Asst Prof	Barber, Kimberly	B	61
PT	Bauman, Carol	M	13,65
PT	Baumgartel, Julie	M	62A
Artist in Res	Bell, Jeremy	D	62A
PT	Bingig, Mariann	B	61
Other	Brickman, Nina	B	63B,48
Prof	Buhr, Glenn	D	10,53
Prof Emeritus	Cabena, Barrie	DIPL	66G
PT	Campion, David	B	65
PT	Castello, Joseph	M	63C
PT	Catlin-Smith, Linda	M	10
PT	Coleman, Cedric	M	64D
Accompanist	De Sousa, Beth Ann	M	13,39,66C
Prof	De'Ath, Leslie	M	66A,39
PT	Edwards, Ross		64C,48
PT	Falkenberger, Kristen	B	33
Assoc Prof	Ferenc, Anna	D	13,13F
PT	Ferretti, Joseph A.	M	66A
PT	Few, Guy	B	63A,49
PT	Finnerty, Rachel	M	33
Accompanist	Froese, Elvera	B	39,66C,36
Artist in Res	Fryer, Simon	DIPL	62C
PT	Gallas, Heidi	M	13
PT	Gemmell, Lori		62E
PT	Grant, Denise	D	37,60
Prof Emeritus	Greene, Gordon K.	D	12A
PT	Greenidge, Evelyn	B	33
PT	Greer, George	B	62D
Prof	Hamilton, Amy	D	64A
PT	Hankins, Barbara	M	64C
PT	Harris, Rob	M	33
Prof	Hatch, Peter	D	13,10
PT	Hiebert, Cynthia	M	66H
PT	Houde, Marc	M	33
	Jackson, Nadina Mackie	DIPL	64D
Assoc Prof	Kaplanek, Jerzy	M	41,62A
PT	Kroetsch, Terence	M	13,66D,66A
PT	Lacoste, Debra	D	12A
PT	Lau, Elaine	M	66A
Prof	Lee, Colin	D	53,33
PT	LeMessurier, Susan	M	33
Assoc Prof	Lichti, Daniel	DIPL	61
PT	Ludolph, Deborah	B	61
PT	Maness, Jane	B	63D
Prof Emeritus	Martens, Victor	B	61
Other	Mason, James	M	64B
PT	McAlister, Anita		63A
PT	McBay, Brian	B	33
Prof Emeritus	McDonald, Boyd	DIPL	66A
PT	McKenna, Terry		70,67D
PT	McKinnon, Taryn	B	33
PT	McKittrick, Cam	M	13
PT	Mieske, Lynda	B	61
PT	Mitchell, Elizabeth	M	33
PT	Montgomery, Joy	M	63B
Prof	Morrison, Charles D.	D	13
PT	Nagtegaal, Marlin	M	66G
PT	O'Donnell, Kevin	B	64A
Prof	Pulford, Paul	DIPL	41,62C,38
Assoc Prof	Purves-Smith, Michael	M	60,37,55,10F
PT	Purves-Smith, Shannon	B	67B
Prof	Santosuosso, Alma	D	12A
PT	Schirm, Ronald	B	47,29
PT	Seabrook, Deborah	M	33
Assoc Prof	Swinden, Kevin J.	D	13,13B,13C
Assoc Prof	Taves, Heather	D	66A,66B
PT	Telner, Susan	D	66A
PT	Thomas, Rachel	B	63C
PT	VanWeelden, Marnie	D	66A
PT	Vascotto, Norma	D	12A,11,20

PT	Veeraraghauen, Lee	M	13
Artist in Res	Vlajk, Christine	M	62B
PT	Wagler, Trevor	M	13
PT	Wiffen, Dave	M	64E
Assoc Prof	Willingham, Lee	D	32,36
PT	Windeyer, Richard	M	34
Asst Prof	Yri, Kirsten	M	12A
PT	Yun, Gerard J.	D	36

AG0650 York University

Department of Music
4700 Keele St/371 Accolade E Bldg
North York Toronto, ON M3J 1P3 Canada
(416) 736-5186   Fax: (416) 736-5321
www.yorku.ca/finearts/music/index.htm
E-mail: zuechl@yorku.ca

4 Year Institution, Graduate School

Master of Arts in Composition, Master of Arts in Ethnomusicology, PhD in Ethnomusicology, PhD in Musicology, Master of Arts in Musicology, Master of Arts in Jazz, Master of Music in Accompanying & Chamber Music, Master of Arts in Popular Music, PhD in Jazz, PhD in Popular Music

Chair: Louise Wrazen, 80A
Dir., Graduate Studies: Lisette M. Canton, 80C
Associate Chair: William Thomas, 80H

PT	Ackerman, Barbara	B	64A
PT	Adams, Mimmie	B	47
	Akrong, Isaac		20B
PT	Beauvais, William	B	70
Prof Emeritus	Beckwith, Sterling	D	12,36,61,12F
PT	Black, Susan		66C,61,60A
PT	Bogle, Stephanie	B	61
Assoc Prof	Bowman, Rob	PhD	14,20G,29A
PT	Brownell, John	M	65,50
PT	Brubeck, Matthew	M	43,53,62C
PT	Burgess, Gareth		20H
PT	Burgess, Lindy		20H
Assoc Prof	Burke, Karen M.	B	61,60A,36,32
PT	Burrowes, Norma		61
PT	Butler, Corey		61
PT	Cado, Michael	M	10A,32,47,70
Assoc Prof	Canton, Lisette M.	D	36,55,60
PT	Caplan, Linda	B	20C
Asst Prof	Chambers, Mark K.	D	38,60,62
PT	Chan, Patty		20C
Prof Emeritus	Clarkson, Austin	D	12,32
Assoc Prof	Coghlan, Michael	M	13,10,29,34,43
PT	Cohen, Judith	PhD	20,55C,55A,32E
PT	Colenbrander, Caroline		32E
	Davidson, Tara		64E
Assoc Prof	De Val, Dorothy	PhD	12
PT	Di Ghent, Rita	M	61
PT	Dunyo, Kwasi		20B
PT	Eisenman, Mark	B	47,66A
Assoc Prof	Elmes, Barry	B	47,29
PT	Esguerra, Ruben		20H
PT	Falco, Frank	B	47,66A
PT	Farrugia, Adrean	B	66A
Prof Emeritus	Gittins, John	M	29,13,47
PT	Graves, Larry		20B
Emeritus	Greer, Albert	B	36,61
PT	Hamper, Robert	B	47
Asst Prof	Henderson, Alan E.	M	47,29,46
PT	Hills, Peggy	B	62A,62B
PT	Hong, Charles	B	20C
Asst Prof	Israelievitch, Jacques		62A,62B,38
PT	Jefferson, Kelly	M	29,64E
Asst Prof	Johnson, Sherry A.		20
PT	Katz, Brian	B	70,53
PT	Koven, Steven	B	53,66A
PT	Lazar, Richard	B	20H
Asst Prof	Levine, Art D.		13
Prof Emeritus	Lidov, David	M	10
PT	Lofsky, Lorne		47,70
PT	Lum, David		63D
PT	MacDonald, James	M	63B,49
Assoc Prof	Marcuzzi, Michael	PhD	32,20H,14
PT	Markoff, Irene	PhD	14,20
PT	Marshall, Sharon		61
Assoc Prof	Martin, Stephanie	M	12A,55,60
PT	McDonald, Lynn	B	61
PT	Melnikoff, Anna	B	20B
Prof	Mott, David	D	13A,10
PT	Naimpally, Ravi	B	20E
PT	Nakhmanovich, Raisa	B	66A,66C
PT	Nelson, Ron		14C
PT	Obermeyer, Janet	B	61
PT	Ormandy, Paul		20H
Prof Emeritus	Otto, Steven	D	11,14,13L
PT	Patterson, Roy	M	47,70
Prof	Petrowska-Quilico, Christina	M	13A,41,66A,66B
Prof	Rahn, Jay	PhD	13,12
Asst Prof	Robbin, Catherine	B	61
PT	Romberg, Barry		65
PT	Roth, Arthur	B	62D
PT	Rymal, Karen	B	66C,61
Prof	Sankaran, Trichy	M	20D
PT	Scannura, Roger		70
PT	Seguin, Philip		63A
PT	Shahouk, Bassam	M	20C
Assoc Prof	Simms, Rob	PhD	20,14
PT	Sinclair, Terrol	B	32
PT	Sinsoulier, Melisande		60A
Assoc Prof	Sokol, Casey	M	13A,66A,53,43
PT	Sue, Phig Choy		20C
	Tait, Edward		62D
Asst Prof	Thomas, William	B	32F,37,38
PT	Turcotte, Kevin	B	47,63A
	Van der Bliek, Rob		12,14C,29
Asst Prof	VanderWoude, Matthew	M	14C
Assoc Prof	Viswanathan, Sundar	M	29,64E,10D,61
PT	Vivian, Jim		47,62D
Assoc Prof	Wait, Patricia	M	41,64C,13A,12A
PT	Wallace, Sharlene		62E
Emeritus	Werren, Philip	M	10F,10,45
Assoc Prof Emeritus	Westcott, William W.	M	10
Asst Prof	Westray, Ron	M	47,63C
PT	Whiteman, Richard	B	66A
PT	Williams, Ray		14C
PT	Williamson, Sacha	B	61
PT	Wilson, Edward		34,35
Prof Emeritus	Witmer, Robert	M	14,20G,29
Assoc Prof	Wrazen, Louise	PhD	12,14
PT	Xia, Vivian		20C
	Yun, Gerard	D	20C
PT	Zhao, Wen	B	20C

AI0050 Bishop's University

Department of Music
2600 College St
Sherbrooke, QC J1M 0C8 Canada
(819) 822-9642   Fax: (819) 822-9661
www.ubishops.ca/ccc/div/hum/mus/
E-mail: jeby@ubishops.ca

3-4 Year Undergraduate Programme, Liberal Arts Institution

Chair: John D. Eby, 80A

PT	Anctil, Gilles	B	65
PT	Beaudry, Genevieve	M	62A
PT	Brouwer, Albert	M	64A
PT	Crooks, Jamie	D	36
PT	Daigneault, Sylvain	M	66A
PT	Desmarais, Gail	M	61
Prof	Eby, John D.	D	11,12A,12C,20G,31A
PT	Eby, Pam	M	66G
PT	Farrugia, Pauline	D	64C,42
	Gang, Eleanor	B	61
PT	Gaudette, Fannie	M	13C,66C
PT	Gauthier, Michael	B	70,29A,47,10D
PT	Jackson, Randy	B	63B
PT	Latulippe, Mario	B	64C
PT	Lepine, Joachim	M	63A
Prof	MacDonald, Andrew	D	13,10F,10,45,70
Prof	Osmun, Ross	D	13,41,42,66A,66B
PT	Stroud, Cheryl	B	66A
PT	Sullivan, Kevin M.	B	47

AI0070 Concordia University

Department of Music, Fac Fine Arts
1455 de Maisonneuve Blvd W
GM 500
Montreal, QC H3G 1M8 Canada
(514) 848-2424 x4555   Fax: (514) 848-3155
music.concordia.ca
E-mail: music@concordia.ca

3 Year Institution

Chair: Christine Beckett, 80A

Assoc Prof	Adams, Liselyn	M	13,12A,41,64A,43
Prof	Austin, Kevin	M	13,10F,10,34,35C
Assoc Prof	Beckett, Christine	D	13,12C,32C,38,62A
	Bhagwati, Sandeep		10
Assoc Prof	Brown, Jeri	B	36,47,61,29
	Chaverdian, Gregory	DIPL	66A
Assoc Prof	Corwin, Mark	D	10F,10,45,34,35C
	Dal Farra, Ricardo		10

Asst Prof	Dimitrov, Georges	D	10
Assoc Prof Emeritus	Ellias, Rod	M	13,47,70,53,29
Assoc Prof	Ellison, Charles	M	47,63A,53,46,29
Prof Emeritus	Homzy, Andrew	M	10,47,29,29A,34
Prof	Jackson, Christopher	M	60,66G,66H,67C
Assoc Prof	Mountain, Rosemary	D	13,10F,10,45,34
Asst Prof	Tsabary, Eldad	D	10B,12A,13C

AI0100 McGill University

Faculty of Education
3700 McTavish St
Montreal, QC H3A 1Y2 Canada
(514) 398-2447   Fax: (514) 398-4529
www.mcgill.ca
E-mail: Russell@education.mcgill.ca

4 Year Program

Program Director: Joan Russell, 80A
Chair, Dept of Integrated Studies in Education: Anthony Pare'

| | Russell, Joan | PhD | 32B,32C,12,12C |

AI0150 McGill University

Schulich School of Music
555 Sherbrooke St West
Montreal, QC H3A 1E3 Canada
(514) 398-4535   Fax: (514) 398-8061
www.mcgill.ca/music
E-mail: dean.music@mcgill.ca

3-4 Year Institution, 2 Year Graduate Institution

Master of Arts in Music Education, Master of Arts in Music Theory, Master of Music in Composition, Master of Music in Performance, PhD in Music Theory, PhD in Composition, PhD in Music Education, Doctor of Music in Composition, PhD in Sound Recording & Theory, PhD in Music Technology, PhD in Musicology, Master of Arts in Musicology, Doctor of Music in Performance, Master of Music in Sound Recording, Master of Arts in Musicology/Gender and Women's Studies, Master of Arts in Music Theory/Gender and Women's Studies, Master of Arts in Music Technology, PhD in Sound Recording, Graduate Diploma in Professional Performance

Dean: Sean Ferguson, 80A
Dir., Graduate Studies: Eleanor Stubley, 80C
Admissions: Patrick O'Neill, 80D
Associate Dean, Administration: Julie Cumming, 80H
Associate Dean, Academic & Student Affairs: Sara Laimon, 80H

Lect FT	Abbott, Patricia		32D,60A
Inst PT	Abdul Al-Khabyyr, Muhammad		63C,29
Inst PT	Aldrich, Simon	DIPL	64C,48
Asst Prof	Algieri, Stefano	M	61
Inst PT	Amirault, Greg	B	70,29
Inst PT	Amirault, Steve		66A,29
Inst PT	Antonio, Garry	D	70
Lect FT	Asly, Monica	B	13C
Inst PT	Azar, Andree		62A
Asst Prof	Barg, Lisa	PhD	12
Assoc Prof PT	Baskin, Ted	M	64B
Inst PT	Beaudry, Pierre		63C
Inst PT	Beaulac, Stephane	M	63A,49
Adj Prof	Bech, Soren	PhD	34,35G
Adj Prof	Begault, Durand	PhD	34,35G
Assoc Prof	Beghin, Tom	D	66E,12
Inst PT	Bergeron, Sylvain	B	67,55
Asst Prof	Biamonte, Nicole	PhD	13
Inst PT	Bibace, Kenny		70
Inst PT	Bluteau, Denis	M	64A
Asst Prof	Bolduc, Remi		64E,29
Lect PT	Boucher, Helene		32A
Assoc Prof	Bouliane, Denys	M	10
Asst Prof PT	Box, James	M	63C
Adj Prof	Braasch, Jonas	PhD	34,35G
Assoc Prof	Brackett, David	D	12,14C
Lect PT	Cain, Jerry	PhD	12
Prof	Caplin, William	PhD	13
Assoc Prof	Cazes, Alain	DIPL	60B,63D,48
Inst PT	Chappell, Eric	B	62D
Inst PT	Chen, Lambert	D	62B,51
Prof	Cherney, Brian	PhD	13,10,12A
Lect PT	Chiasson, Rachelle	PhD	12
Assoc Prof PT	Christie, Carolyn	B	64A
Inst PT	Clayton, Greg		47,70,29
Vstng Prof	Cohen, David		13
Inst	Cook, Peter		34,35G
Asst Prof	Cossette, Isabelle	D	32

Inst PT	Couture, Jocelyn		63A,29
Inst PT	Craig, Sean		29,47
Asst Prof PT	Crowley, Robert	M	64C
Assoc Prof	Cumming, Julie	PhD	12
Asst Prof	Davidson, Thomas	M	13C,66A,13A
Lect PT	De Castro, Margaret		13C
Assoc Prof	De Francisco, Martha	DIPL	34,35G
Lect PT	De Souza, Jordan		66C,39
Assoc Prof	Dean, Kevin	M	63A,29
Inst PT	Denis, Marc		62D
Assoc Prof	Depalle, Philippe	PhD	34
Inst PT	Derome, Denys	DIPL	63B,49
Inst PT	Desgagne, Alain		64C,48
Asst Prof PT	Devuyst, Russell	M	63A
Inst PT	Diamond, Louise	M	66C
Inst PT	DiLauro, Ron		63A,29,47
Inst PT	Dix, Trevor	M	63C,49
Inst PT	Dobby, Tim		70
Asst Prof	Dolin, Elizabeth	DIPL	62C,51
Inst PT	Doxas, Chet		64E,29
Inst PT	Doxas, Jim	B	29,65
Inst PT	Ducharme, Jerome	DIPL	70
Inst PT	Dumouchel, Michael	B	64C,48
Asst Prof	Dunn, Andrew		63A
Inst PT	Dyachkov, Yegor		62C,42
Adj Prof	Epstein, Steven		35G,34
Prof	Ericsson, Hans-Ola	D	66G
Inst PT	Feltham, Scott		62D
Assoc Prof	Ferguson, Sean	D	10,45
Assoc Prof	Fewer, Mark	B	62A
Inst PT	Forget, Normand		64B,48
Lect PT	Freeman, Peter	M	64E,32
Assoc Prof	Fujinaga, Ichiro	PhD	34
Asst Prof PT	Gaudreault, Jean	B	63B
Inst PT	Gauthier, Michael		70,29
Inst PT	Gavrilova, Julia	D	66A,13A
Inst PT	Gearey, Jon		29,70
Emeritus	Gibson, Robert		37,32
Adj Prof	Gilbert, Kenneth	D	67
Inst PT	Godin, Olivier		66C
Inst PT	Gonthier, Esther		66C
Lect PT	Gort, Cristian		36,43
Inst PT	Gossage, Dave		29,64A
Prof Emeritus	Grew, John	D	66G,66H,67
Inst PT	Grott, Dave		29
Assoc Prof	Guastavino, Catherine		32
Inst PT	Guimond, Claire	B	67D
Assoc Prof	Haimovitz, Matt	B	62C
Assoc Prof	Hansen, Patrick J.		61,39
Inst PT	Harboyan, Patil		66A
Asst Prof	Harman, Chris	PhD	10
Asst Prof	Hasegawa, Robert	D	13
Assoc Prof	Hashimoto, Kyoko	DIPL	66A
Assoc Prof	Hauser, Alexis	DIPL	38,60
Inst PT	Hollins, Fraser		29,62D
Inst PT	Howes, Heather		64A
Assoc Prof	Huang, Aiyun	D	65
Prof	Huebner, Steven	PhD	12
Assoc Prof	Hui, Melissa	D	10
Inst PT	Hurley, Brian		62D,29
Assoc Prof PT	Hutchins, Tim	B	38,64A
Assoc Prof	Jarczyk, Jan	DIPL	29,63C,66A
Inst PT	Jennejohn, Matthew	B	67D
Inst PT	Jensen, Christine		29,64E
Inst PT	Jimenez, Carlos	M	70,29
Inst PT	Johnson, Sasha		63D,49
Inst PT	Johnston, Jeffrey		66A,29
Inst PT	Karlicek, Martin		66A
Inst PT	Kennedy, Donny		29,64E,47
Assoc Prof	Kestenberg, Abe		48,64C,64E,64A
Lect PT	Kilianski, Harold		34,35G
Assoc Prof	King, Richard	M	34,35G
Asst Prof PT	Kinslow, Valerie	B	61,55,67
Inst PT	Kirk, Douglas	PhD	67
Assoc Prof	Knox, Hank	M	56,66H,67F,55
Lect PT	Koch, Elizabeth		61
Assoc Prof	Kok, Roe-Min	PhD	12,14
Asst Prof PT	Kolomyjec, Joanne	B	61
Lect PT	Kovacs, Jolan		13C
Inst PT	Kutan, Aline		61
Assoc Prof	Laimon, Sara	D	66A,41
Inst PT	Laing, David	B	65,29
Inst PT	Lambert, Frederic		62B
Inst PT	Lambert, Marjolaine		62A
Inst PT	Lambert, Michel		65,29
Prof PT	Lanza, Alcides	DIPL	12
Assoc Prof Emeritus	Lawton, Richard	M	11,12,63
Asst Prof	Leclair, Jacqueline F.	D	64B,41
Inst PT	Lee, Ranee		61,29
Inst PT	Lee, Vivian		63C
Other	Leive, Cynthia	MLS	16
Inst PT	Leroux, Andre	B	29,64E
Assoc Prof	Leroux, Philippe	DIPL	10
Assoc Prof	Lesage, Jean	DIPL	10
Inst PT	Lessard, Daniel		62D,29
Asst Prof PT	Levesque, Stephane	M	64D
Prof	Levitin, Daniel	PhD	13K
Adj Prof	Lih, Lars	PhD	12
Inst PT	Lizotte, Caroline		62,41
Lect FT	Lorenzino, Lisa	M	32

Inst PT	Lortie, Dominique		67E
Inst PT	Lozano, Frank		29,64E
Asst Prof PT	Lupien, Denise	M	62A
Inst PT	Lussier, Mathieu		67D
Inst PT	MacMillan, Betsy	M	67,55
Inst PT	Mahar, Bill	B	63A,29
Inst PT	Mallette, Marcelle		62A
Inst PT	Mangrum, Martin		64D,48
Inst PT	Manker, Brian		62C
Asst Prof	Marandola, Fabrice	PhD	50,65
Inst PT	Marchand, Jean		66C
Inst PT	Marcotte, Anna-Belle	DIPL	62B
Asst Prof	Mariner, Justin	D	13
Adj Prof	Martens, William	PhD	34,35G
Lect PT	Martin, Cathy	M	12C,16
Inst PT	Martin, David	M	63C
Assoc Prof	Massenburg, George		34,35G
Lect PT	Mather, Pierrette	B	13A,13C
Lect PT	Mativetsky, Shawn		32,65
Inst PT	Maute, Matthias		67C,55
Prof	McAdams, Stephen	PhD	13G,13K,34
Inst PT	McCann, Chris		65,29
Inst PT	McLean, Allan		47,29
Inst PT	McLean, Pierre		66C
Assoc Prof	McMahon, Michael	DIPL	39,40,66C,61,66A
Lect PT	McMillan, Brian	M	12C,16
Assoc Prof	McNabney, Douglas	M	51,62B,42
Assoc Prof	Mdivani, Marina	DIPL	66A,66D
Inst PT	Merkelo, Paul	B	63A
Inst PT	Michaud, Natalie	M	67C,55
Assoc Prof PT	Miller, Dennis		49,63D
Inst PT	Miller, Joel	B	29,64E
Assoc Prof Emeritus	Minorgan, Bruce	M	12A,12
Lect PT	Mitchell, Geoffrey		34,35G
Adj Prof	Montagnier, Jean-Paul	PhD	12
Adj Prof	Mulder, Axel	PhD	34
Inst PT	Napper, Susie		67B
Asst Prof	Neidhoefer, Christoph	D	13,10
Inst PT	Nigrim, Dana		66C
Inst PT	Ouimet, Francois		36
Prof	Palmer, Caroline	PhD	13K
Lect PT	Patterson, Jonathan		39
Inst PT	Pelletier, Louise	M	66C
Inst PT	Pepin, Pierre		62D,29
Lect PT	Petit-Homme, Frederika		60A
Assoc Prof Emeritus	Plaunt, Tom	B	66A
Inst PT	Plouffe, Helene		67A,67B
Asst Prof	Poletaev, Ilya	D	66A
Inst PT	Popescu, Annamaria	DIPL	61
Assoc Prof	Porter, William	D	66G
Assoc Prof	Purdy, Winston	M	61
Lect PT	Rager, Josh	M	29,66A
Prof	Rea, John	PhD	13,10
Inst PT	Remillard, Chantal		67B
Asst Prof PT	Roberts, Richard	B	62A
Asst Prof PT	Robinson, Brian	B	62D
Inst PT	Roney, John	M	29,66A
Adj Prof	Roston, John		34,35G
Assoc Prof	Roy, Andre		38,62B
Asst Prof	Rusch, Rene	PhD	13
Assoc Prof Emerita	Sabourin, Carmen	D	13
Assoc Prof	Scavone, Gary	PhD	34
Prof	Schubert, Peter	PhD	13,13J,36
Assoc Prof PT	Sevadjian, Therese	M	61
Inst PT	Shuter, Cindy	B	64A,48
Inst PT	Simons, Mark	B	67
Inst PT	Stevenson, Francois	B	29,65B
Lect PT	Strauss, Anja		61
Assoc Prof	Strauss, Axel	M	62A
Assoc Prof	Stubley, Eleanor	PhD	12,32
Lect PT	Suh-Rager, Min-Jung		66A,29
Assoc Prof	Sullivan, Joe	M	63A,29,47
Asst Prof PT	Swartz, Jennifer	DIPL	62E,51
Asst Prof	Sylvan, Sanford	B	61
Inst PT	Trottier, Jean-Nicolas		29,63C
Inst PT	Turner, Dave		29,64E
Adj Prof	Verge, Marc-Pierre	PhD	34
Inst PT	Walkington, Alec	M	29,29C,62D
Adj Prof	Waltl, Herbert		34,35G
Inst PT	Wan, Andrew		42,62
Assoc Prof	Wanderley, Marcelo	PhD	34
Prof	Wapnick, Joel	D	32
Asst Prof	Weman, Lena	PhD	67,67D
Assoc Prof	White, Andre	M	65,66A,29A,29
Assoc Prof	Whitesell, Lloyd	PhD	12
Asst Prof	Wild, Jonathan	PhD	10,13
Assoc Prof Emeritus	Williams, Tom	B	38,51,62A
Prof	Woszczyk, Wieslaw	PhD	34,35G
Inst PT	Yazdanfar, Ali		62D
Assoc Prof	Zirbel, John	B	63B
Assoc Prof PT	Zuk, Luba	DIPL	66A

AI0190 Universite Laval

Faculty of Music
Pavillon Louis-Jacques-Casault
1055 Ave du Seminaire
Quebec, QC G1V 0A6 Canada
(418) 656-7061   Fax: (418) 656-7365
www.mus.ulaval.ca
E-mail: doyen@mus.ulaval.ca

3 Year Institution, Graduate School

Master of Music in Composition, Master of Music in Performance, Master of Music in Music Education, Master of Music in Musicology, PhD in Music Education, PhD in Musicology, Master of Music in Instrumental Pedagogy

Dean: Andre Papillon, 80A
Dir., Artist/Performance Series: Sylvie Arseneault, 80F

Inst PT	Bernard, Anne-Marie	M	66C
Inst PT	Bernier, Jean-Sebastien	M	64A
Inst PT	Borowicz, Zbigniew Jozef	DIPL	62D
Inst PT	Bouchard, Jean-Luc	M	50,65
Inst PT	Boucher, Remi	DIPL	70
Inst PT	Brauer, Vincent	M	13C,66D
Inst PT	Brown, Isabelle	M	32I
Inst PT	Champagne, Sebastien	M	66C
Inst PT	Cloutier, Jean	M	34
Vstng Prof	Cote, Gerald	D	14C
Inst PT	Daigle, Paulin	D	13B,13D,13E
Inst PT	De Margerie, Monique	DIPL	66A
Inst PT	Doyon, Pierre	M	64E
Prof	Dube', Francis	M	66A,66B
Inst PT	Dubois, Chantal	M	32A,32B
Prof	Ducharme, Michel	D	39,61
Inst PT	Fortin, Marie	M	66C
Inst PT	Fournier, Patricia	DIPL	61
Inst PT	Fraser, Jo-Anne	M	32
Inst PT	Gagnon, Claude	M	70
Inst FT	Gagnon, Yvaine	M	32B
Inst PT	Gervais, Jean	B	32C
Inst PT	Goulet, Marie-Maude	M	11
Inst PT	Gregoire, Carole	M	12C
Prof	Hamel, Gabriel	DIPL	47,29,70
Vstng Prof	Ichmouratov, Airat	D	38,60B
Inst PT	Jacques, David	M	70
Inst PT	Joly, Rene	B	37
Inst PT	Joyal, Marc	M	66A
Vstng Prof	Kobayashi, Hibiki	M	42,62A
Prof	Lacasse, Serge	D	14C,14D
Inst PT	Laforest, Maurice	M	66A
Inst PT	Laing, David		65
Inst PT	Lambert, Jean-Francois	M	47,13C
Inst PT	Larose, Anne-Marie	DIPL	63B
Inst PT	Larose, Christine	M	32
Inst PT	Le Comte, Louise	DIPL	67C
Prof	Lebens, James C.	D	63C,49,43
Inst PT	Leblanc, Jacques	DIPL	39
Inst PT	Leblond, Louis	M	70
Inst PT	Leclerc, Francois	M	70
Inst PT	Lee, Ranee		29,61
Inst PT	Lemieux, Christiane	M	32
Inst PT	Lessard, Brigitte-Louise	M	32
Inst PT	Levesque, Gerald	M	66A
Asst Prof	Liu-Rosenbaum, Aaron	D	10,34,35G,13,14C
Prof	Mathieu, Louise	D	32G,32I
Vstng Prof	Molzan, Brett	M	42,62A
Vstng Prof	Molzan, Ryan	M	42,62C
Prof	Moreno, Maria Teresa	D	13C
Prof	Morin, Eric	M	10B,10F
Inst PT	Nagels, Lance	DIPL	63D
Inst PT	Neault, Sylvain		29,62
Prof	Nieto-Dorantes, Arturo	DIPL	66A,42
Prof	Papillon, Andre	D	11,41,64A
Prof	Pare, Richard	DIPL	66G,66H,55,42
Prof	Peters, Valerie	D	32C
Inst PT	Pierri, Alvaro	DIPL	70
Vstng Prof	Plourde, Jean-Luc	M	42,62B
Inst PT	Rene, Benjamin	M	11
Prof	Roberge, Marc-Andre	D	12A,12
Inst PT	Robichaud, Clement	M	66C
Inst PT	Roulx, Rene	B	65
Inst PT	Rousseau, Marcel	M	64C
Inst PT	Roussel, Marc	M	66C
Inst PT	Sanheim, Trent	DIPL	63A
Prof	Steprans, Janis	D	64E,47,46
Inst PT	Thibault, Joel	M	64E
Inst PT	Thivierge, Anne	M	64A
Inst PT	Tremblay, Remy	B	61
Inst PT	Trottier, Alain	M	64C
Inst PT	Turgeon, Bruno	M	66C
Prof	Vaillancourt, Josee	M	32,36
Inst PT	Vallieres, Claude	B	61
Inst PT	Vedady, Adrian	DIPL	62D

AI0200 Universite de Montreal
Faculte de Musique
PO Box 6128/Station Centre-Ville
Montreal, QC H3C 3J7 Canada
(514) 343-6427
www.musique.umontreal.ca
E-mail: musique@umontreal.ca

3 Year Institution, Graduate School

Master of Music in Instrumental/Voice Performance, Master of Music in Composition, Master of Music in Conducting, Doctor of Music in Composition, PhD Musicology/Ethnomusicology, Master of Arts Musicology/Ethnomusicology, Doctor in Music Instrumental/Voice Performance, Doctor in Music Performance Conducting, Graduate Diploma: Pro Performance Orchestral Repertory, Graduate Diploma in Professional Performance

Dean: Isabelle Panneton, 80A
Associate Dean: Nathalie Fernando, 80H
Associate Dean: Christiane Laflamme, 80H
Associate Dean: Caroline Traube, 80H

Inst	Alarie, Frederic		62D,29
Inst	Beauchamp, Lise		64B
Assoc Prof	Beaudet, Luce	D	13B,13C,13E
Inst	Beaudoin, Jacques		62D
Inst	Beaudry, Pierre		63D
Inst	Beaugrand, Luc		53,66A,29
Inst	Bedard, Martin		10B
Inst	Belanger, Olivier		34
Prof	Belkin, Alan	D	13,10A
Prof	Bellomia, Paolo	D	60B
Asst Prof	Benoit-Otis, Marie-Helene	D	12
Inst	Bergeron, Sylvain		67B,67G
Inst	Bettez, Michel		64D
Inst	Bluteau, Denis		64A
Inst	Bouchard, Jean-Marc		64E,53
Inst	Bouchard, Lise		63A
Inst	Bourion, Sylveline		12
Inst	Breuleux, Yan		34
Assoc Prof	Briere, Jimmy	D	66A
Inst	Brochu, Paul		65,29
Prof	Caron, Sylvain	D	13,31A,12
Inst	Carpentier, Martin		64C
Inst	Charbonneau, Louis		65
Inst	Chatel, Jean-Louis		63A
Adj Prof	Colin, Marie-Alexis	D	12
Vstng Prof	Dang, Thai Son		66A
Vstng Prof	Daoust, Julie	D	61
Prof	Daoust, Lise	D	64A
Prof	De Medicis, Francois	D	12
Prof	De Stefano, Reno	D	29,12
Inst	Denis, Marc		62D
Inst	Desmarais, Gail		61
Prof	Desroches, Monique	D	14
Assoc Prof	Devito, Albert	D	49,63C
Inst	Di Tomaso, Nick		70
Inst	DiLauro, Ronald	D	47,63A,46
Inst	Dimitrov, Georges		13A,13E
Adj Prof	Dobbins, Francis	D	12
Inst	Donato, Michel		62D,47
Prof	Duchesneau, Michel	D	12
Prof	Durand, Marc	M	66A
Inst	Dyachkov, Yegor		62C
Prof Emeritus	Evangelista, Jose	D	10A,20D
Assoc Prof	Fernando, Nathalie	D	14
Inst	Forget, Georges		10B
Inst	Fradette, Gilbert		65,29
Inst	Gauthier, Michael A.		70
Inst	Gauthier, Thierry		10B
Inst	Gauthier, Tommy		62A,29
Vstng Prof	Gort, Cristian		43
Inst	Gosselin, Nathalie		13K
Prof	Gougeon, Denis	M	10A
Inst	Gregoire, Julien		65
Inst	Gripp, Neal		62B
Inst	Guay, Jean-Francois		64E
Adj Prof	Guertin, Ghyslaine	D	12
Prof	Guertin, Marcelle	D	13,12
Adj Prof	Harbec, Jacinthe	D	12
Inst	Kayaleh, Laurence		62A,42
Inst	Kunz, Jean-Willy		13B,13E
Inst	LaBrosse, Denis		62D,29
Inst	Lacoursiere, Marie-Nathalie		52,67H
Inst	Lalonde, Alain	D	10,13C
Assoc Prof	Landry, Rosemarie	M	61,39
Assoc Prof	Landsman, Vladimir		62A
Inst	Lavoie, Mathieu		34,10C
Inst	Leblanc, Mario		13C,13D
Inst	Leblanc, Suzie		61
Asst Prof	Leclair, Francois-Hugues	D	10
Adj Prof	L'Ecuyer, Sylvia	D	12
Inst	Leduc, Pierre		66A,13B,47
Prof Emeritus	Lefebvre, Marie-Therese	D	12,20G
Inst	Leotar, Frederic	D	14
Prof	Leroux, Robert		65
Inst	Little, Margaret		67A,55B,55D
Inst	Lizotte, Caroline		62E
Prof Emeritus	Longtin, Michel	D	10,13E
Inst	Lussier, Matthieu		64D
Inst	Made Suparta, I Dewa		50,20E
Inst	Maltais, Helene		32
Inst	Mangrum, Martin		64D
Inst	Marcotte, Paul		63B
Inst	Marsolais, Louis-Philippe		63B
Inst	Martel, Helene		61,29
Assoc Prof	Martin, David	M	63C,49
Assoc Prof	McCutcheon, Peter	D	70
Asst Prof	Michaud, Pierre	D	10A,10B
Inst	Mikhaylova, Ekaterina		
Assoc Prof	Moisan, Andre		64C
Inst	Moran, Daniel		66A
Inst	Morel, Vincent		47,36,61
Inst	Napper, Susie		62C,67B
Prof Emeritus	Nattiez, Jean-Jacques	D	12
Inst	Normand, Jean-Francois		64C
Prof	Normandeau, Robert	D	10B
Inst	Overy, Charles		13C
Prof	Panneton, Isabelle	D	13,10A
Inst	Parent, Yolande		61
Inst	Park, Angela		66A
Prof Emeritus	Pepin, Natalie	D	66A
Assoc Prof	Perrin, Raymond	D	36
Inst	Perron, Bruno		70
Asst Prof	Perron, Francis	D	39,66C
Assoc Prof	Perron, Johanne	M	62C,41
Inst	Picard, Paul		65,20H
Prof	Piche, Jean	M	10B
Assoc Prof	Pirzadeh, Maneli	D	66A
Prof Emeritus	Poirier, Rejean	D	66G,66H,55B,55D
Inst	Pozdnyakov, Aleksandr		10F
Assoc Prof	Provencal, Richard		47
Inst	Pucci, Michael		70
Assoc Prof	Puchhammer, Jutta	M	62B,41,51
Vstng Prof	Rheault, Pierre-Daniel		10C,34
Assoc Prof	Richard, Claude	D	62A
Prof	Rivest, Jean-Francois	M	38,60B
Inst	Robert, Anne		62A
Inst	Rousseau, Karine		62B
Inst	Roy, Dany		64E,47
Inst	Santiago, Michelle		66A
Assoc Prof	Saulnier, Jean	D	66A
Inst	Savoie, Adrienne		61
Inst	Secco, Leonardo		10B
Adj Prof	Settel, Zack	D	10B
Inst	Sevigny, Catherine		61
Inst	Shchegolev, Aleksey		13D
Inst	Sirois, Carole		62C
Prof	Smoje, Dujka		
Assoc Prof	Sokolovic, Ana		10A
Vstng Prof	Stevance, Sophie		12
Assoc Prof	Stewart, Paul		66A
Inst	Stone, Simon		64E,47
Inst	Suparta, I Dewa Made		20D
Adj Prof	TellerRatner, Sabina	D	12
Inst	Therrien, Gabrielle		13C
Inst	Todorovski, Catherine		13
Assoc Prof	Traube, Caroline	D	13L,35C,34
Inst	Trottier, Danick	D	12E
Inst	Trottier, Jean-Nicolas		63C,29
Inst	Turovsky, Yuli		62C
Assoc Prof	Vaillancourt, Jean-Eudes	D	41,66D
Prof	Vaillancourt, Lorraine	D	43
Vstng Prof	Verfaille, Vincent		13L,14B
Assoc Prof	Wheeler, Robin		39

AI0210 Univ du Quebec-Montreal
Department de Musique
Succursale Centre A/CS 8888
Montreal, QC H3C 3P8 Canada
(514)987-4174   Fax: (514)987-4637
www.musique.uqam.ca/Page/default.aspx
E-mail: ross.france@uqam.ca

4 Year institution

Director: Claude Dauphin, 80A
Director: Jean-Louis Gagnon, 80A

Lect PT	Angelillo, Vic		20G
Lect PT	Aubin, Stephane		
Prof	Beaudry, Nicole		14
Lect PT	Beaugrand, Luc		
Lect PT	Beaulieu, Cyrille		
Lect PT	Belair, Michel		
Lect PT	Belanger, Marc		
Lect PT	Benoit, Patrick		

Rank	Name	Deg	Codes
Lect PT	Boivin, Luc		20G
Prof	Boky, Colette	DIPL	61
Lect PT	Boudreau, Walter		
Prof	Brassard, Henri	M	66A
Lect PT	Camitsis, Georges		
Lect PT	Carpentier, Gilles		64C
Lect PT	Carpentier, Jean-Pierre		63C
Prof	Carroll, Debbie		33
Lect PT	Cormier, Pierre		
Lect PT	Crago, Bartholemy		70
Prof	Dauphin, Claude	D	32
Lect PT	Denis, Marc	DIPL	62D
Lect PT	Dubois, Chantal		32
Lect PT	Ferland, Louise		61
Prof	Foster, Martin	DIPL	62A
Lect PT	Fraser, Jo-Anne	M	32I
Prof	Gagnon, Jean-Louis	DIPL	63B
Lect PT	Genest, Sylvie		
Prof	Grenier, Monik	M	66A
Lect PT	Harguindey, Jose		
Lect PT	Hebert, Pierre		20G
Prof	Hetu, Jacques	B	10
Prof	Isenberg-Grzeda, Connie	M	33
Prof	Jasmin, Pierre	M	66A
Lect PT	Lacaille, Nathalie		
Lect PT	Lacelle, Diane		
Prof	Lamarche, Andre	M	10
Lect PT	Lauber, Anne		13
Lect PT	Leduc, Yolande		13
Prof	Lefebvre, Claire		33
Lect PT	Lefrance, Manon		
Lect PT	Marion, Pierre		
Lect PT	Martin, Monique		
Lect PT	Moisan, Andre		64C
Lect PT	Ouellette, Antoine		
Lect PT	Panneton, Helene		66H
Lect PT	Parent, Marie-Danielle		
Prof	Paul, Helene	M	12
Lect PT	Pelchat, Andre		64E
Prof	Pierri, Alvaro	DIPL	70
Lect PT	Plante, Gilles		
Lect PT	Plante, Jean-Guy		65
Lect PT	Primeau, Dominique		
Lect PT	Puchammer, Sedillot	M	62B
Lect PT	Ratte, Michel		
Lect PT	Ring, Richard		20G
Prof	Rochon, Gaston		10
Lect PT	Roy, Bruno		14
Lect PT	Samson, Louise		13
Prof	Takacs, Miklos	M	32,36
Lect PT	Thibault, Lorraine		
Lect PT	Thivierge, Jacques		
	Trudel, Louise		
Lect PT	Turp, Richard		
Prof	Vanasse, Guy	DIPL	64A
Lect PT	Villeneuve, Andre		13
Lect PT	Zanella, Jean-Pierre		64E

AI0220 Univ du Quebec-Trois-Riviere
Department of Arts-Music Sec
3351 Blvd Des Forges
Trois-Rivieres, QC G9A 5H7 Canada
(819) 376-5137   Fax: (819) 376-5066
www.uqtr.ca
E-mail: francoise.matte@cgocable.ca

4 Year Institution

Director: Jacques Larocque, 80A
Assistant Director: Dorvalino De Melo, 80H

Rank	Name	Deg	Codes
Lect PT	Beaupre, Odette	M	39,61
Lect PT	Bellemare, Yvon	B	66A,66C
Lect PT	Belleville, Yolande	DIPL	66C
Lect PT	Benoit, Marcel	DIPL	67D,70
Lect PT	Boisvert, Claude	M	10
Lect PT	Carbonneau, Pierre-Marc	B	35B,35C,35D
Lect PT	Carignan, Danielle	DIPL	64A
Lect PT	Chevanelle, Serge	DIPL	63A
Prof	De Melo, Dorvalino	D	60,32C,37,47,64E
Lect PT	Doucet, Denis	M	64C
Lect PT	Dufour, Francine	M	51,62A
Prof	Dussault, Michel J.	DIPL	12A,66A,66B
Lect PT	Dyotte, Claude	DIPL	70
Lect PT	Gagnon-Matte, Francoise	B	66A,66C
Lect PT	Gravel, Manon	B	32B,32A,66B
Lect PT	Jalbert, Sylvain	B	65
Lect PT	Kozlovsky, Danielle Godbout	M	12A
Lect PT	Lagace, Isolde	M	35A,35E,35F
Prof	Larocque, Jacques	DIPL	10,41,48,64E,34
Lect PT	Lavigne, Julie	M	63C
Lect PT	Perrault, Paul	M	45,34,35C,35E,13L
Lect PT	Perrin, Raymond	M	66G
Lect PT	Peterson, Ian	B	62D
Lect PT	Simoneau, Brigitte	M	32B
Lect PT	Vallieres, Claude	B	32

AJ0030 Briercrest College and Seminary
Worship Arts Department
510 College Dr
Caronport, SK S0H 0S0 Canada
(306) 756-3250   Fax: (306) 756-5589
www.briercrest.ca
E-mail: worship.arts@briercrest.ca

4 Year Institution, Graduate School

Master of Divinity in Worship

Dean: David Guretzki, 80A
Coord., Undergraduate Studies: Ruth B. Koop, 80B

Rank	Name	Deg	Codes
Adj	Crawford, Jenn	M	66A,66B,66C,13
Adj	Crawford, Ted	B	65,32B,32C
Asst Prof	De Jager, Ron	M	60A,36,52,61,32D
Assoc Prof	Dirksen, Dale B. H.	D	10,13,32,61,66
Asst Prof	Finch, Scott	D	60A,31A,12A,13A,11
Adj	Harder, Melissa	B	61,11,60A
Adj	Hildebrandt, Darcy	B	66A,66B,66C,13
Other	Koop, Ruth B.	B	13A,31A,35A,35E,61
Asst Prof	Matejka, Merle	M	10,12A,31A,13,29
Inst	Molberg, Keith	M	66A,34D,13,66C,13A
Adj	Pullman, Marlene	DIPL	13A,66A,66B,66D
Adj	Wall, Nathan	B	65
Adj	Winter, Brandon	B	70

AJ0100 Univ of Regina
Department of Music
3737 Wascana Parkway
Regina, SK S4S 0A2 Canada
(306) 585-5532   Fax: (306) 585-5549
www.uregina.ca
E-mail: music@uregina.ca

4 Year Institution, Graduate School

Master of Arts in Music Theory, Master of Music in Composition, Master of Music in Performance, Master of Music in Conducting, Master of Arts in Musicology

Head, Music: Pauline M. Minevich

Rank	Name	Deg	Codes
Inst PT	Ayre, Ron		70
Inst PT	Berthelet, Marie-Noelle	M	64A
Inst PT	Bouffard, Sophie	M	12A,61,11,13C
Inst PT	Burdick, Richard		63B
Asst Prof	Cavanagh, Lynn	D	13B,13E,13F,13J,13I
Prof	Channing, Lynn	DIPL	39,61
Inst PT	Denike, Allan	M	64D
Assoc Prof	Finnsson, Karen	M	12A,64E,64
Asst Prof	Ghiglione, Brent	M	37,60B
Inst PT	Gibbs, Kory	B	50,65
Inst PT	Jacklin, Christopher	B	47,64E
Inst	Johnson, Penny	DMA	66A,66C
Inst PT	Lowe, Cameron	B	62C
Inst PT	Minevich, Eduard		62A
Assoc Prof	Minevich, Pauline M.	D	12A,64C,12C,12D
Inst PT	Newman, Miles	B	63A
Asst Prof	Perron, Alain	D	10A,10B,10C,43,10F
Assoc Prof	Reul, Barbara M.	D	11,12A,12C,12D
Asst Prof	Vanderkooy, Christine	D	66A,66B,66C,13C

AJ0150 Univ of Saskatchewan
Department of Music
28 Campus Dr
Saskatoon, SK S7N 0X1 Canada
(306) 966-6171   Fax: (306) 966-6181
www.usask.ca/music
E-mail: music.uofs@usask.ca

4 Year Institution, Graduate School

Master of Education, Master of Music

Chair/Dir., Institute/Fest/Wksp: Patrick Browne, 80A,80F

Rank	Name	Deg	Codes
Lect PT	Archer, Naida	M	13A,13,66A,66D
Lect PT	Bueckert, Darrell	M	50,65,37
Assoc Prof	Csapo, Gyula	D	13,10,45,10F
Lect	Currie, Neil	D	12A
Lect PT	Day, Gary	M	12A

Directory of Institutions

Lect PT	England, Peter		34
Lect PT	Freisen, Naomi	M	61
Assoc Prof	Gable, Garry	D	61,54,39
Lect PT	Gable, Kathleen	M	66D,66A,66C
Assoc Prof	Gillis, Glen	D	60,32C,37,48,64E
Prof Adj	Halmo, Joan	D	12
Assoc Prof	Harris, Donald	M	32,63,12
Lect PT	Hofmeister, Walter	B	70
Lect PT	Kashap, Philip	M	11,62A
Lect	Kelly, Chris		61,66D
Prof	Kreyszig, Walter	D	12A,12,20G,55
Asst Prof	Langner, Gerald	D	32,36
Lect PT	Linsley, Troy		64E
Asst Prof	McNeill, Dean		63A,29,46,47
Lect	Montalbetti, Barbara		61
Lect PT	Nelson, Joy	B	32A,32B
Lect PT	Nelson, Randi	B	64A
Lect PT	Nicholson, Bonnie	M	66A,66D
Lect	Paterson, Janice		61
Lect PT	Schmidt, Donald	B	63C,63D
Lect PT	Schulte, Gregory	B	66G
Lect PT	Shiplett, Arlene		63B
Assoc Prof	Solose, Kathleen A.	D	66A,66H,66B,66C,42
Lect PT	Wilson, Margaret	M	64C

AK0050 Alaska Pacific University
Department of Liberal Studies
4101 University Dr
Anchorage, AK 99508-4625
(907)564-8291   Fax: (907)562-4276
www.alaskapacific.edu

4 Year Institution

Chair: Marilyn R. Barry, 80A

Adj	Redding, Eric	M	11,36,66A,70,53

AK0100 Univ of Alaska-Anchorage
Department of Music
3211 Providence Dr
Anchorage, AK 99508-4614
(907) 786-1595   Fax: (907) 786-1799
www.uaa.alaska.edu/music
E-mail: aftcs@uaa.alaska.edu

4 Year Institution
Member of NASM

Chair: Timothy C. Smith, 80A

Assoc Prof	Belden, George R.	D	13,12,10,34
Inst	Caudill, Nancy	M	61
Inst	Damberg, John		14,50,65
Inst	Delgado, Derek G.	M	66A
Inst	Egan, Kate	M	61
Inst	Epperson, Dean	M	11,12A,66A,66D,66B
Assoc Prof	Hahn, Mari	D	61,39,54,32D
Inst	Koenig, Laura J.	D	64A
Inst	Li, Tai-Wai	M	32D,40
Inst	Lyons, Shawn	B	70
Inst	Marks, Gary	M	66G
Inst	Munger, Philip		10,13A,33
Inst	O'Connor, Matt T.	M	62D
Assoc Prof	Olivares, Walter G.	M	12A,51,62
Inst	Schweizer, Kiel Jay	M	70
Inst	Smith, Rumi	M	66A
Prof	Smith, Timothy C.	D	11,66A,66B,66C
Asst Prof	Stearns, Roland H.	D	13,70,51
Prof	Strid-Chadwick, Karen	M	13,47,66A,66D,29
Inst	Strock, Kathryn	M	61
Asst Prof	Sweeney, Christopher R.	D	32,63D,63C,32E,32B
Inst	Wardlaw-Bailey, Freya	M	13
Inst	Weeda, Linn	M	11,36,49,63,63A
Prof	Wolbers, Mark	D	60,12A,32C,64C,48
Inst	Woodard, Leigh Ann		64B

AK0150 Univ of Alaska-Fairbanks
Department of Music
PO Box 755660
Fairbanks, AK 99775-5660
(907) 474-7555   Fax: (907) 474-6420
www.uaf.edu/music
E-mail: fymusic@uaf.edu

4 Year Institution, Graduate School
Member of NASM

Master of Arts in Music

Chair: Eduard Zilberkant, 80A
Dir., Summer Programs: Dorli McWayne, 80G

Lect	Aspnes, Jane	M	63B,49
Assoc Prof	Bicigo, James Michael	D	12A,32,37,41,63D
Prof	Butler-Hopkins, Kathleen M.		51,62A,62B
Asst Prof	Cee, Vincent	D	32,29,38,34B,11
Asst Prof	Celaire, Jaunelle R.	D	36,39,40,61
Asst Prof	Gustafson, Karen	D	37,63A,41,11,60B
Lect	Hlashweova, Jamila	M	66C
Assoc Prof	Hopkins, John R.	D	36,39,61,60
Asst Prof	Knapp, Karl D.	D	12A,62C
Lect	McWayne, Dorli	M	48,64A,41
Asst Prof	Palter, Morris	D	12A,29A,42,43,14C
Asst Prof	Post, William Dean	D	13,12A,10A
Lect	Rydlinski, Candy	B	64B
Lect	Rydlinski, George	B	64D
	Watabe, Eileen	M	63B,49
Asst Prof	Watabe, Junichiro	D	64C,64E,48,37,46
Prof	Zilberkant, Eduard	D	66A,66B,66C,66D,41

AL0010 Alabama A & M University
Department of Fine Arts-Music
PO Box 1925
Normal, AL 35762
(256) 372-5512   Fax: (256) 372-5974
www.aamu.edu/music
E-mail: horace.carney@aamu.edu

4 Year Institution, Graduate School, Historically Black College

Master of Education in Music Education

Chair/Coordinator: Horace R. Carney, 80A

Assoc Prof	Carney, Horace R.	D	13,60,10,36
Asst Prof	Hall, Doris S.	D	11,48,64A,64E
Asst Prof	Hawley, Lucrecia	M	11,32,66D
Assoc Prof	Hutson, Danny J.	D	12A,13E,60,63C
Asst Prof	Jordan, Christopher	M	11,61
Assoc Prof	Kruja, Mira	D	66A,66B,13,11
Adj Inst PT	Li, Nina	M	62
Asst Prof	Lott, Peter Tell	M	11,63A
Adj Inst PT	Neely, Dawn Wells	M	61
Adj Inst PT	Nutt, Dorrie	M	63B
Adj Inst PT	Pryor, Cheryl	M	61
Adj Inst PT	Rice, Michael	B	64C,64E
Asst Prof	Wesley, Arthur B.	M	11,37,47,65
Inst	Yates, Derrick	M	11,37,47,63A

AL0050 Alabama State University
Department of Music
PO Box 271
Montgomery, AL 36101-0271
(334) 229-4341   Fax: (334) 229-4901
www.alasu.edu/music
E-mail: mcamacho@alasu.edu

4 Year Institution, Graduate School, Historically Black College
Member of NASM

Master of Music in Music Education

Chair: Martin Camacho-Zavaleta, 80A

Inst	Bell, Isaac	M	47,63C,63D
Assoc Prof	Bristol, Caterina	D	11,12A,64E
Prof	Bristol, Doug S.	D	13,29,63C,47
Asst Prof	Brooks-Lyle, Alma B.	M	13,64A,12B,12A
Prof	Burns, Pamela T.	D	11,32,61

Assoc Prof	Camacho-Zavaleta, Martin	D	66,13
Adj	Cook, Andrew	M	64E
Adj	Crawford, Jeremy	M	11,63D
Adj	Gipson, Crystal	M	11
Asst Prof	Gonzalez-Matos, Adonis	D	66,13A
Inst	Hayes, Tyrone	M	61,11
Asst Prof	Jackson, Gregory	D	65,13,20,10,36
Asst Prof	Johnson, Carly J.	D	63A
Assoc Prof	Jones, Joel C.	D	66,36,13A
Asst Prof	Luchsinger, Brenda	M	11,63B,13A
Adj	Moore, Christine	M	11,32B
Staff	Oliver, James	B	37
Asst Prof	Phillips, Katrina	D	11,64C
Asst Prof	Phillips, Katrina R.	DMA	11,12A,64E
Adj	Povey, Peter	M	62A
Inst	Reeves, M. Bryan	M	37,32E,11,49,60
Asst Prof	Washington-Harris, Kara E.	D	32

AL0200 Auburn University-Auburn
Department of Music
101 Goodwin Music Bldg
Auburn University, AL 36849-5420
(334) 844-4165   Fax: (334) 844-3168
www.auburn.edu
E-mail: slbaird@auburn.edu

4 Year Institution, Graduate School
Member of NASM

Master of Education in Music Education, PhD in Music Education, Specialist in Education in Music Education

Chair: Sara Lynn Baird, 80A

Inst PT	Acker-Mills, Barbara E.	M	11
Prof	Baird, Sara Lynn	D	60A
Lect	Bonds, Eric	D	32C
Asst Prof	Caravan, Lisa	M	62C,62D,32E
Asst Prof	DeGoti, Mark D.	D	63A,49,11
Inst	Dickerson, Shane	M	11,64E,64D
Prof	Garrison, Karen H.	D	11,64A,48
Inst	Gheesling, Laurelie	M	66C
Assoc Prof	Goldstein, Howard A.	D	10F,62A,11,12A,38
Prof	Good, Richard D.	D	37,63D
Asst Prof	Hoch, Matthew	D	61,36,39
Inst	Ikner, W. Joseph	M	70,11
Inst PT	King, Bryan T.	M	11,66
Prof	Knipschild, Ann	D	13,48,64B,64E
Assoc Prof	Kuehne, Jane M.	D	32,32D,32F
Inst	MacDonald, April	M	61,40,39
Assoc Prof	Odom, David H.	D	64C,11
Inst	Pendowski, Michael	D	64E,46,47,11
Lect	Pifer, Joshua K.	D	66A,66C,66D,13C
Prof	Powell, Rosephanye	D	61,36
Prof	Powell, William C.	D	60A,36
Assoc Prof	Rosener, Douglas	M	37,50,65
Assoc Prof	Samolesky, Jeremy	D	66A,66D,13C
Assoc Prof	Schaffer, William R.	D	13,11,63B,49
Assoc Prof	Spurlin, Adam Corey	D	37
Inst PT	Vinson, Nancy	M	11
Prof	Walls, Kimberly C.	D	32,34C,32F,32G
Librarian	Weisbrod, Liza	M	16,66
Assoc Prof	Wood, Matthew P.	D	63D,13A

AL0210 Auburn University-Montgomery
Department of Fine Arts
PO Box 244023
Montgomery, AL 36124-4023
(334) 244-3377   Fax: (334) 244-3740
www.aum.edu
E-mail: mbenson@aum.edu

4 Year Institution

Chair & Dir., Artist Series: Mark F. Benson, 80A,80F

Assoc Prof	Benson, Mark F.	PhD	13,12A,11,65,20
PT	Christensen, James	M	13A,11
PT	DuBose, E. L.	M	11

AL0260 Bevill State Community College
Department of Music
PO Box 800
Sumiton, AL 35148-0800
(205) 648-3271 x 5285   Fax: (205) 648-3311
www.bscc.edu
E-mail: jstallsmith@bscc.edu

2 Year Institution

Adj	Patilla, Michael K.	M	70
Adj	Rizzo, Stephen	M	11,63
Adj	Stallsmith, Becki	B	32,38,50,61,66C
Inst	Stallsmith, John	D	12A,36,47,66,31A

AL0300 Birmingham-Southern College
Department of Music
PO Box 549033
Birmingham, AL 35254
(205) 226-4950   Fax: (205) 226-3058
www.bsc.edu
E-mail: lseigel@bsc.edu

4 Year Institution
Member of NASM

Chair: Lester C. Seigel, 80A
Dir., Preparatory Division: Lucy Victory, 80E

Adj	Baker, James	M	63B
Adj	Bryant, Jennifer	D	61
Adj	Burnham, Jay	B	65
Adj	Candelaria, Leonard	D	63A
Adj Prof Emeritus	Cook, James H.	D	66G
Adj	Denson, Parker	M	64E
Adj Prof Emeritus	DeVan, William	M	66A
Adj	Donaldson, Judy	B	64C
Adj	Hultgren, Craig	M	62C,43
Asst Prof	Kensmoe, Jeffrey	D	61,39,36
Adj	Koonce, Jeff	M	63C
Assoc Prof	Leary-Warsaw, Jacqueline J.	D	61,12A
Adj	Leonard, Katy E.	D	20
Adj	Mazanec, David	M	62D
Adj	Miller, Andrew	D	63D
Adj	Moore, Constance J.	M	66A,66B
Adj	Neal, Mary Elizabeth	M	13A,13B,13C,13D
Adj	Pandolfi, Anne	B	62A,62B
Asst Prof	Posey, Benjamin C.	M	32,37,60B,63A
Adj	Remele, Rebecca	D	10,34
Prof	Seigel, Lester C.	D	60,36,39,66C,13F
Adj	Senasi, Karlo	B	70
Adj	Sharp, Jack	B	64D,64E
Prof	Smith, David J.	D	61,11
Adj	Sullivan, James	M	64B
Adj	Tingle, JoDean	M	66A
Adj	Wienhold, Lisa	B	64A
	Williams, Russell	B	66F

AL0310 Bishop State Comm College
Div. of Humanities-Music
351 N Broad St
Mobile, AL 36603-5833
(251) 690-6416   Fax: (334) 432-2290
www.bscc.cc.al.us
E-mail: mpoellnitz@bishop.edu

2 Year Institution, Historically Black College

Chair: Helen E. Campbell, 80A

Inst	Campbell, Helen E.	D	13A,13,36,61,66
Inst	Poellnitz, Michael	M	12A,47,63,35B
Inst	Swingle, Ira	M	12A,66A

AL0330 Calhoun Community College
Department of Fine Arts
PO Box 2216
Decatur, AL 35609-2216
(256) 306-2500   Fax: (256) 306-2925
www.calhoun.edu
E-mail: hvp@calhoun.edu

2 Year Institution

Chair, Fine Arts & Coord., Music: Holly Powe, 80A

Prof	Cantrell, James	M	35A,35B,35C,35D,46
Prof PT	Cobbs, Jerry	D	61,36,11
Prof PT	Crawley, James	M	63,64
Prof PT	Lanier Miller, Pamela	M	61,11,66A
Prof PT	Moss, Frances	D	11
Prof	Powe, Holly	M	61,13,11,60,47
Prof PT	Valls De Quesada, Margarita	M	41,70

AL0332 Central Alabama Comm College
Department of Music
1675 Cherokee Rd
Alexander City, AL 35010
(256) 215-4326   Fax: (256) 234-0384
www.cacc.edu
E-mail: sgriffin@cacc.cc.al.us

2 Year Institution

Adj Inst	Boncella, Paul		
Inst	Griffin, Stephen W.	M	11,36,37,47,64

AL0335 Chattahoochee Valley Comm Coll
Department of Music & Theatre
2602 College Dr
Phenix City, AL 36869-7960
(334) 291-4987   Fax: (334) 291-4980
www.cv.edu
E-mail: tom.daniel@cv.edu

2 Year Institution

Director, Music & Theatre: Thomas Daniel, 80A
Chair, Language/Fine Arts: Susan Lockwood, 80A

Inst PT	Barraca, Rudy	M	11,63,65
Inst	Daniel, Thomas	D	13,11,47
Inst PT	Smith, Gayle	M	66D,36,61

AL0340 Enterprise State Comm College
Division of Fine Arts
PO Box 1300
Enterprise, AL 36331
(334) 393-2623   Fax: (334) 393-6223
www.escc.edu
E-mail: jjohnson@escc.edu

2 Year Institution

Chair, Fine Arts: Jean Johnson, 80A

	Thomas, Kenneth B.	M	11

AL0345 Faulkner University
Department of Fine Arts
5345 Atlanta Hwy
Montgomery, AL 36109-3323
(334) 272-5820   Fax: (334) 386-7673
www.faulkner.edu
E-mail: mroberson@faulkner.edu

4 Year Liberal Arts, Private University

Dean, College of Arts & Sciences: David Rampersad, 80A
Chair, Fine Arts: Matt Roberson, 80A

Adj	Back, Douglas	M	11,70
Adj	Bender, Sharla A.	M	11,61,66A
Asst Prof	Clements, Allen	D	32D,36,60A,40,61
Asst Prof	Cook, Andrew	M	60B,63,11,47,64
Adj	Gibson, Robbie L.	D	11,70
Adj	Jackson, Gregory	M	11,65
Adj	Jewell, Vickie L.	M	11,37,63B,66A
Adj	Johnson, Carly	D	11,63A
Adj	Nishibun, Tiffany	M	11,61
Assoc Prof	Roberson, Matt	D	12,61
Adj	Rojek, Justin J.	M	11,66,13
Collaborative Pianist	Swears, Marilyn	D	11,54,66A
Adj	Walker, Abigail	M	11,64D

AL0350 Gadsden State Junior College
Department of Music
1000 George Wallace Dr
Gadsden, AL 35901
(205)546-0484
www.gadsdenstate.edu

2 Year Institution

Under Dean: Clifton Osborn, 80A

Prof	McSpadden, George		13,36,49,66A,66G
Prof	Reagan, Billy R.		36,37,41,47,63

AL0400 G C Wallace State Community Coll
Division of Fine Arts-Music
1141 Wallace Dr
Dothan, AL 36303-9234
(334) 556-2256   Fax: (334) 983-3600
www.wallace.edu

2 Year Institution

Dir., Division of Fine Arts: Ralph E. Purvis, 80A

Inst PT	Andrews, Paul		11
Inst PT	Choate, Jim		63D
Inst PT	Dodson, Gordon		70
Inst	Hunter, Rosemary Herlong		13,66A
Inst PT	Mills, Jackie		65
Inst PT	Pina, Juan		63A
	Purvis, Ralph E.		47
Inst PT	Rickey, Shirley		11
Inst PT	Tinsley, David		11,36,61
Inst PT	Tinsley, Janis		61,66A,66B,66D
Inst	Tolar, Ron		13,11,66A,66G

AL0450 Huntingdon College
Department of Music
1500 E Fairview Ave
Montgomery, AL 36106-2148
(334) 833-4457   Fax: (334) 833-4264
www.huntingdon.edu
E-mail: gdavis@huntingdon.edu

4 Year Institution
Member of NASM

Chair: Gene Davis, 80A

Staff	Blankenship, Harold	M	37
Prof	Canfield, Jennifer K.	D	11,32A,32D,66D,32B
PT	Conely, James	D	66A,66G
Prof	Davis, Gene	M	61,36,13C
Prof Emeritus	Glass, James W.	D	61
Prof	Herrick, Dennis R.	D	60,63,34,29A,32C
PT	Hollinger, Curtis	M	64
PT	Manderville, Kevin	D	70
PT	Mayor, Pedro	M	66D
PT	Nishibun, Tiffany	M	13A,61
Prof Emeritus	Rohlig, Harald	D	10,66G,31A
Prof	Serebryany, Vadim	D	66A,12A,13B
PT	Stark-Williams, Turia	M	61,13B
Prof	Williams, Eddy	M	65,13B,32C,37,60B

AL0500 Jacksonville State University
D. L. Walters Department of Music
700 Pelham Rd N
Jacksonville, AL 36265
(256) 782-5559   Fax: (256) 782-5896
music.jsu.edu
E-mail: mcintosh@jsu.edu

4 Year Institution, Graduate School
Member of NASM

Master of Arts in Music, Master of Arts in Music Education

Head: W. Legare McIntosh, Jr., 80A
Assistant Head: Thomas McCutchen, 80H

Assoc Prof Emeritus	Anderson, Carl H. C.	M	13,48,64A,64C
Prof Emeritus	Armstrong, Richard	D	12A,12C,61
Assoc Prof	Baptiste, Renee L.	D	32B,32C,32D,32G,36
Asst Prof	Benson, Jeremy L.	D	64A,64B,12
Asst Prof	Bodiford, Kenneth	M	60,37,63D
Inst	Brandon, Mark	M	32B,32C,64C
Prof Emeritus	Brown, Samuel B.	D	39,61,31A
Lect	Carter, Kenyon W.	M	64E,29
Inst	Cheatham-Stricklin, Teresa	M	13A,11,61,54
Assoc Prof	Collins, Myrtice J.	D	32B,66D,36
Assoc Prof	Corbin, Patricia	D	60A,32D,61,55D,60
Assoc Prof Emerita	Dempsey, O. S.	D	66A,66B,13
Lect	Enghauser, Christopher M.	M	62D,29
Assoc Prof	Faughn, Wendy	D	66A,66B,66C,66D
Inst	Gillespie, Clint	M	60,37,65
Assoc Prof	Gordon, Douglas L.	D	13,34
Lect	Hardin, Larry E.	D	11
Inst	Hosmer, Christopher D.	M	63B,34C
Lect	Jones, Dani R.	D	11,61
Asst Prof	Lambert, David D.	D	63C,29
Assoc Prof	Logsdon, Anthony	D	60,32,64E
Asst Prof Emeritus	Maltese, John	M	11,38,62A
Prof	McCutchen, Thomas	D	65,50
Prof	McIntosh, W. Legare	D	12A,13,66A,66G
Prof	Merriman, John C.	D	11,49,63A,70
Asst Prof	Nevela, Andrew	D	29,35A,35C
Inst	Oft, Eryn	M	64B,64D,12A,12C
Lect	Oliver, Abby	M	62A
Assoc Prof Emerita	Parker, Patricia G.	D	11,66A,66D
Lect	Phillipus, Donna	M	11
Prof Emeritus	Roberts, James E.	D	60,12A,49,63C
Lect	Solomon, Jeffrey	M	63D
Prof	Steward, Gail	D	12A,66A,66D
Inst	Stovall, Jeremy	M	13A,37,41,54
Emeritus	Tyler, George Tracy	M	50,65
Assoc Prof Emeritus	Walters, David	D	13,37,63,60
Lect	Weatherford, Benjamin	M	70,11
Assoc Prof	Wight, Nathan N.	D	61,39
Asst Prof	Woodward, James E.	D	13,10

AL0530 Jefferson State Community College
Department of Music
LA Division
2601 Carson Rd
Birmingham, AL 35215-3007
(205) 856-7900   Fax: (205) 856-6085
www.jeffstateonline.com
E-mail: tarcher@jeffstateonline.com

2 Year Institution

Music Contact: Jessica Kaufhold, 80A

PT	Fitzsimmons, Patricia	D	
PT	Haworth, Laurie	M	11
Inst	Kaufhold, Jessica	M	36,11,13A,13B,13C
PT	Lyons, Lyndel	M	11
PT	Thomas, Michael	M	11
PT	Trucks, Linda	D	
PT	Vines, Lisa	M	11

AL0550 Judson College
Department of Music
302 Bibb St
Marion, AL 36756
(334) 683-5149   Fax: (334) 683-5147
www.judson.edu
E-mail: jransom@judson.edu

4 Year Institution
Member of NASM

Prof	Campbell, Betty	D	61,13C
Adj	Gosselin, Karen	M	32,60,36,40,44
Adj	Hanserd, Mary	D	13,12A
Adj	Hostetter, Elizabeth	D	66A,66D,66C,13,66
Assoc Prof	McManus, Lanny	D	32D,36,12,13E,40
Adj	Street, Deborah	M	63,64

AL0620 Lurleen B Wallace Comm College
Department of Music
PO Box 1418
Andalusia, AL 36420
(334) 222-6591   Fax: (334) 222-6557
www.lbwcc.edu/
E-mail: jbrewer@lbwcc.edu

2 Year Junior Institution

Inst	Brewer, Johnny	M	13A,13B,11,46,13C

AL0630 Lurleen B Wallace Comm College
Department of Music-Greenville
750 Greenville Bypass
Greenville, AL 36037
(334) 881-3100
www.lbwcc.edu

2 Year Junior Institution

Inst	Kennedy, Charles	M	11,70,66A,61

AL0650 Miles College
Department of Music
PO Box 3800
Birmingham, AL 35064
(205) 929-1659   Fax: (205) 929-1619
www.miles.edu
E-mail: jhawkins@miles.edu

4 Year Institution, Historically Black College

Coordinator: Jemmie Peevy Hawkins, 80A

Asst Prof	Chen, Fen-Fang	D	66A,66B,66D,42,66C
Inst	Hampton, Anitra C.	M	12A,32,32G,11
Adj Inst	Hawkins, Jemmie Peevy	D	32,66C
Adj Inst	Jackson, Paul	B	63A
Assoc Prof	Jones, Dani S.	D	61,39,31A,60
	Means, Arthur		37
Adj Inst	Merritt, Romona	M	62,41
Adj Inst	Moss, Patricia J.	M	12A,11
Asst Prof	Ratliff, Phillip	D	13,12A,10F,34
Adj Inst	Thurman, Demondrae	ABD	63C,63D,41
Inst	Western, Daniel	M	64,47,35D,13,29A
	Williams, Bernard	D	36

AL0750 Northeast Alabama Comm College
Department of Music
PO Box 159
Rainsville, AL 35986-0159
(256) 228-6001   Fax: (256) 228-6861
www.nacc.edu
E-mail: knoxd@nacc.edu

2 Year Institution

Music Contact: Daniel Knox, 80A

	Adkins, Kathy		11,36,61,66A
Inst	Knox, Daniel	M	11,70,63,64,13A

AL0800 Samford University
School of the Arts
Division of Music
800 Lakeshore Dr
Birmingham, AL 35229
(205) 726-2851   Fax: (205) 726-2165
www.samford.edu/arts/music
E-mail: klfouse@samford.edu

4 Year Institution, Graduate School
Member of NASM

Master of Music in Church Music, Master of Music in Music Education, Master of Music in Piano Performance & Pedagogy, Master of Music/Master of Divinity (Joint Degree), Master of Divinity emphasis in Church Music

Dean, School of the Arts: Joseph H. Hopkins, 80A
Dir., Graduate Studies: Sarana Chou, 80C
Dir., Preparatory Division: Connie Macon, 80E
Associate Dean, Music: Kathryn L. Fouse, 80H

Lect	Banks, Timothy	D	11
Lect	Berg, Kenneth	M	10
Lect	Cassarino, Richard	M	62D
Asst Prof	Chou, Sarana	M	13,10,34
Assoc Prof	Copeland, Philip L.	D	60,36
Asst Prof	Dalton, Grant B.	D	65,11,32E,47,50
Asst Prof	Davis, Joel	D	10,13,34
Lect	Dorroh, William J.	D	66G
Lect	Doss, Laura	M	61
Lect	Flaniken, Angela M.	M	62B
Asst Prof	Flaniken, Jeffrey Z.	M	62A,13B,32E
Prof	Fouse, Kathryn L.	D	66A,66B
Lect	Gable, Laura Beth	M	66D,34
Lect	Georges, Julia	M	32B
Lect	Henriques, Yurii	M	64A
Lect	Hicks, Judy S.	M	62E
Prof	Hopkins, Joseph H.	D	61
Asst Prof	Kenning, Kristin	D	61,39
Inst	King, Melodie S.	M	66D
Lect	Knight, Stephen B.	M	69
Lect	Koonce, Jeffrey C.	B	63C
Lect	Kozak, Kevin J.	M	63B,13C,41
Lect	Lawhon, Daniel E.	D	66G,44
Prof	Lawhon, Sharon L.	D	61,36
Lect	Lim, Rachel	M	13B
Inst	Macon, Connie	M	66D
Lect	Masri, Tariq	B	64D
Inst	Mathis, Eric L.	M	31A
Lect	McElroy, John	B	63A
Lect	McGinnis, Beth	D	66D,11,12A
Lect	Nordlund, Caroline	M	62A,32E
Prof	Nordlund, Moya L.	D	32,13C
Lect	Nordlund, Samuel	M	62C
Lect	Portis, Vicki	M	32B
Prof	Richardson, Paul A.	D	61,31A
Prof	Richardson, W. Randall	D	61,54
Lect	Robertson, R. Scott	B	63D
Prof	Sanders, Donald C.	D	12A,66A
Lect	Senasi, Karlo	B	70
Lect	Shinn, Barbara A.	M	13C,13B,13A,66D
Prof	Shinn, Ronald R.	D	66A,66C,13B
Asst Prof	Smisek, James J.	D	60B,37,32E
Inst PT	Sullivan, James B.	M	64B
Inst	Szurek, Jaroslaw P.	M	11,16
Lect	Taylor, Terry D.	M	31A
Asst Prof	Viliunas, Brian	M	64C,38,13C,32E,60B
Asst Prof	Villaverde, Christina	M	61
Lect	White, Sallie V.	M	64E

AL0830 Selma University
Department of Music
1501 Lapsley St
Selma, AL 36701
(334) 872-2533   Fax: (334) 872-7746
www.selmauniversity.org

Historically Black College

Prof	Garcia, William Burres	D	

AL0831 Shelton State Junior College
Department of Music
9500 Old Greensboro Rd
Tuscaloosa, AL 35405
(205) 759-1541   Fax: (205)759-2495
www.sheltonstate.edu
E-mail: Gblackshear@Sheltonstate.Edu

2 Year Institution

Inst	Blackshear, Alan	D	37,13,11,29
	Blackshear, Glinda	M	60,11,36,39,61
	Brown, J. F. Mark	D	61,35,36,11
	Coats, Syble M.	M	66A,66D,11,13A

AL0850 Snead State Community College
Department of Music
220 N Walnut St
PO Box 734
Boaz, AL 35957-0734
(256) 593-5120   Fax: (256) 593-7180
www.snead.edu
E-mail: melinda.brooks@snead.edu

2 Year Institution

Chair: Melinda K. Brooks, 80A

Inst	Brooks, Melinda K.	D	11,13,66A,66D
Inst	Lipscomb, Janice		61
Inst	McGee, Michael		37,47,63,64,65
Inst	Sullivan, Keith	B	70,11
Inst	Tidmore, Natasha		36,29

AL0890 Southeastern Bible College
Department of Music
2545 Valleydale Rd
Birmingham, AL 35244-2083
(205) 970-9239   Fax: (205) 970-9207
www.sebc.edu
E-mail: stimothy@sebc.edu

4 Year Institution

Director: Sarah O. Timothy, 80A

Adj	Moore, Kevin	M	11,31
Adj	Spann, Joseph	M	11,13,70,34A,34D
Assoc Prof	Timothy, Sarah O.	M	61,11,36,13,32

AL0900 Southern Union State Comm College
Department of Music
PO Box 1000
Wadley, AL 36276
(256) 395-2211   Fax: (256) 395-2215
www.suscc.edu
E-mail: mmarcades@suscc.edu

2 Year Institution

Music Contact: Michael Marcades, 80A

Inst	Marcades, Michael	PhD	12A,12B,13,32,36

AL0950 Stillman College
Department of Music
PO Box 1430
Tuscaloosa, AL 35403-1430
(205) 247-8046   Fax: (205) 349-4252
www.stillman.edu
E-mail: lparsons@stillman.edu

4 Year Institution, Historically Black College

Chair, Fine Arts: Brock L. Fisher, 80A
Music Area Coordinator: Laura E. Parsons, 80A
Dir., Artist/Performance Series: Phillip Todd Westgate, 80F

Asst Prof	Harrison, Luvada A.	DMA	61,39
Asst Prof	Jung, Hyesook	DMA	66A,66B,66C,13
Asst Prof	Parsons, Laura E.	DMA	63A,63,12A,13A,11
Inst	Thomas, O. T.	M	37,35A,65
Assoc Prof	Westgate, Phillip Todd	DMA	13,36,66A,66G,66C
Inst	Williams, Robert	M	37,46,60

AL1000 Talladega College
Department of Fine Arts & Music
Talladega, AL 35160
(256) 362-0206   Fax: (256) 362-2268
www.talladega.edu
E-mail: lgmcleod@talladega.edu

4 Year Institution, Historically Black College

Chair: Lindy McLeod, 80A

| Assoc Prof | McLeod, Lindy | M | |

AL1050 Troy University
J.M. Long School of Music
University Ave
Troy, AL 36082
(334) 670-3322   Fax: (334) 670-3858
music.troy.edu
E-mail: music@troy.edu

4 Year Institution, Graduate School
Member of NASM

Master of Science in Music Education, Master of Science Focus in Music Industry

Director and Coord., Graduate Programs: Larry Blocher, 80A,80C
Coord., Undergraduate Studies: Carla A. Gallahan, 80B
Coord., Undergraduate Studies: James W. Smith, Jr., 80B
Coord., Graduate Programs: Robert W. Smith, 80C

Adj	Adams, Jacquelyn	D	32D
Adj	Alexander, Jason	D	65
Prof	Allard, Catherine	D	61,42
Asst Prof	Amonson, Christina	D	60A,32D,39
Adj	Bell, James	M	66A
Asst Prof	Blackstock, Adam	D	37,65
Prof	Blocher, Larry	D	32E,37
Adj	Bullock, Robert		34,35
Adj	Burns, Robert	B	62D
Adj	Cutchen, Dovie		62,66A
Adj	Denison, William R.	D	66A,66G
Adj	Foster, Adam	D	32E
Assoc Prof	Franks, Carol	M	13,64A,48
Asst Prof	Fredrick, Samuel	M	11
Asst Prof	Gallahan, Carla A.	M	32,63B
Adj	Georges, Julia	M	64C
Adj	Gibson, Robert L.	D	70
Asst Prof	Huff, Michael H.	D	63A,42,49,67E,37
Asst Prof	Jinright, John W.	D	13,64D,34,64B,66A
Adj	Keeley, Michael	M	63A
Prof Emeritus	Long, John M.	D	
Adj	Mendel, Traci R.	D	13
Adj	Mixon, Laura		36,32
Prof	Orlofsky, Diane	D	32,I2C,36
Asst Prof	Phillips, Timothy S.	D	64C,12,48
Assoc Prof	Smith, James W.	M	63D,32E,11
Assoc Prof	Smith, Raymond H.	M	47,37,34,64E,29
Prof	Smith, Robert W.	M	35,34
Lect	Threadgill, Gwen J.	M	32B,13C,66A,66D
Assoc Prof Emeritus	Vollrath, Carl P.	D	10,11
Adj	Walden, Daniel	M	63D
Assoc Prof	Walker, Mark	D	63D,37,60B
Asst Prof	Ward, Eric	M	65,35
Adj	Webb, Lewis	M	61,36,66A
Adj	Williamson, Andy		70
Asst Prof	Woods, Bret	D	14C,20,34
Lect	Yang, Hui-Ting	D	66A,66C

AL1100 Tuskegee University
Department of Fine & Perf Arts
Band Cottage
Tuskegee Institute, AL 36088
(334) 727-8325   Fax: (334) 724-4295
www.tuskegee.edu
E-mail: duncan@tuskegee.edu

Historically Black College

Chair: Warren L. Duncan, 80A

Barr, Wayne A.		36
Duncan, Warren L.	B	13,11,47,65
Garcia, Lynda K.		66C

AL1150 Univ of Alabama-Birmingham
Department of Music
950 13th St South
Birmingham, AL 35294-1260
(205) 934-7376   Fax: (205) 975-1931
www.music.uab.edu
E-mail: uabmusic@uab.edu

4 Year Institution, Graduate School
Member of NASM

Master of Arts in Education

Chair: Howard L. Irving, 80A
Associate Chair: Paul W. Mosteller, 80H

Adj	Attar, Yaniv	D	70
Adj	Becker, Abraham N.	B	62D
Adj	Bouchillon, Joel	B	35G
Asst Prof	Cho, Won	D	61
Adj	Cochran, Martin	D	63,11
Asst Prof	Fambrough, Gene	D	50,37,65
Adj	Fisher, Chad	B	29
Assoc Prof	Gainey, Denise A.	D	64C,32
Adj	Glaser, Michael P.	B	29
Adj	Haskins, Jodi	B	62A,62B,11
Adj	Hultgren, Craig	M	11,62C
Asst Prof	Hurst-Wajszczuk, Kristine M.	D	61,39
Prof	Irving, Howard L.	D	12A
Adj	Kasman, Tatiana	M	66C,41
Assoc Prof	Kasman, Yakov	D	66A
Asst Prof	Kittredge, Brian	M	36,40
Adj	Koonce, Jeff	M	63C
Adj	Lanter, Mark W.	M	11
Adj	Masri, Tariq	B	64D
Adj	Moon, Brian C.	B	34
Assoc Prof	Mosteller, Paul W.	D	61,11
Adj	Pandolfi, David	B	63B
Prof	Panion, Henry	D	34
Asst Prof	Phillips, Scott L.	D	32F,34,45
Adj	Pino, Carlos E.	M	29
Asst Prof	Price, William M.	D	13,10
Adj	Ratliff, Phillip W.	D	11
Assoc Prof	Reynolds, Jeff W.	D	60,36,39
Asst Prof	Roberts, Steven	D	29,63A,47
Adj	Robertson, R. Scott	B	63D
Adj	Rust, Rosalind	M	66D
Asst Prof	Samuels, Sue	M	37,32E,60B
Adj	Sullivan, James B.	M	64B
Inst PT	Turner, Kevin P.	B	36
Adj	Wienhold, Lisa J.	M	64A
Adj	Wiley, Mathew S.	B	29
Adj	Womack, Sara	M	32B
Asst Prof	Zingara, James	D	63A,37

AL1160 Univ of Alabama-Huntsville
Department of Music
Roberts Hall
Room 102
Huntsville, AL 35899
(256) 824-6436   Fax: (256) 824-6411
www.uah.edu
E-mail: dave.ragsdale@uah.edu

4 Year Institution
Member of NASM

| PT | Avery, Handy | M | 36,60A |
| PT | Balch, Mary W. | M | 64E,64C |

PT	Billmayer, Veneta A.	M	62C
PT	Bounds, Kevin S.	ABD	12A,11,13A
Prof Emeritus	Boyer, D. Royce	D	11,12A,36,61,31A
PT	Branch, Thomas W.	B	50,65
PT	Cavender, James L.	B	70,41,46,62D
Asst Prof	Colwitz, Erin E.	DMA	32B,61,60A,36,32C
PT	Davis, Beth A.	M	32A,32B
PT	Eaton, Alice Butler	B	66A
PT	Gifford, Robert R.	M	64A
PT	Gillies, Peter	D	13C
PT	Guidry, Travis	M	65,50
PT	Hogue, Charles		62B,51
PT	Huff, Mark Y.	M	62D
PT	Leach, Margaret C.	B	61
PT	Loach, Deborah	M	65,50
PT	Miller, David L.	D	66G
PT	Miller, John L.	B	66A
PT	Motz, Steve	B	64E
PT	Newman, Katherine L.	M	62E
PT	Nutt, Dorrie		63B,41
PT	Orton, Billy H.	M	36,60A,60B,61,63C
PT	Park, In-Sook	M	11
PT	Poff, Megan	M	61,11
Asst Prof	Ragsdale, C. David	DMA	37,60,11,64E
PT	Roberts, Ron A.	M	66A,66B
Prof	Sanders, Carolyn I.	D	13A,11,63A
PT	Schneider, Lisa A.	M	11,64B,41
PT	Stone, Elizabeth	B	64A,41
PT	Taylor, Keith A.	M	66A,29B,46
PT	Thomas, Hunter		64D
Adj	Von Spakovsky, Ingrid	M	66A,66D
PT	Waters, Becky	M	10A,11,13C
PT	Watters, Ken G.		29
Adj	Weaver, Phillip E.	B	70,41
Assoc Prof	Wray, Ron E.	DMA	64C,37,13,60
PT	Young, Karen L.	M	61,11,39

AL1170 Univ of Alabama
School of Music
Box 870366
Tuscaloosa, AL 35487-0366
(205) 348-7110   Fax: (205) 348-1473
www.music.ua.edu
E-mail: ssnead@music.ua.edu

4 Year Institution, Graduate School
Member of NASM

Master of Arts in Music Education, Master of Music in Composition, Master of Music in Music Theory, Master of Music in Performance, Master of Music in Musicology, DMA in Composition, DMA in Conducting, DMA in Performance, Doctor of Education in Music Education, Master of Music in Choral Conducting, Master of Music in Wind Conducting, Master of Music in Musicology/Ethnomusicology

Director: Charles G. Snead, 80A
Assistant Director & Dir., Undergraduate Studies: Shelly Meggison, 80B,80H
Dir., Graduate Studies: Linda P. Cummins, 80C
Dir., Summer Programs: Randall Coleman, 80G

Assoc Prof	Biermann, Joanna Cobb	D	12
Prof	Bridges, Scott	D	41,64C
Prof	Cary, Stephen	D	61
Assoc Prof	Cevasco, Andrea	D	33
Inst PT	Chenez, Raymond	D	61
Asst Prof	Coleman, Randall	M	37,60B,32E
Assoc Prof	Cummins, Linda P.	D	12
Asst Prof Emeritus	Drill, Daniel	M	63C
Prof	Engebretson, Noel J.	D	66A
Asst Prof	Fader, Don	PhD	55C,67C,12
Asst Prof	Feeney, Tim	D	65,50
Prof	First, Craig P.	D	13,10,45,34
Prof	Fleming, Susan C.	DMA	61
Prof	Freese, Faythe R.	D	66G,66H,69
Asst Prof	Fulks, Jubal	M	62A
Prof	Gille, Tanya	D	66A
Inst FT	Gordon, Pamela		66D,66C
Inst PT	Gregoire, Jenny		62A
Asst Prof	Hancock, Carl B.	D	32G,32,34
Asst Prof	Houghtaling, Paul	M	39,61
Assoc Prof	Johnson, Marvin	D	13,10,45
Inst PT	Johnson, Michael	M	62D
Inst PT	Kordes, Gesa	D	55
Assoc Prof	Kozak, Christopher M.	M	29,62D
Inst PT	Lanter, Mark	M	65
Asst Prof	Latimer, Marvin E.	D	32D,36,60A
Asst Prof	Mann, Jenny L.	D	64D,12A,13
Prof	McCreery, Carlton	M	38,62C
Assoc Prof	McGuire, Kenneth	D	32
Assoc Prof	Meggison, Shelly	M	64B,11
Librarian	Miller, Cynthia F.	PhD	16
Asst Prof	Molina, Osiris J.	D	64C
Assoc Prof	Noffsinger, Jonathan	D	47,64E,53
Prof	Ozzello, Kenneth B.	D	60B,32C,37
Inst PT	Parrish, Regina T.	D	32
Assoc Prof	Peles, Stephen	D	13
Prof	Penick, Amanda	M	66A
Inst PT	Penick, Pam	D	35E
Prof	Prickett, Carol A.	D	32,33
Prof	Ratledge, John	D	60A,36
Asst Prof	Robinson, Thomas	M	13
Assoc Prof	Schultz, Diane Boyd	D	64A
Inst FT	Segall, Christopher	D	13
Prof	Snead, Charles G.	M	49,63B
Inst PT	Sullivan, Judith	M	62E
Asst Prof	Sweaney, Daniel	M	62B
Assoc Prof	Thurman, Demondrae	M	63D
Asst Prof	Whitaker, Jon	D	63C
Inst FT	Williams, Susan E.	D	61
Inst FT	Witt, Anne C.	D	62,32
Prof	Wolfe, Thomas	M	47,70,29,35B
Asst Prof	Yates, Eric	D	63A

AL1195 Univ of Mobile
Center for Performing Arts
5735 College Parkway
Mobile, AL 36613-2842
(251) 442-2420   Fax: (251) 442-2526
www.umobile.edu
E-mail: amiller@mail.umobile.edu

4 Year Institution

Director & Dean: John Roger Breland, 80A
Associate Dean & Dir., Undergraduate Studies: Al Miller, 80B,80H
Dir., Admissions: Kim Leousis, 80D
Dir., Summer Music Camps: Barbara Laurendine, 80G

Inst PT	Barry, Rebecca	M	29,64E
Inst PT	Breland, Jason	M	36
Adj Prof	Brown, Melba	M	32,61,11,39
Asst Prof	Buhaiciuc, Mihaela	D	39,13,61
Inst PT	Chapman, Stan	M	62D
Inst PT	Crowley, Patrick	B	65
Asst Prof	Davis, Randy	M	37,38,60,13,48
Inst PT	Evers, Carol	M	66
Assoc Prof	Fox, Rebecca	M	13,11,32,66A
Asst Prof	Habib, Mark	M	70
Inst PT	Hall, Beth	B	64A
Asst Prof	Jacobs, Patrick	D	61,39
Inst PT	Johnson, Byron	M	61
Inst PT	King, Adam	B	66A,13,66D,66C
Inst PT	King, Ryan	B	61
Inst PT	Laurendine, Barbara	B	66A,66D
Inst PT	Leday, Eric	M	63D
Inst PT	Lovely, Christopher	M	66A,66C
Inst PT	Merkel, Steve	M	35
Inst PT	Messick, Heather	B	61,43
Asst Prof	Miller, Al	D	60,61,36,43
Adj Prof	Moreland, Wilbur	M	64
Inst PT	Moses, Mark	B	
Asst Prof	Myrick, John	D	32,62A,62B,41,51
Inst PT	Odom, Aaron	M	61
Asst Prof	Plash, Duane	M	13,10,66A,40
Inst PT	Ramirez, Patricia	M	61
Asst Prof	Sanchez, Pete	D	31,43
Inst PT	Sanchez, Scott	B	35
Asst Prof	Small, Allanda	D	61,39
Inst PT	Soo Mauldin, Rosalyn	D	66A,66D
Inst PT	Sylvester, Joyce	M	61
Inst PT	Taylor, William	M	66G
Inst PT	Unger, Susan	B	63B
Inst PT	White, David	B	65
Asst Prof	Wolf, Donald	M	10F,37,46,47,63A
Inst PT	Wolf, Lily	B	54,43
Inst PT	Yu, Enen	M	62A

AL1200 Univ of Montevallo
Department of Music
Station 6670
Montevallo, AL 35115-6670
(205) 665-6670   Fax: (205) 665-6676
www.montevallo.edu/music
E-mail: music@montevallo.edu

4 Year Institution
Member of NASM

Chair: Alan Goldspiel, 80A
Dir., Preparatory Division: Lauren Morgan, 80E

Prof	Ardovino, Joseph	D	63A,37,47,49
Prof	Ardovino, Lori	D	12A,48,64C,64E,67C
Inst PT	Bowles, Adam Alan	D	66C
Inst PT	Burnham, Jay K.	B	65,50
Asst Prof	Doyle, Melinda S.	D	36,60A,40
Inst PT	Evans, Jay	M	63C,63D,42
Inst PT	Faulkner, Lynn	D	66A,66C,66D
Assoc Prof	George, Roderick L.	D	61
Prof	Goldspiel, Alan	D	70,13C,13B,51
Asst Prof	Halliday, Anna Rebecca	D	11,32A,32B
Inst PT	Harrington, Barbara	M	64A,42
Asst Prof	Hoffman, Edward C. 'Ted'	D	11,32C,32E,60B
Assoc Prof	Landers, Joseph	D	10A,10F,13B,13C,13E
Prof	MacCrae, Cynthia Perry	D	66A,66B,66C,66D
Inst PT	McKinney, Matthew	M	34D,34H,35C,35G
Inst PT	Middaugh, Laurie	M	66C,66D
Inst PT	Ortiguera, Joseph	M	11,12A,13B
Inst PT	Pandolfi, David		63B,42
Asst Prof	Sargent, Joseph	D	11,12A,13B,13C
Inst PT	Schlaffer, Machiko Ogawa	M	64B
Prof	Williams, Melanie B.	D	61
Assoc Prof	Wood, Charles E.	D	61,39,12A

AL1250 Univ of North Alabama
Department of Music & Theatre
Box 5040
Florence, AL 35632-0001
(256) 765-4375 Fax: (256) 765-4995
www.una.edu/music
E-mail: dmmccullough@una.edu

4 Year Institution
Member of NASM

Chair: David M. McCullough, 80A

PT	Arcu, Ariana	D	62C
Inst	Bostic-Brown, Tiffany	D	39,61,54,13A
Asst Prof	Brown, Terrance D.	M	39,54,61
Assoc Prof	Cai, Yi-Min	D	66A,66B,66D,66C
Assoc Prof	Elsey, Eddie L.	D	49,13B,63C,63D
Asst Prof	Flores, Yasmin A.	DMA	64C,64E,64D,48,13B
Inst	Flowers, Alan	M	11,12A
PT	Gifford, Gene	M	13A,61,13E
PT	Huff, Mark	D	62D
PT	Jackson, James	D	32E
Assoc Prof	Jones, Lloyd	D	64,37,47,32E,34A
Prof Emeritus PT	Jones, Lloyd E.	D	60B,37,63
PT	Lay, Lara	M	64B
Assoc Prof	Loeppky, Ian R.	D	60,36,41,40
PT	McClellan, Eleanor	M	61
PT	McCoy, Louise	M	66C,66D
Prof	McCullough, David M.	D	32B,63B,32C,32E
Asst Prof	Moyer, Iain	M	65,32E
PT	Nelson, Jessica L.	M	66A,66G,66D
PT	O'Neal, Whitney	M	12A,13A
PT	Stegall, Pat	M	32B,32C
PT	Valentine, Bob	B	70
Inst	Weimann, Viljar P.	M	62A,62B,38,10F
PT	Woodford, Martha	M	66D

AL1300 Univ of South Alabama
Department of Music
LPAC 1072
Mobile, AL 36688-0002
(251) 460-6136 Fax: (251) 460-7328
www.southalabama.edu/music
E-mail: music@jaguar1.usouthal.edu

4 Year Institution
Member of NASM

Chair: Greg Gruner, 80A
Dir., Artist Series: Keith Bohnet, 80F

PT	Barker, John C.		64C,41
PT	Bemis, Jennifer	M	66A,66C,66D
Prof	Bohnet, Andra	D	12A,41,64A,62E,35A
PT	Bohnet, Keith	M	11
Prof	Bush, Jerry Alan	D	66A,66B
PT	Davis, Kevin	M	11,66G,13C
PT	Driskell, Daniel	M	66A,66D
Assoc Prof	Durant, David Z.	D	13,10,34,10A,10B
Assoc Prof	Fresne, Jeannette	D	32A,32B,32C,32D,32I
PT	Gilmore, Robert	M	11,63D
PT	Greenwood, Matthew	M	65,11
Prof	Gruner, Greg	D	37,63D,60B,32E,35
Prof	Heavner, Tracy	D	32E,64E,47,53
Prof	Holm, Robert	M	66A,66B,66C,66D,66H
PT	Imsand, Patrick K.	M	70,11,51

PT	King, Megan	M	61
PT	Leska, Gosia	D	62
Asst Prof	Miller, Ward	M	37,63D,41,32E,60B
Asst Prof	Mindock, Rebecca A.	D	64B,64D,12A,34,42
Asst Prof	Moore, Laura M.	D	36,40,60A,61,66C
PT	Noah, Laura	M	35,65
PT	Noah, Sean	M	62D
Inst	Petersen, William	M	32E,37,63D,60B,49
Inst	Rivera, Luis C.	D	20,32E,41,65,50
Assoc Prof	Rowell, Thomas L.	D	61,39,40
PT	Seebacher, Robert	M	11,38,51
PT	Sunderland, Jose	M	62C
PT	Sylvester, Joyce	M	61
PT	Thwaites, Mary Evelyn Clark	M	11
PT	Wood, Jodi	M	11,63B
Assoc Prof	Wood, Peter J.	DMA	63A,13,49,41
Asst Prof PT	Zoghby, Linda	M	61

AL1350 Univ of West Alabama
Department of Fine Arts
Station 10
Livingston, AL 35470
(205) 652-3515 Fax: (205) 652-3405
www.uwa.edu
E-mail: meb@uwa.edu

4 Year Institution

Prof	Blackwell, Manley	D	11,12A,66A
Prof	Kudlawiec, Nancy A.	D	11,32,66A,12A,13

AL1450 Wallace State Community College
Department of Music
PO Box 2000
Hanceville, AL 35077-2000
(256) 352-8277 Fax: (256) 352-8228
www.wallacestate.edu
E-mail: ricky.burks@wallacestate.edu

2 Year Institution

Chair: Ricky Burks, 80A

Prof	Bean, Robert G.	M	13,37,47,63,29
Assoc Prof	Burks, Ricky	M	48,64,46,29B,37
Staff	Castles, JoAnn		16,34C
Staff	Neal, Mark		65,47,34,35
Assoc Prof	Richter, Tiffany	M	13,36,40,61
Assoc Prof	Sparks, Michael	M	12A,36,66A,31A,34

AR0050 Arkansas Northeastern College
Department of Music
2501 S Division St
Blytheville, AR 72315
(870) 762-1020 Fax: (870) 763-6923
www.anc.edu
E-mail: dhay@smail.anc.edu

2 Year Institution

Music Contact: Dennis Hay

Inst	Hay, Dennis	M	13A,13B,11,66A,66C
Inst	Jensen, Andrew	D	60A,36,11,61,13C

AR0100 Arkansas State University-Beebe
Department of Music
PO Box 1000
Beebe, AR 72012-1000
(501) 882-8766 Fax: (501) 882-8370
www.asub.edu
E-mail: belong@asub.edu

2 Year Institution

Chair: Bill Long, 80A

Asst Prof	Bristow, Brent		
Asst Prof	Long, Bill		

AR0110 Arkansas State University-State U
Department of Music
PO Box 779
State University, AR 72467
(870) 972-2094   Fax: (870) 972-3932
www.astate.edu
E-mail: toconnor@astate.edu

4 Year Institution, Graduate School
Member of NASM

Master of Music in Composition, Master of Music in Performance, Master of Music Education, Master of Music in Choral Conducting, Master of Music in Wind Conducting

Dean: Don Bowyer, 80A
Interim Chair: Ken Hatch, 80A
Dean, Fine Arts: Daniel Reeves, 80A
Dir., Graduate Studies: John Edward Owen, 80C

Adj Inst	Alley, Rob	M	11
Prof	Bartee, Neale	D	60,12A,49,63C
Asst Prof	Bonner, Joe	M	48,64A,20
Prof	Bowyer, Don	D	63C,63D,29,35C,47
Asst Prof	Carey, Matthew	M	54,61
Assoc Prof	Carroll, Kenneth D.	D	29,64E,37,46
Inst	Chandler, Kyle	M	32,36,47,32D,32G
Adj Inst	Clark, Dale	D	64D
Asst Prof	Clark, Lauren Schack	D	66C,66D,66B
Assoc Prof	Collison, Craig	M	11,41,50,65
Assoc Prof	Crist, Timothy D.	D	13,45,10,70
Prof	Dauer, Robin	D	13,11,63B
Inst	Fiala, Joy	M	13,11,32
Asst Prof	Hatch, Ken	D	41,64C,64E,16
Asst Prof	Horton, Ron	M	29
Adj Inst	Julien, Ellis	D	60A
Adj Inst	Kirkscey, Jonathan	M	62C,62D
Assoc Prof	Kyriakos, Marika V.	DMA	61,39
Prof	Miller, Dale	D	60,36,61
Prof	O'Connor, Thomas	D	13,32,47,10A,10F
Assoc Prof	Oliver, Timothy	D	37,32
Adj Inst	O'Neal, Harriet	M	66G,66A
Assoc Prof	Owen, John Edward	D	60,11,63D
Prof	Ross, Daniel F.	D	11,41,64B,64D,72
Adj Inst	Ryan, Kate	M	62A,62B
Asst Prof	Seay, Sandra	M	11,61,32
Asst Prof	Wilson, Chris	D	49,32E,11

AR0200 Arkansas Tech University
Department of Music
WPN 107
407 West Q St
Russellville, AR 72801
(479) 968-0368   Fax: (479) 968-0467
www.atu.edu/music
E-mail: chukill@atu.edu

4 Year Institution
Member of NASM

Chair: Cynthia L. Hukill, 80A
Dir., Summer Music Camp: Christopher Anderson, 80G

Assoc Prof	Anderson, Christopher	D	60,32C,37
Assoc Prof	Barber, Deborah L.	M	34,32B,10D,70,32C
Prof	Barrow, Gary	D	49,63A,63B
Adj	Buck, Casey	M	62
Adj	Buck, Kristina	M	61
Asst Prof	Clements, Barbara	D	61
Asst Prof	Clements, Jon	D	61,39,13C
Adj	Conatser, Brian	M	13A,66A,13B,13C,66C
Adj	Cornwell, Tina	M	32E
Asst Prof	del Grazia, Nicolas M.	D	32E,41,48,64C
Assoc Prof	Futterer, Karen	M	12A,48,64A
Assoc Prof	Futterer, Kenneth	M	10,48,64B,64D,64E
Asst Prof	Gale, Holly Ruth	M	61
Assoc Prof	Hukill, Cynthia L.	D	66A,13
Assoc Prof	Kiehl, Vicky	M	66A,66H,66B,66D,66C
Adj	Lybarger, Lowell H.	D	20,16
Inst	Morris, Gary	M	36,40,60A,61
Assoc Prof	Parker, Philip	M	13,10F,10,65,50
Asst Prof	Reed, Sean Scot	D	63C,47
Assoc Prof	Smith, Timothy	D	13,12A,66A,66C
Adj	Wiggins, Marcus	M	63D

AR0225 East Arkansas Community College
Department of Music
Forrest City, AR 72335-2204
(870) 633-4480   Fax: (870) 633-7222
www.eacc.edu
E-mail: rvowan@eacc.edu

2 Year Institution

Chair: Catherine Cline, 80A

Inst	Carter, Linda		
	Vowan, Ruth A.	M	61,12A,36,39

AR0250 Harding University
Department of Music
HU 10767
Searcy, AR 72149-0001
(501) 279-4343   Fax: (501) 279-4086
www.harding.edu/music
E-mail: music@harding.edu

4 Year Institution
Member of NASM

Chair: Kelly Neill, 80A
Dir., Preparatory Division: Lis Jones, 80E
Dir., Artist/Performance Series: Clifton L. Ganus, III, 80F

Adj	Bristow, Brent	D	64E
Adj	Camp, Cheryl	B	66A
Asst Prof	Carrell, Cynthia T.	D	11,13,32E,37,63A
Assoc Prof	Carrell, Scott	D	10A,13,34A,66A,66B
Prof	Casey, J. Warren	D	10F,11,32,47,64C
Assoc Prof	Chance, Mike	M	32E,37,38,63C,63D
Prof Emerita	Cox, Patricia J.	D	11,32,34C,38,62B
Inst	Eads, Laura	M	61
Prof	Ganus, Clifton L.	D	12A,31A,36,60A
Adj	Gibson, Gerry	M	64B
Adj	Henderson, Jenny	M	66A,32
Asst Prof	Hicks, Charles	M	70
Prof	Hopper, Jeffrey T.	D	66A
Inst	Jones, Lis	M	66A,66C,66D
Asst Prof	Neill, Kelly	D	32D,36,40,61
Asst Prof	Parker, Wesley	M	65,11,20,37
Adj	Robertson, Roki	B	66A
Prof	Shearin, Arthur Lloyd	D	11,36,61
Adj	Williams, Alicia	M	64A

AR0300 Henderson State University
Department of Music
Box 7733
Arkadelphia, AR 71999-0001
(870) 230-5036   Fax: (870) 230-5424
www.hsu.edu/music
E-mail: bucknej@hsu.edu

4 Year Institution
Member of NASM

Chair: James R. Buckner, 80A
Dir., Summer Programs: Steven M. Knight, 80G

Inst PT	Amox, Jennifer	M	64A,20
Assoc Prof	Becraft, Steven C.	D	64C,29A,64E,48,32E
Prof	Buckner, James R.	D	49,63A,32E
Asst Prof	Clardy, Shannon	D	64B
Inst PT	Cranson, Todd	M	63D
Prof	Dimond, Raymond R.	D	47,65,53,13,32E
Prof	Etienne, David	D	11,20,32E
Prof	Evans, David H.	D	13,11,12A,32,48
Asst Prof	Fox, Ryan H	D	36,60A,32D,40
Prof	Higgins, William L.	D	39,61,60A,13C
Inst PT	Jones, Kate	M	62C,62D
Asst Prof	Juhn, Hee-Kyung	D	66A,13C,66G,66C,66B
Inst	Knight, Steven M.	M	37,32E
Inst	Larragoity, Ingrid	M	37,32E,13B,48
Inst PT	Laubach, David	B	63A,49
Inst PT	Laursen, Amy	M	63B,32B
Asst Prof	Lipton, Jamie	D	63D,49,13A
Inst	Molinari, Kyounghwa	M	66A,66C,66D
Prof	Schroeder, Phillip J.	D	13,10
Prof	Sommer, Maralyn		64D
Inst PT	Staskevicius, Algis	M	62A,62B,32E
Assoc Prof	Storm, Laura	D	61
Assoc Prof	Tsao-Lim, May	DMA	66A,66C,66D,66B,13B
Inst PT	Tucker, Jenna	M	61

AR0350 Hendrix College
Department of Music
1600 Washington Ave
Conway, AR 72032-3080
(501) 450-1249   Fax: (501) 450-1437
www.hendrix.edu/music
E-mail: boehm@hendrix.edu

4 Year Institution
Member of NASM

Chair: Norman Boehm, 80A

Inst Adj	Anderson, Robert	M	64B,64C,64D,64E,47
Inst Adj	Austin, Linda	B	61
Inst Adj	Baker, Christian Matthew	D	62A
Inst Adj	Banister, Suzanne	M	61
Prof	Boehm, Norman	D	13,10,12A,66A,11
Inst Adj	Cline, Daniel	M	62C
Inst Adj	Dahlstrand, John	C	62D,51
Inst Adj	Duso, Lorraine	D	64B
Asst Prof	Fannin, Karen M.	D	29,11,13A,47,37
Inst Adj	Fleming, Ansley	M	66G,66A
Prof	Fleming, Nancy P.	D	12A,36,60A
Prof	Griebling, Karen	D	13,10,38,62B,14
Prof	Herrick, Carole	D	63A,63B
Assoc Prof	Krebs, John A.	D	66A,66C,39,11,13
Inst Adj	McDade, Joanne Estelle	M	61,66A
Inst Adj	McVinney, Barry D.	D	47
Inst Adj	Price, Allen	M	46
Inst Adj	Saoud, Erick	M	65,50
Inst Adj	Tucker, Timothy R.	M	61
Inst Adj	Tyson, Liana	D	64A,11,48

AR0400 John Brown University
Department of Music
2000 W University
Siloam Springs, AR 72761
(479) 524-7152   Fax: (479) 238-8580
www.jbu.edu
E-mail: psmith@jbu.edu

4 Year Institution

Chair: Paul B. Smith, 80A

Assoc Prof	Beckman, Linda L.	D	66A,11,10F,34,66C
	Manos, Larry	B	47
Adj Inst	Ostrander, Lonnie	M	66A,66C
Inst	Rollene, Donna	B	61,39
	Smith, Charlie		35G
Assoc Prof	Smith, Paul B.	M	60,36,61
Inst	White, Kayla	M	31,40,61
Prof	Wubbena, Jan Helmut	D	13,66G,12A,11
Prof	Wubbena, Teresa R.	M	13,32,41,16,64

R0425 Lyon College
Department of Music
2300 Highland Rd
Batesville, AR 72501
(870) 307-7332   Fax: (870) 307-7564
www.lyon.edu
E-mail: rstinson@lyon.edu

4 Year Institution

Chair, Language, Literature & Fine Arts: Catherine A. Bordeau, 80A

Adj	Ainanda, Lucy	M	63,64,65
Adj	Healey, Martha M.	M	66
Adj	Musgrave, Helen	B	61
Adj	Reeve, Barbara	M	62
Adj	Stinson, Laura	M	64A
Prof	Stinson, Russell	D	13,11,12A,12,66

AR0500 Ouachita Baptist University
School of Fine Arts-Music Div
410 Ouachita St
Arkadelphia, AR 71998-0001
(870) 245-5128   Fax: (870) 245-5274
www.obu.edu/music
E-mail: gerberg@obu.ed

4 Year Institution
Member of NASM

Chair: Gary G. Gerber, 80A

Adj	Aldridge, Glenda	M	66A
Adj	Bolton, Tom	D	61
Adj	Briggs, John	M	61
Assoc Prof	Cai, Lei	D	66A
Adj	Flora, Sim	D	32,37,47,63,13
Asst Prof	Garrett, Margaret	D	61
Assoc Prof	Gerber, Gary G.	D	36,61,32D,60A
Lect	Glenn, Suzetta	M	61
Inst	Grant, Kristin	M	64A,13A,13B,13C
Adj	Graves, Paul	M	32B
Lect	Haas, Adam J.	D	66A,66D
Prof	Hamilton, Craig V.	PhD	63A,60B,46,37
Inst	Hesse, Robert	M	37,11
Assoc Prof	Hewell, Rob	D	31A,44,11
Prof	Houlihan, Patrick	D	13,10
Inst	Isenhour, Justin	M	63C,63D,11,13C
Prof	Keck, Ouida	D	66A,66B
Vstng Asst Prof	Kolt, Robert P.	D	12,12A,60
Asst Prof	Lewis, Ryan C.	D	65,32E,12A,11
Prof	Secrest, Glenda	D	61
Prof	Secrest, Jon	D	39,61,54
Inst	Stanley, David	M	61,36
Prof	Taylor, Caroline	D	48,64,32E
Adj	Thayer, Heather	M	63B,13C
Lect	Williams, Robin	M	61
Asst Prof Emeritus	Worthen, Mary	M	61,13B,13C

AR0550 Philander Smith College
Department of Music
812 W 13th St
Little Rock, AR 72202-3718
(501) 370-5340   Fax: (501) 370-5278
www.philander.edu
E-mail: ttucker@philander.edu

4 Year Institution, Historically Black College

Chair: Phyllis Ruocco, 80A

Asst Prof	Chapple, Karliss		36
Asst Prof	Ruocco, Phyllis	D	13A,13,11,66A,10F
Asst Prof	Tucker, Timothy	M	61

AR0600 Southern Arkansas University
Department of Music
100 E University
Magnolia, AR 71753
(870) 235-4247   Fax: (870) 235-5005
www.saumag.edu/music
E-mail: dhdykema@saumag.edu

4 Year Institution
Member of NASM

Chair & Dir., Artist/Performance Series: Dan H. Dykema, 80A,80F
Dir., Summer Program: J. P. Wilson, 80G

Adj	Ard, Sharon	M	11,13A
Inst	Britt, Michael J.	M	46,50,65
Prof	Crouse, David L.	D	66A,13C,61,66G,13B
Adj	Davis, Mickey	M	62
Assoc Prof	Dykema, Dan H.	D	13B,11,66A,66D,13C
Adj	Mickey, Brian	M	63A,63B
Inst	Mickey, Sarah	M	37,48,64C,11
Assoc Prof	Shirey, Kim F.	D	32B
Asst Prof	Vickers, Jeffrey E.	M	64,11,64E,64A,12A
Asst Prof	Wilson, J. P.	M	37,63D,63C,32E,60B

AR0700 Univ of Arkansas-Fayetteville
Department of Music
201 Music Bldg
Fayetteville, AR 72701
(479) 575-4701   Fax: (479) 575-5409
www.uark.edu/depts/uamusic
E-mail: rmains@uark.edu

4 Year Institution, Graduate School
Member of NASM

Master of Music in Composition, Master of Music in Music Theory, Master of Music in Performance, Master of Music in Conducting, Master of Music in Music Education, Master of Music in Applied Music, Master of Music in Music History

Chair: Ronda Mains, 80A
Dir., Graduate Studies: Stephen Gates, 80C
Jr. & Sr. High Music Camps: Chalon L. Ragsdale, 80E
Associate Chair: Dale D. Misenhelter, 80H

Rank	Name	Deg	Areas
Prof Emeritus	Bright, Robert M.	M	49,63A
Adj	Burson, Claudia	M	66A
Prof	Cencel, Elaine	M	61
Assoc Prof	Cholthitchanta, Nophachai	D	64C
Inst PT	Delaplain, Theresa	D	64B
Prof	Gates, Stephen	D	41,62C
Prof	Greeson, James R.	D	13,10,70,47
Prof Emeritus	Groh, Jack C.	D	60,36,61
Asst Prof	Hickson, Carolyn R.	M	13,66A
Prof Emerita	Jackson, Barbara G.	D	13,12A,12,55B,67A
Prof Emeritus	Janzen, Eldon A.	M	60,32C,37
Assoc Prof Emeritus	Johnson, Campbell	D	10F,66G
Assoc Prof	Jones, Eddie	D	32,36
Asst Prof	Kahng, Er-Gene	D	62A,62B,41
Asst Prof	Knighten, Christopher	D	32E,37
Vstng Asst Prof	Knighten, Janet W.	M	32C,32E
Vstng Asst Prof	Lacy, Christopher	M	39
Prof	Mains, Ronda	D	64A,32B,32
Prof	Margulis, Elizabeth	D	13
Assoc Prof	Margulis, Jura	M	66A
Assoc Prof	Misenhelter, Dale D.	D	32
Adj	Montgomery, Michael R.	D	62D
Inst	Morris, Stanley	M	64E
Prof	Mueller, Robert K.	D	10,13
Asst Prof	Nedbal, Martin	D	12
Adj	Ortega, Catalina	M	64A
Assoc Prof	Pierce, Benjamin	D	63D
Vstng Asst Prof	Pratchard, Jeremy	M	37
Vstng Asst Prof	Prickett, Todd O.	D	36,32D
Prof	Ragsdale, Chalon L.	M	50,65
Prof	Ramey, Richard C.	M	13A,64D
Assoc Prof	Rulli, Richard J.	D	63A,42,49,41
Prof	Sloan, Gerald H.	M	63C,63D
Prof	Thompson, Timothy F.	D	12A,63B
Prof Emeritus	Umiker, Robert C.	M	48,64C,64E
Prof	Warren, W. Dale	M	60B,32E,37
Assoc Prof	Yoes, Janice	M	61

AR0730 Univ of Arkansas-Fort Smith
Department of Music
5210 Grand Ave
Fort Smith, AR 72913-3649
(479) 788-7530   Fax: (479) 788-7559
www.uafs.edu
E-mail: elizabeth.momand@uafs.edu

4 Year Institution

Chair: Elizabeth B. Momand, 80A

Rank	Name	Deg	Areas
Assoc Prof	Bailey, Don	M	13C,29A,29B,46,64E
Assoc Prof	Booker, Charles L.	M	10,32E,13,60B
Asst Prof	Carter, David	D	64C,64E,48,11
Adj	Dooly, Louann	M	64D,11
Adj	Hayes, Natlynn	M	61
Adj	Hudson, Virginia	M	64A,11
Prof	Husarik, Stephen	D	11,69,12A
Adj	Johnson, Jason	B	32F
Adj	Kenney, Sharon E.	D	61,66D
Adj	Knight, Joshua	M	65,50,11
Adj	Mann, George	M	11
Adj	Mathis, Nancy	M	61
Assoc Prof	Momand, Elizabeth B.	DMA	39,61,32
Assoc Prof	Moore, Rager H.	D	60A,61
Adj	Reyes, William	M	70
Adj	Sanders, Alice	M	66A,66C,66B
Asst Prof	Vangjel, Matthew S.	D	63A,46,13C
Adj	Waynick, Mark	M	11

Asst Prof	White, Edward C.	D	61,39,13
Adj	White, Katherine	D	61,11
Asst Prof	Zacharella, Alexandra	D	63C,63D,11,49,37

AR0750 Univ of Arkansas-Little Rock
Department of Music
2801 S University Ave
Little Rock, AR 72204-1000
(501) 569-3294   Fax: (501) 569-3559
www.ualr.edu/music
E-mail: music@ualr.edu

4 Year Institution
Member of NASM

Dean: Deborah J. Baldwin, 80A
Chair & Dir., Artist/Performance Series: Karen M. Bryan, 80A,80B,80D,80F

Rank	Name	Deg	Areas
Vstng Asst Prof	Allen, Ferris	D	61
PT	Antonetti, Susan	M	64A,48
PT	Austin, Linda B.	B	61
PT	Boccarossa, Jennifer	M	36
Prof Emeritus	Boswell, Ronald L.	M	13,11,29A
Prof	Boury, Robert	D	13,10,11
Prof	Bryan, Karen M.	D	12A,11
Prof	Carenbauer, Michael	M	45,51,70,34
PT	Clardy, Michael	M	64B
PT	Cox, Thomas E.	M	13,47,66A,66D
Assoc Prof Emeritus	Ellsworth, E. Victor	PhD	32,62,38
PT	Finnie, Mary	M	61
PT	Foreman, Carolyn	M	36
PT	Griffin, Nancy W.	M	66D,45
Assoc Prof	Groesbeck, Rolf A.	D	11,12,14,66A,20
Asst Prof	Hakutani, Naoki	D	66A,66D,45
PT	Hearnsberger, Keith	M	11,32
Prof	Holzer, Linda	D	66A,66B,42,15,11
PT	Jorgensen, Richard	M	63A,63B
Assoc Prof	Keating, Bevan T.	D	36,60,61
PT	Kesling, Diane	B	61
Inst	Kincade, Gertrude C.	B	66H,66C,66D
Inst	Law, Charles P.	M	65,50,37
Asst Prof	Lind, Vicki R.	D	32
PT	Maddox, Meredith R.	M	42,62A,62B
Inst	Marinova, Kristina	M	66C
Assoc Prof	Richeson, David T.	M	63A,11,35A
PT	Roitman, Tatiana	D	66A,66D,13
PT	Routen, I. J.	D	11
Assoc Fac	Spencer, James W.		35C,35G
PT	Struthers, Steve		70
PT	Taylor, Greg	M	11
PT	Tenison-Willis, MaryJo	M	11
Asst Prof	Underwood, Michael P.	D	13,37,63
PT	Vick, Joe D.	M	62D,70
Asst Prof	Wen, Andy	D	11,13,64C,64E

AR0800 Univ of Arkansas-Monticello
Division of Music
PO Box 3607
Monticello, AR 71656
(870) 460-1060   Fax: (870) 460-1260
www.uamont.edu/Music/
E-mail: spencer@uamont.edu

4 Year Institution
Member of NASM

Dean: Mark Spencer, 80A
Dir., Summer Programs: John C. Webb, 80G,80H

Rank	Name	Deg	Areas
Prof	Becker, Paul	D	66A,66B,66C,66D,11
Asst Prof	Lobitz, Beverly	M	13E,11,12A,61,13C
Assoc Prof	Meggs, Gary L.	M	60B,64,47,46,29
Assoc Prof	Pack, Lester	M	65,46,47,29,70
Prof	Skinner, Kent	D	60A,36,61,39,54
Inst	Webb, John C.	M	41,32E,37,60B,63
Inst	Windham, Mark	M	11,63,32E,32F,37

AR0810 Univ of Arkansas-Pine Bluff
Department of Music
MS 4956
1200 N Univ Dr
Pine Bluff, AR 71601
(870) 575-8905 Fax: (870) 575-4631
www.uapb.edu
E-mail: baileyr@uapb.edu

4 Year Institution
Member of NASM

Dean: Clifton Orr, 80A

Asst Prof	Bailey, Richard H.	D	34,35C,35G,63A
Prof	Bates, Michael J.	D	36,13,60,12A,66A
Inst	Evans, Darryl	M	32E,47,63D,13A,13B
Asst Prof	Fooster, Harold	M	60,11,37,50,65
Asst Prof	Gordon, Heidi Cohenour	D	61,13C,66D,36
Asst Prof	Graham, John	M	37,64E,64C,48
Assoc Prof	Jackson, Milton	M	13,11,49,63,70

AR0850 Univ of Central Arkansas
Department of Music
201 Donaghey Ave
Conway, AR 72035-5001
(501) 450-3163 Fax: (501) 450-5773
www.uca.edu/music
E-mail: jarvisj@uca.edu

4 Year Institution, Graduate School
Member of NASM

Master of Music in Music Theory, Master of Music in Performance, Master of Music in Conducting, Master of Music in Music Education, Graduate Certificate in Music

Chair: Jeffery W. Jarvis, 80A
Dir., Graduate Studies: Jane Dahlenburg, 80C
Dir., Preparatory Division: Jann D. Bryant, 80E

Prof	Anthony, Carl	D	13,66A
Lect	Antolik, Martha E.	D	61
PT	Banister, Suzanne	D	13C
PT	Biebesheimer, Arlene	D	11
Vstng Lect	Bledsoe, Joshua	M	63C,34
Prof	Brooks, Ricky W.	D	60B,37
Prof	Brown, Carolyn K.	D	64A,48
Inst	Bryant, Jann D.	M	
Vstng Asst Prof	Carichner, Christian Blake	M	63D
Asst Prof	Dahlenburg, Jane	D	12
Asst Prof	Dickinson, Paul J.	D	10,13,43,34
Inst	Dickinson, Stefanie C.	D	66A,13
Inst	Duso, Lorraine C.	D	64B,64D,11
PT	Emerson, Smokey	M	70
Assoc Prof	Erwin, John M.	M	60A,36,40
Asst Prof	Feldman, Stephen B.	DMA	11,41,62C
Asst Prof	Fisher, Ryan A.	D	32D,36
Inst	Franklin, Christine C.	M	66D
Inst	Getzov, Israel	M	38,10F
PT	Hanna, Joan	M	66C
PT	Hatch, Jim	M	62D
Assoc Prof	Holden, Robert	D	61,39
Assoc Prof	Hsu, Linda Y.	D	62A,51
Assoc Prof	Jarvis, Jeffery W.	D	63D,11,12A
Assoc Prof	Johnson, Kelly A.	D	64C
Asst Prof	Jones, R. Larry	M	47,63A
PT	Kotcherguina, Tatiana	M	62B
Prof	Lamar, Jackie B.	D	47,48,64E
PT	Loerch, Suzanne	M	61
Asst Prof	Mayo, Christine H. Donahue	M	61
Lect	Murakami, Kazuo	M	66A,66C
Assoc Prof	Oeste, Wolfgang	D	39,61
PT	Reynolds, Katherine	M	62B
Asst Prof	Rose, Leslie Paige	D	32B,34,32E
Assoc Prof	Rutman, Neil C.	D	66A,66B
Lect	Shires, Brent A.	M	63B,32E,42,49
Inst	Shires, Terrie A.	M	66D
Asst Prof	Smyth, Steven	M	37,47
PT	Stanley, Lynnette	M	66C,32A
Assoc Prof	Tyson, Blake W.	D	50,65
Assoc Prof	Young, Louis G.	D	11

AR0900 Univ of the Ozarks
Department of Music
415 N College Ave
Clarksville, AR 72830-2880
(479) 979-1343 Fax: (479) 979-1453
www.ozarks.edu
E-mail: slgorman@ozarks.edu

4 Year Institution

Music Contact: Sharon L. Gorman, 80A
Chair, Division of Humanities: David Strain, 80A
Dean of Faculty & Vice President Academic Affairs: Daniel L. Taddie

Prof	Gorman, Sharon L.	PhD	12A,66G
Assoc Prof	Lindstrom, G. Mikael	D	13,36
	Taddie, Daniel L.	D	12A,36,61

AR0950 Williams Baptist College
Department of Music
PO Box 3406
Walnut Ridge, AR 72476
(870) 886-6741 x150 Fax: (870) 886-3924
www.wbcoll.edu
E-mail: bmagee@wbcoll.edu

4 Year Institution

Chair: Robert G. Magee, 80A

Prof	Magee, Robert G.	D	12A,60,36,61,31A
Inst	Markowski, Rebecca	M	62A
Inst	Mason, Carl	M	63A
Inst	Pennington, Lynn	M	32,66A,66D
Assoc Prof	Thompson, Christopher K.	D	13A,13,10F,10,66A
Inst	Waddley, Craig	M	41,47

AZ0100 Arizona State University
School of Music
PO Box 870405
Tempe, AZ 85287-0405
(480) 965-3371 Fax: (480) 965-2659
music.asu.edu
E-mail: music@asu.edu

4 Year Institution, Graduate School
Member of NASM

Master of Music in Collaborative Piano, Master of Arts in Ethnomusicology, Master of Music in Composition, Master of Music in Performance, Master of Music in Music Education, Master of Music in Music Therapy, Master of Music in Performance Pedagogy, PhD in Music Education, DMA in Composition, DMA in Conducting, DMA in Performance, Master of Arts in History & Literature, Master of Music in Music Theatre Direction, Master of Music in Musical Theatre, Master of Music Interdisciplinary Digital Media Arts, DMA Interdisciplinary Digital Media Arts

Director: Heather Landes, 80A
Associate Dir., Academic Affairs: Jody D. Rockmaker, 80H

Prof	Aspnes, Lynne A.	D	62E
Prof	Bailey, Wayne A.	D	60
Prof	Britton, David	B	61
Assoc Prof	Buck, Elizabeth	D	64A
Assoc Prof	Buck, Nancy N.	M	62B
Assoc Prof	Campbell, Andrew	D	66C
Assoc Prof	Carpenter, Ellon D.	D	13,13J
Assoc Prof	Cosand, Walter	M	41,66A
Asst Prof	Creviston, Christopher		64E
Vstng Asst Prof	Creviston, Hannah	D	66A,66B,66C
Prof	Crowe, Barbara	M	33
Prof	Demars, James R.	D	13,10F,10
Prof	Doan, Jerry D.	D	61
Prof	Dreyfoos, Dale	M	39
Assoc Prof	Ericson, John Q.	D	63B
Assoc Prof	Feisst, Sabine M.	D	12
Asst Prof	FitzPatrick, Carole	M	61
Lect	Gardner, Joshua	D	64C
Lect	Glassman, Allan H.	D	61
Prof	Hackbarth, Glenn A.	D	13,10F,10,43
Prof	Hamilton, Robert	M	66A
Prof	Hickman, David R.	M	63A
Prof	Hill, Gary W.	M	60,37

Directory of Institutions

Rank	Name	Degree	Areas
Assoc Prof	Holbrook, Amy K.	D	13,13J
Prof	Hudson, James	M	37
Prof	Humphreys, Jere T.	D	32,32G,32E
Assoc Prof	Jiang, Danwen	M	62A
Assoc Prof	Kocour, Michael G.	B	47
Prof	Koonce, Frank W.	M	70
Assoc Prof	Kopta, Anne Elgar		61
Assoc Prof	Landschoot, Thomas V.	M	62C
Asst Prof	Levy, Ben	D	10,13
Prof	Marshall, Kimberly	D	41,66G
Assoc Prof	May, Judy	M	61
Prof	McLin, Katherine E.	D	62A
Assoc Prof	Meir, Baruch	D	66B
Assoc Prof	Micklich, Albie	D	64D
Clinical Asst Prof	Mills, Robert	D	66A
Lect	Moio, Dom	B	29
Asst Prof	Mook, Richard W.	D	14C
Lect	Murillo, Julie	M	33
Assoc Prof	Norton, Kay	D	12
Prof	Oldani, Robert	D	12A,12
Prof	Pagano, Caio		66A
Prof	Reber, William F.	D	39,54,52,66C,60
Assoc Prof	Rio, Robin	M	33
Assoc Prof	Rockmaker, Jody D.	D	13A,13,10,12A,43
Prof	Rogers, Rodney	D	13,10F,10
Assoc Prof	Rotaru, Catalin	M	62D
Prof	Russell, Timothy	D	60,38
Prof/Prac	Ryan, Russell	DIPL	66C
Asst Prof	Saucier, Catherine	D	12A
Prof	Schildkret, David	D	36,60A
Assoc Prof	Schmidt, Margaret	D	32
Assoc Prof	Schuring, Martin	M	64B
Senior Lect	Shellans, Michael	M	14C
Assoc Prof	Smith, Jeffrey B.	D	65
Prof	Solis, Ted	D	12A,20G,14
Prof	Spring, Robert S.	D	64C
Prof	Stauffer, Sandra L.	D	32
Assoc Prof	Sullivan, Jill	D	32
Prof	Sunkett, Mark E.	D	50,65,29A,14
Assoc Prof	Swartz, Jonathan	D	62A
Asst Prof	Swoboda, Deanna	D	63D
Prof Emerita	Thompson, Janice Meyer	D	66A,66B,66D
Asst Prof	Tobias, Evan	D	32C,32F,32G,32H
Lect	Yatso, Toby	M	54
Prof	Yeo, Douglas	M	63C

AZ0150 Arizona Western College

Department of Music
9500 S Ave 8th E
Yuma, AZ 85366-0929
(928) 344-7574   Fax: (928) 344-7730
www.azwestern.edu
E-mail: charles.smalley@azwestern.edu

2 Year Institution

Chair, Social Sciences & Fine Arts: Kathy Watson, 80A

Rank	Name	Degree	Areas
	Bigler, Nathan		61,66A
	Bright, Lorna		66D
	Carlson, Brian	M	64E
	Coz, Brandon		65
	Dallabetta, Amanda		63A,47
	D'Haiti, Maxine		66D,11
	Durham, Franklin		36
	Espinoza, Juan		70
	Jones, Janet	M	38,62A,62C,62B,62D
	Lord, Billy Jean		36
	Lucero, Kerry		62A,62B
	Mitchell, Ian		11
	Moore, Dean		65
	Morrill, Dori	M	63B
	Pollard, Shawn	D	13A,37,11,63D
Prof	Posch, Carl	M	13,11,37,47,63D
	Seale, Sheryl		64A
Prof	Smalley, Charles	D	13C,11,36,61,20G
	Tacke, Tom		11
Prof	Tibbs, Elizabeth J.	D	66A,11,66D
	Woody, John		11
	Wright, Christine	M	64C
	Wright, Randy		32E

AZ0200 Central Arizona College

Department of Music
8470 N Overfield Rd
Coolidge, AZ 85228
(520) 426-4394   Fax: (520) 426-4435
www.centralaz.edu
E-mail: kim_freyermuth@centralaz.edu

2 Year Institution

Chair: G. Kim Freyermuth, 80A

Rank	Name	Degree	Areas
Prof	Bowen, Ron	M	64,70
Prof	Freyermuth, G. Kim	M	36,44,61,47
Prof	Lee, James	M	12A,11,29
Prof	Moore, Rick	M	13,11,37,46,49
Prof	Osteen, Kim	M	11
	Pisciotta, Eva Mae	D	36,61,29A
Prof	Ratz, Arlene	M	66A,66D
Prof	Redmond, James Ryan		34

AZ50 Cochise College

Department of Music
901 N Colombo Ave
Sierra Vista, AZ 85635-2317
(520) 515-5440
www.cochise.edu
E-mail: bellassaim@cochise.edu

2 Year Institution

Music Contact, Lead Faculty: Marc C. Bellassai, 80A,80F

Rank	Name	Degree	Areas
	Bellassai, Marc C.	M	11,12A,66A,66F,66G
Inst	Germond, Melanie		36,61
Inst	Hutchison, Callie		62
Inst	Keyne, Lori V.	D	13B,13C,36,66D
	Kuhn, Michael	M	37,47
	Melito, Matthew	M	70
Inst	Reilley, Duane		64
Inst	Wilkins, Judy		66A

AZ0300 Eastern Arizona College

Department of Music
615 N Stadium Ave
Thatcher, AZ 85552
(928) 428-8233   Fax: (928) 428-8462
www.eac.edu
E-mail: trish.jordahl@eac.edu

2 Year Institution

Chair: Patricia Jordahl, 80A

Rank	Name	Degree	Areas
	Alvarez, Franklin	M	11,51,62,38,13C
	Bishop, Bruce W.	DMA	34,36,61,13,60A
	DeSpain, Geoff	M	37,63,46,47,11
	Fischler, Gail		66A,66B,66C
Inst	Jordahl, Patricia	M	36,54,66D,61,11

AZ0350 Glendale Community College

Department of Performing Arts
6000 W Olive Ave
Glendale, AZ 85302-3006
(623) 845-3720   Fax: (623) 845-3754
www.gc.maricopa.edu/performingarts
E-mail: alyssa.beach@gcmail.maricopa.edu

2 Year Institution

Chair: Donald S. Smith, 80A
Assistant Chair: Charles Hulihan, 80H

Rank	Name	Degree	Areas
Prof	Albury, Robert T.	PhD	13,10
Adj	Baker, Cynthia	M	51,62A,62B
Inst	Buck, Brenda	M	63B
Adj	Buck, Dave	M	70
Adj	Coleman, Matthew	M	32,65
Inst	Edwards, Rachel	M	64B
Inst	Eide, Christina	D	11,66A,66D
Inst	Esler, Robert	PhD	34,35

Adj	Flores, Andrea	M	61
	Gardner, Stefanie	M	12A
Adj	Huggins, Mark	M	11,12A
Inst	Hulihan, Charles	M	70,41,32E,32F
Inst	Hulihan, Theresa	M	64A
Inst	Humbert, William	M	37,64,63,13A,60
Inst Adj	Jennings, Carol	M	61
Adj	Kilstofte, Anne C.	D	11,29A,20
Inst	Nichols, David		35G
Inst	Nottingham, Douglas	D	65,50,45,10B,35
Inst	Ormsbee, Timothy	M	63C,63D
Adj	Reed, William		59
Inst Adj	Roberts, Adam	M	12A,64E,29A
Inst	Schmidt, David	M	47,53,35D,34D
Inst	Smith, Donald S.	D	29A,63A,49
Adj	Taylor, Annie	M	66A,66D
Adj	Thibodeaux, David	M	11
Inst	Weinkum, Harald	M	70
Inst	Yingst, Benjamin	M	64B
	Zemke, Vicki		66C

AZ0400 Grand Canyon University
Department of Music
3300 W Camelback Rd
Phoenix, AZ 85061-1097
(602) 589-2482 x2482   Fax: (602) 589-2492
cola.gcu.edu
E-mail: cofap@gcu.edu

4 Year Institution

Chair: Sheila Corley, 80A
Dean, College Liberal Arts: James Helfers, 80A

Adj	Chao, Barbara	M	64A
Assoc Prof	Corley, Sheila	D	32C,36,39,61
Asst Prof	Doan, Cheryl	M	61
Adj	Gorman, Kevin J.	M	64E
Asst Prof	Gutshall, Christi	M	66A,66B,66D,12A
Inst Adj	Harvey, Julie	M	66A,13
Inst	Kent, Libbie	M	13
Asst Prof	Killian, Joni	M	61
Assoc Prof	Lively, Judy	D	66A,66B
Assoc Prof	Lloyd, Joe	M	32C,37,63A,11,60
Adj	McAllister, Bob	B	63D
Adj	McAllister, DeeAnn	B	32B
Adj	McGlone, Jeff	B	70,13A
Adj	Moio, Dom		65
Assoc Prof	Morrison, Chuck	D	31A
Adj	Pendell, Carter		62A
Adj	Schaeffer, Greg	M	10F

AZ0440 Mesa Community College
Department of Music
1833 W Southern Ave
Mesa, AZ 85202-4822
(480) 461-7000   Fax: (480) 461-7804
www.mc.maricopa.edu/dept/d28
E-mail: music@mcmail.maricopa.edu

2 Year Institution

Chair: Sue Anne Lucius, 80A

Adj	Bartlett, Anthony		63C,29
Prof	Bennett, Glenn	D	36,61
Adj	Bennett, Vicki		61,36
Adj	Brewer, Paul		29
Adj	Broe, Caroline	D	62
Adj	Bromann, Michael		35C,35D
Adj	Christensen, Mary		36
Prof	Clapp, Lawrence	M	66A
Adj	Clausen, Rick		35C,35D
Prof	Conrad, Larry	B	63B
Adj	Counihan, Emma		50,65
Prof	Davis, Daniel W.	B	70
Prof	Durant, Doug	M	13,61
Prof	Forney, Fred	M	63A,46,29A
Prof	Hauan, Catherine	D	61,54
Adj	Hayes, Kelly		64C
Faculty	Hunter, Robert		32E,63A,37,46,29A
Prof	Johnston, Joey	B	36,61
Adj	Killian, Dwight		62D
Adj	Lienert, Keith		
Prof	Lovelady, Hugh	M	64
Prof	Lucius, Sue Anne	M	39,61,54
Prof	Makris, Kristina	B	10,13,35A,29A,61
Adj	Mercer, Bjorn M.		
Prof	Millhouse, Steven	B	62D,47
Adj	Mills, Robert		13,66A,66C

Prof	Moio, Dominick	B	50,65
Adj	Murphy, Brian		38
Adj	Murphy, Tom		65
Prof	Murray, David	M	66A
Prof	Nagell, Ann B.	M	66A
Prof	Nagy, Jennifer	M	61
Prof	Pan, JiaYe		62A
Prof	Peck, Chant	B	35C,35D
Prof Emeritus	Rice, Lorraine	M	66A
Prof	Richardson, Danene	M	13,10
Adj	Sanguinetti, Melanie		64D
Prof	Seagle, Andy	B	35C,35D
Adj	Seifert, James		61,13
Adj	Seymann, Scott		35C,35D
Adj	Shumway, Allyson		61
Prof	Skoldberg, Phyllis	D	62
Adj	Steffen, Christina		64A,41,13
Prof	Summers, George	M	70,13
Prof	Towne, Lora Rost	B	39,61,54,13
Adj	Vela, Gloria		62B
Adj	Vince, Matt		70,35C,35D
Prof	Yandell, Ruth	M	66A,66G,13
Adj	Yandell, Scott		29,35C,35D
Adj	Yanez, Raul		66A

AZ0450 Northern Arizona University
School of Music
PO Box 6040
Flagstaff, AZ 86011-6040
(928) 523-3731   Fax: (928) 523-5111
nau.edu/music
E-mail: todd.sullivan@nau.edu

4 Year Institution, Graduate School
Member of NASM

Master of Music in Performance, Master of Music in Musicology, Master of Music in Music Theory-Composition, Master of Music in Choral Conducting, Master of Music in Teaching, Master of Music in Suzuki Violin/Viola, Master of Music in Piano Accompanying & Chamber Music, Master of Music in Instrumental Conducting, Master of Music in Vocal Performance

Director: Todd E. Sullivan, 80A
Associate Dir., Undergraduate Studies: Rick A. Stamer, 80B
Associate Dir., Graduate Studies: John Masserini, 80C

Assoc Prof	Bergeron, Jonathan	M	64E
Principal Lect	Borden, Rita	M	66A,66C,41
Asst Prof	Brown, Julie Hedges	D	12
Assoc Prof	Brown, Stephen C.	D	13
Lect	Chiang, Janice ChenJu	D	66C,66A,41
Prof	Cloud, Judith	D	61
Prof	Copley, Edith A.	D	60A,36,60
Assoc Prof	Dunn, Stephen J.	D	63A
Asst Prof/Prac	Finet, Christopher	M	29,47,62D
Lect	George, Elizabeth	M	13A,13B,66D
Principal Lect	Gunderson, Margaret	M	61
Senior Lect	Hallberg, Karin	M	62A
Asst Prof	Hamill, Chad	M	14,20
Prof	Hemphill, Steven R.	D	65
Assoc Prof	Holder, Ryan	D	32D,36,60A
Senior Lect	Lapins, Alexander	M	63D
Prof	Leve, James	D	12A,12C
Assoc Prof	Masserini, John	D	64C,41
Assoc Prof	McKay, Emily Hoppe	M	64A,41
Principal Lect	Moore, Kent R.	D	64D
Inst	Peebles, Crystal	M	13,34
Assoc Prof	Pereira, Jose Ricardo	B	61
Lect	Ramos, Mary Ann	D	62C,41
Assoc Prof	Raymond, Deborah	B	61
Prof	Reiprich, Bruce J.	D	13,10,34
Inst	Rich, Shelley	M	62A
Asst Prof	Ross, Nicholas G. M.	D	38,60B
Senior Lect	Russell, Jennifer	D	13
Asst Prof	Saunders, Robert Allen	D	61
Assoc Prof	Scarnati, Blase S.	D	11,12,14
Prof	Scarnati, Rebecca Kemper	D	64B,13,41
Assoc Prof	Schellen, Nando	B	39
Prof	Schmidt, Daniel Joseph	D	60B,37
Assoc Prof	Schwandt, Jacquelyn Joy	M	62B
Prof	Scott, Frank	D	66A,66B
Prof	Scott, Louise H.	D	62A
Principal Lect	Sheeley, Thomas	M	70
Prof	Smith, Timothy A.	D	13,34
Lect	Stamer, Linda	M	32B
Assoc Prof	Stamer, Rick A.	D	32
Inst	Sullivan, Kimberly	B	51,62A
Principal Lect	Sullivan, Nancy	M	63B
Prof	Sullivan, Todd E.	D	11,12,14,20
Lect	Tackitt, Elliott	M	37,32E
Assoc Prof	Vining, David	M	63C,41

AZ0460 Northland Pioneer College
Department of Music
PO Box 610
Holbrook, AZ 86025
(928) 536-6247   Fax: (928) 536-6212
www.npc.edu
E-mail: bobette.welch@npc.edu

2 Year Institution

PT	Beste, Alan	B	46
PT	Darst, John		70,47
PT	Dockendorf, Carl	B	36
PT	Gentry, Scott	B	61,66A
PT	McLane, Brian	M	10D

AZ0470 Phoenix College
Department of Music
1202 W Thomas Rd
Phoenix, AZ 85013-4208
(602) 285-7876   Fax: (602) 285-7275
www.phoenixcollege.edu/music
E-mail: karl.schindler@pcmail.maricopa.edu

2 Year Institution

Director: Karl W. Schindler, 80A

	Allen, Jennifer	M	61
	Apperson, Jim	M	62A,62B
	Bingener, Bonnie	M	66A
	Brown, Ellen		66,13
	Chao, Barbara Davis	M	64A
	Chao, Fred	M	62C
	Chapman, John	M	62D
	D'Ercole, Kendra	D	13
	Dobra, William R.	D	63A,14C
	Dockendorff, Catherine	M	61
	Eckroth, Rachel	M	66A,29B,29A
	Esler, Robert	D	14C
	Graybeal, Dana	M	38
	Haenfler, Eric	M	37
	Hartman, Tony	M	35,34D
	Hawkins, Wes	M	14C,65,50,29A
	Helvey, Emily	D	66A,13
	London, Robert	M	35,14E
	Martinez, Adriana	D	12
	Matsumoto, Shane		35D,35G
	May, Jim		35G
	Messer, Benjamin	M	34
Prof	Miller, Kenny	D	13C,12A,36,40,61
	Perez, Pedro	M	70
	Powers, Bob	M	70
	Ruth, Byron	M	14C,29A,64E
Prof	Schindler, Karl W.	D	10,13,34,12A
	Stenius, Karla		35
	Tomlinson, Dan		65
	Tuttle, Julie	M	13,66
	Weddle, Jamison		35,34D
	Weinkum, Harald	M	62D
	Yancey, James	M	70
Prof	Yoes, Milas	M	12A,29,37,46,63C

AZ0480 Pima Community College
Department of Performing Arts
2202 W Anklam Rd
Tucson, AZ 85709-0015
(520) 206-6826   Fax: (520) 206-6719
www.pima.edu
E-mail: mark.nelson@pima.edu

2 Year Institution

Chair: Mark Nelson, 80A

PT	Boone, Robert	M	63C
PT	Booth, Nancy Davis	M	61,54
PT	Buchholz, Theodore	M	62C
PT	Ceron, Homero	M	65
PT	Chow-Tyne, June	D	66A,66D
Inst	Christofferson, Carol	M	64C,13
PT	Gendler, Anna	M	62A
PT	Guenther, Greg	M	61,39
	Hokin, Harlan B.	D	11
PT	Kasun, Scott	M	34D
PT	Keepe, Michael L.	D	35,64E
PT	Kuhn, Michael	M	29,11,46
PT	McCartney, Ben	M	70
Inst	Nelson, Mark	D	37,13,63D,34
PT	Ng, Jonathan	D	36,61
PT	Pankratz, Timothy	M	12A
Inst	Perry, Eileen	M	66A,13C,66D
PT	Roederer, Jason	D	62D
PT	Ryder, Raymond T.	D	66A,13A,66D
PT	Schwoebel, Sandy	D	64A,48,67D,35A
PT	Solomon, Larry J.	D	13A
PT	Tentser, Alexander	D	66A,38
PT	Valenzuela, Victor	M	63A,63B
PT	Weaver, Ann	M	62A,62B

AZ0490 Scottsdale Community College
Department of Music
9000 E Chaparral Rd
Scottsdale, AZ 85250-2614
(480) 423-6333   Fax: (480) 423-6365
www.scottsdalecc.edu
E-mail: christina.novak@sccmail.maricopa.edu

2 Year Institution

Chair: Christina D. Novak, 80A

	Brewer, Paul	M	11,13,29,32E,47
Adj	Brotman, Justin		62D,10,32E
Adj	Chapman, Polly		54
Adj	Crawford, Stephen L.		61
Adj	Dalbey, Jenna		62C,42
Adj	DeLamater, Elizabeth L.		20,29A,12A,65
Adj	Ehlers, Lisa	M	66D
Adj	Esler, Robert		50,14C,35C,10
Adj	Glenn, Melissa Walker	M	61
Adj	Higgins, Ramsey		35A,35C
Adj	Huff, Cleve		65
Adj	Hulett, Christopher M.	D	37
Adj	Livingston-Hakes, Beth		61,54,13A
Adj	Malito, Jim		35
Faculty	Marschall, Ron		34,35
Adj	Mogerman, Flora		66A,66C
Adj	Norman, Janet	D	66D
Adj	Norman, Jeffery		62B
	Novak, Christina D.	D	11,13,66A,10A,66D
Adj	O'Brien, Andrew C.	M	66A,66D
Adj	Park, Min		62A
Adj	Pearson, Scotty		70,43
Adj	Proudfoot, Carol		61
Adj	Robinson, Doug		63C,63A
Adj	Roper, Scott		14C
Adj	Rosen, Benjamin		35A,35C
Adj	Schumacher, Craig		35G
Adj	Spotts, Cory		35G
Faculty	Stich, Adam	D	36,60A,61,40,13A
Adj	Vacca, Anthony		29A,14C
Adj	Walker, Elaine		34
Adj	Wedington-Clark, Darlene	D	38
Adj	Wegner, Rob		34,35A,35C
Adj	Yanez, Raul		66A,47,14C,29A
Adj	Zawilak, Alexander	D	70,13A,42,41

AZ0500 Univ of Arizona
School of Music
PO Box 210004
Tucson, AZ 85721-0004
(520) 621-1655   Fax: (520) 621-8118
www.music.arizona.edu
E-mail: music@cfa.arizona.edu

4 Year Institution, Graduate School
Member of NASM

Master of Music in Composition, Master of Music in Music Theory, Master of Music in Performance, Master of Music in Conducting, Master of Music in Music Education, Master of Music in Musicology, PhD in Music Theory, PhD in Music Education, DMA in Composition, DMA in Conducting, DMA in Performance

Director: Peter A. McAllister, 80A
Assistant Dir & Dir., Graduate Studies: Rex A. Woods, 80C,80D,80H

Prof	Asia, Daniel I.	M	13,10,43
Asst Prof	Bayless, Robert R.	D	32C,32E,37,60B
Adj Inst	Bontrager, Charles E.	M	38
Assoc Prof	Brobeck, John T.	D	12,55
Assoc Prof	Chamberlain, Bruce B.	D	36
Assoc Prof	Cockrell, Thomas R.	D	38
Asst Prof	Cooper, Shelly	D	32,32A,32B,32G,32H

Asst Prof	Dauphinais, Kristin E.	D	61
Adj Inst	Dauphinais, Michael D.	M	66
Prof	Decker, Pamela A.	D	66G,13
Prof	Dietz, William D.	D	64D,48
Asst Prof	Draves, Tami	D	32G,32H
Prof	Fan, Paula	D	66A,66C
Assoc Prof	Gibson, Tannis L.	M	66
Prof	Hamann, Donald L.	D	32,62,32E,32G
Prof	Hanson, Gregg I.	M	60,37
Prof	Haskell, Jeffrey R.	M	47,46,29,35
Assoc Prof	Hirst, Edmund V. Grayson	DIPL	61
Adj Inst	Horn, Robin Franklin	A	65
Assoc Prof	Katzen, Daniel	M	63B
Lect	Keepe, Michael L.	D	64E
Adj Inst	Keyl, Stephen M.	D	11
Prof	Kirkbride, Jerry E.	M	48,64C
Asst Prof	Luce, Brian A.	D	64A,48
Prof	McAllister, Peter A.	D	32
Prof	McLaughlin, Carrol M.	D	62E
Asst Prof	Milbauer, John P.	D	66
Adj Inst	Moon, Brian A.	D	11
Prof Emeritus	Murphy, Edward W.	D	13,13J
Prof	Neher, Patrick K.	M	62D,51
Assoc Prof	Paiewonsky, Moises	M	63C,46
Prof	Patterson, R. Thomas	M	67D,70
Adj Inst	Pawlak, Keith V.	M	11,16
Asst Prof	Pomeroy, David Boyd	D	13
Prof	Rees, Jay C.	M	37
Prof	Reid, Edward F.	M	63A
Assoc Prof	Robinson, Faye L.	B	61
Prof	Roe, Charles R.	M	39,61
Assoc Prof	Rosenblatt, Jay M.	D	12
Assoc Prof	Rush, Mark	M	51,62A
Assoc Prof	Schauer, Elizabeth	D	36,32D,61
Prof	Sturman, Janet L.	D	14,11
Assoc Prof	Tatman, Neil E.	D	64B,48
Assoc Prof	Thomas, Kelland K.	D	64E
Assoc Prof	Thomas, Kelly Gene	M	63D
Asst Prof	Traut, Donald G.	D	13
Adj Inst	Velez, Gilbert Y.	B	20H
Adj Inst	Veres, Fran A.	M	32
Asst Prof	Votapek, Mark A.	M	62C
Adj Inst	Waggoner, David	M	32
Assoc Prof	Walsh, Craig T.	PhD	10,10B,13,10A
Prof	Weinberg, Norman G.	D	50,65
Prof	Woods, Rex A.	D	66A
Assoc Prof	Xiao, Hong-Mei S.	M	62B
Asst Prof	Zdechlik, Lisa J.	M	66D

AZ0510 Yavapai College
Department of Music
1100 E Sheldon St Bldg 15
Prescott, AZ 86301-3220
(928) 776-2045   Fax: (928) 776-2036
www.yc.edu
E-mail: Roy.Breiling@yc.edu

2 Year Institution

Prof	Breiling, Roy	D	37,38,46,47,63A
Adj Inst	Carter, Edward L.	B	70,53
Adj	Dolatowski, David	D	66A,36,11
Adj Inst	Fisher, Suzanne D.	M	64C
Prof	Fisher, Will J.	D	36,11,66D
Adj	Flurry, Henry	M	66A
Adj	Hepburn, Cathleen	B	61,66A
Adj Inst	Klein, Jim L.	M	36
Adj Inst	Kuhns, Philip A.	D	62A,62B
Prof Emeritus	Longfield, Richard O.	M	13,60,37,38,47
Adj	Mahany, Michael E.	B	66A
Adj Inst	Manz, Paul P.	M	63B,63C
Adj	Mapston, Cindy	B	36
Adj Inst	McGowan, Orpha Ellen	B	64A
Adj Inst	Robertson, Christina N.	M	66A
Adj	Roman, Ed S.	M	61,66A
Adj Inst	Score, Clyde D.		65,70
Adj	Shelley, Bonnie J.	M	61
Adj Inst	Terauchi, Kristi		62C
Adj Inst	Vogel, Michael	M	64B

CA0050 Ali Akbar College of Music
215 W End Ave
San Rafael, CA 94901-2645
(415) 454-6264   Fax: (415) 454-9396
www.aacm.org
E-mail: office@aacm.org

Teaching in the Tradition of the Classical Music of North India

Director: Ben Kunin, 80A

	Chakrovorty, Sumita		61
	Chatterji, Sumita		
	Chaudhuri, Swapan		13A,10,12A,65
	Hamm, Bruce		13A,11,12A
	Harrington, Richard		13A,11,12A
	Harvey, Wallace		
	Jhaveri, Shweta		
	Khan, Alam		
	Khan, Ali Akbar	D	13A,10,11,12A,62
	Khan, Pranesh		13A,10,65
	Kunin, Ben		
	Pomerantz, James		13A,11,12A
	Sahai, Rita		61
	Sharma, Nachiketa		61
	Van Cleave, Brad		13A,11,12A
	Witter, Tim		13A,11,12A

CA0100 Allan Hancock College
Department of Music
800 S College Dr Bldg F
Santa Maria, CA 93454-6399
(805) 922-6966   Fax: (805) 928-7905
www.hancockcollege.edu
E-mail: mengelmann@hancockcollege.edu

2 Year Institution

Dean: Roanna Bennie, 80A
Chair: Marcus W. Engelmann, 80A

	Coehlo, Jerry M.	B	70
	Delore, Deanna	M	61
	Devine, Jeff S.	M	70
Inst	Engelmann, Marcus W.	D	13,10,12A,45,20G
	Foreman, Karen C.		66D,13A
	Keast, Larry	M	66D
	Klinger, Judith	M	61
Inst	Lucas, Ann D.	D	11,12A,20
	Osborne, Charles	M	47
	Rackley, David	M	11
	Severson, Sandi	M	35C
	Stoll, Gregory	M	37

CA0150 American River Community College
Department of Music
4700 College Oak Dr
Sacramento, CA 95841-4217
(916) 484-8357   Fax: (916) 484-8880
www.arc.losrios.edu/~music
E-mail: music@arc.losrios.edu

2 Year Institution

Chair: Ralph Hughes, 80A

Adj	Alkire, Jeff	M	64E
Adj	Allen, Mark	B	64C
Adj	Blumberg, Stephen	D	10
FT	Chun, Eric	B	35
Adj	Crain, Michael	M	34
Adj	Deffner, David	D	66G,13A
Adj	Derthick, Tom	B	62D
FT	Eifertsen, Dyne	M	29,63C,46,47
Adj	Elias, Daniel	M	61
Adj	Gale, Karen	B	64D
FT	Gilman, Joe	D	13,66A,53,29
Adj	Homan, Steve		70
FT	Hughes, Ralph	D	36,61,66A
Adj	Johnson, Robert M.	M	35G,35C
Adj	Kashiwagi, Kerry	B	62D
Adj	Keene, Theresa	M	13A,66A
Adj	Kelly, Aileen	M	62E,12A,66A
Adj	Kennedy, Daniel	D	65
Adj	Kidwell, Curtis		64B
Adj	Lamb Cook, Susan	D	62C
FT	LaPierre, Art	D	36,47,29A,61
Adj	Leathersich, Stacey		11,61
Adj	Limutau, Jacosa	B	47
Adj	Lishman, Steve	M	64E
Adj	Lopes, Gerald	M	38,62D
Adj	Lotter, Rick	B	65
Adj	Macomber, Scott		63A
Adj	Marucci, Mat	A	65
Adj	McMullen, Mike		64E
Adj	McPherson, Sandra		64C
Adj	Nowlen, Peter	B	63B
Adj	Olinyk, George Yuri	M	11,66A,13A
Adj	Perdicaris, Stephen	B	63C
Adj	Peron, Tom		63A
Adj	Phillips, Tom	B	70

Adj	Rink, Shelley	M	66A
Adj	Roach, Stephen	M	63A
Adj	Robinett, Henry		70
Adj	Saraquse, Sandy	M	70
Adj	Scott, Tatiana	M	66A,13
Adj	Sebastian, Mario		65
Adj	Teresi, Cindy		32A
FT	Thompson, Steven D.	D	37,38,63C,11,13A
Adj	Tognozzi, Victoria		62A
Adj	Van Regenmorter, Heidi	B	66A
FT	Van Regenmorter, Merlyn	D	34,35B
Adj	Veligan, Igor		62A
Adj	Yip, Brandon	M	70
Adj	Zucker, Laurel	M	64A

CA0200 Antelope Valley College
Department of Music
3041 W Avenue K
Lancaster, CA 93536-5402
(661) 722-6385   Fax: (661) 722-6390
www.avc.edu
E-mail: bprice@avc.edu

2 Year Institution

Dean, Fine, Performance. & Media Arts: Gary Roggenstein, 80A

Inst PT	Bretz, Jeffrey	B	14C
Inst PT	Carlson, Robert A.	B	35
Inst PT	Counts, Les	M	66
Inst PT	Crocker, John		36
Inst PT	Davila, William	M	70
Inst PT	Dillon, Nathan	B	35,14C
Inst PT	Gregg, Gary	M	63C,29,35
Adj Asst Prof	Heifetz, Robin J.	D	11,20,10A,43,12
Inst PT	Herbeck, Tina	B	35,61
Inst PT	Jang, Jinyoung	M	61
Inst PT	Kang, Leah	M	66D
Inst PT	Kearney, Joe	M	13,70,35
Inst PT	KinKennon, Heather Marie	M	11,60,66,66D
Inst PT	Krumrei, Randall	B	10D
Inst PT	LaCroix, John	M	34,35
Inst PT	Lazarus, Gordon	D	64B,66D
Inst PT	Martindale, Peggy Lee	M	35,39
Inst PT	Matalon, Leon	B	13A,47,53,48
Inst PT	McCullough, Michael	M	13A,11
Inst PT	McCully, Michael	B	35,14C
Inst PT	Meeker, Jared	B	70,34
Prof	Newby, David L.	D	13C,36,38,39
Prof	Price, Berkeley	D	13,37,48,64
Inst PT	Reddish, Debbie	B	13A,66A
Inst PT	Starner, Robert	M	13A

CA0250 Azusa Pacific University
School of Music
901 E Alosta Ave
PO Box 7000
Azusa, CA 91702-7000
(626) 815-3848   Fax: (626) 969-7419
www.apu.edu
E-mail: schoolofmusic@apu.edu

4 Year Institution, Graduate School

Master of Music in Performance, Master of Music in Music Education

Interim Dean: Donald E. Neufeld, 80A
Dir., Undergraduate Studies: Rodney Cathey, 80B
Dir., Graduate Studies: Dennis Royse, 80C
Dir., Institute/Festival/Workshop: John Sutton, 80F

Assoc Prof	Beatty, David	M	47,49,35,63C
Lect	Boocock, William		61
Prof	Browne, Kimasi L.	PhD	12A,14,20
Prof	Cathey, Rodney	DMA	60,36
Asst Prof	Clifft, Al	M	36,60,13
Asst Prof	Clifft, Joel	DMA	66,13C
Assoc Prof	Clousing, Harold	M	61,36
Inst	Edwards, Patricia	DMA	61
Asst Prof	Fedoruk, Claire	DMA	12A
Assoc Prof	Galloway, Melanie	DMA	39,61
Prof	Gray, Donavon D.	DMA	37,44,49,32,48
Lect	Harms, Janet	D	66D,66G
Asst Prof	Hughes, David	DMA	60,36,61
Inst	Jensen, Michelle	M	32,36,55
Asst Prof	Koops, Alexander	DMA	37,32
Asst Prof	Kozubek, Michael	M	70,13A
Asst Prof	Lee, Michael		34
Assoc Prof	McKissick, Marvin L.	M	31A
Prof	Royse, Dennis	PhD	13,12A,32C,11
Asst Prof	Russell, Alex	M	67A,51
Asst Prof	Russell, Christopher	M	38
Prof	Sage, Robert	DMA	66A,12A
Prof	Shackleton, Phil	DMA	13,10,34
Lect	St. Clair, Eniko	M	13
Asst Prof	Sutton, John	DMA	60,31A,36
	Yoder, Roza	M	66A,66B

CA0270 Bakersfield College
Department of Music
1801 Panorama Dr
Bakersfield, CA 93305-1219
(661) 395-4533   Fax: (661) 395-4078
www.bakersfieldcollege.edu
E-mail: jgerhold@bakersfieldcollege.edu

2 Year Institution

Chair: John Gerhold, 80A

Inst PT	Bellah, Mary	B	66D,61
Inst PT	Cervantes, Elizabeth	M	11,13A
Inst PT	Dethlefson, John	B	34
Prof	Gerhold, John	D	13,10,66D,13A
Inst PT	Haas, Karl		70
Inst PT	Heasley, Tim	M	37
Prof	Kean, Ronald M.	D	36,20B,20H
Prof	Martinez, Robby	M	14C
Inst PT	Moore, Vicki	B	12A,11
Inst PT	Pophal, Lee	M	38
Inst PT	Scaffidi, Susan	M	11
Inst PT	Tiner, Kris	M	47,29A,11

CA00 Bethany University
Department of Music
800 Bethany Dr
Scotts Valley, CA 95066-2820
(831) 438-3800   Fax: (831) 438-4517
www.bethany.edu
E-mail: hulse@fc.bethany.edu

4 Year Institution

Chair: Mark Hulse, 80A

Asst Prof	Adkins, Don	D	13,10F,10,12A,62D
PT	Adkins, Kathryn	M	61
PT	Barber, June	M	13A,13,61
PT	Carlton, Jan	M	66A,66D
Prof	Hulse, Mark	D	13,11,32B,32C,61
PT	Inagawa, Kanako	M	66A
PT	Sampson, Larry	M	62,63,64,70

CA0350 Biola University
Conservatory of Music
13800 Biola Ave
La Mirada, CA 90639-0002
(562) 903-4892   Fax: (562) 903-4746
www.biola.edu/music
E-mail: george.boespflug@biola.edu

4 Year Institution
Member of NASM

Director: George Boespflug, 80A

Adj	Anthony, Robert	M	32
Adj	Askew, Jeff	M	31A,70
Adj	Aspling, Carol	B	36,61
Prof	Boespflug, George	D	66A
PT	Craig, Ed	M	32C,32E
PT	Craig, Susan	M	32B
Assoc Prof	Denham, Robert	D	13,10,34,43
Assoc Prof	Feller, Robert	M	11,37,49,63,60
Adj	Garnica, Kevin	D	11,66A,39
Assoc Prof	Hulling, Cliff	M	13,47,50,10A
Asst Prof	Hung, Li-Shan	D	66A,66B,41
PT	Kawamura, Manami	M	41,66A,66C
Adj	Kirkwood, David	M	61
Adj	Kobayashi, Ron	B	29
Asst Prof	Larson, Elizabeth	M	62A,42
Prof	Liesch, Barry	D	11,34,31A

Prof	Lock, William R.	D	60,36,61,31A
Adj	Mumford, Larry	D	10
PT	Owen, Jerri Lee	M	66A,66D
Assoc Prof	Owen, Marlin	M	38,41,51,62,70
Adj	Pantoja, Rique		29,31A
Asst Prof	Park, Angela	D	32
Prof	Robison, Jeanne	D	61,39
Asst Prof	Stewart, Shawna	M	60,36,32
Adj	Tebay, John	M	36
Adj	Watts, Mike		10
PT	Wills, Christopher	M	10,13

CA0400 Cabrillo College

Div. of Visual, Applied, and Perf. Arts
6500 Soquel Dr
Aptos, CA 95003-3119
(831) 479-6464   Fax: (831) 479-5045
www.cabrillo.edu/index.html
E-mail: mirivard@cabrillo.edu

2 Year Institution
Member of MACCC

Dean of Visual, Applied, and Performing Arts: John P. Graulty, 80A
Dir, Artist/Performance Series: John Orlando, 80F
Dir, Summer Theatre Program: Skip A. Epperson, Jr., 80G

Inst PT	Adkins, Donald	D	38,62D,66
	Adkins, Kathryn	M	61,54
Inst	Anderson, Cheryl M.	M	13,36,39
Inst PT	Bidelman, Mark	B	36
Inst	Brown, Ray	M	13,29
Inst	Brown, Susan	M	41,51,62,32
Inst	Bruckner, Susan	M	66A,11
Inst PT	Cantwell, Guy	M	13A,70
Inst	Collins, Philip M.	M	10
Inst	Durland, James		10,34
Inst	Gelman, Stephanie		
Inst	Julin, Patti		
Inst PT	Kvam, Nancy E.	M	32
	Livingston, Lavinia		
	Lopez, Barbara		61,66A,10
Inst PT	McGushin, Michael	M	36
Inst	Nordgren, Jon	M	13,37,46,47,60
Inst	Orlando, John	D	12A,66A
	Parrish, Susan K.	M	11
Inst	Rivard, Michele M.	M	61,34
Inst	Squatrito, Fred	M	13,11,66A
Inst PT	Stewart, James	M	34
Inst	Strunk, Michael J.	B	65,20,20H,50
Inst PT	Trindade, Walter	B	70
Inst PT	Wilson, Steve	M	13,10

CA0450 Calif Baptist University

School of Music
8432 Magnolia Ave
Riverside, CA 92504-3206
(951) 343-4251   Fax: (951) 343-4570
www.calbaptist.edu
E-mail: schoolofmusic@calbaptist.edu

4 Year Institution
Member of NASM

Dean: Gary Bonner, 80A
Associate Dean: Judd Bonner, 80H

Prof	Bonner, Gary	D	36,38,60
Asst Prof	Bonner, Judd	M	36,60
	Brand, Angela	D	66A,12A
Assoc Prof	Clifft, Al	M	13,36,37
Asst Prof	Giorgetti, Marisa	M	61,36
Asst Prof	Holliday, Guy	M	36,37,47
Prof	Howard, Beverly A.	D	13,34A,66G,66A,66H
Asst Prof	Killion, Jamie	M	61,32,31A
Asst Prof	King, Mary J.	D	10,13
Assoc Prof	Miller, Phillip	D	40,66D
Asst Prof	Pickett, Glen	D	10F,66A,66C
Assoc Prof	Reinebach, John	D	61
Vstng Prof	Schafer, Carl	D	32,48,64

CA0500 Calif Institute of Technology

Music Program
MC 2-70
1200 E California Blvd
Pasadena, CA 91125
(626) 395-3295   Fax: (626) 585-9284
www.music-theater-art.caltech.edu
E-mail: cdemesa@caltech.edu

4 Year Institution

Administrator: Cindy De Mesa, 80A

	Bing, Delores M.	M	62,41,42,62C
	Bing, William W.	M	37,47,49,63A
	Elgart, Matthew P.	D	70,42
	Gross, Allen R.	D	38
	Sulahian, Nancy	M	36,40
	Ward, Robert S.	M	66A

CA0510 Calif Institute of the Arts

Herb Alpert School of Music at CalArts
24700 McBean Parkway
Valencia, CA 91355-2340
(661) 253-7817   Fax: (661) 255-0938
www.calarts.edu
E-mail: info@music.calarts.edu

4 Year Institution, Graduate School
Member of NASM

MFA in Specialization in Experimental Sound Practices, MFA in Composition, MFA in Performance, DMA Performer-Composer Program, MFA in Music Tech: Interaction, Intelligence and Design, MFA Performer-Composer Program specialization in African-American Improv Music, MFA Performer-Composer Program, MFA in Jazz Studies

Dean: David Rosenboom, 80A
Dir., Institute/Festival/Workshop: Bob Clendenen, 80F
Associate Dean, Academic Affairs: Susan Allen, 80H
Associate Dean, Accreditation & Special Programs: Jacqueline Bobak, 80H
Associate Dean, Enrollment Management: Julie Feves, 80H,80D
Associate Dean, Academic & Special Projects: Robert Wannamaker

Inst	Allen, Susan	D	41,62E,43,53
Adj	Aplanalp, Woody	M	70
Inst	Berkolds, Paul	D	61,39,40,12A,68
Inst	Bobak, Jacqueline	D	12,42,61,32G
Inst	Bryant, Wanda	D	14
Inst	Carbone, Kathy	M	16
Inst	Carroll, Edward	M	49,63A
Inst	Chaplin, Clay	M	10,34,35G
Inst	Chaudhuri, Swapan	M	20D
Inst	Clendenen, Bob	M	35A,35C
Inst	Dean, Maria	M	61
Inst	Duke-Kirkpatrick, Erika	M	42,62C,51
	Etienne, Pierre		
Inst	Feves, Julie	M	42,64D,48,35A
	Fink, Michael Jon	D	12A,12,35,10
Inst	Fox, Stuart	M	42,70,55B,67G
Adj	Fumo, John	DIPL	47,63A
Inst	Gamma, Lorenz	D	62A
Inst	Gloss, Randy	M	65,20D,50
Inst	Golia, Vinny	B	64,35A,53,47
Adj	Graham, Robin	M	63B
Adj	Grueschow, Andrew	M	20A
Inst	Haden, Charlie	DIPL	47,62D,53
Adj	Holt, Danny	M	66D
Adj	Iles, Alex	B	63C,47
Adj	Johnson, Alphonso	DIPL	70,47
Inst	Johnson, David	M	13A,65,50
Inst	Kapur, Ajay	D	34,20E,45
Inst	Khan, Aashish	C	20
Inst	Knoles, Amy	M	65,50,13A,10B
Inst	Koonse, Larry	B	70,47
Inst	Krieger, Ulrich	M	10,34D,12A,45,64E
Inst	LaBarbera, Joe	DIPL	65,29A,47
Inst	Ladzekpo, Alfred K.	D	20
Inst	Lawluvi, Beatrice	DIPL	20
Inst	LeBaron, Anne	D	10,12,62E
Inst	Lowenstein, Marc	D	13,10,60,39,43
Adj	Mabee, Patricia	M	66H,55B
Inst	Menzies, Mark	D	62A,62B,38,43,60B
Inst	Miller, James	M	63C,49
Inst	Novros, Paul	DIPL	64E,47,29B
Inst	Oles, Darek	B	62D,47
Adj	Pisaro, Kathryn G.	D	12
Inst	Pisaro, Michael J.	D	13,10,12D
Inst	Pourmehdi, Houman	B	65,50,20B

Inst	Powell, William E.	M	48,64C,42,13E
Inst	Ray, Vicki	D	66,42
Inst	Roberts, Sara	M	10,34
Adj	Rofe, Peter	B	62D
Inst	Roitstein, David	M	13C,47,29,66A
Inst	Rosenboom, David		10,43,66A
Inst	Rudich, Rachel	D	64A
Inst	Schrader, Barry	M	13,10,12A,34
Inst	Serfaty, Aaron	DIPL	47,65
Inst	Smith, Wadada Leo	B	63A,29,10,45,53
Inst	Tadic, Miroslav	M	70,47,20F
Inst	Tadmor, Tali	D	66A,66C,31B
Adj	Tornquist, Doug	D	63D
Inst	Trayle, Mark	M	10,34,45
Inst	Uscher, Nancy	D	62B
Inst	Vogel, Allan	D	12A,55B,64B,13C
Inst	Von Schweinitz, Wolfgang	M	10,12
Inst	Vorwerk, Paul	M	60,13C,12A
Inst	Walujo, Djoko	DIPL	20D
Inst	Wannamaker, Robert	D	13,10
Inst	Wenten, I. Nyoman	D	20D
Inst	Wenten, Nanik	M	20D
Inst	Zwartjes, Martijn	DIPL	34

CA0550 Calif Lutheran University
Department of Music-#4000
60 W Olsen Rd
Thousand Oaks, CA 91360
(805) 493-3305   Fax: (805) 493-3904
www.callutheran.edu/music
E-mail: morton@callutheran.edu

4 Year Institution

Chair: Wyant Morton, 80A

Lect PT	Anderson, Marilyn E.	M	61
Lect PT	Barrett, Bill	B	63A
Lect PT	Beerstein, Fred	B	64B
Prof Emeritus	Fritschel, James E.	D	10A,36
Prof	Geeting, Daniel	D	64E,64C,38,11,60B
Lect PT	Geeting, Joyce	D	62C
Lect PT	Granet, Peter		34
Asst Prof	Hart, Michael	M	37,13B,13C,63C,63D
Lect PT	Helms, Elizabeth	M	66C
	Helms, Jessica		66C
Lect PT	Hester, John	B	62D
Lect PT	Hicks, Angela	M	61
Lect PT	Higgins, Scott		65,50
Lect	Johnson, Kyle E.	D	66G,66D
Lect PT	Johnson-Tamai, Eric	B	64D
Lect	Kinsley, Eric B.	D	11,66A,66H,66D
	Kuo, Ruth		66C
Lect PT	LaGuardia, Frank	B	11
Lect PT	MacGillivray, Louise	M	63B
Lect PT	Marfisi, Nancy G.	M	64A
Prof	Morton, Wyant	D	60,36
Lect PT	Phelps, Melissa		62A,62B
Prof Emeritus	Ramsey, Elmer H.	M	63A,38
Prof Emerita	Schechter, Dorothy E.	D	12A,66A,66B,66D
Asst Prof	Spraggins, Mark	D	13,10,34
Prof Emeritus	Swanson, Carl B.	M	66G,31A
Lect PT	Vass, Heidi	M	61
Lect PT	Woodford, Peter		70,47

CA0600 Calif Polytechnic State Univ
Department of Music
One Grand Ave
San Luis Obispo, CA 93407-0326
(805) 756-2406   Fax: (805) 756-7464
www.music.calpoly.edu
E-mail: music@calpoly.edu

4 Year Institution
Member of NASM

Dean: Douglas Epperson, 80A
Chair: W. Terrence Spiller, 80A

Lect PT	Albanese, Brynn		62A
Assoc Prof	Arrivee, David	D	38,13,41,13A,13C
Lect PT	Arthur, Katherine	M	61
Lect PT	Astaire, John	M	65,50
Lect PT	Bachman, James	B	70,41
Prof	Barata, Antonio G.	D	10,34D,35D,35G
Lect PT	Becker, David	B	64E
Prof	Brammeier, Meredith	D	13,11
Lect PT	Castriotta, Gabrielle		64B
Lect PT	Davies, Susan Azaret	M	13,66A,66C
Prof	Davies, Thomas H.	D	13,60,36,61
Asst Prof	D'Avignon, India	M	66A,13
Lect PT	Dodson Galvan, Jennifer	M	63B
Lect PT	Galvan, Santino	B	63D
Lect	Granger, Shelly	B	64A
Asst Prof	Habib, Kenneth S.	D	14,10,13,20B,14C
Lect PT	Hustad, Ken	B	62D
Lect PT	Kreitzer, Jacalyn	M	61
Prof	McLamore, Alyson	D	12A,12,32,16,20G
Asst Prof	McMahan, Andrew	D	60,37,63A,54,34
Lect PT	Nauful, Lisa	M	64B,64D
Prof	Rinzler, Paul	D	13,10,47,66A,29
Prof	Russell, Craig H.	PhD	11,12A,12,67B,70
Lect PT	Sayre, Jennifer	M	62E
Lect PT	Severtson, Paul	M	62A
Lect PT	Shumway, Jeanne	B	62C
Lect PT	Spencer, Barbara		62C
Prof	Spiller, W. Terrence	D	66,11
Lect PT	Swanson, Lucy Jane	B	63B
Lect PT	Waibel, Keith	B	64C
Lect FT	Woodruff, Christopher J.	M	37,13,63A

CA0630 Calif St Polytechnic Univ-Pomona
Department of Music
3801 W Temple Ave
Pomona, CA 91768-2557
(909) 869-3548   Fax: (909) 869-4145
www.class.csupomona.edu/mu/
E-mail: ilevine@csupomona.edu

4 Year Institution

Interim Dean: Sharon Hilles, 80A
Chair: Iris S. Levine, 80A

Assoc Prof	Amaya, Jennifer	M	34
Lect	Anastasia, Stephen	M	61
Lect	Blumberg, Kira	M	62B
Asst Prof	Burdett, John	DMA	32E,37,60B
Prof	Burns, Susan M.	DMA	13A,11,39,61,54
Lect	Cahueque, David A.	D	11,13A,70
PT	Catalano, Roberto	PhD	20
Lect	Clothier, Stephen	M	29,46
Lect	Converse, Mark	B	65
Prof Emeritus	Grasmick, David M.	M	13A,34,63A,29
Lect	Gravelle, Darren	DMA	70
Lect	Harms, Janet	DMA	13A,11,66
Lect	Huff, Lori	M	13A,11,48,64E,32
Lect	Jones, Kelly		10D
Prof	Kopplin, David F.	D	10,20,29,14C,46
Lect	Lamprey, Audrey	M	13A,49,63B
Lect	Lee, Christine	M	51
Prof	Levine, Iris S.	DMA	12A,32,36,60
Lect	Luer, Thomas D.	M	29,46
Lect	Lundgren, Karen E.	B	64A
Lect	Lynch, Kendra	M	61
Lect	Maldonado, Ana Marie	M	13A,62C,20H
PT	Mazzaferro, Tony		60
Lect	Miley, Jeff	B	70
Lect	Millar, Michael W.	D	63C,35E,29A,35A
Lect	Nagle, Lynn	M	61
Lect	Neill, Roger	PhD	10C
Lect	Nelson, Sheri	M	32D
Lect	Norfleet, Dawn	M	14
PT	O'Malley, Sean		35
Prof	Riveire, Janine	DMA	32A,32B,32C
Lect	Schlitt, Bill	M	65,50
Asst Prof	Shpachenko, Nadia	D	66A,66C,66B,66,34D
PT	Silva, Linda		11,64C
PT	Snyder, Vernon G.	DMA	66A
PT	Soto, Robert	M	63C
Lect	St. Clair, Nike'	DMA	36
Assoc Prof	Winer, Arthur H.	M	10D,34D,35G,35,10C
Assoc Prof	Yates, Peter	DMA	11,51,70,13A

CA0650 Calif State Univ-Bakersfield
Department of Music
9001 Stockdale Hwy
Mail Stop MUS 9
Bakersfield, CA 93311-1099
(661) 654-3093   Fax: (661) 654-6901
www.csub.edu/music
E-mail: rprovencio@csub.edu

4 Year Institution

Chair: Robert Provencio, 80A

Inst	Baldwin, Melvin	M	63B
Inst	Boyle, Audrey	M	64A,32
Inst	Cervantes, Ernest	M	65,32

Inst	Chang, Soo-Yeon Park	D	66,42,13A,13C
Inst	Christain, Ron	B	63C,63B
Inst	Clausen, Brett	M	64B,32
Inst	Cope, Roger Allen	B	70,42
Prof	Davis, John Douglas	D	13,10,47,29
	Dethlefson, James		34
Assoc Prof	Ferrell, Rene	M	32B,32C,60A,32D
Assoc Prof	Haney, Joel C.	D	11,12A,41
Inst	Haney, Julia Lawson	M	62A,42
Prof Emeritus	Kleinsasser, Jerome S.	D	11,12A,12,10C
Prof Emeritus	Mehling, Gordon	D	32
Inst	Panelli, Sal	M	63A,32
Inst	Perez, Paul	B	64E
Inst	Provencio, Linda	M	32B
Prof	Provencio, Robert	D	60,32,36
Inst	Sakomoto, Leo	D	37
Inst	Scaffidi, Pete	B	62D
Inst	Sears, Peggy	M	13A,39,61
Inst	Sexton, Norma	D	62C
Inst	Stone, Michael D.	M	32
Inst	Tiner, Kris	M	47,32B
Inst	VanKopp, Kristi	B	64C
Prof	Wildman, Louis	D	65A,65B

CA0800 Calif State Univ-Chico

Department of Music & Theatre
400 W 1st St
Chico, CA 95929-0805
(530) 898-5152   Fax: (530) 898-4082
www.csuchico.edu/mus
E-mail: wjohnson@csuchico.edu

4 Year Institution
Member of NASM

Interim Chair: William Johnson, 80A
Dean, Humanities/Fine Arts: Joel Zimbelman, 80A

Prof	Alexander, Joseph	B	35
PT	D'Augelli, Barbara		64D
PT	D'Augelli, Greg		64E
Lect PT	Dvorin, David	M	13,10,35G,45
PT	Hilsee, Amalie		62
PT	Kinkle, Dan		65
PT	Lundberg, Susan		64B
Asst Prof	McConkey, Michelle	D	32A,32B,32C
PT	Minor, Clark		66A
PT	Pickett, Kyle		38
Prof	Pinckney, Warren R.	D	11,20G,29A,13
Lect PT	Rivas, Anita	JD	35
Prof	Roby, Lloyd	D	32C,49,63D
PT	Ronen, Yael		64A
Lect PT	Roye, Tobin	M	70,13
Lect PT	Sargent, Daniel	B	35C,35G
Assoc Prof	Scholz, David M.	D	36,61,32C,60
Prof	Seppanen, Keith C.	M	13A,35A,35C,35D
Asst Prof	Shkoda, Natalya	D	66,13,13A,13B,12A
Asst Prof	Smith, Hope Munro	D	14,20H,11,12A,12C
Lect PT	Snodgrass, Linda H.	M	61
Prof	Tevis, Royce	D	32,37,63A,60
Lect PT	Weiss, Daun L.	M	61
Prof	Winslow, Michael Rocky	D	29,47,63A
Prof	Winslow, Richard D.	M	49,63A,63B,29A,20G
Prof	Yeh, Ying	M	39,61,12A

CA0805 Calif State Univ-Dominguez Hills

Division of Perf. & Digital Arts
1000 E Victoria St
Carson, CA 90747
(310) 243-3543   Fax: (310) 516-3449
www.csudh.edu
E-mail: rkravchak@csudh.edu

4 Year Institution
Member of NASM

Chair: Richard Kravchak, 80A
Dean: Carol A. Tubbs, 80A

Emeritus	Bialosky, Marshall H.		
Prof	Bradfield, David	M	13,34,66A
Prof Emeritus	Caldwell, Hansonia	D	20G,36
Prof Emeritus	Champion, David	M	
Lect	Davis, Michael	M	63A
Prof	Etcheto, Sally A.	D	11,36,61,54
Assoc Prof	Grasse, Jonathan B.	D	34D,13,20,14C,10
Lect	Greif, Matthew	M	70
Prof	Kravchak, Richard	D	11,64,38,37,32
Lect	Mann, Sylvia Lee	D	32,62,38
Lect	Mitchell, Joseph	M	32,65

Assoc Prof	Moore, Stephen F.	D	13C,29,47,60,66
Lect	Morris, Scott	D	70
Lect	Nivans, David	PhD	14C,29A,20,13,11
Lect	Robinson, Greg	M	32,63D
Lect	Shannon, Jackie	D	63B
Emeritus	Steiner, Frances	D	62C
Prof	Waldrep, Mark	D	34,35C,35D
Lect	Yamamoto, Shirley	M	64A

CA0807 Calif State Univ-East Bay

Department of Music
25800 Carlos Bee Blvd
Hayward, CA 94542
(510) 885-3135   Fax: (510) 885-3461
music.csueastbay.edu
E-mail: mariko.abe@csueastbay.edu

4 Year Institution, Graduate School

Master of Arts in Music

Dir., Graduate Studies: Peter K. Marsh, 80C
Iterim Chair: John Eros

Lect PT	Abraham, Christine	M	61
Lect PT	Athayde, Robert L.	B	66A
Lect PT	Caimotto, Michelle	B	64A
Lect PT	Clements, Tony		63D
Asst Prof	Eros, John	D	32,32E,32B
Lect PT	Flyer, Nina G.	B	62C
Lect PT	Geiger, Jeanne	M	63C,49
Lect PT	Hall, Alan M.		65,29
Asst Prof	Hernandez, Rafael	D	10,13,34
Lect PT	Hicks, Pamela	B	61,39
Lect PT	Highman, Daniel R.	D	10A,12A
Assoc Prof	James, Buddy	D	36,32D,61,60A
Lect PT	Jekabson, Erik	M	63A,29
Lect PT	Klobas, Patrick P.	M	62D
Prof Emeritus	La Rocca, Frank J.	D	13,10F,10
Lect	Maltester, Diane	M	64C
Asst Prof	Marsh, Peter K.	D	14,12,20B,20
Lect PT	Miller, Jeffrey L.	D	13,10
Lect PT	Ortega, Janice D.	M	62E
Lect PT	Pardo, Brian	M	70,29
Lect PT	Ridge, David P.	M	63C
Lect PT	Rivard, Kevin C.	B	63B
Lect PT	Santos, Philip		62A,62B,51
Lect PT	Shearer, Allen R.	D	61,10A
Lect PT	Shidler, Deborah A.	M	64B
Lect PT	Sierra-Alonso, Saul	M	47
Lect PT	Steward, Lee A.	D	61,54
Lect PT	Storch, Arthur L.	M	50,65
Lect PT	Sykes, Jeffrey R.	D	66C,66A
Lect PT	Teicholz, Marc S.	D	70,41
Lect PT	Vasallo, Nicholas R.	D	34D,13A
Prof Emeritus	Wassermann, Ellen	M	41,66A,66D
Lect PT	Weber, Misato	M	66A,66D
Lect PT	Zinn, Daniel L.	B	47,64E,41,29A,11

CA0810 Calif State Univ-Fresno

Department of Music
MS #77
2380 E Keats Ave
Fresno, CA 93740-8024
(559) 278-2654   Fax: (559) 278-6800
www.csufresno.edu/music
E-mail: musicinfo@mail.fresnostate.edu

4 Year Institution, Graduate School
Member of NASM

Master of Arts in Music

Chair: Michael D. Caldwell, 80A
Dean: Vida Samiian, 80A
Dir., Graduate Studies: M. Teresa Beaman, 80C

Inst PT	Aldrich, Rachel	M	64B
Prof	Beaman, M. Teresa	D	13A,13,48,64A,34
Prof	Boone, Benjamin V.	D	13,10,29
Inst PT	Brummel, Jonathan	D	63C
Assoc Prof	Caldwell, Michael D.	D	63A
Assoc Prof	Darling, Matthew H.	D	50,65,14C
Inst PT	DeJong, Brigid	M	61
Inst PT	Durst, Alan Edward		64E,29,32,46,47
Assoc Prof	Froelich, Kenneth D.	D	10,34,43
Inst PT	Gardner, Larry	M	64D
Inst PT	Giersch, Sandra	M	32

Prof	Gilroy, Gary P.	D	13C,10F,60B,37
Lect PT	Hamada, Brian	B	47,65,29A
Prof	Hamre, Anna R.	D	36,60A
Asst Prof	Henriques, Donald A.	D	14,20H
Inst PT	Hensley, David	M	60,61
Inst PT	Hiebert, Lenore	M	66A,13A
Prof	Hiebert, Thomas N.	D	13,63B
Inst PT	Huber, Laurel		66G
Inst PT	Hufft, Bradley	M	14C,13,11
Inst PT	Hull, Edward	M	63D
Prof	Ishigaki, Miles M.	D	48,64C,41,11,14C
Prof	Joseph-Weil, Helene	M	61
Assoc Prof	Karr, John	D	12,14C
Assoc Prof	Loewenheim, Thomas	D	62C,62D,38
Assoc Prof	Mowrer, Tony	D	32D,32,32C
Asst Prof	Radford, Anthony P.	D	61,39,54
Inst PT	Sobieralski, Nathan	D	63A
Asst Prof	Toren-Immerman, Limor	D	62A,62B,13C
Inst PT	VonBerg, Craig	M	29,47,14C
Prof	Werz, Andreas	DIPL	66A,66B,66C,66D
Asst Prof	Whitehead, Corey	D	70,11,14C
Inst PT	Wilke, Adam	M	37

CA0815 Calif State Univ-Fullerton

Department of Music
PO Box 6850
Fullerton, CA 92834-6850
(657) 278-3511   Fax: (657) 278-5956
www.fullerton.edu/arts/music/index.htm
E-mail: mdickey@fullerton.edu

4 Year Institution, Graduate School
Member of NASM

Master of Arts in Music Education, Master of Music in Composition, Master of Music in Performance, Master of Arts in History & Literature, Master of Arts in Piano Pedagogy

Chair: Marc R. Dickey, 80A
Vice Chair: Kimo Furumoto, 80H
Vice Chair: Bongshin Ko, 80H

Adj Inst	Anthony, Robert	M	37
Adj Inst	Baker, Nicole	D	12A,36
Adj Inst	Brightbill, Alvin	M	61
Adj Inst	Chang, W. Michael	B	62B
Adj Inst	Chen, C. Brian	D	62B
Adj Inst	Choate, Ellie	M	62E
Adj Inst	Cole, Thomas	M	32
Assoc Prof	Cunliffe, William H.	D	29,47,41
Prof	Delgado, Eduardo	M	66A
Assoc Prof	Dickey, Marc R.	D	32,37,64
Adj Inst	Domingues, Cameron	D	64D,64E
Adj Inst	Dries, Eric	D	13,13E,13D,29A,66
Asst Prof	Edwards, Alison	M	66A,66C
Adj Inst	Ellwood, Jeff	M	64E,29
Adj Inst	Eschete, Ron	B	29,70
Prof	Fennell, Mitchell	D	60,32,37
Assoc Prof	Ferrandis, Jean	D	64A
Adj Inst	Figueiredo, Virginia Costa	D	64C
Adj Inst	Foster, N. Gary	B	64E
Assoc Prof	Furumoto, Kimo	D	38,39
	Gardner, TK		70
Assoc Prof	Goodrich, Mark J.	D	61
Adj Inst	Greene, Kimberly	M	12A
Adj Inst	Hall, Bianca	M	61
Adj Inst	Hoffman, Michael	B	63C
Adj Inst	Hughes, Luther		29,62D
Asst Prof	Istad, Robert M.	D	36,40
Adj Inst	Jones, Esther		66G
Adj Inst	Keen, Phillip	M	63D
Adj Inst	Kim, Ellen		66D
Adj Inst	Klassen, Masako	D	66A
Assoc Prof	Ko, Bongshin	M	62C
Prof	Koegel, John	D	12,14
Inst	Korzhev, Mikhail	D	66C
Adj Inst	Kreibich, Paul		29,65
Adj Inst	Leyrer, Linda	D	61
Adj Inst	Llewellyn, Raymond	B	32B,37,65
Asst Prof	Lohman, Laura Ann	D	12,14,14C
Adj Inst	Lorbeer, James	B	50
Assoc Prof	Madsen, Pamela	D	13A,13,10
Adj Inst	Mahpar, Steven	M	63B
Adj Inst	Martchev, Valentin	M	64D
Adj Inst	Masters, Martha	D	70
Adj Inst	McGrath, Kenneth	M	65
Adj Inst	Methe, Daniel	M	32
Prof	Miller, Todd	M	49,50,63B,65
Adj Inst	Palmer, Kye	B	63A
Adj Inst	Perkins, Barry		63A
Assoc Prof	Peterson, Christopher	D	32D,36
Adj Inst	Proulx, John	B	66A
Assoc Prof	Prunty, Patricia	M	61
Adj Inst	Pryor, Ryan	M	66A
Prof	Rodgers, Lloyd A.	D	13,10,43
Adj Inst	Rohr, Grant		66A,61,66C
Prof	Rosengren, Hakan	M	64C,41
Adj Inst	Rotter, James	M	64E
Prof	Salem, Ernest	D	13A,41,62A,62B
Adj Inst	Salters, Mark		61,39
Adj Inst	Sanders, Robert		63C,49
Adj Inst	Schaefer, Carl	D	32
Adj Inst	Sellers, Joel	M	63C
Adj Inst	Sharp, Charles		29A,20
Adj Inst	Sharp, Thomas	B	10C,10F
Assoc Prof	Siebenaler, Dennis	D	32B
Adj Inst	Slack, Robert	M	65
Adj Inst	Smith, Janet		61,39
Adj Inst	Thomas, Matthew	D	12A
Prof	Timm, Laurance	D	37,48,64B
Adj Inst	Tinsley, Frederick	M	62D
Adj Inst	Tornquist, Doug		63D
Prof	Tumlinson, Charles	D	47,41,29
Adj Inst	Turner, Richard	M	70
Adj Inst	Unal, Fureya	M	13
Assoc Prof	Walicki, Kenneth J.	D	10,13,34
Prof	Watson, Robert	D	66A,66C
Adj Inst	Watson, Teri	M	66A,66D

CA0825 Calif State Univ-Long Beach

Bob Cole Conservatory of Music
1250 Bellflower Blvd
Long Beach, CA 90840-7101
(562) 985-4781   Fax: (562) 985-2490
www.csulb.edu/~music
E-mail: music@csulb.edu

4 Year Institution, Graduate School
Member of NASM

Master of Arts in Music Education, Master of Arts in Music Theory, Master of Music in Composition, Master of Music in Performance, Master of Music in Opera, Master of Arts in Musicology, Master of Music in Choral Conducting, Master of Music in Jazz Studies, Master of Music in Instrumental Conducting

Chair: Carolyn Bremer, 80A
Director: John Carnahan, 80A
Dir., Graduate Studies: Alicia M. Doyle, 80C

Asst Prof	Anglin, David Ives	D	61,39
Lect PT	Antal, Tom	D	32D
Lect PT	Artemova, Alina	M	61
Lect PT	Asada, Chi	M	66A
Lect PT	Atkinson, James		63B
Prof	Barcellona, John	D	41,64A
Lect PT	Barrera, James	M	64E
Prof	Birkemeier, Richard	D	11,63A,49
Lect PT	Bodnar, Marian	M	61
Prof	Bremer, Carolyn	D	13,10
Lect PT	Brenner, Martin	B	35G
Assoc Prof	Briggs, Ray A.	D	14,29,46,47
Lect PT	Byers, Andrea	M	62A
Lect PT	Campbell, John		64D
Lect PT	Cariaga, Marvellee		61
Lect PT	Carnahan, Deborah	M	64C
Prof	Carnahan, John	M	37
Prof	Carney, Michael	D	65,29,20,50
Lect PT	Carroll, Raynor		65
Prof	Chou, Shun-Lin	D	42,66
Lect PT	Clarke, Axel	M	65
Lect PT	Coleman, Cecilia		66A
Lect PT	Cooper, Rychard	B	35C
Lect PT	Cox, Robin V.	D	13,10
Asst Prof	DeAlbuquerque, Joan	D	32,37
Lect PT	Dickstein, Marcia	M	62E
Assoc Prof	Doyle, Alicia M.	PhD	11,14,20
Lect PT	Drake, Randy	M	65
Lect PT	Duckles, Andrew	M	62B
Lect PT	Dutz, Brad		65
Lect PT	Emerzian, Jimmy	M	29
Lect PT	Eschete, Ron		70
Lect PT	Evans, David	M	63A
Lect PT	Farrell, Brian	M	61
Lect PT	Fornero, Dan		63A
Prof	Forney, Kristine	D	12A,67,11
Asst Prof	Frear, Robert		63A,42
Lect PT	Gamma, Lorenz	D	62A
Lect PT	Garrett, David B.	D	62C
Lect PT	Gerhart, David		65,20H,37,50
Lect PT	Goode-Castro, Helen		64C
Lect PT	Gottlieb, Valentina	D	66A
Lect PT	Grego, Michael	D	64C
Lect PT	Grego, Michele	M	64D
Lect PT	Guter, Christine	M	47,61,32D
Prof	Herman, Martin	D	10F,13,10,34
Prof	Hickman, Roger	D	11,12A,38

Rank	Name	Degree	Codes
Lect PT	Higgins, Michael	M	70
Lect PT	Ignacio, Arnel	M	64C
Asst Prof	Jarvis, Jeffrey S.	M	63A,29
Lect PT	Kronauer, Steven	D	61
Lect PT	LaMarca, Perry	B	10C
Lect PT	Lazarova, Maria	M	61
Lect PT	Lett, Bruce		62D
Lect PT	Lozano, Sal		64E
Lect PT	MacDougall, Tim		61
Lect PT	Maldonado, Greg	M	51,62A,55,62B
Lect PT	Marienthal, Eric		64E
Lect PT	Marsteller, Loren	M	63C,63D
Lect PT	Mason, James	B	64E
Lect PT	Matsumoto, Shigemi	M	61
Prof	Matthews, Justus F.	D	13,10,43,34
Lect PT	McChesney, Bob	B	63C
Prof	Mitchell, Deborah H.	D	32
Asst Prof	Mueller-Stosch, Johannes	D	38,60B
Lect PT	Pehlivanian, Elisabeth	M	61,32D
Lect PT	Peters, Tom	B	62D
	Pilato, Nikk	PhD	63,37,38,32E,60B
Lect PT	Poston, Ken	B	20G,35B,29A
Lect PT	Reichenbach, Bill	B	63C
Lect PT	Reid, Ted	M	32D
Lect FT	Richey, Craig	M	66A,66C,66B
Lect PT	Rose, Linda	B	62A
Lect PT	Rundus, Katharin	D	61
Lect PT	Sabin, Paula	D	12A
Asst Prof	Shockley, Alan	D	13,10
Lect PT	Still, Christopher	M	63A
Lect PT	Stone, Joseph	M	64B
Lect PT	Stout, Ron		63A
Lect PT	Takeya, Kimiyo	DIPL	62A
Assoc Prof	Talberg, Jonathan	D	36
Lect PT	Thaves, Darrin	M	64A
Lect PT	Trapani, Steve	M	63C
Lect PT	Uranker, Mark	B	66A,66D
Lect PT	Urso-Trapani, Rena	M	64A
Prof	Vail, Leland	D	36,61,60
Lect PT	Van Houten, John		49,63D,35A
Lect FT	Verdie' de Vas-Romero, Adriana	D	13
Lect PT	Waites, Althea	M	66A,66D,20G
Lect PT	Washburn, David	M	63A
Lect PT	Weiss, David	DIPL	64B
Lect PT	Wheeler, George	M	10,13
Lect PT	Yun, Chan Ho	D	62A
Prof	Zanutto, Daniel R.	D	32,60
Lect PT	Zibits, Paul	M	62D

CA0830 Calif State Univ-Los Angeles
Department of Music
5151 State University Dr
Los Angeles, CA 90032-8102
(323) 343-4060   Fax: (323) 343-4063
www.calstatela.edu/academic/music/
E-mail: music@calstatela.edu

4 Year Institution, Graduate School
Member of NASM

Master of Music in Afro Latin Music, Master of Arts in Music, Master of Music in Composition, Master of Music in Performance, Master of Music in Conducting, Master of Music in Music Education, Master of Music in Commercial Music

Chair: George DeGraffenreid, 80A
Dir., Graduate & Undergraduate Studies: Jeffrey W. Benedict, 80B,80C

Rank	Name	Degree	Codes
Lect PT	Alancraig, Diane	M	64A
Lect PT	Askren, David	M	29
Prof	Belan, William	D	60,36
Prof	Benedict, Jeffrey W.	DMA	29,47,64E,41
Lect PT	Cepeda, Iris		61
Prof	Connors, David	D	32B,32C,61
Prof	De Castro, Paul	D	14,29,20H,66A
Prof	DeGraffenreid, George	D	32C,32E,32G
Lect PT	Elgart, Matthew	D	70,10,13
Lect PT	Emmons, Tim	M	62D,29
Lect PT	Fernandez, Robert	M	65,50
Assoc Prof	Ford, James	M	63A,29
Lect PT	Goode-Castro, Helen	M	64C
Assoc Prof	Graef, Sara Carina	D	13
Lect PT	Hernandez, Edgar	B	20H
Lect PT	Hoffman, Cathy		61
Prof	Holland, Deborah	M	35,10D
Lect PT	Jones, Randy		63D
Assoc Prof	Kane, Susan W.	D	61
Prof	Kennedy, John M.	D	10,13F,43,10F,13
Lect FT	Kretchner, Darlene	D	32B,32A,32E,32F,32G
Asst Prof	Levinson, Ross	M	35,34A,10C,10D
Lect PT	Lin, ChiaHui	M	66D
Lect PT	Liu, Hui	M	62B
Lect PT	Lozano, Danilo	M	20H
Lect PT	Osika, Geoffrey	B	62D
Lect PT	Pan, Huiyu-Penny	DMA	66A,66D,66B,66C,42
Lect PT	St. Marie, John	M	36
Assoc Prof	Stein, Beverly	D	12,14
Lect PT	Voyement, Jacques	M	63C
Lect PT	Ward, Robert	M	66A
Asst Prof	Wight, Steve	M	35,34A,10C,10D,10F

CA0835 Calif State Univ-Northridge
Department of Music
18111 Nordhoff St
Northridge, CA 91330-8314
(818) 677-3181   Fax: (818) 677-5876
www.csun.edu/music
E-mail: music@csun.edu

4 Year Institution, Graduate School
Member of NASM

Master of Arts in Music, Master of Music in Composition, Master of Music in Performance, Master of Music in Conducting, Master of Arts in Music Industry Administration

Chair: Steve J. Thachuk, 80A

Rank	Name	Degree	Codes
Assoc Prof	Aks, David M.	M	12A,13C,39,60B,62C
Asst Prof	Alviso, Ric	D	11,50
Prof	Baker, Katherine Ramos	D	32,36
PT	Baltz, Ann		39
PT	Beck, Carolyn L.	D	64D
PT	Berg, Robert	M	62B
PT	Bissonette, Gregg S.		65
Prof	Borczon, Ronald M.	M	70,33
PT	Bostrom, Sandra	D	66A,10C,12A,34,65A
PT	Brown, Richard		12
PT	Buckingham, Katisse		29
PT	Buonamassa, John	M	34A,34B,46
PT	Calvert, Phil A.		35C
Asst Prof	Christensen, Carey L.	M	35A
PT	Cooper, Blake		63D
PT	Coye, Gene		29,65
Asst Prof	Daversa, John	DMA	10C,29,63A
PT	Davis, Erica		61
PT	Dearman, John		70
PT	Dell, Kay		32
PT	Dolas, Helen G.		33
PT	Dorsa, James	D	66H,10A,67F,13C,12A
PT	England, George		70
PT	Fasola, Bryan		70
PT	Ferril, Michael J.		62A,42,43
PT	Francis, Edward	M	66A
PT	Fukushima, Gary A.		66A
PT	Garcia, Peter J.		20H
Inst PT	Garrett, Glen R.		29A,11
PT	Gilad, Kimaree T.	M	64B
PT	Glasgow, Scott	M	10C
PT	Grey, Benoit		10C
Prof	Heinen, Julia M.	DMA	64C,42,13C
PT	Hofmann, Richard Glenn	D	63A
PT	Hoover, David E.	M	63B
PT	Howard, Timothy P.		13B,13C,66G
PT	Jaroszewicz, Martin		34
PT	Joyce, David		47
PT	Kasper, Don J.		62D,66D
PT	Keen, Phillip M.	M	63D
PT	Ketchie, Diane		61
PT	Kipp, Sandra		64A
PT	Kirov, Milen		13
PT	Koonse, Larry		70
Asst Prof	Lee, Pei-Shan	DMA	66C
PT	Lewis, Jon L.		65A
PT	Lockart, Rob R.		64E
Prof	Luedders, Jerry D.	M	32,64E
PT	Magnussen, John P.	B	65,13C
PT	Malloy, Andrew Thomas		63C
PT	Malpede, William V.	B	11,46
PT	Mancini, Nick		29,65B
PT	Mankey, Joel R.	B	50
Prof	Marinescu, Liviu	D	10A,13E,13F,10
PT	Marshall, Jason		37
PT	McChesney, Bob H.		63C
PT	Meza, Oscar M.		62D
Asst Prof	Monchick, Alexandra	PhD	12
PT	Mouridian, Linda		62
Prof	Murray, Deanna A.	D	61
PT	Nelson, Josh		29
PT	Nudell, Geoff A.		64E
PT	Oleszkiewicz, Dariusz		62D
PT	Pisano, John J.		70
PT	Pozzi, Dave A.		13C,14C
Prof	Pratt, Gary W.	B	60,37,38,47
PT	Rabe, Gigi 'Gee'	M	11,50
Prof	Rachmanov, Dmitry	D	66A

PT	Ray, Julia J.		32
Prof	Roscetti, Diane	M	42,62C,35A
Prof	Roscigno, John A.	D	38
PT	Rosenn, Jamie		29,70
Inst	Salas, Jacqueline M.	D	66A,66D
Assoc Prof	Sannerud, David	D	39,61
Inst FT	Schliff, Mary A.	M	32
PT	Scott, Judith G.	M	61
Prof	Sellers, Elizabeth A.	M	10C,46,60B
PT	Shear, Howard		63A
PT	Shostac, David J.		64A
PT	Smith, Aaron Todd		65
FT	Smith, Paul A.	M	36,60A
Prof	Stoffel, Lawrence F.	D	32C,37
PT	Stones, Linda M.	D	61
Asst Prof	Surmani, Andrew		35
Prof	Thachuk, Steve J.	D	70
Prof	Toutant, William P.	D	10,11
PT	Weller, Richard A.		65
PT	West, Julie A.	M	32E

CA0840 Calif State Univ-Sacramento

Department of Music
6000 J St
Sacramento, CA 95819-6015
(916) 278-5191   Fax: (916) 278-7217
www.csus.edu/music
E-mail: hills@csus.edu

4 Year Institution, Graduate School
Member of NASM

Master of Music in Composition, Master of Music in Performance, Master of Music in Conducting

Chair & Coord., Graduate Studies: Ernie M. Hills, 80A,80C
Admissions Counselor: Mark E. Allen, 80D
Dir., Fest of New American Music: Stephen F. Blumberg, 80F
Dir., Summer Programs: Jack E. Foote, 80G

Lect	Barbini, William	B	62A,62B
Assoc Prof	Basini, Laura	D	11,12
Prof	Blumberg, Stephen F.	D	13,10
Lect	Bohm, Keith	D	13A,64E
Lect	Bossuat, Judy	M	32E,62
Lect	Britts, Judy	M	32B
Prof	Chopyak, James D.	D	14
Prof	Cionco, Richard M.	M	66A
Other	Cozza, John	D	66C
Lect	Crain, Michael R.	M	20,34
Lect	Deffner, David	D	65B
Lect	Derthick, Thomas	M	62D
Prof	Dilworth, Gary	M	13,63A,20G
Lect	Dixon, Julian	M	63D
Lect	Elias, Joel	M	63C
Prof	Eylar, Leo B.	M	10,12A,38
Prof	Fisher, Robin L.	D	61
Prof	Foote, Jack E.	D	32,64E
Lect	Gilman, Joseph	D	66A,29
Lect	Halseth, Robert E.	D	60,37
Prof	Hills, Ernie M.	D	13,63C
Lect	Homan, Steven	M	29,70
Prof	Kendrick, Donald	D	60,36
Prof	Kennedy, Daniel J.	D	11,65
Prof	Kitka, Claudia B.	M	61
Lect	Kruger, Anna R.	M	62B
Lect	Lotter, Rich	M	29
Prof	Luchansky, Andrew	M	13A,51,62C
Lect	Marsh, Kerry	M	29,36,47
Lect	McMullen, Michael	M	29
Assoc Prof	Metz, Sue	M	32B
Lect	Nowlen, Peter	M	63B
Prof	Peters, Lorna G.	D	66A,66H,13
Lect	Pineda, Gerry	M	29
Prof	Pittman, Deborah M.	M	64C,20G
Lect	Presler, Anna H.	M	13A,51
Lect	Redfield, Clayborn	D	11,32E,37
Prof	Roach, Stephen W.	D	47,29
Prof	Savino, Richard	D	70
Lect	Scott, Tatiana	M	66D
Lect	Shidler, Deborah	M	64B
Lect	Smith, Kirsten	M	66A,66C,66D
Lect	Stevens, Lynn	M	32B
Lect	Swensen, Ian	M	42,62A
Lect	Tau, Omari	M	61,39
Lect	Tulga, Philip	M	29,63C
Lect	Wells, David	M	64D
Lect	Wesner-Hoehn, Beverly	D	62E
Other	Wong, Baldwin	B	72
Prof	Zucker, Laurel	M	64A,20G

CA0845 Calif State Univ-San Bernardino

Department of Music
5500 University Pkwy
San Bernardino, CA 92407-2397
(909) 537-5859   Fax: (909) 537-7016
music.csusb.edu
E-mail: musicadmissions@csusb.edu

4 Year Institution
Member of NASM

Chair: Todd Alan Johnson, 80A

Lect PT	Chang, Jocelyn Hua-Chen	D	66A
Lect PT	Cummins, Danielle Rosaria	D	62A,62B
Lect PT	DeLaO, Armalyn	M	32
Lect PT	Dropkin, Mary	M	62E
Assoc Prof	Fraser, Stacey	D	61,39
Lect PT	Green, Stuart	M	32,70
Lect PT	Hampton, Bradley	B	10D,40
Lect FT	Jester, Erik	M	37,60B,63C
Lect PT	Johansen, Lawrence	M	63A
Assoc Prof	Johnson, Todd Alan	DMA	65,12A,14,50,29A
Lect PT	Kirk, Erin	D	66C,66D
Assoc Prof	Knop, Robert	D	32E,29,64E,11
Lect PT	Lamprey, Audrey	M	63
Lect PT	Long, Gary	M	65
Lect PT	Maldonado, Ana Maria	M	32,62C,51
Prof Emeritus	McFatter, Larry E.	D	13,10F,10,66A
Asst Prof	Menton, Allen W.	D	10,13
Lect PT	Nam, Jason	B	32E
Lect PT	Quintana, Ariel	M	36,32D
Prof	Radomski, James V.	D	11,12A,12,14
Lect PT	Rehfeldt, Phillip	D	64D
Lect PT	Russell, John	M	36,40,32D,60A
Lect PT	Tacchia, Michele	M	38
Lect PT	Tomlinson, Rebecca	D	64A,32B
Lect PT	Undem, Stewart	M	63D
Lect PT	Usher, Jon	D	64C,32
Lect PT	Vance, Scott	M	35B,35C,35D,13L

CA0847 Calif State Univ-San Marcos

Department of Visual & Perf Arts
San Marcos, CA 92096
(760) 750-4174   Fax: (760) 750-3090
www.csusm.edu/vpa
E-mail: bradbury@csusm.edu

4 Year Institution

Music Contact: William Bradbury, II, 80A

Prof	Bradbury, William	D	13,10,11,34,20G
Adj	Corcoran, Catherine T.	M	66D
Adj	Garcia, Eduardo	M	20H,11,70
Prof	Goldberg, Merryl	D	64E,32,11
Adj	Griswold, Randall L.	M	20,11
Assoc Prof	Imara, Mtafiti	D	13,14,64,47,29
Adj	Kostlan, Robert	B	34

CA0850 Calif State Univ-Stanislaus

Department of Music
One University Cir
Turlock, CA 95382
(209) 667-3421   Fax: (209) 664-7027
www.csustan.edu
E-mail: dkavasch@csustan.edu

4 Year Institution
Member of NASM

Chair: Deborah H. Kavasch, 80A
Dean: Daryl Moore, 80A
Dir., Summer Programs: Daniel E. Davies, 80G

Prof	Afonso, Daniel R.	DMA	36,40,13C,32D,60A
Lect FT	Boren, Benjamin J.	M	66A,66B,66C,66D,13B
Lect PT	Brown, Al	D	32E,65,50
Prof	Davies, Daniel E.	D	62C,13A,11,13B
Lect PT	Dennis, Jeannine M.	D	64A
Lect PT	Dubberly, James	M	63C,63D,29A,41
Lect PT	Flores, Richard A.	D	70
Lect PT	Freeman, John S.	M	63A
Lect PT	Gabrielson, David J.	M	65
Lect PT	Harper, Denis B.	B	64B
Prof	Kavasch, Deborah H.	D	10A,13,61,10,10F

Lect PT	Keith, Randall J.	B	62D
Asst Prof	Kelly, Keith	M	29,47,46,41
Lect PT	Marvin, John W.	D	10
Assoc Prof	Mulder, Geoffrey	M	34,35C,35D,12A,62A
Lect PT	Opp, Benjamin A.	M	64D
Assoc Prof	Sims, Stuart	D	37,38,41,60B
Lect PT	Stewart, Kevin J.	B	64E
Prof	Weddle, John W.	D	32C,32B,20G,64C,11
Lect PT	Weichert, Constance E.	M	61
Prof	Wiggett, Joseph	D	61,54,39
Lect PT	Wilson, Elisha K.	M	63B

CA0855 Canada College

Department of Music
4200 Farm Hill Blvd
Redwood City, CA 94061-1030
(650) 306-3336   Fax: (650) 306-3176
canadacollege.net
E-mail: Canada.Humanities@smccd.net

2 Year Institution

Music Contact: David C. Meckler, 80A

Adj	Gunderson, Janice		36
Adj	Kujawsky, Eric	D	38
Inst	Meckler, David C.	D	11,20,12A,10,13A
Adj	Yi, Ann	D	66A,66D,20H

CA0859 Cerritos College

Department of Music
11110 Alondra Blvd
Norwalk, CA 90650-6203
(562) 860-2451   Fax: (562) 467-5005
www.cerritos.edu/music
E-mail: dbetancourt@cerritos.edu

2 Year Institution

Chair: David Betancourt, 80A
Dean, Fine Arts: Connie E. Mayfield, 80A

Assoc Prof	Betancourt, David	D	37,46,38,32E,60B
Adj	Carroll, Don		12A
PT	Chen, Johanna	M	66A,66D
PT	Da Silva, Paul	M	13A,66D,66A
Asst Prof	DeMichele, Anna	D	36,61,13A,38,11
PT	Dillon, Rhonda	M	61,11
PT	Dimond, Theresa	D	65
Prof Emeritus	Erjavec, Donald L.	M	13A,47,29,20G
PT	Gresham, Ann	M	61
PT	Grigoriev, Igor	M	70,53
PT	Gutierrez, Charles	M	34
PT	Hallback, Alan	M	37,63A
	Hart, Victoria	M	61
PT	Immel, Conrad	M	61
PT	Inouye, Fang-Fang Shi	M	66A,66D
Adj	Isaacs, David		70
PT	Kubiak, Paul	M	13A,11
PT	Lee, Sung Ae	D	13A,66A,66D
Asst Prof	Lopez, Christine Sotomayor	D	36,66A,66D,11,66B
PT	Lopez, David F.	B	64C
PT	Marr, John	M	13
PT	Mello, Christopher	M	70
Asst Prof	Nelson, David W.	D	13,13A,10F,10,38
FT	Pritchard, Gary	D	20G,29A,20H,12A
PT	Robertshaw, Manon	M	62C
Adj PT	Russell, Bruce	C	66A,66D
PT	Schreiner, Gregory	M	66A,66D
PT	Schroeder, Lisa	M	64A
PT	Simmons, Jim	M	34
PT	Torres, Martin	M	62D,70
PT	Tsai, Tammy	M	13A,11,62A

CA0900 Chabot College

Department of Music
25555 Hesperian Blvd
Hayward, CA 94545-2447
(510) 723-6829   Fax: (510) 723-6833
www.chabotcollege.edu/music
E-mail: gcarter@chabotcollege.edu

2 Year Institution

Dean: Gary M. Carter, 80A
Coord., Music: Timothy Harris, 80H

Adj	Barrera, Ramiro	B	37
Inst PT	Benkman, Noel	M	11,20,66
Adj	Chou, Yueh	D	64D
Adj	Collins, Allison	M	61,13C
Inst PT	Flores, Rick		13A,70
Prof	Harris, Timothy	M	37,11,12A,32E
Adj	Jekabson, Erik	M	63B,29
Adj	Johnson, Beverly	M	47
Adj	Kennelly, Donald	B	63C
Adj	Lington, Victoria	D	66C
Adj	Matheson, Bryan	B	34D,35
Adj	Ott, Leonard	B	63A
Prof	Palacio, Jon	M	29,46,47,66A
Adj	Rawdon, Kenneth	M	36
Adj	Richman, Glenn	B	62D
Adj	Sanchez, Steve	M	64C
Prof	Schultz, Eric	D	10,13,34
Inst PT	Shannon, William	M	13A,13B,34,63B,35
Adj	Shidler, Deborah	M	64B
Adj	Storch, Arthur	M	65,50
Adj	Weber, Misato	M	66A
Adj	Zinn, Dann	M	64E,29

CA0950 Chaffey College

Department of Music
5885 Haven Ave
Rancho Cucamonga, CA 91737-3002
(909) 652-6071   Fax: (909) 466-2831
www.chaffey.edu
E-mail: gus.gil@chaffey.edu

2 Year Institution

Dean: Michael Dinielli, 80A
Coordinator: John Machado, 80A

PT	Alverson, D. J.	B	35C,35D,35G
Assoc Prof	Aranda, Patrick	M	13A,37,47,63C,29A
Prof	De Dobay, Thomas	D	11,12A,61,66D
Prof PT	Gil, Gustavo	M	36,13,46
PT	Haines, Janice	M	13A,13C,66D
PT	Maldonado, Anna Maria	M	20,11
PT	Rudd, Stephen W.	D	11
PT	Scarano, Robert	M	70
PT	Williams, Nancy	M	66D,16,11

CA0960 Chapman University

College of Performing Arts
Conservatory of Music
1 University Dr
Orange, CA 92866-1011
(714) 997-6871   Fax: (714) 744-7671
www.chapman.edu/music/
E-mail: rickc@chapman.edu

4 Year Institution
Member of NASM

Director: Rick Christophersen, 80A
Chair: Amy Graziano, 80A
Dean, Performing Arts: Dale A. Merrill, 80A

PT	Alexopoulos, Christina	M	61
PT	Alt, David	D	61
PT	Alva, Albert	A	46
PT	Atherton, Peter L.	D	61
PT	Ball, Mindy	B	62E
FT	Becker, Robert	M	62B
PT	Black, David	B	62D
PT	Blanc, Pamela	B	61
PT	Brennan, Christopher	M	66A
PT	Cahueque, David	D	70
PT	Calvo, Francisco	M	11
PT	Campbell, John		64D
PT	Cheng, Clara	M	66C
PT	Cho, Tony	D	66C,39
Assoc Prof	Cogan, Jeff	M	70,34
FT	Coker, Stephen R.	D	36
PT	Dahlin, Christina	M	61
PT	DeHart, Justin	D	65
Assoc Prof	Dehning, Margaret	M	36,61
PT	Dolkas, Bridget	M	62A
PT	Driskill, Kristina	D	61
PT	Fernandez, Robert	M	20
PT	Fielding, Cheryl Lin	D	66C
PT	Fitzpatrick, William		62A
Asst Prof	Fong, Grace	D	66A,66B,66C
Assoc Prof	Frelly, Robert	D	11,32
PT	Gee, Patricia	M	61
Artist in Res	Ghez, Ariana	M	64B

PT	Goeser, Patrick	M	61
PT	Goya, Ruby Cheng	D	66A
Assoc Prof	Graziano, Amy	D	11,12A,12F
PT	Greene, Fred	M	63D
PT	Hall, Timothy		63A
Prof	Hall, William D.	D	
Asst Prof	Heim, Sean	D	13,20
Asst Prof	Holmes, Jeffrey	D	13
Asst Prof	Ivanova, Vera	D	10A,10B,10F,10,66A
PT	Kallay, Aron	D	34
PT	Kao, Janet	M	66A
PT	Kim, Hye-Young	D	66C
PT	Kim, Jennifer L.	D	63B
PT	Kirov, Milen	M	13
Artist in Res	Kitic, Milena		61
PT	Knecht, Karen	MFA	66A
PT	Korzhev, Mikhail	D	66C
PT	Kroesen, Irene	B	62
PT	Lapidis, Rachael	M	12F
PT	Lebow, Roger	M	62C
PT	Lee, Hedy	B	66A
PT	Liu, Vivian	D	66A
PT	Luttinger, Elizabeth	M	13A
PT	Mack, John	M	61
PT	Macy, Elizabeth	D	12
PT	Matsuura, Gary	B	47,64E
PT	McClurg, Bruce	M	61
PT	Min, Beverly	M	66A
PT	Montgomery, Susan	M	61
Assoc Prof	Naidoo, Shaun	D	13
Artist in Res	Neblett, Carol	B	61
PT	Ochs, Hunter	M	34
PT	Palchak, Mary	M	64A
PT	Park, Janice	D	66A
PT	Shaffer, Teren	M	38
PT	Sharp, Thom	B	10C
PT	Sherman, Paul	D	41
PT	Steffens, Lea	D	64C
Asst Prof	Sternfeld, Jessica	D	12A
PT	Stetson, David	M	63C
FT	Terry, Nicholas	M	50,65
Assoc Prof	Thomas, Louise	D	66C
Asst Prof	Vazquez-Ramos, Angel M.	D	60A,36,32D,32B
Asst Prof	Wachs, Daniel Alfred	M	38,60B
PT	Washburn, David	M	49,63
PT	Wells, William	B	66G
PT	Wright-FitzGerald, Jesse	M	13C

CA1000 Citrus College

Department of Fine & Perf. Arts
1000 W Foothill Blvd
Glendora, CA 91741-1885
(626) 914-8580   Fax: (626) 914-8582
www.citrus.cc.ca.us
E-mail: rslack@citruscollege.edu

2 Year Institution

Chair & Dir., Festivals & Summer Programs: Norman Mamey, 80A,80F,80G,80H
Associate Dean: Bernard Bollinger, 80H

	Bagg, Joseph		29B,66A
Adj	Beatty, David	B	63C
Inst	Bollinger, Bernard	M	36,61,54
Adj	Cotter, Steve	M	70,47
	Davis, Charlie		63A
Inst	Eisel, Gunnar	M	10B,12A,13A,14C,29A
	Enos, David		62D
Adj	Ford, Andrew		35,62D
Inst	Galvan, Alex	M	10,13,37,60
PT	Green, Martin	M	11,13H,32D,36,39
	Griffiths, Laura		63B
Inst	Hoehne, Bill	M	10F,12C,64A,13,29
PT	Hynes, Tom	M	13,29,47,53,70
Adj	Ireland, Cathy		61
	Jackson, Joe		63D
Inst	Jaquette, Tim		35A,35C,35D
Adj	Kerr, William		34
Inst	Langford, Bruce	M	11,12A,32D,36,39
	Lee, Janice		61
PT	MacNeil, Robert	B	13A,39,61
Inst	Mamey, Norman	M	66A,10,12A,13,35A
Adj	McChesney, Bob		63C
	McCormick, Corey		62D
	Mixson, Vonnetta		61
Adj	Packer, Michael	B	65
Adj	Praniuk, Ingrid		61
	Schoenbeck, Sara		64D
Adj	Schuricht, Paul	D	
Adj	Scott, Jenni Olson		64A
Adj	Sexton, Bobby	M	66A
	Sherman, Paul		64B
Inst	Shrope, Douglas	B	36,61,60A,40,54
Inst	Slack, Robert	M	47,49,63A,53
Adj	Steinmetz, John		64D,12C

PT	Sushel, Michael	M	10D,66A,66B,11,29A
	Troy, TJ		65
PT	Waddington, Alan		12F,14,29,46,47

CA1020 City College of San Francisco

Department of Music
50 Phelan Ave
San Francisco, CA 94112
(415) 239-3641   Fax: (415) 452-5259
www.ccsf.edu/Departments/Music/
E-mail: mmueller@ccsf.edu

2 Year Institution

Chair: Madeline N. Mueller, 80A

PT	Argenti, Mary A.	M	61
PT	Bernstein, Harry	M	13A,11
PT	Blea, Anthony	M	38,62A,36
PT	Bozina, Robert P.	M	13A,70
PT	Carlson, Lennis Jay	M	70,46,29A
PT	Chui, Eddie	M	66D,13A
PT	Daddy, S. Kwaku	M	20A
Prof	Davis, Bob	M	70,20G
PT	Dilworth, Helen J.	D	61,66D
PT	Enciso, Franz J.	M	13C,66D,11
PT	Fenner, Richard C.	M	62C,66D
Prof	Fergus, Brian S.	M	34,13A
Prof	Ferrara, Lawrence	M	11,70,34C
PT	Fleming, Tod N.	M	65
Emeritus	Grothkopp, William	D	
PT	Hardiman, David A.	M	46,29A,29B
Prof	Hubbell, Judy	M	61,66D,13A
Prof	Hudspeth, Charles M.	M	36,13A,66D
PT	Kamatani, Pamela M.	D	11,13B,13C
PT	Landau, Gregory P.	M	20H
PT	Law, Joshua T.	M	36,61
Prof	Lim, Benedict M.	M	20C,20D,11,66D
Prof	Mauleon-Santana, Rebeca	M	66D,20H,10A
PT	McCarthy, Charles J.	B	64,48
Prof	McFadden, Jim L.	M	66D
PT	Mueller, Gerald A.	M	13B
Prof	Mueller, Madeline N.	M	66D
PT	Pang, Wilma C.	M	66D,11,13A
PT	Shahani, Michael M.	M	39,54,13A
PT	Wynne, Patricia	B	36

CA1050 Claremont Graduate University

Department of Music
925 N Dartmouth Ave
Claremont, CA 91711-4405
(909) 621-8081   Fax: (909) 607-3694
www.cgu.edu/music
E-mail: music@cgu.edu

Graduate Institution

PhD in Music, Doctorate of Church Music, Doctorate of Musical Arts, Master of Arts

Chair: Robert Zappulla, 80A

Adj Prof	Alves, William	D	12C,35C,34D
Adj Prof	Beeks, Graydon	D	37
Adj Prof	Blankenburg, Gayle	M	66A
Prof	Boyer, Peter	D	10,60,35
Adj Prof	Coogan, W. Jack	D	31A
Adj Prof	De Silva, Preethi	D	66A,66H
Adj Prof	Flaherty, Thomas E.	D	10
Adj Prof	Haag, MaryBeth	M	61
Adj Prof	Hagedorn, Katherine	D	20A,20G,14A
Adj Prof	Huang, Hao	D	66A
Adj Prof	Huang, Rachel V.	D	62A,62B
Prof Emeritus	Jackson, Roland	D	13,12
Adj Prof	Lamkin, Michael D.	D	36,38
Adj Prof	Lindholm, Eric	M	13C,38,60B
Adj Prof	Lytle, Gwendolyn	M	61
Adj Prof	Pelev, Todor	D	62A
Adj Prof	Peterson, William	D	66G
	Quintana, Sylvia		
Adj Prof	Robertson, Carey	D	66G
Adj Prof	Rudich, Rachel	D	64A
Adj Prof	Sanders, Jack	M	70
Prof Emeritus	Traficante, Frank	D	13,12A,12
Prof	Van Deusen, Nancy	D	12A,12B,12C,14
Assoc Prof	Zappulla, Robert	D	12A,12C,13,66H

CA1060 Claremont McKenna College
Joint Music Program
890 Columbia Ave
Claremont, CA 91711-3901
(909) 607-3267   Fax: (909) 607-9170
www.scrippscollege.edu/academics/department/music/index.php
E-mail: ckamm@scrippscollege.edu

4 Year Institution

Music Contact: Charles W. Kamm, 80A

| Asst Prof | Cubek, David | D | 38,11,13,60 |
| Assoc Prof | Kamm, Charles W. | D | 36,11,12,60 |

CA1075 Colburn School, The
Conservatory of Music
200 S Grand Ave
Los Angeles, CA 90012
(213) 621-2200   Fax: (213) 625-0371
www.colburnschool.edu
E-mail: info@colburnschool.edu

4 Year Institution, Graduate School
Member of NASM

Artist Diploma, Professional Studies Certificate, Master of Music in Performance

Dean, Conservatory: Richard Beene, 80A
President: Sel Kardan, 80A
Dir., Admissions: Kristi A. Brown, 80D
Dean, CSPA: Robert C. McAllister, 80H,80E
Associate Dean: Kathleen Tesar, 80H,80D

	Bain, Andrew		63B,42
	Baltaian, Sarkis	D	66B
	Beene, Richard		64D,42
	Brooks, Erin		12A
	Brown, Kristi A.		12A
	Coletti, Paul		62B,42
	Duke, Robert		32G
	Garson, Michael		53
	Gilad, Yehuda		64C,38,42
	Goodman, Glenda		12A
Retired Prof	Krehbiel, A. David		63B,42
	Lavner, Jeffrey		66
	Lawrence, Mark		63C,42
	Leonard, Ronald		62C,42
	Liepins, Laura		35A,35F
	Lipsett, Robert		62A
	Lloyd, Peter		62D,42
	Mabee, Patricia		42,55B,66H
	Miller, Bruce E.		13D,13E,13F
	Pearson, Norman		63D,42
	Perry, John		66A,42
	Petitto, Jacqueline		13C
	Ross, Elaine M.	D	13A,13B,13C
	Shihor, Ory		66,66A,42
	Smith, Deborah	M	16
	Steinhardt, Arnold		42
	Turovsky, JoAnn		62E,42
	Ullery, Benjamin		62B
	Van Geem, Jack		65,42
	Vogel, Allan		64B,42,55B
	Walker, Jim		64A,42
	Wilt, James		63A,42
	Zeisler, Nathaniel W.		35A,35F

CA1100 College of Alameda
Department of Music
555 Atlantic Ave
Alameda, CA 94501-2109
(510) 522-7221
alameda.peralta.edu
E-mail: gpearson@peralta.edu

2 Year Institution

Chair: Glen Pearson, 80A
Assistant Dean: Gunther F. Puschendorf, 80H

	Mims, Herbert		
	Pearson, Glen		
	Puschendorf, Gunther F.	D	13A,36,38,66A
	Sparks, David		16,10,66A
	Williams, Loni		

CA1150 College of Marin
Department of Music
835 College Ave
Kentfield, CA 94904
(415) 485-9460   Fax: (415) 454-3194
www.marin.edu
E-mail: tara.flandreau@marin.edu

2 Year Institution (Junior College)

Chair: Tara Flandreau, 80A

Inst PT	Brown, Linda Noble	M	61
Prof	Delaney, Douglas	M	13,11,37,47,64
Prof	Flandreau, Tara	M	12A,13,38,41,62
Prof PT	Ivry, Jessica	M	51,42,62,13C,38
Prof PT	Jarrell, Boyd	M	13,36,40
Prof PT	Kelly, Alex	D	34D
Prof Emeritus PT	Masonson, Norman	M	13A,12A
Prof PT	Schleeter, Bob	B	20G,29A,34D
Prof	Smith, Paul	M	12A,66A,66C,66D,54

CA1250 College of San Mateo
Department of Music
1700 W Hillsdale Blvd
San Mateo, CA 94402-3757
(650) 574-6494   Fax: (650) 574-6485
www.collegeofsanmateo.edu
E-mail: bobrowski@smccd.edu

2 Year Institution

Dean, Business & Creative Arts: Linda Avelar, 80A
Chair: Christine Bobrowski, 80A

Asst Prof PT	Baker, R. Bryan	D	60A,61,36
Prof	Berry, Fredrick J.		
Prof	Bobrowski, Christine	M	45,34,35C
Adj	Devine, Timothy		
Asst Prof PT	Ferguson, Charles Alan	M	10,70
Adj	Fish, Mark		
Asst Prof PT	Galindo, Guillermo	M	45,34,35C
Prof	Galisatus, Michael	M	47,46,63
Adj	Gallagher, Kevin		
Adj	Hanson, Mark		
Asst Prof PT	Hoffmann, Shulamit	M	66A,11
Asst Prof PT	Jackson, Jane	M	13,66A
Adj	Johnson, Keith V.		
Adj	Johnston, Grace		
Asst Prof PT	Klein, Mitchell	M	38,60
Adj	Lim, Benedict		20
Asst Prof PT	Munzenrider, James	M	50,65
Adj	Nichols, James		
Asst Prof PT	Rodriguez-Salazar, Martha	M	13,64A
Asst Prof PT	Santos, John	M	20,65
Asst Prof PT	Williams, Milton H.	M	11,66A

CA1265 College of the Canyons
Department of Music
26455 N Rockwell Canyon Rd
Valencia, CA 91355-1803
(661) 259-7800   Fax: (661) 259-8302
www.canyons.edu/departments/music
E-mail: bernardo.feldman@canyons.edu

2 Year Institution

Chair: Bernardo Feldman, 80A

Adj	Benedict, Les	M	63D
Adj	Bozman, Julissa	M	62A
Assoc Prof	Catan, Daniel	PhD	13A,13,10,11,12A
Adj	Converse, Mark	M	65
Adj	Coulter, Chris	B	62D
Assoc Prof	Feldman, Bernardo	PhD	13A,13,10F,10,11
	Fischer, Stewart R.		46,29A
Assoc Prof	Forbes, Douglas	A	34
Adj	Kearney, Joseph B.	M	10A,29,13B,70
Adj	Kerr, William		64
Adj	Kim, Gloria	D	61,13A,66A

Adj	Lawson, Julie	B	36
Adj	Lawson, Robert	MFA	10,38,41,66A,66D
	Lazerow, Erica	B	61
Adj	Lee, Lydia	M	66A
Adj	LoPiccolo, Joseph	M	70
Assoc Prof	Manji, K. C.	PhD	60,38,49,41,29A
Adj	Quintero, Juan Carlos	M	70,35A
	Schwartz, Agnes Szekely		
Adj	Sherman, Paul	M	64B,60
	Vibe, Andrea	B	61

CA1270 College of the Desert
Department of Performing Arts
43500 Monterey Ave
Palm Desert, CA 92260
(760) 773-2574   Fax: (760) 776-7310
www.collegeofthedesert.edu
E-mail: dromano@collegeofthedesert.edu

2 Year Institution

Dean: Jim Berg, 80A

Adj	Almy, Mark		39,61
Adj	Arizaga, Anthony		70
Adj	Brown, Robert	M	39
Adj	Jacobson, Mikael	M	12A
Adj	Norman, John L.	D	11,13A
Prof	Romano, Darlene	D	36,61,11,13A,40
Adj	Smith, Scott		54,13G
Adj	Stupin, Mary	M	12A,41
	Waddell, Dan	M	66

CA1280 College of the Redwoods
Department of Music
7351 Tompkins Hill Rd
Eureka, CA 95501-9302
(707) 476-4321   Fax: (707) 476-4430
www.redwoods.edu
E-mail: ed-macan@redwoods.edu

2 Year Institution

Area Coordinator: Ed Macan, 80A

Inst PT	Allison, Bill	M	47
Inst PT	Byrd, Joseph	M	14C,10D,12A,13A
Inst PT	Diaz, Reuben		70
Prof	Macan, Ed	D	66A,13A,13B,13C,12A
Inst PT	Newkirk, Brian	M	37
Inst PT	Ryder, Carol	M	36,54,61

CA1290 College of the Sequoias
Department of Music
915 S Mooney Blvd
Visalia, CA 93277-2214
(559) 730-3700   Fax: (559) 730-3894
www.cos.edu
E-mail: lorij@cos.edu

2 Year Institution

Chair, Fine Arts Division: Jeffery A. Seaward, 80A
Lead Instructor, Music: Jeff Bilden

PT	Andre, David	D	38
Prof	Bilden, Jeff	M	37,47,29,63,64
PT	Butts, William	M	46
PT	Cory, Craig	M	11
PT	Grizzell, Janet	M	38,51,62
PT	Kameria, Kim	M	11,32D,35A,35B,35C
PT	Klinder-Badgley, Marcia	D	66
Prof	Lynch, Timothy		13,10,11,14
Prof	Porterfield-Pyatt, Chaumonde	M	11,66A,66G,66D
PT	Raheb, Paul J.	M	61
Prof	Seaward, Jeffery A.	M	13A,36,41,61,54
PT	Snider, Colleen	D	38
PT	Walden, Valerie	D	11

CA1300 College of Siskiyous
Department of Music
800 College Ave
Weed, CA 96094-2806
(530) 938-5315   Fax: (530) 938-5227
www.siskiyous.edu/class/music/
E-mail: schaefer@siskiyous.edu

2 Year Institution

Chair, Performing & Visual Arts: Neil Carpentier-Alting, 80A
Dean, Liberal Arts & Sciences: Joe Zagorsky, 80A

Inst	Abel, Sean	M	13B,13C,20G,29A,34C
Inst	Elliott, Lloyd R.	M	38,61,42
Inst	Schaefer, Elaine	M	13A,36,54,61,40
Inst	Smaga, Svitlana	M	13A,66A

CA1375 Columbia College
Department of Music
11600 Columbia College Dr
Sonora, CA 95370
(209) 588-5100   Fax: (209) 588-5104
columbia.yosemite.cc.ca.us
E-mail: carterj@yosemite.cc.ca.us

2 Year Institution

Music Contact & Dir., Artist/Performance Series: Rod D. Harris, 80F,80A

	Carter, John R.	M	11,12A,36,61,13C
	Harris, Rod D.	D	13A,11,64E,29B,34
	Johnson, Gail	B	66A,66D
	Johnson, Nick	M	38
	Strue, Pattie Jo	M	37
	Woodford, Dorothy	B	66C

CA1400 Compton Community College
Department of Music
1111 E Artesia Blvd
Compton, CA 90221-5314
(310) 900-1600
www.compton.edu
E-mail: pratcliff@elcamino.edu

2 Year Institution, Historically Black College

Lect	Cotton, Wilbur P.		70
Prof	Estrada, Harvey		35
Prof	Leonardo, Manuel	D	11,12A,36,61

CA1425 Concordia University
Department of Music
1530 Concordia W
Irvine, CA 92612-3299
(949) 854-8002 x 1525   Fax: (949) 854-6855
www.cui.edu
E-mail: Music@cui.edu

4 Year Institution, Graduate School

Master of Arts in Education

Chair: Herbert G. Geisler, 80A
Dir., Artist/Performance Series & Dir., Admissions: Jeffrey Held, 80F,80D

PT	Brightbill, Alvin	M	61
Prof	Busch, Michael	D	36,60,13B,32D
PT	Chasin, Richard	B	63A
Staff	Choi, Hyunjoo	D	66C,66G,66D,66A
PT	Christensen, James	M	10
PT	Duquesnel-Malbon, Peggy	B	66A,47
PT	Frey-Monell, Robyn	M	61
PT	Fries, Susan	B	64A
Prof	Geisler, Herbert G.	D	14,32,44,13,31
PT	Gillick, Amy	D	64D,11
PT	Grishkoff, Robert	M	63B
PT	Hare, Matthew	D	62D
Asst Prof	Held, Jeffrey	M	11,12A,37,32E,10F
Asst Prof	Jacobson, Marin	D	36,12A,61,11
PT	Jay, Sarah	B	51

PT	Jessup, Nancy	M	44,32E
PT	Jones, Esther	M	66G
PT	Jordening, Jon	B	31A
PT	Kniss, Karla	M	61
PT	Marzluf, Jonathan	M	64B
PT	Mason, James	B	64C,64E
PT	McDaniel, Carol	D	32B,13C,31A,66G
PT	McGee, Lynnette	M	66C,66A
PT	Raitt, Donovan	M	70
PT	Riffel, Patricia	B	66A,66C
PT	Santana, Lisa	B	62B
PT	Schlitt, William	B	65,50
PT	Thornhill, Margaret	D	64C
PT	Tresler, Matthew	D	36
PT	Tully, Cynthia	B	44
PT	Warren, Charles	M	63D
PT	Wicks, Leonard	AA	63C

CA1450 Contra Costa College
Department of Music
2600 Mission Bell Dr
San Pablo, CA 95860
(510)235-7800   Fax: (510)236-6768
www.contracosta.cc.ca.us
E-mail: worgan@contracosta.cc.ca.us

2 Year Institution

Chair: Wayne Organ, 80A
Performance Program Director: Stephanie Austin, 80F

Prof	Austin, Stephanie	D	36,61,66,40,32
Inst PT	Day, Clinton	M	66A
Inst PT	Galen, Ronald	M	11,70
Inst PT	Griest, Jennifer	M	66
Inst PT	Hunter, Denise	M	36
Inst PT	Letson, Roger	M	61
Inst PT	Murai, Gregory		36
Prof	Organ, Wayne	M	11,13A,13B,13C,34
Inst PT	Walker, Tim	M	34

CA1500 Cosumnes River College
Department of Music
8401 Center Pkwy
Sacramento, CA 95823-5799
(916) 688-7170   Fax: (916) 688-7181
www.crc.losrios.edu
E-mail: parkerg@crc.losrios.edu

2 Year Institution

Chair: Grant Parker, 80A

	Coughran, Steven J.	M	47,20,29A,70
	Erickson, Kurt	M	66,11,13C
PT	Flagg, Darron	JD	36
PT	Hunan, Steve		47,29B,70
PT	Lee-Keller, Derek	PhD	10,10B
PT	Mazzaferro, Jim	M	38
	Parker, Grant	M	13,11,12A,49,37
PT	Robinett, Henry		70
PT	Sands-Pertel, Judith		32A,32B,66
	Smith, Kathryn L.	M	61,36,60A
PT	Tomlinson, Judy	M	66D

CA1510 Cuesta College
Department of Music
PO Box 8106
San Luis Obispo, CA 93403-8106
(805) 546-3195   Fax: (805) 546-3939
www.cuesta.edu
E-mail: bea_anderson@cuesta.edu

2 Year Institution

Chair, Performing Arts: Jennifer Martin, 80A
Dean: Pamela Ralston, 80A

Inst PT	Anderson, Jill	D	61
	Becker, David	B	64E
PT	Budginas, Rudolfas	D	13A,29A
Inst PT	Castro, Chris	M	13A
Inst PT	Davies, Thomas	D	36
PT	D'Avignon, India	D	66A,66C,66D
PT	Gee, Mary Sue	M	61
Inst PT	German, Eugenia	M	66A

PT	Hustad, Ken	M	62D
PT	Irving, Marcy	M	11
Inst PT	Johnson, Dylan	M	11,70
	Knutson, John R.	M	36,13,10
Inst	Martin, Jennifer	M	32E,11,13,48,63C
Inst	McCarley, Ron	M	47,29B
	Miley, Jeff	M	70
Inst PT	Rackley, David	M	11,13
Inst	Stone, George J.	M	13,47,34,66A,35D
PT	Tarantino, Cassandra	M	36,60A
	Voss, Darrell	B	65
Inst PT	Walker, Michael	D	66A,11
Inst PT	Wolf, Aaron	M	29A

CA1520 Cypress College
Department of Music
9200 Valley View St
Cypress, CA 90630-5805
(714) 484-7140   Fax: (714) 952-9602
www.cypresscollege.edu
E-mail: gbeyer@cypresscollege.edu

2 Year Institution

Chair: George Beyer, 80A

	Anthony, Bob		37
	Arcila, Billy		70
Prof	Ball, Sheridan J.	D	36,41,61,13A
PT	Bardin, Joan	M	66A
Prof	Beyer, George	M	47,13A,11,20G
PT	Beyer, LaVaun	M	66A
PT	Buck, Peter		65
Prof	DeCoro, Helena	M	61,66A,11,12A,39
	Deneff, Peter		66A
Assoc Prof	Gallo, Joseph	M	35,34,66A,29,53
	Molina, Jose		34,45
FT	Peterson, Mark	M	66C,66A
	Rodgers, Linda		62,51
	Russell, John K.	M	32D,36,40,60A
PT	Virgoe, Betty	D	66,11,13A,20G
	Weil, Susan		16
	Wheeler, George		34,45
PT	Zacharias, Andrew		34,45,70
PT	Zeidel, Scott	M	70,11

CA1550 De Anza College
Department of Music
21250 Stevens Creek Blvd
Cupertino, CA 95014-5702
(408) 864-8832   Fax: (408) 864-8492
group.deanza.edu/music/
E-mail: glasmanIlan@deanza.edu

2 Year Institution

Dean, Creative Arts Division: Nancy Canter, 80A
Music Department Scheduler: Annamarie Poklewski, 80F

Inst PT	Bandermann, Billie	M	61,36
Inst PT	Brownlee, Jordan	M	70,11
Inst FT	Dunn, Ron	M	70,14
Inst FT	Farrington, Robert	M	41,47,63,64,29A
Inst FT	Glasman, Ilan David	D	36,40,61,11
Inst PT	Hawkins, Michelle	M	36,47
Inst PT	Hicks, Gail	M	66A
Inst FT	Mitchell, Dan	M	11,34
Inst FT	Poklewski, Annamarie	M	13,66A
Inst PT	Russell, John	M	47
Inst PT	Schneider, Jim	M	47
Inst FT	Setziol, Paul	D	13,10
Inst PT	Snyder, Jerrold	M	70
Inst PT	Tayerle, Loren	M	12A,38,41
Inst PT	Thomsen, John David	M	66A,11
Inst PT	Tyler, Steve	M	46

CA1560 Diablo Valley College
Department of Music
321 Golf Club Rd
Pleasant Hill, CA 94523-1529
(925) 685-1230 x 2456   Fax: (925) 288-0936
www.dvc.edu
E-mail: BPeppo@dvc.edu

2 Year Institution

Chair: Bret Peppo, 80A

PT	Aczon, Michael	D	35
PT	Alburger, Mark	D	10,13,38
PT	Allata, Rachid	M	66
Inst	Appell, Glen	M	11,29,46,47
Inst	Bairos, Monte	M	37,41,48,49,50
PT	Bendich, Jon	M	35
Inst	Cook, Bruce	D	66,14,11,20
PT	Creighton, Randall	M	66
PT	Dahl-Shanks, Deborah	M	70
PT	Downey, Wayne		
PT	Emigh, Elizabeth		
PT	Flores, Richard		
PT	Flynt, Ben		66
PT	Forlin, Gino		
PT	Kamprath, Richard	M	34,35
PT	Kester, Nancie	M	66
PT	Kunderna, Jerry	D	11
Inst	Lee, Owen J.	D	13,10
PT	Lewis, Daniel		
PT	Michael, Doug	M	34,35
Inst	Peppo, Bret	M	36,29A,60
PT	Pricco, Evelyen	M	40
PT	Sage, Steve	M	35,70
PT	Scholz, Steve	M	29,66
PT	Simons, Mark		
Inst	Snyder, Rory	M	29,46,47
Inst	Steidel, Mark	M	13,35,34
PT	White, Timothy J.	M	34,35
PT	Wolter, Bill	M	34,35

CA1650 Dominican Univ of California
Department of Music
50 Acacia Ave
San Rafael, CA 94901-2230
(415) 482-3579   Fax: (415) 257-0126
www.dominican.edu
E-mail: singleton@dominican.edu

4 Year Institution

Chair: H. Craig Singleton, 80A
Program Assistant: Rochelle Shaw, 80H

PT	Benedict, Deborah	M	61
PT	Blakey, David		70
PT	Bloom, Joe	M	66A
PT	Burchard, Marcia Earle	M	66A,13
PT	Carey, Pamela Ruth	M	62A
PT	Cox, Natalie	M	62E
PT	Crawford, Ken	B	65
PT	Culbertson, Mark	M	62D
	Dorman, Diana		64C
PT	Lockett, Bonnie	B	64A
PT	Marsh, Marian		61
PT	Nicholas, Julie	M	29,61,47
PT	Oh, June Choi	M	66A
PT	Sagues, Marie	M	12A
PT	Singleton, Beth	M	66G
Prof	Singleton, H. Craig	D	36,61,31A
PT	Stewart, Kevin	B	
PT	Wampner, Barbara	M	62C
PT	Ziedrich, Cheryl	M	66A,66B

CA1700 East Los Angeles College
Department of Music
S2 Building
1301 Avenida Cesar Chavez
Monterey Park, CA 91754
(323) 265-8894   Fax: (323) 267-3717
www.elac.edu
E-mail: gruhnc@elac.edu

2 Year Institution

Chair: Robert B. Dawson, 80A
Dean: Vi Ly, 80A
Instructional Assistant: Charles Gruhn, 80D

Inst PT	Balian, Muriel G.	M	13A,11
Inst PT	Chavez, Robert	M	20H
Inst PT	Chilingarian, Samvel	M	12A,38,62
Inst PT	Coulter, Chris	M	11
Inst PT	Curinga, Nick	M	11
Assoc Prof	Dawson, Robert B.	M	13A,35,13,53
Inst PT	Foley, Megan J.	M	11,13A
	Gruhn, Charles		12,12A
Prof	Hasty, Barbara P.	M	13A,61,66A,36
Inst PT	Hasty, Robert	D	11
Inst PT	Julian, Michael	M	34
Inst PT	Julian, Suzanne	M	66A,11
Asst Prof	Lupica, Anthony J.	D	36,38,13B,70,61
Prof	Martinez, Jesus E.	M	13,29A,37,46
Prof	Nagatani, Chie	D	66A,13,11
Inst PT	Nagatani, Ken	D	70
Inst PT	Nargizyan, Lucy	D	66A,66C
Inst PT	Nunez, John	M	13A
Inst PT	Osuna, Thomas	M	70
Inst PT	Smith, Glenda G.	M	13A,11
Inst PT	Stinson, Lori	B	61
Inst PT	Youngstrom, Kenton	M	70

CA1750 El Camino College
Division of Fine Arts
16007 Crenshaw Blvd
Torrance, CA 90506-0001
(310) 660-3715   Fax: (310) 660-3792
www.elcamino.edu
E-mail: cfitzsimons@elcamino.edu

2 Year Institution

Dean, Fine Arts: Constance Fitzsimons, 80A
Exec Dir., Center for the Arts: Bruce Spain, 80A
Associate Dean, Fine Arts: Diane Hayden, 80H

PT	Aitken, Deborah	M	66A
	Chambers-Salazar, Polli	DMA	66A,66G
PT	Coomber, Robert	M	63C,63D
PT	Dearman, John	M	70
PT	Dillon, Rhonda	M	36,61
Prof	Doyle, William	D	11,37,38,63,60
PT	Dyer, Barbara	D	61
PT	Festinger, Kurt	B	46
PT	Frazier, Virginia	M	62A,62B
PT	Grief, Matt	M	70
PT	Hastings, Richard	B	70
PT	Hovorka, Jamie	M	63A
PT	Hungerford, Grant	M	63A
Prof	Hurd, James L.	D	11,66A,66G
PT	Jaque, Maria	M	64A
PT	Klinghofer, Rhona	M	70
PT	Koba, Dean	M	65
PT	Lobitz, Kristi	M	66A,66G
PT	Luty, Christoph	M	62D
PT	Mack, James	D	64C,64E
PT	Maki, Patricia	M	64A
PT	Martin, Margot	PhD	12A,12B,20,66H,12E
PT	Massey, Mark	M	66A
Inst	Mello, Christopher	D	11,70
PT	Mennemeyer, Bethany	D	62A,62B
PT	Mitchell, Joseph	M	65
PT	Muto, Vicki	D	39,61
Prof	Nachef, Joanna	D	60,11,36,61
Prof	Nosworthy, Hedley	M	36,61
PT	Patterson, Ann	D	29,64B,64E
PT	Roberts, Lois	M	66A,66G
PT	Robertshaw, Manon	M	62C
Inst	Schulz, Patrick	D	13,38
PT	Simons, Diane	B	36
PT	Stannard, Neil	D	66A,66C,66B,62D
PT	Steen, Larry	M	70
Prof	Teter, Francis	D	11,37,38,48,64
PT	Walsh, Peter	M	66A

CA1760 Evergreen Valley College
Department of Music
3095 Yerba Buena Rd
San Jose, CA 95135-1513
(408) 274-6490   Fax: (408) 223-9795
www.evc.edu
E-mail: larry.crummer@evc.edu

2 Year Institution

Dean: Nancy Pawlyshyn, 80A

PT	Andrade, Ken	M	13A,11
PT	Chen, Hsaun-Ya	M	66A,66D
Inst	Crummer, Larry D.	D	20,13,11,14,66A
PT	DiChiacchio, Josh	M	11
PT	Ferguson, James	M	13A,11,70
Inst	Owren, Betty Ann	D	36,61,13C,13A,11
PT	Vereshagin, Alex	M	66A,66D
PT	West, Margaret	M	13A,66A,66D

CA1800 Foothill College
Department of Music
12345 El Monte Ave
Los Altos, CA 94022-4504
(650) 949-7262   Fax: (650) 949-7375
www.foothill.fhda.edu
E-mail: hartwellrobert@fhda.edu

2 Year Institution

Chair: Robert Hartwell, 80A

Inst PT	Adams, Dave	M	37
Inst	Anderson, Mark	M	34,35A,35B,45,35C
Inst	Barkley, Elizabeth F.	D	11,12A,66A,66C,66D
Inst PT	Bhanji, Baomi Butts	D	36
Inst	Davies, Paul	D	13,11,13A,66A,10
Inst PT	Gibson, Michael	M	38
Inst PT	Gove, John	M	46,47
Inst FT	Hartwell, Robert	D	66D,20G,12A
Inst PT	Ramadanoff, David	B	38
Inst PT	Ray, Emily	M	66D,38
Inst PT	Schmidt, Karl	M	36,61
Inst	Stevenson, Janis	M	13A,10,70
Inst PT	Sult, Michael	M	13,70,29,13A

CA1850 Fresno City College
Department of Music
1101 E University Ave
Fresno, CA 93741
(559) 442-4600 x 8462   Fax: (559) 265-5756
www.fresnocitycollege.edu
E-mail: lorence.honda@fresnocitycollege.edu

2 Year Institution

Dean, Fine, Perf. & Communication Arts: Jothany Blackwood, 80A
Chair: Lorence Honda, 80A

PT	Badgley, Clifford	M	66A
PT	Barba, Kathy	B	61
Inst	Cooper, Kevin	D	11,70,13A
Inst	Dana, Julie R.	M	36,61,11
Inst	Dana, Michael	M	29,47,35A,34
PT	Deeter, Gary	M	11
Inst	Engstrom, Dale	M	13A,37,49
Inst	Honda, Lorence	M	13,48,64,29
PT	Hord, John	M	66,66C
PT	Horton, Mathew	M	66A
PT	Klinder-Badgley, Marcia	D	66A
PT	Lizama, Joe	B	65
PT	Morrice, John	M	51
PT	Morton, Nye	B	35C,35D
PT	Nance, Steve	B	70
PT	Nielsen, Robert	M	10,11
Inst	Quercia, Olga	M	66,66C
PT	Ramirez, George	M	20H
PT	Sandersier, Jeffrey	M	38
PT	Sarkisian, Rebecca	B	61
PT	Schramm, David	M	70
PT	VonBerg, Craig	M	34D
PT	Wolfmann, Melissa	M	61,54

CA1860 Fresno Pacific University
Department of Music
1717 S Chestnut Ave
Fresno, CA 93702-4709
(559) 453-2000   Fax: (559) 453-5558
www.fresno.edu
E-mail: music@fresno.edu

4 Year Liberal Arts Institution

Chair: Wayne Huber, 80A

Adj	Aldrich, Rachel		64B
Adj	Blomster, Jennie	M	63B
Adj	DeBenedetto, Patricia	M	32E,37,64E,64C,48
Adj	Doering, Susan J.	D	62A,62B
Asst Prof	Durlam, Zachary D.	D	36,60,32A,32B,40
Adj	Erickson, Janette	M	64A
Prof	Friesen, Milton	M	11,36,70
Adj	Gonzales, Elizabeth		44
Adj	Huber, Laurell	M	66G,66H
Prof	Huber, Wayne	M	37,49,63A,67C,13
Prof	Janzen, Chris	M	47
Prof Emeritus	Klassen, Roy L.	D	36
Adj	Knezovich, Bill	M	64D
Adj	Myers, Brenda		65
Emerita	Payne, Doris		
Adj	Porter, Laura		62E
Prof	Sauer-Ferrand, Deborah	M	12A,61,31A,54
Prof	Saul, Walter B.	D	10A,66A,13,20,10F
Adj	Solomon, Wayne		63C,63D
Adj	Steffen, Arlene	M	66A,66B,66D
Adj	Whitehead, Corey	D	70
Prof	Wulfhorst, Dieter	D	62C,62D,12A,12C,41

CA1900 Fullerton College
Department of Music
321 E Chapman Ave
Fullerton, CA 92832-2095
(714) 992-7296   Fax: (714) 992-7327
music.fullcoll.edu
E-mail: hmejia@fullcoll.edu

2 Year Institution

Dean, Fine Arts: Terrance J. Blackley, 80A
Chair: John Tebay, 80A

PT	Ali, Susan B.	M	61
	Anderson, Dean	M	38,62A
	Aranda, John	M	63A
	Arcila, Billy		70
Inst	Babad, Bruce	M	47,48,64A,64C,64E
	Blackley, Terrance J.	M	66D,46,35
	Brack, Brandon J.		
PT	Brown, Susan Tara	D	61
Asst Prof	Burger, Markus	B	66A
	Calvo, Francisco	M	36,32,12
Inst	Cima, Alex	M	35A,35D,45
Asst Prof	Coletta, Michelle	D	13,64
	Dahlke, Steven	M	61
PT	Delfante, Ernest	M	53
PT	Eisel, Gunnar	M	70
PT	Eubanks, Erdie	M	13A,66A
	Frey-Monell, Robyn	M	61
	Galasso, Mathew	M	11,12A,66A,13
PT	Garvin, Jerry	M	63B,54
PT	Glassman, Bill	M	11
Inst	Griffith, Dorothy S.	M	13A,66A,66H
PT	Grodsky, Michael	M	35A
	Guter, Gerhard		47,61
PT	Harrell, Mary	M	66A,66C,66D
Inst	Jewell, Joe	D	47,70,29
	Johnson, Cory	M	10,47,66A
PT	Johnson, Matt	B	65
	Kao, Janet	M	66A
	Leckrone, Erik	M	65
	Lee, Monica	M	66A,66B
Inst	Linahon, Jim	M	11,63A
PT	Maggs, Patty J.	M	64A
	Maz, Andrew	D	34,10
Inst	Mazzaferro, Anthony	D	13,63,37,12A
PT	McNamara, Ray	M	65
	McRoberts, Gary	D	32,36,66A,20G
Inst	Miller, Bruce	D	13,66
PT	Morris, Scott	M	70
	Polevoi, Randy M.	D	66A,66
	Ragotskie, Scott	B	35G
PT	Ray, Eric	M	70
Inst	Rundus, Katharin	D	36,61
PT	Schmunk, Richard	M	70

Directory of Institutions

	Scott, Michael	M	70
Inst	Shew, Jamie	M	53,60,13A,13B,66D
	Smelser, Nadia	M	61
	Strnad, Frank L.		61
Inst	Tebay, John	M	36,61,66D,66A,12A
Inst	Woll, Greg	D	13,49,63,43
	Wong-Abe, Suzanne	M	66A

CA1950 Gavilan College
Department of Music
5055 Santa Teresa Blvd
Gilroy, CA 95020-9578
(408)847-1400
www.gavilan.edu
E-mail: amarques@gavilan.edu

2 Year Institution

Chair: Arthur Juncker, 80A

	Amirkhanian, Maria	D	66A
PT	Benkman, Noel	M	11,20
	Hicks, G.		
Prof	Juncker, Arthur	M	13,10,12A,41,34
	Lin, C.		
	Marques, Albert		70
	Mello, S.		
	Mollicone, Henry	B	10,12A
	Montoya, Tomas		
	Pruitt, Nate		61
	Quartuccio, Anthony	B	60
	Robb, P.		

CA1960 Glendale College
Department of Music
1500 N Verdugo Rd
Glendale, CA 91208-2894
(818) 240-1000 x 5622   Fax: (818) 549-9436
www.glendale.edu/music
E-mail: pgreen@glendale.edu

2 Year Institution

Chair: Peter Green, 80A

Inst	Balian, Muriel	M	11,66A,66D,36,55D
Prof	Campbell, Jayne E.	D	36,55,61,31A
Inst	Card, Catherine	M	13A,61,11
Inst	Coulter, Chris		11,13A
Prof	Delto, Byron	M	34,70,13A
Inst	Delto, Clare E.	M	10D,54,11,47
Inst	Freemyer, Janice		13A
Prof	Green, Peter	D	13A,66A,36,40
Inst	Ion, Charles	M	61
Inst	Jin, Jungwon	D	66D,13A
	Kupka, Craig	M	10D,46
	Latsabidze, Giorgi	D	66A
Inst	Lu, Alex	M	66A
Inst	Nargizyan, Lucy	D	66D
Inst	Newton, Gregory	M	70,13A,11
Prof	Pflueger, Bethany		13,41
Inst	Primes, Theodora	M	42
	Snyder, Jay R.		35A,35B
Inst	Soto, Jose	M	66A
Prof	Stern, Theodore	D	11,12A,54,13A
Inst	Ter-Kazaryan, Marine	M	66A
Inst	Thallander, Mark		66D,66G
Inst	Zuluaga, Daniel	D	11,70

CA2050 Golden West College
Department of Visual & Perf. Arts
15744 Golden West St
Huntington Beach, CA 92647-4718
(714) 892-7711   Fax: (714) 895-8784
www.gwc.info/campus/music.html
E-mail: chausey@gwc.cccd.edu

2 Year Institution

Chair, Visual & Performing Arts: Henrietta McKee Carter, 80A
Dean, Arts & Letters: David Hudson, 80A

PT	Artemova, Alina V.	D	61,66D
PT	Bales, Ann	M	66A
Prof	Bales, Bruce	DMA	40,61,67,13A,36
Prof	Brodie, Nannette	M	52
PT	Brodie, Trenton		70
Prof	Carter, Henrietta McKee	M	11,61,13A
Inst	Engle, Martha Ramm		12A,11,54
PT	Gottesman, Judith F.	M	66D
Inst	Hausey, Collette J.	D	11,37,41,65
PT	Hernandez, Thomas	M	70
PT	Hughes, Charles M.		35A,35B,35D
PT	Kim, Ellen Y.	M	66A,66D
PT	Kubis, Jon-Michael		34D
Inst	Kubis, Thomas M.	B	10F,13A,29B,46,47
Prof Emeritus	Matthews, Robin L.	M	11,35H
PT	Nivans, David	D	11,13A,20,29A
PT	Robbins, Daniel C.	M	11,13A,10D
PT	Schroder, Lisa	M	64A
PT	Seufert, Dana	M	66C
PT	Sullivan, Shawn		34
PT	Wolzinger, Renah	M	34D
Prof	Wood, Rose Ann	M	13A,13B,13C,11,66D

CA2100 Grossmont College
Department of Music
8800 Grossmont College Dr
El Cajon, CA 92020-1765
(619) 644-7254   Fax: (619) 461-3396
www.grossmont.net/music
E-mail: Derek.cannon@gcccd.edu

2 Year Institution

Co-Chair: Fred Benedetti, 80A
Co-Chair: Derek Cannon, 80A
Dean: Linda Mann, 80A

PT	Anderson, Ken		36,61
PT	Ard, Kenneth	M	66A,29
Prof	Baker, Steve	M	66A,13,29
PT	Beecher, Randy	M	66A,11
Prof	Benedetti, Fred	M	70,53,35B,29
PT	Booth, Doug	B	70,29
PT	Cannon, Derek	M	29,63A,47
PT	Cepeda, Manny	M	20H,13
PT	Gillis, Ron		11,13
PT	Grinnell, Justin	M	11
PT	Grinnell, Melonie		66A,47,61
PT	Hofnockel, Jeff	M	29A
PT	Howe, Martha Jane		61,54
PT	Jordan, Esther	M	36,39,61,54
PT	Kirkell, Lorie	M	32,12A
PT	Klich, Chris	M	29A
PT	Krewitsky, Michael	D	34
Prof	Kurokawa, Paul	M	13,47,63,64
PT	Lim, Philip 'Jay Jay'	B	66A
PT	Lionello, Cathy	M	66C
	Morton, James		29,65
PT	Muresan, Branden A.	M	11,62A
PT	Rodewald, Marion	M	66A,32B
PT	Sperling, Russ		37
PT	Tweed, Pauline	B	66A,61
Prof	Tweed, Randall L.	M	38,36,12A
PT	Wetzel, Robert	M	70
PT	Zwerneman, Jane	D	13

CA2150 Hartnell College
Department of Music
156 Homestead Ave
Salinas, CA 93901-1628
(831) 755-6905   Fax: (831) 759-6052
www.hartnell.edu
E-mail: cchristensen@hartnell.edu

2 Year Institution

Chair: Kathleen Rose, 80A

Inst PT	Aprahamian, Lucik	M	36
Prof	Christensen, Carl J.	D	13,38,37,34G,13A
Inst PT	Collins, Phillip	M	70
Inst PT	Koza, John	M	11
Inst PT	McKee-Williams, Robin	M	61,36
Inst PT	Rudo, Sandy	M	36,61

CA2175 Harvey Mudd College
Department of Hum, SS and the Arts
301 Platt Blvd
Claremont, CA 91711
(909) 621-8022   Fax: (909) 607-7600
www2.hmc.edu/~alves
E-mail: alves@hmc.edu

4 Year Institution

Music Contact: William Alves, 80A

Prof	Alves, William	DMA	10,14,45,34
Asst Prof	Cubek, David	D	38,11,13,60
Assoc Prof	Kamm, Charles W.	D	36,11,12,60

CA2200 Holy Names University
Department of Music
3500 Mountain Blvd
Oakland, CA 94619
(510) 436-1330   Fax: (510) 436-1438
www.hnu.edu
E-mail: hofer@hnu.edu

4 Year Institution, Graduate School

Master of Music in Piano Pedagogy, Master of Music in Vocal Pedagogy, Master of Music in Suzuki Piano Pedagogy, Master of Music in Music Education with Kodaly Emphasis

Prof	Bogas, Roy	M	60,12A,38,66A,66B
Adj	Howe, Eric		61
Lect PT	Kanouse, Monroe	M	39
Lect PT	Keller, Cheryl		61
Asst Prof	Laskey, Anne	M	32A,32B
Lect PT	Matters, Helene		66A,13B,13C
Lect PT	Morant, Trente	B	36
Lect PT	Needleman, Gail	M	13
Lect PT	Smith, Fran	M	13
Lect PT	Spears, Tim		62D
Lect PT	Tchii, Kent	M	66A,66D
Adj	Van Dewark, Vicky	M	61
Asst Prof	Woo, Betty	D	13,12A,66A

CA2250 Humboldt State University
Department of Music
1 Harpst St
Arcata, CA 95521
(707) 826-3531   Fax: (707) 826-3528
www.humboldt.edu/music
E-mail: mus@humboldt.edu

4 Year Institution
Member of NASM

Chair: J. Brian Post, 80A
Dir., Music Academy: Gregg Moore, 80E
Dir., Brass Chamber Music Workshop: Tony Clements, 80F
Dir., Chamber Music Workshop: Alan Geier, 80F
Dir., Sequoia Summer Chamber Music: David Filner, 80G

Lect	Aldag, Daniel	D	63D,29,14C,63C,47
Other	Chernoff, John	M	66C
Prof	Cline, Gilbert D.	D	63A,49,29,67E,63B
Assoc Prof	Cummings, Paul C.	D	32,37,38,64C
Lect PT	Davy, Karen	M	62A,62B,62C,62D,41
Other	Granoff, Gregory J.	B	66F
Assoc Prof	Harrington, Elisabeth	D	39,61,13C
Lect PT	Jacobson, Carol	B	62C
Lect PT	Kaufman, Howard	B	65,20,50
Lect PT	Lambson, Nick	M	70,41,35G
Lect PT	Martin, Mildred	M	62D
Lect PT	Miller, Robin	D	66A
Asst Prof	Mineva, Daniela	D	66A,66B,66C
Prof	Moyer, Cynthia M.	D	13,41,62A,62B
Prof	Muilenburg, Harley	D	36,61,60A,40
Prof	Novotney, Eugene D.	D	14,50,65,20
Lect PT	Pitts, Larry	B	13C
Prof	Post, J. Brian	D	34,35,13,10
Lect PT	Ryder, Carol	M	61,36,11
Lect PT	Ryder, Virginia	M	64,16
Other	Skweir, Michael	B	71,72
Lect PT	Snodgrass, Laura	M	64A,13,35A
Lect PT	Tempas, Fred	B	63D,32B

CA2300 Imperial Valley College
Department of Music
PO Box 158
Imperial, CA 92251-0158
(760) 352-8320 x287   Fax: (760) 355-6205
www.imperial.edu
E-mail: van.decker@imperial.edu

2 Year Institution

Head, Music: Van A. Decker, 80A
Chair: Melani Guinn, 80A

Inst PT	Cannon, Jimmie	M	11,13A,46
Inst PT	Colunga, Richard	D	66D,11
Prof	Davis, Hope	D	13A,12,11,37,13B
Prof	Decker, Van A.	D	11,13A,34D,47,10A
Inst PT	Kofford, Brooke	M	37
PT	Lang, Dennis	B	36
Inst PT	Smith, Ruth	B	13A

CA2390 Irvine Valley College
Department of Music
5500 Irvine Center Dr
Irvine, CA 92618
(949) 451-5366   Fax: (949) 451-5775
www.ivc.edu
E-mail: mtresler@ivc.edu

2 Year Institution

Chair: Matthew T. Tresler, 80A

PT	Azzoni-Dow, Christine	M	66A
FT	Boettger, Susan	D	66A,66D
PT	Breckenridge, Stan	D	12A,13A,14
PT	Campbell, John		64B
PT	Fisk, Peter	M	70
PT	Grishkoff, Rob		63B
PT	Hall, Timothy		63A
PT	Hoffman, Michael	M	63C
PT	Khosrowpour, Iman	M	62A,62B,13B
PT	Leyrer-Furumoto, Linda	M	61,39
FT	Luzko, Daniel	D	13,10F,10,34
PT	Marr, John	M	20
PT	Marzluf, Jonathan	M	64B
PT	Matsuura, Gary	B	53
PT	Mazzaferro, Tony	D	63D
PT	Palchak, Mary	M	64A,13A
PT	Park, Janice	D	66A,42
PT	Parkins, Margaret	D	62C
PT	Peffer, Ed	M	47,29,53
PT	Petersen, Mark		71
PT	Pfiefer, Steve	M	62D
PT	Pile, Randy	D	70
PT	Reisch, Carla	M	11,14,34
FT	Rochford, Stephen M.	D	37,38,11
PT	Schneiderman, John	M	70
PT	Shepherd, Dean	M	66A,66C
PT	Slack, Rob	D	65
PT	Steffens, Lea	D	64C
PT	Toscano, Amy	M	66C
FT	Tresler, Matthew T.	D	36,61,11
PT	Wilsey, Darren	M	34

CA2400 Reedley College
Department of Music
995 N Reed Ave
Reedley, CA 93654-2017
(209) 638-3641   Fax: (209) 638-5040
www.reedleycollege.edu
E-mail: colleen.snyder@reedleycollege.edu

2 Year Institution

Chair: Colleen Snyder, 80A

PT	Basiletti, Sarah	M	13A,66D
PT	Driggers, Doris	M	11
PT	Ellis, Lloyd	M	11,46,47
PT	Fritz, J. Thomas	B	38
PT	Kamerin, Kim	M	10B,35A,36,61
FT	Snyder, Colleen	D	11,29A,37,66D,60

CA2420 La Sierra University
Department of Music
4500 Riverwalk Pkwy
Riverside, CA 92505-3247
(951) 785-2036   Fax: (951) 785-2070
www.lasierra.edu
E-mail: ksmith@lasierra.edu

4 Year Institution
Member of NASM

Chair: Kimo Smith, 80A
Dir., Undergraduate Studies: Barbara Favorito, 80B
Dir., Community Music School: Neddi Yaeger, 80E
Dir., Summer T.I.M.E.: Elvin Rodriguez, 80G

Adj	Barsamian, Aram	M	61,39
Adj	Brennan, David	D	64E,47
Adj	Chan, Celia	D	62E
Adj	Cummings, Daniel	D	60B,38,66D,66A
Adj	Douglass, Jamie	B	65
Adj	Farrell, Frankie	M	34,35
Adj	Glicklich, Martin	D	64A,41
Adj	Hudson, Bruce	M	63B
Adj	Jin, Jungwon	D	66A
Prof	Kaatz, Jeffry M.	D	62C
Adj	Kendall, David	B	35G,63C,63D
Adj	Koster, Charles J.	M	64D
Asst Prof	Lee, Raejin	D	61,39
Adj	Lin, Denny	M	35C
Adj	Liu, Rong-Huey	D	64B
Assoc Prof	Narducci, Kenneth	D	10,37,32E,46,13
Assoc Prof	Ramos, Rene	D	13A,13,12A,12,66A
Asst Prof	Richards, E. Earl	M	32D,36,60A
Prof	Rodriguez, Elvin	D	11,66A,35G,35C
Adj	Rust, Ty	M	67,35C,34
Adj	Santos, E. Giovanni	M	63A
Assoc Prof	Smith, Kimo	D	66A,13A
Adj	Tang, Pin-Fei	M	62C
Adj	Taylor, Lucille	M	62B,41
Prof	Thurber, Donald W.	D	11,32
Asst Prof	Uyeyama, Jason	M	42,51,62A,62B
Adj	Wellwood, William	D	64C
Adj	Zimmer, Lee	B	70

CA2440 Lake Tahoe Community College
Music Program
One College Dr
South Lake Tahoe, CA 96150
(530) 541-4660   Fax: (530) 541-7852
www.ltcc.edu
E-mail: williams@ltcc.edu

2 Year Institution

Dean, Visual and Performing Arts: Diane Lewis, 80A
Chair: Mark D. Williams, 80A

PT	Broscoe, Liz	B	65
PT	Collins, Roger	B	70
PT	Hellberg, Eric	B	65,45
PT	Helwing, Anna	B	66A,61
PT	Mallarino, Larry	M	29,63,13A
PT	Mitchell, Linda	M	36,60A,11,12A,13A
PT	Mori, David	B	65
PT	Parker, Salli	M	66A,13A,11
PT	Rodriguez, Art	B	62D
PT	Smart, Jonathan	M	70
Emeritus	Susens, Sharon K.	M	
Inst	Williams, Mark D.	D	13,36,61,38,34

CA2450 Laney College
Department of Music
900 Fallon St
Oakland, CA 94607
(510) 464-3461
www.laney.edu
E-mail: jlehmann@peralta.edu

2 Year Institution

Chair: Jay Lehmann, 80A
Dean: Ernie Strong, 80A
Assistant Dean: Nathan Strong, 80H

Inst PT	Chew, Sherlyn	M	20D,38
Inst PT	Galen, Ron	B	70
Inst PT	Gove, John	B	13,47,29A
Inst PT	Kinchen, Lucy C.	M	12A,36,61,66A
	Lehmann, Jay	M	60,13,64,63
Inst PT	Navarrete, Jennifer Shaw	M	66A,36
Inst	Pratt, Scott		66A
	Reager, John	M	36,66A,61,12A
	Tsang-Hall, Dale Y.	D	66

CA2550 Long Beach City College
Department of Music, Radio & TV
4901 E Carson St
Long Beach, CA 90808-1706
(562) 938-4838   Fax: (562) 938-4409
www.lbcc.edu
E-mail: pknapp@lbcc.edu

2 Year Institution

Chair: Peter J. Knapp, 80A

Prof	Allen, Nancy	B	34,35B,35C,35D
Inst	Angulo, Skye	M	36,61
Inst PT	Black, David	M	65
Inst PT	Borgers, Ken	B	34,35H
Inst	Brashear, Wayne	M	34,35B
Prof	Burton, Ray	M	35H
Inst PT	Bush, Nathan		29A
Inst PT	Clary, Carol	M	32D
Inst	Durkovic, Timothy	M	66A,66B
Prof	Dustman, Tom	M	36,47,35B
Prof	Fulbright, Marshall T.	M	38,51,48,62,63
Asst Prof	Guiterrez, Charles	B	39,53,46,35B,34
Asst Prof	Hamilton, Brian	M	37,50
Asst Prof	Hersh, Robert	B	35H
Inst PT	Johnson, Roger		38,51,48
Inst PT	Kearney, Kevin	B	66
Prof	Knapp, Peter J.	D	13,10,12A
Inst PT	Krawezyk, Shelly	B	34,35A,35B
Prof	Love, Maurice	M	46,34,35B
Inst PT	Luca, Nancy	B	34,35B,35C,35D
Inst	Martin, Greg	B	34,35A,35B
Inst PT	Pearce, Peter	B	35H
Inst PT	Rodriguez, Elimiano	M	70
Prof	Scott, Gary	D	37,50
Prof	Shaw, George W.	D	47,29,34,35
Inst PT	Simmons, James		29A
Inst PT	Spangler, Pamela	M	11,66A
Inst PT	Teran, Louie		35D,35G
Inst PT	Tim, Raotana	B	34,35A,35B
Inst PT	Winchell, Jill	B	70

CA2600 Los Angeles City College
Department of Music
855 N Vermont Ave
Los Angeles, CA 90029-3500
(323)953-4000 x2880   Fax: (323)953-4013
music.lacitycollege.edu
E-mail: wannerda@lacitycollege.edu

2 Year Institution

Chair: Dan Wanner, 80A

Inst PT	Abbott, Wesley	M	36,61,35B,13
Prof	Blake, C. Marc	D	13,11,34,45,35B
Inst PT	Blomquist, Jane K.	M	36,61,13
Inst PT	Burger, Markus		35A
Inst PT	Carter, Terry	M	70
Inst PT	Dutton, Douglas	M	13A,13,11,66A
Prof	Gengaro, Christine Lee	D	13A,32A,61
Inst PT	Hannifan, Patricia		66G,66A
Prof	Henderson, Luther L.	D	20G,38,62,45
Inst PT	Kahn, Richard	M	34
Prof	Kelly, Kevin J.	D	13
Prof	Kim, Irene	M	13A,61,36
Inst PT	Kozubek, Michael		70
Inst PT	Laronga, Barbara	M	63A,29,47,63
Inst PT	Mitchell, Joseph	M	50,65
Inst PT	Murray, Susannah	D	61
Inst PT	Newton, Gregory	D	70,11
Prof	Park, Christine	M	66A,13A,13B,13C,41
Inst PT	Petitto, Jackie	M	66A
Inst PT	Pozzi, David	M	63,64
Inst PT	Stahl, David		66A
Inst PT	Stuntz, Lori	D	46
Prof	Suovanen, Charles	M	41,70
Inst PT	Sweeney, Cecily	D	66A
Prof	Wanner, Dan	D	13,11,35A,66A
Inst PT	Williams, Leland Page	D	13A,13,66A

CA2650 Los Angeles Harbor College
Department of Music
1111 Figueroa Pl
Wilmington, CA 90744-2311
(310) 233-4429   Fax: (310) 233-4223
www.lahc.edu
E-mail: hiscocm@lahc.edu

2 Year Institution

Chair: Mike Hiscocks, 80A

Inst PT	Babcock, Richard	M	37
Inst PT	Chang, Anita L.	D	66A,13A,11
Inst PT	Favreau, Janet	D	66A,66D,13A,11
Inst PT	Goomas, Steve	M	35C,35G,13L
Inst PT	Gordy, M. B.	M	50
Inst PT	Greif, Matthew	M	70
Inst PT	Hirschelman, Evan	M	70
Inst	Hiscocks, Mike	M	11,13A,61,45,10B
Inst	Keller, Daniel	M	13,10A
Inst PT	Lynch, Kendra	M	61
Inst PT	McMullen, George	M	47,46,10F
Inst PT	Morris, Scott	D	70,13A
Inst PT	Patterson, Ann E.	M	29A,29D,47
Inst PT	Sitterly, James	D	11
Inst	Smith, Byron J.	M	36,35A,35B,61,66

CA2660 Los Angeles Mission College
Music Program
13356 Eldridge Ave
Sylmar, CA 91342-3200
(818) 364-7493
www.lamission.edu
E-mail: sparfetc@lamission.edu

2 Year Institution

Chair: Tobin Sparfeld, 80A

Adj	Canon, Sherri	M	66A,29A
Assoc Prof	Sparfeld, Tobin	D	61,36

CA2700 Los Angeles Pierce College
Department of Music
6201 Winnetka Ave
Woodland Hills, CA 91371-0001
(818) 719-6476   Fax: (818) 710-2943
www.piercecollege.edu
E-mail: aubucham@piercecollege.edu

2 Year Institution

Dean: Donna Mae Villanueva, 80A

Lect	Anthony, Ron	M	70
Lect	Aubuchon, Ann Marie	M	11,66
Lect	Brostoff, Neal	M	11,13
Lect	Danne, Terry	M	36,61
Lect	Domine, James	M	38,70
Lect	Gompertz, Phil	B	45
Prof	Greenberg, Lionel	M	13,10,66A
Lect	Parnell, Dennis	M	11,36,61
Prof	Pawlicki, Michael	M	11,66A,66D
Prof	Piazza, Stephen	M	37,64
Lect	Pinto, David	B	45
Prof	Schneider, John	D	41,45,70,34
Prof	Taylor, Rowan S.	M	13,11
Prof	Warren, James	M	11,61,66A
Lect	Watts, Mike	B	45

CA2710 Los Angeles Southwest College
Department of Music
1600 W Imperial Hwy
Los Angeles, CA 90047-4810
(323) 241-5418
lasc.edu
E-mail: cowarta@lasc.edu

2 Year Institution

Chair: Roland Jackson, 80A

Inst	Blake, Marc C.	D	
Inst	Ingram, Charles	M	
	Jackson, Roland	M	13,12A,12

CA2720 Los Angeles Trade Tech College
Department of Music
400 W Washington Blvd
Los Angeles, CA 90015-4108
(213) 744-9404
www.lattc.edu
E-mail: whiteme@lattc.edu

2 Year Institution

Music Contact: Molly E. White, 80A

Adj	Canon, Sherri D.	M	20,29A,66A
Adj	Ray, Eric J.	M	13A,70
Adj	White, Molly E.	M	66A,13A

CA2750 Los Angeles Valley College
Department of Music
5800 Fulton Ave
Valley Glen, CA 91401-4062
(818) 947-2346
www.lavc.edu
E-mail: arshagmh@lavc.edu

2 Year Institution

Chair: Michael H. Arshagouni, 80A
Dean: Dennis J. Reed, 80A

Inst	Abell, Jan	M	61
Inst	Acosta, Gail	M	62A,62B
Inst	Angebrandt, Lynn	M	62
Asst Prof	Arshagouni, Michael H.	D	13B,13C,12A,66A,36
Prof	Chauls, Robert	D	11,38,66A,10A,39
Inst	Hannifan, Patricia	D	66A
Inst	Heinen, Julia	D	63,64
Inst	Immel, Dean	M	37
Prof	James, Woodrow	D	47,13B,13C
Prof	Julian, Michael	M	35D,35C,35G,13C,13D
Asst Prof	Kahn, Richard	M	10F,13B,34,66A
Inst	Lewis, Ian	M	11,13A
Inst	Lewis, Kate	M	70
Inst	Maddren, Chauncey	M	13A,13B
Inst	Mankerian, Vatche	M	66A
Prof	Mayeur, Robert G.	M	70
Prof	Mertens, Michael	M	13B,11,63,64,37
Asst Prof	Nova, Christian	D	61
Inst	Rydell, Claire	M	13A
Inst	Vaccariello, Lois	M	61

CA2775 Los Medanos College
Department of Music/Recordng Arts
2700 E Leland Rd
Pittsburg, CA 94565-5107
(925) 439-0200   Fax: (925) 439-2692
www.losmedanos.edu
E-mail: kparsons@losmedanos.edu

2 Year Institution

Chair: Silvester Henderson, 80A

Prof	Bachmann, Nancy	M	13A,13B,12A,66A,66B
PT	Beavers, Doug	M	11
Prof	Chuah, Cheong	M	12A,13A,34
PT	Cifarelli, Joan	M	66A,29,13A
PT	Dillenger, Robert	M	12A,13A
Inst	Dorritie, Frank	M	20G,35,34
PT	Hamaker, Robert	M	50,65
Prof	Henderson, Silvester	M	36,40,60A,61,66A
PT	Jekabson, Erik	M	47
PT	Knight, Jonathan	D	12A,13A,60B,63
PT	Maltester, Diane	M	12A,64,41,13C
Prof	Maltester, John	M	37,41,60B,63C
PT	Marrs, Jeff	M	47
PT	Meyer, Kathy	M	64A
PT	Savage, Steve	M	35,34
PT	Shiner, Richard	M	35,34
PT	Smith, Timothy M.	M	60B,38
PT	Thompson, Catherine	M	66
PT	Ting, Damian	M	51,62
PT	Walker, Timm	M	34
PT	Williams, Michael	M	70,12A
Prof	Zilber, Michael	D	11,64E,12A,20G,29

CA2800 Loyola Marymount University
Department of Music/BFAC B103
MS 8347
1 Loyola Marymount Univ Dr
Los Angeles, CA 90045-2659
(310) 338-5386　　Fax: (310) 338-6046
cfa.lmu.edu/programs/music
E-mail: mbreden@lmu.edu

4 Year Institution
Member of NASM

Dean: Bryant Keith Alexander, 80A
Chair: Mary C. Breden, 80A

Prof Emeritus	Arlen, Walter	M	12A
PT	Aviguetero, Anthony	M	11
Prof Emeritus	Avramov, Bogidar	M	38,51,11,10F,60B
Prof	Breden, Mary C.	D	60A,36,32D
PT	Deeter, Constance	M	62D
PT	Dent, Geoffrey	M	14A
PT	Dyer, Barbara J.	D	61
PT	Favreau, Janet	D	66A
PT	Fleischer, Tania	D	66A,42
Prof	Humphreys, Paul W.	D	14A,13A,13B,29A,10A
Clinical Asst Prof	Kocyan, Wojciech	D	66A,13C
PT	Lobitz, Kristi	M	66A,66D
PT	Masters, Martha	D	70
PT	McDermott, Tom	M	13A
PT	Minette, A. J.	B	70
Asst Prof	Miranda, Michael A.	D	11,67G,70,12A,41
PT	Moore, Frances	M	60B,41,62A,67B,38
PT	Robertshaw, Manon	M	62C
Prof Emeritus	Salamunovich, Paul	B	36
Prof	Saya, Mark	D	13B,10A,13D,13E,13F
Prof	Saya, Virginia	D	12A,39,12C,11
PT	Smith, Aaron T.	M	65
PT	Snider, Karl William	D	13A,11,61,40
PT	Talusan Lacanlale, Mary	D	14A

CA2801 Marymount College
Department of Music
30800 Palos Verdes Dr E
Rancho Palos Verdes, CA 90274
(310) 377-5501
www.marymountpv.edu
E-mail: LRaby@marymountpv.edu

2 & 4 Year Institution

Music Contact: Lee Worley Raby, 80A

Adj Prof	Becker, Melinda	M	36,61
Asst Prof	Raby, Lee Worley	D	47,64E,13A,13B,64

CA2810 Masters College, The
Department of Music
21726 Placerita Canyon Rd #13
Santa Clarita, CA 91321-1200
(800) 568-6248 x 2251　　Fax: (661) 362-2720
www.masters.edu
E-mail: music@masters.edu

4 Year Institution

Chair: Paul T. Plew, 80A
Assistant Chair: Carolyn Simons, 80H

Inst	Blackwell, Claire	B	44
Inst	Bloomfield, Ruta	D	66H,11
Inst	Davis, Joel Scott	D	10,13D
Prof	Jones, Kimberlyn	D	39,61,54,53
Prof	Mays, Kenneth R.	D	66
Prof	Opfer, Stephen R.	D	32,37,38,60B,47
Prof	Plew, Paul T.	D	60,36,61,31A
Inst	Rotman, Sam	M	66
Prof	Simons, Carolyn	D	11,20,60A,12
Inst	Webb, Phil		61

CA2840 Mendocino College
Music Program
1000 Hensley Creek Rd
Ukiah, CA 95482-3017
(707)468-3002　　Fax: (707)468-3120
www.mendocino.edu
E-mail: lpfutzen@mendocino.edu

2 Year Institution

Dean, Fine Arts: Susan Bell, 80A

	Allan, Kathryn	M	61,66A,66D
	MacDougall, Elizabeth	M	66A,66D
Prof	Parkinson, John S.	M	37,38,47,49,45
Prof	Pfutzenreuter, Leslie D.	M	11,36,38,39,61
	Simpson, Marilyn	M	61
	Sloane, Marcia	M	13A

CA2900 Merced College
Department of Music
3600 M St
Office IAC-207
Merced, CA 95348-2898
(209) 386-6777　　Fax: (209) 386-6646
www.mccd.edu
E-mail: stephanie.flowers@mccd.edu

2 Year Institution

Chair, Arts Division: Jamey Brzezinski, 80A

Inst	Albano, John	MFA	10D,29,47,70
Inst	Doiel, Mark	MFA	10D,11,12A,13,37
Inst	Nelson, Curt	M	10D,36,40,54

CA2910 Merritt College
Department of Music
12500 Campus Dr
Oakland, CA 94619-3107
(510) 436-2430
www.merritt.edu
E-mail: dmorales@peralta.edu

2 Year Institution

Assistant Chair: Peggy Pawek, 80H

PT	Creese, Anne	M	39
FT	Morales, David	M	13A,11,36,61,66
PT	Smart, Carlos	M	20H
PT	Thomson, George	M	38

CA2950 Mills College
Department of Music
PO Box 9970
Oakland, CA 94613-0970
(510) 430-2171　　Fax: (510) 430-3228
www.mills.edu
E-mail: music@mills.edu

4 Year Womens' Undergraduate College, Co-Ed Graduate School

Master of Arts in Composition, MFA in Performance-Literature, MFA in Electronic Music

Chair & Co-Dir., Center for Contemporary Music: Chris Brown, 80A,80F
Dir., Center For Contemporary Music: Maggi Payne

Inst	Abondolo, Gianna	M	62C
Inst	Abraham, Christine		61
Inst	Abramowitsch, Miriam	B	61
Inst	Adams, Stephen		64E
Inst	Barber, Gregory		64D
Inst	Beitmen, Cynthia	M	55D
Inst	Belove, David		62D
Prof	Bernstein, David	D	13,12A,13J
Inst	Binkley, Paul	M	70
Inst	Bischoff, John		45,10B,12A,13B,20F
Prof	Brown, Chris	M	10B,10A,20,13,14
Inst	Bulwinkle, Belle	M	66A,66C,20F

Inst	Caimotto, Michelle	B	64A
Inst	Carslake, Louise	DIPL	12,55,64A,67
Inst	Cooke, India	M	62A,29
Inst	Cowart, Steed D.	M	10,13,43
Inst	Custer, Beth		10
Inst	Dunlap, Larry		66A
Inst	Dutt, Hank		62B
Asst Prof	Eshleman, Elizabeth	M	61,13C
Inst	Evans, William	D	
Asst Prof	Fei, James		10B,34A
Prof	Frith, Fred	M	10A,10B,53,43,11
Inst	Ganz, Sara	M	61
Inst	Gelb, Philip		64A
Asst Prof	Ghuman, Nalini G.	D	13,12A,12C,12
Inst	Goldberg, Benjamin		64C
Inst	Goodheart, Matthew W.	M	66A
Inst	Gottlieb, Karen	M	62E
Inst	Holm, Molly	M	61,47,53
Inst	Hull, Douglas		63B
Inst	Jeanrenaud, Joan		62C,42
Inst	Jennings, Graeme		40,41,62A,62B,42
Inst	Justen, Gloria		62A
Inst	Kobialka, Daniel	M	62A
Inst	Koregelos, Angela		64A
Inst	Kutulas, Janet		61
Inst	Ladzekpo, C. K.		20A,20B,50
Inst	Levine, Mark		66A
Inst	London, Larry		64C
Inst	Mann, Sharon		66A
Inst	Marshall, Eddie		65
Prof	Mitchell, Roscoe		10,29,53
Inst	Nugent, Thomas	M	64B
Prof	Oliveros, Pauline		10,15
Inst	Olivier, Rufus		64D
Inst	Ortega, Janice	M	62E
Inst	Pardo, Brian		70
Prof	Payne, Maggi	M	10B,35D,35C,35G
Inst	Raskin, Jon		10,64E
Inst	Reed, Elizabeth	M	62C
Inst	Reid, Wendy	M	10
Inst	Rizzetto, Jay	M	63A
Inst	Rose, Thomas	B	64C
Inst	Schmidt, Daniel		72,10E,20D
Inst	Schwartz, Robert		66A,41,42
Inst	Shapiro, Marc		66A
Inst	Soderlund, Sandra	D	66G,66H,12A
Inst	Sonami, Laetitia		10B
Inst	Stuck, Les		10B,34A,13G,35C,10C
Inst	Swallow, John		63C
Inst	Tramontozzi, Stephen		62D
Inst	Wahrhaftig, Peter	M	63D
Inst	Winant, William	M	65,41,42
Inst	Winthrop, Faith		61

CA2960 MiraCosta College
Department of Music
1 Barnard Dr
Oceanside, CA 92056-3820
(760) 795-6816   Fax: (760) 795-6673
www.miracosta.edu/music
E-mail: music@miracosta.edu

2 Year Institution

Chair & Dir., Artist Series: Matt Falker, 80A,80F
Dean: Dana Smith, 80A

Adj	Chang, Wan-Chin	D	66A,66D
Prof	Coobatis, Christy	M	35,34D
Adj	Cratty, William	D	13,66
Prof	Falker, Matt	M	36,66A,47,66D
Adj	Foster, Eric		70
Adj	Gonzales, Mario	M	35G
Prof	Langager, Arlie	D	36,47,40,61
Adj	Lee, Jaeryoung		66D
Adj	Libertino, Dan	M	70
Adj	Lopez, Sarah	D	61
Prof Emeritus	Megill, David W.	D	
Prof Emeritus	Megill, Donald D.	M	
Adj	Muresan, Branden	M	38,62
Adj	O'Brien, Kathleen	M	61
Prof Emeritus	Shepard, James A.	M	
Prof	Siegel, Dan	M	35C,35D,34D,35G
Adj	Traugh, Steven	M	35G

CA2975 Mission College
Department of Music
3000 Mission College Blvd
Santa Clara, CA 95054-1804
(408) 988-2200   Fax: (408) 855-5497
www.missioncollege.org
E-mail: joseph_ordaz@wvmccd.cc.ca.us

2 Year Institution

Division Chair: Jim DeLongchamp, 80A
Chair: Joseph Ordaz, 80A
Dir., Artist Series: Phillip Hawkins, 80F

PT	Brown, George	M	37
PT	Drion, Yoka	M	66A,66D
FT	Hawkins, Phillip	M	11,20H,34,50
FT	Johnson, Keith	D	10,20,34,35,13B
PT	Linduska, Mary	M	61,36
FT	Ordaz, Joseph	M	11,66A,66D,38
Emeritus	Sterling, Eugene	D	
PT	Vargas, Philip	M	70

CA3000 Modesto Junior College
Department of Music-Arts Div
435 College Ave
Modesto, CA 95350-5808
(209) 575-6081   Fax: (209) 575-6086
www.mjc.edu
E-mail: sundquistm@mjc.edu

2 Year Institution

Interim Division Dean: Michael Sundquist, 80A

Prof Emeritus	Boyer, Allen	M	13A,47,61,20G
Inst PT	Chan, Yan-Yan	D	66A,66C
Prof	Chapman, David	M	11,70,20
Inst PT	Colla, Ginger	D	11
Inst PT	Dow, David Charles	M	45,66D,34
Inst PT	Fair, Gary	M	11,37
Inst PT	Grubb, Steve	M	11,66D,66G,66H
Prof	Keller, Daniel B.	M	11,36,60
Prof	Llewellyn, Cherrie	D	11,61,54,39
Inst PT	Maas, Dan	B	46
Prof	Maki, Erik	M	37,11,63,64,65
Prof	Martin, Anne L.	M	11,62,38
Prof	Sabre, Alejandro	D	13,66A
Inst PT	Silvers, Travis	M	70
Prof	Stroud, Stephen	D	11,12A

CA3050 Monterey Peninsula College
Department of Music
980 Fremont St
Monterey, CA 93940
(831) 646-4200
www.mpc.edu
E-mail: sferrantelli@mpc.edu

2 Year Institution

	Anderson, John	D	13,11,37,64A
	Bryant, Richard		
	Ferrantelli, Sal	D	13,36,61
	Hulse, Barney		
	McNamara, Robert		
	Mendenhall, Eddie		
	Schamber, Don		

CA3100 Moorpark College
Department of Music/Dance
7075 Campus Rd
Moorpark, CA 93021-1605
(805) 378-1495   Fax: (805) 378-1499
www.moorparkcollege.edu/departments/
academic/music.shtml
E-mail: jsong@vcccd.edu

2 Year Institution, Community College

Chair: James J. Song, 80A

Adj	Anderson, Marilyn E.	M	39,61,54
Adj	Bateman, Melinda	M	66D
PT	Benson, William	M	62D
PT	Bonds, Nancy	D	64C
PT	Borczon, Ronald	M	70
PT	Boss, Bonnie	M	65
Prof	Bowen, Nathan	M	13,11,10,34
Adj	Burch, Steve	M	13A
Adj	Charnofsky, Jordan	D	70
Adj	Chung, He-Lyun	D	66A,66D
Adj	Corin, Amy R.	D	14,11,13C,12A
PT	Custer, Stephen	D	62C
Adj	Decesare, Mona Wu	M	66A,66D
Adj	Demmond, Edward C.	D	13A,11
PT	Francis, Edward	M	66A
PT	Gilbert, Diane	M	62A,62B
PT	Gillick, Amy	D	64B,64D
PT	Hoover, David	D	63B
Prof	Ingersoll, Orbie D.	M	13A,11
PT	Jang, Jinyoung	M	61
Adj	Julian, Suzanne	M	11,66A,66D
Prof	Keck, Vail	D	36,60,11,13A,61
Prof Emerita	Kessner, Dolly Eugenio	D	
PT	Lancaster, Carol	B	66A
PT	Lockart, Carol	M	64A
PT	Mason, Roger	D	63A
Adj	McMullin, Brendan	M	37,46,47
PT	Newton, Barry	M	62D
PT	Paton, John Glenn	M	61
Prof	Song, James J.	M	60,11,12,38,13
Prof Emeritus	Stemen, James A.	M	
PT	Tholl, Andrew	D	62A,62B
Prof Emerita	Thompson, Joan M.	M	
Adj	Wardzinski, Anthony J.	M	13A,13

CA3150 Mount St Marys College
Department of Music
12001 Chalon Rd
Los Angeles, CA 90049-1526
(310) 954-4266   Fax: (310) 954-1709
www.msmc.la.edu
E-mail: tespinosa@msmc.la.edu

4 Year Institution

Chair: Teresita Espinosa, 80A

Lect PT	Archer, Ed	B	36,40
Prof	Espinosa, Teresita	DMA	11,12A,32,61,20G
Lect PT	Fassnacht, Therese	D	13B,13C,20H,12A
Lect PT	Fierro, Nancy	DMA	66A,66B,66D
Lect PT	McEndarfer, Luke	M	60
Lect PT	Moon, Kathleen	M	32B,32C
Lect PT	Stevens, Delores E.	B	41,66A,66H,66C
Lect PT	Swiatkowski, Chet	M	13B,13C,13E,66A
Lect PT	Swiatkowski, Hak Soon	M	66A,66D
Lect PT	Walker, Christopher	M	13,10,31A
Lect PT	Wanner, Dan	DMA	12A

CA3200 Mount San Antonio College
Department of Music
1100 N Grand Ave
Walnut, CA 91789-1341
(909) 594-5611 x4426   Fax: (909) 468-4072
www.mtsac.edu/instruction/arts/music/
E-mail: kcalkins@mtsac.edu

2 Year Institution

Chair: Katherine Charlton Calkins, 80A

Adj	Adele, David	M	70
Adj	Altmire, Matt	M	50,65
Adj	Anastasia, Stephen	M	61,11
Adj	Anderson, Dennis	M	13
Prof	Barr, Dustin	M	37,11
Prof	Bowen, Robert E.	D	13,10A,29A,34
Adj	Cahow, Matthew	M	11,20G
Adj	Cahueque, David	D	11,13A,13B,13C,70
Prof	Calkins, Katherine Charlton	M	11,12A,20G
Prof	Carroll, Don	D	11,14,29A,20G
Adj	Chevalier, Angelis	M	11,66A
Prof	Chevalier, Jason	M	13A,37,20G
Adj	Domingues, Cameron	M	13A
Prof	Ellwood, Jeffrey	M	29B
Adj	Haddock, Lynette	M	13A
Adj	Haines, Janice	M	66D
Adj	Jones, Jeff	M	13A,11
Adj	Klassen, Masako	M	66D
Adj	Landis, Melissa McIntosh	M	61,36

Adj	LoPiccolo, Joseph	M	14,70
Adj	Martin, Margo	D	11,14
Prof	McIntosh, William	M	36,61
Adj	Meier, Margaret	D	13A,11,66D
Accompanist	Mojica, Porfirio Antonio		
Adj	Myers-McKenzie, Laurl	M	64A,13A
Prof	Rogers, Bruce	M	36,61,60A
Adj	Sanford, Elizabeth	M	61
Adj	Shaw, Roger	M	20G
Adj	Spoor, Aaron	M	20G
Adj	Stephenson, Carol	M	61
Adj	Stier, Greg	M	11
	Stuntz, Lori A.	D	63,47
Prof Emeritus	Toops, Gary	M	13,11,66G
Adj	Varellas, Barbara A.	M	66D
Accompanist	Wiley, Kevin	M	
Prof	Wilkerson, Steve	M	13A,29A
Adj	Worsley, Margaret	M	11
Adj	Zeidel, Scott	M	13A,11,70

CA3250 Napa Valley College
Department of Music
2277 Napa Vallejo Hwy
Napa, CA 94558-6236
(707) 253-3204   Fax: (707) 253-3018
www.musicnapavalley.org
E-mail: ewilkes@napavalley.edu

2 Year Institution

Chair, Arts & Humanities: Erik Shearer, 80A

PT	Cadelago, Harry	M	37,38,60B,49
PT	DiChiacchio, Joshua	D	70
PT	Falconbridge, Vaida	M	61,13C
PT	Galambos, Joe	M	70
PT	Gantt, William	D	47,29B,60B
	Gonzalez, Roberto-Juan	D	11,29A
PT	Khamda, Mazdak	M	66A,66D,32F,35C
PT	Markovich, Kimberly	M	32A
PT	Osten, Mark	M	13
PT	Seagrave, Charles	M	35C,34D
PT	Simpson, Brian	M	65
PT	Van Dewark, Vicky	B	61,54
Prof	Wilkes, Eve-Anne	D	36,61,54,60

CA3258 National University
Department of Arts & Humanities
10901 Gold Center Dr #101
Rancho Cordova, CA 95670-6056
(916) 855-4145   Fax: (916) 855-4398
www.nu.edu
E-mail: jbaker@nu.edu

4 Year Institution

Chair: Janet Ann Baker, 80A

Asst Prof	Lovallo, Lee T.	PhD	11,34B,67F,12A

CA3265 Norco College
Department of Music
2001 Third St
Norco, CA 92860
(951) 372-7000
www.norcocollege.edu
E-mail: vanessa.sheldon@norcocollege.edu

2 Year Institution, Degree in Conjunction with Riverside Community College

Chair, Arts, Humanities & World Languages: Karin Skiba, 80A

Assoc Fac	Kerr, Brady	A	66C,35A,35C,35D,35G
Assoc Fac	Scarano, Robert	B	34D,35G,70
Assoc Fac	Sheldon, Vanessa R.	D	12,13C,13A,62E,66A
Assoc Fac	Valcarcel, David Shawn	M	45,65,35C,13G,66A

CA3270 Notre Dame de Namur University
Department of Music & Vocal Arts
1500 Ralston Ave
Belmont, CA 94002-1997
(650) 508-3429   Fax: (650) 508-3682
ndnu.edu/the-arts/music
E-mail: dlambert@ndnu.edu

4 Year Institution, Graduate School

MFA in Performance, Certificate

Chair: Debra Lambert, 80A,80F,80G

Lect PT	Bart, Sean	B	61
Lect PT	Breeden, Barbara	M	64A
Lect PT	Cancio, Clint	B	61
Lect PT	Chien, Hsueh-Ching	M	39,61
Lect PT	Cook-Perez, Paige	A	52,54
Lect PT	Costigan-Kerns, Louise	M	39,61,66C
Lect PT	Dronkers, Marcelle	M	39,42
Lect PT	Fritsch, Greg	M	39,54
Lect PT	Glover, Daniel	D	66A
Lect PT	Hansen, Thomas	M	66A
Lect PT	Jacobs, Marc	M	39,54
Prof	Lambert, Debra	M	61,39,54
Lect PT	Lester-White, Dottie	B	52,54
Lect PT	Liberatore, William	B	39,54,60,61
Lect PT	Lockert, Daniel	B	66C
Lect PT	Mills, Kate Irvine	M	39,54
Lect PT	Mollicone, Henry	M	10A,12A,39,54,60
Lect PT	Morris, Eric	B	13C,39
Lect PT	Musmann, Lois S.	D	12,39,60,66H
Lect PT	Najar, Michael	M	13G,36,40
Lect PT	Nixon, Justin Taylor	M	61
Lect PT	Patterson, Richard	M	70
Lect PT	Pippin, Donald	D	39
Lect PT	Royce, Matthew M.	M	39,54
Lect PT	Sanders, Steve	B	54
Prof	Schmitz, Michael	D	66A,12A,13,20,41
Lect PT	Solari, Gia	M	52,54
Lect PT	Strawn, Lee	D	12A,39
Lect PT	Urbano, Patricia	M	61
Lect PT	Velickovic, Ljubomir	D	62A,42
Lect PT	Whitfield, Wesla	D	61

CA3300 Occidental College
Department of Music
1600 Campus Rd
Los Angeles, CA 90041-3314
(323) 259-2785   Fax: (323) 341-4983
www.oxy.edu/music
E-mail: music@oxy.edu

4 Year Institution

Chair: Irene Girton, 80A

PT	Addington, Joe		20H
PT	Baltaian, Aroussiak	M	66A,62A
PT	Barskaya, Galina	M	66A,66C
PT	Berman, Ronald	M	70
PT	Bing, William	M	37
PT	Blois, Scott	B	61
PT	Castro, Cesar		20H
PT	Del Russo, Catherine	M	64B
PT	Divers, Timothy	B	63A
PT	Emmons, Timothy	M	62D,47
PT	Garrett, Junko Ueno	D	66A
Prof	Girton, Irene	D	13,34B,34G
Prof	Gross, Allen	D	11,38,60B,42
PT	Hughes, Larry	M	64C,64E
PT	Imamovic, Almer	M	70
PT	Inoo, Yuri	D	65
PT	Johnson, Edmond	M	12A
PT	Karush, Larry	M	66A,53
Asst Prof	Kasunic, David M.	D	12A,12B,12D,11
PT	LaVertu, Desiree	M	36
Adj Asst Prof	Logan, Jennifer	D	10B,13A,13B,13C,35C
Asst Prof	Lorenz, Shanna		14,20G,20H
Adj Assoc Prof	Louchouarn, Bruno E.	D	10C,34H
PT	Lum, Gloria	B	62C
PT	Marsden, Frances	B	
PT	Marsteller, Loren	M	63C
Asst Prof	Myers, Andre K.	D	10A,10B,10F,13
PT	O'Keefe, Stephanie	M	63B
PT	Ormenyi, Dina	M	66D
Inst	Pillich, G. Simeon	M	20,29
PT	Ponce, Alma Mora	M	61
PT	Savedoff, Allen M.		64D
PT	Scivally, Riner	M	70

PT	Shulman, Amy	M	62E
PT	Sonderling, Lawrence	B	62A
PT	Thomas, Diane		61
PT	Tischer, Raymond	D	62B
PT	Tornquist, Douglas	D	63D
PT	Ward, Robert	M	66A
PT	Wetzel, Minor	D	62B
PT	Woodward, Gary	M	64A

CA3320 Ohlone College
Department of Music
43600 Mission Blvd
Fremont, CA 94539-5847
(510) 659-6158   Fax: (510) 659-6145
www.ohlone.edu/instr/mus/

2 Year Institution

Dean, Fine & Performing Arts: Walter Birkedahl, 80A

Inst PT	Cardoza, Don		66A,66C
Inst PT	Carter, Priscilla	M	66A,66C
Inst PT	Clements, Tony		37
Inst PT	Crowell, Ken R.		47
Inst PT	Guzman, Darryl		36
Inst PT	Holmes, Janet		66C,61
Inst PT	Johnson, Tom		35C,35D,35G
Assoc Prof	Keller, Dennis L.	M	36,61,20,11,40
Inst PT	Kendrick, Richard		70
Inst PT	London, Lawrence		13A,11
Asst Prof	McManus, James M.	D	13,45,29A,12A,11
Inst PT	Osborne, Larry		38
Assoc Prof	Roberts, Tim	M	46,14C,10D,13
Inst PT	Torres, Douglas		70
FT	Whitehouse, Jackie		16
Inst PT	Zilli, Carol		32A,32B

CA3350 Orange Coast College
Department of Music
2701 Fairview Rd
PO Box 5005
Costa Mesa, CA 92628-5005
(714) 432-5629   Fax: (714) 432-5609
www.orangecoastcollege.edu
E-mail: rsoto@occ.cccd.edu

2 Year Institution

Chair: Ricardo Soto, 80A

PT	Anderson, Dennis W.	M	34D
Inst PT	Clark, Charles C.	B	61
Inst PT	DeJong-Pombo, Theresa	M	66A
Inst PT	Glenn, Richard B.	M	70
Prof	Gould, Brian	D	12A,66A
Inst PT	Hung, Emily	D	66A
PT	Mayor, Jeff	M	13A
Inst PT	Murdy, David H.	B	70
Asst Prof	Navidad, Paul J.	M	47
PT	Pile, Randy	D	70
Prof	Poshek, Joe	M	13,70
Prof	Rubenstein, Eliza N.	M	40
PT	Smelzer, Nadia		61
Prof	Soto, Ricardo	M	36,61,38
Prof	Wheaton, Dana	M	37,63C,34,53

CA3375 Oxnard College
Department of Music
4000 S Rose Ave
Oxnard, CA 93033-6699
(805) 986-5800 x1912   Fax: (805) 986-5806
www.oxnardcollege.edu
E-mail: jkenney@vcccd.edu

2 Year Institution

Music Contact: James Kenney, 80A
Dean, Fine Arts: Marjorie Price, 80A
Chair: Matilde Sanchez, 80H

PT	Gonzales, Carlos	M	70
	Kenney, James	M	13A,11,14C,66D

CA3400 Pacific Union College
Department of Music
1 Angwin Ave
Angwin, CA 94508-9797
(707) 965-6201   Fax: (707) 965-6738
www.puc.edu
E-mail: lwheeler@puc.edu

4 Year Institution
Member of NASM

Chair & Dir., Artist/Performance Series: Charles Lynn Wheeler, 80A,80F
Dir., Admissions: Craig Philpott, 80D
Dir., Preparatory Division: G. Rosalie Rasmussen, 80E
Dir., Summer Programs: Nancy Lecourt, 80G

PT	Ayres, Rebecca Pollack		64A
PT	Bargas, Nanci		66A
PT	Bell, Charles V.	D	64B
PT	Bennett, John L.		62C
Prof Emeritus	Case, Del W.	D	66G,44,13,12A,36
PT	Davis, Rachelle Berthelsen	M	62A,12A,38
PT	Ford, Anita	AS	66A
PT	Keller, Karlton	M	13,47,48,49,12
Prof Emeritus	Kempster, James	D	11,12A,36,61,31A
PT	Kim, Jin-Hee	D	61
PT	Kramer, Jacob	M	70
PT	Lang, Cynthia	D	38,41,51,62
Prof Emeritus	McGee, William James	D	13,10F,10,66A,34
Prof Emeritus	Mercer, James	D	32C,61,35C
PT	Milholland, John		63C
Prof Emeritus	Peterson, Leroy	M	20,62A
Artist in Res	Raboy, Asher	M	37,13D,10F,13E,11
Assoc Prof	Rasmussen, Bruce	M	60A,36,61,40,66G
Asst Prof	Rasmussen, G. Rosalie	M	32,44,66B,66D,13C
Prof Emeritus	Traver, Ivylyn	M	62A
Prof	Wheeler, Charles Lynn	D	66A,66B,66D,13
PT	Zimmerman, Karen	M	62D

CA3450 Palo Verde College
Department of Music
1 College Dr
Blythe, CA 92225-1118
(760) 921-5500
www.paloverde.edu

2 Year Institution

Dean: William Davila, 80A

	Davila, William	M	13A,11,12A,66A,67D

CA3460 Palomar College
Department of Perf Arts-Music
1140 W Mission Rd
San Marcos, CA 92069-1415
(760) 744-1150 x 2316   Fax: (760) 744-3400
www.palomar.edu
E-mail: kloya@palomar.edu

2 Year Institution

Chair: Peter F. Gach, 80A

Adj	Bell, Ken		37,60
Adj	Biggs, Gunnar	M	60B,47,29A
Adj	Bruck, Douglas	M	38
Adj	Bryan, Karen	M	36,60A
Adj	Bulat, Therese Marie	M	61
Prof	Byrne, Madelyn	D	10,11,34
Adj	Chase, David A.	D	13A,13,12A,36,60
Adj	Dean, Sally		36,60
Prof	Gach, Peter F.	D	66,11,13
Adj	Golden, Arthur	M	70
Adj	Gray, Steven	D	13,66A,66G,66H
Adj	Hammer, Janet		61
Prof	Hawkins, William	M	13A,32A,49,63,29
Adj	Ingber, Jonathan	M	47,60B
Adj	Jaeb, Mary	M	61,60A
Adj	Kuhn, Lynne	M	66A,66D
Adj	Lopez Yanez, Ruth	M	13A,60,66,66C
Adj	Montiel, Brenda F.	D	12A,55,66A,67B,67C
Adj	Pile, Randy		51,70
Adj	Reiner-Marcus, Ullricke	M	62A
Adj	Steinberg, Steve	M	46,47,60B
Adj	Vigo, Silfredo		50
Adj	Walton, Scott	D	29A

Prof	Weller, Ellen	D	12A,55,20,29A,60
Adj	Weller, Robert	M	46,47,66
Adj	Wolf, Scott	M	70,11

CA3500 Pasadena City College
Department of Music
1570 E Colorado Blvd
Pasadena, CA 91106-2003
(626) 585-7216   Fax: (626) 585-7399
www.pasadena.edu
E-mail: jaarnwine@pasadena.edu

2 Year Institution

Dean: James A. Arnwine, 80A

PT	Arnay, David	M	66A
	Arnwine, James A.	D	
PT	Awe, Francis P.	M	20A
PT	Bansal, Juhi	D	13C
PT	Barsamian, Aram V.	M	61
PT	Beck, Laurel D.	M	32A
PT	Berman, Ronald M.	M	70,29
PT	Bernstein, Brandon	D	70
PT	Brenner, Christopher	D	66D
PT	Briggs, Ray	D	20,11,29
Prof	Brinegar, Donald L.	M	13A,36,61,60
PT	Brown, Kevin W.	M	63A
Inst	Carpenter, Charles M.	M	37,50,65
Lect	Castillo, Francisco		64B
PT	Chapman, Karen Benjamin	M	54
Inst	Cole, Daniel	D	10D,35
Assoc Prof	De La Vega, Anne M.	M	61,54,39
PT	Dunbar, Geoffrey	M	35
PT	Durst, Mary	M	61
PT	Fehrenbach, Paula	D	62,62C
Inst	Gates, Steven	D	13
PT	Griffin-Keller, Betty	B	36
PT	Hall, Nadine	M	32A
FT	Herdan, Eric S.	B	16
PT	Hoppe, Frank	M	16
PT	Hsiang, Cynthia H.	D	20D
PT	Hughes, Lawrence P.	M	64C,64E
PT	Jasperse, Gregory P.	M	61,36
PT	Jones, Stephen F.	M	51,70
PT	Joyce, David	M	61,10D
PT	Kakish, Wael	B	20
Inst	Kiss, Boglarka	M	11,12A,64A
PT	Klice, Joseph A.	M	66A,16
PT	Lisek, Carol A.	D	11
PT	Lobitz, Kristi	M	66A
Inst	Luck, Kyle	M	37,47,11
Inst	Matthews, Zachary P.	M	62D,29,34
PT	McLamore, L. Alyson	D	37
PT	Mitchell, Katherine Beth	M	63
PT	Muto, Vicki	M	61
PT	Oka, Betty A.	M	66D,66A
PT	Olson, Jennifer	M	11
PT	Pedrini, Jamie J.	M	64A,48
PT	Penland, Ralph	B	65
PT	Perera, Selina	M	11,20,14C
PT	Petitto, Jacqueline	D	66A
PT	Rodriguez, Bobby H.	D	47
Lect PT	Scivally, Riner	B	70,53
PT	Shaw, Rick	M	62D
Inst	Sills, David	D	62B
Inst	Steed, Brad B.	M	13A,11,16
PT	Stein, Paul A.	M	62A
PT	Stoup, Nicholas	M	65
PT	Taylor, Jack S.	B	37
PT	Thomas, Matthew	M	11
PT	Tull, David	M	65
Inst	Wilkerson, Andrea	M	47,61,29,46,53
Lect PT	Williams, Cynthia B.	D	66A,66D
Lect PT	Williams, Steven J.	M	63C,49
PT	Wright-FitzGerald, Jesse	D	13C
Asst Prof	Young, Phillip D.	D	11,66A,66D
Lect PT	Youngstrom, Kenton D.	M	70
Lect PT	Yslas, Ray V.	B	65
PT	Zoolalian, Linda A.	D	66A,66C

CA3520 Patten University
Department of Music & Worship
2433 Coolidge Ave
Oakland, CA 94601-2630
(510) 261-8500 x7751   Fax: (510) 534-8564
www.patten.edu
E-mail: admissions@patten.edu

4 Year Institution

Chair: William Harrington, 80A

Inst PT	Aron, William	M	64E
Inst PT	Beck, Lucy	M	61
Inst PT	Cruz, Karena	B	64A,66C
Inst PT	Deardorf, Glen	B	70
Inst PT	Fears, Angela	M	13A,13C,64D,16
Inst PT	Friberg, David	M	60
Assoc Prof	Harrington, William	M	32,38,41,63B,31A
Inst PT	Harvey, William	M	63A
Inst PT	Howe, Donald	B	12A,29A,14C,63C
Inst PT	King, Sandi	B	36,61,31A
Inst PT	Klobas, Patrick	B	62D
Inst PT	Krouseup, Jack	B	10,13B,13A,13F,47
Inst PT	Miotke, David	M	66A,66H,66C,13C
Inst PT	Motto, David	B	70
Inst PT	Nasatir, Cary	B	65,42,46
Inst PT	Railsback, Stephanie	B	62B,42
Inst PT	Santos, Philip		62A,42
Inst PT	Wahrhaftig, Peter	B	63D

CA3600 Pepperdine University at Malibu
Division of Fine Arts
24255 Pacific Coast Hwy
Malibu, CA 90265
(310) 506-4462   Fax: (310) 506-4077
www.pepperdine.edu
E-mail: gary.cobb@pepperdine.edu

4 Year Institution
Member of NASM

Coordinator: Gary W. Cobb, 80A
Dean: Rick R. Marrs, 80A
Dir., Artist/Performance Series: Rebecca Carson, 80F
Dir., Summer Programs: Kanet Thomas, 80G

Asst Prof	Board, Ryan A.	D	11,32C,36,31A,60A
Adj	Casale, Maria	M	62E
Vstng Prof	Cason, Tony	M	41,32E,60B,38,12A
Prof	Cobb, Gary W.	D	13,10,12,66G,66B
Adj	Comanescu, Anastasios	M	70
Adj	Cook, Andrew	M	62C
Adj	DeCesare, Mona	M	66A
Adj	Del Russo, Catherine	M	64B
Adj	Dondlinger, Lisa	M	61
Prof	Emelio, Melanie	D	40,61,39
Adj	Fernandez, Alma	M	62B
Adj	Francis, Edward	M	66A
Adj	Gale, Mary	B	64C
Adj	Greenberg-Norman, Susan	M	64A
Assoc Prof	Hanks, N. Lincoln	D	55D,13,10,34,12A
Adj	Hatsuyama, Hiroyo	D	66C
Adj	Hester, John	B	62D
Adj	Higgins, Scott	M	65
Adj	Holben, David	D	63D
Adj	Howard, Elisabeth	M	61
Adj	Lashinsky, Leslie	M	64D
Adj	Lee, Kyung	D	66C,66D
Asst Prof	Lofquist, Louise H.	D	61,66C
Adj	Maier, Lori	B	61
Adj	Malloy, Andrew	M	63C
Adj	McKinney, Dustin	M	63A
Adj	Meyer, Joe	M	63B
Adj	Nicolosi, Ida	M	61,32B
Prof	Parkening, Christopher		70
Prof	Price, Henry P.	D	61,39,12A
Adj	Raynor, Shari	M	66C
Adj	Sahuc, Paul	M	61
Adj	Scanlon, Brian		64E,47
Adj	Schindler, Bonnie		61
Adj	Seminatore, Gerald	D	61
Adj	Thiagarajan, Beverly	D	66C
Adj	Wilkinson, David	M	66C
Adj	Yih, Annie	D	13B,13C
Adj	Youngstrom, Kenton	M	70

CA3620 Pitzer College
Joint Music Program
1030 Columbia Ave
Claremont, CA 91711-3905
(909) 607-3266   Fax: (909) 607-9170
www.scrippscollege.edu/academics/department/music/index.php
E-mail: ckamm@scrippscollege.edu

4 Year Institution, Joint Music Program at Scripps College

Music Contact: Charles W. Kamm, 80A

Asst Prof	Cubek, David	D	38,11,13,60
Asst Prof	Kamm, Charles W.	D	36,11,12,60

CA3640 Point Loma Nazarene University
Department of Music
3900 Lomaland Dr
San Diego, CA 92106-2899
(619) 849-2445   Fax: (619) 849-2668
www.pointloma.edu
E-mail: pkenyon@pointloma.edu

4 Year Institution

Chair: Paul Kenyon, 80A
Dir., Preparatory Division: Philip Tyler, 80E

Lect	Campbell, Glenn	M	62C
Prof	Clemmons, Bill	D	13,34,10F
Asst Prof	Dally, John	M	37,32
Prof	Jackson, Dan	D	31A,36
Assoc Prof	Johnson, Craig	D	61,39,11
Prof	Kenyon, Paul	DMA	66A,66D
Prof	Labenske, Victor	D	66A,66D,12A,10
Lect	Martin, Brenda	M	66A,66D
PT	Moynier, Miles	M	70
Prof	Pedersen, Keith	D	36,11,60A
Assoc Prof	Singler, Juliette	D	61,39
Prof	Tyler, Philip	D	62A,38

CA3650 Pomona College
Department of Music
340 N College Ave
Claremont, CA 91711-4401
(909) 621-8155   Fax: (909) 621-8645
www.music.pomona.edu
E-mail: music@pomona.edu

4 Year Institution

Chair: Alfred W. Cramer, 80A
Dir., Artist/Performance Series: Graydon F. Beeks, Jr., 80F

Prof Emeritus	Bailey, Jon D.	D	60,12A,36,11
PT	Beck, Carolyn		64D
Prof	Beeks, Graydon F.	D	60,12A,37,16,54
PT	Blankenburg, Gayle R.	M	66A,13C
PT	Bovyer, Gary S.	M	64C
Lect PT	Bradford, Bobby L.	B	47,29A
Prof Emeritus	Briggs, Margery S.	M	13,61
PT	Burkhart, Raymond David	D	63A
PT	Castillo, Francisco J.	M	64B
Lect PT	Catlin, Barb A.	M	47
Assoc Prof	Cramer, Alfred W.	M	13,12A,12B
Prof	Di Grazia, Donna M.	D	60,11,12A,36
PT	Dimond, Theresa A.	D	65
PT	Dropkin, Mary C.	B	62E
Prof	Flaherty, Thomas E.	D	13,10,12A,45
PT	Foerch, Ken R.	D	64E
PT	Fogg, Cynthia R.	M	62B
PT	Geiger, Gregory	M	61
Prof	Hagedorn, Katherine J.	D	14,20H,20A
PT	Keen, Phil M.	M	63C
PT	Klein, Stephen T.	M	63D
PT	Kleinecke-Boyer, Ursula Maria	M	61
Prof Emeritus	Kohn, Karl G.	M	13,10,11,12A
PT	Kohn, Margaret S.	B	66A
PT	Lebow, Roger B.	M	62C
Prof	Lee, Genevieve Feiwen	D	66A,13
Assoc Prof	Lindholm, Eric C.	M	13A,60,11,38,41
Prof	Lytle, Gwendolyn L.	M	61,20G
PT	Ondarza, Danielle	B	63B
PT	Pelev, Todor D.	D	62A
Prof	Peterson, William J.	D	11,12A,66G,66H
PT	Price, Holly S.	M	61
Asst Prof	Rockwell, Joti	D	13,14C,11
PT	Rudich, Rachel E.		64A
PT	Sanders, Jack D.	M	70
Vstng Asst Prof	Scheffler, Gibb	D	14,20B,20G
PT	Thornblade, Sarah	M	62D
PT	Tinsley, Frederick D.	M	62D
PT	Wenten, Nyoman	D	20D
PT	Yoshida, Jason	B	70
PT	Young, Phillip D.	D	66A,66C
PT	Zoolalian, Linda A.	D	66A,66C,13C

CA3700 Porterville College
Department of Music
100 E College Ave
Porterville, CA 93257-6058
(559) 791-2255   Fax: (559) 791-2352
www.portervillecollege.edu
E-mail: dhensley@portervillecollege.edu

2 Year Institution

Chair, Fine Arts: James Entz, 80A

Prof	Hensley, David L.	M	11,36
Adj Prof	Hodges, William Robert	PhD	20
Adj Prof	Robinson, Richard	B	66D

CA3750 Rio Hondo College
Department of Music
3600 Workman Mill Rd
Whittier, CA 90601-1699
(562) 908-3471   Fax: (562) 908-3446
www.riohondo.edu
E-mail: jdowney@riohondo.edu

2 Year Institution

Dean: Joanna Downey, 80A

FT	Accardo, Frank	M	70
Prof	Brown, Linda	M	36,40,61
PT	Gresham, Ann	M	61
Prof	Livingston, Jannine	M	66
Prof	Moshier, Steve	M	13,11,12A,34,43
PT	Wyatt, Gwendolyn	D	36,61

CA3800 Riverside Community College
Department of Perf. Arts-Music
4800 Magnolia Ave
Riverside, CA 92506-1242
(951) 222-8793   Fax: (951) 328-3535
www.rcc.edu
E-mail: charles.richard@rcc.edu

2 Year Institution

Chair: Charles Richard, 80A

PT	Alverson, David J.		35G
PT	Anastasia, Stephen	M	61
PT	Byun, John	M	61,36,11
Asst Prof	Curtis, Peter	M	11,70,14,20,29
PT	Dominguez, Bob		65
PT	Duffer, Rodger	M	61,11
PT	Estes, Nancy Bliss		61
PT	Garrett, Karen	B	61,36
PT	Guter, Gerhard	M	34
PT	Holben, David	M	63D
Asst Prof	Humble, Dina M.	M	61,36,11,34,29
PT	Johansen, Judy	M	11,66C
PT	Johansen, Larry	M	63A
PT	Klintworth, Paul	M	63B
PT	Knecht, Jasminka	M	66
PT	Kobernik, Lynnette	M	64B,11
PT	Lau, Sylvia	M	66
PT	Libertini, Richard	B	62D
Assoc Prof	Locke, Gary	B	37,50
PT	Locke, Sheila		37
Assoc Prof	Mayse, Kevin A.	M	37,63A,38
PT	Mayse, Susie	M	11
PT	McNaughton, Barry	M	70
PT	Megas, Alexander	B	34
PT	O'Connor, Philip	M	64C
PT	Paat, Joel	B	66,29
PT	Read, Patrick	M	70
Assoc Prof	Richard, Charles	M	47,64E,29,34,42
PT	Sausser, Darrell	M	11
PT	Schmidt, Steven	D	65,50
PT	Schoenbeck, Sara		64D
PT	Silva, LaVista	B	61
PT	Stover, Jeff		62D
PT	Tabor, Angela	M	11,65
PT	Townsend, Norma	M	66D,11
PT	Tsai, I-Ching	M	66
PT	Uch, Mandeda	M	70
PT	Vliek, Pamela	B	64A,11
PT	Williams, Steve	M	63C

CA3850 Sacramento City College
Department of Music
3835 Freeport Blvd
Sacramento, CA 95822-1318
(916) 558-2551   Fax: (916) 650-2945
www.scc.losrios.edu
E-mail: KnableR@scc.losrios.edu

2 Year Institution

Inst PT	Altman, John	M	35C,35D
Inst PT	Dupertuis, Jeff	M	62,63,64,65,66
Inst PT	Goldsmith, Maryll	M	11,66A
Inst	Irwin, Doreen	M	36,41,66A
Inst	Knable, Robert	M	13,38,34
PT	Lower, Nancy		66
PT	Scagarella, Susan	M	70,66A
Inst	Woody, Gilbert P.		12A
Inst	Young, Donald	M	20H,34,35

CA3920 St Marys College of California
Department of Performing Arts
1928 Saint Mary's Rd
Moraga, CA 94556
(925) 631-4670   Fax: (925) 631-4410
www.stmarys-ca.edu
E-mail: scahill@stmarys-ca.edu

4 Year Institution

Chair: Catherine Davalos, 80A

Lect	Achen, Mori	M	70
Prof	Cawthon, Daniel D.	D	54
Assoc Prof	Davalos, Catherine	MFA	52
Lect	Engle, Rebecca	M	54
Lect	Fettig, Mary	M	64E
Lect	Foster-Dodson, Dawn	M	41
Lect	Freund-Striplen, Pamela	M	62A,62B
Lect	Hambelton, Patrice	B	64A
Lect	Hunter, Denise	M	40
Lect	Maltester, John	M	46
Assoc Prof	Murray, Frank	D	54
Lect	Ridge, David	M	63C
Assoc Prof	Rivera, Lino	D	11,41
Prof	Rokeach, Martin	D	13A,13,11,12A,41
Lect	Striplen, Anthony	M	64C
Lect	Tuning, Mark	M	36,40,61
Lect	Williams, Michael	M	70
Lect	Witon, Renee	M	66A,66D

CA3950 San Bernardino Valley College
Department of Music
701 S Mount Vernon Ave
San Bernardino, CA 92410-2705
(520) 888-6511 x1515   Fax: (520) 223-8319
www.sbccd.org
E-mail: mscully@valleycollege.edu

2 Year Institution

Dean: David Lawrence, 80A
Chair: Mathew Scully, 80A

PT	Berry, Robert C.	D	62D,45
	Beuche, William A.		11
	Catalano, Roberto F.		14,20
	Edwards, Julie		
	Hoglund, Richard E.		
	Lavruk, Alexander E.		66A
PT	Scully, Mathew	M	36,61,13
	Valcarcel, David		45,65,35C,13G,66A
	Yarnelle, E.		
	Yoon, Choon Sil		13

CA3975 San Diego Christian College
Department of Music
2100 Greenfield Dr
El Cajon, CA 92019-1161
(619) 441-2200   Fax: (619) 440-0209
www.sdcc.edu
E-mail: sbranch@sdcc.edu

4 Year Institution

Chair: Stephen F. Branch, 80A

Adj	Allee, Fred	B	65
Assoc Prof	Branch, Stephen F.	D	12A,61,31A,36,40
PT	Gates, Jim	B	70
Adj	Tellinghuisen, Harvey	M	64,63
Assoc Prof	Wilson, Larry K.	M	60,32C,13,66A,36

CA4000 San Diego City College
Department of Visual & Perf Arts
1313 Park Blvd
San Diego, CA 92101
(619) 388-3400
www.sdcity.edu
E-mail: arincon@sdccd.edu

2 Year Institution

Dean: James Dark, 80A
Chair: Alicia Rincon, 80A

Asst Prof	Fenwick, Jerry	M	11,66A,54,29,35
	Gardella, Duane	M	54
Adj	Lawthers, Carol	M	11,32B,61,66A
	Richards, June	M	54
	Rincon, Alicia	M	54
Asst Prof	Robinson, Stephanie	D	35
Adj	Witt, James	M	13A,11,35

CA4050 San Diego Mesa College
Department of Music-C109
7250 Mesa College Dr
San Diego, CA 92111-4998
(619) 388-2809   Fax: (619) 388-5814
www.sdmesa.edu
E-mail: jromeo@sdccd.edu

2 Year Institution

Dean, Humanities: Jonathan Fohrman, 80A
Chair: James Romeo, 80A

PT	Ard, Ken	M	66A,66B,66C,66D
PT	Beecher, Randy	M	66A,66B,66C,66D,12
PT	Boss, Robert		47,62D
PT	Bruck, Douglas	M	13A,13,66A,60
Prof	Chagnon, Richard	M	11,12A,36,61
PT	Cratty, William	D	13A,13,12A,14,32
PT	Elliott, John		34,35C
PT	Frater, Betsy	M	61,66A
PT	Gerard, Mary	M	38
Prof	Korneitchouk, Igor	D	13A,10,11,12A,34
Prof	Lee, Jaeryoung	M	32E,13A,11
PT	Luu, Bing	M	20,12
PT	Magnusson, Robert		47,62D
PT	McDaniel, Alfred	M	61
PT	Pile, Randy	M	70
Prof	Ramstrum, Momilani	D	13
PT	Ratelle, Dan	M	11,12A
Prof	Romeo, James	M	11,37,47,48,29
Prof	Svoboda, George	M	70,12A
PT	Witt, James	M	13A,11,12A,47,62D

CA4100 San Diego State University
School of Music & Dance
5500 Campanile Dr
San Diego, CA 92182-7902
(619) 594-6031   Fax: (619) 594-1692
www.music.sdsu.edu
E-mail: music.dance@sdsu.edu

4 Year Institution, Graduate School

Master of Arts in Music Theory, Master of Arts in Ethnomusicology, Master of Music in Composition, Master of Music in Performance, Master of Music in Conducting, Master of Arts in Musicology, Master of Music in Jazz Studies, Master of Arts in Piano Pedagogy

Director & Community Music School: Donna Conaty, 80A,80E
Dir., Graduate Studies: Kevin M. Delgado, 80C

Prof Emeritus	Almond, Frank W.	D	60,12A,36
PT	Bell, Lori	B	64A
PT	Benedetti, Fred	M	70
Lect	Beteta, Xavier		13
Emeritus	Biggs, Millard R.	D	
PT	Boss, Robert	M	70
Emeritus	Bruderer, Conrad D.	D	66A
PT	Cannon, Derek	M	63A
Staff	Carney, David		34D,35C,35G,72
Prof Emeritus	Chambers, Martin	M	36,61
PT	Chen, Chi-Yuan	B	62B
PT	Cohen, Greg	M	65
Prof	Conaty, Donna	M	64B
Assoc Prof	Delgado, Kevin M.	D	14,20H
Prof	Dutton, Brent	M	13,10F,10,49,63D
Staff	Edington-Hogg, Lynn	B	16
PT	Erb, Jack	B	32
Emeritus	Estes, Russell G.	D	
Staff	Fleming, Becky	B	35E
Emeritus	Flood, John	M	20A,13A,11,65,50
Lect	Fogelquist, Mark		20H
Prof	Follingstad, Karen J.	D	11,66A,66C,66D
Emeritus	Forman, Robert B.	D	
Assoc Prof	Friedrichs, Charles	D	11,37,63C,13A,32
Emeritus	Genzlinger, Cleve K.	M	
Assoc Prof	Helzer, Richard A.	M	29B,29C,66A,47,53
Emeritus	Hogg, Merle E.	D	
PT	Holguin, Mike		65
Asst Prof	Kitelinger, Shannon	M	37,60B
Emeritus	Kolar, J. Mitzi	D	66A,66B,66D
PT	Kurtz-Harris, Jeremy		62D
PT	Kyle, Scott	M	29
Prof	Liebowitz, Marian L.	D	11,41,48,64C,35B
PT	Lohorn, Michiko		66C
PT	Magnusson, Robert		62D
PT	Maril, Travis		62B
PT	Martchev, Pamela		64A
PT	Martchev, Valentin		64B
PT	Mashkovtseva, Elena		62E
Prof	McDonald, Nan	D	13A,32
Prof Emeritus	Mitchell, Danlee G.	M	
Staff	Miyashiro, Ralph		66F
Emeritus	Moe, Jean		
Lect	Nikkel, Laurinda		61
Prof Emeritus	O'Donnell, Terry	D	60,66A,69,54
Prof Emeritus	Peterman, Lewis E.	D	14A,41,55,11
PT	Ransom, Bryan K.	M	37
PT	Rekevics, John	M	64E
PT	Renk, Sheryl	B	64A
Assoc Prof	Rewoldt, Todd	D	13,29,64E
PT	Romero, Celin	B	70
Asst Prof	Rowe, Matthew	B	38,60B
Emeritus	Sheldon, John M.	D	
PT	Shick, Suzanne		66C
PT	Skuster, Sarah		64B
Asst Prof	Smigel, Eric	D	12
Lect	Sokol, Michael	M	39,61
PT	Starr, Eric P.		63C
Prof Emeritus	Stauffer, Thomas D.	M	
Assoc Prof	Thompson, Richard O.	M	47,66A,29A
PT	Tweed, Pauline	B	61
PT	Walujo, Djoko	D	20D
Emeritus	Ward-Steinman, Susan L.	M	
Emeritus	Warman, Harold	M	60,37,49
Prof	Waters, Joseph	D	10,45,34,35C
PT	Wetzel, Robert		70
PT	Wilds, John		63A
Staff	Willis, Debbie		
Prof Emeritus	Yates, Charles	M	
Prof	Yeager, Bill	M	47,63C,29
PT	Zhao, Yao	B	62C

Directory of Institutions

CA4150 San Francisco Conserv of Music
50 Oak St
San Francisco, CA 94102
(415) 864-7326   Fax: (415) 503-6299
www.sfcm.edu
E-mail: abeckett@sfcm.edu

4 Year Institution, Graduate School
Member of NASM

Master of Music in Performance, Master of Music in Conducting, Master of Music in Collaborative Keyboard, Master of Music in Chamber Music, Artist's Certificate, Postgraduate Diploma in Performance

President: Colin Murdoch, 80A
Dean: Mary Ellen Poole, 80A
Dir., Admissions: Melissa Cocco-Mitten, 80D
Dir., Preparatory/Adult Ext. Divisions: Joan Gordon, 80E
Dir., Artist Series: Wei He, 80F

Rank	Name	Degree	Codes
Prof PT	Anderle, Jeffrey	M	64C,48
Prof PT	Anderson, Jeffrey	M	63D
Prof PT	Anderson, Miles	M	
Prof PT	Anderson, Sylvia	M	61
Prof PT	Armer, Elinor	M	10
Prof PT	Asbo, Kayleen	M	32A
Prof	Assad, Sergio		70
Prof	Bach, Timothy	D	12A,41,66C
Prof PT	Baez, Luis	B	64C
Prof PT	Barantschik, Alexander	M	62A
Prof PT	Bates, Mason W.	PhD	12A
Prof	Becker, Daniel	D	10,12A
Prof Adj	Bell, Carey	B	64C
Prof PT	Bennett, William	B	64B
Prof PT	Biancalana, Jeff	B	
Prof Adj	Blumenstock, Elizabeth		67B
Prof PT	Bohlin, Ragnar	M	40
Prof Adj	Brandes, Christine	M	61
Prof PT	Britton, Robert		
Prof PT	Burkhart, David	M	63A
Prof PT	Cahill, Sarah	B	12A
Prof PT	Carey, Milissa	M	39
Prof	Cathcart, Kathryn	M	39
Prof PT	Chessa, Luciano	PhD	12A
Prof PT	Conroy, Thomas	D	12A,13
Prof	Conte, David	D	10,12A,36
Prof	Cook, Catherine	M	61
Prof	Cooper, Darryl	M	39,66C
Prof PT	Craig, Patricia	B	61
Prof PT	Cranna, Kip	PhD	
Prof	Culp, Jennifer	M	42,62C
Prof PT	Day, Timothy	B	64A
Prof PT	DeBakcsy, Erin	M	
Prof PT	DeLuna, Russ	M	64B
Prof PT	Desjardins, Jacques	D	43,60B,13
Prof PT	Dibner, Steven	M	
Prof PT	Ehrlich, Don	D	62B
Prof PT	Engelkes, John	M	63C
Prof PT	Ferrara, Lawrence	M	70
Prof PT	Fettig, Mary	M	29A
Prof	Foglesong, Scott	M	13
Prof	Fonteneau, Jean-Michel	M	62C,42
Prof	Fry, Pamela	M	61
Prof PT	Gardner, Kara	PhD	12A
Prof	Garner, David	B	13,10
Prof PT	Gehrke, Rodney	M	66G
Prof PT	Gladysheva, Alla	M	13,16
Prof PT	Guarneri, Mario	M	49,53,63A
Prof	Harrell, Richard	M	39
Prof PT	Harvey, Susan	PhD	12A
Prof PT	He, Wei	B	62A
Prof PT	Herbert, David	M	65A
Prof	Hersh, Paul		12A,42,62B,66A
Prof PT	Higgins, Timothy	B	63C
Prof	Hohmann, Nikolaus	PhD	
Prof PT	Inouye, Mark	M	63A
Prof PT	Izdebski, Krzysztof	PhD	61
Prof	Jamason, Corey	D	66H,66E,12A,55B
Prof	Jenks, Alden	M	10,45
Prof	Kadarauch, Katie		62B
Prof PT	Kennedy, Matthew	M	12E
Prof	Kromm, Leroy	M	61
Prof PT	Lamott, Bruce	PhD	12A
Prof	Laurance, Emily R.	PhD	12
Prof PT	Lawrence, Mark	B	63C
Prof PT	Lee, Hayoung Heidi	PhD	12A
Prof	Levitz, Jodi	M	41,62B
Prof PT	Luchansky, Andrew	M	62
Prof PT	Luftman, Adam		63A
Prof PT	Mann, Sharon	D	66A
Prof PT	Marvit, Betsy	B	13L
Prof	Mathews, Heather	M	54
Prof	McCray, Mack	M	66A,41
Prof	McLaughlin, Kevin	DMA	16
Prof	Mobbs, Daniel		61
Prof PT	Mohammed, Michael	M	54
Prof PT	Moore, James	M	64B
Prof PT	Morgan, Michael		60
Prof PT	Mussumeli, Bettina		62A,42
Prof	Nagai, Yoshikazu	M	66A
Prof PT	Neale, Alasdair	M	38,60
Prof	Neblett, Sonja	M	13,60
Prof PT	Neilson, Brian	M	
Prof PT	Nies, Bryan	M	54
Prof PT	O'Connell, Jason	M	34
Prof PT	Paiement, Nicole	D	43,60
Prof	Pajer, Curt	D	39
Prof PT	Pardini, Eithne	M	
Prof PT	Paulson, Stephen	B	64D
Prof PT	Pingel, Scott	M	62D
Prof	Plack, Rebecca	PhD	12,61
Prof PT	Pleasure, Ruby	M	61
Prof PT	Prager, Madeline	M	62B
Prof PT	Pragides, Carol	M	
Prof PT	Randolph, Jane		61
Prof PT	Reed, Elisabeth	M	55B
Prof PT	Richman, Yoriko	B	32I
Prof PT	Ring, Jonathan	B	63B
Prof PT	Rioth, Doug		62E
Prof PT	Roberts, Bruce		63B
Prof PT	Roper, Richard	D	
Prof Adj	Sanchez, Steve	M	64C
Prof PT	Savino, Richard	PhD	70
Prof PT	Schroeder, Michael	M	13,38
Prof PT	Siegel, Matthew	M	
Prof PT	Smyla, Adam	M	
Prof	Sokol, Mark		42
Prof PT	Spitzer, John	PhD	12
Prof PT	Stapp, Marcie	B	61
Prof PT	Strauss, Axel	M	62A
Prof	Susa, Conrad	M	10,13D
Prof	Swensen, Ian	B	62A,42
Prof	Tanenbaum, David	B	70,41
Prof PT	Teicholz, Marc	M	70
Prof PT	Tomkins, Tanya		
Prof PT	Tramontozzi, Stephen	M	62D
Prof	Ulloa, Cesar	B	61
Prof PT	Van Geem, Jack	M	65,41
Prof PT	Van Hoesen, Catherine	M	62A
Prof PT	Viskontas, Indre	PhD	
Prof PT	Vobejda, Lori		
Prof PT	Wahrhaftig, Peter	B	63D
Prof PT	Ward, Robert	B	63B
Prof PT	Welcomer, Paul	M	63C,49
Prof PT	Wellborn, William E	D	66B
Prof PT	Zhao, Chen	M	

CA4200 San Francisco State University
School of Music & Dance
1600 Holloway Ave
San Francisco, CA 94132-1722
(415) 338-1431   Fax: (415) 338-3294
musicdance.sfsu.edu
E-mail: smd@sfsu.edu

4 Year Institution, Graduate School
Member of NASM

Master of Arts in Composition, Master of Arts in Music Education, Master of Arts in Music History, Master of Music in Performance, Master of Music in Conducting, Master of Music in Chamber Music

Director: Dianthe M. Spencer, 80A

Rank	Name	Degree	Codes
Lect PT	Bennett, Bruce Christian	PhD	10,13,34,10A,10B
Prof Emeritus	Bielawa, Herbert	D	13A,13,10F,10,45
Lect PT	Biggs, Allen	M	50,65
Asst Prof	Brandes, Christine	B	11,13C,32D,39,61
Lect PT	Calloway, John	D	20A
Prof Emeritus	Camp, Dewey	M	61
Emeritus	Carroll, Donald H.	B	64C
Lect PT	Collins, Anthony	M	63C
Emeritus	Dudley, Anna C.	B	61
Lect PT	Ellison, Paul	PhD	12,31,55
Lect PT	Eshima, Shinji	M	62D
Lect PT	Ferrara, Lawrence David	M	70
Prof	Festinger, Richard	PhD	13,10,45,34
Assoc Prof	Ginwala, Cyrus	D	38,13B,11,60B
Prof Emeritus	Girard, Sharon	D	12A,12,14
Lect PT	Grafilo, Zakarias	D	62A,41,42
Lect PT	Griffiths, Laura	M	64B
Prof Emerita	Hackett, Patricia	M	13A,32
Prof Emeritus	Haderer, Walter	D	62A
Assoc Prof	Hanna, Wendell	D	32B,64D,32
Prof Emeritus	Hopkins, William T.	D	11,12A,12,12F
Prof Emeritus	Jones, William C.	DIPL	66A
Lect PT	Kornfield, Jono	M	13
Prof Emerita	Lee, Patricia Taylor	D	41,66A,66B

Lect PT	Lifsitz, Fred	D	41,62A,42
Prof Emerita	Lindeman, Carolynn A.	D	13A,32,66D,34
Lect PT	Lubin, Renee	M	40,61
Lect PT	Luftman, Adam	M	63A
Lect PT	Lukas, Linda D.	M	64A
Prof Emeritus	McGilvray, Byron	D	60,32C,36
Assoc Prof	Modirzadeh, Hafez	D	14,20,64E
Lect PT	Morgenstern, Inara E.	M	66
Prof	Neve, Vicki	D	66
Prof Emeritus	Nixon, Roger A.	D	10
Prof Emeritus	Peterson, Wayne T.	D	13,10F,10,12A,66A
Prof Emeritus	Rasmussen, Warren	D	32
Emeritus	Renzi, Paul	DIPL	41,64A
Lect PT	Rider, Wendell	M	63B
Prof Emeritus	Roach, L. Leroy	M	32C,49,63,37
Assoc Prof	Seggelke, Martin H.	D	37,41,42,60
Lect	Speight, Andrew	M	29,64E,46,47
Lect PT	Spellman, Zachariah	M	63D
Prof	Spencer, Dianthe M.	D	66A,66D,20G,29
Lect PT	Striplen, Tony	M	64C
Assoc Prof	Suzuki, Dean P.	D	11,12,20G
Lect PT	Tana, Akira	B	65
Prof Emeritus	Tegnell, John Carl	D	36,61
Assoc Prof	Todorov, Jassen	M	62A,35,11
Prof Emeritus	Vanderkamp, Herman A.		66A
Lect PT	Wilson, Sandy	DIPL	41,62C,42
Lect PT	Witzel, James F.	B	70
Prof	Woodward, Roger	D	66
Assoc Prof	Xiques, David	M	13A,13C,36
Lect PT	Yarbrough, Paul R.	DIPL	41,62B,42
Lect PT	Zisman, Michael	B	62D

CA4300 San Joaquin Delta College

Department of Music
5151 Pacific Ave
Stockton, CA 95207
(209) 954-5209   Fax: (209) 954-5755
finearts.deltacollege.edu
E-mail: cjennings@deltacollege.edu

2 Year Institution, Community College

Chair, Fine Arts: Charles R. Jennings, 80A

Adj Inst	Anderson, Seija	M	36,61
	Baer, Matthew Kevin	M	66A,66C,66D
Adj Inst	Barron, Jose	M	41
Inst	Bowen, K. Scott	D	13,36
Adj Inst	Britten, Ruth	D	63B
Adj Inst	Cottin-Rack, Myriam	M	62A,42,41
Adj Inst	Daegling, Sharon	M	16
Adj Inst	DaGrade, Donald	D	64D,64E
Adj Inst	Derthick, Tom	M	62D
Adj Inst	England, Diane	M	61
Adj Inst	Hodgdon, Elizabeth	M	61
Inst	Holton, Arthur	M	37,64C,48,49
Adj Inst	Hunn, Jana	M	62C
Adj Inst	Hunt, Douglas	M	49,48,63D
Adj Inst	Kendrick, Brian	M	46,47,65,54
Adj Inst	Mielbrecht, Marie	M	66D
Adj Inst	Mills, Terry	M	70
Adj Inst	Scott, Caryl Mae	A	64A,66D
Adj Inst	Secor, Robert	M	29
Inst	Simoncic, Max	M	13,10,11
Adj Inst	Swaim, Timothy	M	61
Adj Inst	Villec, John	M	34
Adj Inst	Wells, Mary	M	50,65
Adj Inst	Willenborg, Hal	B	63A
Adj Inst	Won, Mel	M	47
Adj Inst	Ziemann, Mark	B	61

CA4350 San Jose City College

Department of Music
2100 Moorpark Ave
San Jose, CA 95128-2723
(408) 288-3717   Fax: (408) 286-2052
www.sjcc.edu
E-mail: bahram.behroozi@sjcc.edu

2 Year Institution

Coordinator: Bahram Behroozi, 80A
Dean: Patrick Gerster, 80A

Inst	Behroozi, Bahram	M	13A,11,12A,14,70
Inst	Frey, Kevin T.	M	13,11,14,63,53

CA4400 San Jose State University

School of Music and Dance
1 Washington Sq
San Jose, CA 95192-0095
(408) 924-4673   Fax: (408) 924-4773
www.music.sjsu.edu
E-mail: echarris@email.sjsu.edu

4 Year Institution, Graduate School
Member of NASM

Master of Arts in Composition, Master of Arts in Performance, Master of Arts in Music Education, Master of Arts in Music History, Master of Arts in Music Theory, Master of Arts in Conducting, Master of Arts in Jazz Studies

Director: Edward C. Harris, 80A
Dir., Graduate Studies: Gordon Haramaki, 80C
Associate Director: Janet M. Averett, 80H

Asst Prof	Adduci, Kathryn James	D	63
Lect PT	Adduci, Michael D.	D	64B
	Archibeque, Charlene	D	36,40,60A,32D
Prof	Averett, Janet M.	D	38,64,48
Prof	Belet, Brian	D	10,13B,13C,13E,13F
Lect PT	Brook, Sharon D.	M	11,66A,66C,66D
Lect PT	Croft, Mathew	M	63B
Lect PT	D'Ambrosio, Kara Ireland	M	32A,32B
	Dameron, Beth	M	20
	Francis, Patrick	D	70
Prof	Frank, Joseph	M	61
Prof	Furman, Pablo	D	13,10,34,35C
Lect PT	Groce-Roberts, Virginia	M	53
Asst Prof	Haddad, Layna Chianakas	M	61
	Haramaki, Gordon	D	12
Prof	Harris, Edward C.	D	37,60B
Lect PT	Helfgot, Daniel	B	39
Asst Prof	Hollinger, Diana	M	32,60
Lect PT	Hornig, Tom	M	63
	Lease, Gus	D	11
Lect PT	Lemmon, Galen	M	65,50
	Lewis, Jason	B	65
Lect PT	Lewis, Jeffrey	B	29,63A
Assoc Prof	Lington, Aaron	D	29,46,63,29B
Lect PT	Lington, Victoria	D	11,66D
Lect PT	Lockhart, Carolyn	M	64D
Lect PT	Mathews, Rod	B	63D
Prof	Meredith, William	D	12
Assoc Prof	Mok, Gwendolyn	D	66
Lect PT	Moyer, Bruce	M	62D
Lect PT	Nicholeris, Dian	B	62A
	Nies, Bryan	M	38
Lect PT	Payne, Catherine	B	41,64A
Lect PT	Pierson, Scott	B	37
Lect PT	Shifflett, John	M	53,47,62D
Lect PT	Simi, David R.	M	11,66G
Lect PT	Stubbe, Joan	M	11,66D
Lect PT	Sultanov, Namiq	D	66A
Lect PT	Sumares, Frank	M	63,29
Lect PT	Thielen, Karen	M	62E
Lect PT	Tomkins, Tanya	B	62C
Lect PT	Van Dijk, G. Hage	B	34D
Lect PT	Vandivier, Rick	M	70
Lect PT	Wallace, Wayne		47
Lect PT	Wolford, Dale		64E,41

CA4410 Santa Barbara City College

Department of Music
721 Cliff Dr
Santa Barbara, CA 93109-2312
(805) 965-0581   Fax: (805) 730-5164
www.sbcc.edu
E-mail: clark@sbcc.edu

2 Year Institution

Chair: John W. Clark, 80A
Dean, Education: Alice Scharper, 80A

Adj	Brummel, Josephine I.	M	66A,66C
Adj	Camardella, Dominic P.	M	34
PT	Campos, David M.	M	66A
Adj	Carubia, Agatha	M	61
Prof	Clark, John W.	D	13,11,12A,10D
Inst	Dechaine, Nichole P.	D	61
Adj	Dunn, Phyllis M.	M	62
Inst	Heidner, Eric C.	M	37,47,13,29,12A
Adj	Holland, Linda L.	D	13,13A,13C
Prof	Hontos, Margaret Ellen	D	13,13A,12A,20
Adj	Jenkins, Isaac B.		47,36
Prof	Kreitzer, Nathan J.	M	61,36,40,55

Adj	Lowi, Ralph	M	12A,11,62D
Adj	Malvinni, David J.	D	12,20
Inst	Malvinni, Valerie L.	M	62A,62B
Prof	Mooy, James D.	M	45,35C,34,46,64
Inst	Neufeld, Julia R.		
Adj	Redman, Bill M.	M	70
Prof	Scharper, Alice	D	
Inst	Ullom, Jack R.	D	
Inst	Unruh, Elise A.		
Inst	Way, Marshall R.		
Inst	Winard, Kevin R.		
Adj	Wood, Charles H.	D	29A
Inst	Woods, Craig W.		
Adj	Ybarra, Anthony L.		70,53,47

CA4425 Santa Clara University
Department of Music
500 El Camino Real
Santa Clara, CA 95053
(408) 554-4428 Fax: (408) 554-2125
www.scu.edu/music
E-mail: rkathner@scu.edu

4 Year Institution

Chair: Nancy Wait Kromm, 80A

Lect Adj	Barnetson, Ginger K.	M	64C
Lect Adj	Bloom, Claudia	M	62A
Prof	Boepple, Hans C.	M	13,12A,66A,66B,66C
Assoc Prof	Bozina, Robert	M	20H,70,13A,14F,14C
Lect Adj	Carlson, Mimi	M	64A
	Catsalis, Marie-Louise	D	12A,66A
Lect Adj	Clements, Tony	M	63D
Lect Adj	Cromer, Lilianne	M	61
	Cunha, Stephanie	M	61
Lect Adj	Duenas, David	M	70
Lect Adj	Elder, Joshua Ian	M	61
Inst	Flores, David		51,65
	Friedman, Joel Phillip	D	13B,10A,10D,12A
Lect Adj	Fukuda, Ryo	M	62A
Lect Adj	Gelfand, Peter	M	62C
Lect Adj	Haines, Stephanie		61
Lect Adj	Hartman, Scott	M	63B
Lect Adj	Harvey, William	M	63A
Assoc Prof	Kromm, Nancy Wait	M	39,61
Lect Adj	Lin, Melissa		66A
Lect Adj	Ludowise, Kathleen D.	M	61
Prof	McCollough, Teresa	D	13,12A,66A,66B,66C
	McNeely, April A.	M	61
Inst	Moorefield, Bob		37,46
Lect Adj	Moyer, Bruce	M	62D
Lect Adj	Murray, Paul		61
Lect Adj	Perla, James 'Jack'		10A,10B,66A
Assoc Prof	Pier, David G.		14,46
Inst	Plude, Patricia	D	13
Inst	Quist, Pamela	D	13,10,66A,12
Inst	Ray, Emily	M	38,41
Lect PT	Rivard, Michelle	M	61
Lect PT	Seshadri, Jaleen		64B
Lect Adj	Strom, Kirsten	M	64E
Lect Adj	Thielen, Karen	M	62E
Lect Adj	Welch, James	D	66G
Lect Adj	Witzel, James	M	70
	Wyant, Frank	M	65
Lect Adj	Yu, Tian-En		66A

CA4450 Santa Monica College
Department of Music
1900 Pico Blvd
Santa Monica, CA 90405-1628
(310) 434-4323 Fax: (310) 434-3693
www.smc.edu/music
E-mail: smith_james@smc.edu

2 Year Institution

Chair: James E. Smith, 80A
Dean, Curriculum: Jeff Shimizu

PT	Altmire, Matthew	M	65
PT	Alviso, Ric	M	11
PT	Augustine, William		66
PT	Benjamin, Karen		61
PT	Bergman, James		13A,11
PT	Bourquin, Cindy	M	40,29A
PT	Carlson, Mark		13,10
PT	Carter, Terry	M	70
PT	Cheesman, Jimmy		70
PT	Chiang, Nora		66
	Chou, Lin-San		
PT	Dodson, Brent A.	M	20F
PT	Drayton, Leslie	M	29
PT	Druckman, Joel	M	20G
PT	Fiddmont, Keith	M	11,29,13A,46,47
PT	Fredrickson, Don	M	66
Prof	Goodman, David	D	13,10,34
PT	Gordon, Gail R.	M	61
PT	Gray, Gary	M	66
PT	Harmon, Jim		70
PT	Hernandez, Richard		13A
PT	Holt, Drew	M	13A
PT	Kim, Jung Eun	M	66,13A
Assoc Prof	Kozlova, Yulia	D	11,13,41,66
PT	Lepley, Louise	M	66
Prof	Lessing, Arnold	B	70
PT	Madlangsakay, Roselle	M	66
Prof	Martin, James	M	13A,13,11
PT	Mayer, Paul	M	70
PT	McKeown, Kevin	M	37,63,64
PT	Merrifield, Deborah	M	66A
Prof	Mills, Joan G.	M	13,66
PT	Mora, Richard		32E
PT	Oliver, Gale		61
PT	O'Neal, Kevin		29
PT	Parnell, Dennis	M	61,36
PT	Richardson, Donald G.	D	11,12A,61
PT	Richardson, Lisa		20
PT	Schreiner, Gregory	M	66
PT	Schulman, Jory	M	70
Prof	Smith, James E.	D	13,60,36,38
PT	St. Clair, Eniko	M	40
PT	Sterling, Jolanta	M	66A
PT	Takesue, Sumy A.	D	13A,66,12F,13B,13C
PT	Terry, Lesa		29
PT	Titmus, Jon	M	13A,20F
PT	Trabold, William E.	D	61,11,13A,12
Prof	Tuit, Rhoda	M	66,35A
Prof	Turner, J. Frank	M	13A,11,12A,54,13B
PT	Verhoeven, Martine	M	62
PT	Young, Ann		13,67B,11
PT	Zaslove, Diana		61
PT	Zusman, Shanon P.	D	67A,12,11

CA4460 Santa Rosa Junior College
Department of Music
1501 Mendocino Ave
Santa Rosa, CA 95401
(707) 527-4249 Fax: (707) 527-4816
www.santarosa.edu
E-mail: bfriedman@santarosa.edu

2 Year Institution

Dean: Kristeen Abrahamson, 80A
Chair: Bennett Friedman, 80A

Prof	Anderman, Mark	M	13,34,10,70,13A
	Boatright, Ann	M	66A
	Brandeburg, Michael	B	32F
	Burchard, Marcia	M	66A,13B
	Christopulos, Paul	B	70
	Crevelli-Sallee, Monica	M	66A
	Davison, Dorothy	B	13A
	Digman, Gary	M	70
	Dithrich, William		
	Dukes, Leslie D.		66,42,66C
	Earl, R. Daniel	M	36
	Estabrook, Peter	M	29
Prof	Foshee, Anna Harriette	M	66A,66B,66D
Prof	Friedman, Bennett	M	29,53,47
	Gardner, Marvel	B	61
	Hall, Janice	B	61
	Johnson, Will	M	13C
	Jubenville, Suzanne	D	36
	McFadden, James	M	66A
	McLaughlin, Gary		51
	Menke, Carol		61
	Neely, William J.	M	61
	Neese, Bethany		61
Prof	Nelson, Jon	D	12A,11
	Osten, Mark	M	11
	Prenkert, Richard	M	70
	Satloff, Laila		
	Schoenlein, Laila	M	36
	Shepherd, Eugene	M	38
	Sprenger, Curtis	D	36
	Steinbuck, Caroline	M	36
Prof	Wanhoff, Meryl	M	37,46
	Weichel, Cynthia	M	38
	Winett, Kenneth		
	Xenelis, Nick	M	56
	Ziedrich, Cheryl	M	66A

CA4500 Scripps College

Department of Music
1030 Columbia Ave
Claremont, CA 91711-3905
(909) 607-3266 Fax: (909) 607-9170
www.scrippscollege.edu/academics/department/music/index.php
E-mail: music@scrippscollege.edu

4 Year Institution

Chair: Charles W. Kamm, 80A

Lect PT	Blankenburg, Gayle	M	66A,66C
Lect PT	Cronk, M. Sam	M	20
Asst Prof	Cubek, David	M	38,11,60,13
Asst Prof	Harley, Anne	D	61,39,12
Prof	Huang, Hao	D	66A,12,20C,20G,29
Lect PT	Huang, Rachel Vetter	D	62A,11,13A,42
Assoc Prof	Jaquez, Candida	D	14,20,12,41
Lect PT	Johnson, Lindsay	M	12
Assoc Prof	Kamm, Charles W.	D	36,12,40,60
Assoc Prof	Kang, YouYoung	D	13,12,20C,20G
Lect PT	Murray, Susannah	D	61
Lect PT	Rentz, David Joseph	D	13
Lect PT	Simon, Julie	M	66A,66D
Lect PT	Thibodeaux, Tatiana	D	66A,12A,13C,66C

CA4550 Shasta College

Department of Music
PO Box 496006
Redding, CA 96049-6006
(530) 242-7730 Fax: (530) 225-4763
www.shastacollege.edu
E-mail: lgrandy@shastacollege.edu

2 Year Institution

Music Contact: Larry Grandy, 80A
Dean, Arts, Communication & Social Sciences: Ralph W. Perrin, 80A,80B

PT	Corbin, Dwayne	D	38,20
Inst	Fiske, Richard Allen	D	11,38,66A,63
Inst	Grandy, Larry	D	37,47,64,29,14C
PT	Southard, Ellen	M	66C,66D
Inst	Waterbury, Elizabeth	D	36,61,40,13A,39
PT	Woods, William	M	70

CA4580 Sierra College

Department of Music
5000 Rocklin Road
Rocklin, CA 95677
(916) 624-3333
www.sierracollege.edu
E-mail: gmclaughlin@sierracollege.edu

	Briggs, Nancy L.	D	29,10,66,53,20
	McLaughlin, Greg	M	64A,64E,47
	Menmuir, Dorla	M	36,61
	Viemeister, Jane Stave		66A,11

CA4600 Simpson University

Department of Music
2211 College View Dr
Redding, CA 96003-8601
(530) 226-4507 Fax: (530) 226-4863
www.simpsonu.edu
E-mail: dpinkston@simpsonu.edu

4 Year Institution

Chair: Dan Pinkston, 80A

Asst Prof	Corbin, Dwayne V.	D	37,38,65,29
Adj	Hayes, Daun	M	36,61,54
Inst FT	Nichols, Lois J.	M	66,32,44,67B,11
Asst Prof	Pereira, Hoffmann Urquiza	D	36
Assoc Prof	Pinkston, Dan	D	13,12A,14,10,20

CA4625 Skyline College

Department of Music
3300 College Dr
San Bruno, CA 94066-1662
(650) 738-4100 Fax: (650) 734-4404
www.skylinecollege.edu/
E-mail: navarij@smccd.edu

2 Year Institution

Division Dean: Donna J. Bestock, 80A
Music Contact: Jude Joseph Navari, 80A

Asst Prof	Bruno, Zachary	D	11,32,37,47,41
PT	Conrad, Robert	M	13,11,12A,61
PT	Hansen, Julia	M	14,66A,20
PT	Hicks, Gail	M	66A,13A
PT	Ingber, Elizabeth	M	66A,62A,62B
PT	Jackson, Kymberly	M	14C,29,35
PT	Kalanduyan, Danongan		20D
PT	Markovich, Frank	M	70,34
	Millar, Robert R.	M	13A,13,11,12A,66
	Navari, Jude Joseph	D	10,11,13,36,61
PT	Nichols, Jim	B	70
PT	Sacco Belli, Jeanette	M	61
PT	Schwartz, Robert	D	12,66
PT	Williams, Milton H.	D	11,61,29,34

CA4650 Solano College

Department of Music
4000 Suisun Valley Rd
Fairfield, CA 94534
(707)864-7000 Fax: (707)864-0361
www.solano.edu
E-mail: Leocav@ix.netcom.com

2 Year Institution

Inst PT	Acosta, Tim	M	11,63,29A
Inst PT	Aron, William	M	64
Inst	Bump, Delbert	M	13A,13,36,53
PT	Cavanagh, Leo	M	70
PT	Crooks, Mack	D	13,12,66A,34
	Intintoli, Helen	M	36,61,66A,31A,54
Inst PT	Maguire, George	M	54
Inst	Mikolajcik, Walter	M	36,37,47,63,66A
Inst PT	Murphy, Douglas	B	70
PT	Reynolds, Elaine	B	61

CA4700 Sonoma State University

Department of Music
Green Music Center
1801 E Cotati Ave
Rohnert Park, CA 94928-3613
(707) 664-2324 Fax: (707) 664-3469
www.sonoma.edu/performingarts/music
E-mail: brian.wilson@sonoma.edu

4 Year Institution
Member of NASM

Chair: Brian S. Wilson, 80A
Artistic Director, School of Performing Arts: Jeff Langley, 80H

Lect	Afifi, Bob	M	47
Lect	Bauman, Marcia	M	10,14C,34,35
Lect	Bent, Jenny	D	36
Lect	Brooks, Bonnie	B	61
Lect	Burnakus, David	M	61
Lect	Cabalo, Eric	M	70,32E,41
Lect	Celidore, Daniel	M	42,64B
Lect	Collins, Tony	B	63C,63D
Prof	Collinsworth, Andy	D	13A,32,37,41,60B
Lect	Cook, Ken	M	66A,47
Lect	Edelberg, Joe	D	32E,38,42,62A,62B
Lect	Freeman, Kendrick	B	65
Lect	Hammet, Jane	M	61
Lect	Hugo, Cliff		62D
Prof	Johnson, William T.	M	13,10,11,43,12A
Lect	Judiyaba,	M	52,62C
Lect	Knudsen, Kasey		64E
Prof	Langley, Jeff	D	10,14C
Prof	Leibinger, Douglas J.	D	47,29B,63C,10A
Lect	Levitan, Dan	M	62E
Lect	London, Betsy	M	62
Lect PT	Marsh, George		65,50

Lect	Morrow, Lynne	D	39,54,60A,61
Lect	Olivier, Rufus		42,64D
Prof	Palmer, John	D	12,13
Lect	Reynolds, Kathleen	M	64A
Lect	Scott, Dave	M	63A,29A
Lect	Stanley, John	D	32
Lect	Swenson, Ruth Ann	M	61
Prof	Tewari, Laxmi	D	14,13A,61,10E,31D
Prof	Thompson, Marilyn	M	66A,41,42
Lect	Vincent, Randy		70,47
Lect	Wilsey, Jennifer	M	65,50,32E
Prof	Wilson, Brian S.	D	10,37,13,43,60
Lect	Wilson, Ruth	M	32E,42,49,63B
Lect	Witt-Butler, Susan		61
Lect	Zajac, Roy	M	42,64C

CA4850 Southwestern College

Department of Music
900 Otay Lakes Rd
Chula Vista, CA 91910-7223
(619) 421-6700   Fax: (619) 482-6413
www.swccd.edu
E-mail: trussell@swccd.edu

2 Year Institution

Dean: Donna Arnold, 80A
Chair, Performing Arts: Teresa P. Russell, 80A

PT	Academia, Jon	M	66D
Inst PT	Atienza, Anthony	M	66A,36
Inst	Caschetta, Todd	M	20G,11,12,14,50
PT	Delto, Clare	M	61,40
Inst PT	Frigon, Matthew A.	M	70
Inst PT	Green, Wendy	M	61
Inst	Henry, James		34,35A,35B,35C,35D
Inst PT	Jenkins, Jeffry	M	32,66D
Prof	McGregor, Cynthia	D	13,11,34
Prof	Nevin, Jeff	D	63A,20H,10
Prof	Pastrana, Jorge	D	47,46,45,35D,10B
Prof	Russell, Teresa P.	DMA	60,36,61,54,32A
Inst PT	Sacalamitao, Melonie	M	32A,32B,32C,66D,36
PT	Scheidker, Barbara	D	32A,32B
Inst PT	Sobke, Catherine	M	32
Inst PT	Walton, Scott	D	53
PT	Watts, Joel	M	11,66D

CA4900 Stanford University

Department of Music
Braun Music Center
541 Lasuen Mall
Stanford, CA 94305-3076
(650) 723-3811   Fax: (650) 725-2686
music.stanford.edu
E-mail: musicinfo@stanford.edu

4 Year Institution, Graduate School

DMA in Composition, PhD in Musicology, Master of Arts in Music, Science & Technology, PhD in Computer Based Music Theory and Acoustics

Chair: Stephen M. Sano, 80A
Administrative Director: Mario Champagne, 80B,80C
Undergraduate Student Services: Elise Fujimoto, 80B
Grad., Student Services & Admissions: Debbie Barney, 80C,80D

Other	Abel, Jonathan	D	34
Assoc Prof	Applebaum, Mark S.	D	13,10,20G
Senior Lect	Aquilanti, Giancarlo	D	13,10F,60,37,49
Lect PT	Arul, Kumaran	M	66A
Prof Emeritus	Barnes, Arthur P.	D	13,10F,37
Prof	Barth, George	D	13,66A,67C
Prof	Berger, Jonathan	D	13,10,45,34
Prof	Berger, Karol	D	12A,12,13J,12B
Senior Lect	Berger, Talya	D	13,13A,13B,13C
Other	Berners, David P.	D	34
Lect PT	Berry, Fredrick J.	M	47,29A
Other	Bosi-Goldberg, Marina	D	34
Lect PT	Brandenburg, Mark	M	64C
Assoc Prof	Cai, Jindong	M	60,38,43
Lect PT	Catsalis, Marie-Louise	D	61
Prof	Chafe, Chris	D	10,45,34,13L
Lect PT	Chauvel, Marjorie A.	DIPL	62E
Prof Emeritus	Chowning, John M.	D	10,45,34,13L
Lect PT	Clark, Jonathan	B	20H
Lect PT	Clements, Anthony	B	63D
Prof Emeritus	Cohen, Albert	D	12A,12,13J,20G
Lect	Costanza, Christopher	M	62C,41,51
Lect PT	Dahl, Laura	M	66A,66C
Lect PT	Doheny, Anthony J.	D	62A
Lect PT	Dornenburg, John D.	DIPL	41,67A
Lect PT	Ferguson, Charles A.	M	70
Prof	Ferneyhough, Brian	DIPL	10
Lect PT	Fong, Debra	M	62A
Asst Prof	Fujioka, Takako	D	34,13K
Prof Emeritus	Gibson, Marie	B	61
Lect PT	Giovannetti, Claire	M	61
Prof	Grey, Thomas S.	D	13,12A,12
Assoc Prof	Hadlock, Heather L.	D	11,12A,12
Lect PT	Harms, Dawn L.	M	62A
Senior Lect PT	Harrison, Stephen J.	M	62C
Lect PT	Hawley, Alexandra W.	M	64A
Lect PT	Henderson, David D.	M	64E
Other	Hewlett, Walter	D	34
Lect	Hillhouse, Wendy	M	61
Prof Emeritus	Hinton, Stephen W.	D	12A,12
Prof Emeritus	Houle, George L.	D	12A,55,67B
Lect PT	Johnson Hamilton, Joyce	D	63A
Lect PT	Kadis, Jay L.	M	45,35C
Asst Prof	Kapuscinski, Jaroslaw	D	10,20C
Lect PT	Kenley, McDowell E.	D	63C
Asst Prof	Kronengold, Charles	D	12,20
Lect PT	Low, Murray	B	47,66A
Lect PT	Maestre, Janet M.	M	64A
Assoc Prof	Mahrt, William P.	D	12A,55,67E,31A
Lect PT	Martin, Anthony P.	M	67E
Lect PT	Matheson, James	B	64B
Lect PT	McCain, Seward	B	62D
Lect PT	McCarthy, Charles	DIPL	64E
Lect PT	Morgan, Robert Huw	D	66G,60,36
Lect PT	Moyer, Bruce D.	M	62D
Lect PT	Myers, Herbert W.	M	67B,71
Lect PT	Nadel, James	B	41,29
Lect	Nuttall, Geoff	M	62A,41,51
Lect PT	Olivier, Rufus	DIPL	64D
Lect	Ragent, Lawrence S.	B	63B
Prof Emeritus	Ramsey, William H.	D	60,36
Lect	Robertson, Lesley N.	M	62B,41,51
Asst Prof	Rodin, Jesse	D	12
Prof	Sano, Stephen M.	M	60,36,20C,20I
Asst Prof	Schultz, Anna	D	20E,20G,20F
Senior Lect	Schultz, Thomas J.	D	66A
Other	Selfridge-Field, Eleanor	D	34
Lect	Sharp, Robin	M	62A
Other	Slaney, Malcolm	D	34
Prof	Smith, Julius O.	D	34,13L
Prof Emeritus	Smith, Leland C.	M	13,10,12A,34
Lect PT	Sohn, Livia	DIPL	62A
Lect	St. John, Scott	M	62A,41,51
Lect PT	Thornburgh, Elaine	M	66H
Lect PT	Ulman, Erik	D	10,13,12B,62A
Lect PT	Vandivier, Rick	DIPL	70
Lect PT	Veregge, Mark F.	M	50,65
Lect PT	Verplank, William	D	34
Senior Lect	Wait, Gregory A.	B	36,61
Asst Prof	Wang, Ge	D	34,35,13L
Lect PT	Wei, Sharon	DIPL	62B
Senior Lect	Weldy, Frederick R.	D	66A,66C
Lect PT	Worley, John L.	DIPL	63A
Lect PT	You, Daisy	B	67H,20E
Lect PT	Zerlang, Timothy	D	66A,69

CA4950 Taft College

Department of Music
29 Emmons Park Dr
Taft, CA 93268-1437
(661) 763-7771   Fax: (661) 763-7705
www.taftcollege.edu
E-mail: lsmith@taftcollege.edu

2 Year Institution, Music Appreciation Courses Only

Division Chair: Sonya Swenson, 80A

Smith, Lee		11,41,62
Swenson, Sonya		11

CA5000 Univ of California-Berkeley
Department of Music
104 Morrison Hall #1200
Berkeley, CA 94720-1200
(510) 642-2678   Fax: (510) 642-3482
music.berkeley.edu
E-mail: music@berkeley.edu

4 Year Institution, Graduate School

Master of Arts in Composition, Master of Arts in Historical Musicology, Master of Arts in Ethnomusicology, PhD in Historical Musicology, PhD in Ethnomusicology, PhD in Composition

Chair: Benjamin Brinner, 80A

	Antonioli, Laurie A.		61
	Atladottir, Hrabba	M	62A
Asst Prof	Bedrossian, Franck	D	10,13
	Benedict, Deborah	M	61
	Berman, Kenneth M.	M	66A
	Biancalana, Jeff		63A
	Bidwell, Louise B.	M	66A
	Brandes, Christine	M	61
	Brendler, Charlene	M	66H
Prof	Brinner, Benjamin	D	13K,14,20B,20D,11
	Calonico, Robert M.	M	37
Prof	Campion, Edmund	D	20,13,34,35G
	Carslake, Louise	M	67D
	Cheetham, Richard	B	63C
	Chew, Jacqueline	M	66A,66D
	Clegg, Aaron		64A
Prof	Cox, Cindy	D	10,13
Lect	Dana, Christy L.	M	13A,13C,29B,47,29C
	Dangi, Suparna	B	61
Asst Prof	Davies, James	D	11,12A,12E,20A,66A
	Davis, Jeff	M	69
	Didi, Rani		61
	Embloom, George	M	66G
	Engelhart, Cecilia		61
	Fong, Leighton	M	62C
Lect	Fuson, Tim Abdellah		20B
	Gehrke, Rodney P.	D	66G
Lect	Gold, Lisa R.	D	20D
	Goldberg, Michael K.	M	70
	Granger, David W.	M	64D
Prof	Guilbault, Jocelyne	D	11,14,20H
	Gundanas, Susan	B	61
	Heater, Katherine	M	66H,66E
Lect	Johnson, Candace Y.	M	61
	Johnston, Darren	M	63A
	Klein, Laura	B	66A
	Koh, Jonathan	M	62C
Prof	Kuzma, Marika C.	D	36,40,60A,61
Lect	Ladzekpo, C. K.		20A
	Luftman, Adam	B	63A
	MacCallum, John		10B
	Marrs, Jeffrey	M	65
	Martin, Frank		66A
	Massanari, Jeff		70
Asst Prof	Mathew, Nicholas	D	11,12
	Mckenzie, Julie C.	B	64A
Assoc Prof	Melford, Myra J.	B	29,47,53
Prof	Milnes, David	D	38,43,60B
	Moon, Emma	M	64A
	Moore, Carla	M	67B
Prof	Moroney, Davitt	D	11,12,55B,56
	Muscarella, Susan	B	66A
Prof Emeritus	Newcomb, Anthony A.	D	12A,12
Lect	Orland, Michael	B	13A,66D,66A,13C
	Pardo, Brian	M	70
Lect	Pereira, David	D	13B,13H
	Rathke, Sarah	M	64B
	Reed, Elisabeth	M	67A
	Richman, Glenn		62D
Prof Emeritus	Roberts, John H.	D	12,16
Asst Prof	Roberts, Tamara	D	11,14C,14D,20G
	Rose, Ellen Ruth	M	62B
Lect	Rosenak, Karen	D	13A,13C,43
	Seeling, Ellen	B	63A
Lect	Sharp, Irene	B	62C
	Shearer, Allen R.	D	61
	Simon, Benjamin	M	62C
Prof	Smart, Mary Ann	D	11,12,15
	Smiley, Mariko	M	62A
	Sor, Karen Shinozaki		62A
	Sykes, Jeffrey	D	61,66C
	Tamburrino, Maria	M	64A
Prof	Taruskin, Richard	D	11,12
	Tayler, David	D	67D,67G
	Telford, Alicia	B	63B
Asst Prof	Ueno, Ken	D	10,13,34A,34D
Prof	Van Orden, Katherine	D	11,12A,12D,55,67
	Van Proosdij, Hanneke	M	67C
Prof	Wade, Bonnie C.	D	11,14,20C,20E,12G
	Wahrhaftig, Peter	M	63D
	Ward, Robert	B	63B
	Wasley, Martha		66A
Prof	Wessel, David	D	12F,13G,13K,13L
Lect	Wilson, Mark	D	60A
Prof Emeritus	Wilson, Olly W.	D	10,20G,29
	Winant, William	M	65
	Wolford, Dale		64E
	Woo, Betty	M	66A
	Worn, Richard	M	62D
	Zhang, Xiao Feng	B	
	Zinn, Dann		64E

CA5010 Univ of California-Davis
Department of Music
One Shields Ave
Davis, CA 95616
(530) 752-5537   Fax: (530) 752-0983
music.ucdavis.edu
E-mail: baolivier@ucdavis.edu

4 Year Institution, Graduate School

Master of Arts in Composition, Master of Arts in Ethnomusicology, PhD in Ethnomusicology, PhD in Composition, PhD in Musicology, Master of Arts in Conducting, Master of Arts in Musicology

Chair: Henry Spiller, 80A

Asst Prof	Baldini, Christian	D	38,10,13,39
Prof	Bauer, Ross	D	13,10,43,29
Prof Emeritus	Bloch, Robert S.		13,11,41,62A,62B
Prof	Busse Berger, Anna Maria	D	12A,12
Prof Emerita	Charles, Sydney R.	D	12A,12
Lect	Craig, Phebe	M	13C,56,66H
Prof Emeritus	Elkus, Jonathan B.	M	37
Prof Emeritus	Frank, Andrew D.	M	13,10,11
Prof	Hess, Carol A.	D	12,20H
Prof	Holoman, D. Kern	D	60,11,12A,12
Asst Prof	Lee, Katherine In-Young	D	14,12,20C,12D
Assoc Prof	Levy, Beth E.	D	12A,12B,12C,20G
Prof Emeritus	McNeil, Albert J.	M	60,14,32,36
Lect	Nichols, Samuel S.	D	13,10,70,10B
Prof Emeritus	Nutter, David A.	D	12A,12,55
Prof	Ortiz, Pablo	D	13,10,45,29,34
Prof	Owens, Jessie Ann	D	12A,13J,15
Asst Prof	Pelo, Mika	D	10,11,13,43
Prof	Reynolds, Christopher A.	D	12,11
Prof	Rohde, Kurt E.	M	13,10,11,43
Lect	Sabino, Robert	B	10B
Assoc Prof	San Martin, Laurie A.	D	10,13,43,35E
Lect	Slabaugh, Thomas E.	D	37,60,65,50,42
Prof Emeritus	Slawson, A. Wayne	D	13,10,34
Assoc Prof	Spiller, Henry	D	14,12,15,20D,12D
Prof	Thomas, Jeffrey		60,36,12A
Lect	Triest, Amelia	B	13A,13C,66D

CA5020 Univ of California-Irvine
C. Trevor School of the Arts
303 Music & Media Bldg
Irvine, CA 92697-2775
(949) 824-6615   Fax: (949) 824-4914
music.arts.uci.edu/
E-mail: music@uci.edu

4 Year Institution, Graduate School

MFA in Intergrated Composition, Improv and Tech, MFA in Performance, MFA in Collaborative Piano, MFA in Choral Conducting

Chair: David Brodbeck, 80A
Dean: Joseph S. Lewis, III, 80A

Prof	Akagi, Kei	B	53,29,47
Asst Prof	Bauer, Amy M.	D	13,13F,12D
Prof	Bedelian, Haroutune		62A
Lect	Bedelian, Lorna Griffitt	D	66A
Lect	Bosler, Annie J.	D	63B
Prof	Brodbeck, David	D	12
Assoc Prof Emerita	Brown, Rae Linda	D	12,29A
Assoc Prof	Buck, Robin T.	M	39,61
Lect	Choate, Ellie		62E
Lect	Cloud, Patricia	M	64A
Lect	Davis, Jonathan Doane	D	64B
Asst Prof	Dessen, Michael J.	D	10,12D,29E
Lect	Dimond, Theresa		65,50
Prof	Dobrian, Christopher	D	10
Prof Emerita	Fernandez, Nohema		66A

Prof Emeritus	Gilmore, Bernard H.	D	10,13
Lect	Greene, Fred W.	M	63D
Lect	Hare, Matthew	D	62D
Lect	Harnell, Jason		65
Prof Emeritus	Hickok, Robert B.	B	60,36
Prof	Huszti, Joseph B.	M	60,36,61
Lect	Kosmala, Jerzy S.	D	62D
Lect	McKeown, Kevin	M	48
Lect	McMullen, George Edward		63C
Prof	Murata, Margaret K.	D	12A,12
Lect	Oles, Darek	B	62D
Prof	Omoumi, Hossein	D	14
Lect	Owens, Charles Marion	B	47
Lect	Parkins, Margaret Clara	D	62C
Lect	Pinter, Jerry	B	64E
Prof	Reardon, Colleen A.	D	12
Lect	Rodriguez, Bobby	D	63A
Lect	Schneiderman, John H.	B	67D,70
Lect	Scolnik, Nina	B	66A
Prof Emeritus	Slim, H. Colin	D	12
Lect	Stetson, David B.	B	63C
Asst Prof	Sun, Cecilia	D	12
Assoc Prof	Taylor, Darryl G.	D	61
Asst Prof	Tucker, Stephen Earl	D	60,38
Asst Prof	Umezaki, Kojiro	M	10,13,34
Lect	Walker, Amanda Jane	M	64C
Lect	Washburn, David W.	M	63A

CA5030 Univ of California-Los Angeles

Herb Alpert School of Music
2539 Schoenberg Music Bldg
PO Box 951616
Los Angeles, CA 90095-1616
(310) 825-4761   Fax: (310) 206-4738
www.music.ucla.edu
E-mail: m.dean@arts.ucla.edu

4 Year Institution, Graduate School

Master of Arts in Composition, Master of Music in Performance, PhD in Composition, DMA in Conducting, DMA in Performance, Master of Arts in Composition for Visual Media

Chair: Michael Dean, 80A
Vice Chair: Gordon L. Henderson, 80H

Prof	Bourland, Roger	D	13,10
Adj Assoc Prof	Bull, Christoph	M	66G
Prof	Burrell, Kenneth	B	47
Adj Assoc Prof	Carlson, Mark	D	10,13
Lect	Cheng, Gloria	D	12C,12B
Prof	Chernov, Vladimir	M	61
Prof	Chihara, Paul	D	10,13
Lect	Cooper, Chris	B	63B
Lect	Davis, Jonathan	D	64B
Assoc Prof	Dean, Michael	M	61
Lect	Flanagan-Lysy, Margaret		51
Vstng Prof	Franzen, Donald	JD	35A
Prof	Gondek, Juliana	M	61
Prof	Gray, Gary	M	64C
Lect	Hak, Rakefet		39
Adj Asst Prof	Hansen, Judith	M	40
Adj Prof	Hanulik, Christopher	B	62D
Prof	Henderson, Gordon L.	M	37
Assoc Prof	Heuser, Frank	D	32
Adj Assoc Prof	Judkins, Jennifer	D	12B,12C
Prof	Kazaras, Peter	JD	39,54
Prof	Krouse, Ian	D	13,10
Prof	Lee, D. Thomas	D	37,48
Assoc Prof	Lefkowitz, David S.	D	13,10
Prof	Lindemann, Jens	M	63A,49
Prof	Lysy, Antonio	M	62C,42
Prof	Masek, Douglas H.	DMA	64E,64C
Lect	Matsumoto, Kanae	D	66A,66C
Lect	Miller, James	M	63C
Lect	Neill, Lou Anne	M	62E
Prof	Neuen, Donald	M	36,40
Lect	O'Neill, Richard	M	62B
Lect	Peters, Mitchel	M	50,65
Prof	Pogossian, Movses	D	62A,62
Prof	Ponce, Walter	D	66A,66B
Lect	Rodrigue, Jean-Louis	B	
Lect	Sheridan, Patrick	M	63D
Adj Assoc Prof	Snow, Jennifer L.	D	66C
Lect	Steinmetz, John	D	64D,12C
Senior Lect	Stokes, Sheridon		64A
Prof	Stulberg, Neal	D	38,12C
Prof	Sutre, Guillaume		62A,51
Prof	Winter, Robert		12C
Adj Assoc Prof	Yates, Peter F.	D	70

CA5031 Univ of California-Los Angeles

Herb Alpert School of Music
Department of Ethnomusicology
PO Box 951657
Los Angeles, CA 90095-1657
(310) 206-3033   Fax: (310) 206-4738
www.ethnomusic.ucla.edu
E-mail: hrees@arts.ucla.edu

4 Year Institution, Graduate School

Master of Arts in Ethnomusicology, PhD in Ethnomusicology, PhD in Ethnomusicology/Speciality in Systemantic Musicology

Chair: Helen Rees, 80A
Dir., Undergraduate Studies: Munir N. Beken, 80B
Dir., Graduate Studies: Daniel M. Neuman, 80C
Archive Director: Anthony Seeger

Lect	Almario, Justo	B	29,64
Asst Prof	Beken, Munir N.	D	13,10
Asst Prof Adj	Bohanon, George		63C,29
Prof	Browner, Tara C.	D	20G,14A
Prof	Burrell, Kenneth	B	29
Lect	Cameron, Clayton	B	29,65
Lect	Catlin, Amy	D	14,20C,20D,20E
Prof	DjeDje, Jacqueline Cogdell	D	20A,20G,14A
Lect	Guzman, Jesus		20H
Lect	Harrison, Charley	M	29,47
Lect	Hendelman, Tamir	B	29,66A
Lect	Jamieson, Jake	M	20,32
Lect	Janeczko, Jeffrey M.	D	20F,20G,20H
Adj Asst Prof	Kaushal, Abhiman		20E
Prof	Kendall, Roger A.	D	32,13L,12F,12C
Prof	Keyes, Cheryl L.	D	20G,14A
Lect	Khan, Shujaat Husain		20E,62,61
Asst Prof Adj	Kim, Dong Suk	D	20C,62,65
Asst Prof Adj	Ladzekpo, Kobla	M	20A,65
Assoc Prof Adj	Li, Chi	B	20C,62,64,65
Prof	Loza, Steven	D	14A,20H,20G
Lect	Macy, Elizabeth	D	20
Lect	Marshall, Wolf	B	29,70
Assoc Prof Adj	Miranda, Roberto	M	29,62D
Asst Prof Adj	Morrison, Barbara		61,29
Prof	Neuman, Daniel M.	D	20E,14A
Lect	Neuman, Rahul		20F,62
Prof	Newton, James	D	29,10
Lect	Owens, Charles		29,47,64
Prof Adj	Petrovic, Ankica	D	20F,14A,31
Asst Prof Adj	Price, Ruth	B	29,61
Prof	Racy, A. J.	D	20B,14A,14B
Prof	Rees, Helen	D	20C,20D,20E,14A
Prof	Rice, Timothy	D	20E,14A
Asst Prof Adj	Roberson, James	M	20G,61
Lect	Rodriguez, Bobby		29,63A
Prof Emerita	Sakata, Lorraine	D	20B,14A,20E
Lect	Salazar, Lauryn C.	D	20
Assoc Prof	Savage, Roger W. H.	D	12B,12E
Prof	Seeger, Anthony	D	20H,14A,20G,35A,35D
Prof	Taylor, Timothy D.	D	12,14,34
Asst Prof Adj	Varimezov, Ivan S.	B	20F,64
Assoc Prof Adj	Varimezova, Tzvetanka	B	20F,61
Assoc Prof Adj	Weir, Michele	M	61,29
Assoc Prof Adj	Wenten, I. Nyoman	D	20D

CA5032 Univ of California-Los Angeles

Department of Musicology
2443 Schoenberg Music Bldg
Los Angeles, CA 90095-1623
(310) 206-5187   Fax: (310) 206-9203
www.musicology.ucla.edu
E-mail: bvannost@humnet.ucla.edu

4 Year Institution, Graduate School

PhD in Musicology, Master of Arts in Musicology

Chair, Musicology: Robert W. Fink, 80A
Dean, Humanities: David Schaberg, 80A
Dir., Undergraduate Studies, Musicology: Elisabeth C. Le Guin, 80B
Dir., Graduate Studies, Musicology: Olivia A. Bloechl, 80C

Assoc Prof	Bloechl, Olivia A.	PhD	12,12A,12D,20G,31A
Prof Emeritus	Bradshaw, Murray C.	PhD	13,11,12A,13J
Prof Emeritus	Cole, Malcolm S.	PhD	11,12A,12,66G,31A
Prof Emeritus	D'Accone, Frank A.	PhD	12A,12,13J
Asst Prof	Eidsheim, Nina	D	12A,12,13
Prof	Fink, Robert W.	PhD	13,12,34,20G
Prof Emerita	Gollner, Marie L.	PhD	12A,12,13J

Prof Emeritus	Hudson, Richard	PhD	12A,12
Prof	Knapp, Raymond L.	PhD	12A,12
Assoc Prof	Le Guin, Elisabeth C.	PhD	12A,12,62C,67B,15
Prof	Levitz, Tamara	PhD	12A,12,13
Assoc Prof	Morris, Mitchell B.	PhD	12A,12,20G,15
Prof Emeritus	Stevenson, Robert M.	D	12,14,20G,20H
Prof	Taylor, Timothy D.	PhD	14,20,34
Asst Prof	Upton, Elizabeth R.	PhD	12A,12,13J

CA5040 Univ of California-Riverside
Department of Music
900 University Ave
Riverside, CA 92521
(951) 827-7059   Fax: (951) 827-4651
www.music.ucr.edu
E-mail: music@ucr.edu

4 Year Institution, Graduate School

Master of Arts in Ethnomusicology, PhD in Music, Master of Arts in Music Theory-Composition, Master of Arts in Musicology

Chair: Paulo Chagas, 80A
Graduate Advisor: Rogerio Budasz, 80C

Prof	Adams, Byron	D	13,10F,10,12
PT	Amin, Kimberly	M	66A
Lect PT	Beazley, Janet M.	D	55,67
Lect	Bennett, Barbara A.	D	13B,13,11,45,34
PT	Best, Ed	B	65
Lect PT	Bruner, G. Edward	D	11,36
Assoc Prof	Budasz, Rogerio	D	12,20H
PT	Casale, Bill	D	62D
PT	Cato, Ralph Wayne	D	61
Prof	Chagas, Paulo	D	10
Lect	Charloff, Ruth	D	60,11,36,38
Lect PT	Christensen, David	M	66G,69
	Clark, Walter A.	D	12,20H
Lect PT	De Leon, Tagumpay	M	20D,51
Asst Prof	Dicke, Ian	D	10A,10B,10C
Asst Prof	Dicke, Ian	D	10A,10B,10C
PT	Dominguez, Robert		65
Prof Emeritus	Gable, Frederick K.	D	12A,12,31A
Prof Emeritus	Ginter, Anthony F.		12,38
PT	Holt, Eileen	M	64A
Prof Emeritus	Johns, Donald C.	D	12,29
Lect PT	Kaushal, Abhiman	B	20E,65
PT	Koster, Charles	M	64D
Lect PT	Kurai, Tom	B	20C,65
Assoc Prof	Labor, Tim A.	M	10,10A,10B,10C
Lect PT	Lamprey, Audrey	D	13A,63B
Assoc Prof	Lysloff, Rene T.A.	D	14,20,20D,20G
Lect PT	Moore, Frances	M	62,42
Lect PT	Rios, Juan	M	20H,52
Asst Prof	Ritter, Jonathan	D	14,20,20H
PT	Robertshaw, Manon	M	62C
Assoc Prof	Saavedra, Leonora	D	12,20H
PT	Scarano, Robert	B	70
PT	Schroerlucke, Leslie	M	64C
	Sobrino, Laura	B	20H,51
PT	Tomoff, Lisa Geering	B	64B
PT	Valerio, Celia Chan	D	62E
PT	Voin, Camelia	D	61
Lect PT	Whitelaw, Ian		48
Prof	Wong, Deborah	D	14,20,20D,20G,31D
Lect PT	Zebley, Matthew	D	37,46,47

CA5050 Univ of California-San Diego
Department of Music
9500 Gilman Dr
La Jolla, CA 92093-0999
(858) 534-3230   Fax: (858) 534-8502
music.ucsd.edu
E-mail: info@music.ucsd.edu

4 Year Institution, Graduate School

Master of Arts in Composition, Master of Arts in Performance, PhD in Composition, Master of Arts in Computer Music, Master of Arts in Integrative Studies, DMA Contemporary Music Performance, PhD in Computer Music, PhD in Integrative Studies

Chair: Miller Puckette, 80A

Assoc Prof	Balzano, Gerald	D	13A,34,13L,12F,12
Assoc Prof	Borgo, David R.	D	64E,14,29,47
Asst Prof	Burr, Anthony	D	64C,43,13D,14C,12D
Prof	Curtis, Charles	M	13A,41,62C
Prof	Davis, Anthony	B	20G,66A,10,53
Prof	Dresser, Mark	M	62D,29
Assoc Prof	Dubnov, Shlomo	D	34,34B
Prof Emeritus	Farrell, Peter S.	M	13,12A,62C,67A
Prof	Fonville, John	D	13,10,64A,53,43
Assoc Prof	Guy, Nancy	D	14,20D
Prof Emeritus	Harkins, Edwin	D	13A,13,63A,54,43
Asst Prof	Jung, Eun-Young	D	11,12D,14,20C
Prof	Karis, Aleck	M	13,12A,66A,66H,43
Prof	Larson, Philip	M	13A,11,12A,36,61
Assoc Prof	Liang, Lei	D	10,13B,13D,10A,10B
Prof Emeritus	Lytle, Cecil W.	B	66A,29,20G
Prof	Manoury, Philippe	DIPL	10
Prof	Moore, F. Richard	D	10,45,34,35C,13L
Prof	Negyesy, Janos	DIPL	20F,41,62A,43,34
Prof Emeritus	Ogdon, Will L.	D	13,10F,10,12A
Prof	Pasler, Jann C.	D	11,12A,12,12B,12E
Prof Emeritus	Plantamura, Carol	M	12A,55,61,54,43
Prof	Puckette, Miller	D	34,12C
Prof	Reynolds, Roger L.	M	13,10F,10,20G,34
Prof	Schick, Steven	M	11,50,65,43,29
Prof Emeritus	Sollberger, Harvey	M	10F,60,10,64A,43
Prof	Steiger, Rand	M	13,10,34
Assoc Prof	Stevens, Jane	D	11,12A,12
Prof Emeritus	Turetzky, Bertram	M	12A,41,62D,43,29
Prof	Ung, Chinary	D	10,20D,64
Prof Emeritus	Yuasa, Joji	DIPL	10,20D,35H,34,35C

CA5060 Univ of California-Santa Barbara
Department of Music
1315 Music Bldg
Santa Barbara, CA 93106-6070
(805) 893-3261   Fax: (805) 893-7194
www.music.ucsb.edu
E-mail: berkowit@music.ucsb.edu

4 Year Institution, Graduate School

Master of Arts in Composition, Master of Arts in Music Theory, Master of Arts in Ethnomusicology, Master of Music in Performance, PhD in Ethnomusicology, PhD in Music Theory, PhD in Composition, DMA in Performance, PhD in Musicology, Master of Arts in Musicology

Dir., Graduate Studies: Michel Marc Gervais, 80C

Chair: Lee Rothfarb

Senior Lect	Asche, Charles	D	66A,41
Lect	Ballerino, John	D	61,66C
Senior Lect	Bambach, Paul	M	64C,48
Prof	Barlow, Clarence	DIPL	10A,10B,13G
Lect	Bell, Victor		36
Prof	Berkowitz, Paul M.	DIPL	66A,41
Lect	Booth, William	M	63C
Assoc Prof	Brecher, Benjamin	M	61,39
Prof	Callus, Helen	DIPL	62B,41
Assoc Prof	Cooley, Timothy J.	D	20F,20G,14A,14C,14D
Prof Emeritus	Diemer, Emma Lou	D	13,10F,10
Prof	Feigin, Joel	D	10,10A,10F,13D
Prof	Felber, Jill	M	64A,48
Lect	Garber, Neil	M	62D
Prof	Gervais, Michel Marc	B	36,60A,55D,40
Prof	Gross, Steven	D	63B,49
Asst Prof	Hajda, John M.	D	13K,13L,13A,13B,14A
Lect	Haladyna, Jeremy	D	10,43
Lect	Horn, Stuart	M	64B
Prof Emerita	Hsu, Dolores M.	D	12A,12,20D,14A,14B
Lect	Hungerford, Grant	M	63A
Assoc Prof	Katz, Derek	D	12A,12
Lect	Kislenko, Natalia	D	66A,66C,66D
Assoc Prof	Koenig, Robert	M	66C
Prof	Kuchera-Morin, JoAnn	D	13,10F,10,45,13L
Prof	Marcus, Scott	D	14,20B,20E
Lect	Nathan, Jonathan	D	47,50,65
Asst Prof	Novak, David	D	14A,14C,14D,20C
Prof Emerita	Oberacker, Betty	D	66A
Asst Prof	Paul, David	D	12A,12,13B
Lect	Poretsky, Susana	DIPL	61
Prof Emeritus	Prizer, William	D	12A,12
Lect	Radford, Andrew		64D
Lect	Rintoul, Richard	D	38
Prof	Roads, Curtis		10B
Prof	Rothfarb, Lee	D	13J,13I,13B,13E,13
Prof	Rutkowski, Geoffrey	M	41,62C
Lect	Sahuc, Paul N.	M	61,39
Assoc Prof	Tcharos, Stefanie	D	12A,12
Prof	Van Den Toorn, Pieter	D	13,13F,13I
Prof	Yaron, Yuval	DIPL	62A
Lect	Yih, Annie	D	13,13I,13C

CA5070 Univ of California-Santa Cruz
Department of Music-Music Ctr
1156 High St
Santa Cruz, CA 95064
(831) 459-2292   Fax: (831) 459-5584
music.ucsc.edu
E-mail: music@ucsc.edu

4 Year Institution, Graduate School

Master of Arts in Composition, Master of Arts in Ethnomusicology, DMA in Composition, PhD in Cross Cultural Studies, Master of Arts in Performance Practice

Chair: Fredric Lieberman, 80A
Dean: David Yager, 80A

Assoc Prof	Beal, Amy C.	D	12A,12,43,20G
Lect	Brandenburg, Mark	M	64C
Prof	Burman-Hall, Linda C.	D	55B,20D,20F,66H,67C
Asst Prof	Carson, Benjamin Leeds	D	13K,10
Lect	Contos, Paul D.		64E
Prof Emeritus	Cope, David H.	M	13,10,12A
Lect	Cope, Mary Jane	M	66A
Lect	Coulter, William D.	M	70
Prof Emeritus	Dudley, Sherwood	D	13,10F,12A,39
Lect	Elsea, Peter	M	45,35C
Lect	Ezerova, Maria V.	D	66A,66D
Lect	Fromme, Randolph	M	62C
Lect	Green, Barry L.	M	62D
Assoc Prof	Hester, Karlton E.	D	29
Prof Emeritus	Houghton, Edward F.	D	12A,12
Lect	Irvine, Erin	M	64D
Prof	Jones, David Evan	D	13,10
Assoc Prof	Kim, Hi Kyung	D	13,10
Lect	Klevan, Robert B.	D	48,46
Prof	Leikin, Anatole	D	13,12A,66A
Prof	Lieberman, Fredric	D	12,14
Lect	Maginnis, Patrice	M	61
Lect	Malan, Roy	DIPL	62A,62B
Lect	Marsh, George		65
Asst Prof	Merchant, Tanya H.	D	20B,15,12A
Prof	Miller, Leta	D	11,12A,12,64A,67E
Lect	Mitchell, Patricia	B	64B
Prof Emeritus	Mumma, Gordon		12A,45
Prof	Nauert, Paul	D	13,10
Asst Prof	Neuman, Dard A.	D	20E,14F
Lect	Ozgen, Mesut	M	70
Prof	Paiement, Nicole	D	60,36,38
Lect	Poplin, Stan E.		62D,47
Lect	Roper, Richard	D	63A
Prof Emeritus	Schechter, John M.	D	13,14,20H
Lect	Solomon, Wayne	M	63C,63D
Lect	Staufenbiel, Brian	D	61,39
Lect	Sumarna, Undang		20D
Assoc Prof	Treadwell, Nina K.	D	12A,67G,55
Lect	Vollmer, Susan C.	M	63B
Lect	Winant, William K.	M	50,65,43
Lect	Wolfson, Greer Ellison	M	64A

CA5100 Univ of La Verne
Department of Music
1950 3rd St
La Verne, CA 91750-4401
(909) 593-3511 x 4917   Fax: (909) 392-2720
www.laverne.edu/academics/arts-sciences/music/
E-mail: rgratz@laverne.edu

4 Year Institution, Comprehensive University

Chair & Dir., Admissions: Reed Gratz, 80A,80D
Dir., Artist Series: Steven A. Biondo, 80F

Inst PT	Alaniz, Steve		64E,64C
Other	Biondo, Steven A.		34,16,20A
Inst PT	Brown, Pebber		70,62D
Asst Prof	Calhoun, James M.	D	36,40,60
Senior Adj	Catalano, Roberto		14,20
Senior Adj	Chen, Moh Wei	D	66A,66D,13C
Senior Adj	Dominguez, Robert		65
Prof Emeritus	Gothold, Stephen A.	D	36,40,61,60A
Prof	Gratz, Reed	D	13,10,14C,29,11
Inst	Hanawalt, Anita	D	13A,11
Inst PT	Holt, Eileen	M	64A
	Kaplan, Adam		66F
Prof	Lamkin, Kathleen J.	D	12A,11,12,62A,66A
Inst PT	Mack, Jonathan	M	61
Senior Adj	Ryan, Michael	M	70,42,10D
Senior Adj	Stephenson, Carol	M	61,54
Inst PT	Summers, Shane	M	66
Inst PT	Walsh, C. Peter	M	66
Artist in Res	Zhao, Grace Xia	D	66,14,13,66A,66C

CA5150 Univ of Redlands
School of Music
1200 E Colton Ave
Redlands, CA 92373-0999
(909) 748-8700   Fax: (909) 335-5183
www.redlands.edu
E-mail: music@redlands.edu

4 Year Institution, Graduate School
Member of NASM

Master of Music in Composition, Master of Music in Performance, Master of Music in Conducting, Master of Music in Music Education

Dean: Andrew Glendening, 80A
Assistant Dean: Eddie Smith, 80H

Lect PT	Andon, Sarah	M	64A,48
PT	Andrews, Bradford	M	35C,13L
Asst Prof	Baber, Katherine	D	12
Lect PT	Beck, Carolyn L.	D	64D
Lect PT	Blumberg, Kira	M	62B
Lect PT	Brenes, Laura	M	63B
Lect PT	Castillo, Francisco	M	64B
Lect PT	Champion, Kyle	M	62C
Lect PT	Dropkin, Mary	M	62E
Lect PT	Emmons, Timothy	M	70,62D
Asst Prof	Farkas, Pavel	M	38,41,51,62A,62B
Lect	Gee, Patricia	M	61,11
	Glendening, Andrew	D	63C
Lect PT	Green, Stuart	M	29,70
Lect PT	Helms, Nancy	M	52
Asst Prof	Hickey, Katherine M.	D	32,13A,13C,36,40
Prof Emeritus	Keays, James	D	12A,49,63B
Prof	Long, Louanne J.	M	13,66A,66B,66C
Lect PT	Lovell, Stephanie	M	13B
Asst Prof	Martin-Andrews, Nicholle	D	36
Vstng Asst Prof	Modica, Joseph	M	13C,36
Prof	Murphy, Daniel	D	34,35,29
Lect PT	Murphy, Paul R.	D	29,70
Lect PT	Nevin, Kathryn A.	D	64C
Asst Prof	Nguyen, Co Boi	D	38
Lect PT	Prodan, Angelica	D	66A
Prof Emeritus	Rickard, Jeffrey H.	M	10,60,36,31A
Asst Prof	Schindelmann, Marco	M	61
Lect PT	Schlitt, Bill	M	50,65
Asst Prof	Scott, David L.	D	63A,46,37
Lect PT	Skrocki, Jeanne	B	62A
Prof	Smith, Eddie	D	60,32C,37,64E
Lect PT	Snyder, Cindy	M	61
Asst Prof	Suter, Anthony	D	13D,13E,10
Lect PT	Sutherland, Scott	M	63D
Lect PT	Taylor, Joel	B	65
Asst Prof	Tosh, Melissa Denise	D	61,36,39,54
Vstng Lect	Urrutia, Lara	M	66D

CA5200 Univ of San Diego
Music Department
5998 Alcala Park
San Diego, CA 92110-2492
(619) 260-2938   Fax: (619) 260-6875
www.sandiego.edu/music
E-mail: dharnish@sandiego.edu

4 Year Institution

Chair: David D. Harnish, 80A
Dir., Artist/Performance Series: Ronald T. Shaheen, 80F
Dir., Summer Programs: Angela C. Yeung, 80G

Assoc Prof	Adler, Christopher A.	D	10,14,13,10A,20D
Vstng Prof	Basilio, Edwin L.	D	60A,32
Vstng Prof	Etheridge, Kay	D	11,32B,66A,66B,66C
	Harnish, David D.	D	14,20,31,41
Prof	Pfau, Marianne Richert	D	12A,67D
PT	Shaheen, Ronald T.		11,12A,13A,61
Assoc Prof	Yeung, Angela C.	D	13,38,41,42,62C

CA5300 Univ of Southern California
Thornton School of Music
840 W 34th St
Los Angeles, CA 90089-0851
(213) 740-6935   Fax: (213) 740-3217
www.usc.edu/music
E-mail: uscmusic@thornton.usc.edu

4 Year Institution, Graduate School
Member of NASM

Master of Arts in Music History, Master of Arts in Early Music, Master of Music in Composition, Master of Music in Performance, Master of Music in Conducting, Master of Music in Music Education, DMA in Composition, DMA in Performance, DMA in Music Education, DMA in Choral Music, PhD in Musicology, Master of Music in Choral Music, Master of Music in Jazz Studies, DMA in Jazz Studies, Master of Music in Education, DMA in Early Music

Dean: Robert A. Cutietta, 80A
Assistant Dean, Operations: Jeffrey De Caen, 80H
Associate Dean, Doctoral Programs: Debora L. Huffman, 80H,80C
Associate Dean, Administration & Finance: Susan Miltner Lopez, 80H
Assistant Dean, Admission & Student Affairs: Phillip Placenti, 80H,80D
Associate Dean, Advancement: Christopher Sampson, 80H

Rank	Name	Deg	Codes
Adj Inst	Abad, Andy	M	10D,14C
Adj Inst	Allen, Jeffrey L.		10D,14C
Adj Inst	Ancona, Ted		35
Adj Inst	Anderson, Robert J.		10D,14C
Adj Asst Prof	Arnay, David	M	66A,29
Adj Asst Prof	Babor, James	M	65A
Adj Inst	Balic, Adriana	B	61
Adj Asst Prof	Batjer, Margaret		62A
Senior Lect	Biersach, Bill		35
Senior Lect	Blaha, Bernadene	M	66A
Adj Inst	Bowers, Amy	D	63C
Adj Prof	Brinegar, Don	M	61
Prof	Brown, Bruce	D	12A
Adj Inst	Brown, Linda		32
Adj Prof	Burlingame, Jon		35H,10C
Senior Lect	Carver, Lucinda	D	66H
Adj Inst	Castellanos, Gilbert		29,63A
Assoc Prof	Cazan, Ken	B	39
Adj Prof	Chalifour, Martin	B	62A
Adj Asst Prof	Chancler, Ndugu	B	29,65
Adj Inst	Clifft, Joel		66
Adj Asst Prof	Corrigan, Rose	B	64D
Prof	Cravens, Terry	D	63C
Prof	Crockett, Donald	D	13,10F,10
Senior Lect	Cunningham, Steve M.	B	35
Adj Inst	Daversa, John	D	63A
Adj Inst	De More, Christine		12
Adj Asst Prof	Del Monte, Adam		70
Asst Prof	Demers, Joanna	D	12D
Adj Asst Prof	Desby, Neal	M	13,10F
Adj Inst	Dohr, Richard William		10D,14C
Inst	Dougall, Sean		10C
Adj Prof	Dozier, Lamont		10D,14C
Prof	Erskine, Peter C.	D	29,65
Adj Assoc Prof	Farmer, Judith	M	64D
Adj Asst Prof	Farnsworth, Anne	M	61,29
Adj Asst Prof	Feldman, Susan M.	D	62A,67B,12A
Adj Asst Prof	Ferrante, Russell K.		29
Adj Asst Prof	Figueroa, Angel	AA	65,29
Assoc Prof	Fitz-Gerald, Kevin	DIPL	41,66A,66C
Adj Inst	Forman, Bruce		70
Adj Inst	Fox, Rachelle		12A
Adj Asst Prof	Fuller, Parmer	D	61
Adj Inst	Fumo, John	DIPL	63A
Asst Prof	Garver, Andrew	B	35
Assoc Prof	Gilad, Yehuda	DIPL	64C
Asst Prof	Gilbert, Adam	D	12A
Lect	Gilbert, Rotem	D	12A
Asst Prof	Gilfry, Rod		61
Prof	Glaze, Gary	M	61
Lect	Goldman, Jason	M	29
Adj Prof	Goldsmith, Pamela	D	62B
Asst Prof	Goldstein, Mark	D	35
Prof	Gordon, Stewart	D	12A,66A
Prof	Goto, Midori	M	62A,42
Adj Prof	Granat, Endre	M	62A
Asst Prof	Grases, Cristian	D	60A
Adj Prof	Green, Donald	M	63A
Adj Inst	Gronnier, Henry M.		62
Adj Inst	Gutierrez, Charles		35
Lect	Harris, Karin		29
Prof	Hartke, Stephen	D	13,10
Adj Asst Prof	Hayhurst, John		62B
Senior Lect	Head, Brian	M	13,70
Asst Prof	Helfter, Susan	D	11,63B
Senior Lect	Hood, Boyde	M	63A
Adj Assoc Prof	Howard, David	B	64C
Assoc Prof	Hynes, Elizabeth	B	61
Adj Inst	Immel, Dean	M	32
Adj Inst	Johnson, Alphonso		29
Adj Inst	Kallay, Aron T.		66
Senior Lect	Kanengiser, William	M	70
Senior Lect	Kelley, Pat	B	70
Asst Prof	King, Brian	B	10,35H,35
Prof	Kirshbaum, Ralph		62C
Adj Inst	Kirst, Patrick		10C
Adj Inst	Kobza, Tim	M	70,29
Adj Asst Prof	Kojian, Miran	M	62A
Lect	Korb, Kristin	M	62D,29
Lect	Krausas, Veronika	D	13
Assoc Prof	Krieger, Norman	DIPL	66A
Prof	Lauridsen, Morten	D	13,10
Senior Lect	Lavery, Sharon	M	60B
Prof	Lesemann, Frederick	D	13,10F,10,45
Adj Inst	Livingston, Edwin U.		10D,14C
Prof	Livingston, Larry J.	M	60
Asst Prof	Lopez, Kenneth	B	35H,35
Senior Lect	Marsh, Peter	DIPL	41,62
Prof	Mason, Thom	D	47,29
Adj Asst Prof	Matsumoto-Stark, Shigemi	B	61
Prof	McCurdy, Ronald	D	29
Prof	McCurdy, Roy	D	65,29
Assoc Prof	McIlvery, Richard	M	35
Prof	McInnes, Donald	M	62B
Asst Prof	McMunn, Brent	M	39
Adj Asst Prof	McNeely, Joel		10C
Senior Lect	McVeigh, Janice	M	61
Adj Asst Prof	Mendoza, Vince	M	29
Prof	Mintzer, Bob		29
Adj Asst Prof	Moore, David	B	62D
Assoc Prof	Moore, Robert S.	D	13,10
Adj Asst Prof	Morrell, Kristy M.		63D
Adj Asst Prof	Morrison, Leah A.	D	31A,13J,12A,12D
Prof	Muhl, Erica	D	13,10
Assoc Prof	Munzer, Cynthia	B	61
Adj Inst	Muto, Vicki	D	61
Adj Inst	Oleszkiewicz, Dariusz		29
Prof	Page, Tim		12D
Adj Inst	Park, Sung-Hwa		66
Assoc Prof	Pasqua, Alan	B	47,29
Adj Prof	Pearson, Norm	B	63D
Adj Asst Prof	Pereira, Joseph		65
Senior Lect	Perry, Antoinette	M	66A
Adj Inst	Perry, Gail		35
Prof	Perry, John	M	66A
Prof	Pollack, Daniel	M	66A
Adj Inst	Popeney, Mark	DMA	10,13
Prof	Potenza, Frank	B	70,29
Adj Inst	Powers, Michael	M	60B
Adj Prof	Reynolds, H. Robert	M	37
Adj Prof	Rhodes, Cherry	B	66G
Adj Prof	Romero, Jose		70
Adj Asst Prof	Rothmuller, Daniel		62C
Adj Asst Prof	Rotter, James	M	64E
Lect	Roze, Chris	M	13,10
Adj Inst	Ruiz, Otmaro		66A,10
Adj Inst	Rushen, Patrice Louise		10D,14C
Prof	Scheibe, Jo-Michael	D	36,60A
Adj Inst	Schmidt, Eric	B	10C
Asst Prof	Schmunk, Richard	D	34,35
Prof Emerita	Schoenfeld, Alice	DIPL	62A
Adj Inst	Schorsch, Kathleen		61
Adj Inst	Schyman, Garry		10
Adj Prof	Self, James	D	63D
Adj Asst Prof	Serfaty, Aaron		29
Assoc Prof	Shepard, Brian K.	DMA	34,10,13,34C,65
Adj Asst Prof	Sheppard, Robert	M	64E,29
Adj Inst	Sherman, Paul	M	12A
Adj Inst	Shubeck, Scott	D	67
Prof	Simms, Bryan R.	D	12A,12
Adj Inst	Skeen, William		67B
Adj Prof	Smalley, Jack		35H,35
Prof	Smith, Alan	D	41,66A,66C
Assoc Prof	Smith, James	M	70
Adj Inst	Smith, Lisa Kingston	B	32
Prof	Smith, Richard	M	70
Adj Inst	Stolpe, Andrea Kay		10D,14C
Senior Lect	Stoubis, Nick	M	70
Asst Prof	Strimple, Nick	D	12A,60A
Adj Prof	Stumpf, Peter		62C
Adj Asst Prof	Suleiman, Alexander		62C
Adj Asst Prof	Sylvester, Lisa M.	D	61,12A
Adj Assoc Prof	Tennant, Scott	M	70
Assoc Prof	Thatcher, James	D	63B
Assoc Prof	Thomas, John	M	47,29
Prof	Thomas, Ladd	D	66G
Prof	Ticheli, Frank	D	13,10
Senior Lect	Timm, Joel	D	64B
Adj Inst	Tornquist, Douglas V.	M	63D
Adj Assoc Prof	Treadwell, Nina	D	12
Adj Prof	Trembly, Dennis	M	62D
Senior Lect	Trovato, Stephen	B	70
Adj Assoc Prof	Turovsky, JoAnn	M	62E
Adj Inst	Vartanian, Tina M.	D	32
Adj Prof	Vogel, Allan	D	64B
Asst Prof	Voyement, Jacques	M	29
Senior Lect	Walker, James	B	64A

Directory of Institutions

Adj Prof	Watrous, Bill		29
Lect	Weiser, Mark L.	M	13
Adj Assoc Prof	Weiss, David	B	64B
Adj Inst	Wetzel, Don Louis		12
Asst Prof	Whitener, John L.	M	32
Adj Inst	Wilkinson, David B.	M	61
Adj Prof	Winkler, Kathleen	M	62A
Adj Asst Prof	Woodward, Gary	M	64A
Adj Inst	Wu, Tien-Hsin	B	62A
Adj Prof	Xue, Suli	B	62A
Asst Prof	Yang, Mina	D	12
Adj Asst Prof	Young, Chris	M	35H,35
Lect	Young, Paul U.	M	35
Adj Prof	Zukovsky, Michele		64C
Adj Inst	Zusman, Shannon		67A,67B

CA5350 Univ of the Pacific

Conservatory of Music
3601 Pacific Ave
Stockton, CA 95211
(209) 946-2417   Fax: (209) 946-2770
www.pacific.edu/conservatory
E-mail: gongaro@pacific.edu

4 Year Institution, Graduate School
Member of NASM

Master of Music in Music Education, Master of Arts in Music Therapy

Dean: Giulio M. Ongaro, 80A
Dir., Graduate Studies: Ruth Brittin, 80C
Dir., Summer Programs: Stephen Perdicaris, 80G
Assistant Dean: David M. Chase, 80H
Dir., Brubeck Institute: Simon B. Rowe

Lect PT	Ahn, Christina H.	D	13C
Lect PT	Ahn, Jean	D	10A
Lect PT	Blomster, Jennie	M	63B,41,42
Assoc Prof	Brierton, Thomas D.		35A
Prof	Brittin, Ruth	D	32
Lect PT	Brown, Allen	M	50,65
Asst Prof	Cetto, Edward	D	36,32D,13C
Lect PT	Chase, David M.	M	
Prof	Coburn, Robert	D	13,10,45
Prof	Cooper, Rex	D	66A,12A
Lect PT	Cozza, John	D	66A,66C
Lect PT	Crawford, Jeff D.	M	35G,34A,34D
Lect PT	Derthick, Thomas	M	62D,42
Assoc Prof	Ebbers, Daniel	M	61
Lect PT	Flyer, Nina		62C,41,42
Lect PT	Fryer, Nicholas	M	47,29B
Prof	Haffner, James	M	39,61,54
Prof	Hammer, Eric	D	60B,37,32E
Assoc Prof	Hatschek, Keith N.	B	35
Lect PT	Henderson, David	M	64E,42
Assoc Prof	Hsaio, Fei-Lin	D	33
Lect PT	Johnson, Charles	M	34B
Lect PT	Kendrick, Brian	M	65
Lect PT	Kenworthy, Jane	B	35E
Lect PT	Kimball, Paul	M	60A
Lect PT	Krejci, Mathew	M	64A,42,41
Asst Prof	Kuster, Nicolasa	M	64D,42,41
Assoc Prof	Langham, Patrick	M	46,47,29,53
Lect PT	Leong, Sonia	D	66A,41,42
Asst Prof	Miller, Ann Elizabeth	M	62A,42,12A,41
Lect PT	Moes, Brook	M	32E
Lect PT	Myers, Dana	M	35A
Lect PT	Nugent, Thomas	M	64B,41,42
Prof	Ongaro, Giulio M.	D	11,12
Lect PT	Ott, Leonard	M	63A
Lect	Perdicaris, Stephen	M	63C,42
Lect	Perry, Margaret	D	66B,66D,66C,13C
Assoc Prof	Phillips, Burr Cochran	D	61,39
Lect PT	Pineda, Gerry	M	29
Prof	Rose, Francois	PhD	13,10
	Rowe, Simon B.	M	29
Prof	Shands, Patricia	D	64C,42,41
Lect PT	Silvers, Travis	M	70
Lect PT	Stevens, Bill	B	35A
Lect PT	Swope, Monica	M	66C
Lect PT	Tropman, Matt	M	63D
Lect PT	Veligan, Igor		62B,42,62A
Asst Prof	Waldon, Eric	D	33
Prof	Waldvogel, Nicolas		38,60B
Asst Prof	Waltz, Sarah Clemmens	D	11,12
Lect PT	Wentz, Brooke		35A
Prof	Wiens, Frank	M	66A
Prof	Wiens, Lynelle	D	61
Lect	Williams, Barbara	M	32A,32B
Lect PT	Wood, Eric	D	10A,11,20,13A,13E

CA5353 Univ of San Francisco

Department of Performing Arts
2130 Fulton St
San Francisco, CA 94117
(415) 422-5979   Fax: (415) 422-2815
www.usfca.edu/artsci/pa
E-mail: camperia@usfca.edu

4 Year Institution

Co-Coordinator, Music: Alexandra Amati-Camperi, 80A
Co-Coordinator, Music: Francesca M. Rivera, 80A

Prof	Amati-Camperi, Alexandra	D	12A,11,12C,13A,12
Inst PT	Bokar Thiam, Pascal	M	47,20
Inst PT	Burgoyne, Carolyn	M	61
Inst PT	D'Andrea, Daria	M	62A,62B
Inst PT	Fiorentino, Mike		70,62A
Lect PT	Gardner, Kara	D	12,11
Inst PT	Garramone, Suzanne	M	66A
Inst PT	Grissom, Cole		61
	Harbor, Ronald		36
Inst PT	Hayes, Angela	B	61
Lect PT	Hsu, Pattie	D	12,20
Lect PT	Kamatani, Pamela	D	12A,11,12C,13
Inst PT	Lares, Joseph		37
Inst PT	May, Judith	M	61
Inst PT	McWilliams, Paul		36
Asst Prof	Rivera, Francesca M.	M	14,20H,41
Inst PT	Ruscoe, Christopher	M	70
Lect PT	Seeman, Rebecca	D	13A,11,36,38,61
Inst PT	Sheie, Sigrid	M	66A
Inst PT	Zbyszynski, Michael F.	D	34,43

CA5355 Vanguard University

Department of Music
55 Fair Dr
Costa Mesa, CA 92626-9601
(714) 556-3610 x 5272   Fax: (714) 662-5229
www.vanguard.edu
E-mail: jmelton@vanguard.edu

4 Year Institution

Chair & Dir., Undgraduate Studies: James L. Melton, 80A,80B
Dir., Artist Series & Summer Programs: Shree Carter, 80F,80G
Associate Chair: Gregory T. Glancey, 80H
Assistant Chair: Susanne M. Reid, 80H

Adj	Alm, Gina	M	11,66A,66B,66C,66D
Adj	Ball, Mindy	M	62E
Adj	Bottorf, Deane	M	32B
Adj	Chasin, Richard	M	63A,49
	Donnelly, Margaret		
Adj	Dovel, Teresa	B	16
Asst Prof	Foerch, Kenneth	D	46,47,64C,64E
	Fukuda, Joni	M	11,13A,32D,36,61
	Glancey, Gregory T.	D	10F,13,34,35
Adj	Green, Stephen	M	62C
	Grishkoff, Robert		63B
Asst Prof	Jarrell, Erinn	M	13,66A,66B,66C,66D
Adj	Johnson, Ann	M	61
	Johnson, Elizabeth		62A
Adj	Karyagina, Tanya		
	Keen, Phil		63D
Adj	Kress, David	M	61
	Lai, Yun-Ju		61
	Macovei, Felix	B	66C
Adj	Mason-Christianson, Teri	M	64A
Prof	Melton, James L.	D	60,36,31A,32D,35E
	Messenger, Richard	D	32C,36
Adj	Mumford, Lawrence R.	D	10,12,13,10F
	Nigro, Michael		70
	O'Hern, Eilene	M	61
Adj	Park, Jenny		51,66A,66B
Assoc Prof	Reid, Susanne M.	D	11,12A,20,31A
Adj	Schlitt, William	M	65,50
Adj	Scott, Sarah	M	16,66D
	Torres, Martin		62D
Adj	Wondercheck, Debora	M	62C

CA5360 Ventura College
Department of Music
4667 Telegraph Rd
Ventura, CA 93003-3872
(805) 654-6400   Fax: (805) 654-6466
www.venturacollege.edu
E-mail: RLawson@vcccd.edu

2 Year Institution

Chair & Dir., Festival/Guest Artist Series: Robert Lawson, 80A,80F

PT	Bergamo, Janet	M	62C
PT	Del Aguila, Miguel	M	10,66A,13A,11
PT	Drayton, Leslie	M	46,47,29B
PT	Elston, Robert	M	65
PT	Farrell, Jodi	B	61
PT	Fay, Fern	M	66
PT	Franco-Summer, Mariana	M	11,13A,66
PT	Gonzales, Carlos	B	70
PT	Grippo, James	M	20
PT	Hardy, Bruce	D	11,29A,14C
PT	Helms, Elizabeth	B	66C,13A,13C,36,39
Inst PT	Johnson, Ruth	M	13A,66A,66D
Prof	Lawson, Robert	M	13,10,11,66D,12A
PT	Lockart, Carol	M	64A,55
PT	Mateus, Cesar	D	70
PT	Newton, Barry	M	62D,11
PT	Nicholson, David	M	13A,64C
PT	Ottsen, Linda	M	61,39
PT	Porter, Lenore	M	61
PT	Powers, Ollie	D	35G,35C,11,12A,34
PT	Radford, Andy	B	64D
Prof	Taft, Burns	D	13,60,36,66A,38
PT	Titmus, Jon	M	63,11,13A
PT	Viaman, Philip	M	62A

A5400 Victor Valley College
Department of Perf. & Applied Arts
Music
18422 Bear Valley Rd
Victorville, CA 92392-5850
(760) 245-4271   Fax: (760) 245-9744
www.vvc.edu
E-mail: thomas.miller@vvc.edu

2 Year Institution

Chair: Thomas E. Miller, 80A
Dean: Paul Williams, 80A

Prof	Graham, Dave	M	47,13A,11,46,29A
PT	Kirk, Erin	D	11,13A
PT	Linstrom, Tracie	M	66D,66A
Prof	Miller, Thomas E.		13B,13C,36,39,54
PT	Minasian, Linda	D	11,66D,66A
PT	Peloza, Susan	M	62,11,13A,66D
PT	Pridmore, Craig	M	37,49,12
PT	Sternfeld, Barbara	M	11,38,62
PT	Sumner, Richard		70
PT	Tsai, Shang-Ying	D	13A,11,20G
PT	Yancey, Patty	M	11,61,36

CA5500 West Los Angeles College
Music Division
9000 Overland Ave
Culver City, CA 90230-3519
(310) 287-4265   Fax: (310) 841-0396
www.wlac.edu

2 Year Institution, Community College

Chair: Michael Arata, 80A
Vice Chair, Music, Humanities & Philosophy: Joyce Sweeney, 80H

Assoc Prof	DuBois, May	M	11,13A,66A
Inst PT	Festinger, Kurt	B	13A,29,47
Assoc Prof	Sweeney, Joyce	M	12A,13,35A,61
Inst	White, Janice	M	11,13A,36,61,66A

CA5510 West Valley College
Department of Music
14000 Fruitvale Ave
Saratoga, CA 95070-5640
(408) 741-2014   Fax: (408) 741-2059
www.westvalley.edu/music
E-mail: lou_delarosa@wvm.edu

2 Year Institution

Chair: Lou DeLaRosa, 80A

PT	Archer, Esther	M	66A,13A
PT	Bengochea, Sandra	M	61,39,54
Inst FT	Cornejo, Robert Joseph	M	13,11,34C,10,12A
FT	DeLaRosa, Lou	M	13A,13C,12A,11,34C
PT	Dotson, Ronald	ABD	11,34C,66D,14C,12A
PT	Drion, Yoka	M	66D
PT	Forehan, Jeff	M	10B,13A,34D,35G,35D
PT	Hawkins, Michelle	M	60A
Inst FT	Kambeitz, Gus	M	46,37,47,29,13A
PT	Lin, James	D	13A,13B,42,13C,13D
PT	Linduska, Mary	M	61
Inst PT	McChesney, Michael	M	70
Inst PT	Stubbe, Joan H.	M	66D
PT	Taniguchi, Naoki	M	13,66D
PT	Wilson, Jacque Scharlach	M	61

CA5550 Westmont College
Department of Music
955 La Paz Rd
Santa Barbara, CA 93108-1023
(805) 565-6040   Fax: (805) 565-7240
www.westmont.edu

4 Year Institution

Chair: Steve Butler, 80A

Inst PT	Bos, Daniel		70
Prof	Brothers, Grey	D	13,36,61,11,12A
Prof	Butler, Steve		10,13,34,10A,13E
Inst PT	Connolly, James		70
Inst PT	Dechaine, Nichole	D	61
Inst PT	Dickstein, Marcia	M	62E
Inst PT	Douglas, John	M	47,66A
Inst PT	Evans, Michael		63C
Asst Prof	Ficsor, Philip G.	D	62A,38
Inst PT	Gross, Steven		63B
Inst PT	Hatley, Paula		66C
Inst PT	Heidner, Eric	M	63C
Prof	Hodson, Steven R.	D	11,36,60,66A
Inst PT	Hopson, John Casey	M	70
Inst PT	Horn, Stuart	M	64B
Inst PT	Januleviciute, Egle	D	66A
Inst PT	Lafranque, Claude-Lise	M	62A
Inst PT	Levin, Heather	M	66A
Inst PT	Malvinni, Valerie	M	62A,62B
Inst PT	Mooy, James	D	63
Inst PT	Mori, Paul	M	37,64B
Inst PT	Nathan, Jonathan	D	65
Inst PT	Park, Helen	M	64C
Inst PT	Pyron, Nona	M	62C
Inst PT	Radford, Andy	M	64D
Inst PT	Rintoul, Richard		62B
Inst PT	Seo, Seungah	M	66A
Prof	Shasberger, Michael	D	36,31A,38,60,61
Inst PT	Tavera, Celeste	M	39
Inst PT	Thomas, Craig	B	64E
Inst PT	Walter, Laura	M	64A
Inst PT	Wasserman, Joanne		60A

CA6000 Whittier College
Department of Music
PO Box 634
Whittier, CA 90608
(562) 907-4237   Fax: (562) 464-4592
www.whittier.edu/Academics/Music/
E-mail: scook@whittier.edu

4 Year Institution

Chair: Stephen Cook, 80A

PT	Barrientos, Victor	M	65
PT	Black, David	M	62D
Prof	Cook, Stephen	D	66A,35A,34,36,11

PT	Dimond, Theresa	D	65
PT	Ho, Leslie	M	62A,62B
PT	Landis, Melissa McIntosh	M	61
Prof	LeVelle, Teresa	D	13,10,44,42
PT	Livesay, Yumi	D	66A
Prof	Lozano, Danilo	M	47,64A,20,29A,14
PT	Mack, Jonathan	M	61
Prof	Muller, David J.	M	10F,11,12A,60B,64D
PT	Stetson, Stephanie	B	63B
PT	Stone, Joseph	M	64B,64E
PT	Velasco, Edmund	B	64E
PT	Velasco, Wendy	M	62C
PT	Wirtz, Bob		62
PT	Wolf, Scott	D	70

CA6050 Yuba College
Music Program
2088 N Beale Rd
Marysville, CA 95901-7605
(530) 741-6883   Fax: (530) 634-7709
yc.yccd.edu/
E-mail: amiller@yccd.edu

2 Year Institution

Dean: Jay Drury, 80A

Prof PT	Johnson, Joaquina Calvo	M	36,39,61,67B
Prof	Mathews, Robert P.	D	13,64,48,70
Prof	Miller, Allan	D	11,12,37,47,63

CO0050 Adams State University
Department of Music
208 Edgemont Blvd
Alamosa, CO 81102-0001
(719) 587-7621   Fax: (719) 587-7094
www.music.adams.edu
E-mail: ascmusic@adams.edu

4 Year Institution
Member of NASM

Chair: Tracy A. Doyle, 80A

Emeritus	Boyer, Charles G.	D	32,11,32E,37
Adj	Branchal, Nick		20H
Adj	Capocchi, Roberto	M	70
Vstng Asst Prof	Doyle, James	M	46,47,65
Assoc Prof	Doyle, Tracy A.	D	64A,32,32B
Adj	Ferrone, Joe	M	63A
PT	Heersink, Barbara	B	66C,66A
Adj	Janus, Ryan	M	64E
Prof	Keitges, Christine	D	39,61,54
Prof	Lipke, William A.	D	66A,38,67F,66B,66D
Adj	Plesner, Joy	B	62A,62B
Assoc Prof	Schildt, Matthew C.	D	13,10,10D,13E,34
Adj	Starcher, Veronica	B	63B
PT	Troyer, Claire	M	66C
Adj	VanValkenburg, Holly	M	64B
Asst Prof	VanValkenburg, Jamie G.	D	63A,63C,63D,37,41
Asst Prof	Wagstrom, Beth Robison	D	36,40,47,60A
Adj	Weir, Claudia	M	64C

CO0100 Arapahoe Community College
Department of Music
PO Box 9002
Littleton, CO 80160-9002
(303) 797-5867   Fax: (303) 797-5782
www.arapahoe.edu
E-mail: hidemi.matsushita@arapahoe.edu

2 Year Institution

Chair: Hidemi Matsushita, 80A

Inst PT	Ailshie, Tyson	M	11,13,62D,70,29
Inst PT	Chang, Melody Jun Yao	M	35,66A,13
Inst PT	Engberg, Michael	M	13,70,41,35,47
Inst PT	Fiegl, Ryan	M	70
Inst PT	Gale, Robert		64,66A,66F,72
Inst PT	Haarhues, Charles D.	D	10,13,29,70,11
Inst PT	Jacobs, Malcolm		65
Inst PT	Kientz, Ron		36
Inst PT	Knetsch, Rene	M	38,62A,42
Inst PT	Kushnir, Regina	M	13A,66A
Inst PT	Lehn, Steven		63A
Inst PT	Levasseur, Susan	D	61
Inst PT	Lewis, Cecil	M	47,53,64E,37
Inst	Matsushita, Hidemi	D	66A,11,12,15,13
Inst PT	Twitty, Katrina	M	61,39
Inst PT	Yeung, Karay		66A,66D
Inst PT	Yotsumoto, Mayumi	M	61,40,39

CO0150 Colorado Christian University
School of Music
8787 W. Alameda Ave
Lakewood, CO 80226-2824
(303) 963-3130   Fax: (303) 963-3131
www.ccu.edu
E-mail: staylor@ccu.edu

4 Year Institution

Dean: Steven Taylor, 80A

PT	Ambler, Don	B	64C
PT	Bland, Ron	B	29,62D
PT	Broome, Curtis	B	65
PT	Buchwald, Peter	M	64E,35C,35D,10
PT	Delevoryas, Sarah	M	62A,62B
Assoc Prof	Dorn, Mark	M	37,63A,46,60B,49
Assoc Prof	Eychaner, Frank	M	10,32,13,47,60
PT	Fleming, Kyle J.	B	36,11,31A,60A
PT	Gaide, Diana	B	66A
PT	Gallo, Pam	M	66A
PT	Gorklo, Dan	M	70
PT	Harper, Gregory		63C,63D
PT	Hatton, Christopher	DMA	66A
PT	Hope, Colleen	M	32B
PT	Kloetzli, Pamela	M	54
PT	Lepke-Sims, Barbara	M	62E
PT	Lloyd, William	B	42
PT	Macy, John		35C,35D
Prof	Menth, Christelle	D	66,12A,20
PT	Moreland, Irina	D	66A
PT	Motter, Catherine	M	66A,13C
PT	Muench, Felicity	M	70
PT	Niezen, Richard S.	M	62C,62D,13C,13G
PT	Perez-Tetrault, Rachel	M	64A
PT	Reyes, Iris		61
PT	Rutherford, Pearl	B	61
PT	Savery, Robert	B	64D
Prof	Schantz, Allen P.	D	11,12B,13,68
PT	Simpson, Steve	B	63B
Prof	Taylor, Steven	M	39,61,31A,44,13C

CO0200 Colorado College
Department of Music
14 E Cache La Poudre St
Colorado Springs, CO 80903-3243
(719) 389-6545   Fax: (719) 389-6862
www.coloradocollege.edu/academics/dept/music
E-mail: sbburns@coloradocollege.edu

4 Year Liberal Arts Institution

Chair: Ofer Ben-Amots, 80A
Dean of Faculty: Sandra Wong, 80A
Associate Chair & Dir., Festivals: Susan L. Grace, 80F,80H

Prof	Agee, Richard J.	D	13,11,12,66H,67D
PT	Anderson, Diana	M	32B,66A,66G
Assoc Prof	Banagale, Ryan	D	11,12,29,34
PT	Barta, Steve	B	66
Prof	Ben-Amots, Ofer	D	13,10F,10,11,34
PT	Bolger, Jean		20F
PT	Brink, Ann	B	61
Lect	Brink, Daniel	M	13A,13,10F,11,66A
PT	Burns, Judeth Shay		61
PT	Cooper, Peter	M	65
PT	Ding, Monica		64B
PT	Ekberg, Nancy	M	67C
Prof Emeritus	Gamer, Carlton	M	13,10,11,20D,34
Prof	Grace, Michael	D	11,12A,12,55
Lect	Grace, Susan L.	M	41,66A
PT	Hanagan, Joyce		32B
PT	Hansen, Victoria	M	61,54
PT	Head, Joseph	M	62D
Prof Emeritus	Jenkins, Donald P.	M	60,36,39,41,54
PT	Jorgensen, Jerilyn J.		62A,41
PT	Knight, Katharine	M	62C
PT	Lasmawan, I. Made		20D
Prof	Levine, Victoria Lindsay	D	11,20E
PT	Liss, Ann Marie		62E
PT	Matzke, Rex	M	64E,29B

PT	Miller, Dale	M	67D,70
PT	Miller, Margaret	B	62B
PT	Nagem, Paul	B	64A
PT	Neihof, Marc	B	70
PT	Polifka, Joyce E.	B	66A
	Reed, Keith	B	67H
PT	Rowland, Martile		39,61
	Scheffelman, Matthew		63B
Prof	Scott, Stephen	M	10,11,45,43,29
PT	Shelton, Evan	M	62C
PT	Shelton, Frank	M	11,66G
PT	Stevens, Daryll	M	64C,16
PT	Taylor, Tom	B	70,29B,46,47
	Teske, Deborah Jenkins	M	36,40,60A
PT	Van Hoy, Jeremy	B	63C,37
PT	Vieira, Alex	M	64D
	Wilson, Carol		66A,66G
PT	Wilson, Thomas	B	63A

CO0225 Colorado Mesa University
Department of Music
1100 North Avenue
Grand Junction, CO 81501-3122
(970) 248-1163   Fax: (970) 248-1159
www.coloradomesa.edu/music/

4 Year Institution

Head: Calvin Hofer, 80A

Prof	Atkinson, Monte	D	60,32C,36,61,66A
Lect	Bailey, Mary Lindsey	D	64B,11
Adj	Ballif, Kristi	M	64A
Prof	Delmore, Jack	D	36,39,61,54
Adj	Drazek, Jan B.	M	61
Assoc Prof	Elias, Carlos	M	32C,38,62A,62B,51
Asst Prof	Flanigan, Sean G.	D	63C,63D,41,47,35A
Lect	Gustafson, Kirk	D	13,10F,60,62C
Prof	Hofer, Calvin	D	32,37,49,63A,60B
Prof	Houle, Arthur Joseph	DMA	66A,66C,66B,66D
Asst Prof	Kamstra, Darin	M	65,29,13B,47,50
Adj	Law, Cameron	B	62C
Adj	McKim, Christopher Z.	D	61
Adj	Musselman, Diana	M	63B,32B
Lect	Niles, Carol Ann	M	36,61
Adj	Nohe, Eric	M	70
Adj	Pytlewski, Barbara	M	64D
Adj	Raper, Troy	B	62D
Adj	Sothers, Misty K.	M	66A
Adj	Wyse, Philip	M	66H,66D
	Yun, Yeon-Ji	D	62C

CO0250 Colorado State University
Department of Music/Theatre/Dance
120 Univ Center for the Arts
Fort Collins, CO 80523-1778
(970) 491-5529   Fax: (970) 491-7541
www.music.colostate.edu/
E-mail: Todd.Queen@colostate.edu

4 Year Institution, Graduate School
Member of NASM

Master of Music in Performance, Master of Music in Conducting, Master of Music in Music Education, Master of Music in Music Therapy

Chair: Todd Queen, 80A
Assistant Chair, Undergraduate Studies: Paul W. Metz, 80B
Assistant Chair, Graduate Studies: William B. Davis, 80C

Prof Emeritus	Anderson, Edward D.	M	60,36
Inst	Apodaca, Denise R.	M	66B
Assoc Prof	Bacon, Joel	D	66G,12A,66H
Asst Prof	Blake-Oliver, Tiffany Erin	D	61
Assoc Prof	Brewer, Robert G.	D	32C,63D,49
Prof Emeritus	Busch, Stephen E.	D	32,44,66D
Inst	Dameron, Stuart	M	
Asst Prof	David, James M.	D	13,10,10F,63C
Prof	Davis, William B.	D	33,12C
Asst Prof	Ellins, Rachael Starr	M	62E,11
Asst Prof	Ferreira, Copper	M	13
Asst Prof	Ferreira, Wesley	M	64C
Assoc Prof	Francois, Ronald P.	D	62A,42
Asst Prof	Frey, Richard	D	37
Asst Prof	Grapes, Dawn	M	12
Asst Prof	Greenough, Forest G.	D	47,62D,10F,34
Asst Prof	Harper, Greg J.	M	63C
Assoc Prof	Hollenbeck, Eric R.	D	65,50
Asst Prof	Jacobi, Bonnie S.	D	32B,66A,13,32I,32
Asst Prof	Johnson, Erik A.	D	32,32E
PT	Johnson, Sarah	M	33
Prof	Kenney, Wes	M	38,60B
Assoc Prof	Kim, James	D	36,60A
Asst Prof	Lagasse, Blythe		33
Prof	Landreth, Janet M.	D	66A,66B
Assoc Prof Emeritus	Lawson, Charles E.	D	13,64C,41
Prof Emeritus	Lueck, John	D	36,61
Asst Prof	Marx, Steve	M	63A
Asst Prof	Marx, Susan A.	D	61
Prof Emeritus	McCray, James	D	10,32C,12A
Asst Prof	McGuire, John	D	63B,11
Asst Prof	McGuire, John P.	M	63B
Asst Prof	McNeal, Steve W.	M	38,32E
Assoc Prof	Metz, Paul W.	D	13
Asst Prof	Miller, Margaret J.		62B
Prof	Moody, Gary E.	D	64B,13,41,64D
Assoc Prof Emerita	Morrow-King, Janet		61,39,12A
Inst	Mosko, Beth	M	33
Asst Prof	Nicholas, Christopher J.	D	37,60B
Prof Emeritus	Nisbett, Robert	D	13,12A,66C
Asst Prof	Oliver, Murray	M	11
Asst Prof	Olsen, Ryan	D	36,32
Assoc Prof	Queen, Todd	D	39,61
Inst	Rosenholtz-Witt, Jason	M	11
Prof Emeritus	Runyan, William E.	D	10F,12C,12A
Asst Prof	Santinelli, Silvana		66A
Asst Prof	Seesholtz, John C.	D	61,39
Asst Prof	Sinaisky, Ilya	D	66C
Inst	Sletta, Lauren	M	33
Asst Prof	Sommer, Peter J.	M	46,47,64E
Asst Prof	Stanley, Michelle	D	64A
Asst Prof	Stewart, Leslie	M	62A,62B,38,11
Asst Prof	Stroman, Shilo	M	65
Asst Prof	Swindler, Wil J.	M	29,47,64E
Artist in Res	Taylor, Charles Edwin		61
Prof	Thaut, Michael H.	D	12F,33
Asst Prof	Thiem, Barbara	M	41,62C,42
Inst	Tomaszewski, Staci	M	50
Asst Prof	Torres, Adam A.	M	11
Asst Prof	Wilshusen, Nicole	M	33
Asst Prof	Yeager, Katherine	M	11

CO0275 Colorado State University-Pueblo
Department of Music
2200 Bonforte Blvd
Pueblo, CO 81001-4901
(719) 549-2552   Fax: (719) 549-2969
chass.colostate-pueblo.edu/music/
E-mail: jennifer.peters@colostate-pueblo.edu

4 Year Institution
Member of NASM

Chair: Jennifer Shadle-Peters, 80A

Artist in Res	Afanassieva, Veronika	M	62A,42,51
Artist in Res	Artmann, Mary	M	62C,42,51
Staff	Axworthy, Tamra	A	16
Adj Lect	Barto, Betsy	B	61,42
Artist in Res	Beck, Barbara Geiser	M	61,39,54,66C,42
Adj Lect	Cantu, Ben	M	70,41,42
Prof	Chi, Jacob	D	13,38,60B
Adj Lect	Creager, Greg	B	66A
Adj Lect	Crowe, Jason	B	62D,42
Artist in Res	DeLuca, Mike	M	13,64C,11,32
Artist in Res	Dobrotvorskaia, Ekaterina	M	62B,42,51
Artist in Res	Eastin, Brad	M	64E,48,46,47,64C
Artist in Res	Eberhardt, Allan	M	47,63A,46,49,29
Staff	Eickelman, Diane	B	66C,42
Adj Lect	Evans, Mathew J.	M	63B,11,13C,42
Artist in Res	Garibova, Karine	M	62A,42,51
Adj Lect	Hollingsworth, Dina L.	B	64A,64E,29,41,11
Prof	Hudson, Mark E.	D	11,32,60B
Assoc Prof	Ihm, Dana	D	36,40,47,60A
Prof Emeritus	Markowski, Victoria	B	66A,66D,41,42
Asst Prof	Mills, Alan W.	M	37,66A,63A,32E,60B
Staff	Moore, Dennis	B	71,72
Adj Lect	Pannunzio, Sam		66A,53,66D,47
Adj Lect	Plumer, Shirley	B	42,64D
Adj Lect	Quintanar, David		63C,42
Adj Lect	Reid, Nola	M	61,42
Adj Lect	Scott, Carla A.		64B,42
Assoc Prof	Shadle-Peters, Jennifer	D	12A,20,32,36,67
Artist in Res	Sizer, Todd	B	63D,10F,34,42
Artist in Res	Turner, Aaron	M	50,65A,65B,13,41
Adj Lect	Wilkinson, Wayne		70,47,41,42

CO0300 Community College of Aurora
Department of Music
16000 E CentreTech Pkwy
Aurora, CO 80011-9057
(303) 361-7425   Fax: (303) 361-7374
www.ccaurora.edu
E-mail: rich.italiano@ccaurora.edu

2 Year Institution

Coordinator: Richard Italiano, 80A
Chair, Humanities & Fine Arts: Ruthanne Orihuela, 80A

PT	Antony, Trent	B	65
PT	Canton, Jacky	B	64A
PT	Dadian, Clinton M.	M	70
PT	Ernardt, Eric	M	64
PT	Fahrion, Stacy	M	11,66A,66D
Inst	Italiano, Richard	M	13,10,11,66A,66D
PT	Johnson, Kerry	M	61,11
PT	Lewis, Cecil	M	47
PT	SchoederDorn, Jill	D	14
PT	Scott, Jennifer	M	62A,34

CO0350 Fort Lewis College
Department of Music
1000 Rim Dr
Durango, CO 81301
(970) 247-7377   Fax: (970) 247-7520
www.fortlewis.edu
E-mail: jetter_k@fortlewis.edu

4 Year Institution
Member of NASM

Dean: Maureen Brandon, 80A
Chair: Marc A. Reed, 80A

PT	Bara, Paul	M	63C
Assoc Prof	Campi-Walters, Lisa	D	13,12A,66,10A
Vstng Prof	Chiaravalloti, Charissa	D	36,40,60,12A,32D
Inst	Graham, Alta Elizabeth	D	13,10,12A
Assoc Prof	Jetter, Katherine	D	38,62C,62D,13,51
PT	Lambert, Nathan T.	M	10F,11,14C,42,51
Asst Prof	Latta, Jonathan R.	D	10F,47,50,65,20
PT	Livingston, Christi J.	B	66C
Prof Emeritus	Mack-Bervin, Linda	D	11,32D,36,60A
Prof Emeritus	Mann, Rochelle	D	10,11,32,64
PT	Olinger, Kathy A.	B	66C
Asst Prof	Reed, Marc A.	D	63A,63B,49
PT	Steele, Louis L.	M	70
PT	Turner, Veronica R.	M	61,13A,13B,13C,13D
Prof	Walters, Mark A.	D	60,11,48,37,64
PT	White, Richard H.	B	70

CO0400 Front Range Community College
Department of Music
3645 W 112th Ave
Westminster, CO 80030-2105
(303) 404-5590   Fax: (303) 404-2166
www.frontrange.edu
E-mail: kevin.garry@frontrange.edu

2 Year Institution

Chair: Kevin M. Garry, 80A

	Barber-McCurdy, Sarah	D	61
	Cline, James E.	D	70,11
Prof	Garry, Kevin M.	D	70,13A,11,12A,14C
Prof	Mastronicola, Michael	D	61,66A,66D
Inst	Mullins, Steve	D	70,11

CO0550 Metropolitan State Coll of Denver
Department of Music
CB 58
PO Box 173362
Denver, CO 80217-3362
(303) 556-3180   Fax: (303) 556-2714
www.mscd.edu/music
E-mail: music@mscd.edu

4 Year Institution
Member of NASM

Chair: Michael J. Kornelsen, 80A
Assistant Chair: Peter Schimpf, 80H

PT	Adams, Justin	M	66A,46
Asst Prof	Aguilar, Carla E.	PhD	32
PT	Allen, Michael	M	63D
Vstng Prof	Andres, Hoyt	D	13,10
PT	Andrew, Nancy	M	64A
PT	Angerhofer, Thomas Erik	M	61
FT	Bevan, Charla		
PT	Bland, Ronald	B	62D,70
PT	Camp, Marjorie	M	32
PT	Christin, Judith		61
PT	Christoph, Michael E.	M	64D
PT	Cook, Lisa M.	PhD	11,12A,20G,31A,14
PT	Cooper, Peter	M	65
PT	Devine, David	B	70
Vstng Prof	Dufford, Gregory	D	64C,32E
PT	Dupuy, Kathryn D.	M	64B
PT	Ellison, Sue	M	11
PT	Endsley, Gerald		37
PT	Farrell, David E.	D	10,13
PT	Flannery, Katie	M	11
PT	Foster, Mark	M	50,65,32E
PT	Friesen, Peter	M	66C,66D
PT	Garrison, Greg	M	62D
PT	George, Alexander	M	63B
Vstng Prof	Gibson, Joice Waterhouse	M	34B,34C,12A,12C,13A
PT	Gleason, Jeff	M	70
PT	Goldstein, Tamara B.	D	66A,66C,66B,42
PT	Hall, Bob		50
PT	Harris, Mark	B	64E
Vstng Prof	Hengst, Michael	D	63A,37
Asst Prof	Hess, Fred	D	11,13,29
PT	Hoffman, Matt		13C
PT	Jermance, Frank	M	35
PT	Kellogg, Hsing-ay	M	66A
PT	Kirchoff, Leanna	M	66D,13A
Asst Prof	Kish, David	D	37,32E,60B,32
PT	Komodore, Alex	M	70
Prof	Kornelsen, Michael J.	D	36
PT	Kraakevik, Kari	M	13B,13C
Vstng Asst Prof	Krueger, Mary Beth	M	54,61,66C,66D
PT	Krueger, Timothy	D	11
PT	LaQuatra, Jeff	M	70
PT	Lee, Charles	D	62C
Asst Prof	Leiter, Cherise D.	M	11,13,10
PT	Massey, LaDamion	B	36,47
Asst Prof	Matthews, Brandon Stephen	DMA	38,42,32E
Asst Prof	Miles, Ron	M	47,63A,29
Vstng Prof	Miller, R J		34A
PT	Mollenhauer, Shawn	D	20
PT	Pulido, Maria Fernanda Nieto	M	66D
Vstng Prof	Roberts, Gene	M	61
PT	Romaine, Paul	B	65,46
FT	Rooney, Matthew		
PT	Sandim, Carmen	M	29A,66D
PT	Sapegin, Judy	M	32
Asst Prof	Schimpf, Peter		12A
Vstng Prof	Schwarm-Glesner, Elizabeth	M	11
PT	Shannon, Nanette	D	66C,66D
PT	St. Clair, Collette	M	11
PT	Startsev, Mila		66C
PT	Stevens, Phillip	M	62B
FT	Taylor, Mark	B	
Vstng Prof	Thompson, Bradley	D	61
PT	Thompson, Michelle	M	61
PT	Watson, Bradley	M	62A
Prof	Worster, Larry	D	12
PT	Wright, Trudi Ann	PhD	11
PT	Young, Sam	B	13C

CO0560 Naropa University
Department of Music
2130 Arapahoe Ave
Boulder, CO 80302-6602
(303) 444-0202   Fax: (303) 444-0410
www.naropa.edu
E-mail: enapodano@naropa.edu

4 Year Liberal Arts Institution

Chair: Mark Miller, 80A

Prof	Douglas, Bill	M	13,11,12A,36,66A
Asst Prof	Feder, Janet	B	10,70,12A,13A,53
Lect	Houlihan, Mickey		34D,35G
Lect	Kabir, Chaitanya Mahmud	M	20A,31C,20B,20C,20E
Assoc Prof	Miller, Mark	MFA	29,13A,41,47,64A
Lect	Rolle, Nina	B	11,35H
Lect	Stewart, Jon	B	13
Prof	Sussuma, Robert	M	36,55D

CO0600 Northeastern Junior College
Department of Music
100 College Ave
Sterling, CO 80751
(970) 521-6671   Fax: (970) 522-4945
www.njc.edu
E-mail: Celeste.Delgado@njc.edu

2 Year Institution

Dean: Scott Thompson, 80A

PT	Abernathy, Kristina	M	61
Inst	Delgado-Pelton, Celeste	M	13,11,34,36,47
PT	Fennell, Arden		70
PT	Fetzer, Elsie J.	M	36
PT	Lippstrew, Lee		46,34D,35G,35A
PT	Smith, Mary L.		66A

CO0625 Red Rocks Community College
Department of Visual & Perf. Arts
Music Program
13300 W 6th Ave
Lakewood, CO 80228-1255
(303) 914-6428   Fax: (303) 914-6285
www.rrcc.edu
E-mail: stephanie.berg@rrcc.edu

2 Year Institution

Music Program Chair: Stephanie Berg Oram, 80A

Inst PT	Baker, Hill	M	14C,20,65,34B
Prof	Berg Oram, Stephanie	DMA	11,12A,61,34B
Inst PT	Bigelow, Ira	D	11,34B
Inst PT	Cullison, Jonathan	M	62D,10D
Inst PT	Dashevskaya, Olga	M	11,13A,66A,13B
Inst PT	Dorris, Jennifer	M	11,34B
Inst PT	Fouse, Jennifer	M	62C
Inst PT	Jurkscheit, Robert	M	65
Inst PT	Kennedy, P. Kevin	M	61,60,12A,66
Inst PT	LaQuatra, Jeff	M	70
Inst PT	Lucas, Michael	M	37,47,64C
Inst PT	Mongrain, Richard	M	37,47
Inst PT	Paulson, Brent	B	63A,63,64,37
Inst PT	Schulkind, Laura	M	64A
Inst PT	Studinger, Bob	D	11,10,13
Inst PT	Tapia, Doug	B	34,34A,34D,34B
Inst PT	Thayer, Katherine	M	62A,62B

CO0650 Regis University
Department of Fine & Perf. Arts
3333 Regis Blvd
Denver, CO 80221-1154
(303) 964-3609   Fax: (303) 964-5110
www.regis.edu/music
E-mail: mdavenpo@regis.edu

4 Year Institution

Chair: Barbara J. Coleman, 80A
Director, Music Program: Mark Davenport, 80A

PT	Ailshie, Tyson	M	62D
PT	Bartels, Justin	B	63A
PT	Beeson, Catherine	M	62B
PT	Bierhaus, Sarah	D	64B
PT	Cline, James	D	70
Assoc Prof	Davenport, Mark	D	12,55,67C,29A,14C
PT	Ebert, Brian	M	64C
PT	Helble, Mitch	M	70
PT	Hubert, John	M	61
PT	Julyan, Robyn	M	62A
Asst Prof	Kirschstein, Natalie	D	11,20,13A
PT	Koenigberg, Rebecca Anne	D	61,11,54
PT	Lee, Charles	D	62C,41,51,10F,60
PT	Lee, Richard A.	D	66A
PT	Lepke-Sims, Barbara	M	62E
Asst Prof	Notareschi, Loretta K.	D	10,11,13
Emeritus PT	Reyes, Ysmael	M	64A,41,48
PT	Riggs, Ben	M	36
PT	Sabatella, Marc	M	66A,47
Emeritus PT	Segal, Rachel	M	62A
PT	Shannon, Nanette	D	66A,41,66D
PT	Strickland, Caitlin	M	66C
PT	Wollan, Barbara	B	61,36

CO0750 United States Air Force Academy
Fairchild Hall
USAF Academy, CO 80840
(719) 333-2019   Fax: (719) 333-3932
www.usafa.af.mil

4 Year Institution

Department Head: Katherine Harrington, 80A

Inst	Fawcett-Yeske, Maxine	D	11,12,14,16,20
Assoc Prof	Reagan, Ann B.	D	11,12A,12,41,66A

CO0800 Univ of Colorado-Boulder
College of Music
301 UCB
Boulder, CO 80309-0301
(303) 492-6352   Fax: (303) 492-5619
www.colorado.edu/music
E-mail: gradmusc@colorado.edu

4 Year Institution, Graduate School
Member of NASM

Master of Music in Collaborative Piano, Master of Music in Composition, Master of Music in Music Theory, Master of Music in Performance, Master of Music in Conducting, Master of Music Education, PhD in Music Education, DMA in Composition, DMA in Performance, DMA in Performance & Pedagogy, DMA in Choral Literature & Conducting, PhD in Musicology, Master of Music in Music Literature, DMA in Jazz Studies, Master of Music in Performance & Pedagogy, DMA in Instrumental Conducting, DMA in Collaborative Piano

Dean: Daniel Sher, 80A
Associate Dean, Undergraduate Studies: James R. Austin, 80B
Associate Dean, Graduate Studies & Dir., Summer Programs: Steven Bruns, 80C,80G
Assistant Dean, Recruitment & Outreach: Frederick Peterbark, 80D,80H
Dir., Concerts & Cultural Program: Joan McLean Braun, 80F
Associate Dean, Administration: John S. Davis, 80H

Directory of Institutions

Prof	Austin, James R.	D	32
Asst Prof	Bahn, Lina	D	62A
Assoc Prof	Berg, Margaret Haefner	D	32
Inst	Biggs, Dana M.	D	37,32E
Asst Prof	Bird-Arvidsson, Jennifer	M	61
Assoc Prof	Brody, James	M	11,64B
Assoc Prof	Bruns, Steven	D	13
Asst Prof	Burcham, Joel	D	61
Assoc Prof	Caballero, Carlo	D	12
Assoc Prof	Carthy, Nicholas	DIPL	39,54
Inst	Chang, Phillip	D	13
Senior Inst	Cloutier, Robert F.	B	66F
Prof Emerita	Conlon, Joan C.	D	60,36
Inst	Cooper, Peter	B	64B
Prof	Cooperstock, Andrew	D	66A
Lect	Corbus, Dave	B	29A
Assoc Prof	Cremaschi, Alejandro M.	D	66D,66A,66B
Assoc Prof	Davis, John S.	D	47,29,29A,63A
Inst	Drumheller, John	D	29
Assoc Prof	Dunn, J. Michael	M	63D
Artist in Res	Dusinberre, Edward	DIPL	41
Assoc Prof	Eckert, Erika	B	51,62B
Prof Emeritus	Endo, Akira	M	38,60
Assoc Prof	Erhard, Paul	D	11,62D
Prof	Farr, Elizabeth	D	55,66G,66H
Artist in Res	Fejer, Andras	DIPL	62C,41
Asst Prof	Gemmell, Jeffrey S.	D	36,32D,60A
Assoc Prof	Gentry, Gregory R.	DMA	36,60A
Prof	Glyde, Judith	M	11,51,62C
Assoc Prof	Goode, Bradley	M	63A,29A,29B
Assoc Prof	Gunther, John	D	29,45
Prof	Guralnick, Elissa	D	12C
Inst	Harbison, Kevin	B	35G
Lect	Harriman, Janet K.	M	62E
Asst Prof	Heil, Leila T.	D	32D
Asst Prof	Holman, Leigh	D	39,61
Lect	Hsu, Hsing Ay	M	66A
Prof	Ishikawa, Yoshiyuki	D	64D
Lect	Jenkins, Jeff C.	B	29
Asst Prof	Jennings, Christina	D	64A
Assoc Prof	Keister, Jay	D	12
Lect	Keister, Mami Itasaka		20C
Lect	Keller, James		36
Assoc Prof	Kellogg, Daniel	D	10A,10F
Prof	Korevaar, David J.	DMA	66A
Lect	Lasmawan, I. Made		20
Prof	Lehnert, Doris Pridonoff	DIPL	66A
Prof Emeritus	Lehnert, Oswald	DIPL	51,62A,62B
Assoc Prof	Leong, Daphne	D	13,10
Prof	Lewis, Gary J.	M	60B,38
Inst	Lin, Hsaio-Ling	M	66C
Asst Prof	Malin, Yonatan	PhD	13,12
Assoc Prof	Maloy, Rebecca	D	12
Prof	Mason, Patrick		61
Asst Prof	McDonald, Margaret	D	66C
Prof	McMurray, Allan R.	M	60,37
Inst	Miller, Paul V.	D	13
Assoc Prof	Miranda, Martina	D	32
Assoc Prof	Moteki, Mutsumi	D	61
Senior Inst	Mueller, Ronald	B	54
Assoc Prof	Myer, Tom	M	47,64E
Asst Prof	Nguyen, Alexandra	D	66C
Asst Prof	Nytch, Jeffrey C.	D	35A
Asst Prof	Okigbo, Austin	D	31F,20,14
Asst Prof	Pann, Carter N.	D	13,10
Assoc Prof	Peterson, Patti	D	61
Asst Prof	Rickels, David A.	D	32C,32E,32F,32G,32H
Prof	Riis, Thomas L.	D	12,20G
Lect	Rodriguez, Francisco		70
Asst Prof	Roeder, Matthew J.	D	37,32E,60B
Lect	Romaine, Paul	B	65
Assoc Prof	Romero, Brenda M.	D	14
Assoc Prof	Sampsel, Laurie	D	16
Assoc Prof	Sawchuk, Terry M.	M	49,63A
Artist in Res	Schranz, Karoly	DIPL	62A,41
Prof	Sher, Daniel	D	66A
Assoc Prof	Silver, Daniel	M	64C
Prof	Simson, Julie	M	61
Assoc Prof	Smith, Jeremy L.	D	12
Inst	Spera, Nicolo	M	70
Prof Emeritus	Spillman, Robert	M	66A,39
Assoc Prof	Stanley, Bill J.	D	13A,13,63C
Assoc Prof	Theodore, Michael	D	45,34,10
Assoc Prof	Thornton, Michael	B	63B
Prof Emeritus	Toensing, Richard E.	D	13,10,45
Prof	Walter, Douglas		65
Artist in Res	Walther, Geraldine E.		42,62B
Prof	Waters, Keith	D	13
Asst Prof	Wetherbee, Charles	B	62A
Inst	Zemliauskas, Christopher	D	39,61,54

CO0810 Univ of Colorado-Colorado Springs
Department of Music
420 Austin Bluffs Pkwy
PO Box 7150
Colorado Springs, CO 80933-7150
(719) 262-3563   Fax: (719) 262-3146
www.uccs.edu
E-mail: csmith@brain.uccs.edu

4 Year Institution

Chair: Suzanne MacAulay, 80A
Director: Glen Whitehead, 80A

	MacAulay, Suzanne	D	
Lect	Malone, William	M	64E,64C,64A,29A,20
Lect	Rigler, Jane		64A,10B,34D,10
Lect	Skidgel, Sharon		
Inst	Smith, Curtis F.	M	13,34D,36,66A
Asst Prof	Whitehead, Glen	D	63A,47,29,45

CO0830 Univ of Colorado Denver
Music & Entertainment Industry Studies
Campus Box 162
PO Box 173364
Denver, CO 80217-3364
(303) 556-2279   Fax: (303) 556-6612

www.ucdenver.edu/academics/colleges/CAM/programs/meis/Pages/index.aspx
E-mail: start@ucdenver.edu

4 Year Institution
Member of NASM

Chair: Judith A. Coe, 80A
Associate Chair: Frank J. Jermance, 80H

PT	Bigelow, Ira	D	11
PT	Bingham, James	D	35A
PT	Bland, Ron	B	47,62D
PT	Bodaubay, Dina	M	66A,66D
Asst Prof	Bondelevitch, David	M	35C,35D,35G
Asst Prof	Bregitzer, Lorne	M	35C,35D,35G
PT	Buchwald, Peter	M	35C,35D,35G
PT	Buss, Gary	M	11
Assoc Prof	Clark, William F.	M	47,63D,13,49,29
Assoc Prof	Coe, Judith A.	DMA	61,10D,34,14C,12C
PT	Cullison, Jon	M	13,45
Asst Prof	Daniels, Chris	M	35A,29A
Inst	Desai, Nayantara	M	66A,66C,66D
PT	Devine, Dave	M	11
Inst	Ellingson, Peter	M	66,13C,29
Inst	Evans, Lorraine	M	12C
Asst Prof	Gaston, Leslie	M	35C,35D,35G
Asst Prof	Gloor, Storm	M	35A
Inst	Hackel, Erin H.	D	36,13,11,10D
Inst	Hauger, Karin	M	11,13,36
Assoc Prof	Jermance, Frank J.	M	35A
PT	Johnson, Fred	M	35G
PT	Keeble, Carson	M	63C,63D
PT	Kortz, Owen	M	61,10D
Inst	Krause, Douglas	M	13A,11,35A,35B,35C
PT	Lancaster, Michael	M	11
PT	Leder, Matthew D.	M	63A
PT	Levinson, Drew	M	35G
Asst Prof	McGowan, Sean C.	D	13A,13B,13C,13E,29B
Asst Prof	McGuire, Samuel A.	M	35C,35D,35G
PT	Merkel, Jeffrey	M	35C,35D,35G
PT	Moreland, Irina	D	66A,11,12A
Inst	Morell, Drew		70,47,62D
Asst Prof	Musso, Paul J.	M	70,47,53,13A
PT	Neal, Tira	M	35G
PT	Park-Song, Sophia	D	11,13,66A
Inst	Reid, Todd		11,20,29,65
PT	Roberts, Gene	M	61,10D
PT	Schwindt, Dan	M	13C,70
PT	Selter, Scott	M	35G
Inst	Soich, Leslie	M	36,13,11,10D
PT	Soifer, Tyler	M	35G
Assoc Prof	Soocher, Stan	D	35A
PT	Storyk, John	M	35G
PT	Stup, Chris	M	35A,35C,35D,35F
PT	Terkeek, Karen	M	62C
Inst	Tietjen, Linda	M	12C
Inst	Van Schoick, Thomas	M	65
Prof	Walker, Gregory T. S.	D	11,62A,20G,62B,46
Inst	Weng, Pamela	M	13,11,12A,66A
PT	White, Andrew	M	35C
PT	Wright, Bron	M	63C,63D
	Wright, Trudi Ann	PhD	11
Inst	Yamamoto, Travis S.	M	66A,11,13C

CO0900 Univ of Denver
Lamont School of Music
Trevorrow Hall
2344 E Iliff Ave
Denver, CO 80208
(303) 871-6400   Fax: (303) 871-3118
www.du.edu/ahss/schools/lamont/index.html
E-mail: nancy.cochran@du.edu

4 Year Institution, Graduate School
Member of NASM

Master of Music in Suzuki Pedagogy, Master of Arts in Music Education, Master of Arts in Music Theory, Master of Music in Composition, Master of Music in Performance, Master of Music in Conducting, Master of Arts in History & Literature, Master of Music in Piano Pedagogy

Director: Nancy Cochran, 80A
Dir., Admissions: Jerrod J. Price, 80D
Assistant Director: John J. Sheinbaum, 80H

Prof	Baker, Malcolm Lynn	M	47,53,46,29
Inst PT	Ball, Thomas J.	M	63C
Prof	Banducci, Antonia L.	D	12A,12,12C
Inst PT	Bardill, Sara	M	61
Assoc Prof	Bouton, Arthur E.	M	48,64E,41
Inst PT	Brantigan, Kathleen		63D
Inst PT	Brozna, Caitlin	M	
Inst PT	Cahill, Susan	M	62D
Inst PT	Cognata, Chad	B	64D
Prof	Cox, Kenneth	M	39,61,54
Inst PT	Deck, Warren	B	63D
Lect FT	Emerich, Kate	M	61,40
Inst PT	Endsley, Pamela	M	64A
Inst PT	Flemming, Kyle	D	36
Inst PT	Galema, Joseph M.	D	66G
Assoc Prof	Genova, David	M	66A,66B
Assoc Prof	Gertig, Suzanne	M	62E,16,12
Assoc Prof	Glenn, Larry M.	M	39,61,54
Prof	Golan, Lawrence	D	60,38
Inst PT	Gunnson, Eric	M	29,66A
Inst PT	Hanson, David	M	66A,29,35B,10A,10C
Inst PT	Hill, Bill	D	10
Assoc Prof	Hood, Alan	M	63A,29
Prof	Iznaola, Ricardo	M	70,41
Inst PT	Jinkling-Lens, Carol	M	69
Inst PT	Jorgenson, Jeri	M	62A
Inst PT	Joseph, Alan		70,47
Lect PT	Kasch, Catherine Loraine	M	61,40
Inst PT	Kehn, Conrad	M	13,43
Inst PT	Kinzie, John	M	50,65
Inst PT	Kirchoff, Leanna		10A
Prof	Kireilis, Ramon J.	D	11
Inst PT	Knight, Katharine	M	62C,41
Inst	Leathwood, Heidi Brende	M	
Lect FT	Leathwood, Jonathan		70,41,13D,10A,13E
Assoc Prof	Malloy, Chris	D	10,13
Inst PT	Marlier, Mike	M	65B,53,29
Assoc Prof	Martin, Joseph	D	37,63C,63D,41,60
Prof	Mayer, Steven	D	66A,66B
Inst PT	McCullough, Susan	M	63B
Inst PT	Miller, Thomas	M	65
Assoc Prof	Montano, David R.	D	66A,66B,66D,32
Asst Prof	Morelli, Sarah	D	14
Inst PT	Ramsey, James	D	36
Asst Prof	Reynolds, Jeremy W.	D	64C,33,13C,13H
Lect FT	Rybak, Alice	B	66A,66C
Inst PT	Sabatella, Marc	M	13,29B
Assoc Prof	Sailor, Catherine		36,60
Inst	Schulze, Michael	D	35C,35D,35G
Assoc Prof	Sheinbaum, John J.	M	12,13E,11,12A
Prof	Slavich, Richard	M	12A,51,62C,41
Inst PT	Spring, Kathleen	M	62A
Asst Prof	Taavola, Kristin	D	13,13H,13C
Inst PT	Tarr, Carol		62C
Inst PT	Twitty, Katrina	M	61
Inst PT	Vendryes, Basil	M	62B
Inst PT	Von Foerster, Richard	M	13
Inst PT	Walker, Kenneth	M	62D,29
Assoc Prof	Wang, Linda	M	62A,41,42
Inst PT	Whang, Yumi	M	62A
Inst PT	Wickham, Donna	M	29,61

CO0950 Univ of Northern Colorado
School of Music
501 20th St
PO Box 28
Greeley, CO 80639
(970) 351-2993   Fax: (970) 351-1923
www.arts.unco.edu
E-mail: valerie.anderson@unco.edu

4 Year Institution, Graduate School
Member of NASM

Master of Music in Collaborative Piano, Master of Music in Composition, Master of Music in Performance, Master of Music in Conducting, Master of Music in Music Education, Master of Music in History & Literature, Doctorate of Arts in Music, Master of Music in Jazz Studies, Doctorate of Arts in Music Education

Director: H. David Caffey, 80A
Dean: Andrew Svedlow, 80A
Coord., Graduate Music Studies: Robert Ehle, 80C
Assistant Dean: Vergie Amendola, 80H
Associate Director: Charles Hansen, 80H

Asst Prof	Adler, John	DMA	63A,49
Adj	Alexander, Eric		13B,13C,10,13
Prof	Amendola, Vergie	M	66A,66C
Asst Prof	Applegate, Erik	M	29,47
Prof	Barrier, Gray	M	50,65,32E
Prof	Bellman, Jonathan	D	12
Prof	Bolden-Taylor, Diane	M	61
Inst	Brooks, Ronald M.	D	63A
Inst	Brown, Alise	D	32B
Asst Prof	Burleson, Jill	D	60A,36,32D
Assoc Prof	Byrnes, Jason	D	63D,32
Prof	Caffey, H. David	M	29
Assoc Prof	Dahlke, Andrew	D	64E,48
Prof	Darrough, Galen P.	D	60A,36,32D
Inst	Dickensheets, Janice	D	12,34A,14,12B,12A
Prof	Ehle, Robert	D	13,10,13L
Asst Prof	Elwood, Paul	D	10,13
Asst Prof	Faganel, Gal	D	62C,42,35G,51
Prof	Fuchs, Richard	M	62A
Inst	Fuller, Matthew	M	29
	Glen, Nancy L.	D	63B,32B
Prof	Guyver, Russell	D	60B,38
Prof	Hansen, Charles	D	64D
Asst Prof	Harris, Caleb	M	66A,66C
Assoc Prof	Haun, Errol	D	66A,66B
Inst	Heimbecker, Sara	M	12A,11,13A,14C
Assoc Prof	Hesse, Marian	D	63B,49
Inst	Hinkie, William H.	M	32E
Prof	Kauffman, Deborah	D	12A,12C
Inst	Kovalcheck, Steve	M	29
Prof	Landry, Dana	M	29,66A,47
Assoc Prof	Luedloff, Brian Clay	M	39
Prof	Luttmann, Stephen	M	16,12C
Prof	Malde, Melissa	D	61
Assoc Prof	Manring, Lesley	M	61
Prof	Mayne, Richard	D	32E,37
Prof	Mills, Charlotte	D	32,66D
Assoc Prof	Montemayor, Mark	D	32
Prof	Moore, Kathy Bundock	D	62E,13B,13C,13E
Inst	Olson, Jason	M	70
Asst Prof	Reddick, Carissa	D	13
Inst	Rush, Tobias	D	13B,13C,13A
Inst	Sapegin, Judith	M	32B
Prof	Singleton, Kenneth	D	60B,37
Inst	Smith, Michael	M	13A,32,32H
Inst	Throgmorton, Debra	M	66H
Inst	Vaughn, James	B	62D
Asst Prof	Weng, Lei	M	66
Assoc Prof	White, James	M	29,47,65
Prof	Wickham, Nathaniel	D	63C,49,63D
Assoc Prof	Wilson, William	M	61

CO1050 Western State College
Department of Music
Quigley Hall
Gunnison, CO 81231
(970) 943-3054   Fax: (970) 943-2329
www.western.edu
E-mail: mviolett@western.edu

4 Year Institution
Member of NASM

Chair: John M. Wacker, 80A

Directory of Institutions

Prof	Barrett, Robert H.	D	11,47,64,34,29
Lect	Belgiovane, Alicia	M	32D
Lect	Cook, Amanda B.	M	
Prof Emeritus	Kincaid, John	M	49
Lect	Koepsel, Keith	M	32B
Asst Prof	Roberson, Heather D.	D	61,36,11,60A,32D
Lect	Thompson, Amanda	M	65,50
Vstng Prof	Todd, Kenneth W.	M	11,38,51,62
Prof	Violett, Martha Watson	D	11,12,66
Asst Prof	Wacker, John M.	D	60,63,37,49,32E
Lect	Weidman-Winter, Becky	M	64A,41,13

CT0050 Central Connecticut State Univ

Department of Music
1615 Stanley St
New Britain, CT 06050
(860) 832-2912   Fax: (860) 832-2902
www.music.ccsu.edu
E-mail: menochec@ccsu.edu

4 Year Institution, Graduate School
Member of NASM

Master of Science in Music Education

Chair: Charles Paul Menoche, 80A
Dir., Graduate Studies & Summer Programs: Carlotta Parr, 80C,80G
Dean, School of Arts & Sciences: Susan Pease

Lect PT	Adam, Nathaniel	D	13B,13C
Lect PT	Aquino, Diane	M	61,13C
Lect PT	Casey-Nelson, Colleen Mary	M	32
Lect PT	Cheng, Susan	M	66A,66D
Lect PT	Coghlan, Connie	M	65,50
Prof	D'Addio, Daniel F.	DMA	13,32,37,49,63A
Lect PT	Eagleson, Ian	D	20
Lect PT	Fagerburg, Karin	M	62A,62B
Lect PT	Ferrebee, Sarah	B	32B,32C,32D
Lect PT	Fischer, Kenneth	M	66A
Lect PT	Gareau, Larry	M	63,29A
Lect PT	Getter, Joseph	M	14
Lect PT	Gibson, Walter	B	63D
Lect PT	Goldstein, Rich	B	70
Lect PT	Heavner, Tabitha	M	11,13A
Asst Prof	Heller, Lauren B.	D	37,32E,60B,64A
Lect PT	Homann, J. Oliver	M	64B
Assoc Prof	Kershner, Brian	D	10,13,64D
Lect PT	Klein, Benjamin	M	34
Assoc Prof	Knox, Carl	D	64E,29A,46,47
Asst Prof	Kramer, Keith A.	D	13,34
Lect PT	Kumme, Karl	M	32B,32E
Lect PT	Labadorf, Tom	M	64C,48
Lect PT	Ladd, Christopher	M	70
Prof	Laurent, Linda	D	13,12,66A,66D,42
Lect PT	Logan, Christopher	M	63C
Lect PT	Lorenzo, Elizabeth	D	12,11,15,12A
Lect PT	Mast, Murray	M	13A
Lect PT	Maurer-Davis, Jill	M	64A,48
Lect PT	Melito, Tom	M	47
Assoc Prof	Menoche, Charles Paul	DMA	10,12,13,34
Lect PT	Northrop, Jonathan	D	13A,13B,13C,13E
Prof	Parr, Carlotta	D	32A,32B,32C,36,32G
Lect PT	Paxton-Mierzejewski, Adele	M	61
Prof	Perry, Pamela J.	D	32B,32C,36,32D,60A
Lect PT	Pott, Jack	B	61
Prof	Ribchinsky, Julie C.	M	13A,13C,62C,11,38
Lect PT	Roberts, Vera	M	66D
Lect PT	Rosa, Gerard	M	11,62A,12A
Lect PT	Scattergood, Joanne	M	61
Lect PT	Schuttenhelm, Thomas	M	11,13,70,34
Lect PT	Solomon, William	M	32F
Lect PT	Spaulding, Susan	M	63B
Lect PT	Tyler, Edward	M	36
Lect PT	Wiseman, Roy	D	62D

CT0100 Connecticut College

Department of Music
270 Mohegan Ave
New London, CT 06320-4196
(860) 439-2720   Fax: (860) 439-5382
music.conncoll.edu
E-mail: metho@conncoll.edu

4 Year Institution

Chair: Margaret E. Thomas, 80A
Dir., Arts Programming: Robert Richter, 80F

Prof	Althouse, Paul L.	D	11,60A,12A,36
Prof	Anthony, John P.	D	13A,11,12A,66D,66G
Inst Adj	Brown, Thomas	M	63C
Asst Prof Adj	Buttery, Gary	M	63D,37,47
Assoc Prof Emeritus	Church, Frank V.		62C
Vstng Asst Prof	Clark, John	D	11,13,29
Inst Adj	Doughty, Heather	M	63B
Asst Prof Adj	Dygert, James	M	64E
Prof Adj	Harper, Patricia	M	64A
Vstng Inst	Jackson, James	M	38
Asst Prof Adj	Jarvis, Peter	B	65,50
Asst Prof Adj	Johnson, Victor	B	63C
Assoc Prof	Kreiger, Arthur V.	D	13,35C,10,45,34
Asst Prof Adj	Labadorf, Thomas	M	64C
Inst Adj	Lee, Daniel	M	62A,62B
Asst Prof Adj	McCormick, Mark	M	62D
Assoc Prof Adj	McNeish, James	M	70,35C
Inst Adj	Newman, Patrice	M	66A
Asst Prof Adj	Noreen, Rebecca	M	64D
Asst Prof Adj	Ogano, Kumi	M	66A
Asst Prof	Seto, Mark	D	11,12,13A,13C,38
Assoc Prof Adj	Skernick, Linda	M	66H
Asst Prof Adj	Svedaite-Waller, Jurate	M	61
Inst Adj	Talmadge, Samantha	M	61,32
Assoc Prof	Thomas, Margaret E.	D	13,11,12C
Vstng Inst	Torrenti, John	M	66A,66G
Assoc Prof Adj	Van Cleve, Libby	D	64B
Asst Prof	Wilson, James Dale	D	14,20C,12A,12E,29B
Inst Adj	Wong, Y. Alvin	M	62C
Asst Prof Adj	Zhdanovskikh, Maksim	D	61

CT0150 Eastern Connecticut State Univ

Music Program
83 Windham St
Willimantic, CT 06226-2211
(860) 465-5325   Fax: (860) 465-5764
www.easternct.edu
E-mail: raymondla@easternct.edu

4 Year Institution

Dean: Carmen Cid, 80A
Chair: David Pellegrini, 80A

Asst Prof	Ashe, Jennifer	D	11,61
PT	Balough, Teresa	D	20G
Assoc Prof	Belles, David	D	36,40,60,61
Asst Prof	Calissi, Jeff L.	D	37,65B,11
Assoc Prof	Cornicello, Anthony	D	10,34,13,34D,13F
PT	Dina, James L.	M	70
Prof	Hwang, Okon	D	14,66,11,12,13
Assoc Prof	Jones-Bamman, Richard	D	11,14,32,20
Prof	Lemons, Robert M.	D	11,60,32,63A

CT0200 Gateway Community Technical Coll

Department of Music-LWC
60 Sargent Dr
New Haven, CT 06511-5918
(203) 285-2197   Fax: (203) 285-2087
www.gwctc.commnet.edu
E-mail: gw_salyer@commnet.edu

2 Year Institution

Director: Douglas W. Salyer, 80A
Chair, Humanities & Fine Arts: Chester Schnepf, 80A

Prof	Salyer, Douglas W.	D	13,34,12A,36,66

CT0240 Hartford College for Women-UH

Department of Music
1265 Asylum Ave
Hartford, CT 06105-2200
(860) 768-5657   Fax: (860) 768-5693
E-mail: harvey@mail.hartford.edu

2 Year Institution

Director: Peter J. Harvey, 80A

Assoc Prof	Harvey, Peter J.	D	13,12A,36,54,20G

CT0246 Mitchell College
Department of Music
437 Pequot Ave
New London, CT 06320
(860) 701-5000
www.mitchell.edu
E-mail: odonnell_j@mitchell.edu

4 Year Institution

Prof	O'Donnell, Jennifer M.	M	

CT0250 Quinnipiac College
Department of Music
275 Mount Carmel Ave
Hamden, CT 06518
(203) 582-8783
www.quinnipiac.edu
E-mail: luis.arata@quinnipiac.edu

2 Year Institution

PT	Congo, John R.	M	11
Prof	Costanzo, Samuel R.	M	13,11,29A
PT	DeQuattro, Anthony		11,12A
PT	Dickson, Douglas R.	M	11
PT	Landolfi, Dominic J.		70
PT	McEachern, Peter J.		47
PT	Pasqua, Ferdinand A.	D	11
PT	Rossomando, Fred E.		36,11

CT0300 Sacred Heart University
Department of Music
5151 Park Ave
Fairfield, CT 06432-1023
(203) 371-7735   Fax: (203) 365-7634
www.sacredheart.edu
E-mail: music@sacredheart.edu

4 Year Institution, Introductory Courses Only

Director: Joseph Carter, 80A

Inst Adj	Ahlers, Ruth	B	64A,64E
Inst Adj	Andreas, Cassandra	B	61
Inst Adj	Boughton, Janet	B	51,62,41
Inst Adj	Carter, Joseph	M	70,29A,20G,20H,47
Inst Adj	Connolly, Damien	B	20F
Inst Adj	Finley, William	M	61,31A
Inst Adj	Gates, Giacomo	B	61
Inst Adj	Hartley, Brian	M	70
Inst Adj	Johnston, Keith	M	37,63C,63D
Inst Adj	Kolar, Andrew	M	37,65
Inst Adj	Lin, Hui-Mei	D	66A
Inst Adj	Lorenzo, Elizabeth	M	11
Inst Adj	Mazer, Susan	B	13A,13B,13C
Inst Adj	Meyers, Angela	M	66A,11
Inst Adj	Michniewicz, John T.	DMA	36
Inst Adj	Reis, Marzo	M	20G,20H
Inst Adj	Stanley, Justin	D	64C
Inst Adj	Tate, Galen	M	11,35
Inst Adj	Utterback, Joe	D	12A,20G,29A

CT0350 St Joseph College
Department of Fine & Perf Arts
1678 Asylum Ave
W Hartford, CT 06117-2764
(203)232-4571   Fax: (203)233-5695
www.sjc.edu
E-mail: dkeller@sjc.edu

4 Year Institution

Chair: Dorothy Keller, 80A

Adj PT	Brown, Adrianne	M	66A,66B,66C,66D
PT	Cinquegrani, David	M	31A,36,41,12
Adj PT	Giardina, David	B	62,70
PT	Murphy, Susan	M	52

CT0450 Southern Connecticut State Univ
Department of Music
501 Crescent St
New Haven, CT 06515-1355
(203) 392-6625   Fax: (203) 392-6637
www.southernct.edu
E-mail: irvingj2@southernct.edu

4 Year Institution

Acting Chair: Richard A. Gerber, 80A

Inst Adj	Brown-Clayton, Janet	M	36
Asst Prof	Chevan, David	D	11,12A,47,53,29
Inst Adj	Cimino, Matthew	M	61
Inst Adj	Dubowchik, Rosemary	D	11,12A
Prof Adj	Gelineau, Phyllis	D	13A,11
Asst Prof	Gemme, Terese	D	13A,12A,36,66G
Inst Adj	Getter, Joseph	M	11,14
Inst Adj	Johnson, Clifford		11
Inst Adj	Kirsch, Gary	D	37
Asst Prof	Kuss, Mark	D	13,10,45,66A,34
Inst Adj	May, Juliana	M	11,13
Inst Adj	Peterson, Kirsten	D	11
Assoc Prof	Russell, Tilden	D	11,12A,12,41
Inst Adj	Scott, Stanley	D	11,14
Inst Adj	Senedak, Irene	M	66D
Inst Adj	Skelton, Neal	M	70
Inst Adj	Snyder, David	D	11,13
	Stutzman, Walter J.		

CT0500 Trinity College
Department of Music
300 Summit St
Hartford, CT 06106-3100
(860) 297-5122   Fax: (860) 297-5380
www.trincoll.edu
E-mail: pkennedy@trincoll.edu

4 Year Institution

Chair & Dir., Artist Series: Eric A. Galm, 80A,80F

Vstng Lect	Allen, Kristopher	M	47,29A
Inst	Curran, Nancy A.	M	42,66A,66H
Assoc Prof	Galm, Eric A.	D	14,20,20H,50,65
Inst	Melson, Christine	M	13A,13C,36,66C
Prof	Moshell, Gerald	D	60,12A,54
Prof	Platoff, John	D	13,11,14C,12,12F
Asst Prof	Roman, Dan	D	34,70,10A,10F,13
Adj Prof	Rose, John	B	36,66G,69,31A
Prof	Woldu, Gail Hilson	D	11,14C,12A,15

CT0550 Univ of Bridgeport
Department of Music
Arnold Bernhard Ctr
Bridgeport, CT 06601
(203) 576-4407
www.bridgeport.edu
E-mail: jjohnson@bridgeport.edu

4 Year Institution

Master of Science in Music Education

Director: Jeffrey Johnson, 80A

	Arcamone, Dan		70
Adj	Coogan, Chris	B	29,66,47
Adj	DeQuattro, Anthony	M	29A
Adj	Fay, Terrence		63C
Adj	Freas, Thomas	M	63A,35A
Adj	Goetz, Michael	M	62D
Adj	Hannon-Roberts, Emilie	B	61
Adj	Harris, Bill	B	64E,64C
Adj	Interlandi, Silvio	M	62C
Prof	Johnson, Jeffrey	D	10,11,12,13
Adj	Jones, Jeffrey	M	65
Adj	McLafferty, Tim		65
Adj	Schneider, Brandt	M	32
Adj	Smith, Aron	M	66A
Adj	Trapp, Ken	M	32
Adj	Weidlich, Richard	D	61

CT0600 Univ of Connecticut
Department of Music - U-1012
1295 Storrs Rd
Storrs, CT 06269-1012
(860) 486-3728   Fax: (860) 486-3796
www.music.uconn.edu
E-mail: music@uconn.edu

4 Year Institution, Graduate School
Member of NASM

Master of Arts in Historical Musicology, Master of Arts in Music Theory, Master of Music in Performance, DMA in Conducting, DMA in Performance, PhD in History & Music Theory

Chair: Catherine Jarjisian, 80A
Dean: David G. Woods, 80A
Dir., Undergraduate Studies: Peter Kaminsky, 80B
Dir., Graduate Studies: Eric N. Rice, 80C
Dir., Recital Hall: Krik Matson, 80F

Asst Prof	Abramo, Joseph M.	D	32,64E
Lect	August, Gregg	M	62D
Prof	Bass, Richard	D	13
Lect	Blood, Curt	M	48,64C
Lect	Bourne, Thaddeus	B	61
Lect	Case, Greg	M	64E
Lect	Cimino, Matthew	M	61
Lect	Clark, Kenneth	M	66D
Lect	Clayton, Lisa	M	60
Lect	Diaz, Javier	M	65
Lect	Dimock, Nancy	M	64B
Lect	Dion, David	M	32
Assoc Prof	Felder, Harvey	M	38,60B
Lect	Fields, Melinda	M	13A
Prof	Frogley, Alain	D	12
Lect	Frogley, Jane	M	11
Prof	Fuchs, Kenneth	D	10
Asst Prof	Hanzlik, Louis	D	63A
Lect	Haroutunian, Ronald	B	64D
Lect	Hodgdon, Brett	M	61
Lect	Hopkins, Barbara	D	64A
Lect	Hoyle, Robert	M	63B
Lect	Jackson, James	M	63D
Prof	Jarjisian, Catherine	D	32
Prof	Junda, Mary Ellen	D	32,36
Prof	Kaminsky, Peter	D	13,13J,12B
Lect	Logan, Cameron	M	11
Assoc Prof	MacDonald, Earl M.	M	29,47,46
Lect	Mastroianni, John	M	47
Asst Prof	McEvoy, Jeffrey S.	D	61
Lect	McNeill, Marvin	M	37,32E
Lect	Meyer, Robert	M	62B
Prof	Miller, Robert F.	D	34,34D
Prof	Mills, David	D	32C,37,49
Assoc Prof	Neelly, Linda Page	D	32
Prof	Renshaw, Jeffrey	D	60,37,43
Assoc Prof	Rice, Eric N.	D	55,12A,13A,12
Assoc Prof	Rock, Connie	M	61
Asst Prof	Rosenfeld, Julie	M	62A
Lect	Salcedo, Angela	M	66G
Lect	Sanders, George	M	63C,44
Lect	Schlaikjer, Katie	D	62C
Lect	Sienkewicz, Gary	M	63D
Assoc Prof	Spillane, Jamie D.	DMA	36,60A
Asst Prof	Squibbs, Ronald J.	D	13
Prof	Stanley, Glenn	D	11,12A,12,12B
Prof	Stephens, Robert W.	D	32,20A,20G
Asst Prof	Vallecillo, Irma	M	66A,42
Lect	Waters, Willie		61
Lect	Woronecki, Stuart	M	13
Lect	Ziegler, Meredith	M	61

CT0650 Univ of Hartford
The Hartt School
200 Bloomfield Ave
W Hartford, CT 06117-1599
(860) 768-4454   Fax: (860) 768-4441
harttweb.hartford.edu
E-mail: ziccardi@hartford.edu

4 Year Institution, Graduate School
Member of NASM

Master of Music in Suzuki Pedagogy, Diploma, Master of Music in Organ & Liturgical Music, Master of Music in Composition, Master of Music in Music Theory, Master of Music in Performance, Master of Music in Conducting, Master of Music Education, PhD in Music Education, DMA in Composition, DMA in Conducting, DMA in Performance, DMA in Music Education, Master of Music in Piano Accompanying, Master of Music in Music History, Master of Music in Piano Pedagogy, Master of Music in Accompanying

Dir., Undergraduate Studies: Irene H. Conley, 80B
Associate Dean & Dir., Graduate Studies: T. Clark Saunders, 80C,80H
Dir., Admissions: Lynn M. Johnson, 80D
Dir., Hartt Community Division: Mark George, 80E
Dir., Summer Programs: Demaris Hansen, 80G

Prof	Adsit, Glen	M	37
Adj	Andersen, Nancy	B	61
Adj	Arms, Janet	M	64A
Adj	Babal, Gregory	M	66A,66D
	Barefield, Robert C.	D	61
Assoc Prof	Black, Robert	B	62D
Adj	Blood, Curtis	B	64C
Other	Bolkovac, Edward	D	36,60
Prof	Borror, Ronald	D	41,49,63C,67E,55
Assoc Prof	Braus, Ira	D	12A,12
Asst Prof	Caluda, Cherie	M	61
Prof	Carl, Robert B.	D	13,10,45
Adj	Casey, Christopher	B	47,64E
Adj	Chandler, David	B	54,52
Adj	Chapdelaine, Jim		35C
Adj	Cobb, Kevin	M	63A
Adj	Cohn, Sanford	B	61
Assoc Prof	Conley, Irene H.	M	35A,35E
Prof	Davis, Robert H.	M	54
Assoc Fac	Davis, Steve	B	29
Adj	Davison, Susan		35A
Prof	De Moura Castro, Luiz		66A
Adj	Einfeldt, Teri	B	62A
Adj	Ellis, Lief	DIPL	35G
Adj	Faidley-Solars, Elizabeth	M	62A
Adj	Falk, Jodi		52
Prof	Feierabend, John	D	32A,32B
Adj	Felstein, Robert		54
Adj	Ferreebee, Sarah		32D
Adj	Feyer, Paul		61,54
Adj	Flannery, Rebecca	M	62E
Adj	Flores, Carolina	D	32D
Prof	Fonte, Henry	M	54
Assoc Fac	Francis, Margreet	B	66A
Adj	Goldberg, Marc	M	64D
Adj	Goldstein, Richard	M	70,29
Adj	Goodell, Mark		35A
Prof	Gryc, Stephen Michael	D	13,10F,10
Assoc Prof	Hansen, Demaris	D	32A,32B,32G,32H
Asst Prof	Haston, Warren	D	32E,37,32G
Adj	Haynes, Erica		35A,35D,35E,35F
Adj	Herman, Gabe		35C,35D
Adj	Huebner, Elizabeth	B	54
Adj	Jackson, James	M	63D
Adj	Johnson, Barbara C.	M	66A
Adj	Johnston, Randy	B	47,70,53
Adj	Jones, Kevin	M	61
Adj	King, Terry B.	D	51,62C
Adj	Koffman, Carrie	B	64,64C
Assoc Fac	Kosloff, Doris	B	61
Vstng Asst Prof	Kurtz, Justin	M	35C,13L
Adj	Kutner, Michael	D	61
Adj	Ladd, Chris		70
Adj	Lansdale, Katie	D	41,51,62A
Adj	Larson, Steven	M	41,62B
Adj	Laverne, Andrew	B	29
Assoc Prof	Levy, Joanna	M	61
Adj	Lichtmann, Jay	B	63A
Prof	Lucarelli, Humbert	B	41,64B
Prof	Macbride, David	D	13,10
Adj	MacHose, Kathleen		35A
Adj	McBride, Michelle	M	61
Adj	McLean, Rene		29,29A
Adj	Melnick, Marjorie	M	61
Adj	Mendoken, Scott		63D
Adj	Menhart, Donna	M	13
	Metcalf, Steve P.	B	
Assoc Prof	Miller, Anton	M	41,51,62A

Assoc Prof	Miller, Patrick	D	13
Assoc Prof	Moller-Marino, Diana	M	54
Adj	Monteiro, Shawn		29
Adj	Moore, Denise Leetch	B	52
Assoc Fac	Morales, Hilda		52
Asst Prof	Mori, Akane	D	13
Assoc Fac	Morris, Michael	B	54
Adj	Morrison, Johanna		54
Prof	Morrison, Malcolm	B	54
Adj	Myrick, Korby	M	61
Adj	Ngai, Emlyn		62A
Adj	Nikitina, Alla		52
Prof	Nott, Kenneth	D	12A,12,66G
Adj	Oshima, Ayako		64C
Adj	Partridge, Gary	M	38
Adj	Paulus, Carolyn	B	54
Asst Prof	Perkins, Ralph	B	54
Adj	Perlstein, Marla	B	54
Vstng Assoc Prof	Pier, Stephen		52
Adj	Planner, Mark		54
Asst Prof	Porfiris, Rita	M	62B
Prof	Provost, Richard C.	B	41,70
Adj	Quinn, Ann	M	52
Adj	Raiken, Larry		61
Adj	Rauch, Benjamin	B	61,31C
Assoc Fac	Reeves, Nat		29
Adj	Reisman, Leana	M	52,13C
Adj	Reisman, Mickey	M	62A
Adj	Reit, Peter	B	63
Assoc Prof	Reynolds, Geoffrey	D	32B,32C,32D,32F,32G
Adj	Rittner, Phillip	B	54
Assoc Fac	Rivera, Wayne	M	61
Adj	Rowe, Larry	M	52
Adj	Rozie, Edward Rick	B	20G,47,62D,29
Prof	Rust, Alan	M	54
Prof	Rutman, Paul	D	66A
Assoc Prof	Schiano, Michael	D	13,13J,20G,34
Adj	Schuttenheim, Tom	D	10F,13F
Adj	Shearer, Greig	M	64A
Adj	Shelley, Kenneth	D	61
Adj	Smith, Brian R.	D	35E
Prof	Smith, Larry Alan	D	10
Adj	Snyder, Patricia	D	66G
Adj	Spaulding, Sue	M	32E
Assoc Prof	Steen, Kenneth	M	10,13,45
Asst Prof	Stevinson-Nollet, Katie	M	52
Adj	Swann, Kyle	M	61
Adj	Swanson-Ellis, Kathryn		13A
Adj	Tedeschi, John		61
Assoc Prof	Tetel, Mihai	M	62C
Adj	Tomassetti, Gary		35A
Other	Tonkin, Humphrey	B	54
Prof	Toth, Benjamin J.	M	65
Assoc Prof	Turner, Charles	D	12A,12,67
	Unger, Leslie	B	52
Assoc Prof	Viragh, Gabor	M	13
Adj	Viragh, Katalin		13J
Assoc Prof	Watson, W. David	M	54
Adj	Weisman, Bonita		52
Assoc Fac	Westfall, David C.	D	66A,66C
Adj	Wierzbicki, Marishka	M	61
Adj	Wietszychowski, Stanley	M	61
Assoc Fac	Woodard, Peter	M	13B,47,66A,29
Adj	Younse, Stuart	D	32D
Other	Zimmerman, Christopher	M	60,38
Adj	Zimmerman, Stevie	B	54

CT0700 Univ of New Haven

Department of Music
300 Boston Post Rd
West Haven, CT 06516
(203) 932-7101 Fax: (203) 931-6097
www.newhaven.edu
E-mail: gmager@newhaven.edu

4 Year Institution

Coordinator, Music: Guillermo E. Mager, 80A
Assistant Coordinator: Jose M. Garcia-Leon, 80H

Prac_in_Res	Arnold, Roger	M	34
Other	Bonnefond, James L.	M	34
Asst Prof	Celotto, Albert Gerard	M	13,12,66A
Lect	DeGroff, Jason	M	32E,37,46
Assoc Prof	Garcia-Leon, Jose M.	D	11,12A,13,66A,66D
Prof	Kaloyanides, Michael G.	D	12,13,14,20,34
Lect	Krugman, Murray	JD	35,34
Assoc Prof	Mager, Guillermo E.	D	13,12A,34,35,32
Asst Prof	Markiw, Victor R.	D	66,13,12A,66A,11
Asst Prof	Reba, Christopher H.	D	34D,10B,35G,62D,13

CT0750 Wesleyan University

Department of Music
113 Music Studios
Middletown, CT 06459
(860) 685-2598 Fax: (860) 685-2651
www.wesleyan.edu
E-mail: dshore@wesleyan.edu

4 Year Institution, Graduate School

Master of Arts in Music, PhD in Ethnomusicology

Chair: Jane Alden, 80A
Dir., Graduate Studies: Sumarsam, 80C

Adj	Adzenyah, Abraham	M	20A
Assoc Prof	Alden, Jane	PhD	12,55
Adj Asst Prof	Balasubrahmaniyan, B.	PhD	20E
Prof	Braxton, Anthony		10,20G,29
Prof	Bruce, Neely	D	12A,36,20G
Prof	Charry, Eric	PhD	14
Artist in Res	Ebrecht, Ronald	M	36,66G
Artist in Res	Harjito, I.	M	20D
Adj Assoc Prof	Hoggard, Jay	M	20G,29
Prof	Kuivila, Ronald		10,45
Prof Emeritus	Lucier, Alvin	M	10,45,34
Asst Prof	Matthusen, Paula A.	PhD	34,45,10
	McLane, Alec		16
Artist in Res	Nelson, David	PhD	20E
Prof	Slobin, Mark	PhD	12,14
Prof	Sumarsam,	PhD	20D
Prof Emeritus	Winslow, Richard	M	13A,13,10
Assoc Prof	Zheng, Su	PhD	12,14

CT0800 Western Connecticut State Univ

Department of Music
181 White St
Danbury, CT 06810-6845
(203) 837-8350 Fax: (203) 837-8630
www.wcsu.edu/music
E-mail: gobled@wcsu.edu

4 Year Institution, Graduate School
Member of NASM

Certificate, Master of Science in Music Education

Chair: Daniel P. Goble, 80A
Associate Chair & Dir., Graduate Studies: Kevin Isaacs, 80H,80C

Prof	Astrup, Margaret	D	39,61
Prof	Ball, Wesley A.	D	32,32B,13C
Adj	Beals, Andrew	M	64E,41,53
Asst Prof	Begian, Jamie	M	41,70,53,47,29
Assoc Prof	Callaghan, Marjorie S.	D	12A,13,63B
Adj	Chase, Constance	M	61
Adj	Clymer, Richard		63A
Adj	Cuffari, Gina	M	64D,48,11
Adj	Cullen, Christopher	M	64C,41
Adj	Giampietro, Matilda	D	20
Prof	Goble, Daniel P.	D	47,64E,53,29,41
	Greene, James S.	B	29,64E,46
Prof	Hirshfield, L. Russell	D	16,13,66,66B,66A
Prof	Isaacs, Kevin	D	13,60,10,12B,36
Assoc Prof	Jimenez, Fernando	D	60B,37,63C
Adj	Lafreniere, Andy	M	41,70
Prof	Lewis, Eric	M	12A,62B,51,62A,12B
Adj	Lutnes, Patricia	M	66A
Adj	Mansfield, Cynthia	M	32B
Adj	Mazzacane, Roy	M	61
Adj	Metcalf, Lee	M	29A,70
Adj	Morrison, Chris	M	53,70,41
Adj	Noland, David	M	64E,41
Asst Prof	OGrady, Douglas M.	D	13,34,35G,10
Adj	Oviedo, Javier	M	64E,48
Adj	Roberts, Stephen	M	66G
Adj	Rodgers, Andy	M	49,63D
Adj	Ruffels, Dave	M	62D,53,41
Adj	Scott, David	M	47,63A,41
Adj	Siegel, Jeff S.	M	53,41,65,29
Prof	Smith, David	M	13,50,65,34
Adj	Smith, Jeff	M	32E
Adj	Smith, Judith	M	62C,32E,41
Adj	Smith, Patrick	M	65
Adj	Snyder, Mark S.	D	64B,48,11
Adj	Sternberg, Jo-Ann	M	64C,48
Asst Prof	Theisen, Kathleen Ann	M	13,66
Adj	Tomlinson, Peter	B	66A,53,41
Adj	Trudel, Eric	M	61
Prof	Walker, Kerry E.	D	32,48,64A

Directory of Institutions

Adj	Weidlich, Richard H.	D	61
Adj	Weisz, Deborah	M	29,63C
Adj	Westervelt, Dirck	M	20
Adj	Winters, Gregg	M	34A,34B

CT0850 Yale University
School of Music
PO Box 208246
New Haven, CT 06520-8246
(203) 432-1965   Fax: (203) 432-2061
music.yale.edu
E-mail: laura.chilton@yale.edu

Graduate School
Member of NASM

Certificate, Artist Diploma, Master of Music in Composition, Master of Music in Performance, Master Musical Arts in Composition, Master Musical Arts in Performance, DMA in Composition, DMA in Performance

Dean: Robert Blocker, 80A
Deputy Dean: Paul Hawkshaw, 80H
Associate Dean: Michael C. Yaffe, 80H

Asst Prof Adj	Akahoshi, Ole	M	62C
Prof Adj	Aki, Syoko	M	41,62A
Asst Prof Adj	Baty, Janna	M	61
Artist in Res	Beaver, Martin		41
Prof Adj	Berman, Boris	M	66A
Asst Prof Adj	Berry, Paul		
Prof	Blocker, Robert	D	66A,42
Prof Adj	Bresnick, Martin I.	D	10,43
Lect	Brillhart, Jeffrey	M	66G
Assoc Prof Adj	Brooks, Marguerite	M	60,36
Prof Emeritus	Carrington, Simon	M	36
Assoc Prof Adj	Causa, Ettore	M	62B
Prof Emerita	Chookasian, Lili P.		39,61
Vstng Lect	Cross, Richard	B	39,61
Prof Adj	Dean, Allan	M	49,63A
Lect	Dickson, Douglas	M	66C
Assoc Prof Adj	Douma, Jeffrey		
Prof Adj	Duffy, Thomas	D	13,37,47
Prof Adj	Frank, Claude	M	66A
Vstng Prof	Frankl, Peter		66A
Prof Adj	Friedmann, Michael L.	D	13
Artist in Res	Greensmith, Clive		41
Prof Adj	Hahm, Shinik	M	60
Lect	Han, June Young		
Lect	Hartman, Scott	M	63C,41
Prof Adj	Hawkshaw, Paul	D	12
Assoc Prof Adj	Holzer, Robert R.	D	12A
Artist in Res	Ikeda, Kikuei		41
Artist in Res	Isomura, Kazuhide		41
Prof	Jean, Martin D.	D	66G
Vstng Prof	Kang, Hyo		62A,42
Prof Adj	Kavafian, Ani		62A
Prof Adj	Kernis, Aaron Jay		10
Prof Emeritus	Killmer, Richard	D	64B
Lect	Kimball, Eugene	B	35C
Prof Emeritus	Krigbaum, Charles		66G
Prof	Laderman, Ezra	M	10
Prof Adj	Lang, David	D	10
Lect	Malafronte, Judith		61
Lect	Marshall, Ingram	M	10
Assoc Prof Adj	Morelli, Frank	D	64D,41
Prof Adj	Murray, Thomas	B	36,66G
Prof Adj	Oundjian, Peter		41,62A
Asst Prof Adj	Palma, Donald	B	62D
Prof Adj	Panetti, Joan	D	13
Prof Adj	Parisot, Aldo S.	M	62C
Assoc Prof Adj	Parisot, Elizabeth	D	66A,66C
Other	Perlis, Vivian M.	M	20G
Lect	Purvis, William	M	63B
Assoc Prof Adj	Rathey, Markus		
Lect	Roylance, Mike	M	63
Prof Adj	Ruff, Willie H.	M	35,10F,13
Lect	Shaindlin, Tim	M	61
Lect	Sharp, Wendy	M	41
Prof Adj	Shifrin, David	B	41,64C
Assoc Prof Adj	Shimada, Toshiyuki	B	60B
Prof Emeritus	Swallow, John		63C
Lect	Swann, Kyle	M	61
Assoc Prof Adj	Taylor, James R.	M	61
Lect	Taylor, Stephen G.		64B,42
Assoc Prof Adj	Theofanidis, Christopher	D	10
Lect	Van Sice, Robert	M	65
Other	Vees, Jack	M	34
Assoc Prof Adj	Verdery, Benjamin	B	70,41
Lect	Verzatt, Marc		
Prof Adj	Wilson, Ransom	B	41,64A
Prof Adj	Yarick-Cross, Doris	M	39,61
Lect	Yu, Kyung Hak		62A

CT0900 Yale University
Department of Music
PO Box 208310
New Haven, CT 06520-8310
(203) 432-2985   Fax: (203) 432-2983
www.yale.edu/yalemus
E-mail: linette.norbeau@yale.edu

4 Year Institution, Graduate School

PhD in Music Theory, PhD in Music History, Master of Arts

Chair: Daniel Harrison, 80A
Dir., Undergraduate Studies: Kathryn J. Alexander, 80B
Dir., Graduate Studies: Richard L. Cohn, 80C

Prof Adj	Alexander, Kathryn J.	D	13,10,34,43
Asst Prof	Brodsky, Seth	D	12
Prof	Cohn, Richard L.	D	13
Lect	Egan, Dan	M	54
Prof Adj	Friedmann, Michael	D	10,13,66A
Assoc Prof Adj	Hahm, Shinik	D	60
Prof	Harrison, Daniel	D	13
Lect	Harwood, Craig	D	12,14
Prof	Hepokoski, James	D	12
Lect	Herreid, Grant	M	55
Lect	Jolles, Annette	M	54
Asst Prof Adj	Klingbeil, Michael	D	10,13
Lect	Kohane, Sara	M	61
Assoc Prof	Kreuzer, Gundula	D	12
Lect	Kwok, Sarita	M	13C
Prof Adj	Lalli, Richard	D	55,61
Lect	Malafronte, Judith	M	55
Prof	McCreless, Patrick	D	13
Prof Adj	Mealy, Robert	M	55
Asst Prof	Poudrier, Eve	M	13,13I,13F,13K,13J
Assoc Prof	Quinn, Ian	D	13
Prof	Rosand, Ellen	D	12A,12
Lect	Rosenblum, Joshua	M	54
Lect	Sharp, Wendy	M	42
Assoc Prof	Shimada, Toshiyuki	D	38
Prof	Veal, Michael E.	D	14,20A,20G
Assoc Prof	Weiss, Sarah	D	14,20
Prof	Wright, Craig M.	D	11,12A,12

DC0010 American University
Department of Perf Arts-Music
4400 Massachusetts Ave NW
Washington, DC 20016-8200
(202) 885-3422   Fax: (202) 885-1092
www.american.edu
E-mail: nsnider@american.edu

4 Year Institution
Member of NASM

Director: Nancy Jo Snider, 80A

Asst Prof	Abraham, Daniel E.	D	11,12,14C,36,60
	Allison, Linda	D	61
PT	Baldwin, Todd		63C
Artist in Res	Baumgarten, Jonathan	M	64A,42,48
PT	Bayer, Joshua	D	29,20,13,62D,70
Asst Prof	Benadon, Fernando Raul	D	13,34,10
Asst Prof	Berard, Jesus Manuel	M	38,60,13,11
PT	Bolling-May, Joan	M	61
PT	Bowles, Douglas	M	61
PT	Cameron, Scott	M	37,63D,63C
PT	Carrier, Lisa	M	61
PT	Chalifoux, Jeanne	DIPL	62E
PT	Dircksen, Eric	M	64D
PT	Evers, Brooke	D	61
PT	George, Emil	B	63B
PT	Getz, Noah		64E
Artist in Res	Gorenman, Yuliya	M	66A,42
Lect	Heap, Matthew	PhD	13,10,13F
PT	Hollinshead, Barbara		61
PT	Holloway, Greg	M	65
Asst Prof	Kang, Ann Teresa	D	13B,13I
Artist in Res	Kivrak, Osman	D	62B,42,51
	Kopfstein-Penk, Alicia	M	70,12,13C,11
Artist in Res	Lazar, Teri	D	62A,42,51
PT	Malaga, Edgaro	M	62D
Prof Emeritus	Mandel, Alan R.	M	66A
Prof	Mardirosian, Haig L.	D	13,10,66G,11
Prof Emeritus	Mason, Vito	M	36
PT	Mastrian, Stacey	D	61
PT	McCusker, Philip	M	70
Prof Emeritus	McLain, James	B	61
Asst Prof	Medwin, Marc	D	11,29,12,20

PT	Merz, Albert	M	65
PT	Owens, Meg	M	64B
PT	Ozment, Jon	M	66A
Prof	Sapieyevski, Jerzy	M	13,10,45,11,34
PT	Scroggins, Sterling Edward	D	61,16,11
PT	Shioji, Lane	M	64D
PT	Sledge, Sylstea	M	31F,60A
Artist in Res	Snider, Nancy Jo	B	62C,42,51,67B,41
PT	Snitzler, Larry	M	70
PT	Tarr, Jeffrey	D	61
PT	Van Hoose, Matthew	M	66C
Prof Emerita	Vrenios, Elizabeth	M	39,61,54

DC0050 Catholic Univ of America, The

Benjamin T. Rome School of Music
Ward Hall
Washington, DC 20064
(202) 319-5414   Fax: (202) 319-6280
music.cua.edu
E-mail: cua-music@cua.edu

4 Year Institution, Graduate School, Teacher Certification Program
Member of NASM

Artist Diploma, Master of Music in Composition, DMA in Composition, DMA in Chamber Music (Piano), DMA in Sacred Music, Master of Music in Chamber Music (Piano), Master of Music in Orchestral Instruments, Master of Music in Vocal Accompanying, DMA in Vocal Accompanying, DMA in Orchestral Instruments, DMA in Orchestral Conducting, DMA in Vocal Pedagogy, Master of Music in Sacred Music, PhD in Musicology, Master of Music in Piano Pedagogy, Master of Music in Vocal Pedagogy, Master of Arts in Musicology/MS in Library Science, DMA in Piano Performance, DMA in Vocal Performance, DMA in Piano Pedagogy, Master of Music in Orchestral Conducting, Non-Degree Music Teacher Certification, Master of Music in Piano Performance, Master of Music in Vocal Performance

Dean: Grayson Wagstaff, 80A
Assistant Dean, Admissions: Amy Antonelli, 80D,80B
Assistant Dean, Academics: Joseph A. Santo, 80D,80C
Production Manager: Dominic Traino, 80F

Inst PT	Adkins, Elizabeth	D	54,62A
Inst PT	Allphin, Andrew	D	63A,41
Assoc Prof Adj	Antonelli, Amy	D	13
Prof Emerita	Barr, Cyrilla	D	12A,12C
Asst Prof	Battersby, Sharyn L.	D	32B,32C,66D,32D,32H
Lect	Beeson, Robert	D	32E,64E
Lect	Berrocal, Esperanza	D	20H
Inst PT	Bocaner, Lawrence		64C
Vstng Asst Prof	Bower, John E.	D	10A,13C,10F
Inst PT	Bowles, Douglas		61
Prof Emeritus	Braunlich, Helmut	D	13
Inst PT	Bravo, Fabiana	M	61,12A
Inst PT	Breedlove, Graham	M	63A
Vstng Asst Prof	Brock, Jay	M	54
Lect	Catravas, Nicolas	M	
Inst PT	Cho, Michelle	D	64A
Inst PT	Choi, In Dal	D	61
Vstng Asst Prof	Christman, Rick	B	61
Prof	Christman, Sharon Lynn	M	61,39
Inst PT	Chudnovsky, Emil	B	62A
Inst PT	Cigan, Paul	B	64C
Inst PT	Craven, Robert	M	63B
Inst PT	Daval, Charles	M	63A
Inst PT	Figueiroa, Joao Paulo M.	D	70
Inst PT	Filsell, Jeremy	D	66G
Asst Prof	Fitenko, Nikita	D	66A
Inst PT	Fleming, Rachelle	D	61,54
Inst PT	Galvin, Eugene	D	61
Prof Emeritus	Garofalo, Robert	D	32E,37,60B
Assoc Prof	Gatwood, Jody	B	62,62A,41
Inst PT	Gold, Ira	M	62D
Asst Prof	Gorbos, Stephen	D	10
Lect	Grogan, Robert	D	66G
Lect	Grossman, Pauline	B	52
Inst PT	Harris, Turman	M	64D,41
Inst PT	Hearn, Barry	M	63C
Inst PT	Hoffman, Susan	M	54
Lect	Houghton, Rosemarie	M	61
Inst PT	Hurst, Francesca	D	66A
	Hylton, Fleta	M	61
Lect	Johnson, Maurice	B	52
Inst PT	Jones, Vanita	B	64A
Assoc Prof	Kaltchev, Ivo	D	66A
Inst PT	Lilley, Marc Bryan	M	61
Lect	Litzelman, James	D	66A,66B
Vstng Asst Prof	Lovelace, Jason R.	D	10A,13C,10F
Inst PT	Lund, Henriette	D	61
Lect	Mahady, Jim	B	54
Inst PT	Martin, Gregg	M	32E
Prof Emeritus	Mastroianni, Thomas	D	66A,66B
Assoc Prof	Mermagen, Michael	M	62C
Inst PT	Merz, Albert	M	65
Lect	Mitchell, John	M	37
Inst PT	Mondie, Eugene	M	64C
Inst PT	Mulcahy, Craig	B	63C
Prof	Nestor, Leo Cornelius	D	10A,31A,36,40,60A
Inst PT	Nickel, James	B	63B
Lect	O'Brien, Kevin	D	36,13B,60A,40
Inst PT	Ohlson, Laurel	M	63B
Inst PT	Patcheva, Ralitza	D	66A
Vstng Asst Prof	Pedersen, Thomas	B	36,39,54,56,61
Asst Prof	Puricelli, Denise	M	54
Lect	Quinn, Shannon	B	52
Inst PT	Santana, Jose Ramos	M	66A
Asst Prof Adj	Santo, Joseph A.	D	10A,10F,13B,13H,13C
Asst Prof	Searle, David	M	38,39,41
Lect	Short, Shawn	B	52
Prof	Sidlin, Murry	M	38,60B
Prof	Simpson, Andrew Earle	D	10,10F,13,66A,43
Lect	Skeris, Robert	D	31A,36
Assoc Prof	Smith, Michael V.	PhD	60,32,32B,32C,32D
Lect	Souvorova, Katerina	D	66A,66C
Prof Emerita	Steiner, Ruth	D	12A,12,14A
Inst PT	Stolk, Ronald	M	66G
Inst PT	Stovall, Nicholas	M	64B
Inst PT	Strother, Kevin L.	D	61
Assoc Prof	Taylor, Paul	D	13
Vstng Asst Prof	Taylor-Gibson, Cristina	D	12A
Inst PT	Traino, Dominic	M	61
Prof	Wagstaff, Grayson	D	12A,12,12C
Prof	Walter, Elaine R.	D	11,12A,39
Assoc Prof	Weaver, Andrew H.	D	12A,12,12C,62B
Inst PT	Weinhold, Scott	M	64C
Inst PT	Weinreb, Alice Kogan	M	64A
Inst PT	Zukerman, Arianna	B	61

DC0075 Georgetown University

Department of Performing Arts
37th & O Sts NW
108 Davis Ctr, Box 571063
Washington, DC 20057
(202) 687-3838   Fax: (202) 687-5757
www.georgetown.edu
E-mail: deldonna@georgetown.edu

Jesuit Institution

Interim Chair: Hugh Cloke, 80A
Director, Music Program: Anthony R. DelDonna, 80A

	Celenza, Anna H.	PhD	12A,12B,12C,12G
	DelDonna, Anthony R.	PhD	12,12A,12B,12C,12D
Asst Prof	Harbert, Benjamin J.	PhD	14
	Jones, Rufus	D	38,12A
	Stilwell, Robyn	PhD	12,14
	Williams, John Flawn	B	35C,35G,35H

DC0100 George Washington University

Department of Music
801 22nd St NW/Ste B-144
Washington, DC 20052
(202) 994-6245   Fax: (202) 994-9038
departments.columbian.gwu.edu/music/
E-mail: gwmusic@gwu.edu

4 Year Institution
Member of NASM

Chair: Douglas J. Boyce, 80A
Dir., Performance Studies: Robert P. Baker, 80H

Assoc Prof	Ahlquist, Karen	D	12,14
Prof Adj	Albertson, John	B	67B,70,53
Asst Prof	Baker, Robert P.	D	61
PT	Barnet, Lori A.	B	62C,51
Inst Adj	Becker, Gisele	M	36
Asst Prof Adj	Birch, Robert M.	D	49,63A,37,48
Assoc Prof	Boyce, Douglas J.	D	13,10
PT	Burney, Herman	M	62D
Asst Prof Adj	Conlon, Francis	D	39,66A,66C,54
PT	Connell, Joseph C.	B	65
PT	Corella, Gil C.		63D
PT	Crockett, Alison	M	61
Inst Adj	Dahlman, Barbro E.	M	66A,66D
PT	D'Alimonte, Nancia	D	38
PT	Dircksen, Eric	M	64D
PT	Drennen, Edward	B	62A
PT	Edgar, Paul	M	50,65

PT	Fearing, Scott M.	M	63B
PT	Ferguson, Lora	M	64C
PT	Field, Elizabeth	D	62A,67B
Prof Adj	Findley, Mary B.	D	62A,51
Inst Adj	Fraize, Peter W.	M	47,53,64E,29
Assoc Prof	Fritz, Benno P.	D	37,49,60,11
PT	Gascho, Joseph	M	66H
PT	Gilliam, Laura	B	48,67C
PT	Guenther, Eileen Morris	D	66G
Prof	Guenther, Roy J.	D	13E,13F,11,12A
Prof Adj	Hilmy, Steven C.	M	10,45,34
PT	Jones, David	B	64C
PT	Koczela, Jeff	B	62D
Asst Prof Adj	Konstantinov, Tzvetan	M	66A,66C,66D
PT	Krash, Jessica	D	41,66A
Prof Adj	Levy, James D.	M	47,66A,29B
Prof Adj	Lornell, Christopher 'Kip'	D	29A,14
PT	Lucini, Alejandro	B	47,65
PT	Mikolajewski, Alice	M	36,66A,66C,66D
Asst Prof	Montague, Eugene	D	13,34A
PT	Ocampo, Rebecca	D	61
Prof Adj	Peris, Malinee	M	41,66A,51
PT	Reiff, Amy	M	61
Inst Adj	Rojas, Berta	M	70,51
PT	Scarlett, Millicent	M	61
PT	Sciannella, David	M	63C
PT	Seidman, Barbara	M	62E
PT	Stabile-Libelo, Carole	M	64B
PT	Stang-McCusker, Stephani	M	64A
PT	Von Villas, Muriel	M	11,39,54
PT	Wassertzug, Uri	M	62B
PT	Wellman, Steve	B	61
PT	Wilson, Thad	M	63A
Prof	Youens-Wexler, Laura	D	11,12

DC0110 George Washington Univ-Mt Vernon

Department of Music
2100 Foxhall Rd NW
Washington, DC 20007
(202) 625-4541
www.mvc.gwu.edu
E-mail: dboyce@gwu.edu

4 Year Institution

Lect	Allison, Linda	M	36,61
Lect	Blumfield, Coleman		66A
Prof Emeritus	Eckert, William H.	M	13,12A,32A,66G
Lect	Hubner, Carla	M	12A,12,66A,35E
Lect	Maalouf, Janet	M	36,66
Assoc Prof	Mikhalevsky, Nina	D	12A,12B

DC0150 Howard University

Division of Fine Arts-Music
2455 6th St NW RM 3004
Washington, DC 20059
(202) 806-7082   Fax: (202) 806-9673
www.coas.howard.edu/music/index.html
E-mail: groyal@howard.edu

4 Year Institution, Graduate School, Historically Black College
Member of NASM

Master of Music in Performance, Master of Music Education, Master of Music in Jazz Studies

Chair: Guericke Royal, 80A

Lect	Boykin-Settles, Jessica	M	29
Lect PT	Bunn, Michael		63D
Lect	Covington, Charles		29
Assoc Prof	Eichelberger, K. V.	M	61,54
Assoc Prof	Holliday, James T.	D	13A,13,61
Lect	Holloman, Charlotte W.	M	61
PT	Hopkins, Gregory H.	B	61
Prof	Irby, Fred	M	47,49,63A
Prof	Jackson, Raymond T.	D	66A
Asst Prof	Kamalidiin, Sais	D	64A,29
Lect PT	Koczela, Jeffrey L.	M	62D
Lect PT	Kunkel, Gerard F.	B	70
Lect PT	Lewis, Nicholas	M	64C,41
Lect PT	Lovinsky, Joseph	B	63B
Lect PT	Macek, Timothy A.	M	62A,62B
Asst Prof	Mauldin, Mark K.	M	13A,13B,32,63C
Lect PT	Mercer, John	M	35
Assoc Prof	Miller, Connaitre	M	29
Prof	Norris, James Weldon	D	12A,12,36
Assoc Prof	Ohia, Chinyerem	D	13
Lect PT	Owen, Drew	B	62C

Asst Prof	Randolph, Anthony W.	D	10C,11
Lect PT	Reed, Richard		64B
Lect PT	Richards, William W.	M	65
Assoc Prof	Royal, Guericke	M	29,35
Asst Prof	Schultz, Paul	D	63C,13
Prof	Timbrell, Charles	D	66A
Assoc Prof	Walwyn, Karen M.	M	66A
Assoc Prof	Washington, Donna	M	33
Lect PT	Wassertzug, Uri	M	62B
Asst Prof	Young, Charlie	M	64E

DC0170 Levine School of Music

Sallie Mae Hall
2801 Upton St NW
Washington, DC 20008
(202) 686-8000   Fax: (202) 686-9733
www.levineschool.org
E-mail: info@levineschool.org

Community Music School
Member of NASM

President: Peter Jablow, 80A
Dir., Programs & Admissions: Lois Narvey, 80D
Assistant Dean: Maria Mathieson, 80H

	Adkins, Elizabeth	D	62A
	Alekseyeva, Marina	M	66A
	Auer, Frank	B	62A
	Babayan, Naira	D	66A,66C
	Baird, Melinda Lambert	M	66A
	Bartman, Karen	D	66A
	Battistone, Christopher	B	63A,29
	Bavaar, Kathleen	B	54,61
	Bennett, Joyce	B	64A,38
	Bien, Leander	M	66A
	Brinegar, Steve	B	63
	Bullock, Betty	M	66A,39
	Carlson, Risa	M	70
	Chan, Wenyin	M	66A
	Chappell, Jeffrey	M	13,29,66A
	Chiu, Ying-Ting	D	64D
	Cho, Cecilia	D	66A
	Clark, Jacob	D	66A
	Collaros, Rebecca L.	M	13,64A
	Cook, Seth	B	63D
	Cook, Sophia	M	32A
	Cooper, Ted	D	66A,66C
	Cyncynates, Ricardo		62A
	Dahlman, Barbro	B	66A
	Dale, Monica	M	32A,66A
	Davenport, David A.	M	54,66D,66A
	Day-Javkhlan, Alicia	B	62C
	Dievendorf, Matthew	B	70
	Dooley, Ellen	M	64A
	Dotson, Danielle	M	66A
	Drennon, Eddie		62A,29
	Dzuik, Youlee	B	32A
	Eckert, Elizabeth	M	66A
	Efremova, Natalia	M	66A
	Eichhorn, Claire	B	64C
	Ethington, Martha Poleman	M	64A
	Ferguson, Lora	M	64C
	Fernandez, Gerardo		62A
	Findley, Mary	D	62A
	Fisher, Anna		66A,32A
	Fleming, Phyllis	B	62A,62B
	Foard, Sarah	B	62A
	Forrest, Sidney	M	64C
	Freeman, Gregory	M	63C
	Frye, Brian	B	37
	Fuller, Susan	M	62A
	Gabay, Darya	M	66
	Galvin, Eugene	D	64A
	Gerber, Heidi	B	34
	Getz, Noah	D	64E
	Gonzalez, Pepe		29,62D
	Gorenman, Svetlana	D	66A
	Hahn, Hae Soon	M	62A
	Hallsted, Nancy	M	66A
	Han, Jiyon	M	13,66A
	Hare, Andrew	B	65
	Hawkley, Krysta	M	66A,66B
	Horn, Alisa	M	62C
	Hubner, Carla	M	66A
	Hudicek, Laurie	D	66A
	Hylton, Fleta	M	61
	Johnson, Karen	B	41,64A
	Johnston, Susan	B	32A
	Jones, Brian D.		64C
	Ju, Alice	M	62A
	Kanno, Sayaka	D	66A
	Kats, Irina	D	66A
	Katsarelis, Susan	M	62A
	Kelly, Susan	B	62C

	Kemp, Wayne N.	D	61
	Khalsa, Gurjeet	B	32A
	Khoja-Eynatyan, Leon	M	65
	Kostaras, Jimmy	B	64E,64
	Lane, Elizabeth	M	66A
	Lee, Alice E.	M	66A
	Lee, Hyeweon	D	66A
	Lee, Pamela Perec	B	32A
	Little, Robert	D	64C
	Lloyd, Deborah F.	D	66A
	Lundy, Joyce	M	61
	Maring, Eric	M	32A
	McCabe, Amy	M	63A
	McCarthy, Kerry	B	61
	McFarlane, Grace	M	66A
	McFeaters, Jason	M	64E
	McKay, Frances	D	13,10
	McNeely, Carol	M	62A
	Miklhin, Alexandra	M	62A
	Minas-Bekov, Ivan		62A
	Mitchell, Andrew	M	70
	Moore, Marilyn	B	61
	Narvey, Lois	M	66A,66H
	Norris, Paul	M	47,37
	Noyes, Rachel	M	62A
	O'Donnell, Patrick	D	66A,66C
	Oh, Jiyoung	D	66A
	Orlov, Irena	M	66A
	Orozco, Jorge	M	62A
	Ouspenskaya, Anna	M	66A
	Pan, Shelly	M	62A
	Papp, Anne	M	64A
	Patcheva, Ralitza	D	66A,42
	Peh, Alex L.	M	66A
	Perry, Tiffany	M	13,64C
	Platino, Franco	M	70
	Popov, Vasily	D	62C,41
	Prince, Gary	B	70
	Pulliam, Christine	M	66A
	Rampp, Rose K.	B	32A
	Rodriguez, Carlos Cesar	M	66A
	Rogentine, Carole	B	67C
	Rogers, Douglas	M	70
	Rubens, Beth	B	32A
	Ruiz-Bernal, Gabriel	D	66A
	Ryoo, Soyoung	M	66A
	Saelzer, Pablo	M	62A,62B
	Sagripanti, Andrea	M	66A
	Sakamoto, Haruyo	M	66A
	Seidman, Barbara	M	62E
	Sexton, Lucinda	M	32A
	Shaw, Lisa	D	61,36
	Sirotin, Peter	B	62A
	Smith, Tracy Anne	M	70
	Stilwell, Kenneth	M	64B
	Stone, Scott	B	70
	Stricklett, Margaret	M	61
	Suess, Jennifer	M	61
	Sumi, Akiko	B	70
	Sverjensky, Pamela	M	66A
	Sykes, Robert		13,66A,29
	Trail, Julian	M	12A,13,66A
	Turner, Corinne	B	32A
	Ulreich, Eric	B	70
	Van Hoose, Matthew	D	66A
	Vasey, Monika	M	32A
	Vierra, Alice	M	62C
	Volchok, Michail	D	66A
	Whitehead, Patrick		63A
	Whittaker, Billie	M	61,66C
	Williams, Charles	B	61,36
	Wing, Barbara	M	66A
	Wolff, David	B	32D
	Wright, Margaret	M	41,62A,62B
	Yaffe, Carl	M	13,12
	Yang, Emily	D	62C
	Yim, Soyoon	M	66A,66C
	Youn, Gloria	B	66A

DC0250 Trinity University

Fine Arts Program - Music
125 Michigan Ave NE
Washington, DC 20017-1004
(202) 884-9252   Fax: (202) 884-9229
www.trinitydc.edu

4 Year Institution

Chair, Fine Arts: Rebecca Easby, 80A
Dir., Artist/Performance Series: Sergio Buslje, 80F

Lect PT	Buslje, Sergio	M	38,41
Lect PT	Dexter Sawyer, Annetta	M	52
Lect PT	Hurst, Francesca	D	66A
Lect PT	Jagielsky, Kathleen	M	61
Prof Emerita	Shafer, Sharon Guertin	D	13,10F,12A,39,61

DC0350 Univ of the District of Columbia

Music Program
MB 4601
4200 Connecticut Ave NW
Washington, DC 20008-1122
(202)274-5802   Fax: (202)274-5589
www.udc.edu
E-mail: jkorey@udc.edu

4 Year Institution

Dean: Beverly Anderson, 80A
Acting Chair: Judith A. Korey, 80A
Coord., Music Program: William Dee Mandle, 80A

PT	Barton, Leroy	M	64E
PT	Campbell, Derek	M	36,61
PT	Cohen, Bonnie	M	62A
Prof	Cooper, Marva W.	D	11,12A,66A,66B,66C
Assoc Prof	Edwards, George L.	D	11,32C,48,64A,64C
PT	Gelman, Robin	M	64D
PT	Guillen, Jorge	M	70
PT	Holloman, Charlotte	M	61
PT	Hoover, Lloyd W.	M	32,37
Assoc Prof	Jones, Calvin	M	47,62D,63C,63D,29
PT	Jones, William	M	11,36,61,66A,66G
Assoc Prof	Korey, Judith A.	M	13A,13,66A,29,34
PT	Krebill, Kerry	M	60,11
PT	Louis, Kenneth	M	36,61,31A
Prof	Mandle, William Dee	D	13A,13,32B,66A,66D
PT	Mitchell, Clarence T.		63A
PT	Nahm, Dorothea A.	D	66A,66D
PT	Novosel, Steve J.		62D
Assoc Prof	Ormond, Nelda C.	M	39,61
Prof	Roach, Hildred E.	M	20G,66A,66B,66C,66D
PT	Rosario, Lita	D	35A
PT	Snider, Nancy		62C
PT	Stephens, John	D	13,60
PT	Teasley, Tom	M	65
Prof	Van Buren, Harvey	M	13A,13,10F,10,66G

DE0050 Delaware State University

Department of Music
1200 N DuPont Hwy
Dover, DE 19901-2277
(302) 857-6680   Fax: (302) 857-6681
www.desu.edu/department-music
E-mail: yjohnson@desu.edu

4 Year Institution, Historically Black College

	Bryant, Michael	M	65
	Cannon, Maureen McDermott	M	64A
Prof	Davis, Lapointe M.	D	32,48,64
	Edwards, Ricky	B	37
Asst Prof	Gazda, Frank S.	D	63D,37,49,63C,42
Asst Prof	Hoffman, Patrick	D	63A,63B,13,11,49
	Johnson, Randolph J.	M	37,47
Asst Prof	Johnson, Yvonne P.	D	32,66D,62
	Moore, Marilyn	B	61
Assoc Prof	Morrison, Mable R.	M	11,12A,66A,66D
	Rhodes, Aaron		70
Assoc Prof	Tolley, David	D	10,34,35

DE0150 Univ of Delaware

Department of Music
Amy E du Pont Music Bldg
100 Orchard Rd
Newark, DE 19716
(302) 831-2577   Fax: (302) 831-3589
www.music.udel.edu
E-mail: UD-Music@udel.edu

4 Year Institution, Graduate School
Member of NASM

Master of Music in Composition, Master of Music in Performance, Master of Music in Music Education

Chair: Paul D. Head, 80A
Dir., Preparatory Division: Demetrius Delancy, 80E
Business Administrator: Tamara L. Smith, 80F
Associate Chair: Russell E. Murray, 80H

Inst	Allen-Creighton, Esme	M	62B
Asst Prof	Ancona, James	M	37,65
Asst Prof	Anderson, James Allen	DMA	38
Asst Prof	Archambeault, Noel	D	61,39
Prof Emeritus	Arenson, Michael	D	13B,34B
Prof	Barker, Jennifer M.	D	10
Asst Prof	Brandt, Robert	M	61,39
PT	Brown, Brian	M	63D
PT	Burke, Martha	M	32B
Prof	Burton, Suzanne L.	PhD	32C
Assoc Prof Emeritus	Conrad, Jon Alan	D	13C
Assoc Prof	Cottle, W. Andrew	D	11
PT	Cotto, Orlando	B	65B
Asst Prof	Cottrell, Duane	D	36,32D
Assoc Prof	Delbeau, Marie-Christine	M	66A,66D,66B
Assoc Prof	DeMent, Melanie	D	39,61
Asst Prof	Duker, Philip	D	13B,13C
PT	Gaarder, Jon	M	48,64D
Prof	Gao, Xiang	M	62A
Asst Prof	Gentry, Philip	D	12A
PT	Gross, Anne	D	11,12A
PT	Groves, Todd	B	47,64E
Assoc Prof	Grycky, Eileen J.	M	64A,41,48
Assoc Prof	Gythfeldt, Marianne	M	64C,48
Assoc Prof	Hamant, Alan D.	M	14C
Prof	Head, Paul D.	D	36
PT	Marinelli, Michael	D	35A
PT	Marinelli, Vincent J.	M	64C,64E
PT	Meyer, Andreas K.	M	35D
Prof	Murray, Russell E.	D	12A,15,55,67D,67B
PT	Neff, Lyle	D	11
Asst Prof	Nicholson, Chad	D	37,32E
Inst	Nishimura, Julie	B	66C
Asst Prof	Palmer, Thomas	B	47
PT	Paradis, Kristian	M	50
Asst Prof	Price, Harvey	M	50,65,47
Asst Prof	Purciello, Maria Anne	D	12A
PT	Sarro, John	M	35A
Assoc Prof	Sarver, Heidi	M	32C,37
PT	Schweitzer, Kenneth	D	14C
PT	Seglem-Hocking, Sara	M	61
Asst Prof	Shorter, Lloyd	B	48,64B,12A
PT	Skoniczin, Robert	M	63A
Asst Prof	Smith, Blake	D	61,54,39
Assoc Prof	Smith, John David	D	63B,48,49
Asst Prof	Snell, Alden	M	32C,32E
Asst Prof	Stevens, Daniel B.	D	13B,13C
Assoc Prof	Stomberg, Lawrence J.	D	62C,51
Asst Prof	Stone, Brian D.	D	60B
PT	Sullivan, Anne	B	62E
Inst	Taggart, Christian	B	70
PT	Thomas, Craig	M	62D
Asst Prof	Tychinski, Bruce D.	D	63C,63D
PT	Ventura, Anthony C.	B	70

DE0175 Univ of Delaware
Department of Music
Southern Campus
PO Box 627
Georgetown, DE 19947
(302) 856-5400
www.udel.edu
E-mail: 08574@udel.edu

2 Year Institution

Music Contact: Ruth Stomne Mulford, 80A

Inst	Mulford, Ruth Stomne	M	13,11,12A,62A,20G

DE0200 Wesley College
Department of Music
120 North State St
Dover, DE 19901-3875
(302) 736-2300   Fax: (302) 736-2312
www.wesley.edu
E-mail: laganeda@wesley.edu

4 Year Institution

Chair: David Laganella

Assoc Prof	Laganella, David	D	10,13,34,14C,12A
Adj	Redington, Britania		61
Adj	Ryan, Ed		
Adj	Thompson, Gerald		37

FL0040 Baptist College of Florida
Music Program
5400 College Dr
Graceville, FL 32440-3306
(850)263-3261   Fax: (850)263-7506
www.baptistcollege.edu
E-mail: drodom@baptistcollege.edu

Theological Education, 2 & 4 Year Degree Programs

Adj Prof	Branning, Ron	M	63,64
Asst Prof	Cox, Buford	D	13A,12A,66A,66C
Assoc Prof	Glover, Angela	M	66A,66B,66C,66D
Adj Prof	Jones, Emily	M	11,12A,13C,41,70
Prof	Malone, Patrick R.	D	13,66G
Adj Prof	Moon, Kimberle	D	61,54
Adj Prof	Tinsley, David	M	61

FL0050 Barry University
Department of Fine Arts
11300 NE 2nd Ave
Miami Shores, FL 33161-6628
(305) 899-3428   Fax: (305) 899-2972
www.barry.edu
E-mail: amason@mail.barry.edu

4 Year Institution

Adj Prof	Adan, Jose	M	70,13,13C,11,29A
Adj	Ahn, Hyojin		66A
Adj Prof	Camacho, Dionisio	M	66A
Adj Prof	Cicconi, Christopher M.		63
Prof	Coulter, Beverly	D	61
Adj Prof	Daroca, Daniel		66C,61
Adj Prof	Eisenreich, Samuel		64,48,64E
Adj Prof	Furtado, Danial		66A
Adj Prof	Kerr, Hugh	M	12
Adj Prof	Kostic, Dina	M	62A,41,42,51
Asst Prof	Mason, Alan	D	11,12,31B,66A,66C
Adj Prof	Potts, Brian	M	65,50
Asst Prof	Rios, Giselle Elgarresta	D	61,36,60,32,41
Adj Prof	Rodriguez, Hugo Marcos		
Adj Prof	Rondinelli-Eisenreich, Cassandra	D	64A
Adj Prof	Russell, Brian E.	D	70
Adj Prof	Shafer, Karen	M	61
Adj Prof	Vassilev, Mia	D	66A

FL0100 Bethune-Cookman University
Department of Music
640 Dr. Mary McLeod Bethune Blvd
Daytona Beach, FL 32114
(386) 481-2740   Fax: (386) 481-2777
www.bethune.cookman.edu
E-mail: haynesk@cookman.edu

4 Year Institution, Historically Black College

Chair: Kimberly Haynes, 80A

	Brooks, Victoria	M	16
Asst Prof	Grace, Rose S.	DMA	66A,66B,66C,66D
Inst	Harris, Ben	M	34,35C,35G,32F
Asst Prof	Haynes, Kimberly	D	12A,39,61
Asst Prof	Hundley, Marion S.	D	10A,66A,66C,13
Inst	Lawrence, Lisa	M	32,54,61
	Milam, Timothy A.	B	34A,34B,34D,34E
Inst	Orey, Pedro	M	37,50,65
Asst Prof	Paglialonga, Phillip O.	D	64C,41,48,13A,13B
Inst	Poitier, James	M	37,49,63,32F,41
Inst	Polk, Sylvester	M	34,63A,35A,35D,35G
Inst	Rayam, Curtis	B	36,61,40,39
Asst Prof	Simmons, Matthew	D	49,60B,63C,63D
Prof	Steele, Rebecca W.		36,61
Inst	Wells, Donovan V.	M	37,32E
Asst Prof	Westervelt, Todd G.	D	32,12C,63A

FL0150 Brevard Community College
Department of Music
1519 Clearlake Rd
Cocoa, FL 32922
(321) 632-1111   Fax: (321) 433-7194
www.brevardcc.edu
E-mail: lambr@brevardcc.edu

2 Year Institution

Chair: Robert E. Lamb, 80A

Adj	Apelgren, Scott	B	63A
Adj	Baker, Mark	M	61
Asst Prof	Bishop, James	M	12A,37,38,47,64E
Adj	Clew, Nancy	B	64A
Adj	Cockerham, Scott	M	41,70,34
Adj	Cook, Sally	M	66
Adj	Desgrange, Richard	M	62D
Adj	Graham, Patrick	M	64C
Adj	Jevitt, Amy	B	62A,62B
Adj	Juilianna, Anita	B	64B,64D
Assoc Prof	Kim-Quathamer, Chan Ji	D	10,11,13,34
Prof	Lamb, Robert E.	D	36,13,12,60A
Adj	Leasure, Michael	B	29,70
Adj	MacLean, Sherry	B	61
Adj	Markstein, Igor	M	62A,62B
Adj	Markstein, Joan	M	62C
Adj	Quathamer, Mark	M	10,13,34
Adj	Slawson, Brian	DIPL	65
Adj	Waid, Tom	B	63C,63D
Adj	Wilkerson, John	M	63B

FL0200 Broward College
Department of Visual & Perf Arts
3501 SW Davie Rd
Davie, FL 33314-1694
(954) 201-6840   Fax: (954) 201-6605
www.broward.edu
E-mail: bburbach@broward.edu

2 Year Institution

Coordinator: Brock Burbach, 80A
Event Manager: Susan Barnett, 80F
Associate Dean: W Scott Miller, 80H

PT	Abbot, Louis	M	11
PT	Arne, Devin	M	70
PT	Ayick, Paul	M	63A,41
PT	Bertolet, Jay	M	63D
PT	Brubaker, William	M	64D
Asst Prof	Burbach, Brock	D	36,61,40
PT	Capezza, June	M	61,13A,13B,13C
PT	Cavendish, Thomas	D	61
PT	Corinthian, Randy	M	34D,37
PT	Crawford, Richard	M	13B,13C
PT	Dadurka, Jon	M	62D,47
PT	Dawson, Brett	M	63C
PT	Dodd, Susan	M	66A,66C,66D
PT	Feldman, Damira	M	66A
PT	Garritson, Ashley	M	62C
PT	Gregory, Rosalie	M	66A
Asst Prof	Hainsworth, Jason D.	M	11,29,46,47,64E
PT	Jenkins, Neil	M	37
PT	Kleiman, Carey D.	M	34,35A,64,35,32E
PT	Lan, Catherine	M	13B,13C,66D
PT	Luo, Mei Mei	M	62A
PT	Mautner, Roselida	M	40,61,11
PT	Meeroff, Myrna	M	63B
PT	Miska, Renee	M	64A
PT	Murphy, Joanna	M	10,13
PT	Neciosup, Hector	M	65
PT	Pitasi, Dennis	M	66A
PT	Real-D'Arbelles, Giselle	M	11
Asst Prof	Rozman, Jure	D	66A,13,41
Prof Emerita	Scherperel, Loretta	D	13,11,66G
PT	Smith, Tom	M	70
PT	Strattan, Ken	M	11
Asst Prof	Ulibarri, Fernando	M	35,70,47
PT	Weiner-Jamison, Sarah	M	61,11
PT	Wheeler, Candace	D	66,11,32,10,66A
PT	Zeniodi, Zoe	D	38
PT	Zuniga, Rodolfo	M	65,47

FL0350 Chipola College
Department of Music
3094 Indian Cir
Marianna, FL 32446-1701
(850) 718-2301   Fax: (850) 718-2206
www.chipola.edu
E-mail: heidebrechtd@chipola.edu

2 Year Institution

Director & Dir., Artist Series: Joan B. Stadsklev, 80A,80F
Director, Show Choir: Angela S. White, 80G

	Gordon, Stefan	M	61,60A
	Larison, Adam	M	70,11
Inst	Martin, Joshua	D	13,11,66A,66D
	Powell, Daniel	D	11,13,47,63,64
	White, Angela S.	B	36
Inst	Yoshikawa, Christine	D	66A,13A

FL0365 College of Central Florida
Department of Visual & Perf. Arts
3001 SW College Rd
Ocala, FL 34474
(352) 854-2322   Fax: (352) 873-5886
www.cf.edu/departments/instruction/las/music
E-mail: frynsj@cf.edu

2 Year Institution

Director: Jennifer Fryns, 80A

Adj	Bumbach, Matthew	M	66A,61
Adj	Capitano, Gay Lyn	M	66A
	Fryns, Jennifer	D	20,12A
Adj	Harrison, Rosaura		62A
Adj	Jo, Marie		66A
Adj	Klein, Edward		62C
Assoc Prof	McClung, Sam W.	M	60B,37,13,47,46
Adj	Sapochetti, Daniel		63
Assoc Prof	Satterfield, Sarah	D	12A,64A,11,42,48
Adj	Smith, Peter D.	D	70
Adj	Trinckes, John	M	70

FL0400 Daytona Beach Community College
Department of Music
1200 W Intl Speedway Blvd
Daytona Beach, FL 32115-1111
(386) 255-8131
www.daytonastate.edu
E-mail: petersd@daytonastate.edu

2 Year Institution

Chair: Douglas A. Peterson, 80A

Adj	Belden, Carol Beck		66A,66C
Inst	Christeson, Norton M.	D	36,38,39,61
Adj	Forrest, Sam		50
Adj	Graves, James		70
Adj	Kearley, Kandie	D	61
Adj	Levine, Jonathan	M	64E
Adj	McCoy, Steve		66A,66C
Adj	Niemann, Judith A.	M	61
Inst	Peterson, Douglas A.	M	11,37,38,64C
Adj	Peterson, Pamela	M	66A,66D
Adj	Rabe-Meyer, Janet		61
Adj	Schmidt, David A.	M	47,63C,63D
Adj	Stork, David	M	61
Adj	Waidelich, Peter J.	M	49,63A
Adj	Ward, Ann	M	64B
Inst	Zelley, Richard S.		55,66A,66H,67B

FL0450 Eckerd College
Department of Music
PO Box 12560
St Petersburg, FL 33733-2560
(727) 864-8471   Fax: (727) 864-7890
www.eckerd.edu
E-mail: epsteijo@eckerd.edu

4 Year Institution

Coordinator: Joan O. Epstein, 80A

PT	Bygrave, Max	M	63B
PT	Collins, Amy	B	64B
PT	Douglas, Brent	B	41,66A,66C
Prof	Epstein, Joan O.	M	13,11,12A,53,63A
PT	Eubanks, Dawne	B	61
PT	Grissom, Kurt	M	65
PT	Hall, Thomas	M	66G
PT	Harris, Janet	B	64D
PT	Harris, Jonathan	B	70
PT	Irwin, David E.	M	64C,64E,37,41
PT	Klukoff, Ruth	B	62A,62B
PT	Manson, David	D	63D
PT	Neuenschwander, Mark	B	62D
PT	Prescott, Barbara	B	41,64A
PT	Roberts, Dolly	B	62E
Prof	Smith, Marion	D	13,12A,36
PT	Varosy, Zsuzshanna	M	41,62C

FL0500 Edison College-Lee County
Department of Music
8099 College Pkwy SW
Fort Myers, FL 33906-6210
(941) 489-9332   Fax: (941) 489-9482
www.edison.edu
E-mail: tsmith8@edison.edu

4 Year Institution

Dean: Robert Beeson, 80A

Adj	Bendixon-Mahoney, Kristen	M	63B
Adj	Bovbjorg-Neidung, Helen	M	61
Adj	Christman, Ruth	M	64B
Prof	Cornish, Glenn S.	D	13,11,66A
Adj	Day, Geoff	M	62A,62B
Adj	Griffin-Seal, Mary	M	66A,11,66D,13C
Adj	Hall, Elena	M	66A,66D,13C
Prof	Hill, Dennis	D	37,47,64A,64E,29
Adj	Larsen, William H.	M	64A
Adj	Leone, Gary	M	65,11
Adj	Liu, Si-Cheng	M	62C
Adj	Lorenz, Jim	D	66G
Adj	Perry, Skip	M	66A
Adj	Puls, Kenneth	D	70
Adj	Scaruffi-Klispie, Cindy	M	63A
Adj	Schneider, Bernard	M	63C,63D
Adj	Sonnenborn, Kristen	M	64D
Adj	Sundby, Candace	M	61,36
Adj	Trunk, Joseph	M	62D

FL0550 Edward Waters College
Department of Fine Arts
1658 Kings Rd
Jacksonville, FL 32209-6167
(904) 470-8132   Fax: (904) 470-8132
www.ewc.edu
E-mail: timothy.root@ewc.edu

4 Year Institution, Historically Black College

Chair: Timothy Root, 80A

Inst	Brown, Thomas P.	M	
Asst Prof	Fulmer, Daniel		
	Graham, Marques		37
	Huang, Ming Shiow		66A
	McNeely-Bouie, Barbara	M	36

FL0570 Flagler College
Music/Theatre Arts Program
74 King St
St. Augustine, FL 32084
(904) 829-6481   Fax: (904) 826-0094
www.flagler.edu
E-mail: gibbspm@flagler.edu

4 Year Institution

Chair: Phyllis M. Gibbs, 80A
Liason Community Concert Series: Laura Stevenson, 80F

Vstng Prof	Fradley, Kerry		36
Vstng Prof	Fulmer, Daniel	D	11
Vstng Prof	Hache, Reginald		11,66A
Vstng Prof	Reed, James		11
Vstng Prof	Saliba, Raphael	M	11

FL0600 Florida A & M University
Department of Music
1635 M.L. King Jr Blvd
Tallahassee, FL 32307
(850) 599-3334/3341   Fax: (850) 561-2176
www.famu.edu
E-mail: Kimberly.Jackson@famu.edu

4 Year Institution, Historically Black College

Chair: Julian E. White, 80A

Assoc Prof	Bing, Charles S.	M	32C,37,63C,63D
Asst Prof	Chipman, Shelby R.	M	60,32C,37,63A
Assoc Prof	Clark, Wallace	M	12A,32C,37
Prof	Daniels, John	D	13,32C,64A,64C
Prof	Foster, William P.	D	60,37
Assoc Prof	Horn, Goffery C.	D	13A,13
Prof	James, Shaylor L.	D	32C,50,65
Assoc Prof	Johnson, Shirley M.	D	13A,61,66A,66D
Asst Prof	King, Curtis R.	M	13A,13,32,61,62
Asst Prof	Parsons, Longineu	M	47,63A,29
Prof	Roberts, Mary W.	D	66A,66B,66C,66D
Asst Prof	Robinson, Florence	D	12A,66A,66,66D
Asst Prof	Robinson, Marty	M	47,45,63A,29
Assoc Prof	Sarjeant, Lindsey B.	M	47,49,53,46,29
	Sobkowska-Parsons, Joanna		66A
	Toomer, Charlie	M	60,36,61
Asst Prof	White, Dennine	M	32C,37,64A
Prof	White, Julian E.	D	60,32C,37,64A,64B
	Williams, Johnny	B	16

FL0650 Florida Atlantic University
Department of Music
777 Glades Rd
Boca Raton, FL 33431
(561) 297-3820   Fax: (561) 297-2944
www.fau.edu
E-mail: rlautar@fau.edu

4 Year Institution, Graduate School
Member of NASM

Master of Arts in Music

Chair & Dir., Summer Programs: Rebecca Lautar, 80A,80G
Dir., Graduate Studies: Sandra McClain, 80C

Adj PT	Abrams, Ira		35A
Adj PT	Akers, Diana L.	M	66G
Adj PT	Bonsanti, Neal	M	64E,47,46
Adj PT	Brignola, Michael	B	64E
Adj Inst	Brubeck, Cornelia	M	62C
Prof	Burganger-Treer, Judith		66A,66B
Adj PT	Caputo, Charles R.	D	63C
Adj	Carlisle, Stephen M.		35A
Adj	Charles, Benjamin	M	50,65
Prof	Coltman, Heather	D	66A
Adj	Crilly, Neil D.	B	35A
Assoc Prof	Cunningham, James E.	D	14,20,32,11,12A
Inst	Dorchin, Susan	B	61
Prof	Fleitas, Patricia P.	D	60,36,61
Prof	Glazer, Stuart	D	13,10,64
Adj PT	Green, Paul	M	64C
Adj PT	Gutierrez, Alfonso		35C
Adj PT	Hammer, David A.	M	66A
Adj PT	Joella, Benjamin R.	M	12A

Asst Prof	Joella, Laura	D	38,12A,62D,60B
Prof	Keaton, Kenneth D.	D	60,12A,41,67D,70
Adj PT	Kofman, Irena	M	66A
Inst	Kover, Krisztina	M	66A
Adj PT	Lakofsky, Elissa	M	64A
Prof	Lautar, Rebecca	M	11,41,51,62A,62B
Adj PT	Lavender, Robert	M	65
Adj PT	Louise-Turgeon, Anne	D	66A,66C
Vstng Prof	McClain, Sandra	D	61
Asst Prof	Murray, Sean	D	37
Adj PT	Okubo, Mack	M	70
Assoc Prof	Prescott, Kyle	D	37
Adj PT	Rimmington, Rob	M	62D,29
Adj PT	Rossow, David	B	66C
Inst	Rossow, Stacie	D	61,36,13A
Asst Prof	Sanchez-Samper, Alejandro	M	35
Adj PT	Stanley, Brian	M	63A
Prof	Treer, Leonid P.		14,66A,66B,42
Assoc Prof	Turgeon, Edward	D	66A,66B
Assoc Prof	Walters, Timothy	D	13,41,63A,29
Adj Inst	Weisberg, Diane K.	D	62B
Other	Zager, Michael	M	34,35

FL0670 Florida College

Department of Music
119 N Glen Arven Ave
Temple Terrace, FL 33617-5527
(813) 988-5131 x 303 Fax: (813) 899-6772
www.floridacollege.edu
E-mail: barlard@floridacollege.edu

4 Year Private Liberal Arts Institution
Member of NASM

Chair: Douglas Barlar, 80A

	Barlar, Douglas	D	12A,63D,49,32E
	Barlar, Nancy	D	64C,32B,32C,32E,11
	Barlar, Rebecca	M	13,66A,66B,66C
	Bassett, Jenny	B	61,62
	Bassett, Jon	D	36,61,51,38,32D
	Moore, Tim	M	40,61,54
	Payne, Benjamin	M	11,34,13,66A,66D
	Rainwater, Brian	M	60,37,13C,63C,47
	Walker, Darlene	M	66D,66A

FL0675 Florida Gateway College

Department of Music
149 SE College Pl
Lake City, FL 32025
(386) 752-1822 Fax: (386) 754-4755
www.fgc.edu
E-mail: owen.wingate@fgc.edu

2 Year Institution

Dean, Arts & Sciences: Brian Dopson, 80A
Dir., Artist/Performance Series: Joan Fetchen, 80F

Adj	Skoglund, Frances	M	66A,66D,13A,11
Prof	Wingate, Owen K.	M	13,11,12A,61,36
PT	Wuest, Harry		37,47,64,63

FL0680 Florida Gulf Coast University

Bower School of Music
10501 FGCU Blvd S
Fort Myers, FL 33965
(239) 590-7851 Fax: (239) 590-7581
www.fgcu.edu/cas/bsm
E-mail: mvarney@fgcu.edu

4 Year Institution

Director: Cathy Albergo, 80A

Asst Prof	Bahr, Jason	D	10,13,31A,13C,13B
Prof	Baron, Michael	DMA	66A,66C,66B,66D
Adj	Bendixen-Mahoney, Kirsten	M	63B
Adj	Bernardo, Mario	M	64E
Asst Prof	Brown, Trent R.	DMA	36,40,60A
Adj	Carper, Ken	PhD	20
Adj	Castellano, Mark	M	63
Assoc Prof	Chesnutt, Rod M.	PhD	37,38,60,32E,32F
Adj	Christy, Judy	M	64B
Asst Prof	Cole, David	DMA	51

Vstng Prof	Cole, David C.	DMA	38,51,39,62A,32
Assoc Prof	Darnell, Debra Jean	DMA	61,11,39
Adj	Evans, Judith	M	62
Adj	Ferlazzo, Gaetano	M	70
Adj	Frank, Robin Shuford	M	61
Adj	Griffin, William	M	61,13A
Adj	Hess, Debra L.	PhD	12A
Inst	Jones, Troy V.	M	32E,37,65
Adj	Kirton, Suzanne	M	64A
Adj	Koch, Thomas	M	70
Adj	Larsen, Bill	M	64A
Adj	Lilly, Elizabeth	M	62E
Adj	Liu, Si-Cheng	M	62C
Adj	Locke, Randolph	M	61
Adj	Lorenz, James	D	12A
Adj	Mattson, Lisa	M	62B
Adj	May, Tom	M	62C
Adj	McCalla, Aaron	B	63D
Adj	Medlock, Matthew	M	62D
Adj	Neal, Patrick	M	62A
Assoc Prof	Patrick, Louise R.	PhD	32
Adj	Seal, Mary Griffin	M	13A,13C
Adj	Smith, Joanne	M	66A,66B
Adj	Sonneborn, Kristen	M	64D
Adj	Sonneborn, Matthew	B	63A
Adj	Sparrow, Carol	M	61
Asst Prof	Stewart, Tobin E.	D	51,13A,13C
Asst Prof	Thurmaier, David P.	PhD	13,13C,13B,13E,13F
Adj	Votapek, Paul	M	64C
Adj	Zion, Mike	M	63C

FL0700 Florida International Univ

School of Music
SW 107th Ave & 8th St
Miami, FL 33199
(305) 348-2896 Fax: (305) 348-4073
music.fiu.edu
E-mail: garciao@fiu.edu

4 Year Institution, Graduate School
Member of NASM

Master of Music in Composition, Master of Music in Performance, Master of Music in Conducting, Master of Science in Music Education, Master of Music in Jazz, Master of Music in Music Technology

Director: Orlando Jacinto Garcia, 80A
Associate Dir., Graduate Studies and Academic Affairs: Joel Galand, 80C,80H
Associate Dir., Development: Kathleen L. Wilson, 80H

Adj	Aliapoulis, S. Mark	M	36,61
Assoc Prof	Augenblick, John	D	60A,36,11
Adj	Averhoff, Carlos	M	64E,29A
Asst Prof	Benedict, Cathy L.	D	32
Inst	Bernhardt, Barry W.	M	37,47,63A,29A
Adj	Bertolet, Jay	M	63D
Inst	Calloway, Jason	M	62C,43,42
Prof	Campbell, Gary	M	64E,29,53,47
Prof	Davidovici, Robert	M	62A,62B,11
Adj	Diaz, Rebekah	M	61
Assoc Prof	Dolata, David	D	12,67G,55,56,67H
Assoc Prof	Dundas, Robert B.	M	39,61
Adj	Fernandez, David D.	M	29B
Inst	Fuller, Karen	M	35
Assoc Prof	Galand, Joel	D	13J,13
Prof	Garcia, Orlando Jacinto	D	10,34A
Prof	Gekic, Kemal	M	66A
Adj	Gomez-Imbert, Luis	D	62D,43,11
Adj	Grabowski, Robert	M	29A,11
Inst	Hacker, James	B	63A,42,49
Adj	Hancock, Richard K.		64C
Asst Prof	Hardin, Dan	D	16,66G
Adj	Jimenez, Lissette	M	61,12A,13C
Adj	Kauffman, Mary Adelyn	D	66C
Adj	Kerley, Eric	M	63B
Inst	Klotz, Michael	M	62B,42
Adj	Lakofsky, Elissa	M	64A
Adj	Lathrum, Linda	M	32B
Asst Prof	Lindhal, Gregory	D	37,48,60B
Adj	Lippincott, Tom	M	70,51
Inst	Littley, Marcia De Arias	M	62A,42
Asst Prof	Lopez, Jose R.	D	66A,66C,66H,66B
Adj	Lyons, Lisanne	D	47
Asst Prof	Nowak, Grzegorz	D	38,60
Assoc Prof	Orta, Michael	M	66A,29A,29B,47
Inst	Ousley, Larry James	D	62D,46,47,53
Adj	Padron, Rafael	M	70,57
Adj	Pagluica, Domincio	M	63C
Adj	Proctor, Andrew	M	65
Adj	Rackipov, Errol	M	29A,65B,11
Adj	Richards, Lasim	M	63C,35A
Adj	Rose, John E.	M	36
Adj	Ross, Rashawn	B	63A

Assoc Prof	Schmidt, Patrick	D	32
Asst Prof	Sudol, Jacob David	D	34,35,45
Adj	Swanson, Brent	M	12A,14,20
Adj	Szklarska, Kamilla	D	66A,66C,66D
Adj	Tranquilino, Armando	D	13A,13B,13C,34B,12A
Adj	Tripp, Scott	M	13C
Inst	Vitenson, Misha	M	62A,42
Prof	Wilson, Kathleen L.	D	61,54
Adj	Zuniga, Rodolfo	M	65

FL0730 Florida Keys Community College

Department of Music
5901 College Rd
Key West, FL 33040
(305)296-9081   Fax: (305)292-5155
www.fkcc.edu
E-mail: dean.walters@fkcc.edu

2 Year Institution

Chair: G. Gerald Cash, 80A

Adj	Lowe, Emily	M	36,61
PT	Walters, Dean	M	61
PT	Zito, Vincent	M	13A,13

FL0800 Florida Southern College

Department of Music
111 Lake Hollingsworth Dr
Lakeland, FL 33801-5607
(863) 680-4229   Fax: (863) 680-4395
www.flsouthern.edu
E-mail: fscmusic@flsouthern.edu

4 Year Institution

Chair: Brian S. Brink, 80A
Dir., Artist Series: Rob Tate, 80F

PT	Brenner, Laura	M	62B
Assoc Prof	Brink, Brian S.	D	63C,49,34
Asst Prof	Burke, Larry	M	32B,63D,29A,49,35A
PT	Butcher, Paul	M	29B,47,35A,63A
PT	Coash, David	D	65,50
PT	Cole, Pamela	B	66A,66D
PT	Danielsson, Tamara	M	64E
PT	Dominski-Sale, Christina	M	61
Assoc Prof	Fandrich, Rita E.	M	13,66A,66B,10
PT	Fleitz, Patrick	M	66A,11
PT	Gilmer, Melissa	M	61
PT	Haubry, Rebekah	B	66A
PT	Hill, Don-Michael	M	62D
PT	Jacobson, Barbara	M	64A,48
Assoc Prof	Jossim, J.	D	64B,37,32C
PT	Lugo, Edward	M	70
Artist in Res	MacDonald, Robert M.	M	66A,12A,35A,35E,35F
PT	McColley, Stacey	M	64C,48,13
PT	Parrette, Anne		62C
Assoc Prof	Parsche, Paula	M	13,66A,66C,11
Asst Prof	Pranno, Arthur J.	M	62A,38,51,62B,12A
PT	Schaffer, Candler	D	63B
PT	Sedloff, Michael	M	13A,62D
Assoc Prof Emeritus	Sledge, Larry	D	60,12A,31A,36,13
Assoc Prof	Stahl, Diane Willis	M	39,61
Vstng Prof	Svistoonoff, Katherine	DMA	66A,13,12A
PT	Switzer, Mark	D	70
Assoc Prof	Thomasson, John	D	39,61
PT	Thompson, Jack	B	61,39
PT	Traba, Fernando	M	64D
PT	Wansley, Ivan		64C

FL0850 Florida State University

College of Music
122 N Copeland Ave
Tallahassee, FL 32306-1180
(850) 644-3424   Fax: (850) 644-2033
www.music.fsu.edu
E-mail: sbeckman@admin.fsu.edu

4 Year Institution, Graduate School
Member of NASM

Master of Arts in Music, Master of Music in Composition, Master of Music in Music Theory, Master of Music in Performance, Master of Music in Conducting, Master of Music in Music Therapy, Master of Music in Musicology, Master of Music Education, PhD in Music Theory, PhD in Music Education, Doctor of Music in Composition, PhD in Musicology, Master of Arts in Arts Administration, Master of Music in Opera Production, Master of Music in Piano Pedagogy, Doctor of Music in Performance, Master of Music in Jazz Studies, Master of Music in Accompanying

Dean: Don Gibson, 80A
Senior Associate Dean & Dir., Graduate Studies: Seth Beckman, 80C,80H
Associate Dean: William E. Fredrickson, 80H
Associate Dean: Leo Welch, 80H

Asst Prof	Akers, Ruth	PhD	11
Assoc Prof	Amsler, Eva	M	64A
Assoc Prof	Anderson, Leon	M	47,65,29,46
Assoc Prof	Andrews, Pamela	M	51,67A
Assoc Prof	Bakan, Michael	PhD	14,20D,20G
Asst Prof	Barnhart, William	B	29,63A
Prof	Beckman, Seth	D	66A,66C
Assoc Prof	Bish, Deborah	D	64C
Prof	Bowers, Judy	PhD	32,36
Prof	Brewer, Charles E.	PhD	12A,12
Assoc Prof	Brister Rachwal, Wanda	D	61,31A
Prof	Broyles, Michael	PhD	12
Assoc Prof	Buchler, Michael	PhD	13
Assoc Prof	Callender, Clifton D.	PhD	10
Prof	Chapo, Eliot	D	41,51,62A
Librarian	Clark, Dan	M	16
Prof	Clary, Richard	M	48
Prof	Clendinning, Jane Piper	D	13
Assoc Prof	Close, Shirley J.	M	61
Librarian	Cohen, Sarah Hess	M	16
Prof	Corzine, Michael L.	D	66G
Prof	Darrow, Alice-Ann	PhD	33
Prof	Delp, Roy	M	61
Prof	Drew, John	D	49,63C
Prof	Dunnigan, Patrick	PhD	32C,37,60B
Assoc Prof	Ebbers, Paul	M	63D
Prof	Fenton, Kevin	PhD	60,32,36
Prof	Fisher, Douglas	M	39
Prof	Fredrickson, William E.	PhD	32G,32E,32
Assoc Prof	Gaber, Brian	M	47,35
Assoc Prof	Gainsford, Read	D	66A
Other	Garee, Anne	B	66F
Prof	Gerber, Larry	M	36,61
Prof	Geringer, John M.	PhD	34
Prof	Gibson, Don	PhD	13
Assoc Prof	Gregory, Dianne	M	33
Assoc Prof	Gunderson, Frank	PhD	14,20A,20B
	Hargabus, Bruce	DIPL	66F
Other	Hodges, Anne R.	D	35E
Prof	Hoekman, Timothy	D	66A,66C
Assoc Prof	Holzman, Bruce	B	70
Assoc Prof	Jimenez, Alexander	D	38,60B,65A,60,65
Assoc Prof	Jones, Evan	D	13
Assoc Prof	Jordan, Rodney	B	47,62D,29
Prof	Keesecker, Jeffrey	M	64D
Prof	Kelly, Steven N.	PhD	32,37
Assoc Prof	Kennedy, William	M	47,29,64E
Assoc Prof	Koen, Benjamin D.	PhD	14,20B
Prof	Kowalsky, Frank	D	64C
Prof	Kraus, Joseph C.	PhD	13
Prof	Kubik, Ladislav	DIPL	10
Prof	Lata, Matthew	B	39
Other	Lima, Deloise	D	66C
Prof Adj	Louwenaar, Karyl	D	66E,41,66A,66H
Prof	Madsen, Clifford K.	PhD	32,33,12C
Prof	Mastrogiacomo, Leonard	DIPL	66A,66C
Asst Prof Adj	Mastrogiacomo, Norma	M	66A,66C
Assoc Prof	Mathes, James	PhD	13,10
Other	McArthur, Victoria	PhD	66B,66D
Asst Prof	McKee, Paul	M	29,63C
Prof	Meighan, Patrick	M	64E
Assoc Prof	Moore, Christopher	D	63A
Prof	Ohlsson, Eric	D	48,64B
Asst Prof	Okerlund, David	M	61
Assoc Prof	Parks, John	D	65
Assoc Prof	Peterson, William F.	M	10,29
Other	Plack, David	PhD	37
Assoc Prof	Porter, Marcia	D	61

Assoc Prof	Punter, Melanie	DIPL	62D
Asst Prof	Roberts, Marcus	B	29,66A
Assoc Prof	Rogers, Nancy Marie	PhD	13B,13H,13K,13C,13
Assoc Prof	Roman, Mary C.	M	62E,66D
Prof	Ryan, Pamela	D	41,62B
Assoc Prof	Sauer, Gregory D.	M	62C
Prof	Seaton, Douglass	PhD	12A,12D,12C,12
Other	Seaton, Gayle	D	61,54
Assoc Prof	Shaftel, Matthew R.	PhD	13
Prof	Standley, Jayne	PhD	32A,33
Assoc Prof	Stebleton, Michelle	M	49,63B,67E
Asst Prof	Stillwell, Corinne	M	62A,41
	Sung, Benjamin H.	D	62A,62B,41,42
Prof	Thomas, Andre J.	D	60A,32,36
Assoc Prof	Trujillo, Valerie M.	M	66C
Assoc Prof	VanWeelden, Kimberly	PhD	60,32,36
Prof	Von Glahn, Denise	PhD	12A,12
Other	Walworth, Darcy DeLoach	PhD	33
Prof	Welch, Leo	D	70
Asst Prof	Williams, Heidi L.	D	66A
Assoc Prof	Wingate, Mark	D	10,34
Prof	Zwilich, Ellen T.	PhD	10

FL0900 Gulf Coast Community College
Division of Visual and Perf. Arts
5230 W Highway 98
Panama City, FL 32401-1041
(850) 872-3886   Fax: (850) 873-3520
www.gulfcoast.edu
E-mail: robourke@gulfcoast.edu

2 Year Institution

Coordinator: Rusty Garner, 80A
Chair: Rosemarie O'Bourke, 80A

	Garner, Rusty	M	60,11,61,54,64D
	Harrison, Judy	M	13,36,60A,66

FL0930 Hillsborough Community College
Department of Music
2112 N 15th St
Tampa, FL 33605-3548
(813) 253-7684/7686   Fax: (813) 253-7771
www.hccfl.edu
E-mail: khanks@hccfl.edu

2 Year Institution

Head of Music: Kenneth B. Hanks, 80A

PT	Abbott, Carol	M	61,36
PT	Adams, Valerie		51,62A
PT	Audi, Carlos	D	62C
PT	Baker, John		63A
PT	Burge, James	M	37
PT	Collins, Amy	M	64B
PT	Dalmasi, Martin	M	41,64A,64E
PT	Demas, John	B	70
PT	Dillingham, David	M	62A
PT	Eubanks, Dawne	B	61
PT	Glowacki, T. J.	M	62D
Asst Prof	Hanks, Kenneth B.	M	66,13,11
PT	Hernly, Patrick	M	50,65
	Karlin, Brett		36,61
PT	Kwo, Kenneth P. C.	M	62B
PT	Lugo, Edward	M	70,11
PT	Sager, Stephanie	M	61
PT	Stefanov, Emi	M	66A
Asst Prof	Switzer, Mark	D	11,70
PT	Traster, Jeffry	D	63D
PT	Venterini, Maurizio	M	64D
Asst Prof	Winslow, Robert J.	M	66A,46,13,34D,11
PT	Ziegel, Donald	M	63C

FL0950 Indian River State College
Department of Music
3209 Virginia Ave
Fort Pierce, FL 34981-5541
(772) 462-4700   Fax: (772) 462-4796
www.irsc.edu
E-mail: drieth@irsc.edu

2 Year Institution

Dir., Preparatory Division & Music Contact: Dale Rieth, 80A,80E

PT	Daniels, Matthew	M	61
PT	Enyart, John	D	38,62A,51
FT	Jarred, Jennifer	M	33
PT	Kingfield, Edward	M	64C
PT	Kuliush, Tetyana	M	66A
PT	Muldar, Dennis	M	65,50
PT	Oestreich, Martha	M	64A
PT	Pierpoint, Paula	M	61,66A,66D
PT	Posey, Dale	M	62D,29B
Prof	Rieth, Dale	D	13,36,47,61,66A
PT	Sabo, Vyki	M	61,11
PT	Shea, Maurice	M	64
PT	Smukala, Edward	M	64
Assoc Prof	Southall, John K.	D	13,63A,60B,37,32E
PT	Steinke, David	M	13C,13A,13B
FT	Walworth, Darcy	D	33
PT	Weber, Carlyle	M	63A,63B
PT	Whitaker, Jane	M	54,11

FL1000 Jacksonville University
Department of Music
2800 University Blvd N
Jacksonville, FL 32203
(904) 256-7370   Fax: (904) 256-7375
www.ju.edu
E-mail: tharris7@ju.edu

4 Year Institution
Member of NASM

Dean: William Hill, 80A

Asst Prof	Beasley, Kimberly	M	61,54,39
Assoc Prof	Clifton, Artie	M	37,64C
Adj	Dwyer, Laura	M	64A
Adj	Ealum, Ernie	B	62D
Adj	Giddens, Scott	B	66A
Assoc Prof	Harrison, Thomas	D	34D,35,35A,35B,35F
Assoc Prof	He, Jianjun	D	13,34,10
Adj	Ishimaru, Kayo	B	62E
Adj	Krikland, Ricky		65
Adj	Lockwood, Shannon	M	62C
Adj	Moore-Hubert, Edith	M	66
Adj	Morgan, Sean	M	63B
Adj	Reynolds, Don	B	63D
Asst Prof	Ricci, John	M	64E,47,29
Asst Prof	Richardson, Marguerite	M	38,60B,62A,62B
Adj	Sales, Christopher	M	64D
Adj	Siemon, Brittnee	D	61
Asst Prof	Snyder, Timothy	D	36,40,12A,32D,60A
Artist in Res	Starling, Gary		70,29
Asst Prof	Steve, Tony	M	65,50
Assoc Prof	Vincent, Dennis	D	32,34
Asst Prof	Watkins, Scott	M	66A,66D
Adj	Yorio, Joseph	M	64E

FL1100 Lake Sumter Community College
Department of Music
9501US Highway 441
Leesburg, FL 34788-3950
(904) 787-3747   Fax: (904) 365-3501
www.lscc.edu
E-mail: arcarop@lscc.edu

2 Year Institution

Chair: Peter Arcaro, 80A

Inst	Arcaro, Peter	D	13B,11,29A,47
Adj	DeHoog, David	D	13A,29A
Adj	Langford, Jeremy	M	37
Adj	Miller, Michael	M	38,42,62A
Adj	Neas, Michael	M	36,60A
Adj	Saginario, Donald	M	11,32A

FL1125 Lynn University
Conservatory of Music
3601 N Military Trail
Boca Raton, FL 33431-5598
(561) 237-9001   Fax: (561) 237-9002
www.lynn.edu/music
E-mail: music@lynn.edu

4 Year Institution, Graduate School

Master of Music

Dean: Jon Robertson, 80A
Dir., Preparatory Division: Luisa Sanchez de Fuentes, 80E
Assistant Dean: Marc B. Reese, 80H

Artist in Res	Amis, Kenneth	M	63D
Artist in Res	Atkatz, Edward	M	65
Assoc Prof	Barry, Barbara R.	D	12A,12C
Staff	Cherkaoui, Tsukasa	M	16
Artist in Res	Cobb, Timothy	B	62D
Asst Prof	Cole, Carol		62A,42,32E
Assoc Prof	Cole, David	DIPL	62C,42
Asst Prof	Ellert, Michael		64D,41,42
PT	Evans, Phillip	M	66D,42
Artist in Res	Fielding, Ralph W.	M	62B
Artist in Res	Khaner, Jeffrey		64A
Assoc Prof	Leonard, Lisa	M	66B,66D,42
Asst Prof	Lin, Tao	M	66C,42
Artist in Res	Manasse, Jon	M	64C
Prof	McKinley, Thomas L.	D	13,10A,12A,34F
PT	Miller, Gregory	B	63B,42
Artist in Res	Oliveira, Elmar		62A
Assoc Prof	Reese, Marc B.	M	63A,49,41,42,48
Prof	Robertson, Jon	D	60B,38,66A
Artist in Res	Robinson, Joseph	M	64B
Prof	Rust, Roberta	D	42,66A
Staff	Sanchez de Fuentes, Luisa	D	
Asst Prof	Satterwhite, Dan	B	63C,42
PT	Schram, Albert George	D	38
Asst Prof	Shen, Yang	D	66C,66D,13C
PT	Siebert, Renee		64A

FL1300 Miami-Dade College-Kendall
Department of Music, Theatre & Dance
11011 SW 104th St
Miami, FL 33176-3393
(305) 237-2282   Fax: (305) 237-2411
www.mdc.edu/kendall/mtd
E-mail: rbrandon@mdc.edu

4 Year Institution

Chair: Rodester Brandon, 80A

PT	Adan, Jose	M	11,70,13A
PT	Barish, Sheila	B	61
PT	Bonelli, Matt	M	62D,53
Inst	Broderick, James	B	13,63A,53,34
PT	Brown, Eileen Duffy	B	39,61,54
Prof	Brown, James	M	11,12A,38,64C
Assoc Prof	Brubeck, Dave W.	D	13,37,47,63C,49
Assoc Prof	Bumpers, Wayne	M	36,66A,66D,20G,66B
Prof	Bustamante, Linda	D	11,38,51,62C,62D
PT	Ciano, Jack		65
PT	Degooyer, Suzan	B	64A
PT	Driscoll, Katherine	D	66D,66A
PT	Farber, Mitchell		70
PT	Fowler, Lynda	D	66A
Prof	Greco, Eugene A.	D	36,12A,67F,12,67
PT	Hahn, Marjorie	B	63B,49,60
PT	James, William R.	D	66A,66C,66D
PT	McCormick, Thomas	M	64E,20G,29
PT	Molina, Carlos	B	70
PT	Nakashima, Rieko	M	66A,66D
PT	Poltarack, Sanford	A	70
Prof	Pyle, Jane	M	13,11,12A,66A,66B
PT	Pyle, Sally	B	66A
PT	Rice, Betty	M	66G
Prof	Rose, Richard F.	D	11,32B,32C,62D,29
PT	Rutter, Bronwen	M	66A,66H,66C
PT	Santiago, Gabriella	M	62A
PT	Sendler, Greg	M	
PT	Sleeper, Kathryn	M	64D
Prof	Smith, Vernon L.	D	11,36,61
PT	Soto, Christian	M	61
Prof	Tomasello, Randal S.	M	29
Assoc Prof	Vasquez, Hector	D	13,11,12A,66A
PT	Webster, Peter	B	50,65

FL1310 Miami-Dade Comm College-North
Department of Performing Arts
11380 NW 27th Ave
Miami, FL 33167-3418
(305) 323-1450   Fax: (305) 237-1850
www.mdc.edu/north
E-mail: oroca@mdc.edu

2 Year Institution

Prof	Boos, Kenneth G.	D	13,60,36,41,61
	Bredice, Vincent	B	70
	Casselle, Carol	M	61
	Dinino, Aileen	M	62A,62B
Assoc Prof	Douyon, Marcaisse	M	13,10,34
PT	Erastostene, Mario		70,35B
PT	Gold, Maxine		66A
	Gold, Scott		62D
Prof	Hanna, Cassandria	M	13,66A,66D,36
Inst	Kreitner, William	M	47,50,65,53
	Lester, Timothy	M	61
	Mitchell, Teresa L.		64A
	Nagy, Karen	M	61,39
	Osorio, Claudio	M	63A
	Perez-Feria, Willy	B	47,61
Lect	Pitasi, Dennis		66A
PT	Reichgott, Joseph	M	62D
	Remek, Robert	M	66A
	Rutledge, Kevin		36,61
	Selleck, Maria	D	66A
Inst	Steele, Carol	M	61,39
	Valeria, Anna		32B,66D
	Vera, Juan-Carlos	M	70

FL1360 New College of Florida
Division of Humanities-Music
5800 Bay Shore Rd
Sarasota, FL 34243
(941) 487-4360   Fax: (941) 487-4479
www.ncf.edu
E-mail: miles@ncf.edu

4 Year Institution

Chair: Aron Edidin, 80A

Assoc Prof	Clark, Maribeth	D	11,12,14,15
Assoc Prof	Miles, Stephen T.	D	13,10,43

FL1430 Northwest Florida State College
Division Hum., Fine & Perf. Arts
100 College Blvd E
Niceville, FL 32578-1347
(850) 729-5382   Fax: (850) 729-5286
www.nwfsc.edu/Humanities
E-mail: bakerm@nwfsc.edu

2 Year Institution

Chair & Dir., Artist Series: Clifford Herron, 80A,80F

Inst PT	Boudette, Jennifer	M	61
Inst	Domulot, Fred		65
Inst PT	Dunbar, Ulrike		52
Inst	Everitt, Allison	M	13,36,61,55
Inst	Heath, Guy	PhD	11,36,35A
Inst	Hoops, Richard	D	66A
Inst	Horne, Robin	B	64A,48
PT	Jones, Cheryl	M	37,66A,66B,47,61
Inst	Latenser, Tom	M	62D
Inst	Leatherwood, John G.	M	61,11
Inst	Murdock, Kelly	B	52
Inst PT	Nida, Chris	B	70
Inst	Parker, Kara	M	61,36
Inst	Ribando, Jeremy S.	D	61,13
Inst	Schlatter, Carolyn	M	66A,13,11
Inst PT	Spivey, Gary	M	64
Inst	Taylor, Joseph	M	52
Inst	VanDam, Lois	M	66A,36,60A

FL1450 Palm Beach Atlantic University
School of Music & Fine Arts
PO Box 24708
West Palm Beach, FL 33416-4708
(561) 803-2400   Fax: (561) 803-2424
www.pba.edu
E-mail: ken_phillips@pba.edu

4 Year Institution

Dean & Dir., Artist Series: Lloyd Mims, 80A,80F
Chair: Kenneth Phillips, 80A
Dir., Preparatory Division: Patrick Clifford, 80E

Adj	Aliapoulios, S. Mark	M	61,47
Adj	Ashley, Marie	M	61
Adj	Brouwer, Kristin	M	61
Adj	Castiglione, Anita	D	66C,13
Asst Prof	Clifford, Patrick	M	62A,62B,51
Adj	Forte, Michael	B	64C
Assoc Prof	Galer, Suzanne J.	D	61
Adj	Glover, Robert	D	66C
Asst Prof	Grohman, Bryon T.	D	61,36
Assoc Prof	Hayslett, Dennis J.	D	37,32E
Assoc Prof	Holland, Geoffrey	D	60,36
Adj	Holland, Patricia	M	66G
Adj	Horstman, Dorothy Yanes	M	61
Adj	Ivanovic, Predrag	M	63B
Adj	Jaffe, Claudio	D	62,38,62C
Adj	Joyce, Susan	D	66A,66D
Adj	Keith, Anna	M	61
Adj	Kennedy, Sarah	M	64B
Adj	Maloney, Chris	B	70
Adj	McComas, Inez S.	D	64E,13
Prof	Mims, Lloyd	D	61,31A,38
Artist in Res	Mims, Marilyn	B	61,39
Asst Prof	O'Connor, Michael B.	D	12A,11,20,55
Adj	Owens, Janet	M	66D,13,11
Adj	Pagliuca, Domingo	M	63C
Prof	Phillips, Kenneth	D	32
Asst Prof	Pontbriand, Roget	M	45,46,35,10D,10C
Adj	Riter, Tye	M	63A
Adj	Salsbury, Ben	M	51
Adj	Seward, Owen	M	65,11
Adj	Sharon, Robert	D	66C
Adj	Skantar, David	M	70
Adj	Spangler, Martha	B	62D
Adj	Stout, Sara	M	64A
Adj	Taylor, Janda	B	66C
Prof	Thompson, Timothy D.	D	10,13,34,64E
Prof	Woodward-Cooper, Marlene	M	13,66A,66B,66C

FL1470 Palm Beach Community College
Division of Humanities-Music
4200 S Congress Ave
Lake Worth, FL 33461-4705
(561) 868-3316   Fax: (561) 868-3273
www.palmbeachstate.edu
E-mail: webbera@www.palmbeachstate.edu

2 Year Institution

Associate Chair: David L. Gibble, 80H
Associate Dean: Richard Holcomb, 80H
Associate Chair: Michael J. MacMullen, 80H

Assoc Prof	Gibble, David L.	M	29,47,37,53,49
Assoc Prof	Jones, Robert D.	M	66A,66G,66C,66D,34
Assoc Prof	MacMullen, Michael J.	M	13A,11,36,61,54
Prof	Webber, Allen L.	M	13,11,61,10A,66A

FL1500 Pensacola State College
Department of Music & Theatre
1000 College Blvd
Pensacola, FL 32504-8910
(850) 484-1800   Fax: (850) 484-1835
www.pensacolastate.edu
E-mail: dsnowden@pensacolastate.edu

2 Year Institution

Head: Donald Snowden, 80A

Adj	Brown, Ila	B	66A,66C
Prof	Chen, Xiaolun	M	11,36,61
Adj	Coleman, Michael	D	13,10,11,66A,34
Adj	Eddins, Judy	M	11,61
Adj	Fossa, Matthew A.	M	11,64B
Adj	Gibson, Jeannette	M	11
Prof	Jernigan, Richard	M	11,64
Adj	Lujan, Bethany	M	64A
Adj	Millet, Wayne	M	61
Adj	Nagy, Daniel	M	66A,66D
Adj	Onalbayeva, Kadisha	D	11,66
Adj	Pearce, Stephen	M	63A
Adj	Riegle, Dale	B	47,49,63A
Adj	Sherwood, Gertrude	M	61
Assoc Prof	Snowden, Donald	M	37,47,63D,29A
Prof	Stallings, Joe	D	13,11,70,34
Adj	Villines, Roger	M	63A,47,11
Adj	Walker, Abigail	M	11,64D,66D
Adj	Yanovskiy, Leonid	D	62A,62B,38

FL1550 Rollins College
Department of Music
1000 Holt Ave - # 2731
Winter Park, FL 32789-4419
(407) 646-1527   Fax: (407) 646-2533
www.rollins.edu/music/
E-mail: sorr@rollins.edu

4 Year Institution
Member of NASM

Chair: John V. Sinclair, 80A

Artist in Res	Archard, Chuck	M	47,62D,53,29
Adj	Arzillo, Marisa A.	M	61
Adj	Barron, Christine	B	64C
Adj	Blice, Carolyn	M	63B
Adj	Bolves, Keith	M	61
Adj	Carter, Christina	M	60A,61,11
Adj	Concepcion, Elman O.	M	70
Prof	Cook, Gloria	D	66A,66B,13C,11,66C
Adj	Croson, James M.	D	34
Assoc Prof	Crozier, Daniel G.	D	13,10,12A
Adj	Davis, Morgan	B	61
Adj	De Paula, Isidoro	D	66A
Adj	Del Cid, Sandra	M	64A
Adj	Dietz, Tom	M	64C
Adj	Dolske, Christopher C.	M	63A,49,29A
Adj	Edwards, Dawn	M	62E
Adj	Ervin, Richard	M	64D
Adj	Flick, Daniel K.	M	70,13,42
Asst Prof	Foster, Julia	D	39,61
Adj	Gifford, Amy L.	D	61,11,54
Adj	Hawkins, Sherwood M.	B	64B,48
Adj	Higgins, Brenda L.	M	62C,55B
Adj	Hilbun, Aaron Ichiro	D	12A
Adj	Hill, Don-Michael A.	B	62D
Collaborative Pianist	Irei, Norito	M	66A,66C
Adj	Johnson, Daniel	M	65
Adj	Kashnig, Claude	M	63D
Adj	Koelble, Bobby	B	70,42
Prof	Lackman, Susan Cohn	D	13,10,12A,35
Adj	Lee, Rebecca	M	66A
Adj	Lefkowitz, Aaron M.	M	63C,37
Adj	Llyod, Adam	M	61
Adj	LoPresti, Kathleen M.	M	61
Adj	Mozelle, Mary M.	M	66G,66H
Adj	Nicholas, Alexander	M	61
Adj	Owens, Richard R.	M	61,39
Adj	Pattishall, Jeffrey	B	70
Adj	Ray, James	M	66D,34D,60A,35C
Adj	Rayam, Curtis J.	B	61
Artist in Res	Roos, Joni N.	B	62A,62B,51
Adj	Shoopman, Chad	M	10C
Prof	Sinclair, John V.	D	60,32,36,41,38
Adj	Swope, Matthew	M	61
Adj	Valente, Liana	D	61,38,13E,39,12A
Adj	Witmer, Ruth	D	12A,14,20
Adj	Wolf, Gary	D	66A
Adj	Yount, Terry A.	D	66G

FL1570 St Johns River State Coll
Florida School of the Arts
5001 St Johns Ave
Palatka, FL 32177-3897
(386) 312-4300   Fax: (386) 312-4306
www.floarts.org
E-mail: floarts@sjrstate.edu

2 Year Institution

Dean: Alain R. Hentschel, 80A

Prof	Clark, Michael	M	13,12A,36,66,54
Prof	Dando, Lee C.	M	52
Prof	Masterson, Stephanie C.	M	12A,61,54

FL1600 St Leo University
School of Arts & Sciences
PO Box 6665 MC 2127
Saint Leo, FL 33574-6665
(352) 588-8423   Fax: (352) 588-8300
www.saintleo.edu
E-mail: june.hammond@saintleo.edu

4 Year Institution

Coordinator: June C. Hammond, 80A
Dean: Mary T. Spoto, 80A

Asst Prof	Hammond, June C.	D	12A,36,61,66A,37
Adj	Parris, John	M	70
Adj	Payne, Bryon	B	61,62,66A
Adj	Yamaguchi, Yuko	B	66A,66C

FL1650 St Petersburg College
Department of Fine Arts
6605 5th Ave N
St Petersburg, FL 33710-6801
(727) 341-4360   Fax: (727) 341-4744
www.spcollege.edu/spg/music
E-mail: smith.nancy@spcollege.edu

2 Year Institution

Chair: Nancy Smith, 80A

PT	Bannon, John	D	37
PT	Barbanera, William	M	64E
PT	Braccio, Joseph	B	62
PT	Brian, Aric	M	63A
PT	Dixon, Paul	M	66G
PT	Donovick, Jeffery	M	66D,13A,13B,13C,34C
PT	Geyer, Luba	M	62A,62B
PT	Geyer, Oleg	M	62A,62B
PT	Gill, Lynette	M	66A
PT	Hall, Cory	D	66D,66A,12A
PT	Harris, Janet	B	64D
PT	Irwin, David	M	64C
PT	Lawhead, David	M	61
PT	Lugo, Eddy	M	70
PT	Mackle, Anne Kate	M	62E
Inst	Manson, David	M	47,63C,63D,53,34
	Matthews, Mark		10B,13A,34B,35A,70
Inst	Michael, Marilyn	M	39,61
PT	Neuenschwander, Mark		62D
PT	Pate, David	B	64E
PT	Prescott, Barbara	B	64A
PT	Shaw, John	M	50,65
PT	Switzer, Linda		61
Inst	Taranto, Vernon	D	10,11,13B,36,13C
PT	Varosy, Zsuzsanna	M	62C
PT	Wahl, Carolyn	B	63B

FL1675 Santa Fe College
Department of Music
3000 NW 83rd St E-127
Gainesville, FL 32606-6210
(352) 395-5310   Fax: (352) 395-4432
www.sfcollege.edu
E-mail: alora.haynes@sfcollege.edu

2 Year Institution

Chair: Alora D. Haynes, 80A

Adj Asst Prof	Ballengee, Chris	M	11,20
Adj Asst Prof	Barnfather, Samantha	M	13A
Prof	Bingham, Steve	D	11,13A,20,29,64
Adj Asst Prof	Forrester, Sheila	D	10A,13,66D,13D,13E
Adj Asst Prof	Goldblatt, David Nathan	D	13A
Adj Asst Prof	Harris, Melanie	M	36,61
Adj Asst Prof	Holder, Brian	D	11,20,13A,65,50
Adj Asst Prof	Keebaugh, Aaron	M	11,20,13A,63
	Larson, Leon		20H,65
Adj Asst Prof	Rosenshein, Ingrid		11,13A,61,66D,54
Prof	Sandefur, Lynn	M	11,13A,36,40,61
Adj Asst Prof	Smolenski, Scott	M	66A,10,11,13,20
	Stano, Richey		70,10

FL1700 Seminole State College of Florida
Department of Arts & Communication
100 Weldon Blvd
Sanford, FL 32773-6199
(407) 708-2039   Fax: (407) 328-2354
www.seminolestate.edu
E-mail: parkerr@seminolestate.edu

2 Year Institution

Music Coordinator: Robin Lee Parker, 80A
Associate Dean, Arts and Communications: Paul Luby, 80H

	Campbell, Dianna		61,36,40,11,32D
	Ellmore, Laurel	B	61
	Ettinger, Karl Erik	M	66A,11,12A
	Gallo, Patrick	M	66D
	Harmon, Richard		
	Hsu, Yun-Ling	D	66A
	James, Richard	M	11
	Johnson, Daniel	M	12A,13,65
	Lewis, Cheryse McLeod	M	61
	Loos, Brandon	M	63A
	Luciano, Stephen		70
	Mudge, Ashley	M	13,64A
	Parker, Robin Lee	B	66C
	Pattishall, Teresa	M	11,37
	Perinchief, Burt H.	D	61
	Stillwell, Jonathan	M	62C
	Strang, Kevin	M	64C
	Terrell, Maurice		11,29,37,47,60B
	Tschannen, James	M	70
	Whitehead, David	M	61

FL1730 South Florida Community College
Department of Music
600 W College Dr
Avon Park, FL 33825-9356
(863) 784-7201   Fax: (863) 784-7190
www.southflorida.edu/
E-mail: JamesT@southflorida.edu

2 Year Institution

Dean: David Sconyers, 80A

PT	Lewis, Susan	M	61,66A,66G
PT	Smith, D.	M	37

FL1740 Southeastern University
Music Program
1000 Longfellow Blvd
Lakeland, FL 33801-6034
(863) 667-5000   Fax: (863) 667-5200
www.seu.edu
E-mail: dhtindal@seu.edu

4 Year Institution

Chair & Dir., Summer Programs: Danny H. Tindall, 80A,80G
Dir., Artist Series: Edward Bryant, 80F

Assoc Prof	Braamse, Shudong	D	61,13C
Assoc Prof	Bryant, Edward	M	13C,36,61,39,40
Asst Prof	Gardiner, Annabelle	M	62A,62B,51,38
Assoc Prof	Gardiner, Ronald	M	13,62,60B,51,38
Prof	Gordon, Daniel	D	13,32,60A,36
Assoc Prof	Harlan, Paul	D	66A,10,34,35C
Asst Prof	Hulin, Charles J.	D	13,66D,66A,66G
Prof	Seybert, John M.	M	60,66A,32,64E,12
Artist in Res	Tak, Young-Ah	M	66A,60,13A,13B,41
Prof	Tindall, Danny H.	D	36,37,65,11

FL1745 State College of Florida
Department of Fine & Perf Arts
Music Program
PO Box 1849
Bradenton, FL 34206
(941) 752-5351   Fax: (941) 727-6075
www.scf.edu
E-mail: turonc@scf.edu

2 Year Institution

Music Contact: Charles T. Turon, 80A

Adj	Apple, Warren	D	61,66A
Adj	Barbanera, Lisa	M	64A
Adj	Barbanera, William	M	64C,64E
Adj	Bolton, Gregory	B	70
Adj	Brunelle, Felicia	D	62A
Adj	Chandra, Bharat	M	64C
Adj	Choe, Sung	M	66A
Adj	Craven, Todd	M	63A
Adj	Frantz, Nathan	M	62B
Adj	Gershfeld, Tatyana	M	66
Adj	Hawkinson, Carol	M	66A,66G
Adj	Johns, Stephen	M	11
Inst	Lewis, Alexander	D	61,36,39
Adj	Lischetti, Robert	B	61
Adj	Mannino, Marc P.	M	70
Adj	Markaverich, Michael	M	66A
Adj	Miller, John	M	62D,70
Adj	Millner, William	M	37
Adj	Pegis, Damien	M	62A
Adj	Penpraze, Laurie	D	63C,63D,66D,67E
Adj	Reinert, C. Robert	M	64D
Adj	Sarakatsannis, Leonidas N.	D	66A
Adj	Spaulding, Laura	M	61
Adj	Stoltie, James	M	64E
Adj	Streetman, Nancy	M	62C
Adj	Suta, Thomas	M	65,50
Adj	Traba, Fernando	M	64D
Assoc Prof	Turon, Charles T.	M	11,13,66A,66D
Adj	Van Dreel, K.	M	63B
Adj	Von Dassow, Sasha	M	51,62C
Adj	Willis, A. Rexford	M	13,10,70,13A

FL1750 Stetson University
School of Music
421 N Woodland Blvd
Unit 8399
Deland, FL 32723
(386) 822-8950   Fax: (386) 822-8948
www.stetson.edu
E-mail: jwest@stetson.edu

4 Year Institution
Member of NASM

Dean: Jean West, 80A
Counselor, Music Admissions: Tammy C. Shistle, 80D
Dir., Comm School of the Arts: Claudia Gatewood, 80E
Associate Dean: Noel Painter, 80H

Lect	Adams, Ann M.	D	64B,11,32C
Prof	Adams, Bobby L.	D	32,37,60B
Assoc Prof	Alfonzo, Jesus	D	62A,62B
Adj	Bishop, James	M	64E
Assoc Prof	Bjella, David E.	M	41,62C
Lect	Born, Kristie	D	66C
Adj	Brame, Robert	B	34
Prof	Christeson, Jane	M	61,12A,39,36
Adj	Crane, Amy	M	66A
Assoc Prof	de Murga, Manuel	D	10,10F,13E,34,43
Adj	Franks, Russell	M	61,39
Assoc Prof	Gomez, Routa Kroumovitch	M	12A,62A,62B
Lect	Groskreutz, Shannon	M	13
Lect	Haakenson, Matthew A.	M	10A,66G,13,13D,13J
Adj	Heintzen, Ashley	D	64D
Adj	Hodkinson, Sydney P.	D	10A
Prof	Hose, Anthony	M	38,60,35E
Prof	Jones, Boyd M.	D	13,66G
Adj	Kang, Grace	D	41,63B
Adj	Kerney, Marja	M	65
Prof	Kindred, Janis B.	D	13
Adj	Knotts, Clara		32C,32E
Assoc Prof	Larson, Andrew	D	61,36,60A
Assoc Prof	Linney, Lloyd	D	13,61,12A
Adj	Macklin, Thomas		63A
Assoc Prof	Maddox, Craig	D	34,61
Adj	McQuinn, Susan	M	64A
Adj	Miller, Tammy	M	66C,66A,66D
Adj	Mitchell, Rebecca		52
Adj	Muley, Nandkishor	M	20D
Prof	Musco, Lynn A.	D	41,64C
Assoc Prof	Painter, Noel	D	13,10F
Adj	Palmer, Edit	M	13,66A
	Peter, Timothy	D	36
Adj	Rich, Mollie	M	61
Prof	Rickman, Michael	D	66A,12A,66B,66D
Adj	Robinson, Patrece	M	35
Prof	Robinson, Stephen	D	70
Assoc Prof	Schmidt, David	M	49,63C,63D
Prof	Small, Ann R.	D	32,36
Adj	Waid, Tom	B	63D
Asst Prof	Wald, Jean P.	M	16
Adj	West, George	D	47,29A,53
Prof	West, Jean	D	12A,64A
Adj	Wieland, John	M	62D
Assoc Prof	Wolek, Nathan	D	34,11,45

FL1790 Tallahassee Community College
Department of Music
444 Appleyard Dr
Tallahassee, FL 32304-2815
(850) 201-6200   Fax: (850) 201-8044
www.tcc.fl.edu
E-mail: barinear@tcc.fl.edu

2 Year Institution

Dean: Marge Banocy-Payne, 80A

Prof	Beckley-Roberts, Lisa	M	20G,29
Adj	Coates, Gary	B	47,37,46,66F
Adj	Fleischmann, Rob	M	20G
Adj	Norris, Mike	M	36,12A
Adj	Richards, Walter	PhD	20G

FL1800 Univ of Central Florida
Department of Music
4000 Central Florida Blvd
Orlando, FL 32816-1354
(407) 823-2869   Fax: (407) 823-3378
www.music.ucf.edu
E-mail: jeffrey.moore@ucf.edu

4 Year Institution, Graduate School
Member of NASM

Master of Arts in Music

Chair: Jeffrey M. Moore, 80A
Dir., Undergraduate Studies: Kirk Gay, 80B
Associate Chair & Dir., Graduate Studies: Keith Koons, 80C,80H
Associate Vice Provost: Lyman Brodie

Inst	Allen, Donald F.	D	37
Adj	Almeida, Artie	D	32A
Assoc Prof	Almeida, John	M	63A,49
Vstng Inst	Anderson, Thad	D	65,50,34
Adj	Beck, Rosalind	B	62E
Assoc Prof	Boukobza, Laurent	DIPL	66A,66B
Prof	Brunner, David L.	D	60,36,32D,10
Asst Prof	Danielsson, Per	M	29,66A
Adj	Drexler, Richard	B	29
Vstng Inst	Garasi, Michael J.	M	37,60B
Assoc Prof	Garcia, Nora Lee	D	64A,48
Inst	Gay, Kirk	M	50,65,34
Lect	Gennaro, Joe	D	11,12A,20
Adj	Hill, Don-Michael A.	M	62D
Adj	Hsu, Yun-Ling	D	66A,66B,66C,66D
Assoc Prof	Hunt, Jeremy	D	61
Adj	Hunt, Johanna	M	61
Adj	Jordan, Grace	M	32
Adj	Koeble, Robert	B	29
Prof	Koons, Keith	D	64C,48
Assoc Prof	Marosi, Laszlo	D	38,60
Adj	Marshall, Christopher J.	M	10
Asst Prof	Miller, Kelly A.	D	32,36
Prof	Moore, Jeffrey M.	M	65,50
Adj	Morell, Martin		29
Prof	Pherigo, Johnny L.	D	11,41,49,48,63B
Assoc Prof	Potter, Thomas	M	61,39
Adj	Rinaldi, Beverley	M	61
Prof	Rupert, Jeffrey M.	M	29,46
Assoc Prof	Scharron, Eladio	D	70,51
Inst	Schreier, David	M	49,37
Adj	Sisk, Robin	D	63D
Adj	Stanton, Laurel	M	62C
Assoc Prof	Stephenson, JoAnne	D	61

Adj	Strefeler, Jamie	M	64B,48
Inst	Thornton, Robert	M	13C,13A
Asst Prof	Tobias, Scott C.	D	37,32E,60
Assoc Prof	Warfield, Scott A.	D	12,20,11
Assoc Prof	Weremchuk, George	D	64E,48
Asst Prof	Wilkinson, Michael	M	63C,47,29B
Prof	Yonetani, Ayako	D	62A,62B,42

FL1850 Univ of Florida

School of Music
PO Box 117900
Gainesville, FL 32611-7900
(352) 392-0223   Fax: (352) 392-0461
www.arts.ufl.edu/music
E-mail: music@arts.ufl.edu

4 Year Institution, Graduate School
Member of NASM

Master of Music in Composition, Master of Music in Music Theory, Master of Music in Performance, Master of Music in Conducting, Master of Music in Music Education, PhD in Music Education, PhD in Music, Master of Music in Music History & Literature

Director: John A. Duff, PhD, 80A
Coord., Admission/Undergraduate Advising: Mutlu Citim-Kepic, 80B,80D
Dir., Operations: Charles W. Pickeral, 80H

Prof	Basler, Paul	D	13,63B,34
Assoc Prof	Bauer, William I.	PhD	32,34
Inst	Birkner, Chip	M	37
Assoc Prof	Broadway, Kenneth	D	50,65
Assoc Prof	Brophy, Timothy S.	D	32
Prof	Burrichter, Ronald	M	36,61
Asst Prof	Butler, Margaret R.	D	12
Vstng Lect	Casseday, Kevin	M	62D
Assoc Prof	Chobaz, Raymond	D	13,60,38
Prof	Crook, Larry	D	14,50,20H
Prof	Davis, Joyce	D	49,63A
Asst Prof	dos Santos, Silvio J.	D	12
Prof	Duff, John A.	PhD	
	Elezovic, Ivan	M	10,13,34
Assoc Prof	Ellis, Laura	D	66G,69,66H,31
Assoc Prof	Estrin, Mitchell	M	41,64C
Prof	Graham, Elizabeth	D	39,61
Assoc Prof	Helton, Jonathan	D	64E,42,43
Prof	Hoffer, Charles	D	32
Asst Prof	Irchai, Arnold	D	64D
Inst	Jenkins, James E.	B	63D
Prof	Jennings, Arthur	D	11,63C,63D
Prof	Kesling, Will	D	36
Assoc Prof	Koonce, Paul C.	D	13,10
Prof Emeritus	Kushner, David Z.	D	12,12A,12B,12E,20G
Prof Emeritus	Langford, R. Gary	M	37,47,29A
Assoc Prof	Lower, Janna	D	62A
Asst Prof	Martinson, Kenneth	M	62B,51
Assoc Prof	Odom, Leslie S.	D	13,64B
Assoc Prof	Offerle, Anthony	D	39,61
Prof	Oliverio, James C.	D	10,34
Assoc Prof	Orr, Kevin Robert	D	66A,66B,66D,13A,13
Asst Prof	Reed, S. Alexander	D	13,10
Assoc Prof	Richards, Paul	D	13,10
Prof	Robinson, Russell	D	32,36
Prof	Sain, James Paul	D	13,10,34
Assoc Prof	Sharpe, Kevin	D	66A,66C
Assoc Prof	Smith, Brenda	D	61
Assoc Prof	Stoner, Kristen L.	D	64A
Assoc Prof	Thomas, Jennifer	D	12
Asst Prof	Thomas, Steven F.	D	62C
Asst Prof	Tremura, Welson Alves	D	70,20
Asst Prof	Watkins, John M. 'Jay'	M	37
Prof	Waybright, David	D	60,37
Asst Prof	Wilson, Scott	M	29

FL1900 Univ of Miami

Frost School of Music
PO Box 248165
Miami, FL 33124-7610
(305) 284-2241   Fax: (305) 284-6475
www.music.miami.edu
E-mail: eutsey@miami.edu

4 Year Institution, Graduate School
Member of NASM

Master of Music in Multiple Woodwinds, Master of Music in Composition, Master of Music in Music Education, Master of Music in Music Therapy, Master of Music in Musicology, PhD in Music Education, DMA in Composition, DMA in Choral Conducting, Artist Diploma in Keyboard Performance, Artist Diploma in Vocal Performance, Master of Music in Choral Conducting, Master of Music in Studio Jazz Writing, Master of Music in Media Writing-Production, Master of Music in Collaborative Keyboard, Master of Music in Instrumental Performance, Master of Music in Studio Music & Jazz Instrumental Performance, Master of Music in Studio Music & Jazz Vocal Performance, Master of Music in Keyboard Performance, Master of Music in Music Ed with Certification, Master of Music in Sound Recording Arts, Master of Music in Digital Arts & Sound Design, Master of Arts in Arts Presenting, Master of Music in Music Ed with String Pedagogy Emphasis, DMA in Vocal Performance, DMA in Instrumental Conducting, DMA in Studio Music & Jazz Instrumental Performance, DMA in Studio Music & Jazz Vocal Performance, DMA in Collaborative Keyboard, DMA in Keyboard Performance, DMA in Jazz Composition, DMA in Vocal Pedagogy & Performance, DMA in Instrumental Performance, DMA in Instrumental Performance - Multi Woodwinds, PhD in Music Ed with Music Therapy Emphasis, Artist Diploma in Instrumental Conducting, Artist Diploma in Instrumental Performance, Master of Music in Instrumental Conducting, Master of Science in Music Engineering Technology, Master of Music in Vocal Performance, Master of Music in Keyboard Performance & Pedagogy

Dean: Shelton G. Berg, 80A
Associate Dean & Dir., Undergraduate Studies: Kenneth J. Moses, 80B,80H
Interim Associate Dean, Dir., Graduate Studies: Shannon K. De L'Etoile, 80C,80H
Dir., Summer Programs: Esther Jane Hardenbergh, 80G

Lect	Abbati, Joseph S.	B	10B,34A,35C,45,34E
Assoc Prof	Abril, Carlos	D	32,12E
Prof	Asmus, Edward P.	D	32,12F
Prof	Basham, Glenn D.	M	62A
Asst Prof	Bejerano, Martin	M	29,10,66A,53
Asst Prof	Bennett, Christopher	D	34D,34G,34H
Prof	Berg, Shelton G.	M	66A,66C,29,46,47
Lect	Bergeron, Chuck	M	62D,47,29A,46,12A
Other	Blanchard, Terence	D	63A,10,47
Lect	Boardman, Christopher	DIPL	10C,35
Vstng Lect	Boutte, Tony L.	D	61,39
Asst Prof	Chattah, Juan	D	13,10B,10C
Prof	Coffman, Don D.	D	32E,32G
Asst Prof	Collins, Willa	D	12,14C
Lect	Conner, Timothy M.	B	63C,41,42
Prof	Cooper, Frank E.	M	12,66A,66H,67
Asst Prof	de Graaf, Melissa J.	D	12,12A,11
Assoc Prof	De L'Etoile, Shannon K.	D	33
Lect	Denison, Maria Fenty	D	61
Assoc Prof	Donaghue, Margaret A.	D	64C,42
Assoc Prof	Elton, Serona	D	35A,35B,35D,35F,35H
Lect	Flavin, Scott Thomas		62A,51
Prof	Floyd, J. Robert	D	66A
Assoc Prof	Gonzalez, Rene	D	41,70
Prof	Green, Gary D.	M	60,37
Lect	Guerra, Stephen J.	M	10F,29A,29B,47
Adj Asst Prof	Guy, Kathyanne	M	52
Prof	Harbaugh, Ross T.	B	62C
Assoc Prof	Hardenbergh, Esther Jane	D	61
Asst Prof	Hindman, Dorothy Elliston	D	10A,10F,13
Asst Prof/Prac	Hughes, Bryn	D	13
Asst Prof	Johnson, Alan O.	M	61,39
Prof	Kam, Dennis	D	13,10
Lect	Kaminsky, Carol Frances	M	52
Assoc Prof	Kane, Trudy	M	64A,41,48
Lect	Keck, Thomas B.	D	37,60B
Adj Assoc Prof	Keller, Gary W.	M	64E,29,47
Assoc Prof	Kennedy, Karen	D	60A,36
Lect	Kuite, Anne		52
Prof	Lapin, Lawrence	M	13,10,36,47,29
Prof	Lebon, Rachel L.	D	47,61,32,35A,54
Assoc Prof	Leider, Colby N.	D	34A,35C,10B,34D,35G
Assoc Prof	Lesiuk, Teresa L.	D	33,12A
Prof	Lindsay, Gary M.	M	47,64E,29
Lect	Luciani, Dante T.		47,63C,29
Asst Prof	Lynch, Brian	M	63A,10,47,46,29B
Lect	Lyons, Lisanne E.	D	61,29,53,47
Prof	Magnanini, Luciano	DIPL	41,48,64D

Assoc Prof	Mason, Charles Norman	D	10A,10B,10F,34D
Prof	McConnell, Pamela A.	M	62B
Assoc Prof	McLoskey, Lansing D.	D	10A,10F,13,55D
Assoc Prof	Morris, Craig	M	41,49,63A,42
Lect	Moses, Kenneth J.	M	60,37
Prof/Prac	Murciano, Raul	D	35,20H,10C
Lect	Murnak, Raina	D	61
Prof	Oglesby, Donald T.	D	60,12A,36
Assoc Prof	Olah, John J.	M	13,49,63D
Asst Prof/Prac	Overland, Corin T.	D	40,32,60A
Asst Prof	Palmer, Christopher G.	M	35A,35B,35E,35F,35H
Prof/Prac	Pilafian, Sam	B	63D,42
Lect	Pilar, Nobleza Garcia	D	61
Asst Prof	Pirkle, William C.	M	34A,34D,34G,35C,35G
Prof	Posnak, Paul	D	41,66A,66H,66C
Asst Prof	Powell, Brian T.	M	62D,41
Vstng Asst Prof	Redmon, Robynne	M	61
Asst Prof/Prac	Redmond, John	D	35A,35B,35D,35H
Prof	Rodriguez, Santiago	M	66A
Lect	Rucker, Steve P.	M	65,47,29
Lect	Russell, Brian	D	70
Assoc Prof	Sanchez, Rey	M	10D,34C,35A,20G,43
Lect	Schwartz, Paul	M	66C
Assoc Prof	Schwartz-Kates, Deborah	D	12,20H,14
Vstng Asst Prof	Short, Kevin	M	61
Prof	Sidener, Whitney F.	M	47,64E,29
Prof	Sleeper, Thomas M.	M	10F,60,10,38
Lect	Stinson, Scott	D	10A,10F,13D,13F
Asst Prof	Stoyanov, Svetoslav R.	M	65,50,42,43
Vstng Asst Prof	Strauss, Matthew B.	M	65,50
Asst Prof	Takao, Naoko	D	66B,66C,66D
Assoc Prof	Todd, Richard	B	61,39
Lect	Underwood, Dale W.	DIPL	64E
Lect	Walsh, Megan A.	D	66A
Lect	Weiner, Robert A.	M	41,64B
Assoc Prof	Ying, Tian	DIPL	66A
Assoc Prof	Zavac, Nancy C.	M	16,12F
Assoc Prof	Zdzinski, Stephen	D	32,32G,32H,12C,13K

FL1950 Univ of North Florida
Department of Music
1 UNF Drive
Jacksonville, FL 32224-2646
(904) 620-2960   Fax: (904) 620-2568
www.unf.edu/coas/music
E-mail: rtinnin@unf.edu

4 Year Institution
Member of NASM

Chair: Randall C. Tinnin, 80A
Dir., Institute/Festival/Workshop: Nick Curry, 80F
Dir., Institute/Festival/Workshop: Clarence Hines, 80F
Dir., Artist/Performance Series: Charlotte Mabrey, 80F
Dir., Artist/Performance Series: J. B. Scott, 80F
Dir., Artist/Performance Series: Guy Yehuda, 80F
Dir., Summer Programs: Erin K. Bennett, 80G
Dir., Summer Programs: Marcus Dickman, 80G

Adj	Amato, Michelle	M	61
Assoc Prof	Arriale, Lynne	M	66A,29B,46
Asst Prof	Bennett, Erin K.	D	66A,66B,66D
Assoc Prof	Biernacki, Krzysztof K.	M	61,39
Asst Prof	Bovenzi, Michael	D	34,32E,64E
Prof	Brock, Gordon R.	D	37,48,64E,60B,10A
Adj	Cassano, Rhonda	M	64A
Asst Prof	Curry, Nick	D	62C,12,11
Assoc Prof	Dickman, Marcus	D	63D,53,29
Adj	Dwyer, Laura L.	M	64A
Adj	Falkner, Renate M.	M	62B,67B
Adj	Garry, Kevin	M	65
Assoc Prof	Gottlieb, Daniel	B	65,46,34C
Prof Emeritus	Green, Bunky	M	64E,53,29
Prof	Greene, Barry	M	47,70,29
Adj	Hibbard, Jason	M	11,66D
Asst Prof	Hines, Clarence	D	63C,29
Prof Emeritus	Holt, Dennis	D	32
Adj	Ishimaru, Kayo	M	62E
Adj	Lindsay, Jason M.	D	62D
Prof	Mabrey, Charlotte	M	50,65,43,20G
Assoc Prof	Marks, Dennis J.	M	62D,66A,47,29A
Vstng Asst Prof	Mathews, Peter	D	11,12
Adj	Minch, Claudia	M	64B
Adj	Rankin, Charles	M	32,37
Adj	Reid, Kevin	M	63B
Assoc Prof	Scott, J. B.	M	63A,53,47,29A
Assoc Prof	Shiao, Simon	D	51,62A,62B,38
Prof	Smart, Gary	D	13,10F,10,66A,53
Adj	Smart, Marilyn	M	11,39,61
Adj	Smith, Kandie K.	D	61,13
Assoc Prof	Tasher, Cara S.	D	60A,61,36
Adj	Thornton, Paula E.	M	60
Assoc Prof	Tinnin, Randall C.	D	63A,49,37,32E,20
Asst Prof	Yehuda, Guy	D	64C,60B,41,32E

FL2000 Univ of South Florida
College of the Arts
MUS 101
4202 E Fowler Ave
Tampa, FL 33620-7350
(813) 974-2311   Fax: (813) 974-8721
music.arts.usf.edu
E-mail: info@arts.usf.edu

4 Year Institution, Graduate School
Member of NASM

Master of Arts in Music Education, Master of Music in Composition, Master of Music in Music Theory, Master of Music in Performance, Master of Music in Conducting, PhD in Music Education, Master of Music in Jazz Studies, Master of Music in Pedagogy, Master of Music in Chamber Music, Master of Music in Electro-Acoustic Music

Interim Director: Josef W. Knott, 80A
Dir., Undergraduate, Graduate Studies & Admissions: William P. Hayden, 80B,80D,80C
Associate Director: David A. Williams, 80H

Adj Inst	Aagaard, Kathy	M	62B
Assoc Prof	Bass, James K.	D	36
Prof	Brantley, K. Thomas	M	63C
Asst Prof	Brasky, Jill T.	D	13,13B,13C,62A
Adj Inst	Brian, Aric J.	M	11
Asst Prof	Bugos, Jennifer A.	D	32
Prof	Carmichael, John C.	D	37
Asst Prof	Cho, Kyoung	M	61
Assoc Prof	Coble, Jay	M	63A
Adj Inst	Collins, Amy	M	64B
Asst Prof	Diamond, Brad	D	61
Adj Inst	Falwell, Calvin	M	64C
Prof	Fung, C. Victor	D	32G,32,20D
Adj Inst	Gillespie, Valerie	M	64E
Adj Inst	Goodman, Ian P.	M	65
Prof Emerita	Hawkins, Anne	M	13
Assoc Prof	Hayden, William P.	D	62A,62B,51
Prof Emeritus	Heller, Jack J.	D	32,12F
Vstng Asst Prof	Hunsberger, Johnson	M	63D
Assoc Prof	Ivanov, Svetozar D.	D	66A
Assoc Prof	Jaworski, Warren	D	61
Prof Emeritus	Jennings, Vance	D	12A,14A
Prof Emeritus	Jones, Hilton Kean	M	10,35,13,45,66G
Adj Inst	Karr, Andrew	M	63B
Adj Inst	Kehayas, John	M	64D
Prof	Kluksdahl, Scott	M	12A,62C
Asst Prof	Lang, Zoe	D	12
Assoc Prof	Lee, Sang-Hie	D	11,12C
Prof Emeritus	Lewis, James E.	M	13,10F,10,43
Assoc Prof	McCormick, Kim S.	D	64A
Prof	McCormick, Robert	M	50,65
Inst	McCutchen, Matt	D	37
Prof Emerita	Monroe, Annetta Y.	B	61
Assoc Prof	Moore, Janet L. S.	D	32B
Assoc Prof	Moorhead, J. Brian	M	64C
Adj Inst	Moses, Dee	M	11,62D
Adj Inst	Neuenschwander, Mark L.		62D
Adj Inst	Nickelson, LaRue S.		70
Prof	Owen, Charles (Chuck) R.	M	47,29,10
Vstng Asst Prof	Panayotova, Miroslava I.	D	66A
Adj Inst	Posadas, John	M	62A,62B
Adj Inst	Rain, Jack	M	61,39
Asst Prof	Randles, Clinton A.	D	32C,32G,32E
Assoc Prof	Reller, Paul	D	10,34
Emeritus	Reynolds, Jerald M.	M	61
Prof	Robison, John O.	D	13,12A,12,67
Adj Inst	Rottmayer, Chris A.	M	66A
Asst Prof	Scotto, Ciro G.	D	13
Vstng Asst Prof	Sekhon, Baljinder S.	M	10,65,13,34
Assoc Prof	Stuart, Carolyn		62A,62B
Prof Emerita	Summer, Averill V.	D	66A,66D
Prof Emeritus	Summer, Robert J.	D	60,36
Vstng Inst	Tambiah, Dharshini	M	66A
Assoc Prof	Wiedrich, William	D	60,37,43
Prof	Wilkins, Ashby	M	47,29
Assoc Prof	Williams, David A.	D	32E,32G

FL2050 Univ of Tampa
Department of Music
401 W Kennedy Blvd
Tampa, FL 33606-1450
(813) 253-6212 Fax: (813) 258-7241
www.ut.edu
E-mail: tmohn@ut.edu

4 Year Institution
Member of NASM

Dean: Haig L. Mardirosian, 80A
Chair: Jeff Traster, 80A
Coord, Musical Events: David Isele, 80F

Adj	Adams, Lowell	M	51,62C
Adj	Arzillo, Marisa		61
	Blackburn, Bradford	M	13,11
Adj	Brian, Aric		63A,47
Adj	Callahan, Nancy		36
Adj	Coash, David C.	D	65
Adj	Decorso, Theodore	D	11,64
Adj	Demas, John	M	70
Adj	Devlin, Scott		64E
Adj	Geist, Gretchen		61
Adj	Goldstein, Lloyd		62D
Asst Prof	Hebert, Ryan	D	60,36,13C,66G
Adj	Hernly, Patrick		20,65
Prof	Isele, David	D	10F,10,36,61,66G
Adj	Jemmott, Thomas		29,70
Asst Prof	Jung, Hein	D	61
Adj	Liu, Lei	M	62A,62B
Adj	Macar, Robert		29,66A
Adj	Prescott, Barbara		64A
Adj	Reynolds, Jerald		61
Adj	Roberts, Elizabeth 'dolly'		62E
Adj	Robinson, Susan		38
Adj	Rodriguez, Linda M.	M	12A,66A
Adj	Sparrow, Richard		63B
Adj	Strawbridge, Nathan		20,65
Adj	Swartzbaugh, Bill	M	62D
Adj	Swartzbaugh, Tara	M	66A
Assoc Prof	Traster, Jeff	D	37,49,63D,32
Adj	Venturini, Maurizio		64D
Adj	Williams, Dale		66A,66C
Adj	Young, Katherine		64B
	Zamparas, Grigorios	D	66A,66H,12A
Adj	Zegel, Don		63C

FL2100 Univ of West Florida
Department of Music
11000 University Pkwy
Pensacola, FL 32514-5750
(850) 474-2147 Fax: (850) 474-3247
www.uwf.edu/music
E-mail: jspaniola@uwf.edu

4 Year Institution
Member of NASM

Chair: Joseph T. Spaniola, 80A

Assoc Prof	Glaze, Richard T.	M	60,32,37,48,64
Assoc Prof	Lauderdale, Lynne A.	D	12A,66A,66G,66D,66B
Asst Prof	Murphy, Sheila C.	D	61,39,32D
Faculty	Riley, Blake	M	36,60A
Prof	Salanki, Hedi	D	13C,13E,66A,66H,41
Assoc Prof	Spaniola, Joseph T.	DMA	47,46,63D,11,10
Prof	Yanovskiy, Leonid	DMA	62A,62B,38,11,41

FL2120 Valencia Community College
Music Program
PO Box 3028
Orlando, FL 32802-3028
(407) 582-2332 Fax: (407) 582-8917
www.valenciacollege.edu
E-mail: tgifford@valenciacollege.edu

2 Year Institution

Director: Troy S. Gifford, 80A

Assoc Prof	Gerber, Alan E.	M	11,55,61,36
Assoc Prof	Gifford, Troy S.	D	11,13,46,70,10

FL2130 Warner Southern College
Department of Music
13895 US Hwy 27
Lake Wales, FL 33859
(863) 638-7231 Fax: (863) 638-7610
www.warner.edu

4 Year Institution

Chair: Steven L. Darr, 80A

Prof	Darr, Steven L.	D	60,32,36,61
Prof	Johnson, Bryan	M	12A,34
Adj	Loomis, Joy	M	61,66
Adj	Metcalfe, Evelyn	M	13,66
Adj	Thompson, Linda	M	66
Adj	Walton, Madalyn	M	61,32C
Adj	Williams, Harry	M	61

GA0050 Agnes Scott College
Department of Music
141 E College Ave
Decatur, GA 30030
(404) 471-6049 Fax: (404) 471-5087
www.agnesscott.edu
E-mail: tlaird@agnesscott.edu

4 Year Institution

Chair: Tracey Laird, 80A
Dir., Undergraduate Studies: Carolyn Stefanco, 80B
Dir., Admissions: Laura Martin, 80D
Dir., Artist/Perf. Series & Summer Programs: Demetrice Williams, 80F,80G

PT	Black, Amy King	M	63B
PT	Chang, Amy	M	62B
PT	Choi, Wooyoung	M	66A,66D,66C
PT	Curran, Kathryn	M	64C
PT	D'Ambrosio, David	M	66A,66C,48
PT	Denton, Robert	D	66A
PT	Deuson, Nicolas	D	13,34A,34D,35G,70
	Eskew-Sparks, Elise	D	36,40
PT	Goin, Robert	M	62D
PT	Grigsby, Nathan	M	36
PT	Hargrave, Monica	M	62E
PT	Harran, Roy	M	62C
PT	Harris, Anton	M	29,64E
PT	Holland, Greg	M	63A
PT	James, Dawn-Marie	B	61
Prof Emeritus	Johnson, Calvert	D	66G,15,31,66H,12A
PT	Kim, Kyung-Mi	D	66A,66D
PT	Kotan, Emrah	M	65,29A,47
Assoc Prof	Laird, Tracey	D	12,14,11,29A
PT	Lillya, Ann	D	64B,48
PT	Maxwell, Francisca	D	61
PT	Miller, Jody	M	67C
PT	Morris, Stephen	D	12
PT	Ryan, Patrick	M	51
PT	Scarr, Susie	M	63D,63C
Vstng Asst Prof	Solomon, Jason Wyatt	D	10,13
PT	Solomon, Qiao Chen	M	62A,62B,51,41,38
PT	Torre, Robert Anthony	D	12,14
PT	Unger, Ruth Shelly		64D
PT	Via, Kelly	M	64A,48
PT	Zara, Meredith	M	61

GA0150 Albany State University
Department of Fine Arts
504 College Dr
Albany, GA 31705
(229) 430-4849 Fax: (229) 430-0425
www.asurams.edu
E-mail: marcia.hood@asurams.edu

4 Year Institution, Historically Black College, Graduate School

Master of Music Education

Chair: Marcia Mitchell Hood, 80A

PT	Bowie, Lenard C.	D	63A
Assoc Prof	Bynum, Leroy E.	D	12A,39,61
Asst Prof	Decuir, Michael	M	11,20,29,37,47
PT	Hillard, Clair Fox	D	62A
Asst Prof	Hood, Marcia Mitchell	D	66A,60A,32B,36,40
PT	Jones, T. Marshall	D	11,29,47,53

Assoc Prof	Martin, Michael D.	M	11,12A,13C,32,49
Asst Prof	Martin, Michelle Denise	D	11,65,66D,60B
Asst Prof	Puller, Shawn I.	M	11,61,12A,32A,39
Asst Prof	Walker, Christopher G.	D	11,32,64,48
Prof	Walker, Jesse	M	13A,63C,63D,13B,13C
Asst Prof	Weber, Deanna F.	M	13A,13B,13C,13D,61

GA0160 Andrew College

Department of Music
501 College St
Cuthbert, GA 39840
(229) 732-2171   Fax: (229) 732-5994
www.andrewcollege.edu
E-mail: mariaseuffert@andrewcollege.edu

2 Year Liberal Arts Institution

Music Contact: Maria C. Seuffert, 80A

Asst Prof	Seuffert, Maria C.	M	36

GA0200 Armstrong Atlantic State Univ

Department of Art, Mus & Theatre
11935 Abercorn St
Savannah, GA 31419-1909
(912) 344-2556   Fax: (912) 344-3419

www.armstrong.edu/Liberal_Arts/art_music_theatre/amt_welcome
E-mail: finearts@mail.armstrong.edu

4 Year Institution
Member of NASM

Chair: Tom L. Cato, 80A

Prof	Anderson, James N.	D	12A,32,37
Asst Prof	Benton, Carol W.	D	13C,13K,32B,32D,32G
Inst PT	Berquist, Peter	M	62D
Inst PT	Bozeman, Scott	D	63D
Inst PT	Chandler, Chris	M	11
	Estes, Linda	M	11
	Garcia, Jessica	M	63B
Assoc Prof	Hampton, Edwin Kevin	D	13,66
Prof	Harris, Robert	D	12A,60,61,11,32D
Asst Prof	Johnson, Mark	M	32E,37,60B,63C
Inst PT	Johnson, Yvonne P.	M	62
Inst PT	Jones, Lorraine	B	48,64A
Inst PT	Kiene, Kristi	M	64B
Inst PT	Patricio, Raymond	M	64D
Assoc Prof	Primatic, Stephen P.	D	65,13,29,11,47
Inst PT	Reams, John D.	M	64C,11
	Reams, Lisa	M	11
Assoc Prof	Reese, Randall	D	10F,47,64E,10A,13D
Inst PT	Richter, Lois	M	66D
	Schmid, Alice	M	63A
Prof	Schultz, Lucinda D.	D	61
Inst PT	Spradley, Bruce	M	70
Inst PT	Standard, Richard	B	70
	Williams, Ray	B	62D

GA0250 Augusta State University

Department of Music
2500 Walton Way
Augusta, GA 30904-2200
(706) 737-1453   Fax: (706) 667-4937
www.aug.edu/music
E-mail: music@aug.edu

4 Year Institution
Member of NASM

Chair: Angela L. Morgan, 80A

Prof	Banister, Linda	D	11,39,61
PT	Bearden, Gregory	M	11
PT	Brasco, Richard	M	32
PT	Carr, Johnny	M	32B
PT	Cheney, Kathryn	M	63A,13A,11
PT	Choi, Hyangbin	M	66A
Assoc Prof	Crookall, Christine	D	13A,13,62C,12A,41
Asst Prof	Fallin, Nicky G.	M	37,32E,63A,49,60B
Prof	Floyd, Rosalyn	D	13A,13,11,66A,66C
Prof	Foster, Robert	D	13,10,11,47,48
PT	Garman, Barry	D	62D
PT	Henderson, Matthew	M	11,63C,63D

Prof	Hobbins, William	D	32,36,61,11
Prof	Jones, Martin David	D	11,66A,66H,66B,13
PT	Katterjohn, Michael	M	50,65
Prof	Morgan, Angela L.	D	32,38,51,62A
Lect	Myers, Patricia	M	12A,61,11
PT	Nabholz, Fran	M	61
PT	Nord, James	M	66G
PT	Odell, Kelly	M	64B
PT	Park, Clara	D	66A,11
PT	Playford, Louis	D	66C
PT	Purdy, Carl	M	62A,62B,70,51
PT	Ramsey, Laura	M	11,64D
Inst	Scott, Rosemary	M	32A,32B,32C,11
Prof	Shotwell, Clayton	D	12,20,34,11,13A
PT	Tomlin, Laura A.	D	62A,11,13A
PT	Woodruff, Sidney	M	70,11

GA0300 Berry College

Department of Music
2277 Martha Berry Hwy NW
Mount Berry, GA 30149
(706) 232-5374   Fax: (706) 238-7847
www.berry.edu
E-mail: spethel@berry.edu

4 Year Institution
Member of NASM

Chair: Stan Pethel, 80A

Lect	Baker, Ruth	M	11,61
Asst Prof	Carlisle, Kris	D	11,66A,13
Prof	Davis, John E.	M	60,11,37,64A,64E
Adj Inst	Enloe, Luther D.	M	70,11
Adj Inst	Fisher, Mickey	M	64B,64C,64E,48
Lect	Jenkins, Ellie M.	D	63B
Lect	Musselwhite, Harry	M	60,36,39,61
Adj Inst	Nobles, Katherine	B	66D
Adj Inst	Ogrizovic-Ciric, Mirna	M	38,42,62
Prof	Pethel, Stan	D	13,60,10,63C,10F
Adj Inst	Watson, Gwendolyn	M	62C
Adj Inst	Williams, Wade	M	50,65

GA0350 Brenau University

Department of Music
500 Washington St SE
Gainesville, GA 30501
(770) 534-6235   Fax: (770) 534-6777
www.brenau.edu
E-mail: bsteinhaus@brenau.edu

4 Year Institution

Director: Barbara Steinhaus, 80A

	Burns, Portia	B	36
PT	Grissom, Jan	M	61
PT	Hunt, Keena Redding	M	11
Asst Prof	Ivey, Bobby	M	32,36,13C,40
Assoc Prof	Jefcoat, Priscilla	D	13A,66A,10F,12A,13D
Asst Prof	Leaptrott, Ben	M	11,13,39,66A,66B
Prof	Steinhaus, Barbara	D	61,11,39

GA0400 Brewton-Parker College

Division of Music
201 David-Eliza Fountain Cir
Mount Vernon, GA 30445-9999
(912) 583-3136   Fax: (912) 583-2997
www.bpc.edu
E-mail: music@bpc.edu

2 and 4 Year Institution
Member of NASM

Chair: Glenn Fernisse, 80A
Dir., Artist/Performance Series: Pierce Dickens, 80F

Asst Prof	Caston, Ben	D	44,61,31
Adj	Cooper, Ralph	D	66D
Assoc Prof	Dickens, Pierce	D	13A,13B,13C,13E,66A
Prof	Fernisse, Glenn	D	10,63B,34,32E
Adj	Fernisse, Susan	M	32C
Adj	Probst, Christopher	M	63A,63B
Adj	Reed, John	M	32E
Prof Emeritus	Retif, T. N.	D	13E,12A,61,44
Assoc Prof	Smith, Kandie K.	D	61,40
Adj	Weaver, John	M	65

GA0490 Clark Atlanta University
Department of Music
223 James P Brawley Dr SW
Atlanta, GA 30314
(404) 880-8211 Fax: (404) 880-6267
www.cau.edu
E-mail: swillis@cau.edu

4 Year Institution

Chair: Sharon J. Willis, 80A

Assoc Prof	Adams, J. Robert	D	61,14,11,39,40
Inst	Anderson, Juliet V.	M	11,39,61
Asst Prof	Boozer, Mark	M	13C,66A,66B,66D
PT	Camp, James L.	M	37,49,63B,63C,63D
	Floyd, Pharroll	B	65
Asst Prof	Gable, David D.	D	11,12A,12B,13A,16
Inst	Georgieva, Roumena G.	M	62A,62B,38,51
Asst Prof	Halsey, Glynn	M	11,36,40,60A
Adj	Head, John	M	63A
	Lee, LaToya	M	
Inst	Marcus, David	M	10,11,12A,13A,29A
Inst	Parker, Val	M	10,11,13A,34D,29A
Asst Prof	Patterson, James H.	M	29,32,46,63,47
	Powell, Curtis Everett	B	36,13,32,32D
Inst	Warner, Thomas	M	37
Assoc Prof	Willis, Sharon J.	D	10A,11,12,61,13A

GA0500 Clayton State University
Department of Visual & Perf. Arts
2000 Clayton State Blvd
Morrow, GA 30260
(678) 466-4750 Fax: (678) 466-4769
www.clayton.edu/vpa/music
E-mail: susantusing@clayton.edu

4 Year Institution

Chair: Susan Tusing, 80A
Dir., Preparatory Division: Carol W. Payne, 80E
Dir., Artist/Performance Series: Sam Dixon, 80F

Prof	Amos, Shaun	D	60,36,13B,13C,12A
Inst PT	Bartholow, Lisa	M	64A
Asst Prof	Bell, Richard	D	32E,13,38,60B,62D
Collaborative Pianist	Benford, Alexander E.	M	
Inst PT	Black, Amy King	M	11
Inst PT	Hearn, William	D	11,41,70,20
Inst PT	Houghton, Stacey	M	47,29,64E,64C
Asst Prof	Howell, Christina	DMA	61
Asst Prof	Kelly, Kathleen	M	52,54
Inst PT	Kemberling, Nan	M	62C
Inst PT	Lorch, Kimberly	M	11,64B
Asst Prof	Lyman, Kristin M.	D	32,65
Prof	Otaki, Michiko	D	41,66A,66C,66D
Inst PT	Puckett, Michael	M	63D
Inst PT	Pyle, Daniel S.	D	11,66G
Inst PT	Soykan, Betul	M	62A,62B
Inst PT	Toll, Yvonne	M	63A
Assoc Prof	Tusing, Susan	D	66A,66B,13A,13B
Inst PT	Wucher, Jay	M	64
Asst Prof	Young, Shawn David	D	14C,35A,31A,35,11
Prof	Zeller, Kurt-Alexander	D	61,39,12A

GA0525 College of Coastal Georgia
Department of Music
3700 Altama Ave
Brunswick, GA 31520-3644
(912)-264-7235
www.ccga.edu
E-mail: jlemieux@ccga.edu

2 Year Institution

Chair: Watson Holloway, 80A

PT	Nilsson, Donna	M	11,32

GA0550 Columbus State University
Schwob School of Music
4225 University Ave
Columbus, GA 31907-5645
(706) 649-7225 Fax: (706) 649-7369
music.columbusstate.edu
E-mail: schwobmusic@columbusstate.edu

4 Year Institution, Graduate School
Member of NASM

Artist Diploma, Master of Music in Performance, Master of Music in Conducting, Master of Music in Music Education

Director: Fred S. Cohen, 80A
Interim Dean, College of the Arts: Gary S. Wortley, 80A
Dir., Graduate Studies: Andrew Zohn, 80C
Dir., Preparatory Division: Zoran Jakovcic, 80E
Associate Director: Lisa M. Oberlander, 80H

Inst	Bennett, Susan Brady	D	62E
Adj Inst PT	Bullock, Janie Lee	M	66A
Assoc Prof	Chodacki-Ford, Roberta	M	16,12G
Emeritus	Clark, Steve H.	M	66B,66D
Prof	Cohen, Fred S.	D	10,13
Assoc Prof	Coleman, Earl	M	61,13C
Adj Inst PT	Cone, Kimberly	M	61
Asst Prof	DeBruyn, Michelle Murphy	D	61
Adj Prof PT	Diaz, Manuel	M	72
Adj Inst PT	Foor, Morris	M	32E
Adj Inst PT	Ge, Tao	M	10F,13C
Assoc Prof	Golden, Joseph	M	39,66G,11,12
Adj Inst PT	Griffiths, Amy	D	64E,32E,11,47
Assoc Prof	Hansen, Kristen S.	D	13,11,32E
Assoc Prof	Hostetter, Paul K.	D	38,39,60B,43
Vstng Asst Prof	Jakovcic, Zoran	M	62B
Asst Prof	Kobrin, Alexander	D	66A,42
Adj Inst PT	Launius, Michael	M	20
Lect	Lawler-Johnson, Dian	M	61
Adj Inst PT	Maddox, Eric	D	32E,20
Assoc Prof	Martin, Andree	D	64A,11,43,12
Adj Inst PT	May, Luise	M	66D
Vstng Asst Prof	McCabe, Matthew	D	34,13,10
Adj Inst PT	Miller, Andrew	M	63D
Assoc Prof	Murray, Robert P.	D	63A,49
Assoc Prof	Nix, Jamie L.	D	37,60B
Prof	Oberlander, Lisa M.	D	64C,64E
Assoc Prof	Palmer, Bradley E.	D	63C,11,34,32F,41
Asst Prof	Parker, Elizabeth	D	32A,32B,32C,32D
Assoc Prof	Pershounin, Alexander	D	62D,47
Adj Inst PT	Poor, Andrew F.	D	32E
Asst Prof	Powell, Sean	D	32
Prof	Schwartz, Sergiu	DIPL	62A
Prof	Tsolainou, Constantina	M	60
Assoc Prof	Vaillancourt, Paul	D	65,50,13C,43
	Wang, Yien	M	66C
Asst Prof	Warner, Wendy	D	62C,42
Inst	Williams, Richard	M	13B,13C
Prof	Wirt, Ronald	D	13,48,64D,10
Assoc Prof	Zohn, Andrew	D	70,10

GA0600 Covenant College
Department of Music
14049 Scenic Hwy
Lookout Mountain, GA 30750
(706) 820-1560 Fax: (706) 820-0893
www.covenant.edu
E-mail: sarah.dewaters@covenant.edu

4 Year Liberal Arts Institution

Chair & Dir., Undergraduate Studies: Brandon R. Kreuze, 80A,80B

Vstng Prof	Ewing, Rosella	D	12A,61
Adj Prof	Humphries, Stephen	M	13A,20,50,65
Adj Prof	Jobe, Elena	M	66A,66B,66C
Vstng Prof	Kim, Lok	M	38,42,60,66A
Assoc Prof	Kreuze, Brandon R.	D	10,34,13,12C
Vstng Prof	Long, David	M	36,63A,49,55C,40
Vstng Prof	Tahere, David	M	11,54,61

GA0610 Dalton State College
School of Liberal Arts
650 College Drive
Dalton, GA 30720
(706) 272-2528
www.daltonstate.edu
E-mail: ejenkins@daltonstate.edu

Music Contact: Ellie Jenkins, 80A

FT	Jenkins, Ellie	D	11

GA0625 Darton College
Department of Music
2400 Gillionville Rd
Albany, GA 31707-3098
(229) 317-6856   Fax: (229) 317-6650
www.darton.edu
E-mail: jeff.kluball@darton.edu

2 Year Institution

Dean, Humanities: Alysia Ehlert, 80A
Director: Jeff L. Kluball, 80A

Inst PT	Baxter, Jillian	M	65,65B
Inst PT	Campiglia, Paul	M	47,29,53,65
Inst PT	Cochran, Matthew	D	11,70
	Hillard, Claire Fox	D	11,62A,62B,66D,62
Inst PT	Jewell, Jim	M	66B,63A
Inst PT	Jewell, Renee	M	61
	Kluball, Jeff L.	D	37,63,29,13,10
Inst PT	Miller, Richard	M	66A
Inst PT	Myers, Steven	M	63A
Inst PT	Walker, Chris	D	64E
	Walker, Keith H.	M	36,61,60
Inst PT	Young, Scott	M	63B,66D

GA0700 Emmanuel College
Department of Music
212 Spring St
PO Box 129
Franklin Springs, GA 30639
(706) 245-7226 x 2649   Fax: (706) 245-4424
www.ec.edu
E-mail: lboucher@ec.edu

4 Year Institution

Chair & Dean, Arts & Sciences: Leslie H. Boucher, 80A

Prof	Boucher, Leslie H.	D	12,20,13,62,11
Inst	Chitwood, Elizabeth	M	66A,66B,66C
Prof	Goodwin, Mark A.	D	13,32,37,64
Assoc Prof	Pettyjohn, Emma	D	66A,66B,66C,66G,66D
Inst	Rowell, Michael	M	31A,60A,47,36
Assoc Prof	Stark, Deborah	D	12A,54,11,61,40

GA0750 Emory University
Department of Music
1804 N Decatur Rd
Atlanta, GA 30322
(404) 727-6445   Fax: (404) 727-0074
www.music.emory.edu
E-mail: music@emory.edu

4 Year Institution, Graduate School

Master of Sacred Music, Master of Music in Choral Conducting, Master of Music in Organ Performance

Chair: Kevin C. Karnes, 80A
Dir., Undergraduate Studies: Deborah Thoreson, 80B
Dir., Graduate Studies: Eric Nelson, 80C

Inst PT	Albrecht, Tamara	M	11,12A,32A
Prof	Albrecht, Timothy	D	11,12A,66G,31A
Assoc Prof	Andrews, Dwight D.	D	13,14,31A,29
Adj PT	Ardan, Laura	M	64C
Adj PT	Baker, Jan Berry		64E
Assoc Prof	Bertrand, Lynn Wood	D	13,11,12A,12
Adj PT	Bishop, Martha	M	62B,67A
Adj PT	Bonin, Brian P.		61
Adj PT	Cebulski, Michael	M	50,65
Adj PT	Chesarek, Justin	M	65
Adj PT	Cholakova, Elena	D	66C
Adj PT	Christy, Jay		62A
Other	Clinkscales, Joyce	M	16
Adj PT	Cote, Alejandro	M	70
Adj PT	Covey, Jason	M	60,47
Lect	Cox, Melissa	D	11,12,13
Assoc Prof	Crist, Stephen A.	D	12
Adj PT	Deane, Richard	M	63B
Adj PT	Dinkins-Matthews, Patricia A.	D	66C
Adj PT	Eklund, Jason	M	13
Prof	Everett, Steve	D	60,10,41,45,34
Assoc Prof	Everett, Yayoi Uno	D	13
Adj PT	Fairchild, Kay		49,63
Adj PT	Flythe, Bernard	M	63D
Adj PT	Freer, Karen		62C
Adj PT	Frey, Adam		63D
Adj PT	Gordy, Laura	D	66A
Adj PT	Hall, Carl	M	64A
Senior Lect	Hopkin, Teresa	M	39,61
Adj PT	Howard, Brad		61
Adj PT	Hunter, Randy		47,64E
Adj PT	Johnson, Elisabeth Remy		62E
Assoc Prof	Karnes, Kevin C.	D	12,12C
Adj PT	Kenney, Mary	M	62C
Adj PT	Kong, Yinzi		62B
Assoc Prof	Lee, Tong Soon	D	14,20C,20D,14D,14F
Prof	Lennon, John A.	D	13,10
Adj PT	Moore, Michael	M	63D
Lect	Motley, Gary D.	M	29,46,47
Adj PT	Murphy, Paul		62B
Assoc Prof	Nelson, Eric	D	60,36,38,41
Adj PT	Nicholson, Edmon	M	63C
Adj PT	Nitchie, Carl		64D
Adj PT	Pagliarini, Shawn		62A
Adj PT	Paulo, Gary		64E
Adj PT	Philipsen, Dane		64B
Senior Lect	Prior, Richard	D	38,41,42,60B
Adj PT	Qualls, Todd		66A
Adj PT	Ransom, Keiko	M	66A
Prof	Ransom, William		66A
Prof Emeritus	Schisler, Charles	D	11,12
Senior Lect	Stewart, Scott A.	D	37,38,71
Senior Lect	Thoreson, Deborah	M	66B,66C
Adj PT	Tiscione, Mike		63A
Adj PT	Trotz, Amy		63B
Adj PT	Unger, Ruth Shelly	D	64D,11
Adj PT	Wang, Guang		62C
Inst PT	Weaver, Zac	D	13
Senior Lect	Wendland, Kristin	D	13,66A
Adj PT	Williams, Paula		65
Adj PT	Wu, Jessica Shuang		62A
Adj PT	Yancich, Lisa	M	62A
Adj PT	Yancich, Mark	M	65A
Adj PT	Zellers, Jim A.		64A

GA0755 Emory University-Oxford College
Division of Humanities
Oxford, GA 30054
(770) 784-8466   Fax: (770) 784-4660
oxford.emory.edu
E-mail: marchetto@learnlink.emory.edu

2 Year Institution

Music Contact: Maria Archetto, 80A
Chair, Humanities: Adriane Ivey, 80A

Assoc Prof	Archetto, Maria	D	11,12A,12B,13A,20

GA0810 Fort Valley State University
Department of Fine Arts
1005 State University Dr
Fort Valley, GA 31030-4313
(912) 825-6387   Fax: (912) 825-6132
www.fvsu.edu
E-mail: gilesl@fvsu.edu

4 Year Institution, Historically Black College, State & Land Grant

Chair, Fine Arts: Bobby Dickey, 80A
Coord., Music Area: Leonard Giles, 80A

	Cheng, Ya-Hui		
Asst Prof	Giles, Leonard	M	11,32,37,47,63
Asst Prof	Stripling, Allen	M	11,36,66,32,40

GA0850 Georgia College & State University
Department of Music
231 W Hancock St
CBX 66
Milledgeville, GA 31061
(478) 445-8289   Fax: (478) 445-1633
www.gcsu.edu/music
E-mail: victor.vallo@gcsu.edu

4 Year Institution, Graduate School
Member of NASM

Master of Music Education, Masters in Music Therapy

Chair: Victor Vallo, Jr., 80A

Inst PT	Altman, Barbara	M	62C
Asst Prof	Auerbach, Dan J.	D	60,62A,62B,38,51
Inst PT	Bartholow, Lisa	M	64A
Inst PT	Belzer, Katie	D	64C
Inst PT	Brooks, Ipek	M	66A
Inst PT	Caldwell, Ann	D	66A,66D,66G,11
Inst PT	Crook, Joshua	M	63B
Inst PT	Dennison, Jessica	M	61,32D
Inst PT	Enghauser, Chris	M	62D
Inst PT	Fischer, Stephen M.	M	64E
Assoc Prof	Flory, Jennifer Morgan	D	36,32D,15,60A,61
Inst PT	Gnam, Adrian	M	64B
Prof	Greene, Richard C.	D	70,13C,11,13E,12A
Inst PT	Harrell, Jana	B	66C
Inst PT	Holland, Katie	M	64D
Assoc Prof	Horgan, Maureen A.	D	63D,11,49,63C,29A
Asst Prof	Johnson, David H.	D	13,10,10B,10C
Asst Prof	Keith, Douglas	D	33
Inst PT	Lundin, Claudia	M	32E
Assoc Prof	Mercado, Chesley	D	33
Assoc Prof	Mullen, Wendy Anne	D	61,54,39
Prof	Pepetone, Gregory	D	12A,32,66A,66B,66D
Inst PT	Probst, Christopher	M	63A
Inst PT	Rehberg, Nancy	M	61
Inst PT	Robinson, Vicky	D	33
Inst	Ryabinin, Lev	M	66C,66A
Inst PT	Smith, Ryan	M	65,50
Prof	Tolbert, Patti	D	32,65,50
Asst Prof	Towner, Cliff	D	32E,37,47,60B
Prof	Vallo, Victor	D	32,37,60B
Inst PT	Watkins, Russell	M	61

GA0875 Georgia Highlands College
Department of Music
5441 Highway 20 NE
Cartersville, GA 30121
(706) 295-6312   Fax: (706) 295-6610
www.highlands.edu
E-mail: radams@highlands.edu

2 Year Institution

Music Contact: Robert C. Adams, 80A

Asst Prof	Adams, Robert C.	M	11

GA0900 Georgia Institute of Technology
School of Music
840 McMillan St
Atlanta, GA 30332-0456
(404) 894-8949   Fax: (404) 894-9952
www.music.gatech.edu
E-mail: corissa.jones@music.gatech.edu

4 Year Institution, Graduate School

PhD in Music Technology, Master of Science in Music Technology

Director: Frank L. Clark, 80A

Vstng Asst Prof	Arasi, Melissa	D	40,61
Vstng Asst Prof	Brown, Andrea E.	D	37,38,11
Inst	Bull, Catherine	M	64A
Inst	Carter, Kenyon	M	47,64E
Asst Prof	Chordia, Parag	D	34
Inst	Ciaschini, Peter	M	62
Prof	Clark, Frank L.	D	34
Vstng Asst Prof	Diden, Benjamin	M	37,13
Asst Prof	Freeman, Jason A.	D	34
Inst	Knight, Adam	M	70
Assoc Prof	Mendola, Ron	M	38,47
Asst Prof	Moore, Christopher J.	M	37,65
Inst	Sigmon, Susan	M	66A
Assoc Prof	Ulrich, Jerry	D	10,36,32,32D,60A
Asst Prof	Weinberg, Gil	D	34

GA0940 Georgia Perimeter College
Department of Fine Arts
555 N Indian Creek Dr
Clarkston, GA 30021-2361
(678) 891-3555   Fax: (678) 299-4271
www.gpc.edu
E-mail: ssigmon@gpc.edu

2 Year Institution, a Unit of the Univ System of Georgia

Chair: David Koffman, 80A
Dir., Artist/Performance Series: Susan McEwen Sigmon, 80F

PT	Cebulski, Michael	M	50,65
Asst Prof	Chen, Ginger Jui-Wen	D	66A,66D
PT	Cherniansky, Fyodor	M	38
PT	Clements, Emory	M	62D
PT	Farmer, Katherine	M	48,64A
PT	Glicklich, Jocelyn Rose	M	61
Asst Prof	Hughes, Evelyn	M	11,12A,61
PT	Hutchison, Patrick	M	66C
PT	Knapp, Donna	M	64C
Asst Prof	McClary, Michael	M	11,37,47,63
Inst	McLean, Greg	M	13,11,29,10
PT	Melgaard, Connie	M	66C
PT	Mitchell, Brian	M	70
PT	Mitchell, Carol	M	13,66A,66G,66C,66D
Asst Prof	Prudchenko, Slava	M	37,13A,13B,13C
PT	Renn, Rowena S.	M	61
PT	Rice, Alexandria	M	62C
PT	Rogers, Richard	B	63C
Assoc Prof	Sigmon, Susan McEwen	D	13,36,66A,66G,40
PT	Stallings, Jim	M	10
PT	Vogler, Paul	M	46
PT	Warsaw, Benjamin		66A,13
PT	Wheeler, John	M	11
PT	Zezelj-Gualdi, Danijela	D	62A,62B,51

GA0950 Georgia Southern University
Department of Music
PO Box 8052
Statesboro, GA 30460-8052
(912) 478-5396   Fax: (912) 478-1295
class.georgiasouthern.edu/music
E-mail: music@georgiasouthern.edu

4 Year Regional Institution, Graduate School
Member of NASM

Master of Music in Composition, Master of Music in Performance, Master of Music in Conducting, Master of Music in Music Education, Master of Music in Music Technology

Chair: Richard E. Mercier, 80A
Dir., Graduate Studies: Gregory Harwood, 80C

Inst PT	Aceto, Jonathan D.	D	51,62A,11,62B,13E
Inst PT	Balmaceda, Kelly	M	61
Prof	Bryan, Carolyn J.	D	64E,48
Prof	Cionitti, Linda A.	D	48,64C
Inst PT	Dickens, Pierce	D	39,66A,66C,66G
Asst Prof	Doyle, Timothy	M	37
Assoc Prof	Dunham, Robert W.	D	32E,37
Asst Prof	Elisha, Larisa	D	62A,62B,42
Asst Prof	Elisha, Steven K.	D	62C,62D,41,42
Other	Elliott, Margarett	M	66C
Prof	Fallin, Mathew D.	D	50,65
Asst Prof PT	Furry, Stephanie	D	63B,49,33,11
Asst Prof	Gendelman, Martin	D	10,13,70,34A
Assoc Prof	Gnam, Adrian	M	38,60,64B
Assoc Prof	Gregory, Arikka	D	39,61
Prof	Hancock, Kyle	D	39,61
Inst PT	Hancock, Sarah	M	61
Prof	Harwood, Gregory	D	11,12
Prof	Henderson, Allen C.	D	61,39
Inst PT	Horel, Charles	M	10A,70,13A,13C
Asst Prof	Jeffreys, Shannon	D	36,32D
Other	Marshall, Cindy	B	66C
Asst Prof	Mason, Richard	D	63D,49
Asst Prof	McKenzie, Colin	D	37
Prof	Mercier, Richard E.	D	66A,66C,39
Assoc Prof	Murray, David	D	66A,66D

Inst PT	Patricio, Raymond	M	64D
Prof	Pearsall, Tom	D	66A,66B,66D
Prof	Pittman, Daniel	D	11
Other	Ponder, Wemberly	M	66C
Other	Porter, Melana	M	66B
Asst Prof	Rocker, Karla J.	D	66C
Inst PT	Schmid, Alice	M	11,63A
Assoc Prof	Schmid, William	D	63A,46,29,49,47
Asst Prof	Stambaugh, Laura	D	32A,32B,32C,32E,32G
Inst PT	Thibeault, Anna	M	64A,48
Assoc Prof	Thompson, John	D	34,10
Asst Prof PT	Thomson, Susan N.	D	13B,13E,66A,13

GA1000 Georgia Southwestern State Univ
Department of Music
800 GSW Dr
Americus, GA 31709-4693
(229) 931-2204 Fax: (229) 931-2203
www.gsw.edu
E-mail: julie.megginson@gsw.edu

4 Year Institution

Chair & Dir., Artist Series: Julie Megginson, 80A,80F

Adj	Davis, Lisa A.	M	61
Adj	Horan, Sara	M	32,11,61
Asst Prof	Laughlin, Mark	D	66A,13,12A,66D,13B
Assoc Prof	Megginson, Julie	D	61,36,40,60A
Lect	Swope, Richard	M	37,63,49
Lect	Yeung, Alwen	M	11,66C,13C,66D

GA1050 Georgia State University
School of Music
PO Box 4097
Atlanta, GA 30302-4097
(404) 413-5900 Fax: (404) 413-5910
www.music.gsu.edu
E-mail: music@gsu.edu

4 Year Institution, Graduate School
Member of NASM

Master of Music in Composition, Master of Music in Performance, Master of Music in Conducting, Master of Music in Music Education, PhD in Music Education, Master of Music in Piano Pedagogy, Specialist in Education, Master of Music in Jazz Studies

Director: William Dwight Coleman, 80A
Dir., Graduate Studies: Steven A. Harper, 80C
Associate Director: Robert J. Ambrose, 80H

Senior Lect	Albo, Francisco Javier	D	11
Assoc Prof	Ambrose, Robert J.	D	37,32E,60B
Inst PT	Ambrose, Sarah Kruser	M	64A
Inst PT	Andrus, Brice	M	63B
Asst Prof	Baker, Jan Berry	D	64E,11,13E
Inst PT	Bales, Kevin	M	29
Inst PT	Bryant, Curtis	B	13A,10F
Inst PT	Bubacz, Eric	B	63D
Asst Prof	Carlisle, Katie	D	32B,32C
Assoc Prof	Carter, Marva G.	D	12,20G,20,20A
Asst Prof	Clement, Richard	M	61
Inst PT	Clements, Emory Lamar	B	62D
Lect	Clements, Tania Maxwell	M	62B,62A
Prof	Coleman, William Dwight	M	61,39
Lect	Dahl Saville, Lara R.	D	11,64B
Assoc Prof	Demos, Nickitas J.	D	10,43
Inst PT	Dickson, Robert	M	29
Inst PT	Ewing, Monica Emmons	M	35A
Inst	Frackenpohl, David J.	M	29A
Assoc Prof	Fredriksen, Brandt		66A,66C,42
Assoc Prof	Freeman, Carroll		39
Vstng Inst	Freeman, Kay Paschal		61
Assoc Prof	Freer, Patrick K.	D	32D,32C,32G,36,60A
Inst PT	Frey, Adam	M	63D
Inst PT	Funderburk, Wes		47,63C
Asst Prof	Galileas, Christos	D	62A
Assoc Prof	Gallo, Sergio	D	66A,66B,66C,66D
Assoc Prof	Gerber, Stuart W.	D	65,50
Assoc Prof	Greene, Oliver N.		12,20H
Prof Emeritus	Haberlen, John B.	D	60,32D,36
Assoc Prof	Harper, Steven A.	D	13
Assoc Prof	Hartgrove, Kathryn	M	61
Assoc Prof	Haydon, Geoffrey Jennings	D	66A,66F,29B
Inst PT	Hibbard, Mace	M	64E
Vstng Lect	Jones, Steve		35
Asst Prof	Joseph, Deanna	M	36,40

Prof Emeritus	Knox, Charles C.	D	10
Assoc Prof	Long, Kenneth A.	D	13A,64C,64E
Inst	Marshall, Peter M.	D	66C
Inst PT	Martin, Sarah	M	66G
Assoc Prof	McFarland, Mark J.	D	13
Vstng Lect	Milam, Brent	M	13
Inst PT	Minter, Kendall	D	35A
Asst Prof	Mixdorf, Cory Daniel	D	63,63C
Lect	Moulson, Magdalena	B	61
Inst PT	Muszynski, Michael	M	64D
Asst Prof	Norgaard, Martin	D	32E,32F,62A,29E,32
Assoc Prof	Palmer, Michael	M	38,60B
Asst Prof	Pepping, Amanda J.	D	63A,41
Asst Prof	Phillips, Chester B.	D	37
Inst PT	Remy, Elisabeth	M	62C
Inst PT	Rex, Christopher	B	62C
Inst PT	Shakir, Audrey		61
Inst PT	Smith, Rylan	M	70,41
Asst Prof	Sumner Lott, Marie	D	12
Prof	Thompson, Robert Scott	D	10A,10B,10C,45,34
Lect	Vandewalker, David W.	M	37
Vstng Inst	Varnes, Justin	M	65,29
Assoc Prof	Vernick, Gordon Jay	D	47,46,29
Vstng Lect	Welborn, Daniel C.	M	32A

GA1070 Gordon College
Music Program
419 College Dr
Barnesville, GA 30204-1762
(678) 359-5293 Fax: (678) 359-5140
www.gdn.edu/programs/humanities/music.asp
E-mail: jwallace@gdn.edu

2 Year Institution

Music Contact: James A. Wallace, 80A
Chair, Division of Humanities: Edward Whitelock, 80A

Assoc Prof	Boumpani, Neil M.	D	13,37
PT	Calhoun, Valerie J.	M	11
PT	Firkus, Krista	M	61
PT	Glenn, Susan G.	D	64D
PT	Holmes-Davis, Tina	M	64C
PT	Johns, Amy	M	66A,66D,11
PT	Lundy, Alexis	M	11
PT	McKinney, Kelly	M	64A
PT	Mulder, Erin	M	11
PT	Plato, Scott	M	70
PT	Probst, Christopher	M	63A
PT	Rousch, John	M	63D
PT	Smith, Danny	M	47
Assoc Prof	Wallace, James A.	D	36,13C,40,11
PT	Watts, Ronald	M	62C

GA1100 Interdenominational Theo Center
Department of Music
700 MLKJ Dr. SW/Box 429
Atlanta, GA 30314
(404) 527-7729 Fax: (404) 527-0901
www.itc.edu
E-mail: lallen@itc.edu

Theological Seminary

Master of Arts in Church Music, Master of Arts in Church Music/Christian Education, Master of Divinity in Worship Leadership

Prof	Allen, Lisa M.	PhD	20G,32,36,31A
Prof Emerita	Costen, Melva Wilson	PhD	
Adj	Hargrave, Monica		
Collaborative Pianist	King, Janette	M	66A,36
Adj	Rivers, Cynthia	M	66A,66G,66C,31A,36

GA1150 Kennesaw State University
School of Music
1000 Chastain Rd Box 3201
Kennesaw, GA 30144-5591
(770) 423-6151 Fax: (678) 797-2536
www.kennesaw.edu
E-mail: hprice8@kennesaw.edu

4 Year Institution
Member of NASM

Dean: Joseph D. Meeks, 80A
Director: Harry E. Price, 80A
Dir., Summer Programs: Charles Laux, Jr., 80G

Lect	Akerman, Mary S.	M	41,70
Assoc Prof	Alexander, Michael	D	38,60B,12A,35A
Assoc Prof	Blackwell, Leslie	D	36,40,60A
Artist in Res	Bliznik, Karen	M	63A
Inst PT	Boner, Jan	M	32A
Artist in Res	Chesarek, Justin	M	65,47
Asst Prof	Cole, Judith E.	M	11,13C,13A,66C
Asst Prof PT	Creasy, Kathleen	D	32A
Artist in Res	Cronin, Robert	M	64A
Prof	Culvahouse, John N.	D	37,32C,32E,60B
Artist in Res	Curran, George	M	63C
Inst PT	Dolan, Drew	M	11
Inst PT	Dorff, Carolyn	M	61
Assoc Prof	Eanes, Edward	D	12A,11,12C,20G
Artist in Res	Eklund, Jason	M	63B,41
Asst Prof PT	Fleck, Allyson	D	62B,42,13B
Asst Prof PT	Flythe, Bernard	M	32E,63D,41,11
Inst PT	Francis, Kelly A.	D	13B,13C
Inst PT	Funderburk, Wes	M	47
Artist in Res	Gibson, Thomas S.	D	63C,34,41
Inst PT	Grayburn, Margaret	M	32A
Inst PT	Hammond, Barbara	M	32B
Artist in Res	Henry, Robert	D	66A,66B
Artist in Res	Jackson, Tyrone	B	66A,29B,66D,53
Assoc Prof	Kehler, David T.	D	37,60B,11
Assoc Prof	Kim, Helen	M	62A
Assoc Prof	Kirkpatrick, Adam	D	61
Artist in Res	Koch, Elizabeth		64B
Artist in Res	Krueger, Charae	B	62C,42
Asst Prof	Laux, Charles	D	32E,34C,38,62,32C
Inst PT	Lawing, Hollie	B	32E
Lect	Lawless, John	B	65,50
Asst Prof	Lindsey, Douglas	M	63A,41
Artist in Res	Lynn, Catherine D.	D	62B,42
Asst Prof	Mann, Alison	D	40,60A,32C,32D
Inst PT	Marsh, John	D	66D,11
Artist in Res	McFadden, Joseph	B	62D,51
Inst PT	McKee, Angela	M	32A,32B,32G
Inst PT	McKee, Richard	M	32A
Prof	Meeks, Joseph D.	M	13,12A,66,66B
Artist in Res	Miller, Marc	M	62D,47
Inst PT	Mitchell, Jennifer	M	13B,13C,11,10
Artist in Res	Moore, Michael	B	63D
Inst PT	Morehouse, Katherine	D	11,20
Artist in Res	Moremen, Eileen	M	61,39
Prof	Moses, Oral	D	11,36,61
Artist in Res	Najarian, Laura	M	64D
Artist in Res	Philipsen, Dane	M	64B
Artist in Res	Price, Cecilia	D	41
Prof	Price, Harry E.	D	32
Artist in Res	Remy, Elizabeth	B	62E
Prof	Sherr, Laurence E.	D	13,12A,10
Senior Lect	Skelton, Sam	B	64E,47,29
Artist in Res	Smith, Christina		64A
Artist in Res	Sommer, Douglas	M	62D
Inst PT	Talley, Terri	M	32A
Asst Prof	Wadsworth, Benjamin K.	D	13
Artist in Res	Walters, Valerie	M	61
Asst Prof	Warren, John	B	64C,32E,42
Prof Emeritus PT	Watkins, David		66
Inst PT	Weldon-Stephens, Amber	M	32,33
Inst PT	White, Susan	M	66D
Artist in Res	Witte, Tom	B	63B
Lect	Wright, Trey	M	70,47,29A,29B,14C
Prof	Young, James Russell	D	40,39,66C,54
Artist in Res	Young, Jana	M	61
Asst Prof	Yun, Soohyun	D	66A,66B,66C,42

GA1200 La Grange College
Department of Music
601 Broad St
La Grange, GA 30240-2955
(706) 880-8351   Fax: (706) 880-8028
www.lagrange.edu
E-mail: asellman@lagrange.edu

4 Year Liberal Arts Private Institution

Chair: Toni P. Anderson, 80A

Prof	Anderson, Toni P.	D	61,39
PT	Callaway, Patricia	D	61,12A,41
PT	Criswell, James Anthony	M	66G
PT	Duraski, Anne	M	61
PT	Hawkins, Ashley	B	66C
Prof	Johnson, Lee E.	M	10,35B,35A
PT	Mann, George	M	66A
Asst Prof	Ogle, Deborah A.	M	36,13A,60,40,61
Inst	Passmore, Ken	M	66D,66C,65,50
PT	Smith, Brian	B	70
PT	Treadwell, Robin	M	64E

Assoc Prof	Turner, Mitchell	D	13A,13B,13C,13F,13G
PT	Xian, Tracy	D	66A

GA1260 Macon State College
Department of Media, Culture & Arts
100 College Station Dr
Macon, GA 31206-5145
(478) 471-5773   Fax: (478)757-3624
www.maconstate.edu
E-mail: rebecca.lanning@maconstate.edu

4 Year Institution

Head: Rebecca Lanning, 80A

Adj	Cantwell, Terry	M	13A,13,70,51
Adj	Horton, Christian	PhD	20A,11
Asst Prof	Lanning, Rebecca	M	11,36,61
Adj	McNair, Jacqueline	B	66A
Adj	Rule, Tom	M	66A,11

GA1300 Mercer University
Townsend School of Music
1400 Coleman Ave
Macon, GA 31207
(478) 301-2748   Fax: (478) 301-5633
www.mercer.edu/music
E-mail: john.h.dickson@mercer.edu

4 Year Institution, Graduate School
Member of NASM

Master of Music in Performance, Master of Music in Church Music, Master of Music in Choral Conducting, Artist Diploma

Dean: John H. Dickson, 80A
Dir., Undergraduate Studies: Douglas M. Hill, 80B
Dir., Graduate Studies: David C. Keith, 80C
Dir., Grand Opera House Series: Betsy Fitzgerald, 80F
Associate Dean: Stanley L. Roberts, 80H

PT	Albers, Julie		62C
Assoc Prof	Altman, I. H.	D	11,66A
PT	Armstrong, Anne A.	M	66C
PT	Bubacz, Eric	B	63D
PT	Calin, Rachel		62D
PT	Cantwell, Terry	M	70
Asst Prof	Cole, Monty	D	29,32E,46,64C,64E
PT	Dutton, Lawrence	M	62B
PT	Gibson, Tom	D	63C
PT	Gnam, Adrian	M	64B
Assoc Prof	Goff, Carolyn	D	13A,66C,66A
PT	Hanselman, Jay	M	63B
Prof	Hill, Douglas M.	D	60B,32C,37,49,63A
PT	Holland, Katherine N.	D	64D,32,64
PT	Jarriel, Janet		35A
PT	Jensen, Hans Jorgen	DIPL	62C
Assoc Prof	Keith, David C.	D	60A,36
Asst Prof	Kosowski, Richard	D	61,39
Asst Prof	Macklin, Christopher B.	D	12
Assoc Prof	Malone, Martha		39,61
Asst Prof	McCullough, Allen	D	13
Prof	McDuffie, Robert		62A
Assoc Prof	Moretti, Amy Schwartz		62A
PT	Muroki, Kurt		62D
PT	Murphy, Paul		62B
Asst Prof	Pridgen, Elizabeth A.	B	66A,66C
Asst Prof	Reddick, Marcus	D	65
PT	Rehberg, Nancy R.	B	61
PT	Roberts, Marie J.	M	61
Assoc Prof	Roberts, Stanley L.	D	60A,36,31A
PT	Swygert, Jonathan	M	63A
PT	Via, Kelly	M	64A,41

GA1400 Middle Georgia State College
Department of Humanities-Music
1100 Second St
Cochran, GA 31014
(478) 934-3085   Fax: (478) 934-3517
www.mgc.edu
E-mail: rmctyre@mgc.edu

2 Year Institution, with some 4 year degree programs

Music Contact & Dir., Artist Series: Robert A. McTyre, 80A,80F

Inst PT	Cain, Sarah	D	11
Inst PT	Castro, Miguel	M	50,65,11,47
Asst Prof	Clark, Norman Alan	D	11,37,49,64
Inst PT	Foster, Willene	B	66A
Assoc Prof	McTyre, Robert A.	D	11,13,61
Inst PT	Nuss, Patricia	M	11

GA1450 Morehouse College
Department of Music
830 Westview Dr SW
Atlanta, GA 30314-3773
(404) 215-2601   Fax: (404) 215-3479
www.morehouse.edu
E-mail: ubrown@morehouse.edu

4 Year Institution, Historically Black College

Chair: Uzee Brown, Jr., 80A
Dean, Humanities & Social Sciences: Terry Mills

Adj	Brewer, Spencer	M	62C,62D
Prof	Brown, Uzee	D	13,10,61,11
Assoc Prof	Ethridge, William J.	D	11,66A
Asst Prof	Foster, Melvin F.	D	61
Adj	Georgieva, Roumena	M	38
Prof	Grimes, Calvin B.	D	13,10,12,20G,31A
Adj	Howard, Jacqueline	M	11
Inst	Jones, Melvin	M	11,37,29,63A
Adj	Mayfield, Gray	M	64E,37
Adj	Miller, Timothy	M	61
Adj	Moore, Michael	B	63D
Assoc Prof	Morrow, David E.	D	60,11,36,61,66A
Adj	Neely-Chandler, Thomasina	D	31,66D
Adj	Ruffin, W. Floyd	M	66A,11
Asst Prof	Tanner, Robert	D	10,12A,11,65,34
Adj	Wu, Shuang	M	62A,62B

GA1500 North Georgia Coll & State Univ
Department of Performing Arts
322 Georgia Cir
Dahlonega, GA 30597
(706) 864-1423   Fax: (706) 864-1429
www.northgeorgia.edu
E-mail: adavid@northgeorgia.edu

4 Year Liberal Arts Institution

Music Head & Dir., Guest Artist Series: Andy David, 80A,80F,80C
Dir., Graduate Studies: Brandon L. Haskett, 80C

PT	Anderson, Matt	M	70,13C
Prof	Barrow, Lee G.	D	13,60,34
PT	Blalock, James	M	62D,62C
Prof	Broman, John M.	D	36,40,61
PT	Carere, Anthony	M	29
PT	Carter, Kenyon	M	64E,29
Prof	Chapman, Joe C.	D	13,66A,10
Assoc Prof	David, Andy	M	37
PT	David, John	D	65,50
PT	Finlay, Lois	M	66A
PT	Gardner, Valerie	M	62A
PT	Harwood, Andy	M	64C
PT	Harwood, Karen	M	64B,64D
Asst Prof	Haskett, Brandon L.	D	32
PT	Hutcheson, Mary Beth	M	61
PT	Keyser, Catherine	M	64A
PT	Keyser, Timothy	M	63D
PT	May, Susan	M	61
PT	Meier, Steven	M	11,12A,29
Asst Prof	Perry, Mark E.	D	20,12
PT	Sharp, Leanne	M	66D
PT	Sleister, Terry	M	63C

GA1550 Oglethorpe University
Department of Music
4484 Peachtree Rd NE
Atlanta, GA 30319-2737
(404) 261-1441   Fax: (404) 364-8442
www.oglethorpe.edu
E-mail: iray@oglethorpe.edu

4 Year Institution

Director: W. Irwin Ray, Jr., 80A

Inst PT	Arenz, David	M	62A
Inst PT	Buice, David	M	66C,66H,66G,69
Inst	Burgess, Richard	M	70
Inst PT	Ellis, Erin L.	DMA	62C
Inst PT	Hill, Mary Ann	M	61
	Ray, W. Irwin	DMA	60,11,41,36,40
Inst	Runnels, Brent	DMA	66A,11,29,47,13A
Inst PT	Scanling, Paul F.	M	64,37,42,48

GA1600 Paine College
Department of Music
1235 15th St
Augusta, GA 30901-3105
(706) 821-8246
www.paine.edu
E-mail: iholmes@paine.edu

4 Year Institution, Historically Black College

Dean: Curtis E. Martin, 80A
Chair & Dir., Artist Series: Sandra C. Scott, 80A,80F

Asst Prof	Carroll, Kevin	D	10,64,60B,11,13
Asst Prof	Holmes, Isaac	M	60A,11,36,61,39
Other	Johnson, Henry	B	36,66A,46,47,48
Prof	Scott, Sandra C.	D	36,40,60A,32D,66A
Adj Prof	Shaw, A. Herndon	D	11

GA1650 Piedmont College
Department of Music
165 Central Ave
PO Box 10
Demorest, GA 30535-5644
(706) 778-3000   Fax: (706) 778-0701
www.piedmont.edu
E-mail: whinson@piedmont.edu

4 Year Institution, Graduate School

Master of Arts in Music Education, Master of Arts in Teaching in Music Education

Chair: Wallace Hinson, 80A

PT	Bass, Louise	M	66C,66G
PT	Dawkins, Kyle	B	70
PT	Dean, Martin	M	64,48
PT	Ewing, Lee	M	37,63,64
Assoc Prof	Hayner, Joy	M	11,13,66
Prof	Hayner, Phillip A.	D	11,12,66A,66C,66D
Prof	Hinson, Wallace	D	60,36,40
PT	James, Donna Bunn	M	66C
PT	Jones, Rebecca	M	11
PT	LeCroy, Hoyt F.	D	65,32
Prof	Mellichamp, James F.	D	66G
PT	Pilkington, Jonathan	M	61,39,11
Asst Prof	Price, Andrea M.	D	61,39,14
Asst Prof	Ringwall, Lauren	M	32,60,36
PT	Strachan, Heather	B	62,42

GA1700 Reinhardt University
School of Music
7300 Reinhardt Circle
Waleska, GA 30183-2900
(770) 720-5600 x 9221   Fax: (770) 720-9164
www.reinhardt.edu
E-mail: dkm@reinhardt.edu

4 Year Institution, Graduate School

Master of Music in Conducting, Master of Music in Music Education, Master of Music in Piano Pedagogy

Dean: Dennis K. McIntire, 80A

Inst PT	Adams, Alison	M	61
Inst	Anderson, Matthew M.	M	70,13B
Inst PT	Bennett, Susan Brady	B	62E
Inst	Berger, Reverie Mott	D	61,54
Inst PT	Bishop, Marla	M	66A,66D
Inst PT	Bryant, Kelly	M	64A,48
Inst PT	Cantrell, Wanda	M	66C
Asst Prof	Chandler, Chuck	D	61
Inst PT	Cheyne, Donald R.	D	32,72
Inst PT	Flint, Jere	M	38
Inst PT	Fraschillo, Tom	D	37,60B,32E
Assoc Prof	Gregory, M. David	D	32E,37,32F,60B
Assoc Prof	Harper, Tamara W.	D	61,54
Inst PT	Harrison, David E.	M	32E
Inst PT	Henson, Mitchell	D	64E,47,13A
Inst PT	Kennedy, Warren	M	66C
Inst PT	Kieffer, Olivia	M	65,50
Inst PT	Laminack, Emily	M	62A
Prof	Lucktenberg, George	D	66A,66E,66H
Inst PT	Maddox, Harry	B	63D,42
Inst PT	Maddox, Nan	B	62C,42
Inst PT	Martin, Freddie	M	37,32E
Assoc Prof	McIntire, Dennis K.	D	36,13E
Assoc Prof	Naylor, Susan E.	M	13B,66A,13C
Inst PT	Neese, Charity	B	66C
Inst PT	Optiz, Robert	B	29,63A
Asst Prof	Salter, Rebecca	D	61
Inst PT	Sayre, Charles L.	B	10
Inst PT	Sayre, Lisa	B	64B
Inst PT	Seidel, William	M	66G
Prof	Shaw, Martha	D	36,32D,60A
Inst PT	Silva, Ulisses C.	D	62B,11
Inst PT	Smith, Fabia	M	66C
Inst PT	Smith, Miriam	M	62A
Asst Prof	Thomas-Lee, Paula	D	66A,66B,32B
Inst PT	Wallace, Susan	M	66C
Inst PT	Werling, Helen	M	63B
Inst PT	Williams, Melanie	M	66C

GA1750 Savannah State University
Department of Fine Arts-Music
PO Box 20029
Savannah, GA 31404
(912) 356-2248   Fax: (912) 691-5550
www.savannahstate.edu
E-mail: bindhamm@savannahstate.edu

4 Year Institution, Historically Black College

Chair: April Gentry, 80A

Lect	Bindhammer, Heidi		
Adj Inst	Bratcher, Nicholas O.		37
Inst	Shannon, Quynh		66C
Asst Prof	Spicer, Nan		36
Inst	Wright, Arthur		37

GA1800 Shorter University
School of the Arts - Music
315 Shorter Ave
Rome, GA 30165
(706) 233-7247   Fax: (706) 236-1517
www.shorter.edu
E-mail: awingard@shorter.edu

4 Year Institution
Member of NASM

Dean: Alan B. Wingard, 80A
Dir., Artist Series: Jerico Vasquez, 80F

Asst Prof	Bearden-Carver, Julie	M	61,54
Asst Prof	Huey, Daniel J.	M	13,66G
Asst Prof	Jordan-Miller, Rebekah	D	66A,66B
Asst Prof	McCluskey, P. Eric	D	61
Asst Prof	Popham, Deborah	DMA	61,39
Asst Prof	Reams, John	D	13,38,41,64
Asst Prof	Salter, Rebecca A.	D	61
Asst Prof	Tarrant, Fredrick A.	D	11,12,14,20,55
Asst Prof	Vasquez, Jerico	D	66A,66D
Prof	Wingard, Alan B.	D	31A

GA1900 Spelman College
Department of Music
350 Spelman Ln SW Box 312
Atlanta, GA 30314-4346
(404) 270-5476   Fax: (404) 270-5484
www.spelman.edu
E-mail: kjohns10@spelman.edu

4 Year Institution, Historically Black College
Member of NASM

Chair: Kevin P. Johnson, 80A

Adj	Bell, Valda		66C
Asst Prof	Chung, Hyunjung Rachel	D	66A,13,66C
Adj	Clegg, Trey	M	66C
Adj	Dillard, Pamela		61
Adj	Georgieva, Roumena		
Inst	Grissom, Paula		66D
Inst	Jennings, Joseph W.	M	47,64C,29,64E
Adj	Johnson, Clarence J.		37
Prof Emerita	Johnson, Joyce F.	D	13,66
Assoc Prof	Johnson, Kevin P.	D	60,11,32A,32B,34
Adj	Keach, Candace	M	64A
Adj	Kerschner, Jeff	M	65
	McKinney, Kevin	D	13A,10F,11
Inst	McPhail, Ann Marie		
Lect	Robinson, Laura E.	M	61
Assoc Prof	Schenbeck, Lawrence A.	D	11,12A,12C
Adj	Wyatt, Alfred	D	37

GA1990 Thomas University
Department of Music
1501 Millpond Rd
Thomasville, GA 31792-7499
(229) 226-1621   Fax: (229) 226-1653
www.thomasu.edu/actu
E-mail: kbarton@thomasu.edu

4 Year Institution

Chair & Dir., Artist Series: Karl S. Barton, 80A,80F

Inst Adj	Amend, James M.	D	66A,66C
Prof	Barton, Karl S.	D	64,47,12A,34
Inst Adj	Fadell, Rebecca	M	61
Inst Adj	Foster, Adam	D	70
Inst Adj	Pursino, Peter	M	36,40

GA2000 Toccoa Falls College
School of Music
107 N Chapel Dr
Toccoa, GA 30598
(706) 886-6831 x 5263   Fax: (706) 282-6036
www.tfc.edu
E-mail: dstufft@tfc.edu

4 Year Institution
Member of NASM

Director: David Stufft, 80A
Associate Director: Thomas Council, 80H

Inst	Bartholow, Lisa Hanson		
		M	64A
Inst	Byrd, Katie	M	65
Assoc Prof	Council, Thomas	D	31A,61,36,60,40
Inst	Cox, Thomas B.	M	63D
Inst	Davis, Kaylynn	M	62E
Inst	Dean, Martin	M	64C
Inst	Gehle, Keith	B	70
Inst	Hixson, Mary	M	13C,20,40,43
Asst Prof	Jones, David	M	61,39,42
Asst Prof	Lee, You Ju	D	66A,66C,66D,66B
Inst	Little, Marica	M	61

Asst Prof	Morden, James	M	13,11,12A,63A
Inst	Strachan, Heather	B	51,62A,62C
Asst Prof	Stufft, David	M	37,41,47,32,60B
Inst	Wilkes, Jamey	M	11,16

GA2050 Truett-McConnell College

Division Music and Fine Arts
100 Alumni Dr
Cleveland, GA 30528
(706) 865-2134   Fax: (706) 865-5135
www.truett.edu
E-mail: bcaston@truett.edu

4 Year Institution
Member of NASM

Chair: Ben Caston, 80A

Assoc Prof	Caston, Ben	D	36,60A,61
Asst Prof	Costigan, Christopher	D	64C,64E
Adj	Davis, Anna	M	66A,66D
Adj	Garcia, Jose Manuel	D	66A,66D,11,10A
Adj	George, David N.	D	66A
Adj	Kilroe-Smith, Catherine	D	63B
Prof	Lombard, Becky	D	66A,13B,13C,12A,66C
Adj	McKissick, Charles	M	65
Adj	Moore, Ryan		70
Adj	Mourton, Laurie		64A
Adj	Wells, Connie	M	64D

GA2100 Univ of Georgia

Hugh Hodgson School of Music
250 River Rd
Athens, GA 30602-7287
(706) 542-3737   Fax: (706) 542-2773
www.music.uga.edu
E-mail: dmonson@uga.edu

4 Year Institution, Graduate School
Member of NASM

Master of Arts in Music History, Master of Education in Music Education, Master of Music in Composition, Master of Music in Performance, Master of Music in Conducting, Master of Music Education in Music Therapy, Master of Music Education, DMA in Composition, DMA in Conducting, DMA in Performance, DMA in Music Education, Doctor of Education in Music Education, PhD in Music, Master of Music in Music Literature, Specialist in Education in Music Education

Director: Dale E. Monson, 80A
Dir., Graduate Studies: Adrian P. Childs, 80C
Dir., Community/Preparatory Division: Kristin Jutras, 80E
Dir., Artist Series & Summer Programs: Milton Masciadri, 80F,80G
Dir., Institute/Fest/Workshop: Clint 'Skip' Taylor, 80F
Associate Director: Mary A. Leglar, 80H
Associate Director: David A. Starkweather, 80H

Prof	Adams, Timothy K.	M	65
Prof	Ambartsumian, Levon	D	51,62A,62B
Other	Azimkhodjaeva, Shakida		51,62A
Assoc Prof	Ball, Leonard V.	D	13,10,45,34
Prof	Bara, Daniel J.	D	60A,36
Prof	Bilger, David	M	63A
Assoc Prof	Broughton, Gregory	D	36,61
Prof	Burchinal, Frederick	M	39,61
Inst PT	Burton-Brown, David	D	66G
Asst Prof	Bynum, Josh L.	D	63C,63D,13A
Prof	Cedel, Mark	M	60B,38,62B
Assoc Prof	Childs, Adrian P.	PhD	10,13,43
Prof Emeritus	Corina, John H.	D	13,10,64B
Librarian	Coscarelli, William F.	M	16
Asst Prof	Craswell, Brandon	D	63A,49
Prof Emeritus	Crowell, Allen	M	60,36
Inst	D'Angelo, David	M	29,53
Assoc Prof Emerita	Davis, Jolene	D	13,66G,31A
Prof Emeritus	Davis, William	D	13,64D
Inst PT	Deane, Richard	M	63B
Other	Denton, Damon	M	66C
Inst PT	Elton, Nancy H.	D	66
Prof Emeritus	Ennulat, Egbert M.	D	12A,66G,66H
Assoc Prof	Foreman, George C.	D	12
Assoc Prof Emeritus	Frazier, Ivan	D	66A,66B,66D
Asst Prof	Frigo, Connie	D	64E
Lect	Gertsch, Emily	M	13
Prof Emeritus	Graham, Richard M.	D	33,12F
Assoc Prof Emeritus	Grant, Roy	D	33
Prof	Haas, David	PhD	11,12

Prof Emerita	Hair, Harriet	D	11,32,34,12F
Inst PT	Hargrave, Monica E.	M	62E
Assoc Prof Emeritus	Hasbrouck, Calvin	M	63A
Assoc Prof	Heald, Michael	D	62A
Prof Emeritus	Jameson, Philip	D	49,63C
Other	Jones, Scott A.	M	37,60B
Prof	Jones-Reus, Angela	M	64A,48
Assoc Prof	Jutras, Peter J.	PhD	66A,66B,66D,32G
Other	Kelly, Kevin	PhD	16,12
Assoc Prof	Kennedy, Roy	PhD	33
Assoc Prof	Kidula, Jean	PhD	14,20,11,31,12
Assoc Prof	Legette, Roy M.	PhD	32
Prof	Leglar, Mary A.	PhD	32
Assoc Prof Emeritus	Ligotti, Albert F.	M	49,63A
Prof	Link, Dorothea	PhD	11,12
Prof Emeritus	Lowe, Donald R.	D	32,31A
Prof	Lynch, John P.	D	37,60A
Other	Marlow, William	M	35G
Prof	Martin-Williams, Jean F.	D	49,63D
Prof	Masciadri, Milton	M	51,62D
Inst PT	Massey, Taylor	M	64C
Prof	McClellan, David Ray	D	64C,48
Prof Emeritus	McCutchen, Thomas	D	65,46
Inst	Messich, Reid	M	64B
Prof	Monson, Dale E.	PhD	12
Asst Prof	Moody, Philip	D	36,60A,61
Other	Moore, Raymond D.	M	35G
Prof Emeritus	Parker, Olin G.	D	32
Lect	Pierce, Stephanie D.	M	61
Prof Emeritus	Placek, Robert W.	D	32,34
Asst Prof	Pollard, Amy	M	64D,42
Assoc Prof Emeritus	Reinke, Charlotte	M	61
Inst PT	Ritchey, Doris Ellen	D	33,61
Prof	Rivkin, Evgeny	D	41,66A
Assoc Prof	Robinson, Michael C.	D	37,60,32E,60B
Asst Prof	Royo, Johanna	M	32D
Prof Emeritus	Sandor, Edward	D	49,63A
Prof	Satterwhite, H. Dwight		60B,37
Lect	Scott, Arvin	PhD	65
Other	Sheludyakov, Anatoly	M	66C
Asst Prof	Simpson-Litke, Rebecca	PhD	13,14C,20H
Assoc Prof	Snyder, Maggie	M	62B
Asst Prof	Snyder, Philip	D	70
Prof	Starkweather, David A.	D	51,62C
Assoc Prof Emeritus	Stoffel, David N.	D	61,54
Assoc Prof Emeritus	Strahl, Margaret A.	M	11,66A
Emeritus	Sutherland, John	DIPL	70
Assoc Prof	Taylor, Clint 'Skip'	PhD	32
Prof	Thomas, Martha L.	D	66A,66C
Assoc Prof	Thomas, Susan R.	PhD	11,12,14,20H,34A
Assoc Prof	Tingler, Stephanie	D	61
Assoc Prof	Valdez, Stephen	D	29,12
Prof Emeritus	Vogel, Roger C.	PhD	13,10
Prof Emeritus	Waln, Ronald	D	64A
Inst PT	Welty, Susan	B	63B
Asst Prof	Wesolowski, Brian	PhD	32E,32G,29C
PT	Whitwell, John	M	35E,37,60B
PT	Wickes, Frank	M	37,60
Asst Prof	Williams, Natalie	D	10,13
Other	Wright, Kathryn	M	61
Prof	Zerkel, David	M	63D,49
Prof	Zimdars, Richard L.	D	66A,42

GA2130 Univ of West Georgia

Department of Music
1601 Maple St
Carrollton, GA 30118-2210
(678) 839-6516   Fax: (678) 839-6259
www.westga.edu/music
E-mail: musicdpt@westga.edu

4 Year Institution, Graduate School
Member of NASM

Master of Music in Performance, Master of Music in Music Education

Chair: Kevin Hibbard, 80A

Inst PT	Adams, Jan	M	66A,66D
Prof	Bakos, Daniel F.	D	13,47,29
Assoc Prof	Bleuel, John	D	13C,60,64E,64B,64D
Asst Prof	Byrd, Joshua	D	37,10A,13G,48,10F
Inst PT	Byrd, Katherine	M	65,50
Inst PT	Crews, Janice	D	64B
Inst PT	Dodd, Anna	D	63B
Inst PT	Frank, Adam	M	70
Prof	Frazier, Larry R.	D	39,61
Inst PT	Fuller, Melanie	D	64A,48
Assoc Prof	Gingerich, Carol	D	66A,66B,66C
Inst PT	Hays, Sorrel	M	11
Prof	Hibbard, Kevin	D	36,32D,61,60,32C
Inst FT	Hunt, Emily	M	11
Asst Prof	Kramer, Elizabeth A.	D	12A,14,11,13A,62A
Inst PT	Lanier, Michael	M	63A,49

Inst PT	Lawing, Sarah	M	64C
Inst PT	Lowry, Julie	M	61
Asst Prof	McCord, G. Dawn Harmon	D	32B,32C,32A,13C,66D
Asst Prof	Self, Cale	M	37,63C,63D,32E,49
Inst PT	Smith, J. Benjamin	M	64D

GA2150 Valdosta State University
Department of Music
1500 N Patterson St
Valdosta, GA 31698-0115
(229) 333-5804   Fax: (229) 259-5578
www.valdosta.edu/music
E-mail: dfarwell@valdosta.edu

4 Year Institution, Graduate School
Member of NASM

Master of Music in Performance, Master of Music in Music Education

Interim Head, Music: Douglas G. Farwell, 80A
Dir., Graduate Studies: Lyle Indergaard, 80C
Dir., Preparatory Division: Lauren Burns, 80E

Asst Prof	Bradshaw, Eric E.	M	63D,32E,37,60
Prof	Brashier, Joe H.	D	32,37,60
Lect	Burns, Lauren	M	62B,32E,51
Assoc Prof	Cain, Joren R.	D	29,64E
Lect	Campiglia, Paul	M	65,29,71,50,11
Prof	Corbin, Lynn Ann	D	32,61,60A
Prof	Eischeid, Susan	D	64B,11,48,42
Prof	Farwell, Douglas G.	D	63C,49,34,35C,35D
Prof	Goode, Elizabeth	D	64A,48,13
PT	Hardesty, Tamara G.	D	61
Asst Prof	Hsu, Howard	D	38,42,60B
Prof	Indergaard, Lyle	D	66A,66C,66D
Assoc Prof	Johns, Kristen	D	63B,11,42,49
Prof Emeritus PT	Johnson, David Lee	D	61
Prof	Kirk, Kenneth P.	D	63A,49,13,39
Lect	Leavitt, Tod J.	D	62D
Asst Prof	Lowe, Shannon R.	D	64D,48,13
Lect	Lutz, Nina	M	62A,13A
Prof	Mikkelsen, Carol M.	D	61,39
Prof	Morris, J. David	D	65,34,13,50
Assoc Prof	Neal, Paul	D	36,60A,61,60
Assoc Prof	Olson, Jeffrey K.	D	64C,48,64E
Asst Prof	Paoletti, Karl P.	DMA	61
PT	Rowland, Daniel	M	63D
PT	Santiago, Nephtali	M	70,29,11
Prof	Scully, Lawrence L.	D	66,12A
Prof	Shrader, James A.	PhD	60,12A,61,36,39
Asst Prof	Springfield, David	M	29,35G,63C
Inst	Springfield, Maila Gutierrez	M	66C
Lect	Taylor, Steve M.	M	62C,11
PT	Todd, Charles E.	M	11
Lect	Williams, Brent	D	62A,20

GA2175 Waycross College
Department of Music
2001 S Georgia Pkwy
Waycross, GA 31503-9248
(912) 449-7600   Fax: (912) 449-7610
www.waycross.edu
E-mail: wcharact@waycross.edu

2 Year Institution

Chair: Sara E. Selby, 80A

| PT | Character, William | M | 61,66A,70 |

GA2200 Wesleyan College
Department of Music
4760 Forsyth Rd
Macon, GA 31210-4462
(478) 757-5259   Fax: (478) 757-5268
www.wesleyancollege.edu
E-mail: nwhitney@wesleyancollege.edu

4 Year Institution
Member of NASM

Dean: Vivia Fowler, 80A
Chair: Nadine C. Whitney, 80A
Dir., Artist/Performance Series: Michael McGhee, 80F

Prof	Eikner, Edward	M	12A,66A,66C,66D,11
Asst Prof	Hanson, Ellen	M	12A,61,39
Asst Prof	McGhee, Michael	D	13,11,12A,66G,66H
Prof	Whitney, Nadine C.	M	12A,36,61,40,39

GA2300 Young Harris College
Department of Music
1 College St
PO Box 68
Young Harris, GA 30582
(706) 379-5181   Fax: (706) 379-4596
www.yhc.edu
E-mail: ecalloway@yhc.edu

4 Year Liberal Arts Institution
Member of NASM

Chair: Edwin S. Calloway, 80A
Dean, Fine Arts: Ted Whisenhunt, 80A
Dir., Artist/Performance Series: Christopher Sass, 80F

Adj	Barnstead, Scott	M	63C
Prof	Bauman, Jeffrey Milo	M	36,61,54,10F,60A
Adj	Brown, Eric	B	65,32E
Adj	Bryant, John	M	11,13C,63A,20
Assoc Prof	Calloway, Edwin S.	D	13C,35C
Asst Prof	Calloway, Karen E.	M	61,64A
Adj	Campbell, Michael J.	D	60B,47,64E,32E,11
Adj	Covington, Alicia	M	63B
Adj	DeFoor, Cynthia	B	66C,66D,66B,66A
Prof	DeFoor, Keith	D	66G
Adj	Denmon, Alan	M	11,13A,13B,32C,32E
Prof Emerita	Fox, Mary Ann	M	66A
Prof Emeritus	Fox, William	M	
Adj	Hooper, Terry	M	61
Asst Prof	Knepp, Richard	M	70,41,12A
Asst Prof	Land, Mary	M	37,32
Asst Prof	Miller, Leigh	D	13A,13B,64C
Adj	Peebles, William	D	64D
Adj	Ramsay, Ginger	M	64B
Adj	Richardson, Vernal	D	32E
Adj	Rittenhouse, Kerry	D	32E
Adj	Seis, Catherine	D	32B
Adj	Star, Cheryl	M	64A
Adj	Stooksbury, Laura	M	61
Asst Prof	Wayman, John B.	D	32,36,61
Adj	Wildman, Simon	M	63D

GU0500 Univ of Guam
Department of Music
UOG Station
Mangilao, GU 96923
(671) 735-2700   Fax: (671) 734-3575
www.uog.edu
E-mail: smbed@guam.net

4 Year US Land Grant Institution

Music Contact: Cynthia B. Sajnovsky, 80A
Dean, College of Liberal Arts & Social Sciences: Mary Spencer, 80A

Adj Inst	Batimana, Ching		65
Assoc Prof	Bednarzyk, Stephen C.	D	60,37,64C,66A
Adj Inst	Goldhorn, Jan	M	64A
Prof	Johnson, Randall	D	11,36,47,61,64E
Adj Inst	Laguana, Carlos	M	70
Prof	Sajnovsky, Cynthia B.	D	13A,12A,20C,66D,67C

HI0050 Brigham Young Univ-Hawaii
Department of Fine Arts-Music
55-220 Kulanui St #1953
Laie, HI 96762
(808) 675-3892   Fax: (808) 675-3900
academics.byuh.edu/finearts
E-mail: mccarres@byuh.edu

4 Year Institution

Chair: David Kammerer, 80A

PT	Bai, Pauline	M	62C
PT	Belnap, Lila	B	61
Prof	Belnap, Michael	M	36,39,40,54,61
Asst Prof	Bradshaw, Daniel	D	13D,42,41
PT	Chandler, Lloyd	B	50

PT	Cook, Lawrence	M	48,64A,64C,64E
Assoc Prof	Duerden, Darren	D	32E,65,50,47,11
PT	Duerden, Jennifer	M	11,66A,66C,66D
PT	Goldsmith, Robert		70
PT	Jang, Iggy	B	62A
Asst Prof	Kammerer, David	M	10F,37,35B,63A,13C
PT	Kammerer, Elizabeth	B	61,36
PT	Kim, Linda	M	66A
PT	Lin, I-Bei	D	62C
PT	Luscher, Alexia	M	62A,62B
Assoc Prof	McCarrey, Scott	D	66A,66B,13E,12A,11
PT	McCarrey, Stacy	M	66A,66C,66D
Asst Prof	Mooy, Mary Annaleen	M	60A,32D,36
PT	Nakashita, Sonomi	B	66A
Prof Emeritus	Ottley, Jerold	D	32D,36,60A
Emeritus	Ottley, JoAnn	B	39,61
PT	Pernela, Nathan	M	62B
PT	Stone, Geoff	M	62D

HI0060 Chaminade University of Honolulu
Department of Music
3140 Waialae Ave
Honolulu, HI 96816-1510
(808) 735-4865   Fax: (808) 739-4647
www.chaminade.edu
E-mail: tcarney@chaminade.edu

4 Year Institution

Chair: Timothy F. Carney, 80A

Vstng Assoc Prof	Bouffier, Robert	B	
FT	Carney, Timothy F.	D	36,11,13A,54,61
Assoc Prof	Morris, Gary		
Prof	Ozaki, Yukio	M	
Prof	Takeda, Walter N.	M	

HI0110 Hawaii Pacific University
Department of Arts & Humanities
Music
1188 Fort St Mall #430
Honolulu, HI 96813-2882
(808) 544-0887   Fax: (808) 544-1424
www.hpu.edu
E-mail: tmccreary@hpu.edu

4 Year Institution

Chair: Teresa J. McCreary, 80A

	Hennessey, Patrick D.	PhD	37,47,29A,12A,63C
	McCreary, Teresa J.	PhD	37,13A,13C,38,47
	Stern, Kalai	M	11,36,40,13A,13C
	Yoo, Esther	D	36

HI0120 Honolulu Community College
Department of Music
874 Dillingham Blvd
Honolulu, HI 96817-4505
(808) 845-9415   Fax: (808) 845-9416
honolulu.hawaii.edu/
E-mail: lmount@hawaii.edu

2 Year Institution

Music Contact: Lorna Mount, 80A

Lect PT	Mount, Lorna	M	13A,11,12A,70,36

HI0150 Kapi'olani Community College
Department of Humanities
4303 Diamond Head Rd
Honolulu, HI 96816-4421
(808)734-9255   Fax: (808)734-9151
kapiolani.hawaii.edu
E-mail: anne@hawaii.edu

2 Year Institution

Music Coordinator: Anne Craig Lum, 80A

Lect PT	Aamodt, Rucci R.	M	32,11,66A,66D
Asst Prof	Doo, Lina J.	M	11,61,36,54,20
Assoc Prof	Lum, Anne Craig	M	66D,66A,64A,45,66C
Lect PT	Nago, Stuart H.	B	70

HI0155 Kauai Community College
Department of Music
3-1901 Kaumualii Hwy
Lihue, HI 96766-9500
(808)245-8269   Fax: (808)245-8820
www.kauaicc.hawaii.edu
E-mail: shep@hawaii.edu

2 Year Institution

Chair: Gregory Shepherd, 80A

PT	Kinnaman, Hal	B	70
PT	McIntosh, Lawrence	M	37
Prof	Shepherd, Gregory		

I0160 Leeward Community College
Department of Music
96-045 Ala Ike St
Pearl City, HI 96782-3366
(808) 455-0350   Fax: (808) 455-0638
www.lcc.hawaii.edu
E-mail: frary@hawaii.edu

2 Year Institution, Music Certificate Program

Chair, Division of Arts & Humanities: James West, 80A

Prof	Frary, Peter Kun	M	13,11,12A,70,34
PT	Kane, Dreena	B	20D
Prof	Kim-Infiesto, Marilyn Liu	M	36,61,12A,32,13A
Assoc Prof	Minasian, Mark		11,12A,29,34,35
Asst Prof	Pfeiffer, Ruth Imperial	M	13A,12A,32,36,66

HI0200 Univ of Hawaii-Hilo
Department of Performing Arts
200 W Kawili St
Hilo, HI 96720-4091
(808) 974-7304   Fax: (808) 974-7736
www.uhh.hawaii.edu/academics/perfarts
E-mail: jpjohnso@hawaii.edu

4 Year Institution

Chair: Jacquelyn Pualani Johnson, 80A

Lect	Boyd, Don E.	B	66A
Lect	Horst, Amy S.	M	36,13
Asst Prof	Howell, Matthew	D	36,38,40
Prof	Johnson, Jacquelyn Pualani	M	54
Assoc Prof	Lee, Richard A.	D	13,10,12A,64E,64A
Inst	Staton, Celeste A.	DIPL	52
Lect	Veilleux, Trever L.	B	46

HI0210 Univ of Hawaii-Manoa
Department of Music
2411 Dole St
Honolulu, HI 96822-2329
(808) 956-7756   Fax: (808) 956-9657
www.hawaii.edu/uhmmusic
E-mail: uhmmusic@hawaii.edu

4 Year Institution, Graduate School
Member of NASM

Master of Arts in Music Education, Master of Arts in Ethnomusicology, Master of Music in Composition, Master of Music in Performance, PhD in Music, Master of Arts in Musicology

Dean: Peter Arnade, 80A
Chair: Laurence Paxton, 80A
Dir., Undergraduate Studies: Jane Moulin, 80B
Dir., Graduate Studies: Lesley A. Wright, 80C
Associate Chair: Thomas Yee, 80H

Lect	Aamodt, Rucci R.	M	32,66
Lect	Barrett, Paul	M	64D
Lect	Bingham, Martina	M	61
Prof	Bingham, Thomas	M	32E,37,60
Asst Prof	Boeckman, Jeffrey	D	37,60B
Lect	Byerlotzer, Jason L.	M	63C
Lect	Casano, Steven	M	13A,13B,13C,13D
Lect	Dinion, Steve	M	65A,65B
Asst Prof	Felpe, Miguel	D	36
Lect	Gallagher, John P.	M	62D
Prof Emeritus	Greenberg, Marvin	D	32
Lect	Hafner, Kenneth A.	M	63A
Prof Emeritus	Hines, Robert S.	D	36
Assoc Prof	Hoover, Maya	D	61
Asst Prof	Itoh, Takuma	D	10A,13A,13B,13C,13D
Lect	Jang, Ignace	DIPL	62A
Prof Emerita	Johansson, Annette	M	61
Lect	Johnson, Lynne	M	11,12A
Lect	Junker, Jay	B	20G
Lect	Kaneshiro, Norman	DIPL	20D
Asst Prof	Korth, Jonathan	D	66A,66B,66C
Prof Emeritus	Kudo, Takeo	D	10A,10F,13,20D
Prof	Lau, Frederick C.	D	14A,38,43,64A,20C
Prof	Lee, Byong Won	D	20A,20D,14A
Lect	Li, Bichuan	M	66A,66D
Assoc Prof	Lin, I-Bei	D	62C,41,42,13A
Assoc Prof	Loong, ChetYeng	D	32
Prof Emeritus	Lum, Richard	M	37
Prof Emeritus	Lyddon, Paul W.	M	66
Lect	McCulloch, Doug	M	13A,13B,13C,13D
Prof Emeritus	McKay, Neil	D	10,13
Prof	McLain, Barbara	D	32
Assoc Prof	McQuiston, Kate	D	12A,12B,12C
Lect	Medeiros, Peter	B	20I
Prof	Miyamura, Henry	M	32C,38,64C
Lect	Miyashiro, Darin	DIPL	20C
Prof	Moulin, Jane	D	20D,14A,55,67A
Prof	Mount, John	M	39,61
Lect	Mount, Megan M.	B	61
Lect	Nahulu, Nola A.	M	36,20I
Lect	Nakamura, Gwen H.	M	37,64E
Lect	Ochi-Onishi, Susan M.	M	64B
Prof Emeritus	Okamura, Grant K.	M	60,32C,37,63A
Asst Prof Emeritus	Osborne, Thomas	D	10A,10F,13,43
Lect	O'Sullivan, Ian	M	70
Lect	Padilla, Reginald A.	M	47
Lect	Parrish, Jonathan L.	M	63B
Prof	Paxton, Laurence	M	39,61,54
Lect	Ricer, Thomas	D	63D
Prof Emeritus	Russell, Armand	D	10,13
Lect	Saiki-Mita, Sabrina	M	64A
Asst Prof	Sala, Aaron J.	M	14A
Lect	Schutz, Rachel	M	61
Lect	Shamoto, Masatoshi	DIPL	20D
Prof Emeritus	Shipwright, Edward	D	66
Lect	Skurtu, Jasmine J.	B	70
Prof Emeritus	Smith, Barbara B.	M	20I,20C,14
Lect	Takamine, Victoria	M	20I
Prof Emeritus	Trimillos, Ricardo D.	PhD	20D,20I,14D,14A,14F
Lect	Wang, Rosy	M	66A
Lect	Wenderoth, Valeria	D	12A
Lect	Womack, Anna	M	62B
Prof	Womack, Donald Reid	D	10,13,13E,10A,10F
Prof	Wright, Lesley A.	D	11,12
Lect	Yamashita, Wendy	D	66B
Prof Emeritus	Yasui, Byron K.	D	70,10A,10F,13,20B
Prof	Yee, Thomas	D	13C,66A,66C,66B
Lect	Yukumoto, Todd	M	64E
Lect	Zuttermeister, Noenoelani		20I

HI0300 Windward Community College

Music Program
45-720 Keaahala Rd
Kaneohe, HI 96744-3528
(808) 235-7400   Fax: (808) 247-5362
www.wcc.hawaii.edu
E-mail: moffat@hawaii.edu

2 Year Institution

Dean: Richard D. Fulton, 80A
Chair, Humanities: Bennet T. Moffat, 80A

Inst	Faltstrom, Gloria V.	M	13A,11,66D,61,36
Inst	Loo, Ronald	M	70

IA0050 Ashford University

Department of Music
400 N Bluff Blvd
Clinton, IA 52732-3910
(563) 242-4023   Fax: (563) 242-2003
www.ashford.edu
E-mail: rob.engelson@ashford.edu

4 Year Institution

Chair & Dir., Artist/Performance Series: Robert A. Engelson, 80A,80F,80H
Dir., Admissions & Summer Programs: Curt Lowe, 80D,80G

Prof	Engelson, Robert A.	D	13,60,11,36,54
Adj	Engelson, Thea	D	61,66A
Adj	Little, Steve		37

IA0100 Briar Cliff University

Department of Music
3303 Rebecca St
Sioux City, IA 51104
(712) 279-5567   Fax: (712) 279-5486
www.briarcliff.edu
E-mail: mary.day@briarcliff.edu

4 Year Institution

Chair: Mary Day, 80A

Assoc Prof	Burton, Sean Michael	D	36,61,41,11,13D
Assoc Prof	Day, Mary	D	41,61,67,31A,39
Inst	Gibson, Robert	M	47,49
Asst Prof	Owens, Jeremy	D	11,12A,66
Inst	Salyards, Shannon	M	61
Prof	Steinbach, Richard	DMA	13,10,66,34

IA0150 Buena Vista University

Department of Music
610 West 4th St
Storm Lake, IA 50588
(712) 749-2131   Fax: (712) 749-2037
www.bvu.edu
E-mail: klee@bvu.edu

4 Year Institution

Chair: Michael Whitlatch, 80A

Asst Prof	Bertrand, Jerry	M	63A,37
PT	Hinkeldey, Jeanette	M	13,64B,64D,66
Asst Prof	Keeler, Paula	D	32,36,39,41,61
Assoc Prof	Klee, Wendy A.	D	10C,29A,34D,35A,47
PT	Larson, Deanna	M	66C
PT	Thorson, Lee	M	62C,62D

IA0200 Central College

Department of Music
Campus Box 6100
812 University
Pella, IA 50219
(641) 628-5236   Fax: (641) 628-5395
www.central.edu
E-mail: abeld@central.edu

4 Year Institution
Member of NASM

Chair: Mark A. Babcock, 80A

Assoc Prof	Babcock, Mark A.	M	36,40,66G,13
Inst PT	Berimeladze, Tariel		
Prof	Breckenridge, Carol Lei	D	11,66A,66B,66C,66H
Inst PT	Crumley, Terri L.		61
Asst Prof	Dahl, Stanley E.	M	50,65,34,65A,65B
	Doggett, Cynthia Krenzel	D	12A,20,48,64C,64E
Inst PT	Doggett, Thomas J.	M	64A
Inst PT	Driscoll, Matthew	M	63A,63C,63D
Inst PT	Eekhoff, CharLee		66A
Asst Prof	Espinosa, Gabriel	M	47,53,29,40
	Kovacovic, Paul	D	10,12A,66A,66C
Inst PT	Lane, Stephen S.		

Asst Prof	Lutch, Mitchell B.	M	10F,32E,37,60
	Myers, Ty		13,38
Assoc Prof	Nielsen, John		44,32
Inst PT	Odem, Susan K.	M	64B,64D
Inst PT	Pedde, Dennis R.	D	63A
Prof	Petrie, Anne M.	D	39,61
Vstng Asst Prof	Phoenix-Neal, Diane	DMA	62,11,12,51
Inst PT	Watts-Foss, Mary		62A

IA0250 Clarke College
Department of Music
MS 1726
1550 Clarke Dr
Dubuque, IA 52001
(563) 588-6359   Fax: (563) 588-6789
www.clarke.edu
E-mail: ladonna.manternach@clarke.edu

4 Year Institution
Member of NASM

Chair: LaDonna Manternach, B.V.M., 80A

Inst	Burns, Brian E.	M	36,12A,32C,32D,60
Adj Inst	Cornils Luke, Peg	M	64A
Adj Inst	Dickey, Thomas Taylor	D	60,64D
Assoc Prof	Dunker, Amy	D	13,10,63A,41,49
Adj Inst	Enabnit, Brian	B	63C,63D
Asst Prof	Han, Sang-In	D	61,11
Adj Inst	Huckleberry, Heather	M	11,64B
Inst Adj	Iwasaki, Masahiro	B	65
Inst Adj	Klinebriel, Jill	B	16,54
Staff	Kubesheski, Cindy	B	16
Asst Prof	Lease, Nancy	M	12A,66,11
Asst Prof	Manternach, LaDonna	D	61,32B
Adj Inst	McConnell, Miles		11,70
Adj Inst	Nichols, Beverly	M	66
Inst	Resnick, David	M	10B,10F,13A,37,48
Adj Inst	Strizic, Owen	M	62

IA0270 Clinton Community College
Department of Music
1000 Lincoln Blvd
Clinton, IA 52732-6224
(563) 244-7001   Fax: (563) 242-7868
www.eicc.edu/ccc/index.html

2 Year Institution

Dir., Artist/Performance Series: Tim Sievers, 80F,80A

Adj	Rogers, Maurice L.	M	

IA0300 Coe College
Department of Music
1220 1st Ave NE
Cedar Rapids, IA 52402-5092
(319) 399-8521   Fax: (319) 399-8209
www.coe.edu
E-mail: btiede@coe.edu

4 Year Institution
Member of NASM

Chair: Marc Falk, 80A
Dir., Recruiting: Robert Benson, 80D

	Adkins, Richard C.		16,71,66F
PT	Benson, Robert	B	34D,35G
PT	Brumwell, Gretchen	M	62E
Prof	Carson, William S.	D	60B,37,12A,32E,64C
Assoc Prof	Dangerfield, Joseph Allen	D	10,13,66A,38,43
PT	Dockendorf-Boland, Janice		64A
Assoc Prof	Falk, Marc	D	36,11,12A,60A,40
PT	Fields-Moffitt, Rebecca	M	32D
PT	Fleer, Lesley	B	64B
PT	Harris, C. Andrew	M	63B
PT	Hoffman, Beth	M	62A
PT	Kimber, Michael	D	62B
PT	Lawrence, Alan	M	65
PT	Mallory, Jason	M	61,13C
Prof	Marrs, Margie V.	M	61,13A,13C
PT	Morton, R. Gregory	D	64D,64E
PT	Naylor, Al	M	63A
PT	Pearson, Ryan	B	70

PT	Phelps, Amy	D	62C,42
PT	Reznicow, Joshua	B	32E
PT	Schendel, Todd	D	63C
Asst Prof	Shanley, Steven	M	32,46,47,53
PT	Stang, Sharon Kay	M	66A,66C,66B
PT	Titus, Julia	M	11,66A,66D
PT	Von Kamp, Rebecca		61
PT	Wagor, Richard	M	62D
PT	Wiebe, Laura	M	36,11
Adj Prof	Wolgast, Brett	D	66A,66G,13,12A
PT	Wolgast, Marita		66A
PT	Yeats, Robert E.	M	63D

IA0400 Cornell College
Department of Music
PO Box 2626
600 1st St SW
Mount Vernon, IA 52314-1098
(319) 895-4228   Fax: (319) 895-5926
www.cornellcollege.edu/music/
E-mail: jmartin@cornellcollege.edu

4 Year Institution

Chair: James Martin, 80A
Dir., Music Festival: Martin Hearne, 80F

PT	Acevedo-Hernandez, Victor	D	64C
PT	Bennett, Michelle	D	62B
PT	Bogert, Nathan	M	64E
PT	Brumwell, Gretchen	M	62E
PT	Caraway, Dan		70
Prof	Chamberlain, Donald J.	D	13,10F,10,11,47
PT	Driscoll, Matthew	M	63C,63D
PT	Ellis, James	D	62C
PT	Fuller, Marcia	M	64A
PT	Hakken, Lynda S.	D	66G,13,66C,66A,11
Assoc Prof	Hearne, Lisa	D	36,61,40
Prof	Hearne, Martin	D	37,38,50,60
PT	Kim, Miera	M	62A
PT	Lawrence, Alan	M	65
Prof	Martin, James	D	13,66A,66B,20G
PT	Morton, R. Greg	D	64D
PT	Schultz, Steve	M	63B
Assoc Prof	Stilwell, Jama Liane	D	11,12,20G,13,64A
PT	Strabala, Joyce	M	66A
PT	Thompson, James	M	61
PT	Thull, Jonathan	D	39,61,54
PT	Van Houzen, Aren	D	63A
PT	Wagor, Rich	M	62D

IA0420 Des Moines Area Community College
Ankeny Campus-Music
2006 S Ankeny Blvd
Ankeny, IA 50021-8995
(515) 964-6633   Fax: (515) 964-6830
www.dmacc.edu/music
E-mail: jcloos@dmacc.edu

2 Year Institution

Chair: James C. Loos, 80A
Dean, Div. of Science & Humanities: James W. Stick, Jr., 80A

Inst PT	Beach, Sue Odem	M	64,13,11
Inst PT	Bostwick, Stacey	M	11,65
Inst PT	Davis, Scott	M	29A,47,63A
Inst PT	Gould, Brooke	M	20
Inst PT	Harrison, Joy	M	11,61
Inst PT	Jones, Daniel	M	63
Inst	Loos, James C.	M	11,61,66A
Inst PT	Lundak, Gayle	M	11
Inst PT	Miranda, Charles	M	11,62A,62B
Inst PT	Powell, Aaron	M	70,36
Inst PT	Svengalis, Judy	D	32B,66A

IA0425 Des Moines Area Community College
Boone Campus-Music
1125 Hancock Dr
Boone, IA 50036-5326
(515) 432-7203 Fax: (515) 433-5033
www.dmacc.edu
E-mail: shoifeldt@dmacc.edu

2 Year Institution

Music Contact: Steven Hoifeldt, 80A
Provost: Vivian Brandmeyer

| Adj Inst | Crawley-Mertins, Marilee | M | 11,66A,66D,34 |
| Adj Inst | Hoifeldt, Steven | M | 61,11,40 |

IA0450 Divine Word College
Department of Music
102 Jacoby Dr SW
Epworth, IA 52045
(319) 876-3354 Fax: (319) 876-3407
www.dwci.edu
E-mail: heitzman@dwci.edu

4 Year Institution, Seminary

Chair: Jill M. Heitzman, 80A
Academic Dean: Mathew Kanjirathinkal

| PT | Do, Bang Lang | D | 66A,66C |
| Asst Prof | Heitzman, Jill M. | M | 61,64A,66A,11 |

IA0500 Dordt College
Department of Music
498 4th Ave NE
Sioux Center, IA 51250-1697
(712) 722-6000 Fax: (712) 722-1185
www.dordt.edu
E-mail: kdemol@dordt.edu

4 Year Institution

Co-Chair & Dir., Artist/Performance Series: Karen DeMol, 80A,80F
Co-Chair: Benjamin Kornelis, 80A

Adj	Carlson, Andrea	B	63B
Adj	Casey, John	M	62D
Adj	Dahn, Luke	D	10
Adj	DeHaan, Pam	M	61,64E
Prof Emerita Adj	DeMol, Karen	D	64C,13C
Adj	Dibley, Charles	M	
Adj	Frens, Jennifer	B	62A,62B
Adj	Geerlings, Matthew	M	66G
Adj	Gibson, Beverly	D	64C
Adj	Gunderson, Geoff	B	70
Adj	Hallberg, Carol	B	32B
Adj	Hillyer, Timothy	M	65
Adj	Kocher, Stephanie	M	64A
Prof	Kornelis, Benjamin	D	20,32D,36,60A,40
Adj	Linder, Kevin	B	63A,46
Inst	MacInnis, John	M	12,13A,13B,11
Adj	Melik-Stepanov, Karren	D	62C
Inst	Miedema, Bradley	M	32E,37,38,60B
Adj	Miedema, Lisa	B	62A
Adj	Schaaf-Walker, Leah	M	64D
Adj	Shoemaker, Vance	B	63C,63D
Adj	Stanichav, Kristi	M	64B
Adj	Synder Jones, Norma	M	66A,66B
Adj	Vogel, Debora	M	61
Adj	Vorhes, Anna	M	62E
Adj	Wielenga, Mary Lou	M	66A,66D,66G

IA0550 Drake University
Department of Music-FAC 260
2507 University Ave
Des Moines, IA 50311-4516
(515) 271-3975 Fax: (515) 271-2558
www.drake.edu/artsci/Music_Dept/index.html
E-mail: clarence.padilla@drake.edu

4 Year Institution
Member of NASM

Chair: Clarence S. Padilla, 80A
Dir., Preparatory Division: M. Christine Schneider, 80E

Lect PT	Albanese, Janet	M	35E
Lect PT	Albaugh, John	B	29,70
Lect PT	Altemeier, David	B	62D
Prof	Beckmann-Collier, Aimee	D	60,36,40
Lect PT	Blanner, Christine Fortner	M	61
Lect PT	Bloomberg, Jennifer Wohlenhaus	M	64B
Lect PT	Bridson, Paul		63C
Lect PT	Brizzi, Paul D.	M	32
Lect PT	Brookens, Justin		63A
Prof	Classen, Andrew B.	M	47,49,63A,29
Lect PT	Corpus, Edward	M	61
Lect PT	Crabbs, David	B	70
Assoc Prof	Cravero, Ann	D	39,61
Prof	Dougherty, William P.	D	13,10F,10,34
Assoc Prof	Freeman-Miller, Leanne	M	61
Lect PT	Gale, Timothy M.	M	64D
Lect PT	Giunta, Cynthia	M	66D,66C,66A
Lect PT	Harris, Ruth	M	66G
Lect PT	Jacobsen, Chad		29,35G
Lect PT	Jensen, Jeff	M	62D
Lect PT	Kizilarmut, John	B	65
Lect PT	Leo, Nick	B	66A
Lect	Maday, Casey	D	63C
Asst Prof	Marrs, Leslie	D	64A,48,13A
Asst Prof	McGrannahan, Grady	M	63C,37,63D
Lect PT	McIntyre, Guinevere	M	63B
Prof	Meunier, Robert W.	M	60B,37,65,32E
Asst Prof	Mori, Akira	M	38,51,11
Prof	Padilla, Clarence S.	M	64C
Lect PT	Peichl, Dan	B	63B
Asst Prof	Plum, Sarah A.	D	62A,62B,11,42
Assoc Prof	Romain, James P.	D	64E,29A,35A,29,47
Assoc Prof	Roth, Nicholas	D	66A,66B,66C,66
Lect PT	Ryker, Andrew	M	61
Assoc Prof	Saylor, Eric A.	D	20,12A
Lect	Schneider, M. Christine	M	13
Lect PT	Schumacker, Meghan	M	64E
Lect PT	Short, Michael	M	63D
Asst Prof	Sidon, Ashley Sandor	D	62C,32E,41
Asst Prof	Sletto, Thomas A.	M	32
Lect PT	Stanfield, Ashley		62A,62B
Lect PT	Strohmaier, Chris	B	63A
Asst Prof	Uchida, Rika	D	13,66A,66C,66D
Lect PT	Vanderpool, Linda	M	36
Lect PT	Wheeler, Joyce		64C

IA0600 Graceland University
Department of Music
1 University Place
Lamoni, IA 50140
(641) 784-5270 Fax: (641) 784-5487
www.graceland.edu
E-mail: templetn@graceland.edu

4 Year Institution

Chair: Jack Ergo, 80A

Inst PT	Altemeier, David	B	62D
Inst PT	Beland, Sarah	M	64A
Inst PT	Cox, Kerry	B	62A,62B
Assoc Prof	Ergo, Jack	M	20,31A,38,66A
Inst PT	Finkelshteyn, Tracy	D	62A
Inst PT	Gould, Brooke	M	64B,64C,64D,64E
Prof	Hart, Thomas J.	D	60,36,12A
Inst PT	Jeffers, Amy	M	61
Inst PT	Johnson, Christine	B	62A
Inst FT	Perez, Frank	M	37,47,32,29,63C
Inst PT	Peters, Michael	B	63A,63B
Inst PT	Pickering, Melinda C.	B	66D

IA0650 Grand View University
Department of Music
1200 Grandview Ave
Des Moines, IA 50316-1529
(515) 263-2958   Fax: (515) 263-6192
www.grandview.edu
E-mail: kduffy@gvc.edu

4 Year Institution

Chair: Kathryn Ann Pohlmann Duffy, 80A

Adj Prof	Brauninger, Eva	M	62D
Adj Prof	Dahl, Stanley	M	65
Prof	Duffy, Kathryn Ann Pohlmann	D	11,12,13,36,60
Adj Prof	Harms, Lois	M	64C,66
Adj Prof	Harrison, Joy	M	32B,61
Adj Prof	Miranda, Charles	M	62A,62B,11
Adj Prof	Morgan, John	M	64D
Adj Prof	Nielsen, John	M	61,32
Adj Prof	Odem, Susan	M	64D,20,64B,64E
Adj Prof	Powell, Aaron	M	70,13A
Adj Prof	Siebert, Sonya	M	66
Adj Prof	Thimmesch, Richard	M	13B,13C,32E,37,47
Adj Prof	Witt, Jeanne	M	64A

IA0700 Grinnell College
Department of Music
1108 Park St
Grinnell, IA 50112
(641) 269-3064   Fax: (641) 269-4420
www.grinnell.edu/academic/music
E-mail: poynterp@grinnell.edu

4 Year Institution

Chair: Jennifer Williams Brown, 80A

	Anderson, Claudia		64A,48
PT	Bogert, Nathan	M	64,63
Assoc Prof	Brown, Jennifer Williams	D	12,55,67,66H
PT	Bryant, Linda	M	66G
PT	Buck, Fred		
Asst Prof	Cha, Jee-Weon	D	13,12B
PT	Chang, Yoo-Jung	M	62C
PT	Clower, Rob	D	
PT	Cunningham, Blaine E.	M	63C,63D
PT	Dunn, Robert	M	70,62D
PT	Eidbo, Ashley	M	62D
PT	Espinosa, Gabriel	M	66A,47,61
Assoc Prof	Gaub, Eugene	D	13,12A,66A,11
Lect	Gaub, Nancy McFarland	M	62A,13C,41
Lect	Grimm, Marlys		66C
Assoc Prof Emeritus	Hays, Elizabeth	D	12,55,66H
PT	Henderson, Lisa	M	61
PT	Jones, Barry		36
PT	Kelley, Marvin	M	61
Lect	Lutch, Mitchell	D	37
PT	Maahs, Kristin	B	62C,51
Assoc Prof	McIntyre, Eric L.	D	10,38,60,12A,13
PT	McIntyre, Guinevere	M	63B
PT	Oxley, Michael		61
Lect	Pawlak, Michael	B	65,50
Asst Prof	Perman, Anthony	D	14,20
Asst Prof	Phillips, Damani	D	29,47
PT	Ponton, Lisa	M	62B
PT	Rivadeneira, Barbara		66A
Prof	Rommereim, John Christian	D	60,10,36,61
PT	Smith, Pat	B	70
PT	Swartz, Craig	M	63A
Prof	Vetter, Roger R.	D	11,14
PT	Vetter, Valerie	M	20D
Lect	Westphalen, Melinda	D	66A,66D
PT	Wohlenhaus, Jennifer	M	64B,64D
PT	Young, Colin	M	64E,64C
Lect	Zubow, Zachariah	D	13

IA0750 Indian Hills Community College
Department of Music
525 Grandview Ave
Ottumwa, IA 52501-1359
(641) 683-5223   Fax: (641) 683-5206
www.ihcc.cc.ia.us
E-mail: Michael.Philipsen@indianhills.edu

2 Year Institution

Chair: Michael D. Philipsen, 80A
Dean: Darlas Shockley, 80A

Inst	Diebold, Becky	B	61
Inst	McPartland, Dennis	B	65
Inst	Philipsen, Michael D.	M	13,11,36,61,66A
Inst	Sharp, David	M	13,11,47,64
Inst	Upton-Hill, Diana	M	36

IA0790 Iowa Central Community College
Department of Music
One Triton Circle
Fort Dodge, IA 50501
(800) 362-2793   Fax: (515) 576-2795
www.iccc.cc.ia.us
E-mail: schreier@iowacentral.edu

2 Year Institution

Dean, Humanities & Language Arts: Jennifer Condon, 80A
Coord., Performing Arts: Thomas Wilson, 80A

Inst PT	Baker, Sidney	M	11,62
Inst	Bloomquist, Paul	M	11,63,60B,13,37
Inst PT	Hopkins, Karen	M	66A
Inst PT	Lehman, Shari	B	66A
Inst PT	Morrical, Sharon	B	61
Inst PT	Naeve, Denise	M	61,66A,13
Inst PT	Ober, Jeremy	B	70
Prof	Schreier, Kathleen	M	13,11,36,54
Inst PT	Simon, Dennis	B	66A,13
Inst PT	Smith, Jeremy	B	65
Inst PT	Smith, Tara	M	64
Inst	Vermeer, Cassidy	B	52

IA0800 Iowa Lakes Community College
Department of Music
300 S 18th St
Estherville, IA 51334-2721
(712) 362-2604   Fax: (712) 362-8363
www.iowalakes.edu/music
E-mail: cayres@iowalakes.edu

2 Year Institution

Chair: Carol Ayres, 80A
Dean: Mary Larcheid, 80A

Prof	Ayres, Carol	M	11,37,47,64,29A
PT	Batz, Nancy J.	M	61
Assoc Prof	Fuelberth, Brett J.	M	13,36,47,44
PT	Lambert, Gary		70
PT	Schilling, Arnie	M	66A,66D

IA0850 Iowa State University
Department of Music
Music Hall
Room 149
Ames, IA 50011-2182
(515) 294-5364   Fax: (515) 294-6409
www.music.iastate.edu
E-mail: mgolemo@iastate.edu

4 Year Institution
Member of NASM

Chair: Michael Golemo, 80A
Dir., Undergraduate Studies: Kevin Schilling, 80B

Prof Emeritus	Bleyle, Carl O.	D	
Assoc Prof	Bovinette, James	D	47,63A,29
Lect	Bronson, Janci	M	66A,66B,66D
Adj Asst Prof	Bryden, Kristy	D	13,10A,10F,34A,34H
Prof Emeritus	Burkhalter, N. Laurence	D	
Lect	Coley, Matthew	M	65,50
Assoc Prof	Creswell, Mary	D	61,39
Prof Emeritus	Darlington, Mahlon S.	M	
Prof Emeritus	David, William M.	D	
Vstng Prof	Estes, Simon	B	39,61
Lect	Foss, Mary	M	62E
Lect	Giles, Michael S.	M	64E,47
Asst Prof	Giles, Sonja	D	64A,41,42
Lect	Goble, Jodi	M	61
Prof	Golemo, Michael	D	37,60,64E,32
Asst Prof	Harrison, Jacob G.	D	38,60

Prof Emerita	Haug, Sue	D	
Assoc Prof	Hopkins, Christopher	D	13,10B,34,10,67A
Asst Prof	Huang, Mei-Hsuan	D	66A
Lect	Judge, Kevin	M	64D
Lect	Kortenkamp, Peter	D	63D
Asst Prof	Marinic, Boro	M	13,62A,62B
Prof Emeritus	Messenger, Joseph	D	
Asst Prof	Oakes, Gregory	D	64C
Lect	Peyton, Heather	M	64B
Prof Emeritus	Prater, Jeffrey L.	D	
Lect	Richards, Erik W.	D	37,32E
Prof	Rodde, James	D	36,60,32D
Lect	Rodde, Kathleen	M	36,66A,66C
Prof	Simonson, Donald R.	D	39,61,13L,34C,34D
Asst Prof	Steele, Natalie	D	32
Prof	Stuart, David H.	D	63D,42,34A,34C,11
Prof	Sturm, Jonathan	D	12A,11,20G,20
Lect	Sturm, Julie	D	13
Prof Emeritus	Swift, Arthur	D	
Assoc Prof	Tam, TinShi	D	69,66G,11,34B,66D
Lect	Tener, James R.	M	61
Prof	Work, George P.	M	51,62C,62D,13
Prof Emerita	Zeigler, Lynn J.	M	

IA0900 Iowa Wesleyan College
Department of Music
601 N Main
Mount Pleasant, IA 52641
(319) 385-8021 x 6351   Fax: (319) 385-6286
www.iwc.edu
E-mail: djohnson5@iwc.edu

4 Year Institution

Chair: David A. Johnson, 80A

Prof	Brown, L. Joel	D	13,12A,14,66,11
	Coberly, Ron	M	63C
Assoc Prof	Edwards, Jason R.	D	64,13,10,32E
Inst PT	Frakes, Louise	D	32A,32B
Inst PT	Freyenberger, Denise	B	62
Prof	Johnson, David A.	D	60,32,37,47,65
Inst PT	McConnell, Robert	M	38
Assoc Prof PT	Moehlman, Carl B.	M	13,12A,44,66G,31A
Inst PT	Murphy, Derrick	D	63A
Inst PT	Riepe, Heidi	B	66A
Inst PT	Rod, Steve	M	63B
Inst PT	Swygard, Craig	M	62D

IA0910 Iowa Western Community College
Department of Music
2700 College Rd
Council Bluffs, IA 51503-0567
(712) 325-3726   Fax: (712) 388-6809
www.iwcc.edu/programs/departments/Music.asp
E-mail: mmisfeldt@iwcc.edu

2 Year Institution

Chair: Arla Clausen

	Bartels, Bruce	M	37
	Clausen, Arla	B	36,61
	Fiscus, Gary	B	61
	Hamling, Phyllis	M	61
	Hammiel, Chris	B	63A
	Haneline, Stacie	M	66A,11
	Hitt, Barry	B	63A
	Hitt, Christine	M	66A,47,53,46
	Larish, Charles	M	34
	Lawson, Dianne	M	66A,11
	Lawson, Ronald S.	M	63C,65,11,50
	Roberts, Kate	M	61,11
	Scheffler, Jeff	B	70,11
	Singer, Leigh Ann	M	41,64A,64E
	VanNordstrand, Shelby	M	12A,13,61

IA0930 Kirkwood Community College
Music Program
6301 Kirkwood Blvd SE
Cedar Rapids, IA 52406
(319) 398-4956   Fax: (319) 398-7135
www.kirkwood.edu
E-mail: abareis@kirkwood.edu

2 Year Institution

Dean: Jennifer Bradley, 80A

	Barclay, Martin	M	61
Inst	Berimeldze, Tariel	M	70
Prof	Feldkamp, Timothy L.	DMA	13,41,47,64
Inst	Gibson, Gary		70
Inst	Harris, Charles	M	63B
Inst	Ho, Hsing-I		64A
	Hoffman, Beth	M	62A
Inst	Holmes, Allison	M	61
Inst	Kimber, Michael	D	62B
Inst	Nichols, Lena	M	61
Inst	Pedde, Dennis	D	63A,63B,63C,63D
Inst	Rodenberg, Elise	M	64A
Prof	Salucka, Ray	M	13,36,60,11,47
Inst	Shaw, Laura	D	62C
Inst	Tauscheck, Jonathan	M	66A
Inst	Towey, Dan		70
Inst	Welch, Jeanette	M	62D
Inst	Western, Bruce	M	64E
Inst	Whipple, William P.	M	66A
Asst Prof	Zamzow, Beth Ann	PhD	13,41,42,37,12

IA0940 Loras College
Department of Music
1450 Alta Vista
Dubuque, IA 52001
(563) 588-7280   Fax: (563) 557-4086
www.loras.edu
E-mail: marycarol.harris@loras.edu

4 Year Institution

Chair, Division of Communication & Fine Arts: Mary Carol C. Harris, 80A

Adj	Carroll, Nancy A.	M	64A
Prof	Carroll, Roy W.	D	66,13,12,11,31A
Adj	Duchow, Ann L.		62A,62B
Assoc Prof	Hughes, Brian L.	M	60,11,32,37,47
Adj	Iwasaki, Masahiro		65
Inst	Kotowich, Bruce J. G.	D	61,36,31
Adj	McClure, Michelle	M	66A
Adj	Sacchini, Louis V.	D	64C,64E
Adj	Wall, Donna		61

IA0950 Luther College
Department of Music
700 College Dr
Decorah, IA 52101
(563) 387-1208   Fax: (563) 387-1076
www.luther.edu

4 Year Institution
Member of NASM

Dir., Festival: Daniel Baldwin, 80F
Dir., Festival: Allen Hightower, 80F
Dir., Festival: Fred Nyline, 80F
Dir., Festival: John F. Strauss, 80F
Dir., Summer Programs: David Judisch, 80G
Assistant Chair: Beth Ray Westlund, 80H

Prof	Andereck, Edwin	D	61
Asst Prof	Armstrong, Heather M.	D	13B,64B,32E
Inst PT	Ashcraft, Eric	M	61
Prof	Baldwin, Daniel	D	60,41,38
Inst PT	Benjamin, Ann	M	62E
Inst PT	Bourcier, Tom	M	47,10A
Asst Prof	Britton, Jason	D	13,12A,70,13I
Inst PT	Brumbelow, Rosemary	M	64C
Prof Emeritus	Butler, Bartlett	D	
Assoc Prof	Chesher, Michael	D	32E,42,64C,64E
Asst Prof	Engelsdorfer, Amy L.	M	13,13D
Inst PT	Erdahl, Rolf	D	62D,32E
Inst	Fordice, William	M	32,60A
Prof Emeritus	Fox, Ronald	D	
Inst PT	Geary, Michael	M	65,50,32E

Assoc Prof	Griesheimer, James	D	12,11,13
Assoc Prof	Guzman, Juan-Tony	D	32,47,14,29,20
Assoc Prof	Hester, Carol	D	64A,32E
Prof	Hightower, Allen	D	36,32D,60
Inst PT	Hightower, Kristin	D	61
Inst PT	Hu, Xiao	D	66A,66D
Assoc Prof	Huang, Du	D	66A,66D
Inst PT	James, Helen	D	64D
Asst Prof	Joyce, Brooke	D	10,13,34,12
Prof	Judisch, David	D	39,61,32D
Assoc Prof	Kanakis, Karen	D	61,39
Inst PT	Kominami, Miko	M	66A,13
Prof Emeritus	Kuhlman, William	M	
Assoc Prof	Kutz, Eric A.	D	62C,32E,42
Inst PT	Lassetter, Jacob	D	61,39
Inst	Lingen, Peter		42,67G,70
Inst PT	Martin, Linda	M	36,13,32B
Assoc Prof	Martin, Spencer L.	D	62A,62B,51,38
Other	Mix, Ryan	M	66F
Prof Emeritus	Monhardt, Maurice	D	
Inst PT	Moss, Gary	D	61,13C
Prof Emeritus	Noble, Weston H.	M	
Prof	Nyline, Fred	M	37
	O'Brien, Michael S.		
Assoc Prof	Paul, Jessica	D	66C
Asst Prof	Peter, Sandra K.	D	60,36
Assoc Prof	Peterson, Gregory M.	D	44,66G,31A
Inst PT	Petraborg, Kirsti J.	D	62B
Assoc Prof	Ray Westlund, Beth	D	61
Inst	Reed, Kathryn	M	13C,55,66H
Inst PT	Shaffer, Rebecca Boehm	D	63B,49,12A,32E,13C
Assoc Prof	Smith, Michael K.	D	42,63C,63D,49
Inst PT	Steeds, Graham	M	63A
Prof	Strauss, John F.	D	66A
Prof	Strauss, Virginia F.	D	62A,13C,13D
Inst PT	Struve, Jonathon Paul	M	61
Vstng Inst	Travers, Tarn	M	62A
Inst PT	Ware, Rachel J.	M	61
Assoc Prof	Wharton, Marjorie R.	D	66A,66D
Asst Prof	Whitfield, Andrew D.	D	61,39
Inst	Williams, Susan	M	61

IA1100 Morningside College

Department of Music
1501 Morningside Ave
Sioux City, IA 51106-1717
(712) 274-5210   Fax: (712) 274-5280
www.morningside.edu
E-mail: dooley@morningside.edu

4 Year Institution
Member of NASM

Chair: Gail Dooley, 80A

Prof	Dooley, Gail	D	61
Vstng Inst	Hutchins, Tony	M	11,29A,63B,63C,32E
PT	Kisor, Justin	B	63A
PT	Langley, Mike	B	70
PT	Lundberg, Steve	B	61
Prof	March, James J.	D	66A,66B,66C,12A
PT	March, Kathryn Lucas	D	13C,66A,66D,66C
PT	May-Patterson, Eleanor	M	32E,62A,62B
PT	O'Leary, Jay	D	64B,64D
PT	Salyards, Shannon	M	61,39
PT	Saulsbury, Kate	M	61,39,66D
PT	Shirley, Ellen	M	64A
Assoc Prof	Shufro, Joseph L.	M	10F,13E,34,38,62C
PT	Smith, Ron	M	65,50
Asst Prof	Watson, Tim M.	M	32D,47,36,60A
Asst Prof	Wilson, Jill	M	63B,36,32B,60,13C
Vstng Asst Prof	Wise, Wilson	M	64C,13B,32E,37,60B

IA1140 Mount Mercy College

Department of Music
1330 Elmhurst Dr NE
Cedar Rapids, IA 52402-4763
(319) 363-8213   Fax: (319) 363-5270
www.mtmercy.edu
E-mail: dkleink@mmc.mtmercy.edu

4 Year Liberal Arts Institution

Dean: Buelane Daugherty, 80A
Chair: Daniel E. Kleinknecht, 80A

PT	Benya, Susan	D	37,13,11
Assoc Prof	Kleinknecht, Daniel E.	D	60,32,36,61
Prof Emeritus	Medley, William R.	M	66A
PT	Nickel, Tony	B	66A
PT	Wachsmuth, Karen	D	13,11,12A,66A

IA1170 North Iowa Area Community College

Department of Music
500 College Dr
Mason City, IA 50401-7213
(515) 421-4241   Fax: (515) 424-1711
www.niacc.edu
E-mail: backlwil@niacc.edu

2 Year Institution

Chair: William Backlin, 80A

Inst	Backlin, William	M	13,66
Inst PT	Everist, Rachel	B	66
Inst PT	Fleming, Mark		70
Inst	Klemas, John	M	37,47,63,64,65
Inst PT	Koehner, Leon	M	66,11
Inst PT	Lubke, Sarah		61
Inst	Ryner, Jayson	M	32C,36,61,11,13C

IA1200 Northwestern College

Department of Music
101 7th St SW
Orange City, IA 51041
(712) 707-7062   Fax: (712) 707-7068
www.nwciowa.edu/music
E-mail: nverburg@nwciowa.edu

4 Year Liberal Arts Institution

Chair: Luke Dahn, 80A

	Casey, John	M	62D
Lect	Crippin, Glee	M	61,60A
Asst Prof	Dahn, Luke	D	66A,13B,13C,13D,13E
Lect	DeHaan, Pam	M	64E
Lect	DeHaan, Sue	M	64A
Lect	Dibley, Charles	M	63D
Lect	Ewing, Randy	B	32C
Lect	Foughty, Sharon	M	32B
Lect	Gibson, Beverly	D	64C
Lect	Hillyer, Tim	M	65,50
Asst Prof	Holm, Thomas	D	12A,36,11,60,61
Lect	Hutchinson, Chad	M	11,38,51
Assoc Prof	Josselyn-Cranson, Heather	D	66A,31A,10,20
Asst Prof	Kang, Juyeon	D	66A,66D,66C,13C
Lect	Linder, Kevin	B	63A
Lect	Lodine, Emily	M	61
Assoc Prof	McGarvey, Timothy	D	37,60,32E,41,29A
Lect	Melik-Stepanov, Karren	D	62C
Lect	Miedema, Lisa	B	62A,51
Lect	Moeller, Cindy R.	M	61
Lect	Reeve, Jay A.	M	62B
Lect	Shoemaker, Vance	B	63C
Lect	Swanson, Karin	M	64B
Lect	Vander Hart, Gary	B	70
Lect	Vorhes, Anna	M	62E
Lect	Westerholm, Joel M.	D	70
Lect	Wielenga, Mary Lou	M	66A,66G,66D

IA1300 St Ambrose University

Department of Music
518 W Locust St
Davenport, IA 52803-2829
(563) 333-6145   Fax: (563) 333-6243
www.sau.edu/music
E-mail: campbellwilliamg@sau.edu

4 Year Institution

Chair: William G. Campbell, 80A
Dir., Admissions: Meg Halligan, 80D
Dir., Artist Series: Lance Sadlek, 80F

PT	Bawden, Susan	M	64D
Prof	Bechen, Gene	D	37,32E,60,32
PT	Bobe, Larry	M	63C,63D
Assoc Prof	Campbell, William G.	PhD	10,13,20,34
PT	Engelson, Thea	D	40,61,54
PT	Fudge, James	M	62A,11
PT	Gast, Gene	B	63A
Prof	Haan, Keith A.	D	60,36,32D,61,40
PT	Hadesbeck, Robert	M	64C
PT	Harris, Mitzi	B	32B
PT	Hyland, Judy	M	13A,66C,11
Asst Prof	Lee, Marian Y.	DMA	66A,66B,66C,13C,11
PT	Lopez, Tewanta	B	66A

PT	Peterson, Jeff	M	64E
PT	Pierson, Rod	M	46
PT	Price-Brenner, Kevin	M	38
PT	Sanborne, Deborah	M	12,66G,66C,11
PT	Seedorf, Bethany	M	64B
PT	Stodd, Janet	M	64A
PT	Tucker, Kerry	B	70
PT	Van Speybroeck, Jennifer	B	63B
PT	VanEchaute, Michael	B	70
PT	Zeglis, Brian	M	65

IA1350 Simpson College
Department of Music
701 North C St
Indianola, IA 50125-1297
(515) 961-1637   Fax: (515) 961-1498
www.simpson.edu

4 Year Institution
Member of NASM

Chair: Maria DiPalma, 80A
Dir., Admissions: Raelene Best, 80D

Prof	Albrecht, Ronald	D	13A,13,66A,11
Asst Prof	Benoit, John	D	13,11,63C,10F,55
Adj	Benoit, Linda	B	62
Inst	Best, Raelene	M	66A
Inst	Brown, Bruce	M	70
Asst Prof	Camwell, David J.	D	32C,46,47,64E,48
Asst Prof	Croskery, Virginia	D	61,20
Prof	DiPalma, Maria	D	12A,39,61
Asst Prof	Eckerty, Michael	D	64D,32C,37,60,48
Adj	Gravander, Carl	M	66G
Adj	Gruber, Rebecca C.	D	61
Adj	Hedquist, Seth	B	70
Adj	Helton, Kimberly	D	64A
Adj	Husted, Audrey	B	63A
PT	Larsen, Robert L.	D	12A,36,39,66A,66C
Adj	McCombs, Steven	M	65
Inst	McMillin, Timothy A.	M	60,36,61,32D,12A
Adj	Odem, Susan	M	64B,64D
Inst	Park, Jin Young	D	66A,66C
Assoc Prof	Patterson, Michael R.	D	12A,32B,66A,13,10
Inst	Poulsen, James	M	13,66A,66C,10
Adj	Powell, Aaron	M	70
Asst Prof	Roberts, Kimberly	D	61
Adj	Short, Michael	M	63D
Adj	Thomson, Jacqueline	M	61
Adj	Voigts, Kariann	M	64C
Adj	Wilson, Mike	M	63B

IA1390 Southeastern Community College
Department of Music
1500 West Agency Road
PO Box 180
West Burlington, IA 52655-0180
(319) 752-2731   Fax: (319) 752-4957
www.secc.cc.ia.us
E-mail: lpirtle@scciowa.edu

2 Year Institution

Chair: R. Leigh Pirtle, 80A

Inst	Ahern, Rebecca	B	61,66A
Inst	DeVilbiss, Gloria	B	61,41,36
Inst	Hinesley, Terry	B	70
Inst	Pirtle, R. Leigh	M	66A,66G,66B,66C
Inst	Scott, David	B	65
Inst	Wolf, Lee A.	B	66F

IA1400 Southwestern Community College
School for Music Vocation
1501 W Townline St
Creston, IA 50801
(641) 782-7081   Fax: (641) 782-3312
www.swcciowa.edu
E-mail: lmattson@swcciowa.edu

2 Year Institution

Music Contact & Dir., Summer Programs: Jeremy Fox, 80A,80F,80G
Dir., Artist/Performance Series: Jason Smith, 80F

	Crabbs, David		70
	Fox, Jeremy		13,10F,37,50,34
	Gettys, Joel		65
	Greene, Doug		11
	Howe, Ryan		13A,13B,13C
	Krieger, Eric		62D
	Mattson, Lucas		47,66
	Roth, Lisa		53,61,46,13A,13B
	Smith, Jason		13,36,61,60A
	Smith, Vern		53
	Thomson, Jacqueline		13,36,61,60A

IA1450 Univ of Dubuque
Department of Fine & Perf. Arts
2000 University Ave
Dubuque, IA 52001-5099
(563) 589-3564   Fax: (563) 589-3433
www.dbq.edu
E-mail: cbarland@dbq.edu

4 Year Institution

Chair: Charles J. Barland, 80A

Assoc Prof	Barland, Charles J.	D	13,11,31A,66A,36
Adj	Boone, Bridgett	B	40
Adj	Burns, Elaina Denney	D	66A,66C
Adj	Do, Bang Lang	D	66A,66C
Adj	Eby, Kristen	M	44,61,40,36,13
Adj	Encke, William	B	70,46,47,29
Adj	Iwasaki, Masahiro	M	65
Adj	Mackie, Doug	M	52
Adj	Martin, Robert		41
	Mason, Craig	M	37
Adj	Muehleip, Marc	B	35
Assoc Prof	Ressler, Amy	M	54,53
Adj	Sherry, James Wallace	D	29,63A
Adj	Stevens, Deborah	M	20
Adj	Woodin, Nancy	B	66A,66C

IA1550 Univ of Iowa
School of Music
375 CSM5
Iowa City, IA 52242-1795
(319) 335-1603   Fax: (319) 335-2637
music.uiowa.edu
E-mail: music@uiowa.edu

4 Year Institution, Graduate School
Member of NASM

Master of Arts in Composition, Master of Arts in Performance, Master of Arts in Music Education, Master of Arts in Music Theory, PhD in Music Theory, PhD in Composition, PhD in Music Education, DMA in Conducting, PhD in Music History & Musicology, PhD in Music Literature, Master of Arts in Conducting, Master of Arts in Music History & Musicology, DMA in Performance & Pedagogy

Director: David Gier, 80A
Associate Dir., Undergraduate Studies: Benjamin A. Coelho, 80B,80H
Associate Dir., Scheduling, Facilities & Technology: Daniel Moore, 80B,80H
Associate Dir., Graduate Studies & Admissions: Christine S. Getz, 80C,80D,80H
Associate Director: Kristin Thelander, 80H

Prof	Adamek, Mary	D	33
Assoc Prof	Agrell, Jeffrey	M	63B
Lect	Allen, Jonathan	D	49,63C
Asst Prof	Arndt, Matthew J.	D	13
Assoc Prof	Arnone, Anthony R.	M	62C
Prof	Coelho, Benjamin A.	M	64D,13
Asst Prof	Cohen, Mary L.	PhD	32
Assoc Prof	Conklin, Scott A.	D	62A
Asst Prof	Cook, Robert C.	PhD	13
Lect	Dreier, James	M	65
Prof	Eckert, Michael	D	13,10A
Asst Prof	Esposito, Nicole	M	64A
Prof	Fink, Katherine Ann	D	61
Assoc Prof	Fritts, Lawrence	D	13
Prof	Getz, Christine S.	PhD	12A,12
Prof	Gfeller, Kate	D	33
Prof	Gier, David	D	49,63C
Prof	Gompper, David	D	13,10
Lect	Grismore, Steven D.	M	29
Asst Prof	Hand, Gregory	D	66G,66H
Lect	Harvey, Trevor	PhD	14
Assoc Prof	Heidel, Richard Mark	D	37
Assoc Prof	Huckleberry, Alan R.	D	66A,66B,66C,66
Asst Prof	Iverson, Jennifer	D	13

Vstng Asst Prof	Johnson, Laura	MFA	39
Lect	Jones, Susan	M	61
Prof	Jones, William LaRue	DMA	60,38
Assoc Prof	Joselson, Rachel	ABD	61
Prof	Kastens, Kevin	M	37
Prof	Lecuona, Rene	M	66A
Assoc Prof	Manning, John	M	63D
Prof	Mead, Maurita Murphy	D	64C
Prof	Moore, Daniel	M	50,65
Prof	Muriello, John R.	DMA	61
Prof	Nosikova, Ksenia	D	66A
Lect	Oakes, Elizabeth	M	51
Assoc Prof	Orhon, Volkan	M	62D
Asst Prof	Parker, Andrew	D	64B
Lect	Parsons, Donna S.	PhD	14C
Asst Prof	Puderbaugh, David J.	D	36
Prof	Rapson, John	M	47
Lect	Rhoads, Shari	B	61,66C
Prof	Rutledge, Christine	M	62B
Lect	Sandy, Brent	B	29
Asst Prof	Schendel, Amy	D	63A
Vstng Asst Prof	Sifford, Jason	DMA	66B,66D,66,29B,66A
Prof	Stalter, Timothy J.	DMA	36
Prof	Swanson, Stephen	M	61
Prof	Titze, Ingo R.	D	61
Adj Assoc Prof	Tsachor, Rachelle P.	M	
Prof	Tsachor, Uriel	D	66A
Assoc Prof	Tse, Kenneth	M	64E
Vstng Asst Prof	Van Herck, Bert	PhD	13
Adj Asst Prof	Walker, Joey	M	33
Asst Prof	Wehr, Erin	PhD	32B,32C,32E
Assoc Prof	Wilson Kimber, Marian	PhD	12
Assoc Prof	Wolfe, Katherine	M	62A
Vstng Asst Prof	Wolgast, Brett	DMA	66G
Vstng Assoc Prof	Wyman, Wayne	M	61,66C

IA1600 Univ of Northern Iowa
School of Music
115 Russell Hall
Cedar Falls, IA 50614-0246
(319) 273-2024   Fax: (319) 273-7320
www.uni.edu/music
E-mail: music@uni.edu

4 Year Institution, Graduate School
Member of NASM

Master of Arts in Music, Master of Music in Composition, Master of Music in Performance, Master of Music in Conducting, Master of Music in Music Education, Master of Music in Music History, Master of Music in Jazz Pedagogy, Master of Music in Piano Pedagogy & Performance

Director: John Vallentine, 80A
Associate Dir., Undergraduate Studies: Alan W. Schmitz, 80B
Associate Dir., Graduate Studies: Julia K. Bullard, 80C

Asst Prof	Altstatt, Alison	D	12
Asst Prof	Barrett, Korey J.	D	61,66C
Asst Prof	Barry, Thomas	M	64B,64E,35C
Asst Prof	Botkin, Sean	M	66A
Asst Prof	Boyd, Melinda J.	D	12
Inst	Brich, Jeffrey	M	61
Asst Prof	Buckholz, Christopher John	D	63C,29,41,11
Assoc Prof	Bullard, Julia K.	D	62
Prof	Burkhardt, Rebecca L.	D	13,38,60
Asst Prof	Camilli, Theresa Chardos	M	66B,32
Assoc Prof	Chenoweth, Jonathan N.	D	11,41,62C
Asst Prof	Droe, Kevin	D	32
Prof	Floyd, Angeleita S.	D	48,64A
Prof	Funderburk, Jeffrey	D	49,63D,72
Asst Prof	Galyen, S. Daniel	D	37,41,32E,60B,32
Prof	Grabowski, Randy	D	63A
Prof	Guy, Robin	D	66C,66D
Assoc Prof	Halgedahl, Frederick	M	41,62A
Asst Prof	Hines, John T.	D	61
Assoc Prof	Hogancamp, Randy	M	50,65
Prof	Johnson, Ronald	D	60,37
Asst Prof	McCandless, Amanda	D	64C,64
Assoc Prof	McDonald, Jean	D	61
Assoc Prof	Merz, Christopher Linn	M	64E,47,29
Inst	Meyer, Dyan	M	36,60A
Assoc Prof	Morgan, Leslie		61
Prof	Rachor, David J.	D	11,64D,64E,72
Prof	Schmitz, Alan W.	D	13,10
Prof	Schwabe, Jonathan C.	D	13,10,29
Assoc Prof	Shepherd, William	M	11,32C,37
Asst Prof	Su, Yu-Ting (Tina)	D	63B,49
Assoc Prof	Swanson, Michelle	M	32
Prof	Vallentine, John	D	32,37,64C
Asst Prof	Vorobiev, Dmitri	D	66A
Inst	Walden, Sandra	M	39,11,61
Prof	Washut, Robert	D	13,47,29
Asst Prof	Wiles, John L.	D	36,60A,61,32

IA1750 Waldorf College
Department of Music
106 S 6th St
Forest City, IA 50436
(641) 585-8177   Fax: (641) 585-8194
www.waldorf.edu
E-mail: music@waldorf.edu

4 Year Liberal Arts Institution

Chair: Glen T. Wegge, 80A
Dir., Artist Series: Kristin Jonina Taylor, 80F

Asst Prof	Buffington, Blair	M	61,36,40,32A,60A
Prof Emeritus	Creswell, Bradley	D	61,60A
Asst Prof	Dodson, Brent	D	63,64,37,60B,48
Inst	Farndale, Nancy	B	64B,64D,66G
Prof Emeritus	Schmidt, Timothy R.	D	13B,31A,66A,66H
Asst Prof	Taylor, Kristin Jonina	D	12A,20,66A,66D,66
Assoc Prof	Wegge, Glen T.	D	13C,13B,13G,64C

IA1800 Wartburg College
Department of Music
100 Wartburg Blvd
Waverly, IA 50677
(319) 352-8300   Fax: (319) 352-8501
www.wartburg.edu/music
E-mail: eric.wachmann@wartburg.edu

4 Year Institution
Member of NASM

Chair: Eric Wachmann, 80A

Prof	Andrews, Jane E.	D	32,36
Senior Lect	Beane, Diane	M	66A
Lect	Bieber, Elizabeth	M	61
Prof	Black, Karen	D	13C,31A,36,66G
Senior Lect	Braaten-Reuter, Laurie		66A,66C,66D
Lect	Brumwell, Gretchen	M	62E
Lect	Burak, Jeff	M	70
Senior Lect	Cawley, Dominique	M	64A
Lect	Chenoweth, Jonathan	M	62C
Senior Lect	Gast, Daniel	M	61
Senior Lect	Gast, Rosemary	M	61
Senior Lect	Graham, Jack	M	64C,48
Prof	Hancock, Craig A.	D	37,60B,63C,63D,72
Asst Prof	Harms, Melanie	M	33
Senior Lect	Harris, Charles	M	63B
Senior Lect	Jacobson, Alan	M	47,65
Senior Lect	Jensen, Michael	M	61
Asst Prof	Kaplunas, Daniel	D	38,62C,62B,51,60
Asst Prof	Larson, Jennifer	D	39,61
Lect	Lehmann, Mark	M	61
Senior Lect	Morton, Gregory	D	64B,64D
Asst Prof	Muntefering, Scott	D	32,63A,49
Assoc Prof	Nelson, Lee D.	D	36,60A
Assoc Prof	Pfaltzgraff, Brian	D	61,39
Lect	Pfaltzgraff, Carita	M	61
Prof	Reuter, Ted A.	D	12A,66A
Senior Lect	Reuter-Riddle, Pat	M	13A,66A
Lect	Scheffel, Rich	M	63D,32E
Prof	Survilla, Maria Paula	D	13,12A,14
Prof	Torkelson, Suzanne	D	11,66A,66B,66C
Prof	Wachmann, Eric	D	13,64C,48
Senior Lect	Williams, Jane	M	64E,48
Asst Prof	Wilson, Geoffrey	D	12A,13,66A,10F

IA1950 William Penn College
Department of Fine Arts
201 Trueblood Ave
Oskaloosa, IA 52577-1757
(515)673-1063   Fax: (515)673-1396
www.wmpenn.edu
E-mail: meinerta@wmpenn.edu

4 Year Liberal Arts Institution

Dean: Thomas Haas, 80A
Interim Chair: Jared Pearce, 80A

Inst	Cressley, Scott	M	37
Emeritus	Eliason, Linda J.	M	
Asst Prof	Meinert, Anita	B	64C,66A,66C,54
Emeritus	Wormhoudt, Pearl	M	

ID0050 Boise State University
Department of Music
1910 University Dr
Boise, ID 83725
(208) 426-1772   Fax: (208) 426-1771
www.boisestate.edu/music
E-mail: markrhansen@boisestate.edu

4 Year Institution, Graduate School
Member of NASM

Master of Music in Performance, Master of Music in Music Education

Chair: Mark R. Hansen, 80A
Dir., Graduate Studies: Jeanne M. Belfy, 80C
Associate Chair: Linda Kline Lamar, 80H

PT	Apel, Ted R.	D	34
Prof	Baldwin, John	D	13,50,65
Prof	Belfy, Jeanne M.	D	11,12,64B
Prof	Berg, Lynn	D	61
Assoc Prof	Bratt, Wallis	M	13,10
Assoc Prof	Brown, Marcellus	M	37,60B
PT	Calas, Tiffany	M	61
Asst Prof	Farmer, Dawn	M	32
PT	Galvin, Nancy	M	66A
Assoc Prof	Goodman, James A.	D	32B,32C,32D,32F
Prof	Hansen, Mark R.	DMA	66A,13E,11,66G
PT	Harrison, James	M	65
PT	Helton, Johann	D	70
PT	Hodges, Betsi	D	11
Asst Prof	Hodges, Brian D.	D	62C,11,42
Assoc Prof	Jirak, James	M	36,32D,60A
PT	Khan, Lori Conlon	M	32B
Assoc Prof	Lamar, Linda Kline	M	13,62B,41
Prof	Mathie, David	D	63C,32E,63D,49
Assoc Prof	Molumby, Nicole L.	D	64A,32E,32I,13C
PT	Moreau, Barton	D	13,11,66C,66D,66A
Assoc Prof	Moreau, Leslie M.	D	64C,13A,13B,48
PT	Oberbillig, Janelle	M	64D
PT	Olsen, Ryan	B	61
Prof	Parkinson, Del	D	66A,66B
Asst Prof	Porter, Michael C.	D	36
Asst Prof	Purdy, Craig Allen	M	41,42,51,62A,38
PT	Raynes, Christopher	D	61,39,54
PT	Rodriguez, Jose	M	64C
PT	Rowley, Jill	M	62A
Assoc Prof	Rushing-Raynes, Laura	D	61,39,54
Assoc Prof	Samball, Michael L.	D	11,12A,29A,35A
Prof	Saunders, David E.	D	63B,60B,13E,12A
PT	Smith, Chuck	M	29,66A
PT	Stamps, Justin	M	63A,11
Asst Prof	Tornello, Joseph	M	37
PT	Winkle, Carola	M	64C,32
PT	Winkle, William	D	63D,49
PT	Zuroeveste, Rodney	M	64C

ID0060 Brigham Young Univ-Idaho
Department of Music
246 Snow Bldg
Rexburg, ID 83460-1210
(208) 496-4951   Fax: (208) 496-4953
www.byui.edu/Music/
E-mail: callk@byui.edu

4 Year Institution
Member of NASM

Chair: Kevin Call, 80A
Dir., Artist/Performance Series: Don Sparhawk, 80F

Adj	Adams, George	D	64D
FT	Allen, Stephen	D	66A,66C,66B
FT	Ashby, Eda	D	36,61,32D
FT	Ashton, Ted	M	41,62A,32E
FT	Ballif, Adam	D	32C,32E,64C
PT	Barton, David	M	32E
FT	Bascom, Brandon R.	D	32F,66A,66C
Adj	Bjornn, Marsha	B	66A
PT	Blanchard, Carol	B	66D
Adj	Broadbent, Michelle	M	61
FT	Brower, Kevin	D	36,61,32D
PT	Brower, Nori	M	13C,36
FT	Brown, Darrell	M	32E,65,50
FT	Call, Kevin	D	38
Adj	Cherrington, Joseph	M	61
PT	Clark, Paula	M	66A,66C
PT	Coates, Atina	B	36,61
PT	Davis, Mindy	B	31A
Adj	Dresen, Steven	M	61
Adj	Fife, Melissa	M	61
PT	Hansen, Cheryl	B	66D
FT	Hansen, Dallin	M	62A,32E
PT	Hansen, Lisa	B	66D
Adj	Hinck, David	M	61
Adj	Hinck, Julie	B	66A
FT	Kempton, Randall	D	61,36
FT	Kerr, Daniel	D	10A,13,66G,10F
PT	Kimball, Newel	B	70
FT	Klein, Jon	D	11,63B
PT	Lassen, Emily	B	66D
Adj	Lawrence, Jay	M	65
FT	Linford, Jon	D	39,61,32D
FT	Luke, Nadine	D	13A,13B,13C,64A
Adj	Lyman, Rebecca	M	62C
PT	May, Ed	D	70
PT	McNiven, Lisa	M	12A,62B
FT	Mecham, Bryce	M	63C,41,32E
PT	Mecham, Jessica	M	11,20
FT	Miller, Aaron D.	M	47,62D
FT	Moore, Matthew	M	34,41,63D
Adj	Morris, LoriAnn		66A
FT	Nielsen, Ryan	M	29,46,47,63A
FT	Olsen, David	D	32D,39,61
Adj	Olsen, Rebecca	M	61
Adj	Pack, Shari	B	61,62E
Adj	Parkinson, Rebecca	B	66G
Adj	Peck, Andrew	M	61
PT	Peck, David	D	12A,12B,12C,61
Adj	Phillips, Keith		66A
PT	Skinner, Josh	ABD	12,13A,13B,13C,62D
PT	Skinner, Kate	ABD	12,13A,13B,13C,61
PT	Smoot, Lonna Joy	M	61
FT	Soelberg, Diane	M	48,64B,60
FT	Taylor, David L.	D	50,65
FT	Tueller, Robert F.	D	38,62C,67B
FT	Watkins, Mark	D	47,48,64E
PT	Wayne, Barbara	M	70
Adj	Weisse, Lisa		62A
PT	Wilcox, Eileen	M	66D

ID0070 College of Idaho, The
Department of Music
2112 Cleveland Blvd
Caldwell, ID 83605-4432
(208) 459-5275   Fax: (208) 459-5885
www.collegeofidaho.edu/academics/music
E-mail: eearl@collegeofidaho.edu

4 Year Institution

Chair: Mari Jo Tynon, 80A
Dir., Preparatory Division: Sylvia Hunt, 80E,80F
Dir., Artist Series: David Johnson, 80F
Dir., Artist Series: Sam Smith, 80F

PT	Corkey, Jim	M	10
Prof	Derry, Lisa	D	13,10,34,66A,66B
PT	Griffiths, Curt	B	37
PT	Hunt, Sylvia	M	66G,66C
Artist in Res	Johnson, David	M	13A,41,62B,42,51
PT	Kassel, Philip	M	13
PT	Mayhew, Sandon	B	47,64E
Asst Prof	Moulton, Paul F.	M	11,12A,32,14
PT	Nielsen, Aage	M	64C
Inst	Rogers, Sean	B	36,39,60,66A,66G
PT	Saunders, Marianne	D	47
Artist in Res	Smith, Sam		62C,51,38
PT	Towery, Randy	B	63A
Artist in Res	Trabichoff, Geoffrey	M	62A
PT	Turner, George	D	63D
Prof	Tynon, Mari Jo	D	39,61,54
PT	Viertel, Breton	M	62D
PT	Walker, Rob	B	46
PT	Wells, Robyn	M	66A,66B,66C
PT	White, Carol	M	64A

ID0075 College of Southern Idaho
Department of Music
315 Falls Ave
PO Box 1238
Twin Falls, ID 83303-1238
(208) 733-9554   Fax: (208) 736-3015
www.csi.edu
E-mail: cbragg@csi.edu

2 Year Institution

Chair Fine Arts: Christopher Bragg, 80A

PT	Casperson, Joseph	M	36
PT	Clark, Serena Jenkins	B	40,61
PT	Conley, Gene		46
PT	Davis, Diane	M	61,66A
PT	Gerrish, Jo		64A
PT	Hadley, Theodore	M	38
Prof	Halsell, George K.	D	13,37,63,11,71
PT	Harris, Kathy		62A
Asst Prof	Jensen, Brent	M	29A
PT	Johnson, Hubert		64C,64D
PT	Jones, Colby		11
PT	Loranger, Gene		70
PT	McCarty, Daniel J.		64C,64E
Asst Prof	Miller, Sue	M	13,32B,66
PT	Nelsen, Jack	M	11,32B
PT	Nye, Karmelle		66D
PT	Oppelt, Maren		11
PT	Pugh, Paul William	D	46
PT	Spelius, Susan M.	M	11,66D,13B,13C
PT	Wong, K. Carson	M	36,61

ID0100 Idaho State University
Department of Music
921 S 8th Ave. Stop 8099
Pocatello, ID 83209-8099
(208) 282-3636   Fax: (208) 282-4884
www.isu.edu/music
E-mail: music@isu.edu

4 Year Institution, Graduate School
Member of NASM

Master of Music in Music Education

Chair: Thom Hasenpflug, 80A
Dir., Undergraduate Studies: Diana Livingston-Friedley, 80B
Dir., Community/Preparatory Division: Kori Bond, 80E

PT	Adams, George C.	D	64D
PT	Adams, Michelle	M	66D,13C
Prof	Anderson, Scott E.	D	36,40,60A,61
PT	Attebery, Brian	D	62C
PT	Banyas, Thomas P.	M	63A
Prof	Bond, Kori	D	12A,66A,66B,66C
Prof	Brooks, John Patrick	D	60B,37,63C,47,63D
PT	Cha, Keum Hwa	D	62A
PT	Colby, Donald	M	62D
PT	Drake, James	D	66G
Prof	Earles, Randy A.	D	13,20G
Lect	Friedley, Geoffrey A.	M	61,11,12A
Assoc Prof	Hasenpflug, Thom	D	65,13,20,10,50
PT	Helman, Michael	M	63B,11
Asst Prof	Helman, Shandra K.	D	64C,13C,48,20,64E
PT	Hughes, Susan K.	B	64B
Prof	Lane, Kathleen	M	39,61,36
Assoc Prof	Livingston-Friedley, Diana	D	61
PT	LoPiccolo, John	M	11
PT	Neiwirth, Mark	C	66A
PT	O'Brien, William J.	M	70
Lect	Sorensen, Julie	D	13
Asst Prof	York, Kevin	M	37,47,34,32E
PT	York, Molly	D	64A

ID0130 Lewis-Clark State College
Division of Humanities
500 8th Ave
Lewiston, ID 83501-2691
(208) 792-2307   Fax: (208) 792-2324
www.lcsc.edu
E-mail: bpercont@lcsc.edu

4 Year Institution

Division Chair: Mary Flores, 80A
Coordinator: William J. Perconti, 80A

	Bell, Tim	M	70
	Pals, Joel	M	36
Prof	Perconti, William J.	D	13,11,47,64

ID0140 North Idaho College
Department of Music
1000 W Garden Ave
Coeur D Alene, ID 83814-2161
(208) 769-3300   Fax: (208) 769-7880
www.nic.edu
E-mail: DKMoerer@nic.edu

2 Year Institution

Dir., Summer Programs: Jay Lee, 80G

	Aiken, Barry		66A,66C
	Carlson, Ernie		63C
	Cathey, Jill		64B
	Cox, Daniel R.		50,65,53,11
	Dawson, Andrea	M	61
	Gordon, Rachel		64A
	Grove, Paul		51,70
	Hekmatpanah, Kevin		62C
	Jones, Terry		37,47,49,63A,29
	Mathes, Gerard		13,11,13J,62A,34
	Mendez, Max		61,36,42,47
	Miller, Charles		51,70
	O'Dell, Debra		66A,66C,11,66D,12A
	Rutley, Thom		62D
	Sandford, Tim		63C
	Sescilla, Mark Christopher		64C
	Strobel, Larry		63B
	Wood, Tim		64E

ID0150 Northwest Nazarene College
Department of Music
623 Holly St
Nampa, ID 83651
(208) 467-8413   Fax: (208) 467-8360
www.nnu.edu
E-mail: lsrichardson@nnu.edu

4 Year Institution
Member of NASM

Chair Art & Music: Barry Swanson, 80A

Assoc Prof	Christopher, Casey R.	D	11,29B,34,35,37
Prof	Hughes, Walden D.	D	12A,41,42,66
Assoc Prof	Marlett, Judy	D	32,36,39,54,60A
Assoc Prof	Swanson, Barry	D	31,36,40
Asst Prof	Turner, George	M	10,13,60B,63C,63D

ID0250 Univ of Idaho
Lionel Hampton School of Music
Music Bldg
Room 206
Moscow, ID 83844-4015
(208) 885-6231   Fax: (208) 885-7254
www.uidaho.edu/class/music
E-mail: music@uidaho.edu

4 Year Institution, Graduate School
Member of NASM

Master of Arts in Music History, Master of Music in Composition, Master of Music in Performance, Master of Music in Music Education, PhD/EDD in Education Emphasis Music Education, Master of Music in Accompanying, Master of Music in Piano Pedagogy & Performance

Director: Kevin Woelfel, 80A
Dir., Artist Series: Mary DuPree, 80F
Assistant Director: Susan M. Hess, 80H

Lect	Anderson, Jon	M	13C,47,66A,66E
Assoc Prof	Bathurst, Pamela	M	61
Emeritus	Bauer, Leroy	M	62B
Asst Prof	Bilderback, Barry T.	D	11,12A,20B,12C,14A
Adj Asst Prof	Billin, Susan	M	66G,66D
Prof	Bukvich, Daniel J.	M	13,10,47,50,65
Lect	Cline, Everett Eugene	M	61,66
Prof	Cole, Roger	D	11,64C
Assoc Prof	Cseszko, Ferenc	D	38,62A,62B,41
Assoc Prof	Dickow, Robert H.	D	13,10,63B,34
Emeritus	DuPree, Mary	D	12A,12,43,14C
Asst Prof	Elgersma, Kristin M.	D	66A,66B,66C
Assoc Prof	Enloe, Loraine D.	D	32E,64,37,64C,32C

Asst Prof	Ferrill, Kyle	D	61,40
Asst Prof	Garrison, Leonard	D	64A,13,12,13B,13C
Assoc Prof	Gemberling, Alan	M	37,63C,47,60,41
Emeritus	Hahn, Richard	M	64A,12A
Assoc Prof	Hess, Susan M.	D	64D,32E,41
Lect	Hungerford, Delores	D	32B,64C
Asst Prof	Jackson, Dennis C.	D	39,61
Emeritus	Klimko, Ronald	M	13,64D
Lect	Krone, Claudia	M	61
Assoc Prof	Lawrence, Torrey	D	63D,37
Emeritus	Lockery, Glen	M	36,61
Emeritus	Logan, Norman	M	36
Prof Emeritus	Mauchley, Jay	D	66A,66C
Emeritus	Mauchley, Sandra	M	66A,66H,66B,66D
Prof	Murphy, James L.	D	13
Asst Prof	Murphy, Michael	D	36,40,32D,12A,32C
Assoc Prof	Padgham Albrecht, Carol	D	11,12A,64B,32E,41
Emeritus	Peterson, Floyd	D	13,12A
Prof	Reid, James	M	11,41,70
Asst Prof	Sielert, Vanessa	D	64E,47
Assoc Prof	Sielert, Vern	D	47,63A,29
Asst Prof	Soto, Amanda C.	M	14,20H,32B,32G,32H
Emeritus	Spevacek, Robert	D	60,37,63D
Lect	Walker, Garry	M	32E,32G
Emeritus	Walton, Charles	M	61
Prof Emeritus	Wharton, William	D	13,41,62C,62D
Asst Prof	Wilson, Miranda	D	13C,41,42,62D,62C
Prof	Woelfel, Kevin	M	35A,35,63A,35E,35B
Asst Prof	Yang, Rajung	D	66A,66C,66H,42
Asst Prof	Zavislak, Kay	D	66A

IL0100 Augustana College
Department of Music
639 38th St
Rock Island, IL 61201
(309) 794-7233   Fax: (309) 794-7433
www.augustana.edu
E-mail: jonhurty@augustana.edu

4 Year Institution
Member of NASM

Chair: Jon Hurty, 80A
Assistant Chair & Dir., Admissions: Margaret J. Ellis, 80D,80H
Dir., Artist Series: Clyde Andrew Walter, 80F

PT	Baldwin, Gail	M	66,66A
Asst Prof	Bancks, Jacob	PhD	10,10F,43,13,12A
PT	Barclay, Martin	D	61
PT	Bawden, Sue	B	64D
Prof	Culver, Daniel	D	13,60B,12,38
Adj Prof	Dakin, Deborah	D	11,62B,62A
PT	DeWitt, Dortha	M	62A
PT	Dreier, James	M	65,50
Assoc Prof	Ehrlich, Janina	D	11,12,41,62C
Asst Prof	Elfline, Robert	D	66A,11,13
FT	Ellis, Margaret J.	M	13C,11,63A
PT	Grismore, Steve	M	70
FT	Hall, Randall	D	64E,13
Adj Prof	Hand, Angela R.	D	61,11
Prof	Hildreth, John W.	D	11,14,20
Prof	Hurty, Jon	D	36
Adj Prof	Hurty, Sonja	M	36,61,13C
Assoc Prof	Jaeschke, Rick	D	32,37,34
Artist in Res	Keehn, Samantha	D	63C,63D,11
PT	Lambrecht, Cynthia A.	M	64B,11
Assoc Prof	Lambrecht, James M.	D	37,49,63A,60B,13C
Prof	Neil, Mary	D	13,66A,66C,66B
PT	Oliver, Tony	D	65,50
Adj Prof	Ott, Joseph	B	53,47,29A
PT	Palmer, Gary	M	62D
Prof	Peterson, Larry	M	66A,66C,11
Prof	Pfautz, John S.	D	39,61,31
PT	Pobanz, Randy	M	70
Asst Prof	Rayapati, Sangeetha	D	11,61
Vstng Asst Prof	Schmidt, Charles	D	11,66A,13
PT	Schwaegler, Susan	M	64C,48
Artist in Res	Scott, Chris	M	36,61,13C
PT	Stodd, Janet	M	48,64A
Prof	Stone, Susan E.	D	13,62A
Vstng Inst	Tendall, Rosita	M	32
Asst Prof	Zemek, Michael D.	D	32,36,60A

IL0150 Aurora University
Department of Music
347 S Gladstone Ave
Aurora, IL 60506-4892
(630) 844-6862   Fax: (630) 844-7830
www.aurora.edu
E-mail: music@aurora.edu

4 Year Institution

Chair: Lisa M. Fredenburgh, 80A

Inst	Abernathy, Jennifer	B	41
Inst	Areyzaga, Michelle	B	61
Asst Prof	Baum, Joshua	D	61,11,39,12
Inst	Chi, Sungha	M	66C
Inst	Edwards, Geoff	PhD	11
Assoc Prof	Fredenburgh, Lisa M.	D	36,11,40,60A
Inst	Hagglund, Heidi	M	64A,41
Inst	Larson, Richard	M	70,41
Inst	Moore, Joel	M	64E,64C
Asst Prof	Pastorello, Cristian	D	66A,66B,66C,11,13
Assoc Prof	Plummer, Mark W.	D	36,32D,40
Inst	Wood, Rose Marie	M	66A

IL0275 Benedictine University
Department of Fine & Perf. Arts
Scholl Hall
5700 College Rd Rm 105
Lisle, IL 60532-2851
(630) 829-6325
www.ben.edu/music
E-mail: lloubriel@ben.edu

4 Year Liberal Arts Institution

Chair: Luis E. Loubriel, 80A

PT	Bishop, Dawn	B	62E
PT	Castaneda, Ricardo	B	64B
PT	Fort, Kevin	M	66A,42
	Infusino, Patrick	M	11,64E,13C
PT	Kreft, Anne	M	64A,11
Prof	Legutki, Allen R.	PhD	37,38,32
Prof	Loubriel, Luis E.	DMA	11,13A,34,63,35
PT	Mallak, Augustine	M	13
PT	Moore, Nancy	B	62C
	Moulder, John	M	14C,29,70
PT	Noguera, Darwin	M	66A,42
Prof Emeritus	Palmer, John M.	M	66A,66G
PT	Pastor, Juan	B	65
PT	Stampfl, Aaron	DMA	66A
Prof	Tait, Alicia Cordoba	DMA	20,12A,15,35,11
PT	VerHoven, Victoria K.	M	61
Adj	Watkins, Wilbert O.	PhD	36,40,32

IL0300 Black Hawk College
Department of Music
6600 34th Ave
Moline, IL 61265-5870
(309) 796-5478   Fax: (309) 796-5357
www.bhc.edu
E-mail: palomakij@bhc.edu

2 Year Institution

Chair, Communication & Fine Arts: Michelle Johnson, 80A

Adj Inst	Blucker, James	M	63C
Adj Prof	Bowlin, Ellen	D	66A,66G,66C
Adj Inst	Carlin, Pete	M	11
Adj Inst	Clark, Rich	M	11
Prof	Crockett, C. Edgar	D	13,10,47,35,63A
Adj Inst	Croegaert, Roxanne	M	38
Adj Prof	Crowder, James	M	37
Adj Inst	Ewoldt, Virginia	B	62C
Adj Prof	Fudge, James	D	11,62
Adj Prof	Fudge, Tamara	D	61
Adj Prof	Grismore, Steve	M	70
Adj Inst	Gustofson, Don	B	66A,70
Adj Inst	Hanson, Terry	B	65
Adj Inst	Kendrick, Corey	B	46
Adj Inst	Little, Steve	B	63A
Adj Inst	Minard, Juliet	M	11
Adj Inst	Morton, Ron	M	63D
Adj Inst	Oelschlaeger-Fischer, Curtis	M	11

Prof	Palomaki, Jonathan	M	12A,32B,36,70,61
Adj Prof	Pobanz, Randy	M	70
Adj Prof	Schwaegler, Susan	M	64C
Adj Prof	Stodd, Janet	M	64A
Adj Prof	Stukart, Lynne	M	64A,11
Adj Inst	Turner, Randin	A	66C

IL0350 Blackburn College

Department of Performing Arts
700 College Ave
Carlinville, IL 62626
(217) 854-3232 x 4264   Fax: (217) 854-3713
www.blackburn.edu
E-mail: performingarts@blackburn.edu

4 Year Institution

Chair: Elizabeth W. Zobel, 80A

Adj PT	Chan, See Tsai	D	66A,66G,13
Adj PT	Haglund, Richard	M	11,13
Adj PT	Kim, Junghyun	D	66A
Adj PT	Smith, Neal	D	37
Adj PT	Warnock, Matthew	D	29,70
	Zobel, Elizabeth W.	D	12,13,36,60,61

IL0400 Bradley University

Department of Music
1501 W Bradley Ave
Peoria, IL 61625
(309) 677-2595   Fax: (309) 677-3871
www.bradley.edu
E-mail: dvroman@bradley.edu

4 Year Institution
Member of NASM

Chair: David Vroman, 80A

Inst PT	Anderson, Carl		35
Inst PT	Archbold, Timothy	M	62C
	Attanaseo, Jeremy	M	62D
Inst PT	Bonner, Peggy	M	50,65
Prof	Dzapo, Kyle J.	D	12A,12,64A
Librarian	Fuertges, Dan H.	B	16
Assoc Prof	Heinemann, Steven	D	13,10,64C
Inst PT	Hull, Michael	M	70
Prof	Jost, John R.	D	60,36,61,38
Prof	Kaizer, Edward	D	11,12A,66A,66B
Lect	Kaizer, Janet	M	66A,66D
Assoc Prof	Kelly, Todd	M	32,47,63A,35
Inst PT	Kielson, Lisette	M	67,55
Inst PT	King, Andy	M	38
Inst PT	Larson, John	M	34
Lect	Liebenow, Marcia Henry	M	62A,62B
Inst PT	Miller, Ryan	M	63C
Other	Molina, Andrea	M	66C
Prof PT	Orfe, John	D	10,13
Inst PT	Rimington, James	D	32,61
Inst PT	Robock, Alison	D	64B,11
Inst PT	Roman, Joe	M	32C
Inst PT	Salazar, Shirley	M	61
Other	Sloter, Molly	M	66C
Inst PT	Solomonson, Terry	M	63D
Prof	Vroman, David	D	60,32,37,63B
Assoc Prof	Walters, Kerry E.	M	61,32,39
Inst PT	Wanken, Matthew	M	32E
Inst PT	Wessler, Peter	M	62
Inst PT	Wright, Gina	M	61
Inst PT	Zimmerman, Keith	M	64E

IL0420 Carl Sandburg College

Music Program
2400 Tom L. Wilson Blvd
Galesburg, IL 61401-9574
(309) 341-5317   Fax: (309) 341-5471
www.sandburg.edu
E-mail: jhutchings@sandburg.edu

2 Year Institution

Coordinator: James Hutchings, 80A
Associate Dean, Humanities: Carol Petersen, 80H

Inst PT	Domenici, Gianna	B	39,61
Inst PT	Harlan, Mary	M	66A,66G
Inst FT	Hutchings, James	M	11,13B,12A,61,13A
Inst PT	Jackson, Stephen	M	48,11,20,41,47
Inst PT	McCord, Vicki	M	29A,29B
Inst PT	Mohr, Bette	M	66G
Inst PT	Nelson, Bruce	B	70
Inst PT	Olszewski, Thomas	M	63,64,62D
Inst PT	Polay, Louise	B	62A
Inst PT	Robbins, Cheryl	M	61,66A
Inst PT	Triplett, Isaac	M	65
Inst PT	Wanken, Matthew	M	12A,13A,13B,13C

IL0450 Chicago City College

Olive-Harvey College
10001 S Woodlawn Ave
Chicago, IL 60628-1645
(773) 291-6530   Fax: (773) 291-6304
oliveharvey.ccc.edu
E-mail: jyounge@ccc.edu

2 Year Institution

Chair: J. Sophia Younge, 80A

Prof	Johnson, Cornelius	M	13A,66A,11,36,20
Prof	Scully, Joseph D.	M	13A,11,36,20
Prof	Younge, J. Sophia	M	13A,66A,11,36

IL0550 Chicago College of Perf Arts

Roosevelt University
430 S Michigan Ave
Chicago, IL 60605-1394
(312) 341-3785   Fax: (312) 341-6358
ccpa.roosevelt.edu
E-mail: lberna@roosevelt.edu

4 Year Institution, Graduate School
Member of NASM

Graduate Diploma in Performance, Master of Music in Composition, Master of Music in Performance

Director & Associate Dean: Linda Berna, 80A,80H
Dean, Performing Arts: Henry Fogel, 80A

Lect PT	Alger, Neal	B	47,70
Lect PT	Alvarez, Ruben		47,65
Lect PT	Anderson, Andrew	M	62D
Lect PT	Azabagic, Denis	B	70,42
	Berna, Linda	D	13,12
Lect PT	Berry, Steve	B	47,63C
Lect PT	Best, Michael	M	61
Asst Prof	Brewer, Wesley D.	D	32E,32F
Assoc Prof	Brown, Dana L.	D	66C
Lect PT	Bullen, Sarah		62E
Adj	Burlingame-Tsekouras, Jill	M	
Lect PT	Capshaw, Reed	M	63C
Lect PT	Carey, Tanya L.	D	62C
Lect PT	Chase, Roger		62B,42
Lect PT	Chellis, Matthew W.	M	61
Assoc Prof Emeritus	Chen, Donald	D	60B,13
Assoc Prof	Choi, Kyong Mee	D	10,13,66G
Asst Prof	Choi, Winston	D	66A
Adj	Christ, Linden	M	36
Lect PT	Clarey, Cynthia	M	61
Lect PT	Clevenger, Dale	B	63B
Lect FT	Crayton, Mark	M	61,36
Lect PT	Eggert, Andrew	M	39
Lect PT	Ellefson, Peter		63C
Lect PT	Farouk, Wael	D	66A
Lect PT	Favario, Giulio	M	66C
Lect PT	Ferneding, Mary Jo	M	32
Lect PT	Flint, Gregory	B	63B,42
Lect PT	Floeter, John	M	62D
	Fogel, Henry		35E
Assoc Prof	Folse, Stuart J.	D	13
Lect PT	Friedman, Jay	B	63C,38
Lect PT	Gage, Yvonne		61
Lect PT	Gailloreto, Jim	M	47,64E
Lect PT	Garcia, Paulinho		47,70
Lect PT	Garcia, Victor		61
Lect PT	Garling, Tom	M	29B,63C
Assoc Prof	Garrop, Stacy	D	10,13
Lect PT	Giles, Sevgi	M	66A,66D
Asst Prof	Gilmore, Scott	B	39,61
Lect PT	Gluzman, Vadim	B	62A,42
Adj	Goldston, Christopher	M	66D
Lect PT	Guastafeste, Joseph		62D

Lect PT	Gunn, Jennifer	B	64A
Prof	Haddon, Judith	B	61
Lect PT	Hansen-Jackson, Dionne	M	64A
Lect PT	Harris, Roger	B	47,66A
Lect PT	Harrison, Edward	M	65,50
Lect PT	Hersh, Stefan	B	62A,42,38
Assoc Prof	Hill, Cheryl Frazes	D	32,36,60A
Lect PT	Hirschl, Richard	M	62C,42
Lect PT	Holloway, David	M	61
Lect PT	Huang, Kuang-Hao	D	66A
Lect PT	Hurlburt, Sean	M	64E
Assoc Prof	Hussey, William G.	D	13
Lect PT	Ingram, Roger		47,63A
Lect PT	Izotov, Eugene	M	64B
Lect PT	Jee, Patrick	B	62C
Lect PT	Johnson, Henry		47,70
Lect PT	Karpinos, Vadim	B	65
Assoc Prof	Kimmel, Pamela J.	M	13A,70
Asst Prof	Kwon, Yeeseon	D	66A,66B,66D,66
Lect PT	Lakirovich, Mark	B	62A
Lect PT	Lattimore, Jonita	M	61
Prof Emerita	Lazar, Ludmila	D	66A,66B
Lect PT	Lin, Jasmine	B	62A
Lect PT	Liu, Meng-Chieh	B	66A
Lect PT	Liu, Yang	B	62A
Prof	Marcozzi, Rudy T.	D	13A,13,13J
Lect PT	Mason, Scott	B	13B,13C,53,29
Lect PT	McGill, David	M	64D
Lect PT	McLean, John	M	47,70,29
Lect PT	Mertens, Paul	B	47,64E
Lect PT	Michel, Dennis	M	64D,42
Lect PT	Michel, Peggy	M	64B,42
Lect PT	Mikowsky, Solomon	D	66A
Inst	Moe, Judy	M	32
Lect PT	Moliner, Eugenia	B	42,64A
Lect PT	Morrow, Jeff	B	47,61
Lect PT	Moulder, John	M	47,70
Lect PT	Neuman, Lawrence	M	62
Asst Prof	Niedermaier, Edward G.	D	13B,13C,13E
Lect PT	Nieman, Adam	D	66A
Adj	O'Brien, Susan	M	39
Lect PT	Ogura, Yukiko		62B
Lect PT	Osorio, Jorge Federico		66A
	Owen, Wesley	B	66F
Adj	Palfrey, Rossman	M	70
Lect PT	Pavlovska, Jana		66A
Lect PT	Philbrick, Channing P.	M	63A
Lect PT	Pokorny, Gene	B	63D
Adj Inst	Polancich, Ronald	M	32
Lect PT	Ramey, Samuel	B	61
Assoc Prof	Reish, Gregory N.	D	12A
Lect PT	Ridenour, Mark	M	63A
Lect PT	Robertello, Thomas		64A
Lect PT	Rosenberg, Marlene	B	62D
Asst Prof	Roust, Colin	D	12
Lect PT	Schaefer, Lora	B	64B
Prof	Schrader, David D.	D	12,51
Lect PT	Schuchat, Charles	B	63D,49
Lect PT	Sharp, John	M	62C
Lect PT	Simon, Fred	B	47,66A
Lect PT	Smith, Gregory	B	64C
Lect PT	Smith, Mike	B	64E,29
Lect PT	Sobol, Deborah	B	66A,42
Lect PT	Soluri, Theodore	M	64D
Prof	Squires, Stephen E.		60B,37
Lect PT	Stilwell, Richard	M	61
Lect PT	Strauss, Michael	M	62B
Lect PT	Taylor, David	M	62A
Adj	Thomson, John	M	32
Lect PT	Trompeter, Jim W.	B	47,66A
Asst Prof	Wertico, Paul		65,29
Lect PT	Wilkes, Corey		63A
Lect PT	Wilson, Cheryl	B	47
Lect PT	Xu, MingHuan	D	62A
Lect PT	Yeh, John Bruce	B	64C
Lect PT	Yu, Yuan-Qing	M	62A
Lect PT	Zimmerman, Charlene	B	64C,42

IL0600 Chicago State University
Department of Music
9501 S King Dr
Chicago, IL 60628-1598
(773) 995-2155   Fax: (773) 995-2156
www.csu.edu/Music/
E-mail: music@csu.edu

4 Year Institution
Member of NASM

Dean: David Kanis, 80A
Chair: Mark Smith, 80A

Lect PT	Bridges, Cynthia	M	
Lect PT	Butters, Steven	M	65,50
Lect PT	DeSanto, Donn	B	62D
Lect PT	Felton, Jukube	M	13A,29
Prof	Florine, Jane Lynn	D	11,12A,12,20A,64A
Lect	Gessner, Dave	B	66A,29
Assoc Prof	Haefliger, Kathleen	M	16
Assoc Prof	Hendricks, James	M	13A,47,66A,66D,29
Lect	Hines, Tyrone	M	63C,63D,46
Lect	Kuchar, Evan	M	13,11
Lect	LeClair, Ben	M	61,39
Lect	Manson, Michael	M	62D
Lect	Matthews, Todd	B	62A,62B
Lect	Norman-Sojourner, Elizabeth	M	61,39,12
Lect PT	Offard, Felton	M	13A,11,47,70,29A
Asst Prof	Raynovich, William Jason	D	13,10,34
Lect PT	Schulz, Blanche	M	61
Prof	Smith, Mark	M	13A,50,65,29,20G
Prof	Stevenson, Roxanne	M	13A,20G,32,37,64
Prof	Sudeith, Mark A.	D	13,66A,66G,66C
Asst Prof	Whitted, Pharez	M	63A,29,47,49
Assoc Prof	Williams, Deborah	M	32C,36,61,32D

IL0630 College of Du Page
Department of Music
425 Fawell Blvd
Glen Ellyn, IL 60137
(630) 942-3008   Fax: (630) 790-9806
www.cod.edu
E-mail: kesselma@cdnet.cod.edu

2 Year Institution

Coord,. Fine Arts Programs: James Kampert, 80A
Associate Dean: Cathryn Wilkinson, 80A
Associate Dean, Fine Arts: Alain Hentschel, 80H

Emeritus	Bauer, Harold	D	
Prof	Kesselman, Lee R.	M	13,10,36,54,60
Prof	Paoli, Kenneth N.	D	13,10,11,35,34
Prof	Tallman, Thomas J.	D	13,11,47,63,29
Assoc Prof	Ward, Larry F.	D	11,20,14

IL0650 College of Lake County
Department of Music
19351 W Washington St
Grayslake, IL 60030-1148
(847) 543-2040   Fax: (847) 543-3040
www.clcillinois.edu
E-mail: mflack@clcillinois.edu

2 Year Institution

Music Contact: Michael Flack, 80A
Dean: Roland G. Miller, 80A

Inst PT	Barclay, Timothy R.	M	13A,64E,46,47
Inst PT	Bornovalova, Olga	M	66A,66D
Inst PT	Buglio, Patricia L.	M	61
Inst PT	Catalano, Frank K.	B	64E,47
Inst PT	Cizewski, Kathleen	M	66A,66D
Prof	Clency, Cleveland	D	11,66,40,36
Inst PT	Delay, Jeffrey S.	B	61
Prof	Flack, Michael	D	11,66,13,29,32B
Inst PT	Flippo, David	D	66A
Inst PT	Fuhrmann, Melanie J.		61
Inst PT	Hibbard, Dave	M	11,47,46
Inst PT	Jennings, David J.	M	11,65,13
Inst PT	Keeler, Elden L.	M	11,65,13
Inst PT	Klipp, Barbara A.	M	13A,11,64A
Inst PT	Li, Lei	M	13A,11,66A,66D
Inst PT	Lundholm, Susan L.		61
Inst PT	Mose, John	M	37,63C,63D
Inst PT	Ness, David J.	M	70,11,13
Inst PT	O'Callaghan, Brien	M	70
Inst PT	Ponce, Julie	M	11
Inst PT	Purnell, Tom F.	M	11,66A
Inst PT	Ray, Chris	M	62D
Inst PT	Tisch, Don	M	70
Inst PT	Turska, Joanna	M	64A

IL0720 Columbia College Chicago
Department of Music
600 S Michigan Ave
Chicago, IL 60605-1996
(312) 369-6300 Fax: (312) 369-8078
www.colum.edu/music
E-mail: music@colum.edu

4 Year Institution, Graduate School

MFA - Music Composition for the Screen

Chair: J. Richard Dunscomb, 80A
Dean: Eliza Nichols, 80A
Dir., Undergraduate Studies: H. E. Baccus, 80B
Dir., Admissions: Murphy Monroe, 80D
Associate Chair: Rosita M. Sands, 80H

Adj	Alvarez, Ruben		47
Adj	Anderson, Dan		62D,63D,29
Adj	Axelrod, Lawrence		13A
Adj	Baccus, H. E.		61
Asst Prof	Bakkum, Nathan	PhD	20,12
Adj	Ballmaier, Robert		13A,13C
Asst Prof	Balter, Marcos	PhD	10,13
Adj	Barnes, Rich		34D
Adj	Boris, William		70,29
Adj	Borja, Eric		34D
Adj	Bradfield, Bart	M	36
Adj	Cameron, Janet		13A
Adj	Carlson, Sharon		61
Adj	Carreira, Jonathan		13A
Adj	Cerqua, Joe		13,13C
Assoc Prof	Chang, Gary	M	10C
Adj	Coulson, Bette		66
Adj	Crawford, Raphael		63C
Adj	Deadman, Carey		38
Adj	Delin, Diane		29,62A,10
Adj	Donaldson, Frank		66,47,65
Adj	Duchak, Roberta		61
Adj	Edwards, Timothy D.	D	13,34D
Adj	Fawcett, Derek		61
Adj	Forte, Chris		70
Adj	Galasek, Judith		
Adj	Goldston, Chris		66,13
Adj	Grant, David	D	13
Adj	Greenspan, Stuart	B	13,35G
Adj	Gunther, Thomas		66
Senior Lect	Hall, Scott		29,46,47
Adj	Harris, Jarrard		46
Adj	Hicks, Jarrett		65
Adj	Hipskind, Tom		29
Adj	Hmura, Harry		70
Asst Prof	Huydts, Sebastian		66
Adj	Jones, Fernando		70
Adj	Kowalkowski, Paula		13
Adj	Lerner, Peter		29,70,10
Asst Prof	Levinson, Ilya	PhD	13,10
Assoc Prof	Lo Verde, Carol		61
Assoc Prof	Lofstrom, Douglas		60B,10
Adj	Luxion, Dennis		66
Assoc Prof	MacDonald, James M.	M	13
Adj	Mann, Hummie		10C
Prof	McHugh, David	M	10C
Adj	McReynolds, Clifton		13
Adj	Morehead, Patricia	M	10F,10,64B
Adj	Morrison, Audrey		29,63C
Adj	Neale, Donald		66A
Adj	Owens, Walter		36
Adj	Paris, John		13
Adj	Reinhart, Robert		10A
Adj	Rizzo, Rick		37
Adj	Ruiz, Norman		70
Prof	Sands, Rosita M.	PhD	14,12,20
Adj	Saxe, Peter		29,66,53
Adj	Schultze, Andrew W.	M	61
Adj	Sevilla, Tiffany		10,34
Senior Lect	Seward, Philip		13,13B,13C,13E
Adj	Tremulis, Nick		37
Adj	Vinick, Russ		60
Adj	Webb, Chuck	B	70
Senior Lect	Wilsyn, Bobbi		61
Adj	Winograd, Barry		29,12
Adj	Winters, Ellen		29,61
Adj	Yang, Fengshi		10A,13
Senior Lect	Yerkins, Gary		34

IL0730 Concordia University
Department of Music
7400 Augusta St
River Forest, IL 60305-1499
(708) 209-3060 Fax: (708) 209-3176
www.cuchicago.edu
E-mail: crfmusic@cuchicago.edu

4 Year Institution, Graduate School

Master of Arts in Music, Master of Church Music

Chair: Steven F. Wente, 80A
Dean: Gary Wenzel, 80A
Dir., Preparatory Division: Craig Sale, 80E

Adj	Artinian, Annie	M	66A
Adj	Beatty, Sarah	M	61
Adj	Bezaire, Fionna	M	66A,66D
Asst Prof	Boyer, Maurice C.	M	13C,36,38,44
Asst Prof	Brown, Charles P.	M	36,60,32
Adj	Burson, John	B	63A
Adj	Coffman, Elizabeth	M	62A,62B
Adj	Everson, Robert	M	65
Adj	Fackler, Barbara Ann	M	62E
Adj	Fackler, Dan	B	63B
Prof	Fischer, Richard R.	D	37,60B
Adj	Fudala, Cynthia T.	M	64A
Adj	Garrison, Kirk	M	47,53
Adj	Gildow, Kurtis	M	63D
Adj	Hanna, Judith	M	62D
Adj	Henry, Paul	M	70
Adj	Honigschnabel, Maria	M	66A
Adj	Howard, Billie	M	66A
Adj	Huang, Kuang-Hao	M	66A,66C
Adj	Jenne, Natalie	D	66H
Adj	Kasten, Martha	M	61
Asst Prof	Kohrs, Jonathan A.	M	10,36,11,31A,34
Adj	Krout-Lyons, Susan	M	61
Adj	Lano, Matthew	M	64D
Adj	Marquardt, John	M	64C
Adj	Michel, Peggy	M	64B
Adj	Monson, Anne	B	62C
Adj	Morlan, Emily Jane	M	66A
Adj	Phillips, Christine	M	64B
Adj	Port, Donna	B	64A
Adj	Rodriguez, Joseph	M	63D,63C
Adj	Ruthrauff, Jeremy	B	64E,41
Adj Asst Prof	Sale, Craig	M	66A,66B,66D,66C
Prof	Stahlke, Jonathan E.	D	13,10,38,10F
Adj	Thomen, Willard	M	61
Prof	Wente, Steven F.	D	13,66G,12A,31A

IL0750 DePaul University
School of Music
804 W Belden Ave
Chicago, IL 60614-3214
(773) 325-7260 Fax: (773) 325-7263
music.depaul.edu
E-mail: pmikos@depaul.edu

4 Year Institution, Graduate School
Member of NASM

Master of Music in Composition, Master of Music in Performance, Master of Music in Music Education, Master of Music in Applied Music, Master of Music in Jazz Studies

Dean: Donald E. Casey, 80A
Dir., Admissions: Ross Beacraft, 80D
Dir., Preparatory Division: Susanne R. Baker, 80E
Dir., Summer Programs: Jacqueline Kelly-McHale, 80G
Associate Dean, Academics: Judy Iwata Bundra, 80H
Associate Dean, Administration: Rob W. Krueger, 80H

Lect	Baker, Susanne R.	D	66D
Assoc Prof	Balderston, Stephen	M	62C
Lect	Barris, Robert A.	M	64D
Lect	Behling, John F.	D	11
Lect	Bentley, Julia	DIPL	61
Lect	Berry, Brandi	M	42
Lect	Bimm, Greg L.	M	32C
Lect	Bitticks, Meret	M	32E
Lect	Bogojevic, Natasha		11
Lect	Bolles, Marita	D	10A
Lect	Bridges, Alban Kit	D	39
Asst Prof	Brucher, Katherine	D	14A,20
Lect	Bruno, Anthony	B	32E
Lect	Buchman, William	B	64D

Assoc Prof	Bundra, Judy Iwata	D	32
Assoc Prof	Bunnell, Jane E.	B	61
Lect	Byrne, Elizabeth		61
Lect	Campos, Wagner		64C
Lect	Carrillo, Oto G.	M	63B
Prof	Casey, Donald E.	D	32
Lect	Clark, Joseph	M	13C
Lect	Coffman, Timothy J.	B	29,63C
Lect	Colby, Mark S.	M	64E
Lect	Colnot, Cliff C.	D	38
Lect	Combs, Larry R.	M	64C
Lect	Cook, Susan C.	M	64E
Lect	Cooley, Floyd O.	B	63D
Lect	Cunningham, Mark T.	B	35E
Lect	Damoulakis, Marc H.		65
Assoc Prof	DeRoche, Julie R.	B	64C
Lect	Dirks, Jelena M.	M	64B
Lect	Dirks, Karen	B	62B
Lect	Dufour, Mathieu T.		64A
Lect	Elias, Cathy A.	D	11,12A,12C
Lect	Embree, Marc A.	M	61,32B
Lect	Epstein, Nomi R.	D	13C
Lect	Farina, Geoff	M	11
Lect	Fisher, Mark	M	63C,63D
Lect	Gallo, Donna	M	32F
Lect	Gallo, Franklin J.	M	32C,32D
Lect	Garrison, Kirk A.	M	46
Lect	Grant, David	D	13C
Lect	Grau-Schmidt, Anna K.	B	11,12A
Lect	Green, Michael C.	M	65
Vstng Asst Prof	Grives, Steven Matthew	D	36,40
Lect	Hall, Crystal	M	32E
Assoc Prof	Hall, Dana	M	14,29
Lect	Hanna, Alexander	B	62D
Lect	Heath, Jason	M	62D
Lect	Henes, John M.	B	
Lect	Hersh, Julian E.	M	42
Lect	Hirt, Linda L.	M	66C
Lect	Hovnanian, Michael J.	B	62D
Lect	Hutchinson, Nicholas	D	61,66C
Lect	Hutter, Greg J.	D	13C,13D,10A,11
Lect	Hwang-Hoesley, Jae W.	D	66D
Lect	Izotov, Eugene A.	B	64B
	Johnson, Alyce	M	64A
	Johnston, Margaret	M	32C,32E
Asst Prof	Jones, Christopher	D	10,13
Lect	Jones, Trevor	M	32C,32D
Prof	Kaler, Ilya	D	62A
Assoc Prof	Kaler, Olga D.	D	62A
Lect	Kassinger, Robert C.	B	62D
Lect	Kawaller, Meaghan	M	32E
Asst Prof	Kelly-McHale, Jacqueline	D	32
Lect	Kimel, Neil	B	63B
Lect	Kosower, Paula	D	62
Lect	Kowalkowski, Jeffrey F.	D	10,11
Lect	Kozakis, Michael J.	M	65,50
Lect	Langenberg, Kelly		32E
Prof	Lark, Robert J.	D	29,63A,47
Lect	Larsen, Tage	B	63A
Lect	Laughlin, Tina	M	32E
Lect	Lee, Matt	M	63A,32E
Lect	Lemons, Chris H.	D	11
Asst Prof	Lewanski, Michael A.		41,43
Lect	Marshall, Ruth	M	32E
Asst Prof	Matta, Thomas		63C,29
Lect	Maxwell, Mark A.		70
Lect	McMunn, Ben	M	32E
Prof	Miller, Tom D.		35C
Lect	Millstein, Eric J.	M	65
Assoc Prof	Mosteller, Steven	M	39,61
Lect	Moy, Jason	M	55B,66H
Lect	Murphy, Shawn		35B
Assoc Prof	Neidlinger, Erica	D	36,32E
Lect	Nicholson, Daniel	M	32E
Asst Prof	Oh, Seung-Ah	D	10,13,13F,10A
Lect	Palmieri, Bob	M	70
Lect	Payson, Al E.		65
Lect	Peot, Deborah L.	M	32
Lect	Perrillo, Ron J.		46,66A
Lect	Pituch, David A.	D	64E,11,12A
Lect	Randruut, Avo	M	20A
Lect	Rivera, Nicole		33
Lect	Rizzer, Gerald M.		11
Lect	Rummage, Robert F.	M	46,65
Lect	Rzasa, Karl		32E
Assoc Prof	Salzenstein, Alan N.	JD	35
Lect	Sato, Junichi S.	M	66D
Lect	Sill, Kelly	B	62D
Prof	Silverstein, Harry		39
Lect	Sincaglia, Nicolas W.	B	35C
Lect	Smelser, Jim	M	63B
Lect	Snoza, Melissa	M	35B
Lect	Soderstrom, Erik	JD	35
Prof	Solomonow, Rami	M	62B
Lect	Stampfl, Aaron	DIPL	66D
Lect	Staron, Michael	M	11
Lect	Steinman, Daniel B.	B	35G
Lect	Stolper, Mary	M	64A
Lect	Sugimura, Kyomi	M	66A
Assoc Prof	Sung, Janet		62A

Lect	Sylvester, Michael	M	61
Lect	Tashjian, B. Charmian	D	11
Lect	Taylor, Brant	M	62C
Lect	Tiffin, Corey	B	32E
Assoc Prof	Vatchnadze, George	M	66A
Lect	Vernon, Charles G.	M	63C
Assoc Prof	Westerberg, Kurt H.	D	13,10,11
Lect	Williams, Bradley	M	29A
Lect	Zupko, Mischa	D	11

IL0780 Dominican University

Music Discipline
7900 W Division St
River Forest, IL 60305
(708) 366-2490   Fax: (708) 366-5360
www.dom.edu
E-mail: goetzsota@dom.edu

4 Year Institution

Chair: Germaine Goetz-Sota, 80A
Dean, Liberal Arts: Hugh Mcelwain, 80A

Adj	Gallagher, Patty		
Adj	Guccione, Rose		
Adj	McLaughlin, Michael		
Adj	Papatheodorou, Devovora	M	66A,66B
Adj	Sauer, Maureen		61
Adj	Sayre, Paul		
Prof Emeritus	Steffen, Cecil	M	13,66A,66D
Prof Emeritus	Stohrer, Baptist	D	12A,12,61

IL0800 Eastern Illinois University

Department of Music
600 Lincoln Ave
Charleston, IL 61920
(217) 581-3010   Fax: (217) 581-7137
www.eiu.edu/~music
E-mail: music@eiu.edu

4 Year Institution, Graduate School
Member of NASM

Master of Arts in Music

Chair: Jerry L. Daniels, 80A
Graduate Coordinator: Marilyn J. Coles, 80C
Dir., Community Music Program: Mary M. Smith, 80E

Inst	Borah, Bernard	D	13,64D
Asst Prof	Cheetham, Andrew	D	63A,47,66A,11
Prof	Coles, Marilyn J.	D	61
Inst	Conrad, Kent R.	M	66A,66C,66D
Asst Prof	Cromwell, Anna L.	D	62A,62B,41
Prof	Daniels, Jerry L.	M	61
Inst	Decker, Bradley	D	13,10
Asst Prof	Eckert, Stefan	D	13,13J,13E
Prof	Fagaly, Sam W.	D	64E,47,29,48
Inst	Florea, Luminita D.	D	12
Inst	Francis, Joseph Corey	M	37
Inst	French, Todd M.	M	63D,32E
Inst	Hesse, Scott A.	M	70
Inst	Jakubiec, Aaron F.	D	11,64B,13B
Asst Prof	Jensen, Gary J.	M	32A,32B,32H,32C
Inst	Johnson, Rebecca R.	D	64A,48
Assoc Prof	Johnston, Paul R.	M	46,29,53
Inst	Killen, Seth R.	M	61,54
Asst Prof	Larson, Danelle	D	32E,37
Inst	Lee, April	M	36,11
Inst	McBain, Jeremy	D	11
Inst	McBain, Katherine C.	D	63B,41,11
Prof	Poulter, Patricia S.	D	32
Inst	Robertson, Jemmie	D	63,11
Assoc Prof	Rossi, Richard Robert	D	60A,36,38,66G
Inst	Rubel, Mark B.	B	34
Asst Prof	Ryan, Jamie V.	M	65,50
Inst	Ryan, Kathreen A.	D	11
Inst	Schuette, Rebecca C.	M	32
Inst	Smith, Mary M.	D	64C
Asst Prof	Teicher, Susan C.	D	66A
Inst	Tucker, Nick	M	62D
Inst	Yu, Ka-Wai	M	62C,11,13B

IL0840 Elgin Community College
Music Program
1700 Spartan Dr
Elgin, IL 60123-7189
(847) 214-7240   Fax: (847) 214-7757
www.elgin.edu
E-mail: dmaki@elgin.edu

2 Year Institution

Dean: Ruixuan Mao, 80A
Associate Dean: Mary Hatch, 80H

Adj	Bernhard, Kathryn M.		
Adj	Bettcher, Mark T.		
Adj	Buglio, Patricia L.	M	61
Adj	Butters, Steven G.	M	65,50
Inst	Cates, Deanna S.		
Adj	Curtis, Robert C.		
Adj	Dieffenbach, Larry S.		
Adj	Dzhuryn, Nazar	M	62C
Adj	Freedland, Debra R.	M	64B
Adj	Hughes, Constance M.		
Adj	Hunt, Jeffrey S.		
Adj	Joyce, Michael		
Adj	Koehler, Reimund G.		
Adj	Kull, James A.	M	32E
Adj	Lewis, D. Andrew		
Adj	Lienert, Keith A.		
Prof	Maki, Daniel H.	M	13,11,37,64A,66D
Adj	McIntyre, Daniel P.		
Adj	Metlicka, Scott D.	M	32E
Adj	Mo, Sung Hoon		
Adj	Oper, Linda L.		62A
Adj	Richter, Julia M.		
Adj	Salter, Michael A.		
Adj	Semanic, Paul A.		
Adj	Shaffer, Timothy William	M	62D
Prof	Slawson, John G.	D	60,12A,36,38,54
Adj	Szabo, Natalie		

IL0850 Elmhurst College
Department of Music
190 S Prospect Ave
Elmhurst, IL 60126-3296
(630) 617-3515   Fax: (630) 617-3738
public.elmhurst.edu/music
E-mail: griffinp@elmhurst.edu

4 Year Institution

Chair: Peter J. Griffin, 80A
Dir., Preparatory Division: Timothy O. Hays, 80E
Dir., Jazz Festival: Douglas Beach, 80F

Teach Assoc	Babbitt, Frank	M	62A,62B
Teach Assoc	Badea, Remus	M	62A,62B
Inst Adj	Baker, Andrew	B	63C,47
Asst Prof	Beach, Douglas	B	47,53,71,29,35
Teach Assoc	Benway, Joel	M	63B
Teach Assoc	Birkeland, Roger	M	64E
Inst Adj	Bisesi, Gayle	B	47,61
Teach Assoc	Blackburn, Gregory	M	64A
Teach Assoc	Brown, Jennie	D	64A,41,42
Teach Assoc	Camp, Linda	M	66A
Inst Adj	Caruso, Frank		66A
Inst Adj	Christiansen, David	M	66G,31A
Teach Assoc	Colby, Mark	M	64E,53
Inst Adj	Crosson, Gail	M	32,64C
Teach Assoc	Deadman, Randall	M	63A,10
Teach Assoc	Dennis, Susan	M	54,61
Teach Assoc	Deutsch, Jeff	B	61
Asst Prof	DeVasto, David	PhD	10,13,32E,66
Teach Assoc	Dixon, Virginia	M	62D
Inst Adj	Dorhauer, John	M	20A,13,63A
Teach Assoc	Freedland, Debra	M	64B
Teach Assoc	Gabriel, Edgar	M	62A,62B,45
Teach Assoc	Garling, Tom	M	47,63C
Inst Adj	Greene, Gary A.	PhD	32
Assoc Prof	Griffin, Peter J.	D	32,37,60B,63C,63D
Prof	Grimes, Judith	M	60,14,32,37
Inst Adj	Haebich, Kenneth	M	62D,10A,10F
Prof	Harbold, Mark A.	PhD	13,10F,10,16,12A
Prof	Hays, Timothy O.	PhD	13,62D,45,34,35
Inst Adj	Hennel, Daniel	M	13,66A
Teach Assoc	Hirna, Olena	M	62A,62B
Teach Assoc	Hixson, Wesley	M	70
	Houston, James	M	66F
Teach Assoc	Howell, Todd	B	65
Inst Adj	Jones, Josh	D	61
Inst Adj	Junokas, Michael	M	10A,10B,13,34
Teach Assoc	Kawaller, Meaghan	M	64C
Teach Assoc	Kee, Soyoung	D	66A,11
Asst Prof	Kellan, Ross	M	60,32,37,11,13
Teach Assoc	Leddy, Thomas	B	65
Teach Assoc	Lee, Kari	M	63A
Inst Adj	Lee, R. Matthew	M	63A
Inst Adj	Lualdi, Brenda	M	61,54
Teach Assoc	Lustrea, Robert	M	63D
Teach Assoc	Macdonald, James	M	36,41
Inst Adj	Maimonis, Nina	M	32
Teach Assoc	Masters, Barbara	M	66A,66G,66H
Inst Adj	Mather, Jennifer	M	61
Asst Prof	May, Joanne	M	13,38,42
Inst Adj	Miller, Bryan	M	37
Prof	Moninger, Susan	M	36,40,47,61
Teach Assoc	Moore, Edward	M	62C
Teach Assoc	Morong, Eric	B	37
Teach Assoc	Moser, Janet	M	66A,66D,32A,32
Teach Assoc	Pickering, Amy	M	61
Inst Adj	Pinto, Mike	M	70,53,47
Inst Adj	Portolese, Frank	B	70,53
Teach Assoc	Regan, Lara	M	64E
Inst Adj	Rummage, Robert	M	50,65,53
Teach Assoc	Ryan, P. Dianne	M	64D
Teach Assoc	Skidgel, Wesley	M	63A,32E
Teach Assoc	Spurr, Ken	M	66A,46,47
Inst Adj	Stark, Cynthia	M	63D,49
Inst Adj	Streder, Mark	B	13,66A,53,34,45
Inst Adj	Suvada, Steve	M	70,41,20
Inst Adj	Tallman, Donna	M	36,60A,44
Inst Adj	Towner, John	B	45,34
Inst Adj	Uddenberg, Scott	M	61,54
Inst Adj	Unrath, Wendy	M	66A,66D,12A,11

IL0900 Eureka College
Department of Music
300 E College Ave
Eureka, IL 61530
(309) 467-6397   Fax: (309) 467-6891
www.eureka.edu
E-mail: jdhenry@eureka.edu

4 Year Institution

Dean: Philip Cavalier, 80A
Music Contact: Joseph D. Henry, 80A

Inst	Bates, Pamela	M	12A,13,66A,66C,66D
Assoc Prof	Henry, Joseph D.	D	12A,20G,36,40,32C
Lect	Wright, Gina	M	61

IL1050 Greenville College
Department of Music
315 E College Ave
Greenville, IL 62246
(618) 664-2800 x 6560   Fax: (618) 664-6580
www.greenville.edu
E-mail: jeff.wilson@greenville.edu

4 Year Institution

Chair: Jeffrey S. Wilson, 80A

Adj	Archibald, William	B	64E
Adj	Boese, Jessica	M	64C
Adj	Briles, Charity	M	38,62A,62B
Adj	Briles, Travis	B	35
Artist in Res	Casas, Jorge	B	62D,47,10D
Adj	Cosentino, Mike	B	70
Adj	DeJaynes, Luke	B	65,35C
Asst Prof	Erickson, Gary	M	34B,10A,13G,31A,35D
	Fairbanks, Will	M	37,63A,46,49,63B
Assoc Prof	Marsch, Debra	M	12A,61
Adj	Marshall, Lynda	M	61,36
Adj	Porter, Miriam	M	61
Adj	Ritter, Stacey	M	61
Assoc Prof	Stampfli, L. Thomas	D	66A,66B,66D,66C
Inst	Sunderland, Paul	M	29B,31A,43,70
Adj	Todd, Sarah	M	66A,66C,66D
Asst Prof	Weiss, Louise	M	13A,32B,48,64A,66C
Prof	Wilson, Jeffrey S.	D	60,36,61,40,31A
Assoc Prof	Woods, Chris P.	D	13A,10F,13C,49,63

IL1080 Harold Washington College
Department of Music/Humanities
30 E Lake St
Chicago, IL 60601
(312) 553-5720   Fax: (312) 553-5721
www.hwcmusic.com
E-mail: mshevitz@ccc.edu

2 Year Institution, Community College

Coordinator: Matthew Shevitz, 80A

Inst	Florez, Anthony	M	11,34,65,70,13
Inst	Laymon, Michael	M	11,13,35,63C
Assoc Prof	Shevitz, Matthew	DMA	11,13,29,47,46
Asst Prof	Tapanes-Inojosa, Adriana	D	11,20,36,12,66

IL1085 Harper College
Department of Music
1200 W Algonquin Rd
Palatine, IL 60067-7398
(847) 925-6568   Fax: (847) 925-6582
harpercollege.edu/libarts/mus/dept
E-mail: kstoesse@harpercollege.edu

2 Year Institution
Member of NASM

Chair: Gregory G. Clemons, 80A
Community Music Center: Henrietta Neeley, 80E
Cultural Arts Concert Series: Thomas J. Stauch, 80F

Adj Prof	Aglinskas, Peter	M	70,14C
Prof Emerita	Albergo, Cathy	D	66A,66B,66D
Adj Prof	Amano, Hideko	D	64A
Adj Prof	Anderson, Collin	D	64D
Adj Prof	Baumann, Keith	C	62
Adj Prof	Biggerstaff, Corey	M	62D
Adj Prof	Bornovalova, Olga	D	66A,66B,66D
Assoc Prof	Bowker, Barbara E.	PhD	13,11,13B,13C,12A
Other	Byrley, Michael	C	66F
Adj Prof	Capshaw, Reed	M	63C,63D
Adj Prof	Chang, Helen	M	66A
Prof	Clemons, Gregory G.	M	37,63A,41,13
Adj Prof	Davis, Michael	M	63A
Adj Prof	Dennis, Susan	M	61,54,40
Adj Prof	Duncan, Steven	M	63C
Adj Prof	Espel, Ann	M	36
Adj Prof	Filliman, Timothy	M	61
Adj Prof	Fleer, Suzanne	M	66A,66D
Adj Prof	Freedland, Debra	M	64B
Adj Prof	Gabriel, Edgar	M	62A,53,51
Adj Prof	Groner, Brian	DIPL	38
Adj Prof	Hedberg, Jeffrey	M	61,63A
Adj Prof	Huerta, Edgar		70
Adj Prof	Kemp, Edward	M	36
Other	LaBorn, John	C	66F
Adj Prof	Lee, Chiayi	D	66C
Adj Prof	Lee, Sang-Eun	M	62A,42
Adj Prof	Lim, Cheryl	M	66A,66D
Adj Prof	Lundholm, Susan	M	61
Prof Emeritus	Makas, George	D	13,62A
Adj Prof	Mrozinski, Lavonne	M	66A,66D
Adj Prof	Mrozinski, Mark	M	66A,66D
Adj Prof	Neeley, Henrietta	M	62A,11,42,62B
Adj Prof	Niehoff, Carolyn	M	61
Adj Prof	Pazin, Eugene	M	62A
Adj Prof	Peyton, Claudia	C	
Adj Prof	Porter, William Anthony	M	62C,42
Adj Prof	Razaq, Janice L.	D	66A,66B,66D
Adj Prof	Ritzenthaler, Maria	M	62B,41,42
Adj Prof	Robinson, Ian	B	64E
Adj Prof	Ross, Paul	M	65,50
Adj Prof	Ruthrauff, Jeremy	M	64E
Prof Emeritus	Ryberg, J. Stanley	PhD	13B,13C,12A,63C,63D
Adj Prof	Sbarboro, Kathlyn	M	66A,66D
Adj Prof	Schroeder-Garbar, Lacy	M	64C
Adj Prof	Scorza, Darren	M	65
Adj Prof	Shaffer, Timothy	M	62D
Adj Prof	Sidhu, Inderjeet	M	10E
Adj Prof	Spurr, Kenneth	B	66A,53,29,47
Prof	Stauch, Thomas J.	D	36,40,61,32D,11
Adj Prof	Stiernberg, Donald	B	62
Adj Prof	Suvada, Steven	M	70,34,35
Adj Prof	Tashjian, Charmian	D	13A,13B,13C
Prof Emeritus	Tillotson, J. Robert	D	37,13,41,64C
Adj Prof	Toledo, Patricia	M	61
Adj Prof	Towner, John	M	34,35
Adj Prof	Vazquez, Steven	M	70
Adj Prof	Von Pechmann, Lisa	M	63B
Adj Prof	Walgren-Georgas, Carol	M	66A,66D
Adj Prof	Westlake, Walton	M	61
Adj Prof Emeritus	Winkler, Frank	M	38
Adj Prof	Wood, Kevin	M	63A

IL1090 Illinois Central College
Music Program
1 College Dr
East Peoria, IL 61635-0001
(309) 694-5113   Fax: (309) 694-8505
www.icc.edu
E-mail: tjones@icc.edu

2 Year Institution, Public Community College

Associate Dean: Jeffrey Hoover, 80A
Teaching Chair: Tony Jones, 80H

Inst PT	Arvin, Tammy J.	M	13,64C
Inst PT	Conroy, Brenda	M	66A,66D
Inst PT	Cooksey, Denise	M	64A
Inst PT	Dahlem, Justin	M	64D
Inst PT	Dexter, Mary	B	52
Inst PT	Dorough, Prince	D	11
Inst PT	Etzel, Laurel	M	11,63B
Inst PT	Ford, Douglass	M	65
Asst Prof	Harms, Lawrence	M	11,47,64C,64E,29A
Inst PT	Hughes, Laura Weaver	M	61
Inst PT	Hull, Michael	M	70
Inst	Jones, Tony	M	37,63,13A,11
Inst PT	Moder, Jennifer	M	29A
Asst Prof	Oh, Annette	D	11,61,36,13B,13C
Inst PT	Sheldon, Robert	M	37
Inst PT	Smith, Sally	M	66G
Inst PT	Somer, Gena		36
Inst PT	Trang, Grace	M	66A,66D
Inst PT	Walker, James E.	M	11

IL1100 Illinois College
Department of Music
1100 W College Ave
Jacksonville, IL 62650
(217) 245-3491   Fax: (217) 245-3470
www.ic.edu/music
E-mail: timothy.kramer@mail.ic.edu

4 Year Institution

Chair: Timothy Kramer, 80A
Program Chair, Fine Arts Series: Garrett N. Allman, 80F

Assoc Prof	Allman, Garrett N.	D	13,66C,38,66A,60B
PT	Brazzel, Russel	M	70,12A
PT	Burchard, Brett	B	62A
PT	Cochran, Shelley	B	64A
PT	Cox, Kris	M	32B,32C
PT	DelGiorno, Nichol	M	66G
PT	Fulton, Judy	M	32B,32C
Inst	Gramelspacher, Addie	M	39,61
PT	Hume, John	M	32E,63A,63B
PT	Kozelka, David	B	63B
Prof	Kramer, Timothy	D	13,10F,10A,10B
PT	Magliocco, Hugo	D	63D,63C
PT	McCandless, Marty	B	64C,64E,32E,47,41
Asst Prof	Musgrove, Abby R.	D	36,40,11,32C,32D
PT	Phillips, Susan	B	62C
PT	Stahel, Ann Marie	M	37
PT	Stellar, Krista	B	64B
PT	Vortman, Karma K.	B	66A,66C

IL1150 Illinois State University
School of Music
Campus # 5660
Normal, IL 61790-5660
(309) 438-7633   Fax: (309) 438-5833
www.cfa.ilstu.edu/music
E-mail: music@ilstu.edu

4 Year Institution, Graduate School
Member of NASM

Master of Music in Collaborative Piano, Master of Music in Composition, Master of Music in Performance, Master of Music in Music Education, Master of Music in Music Therapy

Director: Stephen Parsons, 80A
Coord., Graduate Programs: Angelo L. Favis, 80C
Assistant Director: Tim Fredstrom, 80H

Assoc Prof	Aduonum, Ama Oforiwaa Konadu	D	20,11
Inst	Austin, Debra	M	61
Assoc Prof	Babbitt, Mark	D	63C
Asst Prof	Belongia, Daniel A.	D	60,37
Prof	Block, Glenn	D	60,38
Inst	Bock, Susan V.	M	33
Prof	Borg, Paul	D	13A,13,11,12A,12
	Carlson, Karyl K.	D	36,60A
Assoc Prof	Collier, David L.	DMA	50,65
Asst Prof	Crimmins, Andrea	M	33
Inst	Dicker, Judith	M	64B
Prof	Dicker, Michael H.	M	11,48,64D
Inst	Faux, Tom	D	11,20
Assoc Prof	Favis, Angelo L.	D	70
Assoc Prof	Fredstrom, Tim	D	32D,36,60A,32
Assoc Prof	Gentry, Sarah	D	13,62A,62B
Inst	Graham, Sarah J.	D	36,60A
Assoc Prof	Gresham, David	D	48,64C
Lect	Hart, Kevin	M	13,66A
Asst Prof	Horst, Martha C.	D	13,10
Assoc Prof	Koch, John M.	M	61
Prof	Koehler, William	D	32B,32C,62D
Assoc Prof	Labonville, Marie E.	D	11,12A,12,20D
Prof	Larsen, Arved	D	13,12A,63C
Asst Prof	Lewis, Katherine J.	D	11,62B
Prof	Major, Amy Gilreath	D	63A
Prof	Major, James E.	D	36,40,32D
Inst	Manfredo, Joseph	D	32E,60B,37,32
Assoc Prof	Marko, Thomas	D	47,29
Asst Prof	Marshack, Rose	M	34,35A
Assoc Prof	McCord, Kimberly A.	D	32B,32C,32F,29A,32A
Assoc Prof	Morenus, Carlyn G.	D	66A,66D
Prof	Neisler, Joseph	D	11,63B
Asst Prof	Nolen, Paul	D	64E,29A
Asst Prof	Ransom, Adriana LaRosa	D	11,62C
Prof	Risinger, Kimberly	D	64A
Assoc Prof	Ropp, Cindy	D	33
Asst Prof	Rummel, Andrew	M	63D
Inst	Russell, Joshua D.	D	66A
Asst Prof	Schimmel, Carl W.	D	10A,13
Inst	Schuetz, Daniel	D	61
	Smith, Elizabeth Lena	D	13
Assoc Prof	Smith, Matthew	D	34
Prof	Snyder, David W.	D	32,37
Prof	Steele, Stephen K.	D	60,32,37
Asst Prof	Tonnu, Tuyen	D	66A,66B,13B,13C
Prof	Vought, J. Michelle	D	39,61

IL1175 Illinois Valley Community College
Department of Music
815 N Orlando Smith Ave
Oglesby, IL 61348-9692
(815) 224-2720
www.ivcc.edu
E-mail: Jeff_Anderson@ivcc.Edu

Introduction Courses Only

Head: Michael J. Pecherek, 80A

Inst	Pecherek, Michael J.	M	13,60,11,38,62C

IL1200 Illinois Wesleyan University
School of Music
PO Box 2900
Bloomington, IL 61702-2900
(309) 556-3061   Fax: (309) 556-3121
www.iwu.edu/music
E-mail: mpelusi@iwu.edu

4 Year Institution
Member of NASM

Director: Mario J. Pelusi, 80A
Coordinator, Music Admissions: Laura Dolan, 80D
Dir., Summer Programs: Nina Gordon, 80F,80G
Dir., Guest Artist Series: David J. Vayo, 80F
Coord., Operations: Stephanie Kohl Ringle, 80H

Inst PT	Anderson, Mark	M	70
Assoc Prof	Bondurant-Koehler, Shela	D	32
Inst PT	Bryant, Deanne	B	32B,32C,32D,32E
Inst PT	Buck, Lynn	M	32E
Asst Prof	Burt, Patricia A.	M	13A,66A,66D,13B,13C
Inst PT	Church, Gretchen	M	66C
Asst Prof	Cook, Kent	D	66A,66D
Inst PT	Dale, Sarah	B	66C
Assoc Prof	Delvin, Robert	M	16
Inst PT	Dixon, Nellie	M	64D
Inst PT	Doran, Joy	M	66C,66A,66D
Prof	Eggleston, Steven	M	60B,37,38,63A
Prof	Farquharson, Linda J.	D	39,61
Inst	Ferguson, Eva	M	66C,66D
Prof	Ferguson, J. Scott	D	60A,36,61
Asst Prof	Garrett, Roger	M	37,64C,60B,41,35D
Assoc Prof	Gordon, Nina	D	62C,42
Prof	Green, Jonathan D.	D	36
Inst PT	Green, Tricia	B	64C
Inst PT	Gresham, Momoko	M	66C
Inst PT	Hepner, Jae Lyn	B	64A
Inst PT	Hill, Doris	M	66G,66H
Prof	Hishman, Marcia	M	66C,66A
Inst PT	Huang, Chen-Yu	M	62E
Inst	Hudson, William	M	55D,61
Inst PT	Johnson, Daniel	M	32A,32B,32C,32D,32E
Inst PT	Jones, Trevor	M	62D
Inst PT	Klotzbach, Susan	D	66C,13A,13B,13C
Staff	Krippenstapel, George	M	66F
Inst PT	Langenberg, Kelly	M	63B
Inst PT	Legner, Amanda	M	65
Inst	Mangialardi, Robert	M	61,39
Assoc Prof	Mazo, Vadim	M	41,42,62A,62B,51
Assoc Prof	Moham, Carren D.	D	20G,61
Inst PT	Mulliken, Erin	M	66A,66D
Inst PT	Nelson, Lisa	M	62A
Inst PT	Olive, Jordan	M	63A
Prof	Pelusi, Mario J.	D	10A,10F,13,43,29B
Asst Prof	Pitchford, Timothy	D	63C,29A,46,47,53
Asst Prof	Plazak, Joseph S.	D	13
Asst Prof	Ponce, Adriana	D	12A,11,20
Inst PT	Pounds, Nancy	M	66C
Assoc Prof	Press, Stephen D.	D	12A,12E
Inst	Risinger, Ed	M	63D,32E,37
Inst PT	Schuetz, Jennifer Hilbish	D	61
Inst PT	Scifres, Maxie	M	66C
Assoc Prof	Scifres, Sam G.	D	61
Inst PT	Swallow, Dan	M	37
Inst PT	Swilley, Daniel	M	10,13,34,13A,13B
Prof	Vayo, David J.	D	10F,10,10D,10B,10A
Inst PT	Vogt, Elaine	M	66A,66C
Inst PT	West, Jill	M	64B,64D
Inst PT	West, Rachel	B	66C
Assoc Prof	West, William	M	13,64A,64E,41,67E
Inst PT	Wtizig, Lu	M	66C
Inst PT	Zimmerman, Keith	M	64E,41

IL1240 John A Logan College
Music Program
700 Logan College Rd
Carterville, IL 62918
(618) 985-3741   Fax: (618) 985-2248
www.jalc.edu

2 Year Institution

Music Contact: Nathan D. Arnett, 80A
Chair, Humanities: Gayle Pesavento, 80A

Inst	Arnett, Nathan D.	M	11,13C,32A,36,40
Inst	Gardner, Richard	M	11,66D
Inst	Hanes, Michael	M	46
Inst	McHaney, David	M	38
Prof Emerita	Sala, Karen	M	13A,13B,13E,13F,61
Inst	Watson, Marva	B	66A,66B,66C,11,12A

IL1245 John Wood Community College
Department of Fine Arts
1301 S 48th St
Quincy, IL 62305
(217) 224-6500   Fax: (217) 224-4208
www.jwcc.edu/instruct/music/default.htm
E-mail: declueg@jwcc.edu

2 Year Institution

Chair: Gary L. Declue, 80A

Assoc Prof	Basinger, Rhonda	A	13,11,66
	Declue, Gary L.	M	12A,13A,11,61,36

IL1250 Joliet Junior College
Department of Fine Arts-Music
1215 Houbolt Rd
Joliet, IL 60431-8938
(815) 280-2232   Fax: (815) 280-6739
www.jjc.edu
E-mail: chmorgan@jjc.edu

2 Year Institution

Chair & Dir., Artist/Performance Series: Charles Morgan, 80A,80F

Asst Prof	Broderick, Daniela	D	11,66A,66D,20G,54
Prof	Liley, Thomas	D	13,12A,64
Prof	Morgan, Charles	M	13A,60B,37,47,63
Asst Prof	Nuccio, David A.	M	11,29A,34,54,66A
Prof	Spencer, Philip	M	20,61,66A,36,60A

IL1300 Judson University
Department of Music
College of Liberal Arts & Sciences
1151 N State St
Elgin, IL 60123-1498
(847) 628-1110   Fax: (847) 628-2043
www.judsonu.edu/Undergraduate/Music/Overview
E-mail: cgross@judsonu.edu

4 Year Institution

Chair: Ernest H. Gross, III, 80A
Assistant Chair & Dir., Preparatory Division: Robert P. Kania, 80E,80H,80G

Inst	Bishop, Jean	B	64A
Inst	Davies, Karl	M	62B
Inst	Downey, Gwyn	B	64D
Inst	Folker, Michael	M	65
Inst	Frederick, Jeremiah	M	63B
Inst	Freedland, Debra	M	64B
Assoc Prof	Gross, Ernest H.	D	37,49,60B,63D,12A
Inst	Hayes, Tara	M	62A
Inst	Hinkle, Laura	M	62,32E
Asst Prof	Hong, Sojung Lee	D	66A,66D,66B,42,66C
Inst	Huff, Adam	M	70
Asst Prof	Jones, Joshua	M	61,11,39,54
Assoc Prof	Kania, Robert P.	D	66A,13
Inst	Lemons, Nancy	B	66A,13B
Inst	Newby, Joanna	M	62A,62B
Inst	Rider, Daniel	M	64C,64E
Inst	Shaffer, Timothy	M	62D
Inst	Steuer, Jeff	M	32B
Prof	Voelker, Dale	D	13A,13B,60A,36,66G
Inst	Weber, Robert	B	62C,51
Inst	Wrighte, Michelle	M	61

IL1330 Kankakee Community College
Division Humanities and Social Sc
100 College Dr
Kankakee, IL 60901
(815) 802-8700   Fax: (815) 802-8101
www.kcc.edu
E-mail: spfaff@kcc.edu

2 Year Institution

Assoicate Dean: Mark Lanting, 80H

Adj	Ebert, Shari E.	B	11,20

IL1340 Kishwaukee College
Music Program
21193 Malta Rd
Malta, IL 60150-9600
(815) 825-2086 x 209   Fax: (815) 825-2072
www.kishwaukeecollege.edu
E-mail: gary.mattin@kishwaukeecollege.edu

2 Year Institution

Dean: Ann Busse Tucker, 80A

Adj Inst	Francini, Kerri		
Adj	Hwang, Mary		
Adj Inst	Johnson, Gary		
Adj Inst	Mattin, Gary		
Adj Inst	Whiting, Jennifer		

IL1350 Knox College
Department of Music
2 East South St
Galesburg, IL 61401
(309) 341-7208   Fax: (309) 341-7090
www.knox.edu/Academics/Courses-of-Study/Music.html
E-mail: bpolay@knox.edu

4 Year Institution

Chair: Bruce Polay, 80A
Dir., Artist Series: Nicole Malley, 80F

Inst	Clark, Amber L.	B	66A,66G,66B
PT	Clemens, Julie	M	36
PT	Cominskey, Millie M.	M	62B
PT	Cooksey, Denise		64A
PT	Crawford, Andy J.	B	70,47
Asst Prof	Day-O'Connell, Jeremy	D	13
Asst Prof	Day-O'Connell, Sarah K.	D	12,14,66A,66E
PT	Dillon, Jake R.		65
PT	Faust, Sharon K.	M	64B
PT	Filzen Etzel, Laurel Kay	M	63B,60B,37
PT	Filzen, Sherill	B	63B
PT	Fowler, Garold	B	62D
PT	Godsil, Dan	B	66A,48,49
PT	Harlan, Mary E.		66A
PT	Hart, Kevin M.	M	29B,53,66A,47,65
PT	Haynes, Justin	B	64E
PT	Hoffman, David	D	47,63A,66A
PT	Jackson, Steve	D	62D
PT	Kellert, Carolyn	M	32C,32D,61
Prof	Lane, Laura L.	D	12A,60,36,40,61
PT	Lewis, Gregory		61
PT	Lyle, Anne K.	M	64D
PT	Mack, Ashlee	B	66A
PT	Malley, Kevin J.	B	64E,47
Inst	Malley, Nicole	M	12A,20,47,29,31F
PT	Marassa, Jill	M	64C
Lect	Maxfield, Lynn M.	M	61
PT	McCord, Semenya	B	61
PT	Miller, John A.	M	47,70
PT	Mindemann, John	M	63C
Lect	Moran, Sarah E.		61
PT	Pahel, Tim A.	M	36,60
PT	Petrie, Dean	M	63D
PT	Pobanz, Randy F.	M	70
Prof	Polay, Bruce	D	10A,10F,12A,13B,60B
PT	Polay, Louise	B	62A
PT	Suda, Carolyn W.	M	11,42,51,62C
PT	Zeglis, Brian M.	M	65

IL1400 Lake Forest College
Department of Music
555 N Sheridan Rd
Lake Forest, IL 60045-2399
(847) 735-6147   Fax: (847) 735-6097
www.lakeforest.edu
E-mail: ksiebert@lakeforest.edu

4 Year Institution

Chair: Donald C. Meyer, 80A

Asst Prof	Amrein, Emilie	D	36,12A,13C,60,11
PT	Anno, Mariko	D	20C,64A
PT	Arden, Cynthia	M	62A
PT	Baur, James	M	70
Prof Emerita	Bowen, Ann D.	D	
PT	Bowers, Sally	B	64A
PT	Cox, Jim	M	62D
Asst Prof	Edgar, Scott N.	D	37,32,11,13A
PT	Faller, Richard	B	63D
PT	Gottlieb, Elizabeth	M	61
PT	Harvell, Matthew	B	64D
PT	Hoffman, David E.	M	61
PT	Knowles, Debbie	M	65,11
PT	Lee, Soo Young	D	66A
Prof Emerita	Levin, Rami Y.	D	13,11,38,10A
PT	Merva Robblee, Carolyn	M	64C
Assoc Prof	Meyer, Donald C.	PhD	13,12A,10,34
PT	Mosher, Ellen	M	66A
PT	Naito, Shoji	M	70
PT	Paliga, Mitchell L.	M	64E,47,29A

PT	Phillips, Christine	M	64B
PT	Puccini, Dorival	M	63A
PT	Ranieri, Anthony	B	66A
PT	Van De Graaff, Kathleen	M	61,39
Asst Prof	Wallin, Nicholas L.	D	38,13,11,20
PT	Webber, Sophie C.	D	62C,20,12A
PT	White, Christopher E.	D	66A
PT	Whitney, Valerie	M	63B

IL1500 Lewis and Clark Community College

Department of Music
5800 Godfrey Rd
Godfrey, IL 62035
(618) 468-4731   Fax: (618) 468-4707
www.lc.edu
E-mail: spstanard@lc.edu

2 Year Institution

Chair & Dir., Undergraduate Studies: Susan Parton-Stanard, 80A,80B,80F
Coord., Music Preparatory Division: Teresa Ann Crane, 80E

PT	Banks, Matthew	B	37
PT	Brame, Steven	B	63C,63D
PT	Brannan, Victoria	B	62
PT	Clemens, Peter	M	70
Asst Prof	Crane, Teresa Ann	D	66C,61,66,66A,11
PT	DeVaney, Fred	M	62D
PT	Dolbashian, Edward	M	38
PT	Drillinger, David	M	63
Asst Prof	Hussey, Peter	M	65,20,11,50,12A
PT	Jarden, Timothy	M	47,46
PT	Likes, Susan	B	64A
PT	Magurany, John	M	70
PT	Mattison, Travis	M	70,11,13A
PT	McHugh, Barbara	B	32A,36
Asst Prof	Michael, Louis	M	29,66A,13,11,34A
PT	Pancella, Peter	B	62A,62B,51
Asst Prof	Parton-Stanard, Susan	M	61,40,36,11,32D
PT	Schroeder, Waylon	B	64B,64E
PT	Shultz, Bud	M	64C,64E
PT	Stillwell, Roy	D	66G,66A,11
PT	Taylor, Mitchell	M	20,61,34B

IL1520 Lewis University

Department of Music
One University Pkwy
Romeoville, IL 60446
(815) 836-5619   Fax: (815) 836-5540
www.lewisu.edu
E-mail: siskla@lewisu.edu

4 Year Institution

Chair: Lawrence T. Sisk, 80A

Inst	Bennett, Cynthia	M	63A
Inst	Bowlby, Timothy	D	13,10
Inst	Brown, Zorriante	M	40
Inst	Drake, Thomas	M	37
Inst	Evans, Brett	M	63D
Inst	Ferraris, Robert		62D
Inst	Holst, Robert I.	D	12A,12,61
Inst	Jacobson, Steve	M	47,70
Inst	Lim, Christine	M	66A
Inst	Lowery, Christopher	M	14
Prof	McFerron, Mike	DMA	13A,13,10F,34,10
Inst	McGrath, Casey	M	62A,62B
Inst	Moore, Joel	M	64E,29A
Inst	O'Brien, Nancy		62E
Inst	Payne, Mary	M	64C
Inst	Peeples, Terrance P.	M	65,14C,11,50
Inst	Scherer, Paul	M	29B,66A
Prof	Sisk, Lawrence T.	D	38,12A,36,31A
Inst	Swearingen, Elaine	M	61
Inst	Tempas, Laurel	B	64A
Lect	Velazquez, Paulette	M	63B

IL1550 Lincoln Christian College

Department of Music
100 Campus View Dr
Lincoln, IL 62656-2111
(217) 732-3168 x 2254   Fax: (217) 732-1729
www.lincolnchristian.edu
E-mail: jcolleen@LincolnChristian.edu

4 Year Institution

Chair & Dir., Summer Programs: Jeffrey Colleen, 80A,80G

Assoc Prof	Allison, James	M	12A,61
Prof	Colleen, Jeffrey	M	13,10,36,66A,31A
Assoc Prof	Gaff, Isaac	M	34,13G,13,35C,35G
Assoc Prof	Jones, Sue	M	42,66A,66C,66D,13C
Inst PT	Storm, Linda	M	66A,66G,66B,44

IL1600 Lincoln College

Department of Music
300 Keokuk St
Lincoln, IL 62656
(217) 732-3155   Fax: (217) 732-3715
www.lincolncollege.edu
E-mail: ddietz@lincolncollege.edu

2 Year Institution

Chair, Fine Arts: Dan McLaughlin, 80A

Inst	Boehmke, Erik A.	M	63A,66,47,37,49
Inst	Dietz, Diane		61
	Woger, Scott	M	13,11,66A,47

IL1610 Lincoln Land Community College

Music Program
5250 Shepherd Rd
Springfield, IL 62794-9256
(217) 786-2240   Fax: (217) 786-2340
www.llcc.edu
E-mail: david.laubersheimer@llcc.edu

2 Year Institution

Dean, Arts & Humanities: David Laubersheimer, 80A

PT	Brazzel, Russell	M	70
PT	Calandrino, Jo		70
PT	Cohill, Gregory	M	64C,64E
PT	Ecklund, George	B	66A
PT	Edwards, Alice	M	66A,66G
PT	Edwards, Denise	M	13,66A
PT	Finn, Danielle	B	64A
PT	Greenwald, Fred	M	63A,63B,37
PT	Hamilton, Sue	M	61
Asst Prof	Hartman, Jane	M	13,11,66A,46,47
PT	Horvath, Maria	D	66A,66C,13,66D,11
PT	Kimball, Roger	B	64E,64C
Prof	Lanham, Barbara	M	13A,36,66A,66D
PT	Philbrick, Rebekah	B	63D
PT	Philbrick, Tom		61
PT	Pitt-Kaye, Melinda	M	61,11
PT	Pruitt, David	M	65
PT	Reichart, Alan	M	63C

IL1612 Lincoln Trail College

Department of Music
11220 State Highway 1
Robinson, IL 62454-5707
(618) 544-8657   Fax: (618) 544-3957
www.iecc.edu/ltc
E-mail: newliny@iecc.edu

2 Year Institution

Director, Performing Arts: Yvonne Newlin, 80A,80E

Inst PT	Brewer, Aaron	B	70
Inst PT	Downes, Greg	B	63
	Franklin, Jeshua	M	61,66D,10D
Inst PT	Harris, Brenda	M	66,32A
Inst PT	Hilderbrand, Monica	B	61,62

Inst PT	Miller, Becky	B	36,32B,32C
Inst FT	Newlin, Yvonne	M	13,60,37,66,47
Inst PT	Nichols, Sandra	M	11,32E,66A
Inst PT	Piersall, Janie	B	32A,32B,66A
Inst PT	Reedy, Hillary	B	32,65
Inst PT	Richardson, Tracy	M	33
Emeritus	Runyan, Donald	PhD	36,32D,61
Emerita	Shimeo, Barbara	B	61,36
Inst PT	Strieby, Ken	B	37,46
PT	Tracy, Gina	B	61
Inst PT	Wesley, Dee	B	66,32B

IL1615 Loyola University

Department of Fine Arts & Perf. Arts
6525 N Sheridan Rd
Chicago, IL 60626-5311
(773) 508-7510   Fax: (773) 508-7515
www.luc.edu/dfpa/index.html
E-mail: cjurgensmeier@luc.edu

4 Year Institution

PT	Asche, Kyle		42
PT	Burns, Scott	M	47
PT	Dillon, Robert		65
PT	DiOrio, Andrea		64C
FT	Garcia, Victor		63A
PT	Hedegaard, Kirsten		61,40
PT	Holman, Colin	D	38,12A
PT	Hwang, Christine	D	11,66D
FT	Kang, Haysun	D	11,66A,66D
PT	Koidin, Julie	D	64A
PT	Kornick, Rebecca	D	13
	LeClair, Benjamin		61
FT	Leone, Gustavo	D	10,13
PT	Lowe, Frederick W.	D	37,46
PT	McHugh, Kelli M.		61
FT	Molinaro, Anthony G.	M	66A,29,13A,13B,13D
PT	Smith, Cameron		66A
PT	Suvada, Steve	M	70
PT	Xu, MingHuan		42

IL1650 MacMurray College

Department of Music
447 East College Ave
Jacksonville, IL 62650
(217) 479-7000   Fax: (217) 479-7078
www.mac.edu
E-mail: laurie.lewis@mac.edu

4 Year Institution

Chair: Jay Peterson, 80A

Inst PT	Benz, Terri	B	61,66A,36
Inst PT	Lyon, Kristine	D	61,66A
Prof Emeritus	Peterson, Jay	D	13,12A,14,66A,66G

IL1740 McKendree University

Department of Music
701 College Rd
Lebanon, IL 62254-1212
(618) 537-6922   Fax: (618) 537-6570
www.mckendree.edu
E-mail: nypma@mckendree.edu

4 Year Liberal Arts Institution

Dean: Christine Bahr, 80A
Head of Music: Nancy S. Ypma, 80A

PT	Allen, Greg	M	32E
PT	Aymer, Justin	M	35C,35D
Inst	Boggs, David G.	M	37,32E,60B
PT	Brewer, Curt	M	70
PT	Byrkit, Douglas	M	62D
PT	Connor, Mark	D	13
PT	Dugger, Clay	M	32E
PT	Favazza, Kathleen	M	61,20
PT	Fisher, Yuko	M	62A,62B,62C,41
PT	Galbraith, Connie	B	64C,42
PT	Gartley, Jennifer	D	64A
PT	Groome, Frank	M	63B
PT	Gustafson-Hinds, Melissa	D	64B
PT	Harres, Debra	M	61
PT	Hettenhausen, Amy	M	32E

PT	Kim, Soyeon	M	66
PT	Mandel, Nathan	D	64E
PT	Marble, Troy	M	63D
Inst	Mayhue, Terence C.	M	47,65
PT	Miller, Heather	M	66,13A
PT	Newman, Jill	M	35A
PT	Peterson, Ben	M	63A
PT	Smith, Dean W.	M	63C
PT	Washburn, Rodney	B	32E
Asst Prof	Wilhelm, Philip	D	64D,32,40,11
Prof	Ypma, Nancy S.	D	12A,36,66G

IL1750 Millikin University

School of Music
1184 W Main St
Decatur, IL 62522-2039
(217) 424-6300   Fax: (217) 420-6652
www.millikin.edu/music
E-mail: swidenhofer@millikin.edu

4 Year Institution
Member of NASM

Director & Dir., Preparatory Division: Stephen B. Widenhofer, 80A,80E

Assoc Prof Adj	Baer, Solomon	D	64C
	Baird, John	B	66F
	Beck, Chuck	B	66F
Adj Asst Prof	Borders, Ann	M	61
Lect	Brunk, Jeremy	M	13,12,65,10
Assoc Prof	Burdick, David H.	D	10,13,34,70,35
Assoc Prof	Carberg, Daniel J.	D	61,55B
Asst Prof Adj	Choi, Chee Hyeong	D	66D
Asst Prof Adj	Chung, Sharon	M	62B
Assoc Prof Adj	Cobb, Susan	D	66A,66B,66D
Inst Adj	Creighton, Elizabeth	B	66C
Asst Prof Adj	Daniels, Frances	M	61
Asst Prof	Dean, Ronnie	B	35C,35D
Adj Asst Prof	Flores, Amy	M	41,62C
Assoc Prof	Forbes, Guy	PhD	32,36
Prof Adj	Gibbons, Bruce L.	D	66A,66C
Assoc Prof	Gibbons, Helen	D	13,61
Assoc Prof	Glencross, Laurie A.	D	13,41,64A
Lect	Hesse, Ted	M	13,36,61
Prof	Holmes, Brad	D	60,32C,36
Asst Prof Adj	Holmes, Elizabeth	M	36,61
Prof	Hornbacker, Georgia	M	62A
Assoc Prof Adj	Huff, Sharon	D	63D,32E
Inst Adj	Jang, Hue Jeong	D	66D
Assoc Prof	Justison, Brian	M	29A,50,65
Inst Adj	Krolikowski, Lucas	B	41,70
Asst Prof Adj	Leese, Matthew	D	61
Artist in Res	Long, Kevin	M	54,13
Prof	Luxner, Michael	PhD	13,38
Asst Prof	Mallard, Manley	M	41,70,34
Assoc Prof Adj	Mancinelli, Judith	M	66A,66C
Inst Adj	Morgan, Nicole	M	61
Prof	Nicholson, Tina	M	13,64B
Lect	Oeck, Cynthia	M	61
Inst Adj	Pope, Andrea	M	61
Asst Prof Adj	Rai, Diana	M	62D
Assoc Prof	Rask, Perry J.	D	47,64E,29
Assoc Prof	Reyman, Randall	M	47,63A,53,29
Inst Adj	Robertson, Christine	M	61
Inst Adj	Schaller, Edward	M	62D
Asst Prof Adj	Schepper, Stephen	D	63B
Inst Adj	Sepulveda, Richardo	M	61
Prof	Shaw, Gary R.	D	10F,60,37,63C
Inst Adj	Shoemaker, Elizabeth	D	64
Assoc Prof	Smith, Neal	D	32E,37,32C,13
Asst Prof	Stimeling, Travis D.	D	12,63D,12D,14
Lect	Stone, Terry	M	61,39
Inst	Talbott, Matthew	M	35
Asst Prof	Tu, Ming	D	32A,32B
Asst Prof Adj	Van der Loo, Marion	M	61
Prof	Widenhofer, Stephen B.	D	47,35A
Assoc Prof Adj	Yadeau, Lois J.	M	61
Assoc Prof	YaDeau, William Ronald	D	13,66A,66D

IL1800 Monmouth College
Department of Music
700 E Broadway
Monmouth, IL 61462-1963
(309) 457-2382   Fax: (309) 457-2310
department.monm.edu/music/default.htm
E-mail: betts@monmouthcollege.edu

4 Year Liberal Arts Institution

Chair: James E. Betts, 80A

Lect	Alderson, Erin	M	11,13A,32E,37,64
Prof	Betts, James E.	D	13,20,29A,63,34
PT	Debes, Pier	B	36
PT	Godsil, Daniel	B	66A,66D
PT	Jackson, Stephen	D	47,62D
PT	Mendoza, Juan Carlos	M	61
PT	Meuth, Alison	B	61
Assoc Prof	Moschenross, Ian	D	12A,13E,20,66A,66G
Asst Prof	Pahel, Timothy	M	32,36,61,12A
Lect	Suda, Carolyn	M	11,12A,62C,38,42
PT	Suda, David	D	62A
PT	Wanken, Matthew	M	37
PT	Zeglis, Brian	M	65

IL1850 Moody Bible Institute
Department of Music
820 N La Salle Blvd
Chicago, IL 60610-3214
(312) 329-4080   Fax: (312) 329-4098
www.moody.edu
E-mail: cynthia.uitermarkt@moody.edu

4 Year Institution
Member of NASM

Chair: Cynthia D. Uitermarkt, 80A

Inst PT	Bailey, Marie	M	61
Inst PT	Dahman, Jamie	D	61
Inst PT	Fackler, Dan	B	63B
Prof	Gauger, David	M	37,38,45,63A
Inst PT	Hassler, Desiree	D	61
Inst	Hong, Xiangtang	M	60A,31A,36,44,11
Asst Prof	Jang, Jae Hyeok	D	13,10,31A
Asst Prof	Jennings, Jori Johnson	D	61,32B
Inst PT	Kellogg, Lydia	M	66A
Inst PT	Kellogg, Robbie	M	70
Assoc Prof	Lee, Brian	D	66A,11
Assoc Prof	Lynerd, Betty Ann	D	31A,44,36
Inst PT	Mattix, Daniel J.	M	11
Prof	Naegele, Elizabeth M.	D	13A,13,66A,66G,11
Prof	Rownd, Gary	D	13A,66A,66D,11
Prof	Singley, H. E.	D	66A,66G,11,36,31A
Inst PT	Stafford, Timothy	M	60A,11
Prof	Strandt, Terry W.	D	12A,61,29
Prof	Uitermarkt, Cynthia D.	D	13A,13,66A,31A
Prof	Whang, Un-Young	D	13,66A,66B

IL1890 Moraine Valley Community College
Department of Fine Arts
10900 S 88th Ave
Palos Hills, IL 60465-2175
(708) 974-5215   Fax: (708) 974-5366
www.morainevalley.edu
E-mail: thomasn@morainevalley.edu

2 Year Institution

Coordinator: Nicholas Thomas, 80A

PT	Becker-Billie, Elisa	D	61
PT	Bratt, Douglass F.	M	50,47,65A,65B,46
PT	Broderick, Daniela C.	M	11,66A,66D
PT	Burns, Timothy	B	70,47
PT	Carlson, Tammi	M	13F,11,64A
PT	Dorris, Dennis	M	66A
PT	Forlenza, Ray	M	37
PT	Gerrish, June	M	66A,11
PT	Goldberg, Julie	D	70
PT	Hearne, Clarice	M	61
PT	Holt, Beverly	B	66A,66G,66C
PT	Kaminski, Imelda	M	62A,51
PT	Kelly, Linda	M	70
PT	Koranda, Ann	M	66A,66G,66C
PT	Mallady, Joan	M	66A,66D
PT	Norton, John	M	64C,11
PT	Picard, Annie	D	61
PT	Ray, Jeff	B	61
FT	Reifsnyder, Robert	D	11
PT	Shaw, Kimberly	M	64E
FT	Thomas, Nicholas	M	60A,66D,13A,36,61
PT	Thornton, Jim	M	66A,66D
PT	Tumino, Joe	M	63D,11
PT	Vaughn, Jeanne	B	61
PT	Wieneke, Erin	M	61

IL1900 Morton College
Department of Music
3801 S Central Ave
Cicero, IL 60804-4306
(708) 656-8000 x2231   Fax: (708) 656-3297
www.morton.edu
E-mail: John.Warren@morton.edu

2 Year Institution

Music Contact: John Warren, 80A

Inst PT	Asche, Kyle	M	70
Inst PT	Fagerberg, Kaj	M	63C,63D
Inst PT	Hutchinson, Raymond	M	66A,63A,63B,11
Inst PT	Knickerbocker, Sharon	M	66A,66B,66C,66D
Inst PT	Kukec, Catherine	B	11,41,47,50,48
Emeritus	Kukec, Paul E.	M	13A,13,12A,36,66A
Inst PT	Lauer, Eileen	M	61,11,20
Inst PT	Maxfield, Jessica	DMA	64A,64C,64E
Inst PT	Pidluski, Eric	M	62A,62B
Inst PT	Policastro, Joseph	M	62D
Inst PT	Roman, Brent	B	65A,65B
Inst PT	Sterba, Lydia	M	66A
Inst PT	Tu, Gary	B	70
Inst FT	Warren, John	M	36,11,12A,13B,13C
Inst PT	Watson, Rita	M	61,66A

IL2000 National-Louis University
Department of Music
5202 Old Orchard Rd
Suite 300
Skokie, IL 60077-4409
(847) 256-5150   Fax: (847) 256-1057
www.nl.edu
E-mail: EOlin@nl.edu

4 Year Institution

Chair: Elinor Olin, 80A

Assoc Prof	Olin, Elinor	D	11,12A,12,64A
Inst PT	Tyler, Paul	D	14,20
Inst PT	Vaughn, Michael	D	12A,12,32A,66A

IL2050 North Central College
Department of Music
30 North Brainard St
Naperville, IL 60540-4607
(630) 637-5372   Fax: (630) 637-5140
northcentralcollege.edu/
E-mail: rmwis@noctrl.edu

4 Year Institution

Chair: Ramona M. Wis, 80A
Dir., Preparatory Division: Ann Waldron, 80E

Inst PT	Adams, Joel	B	46,63C
Inst PT	Bennett, Marie Micol	M	64A,48,41,13A,42
Inst PT	Blanchet, George A.	B	65
Inst PT	Borla, Janice	B	53,29,29A,29B
Inst PT	Christian, Kathy P.	M	66A
Inst PT	Cox, James	B	47,62D
Inst PT	Davis, Art	M	63A,14,29A,29B
Inst PT	DiOrio, Andrea R.	M	64C,11,42,43
Inst PT	Dunafin, Cathy A.	M	32
Inst PT	Dymit, Thomas E.	B	61
Inst PT	French, Chelsea	M	63C,63D
Inst PT	Gallagher, Mara	B	62A,51
Inst PT	Gildow, Kurtis C.	M	63D
Inst PT	Grant, David	D	13C
Inst PT	Grives, Julie	M	39,61

Directory of Institutions — Page 137

Inst PT	Grizzell, Paul W.	M	61
Inst PT	Hemenway, Langston	D	11,32E,37,41
Asst Prof	Kirk, Jonathon J.	D	13,10,20,34
Inst PT	Korbitz, Angela Presutti	M	61
Inst PT	Langenberg, Claire Coyle	M	62C
Inst PT	Lowry, Paul	M	63A
Inst PT	Luchs, Nicole	M	62E
Prof	Martinez, Jeordano S.	M	12A,36,39,54,38
Inst PT	McLean, John T.	M	70,29,53
Inst PT	Mielcarz, Kelly	B	32,32D
Inst PT	Miller, Jeremy	B	62D
Adj Inst	Mouse, Eugene	B	53,47,29A,29B
Inst PT	O'Connell, Daniel P.	M	63B
Adj Assoc Prof	Ogden Hagen, Linda	M	61
Inst PT	Paliga, Mitch L.	M	64E,29A,41,47,48
Inst PT	Richter, Kimberlie J.	M	13A,61,64E,29
Inst PT	Schopp, James A.	D	61
Inst PT	Schutt, Jackie T.	M	32,13C,36
Inst PT	Stirtz, Bradley	M	65B
Prof	Van Oyen, Lawrence G.	D	13,64E,37
Adj Asst Prof	Vanderwall, Barbara S.	M	66A
Inst PT	VerHoven, Victoria	M	61
Inst PT	Wahlund, Ben	M	65
Inst PT	Waldron, Ann	M	66A,66B
Inst PT	Warfel, Jon R.	M	66C
Inst PT	White, Chris	D	66A,13F,29A,29B,29C
Prof	Wis, Ramona M.	D	60A,42,32D,36
Inst PT	Wlazlo, Tricia L.	M	64B

IL2100 North Park University
School of Music
3225 W Foster Ave
Chicago, IL 60625-4810
(773) 244-5623   Fax: (773) 279-7310
www.northpark.edu/music
E-mail: rolthafer@northpark.edu

4 Year Institution, Graduate School
Member of NASM

Master of Music in Collaborative Piano, Master of Music in Performance

Chair: Craig R. Johnson, 80A
Dir., Operations: Rebecca Olthafer, 80D
Dir., Events/Communications: Karen Dickelman, 80F
Dir., Summer Programs: Joseph Lill, 80G

Inst PT	Anderson, Collin	D	64D
Inst PT	Anderson, Elizabeth	M	62C
Inst PT	Basney, Nyela	M	39
Prof	Bauer, Karen	D	61
Inst PT	Bensdorf, Naomi	M	64B
Inst PT	Bentley, Julia	M	12A,12C
Inst PT	Bershad, Kara	M	62E
Emeritus	Burswold, Lee	D	
	Byrd-Anderson, Shelley	B	66F
Inst PT	Coleman-Evans, Felicia	M	61,40
Inst PT	Condon, Clay	M	65
Assoc Prof	Davids, Julia L.	D	36,40
Inst PT	Eckhardt, Janet	M	66A,66D
Inst PT	Goldberg, Julie	D	70,41
Inst PT	Gratteau, Phil	M	65
Inst PT	Holman, Colin	D	12A
Assoc Prof	Hudgens, Helen	D	13,31,12A
Inst PT	Huntington, Ellen	D	64A
Inst PT	Jefferson, Thomas	D	66A,66D
Prof	Johnson, Craig R.	D	13C
Inst PT	Kelly, Stephen	B	36,66A
Inst PT	Koeller, David	D	20
Inst PT	Kosower, Paula	D	62C
Inst PT	Kotze, Michael	M	39
Inst PT	Krause, Philip	D	39,12C
Inst PT	Lahti, Carol	M	62A
Inst PT	Langenberg, Kelly	M	63B
Inst PT	Lasareff-Mirinoff, Claudia	M	41,42
Inst PT	Lawson, Peter K.	M	62D
Assoc Prof	Lill, Joseph	D	47,49,63A,37,42
Inst PT	Lill, Michael	B	65
Inst PT	MacAyeal, Gregory	M	12C
Inst PT	McBride, Michael S.	D	10,34,13,31,12A
Inst PT	Morrison, Audrey	M	63C,63D
Inst PT	Nelson, Leon	M	66G
Inst PT	Offard, Felton	M	70
Asst Prof	Olthafer, Rebecca	D	11
Inst PT	Picard, Annie	D	61
Inst PT	Pikler, Charles	B	62A,51,42,62B
Inst PT	Ray, Jeffrey	M	61
Inst PT	Scharf, Scott L.	M	13
Prof	Shofner-Emrich, Terree	D	66A,39,66B,66C,66D
Inst PT	Tenegal, George	M	66C
Inst PT	Toyonaga, Shiho	M	62B,51
Inst PT	Tropp, Thomas	M	36
Inst PT	Watkins, Ron	B	61
Inst PT	White, Christopher	D	66A
Inst PT	Wilder, Ralph	M	64C,32E,64E,11,42
Inst PT	Yonan, David	M	62A,62B
Prof	Zelle, Tom	D	60B,38

IL2150 Northeastern Illinois University
Department of Music
5500 N St Louis Ave
Chicago, IL 60625-4625
(773) 442-5900   Fax: (773) 442-5910
ww.neiu.edu
E-mail: r-shaynecofer@neiu.edu

4 Year Institution, Graduate School

Master of Arts in Music, Master of Arts in Music Education, Master of Arts in Pedagogy

Chair: R. Shayne Cofer, 80A
Coord., Graduate Studies & Asst. Chair: Phyllis A. Hurt, 80C,80H

Prof Emeritus	Anderson, Charles A.	D	66A
PT	Anderson, Collin J.	D	64D
PT	Bulmer, Jared S.	M	63D
Lect	Burton, Rachel Anne	M	52
Prof	Chang, Peter M.	D	11,14,12,42
Prof	Cofer, R. Shayne	D	32,37,49
Prof Emeritus	Combs, Ronald	D	39,61
Lect	Condon, Clay	M	65,50,11
PT	Cowan, Kathryn Jean	M	61,11
PT	Dzhuryn, Nazar V.	M	62C
PT	Farrell, Jamie	M	52
Lect	Gerritson, Sasha L.	M	11,13C,39,13A
PT	Gorgojo, Jamie	M	62A,62B
Lect	Groner, Brian	M	62A,38
	Gurin, Shelley Foster	D	13A,32E
Asst Prof	Heath, Travis M.	D	49,63A
PT	Hibbard, Sarah	D	11
Prof	Hurt, Phyllis A.	D	12A,61,54
PT	Keys, Keven	M	61
PT	Kim, Kay	D	66C
Prof	Komaiko, Libby A.	B	52
PT	Kowalkowski, Jeffrey F.	D	11
PT	Leifer, Lyon	M	64A
PT	Linsner, Arthur F.	M	63C
Prof Emeritus	Lucas, James A.	D	11
Prof	Mach, Elyse J.	D	11,66D,66B
Assoc Prof	Mandrell, Nelson E.	D	13,10,45,34
PT	Mayne, Anna	M	63B
Lect	Melton, Michael D.	M	36,40,32D,61,60A
PT	Myintoo, Sylvia C.	M	62A,11
Asst Prof	Owen, Christopher S.	D	36,32D
PT	Reminick, David M.	M	64E
Lect	Ruiz, Irma	B	52
PT	Sarchet, Gregory B.	B	62D
Lect	Snow, Lydia F.	M	32B,20
Prof Emeritus	Speake, Constance J.	D	11,32
Asst Prof	Sperrazza, Rose U.	D	64C,48,13H
Prof	Stifler, Venetia C.	D	52
Asst Prof	Tang, Susan	D	66A
PT	Teruel, Hugo	M	11
Lect	Tiana, Mayo	M	29,46,47,10F
Lect	Torosian, Brian L.	D	70,11,13H
PT	Weber, Angela	M	11

IL2200 Northern Illinois University
School of Music
Music Bldg 140
1425 W Lincoln Highway
De Kalb, IL 60115-2828
(815) 753-1551   Fax: (815) 753-1759
www.niu.edu/music
E-mail: paulbauer@niu.edu

4 Year Institution, Graduate School
Member of NASM

Graduate Certificate in Performance, Master of Music in Performance, Master of Music in Music Education, Master of Music Individual Studies

Director: Paul D. Bauer, 80A
Assistant Director & Dir., Graduate Studies: Janet J. Hathaway, 80C,80H

Assoc Prof	Arania, Orna	D	61
Prof	Barrett, Gregory M.	D	48,64C
Prof	Bauer, Paul D.	D	49,63C
Assoc Prof	Beyer, Gregory S.	D	50,65
Assoc Prof	Bough, Thomas	D	37
Asst Prof	Bradfield, Geoffrey	M	64E,29

Prof	Carter, Ronald	M	47,29
Applied Artist	Castaneda, J. Ricardo	M	64B
Prof Emeritus	Chappell, Robert	M	20B,29
Assoc Prof	Cosenza, Glenda L.	D	32
Applied Artist	Davis, Art	M	63A,29
Asst Prof	Devroye, Anthony	M	62B,51
Assoc Prof	Doherty, Mary Lynn	D	32
Prof Emeritus	Fairfield, John	M	11,63B
Prof	Fleisher, Robert J.	D	13,10
Applied Artist	Floeter, John	B	62D
Applied Artist	Garling, Tom	M	29,63C
Prof	Goldenberg, William	D	66A,66C,41
Inst	Griffin, Jennifer J.	M	11,61
Assoc Prof	Haque, Fareed	B	70,53,29
Prof	Hart, Brian J.	D	12A,12
Assoc Prof	Hathaway, Janet J.	D	12A,55,67,12C
Inst	Hatmaker, J. E.	D	13,10
Prof	Holly, Richard	M	50,65,29
Prof	Johnson, Eric	D	60,36
Assoc Prof	Kim, JeongSoo	D	66A,66B
Assoc Prof	Klonoski, Edward	D	13
Prof Emeritus	Koehler, William	D	66A,66C
Asst Prof	Lee, Cheng-Hou	M	62C,51
Asst Prof	Magniere, Blaise	M	62A,51
Assoc Prof	Maki, David J.	D	13
Asst Prof	Matos, Lucia Regina	D	38,39,60B,66G,66H
Prof	Middleton, Peter	M	45,64A,34,35C,13L
Applied Artist	Moeller, Jeremy	M	63C
Applied Artist	Montzka, Ann	M	62A,62B
Applied Artist	Moore, Rich	M	64E,29
Prof	Myers, Myron	M	39,61
Assoc Prof	Novak, John K.	D	13
Applied Artist	Perrella, Anthony	M	39
Assoc Prof	Phelps, James	D	10,45,34
Applied Artist	Pickens, Willie	B	66A,29
Prof	Ponzo, Mark	D	49,63A
Prof Emerita	Ragains, Diane	M	61
Applied Artist	Rhodes, Amy Patricia	M	64D
Assoc Prof PT	Schuchat, Charles	B	63D,49
Applied Artist	Sill, Kelly	B	62D,29
Prof	Sims, Robert	M	61
Applied Artist	Smelser, Linc	M	62C
Prof	Tacke, Mathias	DIPL	62A
Assoc Prof	Teague, Liam	M	20H
Assoc Prof	Villanueva, Rodrigo	M	29,47
Asst Prof	Wang, Jui-Ching	D	32,20
Asst Prof	Wang, Marie	M	62A,51
Prof	Wooten, Ronnie	D	32,37

IL2250 Northwestern University

Bienen School of Music
711 Elgin Rd
Evanston, IL 60208-1200
(847) 491-7575   Fax: (847) 491-5260
www.music.northwestern.edu
E-mail: musiclife@northwestern.edu

4 Year Institution, Graduate School
Member of NASM

Graduate Certificate in Performance, Master of Music in Music Theory, Master of Music in Performance, Master of Music in Conducting, Master of Music in Music Education, Master of Music in Musicology, Master of Music in Music Ed. & Piano Pedagogy, Master of Music in Music Ed. & String Pedagogy, Master of Music in Piano Performance & Collaborative Arts, Master of Music in String Performance & Pedagogy, PhD in Music Education, Doctor of Music in Composition, Doctor of Music in Conducting, Doctor of Music in Piano Performance & Collaborative Arts, PhD in Music Theory & Cognition, Doctor of Music in Piano Performance & Pedagogy, PhD in Musicology, Doctor of Music in Conducting, Doctor of Music in Performance, Master of Music in Jazz Pedagogy, Master of Music in Piano Pedagogy & Performance

Dean: Toni-Marie Montgomery, 80A
Assistant Dean, Academic Affairs & Graduate Studies: Stephen Hill, 80C
Assistant Dean, Admission & Student Affairs: Linda Garton, 80D,80B,80C
Director of Admissions: Ryan O'Mealey, 80D
Associate Dean, Administration & Finance: Rene E. Machado, 80H

Senior Lect	Alltop, Stephen W.	D	60,38
Lect	Almond, Frank	M	62A
Lect	Alvarez, Ruben		65
Assoc Prof	Ashley, Richard	D	13,10,29
Assoc Prof	Austern, Linda	D	12
Lect	Barnewitz, William		63B,42
Assoc Prof	Barrett, Janet R.	D	32
Lect	Barston, Gilda R.		62
Prof	Bauman, Thomas	D	12
Lect	Bennett, Rebecca K.	PhD	12A
Lect PT	Bloom, J. Lawrie	M	64C
Lect	Boen, Jonathan C.	M	63B
Senior Lect	Boldrey, Richard L.	B	61
Assoc Prof	Bosits, Marcia L.	D	66A,66D
Lect	Boyd, Bob		32D
Assoc Prof	Brunssen, Karen	B	61
Senior Lect	Buccheri, Elizabeth	D	66B
Prof	Butler, Barbara	B	63A,49
Assoc Prof	Butler, Mark J.	PhD	13
Asst Prof	Byros, Vasili	PhD	13
Assoc Prof	Chow, Alan	M	66A
Lect PT	Cifani, Elizabeth	M	62E,51
Assoc Prof	Cohen, Steven	B	64C
Lect PT	Darling, Alan T.	M	66A
Lect	Davies, Drew Edward		12A
Lect	Davis, Caroline	PhD	13C
Lect PT	Dawson, Julian S.	DIPL	66A
Prof	Dobroski, Bernard J.	D	32H,63D,32,60,35E
Senior Lect	D'Ortenzio, Marie Michuda	M	54
Lect PT	Drews, Richard	M	39,61
Senior Lect	Farris, Daniel J.	M	47,37,60B,60
Senior Lect	Foster, Melissa		61
Prof	Geyer, Charles	M	63A,49
Asst Prof	Giles, James	D	66A
Assoc Prof	Gjerdingen, Robert	D	13,13J,20G
Prof	Goines, Victor L.	M	47,64E
Lect	Goll-Wilson, Kathleen		32E
Lect PT	Graef, Richard	M	64A
Lect PT	Grimm, Leslie	M	64C
Asst Prof	Hall, Bruce	M	61,36,40
Adj Asst Prof	Hall, Sunny Joy Langton	B	61
Lect	Hanford, Robert A.		62A
Senior Lect	Hansen, Kurt R.	M	61,54
Lect	Hansen, Theresa Brancaccio	M	61
Prof	Harris, Robert A.	D	60,36
Lect	Hasty, Robert G.	D	41,38
Lect	Hawes, Randell D.	M	63C
Prof	Hemke, Frederick	D	64E
Lect PT	Henes, John	B	
Lect PT	Henoch, Michael L.		64B
Lect	Henriquez, Carlos G.		47
Asst Prof	Hickey, Maud	D	32
Assoc Prof	Hinchman, Pamela	M	61
Lect	Hostetler, Scott	M	64
Lect	Hsiao, Annie C.	D	66A
Prof	Hyla, Lee	M	10
Lect	Jenkins, Jennifer R.	D	12A
Prof	Jensen, Hans Jorgen	DIPL	62C
Lect	Jones, Willie		65
Lect PT	Kan-Walsh, Karen	D	66D
Assoc Prof Adj	Kemper, Margaret M.	M	66G,31A
Lect	Keys, Kevin M.	M	11
Lect	Kirk, Lewis	B	64D
Assoc Prof	Kjelland, James	D	60,32C,38,62
Lect	Kosower, Paula	M	62C
Lect	Kraus, Philip	D	39
Prof PT	Kujala, Walfrid	M	64A
Prof	Lesenger, Jay	M	39
Senior Lect	Lyashenko, Natalia E.	D	11
Lect	Madsen, Christopher	DIPL	47
Lect	Martin, Chris		42
Lect	Martin, Peter H.	M	32E
Prof	Martin, Rex	M	63D,49
Lect	Mason, Elliot J.	B	47
Lect	Mercer, Christopher A.	D	34A,34D
Lect	Millard, Christopher		41
Asst Prof PT	Milton, Blair	M	62A
Lect	Molenaar, Mary Beth	D	66B
Lect	Morgan, Robert	C	42
Lect	Mosbey, Jerad M.	M	66C
Lect	Moulder, John P.	M	29,70
Prof PT	Mulcahy, Michael	DIPL	63C
Asst Prof	Naroditskaya, Inna	D	12
Assoc Prof Emeritus	Ockwell, Frederick	M	60,39,54
Lect	Osborn, Susan R.	D	66D
Lect PT	Pegis, John		62C
Lect	Philbrick, Channing	M	41
Senior Lect	Piagentini, Susan M.	PhD	13C,13H,13K,13
Lect	Pikler, Charles		41
Lect PT	Raimi, Max		41
Lect	Reinhart, Robert A.	M	13A
Prof	Ribeiro, Gerardo	DIPL	62A
Lect	Robblee, Timothy	D	37,47,32E
Senior Lect	Rosenberg, Jesse	D	12
Lect	Rosenberg, Marlene	M	62D
Lect PT	Ross, James R.	M	65
Lect	Shapiro, Gail S.	M	39
Lect	Smith, Kenneth	M	61
Lect PT	Spencer, Stacia C.		32B,62A,62B
Lect	Sugihara, Masahito	D	64E
Lect	Tacke, Mathias	M	42
Lect	Tejada, Rob		32E
Asst Prof	Thomalla, Hans Christian	D	10
Prof	Thompson, Mallory	D	60,37
Prof	Vamos, Almita	D	62A
Prof	Vamos, Roland	D	62B
Senior Lect	Waller, Anne	M	70
Assoc Prof	Wang, Sylvia	D	66,41
Prof	Webster, Peter R.	D	32
Lect	Weller, Amy G.	D	60A
Prof	Williams, Gail	M	63B
Lect	Wint, Suzanne	M	20
Assoc Prof	Wu, She-e	M	65

Prof	Yampolsky, Victor	DIPL	38,60
Assoc Prof	Yim, Jay Alan	D	13,10
Lect	Yoo, Soyeon Park	D	66A
Lect	Young, Susan	C	32D

IL2300 Olivet Nazarene University
Department of Music
One University Ave
Bourbonnais, IL 60914
(815) 939-5110   Fax: (815) 939-5112
music.olivet.edu
E-mail: dreddick@olivet.edu

4 Year Institution
Member of NASM

Chair: Don Reddick, 80A

Prof	Anderson, H. Gerald	D	66A,66C,66D,12A
Prof	Ball, Karen	D	10A,66A,66B,13B,13C
Adj	Barnlund, Anna	M	61
Prof	Bell, Jeff	D	36,61,54,60
Adj	Benson, Katherine	M	64A,41,44
Adj	Comer, Sonya	B	66A
Assoc Prof	Dalton, Martha	M	36,61
Adj	Franken, Fred	M	70
Adj	Hopkins, Harlow	D	64C
Adj	Jacklin, Matt	D	65,50
Adj	Jacklin, Rachel	M	62A,62B
Adj	Luzeniecki, Jerry	M	64E
Adj	Lynch, Charles	D	62E
Adj	Marcotte, Tracy	B	64C
Adj	McMichael, Stacy	M	62D
Prof	McMullian, Neal	D	13B,32E,64D,60,37
Prof	Nelson, Timothy	D	13,10F,66A,66G
Adj	Poquette, Linda	B	66A
Prof	Reddick, Don	D	32E,46,34,13A
Adj	Reichenbach, Brian	M	63A
	Schmalzbauer, Julie A.	D	64B
Asst Prof	Schultz, Ryan	B	37,63C,36
Adj	Semmes, Carol	M	62C
Adj	Tung, Margaret M.	D	63B
Adj	Welch, Kay	M	61
Adj	Williams, Heather	B	66A
Prof	Woodruff, Neal	D	60,36,38,61,12A
Artist in Res	Young, Ovid	M	66A,66C,10A

IL2310 Olney Central College
Music Program
305 Northwest St
Olney, IL 62450-1043
(618) 395-7777   Fax: (618) 392-3293
www.iecc.edu
E-mail: downess@iecc.edu

2 Year Institution

Music Contact: Suzanne Downes, 80A
Dean: Kristi Urfer, 80A

FT	Downes, Suzanne	M	66D,47,11,37,65
PT	Henry, Ruth	DIPL	61,66A,54
PT	Michels, Joyce	B	62

IL2350 Parkland College
Department of Music
2400 W Bradley Ave
Champaign, IL 61821-1806
(217) 351-2392   Fax: (217) 373-3899
www.parkland.edu
E-mail: tschirmer@parkland.edu

2 Year Institution

Chair, Music: Timothy Schirmer, 80A
Chair, Fine & Applied Arts: Barbara Wilson, 80A
Dir., Artist/Performance Series: Randi Hard, 80F

PT	Engberg, Kristina L.	M	66D,11,13,34B
PT	Hart, Kevin	D	47,65
PT	Hutchens, John	M	47,64
PT	Kaye, Jordan	B	70
PT	Koblyakov, Lev	D	13,12A,34B
PT	Marshall, Jeffrey	M	37,41
PT	Parkhurst, Raymond	M	11
PT	Ranney, Jack	M	38,51,62
Prof	Roubal, Peter	D	13,10,34B,47
PT	Rubel, Mark	B	45,35C,35D
Prof	Schirmer, Timothy	D	13,10,34B,54
PT	Trauth, Vincent	M	66D,11
PT	Zachow, Barbara	M	36,20G

IL2400 Principia College
Department of Music
1 Maybeck Place
Elsah, IL 62028-9720
(618) 374-5009   Fax: (618) 374-5911
www.prin.edu/college/academics/departments/
   music/index.htm
E-mail: jim.hegarty@prin.edu

4 Year Institution

Dir., Summer Programs & Artist Series: Marie Jureit-Beamish, 80F,80G
Chair: James Hegarty

Assoc Prof	Hegarty, James	M	10A,29A,34D,47,13A
Prof	Jureit-Beamish, Marie	D	38,64A,66A,10F,11
Prof	Near, John R.	D	11,12A,12C,66G
Asst Prof	Parker, Laura M.	M	13A,41,42,62A,66A
Prof Emerita	Rockabrand, Sarah	M	36,61,60A

IL2450 Quincy University
Div. of Fine Arts & Communication
1800 College Ave
Quincy, IL 62301-2699
(217) 228-5203   Fax: (217) 228-5257
www.quincy.edu
E-mail: bschlepp@quincy.edu

4 Year Institution

Dean: Barbara Schleppenbach, 80A

Artist in Res	Gehrich, Leonora S.	M	66A,66C,66D
Lect PT	Machold, William	M	65
Prof	Margaglione, Louis A.	M	64,13A,13C,11
Vstng Asst Prof	Means, Allen	M	36,61,63D,63C
Artist in Res	Parke, Steve	M	10,47,63A,29A,35A
Vstng Asst Prof	Stollberg, Amy	M	61

IL2500 Rend Lake College
Department of Music
468 N Ken Gray Pkwy
Ina, IL 62846
(618) 437-5321   Fax: (618) 437-5677
www.rlc.edu
E-mail: alstats@rlc.edu

2 Year Institution

Music Contact: Sara Alstat, 80A

Assoc Prof	Alstat, Sara	M	11,13A,13C,36,61
Adj	Gibbs, Brett	M	61,13
Adj	Mikulay, Mark	M	37,66A
Adj	Phifer, Larry	M	11
Adj	Williamson, Amber		11

IL2510 Richland Community College
Department of Music
1 College Park
Decatur, IL 62521-8512
(217) 875-7200 x 342   Fax: (217) 875-6961
www.richland.edu
E-mail: sbond@richland.edu

2 Year Institution

Dean: Lily Siu, 80A

	Anderson, Christopher		
	Beyt, Christopher	DMA	11
PT	Shabani, Afrim	M	11,10,13,34B,13C

IL2560 Rock Valley College
Division of Art & Music
3301 N Mulford Rd
Rockford, IL 61114-5640
(815) 912-3312   Fax: (815) 921-3439
www.rockvalleycollege.edu
E-mail: m.youngblood@rockvalleycollege.edu

2 Year Institution

Chair & Dir., Artist/Performance Series: Michael Beert, 80A,80F
Associate Dean: Michael Youngblood, 80H

Prof	Beert, Michael	M	11,12A,13,38,20
Prof	Durst, Dean	M	11
Assoc Prof	Laprade, Paul	M	13C,36,61,66D,32
Assoc Prof	Stein, Ken J.	M	11,13B,20,47,64E

IL2650 St Xavier University
Department of Music
3700 W 103rd St
Chicago, IL 60655-3105
(773) 298-3421   Fax: (773) 298-3429
www.sxu.edu
E-mail: coutts@sxu.edu

4 Year Institution
Member of NASM

Dean, Arts & Sciences: Kathleen Alaimo, 80A
Chair: Greg A. Coutts, 80A
Dir., Admissions: Andrea Caruso, 80D

Lect PT	Baxter, Brett	M	65
Lect PT	Becker, Michael	M	20
Lect PT	Bibzak, Ray	M	64D,64B
Prof	Bickel, Jan	D	39,61
Lect PT	Brady-Riley, Carolyn	M	39,61
Lect PT	Carney, Peter	M	11,29
Lect PT	Chin, Pablo	D	10A,13
Assoc Prof	Coutts, Greg A.	D	13,10,34
Lect PT	Downey, Mark	M	66G
Lect PT	Eckert, Stacy	M	36,39,61
Lect PT	Foley, Laura	B	62D
	Horcher, Nick		66F
Lect PT	Hsu, Chia-Ying	D	62A,62B
Lect PT	Jirosek, Peter	M	63B
Lect PT	Kropidlowski, Monica	M	66A,66D
Assoc Prof	Lee, Patricia	M	66A,66H,66B,66C,66D
Asst Prof	Malecki, Jeffrey	D	37,60B,63C,63D,38
Lect PT	Mantell, Emily	B	62C
Lect PT	Miller, M. Frederick	M	70,47
Assoc Prof	Morris, Martha M.	M	12A,32,64A
Lect PT	Nuccio, David	M	11
Lect PT	Olive, Jordan	M	63A
Lect PT	Regan, Lara		64E,64C
Lect PT	Surma, Dan	M	66A,66D
Lect PT	Swisher, Martha	M	36,60A

IL2730 Sauk Valley Community College
Department of Music
173 Illinois Route 2
Dixon, IL 61021-9110
(815) 288-5511   Fax: (815) 288-1880
www.svcc.edu
E-mail: murrayk@svcc.edu

2 Year Institution

Adj	Bressler, Mark		37,63
Adj	Fischbach, Tim C.	A	61,66A,66G
Adj	Hulteen, Rhonda L.	B	66
Adj	Johnson, Gary V.		13,13C,29,34
Asst Prof	Murray, Kris A.	M	36,70,11,51
Adj	Nunemaker-Bressler, Emily B.		64
Adj	Rogiewicz, Thomas	M	65

IL2750 Sherwood Community Music School
Columbia College Chicago
1312 S Michigan Ave
Chicago, IL 60605
(312) 369-3100   Fax: (312) 427-6677
www.colum.edu/sherwood
E-mail: sherwood@colum.edu

Community Music School

Operations Manager: Christopher Gorcik, 80D

Abe, Christie-Keiko	PhD	62A,66E
Baker, Jessica	B	32A
Bartolomeo, Andrea	M	66A
Bartolomeo, Luke	M	66A
Benham, Jeremiah	M	70
Benmann, Martine	M	62C
Blaszak, Emilia	M	62A,62B
Bubanj, Marija	M	62A,62B
Bukvich, Ivana	M	66A
Burns, Chelsea R.	B	66A,66D
Burns, Stephen	M	60B
Caldwell, Philip	M	61
Carpenter, Andrew	M	64E
Chadwick, John	M	37
Coulson, Bette	M	66A
Cross, Sandra	M	32A,61
Davidson, Thalia	M	66A
Delaplane, Marjorie	M	66A
Dutton, Kristina	B	62A
Eakin, Kate	M	64B
Faith-Slaker, Aubrey	M	66A,66D
Fenster, Laura	M	66A
Flores, Lisa		32A
Frederick, Jeremiah	M	63B
Fry, Mark	M	63C
Galvez, Luis	B	61,36
Goethe-McGinn, Lisa	M	64A
Goldston, Christopher	M	66A
Gonzalez, Tamara	M	62A
Gorcik, Christopher	B	62D
Gray, Terrance	B	62A
Guccione, Rose		39
Harris, Jarrard	M	29
Hedlund, Kristin	B	60B
Hicks, Jarrett	M	32B,32C,32E,65
Hitsky, Seth	B	32A
Huntley, Yvonne	M	66A,66D
Iwata, Nanae	M	62A
Jefferson, Thomas	D	36,66D
Jones, Kimberly		61
Kirchner, Walter	B	39,61
Knecht, John	B	65
Kuller, Ronnie	B	32A
Kwon, Yeeson	D	66A
Lauterbach, Megan	M	66A
Lessie, Erica	M	62C
Levitin, Susan	B	48,64A
Martell, Mary	B	60A
McIntyre, Sarah Elizabeth	B	32D
McKinney, Brian	M	63A
Muhly, Alexa	M	62C
Mundy, Paul	B	64E
Nichols, Margaret	M	66A
Papatheodoroa, Devvora	M	66A
Regester, Kristen	B	32A,65
Rizzer, Gerald	M	66A,13,10
Saad, Olga	B	54
Saltzman, Peter	B	66A
Sherman, Bob	M	70
Smith, Sonja	B	66A
Stanford, Ann	M	64C
Tam-Wang, Erica	M	66A
Trejo, Kyndell	B	15
Van Duyne, Lisa	B	66A,66D
Weber, Jonathan	M	63A

IL2775 South Suburban College

Department of Music
15800 S State St
South Holland, IL 60473
(708) 596-2000   Fax: (708) 210-5797
www.southsuburbancollege.edu
E-mail: ajackson@southsuburbancollege.edu

2 Year Institution
Member of NASM

Dean: Debra Hingst, 80A
Chair: Albert Jackson, 80A

PT	Bibzak, Ray	M	64B,64D
PT	Bourgeois, Marilyn	M	66A
PT	Brath, Jeff	M	63A
PT	Carter, Joyce	M	61
Inst	Chou, Godwin	M	10A,13,66A,66,10
PT	DeYoung, William	B	66A,66G
PT	Ellison, Glenn	M	11,65
PT	Gawthorp, Kevin	B	64
PT	Hanzelin, Fred	D	13,34,11,10
Inst	Hoefle, Andrew	M	11,37,47,63D,29
Inst	Jackson, Albert	M	13A,11,36,61
PT	Kaplan, Sara	M	63B,13A
PT	Kelley, Linda		70
PT	Kirk, Betty	D	61
	Kleis, Lisa		62D
	Kwok, Daniel		62A,62B
PT	Lee, Christina	M	61
	Lewis, Kimberly		66D
PT	Lowezyk, Victoria	M	61
	Madonia, Michael	M	63A
	McGrath, Michael		63A
PT	Miller, Fred	M	70,47,14C
PT	Patterson, Lisa D.	D	64A
	Sluis, Joyce		66A
PT	Tritt, Terry	B	64E
	Ulreich, Douglas		11
PT	Weber, John	M	63D

IL2800 Southeastern Illinois College

Department of Music
3575 College Rd
Harrisburg, IL 62946-4925
(618) 252-5400 x2235   Fax: (618) 252-3062
www.sic.edu
E-mail: kurt.miyashiro@sic.edu

2 Year Institution, Intro Courses Only

Dir., Artist/Performance Series: Bruce Boone, 80F
Dir., Artist Series & Summer Programs: Kellye Whitler, 80F,80G

Inst PT	Clark, Matt	M	70
Inst PT	Green, Tim	B	36,63
Inst PT	Herman, Cheryl	B	36,54,66A,64
Inst	Miyashiro, Kurt	PhD	13,10A,34,10C

IL2900 Southern Illinois Univ-Carbondale

School of Music
Altgeld Hall 103
1000 S Normal Ave
Carbondale, IL 62901
(618) 536-8742   Fax: (618) 453-5808
music.siuc.edu
E-mail: jwagner@siu.edu

4 Year Institution, Graduate School
Member of NASM

Master of Music in Opera-Music Theatre, Master of Music in Collaborative Piano, Master of Music in Performance, Master of Music in Music Education, Master of Music in History & Literature, Master of Music in Music Theory-Composition, Master of Music in Piano Pedagogy

Director: Jeanine F. Wagner, 80A
Assistant Director & Coord., Undergraduate Studies: Susan G. Davenport, 80B,80H
Coord., Graduate Studies: Frank L. Stemper, 80C

Assoc Prof	Allison, Robert	D	63A,29
Prof	Barta, Michael	DIPL	12A,62A,62B
Assoc Prof Emeritus	Beattie, Donald P.	M	66B,66D
Lect	Bell, Cully	M	66B,66D
Prof	Benyas, Edward M.	M	60,38,64B
Lect	Benyas, Kara	M	66C
Prof Emeritus	Best, Richard W.		39,61
Prof	Breznikar, Joseph	M	70
Assoc Prof	Brown, Philip	M	62D,29,35
Lect	Brozak, George A.	D	37,32H
Asst Prof Emeritus	Carter, Clarence	M	39,61
Lect	Coloton, Diane S.	D	61,39
Vstng Lect	Combest, Chris	D	63D,13B
Senior Lect	Coulter, Ronald E.	M	65,10B,50
Asst Prof	Davenport, Susan G.	D	36
Prof Emeritus	Delphin, Wilfred	D	66A
Asst Prof	Dillard, David A.	D	61
Prof	Fink, Tim J.	M	39,61
Senior Lect	Ginther, Kathleen C.	D	13,10
Prof Emeritus	Hanes, Michael D.	M	37,50,65
Assoc Prof	Johnson, Maria V.	D	14
Asst Prof	Kato, Yuko	D	66A
Lect	Kelley, Richard P.	M	64E
Assoc Prof	Lee, Junghwa	D	66A
Assoc Prof	Lenz, Eric	D	13,62C
Assoc Prof Emerita	Lord, Suzanne	D	64A,12A
Collaborative Pianist	Lyons, David P.	D	66C
Assoc Prof	Mackey, Melissa A.	D	64D,12A
Prof	Mandat, Eric P.	D	13,64C,64E
Lect	McCluskey, Eric	M	61
Prof Emeritus	Mochnick, John	D	36,41
Asst Prof	Morehouse, Christopher L.	D	37
Lect	Palermo, Joseph M.	M	70
Lect	Petillot, Aurelien	D	62B,62A,42,11,12A
Senior Lect	Pitchford, Timothy	D	63C
Senior Lect	Presar, Jennifer	M	63B,13B,13C,13
Emeritus	Romersa, Henry J.	M	35
Prof Emerita	Simmons, Margaret R.	M	61,66C
Prof	Stemper, Frank L.	D	13,10,43
Asst Prof	Stover, Pamela J.	D	32,13A
Lect	Transue, Arlene M.	M	39,61
Assoc Prof	Transue, Paul A.	DMA	66C,39
Prof	Wagner, Jeanine F.	D	39,61
Prof Emerita	Webb, Marianne	M	66G
Prof Emeritus	Weiss, Robert L.	D	63C
Senior Lect	Worthen, Douglas	D	12A,64A
Lect	Zimmermann, Carlyn	M	36

IL2910 Southern Illinois Univ-Edwardsvle

Department of Music
Box 1771
Edwardsville, IL 62026
(618) 650-3900   Fax: (618) 650-5988
www.siue.edu/artsandsciences/music/
E-mail: atallan@siue.edu

4 Year Institution, Graduate School
Member of NASM

Certificate, Master of Music in Performance, Master of Music in Music Education

Chair: Audrey Tallant, 80A

Assoc Prof	Anop, Lenora Marya	D	62A,41,51,42
Assoc Prof	Archer, Kimberly K.	D	10,13,32E,10A,10F
Prof	Bell, John	D	32,32C,37,60B
Assoc Prof	Chin, Huei Li	D	66A,66B,66D
Prof	Coan, Darryl	D	13,32,62E,67
Prof	Haydon, Rick	M	70,29,35G,53,47
Prof	Hinson, James M.	D	48,64C,64E,42
Prof	Ho, Allan	D	13,12A,12
Prof	Knapp, Joel	D	60,36,40
Prof	Korak, John	D	60,37,63A,49,42
Prof	Mishra, Michael	D	10F,60,38
Asst Prof	Pineda, Kris	D	66A,66C,41
Asst Prof	Schapman, Marc	D	39,61
Assoc Prof	Simidtchieva, Marta	D	38,42,41,51,62C
Assoc Prof	Smith, Deborah	D	32,32I
Prof	Tallant, Audrey	M	11,35
Asst Prof	Truckenbrod, Emily	D	61
Assoc Prof	Wells, Prince	M	13,11,29,35

IL2970 Southwestern Illinois College
Department of Music
2500 Carlyle Ave
Belleville, IL 62221-5859
(618) 235-2700   Fax: (618) 235-1578
www.swic.edu
E-mail: darice.palmier@swic.edu

2 Year Institution

Chair: Darice Palmier, 80A

Inst PT	Anop, Lenora	M	62A
Inst PT	Aulenbacher, Dennis	M	35C
Inst PT	Birkner, Tom	D	53
Inst PT	Bolen, Jerry	M	65,20
Inst PT	Briskovich, Zebadiah	M	62D
Inst PT	Buckley, Chris	B	62D
Inst PT	Drennan, Jennifer	M	11,14C,20
Inst PT	Favazza, Kathleen	M	61
Inst FT	Fleming, Gail H.	D	11,36,66A,40,20
Inst PT	Friedel, Aileen	B	62C
Inst PT	Harres, Debra	M	61
Inst PT	Hinds, Evan	B	65
Inst FT	Hucke, Adam	M	11,13A,29A,63A,47
Inst PT	Hunter, Barbara	M	63B
Inst FT	Jacobs, Ed	M	63D,11,13A,37,46
Inst PT	King, Matthew	B	62A
Inst PT	Knoeloch, Glenn	M	11
Inst PT	Long, Gail	M	66D
Inst PT	Marble, Jamie	M	20,11
Inst PT	Mattison, Travis	M	70,11
Inst PT	Mehrmann, Dan	M	34D,35H
Inst PT	Nix, Kathy	M	35A
Inst FT	Palmier, Darice	M	66A,66D,11,13A,66C
Inst PT	Scott, Janet	M	64A
Inst PT	Shelley, Kim S.	M	65
Inst PT	Smolik, Vicky	M	11,63A,10D,35D
Inst PT	Swagler, Jason	M	64E
Inst PT	Tonnies, Mary Kaye	M	35D

IL3100 Trinity Christian College
Department of Music
6601 W College Dr
Palos Heights, IL 60463-1768
(708) 239-4874   Fax: (708) 239-4890
www.trnty.edu
E-mail: music@trnty.edu

4 Year Institution

Chair: Mark Peters, 80A

PT	Armandi, Richard	M	63C,63D
Prof	Austin, Kenneth L.	D	13,32C,37,49,46
PT	Brown, Michael	M	61
PT	Kramer, Janet	M	50,65
PT	Mantell, Emily Lewis	M	62C
PT	Mantell, Matthew	M	51,62A,62B
PT	Miller, Fred	M	70
PT	Miller, June Entwisle	M	36,32B
PT	Palmore, James	B	36
Assoc Prof	Peters, Mark	D	11,20,13E,12
PT	Shin, MinKyoo	M	13C,66A,66D,66G
PT	Sopata, Kimberly	M	48,64A
PT	Sugihara, Masahito	D	48,64E
Prof	Van Wyck, Helen J.	D	13,60A,11,36,32D
PT	Zupko, Mischa	D	10,66A

IL3150 Trinity International University
Department of Music
2065 Half Day Rd
Deerfield, IL 60015
(847) 317-7035   Fax: (847) 317-4786
www.tiu.edu/
E-mail: music@tiu.edu

4 Year Institution

Chair: Don P. Hedges, 80A

Adj	Agnew, Joseph	M	63D
Assoc Prof	Alcorn, Allison A.	D	10E,11,12A,20,31A
Adj	Baker, Allison	M	64B,64D
Emeritus	Bell, Jacqueline H.	M	
Adj	Duggan, Ann	M	62A,62B
Emeritus	Faugerstrom, Morris	D	
Adj	Finton, Charles	M	63A
Adj	Hacker, John	B	61
Adj	Hagglund, Heidi	M	64A
Adj	Harris, Jarrard	M	64E
Prof	Hedges, Don P.	D	13,31A,11,39
Adj	Lustrea, Robert	M	63C,63D
Assoc Prof	Posegate, Stephen C.	D	32,37,49,34
Adj	Ruiz, Norman	B	70
Prof	Satre, Paul J.	D	36,66A,66G,60,13
Adj	Selvaggio, Frederick	D	65
Adj	Shaffer, Timothy	B	62D
Adj	Snow, Andrew	M	62C
Lect	Swinson, Beth Ann	B	61,39,41
Lect	Teichler, Robert Christopher	D	47,10,38
Adj	Velleur, Melody	B	63B
Adj	Woodrum, Jennifer	M	64C

IL3200 Triton College
Department of Music
2000 N 5th Ave
River Grove, IL 60171-1907
(708) 456-0300   Fax: (708) 583-3140
www.triton.edu/music
E-mail: pjermiho@triton.edu

2 Year Institution

Dean: Jonathan Paver, 80A

	Duncan, Steven	M	11,63C
	Groeling, Charles	D	32,37
	Jermihov, Peter	D	36,13
	Koehler, Raymund	M	29,66
	Magnone, Steve		50,65
Emeritus	Schlabach, Eugene	D	11,12A,66A
	Staron, Michael	M	13,11,29,62D
	Yoelin, Shelley	M	13A,13,37,47,64E

IL3250 Univ of Chicago
Department of Music
Goodspeed Hall
1010 E 59th St
Chicago, IL 60637-1512
(773) 702-8484   Fax: (773) 753-0558
music.uchicago.edu
E-mail: music@uchicago.edu

4 Year Institution, Graduate School

Master of Arts in Composition, Master of Arts in Ethnomusicology, Master of Arts in History & Theory, PhD in Ethnomusicology, PhD in Composition, PhD in History & Music Theory

Chair: Martha Feldman, 80A
Dir., Undergraduate Studies: Steven M. Rings, 80B
Dir., Graduate Studies: Melvin L. Butler, 80C
Dir., Graduate Admissions: Travis A. Jackson, 80D
Dir., Student Performance Programs: Barbara Schubert

Prof Emeritus	Blackwood, Easley R.	M	10F,13L
Prof	Bohlman, Philip V.	D	14,20G
Lect	Briggs, Amy	D	41,13
Asst Prof	Butler, Melvin L.	D	14,20
Prof	Christensen, Thomas	D	13,13J,12D
Prof	Feldman, Martha	D	11,12A,12,15
Prof Emeritus	Gossett, Philip	D	12A,12
Assoc Prof	Hoeckner, Berthold	D	11,12,12A
Assoc Prof	Jackson, Travis A.	D	29,20,29D,29E,14
Senior Lect	Kallembach, James	D	36,60A
Prof	Kendrick, Robert L.	D	11,31,12,14
Asst Prof	Mason, Kaley R.	D	14,20
Prof	Ptaszynska, Marta	M	13,10,10F
Prof	Ran, Shulamit		10
Asst Prof	Rings, Steven M.	D	13
Prof	Robertson, Anne Walters	D	11,12A,12
Senior Lect	Sandroff, Howard	M	10,45,34,13L
Senior Lect	Schubert, Barbara	M	38,41,60,43
Assoc Prof	Zbikowski, Lawrence	D	13,12A,13J,29C

IL3300 Univ of Illinois

School of Music
1114 W Nevada St
Urbana, IL 61801-3859
(217) 333-2620   Fax: (217) 244-4585
www.music.uiuc.edu
E-mail: griggs@illinois.edu

4 Year Institution, Graduate School
Member of NASM

Artist Diploma, Master of Music in Composition, Master of Music in Music Theory, Master of Music in Conducting, Master of Music in Musicology, Master of Music Education, PhD in Music Education, DMA in Composition, Doctor of Education in Music Education, DMA in Choral Music, DMA in Performance & Literature, Master of Music in Vocal Accompanying & Coaching, PhD in Musicology, Master of Music in Choral Music, Master of Music in Piano Pedagogy, Master of Music in Performance & Literature, DMA in Vocal Accompanying & Coaching

Director: Karl P. Kramer, 80A
Associate Director & Dir., Undergraduate Studies: Edward Rath, 80B,80H
Coord., Graduate Studies: Michael J. Cameron, 80C
Assistant Dir., Enrollment Mgt & Public Engagement: Joyce L. Griggs, 80D,80E,80G
Asst. Dir., Operations: Paul Redman, 80H

Prof	Alexander, Charles Reid	D	66B,66D,66A
Other	Allen, David	M	34
Assoc Prof	Alwes, Chester	D	36,60A
Inst	Asnawa, I Ketut Gede	M	20D
Asst Prof	Bashford, Christina	D	12A,12C,12D,42,51
Prof	Bergonzi, Louis	D	32E,38,62,32G,60B
Other	Bernhardsson, Sigurbjorn	M	51,62A
Vstng Lect	Bhattacharya, Subrata	B	20E
Vstng Asst Prof	Blume, Philipp G.		13,10,10A,10F
Other	Bresler, Liora	D	32
Assoc Prof	Bridgewater, Ronald S.		47,64E,29
Assoc Prof	Browning, Zack D.	D	13,10,43
Assoc Prof	Buchanan, Donna A.	D	20F,12,14
Vstng Lect	Bunch, James D.	M	10A
Prof	Cameron, Michael J.	M	62D,51,41
Asst Prof	Carrillo, Teofilo	B	63A
Assoc Prof	Chasanov, Elliot L.	M	63C,49,41
Vstng Inst	Chen, Yao	D	10A
Assoc Prof	Coleman, Barrington		36,61
Vstng Lect	Conde, Moussa		20A
Prof	Davis, Ollie Watts	D	61,36
Prof	Dee, John	B	64B,42
Assoc Prof	DeNardo, Gregory F.	D	32
Prof	Diazmunoz, Eduardo	M	39,43,60B
Assoc Prof	Ehlen, Timothy	D	66A,41
Assoc Prof	Flores, Ricardo	M	65,50
Other	Ganatra, Simin	B	51,62A
Assoc Prof	Garnett, Guy E.	D	10,34,13
Assoc Prof	George, Roby G.	D	37,60B
Assoc Prof Emeritus	Grant, Joe W.	D	60,32,36
Assoc Prof	Grashel, John W.	D	32
Asst Prof	Gray, Lawrence	M	29,62C,62D
Assoc Prof	Gunn, Julie	D	66C
Prof	Gunn, Nathan	B	61
Assoc Prof	Haken, Rudolf	M	62B,51,41
Inst	Harris, Dawn	M	61
Assoc Prof	Harris, J. David	M	64C,48,41
Assoc Prof Emerita	Harwood, Eve E.	D	32
Other	Haymon-Coleman, Cynthia	B	61
Prof	Heiles, William H.	D	66A,66H,41
Assoc Prof	Helmrich, Dennis	M	66A,66C
Vstng Asst Prof	Hendricks, Karin S.	D	32G
Asst Prof	Herrera, Luis Ricardo	M	61
Lect	Hickey, Joan B.	B	47,66B,29
Prof	Hobson, Ian	D	38,41,66A
Vstng Lect	Holmes, J. Michael	M	64E
Asst Prof	Jostlein, Thomas	B	63B
Assoc Prof	Keeble, Jonathan	D	64A,48
Prof	Kinderman, William A.	D	12
Asst Prof	Kouzov, Dmitry	DIPL	62C
Prof	Kramer, Karl P.	D	42,43
Vstng Asst Prof	Leyva, Jesse	M	60B,37,32E
Assoc Prof	Lund, Erik R.	D	13,10,43
Assoc Prof	Lupu, Sherban	B	51,62A,41
Prof Emeritus	Machala, Kazimierz W.	D	63B,49,41
Asst Prof	Magee, Gayle Sherwood	D	12A
Assoc Prof	Magee, Jeffrey	D	12,20G,29A
Assoc Prof	McGovern, Timothy S.	M	64D,48,41
Assoc Prof	McNeill, Charles	M	29
Assoc Prof	Milenkovich, Stefan	DIPL	62A
Assoc Prof	Moersch, Charlotte Mattax	D	67F,66H,12A,55C,12
Assoc Prof	Moersch, William	M	65,50
Assoc Prof	Moore, Mark E.	M	63D,49,41
Prof Emeritus	Nettl, Bruno		14,20G
Asst Prof	Prescott, Anne	D	20D
Prof	Pugh, James	B	63C
Asst Prof	Rath, Edward	D	66A,41
Assoc Prof	Redman, Yvonne Gonzales	B	61
Prof	Richtmeyer, Debra A.	M	64E,48,41
Vstng Asst Prof	Rios, Fernando	D	20H
Asst Prof	Robinson, Dana M.	D	66G
Prof	Romm, Ronald	M	63A,41
Other	Rostad, Masumi	M	51,62B
Assoc Prof	Schleicher, Donald J.	M	60B,38
Lect	Schleis, Thomas H.	M	39
Vstng Asst Prof	Schulze, Hendrik	D	12A
Vstng Lect	Seo, Ju Ri	M	10A
Prof	Siena, Jerold	DIPL	61,39
Assoc Prof	Solis, Gabriel	D	12,20G
Assoc Prof	Stephens, John C.	M	29,46,47
Prof	Stoltzfus, Fred A.	D	60A,36
Prof	Stone, Sylvia	M	61
	Sweet, Bridget Mary	M	32,11,60A
Asst Prof	Syer, Katherine R.	D	12B
Vstng Inst	Talbot, Brent	M	32E
Assoc Prof	Taube, Heinrich K.	D	13,10,34
Assoc Prof	Taylor, Stephen A.	D	13,10
Asst Prof	Tharp, Reynold	D	10F
Asst Prof	Thibeault, Matthew	D	32C,32F
Prof	Tipei, Sever	D	13,10,34
Assoc Prof	Tsitsaros, Christos	D	66B,66D
Prof	Turino, Thomas R.	D	11,20A,20H,14
Other	Vamos, Brandon	M	51,62C
Vstng Lect	Walburn, Jacob A.	M	63A,29
Prof	Ward, Tom R.	D	11,12
Vstng Lect	Wilson, Glenn	M	64E
Prof	Wyatt, Scott A.	M	13,10,34,45
Asst Prof	Yampolsky, Philip	M	20D
Assoc Prof	Yeung, Ann M.	D	62E,51

IL3310 Univ of Illinois-Chicago

Department of Performing Arts
1040 W Harrison St - MC 255
Chicago, IL 60607-7130
(312) 996-2977   Fax: (312) 996-0954
www.uic.edu/depts/adpa
E-mail: dpa@uic.edu

4 Year Institution

Chair: Michael J. Anderson, 80A
Coordinator: William Kaplan, 80A
Dir., Artist/Performance Series: Theodore Edel, 80F

	Adams, Ernie		47,65
Assoc Prof	Anderson, Michael J.	D	13A,60,36
	Barilari, Elbio Rodriguez		20H
	Becos, Pelarin	M	10,13,13C
	Brown, Ari		64E,29
	Bukvich, Ivana		66A
	Cohan, Ryan		47,66A
Lect	Cohen, Joel D.	M	65
Assoc Prof	Collerd, Gene J.	M	13A,60,37,64C
Assoc Prof	Davis, Orbert	M	47,63A
Prof	Edel, Theodore	D	11,66A,12A
	Floeter, John		62D
	Goldston, Christopher	M	66A
Teach Assoc	Huang, Hai Tao	B	13A,63A
Prof	Kaplan, William	D	13,12A,64D
	Lewis, Andrew		36
Lect	Milanovich, Donna Z.	M	64A
	Miller, Stewart		62D,29
	Mitchell, Nicole		29,29A,64A
	Moran, Nick		64
	Morrison, David	M	37
Lect	Pickering, Amy J.	M	61
	Rosenberg, Ruth Emily	D	20F,15,14
Assoc Prof	Saunders, Harris S.	D	11,12A,12
	Tot, Zvonimir	D	29,13,13C,70,47
Assoc Prof Emeritus	Wang, Richard A.	M	10F,12A,47,53,29

IL3370 Univ of St. Francis

Department of Music & Perf. Arts
500 Wilcox St
Joliet, IL 60435-6169
(815) 740-3219   Fax: (815) 740-4285
www.stfrancis.edu
E-mail: pbrannon@stfrancis.edu

4 Year Institution

Chair & Dir., Artist Series: Patrick V. Brannon, 80A,80F
Dir., Artist Series: Clarice Hearne, 80F

Adj	Bennett, Cindy	M	63,32B
Prof	Brannon, Patrick V.	D	14,12A,36,60A,40
Adj	Diab, Mary Beth	M	66A,66C,66B,66D

Adj	Fon-Revutzky, Gerik	M	64
Asst Prof	Hearne, Clarice	M	61,39
Adj	Jaskowiak, Jeffrey	B	34H,34D,34G
Adj	Johansen-Werner, Bonnie	M	10A,13
Prof	Kase, Robert	D	63
Adj	Lin, Kelvin	D	62A
Adj	Peeples, Terry	M	65
Adj	Pierard, George	M	32C,32E
Adj	Ray, Jeffrey	B	61
Adj	Salazar, Dennis A.	M	70
Adj	Stumpf, Robert	M	36,13
Adj	Thomen, Willard	M	61,11

IL3400 Univ of St. Mary of the Lake

Department of Music/Mundelein Sem
1000 E Maple Ave
Mundelein, IL 60060-1174
(847) 970-4877   Fax: (847) 566-2583
www.vocations.org
E-mail: lcerabona@usml.edu

Introductory Courses Only

Director: Linda M. Cerabona

Inst	Cerabona, Linda M.		11,13A,20A,31A,32D
Prof Emeritus	Wojcik, Richard J.	M	11,12A,36,61,31A

IL3450 VanderCook College of Music

3140 S Federal St
Chicago, IL 60616
(312) 225-6288   Fax: (312) 225-5211
www.vandercook.edu
E-mail: cmenghini@vandercook.edu

4 Year Institution, Graduate School
Member of NASM

Master of Music Education

President: Charles T. Menghini, 80A
Dean, Undergraduate Studies: Stacey L. Larson, 80B
Dean, Graduate Studies: Ruth Rhodes, 80C

Inst PT	Abramovitch, Ruti	D	66A
Inst PT	Bach, Anne	B	64B
Inst PT	Becker, Michael	M	14,12A
Inst PT	Bistrow, Douglas	B	62D
Assoc Prof PT	Campbell, Bonnie H.	D	64C
Librarian	DeLand, Robert	M	16
Asst Prof	Eccles, David F.	ABD	51,32E,38
Inst PT	Goldberg, Julie	D	70
Asst Prof PT	Hall, Michael L.	D	62A,62B
Assoc Prof	Hung, Yu-Sui	D	66A,66D,13C
Inst PT	Jirousek, Peter	M	63B
Asst Prof	Kidonakis, Tony G.	M	64E,47
Inst PT	Korbitz, Ronald S.	M	11
Assoc Prof	Krupa, Mary Ann	M	13,54,66A
Inst PT	Kuhn, Bret	B	65
Assoc Prof	Larson, Stacey L.	M	32E,37,60B
Prof	Lepper, Kevin	M	65,50
Inst PT	Martorano, Joseph P.	M	61
Inst PT	Meir, Eran	M	62C
Prof	Menghini, Charles T.	D	60,37,32
Asst Prof	Palese, Richard	M	32,34
Asst Prof PT	Presutti Korbitz, Angela	M	61
Prof	Rhodes, Ruth	M	48,64C,32
Prof	Rosenthal, Roseanne K.	D	12C
Assoc Prof PT	Schuman, Leah	D	63A,49
Prof	Sinclair, Robert L.	D	36,32,60A
Inst PT	Smith, Emily M.	M	64D
Inst PT	Stingley, Mary-Christine	M	64A
Asst Prof	Tsai, I-Hsuan	D	66C
Inst PT	Young, Michael		63C,63D

IL3500 Western Illinois University

School of Music
1 University Circle
Macomb, IL 61455-1390
(309) 298-1544   Fax: (309) 298-1968
www.wiu.edu/music
E-mail: b-shanklin@wiu.edu

4 Year Institution, Graduate School
Member of NASM

Master of Music in Composition, Master of Music in Performance, Master of Music in Conducting, Master of Music in Music Education, Master of Music in Musicology, Master of Music in Piano Pedagogy, Master of Music in Jazz Studies

Dean: William Clow, 80A
Director: Bart Shanklin, 80A
Dir., Graduate Studies: Brian Locke, 80C
Dir., Summer Programs: Michael J. Fansler, 80G
Assistant Director & Dir., Undergraduate Studies: Moises Molina, 80H,80B

Inst	Andrews, Adrianna	M	32
Inst	Andrews, Linda	M	66G
Other	Arakawa, Jasmin	M	66C
Prof	Bean, Matt	D	61,54
Inst	Blankenship, Courtney	M	35A
Prof	Briney, Bruce C.	D	63A
Asst Prof	Brown, Jeffrey A.	D	66,66A,66D
Inst	Brown, Joseph	D	11
Asst Prof	Brown, Laura E.	D	33
Prof	Caldwell, James M.	D	13,10,45
Asst Prof	Cangro, Richard	D	32E,11
Assoc Prof	Chasteen, Terry L.	M	61
Prof	Cooper, John	D	29,63A
Prof	Ericson, Michael	M	13B,13C,64B,48
Assoc Prof	Fansler, Michael J.	M	37,60B,32E
Prof	Faust, Randall E.	D	63B,10,63,13,49
Prof	Ginsberg, Eric	M	64C
Inst	Hand, Angela R.	D	61,39
Asst Prof	Hardeman, Anita	D	66G,12A,66A
Prof	Huff, Douglas M.	D	64D,12A,11,48
Inst	Hughes, Matthew	M	62D,20,29
Assoc Prof	Hughey, Richard	D	38,60B
Assoc Prof	Jones, Jennifer D.	M	33
Other	Joo, Narae	M	66C
Assoc Prof	Karn, Kitty	M	61,54
Assoc Prof	Kurasz, Rick	M	65,20
Prof	Lapka, Christine	D	32,11,12C
Assoc Prof	Locke, Brian	D	11,20F,12
Asst Prof	McMurtery, John M.	D	64A,48
Asst Prof	Megginson, Charolette	M	61
Assoc Prof	Mihai, Julieta		62A,51
Assoc Prof	Mindeman, John	M	63D,63C,49,29
Prof	Molina, Moises	D	62C,51
Assoc Prof	Nichols, Kevin A.	M	65,20
Prof	Paccione, Paul	D	13,10,43,20G
Assoc Prof	Romig, James	D	13,13F,10A,10
Other	Seo, Minjung	D	66C
Prof	Shanklin, Bart	D	61,60A,36,32D
Assoc Prof	Sharpe, Rod L.	M	16
Assoc Prof	Solomonson, Terry	M	11,63D,35C,35D,35G
Prof	Stegall, James C.	D	36,32D,60A
Assoc Prof	Stryker, Michael S.	M	66A,29
Assoc Prof	Szabo, Istvan	M	62B,51
Asst Prof	Thomas, Matthew J.	D	37,60B
Assoc Prof	Thompson, Lynn	M	61,54,39,36
Inst	Turner, George	M	29,70
Prof	Vana, John	M	64E,29A
Prof	Walker, Tammie Leigh	D	66D,66A,12A

IL3550 Wheaton College

Conservatory of Music
501 College Ave
Wheaton, IL 60187-5593
(630) 752-5099   Fax: (630) 752-5341
www.wheaton.edu/conservatory
E-mail: michelle.nash@wheaton.edu

4 Year Institution
Member of NASM

Dean: Michael Wilder, 80A

Lect	Anderson, Andrew	D	62D
Lect	Baddorf, Donald	B	34,35C
Lect	Bauer, Elizabeth	D	32A,32B,32C
Lect	Bazan, Michael	B	64E,29
Lect	Boyd, Robert	M	32D
Lect	Brown, Jennie S.	D	64A,12A,13C,42
Assoc Prof	Buis, Johann S.	D	12,20,11
Lect	Chiu, Cornelius	M	62A
Lect	Cockle, Katherine G.	M	11
Lect	Cottle, Melanie	B	63B
Lect	Davis, James	M	63A
Prof	Edwards, Karin	D	66A
Assoc Prof Emeritus	Evans, Margarita	M	61
Lect	Folker, Michael	M	65
Assoc Prof Emeritus	Funk, Curtis H.	D	13,32
Lect	Gamez, Denise	M	61
Lect	Gemmill, Matthew	M	11
Lect	Gillan, Lucas	B	65
Asst Prof	Gordon, David M.	D	13,10
Lect	Griffin, Rose	D	13
Lect	Harrison, Kevin	M	63D

Assoc Prof	Hart, Carolyn	D	61
Lect	Hollinger, Deborah	M	66A,11,66D
Assoc Prof	Holman, Sarah	D	39,61
Prof	Hopper, Mary	D	60,36
Prof	Horn, Daniel Paul	D	66A,66C
Assoc Prof	Joiner, Lee	D	51,62A,62B
Prof	Kastner, Kathleen	D	13A,13,50,65,20
Lect	Kim, Misook	D	13
Lect	Lim, Cheryl	D	66A,66D
Lect	Lorimer, Christopher	M	61
Lect	Mangin, Andy	MFA	39
Lect	Mindeman, John	M	63C
Lect	Montzka Smelser, Ann	M	32C,62
Lect	Moshier, Josh	B	29,10C,47
Asst Prof	Okpebholo, Shawn E.	D	13,10
Assoc Prof	Payne, Tony L.	D	10,34
Prof Emeritus	Phemister, William	D	66A
Lect	Pierson, Steve	D	63,11
Lect	Polifrone, Sharon	M	42
Lect	Ramsdell, Steve	M	70
Asst Prof	Sanchez, Paul	M	66A
Prof	Saylor, Jonathan	D	12A,64D,41
Assoc Prof	Schwartz, Terry R.	D	37,63A
Lect	Schweitz, Kurt	M	62D,46
Lect	Seeman, Faye	M	62E
Lect	Simmons, Sunshine	M	64C
Lect	Sjobring, Steve	B	62A
Lect	Smelser, Linc	M	62C
Assoc Prof	Sommerville, Daniel A.	D	38,10,60B
Lect	Sterling, Robin	M	61
Lect	Stevenson, Deborah	M	64B
Lect	Sullivan, Anne	M	64A
Prof	Sundberg, Gerard	D	36,61
Lect	Tehan, Julie	M	62C
Lect	Torosian, Brian	D	70,32E
Asst Prof	Trotter, John William	D	36,60A
Lect	Trowbridge, Cynthia	M	66C
Lect	Vanderwerf, Paul	D	62A,62B
Lect	Walford, Maria	D	61
Lect	Wheatley, Greg	M	13
Prof Emeritus	Whitaker, Howard	D	13,10F,10,64C
Prof Emeritus	Wiens, Paul W.	D	13C,60A,36
Lect	Williams, Brad		29
Assoc Prof	Yontz, Timothy	D	32E,37,63A,32
Lect	Zafer, Paul	M	62A,51
Assoc Prof Emeritus	Zimmerman, John	M	13,66A
Prof	Zimmerman, R. Edward	D	11,66G,66H,31A

IN0005 American Conservatory of Music

252 Wildwood Rd
Hammond, IN 46324
(219) 931-6000   Fax: (219) 931-6089
www.americanconservatory.edu
E-mail: registrar@americanconservatory.edu

4 Year Institution, Graduate School

DMA in Music, Master of Music

Dean: Fr. Daniel Gorham, 80A
Registrar: Mary Ellen Newsom, 80D
Dir., Admissions: Edwin Thomas, 80D
Dean, Extension Division: Paul Jordan, 80E
Chairman: Otto Schulze
President: Theodora Schulze

	Baker, William	D	12,13,60,36,39
	Bershad, Kara	M	62E
	Bruk, Elfrida	DIPL	66A,13,31B,66C,66H
	Cademcian, Gerard	M	66A,31A,31B,67F,13
	Chen, Chia-Chi	D	33
	Chung, Hsieh	D	33
	Combs, Ronald	D	61,13
	Geller, Ian R.	D	61,10A,60,36
	Gonzalez, Fr. George	D	11,14,20,66G,32
	Gorham, Fr. Daniel	D	31A,33,61
	Hansen, Jack	M	66A,13,61
	Harris, Roger	B	10B,13,29,47,66A
	Henry, Paul	M	70,13
	Hohman, Frederick	D	66G
	Hollingsworth, Devon	M	10A,12,13,32,66G
	Hoppmann, Kenneth	D	10,16,20F,35A,66
	Jacob, Jeffrey	M	66A
	Ji, Ming Sheng	D	33
	Jordan, Paul	D	10A,61,13,20F,31A
	Kho, Julia	D	61
	Kilburn, Ke-Yin	D	33,66A,66B,13
	Lee, Ki Joo	M	62A
	Levitan, Susan	M	64A
	Lin, Chen-Chi	D	33
	Liu, Hsien-Ping	D	33
	Mallinger, Patrick	M	64E,64C
	Matesky, Elisabeth	M	62A
	McKenna, Fr. Edward	M	10,62A,16,31A,11
	Milosavljevic, Svetozar		68,60B
	Moravec, Andriana	B	62A,62B
	Newsom, Mary Ellen	D	12,14,32,61,62
	Nitschke, Brad	D	11,12,13,60,63
	Park, Sang Eui	D	10,60,12,13,31A
	Prince, Curtis L.	D	10,12,20G,65,47
	Reid, Steven	D	63A,36,37,38,13
	Robinson, Curtis	DIPL	13,16,29,34,35
	Schulze, Otto	DIPL	62A,67,10,13,36
	Schulze, Theodora	DIPL	61,10A,13,50,51
	Slavin, Peter	D	10,13,66,66A,11
	Smith, Roy C.	D	61,11,10A,60,36
	Snukst, Penny	M	33,13,31A
	Spicer, Nan	D	61,60A,66A,66G,31A
	Thomas, Edwin	D	65,11,12,32,60
	Vargas, Luis	M	62B
	Webb, Charles	M	62C,62D
	Willy, Alan	M	66A,66G,70,13
	Wong, Wing Ho	D	33
	Yang, Hao	B	33
	Yubovich, Benjamin	D	60,16,12,13,14

IN0010 Ancilla College

Department of Music
PO Box 1
Donaldson, IN 46513
(574) 936-8898   Fax: (574) 935-1773
www.ancilla.edu
E-mail: roba.kribs@ancilla.edu

2 Year Institution

Academic Dean: Joanna Blount, 80A
Dir., Artist/Performance Series: Clara Woolley, 80F

| PT | Woolley, Clara | M | 13,11,32,66A,66G |

IN0100 Anderson University

School of Music, Theatre & Dance
1100 E 5th St
Anderson, IN 46012
(765) 641-4450   Fax: (765) 641-3809
www.anderson.edu
E-mail: jewright@anderson.edu

4 Year Institution, Graduate School
Member of NASM

Master of Music in Music Education

Dean & Dir., Graduate Studies: Jeffrey E. Wright, 80A,80C
Dir., Summer Programs: Joan Lynette Brandon, 80G
Assistant Chair: Susan Lynnette Taylor, 80H

PT	Archibald, Becky H.	B	10D
PT	Ballard, Jeffrey D.	D	61
Assoc Prof	Brandon, Joan Lynette	M	32B,36,32C,32D
PT	Brewer, Mary Kathryn	M	61
Prof	Brooks, Jonathan E.	D	13,10A
PT	Chan, Ken	M	66C
Prof	Chappell, Rebecca Ann	D	64C,64E,35A,64D
PT	Edie, Rebecca L.	M	66A,66C
PT	Fan, Heaven H.	D	62E
PT	French, Pamela A.	M	64B
Prof	Frieling, Randall J.	D	66A,66C,66D,66G
Assoc Prof	Goetzinger, Laurel E.	M	61,39,54
PT	Hachiya-Weinrer, Jane	B	52
PT	Helsley, Jack	M	62D
Asst Prof	Holmes, Christopher	M	12A,12C,20,11
PT	Huntoon, Diana	M	61
Asst Prof	Huntoon, John Richard	M	63C,63D,47,37,49
PT	King, Douglas	B	52
Asst Prof	Kumi, Gert	M	62A,38
PT	Li, Li	M	62B,38
PT	Moore, Gary A.	B	70
Prof	Murray, Mark S.	D	29,63A,34,35
Assoc Prof	Murray, Michele C.	M	13A,13B,13C,66D
PT	Oh, Kyung-Nam	D	62C,38
PT	Potaczek, Amanda Lee	B	10D,35A
PT	Potaczek, Steven A.	B	35A
PT	Rice, Suzanne	M	63B
PT	Robbins, David	B	65
Prof	Robertson, Fritz S.	D	39,61
Prof	Rodgers, Reginald G.	D	66A,66B,66D
PT	Scagnoli, Joseph R.	B	65,50
PT	Shaver, Cynthia L.	B	32E
PT	Shepard, Kenny	B	52
PT	Silveus, Debra L.	B	52
Prof	Sowers, Richard L.	D	60A,36,32D
PT	Stanek, Emily	M	64A

PT	Stanek, Mark	D	70,13B,13C,41
Asst Prof	Steele, Shauna	M	52
PT	Tashpulatov, Oyber N.	B	52
Prof	Taylor, Susan Lynnette	D	32E,37,48,60B
Prof	Wright, Jeffrey E.	D	31A,32G

IN0150 Ball State University

School of Music
2000 University Ave
Muncie, IN 47306-0410
(765) 285-5400   Fax: (765) 285-5401
www.bsu.edu/music

E-mail: jwscheib@bsu.edu

4 Year Institution, Graduate School
Member of NASM

Artist Diploma, Master of Arts in Music, Master of Music in Composition, Master of Music in Music Theory, Master of Music in Performance, Master of Music in Conducting, Master of Music in Music Education, Master of Music in Woodwinds, Master of Music in Piano Performance & Pedagogy, MFA, Master of Music in History-Musicology, Doctorate of Arts in Music, Doctor of Arts in Conducting, Doctor of Arts in Piano Chamber Music/Accompanying, Master of Music in Piano Accompanying & Chamber Music, Doctorate of Arts in Music Education, Doctor of Art in Performance, Master of Music in Multiple Woodwinds

Dean, Fine Arts: Robert A. Kvam, 80A
Director: John W. Scheib, 80A
Coord., Undergraduate Programs: Keith K. Kothman, 80B
Coord., Undergraduate Admissions & Scholarships: Keith Sweger, 80B,80D
Coord., Graduate Programs: Linda L. Pohly, 80C
Associate Director: Ryan M. Hourigan, 80H
Associate Dean, Fine Arts: Michael O'Hara, 80H

PT	Alder, Alan	M	40
Prof	Atherton, Leonard	M	60B
PT	Atherton, Susan	M	32
Asst Prof	Berger, Gene P.	D	49,41,63B
Asst Prof	Braun, Joel	M	62D,51
PT	Burkart, Rebecca L.	D	11
Asst Prof	Buselli, Mark	M	63A,29,47
Prof	Caneva, Thomas	D	37,48
FT	Colston, Daniel	M	62B
Assoc Prof	Crawford, Elizabeth A.	D	64C,35F
Asst Prof	Crow, Andrew	D	36
Assoc Prof	DiGiallonardo, Richard L.	M	34
PT	Edwards, Stacey	M	11
Prof	Ester, Don P.	D	32
Assoc Prof	Everett, Paul	M	49,63A,41
Asst Prof	Fishell, John C.	M	13L,34D
Asst Prof	Gerrity, Kevin W.	D	32
FT	Hall, Michael	M	38
Assoc Prof	Helton, James Caton	D	66A,66C
Asst Prof	Hendricks, Karin S.	D	32E
FT	Hicks, Ann M.	M	32
PT	Hourigan, Amy	B	32
Assoc Prof	Hourigan, Ryan M.	M	32
Assoc Prof	Inks, Kimberly	D	32B
FT	Johnson, Derek Martin		13
Assoc Prof	Kaplan, Amelia S.	PhD	10,13
Assoc Prof	Karna, Duane	D	36
PT	Karna, Kathy	D	62E
Assoc Prof	Kilburn, Ray	D	66A
Prof Emeritus PT	Koriath, Kirby L.	D	66G,66H,31A,34
Assoc Prof	Kothman, Keith K.	D	10B,10,34,13,35C
PT	Kothman, Mary	M	62A
PT	Lautzenheiser, Tim N.	D	32
Assoc Prof	Levitt, Joseph	D	39
Asst Prof	Lyon, Matthew	M	49,63D
Prof	Mantione, Meryl E.	D	61
Assoc Prof	Maurer, Kathleen M.	M	61
Assoc Prof	McConnell, Roger	M	11
Prof Emeritus PT	McWilliams, Larry	M	47,29
Prof	Mueller, Erwin	D	50,65
Assoc Prof	Nagel, Jody	D	13,10,45,35C
Asst Prof	Opie, Peter	M	62C
Asst Prof	Oravitz, Michael	M	13,10
Prof	Palmer, Robert	D	66A,66C
Prof	Platt, Heather	D	11,12,12A
Prof	Pohly, Linda L.	D	11,12,14,12A
Assoc Prof	Pounds, Michael S.	DMA	10,34D,13,45,34
Assoc Prof	Priebe, Craig	M	61,39
Prof	Reilly, Paul C.	M	41,70,67D
PT	Rhinehart, James	D	11
Prof	Rhoden, Lori E.	D	66A,66B,66D
Prof	Richter, Elizabeth	M	41,66E,66D
Asst Prof	Routenberg, Scott	D	29,66A
Assoc Prof	Scheib, John W.	D	32,32E
Assoc Prof	Seidel, John	D	49,63C
FT	Shimazaki-Kilburn, Yoko	M	61
PT	Smith, Tawnya D.	M	32
Assoc Prof	Steib, Murray	D	11,12,12A
Asst Prof	Sweeney, Aryn D.	D	64B
Prof	Sweger, Keith	D	48,64D,42
Prof	Trawick, Eleanor	D	10,13,13F,13H,13L
Assoc Prof	Vayman, Anna	M	62A
Asst Prof	Vondran, Shawn	D	37,60B
Assoc Prof	Watanabe, Mihoko	D	64A,20
PT	Wolfe, Anne Marie	D	63D,64,32E,10F,60B
Assoc Prof	Wolfe, George	D	64E,48
Prof	Zhong, Mei	D	61

IN0200 Bethel College

Department of Music
1001 Bethel Circle
Mishawaka, IN 46545
(574) 807-7575   Fax: (574) 807-7806
www.bethelcollege.edu
E-mail: music@bethelcollege.edu

4 Year Institution

Chair: Robert Ham, 80A

Assoc Prof	Garrett, Victoria	M	61
Assoc Prof	Ham, Marilynn	M	66A,66C
Assoc Prof	Ham, Robert	M	32D,36,40
Adj	Hostetler, Jill		36,40,61
Prof	Kendall, Michael	D	60,37,32,20,34
Prof	Klopfenstein, Reginald	D	13A,12A,47,50,65
Assoc Prof	Pennix, Derrick A.	D	61,39
Assoc Prof	Rhein, Robert	D	10A,66A,11,12A,13
Assoc Prof	Warkentien, Vicky	D	13,66,41,51,38

IN0250 Butler University

Jordan College of Fine Arts
4600 Sunset Ave
Indianapolis, IN 46208-3443
(317) 940-9231   Fax: (317) 940-9658
www.butler.edu/music
E-mail: dbloin@butler.edu

4 Year Institution, Graduate School
Member of NASM

Master of Music in Composition, Master of Music in Music Theory, Master of Music in Performance, Master of Music in Conducting, Master of Music in Music Education, Master of Music in Music History, Master of Music in Pedagogy

Chair: Daniel Bolin, 80A
Interim Dean: Michelle Jarvis, 80A
Assistant Chair & Dir., Graduate Studies: Eric Stark, 80C,80H
Interim Associate Dean: Owen Schaub, 80H

Assoc Prof	Bolin, Daniel	D	32,11
Asst Prof	Boyd, Kathleen E.	D	66A
Inst PT	Brightman, Nicholas	M	64E,72
Assoc Prof	Brimmer, Timothy	D	60,32,36,34
Inst PT	Bringerud, Catherine	M	66C
Inst PT	Briscoe, Anna	M	66A
Prof	Briscoe, James R.	D	12A,14,12C,12
Assoc Prof	Brooks, Davis H.	D	62A
Assoc Prof	Brooks, Lisa E.	D	62A
Inst PT	Childs-Helton, Sally	D	20
Assoc Prof	Clark, Richard A.	M	38,60
Inst	Crabiel, Jon	M	65,13A
Prof	DeRusha, Stanley	M	32E,11,60B
Assoc Prof	Dimmick, Penny	D	32,65,34
Asst Prof	Eyerly, Sarah J.	D	12,13A,14A,15
Assoc Prof	Felice, Frank	D	10,10B,10D,34D,13D
Inst PT	Gerber, Tom	M	13,66H
Inst PT	Gilgallon, Mark	M	61
Assoc Prof	Gillespie, Jeffrey L.	D	13
Prof	Grechesky, Robert	D	60,32
Assoc Prof	Grubb, William	D	62C
Inst PT	Guelce, Sayuri	M	66D
Prof	Gullickson, Andrea	D	64B
Inst PT	Hetrick, Craig	M	65
Inst PT	Hinton, Heather	D	66G
Asst Prof	Jones, Melvin Rusty	D	13
Assoc Prof	Kelton, Mary Katherine	D	61
Inst PT	Kunda, Keith	D	13
Assoc Prof	Leck, Henry	B	60,36,32
Assoc Prof	Lewis, Gail D.	D	63B,13
Inst	McCullough, David	M	37,32

Inst PT	Miller, Alan	M	63A
Assoc Prof	Miranda, Julianne M.	M	66C,66D
Inst PT	Mobley, Jenny	M	66A,66D
Inst PT	Moratz, Karen	M	64A
Prof	Mulholland, James Q.	M	11,61
Assoc Prof	Murray, David	M	62D,11
Inst PT	Muston, Wendy	B	62E
Inst PT	Nobles, Ron		62
Asst Prof	Pivec, Matthew	M	29,64E
Inst PT	Queen, Jeffrey	M	65
Inst PT	Rickards, Steven	D	61
Inst PT	Rodin, Jared	M	63C
Inst PT	Rossi, Achille	B	64C
Inst PT	Sanborn, Timothy	D	13
Prof	Schelle, Michael	D	13,10,43,10F
Inst PT	Schmid, John	M	54
Inst	Scott, Mary Anne Spangler	M	61,39
Prof	Shapiro, Laurence	M	62A
Inst PT	Smith, Don	M	66D
Inst PT	Smith, Malcolm	D	64B
Assoc Prof	Spaniol, Douglas E.	D	64D,37
Inst	Stark, Eric	D	36
Inst PT	Stormes, Sheridan	M	61
Inst PT	Terrell, Brett	M	51,70
Prof	Thickstun, Karen	M	66A,66D
Inst PT	Walters, Gary	M	66A,47
Inst PT	West, Cheryl	M	40,32
Inst PT	Williams, Melissa	M	63D
Inst PT	Wright, John	M	40

IN0300 Christian Theological Seminary

Church Music, Religion and the Arts
1000 W 42nd St
Indianapolis, IN 46208-3301
(317) 931-2350   Fax: (317) 931-2399
www.cts.edu
E-mail: jkrauser@cts.edu

Prof	Brown, Frank Burch	D	12A,66A,12B,10
Prof	Junker, Tercio	D	60A,36,31A,32D,10E
PT	Powell, Jason	D	20F,20H,31A,66A,66G

IN0350 DePauw University

Green Center for the Performing Arts
605 S College Ave
Greencastle, IN 46135-0037
(765) 658-4380   Fax: (765) 658-4042
www.depauw.edu/music
E-mail: markmccoy@depauw.edu

4 Year Institution
Member of NASM

Dean: D. Mark McCoy, 80A

Prof	Balensuela, Matthew	D	11,12A
Prof	Barber, Amy Lynn	D	65,50
Adj Prof	Beckel, James A.	B	63C
Asst Prof	Brockmann, Nicole M.	D	62B,32I,13C
Adj Prof	Carkeek, Maureen M.	M	66A
Asst Prof	Clodfelter, John D.	B	66A,66C,66D
Adj Prof	Coburn, Pamela	M	61
Prof	Cymerman, Claude	DIPL	66A
Adj Assoc Prof	Danforth, Robert B.	B	63B
Adj Assoc Prof	Dugan, Gregory S.	B	62D
Prof	Edberg, C. Eric	D	41,62C,13A
Prof	Edwards, Carla Grace	D	66G,13F
Asst Prof PT	Foster, Daniel	M	47
Prof	Foy, Leonard C.	M	63A,49,29
Adj Asst Prof	Grammel, Deborah Lynn	M	52
Adj Asst Prof	Helsley, Jack D.	M	62D
Assoc Prof	Hopson, Amanda	D	66A
Asst Prof	Jennings, Kerry L.	DMA	61
Prof	Jetton, Caroline K.	D	32
Asst Prof PT	Kim, Wonmin	M	66A
Asst Prof PT	Kramer, Katya	M	66A
Asst Prof	Lanzrein, Valentin Christian	D	61,66C
Inst	Lynch, Christopher	M	11,12A
Adj Asst Prof	McCoy, Darcy	D	66A,66C,12A,66B
Adj Asst Prof	Moore, Harriet T.	M	62E,70
Adj Asst Prof	Pare', Barbara A.	M	61,40
Prof	Pare', Craig T.	D	32,37,65,60
Inst PT	Pejril, Veronica	B	32F
Asst Prof	Perkins, Scott	D	10,13
Assoc Prof	Phang, May	D	66A,66B
Asst Prof PT	Rachford, Natalia	M	66A
Adj Prof	Reynolds, Anne B.	B	64A,41
Asst Prof	Ristow, Gregory C.	M	36,40
Prof	Rizner, Dan Joseph	M	41,62A

Prof	Salman, Randy Keith	M	47,64C,64E,29
Asst Prof	Sirotkin, Leonid	M	64B
Prof	Smith, Caroline B.	M	61
Prof	Smith, Orcenith George	M	60,38,63D
Adj Prof	Spicknall, John	D	66A
Assoc Prof	Spiegelberg, Scott C.	D	13
Asst Prof PT	Stepp, Scotty	M	64E
Adj Asst Prof	Stolle, Kara M.	M	64D,41
Adj Inst	Williams, Alexander W.	B	70

IN0400 Earlham College

Department of Music
801 National Rd W
Richmond, IN 47374-4095
(765) 983-1200 x 1410   Fax: (765) 983-1247
www.earlham.edu/music
E-mail: culvebi@earlham.edu

4 Year Institution

Chair: William Culverhouse, 80A

PT	Bailey, Rex	M	70
PT	Begel, Rich	M	63C,47
Asst Prof	Benamou, Marc	D	14,12,20,20D,12B
PT	Bergman, Elaine		64A
PT	Cozart, Keith	B	65,50
Asst Prof	Culverhouse, William	D	36,12A,60
PT	Denham, Ellen Louise	B	61
PT	Diamond, David	D	63A
PT	Estes, Charlie	B	70
Prof	Graves, Daniel H.	D	11,12A,36,60,41
PT	Hayase, Takako	D	66A
	Lardinois, John		62A,62B
PT	Madsen, Jessica	M	66A
PT	Neumayr, Anton	B	62D
PT	Parcell, Renee	B	63B
	Piper, Patrick		66A,53
	Piper, Shenita		36
PT	Polanco-Safadit, Pavel	M	66,53,46,47
PT	Ray, Kathryn		64B
PT	Roesch, Erin R.		64C
PT	Shikaly, Al	B	64E,48,66
Asst Prof	Tobey, Forrest	D	38,47,13,34
Prof Emeritus	Vail, Eleanore	M	11,12A,66A
PT	Wheatley, Jennifer	B	62C

IN0500 Franklin College

Department of Music
101 Branigin Blvd
Franklin, IN 46131
(317) 738-8271   Fax: (317) 738-8242
www.franklincollege.edu
E-mail: kburke@franklincollege.edu

4 Year Liberal Arts Institution

Chair: Kevin R. Burke, 80A

Asst Prof	Burke, Kevin R.	D	12,13,20,42,63B
Adj Lect	DeForest, Eric P.	D	61
Adj Lect	Gries, Rachel	M	62A,51
Asst Prof	Hayes, Casey J.	D	36,32,11
Adj Lect	Hoeflicker, Cale	ABD	70
Adj Lect	Lapin, Geoff	M	62C
Lect	Mendoza, Eleanor	M	61
Adj Lect	O'Neal, Andrea	B	66A,66D
Adj Lect	Piccirillo, Lauren	M	64
Staff	True, Janice	B	66C

IN0550 Goshen College

Department of Music
1700 S Main St
Goshen, IN 46526
(574) 535-7361   Fax: (574) 535-7949
www.goshen.edu
E-mail: music@goshen.edu

4 Year Institution

Co-Chair: Debra Brubaker, 80A
Co-Chair: Matthew Hill, 80A
Dir., Artist Series: Brian Wiebe, 80F

Prof	Brubaker, Debra	D	39,61,36,31A,20
	Fashun, Christopher H.	M	38,65,32,47,62B

Prof	Hill, Matthew	D	66A,66B,11,12A
Asst Prof	Hochstetler, Scott	D	36,61,60
Assoc Prof	Lapp, Beverly K.	M	66B,66A,11,66C
Prof Emeritus	Oyer, Mary K.	D	
Asst Prof	Seitz, Christine L.	M	13,66C,34
Prof Emeritus	Sherer, Kathryn	M	
Prof Emeritus	Sherer, Lon	D	
Assoc Prof	Soroka, Solomia	D	13,62A,41
Lect PT	Stegmann, Matthias	M	70,35G
Assoc Prof	Thaller, Gregg	D	65,32,13C,38
Asst Prof	Thogersen, Chris	M	66A,66G,32B,31A

IN0650 Hanover College

Department of Music
PO Box 890
Hanover, IN 47243
(812) 866-7342   Fax: (812) 866-7114
www.hanover.edu/academics/programs/music/
E-mail: hollis@hanover.edu

4 Year Institution

Chair: C. Kimm Hollis, 80A
Dir., Admissions: John Reister, 80D

Assoc Prof	Batchvarova, Madlen T.	D	60A,36,61,66A,12A
Prof	Hollis, C. Kimm	D	13,66A
Assoc Prof	Mruzek, David M.	D	11,37,38,47
	Plaster, Amos		66F

IN0700 Huntington University

Department of Music
2303 College Ave
Huntington, IN 46750
(260) 359-4262   Fax: (260) 359-4249
www.huntington.edu
E-mail: nbarnes@huntington.edu

4 Year Institution

Chair: George W. Killian, Jr., 80A

Adj	Burkett, Darlene	M	44,66G
Adj	Burkett, Phil L.	D	31
Adj	Clancy, Eric	B	47,29,53
Adj	Gardner, John	M	64C
Assoc Prof	Killian, George W.	D	60A,32,36
Adj	Killian, Joni	M	61,36,39
Adj	Lewellen, Michael		63B
Asst Prof	Lynn, Robert	D	13,37,38,62C,63D
Adj	MacKay-Galbraith, Janet	M	64A
Adj	Rowley, Terra	M	32B
Adj	Schleiffer, Marlene J.	D	10,64B
Adj	Schurger, Phillip	M	70,10
Adj	Smith, Elizabeth		13C,62A
Prof	Spedden, Patricia R.	D	66A,66B,13,66C,66D
	Spitler, Justin		34
Adj	Walter, Matt	B	63A
Adj	Wutke, Drew	B	66D,66C

IN0800 Indiana State University

School of Music
Landini Ctr for Perf. & Fine Arts
300 N 7th
Terre Haute, IN 47809
(812) 237-2771   Fax: (812) 237-3009
www.indstate.edu/music
E-mail: Nancy.CobbLippens@indstate.edu

4 Year Institution, Graduate School
Member of NASM

Master of Music in Performance, Master of Music in Conducting, Master of Music in Music Education

Director: Nancy Cobb Lippens, 80A
Dir., Graduate Studies: Douglas Keiser, 80C

Prof	Balensuela, Peggy	D	61
Assoc Prof	Ballard, Dennis L.	D	32
Inst	Boone, Christine	D	13
Prof	Bro, Paul	D	48,64E
Other	Browne, Lynette	D	66B
Assoc Prof	Buchanan, Scott	D	36,60
Asst Prof	Carlisle, Mark R.	D	36,61
PT	Claybrook, Kara	M	61
Assoc Prof	Davis, Colleen	D	61
Assoc Prof	Davis, William	D	38,62A,62B
Asst Prof	Dean, Terry Lynn	D	11,12A,13
PT	Dimick, Glen	M	63D
PT	Edwards, Julie	M	13,12A
Other	Fallon, Kelly	B	35,67,71,72
Prof	Finnie, Jimmy	D	50,65
Prof	Fowler, Kurt	D	62C,11,12A,51
PT	Gallagher, Todd	M	62D
Assoc Prof	George, Roby	D	37,60
PT	Gunn, Katherine	M	64B,32
Assoc Prof	Keiser, Douglas	D	37,32
Prof	Kilp, Brian T.	D	63B,13
Other	Krasnican, Martha	M	66C
Prof	Lippens, Nancy Cobb	DMA	10,13,36
Asst Prof	Luebke, Linda M.	M	32
PT	Mannell, David B.	M	61
PT	McPike, Brent G.	D	70
Prof	Mitchell, Randall	D	63C
PT	Niiyama, Kelley	M	64C
PT	Pennington, Curt	M	13,66D
Assoc Prof	Piechocinski, Janet	D	66D
Assoc Prof	Piechocinski, Theodore J.	JD	35
PT	Powers, Daniel	M	10
PT	Roseland, Chad	M	13,64D
Prof	Simms, Beverley	D	66A,66D
Prof Emeritus PT	Spicknall, John P.	D	12A,47,64C
PT	Strawn, Logan	M	62B
Inst	Vincent, Jennifer J.	M	32
Inst	Waugh, Robert	M	63A,47
PT	Williams, John J.	M	37
Assoc Prof	Wilson, Joyce	D	11,64A

IN0900 Indiana Univ-Bloomington

Jacobs School of Music
1201 E Third St
Bloomington, IN 47405
(812) 855-2435   Fax: (812) 856-5006
www.music.indiana.edu
E-mail: wennerst@indiana.edu

4 Year Institution, Graduate School
Member of NASM

Performer Diploma Orchestral Studies, Performer Diploma Solo Performance, Master of Music in Computer Music Composition, Master of Music in Early Music, Artist Diploma, Master of Music in Music Theory/Master of Library Science, Master of Music in Composition, Master of Music in Music Theory, Master of Music in Performance, Master of Science in Music Education, Master of Music Education, PhD in Music Theory, PhD in Music Education, Doctor of Music in Composition, PhD in Musicology, Master of Arts in Musicology, Master of Music in Choral Conducting, Doctor of Music Education, Doctor of Music in Music Literature & Performance, Master of Music in Jazz Studies, Master of Music in Wind Conducting, Specialist in Music: Music Education, Master of Music in Orchestral Conducting, Master of Arts in Musicology/Master of Library Science, Master of Music in Organ & Sacred Music, Doctor of Music in Early Music, Doctor of Music in Organ & Sacred Music, Doctor of Music in Choral Conducting, Doctor of Music in Orchestral Conducting, Doctor of Music in Wind Conducting

Dean: Gwyn Richards, 80A
Dir., Undergraduate Studies: Lissa F. May, 80B
Dir., Graduate Studies: Eric J. Isaacson, 80C
Executive Associate Dean: Eugene O'Brien, 80H
Associate Dean, Instruction: Mary H. Wennerstrom, 80H

Assoc Prof	Adams, Kyle	PhD	13
Asst Prof	Allen, Jeremy	M	62D,29
Specialist	An, Chun Chi		52
Prof	Arad, Atar	DIPL	62B
Assoc Prof	Arvin, Gary	M	61
Adj Lect	Asai, Rika	M	12
Prof	Auer, Edward	B	66A
Prof	Bae, Ik-Hwan		42,62A
Prof	Baker, David N.	M	47,29
Prof	Baker, W. Claude	D	10
Prof	Battersby, Edmund	M	66A
Senior Lect	Bell, Joshua	DIPL	62A
Adj Lect	Bellisario, Kristen	M	11
Prof	Bernhardsson, Sigurbjorn	M	62A,42
Prof	Bitetti, Ernesto	DIPL	70
Prof	Bloom, Myron		63B
Assoc Prof	Bobo, Kevin A.	M	65
Adj Lect	Bogard, Emily	M	60A
Prof	Brancart, Evelyne	DIPL	66A
Prof	Bransby, Bruce	B	62D
Prof	Brendel, Wolfgang	DIPL	61

Directory of Institutions

Title	Name	Degree	Codes
Assoc Prof	Brenner, Brenda L.	D	62A,32E
Vstng Lect	Brown, Craig	B	62D
Prof	Burkholder, J. Peter	PhD	12
Prof	Campbell, James	B	64C
Academic Specialist	Carballo, Kimberly	M	39
Asst Prof	Cartledge, David O.	D	66A
Prof	Cesbron, Jacques		52
Senior Lect	Chen, Chih-Yi	M	66C
Adj Lect	Christiansen, Corey M.	M	70,29
Adj Prof	Clevenger, Dale	B	63B
Adj Lect	Climis, Sarah	M	11
Prof	Cohen, Arnaldo	B	66A
Assoc Prof	Colon, Emilio W.	M	62C
Adj Lect	Contino, Adriana	B	62C
Senior Lect	Cook Glen, Constance		11
Prof	Cord, Edmund	B	63A
Academic Specialist	Cuccaro-Penhorwood, Costanza	B	61
Academic Specialist	Di Bacco, Giuliano	PhD	12A,13J
Asst Prof	DiOrio, Dominick	DMA	60A,36
Prof	Dzubay, David	D	10,43
Prof	Eban, Eli	DIPL	64C
Prof	Edlina-Dubinsky, Luba	M	66A
Prof	Effron, David	M	60,38
Prof	Ellefson, Peter E.	M	63C
Prof	Elliott, Paul	M	61,67H,55
Prof	Fagen, Arthur H.	DIPL	60,38
Prof	Fishell, Janette S.	D	66G
Prof	Fleezanis, Jorja		62A
Asst Prof	Ford, Philip	PhD	12
Vstng Asst Prof	Freeze, Timothy	PhD	12
Prof	Freund, Don	D	10
Prof	Fuks, Mauricio	DIPL	62A
Prof	Ganatra, Simin	B	62A,42
Prof	Gass, Glenn	D	20G,11
Assoc Prof	Gault, Brent M.	PhD	32
Prof	Gazouleas, Edward	B	62B
Assoc Prof	Gershman, Jeffrey D.	D	37
Asst Prof	Gibson, John	PhD	10B
Assoc Prof	Gillespie, Luke O.	D	11,29
Prof	Gillespie, Wendy	B	67A,55
Assoc Prof	Goldberg, Halina	PhD	12
Asst Prof	Gray, William Jon	D	60,36
Adj Lect	Grieb, Scott	M	11
Adj Lect	Guntren, Alissa	M	11
Prof	Haguenauer, Jean-Louis	B	66A
Prof	Harbison, Patrick L.	M	47,29
Prof	Harrison, Robert J.	D	61
Prof	Hart, Mary Ann	M	61
Prof	Hass, Jeffrey E.	D	10B
Assoc Prof PT	Havranek, Patricia	MFA	61
Adj Lect	Hoeprich, Eric	DIPL	64C,67H
Senior Lect	Hollinden, Andrew J.	M	11,29
Asst Prof	Hood, Mark	B	35C,35G
Assoc Prof	Hook, Julian L.	PhD	13
Senior Lect	Hopper, Alice R.	M	61
Assoc Prof	Horlacher, Gretchen G.	PhD	13
Assoc Prof	Horne, Brian	D	61
Prof	Houghton, Steve		47,65
Adj Assoc Prof	Huff, Walter	M	36,60A
Adj Lect	Huseynova, Aida N.	PhD	11
Adj Lect	Im, Sung-Mi	M	42
Assoc Prof	Isaacson, Eric J.	PhD	13,34
Assoc Prof	Ivanovitch, Roman M.	PhD	13
Vstng Lect	Jankovic, Petar S.	M	70
Adj Lect	Jensen, Espen	M	20H
Asst Prof	Johnston, Blair	PhD	13
Prof	Jorgensen, Estelle R.	PhD	32
Adj Lect	Kalis, Dawn	M	67F
Adj Asst Prof	Kallaur, Barbara	M	67D
Prof	Kaplan, Mark S.	B	62A
Adj Assoc Prof	Karp, Benjamin	M	62C
Academic Specialist	Kazimir, David	B	66G,69,71
Prof	Kerr, Alexander	B	62A
Prof	Kielian-Gilbert, Marianne	PhD	13
Prof	Kim, Eric	M	62C
Prof	Klug, Howard D.	M	64C
Prof	Kubiak, Teresa	M	61
Adj Lect	Kwapis, Kris	D	67
Prof	Lenthe, Carl	B	63C
Asst Prof	Leon, Javier F.	D	14,20H
Prof	Liotta, Vincent J.	M	39
Prof	Long, Michael	PhD	12
Prof	Ludwig, William	M	64D
Prof	Lukas, Kathryn	M	64A
Prof	Mardirossian, Kevork M.	DIPL	62A
Prof	May, Lissa F.	D	32
Adj Asst Prof	McClain, Washington	M	67D
Prof	McCraw, Michael	M	67D,55C,55
Prof	McDonald, Susann	DIPL	62E
Asst Prof	McKinnie, Douglas	PhD	35C,35G
Assoc Prof	McLean, Kathleen	DIPL	64D
Senior Lect	McNair, Sylvia	M	61
Vstng Academic Spec	Medina, Lindsay	M	35A
Prof	Melamed, Daniel R.	PhD	12
Assoc Prof	Miksza, Peter J.	PhD	32
Prof	Montane, Carlos	B	61
Adj Prof	Murphy, Heidi Grant	B	61
Prof	Murphy, Kevin	M	39
Assoc Prof	Murphy, Otis	D	64E
Assoc Prof	Muxfeldt, Kristina	PhD	12
Assoc Prof	Naoumoff, Emile	DIPL	66A
Prof	Nelsen, Jeffrey	B	63B
Senior Lect	Neriki, Reiko S.	M	66A
Prof	Neriki, Shigeo	DIPL	66A
Assoc Prof	Neswick, Bruce	M	66G
Prof	Noble, Timothy R.	M	61
Prof	North, Nigel	DIPL	67G,55
Prof	O'Brien, Eugene	D	10
Assoc Prof	Ossi, Massimo M.	PhD	12
Vstng Asst Prof	Park, Angela	D	66C,64
Adj Lect	Pearse, Linda	M	67E
Prof PT	Penhorwood, Edwin L.	D	39
Prof	Perantoni, Daniel T.	M	63D
Assoc Prof	Phan, P. Q.	D	10
Asst Prof PT	Phelps, Mark D.	M	61
Adj Lect	Phillips, Lee	M	66C
Prof	Poulimenos, Andreas	M	61
Prof	Pratt, Stephen Wayne	M	37
Prof	Pressler, Menahem	DIPL	66A
Vstng Asst Prof	Reger, Jeremy J.	D	66C,61
Prof	Richards, Gwyn	M	36
Prof	Ritchie, Stanley	DIPL	67B,55C
Assoc Prof	Robertello, Thomas J.	B	64A
Adj Assoc Prof	Roe, Roger A.	M	64B
Prof	Rommel, John D.	B	63A
Prof	Rostad, Masumi Per	M	62B,42
Adj Lect	Ruhstrat, Desiree	DIPL	62A
Academic Specialist	Sales, Doricha	M	52
Assoc Prof	Samarotto, Frank	PhD	13
Senior Lect	Schrock, Scharmal	M	61
Senior Lect Adj	Segal, Uriel	B	38
Prof	Seraphinoff, Richard M.	M	67E
Asst Prof PT	Shaver, Stephen R.		66F
Prof	Shaw, Karen	D	66A
Prof	Simpson, Marietta	M	61
Asst Prof	Smedley, Eric M.	D	37
Assoc Prof	Smith, Ayana	PhD	12
Senior Lect	Sparks, Thomas G.		72
Assoc Prof	Spiro, Michael E.	B	62
Prof	Starker, Janos	DIPL	62C
Prof	Stewart, M. Dee	M	63C
Prof	Stiles, Patricia J.	M	61
Academic Specialist	Stillman, Fallon	M	35C,35G
Assoc Prof	Strand, Katherine D.	PhD	32B,32C,32H,32G
Prof	Strauss, Konrad	M	35C,35G
Prof	Strommen, Linda	M	64B
Senior Lect	Stucker, Michael D.	AS	35C,35G
Prof	Stumpf, Peter	DIPL	62C
Adj Lect	Swaney, Susan	M	36
Assoc Prof	Szmyt, Elzbieta M.	M	62E
Academic Specialist	Tadey, Anthony	B	35C,35G
Prof	Tafoya, John J.	M	65
Adj Lect	Tai, FanFen	D	62E
Assoc Prof	Tartell, Joey	M	63A
Asst Prof PT	Taylor, Karen M.	D	66A,66B
Specialist	Ter-Grigor'yan, Irina	M	52
Asst Prof	Travers, Aaron	PhD	10
Specialist	Tzvetkov, Atanas	D	70
Asst Prof PT	Umeyama, Shuichi	M	39
Prof	Vamos, Brandon	M	62C,42
Prof	Vaness, Carol T.	M	61
Prof	Verdy, Violette		52
Prof	Vernon, Michael		52
Adj Lect	Vollmer, Jeffrey	M	11
Asst Prof	Wallarab, Brent K.	M	29,47
Assoc Prof	Walsh, Thomas P.	D	64E
Lect	Wang, Guoping	DIPL	52
Vstng Asst Prof	Wang, Liang-yu	D	66C,62
Adj Prof	Ward-Steinman, David	D	10,11
Prof	Ward-Steinman, Patrice Madura	D	32G,32D,32,29,47
Adj Asst Prof	Warren, Alicyn	PhD	10B
Prof	Watts, Andre	B	66A
Prof	Wennerstrom, Mary H.	PhD	13
Academic Specialist	Wieligman, Thomas	M	37,38,43,46
Prof	Wise, Patricia	B	61
Prof	Woodley, David C.	M	37
Prof	Wright, Elisabeth B.	B	66H
Prof	Wyrczynski, Stephen	DIPL	62B
Vstng Asst Prof	Yeary, Mark	PhD	13
Prof	Young, Christopher	D	66G
Asst Prof	Zanovello, Giovanni	PhD	12
Prof	Zegree, Stephen	D	36,47,40
Prof	Zweig, Mimi	B	62B

IN0905 Indiana Univ-Purdue Univ
Department of Music
2101 E Coliseum Blvd
Fort Wayne, IN 46805-1499
(260) 481-6714   Fax: (260) 481-5422
www.ipfw.edu
E-mail: beanr@ipfw.edu

4 Year Institution
Member of NASM

Chair: Robert D. Bean, 80A

PT	Agen, Kristine	B	33
PT	Ator, Irene S.	B	66G
Assoc Prof Emeritus	Ator, James	D	13,10,48,64E,29
PT	Bardi, Elena	B	66C
Prof	Bean, Robert D.	D	13A,66A,66B,66C,66D
PT	Bickley, Ashlee Beth	M	61
Assoc Prof	Bookout, Melanie	D	11,12A,12,55,67A
PT	Busarow, Jonathan	M	61
Lect	Cooke, David	M	38,60B,49,63C
PT	Donnell, Julie	M	61
Lect	Farlow, Peggy	M	33
PT	Ferguson, Robert	M	70
PT	Fisher, Daniel	B	34D
PT	Freeman, Christine L.	M	13A,66C,66A
PT	Gallagher, Mitchell	B	35A
PT	Gnagey, Sam	B	63D
Lect	Greider, Cynthia S.	M	64C,41
PT	Hahn, Carol G.	M	66D,66A
Assoc Prof	Haritun, Rosalie	D	11
PT	Hastings, Gena M.	M	32B
PT	Hinsey, Jackie	B	33
PT	Hunsinger, Melita	M	62C
Assoc Prof	Jackson, Nancy	D	33
PT	Johnson, Adam	D	63C
Lect	Johnson, Kenneth W.	D	13B,12A
PT	Kennedy, Patricia E.	D	13C,32D
PT	Klickman, William	M	38,32E
PT	Lautzenheiser, Tim	D	32
Lect	Lewellen, Michael	M	63B
Lect	Lydy, Laura	M	70,41
PT	MacDonald, Campbell	B	64C
Prof Emeritus	Meyers, Joseph	D	39,61
Asst Prof	Mitchell, Aaron Paul	D	32D,36,40,60A
PT	North, Geoffrey	D	13B,13C
Asst Prof	Outland, Joyanne	D	13,66A,66D,66B
PT	Piekarski, Kevin J.	B	62D
PT	Reeves, Derek	M	62A,62B
Assoc Prof	Resch, Barbara	D	32B,32C
Assoc Prof Emeritus	Robertson, Masson	D	13,66A,66B,66C
Asst Prof	Rutkowski, Chris	D	13,34D
Asst Prof	Savage, Samuel T.	D	61,39
PT	Schwaberow, Denise	B	33
Lect	Schweikert, Eric	B	65
Lect	Severs, Alan R.	M	63A,41
PT	Stachofsky, Mark	M	61
PT	Streeter, David	M	46,48
Vstng Inst	Tembras, Dan	D	32E,37,60B
Asst Prof	Tescarollo, Hamilton	D	66A,66B,66C
PT	Trentacosti, Marcella	M	62A
PT	Trentacosti, Michael J.	M	64D
Assoc Prof	Vernon, James Farrell	D	64E,47
Lect	Volk, Jennifer Regan	M	64A
PT	Walley, Steve	M	13G,34,10D
Asst Prof	Wright-Bower, Linda	M	33

IN0907 Indiana Univ-Purdue Univ
Department of Music & Arts Technology
535 W Michigan St
Room 352
Indianapolis, IN 46202
(317) 274-4000   Fax: (317) 278-2590
music.iupui.edu
E-mail: nmthomps@iupui.edu

4 Year Institution, Graduate School, State-Sponsored

Master of Science in Music Therapy, Master of Science in Music Technology

Chair: Fred J. Rees, 80A
Head, Graduate Studies: G. David Peters, 80C
Dir., IUPUI Music Academy: EJ Choe, 80E

Lect PT	Albright, Bruce Randall	M	20G
Adj	Allee, Steve		66A,47,35A,53
Lect	Alvarado, John	M	41,70
Lect PT	Anderson, Elizabeth Rene	M	61
Lect PT	Babb, Douglas		45
Prof	Bailey, Darrell	D	11
Lect PT	Baranyk, David S.	M	70
Inst PT	Bowman, Sean	B	63A
Lect PT	Brooks, Beth	M	32F
Asst Prof	Burns, Deb S.	D	33,12
Adj	Byrket, Patrick S.	M	11
Asst Prof	Choe, EJ	D	13,11,32A,32B,66
Adj	Chung, Miri	M	62A,62B,33,51
Lect PT	Copeland, David	M	37
Prof	Deal, W. Scott	D	34,65
Adj	Dimick, Glen	D	63D
Lect	Drews, Michael R.	D	13A,13B,13C,13E,11
Adj	Helsley, Jack		46,47,62D
Adj	Hetrick, Loy	M	63C,63D
Adj	Hopkins, Alice	M	61,66A
Lect PT	Janke, Tom J.	M	34,62D
Lect PT	Koenig, Mark	M	34,63A
Lect PT	Laranja, Ricardo	M	34D,35C
Asst Prof	Lindsey, Roberta	D	11,13A,34C,34B,14A
Lect PT	Mannell, David	M	11,61,36,32B
Adj	Marcus, Aaron		64E,47
Other	Marshall-McClure, Clara	M	11
Lect	Meng, Chuiyuan	M	34A,66A,34G
Lect PT	Mullins, Debra		66A,34C
Lect	Munson, Jordan	M	45,53,13A
Adj	Murphy, Steve		66A,66B,54
Prof	Peters, G. David	D	34,12C,12,35C,35A
Adj	Redmond, Michael		11
Prof	Rees, Fred J.	DMA	34,12C,35C,32,12
Adj	Schreibman, Janice		12,33
Adj	Scull, Erik	M	34D
Lect PT	Sowers, Jodi L.	M	11,64A,41
Adj	Stapleton, Chip		29A,64E,14C,11
Lect PT	Stokes, Jennifer	M	66A,66B,66D,11,66C
Asst Prof	Vander Gheynst, John R.	D	29A,10A,63,34D,35A
Adj	Walker, Regina	M	39,40
Asst Prof	Walker, Richard L.	M	65,35,34A,50,37
Adj	Williams, Sandy		70,47,46
Lect PT	Witte, Diane	M	66A,66B,66D
Adj	Wynn, Julie		34F,66A,66B

IN0910 Indiana Univ-South Bend
E. M. Raclin Sch of the Arts-Music
1700 Mishawaka Ave
PO Box 7111
South Bend, IN 46634-1700
(574) 520-4134   Fax: (574) 237-4317
www.iusb.edu
E-mail: musicsb@iusb.edu

4 Year Institution, Graduate School

Artist Diploma, Master of Music in Composition, Master of Music in Performance

Dean, School of the Arts: Marvin V. Curtis, 80A
Coordinator: Jeffrey Wright, 80A
Dir., Graduate Studies: John S. Mayrose, 80C

Lect	Badridze, Ketevan	M	66A
Adj Lect	Capshaw, Reed	M	63C,63D
Lect	Cooper, Jameson	M	62A,38,60B
Asst Prof	Douglas, Kenneth	D	32,37,60B
Asst Prof	Duce, Geoffrey	DMA	13,66A,66C,66D
Adj Lect	Emery, Marian L.	M	13A
Adj Lect	French, Chris	M	64E,64C
Adj Lect	Hochstetler, Tim	B	70
Adj Lect	Hovan, Rebecca	M	64A
Adj Lect	Inglefield, Deb S.	M	63B
Adj Asst Prof	Kam, Genna	D	11,66D
Adj Lect	Kizer, Kay	M	10B
Adj Lect	Kuehner, Eric L.	B	64
Lect	Li, Darren Si-Yan	M	62C
Vstng Asst Prof	Limbert, Thom	D	10,13,20
Adj Lect	Mather-Stow, Andrea	B	64B
Adj Lect	Mayer, Deborah L.	M	61
Asst Prof	Mayrose, John S.	D	10,13
Asst Prof	McCormack, Jessica D.	D	61,39,12,15,67H
Assoc Prof	Muniz, Jorge	D	10A,13,10B,10,43
Lect	Murphy, Jacob P.	M	62A
Adj Asst Prof	Phillips, Edward D.	D	63A,35E
Adj Asst Prof	Roth, Jonathan D.	D	11
Adj Asst Prof	Rusche, Marjorie M.	D	10,13
Adj Lect	Schleicher, Elizabeth	M	61
Adj Lect	Seitz, Christine	M	11
Adj Lect	Stegmann, Matthias	M	70
Adj Lect	Thompson, Douglass	M	65
Lect	Tidaback, Darrell	M	62D,10B,47
Prof	Toradze, Alexander D.	M	66A
Lect	Vargas, Luis Enrique	M	62B
Adj Lect	Wade, Michael	M	36
Adj Asst Prof	Weiss, Celia	M	66C
Asst Prof	Wright, Jeffrey	D	12
Adj Asst Prof	Young-Davids, Suzann	D	62E

IN1010 Indiana University-Southeast
Department of Music
4201 Grant Line Rd
New Albany, IN 47150-2158
(812) 941-2655   Fax: (812) 941-2660
www.ius.edu/music
E-mail: semusic@ius.edu

4 Year Institution

Chair & Preparatory Division: Joanna Goldstein, 80A,80E

Adj	Acker, Gregory	M	20
Adj	Albrecht, Ken		63B
Adj	Amend, Jerome	M	63A,49
Adj	Baugh-Bennett, Grace	M	66A
Adj	Bohannon, Helen	M	62A
Adj	Brown, Christine A.	M	11,66A,13,66B
Adj	Brown, Sharon L.	M	61
Adj	Casper, Meghan	M	62B
Adj	Cumberledge, Melinda	M	61,39
Adj	Curry, Paul		14C
Adj	DaSilva, Mario	M	70
Adj	Dickinson, Marci	M	66A,13A
Adj	Fortin, Nicholas		62A
Adj	Frank, Mary Lou	M	11,13A
Prof	Goldstein, Joanna	D	13,66A,66C,38,11
Adj	Gross, Louis E.	M	64C
Adj	Grossman, Andrea	M	11,66A,13A,66D
Adj	Haertel, Tim	M	35C,35G
Adj	Hamilton, Janet	D	11,66G
Adj	Jamner, Margaret	M	64A
Adj	Johanningsmeier, Scott	B	34
Adj	Johnson, Daryl		63D
Adj	Johnson, Trevor	M	64B
Adj	Kemp, Mildred	M	63C,63D
Adj	Mattingly, Stephen	D	70
Adj	McClure, Carol	M	62E
Adj	McMahel, Donald	D	37,38,60B
Adj	Moore, John S.	M	64E
Adj	Niren, Ann Glazer	D	11,12A
Adj	Olsen, Karl	M	62D
Adj	Onwood, Susannah	M	62C
Adj	Rebilas, Richard P.	M	61
Adj	Reigler, Susan		11
Adj	Soren, Roger	M	64D
Adj	Tate, Mark	M	65

IN1025 Indiana Wesleyan University
Division of Music
4201 S Washington St
Marion, IN 46953-4974
(765) 677-2152   Fax: (765) 677-2620
www.indwes.edu/Academics/CAS/Division-of-Music/
E-mail: todd.guy@indwes.edu

4 Year Liberal Arts Institution

Chair: Todd Guy, 80A

Asst Prof	Brautigam, Keith D.	D	61,39
Assoc Prof	Dawson, Lisa	D	61,39
Asst Prof	Flanagin, Michael	M	37,63A,63B,41,60B
Prof	Guy, Todd	D	36,31A,61,60A,11
Asst Prof	Huff, Christina	M	32A,32B,32C,11,36
Assoc Prof	Huntington, Tammie M.	D	61,39
Inst	Johnson, Ken	M	13E,70
PT	Kraft, James	D	63C,63D
Prof	Lessly, Chris Ann	D	32,41,48,64C,64E
Prof	Maher, John	D	13,12A,66G,16,34
Asst Prof	Miller, Peter	M	61,11
Assoc Prof	Park-Kim, Phoenix		66A,66D,66C
PT	Patton, Richard	D	61
Prof	Rickey, Euni	D	66A,66D,66B,66C
PT	Rojas, Ner	M	70
Assoc Prof	Syswerda, Todd	D	13A,13,10,11,10F
Asst Prof	Thompson, Jason	M	38,62A,62B,51,62C
PT	Westfall, Ben		35G
PT	Whitford, Trudy	M	64A,11
Prof	Wooldridge, Marc	D	13
Assoc Prof	Yoder, Tim	D	31A
Inst	Zimmerman, Tim	M	63A

IN1050 Manchester College
Department of Music
604 E College Ave
North Manchester, IN 46962-0164
(260) 982-5426   Fax: (260) 982-5043
www.manchester.edu
E-mail: cphumphries@manchester.edu

4 Year Institution

Dir., Summer Programs: Stuart Jones, 80G

Adj	Chambers, James Alan	M	61,13A,36
Adj	Dockter, Larry	M	47,63A,65
Adj	Donner, Ann	M	64A
Adj	Donner, George	M	64B
Asst Prof	Gindin, Suzanne B.	M	32,37,38,41,63B
Adj	Gratz, Robin	M	66G
	Jeoung, Ji-Young	D	66C
Adj	Jones, Robert	M	64C
Adj	Kummernuss, Linda	M	62A
Assoc Prof	Lynn, Debra J.	D	60,36,61,40,39
Prof	Planer, John H.	D	20,12,13,14,61
Adj	Sloan, Chikako	M	66A
Adj	Streator, Carol	M	61,13C
Adj	VanCleave, Timothy	M	65

IN1100 Marian University
Department of Music
3200 Cold Spring Rd
Indianapolis, IN 46222-1997
(317) 955-6109   Fax: (317) 955-6448
www.marian.edu
E-mail: jlarner@marian.edu

4 Year Institution

Chair: James M. Larner, 80A

Lect PT	Babb, Douglas		14C
Inst	Bain, Clare	M	36,31A
Inst PT	Bowling, Jeanne	B	61
Inst	Dembar, Braham		65
Inst PT	French, Pam	M	64B
Emeritus	Gallagher, Mary Gloria	M	62,66A,66G
Inst	Gardner, Charles	M	31A
Lect PT	Gerber, Thomas	M	12A,66A
Inst PT	Harris, Matthew W.	M	65
Inst PT	Hearn, Elizabeth	M	32
Inst	Hearn, Sidney T.	D	32,32E,34,37,63A
Inst PT	Hoover, Brian	B	63A
Inst PT	Johns, Brian	B	70
Inst	Johnston, James W.	D	60,62A,66A
Assoc Prof	Kern, Philip	M	13,10F,36,54,66A
Prof	Larner, James M.	D	12A,48,10E,64A,29A
Inst PT	Medley, Nathan		61
Inst	Meyer, Thomas	M	64A,64C
Inst	Moran, Margaret A.	M	63B
Inst PT	Ortwein, Mark	B	64B
Inst PT	Rickards, Steven	D	61
Inst PT	Stallings, Charles		66A
Inst	Whipkey, Steve	M	66A,66C,47
Inst	Williams, Melissa	M	63D
Emeritus	Wirtz, Ruth Ann	M	66A
Inst PT	Young, Jay		64A,64C,64E

IN1250 Oakland City University
Department of Music
143 Lucretia St
Oakland City, IN 47660
(812) 749-4781   Fax: (812) 749-1233
www.ocu.edu
E-mail: cspitler@oak.edu

4 Year Institution

Chair, Arts & Sciences: Michael Atkinson, 80A
Chair & Dir., Undergraduate Studies: Carolyn Spitler, 80A,80B

Asst Prof	Graham, Brenda J.	D	13A,32,37,62,31A
Adj	Retana, Cynthia	B	61
Assoc Prof	Spitler, Carolyn	M	64A,66A,13B,13C,66G

IN1300 Purdue University
Rueff School of Visual & Perf. Arts
Music
552 West Wood St
West Lafayette, IN 47907-2002
(765) 494-3708   Fax: (765) 496-2784
www.purdue.edu/music
E-mail: hbulow@purdue.edu

4 Year Institution

Chair/Head: Harry T. Bulow, 80A

Adj	Applegate, Janice	M	32
Adj	Bodine, Gerald B.	D	13
Assoc Prof	Brown, Helen F.	D	13A
Adj	Bulow, Ellen	PhD	11
Prof	Bulow, Harry T.	PhD	10,13,34,13A
Adj	Deagan, Gail	M	13,20
Adj	Dubikovsky, Nadya	M	32
Asst Prof	Hund, Jennifer L.	PhD	12,66A,12A,11
Adj	Monical, Dwight	M	13,11
Prof	Riley, Martha C.	D	32
Adj	Seybold, Donald	M	29A
Prof	Sudano, Gary R.	D	12A
Adj	Sutton, Leslie	B	32
Adj	Weiss, Daniel	M	29A,13

IN1310 Purdue University
Department of Univ Bands
Elliot Hall of Music
712 3rd St
West Lafayette, IN 47907-2005
(317) 494-0770   Fax: (317) 496-2822
www.purdue.edu/BANDS
E-mail: bandsinfo@purdue.edu

4 Year Institution

Chair: Jay S. Gephart, 80A

PT	Anderson, Jeff	B	70
PT	Boyd, Ned	M	64E
PT	Brandfonbrener, Amy	M	62B
PT	Colwell, Lynn	B	63D
Inst	Cox, Ishbah	M	37,60B
PT	Danby, Judd	D	10,13,29B,10A,13F
PT	Edwards, Celeste	B	64A
Prof	Gephart, Jay S.	M	37,60B
PT	Howard, Sharon	B	64C
Asst Prof	Jones, Max	M	37,60B
PT	Knepper, Bruce	M	63A
Assoc Prof	Nave, Pamela J.	D	37,65,50
PT	Spicknall, Sharry	B	62A
Assoc Prof	Trout, Marion T.	D	37,47,53
PT	Whiteley, Dan	D	66A

IN1350 St Josephs College
Department of Music
PO Box 942
Rensselaer, IN 47978
(219) 866-6203   Fax: (219) 866-6100
www.saintjoe.edu
E-mail: robbt@saintjoe.edu

4 Year Institution, Graduate School

Master of Arts in Church Music

Chair: Robb G. Thiel, 80A
Dir., Summer Programs: Steve Janco, 80G

Lect PT	Amsler, Audrey	B	64E
Assoc Prof	Berger, Sally	M	64A
Lect PT	Bier, Ken	M	70
Lect PT	Earnest, James	M	64C
Assoc Prof Emeritus	Egan, Anne Marie	M	66A
Prof	Egan, John B.	D	13,66,66G,11
Asst Prof	Ford, Kelly	M	36,61,60A,12,64E
Lect PT	Fragomeni, Richard	D	31A
Asst Prof	Geraci, Paul	D	13,10,29,63A,32B
Prof Emeritus	Heiman, Lawrence F.	D	12A,31A
Lect PT	Hobbs, Sandy	M	13
Lect PT	Hughes, Patricia	D	31A
Lect PT	Janco, Steve	D	31A
Lect PT	McIntyre, John	D	13,10,60,36
Lect PT	Nennmann, Jill	D	66G
Lect PT	Ritchie, Michael	M	63D
Lect PT	Shedd, Kylie	B	66A
Lect PT	Smith, Cherie	B	61,66A
Assoc Prof	Thiel, Robb G.	M	10F,60B,32,37,65

IN1400 St Mary of the Woods College
Department of Music & Theatre
3301 St Marys Rd
St Mary of the Woods, IN 47876
(812) 535-5016   Fax: (812) 535-4613
www.smwc.edu
E-mail: jmcintyre@smwc.edu

4 Year Institution
Member of NASM

Master of Arts in Music Therapy

Chair: John McIntyre, 80A

Vstng Asst Prof	Boswell, Michael	M	39,61,12A
Assoc Prof	Boyle, Sharon	M	33,70
Vstng Asst Prof	Endris, Robert R.	M	60,32B,36
Inst	Maurey, Ronald D.	B	66
Assoc Prof	McIntyre, John	DMA	13,34,12A,36,10
Assoc Prof	Prescott, Steve C.	DMA	32E,11,60B,64,37
Assoc Prof	Richardson, Tracy	M	33

IN1450 Saint Mary's College
Department of Music
Office 313
Moreau Center for the Arts
Notre Dame, IN 46556
(574) 284-4632   Fax: (574) 284-4884
www3.saintmarys.edu/music
E-mail: lthomas@saintmarys.edu

4 Year Institution
Member of NASM

Chair: Laurel A. Thomas, 80A
Dir., Artist/Performance Series & Summer Programs: Richard Baxter, 80F,80G

Lect PT	Allen, Steve	M	63A
Lect PT	Barrier, Dawn	M	64B
Lect PT	Budzinski, Thomas	M	64
Lect PT	Butler, Beverly	M	66A,66C,66D
Lect PT	Catello, Darlene	M	66H
Lect PT	Daugherty, Helene	M	63C
Lect PT	Emmons, Deanna	M	64E
Lect PT	Forsythe, Dawn	M	64
Lect PT	Frisk, Nora	M	62B
Lect PT	Glashauser, Jason	M	63
Lect PT	Hayden, Paulina	M	32B
Prof	Jacob, Jeffrey	D	11,66A,66B
Lect PT	Klinedinst, Sherry	B	66C
Lect PT	Kuehner, Denise	M	32E
Lect PT	Kuehner, Eric	M	64D
Lect PT	Lee, Jaesung	M	62A
Lect PT	Lynch, Charles	M	62E
Prof	Menk, Nancy L.	D	60,36,40
Prof	Munn, Zae	D	13,10F,10,43
Asst Prof	Party, Daniel	D	14C,12A,11,20H
Lect PT	Phipps, Dennis	M	32C
Lect PT	Russell, Carol	M	62C
Lect PT	Russell, Scott	D	63B,13B,13C
Lect PT	Sanchez, Samuel L.	M	65
Lect PT	Schilling, Korin	M	64A
Assoc Prof	Thomas, Laurel A.	D	39,61
Lect PT	Tidaback, Darrel	M	62D
Lect PT	Wachs, Dean	B	70
Lect PT	Warner, Michele	M	61
Lect PT	Woodland, Betty	D	61,66

IN1485 Trine University

Department of Music
1 University Ave
Angola, IN 46703
(260) 665-7537   Fax: (260) 665-4558
www.trine.edu
E-mail: kaysm@trine.edu

Private, Non-Denominational Institution

Chair: Mark Kays, 80A
Dean, Arts & Sciences: John Shannon, 80A

Adj	Babb, Mark	M	36
Inst	Kays, Mark	M	12A,13B,37,47,60B

IN1560 Taylor University-Upland

Department of Music
236 W Reade Ave
Upland, IN 46989
(765) 998-5232   Fax: (765) 998-4735
www.taylor.edu
E-mail: alharrison@taylor.edu

4 Year Institution, Evangelical Christian, Interdenominational
Member of NASM

Chair: Albert D. Harrison, 80A
Dir., Artist/Performance Series: Judy Kirkwood, 80F

Adj PT	Anderson, Jeff	M	47,29
Adj PT	Arbogast, Jennifer	M	61
Prof	Bade, Christopher	D	11,38,48,64,12A
Adj PT	Barber, Julie	M	66A,61,40,12A
Adj PT	Brewer, Mary Kathryn	M	61
Prof	Collins, Dana L.	D	10,12A,34,35C,13
Adj PT	Fata, Patrick	M	66A
Adj PT	Fiene, Darrel J.	B	62D
Adj PT	Gilbert, Karl	B	65,50
Adj PT	Grile, Kathy	M	66A,66B,13A
Adj PT	Guebert, Carolyn	B	61
Prof	Harrison, Albert D.	D	60B,37,47,63D,32E
Prof	Harshenin, Leon A.	D	66A,13B
Adj PT	Jenkinson, Janet	B	66A
Adj PT	Johnson, Jamie	M	70
Adj PT	Kothman, Mary	M	62A
Adj PT	Kunda, Keith	D	13B,13C,10F
Prof	Kwan, Eva	D	12A,32,44,20
Adj PT	Maxfield, Adele	M	62
Adj PT	Mordue, Mark	M	63B
Adj PT	Oh, Kyung-Nam	M	62C,42
Prof	Rediger, JoAnn K.	D	36,31A,60A,11,40
Adj PT	Rice, Suzanne	M	63D
Prof	Robertson, Patricia	D	39,61,32D
Adj PT	Singer, Douglas Michael	M	66C
Adj PT	Sloan, Chikako	M	66A
Adj PT	Stanek, Mark	D	70
Adj PT	Todd, Sheila	B	66C
Adj PT	Trubow, Valentina	M	61,13C,13B
Adj PT	Walley, Steve	M	66A
Prof	Whipple, Shederick Lee	D	61,39
Adj PT	Whitford, Keith	M	63A
Adj PT	Whitford, Trudy	M	64A,41
Adj PT	Whitlock, Christina	M	11

IN1600 Univ of Evansville

Department of Music
1800 Lincoln Ave
Evansville, IN 47722-0001
(812) 488-2754   Fax: (812) 488-2101
www.evansville.edu/areasofstudy/music/

E-mail: music@evansville.edu

4 Year Institution
Member of NASM

Chair: Thomas Josenhans, 80A
Coord., Music Admissions: Christi Peach, 80D

Asst Prof	Butturi, Renato	M	70,11,67G,47,29
Prof	Dallinger, Carol	M	62A,13A,62B,51
Inst	Erickson, Ross	M	65,50
Prof	Fiedler, Anne	M	13B,13C,66A
Asst Prof	Groulx, Timothy J.	D	13B,13C,32
Asst Prof	Jordan, John M.	D	12A,11,31A,20
Assoc Prof	Josenhans, Thomas	D	64C,13B,13C,64E,41
Prof Emeritus	Lacy, Edwin	D	64D
Assoc Prof	Malfatti, Dennis	D	36,40,31A
Asst Prof	Murphy, Kathleen	D	33,32B,66D
Prof Emeritus	Reed, Douglas	D	66G,66H,13D,31A
Asst Prof	Rike, Gregory	D	61,42
Inst Adj	Rinne, Erzsebet Gaal	D	62E
Inst	Robertson, Elizabeth A.	D	64B,11,41
	St. John, Brian	D	38,62A,62B,60B
Asst Prof	Steinsultz, Kenneth	D	63D,37
Inst	Thompson, Shauna	M	64A
Inst Adj	Truitt, Elizabeth	M	61
Assoc Prof	Truitt, Jon	D	61,39
Assoc Prof	Ungar, Garnet	D	66A,66C,66D
Inst Adj	Veazey, Lee	M	62D
Adj Inst	Williams, William Richard	M	61
Inst Adj	Wingert, Jennifer	M	62C
Prof	Wylie, Mary Ellen	D	33
Assoc Prof	Zifer, Timothy	D	47,63A,29A,49
Inst	Zyla, Marc	M	63B

IN1650 Univ of Indianapolis

Department of Music
1400 E Hanna Ave
Indianapolis, IN 46227-3697
(317) 788-3255   Fax: (317) 788-6105
music.uindy.edu
E-mail: labensg@uindy.edu

4 Year Institution
Member of NASM

Dean: Daniel H. Briere, 80A
Chair: Kathleen M. Hacker, 80A
Dir., Preparatory Division & Summer Programs: Rebecca E. Sorley, 80E,80G

Adj	Allee, Steve		66A
Adj	Bellman, David	B	64C
Assoc Prof	Berners, John	PhD	10,13
Adj	Berns, Paul S.	M	65,50
Adj	Blosser, Dan C.	B	61
Adj	Brewer, Jane	M	32
Adj	Burgeson, Eric	B	64E
Inst	Chan, Jacklyn	M	66A,66D
Adj	Chan, Susan	M	62B
Adj	Choi, Minju	D	66A,66D
Asst Prof	Clark, Brenda J.	PhD	32,11,37
Adj	Dimick, Glen M.	D	63D,41,49
Adj	Eggleston, Amy	M	39
PT	Franke, Dean		62A
Adj	French, Pamela Ajango	M	64B
Adj	Gerber, Thomas E.	M	11,66H,55B,12A
Adj	Gilgallon, Mark T.	M	61
Adj	Gross, Cathryn A.	M	64C
Assoc Prof	Hacker, Kathleen M.	D	61,39
PT	Hague, Joylyn	M	70
Adj	Hansen, Peter		62D
PT	Hoegberg, Elisabeth Honn	PhD	61,13A,13B
Adj	James, Matthew C.	M	32E
Adj	Kane, Scott	M	66A
Adj	Kelsaw, Geoffrey L.	B	36,61
Asst Prof	Kim, Ariana	D	62A,11,38,32E
Assoc Prof	Krasnovsky, Paul J.	D	60A,36,40
PT	McCafferty, Dennis S.	M	62C,41
Assoc Prof	Miedema, Harry F.	M	47,64E,29,53
Adj	Nichols, Peter W.	B	44
Adj	Ortwein, Mark T.	M	64D,64E
Asst Prof	Parr, Sharon M.	D	11,66A,66D,12A
Adj	Petricic, Marko	D	12A,66G
Adj	Plexico, Byron K.	M	62B
Adj	Powell, Larry	M	63A,42
Prof	Ratliff, Richard J.	D	13,66A,12D
Adj	Reiner, Art		50,65
Adj	Reynolds, Anne	B	48,64A
Adj	Rickards, Steven	D	61
Adj	Samuelsen, Roy	M	61
Adj	Schlabach, Blake	B	63C
Asst Prof	Schmutte, Peter J.	M	36,45,35C,35G,34
Adj	Sorley, Darin S.	M	63B
Assoc Prof	Sorley, Rebecca E.	D	66A,66C,66B,66D
Adj	Sowers, Jodi L.	M	64A,11
Assoc Prof	Spinazzola, James M.	D	37,41,60B
Adj	Tudek, Thomas S.	D	41,70
Adj	West, Cheryl E.	M	32D
Inst	Westra, Mitzi	D	61,13A,11,44
	Wittman, Jesse C.	B	29

IN1700 Univ of Notre Dame
Department of Music
105 Crowley Hall
Notre Dame, IN 46556-5643
(574) 631-6211   Fax: (574) 631-4539
music.nd.edu
E-mail: music@nd.edu

4 Year Institution

Chair: Louis MacKenzie, 80A
Undergraduate Advisor: Peter H. Smith, 80B

Specialist	Beudert, Mark	D	61
Prof	Blachly, Alexander	D	60,12,36,55,12A
Assoc Prof	Blacklow, John	D	66A,66C
Prof Emeritus	Bower, Calvin	D	12A,12
Assoc Prof	Buranskas, Karen	M	41,62C
Prof Emeritus	Cerny, William J.	M	12A,41,66A,66C
Prof	Cramer, Craig	D	12A,66G
Prof	Dye, Kenneth W.	D	10,37
Assoc Prof	Frandsen, Mary E.	D	12A,12
Prof Emeritus	Haimo, Ethan	D	13,10,10F
Asst Prof	Jarjour, Tala	D	12,20
Assoc Prof	Johnson, Paul	D	13,10,34
Specialist	Lancaster, Stephen J.	D	61
Prof Emeritus	Leahy, Eugene J.	D	11,12A,12
Assoc Prof Emeritus	Maloney, Patrick H.	M	11,61
Specialist	Park, Tricia	M	62A,42,41
Assoc Prof	Plummer, Carolyn	M	62A,42,41
Asst Prof	Redwood, Andre	D	13
Assoc Prof	Resick, Georgine	B	39,61
Assoc Prof	Smith, Peter H.	D	13
Asst Prof	Stowe, Daniel	M	12,36,38
Prof	Youens, Susan	D	12A,12

IN1750 Valparaiso University
Department of Music
1709 Chapel Dr
Valparaiso, IN 46383-6493
(219) 464-5454   Fax: (219) 464-5244
www.valpo.edu/music
E-mail: music@valpo.edu

4 Year Institution
Member of NASM

Chair: Joseph A. Bognar, 80A
Dean, Arts & Sciences: Jonathan Kilpinen, 80A
Dir., Center for the Arts: Jeff Hazewinkel, 80F

Assoc Prof Emeritus	Bernthal, John P.	D	13,66G
Assoc Prof	Bognar, Joseph A.	D	66A,13,66H,66G
Adj Asst Prof	Brown, Jeffrey C.	M	47,50,65,11
Assoc Prof	Brugh, Lorraine S.	D	36,31A,66G
Prof	Cock, Christopher M.	D	60,36,61
Lect	Cock, Maura	M	61,60A
PT	Deforest, June D.	M	62A
Prof	Doebler, Jeffrey S.	D	11,32,37
PT	Evans, Bruce	M	62D
Prof	Ferguson, Linda C.	D	12A,20G,11
PT	Foster, William	M	66A
Prof	Friesen-Carper, Dennis	D	60,10,41,38
PT	Fudala, Cynthia	M	64A
PT	Gartshore, Sarah	M	61
PT	George, John Brian	M	66G
PT	Graef, Becky	M	66A,66D,13A
Asst Prof	Grodrian, Ericka	D	11,13C,49,63B
PT	Hollander, Jeffrey M.	D	12A,15,11,12
PT	Ingle, Jennet	B	64B,48
PT	Kirkland, Denise	M	64C
PT	Klapis, Ralph	B	61,39
PT	Konsbruck, James	M	70,35G
PT	LeePreston, Nicole	M	66A,66C
Assoc Prof Emerita	Lewis, Marcia	D	61,35
PT	Lynch, Charles	D	62E
PT	Machavariani, David	M	62C
Asst Prof	Maugans, Stacy	D	48,64E,13A
PT	Oram, Virginia	M	61
PT	Riley, Mary Lee	M	66A
PT	Scheck, Carey	M	66A
PT	Schreckengost, John	M	63B,49,11
PT	Serna, Phillip Woodrow	D	62D,67A,70,67B
PT	Smith, Emily	M	64D
PT	Smucker, Angela Young	M	36,61
Vstng Inst	Smucker, Peter	M	13
PT	Steck, Charles	M	63A
PT	Takarabe, Clara	M	62A,62B
PT	Watson, Richard	M	63D,49
PT	Wells, Matthew	M	61
Artist in Res	Yu, Yuan-Qing	M	62A

IN1800 Vincennes University
Department of Music
1002 N 1st St
Vincennes, IN 47591-1504
(812) 888-4175   Fax: (812) 888-5531
www.vinu.edu

2 Year Institution

Co-Chair: Dan Miller, 80A
Co-Chair: Lisa Miller

	Avanesian-Weinstein, Karina	M	66A
	Bossard, Claudia M.	D	66A
	Chan, Joni	M	66A
	Franklin, Virgil	M	34D,13A,34
Asst Prof	Howell, Michael W.		41,67D,70
Asst Prof	Jackson, Sharon Sue	M	37,50,65,65B
	Latta, Matthew	M	61,32B,36,54
	Lewis, Jeremy		34D,34H
	Lowry, Lisa M.	D	61
Asst Prof	Mercer, Scott A.	M	13A,13,47,61,53
Prof	Miller, Dan	D	12A,36,44,61
Asst Prof	Miller, Lisa		32,61,54,12A
Asst Prof	Parman, David L.	M	41,62C,62D,70,20G
	Sulliman, Jason M.	M	63,49,47
	Trail, Robert		70
	Weinstein, Tony	M	66A
	Welte, DeEtta		66A,66C

IN1850 Wabash College
Department of Music
301 W Wabash Ave
Crawfordsville, IN 47933-2428
(765) 361-6089   Fax: (765) 361-6341
www.wabash.edu/academics/music
E-mail: hulenp@wabash.edu

4 Year Institution

Chair: Peter Lucas Hulen, 80A

PT	Abel, Alfred	B	62A,62B,38,48
PT	Baranyk, David	M	65,70
Prof Emeritus	Bennett, Lawrence E.	D	11,12A,12,13A
Asst Prof	Bowen, Richard L.	D	36,12,12A,11,12B
PT	Colwell, Lynn	B	63C,63D
PT	Dugan, Greg	B	62D
PT	Everett, Cheryl		66A,66G
Assoc Prof	Hulen, Peter Lucas	D	13,10,34,34A,41
PT	Lowry, Lisa	D	61
Assoc Prof	Makubuya, James	D	13A,13C,11,14,20
PT	Marlatt, Margot	M	62C
PT	Moore, Christopher	B	64E
PT	Norton, Diane M.	M	66A,66H
PT	Pazera, Scott	M	47
PT	Purkhiser, Beth		64C,64E
Vstng Asst Prof	Strandberg, Kristen	M	11,12,13A

KS0040 Allen County Community College
Department of Music
1801 N Cottonwood St
Iola, KS 66749-1607
(620) 365-5116 x 258   Fax: (620) 365-7406
www.allencc.edu
E-mail: CSmith@allencc.edu

2 Year Institution

Chair: Gary Tebbets, 80A

Adj	Gifford, Jewell A.		
Inst	Lammers, Ed	M	46,37,65,63,11
Adj	Smith, Craig Steven		
Inst	Summers, Michelle		61
Adj	Summers, Stanley Bryan		
Inst	Tebbets, Gary	M	12A,11,36,54,62

KS0050 Baker University
Department of Music and Theatre
PO Box 65
Baldwin City, KS 66006
(785) 594-8478   Fax: (785) 594-4546
www.bakeru.edu
E-mail: music@bakeru.edu

4 Year Institution
Member of NASM

Chair: Trilla R. Lyerla, 80A
Dir., Summer Programs: Lynda Lewis, 80G

Inst PT	Becker, Thomas R.	M	70,13
Inst PT	Cooper, William	M	63A
Inst PT	Funkhouser, James	B	63B,10
Asst Prof	James, Ray	M	37,63D,32E,49
Inst PT	Kraus, Nanette	B	66C,66D
Asst Prof	Liston, Robin	D	32A,32B,12A,11
Prof	Lyerla, Trilla R.	D	13,66A,66B,20
Inst PT	McKinney, Lori	B	38,62A,62B
Prof	Parr, J. D.	D	37,47,48,64,29
Inst	Potterton, Matthew	D	60,36,32D
Inst PT	Renyer, Erinn	M	62C,62D,51,42
Inst PT	Riley, Steve	B	65,50,10
Inst	Ziegler, Marci	M	61,66F,39

KS0060 Barclay College
Department of Music
607 Kingman Rd
Haviland, KS 67059
(620) 862-5252 x 52   Fax: (620) 862-5403
www.barclaycollege.edu
E-mail: jared.ross@barclaycollege.edu

4 Year Institution, Bible College

Chair: Jared Ross, 80A

Asst Prof	Ross, Jared	M	13,60,31A,36,61

KS0100 Benedictine College
Department of Music
1020 N 2nd St
Atchison, KS 66002
(913) 367-5340 x2598   Fax: (913) 360-7301
campus.benedictine.edu/music
E-mail: ruthk@benedictine.edu

4 Year Institution
Member of NASM

Chair: Ruth E. Krusemark, 80A

Asst Prof	Greco, Christopher J.	DMA	13,10,64,64E,13F
Asst Prof	Hanman, Theodore	M	65,60B,47,37,32E
Prof Emerita	Kew, Margaret Davis	M	51,62,66A
Asst Prof	Krusemark, Ruth E.	D	13,10,66A,66G,66D
Assoc Prof	Minter, Karen	D	12A,39,61
Lect	Riley, Jason		70
Prof Emeritus	Schultz, Blaine	M	66A
Lect	Shepard, Matthew C.		38
Lect	West, Lara L.	D	40,11,66D,66G,20

KS0150 Bethany College
Department of Music
335 E Swensson St
Lindsborg, KS 67456-1895
(785) 227-3380 x 8235   Fax: (785) 227-2004
www.bethanylb.edu
E-mail: music@bethanylb.edu

4 Year Institution
Member of NASM

Chair: Daniel J. Masterson, 80A

Adj PT	Bell, MaryLynn	M	32B
Adj PT	Bishop, Genevieve	B	66A
Adj PT	Brunelli, Stephanie	D	66A,12A,13,13B
Adj PT	Cooley, Brian	B	64D
Asst Prof	Frisbie, Jodi	M	61,36,39,13C
Prof Emeritus	Higbee, David	D	48,64E
Adj PT	Holbrook, Ashley	B	62D,62C
Adj PT	Jirak, Steve	B	70
Adj PT	Koshgarian, Richard	D	38,51,63C,63D
Adj PT	Kranzler, Dean	M	65,50
Assoc Prof	Masterson, Daniel J.	D	13,41,66A,66B,42
Adj PT	Neufeld, Hannah	M	61
Adj PT	Patterson, Paula	B	64A
Adj PT	Steinberg, A. Jay	M	64C,12A
Adj PT	Stultz, Rachel	M	62A,62B
Assoc Prof	Talbott, Doug	M	10F,32E,37,47,49
Prof Emeritus	Thorstenberg, Roger W.	M	63A,63B
Asst Prof	Turnquist-Steed, Melody	D	11,13C,31,44,66G
Adj PT	Wiggins, David	M	32B

KS0200 Bethel College
Department of Music
300 E 27th St
North Newton, KS 67117
(316) 284-5269   Fax: (316) 284-5286
www.bethelks.edu
E-mail: kschlab@bethelks.edu

4 Year Institution

Chair: Karen Bauman Schlabaugh, 80A
Dir., Preparatory Division: Danika Bielek, 80E

Inst Adj	Baxter, David	B	63A
Inst Adj	Buskirk, Kay	M	62B
Asst Prof	Chun, Soyoun Lim	D	61,39
Inst Adj	Danders, Dennis	M	62D
Prof	Eash, William	D	60,36
Inst Adj	Glanton, Howard	M	70
Inst Adj	Hague, Zach	M	64D
Prof Adj	Johnson, Nancy S.	M	62A
Assoc Prof Emeritus	Kasper, Kathryn	M	39,61,54,13C
Inst Adj	Kaufman, Roseann Penner	D	66G,66H
Prof Emeritus	Kehrberg, Donald A.	D	64B,37,32
Inst Adj	Kranzler, Dean	M	65
Prof Emeritus Adj	Moyer, J. Harold	D	10
Asst Prof	Pisano, James	M	64C,64E,47,53,13
Prof	Schlabaugh, Karen Bauman	D	13,66A,66B,66C,12A
Inst	Shade, Timothy	M	63D,38,37,13C,32E
Inst Adj	Shaffer, Kristin	M	64A
Inst Adj	Stanley, Parker	M	62C
Inst Adj	Thompson, Cindy	M	64B

KS0210 Butler Community College
Department of Music
901 S Haverhill Rd
El Dorado, KS 67042-3225
(316) 321-2222   Fax: (316) 322-3109
www.butlercc.edu
E-mail: lpatton@butlercc.edu

2 Year Institution

Dean: Larry Patton, 80A
Lead Faculty: Valerie Lippoldt-Mack, 80H

Inst	Anderson, Kris	M	52
Inst	Garber, Ron	M	11,12A,36,41,61
Inst	Knudsen, Joel	M	13,11,66
Inst	Lewis, Roger	M	13,10,37,47,53
Inst	Lippoldt-Mack, Valerie	M	11,36,61,32I,52
Inst PT	Pickerell, Kevin	M	63A,37
Inst PT	Scherling, John	M	11
Inst PT	Tichgraeber, Heidi		11,61
Inst	Udland, Matt	M	11,36,43,61
Inst	Wesche, Nancy		36,61,11

KS0215 Central Christian College
Department of Music
1200 S Main St
PO Box 1403
Mc Pherson, KS 67460-5740
(620) 241-0723   Fax: (620) 241-6032
www.centralchristian.edu
E-mail: Jacob.Kaufman@centralchristian.edu

2 and 4 Year Institution

Dean: Jerry Alexander, 80A
Chair: Jacob Kaufman, 80A
Dir. Artist/Performance Series: Sylvia Wolcott, 80F

	Dawson, Shane		70
	Janssen, Brett	M	66,13
	Kaufman, Jacob	M	70
	Mackey, Ryan	M	34
Emeritus	Mason, Don	D	36
	Moore, Alison	M	36,61
	Seymore, Sam	D	66A
Emerita	Wolcott, Sylvia		36,66
	Zyskowski, Ginger	M	65

KS0225 Cloud County Community College
Department of Music
PO Box 1002
Concordia, KS 66901-1002
(785) 243-1435 Fax: (785) 243-1043
www.cloud.edu
E-mail: emiller@cloud.edu

2 Year Institution

Chair: Nick Jones, 80A

Prof PT	Hartzel, Marcie	B	66
Prof	Miller, Everett F.	D	11,36,34,70,20
Prof	Sieben, Patrick	M	37,20,13,46,11

KS0250 Coffeyville Community College
Department of Music
400 West 11th
Coffeyville, KS 67337
(316) 251-7700 Fax: (316) 251-7798
www.coffeyville.edu
E-mail: jeremyk@coffeyville.edu

2 Year Institution

	Boatman, Amy		66C
	Gray, John	B	36,13,61
Prof	Kirk, Jeremy	M	37,13,20A,50,65

KS0265 Dodge City Community College
Department of Music
2501 N 14th Ave
Dodge City, KS 67801-2316
(620) 227-9384 Fax: (620) 227-9411
www.dc3.edu
E-mail: fdurant@dc3.edu

2 Year Institution

Division Chair: Dana Waters, 80A

Adj	Ahern, Patty		32B
Adj	Falcon, Richard		70
Assoc Prof	McKinney, David	D	13,37,63D,64,29
Adj	Mickey, Wendy		62
Asst Prof	Reese, Jodi	D	36,11,13C,61,60A
Inst	Thomas, Joel Wayne	D	11,13,29,66
Adj	Westmacott, John		65

KS0300 Emporia State University
Department of Music
1200 Commercial St
Box 4029
Emporia, KS 66801-5087
(620) 341-5431 Fax: (620) 341-5601
www.emporia.edu/music
E-mail: acomstoc@emporia.edu

4 Year Institution, Graduate School
Member of NASM

Master of Music in Performance, Master of Music in Music Education

Chair: Allan D. Comstock, 80A
Dir., Preparatory Division: Melinda Groves, 80E

Asst Prof	Bassett, Dennis	D	61
Inst	Bergman, Catherine	D	64A,13C
Lect	Budke, Tiffany	M	66A,66C,11
Assoc Prof	Comstock, Allan D.	D	11,64B,64D,12A
Assoc Prof	Cuellar, Martin	D	66A,66B,66C,66D
Asst Prof	Freeze, Tracy	D	65,50,20,34D
Inst	Garritano, Andrea	M	11,61
Inst	Gay, Nathan	M	63C,63D,60B,37
Lect	Groves, Melinda		66D
Assoc Prof	Houchins, Andrew	D	13,10,34D
Inst	Krueger, Carol J.	D	13C,60,36,32D
Inst	Mayo, Susan	M	62C,62D
Inst	McCarty, Diane	M	32
Assoc Prof	McConkie, Dawn	D	32,64C,64E
Prof	Miller, Marie C.	D	32A,32B,66A
Assoc Prof	Speedie, Penelope A.	D	39,61
Inst	Starr, Jeremy A.	D	38,62A,62B,11
Prof	Ziek, Gary D.	D	60,37,63A
Inst	Ziek, Terrisa A.	M	32B,63B

KS0350 Fort Hays State University
Department of Music & Theatre
600 Park St
Hays, KS 67601
(785) 628-4226/4533 Fax: (785) 628-4227
www.fhsu.edu/music
E-mail: brcline@fhsu.edu

4 Year Institution
Member of NASM

Chair: Benjamin Cline, 80A
Dir., Summer Programs: Ivalah Allen, 80G

Asst Prof	Allen, Ivalah	D	61,39,12A,20F
Assoc Prof	Andrews, Laura J.	D	32B,32C,32A,32G,32H
Prof Emerita	Boire, Paula L.	D	61,20F
Asst Prof	Cline, Benjamin	M	51,62C,62D,38
Asst Prof	Crull, Terry	D	11,36,40,60A
Asst Prof	Dawson, Bradley J.	M	47,49,63A,29
Assoc Prof	Huber, John	D	13,66A,66D
Asst Prof	Jordan, Jeff	D	37,32E,60B,63B,10
Inst PT	Kranzler, Dean	M	65,50
Asst Prof	Means, Matthew L.	M	11,62A,62B,41,42
Asst Prof	Perniciaro, Joseph C.	D	39,61
Assoc Prof	Pisano, Kristin	D	11,64C,64E,12A,14C
Asst Prof	Ravitskaya, Irena	D	66A,66B,66C,66D,66G
Asst Prof	Rolls, Timothy	D	10,13,34,35C,35G
Inst	Shepard, Hilary	M	64A,11,20
Inst	Weaver, Lane	D	11,63D,37,49
Inst PT	Werth, Kay	M	64B,64D,48,64A

KS0400 Fort Scott Community College
Department of Music
2108 S Horton St
Fort Scott, KS 66701-3140
(620) 223-2700 Fax: (620) 223-4927
www.fortscott.edu
E-mail: gregt@fortscott.edu

2 Year Institution

Chair: Gregory E. Turner, 80A

Adj	Adams, Greta	B	62C,62D,61
Inst	Bailey, Ronda J.	M	13A
Adj	Bennett, John	M	70
Adj	Fox, James	B	63
Inst	Laflen, Betty Jo	M	11,13C,32B,37,64
Adj	Salsbury, Karen	M	62A,62B
Inst	Turner, Gregory E.	D	13,38,36,60,61

KS0440 Garden City Community College
Department of Music
801 Campus Dr
Garden City, KS 67846-6333
(620) 276-7611 Fax: (620) 276-0478
www.gcccks.edu
E-mail: clay.wright@gcccks.edu

2 Year Institution

Director, Fine Arts: Larry Walker, 80A
Chair: J. Clay Wright, 80A
Dir., Artist Series/Preparatory Division: Carolyn Klassen, 80E,80F

	Klassen, Carolyn	M	66,34,13,20F
	McAllister, James	M	37,10A,63,60B,32C
	Wright, J. Clay	M	11,13,36,40,61

KS0500 Hesston College
Department of Music
PO Box 3000
Hesston, KS 67062
(620) 327-8141   Fax: (620) 327-8300
www.hesston.edu
E-mail: bradleyk@hesston.edu

2 Year Institution

Chair: Bradley Kauffman, 80A
Dir., Artist Series: Matthew Schloneger, 80F

Inst	Glanton, Howard	M	70
Inst	Kauffman, Bradley	M	13,36,37
Inst	Rodgers, Kenneth	M	66G,66A,66D,66C,11
Inst	Schloneger, Matthew	M	61,54,11

KS0550 Hutchinson Comm Junior College
Department of Fine Arts
1300 N Plum St
Hutchinson, KS 67501-5831
(316) 665-3500   Fax: (316) 655-3310
www.hutchcc.edu
E-mail: Allsupn@hutchcc.edu

2 Year Institution

Chair: William T. Brewer, 80A

	Allsup, Neal	M	11,12A,36,60,61
	Batchelor, Daryl	M	47,63A,29,29A
	Hearn, Priscilla	M	66A,11,12,66D,13C
	Pelischek, Jeff	M	11,37,48,64C,64E

KS0560 Independence Community College
Department of Music
PO Box 708
Independence, KS 67301
(620) 331-4100   Fax: (620) 331-9022
www.indycc.edu
E-mail: erutherford@indycc.edu

2 Year Institution

Music Contact: Eric D. Rutherford, 80A
Dean of Instruction: Peggy Forsberg

	Forsberg, Peggy		37
Adj Prof	Hamlin, John	B	70
Adj Prof	Hille, Regina	M	66A,66G
	Rutherford, Eric D.		61
Assoc Prof	Webber, Kelly Marie	D	11,13A,12A,61,60A

KS0570 Johnson County Community College
Department of Music
12345 College Blvd
Overland Park, KS 66210-1283
(913) 469-8500   Fax: (913) 469-2588
www.jccc.edu
E-mail: mmorelan@jccc.edu

2 Year Institution

Dean, Liberal Arts: Bill Lamb, 80A
Assistant Dean, Arts & Humanities: Michael D. Garrett, 80H

Adj	Auwarter, Douglas	A	50,65
Adj	Brown, Debra	M	11,34B
Adj	Dolnik, Nata	M	66A
Adj	Fitzer, Harvey	B	70
Adj	Isaac, James	M	48,64
Adj	Kennedy, Nancy	M	11,61
Adj	Khadavi, Linda	D	13,66A
FT	Moreland, Michael	M	10A,10B,34D
Adj	Murray, Alan	M	61
Adj	New, Laura	M	13

Adj	Olvera, Victor	D	10B,34D
Adj	Pretzel, Mark W.	D	66A,66
FT	Stinson, Ron	ABD	29,37,41,46,47
FT	Teal, Terri	ABD	11,40,61,36
Adj	Wilcken, Geoff	M	11

KS0590 Kansas City Kansas Community Coll
Department of Music
7250 State Ave
Kansas City, KS 66112-3003
(913) 288-7634   Fax: (913) 288-7638

www.kckcc.edu/academics/academicDivisions/humanitiesFineArts/music
E-mail: cwalker@kckcc.edu

2 Year Institution

Dean, Humanities & Fine Arts: Cherilee Walker, 80A

Adj Inst	Augustine, Shari	M	52
Adj Inst	Baumgarnder, Brad	M	34D,32F,35C,35D
Adj Inst	Chittum, John	M	34D,32F,35C,35D
Prof	Corbett, Ian	D	10,34,35D,35G,13G
Adj Inst	Dalton, Lester	M	11
Adj Inst	Fleeman, Rodney	B	70
Adj Inst	French, Nell	M	62A,62B
Prof	Gammon, Richard	M	32F,34D
Adj Inst	Huston, Spencer	M	11,66A
Adj Inst	Jackson, Brett	M	64
Adj Inst	Jackson-Legris, Erin	M	61
Adj Inst	Johnson, Richard	D	13G,32F,34D,35C,35D
Adj Inst	Kim, Nahyun	M	66A,66D
Adj Inst	LaBarr, Sarah	M	61
Prof	Mair, Jim	M	11,47,53,46
Adj Inst	Miller-Brown, Donna	M	34D,32F,35C,35D
Adj Inst	Moder, Jennifer	M	11,13A
Adj Inst	Molloy, Steve	M	63
Adj Inst	Pixton, Clayton	M	34D,32F,35C,35D
Asst Prof	Pope, Jerry	M	13,66A,11
Adj Inst	Smart, David	M	11
Inst	Stafford, John		36,40,47,11,13A
Adj Inst	VanWick, Brad	M	34D,32F,35C,35D
	Walker, Cherilee	D	36,13,11,61,29A
Adj Inst	Welge, Jurgen		65,46,47
Adj Inst	Wichael, Scott	M	13A,61
Adj Inst	Wijnands, Aberham	M	66A,66F,62D

KS0650 Kansas State University
School of Music, Theatre & Dance
109 McCain Auditorium
Manhattan, KS 66506-4702
(785) 532-5740   Fax: (785) 532-6899
www.ksu.edu/music
E-mail: mus@ksu.edu

4 Year Institution, Graduate School
Member of NASM

Master of Music in Performance, Master of Music in Music Education, Master of Music in History & Literature, Master of Music in Music Theory-Composition

Director: Gary Mortenson, 80A
Dir., Undergraduate Studies: Paul B. Hunt, 80B
Dir., Graduate Studies: Frederick Burrack, 80C
Associate Director: Kurt Gartner, 80H

Inst	Arrington, Amanda	M	54,66A,66C
Inst	Britt, Joshua	D	13A
Assoc Prof	Burrack, Frederick	D	32,12B,11,32,37
Prof	Cochran, Alfred W.	D	12A,13A,13B,13E
Prof	Cooper, Cora	D	51,62A,62B
Assoc Prof	Dobrzanski, Slawomir Pawel	D	66A,66C,66B
Inst	Dunn, Neil	M	65,50
Asst Prof	Fassler-Kerstetter, Jacqueline	D	63B,13E,13B
Assoc Prof	Ganz, Dale	D	61
Assoc Prof	Gartner, Kurt	D	65,20H,47,50
Prof	Goins, Wayne	D	46,47,70,29
Inst	Holmberg, Teri	M	33
Assoc Prof	Houser, Virginia	D	66A,66B,66D
Prof	Hunt, Paul B.	D	63C,12A,29A
Prof	Kerstetter, Tod	D	13A,48,64C,13B
Asst Prof	Large, Karen McLaughlin	D	13,11,64A,13A,48
Inst	Lewis, Gordon R.	M	62D,47,42,46
Asst Prof	Lewis, Nora A.	D	64B,12A,11
Inst	Linn, Don	M	37,32E,10F
Prof	Littrell, David	D	38,41,62C,62D,13A
Asst Prof	Maxwell, Steven	D	63D,11,41

Inst	Maxwell, Susan	D	13A,13B,64D
Inst	McCoy, Matthew T.	M	32
Prof	Mortenson, Gary	D	63A,49
Inst	Mortenson, Kristin	M	13A,13B
Asst Prof	Oppenheim, Joshua	D	32D,36
Assoc Prof	Parker, Craig B.	D	12A,63A,12
Asst Prof	Payne, Phillip	D	32
Asst Prof	Pickering, David C.	D	66A,66G,66H,13,12A
Assoc Prof	Pittman, Reginald L.	D	39,61,54
Inst	Richt, Cheryl	M	61
Inst	Robinson, Elizabeth	D	11
Asst Prof	Rosine, Amy	D	61,54
Asst Prof	Thompson, Patricia A.	D	61
Prof	Tracz, Frank	D	60B,37,32E
Assoc Prof	Weston, Craig A.	D	10A,10B,13,34
Asst Prof	Wytko, Anna Marie	D	64E,13A,48
Asst Prof	Yu-Oppenheim, Julie	D	32D,36,60A

KS0700 Kansas Wesleyan University
Department of Music
100 E Claflin Ave
Salina, KS 67401-6196
(785) 827-5541 x 5214   Fax: (785) 827-0927
www.kwu.edu/academics/undergraduate-programs/music
E-mail: hakoda@kwu.edu

4 Year Institution

Chair: Ken Hakoda, 80A

Asst Prof	Bernard-Stevens, Sarah	M	37,38,13,64D
Inst	Beyer, Douglas A.	M	62A,62B
Inst	Blehm, Denise		62B
Inst	Cardinal-Dolan, Michelle		61
Inst	Davis, John		62D
Asst Prof	Hakoda, Ken	M	36,38,32
Inst	Hernandez, Teresa		62C
Adj PT	Kranzler, Dean	M	65
Inst	Lowe, David	D	62B
Asst Prof	Mangrum, Leslie	M	61,36,39,12A
Assoc Prof	McMosley, William F.		46,32
Inst	Modin, Lindsay		64B
Inst	Morgenstern, Julia		64A
Inst	Tuzicka, William		61,36
	Weber, Judy		66C

KS0750 Labette Community College
Department of Music
200 S 14th St
Parsons, KS 67357
(620) 820-1021   Fax: (620) 421-2786
www.labette.edu/dept/music/music.htm
E-mail: christopherl@labette.edu

2 Year Institution

Director: Christopher M. Langsford, 80A

Assoc Prof	Head, Russell		10B,10D,34,35,45
Assoc Prof	Langsford, Christopher M.	M	36,32,11,12,13
Adj	Nelson, Scott	B	38
PT	Penner, Ruth	B	66C
Adj	Roach, Rebecca	B	64
Adj	Roach, Seth	M	65,66,29,70,50
Asst Prof	Walker, Elizabeth	M	39,61,54,35,34C

KS0900 McPherson College
Department of Music
1600 E Euclid St
PO Box 1402
McPherson, KS 67460-1402
(620) 242-0400   Fax: (620) 241-8443
www.mcpherson.edu/music/
E-mail: norrisj@mcpherson.edu

4 Year Institution

Chair: Joshua L. Norris, 80A

Assoc Prof	Bowman, J. D.	M	12A,11
Prof	Gustafson, Steven	D	61,66G,40,13B,36
Inst	Janzen, Dorothy		66
Inst	Kennedy, Rebecca	B	70
Inst	Knopp, Shawn	M	64
Asst Prof	Norris, Joshua L.	D	36,60,13,32

KS0950 Neosho County Community College
Department of Music
800 W 14th St
Chanute, KS 66720
(620) 431-2820   Fax: (620) 431-0082
www.neosho.edu
E-mail: dksmith@neosho.edu

2 Year Institution

Chair: David K. Smith, 80A

	Smith, David K.	M	36,11,61,13,66A

KS0980 Newman University
Department of Fine Arts
3100 McCormick St
Wichita, KS 67213-2008
(316) 942-4291
www.newmanu.edu
E-mail: zoglemand@newmanu.edu

4 Year Institution

Chair, Division of Arts & Letters: Susan Crane, 80A
Director, Music: Deanne Zogleman, 80A

Adj	Baxter, David A.	B	63,37
Adj	Baxter, Sarah M.	M	62
Adj	Graves, Paul	B	13,61
Adj	Hanne, Matt	M	61
Adj	Olivier, Thomas	M	70,13
Inst	Pracht, Carole	B	66A,66G,66C
Lect	Thompson, Cindy	B	64
Inst	Zogleman, Deanne	B	12A,13,20G,36,40

KS1000 Ottawa University
Department of Music
1001 S Cedar St # 8
Ottawa, KS 66067-3341
(785) 242-5200 x 5552   Fax: (785) 242-7429
www.ottawa.edu
E-mail: roger.kugler@ottawa.edu

4 Year Institution

Chair: Roger T. Kugler, 80A

Vstng Prof	Anderson, Jeff	D	36,32D,60A
Adj Prof	Baggett, Brian		70
Adj Prof	Baker, Kristi A.	M	66A
Adj Prof	Blachly, Barbara	M	44
Adj Prof	Chuang, Chun-Chien	M	62A
Adj Prof	Groschang, Sascha	M	62C
Assoc Prof	Kugler, Roger T.	D	32E,63,13,37
Adj Prof	Mallory, Keith	M	65,50
Asst Prof	McDonald, Steven	M	66,38,60B,12A,41
Adj Prof	McKemy, Bill	M	62D
Adj Prof	Ryan, Anna	M	61
Assoc Prof	Wilkinson, Todd R.	D	47,64E,29,32E
Adj Prof	Wohletz, Jeremy	M	64

KS1050 Pittsburg State University
Department of Music
1701 S Broadway
Pittsburg, KS 66762-7511
(620) 235-4466   Fax: (620) 235-4468
www.pittstate.edu/music
E-mail: music@pittstate.edu

4 Year Institution, Graduate School
Member of NASM

Master of Music in Pedagogy, Master of Music in Performance, Master of Music in Music Education, Master of Music in Choral Conducting, Master of Music in Wind Conducting

Chair & Dir., Graduate Programs: Russell L. Jones, 80A,80C
Dir., Artist/Performance Series: Susan J. Marchant, 80F

PT	Beard, Charles	M	64C,64E
Assoc Prof	Britz, Joanne M.	D	64C,64E,41
Inst	Clanton, James	M	65
Asst Prof	Deats, Carol	D	32B,63B
Assoc Prof	Fuchs, Craig		60B,37,32E
PT	Gerstenkorn, Lisa M.	M	61
Assoc Prof	Hastings, Stella	M	38,13B,13C,66D
Prof	Hastings, Todd J.	DMA	63A,29,11,41,42
PT	Herren, Matthew	M	62C,62D
Inst	Howle, Patrick	M	61,39
Prof	Hurley, David R.	D	12,20,64B
Prof	Jones, Russell L.	D	32,64D
Inst	Kehle, Lori	B	66D
Prof	Kehle, Robert G.	M	11,47,29,63C
PT	Kirkendoll, Mary	D	41,64A
Prof	Marchant, Susan J.	D	36,66G,66H,60A
Assoc Prof	Montague, Matthew G.	D	32,36,60A,11
Assoc Prof	Natenberg, Reena Berger	D	66A,66C,41
Assoc Prof	Ross, John C.	D	13,10,10F
Assoc Prof	Whitten, Douglas	M	37,63D,32E,11,49

KS1110 Seward County Community College
Department of Music
PO Box 1137
Liberal, KS 67905-1137
(316) 629-2683   Fax: (316) 626-3005
www.sccc.edu/academics/divisions/humanities/
   music/index.html
E-mail: dworkman@sccc.edu

2 Year Institution

Chair: John Loucks, 80A
Head: Darin D. Workman, 80A

	Silva, Magda Y.		61
Inst	Workman, Darin D.	M	60,32,37,47,64

KS1200 Southwestern College
Department of Music
100 College St
Winfield, KS 67156-2499
(620) 229-6272   Fax: (620) 229-6335
www.sckans.edu
E-mail: timothy.shook@sckans.edu

4 Year Institution
Member of NASM

Chair: Timothy Shook, 80A

Asst Prof	Gardner, David B.	D	36,60,61,60A,54
PT	Granberry, Marsha	M	32
PT	Hoeffgen, Thomas E.	B	70
Asst Prof	Jones, Michael C.	M	47,63A,63B,63C,13
PT	Leland, James	D	66G,66H
Prof	Shook, Timothy	D	66A,66B,66D,13
Asst Prof	Stevens, Daniel B.	M	38,41,37,62,51
PT	Williamson, Melissa	B	64A,48,13

KS1250 Sterling College
Department of Music
125 W. Cooper
Sterling, KS 67579
(800) 346-1017 x 382   Fax: (620) 278-4414
www.sterling.edu/academics/academic-departments/music
E-mail: bnix@sterling.edu

4 Year Institution

Chair: Brad K. Nix, 80A,80E

Inst PT	Boyd, Bruce	M	62A,62B,70,32E,62C
Asst Prof	Clark, Mark	M	36,32D,13,40
Inst PT	Esau, Matt	M	65,50
Asst Prof	Martin, Blair	M	13C,37,46,41,32
Inst PT	McClard Kirk, Jennifer	M	32E,64A,64C
Assoc Prof	Nix, Brad K.	D	66B,66A,66C,10F,66D
Inst PT	Settle, David		61,32D

KS1300 Tabor College
Department of Music
400 S Jefferson St
Hillsboro, KS 67063-1753
(620) 947-3121   Fax: (620) 947-2607
www.tabor.edu
E-mail: richardc@tabor.edu

4 Year Institution, Member of NCATE
Member of NASM

Chair & Dir., Undergraduate Studies: Richard E. Cantwell, 80A,80B
Dir., Preparatory Division: Sheila Litke, 80E

Prof	Cantwell, Richard E.	D	13,60,10A,37,38
Inst PT	Epp, Paul	B	63A
Inst PT	Johnson, Nancy	B	62
Inst PT	Johnston, Steve	B	70
Inst PT	Kranzler, Dean	B	65
Assoc Prof	Litke, Sheila	D	66,13,66A,66B,13A
Asst Prof	Swartzendruber, Holly	D	61
Inst PT	Vincent, Stephen	B	66G
Assoc Prof	Vogel, Bradley D.	D	60,32B,36,61,31A

KS1350 Univ of Kansas
School of Music
460 Murphy Hall
1530 Naismith Dr
Lawrence, KS 66045-3102
(785) 864-3436   Fax: (785) 864-5866
www.music.ku.edu
E-mail: music@ku.edu

4 Year Institution, Graduate School
Member of NASM

Master of Music in Composition, Master of Music in Music Theory, Master of Music in Performance, Master of Music in Conducting, Master of Music in Church Music, Master of Music in Music Education, Master of Music in Musicology, Master of Music in Opera, Master of Music Education in Music Therapy, PhD in Music Theory, PhD in Music Education, DMA in Composition, DMA in Conducting, DMA in Performance, DMA in Church Music, DMA in Choral Conducting, PhD in Musicology, Master of Music in Piano Accompanying

Dean: Robert L. Walzel, 80A
Associate Dean: Martin Bergee, 80H
Assistant Dean: Dina Pannabecker Evans, 80H
Associate Dean: Paul W. Stevens, 80H

Prof	Barnes, James	M	10F,10,12A
Prof	Bauer, Michael J.	D	36,66G,66H,31A
Prof	Bergee, Martin	D	32
Assoc Prof	Berghout, Elizabeth	D	66G,69
Asst Prof	Broxholm, Julia A.	D	61
Prof Emeritus	Bushouse, M. David	M	
Prof	Castle, Joyce	M	61
Assoc Prof	Chun, Peter	D	41,62B
Prof	Clair, Alicia A.	D	32,33
Assoc Prof	Colwell, Cynthia	D	32
Asst Prof	Dakon, Jacob M.	D	32,33
Assoc Prof	Daugherty, James F.	D	32,36
Asst Prof	Davidson, Michael	D	63C
Asst Prof	Dohoney, Ryan	D	12
Prof	Duerksen, George L.	D	32,33
Other	Eversole, Tom	B	72
Asst Prof	Farah, Mariana	D	36
Assoc Prof	Fedele, David	M	64A
Assoc Prof	Ferrell, Mark T.	M	39,61,66C
Prof	Foster, Robert E.		32E
Prof	Gailey, Dan J.	M	47,29
Other	Gibbs, George E.	M	16
Prof	Gnojek, Vincent	M	47,64E
Assoc Prof	Haaheim, Bryan Kip	D	10B
Assoc Prof	Hedden, Debra Gordon	D	32
Prof	Higdon, James M.	D	66G,66H,31A
Prof	Johnson, Christopher	D	32
Asst Prof	Jung, Ji Hye	M	65
Prof	Laird, Paul R.	D	12A,12,55B,55C
Prof	Laut, Edward A.	M	41,62C
Assoc Prof	Leisring, Stephen W.	M	63A
Assoc Prof	Marco, Margaret	D	64B,13
Assoc Prof	McGee, Deron	D	13,34
Assoc Prof	Mendez, Genaro	D	61
Assoc Prof	Murphy, Scott	D	13
Asst Prof	Neely, David L.	M	38
Asst Prof	Pierce, Forrest D.	D	13,10,43

Asst Prof	Popiel, Paul W.	D	37,60B
Prof	Reber, Richard	M	66A
Assoc Prof	Register, Dena M.	D	33
Inst	Rice, Laurence E.	M	62D
Assoc Prof	Schwartz, Roberta Freund	D	12
Other	Smith, James A.	M	16
Lect	Smith, Matthew O.	D	37
Prof	Smith, Scott McBride	D	66B
Asst Prof	Spooner, Steven	D	66A
Prof	Stephens, John A.	D	39,61
Asst Prof	Stevens, Paul W.	D	49,63B
Assoc Prof Emeritus	Stidham, Thomas M.	M	60,37
Assoc Prof	Stomberg, Eric W.	D	64D
Asst Prof	Street, D. Alan	D	13
Lect	Toulouse, Sharon	M	37
Asst Prof	Tucker, Carlton	M	36
Prof	Watson, Scott C.	M	11,49,63D
Prof	Winerock, Jack H.	D	66A
Assoc Prof	Wong, Ketty	D	14
Assoc Prof	Zelnick, Stephanie	D	64C

KS1375 Univ of Saint Mary
Department of Fine Arts-Music
4100 S 4th St
Leavenworth, KS 66048-5082
(913) 682-5151 x 6460   Fax: (913) 758-6140
www.StMary.edu
E-mail: krusemarkw@stmary.edu

4 Year Liberal Arts Institution

Chair & Dir., Undergraduate Studies: William Krusemark, 80A,80B

Prof Emerita	Callahan, Anne	M	31A
Prof	Krusemark, William	D	36,39,61,54,11
Asst Prof	Proctor, Freda	M	66,64A,13,37,41

KS1400 Washburn University
Department of Music
1700 College Ave
Topeka, KS 66621-0001
(785) 670-1511   Fax: (785) 670-1042
www.washburn.edu/cas/music
E-mail: annmarie.snook@washburn.edu

4 Year Institution
Member of NASM

Chair: Ann Marie Snook, 80A

Lect	Averrett, Michael	M	63A
Lect	Benda, Karen L.	D	64C,48
Adj Asst Prof	Bickers, Elisa	M	66G
Prof	Ding, Xiaoli	D	66A,66B,66D,20
Adj Inst	Fuller, Mark	M	61
Adj Inst	Fullerton, Kevin T.	M	14C,12A,29A,63D,11
Adj Asst Prof	Hearrell, Steve	B	70
Adj Inst	Huff, Kelly A.	M	12A
Assoc Prof	Hunt, Catherine	D	32A,32B,32C
Adj Inst	Jeon, Hyerim	M	62C
Prof	Kellim, Kevin	D	60A,36,61
Asst Prof	Kelts, Christopher M.	D	38
Adj Inst	Krutz, Kim	M	64D
Adj Inst	Labovitz, Sarah J.	D	37
Adj Inst	Lewis, Gordon R.	M	62D
Adj Inst	Marshall, Jean V.	M	11
Adj Inst	Mathias, Brian	M	66G
Prof	McQuere, Gordon	D	13
Prof	Meador, Rebecca	D	13,64A
Assoc Prof	Morgan, Tom T.	D	50,65,13C
Adj Inst	Neufeld-Smith, Cynthia	D	66C
Asst Prof	Norman, Mark	M	37,41,60B,63D
Adj Inst	Reist-Steiner, Tabitha	M	62E
Prof	Rivers, James	DIPL	11,66A,66C,10
Asst Prof	Seitz, Diana	D	62A,51
Adj Inst	Smith, Linda S.	M	11
Assoc Prof	Snook, Ann Marie	D	61
Assoc Prof	Snook, Lee	D	61
Adj Inst	Staerkel, Todd C.	M	61
Lect	Stoner-Hawkins, Sylvia Frances	D	61,39
Adj Inst	Strait, Cindy J.	B	66D
Adj Inst	Taggart, Charlotte A.	M	11
Adj Inst	Vellenga, Curtis W.	M	63B
Adj Assoc Prof	Wallace, Virginia V.	M	66A
Adj Inst	Woolsey, Katherine E.	M	64B
Adj Inst	Zawacki, Karen A.	M	63C

KS1450 Wichita State University
School of Music
Wiedemann Hall, Room 116
1845 Fairmount St
Wichita, KS 67260-0053
(316) 978-3500   Fax: (316) 978-3625
www.wichita.edu/music
E-mail: russ.widener@wichita.edu

4 Year Institution, Graduate School
Member of NASM

Master of Music in Performance, Master of Music in Conducting, Master of Music in Music Education, Master of Music in History & Literature, Master of Music in Opera, Master of Music in Music Theory-Composition, Master of Music in Pedagogy

Director: Russell D. Widener, 80A
Dir., Graduate Studies: Mark Foley, 80C
Dir., Institutes: Wendy L. Hanes, 80F
Dir., Summer Programs: Elaine D. Bernstorf, 80G

Asst Prof	Aranovskaya, Alla	DMA	62A
Asst Prof	Banke, Andrea E.	M	48,64B
Assoc Prof	Baxter, Deborah	DMA	61
Prof	Bees, Julie	DMA	66A
Assoc Prof	Bernstorf, Elaine D.	D	32A,32B
Asst Prof	Black, Phillip	M	49,63D
Inst PT	Blauer, Matt		63C
Inst PT	Brody, David C.	M	70
Prof	Coats, Sylvia	DMA	66B,66D
Assoc Prof	Consiglio, Catherine	M	62B,51,41
	Crane, Alan	B	66F
	Crane, Rachel L.	M	16
Prof	Crum, Dorothy E.	DMA	61
Assoc Prof	Davis, Lynne	M	66G
Vstng Asst Prof	Deibel, Geoffrey	DMA	64E,46
Inst PT	Edwards, Eric F.	M	20F,11
Inst PT	Fear, Judith	M	66A,66C
Prof	Foley, Mark	DMA	62D,29,13
	Giray, Selim	D	62A,62B,51,42,38
Asst Prof	Goering, John	M	29,20,66A
Inst PT	Gray, Sterling	B	70
Asst Prof	Hanawalt, Michael	PhD	36
Inst PT	Hoover, Tracy	M	67B
Asst Prof	Hunsicker, David	D	63A
Asst Prof	Jankauskas, Sarunas	D	64C
Prof	Johnson, John Paul	PhD	32,36
Assoc Prof	King, Marie A.	M	39,54
Asst Prof	Lacy, Randolph A.	D	61
Assoc Prof	Laycock, Mark Andrew	DMA	38,60B
Prof	Markovich, Victor A.	D	37,60B
Prof	Mays, Walter A.	DMA	13,10
Asst Prof	Mozzani, Pina	D	61
Asst Prof	Oakes, Scott	M	64D
Asst Prof	Oare, Steven	D	32E,32B,32C
Asst Prof	Owens, Craig	B	47,70,53,29A,20G
Vstng Prof	Popp, Harold	DMA	12A,12C
Prof	Roush, Dean	DMA	13,10F,10,34
Asst Prof	Scholl, Gerald	M	65,50,11
Prof	Shelly, Frances	DMA	64A,41
Asst Prof	Shukaev, Leonid	DMA	62C
Prof	Smith, Nicholas	DMA	63B,49,12A
Assoc Prof	Starkey, Linda	M	61,54,39
Asst Prof	Sternfeld-Dunn, Aleksander	D	10A
Inst PT	Sternfeld-Dunn, Emily	D	61
Inst PT	Strecker, Scott	M	63A
Assoc Prof	Trechak, Andrew	D	66A
Inst PT	Vance, Jeanne	M	32C
Prof	Widener, Russell D.	D	63C
Inst PT	Wiebe, Jill	M	62E
Prof	Wine, Thomas	D	32,36,60A

KY0050 Alice Lloyd College
Department of Music
100 Purpose Rd
Pippa Passes, KY 41844
(606) 368-6082   Fax: (606) 368-6216
www.alc.edu

4 Year Institution

Music Contact: Bryan Bolton, 80A

Asst Prof	Bolton, Bryan	M	11,13A,32,36,61

KY0100 Asbury University

Department of Music
One Macklem Dr
Wilmore, KY 40390-1198
(859) 858-3511 x 2250   Fax: (859) 858-3921
www.asbury.edu
E-mail: mark.schell@asbury.edu

4 Year Institution
Member of NASM

Chair: Mark Schell, 80A
Dir., Artist/Performance Series: Donald Zent, 80F

Adj	Beavers, Clyde	D	62D
Adj	Beers, Al	M	70
Assoc Prof	Bell, Vicki	D	13,10,36
Emerita	Bowles, Virginia	M	61
Adj	Bracken, Patricia	D	61
Adj	Bryant, Robert	M	62D
Adj	Burgess Amstutz, Cheryl	M	63B
Adj	Drewek, Doug	D	64C,64D
Assoc Prof	Flanigan, Glen	M	11,32C,41,47,63D
Assoc Prof	Holz, Beatrice	D	32B,36,39,61,32D
Prof	Holz, Ronald	D	12,38,41,49,10
Adj	Johnson, Timothy	M	34
Adj	Kerns, Brad	M	63C
Adj	Kirsh, Kristy	M	64A
Adj	Koehn, Daniel	M	61
Adj	Koehn, Renita	D	61
Adj	Nardolillo, Jo	D	62A,62B
Adj	Pickerill, Linda	M	66A,66C
Adj	Rector, Arlene	M	62E
Adj	Roller, Jonathan	D	11,10F
Adj	Schell, Cheryl	B	44
Prof	Schell, Mark	D	44,66G,31A
Adj	Strouse, Greg	M	65
Adj	Wilder, Mary Ann	M	66A,66C,66D,13A,13B
Adj	Wood, Dawn	M	61
Prof	Zent, Donald	D	13E,66B,66A,66C,66D

KY0150 Asbury Theological Seminary

Department of Music
204 N Lexington Ave
Wilmore, KY 40390-1129
(859) 858-3581   Fax: (859) 858-4509
www.asburyseminary.edu/
E-mail: bill.goold@asburyseminary.edu

4 Year Institution, Graduate School

Master of Arts in Church Music

Chair: William C. Goold, 80A

Inst Adj	Beers, Alva E.	M	70
Inst Adj	Bowles, Virginia B.	M	61
Inst Adj	Bracken, Patricia	D	61
Prof	Goold, William C.	D	60,12A,36,61,31A
Inst Adj	Harstad, Bonnie	M	66A
Inst Adj	McCardle, Dennis	M	31A
Prof	Whitworth, Albin C.	D	13A,13,10,36,66

KY0200 Ashland Community College

Department of Music
1400 College Dr
Ashland, KY 41101-3617
(606) 329-2999   Fax: (606) 325-8124
www.ashland.kctcs.edu
E-mail: dguilds0002@kctcs.edu

2 Year Institution

Chair: Barbara Nicholls, 80A

PT	Doss, Robert	M	36
Prof	Jackson, L. Max	M	13,11,36,66A
PT	Trumbore, Lisa	M	13A,32B

KY0250 Bellarmine University

Department of Music
2001 Newburg Rd
Louisville, KY 40205-0671
(502) 452-8224   Fax: (502) 452-8451
cas.bellarmine.edu/music
E-mail: rburchard@bellarmine.edu

4 Year Institution

Director: Richard Burchard, 80A
Dir., Preparatory Program: Meme Tunnell, 80E

Inst	Aaron, Kathryn	B	55,61
Inst	Alberts, Katherine	M	64B
Inst	Apple, Trent	JD	35A,35E
Inst	Bizianes, Chris	B	35C,35D
Inst	Bouras-Recktenwald, Christina	M	61
Inst	Brisson, Philip	D	66G
Assoc Prof	Burchard, Richard	M	10,13,20,34,35
Inst	Clark, Dave	M	29B,47,53,64E
Inst	Culligan, Paul	B	47,65
Inst	Diallo, YaYa	D	20A,65
Inst	Eberenz, Gina	M	32A,32B,32C
Inst	Falfalios, Anatasi	B	63C
Inst	George, David Alan	B	66A,66C
Inst	Harris, Kim	M	12A,62B,62C
Inst	Hayden, Ron	B	70
Inst	Hildreth, Todd	B	14,34,47,66A
Inst	Hodges, Brian	M	48,64A,64C
Asst Prof	Kirkpatrick, Leon	M	37,38,41,51,60B
Inst	Lawrence, Barry	B	61
Inst	Lawson, Matthew	B	13A,63A
Inst	Light, Daniel	M	66A
Inst	Lord-Powell, Karen	M	62A
Inst	Neumann, Kyle	B	34
Inst	Oliver, Alise M.	M	63B
Inst	Plummer, William	M	13A
Inst	Recktenwald, James	M	63A
Inst	Richardson, Marc	M	63D
Inst	Sherman, Jeff	B	47,53,70
Assoc Prof	Simpson, Alexander T.	D	11,12A,36,44,60A
Inst	Smith, Demond	M	50,65
Inst	Stephens, Sonny	B	47,62D
Inst	Tunnell, Meme	M	13B,66A,66B,66D
Inst	Walker, Dave	B	70,67D,67H
Inst	Wellman, Wayne	M	64D
Inst	Wilson, Leslie	M	35C

Y0300 Berea College

Department of Music
CPO # 2194
Berea, KY 40404-0001
(859) 985-3466   Fax: (859) 985-3994
www.berea.edu/music
E-mail: kathy_bullock@berea.edu

4 Year Institution

Interim Chair: Kathy Bullock, 80A
Dir., Admissions: Luke Hodson, 80D
Dir., Artist/Performance Series: Randall Roberts, 80F

Prof	Bolster, Stephen C.	D	60,32D,36,40,61
Lect PT	Bratton, Tripp	B	65,50
Prof	Bullock, Kathy	D	11,20A,36,13A,13C
Lect PT	Calkins, Mark	D	61,54
Lect PT	Hedger, John	M	70
Lect PT	Jones, Colette	M	32B,11,66A,66D
Lect PT	Kramer, Atossa	M	13C,48,64C,66A,67C
Prof	Lewis, Robert J.	M	13B,11,66A,66B,66D
Asst Prof	Rhodes, Ann G.	D	11,12A,61,32D,29A
Lect PT	Shirar, Ryan	M	66,66C
Lect PT	Stevens, Dwana F.	M	64A,64E
Assoc Prof	Turner, Charles	D	32,37,63,47,41
Lect PT	White, Al	M	70,51

KY0350 Brescia University
Department of Music
717 Frederica St
Owensboro, KY 42301
(270) 685-3131 Fax: (270) 686-6422
www.brescia.edu
E-mail: maryh@brescia.edu

4 Year Institution

Chair: Mary Henning, 80A

Assoc Prof	Henning, Mary	M	20,44,32,36
Adj	Hudson, S.	D	11,13,36

KY0400 Campbellsville University
School of Music
UPO 792
1 University Dr
Campbellsville, KY 42718-2799
(270) 789-5269 Fax: (270) 789-5524
www.campbellsville.edu/music
E-mail: jrgaddis@campbellsville.edu

4 Year Institution, Graduate School
Member of NASM

Master of Arts in Music, Master of Music in Performance, Master of Music in Conducting, Master of Music in Church Music, Master of Music in Music Education, Master of Music in Musicology, Master of Music in Piano Pedagogy

Dean & Dir., Graduate Studies: J. Robert Gaddis, 80A,80C
Assistant Dean & Dir., Undergraduate Studies: Alcingstone DeOliveira Cunha, 80H,80B

Asst Prof	Bersaglia, G. Scott	D	13A,60,37
Prof	Bradley, Mark	D	12C,32G,36,39,61
Asst Prof	Budai, William H.	M	66A,66B,66D
Inst	Cho, Wan-Soo	M	62B,51
Staff	Cundiff, Larry		66F
Asst Prof	Cunha, Alcingstone DeOliveira	D	31A,36
Adj	Davis, Judith Chen	M	66A
Adj	Davis, Michael W.	M	62A
Adj	DeAlmeida, Saulo	M	62C,42
Adj	Farmer, Joni		63B
Asst Prof	Floyd, C. Chad	M	37,65,50
Prof	Gaddis, J. Robert	D	60,32,51,63D,38
Asst Prof	Hedrick, David	D	61,32
Inst	Hodge, R. Matthew	M	11,13A
Adj	Irwin, Donna	D	32
Adj	Johnson, Trevor	M	64B
Asst Prof	Land, W. Reese	M	11,13A,41
Adj	Levine, Andrea	C	64C
Assoc Prof	McArthur, Lisa R.	D	13,48,64A,12A,12F
Adj	McDonald, Heather	M	64E
Prof	Moore, James Walter	D	34,13,10,70
Inst	Moura, Juliana	M	61
Adj	Olsen, Karl	M	62D
Prof	Roberts, Wesley	D	12,14,31,66
Adj	Santos, Denis Almeida	M	64A,13
Inst	Tinnell, Jennifer L.	M	37,63C,32E,47

KY0450 Centre College
Department of Music
600 W Walnut St
Danville, KY 40422-1309
(859) 238-5424 Fax: (859) 238-5467
www.centre.edu/majors/music
E-mail: sallie.bright@centre.edu

4 Year Institution

Chair: Barbara L. Hall, 80A
Dir., Artist/Performance Series: Steve Hoffman, 80F

Vstng Inst	Atchison-Wood, Dawn	M	61
Adj	Baker, Sherry H.	M	63B
Adj	Binford, Patrick	M	62C
Assoc Prof	Bitensky, Laurence S.	D	13,10
Adj	Bryant, Bob	M	63D
Adj	Bryant, David	D	64D
Adj	Cook, Elaine	M	62E
Adj	Drewek, Douglas Alexand	M	64E,64C,47
Prof	Hall, Barbara L.	D	13,12A,12,36,60
Adj	Harrod, John		
Adj	Hawkins, Chase	M	63A
Adj	Heersche, Kim	M	64B
Adj	Hill, Colin	M	65
Asst Prof PT	Jones, Jeff	D	66G,66H,66A
Vstng Inst	Kano, Mark A.		61,39
Adj	Karr, Kathy	M	48,64A
Assoc Prof	Link, Nathan	D	12A,14C
Vstng Asst Prof	Loeb, Jaemi	D	38,13A,41,42,60B
Vstng Inst	Saunders, Meg	B	62A,62B,41
Adj	Scott, Jerry		
Adj	Spoonamore, Dudley	M	63C
Vstng Inst	Wolfe, Elizabeth	M	66A,66C
Vstng Inst	Worley, Dan	D	70,10A,10B,10C,34B

KY0550 Eastern Kentucky University
Department of Music
521 Lancaster Ave
Richmond, KY 40475
(859) 623-3266 Fax: (859) 622-1333
www.music.eku.edu
E-mail: rob.james@eku.edu

4 Year Institution, Graduate School
Member of NASM

Master of Music in Performance, Master of Music in Conducting, Master of Music in Music Education, Master of Music in Music Theory-Composition

Chair & Dir., Summer Programs: Robert R. James, 80A,80G
Dir., Summer Programs: Ben Walker, 80G
Assistant Chair & Dir., Graduate Studies: Karin M. Sehmann, 80H,80B,80C

Prof	Allison, Joseph	D	11
Asst Prof	Brumfield, April	M	35A
Assoc Prof	Byrd, Richard W.	D	13,63A
Asst Prof	Carucci, Christine	D	64D,32
Assoc Prof	Couvillon, Thomas M.	D	13,10B,10A,10,13F
Prof	Crosby, Richard A.	D	66A,66D,12A
Assoc Prof	Davis, Dennis	D	70,45,34
PT	Engstrom, Greg	D	11
Asst Prof	Haddix, Ken	D	37,63C
Prof	Hensley, Hunter C.	D	36,61,60A,55,32D
PT	Ignatiou, Connie	M	64B
PT	James, Candace	M	11
Prof	James, Robert R.	M	35,34
Assoc Prof	Jasinski, Nathan David	D	62C,32E,38,42,13A
Assoc Prof	Kean, Kristen	D	64A,13A,13,42,48
Asst Prof	Koontz, Jason	D	50,65,14,34B
PT	Martin, Canarissa	B	66C
PT	Maturani, Marilyn Muns	M	11
Asst Prof	Mulholland, Jeremy	M	62A,62B,38,60B
Lect	Munson, Chris	M	35
Asst Prof	Nelson, Larry	D	64E,53,29,47,29A
Prof	Rhoades, Connie A.	D	64C,64E,20G
Staff	Risk, Lee		72
Vstng Asst Prof	Saunders, Meg	M	62A
Asst Prof	Scarambone, Bernardo	D	66A,66D,66B,66,66C
Prof	Schmann, Phillip M.	D	11,63B
PT	Schneiders, Carson	M	66
Prof	Sehmann, Karin M.	D	32
Staff	Sexton, Greg		66F
PT	Stites, Nathan	M	66C,66D
PT	Stone, Michael	M	11
PT	Taylor, Rachel		66
Asst Prof	VanFleet, Joseph	D	63A
PT	Walker, Ben	M	66C
Assoc Prof	Waters, Richard	D	36,60A,32D,40
PT	Westbrook, Randy	D	66C,12,11
Asst Prof	Willett, Jim R.	M	13,63D
Prof	Wolf, Joyce Hall	D	61,39

KY0600 Elizabethtown Community College
Division of Humanities
600 College Street Rd
Elizabethtown, KY 42701
(270) 706-8448 Fax: (270) 769-0736
www.elizabethtown.kctcs.edu/
E-mail: camille.hill@kctcs.edu

2 Year Institution

Chair, Music: Camille Hill, 80A

Inst PT	Day, John	M	11
Prof	Hill, Camille	D	13A,11,36,61,66D
Inst PT	Monroe, Marc	M	11
Inst PT	Shank, Kevin	M	11,37

KY0610 Georgetown College
Department of Music
400 E College St
Georgetown, KY 40324-1696
(502) 863-8100   Fax: (502) 868-8888
spider.georgetowncollege.edu/music
E-mail: Sonny_Burnette@georgetowncollege.edu

4 Year Institution

Chair: Sonny Burnette, 80A

PT	Binford, Patrick	M	62C
Prof	Burnette, Sonny	D	13,47,64E,34
Assoc Prof	Campbell, John W.	D	60,11,32,61,36
PT	Flygstad, Jana	M	64A
PT	Fogler, Michael	M	70
Asst Prof	Hayashida, Mami	D	66A,66G,66D
Asst Prof	Hunnicutt, Heather Winter	D	61,32,11
Prof	LaRue, Peter	D	60,11,32,37,63D
PT	Lewis, Eloise	M	62A
Prof	Lewis, H. M.	D	10F,11,12A,49,63A
PT	McElroy, Dennis	M	64C
PT	Miller, Rebecca C.	M	61
PT	Tate, Mark	M	47,65

KY0650 Kentucky Christian University
School of Music
100 Academic Pkwy
Grayson, KY 41143-2205
(606) 474-3290   Fax: (606) 474-3157
www.kcu.edu
E-mail: mdeakins@kcu.edu

4 Year Christian Liberal Arts Institution

Dean: Mark Deakins, 80A
Dir., Artist/Performance Series: Daniel Bell, 80F

Asst Prof	Bell, Daniel	M	61
Prof	Deakins, Mark	D	13A,60,36,31A,40
Prof	Golightly, John Wesley	D	12A,31A,66,34,13D
Adj	Hatfield, Clancy	M	70
Adj	Norden, Gene	M	64
PT	Tompkins, Ruth	M	66A
PT	Venettozzi, Vasile	M	61

KY0700 Kentucky Mountain Bible College
Department of Music
PO Box 10
Vancleve, KY 41385-0010
(606) 666-5000   Fax: (606) 666-7744
www.kmbc.edu

4 Year Institution

Chair: John W. Finney, 80A

Assoc Prof	Finney, John W.	M	13,12A,36,61,66A
Inst	Shuck, Carla	B	
Inst	Wisler, Jay	B	

KY0750 Kentucky State University
Department of Music
400 East Main St
Frankfort, KY 40601
(502) 227-6496   Fax: (502) 227-5999
www.kysu.edu
E-mail: barbara.buck@kysu.edu

4 Year Institution, HBCU
Member of NASM

Area Coordinator: Louis Bourgois, III, 80A
Division Chair: Barbara Buck, 80A

Asst Prof	Bailey, Kalomo	M	37,32E
Prof	Bourgois, Louis	D	11,12A,49,63D,34
Assoc Prof	Buck, Barbara	D	32A,32B,32C,32D,61
Assoc Prof	Butler, Hunt	M	47,48,64,53,29A
Assoc Prof	Griffin, Robert	M	13A,11,50,65
Assoc Prof	Johnson, Barry	D	13,10F,10,11
Prof	Richard, Leon	D	49,63A,63B
Assoc Prof	Smith, Andrew W.	M	39,61
Prof Emeritus	Smith, Carl H.	D	60,32B,32C,36
	Tsangari, Victoria		

KY0800 Kentucky Wesleyan College
Department of Music
3000 Frederica St
Owensboro, KY 42301
(270) 852-3620   Fax: (270) 926-3196
www.kwc.edu
E-mail: peoakley@kwc.edu

4 Year Institution

Chair: Diane K. Earle, 80A
Dir., Admissions: Paul E. Oakley, 80D

Prof	Earle, Diane K.	D	11,66
Assoc Prof	Jewett, Dennis A.	M	61,31A,32,36
Assoc Prof	Laughrey, Gary	M	64,32F,12A,13
Inst	Malone, Joy	M	66A,66C
Prof	Oakley, Paul E.	M	61,31A,36
Assoc Prof	Pederson, Steven A.	M	37,41,47,64
Inst	Pope, Beth	M	61
Inst	Thorpe, Clyde	M	70,42

KY0860 Lindsey Wilson College
Department of Music
210 Lindsey Wilson St
Columbia, KY 42728-1223
(502) 384-2126   Fax: (502) 384-8050
www.lindsey.edu
E-mail: reynolds@lindsey.edu

4 Year Institution

Chair, Humanities Division: Tim McAlpine, 80A

Assoc Prof	Chafin, Gerald	D	60A,11,32,36,44
Prof	Reynolds, Robert	D	13A,13,11,66A,20G

KY0900 Morehead State University
Department of Music/Theatre/Dance
106 Baird Music Hall
Morehead, KY 40351-1689
(606) 783-2473   Fax: (606) 783-5447
www.moreheadstate.edu/music
E-mail: music@moreheadstate.edu

4 Year Institution, Graduate School
Member of NASM

Master of Music in Performance, Master of Music in Music Education

Interim Chair: L. Curtis Hammond, 80A
Coordinator, Graduate Studies: David W. Oyen, 80C

Prof	Baker, Stacy A.	D	63D
Asst Prof	Baruth, Lori E.	M	13B,13C,64C
Asst Prof	Blair, Suanne Hower	M	12A,62C,62D,62E
Lect	Bromley, Tanya M.	M	32
Prof	Creasap, Susan D.	D	32E,37
Assoc Prof	Detweiler, Greg J.	D	60,36,61,40
Inst	Eastwood, Deb A.	D	13A,13B,13C,63A
Asst Prof	Escalante, Roosevelt	D	13B,13C,32D,36
Lect	Flippin, Jay	M	11
Other	Gibbs, Don	DIPL	66F
Assoc Prof	Ginn, Glenn A.	M	29,70
Assoc Prof	Grice, June	D	32A,32B,32C,32G,32H
Assoc Prof	Hammond, L. Curtis	D	63B,12A
Lect	Hartke-Towell, Christina	B	38,62A,62B
Inst	Hsieh, Chialing	M	66C
Prof Emeritus	Keenan, Larry W.	M	11,66A,66G,66D,66H
Lect	Kuo, Ming-Hui	M	65B
Assoc Prof	Little, Ricky R.	D	61
Asst Prof	Mann, William P.	D	63C
Asst Prof	Mason, Brian S.	M	50,65
Prof	McBride, M. Scott	D	60B,32,10F,63C,37
Prof	Miles, Richard B.	D	60,37
Assoc Prof	Oddis, Frank A.	M	50,65
Assoc Prof	Oyen, David W.	D	13,48,64D
Assoc Prof	Prindle, Roma	D	39,61
Asst Prof	Roseman, Jacob	D	12A
Vstng Asst Prof	Roseman, Molly	D	66A,66D

Assoc Prof	Snyder, Steven D.	D	13,47,66A,29
Assoc Prof	Taylor, Paul F.	D	66A,66H,66C,66D
Prof	Towell, Gordon L.	D	47,64E,53,29
Assoc Prof	Viton, John	D	13,64B
Lect	Wells, Jesse R.	B	11,53,62A,70
Assoc Prof	Wing, Gregory	M	63A
PT	Young, Michael J.	M	66C

KY0950 Murray State University
Department of Music
504 Fine Arts Bldg
Murray, KY 42071-3342
(270) 809-4288   Fax: (270) 809-3965
www.murraystate.edu/music
E-mail: msu.music@murraystate.edu

4 Year Institution, Graduate School
Member of NASM

Master of Music Education

Chair & Dir., Graduate Studies: Pamela S. Wurgler, 80A,80C

Prof	Almquist, Bradley L.	D	60,32,36,13C
Assoc Prof	Aucoin, Amy	D	32,36,60A,13C
Prof	Baker, Sonya G.	D	61
Prof	Black, Randall	D	61
Asst Prof	Ciach, Brian	D	10,13
Prof	Conklin, Raymond L.	M	49,63C,63D
Inst PT	D'Ambrosio, Christina	D	66D
Assoc Prof	D'Ambrosio, Michael	D	13,10
Prof	Dressler, John C.	D	12A,63B,11,12C
Assoc Prof	Erickson, Scott	M	48,64B,64D,64E
Assoc Prof	Fannin, John E.	M	32,37,10F
Asst Prof	Field, Tana	D	61
Asst Prof	Gianforte, Matthew P.	D	66A,66D,66B,66,12A
Inst PT	Han, Jinhee	M	62C,62D
Asst Prof	Hill, John E.	D	50,65
Asst Prof	Hill, Todd E.	D	63D,46,47
Assoc Prof	Johnson, Dennis	M	60,37,38
Assoc Prof	Locke, Scott A.	D	64C,11,20
Inst PT	Madison, Vicki	M	32
Inst PT	Millsap, Kyle	D	63A,49
Assoc Prof	Mitchell, Christopher	D	61,39
Vstng Asst Prof	Park, Meeyoun	D	66C,66D
Asst Prof	Park, Sue-Jean	D	62A,62B,41
Prof	Rea, Stephanie	D	64A,13
Assoc Prof	Swisher, Eric	D	63A,49
Inst PT	Thacker, Hope	D	61
Other	Thile, Scott		66F,72
Inst PT	Turner, Tammy	D	11,12
Inst PT	Webster, Brent	B	70
Inst PT	Woodring, Mark	M	63A,49
Lect	Wray, David	D	35
Lect	Wu, Angela	D	66C,66D
Prof	Wurgler, Pamela S.	D	32

KY1000 Northern Kentucky University
Department of Music
Fine Arts 253
Nunn Dr
Highland Heights, KY 41099
(859) 572-6399   Fax: (859) 572-6076
music.nku.edu
E-mail: sanderk@nku.edu

4 Year Institution
Member of NASM

Chair: Kurt L. Sander, 80A
Dir., Preparatory Division: Toni Sheffer, 80E
Assistant Chair: David L. Dunevant, 80H

Adj	Asefiev, Boris	M	62D
Adj	Aufmann, Ronald	B	64C
Adj	Barton, Katie	M	36
Prof	Belland, Diana R.	D	66A
Adj	Belland, Douglas	D	11,14C
Adj	Breneman, Marianne Leitch	M	11,64C,32E,64B
Adj	Burdette, Joy	M	61
Adj	Burkhead, Phillip	M	29
Adj	Buzza, Scott	M	13C
Adj	Chang, Ya-Liang	D	66D
Adj	Clary, Philip	M	13C
Adj	Dean, Myron	M	11
Artist in Res	Dong, Kun	M	62B
Adj	Dorff, Dan	M	65
Assoc Prof	Dunevant, David L.	M	12A,63C
Adj	Galyon, Joseph	D	66A
Adj	Ginn, Stan	B	42,50,65
Adj	Grant, Margaret	D	13,64B
Prof Emeritus	Gresham, Jonathan	D	49,63A,41
Prof	Grout, Gayle		61
Adj	Gwynne, Michelle	M	62E
Prof Emeritus	Hagner, Carolyn Zepf	M	66A,66B,66C
Adj	Hinkle, Russ	M	64D
Asst Prof	Hogg, Wiliiam	M	29,64E
Adj	Jackson, William	M	62D
Adj	Jensen, Richard	B	65
Assoc Prof	Johnston, Gary	M	10F,11,34
Adj	Jordan, L. Thomas	B	11,34
Adj	Karas, Ted	B	70
Assoc Prof	Karrick, Brant	D	37,60B,32E
Asst Prof	Knechtges, Eric T.	D	10,13
Prof Emeritus	Koplow, Philip	D	13,10
Lect	Lang, Scott	M	50,65
Artist in Res	Lange-Jensen, Catherine	M	62C,41
Adj	Lee, Owen	B	62D
Prof Emerita	Martin, Nancy D.	M	61
Adj	Nam, Esther Hyun	D	61
Adj	Nam, Song Hun	M	66D
Adj	Olt, Timothy	M	63D
Assoc Prof	Pennington, Randy	D	60,36,47
Adj	Perlove, Nina	D	64A,12A
Artist in Res	Polusmiak, Sergei	D	66
Adj	Pratt, Holly	M	20
Artist in Res	Rafferty, Alan	M	62A
Asst Prof	Restesan, Francis'c	M	38,51,39,62A
Asst Prof	Rodriquez, Raquel H.	D	37,42,63A
Assoc Prof	Sander, Kurt L.	D	10,13
Adj	Scheider, Karen	B	63B
Adj	Schneider, David	D	13,13E
Adj	Schowalter, Elise Anne	M	13A,13B
Lect	Sheffer, Toni	B	66C
Adj	Steva, Elizabeth Ryland	D	62,11,12
Adj	Van Pelt, Michael		64A
Adj	Webber, David	M	32E
Emeritus	Westlund, John	D	36
Adj	Winner, Andrew	M	70,41
Artist in Res	Wojtowicz, Joanne	M	62A,41
Adj	Wolverton, Peggy	M	32B
Prof	Wolverton, Vance D.	D	32D
Adj	Wyatt, Scott	D	61
Adj	Zappa, John	M	29A

KY1100 Pikeville College
Department of Music
147 Sycamore St
Pikeville, KY 41501
(606) 432-9200   Fax: (606) 432-9328
humanities.pc.edu
E-mail: jfreeman@pc.edu

4 Year Institution, Electives courses only

Chair., Dir, Music Ensembles: William B. Daniels, 80A
Assistant Chair: Margaret B. Andraso, 80H

Asst Prof	Andraso, Margaret B.	M	11,36,61,63A
Asst Prof	Bustamante, Tamara A.	D	36,11,13,66C,66A
	Daniels, William B.	M	32B,37,47,49,63
Inst	Freeman, Janean	M	61,11

KY1150 St Catharine College
Department of Music
2735 Bardstown Rd
St Catharine, KY 40061-9435
(859) 336-5082   Fax: (859) 336-5031
www.sccky.edu
E-mail: ttedder@sccky.edu

4 Year Institution

Chair: Teresa C. Tedder, 80A

	Tedder, Teresa C.	M	10A,10C,10F,66A,11

KY1200 Southern Baptist Theo Seminary
School of Church Music & Worship
2825 Lexington Rd
Louisville, KY 40280-1812
(502) 897-4115   Fax: (502) 897-4066
www.sbts.edu
E-mail: tbolton@sbts.edu

Graduate School
Member of NASM

DMA in Church Music, Master of Music, Master of Church Music, Doctor of Music Ministry, Master of Divinity in Church Music, Master of Divinity in Worship, Master of Arts in Worship

Dean: Thomas W. Bolton, 80A
Dir., Artist Series: Sandra L. Fralin, 80F

Prof	Bolton, Thomas W.	D	61,31A,36,12A
Assoc Prof	Brewton, Greg	D	31A
Prof	Crookshank, Esther R.	D	12,14,62
Adj	Fralin, Sandra L.	D	12A
Adj	Gregory, David	D	61,16,12
Prof	Hinson, G. Maurice	D	12A,66A,31A,66B,66C
Inst	Kim, Myung Whan	M	13
Adj	Lancaster, Linda K.	D	32A,32B
Prof	Landgrave, Phillip	D	10,35C,31A
Inst	Norberto, Jezimar	M	70
Inst	Park, Dong Hoon	M	61
Adj	Platt, Nathan	D	13,60,61,31A
Adj	Priest, Charles	D	13
Inst	Richey, Marc	M	35C
Prof	Sherman, Mozelle C.	D	39,61
Prof	Smith, G. D.	D	13,60,38,63A
Adj	Sones, Rodney	D	61
Assoc Prof	Stam, Carl L.	M	36,31A
Prof	Turner, Ronald A.	D	13,61
Prof	Turner, Sandra	D	66A,66D,66B,66G
Inst	Valle, Amy	M	66A,66D
Inst	Vaughn, Donna	B	44

KY1300 Thomas More College
Department of Music
333 Thomas More Pkwy
Crestview Hills, KY 41017
(859) 341-5800   Fax: (859) 344-3345
www.thomasmore.edu
E-mail: stephen.goforth@thomasmore.edu

4 Year Institution

Director: Stephen C. Goforth, 80A

Lect	Goforth, Stephen C.		11,36,60A,61,12A
Lect	Wells, Rebecca Schaffer		13A,13B,13C,13D,13E
Adj	Winner, Andrew		70

KY1350 Transylvania University
Music Program
300 N Broadway
Lexington, KY 40508
(859) 281-3546   Fax: (859) 233-8797
www.transy.edu
E-mail: gpartain@transy.edu

4 Year Institution

Director: Gregory L. Partain, 80A

Inst PT	Acord, Michael D.	M	64C
Prof	Anderson, Gary L.	D	60A,12A,36
Prof	Barnes, Larry J.	D	13,10,29A,34,14C
Inst PT	Beavers, Clyde E.	D	62C
Inst PT	Binford, Joanna	M	62A,62B,41
Inst PT	Bromley, Tanya M.	M	63A
Inst PT	Calkins, Mark R.	M	61
Inst PT	Cox, Rachel	M	61,36
Inst PT	Davis, Meredyth P.	M	66C
Inst PT	De Aeth, Ross	B	67H
Inst PT	Eaton, Angela S.	M	66C,66A
Inst PT	Elliott, Merrilee	M	64A
Inst PT	Evans, Valerie L.	M	63C,47
Inst PT	Gray, Julie	M	64D
Inst PT	Griffith, Ben	B	66F
Prof	Hawkins, Ben	D	60B,32,37,38,63B
Inst PT	Hedger, John R.	B	70
Inst PT	Heershe, Kim	M	64B
Inst PT	Louder, Earle	D	63D
Prof	Partain, Gregory L.	D	11,41,66A,66B,12A
Inst PT	Patrick, Lee	D	64E
Inst PT	Rector, Arlene	M	62E
Inst PT	Strouse, Greg	M	65,50
Inst PT	Tice, Loren C.	M	11,66A,66H,66C,66G

KY1400 Union College
Department of Music
310 College St
Barbourville, KY 40906
(606) 546-1625
www.unionky.edu
E-mail: tjmcf@unionky.edu

4 Year Institution

Chair: Thomas J. McFarland, 80A

Asst Prof	Gandy, V. Gay	D	36,61,13A,13C,11
Inst PT	McFarland, Kay Dawn	M	66
Prof	McFarland, Thomas J.	D	60,12A,32E,49,63
Inst PT	Oliver, Jon	M	32B
Inst PT	Sizemore, Mark	M	48,64,46

KY1425 Univ of the Cumberlands
Department of Music
7525 College Station Dr
Williamsburg, KY 40769
(606) 539-4332   Fax: (606) 539-4332
www.ucumberlands.edu
E-mail: jeff.smoak@ucumberlands.edu

4 Year Institution

Chair: Jeff C. Smoak, Jr., 80A

Asst Prof	Corcoran, James R.	M	65,34,11,50
Prof	Etter, David D.	D	36,61,31A,60
PT	Fox, Dana	M	64B
PT	Logan, Brian	M	64D
Assoc Prof	Majors, Gayle	M	32,66,11
Inst	McFarland, Kay Dawn	M	11,66A,66C,66D
Prof	Smoak, Jeff C.	D	32,36,61,40,43
PT	Stegner, John M.	M	32D,61
Assoc Prof	Sudduth, Steven	D	13,32E,37,60B,63C
Assoc Prof	Threlkeld, David M.	M	11,12A,47,48,64
Asst Prof	Tuck, Patrick M.	D	10,13,49,63A,63B

KY1450 Univ of Kentucky-Lexington
School of Music
105 Fine Arts Bldg
465 Rose St
Lexington, KY 40506-0022
(859) 257-4900   Fax: (859) 257-9576
www.uky.edu/FineArts/Music
E-mail: skipgray@uky.edu

4 Year Institution, Graduate School
Member of NASM

Master of Arts in Music Theory, Master of Music in Composition, Master of Music in Performance, Master of Music in Conducting, Master of Music in Music Education, PhD in Music Theory, PhD in Music Education, DMA in Composition, DMA in Conducting, DMA in Performance, Master of Music in Sacred Music, PhD in Musicology, Master of Arts in Musicology

Director: Harold R. 'Skip' Gray, 80A
Dir., Undergraduate Studies: Elizabeth Packard Arnold, 80B
Dir., Graduate Studies: Lance Brunner, 80C
Dir., Preparatory Division: Daniel Mason, 80E
Associate Director: Karen Bottge, 80H

Prof	Arnold, Ben	D	12,12A
Asst Prof	Arnold, Elizabeth Packard	D	61,39
Asst Prof	Atchison, Scott-Lee	M	37,63A
Prof	Baber, Joseph W.	M	13,10
Asst Prof	Baker, Michael	D	13,13C,13E,13G,13I
Assoc Prof	Bender, Dennis	D	61
Assoc Prof	Birdwell, Cody	D	48,60B
Asst Prof	Bottge, Karen	D	13
Assoc Prof	Boulden, George	M	37,60,32E
Assoc Prof	Brunner, Lance	D	12A,12
Prof	Campbell, James B.	M	65,50
Assoc Prof Emeritus	Clarke, W. Harry	M	60,32E
Asst Prof	Clay, Angelique	D	61
Assoc Prof	Clodfelter, Mark	M	63A,41
Inst PT	Cook, Elaine Humphreys	M	62E
Asst Prof	Dailey, Raleigh K.	D	29,46
Inst PT	DiMartino, Vincent	M	63A,41
Prof	Domek, Richard C.	D	13,13J

Assoc Prof	Elliott, David	M	49,63B
Inst PT	Glixon, Beth	D	12
Prof	Glixon, Jonathan	D	12,55
Asst Prof	Gooding, Lori	D	33
Prof	Gray, Harold R. 'Skip'	D	63D,49,41
Assoc Prof	Hallman, Diana R.	D	12,20A
Asst Prof	Hennings, Dieter	M	70
Prof Emeritus	Hersh, Alan	D	66A,66B,66C,41
Assoc Prof	Hetzel, Lori	D	32,36,32D
Assoc Prof	Hobbs, Julie	D	64A,48
Assoc Prof	Holm-Hudson, Kevin	D	13F,13,10A,13E,13H
Asst Prof	Hudson, Michael	D	32
Assoc Prof Emeritus	Jackson, Cliff	B	61,66C
Prof	Johnson, Jefferson	D	60,40,36,42
Assoc Prof	Karp, Benjamin	M	41,62C,42
Inst PT	Karp, Margaret B.	M	62A,62B
Lect	Kern, Bradley	M	63C,41
Asst Prof	Kwon, Donna L.	D	12,20
Asst Prof	Lander, Deborah R.	D	62B,42
Prof	Lawrence, Cynthia	M	61,39
Lect	Lindsay, Tedrin Blair	D	61,66C
Prof	Lugo, Noemi	D	61
Assoc Prof	Mason, Daniel	M	62A,62B,41
Prof	McCorvey, Everett	D	61,39
Lect	McVay, Vicki	D	66D,13,66B,13C
Inst PT	Mieses, Nermis	M	64B,13C,41
Assoc Prof	Nardolillo, John	M	38,60B
Inst PT	Olsen, Karl	M	62D
Inst PT	Osland, Lisa	M	64E,41,47
Prof	Osland, Miles	M	47,64E,29,53,48
Prof	Pen, Ronald	D	20G,29A,12A,12
Lect	Penn, Stephen T.	M	61,66C
Prof	Robinson, Schuyler	D	13,66G,66H,31A
Assoc Prof	Simpson, Peter	M	13,64D,41
Prof	Sogin, David	D	32
Prof	Voro, Irina	D	66A,66B
Lect	Walker, Erin	D	12,20,50,65
Prof	Wang, Cecilia	D	32,12C
Assoc Prof Emeritus	Warren, Dale E.	M	63C,41
Assoc Prof	Wright, Scott	D	64C,41,48
Asst Prof	Yinger, Olivia	D	33

KY1460 Univ of Kentucky-Louisville

Jefferson Community College
109 E Broadway
Louisville, KY 40202-2005
(502)584-0181   Fax: (502)584-0181
www.jcc.kctcs.edu
E-mail: william.lites@kctcs.edu

2 Year Institution

Chair: Wesley Lites, 80A

PT	Dasilva, Mario	M	47,70,20H,29
Prof	Doran, David Stephen	M	13A,13,10,11,12A
Asst Prof	Jones, M. Douglas	M	20G,67D,70
PT	Morrison, Linda	D	11,32,36,66A,66G

KY1500 Univ of Louisville

School of Music
2301 South Third St
Louisville, KY 40292
(502) 852-6907   Fax: (502) 852-0520
www.louisville.edu
E-mail: doane@louisville.edu

4 Year Institution, Graduate School
Member of NASM

Master of Music in Composition, Master of Music in Music Theory, Master of Music in Performance, Master of Music Education, Master of Music in Music History & Literature

Dean: Christopher Doane, 80A
Dir., Undergraduate Studies: Anne Marie DeZeeuw, 80B
Acting Dir., Graduate Studies: Krista B. Wallace-Boaz, 80C
Dir., Community Music Program: Stephen P. Mattingly, 80E
Associate Dean: Naomi J. Oliphant, 80H

Asst Prof	Acklin, Amy	D	32E,37,60B
Inst PT	Albrink, Emily	M	61
Prof	Amchin, Robert A.	D	32B,32H,32A
Prof	Ashworth, John	D	12A,55,66H,67
Asst Prof	Banks, Ansyn P.	D	63A,29
Asst Prof	Biran, Dror	D	66A
Asst Prof	Bowles, Shannon	M	33
Prof	Byrne, Gregory	D	65,37,50
Inst PT	Christensen, Jean M.	D	12,29A
Inst PT	Connerley, Jim L.	M	47
Inst PT	Dell Aquila, Paul	M	13E
Inst PT	DeStefano, Dominic	M	62B
Prof	DeZeeuw, Anne Marie	D	13
Inst PT	Dierks, Deborah	M	66C
Prof	Doane, Christopher	D	32
Inst PT	Durbin, Timothy T.	D	32E
Inst PT	Elmore, Doug	M	32B,32C
Inst PT	Ensel, Amy	M	32E
Inst PT	Fitzgerald, Chris	M	29B,13
Inst PT	Gottlieb, Donald	B	64A
Inst PT	Griffin, Karen K.	M	66D
Prof	Hatteberg, Kent E.	D	36,60
Inst PT	Hausmann, John P.	M	12A
Prof	Heim, D. Bruce	M	63B,49,42
Inst PT	Hutchinson, Jean Leslie	M	12A
Inst PT	Ibershoff, Emily	M	33
Inst	Jones, Douglas	M	32
Assoc Prof	Jones, John R.	M	49,63D,42
Inst PT	Karr, Kathy	M	64A,48
Inst PT	Karr, Matthew L.	M	64D
Inst	King, Sidney	B	62D,41
Prof	Koerselman, Herbert L.	D	63A,32B
Prof	LaBarbera, John P.	B	47,35A,35C
Inst PT	Lee, Bomi	M	36
Assoc Prof	Lloyd, Kimcherie	M	60,39,38
Inst PT	Lynn, Mark J.	M	63A
Inst PT	Lynn, Mark J.	D	37
Inst PT	MacWilliams, Brittany K.	M	62A
Inst PT	Mattingly, Stephen P.	D	70
Inst PT	McCanless, Clinton T.	M	63D
Inst PT	McClure, Carol	M	62E
Inst PT	McCord, Adam R.	M	64E
Inst PT	Mulhall, Sean	M	12A
Inst PT	Nije, Marilyn	M	64C
Inst PT	Noble, Steve L.	M	12A
Prof	Oliphant, Naomi J.	D	66A
Prof	Ong, Seow-Chin	D	12
Inst PT	Paxton, Alexis G.	M	36
Inst PT	Potochnic, Jennifer	M	64B
Inst PT	Purcell, Julia	M	33
Prof	Rafferty, J. Patrick	B	62A,51
Inst PT	Ramach, Michael E.	M	54,12A
Inst PT	Ratti, Linda	M	32E
Inst PT	Ritz, John	D	10B,53
Prof	Rouse, Steve	DMA	10
Prof	Satterwhite, Marc	D	13,10
Inst	Shadle, Douglas W.	D	12A
Assoc Prof	Shuster, Brett A.	D	42,63C,49,67E
Prof	Speck, Frederick A.	D	10,37,43
Inst PT	Sprowles, Michael David	M	12A
Prof	Tidwell, Dallas	M	64C,48,42
Prof	Tidwell, Edith		61
Inst PT	Tiemann, Jason E.		47,65
Prof	Tolson, Gerald H.	M	32,47,29,14C
Prof	Tracy, Michael	M	47,64E,42
Prof	Tunnell, Michael	D	49,63A,42
Inst PT	Vasconcellos, Renato	M	20H,34C
Inst PT	Wagner, Craig	B	70,47
Assoc Prof	Wallace-Boaz, Krista B.	D	66D
Asst Prof	Weeks, Daniel	M	61
Inst PT	Wheeler, Tyrone		47,62D
Inst PT	White, Christopher T.	M	12A,34D
Asst Prof	Wolek, Krzysztof	D	10B
Inst PT	Worley, Daniel T.	D	10,10F
Prof	York, Paul	M	51,62C,42

KY1540 West Kentucky Comm & Tech College

Department of Music
PO Box 7380
Paducah, KY 42002-7380
(502) 554-9200   Fax: (502) 554-6310
www.westkentucky.kctcs.edu
E-mail: norman.wurgler@kctcs.edu

2 Year Institution

Chair, Humanities: Sharla Krupansky, 80A
Coordinator, Fine Arts: Norman F. Wurgler, 80H

Inst PT	Heath, Malissa	M	11,66D,32B,13,12A
Inst PT	Hollis, Brenda	M	32B,20,11
Inst PT	Julian, Ester	M	32B
Inst PT	Leslie, Tracy	M	32B
Inst PT	Turner, Tammy	D	29A,11,32B
Prof	Wurgler, Norman F.	M	11,36,20G,61,54

KY1550 Western Kentucky University
Department of Music
1906 College Heights Blvd., #41029
Bowling Green, KY 42101-1029
(270) 745-3751   Fax: (270) 745-6855
www.wku.edu/Music
E-mail: music@wku.edu

4 Year Institution, Graduate School
Member of NASM

Master of Arts in Music Education

Chair: Mitzi Groom, 80A
Dean, Potter College: David Lee, 80A

Vstng Asst Prof	Adam, Jennifer	D	32D,13C,36
Assoc Prof	Alvarez, Heidi Pintner	D	64A,13B,41
Inst	Belcher, Debbie	M	11
Asst Prof	Berry, Mark S.	M	65,50,41
Inst	Berry, Sarah	M	62C
PT	Blakeman, Lee	M	63C,13C,11,41
PT	Brennan-Hondorp, Jennifer J.	M	61
Asst Prof	Bright, Jeff R.	D	37,32E,34
Asst Prof	Cipolla, John M.	M	41,64C,64E
PT	Cron, Nancy	M	61
PT	Dockery, Darryl D.	M	32B
PT	Doughty, Ryan	M	11
PT	Gibson, David	M	11,61
Prof	Groom, Mitzi	D	32,69,66G
Asst Prof	Hondorp, Paul	D	36,60A,32D,61,40
PT	Hussung, Lisa	M	61,11
PT	Johnson, Patricia	M	11,13C
Prof	Kallstrom, Michael	D	13,10
Asst Prof	Kelly, Liza	D	61,39
Inst	Lin, Ching Yi	M	62A
PT	Lloyd, Leslie	M	32B
Inst	Martin, John	M	70,11,34B,34G,41
PT	Paugh, Rob	M	32B
Inst	Polk, Ben	M	11
Asst Prof	Polk, Kristin	D	64B,64D,32E,13A,13B
PT	Pope, Beth	M	61
Assoc Prof	Pope, Wayne	D	39,61,41
PT	Powell, Clay	M	32
PT	Reed-Lunn, Rebecca	B	62B,11
Assoc Prof	Schallert, Gary	D	37,60B
Prof	Scott, Marshall	D	41,47,63A,29
Prof	Scott, William	D	62D,38,41
PT	Speer, Alesia L.	M	66A,66C
Prof	Speer, Donald R.	D	66B,66C,66D
Inst	Stein, Ken	B	66G
Asst Prof	Stites, Joseph	M	32C,37
Prof	Swanson, Robyn	D	32A,32B,32G,32H
Assoc Prof	Wolinski, Mary E.	D	12A,11
PT	Woodward, Todd	M	11

LA0030 Bossier Parish Community College
Department of Perf. Arts-Music
6220 E Texas St
Bossier City, LA 71111
(318) 678-6146   Fax: (318) 678-6424
www.bpcc.edu/
E-mail: mhart@bpcc.edu

2 Year Community College

Inst	Chandler, Gulya	M	66A,66C,66D,11,12A
	Hart, Michael D.	D	37,63A,11,13,47

LA0050 Centenary College of Louisiana
Hurley School of Music
2911 Centenary Blvd
Shreveport, LA 71104
(318) 869-5235   Fax: (318) 869-5248
www.centenary.edu/music
E-mail: music@centenary.edu

4 Year Institution
Member of NASM

Dean: Gale J. Odom, 80A

Lect PT	Aiken, Janice	M	61
Lect PT	Allen, Christopher	B	62D
Lect PT	Bridges, Theresa	M	64B
Lect PT	Brown, Leon	M	70
Lect PT	DeRousse, Cathy	M	66A
Prof	English, Horace	D	61
Lect PT	Gabriel, Adrienne Moffitt	M	62B
Asst Prof	Gabriel, Todd A.	D	10,13,38
Lect	Grosz, Gay	D	66A,66C
Lect PT	Haas, Peter	B	62D
Lect	Hobson, David	D	36,11,31A,12A
Lect PT	Horak, Sally	M	64A
Lect PT	Hundemer, Thomas	M	63B,16,10A
Lect PT	Maynard, Robert	B	64E,47
Prof	Odom, Gale J.	D	61
Lect PT	Phillips, Tom	M	64C
Lect PT	Ratcliff, Joy	M	66D
Lect PT	Scarlato, Michael	M	63A
Assoc Prof	Smith, Ross	D	11,66A,13A,13B,13C
Lect PT	Teague, Chan	B	50,65
Lect PT	Vaska-Haas, Kristina	M	62C
Lect PT	Watson, Holly	D	66G
Lect	Wikan, Cory	M	36,60A

LA0080 Delgado Community College
Department of Music & Music Business
615 City Park Ave
New Orleans, LA 70119-4326
(504) 671-6373   Fax: (504) 483-1953
www.dcc.edu
E-mail: sedwar@dcc.edu

2 Year Institution

Head Instructor: Steven C. Edwards, 80A

PT	Boyd, Jesse	M	11,13,29,62,70
PT	Branch, Kirk	M	66A
Asst Prof	Cho, Peter	M	13,34,35,47,66A
PT	Connors, Lori	M	35A
Prof	Edwards, Steven C.	M	11,12,36,40,61
Inst	George, Kevin	M	11,13,34,35
PT	Laky, Beth	JD	35A
PT	Maurreau, Robert	B	65
Inst	McDermott, Sheila	M	11,13,61,66D
PT	Rose, Brent	M	29B,64
PT	Settoon, Donna	B	66A,66D
PT	Skinkus, Michael	M	65
PT	Wadsworth, Amanda	M	11,66A,66D
PT	Walters, Corinne	M	11
PT	Williams, Jamelle	M	63
PT	Zeller, Jared	B	35

LA0100 Grambling State University
Department of Music
GSU Box 4258
Grambling, LA 71245
(318) 274-2682   Fax: (318) 274-4089
www.gram.edu
E-mail: pannell@gram.edu

4 Year Institution, Historically Black College
Member of NASM

Chair: Larry J. Pannell, 80A

Asst Prof	Bogdan, Valentin Mihai	DMA	66A,10,35A
Inst	Hawthorne, Leroy	M	70,20G,16,47
Asst Prof	Hendrix, Michael	M	37,63C
Inst	Lacy, Charles	M	37,63D
Asst Prof	Pannell, Larry J.	D	64,34,35C,37,32
Asst Prof	Ransom, McCoy	M	13,66A,66G,66C
Asst Prof	Roebuck, Nikole D.	M	32,64C
Assoc Prof	Rubrecht, Karl	D	66A
Asst Prof	Spencer, Malcolm	M	63,37
Asst Prof	Tao, Ye	M	51,38
Inst PT	Teague, William C.	B	65
Asst Prof	Wimberly, Brenda	M	36,61

LA0150 Louisiana College

Department of Music
PO Box 604
Pineville, LA 71359
(318) 487-7336   Fax: (318) 487-7337
www.lacollege.edu
E-mail: miller@lacollege.edu

4 Year Institution

Dean: Fred Guilbert, 80A
Coordinator: Gabriel Miller, 80A

Adj Inst	Cauley, Susan	M	66G
Artist in Res	Chou, Mei-En	M	66A,66B,66C,12A
Adj Inst	Cockerham, Barbara	M	61
Prof	Frey, Loryn E.	DMA	12A,39,61
Adj Inst	Guilbert, Fred	D	36
Inst	Hunter, Andrew	M	37,65,32
Asst Prof	Miller, Gabriel	D	12
Adj Inst	Rivet, Joe	M	37,63
Adj Inst	Turner, Randy	M	11
Prof	Yang, Ben Hoh	PhD	13,66A,66C

LA0200 Louisiana State University

College of Music & Dramatic Arts
102 School of Music Bldg
Baton Rouge, LA 70803-2504
(225) 578-3261   Fax: (225) 578-2562
www.music.lsu.edu
E-mail: wdelony@lsu.edu

4 Year Institution, Graduate School
Member of NASM

Master of Music in Collaborative Piano, Master of Music in Composition, Master of Music in Music Theory, Master of Music in Performance, Master of Music in Conducting, Master of Music in Music Education, Master of Music in Musicology, PhD in Music Theory, PhD in Composition, PhD in Music Education, DMA in Conducting, DMA in Performance, PhD in Musicology, Master of Music in Jazz Studies, Master of Music in Piano Pedagogy

Dean: Laurence D. Kaptain, 80A
Assistant Dean: Carol W. Larsen, 80B,80D,80H
Dir., Graduate Studies: Lori E. Bade, 80C,80D
Dir., Festival of Contemporary Music: Stephen David Beck, 80F
Associate Dean: Willis Delony, 80H,80B,80C

Prof	Bade, Lori E.	D	61
Asst Prof	Bartolome, Sarah J.	D	32
Asst Prof	Bazayev, Inessa	D	13
Asst Prof	Beavers, Gabriel	M	64D
Prof	Beck, Stephen David	D	10,45,34
Asst Prof	Borowitz, Michael J.	M	39
Asst Prof	Boutwell, Brett N.	D	12
Prof	Byo, James L.	D	32
Prof	Campbell, Griffin M.	D	64E
Prof	Constantinides, Dinos	D	10
Prof	Delony, Willis	D	47,11
Assoc Prof	Dietz, Brett William	D	65
Assoc Prof	DiLutis, Robert A.	M	64C
Other	Frazer, Dianne	M	66C
Prof	Fulton, Kenneth	D	60,36
Assoc Prof	Giger, Andreas	D	12
Prof	Grayson, Robert E.	M	61,39
Other	Grimes, Janice	M	66C
Prof	Grimes, William F.	D	47,29
Prof	Gurt, Michael	M	66A
Other	Harris, Rachel	D	11
Asst Prof	He, Lin	D	62A
Other	Houser, Kimberly A.	D	62E
Inst	Howe, Blake	D	12A
Asst Prof	Jesse, Dennis	M	61
Prof	Kaptain, Laurence D.	D	65
Prof	Kemler, Katherine A.	D	64A
Inst	King, Roy M.	M	37
Assoc Prof	Lilleslatten, Espen	M	62A
Asst Prof	Little, Jeannie E.	M	63C
Asst Prof	McBride-Daline, Matthew S.	M	62B
Assoc Prof	McDonough, James D.	M	39
Assoc Prof	McFarland, Alison	D	12
Inst	Melley, Eric	M	37,60B
Asst Prof	Olesen, Bradley C.	D	32D
Prof	O'Neill, Patricia A.	M	61
Assoc Prof	Orgel, Seth H.	M	63B
Assoc Prof	Orman, Evelyn	D	32
Prof	Parker, Dennis N.	M	62C
Adj	Parker, Everett G.	M	36
Other	Patrick-Harris, Terry	M	61
Assoc Prof	Peck, Robert W.	D	13
Prof	Perry, Jeffrey	D	13
	Petzet, John M.	D	11,36
Asst Prof	Pike, Pamela D.	D	66B,66D
Assoc Prof	Riazuelo, Carlos	M	38,60B
Prof Emeritus	Ross, Ronald	D	
Prof	Ryon, James M.	M	63C
Asst Prof	Shaw, Brian	D	63A,47
Assoc Prof	Sims, Loraine	D	61
Asst Prof	Sioles, Gregory	M	66A
Prof	Skillen, Joseph	D	63D
Prof	Smyth, David H.	D	13
Prof	Spillman, Herndon	D	66G
Other	Vandermark, Mark S.	B	72
Assoc Prof	Wei, Yung-Chiao	M	62D
Assoc Prof	West, James R.	D	63A

LA0250 Louisiana Tech University

Department of Music
PO Box 8608
Ruston, LA 71272-0034
(318) 257-4200   Fax: (318) 257-4571
performingarts.latech.edu/music
E-mail: sorensen@latech.edu

4 Year Institution
Member of NASM

Coordinator: Randall J. Sorensen, 80A

Assoc Prof	Alexander, Joe L.	D	10,13,63D,10A,49
Asst Prof	Budds, Cain	D	70,11,13A,13B,13C
Assoc Prof	Gibbs, Lawrence	M	11,29A,37,47,64C
Asst Prof	Lyons, Greg	M	32E,65,50
Asst Prof	Maxedon, Lisa M.	D	61,11,39
Assoc Prof	Moegle, Mary Steele A.	D	11,66A,66C,66D
Asst Prof	Robken, Jim	M	37,60B
Inst PT	Sorensen, Ann	M	62A,62B,62C,62D
Assoc Prof	Sorensen, Randall J.	D	63A,63B,13,13B,13A
Asst Prof	Teets, Sean	D	60A,61
Asst Prof	Thompson, Laura	D	32C,32D,36,60A,61

LA0300 Loyola University

College of Music & Fine Arts
6363 Saint Charles Ave
New Orleans, LA 70118-6143
(504) 865-3037   Fax: (504) 865-2852
music.loyno.edu
E-mail: decuir@loyno.edu

4 Year Institution, Graduate School
Member of NASM

Master of Music in Performance, Masters in Music Therapy

Associate Dean: Anthony Decuir, 80A
Dir., Graduate Studies: H. Jac McCracken, 80C
Dir., Admissions: Allison R. Halperin, 80D
Dir., Preparatory Division: Elizabeth M. Floyd, 80E
Associate Dean: Georgia Gresham, 80H

Inst PT	Adams, Patti	M	64A
Inst PT	Andrews, Susan	M	64D
Prof Emeritus	Angeles, L. Dean	M	38,32E,60B
Staff	Asano, Yuiko	M	66C
Inst PT	Atwood, James H.	M	65
Inst PT	Bond, Mona	M	61
Asst Prof	Botelho, Paul J.	D	34
Vstng Prof	Bourgeois, John	B	60
Inst PT	Boyd, Jesse	B	62D
Assoc Prof	Clark, Alice V.	D	12A,11,31A,12
Inst PT	Crutti, John A.	B	35G
Assoc Prof	Dagradi, Anthony	M	64,64E,29
Vstng Prof	Davis, Gregory	B	35
Inst PT	Davis, Mark J.	D	35
Prof	Decuir, Anthony	D	61,33
Emeritus	Erb, Helen	M	64B
Emeritus	Erb, Richard	B	63C
Staff	Evans, Dane	M	66C
Inst PT	Floyd, Elizabeth M.	M	66D
Assoc Prof	Frazier, Meg Hulley	D	36
Asst Prof	Frohnmayer, Ellen Phillips	M	61
Prof	Frohnmayer, Philip	M	61
Artist in Res	Gabour, James	M	34E
Inst PT	Glynn, Mark D.	M	35A
Asst Prof	Goertzen, Valerie Woodring	D	12
Asst Prof	Hansen, Alicia S.	M	16
Prof	Hebert, Joseph G.	D	32,37,46,35
Prof	Hinderlie, Sanford E.	M	13

Prof	Horne, William P.	D	13
Prof	Kvet, Edward J.	D	32
Inst PT	Lambert, Lerene	M	66B
Inst PT	Leblanc, Stuart W.	M	70
Staff	Leerstang, Carmen	M	66C
Asst Prof	MacKay, James S.	D	13,10
Prof	Mahoney, John A.	M	29
Vstng Prof	Marsalis, Ellis	M	35A,29
Inst PT	Maureau, Wayne	B	29
Inst PT	Mayes, Frank	B	29
Assoc Prof	McCracken, H. Jac	M	66A
Inst PT	Miller, Greg F.	M	63C
Inst PT	Montequt, Dreux	M	61
Staff	Morelock, David	M	39
Prof	Murphy, John	D	66A,66B
Asst Prof	Nisbet, Allen	M	62C
Vstng Prof	Olander, Virginia	M	32
Inst PT	Owen, Bruce M.	M	62B
Inst PT	Rankin, John B.	M	70
Inst PT	Rausch, Carol E.	M	39
Inst PT	Reeks, John	M	64C
Asst Prof	Saslaw, Janna K.	D	13
Inst PT	Seeger, Brian	M	70
Inst PT	Smith, Karen B.	M	66A
Prof	Snyder, John	D	35
Inst PT	St. Julien, Marcus	D	13B,13C,61,66G
Prof Emeritus	Swanzy, David	D	32
Inst	Thiaville, Amy L.	M	62A,42
Inst PT	Vanvoorhees, Rachael F.	M	62E
Inst	Vega, Victoria P.	D	33
Inst PT	Vidacovich, John	B	65
Asst Prof	Volz, Nick R.	D	63A
Inst PT	Walsh, James	D	13

LA0350 McNeese State University
Department of Performing Arts
Box 92175
Lake Charles, LA 70609
(337) 475-5028   Fax: (337) 475-5063
www.mcneese.edu/performingarts
E-mail: mbuckles@mcneese.edu

4 Year Institution
Member of NASM

Master of Music Education

Chair: Michael Buckles, 80A
Assistant Chair: William G. Rose, 80H
Assistant Chair: Jan Scott, 80H

Asst Prof	Benoit, Lonny	M	65
Assoc Prof	Buckles, Michael	D	32E,62A
Assoc Prof	Hand, Judith	D	48,64A
Asst Prof	Jacobs, Jay N.	D	37,41,42,48
Assoc Prof	Jones, William Darryl	D	32C,36
Asst Prof	Lauderdale, Rod	M	11,63B
Prof	Lemke, Jeffrey J.	D	32,37,60
Asst Prof	Lines, Carol F.	D	61
Asst Prof	Morita, Lina	D	13C,41,66A,66C,66D
Asst Prof	Proksch, Bryan	D	13
Assoc Prof	Rose, William G.	M	13,49,34,63D,63C
Assoc Prof	Scott, David R.	M	12A,49,63A
Asst Prof	Scott, Jan	M	32B,48,64B,64D,64C
Asst Prof	Smithey, David B.	D	11,61
Artist in Res	Sylvester, Eric	B	70
Asst Prof	Vogt-Corley, Christy L.	D	66A,66B,66C,66D

LA0400 New Orleans Baptist Theo Seminary
Division of Church Music Ministries
3939 Gentilly Blvd
New Orleans, LA 70126-4858
(504) 282-4455   Fax: (504) 816-8033
www.nobts.edu/music
E-mail: musicdivision@nobts.edu

4 Year Institution, Graduate School
Member of NASM

Master of Music in Church Music, DMA in Church Music

Chair: Greg Woodward, 80A

Prof	Ferrington, Darryl	D	13A,36,32,31A
Prof	Gabrielse, Kenneth J.	D	60,36,31A,12A
Prof	Harlen, Benjamin	D	10A,31A,13B,13C,13D
Prof	Lombard, Becky	D	13,12A,66A,66G,12C
Prof	Sharp, Michael D.	D	66A,66B,31A,34,10A
Asst Prof	Steele, Edward L.	D	12A,13A,13B,13C,61
Asst Prof	Woodward, Greg	D	60

LA0450 Nicholls State University
Department of Music
PO Box 2017
Thibodaux, LA 70310
(985) 448-4600   Fax: (985) 448-4674
www.nicholls.edu/perform
E-mail: carol.britt@nicholls.edu

4 Year Institution
Member of NASM

Director: Carol Britt, 80A

PT	Alexander, James	B	62A,62B
Assoc Prof	Britt, Carol	D	13,11,12A,66D
Inst	Guenoit, Eric	M	60B,11,37,65,50
PT	Haynes, Casey	B	66C
Prof	Klaus, Kenneth S.	D	60A,11,36,61,40
Inst	Mendoza, Cristina	M	63,46,49,11,41
Inst	Sammarco, Donna	M	66A,66B,66C
Assoc Prof	Soares, Luciana	D	66A,66C,13F,51,13C
Inst	Torres, Gregory J.	M	60B,11,37,34B,32B
Inst	Van Regenmorter, Paula	D	64,12A,11,48,20

LA0550 Northwestern State Univ of Louisiana
School of Creative & Perf. Arts
140 Central Ave
Natchitoches, LA 71497
(318) 357-4522   Fax: (318) 357-5906
music.nsula.edu
E-mail: brent@nsula.edu

4 Year Institution, Graduate School

Master of Music

Chair: William Brent, 80A
Dir., Summer Programs: Jeffrey Mathews, 80G
Assistant Chair: Burt Allen, 80H

Prof	Allen, Burt	D	36,60A,60,34,61
Assoc Prof	Allen, Christine	D	66A,66D
Assoc Prof	Bakenhus, Douglas	D	13B,38,60B,64D
Assoc Prof	Brent, William	M	37,72
Inst	Brouillette, Luke	B	70
Asst Prof	Christopher, Paul	D	10,13,51,62C,62D
Prof	Coreil, Kristine	D	63B,13,41
Inst	Deville, Mary	D	66G,12
Asst Prof	Dill, Patrick	D	39,61
Asst Prof	Dunn, John	M	13B
Asst Prof	Forsyth, Paul	D	64E,48
Assoc Prof	Green, Kenneth	M	37,65,41
Asst Prof	Handel, Greg	D	32
Emeritus	Jennings, Shirley	M	62E
Asst Prof	Joy, Sharon	D	32A,32B,32H,32G,32
Inst	Kuroda, Elena	M	66C,66D
Asst Prof	Kuroda, Masahito	M	63D
Assoc Prof	Kurti, Andrej	D	62A
Assoc Prof	Mathews, Jeffrey	D	37,32C
Prof	McDermott, Dennette Derby	D	13,64A
Asst Prof	McKeithen, Steven	M	11,32,37
Assoc Prof	McLaren, Malena	D	12,64C,64E,47
Assoc Prof	Rodriquez, Galindo	M	63A,41,47
Assoc Prof	Rorex, Michael	M	36,39,61
Assoc Prof	Sanders, Terrie	M	61,66D
Prof	Thompson, J. Mark	D	49,63C
Asst Prof	Yang, Frances K.	D	66

LA0560 Our Lady of Holy Cross College
Department of Music
4123 Woodland Dr
New Orleans, LA 70131-7337
(504) 394-7744   Fax: (504) 391-2421
www.olhcc.edu
E-mail: Rgitz@olhcc.edu

4 Year Institution

Dean: Raymond Gitz, 80A
Dir., Artist/Performance Series: Julie Nice, 80F

Prof	Gitz, Raymond	D	12A,66A,31A
Lect	Nice, Julie	M	61
Lect	Scully, Francis	M	13A,12A,11

LA0600 St Joseph Abbey Seminary College
Music Program
75376 River Rd
St Benedict, LA 70457
(985) 892-1800
www.sjasc.edu

4 Year Undergraduate Institution Seminary

Coordinator: Sean B. Duggan, 80A
Dir., Artist/Performance Series: Peter E. Hammett, 80F

Duggan, Sean B.		MFA	11,12A,36,66,31A

A0650 Southeastern Louisiana University
Department of Fine & Perf. Arts
SLU Box 10815
Hammond, LA 70402-0815
(985) 549-2184   Fax: (985) 549-2892
www.selu.edu/music
E-mail: kenneth.boulton@selu.edu

4 Year Institution, Graduate School
Member of NASM

Master of Music in Music Theory, Master of Music in Performance

Interim Head: Kenneth Boulton, 80A
Coord., Undergraduate Programs: David Bernard, 80B
Coord., Graduate Programs: Glen J. Hemberger, 80C
Dir., Community Music School: Jivka Jeleva, 80E

Lect	Anthon, Gina	D	32B
Lect	Barry, JoAnne	M	12C
Prof Emeritus	Barzenick, Walter	M	
Asst Prof	Bernard, David	D	61
Lect	Besharse, Kari	D	11,13C
Assoc Prof	Boulton, Kenneth	D	66A,66B,66D
Lect	Bryan, David	M	13G,13C,70
Lect	Buerkle, Suzanne	M	64A
Lect	Callaway, Dan T.	M	63B
Lect	Cassin, Daniel	M	62C
Lect	Ciraldo, Rachel Taratoot	M	64A
Lect	Cunev, Irina	M	66C
Lect	Cvetkov, Vasil	D	66D,13
Inst	Effler, Charles E.	M	66C,39,13C
Lect	Estoque, Kevin S.	M	65,50,46,20H
Prof Emeritus	Evenson, David N.	D	66A,66D
Inst	Frechou, Paul A.	M	64C,37,32C,32E
Lect	Gallion, Brian	D	63D
Lect	Gauthreaux, Guy G.	D	65
Lect	Hanson, Brian L.	M	11
Assoc Prof	Hemberger, Glen J.	D	60B,32C,37,63C,47
Assoc Prof	Johansen, David A.	DMA	63C,11,63D,49
Assoc Prof	Jones, Henry S.	D	66A,66B,66D,13C
Inst	Kerber, Patrick C.	M	70,11
Lect	Kmiecik, Thomas	M	64C
Lect	Lawrence, Kenya L.	M	36,32B
Prof Emeritus	McCormick, David	D	
Lect	Morrow, Jo L.	M	11,66D
Lect	Morse, Dana	M	66D,66A
Lect	Nash, Robert	D	62D,11
Lect	Piattoly, Lindsay	M	36
Inst	Place, Logan B.	D	63A,37,12A
Prof Emeritus	Priez, Robert G.	M	
Assoc Prof	Ratliff, Joy	D	61
Asst Prof	Rowe, Alissa	D	36,61,60A
Assoc Prof	Rushing, Steven J.	D	61
Lect	Schepker, Kay	M	61
Assoc Prof Emerita	Schrock, Scharmal K.	M	61
Inst	Schuessler, Philip T.	D	13
Inst	Schwartz, Richard A.	D	29,47,64E,11,46
Lect	Stolz, Lissa J.	M	64B
Prof	Suber, Stephen C.	D	13,10,11
Assoc Prof Emerita	Vogt, Harriet	M	61
Inst	Voldman, Raisa	M	66C
Prof	Voldman, Yakov	D	60,32C,38,51,62
Prof Emeritus	Voorhees, Jerry L.	D	48,64D,72
Prof Emeritus	Wilcox, James H.	D	

LA0700 Southern University and A & M
Department of Visual & Perf Arts
Southern Branch Post Office
Baton Rouge, LA 70813
(225) 771-3440   Fax: (225) 771-2495
www.subr.edu

4 Year Institution, Historically Black College
Member of NASM

Coordinator, Music: Frank White, 80A

Assoc Prof	Batiste, Alvin	M	64A,64C,29,47,35A
Asst Prof	Beckford, Richard		11,36,66G,13
Asst Prof	Chemay, Frank	M	10,63D,10F,11,49
Prof	David, Myrtle	M	11,66A,66B,66C,66D
Prof	Greggs, Isaac	M	37,63A,46
Inst	Heinzen, Craig		11,63A,63B
Inst	Jackson, Herman		65,29,50
Inst	James, Judy A. G.		11,32,32I,66D
Asst Prof	Lloyd, Charles	M	13,39,11,66D
Inst	Paige-Green, Jacqueline		61,39,11
Lect	Render, Charles		62
Prof	Ryder, William H.	D	11,32,64,13
Inst	Turner, Leon		11,61
Assoc Prof	White, Frank	M	13,39,66A,11,60
Assoc Prof	Williams, Oscar	M	12A,64,11,29A

LA0720 Southern University-New Orleans
Division of Music
6400 Press Dr
New Orleans, LA 70126
(504) 286-5208   Fax: (504) 286-5131
www.suno.edu
E-mail: Mpierce@suno.edu

4 Year Institution, Historically Black College

Adj Prof	Carbonara, David	M	38,41,51,62
Assoc Prof Emeritus	Dickerson, Roger	M	10F,10,12A,36,29
Adj Prof	Fleury, August	M	63,37
Assoc Prof	Jordan, Edward	M	11,20G,37,47,64
Adj Prof	Jordan, Rachel	M	11,62A
Assoc Prof	King, Valeria G.	M	13,60,12A,12,20G
Adj Prof	Pierce, Michael	M	37,41,64A,11
Adj Prof	Stewart, Shirley	M	11,36,61,31A,32

LA0750 Tulane University
Newcomb Department of Music
6823 St. Charles Ave
New Orleans, LA 70118
(504) 865-5267   Fax: (504) 865-5270
www.tulane.edu/~music
E-mail: music@tulane.edu

4 Year Institution, Graduate School

Master of Arts in Composition, Master of Arts in Music Science & Technology, Master of Arts in Jazz Studies: Music Culture of New Orleans, Master of Arts in Musicology, Specialization in New Orleans Music, MFA in Performance, MFA in Musical Theatre

Chair: Barbara M. Jazwinski, 80A

Prof	Baron, John H.	D	12A,12,20F,20G,31B
Prof/Prac	Barreiro, Elias	M	70
Vstng Asst Prof	Dobry, John T.	M	10A,13B,47
Vstng Inst	Doheny, John	B	46,47
Prof/Prac	Guild, Jane E.	M	13A,13,61
Assoc Prof	Howard, Michael	M	61,54
Prof	Jazwinski, Barbara M.	D	13,10,43
Prof/Prac	Jensen, Joan F.	M	66A,66D,13A
Assoc Prof	Joyce, John J.	D	11,12,29
Vstng Inst	Landis, Stella Baty	M	12A,11
Prof/Prac	Lovett, Rita	M	61,54
Prof	Lushtak, Faina	M	66
Asst Prof	Raybon, Leonard	D	36,61,60A,54
Prof/Prac	Weilbaecher, Daniel	D	66A,13A

LA0760 Univ of Louisiana-Lafayette
School of Music
PO Box 41207
Lafayette, LA 70504-1207
(337) 482-6016   Fax: (337) 482-5017
music.louisiana.edu
E-mail: garth@louisiana.edu

4 Year Institution, Graduate School
Member of NASM

Master of Music in Performance, Master of Music in Conducting, Master of Music in Music Education, Master of Music in Music Theory-Composition, Master of Music in Pedagogy & Performance

Director: Garth Alper, 80A
Coord., Graduate Studies: Andrea Kapell Loewy, 80C

Prof	Alper, Garth	D	66A,29,35
Inst	Blaney, Michael S.	M	38,62A
Inst	Breaux, Troy Jude	M	37,65,50
Assoc Prof	Daniel, Margaret H.	M	61
Adj	Devillier, Danny S.	M	65
Prof	DeWitt, Mark F.	D	14,29A,13C,20G
Adj	Gambino, Kyle A.	M	64C
Assoc Prof	Garcia, Susanna P.	D	66A,66B
Adj	Gaudino, Brian J.	M	70
Assoc Prof	Haygood, James	D	32,36
Prof	Hilliard, Quincy C.	D	13,10,32C
Adj	Hochkeppel, Robin M.	M	64B,64D
Assoc Prof	Hochkeppel, William J.	D	37,32C
Inst	Huang-Davie, Yuling	D	66C
	Kennedy-Dygas, Margaret	D	61,39
Asst Prof	Kulp, Jonathan	D	12A,12
Inst	Landry, Scott P.	M	63D
Lect	Lein, Susan E.	D	66A
Inst	Lim, Chan Kiat	M	66
Prof	Loewy, Andrea Kapell	D	13,64A
Assoc Prof	Luckey, Robert	D	47,64E,29
Assoc Prof	Morton, Paul D.	D	63A
Adj	Morton, Susan	M	62C
Adj	Nash, Robert	D	62D
Prof	Reichling, Mary	D	32,66D
Asst Prof	Roche-Wallace, Catherine	D	13,63B
Inst	Roy, Shawn	M	61,39
Inst	Taylor, Brian S.	M	37,32C,60
Other	Whitmire, Sam D.		66F
Asst Prof	Willey, Robert K.	D	13,34,35,10B,45

LA0770 Univ of Louisiana-Monroe
Division of Music
Biedenhard Hall
700 Univ Ave
Monroe, LA 71209-0250
(318) 342-1570   Fax: (318) 342-1599
www.ulm.edu
E-mail: long@ulm.edu

4 Year Institution, Graduate School
Member of NASM

Master of Music in Performance, Master of Music in Conducting, Master of Music in Music Education, Master of Music in Music Theory-Composition

Director: Derle R. Long, 80A
Associate Dean: Matthew H. James, 80H

Assoc Prof	Anderson, Larry R.	M	47,50,65
Asst Prof	Boldin, James E.	D	63B,12A,11
Asst Prof	Chandler, Deborah L.	D	36,60,40
Assoc Prof	Clark, Mark Ross	D	39,54,61,11
Assoc Prof	Gibson, David	M	13,64B,64D,29A
Asst Prof	Gibson, Marilyn	D	11,63A,49
Asst Prof	Humes, Scot A.	D	64C,64E,11
Prof	James, Matthew H.	D	61,13D,39,54,60A
Asst Prof	Long, Derle R.	D	60,32E,37
Prof	Lunte, Sandra K.	D	13A,64A,48
Inst	McCleery, Mark	M	11,41,62C,62D
Asst Prof	McClung-Guillory, Deborah	M	66A,66B,66D
Asst Prof	Mobley, Mel	D	65,13
Assoc Prof	Nabors, Louis A.	M	36,61
Prof Emeritus	Nichols, William		
Asst Prof	Rinehart, Jason	D	60B,37,38,41
Assoc Prof	Seiler, Richard D.	D	66A,66C,13A,13D
	Sumner, Daniel	M	32B,32C,32D,32G
Prof	Thompson, Christopher	D	41,62A,62B,11
Assoc Prof	Vangelisti, Claire	D	61,11
Asst Prof	White, Coralie	M	11,66A,66D

LA0800 Univ of New Orleans
Department of Music
Lakefront Campus
New Orleans, LA 70148
(504) 280-6381   Fax: (504) 280-6098
www.music.uno.edu/
E-mail: unomusic@uno.edu

4 Year Institution, Graduate School
Member of NASM

Master of Music in Composition, Master of Music in Performance, Master of Music in Conducting, Master of Music in Jazz Studies

Chair: Robin Williams, 80A
Dir., Graduate Studies: Victor Atkins, 80C
Associate Chair & Dir., Undergraduate Studies: James Hamman, 80H,80B

Asst Prof	Atkins, Victor	B	29B,46,47,66A
Adj	Benko, Ron	M	63A
Prof	Blancq, Charles C.	D	29A,12A
Asst Prof	Carson, Caroline	D	11,36,32D,60A
Adj	Chase, Leah	B	61
Adj	Christopher, Evan	M	64C,47
Adj	Davis, Troy		65,47
Adj	Dearie, Megan	M	61
Adj	Fischer, Thomas	B	64C
Adj	Guerin, Roland	B	62D,47
Asst Prof	Hamman, James	D	11,12A,13A,55B,66G
Adj	Harrison, Kelvin	M	64E
Asst Prof	Hayes, Beth Tura	M	34A,34B,32,11
Inst	Kelly, Frankie J.	D	66C,40,41,42,11
Adj	Mackie, Henry	M	70,29A,29B,47
Adj	Marsalis, Delfeayo	M	63C
Adj	Marsalis, Jason		65
Prof	Masakowski, Steve	A	70,35B,35C,29B,47
Adj	Matherne, Karl	M	61
Adj	Mayfield, Irvin		63A,46
Adj	Morris, William J.	M	62D
Adj	Nunez, Robert		63D
Adj	Pate, Molly	M	63B
Assoc Prof	Peterson, Edward	M	47,64C,29B
Adj	Rankin, John	M	70
Adj	Reynolds, Steve	B	34D,35C,35D,35G
Adj	Rhody, Matthew	B	62A
Adj	Rose, Brent	M	64C,29A,13A,13B,13C
Adj	Schettler, Sarah M.	D	64A
Adj	Schettler, William	M	62D
Adj	Scott, Cindy	M	61,40
Asst Prof	Seeger, Brian	M	35A,35B,35C,47,70
Prof	Sieg, Jerry	D	10A,10F,13,12A
Assoc Prof	Taylor, Charles L.	D	37,60B,64C,32C,32E
Adj Prof	Westfall, Kathleen	DMA	61
Prof	Williams, Robin	D	66A,66B,66D,66C

LA0900 Xavier Univ of Louisiana
Department of Music
1 Drexel Drive
New Orleans, LA 70125
(504) 520-7597   Fax: (504) 520-7927
www.xula.edu
E-mail: tturner5@xula.edu

4 Year Institution, Historically Black College
Member of NASM

Chair: Timothy R. Turner, 80A

Asst Prof	Ballard, Marcus	D	64,12A
Inst	Barrientos, Carlos	M	70
Artist in Res	Delphin, Wilfred	D	66A,66B,66C,66D
Inst	Griffin, Ivan	M	61
	Haynes, Juliana	M	63A,11
Inst	Hicks, Gregory	M	63C,63D
Inst	Lorenz, Nena	M	65A,65B
Asst Prof	Mok, April H.	D	10,66G
Inst	Rahming, Dara	M	61,39
Inst	Stevens, Mitchell	M	61,36
Assoc Prof	Turner, Timothy R.	D	13G,10F,32E,34,37
Prof	Ware, John Earl	D	11,36,39,41,61
Inst	Woolf, Vance	M	63A
Inst	Yamada, Sojiro	M	62A,62B,62C,62D
Inst	Zinninger, Heather	M	64A

MA0100 Amherst College
Department of Music-2258
PO Box 5000
Amherst, MA 01002-5000
(413) 542-2364   Fax: (413) 542-2678
www.amherst.edu/music
E-mail: smfarnham@amherst.edu

4 Year Institution

Chair: Eric Sawyer, 80A
Dir., Artist/Performance Series: Sara R. Leonard, 80F

Inst	Chernin, Mallorie	M	36,40
Inst	Diehl, Bruce P.	M	29,64E,47,46
Asst Prof	Engelhardt, Jeffers	D	20,33,12
Prof	Kallick, Jenny L.	D	13,12A,39,41,12
Asst Prof	Robinson, Jason	D	12,13,14,34
Assoc Prof	Sawyer, Eric	D	10,13,34,43
Prof	Schneider, David E.	D	12,64C,43,13,41
Inst	Swanson, Mark L.	M	60B,38,66A,41

MA0150 Anna Maria College
Music Program
50 Sunset Ln
Paxton, MA 01612-1198
(508) 849-3441   Fax: (508) 849-3254
www.annamaria.edu
E-mail: rsherwin@annamaria.edu

4 Year Institution
Member of NASM

Chair & Associate Dean: Ronald G. Sherwin, 80A,80C,80F,80H

PT	Carroll, Amy	M	41
PT	Clark, Jonathan	M	11,49,63A
Assoc Prof	Connors, Maureen	M	13A,66A,66C
Assoc Prof	Greene, Roger W.	M	13,34,66A,13A,10F
PT	Grudechi, Kevin	M	41
PT	Hart, Peter	M	61
Asst Prof	Houze, Reginald M.	D	10F,36,37,60,63D
PT	Irving, Silvia	M	61
PT	Lefebvre, Matthew T.	M	64E
Asst Prof	MacDonald, Mary Carla	M	33
PT	Nigro, Christine	D	62C
PT	Noone, Elizabeth	M	66A,66D,11,13A,20B
PT	Pierce, Bradley	M	34D,35D,35G
PT	Rawston, Amy	M	62A
Assoc Prof	Ritchey, Mary Lynn	D	61,36,60A,40,11
Asst Prof	Sherwin, Ronald G.	D	11,31A,60A,36,32
PT	Skop, Stephen	M	47
PT	Struyk, Pieter	B	13A,65A,65B
Prof	Summer, Lisa	M	33

MA0200 Assumption College
Department of Art, Mus & Theatre
500 Salisbury St
Worcester, MA 01615-0005
(508) 767-7304   Fax: (508) 767-7342
www.assumption.edu
E-mail: mgraveli@assumption.edu

4 Year Institution

Chair: Michelle Graveline, 80A

Lect	Burke, Thomas	M	35H
Lect	Clemente, Peter	M	11,13A,13,70,20
Lect	Cushing, Diane	M	61
Prof	Graveline, Michelle	D	15,13,36
Lect	Hopkins, Bruce	M	37
Prof	Lamothe, Donat	D	12A,67C,20G,20H
Lect	Sulski, Peter	M	41,62A,62B
Vstng Prof	Tivnan, Brian	M	54

MA0250 Atlantic Union College
Department of Music
PO Box 1000
South Lancaster, MA 01561
(978) 368-2100   Fax: (978) 368-2011
www.auc.edu
E-mail: music@auc.edu

4 Year Institution
Member of NASM

Chair: Kaestner Robertson, 80A
Dir., Thayer Performing Arts Center: Carol Swinyar, 80E

Inst PT	Esham, Faith L.	M	61
Inst PT	Imperio, Roy	M	66A,66B,41,66C,11
Inst PT	Lion, Na'ama	D	41,64A,67D
Prof Emeritus	Merriman, Margarita L.	D	13,10,66A
Inst PT	Raney, Earl	B	37,63A
Prof	Robertson, Kaestner	D	66A,13,36,66B,66C
Inst PT	Swinyar, Carol	M	32

MA0255 Babson College
Division of Arts & Humanities
231 Forest St.
Babson Park, MA 02457
(781) 239-4598
www3.babson.edu/Academics/Divisions/ahhs/default.cfm
E-mail: graham.sandraj@gmail.com

4 Year Institution

Chair: Mary Pinard, 80A

Inst	Graham, Sandra J.	D	14,20A,20G,31F

MA0260 Berklee College of Music
1140 Boylston St
Boston, MA 02215-3695
(617) 266-1400   Fax: (617) 247-9886
www.berklee.edu
E-mail: academicaffairs@berklee.edu

4 Year Institution

President: Roger H. Brown, 80A
Dean, Music Technology Division: Stephen Croes, 80A
Dean, Professional Education Division: Darla Hanley, 80A
Dean, Professional Writing Division: Kari H. Juusela, 80A
Dean, Professional Performance Division: Matt Marvuglio, 80A
Vice President Academic Affairs, Dean of Students: Lawrence E. Bethune, 80D,80H
Senior Vice President Academic Affairs/Provost: Lawrence J. Simpson, 80H
Gary Burton Chair in Jazz: Joe Lovano

Asst Prof	Abraham, Deborah	PhD	
Assoc Prof	Abraham, Michael	B	35C
Assoc Prof	Adams, Kristine	M	13A,13
	Adderley, Cecil L.	PhD	32E,32F,32G,62A,64C
Inst	Agatiello, Gustavo	B	65
Assoc Prof	Aldrich, Jon	B	10
Assoc Prof	Alexander, Prince Charles	B	34,35C,35G
Assoc Prof	Alhadeff, Peter	PhD	35A
Assoc Prof	Allen, Jodi Leigh	M	
	Allison, Elizabeth Catherine	M	32
Inst	Amy, Robynn	B	63
Prof	Anderson, Dean	M	65
Asst Prof	Andrews, Jennifer	B	
Assoc Prof	Anger, Darol		62A
	Appleman, Richard	B	62D
Asst Prof	Appleman, Tom	B	13C
Prof	Applin, Richard	M	10
Asst Prof	Arcaro, John	B	66A
Assoc Prof	Aronson, Abigail	M	70
Asst Prof	Arzigian, Arleen	M	
Assoc Prof	Baboian, John	M	70
Assoc Prof	Bailey, Sheryl	B	70
	Baione, Larry	M	70
Prof	Banfield, William	D	
Asst Prof	Bares, William	PhD	13A,13B
Asst Prof	Bargfrede, Allen	JD	35
Assoc Prof	Barnett, Janie	B	61
Assoc Prof	Barrett, Darren	M	47
Asst Prof	Barry, Kevin		47
Assoc Prof	Bartlett, Bruce		70
Asst Prof	Baust, Jeffrey P.	DMA	34
Prof Emeritus	Bavicchi, John	B	10
Prof	Beard, Jackie		64

Title	Name	Degree	Codes
Prof	Beasley, Walter	B	47
Assoc Prof	Beauregard, Jennifer	PhD	
Prof	Bedner, Edward C.	M	66A
Assoc Prof	Bell, Larry	PhD	10
Asst Prof	Bellotti, Sergio		65
Inst	Belz, Kevin	B	70
Asst Prof	Bennet, Pratt H.T.	B	13A
Asst Prof	Bennett, Deborah	M	
Prof	Benoff, Mitchell J.	M	35C
Asst Prof	Bent, Catherine	M	13C,62C
Staff	Berger, Brad	B	34,35C,35G
Prof	Bermejo-Greenspan, Mili		61
	Biederwolf, Kurt J.	B	45,35C
Prof	Bierylo, Michael	B	45,35C
Assoc Prof	Biviano, Franklin Lin		47
Asst Prof	Bjorck, Andreas		10C
Assoc Prof	Blake, Joey	B	61
Asst Prof	Blanco, Leo	M	66A
Prof	Blazar, Sally	PhD	13A
Asst Prof	Blinman, Chad		35C,35G
Asst Prof	Block-Schwenk, Kevin	M	35
Asst Prof	Blomquist, Edwin	JD	35A
Assoc Prof	Bouchard, Frederick	B	
Prof	Boulanger, Richard	PhD	45,35C
Assoc Prof	Bowden, Dan B.	B	70
Prof	Brackeen, JoAnne		66A
Assoc Prof	Brandao, Fernando	M	47
	Brass, Kenneth	M	35
Assoc Prof	Bresler, Ross	PhD	13A
Assoc Prof	Brigida, Michael A.		45,35C
Asst Prof	Brindell, Sarah	B	10
Assoc Prof	Broadley-Martin, Sharon		47
Assoc Prof	Brown, Sharon	M	61
Assoc Prof	Browne, Whitman		62D
Asst Prof	Buda, David		62D
Asst Prof	Byers, Eric	M	13A
Prof	Callahan, David	M	10
Asst Prof	Camara, Mohamed Kalifa		65
Assoc Prof	Candelaria-Barry, Consuelo	B	47
Inst	Capozzoli, Andrea	B	61
Asst Prof	Carballeira, Andy	B	
Asst Prof	Carbone, Anthony P.		35C
Asst Prof	Carlberg, Frank T.	M	66A
	Carlin, Dan	B	10C
Asst Prof	Carr, Karen	B	61
Prof	Carrington, Terri Lyne	B	65
Prof	Cassara, Charles	M	13A,13
Asst Prof	Castillo, Ramon	PhD	10
Assoc Prof	Castrillo, Manuel E.		65
Asst Prof	Cattaneo, Susan K.	B	10
Asst Prof	Cecco, Jerry		47,49
Assoc Prof	Cecere, Dennis		47
Prof	Cervenka, Ken	B	63
Assoc Prof	Chadwick, Donna	M	33
	Chase, Allan	M	13C
Asst Prof	Chase, Corinne Sloan	B	13A,13
Asst Prof	Chase, Jon		10,35C,35G
Assoc Prof	Chase, Linda J.	M	
Prof	Christian, Armstead R.	B	61
Assoc Prof	Christopherson, Robert	B	66A
Asst Prof	Cifelli, Kristin	B	61
Prof	Clark, David W.	M	62D
Assoc Prof	Clark, Ronald	M	
Assoc Prof	Clark, Suzanne M.	M	13A,13
Asst Prof	Cline, Rebecca	B	47
Prof	Codding, Peggy	PhD	33
Assoc Prof	Cohen, Alla Elana	M	10
	Coia-Gailey, Susan M.		
Prof	Cokkinias, Peter L.	DMA	64
	Colatosti, Camille	PhD	15
Prof	Coroniti, Joseph	PhD	13A
Prof	Covell, Jeffrey	B	66A
Prof	Crook, Harold	B	13A,13
Assoc Prof	Cudmore, Faye	M	
Prof	Da Silva, Jetro	M	47
Assoc Prof	Dahlgren, Winnie	M	13B
Prof	Dale, Stephen	M	13A,13
Prof	Damian, Jon	B	70
Prof	Davis, Richard	B	10
Assoc Prof	Davis, Suzanne	M	66A
Assoc Prof	Dean, Suzanne B.	M	35B
Assoc Prof	Del Nero, Paul	M	13A,13
Assoc Prof	Denisch, Beth	PhD	13,10F,10,15
Assoc Prof	Dennard, Kenwood	B	65
Assoc Prof	Dennehy, Martin J.	M	35A
Prof	DeOgburn, Scott	B	13A,13
Asst Prof	Diaz, Ernesto		65
Assoc Prof	DiCenso, David		65
Assoc Prof	DiFusco, Salvatore		70
Prof	DiMuzio, Richard J.	DMA	13A,13
Prof	Doezema, Robert	M	
Inst	Doherty, Keith	M	
Asst Prof	Dolan, Anastasia		61
Asst Prof	Doms, David	B	34
Prof	Dorenfeld, Jeffrey	B	35A
Prof	Eastman, George	PhD	13A
Assoc Prof	Edelstein, Andrew S.	B	35C
Assoc Prof	Elliott, Bill		10,35C,35G
Inst	Ellis, Brian	B	47
Asst Prof	Elmen, Paul	B	47,49
Prof	Elowsky-Fox, Jennifer	M	66A
Prof	Epstein, Marti J.	DMA	10
Prof	Evans, Richard L.	M	
Asst Prof	Fabrizio, Louis	M	35
Assoc Prof	Faieta, John	M	63
Prof	Farquharson, Michael	M	13
Asst Prof	Fawson, Christine	B	63
Assoc Prof	Felts, Randolph C.	B	13A,13
Asst Prof	Ferrara, Dominick J.	PhD	32
Prof	Fessler, Scott	M	10
Prof	Fewell, A. Garrison	B	70
Prof	Fialkov, Jay	B	35
Prof	Finn, Jon	B	70
Prof	Finn, Lawrence	B	65
Prof	Fiuczynski, David	B	70
Asst Prof	Flanagan, Richard	M	65
Asst Prof	Fontaine, Paul		47
Assoc Prof	Foster, Stephen Wolf	PhD	13A
Assoc Prof	Francese, Ellen	M	
Prof	Free, Scott	M	10,29
Assoc Prof	Freeman, Jack	B	10C
Assoc Prof	French, Mark	M	70
Assoc Prof	Friedman, Arnold J.	PhD	10,62C,13
Prof	Friedman, Jeffrey A.	B	10,29
Assoc Prof	Friesen, Eugene		62
	Fritze, Gregory P.	M	10
Assoc Prof	Froman, Ian	M	65
Asst Prof	Fujita, Tomohisa	B	70
Assoc Prof	Funkhouser, John	M	
Assoc Prof	Gaboury, Tony	M	70
Assoc Prof	Gagne, Jeannie	M	61
Assoc Prof	Galeota, Joseph	B	65
Asst Prof	Galindo, Jeffrey A.	B	13A,13
Prof	Gardner, Peter S.	M	13A
Prof	Gardony, Laszlo	M	66A
Assoc Prof	Garzone, George		64
Prof	Gates, Gerald		13,10
	Germain, Anthony	B	13A,13
Prof	Gertz, Bruce		62D
Assoc Prof	Gilmore, David	B	70
Prof	Ginenthal, Robin	B	13A,13
Staff	Gitt, Bill	B	34,35C,35G
Other	Glaser, Matthew	M	62
Assoc Prof	Goines, Lincoln	B	62D
Prof	Goodman, Gabrielle A.	B	61
Prof	Goodrick, Mick	B	70
	Gorder, Donald C.	JD	35A
Prof	Gorham, Linda J.	M	35
Asst Prof	Govoni, Dino		64E
Assoc Prof	Greenblatt, Richard	B	13C
Prof	Grudzinski, Richard	M	10,10B
Prof	Gubanov, Yakov	PhD	
Prof	Gullotti, Robert	B	65
Asst Prof	Haas, Janet	B	32
Assoc Prof	Haddad, Jamey		65
Prof	Hadden, Dudley 'Skip'	M	65
Prof	Hagon, John	M	32
Asst Prof	Hampton, Herman	M	47
Inst	Hansen, Charles	B	70
	Hanser, Suzanne	PhD	33
Asst Prof	Harrigan, Robert		70
Prof	Harrington, Danny	M	13A,13
	Harrington, E. Michael	D	35,10,20,14
Prof	Harrington, Jeff	M	64
Asst Prof	Harris, Alonzo	M	13B
Asst Prof	Harris, David	B	13B
Assoc Prof	Hart, Richard	M	70
Asst Prof	Hatfield, D. J.	PhD	
Assoc Prof	Hatfield, Gaye Tolan	B	13A,13
Assoc Prof	Haupers, James Mitch	M	13A,13
Assoc Prof	Hazilla, Jon	B	65
Asst Prof	Heck, Steve		66A
Assoc Prof	Hernandez, Bernardo	DIPL	10,35G,35C
Prof	Heyman, Michael B.	PhD	
Assoc Prof	Hlady, Craig M.	B	70
Assoc Prof	Hoffmann, Russell	M	66A
Assoc Prof	Hogarth, Thaddeus	B	70
	Hojnacki, Thomas W.	M	13B
Assoc Prof	Holland, Jonathan Bailey	PhD	10A,10F,13A,10
Prof	Hollender, David A.	M	47
Assoc Prof	Holstedt, Lucile	M	13
Prof	Hopkins, Gregory	B	10,29
Assoc Prof	Howard, David R.	M	10,35C
	Howe, Melissa	D	62
Prof	Howland, Kathleen	PhD	33
Assoc Prof	Huergo, Fernando A.		62D
Inst	Hunt, Steven		66A
Asst Prof	Hurst, Derek	PhD	10
Prof	Ihde, Mike	B	70
	Inserto, Ayn	M	13B
	Israel, Yoron	M	65
Asst Prof	Itzler, Neal L.	B	47
	Jackson, Isaiah	PhD	10
	Jaczko, Robert	B	35C
Asst Prof	Jenkins Ainsworth, Jodi	B	61
Asst Prof	Jenson, Matthew	M	66A
Asst Prof	Jeon, Hey Rim	M	66A,13B
Asst Prof	Johnson, Andrea	M	35
Prof	Johnson, David	B	13A,13
Assoc Prof	Johnson, Douglas	M	66A

Directory of Institutions

Title	Name	Deg	Code
Assoc Prof	Johnson, Michael	DMA	
Assoc Prof	Johnson, Scott	B	70
Prof	Kachulis, James A.	M	10
Assoc Prof	Kai, Kudisan	B	61
Assoc Prof	Kalogeras, Alexandros	PhD	10
Asst Prof	Karam, Christiane	M	61
Prof	Kasper, Julien	M	70
Assoc Prof	Katz, Bruce	M	13A,13
Prof	Katz, Darrell	M	13A,13
Prof	Katz, Sheila H.	PhD	
Prof	Kaufman, Robert		65
Assoc Prof	Kaufman, Steve	M	
Asst Prof	Kellar, Stephanie	M	35
	Kellogg, John	JD	35
Prof	Kelly, James		70
Assoc Prof	Kelly, Kathryn	M	13C
Asst Prof	Kenehan, Garrett	PhD	33
Assoc Prof	Kerensky, Pam	B	35
Asst Prof	Keys, Scarlet	B	10,10D
Asst Prof	Khare, Kimberly	M	33
Prof	Kidd-Szymczak, Deanna	M	32
	Kim, Chi Gook	M	33
Asst Prof	Kirby, Steven	M	13B
Assoc Prof	Kiros, Teodros	PhD	
Assoc Prof	Klein, Jonathan	B	35B
Assoc Prof	Klein, Wendy L.	M	10,35C
Assoc Prof	Kocandrle, Mirek	B	10,35C
Inst	Kohler, Mark	B	47
Prof	Kohn, Douglas C.	PhD	
Asst Prof	Kott, Sandra	M	62
Assoc Prof	Kress, Richard	M	13A,13
Asst Prof	Kukrechtova, Daniela	PhD	
Prof	Kulenovic, Vuk	PhD	10
Asst Prof	Kyles, Jerome Kwame	B	61
Prof	Lada, Tony	B	63
Prof	LaFitte, Barbara	M	64
Assoc Prof	Landay, Lori	PhD	
Asst Prof	Lange, Magaret	PhD	35A
Asst Prof	Langol, Stefani	M	32
Asst Prof	Lappin, Donald P.	B	70
Asst Prof	Largent, Jeffrey		35C
Inst	Leathers, Gwendolyn	B	61
Prof	Leclaire, Dennis	M	10,63B
Assoc Prof	LeClaire, Shannon L.	DMA	64
Asst Prof	Lee, Abe	B	10A,10D,35C,35G
Assoc Prof	Lee, Rosey	D	13C
Asst Prof	Lehmann, Bertam	M	65
Prof	Leonard, Neil	B	35C
Asst Prof	Leonhart, Carolyn	B	61
Assoc Prof	LeVines, T. Allen	M	10
Assoc Prof	Lewis, Brian	M	13A,13
Assoc Prof	Lewis, Charles A.	M	63A
Asst Prof	Liaropoulos, Panagiotis	DMA	10A,10F
Asst Prof	Limina, David		66A
Assoc Prof	Lipsius, Fred		64
Assoc Prof	Lissance, Alizon J.		13A,13
Prof	List, Andrew	PhD	10
Assoc Prof	Lockwood, John K.	B	62D
Assoc Prof	Lorrey, Haidee	M	
Prof	Lovano, Joe		64E
Asst Prof	Lovely, Valerie	JD	35A,35E
Assoc Prof	Lowell, Richard L.		10,29
Prof	Lowery, Daryl	B	13
Asst Prof	Lucas, Elena	M	10
Assoc Prof	Lucia, Joyce	M	61
Assoc Prof	Lucie, Edwin J.	M	62D
Prof	Lueth, Faith	M	32
Asst Prof	Maccow, Winston		47
Asst Prof	MacLean, Stephen	A	34,35C
Assoc Prof	Macrae, Craig	PhD	13
Assoc Prof	Mahdi, Ronald O. A.	B	47
Assoc Prof	Mallet, Alain	B	47
Asst Prof	Maness, G. Andrew		70
Assoc Prof	Mangini, Michael		65
Assoc Prof	Marasco, John	B	70
	Mash, David S.		
	Mason, Mike	M	
Prof	Matsuoka, Yumiko	B	13A,13
Assoc Prof	McAllister, Margaret	PhD	10,13,34H,10A,34
Asst Prof	McArthur-Brown, Gail	B	10,35C,35G
Assoc Prof	McCluskey, Kevin	B	35
Prof	McCormick, Scott	PhD	29B,32F,32H,20G,34G
Prof	McDonnell, Donald	PhD	10
Prof	McElroy, Donna	B	61
Prof	McGah, Thomas J.	M	10
Prof	McGann, John	B	62
Prof Emeritus	McGhee, Andy		64
Prof	McGrath, Edward J.	M	12A
Assoc Prof	McKelvey, Berke	B	13C
Asst Prof	Mendelson, Richard		35C
Asst Prof	Mendelson, Ruth J.	B	10F
Prof	Mendoza, Victor	B	65
Prof	Menon, Rekha	PhD	
Assoc Prof	Merrill, Amy	M	
Inst	Michaud, Shaun	B	70
Asst Prof	Michelin, Nando	DIPL	66A
Assoc Prof	Miglio, Joseph	PhD	35
Assoc Prof	Miller, Gary	PhD	
Assoc Prof	Miller, Jane		70
Assoc Prof	Miller, Tim	M	70
	Mirowitz, Sheldon P.	B	10F
Assoc Prof	Moebus-Bergeron, Susanne	M	13A
Prof	Molinari, Raffaele 'Lello'	M	47
Prof	Moltoni, Giovanni	M	13
Assoc Prof	Moniz, Michael	M	33
Prof	Monseur, George	M	10,60
Assoc Prof	Montgomery, Dennis	B	47
Assoc Prof	Monzon, Ricardo		65
Assoc Prof	Moody, Duane	M	61
Prof	Moorhead, Jan Paul	M	35C
Prof	Mooter, Gregory G.	B	62D
Assoc Prof	Moral, Carmen	M	10
Prof	Moretti, Daniel D.	B	10
Prof	Morgenstein, Rod	B	65
Prof	Morris, Daniel	B	62D
Assoc Prof	Morris, Nancy	M	47
Asst Prof	Moss, Michael	M	35C
Prof	Mulholland, Joseph	M	13A,13
Asst Prof	Mulroy, John	M	66A
Assoc Prof	Mulvey, Bob		10,35
Inst	Mungo, Nichelle	B	61
Asst Prof	Musella, Joseph		70
Asst Prof	Netto, Alberto	B	65
Asst Prof	Newsam, David		70
Staff	Newsom, Daniel	B	32
	Nicholl, Matthew J.	M	13
Prof	Nifong, Bruce	M	47
Asst Prof	Noya, Francisco	M	10
Assoc Prof	Noyes, Christopher R.	B	34
Assoc Prof	O'Brien, John	M	35
Staff	Odgren, Jim	B	64
Prof	Okoshi, Tiger	B	63A
Assoc Prof	Okumura, Lydie	M	13A,13
Prof	Olmstead, R. Neil	M	66A
Prof	Olson, Mia	M	13A,13
Prof	Osby, Greg	B	47
Asst Prof	Paduck, Ted	B	34,35C,35G
Asst Prof	Pampinella, Paul	B	61
Prof	Paraskevas, Apostolos	DMA	10
Prof	Passarelli, Lauren	B	70
Assoc Prof	Passaretti, Sumalee	M	
Prof	Pattison, C. Pat	M	12A
Assoc Prof	Patton, Robert	B	13A,13
Asst Prof	Payack, Peter	B	35A
Prof	Peckham, Anne	M	61
Assoc Prof	Peckham, Charles R.	M	70
Asst Prof	Pejrolo, Andrea	PhD	34,10C,10,35C,35G
Asst Prof	Peknik, Patricia	M	
Assoc Prof	Pellitteri, Marcello	M	47
Assoc Prof	Pendarvis, Janice	B	61
Other	Perez, Danilo	B	
	Perricone, Jack	M	10
Assoc Prof	Perricone, Rebecca	M	
Asst Prof	Perry, Jeffery S.	M	10B,34
Inst	Person, Philip	B	13C
Assoc Prof	Peterson, James L.	B	70
Prof	Peterson, Ralph	B	65
Prof	Pezanelli, Jack	M	70
Asst Prof	Pfeiffer, Dale	B	61
Inst	Philip, Annette	B	61
Assoc Prof	Phillips, Margaret A.	M	64D,64
	Pierce, Bill	B	64
Prof	Pierce, John		47
Prof	Pilkington, Robert	B	10,29
Assoc Prof	Plainfield, Kim		65,29
	Plante, Alison	B	10C
Asst Prof	Platow, Beth	M	
	Plsek, Thomas	M	63C,63D
Assoc Prof	Pomeranz, Felice	M	62E,62
Asst Prof	Poniatowski, Mark	M	10,35C,35G
Assoc Prof	Potter, Jane	B	13C
Prof	Prosser, Steve	JD	13A,13
	Pullig, Kenneth	B	10,29
Assoc Prof	Pusztai, Tibor J.		
Prof	Qualliotine, Armand Guy	PhD	10
Prof	Raberg, Bruno	B	47
Assoc Prof	Rabson, Miriam		62
	Radley, Roberta	B	13A,13
Assoc Prof	Ragazzi, Claudio	B	10C
Asst Prof	Ramsay, James Ross	B	66A
Prof	Ramsay, John P.		65
Assoc Prof	Ramsey, Jeffery Evans	B	61
Prof	Reasoner, Eric	B	10
Assoc Prof	Reeder, Raymond	B	61
Assoc Prof	Reich, Stephanie	PhD	
Assoc Prof	Reid, Ronald I.	B	35B
	Repucci, John	B	62D
Asst Prof	Reuter, Eric Lehman	B	34,35C,35D
Assoc Prof	Reyes, James E.	M	10
Assoc Prof	Rhea, Thomas L.	PhD	34
Assoc Prof	Richardson, Diane	PhD	61
Asst Prof	Rinaldi, Jason P.	M	35C
Assoc Prof	Ringquist, Mikael	B	65
Prof	Rochinski, Stephen		13A,13
Assoc Prof	Rodriguez, Alex	B	34,35C,35G
Assoc Prof	Rogers, Joseph	B	70
Assoc Prof	Rogers, Susan	PhD	35C,13K,13L
Assoc Prof	Rold, Julie	M	13A
Prof	Rolfe, Wendy	DMA	64
Asst Prof	Romeu, Emma	B	

Assoc Prof	Roos, Randy	B	70
Assoc Prof	Rosen, Josh	M	66A
Prof	Rossi, Marc W.	M	66A
Prof	Russell, George	M	29
Asst Prof	Ryan, Charlene	PhD	32
Prof	Saindon, Ed	B	65
Assoc Prof	Samuels, David A.	B	47,65B
Prof	Santerre, Joseph	B	62D
Prof	Santisi, Ray		66A
Prof	Santoro, David N.		47
Assoc Prof	Santoro, Stephen	B	61
Prof	Santos, Jackie		65
Prof	Saunders, Bruce	M	70
Prof	Savage, Ron	M	65
Asst Prof	Schachnick, Gilson	B	13C
Asst Prof	Schachter, Daniela	B	66A,61
Prof	Scheuerell, Casey		65
Assoc Prof	Schlink, Robert	B	47
Emeritus	Schmeling, Paul	B	66A
Prof	Schmidt, Fred	M	10,35
Prof	Schultz, Willis Jackson	B	10,29
Prof	Scism, William	B	10,29
Assoc Prof	Scott, David	M	61
Prof	Scott, Maggie		61
Prof	Scott, Michael	B	13A,13
Prof	Seidman, Mitch	M	13
Assoc Prof	Sever, Ivan	B	35C,35D,10C
Prof	Shapiro, Jan	M	61
Assoc Prof	Sher, Ben		70
Asst Prof	Shilansky, Mark	M	13A,13
Assoc Prof	Shumate, Curtis	B	70
Prof	Sifter, Suzanna	M	66A
Assoc Prof	Silvio, Will	B	13B
Asst Prof	Simos, Mark	B	10,10D
Inst	Skeete, Sean	B	47
Assoc Prof	Skoler, Harry	M	64
Assoc Prof	Slye, Lorree	B	61
Asst Prof	Smith, Barry	M	62D
Assoc Prof	Smith, Daniel Ian	M	13A,13
	Smith, James Russell	D	10
Prof	Smith, Joseph	M	10
Assoc Prof	Smith, Langston 'Skip'		47
Assoc Prof	Smith, Neal	B	65
Assoc Prof	Smith, Tony 'Thunder'	B	65
Assoc Prof	Snodgrass, Ann A.	PhD	13A
Assoc Prof	Sorrento, Charles J.	M	61
Assoc Prof	Squire, Anne	M	
Prof	Stagnaro, Oscar		62D
Asst Prof	Stallworth, Lenny		47
Asst Prof	Stearns, Loudon	B	10,35C,35G
Assoc Prof	Steele, Nalora L.	B	32
Assoc Prof	Stein, John	M	13B
Prof	Stein, Thomas A.	M	35
Assoc Prof	Stevens, John L.	M	10
Assoc Prof	Stewart, Diane		61
Prof	Stewart, Louis	PhD	10
Assoc Prof	Stiller, Paul	B	13A
Prof	Stinnett, Jim	B	10,35C
	Stoloff, Bob	B	61
Assoc Prof	Stone, Robin	M	70
Prof	Stout, Jeffrey	M	63
Assoc Prof	Strickland, Stanley Leon	M	61
Assoc Prof	Stump, Joseph		70
Assoc Prof	Sweet, Michael	B	10C
Asst Prof	Sykes, Jerilyn	M	10,35C
Asst Prof	Taft, Kenneth	B	70
Prof	Tamagni, Robert	B	65
Assoc Prof	Tanksley, Francesca	M	66A
Asst Prof	Tarulli, Scott	B	70
Prof	Tate, Henry Augustine	PhD	12A
Prof	Taylor, Livingston		61
Assoc Prof	Taylor, Valerie	DMA	10
Asst Prof	Thomas, Ben	PhD	
Prof	Thomas, Bruce	B	66A
Assoc Prof	Thomas, Gates	B	10D
Assoc Prof	Thomas, John		70
Asst Prof	Thomas, Omar	M	13
Prof	Thomas, Rob		62
	Thompson, Dan	B	35C
Asst Prof	Thompson, William C.	B	13A
Prof	Thorson, Lisa	M	61
	Tiberi, Frank		64
	Tiernan, Stephany	M	66A
Prof	Tomassi, Edward		13A,13
Assoc Prof	Trester, Francine G.	PhD	10
Assoc Prof	Tronzo, David		70
Asst Prof	Turnbull, Kai	B	34
Assoc Prof	Ungar, Leanne	B	34,35C,35G
Prof	Van Duser, Guy	B	70
Prof	Vitti, Anthony		62D
Prof	Vose, David	M	13A
Prof	Wacks, Karen S.	M	33
Assoc Prof	Wagner, Paul	B	64
Prof	Walker, Mark		65
Prof	Wallis, Victor E.	PhD	
Asst Prof	Walsh, Marty	B	47
Prof	Ward, Wayne	M	32
Assoc Prof	Wardson, Greg		66A
Asst Prof	Wark, Stephen	B	13A,13
Assoc Prof	Wartofsky, Michael	M	13A,13

Prof	Watson, Lawrence		61
Assoc Prof	Watters, August	B	13A,13
Prof	Webber, Stephen	M	35C
Asst Prof	Wedding, Alison	B	61
Prof	Weigert, David	B	47
Asst Prof	Weinstein, Michael	PhD	10
Prof	Welwood, Arthur	M	10
Asst Prof	Wernick, Diane	M	47
Assoc Prof	Wessel, Mark	B	35C
Assoc Prof	Wheatley, Jon		70
Prof	White, Mark	M	70
Assoc Prof	Wild, Wayne	PhD	
Prof	Wilkes, Steven M.	B	65
Prof	Wilkins, Carolyn	M	47
Prof	Wilkins, Donald		35H
Assoc Prof	Wilkins, John	B	70
Asst Prof	Williams, Jeff	B	34,35C
Prof	Williams, Julius P.	M	10
Asst Prof	Williams, Michael M.	PhD	
Prof	Williams, Mike	B	70
Prof	Willmott, Bret	B	70
Inst	Wilson, Darcel		13C
Prof	Wilson, Phil		63
Prof	Winter, Robert	B	66A
Assoc Prof	Witmyer, Clyde	M	10
Prof	Wright, Kathryn M.	M	61
Assoc Prof	Wyner, Jonathan	B	34,35C,35G
Prof	Zambello, Kenneth	B	47
Assoc Prof	Zeltsman, Nancy	B	65B
Asst Prof	Zigo, Julie Buras	B	33
Assoc Prof	Zocher, Norman	B	70
Asst Prof	Zoffer, David	M	10,35C,35G
Prof	Zonce, George	B	47

MA0280 Berkshire Community College
Department of Music
1350 West Street
Pittsfield, MA 01201
(413) 499-4660   Fax: (413) 447-7840
www.berkshirecc.edu
E-mail: eshanaha@berkshirecc.edu

2 Year Institution

Chair & Program Advisor: Ellen Cooper Shanahan, 80A
Dir., Preparatory Division: Tracy Wilson, 80E

Inst PT	Bazinet, Ryan	M	11,20
Inst PT	Broad, Daniel	B	62D
Inst PT	Brown, David	M	70
Inst PT	DeCandia, Arthur J.	B	61
Inst PT	Granat, Zbigniew	D	13A,13,11
Inst PT	Hohlstein, Marjorie Rahima	DMA	66,13,66A
Inst PT	Link, Jeffrey	B	13,34,47
Inst PT	Livermore, Allen	M	47,64E,29
Inst PT	MacDonald, Kathleen	M	61
Inst PT	Murray, Stephen	D	13
	Rabuse, Brian	M	70
Inst PT	Renak, Amy	B	66A
Inst PT	Rose, Lloyd	B	34
Asst Prof	Shanahan, Ellen Cooper	M	13,12A,36,54,29A
Inst PT	Wilson, Tracy		

MA0330 Boston College
Department of Music
140 Commonwealth Ave
Chestnut Hill, MA 02467
(617) 552-4843   Fax: (617) 552-3807
www.bc.edu/schools/cas/music
E-mail: musicdep@bc.edu

4 Year Institution

Chair: Michael J. Noone, 80A
Assistant Chair: Jeremiah McGrann, 80H

Senior Lect	Finney, John R.	M	60,36,38,66G
Asst Prof	Gawlick, Ralf	D	13A,13,11
Asst Prof Adj	Hebert, Sandra M.	D	13A,13,66A,66B
Prof	Kennedy, T. Frank	D	11,12,31A,20H
Prof	Lee, Thomas Oboe	D	13,10,29B
Assoc Prof	McGrann, Jeremiah	D	11,12,20G
Assoc Prof	Noone, Michael J.	D	11,12,31

MA0350 The Boston Conservatory

8 The Fenway
Boston, MA 02215-4006
(617) 536-6340   Fax: (617) 912-9110
www.bostonconservatory.edu
E-mail: music@bostonconservatory.edu

4 Year Institution of Music, Dance and Theater, Graduate School
Member of NASM

Certificate, Artist Diploma, Master of Music in Composition, Master of Music in Performance, Master of Music in Conducting, Master of Music in Music Education, Master of Music in Opera, Master of Music in Music History, Master of Music in Musical Theatre

President: Richard Ortner, 80A
Director: Karl Paulnack, 80A
Associate Director: Lawrence Isaacson, 80H
Dean, Academic Affairs: James O'Dell, 80H

	Abbate, Elizabeth	D	12A
	Aleo, Keith	M	65
	Alexander, Michelle	D	61
	Alms, Anthony		12A
	Altenbach, Andrew	M	39
	Amis, Kenneth	M	63D
	Anderson-Collier, Jean	D	61
	Baroni, Melissa		61
	Bass, Jonathan	M	66A
	Bernard, Rhoda J.	D	32
	Bewick, Bonnie	B	62A
	Billingsley, Monique Phinney	B	61
	Bobo, Ann	B	64A
	Bolter, Norman		63C
	Brady, Sarah	M	64A
	Brown, Lila R.	B	62B
	Bulli, Marilyn	D	61
	Caliri, Lisa	B	66,66A
	Chang, Lynn	B	62A
	Chuang, Ya-Fei	DIPL	66A
	Cohler, Jonathan	B	64C
	Coticone, Geralyn	B	64A
	Cotten, William	M	61
	Cutter, William	D	60A,60
	Dalton, James	M	13B,13C,20
	Deal, Kerry	D	61
	Dellal, Pamela	B	61
	Eissenberg, Judith	M	41
	Emery, Steven	M	63A
	Epstein, Eli	B	63B
	Faieta, John J.	M	63C
	Foley, Joe	M	63A
	Folsom, Rebecca L.	D	61
	Francoeur-Krzyzek, Damien	M	61
	Frengel, Michael	M	13
	Goldstein, Sara	M	61
	Gregg, Thomas	D	61
	Grimes, John	M	65
	Gurin, Vladimir		13B
	Halloran, Stephen	D	13B,13C
	Hangen, Bruce		61
	Hewitt, Eric	M	48
	Hida, Kyoko	B	64B
	Holt, Joseph	B	62D
	Honeysucker, Robert	M	61
	Hughes, Curtis K.	D	10
	Hurel, Pierre		53
	Isaacson, Lawrence	M	63C
	Jannett, Victor	M	61
	Javore, James	M	61
	Kelton, Anne	M	32
	Kim, Sun Ho		61
	Lefkowitz, Ronan	B	62A
	Leventhal, Sharan	M	62A
	Levinson, Max	DIPL	66A
	Levy, Benjamin	D	62D
	Lewin, Michael	M	66A
	Marchand, Rebecca	D	12A
	Mark, Andrew	M	62C
	Matczynski, Leonard		62B
	McAneny, Marc		13
	Moll, Brian		39
	Morejon, Adrian	M	64D,42
	Muresanu, Irina	D	62A
	Murphree, John	M	13
	Noren, Rictor	M	62B
	Norsworthy, Michael	M	64C
	Owen, Kevin	B	63B
	Pape, John W.		39
	Paulnack, Karl	D	66C
	Pavasaris, Walter	M	32
	Placci, Markus	DIPL	62A
	Price-Glynn, Cynthia	M	62E
	Radnofsky, Kenneth	M	64E
	Rider, Rhonda	M	41,62C
	Rogers, Martha		13,32I
	Rojahn, Karolina		13
	Rojahn, Rudolf	M	13B,13C
	Ruymann, Karen		12A
	Saunders, Mary	M	61
	Seitz, Elizabeth	D	12
	Shea, Merrill	B	61
	Sheena, Robert	M	64B,63B
	Sheldon, Elisabeth	B	61
	Siders, Thomas	M	63A
	Silverstein, Joseph		62
	Solomon, Samuel Z.	M	65
	Stadelman-Cohen, Tara	M	61
	Strauss, Michael	B	61,66C
	Subera, Angel		63A
	Swafford, Jan	D	12A
	Tapping, Roger		42,62A
	Thom, Patty J.	M	61
	Toote, Linda	M	64A
	Troup, Nathan		
	Udagawa, Yoichi	B	60
	Vores, Andy	B	10,13B
	Voth, Alison	M	61
	Warshaw, Dalit Hadass	D	10,13,66A,10F,13E
	Watchorn, Peter G.		12A
	Weber, Janice	M	66A
	Willer, Beth C.	M	36
	Wilson, Kevin	M	61
	Wolfe, Lawrence		62D
	Woo, Jung-Ja	DIPL	66A
	Wright, Kathryn	M	61
	Zdorovetchi, Ina		62E
	Zeltsman, Nancy	M	65

MA0400 Boston University

College of Fine Arts
855 Commonwealth Ave
Boston, MA 02215-1303
(617) 353-3341   Fax: (617) 353-7455
www.bu.edu/cfa
E-mail: rdodson@bu.edu

4 Year Institution, Graduate School
Member of NASM

Certificate, Master of Music in Historical Performance, Master of Arts in Music, Master of Music in Composition, Master of Music in Music Theory, Master of Music in Performance, Master of Music in Conducting, Master of Music in Music Education, Master of Music in History & Literature, DMA in Composition, DMA in Performance, DMA in Music Education, Master of Music in Sacred Music, PhD in Musicology, Master of Music in Music Education (Distance Education), DMA in Music Education (Distance Education), DMA in Historical Performance, DMA in Conducting

Dean: Benjamin Echenique Juarez, 80A
Assistant Dean, Enrollment: Patricia Mitro, 80H,80D
Acting Dir., Opera Programs: William Lumpkin

Asst Prof	Abe, Marie	D	14
Lect	Abigana, Brett	D	13
Lect	Abreu, Aldo	M	67C
Lect	Aghababian, Vartan	D	13
Lect	Alexander, Michelle	D	61,66C
Lect	Amis, Ken	M	63D
Assoc Prof	Amlin, Martin	D	13,10
Assoc Prof	Ansell, Steven	B	62B
Assoc Prof	Barker, Edwin	B	62D
Lect	Basrak, Cathy	M	62B
Lect	Beattie, Michael	M	61
Lect	Bill, Jennifer	D	64E
Assoc Prof	Bitzas, Penelope	M	61
Lect	Budnick, Eve	M	66C
Asst Prof	Bunbury, Richard R.	D	12,66G,32H,31A,32
Asst Prof	Burton, Deborah	D	13
Lect	Casinghino, Justin	D	13,10
Lect	Chang, Lyn	B	62A
Lect	Chapman, Peter	M	63A
Assoc Prof	Clodes-Jaguaribe, Maria	D	66A
Prof	Coehlo, Victor	D	12
Prof	Conkling, Susan W.	D	32D,36,32C,32F,32G
Prof	Cornell, Richard	D	13,10
Lect	Coticone, Geralyn	B	64A
Assoc Prof	Daniels, Sharon	B	61
Asst Prof	Dansereau, Diana R.	D	32E,32G
Prof	de Quadros, Andre F.	M	32
Asst Prof	Demler, James R.	M	61
Prof	Dibonaventura, Anthony	DIPL	66A
Lect	Dona, Daniel	D	62B,42
Asst Prof	Dorfman, Jay	D	32E,32G
Lect	Durham, Gary	M	61
Prof Adj	Dwyer, Doriot	B	64A

Lect	Eskin, Jules	B	62C
Assoc Prof	Eustis, Lynn	D	61
Assoc Prof	Everson, Terry	M	63A
Lect	Ferillo, John	M	64B
Assoc Prof	Fineberg, Joshua	D	10B,10A
Lect	Freiberg, Sarah	M	67B
Lect	Fryer-Davis, Carolyn	M	62D
Vstng Assoc Prof	Gallagher, Sean	D	12
Lect	Gazouleas, Edward	M	62B
Lect	Genis, Timothy	B	65A
Lect	Genovese, John	DMA	13,10
Lect	Goldstein, Gila	D	66A
Lect	Goldstein, Joanna	M	64A
Asst Prof	Goodrich, Andrew M.	D	32E,32G
Lect	Haroutunian, Ronald	M	64D
Assoc Prof	Headrick, Samuel P.	D	13,10,45
Assoc Prof	Heimarck, Brita Renee	D	12
Lect	Heiss, John	M	64A
Lect	Henegar, Gregg	B	64D
Assoc Prof	Higgins, Lee D.	D	32E,32G
Lect	Hobson-Pilot, Ann	D	62E
Prof	Hoffman, Phyllis	M	61
Prof	Hoose, David M.	M	60,38
Lect	Ianni, Davide	D	10B
Lect	Ingles, Greg	M	67E
Lect	Jarrett, Scott	D	36
Lect	Jeppesen, Laura	M	67B
Lect	Jepson, Angela	M	39
Vstng Prof	Johnson, Marc Thomas	M	62C,42
Prof	Jones, Anne Howard	D	60,36
Lect	Kelley, Frank	M	39
Assoc Prof	Keyes, Bayla	M	62A
Asst Prof	Kibbe-Hodgkins, Shiela	M	66C,66A
Assoc Prof	Kopp, David	D	13,10
Lect	Koppel, Mary Montgomery	D	10
Asst Prof	Kos, Ronald P.	D	32
Lect	Krimsier, Renee J.	M	64A
Prof Emeritus	Kroll, Mark	M	66H,66E,12,67F,13
Lect	Krueger, Christopher	M	67E
Lect	Lacarme, Alexandre	M	62C
Assoc Prof	LaCourse, Michelle	M	62B
Lect	Langfur, Gabriel	M	63C
Lect	Larson, Matthew	D	39
Lect	Levenson, Warren	M	70
Lect	Levy, Benjamin	M	62D
Vstng Artist	Lewin, Michael	M	66A,66D
	Liddell, Catherine	M	67G
Assoc Prof	Lin, Lucia	M	62A
Lect	Lister, Rodney	D	10,13
Lect	Lowe, Malcolm		62A
Assoc Prof	Lucas, Don	M	63C
Assoc Prof	Lumpkin, William	D	39
Lect	Mackey, Richard	M	63B
Asst Prof	Mantie, Roger	D	32
Adj Prof	Martins, David J.	M	48
Adj Assoc Prof	Mazurkevich, Dana Pomerantz	DIPL	62A
Prof	Mazurkevich, Yuri	DIPL	62A
Lect	McEwen, Mark	M	63B
Assoc Prof Emeritus	McIntyre, Joy	M	61
Lect	Menaul, Richard A.	M	63B
Lect	Merfeld, Robert	M	66A
Lect	Metcalfe, Scott	D	12
Lect	Miller, Mark	M	38
Lect	Mizuno, Ikuko	B	62A
Lect	Muratore, John	M	70
Assoc Prof	Nagy, Linda Jiorle	D	66A,66B
Lect	Nangle, Richard	D	10,70
Prof Emeritus	Neikrug, George	DIPL	62C
Lect	Nelsen, Suzanne	M	64D
Assoc Prof	Nersesiyan, Pavel	D	66A
Asst Prof	Nez, Catherine Ketty	D	10,66A,10A
Assoc Prof	Nicolucci, Sandra	D	32
Lect	Oft, Toby	M	63C
Lect	Orleans, James B.	B	62D
Lect	Ostling, Elizabeth	M	64A
Vstng Scholar	Palmer, Anthony J.	D	32
Prof Adj	Parnas, Leslie		62C
Prof	Pearlman, Martin	M	55,67F
Asst Prof	Peattie, Thomas A.	D	12
Lect	Poeschl-Edrich, Barbara	D	62E
Assoc Prof Adj	Pomfret, Bonnie	D	39,61
Assoc Prof	Pope, Jerrold	D	61
Lect	Price, Andrew	D	64B
Lect	Pyle, Robinson	M	67E
Lect	Radnosfky, Kenneth	M	64E
Lect	Raffo, Laura	M	39
Lect	Ranti, Richard J.	M	64C
Lect	Reeves, Matthew	D	10
Assoc Prof	Reynolds, Michael	M	62C
Lect	Rider, Rhonda	M	62C
Prof	Rifkin, Joshua	M	12
Adj Assoc Prof	Ritscher, Karen	M	62B
Lect	Rolfs, Thomas C.	M	63A
Lect	Roylance, Mike R.	B	63D
Lect	Ruggiero, Mathew	D	64D
Prof	Ruske, Eric	B	63B
Lect	Schachman, Marc H.	D	67D
Vstng Assoc Prof	Schepkin, Sergey	M	66A
Lect	Seeber, Todd M.	B	62D
Prof	Sharon, Boaz	M	66A
Lect	Sheehan, Aaron	M	67H
Lect	Sheena, Robert	M	64B
Prof Emeritus	Sheveloff, Joel L.	D	12A,12
Lect	Sholes, Jacquelyn	M	12
Lect	Siders, Tom	M	63A
Prof	Sloane, Ethan	D	64C
Lect	Smith, Andrew	D	13
Lect	Snider, Jason	M	63B
Lect	Solomon, Sam	M	65
Lect	Sommerville, James	M	63B
Lect	Starkman, Jane	M	67B
Lect	Stevens, Jeffrey	M	66C,39
Lect	Stovall, John	M	62D
Lect	Sullivan-Friedman, Melinda	M	39
Assoc Prof	Sykes, Peter	D	66G,67F
Lect	Toote, Linda	M	64A
Lect	Troup, Nathan	M	39
Asst Prof	Uribe, Patrick Wood	D	12
Assoc Prof	Voth, Allison	M	39
Asst Prof	Wallace, John H.	D	10,13
Assoc Prof Emeritus	Weale, Gerald	D	13
Lect	Weigt, Steven	D	13
Lect	Wolfe, Lawrence	B	62D
Assoc Prof	Yudkin, Jeremy	D	12
Asst Prof	Yust, Jason	D	13
Adj Assoc Prof	Zaretsky, Michael	DIPL	62B
Prof	Zazofsky, Peter	B	62A
Lect	Zhou, Jessica	M	62C

MA0500 Brandeis University

Department of Music
MS051
415 South St
Waltham, MA 02454-9110
(781) 736-3310   Fax: (781) 736-3320
www.brandeis.edu/departments/music
E-mail: kagan@brandeis.edu

4 Year Institution, Graduate School

PhD in Music Theory-Composition, PhD in Musicology, Master of Arts in Music Theory-Composition, Master of Arts in Musicology, MFA in Music Theory-Composition, MFA in Musicology

Chair: Mary Ruth Ray, 80A
Dir., Undergraduate Studies: Sarah Mead, 80B
Dir., Graduate Studies: Eric Chafe, 80C
Dir., Graduate Studies: Yu-Hui Chang, 80C

Prof Emeritus	Boykan, Martin	M	13,10,12A,10A,13A
Lect	Brown, Whitman P.	D	10A,13A,13B
Prof	Chafe, Eric	D	13A,11,12A,12,13J
Prof	Chang, Yu-Hui	D	10A,10F,13B,13D,13F
Prof	Chasalow, Eric	D	13,10A,10B,11,29A
Asst Prof	Coluzzi, Seth	D	10D,11,13A,12A,12C
Prof/Prac	Eissenberg, Judith	M	41,62A,11
Prof/Prac	Gordon, Joshua	M	11,41,42,62,62C
Lect	Hall, Thomas	B	53,64C
Assoc Prof/Prac	Hampton, Neal	M	60,37,38,41,48
Prof	Keiler, Allan R.	D	11,12A,12D,13E,13J
Lect	Lucas, Ann E.	D	14,11,20,20B,12A
Prof Emeritus	Marshall, Robert L.	D	12
Lect	McAneny, Marc	M	13B,13E,13F,10A
Assoc Prof/Prac	Mead, Sarah	M	55B,55D,67A,67
Assoc Prof/Prac	Nieske, Robert	M	10,47,62D,53,46
Prof	Olesen, James D.	D	60,36,55D
Prof	Rakowski, David	D	13,10,12A
Prof/Prac	Ray, Mary Ruth	B	41,62B,11
Prof Emeritus	Shapero, Harold S.	M	10A,13A,10B,13B,13G
Lect	Souza, Thomas	M	60B,64C,37,32,46
Prof/Prac	Stepner, Daniel	DIPL	41,62A,11
Prof Emeritus	Wyner, Yehudi	M	10F,10,41

MA0510 Bridgewater State University

Department of Music
Maxwell Library, Rm 312
10 Shaw Rd
Bridgewater, MA 02325
(508) 531-1377   Fax: (508) 531-1772
www.bridgew.edu
E-mail: ssachdev@bridgew.edu

4 Year Institution, Graduate Institution

Master of Arts in Teaching Specialization Music

Chair: Salil Sachdev, 80A

Rank	Name	Degree	Codes
Vstng Lect	Acsadi, Daniel	M	70,11
Vstng Lect	Amon, Jonathan T.	M	64E,70
Vstng Lect	Aston, Spencer	D	63A,11
Vstng Lect	Bizinkauskas, Maryte	M	61,11
Vstng Lect	Bohn, James		11,34
Vstng Lect	Campbell, Roy	B	11,10F,38,46,47
Vstng Lect	Conroy, Gregory	M	50,65
Vstng Lect	Daly, Rachel	M	63B,11
Vstng Lect	Ferrante, Martina	M	61
Vstng Lect	Fishman, Guy	D	11,62C
Vstng Lect	Guzasky, G. Frederick	D	66A,66D
Vstng Lect	Hay, James	B	11,12A,66A,66B
Vstng Lect	Holland, Heather	M	61
Prof	Kreiling, Jean L.	D	13A,11,12A,12,66D
Vstng Lect	Krishnaswami, Donald	M	11,12A,62A,62B,51
Vstng Lect	Lai, Juliet	M	11,64C
Vstng Lect	Leschisin, Taras	M	61
Vstng Lect	Lieurance, Barbara	M	66A,66D
Vstng Lect	Lorance, Elana	M	64B
Vstng Lect	McQuarrie, Sarah	D	32
Vstng Lect	Milenkovic, Vladan	M	29,66A,66D
Vstng Lect	Milham, Edwin M.	M	11,61
Vstng Lect	Milstein, Amir	M	11,20H
Vstng Lect	Mouffe, Jerome	DMA	70,11
Asst Prof	Nemko, Deborah G.	D	66A,66C,66D,11
Prof	Nicholeris, Carol A.	D	10A,13D,13A,36,13
Vstng Lect	Perez, Miguel	D	11,62A,51
Asst Prof	Running, Donald	D	37,38,46,47,11
Assoc Prof	Sachdev, Salil	D	10,13A,20A,50,13B
Vstng Lect	Strong, Bent		70,11
Vstng Lect	William, Jacob		70
Assoc Prof	Young, Steven	D	36,11,55,66A,20G
Vstng Lect	Zook, Donald	M	64A

MA0600 Cape Cod Community College
Department of Music
2240 Iyanough Rd
West Barnstable, MA 02668
(508) 362-2131 x4350   Fax: (508)375-4020
www.capecod.edu
E-mail: mcolby@capecod.edu

2 Year Institution

Rank	Name	Degree	Codes
Teach Assoc	Banner, Lucy	M	66A,66G,66H,66B,66C
Teach Assoc	Casper, Richard	M	66A
Teach Assoc	Cosgrove, Nancy	M	66A,66G,66H,66B,66C
Teach Assoc	Crosby, Karen	B	66A
Teach Assoc	Drifmeyer, Fred	M	66A,66C
Teach Assoc	Hagon, Darlene	M	61
Teach Assoc	Harrigan, Wilfred	B	64C,64E
Teach Assoc	Hoopes, Katherine	M	62A,62B
Teach Assoc	Kelly, Elizabeth	M	11,61
Teach Assoc	Machon, Allen	M	63A
Teach Assoc	Scott, Joseph	M	67D,70
Teach Assoc	Slovak, Loretta	M	66A
Teach Assoc	Snyder, Maria	M	66A
Teach Assoc	Spencer, Sandy	B	62C
Teach Assoc	Stevens, Anthony	M	64C,64E
Teach Assoc	Tipton, Elizabeth	M	66A
Teach Assoc	Wingett, Joy	B	62A

MA0650 Clark University
Department of Vis/Perf Arts-Music
950 Main St
Worcester, MA 01610-1477
(508) 793-7349   Fax: (508) 793-8844
www.clarku.edu/departments/clarkarts/music/
E-mail: bkorstvedt@clarku.edu

4 Year Institution

Director: Benjamin M. Korstvedt, 80A

Rank	Name	Degree	Codes
Lect PT	Allard, James	B	64E,47
Lect PT	Anderson, Juliana	M	61
Asst Prof	Aylward, John J.	D	10A,10B,13
Lect PT	Blumhofer, Jonathan	D	10,12
Lect PT	Boothman, Donald	M	61
Lect PT	Bresniak, Chester	M	64C
Lect PT	Busby, Stepanie	M	64D
Lect PT	Cain, Richard	M	62D,37
Prof Emeritus	Castonguay, Gerald	D	12A,12
Lect PT	Clark, Jon	M	63A
Lect PT	Cole, Deb	M	63B
Lect PT	Connors, Michael	M	65
Lect PT	D'Angelo, Joe	B	70
Prof Emeritus	Fuller, Wesley M.		13,10,34
Lect PT	Halko, Joe	B	64B
Lect PT	Johnson, Kallin	M	66D
Assoc Prof	Korstvedt, Benjamin M.	D	12A,12B,12C,12D
Lect PT	Kraus, Tracy	M	64A
Lect PT	Kustanovich, Serafima	M	66A,66C,41
Assoc Prof	Malsky, Matthew	D	10A,10B,34,13,10
Lect PT	Milgate, Brooks	M	66A
Lect PT	Noel, Christine	D	36,60
Lect PT	Provost, Sarah	M	29A
Lect PT	Rudolph, Shay	M	62C
Lect PT	Sullivan, Robert	M	70
Lect PT	Sulski, Peter	B	62A,62B,60B,38
Lect PT	Weeks, Douglas	D	63C

MA0700 College of the Holy Cross
Department of Music
1 College St
PO Box 151A
Worcester, MA 01610
(508) 793-2296   Fax: (508) 793-3030
www.holycross.edu
E-mail: skorde@holycross.edu

4 Year Institution

Chair: Shirish Korde, 80A

Rank	Name	Degree	Codes
Asst Prof	Arrell, Christopher A.	D	10,13,34A,34D
Lect PT	Ashe, Jennifer	D	11,61,55D,40
Vstng Prof	Bandem, I Made		20D
Lect PT	Bob, Sarah	M	66A
Lect PT	Cela, Orlando	M	64A
Artist in Res	Christie, James David		66G,66H,31A
Lect PT	Culver, Eric	D	11,60,10F,38,41
Vstng Inst	DiCenso, Daniel J.	D	11,12
Prof	Golijov, Osvaldo	D	20G,13,10,11,12A
Lect PT	Gregory, Rohan		62A,62B
Lect PT	Halko, Joseph	B	64B
Lect PT	Hanshaw, Marian C.	M	66A
Lect PT	Hopkins, Bruce	M	63A
Lect PT	Karass, Alan M.	M	11,16
Prof	Korde, Shirish	M	13,10,14,20,29
Lect PT	Lai, Juliet	M	64C
Assoc Prof	Lieberman, Carol	D	62A,13,12A,67,62
Lect PT	Mindell, Pamela Getnick		11,36,40
Lect PT	Monaghan, Michael	M	47,64A,64E,53,29
Lect PT	Mountain, Toby	D	34,14C
Lect PT	Muller-Szeraws, Jan	M	62C,42
Lect PT	Struyk, Pieter	B	65
Lect PT	Sullivan, Robert		67B,70
Lect PT	Sulski, Peter	B	62B,62A,42
Lect PT	Vleck, Marsha	M	61
Assoc Prof	Waldoff, Jessica	D	11,12
Lect PT	Weeks, Douglas	D	63C

MA0750 Dean College
Department of Music
99 Main St
Franklin, MA 02038
(508) 541-1823   Fax: (508) 541-1989
www.dean.edu
E-mail: mschmidt@dean.edu

2 Year Institution

Division Chair & Dir., Summer Programs: Myron Schmidt, 80A,80G

Rank	Name	Degree	Codes
Adj Inst	Classen, Jeffrey	M	
Adj Inst	Goldman, Robert J.	M	
Adj Inst	Lonati, Marianne	M	54
	Sartini, Michael R.		65A

MA0800 Eastern Nazarene College
Department of Music
23 East Elm Ave
Quincy, MA 02170
(617) 773-6350   Fax: (617) 773-6324
www.enc.edu
E-mail: Lambert.Brandes@enc.edu

4 Year Institution

Chair: Lambert Brandes, 80A
Dean: David Kale, 80A
Dir., Artist/Performance Series: Brady Millican, 80F

Adj	Bell, S.		41
Adj	Berman, Gayle	M	61
Prof	Brandes, Lambert	M	13,66G,13L
Adj	Broms, E.		70,53
Adj	Danton, Jean	M	61
Adj	Feeney, Timothy P.	D	65
Adj	Gilliam, C.		35G
Adj	Hewett, E.		64E
Adj	Kidd, Murray	M	61
Adj	Leighton, Mark	M	70
Prof Emeritus	Marple, Olive	B	13,12A,66A
Adj	McGowan, M.		64C
Prof	Millican, Brady	D	13,11,12A,66A,66C
Adj	Robinson, D.		63C
Assoc Prof	Shetler, Timothy	M	60,32C,36,61
Adj	Sorg, A.		63A
	Spiradopoulos, S.		63B
Adj	Webb, A. H.		62A
	Wooster, E.		
Adj	Zook, D.		64A

MA0850 Emerson College
Department of Perf. Arts
10 Boylston Pl 5th Fl
Boston, MA 02116
(617) 824-8780
www.emerson.edu/performing_arts/index.cfm
E-mail: scott_wheeler@emerson.edu

4 Year Institution

Coordinator: Scott Wheeler, 80A

PT	Beck, Gina		61
PT	Brennan, Maureen		54
PT	DeSiro, Lisa		66
PT	Durham, Gary D.		61
PT	Frank, Jane Ring		61
Inst PT	Gordon, Todd	M	61
PT	Hofbauer, Eric		29A
PT	King, Fredericka		20G,20H
PT	Kreutz, Michael		61
PT	Murray, Pamela		61
PT	Nicholas, Scott		61,66A
PT	Stornetta, Catherine		60A,32D,36
PT	Sullivan, Daniel		61
Asst Prof	Wheeler, Scott	D	13,60,10,54,43

MA0900 Emmanuel College
Department of Performance Arts
400 The Fenway
Boston, MA 02115-5725
(617) 264-7772   Fax: (617) 735-9801
www.emmanuel.edu
E-mail: schnauth@emmanuel.edu

4 Year Institution

Co-Chair: Thomas Schnauber, 80A,80H

Inst	Evans, Timothy	M	40,66A,61
Asst Prof	Gagnon, Scott R.	M	54
Asst Prof	Schnauber, Thomas	PhD	10A,10C,13A,11,10F

MA0930 Fitchburg State University
Department of Humanities-Music
160 Pearl St
Fitchburg, MA 01420-2697
(978) 665-3276   Fax: (978) 665-3274
www.fitchburgstate.edu
E-mail: alima4@fitchburgstate.edu

4 Year Institution

Assoc Prof	Caniato, Michele	D	10,38,29,13,47
Prof	Dinda, Robin	D	10,11,13,29,66G
Prof	Fiske, Jane	D	11,15,32,66
Assoc Prof	Ness, Marjorie S.	D	11,20,32,36,66G

MA0950 Gordon College
Department of Music
255 Grapevine Rd
Wenham, MA 01984
(978) 867-4364   Fax: (978) 867-4655
www.gordon.edu/music
E-mail: music@gordon.edu

4 Year Institution
Member of NASM

Chair: C. Thomas Brooks, 80A
Dir., Graduate Studies Music Education: Kenneth H. Phillips

Prof	Brooks, C. Thomas	M	60A,36,40,61
Prof	Brooks, Susan G.	M	13,39,61
PT	Brunner, Norma	M	66A
Prof	Brunner, Roy	D	13,10,66G,66H,31A
PT	Bulger, Mary	M	61
Asst Prof	Buswell, James	B	62A,42,38
Asst Prof	Chung, Mia	D	13,66A,66B
PT	Clark, Heidi	M	61
PT	DiDonato, Alicia	M	64A
PT	Dirmeier, Kristen	M	63B
Asst Prof	Doneski, Sandra	M	32,36,13
PT	Fass, YuChing	M	66A
PT	Hagen, Susan	M	62D
PT	Halpern Lewis, Emily	B	62E
PT	Hart, Craig	M	61
PT	Hawryluck, Alan	M	62A,62B
PT	Kent, Heather	M	64A
PT	Kirkley, William	M	64C
PT	Lueth, Faith	M	36
PT	Markowitz, Audrey	M	64B
PT	Mayo, Thomas	M	62B
PT	Monroe, Michael	M	66A,66C
PT	Myers, Terry	M	64D
Asst Prof	Ou, Carol	D	62C,42
PT	Patterson, David	M	70
PT	Phillips, Holland	M	62A
Prof	Phillips, Kenneth H.	D	32
PT	Polyakov, Alina	D	66A
Prof	Rox, David	D	10F,60,32,37,41
PT	Schulz, Robert	M	65
PT	Sienkiewicz, Frederick	M	63A
PT	Spellissey, Gary	M	50,65
PT	Weiler, Ella Lou	M	62B

MA1000 Hampshire College
Music Program
893 West St
Amherst, MA 01002
(413) 559-5586   Fax: (413) 559-5481
www.hampshire.edu
E-mail: dwarner@hampshire.edu

4 Year Institution

Music Contact: Daniel C. Warner, 80A

Assoc Prof	Ehrlich, Martin L.		29,13B,13C
Inst	Ginsberg, Elaine Broad	D	36
Assoc Prof	Miller, Rebecca S.	D	14,13A,20F,31B,35H
Asst Prof	Oba, Junko	D	13B,13C,20C
Inst	Randall, Thomas	M	47,57,72,70
Prof	Warner, Daniel C.	D	13,10A,10B,12D,34

MA1050 Harvard University
Department of Music
North Yard
Cambridge, MA 02138
(617) 495-2791   Fax: (617) 496-8081
music.fas.harvard.edu
E-mail: musicdpt@fas.harvard.edu

4 Year Institution, Graduate School

PhD in Historical Musicology, PhD in Ethnomusicology, PhD in Music Theory, PhD in Composition, Master of Arts in Performance Practice

Chair: Alexander Rehding, 80A

Other	Beaudoin, Richard A.	D	13,12D,10
Lect	Clark, Andrew G.	M	36,60
Assoc Prof	Clark, Suzannah	D	13,12D

Rank	Name	Deg	Codes
Lect	Cortese, Federico		38,12A,12B
Prof	Czernowin, Chaya	D	10
Prof	Hasty, Christopher	D	13,10,12A,13J
Lect	Johnson, Jill		52
Prof	Kelly, Thomas Forrest	D	11,12A,12,13J
Prof	Levin, Robert	D	41,66
Prof	Monson, Ingrid		14,12,29
Prof	Oja, Carol J.	D	12,12A
Lect	Post, Olaf		12A,12B
Prof	Rehding, Alexander	D	13,12A,12B,12C,12G
Asst Prof	Revuluri, Sindhumathi	D	12,12A,12C,14C,20D
Prof	Shelemay, Kay K.	D	12,14
Prof	Shreffler, Anne C.	D	12,12A
Other	Stepner, Daniel	D	41
Prof	Tutschku, Hans	D	10,10B
Assoc Prof	Wolf, Richard	D	12,14
Prof Emeritus	Wolff, Christoph	D	12A,12,12C

MA1100 Holyoke Community College

Department of Music
303 Homestead Ave
Holyoke, MA 01040
(413) 552-2291   Fax: (413) 552-2045
www.hcc.edu
E-mail: ebrill@hcc.edu

2 Year Institution
Member of NASM

Chair: Elissa Brill Pashkin, 80A

Rank	Name	Deg	Codes
PT	Boggs, Isabelle	M	20,64C,62A,62B
Adj	Bostock, Anne	M	66A,66C
PT	Bostock, Matthew	M	12,13A
Adj	Clay, Sarah	B	61
Inst	Cogen, Ellen	M	61,40,36,13A,54
PT	Cunningham, Geoffrey A.	M	13A,37
PT	De Fremery, Phillip	B	70
Prof	Ferrier, Robert	M	70,53,29,13C
PT	Grimaldi, Peter	M	63A,47
PT	Kidwell, David	M	38
PT	Kolek, Adam J.	M	13
PT	LaCreta, Joseph	M	70,13A
PT	Levine, Theodore	B	64E,29A
PT	Maes, James	B	66A,66G,66C,66D,11
PT	Mason, John	M	70,35C,35G
PT	Mast, Murray K.	M	50,65
Prof	Pashkin, Elissa Brill	D	13,10
PT	Ruby, Eileen	M	61
PT	Swist, Christopher	M	65,35C
Adj	Szlosek, Elaine Saloio	M	64A
Adj	Wade, Adrienne Sambo	M	62C
Adj	Weeks, Rudi	B	62D
Adj	Whittle, Ralph	B	66A

MA1175 Longy School of Music

of Bard College
27 Garden St
Cambridge, MA 02138
(617) 876-0956   Fax: (617) 876-9326
www.longy.edu
E-mail: music@longy.edu

4 Year Institution, Graduate School
Member of NASM

Master of Music in Collaborative Piano, Graduate Diploma in Performance, Artist Diploma, Master of Music in Composition, Master of Music in Performance, Master of Music in Opera, Master of Music in Early Music Performance, Master of Music in Dalcroze Eurhythmics

Dean, Conservatory: Wayman Chin, 80A
President: Karen Zorn, 80A
Dir., Admissions: Alex Powell, 80D
Dir., Community Programs: Miriam Eckelhoefer, 80E
Associate Dean: James Moylan, 80H
Assistant Dean: Karyl Ryczek, 80H

Rank	Name	Deg	Codes
	Aldins, Peter	M	13
	Amis, Kenneth	M	63D
	Amper, Leslie	M	66A
	Ausch, Adriana	M	32I
	Belov, Anton	M	61
	Bennes, Gaye	M	
	Benoit, Aline	M	
	Blackburn, Ruth	M	11
	Bolter, Norman		63C
	Bose, Judith	D	32
	Bossert, Laura	M	62A,62B
	Brust, Paul W.	D	10,13,43
	Bryant, Dave	B	47
	Cardone, Alissa	B	32I
	Carrai, Phoebe	M	67B
	Cassino, Peter	M	47,29
	Cheever, Olivia	D	
	Chin, Wayman	M	66A,66C,42
	Cohler, Jonathan	B	64C
	Cutting, Linda	M	12
	Delache-Feldman, Pascale	DIPL	62D
	Dudas, Libor	D	12
	Emery, Steven	M	63A
	Enman, Thomas	M	66C,12A,54,66A,61
	Entwistle, Erik	D	12A,12C
	Evans, Peter J.	D	13
	Fitch, Frances	M	12C
	Freundlich, Douglas	D	67G
	Gabrieli, Anna	M	61
	Galindo, Jeffrey	B	63C
	Granados, Marco	M	64A
	Gullotti, Bob	B	65
	Hammer, Stephen	B	67D
	Hershey, Jane		67A
	Hicks, Calvin	D	29
	Hillyer, Raphael	M	62B
	Hinton, Hugh D.	D	66A
	Hodgkinson, Randall	M	66A
	Honeysucker, Robert	M	61
	Hopkins, Gregory	B	63A
	Huhn, Franziska	M	62E
	Inserto, Ayn	M	10D
	Ishizuka, Eiko	B	32I
	Jackson, Isaiah	D	12F
	Jojatu, Mihail	B	62C
	King, Terry	D	62C
	Kohlhase, Charlie		47
	Lakirovich, Mark		62A,62B
	Latts, Ginny	B	32I
	Lifson, Ludmilla	M	66A
	Lindblad, Sonja	M	67C
	Lion, Na'ama	D	67D
	Lockwood, John	B	62D
	Lowe, Malcolm		62A
	Maiben, Dana	M	67B
	Majerfeld, Paula	M	62B
	Marchand, Rebecca G.	D	12A,31A,12E
	Mastrodomenico, Carol	M	61
	Masuko, Takaaki	B	65
	Merfeld, Robert	M	66A,66C
	Moll, Brian	M	66C,66A
	Monahan, Laurie	M	61,55
	Morris, Joe		70
	Morrison, John H.	D	10,13
	Mulvey, Vanessa Breault	M	64A
	Murrath, Dimitri	M	62B
	Nelsen, Suzanne	M	64D
	Parker, Lisa	M	32I
	Parker-Brass, Myran	M	32
	Patterson, David	M	70
	Pellicano, Julian	M	38,60B
	Pierce, Ken	M	67H,52
	Radnofsky, Kenneth	M	64E
	Rife, Jean	B	67E
	Roll, Donna	B	39
	Rosenblith, Eric	DIPL	62A
	Rudolph, Roy	M	16
	Ruggiero, Matthew	D	64D
	Ryczek, Karyl	M	61,40
	Schwartz, Andrew	M	67D
	Schwendener, Ben	B	13
	Scolnik, Julia	M	64A
	Serkin, Peter		66A
	Sheena, Robert	M	64B
	Shlyam, Eda Mazo	D	66A
	Shoemaker, Michelle N.	D	12A,64,11,64C
	Snider, Jason	M	63B
	Sommerville, James	M	63B
	Strickland, Stan	M	64E
	Struss, Jane		12
	Sykes, Peter	M	66G,66H
	Totenberg, Roman	DIPL	62A
	Trout, Anne	M	67B
	Tucker, Melissa	B	32I
	Van Buskirk, Jeremy	M	10B
	Van Dyck, Thomas	M	62D
	Vilker, Sophia	DIPL	66A
	Vincent, Kate	M	43
	Wakao, Keisuke	DIPL	64B
	Wayne, Michael	M	64C
	West, Jayne	M	61
	Willoughby, Robert	M	64A
	Yasuda, Noriko	B	39
	Zakarian, Sylvie	M	65
	Zorn, Karen	M	66A

MA1185 Massachusetts College of Lib Arts

Department of Fine & Perf Arts
375 Church St
North Adams, MA 01247-4100
(413) 662-5255   Fax: (413) 662-5047
www.mcla.edu
E-mail: Christine.Condaris@mcla.edu

4 Year Institution

Music Contact: Christine Condaris, 80A

| Prof | Condaris, Christine | PhD | 12,14,36 |
| Asst Prof | Dilthey, Michael R. | D | 10,13,34 |

MA1200 Massachusetts Inst of Technology

Department of Mus & Theater Art
77 Massachusetts Ave
Room 4# 246
Cambridge, MA 02139-4307
(617) 253-3210   Fax: (617) 253-4523
web.mit.edu/afs/athena.mit.edu/org/m/mta/www
E-mail: jhlyons@mit.edu

4 Year Institution

Chair: Janet Sonenberg, 80A

Prof	Bamberger, Jeanne	M	13H,13K,13G,32F,13
Prof	Child, Peter	D	13,10
Lect	Cutter, William C.	D	36
Senior Lect	Deveau, David	M	11,41,66A
Prof	Harbison, John H.	M	13,10,12A
Prof	Harris, Ellen T.	D	13,11,12A,12
Lect	Harris, Fred	D	37,47
Lect	Harvey, Mark	D	11,29
Prof	Lindgren, Lowell	D	12A,20G
Asst Prof	Makan, Keeril	D	10,10F,34,13
Senior Lect	Marks, Martin	D	11,12A,54
Lect	Neff, Teresa M.	D	13,11
Lect	Rife, Jean	B	48,63B
Senior Lect	Ruckert, George	D	13A,11,20G,20D,20F
Lect	Ruehr, Elena	D	13,10,34
Lect	Shadle, Charles	M	66A
Assoc Prof	Tang, Patricia	D	20,11,13
Prof	Thompson, Marcus	D	41,62
Prof	Vercoe, Barry	D	13,10,45,34
Senior Lect	Wood, Pamela	M	13A,11
Prof	Ziporyn, Evan	D	13,10,20D,64C,29

MA1350 Mount Holyoke College

Department of Music
50 College St
South Hadley, MA 01075
(413) 538-2306   Fax: (413) 538-2547
www.mtholyoke.edu
E-mail: lladerac@mtholyoke.edu

4 Year Institution

Chair: Linda C. Laderach, 80A

Prof Emeritus	Bonde, Allen R.	D	10
Lect	Cobb, Cheryl	M	61
Inst PT	De Fremery, Phillip	B	70
Inst PT	Dennis, Sandra	B	66A
Lect	Eisenstein, Robert	M	67,34A
Inst PT	Gionfriddo, Mark	M	66A,47,34A
Prof	Greenbaum, Adrianne	M	64A,67D
Inst PT	Hale, Alison	D	64A
Inst PT	Jeffries, Jean	B	61,41,49
Inst PT	Lach, Malgorzata	M	70,13A
Prof	Laderach, Linda C.	M	51,62A,62B,67B
Inst PT	Levine, Ted	B	64E
Inst PT	Lipkens, Kirsten	B	64B
Prof	Litterick, Louise	D	13,12A,12
Inst PT	Malek, Eugenie	M	66A
Inst PT	Miller, Mary Ellen	M	64C
Lect	Ng, Tian Hui	M	38,60,12A
Assoc Prof	Omojola, Olabode	D	14,20
Inst PT	Ruby, Eileen	B	61
Assoc Prof	Sanford, David	D	13,10,29A
Prof	Schipull, Larry D.	D	13,66G,66H
Inst PT	Schnitzer, Dana	M	61
Vstng Lect	Schween, Astrid	M	62C
Prof	Spratlan, Melinda K.	D	61
Prof	Steigerwalt, Gary	D	66A,13A

MA1400 New England Conservatory

290 Huntington Ave
Boston, MA 02115
(617) 585-1100   Fax: (617) 262-0500
www.necmusic.edu
E-mail: admission@necmusic.edu

4 Year Institution, Graduate School
Member of NASM

Diploma, Master of Music in Historical Performance, Master of Music in Composition, Master of Music in Music Theory, Master of Music in Performance, Master of Music in Conducting, Master of Music in Musicology, Master of Music in Opera, DMA in Music Theory, DMA in Composition, DMA in Performance, Master of Music in Choral Conducting, Master of Music in Vocal Pedagogy, Master of Music in Jazz Studies, Master of Music in Chamber Music, Master of Music in Accompanying, Master of Music in Wind Conducting, Master of Music in Orchestral Conducting, Master of Music in Contemporary Improvisation

Dean, Students: Thomas Handel, 80B
Dean: Tom Novak, 80H

Abigana, Brett K.		13A,13C
Abreu, Aldo	M	67B
Ahlbeck, Laura	M	64B
Anderson, Jean	D	66C
Astafan, Marc	M	39
Barron, Ronald	B	63C
Baxtresser, Jeanne	B	64A
Bergonzi, Jerry	B	29,64E,47
Biss, Paul		41
Blaich, Tanya	M	66C
Blake, Ran	B	29,66A,53
Bolter, Norman		41,63C
Breese, Gretchen	M	
Brink, Robert		62A
Brofsky, Natasha		62C
Brubaker, Bruce	D	66A
Buda, Frederick	B	65,29
Burdick, Paul	M	13G,13,34,32
Buswell, James		41,62A
Buys, Douglas	M	13
Bybee, Luretta		61
Byun, Wha-Kyung	M	66A
Cain, Michael D.	M	29,66A,34,31,20
Carlberg, Frank	M	66A,47
Chaffee, Gary	M	29,65
Chandler, Jean	D	
Chapman, Lucy	M	41
Chapman, Peter	M	63A
Chase, Allan S.	M	47,29,53,64E
Chodos, Gabriel	M	66A
Churchill, Mary-Lou	B	62
Cogan, Robert	M	13,10
Coleman, Anthony	M	53,29
Cotten, William	D	61
Craig, Patricia	B	61
Cutter, William	D	36
Dalton, Dana	M	66A,12A,12,66C
Dash, Robin	M	
Davidson, Lyle	M	13,32
Decima, Terry	M	61,66C
Dillon, Cheryl	B	
Drury, Stephen	B	66A,43,12
Drury, William	M	60,48
Eade, Dominique	DIPL	61,53,47,29
Emery, Steven	M	63A
Epstein, Frank B.	M	41,65
Escot, Pozzi	M	13
Eubanks, Robin	B	63C
Feldman, Ronald	B	62C
Ferrillo, John	DIPL	64B
Fisk, Eliot	M	70
Fiuczynski, David	B	47
Flanagan, Sean	D	13
Fortunato, D'Anna	M	61
Francoeur-Krzyzek, Damien		66C
Fried, Miriam		62A
Gandolfi, Michael	M	10
Garzone, George	B	47,29,64E
Gazouleas, Ed	B	62
Gibbons, John	B	41,66H,67
Goodman, Andrea	D	36
Graybill, Roger	D	13
Greenwald, Helen	D	12
Greer, John	M	39
Haber, Carol	M	61
Haddad, Jamey		29,20,65
Hallmark, Anne Vaughan	M	12A
Handel, Thomas	D	12A,13B
Harlan, Evan	M	29
Harris, David		47

Hart, Billy		29,65
Hayward, Andre	B	63C,29
Hazilla, Jon	B	65
Heiss, John C.	M	10,12A,41,43
Henegar, Gregg	DIPL	64D
Hobson-Pilot, Ann	M	62E
Hodgkinson, Randall	M	66A
Holland, Dave		62D,47,29
Hudgins, Will	M	65
Huhn, Franziska	AD	62E
Inserto, Ayn	M	29A
Jochum von Moltke, Veronica	M	66A
Jones, J. Franklin	M	
Kambouris, Panagiota A.	M	
Kashkashian, Kim	B	62B
Katz, Martha	B	62B
Katz, Paul	D	62C
Katzen, Daniel	M	63B
Keppel, Patrick	M	
Kim, Yeesun	DIPL	41,62C
Kitchen, Nicholas	DIPL	41,62A
Klein, James A.	D	
Korsantia, Alexander	M	66A
Krimsier, Renee	M	41
Krueger, Christopher	B	64A,64E
Labaree, Robert	D	12A
LaBron, Wendy	M	
Leake, Jerry	B	20A,20E,47,65
Ledbetter, Steven	D	12A
Lee, Hsin-Bei	D	66C
Lepson, Ruth	M	
Lesser, Laurence	M	62C
Lieberman, Amy	M	36
Lockwood, John	B	62D,29
Lowe, Malcolm		62A
Mackey, Richard	B	63B
Mallia, John	D	10B,10,34
Martin, Thomas	M	64C
McBee, Cecil	B	29,47,62D
McCoy, Marilyn L.	D	12A
McEwen, Mark	B	64B
McNeil, John		29,47,63A
Menkis, Jonathan	B	63B
Miljkovic, Katarina	D	13C,13B,12A,12
Misslin, Patricia	M	61
Moriarty, John	B	39
Morris, Joe		29,47,70
Moses, Robert		47,65,29
Motobuchi, Mai	M	62B
Netsky, Hankus H.	D	29,13C,47,53,20F
Nieske, Robert	M	29,47
Nordstrom, Craig	M	64C
Novak, Tom	M	41
Nubar, Lorraine	M	61
Orleans, James	B	62D
Ou, Carol	D	41
Page, John	M	38,51
Palma, Donald	B	37,62D
Pearson, Mark	M	61
Peltz, Charles	M	48,60B
Perez, Danilo	B	29
Peyton, Malcolm C.	M	10
Pruiksma, Rose A.	D	12A
Radnofsky, Kenneth	M	64E
Rakich, Christa	M	66G
Rakowski, David	D	10
Ranti, Richard		64D
Richter, Magdalena	M	62
Rife, Jean	M	63B
Ringquist, Mikael	B	47,65
Rivera, Angel Ramon	M	66B
Robison, Paula	B	64A
Rodland, Carol	M	62B
Rolfs, Thomas	M	63A
Rosenbaum, Victor	M	41,66A
Row, Peter	D	14,12,13
Rowe, Elizabeth	B	64A
Roylance, Mike	B	63D
Samuels, David	B	29
Sandler, Felicia A.	D	13
Santovetti, Francesca		
Schaphorst, Kenneth	D	29
Schlueter, Charles	B	63A
Schwendener, Benjamin	B	29
Scripp, Lawrence	M	12
Sebring, Richard	B	63A
Seeber, Todd	B	62D
Senders, Warren		32
Sheena, Robert	M	64B
Sher, Benjamin	M	47
Sherman, Russell	B	66A
Skok, Heidi	B	61
Smith, Fenwick	B	64A
Smith, Gregory E.	D	64C
Smucker, Greg		39
Snider, Jason	M	63B
Sommerville, James		63B
Squire, Anne	M	
St. Laurent, Mark	M	61
Stagnaro, Oscar	M	29
Steele, Timothy	M	39
Stein, Deborah	D	13
Stokes, Katarina Markovic	D	12
Stoltzman, Richard	M	64C
Stovall, Sia Liss	M	
Stowe, Cameron	D	66C
Strauss, Michael	M	66C
Sullivan, Melinda	B	39
Sullivan, Robert P.		70
Svoboda, Richard	B	64D
Swanson, Donald	B	39
Swenson, Daniel	DMA	35E
Sykes, Peter	M	66G
Tapping, Roger	M	41,42
Teeters, Donald	B	12
Thompson, Marcus	D	41,62
Tong, Kristopher	M	41
Truniger, Matthias	D	13
Tyson, John	M	67B
Ushioda, Masuko	DIPL	62A
Vallecillo, Irma	M	66C
Vij, Andrea	M	
Vilker-Kuchmen, Valeria	B	62A
Wakao, Keisuke	DIPL	64B
Weilerstein, Donald	M	62A
Weilerstein, Vivian Hornik		66A
Weinmann, Patricia	M	39
Werntz, Julia	D	10
Wilkes, Steve		65
Wolfe, Lawrence	B	62D
Wright, Ben	B	63A
Wyneken, Daniel	M	39
Yeo, Douglas	M	63C
Zander, Benjamin	B	41,62C
Zaritzky, Gerald	M	13
Ziegler, Delores	M	61
Zocher, Norman M. E.	M	29

MA1450 Northeastern University
Department of Music
351 Ryder Hall
360 Huntington Ave
Boston, MA 02115
(617) 373-2440   Fax: (617) 373-4129
www.music.neu.edu
E-mail: b.alter@neu.edu

4 Year Institution

Master of Science in Music Industry Leadership

Chair: Anthony De Ritis, 80A
Graduate Coordinator: Richard Strasser, 80C

Inst FT	An, Won-Hee	D	11,60B,66
Inst FT	Anderson, James	B	34D,35
Assoc Prof	Asai, Susan M.	D	14,20D,20H
Inst PT	Bennett, Evan	D	38
Assoc Prof	Brown, Leonard	D	11,14,64E,29A,12E
Inst FT	Ciucci, Alessandra	D	14C,14F,20B,20H
Asst Prof	De Ritis, Anthony	D	35,62B,34,45
Inst	Durant, Douglas F.	D	13,10,11,12A
Inst	Feinstein, Allen G.	M	13,10F,60,37,48
Inst FT	Frengel, Mike	D	10B,34,35
Inst PT	Hatfield, Bradley	M	35A,10B
Inst PT	Herlihy, David	D	35A
Inst FT	Hichborn, Jon		35A,35D,35F
Inst FT	Ho, Hubert	D	10,13,13K,11
Prof	Jacobson, Joshua R.	D	11,12A,36,13,31B
Assoc Prof	Janikian, Leon C.	M	35,34,64C
Inst FT	Kim, Rebecca Y.	D	11,13F
Inst FT	Kroll, Mark	D	11,66H
Inst PT	Landgrebe, Junauro	B	11,14C,41
Inst PT	Lyons, Robert	B	35D,35H
Inst FT	MacCallum, John	D	10B,34
Asst Prof	McDonald, Matthew	D	13
Prof	Miller, Dennis H.	D	13,10,45,34
Inst PT	Peabody, Martha	M	61,33,13C
Assoc Prof	Poriss, Hilary	D	12A
Assoc Prof	Price, Emmett G.	D	14,29,66A,47
Inst FT	Robinson, Brian	D	11,12A
Prof	Ronkin, Bruce	DMA	64E,34,35
Artist in Res	Rose, Gil B.	D	60,38,41,13A
Inst PT	Smith, Joel L.	M	47,29
Assoc Prof	Smith, Ronald B.	D	34
Inst PT	Stadnicki, Tisha	B	36,61
Inst FT	Strand, Julie	D	20A,20D,11
Assoc Prof	Strasser, Richard	D	35A,35F
Inst PT	Thomas, Caryl Beth	M	33
Prof	Tick, Judith	D	12,20G
Inst FT	Ward, Robert J.	M	70,11,13,20G

MA1500 Northern Essex Community College
Department of Music
100 Elliot St
Haverhill, MA 01830
(978) 556-3223   Fax: (978) 556-3013

www.necc.mass.edu/academics/courses-programs/areas/arts/music/
E-mail: klanger@necc.mass.edu

2 Year Institution

Coordinator: Kenneth P. Langer, 80A

Inst	Beatrice, Anthony B.	M	37
Inst	Buchierre, Alisa	M	11,13C,36
Inst	Dietrich-Hallak, Christine	M	66D
Prof	Finegold, Michael G.	M	13,11,29
Prof	Langer, Kenneth P.	D	10A,10B,13,34D,11
Inst	Lecuyer, Michael P.	M	13,47,34

MA1550 Our Lady of the Elms College
Division of Humanities & Fine Arts
291 Springfield St
Chicopee, MA 01013
(413) 594-2761   Fax: (413) 594-3951
www.elms.edu
E-mail: canalesm@elms.edu

4 Year Institution

Chair, Humanities & Fine Arts: M. Cristina Canales, 80A

Lect	Bakriges, Christopher	PhD	29,14D,12B,20,31G
Inst PT	Feldheim, Michelle	M	66A
Inst PT	Romeo, Tony B.	B	36
Inst PT	Simonds, Judy	M	70

MA1560 Pine Manor College
Music Program
400 Heath St
Chestnut Hill, MA 02467
(617) 731-7000   Fax: (617) 731-7199
www.pmc.edu
E-mail: ambushjune@pmc.edu

4 Year Liberal Arts Institution

Coord., Performing Arts: Mahala Beams, 80A

Dean: Nia Chester, 80A

PT	Abbey, Gail	M	61,36
PT	Ambush, June	M	32
Prof	Beams, Mahala	M	11,12A,66A,13A
PT	Trout, Susan	B	61

MA1600 Regis College
Department of Music
235 Wellesley St
Weston, MA 02193
(718) 768-8326   Fax: (718) 768-7030
www.regiscollege.edu
E-mail: sheila.prichard@regiscollege.edu

4 Year Institution, Intro Courses Only

Chair & Dir., Undergraduate Studies: Sheila Grace Prichard, 80A,80B
Dir., Summer Programs: Rosemary Noon, 80G

PT	Henry, Colleen	M	66C
PT	Maskell, Kathleen D.	B	66D
PT	Paik, Wanda	M	66A
Assoc Prof	Prichard, Sheila Grace	D	36,44
PT	Radlo, Dolores	M	41
PT	Stedry, Patricia	B	61
PT	Vercoe, Elizabeth	D	12

MA1650 Salem State College
Department of Music
71 Loring Ave
Salem, MA 01970-5353
(978) 542-6296   Fax: (978) 542-7507
www.salemstate.edu/music
E-mail: mgrenfell@salemstate.edu

4 Year Institution

Chair: Mary-Jo Grenfell, 80A
Dir., Summer Programs: Abraham L. Finch, 80G

Assoc Prof	Aldrich, Mark L.	D	37,32E,32F,34D,60B
Adj	Bradshaw, Robert J.	M	10A,10C,10F,35A,35G
Adj	Clancy, Todd A.	M	47,11,70
Adj	Finch, Abraham L.	M	32A,50,65A,65B
Adj	Gall, George G.	M	44
Assoc Prof	Grenfell, Mary-Jo	M	12A,32,38,41,42
Prof	Hillyer, Dirk M.	D	63B,11,12A,13E,13F
Adj	Kanda, Sanae	D	10A,42,66A,66C,66D
Adj	Kirby, Steven	M	41
Asst Prof	Kvetko, Peter J.	D	14,13A,14C,20E,41
Adj	Palance, Thomas M.	M	29,46,47,63A
Adj	Routhier, Christine	M	33
Adj	Shane, Lynn	M	11,61,32B,32D,36
Adj	Soll, Beverly A.	D	11,66A,66C
Assoc Prof	Swanson, Philip	D	63C,10A,13B,13C,13F
Adj	Testa, Michael	M	34,34D
Assoc Prof	Wood, Gary F.	D	36,61,60,13A

MA1700 Simmons College
Department of Art & Music
300 The Fenway
Boston, MA 02115-5898
(617) 521-2268   Fax: (617) 521-3199
www.simmons.edu
E-mail: marcia.lomedico@simmons.edu

4 Year Institution

Chair: Margaret Hanni, 80A

Prof	Slowik, Gregory	D	13,11,12A,66A,66C

MA1750 Smith College
Department of Music
144 Green St - Sage Hall
Northampton, MA 01063
(413) 585-3150   Fax: (413) 585-3180
www.smith.edu/music
E-mail: lshaughn@smith.edu

4 Year Institution

Chair: Richard J. Sherr, 80A
Assistant Chair: Karen Smith-Emerson, 80H

Prof	Atlas, Raphael	D	13A,13,13F,13D
Lect	Baldwin, Joseph	M	36,60
Prof	Bloom, Peter A.	D	12A,12
Prof	Bryden, Jane G.	M	61
Assoc Prof	Gordon, Judith	B	66A,42
Lect	Hanick, Conor	M	66A,42
Senior Lect	Hirsh, Jonathan M.	D	60,36,38
Senior Lect	Moss, Grant R.	D	66G,66H,44
Lect	Pelletier, Marie Volcy		62C,42
Assoc Prof	Pitchon, Joel L.	M	62A,41,42
Lect	Robinson, Stephanie	D	10B
Prof	Sarkissian, Margaret	D	14,20D
Prof	Sherr, Richard J.	D	12A,12
Prof	Smith-Emerson, Karen	M	61
Asst Prof	Soper, Kate	D	10,10B
Assoc Prof	Waksman, Steve M.	D	29A,14C
Prof Emeritus	Wheelock, Donald	M	10

MA1850 Springfield College
Department of Music
263 Alden St
Springfield, MA 01109-3797
(413)788-3277
www.spfldcol.edu
E-mail: christopher_haynes@spfldcol.edu

4 Year Institution

Dir, Music Program: Christopher A. Haynes, 80A

PT	Sanchez, Scott R.		70
Inst	Schane-Lydon, Cathy		10,36,66
Prof Emeritus	Vickers, Gilbert		
PT	Watson, Nessim		12E

MA1900 Tufts University
Department of Music
20 Talbot Ave
Medford, MA 02155
(617) 627-3564   Fax: (617) 627-3967
www.tufts.edu/as/music
E-mail: lucille.jones@tufts.edu

4 Year Institution, Graduate School

Master of Arts in Music

Chair: Joseph Auner, 80A

Lect	Auner, Edith	M	13A,13,42
Lect PT	Barwell, Nina	M	64A,41
Lect PT	Berman, Donald L.	M	43
Prof	Bernstein, Jane A.	D	11,12A,12,12C
Asst Prof	Campana, Alessandra	D	12,12A,11
Lect	Coleman, David F.	M	36
Lect PT	Drummond, Barry	M	20D
Lect PT	Hershey, Jane	M	67,55
Asst Prof	Jankowsky, Rich	D	14,31C,20B,14F
Lect PT	Lehrman, Paul D.	M	35C,34,35B,45,45
Assoc Prof	Locke, David	D	11,14,20A
Lect PT	Mastrodomenico, Carol	M	61,39,54
Lect PT	McCann, John	M	13A,11,37
Prof	McDonald, John	D	13A,10,12A,43,13
Lect PT	McLaughlin, Michael G.	M	66A,41
Lect PT	Michelin, Nando		46,66A
Lect PT	Morris, Steven	M	39,61,66C
Asst Prof	Pennington, Stephen	D	12D,29A,29E,15,12
	Rogan, Michael J.	M	16
Prof	Schmalfeldt, Janet	D	13,12A,13J,13L
Lect	Smith, Joel Larue	M	29,47,10,53,13A
Assoc Prof	Summit, Jeffrey	D	20F,31B,14A,14D
Lect	Ullman, Michael	D	20G,29A

MA2000 Univ of Massachusetts Amherst
Department of Music & Dance
Fine Arts Center-273 East
151 Presidents Dr.
Amherst, MA 01003-9330
(413) 545-2227   Fax: (413) 545-2092
www.umass.edu/music
E-mail: mkushick@music.umass.edu

4 Year Institution, Graduate School
Member of NASM

Master of Music in Collaborative Piano, Master of Music in Composition, Master of Music in Music Theory, Master of Music in Performance, Master of Music in Conducting, Master of Music in Music Education, PhD in Music Theory, PhD in Music Education, Master of Music in Music History, Master of Music in Jazz Composing/Arranging

Chair & Dir., Graduate Studies: Jeff R. Cox, 80A,80C
Dir., Undergraduate Studies: Nikki R. Stoia, 80B
Dir., Admissions: Christopher T. Thornley, 80D
Associate Chair & Dir., Summer Programs: John A. Jenkins, 80G,80H
Dir., Dance: Billbob Brown, 80H
Dir., Publicity & Fundraising: Marilyn M. Kushick

Senior Lect	Arslanian, Paul P.	B	66C
Lect	Auerbach, Brent	D	13
Senior Lect	Berlin, Eric M.	B	63A
Lect	Bottomley, John	D	63D
Asst Prof	Brown, Billbob	M	52
Assoc Prof	Brown, T. Dennis	D	32,20G,29A,34
Lect	Buskey, Sherry	M	10,11
Lect	Chang, Elizabeth E.	M	62A
Lect	Chenette, Timothy	M	13
Lect	Cheung, Teresa	M	38
Prof	Cohen, Fredric T.	B	11,38,64B
Lect	Dennis, Paul A.	M	52
Vstng Lect PT	Eisenstein, Robert	M	12A,55B,67
Inst PT	Ferrier, Robert A.	M	70
Other	Hannum, Thomas P.	M	37,50
Prof	Hill, Willie L.	D	32,29
Lect	Hite, William	M	61
Prof	Holmes, Jeffrey W.	M	10,47,46,29
PT	Hooper, Jason	M	13
Prof	Jenkins, John A.	D	11,37
Senior Lect	Jenkins, Miriam R.	M	11
Senior Lect	Jensen-Hole, Catherine	M	47,61,29
Lect	Johnson, Amy S.	M	61
Other	Juengling, Pamela K.	M	16
Prof	Karpinski, Gary S.	D	13,13J
Lect	Kataoka, Ayano	M	65
Prof	Klock, Laura C.	M	63B
Prof	Klock, Lynn E.	M	64E
Asst Prof	Knyt, Erinn	D	12A
Senior Lect	Krueger, Christopher	B	64A
Other	Kushick, Marilyn M.	M	35E
Asst Prof	Lehmberg, Lisa J.	D	32B
Lect	Lockwood, Kathryn	M	62B
Prof	Macchia, Salvatore	D	10,62D
Prof	May, Ernest D.	D	12A,12,66G
Lect	Melnick, Marjorie L.	M	61
Asst Prof	Miller, James Patrick	M	37,32,60B
Asst Prof	Paparo, Stephen A.	D	32D
PT	Savenkova-Krasin, Ludmila V.	M	66C
Lect	Schultz, Robert D.	M	13
Prof	Shank, Nadine E.	M	66A,66C,66D
Senior Lect	Smar, Benedict J.	D	32E,32G
Lect	Spiridopoulos, Gregory	M	63C
Senior Lect	Stoia, Nikki R.	M	
Prof	Sussman, Michael	M	41,64C
Vstng Asst Prof	Thornton, Tony	D	36
Lect	Vacanti, Tom L.	M	52
Asst Prof	Vonsattel, Gilles	M	66A
Senior Lect	Walt, Stephen J.	M	64D,41
Lect	Webb, Richard	M	32E

MA2010 Univ of Massachusetts Boston
Department of Perf Arts-Music
100 Morrissey Blvd
Boston, MA 02125-3393
(617) 287-5640   Fax: (617) 287-5686
www.umb.edu/academics/cla/performarts/
E-mail: performing.arts@umb.edu

4 Year Institution

Chair: Robert Lublin, 80A

Adj	Cooper, Jessica	M	39,61
Lect PT	Giessow, David	M	36,39,61,32B,32C
Other	Halco, Terry	B	36
Adj	Hamlin, Seth	M	63C,63D
Adj	Holman, Andrew	M	66G
Adj	Howarth, Anne	M	63B
Lect PT	Janson, Peter	M	70,29,11,20,47
Adj	Lawlor, Catherine	M	66A,66D
Adj	Lee, Joo-Mee	D	62A
Adj	Liaropoulos, Panagiotis	D	66,11
Adj	Manikam, Seelan	DIPL	63A
Lect PT	McFarland, Timothy	M	13,11,66A
Prof	Mitchell, Jon	D	10F,60,32,38
Assoc Prof	Oleskiewicz, Mary	D	11,12A,12,14B,64A
Prof	Patterson, David N.	D	13,10,11,20G,34
Adj	Perrett, Mario	B	64E
Adj	Platz, Eric	M	65
Lect PT	Rink, Jeffrey	D	36
Adj	Rosinski, Jessi	M	64A
Adj	Scrima, Vin	B	62D
Lect PT	Stubbs, Frederick	M	11,14
Adj	Taylor, Priscilla	M	13,10,62C,41
Adj	Van Slyck, Trudi	DIPL	66A
Adj	Woolweaver, Scott	M	38,41,51,62B,62A

MA2020 Univ of Massachusetts Dartmouth
Department of Music
285 Old Westport Rd
North Dartmouth, MA 02747-2300
(508) 999-8568   Fax: (508) 910-6587
www.umassd.edu/cvpa/undergraduate/music
E-mail: dowens1@umassd.edu

4 Year Institution

Dean: Adrian R. Tio, 80A

Lect PT	Boateng, Kwabena	B	20B
Lect PT	Britto, Richard	M	64E,11,46
Lect PT	Brown, Wes	B	62D,36
Lect PT	Cienniwa, Paul D.	D	12A,12,11,34B
Lect PT	Cobert, Claude	M	64A,11,12A
Lect PT	Eckert, Jamie D.	M	50,65
Lect PT	Farzinpour, Peyman	M	11,12A,13B
Lect PT	Gauvin, Marcelle	B	61,13A,11
Adj	Harjito, I. M.	DIPL	20D
Lect PT	Harrison, John	B	47,66A
Prof	Hartigan, Royal	D	14,20
Adj	Hay, James	DIPL	66C
Adj	Kingsland, William	M	63D
Adj	Mazonson, Eric	M	66C
Lect FT	McWain, Andrew J.	M	29,10,13B
Lect PT	Monte, Charlene	M	62
Lect PT	Monte, Michael		64
Lect PT	Monte, Tobias	M	37,49,60,63A
Lect FT	Nelson, Marie	M	32A,32B,32C,66D
Adj	Poudrier, Chris	B	65,47
Lect PT	Richard, Matthew	B	47
Lect PT	Riley, William	M	70,11,13C
Adj	Ringwald, Ilana	M	62A
Adj	Robitaille, James	DIPL	70,47
Lect PT	Tanaka, Rieko	M	66C,13C,66A,66D
Lect FT	Wang, Jing	M	34,13B,13E,13F
Lect PT	William, Jacob	M	29A,34
Adj	Zhang, Weihua	D	66C
Lect PT	Zhou, Tianxu	M	36,61,12A

MA2030 Univ of Massachusetts Lowell
Department of Music
35 Wilder St
Suite 3
Lowell, MA 01854-0383
(978) 934-3850   Fax: (978) 934-3034
www.uml.edu/music
E-mail: amy_dinsmore@uml.edu

4 Year Institution, Graduate School
Member of NASM

Master of Music in Sound Recording Technology, Master of Music in Music Education, Master of Music in Teaching

Chair: John F. Shirley, 80A

Adj	Angelli, Paul		35C
Adj	Bates, Tom	D	35C
Adj	Bedford, Judith	M	64D
	Bell, Peter J.	M	10,13,31A,34
Adj	Bennett, Janice	M	64B
Adj	Berger, Mark	M	62B
Adj	Bettencourt, Blair	M	32E
Adj	Bohn, Hans		63C
Adj	Buda, Fred	B	65
Adj	Carman, William		35C
Adj	Casano, Joe	B	63A
Asst Prof	Case, Alexander	M	35C,47,13L
Lect	Castillo, Ramon	M	35A
Adj	Cleveland, Mark	M	61
Asst Prof	Crain, Timothy M.	D	12,20,29A,11
Adj	Fischer, Jeffrey	B	50,65
Adj	Fryer, Carolyn		62D
Adj	Gabriel, Charles M.		62D,13C,47
Adj	Giampa, Janice	M	61,39
Adj	Goodridge, Andrew	M	66C,66D
Prof	Greher, Gena R.	D	32,32H,34A
Adj	Huber, Deborah	M	37,60B
Adj	Jeon, Hey Rim		66A
Adj	Jones, Keith D.	D	35C
Adj	Keroack, Marc	M	32E
Adj	Kirklewski, Duff		35C
Adj	Lally, Peter		35A
Adj	Latham, Mark	M	38,60B
Adj	Lattini, James	M	65,47
Adj	Lee, Christopher		13A,13B,13C
Adj	Leonard, Rebecca	M	64C
Prof Emeritus	Lloyd, Gerald J.	D	10,13,10A
Adj	Lutz, Daniel	B	37,46
Lect	Malone, Thomas	D	20,32D,60A
Adj	Markow, Elliott	B	62A,62B
Prof	Martins, David	M	37,64C,60,42
Prof	McGahan, Christopher	D	11,13A,36
Prof Emeritus	Mele, Anthony	M	66A
Adj	Michaels, Mark	M	70
Lect	Michaelsen, Garrett	D	12A,13
Adj	Michaud Martins, Ellen	M	63B
Lect	Millard, Joshua P.	D	13B,13C,41,47
Prof	Moylan, William D.	D	35C,13E
Adj	Nagle, Donna	M	32
Adj	Nangle, Richard P.	D	13B,13C,13D,13E,13F
Adj	O'Connell, Brian	M	32D,60A
Adj	Platt, Walter	B	47,46
Adj	Prichard, Laura D.	D	12A
Adj	Reid, Kenneth	M	64E
Adj	Rivas, Aristides	M	62C
Prof	Roberts, Kay George	D	60,38,51
Lect	Rohlfing, Mimi	M	61,36,47,40
Adj	Rosenberg, Aaron H.	D	13,66D
Lect	Ruby, Meg	M	41,42,47,66A
Asst Prof	Ruthmann, Alex	D	32,34A
Adj	Schilling, Richard	M	70,47
Prof	Shirley, John F.	D	35C
Prof Emeritus	Smith, Stuart	D	13,29B,35C
Adj	Stover, Jerome		63D
Assoc Prof	Telesco, Paula	D	13,13H,13C
Vstng Lect	Testa, Mike	B	35C
Adj	Thibodeau, David	M	35C
Adj	Wheatley, Jon	B	70,47
Adj	Whittaker, Mark	B	35C
Assoc Prof	Williams, Alan	D	35C,35A,20

MA2050 Wellesley College
Department of Music
106 Central St
Wellesley, MA 02481-8203
(781) 283-2077   Fax: (781) 283-3687
www.wellesley.edu/Music/home.html
E-mail: mchristi@wellesley.edu

4 Year Institution

Director: Marion Dry, 80A,80D
Concert Manager: Jennifer L. Hughes, 80F

Inst PT	Adams, Kris	M	29,61
	Akahori, Eliko	M	66C
Inst PT	Aldrich, Fred	B	63B
Asst Prof	Barzel, Tamar	D	14
Asst Prof	Bhogal, Gurminder	D	
Inst PT	Bossert-King, Laura	M	62A,62B
Inst PT	Boyd, Kathleen A.	M	64A
Other	Bristah, Pamela	M	16
Prof	Brody, Martin	D	13,10,12A
Inst PT	Christie, James	M	66G,66H
Inst PT	Cleverdon, Suzanne	M	66H,66B
Inst PT	Collver-Jacobson, Glorianne	B	67G,70
Inst PT	Couture, Robert F.	M	63C
Inst PT	Dry, Marion	M	61
Prof	Fisk, Charles	D	13A,13,12A,66A
Assoc Prof	Fontijn, Claire	D	12A,12
Inst PT	Fuller, Gale	M	61
Other	Graham, Lisa E.	D	36,60
Other	Hampton, Neal	M	60,38
Other	Harris, David		63C
Inst PT	Henry, Mark	M	62D
Inst PT	Hodgkinson, Randall	M	66A
	Hopkins, Greg J.		63A
Emeritus	Jander, Owen	D	11,12A,12
Inst PT	Jeppesen, Laura	M	55,67A,67B
Inst PT	Johnson, Doug	M	66A,29B
Asst Prof	Johnson, Jenny O.		10,13
Inst PT	LaFitte, Barbara	M	64B,42
Inst PT	Langone, Steve M.	B	65
Inst PT	Matasy, Katherine V.	M	64C,64E,68,42
Inst PT	Matthews, Andrea	B	61
	McGinnis, Tracy L.		64D
Inst PT	McNutt, Craig	M	65
Inst PT	Miller, Cercie		64E,47
Inst PT	Russell, David	D	62C
	Russian, Dana S.		63A
Other	Sauer, Karen	M	66C
Inst PT	Shapiro, Lois	D	66A
Inst PT	Sheehan, Aaron	M	61
Inst PT	Starkman, Jane E.	M	67B
Other	Stumpf, Suzanne	B	41,67D,64A
Other	Talroze, Olga W.	B	66C
Inst PT	Tang, Jenny	M	66A,66C,13
Other	Thornblade, Rebecca E.		62C
Inst PT	van Dongen, Antoine	B	62A
Other	Washington, Kera M.	M	20H
Inst PT	Zajac, Tom	M	67C,67D,55
Other	Zdorovetchi, Ina		62E
Inst PT	Zeitlin, Paula H.	M	62A,47

MA2100 Westfield State University
Department of Music
577 Western Ave
Westfield, MA 01086
(413) 572-5356   Fax: (413) 572-5287
www.westfield.ma.edu/music
E-mail: klavoie@westfield.ma.edu

4 Year Institution, Graduate School

Master of Education in Music Education

Chair: Sonya R. Lawson, 80A

Lect PT	Argiro, James		35C,35H,46,10C
Lect PT	Atherton, Timothy	B	63C,63D,29A
PT	Bailey, Scott	M	66C,66D,11
Lect PT	Blanchard, Scott	M	13C
Lect PT	Boggs, Isabelle	M	20,64C
Assoc Prof	Bonacci, Andrew	D	10,13,10A,10F
Asst Prof	Bonacci, Mary Brown	D	61,11,13A
Lect PT	Bostock, Matthew	M	13A,11,12A
Prof Emeritus	Corson, Floyd W.	D	
Inst PT	Coutsouridis, Peter	D	65,41,29A,11,13B
Prof Emeritus	Davidovich, Theodore C.	D	60A,11,36
Lect PT	DeFemery, Philip	B	70
PT	Dostal, Jeffrey	B	62D
Prof Emerita	Dower-Gold, Catherine A.	D	
Lect PT	Ducharme, Jay	M	34
PT	Ducharme, Karen	B	66C
Lect PT	Gannon, Thomas	M	13A,63B
Lect PT	Gertsenzon, Galina	M	66A,66D,13A
PT	Gilwood, Deborah	M	66C
Prof Emeritus	Koury, Daniel J.	D	
PT	LaCreta, Joseph	M	70
Assoc Prof	LaVoie, Karen R.	D	13C,60B,37,63A
Assoc Prof	Lawson, Sonya R.	D	12A,62B,29A,12,20
Lect PT	Levine, Theodore	B	64E,46,29A
PT	Mason, John	M	70
Lect	Orgill, Edward	M	20,64E
PT	Rice, Nancy	M	66C
Lect PT	Rippere, Mathew	M	61
Prof Emeritus	Rogers, George L.	D	32
PT	Sambo, Adrienne	B	62C
Lect PT	Szlosek, Elaine Saloio	M	64A
Lect PT	Taylor, Allan	M	13E,66G,36

MA2150 Wheaton College
Department of Music
26 East Main St
Norton, MA 02766-2322
(508) 285-3570   Fax: (508) 286-3565
www.wheatoncollege.edu/Acad/Music/
E-mail: nmilka@wheatoncollege.edu

4 Year Institution

Chair: Matthew H. Allen, 80A
Provost: Linda Eisenmann, 80H

Assoc Prof	Allen, Matthew H.	D	14C,20E,20H,31,14
Inst PT	Amper, Leslie	M	66A,66D
Inst PT	Britto, Richard		47,64E
Inst PT	Cashen, Jeffrey A.	M	70
Prof PT	Der Hohannesian, Seta	B	41,64A
Inst PT	Falls, Sheila E.	B	41,62A
Prof Emeritus	Fassett, Charles K.	M	60,11,12A,36
Inst PT	Hann, Dan	B	65
Assoc Prof	Harbold, Tim	M	60,36,45
Inst PT	Irkaeva, Zarina S.	B	62E
Asst Prof	MacPherson, William A.	D	11,12,66G,66H
Inst PT	Mouradjian, Joanne	M	61
Inst PT	Raney, Earl L.	B	49,48,63A
Inst PT	Ringwald, Ilana	M	62B
Inst PT	Romanul, Lisa K.	B	66A
Prof Emeritus	Russell, Carlton T.	D	11,12A,66G,31A
Inst PT	Searles, Julie	M	14,14C,20H,20G
Prof	Sears, E. Ann	D	12A,66A,29A,20G
Assoc Prof	Urban, Guy	M	13,60,11,66A

MA2200 Wheelock College
Department of Music
200 Riverway
Boston, MA 02215-4104
(617)734-5200   Fax: (617)566-7369
www.wheelock.edu
E-mail: lclarke@wheelock.edu

4 Year Institution

Chair: Leo W. Collins, 80A

Inst PT	Brown, Leonard	D	20G,20H,29
Asst Prof	Clarke, Leland	D	32A,32B,66A,66B
Prof	Collins, Leo W.	D	12B,31A,20G
Asst Prof	Staab, Jane	M	39,54
Inst	Weinstein, Michael	D	13A,11,12A,49

MA2250 Williams College
Department of Music
54 Chapin Hall Dr
Williamstown, MA 01267-2687
(413) 597-2127   Fax: (413) 597-3100
music.williams.edu
E-mail: w.anthony.sheppard@williams.edu

4 Year Institution

Chair: W. Anthony Sheppard, 80A

Prof	Bloxam, Jennifer	D	11,15,12
PT	Botts, Nathan	M	63A,41
PT	Caproni, Christopher	M	37
Vstng Inst	Dilthey, Michael R.	D	12
Vstng Asst Prof	Dosunmu, Oyebade A.	D	14,20
Artist in Res	Feldman, Ronald	B	60B,38,41,42
PT	Genova, Joana		62A,41
PT	Gold, Matthew	M	50,65,43,41
Assoc Prof	Gollin, Ed	D	13
Vstng Asst Prof	Haringer, Andrew	D	12,11
PT	Hebert, Floyd	M	64A,41
Assoc Prof	Hirsch, Marjorie	D	11,12,15,20G
Artist in Res	Jaffe, Andy W.	M	29,46,47
PT	Jenkins, Carl	M	64B,41
Prof	Kechley, David S.	D	10A,10F,13A,13B,13D
PT	Kibler, Keith E.	D	61,40
PT	Kolodny, Michael		64E,41
Artist in Res	Kurkowicz, Joanna	M	41,62A,43
PT	Lawrence, Edwin	B	13C,66A,66G,66H,66C
PT	Lewis, Bernice		10,40
PT	Martula, Susan	M	64C,41
PT	Meehan, Conor		65,41
Other	Michelin, Rob	M	50
Other	Miller, Heidi Johanna	D	46
PT	Morse, Elizabeth		62E,41
Vstng Artist	Muparutsa, Tendai	D	20A,20B
PT	Nafziger, Erin		61,40
PT	Nazarenko, John	M	66A,41
PT	Neu, Ah Ling	B	62A,41
PT	Parke, Nathaniel	M	62C,43,41
PT	Phelps, Robert	M	70,41
PT	Pierce, Laura	B	61,40
Vstng Inst	Prindle, Daniel	M	12
PT	Ryer-Parke, Kerry	B	61,40
PT	Sharpe, Avery G.	B	62D,41,36
Prof	Sheppard, W. Anthony	D	12A,20C,14C,12D,20G
PT	Stephan, Michael	M	63D,41
Artist in Res	Stevenson, Doris J.	M	41,66A,66C,42,43
PT	Sungarian, Victor		63B,41
Assoc Prof	Velazquez, Ileana Perez	D	10,13,34D
PT	Walt, Marlene	B	61,40
PT	Walt, Stephen	D	48,64D,43,41
Artist in Res	Wells, Bradley C.	D	13C,36,40,60A,61
PT	Wheeler, John		63C,41
PT	Wright, Elizabeth	M	66A,66C,41
PT	Zimmerman, Robert		62D,41

MA2300 Worcester State College
Department of Visual & Perf Arts
486 Chandler St
Worcester, MA 01602-2832
(508) 929-8000   Fax: (508) 929-8166
www.worcester.edu
E-mail: mhachey@worcester.edu

4 Year Institution

Chair & Dir., Undergraduate Studies: Michael C. Hachey, 80A,80B,80F

Prof	Martin, Kyle	DMA	13A,13,11,66,35B
Prof	Nigro, Christie	PhD	13A,11,12A,36,62A
Prof	Sahagian, Robert	PhD	11,12A

MD0050 Allegany College
Department of Humanities-Music
12401 Willowbrook Rd SE
Cumberland, MD 21502-2596
(301) 784-5000   Fax: (301) 724-1349
www.allegany.edu

2 Year Institution

Chair: Jim Zamagias, 80A

PT	Grew, Melody A.	M	11,32,36,61,66A

MD0060 Anne Arundel Community College
Department of Performing Arts
101 College Pkwy
Arnold, MD 21012-1857
(410) 777-7019   Fax: (410) 777-7553
www.aacc.edu
E-mail: dbbyerly@aacc.edu

2 Year Institution

Coordinator, Music: Douglas Byerly, 80A
Chair, Performing Arts: Barbara Marder, 80A
Circulation Manager: Helen Smith Tarchalski

PT	Ascione, Ray A.	M	47,64C,64E
Adj	Barcellona, Mary Anne		61
PT	Barron, Fran	M	32
PT	Bazala-Kim, Allison	D	62C
PT	Binneweg, Anna	D	38,39
PT	Briante, Kate	M	39,61
FT	Byerly, Douglas	M	13,36,39
PT	Chestnut, Louise	M	10,62B
FT	Edwards, T. Matthew	D	66A,13,66C,12,36
PT	Gollmer, James W.	M	63B
PT	Green, Elizabeth	D	66A,66D
PT	Greene, Joy	M	61
PT	Hildebrand, Virginia	M	70,67D
PT	Hiscox, Julie	M	61
PT	Holmes, Daniel	M	61
PT	Kinsley, Diane	M	66A,66D
PT	Knepp, Marty	M	29,47
PT	Mattingly, Douglas	M	13,29,35,70
FT	McCollum, Jonathan Ray	D	12,13,20,55,63C
PT	McCollum, Kimberly	M	62A
PT	Moses, Leonard	D	10
PT	Mutchnik, Ronald	M	62A
Adj	Pallett, Bryan		70
Adj	Pascuzzi, Greg		10,63A
PT	Pitta, Tom	M	62D
PT	Raifsnider, Chrisoper J.	D	12,13,64C
PT	Ray, Frederic	M	61
PT	Tarchalski, Helen Smith	M	66A,66D
PT	Wade, Melinda	M	64A
PT	Wardenski, Ian	D	70
PT	Weidner, Raymond	D	12,13,36

MD0095 Chesapeake College
Department of Music
PO Box 8
Wye Mills, MD 21679-0008
(410) 822-5400 x 206   Fax: (410) 827-5814
www.chesapeake.edu
E-mail: bcutsforthhuber@chesapeake.edu

2 Year Institution

Music Contact: Bonnie Cutsforth-Huber, 80A

Assoc Prof	Cutsforth-Huber, Bonnie	D	13A,13,11,12A,13B

MD0100 College of Notre Dame of Maryland
Department of Music
4701 N Charles St
Baltimore, MD 21210-2404
(410) 532-5386   Fax: (410) 435-5937
www.ndm.edu
E-mail: dfirmani@ndm.edu

4 Year Institution

Interim Chair: Domenico Firmani, 80A

Assoc Fac	Bisson, Mary	M	63B
Assoc Fac	Fleming Peters, Lori		62E
Assoc Fac	Goode, Dana	M	41
Assoc Prof	Izdebski, Christy	D	12A,32,66A,66D,36
Assoc Fac	Lande, Vladimir	M	64B
Assoc Fac	Peters, Braxton	M	61
Assoc Fac	Platino, Franco	M	70
Prof	Ragogini, Ernest	D	13,12A,66A,12C
Assoc Fac	Rehwoldt, Lisa	D	13,12A,66A
Assoc Fac	Suggs, Robert	D	63A
Assoc Fac	Weglein, Carolyn	M	60,36,66G
Assoc Fac	White, Rosemary	M	64A
Assoc Fac	Wirth, Julius	M	62B

MD0150 Columbia Union College
Department of Music
7600 Flower Ave
Takoma Park, MD 20912-7796
(301) 891-4025   Fax: (301) 576-0181
www.wau.edu
E-mail: music@wau.edu

4 Year Institution

Adj	Almargo, Brandon	M	63A
	Baccus, Jessica	B	32
Adj	Bazala Kim, Alison E.	D	62C,41
Adj	Bilinski, Janusz	M	62D
Adj	Carson, Mark	M	65
Adj	Cockson, Aaron	M	63B
Asst Prof	DiPinto, Mark	D	66A,66B,66C,13C
Adj	Feasley, William	M	70
Adj	Findley, Susan	B	64B
Asst Prof	Hawes, Preston	M	62A,38
Adj	Jones, David C.	M	63A
Adj	Jones, Steve	B	70
Adj	Jones, Vanita	B	41,64A
Adj	Ko, Priscilla	M	66
Asst Prof	Lau, Daniel	D	66A,66B,66C,12A
Adj	McGinness, John	M	63C
Adj	Mueller, Geri	M	67B
Adj	Namoradze, Medea	D	61
Prof	Rittenhouse, Virginia Gene	D	38,62A,66A,32I
Adj	Surowiec, Jozef	M	61
Adj	Thurlow, Deborah	M	61
Adj	Tomenko, Keri	M	62A
Asst Prof	Warren, Ron	D	10F,10,66C
Adj	Willey, Mark	B	13,66G
Assoc Prof	Wilson, Bruce	M	63C,63D,49,37,32C
Adj	Yuzefovich, Victor	D	12A,12,62B,32I

MD0170 Community Coll of Baltimore Cnty
Department of Music-Catonsville
800 S Rolling Rd
Baltimore, MD 21228-5317
(410) 455-4177   Fax: (410) 455-5134
www.ccbcmd.edu
E-mail: wwatson@ccbcmd.edu

2 Year Institution

Adj	Allen, Frances	DIPL	13A,66A
Adj	Britt, Michael	M	66A,66G
Adj	Distefano, Donna	M	65
Adj	Gatto, Angelo	M	38,62
Adj	Greenberg, Barry	M	61,66A
Adj	Harrell, James	M	70
Adj	Houston, James	M	66A,66G
Adj	Koomson, Nathaniel	M	66A
Adj	Spicer-Lane, Anita	M	11,61
Adj	Starr, Lucia	DIPL	61
Adj	Thurston, Andrew	M	70
Adj	Valliant, James	M	61,66A

MD0175 Community Coll of Baltimore Cnty
Music Program-Essex Campus
7201 Rossville Blvd
Baltimore, MD 21237-3899
(443) 840-1942   Fax: (443) 840-1250
www.ccbcmd.edu
E-mail: pcrossman@ccbcmd.edu

2 Year Institution
Member of NASM

Music Program Coordinator: Patricia Crossman, 80A
Chair, Performing Arts & Humanities: William E. Watson, 80A
Dir., Artist/Performance Series: Monica D. Otal, 80F

Asst Prof PT	Barczyk, Cecylia	M	62C
Prof PT	Comotto, Brian	M	10,35C,35D,35G,66A
Prof	Crossman, Patricia	M	66A,66C
Asst Prof PT	Dickenson, Andrew	M	11,70
Prof PT	Dimmock, Megan	M	61
Prof PT	Elliott, William	M	65
Prof PT	Fletcher, Ashton	M	62D,46,47
Prof	Gretz, Ronald	M	13A,13,66A,66C,54
Asst Prof PT	Hood, Gary	B	35A,35F
Prof PT	Hulbert, Jarl O.	D	66A
Prof PT	Lawler, Douglas	M	10,54
Asst Prof PT	Lewis, Andrew	M	11,66A,66C
Asst Prof PT	Lewis, Daniel	M	11,13,66D,70
Prof PT	Lindquist, Arne	M	36,61
Asst Prof PT	Mazziot, Nicholas	M	63C,63D
Asst Prof PT	Muller, Janet	M	64A
Assoc Prof	Otal, Monica D.	M	36,61,11
Prof PT	Peters, Braxton	M	61
Asst Prof PT	Schneckenburger, Brian	M	63A
Prof PT	Stockton, Rachel	M	62A
Asst Prof PT	Suchy, John	B	35C,34D
Prof PT	Teter, Eston	M	66A
Prof	Watson, William E.	D	10,47,14C,20
Prof PT	Winter, Robert	M	70,11
Asst Prof PT	Wittstadt, Kurt	M	11,42,63B
Prof	Wolfe, Chris	M	13A,60,37,64C,64E

MD0200 Coppin State College
Department of Visual and Performing Arts
2500 W North Ave
Baltimore, MD 21203
(410) 383-5997
www.coppin.edu
E-mail: ghyatt@coppin.edu

4 Year Institution, Intro Courses Only, Historically Black College

Chair: Garey A. Hyatt, 80A

Asst Prof	Barnes, Hugh W.	M	37
Asst Prof	English, Wendell L.	B	36
	Hyatt, Garey A.	D	

MD0300 Frederick Community College
Department of Music
7932 Opossumtown Pike
Frederick, MD 21702
(301) 846-2512   Fax: (301) 624-2878
www.frederick.edu
E-mail: jholly@frederick.edu

2 Year Institution

Chair: Janice Holly, 80A
Program Manager: Paula Chipman, 80H

Inst PT	Armstrong, Laura D.	D	64C
Inst PT	Ayoub, Jason	M	63B
Inst PT	Ballard, Timothy Marshall	D	61
Inst PT	Ballard-Ayoub, Anne Claire	M	11,64D
Inst PT	Burns, Howard	M	47
Asst Prof	Chipman, Paula	D	61,13A,13C
Inst PT	Fleming, Lynn	M	62D
Inst PT	Gonzalez, Adam	M	62C
Inst PT	Gray, Serap Bastepe	M	70,13A
Inst PT	Gresock, Mary	M	61
Inst PT	Herron, Greg	B	65
Prof	Holly, Janice	D	13B,11
Inst PT	Hontz, James	D	70
Inst PT	Hyun, Suk-Yi	D	66A
Inst PT	Lee, Alice	D	66A
Inst PT	Linton, Larry	B	64C
Inst PT	Lovely, Aaron	M	63C,63D,37
Inst PT	Loy, David	M	13C,61
Inst PT	Millar, Cameron	M	13A,34B,35C,13C,34D
Inst PT	Mowbray, Candice	M	70
Inst PT	Pursell, John	D	63A
Inst PT	Rokosny, Dana	M	62B
Inst PT	Rundlett, Jennifer	M	64A,11,41
Inst PT	Staininger, Lynn L.	M	36,66A,13B,40,61
Inst PT	Thomas, Anita	M	47
Inst PT	Tung, Alice	M	62B
Inst PT	Tung, James	B	62A
Inst PT	Wickelgren, John	D	66A,13C,66C,66D
Inst PT	Wilcox, Fred J.	M	62A,62B

MD0350 Frostburg State University
Department of Music
101 Braddock Rd
Frostburg, MD 21532-2303
(301) 687-4109   Fax: (301) 687-4784
www.frostburg.edu/dept/music
E-mail: mgallagher@frostburg.edu

4 Year Institution

Chair: Mark Gallagher, 80A
Dean, College of Liberal Arts: Joseph M. Hoffman, 80A

Lect	DeWire, James	D	66
Prof	Dixon, Joan DeVee	D	66,31A,35
Assoc Prof	Gallagher, Mark	D	64C,48,13,12A
Prof	Grolman, Ellen K.	D	12A,62C
Inst FT	Horner, Ronald	D	65,20,50
Asst Prof	Klickman, Philip	M	63B,37,32E,60B
Inst PT	Lyons, James H.	D	11,20,32B
Inst PT	Madsen, Brent	M	63A
Inst PT	Madsen, Emily K.	D	64B,64D
Inst PT	McManus, Kevin	M	63B,63C,63D,49
Inst PT	Mihai-Zoeter, Mariana	M	61,39
Inst PT	Murchison, Pamela	M	64A,48,20,15
Inst PT	Phillips, Gary J.	M	20
Inst PT	Sise, Patrick	M	70,41
Prof	Soderberg, Karen	D	61,36,40,32D,60A
Inst PT	Soebbing, Steven	D	61,20,15
Lect	Weber, Brent M.	M	64E,64D,29,47,20

MD0360 Garrett College
Department of Music
687 Mosser Rd
Mc Henry, MD 21541
(301) 387-3093   Fax: (301) 387-3055
www.garrettcollege.edu

2 Year Institution

Director, Arts & Sciences: Vivian Broaddus, 80A
Administrator: Gerald McGee, 80A

Directory of Institutions Page 189

	Hogue, Harry	M	70,12A,63D,13,11
	Reckner, Lillian	M	66,61,65
	Thayer, Fred	CERT	

MD0400 Goucher College
Department of Music
1021 Dulaney Valley Rd
Baltimore, MD 21204
(410) 337-6276   Fax: (410) 769-5063
www.goucher.edu/music
E-mail: kgratz@goucher.edu

4 Year Liberal Arts Institution

Chair: Kendall Kennison, 80A
Coordinator, Summer Programs: Ashton Nicolas, 80G

PT	Bakkegard, Karen	B	63B
PT	Bob, Joan	M	62B
PT	Bonsiero, Philip		68
PT	Boyle, E. C. McGregor	D	70
Inst	Chappell, Jeffrey	M	47,66A,29,29B,10
PT	Crawford, Wesley	B	65
PT	Evans, David	B	67H
PT	Fedderly, Carolyn	M	64D
PT	Gettes, Gretchen	M	62C
Lect	Greenwood, Joanna E.	M	12,20
PT	Hall, Thomas E.	D	36
Inst	Hartzell, Richard	M	61,39,54
PT	Jeng, Rhoda	D	66A
Assoc Prof	Kennison, Kendall	D	13,10
Asst Prof	Kim, Hyun Kyung	D	34
Asst Prof	Koehler, Elisa C.	D	38,63A,60,11,13A
PT	Lane, Mathew	M	13A,13C,66A,66C
PT	LaVorgna, David	M	64A,42
PT	Myers, Benjamin C.	D	62C
PT	Nevius, Sheila	M	64E
PT	Poling, Mary	M	64B
PT	Ridgeway, Betty	M	61
PT	Robinson, N. Scott	D	65
PT	Ruas, Laura	M	62D
PT	Vaupel, Lisa	M	62A,42
PT	Wang, Hsiu-Hui	D	66A,66C,42
Prof	Weiss, Lisa G.	D	13A,11,42,66A,66C
PT	Winter-Jones, Kristin	M	64A
Lect	Wolfe-Ralph, Carol	D	13,66A
Asst Prof	Wright, Geoffrey	D	10,34
PT	Yankee, Steve	B	70
PT	Young, Alice	M	62B

MD0450 Hagerstown Community College
Department of Music
11400 Robinwood Dr
Hagerstown, MD 21742-6514
(301) 790-2800 x380   Fax: (301) 393-3680
www.hagerstowncc.edu
E-mail: jamarschner@hagerstowncc.edu

2 Year Institution

Chair: Terrie Karn Angle, 80A
Music Contact: Joseph A. Marschner, 80A

PT	Domenico, Tony	B	32A,47
PT	Galvin, Mindy		64C
PT	Grab, Charles		63
PT	Jenkins, E. Morgan	M	64A,64E,70,29B
PT	Lundblad, Genevieve	B	32A,11,33
FT	Marschner, Joseph A.	M	11,45,70,34
PT	Moss-Sanders, Korby L.	M	66A
PT	O'Connor, Brad M.		65
PT	Sincell-Corwell, Kathryn	B	36,61
PT	Stotelmyer, Deborah L.		62
PT	Warner, C. David	D	54
PT	Webber, Danny R.	B	11,70,13

MD0475 Harford Community College
Department of Music
401 Thomas Run Rd
Bel Air, MD 21015-1627
(443) 412-2291   Fax: (443) 412-2180
www.harford.edu
E-mail: plabe@harford.edu

2 Year Institution, Community College

Dean of Visual, Perf. & Applied Arts: Paul E. Labe, Jr., 80A

Adj	Anderson, Timothy		62C
FT	Anderson-Himmelspach, Neil	D	10A,13,14C,34,62D
Adj	Bair, Sheldon E.	M	38
Adj	Cunneff, Philip B.	B	13A,65,29A,14C
Adj	Dimmock, Herb R.		36
Adj	Dorsey, Roland W.	A	62D
Adj	Folus, Brian H.	B	62D,62A,62C
Adj	Gray, Madeleine C.		61
Adj	Hontz, James R.	M	70
Adj	Kooken, Brian		70
Adj	Kotter, Laurie		64A
FT	Labe, Paul E.	M	13,10A
Adj	Lipa, Noella P.		64C
Adj	Molina, Linda	M	62A,12A,20
Adj	Murphy, Bill S.	M	12A
Adj	Pastelak, Marianne	B	61,40
Adj	Russell, Benjamin A.		47,64E,14C
Adj	Satava, Joseph F.	D	66A,66D
Adj	Sharnetzka, Charles S.	M	37,12A,63A
Adj	Sharnetzka, Sandra		63B
Adj	Vatz, Shaina V.		61

MD0500 Hood College
Department of Music
401 Rosemont Ave
Frederick, MD 21701
(301) 696-3782   Fax: (301) 694-7653
www.hood.edu
E-mail: nlester@hood.edu

4 Year Liberal Arts Institution

Chair: Wayne L. Wold, 80A

Inst PT	Aaland, Jan	B	61
Inst PT	Ayoub, Anna Claire	M	64D
Inst PT	Bazala Kim, Alison	D	62C
Inst PT	Beachley, Laine	B	66A
Inst PT	Dodson, Lisa	M	61
Inst PT	Duree, David		64C,64E
Inst PT	Fleming, Lynn	M	62D
Inst PT	Hinkley, Brian		63,49,48
Prof Emeritus	Lester, Noel K.	D	66A
Inst PT	Lewis, Kevin	B	47
Inst PT	Markow, Roseann	M	62A,62B,51
Inst PT	Porter-Borden, Catherine		61
Inst PT	Powell, William	D	66A
Inst PT	Simms, William	M	67G,70,55
Inst PT	Smith, Leroy	B	40
Inst PT	Spicher, Barbara		64A
	Staininger, Lynn	M	36,40
Inst PT	Stanley, Ed	M	64B
Asst Prof	Verzosa, Noel	D	12,11
Assoc Prof	Wold, Wayne L.	D	13,66G,66H,10
	Wright, Elaine	M	66A,66B

MD0520 McDaniel College
Department of Music
2 College Hill
Westminster, MD 21157
(410) 857-2552   Fax: (410) 871-3355
www.mcdaniel.edu/3479.htm
E-mail: mboudrea@mcdaniel.edu

4 Year Institution

Chair: Margaret A. Boudreaux, 80A

Lect PT	Anderson, Tim H.	B	62C
	Andrews, Rachel	B	66C
Assoc Prof	Armstrong, Robin E.	D	11,14,29A,12,12A
Prof	Boudreaux, Margaret A.	D	60,12A,32D,36
Lect	Byrd, Eric B.	M	36,66A,29
Prof	Caldwell, Glenn G.	D	13,29B
Lect PT	Currie, Nicholas W.	B	62A
Lect PT	Dix, Ted	M	66G,13C
Lect PT	Duree, David T.	B	64C,64E
Senior Lect	Eckard, Steven C.	B	47,62D,29
Senior Lect	Engler, Kyle C.	M	39,61,54
Lect PT	Fleming, Lynn	M	62D
Lect PT	Griffith, Lynne	M	63B
Lect PT	Hooks, Norma R.	B	64D
Lect PT	Horneff, Donald C.	B	66F,66C,66D,66H,32E
Lect PT	Jenkins, Tim G.	B	70,41
Senior Lect	Kirkpatrick, Linda M.	D	60,37,41,48,64A
Senior Lect	Kreider, David G.	B	11,66A,66G,66B,66D
Lect PT	Lortz, Mark E.	M	32E
Lect PT	Markovic, Lorriana	D	61

Lect PT	Murray, Kathrin	M	70,41
Lect PT	Niles, Melinda Smith	B	64B
Lect PT	Reider, Nick	B	63A
Lect PT	Ryon, James P.	D	63C
Lect PT	Seligman, Jonathan D.	M	50,65,32E
Lect PT	Swan, Steve	B	64E
Lect PT	Tung, Alice Clair	M	62B,41
Lect PT	Wirth, Elijah G.	M	63D

MD0550 Montgomery College
Department of Music
51 Mannakee St
Rockville, MD 20850-1101
(240) 567-5209   Fax: (240) 567-7553
www.montgomerycollege.edu
E-mail: jay.crowder@montgomerycollege.edu

2 Year Institution
Member of NASM

Chair: Jarrell Crowder, 80A

Inst	Alvi, Diba N.	D	61
Inst	Appleman, Harry	B	66A
Prof	Avery, Dawn	M	20,42,62C
Inst	Badolato, James V.	D	13B
Assoc Prof	Boyer, Justin	M	13B,13C,10A
Inst	Brown-Stanford, Deborah	D	66A
Inst	Carrier, Lisa	M	61
Inst	Churchill, Steve	M	64C,64E,64B
Inst	Cook, Seth	M	63C,63D
Inst	Cresci, Jonathan	D	63A,34D,13C,34C,14C
Assoc Prof	Crowder, Jarrell	D	66A,66D,54
Inst	Crowson, James	M	70
Inst	Czarkowski, Stephen	M	38,62C,13A
Inst	Dinitz, Mark	M	65
Prof	Donnelly, Molly	D	36,61,42
Inst	Fleming, Lynn	M	62D
Inst	Giambussso, Scott		62D
Inst	Gibson, Christina Taylor	D	14C
Prof	Harris, Ward	M	11,14C,12A
Inst	Hilton, Suzanne	M	11,13A,34C
Inst	Hughes-Lopez, Jennifer	M	61
Inst	Jaskot, Matthew		10A
Inst	Jones, Vanita	M	64A,41
Inst	Kim-Medwin, Sungah	D	66A,66D
Inst	Krohn, Ken	M	65
Inst	Larrance, Steve		65
Inst	Lindekugel, Denise	M	11,13A
Inst	Mancini, Meredith	M	62E
Assoc Prof	Mangels, Jeffrey W.	D	13A,34C,11,13C,34D
Inst	Mathieu, Phil	B	70
Inst	McCool, Jason	M	14C
Inst	Mentzel, Michael	M	61
Inst	Nazarenko, Dmitri	M	66A
Inst	Patterson, Vincent L.	D	48,64C
Inst	Pinney, Greg	M	62A,62B
Inst	Prossaird, Didier		66A,20
Inst	Rosado, Sara	D	66A,13A
Prof	Saelzer, Pablo	M	11,13A,13C,38,62A
Inst	Sheffer, Jake		70
Inst	Solomon, Evan	M	13A,13B
Inst	Stevans, Joy	M	61
Assoc Prof	Trask, Alvin	M	63A,53,29A,14C,47
Inst	Vardanian, Vera	M	62A
Inst	Wang, Pin-Huey	D	66A,66D
Inst	Warren, Ron	D	20
Inst	Watermeier, Ethan	M	61
Inst	Yang, Tzi-Ming	D	66A,66D

MD0600 Morgan State University
Department of Music
1700 E Cold Spring Ln
Baltimore, MD 21251
(443) 885-3286
www.morgan.edu
E-mail: eric.conway@morgan.edu

4 Year Institution, Graduate School, Historically Black College
Member of NASM

Master of Science in Music Education

Chair: Eric Conway, 80A
Dean: Burney J. Hollis, 80A

Lect	Aldana, Milton		63C,13,12A
Adj	Cameron, Wayne		63A
Prof	Conway, Eric	D	13,66A
Adj	Cooke, Julia		61
Lect	Mahonske, Adam	D	13
Adj	Markovic, Lorriana	D	61
Prof	McCullam, Audrey	M	13,32B,32C,66A,66D
Inst	Miles, Melvin N.	M	60,37,47,49,63A
Asst Prof	Olson, Margaret	D	61,39
Lect	Rowe, Devonna	M	61
Adj	Russo, Tadd		34
Adj	Singer, Mark		62A
Lect	Springer, Samuel	D	66A,39
Lect	Stringer, Vincent Dion	M	61,39
Lect	Thesen, Anita	D	64A,12A
Adj	Williams, Larry		63B
Adj	Willoughby, Malcolm		61
	Yacoub, Allison	M	64C,32E,20

MD0610 Mount St Marys University
Department of Visual & Perf Arts
16300 Old Emmitsburg Rd
Emmitsburg, MD 21727
(301) 447-5308   Fax: (301) 447-7401
www.msmary.edu
E-mail: venzin@msmary.edu

4 Year Institution

Chair: Andrew Rosenfeld, 80A

Lect PT	Armato, John	M	70
Asst Prof	Carlson, Mark	D	63,11,12,13,37
Lect PT	Distefano, Donna	M	65
Lect PT	Fields, Victor	M	66A
Lect PT	Pursell, John	M	63A
Lect PT	Regan, Joseph	M	61
Assoc Prof	Rosenfeld, Andrew	DMA	11,12,13,20F,36
Lect PT	Rundlett, Jennifer	M	64A
Lect PT	Simms, William	M	70
Lect PT	Sweigart, Suzanne	M	66A,61
Lect PT	Wickelgren, John	DMA	66A

MD0650 Peabody Conservatory of Music
Johns Hopkins University
1 E Mount Vernon Pl
Baltimore, MD 21202-2308
(410) 234-4500   Fax: (410) 659-8129
www.peabody.jhu.edu
E-mail: blambert@jhu.edu

4 Year Institution, Graduate School
Member of NASM

Master of Arts in Audio Sciences, Master of Music in Composition, Master of Music in Performance, Master of Music in Conducting, Master of Music in Music Education, Master of Music in Musicology, DMA in Composition, DMA in Conducting, DMA in Performance, Master of Music in Pedagogy & Performance, Master of Music in Piano Ensemble Arts, Master of Music in Music Theory Pedagogy, Master of Music in Computer Music

Dean/Deputy Director: Mellasenah Y. Morris, 80A,80H
Director, Peabody Institute: Jeffrey N. Sharkey, 80A
Associate Dean, Academic Affairs: Paul Mathews, 80H
Assoc. Dean, Student Affairs: Katsura Kurita

	Abadey, Nasar		29
	Adams, Clinton	M	13C
	Adashi, Judah E.	D	13,10
	Ahn, Suhnne	D	12
	Alvi, Diba N.	D	61
	Archibald, Elizabeth	D	12
	Barta, Steven E.	M	64C
	Bartlett, Carol A.	DIPL	52
	Bastepe-Gray, Serap E.	M	70
	Benjamin, Thomas	D	13
	Bettison, Oscar	D	10
	Blades, Jennifer A.	M	39
	Bollenback, Paul		29
	Boyle, McGregor	D	10B,34
	Browder, Risa	B	67B
	Bruce, Garnett R.	B	39
	Brunyate, Roger	M	39
	Bryn-Julson, Phyllis	M	61
	Burgstaller, Josef	M	63A
	Busching, Marianna	M	61
	Campora, Randall S.		63C
	Cardany, Audrey	D	32
	Chang, Li Kuo		62B
	Chester, Ray G.	B	70
	Chiang, Victoria	M	62B

Clayton, Jay	B	29
Cornett, Eileen	M	66C,39
Cornett, Stanley O.	D	61
Cudek, Mark	M	55
Danchenko, Victor	DIPL	62A
Danchenko-Stern, Vera	M	
Falby, Vern C.	D	13
Fedderly, David T.	B	63D
Ferber, Alan	B	29
Fetter, David J.	M	63C
Field, Richard L.	M	62B
Fleisher, Leon		66A
Formanek, Michael		29,46
Fulton, Ruby	D	13
Gajger, Melina	M	62A
Ganz, Brian	DIPL	66A
Giarusso, Richard	D	12
Gingerich, John M.	D	12
Gold, Ira J.	M	62D
Goodwin, Linda G.	M	35A,35E
Graham, Patricia S.	M	13A,66D
Graves, Denyce	B	61
Gray, Julian F.	M	70
Greenberg, Herbert	B	62A
Gretz, Ronald	M	
Hahn, Marian	M	66A
Hardaway, Travis	D	13,10F
Hardy, David	B	62C
Harp, James	M	
Henry, Rebecca S.	M	62B
Hersch, Michael	M	10
Hildebrand, David K.	D	12
Hoffman, Edward W.	M	63A
Hong, Ah Young	M	61
Huang, Juan	D	35C
Inglefield, Ruth K.	D	62E
Jacobson, Katherine	M	42
Janello, Mark	D	13
Johansen, Ken	D	13A,66D
Johnson, Lura	M	13A,66D
Johnson, Paul L.	M	62D
Johnson, Shawn F.	D	35C,35G
Jones, Thomas A.		35C
Justen, Wolfgang H.	D	
Kannen, Michael	B	41,42
Kellner, Steven	B	63D
Khannanov, Ildar	D	13
Kim, Soovin	B	12A
Klickstein, Gerald	M	70
Knopp, Seth D.	B	41,42
Kolker, Phillip A.	M	64D
Lambros, Maria	M	41,42
Levy, Byron	D	
Levy, Sharon G.	D	13,12A
Lin, Jolie	D	13,12A
Liotti, Ernest J.	B	
Lisicky, Sandra	M	64B
Locke, John G.	B	65,32E
Lopez-Gonzalez, Monica	D	12
Louie, Gary	B	64E
Loup, Francois	DIPL	61
Lyons, Matthew	B	35
MacDonald, Michael	B	35D
Mack, Ellen	M	66A,66C
Marvine, Jane	M	64B
Mastrian, Stacey L.	D	61
Matchim, David	M	32E
Mathews, Paul	D	13
Mazurek, Drew	B	35C,35G
McGill, Anthony B.	B	64C
Meier, Gustav	DIPL	60
Meister, Blake	B	29
Melancon, Violaine M.	DIPL	41,62A
Metcalfe, Scott	M	35C,35G
Moon, Yong Hi	DIPL	66A
Moran, John	D	67A,12A
Muckenfuss, Robert W.	D	66C
Munds, Philip C.	B	63B
Murai, Hajime Teri	M	60,38
Murphy, Timothy	M	29,47
Needleman, Katherine	B	64B
Norris, Alexander	D	29,47
Olin, James R.	B	63C
Oorts, Paul	D	
Orlando, Courtney Sian	D	13C
Orth, Scott		35C
Ottervik, Jennifer	M	12C
Palmer, Patricia	M	
Parker, Harlan D.	D	60,32
Parker, Laura J.	D	32
Pasternack, Benjamin	DIPL	66A
Pearl, Adam J.	M	67F
Peled, Amit	B	62C
Pevac, Karen	M	
Piccinini, Marina	M	64A
Polochick, Edward L.	M	60,36
Popoli, Gary	D	
Puckett, Joel W.	D	13
Puts, Kevin M.	D	10
Rainbolt, Steven	D	61
Robbins, Hollis	D	
Roberts, Gwyn	B	67C
Rockefeller, John D.	D	
Rothbaum, Christiane	M	
Seter, Ronit	D	12
Shade, Neil Thompson	B	35C
Sharp, William	M	61
Shtarkman, Alexander	D	66A
Skidmore, David	M	65
Slutsky, Boris	M	66A
Smooke, David	D	13
Snyder, Sarah A.	M	
Sokoloff, Laurie	DIPL	64A
Sprenkle, Elam Ray	D	13,12A
Stepansky, Alan	B	62C
Stone, Richard	B	67G
Stone, Stephen C.	D	13
Sutherland, Donald S.	D	66G
Talle, Andrew	D	12
Tetreault, Edward	M	35C,35G
Thakar, Markand	D	60
Thomas, Gary		47,29
Thorndike, Oliver	D	
Thursby, Stephen	D	12
Tolbert, Elizabeth D.	D	14
Tremblay, Christian	D	62A
Tseng, Keng-Yuen	B	62A
Van Sice, Robert	M	65B
Vogt, Sebastian	M	
Walker, John C.	D	66G
Warner, Tony		35G
Webber, Janice E.	M	64C
Weisner, Jeffrey D.	M	62D
Weiss, Susan F.	D	12A,12
Wells, Alison	D	62C,42
Wile, Kip D.	D	13
Wright, Geoffrey	M	45,34,10B
Young, Gene	B	43

MD0700 Prince Georges Community College
Department of Music
301 Largo Rd
Largo, MD 20774-2199
(301) 322-0955 Fax: (301) 322-0549
www.pgcc.edu
E-mail: njudy@pgcc.edu

2 Year Institution, Introductory Courses Only

Chair: Ned Judy, 80A
Dir., Artist/Performance Series: Susan Ricci-Rogel, 80F

PT	Battle, Detra	M	61
PT	Dumm, Mary Elizabeth	M	13A,13,11,66A
Assoc Prof	Judy, Ned	M	13,29,66,34,47
PT	Jurek, Shaun	B	70
PT	Kirkeby, Gary	M	12A,11,61
PT	Linnenbom, Harriett	M	13A,11,66A,66D
PT	Maley, Marshall	M	50,65
PT	Martin, Flora	M	11,36,61
PT	Melkonyan, Magdalina	D	66A,11
PT	Muncy, Robert	M	64A,64E
PT	Park, Kyunghee	D	61
PT	Ricci-Rogel, Susan	M	11,66A,66C
Assoc Prof	Shumway, Angelina	M	11,66D,61,13A
PT	Tucker, Kenneth		66F
PT	Yoo, Hyun Hanna	D	62A

MD0750 St Marys College of Maryland
Department of Music
18952 E Fisher Rd
St Marys City, MD 20686
(240) 895-4498 Fax: (240) 895-4958
www.smcm.edu/music
E-mail: MusicDepartment@smcm.edu

4 Year Institution

Chair: David Froom, 80A
Artistic Dir./Head Performance Activities: Jeffrey Silberschlag, 80F

PT	Adelsberger, Andrew	M	61
PT	Babcock, Beverly		66C,66D
PT	Bourne, Brian	M	63D
PT	Bunn, Michael	M	63D
PT	Cueto, Jose	M	62A
PT	Daglar, Fatma	M	64B
Prof	Froom, David	D	13,10A,10B,10F
PT	Ganz, Brian	M	66A
PT	Garth, Eliza	M	66A

PT	Greitzer, Deborah	M	41,64D,42
PT	Johnson, Karen	M	64A
Assoc Prof	Lambert, Sterling	PhD	12,13B
Assoc Prof	Lawrence, Deborah	PhD	12,20
PT	Malaga, Ed	M	62D
PT	McFarland, Joan	M	61
PT	Murphy, Janice	M	64C
PT	Orban, Suzanne	M	62C
PT	Rende, Jennifer	M	62B
PT	Roman, Orlando	M	70
Prof	Silberschlag, Jeffrey	M	29A,35A,60,38,63A
PT	Spinelli, Donald	M	50,65
PT	Stapleson, Donald	M	46,47,64E,13C
PT	Valerio, Anthony	M	63B
Prof	Vote, Larry	M	60,32,36,61

MD0800 Salisbury University

Department of Music
200 Fulton Hall
1101 Camden Ave
Salisbury, MD 21801
(410) 543-6385   Fax: (410) 548-3002
www.salisbury.edu/MusicDept
E-mail: lecockey@salisbury.edu

4 Year Institution

Chair: Linda E. Cockey, 80A

Lect FT	Bowden, Derek	M	11,66D,66A
Lect PT	Clark, Colleen	M	34A,34D
Prof	Cockey, Linda E.	D	12A,66A,66B,13E
Asst Prof	Cumming, Danielle	D	70,11,41
Lect FT	English, Christopher	B	11
Assoc Prof	Folger, William M.	D	60A,36,40,54
Lect FT	Knier, Lawrence	M	37,13C,63,13K,11
Assoc Prof	Lew, Jackie Chooi-Theng	D	32A,32B,20,32C,66
Lect FT	Murasugi, Sachiho	M	62A,62B,11,13A,51
Lect FT	Nichols, Edward	M	65A,65B,11,34A,34B
Inst PT	Paskova, Lyubov	M	66A,66D
Assoc Prof	Schoyen, Jeffrey G.	D	62C,38,13A,11,62D
Inst PT	Sterling, Amy	M	64C,64E,64B,64D,64A
Prof	Tabor, Jerry N.	D	13,10,29B,47,11
Asst Prof	Wright, John Wesley	M	61,39
Inst PT	Zimmer, Susan	M	66A,66C,11,66G

MD0850 Towson University

Department of Music
8000 York Rd
Towson, MD 21252-0001
(410) 704-2839   Fax: (410) 704-2841
www.towson.edu/music
E-mail: mcriss@towson.edu

4 Year Institution, Graduate School
Member of NASM

Master of Music in Composition, Master of Music in Performance, Master of Science in Music Education

Chair: Eileen M. Hayed, 80A
Dir., Graduate Studies: Luis C. Engelke, 80C
Dir., Graduate Studies: Dana Rothlisberger, 80C
Dir., Admissions: Mary Ann Criss, 80D
Dir., Summer Programs: Melissa McCabe, 80G
Assistant Chair: William Kleinsasser, 80H

PT	Afonasyeva, Yekaterina	M	66D,36,66C
PT	Amato, Patricia	M	36,39
Assoc Prof	Anthony, James	D	11,12,16
Assoc Prof	Ballou, David L.	M	29,53,63A,29A,36
Prof	Barczyk, Cecylia	M	41,62C,32E,51
PT	Barksdale, Alicia	M	32A
PT	Bayes, Michael	B	64E
PT	Bickham, Teri	M	61,39
PT	Brenzel, Darryl L.	B	64E
PT	Brown, Joe Davis	M	63D
PT	Buchanan, Douglas	D	13
PT	Bunn, Michael	M	63D
PT	Cabot, Jennifer C.	M	61
PT	Chiao, Faye	M	13
Assoc Prof	Collister, Phillip	D	61,36,39
PT	Cooke, Julia	M	61
PT	Correlli, Christopher	M	32D
PT	Craig, Mark	M	32E,65
PT	Crawford, Lawrence E.	D	13,66A
Prof	Crawford, Leneida	D	61,39
Other	Criss, Mary Ann	M	
PT	Daglar, Fatma	M	64B,48
Prof	Decker, Michael	M	70,35A,41,47
PT	Derrickson, Keith W.	M	32B
PT	Dierker, John	B	63A,47,53
PT	Dillon, Christopher	D	13
PT	Dvoskin, Victor	B	62D
PT	Eberhardt, Terry N.	M	61
Assoc Prof	Engelke, Luis C.	D	63A,49
PT	Engler, Kyle C.	M	61
PT	Ewell, Laurel A.	D	64A
Prof	Ewell, Terry B.	D	64D,13,64E
PT	Finck, Gabrielle	M	63B
Lect	Fine, R. Samuel	M	12A
PT	Fritts, C. Nelson	D	32
Prof	Hayes, Eileen M.	D	14
PT	Herberman, Steve	B	70
PT	Hernandez, Rene	B	63A,49
PT	Hevia, Lonnie	D	13,13E,13C,10
PT	Holmes, Michael	M	12A
PT	Hong, Ah Yong	M	61
Asst Prof	Howard, Jeffrey	D	62A,41,51
PT	Hultgren, Lori	M	61
PT	Hynson, Bernard	M	32E
PT	Inger, Leah	M	61
Prof	Jothen, Michael	D	32
PT	Jung, Eunice	M	66C
PT	King, Troy	M	70,51
Asst Prof	Kirilov, Kalin	D	13
Prof	Kleinsasser, William	D	10,43
PT	Lackey, Mark A.	D	13
PT	Lagana, Tom	M	70,29A,51
PT	Larson, Nancy	M	12A
Asst Prof	Leach, Brenda	D	38,11,66G
Assoc Prof	Leshnoff, Jonathan	D	13,10
Assoc Prof	Levin, Marguerite	M	64C
Assoc Prof	Luchese, Diane	D	13
Prof	Magaldi, Cristina	D	14C,12A,14,20G,20H
Asst Prof	Mannix, Natalie K.	D	63C,63D,41
PT	Mathews, Teri	M	36
Asst Prof	McCabe, Melissa	D	32
PT	McFalls, James	M	63C,29A,46
Assoc Prof	Mengelkoch, Eva	D	66A,66C,66B,66H,66E
Other	Miliauskas, John	M	37
Assoc Prof	Mueller, Alicia K.	D	32
PT	Murphy, Timothy	M	29,66A,66H
PT	Nichols, Sara	M	64A,48
PT	Norwitz, Sherrie	M	62B
Prof	Phillips, Gerald	D	11,61
PT	Poissant, Michael	M	12A
PT	Ragsdale, Jeremy	M	61,47
PT	Redman, Will	D	12,13
PT	Reed, Jeff	B	62D,47
Prof	Reyes, Reynaldo	M	66A,66C,66B
Lect	Robinson, N. Scott	M	12A,14C,50
Prof	Rothlisberger, Dana	D	32C,37
Asst Prof	Roulet, Patrick E.	D	50,65,66C
PT	Roulet, Rachel	M	66C
PT	Russo, Frank	AA	65
Prof	Schmidt, Carl B.	D	11,12
PT	Sheehan, Aaron	M	61
PT	Szabo, Zoltan	D	62A
PT	Tetreault, Edward	M	35
PT	Trudel, Eric	B	47,53
PT	Van Evera, Angeline Smith	M	12A,12C
PT	Wilson, Granberry	M	61
PT	Winfield, Jeffrey	M	36
PT	Zolper, Stephen T.	D	13

MD0900 United States Naval Academy

Department of Music/Music Activities
Alumni Hall
675 Decatur Rd
Annapolis, MD 21402-1309
(410) 293-2439   Fax: (410) 293-3218
www.usna.edu/Music
E-mail: woodall@usna.edu

4 Year Institution

Chair: Aaron Smith, 80A

	Bauchspies, Cindy	B	31A,36
	Maxwell, Monte	M	66G,38,36,31A,51
	Scott, Karla	M	36,31A
	Smith, Aaron	D	31A,36,54,40

MD1000 Univ of Maryland-Baltimore Cnty

Department of Music
1000 Hilltop Cir
Baltimore, MD 21250
(410) 455-2942   Fax: (410) 455-1181
www.umbc.edu
E-mail: velli@umbc.edu

4 Year Institution

Chair: E. Michael Richards, 80A
Associate Chair: Joseph C. Morin, 80H

Inst PT	Bange, Darren R.	M	63C
Inst PT	Beck, Gina C.	M	20D
Lect	Beith, Nancy S.	M	66D
Inst PT	Cameron, Wayne C.	M	38,41,63A
Asst Prof	Cella, Lisa M.	D	64A,13C,41
Inst PT	Dove, Barry B.		65
Prof	Dusman, Linda J.	DMA	10,13
Inst PT	Forshee, Zane F.	M	70
Inst PT	Franklin, Rachel F.	D	66A,66D
Asst Prof	Goldstein, Thomas	M	47,50,65
Inst PT	Hall, Michael J.	M	63C
Inst PT	Hawley, Thomas E.	D	66G
Inst PT	Hossain, Hamid	M	20D
Other	Jackson, Janice R.	M	61
Asst Prof	Kim-Boyle, David	D	34,35C,35G
Inst PT	King, Thomas D.	B	61
Inst PT	Ladd, Gita	B	41,42,62C
Inst PT	Lagana, Thomas V.	M	70
Adj Assoc Prof	Lambros, Maria	M	62B,42
Inst PT	Lande, Vladimir	M	64B
Inst PT	Love, Jason L.	M	60
Inst PT	Markovic-Prakash, Lorriana	D	61
Lect	Morin, Joseph C.	D	12
Inst PT	Pollauf, Jacqueline M.	B	62E
Assoc Prof	Richards, E. Michael	D	64C,60,41,38
Inst PT	Ruas, Laura M.	M	41,42,62D
Assoc Prof	Rubin, Anna I.	D	10,34
Asst Prof	Smith, David	M	36,39,60,61
Prof	Smith, Stuart Saunders	D	13,10
Inst PT	Tanosaki, Kazuko	D	13,20C
Inst PT	Tremblay, Christian	D	41,42,62A
Inst PT	Villanueva, Jari	M	47
Lect	Wonneberger, Alan A.	B	34D
Asst Prof	Yoshioka, Airi	D	32,41,51,62A

MD1010 Univ of Maryland

School of Music
2110 Clarice Smith Center
College Park, MD 20742-1620
(301) 405-5549   Fax: (301) 314-9504
www.music.umd.edu
E-mail: musicadmissions@umd.edu

4 Year Institution, Graduate School
Member of NASM

Master of Arts in Music Education, Master of Arts in Music Theory, Master of Arts in Ethnomusicology, Master of Music in Composition, Master of Music in Performance, Master of Music in Music Education, PhD in Ethnomusicology, PhD in Music Theory, PhD in Music Education, DMA in Composition, DMA in Conducting, DMA in Performance, PhD in Musicology, Master of Arts in History & Literature

Director: Robert L. Gibson, 80A
Dir., Graduate Studies: Gerald Fischbach, 80C
Associate Director: Lori DeBoy, 80H
Associate Director: Michael P. Hewitt, 80H

Adj Lect	Adkins, Elizabeth	D	62A
Adj Lect	Ames, Anthony	M	65
Adj Lect	Baldwin, Tom	B	62D
Prof	Balthrop, Carmen A.	M	61,39
Lect PT	Cavallaro, Giorgia	M	70
Adj Lect	Cigan, Paul		64C
Prof	Cossa, Dominic	M	39,61
Prof	Dedova, Larissa	D	66A
Prof	DeLio, Thomas	D	13,10
Assoc Prof	DiLutis, Robert	M	64C
Vstng Asst Prof	Doyle, Jennifer	D	32
Adj Lect	Dudley, Christopher	B	63C
Adj Lect	Dumaine, Stephen	B	63D
Adj Lect	Edwards, Mahiri		20A,20B
Asst Prof	Elpus, Kenneth	D	32D,32G,36
Prof	Elsing, Evelyn	M	41,62C
Lect PT	Evans, William	M	34
Prof	Fischbach, Gerald	D	62A
Adj Lect	Foster, Daniel	DIPL	62B
Assoc Prof	Fry, James	D	13,10F,10
Adj Lect	Fuller, Sarah	M	62E
Assoc Prof	Gekker, Chris	M	70,29
Prof	Gibson, Robert L.	D	13,10,45,43
Artist in Res	Gilliam, Jauvon	B	65
Lect	Goldman, Aaron	B	64A
Assoc Prof	Gowen, Bradford	M	66A
Artist in Res	Guilford, Matthew	M	63C
Prof	Haggh-Huglo, Barbara	D	12A,12
Asst Prof	Haldey, Olga	D	12,12A,11,14
Assoc Prof	Hanninen, Dora A.	D	13
Artist in Res	Heinemen, Sue	M	64D
Adj Lect	Hendrickson, Steven	B	63A
Assoc Prof	Hewitt, Michael P.	D	60,32,38
Assoc Prof	Hill, Mark	M	64B
Adj Lect	Hinkle, Lee	D	65,50
Lect PT	Holly, Janice E.	M	12C
Adj Prof	Huglo, Michel	D	12A
Adj Lect	Jones, David	B	64C
Adj Lect	Kellner, Steve	M	63D
Assoc Prof	King, Richard G.	D	11,12A,12,20G,12C
Adj Lect	Kunkel, Gerald	B	70
Inst	Layton, Richard Douglas	D	13
Lect	Lee, Justina	M	39
Prof	Mabbs, Linda	M	39,61
Prof	Maclary, Edward	D	60A,36
Prof Emeritus	Major, Leon	B	39
Adj Lect	McReynolds, Timothy	D	66C,66A
Assoc Prof	Miller, Gregory	B	49,63B
Assoc Prof	Montgomery, Janet	D	32,32A,32B
Prof	Montgomery, William L.	D	41,64A
Prof	Moss, Lawrence	D	10,13,10F
Adj Lect	Mulcahy, Craig	B	63C
Assoc Prof	Murdock, Katherine	B	62B
Adj Lect	Okamoto, Kyoko	B	20C
Adj Lect	Olcott, Nicholas	B	39
Adj Lect	Oppelt, Robert	B	62D
Lect	Osterloh, Elijah	M	37
Adj Lect	Ozment, Jon	M	66A
Prof	Page, Cleveland	D	66A,66B
Lect	Patterson, Benjamin	B	63C
Adj Lect	Powell, Timothy J.		64E
Prof Emeritus	Provine, Robert C.	D	12,14
Lect	Randall, Martha	M	61,39
Adj Lect	Redd, Chuck		65
Adj Prof	Regni, Albert G.	M	64E
Asst Prof	Rios, Fernando	D	20H
Assoc Prof	Ross, James	DIPL	38,60B
Prof	Salness, David	DIPL	62A,41
Emeritus	Sandstrom, Boden	D	14,15
Lect	Shin, Eric	B	65
Prof	Sloan, Rita	M	66C,66A,41
Adj Lect	Slowik, Kenneth	D	67A
Assoc Prof	Sparks, L. Richmond	D	37,60B
Assoc Prof	Stern, James	D	62A,41,42
Adj Lect	Suadin, I. Ketut	B	20I
Adj Lect	Teie, David	M	62C
Adj Lect	Trahan, Kathleen	M	64A
Assoc Prof	Tsong, Mayron K.	D	13A,66A,66
Prof	Vadala, Christopher	M	47,64E,53,29
Lect	Volchok, Mikhail	D	66A
Assoc Prof	Votta, Michael	D	60B
Asst Prof	Warfield, Patrick R.	D	12
Prof	Wexler, Richard	D	12A,12,55,29A
Assoc Prof	Wilson, Gran	M	61,39
Assoc Prof	Wilson, Mark	D	13,10F,10
Prof	Witzleben, J. Lawrence	D	14,20,20C
Prof	Ziegler, Delores	M	61,39
Adj Lect	Zimmerman, Daniel		12A

MD1020 Univ of Maryland-Eastern Shore

Department of Fine Arts, Music
Ella Fitzgerald Ctr for Perf. Arts
Princess Anne, MD 21853
(410) 651-6487   Fax: (410) 651-7959
www.umes.edu
E-mail: ersatchell@umes.edu

4 Year Institution

Chair: Ernest R. Satchell, 80A

Inst	Harleston, Sheila C.	D	60,36,66A,66D
Inst	Knier, Veronica T.	M	13B,13E,66
Inst	Lamkin, John R.	D	10F,37,47,63

MD1050 Washington Bible College
Department of Music
6511 Princess Garden Pkwy
Lanham, MD 20706-3538
(301) 552-1400   Fax: (301) 552-2775
www.bible.edu
E-mail: jwood@bible.edu

4 Year Institution

Chair: Janice Kilgore Wood, 80A

FT	Kilgore Wood, Janice	D	13C,66A,36,66B,31A
Adj	Mentzel, Michael G.	D	61
Adj	Reynolds, David B.	M	70
Adj	Smith, Bruce	M	65
Adj	Walker, Angela	M	61
Adj	Wolfe-Ralph, Carol	D	66A,66G,66B,66C,12A

MD1100 Washington College
Department of Music
300 Washington Ave
Chestertown, MD 21620-1438
(410) 778-7838   Fax: (410) 810-7160
www.washcoll.edu
E-mail: kschweitzer2@washcoll.edu

4 Year Institution

Chair: Kenneth Schweitzer, 80A
Dir., Artist/Performance Series: Kate Bennett, 80F

Lect	Anderson, Catherine Sentman	M	61
Lect	Anthony, Tom		70,62D
Lect	Buxton, Donald	M	51
Lect	Buxton, Merideth	M	62A,62B
Prof	Clarke, Garry E.	M	13,10F,10,12A
Lect	Crossen-Richardson, Phyllis	D	64
Lect	Harvey, Anthony	B	70
Lect	Kim, Eun Hae	D	66A
Lect	Kim, Grace	M	66A
Asst Prof	Leupold, John K.	D	13
Asst Prof	McCollum, Jonathan	D	63C,63D,11,12,20
Asst Prof	Schweitzer, Kenneth	D	20,29,34,35,11
Lect	Wharton, Keith	B	63A

ME0150 Bates College
Department of Music
Olin Art Center
75 Russell St
Lewiston, ME 04240-6044
(207) 786-6135   Fax: (207) 786-8335
www.bates.edu
E-mail: aodom@bates.edu

4 Year Institution

Chair: James P. Parakilas, 80A
Chair, Concert Committee: Gina Andrea Fatone, 80F

PT	Albert, Michael		64B
PT	Antonacos, Anastasia	D	66A
PT	Boardman, Gregory	B	20G,62A
PT	Butler, Erica E.	B	20H
Asst Prof	Chapman, Dale E.	D	12,13,29
PT	Chute, Christina	M	62C
PT	Corrie, John H.	M	13C,36,61,66G,66H
PT	Ebersold, Timothy	B	64D
Asst Prof	Fatone, Gina Andrea	D	13,14,20,20D
PT	Furman, Carol	B	64C,48
PT	Furman, John	B	63A,49
Artist in Res	Glazer, Frank		66A
PT	Grover, Stephen		65,66
PT	Jerosch, Anita	M	63D
PT	Jerosch, Sebastian	M	63C
PT	Labrecque, Kenneth J.	M	70
PT	Landis, Margery	M	63B
PT	LaPerna, Eric		20B
PT	Libby, Amos	B	20E,20B
PT	Loughman, Greg	B	62D
Prof	Matthews, Bill	D	13,10,29,34
Asst Prof	Miura, Hiroya	D	10,13,38
PT	Naruse, Chiharu		66A
Prof	Parakilas, James P.	D	13,11,42,12
PT	Pontbriand, David		20E
PT	Rubino, George		62D
PT	Scarpelli, Bonnie D.	B	61
	Shostak, Anthony	B	20G
PT	Snow, Thomas	M	29,47,46,66A
PT	Tripp, Krysia	M	64A
PT	Wells, David	B	64E
Asst Prof	Woodruff, Jennifer A.	D	13,14

ME0200 Bowdoin College
Department of Music
Gibson Hall
9200 College Station
Brunswick, ME 04011-8492
(207) 725-3321   Fax: (207) 725-3748
www.bowdoin.edu
E-mail: rgreenle@bowdoin.edu

4 Year Institution

Chair: Robert K. Greenlee, 80A
Dean for Academic Affairs: Cristle Collins Judd, 80A

PT	Adams, Julia		62B
PT	Antolini, Anthony		36,13A,66D
PT	Astrachan, Christina		61
PT	Beacham, Karen		64C
Asst Prof	Birenbaum Quintero, Michael		14,20H,31F
PT	Bowder, Naydene		66A,66H
PT	Chute, Christina	M	62C
PT	Cornils, Ray		66G
PT	Fogg, Matthew		66A
PT	Graffam, Allen		63A
Prof	Greenlee, Robert K.	D	60,36,12A,12,55
PT	Grover, Steve		65,66A
Prof	Hunter, Mary K.	D	13A,13,11,12A,12
PT	Jerosch, Anita		63,49
PT	Johnson, Timothy		61
PT	Johnstone, John		70
PT	Joseph, David		64D
PT	Kecskemethy, Stephen		62A
PT	Lopez, George		66A,38,42
PT	Loughman, Greg	B	62D
PT	Mauceri, Frank		47,64E
Asst Prof	McMullen, Tracy		29,15,12,53,14A
PT	McNerney, Kathleen		64B,48
PT	Monke, Kirsten		62B
PT	Morneau, John P.		37,64C,64E
PT	Moulton, Joyce		66A,66B,66C
PT	Peltola, Gilbert		64C,64E
PT	Pierce, Karen		61
PT	Scarpelli, Bonnie		61
Prof Emeritus	Schwartz, Elliott S.	D	10F,10,11,12A,41
Asst Prof	Shende, Vineet	D	10,13,20C,20E,31E
PT	Stein, Dean A.		62A,51
PT	Tripp, Krysia		64A
PT	Watkinson, Christopher L.		13L,34D,35D,35G
PT	Wittner, Gary		70

ME0250 Colby College
Department of Music
5670 Mayflower Hill
Waterville, ME 04901-8856
(207) 859-5671   Fax: (207) 859-5635
www.colby.edu/music
E-mail: vlwood@colby.edu

4 Year Institution

Chair: Jonathan F. Hallstrom, 80A
Coord., Artist/Performance Series, Academic Secretary: Vivian Lemieux, 80F
Dir., Summer Programs: Jacques R. Moore, 80G

Other	Albert, Michael P.	M	64B
Other	Bates, Jennifer	M	61
Other	Beacham, Graybert	M	62A,62B
Other	Bishop, Richard	B	70
Assoc Prof	Borgerding, Todd Michael	D	13,12A,55B
	Buzy, Marilyn		65
Other	Capps, Angela	M	64D
Other	Dimow, Carl	B	70
Other	Ericson, Margaret D.	M	16
Other	Fields, D. Loren		63B
Other	French, Annabeth	B	61,66G
Assoc Prof	Funahashi, Yuri Lily	D	66A
Assoc Prof	Hallstrom, Jonathan F.	D	13,60,10,38,45
Other	Jerosch, Sebastian	B	63C
Other	Leighton, Mark	M	70
Prof	Machlin, Paul S.	D	12A,36,20G,29A
	Macksoud, Mark G.		65
Other	Maroon, Gayle E.	B	66A
Asst Prof	Nuss, Steven R.	D	13,14

Directory of Institutions

Other	Rabata, Nicole		64A
Other	Ross, Paul	DIPL	62C
Assoc Prof	Saunders, Steven E.	D	11,12A,12,66H
Other	Thomas, Eric B.	B	37,47,64C,64E,53
Other	Tipton, Mark	M	63A
Other	Westin, Joann		66A

ME0270 College of the Atlantic
Department of Music
105 Eden St
Bar Harbor, ME 04609
(207) 288-5015   Fax: (207) 288-2328
www.coa.edu
E-mail: jcooper@coa.edu

4 Year Institution

Chair, Music & Media: John H. Cooper, 80A

FT	Andrews, Nancy	M	35B,35C,35F,45,20G
PT	Beal, Elmer	M	14
PT	Bennett, Michael	B	65,50
PT	Colter, Nancy	B	66A
FT	Cooper, John H.	M	10,29,13,64E,10F
PT	Morse, Kevin	B	70
PT	Sellers, Lucy Bell	B	54
PT	Wallace, Thomas	B	36,61

ME0340 Univ of Maine-Augusta
Department of Music
46 University Dr
Augusta, ME 04330
(207) 632-3385   Fax: (207) 621-3293
www.uma.edu
E-mail: timothy.weir@maine.edu

4 Year Institution

Dean: Greg Fahy, 80A
Coordinator: Tim Weir, 80A

Lect	Clancy, Gary		47,70,53,35
Lect	Drown, Steve	B	35G,34D
Lect	Espinoza, Andres	M	47,65
Lect	Fogg, Matthew	B	66A,13
Lect	Gallagher, Marcia		36,61
Lect	Grover, Steve	B	47,65,66A,29,13
Lect	Hughes, Scott	B	70,47
Lect	Jenkins, Pamela	M	64A,64C,64E,32,13E
Lect	Jerosch, Anita	M	32,12A,13A
Lect	Jerosch, Sebastian	B	63C,11
Lect	Johnson, Timothy	B	36,61
Lect	Loughman, Greg	B	70
Lect	Mauceri, Frank	D	10,13,12B
Prof	Moseley, William	M	12A,47,64A,35C,29
Prof	Nelson, Richard	D	10,34,13,29,47
Lect	Saeverud, Trond	D	62
Lect	Thompson, Bob	B	47,70,53,35
Prof	Weir, Tim	D	47,63A,29,32E
Lect	Wells, David	M	47,64E

ME0410 Univ of Maine-Farmington
Department of Visual & Perf Art
238 Main St.
Farmington, ME 04938-1911
(207) 778-7072   Fax: (207) 778-7247
www.umf.maine.edu
E-mail: pane@maine.edu

4 Year Institution

Chair: Sarah R. Maline, 80A

Prof	Aguilar, Gustavo	D	53,34D
Prof	Carlsen, Philip	D	13,10,29A,38,34
Lect	Jerosch, Anita	M	37,63C
Lect	McInnes, Bruce G.	M	36
Prof	Pane, Steven	D	12A,66A,12,12B,11
Lect	Saeverud, Trond	M	38,62A

ME0420 Univ of Maine-Fort Kent
Department of Performing Arts
23 University Dr
Fort Kent, ME 04743-1292
(207) 834-7506   Fax: (207) 834-7503
www.umfk.maine.edu
E-mail: brickman@maine.edu

4 Year Institution

Chair, Arts & Humanities: Scott T. Brickman, 80A

Assoc Prof	Brickman, Scott T.	D	14C,13,32B,10B,66D

ME0430 Univ of Maine-Machias
Department of Music
201 Powers Hall
9 O'Brien Ave
Machias, ME 04654-1397
(207) 255-1229   Fax: (207) 255-4864
www.umm.maine.edu
E-mail: gnichols@maine.edu

4 Year Institution, Also Offering 2 Year Programs & Degrees

Chair, Arts & Letters: Kay Kimball, 80A

Adj	Caya, Patricia	M	61
Adj	Cook, Alan		70,47
Emeritus	Guy, Christine	B	61
Inst	Ingalls, Duane	B	65,53,46
Adj	Lapham, Barbara		62C
Adj	NeCastro, Vicki	B	66A
Assoc Prof	Nichols, Eugene C.	M	13,36,37,46,12A
Adj	Saeverud, Trond	D	11,13A,41,36

ME0440 Univ of Maine-Orono
School of Performing Arts-Music
5788 Class of 1944 Hall
Orono, ME 04469-5788
(207) 581-4700   Fax: (207) 581-4701
www.umaine.edu/spa
E-mail: music@maine.edu

4 Year Institution, Graduate School
Member of NASM

Master of Music in Performance, Master of Music in Music Education

Chair: Beth Wiemann, 80A

Inst PT	Adams, James		62D
Assoc Prof	Artesani, Laura	D	12A,66C,15,32B,32C
Inst PT	Barrett, Dan	D	13E,63C
Inst PT	Birch, Kevin		66G,66H
Assoc Prof	Burt, Jack W.	D	13C,49,63A
Inst PT	Corliss, Heidi E.	M	36
Prof	Cox, Dennis K.	D	60A,12A,36
Inst PT	Downing, Elizabeth A.	M	64A,42
Prof	Farnham, Curvin G.	M	60B,32E,37
Prof	Hall, Louis O.	D	60,32,64B,64E
Prof	Hallman, Ludlow B.	M	36,61,39
Inst PT	Hwalek, Ginger Y.	D	42,66D
Inst PT	Kenefic, Richard	M	70
Assoc Prof	Lidral, Karel	D	13B,47,64E,29B
Inst PT	MacDonald, Elizabeth	M	64D
Prof	Marrs, Stuart	D	12A,65,50,34
Prof	Ogle, Nancy Ellen	M	39,61
Inst PT	Pendleton, Karen A.	M	61
Inst PT	Sargent, Glen		64E
Inst PT	Silver, Noreen	D	42,32E,13C,62C
Prof	Silver, Phillip A.	D	12A,66C,66A,11
Inst PT	Sly, Marcia Gronewold	M	61
Inst PT	Solomon, Marisa	D	13C
Assoc Prof	Voronietsky, Baycka	M	66A,66B,66C,13A
Lect	White, Christopher G.	M	37,60,32E
Prof	Wieck, Anatole	D	38,62A,62B,11
Prof	Wiemann, Beth	D	10F,64C,34,10A,13D
Inst PT	Wubbenhorst, Thomas M.	D	50,65

ME0500 Univ of Southern Maine

School of Music
Corthell Hall
37 College Ave
Gorham, ME 04038
(207) 780-5265   Fax: (207) 780-5527
www.usm.maine.edu/mus
E-mail: music@usm.maine.edu

4 Year Institution
Member of NASM

Master of Music in Composition, Master of Music in Performance, Master of Music in Conducting, Master of Music in Music Education, Master of Music in Jazz Studies

Interim Director: Scott Harris, 80A
Dir., Music Promotions: Mary E. Snell, 80F
Dir., Summer Programs: Monique M. Larocque, 80G

Adj	Astrachan, Christina	M	61
Adj	Austin, Trent R.		63A
Assoc Prof	Boden, John C.	M	63
PT	Boyer, Neil V.	B	64B
Adj	Bucci, Thomas	M	66A
Assoc Prof	Chickering, Ellen	M	61
Asst Prof	Christiansen, Paul V.	D	12
Prof Emeritus	Cole, Ronald F.	D	12A,12,66A
Adj	Cornils, Ray		66G
PT	Crook, Keith R.	M	13,70
Adj	Diehl, Brian L.		63C
Prof	Fithian, Bruce S.		39,12A,61
Lect PT	Goodrich, Jara S.	B	62E
Adj	Goulet, David		61
Adj	Grammar, Kathleen		61
PT	Gunn, Nancy E.	D	13
Adj	Harris, Les		65
Assoc Prof	Harris, Scott	D	13
Adj	James, Judith R.	M	61
Assoc Prof	Kargul, Laura J.	D	66A
PT	Kaschub, Alan R.	M	13
Assoc Prof	Kaschub, Michele E.	D	32
PT	Keef, Ardith A.	M	13A,11,64D
PT	Kissack, Christine W.	M	66B,66D
Assoc Prof	Lehmann, Robert A.	M	60,62
Adj	Liva, Ferdinand R.		62A,62B
PT	Manduca, Mark W.	M	63C,11
Prof	Martin, Peter J.	D	60,32C,37
Adj	Milnarik, Michael S.		63D
Assoc Prof	Oberholtzer, Christopher W.	M	29,47,63C
Adj	O'Dell, Timothy J.	D	29,64E
Assoc Prof	Packales, Joseph	D	13,10F,10
Assoc Prof	Parchman, Thomas	D	13A,13,64C
Adj	Reichert, Ed C.		54
Adj	Rines, Elizabeth B.		63A
Adj	Rosenblum, Jean K.		64A
Adj	Rounds, William	B	62C
Prof	Russell, Robert J.	D	12A,36,60
Adj	Smith, Malcolm S.		61
Lect PT	Smith, Nancy	B	65,50
Adj	Snow, Michelle H.	M	47,61
Asst Prof	Sonenberg, Daniel M.	D	10A,13F,13C,10,13
Lect PT	Street, William	B	64E
Adj	Suchanek, Bronislaw	B	47,62D
PT	Vaillancourt, Scott J.		13A,12A
Adj	Wittner, Gary D.		70
Adj	Yauger, Margaret		61

MI0050 Adrian College

Department of Music
110 S Madison St
Adrian, MI 49221
(517) 264-3868   Fax: (517) 264-3521
www.adriancollegemusic.org
E-mail: thodgman@adrian.edu

4 Year Liberal Arts Institution

Chair: Thomas Hodgman, 80A

PT	Benton, Robert	M	63D
PT	Bitz, Lori	M	42,63A
PT	Conway, Colleen	D	32,63B
PT	Day, David	M	63C
Assoc Prof	Dodson, John	M	10,12,38
PT	Eder, Kristen	D	61
Asst Prof	Ford, Peter	M	13
PT	Ford, Shannon	M	64C,64E
PT	Gartz, Michael	M	66C,66G
PT	Graber, Eric	M	61
PT	Green, Donna	M	61
PT	Hill-Kretzer, Kelly	M	20,64A
Prof	Hodgman, Thomas	D	32,36,40
PT	Johnson, Cecilia	M	62,51
Asst Prof	Kantorski, Valrie	M	66A,66D
PT	Keaster, Aaron	M	62D
PT	Kim, Minjung	D	66A,66C
Asst Prof	Kretzer, Scott	M	37,41,65
PT	Lange, Richard	M	41,70
Asst Prof	Major, Elizabeth	M	11,39,61
Assoc Prof	Marks, Martin	D	37,46,32
PT	Marks, Melissa	M	64B
PT	Raschiatore, Lisa C.	D	13A
PT	Smith, Sue	M	52,54

MI0100 Albion College

Department of Music
611 E. Porter St
Albion, MI 49224
(517) 629-0481   Fax: (517) 629-0784
www.albion.edu/music
E-mail: music@albion.edu

4 Year Institution
Member of NASM

Chair: Samuel D. McIlhagga, 80A

Assoc Prof	Abbott, David	D	12A,66A,42
Inst Adj	Abo, Takeshi	M	62A,62B,51
Prof	Balke, Maureen	D	13C,39,61
Prof	Ball, James	D	29A,38,47,63D,60B
Inst Adj	Benner, Emily	M	61,39
Inst Adj	Cetkovic, Igor	M	62C
Inst Adj	Doyle, Robert	M	61
Inst Adj	Duda, Cynthia M.	M	64D
Inst Adj	Grafius, Ellen	B	62E
Inst Adj	Hoksbergen, Ross	M	63A
Vstng Asst Prof	Jensen-Abbott, Lia	D	13,66A
Inst Adj	King, John	M	61
Inst Adj	Lee, A. Ram	M	66C
Inst Adj	Livesay, Jackie	M	66G
Assoc Prof	McIlhagga, Samuel D.	M	10F,37,14C,32E
Inst Adj	Merciers, Meghan	M	64C
Inst Adj	Otto, James	M	63B
Inst Adj	Palmer, Dan	B	70
Asst Prof	Parr, Clayton G.	DMA	36,40,60A,32D
Inst Adj	Renteria, Gabriel		64B
Inst Adj	Solero, Elena	M	66C
Inst Adj	Streng, Bobby	M	64E
Inst Adj	TenBrink, Karen	M	36
Inst Adj	Williams, Larry	B	41,70
Inst Adj	Wulff, Steve	M	65,50

MI0150 Alma College

Department of Music
614 W Superior St
Alma, MI 48801
(989) 463-7167   Fax: (989) 463-7979
www.alma.edu
E-mail: rileyr@alma.edu

4 Year Institution
Member of NASM

Chair: Raymond G. Riley, 80A

Artist in Res	Abo, Takeshi	D	62A,51
Inst PT	Burdick, Barbara E.	D	61
Asst Prof	Gross, Murray	D	38,13,60B,10,20
Inst PT	Melendez, Carlos	B	47,70
Prof	Messing, Scott	D	11,12A,66A,16,13A
Vstng Inst	Miller, Tess Anissa	DMA	64A,11,41
Prof	Nichols, Will	D	60,36,61,39
Artist in Res	Patterson, Anthony	B	66A,66C
Inst PT	Riley, Kathleen	M	66D
Prof	Riley, Raymond G.	D	66A,13,34,34H
Inst	Walker, Vicki	M	61
Asst Prof	Zerbe, David	M	65,37,50,32C,32E

MI0200 Alpena Community College
Department of Music
666 Johnson St
Alpena, MI 49707
(989) 358-7229
www.alpenacc.edu
E-mail: beyerl@alpenacc.edu

2 Year Institution, Introduction Courses Only

Music Contact: Loretta Beyer, 80A

	Beyer, Loretta	B	13,66A,32B,11
	Hubbard, Mary Ann	M	41,64A
	Schubert, John	M	11,47,13G

MI0250 Andrews University
Department of Music
207 Hamel Hall
Berrien Springs, MI 49104-0230
(269) 471-3555   Fax: (269) 471-6339
www.andrews.edu/Music
E-mail: music@andrews.edu

4 Year Institution, Graduate School
Member of NASM

Master of Arts in Music, Master of Music in Performance, Master of Music in Conducting, Master of Music in Music Education

Music Contact: Carlos Flores, 80A

Asst Prof	Caceres, Marcelo	M	66A,66B,66C,66D
Assoc Prof	Doukhan, Lilianne	D	12A,12,14,31A,12C
Prof	Flores, Carlos	D	13,10,35,34,10F
Asst Prof	Gonzalez, Claudio	D	38,60B,10F,20,12A
Asst Prof	Lindsay, Julia	M	11,61,54,39
Assoc Prof	Logan, Kenneth	D	66G,34,10,10F,31A
Asst Prof	Mitchell, Alan	M	60,32,37,49,48
Prof	Trynchuck, Carla	M	62,41,51
Assoc Prof	Zork, Stephen	M	36,61,60,10,39

I0300 Aquinas College
Department of Music
1607 Robinson Rd SE
Grand Rapids, MI 49506-1799
(616) 632-2413   Fax: (616) 732-4487
www.aquinas.edu
E-mail: mccarbar@aquinas.edu

4 Year Liberal Arts Institution, Graduate School

Master of Arts in Teaching, Masters in Education

Chair: Barbara Witham McCargar, 80A
Dir., Summer Programs: Paul S. Brewer, 80G
Associate Provost: Nanette Clatterbuck, 80H

Lect	Alley, Gregory	M	63A,32E
Lect	Anzivino, Steve	B	65,50,43
	Austin, Paul	D	63B
Lect	Bergeron, Andrew	M	70,41
Adj Asst Prof	Biser, Larry	M	34B,12A,40,66G
Lect	Blakemore, Linda	M	32E
	Bohnhorst, Brendan	ABD	63D
	Bratton, Susanna	M	64C
Assoc Prof	Brewer, Paul S.	D	60B,37,32E,29,63C
Lect	Connell, Robin	D	66A,13
	Erickson, Thomas	M	62D
Lect	Hillyard, Mary	B	62C
Asst Prof Adj	Hurd, Mary	M	66A,66B,66C,66D,13A
	Hyde, Edye Evans	M	61
	Hyde, Michael	B	70
	Joslin, Art	D	61
	Karamanov, Vincent	B	64D
	Lockwood, Tom	M	64E,70
Asst Prof Adj	MacNaughton, Roger	B	66A,13G,32F
Lect	Maret, Carmen	M	64A
Assoc Prof	McCargar, Barbara Witham	M	11,61,39
	Redmon, Nursun	M	62A,62B
Lect	Redmon, Steve	M	32E,51
	Rehl, Mark	A	35G
	Sherman, Ellen	M	64B
Lect	Sinigos, Louis	M	65,50,43

	Streng, Richard	M	32E
Lect	Wakeman, Forrest	ABD	66A
Assoc Prof Adj	Webb, Mark	D	63,32C,32D,32E,11
Lect	Wells, Greg	M	32E
Assoc Prof Emeritus	Williams, Catherine	M	66A,13C
Senior Lect	Wiltse, Stephanie	A	44

MI0350 Calvin College
Department of Music
1795 Knollcrest Circle SE
Grand Rapids, MI 49546-4404
(616) 526-6253   Fax: (616) 526-6266
www.calvin.edu
E-mail: music@calvin.edu

4 Year Liberal Arts Institution
Member of NASM

Chair: Bert Polman, 80A
Music Events Coordinator: Heather H. Rodgers, 80F
Dir., Special Events: Jeff Stob, 80F

Adj	Akins, Keaton Damir		47
Adj	Alley, Greg	M	63A
Adj	Bays, Jay	B	66C,61
Adj	Beck, Matt		65
Adj	Brettschneider, William	B	70
Adj	Britsch, Richard	B	63B
Adj	Brown, Jill Marie	M	48,64A
Adj	Burch, Dwight	M	63D
Adj	Colpean, Elizabeth		62E
Adj	DeYoung, Tim	B	64D
Asst Prof	Engle, Tiffany J.	D	64E,60B,37,32E
Prof	Fuentes, David	D	13,10F,10
Adj	Gomez, Kathleen	M	64B
Asst Prof	Hash, Phillip M.	D	32
Adj	Hoisington, Linda	M	66A
Adj	Hovnanian, Michael Aram	M	62D
Adj	Huizenga, Trudi	D	61
Prof	Kim, Hyesook	D	66A,66B,11,42
Adj	Krummel, Karen	M	62C
Adj	Malefyt, Norma	AB	66A
Adj	Martin, David J.	M	70
Adj	Mustert, Betty	M	66A
Assoc Prof	Navarro, Joel Magus P.	M	36,60A
Asst Prof	Nordling, Robert	B	38
Prof	Polman, Bert	D	31,11,20
Assoc Prof	Reimer, David	D	11,32E,42,62A,41
Prof	Sawyer, Charsie Randolph	D	61,36
Adj	Scanlan, Roger	D	61
Prof	Shangkuan, Pearl	D	60A,36
Assoc Prof	Steele, Timothy	D	11,12
Adj	Tolbert, Clinton		36
Adj	Van Kooten, Jan	M	13
Adj	VanBecker, Leslie	M	62B
Adj	Vandenberg, Lavonne	B	66A
Adj	Varineau, Gwen	B	66C
Adj	Varineau, John	D	64C
Adj	Walhout, Lisa	M	61
Adj	Walvoord, Jennifer R.	D	62A
Adj	Werkema, Jason	D	70
Adj	Wiltse, Stephanie	A	44
Prof	Witvliet, John	D	36,31A
Asst Prof	Wolters-Fredlund, Benita	D	13,11,12A
Adj	Wunder, Patricia	M	62A

MI0400 Central Michigan University
School of Music
Music Bldg
Room 162
Mount Pleasant, MI 48859
(989) 774-3281   Fax: (989) 774-3766
www.music.cmich.edu
E-mail: zeneb1ms@cmich.edu

4 Year Institution, Graduate School
Member of NASM

Master of Music in Composition, Master of Music in Performance, Master of Music in Conducting, Master of Music in Music Education, Master of Music in Piano Pedagogy

Director: Randi L. L'Hommedieu, 80A
Coord., Graduate Studies: Daniel L. Steele, 80C
Dir., Music Events: John Jacobson, 80F
Assistant Director: MaryBeth Minnis, 80H

Assoc Prof	Batcheller, James C.	D	37
Asst Prof	Batzner, Jay C.	DMA	13,10,34,10A,13F
Asst Prof	Binkley, Lindabeth	D	64B,41,48,11
Assoc Prof	Bonnell, Bruce M.	D	63B
	Burgess, Scott		34,34D
Prof Emeritus	Caldwell, J. Timothy	M	61,32I
Prof	Campbell, Jennifer L.	D	11,12,20
Prof	Clifton, Keith E.	D	12,11,20
Prof	Cox, Mark	D	63D,41
Lect	DeRoche, Brad	D	70
Prof	Egler, Steven	D	12A,66H,66G,31A
Assoc Prof Emerita	Enman, Cora	M	39,61
Lect	Fedewa, Edward	M	62D
Assoc Prof	Fiste, James A.	D	62C
Assoc Prof	Gamble, Sue G.	D	32B,32C,32H,32
Prof	Gillingham, David R.	D	13A,13,10F,10
Prof	Gumm, Alan	D	13A,32
Asst Prof	Harding, Scott R.	D	10A,13C,29A,65,13A
Asst Prof	Henderson, Donald O.	D	61
Lect	Holland, David	M	62B,42,51
Prof Emeritus	Horton, Dennis	D	10F,63A
Assoc Prof	Kiesgen, Mary Stewart	M	39,61
Lect	Kitchen, Jennifer	M	13
Lect	Kressler, Jeffrey	M	66A
Prof	Lee, Seunghee	D	62A,51
Prof	L'Hommedieu, Randi L.	D	32,11
Prof	Lindahl, Robert	D	49,63C,29
Lect	Lindahl, Susan	M	11
Prof	Mascolo-David, Alexandra	D	66A,66B,66D
Prof	Maurtua, Jose Luis	D	13A,13,10F,60,10
Asst Prof	Minnis, MaryBeth	M	41,48,64D
Lect	Mocny, Timothy S.	M	11
Asst Prof	Mueller, Neil	D	63A
Prof	Nash-Robertson, Nina	D	60,36
Prof	Nichol, John	M	47,48,64E,29
Assoc Prof	Smith, Robbie Malcolm	M	47,29A
Prof	Spencer, Andrew	D	50,65
Prof	Steele, Daniel L.	D	13A,32
Lect	Stone, Sarah	M	61
Asst Prof	Stoner-Cameron, Elizabeth	D	61
Asst Prof	Tang, Zhihua	D	66C
Assoc Prof	Tucker, Eric Hoy	D	61,39
Inst	Wheeler, Kathy	M	32
Prof	White, Joanna Cowan	D	41,64A
Prof	White, Kennen D.	D	41,64C
Prof	Wiley, Adrienne E.	D	66B,66D
Prof	Williamson, John E.	M	60,37
Prof Emeritus	Woods, Carlton	D	38,60
Lect	Wu, Hai-Xin	M	62A,51

MI0450 C.S. Mott Community College

Department of Music
1401 E Court St
Flint, MI 48503-6208
(810) 762-0459   Fax: (810) 762-5613
www.mcc.edu

2 Year Institution

Dean: Mary Cusack, 80A

Adj Prof	Coviak, James	M	41,65B
Adj Prof	Duquaine, Kenneth	M	11,29A
Adj Prof	Floden, Andrea	B	11,66D
PT	Hill, John	M	11,29A,62D
Inst	Iwanusa, Charles	M	13,10,11,47,29
Adj Prof	MacDonald, Laurence E.	M	11,12A,66A,66D
Adj Prof	Nieuwenhuis, Bruce	M	11
Adj Prof	Nieuwenhuis, Mary	M	13A,11,36,61
Inst	Procopio, Mary J.	D	11,20,37,64
Adj Prof	Richardson, Holly	M	11,66A
Adj Prof	Yancho, Mari	M	11,70,41
Adj Prof	Yon, Franklin	M	63,47,29A,11

MI0500 Concordia University

Department of Music
4090 Geddes Rd
Ann Arbor, MI 48105-2750
(734) 995-7300   Fax: (734) 995-4610
www.cuaa.edu
E-mail: schula@cuaa.edu

4 Year Institution

Director of Choirs: Brian L. Altevogt, 80A
Dean, Arts and Sciences: Robert McCormick, 80A
Director, Instrumental Activities: Matthew Wolf, 80A

Adj	Alfano, Karen		61
	Altevogt, Brian L.	M	36
Adj	Camino, Suzanne		20
Adj	Clemans, Holly		64A
	DeMarsh, Joe		63D
Adj	Dobbins, Sean		65,47
	Fisher, Jenny		66A
Adj	Hellick, Gary		63D
	Hellick, Melanie		63B
Adj	Hildebrandt, Lorna Young		61
Assoc Prof	Lipp, Carolyn	D	14,66A,66H,66B
	McCormick, Robert		60
Adj	Moorehead-Libbs, Jean	D	63A
	Muehlig, Carol		66G
	Nelson, Rob		70
Adj	Reynolds, Kristen		64B
	Schankin, Nora		64D
Adj	Sommerfield, Janet	M	64C,64E
Asst Prof	Wolf, Matthew	M	48,13,60,32H

MI0520 Cornerstone University

Division of Fine Arts
1001 E Beltline Ave NE
Grand Rapids, MI 49525-5897
(616) 222-1545   Fax: (616) 254-1645
www.cornerstone.edu
E-mail: music@cornerstone.edu

4 Year Institution
Member of NASM

Inst PT	Bouwman, Aaron	M	36,40
Inst PT	Claar, Elizabeth	D	66G
Inst PT	Clapp, John	M	64D
Inst PT	Gilman, David	B	35A
Inst PT	Gomez, Kathleen	M	64B
Inst PT	Heddens, Jared	B	37
Inst PT	Hill, Heather	M	64A
Inst PT	Holmes, Phil	M	61
Inst PT	Johnson, Amy	M	66D
Inst PT	Longer-Schreck, Corlyn	M	61
Inst PT	Marshall, Jonathan	M	70
Inst PT	McNeil, Carol	M	32B
Inst PT	Miller, Randy	B	34
Inst PT	Peck, Thomas	M	32C,32E
Inst PT	Rowsey, Les	M	32C,32D
Inst PT	Speck, Matthew	B	61
Asst Prof	Stockdale, Michael	M	70,53,13B
Asst Prof	VanDessel, Joan	D	12A,13D,37,64C,48
Assoc Prof	VanDessel, Peter	M	13C,66A,66D,13E
Inst PT	Varineau, John P.	M	60
Inst PT	Wagner, Kathy	B	61,54
Inst PT	Walters, Kent	D	36,60A
Inst PT	Westerholm, Matthew	B	53,66A
Inst PT	Winn, Jack	D	32B

MI0550 Delta College

Department of Music
1961 Delta Rd
University Center, MI 48710-0001
(989) 686-9000   Fax: (989) 686-8736
www.delta.edu
E-mail: brderoch@delta.edu

2 Year Institution

Asst Prof	DeRoche, Brad	D	70

MI0600 Eastern Michigan University

Department of Music & Dance
Alexander Music Bldg
Room N101
Ypsilanti, MI 48197-9960
(734) 487-0244   Fax: (734) 487-6939
www.emich.edu/music/
E-mail: dwinder@emich.edu

4 Year Institution, Graduate School
Member of NASM

Master of Music in Composition, Master of Music in Performance, Master of Music in Music Education, Master of Music in Piano Pedagogy

Head: Diane L. Winder, 80A
Coordinator of Advising: David M. Pierce
Assistant Vice President for Academic Affairs: David O. Woike

Prof	Amos, C. Nelson	D	12A,12,67D,70
Prof	Babcock, Donald J.	D	47,63C,63D
Asst Prof	Cass, Howard	D	42,10F
Assoc Prof	Dorsey, John F.	M	65,50
Prof	Eggers, Carter	M	49,63A
Asst Prof	Everett, Beth	D	36,60,32D
Assoc Prof	Foster, Daniel	M	62A,62B
Prof	Gajda, Anne	M	66A,66B,66D
Prof Emeritus	Gurt, Joseph	M	66A,66C
Prof	Iannaccone, Anthony J.	D	10A,38,13,10,12A
Asst Prof	Jackson, Sandra	M	64C
Lect PT	Justice, Roberta	M	33
Prof Emeritus	Kalib, Sylvan	D	13
Prof Emerita	Kirkland, Glenda	M	61
Asst Prof	Knopps, Amy	D	32E,37
Staff	Lehman, Paul R.	M	66F
Prof	McNamara, Joann	M	52
Prof Emerita	Meretta, Kristy	M	64B
Asst Prof	Merrill, Theresa R.	D	33
Prof	Miller, Kevin D.	M	60,32,38
Lect PT	Myers-Brown, Ruth	M	62E
Asst Prof	Nam, MeeAe Cecilia	DMA	61
Lect PT	Pappas, Mark		13,29
Asst Prof	Peavler, Robert	D	61
Prof	Pedersen, Gary	D	66A,66B,66C,66D
Prof	Pierce, David M.	D	12A,64D
Lect	Pierce, Denise Root	M	63B
Prof	Prince, J. Whitney	D	13
Prof	Saker, Marilyn	D	13,12A
Asst Prof	Schneider, Mary K.	D	37
Assoc Prof	Schoenhals, Joel	D	12A,66A
Asst Prof	Simmons, Phil	M	52
Asst Prof Emeritus	Smith, John Robert	M	13A
Prof	Stone, Julie	D	64A,48
Lect PT	Thiele, Margaret	M	32A,32B
Lect PT	Wagner, James	D	66G
Lect PT	Weller, Derek	M	62D
Assoc Prof	Wilkinson, Sherry	M	52
	Winder, Diane L.	D	62C
Prof	Woike, David O.	D	37,32E,32C
Prof	Zirk, Willard	D	13,49,63B

MI0650 Ferris State University
Music Center
820 Campus Dr
Big Rapids, MI 49307
(231) 591-2501
www.ferris.edu
E-mail: arroec@ferris.edu

4 Year Institution

Chair: Cate Arroe, 80A

Asst Prof	Arroe, Cate	D	20,36,66
Asst Prof	Cohen, Richard Scott	D	11,37,38
Assoc Prof	Cronk, Daniel L.	M	34,35
Assoc Prof	Dempsey, Harry J.	M	11,35
Asst Prof	Moresi, Matthew S.	M	11,46,66
Vstng Asst Prof	Skornia, Dale E.	D	11,32B,37,64

MI0700 Gogebic Community College
Department of Music
E-4946 Jackson Rd
Ironwood, MI 49938
(906) 932-4962
www.gogebic.cc.mi.us
E-mail: Alex.Marciniak@gogebic.edu

2 Year Institution

| Asst Prof | Marciniak, Alex B. | M | 13A,37,66A,13,11 |

MI0750 Grace Bible College
Worship Arts Department
1011 Aldon St SW
Grand Rapids, MI 49509
(616) 538-2330   Fax: (616) 538-0599
www.gbcol.edu
E-mail: jwerkema@gbcol.edu

4 Year Institution

Chair: Jason R. Werkema, 80A

Asst Prof	Bobbitt, Kayleen	M	11,66,13,40
Adj Prof	Dykstra, Crisi	B	61
Adj Prof	Longhin, Daniel	D	31A
Adj Prof	Post, Corey	B	65
FT	Profitt, Tommee	B	34,31A
Adj Prof	Sloothaak, Bea	A	62
Prof	Werkema, Jason R.	PhD	70,13,29,34

MI0850 Grand Rapids Comm College
Department of Music
143 Bostwick Ave NE
Grand Rapids, MI 49503
(616) 234-3940   Fax: (616) 234-3973
www.grcc.edu
E-mail: KKOLEHOU@grcc.edu

2 Year Institution

Chair: Kevin J. Dobreff, 80A
Dir., Preparatory Division: Malcolm Brannen, 80E

Inst Adj	Asper, Lynn K.	M	49,63A
	Barton, Stephen	D	36,40,11,12A,61
Inst Adj	Bergeron, Andrew	B	70,13A,13D
Inst Adj	Bokhout, William	B	61
Staff	Bos, Ken	D	66C,66A,66D
Inst Adj	Bosscher, Scott	M	61,13C
Prof	Brannen, Malcolm	M	62A,62B,38,32A
Inst Adj	Bristol, Cynthia	M	11,66A,20
Inst Adj	Britsch, Richard	B	63B
Inst Adj	Bylsma, Ruth	M	64A
Inst Adj	Connell, Robin L.	D	13D
Inst Adj	Crawford, Michael	M	62D,20
Asst Prof	DeWitt, Debora	D	66,12
Prof	Dobreff, Kevin J.	M	20F,61,67C,55D,13C
	Doyle, Michael	M	46,47
Inst Adj	Elzinga, Cameo	M	66D
Inst Adj	Eppinga, Alicia	B	62C
Prof	Gillan, Michael	M	11,37,63C,63D,47
Inst Adj	Gomez, Kathleen	B	64D
Inst Adj	Grinwis, Brandan	M	65,50,13A
Inst Adj	Hay, David	B	62D
Prof	Heldt, Tim	B	34D,35D,35G
	Kacos, Lisa	M	13A,13C
Inst Adj	Marshall, Jonathan	M	13A,70
Inst Adj	Michewicz, Michael	M	64E,46
Prof	Morris, Brian	M	70,13,34D
	Penning-Koperski, Diane	M	61
Inst Adj	Scanlan, Mary	D	66A,66H,66C,66D,20F
Inst Adj	Schwanda, Grace	M	11
	VanBecker, Leslie	M	62A
Prof	VanRandwyk, Carol A.	D	13,13C,66A,13D
Inst Adj	Varineau, John	M	64C
Inst Adj	Wallace, Roy	B	34D
	Wells, Yelena	D	66A,66D,20

MI0900 Grand Valley State University
Department of Music
1 Campus Dr
Allendale, MI 49401-9403
(616) 331-3484   Fax: (616) 331-3100
www.gvsu.edu/music
E-mail: phippsda@gvsu.edu

4 Year Institution
Member of NASM

Chair: Danny K. Phipps, 80A
Assistant Chair: Kevin Tutt, 80H

PT	Bergeron, Andrew	M	13C
PT	Bergseth, Heather	M	11,12
Other	Bliton, Nathaniel	M	72,34
Affiliate	Britsch, Richard	M	63B
Affiliate	Byrens, Robert	M	62B
Prof	Campbell, Arthur J.	D	64C,64E,13
Affiliate	Carlson, Paul	M	63D
PT	Clapp, John	M	64D
Assoc Prof	Copenhaver, Lee R.	D	13,11,12A,38,62C
Affiliate	Crowell, Gregory	D	13,12,66G,66H
PT	De.La Barrera, Carlos	M	70
PT	DeBoer, Jack	M	11,13A,12A
PT	Drost, Michael	M	46,47,29
Assoc Prof	Duitman, Henry E.	D	51,38,32E,41
Prof	Feurzeig, Lisa	D	12C,12A,20
PT	French, Allen	M	63B
Affiliate	Froncek, Tim		29,65,29A,47,46
PT	Gaffke, Todd	M	64E,41
Asst Prof	Gibbs, Beth	D	32
Affiliate	Good, Kevin	M	32E

PT	Gordillo, Richard	M	37
PT	Gordon, Patricia	M	11,32B
PT	Hovnanian, Michael	M	62D
Vstng Asst Prof	Jin, Min	D	61
PT	Johnson, Amy E.	M	66D,66B
Affiliate	Kanter, Chris	M	64A
PT	Kloosterman, Jill	M	66D
PT	Lockwood, Tom	M	62D
Asst Prof	Lupis, Giuseppe	D	66A
Assoc Prof	Mahave-Veglia, Pablo	D	42,62C,55B
Assoc Prof	Marlais, Helen	D	66A,66B
PT	Marquez-Barrios, Victor	D	29A,20
Prof	Martin, Barry	M	60,37,32
Asst Prof	Martin, John T.	M	37
Asst Prof	Maytan, Gregory	D	62A
PT	Maytan, Sandra	M	32
PT	Metzler, James	M	11,36
Asst Prof	Nichol, Jonathan	D	64E
Prof	Norris, Charles	D	32D,32G,36
Prof	Phipps, Danny K.	D	64D,12A,12C,13E
Assoc Prof	Pool, Ellen	M	32D,36,60A
PT	Renter, David	D	11,13,29
Assoc Prof	Ryan, William E.	D	10,43
Assoc Prof	Schriemer, Dale	B	61
Prof	Schuster-Craig, John	D	13E,12A,13F,13B
PT	Secor, Greg	M	65
Assoc Prof	Stieler, Kathryn	M	61
Prof	Stoelzel, Richard	M	63A,49
PT	Stumpo, Ryan		66
Affiliate	Swantek, Paul	M	11
PT	Thompson, Anne	M	32
Assoc Prof	Tutt, Kevin	D	37,32E,32G
Prof Emerita	Vanden Wyngaard, Julianne	B	66A,66B,66C
PT	Varineau, John	D	64C
Assoc Prof	Vavrikova, Marlen	D	64B
PT	Veenstra, Kimberly	D	11,12,13
PT	Watson, Jed	M	11
PT	Wilkinson, Leslie		11
Assoc Prof	Williams, Mark	D	63C,49,41

MI0910 Great Lakes Christian College
Department of Music
6211 W Willow Hwy
Lansing, MI 48917-1231
(517) 321-0242   Fax: (517) 321-5902
www.glcc.edu
E-mail: ehetrick@glcc.edu

4 Year Institution

Chair: Esther A. Hetrick, 80A

Prof	Apple, Ryan	M	13,12,70,11
PT	Beavers, Judith	B	66A,41
Prof	Hetrick, Esther A.	D	61,60,31A,36,32B

MI0950 Henry Ford Community College
Department of Perf Arts-Music
5101 Evergreen Rd
Dearborn, MI 48128
(313) 845-9634   Fax: (313) 845-9658
www.hfcc.edu
E-mail: kdewey@hfcc.edu

2 Year Institution

Inst	Dewey, Kevin		

MI1000 Hillsdale College
Department of Music-Howard Hall
79 E. College St
Hillsdale, MI 49242
(517) 607-2590   Fax: (517) 607-2899
www.hillsdale.edu
E-mail: cheryl.thomas@hillsdale.edu

4 Year Institution

Chair: James A. Holleman, 80A
Coordinator: Cheryl Thomas, 80A
Dir., Artist/Performance Series: Diana Kies, 80F

Inst Adj	Bixler, Judith	M	62A
Adj	Clark, Renee Cherie	M	66A
Assoc Prof	Holleman, James A.	M	60,11,36,38
Inst Adj	James, Dean G.	M	66G

Applied Artist	Jones, Eric W.	M	32E,37,50,65
Inst Adj	King, Bill	D	64C
Assoc Prof	Knecht, Melissa Gerber	D	11,32,42,62A,62B
Inst	Krogol, D.J.	B	20F,67E
Inst Adj	Lockwood, Tom	M	62D,64E
Applied Artist	McCourry, Christopher C.	DIPL	29,42,63A
Inst Adj	Newton, Steve	M	64D
Applied Artist	Osmond, Melissa	B	61,39
Inst Adj	Peshlakai, David	M	42,62C
Inst Adj	Reynolds, Kristin	M	64B
Inst Adj	Spangler, Douglas	M	66A
Inst Adj	Swora, Matthew	M	62D
Asst Prof	Waddell, Rachel Lynn	D	11,12,32E,42,64A
Inst Adj	Williams, Larry	B	70
Inst Adj	Wood, Michael	M	32E,63B
Applied Artist	Wyse, Debbi	B	66A

MI1050 Hope College
Department of Music
PO Box 9000
Holland, MI 49422-9000
(616) 395-7650   Fax: (616) 395-7182
www.hope.edu/academic/music/
E-mail: hodson@hope.edu

4 Year Institution
Member of NASM

Chair: Robert Hodson, 80A
Dean: William D. Reynolds, 80A

Prof Emeritus	Aschbrenner, Charles C.	M	66A,32I
PT	Claar, Elizabeth	D	13
PT	Clapp, John	M	64D
Asst Prof	Clark, Adam	D	66,66A,66C,66B,66D
Adj	Corbato, Barbara	M	62B
PT	Cosgrove, Julia	M	61
Prof	Coyle, Brian	D	47,29,53
Prof	Craioveanu, Mihai	M	11,62A,41
Adj	DeBoer, James	M	32
Assoc Prof	Dykstra, Linda	M	61
PT	Erskine, John K.	B	35C,35D,34
PT	Hoats, Charlie		70,62D
Assoc Prof	Hodson, Robert	D	13,29B,47
Asst Prof	Hornbach, Christina M.	D	32,13C
	Hoyer, John	M	16
PT	Hyde, Edye	B	61
PT	Hyde, Michael	B	70
Asst Prof	Kim, Jungwoo	M	61
PT	Kolean, Lora Clark	B	66D
Assoc Prof	Le, Andrew	D	66A
Prof	Lewis, Huw R.	D	13D,66G,66H,31A
PT	Lockwood, Tom	M	64E
Adj	Malfroid, Larry		70
PT	Martin, David	M	70
PT	Peterson, Erich	M	63B
Assoc Prof	Piippo, Richard	M	38,41,51,62C,10F
PT	Pilon, Sherri	M	61
Assoc Prof	Randel, Julia	D	12,20
Prof	Richmond, Brad	D	36,40,60A,61
PT	Schekman, Joel	M	64C
PT	Secor, Greg	M	50,65,32E
Prof Emeritus	Sharp, Stuart	D	61
Adj	Sooy, Julie	M	64A,48
Asst Prof	Southard, Robert G.	D	37,60B,41,11
PT	Southard, Sarah	M	64B,11
PT	Spencer, Daniel	M	63C,63D
PT	Straus, Melissa	D	62D
Adj	Strouf, Linda Kay	M	11,66D
Adj	Talaga, Steve	M	66A,29A,29B,29C,10
PT	VanLente, Mike	B	65
PT	Veenstra, Kim	M	13
PT	Waldvogel, Martha	M	62E
Adj	Wolfe, Jennifer	M	13C,66C,12A,11

MI1100 Jackson Community College
Department of Music
2111 Emmons Rd
Jackson, MI 49201
(517) 787-0800   Fax: (517) 796-8632
www.jccmi.edu
E-mail: DouglasRonaldL@jccmi.edu

2 Year Institution

Music Contact: Ronald L. Douglass, 80A

Prof	Douglass, Ronald L.	M	13,37,41,63,29
PT	Drayton, Joanne	B	61
Prof	Drayton, Keith	M	13,11,36,32,61

MI1150 Kalamazoo College
Department of Music
1200 Academy St
Kalamazoo, MI 49006-3291
(269) 337-7070   Fax: (269) 337-7251
www.kzoo.edu/music
E-mail: tung@kzoo.edu

4 Year Institution

Chair: Leslie Thomas Tung, 80A

PT	Cristy-Couch, Martha	B	66F
PT	Decker, Douglas	M	35C
PT	Di Salvio, Ron	M	66A
PT	Drake, Jennifer	B	66A
Assoc Prof	Evans, Thomas	D	37,47,63C,29A,32
PT	Garrett, Christopher	M	63B
PT	Garrett, Dawn	M	64C
PT	Geiman, Keith	M	63A
PT	Grafius, Ellen	M	62E
PT	Guthrie, Beverly	B	64B
PT	Guthrie, Mark	B	65
PT	Koebel, Carolyn	M	65,50
Asst Prof	Koehler, Andrew	M	60,38,62A,62B,12A
PT	Kramer, Jason	M	64D
PT	Lakers, Janice	M	61
PT	Morgan, Kenyon	M	64E
PT	Schreck, Corlyn	M	61
	Schumaker, Adam	M	10A,10B,10C,10D,70
Assoc Prof	Tan, Siu-Lan	D	12F
PT	Tikker, Timothy	M	66G
Prof	Tung, Leslie Thomas	D	12A,66A,66C,66E,13
Assoc Prof	Turner, James	M	36,61
PT	Wong, Betsy	M	64A

MI1160 Kellogg Community College
Department of Music
450 North Avenue
Battle Creek, MI 49017-0280
(269) 965-3931 x 2207   Fax: (269) 965-0280
www.kellogg.edu/performart
E-mail: blanchardg@kellogg.edu

2 Year Institution, Community College

Music Contact: Gerald J. Blanchard, 80A
Dean: Kevin Rabinau, 80A
Chair, Arts & Communication: Barbara Sudeikis, 80A

Adj	Adams, Mark		63A
	Blanchard, Gerald J.	M	11,36,13,60A,61
	Brown, Nancy		66C
Adj	Cary, Kathy		66G
Adj	Channells, Janet		63B
Adj	Cleland, Sara		66A
Adj	Hirleman, Laura		64C,64E
	Johnkoski, Stephen V.		
Adj	Krontz, Paula		66A
Adj	Ochiltree, Larry		65
Adj	Picard, Betty	M	60A,61
	Throop, Barbara Chandler		66C
Adj	Wells, Mark		61,66

MI1180 Lake Michigan College
Department of Music
2755 E Napier Ave
Benton Harbor, MI 49022-1881
(269) 927-8100 x 5237   Fax: (269) 927-6587
www.lakemichigancollege.edu
E-mail: hendrick@lakemichigancollege.edu

2 Year Institution

Director: Daniel Hendrickson, 80A

Inst PT	Baker, Ron	D	11
Inst PT	Bomer, Delain	M	11,63B
Inst PT	Brumbelow, Denise	M	64E,64C
Inst PT	Bubar, Lisa	B	64D
Inst PT	Churchill, Marc	M	65
Inst PT	Cook, Luke	B	62C
Inst PT	Davids, Suzann	D	62E
Inst PT	Flyger, Paul	M	66A,66D,11
Inst PT	Gibson, Chris	M	64A,32B
Inst	Hendrickson, Daniel	M	11,12A,36,37,61
Inst PT	Kraus, James	M	66G,13A,66A
Inst PT	Krueger, Bradley	M	61
Inst PT	Lunn, Robert A.	D	13,70
Inst PT	McCarthy, Daniel	M	63A
Inst PT	Mitchell, Alan	M	63D
Inst PT	Mow, Paul	M	61
Inst PT	Oeseburg, Beth	M	62A,62B
Inst PT	Pantaleo, Patrick	B	70
Inst PT	Randles, Edward	M	62D
Inst PT	Reuss, Dale	M	37
Inst PT	Slabaugh, Stephen	M	47,63A

MI1200 Lansing Community College
Humanities & Perf. Arts-Music 5100
PO Box 40010
Lansing, MI 48901
(517) 483-1018   Fax: (517) 483-1473
www.lcc.edu
E-mail: potesc@lcc.edu

2 Year Institution, Transfer Associate Programs

Dean: Gary Knippenberg, 80A
Chair: Michael A. Nealon, 80A
Director: Cesar I. Potes, 80A

Inst PT	Alhaddad, Frederick I.	M	13,10,66
Inst PT	Anderson, Marcia H.		64C
Inst PT	Bastian, William M.	B	66A,29
Inst PT	Bondar, Liudmila E.	D	66D,13C
Inst PT	Bowen, Meredith Y.	M	36,20,13
Inst PT	Cirlin, Sunny		62A
Inst PT	Clark, Roger R.	B	35A,35F
Inst FT	Cryderman-Weber, Molly	M	12,20,13B,13,65
Inst PT	Daniels, Michael T.		65,35A
Inst PT	Endahl, John R.		37
Inst PT	Erickson, Lydia K.	M	61
Inst PT	Faiver, Rosemary T.	M	32B,66D
Inst PT	Fedewa, Edward W.	M	62D
Inst PT	Gewirtz, Jonathon D.	M	47,64E,29A
Inst PT	Hiranpradist, Barbara	D	11,32B,20
Inst PT	Kim, Yoo-Jung	D	66A,66C,66D
Inst PT	Lange, Stephen R.	D	66G,61
Inst PT	Lewis, Elizabeth A.	M	50,65
Inst PT	Novenske-Smith, Janine L.		61,36
Inst PT	Pierce, Marilyn	M	61
Inst FT	Potes, Cesar I.	D	13,10,11,34
Inst PT	Rollins, Christopher	B	70,51
Inst PT	Siivola, Carolyn	M	32B
Inst PT	Sinder, Philip	M	66G,61
Inst FT	Sjoquist, Doug P.	M	
Inst PT	Starr, Jeff M.		70
Inst PT	Stoyanov, Simeon N.	M	63C
Inst PT	Therrian, Dennis	B	66A,34

MI1250 Macomb Comm College-Center Campus
Department of Music
44575 Garfield Rd
Clinton Township, MI 48038-1139
(586) 286-2045   Fax: (586) 286-2068
www.macomb.edu
E-mail: cookt@macomb.edu

2 Year Institution

Chair: Melanie Bartlett, 80A

Prof	Cook, Thomas	M	13,12A,38,63C
Inst PT	Huntington, Lawrence	M	47,29B
Prof	Scott, Stuart	D	40,36,61
Prof	Stella, Martin	D	13,11

MI1260 Madonna University
Department of Music
36600 Schoolcraft Rd
Livonia, MI 48150-1176
(734) 432-5709   Fax: (734) 432-5393
www.madonna.edu
E-mail: lpopoff-parks@madonna.edu

4 Year Liberal Arts Institution, Roman Catholic

Chair: Linette A. Popoff-Parks, 80A

Inst Adj	Biskupski, Grazyna	M	62A,62B
	Biskupski, Tadeusz	D	62C
Asst Prof Adj	Brown, Jenine	ABD	13D,13E

Asst Prof Adj	Chen, Ann A.	D	66A,66B
Inst Adj	Cushman, Kevin	M	60,13C
Inst Adj	James, Joshua	D	32E,47
Lect Adj	Kelly, Velda	M	62A
Assoc Prof	Masri-Fletcher, Patricia	M	62E
Adj Assoc Prof	Meehan, Linda Pearce	D	61
Inst Adj	Moon, Brian	M	63A
Asst Prof Adj	Moslak, Judy	M	32,66A
Prof	Popoff-Parks, Linette A.		13,66A,66B,66C
Asst Prof Adj	Raschiatore, Lisa	C	64C,41
Asst Prof Adj	Raymond, Diane	D	32B
Asst Prof Adj	Rottenberg, Helene	M	70,11
Inst Adj	Sklut, Thomas		35A,35E
Prof	Wagner, David O.	D	12A,13B,13C,35,66G
Adj Inst	White, Karin	M	32B,32E,32D
Asst Prof Adj	Wilt, Kevin	M	10A,10C,10F,34
Assoc Prof	Wiltsie, Barbara	M	61,39,54

MI1300 Marygrove College

Department of Music
8425 W McNichols Rd
Detroit, MI 48221-2599
(313) 927-1383   Fax: (313) 927-1345
www.marygrove.edu
E-mail: jclark@marygrove.edu

4 Year Liberal Arts Institution

Chair: Patrick Regan, 80A

Asst Prof	Burton, Christopher	M	66A,66C
Assoc Prof	Duncan, Ellen	M	13A,13,60,36,40
Assoc Prof	Grover, Elaine	M	13A,13,66A,66G,31A
Adj	Krenek, Catherine	M	32B,32C
	McDonald, Shawn	B	61,66C,39
Adj	Nelson, Troy	M	32
Inst	Regan, Patrick	M	61,39,54
Adj	Rogers, Caroline	M	61
Asst Prof	Stanton, Geoffrey	D	13,10,45,34
Prof	Vanderbeck, Sue Ann	M	11,12A,66A,66B,66D
Adj	Waldon, Reed	M	70

MI1400 Michigan State University

College of Music
Music Building
333 W Circle Dr., Rm 102
East Lansing, MI 48824-1043
(517) 355-4583   Fax: (517) 432-2880
www.music.msu.edu
E-mail: forger@msu.edu

4 Year Institution, Graduate School
Member of NASM

Master of Music in Collaborative Piano, Graduate Diploma in Performance, Master of Music in Composition, Master of Music in Music Theory, Master of Music in Performance, Master of Music in Conducting, Master of Music in Music Education, PhD in Music Education, DMA in Composition, DMA in Conducting, DMA in Performance, Master of Arts in Musicology, Master of Music in Piano Pedagogy, Master of Music in Jazz Studies

Dean: James Forger, 80A
Associate Dean, Undergraduate Studies: Michael Kroth, 80B
Associate Dean, Graduate Studies: David C. Rayl, 80C,80H
Dir., Admissions: Ben Ebener, 80D
Exec. Dir., Community Music School & Assoc. Dean Outreach & Engagement: Rhonda Buckley, 80E,80H

Prof	Bagratuni, Suren	D	62C
Asst Prof	Bartig, Kevin	D	12A
Assoc Prof	Berlinsky, Dmitri	M	62A
Asst Prof	Bosse, Joanna	D	12A,14
Specialist	Buckley, Rhonda	M	
Prof	Budrow, Jack	D	62D
Assoc Prof	Burgett, Gwendolyn	M	65,50
Asst Prof	Callahan, Michael R.	D	13
Asst Prof	Cannon, Cormac	D	37
Asst Prof	Charles, Etienne	M	29,63A,47
Asst Prof	Dease, Michael	M	29,63C
Specialist	Ebener, Ben	M	
Assoc Prof	Eberle, Jan	M	64B
Assoc Prof	Fillmore, Molly	M	61
Prof	Forger, James	M	64E
Assoc Prof	Fracker, Richard	M	61
Assoc Prof	Gaboury, Janine	M	41,49,63B
Prof	Gandelsman, Yuri	D	62B
Inst	Gelispie, Randle		29,65
Assoc Prof	Helton, Melanie	M	61
Prof	Hutcheson, Jere T.	D	10
Assoc Prof	Illman, Richard	M	63A
Assoc Prof	Jennings, Harlan	D	61
Prof	Kratus, John	D	32
Assoc Prof	Kroth, Michael	M	64D,41
Prof	Largey, Michael	D	12,14,20
Assoc Prof	Lightfoot, Peter W.	M	61
Asst Prof	Lim, Sangmi	D	66A
Assoc Prof	Lorenz, Ricardo	D	10
Prof	Lulloff, Joseph	M	42,64E
Prof	Lyras, Panayis	M	66A
Assoc Prof	Madden, John	M	37,32
Asst Prof	Masri-Fletcher, Patricia	M	62E
Lect	McLellan, Ray	D	69
Prof	Moriarty, Deborah	M	66A
Asst Prof	Nathan, Alan	B	66A,66C
Prof	Newman, Ronald	D	13
Asst Prof	Nispel, Anne	M	61
Prof	Noe, Kevin	M	38,43,60B
Assoc Prof	Oien, Theodore	M	64C
Assoc Prof	Ordman, Ava	M	63C,49
Assoc Prof	Palac, Judith A.	M	32
Asst Prof	Polischuk, Derek Kealii	D	66A,66B,66D,38,29
Asst Prof	Prouty, Kenneth E.	D	12,14,29
Asst Prof	Ray, Marcie	D	12A,15
Prof	Rayl, David C.	D	36,60A
Prof	Reed, Jonathan I.	D	60A,32C,36
Asst Prof	Rivera, Diego	B	29,64E,53
Assoc Prof	Robinson, Mitchell	D	32
Prof	Ruggiero, Charles	D	13,10
Prof	Sedatole, Kevin	D	37,60B
Prof	Sherman, Richard	M	64A
Prof	Sinder, Philip	M	63D
Assoc Prof	Sly, Gordon C.	D	13
Prof	Snow, Sandra	D	32D,36
Asst Prof	Sohn, Minsoo	D	66A
Assoc Prof	Sullivan, Mark	D	10,12B,34
Inst	Taggart, Bruce F.	D	13,34
Prof	Taggart, Cynthia Crump	D	32
Prof	Thomas, Reginald	M	29,66A,53
Assoc Prof	VanHandel, Leigh A.	D	13,13K,13G
Prof	Verdehr, Walter	D	62A
Assoc Prof	Wagner, Corbin	M	63B
Assoc Prof	Wang, I-Fu	B	41,62A
Inst	Weber, Jonathan	M	65,50
Prof	Whitaker, Rodney		47,29,62D

MI1450 Michigan Technological University

Department of Visual & Perf. Arts
1400 Townsend Dr
Houghton, MI 49931-1295
(906) 487-2067
www.vpa.mtu.edu
E-mail: rheld@mtu.edu

4 Year Institution

Chair: Roger L. Held, 80A
Dir., Preparatory Division: Elizabeth C. Meyer, 80E

Asst Prof	Anderson, Jared	D	36,40,11,12A
Adj	Byykkonen, Susan E.	B	66,36
Inst	Enz, Nicholas J.	B	37,41,64E,47
Assoc Prof	Irish, Michael J.	M	13,47,45,53,29
Adj	Meyer, Elizabeth C.	D	38,62A,62B,10A
Asst Prof	Neves, Joel	D	38,39,42,20G

MI1500 Monroe County Community College

Department of Music
1555 S Raisinville Rd
Monroe, MI 48161-9047
(734) 384-4152   Fax: (734) 384-4192
www.monroeccc.edu
E-mail: pdorcey-naber@monroeccc.edu

2 Year Institution

Dean, Humanities & Social Sciences: R. Bruce Way, 80A

Adj	Brodie, Catherine	M	36
Adj	Felder, Mark	M	37
Adj	Goss, Kim	M	29A
Adj	Schroeder, Joy A.	PhD	32B,13A,13C

MI1550 Muskegon Community College
Creative & Performing Arts-Music
221 S Quarterline Rd
Muskegon, MI 49442
(231) 777-0324   Fax: (231) 777-0255
www.muskegoncc.edu
E-mail: scott.cutting@muskegoncc.edu

2 Year Institution

Coordinator, Music Program: W. Scott Cutting, 80A

Inst Adj	Brechting, Gail	M	60B,63C,37
Inst	Cutting, W. Scott	M	13,11,66A,66D,34D
Inst Adj	Gilson, Catherine	M	36,60A
Inst Adj	Hoogenstyn, Don	M	11,12A
Inst Adj	Meyers, Dan	M	60B,38
Inst Adj	Smith, Jennifer	M	36,61,66

MI1600 Northern Michigan University
Department of Music
1401 Presque Isle Ave
Marquette, MI 49855-5365
(906) 227-2563   Fax: (906) 227-2165
www.nmu.edu/music
E-mail: dgrant@nmu.edu

4 Year Institution
Member of NASM

Head: Donald R. Grant, 80A

Assoc Prof	Engelhart, Robert	D	39,61,36,11
Assoc Prof	Flaherty, Mark	D	47,63A,29A,34,63B
Prof	Grant, Donald R.	D	64B,64C,64D,64E,13
Inst	Green, Sharon	M	32,61,70
Assoc Prof	Grugin, Stephen	D	37,63D,12A,32C,32E
Prof	Redfern, Nancy	D	66,11,66D,66B,66G
Asst Prof	Rhyneer, Barbara	D	60,38,41,62,11
Prof	Slotterback, Floyd	D	60,36,11
Prof	Strain, James A.	D	65,13,41,11
Prof	Tate, Elda Ann	D	13,10E,41,64A

MI1650 Northwestern Michigan College
Department of Music
1701 E Front
Traverse City, MI 49684
(231) 995-1338   Fax: (231) 995-1696
www.nmc.edu/music/
E-mail: mpuchala@nmc.edu

2 Year Institution

Chair: Mark Puchala, 80A

Adj	Beery, John	M	32,37,47,63,11
Adj	Bragle, John	M	36
Adj	Davis, Mike		11
Adj	Gentry, Ron	M	61
Adj	Hathaway, Matt		
	Holland, David		62B,42,51
Adj	Hunter, Michael	B	47,63C,29,64E
Adj	Husser, David		
Adj	Novak, Brad		65
Adj	Pavelek, Robert		
Adj	Podolka, Deborah		
Prof	Puchala, Mark	M	12A,36,61,34,41
Adj	Quick, Steve		
PT	Sorenson, Scott	PhD	63,46,37
Adj	Tarczon, Philip		
Adj	Tilley, Marilyn		
PT	Tomlin, Charles	B	70
PT	Vogel, Dorothy	M	66D,11
PT	Warne, David	M	50,65,20
Adj	Weston, Beth		
Adj	Williams, Christine		

MI1700 Oakland Comm Coll-Orchard Ridge
Department of Music
27055 Orchard Lake Rd
Farmington Hills, MI 48334
(248) 522-3590   Fax: (248) 522-3696
www.oaklandcc.edu
E-mail: jmgarcia@oaklandcc.edu

2 Year Institution

Chair: Nick J. Valenti, 80A

Adj Prof	Blaszkiewicz, Michael J.	M	70
Prof Adj	Culver, Jerry	D	36,13C,60
Adj Prof	Dennis, Thomas A.	D	12A,66A,46
Prof Adj	Feinberg, Henry A.	M	12A,10
Prof Adj	Gallet, Coralie	M	61
Prof Adj	Goslin, Gerald H.		61,66A,20
Prof Adj	Phipps, Juanita K.	M	66A
Prof Adj	Troxtel, Diane C.		12A

MI1750 Oakland University
Department of Music/Theatre/Dance
207 Varner Hall
Rochester, MI 48309-4401
(248) 370-2030   Fax: (248) 370-2041
www.oakland.edu/mtd
E-mail: mtd@oakland.edu

4 Year Institution, Graduate School

Master of Music in Performance, Master of Music in Conducting, Master of Music in Music Education, PhD in Music Education, Master of Music in Pedagogy

Chair: Jacqueline H. Wiggins, 80A
Program Director, Music: Michael A. Mitchell, 80H

Inst PT	Abrahams, Daniel	M	60B
Inst PT	Allvin, Kerstin	M	62E
Asst Prof	Blair, Deborah V.	D	32B,32C,12B,12F,32D
Inst PT	Bland, Barbara	M	61
Inst PT	Bloom, Bradley	D	60A
Asst Prof	Brown, Miles	M	62D,47,29A,29B,46
Inst PT	Cafagna, Carl	M	47,40
Inst PT	Catallo, Jennifer Kincer	M	32B
Inst PT	Chandler, Vincent Arvel	M	63C
Assoc Prof	Cunningham, Gregory M.	D	60B,38,37
Inst PT	Dantzler, Alta	D	61
Asst Prof	Dantzler, Drake M.	D	61,39
Inst PT	Dehaven, Frederic	M	66G,66H
Inst PT	Deleury, Nadine	M	62C
Asst Prof Adj	Diggory, Edith	D	61
Inst PT	Dobbins, Sean	B	47,65,29
Inst PT	Flanigan, Nina	M	32
Inst PT	Graser, Daniel	M	64E
Inst PT	Hall, John	M	70
Inst PT	Hammond, Rebecca	M	64B
Inst PT	Happel, Rebecca	D	66A,66C
Inst PT	Herald, Terry	M	35G,35C,11
Inst PT	Hoag, Bret	M	70,41,11
Asst Prof	Hoag, Melissa E.	D	13B,13C,13D,13E,13F
Inst PT	Janowsky, Maxim	M	62D
Inst PT	Jeyasigam, Sam	M	65
Inst PT	Kaarre, Lois	M	66D,66C
Assoc Prof	Kidger, David M.	D	12A
Inst PT	Kieme, Mark	B	64E
Assoc Prof	Kroesche, Kenneth	D	63D,63C,49,37
Inst PT	MacNair, Alan	M	38
Inst PT	Maloney, Melissa	M	61
Inst PT	Maslanka, Daniel	B	65,50
Inst PT	Milicevic, Zeljko	M	32E
Assoc Prof	Mitchell, Michael A.	D	60A,36,11
Asst Prof	Payette, Jessica	D	12A,12C
Inst PT	Rowin, Elizabeth	M	62A,62B,42
Inst PT	Schauert, Paul W.	D	20,11
Inst PT	Schoon, Marcus	M	32E,64D
Assoc Prof	Shively, Joseph L.	D	32G,34,11,32,32C
Inst PT	Shively, Victoria	M	13B,13C,12A
Inst PT	Siciliano, Mary	M	66A,66C,66B
Inst PT	Simmons, Gordon	B	63A
Inst PT	Soroka, Michele R.	B	13B,13C
Inst PT	Sparfeld, Amanda	M	64A
Inst PT	Sparrow, Sharon W.		64A,48
Asst Prof	Stoffan, George C.	D	64C,48,42,32E
Inst	Stone, Mark	M	20,50
Inst PT	Tait, Kristen N.	D	11,35A
Inst PT	Washington, Nadine	M	61
Inst PT	Weed, Tad		66A,29,47
Prof	White, John-Paul	M	61

Inst PT	White, Phyllis	M	11,13A
Inst PT	White, William	M	63A,29
Prof	Wiggins, Jacqueline H.	D	12F,32B,32G
Inst PT	Xydas, Spiros	M	32E
Inst PT	Zook, Jeffrey	M	64A

MI1800 Olivet College
Department of Performing Arts
Music Program
320 S Main St
Olivet, MI 49076
(616) 749-7660   Fax: (616) 749-7695
www.olivetcollege.edu
E-mail: tflynn@olivetcollege.edu

4 Year Institution

Program Director & Chair: Timothy Flynn, 80A

Adj	DeRosa, Julia	M	61,39,13C
Assoc Prof	Flynn, Timothy	D	10A,12,36,39,13
Adj	Forquer, Ty	M	65,50,13C
Asst Prof	Furman, Lisa J.	D	37,60B,11,13,32
Adj	Gewirtz, Jonathan	M	47,64E,64C,11,29
Adj	Henson, Bill	M	61,39,13C
Adj	Humphrey, Roger G.		70
Assoc Prof	Kime, Ramona	D	62,66A,66D,66H
Adj	Noble, James	M	32
	Ritzenhein, Mark	B	72
Adj	Suhusky, Craig	M	64C
Adj	Young, James	D	63A

MI1830 Rochester College
Department of Music
800 W Avon Rd
Rochester Hills, MI 48307-2704
(248) 218-2000   Fax: (248) 218-2045
www.rc.edu
E-mail: jbentley@rc.edu

4 Year Liberal Arts Institution

Director: Joe Bentley, 80A

Prof	Bentley, Joe	D	12A,32D,60,36
Inst Adj	Gunn, Lorrie	M	62A
Inst Adj	Hoag, Bret	M	70,20
Inst Adj	Hughes, Julayne	M	11,13A
Inst Adj	Irvine, Mary	M	61
Inst Adj	Joul, Susan	M	62C
Inst Adj	Lewis, Walter	M	63B
Inst Adj	Pitts, Frank	M	61
Inst Adj	Randall, Jean	D	66A,13D,13E,13B
Inst Adj	Thoma, August	M	32E,37,64C
Inst Adj	Yoon, Hye	M	61

MI1850 Saginaw Valley State University
Department of Music
7400 Bay Rd
University Center, MI 48710-0001
(989) 964-4159   Fax: (989) 964-7104
www.svsu.edu
E-mail: music@svsu.edu

4 Year Institution
Member of NASM

Chair: Jane C. Girdham, 80A

Applied Artist	Andrews, Rachel	D	61
Applied Artist	Angelo, Carl	D	66
PT	DeMull, Mark	M	65
PT	DeRoche, Brad	D	70
PT	Fairfield, Patrick K.	D	11,15,20,70
PT	Flegg, Mark	D	63A
PT	Franklin, Kip	M	64C
Prof	Girdham, Jane C.	D	11,12A,13B,13C,13E
Artist in Res	Hall, Jeff	B	47,64C,64E,66A,29B
PT	Leppert-Largent, Anna	M	11,66A
PT	Littel, Sue	M	64E
PT	Meyer, Julie	D	61
Prof	Nisula, Eric	D	11,55,67
PT	Penkala, Dan	B	70
Prof	Peretz, Marc	D	11,32,66D,34
Asst Prof	Simons, Kevin	M	61,36,32D,60A

PT	Soehnlen, Edward J.	D	11,66A,66G
PT	Stott, Susan	M	61
PT	Weyersberg, Roger	M	63C,63D
Assoc Prof	Wollner, William	M	11,13B,37,63B,60B
PT	Zantow, Thomas	M	64D

MI1900 Schoolcraft College
Department of Music
18600 Haggerty Rd
Livonia, MI 48152-3932
(734) 462-4400   Fax: (734) 462-4495
www.schoolcraft.cc.mi.us
E-mail: dmoreloc@schoolcraft.edu

2 Year Institution

Adj Prof	Bossart, Eugene	M	41,66A,66C
Adj Prof	Harden, Shirley	M	11
Prof	Morelock, Donald	M	13,11,12A,66A,66B
Asst Prof	Nissen, James	D	13A,13,37,34
Prof	Polot, Barton L.	D	10A,10B,10F,12,13
Adj Prof	Wotring, Linda	M	11,32A,32B,66A,66B

MI1950 Siena Heights University
Department of Music
1247 E Siena Heights Dr
Adrian, MI 49221-1755
(517) 264-7899   Fax: (517) 265-3380
www.sienaheights.edu
E-mail: mlorenz@sienaheights.edu

4 Year Institution

Chair: Susan Matych-Hager, 80A

Adj	Bitz, Lori	M	46
Adj	Deatrick, Linda	M	63B,66D
Assoc Prof	Ezoe, Magdalena	M	66A,13,12B,12A,41
Adj	Ford, Shannon	M	64C,64E
Adj	Hill, Kelly	M	64,38
Adj	Johnson, Cecilia	M	62A,62B
Asst Prof	Lorenz, Michael L.	M	13,47,63,29,34
Assoc Prof	Matych-Hager, Susan	M	12A,32,36,61
Adj	Schiller, Andrew	B	70
Adj	Swora, Matthew	M	62C,62D
Adj	Wagner, Lauren	M	61

MI1985 Southwestern Michigan College
Department of Fine & Perf. Arts
58900 Cherry Grove Rd
Dowagiac, MI 49047-9726
(269) 782-1000   Fax: (269) 782-8414
www.swmich.edu
E-mail: mdombrosky@swmich.edu

2 Year Institution

Chair: Marc Dombrosky, 80A
Dean: Elaine Foster, 80A

PT	Brown, Breighan M.	M	12A
Inst	Carew, David	M	36,61,40,32D,13C
PT	Crouch, Jay	M	63A,29
PT	Gartshore, Sarah	M	61
PT	Gibson, Christina	M	64A
PT	Keech, Christopher	B	64C,64E,37,48,47
PT	Keller, Deborah	M	66A,66C,66G
Inst	Korzun, Jonathan	D	32E,37,47,13
PT	Mow, Paul	M	61,54
PT	Ripley, Randal	B	65,50
PT	Roll, Marcus	M	61
PT	Whitaker-Auvil, Melissa	M	11,61

MI2000 Spring Arbor University
Department of Music
106 East Main
Spring Arbor, MI 49283
(517) 750-1200   Fax: (517) 750-3410
www.arbor.edu
E-mail: bbrown@arbor.edu

4 Year Liberal Arts Institution

Chair: J. Bruce Brown, 80A

Inst PT	Andrews, Mary	D	61
Prof	Brown, J. Bruce	D	13,10,11,34,51
Inst PT	Brundage, Cynthian	M	61
Inst PT	Feinberg, Joseph	M	62D
Inst PT	Harter, Melody		66A
Asst Prof	Heydenburg, Audrejean	M	11,12A,66A,66B,66C
Inst PT	Jones, Stacey		65
Inst PT	Kim, Ji Hyun	M	62A,62B
Prof	Livesay, Charles	D	60,32D,36,40,61
Inst PT	McInchak, Kellie	M	64C
Inst PT	Nebelung, Russell	M	70
Inst PT	Olin, Marissa H.		48,64A
Inst PT	Popham, Phillip F.	M	64B,10B,13C
Inst PT	Runyon, Renee		66A,66C
Inst PT	Slezak, Heide Marie	M	61
Inst PT	Teager, Michael	M	11,20
Asst Prof	Teichmer, Shawn	M	32,60,64,12A,11
Inst PT	Walbridge, William		70
Assoc Prof	Walrath, Brian	D	11,12A,65,31,34
Inst PT	Williams, Larry		70

MI2100 Univ of Michigan-Ann Arbor
School of Music, Theatre, & Dance
1100 Baits Dr
Ann Arbor, MI 48109-2085
(734) 764-0584   Fax: (734) 615-6616
www.music.umich.edu
E-mail: ckndll@umich.edu

4 Year Institution, Graduate School
Member of NASM

Master of Music in Collaborative Piano, Master of Arts in Composition, Master of Arts in Music Theory, Master of Music in Composition, Master of Music in Performance, Master of Music in Conducting, Master of Music in Church Music, Master of Music in Music Education, PhD in Music Theory, PhD in Music Education, DMA in Composition, DMA in Conducting, DMA in Performance, PhD in Music Theory-Composition, PhD in Musicology, Master of Arts in Musicology, Master of Music in Chamber Music, Master of Music in Arts Administration, Master of Music in Piano Pedagogy & Performance, Specialist in Music: Ethnomusicology (Graduate), Master of Music in Improvisation, Master of Music in Early Keyboard Instruments, Master of Music in Keyboard Instruments, Master of Music in Wind Instruments, DMA Piano Pedagogy & Performance, Master of Arts in Media Arts

Dean: Christopher Kendall, 80A
Chair, Theatre & Drama: Priscilla Lees, 80A
Associate Dean, Academic Affairs: Melody Lynn Racine, 80B,80H
Associate Dean, Graduate Studies: Steven M. Whiting, 80C,80H
Associate Dean, Faculty Affairs: Daniel Washington, 80H

Asst Prof	Adams, Catherine W.	M	54,60A
Assoc Prof	Allen, Geri	M	29
Asst Prof	Ball, Steven	D	69
Lect	Benson, Kelley	M	66A,66B
Assoc Prof	Berick, Yehonatan M.	B	62A
Assoc Prof	Berofsky, Aaron	M	62A
Asst Prof	Bishop, Andrew	D	29
Prof	Blackstone, Jerry O.	D	60,36
Assoc Prof	Boerma, Scott	M	60,37
Prof Emeritus	Bolcom, William E.	D	10
Prof	Borders, James M.	D	12,14B,71
Asst Prof	Burrow, Chad E.	M	64C
Prof	Campbell, William	M	63A
Assoc Prof	Castaldo, Kay		61
Assoc Prof	Castro, Christi-Anne Salazar	M	12
Prof	Chambers, Evan	M	10,45
Assoc Prof	Cheek, Timothy Mark	D	66C,39,61
Assoc Prof	Clague, Mark A.	B	12
Lect	Coade, Caroline	M	62B
Lect	Collier, Katherine	M	66A
Assoc Prof	Conway, Colleen	D	32
Assoc Prof	Corey, Jason	D	34
Assoc Prof	Crawford, Penelope	M	67F
Asst Prof	Cruz, Gabriela G.	D	12
Prof Emeritus	Culver, Robert L.	M	32,62B
Prof Emeritus	Dapogny, James	D	
Prof	Daugherty, Michael	D	10
Asst Prof Emeritus	De Puit, Gerald	B	54
Asst Prof	DeJesus, Ron		52,54
Lect	Ding, Ian	M	65
Assoc Prof	Dorsey, Rodney	M	60,37
Prof	Elliott, Anthony D.	B	62C
Assoc Prof	Ellis, John S.	D	66A
Asst Prof	Essl, Georg	D	34
Prof	Everett, Walter T.	D	13
Asst Prof	Fitzpatrick, Kate R.	M	32
Asst Prof	Fournier, Karen J.	D	13
Prof	Fulcher, Jane	PhD	12,12A
Prof	Gannett, Diana	D	62D
Assoc Prof	Garrett, Charles	M	12
Assoc Prof	Geary, Jason D.	D	12
Assoc Prof	Gilbert, Daniel	M	64C
Assoc Prof	Goodrich, Linda	B	54
Assoc Prof	Gosman, Alan	D	13
Assoc Prof	Gould, Michael	D	50
Asst Prof	Gramley, Joseph	D	65
Prof	Greene, Arthur	D	66B
Asst Prof	Grijalva, Robert	M	66F
Prof	Guck, Marion A.	D	13
Asst Prof	Gurevich, Michael	PhD	34
Prof	Haithcock, Michael	M	60,37
Prof	Halen, David		62A
Prof	Hall, Patricia	D	13
Assoc Prof	Harding, Christopher	M	66A,66C,66D
Lect	Hayden, Marion	M	29,62D
Assoc Prof	Helton, Caroline	D	61
Prof	Herseth, Freda	M	61
Asst Prof	Ho, Meilu	D	12
Assoc Prof	Holland, Joan	B	62E
Assoc Prof	Hopkins, Michael	D	32
Assoc Prof	Hurst, Robert	B	29
Assoc Prof	Jackson, David Lee	M	63C
Prof	Jennings, Andrew W.	B	62A
Lect	Johns, Michele S.	D	66G
Prof	Kaenzig, Fritz	M	63D
Prof	Kane, Angela	PhD	52
Prof	Katz, Martin E.	B	41,66C
Prof	Kendall, Christopher	M	60B
Lect	Kennedy, Bryan		63B
Prof	Kibbie, James W.	D	66G
Prof	Kiesler, Kenneth	M	60B,38
Prof	King, Nancy Ambrose	D	64B
Adj Lect	Kirschenmann, Mark	D	47
Assoc Prof	Kirshner, Andrew	D	34
Prof	Korsyn, Kevin E.	D	13
Asst Prof	Kuster, Kristin P.	D	10
Prof	Lam, Joseph S. C.	D	14
Lect	Lees, Christopher	M	60B
	Lees, Priscilla	D	
Prof	Lindsay, Priscilla	M	54
Asst Prof	Lucas, William G.		63A
Assoc Prof	Lusmann, Stephen	M	61
Assoc Prof	Lyman, Jeffrey	D	64D
Assoc Prof	Madama, Mark	B	54
Prof	Mason, Marilyn	D	66G
Prof	McCarthy, Marie F.	D	32
Prof	Mead, Andrew W.	D	13A,13
Assoc Prof	Mengozzi, Stefano	D	12
Lect	Molina, Stephen	B	62D
Prof	Monts, Lester P.	D	12
Assoc Prof Emerita	Morris, Joan		54
Prof	Nagel, Louis B.	D	66A
Prof	Olsen, Stanford	B	61
Assoc Prof	O'Modhrain, Sile	PhD	34
Asst Prof	Ovalle, Jonathan		65
Prof	Parmentier, Edward L.	M	12A,12,66H
Assoc Prof	Pelton, Carmen	B	70
Lect	Petty, Judith V.		13
Assoc Prof	Petty, Wayne C.	D	13A,13
Asst Prof	Piper, Scott	D	61
Prof	Porter, Amy	M	64A
Assoc Prof	Racine, Melody Lynn	M	61,54
Lect	Ricotta, Charles		65,37
Assoc Prof	Rodriguez, Carlos Xavier	D	32
Asst Prof	Rogers, Eugene C.	M	36
Assoc Prof	Rowe, Ellen H.	M	47,29,66A
Prof	Rush, Stephen J.	D	52,34A
Assoc Prof	Santos, Erik	D	10,34A,45
Assoc Prof	Sarath, Ed	M	46,29
Assoc Prof	Satyendra, Ramon	D	13
Prof	Schoenfield, Paul	D	10
Prof	Schotten, Yizhak		62B
Assoc Prof	Serbo, Rico	B	61
Assoc Prof	Sheil, Martha	B	61
Prof	Sheng, Bright	D	13,10
Prof	Shipps, Stephen	M	62A
Prof Emeritus	Shirley, George I.	B	39,61
Prof	Sinta, Donald J.	M	64E
Assoc Prof	Skadsem, Julie A.	D	32D,32
Prof	Skelton, Logan	D	66A
Prof	Stein, Louise K.		12
Lect	Sutherland, Enid		62C
Assoc Prof	Swedberg, Robert M.	M	61
Lect	Travers, Martha	D	29

Prof Emeritus	Udow, Michael W.	D	65
Assoc Prof	Unsworth, Adam	M	63B
Asst Prof	Vojcic, Aleksandra	PhD	13
Lect	Votapek, Kathryn	M	62A
Assoc Prof	Wagner, Brent	M	54
Prof	Washington, Daniel	M	61
Prof	West, Stephen		61
Asst Prof	Westphal, Cynthia	M	54
Prof	Whiting, Steven M.	D	12
Prof	Wiley, Roland J.	D	12A
Assoc Prof	Wilson, Dennis E.	D	63C,29,47

MI2110 Univ of Michigan-Dearborn

LPA-Music
4901 Evergreen Rd
Dearborn, MI 48128-2406
(313) 593-5077   Fax: (313) 593-5552
www.umd.umich.edu
E-mail: rischarr@umd.umich.edu

4 Year Institution

Chair, Literature, Philosophy and Arts: Susan N. Erickson, 80A
Music Contact: Richard A. Rischar, 80A

Inst PT	Caron-Gatto, Lisa J.	M	66D
Inst PT	Johnston, Jesse A.	PhD	11,12A,29A
Inst PT	Nissen, James C.	D	11,12A
Assoc Prof	Rischar, Richard A.	PhD	12,29,40,14,20
Inst PT	Roberts, Brian S.	M	70

MI2120 Univ of Michigan-Flint

Department of Music
French Hall 126
303 E Kearsley St
Flint, MI 48502-2186
(810) 762-3377   Fax: (810) 762-3326
www.umflint.edu/music
E-mail: chumov@umflint.edu

4 Year Institution
Member of NASM

Chair: Lois L. Alexander, 80A
Dean: DJ Trela, 80A
Associate Dean: Ricardo Alfaro, 80H
Assistant Dean: Roy Barnes, 80H

Assoc Prof	Alexander, Lois L.	D	63D,49,12,32
PT	Carr, Julie Anne	M	61,11
PT	Cavallini, Francesco	M	70
PT	Cech, Jessica	M	64A,11,12A
PT	Chaney, Carol	M	34
PT	Coviak, James	M	50,65
PT	Dahman, Jamie	D	61
Asst Prof	DiBlassio, Brian	M	47,13,43
PT	Douglass, Mark	M	11
PT	Duquaine, Kenneth	M	64,13E
PT	Hall, Amy	M	32
Asst Prof	Heidenreich, Christopher	D	37,49,11,10F
PT	Hill, John	M	65
Asst Prof	Hristova, Gabriela	D	36,60
PT	Kaye, G. Donald	M	66G
PT	Leshchinskaya, Ida	M	66A
PT	Pitts, Frank		66D
PT	Price, Jeffrey	M	64E,11
PT	Prouty, Patrick	M	47,13,43,10
Asst Prof	Salvador, Karen	D	32
PT	Schuster, James	M	63B
PT	Wright, Joseph	M	64C,11
PT	Yancho, Mari	M	70
PT	Zimmerman, Dean	M	64D

MI2200 Wayne State University

Department of Music
1321 Old Main
4841 Cass Ave
Detroit, MI 48202
(313) 577-1795   Fax: (313) 577-5420
www.music.wayne.edu
E-mail: music@wayne.edu

4 Year Institution, Graduate School
Member of NASM

Master of Arts in Music, Master of Music in Performance, Master of Music in Conducting, Master of Music in Music Education, Master of Music in Music Theory-Composition, Master of Music in Jazz Performance, Graduate Certificate in Orchestral Studies

Chair: John D. Vander Weg, 80A
Academic Advisor: Maurice Draughn, 80B
Associate Chair & Dir., Undergraduate Studies: Norah Duncan, IV, 80B,80H
Dir., Graduate Studies: Mary A. Wischusen, 80C

PT	Adams, Dwight		63A
Asst Prof	Anderson, Jonathan	D	10,13
PT	Applegate, Geoffrey	M	62A
PT	Ball, Gerrie	M	66C,66D
PT	Benson, George		29,64E
Assoc Prof	Bianchi, Douglas	M	37,13,60B
Assoc Prof	Braunschweig, Karl	D	13
Assoc Prof	Brockington, Frances N.	M	61,39
PT	Brzozowski, Kazimierz		66A
PT	Burdette, Glenn E.	D	12,66A,66H
Assoc Prof	Butler, Abigail	D	32
PT	Carryer, Steven J.	M	70,29
PT	Chanteaux, Marcy K.	B	62C
PT	Claeys, Keith	M	65
PT	Coade, Caroline	M	62B
Assoc Prof	Collins, Christopher	M	47,64E,29A,35
Assoc Prof	Conway, Robert	D	66A,66B,66D,12A
Lect	Court, Tom		34
PT	Custer, Gerald	D	36,60A,13
PT	DiChiera, David	D	39
PT	Dobbins, Sean		29
PT	Draughn, Maurice	M	62E,66G
Asst Prof	Duchan, Joshua S.	D	14
PT	Duensing, Dorothy	M	61
Assoc Prof	Duncan, Norah	D	36,13C,66G
PT	Dyament, Lee	M	70
PT	Finlay, Gordon J.		61
PT	Flegg, Mark	D	63A,32E
PT	Foreman, Kelly	D	14
PT	Fusik, James	M	64E
PT	Gebhart, Gail Y.	M	66A
PT	Guinn, John R.	M	12
PT	Hanoian, Scott	M	36,60A
Prof Emeritus	Hartway, James	D	13A,10,10F,66D,13B
PT	Hellick, Gary J.	M	63C
PT	Hutchinson, Larry	M	62D
PT	Janowsky, Maxim	B	62D
PT	Jennings, David	B	63A
PT	Karloff, Michael	M	47,46,29,66A
PT	Keller, Paul		62D
PT	Kischuk, Ronald K.	B	63C,29
PT	Koukios, Ann Marie	D	36,12A,66D
Prof Emeritus	Labuta, Joseph	D	60,32
PT	Lane, Betty D.	M	61,39
PT	Larson, Laura A.	B	64A
Prof	Markou, Kypros L.	M	10F,38,62A
PT	Mastrogiacomo, Steven J.	M	66A
Asst Prof	Matthews, Wendy K.	PhD	32,32E
PT	May, Eldonna	D	11,12
Lect	McCaskill, Janet L.	M	63D,32E,60B,32C
PT	Meyer, Lisa M.	M	32
Prof Emeritus	Michaels, Matthew		47,66A,29
Asst Prof	Miller, Russell	M	29,64
Adj Assoc Prof PT	Molina, Steven R.	M	62D
PT	Monear, Clifford E.		29,66A
Adj Inst PT	Naylor, Michael L.	D	14
PT	Newsome, Charles	M	29,46,47,70
PT	Nulty, Dennis	M	63D
PT	Oien, Theodore		64C
PT	Paquette-Abt, Mary	PhD	12
PT	Parker, Gene	B	29
PT	Pipho, Robert S.		47,29,66A
PT	Pituch, Karl	B	63B
PT	Platter, Donald R.	M	37,32
PT	Pliskow, Dan J.		62D,29
Adj Asst Prof PT	Prowse, Ronald H.	D	66G
PT	Rattner, Richard D.		35A
Assoc Prof Emeritus	Richards, Doris	M	66A,66D
PT	Roberts, Brian	M	70
PT	Rodgers, Ernest E.	M	64E,29,47
Assoc Prof	Roelofs, Laura Leigh	D	62A,32E,41,11
PT	Ryan, James		65,29

PT	Schoendorff, Matthew	D	10
PT	Schoon, Marcus	M	64D
PT	Shapiro, Stephanie	M	64B
Asst Prof	Stephens, Emery	D	61
PT	Tanau, Marian	M	62A
PT	Taylor, David B.		29,65
PT	Terry-Ross, Patricia	M	62E
Prof	Tini, Dennis J.	M	60,36,29,35
Assoc Prof Emeritus	Tuohey, Terese M.	D	32,32E
Prof	Vander Weg, John D.	D	13B,13F,13E,13
PT	Vander Weg, Judith B.	M	62C
PT	VanValkenburg, James	B	62B
Adj Asst Prof PT	Ventura, Brian J.	B	64B
PT	Waldon, Stanley H.	D	32,66D
PT	Williams, Robert S.		64D
Assoc Prof	Wischusen, Mary A.	D	12A,12,14C
PT	Wu, Hai-Xin	B	62A

MI2250 Western Michigan University
School of Music
1903 W Michigan Ave
Kalamazoo, MI 49008-5434
(269) 387-4667 Fax: (269) 387-1113
www.wmich.edu/music
E-mail: david.colson@wmich.edu

4 Year Institution, Graduate School
Member of NASM

Master of Music in Composition, Master of Music in Performance, Master of Music in Conducting, Master of Music in Music Education, Master of Music in Music Therapy

Director: David J. Colson, 80A
Assistant Director: Margaret J. Hamilton, 80H
Associate Director: Kevin West, 80H

Assoc Prof	Adams, Richard	D	10,49,13L,13,10F
Other	Campos, John	M	35C,35D
Prof	Code, David Loberg	D	13
Prof	Colson, David J.	D	10,65,60
Asst Prof	Councell-Vargas, Martha	D	64A,48
PT	Cowan, Elizabeth		61
Asst Prof	Cowan, Scott M.	D	11,47,63,29
Prof	Curtis-Smith, Curtis O.	M	10,14,66A,20G
PT	Davis, Duane Shields	M	29,61
Prof	Fedotov, Igor	D	51,62B
Assoc Prof	Fitzgerald, Gregory	M	16
Assoc Prof	Foulk, Lin	M	63B,15,41,48,49
Prof	Gauthier, Delores	D	32
PT	Griffin, John C.	D	10,13,13C,66C
PT	Hall, Keith	M	29,65
Other	Hamilton, Margaret J.	M	63B,32,13,35E
PT	Harrell, Greg	M	61
Other	Hong, Yat-Lam	D	66F
PT	Hovnanian, Stephanie	M	64C
PT	Humiston, Robert G.	D	13
Prof	Jacobson, Daniel C.	D	11,12A,12,34
Prof	Jones, Stephen	D	49,63A,20G
Asst Prof	Kness, Karen	D	61
Prof	Knific, Renata	M	51,62A
Prof	Knific, Thomas	M	47,51,62D,46,29
Prof	Kynaston, Trent	M	47,64E,46,29
Prof	Little, David	D	39,61,54
Other	Little, Julie Evans	M	13
Prof	Lychner, John	D	32,37
PT	Mannion, Grace	M	61
Assoc Prof	Miller, Michael	D	13,48,64B
PT	Montgomery, Annette	M	32E
Other	Montgomery, David L.	M	32,37
Prof	Moonert, Judy	M	14,50,65
Asst Prof	Oliver, Ronald D.	D	36,60A,32D
Asst Prof	Prewitt, Kenneth	D	39,61
Assoc Prof	Ratner, Carl J.	M	39,61,54
Prof	Ricci, Robert	D	13,10F,12B,29
Prof	Roederer, Silvia	D	66A,66B,66C,66D
Assoc Prof	Rose, Gwendolyn	D	13,48,64D
Assoc Prof	Roth, Edward	M	33
PT	Schrock, Karl	D	66G
PT	Schumaker, Adam T.	M	10,11
	Scoles, Shannon	M	13C
Prof	Sims, Lori E.	M	66
Prof	Smith, David S.	D	32
Asst Prof	Smith, Kenneth H.	D	32,34,12F
Prof	Spradling, Robert	D	60,37
Assoc Prof	Steel, Matthew	D	12A,12,14,55
PT	Stoner, Elizabeth	D	61
Prof	Thornburg, Scott	M	13A,13,49,63A
Prof	Uchimura, Bruce	M	60,51,62C
Other	Uchimura, Susan	M	66A,66B,66C
PT	Wheaton, Michael		29
Assoc Prof	Wicklund, Karen	D	61
Prof	Wilson, Brian		33

Prof	Wolfinbarger, Steve	D	49,63C,29A
Prof	Wong, Bradley	M	48,64C

MN0040 Anoka Ramsey Community College
Department of Music
11200 Mississippi Blvd NW
Coon Rapids, MN 55433-3470
(763) 422-3534 Fax: (763) 422-3341
www.anokaramsey.edu
E-mail: melissa.bergstrom@anokaramsey.edu

2 Year Institution

Chair: Melissa Bergstrom, 80A

Inst FT	Anderson, Eric	M	11,41
Inst FT	Bergstrom, Melissa	M	36,40,12A,38,61
Inst FT	Bergstrom, Samuel	M	20,32,37,41,47
Inst FT	Clark, Evan	M	63D
Inst PT	Duncan, Preston	M	64E
Inst PT	Gaudette, Nicholas	M	38,62D
Inst PT	Giddings, Lorelei	M	64B
Inst PT	Glenn, Brian	A	65
Inst PT	Gudmundson, Paula	M	64A,64,12A,14
Inst PT	Jenson, Joyce	M	66
Inst PT	Joseph, Richard	M	11,61
Inst PT	Kajiwara, Greg	M	64C
Inst PT	Kern, Stacy J.	D	64D
Inst PT	Lindenfelser, Kathryn	M	11,20,33
Inst PT	Noraker, Dan	M	63D
Inst PT	Olson, John	M	63C
Inst PT	Perkins, Richard	M	13
Inst PT	Salvo, Joel	M	62C,11
Inst FT	Senn, Geoff	M	29A,63A,34,41,11
Inst PT	Toliver, Nicki Bakko	M	11,13,40,61
Inst PT	VanBurkleo-Carbonara, Natalie	B	62A,62B
Inst PT	Vanselow, Jason	D	20,70

MN0050 Augsburg College
Department of Music
2211 Riverside Ave
Minneapolis, MN 55454-1338
(612) 330-1265 Fax: (612) 330-1264
www.augsburg.edu/music
E-mail: musicdept@augsburg.edu

4 Year Institution
Member of NASM

Chair: Robert J. Stacke, 80A

Inst PT	Anderson, Trudi J.	M	64A,48
Inst PT	Barber, Matthew C.	B	65,50
Inst PT	Barnett, Carol	M	10
Inst PT	Bretschger, Fred	M	62D
Asst Prof	Buck, Michael W.	D	32
Inst PT	Comeaux, Garrick	M	11
Inst PT	Dahlgren, Marv	B	65
Assoc Prof	Dawe, Jill A.	D	13,66A,66B,66D
Asst Prof	Diamond, Douglas	M	60B,38,51,12A
Inst	Doak, Bridget A.	D	33
Inst PT	Druck, Susan S.	M	61
Inst PT	Erickson, Lynn M.	D	63A
Inst PT	Fried, Janet Gottschall	B	61,39
Prof Emeritus	Gabrielsen, Stephen M.	D	
Inst PT	Gerth, Jennifer L.	M	64C
Inst PT	Grundahl, Nancy J.	M	36
Assoc Prof	Hendrickson, Peter A.	D	60,36,13,66G
Inst PT	Holroyd, Megan Calgren	M	11,35
Inst PT	Horozaniecki, Mary A.	B	62A,62B
Inst PT	Hutton, Joan	M	64E
Inst PT	Jacobson, James	M	62C
Assoc Prof	Kagin, Roberta S.	M	33,11
Assoc Prof	Kantar, Ned D.	D	13C,35
Inst PT	Kienzle, Kathy	M	62E
Assoc Prof	Klemp, Merilee I.	D	12A,12,64B,48,40
Inst PT	Kraut, Rena	M	64C
Inst PT	Lund, Steve	B	63C,63D
Inst PT	McGuire, K. Christian	M	11,47
Inst PT	Merz, Laurie	M	64D
Inst	Meyer, Peter	M	33
Inst PT	Milenkovic, Vladan	M	29,20
Inst PT	Penning, Rick	D	61
Inst PT	Raths, O. Nicholas	D	70,51
Assoc Prof	Stacke, Robert J.	D	37,47,29
Inst PT	Stern, Andrea	M	62E
Asst Prof	Thompson, Sonja K.	M	61,39,54,41,42
Inst PT	Webb, William	B	33
Inst PT	Wettstein Sadler, Shannon Leigh		66A,66C,13F
Inst PT	Williams, Yolanda	D	29A,20
Inst PT	Wilson, Matthew	M	63B

MN0150 Bemidji State University
Department of Music
1500 Birchmont Dr NE #16
Bemidji, MN 56601-2600
(218) 755-2915   Fax: (218) 755-4369
www.bemidjistate.edu
E-mail: jhaworth@bemidjistate.edu

4 Year Institution
Member of NASM

Chair: Janice Haworth, 80A

Assoc Prof	Carlson, Stephen J.	D	66A,66B,66C
Vstng Inst	Gallagher, Fulton	D	61
Vstng Inst	Gaston, Greg	B	34,11
Vstng Inst	Hanson, Melanie	D	62A,13
Vstng Inst	Hanson, Michael	D	64C
Assoc Prof	Haworth, Janice	D	32A,32C,32B,36,20A
Prof	Logan, P. Bradley	D	60A,36,32D,40
Prof	Lyren, Delon	D	63A,63B,49,45
Vstng Inst	Maxwell, Margaret	M	66A,66H,66G
Vstng Inst	Nelson, Susan	M	64A
Asst Prof	Renbarger, Cory James	D	39,61
Vstng Inst	Reznicek, Steven	M	36,32B,32C
Vstng Inst	Samsa, Louis		70
Vstng Inst	Sundeen, Eric	B	50,65
Asst Prof	Svanoe, Erika K.	D	64C,60B,37,32E,45
Vstng Inst	Wagner, Linda	M	61

MN0200 Bethany Lutheran College
Department of Music
700 Luther Dr
Mankato, MN 56001-4436
(507) 344-7300   Fax: (507) 344-7376
www.blc.edu
E-mail: dmarzolf@blc.edu

4 Year Liberal Arts Institution

Fine Arts Administrator: Lois Jaeger, 80A
Chair: Dennis Marzolf, 80A
Dean, Academic Affairs: Ronald Younge

Adj Prof	Balge, Bethel	B	66A
Adj Prof	Burns, Logan		70
Prof	DeGarmeaux, Mark	M	31A
Adj Prof	Draper, Charles		65
Adj Prof	Fredrickson, Ann	M	61,36,39,54,13C
Adj Prof	Giles, Ruth		64A
Adj Prof	Hermanson, Erik	B	46
Adj	Kresnicka, Judith	M	12A,66G,55C
Adj Prof	Lindberg, John	D	64D
Prof	Lo, Adrian	M	12A,37,38,47,62
Prof	Marzolf, Dennis	M	60,36,31A,61,54
Adj Prof	Matzke, Laura	B	66A,66G,66C,68,31A
Adj Prof	Merseth, Megan	M	61
Adj Prof	Moxness, Paul	D	64C,64E
Adj Prof	Nuessmeier, Tom	B	63
Adj Prof	Rodgers, Joseph	D	62C
Prof	Tollefson, Tim	M	13,10A,34
Adj Prof	Wayne, Nicholas	M	61,13C
Adj Prof	Wurster, Kathryn	M	61

MN0250 Bethel University
Department of Music
3900 Bethel Dr
Saint Paul, MN 55112-6999
(651) 638-6400   Fax: (651) 638-6001
www.bethel.edu
E-mail: music@bethel.edu

4 Year Institution

Chair: Jonathan Veenker, 80A

PT	Allen, Ben	B	61
PT	Allmann, Kimberly	M	63B
PT	Anderson, Trudi	M	64A
PT	Banti, Mary	M	64D
Emeritus	Berglund, Robert	D	
PT	Bradley-Vacco, Lynda	D	38,62A,62B,51
PT	Brath, Wally	B	46
PT	Brueske, Jeffrey	M	46
PT	Crittenden, David	D	70
PT	Crowe, Gary	M	64E
PT	Goold, Stephen P.	B	46
PT	Hanson, Angela	D	62A
PT	Harms, Jason	B	47
PT	Heberlein, Yuko	M	62A
Prof	Johnson, Herbert	D	11,66A,66B,66C
PT	Kausch, Mark L.	M	62D
PT	Li, Juan	D	66A,66D
PT	Madison, Jeffrey	D	61
PT	Madura, Julie	B	64B
PT	Oie, Cheryl	B	61
Prof	Port, Dennis	D	60A,36
Assoc Prof	Poulson, Ruby Ann	D	61
PT	Povolny, John	M	65
PT	Reimers-Parker, Nancy	D	36
Prof	Rhoads, Mark	D	11,32,31A
Prof	Self, Stephen	D	12A,66A,66G
PT	Shull, Kevin	M	44
PT	Sohriakoff, Pam	M	66C
Prof	Thompson, Steven	D	37,60B,63A,32E,49
PT	Urban, Emily	B	66C
PT	Urban, Marshall	M	61
Assoc Prof	Veenker, Jonathan	D	13,10F,10
PT	Victorsen, Catherine	M	62E
PT	Wang, Hong	D	62C
PT	Wyland, Richard	M	64C
PT	Zimmerman, Larry		63D,63C

MN0300 Carleton College
Department of Music
1 N College St
Northfield, MN 55057-4001
(507) 222-4347   Fax: (507) 222-5561
www.carleton.edu
E-mail: music@carleton.edu

4 Year Institution

Co-Chair: Lawrence Archbold, 80A
Co-Chair: Melinda Russell, 80A
Dir., Artist/Performance Series: Ronald Rodman, 80F

Senior Lect PT	Allen, Benjamin	M	61
Lect PT	Anderson, Gwen	M	63B,42
Prof	Archbold, Lawrence	D	11,12A,66G,15,12D
Senior Lect PT	Bryce, Jackson	D	64D
Prof	Burnett, Lawrence E.	D	36,40,31F,61,13A
Lect PT	Caviani, Laura	M	66A
Senior Lect PT	Deichert, Lynn	M	63A
Senior Lect	Ellinger, John	B	41,34,70
Senior Lect PT	Ericksen, Elizabeth	M	62A,62B,42
Asst Prof	Flory, Andrew	D	12A,29A
Asst Prof	Freeman, Alexander	D	10,13,11
Senior Lect PT	Hall, Janean	M	66G,66H
Lect PT	Hong, Gao		20C,20E
Senior Lect PT	Horozaniecki, Mary B.	B	62A,62B,42
Senior Lect PT	Huber, Kenneth	M	66A
Senior Lect PT	Jamsa, Martha	M	64A
Senior Lect PT	Johnson, Jay L.	M	65,50,42
Prof Emeritus	Kelly, Stephen K.	D	12A,55,29A
Lect PT	Kent, Patricia	M	61
Senior Lect PT	Klemp, Merilee	D	64B
Inst PT	Kreitzer, Mark	M	20G
Senior Lect PT	Krusemeyer, Mark	D	67B
Prof	London, Justin	D	13,12B,12F,20G,12A
Lect PT	Martin, Constance	M	62D
Senior Lect PT	Martz, Mary	B	61
Prof Emerita	Mayer, Anne B.	M	13A,41,66A,12A
Inst PT	McCright, Matthew	D	66A,66C,66B
Asst Prof	Melville, Nicola	D	66A,41
Senior Lect PT	Niemisto, Elinor	M	62E
Senior Lect PT	Olsen, Nina	D	64C,42
Senior Lect PT	Penning, Rick	D	61
Prof Emeritus	Rhodes, Phillip	M	13A,13,10,11
Prof	Rodman, Ronald	D	13,37,63C,63D,12D
Lect PT	Rosenberg, Thomas	M	62C,41
Prof	Russell, Melinda	D	14
Senior Lect PT	Saunders, David	M	41,64E
Lect PT	Schilling, Travis	B	62D
Vstng Asst Prof	Semanik, Timothy	D	38
Senior Lect PT	Singley, David	M	70,47,41
Prof	Valdivia, Hector	D	10F,60,11,38,41
Senior Lect PT	Whetstone, David		20D
Senior Lect	Widman, Marcia	M	66A

MN0350 Coll of St Benedict/St Johns Univ
Department of Music
37 College Ave S
Saint Joseph, MN 56374-2001
(320) 363-5796   Fax: (320) 363-2504
www.csbsju.edu/music
E-mail: eturley@csbsju.edu

4 Year Institution, Joint with St. Johns University
Member of NASM

Dean: Joseph DesJardins, 80A
Dean: Richard Ice, 80A
Chair: Edward L. Turley, 80A
Dir., Artist/Performance Series: Brian Jose, 80F
Dir., Institute/Festival/Workshop: Deborah Lehman, 80F

Asst Prof	Arnott, J. David	D	38,62A,62B,51
Asst Prof	Campbell, Brian G.	D	13,10A,20,12B,10F
Lect	Cudd, Patti	D	65,32E,50
Inst PT	Dennihan, James	D	66A
Inst PT	Dirlam, Richard	D	64E,48
Inst PT	Drontle, Lisa	M	66A
Inst PT	Fedele, Andrea	D	64B,64A
Assoc Prof	Finley, Carolyn Sue	D	39,61
Inst PT	Hagen Givens, Marcie	D	61
	Handel-Johnson, Brenda		36
Inst PT	Heywood, Andre'	M	36
Assoc Prof	Kasling, Kim R.	D	12A,66G,31A,66A
	Kasling, Tess	M	16
Inst PT	Kausch, Mark	M	62D
Asst Prof	Kent, Patricia A.	D	61
Prof	Koopmann, Robert	D	66
Inst PT	Magney, Lucia	D	62C,62D,32E,42
Asst Prof	Pauley, John-Bede	D	61,13,11
Inst PT	Rassier, Daniel	M	63,37
Inst PT	Raths, O. Nicholas	D	70,13C
Assoc Prof	Theimer, Axel K.	D	60A,36,61,32D
Asst Prof	Thornton, Bruce	D	60B,41,47,64
Prof	Turley, Edward L.	D	11,66A,66B,66C
Assoc Prof	Walker, Gregory	D	13,10,45,34
Prof	White, Dale A.	D	60B,37,41,32E,63
Inst	Zahn, George	M	32

MN0450 College of St Scholastica
Department of Music
1200 Kenwood Ave
Duluth, MN 55811
(218) 723-6194   Fax: (218) 723-6290
www.css.edu/x3330.xml
E-mail: lhouse@css.edu

4 Year Institution

Chair: LeAnn House, 80A

Adj	Aerie, Josh	M	62C
Asst Prof	Amundson, Bret	DMA	32,36,60A
Inst	Bastian, William	M	39,61,11
Adj	Chelseth, Gretchen		66A
Asst Prof	Connelly, Marianne	M	37,32,47,64,60B
Asst Prof	Craycraft, Jeremy	D	20,50,34,65
Adj	Craycraft, Nicole		62A
Prof	House, LeAnn	D	13,12,66
PT	Kaiser, Tyler	B	70,10,13
Adj	Lanzer, Kate J.	D	66A
Adj	Lemire, Janell		62E
Adj	Martin, Edward		67G
Adj	Osborn, Vince	M	62D
Prof	Schwarze, Penny	D	12A,11,38,62A,67A
Adj	Van Brunt, Laurie	M	64B
Asst Prof PT	Vosen, Elyse Carter	D	14,15

MN0600 Concordia College
Department of Music
901 S 8th St
Moorhead, MN 56562
(218) 299-4414   Fax: (218) 299-3058
www.cord.edu/music
E-mail: chabora@cord.edu

4 Year Institution
Member of NASM

Chair: Robert J. Chabora, 80A
Associate Dir., Music Organizations: Kent Loken, 80E
Associate Dir., Music Organizations: Gordon Moe, 80E
Office of Cultural Events: Timothy Wollenzein, 80F

Inst	Beyers, Foster	M	38,60B
Prof	Breedon, Daniel	D	13,10,12A,14
Emeritus	Buckley, Wendell	D	61
Inst PT	Cessor, Tyler	M	64E
Prof	Chabora, Robert J.	D	66A,66B,66D,11,13
Prof Emeritus	Childs, David T.	D	13,12A
Assoc Prof	Clausen, Rene	D	60,36
Inst PT	Clemenson, Andrew	B	65
Inst PT	Coates, Michael	M	70
Assoc Prof	Cohen, Joanne	M	32,51,62A,62B
Inst	Culloton, Michael		36,12A
Asst Prof	Dickey, Nathaniel H.	M	37,63C,63D,32E,49
Inst PT	Dietzler, Judy	D	66A
Prof	Eyler, David	D	32,50,65,42
Inst PT	Ferreira, David	D	66A,47
Inst PT	Fogderud, Marla G.	D	61
Inst PT	Foster, Shimmer	M	66A
Inst PT	Gruber, Nikolas	M	70
Asst Prof	Haberman, Peter J.	D	37,32E
Inst	Hagen, Julie	M	32,36
Assoc Prof	Halverson, Peter	D	61
Assoc Prof	Hamilton, David	M	61,12A
Asst Prof	Hamilton, Gregory	D	62C
Lect	Hamilton, Karen	M	61
Inst PT	Hamilton, Kate	M	62B
Inst PT	Hammerling, Margaret	B	64A
Assoc Prof	Harris, Debora	M	64A
Prof	Hershberger, Jay	D	66A
Inst	Hindemith, Paul B.	D	61
Inst PT	Horan, Rachel	B	61
Inst PT	Huttlin, Edward	D	63C
Asst Prof	Janz, Holly A.	D	61
Inst PT	Johnson, Peggy J.	D	13
Assoc Prof	Knudsvig, Peter	D	63A
Inst	Linde-Capistran, Jane	M	41,62A,62B
Asst Prof	Makela, Steven L.	D	10A,10B,13,10,34D
Inst	McCallum, Kyle	B	64D
Inst PT	Mercer, Amy	B	66
Assoc Prof	Meyer, Jeffrey	D	12A,13,11,14,20
Inst	Narum, Jessica	M	13
Asst Prof	Nash, Anne Jennifer	D	61
Inst PT	Neill, Douglas	M	62D
Inst PT	Nustad, Corinne	M	66A
Inst PT	Peterson, Jennifer	B	64B
Asst Prof	Peterson, Russell	M	47,48,64D,64E,35G
Inst PT	Prigge, Sarah	M	66A
Assoc Prof	Rauschnabel, June	M	44,61
Prof Emeritus	Richmond, Thomas	D	13,10,11,12A
Lect	Sawyer, Lisa Lee	D	13,61,66A
Lect	Schramm, Barbara	M	61
Inst PT	Sulich, Stephen	M	39
Asst Prof	Thrasher, Lucy	M	61,39
Inst PT	Wakefield, Karin	M	63B,66A
Assoc Prof	Wakefield, Leigh	D	64C
Inst PT	Westgard, Jessica	B	44
Prof	Worth, David	D	66A

MN0610 Concordia University - St. Paul
Department of Music
275 Syndicate St N
St. Paul, MN 55014
(651) 641-8828   Fax: (651) 603-6260
www.csp.edu
E-mail: dmennicke@csp.edu

4 Year Liberal Arts Institution

Dean, College of Arts & Sciences: David Lumpp, 80A
Chair: David Mennicke, 80A
Assistant Chair: Monica Murray, 80H

Adj Prof	Bartz, Karen	M	66A,66D
Adj Prof	Betinis, Abbie	M	10
Adj Prof	Bujak, Ewa	M	62A,62B
Adj Prof	Chacholiades, Linda P.	M	11,20,12A
Prof Emeritus	Eggert, John	D	10,13,31A,66G
Adj Prof	Elsbernd, Jerome	M	61
Adj Prof	Fahy, Alison	M	32E,51
Adj Prof	Griffin, Andrew	B	36
	Henry, Joseph W.	D	11
Adj Prof	Hilson, Keith	M	63C,63D
Adj Prof	Isakson, Aaron	M	32E,37,50,60B,65
Adj Prof	Kennard, Jennifer C.	D	64A
Adj Prof	Kennedy, Nathan	D	13A,13B,13C,13D,13F
Adj Prof	Lammers, Paula	M	29,61
Adj Prof	Langlois, Kristina	D	66G
Adj Prof	Levin, Oleg	D	66A
Adj Prof	Livingston, Don	JD	66H
Adj Prof	Mathis, Carolynne	M	32E,44,65
Prof	Mennicke, David	D	31A,32,60,61

Assoc Prof	Murray, Monica	JD	11,13A,61
Adj Prof	Parker, Nancy	D	11,20,32D
Adj Prof	Richards, Rebekah	M	66C
Adj Prof	Rossmiller, Adam	D	29,47
Adj Prof	Roth, John	M	34,40,41,70
Adj Prof	Rubin, Jennifer	M	62D
Prof Emeritus	Schenk, Kathryn E.	D	11,66A,66H
Adj Prof	Schimming, Paul	D	32E,64E,64C
Adj Prof	Seerup, Mark	B	64D
Adj Prof	Senn, Takako Seimiya	D	63A
Term Prof	Speer, Shari	M	36,39,61
Adj Prof	Wang, Hong	D	64C
Adj Prof	White, Bill	M	47
Adj Prof	White, Kim	M	32A,32B

MN0620 Crossroads College

Department of Music
920 Mayowood Rd SW
Rochester, MN 55902-2382
(507) 288-4563   Fax: (507) 288-9046
www.crossroadscollege.edu
E-mail: bdunbar@crossroadscollege.edu

4 Year Institution

Chair: Brian Dunbar, 80A

Inst PT	Carey, Kevin		70
Inst PT	Carriere, Marilyn	M	66A,66D
Prof PT	Collins, Kimberly	M	61
Prof	Dunbar, Brian	M	10,13,36,34,60A

MN0625 Crown College

Department of Music
8700 College View Dr
St. Bonifacius, MN 55375
(952) 446-4231   Fax: (952) 446-4149
www.crown.edu
E-mail: music@crown.edu

4 Year Liberal Arts Institution

Chair: Gene Rivard, 80A

Adj	Bouissieres, Ben	B	70
Adj	Hathaway, Cheryl	B	32B
Adj	Hawkins, Allan	M	61,32C,32D
Adj	Hawkins, Kay	B	66A
Adj	Hryniewicki, Donna	D	64A,48
Adj	Kruse, Lacey	M	66A,65
Adj	Patterson, Chris	M	61
Adj	Rieken, Justin	B	70
Prof	Rivard, Gene	D	13,10F,49,63,31A
Prof	Smith, Kevin	D	36,60,40,10A
Adj	Ten Brink, Jonathan	M	12A,61
Adj	Thomas, Jennifer	B	51,62A,62B
Adj	Warren, Jeffrey	M	41,70
	Wohlgemuth, J. Leigh	B	32A
Adj	Yannie, Mark	M	46,64C,64E

MN0750 Gustavus Adolphus College

Department of Music
800 W College Ave
Saint Peter, MN 56082-1485
(507) 933-7364   Fax: (507) 933-7041

www.gustavus.edu/oncampus/academics/music/index.html
E-mail: smoore@gustavus.edu

4 Year Institution
Member of NASM

Dean: Mark Braun, 80A
Chair: D. Scott Moore, 80A
Dir., Preparatory Division: Rebekah Richards, 80E
Dir., Artist/Performance Series: Al Behrends, 80F

Assoc Prof	Aune, Gregory	D	60A,36,32D
Asst Prof PT	Budde, Paul J.	D	63D,49,32C
Vstng Inst PT	Clinefelter, Molly	M	61
Asst Prof	Dean, Brandon	D	36,13,20,32D,34B
Inst PT	DeVoll, James	M	64A,48
Inst PT	Engebretson, John	M	64E
Asst Prof PT	Erdahl, Rolf	D	62D
Inst PT	Erickson-Lume, Sarah	M	64B
Inst PT	Gustafson, Beverly	M	67,55
Asst Prof PT	Hess, Jeffery	D	61
Inst PT	Hill, Paul	M	65,50
Prof	Jorgensen, Michael	D	61,11,32D,14C
Asst Prof	Knoepfel, Justin	D	62B,62A,38,42,13
Emeritus	Lammers, Mark E.	D	12C
Inst PT	Leibundguth, Barbara	M	64A
Asst Prof	Lin, Ruth	D	38,13
Inst PT	Mautner-Rodgers, Sharon	B	62C
Asst Prof PT	McConnaughey, Rebecca H.	D	61
Inst PT	McGuire, James		70
Asst Prof	Meffert-Nelson, Karrin	D	64C,37,48,32E,12A
Asst Prof	Moore, D. Scott	D	49,14C
Prof	Nimmo, Douglas	D	60B,37,32C,32E
Prof	Orpen, Rick	D	13,70,34,10
Assoc Prof	Oshima-Ryan, Yumiko	D	66A,66B,13C
Prof PT	Pesavento, Ann	D	64D,42
Inst PT	Richards, Rebekah	M	66B
Inst PT	Smith, Christina	B	61,54
Assoc Prof	Snapp, Patricia	D	61,39,40
Inst PT	Studt-Shoemaker, Lauren	M	32
Inst PT	Tracy, Phala		62E
Assoc Prof	Wang, Esther	D	66A,66C,11
Inst PT	Wilson, Matt	M	63B
Asst Prof PT	Winterfeldt, Chad	D	66G,44,12
Asst Prof	Wright, Steve	D	47,63A,35,46,10
Inst PT	Zimmerman, Larry	M	63C,63D,49

MN0800 Hamline University

Department of Music
Mail #16
1536 Hewitt Ave
Saint Paul, MN 55104-1284
(651) 523-2296   Fax: (651) 523-3066

www.hamline.edu/cla/acad/depts_programs/music/index.html
E-mail: rallison@hamline.edu

4 Year Institution, Graduate School
Member of NASM

Master of Arts in Education, Master of Arts in Liberal Studies

Chair: Rees Allison, 80A
Interim Dean, College of Liberal Arts: John Matachek, 80A

Prof	Allison, Rees	D	12A,66A,66H
Inst PT	Anderson, Marc		65
Inst PT	Black, Marjorie	M	63B
Inst PT	Brudnoy, Rachel		64B
Inst PT	Carbaugh, Deborah	M	61
Prof	Chu, George	D	13,36,61
Inst PT	Crittenden, David	M	70
Inst PT	Gerberg, Miriam	M	20
Inst PT	Gilroy, Debra	M	61
Prof	Greene, Janet E.	D	32E,13A,37,64C
Inst PT	Hara, Craig	M	63A
Asst Prof	Harris, Zacc	B	62D,70
Inst PT	Hepola, Ralph		63D
Inst PT	Janda, Susan	M	62B
Inst PT	Kausch, Mark	M	62D
Inst PT	Kemperman, William	M	65
Inst Adj	Koziol, John		47,48
Inst PT	Lund, Steven	M	63C
Inst PT	Marcus, Edward		10
Inst PT	Morris, Amy	M	64A
Inst PT	Parsons, Charles		66G
Inst PT	Sick, Stella B.	D	66A
Inst PT	Smith, Carole Mason		64D
Assoc Prof	Thomsen, Kathy	D	66A,66D,11
Inst PT	Thomson, Christopher		64E
Inst PT	Victorsen, Catherine	M	62E
Inst PT	Watson, Virginia	M	62A
Assoc Prof	You, Yali	D	38,41,62C,11,12A

MN0850 Hibbing Community College

Department of Music
1515 E 25th St
Hibbing, MN 55746
(218) 262-6729
www.hibbing.tec.mn.us
E-mail: dorothysandnessh@hibbing.edu

2 Year Institution

Inst	Sandness, Dorothy		11,20G

MN0900 Itasca Community College
Department of Music
1851 East Highway 169
Grand Rapids, MN 55744-3397
(218) 322-2379
www.itascacc.edu
E-mail: maria.annoni@itascacc.edu

2 Year Institution, Intro Courses Only

Music Contact: Maria T. Annoni

Inst PT	Annoni, Maria T.	PhD	11,13A,13B,70,14C

MN0950 Macalester College
Department of Music
1600 Grand Ave
Saint Paul, MN 55101
(651) 696-6808   Fax: (651) 696-6785
www.macalester.edu/music
E-mail: mazullo@macalester.edu

4 Year Institution

Inst PT	Anderson, Stella N.	B	62A,62B
Prof Emeritus	Betts, Donald	D	66A,10
Inst PT	Brooks, Barbara J.	M	66A
Inst PT	Brudnoy, Rachel	B	64B
	Bryant, Lei Ouyang		20
Inst PT	Chen, Claudia S.	M	66A
Inst PT	Dahl, Christine E.	M	66A
Inst PT	Erickson, Lynn M.	D	63A
Inst PT	Flegel, James	M	70
PT	Franklin, Cary J.		10,37,38,42,60B
Inst PT	Galhano, Clea	M	67C
Inst PT	Gaynor, Rick G.	M	63C
Inst PT	Gilbert, Jan M.	D	13A,13C,10
Inst PT	Griffith, Joan E.	B	47,70,29,10,62D
Inst PT	Hanson, Shelley J.	D	64C
Inst PT	Hart Stoker, Catherine		52
Inst PT	Hauser, Michael S.	B	70
Inst PT	Hey, Phillip	M	65
Inst PT	Horozaniecki, Mary Budd	B	62A
Inst PT	Jamieson, Robert		67A
Inst PT	Jamsa, Martha N.		64A
Inst PT	Kaehler, Winston H.	D	66G,66H
Inst PT	Keel, Gregory		64E
Inst PT	Kimball, Steve T.	B	65
Inst PT	Lemen, Caroline M.	M	63B
Prof	Macy, Carleton	D	13,10,67,55,47
Inst PT	Maybery, Paul	M	63D
Prof	Mazullo, Mark	D	12,66
Inst PT	Mensah, Sowah	M	12A,20A,10
Inst PT	Nichols, Laura L.	M	61
Inst PT	Peterson, Robert L.	D	36,61,60A
Inst PT	Rosenberg, Thomas A.	M	62C
Inst PT	Schmidt, Michael P.	M	61,64D,32
Inst PT	Ullery, Charles	B	64D
Inst PT	Weinbeck, Benedict J.		66
Inst PT	Whetstone, David S.		20D

MN1000 Minnesota State Univ-Mankato
Department of Music
202 Performing Arts Center
Mankato, MN 56002-0005
(507) 389-2118   Fax: (507) 389-2922
www.mnsu.edu
E-mail: music@mnsu.edu

4 Year Institution, Graduate School

Master of Music in Performance, Master of Music in Music Education, Master of Music in Choral Conducting, Master of Music in Wind Conducting

Chair: Karen A. Boubel, 80A
Dir., Artist/Performance Series: Dale F. Haefner, 80F

Prof	Aloisio, Gerard S.	DMA	11,49,63C
Prof	Boubel, Karen A.	D	13,10,34,13C,10A
Prof	Dickau, David C.	D	60,36,45,34
Prof	Duckett, Linda B.	D	13,66G,66H
Inst	Haefner, Dale F.	M	66D,35
Assoc Prof	Julian, Kimm D.	D	61
Prof	Lindberg, John E.	D	12A,12C,48,64D,72
Inst PT	Lindberg, Martha	M	64B
Inst PT	McGuire, James	M	70
Asst Prof	Meitin, A. Richard	JD	35
Prof	Moxness, Diana	D	32B,61
Assoc Prof	Moxness, Paul	D	13A,32,64E
Inst PT	Orpen, Rick	D	65
Asst Prof	Rodgers, Joseph W.	D	38,62C,13,62D
Assoc Prof	Roisum Foley, Amy K.	M	37
Inst PT	Sappa, Emily	M	64A
Prof	Snapp, Doug R.	D	46,47,63A,29
Prof	Viscoli, David A.	DMA	66A,66H,66C

MN1030 Martin Luther College
Department of Music
1995 Luther Ct
New Ulm, MN 56073-3965
(507) 354-8221   Fax: (507) 354-8225
www.mlc-wels.edu
E-mail: noltejp@mlc-wels.edu

4 Year Institution

Chair: John P. Nolte, 80A
Dir., Artist/Performance Series: Lance Hartzell, 80F
Dir., Summer Programs: John E. Meyer, 80G

Inst	Balge, Bethel A.	B	66A
Prof	Bauer, David T.	M	13A,34,66A,66G
Inst	Boeder, Bethel J.	B	36,66A
Inst	Haugen, Jennifer E.	M	61
Inst	Martens, Judith L.		66A
Prof	Moldenhauer, Kermit G.	D	13A,36,66G,31A,60A
Inst	Nolte, Brent J.	M	66G,63
Prof	Nolte, John P.	D	13A,32D
Inst	Nolte, Lanita M.	B	66A,66D
Inst	Ohm, Carlotta L.	B	66A
Prof	Potratz, Robert C.	B	11,12A,66G,13A
Inst	Schubkegel, Joyce C.	M	66G,66A
Prof	Shilling, Ronald L.	M	66G
Inst	Thiesfeldt, Jeneane M.	B	66G,66A
Inst	Vagel, Marianne E.	B	66A
Prof	Wagner, Wayne L.	D	13A,32,36,66G,66D
Inst	Wiechman, Elizabeth J.	B	66A,66G
Inst	Wurster, Kathryn M.	M	61
Prof	Wurster, Miles B.	M	37,13A,64,65

MN1050 Minneapolis Comm & Tech College
Department of Music
1501 Hennepin Ave
Minneapolis, MN 55403-1710
(612) 659-6000   Fax: (612) 659-6128
www.minneapolis.edu
E-mail: stephen.solum@minneapolis.edu

2 Year Institution

Chair: Stephen Solum, 80A

Adj	Bregman, Jacqueline		62A
Adj	Giddings, Lorelei	M	64B
Adj	Gilroy, Debra		61
Adj	Greer, Sarah		61
Adj	Haskin, Steven		70
Adj	Heller, Brian	B	10B,34,12A,35B,35G
Adj	Hryniewicki, Donna		64A
Adj	Keys, Jeff		63A
Adj	King, Jeffrey		64C,64E
Adj	Krislov, Donna	M	66A
Adj	Langley, DeeAnna		68
Adj	Ouska, Jim		70
Adj	Pauly, Elizabeth	D	61,60A,11,36,13A
	Solum, Stephen	D	13,20G,10,35G,34
Adj	Thompson, Floyd		65
Adj	Ultan, Jacqueline		62C
Adj	Williams, Yolanda	D	12A,20,47,29A,41

MN1100 Minn St. Comm & Tech Coll-Fergus Falls
Department of Music
1414 College Way
Fergus Falls, MN 56537-1000
(218) 736-1500   Fax: (218) 736-1510
www.minnesota.edu
E-mail: teresa.ashworth@minnesota.edu

2 Year Institution

Chair: Teresa Ashworth, 80A

Inst	Ashworth, Teresa	M	61,36,40,20,13C
Inst	Carlson, Dan	M	11,35A,37,46,63
	Embretson, Deborah	M	61,66D,11,20,66C
Inst	Lundberg, Erika	B	66A,66B,66C
Inst	Stoddard, David	M	70,13I
Inst	Trosvig, Michael	M	10A,13

MN1120 Minnesota State Univ Moorhead
Department of Music
1104 7th Ave S
Moorhead, MN 56563
(218) 477-2101   Fax: (218) 477-4097
www.mnstate.edu
E-mail: music@mnstate.edu

4 Year Institution
Member of NASM

Chair: Tom Strait, 80A

PT	Adams, Julie R.	M	61,32B
PT	Allebach, Robin K.	M	61
Prof	Blunsom, Laurie	D	12
Assoc Prof	Carter, Allen L.	D	13,10F,65,47
PT	Chen-Beyers, Christina	D	38
Assoc Prof	Dufault, Jenny E.	D	32B,39,61
PT	Ferreira, David C.	D	40
Asst Prof	Grise', Monte	D	64E,32E,47,37,60B
PT	Gurney, James F.	B	61
Prof	Gwiazda, Henry	D	13,10
PT	Halverson, Janelle C.	M	32B
PT	Harris, Debora	M	64A,48
Asst Prof	Izzo, Jeffrey	D	35A
Assoc Prof	Jackson, Ryan D.	B	34,35C,35D
Asst Prof	Krajewski, Michael J.	M	70,47,29
PT	Larson, Jon D.	M	62A,62B
Asst Prof	Mahraun, Daniel A.	D	61,36,60A,40
Prof	Manno, Terrie	D	66A,66B,66C,66D
PT	Mattison, Nate	B	66F
PT	Nagel, Sue S.	B	66A
PT	Neill, Douglas A.	B	70,62D
PT	Nelson, Elise	M	62C
Assoc Prof	Nesheim, Paul J.	D	36,40,60A
PT	Peterson, Jennifer L.	B	64B
Asst Prof	Rolsten, Kathy	PhD	32A,32B,32D,36,61
Prof	Rothlisberger, Rodney	D	32D,36,66G
PT	Rudolph, Jon	B	70,47
PT	Schroeder, Jerry		66F
Prof	Strait, Tom	D	63A,29,63B,47
PT	Tesch, Catherine	D	64C
Prof	Tesch, John	D	32E,37,63C,11
Assoc Prof	Williams, Kenyon C.	D	65,50,20

MN1175 Minn West Comm and Tech College
Department of Music
1450 College Way
Worthington, MN 56187-0107
(507) 372-3400   Fax: (507) 372-5801
www.mnwest.edu
E-mail: eric.parrish@mnwest.edu

2 Year Institution

Chair: Eric Parrish, 80A

	Lang, Linda	B	66,36
	Parrish, Eric	M	11,13,36,61

MN1200 Normandale Community College
Department of Music
9700 France Ave S
Bloomington, MN 55431-4309
(952) 358-8200   Fax: (952) 358-8101
www.normandale.edu
E-mail: Robert.Gronemann@normandale.edu

2 Year Institution
Member of NASM

Chair: Robert Gronemann, 80A

PT	Ahn, Hyeson Sarah	D	66A,66D
Inst	Gronemann, Robert	M	66A,13
PT	Hess, Jeffrey	D	61,34,32,11
Inst	Jaros, Marc	D	12,36,20,40

Inst	Kurschner, James	M	37,64E,41,66D
Inst	Moe, Aaron	M	29,47
PT	Munoz, William	D	63A
PT	Oden, Wade	M	70
Inst	Pinsonneault, Ona	D	64C

MN1250 North Central University
Department of Music
910 Elliot Ave South
Minneapolis, MN 55404-1322
(612) 343-4700   Fax: (612) 343-4778
www.northcentral.edu
E-mail: finearts@northcentral.edu

4 Year Institution

Dean, College of Fine Arts: Larry Bach, 80A
Chair: David Collins, 80A

Adj	Allison, Ian	B	62D
Adj	Arellano, Kristina	B	66A
Assoc Prof	Bach, Larry	M	60,36,61
Assoc Prof	Collins, David	M	31A,61,36,46
Adj	Collins, Linda	B	66A
Adj	Droba, Romalee	B	61,66A
Adj	Dwyer, Mac	B	43
Adj	Ford, William	D	64E,48
Adj	Hentges, Londa		14C
Prof	Johnson, Herbert	D	12A,13,31A,66B,66C
Assoc Prof	Kersten, Joanne	M	13,66A,32B
Adj	Kisilevitch, Miroslava	D	66A
Adj	Lewis, Lori	M	61
Adj	May, Pam	B	66A,61
Adj	Miller, Ken	D	62C,51
Adj	Miller, Zach	B	65
Assoc Prof	Norberg, Rebecca	M	61,54,12A,11
Adj	Norris, Phil	D	63A
Adj	Osterhause, Sharon	B	62A
Asst Prof	Pedde, David	B	66A,10B,14C,31A
Adj	Pettis, Paula	M	64A
Adj	Shu, Peter	B	66A,47
Prof	Thomas, Wayne	B	35G
Adj	Thulin, Jeanette	B	36
Adj	Tomlinson, Mike	M	61
Adj	Tompkins, Joshua	D	66A
Adj	Warren, Jeff	M	70
Adj	Wegenke, Wendy	M	61
Adj	Wilson, Ken		70,43
Adj	Wipf, Elaine	M	66A,66B
Adj	Young, David		70

MN1260 North Hennepin Community College
Department of Music
7411 85th Ave N
Brooklyn Park, MN 55445-2231
(763) 424-0792   Fax: (763) 424-0929
www.nhcc.mnscu.edu
E-mail: Karla.Miller@nhcc.edu

2 Year Institution

Dean, Instruction: Jerry Sandvick, 80A

	Anderson, Kristian		
	Bender, Judy		61
Inst PT	Borgstrom, Steven		
	MacLaughlin, Heather		
	Mantini, David		
FT	Miller, Karla	M	13A,11,36,61,66A

MN1270 Northland Comm & Tech College
Department of Music
1101 Highway 1 E
Thief River Falls, MN 56701
(218) 681-0733   Fax: (218) 681-0724
www.northlandcollege.edu
E-mail: lsamuelson@northlandcollege.edu

2 Year Institution

Dean: Norma Konschak, 80A
Director: Linda Samuelson, 80A

PT	Hagen, Cathy	B	66A
PT	Lunsetter, Gene	B	70
PT	Martell, Vanessa	M	61,12A,36
	Samuelson, Linda	M	13,20,37,46,64

MN1280 Northwestern College
Department of Music
3003 Snelling Ave N
F2219
Saint Paul, MN 55113-1501
(651) 631-5218   Fax: (651) 628-3368
www.nwc.edu
E-mail: jwkolwinska@nwc.edu

4 Year Institution
Member of NASM

Chair: Jeremy Kolwinska, 80A
Dir., Preparatory Division: Julie J. Johnson, 80E

Adj	Alexander, Joel	M	65,50
Adj Inst	Benham, John	D	20
Prof	Danek, Leonard P.	D	13,10,66G
Assoc Prof	Eikum, Carol L.	M	61
Adj	Frisch, Michele	B	41,64A
Adj	Frisch, Roger	M	62A,41
Asst Prof	Geston, Mary K.	D	40,32D,60A,32C,36
PT	Grimes, Sonja	M	66C
Asst Prof	Herlihy, John S.	M	60B,49,37,46
Adj	Hood, Heather	D	31A
Inst FT	Hutchings, Doreen L.	M	61,39
Adj	Isomura, Sachiya	B	62C
Adj	Johnson, Melody	M	11
Prof	Kelley, Cheryl K.	D	13,32,48,64D
Assoc Prof	Kolwinska, Jeremy	D	63C,63D,11,63B
Asst Prof	Kozamchak, David M.	M	38,51,62A,62B,41
Assoc Prof	Lange, Richard A.	D	66A,66B,66C
Adj	Larsen, Catherine	M	61
Adj	Larson, Glen	M	70
Adj	Leverence, Dan	B	43
Assoc Prof	Loeffler, Rodney J.	M	32E
Prof	Norris, Philip E.	D	10F,11,32E,63A,31A
Adj	Osterhouse, Carl	B	62D
Assoc Prof	Robinson, Kathleen E.	D	31A,11,12A,13C
Lect	Rogers, Barbara J.	DMA	66A,66D,66C
Assoc Prof	Sawyer, Timothy K.	M	60,36
Adj	Scholl, Janet	M	64C
	Scovill, Janet R.		66C
Adj	Victorsen, Catherine	M	62E
Adj	Warren, Jeff	M	11
Adj	Wilson, Matthew	M	63B
Adj	Woelfle, Colin	B	64E

MN1285 Ridgewater College
Department of Music
2101 15th Ave NW
Willmar, MN 56201
(320) 222-7576   Fax: (320) 222-8067
www.ridgewater.edu

2 Year Community and Technical College

Music Contact: Darcy Lease Gubrud, 80A

Inst	Gubrud, Darcy Lease	M	13,11,36,61,40
Inst	Kochis, Jane	M	66A,66C,11

MN1290 Riverland Community College
Department of Music
1900 8th Ave NW
Austin, MN 55912
(507) 433-0547   Fax: (507) 433-0515
www.riverland.edu
E-mail: sblanken@riverland.edu

2 Year Institution

Music Contact: Scott E. Blankenbaker, 80A
Dean, Liberal Arts: Jan Waller, 80A

Inst	Blankenbaker, Scott E.	M	11,13,61,36
Inst PT	Conway, Mark		70
Inst PT	Davis, Tim	M	63
Inst PT	Erickson, Neal	M	66G
Inst PT	Larson, Lynee	B	66A,66D
Inst PT	Radloff, Susan	B	62A,62B
Inst PT	Wangen, Peter	B	65

MN1295 St Catherine University
Department of Music & Theater
2004 Randolph Ave
Saint Paul, MN 55105-1794
(651) 690-6690   Fax: (651) 690-8819
www.stkate.edu/academic/music/
E-mail: pcconnors@stkate.edu

4 Year Institution

Chair: Patricia Cahalan Connors, 80A

Asst Prof	Allison, Adrian	D	12,20
Adj PT	Bujak, Ewa	M	38,62B,62A
Prof	Connors, Patricia Cahalan	D	36,55D,60
Prof	Goter, Arlene	D	66A,66B,13,66D
Adj PT	Morris, Amy	M	64A
Adj PT	Pauly, Elizabeth	D	61
Adj PT	Thygeson, Jeffrey	M	70
Adj PT	Tierney, Joanne	B	66A
Asst Prof	Tigges, Kristie M.	M	61,11
Adj PT	Van Nostrand, Carol	D	66A
Adj PT	Vazquez, Anna	D	62C

MN1300 St Cloud State University
Department of Music-PAC 238
720 4th Ave S
Saint Cloud, MN 56301-4498
(320) 308-3223   Fax: (320) 308-2902
www.stcloudstate.edu/music
E-mail: music@stcloudstate.edu

4 Year Institution
Member of NASM

Dean & Dir., Summer Programs: Dennis Nunes, 80A,80G
Chair: Terry L. Vermillion, 80A
Dir., Artist/Performance Series: Jessica Ostman, 80F

Emeritus	Abbott, Thomas	M	14,61
Emeritus	Allen, Thomas O.	D	66A,66B,66D
Inst	Barsness, Erik	M	65
Inst	Bird, Gary	D	63D
Inst	Bot, Mary Jo	M	36
Inst	Budde, Paul	M	32C
Asst Prof	Carucci, Christine	M	32C,11
Inst	Dalton, Phoebe A.	B	62C
Inst	Deiderichs, Patty	M	63B
Inst	Dennihan, James	D	66A
Emeritus	Echols, Charles	D	66H,12A,66A,66G
Emeritus	Ernest, David J.	D	13A,11,64B
Inst	Fedele, Andrea		64B
Asst Prof	Ferrell, Matthew	M	36,60A
Emeritus	Flom, James H.	D	13A,11
Emeritus	Frohrip, Kenton R.	D	29A,35,63A
Emeritus	Fuller, Stephen		60A,11,20D,31A
Prof	Gast, Kim	D	47,64E,29
Prof	Givens, Hugh	D	39,61
Emeritus	Gyllstrom, Mabeth	D	61
Prof	Hansen, Richard K.	D	60B,37,20G,12A
Inst	Hawkins, Allan	M	36
Inst	Heine, Bruce	B	62D
Emeritus	Johnson, James R.	D	13,11,12
Prof	Judish, Marion	D	62A,62B
Prof	Krause, Melissa M.	D	13,64A,10A,10F
Inst	Kraut, Rena		64C
Prof	Layne, R. Dennis	D	11
Inst	Manik, Rich		13
Inst	Merz, Laurie	M	64D
Emeritus	Miller, Joan	M	20D,11,32B
Prof	Miller, Scott L.	D	13,10A,10B,10C,34
Emeritus	Moore, Albert L.	D	49,63B,63A,11
Inst	Nelson, Gregory	B	62C
Prof	O'Bryant, Daniel K.	D	38,60B,62D
Inst	Okwabi, Tori		64C
Inst	Parker, Nancy	M	32B
Inst	Peterson, David		63C
Inst	Roessler, Brian		62D
Inst	Senn, Takako	M	63A
Prof	Smale, Marcelyn	D	32A,13C,66D,32B,32D
	Springer, Mark	D	63D,63C
Staff	Tuomaala, Glen	M	37
Asst Prof	Twombly, Kristian	D	10B,34H,12B,10,11
Prof	Vermillion, Terry L.	D	65,50
Prof	Verrilli, Catherine J.	D	61,20B
Inst	Wartchow, Brett	M	13
Inst	Wazanowski, Charles	M	63D
Prof	Wilhite, Carmen	D	66A,66B,66C

MN1400 St Marys University of Minnesota

School of the Arts-Music
700 Terrace Hts #1447
Winona, MN 55987
(507) 452-4430 x 1598   Fax: (507) 457-1611
www.smumn.edu
E-mail: music@smumn.edu

4 Year Liberal Arts Institution, Graduate School

Master of Education in Music Education, Master of Arts in Arts Administration

Dean: Michael Charron, 80A

PT	Bartz, Tammy	B	63B
PT	Hanson, Sylva	M	32B,64C
PT	Heukeshoven, Eric	B	63C,63D,34,10
Assoc Prof	Heukeshoven, Janet	D	37,32,60,11,41
PT	Huus, Brett	B	35
PT	Kirk, Caroline	M	11,66A,66B,66D
PT	Knutson, James	M	65
PT	Matson, Jan	M	61
PT	Matzke, Kathleen	B	61
PT	McGuire, Dennis	M	70,50,29
PT	Mundy, John	M	70
PT	O'Shea, Lindsy	M	61
Assoc Prof	O'Shea, Patrick	D	60,12A,36,61,10A
Assoc Prof	Paulson, John C.	D	47,64,29,34,35
PT	Welch, Jennifer	B	64

MN1450 St Olaf College

Department of Music
1520 St. Olaf Ave
Northfield, MN 55057-1098
(507) 786-3180   Fax: (507) 786-3527
www.stolaf.edu/depts/music
E-mail: music@stolaf.edu

4 Year Liberal Arts College
Member of NASM

Chair: Alison Feldt, 80A
Dir., Summer Programs: Michelle Egeness, 80G
Associate Dean, Fine Arts: Dan F. Dressen, 80H
Assistant Chair: P. Andrew Hisey, 80H
Manager, Music Organizations: B. J. Johnson

Prof	Amundson, Steven	M	13,60B,38,10A
Prof	Armstrong, Anton	D	60A,36,61
Asst Prof	Aspaas, Christopher	D	36,61,60A,32D
Asst Prof	Atzinger, Christopher	D	66A,66B,66D,66C
Prof	Berger, Linda	D	32
Vstng Asst Prof	Byl, Julia S.	D	20
Prof Emeritus	Campbell, Arthur	D	10,13
Prof	Carter, David	D	11,41,62C,42
Asst Prof	Castro, David R.	D	13
Inst PT	Caviani, Laura	M	66A
Prof	Christensen, Beth	M	16
Inst PT	Claussen, Kurt	M	64E,42
Inst PT	Clift, Anna	M	62C,42
Prof	Dressen, Dan F.	D	61
Assoc Prof	Eaves-Smith, Margaret	M	61
Assoc Prof	Een, Andrea	D	42,62A,62B
Emeritus	Engen, Helen	B	61
Assoc Prof	Feldt, Alison	D	61
Prof	Ferguson, John	D	36,66G,31A
Prof Emeritus	Forsberg, Charles	D	13
Inst	Gorman, Tracey	M	61
Prof Emeritus	Graber, Kenneth	D	66A
Prof	Gray, Charles	M	42,62A,62B
Artist in Res	Hagedorn, David	D	13A,65,50,47,13B
Prof	Hanson, Alice	D	12A
Vstng Prof	Hanson, J. Robert	D	63A
Assoc Prof	Hardy, Janis		61,39,54
Inst PT	Hey, Phillip	B	65
Assoc Prof	Hisey, P. Andrew	D	66A,66B,66D
Assoc Prof	Hodel, Martin	D	38,63,42
Prof	Hoekstra, Gerald	D	12A,55,29A
Inst PT	Holt, Anthony	M	61
Prof Emerita	Jennings, Carolyn	M	66A
Prof Emeritus	Jennings, Kenneth	D	60A,61,36
Inst PT	Jensen, Rachel	B	62A
Artist in Res	Johnson, Sigrid	M	36,61
Inst PT	Kelley, Mark	B	64D
Inst PT	Kienzle, Kathy	M	62E
Inst PT	Lee, Nancy	B	32D
Inst PT	Maeda, Dana	M	64B,42
Inst PT	Mahr, Jill	M	44,64A
Prof	Mahr, Timothy	D	60B,37,10
Inst PT	Martz, Mary	B	61
Inst PT	McCleary, Harriet C.	DMA	61
Prof	McKeel, James	M	61,39,54
Assoc Prof	McWilliams, Kent M.	D	66A,66C,66D,66E
Asst Prof	Merritt, Justin W.	D	10,13,43,13A,34
Inst PT	Niemisto, Elinor	M	62E
Assoc Prof	Niemisto, Paul	D	49,63C,63D,37,42
Inst PT	Oliveros, Nancy	M	62A
Inst PT	Ousley, Paul	M	62D
Assoc Prof	Owens, Kathryn Ananda	DMA	66A,66C,66D,66E,66B
Prof	Paddleford, Nancy	D	66A,66C,66B,66D
Emeritus	Paulsen, Donna	B	66A
Inst PT	Petruconis, Michael	M	63B
Prof Emerita	Polley, Jo Ann	D	38,48,64C
Asst Prof	Qian, Jun	D	42,64C,48
Asst Prof	Ramirez, Catherine	ABD	13A,64A,48,42,13B
Artist in Res	Rodland, Catherine	DMA	13,66G
Emerita	Sahlin, Kay	B	64A,42
Prof Emeritus	Scholz, Robert	D	36,61,60A
Inst PT	Scholz-Carlson, Miriam	B	
Inst PT	Shows, Ray	M	62A,62B
Assoc Prof	Smith, Robert C.	D	61
Vstng Artist	Thomas, Darrin	B	36
Prof Emeritus	Wee, A. Dewayne	D	66A
Prof Emeritus	Wee, Theo R.	M	66A,66G,66D
Vstng Prof PT	Westermeyer, Paul	D	31A
Inst PT	Wilkerson, Karen	M	61
Inst PT	Winslow, Herbert	B	63B
Inst PT	Wolf, Annalee	M	62B
Inst PT	Zimmerman, Larry	M	63C,63D

MN1500 Southwest Minnesota St Univ

Music Program
1501 State St
Marshall, MN 56258
(507) 537-7103   Fax: (507) 537-7014
www.smsu.edu
E-mail: john.ginocchio@smsu.edu

4 Year Institution
Member of NASM

Coordinator: John Ginocchio, 80A
Chair, Art, Music, Speech & Theatre: Jan Loft, 80A

PT	Alvarado, Julieta	M	66A,66H
PT	Anderson, Ross	B	53
PT	Demaris, Mary Kay	M	61,60A
PT	Funk, Dana	B	66A
Asst Prof	Ginocchio, John	D	37,13,47,32E,60B
PT	Lothringer, Peter	D	70,10A,13
PT	Nester, Holly	M	64A
PT	Peterson, David	M	63C,63D
PT	Przymus, Chad	B	65
Prof	Rieppel, Daniel	D	66A,11,38,66C,12
PT	Schimming, Paul	D	64C
PT	Steuck, Beth	B	63B,66A
PT	Tabaka, Jim	M	70,20,12A
PT	Vondracek, Tom	B	63A
PT	Wright, Lon	B	64D,64E,64B

MN1590 Univ of Minnesota-Crookston

Department of Music & Theatre
2900 University Ave
Crookston, MN 56716
(218) 281-8266   Fax: (218) 281-8050
www.crk.umn.edu
E-mail: gfrench@mail.crk.umn.edu

2 and 4 Year Technical Institution

Director: George E. French, 80A

Assoc Prof	French, George E.	M	36,37,66A,66G,54
Lect	Kent, James		32A

MN1600 Univ of Minnesota Duluth

Department of Music
212 Humanities Bldg
1201 Ordean Ct
Duluth, MN 55812
(218) 726-8208   Fax: (218) 726-8210
www.d.umn.edu/music
E-mail: umdmusic.d.umn.edu

4 Year Institution, Graduate School
Member of NASM

Master of Music in Performance, Master of Music in Music Education

Chair: Jefferson Campbell, 80A
Dir., Graduate Studies: Thomas R. Muehlenbeck Pfotenhauer, 80C

Inst	Barnard, William		70,29,42
Inst PT	Bombardier, Bradley A.	M	64C,64E,11
Asst Prof	Booker, Adam	D	29,41,46,62D
Inst PT	Booker, Sally	M	13C,66A
Inst PT	Bromme, Derek	M	63C
Inst PT	Broscious, Timothy L.	M	10E,65
Asst Prof	Campbell, Jefferson	D	11,64D,34
Asst Prof	Chernyshev, Alexander	D	66A,66D
Inst PT	Cooper, Jim	B	70
Asst Prof	Eaton, Daniel	M	37,63D,49
Asst Prof	Edmund, Carina	D	32
Asst Prof	Edmund, David	D	32
Assoc Prof	Frane, Ryan	M	29,47,66A,46
Teach Assoc	Graupmann, Jennifer	M	61
Asst Prof	Gudmundson, Paula	D	11,13B,64A
Inst PT	Holstrom, Jacqueline	M	66A,66C
Asst Prof	Husby, Betsy	D	62C
Assoc Prof	Inselman, Rachel	M	61
Inst PT	Jonker, Jacob	M	70,41
Asst Prof	Koshinski, Eugene	M	47,65,29,20G,35
Prof	Kritzmire, Judith A.	D	32
Inst PT	Kulas, Katherine F.	M	61
Inst PT	Lemire, Janell	B	62E
Asst Prof	Lipke-Perry, Tracy D.	D	66A,66C
Inst PT	Liu, Te-Chiang	M	62A,62B,41
Inst PT	McConico, Marcus	M	61
Inst FT	Metts, Calland	M	61,36
Inst FT	Mokole, Elias	M	61
Asst Prof	Muehlenbeck Pfotenhauer, Thomas R. 63A,47,29,11,11		DMA
Asst Prof	Muehlenbeck, Bettina	D	12A
Inst PT	O'Hara, Thomas	B	70
Assoc Prof	Perrault, Jean R.	M	60,62A,62B,62C,38
Inst FT	Pierce, Alice O.	M	61,39
Inst PT	Pierce, John	M	61
Inst PT	Pospisil, James	M	63B
Prof	Rubin, Justin H.	D	13,34,66G,10,66A
Prof	Schoen, Theodore A.	D	64C,64E,41,10F
Asst Prof PT	Scott, Laurie		13A,13C,64A
Asst Prof	Thielen-Gaffey, Tina	M	36,61,40,32
Inst PT	Van Brunt, Laurie	M	64B
Prof	Whitlock, Mark	D	32,37,49,63C,63D
Prof	Wold, Stanley R.	D	60A,36,40,61

MN1620 Univ of Minnesota-Morris
Music Discipline
600 E 4th St
Morris, MN 56267
(320) 589-6251   Fax: (320) 589-6253
www.morris.umn.edu/academic/music/
E-mail: seggelke@morris.umn.edu

4 Year Institution

Inst PT	DeJong, Diane	B	61
Inst	DuHamel, Ann M.	M	66
Inst PT	Flegel, James	D	70
Inst	Hanson, Melissa	M	61
Inst PT	Helder, Annette	B	66A
Assoc Prof	Hodgson, Ken	D	36,61,34D,11,60A
Inst PT	Klemetson, Roxanne	M	66A
Inst PT	Miller, Kristi	B	61
Inst PT	Morken, Randy A.	B	66A,66G
Asst Prof	Odello, Denise	D	11,12,64B,14,20
Inst PT	Odello, Mike	B	63D,72,49
Inst PT	Richards, Jeanne	B	64A,67C,48
Assoc Prof	Richards, Richard	D	13
Inst PT	Rossmiller, Adam	D	63A
Inst PT	Salvo, Joel	M	62
Inst PT	Schwagerl, Renee	B	63B
Inst PT	Svendsen, Dennis	D	65
Inst PT	Varpness, Lee	B	63C,63D

MN1623 Univ of Minnesota-Twin Cities
School of Music
2106 S 4th St
Minneapolis, MN 55455-0437
(612) 626-1882   Fax: (612) 626-2200
www.music.umn.edu
E-mail: menken@umn.edu

4 Year Institution, Graduate School

Master of Arts in Composition, Master of Arts in Music Education, Master of Arts in Music Theory, Master of Music in Performance, PhD in Music Theory, PhD in Composition, DMA in Conducting, DMA in Performance, PhD in Music, PhD in Musicology, Master of Arts in Musicology, Master of Music in Choral Conducting, Master of Music in Wind Conducting, Master of Music in Orchestral Conducting, Master of Music in Collaborative Piano/Coaching, DMA in Collaborative Piano/Coaching, Master of Music in Suzuki Ped & Violin Performance

Director: David E. Myers, 80A
Associate Director & Dir., Undergraduate Studies: Scott D. Lipscomb, 80B,80H
Dir., Graduate Studies: Peter Mercer-Taylor, 80C
Assistant Director: Anne Barnes, 80H

Assoc Prof	Addo, Akosua O.	D	32
Prof Emeritus	Argento, Dominick J.	D	13,10F,10,12A
Prof	Artymiw, Lydia	B	66A
Prof	Ashworth, Thomas	M	41,63C
Prof	Baldwin, David B.	D	41,49,63A
Prof	Billmeyer, Dean W.	D	66G,66H
Prof	Bjork, Mark	B	41,62A
Adj	Bogorad, Julia A.	M	64A
Adj	Bordner, Gary	M	63A
Prof	Braginsky, Alexander	D	66A
Assoc Prof	Bribitzer-Stull, Matthew	D	13
Adj	Brown, Christopher C.	B	62D
Adj	Campbell, Steven	B	63D
Prof	Cherlin, Michael	D	13,13J
Assoc Prof	Currie, Gabriela	D	12
Lect	Currie, Scott	M	14
Prof	Damschroder, David	D	13,13J
Assoc Prof	Davis, Immanuel	M	64A
Assoc Prof	DeHaan, John D.	M	61
Assoc Prof	Del Santo, Jean	M	61
Inst	Diem, Timothy W.	D	37,41
Prof	Dillon, James	B	10
Prof Emeritus	Fetler, Paul	D	13,10F,10
Asst Prof	Fiterstein, Alexander	M	64C
Adj	Gast, Michael	B	63B
Assoc Prof	Gopinath, Sumanth	D	13
Prof	Grayson, David	D	12
Prof Emeritus	Haack, Paul	D	32
Assoc Prof	Hamann, Keitha Lucas	D	32
Assoc Prof	Harness, Kelley	D	12,14
Adj	Hey, Philip	D	65
Vstng Assoc Prof	Huovinen, Erkki	D	12
Assoc Prof Emeritus	Kagan, Alan L.	D	12A,12,14
Adj	Kienzle, Kathy	M	62E
Adj	Kierig, Barbara G.	M	61
Assoc Prof	Kim, Young-Nam	M	41,62A
Prof	Kirchhoff, Craig	M	60,37,41
Adj	Kogan, Peter	B	65A
Prof	Konkol, Korey	M	41,62B
Prof Emeritus	Laudon, Robert	D	11,12A,12,66H
Adj	Lemen, Caroline	M	63B
Assoc Prof	Lipscomb, Scott D.	D	32
Assoc Prof	Lovelace, Timothy	D	66C
Prof	Lubet, Alex	D	13,10
Assoc Prof	Luckhardt, Jerry	M	60,37,41
Adj	Maloney, Timothy	D	16
Prof Emerita	Maurice, Glenda A.	M	61
Prof	Mazzola, Guerino	D	13
Adj	McCullough, Brian	B	
Assoc Prof Emeritus	McNab, Duncan	D	66A
Assoc Prof	Mehaffey, Matthew W.	D	36,13A
Adj	Mensah, Sowah	M	50
Assoc Prof	Mercer-Taylor, Peter	D	12
Assoc Prof	Meza, Fernando	M	50,65
Adj	Miller, John	M	64D
Prof	Myers, David E.	D	32
Adj	Nielubowski, Norbert	B	64D
Prof	O'Reilly, Sally	M	41,62A
Assoc Prof	Painter, Karen	D	12
Adj	Radovanlija, Maja	M	70
Asst Prof	Rahaim, Matthew	D	14
Adj	Reeve, Basil	B	64B
Prof	Remenikova, Tanya	M	41,62C
Assoc Prof	Romey, Kathy Saltzman	D	36
Lect	Rousseau, Eugene E.	D	41,64E
Adj	Schwartzberg, Edward	M	33
Assoc Prof	Shaw, Paul	D	66A
Prof	Shockley, Rebecca P.	D	66A,66B,66D
Asst Prof	Silverman, Michael	D	33
Asst Prof	Sindberg, Laura K.	D	32E
Asst Prof	Smith, Mark Russell	B	38
Lect	Snow, John	M	64B
Assoc Prof	Sorenson, Dean P.	M	47
Adj	Sutrisno, Joko	B	42
Prof Emeritus	Sutton, Everett L.	D	39
Adj	Tranter, John	D	63D
Adj	Turner, Thomas	B	62B
Adj	Ullery, Charles	B	64D
Assoc Prof	Walsh, David	M	39
Prof Emeritus	Ware, Clifton	D	61

Prof Emeritus	Weller, Lawrence	M	61
Adj	Wyatt, Angela	M	64E
Asst Prof	Zabala, Adriana	M	61
Prof Emerita	Zaimont, Judith Lang	D	10
Assoc Prof	Zaro-Mullins, Wendy	D	61
Asst Prof	Zawisza, Philip David	M	61

MN1625 Univ of St. Thomas
Department of Music
BEC 9
2115 Summit Ave
Saint Paul, MN 55105-1096
(651) 962-5850   Fax: (651) 962-5876
www.stthomas.edu/music
E-mail: mjgeorge@stthomas.edu

4 Year Institution, Graduate School
Member of NASM

Master of Arts in Music Education

Chair: Matthew J. George, 80A
Dir., Graduate Studies: Angela Broeker, 80C
Assistant Chair: Douglas Orzolek, 80H

Adj PT	Allaire, Denis	B	47
Adj PT	Auerbach, David	M	62B
Adj PT	Balder, Patrick	M	35C,35G
Adj PT	Bartus Broberg, Kirsten A.	D	13,10
Adj PT	Berget, Paul	M	67G
Adj PT	Bodner, Jessica	M	62B
Assoc Prof	Broeker, Angela	D	60A,36
Adj PT	Broeker, Jay	B	32
Adj PT	Brown, Aaron	M	36,31A
Adj PT	Brudnoy, Rachel	M	64B
Assoc Prof	Bryan, Alan	D	11,39,61,54
Adj PT	Budde, Paul J.	D	13
Adj PT	Cadwell, Jennifer	M	44
Adj PT	Capener, Debra A.	D	61
Adj PT	Chong, Daniel	M	62A
Clinical Asst Prof	Cole, Steven	M	35
Asst Prof	Cornett-Murtada, Vanessa	D	66A,13,12A,66B
Adj PT	Douglas, Peter	M	64D
Adj PT	Garvin, Jane	M	64A
Prof	George, Matthew J.	D	60,41,37
Adj PT	Gerth, Jennifer	M	64C
Asst Prof	Gleason, Bruce	D	32,14A
Adj PT	Griffith, Joan	M	11,70,29
Adj PT	Haugen, Ruben	M	64E
Adj PT	Hauser, Michael	M	70
Adj PT	Hisey, Andrew	D	66A
Adj PT	Itkin, Ora	M	66A
Adj PT	Jenkins, David	D	66G,31A
Adj PT	Jensen, John	M	66A
Asst Prof	Johnson, Shersten	M	13,10
Adj PT	Jorstad, Dede	M	61
Prof	Kachian, Christopher	D	11,70,20
Adj PT	Kemperman, William	B	65
Adj PT	Kim, Karen	M	62A
Adj PT	Kim, Kee-Hyun	M	62C
Adj PT	Mensah, Sowah	M	20
Adj PT	Miller, Lydia	M	62A
Adj PT	Morgan, Stephen	B	70
Asst Prof	Orzolek, Douglas	D	11,32,37,60
Adj PT	Reed, W. Joseph	D	61
Adj PT	Rinear, Jeffrey	B	47
Assoc Prof	Schmalenberger, Sarah	M	12A,63B,12,67E,14
Adj PT	Schons, Suzanne	D	66D
Adj PT	Schroepfer, Mark	M	35
Adj PT	Schulz, Paul	M	64C
Adj PT	Skaar, Trygve	M	63D
Adj PT	Stern, Andrea	M	62E
Adj PT	Tchekmazov, Andrey	M	62C
Adj PT	Thygeson, Jeffrey K.	M	70
Adj PT	Titus, Anthony	M	35
Adj PT	Vickery, Robert	M	36
Adj PT	Volpe, Christopher	B	63A,41
Adj PT	Zimmerman, Larry	M	63C,63D
Adj PT	Zocchi, Michael	M	13,10

MN1630 Vermilion Community College
Department of Music
1900 E Camp St
Ely, MN 55731-1918
(218) 365-3256   Fax: (218) 365-7207
www.vcc.edu
E-mail: s.skelton@vcc.edu

2 Year Institution

	Skelton, Sara	M	61,66A

MN1700 Winona State University
Department of Music
PO Box 5838
Winona, MN 55987-5838
(507) 457-5250   Fax: (507) 457-5624
www.winona.edu/music
E-mail: dmohr@winona.edu

4 Year Institution
Member of NASM

Chair: Deanne Mohr, 80A
Dean, Liberal Arts: Ralph Townsend, 80A

Assoc Prof	Brisson, Eric	D	13A,13B,13C,13E,66C
Prof	Draayer, Suzanne Collier	D	39,61,11
PT	Filipovich, Natalie	M	62A,62B,32E
PT	Henke, Corey	M	63B
PT	Hindson, Harry	D	64D,64E,48
PT	Krause, Kristi	B	64B,41
Prof	Lovejoy, Donald G.	D	37,63A,41,60,32E
Prof	MacDonald, R. Richard	D	47,50,65,32E
PT	Martin, Sharon	M	64A,48
Prof	Mechell, Harry A.	D	60,36,32D,61,54
PT	Mechell, Lauren	B	66D
PT	Merchlewitz, Brenda	M	32B
Prof	Mohr, Deanne	D	66A,66C,66B,13B,13C
PT	Mundy, John	M	13A,11
Asst Prof	Neidhart, Gregory	M	35A,35E,10C
PT	Price, Larry	B	47
Prof	Schmidt, Catherine M.	D	32B,14,32A
Assoc Prof	Sheridan, Daniel	D	64C,60,32C,13A,11
PT	Strom, Jeffrey	M	32E
Prof	Vance, Paul	D	12A,62D,38,51,62C
PT	Wheat, James R.	D	63C,63D

MO0050 Avila University
Department of Music
11901 Wornall Rd
Kansas City, MO 64145-1007
(816) 501-3651   Fax: (816) 501-2442
www.avila.edu
E-mail: Amity.Bryson@Avila.edu

4 Year Institution

Chair: Amity H. Bryson, 80A

Inst PT	Beauregard, Jenny	D	61
	Bryson, Amity H.	D	36,61,60A,15,32D
Inst PT	English, Joseph R.	B	70
Inst PT	Hendrix, Suzanne R.	D	61
Inst PT	Johnson, Kari M.	M	66A,66B,13
	McCarty, Patrick	M	11,32E,37,65,50
Inst PT	Memmott, Jenny	M	66A,66C,33
Inst PT	Scrivner, Matthew	M	61,12,13
Inst PT	Sproul Pulatie, Leah	M	10,13
Inst PT	Titus, Jamie	D	64A,12,13,48
Inst PT	Walker, Anne E.	D	61

MO0060 Calvary Bible College
Department of Music
15800 Calvary Rd
Kansas City, MO 64147-1303
(816) 322-0110 x1342   Fax: (816) 331-4474
www.calvary.edu
E-mail: tom.stolberg@calvary.edu

4 Year Institution

Chair: Tom Stolberg, 80A
Dir., Preparatory Division: Teresa Purinton, 80E

Asst Prof	An, Haekyung	D	61
Adj Inst	Belcher, Jeff	B	37,70
Adj Inst	Bluebaugh, Diana	M	66A
Assoc Prof	Christopher, Un Chong	M	11,12A,13,66A,66C
Adj Inst	Huang, Alice	M	62C
Adj Inst	Jeffrey, Bobbie	M	54
Adj Inst	Lin, Chloe	M	62A,62B,62C,38
Assoc Prof	Stolberg, Tom	D	10F,34,31A,32B,60

MO0100 Central Methodist University
Swinney Music Conservatory
411 Central Methodist Sq
Fayette, MO 65248
(660) 248-6317   Fax: (660) 248-6357
www.centralmethodist.edu
E-mail: dwaggone@centralmethodist.edu

4 Year Institution
Member of NASM

Dean: Dori Waggoner, 80A
Dir., Admissions: Mara Bowen, 80D

Adj Prof	Arnold, Tom	M	61
Asst Prof	Atteberry, Ron	M	10F,36,61,10A
Adj Prof	Baughman, Melissa	M	61
Adj Prof	Bennett, Larry	M	32E,63D,63C,41
Adj Prof	Head, Kelley	M	66D
Adj Prof	Jordan, DJ	M	61
Adj Prof	Lambson, Jeanne	B	62
Adj Prof	Lordo, Jacqueline L.	M	11,63D
Adj Prof	McLouth, Ryan	M	53,70
	Muniz, Jennifer	D	66A,66D,13C,13E
Adj Prof	Muniz, Jorge	D	10A,10F
Assoc Prof	Perkins, John D.	D	63A,63B,12A,42,49
Assoc Prof	Quigley-Duggan, Susan E.	D	61,39
Adj Prof	Ross, Donald	B	64D,64B
Adj Prof	Shroyer, Jo Ellen	M	64A,64C,64E
Adj	Shroyer, Ronald L.	D	64A,64C,64E,64
Adj Prof	Spayde, Ruth	B	66G
Asst Prof	Vandelicht, Roy D. 'Skip'	M	32,37,60B,64A,47
Asst Prof	Waggoner, Dori	D	13E,10F,64A,37,13C
Adj Prof	Warden, Loyd	M	53,65
Asst Prof	Westfall, Claude R.	D	32B,32D,36,60A,70

MO0200 College of the Ozarks
Department of Music
PO Box 17
Point Lookout, MO 65726
(417) 334-6411   Fax: (417) 335-2618
www.cofo.edu
E-mail: gerlach@cofo.edu

4 Year Institution

Chair, Performing & Professional Arts: Mark Young, 80A

PT	Becker, Tia	M	70
Inst	Busch, Gregg		11,13A,31A,36,61
PT	Droke, Marilyn	M	13A,32B,44
PT	Erickson, Margaret		66C
PT	Franks, Kendra	M	61
Prof	Gerlach, Bruce	D	13,10,11,54,66G
PT	Goldapp, James	M	64
Asst Prof	Huff, Dwayne	D	11,66A,66B,66C,66D
Assoc Prof	Jesse, Lynda	M	32D,36,54,60,61
PT	Lohman, Al	M	65,46,47
PT	MacMasters, Dan	M	70
PT	Mizell, John	D	61
PT	Nichols, William	M	66A,66D
PT	Smither, Robert	M	63
PT	Suh, Elizabeth	M	62

MO0250 Cottey College
Department of Music
1000 W Austin Blvd
Nevada, MO 64772-2763
(417) 667-8181   Fax: (417) 667-8103
www.cottey.edu
E-mail: mashmore@cottey.edu

Independent 2 Year Womens College
Member of NASM

Coordinator: Michel Ashmore, 80A

Assoc Prof	Ashmore, Michel	M	11,66A,13A
Adj Asst Prof	Johnson, Gary	M	41,46,63,65
Prof	Kiel, Dyke	D	13B,13C,64
Adj Inst	Morgan, Lauren R.	B	62A,62B,62C,62D,51
Prof	Spencer, Theresa Forrester	M	36,40,61,14C

MO0260 Crowder College
Department of Music
601 Laclede Ave
Neosho, MO 64850-9165
(417) 455-5634/455-5620   Fax: (417) 455-5539
www.crowder.edu/humanities/music.php
E-mail: kierstinbible@crowder.edu

2 Year Institution

Music Contact: Kierstin Michelle Bible, 80A

Adj	Abercrombie, Marilyn	M	66A,66D
Inst	Bible, Kierstin Michelle	D	36,61,12A,13A,54
Inst	Ensor, Robert	M	12A,47,66A,66C,54
Adj	Youngs, Jennifer	B	61

MO0300 Culver-Stockton College
Department of Music
One College Hill
Canton, MO 63435
(573) 288-6346   Fax: (573) 288-6617
www.culver.edu
E-mail: azirnitis@culver.edu

4 Year Institution
Member of NASM

Chair & Dir., Artist Series: Anda Zirnitis, 80A,80F

Assoc Prof	Baker, Kevin L.	D	36,32D,61,60,32
Adj	Beland, Sarah	M	64A
Inst PT	Brewer, Abbie C.	M	66A,66D
Prof	Dieker, R. Joseph	D	64C
Asst Prof	Hollinger, Trent A.	D	64,37,13C,13A,60B
Adj	Machold, William	M	65
Prof	Mathieson, Carol Fisher	D	12A,39,61,31A,11
Adj	Mazzoccoli, Jesse	B	70
Prof Emeritus	McSpadden, Larry D.	M	36,61
Adj	Polett, Jane	M	62A
Assoc Prof	Polett, Thomas C.	D	63,47,32,13,20
Adj	Reeve, Douglas	M	62C,62D
Adj	Van Houzen, Aren	D	63A
Prof	Zirnitis, Anda	D	13,66A,66C,66D

MO0350 Drury University
Department of Music
900 N Benton Ave
Springfield, MO 65802-3712
(417) 873-7296   Fax: (417) 873-7898
music.drury.edu
E-mail: asorenson@drury.edu

4 Year Institution

Chair: Allin Sorenson, 80A

PT	Barnes, Darrel	M	62B,62A,63B
PT	Becker, Tia	B	70
Assoc Prof	Bomgardner, Stephen D.	D	61,39,12A,11
PT	Brewer, Suzann	M	64C
Prof	Cassity, Michael	D	33
Asst Prof	Claussen, Tina	D	47,64E,46,29
PT	Cowens, Kathleen	M	64A,48
PT	Echols, Carol	M	66A,66D,66B
Inst	Harris, Duane	M	32,36,61,12A
PT	Hendry, Robin	B	65
PT	Jackson, Rosemary	M	61
Prof	Julian, Tijuana	D	63A,49,20G
PT	Kim, Sungsil	M	66A
Asst Prof	Koch, Christopher	D	37,38,60B
PT	Koch, Danielle	M	11
PT	Lair, Christopher	M	63D
PT	Moulder, Earline	D	66A,66G
Assoc Prof	Sharpe, Carlyle	D	13,10F,10
PT	Smith, Carolyn	M	61
Prof	Sorenson, Allin	D	60,11,36,61
PT	Southern, Lia	D	64D
PT	Spiegelman, Ron	M	60B,35E
PT	Stacy, Barry	B	66A
PT	Strickler, John	M	70
PT	Swanson, Bob	M	63C
PT	Trtan, Jacqueline	B	51,62C

MO0400 Evangel University
Department of Music
1111 N Glenstone Ave
Springfield, MO 65802
(417) 865-2815 x 7211   Fax: (417) 865-9599
www.evangel.edu
E-mail: kolstadm@evangel.edu

4 Year Institution
Member of NASM

Chair & Dir., Summer Programs: Michael L. Kolstad, 80A,80G
Dir., Graduate Studies: Richard Honea, 80C
Dir., Artist Series: Linda Ligate, 80F

PT	Blair, Starla	M	32E
PT	Boston, Marilyn	M	66A,66D
PT	Cole, Kathryn	M	61,13A,13C
PT	Cowens, Kathy	M	64A,41
Prof	Dissmore, Larry	D	60,38,51,62A,62B
PT	Donaldson, Doree	M	66A,13C
PT	Elliot, William	M	62C
Asst Prof	Griffin, Joel	M	64E,46,47,13A,13B
Inst	Griffin, T. Joel	M	29,31A,47,64E
PT	Gutierrez, Dawn	M	61
PT	Hammar, Christine		44
PT	Harrison, Clint	B	70
PT	Hendry, Robin	B	65
PT	Hensley, Maria	M	64B
Prof	Honea, Richard	D	36,61,60A
PT	Jackson, Eric	M	63B
Prof	Kolstad, Michael L.	D	49,63C,63D,47,34
PT	Lawley, Mark	M	61
Prof	Ligate, Linda	D	12A,66A,31A
PT	Matrone, Tom	M	31
PT	Moore, Matthew	B	34
Assoc Prof	Morris, Gregory	D	11,66A,66B,13
PT	Porter, Mark	M	34B
PT	Ramey, Kara	M	61
PT	Robison, Riley	B	62D
Asst Prof	Salazar, Jason	M	34,13,35,43,47
PT	Shudy, Deryk	M	63D
PT	Slater, Sheri	D	11,48,64C
Assoc Prof	Smith, Susan	M	16,61,12A
PT	Wildman, Randall	M	66D
Assoc Prof	Wilkins, Sharon	M	32,36,66A
PT	Wootton, Tim	M	63A,49

MO0500 Hannibal La Grange College
Department of Music
2800 Palmyra Rd
Hannibal, MO 63401
(573) 629-3161   Fax: (573) 221-6594
www.hlg.edu
E-mail: jbooth@hlg.edu

4 Year Institution

Chair: John D. Booth, 80A

Prof	Booth, John D.	D	12,44,61,31A,70
Asst Prof	Corkern, David	M	46,63A,37,47,10F
Adj	Ferguson, John	B	62,51
Asst Prof	Griffen, Jane	M	60A,32A,32B,36,61
Adj	Meade, Karen	M	32,11,66A,66G
Adj	St. Juliana, Linda	M	32
Adj	Sweets, Nancy	B	37,65,64,66A
Inst	Woodworth, Jessica A.	B	11,34,13,66A

MO0550 Jefferson College
Department of Music
1000 Viking Dr
Hillsboro, MO 63050-2440
(636) 797-3000   Fax: (636) 789-4012
www.jeffco.edu
E-mail: mselsor@jeffco.edu

2 Year Institution

Division Chair: Shirley Dubman, 80A
Dean: Mindy Selsor, 80A

PT	Bell, Richard L.	M	
PT	Boemler, Cathy	M	66A,66B,66C,66D
PT	Bratic, Dean	M	62D
PT	Hodge, Randy	M	37,64E
PT	Howard, Robert C.	M	36,40
PT	Kremer, Kelly	M	11
Prof	McCready, Matthew A.	D	11,12A,63,13A,20
PT	McKee, Holly	B	66C
PT	McNair, Linda	M	62A,11
PT	Pappas, J.	M	65,11,34
PT	Sikes, Ron	M	65
PT	Stoub, Amy	M	62A
PT	Torlina, Mark	M	62
PT	Trautwein, Mark	M	11
Asst Prof	Vanderheyden, Joel	D	64E,46,47,29,13
PT	Vaughan, Laura	M	61,66D

MO0600 Lincoln University
Department of Fine Arts
820 Chestnut St
Jefferson City, MO 65102-0029
(573) 681-5280   Fax: (573) 681-5004
www.lincolnu.edu
E-mail: govangd@lincolnu.edu

4 Year Institution, Historically Black College
Member of NASM

Asst Prof	Gamblin-Green, Michelle	M	36,43
Assoc Prof	Grey, Meg	D	11,12A,32,66A,66G
Asst Prof	Harper, Rhonda	M	37,46,47
Prof Emeritus	Houser, Steven	D	13,12A,12,64
Asst Prof	Johnson, Michael	D	32,29
Prof Emeritus	Mitchell, Charlene	M	32B,66A,66C,66D
Prof Emeritus	Mitchell, Robert	M	13,32,36
Prof	Robertson, Ruth M.	D	36,39,61
Asst Prof	Smith, Derek T.	D	11,13,29
Asst Prof	Zambito, Pete I.	D	65,31

MO0650 Lindenwood University
Department of Music
209 S Kingshighway St
Saint Charles, MO 63301-1693
(636) 949-4506   Fax: (636) 949-4505
www.lindenwood.edu/arts/music/index.html
E-mail: PGrooms@lindenwood.edu

4 Year Institution, Graduate School

Master of Arts in Education

Dean, Fine & Preforming Arts: Joseph Alsobrook, 80A
Chair: Pamela Grooms, 80A
Dir., Graduate Studies: David N. Wallis, 80C

Asst Prof	Alsobrook, Joseph	M	10F,32E,37,34F,35A
Inst Adj	Anderson, Danna	M	61
Asst Prof	Barudin, Jeffrey E.	D	65
Inst Adj	Bittner, Groff S.	M	66A,66D
Inst Adj	Blackmore, Lisa	D	49,63A,63B
Asst Prof	Briones, Marella	M	61,11,36,32B,39
Inst Adj	Bryant, Mary	M	64C
Inst Adj	Ditiberio, Lisa	M	64A
Inst Adj	Frederickson, Matthew	M	63D,32E,49,63C
Asst Prof	Grooms, Pamela	M	12A,20,32D,60,66
Adj	Heyl, Jeffrey	D	61
Inst Adj	Kimler, Wayne	M	51,70
Inst Adj	McClellan, John	M	70
Inst Adj	Pittman, Dwight	M	62D
Inst Adj	Rubenstein, Natasha	M	62C
Inst Adj	Thierbach, Susie	D	62A,62B
Assoc Prof	Wallis, David N.	D	36,10A,11,13,32D
Inst Adj	Williams, R.	M	62
Asst Prof	Williams, Shane	M	11,13,32E,38,41
Inst Adj	Woebling-Paul, Cathy	M	64B

MO0700 Maryville University
Department of Music/Music Therapy
650 Maryville Univ Dr
Saint Louis, MO 63141
(314) 529-6537/529-9441
www.maryville.edu
E-mail: phenderson@maryville.edu

4 Year Institution, Graduate School (Music Therapy only)

Master of Music Therapy

Chair, Music Therapy: Cynthia Briggs, 80A
Chair, Music: Peter Henderson, 80A

Adj	Adams, Robert L.	D	11,12A,12,66A
Adj	Amato, Beatrice	B	33
Asst Prof	Briggs, Cynthia	D	33
Adj	Connor, Mark	D	13,20,41,47
Adj	Edmonds, Kristin	M	61
Adj	Elstner, Erin	M	65
Adj	Garcia, Tim	M	34
Adj	Gerdes, John	M	10F,29A,63
Asst Prof	Henderson, Peter	D	12A,13,42,66A
Adj	Honnold, Adrianne	M	12A,64E
Adj	Hotle, Dana	M	11,64C
Adj	Jenkins, Jack	M	33,36,60
Adj	Kasica, John	B	65
Asst Prof	Kwoun, Soo Jin	D	33,61,66A
Adj	Mosby, Todd		70
Adj	Peterson, Melissa	M	61
Adj	Rocchio, Karen	M	66A
Adj	Rubright, Dan	M	70
Adj	Self, Susanna	M	64A
	Summers, Debora	M	33
Adj	Weber, Susan	M	33

MO0750 Mineral Area College
Department of Music
PO Box 1000
Park Hills, MO 63601
(573) 431-4593   Fax: (573) 518-2230
www.mineralarea.edu
E-mail: kwhite@mineralarea.edu

2 Year Institution

Music Contact: Greg Graf, 80A

Adj Inst	Adkins, Scottye	M	61
Adj Inst	Cox, Kyle	B	50
Adj Inst	Goldsmith, Michael	M	11,13,66A
Inst	Graf, Greg	M	36,40,60,11
Adj Inst	Howard, Chris	B	47,70
Adj Inst	Roed, Tom	M	13,11,66A
Adj Inst	Schunks, Dan	B	47,37
Inst	White, Kevin	D	13,10F,10,63A,53

MO0775 Missouri State University
Department of Music
901 S National
Springfield, MO 65897
(417) 836-5648   Fax: (417) 836-7665
www.missouristate.edu/music
E-mail: music@missouristate.edu

4 Year Institution, Graduate School
Member of NASM

Master of Music in Performance, Master of Music in Conducting, Master of Science in Music Education, Master of Music in Music Education, Master of Music in Music Theory-Composition, Master of Music in Pedagogy

Chair: Julia C. Combs, 80A
Dir., Graduate Studies: Robert C. Quebbeman, 80C

PT	Aho, Kyle	M	11,66A,47
PT	Augustson, Darice E.		62E
PT	Beisswenger, Donald A.	D	20
PT	Brammer, Ron L.	M	37
Assoc Prof	Cameron, James Scott	D	37,50,65
Prof	Casey, Lisa R.	M	13,63B
Prof	Casey, Michael R.	M	49,63A,60,54
Asst Prof	Chapman, Carol L.	M	61
Assoc Prof	Chesman, Jeremy A.		13,66G,69
Prof	Collins, Peter F.	D	66A,66D,66B
Prof	Combs, Julia C.	D	64B,13B,12A,11,13C
PT	Daucher, Tim		62A
PT	Hamilton-Jenkins, Leah		61
Prof	Hamm, Randall P.	M	47,64E,29
Asst Prof	Hausback, Jason	M	63C,47
Prof	Hays, David R.		62A,51
Assoc Prof	Hellman, Daniel S.	D	32
Prof	Heyboer, Jill L.	D	64A
Asst Prof	Homburg, Andrew H.	D	32
Asst Prof	Hong, Hye Jung	D	13,66A
Prof	Hoover, Jerry W.	M	60B,37,46
Prof	Libby, Cynthia Green	D	13,64B,64D,20,48
PT	Loffler, Robert	M	63D
PT	Luellen, Heather M.		54
Prof	Muchnick, Amy Faye	M	11,12A,62B,41
PT	Murray, Kathy	M	13B,13C
Prof	Murray, Michael F.	D	10,13
Prof	Murray, Michael A.	D	13,51,62C
Prof Emerita	Owens, Rose Mary	D	11
Prof	Parsons, James B.	D	12
Asst Prof	Patterson, Paula K.	D	39,61
Assoc Prof	Payne, Richard Todd	D	61
Prof	Peters, Grant S.	D	63A
Prof	Prather, Belva W.	D	60B,48,64A
Prof	Prescott, John S.	D	13,10,20
Prof	Quebbeman, Robert C.	D	38,64C,60
PT	Scott, Vicky		32B,32C
PT	Shelton, Adam	M	11,64E
PT	Smith, Carolyn J.	M	61
PT	Southern, Lia M.	M	64D
PT	St. Pierre, Laurine Grace	D	61
Prof	Storochuk, Allison M.	D	64C,13,48
PT	Strickler, John A.	M	70
PT	Stubbs, Sue A.	M	62D
Prof	Su, Wei-Han	D	66
PT	Taylor, Amanda	D	61
Assoc Prof	Thompson, Christopher E.	D	66C,61
Prof	Webb, Guy B.	D	60,36,61
Asst Prof	Wilcox-Daehn, Ann Marie	D	39,61

MO0800 Missouri Southern State Univ
Department of Music
3950 E Newman Rd
Joplin, MO 64801-1512
(417) 625-9318   Fax: (471) 625-3030
www.mssu.edu/academics/arts-sciences/music/
E-mail: macomber-j@mssu.edu

4 Year Institution

Head, Music: Jeffrey R. Macomber, 80A

Adj	Austin, Glenda K.	M	
Adj	Carlson, Paul B.	D	62A
Prof	Carnine, Albert J.	D	11,61
Asst Prof	Cifelli, Cheryl L.	D	64C,64D,12A,11,13E
Assoc Prof	Clark, Charles 'Bud'	M	36,61,54
Adj	Cunningham, Jeffrey N.	M	64E
Asst Prof	Fronzaglia, Brian	D	65
Adj	Harrell, Wayne	D	63B
Adj	Holt, Matthew K.	M	66C
Adj	Jardon, Gloria J.	M	66A
Adj	Jobson, Krista	M	64A
Adj	Leiter, Joseph W.	M	70
Assoc Prof	Liu, Kexi	D	11,51,62A,62B
Asst Prof	Macomber, Jeffrey R.	D	10,11,12A,32E,63D
Adj	Martin, CarolAnn F.	D	62C,62D
Adj	Murphree, Martin R.	M	61
Asst Prof	Raymond, Rusty	M	37,63A,60B
Assoc Prof	Smith, Susan K.	D	61,13C
Asst Prof	Snodgrass, Debra D.	B	32B
Adj	Snodgrass, William G.	M	20
Adj	Wildman, Randall D.	M	66D
Prof	Wise, Phillip C.	D	29,32

MO0825 Missouri Univ of Science & Tech
Department of Performing Arts
127 Castleman Hall/1870 Miner Cr
Rolla, MO 65409-0670
(573) 341-4185   Fax: (573) 341-6992
alp.mst.edu/music/
E-mail: performingarts@mst.edu

Introductory Courses Only

Chair: W. Lance Haynes, 80A
Vice Provost, Academic Affairs: Phillip Whitefield

Asst Prof	Cesario, Robert James	D	37,38,60B,41
Lect PT	Cress, David	M	47,54,63
Lect	Francis, Lorie	M	11,12A,13,36,66A
Prof Emeritus	Kramme, Joel I.	M	11,36,55,67,12A
Lect PT	Midha, Chris	B	
Lect PT	Stevens, Frankie	M	62A,62B

MO0850 Missouri Western State University
Department of Music
4525 Downs Dr
Saint Joseph, MO 64507-2294
(816) 271-4420   Fax: (816) 271-5974
www.missouriwestern.edu/music
E-mail: gilmour@missouriwestern.edu

4 Year Institution, Graduate School

Member of NASM

Masters of Applied Integrated Media

Chair: F. Matthew Gilmour, 80A

Adj	Agnew, Shawn	M	61,54
Prof Emeritus	Anderson, Jerry L.	M	66A,66B,66C,66D
Asst Prof	Austin, Michael	D	34,35C,13,35,10
Adj	Auwarter, Doug	B	65
Adj	Baskin, Jason	M	11,65,34
Adj	Becerra, Janelle		32A,32B
Adj	Bell, John	M	32,38,63B
Assoc Prof	Benz, David	D	61,39,40
Assoc Prof	Carter, Susan	D	61,40,54,39
Assoc Prof	Edwards, Matthew	D	66A,66B,66C,66D,13
Adj	Fink, Simon B.	D	11
Adj	Foster, Brenda	B	66A,66C
Prof	Gilmour, F. Matthew	D	13,10,11,12A,34
Adj	Glise, Anthony	M	70,41,42
Asst Prof	Hale, Roger	D	60A,61,40,36
Asst Prof	Harrelson, Lee	D	13,63D
Adj	Haynes, Greg	D	65
Adj	Heinz-Thompson, Leslie	M	61,11
Asst Prof	Hinton, Jeffrey	M	60,32C,37,64E
Adj	Holeman, Kathleen	M	61,40,42
Adj	Ju, Ara	M	66C,66D
Adj	Kessler, Stan	M	35A,35
Adj	Kew, Craig	B	62D
Asst Prof	Long, Bob	M	29,64E,47
Prof Emeritus	Mack, William G.	M	60,32C,37,49,63A
Prof Emeritus	Matthews, Michael K.	D	13A,13,10F,47,63C
Asst Prof	May, Nathanael A.	D	66,66B,66C,66D
Adj	McMurray, William	M	12A,11
Assoc Prof	McNeela, Rico		38,11,62A,62B,60
Adj	Molloy, Steve	M	63A,11
Adj	Ragland, Janice	M	61,36,32C
Adj	Riley, Jason	B	70
Prof	Rogers, Dennis G.	D	32,65
Adj	White, Jennifer	M	61
Adj	Yeager, Richard F.	M	37,48,64
Adj	Zuptich, Lory Lacy	M	64A

MO0950 Northwest Missouri State Univ

Department of Music
800 W University
Maryville, MO 64468-6001
(660) 562-1315   Fax: (660) 562-1900
www.nwmissouri.edu/dept/music
E-mail: music@nwmissouri.edu

4 Year Institution, Graduate School
Member of NASM

Master of Science in Ed Teaching: Music

Chair: Ernest Woodruff, 80A

Inst	Badami, Charles A.	D	66C,66A,66D,11
Asst Prof	Bates, Vincent C.	D	63B,32B,32C,11
Adj	Carter, Monty	M	62A,62B,38
Assoc Prof	Dunnell, Rebecca	D	64A,12A,14,11,20
Prof	Gibson, Christopher A.	D	11,64B,64C,64D,64E
Prof	Kramer, Ernest Joachim	D	13,10,11,66A,66H
Assoc Prof	Lanier, Brian	D	32D,36,60A,61
Adj	Maret, Kevin	M	65,47
Assoc Prof	Olson, Anthony	D	11,66A,66G,66D
Asst Prof	Overmier, Douglas R.	D	60B,60A,37,47,10
Adj	Peng, Yan	M	61
Asst Prof	Phillips, Sheila A.	D	36,11
Assoc Prof	Richardson, William	D	47,63A,11
Assoc Prof	Shannon, Pamela	D	11,61
Prof	Town, Stephen	D	13,61,36
Prof	Woodruff, Ernest	D	11,32E,63D

MO1000 Park University

Department of Music
8700 NW River Park Dr
Parkville, MO 64152
(816) 584-6550   Fax: (816) 584-6551
www.park.edu/icm
E-mail: istas@park.edu

4 Year Institution

Director: Stanislav Ioudenitch, 80A

Adj Inst	Berg, Steve	M	37
Adj Inst	Cox, Bradley	M	13J,66A
Adj Inst	Horsley, Paul J.	M	12A,66A
Assoc Prof	Ioudenitch, Stanislav	M	66A
Adj Inst	Ioudenitch, Tatiana	M	66A
Adj Inst	Ito, Kanako	M	51,62A
Adj Inst	Jacobs, Gene	M	60B
Adj Inst	Lisovskaya-Sayevich, Lolita	M	66C
Adj Inst	Oberle, Curtis P.	M	11,70
Adj Inst	Sandomirsky, Gregory	M	51,66A
Prof	Sayevich, Ben	M	51,62A
Adj Inst	Schaefer, John	M	66G
Adj Inst	Sims, Lamar	M	20B,66A
Assoc Prof	Storey, Martin	M	51,62C
Prof	Sultanova, Marina	M	66A

MO1010 Rockhurst University

Department of Music
1100 Rockhurst Rd
Kansas City, MO 64110-2508
(816) 501-4000 x 4741   Fax: (816) 501-4169
www.rockhurst.edu
E-mail: victor.penniman@rockhurst.edu

4 Year Institution

Director, Music Program: G. Victor Penniman

Adj	Christopher, Un Chong	M	61
Adj	Chung, Jiyun	M	66A
Adj	Egger, Cynthia	M	70
Prof	McDonald, Timothy L.	D	11,12A,36,20G
Assoc Prof	Penniman, G. Victor	D	55,12A,62,11,36

MO1100 St Louis Comm Coll-Florissant

Department of Music
3400 Pershall Rd
Saint Louis, MO 63135-1408
(314) 513-4493   Fax: (314) 513-4080
www.stlcc.edu
E-mail: phigdon@stlcc.edu

2 Year Institution

Chair: Paul Higdon, 80A

Adj Inst	Anderson, Alerica		36
Assoc Prof	Higdon, Paul	D	13,66A,66B,11,66D
Adj Inst	Ivy, Allen	M	60,38,51,64A
Adj Inst	Jones, Christine	M	11,66
Adj Inst	Monier, Shelly	M	13
Adj Inst	Strathman, Marc	M	29A

MO1110 St Louis Comm Coll-Forest Park

Department of Music
5600 Oakland Ave
Saint Louis, MO 63110-1316
(314) 644-9769   Fax: (314) 951-9406
www.stlcc.edu
E-mail: tzirkle@stlcc.edu

2 Year Institution

Music Coordinator: Thomas Zirkle, 80A

Adj Inst	Bemberg, Stephanie		12A,66A
Adj Inst	Crews, Joel		29A
Adj Inst	Laufersweiler, Jonathon		70
Adj Inst	Perry, Talya		61,66A
Adj Inst	Potthoff, Joseph		
Adj Inst	Quinn, Kelly		29A
Adj Inst	Renner-Hughes, Marty		12A,36,54
Adj Inst	Thomas, Steven		
Assoc Prof	Zirkle, Thomas	D	65,65B

MO1120 St Louis Comm College-Meramec
Department of Music
11333 Big Bend Rd
Saint Louis, MO 63122-5720
(314) 984-7639   Fax: (314) 984-7254
www.stlcc.edu/Programs/Music
E-mail: dwerner@stlcc.edu

2 Year Institution

Chair: Donna Werner, 80A
Music Coordinator: Gary Gackstatter, 80H
Music Coordinator: Gerald C. Myers, 80H

Inst PT	Benedick, Kristi	M	14C
Inst PT	Boedges, Bob	M	46,14C
Inst PT	Conley, Cheryl	M	66D
Asst Prof	Gackstatter, Gary	M	37,11,38
Inst PT	Honnold, Adrianne	M	14C
Inst PT	Hotle, Dana	M	11
Inst PT	Melman, Mort	M	70
Asst Prof	Myers, Gerald C.	D	11,36,40,54,13
Inst PT	Pittman, Dwight	M	14C
Inst PT	Quinn, Kelly	M	11
Inst PT	Ross, Laura	M	11
Inst PT	Schmidt, Susan	M	66D
Inst PT	Vaccaro, Brian	M	47,14C
Inst PT	Whittemore, Joan	D	61

MO1250 St Louis University
Department of Fine & Perf Art-Mus
221 N Grand Blvd
Saint Louis, MO 63103-2006
(314) 977-2410   Fax: (314) 977-2999
www.slu.edu
E-mail: hughesrl@slu.edu

4 Year Institution

Chair: James J. Burwinkel, 80A

Assoc Prof	Becker, Jeral Blaine	D	61,36,11,60,39
Inst PT	Becker, Wanda	B	51
Inst PT	Burke, Leon	D	61
Inst PT	Burkhart, Annette	M	66A
Inst PT	Daniels, Mathew	B	70
Inst PT	Danner, Zachary	M	63C
Assoc Prof	Dees, Pamela Youngdahl	D	66A,66B,66C,11,12A
Inst PT	Friedel, Aileen	B	62C
Prof Emeritus	Guentner, Francis J.	M	
Asst Prof	Hughes, Robert L.	D	12A,29,13,29A,29E
Adj Prof	Johnson, Aaron E.	D	10A,34D,13,70
Inst PT	Leonhardt, Julie	B	62,51
Adj Prof	Lim, Jennifer	D	66A,66D
Adj Prof	Rotola, Albert	D	11,12A
Inst PT	Rowbottom, Terree	M	61
Inst PT	Saunders, Ruth	M	66A,66H
Inst PT	Scanlon, Patricia A.	B	61
Inst PT	Scott, Janet	M	64A
Inst PT	Stubbs, Susan A.	M	62D
Inst PT	Stubbs, Thomas L.	B	65
Adj Prof	Weber, Mary	M	63A,13,11

MO1350 St Paul School of Theology
Department of Music
5123 E Truman Rd
Kansas City, MO 64127-2440
(816) 483-9600   Fax: (816) 483-9605
www.spst.edu
E-mail: spst@spst.edu

Graduate School of Theology

Chair: Sujin Yoon, 80A

	Yoon, Sujin	M	36,66G,66H,31A,60A

MO1500 Southeast Missouri State Univ
Department of Music
1 University Plz
Cape Girardeau, MO 63701-4710
(573) 651-2141   Fax: (573) 651-2431
www.semo.edu
E-mail: cgoeke@semo.edu

4 Year Institution, Graduate School
Member of NASM

Dean, Liberal Arts: Francisco X. Barrios, 80A
Chair: Christopher L. Goeke, 80A
Dean, Graduate School: William Eddlman, 80C
Dir., Preparatory Division: Rebecca L. Fulgham, 80E
Associate Dean: Rhonda Weller-Stilson, 80H

Assoc Prof	Christensen, Brandon J.	D	62A,62B,42,11
Assoc Prof	Conger, Robert B.	D	60B,32C,63C,63D
Inst PT	Contrino, Joseph L.	M	65,29A,13A,13C
Asst Prof	Durow, Peter J.	PhD	36,32D,60A
Prof	Edgerton, Sara A.	D	11,12A,38,62D,62C
Prof	Fruehwald, Robert D.	D	13,10,45,64A
Prof	Fulgham, Marc S.	D	11,49,63A,63B
Prof	Goeke, Christopher L.	D	39,41,61,54
Assoc Prof	Hendricks, Steven	D	32,37,34,36
Assoc Prof	Jones, Leslie I.	DMA	61,39,11,54
Inst PT	Kelley, Charles	B	63D
Inst	Mims, Mary	M	32A,32B
Asst Prof	Mizicko, Shane J.	D	11,50,65A,65B,65
Assoc Prof	Noonan, Jeffrey	D	12A,14,67D,70,20G
Inst	Reuter, Jessica M.	M	63B
Asst Prof	Reynolds, Martin C.	D	37,63C,41,47,32E
Inst PT	Ross, Laura Guyer	M	64B,64D
Asst Prof	Schmidt, Timothy A.	D	61,39,54
Inst PT	Shaffer, Lori	B	61
Prof	Sifferman, James P.	D	11,66A,66D
Inst	Thompson, Paul	M	11,41,64A,29A,55C
Inst	Yount, Matthew W.	M	11,66C

MO1550 Southwest Baptist University
Department of Music
1600 University Ave
Bolivar, MO 65613-2496
(417) 328-1644   Fax: (417) 328-1637
www.sbuniv.edu/music
E-mail: mhicks@sbuniv.edu

4 Year Institution
Member of NASM

Chair: Martha K. Hicks, 80A
Dean: Jeffery L. Waters, 80A

PT	Baker, Marc	M	65
PT	Bowdidge, Mark	D	66G
Prof	Brown, Kathy	D	32B,61
PT	Bruner, Regina	M	64C
PT	Burgher, R. Catherine	B	40
Assoc Prof	Campbell, Andy	M	36,61,13C
Asst Prof	Carney, Robert D.	D	66A,66B,66C,11,13C
PT	Draper, Michelle	M	64A,48
PT	Glidwell, Delrae	B	32B,32C,13A
PT	Harrison, Carol	M	62A,62B
Prof	Hicks, Martha K.	D	31A,11,60,13C,32B
Assoc Prof	Hopwood, Brian	D	32E,37,38,63
PT	Jackson, Eric	M	63B
Prof	Jones, Melinda	D	66A,66D,66B,13B,13C
Assoc Prof	Knupps, Terri L.	D	12A,20,63C,63D,42
PT	Miller, Sara	M	66D
PT	Price, Matt	B	62C,62D
PT	Roberts, Melissa	D	66A,66D
PT	Strickler, John	M	70
Prof	Tarrant, James	D	36,60A,35,42,66A
Prof	Waters, Jeffery L.	D	13B,47,64
Prof	Waters, Renee	D	13,10,66A,34,11
PT	Wooderson, Joseph	M	11,61
PT	Wootton, Tim	M	63A

MO1650 Stephens College
Department of Perf Arts-Music
1200 E Broadway
Columbia, MO 65215
(573) 876-7194   Fax: (573) 876-7248
www.stephens.edu
E-mail: cnichols@stephens.edu

4 Year Women's College

Chair: Rob Doyen, 80A

Archer, Kelly	B		13A,66A
Doyen, Rob			
Elliot, Mike	B		61,54
Ellsworth-Smith, Pamela	M		61,54
Morrison, Harry	M		61,54

MO1710 Three Rivers Community College
Department of Music
2080 Three Rivers Blvd
Poplar Bluff, MO 63901
(573) 840-9639   Fax: (573) 840-9603
www.trcc.edu
E-mail: cwhite@trcc.edu

2 Year Institution

Division Chair: Steven D. Lewis, 80A

Inst PT	Allen, Tom	M	70,32B
Inst PT	Becker, Pam	M	61
Inst PT	Book, Andee	M	61
Inst PT	Renshaw, Kenneth	M	66A,66D
Inst PT	Rybolt, Scott	M	64
Inst FT	White, Cindy	M	64,13,36,61,66A
Inst FT	White, William	M	11,37,47,65,63

MO1780 Truman State University
Department of Music
100 E Normal St
Kirksville, MO 63501-4221
(660) 785-4417   Fax: (660) 785-7463
www.truman.edu
E-mail: music@truman.edu

4 Year Institution, Graduate School
Member of NASM

Master of Arts Education in Music Education, Master of Arts in Music

Chair: Jay C. Bulen, 80A
Dir., Artist/Performance Series: Winston Vanderhoof, 80F

Inst PT	AuBuchon, Elaine	M	64B,64D,11
Asst Prof	AuBuchon, Tim	M	29,46,47
Prof	Bulen, Jay C.	D	12C,12A,63C
Assoc Prof	Bump, Michael	D	65,50
	Coggins, Janet	M	66C
Prof	Collett, Jacqueline L.	D	32,36,61,39
Prof	Gooch, Warren P.	D	10,13,10A
Asst Prof	Gran, Charles	D	11,13,34,10
Prof	Hueber, Thomas E.	D	39,61
Assoc Prof	Jennings, Mark D.	D	60,36,61
Prof	Jones, Gregory R.	D	11,63A,49
Asst Prof	Krebs, Jesse D.	D	11,64C,13D,48
Asst Prof	Kubin, Brian	D	62C,13,51,62D
PT	Kubus, Daniel	M	66C
Prof	McClure, Sam	D	13,38,62A,62B
Prof	McKamie, David W.	D	13,12A,66A
Inst PT	McKamie, Shirley	M	11,66D,66H
Asst Prof	Mickey, Patricia A.	M	63B,11,13D
Prof	Moore, Julianna	D	13,48,64A
	Peterson, Dan L.	M	37,65
Asst Prof	Radoslavov, Ilia G.	D	66C,66A,66D,66B
Prof	Rice, Marc	D	11,12A,14C
Inst PT	Robertson, Phyllis	D	61
Inst PT	Seward, Steve K.	B	63D
Prof	Smith, Randall A.	D	13,64E
Prof	Trimborn, Thomas J.	D	60,11,32

MO1790 Univ of Central Missouri
Department of Music
Utt Music Bldg
Rm 109
Warrensburg, MO 64093
(660) 543-4530   Fax: (660) 543-8271
www.ucmo.edu/music
E-mail: smoore@ucmo.edu

4 Year Institution, Graduate School
Member of NASM

Master of Arts in Performance, Master of Arts in Music Education, Master of Arts in Conducting, Master of Arts in Music Theory-Composition, Master of Arts in Piano Pedagogy, Master of Arts in History & Literature, Master of Arts in Kodaly

Chair: J. Steven Moore, 80A
Dir., Artist/Performance Series: Jeff H. Imboden, 80F
Dir., Music Camp: Scott C. Lubaroff, 80G
Dir., Piano Institute: Mia M. Hynes

Prof	Aaberg, David E.	D	47,29,10
Adj	Adams, David	M	39,61
Adj	Armetta, Joseph F.	M	70
Prof	Bersin, Michael D.	D	11,12A,62C,62D
Prof	Brothers, Lester D.	D	11,12A,12C
Assoc Prof	Check, John D.	D	13
Prof	Fenley, J. Franklin	D	11,12A,64A
Prof	Gai, James R.	D	20,64C,64E
Adj	Gregory, Jon M.	M	63D
Adj	Hartman, Lee	M	13A
Assoc Prof	Honour, Eric C.	D	10,34,13,13F,35C
Prof	Hynes, Mia M.	D	66A,66B,66D
Adj	Isaac, James G.	M	64E,47
Assoc Prof	Lawrence, Robert J.	D	32,36,11,47
Assoc Prof	Lubaroff, Scott C.	D	37,32E,10F,60
Assoc Prof	Maltas, Carla Jo	D	32,32B
Assoc Prof	Mattson, Sheri	D	11,64B,64D
Adj	McBain, Mike	M	65
Adj	McIntire, David D.	D	34,35A
Prof	Moege, Gary R.	D	11,63B,70,71,12A
Prof	Moore, J. Steven	D	37,32E,60B
Inst	Oyster, Roger	M	63C
Assoc Prof	Roden, Stella D.	D	61,11
Assoc Prof	Rutland, John P.	D	38,62A,62B
Prof	Sekelsky, Michael J.	D	37,50,65
Asst Prof	Sentgeorge, Aaron Jacob 'Jake'	ABD	61,35C
Prof	Stagg, David L.	D	11,37,63C
Asst Prof	Tian, Tian	ABD	66A
PT	Villaveces, John	ABD	66C
Assoc Prof	Wenger, Alan J.	D	11,63A
Asst Prof	Zabriskie, Alan N.	D	11,40,36,60A

MO1800 Univ of Missouri
School of Music
140 Fine Arts Bldg
Columbia, MO 65211
(573) 882-2606   Fax: (573) 884-7444
music.missouri.edu
E-mail: shayr@missouri.edu

4 Year Institution, Graduate School
Member of NASM

Master of Music in Collaborative Piano, Master of Arts in Music Education, Master of Arts in Music History, Master of Education in Music Education, Master of Music in Composition, Master of Music in Music Theory, Master of Music in Performance, Master of Music in Conducting, Master of Music in Jazz Performance & Pedagogy, Master of Music in Piano Pedagogy, PhD in Curriculum & Instruction (Music Education)

Director: Robert Shay, 80A
Coordinator, Admissions: John Slish, 80D
Dir., Preparatory Division: Jonathan Kuuskoski, 80E
Dir., Preparatory Division: Erica Manzo, 80E
Associate Director: Janice K. Wenger, 80H
Associate Director: Dan L. Willett, 80H

Assoc Prof	Akhmadullin, Iskander	D	63A
Adj PT	Andes, Tom	B	66A
Asst Prof	Baumgartner, Christopher	D	37,60B
Adj Asst Prof	Bolshakova, Natalia	D	66C
Prof	Budds, Michael J.	D	12A,11,29
Adj Asst Prof	Carlson, Maureen A.	D	61
Prof	Crabb, Paul	D	36,60A

Vstng Asst Prof	Dade, Alice K.	M	64A
Assoc Prof	Dolbashian, Edward	M	60B,38
Assoc Prof	Dolezal, Darry	M	62C,42
Assoc Prof	Freund, Stefan	D	13,10
Assoc Prof	Gaines, Julia	D	65,50
Assoc Prof	Garritson, Paul W.	M	64C,48
Asst Prof	Gibson, Maya	D	12
Adj Asst Prof	Glise, Anthony	M	70
Assoc Prof	Harrell, Ann	M	61
Asst Prof	Howe, Timothy E.	D	63C,63D
Asst Prof	Jensen, Susan	M	62A,42
Asst Prof	Kuuskoski, Jonathan	D	35
Asst Prof	Lackey, William J.	D	10B,34
Asst Prof	Mabary, Judith A.	D	12A,20,11
Asst Prof	Major, Marci L.	D	32D,60A
Assoc Prof	Manzo, Angelo	D	63D
Adj Asst Prof	Manzo, Erica	D	13,64C
Prof	McKenney, W. Thomas	D	13,10,34D
Assoc Prof	Minturn, Neil	D	13
Assoc Prof	Miyamoto, Peter M.	DMA	66,13,42
Assoc Prof	O'Neal, Thomas	D	11
Vstng Asst Prof	Pellegrin, Richard S.	M	13
Prof	Perna, Leslie	M	62B,42
Prof	Platt, Melvin C.	D	32
Adj Asst Prof	Ryan, Sarah E.	M	13,66D
Assoc Prof	Saguiguit, Leo C.	M	64E,48
Asst Prof	Savvidou, Paola	D	66A,66B
Assoc Prof	Seitz, Christine	M	39,11
Adj Asst Prof	Seitz, Paul T.	D	13A,13B,13C
Prof	Shay, Robert	D	12
Asst Prof	Shonekan, Stephanie	D	14,20
Asst Prof	Silvey, Brian A.	D	32E,60B
Prof	Sims, Wendy L.	D	32A,32B,32G
Asst Prof	Snow, Bradley	D	37,60B
Prof	Spence, Marcia L.	D	63B,49
Vstng Asst Prof	Stone, Maya K.	D	64D
Adj Asst Prof	Stubbs, Sue	M	62D
Prof	Szekely, Eva D.	M	62A,51
Adj PT	Tate, Brian	M	11,34
Prof	Todd, Jo Ella	M	61
Adj Assoc Prof	Urton, Dan	M	61
Prof	Wenger, Janice K.	D	66C,66A,66H,66E
Asst Prof	White, Arthur	D	47,64C,29B
Assoc Prof	Willett, Dan L.	M	64B,48

MO1810 Univ of Missouri-Kansas City

Conservatory of Music & Dance
4949 Cherry St
Kansas City, MO 64110-2229
(816) 235-2900   Fax: (816) 235-5265
conservatory.umkc.edu
E-mail: wittep@umkc.edu

4 Year Institution, Graduate School
Member of NASM

Master of Arts in Music, Master of Music in Composition, Master of Music in Music Theory, Master of Music in Performance, Master of Music in Conducting, Master of Music in Musicology, Master of Music Education, DMA in Composition, DMA in Conducting, DMA in Performance, IPHD in Music Education, Master of Arts in Music Therapy, Performer's Certificate, Artist's Certificate

Dean: Peter Witte, 80A
Associate Dean & Dir., Undergraduate Studies: Sabrina Madison-Cannon, 80B,80H
Dir., Preparatory Division: Mara Gibson, 80E
Associate Dean & Dir., Graduate Studies: William A. Everett, 80H,80C
Associate Dean: Mary Pat Henry, 80H
Associate Dean: James W. Snell, 80H
Associate Dean: Robert W. Weirich, 80H

Asst Prof	Abbott, Gary Bernard		52
Prof Emeritus	Abelson, Norman		61
Asst Teaching Prof	Abner, Marita	M	64D
Adj Assoc Prof	Ackerly, Olga	PhD	12A
Adj Inst	Auwarter, Doug	M	47
Adj Inst	Barham, Terry	D	32D
Prof Emerita	Bashar, Inci	B	61
Asst Prof	Bazell, Marciem	M	39
Assoc Prof Emerita	Bean, Shirley Ann	D	13A,13B,13C,13D,13E
Other	Beck, Robert T.	M	35G
Asst Prof	Belgrave, Melita	D	33
Inst Adj	Bell, Valerie	M	51,62
Prof	Benjamin, Keith	D	63A
Adj Assoc Prof	Bickers, Elisa	D	66G
Asst Teaching Prof	Bishop, Barbara A.	M	64B
Prof	Bode, Robert	D	60A,36,61
Inst Adj	Borja, Jonathan	D	12A
Inst Adj	Bowman, Bob		29,62D
Assoc Prof Emeritus	Brown, Hugh M.		41,62A,62B
Adj Prof	Campbell, Douglas	PhD	41
Prof	Carl, Jane	D	64C
Prof	Chen, Yi	D	10
Adj Inst	Christopher, Un Chong	M	61
Prof	Cole, Vinson	DIPL	61
Assoc Prof	Davis, JoDee	D	63C
Assoc Prof	Davis, Steven D.	M	60B
Assoc Prof	De Launay, Anne M.	D	61,12A
Adj Inst	Dekker, Steve	M	63C
Assoc Prof Emeritus	Ditto, John A.	D	66G,31A
Prof Emeritus	Ehly, Ewald	D	60A,61,36
Asst Teaching Prof	Elswick, Beth L.	D	13A,13B,13C,13D
Asst Prof Adj	Embrey, Danny		29
Adj Inst	English, Nicole	M	52
Prof	Enyeart, Carter	M	62C
Prof	Everett, William A.	PhD	12A
Assoc Prof	Feener, Raymond	D	61
Assoc Prof	Fieldman, Hali	PhD	13
Adj Inst	Fillingim, Debra K.	M	32B
Adj Inst	Fleeman, Rod		70
Adj Prof	Geller, Noah	M	62A
Prof	Genualdi, Joseph	DIPL	62A
Adj Asst Prof	Gibson, Mara	D	10
Adj Prof	Gippo, Jan	M	41
Assoc Prof	Granade, S. Andrew	PhD	12A
Assoc Prof	Groene, Robert W.	PhD	33,13L
Assoc Teaching Prof	Hackleman, Martin		63B
Adj Assoc Prof	Halley, Gustavo	D	61
Assoc Prof Emeritus	Hamilton, Alexander W.	D	32
Assoc Prof	Hanson-Abromeit, Deanna	PhD	33
Adj Inst	Harrel, Shawn	M	32B
Assoc Prof Emeritus	Hehr, Milton G.	PhD	13,10F,12A
Prof	Henry, Mary Pat	M	52
Asst Prof	Hiett, Dee Anna		52
Assoc Teaching Prof	Higdon, Patricia	M	66C
Asst Prof	Honisch, Erika	D	12
Adj Prof	Kail, Jeffrey E.	B	62D
Adj Inst	Kessler, Stan		63A
Assoc Prof	Kim, Benny	M	62A
Prof Emeritus	Klausner, Tiberius		41,62A
Prof Emeritus	Knoll, Richard C.		61
Adj Assoc Prof	Kushner, Karen	M	66A
Adj Inst	Lammers, James	B	70
Prof Emerita	Lathom-Radocy, Wanda	PhD	33
Assoc Prof	Lee, Scott	M	62B
Prof Emeritus	Leisenring, John R.	D	41,63C,63D
Asst Teaching Prof	Lidge, Kenneth	D	13,11
Asst Teaching Prof	Lorek, Mary Jo	PhD	13
Assoc Prof	Madison-Cannon, Sabrina	M	52
Adj Prof	Mahoney, Billie	M	52
Prof	McIntyre, Robert John	M	66A
Adj Inst	McKee, Lindsey L.	B	61
Adj Prof	McLaurin, Christopher	DIPL	65
Prof	Mobberley, James C.	D	10A,10B,10F
Assoc Prof	Morehouse, Dale	M	61
Inst	New, Laura L.	M	13C
Assoc Prof	Niedt, Douglas Ashton	B	70
Adj Asst Prof	Oldham, Ryan P.	D	11
Prof	Olson, Robert H.	D	60B,38
Assoc Prof	Parisi, Joseph	D	32E,32F,37
Prof Emerita	Petersen, Marian F.		13,12A
Assoc Prof	Petrella, Diane Helfers	D	66A,66B,66D
Adj Asst Prof	Petrella, Nick E.	D	65
Assoc Prof	Posses, Mary	D	64A,42
Prof Emerita	Rich, Ruth Anne	D	66A
Asst Teaching Prof	Rivera, Natalia	D	40
Prof	Robinson, Charles R.	PhD	36,32D,32H
Assoc Prof Emerita	Ross-Happy, Linda Mae	D	66D
Prof	Rudy, Paul	D	10A,10B,10C,10F
Prof Emeritus	Shatzkin, Merton T.	PhD	13,12A,62A
Assoc Prof	Sherburn, Rebecca	D	61
Assoc Prof	Simpson, Reynold	D	13
Assoc Prof	Snell, James W.	D	65
Asst Prof	Soder, Aidan L.	D	61
Assoc Prof	Solose, Jane M.	D	66A,66H
Prof Emerita	Sommers, Joan C.		68
Prof Emeritus	Sommers, Paul B.		61
Adj Inst	Spaits, Gerald K.	A	62D
Assoc Prof	Stein, Thomas G.	M	63D
Adj Inst	Strong, Michael		52
Other	Swafford, Kent		66F
Inst	Thomas, Daniel A.	M	64E,47,53
Adj Prof	Thompson, Lee D.	D	66C
Asst Prof	Tice, Ronald	B	52
Adj Inst	Timmons, Jeff D.	M	64E
Assoc Prof	Timmons, Timothy	M	64E
Adj Asst Prof	Titterington, Beth	M	32H
Asst Teaching Prof	Tyrrell, Sarah	D	12A,20
Adj Inst	Warren, Michael		50
Prof	Watson, Robert M.	B	29A,29B,29C,47,64E
Prof	Weber, Paula B.	M	52
Prof	Weirich, Robert W.	D	66A
Adj Asst Prof	Wijnands, Bram	B	66A
Adj Asst Prof	Wilder, Roger M.		66A
Assoc Prof	Williams, Lindsey R.	D	32E,60B,32H,32G,63C
Asst Prof	Williams, Richard Lee	M	66C,61
Prof	Zhou, Long	D	10

MO1830 Univ of Missouri-St. Louis
Department of Music
One University Blvd
Saint Louis, MO 63121-4400
(314) 516-5981   Fax: (314) 516-6593
www.umsl.edu/~umslmusic/
E-mail: umslmusic@umsl.edu

4 Year Institution, Graduate School
Member of NASM

Master of Music Education

Chair: Robert W. Nordman, 80A
Dean, Fine Arts & Communication: James Richards, Jr., 80A
Dir., Graduate Studies: Fred Willman, 80C
Assistant Chair: Barbara Harbach, 80H

Assoc Prof	Baldwin, Kurt	M	51,62C
Lect PT	Beeson, D. Allen	B	29B
Lect PT	Blackmore, Lisa	D	63A
Lect PT	Bowermaster, Tod	B	63B
Asst Prof	Brandes, Gary W.	M	37,60,32E
Lect PT	Cairns, Whitney	M	13C
Asst Prof	Cairns, Zachary	D	13
Lect PT	Cowell, Kimberly S.	M	32B
Lect PT	Davenport, Roger N.	B	63C,63D
Lect PT	Davis, Jan	D	32E
Lect PT	Derham, Billie	M	66A,66D
Lect PT	Dunlap, Phil	M	29A
Lect PT	Fleming, Gail	D	32B,32C
Specialist PT	Fry, Daniel	M	66C
Assoc Prof PT	Haggans, Kathryn	D	36,61
Prof	Harbach, Barbara	D	66G,67F,15,66H,34A
Lect PT	Hartenberger, Aurelia	D	20,32
Assoc Prof	Henry, James	D	36,40,60A,32D,10F
Lect	Henry, Matthew	M	65,50
Specialist PT	Hironaka-Bergt, Mieko	M	66C
Lect PT	Homann, Ann		64B
Lect PT	Honnold, Adrianne L.	M	64C
Lect PT	Howard, Robert	M	38
Asst Prof Emeritus	Hylton, Doris	M	32B,13A,13C
Prof Emeritus	Hylton, John B.	D	32D
Lect PT	Jones, Hugh	M	29B
Lect PT	Kasica, Paula J.	B	64A
Lect PT	Kehner, Kenneth W.	B	66A
Lect PT	Langerak, Terri	B	62E
Assoc Prof	Markou, Stella	D	61,39,40
Assoc Prof	McGrosso, John	M	51,62A
Assoc Prof	Mendoza, Joanna	M	62B
Prof Emeritus	Miller, Kenneth E.	D	32
Assoc Prof	Mishra, Jennifer	D	32
Prof Emeritus	Mitchell, Evelyn		66A
Lect PT	Morton, Stephen C.	M	61
Lect PT	Mottl, Robert O.	M	64D
Assoc Prof	Nordman, Robert W.	M	32E
Prof Emeritus	Perris, Arnold	D	
Specialist PT	Pyron, Donna N.	B	66C
Prof Emeritus	Ray, Robert	B	20G,36,66A
Prof	Richards, James	D	10F,60,38
Lect PT	Rosenkoetter, Alan C.	B	70
Asst Prof	Sakharova, Julia	M	62A,42
Lect PT	Smith, John	M	36
Lect PT	Stubbs, Sue	M	62D
Prof	Touliatos-Miles, Diane	D	11,12A,12,29A
Prof Emeritus	Turpin, Douglas	D	32
Lect PT	Voskoboynikova, Alla	M	66A
Lect PT	Werner, Susan	M	61
Artist in Res	Widner, James	M	46,29B,29C,47
Prof	Willman, Fred	D	32,34
Lect PT	York-Garesche, Jeanine	M	64C

MO1900 Washington University
Department of Music
CB 1032
1 Brookings Dr
St. Louis, MO 63130
(314) 935-5581   Fax: (314) 935-4034
music.wustl.edu
E-mail: music@artsci.wustl.edu

4 Year Institution, Graduate School

Master of Arts in Composition, Master of Arts in Music Theory, PhD in Music Theory, PhD in Musicology, Master of Arts in Musicology, Master of Music in Keyboard Studies, Master of Music in Vocal Performance

Chair: Dolores Pesce, 80A
Dir., Undergraduate Studies: Patrick L. Burke, 80B
Dir., Graduate Studies: Robert Snarrenberg, 80C

Lect	Aldrich, Nicole P.	D	36,40,60
Senior Lect	Armistead, Christine	M	39,61
Adj PT	Baldus, Kara A.	B	66A
Adj PT	Barnum, Justin	M	62A
Adj PT	Becker, Christopher A.	M	47
Emeritus	Bolduan, Kathleen	D	13A,13
Assoc Prof	Burke, Patrick L.	D	14
Adj	Burkhart, Annette M.	M	66A,66D
Adj PT	Carlin, Maryse	M	66A,66H
Prof	Carlin, Seth A.	M	66A,67C
Adj PT	Carnes, Maurice J.		47
Adj PT	Clark, Charlene K.	B	62A
Adj PT	Claude, Henry	B	65
Asst Prof	Decker, Todd R.	D	12,12A
Lect	Demarinis, Paul	M	29A
Adj PT	Garritson, Paul W.	M	64C
Adj PT	Geary, Sandra	B	66A
Adj PT	Gianino, Kevin	B	65
Asst Prof	Gill-Gurtan, Denise	D	14
Adj PT	Gott, Andrew	M	64D
Adj PT	Hanser, Kirk	M	70
Adj	Hintz, Gail	M	66C
Adj PT	Honnold, Adrianne L.	M	64E
Adj PT	Hsieh, Annie	M	66A
Adj PT	Iticovici, Silvian	M	62A
Adj PT	Jarvi, Steven	M	38
Asst Prof	Kennedy, Martin P.	D	10,13
Adj	Kirkpatrick, Amanda	M	66A,66D
Prof	Kurtzman, Jeffrey	D	12A,12
Adj PT	Lemire, Carole E.	B	63B
Senior Lect	Lenihan, William	B	70,29
Adj PT	Macdonald, Elizabeth	M	41,62C
Adj PT	Martin, Don R.	B	62D
Adj PT	Miller-Campbell, Tamara J.	M	61
Prof	Monson, Craig	D	12A,12
Adj PT	Myers, Timothy R.	B	63C
Adj PT	Noonan, Jeffrey J.	D	67D
Adj PT	Ocel, Timothy	B	61
Adj PT	O'Donnell, Richard L.	DIPL	45
Prof	Pesce, Dolores	D	12A,12,13J
Adj PT	Price, Jane E.	M	62A
Adj	Prince, Noel	M	61
Adj PT	Raedeke, Barbara A.	D	66G
Adj PT	Reycraft, Jonathan W.	M	63C
Adj	Rosenkoetter, Alan	B	70
Adj PT	Ross, Laura	M	64B
Adj PT	Ruggles, Nathan	B	61
Adj PT	Sasse, Christine T.	M	62A
Assoc Prof	Schmelz, Peter	D	12,12A
Adj	Smith, Denise A.	M	61
Adj PT	Smith, Janice M.	B	41,64A
Assoc Prof	Snarrenberg, Robert	D	13,13J
Adj PT	Sparks, Dee	B	62B
Asst Prof	Stefaniak, Alexander	D	12,12A
Asst Prof	Steinbeck, Paul	D	13
Adj PT	Tash, Sharon	B	66C
Adj PT	Taylor, Sue	D	12A
Adj	Varvel, Vince	B	70
Adj PT	Weber, Mary	M	63A
Adj PT	Wheeler, Ben A.	M	47,62D

MO1950 Webster University
Department of Music
470 E Lockwood
Saint Louis, MO 63119
(314) 968-7032   Fax: (314) 963-6048
www.webster.edu/music
E-mail: jeffreycarter67@webster.edu

4 Year Institution, Graduate School
Member of NASM

Master of Arts in Music, Master of Music in Composition, Master of Music in Performance, Master of Music in Church Music, Master of Music in Music Education, Master of Music in Jazz Studies, Master of Music in Orchestral Performance

Chair: Jeffrey Richard Carter, 80A
Assistant Chair & Dir., Graduate Studies: Glen Bauer, 80C,80H

Adj	Akin, Willie	B	29
Adj	Ayllon, Robert	M	12A
Assoc Prof	Bauer, Glen	D	13,12,12A
Adj	Black, David	M	29,70
Prof Emerita	Bowers, Kathryn Smith	D	11
Adj	Braig, Christopher	B	47
Adj	Branum, Justin	M	62A
Adj	Bridges, Duane	M	43
Adj	Bryant, Ron		66C
Adj	Byrne, Tom	M	29,70
Assoc Prof	Carter, Jeffrey Richard	D	60A,36,61,13A
Adj	Cereghino, Rosemarie		61
Assoc Prof	Chamberlin, Robert	M	13,10F,10,45

Asst Prof	Colletti, Carla	D	13
Assoc Prof	Davis, Paul G.	D	60B,37,38,32E
Assoc Prof	DeMarinis, Paul	B	64E,53,29
Adj	Dunlap, Phillip	M	35,66A
Adj	Eastman, Patricia	M	13A,13B,13C,66A
Adj	Elstner, Erin	M	65,50
Adj	Garcia, Tim	M	13G
Adj	Garesche, Jeanine	M	64C
Prof	Gaspar, Carole	M	12A,61
Adj	Gianino, Kevin	B	65
Adj	Harris, Erik	M	62D
Asst Prof	Hart, Martha J.	M	61
Adj	Hartenberger, Aurelia	D	32B,32C,32G,32H
Adj	Hungerford, Jay	M	62D,29
Adj	Kaminsky, Joseph	M	62A
Adj	Karpowicz, Mike	M	29,41
Adj	Kasica, Paula	M	64
Adj	Keller, Merry	M	31A,32D,13
Adj	Koesterer, Karl	M	66A
Adj	Kulosa, Kenneth	M	62C
Adj	Lackschewitz, Anna	M	62B
Prof Emeritus	Larson, Allen C.	D	13,60,12A,38
Adj	Lennon, Debby	M	36,61,29,47
Adj	Martin, James	D	11,37,47,63D
Adj	Martin, Susan Ryan	M	66A
Adj	Mayo, Nancy		66C
Adj	McClellan, John	M	42,70
Adj	McDaniel, Jane	B	66A
Adj	Minear, Carolyn	D	32
Adj	Montgomery, Alice	M	61
Adj	Nalesnik, David A.	M	13B,13C
Adj	Naylor, Earl	M	13C
Adj	Nehre, Heather	M	12A
Adj	Nelson, Alice	M	39
Adj	Neske, Joe	B	13D,13E
Adj	Nordhorn, Johanna	M	61
Adj	Pace, Matthew	D	10,13
Adj	Parkin, Vera L.	M	66A,66C
Adj	Partridge, William	M	66G
Adj	Patterson, Heather	M	61
Asst Prof	Patterson, Trent A.	D	60A,61,32,36,39
Adj	Pavelka, Dee	M	61
Assoc Prof	Portnoy, Kim	M	10F,10,29
Adj	Price, Ruth	D	66A
Adj	Richardson, Neal	M	11,13C
Adj	Ring, Eric	D	64D,48,13C
Adj	Rolf, Alison	M	62A
Assoc Prof	Schene, Daniel	M	66A,42
Prof	Schenkel, Steve	D	12A,31,45,29,35
Adj	Schlamb, Peter	M	47
Adj	Schmidt, Carol	M	66A,29
Adj	Sims, Gary	M	61
Adj	Smith, Victoria	M	61
Prof Emeritus	Stallings, Kendall	D	13,10
Adj	Taylor, Amanda	M	61
Adj	Taylor, Sue	M	62E
Adj	Thayer, Marc	M	35A
Adj	Thierbach, Sue Ellen	D	62A
Adj	Thomas, John	M	13B,13C,63B
Adj	Thorn, Becky	M	11
Adj	Trinkle, Karen M.	M	12,15,12A
Adj	True, Carolbeth	B	66A,29
Adj	Vince, Donna	M	66A,66B
Adj	Von Hombracht, Willem		29,62D
Adj	Waggoner, Robert	M	32E
Adj	Wheeler, Ben	M	47
Adj	Woelbling-Paul, Cathleen	M	64B

MO2000 William Jewell College

Department of Music
500 College Hill
Liberty, MO 64068-1896
(816) 781-7700 x 5204   Fax: (816) 415-5097
www.jewell.edu
E-mail: colemani@william.jewell.edu

4 Year Institution
Member of NASM

Chair & Dir., Institute/Festival.Workshops: Ian D. Coleman, 80A,80F
Dir., Preparatory Division: Nicole Murray, 80E

Inst PT	Albright, James	B	62D
Prof	Brandolino, Tony	D	62A,38,42
Inst PT	Brown, Elaine K.	M	41,64A
Inst PT	Bryan, Stephanie	B	63C,63D
Inst PT	Carter, Jay	M	55,61
Inst PT	Carter, Monty	M	62B,42
Inst PT	Cohick, Mark	B	64E,64D,64B
Prof	Coleman, Ian D.	D	13,10,34
Inst PT	Cunningham, Randall	D	64C
Inst PT	De Marchi, Ray	M	65
Emeritus	Epley, Arnold	D	60A,32C,36,61,40
Inst PT	Grimm, James	M	70,35A
Inst PT	Haney, Kristee		61

Inst PT	Johnson, Tracey	M	66A,66D,13C
Emerita	Ma, Shuhui Nettie	D	62E
Asst Prof	Maglione, Anthony	D	36,32D,60
Inst PT	Myers, Allen	D	35A,66A,29
Prof	Permenter, Calvin	D	66A,66B,66C
Inst PT	Peters, Shelley	M	63B
Inst PT	Posey, Ann	M	66A,66H
Inst PT	Ray-Carter, Trilla	B	51,62C,42
Emeritus	Riddle, Donald	M	34,35C
Assoc Prof	Rigler, Ann Marie	D	66A,66G,31A,12A,12C
Inst PT	Risser, Martha	M	32B
Asst Prof	Schaefer, Phillip	M	37,47,49,63A
Inst PT	Tannehill, Sarah	M	61
Inst PT	White, Christie		44
Prof	Witzke, Ron	D	39,61

MO2050 William Woods University

Division of Visual, Perf. & Com. Art
One University Ave
Fulton, MO 65251-1098
(573) 592-4367   Fax: (573) 592-1623
www.williamwoods.edu
E-mail: pclervi@williamwoods.edu

4 Year Institution

Chair: Paul Clervi, 80A

Asst Prof	Potter, Joe	M	66A,66G,35H,54,35E
Inst	Railton, Marlene	M	36,61
Inst	Talbert, Rebecca	M	61,66A,13,12A,11

MS0050 Alcorn State University

Department of Fine Arts
1000 ASU Dr # 29
Alcorn State, MS 39096-9400
(601) 877-6261   Fax: (601) 877-6262
www.alcorn.edu/finearts/
E-mail: lkonecky@alcorn.edu

4 Year Institution, Historically Black College
Member of NASM

Chair: Larry Konecky, 80A

Inst	Gordon, Tony A.	M	66A,66D,66B,66C,11
Inst	Griffin, Samuel S.	M	60,37,63D
Asst Prof	Johnson, Byron	D	13A,13B,13C,61,39
Prof	Konecky, Larry	D	13,62,70,34
Prof	Lee, Donzell	D	12A,32,66A
Prof	Miller, David	D	13,47,46,29
Asst Prof	Murray, Renardo	D	37,32,63,13A
Inst	Schaffer, Donna	M	36,61,60A
Asst Prof	Wesley, Charles E.	M	36,61,12A,11

MS0100 Belhaven University

Department of Music
1500 Peachtree St
Jackson, MS 39202-1789
(601) 974-6471   Fax: (601) 974-6499
www.belhaven.edu
E-mail: ssachs@belhaven.edu

4 Year Institution
Member of NASM

Chair & Dir., Artist Series: Stephen W. Sachs, 80A,80F

PT	Bateman, Nancy	M	62C
PT	Bonds, Dennis	M	70,47
PT	Brown, Richard	M	62D,70
PT	Cheesman, Sybil	M	64A
PT	Cranford, Dennis	D	13C
PT	Davis, Lisa	M	63B
PT	Davis, Mark	M	63D
PT	Durham, Carol	M	66G
PT	Everitt, Gena	M	61
PT	Geihsler, Rebecca	D	61,12A,14C
Assoc Prof	Girtmon, Paxton	D	37,47,64E,10F,60
PT	Graves, Kenneth	M	64C
Asst Prof	Hong, Sylvia	M	66A,66D
PT	Houghton, Amy	M	70,42
PT	Hrivnak, Christine	M	61
PT	Mangrum, Amanda	M	62E
PT	Mapes, Randy	M	64B,64D

PT	Rockwell, Owen	M	65,50
PT	Sachs, Carolyn Reed	M	66B
Prof	Sachs, Stephen W.	D	66A,66C,38
Assoc Prof	Sauerwein, Andrew Mark	D	13,10,29B,43,64B
Prof	Shelt, Christopher A.	D	60A,36,31A,61,40
PT	Sprow, Margaret	M	31A
PT	Turner, Lloyd	M	63A
Asst Prof	Xie, Song	M	62A,62B,51,42

MS0150 Blue Mountain College

Department of Music
201 W Main
PO Box 160
Blue Mountain, MS 38610
(662) 685-4771 x 163   Fax: (662) 685-4776
www.bmc.edu
E-mail: jkantack@bmc.edu

4 Year Private Institution

Chair: James Andre, 80A
Music Contact: Jerri Lamar Kantack, 80A

Asst Prof	Kantack, Jerri Lamar	D	60,36,61,12A,32
Asst Prof	Wimberly, Larry	D	11,13A,31A,34E,46

MS0200 Copiah-Lincoln Comm College

Department of Music
PO Box 649
Wesson, MS 39191-0649
(601) 643-8431   Fax: (601) 643-8212
www.colin.edu/
E-mail: Brad.Johnson@colin.edu

2 Year Institution

Chair, Fine Arts: Brad Johnson, 80A

Inst	Furlow, Shaw	M	13,11,10,37,47
Inst	Harris, B. Joan	M	11,12A,66
Inst	Johnson, Brad	M	60,11,36,44,61
Adj	Klasinc-Loncar, Natasa	M	70
Inst	Riley, Denise	M	13,36,61
PT	Russell, Steve	M	66C
PT	Stewart, Stanley W.	M	11,37,47,49,48
Adj	Warren, Chris	M	65,50

MS0250 Delta State University

Department of Music
DSU Box 3256
1003 W Sunflower Rd
Cleveland, MS 38733
(662) 846-4615   Fax: (662) 846-4605
www.deltastate.edu
E-mail: phankins@deltastate.edu

4 Year Institution
Member of NASM

Interim Chair: Charles Mark Butler, 80A
Interim Dean, Arts and Sciences: Paul Hankins, 80A

Inst	Armstrong, Joshua	M	65,50,37,41
Prof	Buchanan, Mary Lenn	D	39,61
Prof	Butler, Charles Mark	D	63B,32B,13E,13B,66G
Asst Prof	Collins, Shelley	D	11,64A,12A,48
Inst	Cummins, Nicholaus B.	M	36,60A,32D,40
Prof	Fosheim, Karen	D	66A,13B,50,20A,10F
Prof	Hankins, Paul	D	63A,41,47,32E
Asst Prof	Herron, Teri A.	D	61,11
Asst Prof	Mark, Douglas L.	D	49,63C,63D,41
Inst	Moore, Joe D.	M	37,32E,60B
Asst Prof	Payton, Chad	D	11,13C,61
Asst Prof	Pimentel, Bret R.	D	64,29,64B,11,64C
Asst Prof	Shimizu, Kumiko	D	66C,66A
Assoc Prof	Shin, Jung-Won	D	66A,66D,66B,66C,13B

MS0300 Hinds Community College

Department of Music
PO Box 1100
Raymond, MS 39154-1100
(601) 857-3271   Fax: (601) 857-3458
www.hindscc.edu/Departments/music/default.aspx
E-mail: bsrhines@hindscc.edu

2 Year Institution

Chair: Robert Cheesman, 80A

	Ballard, Alice	M	66A,66G,66D,11
PT	Berthold, Sherwood	M	65
	Cheesman, Robert	M	63,46,34
	Crosby, Tracy	M	63C,11,13
	Davis, Clarissa	D	11,61
	Fletcher, Terry W.	M	36,61,12A
	Ingwerson, John	D	70,11
	Joseph, Jane	M	11,66A
	Manchester, John	D	13,34,11
	Mapes, Randy K.	M	64,37
	Sprayberry, Shane	M	37,11

MS0320 Itawamba Community College

Department of Music
602 W Hill St
Fulton, MS 38843-1099
(662) 862-8303   Fax: (662) 862-8036
www.iccms.edu
E-mail: rcpatrick@iccms.edu

2 Year Institution

Dir, Institute/Festival/Workshop: David East, 80F

Inst	Cass, Patrick	D	13,11,47,64,70
	Cogdell, Jerry	M	13,11,50,63,54
Inst PT	Cogdell, Robyn	B	36,54
Inst	Davis, Karen	M	11,36
Inst	East, David	M	37,47,48,63C
Inst	Myers, Jeff	M	11,66,13
Inst PT	Steele, Cathy	B	52

S0350 Jackson State University

Department of Music
PO Box 17055
Jackson, MS 39217
(601) 968-2141   Fax: (601) 968-2568
www.jsums.edu
E-mail: anissa.r.hampton@jsums.edu

4 Year Institution, Graduate School, Historically Black College
Member of NASM

Master of Music Education

Interim Chair: Darcie Bishop, 80A
Dir., Graduate Studies: Johnny Anthony, 80C

Assoc Prof	Anthony, Johnny	D	32C,37,49,63
Assoc Prof	Bishop, Darcie	D	11,41,49,63A
Assoc Prof	Blaine, Robert	D	11,38,32E,63C,60B
Vstng Prof	Brooks-Smith, Emma	D	32A,32B,32C,32G
Inst	Castilla, Willenham	M	36,31,32D,61
Asst Prof	Galbreath, Loretta J.	M	36,40,47,61
Inst	Hollinger, Lowell	M	11,13A,32C,48,64E
Vstng Asst Prof	Jordan, Rachel	M	62A,11,13A,13B,42
Asst Prof	Laubengayer, Karen	D	66A,66B,66C,66D
Adj Inst	Lewis, Andrew J.	M	66A,66C
Inst	Lewis-Hale, Phyllis	M	61,39,32D
Inst	Mitchell, Adrian	M	11,63A,37,32C,49
Asst Prof	Murray, Renardo	M	37,11,32C,49,63D
Inst	Rockwell, Owen P.	M	11,32C,37,65A,65B
Asst Prof	Taylor, Dowell	M	11,13C,34
Prof	Thomas, Russell	PhD	47,64E,29,13
Assoc Prof	Ware, David N.	D	63A,34C,47,11,13B
Asst Prof	Zackery, Harlan H.	M	11,66A,66B,66C,66D

MS0360 Jones County Junior College
Department of Music
900 S Court St
Ellisville, MS 39437-3901
(601) 477-4094   Fax: (601) 477-4202
www.jcjc.edu
E-mail: susan.smith@jcjc.edu

2 Year Institution, Junior College

Chair: Susan A. Smith, 80A

Inst	Barr, Sammy	M	37,65
Inst	Boyd, Michael	D	70,62D,41,10,11
Inst	Brown, Jeff	M	37,65,50,46
Inst	Guiles, Kay	M	11,66A,66D,66G
Inst	Johnson, Nikki	M	11,61,54,36
Inst	Johnson, Victoria	D	11,66A,66D
Inst	Newell, Meri	M	11,32,64,37,48
Inst	Nichols, Clinton	D	61
Inst	Pickering, Matthew	M	63,37,11,49,60B
Inst	Richards, Patrick	M	41,49
Inst	Sanchez, Theresa	D	11,66
Inst	Smith, Susan A.	D	61,40,13,36,13B
Inst	Taylor, Mark A.	D	36

MS0370 Meridian Community College
Department of Music
910 Highway 19 N
Meridian, MS 39307-5801
(601) 483-8241   Fax: (601) 482-3936
www.mcc.cc.ms.us
E-mail: tbrand@meridiancc.edu

2 Year Institution

Chair, Fine Arts: Todd Brand, 80A
Chair, Music: Carey Smith, 80A

Inst	Brantley, Mitch	M	11,41,70
Inst	Hurst, Twyla	M	13A,36,61,66D
Inst	Miles, Tammy	M	13,66A,66C,36
Inst	Smith, Carey	M	63,64,65,11,13

MS0385 Millsaps College
Department of Performing Arts
1701 N State St
Jackson, MS 39210
(601) 974-1422   Fax: (601) 974-1393
www.millsaps.edu
E-mail: smithel@millsaps.edu

4 Year Institution

Acting Chair: Elise Smith, 80A
Dir., Artist Series: Lynn Raley, 80F

Assoc Prof	Coker, Cheryl W.	D	15,61
Prof	Coker, Timothy C.	D	13,60,32,36,66A
Inst PT	Durham, Carol	M	66G
Asst Prof	Heard, Rachel P.	D	66
Inst PT	Martin, James	M	61
Inst PT	Moritsugu, Jim	M	64C
Assoc Prof	Raley, Lynn	D	66A,12A,29
Inst PT	Sudderth, Janette	M	66A,62C
Inst PT	Szlubowska, Danuta	M	66A
Inst PT	Turner, James	M	70
Inst PT	Wenberg, Jon	M	64D
Inst PT	Xie, Song	M	62A,62B

MS0400 Mississippi College
Department of Music
Box 4021
Clinton, MS 39058
(601) 925-3440   Fax: (601) 925-3945
www.mc.edu
E-mail: meaders@mc.edu

4 Year Institution, Graduate School
Member of NASM

Master of Music in Performance, Master of Music in Conducting, Master of Music in Music Education, Master of Music in Music Theory-Composition, Master of Music in Vocal Pedagogy

Chair: James M. Meaders, 80A

Inst	Adams, Nell	D	61,12A
PT	Berthold, Sherwood	M	65A,65B
PT	Cheeseman, Sybil	M	64A
Asst Prof	Dacus, Edward	D	12A,61
PT	Dacus, Viola	D	61
PT	Durham, Carol S.	M	66G,66A,66C,66H,12A
Asst Prof	Knupp, Robert	D	66G,13I,13B,66A
PT	Linehan, Wayne	M	63A
Asst Prof	Meaders, James M.	D	60A,36,61
Assoc Prof	Oswalt, Lewis	D	12A,13,31A
PT	Randman, Bennett	M	62C
Asst Prof	Rice, Dana R.	D	61,39
PT	Rice, Patton	M	61
Prof	Sclater, James	D	13E,10F,10,13C
PT	Song, Xie	M	62A,62B
Inst	Sparkman, Carol Joy	M	66C,66D,36,66A
PT	Taylor, Janet	M	13B,13C,66A
PT	Taylor, Ralph	D	66A
PT	Tucker, Craig	M	63C
Asst Prof	Walston, Patricia	M	11,66A,66B
PT	Wicker, Charles	M	46
Assoc Prof	Williams, Bonnie Blu	D	11,32
Asst Prof	Willoughby, Angela	D	12A,66A,66B
Asst Prof	Young, Craig S.	D	60B,37,63,64

MS0420 Mississippi Gulf Coast College
Department of Music
PO Box 548
Perkinston, MS 39573
(601)928-6211   Fax: (601)928-6386
www.mgccc.edu
E-mail: stacy.fore@mgccc.edu

2 Year Institution

Dean, Fine Arts: Kathryn Lewis, 80A

FT	Allen, David	B	37,63A,65
FT	Braun, Kathleen	M	52
FT	Burnside, Joanna	D	13,12A,66
PT	Cook, Gary	M	63
FT	Dueitt, David P.	M	37,48,64,65
PT	Hardin, Jane L.	M	61
PT	Klasinc, Natasa	M	70
FT	Myrick, Kenny	M	44,64
FT	Smith, Marilyn	B	36,32A,32B
FT	Taylor, Clifton	M	13,47,49,63C,37

MS0500 Mississippi State University
Department of Music
PO Box 9734
Mississippi State, MS 39762-9734
(662) 325-3070   Fax: (662) 325-0250
www.MsState.edu
E-mail: mbrown@CollEd.MsState.Edu

4 Year Institution
Member of NASM

Head: Michael R. Brown, 80A
Assistant Head: Lana Kay Johns, 80H

Asst Prof	Aarhus, Craig	D	37,60
Asst Prof	Baker, Jason	M	65
Prof	Brown, Michael R.	D	11
Prof	Damm, Robert J.	D	32
Prof	Edwards-Henry, Jacqueline	D	13,66A,66B,66C
Inst	Falcone, Sheri A.	M	64
Assoc Prof	Human, Richard	D	63C,11
Prof	Johns, Lana Kay	D	13A,11,64A
Asst Prof	Kirkland, Anthony B.	D	63A,42,49,67E,11
Inst	Lance, Elva Kaye	M	37,46
Inst	Murphy, Karen Lee	D	66B,66C
Asst Prof	Packwood, Gary D.	D	36
Assoc Prof	Pattila, Michael	D	11
Asst Prof	Ross, Ryan M.	PhD	12
Assoc Prof	Sebba, Rosangela Yazbec	D	66A
Asst Prof	Sobaskie, James William	D	13,13E,10F,13I,12
Assoc Prof	Taylor, Clifton	D	60,37,47
Asst Prof	Warfield, Tara	D	61,39
Lect	Webb, Adam	D	61,39

MS0550 Mississippi University for Women
Department of Music & Theatre
1100 College St W-1030
Columbus, MS 39701
(662) 329-7341   Fax: (662) 241-7815
www.muw.edu/music
E-mail: jvmortyakova@as.muw.edu

4 Year Institution
Member of NASM

Chair: Julia V. Mortyakova, 80A

Assoc Prof	Allen, James O.	M	11,12A,16,66A,66C
Vstng Inst	Browning, Doug	DMA	32,40,42,47,60
Vstng Asst Prof	Dunn, Cherry W.	DMA	61,39,15
Prof	Montalto, Richard Michael	DMA	13,12A,35,10,13F
Asst Prof	Mortyakova, Julia V.	D	66A,66D,66B,66C,12B
Asst Prof	Osburn, Carmen E.	M	33
Inst	Segrest, Linda H.	M	13A,13B,66A,66D,13C

MS0560 Mississippi Valley State Univ
Department of Fine Arts - Music
14000 Hwy 82 W #7255
Itta Bena, MS 38941-1400
(601) 254-3682   Fax: (601) 254-3485
www.mvsu.edu
E-mail: dhart@mvsu.edu

4 Year Institution, Historically Black College
Member of NASM

Acting Chair: Lawrence C. Horn, 80A

PT	Burkhead, Ricky	M	65A,65B,50,65
Prof	Goldman, Lawrence	D	66A,66D,66,11,66C
Assoc Prof	Horn, Lawrence C.	D	11,32A,48,64
Inst	Milton, Kenneth	M	11,47,49,63A,63B
Asst Prof	Moss, Orlando	M	13,60,36,61
Asst Prof	Schreiber, Paul	D	10,13,34,10B,10A
Asst Prof	Tramiel, Leonard	M	60,11,37,63C,63D

MS0570 Northeast Mississippi Comm Coll
Department of Music
101 Cummingham Blvd
Booneville, MS 38829
(662) 720-7320   Fax: (662) 728-1165
www.nemcc.edu
E-mail: rharris@nemcc.edu

2 Year Institution

Chair: Ray Harris, 80A
Dean & Dir., Artist/Performance Series: Larry J. Nabors, 80A,80F
Dir., Institute/Festival/Workshop: Angie D. Langley, 80F

Inst	Anderson, Kathy T.	M	36,40,61
Inst	Beghtol, Jason W.	M	37,13A,46,63,49
Inst	Dunn, Christopher	M	11,35,70
Inst	Forsythe, Jada P.	M	11,64C,64E,37,48
Inst	Harris, Ray	D	11,36,66,54
Adj	Hester, Charlotte	M	61
Inst	Mattox, Amanda M.	D	64,13,11
Inst	Mitchell, Bryan P.	M	11,37,46,65,50
Adj	Monroe, Martha Frances	M	11
Inst	Schager, Christopher J.	M	54
Inst	Stone, William S.	D	54

MS0575 Northwest Mississippi Comm College
Department of Music
4975 Highway 51 North
Senatobia, MS 38668
(662) 562-3334   Fax: (662) 560-1118
www.northwestms.edu
E-mail: ksipley@northwestms.edu

2 Year Institution

Director: Kenneth L. Sipley, 80A

Inst	Bishop, Saundra	D	13A,36,66A,66D,13B
	Mixon, John	M	37,11,63
	Sipley, Kenneth L.	D	11,12A,13A
	Ungurait, John B.	M	37,65,62D,46,50
	VanDyke, Susanne	M	36,61,13B,13C

MS0580 Pearl River Community College
Department of Fine Arts & Comm
101 Highway 11 N
Poplarville, MS 39470-2216
(601) 403-1180   Fax: (601) 403-1138
www.prcc.edu
E-mail: arawls@prcc.edu

2 Year Institution

Chair: J. Archie Rawls, 80A

	Bass, Michael	M	11,49,37,63
	Hill, Kyle W.	D	13B,11,37,50,65
	Hunt, Trevor	M	11,70,13C,13G
	Jones, Pamela	D	11,61,13C
	McKellip, Hope	M	11,66
	Rawls, J. Archie	M	13,11,64,46,48
	Tyson, LaDona	M	11,40,36,61

MS0600 Rust College
Department of Music
150 Rust Ave
Holly Springs, MS 38635
(662) 252-4661
www.rustcollege.edu
E-mail: syoliver@rustcollege.edu

4 Year Institution, Historically Black College

Music Contact: Norman Chapman, 80A
Chair, Humanities Division: Sylvester Oliver, 80A

Assoc Prof	Chapman, Norman	D	13A,13,12A,66A
Asst Prof	Jones, Zebedee	M	13A,32,36,66A
Assoc Prof	Oliver, Sylvester	D	12A,20G,37,46
	Weatherall, Maurice	M	64C,37

MS0650 Tougaloo College
Department of Music
500 W County Line Rd
Tougaloo, MS 39174
(601) 977-7758   Fax: (601) 977-7824
www.tougaloo.edu
E-mail: amontgomery@tougaloo.edu

4 Year Institution

Dean: Andrea Montgomery
Chair: Jessie Primer, III

Assoc Prof	Castilla, Kathy	M	11,36,61
Inst	Jenkins-Turner, Christy		
Asst Prof	Montgomery, Andrea	D	
Inst	Primer, Jessie		
Asst Prof	Walker, Gerald	D	

MS0700 Univ of Mississippi
Department of Music
164 Music Bldg
PO Box 1848
University, MS 38677-1848
(662) 915-7268   Fax: (662) 915-1230
www.olemiss.edu/depts/music/
E-mail: mugates@olemiss.edu

4 Year Institution, Graduate School
Member of NASM

Master of Music in Performance, Master of Music in Music Education, PhD in Music Education, Master of Music in Choral Conducting

Chair: Charles R. Gates, 80A
Dir., Graduate Studies: Alan L. Spurgeon, 80C
Assistant Chair: Julia Aubrey, 80H

Assoc Prof	Aubrey, Julia	M	39,61
Asst Prof	Aubrey, Robert	D	32B,11
Assoc Prof	Balach, Nancy Maria	M	61
Assoc Prof	Burkhead, Ricky	M	50,65
Inst PT	Carlisle, David	M	11
Asst Prof	Dale, Randall N.	M	37
Assoc Prof	DeJournett, William	D	37,12B,11
Assoc Prof	Dor, George	D	14,20
Asst Prof	Everett, Micah P.	D	63C,63D,13C,41,49
Inst PT	Falkner, Dianne	D	32B
Assoc Prof	Foulkes-Levy, Laurdella	D	13
Inst PT	Friedman, Stanley Arnold	D	10
Inst PT	Gaston, Susan Deaver	M	41,62C,62D
Prof	Gates, Charles R.	D	63A,11
Inst PT	Gilbert, Robert	M	63B
Assoc Prof	Hominick, Ian G.	D	66A,66D,41
Prof Emeritus	Irvin, Wade	D	64D,64E
Asst Prof	Johnston, Amanda J.	M	66C,61
Assoc Prof	Latartara, John	D	13,34
Inst PT	Miles, Charles F.	M	11
Asst Prof	Milton, Jos	D	61
Asst Prof	Paney, Andrew S.	D	32B,13A,66A,32A
Accompanist	Park, Adrienne	M	66C
Inst PT	Piecuch, Katherine H.	D	64B
Prof	Riggs, Robert D.	D	12A,12B,41,62A,62B
Assoc Prof	Robinson, Bradley C.	D	61
Inst PT	Robinson, Jennifer	M	61
Prof	Rodgers, Stacy D.	M	66A,66B,56C
Asst Prof	Rowlett, Michael T.	D	64C,11,41
Assoc Prof	Schuesselin, John C.	D	63A,49
Prof	Spurgeon, Alan L.	D	32
Assoc Prof	Spurgeon, Debra L.	D	32C,36
Prof	Steel, David	D	14,66H,55,66G
Prof	Trott, Donald L.	D	61
Prof Emeritus	Vernon, Ronald	D	38
Inst PT	Wang, Diane	M	64A,66D
Collaborative Pianist	Welch, Nancy	M	66C
Prof	Willson, David	M	37,60B
Assoc Prof	Worthy, Michael D.	D	32C,32E,32G,47

MS0750 Univ of Southern Mississippi, The
School of Music
118 College Dr #5081
Hattiesburg, MS 39406-0001
(601) 266-5543   Fax: (601) 266-6427
www.usm.edu/music
E-mail: michael.a.miles@usm.edu

4 Year Institution, Graduate School
Member of NASM

Master of Music in Performance, Master of Music in Conducting, Master of Music in History & Literature, Master of Music Education, PhD in Music Education, DMA in Composition, DMA in Conducting, DMA in Performance & Pedagogy, Master of Music in Piano Accompanying, Master of Music in Woodwind and Pedagogy, Master of Music in Music Theory & Composition

Director: Michael A. Miles, 80A
Coordinator, Undergraduate Studies: J. Taylor Hightower, 80B
Coordinator, Graduate Studies: Douglas Rust, 80C
Dir., Artist Series: Jay L. Dean, 80F
Dir., Artist Series: Gregory Fuller, 80F
Dir., Artist Series: Hsiaopei Lee, 80F
Dir., Artist Series: Alexander Russakovsky, 80F
Dir., Summer Programs: Catherine Rand, 80G
Dir., Summer Programs: John A. Wooton, 80G
Associate Director: Nicholas A. Ciraldo, 80H

Vstng Asst Prof	Alvarez, Euridice	ABD	64B
Assoc Prof	Beard, R. Daniel	D	13
Asst Prof	Bergman, Jason	D	63A
Assoc Prof	Brumbeloe, Joseph	D	13
Asst Prof	Ciraldo, Nicholas A.	DMA	70
Assoc Prof	Davis, Kimberley M.	D	61
Prof	Dean, Jay L.	D	60,38,39
Vstng Asst Prof	Elder, Ellen	D	66A,66C,66D
Assoc Prof	Flanery, John	D	36
Prof	Fuller, Gregory	D	60,36
Prof	Goertzen, Christopher	D	12
Prof	Gwozdz, Lawrence S.	D	64E
Prof	Hafer, Edward	D	12,12A
Assoc Prof	Hightower, J. Taylor	D	61
Asst Prof	Holden, Jonathan	D	64C,41
Collaborative Pianist	Kim, Joo-Hae	D	66C
Assoc Prof	Kyle, Maryann	D	61,39
Assoc Prof	Lee, Hsiaopei	D	62B,62A
Prof	Leventhal, Lois A.	D	66A,66C,66D
Asst Prof	Lucas, Heidi	D	63B
Assoc Prof	Machado, Marcos	D	62D
Asst Prof	McIlwain, William Benjamin	D	63C,49
Assoc Prof	Mezzadri, Danilo	D	64A,12E,48
Prof	Miles, Michael A.	D	38
Vstng Inst	Miles, Stacey	M	32B
Assoc Prof	Moak, Elizabeth W.	D	66A,66D,66C
Prof	Moser, Steven R.	D	60,32C
Assoc Prof	Panella, Lawrence	M	29,64E,47
Collaborative Pianist	Park, Eun-Hee	D	66C
Vstng Inst	Parker, Webster	D	32D
Assoc Prof	Perry, Richard H.	D	49,63D
Assoc Prof	Rand, Catherine	D	60,32C,37
Assoc Prof	Redfield, Stephen C.	D	62A,51
Assoc Prof	Russakovsky, Alexander	D	62C
Asst Prof	Rust, Douglas	D	13
Asst Prof	Schlegel, Amanda L.	D	32
Asst Prof	Schuman, Mohamad	D	37,32E
Prof	Smith, Larry Dearman	D	44,61
Inst	Standland, James	D	37,32E
Asst Prof	Waymire, Mark D.	D	32A,32B,32C
Assoc Prof	Woolly, Kimberly A.	D	64D,12A,41,48,72
Prof	Wooton, John A.	D	50,65
Staff	Young, Lonnie		66F,72
Prof Emeritus	Zaninelli, Luigi	M	10

MS0850 William Carey University
Winters School of Music
WCU Box 14
498 Tuscan Ave
Hattiesburg, MS 39401
(601) 318-6175   Fax: (601) 318-6176

www.wmcarey.edu/Academics/Music/196/WintersSchoolofMusic.shtm
E-mail: music@wmcarey.edu

4 Year Institution
Member of NASM

Master of Music in Music Education

Dean: Donald R. Odom, 80A
Dir., Preparatory Division: Ellen P. Elder, 80E

Inst	Beard, Christine	M	32H
Inst	Cameron, Wes		11,63,64,65,34
Prof	Cotten, Paul	D	33
	Elder, Ellen P.	D	66A,66B,66D,66C
Inst	Hunt, Justin Trevor	M	70
Prof	Keever, Howard	D	10A,10D,13A,13B,13D
Prof	Malone, Mark H.	D	32A,32B,32C,32D
Prof	Odom, Donald R.	D	36,13C,11,32D,60A
Inst	Pierce, James	M	33
Assoc Prof	Roberts, Connie	D	39,61
Assoc Prof	Vail, Kathy	M	66A,66G,69,44
Prof	Winters, Donald Eugene	D	61,31A,12A,60A

MT0075 Carroll College
Department of Fine & Perf Arts
1601 N Benton Ave
Helena, MT 59625
(406) 447-4807   Fax: (406) 447-5476
www.carroll.edu
E-mail: rpsurny@carroll.edu

Catholic Liberal Arts College

Music Contact: Robert D. Psurny, Jr., 80A

Inst Adj	Mattson-Hill, Jodi	M	32B
Assoc Prof	Petersen, Lynn	PhD	10A,11,13A,66A,47
Assoc Prof	Psurny, Robert D.	DMA	29A,36,40,54,61

MT0100 Dawson Community College
Department of Music
300 College Dr
Glendive, MT 59330-0421
(406) 377-3396   Fax: (406) 365-5928
www.dawson.cc.mt.us
E-mail: Lisa_S@dawson.edu

2 Year Institution

Chair, Humanities Division: Jim Schultz, 80A

FT	Shields, Lisa	M	13,36,37,64E

MT0175 Montana State University-Billings
Department of Music
1500 University Dr
Billings, MT 59101-0298
(406) 657-2350   Fax: (406) 657-2051
www.msubillings.edu/cas/music/
E-mail: berickson@msubillings.edu

4 Year Institution
Member of NASM

Chair: Dorothea Cromley, 80A
Dean: Tasneem Khaleel, 80A

PT	Adcock, Elizabeth	B	70
Asst Prof	Barfield, Susan	D	32A,32B,32C
Prof	Behm, Gary	D	37,64C,64E,64A
Prof	Cromley, Dorothea	M	12A,66A,66B
PT	Dalbey, Laura	B	62
PT	Devitt, Matthew	B	65
Asst Prof	Fenderson, Mark W.	D	11,37,63A,63B
PT	Gilstrap, Kenneth	B	35G
PT	Hansen, Kathleen	B	13,20
PT	Kestner, Luke	M	50,65
PT	Letson, Amy	B	62B
PT	Logan, Susan	B	64B
Assoc Prof	Nagel, Douglas	M	61,36,60A,13C
Prof	Robertson, James D.	D	13,60B,63C,63D,47
PT	Zuidema, Jeannie	M	13E,66D

MT0200 Montana State University-Bozeman
Department of Music
PO Box 173420
Bozeman, MT 59717-3420
(406) 994-3562   Fax: (406) 994-6656
www.montana.edu/music
E-mail: music@montana.edu

4 Year Institution
Member of NASM

Interim Director: Gregory D. Young, 80A

Assoc Prof	Aamot, Kirk C.	D	36,40,32D,60A
Adj Assoc Prof	Ahn, Angella	M	62A,62B
Adj Inst	Baker, Frederick	B	35G
Prof	Bartholomew, Douglas	D	13
Asst Prof	Biber, Sarah J.	M	13B,41,62C
Adj Inst	Charles, David	M	14,20,47
Prof	Croy, Elizabeth	M	61
Adj Inst	Espinosa, Angela G.	B	62E
Adj Inst	Ford, Jonathan	B	62D
Adj Asst Prof	Funk, Eric	M	10A,10F,60,29,13
Adj Asst Prof	Gosswiller, Julie	M	13C,66D,66A
Assoc Prof	Harney, Jon M.	D	36,39,40,61
Asst Prof	Harney, Kristin	M	32
Prof Emeritus	Hickman, Lowell	M	36,61,63A
Adj Asst Prof	Jacobson, Mary Ann	D	64C,14C,41
Prof Emeritus	Johnston, Glen	M	46,64C
Prof	Jonsson, Johan	M	62A,12A
Prof	Leech, Alan B.	M	64D,64E,20,64,42
Adj Prof	Leech, Karen	M	64A,42
Adj Inst	Linnerooth, Sherry	M	63B,41
Assoc Prof	Makeever, Gerald	M	13A,42,63A
Asst Prof	McGarity, Kristin A.	D	10B,34,64B
Asst Prof	Versaevel, Stephen	M	65,50,14C
Adj Asst Prof	Videon, Michael	M	70,41
Assoc Prof	Yost, Laurel	M	66A,66B,66C,12A
	Young, Gregory D.	D	13,64C

MT0300 Northern Montana College
Department of Music
PO Box 7751
Havre, MT 59501
(800) 662-6132   Fax: (406) 265-3777
www.msun.edu
E-mail: wiberg@msun.edu

2 and 4 Year Institution

Music Contact: Janice Wiberg, 80A

Prof	Wiberg, Janice	D	13,12A,32,36,66

MT0350 Rocky Mountain College
Department of Music
1511 Poly Dr
Billings, MT 59102-1739
(406) 657-1000   Fax: (406) 259-9751
www.rocky.edu
E-mail: harts@rocky.edu

4 Year Institution

Chair: Steven R. Hart, 80A

Prof Emeritus	Binckes, Fred B.	D	13,10,11,66G
Prof	Bratz, Jennifer	M	66
Adj	Coefield, Carolyn	M	61
Adj	Dutton, John		63B
Prof	Hamm, Samuel J.	D	12A,13,63D
Inst	Hammond, Tony	B	37,47,32
Assoc Prof	Hart, Steven R.	D	36,61,32D
Adj	Kestner, Luke		65
Adj	Linde, Laurel	M	64C
Adj	Logan, Susan	M	64B
Adj	Micheletti, Joan	M	32B
Adj	O'Toole, Elizabeth A.		64A
Adj	Tracy, Randy	M	62A
Adj	Troxel, Jeffrey C.		70

MT0370 Univ of Great Falls
Department of Music
1301 20th St S
Great Falls, MT 59405-4934
(406) 791-5377   Fax: (406) 791-5395
www.ugf.edu
E-mail: jcubbage@ugf.edu

4 Year Institution

Chair: John Cubbage, 80A

PT	Aikens, Bill	M	64B
PT	Bailey, Shad	D	32B
PT	Briant, Peter	B	66F
PT	Brown, Douglas	B	64D
Prof	Cubbage, John	D	13,12A,66A,10A
PT	Eyles, Amy	M	64A
PT	Gemberling, John	M	47,29,63
PT	Hancock, Cindy	M	66A,66G
PT	Johnson, Gordon	M	60
PT	Mathes, Adam	M	62B
PT	Muller, Irina	M	62A
PT	Murdick, Nick	M	63B
PT	Nicholls, Bud	B	37
PT	Nilson, Shawnda	M	64E
PT	Papoulis, Mary	D	62A
PT	Raines, Sarah	B	40,61
PT	Ritter, Paul	M	36
PT	Sontz, Allison	B	64C
PT	Suits, Sue	B	66A
PT	Suits, Thad	M	62C
PT	Varner, Ed	M	32B,37,65
PT	Wenger, Fred	B	63C
PT	Wenger, Laurie	B	65
PT	Young, Mike	M	70

MT0400 Univ of Montana
School of Music
32 Campus Dr
Missoula, MT 59812-7992
(406) 243-6880   Fax: (406) 243-2441
www.umt.edu/music
E-mail: griz.music@umontana.edu

4 Year Institution, Graduate School
Member of NASM

Master of Music in Performance, Master of Music in Music Education, Master of Music in Musical Theatre, Master of Music in Composition/Music Technology

Dean, College of Visual & Perf. Arts: Stephen Kalm, 80A
Director: Maxine Ramey, 80A

Prof	Baldridge, Margaret Nichols	D	62A,62B,51
Prof	Basinski, Anne	M	61,54,39
Prof	Boyd, Fern Glass	M	12A,51,62C,11

Prof	Boyd, Lance	M	47,63C,63D,53,29
Inst PT	Brandt, Jeffrey	M	14C
Assoc Prof	Cavanaugh, Jennifer Gookin	D	64B,64D,13
Assoc Prof	Cody, David	D	36,61,54,39,60A
Asst Prof PT	Cooper, Nancy Joyce	D	13,66G,66H,69
Asst Prof PT	Eriksson, Johan	M	64E,29
Asst Prof	Gray, Lori F.	M	32,12F
Asst Prof	Griggs, Kevin D.	D	37,60B,32E
Asst Prof	Hahn, Christopher	D	66A,66B,66C,66D
Prof	Hesla, Steven	M	66A,66B,66C,66D
Asst Prof PT	Heuermann, Beryl Lee	D	10A
Inst PT	James, Creighton	M	61
Assoc Prof	James, Kimberly Gratland	D	61,40,13
Prof	Kalm, Stephen	D	61
Asst Prof	Kirkpatrick, Christopher	D	64C,48
Prof	Ledbetter, Robert	D	37,50,65,20H,14C
Inst PT	Logan, Roger	B	63B
Inst PT	McNally, Patrick	D	62D
Assoc Prof	Millan, Luis	D	38,70,60B,13
Assoc Prof	Nichols, Charles Sabin	PhD	10A,10B,10,45,34
Asst Prof	Peterson, Dean	M	60A,32D,36,40
Prof	Ramey, Maxine	D	64C,48
Asst Prof	Randall, James	D	12,14,20,11
Prof	Schuberg, Margaret	M	13,48,64A
Asst Prof	Smart, James	D	37,63A,32E,60B
	Tapper, Robert	M	29,63C,46,47
Prof	Williams, Patrick C.	M	10A,13,13C,13D,10

MT0450 Univ of Montana-Western

Department of Music
710 Atlantic Ave
Dillon, MT 59725
(406) 683-7242   Fax: (406) 683-7493
www.umwestern.edu
E-mail: e_mastandrea@umwestern.edu

4 Year Institution

Chair: Eva Mastandrea, 80A

	Brewer, Bert R.	D	36,61
	Garard-Brewer, Gay	D	66A,32
	Hong, Martha	M	61,54
Asst Prof	McCabe, Brent Poe	D	37,11,32E,70

NC0050 Appalachian State University

Mariam C Hayes School of Music
Broyhill Music Center
Boone, NC 28608
(828) 262-3020   Fax: (828) 262-6446
www.music.appstate.edu
E-mail: peltowl@appstate.edu

4 Year Institution, Graduate School
Member of NASM

Master of Music in Performance, Master of Music in Music Education, Master of Music Therapy

Dean: William L. Pelto, 80A
Dir., Graduate Studies: Jennifer Sterling Snodgrass, 80C
Dir., Preparatory Division: Edward Allison, 80E
Associate Dean: Jay Craig Jackson, 80H

Adj Inst	Abrams, Ira	D	35,35A,35E
Adj Inst	Allison, Edward	M	11,32E
Prof	Amaya, Joseph	D	39,61
Assoc Prof	Au, Hiu-Wah	D	13
Prof	Bargerstock, Nancy E.	D	51,62A,42,62B
Adj Inst	Bartlett, Jacquelyn	B	62E
Prof	Beebe, Jon P.	D	13,48,64D,32E,42
Assoc Prof	Bell, Joby	D	66G,66H,36,31A
Adj Inst	Berry, Rodney	M	47,11
Asst Prof	Blaha, Christopher	D	63D
Prof	Boye, Gary	D	16
Adj Inst	Brendle, Ron	M	62D
Adj Inst	Cassini, Corinne	M	
Adj Inst	Chapman, Alicia	D	55C,64B,32E
Assoc Prof	Cheeseman, Andrea L.	D	64C,32E
Adj Inst	Dilling, Rick	B	65
Prof	Falvo, Robert J.	D	65,50
Assoc Prof	Fankhauser, Gabe	PhD	13
Adj Inst	Greene, Mary Gayle	M	61
Adj Inst	Griffin, Tammy	M	61
Prof	Harbinson, William G.	D	13,34
Adj Inst	Hayes, Christina	D	66A,66C,66D
Adj Inst	Hedgepeth, Byron	M	65,50
Prof	Hopkins, Stephen M.	D	36,60A,32D
Prof	Jackson, Jay Craig	D	60,32E
Prof	James, Douglas	D	70,51
Assoc Prof	Kallestad, Scott	D	32E,64E
Prof Emeritus	Kindt, Allen	D	66A,66B
Inst	Koontz, Eric E.	D	62B,62A,67A,42,51
Adj Inst	Larson, Linda L.	D	36
Lect	Leist, Christine	D	33
Adj Inst	Lesbines, Melissa	M	11,66A,66C
Asst Prof	Leslie, Drew	D	63C,49,42,41
Asst Prof	Licata, Thomas V.	D	13
Prof Emeritus	Logan, Joseph C.	D	12A,32,36,61
Prof	Lurie, Kenneth P.	D	13A,62C,42
Assoc Prof	Mansure, Victor N.	D	12
Inst	McCutchen, Keith	M	36
Prof	McKinney, Cathy	D	33
Prof	McKinney, Harold	D	63C,49
Prof	Meister, Scott R.	D	10,65,43,50
Prof	Miller, Douglas	D	64C
Assoc Prof	Mills, Susan W.	D	20,32B,32C,61,36
Prof Emeritus	Muegel, Glenn	D	13,41,62A,62B
Prof Emeritus	Newton, Jack	D	47,41,64C,72,35
Lect	Outland, Randall	M	61
Adj Inst	Page, Andy	M	29A,29B,70
Asst Prof	Park, Chung	D	38,62A,62B,51,60
Prof Emeritus	Parker, Clinton R.	D	11,61
Prof Emeritus	Paul, Philip	D	13,36,63B
Prof	Pedigo, Julia A.	D	61
Prof	Pelto, William L.	D	13
Prof	Phelps, Joe F.	M	63A
Assoc Prof	Porterfield, Priscilla J.	D	61,36
Inst Adj	Price, Hannah E.		13
Prof	Reynerson, Rodney T.	D	66A,66C,66D,11,41
Asst Prof	Richardson, Kevin	D	37,32E
Adj Inst	Rippy, Sylvia	M	32E,66D
Adj Inst	Roberts, Shawn M.	D	11,65
Prof	Robertson, Karen	D	49,63B,42,41
Prof	Rose, Sarah Elizabeth	D	32,33
Assoc Prof	Ross, John Stanley	D	37,32E
Assoc Prof	Runner, Lisa	D	32B
Assoc Prof	Schneeloch-Bingham, Nancy	D	64A,48,32E
Adj Inst	Schwantes, Melody	D	33,11
Adj Inst	Selle, William	B	38
Assoc Prof	Semmes, Laurie R.	D	14,20
Prof	Shagdaron, Bair	D	66A,66C,66D
Assoc Prof	Shulstad, Reeves	D	12,14,20
Accompanist	Slingland, Susan	D	66C
Assoc Prof	Snodgrass, Jennifer Sterling	PhD	13,13F,13C,13H,13G
Prof Emeritus	Spencer, William G.	D	60,32,64D,65
Adj Inst	Spuller, John	B	62D
Assoc Prof	Stokes, James M.	D	63A,49,41,42
Prof Emeritus	Unsworth, Arthur E.	D	20G,35
Assoc Prof	Wangler, Kim L.	M	35,64D,35A
Prof Emerita	White, Lynn	D	48,64,67
Adj Inst	Whitener, Edward	M	32E
Adj Inst	Witcher, William	M	32E
Prof	Wright, Todd T.	M	29,47
Assoc Prof	Wynne, Scott	M	35G,35D,35C,35

NC0100 Barton College

Department of Comm & Perf Arts
PO Box 5618
Wilson, NC 27893-7000
(919) 399-6492   Fax: (919) 399-6571
www.barton.edu
E-mail: pmcconnell@barton.edu

4 Year Institution

Chair: Patrick McConnell, 80A
Dir., Admissions: Amanda H. Metts, 80D

Assoc Prof	Bostick, D. Jane	M	66A,11
Staff	Peterson, Mark	M	36,38,66G,66A
Lect PT	Spell, Cindy	M	70
Asst Prof	Valera, Philip	M	34D,35G,35C,35D,13L
Lect Adj	Winstead, Elizabeth	M	61,11

NC0200 Bennett College

Department of Visual & Perf. Arts
900 E Washington St
Greensboro, NC 27401
(336) 273-4431   Fax: (336) 517-1500
www.bennett.edu
E-mail: slwhite@bennett.edu

4 Year Institution, Historically Black College

Chair: Stephanie Lawrence-White, 80A
Division Chair, Humanities: Steve Willis, 80A
Dir., Festival/Artist Series: Valerie Johnson, 80F

Adj Prof	Dunn, Kimberly	M	61
Inst	Johnson, Valerie	M	60,36,61
Inst	Joyner, Rochelle	M	11,66A,66D
Assoc Prof	Lawrence-White, Stephanie	PhD	12A,66A,12C,20F,66B
Assoc Prof	Parker, Linda	PhD	11,32,44,13,64

NC0220 Blue Ridge Community College
Department of Music
180 W Campus Dr
Flat Rock, NC 28731-4728
(828) 694-1860   Fax: (828) 694-1690
www.blueridge.edu
E-mail: kevina@blueridge.edu

2 Year Institution

Dir., Artist/Performance Series: Kevin Ayesh, 80F
Associate Dean: David Davis, 80H

Inst	Ayesh, Kevin	D	13,11,12A,66A,66D
Inst PT	Davis, Gladys	M	66D,61
Inst PT	Morgan, Christopher	B	70
Inst PT	Spence, Stephen	M	11

NC0250 Brevard College
Department of Music
1 Brevard College Dr
Brevard, NC 28712
(828) 884-8211   Fax: (828) 884-3790
www.brevard.edu
E-mail: franklll@brevard.edu

4 Year Institution
Member of NASM

Music Contact: Laura L. Franklin, 80A
Chair, Fine Arts: Michael Mihalyo, 80A

Inst	Asbill, M. Miller	D	37,32E
PT	Black, Larry	M	63A
PT	Caltvedt, Emily	B	64B
PT	Franklin, Kenneth	B	37
Assoc Prof	Franklin, Laura L.	D	50,65,20,32E
Asst Prof	Gresham, David Allen	D	61,11,34,13
Asst Prof	Gresham, Kathryn	D	61,39
PT	Huntley, Lawrence	M	32
Prof	McDowell, Laura	D	12C,12A,66D,67C
PT	Mowad, Lou	B	70,57
PT	Murray, Janice	M	66A,66C,66D,13
PT	Palmer, Katherine	M	66A
PT	Palmer, Robert	D	13A,13B,13C
Asst Prof	Porter, Michael	M	36,40,60,61,32D
PT	Posnock, Jason	M	62A,62B,32E
PT	Steele, Charlie W.	D	66G
Asst Prof	Wilson, Stephen K.	M	47,29,63

NC0300 Campbell University
Department of Music
PO Box 70
Buies Creek, NC 27506
(910) 893-1495   Fax: (910) 893-1515
www.campbell.edu
E-mail: whitley@mailcenter.campbell.edu

4 Year Institution

Chair: H. Moran Whitley, 80A
Dir., Artist/Performance Series: Barbara D. Hudson, 80F

Inst PT	Buckner, Janice	D	66A
Inst PT	Hester, Danny	D	66G
Inst	Hudson, Barbara D.	M	63C,63D
Inst PT	LeGrand, Catherine M.	M	64A
Inst PT	Martin, Don	M	64C,64E
Asst Prof	McKee, Richard	D	12A,66A
Asst Prof	Morrow, Phil J.	D	60,36,31A,61
Inst PT	Parashevov, Milen	D	70
Inst PT	Schaffer, Amanda	M	66A
Asst Prof	Thomas, Sally	D	61
Asst Prof	Whitley, H. Moran	D	32,31A,13
Assoc Prof	Wilson, Dwayne	D	48,60,65
Inst PT	Winter, Allen	M	63B
Inst PT	Wishart, Betty	M	66A

NC0350 Catawba College
Department of Music
2300 W Innes St
Salisbury, NC 28144
(704) 637-4345   Fax: (704) 637-4268
www.catawba.edu
E-mail: rpannell@catawba.edu

4 Year Institution

Chair: Renee McCachren, 80A
Dir., Community Music Program: Julie Rhyne Chamberlain, 80E

Adj	Bartz, Martha	B	61
Adj	Belflowers, Timothy	D	44
Asst Prof Emeritus	Carlton, Elizabeth	M	32,66A,66B,66D
Assoc Prof	Chamberlain, Julie Rhyne	D	66A,66B,66C,66D,11
Adj	Duckworth, James	M	70
Assoc Prof	Etters, Stephen C.	D	60,32,37,63D,13A
Assoc Prof	Fish, David Lee	D	35,14,34,20C,29
Staff	Harper, Erin Michelle	M	66A,66C,66D
Adj	Jewett, Dennis A.	M	61
Adj	MacLeod, Scott	M	61
Prof	McCachren, Renee	D	13,12A,66A,13E,13J
Adj	Meachum, Jay	M	63A
Adj	Mosher, Jimm		35D,35G,34D
Adj	Murray, Jack T.	M	64A,64C,64E
Vstng Artist	Naff, George	D	37
Assoc Prof	Oakley, Paul E.	M	36,40,61,11
Adj	Pier, Christina	M	61
Artist in Res	Reed, Dennis	B	43
Adj	Sang, Barry R.	D	63B
Adj	Schuttenberg, Emily Amanda	M	66A,66C,66D
Adj	Sellitti, Anne	M	62C,62D
Adj	Skidmore, Dan	M	62A,62B
Adj	Stein, Daniel C.	M	61
Adj	Stine, Maria W.	M	64B,64D
Adj	Zlotnick, Peter	M	50,65

NC0400 Chowan University
Department of Music
1 University Place
Murfreesboro, NC 27855
(252) 398-6201   Fax: (252) 398-6213
www.chowan.edu
E-mail: parkeg@chowan.edu

4 Year Institution

Chair: Gregory B. Parker, 80A

Assoc Prof	Butrico, Michael	M	32E,37,46,60B,63
Assoc Prof	Guthrie, James M.	D	13,10,34,66G,66H
Adj	Maddox, Shelley	M	61
Asst Prof	Moser, Bruce	D	12,66A,66B,13,66D
Adj	Nappi, Chris	B	65
Adj	Nesbit, James	B	64
Prof	Parker, Gregory B.	D	36,61,60A,40,32D
Adj	Porter, John	B	70
Other	Pressnell, Paula B.	B	66C,66A,66D

NC0450 Coastal Carolina Comm College
Department of Music
444 Western Blvd
Jacksonville, NC 28546-6816
(910) 455-1221 x 6227   Fax: (910) 455-7027
www.coastalcarolina.edu/
E-mail: nakamaeA@coastalcarolina.edu

2 Year Institution

Music Contact: Ayumi Nakamae, 80A

PT	Kuhn, Stephanie	M	64C,11
PT	Lopez, Michael	M	11,63C,63D
PT	Ludwig, Mary	M	11
PT	McLamb, Victoria	M	64A
PT	McWilliams, Bernard	D	62A,62B
Inst	Nakamae, Ayumi	D	61,36,40,67F
Inst	Perkins, Andrew	M	10A,13A,20G,46,11
Inst	Schmidt, James	D	66A,29A,66D,47,11
PT	Shaar, Erik	D	62C,62D
PT	Spell, Cindy	M	70,11
PT	Stubbs, Fletcher	M	64E
PT	Taliaferro-Jones, Gene	M	11,37
PT	Taylor, Earl	M	65A,65B

NC0500 College of the Albemarle

Department of Music
PO Box 2327
Elizabeth City, NC 27909
(252) 335-0821   Fax: (252) 335-2011
www.albemarle.edu
E-mail: steve_raisor@albemarle.edu

2 Year Institution

Chair, Fine Arts: Gale Flax, 80A
Music Contact, Dir., Summer Programs: Steve C. Raisor, 80G

PT	Middleton, R. Hugh	D	11,66A,66C
FT	Raisor, Steve C.	D	11,13,37,47,70

NC0550 Davidson College

Department of Music
Box 7131
Davidson, NC 28035-7131
(704) 894-2357   Fax: (704) 894-2593
www.davidson.edu
E-mail: jestasack@davidson.edu

4 Year Institution

Interim Chair: Mauro Botelho, 80A
Dir., Artist/Performance Series: Alan Black, 80F

Adj	Bartlett, John	M	63C
Art Assoc PT	Black, Alan	M	62C,42
Assoc Prof	Botelho, Mauro	D	13,11,20H
Adj	Bradford, Lovell	M	66A,47
Adj	Brown, Patrick	M	64E,47
Adj	Cice, Erica	B	64B
Art Assoc PT	Culpepper, Jacquelyn	M	39,61
Vstng Asst Prof	Fenimore, Ross	D	11,12,14C,14D
Adj	Ferdon, Jeff	B	62D
Art Assoc FT	Gilliam, Christopher	D	39,61
Adj	Hofsess, Dustin	B	70
Adj	Hood, Joshua	M	64D
Adj	Hunter, Mario	M	64C,41,42
Art Assoc PT	Lawing, Cynthia	M	66A,66D
Prof	Lawing, William D.	D	29A,47,63A,34D,49
Prof	Lerner, Neil	D	11,12,34H,66H
Art Assoc PT	Palmer, David	D	66A,66C
Adj	Portone, Frank	B	63B
Art Assoc PT	Rowland, Michael	M	66C,66G
Adj	Singleton, Jon		70
Adj	Snow, Adam	M	65
Prof	Stasack, Jennifer	D	10,20,31G
Adj	Teixeira, Robert	M	70
Art Assoc PT	Thornton, Diane B.	M	39,61
Adj	Vadlamani, Mallika	M	61
Adj	VanArsdale, Christine	B	62E
Assoc Prof	Villa, Tara Towson	D	11,38,60B
Art Assoc PT	Warren-Green, Rosemary		62A
Adj	Whitehead, Amy Orsinger	M	64A
Adj	Whitehead, Geoffrey	D	63D

NC0600 Duke University

Department of Music
105 Biddle Music Bldg
PO Box 90665
Durham, NC 27708-0665
(919) 660-3300   Fax: (919) 660-3301
www.music.duke.edu
E-mail: duke-music@duke.edu

4 Year Institution, Graduate School

Master of Arts in Composition, PhD in Composition, PhD in Musicology, Master of Arts in Performance Practice, Master of Arts in Musicology

Chair: Jane Hawkins Raimi, 80A
Dir., Undergraduate Studies: Susan Dunn, 80B
Dir., Graduate Studies: Philip Rupprecht, 80C

Prof/Prac	Bagg, Jonathan E.	M	62B,42
Prof	Berliner, Paul F.	D	20A,14A,14F,14B,31F
Post Doc Assoc	Bonus, Alexander	D	55,12
Prof	Brothers, Thomas	D	12A,12C,12E,29
Assoc Prof/Prac	Brown, John V.		62D,47,29A,29B,29C
Lect PT	Byrne, Laura S.	M	62E
Lect PT	Cotton, Sandra M.	D	61
Prof/Prac	Davidson, Harry L.		38,11
Post Doc Assoc	Davis, Daniel	D	10,14,15,20A
Lect PT	Duarte, Derison	M	66A,66B
Prof/Prac	Dunn, Susan		61,39
Lect PT	Eagle, Don J.		63A
Lect PT	Elliott, Rachael	M	64D
Lect PT	Fancher, Susan L.	D	64E
Lect PT	Finucane, David A.	B	53,64E
Prof	Gilliam, Bryan	D	11,12A,12B,12C,12D
Lect PT	Gilmore, Jimmy J.	M	64C
Lect PT	Greenberg, Susan R.	B	66A
Lect PT	Hanks, John B.	B	65
Prof/Prac	Hawkins Raimi, Jane	B	66A,42
Inst	Heid, David	M	66A,66C
Prof	Jaffe, Stephen	M	13,10F,10
Emeritus	Jeffrey, Paul H.	B	47,29
Assoc Prof/Prac PT	Jensen, Penelope C.	M	61
Assoc Prof/Prac	Kelley, Anthony M.	D	11,13,29,10A,10C
Lect PT	Kris, Michael A.		63C
Prof/Prac	Ku, Hsiao-Mei	M	62A
Lect PT	Lail, H. Wayne	B	61
Lect PT	Lile, Drew		70
Prof	Lindroth, Scott A.	D	13,34D,34H,10A,10B
Lect	Linnartz, Elizabeth Byrum	D	61
Lect PT	Liu, Pei-Fen	M	66A
Assoc Prof/Prac	Love, Randall M.	M	66A,66E,42
Assoc Prof	McCarthy, Kerry R.	D	12A,12C,31A,55
Assoc Prof	Meintjes, Louise	M	20A,14A,14C,14D,14F
Vstng Asst Prof/Prac	Mosenbichler-Bryant, Verena	D	37,11
Lect PT	Newsome, Bo N.	M	64B
Lect PT	Paolantonio, Edmund J.		66A
Prof/Prac	Parkins, Robert		66G,13A,13B,13C
Prof/Prac	Pritchard, Eric N.		62A,42
Prof/Prac	Raimi, Frederic B.	M	62C,42
Lect PT	Reed, Randy	M	70
Assoc Prof	Rupprecht, Philip	D	12A,12D,13E,13F
Prof Emeritus	Silbiger, Alexander	D	12A,12B,12C,13J
Lect PT	Simmons, Bradley E.		50
Asst Prof	Supko, John	D	10A,13B,13C,13D,10B
Prof	Todd, R. Larry	D	12A,13J,12C,13E,13I
Assoc Prof/Prac	Troxler, Rebecca	M	13A,64A,42,67D
Assoc Prof	Waeber, Jacqueline	D	11,12A,12B
Lect PT	Warburg, Claudia E.	M	62A
Librarian	Williams, Laura	M	16
Prof Emeritus	Williams, Peter F.	D	12A,12,14B
Prof/Prac	Wynkoop, Rodney A.	D	13,60,36
Inst PT	Zimmerman, Robert R.		10,13

NC0650 East Carolina University

School of Music
102 A.J. Fletcher Music Ctr
Greenville, NC 27858-4353
(252) 328-6851   Fax: (252) 328-6258
www.ecu.edu/music
E-mail: music@ecu.edu

4 Year Institution, Graduate School
Member of NASM

Master of Music in Composition, Master of Music in Music Theory, Master of Music in Performance, Master of Music in Church Music, Master of Music in Music Education, Master of Music in Piano Pedagogy, Master of Music in String Pedagogy, Master of Music in Jazz Studies, Master of Music in Accompanying, Master of Music in Composition/Music Technology

Interim Dean: J. Christopher Buddo, 80A
Associate Director: Robert Scott Carter, 80H
Associate Director: Christopher Ulffers, 80H

Assoc Prof	Bair, Jeffery J.	D	64E,42,29A
Prof	Bath, Joanne	M	62A,32A
Prof	Broussard, George L.	D	42,63C,29A
Prof	Buddo, J. Christopher	D	62D,38,39
Prof	Burroughs, Mary	D	42,63B,13C
Assoc Prof	Carlin, Kerry	D	66A,66B,66D
Assoc Prof	Carr-Richardson, Amy	D	13
Prof	Carter, Robert Scott	D	60B,37,41,32E
Tchg Inst PT	Clark, John Charles	M	61
Asst Prof	Copeland, Rachel		61
Assoc Prof	Crane, Andrew	D	60A,36
Assoc Prof	Dashiell, Carroll V.	M	47,62D,29
Tchg Asst Prof	Faris, Marc R.	D	13,10D,11
Tchg Inst PT	Finkelshteyn, Leonid	M	62D
Prof	Frank, Elliot		70,42
Tchg Inst PT	Garner, Catherine H.		66C
Tchg Inst PT	Gilliam, Alisa	M	66C
Assoc Prof	Gregorian, Ara		62A,62B,42
Assoc Prof	Gruber, Emanuel	M	62C,42
Tchg Inst	Guberman, Daniel	D	11,13
Prof	Gustafson, Christine		42,64A
Prof	Hairston, Michelle P.	D	33
Tchg Inst PT	Hanseler, Ryan	M	29,66A
Assoc Prof	High, Linda	D	32

Asst Prof	Hochman, Benjamin D.	M	66A
Assoc Prof	Huener, Thomas J.	D	13,63A,55B
Assoc Prof	Hurley, Gregory	D	32
Prof	Jacobs, Edward	DMA	10A,10B,13,43
Asst Prof	Juchniewicz, Jay	D	32E
Asst Prof	Kim, Hye-Jin	M	62A,62B,42
Assoc Prof	Kramar, John S.	M	61,54,39
Assoc Prof	McCaslin, Tom R.	M	63D,42
Assoc Prof	Memory, Barbara	D	33
Inst PT	Meyers, Carolyn	M	61
Assoc Prof	Moll, Kevin N.	D	12,55,67A,12A,12B
Asst Prof	Monroe, Douglas		64C,42
Inst PT	Myers, Carolyn	M	61
Inst PT	Nappi, Chris	M	65,50
Lect	Nelson, Jocelyn C.	D	70,12A,67H,11
Inst	Newsome, Bo	B	64B,13C
Prof	O'Brien, John B.	D	66A,66D,66H,55
Asst Prof	Reardon, Melissa	M	62B,42
Assoc Prof	Rey, Mario	D	14,13,20H
Asst Prof	Rhodes, Jami	D	61
Assoc Prof	Richardson, Mark Douglas		13,10A
Asst Prof	Richter, Jorge Luiz	D	60B,38,42,62A,62B
Tchg Inst PT	Sawyer, Scott	B	29,70
Tchg Inst PT	Scanlon, Andrew	M	66G,31
Asst Prof	Sekino, Keiko	D	66A,66C
Assoc Prof	Smith, Perry	D	61
Asst Prof	Solomon, Mimi	M	66A
Asst Prof	Staub, William D.	M	37,32E
Tchg Inst PT	Stellrecht, Eric	M	66A,66C,13C
Prof	Taggart, Mark Alan	D	13,10
Prof	Theurer, Britton	D	63A,42
Assoc Prof	Ulffers, Christopher	M	12A,64D,11
Prof	Wacker, Jonathan D.	D	50,65,29
Asst Prof	Wacker, Lori	D	13,11
Asst Prof	Wagoner, Cynthia L.	D	32E,32C
Assoc Prof	Ward, Jeffrey	D	32D,36

NC0700 Elizabeth City State University-UNC
Department of Music
1704 Weeksville Rd
Elizabeth City, NC 27909
(252) 335-3359   Fax: (252) 335-3779
www.ecsu.edu/academics/artshumanities/music/index.cfm
E-mail: rnewson@mail.ecsu.edu

4 Year Institution, Historically Black College

	Brock, Joplin		37
	Brock, Tomisha		37
Asst Prof	Campbell, Todd A.	M	35G,34D,35D,65,35C
	DuBeau, Pete	M	63D
Artist in Res	Forrester, Ellard		65,37
	Gonko, Daniel	M	35D,35G
Assoc Prof	Hellmann, Mary	D	66A,66D,12A
Asst Prof	Hines, Billy C.	M	13A,36,61
Asst Prof	Jackson, Douglas A.	M	63A,35
Prof	Knight, Gloria J.	D	32,36,61
Artist in Res	LeFlore, Maurice	M	64E,37
Prof	Palestrant, Christopher	D	13,10
Asst Prof	Parnell, Janine	D	62A,32
Asst Prof	Swan, Walter R.	D	61

NC0750 Elon University
Department of Music
2800 Campus Box
203 N Williamson Ave
Elon, NC 27244
(336) 278-5600   Fax: (336) 278-5609
www.elon.edu/music
E-mail: mbuckmaster@elon.edu

4 Year Institution

Chair: Matthew Buckmaster, 80A
Dean: Alison Morrison-Shetlar, 80A
Dir., Artist/Performance Series: Jeff Clark, 80F

	Beck, Lynn	M	13,63B
Inst PT	Bennett, Wayne	M	63A
Inst FT	Bowers, Michael	M	34,35
Inst PT	Brito, Ramon	M	66
Asst Prof	Buckmaster, Matthew	D	63D,29,63C,49,32
Inst PT	Carter, LisBeth	M	61,39
Inst PT	Celona-VanGorden, Julie	D	61
Asst Prof	Coleman, Todd	D	10,34,62D,35G,45
Lect	Cornelius, Polly Butler	D	61
Inst PT	Cykert, Linda	M	64A,41
Inst PT	DiCamillo, Matthew	M	61
Inst FT	Dollak, Haidee	B	66C
Inst PT	Dollar, Kevin	M	70

Prof	Erdmann, Thomas R.	D	11,38,13E,13F,63A
Prof	Fischer Faw, Victoria	D	12,66A,66B,41
Assoc Prof	Futrell, Stephen A.	D	36,32D,60,35C,40
Inst FT	Hankins, Tyson	M	66C
Inst PT	Harwood, Carey	D	70
Inst PT	Henderson, Pamela	M	61
Assoc Prof	Hogan, Hallie Coppedge	D	39,61
Asst Prof	Knight, Gerald R.	D	36,60,61,32
Inst	Larocco, Sharon Moss	M	66C,66D
Assoc Prof	Metzger, Jon	M	65,29,47,50,53
Inst PT	Newton, Joseph	D	70,53,29
Inst PT	Novine-Whitaker, Virginia	M	64E,41
Inst PT	Robert, James	M	65,11,50
Lect	Sawyer, Tony	M	37,65,34
Assoc Prof	Shimron, Omri D.	D	13,66A,66D
Inst PT	Skidmore, Dan	D	62A,51
Inst PT	Skogen, Meaghan	M	62C,13,41
Inst PT	Summers, Billy	D	66A,66C,66D,66G
Inst PT	Turanchik, Thomas	M	64B,64C,64D,48

NC0800 Fayetteville State University
Department of Perf & Fine Arts
1200 Murchison Rd
Fayetteville, NC 28301
(910) 672-1571   Fax: (910) 672-1572
www.uncfsu.edu
E-mail: elamb@uncfsu.edu

4 Year Institution, Historically Black College

Chair: Earnest Lamb, 80A
Coordinator, Artist Series: Don Parker, 80F

Artist in Res	Chambers, Timothy	M	37,48,64,60B
Asst Prof	Finn, Neal	D	10A,10F,29A,47,63C
Adj	Knibbs, Lester A.	D	11,66C
Assoc Prof	Lamb, Earnest	D	12A,32C,51,62
Assoc Prof	Linch-Parker, Sheryl	D	13A,32B,32C,49,63C
Assoc Prof Emeritus	Owens, Robert	D	11,66D,66G
Assoc Prof	Parker, Don	D	13,50,65,29
Inst	Payton, Denise	M	20A,36,39,60A,61
Assoc Prof	Williams, Robert	D	11,12A,36,61

NC0805 Fayetteville Tech Comm College
Department of Music
PO Box 35236
Fayetteville, NC 28303-0236
(910) 678-8295   Fax: (910) 678-8477
www.faytechcc.edu
E-mail: hoganl@faytechcc.edu

2 Year Institution

Chair, Humanities & Social Science: Larry Hogan, 80A

Inst	Black, Elizabeth P.	M	11,29A,20G

NC0850 Gardner Webb University
Department of Fine Arts
Box 7298
Boiling Springs, NC 28017
(704) 406-4448   Fax: (704) 406-3920
www.gardner-webb.edu
E-mail: psparti@gardner-webb.edu

4 Year Institution
Member of NASM

Chair: Patricia C. Sparti, 80A
Dir., Summer Programs: Roger G. Gaddis, 80G

Inst Adj	Bennett, Elizabeth S.	M	66A,66G
Prof	Billings, Carolyn A.	D	13,12,66A,66B
Inst Adj	Black, Alan R.	M	62C
Inst Adj	Boboc, Monica	M	
Inst Adj	Campbell, Bob	M	63B,49
Adj	Cice, Erica	B	64B
	Cole, Mark R.		32
Inst	Etter, Paul J.	M	60A,36,44,60,31A
Prof	Fern, Terry L.	D	11,39,61,54,69
Inst Adj	Gregg, Nan F.	B	11,61
Asst Prof	Harrelson, Patricia A.	M	61
Inst Adj	Hudson, Timothy	M	63A
Adj	Lupanu, Calin	M	62A,51
	Misenheimer, Aaron L.	M	32E,34,11,63,49

Adj	Moore, Norman	M	65A,65B
Inst Adj	Pease, Janey L.	M	66A,66G
Inst PT	Pickard, Jason A.	M	70
Assoc Prof	Sparti, Patricia C.	D	13,60,38,63D
Adj	Stowe, Samuel P.	M	11,48,64A
Prof	Summers, C. Oland	M	32,63C,64D,65,72
Inst Adj	Swic, Piotr T.	M	62A
Adj	Trexler, Henry	B	62D
Assoc Prof	Whitfield, James M. (Matt)	D	10A,13,37,10F,10

NC0860 Gaston College
Department of Music
201 Highway 321 S/Box 45
Dallas, NC 28034-1402
(704) 922-6346   Fax: (704) 922-6440
www.gaston.edu
E-mail: jones.marcene@gaston.edu

2 Year Institution

Chair: Gary Freeman, 80A

PT	Denson, Keith		11,29,12A
PT	Eagle, Keith		11
	Freeman, Gary	M	
PT	Hiscock, Fred		11,29
PT	Kirk, Elizabeth		11,20G
FT	Porter, Judith		11,20G

NC0900 Greensboro College
Department of Music
815 W Market St
Greensboro, NC 27401-1823
(919) 272-7102   Fax: (919) 271-6634
www.greensboro.edu
E-mail: brothertonj@greensboro.edu

4 Year Institution

Chair: Jane Grant McKinney, 80A
Associate Chair: Jonathan P. Brotherton, 80H

Prof	Brotherton, Jonathan P.	D	36,13C,32D
Inst PT	Campbell, Alicia M.	D	64A
Inst PT	Canter, Jacqueline S.	M	61
Assoc Prof	Clegg, Neill M.	M	10F,12A,64,53,29A
Inst PT	Crawford, Pete	B	32E,65
Inst PT	Fitzpatrick, Stuart L.	M	63B
Assoc Prof	Fox, David E.	D	66A,12A,66D,43,11
Inst PT	Gambetta, Charles L.	D	38,60B,13,62D
Inst PT	Hubbard, Eve P.	M	51,62A
Inst PT	Hyslop, Greg	B	70
Inst PT	Kassner, Karl J.	M	63A
Inst PT	Lane, Roger	D	32B,32F
Prof	McKinney, Jane Grant	D	32C,13B,32D,39
Inst PT	Mintz, Randy	B	63D
Inst PT	Murph, Charles	M	72
Inst PT	Sperry, Tara	M	61
Other	Springs, Benjy L.	B	37,47
Inst PT	Summers, Kim G.	M	65,50
Inst PT	Ware, Steve	B	63D
Inst PT	Wulfeck, David	M	63C

NC0910 Guilford College
Department of Music
5800 W Friendly Ave
Greensboro, NC 27410-4108
(336) 316-2430   Fax: (336) 316-2959
www.guilford.edu
E-mail: tlindeman@guilford.edu

4 Year Institution

Chair: Timothy H. Lindeman, 80A

Lect PT	Bass, Eddie	D	10
Lect PT	Bumgardner, James	M	61
	Carter, Brian	M	62C
Lect PT	Chamis, Michael	B	70
Lect PT	Fancher, Susan	D	64C
Lect PT	Gambetta, Charles		62D
Lect PT	Hayes, Andrew	D	29A,47
Lect PT	Hodges, Betsi	M	66A
Lect PT	Hyslop, Greg	B	70,29
Prof	Lindeman, Timothy H.	D	13,12A,66A,20
Asst Prof	Looker, Wendy	M	60,36,70,12A,13A
Lect PT	Parker, Michael	M	66A,66C
Lect PT	Puterbaugh, Parke	M	12E
Lect PT	Rorie, Alfonso	B	50
Lect FT	Rowan, Kami	M	70,11,51,12E
	Saake, Garrett		
Lect PT	Sykes, Jean	M	62A,62B
Lect PT	Sykes, Wiley	M	65

NC0915 Guilford Tech Community College
Department of Commun/Fine Arts
PO Box 309
Jamestown, NC 27282-0309
(910) 334-4822
www.gtcc.edu
E-mail: mrwheeler@gtcc.edu

2 Year Institution

Chair: Mark Wheeler, 80A

Inst PT	Cobb, James	D	11,36,66G
Inst PT	Fields, Tami	M	11,36
Inst PT	Mazzatenta, Mark	M	29A
Inst	Wheeler, Mark	D	11,12A,20G

NC0930 High Point University
Department of Music
833 Montlieu Avenue
High Point, NC 27262
(800) 345-6993
www.highpoint.edu
E-mail: mfoster@highpoint.edu

Chair: Marc A. Foster, 80A

Inst	Canter, Jacqueline		61
Inst	Copeland-Burns, Carla	M	64A
	Dills, Marcia	M	66
Prof	Foster, Marc A.	D	36
	Frye, Danny	M	65,50,37,65B,32C
Inst	Hall, Carolyn F.		
Inst	Hudson, Timothy		63,38
Inst	McHugh, Steve		65
	Schlimmer, Alexa Jackson	D	39,61
Inst	Stevens, Laura	M	64A
Inst	Thee, Lawrence	M	64B,64C,64D,64E

NC1000 Johnson C Smith University
Department of Music
100 Beatties Ford Rd
Charlotte, NC 28216-5302
(704) 378-1474   Fax: (704) 371-6752
www.jcsu.edu
E-mail: cweise@jcsu.edu

4 Year Institution, Historically Black College

Chair: Gregory T. Thompson, 80A

Inst	Thompson, Bruce A.	M	36,13,66A,61
Assoc Prof	Thompson, Gregory T.	D	66A,66C,12A,31A
Asst Prof	Weise, Christopher	D	13,10,34,35

NC1025 Laurel University
Music Program
1215 Eastchester Dr
High Point, NC 27265
(336) 887-3000   Fax: (336) 889-2261
www.laureluniversity.edu
E-mail: drenfroe@laureluniversity.edu

4 Year Institution

Chair: Dennis C. Renfroe, 80A

Prof	Renfroe, Dennis C.	D	11,12A,32,36,63

NC1050 Lees-McRae College
Department of Performing Arts
PO Box 128
Banner Elk, NC 28604
(828) 898-8721   Fax: (828) 898-8814
www.lmc.edu
E-mail: speerj@lmc.edu

4 Year Institution

Director: Janet Barton Speer, 80A

	Addamson, Paul		66A,66C,66D,13A,13
	Burgess, Stacey		52
	Crabtree, Kacy E.		52,35E
	Hannah, Mike		35H,66C
	Parrish, Steve		61,54
	Speer, Janet Barton		35H,54,35E
	Taylor, James		41,36,61,31A,11

NC1075 Lenoir Community College
Department of Arts & Sciences
PO Box 188
Kinston, NC 28502-0188
(252) 527-6223   Fax: (252) 233-6889
www.lenoircc.edu
E-mail: ccrossland@lenoircc.edu

2 Year Institution

Dean, Arts & Sciences: John Paul Black, 80A
Dir., Artist/Performance Series: Carolyn M. Crossland, 80F

Inst	Crossland, Carolyn M.	M	13A,11,32A,36,32B
Inst	Maddox, Timothy	M	11,13A,13B,13C,13D

NC1100 Lenoir-Rhyne University
Music Program
PO Box 7355
Hickory, NC 28603-7355
(828) 328-7147   Fax: (828) 328-7037
mus.lr.edu
E-mail: nigrellic@lr.edu

4 Year Institution

Chair: Jennifer Heller, 80A

Accompanist	Borman, Jeana	M	
Artist in Res	Burbank, Judith	D	61
Prof	Cheek, John	D	13,11,66A,20G
Inst PT	Cline, Rick	M	65,50
Inst	Hinson, Amalie	D	32D,32B
Assoc Prof	Jowers, Florence	M	36,44,66G
Prof	Kiser, Daniel W.	D	13A,10F,60B,37,63A
Inst PT	Merritt, Frank	M	63A,63B,32
Inst PT	Murray, Jack	M	64C,64E
Prof	Nigrelli, Christopher	D	12A,47,44,63C,63D
Inst PT	Ross, John G.	M	12,60
Inst PT	Ross, Sally	M	62C,62D
Inst PT	Rozukalns, Thelma	D	32D
Inst PT	Smith, Ada	M	32B
Inst PT	Smith, Robert	M	11,13,66G
Inst PT	Steadman, Robert	M	70
Inst PT	Thomason, Jo Carol	B	44
Prof	Weber, Paul	D	60,36
Inst PT	Wortmann, David	M	41

NC1150 Livingstone College
Department of Music
701 W Monroe St
Salisbury, NC 28144
(704) 216-6048   Fax: (704) 216-6143
www.livingstone.edu
E-mail: GCallahan@livingstone.edu

4 Year Institution, Historically Black College

Chair: Gary L. Callahan, 80A

Assoc Prof	Callahan, Gary L.	D	48,64,32,46
Inst	Dean, Curtis	M	35,54
Asst Prof	Harrison, Joanne K.	M	13,66G,31A,66A
Asst Prof	Miller, DaVaughn	M	36,13E,20B,60
Asst Prof	Moore-Mitchell, Teresa	M	61,11
Adj Prof	Palmer, David	M	63,47
Asst Prof	Sessoms, Sydney	M	13E,32E,37,60B,11

NC1200 Louisburg College
Division of Visual & Perf Arts
501 North Main St
Louisburg, NC 27549
(919)496-2521   Fax: (919)496-1788
www.louisburg.edu
E-mail: aadkins@louisburg.edu

2 Year Institution

Chair: Gayle Green, 80A

Inst	Adkins, Angela		36
Inst PT	Powell, Glendora		

NC1250 Mars Hill College
Department of Music
Box 6693
Mars Hill, NC 28754
(828) 689-1209   Fax: (828) 689-1211
www.mhc.edu/music
E-mail: jreed@mhc.edu

4 Year Institution
Member of NASM

Chair: Joel F. Reed, 80A,80F
Dir., Artist Series: Julie T. Fortney, 80F
Dir., Summer Programs: John A. Entzi, 80G
Dir., Summer Programs: Marie Nicholson, 80G
Dir., Summer Programs: Michael L. Robinson, 80G
Dir., Summer Programs: James Sparrow, 80G

Asst Prof	Adkins, Cathy L.	M	12A,66G
Inst Adj	Alford, Steve W.	M	64E,47,53
Inst	Ammons, Anthony	M	63B
Inst	Anderson, Jennifer J.	M	64D
Inst Adj	Aquilino, Dominic	M	61,54
Inst Adj	Babb, Tim	D	32A
Inst	Babelay, Paul	M	65
Inst Adj	Carpenter, Ron		63D
Inst Adj	Entzi, John A.	M	63A,49
Prof	Fortney, Julie T.	D	11,61,34C
Inst Adj	Jenkins, Cara M.	M	64B,48
Inst Adj	Lemmons, Frederick	M	64C,64E,48
Inst	Long, Rebecca	M	13A,13B,13C
Inst	Mullinix, Kelli	M	60A,36
Prof	Reed, Joel F.	D	20G,60A,36,61,31A
Inst	Robinson, Michael L.	B	32E,60B,37
Inst Adj	Roop, Cynthia M.	M	64A,32A,32E,13C,41
Inst Adj	Smathers, Robin H.	B	32B
Assoc Prof	Sparrow, James	DMA	63D,32E,41,63C,63
Adj	Spence, Gary	B	70,20G
Inst Adj	Starkey, David C.	M	61,39,54
Assoc Prof	Sumpter, Teresa L.	D	66A,66B,66D,66C
Assoc Prof	Theisen, Alan	PhD	13,10,34,35G,64E
Assoc Prof	Tinkel, Brian C.	D	65,50,42

NC1300 Meredith College
Department of Music
3800 Hillsborough St
Raleigh, NC 27607-5298
(919) 760-8536   Fax: (919) 760-2359
www.meredith.edu/music/
E-mail: pagef@meredith.edu

4 Year Institution
Member of NASM

Chair: Fran M. Page, 80A
Dir., Community Division: Tom L. Lohr, 80E

Inst Adj	Carter, Lisbeth	M	61
Inst Adj	Cherry, Janet	M	66G,66A
Inst Adj	Chung, Carol	M	62A
Inst Adj	Dunson, Judith	B	70
Asst Prof Adj	Evans, Margaret	D	66A

Inst Adj	Findlay-Partridge, Marta C.	M	62A
Inst Adj	Garriss, Margaret	M	62A
Asst Prof Emerita Adj	Garriss, Phyllis	M	41,62A
Adj Inst	Gilmore, Jimmy	M	37,64C
Inst Adj	Hudson, Virginia	M	62C
Inst Adj	Jolly, Donna	M	66A
Inst Adj	Jong, Pin Pin	M	66A
Inst Adj	Lohr, Tom L.	M	66A,10A
Assoc Prof	Lyman, Kent M.	D	66A,66B,12A
Prof	Lynch, W. David	D	66G
Inst Adj	MacDonald, Austin	M	63B
Inst Adj	Nelson, Pamela	M	64A,48
Prof	Page, Fran M.	D	36,32
Inst Adj	Perry, Robert	M	63,64
Inst Adj	Riva-Palacio, Nancy	M	66A
Inst Adj	Rupp, Emily	M	62D
Inst Adj	Stephenson, Angela	M	66A
Inst Adj	Stephenson, Edward	B	70
Prof	Vaglio, Anthony J.	D	13,10,32,34
Asst Prof	Waddelow, Jim M.	D	41,62,38,32E
Prof	Williams, Ellen	D	12A,39,61
Inst Adj	Wilsden, Melanie	M	64B

NC1350 Methodist University
Department of Music
5400 Ramsey St
Fayetteville, NC 28311-1420
(919) 630-7100   Fax: (919) 630-7513
www.methodist.edu
E-mail: kdippre@methodist.edu

4 Year Institution

Chair: Keith Dippre, 80A
Dean, Arts & Humanities: Emily Powers Wright, 80A

Inst PT	Bullock, Tunisia	M	64A
Assoc Prof	Dippre, Keith	D	13,11,10,47,34
Inst PT	Dumas, Charles	B	64C,64E
Inst PT	French, Shannon	M	61
Inst PT	Grigoryan, Gayane	M	62A
Inst PT	Hardee, Kelly Ann	M	63D
Inst PT	Hrivnak, Michael	M	63B
Inst PT	Jordan, Jason	M	65
Inst PT	Kenny, Megan	M	62A
Asst Prof	Marosek, Scott	D	12,66A,66B
Asst Prof	Martin, Michael D.	M	32,36
Inst PT	Pino, Brad	M	63D
Inst PT	Roehrich, Matthew	M	64E
Inst PT	Smith, William D.	M	70,11
Inst PT	Sparzak, Monica	D	66G
Inst PT	Stam, Martin	M	62D
Inst PT	Walker, Skip	M	65
Asst Prof	Wells, Larry	D	32,63A
Inst PT	Winstead, Elizabeth	M	61,12A

NC1400 Mitchell Community College
Department of Music
500 W Broad St
Statesville, NC 28677
(704) 978-5425   Fax: (704) 978-5408
www.mitchellcc.edu
E-mail: jpardue@mitchellcc.edu

2 Year Institution, Community College

Prof	Brown, Beverly	M	11,29A,47,37,64C
Adj	Cedeno, Eduardo	M	62A,13A
Adj	Pardue, Dan	M	36,61
Prof	Pardue, Jane	M	36,66A,66D,13A,13B
Adj	Phillips, Timothy	M	63A,63C
Adj	Smith, Kathleen	M	11,13A

NC1450 Montreat College
Department of Music
310 Gaither Circle
Montreat, NC 28757
(828) 669-8011   Fax: (828) 669-9554
www.montreat.edu
E-mail: kauman@montreat.edu

4 Year Liberal Arts Institution

Director: Kevin Auman, 80A

Inst	Auman, Kevin	B	34,35
Adj	Carleton, Sharon	M	66G,66A
Adj	Entzi, Karen	M	62,11,41
Adj	Lorenz, Kevin	D	70,41
Adj	McCoy, Jane	M	61
Adj	Moore, Anthony	D	10F,13G,13E
Adj	Myers, Michael	B	64,13G
Adj	Schermerhorn, David	B	34D,34E,35C
Prof	Stackhouse, Eunice Wonderly	D	13,66A,66B,66D,66C
Inst	Wilds, Timothy	M	61,31A,36,40

NC1500 Mount Olive College
Department of Music
634 Henderson St
Mount Olive, NC 28365-1299
(919) 658-2502   Fax: (919) 658-7830
www.moc.edu
E-mail: a1armstrong@moc.edu

4 Year Institution

Chair: Alan Armstrong, 80A

Prof	Armstrong, Alan	PhD	12A,14B,13,62C,66A
Inst	Burnham, Stuart	M	12A,13C,66A,20
Asst Prof	Kerstetter, Kathleen	PhD	32,49,34,64A
Asst Prof	Poniros, Risa	D	32B,40,36,61

NC1550 North Carolina A&T State Univ
Department of Music
1601 E Market St
Greensboro, NC 27420
(336) 334-7926   Fax: (336) 334-7484
www.ncat.edu/~music
E-mail: jphenry@ncat.edu

4 Year Institution, Historically Black College
Member of NASM

Chair: William C. Smiley, 80A

	Alexander, Travis		12A,36,40,66
	Curtis, Ann	M	66D
Assoc Prof	Day, Michael	D	11,32E,32F,63A,63B
	Elkins, Christina	D	61
	Hall, Van-Anthoney		11,12D,40,42,61
	Henry, John P.	D	13,63D
	Lasley, Michael		50,65
	Millsapp, Brian		37,49,60B
	Moffett, C. Mondre		63A,10F,29A,47,31F
	Ruff, Kenneth	D	37
Prof	Smiley, William C.	D	10B,35C,35G,45
	Stephenson, Michael		64,48,64E

NC1600 North Carolina Central University
Department of Music
1801 Fayetteville St
Durham, NC 27707-3129
(919) 530-6319   Fax: (919) 530-7540
www.nccu.edu
E-mail: dmccullers@nccu.edu

4 Year Institution, Historically Black College

Interim Chair: Byron Tymas, 80A

Assoc Prof	Bailey, Candace L.	D	12,29D,15,11,12A
Asst Prof	Banks, Richard	M	39,61,60A
Lect Adj	Bordon, Wellington	B	35D,35G
Lect Adj	Brown, Damon	M	62D
Artist in Res	Calderazzo, Joey		66A,66C,46,47
Lect	Clemons, Kawachi A.	M	35A,35D,35E
Artist in Res	Douthit, Pat		35
Librarian	Faison, Vernice	M	16
Lect Adj	George, Arnold E.	M	47,45,64,34,13
Artist in Res	Green, Elvira	B	39,61
Lect Adj	Halverson, Pamela	M	63,60B
Assoc Prof	Harrell, Paula D.	D	32,66A,66G,66D,31A
Lect Adj	Heitzenrater, John	M	64D,20C,20D,20E
Vstng Lect	Helm, Lenora Zenzalai	M	61,47
Asst Prof	Holley, Timothy	D	14,62,62C,20G
Inst	Horton, Brian	M	64E,46
	Hulme, Lance	D	13,12A
Lect Adj	Kelly, Maureen	M	64A

Artist in Res	Marsalis, Branford		47,46,64E
Artist in Res	Martin, Christopher		35
Lect Adj	Meachum, Jay	M	63A
Lect Adj	Paolantonio, Ed	M	66A,67F
Lect	Reid, Jorim	M	37
Assoc Prof	Simpson, Brennetta	D	32B,32A,32D
Lect	Taylor, Thomas	M	65
Lect Adj	Thai, Mei-Chuan Chen	D	64C
Inst	Trowers, Robert	M	63C,63D,46,29A
Lect Adj	Truckenbrod, Steve	D	63D
Asst Prof	Tymas, Byron	M	11,46,70,47,41
Assoc Prof	Wiggins, Ira T.	D	47,64A,64E,29,46
Lect Adj	Wilson, Grover	M	11,36,66A,66C,66D

NC1650 Univ of North Carolina School of the Arts

School of Music
1533 S. Main St
Winston Salem, NC 27127-2738
(336) 770-3255   Fax: (336) 770-3248
www.uncsa.edu
E-mail: urbanikm@uncsa.edu

4 Year Institution, Graduate School

Certificate, Diploma, Master of Music in Performance

Dean: Wade P. Weast, 80A
Assistant Dean & Dir., Undergraduate Studies: David Winkelman, 80B,80H
Associate Dean & Dir., Graduate Studies: Michael S. Rothkopf, 80C,80H
Assistant Dean & Dir., Enrollment: Steven R. LaCosse, 80D,80H

	Allbritten, James	M	36,61,39
	Bartlett, Jacquelyn		62E
	Beck, John R.	M	50,65
	Beres, Karen E.		13A,66D
	Browne, Sheila A.	M	62B
	Coelho, Tadeu	D	64A,41
	Dillon, Lawrence M.	D	13A,13,10,43
	Dodds, Michael R.	D	12
	Driscoll, Robert	M	64B
	Espina-Ruiz, Oskar	D	64C,42
	Ferri, John P.	D	13
	Forshee, Zane	M	70
	Frazelle, Kenneth	M	13,10F,10
	Gagnon, Allison	D	66C
	Johnson, Sarah	B	62A
	Jolley, David	M	49,63B
	LaCosse, Steven R.	M	39,12A
	Larsen, Eric	M	41,66A
	Lawrence, Kevin	M	62A,41
	Olsen, Timothy	D	66G
	Orenstein, Janet	DMA	62A,42
	Ransom, Matt W.		63D
	Rocco, Robert P.		66C,13
	Rose, Saxton		48,64D,41
	Rothkopf, Michael S.	D	45,35C,35G
	Rudkin, Ronald	M	47,29,53
	Saxton, Judith	M	63A
	Sharpe, Paul	M	41,62D
	Shteinberg, Dmitri	D	66A
	Siebert, Glenn	M	61
	Sullivan, Taimur	M	64E
	Taylor, Marilyn S.	M	61
	Troy, Matthew	M	60B
	Ward, Angela		61
	Weast, Wade P.	D	13
	Whitehouse, Brooks	D	62C
	Winkelman, David	D	13

NC1700 North Carolina State University

Department of Music
Campus Box 7311/Cates Ave
Raleigh, NC 27695
(919) 515-2981   Fax: (919) 515-4204
www.ncsu.edu/music/index.html
E-mail: lydia_coffman@ncsu.edu

4 Year Institution

Director: J. Mark Scearce, 80A
Associate Director: Randolph M. Foy, 80H
Assistant Director: John A. Fuller, 80H

PT	Arnold, Alison E.	D	11,20,20E,14
Adj	Beckman, Gary D.	D	12A,67G,11,35A,35B
Adj Inst	Boone, Mary E.	M	64A
Adj Inst	Foureman, Jason		
Prof	Foy, Randolph M.	D	11,12A,38
Assoc Prof	Fuller, John A.	D	37,13C
Assoc Prof	Garcia, Paul D.	D	37,46,50,65
Adj Inst	Jivaev, Anton		62A
Asst Prof	Kleiankina, Olga	D	66
Asst Prof	Koch, Thomas	D	13,12A
Prof	Kramer, Jonathan C.	D	11,12A,20D,20A,62C
Asst Prof	Leaf, Nathan	D	36,60A,61
	Leechford, Wayne	M	64E
Asst Prof	Parker, Wesley	M	65,47
Adj Inst	Pederson, John		64D
PT	Petters, Robert B.	D	60,11
Prof	Scearce, J. Mark	D	13,10
Adj Inst	Seiger, Jennifer	M	61
PT	Sprague, John L.	D	65,67E
Adj Inst	Suarez, Luciano		
PT	Turner, Kristin Meyers	D	12A
Adj Inst	Wang, Lin-Ti		
Prof	Waschka, Rodney A.	D	10,12A,13F,10B,13

NC1750 North Carolina Wesleyan College

Department of Music
3400 N Wesleyan Blvd
Rocky Mount, NC 27804-8677
(252) 985-5100   Fax: (252) 977-3701
www.ncwc.edu
E-mail: gheavner@ncwc.edu

4 Year Institution

Chair: Michael McAllister, 80A

Adj	Johnston, Ben	M	13,10
Adj	Lohr, Tom L.	M	11
Adj	McAllister, Elizabeth	M	12A,41,48,64C,64E
Asst Prof	McAllister, Michael	M	13,10F,60,11,47
Adj	Pace, Mark	M	66G,36,61

NC1800 Peace College

Department of Music
15 E Peace St
Raleigh, NC 27604
(919) 508-2000   Fax: (919) 508-2326
www.peace.edu
E-mail: vvance@peace.edu

4 Year Liberal Arts Institution for Women

Chair: Virginia L. Vance, 80A

Inst PT	Laird, Scott	M	60,34
Asst Prof	Laufer, Milton R.	D	66A,13C
Inst PT	Martin, Melissa	D	61
Inst PT	Noel, John	D	11
Assoc Prof	Smith, James S.	M	36,41,61
Inst PT	Turner, Kristen	M	12A
Assoc Prof	Vance, Virginia L.	M	13,66G

NC1900 Pfeiffer University

Department of Music & Fine Arts
PO Box 960 Hwy 52N
Misenheimer, NC 28109-0960
(704) 463-1360   Fax: (704) 463-1363
www.pfeiffer.edu
E-mail: David.Kirby@fsmail.pfeiffer.edu

4 Year Institution
Member of NASM

Chair: David S. Kirby, 80A

Inst	Campbell, Robert	M	63B,49
Inst	Conn, Troy	M	70
Asst Prof	Harrill, Stephen	M	61,41,44
Inst	Harvey, Brent M.	D	63C,63D,41
Inst	Hedrick, Carmella	M	64A,41
Assoc Prof	Judge, Joseph	M	36,61,31A,40
Asst Prof	Kirby, David S.	D	12A,64C,64E,64D,41
Prof	Palmer, David	D	13A,66A,13B,13C,66G
Prof	Raines, Jean	D	12A,11,66A,32
Inst	Rhodes, Edward	M	65,50
Inst	Smith, Rusty	M	63A,41,46,47

NC1950 Piedmont International Univ
School of Arts and Sciences
Department of Music
420 S Broad St
Winston Salem, NC 27101-5133
(336) 714-7983   Fax: (336) 725-5522
www.piedmontu.edu
E-mail: smithr@piedmontu.edu

4 Year Institution

Dean/Chair: Ronald Smith, 80A

FT	Cole, Darlyn	M	61,66D,60A,11,13
FT	Lucas, Adonna	M	13,36,64A,66,31A
Adj	Mikkola, Gary	M	70,64
FT	Smith, Ronald	DMA	37,32,63,12A
Adj	White, Pat	M	66A

NC2000 Queens University of Charlotte
Department of Music
1900 Selwyn Ave
Charlotte, NC 28274-0001
(704) 337-2213   Fax: (704) 337-2356
www.queens.edu
E-mail: steelea@queens.edu

4 Year Institution
Member of NASM

Interim Chair: Emily Seelbinder, 80A
Dir., Preparatory Division: Angela Steele, 80E

PT	Brown, Chris	M	63A
PT	Burns, Elizabeth	M	62C,62D
PT	Carter, Drew	M	37
PT	Cordell, Tim	D	12A
PT	Costa, Jennifer	M	66A,66C
PT	Crutchfield, Jonathan	D	36
PT	Edmonds, Carol	M	66D
Assoc Prof	Engen, Rebecca	D	33
PT	Gilbody, Mila	M	62A
PT	Gilpin, Shirley	M	64A,48
Prof	Glenn, James H.	D	36,61,60A,11,12A
PT	Harris, Amy	M	66A
PT	Hines, David	M	66A
PT	Hiscock, Fred	M	64E
PT	Irmiter, Kay	D	61
PT	Johnson, Meg	B	33,44
PT	McCain, Alisa	M	61
Prof Emerita	McClain, Frances	D	33,44
Asst Prof	Miller, Elaine	M	13C,66A,66C,66B,13A
PT	Morrison, Marian	M	66A
Prof	Nitsch, Paul A.	D	41,66A,66H
PT	Parks, John	B	70
Asst Prof	Pasiali, Varvara	D	33,53
PT	Pereira, Ernest	D	62A
PT	Postle, Matthew W.	D	47,29A
Asst Prof	Rhyne-Bray, Constance	M	39,61,20
PT	Rydel, Robert	B	63B
PT	Sesler, Betsey	B	62E
PT	Soto, Leonardo	M	65
PT	Teixeira, Robert	M	70,41
PT	Ulaky, Hollis	B	64B
PT	Watson, Nancy	M	66G
PT	Whalen, Margaret F.	M	11,12A,20B,29A

NC2050 Rockingham Community College
Department of Music
PO Box 38
Wentworth, NC 27375
(336) 342-4261 x2131
www.rockinghamcc.edu
E-mail: hardenp@rockinghamcc.edu

2 Year Institution

Music Contact: Patricia A. Harden, 80A

Asst Prof	Harden, Patricia A.		11

NC2150 St Augustines College
Department of Music
1315 Oakwood Ave
Raleigh, NC 27611
(919)828-4451 x313   Fax: (919)834-6473
www.st-aug.edu
E-mail: eopoole@st-aug.edu

4 Year Institution

Chair: Eric Poole, 80A

Adj	Brown, Charles V.	M	50,65
Adj	Edwards, Robert		63A
Prof	Jeffreys, Harold L.	D	10F,32,64C,65,46
	Kang, Sooyoung		66A,13
	Poole, Eric	M	13,60,20G,36,41
	Woods, William		37
Adj	Wulfeck, David	M	63D

NC2205 Salem College
School of Music
601 S Church St
Winston Salem, NC 27101-5376
(336) 721-2636   Fax: (336) 721-2683
www.salem.edu
E-mail: barbara.lister-sink@salem.edu

4 Year Institution
Member of NASM

Artistic Director: Barbara Lister-Sink, 80A
Dir., Community Music School: Thomas S. Swenson, 80E
Associate Director & Chair: Cristy Lynn Brown, 80H

Asst Prof	Brown, Cristy Lynn	M	61,15,54
Adj Asst Prof	Cirba, Anita	M	63A
Inst	Duran, Sally	B	62E
Inst Adj	Fox, Frances	B	63C
Inst Adj	Lampidis, Anna	D	64B,48
Prof	Lister-Sink, Barbara	DIPL	66A,66B,66C,42
Inst Adj	Michels, Maureen	M	62B
Assoc Prof	Olsen, Timothy	D	66G,31A,66H,42,56
Inst Adj	Perkins, Susan	M	62A
Asst Prof Adj	Reuter-Pivetta, Debra	B	64A
Asst Prof	Rothrock, Donna K.	D	16,32E,63D
Asst Prof Adj	Sellitti, Anne	M	62C,51
Asst Prof	Sepulveda, Sonja	D	36,47,13,60
Asst Prof	Swenson, Thomas S.	D	13A,66B,35C,34,32
Asst Prof Adj	Taylor, Sam	M	70
Inst Adj	Young, Eileen	M	64C
Adj Asst Prof	Zigler, Amy E.	D	12A,15

NC2210 Sandhills Community College
Music Program
3395 Airport Rd
Pinehurst, NC 28374-8283
(910) 692-6185   Fax: (910) 692-2756
www.sandhills.edu
E-mail: haleyt@sandhills.edu

2 Year Institution

Chair, Fine Arts: Timothy R. Haley, 80A

Inst	Book, A. Ryan	M	70,12A,13,41
Prof	Haley, Timothy R.	M	11,13A,46,34C,34A
Inst PT	Thomas, Jennifer	M	66
Prof	Wilson, Frances	M	13A,36,61,11

NC2300 Shaw University
Department of Visual & Perf Arts
118 E South St
Raleigh, NC 27601
(919) 546-8353   Fax: (919) 546-8209
www.shawuniversity.edu
E-mail: ghatcher@shawu.edu

4 Year Institution, Historically Black College

Chair: George Hatcher, 80A

PT	Barley, Leroy	M	63A,63B
Asst Prof	Brown, Charles	M	37,47,65
Assoc Prof	Cornwall, Lonieta	D	13,60,36,66D
Asst Prof	Hatcher, George	M	11,12A
Asst Prof	Hunnicutt, Bradley C.	D	13,66,34,13A,13E
PT	Jeffreys, Harold	D	64
PT	Larson, Anne	M	64A
PT	Shah, Nikita	D	61
PT	Wulfeck, David	M	63D

NC2350 Southeast Baptist Theo Seminary
Department of Music
PO Box 1889
Wake Forest, NC 27587-1889
(919) 761-2316   Fax: (919) 761-2315
www.sebts.edu
E-mail: jboozer@sebts.edu

4 Year Institution, Graduate School

Master of Church Music, Master of Divinity in Worship Leadership

Music Contact & Dir., Graduate Studies: John E. Boozer, 80A,80C
Music Contact & Dir., Undergraduate Studies: Joshua A. Waggener, 80A,80B

Adj Prof	Baker, Dale	M	50,65
Prof	Boozer, John E.	D	60,20,36,31,61
Adj Prof	Boozer, Pat	M	10,32B,66A,13A,13B
Adj Prof	Bullock, Karen	M	66A,13A,66C
Adj Prof	Cherry, Diana	M	64A
Adj Prof	Day, Derek	M	70
Asst Prof	Durham-Lozaw, Susan	M	13A,13B,13C,61
Adj Prof	Garris, Margaret E.	M	62
Assoc Prof	Godwin, Nannette Minor	D	31,66A,66G,32B
Adj Prof	Johnson, Ben S.	D	61,12A,31
Adj Prof	Kris, Mike	M	63C
Prof	Nelson, David P.	D	31A
Adj Prof	Waggener, Joshua A.	M	12A,38,13E

NC2370 Surry Community College
Music Program
630 South Main St
Dobson, NC 27017
(336) 386-3425   Fax: (336) 386-3418
www.surry.edu
E-mail: mabryd@surry.edu

2 Year Institution

Chair, Humanities & Social Sciences: Danajean Mabry, 80A

Inst	Smith, Angie		11,36

NC2400 Univ of North Carolina-Asheville
Department of Music-CPO #2290
024 Lipinsky Hall
1 Univ Heights
Asheville, NC 28804-3251
(828) 251-6432   Fax: (828) 253-4573
www.unca.edu
E-mail: kirby@unca.edu

4 Year Institution

Chair: Wayne J. Kirby, 80A

Inst Adj	Barnes, Michael	B	70
Asst Prof Adj	Belcher, Deborah	D	66A
Inst Adj	Bracchitta, Ian	B	62D
Asst Prof Adj	Coppenbarger, Casey	M	63A
Asst Prof Adj	Coppola, Thomas	M	66A,66D,10C,29
Asst Prof	Entzi, John A.	D	37,63B,41
Asst Prof	Galloway, Melodie		36
Asst Prof Adj	Kim, Hwa-Jin	D	66A
Prof	Kirby, Wayne J.	D	10,45,34,35,62D
Asst Prof Adj	Lampert, Judi	M	64A
Assoc Prof	McKnight, Charles M.	D	13,12A
Inst Adj	O'Farrell, Elsa		66C,66A
Inst Adj	Redman, Inez	B	62A,62B,42
Inst Adj	Richmond, Matthew	M	50,65
Asst Prof Adj	Stevenson, David		70
Asst Prof Adj	Sullivan, Aimee M.	M	64C,64E
Inst Adj	Templon, Paul	M	66A,66C,36
Inst Adj	Weinberg, Charles	B	35G
Asst Prof	Wilken, David M.	D	63C,46,47,10A

NC2410 Univ of North Carolina-Chapel Hill
Department of Music
104 Hill Hall CB #3320
Chapel Hill, NC 27599-3320
(919) 962-1039   Fax: (919) 962-3376
music.unc.edu
E-mail: mkatz@email.unc.edu

4 Year Institution, Graduate School

PhD in Musicology, Master of Arts in Musicology

Chair: Mark Katz, 80A
Dir., Undergraduate Studies: Merida Negrete, 80B
Academic Graduate Admissions: Mark Evan Bonds, 80C,80D
Dir., Graduate Studies: David F. Garcia, 80C
Associate Chair, Academic Studies: Annegret Fauser, 80H
Associate Chair, Applied Studies: Richard E. Luby, 80H

Asst Prof	Alamo, Juan	D	29,65,50
Assoc Prof	Anderson, Allen L.	D	10A,13B,13D,13E,13F
Lect PT	Anderson, Robert	B	62D
Asst Prof	Anderson, Stephen	D	10,29
Prof	Bonds, Mark Evan	D	11,12
Lect PT	Brackett, John	D	13,14C
Lect PT	Byrne, Laura	M	62E
Prof	Carter, Timothy	D	12,13
Lect PT	Davis, Dan	M	47,65
Prof	De Wetter-Smith, Brooks	D	64A,29A
Lect PT	Duarte, Derison	M	66A
Prof	Fauser, Annegret	D	12,15
Asst Prof	Feldman, Evan	D	37,60B
Prof	Finson, Jon W.	D	11,12
Lect PT	Finucane, Dave	B	64E
Lect	Fischer, Jeanne	D	61
Lect PT	Foureman, Jason	M	47,62D
Other	Fuchs, Jeffrey W.	M	32E,37
Asst Prof	Garcia, David F.	D	12,14,20
Lect PT	House, Nicole	M	61
Assoc Prof	Huff, Daniel M.	D	32,36
Prof	Kalam, Tonu	M	60B,38
Asst Prof	Katz, Mark	D	12,14,20,34
Prof	Ketch, James E.	M	47,63A,46,29
Lect PT	Klausmeyer, Sue T.	D	36
Prof	Klebanow, Susan	D	60,36
Lect	Kris, Michael	M	63A
Prof	Luby, Richard E.	D	41,51,62A,67A
Assoc Prof	MacNeil, Anne E.	D	12,15
Lect PT	Martin, Melissa	D	61
Lect PT	McAfee, Andrew	M	63B
Lect PT	McChesney, David	D	63A
Lect	McClure, Matthew	M	37,64E
Prof	Moeser, James	D	12B
Lect	Moeser, Susan	D	66G
Lect PT	Moore, Andrea	M	61
Prof	Nadas, John L.	D	12
Asst Prof	Ndaliko, Cherie Rivers	D	10C,12,14
Assoc Prof	Neal, Jocelyn	M	13,20G,34,14C
Prof	Neff, Severine	D	13
Lect PT	Negrete, Merida	M	32,13
Prof	Oehler, Donald L.	B	41,42,43,48,64C
Assoc Prof	Otten, Thomas J.	D	66A,66E,66H
Lect PT	Paolantonio, Ed	M	66A,47
Lect PT	Partridge, Hugh	M	64D
Lect PT	Pederson, John	B	64D
Lect PT	Peroutka, Leah	M	62A
Prof	Rhodes, Terry Ellen	D	61
Lect	Robinson, Bobb	D	39,61
Lect PT	Savage, Matt	M	65
Lect PT	Schultz, Michael	B	64B
Lect PT	Sparks, Tim	M	61
Lect PT	Stewart, Billy	B	70
Prof	Toppin, Louise	D	61
Assoc Prof PT	Vandermeer, Philip R.	D	14,16
Lect PT	Vial, Stephanie	D	62C
Asst Prof	Weisert, Lee	D	13,10
Prof	Wissick, Brent S.	M	55,51,62C,67A,67E
Asst Prof	Yang, Clara	D	66A,66B,13

NC2420 Univ of North Carolina-Charlotte
Department of Music
9201 University City Blvd
Charlotte, NC 28223-0001
(704) 687-2472   Fax: (704) 687-6806
www.music.uncc.edu
E-mail: dlshrops@email.uncc.edu

4 Year Institution, Graduate School

Chair: Royce E. Lumpkin, 80A
Dir., Undergraduate Studies: James A. Grymes, 80B

Asst Prof	Allemeier, John	D	13,10,34
Asst Prof	Arreola, Brian	M	61,39
PT	Bartlett, Jacquelyn	M	62E
PT	Boyd, Frederick	M	63D,63C
Asst Prof	Campbell, Will	D	46,47,53,64E
PT	Cannon, Carey	M	60A
PT	Champney, Morgen	M	32E
PT	Cloer, John	D	11
Assoc Prof	Deeter, Alissa Walters	D	61
PT	Dior, Jennifer	B	64A
Lect	Dior, Rick	B	50,65
PT	Dover, Cory	B	37
PT	Fensom, Chris	M	63A,49
PT	Ferdon, Ellen		62B
PT	Ferdon, Jeffrey	B	62D
PT	Freidline, Noel	M	40,47,35A
Asst Prof	Frisch, Miranora O.	D	62C,11
Assoc Prof	Grymes, James A.	D	12,12A,11
Assoc Prof	Haldeman, Randy	D	36,32D
PT	Hildreth, Tom	M	62D
PT	Holland, Sandra Renee	M	60A
PT	Hood, Joshua	M	64D
Prof	Lumpkin, Royce E.	D	63C,49
PT	Manceaux, Reese	M	64E
Assoc Prof	Marks, Laurence L.	D	37,64C,32C,41
PT	Pickney, Linda M.		63B,32E,38
Assoc Prof	Price, Jeffrey	D	61,66D
Prof	Russell, David	M	62A
PT	Sadak, John	M	64C,11
Assoc Prof	Savage, Dylan C.	D	66A,66B,66C
PT	Savage, Susan	D	64B
Assoc Prof	Spano, Fred P.	D	32B,32D,32G,32
PT	Springer, Alisha	M	66D
Staff	Underwood, Greg	B	66C
PT	Vaughan, Charles	B	70,41
Asst Prof	Whitaker, Jennifer A.	D	32E,37
PT	Yost, Jacqueline	D	13,66G

NC2430 Univ of North Carolina-Greensboro

School of Music, Theatre & Dance
PO Box 26170
Greensboro, NC 27402-6170
(336) 334-5789   Fax: (336) 334-5497
performingarts.uncg.edu
E-mail: music@uncg.edu

4 Year Institution, Graduate School
Member of NASM

Master of Music in Composition, Master of Music in Music Theory, Master of Music in Performance, Master of Music in Conducting, Master of Music in Music Education, PhD in Music Education, DMA in Conducting, DMA in Performance, Master of Music in Vocal Pedagogy, Master of Music in Accompanying

Dean: John J. Deal, 80A
Associate Dean & Dir., Graduate Studies: William P. Carroll, 80C,80H
Dir., Summer Music Camp: John R. Locke, 80G

Asst Prof	Allen, Aaron S.	D	12
Prof	Askew, Dennis	D	63D
Assoc Prof	Bagley, Marjorie H.	M	62A
Assoc Prof	Barret, Mary Ashley	D	64B
Prof Emeritus	Bass, Eddie C.	D	13,10
Assoc Prof	Bracey, Robert D.	D	61
Lect PT	Brown, Craig	B	62D
Prof	Burke, Kelly J.	DMA	64C
Prof	Burns, Michael J.	D	64D
Assoc Prof	Capuzzo, Guy	D	13
Asst Prof	Carr, James H.	D	14
Assoc Prof	Carroll, Gregory D.	D	13,10,11
Prof	Carroll, William P.	D	60,36
Prof Emeritus	Cox, Richard G.	D	36,60A
Prof Emeritus	Darnell, Robert	M	66A,66D
Prof	Deal, John J.	D	32,34
Prof	DiPiazza, Joseph	D	66A,66C
Assoc Prof	Douglas, Gavin D.	D	14,20D
Assoc Prof	Douglass, James B.	D	66C
Asst Prof	Eby, Chad	M	46,47,29
Assoc Prof	Egekvist, Deborah	D	64A
Assoc Prof	Engebretson, Mark	D	10
Assoc Prof Emeritus	Eskey, Kathryn F.	D	13,66G
Assoc Prof	Ezerman, Alexander	D	62C
Prof Emeritus	Garlington, Aubrey S.	D	12,12A
Assoc Prof	Geraldi, Kevin M.	D	37
Prof	Gray, Patricia	D	32G
Assoc Prof	Haines, Steve J.	M	29,62D
Assoc Prof	Harley, Andrew	D	66C
Prof Emeritus	Hart, Lawrence	D	66A
Prof	Hartmann, Donald	D	39,61

Prof Emeritus	Hill, Barbara F.	D	66A
Prof	Hodges, Don	D	32
Prof	Holley, David	M	39,61
Assoc Prof Emeritus	Hunkins, Arthur B.	D	13,10,45,34
Lect	Jarrett, Jack	D	38
Assoc Prof	Keathley, Elizabeth L.	D	12A,12
Asst Prof	Keeton, Kristopher	M	65
Prof Emeritus	Kiorpes, George A.	D	66A,66B,66C
Prof	Kohlenberg, Randy	D	32,63C
Lect PT	Lash, Andre D.	D	66G
Assoc Prof	LeFevre, Carla	D	61
Prof	Locke, John R.	D	60,32C,37
Asst Prof	Lopez, Fabian E.	D	62A
Prof Emeritus	Lynam, Charles A.	D	61
Asst Prof	MacLeod, Rebecca	D	32
Prof Emerita	Marsh, Carol	D	12A,12,55,67
Prof Emerita	McCrickard, Eleanor	D	12
Assoc Prof	McKoy, Constance L.	D	32B,32A,20A,32
Prof	Nelson, David L.	D	13,60,37
Assoc Prof	Nolker, D. Brett	D	32D
Assoc Prof	O'Brien, Clara	M	61
Assoc Prof	Pack, Abigail	D	63B
Assoc Prof	Priore, Irna	D	13,13I
Assoc Prof	Rawls, Scott	D	62B
Assoc Prof	Ricci, Adam	D	13
Asst Prof	Rubinoff, Kailan	D	67D,14,12
Assoc Prof	Rutty, Alejandro	D	10
Prof	Salmon, John C.	D	66A,66C,29A
Lect	Scott, Levone Tobin	M	61
Prof Emeritus	Sherbon, James W.	D	32
Assoc Prof	Sink, Patricia E.	D	32
Prof	Stewart, Paul B.	D	66A,66C
Assoc Prof	Stusek, Steven C.	D	64E
Asst Prof	Taylor, Anthony	D	64C
Lect	Taylor, Thomas E.	M	65
Assoc Prof	Teachout, David J.	D	32
Asst Prof	Titus, Joan M.	D	12
Prof Emeritus	Tollefson, Arthur R.	D	66A
Assoc Prof	Walker, Nancy L.	D	61
Assoc Prof	Walter, Jennifer Stewart	D	32E,37
Assoc Prof	Wells, Robert A.	D	61
Prof	Williams, J. Kent	D	13,34
Prof	Willis, Andrew S.	DMA	66A,66H,66C
Assoc Prof	Young, Welborn E.	D	36,60
Inst	Zandmane, Inara	D	66C

NC2435 Univ of North Carolina-Pembroke

Department of Music
PO Box 1510
Pembroke, NC 28372-1510
(910) 521-6230   Fax: (910) 521-6390
www.uncp.edu/music
E-mail: tim.altman@uncp.edu

4 Year Institution, Graduate School
Member of NASM

Master of Arts in Teaching Specialization Music, Master of Arts in Music Education

Chair: Timothy Altman, 80A
Dir., Graduate Studies: Valerie A. Austin, 80C
Dir., Admissions: Jackie Clark, 80D
Dir., Artist/Performance Series: Tracy Richard Wiggins, 80F
Dir., Summer Programs: William H. Gash, 80G

Assoc Prof	Altman, Timothy	D	60,32,37,63A,63B
PT	Amendola, James	M	32B
Prof	Arnold, Larry	D	10,29A,13,34A,62D
Asst Prof	Austin, Valerie A.	D	32,55
Asst Prof	Davis, Hal	B	61,54
PT	Day, Derek	M	70,41
PT	DeVaney, Camille	M	66G
PT	Ding, Jian	M	62C
Asst Prof	Hersey, Joanna R.	D	10F,63C,63D,12A
PT	Kenny, Megan	M	62A,62B,51
Lect	Kim, Jaeyoon	D	61,60A,36
PT	Kim, Seung-Ah	D	11,66D,66C
Assoc Prof	Maisonpierre, Elizabeth	D	11,13,66A,66B,66D
Lect	Maisonpierre, Jonathan	D	11,66A
PT	Matson, Erin	M	61
PT	Orr, Emily G.	D	64A
PT	Panepinto, Tom	D	63B
Asst Prof	Rivera, Jose	D	32,36,61,60
Lect	Spitzer, David Martin	M	37,11,64E
Lect	Thomas, Tracy	M	61
Lect	Vandermeer, Aaron D.	M	29,35,47
Lect	Wiggins, Tracy Richard	D	65,11,37,50

NC2440 Univ of North Carolina-Wilmington
Department of Music
601 S College Rd
Wilmington, NC 28403-3201
(910) 962-3390   Fax: (910) 962-7106
www.uncw.edu/music
E-mail: uncwmus@uncw.edu

4 Year Institution
Member of NASM

PT	Bailey, Steve	B	62D
Prof	Bongiorno, Frank	D	47,64E,29
Prof	Chambers, Joseph	B	29
PT	De Ratmiroff, Marina	M	61
Prof	Errante, Steven	D	13,10F,60,10,38
PT	Furr, Barbara	M	12A,66A,66D
Prof	Hickman, Joe Eugene	D	60,36,41,61
PT	Izdebski, Pawel	M	61
PT	Johns, Christopher	M	62C,13A
Assoc Prof	Johnson, Daniel C.	D	32,63D,34,32B,63C
Assoc Prof	King, Nancy	M	61
Asst Prof	LaCognata, John P.	D	37,49,63
PT	Loparits, Elizabeth	M	66C,11
Prof	Martin, Sherrill	D	12A,66A,66B,20G
PT	Miller, Jessica	M	64B
Prof	Nathanson, Robert	M	70,11,13A
PT	Nelson, Valanda	M	64D
Assoc Prof	Rack, John	D	32,65,29A
Lect	Russell, Robert A.	B	70,29
Assoc Prof	Salwen, Barry	D	11,66A,66B,66D
Assoc Prof	Shynett, Jerald	M	29,63C
PT	Waddell, Mike	M	64B,64C,64D,11,32
Assoc Prof	White, Mary Joanna	D	64D
PT	Whittington, Andy	M	66A,29
PT	Zezelj-Gualdi, Danijela	D	62A,62B,13C

NC2500 Wake Forest University
Department of Music
PO Box 7345
Winston Salem, NC 27109-7345
(336) 758-5364   Fax: (336) 758-4935
www.wfu.edu/music
E-mail: brehmcj@wfu.edu

4 Year Institution

Chair: Stewart Carter, 80A

Adj	Bates, Susan	M	66,66H
Adj	Beck, John	M	65
Adj	Bills, Mary Ann	M	66A
Prof	Borwick, Susan Harden	D	13,12,31,10,15
Other	Bowen, Charles Kevin	D	37,47,49,63A
Adj	Campbell, Robert	B	63B
Assoc Prof	Carrasco, Jacqui	D	62A,62B,51,41,14
Adj	Carter, Selina	B	62C,67A
Prof	Carter, Stewart	D	13,11,12A,55,67
Adj	Dharamraj, Fabrice B.	M	62A
Senior Lect	Dixon, Patricia	M	70,20H
Adj	French, Brian	M	63C
Prof	Goldstein, Louis	D	11,66A
Assoc Prof	Gorelick, Brian	D	60A,36,55D
Other	Hagy, David	D	11,38,51
Assoc Prof	Heard, Richard	M	61,20G
Adj	Hoirup, Marlene	M	66A,66C
Other	Holcomb, Teddy	B	37
Adj	Howland, Pamela	D	11
Lect	Inkman, Joanne	D	66A,66C,66D,13A
Prof	Kairoff, Peter	D	11,66A
Adj	Kendrick, Matt		46,53
Adj	Lampidis, Anna	M	64B
Prof	Levy, David B.	D	13,11,12A
Senior Lect	Levy, Kathryn	B	48,64A
Adj	Libera, Rebecca	M	64D
Prof	Locklair, Dan	D	13,10,11,31A,66G
Other	Morgan, Philip		37,47,50,11
Prof	Radomski, Teresa	M	61,54
Adj	Ransom, Matt	B	63D
Adj	Rifas, Helen	M	62E
Adj	Spuller, John	B	62D
Other	Tingen, Jolie	M	34
Adj	Trautwein, Barbara	M	64
Adj	Young, Eileen M.	D	64C,64E,41,64,12A

NC2525 Wake Tech Community College
Department of Fine Arts
9101 Fayetterville Rd
Raleigh, NC 27603
(919) 866-5194
www.waketech.edu
E-mail: slschlesinger@waketech.edu

2 Year Community College

Dean: Gayle Greene, 80A
Music Contact: Scott L. Schlesinger, 80A

Inst	Gilleland, Katharine	D	66G,11,13A,29A,36
Inst	Schlesinger, Scott L.	D	66G,11,13A,29A,36

NC2550 Warren Wilson College
Department of Music
PO Box 9000
Asheville, NC 28815-9000
(828) 298-3325   Fax: (828) 299-4841
www.warren-wilson.edu/~music/
E-mail: wgaughan@warren-wilson.edu

4 Year Institution

Chair: Warren J. Gaughan, 80A

PT	Erbsen, Wayne	M	20G,70
	Gaughan, Warren J.	D	47,13,66A,46,29
PT	Jamison, Phil A.	M	72,70,20G
	Kehrberg, Kevin	D	12,14C,20,60A,62D
PT	McCoy, Jane O.	M	61,16,40
	Williams, Steven	D	11,54,39,66G

NC2600 Western Carolina University
School of Music
253 Coulter Building
Cullowhee, NC 28723
(828) 227-7242   Fax: (828) 277-7162
music.wcu.edu
E-mail: wpeebles@wcu.edu

4 Year Institution, Graduate School
Member of NASM

Master of Arts in Education, Master of Music in Performance, Master of Arts in Teaching

Dean, College of Fine & Perf. Arts: Robert Kehrberg, 80A
Director: William L. Peebles, 80A
Coordinator, Graduate Studies: Mary K. Bauer, 80C
Assistant Director: Amy K. Cherry, 80H
Associate Dean: John T. West, 80H

Asst Prof	Adams, Andrew	D	66C,11,66A,66D
Lect PT	Aquilino, Dominic	M	61
Asst Prof	Armfield, Terri E.	D	64B,13
Assoc Prof	Bauer, Mary K.	D	61
Assoc Prof	Bennett, Travis	D	63B,13B,13C
Emeritus	Buckner, Bob	B	37
Inst	Cherry, Amy K.	D	11
Assoc Prof	Cherry, Daniel E.	D	63C
Lect PT	Colvin, Maura	M	32B
Prof	Frazier, Bruce H.	D	10C,10F,35
Prof	Gaetano, Mario A.	D	50,65,11
Lect PT	Hedberg, Kristen	M	61
Lect PT	Henigbaum, William	B	62,38
Lect	Henley, Matthew	M	37
Prof Emeritus	Holquist, Robert A.	D	32C,36,55D,32D
Asst Prof	Lancaster, Michael	D	60A,55D,61,36,32D
Assoc Prof	Martin, Bradley	D	11,66A
Assoc Prof	Martin, William	D	61,11
Prof	Peebles, William L.	D	64D,20D
Asst Prof	Reitz, Christina L.	D	12,66A,12A
Assoc Prof	Schallock, Michael G.	D	32E,63D,60B
Lect PT	Shea, Joy	M	20D,11
Vstng Asst Prof	Sink, Damon W.	DMA	10,13,34,34B,13I
Prof	Spell, Eldred	D	64A,72
Asst Prof	Starnes, David	B	37
Assoc Prof	Thompson, Shannon	D	64C,11
Prof	Ulrich, Brad	D	63A
Lect PT	Wadopian, Eliot	B	62D
Prof	West, John T.	D	32E,37,60B
Assoc Prof	Wlosok, Pavel	M	47,13F,29,66A
Assoc Prof	Wohlrab, Stephen	M	70,35A

NC2640 Wilkes Community College
Department of Music
PO Box 120
Wilkesboro, NC 28697-0120
(336) 838-6200
www.wilkescc.edu
E-mail: carrie.custer@wilkescc.edu

2 Year Institution

Dean: Blair M. Hancock, 80A
Chair: Julie Mullis, 80A

| Inst | Bangle, Jerry | M | 13,11,38,53,29 |
| Inst | Swaim, Doris | M | 32A,36,61,66D |

NC2650 Wingate University
Department of Music
220 N. Camden St.
Wingate, NC 28174-0159
(704) 233-8312   Fax: (704) 233-8309
www.wingate.edu/academics/music
E-mail: robost@wingate.edu

4 Year Institution
Member of NASM

Chair: Ronald D. Bostic, 80A

Prof	Asti, Martha S.	D	12A
Prof	Blizzard, John T.	D	61
Inst	Bostic, Polly T.	M	66A,66D,66G
Prof	Bostic, Ronald D.	D	60,12A
Lect PT	Griffin, Christopher	D	63B,13C
Lect PT	Hann, Gordon	B	63A
Lect PT	Howard, Sabrina	M	62
Lect PT	Humphries, Tracy	M	64D
Lect PT	Hunter, James	M	70
Prof Emerita	Hutton, Judy F.	D	13,66A,66B,66C,66D
Asst Prof	Lein, Melinda	D	61,12
Lect PT	Markgraf, David	M	65
Assoc Prof	Martin, Jessie Wright	D	61,39
Lect PT	Maughan, Sarah	M	61
Lect PT	Murray, Jack	M	64A
Asst Prof	Perry, Dawn A.	D	63C,32E,37,47,60B
Assoc Prof	Potter, Kenney	D	36,13C,60A
Lect PT	Wyrick, Ginger	M	36,32B

NC2700 Winston-Salem State University
Department of Fine Arts-Music
PO Box 19432
Winston-Salem, NC 27110-0001
(336) 750-2520   Fax: (336) 750-2522
www.wssu.edu

4 Year Institution, Historically Black College
Member of NASM

Dean, College of Arts & Sciences: Charles W. Ford, 80A
Chair: Charles E. Hicks, 80A

Inst	Armstrong, James E.	M	63A,13A,37,46,49
Inst	Artimisi, Tony	M	35,65
Asst Prof	Belfield, Roy L.	D	66G,36,60A,10F,12A
Inst PT	Boudreault, Mary	M	63B,13A,13D,13E,13B
Inst	Burke, D'Walla Simmons	M	60A,36,61
Inst PT	Crump, Jason	M	11
Inst PT	Douthit, LaTika	M	11,37,64A
Inst PT	Federle, Yong Im Lee	D	66A,66D
Inst PT	Ford, Ronnal	M	64,64B,11,64D,62A
Inst PT	Gambetta, Charles	D	11,12E
Inst PT	Harvey, Brent	D	11,63D
Inst PT	Heard, Richard	M	61
Prof	Hicks, Charles E.	D	
Asst Prof	Judson, Tohm	D	10B,62D,70,34,35
Prof	Legette, Lee David	D	11,32B,37,47,64E
Inst PT	Lewis, Cheryse M.	M	61
Assoc Prof	Magruder, Michael	D	10F,37,64C
Inst	Mietus, Raymond	M	13A,37,50,65
Inst	Mood, Aaron	M	66C
Inst	Moore, Deena	M	61
Inst PT	Moore-Mitchell, Teresa A.	M	11,61
Asst Prof	O'Connell, Debora S.	D	32
Asst Prof	Placilla, Christina D.	D	12A,20,38,62A,62B
Inst	Rice, Karen	M	66A,66C,66D
Inst PT	Tillman, Joshua	M	63A,11
Asst Prof	Wiggins, Donna	D	12C,32,32G

ND0050 Bismarck State College
Department of Music
1500 Edwards Ave
Bismarck, ND 58506-5587
(701) 224-5438   Fax: (701) 224-5472
www.bismarckstate.com
E-mail: john.darling@bsc.nodak.edu

2 Year Institution

Chair, Arts & Communication: Michelle Lindblom, 80A

Adj	Bauman, Clyde	B	61
Assoc Prof	Darling, John A.	D	37,60B,47,13,41
Adj	Eckroth-Riley, Joan	M	32
Adj	Eichhorst, Diane	B	13C,66
Adj	Fuzesy, Brianne	B	11,63,42
Adj	Gray, Arlene	B	66
Asst Prof	Hagerott, Dawn	M	40,61,11
Adj	Klein, Doug	B	70,41
Adj	Martinez, Everaldo	D	62,51
Adj	Miller, Andrew	M	36,60A,40,13C
Adj	Peske, Robert	B	50,65
Adj	Rehberg, Jeanette	B	11,64,42

ND0100 Dickinson State University
Department of Music
291 Campus Dr
Dickinson, ND 58601
(701) 483-2307   Fax: (701) 483-2006
www.dickinsonstate.edu
E-mail: timothy.justus@dsu.nodak.edu

4 Year Institution

Asst Prof	Burns, Carolyn	D	32,20,14,55B
Asst Prof	Compton, Michael	M	64,37,41,47,60B
Inst	DyKema, Laurae	B	61
Inst	Heley, Ruth	B	61
PT	Hewson, Cheryl	M	66C
Inst	Keogh, Priscilla	B	38
Inst	McKirdy, Colleen	M	66A,66B,66C
Asst Prof	Nozny, Brian	M	13,10A,10F,34A,34B
PT	Nozny, Rachel	M	64A,13C
Asst Prof	Southard, Bruce	D	36,60A,12A,61,60
PT	Vranna, Jeff	M	11

ND0150 Jamestown College
Department of Music
6031 College Ln
Jamestown, ND 58405
(701) 252-3467   Fax: (701) 253-4318
www.jc.edu
E-mail: rwalenti@jc.edu

4 Year Institution

Chair: Richard L. Walentine, 80A

Inst	Braunagel, Jesse	B	63
Inst	Christianson, Tom	M	65
Asst Prof	McDermid, Aaron	ABD	36,60A,61,11,32
Assoc Prof	Schneider, Benjamin D.	ABD	37,38,60B,64,32
Inst	Villareal, Leanne	M	61
Prof	Walentine, Richard L.	D	61,54,13A,39,12A
Prof	Wojnar, William A.	D	12A,66A,66G,31B,31A

ND0250 Minot State University
Division of Music
500 University Ave W
Minot, ND 58707-0001
(701) 858-3185   Fax: (701) 858-3823
www.minotstateu.edu/music
E-mail: kenneth.bowles@minotstateu.edu

4 Year Institution, Graduate School
Member of NASM

Master of Music Education

Chair: Kenneth E. Bowles, 80A

Vstng Asst Prof	Alme, Joseph	M	63C,63D,37,60
Lect PT	Anderson, Dianna M.	D	13,66
Assoc Prof	Anderson, Erik	D	62D,62C,13,51,29
Inst	Boren, Mark	M	63A,63B,13A,41
Assoc Prof	Bowles, DeVera	D	61,39
Prof	Bowles, Kenneth E.	D	36,61,39,60,32C
Lect PT	Collins, Cherie	M	61,36,32D,64B
Lect PT	Demme, Elizabeth	D	66A
Asst Prof	Estes, Adam	D	46,47,64E,64C,64D
Lect PT	Files, Kari	M	66G
Inst	Petrik, Rebecca	M	32,13A,61,70,36
Prof	Rumney, Jon	D	13,38,41,62A,62B
Assoc Prof	Simons, Dennis	D	11,13,20,38
Lect PT	Simons, Penelope	D	66A,66H
Lect PT	Veikley, Avis	M	65,50,62E
Lect PT	Watson, Richard	M	14C,20G

ND0350 North Dakota State University
School of Music
Department 2334
PO Box 6050
Fargo, ND 58108
(701) 231-7932   Fax: (701) 231-2085
www.ndsu.nodak.edu/finearts
E-mail: EJ.Miller@ndsu.edu

4 Year Institution, Graduate School
Member of NASM

Master of Music in Performance, Master of Music in Conducting, Master of Music Education, DMA in Conducting, DMA in Performance

Director, Fine Arts: John Miller, 80A
Dir., Graduate Studies: Jo Ann Miller, 80C
Assistant Dir., Fine Arts: Bill R. Law, 80H

Assoc Prof	Brekke, Jeremy	D	63,37,49,63A,47
Lect	Burggraff, Allison	M	62A
Lect	Chen-Beyers, Christina	D	64B
Lect	Coates, Michael	M	70
Prof	Froelich, Andrew I.	D	13,12A,66A,66H
Lect	Geston, Janet	M	66C
Prof	Groves, Robert W.	D	11,12A,66A,20G,66H
Staff	Heaford, Christian	B	66F
Lect	Helm, Michael	B	66A
Lect	Hoffelt, Tim	B	70
Assoc Prof	Johnson, Sigurd	D	65,50,37
Assoc Prof	Jones, Robert J.	D	39,61,54,14
Asst Prof	Kang, Cecilia	D	64C,13
Lect	Law, Bill R.	M	62D,29
Assoc Prof	Mack, Kyle	D	60,37,47,63C,29
Prof	Miller, Jo Ann	D	60,36,40,56
Prof	Miller, John	D	13,34
Lect	Moe, Charlotte	D	32B,32D,36
Lect	Nagel, Susan	M	66C
Lect	Neill, Doug A.	M	63D
Lect	Nelson, Elise Buffat	M	62C,41,42
Lect	Noone, Katherine	D	61,54
Assoc Prof	Olfert, Warren	D	60,32C,37,63C
Lect	Olson, Michael	M	66G
Prof	Olson, Robert	D	39,61,54
Lect	Orozco, Eduardo	M	12A
Assoc Prof	Patnode, Matthew A.	D	64E,64A,29,48,47
Lect	Poehls, Jenny	M	64A
Lect	Prigge, Sarah	D	12A,66D
Lect	Stine, Steve	B	70
Prof	Sublett, Virginia	D	61,39,54
Lect	Tackling, Sebastian	B	64D
Lect	Vigesaa, Erik	M	63B
Assoc Prof	Weber, Michael J.	D	60,54

ND0400 Univ of Mary
Department of Music
7500 University Dr
Bismarck, ND 58504
(701) 355-8301   Fax: (701) 255-7687
www.umary.edu/music
E-mail: music@umary.edu

4 Year Institution

Chair: Thomas Porter, 80A

Inst	Augustadt, David W.	B	70
Inst	Bernier, Lucas	M	65,50,11,34
Inst	Bohlen, Tara M.	B	62A,62B
Lect	Boyd, Sara	M	64D
Inst	Candee, Jan	B	66A,66D,66G,32B,11
Inst	Ehrmantraut, Ben R.	B	62D

Prof	Gowen, Dennis	M	37,49,63A,63B,60
Inst	Gowen, Rhonda	M	66A
Assoc Prof	Henjum, Katherine	M	61,40,13C
Inst	Land, Michael	D	13C,66A
Inst	Martinez, Everaldo	M	62A,62B,62C,51,38
Inst	Mertz, Tonya	M	64B
Inst	Palecek, Brian	D	11
Lect	Peske, Robert T.	M	70
Prof	Porter, Thomas	D	36,13B,10A,32D,31A
Lect	Prebys, Marylee A.	M	66A,66B,12A
Asst Prof	Sandberg, Scott	D	64,13B,13C,11,48
Asst Prof	Williams, Anthony N.	M	29,47,63C,63D

ND0500 Univ of North Dakota-Grand Forks
Department of Music
3350 Campus Rd Stop 7125
Grand Forks, ND 58202
(701) 777-2644   Fax: (701) 777-3320
arts-sciences.und.edu/music
E-mail: michael.wittgraf@und.edu

4 Year Institution, Graduate School
Member of NASM

Master of Music in Pedagogy, Master of Music in Composition, Master of Music in Performance, Master of Music in Conducting, Master of Music in Music Education, PhD in Music Education

Chair: Michael A. Wittgraf, 80A
Dir., Graduate Studies: Gary Towne, 80C

Lect	Barbu, Simona	D	62C,62D
Lect	Berry, Whitney	M	13
Assoc Prof	Blackburn, Royce F.	D	61,54,39
Prof	Blake, Michael	M	13A,50,53,65
Lect	Boschee, Sharon	M	64A
Assoc Prof	Bronfman, Joshua	M	36,40,32D,60A
Lect	Brooks, William Robert	M	37
Lect	Chen-Beyers, Christina	M	64D
Assoc Prof	Christopherson, Anne	D	39,61
Librarian	Clifton, Felecia		16
Assoc Prof	Dearden, Katherine Norman	D	32C
Asst Prof	Drago, Alejandro M.	D	38,62
Lect	Eylands, Kristian	M	70
Lect	Fogderud, Marla	D	61
Lect	Gable, Christopher	D	13,10
Assoc Prof	Ingle, Ronnie	M	49,63A,47
Assoc Prof	Keyser, Dorothy	D	11,12A,14
Asst Prof	Knight, Andrew	D	33
Lect	Lawrence, Wesley	D	61
Assoc Prof	Lewis, Barbara E.	D	12F,12C,32A,32B
Asst Prof	Masko, Meganne	M	33
Lect	Nelson, Kayla	M	63B
Lect	Pinkerton, Louise	M	61,12A
Prof	Popejoy, James R.	DMA	37,60B,32E
Lect	Popejoy, Melanie	M	36
Lect	Pugh, Joel	D	63C,63D,11
Assoc Prof	Rheude, Elizabeth A.	M	41,64C,64E
Lect	Schott, Kimberly	M	66A,66D
Prof	Towne, Gary	D	12A,55,12C
Lect	Williams-Kennedy, Maria	B	61
Prof	Wittgraf, Michael A.	D	10,13,34,10A,10B

ND0600 Valley City State University
Department of Music
101 SW College St
Valley City, ND 58072-4024
(701) 845-7272   Fax: (701) 845-7264
music.vcsu.edu
E-mail: diana.skroch@vcsu.edu

4 Year Institution
Member of NASM

Chair, Fine Arts & Dir., Undergraduate Studies: Diana Skroch, 80A,80B
Dir., Community School for the Arts: Shari Larson, 80E

Asst Prof	Adams, James M.	D	35G,37,47,49,53
Lect	Allebach, Robin	M	39,61
Prof	Hagen, Sara L.	D	13B,32B,32C,35A
Lect	Hammerling, Margaret	B	64A
Prof	Klingenstein, Beth Gigante	D	12A,66B,66D
Asst Prof	Levy, Leesa	D	60
Lect	Meyers, Nicholaus S.	M	65,50
Lect	Namminga, Jaime	M	13C,66C,66A
Asst Prof	Redfearn, Christopher	D	36,40,60A,61
Lect	Rudolph, Jon	B	11,13A,70
Lect	Sidoti, Vincent	D	10,13B
Prof	Skroch, Diana	D	11,66D
Prof	Variego, Jorge	M	10,13B,48,64C,64B

NE0040 Central Comm College-Columbus
Department of Music
PO Box 1027
Columbus, NE 68602-1027
(402) 564-7132   Fax: (402) 562-1201
www.cccneb.edu
E-mail: jcurry@cccneb.edu

2 Year Institution

Chair: Jeffrey P. Curry, 80A

	Curry, Jeffrey P.	D	11,13C,32,37,49
	Kitson, Jeffrey	M	11,13,36,40,61

NE0050 Chadron State College
Department of Music
1000 Main St
Chadron, NE 69337
(308) 432-6375   Fax: (308) 432-6071
www.csc.edu/music
E-mail: jrutter@csc.edu

4 Year Institution

Chair: Joel T. Schreuder, 80A
Dir., Cultural Programming: Shellie Johns, 80F

Adj Inst	Beutler, Marian	M	61,66A
Lect	Carey, Charles	M	11,13A,70
Assoc Prof	Lambert, Adam E.	D	32E,37,60B,63,49
Adj Inst	Lambert, Michelle		63C
Assoc Prof	Margetts, James A.	D	66,12A,13,32A
Assoc Prof	Schaefer, G. W. Sandy	D	14C,46,65,29,35
Assoc Prof	Schreuder, Joel T.	D	60A,36,61,40,32D
	Stephens, Loren		11,64A
Asst Prof	Stephens, Michael	D	10,29,46,13,64
Asst Prof	Taylor, Una D.	D	36,61,32B,11,40

NE0100 College of St Mary
Department of Music
7000 Mercy Rd
Omaha, NE 68106
(402) 399-2622   Fax: (402) 399-6222
www.csm.edu
E-mail: mburnett@csm.edu

4 Year Institution, Graduate

Director: Marty Wheeler Burnett, 80A

Assoc Prof	Burnett, Marty Wheeler	D	12A,13,66A,36,66G
PT	Castellote, Javier	M	70
PT	Fagan, Leslie M.	D	64A
PT	Gamerl, Darci	M	64B
PT	Jensen, Janeen	M	61
PT	Kallstrom, Wayne	D	66A,66G,12A
PT	Klinghammer, John	D	64C
PT	Lim, Margaret	M	62C
PT	Pruss, Melissa	B	62A

NE0150 Concordia University
Department of Music
800 N Columbia Ave
Seward, NE 68434-1556
(402) 643-7282   Fax: (402) 643-3671
www.cune.edu/music
E-mail: music@cune.edu

4 Year Institution
Member of NASM

Chair: Kurt E. Von Kampen, 80A

Adj	Avey, Kevin		70
Adj	Beal, Kaylene	B	63B
Adj	Blersch, Carla	M	66A
Prof	Blersch, Jeffrey	D	13,36,66G
Adj	Bou, Emmy	M	66A,61
Adj	Dickson, Adrienne C.		61
Adj	Farr, Sarah	M	61
Asst Prof	Grimpo, Elizabeth	D	11,13,66A
Adj	Herbener, Catherine	M	66A
Assoc Prof	Herl, Joseph	D	12,13,31A
Adj	Jacobs, Nicole	B	33
Adj	Johnson, Ryann	M	64B,64D
Adj	Keelan, Michael	M	62A,62C
Adj	Keele, Jeffrey		61
Adj	Kelly, Thomas	M	63A
Adj	Kite, Jessica	M	44
Adj	Krutz, Jim	B	65
Adj	McMahan, Cassandra		32B
Inst	Nichols, Christopher Robert	DMA	64C,64E,38
Prof	Ore, Charles	D	66G
Asst Prof	Prochnow, Peter	M	31A,35G
Asst Prof	Schultz, Andrew J.	M	29,37,60B,63A
Adj	Schultz, Wendy E.	D	49,63D
Adj	Thiemann, Amy	M	64A
Adj	Varilek, Stephanie R.		61
Adj	Von Kampen, David	M	10
Assoc Prof	Von Kampen, Kurt E.	D	36,60A,32

NE0160 Creighton University
Music Program
2500 California Plz
Omaha, NE 68178
(402) 280-2509   Fax: (402) 280-2320
www.creighton.edu
E-mail: fhanna@creighton.edu

Private, 4 Year Institution

Chair: Frederick Hanna, 80A
Dean: Robert Lueger, 80A

Inst PT	Bircher, Craig	B	63A
Inst PT	Bircher, Mary	B	62E
Asst Prof	Breland, Barron	D	13,36
Inst PT	Eaton, Wendy	M	61
Inst PT	Eden, Gregg	D	70
Inst PT	Gamerl, Darci	M	64B,32E,67H
Inst PT	Gaver, Angie	M	64C
Assoc Prof	Hanna, Frederick	D	13,37,38,10
Inst PT	Ono, Momoro	D	66A
Inst PT	Owens, Diane	M	61
Inst PT	Plenert, Keith	M	62A,62B
Assoc Prof	Seitz, Carole J.	M	39,61,11
Asst Prof	Sheftz, Stephen Walter Robert	M	36
Inst PT	Shogrin, Tina	B	64A
Inst PT	Trussell, Adam	B	64D
Inst PT	Valentine, Claudette	D	66A,36,66D
Inst PT	Wilmeth, Margaret	B	62C
Inst PT	Wise, Jay	D	63C

NE0200 Doane College
Department of Music
1014 Boswell Ave
Crete, NE 68333
(402) 826-8256   Fax: (402) 826-8278
www.doane.edu
E-mail: jay.gilbert@doane.edu

4 Year Institution

Chair & Dir., Artist/Performance Series: Jay W. Gilbert, 80A,80F

Inst PT	Baxter, Kara	M	46,47,62
Inst PT	Behrmann, Candice		64A
Inst PT	Boye, David	M	70
Asst Prof PT	Breckbill, David	D	12,66C
Inst PT	Carpenter, William	M	66C
Inst PT	Cogdill, Susan	M	36
Inst PT	Dalby, Kathy	M	32E
Inst PT	DeAmbrose, Marci Malone	M	61
Inst PT	Farr, Sarah	M	61
Assoc Prof	Ferguson, Dianne S.	M	13,66A,66C,66D
Prof	Gilbert, Jay W.	D	37
Inst PT	Guevara, Amy	M	61
Inst PT	Hildebrand, Janet N.		64C
Inst PT	Houk, Chad M.	M	66C
Inst PT	Johnson, Jeremiah	M	66A,66C
Inst PT	Johnson, Ryann P.	M	64B,64D
Inst PT	Keele, Jeffrey		61
Inst PT	Kelly, Tom	M	63
Inst PT	Krutz, James	M	65
Inst PT	Lingren, Allison	M	66C
Asst Prof	Ohlman, Kathleen	M	32B,32C,32D,32E
Asst Prof	Runestad, Kurt	D	36,32D,60A,47
Inst PT	Sands, Tracy	M	62,38
Inst PT	Schmidt, Nolan	M	32D
Inst PT	Smith, Hannah	D	61,39
Inst PT	Temme, Diane	M	66A
Inst PT	Ulmer, Enoch	M	61
Inst PT	Von Kampen, David W.	B	47

NE0250 Grace University
Department of Music
1311 S 9th St
Omaha, NE 68108-3629
(402) 449-2800   Fax: (402) 341-9587
www.graceuniversity.edu
E-mail: gzielke@graceu.edu

4 Year Institution

Chair: Gregory D. Zielke, 80A

Adj	Austin, Joshua	B	65
	Bircher, Mary		62E
Adj	Brophy, Nicholas	B	70
Adj	DeVries, Anne	B	61
Adj	Haar, Mark	B	62D
Adj	Hartwig, Judy	M	32B
Adj	Heil, Teri	M	66A,13,11
Adj	Hess, Rick	M	62
Assoc Prof	James, Jeffrey R.	M	13,60,32,37,63
Adj	McClure, Ryan	M	31A
Adj	Oreskovich, Kristina	M	61
Adj	Reimer, Joyce L.	M	44,66A,66G
Adj	Schultz, James	M	61
Adj	St. Claire, Jason	M	36
Adj	Temple, Robert P.	M	61
Prof	Zielke, Gregory D.	D	60,32C,36,61,31A

NE0300 Hastings College
Department of Music
PO Box 269
Hastings, NE 68902-0269
(402) 461-7448   Fax: (402) 461-7428
www.hastings.edu
E-mail: rkoozer@hastings.edu

4 Year Institution
Member of NASM

Chair: Robin R. Koozer, 80A

PT	Aikin, Diane	M	66G,13A
Prof	Jensen, Byron W.	D	13B,38,12A,62,32C
Asst Prof	Johnson, Deborah S.	M	13A,11,48,64A,13B
PT	Klentz, Richard	M	70
Prof	Koozer, Robin R.	D	36,61
PT	LaBrie, Jesse	M	61,36
Assoc Prof	LaChance, Marc	D	63C,63D,13,10F,29
Assoc Prof	Laing, Daniel R.	D	60B,37,49,63A,63B
PT	Michalek, Thomas	M	32B,32A
Prof	Moore, Ruth	M	66A,66B,66C
Prof	Mountford, Fritz	D	32C,36,60A,10,20
Asst Prof	Murphy, Cynthia	B	16,66A,66D,13
PT	Parker, Phillip	M	65
Prof	Rhodes, Debra	D	12A,64,48
Prof	Smith, Charles	D	36,39,61,54
Prof	Sokasits, Jonathan F.	D	66A,66D,66B,42,12A
Prof	Watter, Hillary	D	61

NE0400 Midland University
Department of Music
900 N Clarkson
Fremont, NE 68025
(402) 721-5480   Fax: (402) 727-6223
www.midlandu.edu
E-mail: logue@midlandu.edu

4 Year Institution

Chair: Eric J. Richards, 80A

Inst	Aleksander, Elizabeth	M	64C,12A
Inst	Bushong, Claire B.	D	12A,13B,13C,66A,66G
Inst	Erickson, Steve	M	63A
Inst	Logue, James	M	36,40
Inst	Mullins, Devoyne	M	32B
Inst	O'Leary, Jed	M	62,64
Asst Prof	Richards, Eric J.	D	63C,37,10A,13B,47

NE0450 Nebraska Wesleyan University
Department of Music
5000 Saint Paul Ave
Lincoln, NE 68504-2794
(402) 465-2269   Fax: (402) 465-2179
www.nebrwesleyan.edu
E-mail: jjh@nebrwesleyan.edu

4 Year Private Institution
Member of NASM

Chair & Dir., Undergraduate Studies: Jana Holzmeier, 80A,80B

Inst	Bacon, Boyd	M	13,36,61,40
Inst PT	Bacon, Masako	D	66G
Inst PT	Besch, Joyce	M	64D
Inst PT	Bobenhouse, Elizabeth	M	41,64A
Adj Inst	Carnes, Donna	M	62A
Inst PT	Guevara, Amy	M	61
Asst Prof PT	Haist, Dean	M	47,63A,29
Inst PT	Henderson, Jean	D	13A,13B,13C,13D,10A
Assoc Prof	Holzmeier, Jana	D	61
Prof	Jones, Larry E.	D	66A,66B
Inst PT	Jones, Richard	B	50,65,34,70
Adj Inst	Krogh, Dawn Pawlewski	D	61,39
	Manner, Mollie		66C
Adj Inst	Mausolf, Susan	M	64B
	Morris, Richard		66C
Inst PT	Ricker, Richard	M	63B
Adj Inst	Schernikau, Burt	M	32B,61
	Schlater, Lynn		66C
Inst FT	Sheldon, Janene	D	61,32B,36,40,16
Asst Prof	Spilker, John D.	D	12
Inst PT	Vogt, Nancy	D	63C,63D,11
Inst PT	Wyman, Tamara	M	66A,66D
Prof	Wyman, William A.	D	36,39,61,60,40
Adj Inst	Young, David	M	32E
Inst PT	Zaev, Pance	M	64C,64E,48
Assoc Prof	Zitek, Sam	D	37,64E,60B,32E

NE0460 Northeast Community College
Department of Music
801 E Benjamin Ave
Norfolk, NE 68702-0469
(402) 844-7354   Fax: (402) 844-7402
www.northeast.edu
E-mail: lindab@northeast.edu

2 Year Institution

Chair: Linda Boullion, 80A

FT	Beardslee, Tony	B	35C,35D,35G,34D,34E
FT	Boullion, Linda	D	13,11,40,36,61
PT	Hilson, Mike	B	70
PT	Klee, Michael	M	65,11
FT	Miller, Tim	B	35C,35D,35G,34D,34E
FT	Neuharth, Randall	D	11,37,47,63
FT	Schultz, Margaret	M	13C,66A,66C,11,32B
FT	Skogstoe, John	M	35H,34E

NE0500 Peru State College
Department of Music
PO Box 10
Peru, NE 68421
(402) 872-2368   Fax: (402) 872-2412
www.peru.edu
E-mail: tediger@peru.edu

4 Year Institution

Chair: Thomas L. Ediger, 80A

Asst Prof	Bartlett, Jacob Kenneth	D	36,61,11
Adj	DeFrain, Debbie	M	66A,11,32B
Prof	Ediger, Thomas L.	D	13,12A,32,36,66
Asst Prof	Fortney, Patrick	D	60,37,47
Asst Prof	Meints, Kenneth	M	63,20,65,35A,32
	Sheedy-Gardner, Anne	M	64
Adj	Snyder, Randall	D	14C

NE0525 Southeast Comm College-Beatrice
Department of Music
4771 W Scott Rd
Beatrice, NE 68310-9802
(402) 228-8266   Fax: (402) 228-2218
www.southeast.edu
E-mail: khoppmann@southeast.edu

2 Year Institution

Inst PT	Boesiger, Kevin	B	36,54
Inst	Douglass, Mary	D	54
	Hoppmann, Ken J.	D	66A,66B,20,66C,12A
Inst PT	Zimmerman, Kimberly	B	61,66C

NE0550 Union College
Department of Music
Fine Arts
3800 S 48th St
Lincoln, NE 68506
(402) 486-2553   Fax: (402) 486-2528
www.ucollege.edu
E-mail: b2forbes@ucollege.edu

4 Year Institution

Chair: Bruce Forbes, 80A

Prof	Lynn, Daniel	D	60A,61,36,32C,32D
Assoc Prof	Restesan, Frank	D	38,13C,62A,51,12A
Prof	Wells, Ryan	D	13,66A,66B,66C

NE0590 Univ of Nebraska-Kearney
Department of Music
2506 12th Ave
Kearney, NE 68849
(308) 865-8618   Fax: (308) 865-8806
www.unk.edu/acad/music
E-mail: cislerv@unk.edu

4 Year Institution, Graduate School
Member of NASM

Master of Arts in Education: Music Education

Chair: Valerie C. Cisler, 80A
Associate Dean: Ronald Crocker, 80H

Prof	Bauer, David	D	36,61,60A,32D
Asst Prof	Beard, Michael R.	M	37,32C
Asst Prof	Bierman, Duane	D	37,65,50
Adj PT	Bircher, Mary W.	B	62E
Prof	Buckner, Nathan	D	66A,66C,66D,13B,13C
Asst Prof	Campbell, Sharon O'Connell	D	61
Assoc Prof	Chen, Ting-Lan	D	11,13B,62A,62B,13C
Prof	Cisler, Valerie C.	D	66A,66B,66D
Prof	Cook, James	D	11,66A,66D
Prof	Crocker, Ronald	D	11,38,65
Staff	Curry, Nancy	M	66C
Lect	Fletcher, Seth	D	63D,63C,13B,13C,11
Prof	Foradori, Anne	D	39,61,54
Assoc Prof	Freedman, Deborah	D	11,12A,38,63B
Assoc Prof	Harriott, Janette	D	32A,32B,11
Staff	Johnson, Mick	B	66F
Assoc Prof	Mitchell, Darleen C.	D	13,10,15,43,12B
Adj PT	Musick, Marilyn J.	D	66G
Prof	Nabb, David	D	64,11,12A,48
Adj PT	Nabb, Franziska	M	64A
Prof	Payne, James	D	11,63A,63B,46,35A
Asst Prof	Rogoff, Noah T.	D	62C,62D,13A,13B
Adj PT	Sales, Gregory	B	70
Prof	Schaaf, Gary D.	M	52
Staff	Scholwin, Richard M.	M	35C,35G,34D
Adj PT	Tincher, Brenda M.	B	66D
Asst Prof	White, Andrew R.	D	61

NE0600 Univ of Nebraska-Lincoln
School of Music
PO Box 880100
Lincoln, NE 68588-0100
(402) 472-2503   Fax: (402) 472-8962
music.unl.edu
E-mail: jrichmond2@unl.edu

4 Year Institution, Graduate School
Member of NASM

Master of Music in Composition, Master of Music in Music Theory, Master of Music in Performance, Master of Music in Music Education, DMA in Composition, DMA in Conducting, DMA in Performance, PhD in Music, Master of Music in Choral Conducting, Master of Music in Music History, Master of Music in Piano Pedagogy, Master of Music in Jazz Studies, DMA in Jazz Studies, Master of Music in Instrumental Conducting, Master of Music in Orchestral Conducting, Master of Music in Woodwind Specialties, Graduate Certificate in Music Entrepreneurship

Interim Associate Dean: John R. Bailey, 80A
Associate Dean, Fine Arts: Christin J. Mamiya, 80A
Dean, Fine Arts: Charles 'Chuck' O'Connor, 80A
Director, Music: John W. Richmond, 80A
Associate Director, Music: Glenn E. Nierman, 80H

Prof	Anderson, Scott	D	63C,42
Prof	Bailey, John R.	D	64A,42,12A
Assoc Prof	Barber, Carolyn	D	60,37
Prof	Barger, Diane C.	D	42,64C
Prof	Barnes, Paul	D	66A
Asst Prof/Prac	Bazan, Dale E.	D	32E,32F,32G,32H,34
Asst Research Prof	Beaver, Gregory	DIPL	62C,42
Assoc Prof	Becker, Karen A.	D	62C,42,13C
Senior Lect	Belflower, Alisa	M	61,54
Lect	Bircher, K. Craig	M	63A
Lect	Bouffard, Peter P.	M	70
Prof	Breckbill, Anita	D	16
Lect	Bush, Doug W.	M	32E,37
Assoc Prof	Bushard, Anthony J.	D	12,29A
Assoc Prof	Butler, Kate S.	M	61,39
Assoc Prof/Prac	Chang, Ann	D	66A,66E
Prof	Clinton, Mark K.	DMA	66A
Lect	Damuth, Laura	D	12A
Prof	Eklund, Peter A.	D	60,32D,36
Senior Lect	Falcone, Anthony M.	M	37,65,50
Asst Research Prof	Fischer, Rebecca J.	DIPL	62A,42
Assoc Prof	Foley, Gretchen C.	D	13
Assoc Prof	Fuelberth, Rhonda J.	D	32D,36
Senior Lect	Fuller, Craig	B	63D
Assoc Prof	Haar, Paul	D	29,64E
Assoc Prof	Hanrahan, Kevin G.	D	61
Prof	Harler-Smith, Donna D.	M	61
Assoc Prof	Hibbard, Therees Tkach	D	36,60A
Assoc Prof	Kleppinger, Stanley V.	D	13,63A,37,12C
Lect	Larson, Tom	M	29A
Asst Prof	Lee, Damon Thomas	D	10A,10B,10C,10F,34A
Prof	Lefferts, Peter M.	D	11,12A,12
Assoc Prof	Levine, Susan	M	52
Assoc Prof	Marks, Christopher	D	66G,66H,13
Assoc Prof	Mattingly, Alan F.	D	63B,13,42
Lect	Mattingly, Jacqueline	D	63B,12B
Asst Prof	McCray, Jeffrey	D	64D,13
Prof	McMullen, William W.	D	13,12A,64B
Assoc Prof	Moore, Brian	D	32,34
Assoc Prof	Neely, David C.	M	62A,62B
Prof	Nierman, Glenn E.	D	32
Artist in Res	Polochick, Edward	M	36
Assoc Prof	Potter, Clark E.	M	62B
Asst Prof	Reimer, Jamie M.	D	61,39
Assoc Prof	Richards, Eric	D	47,10A,10D,13G
Prof	Richmond, John W.	D	32D,32G,36,32
Prof	Rometo, Albert A.	M	65
Prof	Shomos, William	D	39,61
Asst Research Prof	Sirota, Jonah B.	DIPL	62B,42
Prof	Starr, Pamela	D	12A,12
Asst Prof	Sturm, Hans	D	51,62D
Assoc Prof	White, Darryl A.	D	63A,29
Prof	White, Tyler G.	D	10,38
Assoc Prof	Woody, Robert H.	D	32B,12F
Assoc Prof	Wristen, Brenda	D	66A,66B,66D
Asst Research Prof	Yoon, Hyeyung	DIPL	62A,42

NE0610 Univ of Nebraska-Omaha

Department of Music
60th Dodge
Omaha, NE 68182-0245
(402) 554-2251   Fax: (402) 554-2252
music.unomaha.edu
E-mail: mberke@mail.unomaha.edu

4 Year Institution, Graduate School
Member of NASM

Master of Music in Performance, Master of Music in Conducting, Master of Music in Music Education

Dean: Gail Baker, 80A
Chair: Melissa Berke, 80A
Dir., Artist/Performance Series: Greg Perdue, 80F

Prof	Bales, Kenton W.	D	13,10,43,34
Inst PT	Barnette, Mark	M	63D
Assoc Prof	Beard, Christine E.	D	64A,48,11,13
Prof	Berke, Melissa	D	32A,32B
Inst PT	Cosby, Tom	M	64B
Inst PT	Dewater, Jason	M	63B
Inst PT	Divis, Judy	M	62B
Inst PT	Domonkos, Jason	B	65
Inst PT	Dunsmore, Matthew	M	63D
Inst PT	Eaton, Wendy	M	61
Prof	Foltz, Roger	D	13,10
Inst	Ford, Barry M.		13,20
Inst PT	Hall, Andy		62D
Assoc Prof	Harden, Matthew C.	PhD	36,60A,32D,40
Inst PT	Hartwig, Judy	M	32B
Inst PT	Heavin, Hadley	M	70
Inst PT	Hillyer, Tim	B	65
	Holloway, Peggy A.	D	61,32B,15,36,40
Inst PT	Homan, Jim W.	B	34D
Inst PT	Humphrey, AnDrue R.	B	34
Prof	Johnson, James D.	D	66A,66G,69
Inst PT	Johnson, Jason K.	M	63A
Inst PT	Kallstrom, Wayne	D	66G
Inst PT	Knott, Sarah	B	61
Inst PT	Koenig, Paul	B	61
Prof	Low, David G.	D	12A,62C
Assoc Prof	Madsen, Peter C.	D	63C,47,29,49
	Maring, Marvel A.		16
Inst PT	Meints, Ruth	M	62A
Inst PT	Misfeldt, Mark	B	66A
Inst PT	Murray, Dana A.	B	65
Inst PT	Nichols, Cynthia	M	64C
Inst PT	Palmer, Richard	D	61
Inst PT	Pettit, Darren	M	64E,47
Assoc Prof	Roland, Tomm	D	65,20,34H,50
Prof	Saker, James	D	32E,37,60B
Inst PT	Salyards, Shannon	M	61
Inst PT	Scheffler, Jeff E.	B	70
Asst Prof	Snyder, Courtney	D	37
Inst PT	Trussell, Adam		66D
Inst PT	Vondra, Nancy	M	32B
Inst PT	Weiser, Kimberly	M	40,61
Inst PT	Wolcott, William A.	B	62A
Inst PT	Wychulis, Kathleen	M	62E
Inst PT	Yoshida, Ken	B	65

NE0700 Wayne State College

Department of Music
1111 Main St
Wayne, NE 68787
(402) 375-7359   Fax: (402) 375-7460
www.wsc.edu
E-mail: lichris1@wsc.edu

4 Year Institution, Graduate School

Master of Science in Music Education

Chair: Linda Christensen, 80A

Adj	Angeroth, Kathi	B	62
Assoc Prof	Bohnert, David A.	D	63A,60B,37,11,32E
Asst Prof	Calkin, Joshua	M	63D,37,11,49,63C
Adj	Calkin, Lauren	B	65
Assoc Prof	Christensen, Linda	D	66A,66D,34,66B,11
Adj	Derechailo, Melissa	D	63B,11,35
Asst Prof	Hepworth, Elise M.	D	32D,61,32B,32C,11
Adj	Jeffries, Curt	M	11
Adj	Kolbeck, Brandi	M	32B
Asst Prof	Kolbeck, Karl F.	D	12A,72,48,64,11
Assoc Prof	Lofgren, Ronald R.	D	11,32D,36,60A,61
Adj	O'Leary, Jed	M	11
Staff	Pfaltzgraff, Philip	M	66C,11,42,12A
Adj	Weber, Bradley	M	65,50

NE0710 Western Nebraska Comm College

Department of Music
1601 E 27th St
Scottsbluff, NE 69361-1815
(308) 635-6046   Fax: (308) 635-6100
www.wncc.cc.ne.us
E-mail: johnsonn@wncc.edu

2 Year Institution

	Johnson, Nathaniel	D	60,37,64C,64E
Inst	Stinner, Rita	M	13,36,20G

NE0720 York College

Department of Music
1125 E 8th St
York, NE 68467
(402) 363-5610   Fax: (402) 363-5713
www.york.edu
E-mail: croush@york.edu

4 Year Institution

Chair: Clark Roush, 80A

Inst	Dickson, Adrienne	M	61
Inst	Fraser, Amy	B	13C
Inst	Nestor, Gayleen	M	66A
Prof	Roush, Clark	D	11,12A,13A,32C,32B

NH0050 Colby-Sawyer College

Department of Fine & Perf Arts
541 Main St
New London, NH 03257
(603) 526-3661   Fax: (603) 526-2135
www.colby-sawyer.edu
E-mail: colbyweb@colby-sawyer.edu

4 Year Institution

Chair: Brian Clancy, 80A

Adj Asst Prof	Cancio-Bello, Susan	M	11,54,61,36,33
Asst Prof	Robinson, Gary	B	70
Asst Prof	Sanborn, Pamela	B	11

NH0100 Dartmouth College

Department of Music
6187 Hopkins Center
Hanover, NH 03755
(603) 646-2520   Fax: (603) 646-2551
www.dartmouth.edu/~music
E-mail: ted.levin@dartmouth.edu

4 Year Institution, Graduate School

Master of Arts in Digital Musics

Chair: Michael Casey, 80A
Dir., Hopkins Center: Jeffrey H. James, 80F
Dir., Artist/Performance Series: Margaret A. Lawrence, 80F

Lect PT	Atherton, Timothy E.	B	63C,41,42
Lect PT	Baldini, Donald J.	B	62D
Lect PT	Boyer, Neil V.	M	64B
Lect PT	Burkot, Louis G.	D	36,61,39
Lect PT	Carroll, Ed J.	M	63A,41
Asst Prof	Casal, David Plans	D	10B,10F,34,13,35
Prof	Casey, Michael	D	10B,10F,34,13,35
Lect PT	Cassidy, Marcia	M	62A,62B,41
	Cunningham, Walt	B	36
Vstng Prof	Diamond, Jody	M	14,53,43
Assoc Prof	Dong, Kui	D	13,10,20D,45,43
Lect PT	Duff, Robert P.	D	36,60,10A,40,13C
Lect PT	Dunlop, John	M	62C,41
	Fielding, Crystal	B	66F
	Fisken, Patricia B.	M	16
	Glasgo, Don	M	47
Adj Asst Prof	Haas, Frederick L.	B	64E,66A,29A,29B,47

Lect PT	Halloran, Jan	M	64C
Lect PT	Haunton, Thomas C.	B	63B,42
Lect PT	Hayes, Gregory M.	M	66,41,42
Prof	Levin, Theodore C.	D	14
	Marsit, Matthew	B	37
Lect PT	Mellinger, Erma	M	61
Lect PT	Muratore, John D.	M	67A,70
Lect PT	Newsam, David R.	B	47,70
Lect PT	Ogle, Alex	M	64A,41,42
Prof	O'Neal, Melinda P.	D	60,11,36
Lect PT	Perkins, Douglas	D	65,50
Prof	Pinkas, Sally	D	66A,67C
Assoc Prof	Polansky, Larry	M	13,10,45,34
Lect PT	Polk, Janet E.	M	64D,41,42
Lect PT	Princiotti, Anthony F.	D	62A,38
Assoc Prof Adj	Shabazz, Hafiz F.	M	14,50
Assoc Prof	Summers, William J.	D	12A,12,67C
Assoc Prof	Swayne, Steven R.	D	12A,12,39,54
Lect PT	Topel, Spencer	D	10B,10F,34,13,35

NH0110 Franklin Pierce University
Department of Music
40 University Dr
Rindge, NH 03461
(603) 899-4006   Fax: (603) 899-1188
www.franklinpierce.edu
E-mail: scharfpe@franklinpierce.edu

4 Year Institution

Co-Coordinator: David E. Brandes, 80A
Co-Coordinator: Louis Bunk, 80A
Co-Coordinator: Paul E. Scharfenberger, 80A

Prof	Brandes, David E.	M	13,10F,60,36,66G
Asst Prof	Bunk, Louis	M	34,10,11,13,43
Lect	Hyman, Victor G.	B	70
Lect	Johnson, Robert	DIPL	66A
Lect	Nolan, Denise G.	M	48,64A,11,13C
Lect	Oster, Floyd		63A,49
Lect	Page, Richard L.	B	47,64E,29
Lect	Sanchez, Scott	M	70
Assoc Prof	Scharfenberger, Paul E.	M	12,67C,43,55,15
Lect	Schwartz, Cornelia	M	62A
Lect	Sharrock, James	M	64B
Lect	Swist, Christopher	M	65,50
Lect	Yanish, Dorothy	M	61,13C

NH0150 Keene State College
Department of Music
229 Main St
Keene, NH 03435-2402
(603) 358-2177   Fax: (603) 358-2973
www.keene.edu
E-mail: music@keene.edu

4 Year Institution
Member of NASM

Dean: Nona Fienberg, 80A
Chair: Maura Glennon, 80A
Dir., Arts Center: William Menezes

Artist in Res	Baldini, Donald	B	38,47,62D,29A
Adj PT	Boccia, James	M	63A,49
Adj FT	Broad-Ginsberg, Elaine	D	13,31B,10A,36
Asst Prof	Chesebrough, James C.	D	37,60,32,63D,32E
Adj PT	Cohen, Flynn	M	13,12
Adj FT	Cushing, Diane	M	36,61,54,11
Assoc Prof	Darby, Joseph E.	D	12
Adj PT	Flemming, Joy	M	64D,48
Adj PT	Gerstin, Julian	D	20
Asst Prof	Gilligan, Heather M.	DMA	13,10A
Prof	Glennon, Maura	D	66A,66C,66D,66H
Adj PT	Henkel, Sussan	M	64B
Asst Prof	Howard, Sandra	D	32,36,40
Adj PT	Krause-Hardie, Rebecca	B	63B
Prof	Lehman, Carroll	D	40,39,61
Adj PT	Lehninger, Marcia	M	11,20H,62A,62B
Prof	Lezcano, Jose	D	41,70,20H
Artist in Res	Loring, George	M	66A,66B,66D,66H
Adj FT	Mann, Ted	M	70,14C,13D
Adj PT	Matathias, Robin	M	64A,48
Adj PT	Matthews, Andrea	M	13A,32
Adj PT	Mullett, Scott		53,47,29B
Adj PT	Rogers, Timothy	M	66D,11
Adj PT	Stevens, Pamela	B	61
Adj FT	Swist, Christopher	M	50,65,13,10
Prof	Sylvern, Craig	DMA	64E,34,32F,10,48
Adj PT	White, R. Scott	M	66A,66G

NH0250 Plymouth State University
Department of Music, Thtr & Dance
MSC #37
17 High St
Plymouth, NH 03264-1595
(603) 535-2334   Fax: (603) 535-2645
www.plymouth.edu/mtd
E-mail: MTD_dept@mail.plymouth.edu

4 Year Institution

Master of Music in Piano Pedagogy

Chair: Jonathan C. Santore, 80A
Dir., Artist/Performance Series: Diane Jeffrey, 80F
Vice Chair: Kathleen H. Arecchi, 80H

Adj	Alba, James J.		70
Prof	Arecchi, Kathleen H.	D	61,54
Other	Blood, Charles F.	M	66C
Adj	Boccia, James	M	63A
Lect	Chesebrough, Constance D.	M	66C,66A
Adj	Cole, Victoria	M	61
Adj	Coppola, A. J.	B	64D
Prof	Corcoran, Gary J.	D	37,60B,63A,32E
Adj	Corcoran, Kenda	M	64B
Other	DiBiase, Allan	D	66C
Adj	Dionne, Aubrie	B	64A
Adj	Ellsworth, Rodger		62
Adj	Gibson, Deborah	M	64C
Adj	Gilmore, Timothy	B	50,65
Prof	Graff, Carleen	D	66A,66D,66B
Adj	Masterson, Kyle	M	61
Other	McCarthy, Justin	D	66C
Adj	Melloni, Romeo	M	13
Adj	Munton, Amanda	M	61
Lect	Oliver, Holly E.	M	32B,32C,13A
Prof	Perkins, Daniel R.	D	36,61,12A,32D,60A
Prof	Pfenninger, Rik C.	D	64E,29,35,32E,10B
Adj	Robinson, Thomas S.	B	66A,46,47,29
Prof	Santore, Jonathan C.	D	13,10
Prof	Swift, Robert F.	D	11,32,36
Adj	Templeton, Peter	B	66A,66D
Adj	Ward, Margaret S.	B	63B
Other	Whitworth, Amanda E.	M	52
Adj	Williams, Don	M	62D

NH0300 Rivier College
Department of Art
420 Main St
Nashua, NH 03060-5086
(603) 897-8276   Fax: (603) 897-8817
www.rivier.edu
E-mail: cldavis@rivier.edu

4 Year Institution

Coordinator: Clifford Davis, 80A

Lect	Adams, Gerard	B	70
Lect	Cannava, Ruth	M	11
Lect	Cavanar, Mary	M	32
Prof	Couture, Marie	M	11,16
Lect	Harvey, Anne	B	66A
Lect	Koenig, Chris	M	11
Lect	LeBlond, Gerald	M	66A,66B
Lect	McCartney, Lynn R.	M	61,11
Lect	Oliver, Brenda	M	11,32
Lect	Polcari, Jeanne	M	66A,66B,10A

NH0310 St Anselm College
Department of Fine Arts
100 St Anselm Dr
Manchester, NH 03102
(603) 641-7000   Fax: (603) 641-7116
www.anselm.edu
E-mail: lcleveland@anselm.edu

4 Year Institution

Chair: Lisa A. Cleveland, 80A

PT	Camera, Bede C.	M	36
Asst Prof	Cleveland, Lisa A.	D	13,11,29A,66
Asst Prof	Parr, Sean M.	D	12

NH0350 Univ of New Hampshire
Department of Music
Paul Creative Art Center
30 Academic Way
Durham, NH 03824
(603) 862-2404   Fax: (603) 862-3155
www.unh.edu/music
E-mail: nicholas.orovich@unh.edu

4 Year Institution, Graduate School
Member of NASM

Master of Arts in Music

Chair: Nicholas Orovich, 80A
Dir., Graduate Programs: Daniel Beller-McKenna, 80C
Dir., Admissions: Alexis Zaricki, 80D
Coord., Music Events: Susan Adams, 80F
Dir., Center for Teaching Excellence: Victor Benassi

Assoc Prof	Annicchiarico, Michael	D	13B,13C,13E,10
Res Artist	Baker, Sharon	M	61
Assoc Prof	Beller-McKenna, Daniel	D	12A,12C,11,14C
Res Artist	Betts, Kendall	B	63B
Res Artist	Blood, Elizabeth P.	D	66C,66D
Assoc Prof	Boysen, Andrew A.	D	37,60B,10F
Res Artist	Bravar, Mimi	D	62B,41
Assoc Prof	Cook, Jenni	D	61,11
Assoc Prof	DeTurk, Mark	D	32C,32E,32G
Assoc Prof	Dobbins, Lori E.	D	13B,11
Assoc Prof Emerita	Edward, Ruth	M	66A,66B
Assoc Prof	Eshbach, Robert	M	11,62A,41
Lect	Goodwin, Casey S.	M	37,32D,47,60B
Asst Prof	Gunlogson, Elizabeth	D	64C,13B
Res Artist	Harris, Les	B	65
Asst Prof	Haskins, Robert	D	12A
Res Artist	Herlehy, Margaret	B	64B
Res Artist	Hunter, John	B	62D
Prof	Kempster, William G.	D	36,32C
Lect	Kies, Arlene	M	66A,66B,66C
Prof	Kies, Christopher	D	13B,10,66A,13F
Res Artist	Merrill, Paul	M	66C,66D
Res Artist	Newsam, David R.	B	70
Adj	Noseworthy, Susan	M	32B
Prof	Orovich, Nicholas	M	13C,37,63C,63D
Res Artist	Polk, Janet	M	64D,48
Prof Emeritus	Polk, Keith	D	11,12A,12C,63B
Lect	Pruiksma, Rose	D	12
Prof	Ripley, David	M	61,39
Prof Emeritus	Rogers, John E.	M	13B,10,13D,13E,13G
Prof	Seiler, David E.	M	47,48,64C
Res Artist	Shilansky, Mark G.	M	66A
Assoc Prof Emeritus	Sir, Neil	M	10A,13
Res Artist	Smith, Nancy A.	B	50,65
Res Artist	Sokolov-Grubb, Silvana I.	M	66C,66D
Prof	Stibler, Robert	D	11,63A,67C,49,67E
Lect	Upham, David	D	38
Assoc Prof	Urquhart, Peter W.	D	12C,13B,12A
Prof	Vagts, Peggy A.	M	64A
Assoc Prof	Veal, Larry	M	11,62C,13A,41
Lect	Vigil, Ryan H.	M	13
Assoc Prof Emeritus	Wing, Henry	D	36,40,61
Lect	Zielinski, Mark D.	M	32

NJ0020 Bergen Community College
Div of Arts, Humanities & Wellness
400 Paramus Rd
Paramus, NJ 07652-1508
(201) 447-9279   Fax: (201) 612-5240
www.bergen.edu
E-mail: lmarcel@bergen.edu

2 Year Institution

Dean: Amparo Codding, 80A
Academic Chair: Linda A. Marcel, 80A

Asst Prof	Amico, Stephen	D	11,14
Asst Prof	Krikun, Andrew		35A,10D,47,14,20
Prof	Marcel, Linda A.	D	12B,66A,66D,32,11
Asst Prof	Sheehan, Dan		35,35G

NJ0030 Brookdale Community College
Department of Music
765 Newman Springs Rd
Lincroft, NJ 07738-1543
ux.brookdalecc.edu/fac/music/
E-mail: jaccurso@brookdale.cc.nj.us

2 Year Institution

Chair: Joseph Accurso, 80A

Assoc Prof	Accurso, Joseph	M	13A,13,60,10,35B
Prof	Benham, Helen	M	13A,66A,66H,66B,66C

NJ0050 Caldwell College
Department of Music
120 Bloomfield Ave
Caldwell, NJ 07006-6109
(973) 618-3587   Fax: (973) 618-3467
www.caldwell.edu
E-mail: nchildress@caldwell.edu

4 Year Liberal Arts Institution

Chair: Nan Childress Orchard, 80A
Dir., Admissions: Rebecca Vega, 80D
Dir., Artist Series: Laura Greenwald, 80F

Adj	Charsky, Thomas	M	32B,11
Assoc Prof	Childress Orchard, Nan	D	66,13,54
Prof	Greenwald, Laura	D	36,13C,61,39
Prof	Middleton, Robert M.	M	47,29,64,13,11
Adj	Orchard, Joseph T.	D	12A
Adj	Rafal, Jeremy	D	11,20
Inst FT	Vega, Rebecca	M	32,37,11,64A,60B
Adj	Wramage, Gregg	D	10A,10F,11

NJ0060 Camden County College
Department of Music
PO Box 200
Blackwood, NJ 08012-0200
(856)227-7200   Fax: (856) 374-4969
www.camdencc.edu
E-mail: jrowlands@camdencc.edu

2 Year Institution

Assistant Dean: Judith Rowlands, 80H

	Billingsley, Michael		13,12A

NJ0100 Centenary College
Department of Music
207 Main St
Hackettstown, NJ 07840-2100
(908)852-1400
www.centenarycollege.edu
E-mail: wallnauc@centenarycollege.edu

4 Year Institution

Adj Prof	Idenden, John	M	13A,11,12A,61,66A

NJ0175 The College of New Jersey
Department of Music
PO Box 7718
Ewing, NJ 08628-0718
(609) 771-2552 or 2551   Fax: (609) 637-5182
www.tcnj.edu/~music
E-mail: music@tcnj.edu

4 Year Institution
Member of NASM

Chair: Gary Fienberg, 80A
Dean, School of Arts & Communications: John C. Laughton, 80A
Interim Dean, School of Arts & Communications: Taras Pavlovsky, 80A
Program Admissions: Susan O'Connor, 80D

PT	Alms, Anthony	D	12A
PT	Amoriello, Laura	M	66A
PT	Balog, George	M	37,32
PT	Blose, Dennis	M	37,32
PT	Brown, Brian	M	63D,41
PT	Chao, Joanna K.	D	66A,13C,13B
PT	Clark, Chris	M	62D
PT	Conklin, Michael	M	11,29A
PT	Day, James G.	M	32E
PT	Day, James M.	D	70,42
PT	Demitry, E. Hope	M	32
Other	Dempf, Linda	D	16
PT	DiGiacobbe, David	M	64A,41
PT	Donald, Scott	D	66A
Asst Prof	Fienberg, Gary	D	63A,29A,47,49
PT	Gale, Robert	B	63C
Assoc Prof	Guarino, Robert	M	61,55,39
Asst Prof	Guerrini, Susan C.	D	32
PT	Hala, James	B	63A
Assoc Prof	Heisler, Wayne H.	D	12A,14,20
Assoc Prof	Hickman, Suzanne L.	D	61
	Holland, Margaret	M	32
PT	Hughes, Winston	M	32
Other	Kalinowski, Mark		35C,35G
Asst Prof	Kanamaru, Tomoko	D	66A,66B,66C,66D
Other	Kroth, Richard	B	35E,35D
PT	MacMullin, Dennis	M	64D,32
PT	Mao, Ruotao	M	62A,62B,42
FT	McDonnell, John	M	36,32
Assoc Prof	McKinney, Roger W.	M	64C,12A,48
Prof	McMahan, Robert Y.	D	13B,13C,13F,10B,10A
PT	Mehrtens, Kathryn	M	63B
Asst Prof Emeritus	Mendoza, Michael D.	D	60A,32D,36
PT	Mitchell, Kathleen	M	64E
PT	Moliterno, Mark	D	61
PT	Moyer, Kathryn	M	61
Asst Prof	Nakra, Teresa Marrin	D	13,34,10B
Other	O'Connor, Susan	M	
Prof Emeritus	Parrish, Robert E.	D	54,34
PT	Recktenwald, Karl	M	32
	Reimer, Robert	M	32
Asst Prof	Russell, Ralph Anthony	D	13,29A,12E
PT	Schneider, David	B	64B
PT	Sciarrotta, Jo-Ann	M	32
Asst Prof Emeritus	Silvester, William	D	60B,32,37
PT	Sirbaugh, Nora	D	61
PT	Suabedissen, Gary	M	32
PT	Szepessy, David	M	62C
PT	Tarantiles, Andre	M	62E
Asst Prof	Tate, Philip	D	38,60B,32
PT	Trigg, William	M	65,41
PT	Wilkinson, Carlton J.	D	13

NJ0200 College of St Elizabeth
Department of Music
2 Convent Rd
Morristown, NJ 07960
(973) 539-1600
www.cse.edu
E-mail: twalters@cse.edu

4 Year Institution

Chair: Teresa Walters, 80A

	Alvey, Mary		66A
Asst Prof	Caputo, Michael		12A,14,37,64,20G
Inst	Cluthe, Betty		61
Inst	Grayson, W. Norman	M	66A,66G
Inst	Oddsen, Kristine		64A
Inst	Ruggles, Patricia		61
Assoc Prof	Walters, Teresa	D	13,60,11,12A,36

NJ0250 County College of Morris
Department of Music
214 Center Grove Rd
Randolph, NJ 07869
(973) 328-5430   Fax: (973) 328-5445
www.ccm.edu
E-mail: scook@ccm.edu

2 Year Institution

Chair: Marielaine Mammon, 80A

Prof	Caputo, Michael		12A,14,37,48,64
Prof	Gorman, John	M	13,66A
Prof	Gradone, Richard		13,12A,12,47,63A
Prof	Mammon, Marielaine	M	12A,32,36,41,61

NJ0300 Drew University
Department of Music
36 Madison Ave
Madison, NJ 07940
(973) 408-3422   Fax: (973) 408-3768
www.depts.drew.edu/music
E-mail: tweston@drew.edu

4 Year Institution

Dean: Paolo Cucchi, 80A
Chair: Trevor L. Weston, 80A
Dean, Admissions: Mary Beth Carey, 80D
Dir., Artist/Performance Series: Lydia Hailparn Ledeen, 80F
Dir., Cont. Ed & Special Programs: Cathy Messmer, 80F
Dir., Inst/Fest/Wksp/Summer Music: Virginia Schulze-Johnson, 80F
Associate Dean: Edward Domber, 80H
Associate Dean, Theological School: Anne B. Yardley, 80H

Adj Asst Prof	Carter, Elise		64A
Adj Lect	Hilton, Ellis		
Adj Lect	Iskowitz, David		
Prof	Ledeen, Lydia Hailparn	D	11,12A,15,12C
Prof	Lowrey, Norman E.	D	13A,13,10,45,34
Assoc Prof	Nair, Garyth	M	36,38,61,60,13C
Adj	Riffel, William	M	70,53
Adj Lect	Saltzman, James A.		64E,29,13C
Adj Asst Prof	Schulze-Johnson, Virginia	D	41,47,48,64A,42
Asst Prof	Sprout, Leslie A.	PhD	12A,12C,13A,12
Assoc Prof	Weston, Trevor L.	D	11,20B,13,10
Prof	Yardley, Anne B.	D	12,14,31,55

NJ0400 Fairleigh Dickinson Univ-Madison
Department of Visual & Perf. Arts
285 Madison Ave
Madison, NJ 07940
(973) 443-8638
www.fduarts.org
E-mail: alcmusic@fdu.edu

4 Year Institution

Music Contact: Allen L. Cohen, 80A

Prof	Cohen, Allen L.	DMA	13,10,54,39,36
PT	Girardi, Steve	M	70
PT	Karpatova, Mariana	M	61
PT	Parrish, Clifford	M	66
PT	Stanley, Justin	D	64C

NJ0500 Felician College
Department of Art & Music
262 S Main St
Lodi, NJ 07644-2117
(201) 559-6150
www.felician.edu
E-mail: gordonb@felician.edu

4 Year Institution

Chair: Barbara N. Gordon, 80A

Adj	Anderson, Matthew	M	13A
Adj	Conti, Michael	D	13A,13C
Adj	Estavez, Evelyn	B	62A
Adj	Fanella, Keith	B	70
Assoc Prof	Gordon, Barbara N.	PhD	11,36,60A,66D,61
Adj	Mihalik, Denise	M	61
Adj	Moore, Corey	M	47,60,64E
Adj	Pike, Lisa	D	63B
Adj	Suzuki, Yuko	M	66A
Asst Prof	Thompson, Douglas S.	D	13,10,12A,34
Adj	Zarro, Domenico E.	D	50,65

NJ0550 Georgian Court University
Department of Art & Music
900 Lakewood Ave
Lakewood, NJ 08701
(732) 987-2624   Fax: (732) 987-2058
www.georgian.edu
E-mail: jzec@georgian.edu

4 Year Institution

Program Director: John Zec, 80A

Adj Lect	Appello, Patrick	M	70,67G,13B,13A,12A
PT	Arndt, Wayne	M	62C
Lect	Dohrmann, Diana	D	32C,32D
Lect	Finkelstein, Marc	D	32A,32B,66A,70
Lect	Kadetsky, Mark	D	62D,51,11
PT	Kovalsky, Vladislav D.	D	66A
Lect	LaGruth, Anthony	M	11
Lect	Lesser, Jeffrey	M	32E,63,10,32C,32F
Lect	Levine, Barry	M	11,64C,64E,29A
Lect	Malamut, Myra Lewinter	M	11,64A,67B,20G,13A
	Mattox, Zeritta		36
Lect	McGee-Daly, Kathleen	M	62A,62B
Lect	Mulhall, Karen	B	36,66A
Lect	Myers-Tegeder, Christine	M	11,60
Inst	Pillion, Ed	B	65
Lect	Schoenberg, Kathe	M	61,36
Inst	Stauch, Michael	B	66A,66G
Lect	Williamson, Steven C.	M	60A,61,36
Lect	Wittemann, Wilbur	B	37,63,47,60B
Lect	Zec, John	D	12A,31,66G,13,11

NJ0700 Kean University
Conservatory of Music
1000 Morris Ave
Union, NJ 07083
(908) 737-4330   Fax: (908) 737-4333
www.kean.edu/KU/Music
E-mail: music@kean.edu

4 Year Institution
Member of NASM

Dean: George Z. Arasimowicz, 80A
Chair & Dir., Concert Artist Program: Anthony Scelba, 80A,80F
Dir., Preparatory Division: Kathryn Roselli, 80E
Dir., Summer Programs: Susannah Chapman, 80G
Assistant Chair: Lyn Schraer-Joiner, 80H

PT	Adams, Elma	M	66D
Applied Artist	Ahuvia, Saar	M	66C,11
PT	Anderson, Lois	M	66A
Affiliate Artist	Andrews, Deborah	D	61,54
PT	Avidon, Scott	M	11
Concert Artist	Baek, Na-Young	D	62C
Concert Artist	Banaszek, Maurycy	M	62B
Applied Artist	Bedo, Maria	M	61
Applied Artist	Bove, Andrew	M	63D
Applied Artist	Bryant, Jerry	M	63A
Concert Artist	Bumcrot, Charles	B	63A,49,11
Applied Artist	Byun, Jin Hwan	M	61
Concert Artist	Caballero, Jorge	M	70,51
PT	Calderone, Kathleen	M	11
Concert Artist	Chapman, Susannah	D	62C,42,11
Assoc Prof	Chen-Hafteck, Lily	D	32
Applied Artist	Cohen, Lynne	M	64B,11
Concert Artist	Cohen, Warren	M	38
Asst Prof	Connors, Thomas	D	37,11,32E,60B
PT	Daly, Kathleen	B	62A,32E,11
Concert Artist	Frankel, Joanna	M	62A,62B,42
Concert Artist	Franzetti-Brewster, Allison	M	66C,41,13A,13B,13C
Concert Artist	Fusco, Andrew	B	64E,47,29,46
PT	Getke, Richard	M	54
PT	Hafteck, Pierre	M	11,46,47
Prof	Halper, Matthew R.	D	10,13,34
Concert Artist	Hansen, Lisa	M	64A,42
Concert Artist	Harris, Katherine	M	61
Affiliate Artist	Hermalyn, Joy	M	61
Applied Artist	Herr, Andrea	M	64D
Applied Artist	Ho, Stephanie	M	66A,66C,11
Concert Artist	Hobson, Richard	M	61
Affiliate Artist	Hudson, Hope A.	D	61,54
Concert Artist	Kim, Andrea	M	66A
PT	Kroik, Anna	M	66D
PT	Langan, David	M	61
PT	Lenney, James	M	11,32
PT	Leshowitz, Myron	M	66D
PT	Lorenzetti, Kristen	M	11,32
Prof	Marchena, Martha	D	66A,66C
Concert Artist	Martinez, Gabriela	M	66A,66D,42
Applied Artist	Mazzocchi, Anthony	M	63C,63D
Applied Artist	McKenzie-Stubbs, Mary E.	M	61,11
Concert Artist	Milovanovic, Biljana	D	66A,66H,13C
PT	Moulton, Elizabeth	M	11
Concert Artist	Musto, James	M	65,50
PT	Noble, Jason L.	M	11
PT	Pearson, Holly	B	11
PT	Pike, Lisa	D	63B,11
PT	Rocco, Robert	M	11,13A,13B,10A
Applied Artist	Rodriquez, Jose	M	62D
PT	Roselli, Kathryn	B	
Prof	Scelba, Anthony	D	12A,13E,11,62D
Asst Prof	Schraer-Joiner, Lyn	D	32,11,13A,60
Concert Artist	Sobieski, Dorothy	D	38
Applied Artist	Sokol, Jill	M	63A
Concert Artist	Stewart, Victoria	M	62A,42
PT	Svorinich, Victor	M	11
Concert Artist	Sweet, Brennan	M	62A,42
Prof	Terenzi, Mark J.	D	36,40,60A,13C
Applied Artist	Thoma, James	M	65
PT	Turrin, Joseph	B	10,10C
PT	Van Hoven, Valerie	B	61,54
	Van Kekerix, Todd	M	66A,66D
PT	Yoselevich, Gerald	M	11

NJ0750 Mercer County Community College
Department of Music
PO Box B
Trenton, NJ 08690-0182
(609) 570-3716   Fax: (609) 570-3834
www.mccc.edu
E-mail: kellyj@mccc.edu

2 Year Institution

Chair: James J. Kelly, 80A

Adj Inst	Allesee, Eric	M	66A,13C
Adj Inst	Corvino, William	B	11,70
Adj Inst	Gottlieb, David	M	10,13A,13B,34D,64E
Adj Prof	Grubb, Jay	JD	14C,35A
Adj Inst	Hornick, Scott J.	M	62D
Adj Prof	Jurcisin, Mark	D	10,13A,13B,13C,11
Prof	Kelly, James J.	M	12A,13,29A,47,70
Adj Inst	Kramer, Steven	B	66A
Prof	Kulpa, John	D	11,13A,13B,13C
Adj Inst	Mekler, Joseph	B	65,50
Adj Prof	Mowitz, Ira	M	10,13A,13B,41,66A
Adj Inst	Robinson-Martin, Trineice	D	11,12A,29,61
Adj Inst	Seeman, Sharon	B	64A,64B,64C,64D,11
Adj Prof	Sharples, Pamela	M	13C,36,66A,66C
Adj Prof	Sirbaugh, Nora	D	12A,39,61
Adj Inst	Tsai, Kevin		62A
Adj Prof	Woodruff, Louis	D	60,11,37

NJ0760 Monmouth University
Department of Music/Theatre Arts
400 Cedar Ave
West Long Branch, NJ 07764
(732) 571-3442   Fax: (732) 263-5330
www.monmouth.edu
E-mail: dtripold@monmouth.edu

4 Year Institution

Chair: David Tripold, 80A

Adj	Baer-Peterson, Jamie	M	61
	Boyd, Bob	M	65
	Dubois, Laura	M	10A,11,32E,66
Adj	Foster, Linda	M	66A,66D
Prof	Frangipane, Ron	M	13,10F,60,10,12A
Prof	Gillette, Michael	M	11,62E,32E
Adj	Jenner, Bryan	M	11,37
Adj	Jupinka, Nick	M	66A
Adj	Leone, Aaron	M	70
Adj	Muller, Marc	M	61
Adj	Myrick, Kathleen	M	61
Adj	Powers, Kathleen	M	66A
Prof	Rotella, Gloria	D	32,66A,66D
Adj	Scialla, Carmen J.	D	11
Adj	Synott, Adrian	M	62D
Adj	Tafrow, Tony	M	63
Assoc Prof	Tripold, David	PhD	13,12A,32,31A,33
Adj	Tupik, Justin	M	70
Adj	Wilson, Mark	M	61,13A
Prof	Wurzbach, George	M	34,35

NJ0800 Montclair State University

John J. Cali School of Music
One Valley Rd
Montclair, NJ 07043
(973) 655-7212   Fax: (973) 655-5279
www.montclair.edu/music
E-mail: music@mail.montclair.edu

4 Year Institution, Graduate School
Member of NASM

One Year Performer's Certificate, Artist Diploma, Master of Arts in Performance, Master of Arts in Music Education, Master of Arts in Music Therapy, Master of Arts in Music Theory-Composition

Academic Administrator: Gina L. Balestracci, 80B,80C,80D,80G
Dir., Preparatory Division: Marla Meissner, 80E
Dir., Preparatory Division: Letitia G. Stancu, 80E
Concert Manager: Martha L. Learner, 80F

Rank	Name	Degree	Codes
Assoc Prof	Abrams, Brian	D	33
Inst PT	Adelson, Andrew D.	M	64A
Inst PT	Alesi-Pazian, Melody	M	11
Asst Prof	Axelson, Shelley	D	32,64
Inst PT	Baer, Seth R.	M	64D
Inst PT	Baltazar, Crystl S.	M	66B,66C
Inst PT	Batchelder, Donald	M	63A,49
Inst PT	Benson, Steve C.	M	70,47
Inst PT	Bernhardt, Valerie	M	61
Inst PT	Billman, Nancy S.	M	63B
Inst PT	Brown, Kevin E.	M	62D
Asst Prof	Buchanan, Heather J.	M	32D,36,40,60A
Inst PT	Bumcrot, Charles F.	M	63A
Inst PT	Burnett, J.D.	M	32D,60A
Adj	Burns, Patrick J.	M	13A,13,10
Adj	Butts, Robert W.	M	11
Inst PT	Centanni, Barry C.	M	65
Inst PT	Cinelli, Dennis J.	M	67G,70
Adj	Clarkson, Amy LYN	M	33
Adj	Coco, Joseph W.	M	11
Inst PT	Cohen, Paul	D	64E,48
Adj	Colson, Steve	M	20,66D
Inst PT	Cordell, Angela	M	63B
Prof	Craig, Mary Ann	D	32,37,63D,49
Inst PT	Cukrov, Martina	M	66C
Inst PT	Cukrov, Terezija	M	66C
Inst PT	Darling, Sandra	M	61
Prof	Delorenzo, Lisa	D	32,66D
Inst PT	Dibari, Keriann K.	M	42,64C
Asst Prof	Dolp, Laura A.	D	12
Assoc Prof	Drummond, Dean J.	M	13,43,10
Adj	Ellias, Marjorie K.	M	33
Inst PT	Ernest, Lorraine K.	M	61
Adj	Farrell, Diane	M	11
Inst PT	Ferber, Alan D.	M	63C
Inst PT	Franzetti, Allison G.	M	66C
Prof	Gall, Jeffrey C.	M	55,61,12A,12,39
Inst PT	Gillis, Peter R.	D	61
Assoc Prof	Goodman, Karen D.	M	33
Inst PT	Ham, Jason D.	M	63D
Inst PT	Hart, Billy W.	M	65,29C
Inst PT	Heller, Marsha	M	48,64B
Prof	Ho, Ting	D	13,10,45,43
Inst PT	Hogan, Lisa	M	11
Asst Prof	James, Clay	D	54
Other	Jiang, Yi-wen	DIPL	62A,42
Asst Prof	Jodoin, Aaron D.	M	46
Inst PT	Johns, Steven S.	M	65,47
Inst PT	Kebuladze, Tatyana	M	66A,66D,66C
Inst PT	Kim, Mansoon H.	D	66B,66C
Inst PT	Kim, Soyeon	M	66C
Inst PT	Kolker, Siobhan	M	61
Inst PT	Korneev, Dmitri V.	M	66C
Inst PT	Kucharsky, Boris	M	62A,42
Assoc Prof	Kunkel, Jeffrey	D	32,47,29,53,46
Inst PT	Lamar, Gregory A.	M	61
Inst PT	Larkin, Christopher J.	M	39
Other	Li, Honggang	DIPL	62B,42,62A
Other	Li, Weigang	DIPL	62A,42
Inst PT	Lipsey, Michael S.	M	65,50
Adj	Lopato, David	M	29A
Inst PT	Lord, Albert P.	M	66F
Inst PT	Louprette, Renee A.	D	66G
Inst PT	Mallimo, Katherine	M	66C
Adj	Manzo, V.J.	M	34
Adj	Markiewicz, Larry	M	32E
Inst PT	Mazzocchi, Anthony J.	M	63C,49
Asst Prof	McCauley, Thomas E.	D	37,60B,32
Inst PT	McKnight, Linda	M	62D,51
Inst PT	Meissner, Marla	D	13A,13,20G
Inst PT	Mills, Jesse A.	M	42,62A
Inst PT	Minichiello, Molly J.	M	32E
Inst PT	Moring, Bill F.	M	46,47,62D
Inst PT	Mulvaney, Thomas	M	65
Adj	Mumm, Daniel C.	DIPL	32E
Adj	Olsen, Eric	D	13A,13B,13C,66D
Inst PT	O'Neill, Darren D.	M	70,12C
Asst Prof	Oosting, Stephen	D	61,54
Inst PT	Overton, LeAnn L.	M	66C
Inst PT	Pakman, Mark	M	66A,66C
Inst PT	Palatucci, John	M	63D
Inst PT	Palma, Susan	M	64A,42
Adj	Parody, Caroline D.	M	66D,61
Inst PT	Pinto, Mary	M	66C
Adj	Reich, Amy J.	D	13A,13B,13C
Prof	Rendleman, Ruth	D	13,66A,66B
Asst Prof	Richards, Scott D.	M	10D,13B,13C,54
Inst PT	Rivera, Jennifer M.	M	61
Inst PT	Ross, Holli	M	40,61
Inst PT	Ryan, Steven	M	66C
Inst PT	Samaras, Stephanie	M	61
Inst PT	Scott, Jeffrey	M	63B,42
Inst PT	Searing, Harry G.	M	64D
Inst PT	Shih, Gloria	M	66C
Inst PT	Shrut, Arlene	M	66C
Prof	Singer, David	DIPL	41,48,64C,11
Inst PT	Smith, James	M	66C
Adj	Smith, Joseph R.	D	11
Inst PT	Smylie, Dennis H.	M	64C,42
Adj	Stancu, Letitia G.	M	11
Inst PT	Stewart, Peter A.	B	61
Inst PT	Swope, Anastasia E.	M	61
Inst PT	Tarantiles, Andre C.	M	62E
Inst PT	Toth, Gwen J.	M	66H
Inst PT	Turner, Kyle	M	63D,42
Adj	Turrin, Joseph E.	M	11,13,10C
Other	Tzavaras, Nicholas G.	DIPL	62C,42
Adj	Valiente, Jessica L.	M	20
Adj	VanHoven, Valerie S.	M	61
Inst PT	Wilson, James	M	61
Inst PT	Witek, Tanya D.	M	64A
Assoc Prof	Witten, David	D	13B,12A,66A,66B,66C
Adj	Yun, Francis Y.	D	13A,13B,13C

NJ0825 New Jersey City University

Department of Music/Dance/Theatre
2039 Kennedy Blvd
Jersey City, NJ 07305-1597
(201) 200-3151   Fax: (201) 200-3130
www.njcu.edu
E-mail: mkim@njcu.edu

4 Year Institution, Graduate School
Member of NASM

Master of Arts in Music Education, Master of Music in Performance

Dean: Barbara Feldman, 80A
Chair: Min Kim, 80A

Rank	Name	Degree	Codes
Asst Prof	Baker, Wilbur	D	11,32
Asst Prof	Bernard, Gilles	D	13,12A,49,63C,63D
Adj	Burns, Patrick	M	37
Asst Prof	Connolly, Donna	D	39,40,54,61
Adj	Cornut, Sebastien	M	66,66A,66C
Adj	Crawford, Steven		66C
Asst Prof	Crespo, Fabra Desamparados	D	10,13,34
Asst Prof	Dalio, Marc G.	M	54,61
Adj	DiPinto, John	M	54
Prof	Dubbiosi, Stelio	D	13,10F,66A,66G
Adj	Duran, Amy	M	54
Adj	Eulau, Andrew	M	29,62D
Adj	Farnham, Allen	M	29A,29B
Adj	Fink, Kathleen	M	64A,41
Adj	Firestone, Adria	M	39,61
Adj	Foerster, Frank	M	62A,62B
Adj	Forderhase, Jerry	D	61
Adj	Giannascoli, B. Greg	M	65
Adj	Goetz, Sariva		54
Adj	Green, Maria	M	11,32
Adj	Hammond, Gary	M	66C
Adj	Hancock, John		61
Adj	Heckman, Rick	M	64
Adj	Heller, Marsha	M	64B
Adj	Herr, Andrea	M	64D
Adj	Hirsch, Michael	M	10,54
Adj	Horner, Tim	M	29,65
Adj	Hunter, Billy	M	63A
Adj	Janelli, Ron	M	64
Prof	Joffe, Edward	D	41,47,48,64
Adj	Kelly, Sondra		61
Adj	Kent, Adam	D	66A,42
Adj	Ketter, Craig	M	66A,66C,42
Adj	Kim, Lisa	M	62A
Assoc Prof	Kim, Min	D	13,12,66A,66B,41
Adj	Kim, Yong Tae	M	41,62A
Adj	Kirchner, William	M	29A
Adj	Kosma, Lou	M	38

Adj	Lee, Christopher		62A
Adj	LeMay, Lisa A.		61
Assoc Prof	Lowenthal, Richard	M	63A,53,46,29
Adj	Magnarelli, Joe	M	29,63A
Adj	Maiullo, David	M	66C
Adj	Malach, Robert	M	64E
Adj	Mayfield, David C.	M	66C
Adj	McConnell, Michele	M	61
Adj	McDevitt, Duane		54
Adj	Meyers, Paul	M	70,29
Adj	Miller, Richard		70
Adj	Mina, Niloofar	M	20
Adj	Moe, Sharon	M	63B
Adj	Morales-Matos, Rolando		65
Adj	Morino, Ayako	M	66A,42
Adj	Mosello, Joe	M	63A
Adj	Nicolson, Mark	M	61
Adj	Pato-Lorenzo, Cristina	D	61
Adj	Peck, Daniel	M	63D
Adj	Phillips, Patricia		61
Asst Prof	Prowse, Robert W.	D	36,40,61,12A
Adj	Rezende Lopes, Joao Luiz	M	70
Adj	Robertson, Paul	M	65,11
Adj	Roldan, Francisco		70
Asst Prof	Romeo, Robert	M	50,65
Asst Prof	Rosado, Ana Maria	D	70,41,11,12A
Adj	Rowell, Frances	M	62C
Adj	Schwartz, Andrew	M	35
Adj	Sherman, Mark	M	65B
Adj	Shin, Aera	M	66A,42
Adj	Smith, Arnold	M	29A
Adj	Spinetti, Sharon		61
Adj	Venable, Catherine Anne	M	66C
Adj	Vitro-Wickliffe, Roseanne		29,61
Assoc Prof	Warren, Maredia D. L.	D	13,11,32
Adj	Wilson, Jeanne	M	64A,48
Adj	Zaidan, Raouf G.	D	61

NJ0850 Princeton Theological Seminary
Department of Music
PO Box 821
Princeton, NJ 08542-0803
(609) 497-7890   Fax: (609) 497-7893
www.ptsem.edu
E-mail: martin.tel@ptsem.edu

2 Year Institution

	Tel, Martin	M	36,66G,31A

NJ0900 Princeton University
Department of Music
310 Woolworth Ctr
Princeton, NJ 08544-1007
(609) 258-4241   Fax: (609) 258-6793
www.music.princeton.edu
E-mail: mham@princeton.edu

4 Year Institution, Graduate School

PhD in Historical Musicology, PhD in Music Theory, PhD in Composition, MFA in Composition, MFA in Historical Musicology, MFA in Music Theory

Chair: Steven Mackey, 80A
Dir., Admissions & Graduate Studies: Wendy B. Heller, 80C,80D
Dir., Admissions & Graduate Studies: Barbara A. White, 80C,80D
Department Manager: Marilyn Ham

Prof	Agawu, V. Kofi	D	12
Prof Emeritus	Babbitt, Milton	M	13,10
Senior Lect	Branker, Anthony D.J.	M	47,29,46
Prof	Burnham, Scott	D	13,12A
Assoc Prof	Heller, Wendy B.	D	12A,12,39,14A
Lect	Isaacs, Robert		36,61
Prof Emeritus	Jeffery, Peter	D	11,12A,12,31A
Prof	Lansky, Paul	D	13,10,45,34
Prof Emeritus	Levy, Kenneth	D	11,12A,12
Prof	Mackey, Steven	D	13,10F,10,11,41
Asst Prof	Manabe, Noriko	D	12
Prof	Morrison, Simon	D	13,12A,12,11
Senior Lect	Pratt, Michael	B	60,38,43,39
Prof Emeritus	Randall, James K.	M	13,10
Prof Emeritus	Spies, Claudio	M	13,60,10,39
Senior Lect	TangYuk, Richard		36,39,40
Assoc Prof	Trueman, Daniel		13,10B,10
Assoc Prof	Tymoczko, Dmitri		13
Assoc Prof	Wegman, Rob		11,12A,12,20G
Prof Emeritus	Westergaard, Peter	M	13,60,10,39
Assoc Prof	White, Barbara A.	D	13A,10,13,10F,43

NJ0950 Ramapo College of New Jersey
School of Contemporary Arts
505 Ramapo Valley Rd
Mahwah, NJ 07430-1623
(201) 684-7368   Fax: (201) 684-7598
www.ramapo.edu
E-mail: rojohnso@ramapo.edu

4 Year Institution

Chair: Roger O. Johnson, 80A
Dean: Steven Perry, 80A

Asst Prof	Brandon, Mack	M	10B,31F,36,41
Adj	Cohen, Alan	M	34D,35G
Adj	Cotroneo, P. J.	M	29,70,13
Assoc Prof	Fikentscher, Kai	D	14,20,45
Prof	Johnson, Roger O.	M	12,14C,35A
Assoc Prof	Jones, Arnold	M	13,20G
Asst Prof	Lutter, Lisa	D	36,61,54,12A
Adj	Schlicht, Ursel	D	13,14,15,53
Adj	Sorce, Richard P.	D	10D,13,34D
Adj	Washington, Shirley	M	35

NJ0975 Raritan Valley Community College
Department of Visual & Perf Arts
PO Box 3300
Somerville, NJ 08876-1265
(908) 218-8876   Fax: (908) 595-0213
www.raritanval.edu
E-mail: atsubota@raritanval.edu

2 Year Institution

Chair, Visual & Performing Arts: Ann Tsubota, 80A
Coord., Performing Arts: James Anthony Strong, 80H

Adj	Barbee, Larry	B	13A,47,70,29
Adj	Eckhart, Michael	M	13A,34,70
Adj	Hudson, Stephen	M	66A,66B,66C,11
Adj	Loehrke, John	B	11,62D,47,29B
Adj	Nelson, Margaret	M	13A,66C,66D
Adj	Reynolds, Sharon	B	61
Inst	Sichel, John	D	13,10,11,12A,36
	Strong, J. Anthony	M	
Asst Prof	Strong, James Anthony	M	13,12A,66,11,54

NJ0990 Richard Stockton College, The
School of Arts & Humanities
PO Box 195
Pomona, NJ 08240
(609) 652-4505   Fax: (609) 652-4550
www2.stockton.edu
E-mail: vaughnb@Stockton.edu

4 Year Institution

Dean, Arts & Humanities: Robert S. Gregg, 80A
Dir., Artist/Performance Series: Michael P. Cool, 80F

Adj	Murawski, Marianne	D	14,11,20
Prof	Olsen, Lance	D	13A,13,11,34
Prof	Vaughn, Beverly Joyce	D	36,11,13A,20G,61

NJ1000 Rider University
School of Fine & Performing Arts
2083 Lawrenceville Rd
Lawrenceville, NJ 08648-3001
(609) 895-5481   Fax: (609) 896-5232
www.rider.edu
E-mail: rife@rider.edu

4 Year Institution

Chair: Jerry E. Rife, 80A

Assoc Prof	Allen, Stephen Arthur	D	13,11,12A,12,20
Adj	Bempechat, Paul-Andre	D	11,12A
Adj	Brosius, Amy T.	D	11,12,13,20,12A
Adj	Burton, Justin D.	M	12
Adj	Coker, Warren	D	13A

Adj	Ernst, John	M	13,13C
Adj	Hedden, Laura	D	12
Adj	Kenworthy, Dan	D	12
Adj	Lauffer, Peter	M	13,13C
Adj	Mateiescu, Carmen	D	13,13C
Adj	Orr, Philip	M	36,66A
Adj	Reeves, Nicholas		13F
Prof	Rife, Jerry E.	D	13,11,12A,12,37

NJ1050 Rowan University
Department of Music
201 Mullica Hill Rd
Glassboro, NJ 08028-1701
(856) 256-4555   Fax: (856) 256-4644
www.rowan.edu/fpa/music/
E-mail: rawlinsr@rowan.edu

4 Year Institution, Graduate School
Member of NASM

Master of Arts in Music Education, Master of Music in Composition, Master of Music in Performance, Master of Music in Conducting, Master of Music in Jazz Studies

Dean: Jon Robert Cart, 80A
Interim Chair: Richard J. Dammers, 80A
Coord., of Field Experience Music Ed.: Lawrence De Pasquale, 80E

Assoc Prof	Appleby-Wineberg, Bryan K.	D	63A
Adj	Atanasiu, George	M	62C
Adj	Atanasiu, Lenuta	M	62A
Adj	Barnes, Jonathan	M	11
Adj	Belzer, Terrence		64B
Adj	Betz, Brian	M	11
Adj	Boguslavsky, Lidia	D	66A
Adj	Breuninger, Tyrone		41,63D
Adj	Brown, Brian	M	63D
Adj	Carney, Sandra L.	M	61
Adj	Carroll, Richard P.	M	64D
Adj	Castelli, James A.	D	10A
Adj	Chu, Brian	M	61
Adj	Cox, Carl	M	64E
Assoc Prof	Dammers, Richard J.	M	32,32E,32F
	De Pasquale, Lawrence	M	11,12A
Prof	DiBlasio, Denis	M	10F,47,64E,53,29
Adj	Earley, Robert		63A
Adj	Edggett, Bryan	D	63A
Adj	Friedman, Eve A.	D	12A
Artist in Res	Garrison, Jon		61
Adj	Gephardt, Donald L.	D	64C,32E,32G
Adj	Giacabetti, Tom		41,53,70
Assoc Prof	Granite, Bonita	M	14,20D,61
Prof	Greenspan, Bertram	D	62A,51,12A,12
Adj	Guida, John	M	64E
Adj	Herzog, James	M	63A
Adj	Kelley, Darin	M	63A
Adj	Kim, Thomas	D	36,60A
Adj	Kramer-Johansen, Karl		63B
Prof	Levinowitz, Lili	D	32,32A,32B
Adj	Linn, Richard	M	63C
Librarian	Lipartito, Robert	M	16
Adj	Lustig, Andrea	M	13
Asst Prof	Mapp, Douglas	M	62D,47,53,34
Prof	Mayes, Joseph	M	41,67,70
Adj	Mayes, Kathleen	M	11
Adj	Mesterhazy, George		66A
Adj	Miceli, Anthony		53,65B
Adj	Miller, Jim D.		65
Librarian	Morris, Marjorie	M	16
Prof	Oliver, Harold	D	13,10F,10,41,53
Adj	Pace, Roberto J.	M	12A
Prof	Pastin, John R.	D	37,60,29,46,48
Adj	Piccone, James	M	13,10,34
Asst Prof	Plant, Lourin	M	60,36,41,61
Adj	Rabbai, George		63A,53,46
Adj	Rawlins, Nancy	D	66D,66G,13,12
Prof	Rawlins, Robert	D	13,12
Adj	Roselle, Herbert	M	63A
Adj	Rowe, Kimberly	M	62E
Adj	Salicondro, Anthony		64
Asst Prof	Scarpa, Salvatore	M	60,38,41,63C
Adj	Spalding, Ben A.	M	60A
Prof	Stewart, Lawrence	D	13,64D
Prof	Stieber, Marian	M	39,61
Adj	Suzuki, Rie	D	64C
Asst Prof	Tomasone, Adeline	D	64A,41
Adj	Traub, Thomas	M	34
Adj	Trigg, William	M	65
Adj	Vezinho, Ed	M	10F
Asst Prof Emeritus	Wade, Thomas	M	13,66D
Prof	Witten, Dean	M	65,50
Adj	Yurko, Bruce		10
Prof	Zuponcic, Veda	M	66A,66B

NJ1100 Rutgers the State Univ-Camden
Department of Fine Arts-Music
314 Linden St
Camden, NJ 08102-1403
(856) 225-6176   Fax: (856) 225-6330
finearts.camden.rutgers.edu/music_home.php
E-mail: schiavo@camden.rutgers.edu

4 Year Institution

Chair & Dir., Artist Series: Joseph C. Schiavo, 80A,80F
Dir., Institute/Festival/Workshop: Julianne C. Baird, 80F

	Akinskas, Joseph	M	32,63
Lect PT	Arnarson, Stefan Orn	M	34A,34D,35C,62,38
Prof	Baird, Julianne C.	D	12A,12C,40,61,67E
	Bunch, Ryan	M	12
	Cain, Michael	M	29
Lect PT	Heffernan, Michele	M	11,13C,29,33,66A
Inst PT	Lally, Laurie A.	B	66A
	Polack, Eric	B	29A
Prof	Schiavo, Joseph C.	D	13B,13D,12A,13F,13
Inst PT	Velykis, Theodore	B	20,70
Prof	Zaki, Mark	D	10,34,10B,34D,10A
Lect PT	Zavadsky, Julia	M	11,13A,36,60A

NJ1130 Rutgers the State Univ-New Brnswk
Mason Gross School of the Arts-Music
Douglass Campus
81 George St
New Brunswick, NJ 08901-1411
(732) 932-9302   Fax: (732) 932-1517
www.masongross.rutgers.edu/music
E-mail: robert.aldridge@rci.rutgers.edu

4 Year Institution, Graduate School
Member of NASM

Master of Music in Performance, Master of Music in Conducting, Master of Music in Music Education, Master of Arts in History & Theory, DMA in Conducting, DMA in Performance, DMA in Music Education, PhD in Music Theory-Composition, PhD in Musicology, Master of Arts in Music Theory-Composition, Master of Arts in Musicology, Master of Music in Jazz Studies, Master of Music in Collaborative Piano Performance, DMA in Collaborative Piano Performance

Director: Robert Aldridge, 80A
Dean, Mason Gross School: George B. Stauffer, 80A
Dir., Undergraduate Studies: Ellen Leibowitz, 80B
Dir., Graduate Studies: Karina Bruk, 80C
Deputy Director: Darryl J. Bott, 80H

Lect PT	Abel, Alan		65
Prof	Aldridge, Robert	D	13,10
Lect PT	Allen, Stephen A.	D	63D
Lect PT	Baer, Alan J.	M	63D
Prof	Berz, William L.	D	32,37
Assoc Prof	Bittmann, Antonius O.	D	12,66G
Lect PT	Blumenfeld, Jonathan	M	64B
Clinical Asst Prof	Bott, Darryl J.	B	32,37
Assoc Prof	Bowen, Ralph	M	47,64E,29
	Bruk, Karina	D	66A,42
Assoc Prof	Chama, Eduardo	M	61
Lect PT	Chang, C. J.	M	62B
Lect PT	Chapman, David F.	M	11,12A
Clinical Asst Prof	Chase, Shannon M.	D	36
Prof Emeritus	Chenoweth, Gerald	D	13,10
Prof Emeritus	Chrisman, Richard		13,10F,13J
Lect PT	Ciulei, Lenuta	M	62A
Lect PT	Cobb, Timothy		62D
Lect PT	Cohen, Paul	D	64E
Prof	Cowell, Stanley	M	66A
Asst Prof	Cypess, Rebecca	D	12,66E,66H,56
Lect PT	Davis, Kenneth	M	62D,29
Asst Prof	Doll, Christopher	D	13
Lect PT	Earley, Robert W.	M	63A,41
Lect PT	Elliott, David J.	D	32
Lect PT	Epstein, Daniel	M	66A
Lect PT	Feller, Bart	B	64A
Lect PT	Fussell, Charles	M	13,10
Lect PT	Gage, Darren J.		34
Prof	Gardner, Patrick	D	60A,36
Clinical Asst Prof	Gilmore, Pamela A.		39
Assoc Prof	Gonzalez-Palmer, Barbara	M	66C
Prof	Grave, Floyd	D	11,12A,12,13J
Lect PT	Gross, Mark	M	64E,29A
Lect PT	Gustafson, Nancy J.	M	39,61
Assoc Prof	Hackworth, Rhonda S.	D	32B,32C,32A,36,32

Prof	Hallmark, Rufus	D	12,12A
Assoc Prof	Herwig, Conrad	B	29,63C
Lect PT	Hinata, Kaoru	D	64A
Prof	Hoffmann, Paul K.	M	66A,43
Inst	Howland, Patricia L.	M	13
Lect PT	Hughes, Nathan N.	M	64B
Assoc Prof	Hurd Hause, Maureen L.	D	64C
Assoc Prof	Johns, Kynan	M	38,60B
Prof	Johnson, Douglas	D	12A,12
Lect PT	Juris, Vic		70,29
Lect PT	Kataja-Urrey, Taina	DIPL	61
Lect PT	Katona, Brian	M	13C
Lect PT	Kopelman, Mikhail	D	62A
Lect PT	Krauss, David B.	M	63A,41
Assoc Prof	Kwon, Min	D	66A
Lect PT	Levesque, Craig	D	13
Lect PT	Lewis, Victor		65,29
Assoc Prof	Lundeen, Douglas	D	12A,63B
Lect PT	Magnarelli, Joe A.	M	63A,29
Lect PT	Muckey, Matthew I.	M	63A
Lect PT	Mumm, Craig	M	62B
Assoc Prof	Nicosia, Judith	M	61
Lect PT	Nye, Roger	B	64D
Lect PT	O'Connell, William	M	29
Lect PT	Phillips, Jessica J.	M	64C
Lect PT	Phillips, Todd		62A
Lect PT	Powell, Michael E.	B	63C,41
Lect PT	Quint, Philippe		62A
Assoc Prof	Rao, Nancy	D	13
Lect PT	Reed, Eric	M	63B
Lect PT	Retzko, Barbara		36
Inst	Riedel, Kimberly	D	13G,34
Lect PT	Rojak, John		63C,41
Lect PT	Smith, Angela	M	64D
Inst	Smith, Timothy G.	B	37
Lect PT	Spitz, Jonathan	B	62C
Lect PT	Sprott, Weston	M	63C
Prof	Stauffer, George B.	D	12A,66G
Lect PT	Tompkins, Joseph H.	M	65
Lect PT	Trautman, Mark A.		66G,41
Lect PT	Urban, Tim	M	13C
Prof	Urrey, Frederick E.	M	61
Prof Emeritus	Whitener, Scott	D	60,49
Assoc Prof	Williams, Kraig	D	37,60B
Lect PT	Zerna, Kyle	M	65A
Lect PT	Zori, Carmit	M	62A

NJ1140 Rutgers the State Univ-Newark

Department of Arts, Culture & Media
Music Bradley Hall Rm 213
110 Warren St
Newark, NJ 07102
(973) 353-5119   Fax: (973) 353-1392
www.newark.rutgers.edu
E-mail: jfloreen@earthlink.net

4 Year Institution, Graduate School

Master of Arts in Jazz Studies

Coordinator, Music: John E. Floreen, 80A
Chair: Ian D. Watson, 80A
Dir., Graduate Studies: Lewis R. Porter, 80C

Lect PT	Chen-Maxham, Li-Chan	M	61
Lect PT	Cochrane, Michael	M	66A,29
Prof	Floreen, John E.	D	12,36,66G
Assoc Prof	Howland, John L.	D	10,12,20,29,29A
Prof	Martin, Henry	D	13,10,12,29,29A
Lect PT	McAdoo, Susan	D	13,61,36
Lect PT	Miller, Elizabeth	M	62A
Lect PT	Narum, Leighann	M	70
Prof	Porter, Lewis R.	D	13,12,29,29A

NJ1160 Seton Hall University

Department of Music
400 S Orange Ave
South Orange, NJ 07079-2646
(201) 761-9474
www.shu.edu
E-mail: maribel.landrau@shu.edu

4 Year Institution

Music Contact: Dena Levine, 80A

	Colosimo, Murray B.	M	64C,38
Adj	Hakim, William J.	M	62A,62B
Adj	Hamersma, Carol	M	11,14C,29A,70
Adj	Harada, Tomoko	M	66A
Adj	Hashimoto, Ayumi	M	66A
Adj	Lawler, Daniel	M	61
Assoc Prof	Levine, Dena		11,66D,66A
Adj	Masuzzo, Dennis		62D
Adj	Newland, Martha	M	61
Adj	Nowik, John	M	66G
Adj	Purviance, Douglas	M	63C
Adj	Scime, Gregory	B	66A
Adj	Sfraga, Debbie	M	32,37,47,64
Asst Prof	Stamps, Jack W.	D	10,34
Faculty	Thurmond, Gloria J.	D	61,31
Adj	Tramm, Jason	D	36,40,60A
Asst Prof	Waters, Robert F.	D	20F
Adj	Weber, Glenn	B	65,50

NJ1350 Westminster Choir College

Rider University School of Music
101 Walnut Ln
Princeton, NJ 08540-3899
(609) 921-7100   Fax: (609) 921-8829
www.rider.edu/wcc
E-mail: wccdeanoff@rider.edu

4 Year Institution, Graduate School
Member of NASM

Master of Music in Composition, Master of Music in Music Education, Master of Music Education, Master of Music in Sacred Music, Master of Music in Choral Conducting, Master of Music in Vocal Pedagogy, Master of Music in Voice Pedagogy & Performance, Master of Music in Organ Performance, Master of Music in Piano Pedagogy & Performance, Master of Music in Piano Accompanying & Coaching, Master of Music in Piano Performance

Dean/Director: Robert L. Annis, 80A
Dir., Continuing Education: Scott Hoerl, 80E
Associate Dean: Marshall Onofrio, 80H

Adj Inst	Abrahams, Ellen M.	D	32
Assoc Prof	Abrahams, Frank E.	D	32
Adj Asst Prof	Amoriello, Laura	M	66D
Prof	Annis, Robert L.	M	64C,43
Asst Prof	Arneson, Christopher P.	M	61
Adj Prof	Ashbaker, Susan	M	61,39
Prof Adj	Baldwin, Dalton	B	66A,66C
Prof	Bartle, Barton	D	13,34
Adj Assoc Prof	Barton, Ena	B	66A
Adj Inst	Bordignon, Paolo	D	66G
Adj Assoc Prof	Boyle, Benjamin C. S.	PhD	10,64A,13
Adj Asst Prof	Brandau, Ryan James	D	36,60A
Asst Prof	Cape, Janet	M	32,34
Asst Prof	Carey, Christian B.	D	13
Adj Asst Prof	Catania, Claudia	M	61
Adj Inst	Chebra, Tracy Richards	B	61
Prof	Christiansen, Lindsey	M	61
Assoc Prof	Chyun, Mi-Hye	M	16
Prof	Clarfield, Ingrid	M	66A,66B
Adj Asst Prof	Cochran, Timothy	D	12
Adj Asst Prof	Conte, Peter Richard		66G
Prof	Cusack, Margaret	M	61
Assoc Prof	Eley, Elem	M	61
Adj Asst Prof	Eley, Miriam	M	66A
Adj Inst	Ellis, Rochelle	B	61
Adj Asst Prof	Esham, Faith	M	61
Adj Asst Prof	Evans, Harold	M	61
Assoc Prof	Faracco, Thomas	M	61
Adj Asst Prof	Frantz, Charles	D	12
Adj Asst Prof	Froysland-Hoerl, Nancy	M	61
Adj Assoc Prof	Gal, Zehava	DIPL	61
Assoc Prof	Goldsworthy, James	D	66A
Adj Asst Prof	Helvering, R. Douglas	D	13
Prof	Hemmel, Ronald A.	D	13,10,34D,13L
Adj Inst	Hobbs, William	M	39
Assoc Prof	Holcomb, Al	D	32,36,60A
Adj Inst	Hudson, Stephen	M	29,66D
Asst Prof	Hung, Eric Hing-tao	D	12,14
Adj Asst Prof	Johnson, Katherine L.	M	61
Adj Asst Prof	Jonck, Rachelle	B	61
Assoc Prof	Jordan, James	D	66G,36,13,60
Prof	Kawarsky, Jay A.	D	13
Adj Asst Prof	Kemp, Julia	B	61
Adj Inst	Klein, Laura	M	66
Prof	Kosar, Anthony	D	13
Adj Asst Prof	Lauffer, Peter	M	66D
Prof	Lehrer, Phyllis	M	66A,66B
Adj Asst Prof	Lewis, Matthew	D	66G
Adj Asst Prof	Liefer, David		66
Adj Assoc Prof	Livingston, Lillian	B	66A,66B
Adj Inst	Loughran, Robert	M	62A,32E
Adj Inst	Maher, James	M	32
Adj Asst Prof	Mariman, Devin	M	61
Adj Inst	Martinez, Taione	B	31,36

Adj Asst Prof	Massie, Robin	M	61
Adj Asst Prof	Mateiescu, Carmen	D	13
Adj Inst	McBride, Nick	M	32
Asst Prof	McCarther, Sean	D	61
Adj Asst Prof	McDonnell, John	M	36
Adj Asst Prof	McKenzie, Art	M	32,54
Assoc Prof	Megill, Andrew	M	60
Prof	Miller, Joe	D	36,60A
Assoc Prof	Mirchandani, Sharon	D	13,12
Adj Assoc Prof	Moliterno, Mark		61
Assoc Prof	Morrison, Alan	M	66G
Asst Prof	Morrow, Sharon	D	32
Prof	Onofrio, Marshall	D	13,10,29,34,32E
Adj Asst Prof	Onofrio, Susan	M	32
Adj Asst Prof	Page, Carolann	B	54,61
Asst Prof	Parente, Thomas	D	66A,66D,32I
Assoc Prof	Penna, J. J.	D	66C
Prof	Phillips, Joel	D	13,10,34
Assoc Prof	Pilkington, Steve	D	36,31A
Adj Asst Prof	Poltorak, Agnes	M	66D
Asst Prof	Price, Kathy Kessler	D	61
Asst Prof	Quist, Amanda R.	D	32D,36,60
Prof	Rice, Laura Brooks	M	39,61
Asst Prof	Rieger, Eric	M	61
Adj Asst Prof	Rothfuss, Guy	M	61
Adj Asst Prof	Scheide, Kathleen	D	66G,12A,67F,66H
Adj Asst Prof	Scurto-Davis, Debra	M	61
Adj Inst	Shaw, Kathleen	B	44
Adj Prof	Sheftel, Paul	M	66B
Asst Prof	Shelton, Tom	M	31,32,36,60A
Adj Assoc Prof	Stoloff, Betty	M	66A,66B,66D
Adj Asst Prof	Sutton, Elizabeth		61
Assoc Prof	Sweet, Sharon	M	61
Assoc Prof	Thomas, Nova	M	61,54
Adj Asst Prof	Urban, Timothy	PhD	13
Adj Inst	Walker, Charles	B	61
Adj Asst Prof	Wolf, Sally	M	61
Adj Prof	Wright, Peter	D	54
Prof	Young, Stefan	D	13,10
Asst Prof	Zorn, Amy	M	61

NJ1400 William Paterson University

Department of Music
300 Pompton Rd
Wayne, NJ 07470-2103
(973) 720-2315   Fax: (973) 720-2217
www.wpunj.edu
E-mail: friersoncampbellc@wpunj.edu

4 Year Institution, Graduate School
Member of NASM

Master of Music in Music Education, Master of Music in Jazz Studies, Master of Music in Music Management

Chair: Carol Frierson-Campbell, 80A
Dir., Graduate Studies: Timothy Newman, 80C
Dir., Artist/Performance Series: Gary Kirkpatrick, 80F

Adj	Arnold, Horacee		29
Adj	Bassler, Samantha Elizabeth	D	13A,13B
Adj	Bertoncini, Gene		29
Prof	Bryant, Stephen	M	60,36,61
Adj	Capetandes, Gary	B	63C
Adj	Charsky, Thomas	M	32B,11
Adj	Clark, Richard	M	63C
Adj	Coll, Peter	D	12A
Asst Prof	Dackow, Sandra K.	D	62
Adj	Dassinger, George		35A
Asst Prof	Davis, J. Craig	D	37,63A,41
Adj	Davol, Sarah	M	64B
Prof	Demsey, David	D	64E,29
Assoc Prof	Demsey, Karen B.	D	64A,48,12,11,12A
Adj	Donelian, Armen	B	29
Adj	Fagnano, Frank	M	35C
Prof	Falk Romaine, Diane	D	32
Adj	Fay, Edmund	M	65,34
Adj	Ferrari, John	D	13A,11,50,65
Adj	Fink, Gary	M	35C
Assoc Prof	Frierson-Campbell, Carol	D	32,63B,60
Adj	Gage, Darren J.	D	13
Adj	Gennarelli, Franco	B	62
Adj	Gray, Robert	M	64D
Adj	Gribbroek, Michael	M	11
Prof	Guptill-Crain, Nan	M	61,36
Adj	Guthrie, Karl	D	35
Adj	Handy, Gabriel		70
Adj	Helms, Warren	M	66C
Adj	Herring, Vincent	B	64E,29,47
Adj	Himmelhoch, Seth	B	70
Adj	Irwin, Frederick	D	36,60A
Inst	Jarvis, Peter	M	65,50
Adj	Jones, David	D	32
Assoc Prof	Kerzner, David	M	35C
Adj	Kirkpatrick, Elka	M	66D
Prof	Kirkpatrick, Gary	M	66A,66B,66D
Prof	Kresky, Jeffrey	D	13,10F,11,66D
Adj	Lamy, Andy	B	64C
Adj	Larson, Dave		63A
Adj	LaSpina, Steven	B	29A,47,62D,29
Adj	Leeds, Steve	M	35
Prof	Link, John	D	13,10F,10,34
Adj	Mabern, Harold		29
Asst Prof	MacDonald, Payton	D	65,50,43
Adj	Marano, Nancy	B	61,29
Prof	Marcone, Stephen		35
Asst Prof	McGuinness, Peter	M	13,10,29,41
Adj	McLaurine, Marcus	B	29
Adj	McNeely, James	B	29B
Adj	Mendoza, Chico		47
Adj	Meyers, Paul	B	70,29
Adj	Miller, Ivan	M	63A
Assoc Prof	Miller, Mulgrew	B	29
Adj	Mosca, John		29
Asst Prof	Neubert, Nils	M	61
Asst Prof	Newman, Timothy	D	47,63,29A
Adj	Nordstrom, Erland	D	32E,11
Adj	Norton, Kevin	M	29
Adj	Noyes, James R.	D	64E
Adj	O'Connor, Margaret	D	11,32
Adj	Paterno, Matthew	B	63
Adj	Pavese, Frank	M	66D
Adj	Perry, Rich	B	64E,47
Adj	Philp, David	M	35
Adj	Pike, Lisa F.	D	63B
Adj	Reeves, Janet	B	66D
Adj	Rizzo, Jacques	D	32
Adj	Rogers, Dave	B	29,63A
Assoc Prof	Rogers, Lynne	D	13
Adj	Roggen, Ann	M	62B,41
Adj	Ruedeman, Tim	M	64E
Adj	Scott, Paul	M	63D
Adj	Simpson, Scott	M	11
Adj	Taber, Randy	B	35C
Adj	Terry, Clark		47
Adj	Thomas, Robert	D	13
Adj	Thompson, John	M	62
Adj	Van Dyke, Gary	M	65,50
Adj	Verdicchio, Linda	M	32
Adj	Weidman, James		29,66A
Assoc Prof	Weisberg, David	D	13

NM0100 Eastern New Mexico University

Department of Music
ENMU Station 16
1500 S Ave K
Portales, NM 88130
(575) 562-2377   Fax: (575) 562-4480
www.enmu.edu/music
E-mail: dustin.seifert@enmu.edu

4 Year Institution
Member of NASM

Chair: Dustin Seifert, 80A

Asst Prof	Bradfield, Ann	D	29,46,47,64A,64E
Assoc Prof	Carr, Tracy A.	D	64B,12A,41,64D,11
Assoc Prof	Dal Porto, Mark	D	10,13,66A,34,13A
Assoc Prof	Ellzey, Michael R.	D	63A,13,32E
Inst	Gelbwasser, Kimberly A.	D	61
	Laubenthal, Jennifer	D	64C,11,13A
Prof	Olsen, John F.	D	66A,66B,66D
Inst	Pachak-Brooks, Cheryl	M	66B,66D,66A,66C
Assoc Prof	Paulk, Jason	D	60A,32C,36
Inst	Paulk, Kayla Liechty	M	66A,66C,66B,66D
Inst	Rutland, Neil	M	37,50,65,35D
Inst	Seifert, Dustin	M	37,63C,63D,60B,32E
Asst Prof	Vest, Jason	D	61,39
Prof	Wozencraft-Ornellas, Jean	DMA	39,61

NM0150 New Mexico Highlands University

Department of Music
PO Box 9000
Las Vegas, NM 87701
(505) 454-3359   Fax: (505) 454-3014
www.nmhu.edu
E-mail: agarcianuthman@nmhu.edu

4 Year Institution

Chair & Assistant Dean: Andre Gracia-Nuthmann, 80A,80H
Dean: Celestino 'Tino' Mendez, 80A

Asst Prof	Dutoit, Tatiana Grecic		
Assoc Prof	Gracia-Nuthmann, Andre	M	13,60,36,55,61
	Harrington, Edward		
Assoc Prof	Leger, James K.	M	10,60,12,14,38

NM0200 New Mexico Junior College
Department of Music
5317 Lovington Hwy
Hobbs, NM 88240
(575) 492-2844   Fax: (575) 492-2838
www.nmjc.edu
E-mail: yswong@nmjc.edu

2 Year Institution

Music Contact: Yau-Sun Wong, 80A

PT	Ball, Julia	B	64
PT	Harlin, Juston	M	61
PT	Hines, Joan		66A
PT	Patman, Rebecca	M	11,66A
PT	Turner-Tsonis, Anne	B	61
PT	Walton, Michele	B	66A
Prof	Wong, Yau-Sun	D	11,60,13B,36,37

NM0250 New Mexico Military Institute
Department of Music
101 W College Blvd
Roswell, NM 88201
(575) 624-8443   Fax: (575) 624-8136
www.nmmi.edu
E-mail: thorp@nmmi.edu

Military Junior College

Chair: Steven Thorp, 80A

Asst Prof	Lamb, William	M	13,11,37,47,63
Assoc Prof	Thorp, Steven	M	13,11,36,61,40

NM0300 New Mexico State University
Department of Music
1500 University Dr
Carlsbad, NM 88220
(505) 885-8831   Fax: (505) 885-4951
carlsbad.nmsu.edu
E-mail: mbuckholz@cavern.nmsu.edu

2 Year Institution

Chair: Barbara Carey, 80A

Inst PT	Carey, Barbara		61,66A
Inst PT	Clark, Martha	B	62A,67B

NM0310 New Mexico State University
Department of Music
Box 30001 MSC 3F
Las Cruces, NM 88003
(505) 646-2421   Fax: (505) 646-8199
music.nmsu.edu/home.php
E-mail: music@nmsu.edu

4 Year Institution, Graduate School
Member of NASM

Master of Music in Performance, Master of Music in Conducting, Master of Music in Music Education

Chair: Lon W. Chaffin, 80A

Inst	Albela-Vega, Daniel	M	62A
Prof	Alt, Jerry A.	D	36,61,60
Prof	Borchert, Laroy	D	13,32,64C
Assoc Prof	Bugbee, Fred	D	65,13
Prof	Clark, William D.	D	32,37
Inst	Espy, Blake	M	62A
	Fels, Carl		64B
	Fitzgearld, Gayl		13
	Gunnarson, Eike	M	61
Inst	Hill, Monty K.	M	37,32
Assoc Prof	Hughes, Christopher A.	D	37,60B,32E,63A,38
Asst Prof	Joy, Nancy	M	63B,49,13A,11
Assoc Prof	Kaplan, Allan Richard	D	11,63C,53
Prof	Klein, Lonnie	D	11,38,41,60
	Klement, David A.		10,36
Lect PT	Loman, Janet	D	66G,66H
Inst	Martinez, Jorge	M	62B
	Pias, Ed	D	65,20
Assoc Prof	Romero, Frank	D	63A,47,72,34
Assoc Prof	Rowe, Martha	D	61
Prof	Shearer, James E.	D	63D,12A,11
Asst Prof	Spitzer, Laura	D	66A,66B,66C
Inst	Taylor, Rhonda	D	64E,13
Prof	Van Winkle, Kenneth	D	37,60
Asst Prof	Van Winkle, Lisa K.	D	64A,35A
Lect PT	York, Lela	M	66A
	Zimmerman, Andrew N.		61

NM0350 New Mexico Tech
Music Program
801 Leroy Place
Socorro, NM 87801
(505) 835-5445   Fax: (505) 385-5544
www.nmt.edu
E-mail: ddunston@nmt.edu

4 Year Institution

Director: Douglas E. Dunston, 80A

Inst PT	Barrientos, Paul	B	11,36,61
Assoc Prof	Dunston, Douglas E.	D	10B,36,38,47,54

NM0400 San Juan College
Department of Music
4601 College Blvd
Farmington, NM 87402-4609
(505) 566-3386   Fax: (505) 566-3385
www.sanjuancollege.edu/pages/2357.asp
E-mail: cochranek@sanjuancollege.edu

2 Year Institution

Co-Chair: Keith A. Cochrane, 80A
Co-Chair: Linda Edwards, 80A

Prof	Cochrane, Keith A.	D	60,12A,32B,37,47
Inst PT	Collins, Cheryl	D	66A,66C,66D
Inst PT	Collins, David	B	61
Asst Prof	Edwards, Linda	M	60,36,41,61,54
Inst PT	Kidd, Christine	B	13A,61,11
Inst PT	Lovato, James	B	35C
Inst PT	Mietz, Joshua	D	64C,64E,13,38
Inst PT	Nogarede, Steve	B	50
Inst PT	Peck, Gordon	B	70,13G
Inst PT	Pope, Cathy	D	62A
Inst PT	Shirley, Hank	A	65,50
Inst PT	Stovall, Leah	B	13A
Inst PT	Wood, Patty	B	66A

NM0425 Santa Fe University of Art and Design
Department of Contemporary Music
1600 St Michaels Dr
Santa Fe, NM 87505-7615
(505) 473-6196   Fax: (505) 473-6021
www.santafeuniversity.edu/
E-mail: cmp@csf.edu

4 Year Institution, Contemporary Music Program

Director: Steven E. Paxton, 80A

Adj Inst	Capocchi, Roberto	B	70

NM0450 Univ of New Mexico
Center for the Arts-Music
MSC04 2570
1 University of New Mexico
Albuquerque, NM 87131-0001
(505) 277-2126   Fax: (505) 277-4202
music.unm.edu
E-mail: polansky@unm.edu

4 Year Institution, Graduate School
Member of NASM

Master of Music in Performance, Master of Music in Conducting, Master of Music in Music Education, Master of Music in Musicology, Master of Music in Music Theory-Composition, Master of Music in Choral Conducting, Master of Music in Accompanying, Master of Music in Music History & Literature

Chair: Steven Block, 80A
Dean: Kymberly Pinder, 80A
Undergraduate Advisor: Keith M. Lemmons, 80B
Graduate Coordinator: Colleen Sheinberg, 80C
Dir., UNM Music Preparatory School: Julia Hoffman, 80E
Associate Chair: Eric Lau, 80H

Lect	Anthony, Michael		70
Lect	Balagurchik, James	M	13
Lect	Barlow, Carla	M	13,10,34
Asst Prof	Bashwiner, David M.	D	13,10
Prof	Block, Steven	D	13A,13,10F
Assoc Prof	Carlow, Regina	D	32
Prof	Chapdelaine, Michael	M	70,41
Lect	Collins, Lisa	M	62
Lect	Dalagar, Martha	M	66A
Prof	Dalby, Bruce	D	32C,47,12
Lect	Davies-Wilson, Dennis	M	12
Lect	Davis, Daniel	M	11
Assoc Prof	De Los Santos, Carmelo	D	62A
Lect	Delgado, Jan	M	62C
Lect	Eisfeller, Anne	M	62E
Prof	Ellingboe, Bradley	M	36,61
Lect	Feldberg, David	M	43,62A,60B
Assoc Prof	Fredenburgh, Kim	M	62B,51
Lect	Geist, Doug		35G,35C
Asst Prof	Gilbert, Peter A.	D	10,13
Prof	Hermann, Richard	D	13A,13
Prof	Hinterbichler, Karl	D	12A,12,63C,63D
Prof	Hix, Michael T.	D	61,13A,12A,12
Lect	Hoffman, Julia	M	32
Vstng Asst Prof	Houghtalen, Brandon	D	60B,64
Asst Prof	Hurtado, Jose-Luis	D	10,13,32B
Lect	Jones, Judy	M	10
Lect	Kempter, Susan	M	62,32A,32B,32C
Assoc Prof	Kostur, Glenn	M	47,29
Assoc Prof	Lau, Eric	D	64E
Lect	Lau, Jennifer	D	64A,11
Prof	Lemmons, Keith M.	M	64C,41
Lect	Lombardi, Paul	M	10,13
Lect	MaCaskie, Stuart	B	66A
Asst Prof	Marchiando, John R.	DMA	63A
Assoc Prof	Ney, Leonard Scott	M	50,65
Asst Prof	Obermueller, Karola	D	10,13
Lect	Otero, Erica	D	32A,32B
Prof	Perez-Gomez, Jorge	D	60,38,39
Lect	Pincock, Christian P.	M	29
Prof	Piper, Jeffrey S.	M	49,63A
Assoc Prof	Potter, Valerie	M	64A,41,48
Assoc Prof	Pyle, Pamela Viktoria	M	66A,66C
Assoc Prof	Repar, Patricia Ann	D	10,45
Prof	Rombach-Kendall, Eric	M	32C,37
Assoc Prof	Schepps, David M.	M	62C,41
Asst Prof	Shaw, J.D.	M	63B,63
Lect	Sheinberg, Art	M	62D,32C
Vstng Lect	Sheinberg, Colleen	M	55
Lect	Shepperson, Sam	B	61
Prof Emeritus	Shultis, Christopher	D	12,12B,10
Lect	Silva, Ben	B	70
Assoc Prof	Simons, Chad P.	D	37
Prof	Steinbach, Falko	M	66A,66C,66B
Lect	Swalin, Paula	M	61
Lect	Tatum, Mark	M	62D,29A
Lect	Thevenot, Maxine R.	D	11,36
Lect	Turner, Denise	B	64D,48
Prof Emerita	Tyler, Marilyn		39,61
Assoc Prof	Umphrey, Leslie	M	61,39
Prof	Vigneau, Kevin	D	64B,13A,13
Lect	Ward, Arlene	M	66D,66G
Asst Prof	White, Richard	D	63D
Assoc Prof	Williams, Maria	D	14,20H,20G

NM0500 Western New Mexico University
Expressive Arts Dept - Music
1000 W College Ave
PO Box 680
Silver City, NM 88062-0680
(505) 538-6614   Fax: (505) 538-6619
www.wnmu.edu
E-mail: eldera@wnmu.edu

4 Year Institution

Chair: Ralph D. Converse, 80A

Adj Inst	Branch, Robert	B	34,70
Asst Prof	Converse, Ralph D.	M	64,41,38,48,29
Adj Inst	Cunningham, Chuck	B	66A,66G,32D,36,40
Adj Inst	Edgar, Donna	B	64A
Adj Inst	Horvath, Juliane	M	66A,66C
Adj Inst	Lamb, William	B	61,63,32E
Adj Inst	Sullivan, Eileen	B	62

NV0050 Univ of Nevada-Las Vegas
Department of Music
4505 S. Maryland Pkwy
PO Box 455025
Las Vegas, NV 89154-5025
(702) 895-3332   Fax: (702) 895-4239
music.unlv.edu
E-mail: jonathan.good@unlv.edu

4 Year Institution
Member of NASM

Master of Music in Performance, Master of Music in Conducting, Master of Music in Music Education, DMA in Performance, Master of Music in Music Theory-Composition

Chair: Jonathan E. Good, 80A
Dean: Jeffrey Koep, 80A
Coordinator, Graduate Studies: Andrew Smith, 80C
Dir., Artist/Performance Series: Larry Henley, 80F
Dir., Artist/Performance Series: Lori James, 80F
Associate Chair: William Bernatis, 80H

Prof	Anderson, Alfonse	D	61
Prof	Baley, Virko	M	10,13
Assoc Prof	Barone, Anthony	D	12,12A,12C
Assoc Prof	Bernatis, William	M	13A,13,49,63B
PT	Brown, Daniel R.	D	63D,41
Assoc Prof	Burkett, Eugenie I.	D	32,32E,32G
Prof	Caplan, Stephen	M	64B,42,11
PT	Cho, Yuri	D	62A
Vstng Lect	Cobo, Ricardo	M	70,13B
PT	Cook, Gary	D	65
PT	Devol, Luana	M	61,39
PT	Douglass, Zane S.	D	37
PT	Dresel, Bernie	M	29
PT	Firak, Paul	M	62D
Assoc Prof	Fitzpatrick, Tod M.	D	61,39
Vstng Lect	Foley, Charles F.		35C,35G
PT	Glennie, Kim	M	62E
Prof	Good, Jonathan E.	M	60B,32,37,32E
Asst Prof	Grim, Jennifer	D	64A,42,41
Prof	Gronemeier, Dean	D	65
Prof	Hanlon, Kenneth	D	13B,13D
PT	Heppner-Harjo, Tianna	M	62B,32E,42
PT	Hesselink, Paul	D	66G
Asst Prof	Hoft, Timothy	D	66A,66C
PT	Ivy, Julie	M	13C,13B
PT	Jensen, Jocelyn	D	36,13B,13C
Lect	Jones, Timothy	D	65,12A
Vstng Lect	Kaupp, Gil	M	35C,35G,63A
Prof Emerita	Kimball, Carol		12A,61
Assoc Prof	Krysa, Taras	M	38,60B
Assoc Prof	LaBounty, Anthony	M	37,32E
PT	Lano, Joe		70
Vstng Lect	Latour, Michelle R.	D	61
Asst Prof	Le, Weiwei	M	62A,42
Prof	Leslie, Tom	M	37,60B
Asst Prof	Lister, Linda J.	D	61
Assoc Prof	Loeb, David	M	29,10,47
PT	Manning, Sheri	M	32E
PT	McArthur, Mark	M	64E,42
Vstng Lect	McCann, Karen	D	61,66C
PT	McEnaney, Rick		32E
PT	McIntosh, Jim	M	11
Assoc Prof	McKay, Janis	D	13,41,55,64D
Assoc Prof	Mueller, Susan	M	32A,32B
PT	Pellegrino, Larry	M	11

Assoc Prof Emeritus	Peterson, Douglas	D	11
PT	Rasmussen, Kurt	M	65
PT	Riske, Barbara	M	66A,66D
Assoc Prof	Smith, Andrew	D	62C
PT	Stephen, Anne	M	32D
PT	Stopa, Alex	D	12A,65
Assoc Prof	Sturm, Marina	D	64C,42
Assoc Prof	Suk, Mykola	M	66A,66B
Asst Prof	Tanouye, Nathan	B	29,63C,47
Assoc Prof	Taranto, Cheryl	D	16,12A,12C
PT	Trinkle, Steven W.	M	63A,41,42,38,13A
Asst Prof	Warrington, Thomas	M	62D,47,29
Asst Prof	Weiller, David B.	M	60A,32D,36
PT	Yonely, Jo Belle		61,29

NV0100 Univ of Nevada-Reno
Department of Music
#226
Reno, NV 89557-0049
(775) 784-6145   Fax: (775) 784-6896
www.unr.edu/cla/music/
E-mail: alenz@unr.edu

4 Year Institution, Graduate School
Member of NASM

Master of Arts in Music, Master of Music in Performance, Master of Music in Music Education

Dir., School of the Arts: Larry M. Engstrom, 80A
Chair: Andrea Lenz, 80A
Dir., Artist/Performance Series: C. J. Walters, 80F

Assoc Prof	Ake, David	D	12,20,29A,14,66A
Inst	Altieri, Jason	D	38
Asst Prof	Atapine, Dmitri	D	62C,42,11
Inst	Corey, Horace E.	M	13A,11,41,70
Assoc Prof	DeBoer, Katharine	D	39,61
Prof	Ehrke, David	D	13C,64C,64E,41
Prof	Engstrom, Larry M.	D	63A
Assoc Prof	Epstein, Peter	M	47,20,64E
Inst	Halt, Hans	M	29B,62D,66A
Assoc Prof	Heglund, Andrew	D	65,46,50,47
Assoc Prof	Lenz, Andrea	M	13,64B,66C
Prof	McGrannahan, A. Graydon	D	37,32C,41,63C,63D
Asst Prof	Niebur, Louis	D	12,20,14,11
Inst	Perrotte, Jean-Paul	M	10,13B,13F,13G,13E
Inst	Pollard, Catherine	M	32
Asst Prof	Sant'Ambrogio, Stephanie	M	62A,62B
Inst	Stevens, Damon B.	D	39,66A,66C,66D
Prof	Winn, James	D	66,13,10
Inst	Wolff, Lisa	D	36,40,61,13C

NV0125 Truckee Meadows Comm College
Department of Visual & Perf Arts
7000 Dandini Blvd
Reno, NV 89512-3999
(775) 789-5672   Fax: (775) 674-4853
tmcc.edu/vparts
E-mail: jfrederick@tmcc.edu

2 Year Institution, Transferable Degrees

Chair: Paul Aberasturi, 80A
Dean: John Adlish, 80A

Prof	Gifford, Tell	PhD	11,12A,13,66A
Prof	Owens, Theodore	M	10,11,12A,61,54

NV0150 Western Nevada Community College
Department of Music
2201 W College Pkwy
Carson City, NV 89703-7316
(775) 445-4249   Fax: (775) 887-3154
www.wnc.edu
E-mail: arrigots@wnc.edu

2 Year Institution

Artistic Dir., of Performing Arts: Stephanie Arrigotti, 80A
Chair of Communications/Fine Arts: Michon Mackidon, 80A

Prof	Arrigotti, Stephanie	M	13A,11,66A,66B,66D
Lect PT	Blankenship, William	M	11
PT	Bugli, David		66A
PT	Davis, William		11
PT	Farnsley, Stephen		64,63
Lect PT	Lachew, Joseph	B	70
PT	Melendres, Henry		
PT	Peebles, Stew		61
PT	Shipley, John		66A,34,14C
Lect PT	Zabelsky, Bill	M	36,47

NY0050 Adelphi University
Department of Music
PAC 207
1 South Ave
Garden City, NY 11530-0701
(516) 877-4290   Fax: (516) 877-4286
www.adelphi.edu

E-mail: clemen@adelphi.edu

4 Year Institution

Director: Michael Hume, 80A

Adj	Abayev, Alexander		41
Asst Prof	Boquiren, Sidney M.	D	10A,13A,20D,31A,10F
Adj	Borbely, Adrienne		66A
Adj	Chang, Shirley		64B
Adj	Comparone, Elaine		66H
Adj	Demilo, Brad		63B
Adj	Di Vittorio, Salvatore		10A,38
Adj	Dougherty, Patrick		63A
Adj	Fredericks, Jim		61
Adj	Frutkoff, Peter		32E,63,64
Adj	Goodman, Jonathan		61
Adj	Gustavson, Mark		64C
Adj	Hume, Michael	M	61,36
Adj	Lampert, Steven		29A,29B
Adj	Litroff, Scott		64E
Adj	Lobenstein, David		29,47
Assoc Prof	Lyndon-Gee, Christopher	D	10A,14A,38,39,42
Prof	Moravec, Paul	D	13,10
Adj	Muncil, Donna		64D
Asst Prof	Newlin, Georgia A.		11,12A,13C,32,36
Adj	Olsen, Gayle		61
Adj	Ratner, Jody		62B
Adj	Renoud, Doug		37
Adj	Riley, William		12A
Adj	Salerno, Steven		29,47,70
Adj	Sepe, Deborah		62C
Adj	Sole, Meryl	M	29A,29B
Adj	Sullivan, Dennis	M	50
Adj	Taffet, Robert S.		62D
Adj	Von Goerken, Lisa C.		61
Adj	Wetherill, Linda Marie		64A,20
Adj	Witmer, Larry		63C
Adj	Younger, Brandee		62E
Adj	Zito, William	B	67G,70

NY0100 Alfred University
Division of Performing Arts
One Saxon Dr
Alfred, NY 14802-1222
(607) 871-2562   Fax: (607) 871-2587
las.alfred.edu/performing-arts/music/
E-mail: flantz@alfred.edu

4 Year Institution

Chair: J. Stephen Crosby, 80A
Dean: William Hall, 80A
Dir., Artist/Performance Series: Daniel Napolitano, 80F

Assoc Prof	Angier, D. Chase	M	52
Inst PT	Buckwalter, Laurel G.	M	66A,66B,66C,69
Prof	Crosby, J. Stephen	M	54
Prof	Crosby, Luanne M.	D	11,36,61,54
Assoc Prof	Fantova, Marketa	M	34
Asst Prof	Foster, Christopher	D	36,63,13A,47,41
Tech Dir	Hamm, Zachary D.	M	54
Assoc Prof	Lantz, Lisa E.	D	11,38,51,62,13A
Inst PT	O'Connor, Peter J.	M	66A,66C
Prof	Prophet, Becky B.	D	54

NY0150 Bard College

Conservatory of Music
30 Campus Rd
Annandale On Hudson, NY 12504
(845) 758-7196   Fax: (845) 758-7440
www.bard.edu/conservatory
E-mail: conservatory@bard.edu

4 Year Liberal Arts College, Graduate School, 5 year Double Degree Conservatory

Master of Music

Director: Robert Martin, 80A
Coord., Conservatory Admissions: Nathan Madsen, 80D
Dir., Prepartory Division: Fu-chen Chan, 80E
Associate Director: Melvin Chen, 80H

	Albach, Carl	M	63A
	Baer, Alan	M	63D
	Bers, Edith	M	61
	Chan, Fu-chen		
	Chen, Melvin	D	66A,42,38
	Corliss, Frank	M	66C
	Dallesio, Richard	M	64B
	Danilow, Marji	B	62D
	Denk, Jeremy	M	66A
	Drucker, Eugene	M	62A
	Farberman, Harold	M	60B
	Flax, Laura	M	64C,42
	Gibbs, Christopher	D	12
	Goldberg, Marc	M	64D,42,48
	Halle, John	D	13,11
	Iwama, Kayo	M	61,66C
	Jiang, Yi-wen	M	62A,42
	Kavafian, Ida	M	62A,42
	Kim, Soovin	M	62A
	Krakauer, David	M	64C,42
	Landsman, Julie	M	63B
	Lang, Jeffrey	M	63B
	Li, Weigang	M	62A,42
	Misslin, Patricia	M	61
	Nubar, Lorraine	M	61
	O'Connor, Tara	D	64A,42
	Rojak, John	M	63C,42,49
	Serkin, Peter		66A
	Shao, Sophie	M	62C
	Smukler, Laurie	M	62A,42
	Steinhardt, Arnold	M	62A
	Tenenbom, Steven	M	62B,42
	Tower, Joan	D	10,43
	Tree, Michael	M	62B
	Tsontakis, George	D	10
	Upshaw, Dawn	M	61
	Weller, Ira	M	62B,42
	Wiley, Peter	M	62C,42

NY0200 Barnard College

Department of Music
3009 Broadway/Box 37
New York, NY 10027
(212) 854-5096   Fax: (212) 854-7491
www.barnard.edu/
E-mail: garcher@barnard.columbia.edu

4 Year Institution

Director: Gail Archer, 80A

Lect	Archer, Gail	D	36,12A
	Gallet, Coralie	M	61,13
Assoc Fac	McMahan, Jane	M	61
	Mongiardo-Cooper, Josephine	M	61
	Ninoshvili, Lauren	D	14,66A

NY0250 Baruch College

Department of Fine & Perf Arts
Box B7/235
55 Lexington Ave
New York, NY 10010
(646) 312-4052   Fax: (646) 312-4051
www.baruch.cuny.edu
E-mail: anne.swartz@baruch.cuny.edu

4 Year Institution

Chair, Music: Anne Swartz, 80A
Deputy Chair: Andrew Tomasello, 80H

Lect Adj	Bayer, Michelle	B	35B
Assoc Prof	Hill, George R.	D	11,12A,12,16
Prof	Lambert, Philip	D	13A,13,11,12A
Prof	Olan, David M.	D	13,10,11
Lect Adj	Parker, Teresa B.	M	36
Prof	Saloman, Ora Frishberg	D	11,12A,12
Assoc Prof	Slavin, Dennis	D	11,12
Prof	Swartz, Anne	D	11,12A,12
Assoc Prof	Tomasello, Andrew	D	11,12,14,29A,35
Asst Prof	Wollman, Elizabeth L.	D	11,14C,14,15,20

NY0270 Borough of Manhattan Comm College

Department of Music
199 Chambers St
New York, NY 10007
(212) 220-1464   Fax: (212) 220-1285
www.bmcc.cuny.edu
E-mail: hmeltzer@bmcc.cuny.edu

2 Year Institution

Chair: Howard S. Meltzer, 80A

Prof	Anderson, Douglas K.	D	13,10F,60,10,38
Lect Adj	Anderson, Frank		36,61
Asst Prof Adj	Bartow, James	M	11,20A,20G,29A,70
Lect Adj	Briggs, Kurt	M	11,62A
Lect Adj	Brown, Charles		36,61
Asst Prof Adj	Free, Christine	D	36,61
Lect Adj	George, Rosemary	M	66A,61,12A,11
Lect Adj	Goeke, Matthew	M	11,62C
Assoc Prof	Hollerbach, Peter	D	13A,11,14,47,70
Asst Prof Adj	Keenan, Maureen	M	11,13,64A
Lect Adj	Kim, Jean	M	11,13,66A,66C
Lect Adj	Lehman, Stephanie	M	65,11,13
Lect Adj	Litera, Ina	M	11,62
Assoc Prof	Meltzer, Howard S.	D	11,13,12,66A,63
Assoc Prof	Moorman, Joyce E.	D	11,13,20A,34D,66
Lect Adj	Moorman, Wilson	M	11,20,65,29
Lect Adj	Parran, John D.	M	11,13,20,29,64
Asst Prof Adj	Raval, Shanti	D	64C,11,20
Lect	Reeves, Bethany	M	11,36,39,60A,61
Asst Prof Adj	Rhodebeck, Jacob	D	66A,66C,11,13
Lect Adj	Robinson, Rick	M	11,13,65,32
Lect Adj	Rothshteyn, Eleonora		66C,11
Prof	Yau, Eugenia Oi Yan	D	11,36,61,40,60A

NY0280 Bronx Community College

Department of Art & Music
University Ave W 181 St
Bronx, NY 10453
(718) 289-5252   Fax: (718) 289-6433
www.bcc.cuny.edu/artmusic
E-mail: ruth.bass@bcc.cuny.edu

2 Year Institution

Chair, Art & Music: Ruth Bass, 80A
Deputy Chair: Tom Cipullo, 80H

Prof	Cipullo, Tom	M	13A,13,10,36,61
Assoc Prof	Yarmolinsky, Benjamin	D	13A,13,10,45,70

NY0350 Broome Community College

Department of Music
PO Box 1017
Binghamton, NY 13902-1017
(607) 778-5000   Fax: (607) 778-5394
www.sunybroome.edu
E-mail: kinney_m@sunybroome.edu

2 Year Institution

Chair: Michael Kinney, 80A

Inst	Alfonsetti, Louis	M	47
Inst	Bachman, Jerome	M	29,47
Inst	Cerniglia, Richard C.	B	35C
Inst	Dawe, Brenda M.	M	13C,61
Asst Prof	Grahame, Gerald	M	36,61
Inst	Greaves, Robert	B	34
Inst	Kennedy, Laura H.	M	66A
Prof	Kinney, Michael	D	13,10,11

Inst	Lalli, Marcus	M	35C
Inst	Maiolo, Georgetta	B	64A
Inst	Roma, Joseph	M	65
Inst	Smith, Vincent	M	64A
Inst	Stalker, Stephen	M	62C
Inst	Sweeny, Paul	M	70

NY0400 Canisius College

Department of Fine Arts - Music
2001 Main St
Buffalo, NY 14208
(716) 888-2536   Fax: (716) 888-2402
www.canisius.edu
E-mail: caryj@canisius.edu

4 Year Liberal Arts Jesuit Institution

Chair of Fine Arts, Dir., Music & Artist Series: Jane G. Cary, 80A,80C,80F

Adj Prof	Accurso, Robert	B	65
Adj Prof	Aquina, Carmen	M	13
Adj Prof	Aylward, Ansgarius	M	60B,38,41,62A
Adj Prof	Barnum, Ellen M.	M	12A,64D,15
Adj Prof	Bennett, Dana	M	63B
Adj Prof	Biddle, Paul D.	M	60B,37
Prof	Cary, Jane G.	M	11,12A,66H
Adj Prof	Colquhoun, Michael	D	10,20
Adj Prof	Eckenrode, Bryan	M	62C
Assoc Prof	Falkenstein, Richard	D	11,12A,70
Adj Prof	Fuchs, Stuart	M	70
Adj Prof	Gormley, Lon	B	63C,63D
Adj Prof	Gregory, Cristen	M	35A
Adj Prof	Hardcastle, Geoffrey C.	M	63A
Adj Prof	Harris, Carole J.	D	13A,13B,13C,13D
Adj Prof	Keenan-Takagi, Kathleen D.	D	32,36,12
Adj Prof	Malkiewicz, Martha	M	11,64D
Adj Prof	Martin, Roland E.	M	66G
Adj Prof	Mattix, Anna	M	64B
Adj Prof	Reeds, Elizabeth	B	41,64A
Adj Prof	Salathe, Leslie	M	62A,62B
Adj Prof	Schiavone, David C.	B	47,48,64C,64E
Adj Prof	Schmid, Karen	M	66A
Adj Prof	Scinta, Frank	M	61,31A,32C,36
Adj Prof	Shurtliffe, Brett	M	62D
Adj Prof	Thomas, Suzanne M.	B	62E
Adj Prof	Thorburn, Melissa R.	M	61,39
Adj Prof	Vehar, Persis Parshall	M	10,66A
Adj Prof	Wright, James	M	61

NY0450 Cayuga County Community College

Department of Music
197 Franklin St
Auburn, NY 13021
(315) 255-1743   Fax: (315) 255-2117
www.cayuga-cc.edu
E-mail: keeler@cayuga-cc.edu

2 Year Institution

Music Contact: Michael Cortese, 80A
Chair, English & Humanities: Steve Keeler, 80A

Adj	Bailey, Sally	M	66A,66B,66C,66D
Adj	Bellamy, Amy J.	M	11,29A,36,61
Asst Prof	Cortese, Michael	M	10,11,20,34,47

NY0500 City Univ of New York-Brooklyn

Conservatory of Music
2900 Bedford Ave
Brooklyn, NY 11210-2889
(718) 951-5286   Fax: (718) 951-4502
www.bcmusic.org
E-mail: brucem@brooklyn.cuny.edu

4 Year Institution, Graduate School

Master of Music in Composition, Master of Music in Performance, Advanced Certificate in Music Education, Master of Arts in Performance Practice, Master of Arts in Musicology, Master of Arts in Music Teaching

Director: Bruce C. MacIntyre, 80A
Dir., Undergraduate Studies & Acting Dir., Center for Computer Music: Douglas H. Cohen, 80B
Dir., Graduate Studies: Stephanie Jensen-Moulton, 80C
Dir., Preparatory Division: Diane M. Newman, 80E
Dir., Inst. for Studies in American Music: Jeffrey J. Taylor, 80F
Assistant Director: Emily A. Moss, 80H

Adj Assoc Prof	Abrams, Brian	D	32H
Adj Lect	Allen, Eddie	B	63A,29
Prof	Allen, Ray	D	11,20G,29A,20H
Prof	Atlas, Allan	D	13,12A,12
Assoc Prof	Barrett, Richard	DIPL	39,61,60
Adj Assoc Prof	Begelman, Igor	M	64C
Asst Prof Adj	Biegel, Jeffrey	M	66A
Adj Lect	Blake, Daniel	M	11,13
Assoc Prof Adj	Bonvisutto, Bruce	M	63C
Adj Lect	Braunstein, Riki	M	32
Asst Prof Adj	Braverman, Frederick	M	63C
Other	Brunner, George	M	34,35C,10B
Adj Lect	Cassara, Frank	M	65,50
Assoc Prof Adj	Chai, Liang	M	62A
Adj Lect	Christensen, Donald	M	32E,64C,64
Lect	Cohen, Douglas H.	D	13,10,11,34
Adj Asst Prof	Cohen, Paul	M	64E
Adj Lect	Corn, Paul	M	37,47
Assoc Prof Adj	Cultice, Thomas	M	61
Asst Prof Adj	Cutler, Sara	B	62E
Adj Lect	Davis, D. Edward	M	11,13
Asst Prof Adj	Diez, German	M	66A
Prof Adj	Dunn, Mignon	B	61
Asst Prof	Eckardt, Jason K.	D	10,10F,13
Asst Prof Adj	Eguchi, Akira	M	66A,66C
Adj Asst Prof	Ellis, Monica	M	64D
Prof Adj	Feldman, Marion	M	62C
Adj Lect	Feltman, Joshua	M	11,13,43
Asst Prof Adj	Frandsen, Lars	DIPL	41,70
Adj Lect	Freyberg, Victoria	M	66A
Adj Asst Prof	Fruehauf, Tina	D	11,12
	Gallagher, Maureen	D	62B
Assoc Prof	Geers, Douglas E.	DMA	10A,10B,10F
Prof Adj	Goldberg, Bernard	DIPL	41,64A
Adj Lect	Gould, David	M	41,64C
Adj Asst Prof	Griffin, Stephanie	D	62B
Asst Prof	Grubbs, David	D	10C,12,34
Adj Lect	Gubrud, Irene	B	61
Prof	Hager, Nancy M.	D	13,11,12A,12
Adj Lect	Harte, Monica	M	61,39
Prof	Hedwig, Douglas F.	D	49,63A,63D
Assoc Prof Adj	Hindell, Leonard	M	64D
Asst Prof Adj	Hirsh, Jules	M	62D
Assoc Prof Adj	Howard, Howard	B	63B
Adj Lect	Ingliss, Robert B.	B	64B
Adj Lect	Ivanov, Kalin H.	M	41,62C
Asst Prof	Jensen-Moulton, Stephanie	M	11,12,12E
Asst Prof Adj	Jones, Harold	DIPL	64A
Asst Prof Adj	Kaminski, Michael	D	66G
Prof Adj	Kang, Hyo	DIPL	62A
Prof	Kawasaki, Masao	DIPL	41,62A,62B
Adj PT	Kent, Adam S.	D	66A
Prof	Leon, Tania	M	10,38,41,60
Adj Asst Prof	Lewis, Alexandra M.	D	11,12,13C,66D
Assoc Prof Adj	Lucarelli, Bert	B	64B
Prof	MacIntyre, Bruce C.	D	12A,12,36
Adj Asst Prof	Makarina, Olga	M	61
Adj Lect	Manabe, Noriko	M	14,12E,20
Assoc Prof Adj	McCaffrey, Patricia	M	61
Adj Lect	Morales-Matos, Rolando	M	65
Adj Lect	Morris, Anthony	M	62D
Asst Prof	Moss, Emily A.	D	32,48,64D,60B
Adj Lect	Mundinger, Gretchen	M	61
Other	Newman, Diane M.	M	
Adj Lect	Oldham, Barbara	M	41,63B
Prof	Oppens, Ursula	M	66,41,42,43
Assoc Prof	Palmquist, Jane E.	PhD	32,11
Adj Prof	Panteleyev, Vladimir	D	62C
Adj Lect	Parodi, Jorge	M	39,40,41,66C
Inst	Peterson, Vince	M	36,60A,32D,13,11
Assoc Prof Adj	Powell, Michael	B	63C
Assoc Prof	Raphael, Honora	M	16
Asst Prof Adj	Reichert, Matthew R.	M	62A
Adj Asst Prof	Rojak, John	B	63C,63D
Asst Prof Adj	Rojas, Marcus	B	63D
Assoc Prof	Rothman, George	M	38,42,60B
Adj Lect	Schnaible, Mark	M	61
Adj Lect	Seldess, Zachary	M	11,13
Adj Asst Prof	Silverman, Marissa	D	32
Assoc Prof Adj	Sperry, Paul	M	61
Assoc Prof Adj	Tanaka, Naoka	DIPL	62A,62B
Assoc Prof Adj	Taylor, Jane	B	64D
Asst Prof	Taylor, Jeffrey J.	D	12,11,29A
Adj Asst Prof	Thorman, Marc	D	10,13,12A,20,14C
Assoc Prof	Washington, Salim	M	47,46,29,29B
Lect Adj	Willson, Brian S.	M	65,11
Other	Wood, Zeno D.	B	66F,13C
Assoc Prof Adj	Woodruff, William	M	61
Adj Assoc Prof	Zlotkin, Fred	D	41,62C

NY0550 City Univ of New York-City Coll

Department of Music
160 Convent Ave
New York, NY 10031
(212) 650-5411   Fax: (212) 650-5428
www.ccny.cuny.edu/music
E-mail: music@ccny.cuny.edu

4 Year Institution, Graduate School

Master of Arts in Composition, Master of Arts in Historical Musicology, Master of Arts in Performance, Master of Arts in Music Theory, Master of Arts in Jazz Studies

Chair: Stephen Jablonsky, 80A
Acting Dean: Geraldine Murphy, 80A
Dir., Artist/Performance Series: Alison Deane, 80F
Assistant Chair: Dan Carillo, 80H

Asst Prof	Carillo, Dan	M	47,13,46,10,29
Assoc Prof	Deane, Alison	M	66,41,42
Prof	Del Tredici, David	M	60,10
Lect	Gallon, Ray	M	29,11
Prof	Hanning, Barbara Russano	D	13A,11,12A,12
Assoc Prof	Holober, Michael	M	66A,29,10,46,47
Assoc Prof	Jablonsky, Stephen	D	11,63A,10A,10F,13
Assoc Prof	Kozel, Paul	M	10,45,35
Lect	Krasner, Orly	D	12
Assoc Prof	O'Donnell, Shaugn	PhD	13,10,12
Prof	Patitucci, John		10,46,47,51,50
Assoc Prof	Perl, Jonathan	B	45,35B,35C,35D
Assoc Prof	Pieslak, Jonathan	M	10,13
Asst Prof	Pittson, Suzanne	M	29,61
Assoc Prof	Reeves, Scott	M	13,47,53,29
Adj Asst Prof	Steele, Janet	M	13A,55,61,66A,36

NY0600 City Univ of New York-Grad Center

PhD/DMA Programs in Music
365 Fifth Ave
New York, NY 10016
(212) 817-8590   Fax: (212) 817-1529
web.gc.cuny.edu/Music
E-mail: music@gc.cuny.edu

Graduate School

PhD in Historical Musicology, PhD in Ethnomusicology, PhD in Music Theory, PhD in Composition, DMA in Composition, DMA in Performance

Executive Officer: David Olan, 80A

Assoc Prof	Allen, Ray	D	20G
Asst Prof	Anson-Cartwright, Mark	D	13
Prof	Atlas, Allan W.	D	12A,12
Asst Prof	Bauer, William R.	D	12A,29A
Asst Prof Adj	Blazekovic, Zdravko	D	12G
Prof	Blum, Stephen	D	12,14
Prof	Brown, Royal	D	10C
Assoc Prof	Burke, Richard	D	12
Prof	Burnett, Henry	D	12,14
Assoc Prof	Burstein, L. Poundie	D	13
Assoc Prof	Carey, Norman	D	13,42
Prof	Corigliano, John	B	10F,10
Asst Prof Adj	Cowdery, James R.	D	20F
Assoc Prof	Deane, Allison	M	66A
Prof	DeFord, Ruth	D	12
Prof	Del Tredici, David	M	10F,10
Asst Prof	Eckardt, Jason	D	10
Prof	Hampton, Barbara	D	14
Prof	Hanning, Barbara	D	12A,12
Asst Prof	Hollerbach, Peter D.	D	14
Prof	Howe, Hubert S.	D	13,10B
Asst Prof	Jenkins, Chadwick	D	12
Prof	Kahan, Sylvia	D	66A,12A
Prof	Kawasaki, Masao	DIPL	62A,62B
Prof	Kramer, Richard	D	12A,12
Prof	Lambert, Philip	D	13,13F
Prof	Leon, Tania	M	10,60
Prof	MacIntyre, Bruce C.	D	12
Asst Prof Adj	Mackenzie, Barbara Dobbs	D	12,34
Prof	Manuel, Peter G.	D	14,20C,20H
Assoc Prof	Nichols, Jeff	D	10A,13E,10F
Asst Prof	Oates, Jennifer Lynn	D	12,16,12A,12C
Assoc Prof	O'Donnell, Shaugn	D	13F,14C
Prof	Olan, David	D	10F,10,10B
Prof	Oppens, Ursula	DIPL	66A
Prof	Orenstein, Arbie	D	12A
Prof	Peress, Maurice	M	60,38
Asst Prof	Pieslak, Jonathan	D	13F
Asst Prof Adj	Piza, Antoni	D	20F
Prof	Ritt, Morey	M	66A
Prof	Rothstein, William	D	12A
Adj	Rudman, Jessica		13A
Prof	Saloman, Ora Frishberg	D	12A,12
Prof	Saylor, Bruce	D	10F,10
Prof	Sheldon, Paul	D	64C,64E
Assoc Prof	Slavin, Dennis	D	12A,12
Asst Prof	Spicer, Mark	D	13,14C
Assoc Prof	Stone, Anne	D	12A,12
Prof	Straus, Joseph N.	D	13
Prof	Sugarman, Jane	D	14
Prof	Swartz, Anne	D	12A,12
Prof	Taylor, Jeffrey	D	29
Assoc Prof	Tomasello, Andrew	D	12,14,29A

NY0625 City Univ of New York-Hunter Coll

Department of Music-416N
695 Park Ave
New York, NY 10065
(212) 772-5020   Fax: (212) 772-5022
www.hunter.cuny.edu/music
E-mail: music@hunter.cuny.edu

4 Year Institution, Graduate School

Master of Arts in Music, Master of Arts in Teaching in Music Education

Chair: Ruth DeFord, 80A
Dir., Undergraduate Studies: Mark Spicer, 80B
Dir., Graduate Studies: L. Poundie Burstein, 80C

Vstng Asst Prof	Aksoy, Ozan	D	20
Vstng Assoc Prof	Argyros, Maria	M	61
Assoc Prof Adj	Bartow, James	M	20A,20G,70
Lect Adj	Benavides, Raul	M	12A
Asst Prof	Blundell, Reuben E.	D	38,11
Assoc Prof	Bobetsky, Victor V.	D	11,12A,62E
Assoc Prof	Burke, Richard N.	D	11,12A,12,20G
Asst Prof	Burleson, Geoffrey	D	66A,13,12A,66,42
Assoc Prof	Burstein, L. Poundie	D	13A,13
Asst Prof Adj	Burwasser, Daniel	D	32
Asst Prof	Cabrini, Michele	D	12B,12A,13B,11,12
Lect	Coppola, Catherine	D	11,12A
Prof	DeFord, Ruth	D	11,12A,12,12C
Lect Adj	DeMotta, David	M	13
Lect Adj	Dumbauld, Benjamin	M	20
Asst Prof	Ewell, Philip	D	13,13F,13I,62C
Teach Fellow	Fleming, Drew	M	13
Lect Adj	Gabrielsen, Dag	M	10,11
Teach Fellow	Garvey, Bradford	M	20
Prof	Gonzalez, Susan	D	11,61,54
Asst Prof Adj	Graff, Steven	D	41,66A
Vstng Lect	Hammond, Gary	M	11,66A,66D
Prof	Hampton, Barbara L.	D	14,20G,29A
Vstng Lect	Ishida, Nobuyuki	M	66C
Lect Adj	Jackson, D. D.	M	29,47
Lect Adj	Katz, Judith	M	64
Vstng Lect	Keberle, Ryan	M	29,47,11,13,63
Lect Adj	Leibensperger, Peter	M	13
Lect Adj	Mahinka, Janice	M	20
Assoc Prof	Mahoney, Shafer	D	13A,13,10
Asst Prof Adj	Millioto, Thomas	D	70
Prof	Mueller, Paul F.	D	10F,60,11,12A,36
Asst Prof Adj	Nguyen, Quynh	M	11,66A
Lect Adj	Noriega, Scott	M	11
Asst Prof Adj	Noyes, James	M	64E
Asst Prof Adj	Overholt, Sara	D	70
Lect Adj	Owens, Priscilla	M	47,29
Lect Adj	Rupcich, Matthew	M	60A
Assoc Prof	Spicer, Mark	M	13A,13
Lect Adj	Stokes, Jordan	M	11
Lect Adj	Terrigno, Loretta	M	13
Prof	Thompson, Jewel	D	13A,13
Lect PT	Wetzel, James	M	36,60A
Lect Adj	Williamson, Emily	M	20
Teach Fellow	You, JaeSong	M	13
Lect PT	Zalantis, Helen	M	32

NY0630 City Univ of New York-J Jay Coll
Department of Art and Music
899 Tenth Ave
New York, NY 10019
(212) 237-8325   Fax: (212) 237-8333
www.jjay.cuny.edu/departments/art
E-mail: lfarrington@jjay.cuny.edu

4 Year Institution

Chair: Lisa Farrington, 80A

Adj	Barger, Laura		
Adj	Barger, Laura Alison		
Adj	Beliavsky, Daniel		
Asst Prof	Bierman, Benjamin	PhD	63A,10,13,34,35
Adj	Dinnerstein, Noe		14
Assoc Prof	Greenberg, Laura		13,10,66A,66D,11
Adj	Hatchett, Yvonne		
Assoc Prof	Lapidus, Benjamin	PhD	14,70,20H
Adj	Lupo, Michael		
Prof	Manuel, Peter	PhD	14
Adj	Sheppard, Gregory		
Adj	Stoessinger, Carolyn		
Adj	Thomas, Samuel		

NY0635 City Univ of New York-Lehman Coll
Department of Music
250 Bedford Park Blvd W
Bronx, NY 10468
(718) 960-8247   Fax: (718) 960-7248
www.lehman.edu/deanhum/music
E-mail: music.department@lehman.cuny.edu

4 Year Institution, Graduate School

Master of Arts in Music Teaching

Chair: Bernard Shockett, 80A

Prof	Battipaglia, Diana M.	D	11,32,36,66A,38
Prof	Corigliano, John	B	10F,10,11,54
Prof	Hyatt, Jack	D	13,63A
Lect	Prince, Penny	M	32,66A,66B,66C
Prof	Tilley, Janette M.	D	12A,11,12

NY0640 City Univ of New York-Medgar Ever
Department of Music
1650 Bedford Ave
Brooklyn, NY 11225-2201
(718) 270-4927   Fax: (718) 270-4828
www.mec.cuny.edu
E-mail: ebarnes@mec.cuny.edu

4 Year Institution

Chair: Elendar Barnes, 80A
Co-Coordinator: Verna Green, 80H
Co-Coordinator: Moses Phillips, 80H

Prof	Barnes, Elendar	M	
Lect	Green, Verna	D	20A,20H,32D,32E,36
Inst	Johnson, Alfred	M	34,35
Lect	McMillan, Glenn	M	14A,14B
Lect	Mitchell, Roman	M	29A,29B,66A,66B
Lect	Phillips, Moses	M	12,13A,13B,13C,64A

NY0642 City Univ of New York-Queens Coll
Aaron Copland School of Music
65-30 Kissena Blvd
Flushing, NY 11367
(718) 997-3800   Fax: (718) 997-3849
www.qc.cuny.edu/music
E-mail: edward.smaldone@qc.cuny.edu

4 Year Institution, Graduate School

Master of Arts in Composition, Master of Arts in Historical Musicology, Master of Arts in Performance, Master of Arts in Music Theory, Master of Science in Music Education, Master of Arts in Jazz Performance & Composition

Acting Chair: Edward Smaldone, 80A,80G
Associate Chair & Dir., Undergraduate Studies: Henry Burnett, 80B,80H
Dir., Undergraduate Performance Studies: Morey Ritt, 80B
Dir., Graduate Studies & Admissions: William Rothstein, 80C,80D
Admissions, Graduate Performance: Marcy Rosen, 80D
Associate Chair: Hubert S. Howe, Jr., 80H
Asst. to the Chair: Jonathan Allan Irving

Asst Prof	Anson-Cartwright, Mark	D	13
Vstng Asst Prof	Berkman, David		29,66A
Emeritus	Brings, Allen	D	13,11
Emeritus	Burkhart, Charles L.	M	13A,13,66A
Prof	Burnett, Henry	D	12,14
Emeritus	Eberl, Carl		60
Prof Emeritus	Eisman, Lawrence W.	D	11,32
Assoc Prof	Gagne, David	D	13
Emeritus	Goodman, Joseph		13
Assoc Prof	Hart, Antonio	M	29,64E
Emeritus	Heath, James		29
Prof	Howe, Hubert S.	D	13,45,34
Asst Prof	John, James A.	DMA	36,40,60A
Prof	Jolley, David		13C,63
Emeritus	Kamien, Roger		11,13
Emeritus	Kouguell, Alexander		62C
Emeritus	Kraft, Leo	M	12,13
Emeritus	Lerner, Edward	D	12
Asst Prof	Lipsey, Michael	M	37,50,65
Prof Emeritus	Mandelbaum, Joel	D	13,60
Prof	Mossman, Michael	M	29,35B,63A
Emeritus	Musgrave, Thea		10
Vstng Assoc Prof	Neidich, Charles		64C
Assoc Prof	Nichols, Jeff W.	D	10,10F,13
Lect	Nitzberg, Roy J.	D	13A,13B,13C,13D
Prof	Orenstein, Arbie	D	13A,13,11,12A
Vstng Asst Prof	Overholt, Sherry	D	39,61
Prof	Peress, Maurice		60,38,39
Lect	Pershing, Drora		13,12A
Prof	Phillips, Daniel		62A
Prof	Ritt, Morey	M	66A
Emeritus	Rorick, William		16
Prof	Rosen, Marcy		62C,42
Prof	Rothstein, William	D	13
Assoc Prof	Sang, Richard C.	D	32C,37
Prof	Saylor, Bruce S.	D	13,10F,10
Emeritus	Schachter, Carl	M	13,12A
Asst Prof	Schober, David	D	13,10A,66A,10
Prof	Smaldone, Edward	D	13,10,10F,11
Assoc Prof	Smith, Janice P.	D	32B,32F
Assoc Prof	Stone, Anne		12
Emeritus	Weinberg, Henry	D	10,13
Emeritus	White, Robert		60A,61
Asst Prof	Wilbourne, Emily	D	12A,12E
Emeritus	Wright, Helen		32

NY0644 City Univ of New York-Staten Isl
Department of Perf & Creat Arts
IP 203
2800 Victory Blvd
Staten Island, NY 10314-6609
(718) 982-2520   Fax: (718) 982-2537
www.csi.cuny.edu
E-mail: george.sanchez@csi.cuny.edu

4 Year Institution

Coordinator: Sylvia Kahan, 80A
Chair, Performing & Creative Arts: George Sanchez, 80A

Asst Prof Adj	Alexander, Marina	M	36,12A,12C,60A
Asst Prof	Bauer, William R.	D	10F,12A,12C,13
Lect Adj	Brown, Edward	M	70,41
Asst Prof Adj	Carlon, Paul	D	29A,64E
Lect Adj	Clive, David	M	65
Asst Prof Adj	Dorin, Ryan	D	13
Lect Adj	Fluchaire, Olivier	M	62A,62B,11,13A,42
Lect Adj	Heimur, Elena	M	61,66A,66D
Asst Prof	Kahan, Sylvia	D	12A,12C,66,13A,13C
Asst Prof	Keberle, David S.	D	10,10B,64C,42,13A
Lect Adj	Keller, Justin	M	29A
Lect Adj	Magnani, Victor A.	M	29A
Lect Adj	Morreale, Michael	M	11,63A,29A,47,13A
Asst Prof Adj	Oh, Yoojin	D	11,42,66
Lect Adj	Prisco, Peter	B	70,62D
Asst Prof Adj	Raickovich, Milos	D	11,13A,20
Asst Prof Adj	Rapport, Evan	D	20
Lect Adj	Sirotta, Michael	M	20
Lect Adj	Tancredi, Dominick	B	13A,29A
Lect Adj	Wechesler, David J.	M	11,13A,29A,41,64A
Asst Prof Adj	Yourke, Peter	D	11

NY0646 City Univ of New York-York College

Department of Perf. & Fine Arts
Music
94 20 Guy Brewer Blvd #1A12
Jamaica, NY 11451
(718)262-2412
www.york.cuny.edu
E-mail: tzlabinger@york.cuny.edu

4 Year Institution

Chair: Tim Amrhein, 80A
Coordinator, Music: Tom Zlabinger, 80A

Adj Lect	Adams, Mark	B	13,66
Adj Lect	Billingslea, Sandra	B	11
Other	Cuenca, Sylvia	B	65
Adj Lect	Dixon, Walter	B	13A,72
Other	Dugard, Freddy	B	65
Adj Lect	Espar, Michael	M	32F,34,35
Adj Lect	Fink, Katherine	B	11,12
	Koza, Matt	B	13A,64C,64E
Other	Lindsey, Gerald	B	62D
Adj Lect	Quash, Jonathan	B	36,54,61
Other	Samu, Lex	M	63A
Adj Lect	Uzeki, Yoichi	M	66
Other	Yao, John	M	63C
Other	Ziemba, Chris	M	66
Lect	Zlabinger, Tom	M	62D,29,14,20,47

NY0650 Colgate University

Department of Music
13 Oak Dr
Hamilton, NY 13346-1338
(315) 228-7642   Fax: (315) 228-7557
www.colgate.edu
E-mail: jswain@colgate.edu

4 Year Institution

Chair: Joseph P. Swain, 80A
Dir., Artist/Performance Series: Roberta Healey, 80F
Dir., Summer Festival: Laura Klugherz, 80G

PT	Balestra, Richard	M	70
PT	Campbell, Laura	M	64A
Assoc Prof	Cashman, Glenn	D	47,64E
Prof	Cheng, Marietta	M	13,60,11,36,38
PT	Cleveland, Michael	B	62A
PT	Crafton, Colleen	M	63C
PT	Decock, Murray	D	66A
PT	Dudgeon, Ralph	D	63A
Prof	Godwin, Joscelyn	D	12A,12
PT	Heyman, Steven	D	66A
PT	Johns, James		47
PT	Kimme, Glenn	M	66C,66G
Prof	Klugherz, Laura	D	13,11,41,62A,62B
PT	Koen, Kerry	M	66C,66A
PT	Montalbano, Richard		66A
Prof Emeritus	Morrill, Dexter G.	D	10,45,29A,34
PT	Pilgrim, Neva	M	61
PT	Pugh, Darryl	M	62D
PT	Rabin, Barbara	M	64C
PT	Renard-Payen, Florent	M	62C
PT	Rosenfeld, Steven	D	66A
Prof Emeritus	Skelton, William	M	14,20D,38,64D
PT	Skovenski, Michael	M	64B
Emeritus PT	Slater, Vivien H.	M	66A
PT	Snedeker, Gretchen	M	63B
	Stern, Jeffrey S.		36,61
PT	Stockham, Jeff	M	63A,47
Assoc Prof	Swain, Joseph P.	D	13,12B,12F,12C

NY0700 College of St Rose, The

Department of Music
Massry Center for the Arts
432 Western Ave
Albany, NY 12203
(518) 454-5178   Fax: (518) 454-2146
www.strose.edu
E-mail: hansbror@strose.edu

4 Year Institution, Graduate School

Master of Science in Music Education

Chair & Dir., Summer Programs: Robert S. Hansbrough, 80A,80G
Coord., Music Education & Undergraduate Studies: Joseph A. Eppink, 80B
Dir., Graduate Studies: Bruce Roter, 80C
Dir., Artist Series: Yvonne Hansbrough, 80F

Asst Prof	Bebe, David M.	D	38,13,42,62C
Artist in Res	Beer, Lucille	M	61
Assoc Prof	Eppink, Joseph A.	D	32B,66G,66H,32C,32A
Prof	Evoskevich, Paul	M	47,64E,53,29,42
Prof	Hansbrough, Robert S.	D	32E,42,37,65
Assoc Prof	Hansbrough, Yvonne	D	64A,67D,12A,42
Assoc Prof	Harwood, Susan	D	39,36,61,40
Assoc Prof	Johnston, Dennis	D	32E,12C,49,63A,60B
Vstng Inst	Kelly, Gary	B	35,34,62D,43
Asst Prof	Kim, Young	D	13B,13C,66A,66D
Prof	Levi, Michael	D	36,29B,13,60A,32D
Asst Prof	Lister, Michael C.	D	32D,32C,55D,36,13
Asst Prof	McLowry, Sean	D	34D,35G,34E,34F,34H
Assoc Prof	Nelson, Mary Anne	M	34,35
Assoc Prof	Roter, Bruce	D	10,13,12A,64C
Vstng Asst Prof	Thomas, Robert E.	D	10,13A,13B,13C,13D
Asst Prof	Wise, Sherwood W.	D	64B,48,13,64D,42

NY0750 Columbia University

Department of Music-MC 1813
621 Dodge Hall
2960 Broadway
New York, NY 10027-6902
(212) 854-3825   Fax: (212) 854-8191
www.music.columbia.edu
E-mail: amg59@columbia.edu

4 Year Institution, Graduate School

PhD in Historical Musicology, PhD in Ethnomusicology, PhD in Music Theory, DMA in Composition

Chair: Aaron A. Fox, 80A
Dir., Undergraduate Studies: Bradford Garton, 80B
Dir., Graduate Studies (Spring Term): Walter Frisch, 80C
Dir., Graduate Studies (Fall Term): George E. Lewis, 80C
Assistant Chair & Dir., Graduate Studies: Ellie M. Hisama, 80H,80C

Teach Assoc	Bailen, Eliot T.	D	62C,41
Prof Emeritus	Bent, Ian	D	11,12A,12,13J
Assoc Prof	Boynton, Susan	D	11,12A,12,12B
Lect	Bradley-Kramer, Deborah	D	11,12A,41
Prof Emeritus	Christensen, Dieter	D	14,14A,12C
Lect	Ciucci, Alessandra	D	11,14,15,14C,20B
Assoc Prof	Cohen, David E.	D	13,12A,13J
Librarian	Davis, Elizabeth	M	16
Prof	Dubiel, Joseph	D	10,11,13
Prof	Edwards, George H.	MFA	13,10,11
Assoc Prof	Fox, Aaron A.	D	14,20G,12E
Prof	Frisch, Walter	D	11,12A,12
Prof	Garton, Bradford	D	10,11,45,34
Assoc Prof	Gerbino, Giuseppe	D	11,12A,12
Asst Prof	Gray, Ellen	D	14A,14E,15,20F,14D
Asst Prof	Henson, Karen A.	D	11,15,39,12A,12B
Prof	Hisama, Ellie M.	D	15,13E,12A,10B,13F
Prof	Lerdahl, Fred	MFA	10,12F,11
Asst Prof	Levy, Fabien	D	10A,10F,13E,13F
Prof	Lewis, George E.	B	10A,10B,12E,29E,34H
Lect	Milarsky, Jeffrey F.	M	38,10F,60
Prof	Murail, Tristan C.		10,34,13L,12F,10F
Lect	Ostbye, Niels J.	DIPL	66A
Prof Emeritus	Perkins, Leeman L.	D	11,12,31A,36
Lect	Pilzer, Joshua	D	11,14,20C
Lect	Silverberg, Laura Gail	D	11,12
Prof	Sisman, Elaine	D	12,11,12A,12B
Lect	Skelly, Michael	B	66A
Assoc Prof	Washburne, Christopher	D	14,29,47
Lect	Wilbourne, Emily	D	11,12,15,20F

NY0850 Concordia College

Department of Music
171 White Plains Rd
Bronxville, NY 10708
(914) 337-9300   Fax: (914) 395-4500
www.concordia-ny.edu
E-mail: jason.thoms@concordia-ny.edu

4 Year Institution

Chair: Jason A. Thoms, 80A

Adj PT	Charupakorn, Joseph		70
Adj PT	Dermody, Joseph	M	62B
Adj PT	Foss, Treva M.	M	61,20

Adj PT	Laine, Karin	M	61
Adj PT	Reiss, Deborah	M	44,40,31A,66C
Asst Prof	Thoms, Jason A.	D	36,32D,61,55D,12A

NY0900 Cornell University
Department of Music
101 Lincoln Hall
Ithaca, NY 14853-4101
(607) 255-4097   Fax: (607) 254-2877
music.cornell.edu
E-mail: musicinfo@cornell.edu

4 Year Institution, Graduate Program

DMA in Composition, DMA in Performance Practice, PhD in Musicology

Dean, College of Arts: Peter Lepage, 80A
Chair: Steven Pond, 80A
Dir., Undergraduate Studies: Chris Younghoon Kim, 80B
Dir., Graduate Studies: Neal Zaslaw, 80C

Prof Emeritus	Bilson, Malcolm	D	66A,66E
Prof	Bjerken, Xak	D	66A,42,43
Prof	Boettcher, Bonna	D	16,12A,12C
Asst Prof	Ernste, Kevin	D	10B,10A,34
Prof	Groos, Arthur	D	12
Senior Lect	Haines-Eitzen, John	DIPL	62C,42
Prof	Harris-Warrick, Rebecca	D	11,12,52
Assoc Prof Emeritus	Hatch, Martin	D	14,20B,20D,20E
Asst Prof	Hicks, Andrew	D	12A,13J
Prof Emeritus	Hsu, John	D	42,62C,67A,38,60B
Prof Emeritus	Husa, Karel	D	10F,60,10A
Prof	Kellock, Judith	M	61
Asst Prof	Kim, Ariana	D	62A,62B
Assoc Prof	Kim, Chris Younghoon	M	38,41,42,60
Lect	Lewandowski, Annie	M	53,66A
Senior Lect	Merrill, Paul	M	46,47,29B,29C,63A
Lect	Miller, Christopher J.		20D,14D
Prof Emerita	Monosoff, Sonya	DIPL	41,62A,62B,67B
Asst Prof	Moseley, Roger S.	D	12,13,14D,34H
Lect	Pepinsky, Juliana May		64A
Assoc Prof	Peraino, Judith A.	D	12A,12D,15
Asst Prof	Piekut, Benjamin	D	12A,12D,12E
Assoc Prof	Pond, Steven	D	14,29
Prof	Richards, Annette	D	12,13A,13B,66G
Prof Emeritus	Rosen, David	D	12A,12B,12C
Lect	Rowehl, John	M	36,40,60A
Prof	Sierra, Roberto	M	10A,10F,13B,13F
Prof Emeritus	Sokol, Thomas A.	M	60,36,40
Prof Emeritus	Stith, Marice W.	M	37,63
Prof	Stucky, Steven	D	10,13B,13D,13F,43
Prof	Tucker, Scott	M	60,36,40,13A,20A
Assoc Prof	Turner, Cynthia Johnston	D	60,37,41,42,38
Prof	Webster, James	D	12,13B,13D,13I
Lect	Yampolsky, Miri	DIPL	42,66A
Assoc Prof	Yearsley, David	D	12,13,11,66H,66G
Prof	Zaslaw, Neal	D	12,55B

NY0950 Corning Community College
Department of Music
1 Academic Dr
Corning, NY 14830-3297
(607) 962-9298   Fax: (607) 962-9456
www.corning-cc.edu
E-mail: lbleile1@corning-cc.edu

2 Year Institution, Intro Courses Only

Chair & Dir., Artist Series: Loueda Bleiler, 80A,80F

| Inst | Bleiler, Loueda | M | 11,12A,13A,13B,36 |

NY1050 Dutchess Community College
Department of Vis/Prf Arts & Comm
53 Pendell Rd
Poughkeepsie, NY 12601-1512
(845) 431-8625   Fax: (845) 431-8629
www.sunydutchess.edu

E-mail: christopher.brelloc@sunydutchess.edu

2 Year Institution

Music Contact: Christopher Brellochs, 80A
Chair: Joe V. Cosentino, 80A

Adj Lect	Armstrong, Jeff	M	11
Adj Lect	Avakian, Helen	M	70
Asst Prof	Brellochs, Christopher	D	47,10,13,12,64E
Adj Lect	Gerbi, Elizabeth	B	36,40,61
Adj Lect	Ham, Lawrence	B	53,29
Adj Lect	Kaczynski, Marrisa	M	38
Adj Lect	Knauth, Dorcinda	D	11,66

NY1100 Eastman School of Music
26 Gibbs St
Rochester, NY 14604-2599
(585) 274-1000   Fax: (585) 274-1088
www.esm.rochester.edu
E-mail: info@esm.rochester.edu

4 Year Institution, Graduate School
Member of NASM

Master of Music in Early Music, DMA in Piano Accompanying & Chamber Music, Master of Arts in Music Theory Pedagogy, Master of Arts in Composition, Master of Arts in Music Education, Master of Arts in Music Theory, Master of Arts in Ethnomusicology, Master of Music in Composition, Master of Music in Conducting, Master of Music in Music Education, Master of Music in Opera, PhD in Music Theory, PhD in Composition, PhD in Music Education, DMA in Composition, DMA in Conducting, DMA in Music Education, Master of Music in Jazz Studies & Contemporary Media, DMA in Performance & Literature, DMA Jazz Studies & Contemporary Media, PhD in Musicology, Master of Arts in Musicology, Master of Music in Performance & Literature, Master of Music in Piano Accompanying & Chamber Music, DMA in Early Music

Joan & Martin Messinger Dean: Douglas Lowry, 80A
Associate Dean, Graduate Studies: Marie Rolf, 80C,80H
Associate Dean, Admissions: Matthew Ardizzone, 80D
Associate Dean, Community & Continuing Education: Howard Potter, 80E
Associate Dean, Academic & Student Affairs: Donna Brink Fox, 80H,80B
Senior Associate Dean, Administration: Michele Gibson, 80H
Executive Associate Dean: Jamal J. Rossi, 80H

Prof	Agostini, Federico	M	62A
Asst Prof	Anderson, Michael Alan	D	12,12A,14F
Prof	Antonova, Natalya	M	66A
Assoc Prof PT	Athayde, Juliana	M	62A
Prof	Azzara, Christopher D.	D	32E,32G
Assoc Prof	BaileyShea, Matthew	D	13B,13E,13F,13I
Prof	Baldo, Jonathan	D	
Prof	Barr, Jean M.	D	66C,42
Asst Prof	Bazler, Corbett	D	12
Asst Prof PT	Beaudette, Sylvie	D	42,66C
Prof Emeritus	Beck, John	M	65
Inst PT	Becker, Kristina	M	
Inst PT	Bezuidenhout, Kristian	M	66H
Prof	Blakeslee, Lynn	B	62A,42
Prof	Boyd, Bonita	B	64A
Assoc Prof PT	Brickman, David	B	62A
Prof	Bride, Kathleen	M	62E
	Brock, Jay D.		54
Prof	Brown, Matthew	D	13B,13D,13I,13J
Asst Prof PT	Burch, Jennifer	B	63B
Inst PT	Burgess, Geoffrey	D	67D
Prof	Burritt, Michael	M	65
	Bush, Abra K.	D	61
Assoc Prof PT	Cahn, William	B	65
Assoc Prof	Campbell, Jeff	D	29A,29B,29C,62D,47
Prof	Caramia, Anthony	M	66A,66B,66D
Prof	Castleman, Charles	M	62A
Prof	Ciesinski, Katherine	M	61
Vstng Inst PT	Conrod, Derek	B	63B
Inst PT	Couderc, Valerie	M	
Prof	Covach, John	D	13,13A,13J,10D
Assoc Prof	Cowdrick, Kathryn	M	61
Inst	Curlee, J. Matthew	M	13A,13B,13C,13D,13K
Asst Prof PT	Curren, Christina	B	
Prof	Daigle, Steven	M	61,39
Prof	Danko, Harold	B	29A,29B,29C,66A,47
Prof	Doane, Steven	M	62C
Prof	Dobbins, William	M	29B,29C,10A,10F,46
Asst Prof PT	DuBois, Peter	M	66G
Prof	Dunsby, Jonathan	D	13F,13I,13K
Assoc Prof	Elisi, Enrico	D	66A,66C
Asst Prof PT	Elliott, Rosemary	M	62C
Assoc Prof	Esse, Melina	D	12A,12B,12D,14C,15
Assoc Prof	Falli, Caterina	M	
Asst Prof	Fetter, John	M	32E
Prof	Fox, Donna Brink	D	32A,32B,32C,32G
Inst PT	Frank, Bruce	D	13B,13C,13D,13H,13I
Asst Prof PT	Freer, Elinor	D	66C,42
Assoc Prof	Freitas, Roger	D	12A,12C,12D,15
Asst Prof PT	Garver, Beryl	M	66C
Asst Prof	Goldman, Edward 'Ted'	D	13K,13C,13B,10A,10F
Prof	Goluses, Nicholas	D	70

Asst Prof PT	Gourfinkel, Anna	M	66C
Assoc Prof	Grant, Kenneth	B	64C,42
Asst Prof	Greitzer, Mary	D	13C,13D,13E,13F,13H
Prof	Grunow, Richard F.	D	32E,32G
Assoc Prof	Guerrero, Jean	D	13B,13E,13F,13J
Prof	Harris, Alan	M	62C
Assoc Prof PT	Harrow, Anne Lindblom	M	64A,42
Assoc Prof	Harry, Don	B	63D,49
Prof	Headlam, David	D	13F,13G,13L,34A,34B
Prof	Hess, Benton	B	61,39
Prof	Higgs, David	M	66G
Prof	Humpherys, Douglas	D	66A
Prof	Hunt, John	M	64D
Asst Prof PT	Hwang, Margery	M	42
Asst Prof	Jakelski, Lisa	D	12A,12E,12B,12C,14F
Assoc Prof	Jenkins, Clay	M	29B,29C,63A,47
Assoc Prof	Kellogg, Mark	B	63C,42
Assoc Prof PT	Kemp, Kathleen	M	62C
Inst PT	Kennedy, Stephen	M	55D,66G
Prof	Killmer, Richard	D	64B
Asst Prof PT	Kodzas, Peter	D	42
Prof	Kopelman, Mikhail	D	62A
Assoc Prof	Koskoff, Ellen	D	14,15,20G,20D,31
Prof	Kowalke, Kim H.	D	12A,12B,12C,12D,15
Prof	Krysa, Oleh	D	62A
Asst Prof PT	Kurau, Pamela	D	
Prof	Kurau, Peter	M	63B
Asst Prof	Kyker, Jennifer	D	14,14C,20,20A
Prof	Laitz, Steven	D	13B,13C,13H,13I
Prof	Lenti, Vincent	M	66A
Asst Prof	Lin, Chien-Kwan	M	64E
Asst Prof PT	Liperote, Kathy	D	32E,32G
Prof	Liptak, David	D	10
Prof	Locke, Ralph P.	D	12A,12B,12C,12D
Prof	Lowry, Douglas	M	37,38,10A,10B,10C
Assoc Prof	Lubman, Bradley	M	43,38,60B
Prof	Macey, Patrick	D	12A,12C,55D
Asst Prof	Mackin, Glenn	D	
Asst Prof PT	Manasse, Jon	M	64C
Prof	Marcellus, John	D	63C
Asst Prof	Martins, Jose Oliveira	D	13B,13E,13F
Prof	Marvin, Elizabeth W.	D	13A,13C,13F,13G,13K
Assoc Prof	Marvin, William	D	13A,13B,13C,13H,13I
Assoc Prof PT	Matson, Melissa	M	62B
Assoc Prof	McHugh, Ernestine	D	31G
Prof	McIver, Robert	D	61
Prof	Meconi, Honey	D	12A,12,55
Prof	Miller, Russell	D	61
Asst Prof	Monahan, Seth	D	13B,13C,13D,13E
Inst	Moritz, Alison	M	39
Prof	Morris, Robert D.	D	10,12,13,20E,31E
Inst	Morrow, Matthew	D	12A,12B,12D
Assoc Prof	Ninomiya, Ayano	M	62A,42
Inst PT	Nissly, Jacob	M	65
Prof	O'Dette, Paul	D	55,56,67G
Asst Prof	Opalach, Jan	B	61
Assoc Prof	Pedersen, Jean	D	
Prof	Penneys, Rebecca	M	66A
Asst Prof PT	Pillow, Charles	M	64E
Prof PT	Porter, William	D	66G,66H
Assoc Prof PT	Prosser, Douglas	B	63A,42
Asst Prof	Remmel, Rachel	D	
Inst PT	Richards, Wade	B	32
Prof	Ricker, Ramon	D	64C,64E
Asst Prof	Rivello, David	M	46
Assoc Prof	Rodland, Carol	M	62B
Prof	Rolf, Marie	D	13B,13F,13H
Asst Prof PT	Ross, Charles	B	65A
Prof	Rossi, Jamal J.	D	64E
Prof	Sanchez-Gutierrez, Carlos	D	10
Prof	Scatterday, Mark	D	37,38,60
Assoc Prof	Scheie, Timothy	D	
Prof	Schindler, Allan	D	10A,10B,10C,34H
Prof PT	Shane, Rita	B	61
Asst Prof	Silvey, Philip E.	D	32D,32G
Asst Prof	Slominski, Johnandrew	D	13B,13C,13E,13H
Asst Prof	Sneider, Robert	B	29,70
Prof	Snyder, Barry	M	66A
Asst Prof	Stanley, Ann Marie	M	32B,32G,32H
Assoc Prof	Steingrover, Reinhild	D	
Vstng Assoc Prof PT	Suadin, I. Ketut	DIPL	20D
Prof	Swensen, Robert	M	61
Assoc Prof	Taylor, George		62B
Asst Prof PT	Tchekina, Tatiana	B	66C
Inst	Teal, Kimberly Hannon		12,14C
Assoc Prof	Temperley, David	D	13B,13G,13K
Assoc Prof	Terefenko, Dariusz	D	13B,13D,13E,13H,29
Asst Prof PT	Thielmann, Christel	B	55,56,67A
Prof	Thompson, James	B	63A,42
Assoc Prof PT	Thompson, Rich	M	65
Prof Emeritus	Thym, Jurgen	D	12A,12B,12C
Prof	True, Nelita	D	66A
Prof	VanDemark, James	B	62D
Prof	Varon, Neil	M	38,60
Prof	Wason, Robert W.	D	13B,13D,13F,13J,29C
Assoc Prof	Watkins, Holly	D	12A,12B,12D,13J,14C
Prof	Webber, Carol	B	61
Prof	Weinert, William	D	36,38,60
Inst PT	West, Glenn A.	M	20A
Prof Emerita	Wheelock, Gretchen A.	D	12A,12B,12C,12D,15
Assoc Prof	Ying, David	D	42,62C
Assoc Prof	Ying, Janet	B	62A,42
Assoc Prof	Ying, Phillip	M	42,62B
Assoc Prof PT	Zager, Daniel	D	16,12C
Assoc Prof	Zohn-Muldoon, Ricardo	D	10,20H

NY1150 Elmira College

Department of Music
One Park Place
Elmira, NY 14901
(607) 735-1948   Fax: (607) 735-1758
www.elmira.edu
E-mail: mspicer@elmira.edu

4 Year Institution

Dean: Stephen Coleman, 80A
Dir., Admissions: Brett Moore, 80D

Lect PT	Coccagnia, Lou	M	64C,64E
Lect PT	Haskell, Peter	B	70
Lect PT	Kelley, Scott	M	37,63A
Lect PT	LaBar, Dan	D	66A
Lect PT	Matthews, Margaret	M	62A,62B,62C
Lect PT	Seeley, Jeffery	D	11,20,36
Prof	Spicer, Mark J.	D	13,11,64A,66A,20G
Lect PT	Stewart, Kasey	M	61

NY1200 Erie Community College-City

Department of Liberal Arts & Hum
121 Ellicott St
Buffalo, NY 14203
(716) 842-2770   Fax: (716) 851-1129
www.ecc.edu
E-mail: mcguigan@ecc.edu

2 Year Institution, Intro Courses Only

Chair: Kathleen McGuigan-Sadoff, 80A

Asst Prof PT	Grant, Joyce		13A,20G,29A
Inst FT	Kee, Edna Gayles		13A,36

NY1210 Erie Comm College-North

Liberal Arts/Humanities
6205 Main St
Williamsville, NY 14221
(716) 851-1318   Fax: (716) 851-1429
www.ecc.edu
E-mail: stencel@ecc.edu

2 Year Institution

Chair: Paul L. Stencel, 80A

Adj	Grant, Joyce	D	12,13A,36
Adj	Piontek, Gregory	M	12A,47,29
Prof	Stencel, Paul L.	D	13A,11,12A,41,47

NY1220 Erie Comm College-South

Liberal Arts/Humanities
4041 Southwestern Blvd
Orchard Park, NY 14127
(716) 648-5400   Fax: (716) 851-1629
www.ecc.edu
E-mail: mahoney@ecc.edu

Introduction Courses Only

Chair: Alan G. Schmidt, 80A

Assoc Prof	Barber, Jerome	M	70
Prof	Schmidt, Alan G.	M	13A,12A,47,20G,29A
Vstng Asst Prof	Schmidt, Doris D.	B	13A

NY1250 Finger Lakes Community College
Department of Music
4355 Lakeshore Dr
Canandaigua, NY 14424-8347
(585) 394-3500   Fax: (585) 394-5005
www.flcc.edu
E-mail: draskoi@flcc.edu

2 Year Institution

Chair: Ines Draskovic, 80A

	Arnold, Mark	M	13A,11,70
	Barbuto, Robert	M	66A,29
	Belec, Jonathan	B	35C
	Christiansen, Gregg	M	66A
	Cushman, Cathy	M	66A,13A,13
	DeWitt, Donald	B	64C,64E,64A
	Draskovic, Ines	D	66A,13A,13C,13
	Dreger, Neil	B	62D
	Gillard, Maria	B	61
Adj	Ko, EunMi	DMA	11,66A
	Maxfield, Dennis	M	36
	McGuire, David	D	13,10,12A,13A,47
	Pritchard, Jillian	M	65,50
	Ralston, Jeananne	M	66A
	Sisbarro, Jennifer L.	M	13A,11,61
	Smith, Geoff	M	47,11,35A,35B,35C
	Snyder, Craig	B	70,29

NY1275 Five Towns College
Department of Music
LIE Exit 50
305 N Service Rd
Dix Hills, NY 11746-2172
(631) 424-7000 x 2110   Fax: (631) 656-2172
www.ftc.edu
E-mail: jill.millerthorn@ftc.edu

4 Year Institution, Graduate School

Master of Music in Music Education, DMA in Performance, DMA in Music Education, DMA in Music History & Literature, Master of Music in Music History, DMA in Composition/Arranging, Master of Music in Composition/Arranging, Master of Music in Jazz/Commercial Music Performance, Master of Music in Music Technology

President: Stanley Cohen, 80A,80B,80E
Chair: Jeffrey S. Lipton, 80A,80B
Dir., Graduate Studies: Jill Miller-Thorn, 80C

Prof PT	Alstadter, Judith	D	66A
Asst Prof	Ballin, Scott	M	66A,66D
Asst Prof PT	Barkan, Paul Michael	M	34
Asst Prof PT	Birnbaum, Melanie	D	61
Asst Prof PT	Bobulinski, Greg	B	63A
Asst Prof PT	Carrott, Bryan	B	65
Prof	Cohen, Stanley	D	14C,32,46,47,64
Assoc Prof PT	Cook, Kenneth	D	12C,13,29A
Inst PT	Cummings, Azande	M	65
Prof	Dailey, Jeff	D	12,32
Assoc Prof Emeritus	DiPippo, Angelo	M	10C,10D,68
Prof	Drake, Erwin	B	10D
Prof Emeritus	Evans, Lee	D	66A,66D
Assoc Prof PT	Friese, Kenneth	M	60A,61
Assoc Prof	Gleason, Stephen	M	10D,12A,13B,14C,34D
Asst Prof PT	Hansen, Peter	M	34
Asst Prof	Karahalis, Dean	D	32E,37
Prof Emeritus	LaRosa, Joseph	D	60
Prof	Lipton, Jeffrey S.	M	12A,13B,32C,36,61
Prof	Miller-Thorn, Jill	D	10A,10F,13,66D,12C
Assoc Prof	Moon, Hosun	D	11,66,13B,32D,36
Assoc Prof	Pagano, Stephen	M	13C,61
Asst Prof PT	Patton, Jeb	M	10,13B,29B,29C,66A
Prof	Rogine, Peter	M	13C,29,47,70
Inst PT	Romano, Tony	B	70
Asst Prof PT	Romeo, Arthur	M	14C,29A
Assoc Prof PT	Rose, Bernard	D	14C,29A,32E
Assoc Prof	Saulter, Gerry	M	12A,13C,70,42,41
	Silverberg, Marc E.		36
Assoc Prof	Somma, Sal	M	32B,32C
Asst Prof	Spaneas, Demetrius	M	10,29,46,64E,10F
Prof	Yeston, Maury	D	10D,54

NY1300 Fordham University
Department of Art History & Music
441 E Fordham Rd
Bronx, NY 10458
(718) 817-4890   Fax: (718) 817-4829
www.fordham.edu/art_hist_music
E-mail: jisaak@fordham.edu

4 Year Institution

Chair: JoAnna Isaak, 80A
Dean, Rose Hill: Michael Latham, Ph.D, 80A
Dean, Lincoln Center: Robert R. Grimes, S. J.

Asst Prof	Bianchi, Eric	PhD	11,12A,12G,13J,31
Asst Prof	Gelbart, Matthew	D	12A,13J,14A,14D,20F
Assoc Prof	Grimes, Robert R.	PhD	12,14,20
Prof	Kramer, Lawrence	PhD	12
Lect	Minotti, Robert	M	36
Asst Prof	Ott, Daniel	D	12A,29A,54,13B,13C
Prof	Stempel, Larry	PhD	13,12,54,29
Lect	White, Barry R.	D	37,38
Lect	Yaraman, Sevin H.	PhD	13,14,12

NY1350 Hamilton College
Department of Music
198 College Hill Rd
Clinton, NY 13323-1218
(315) 859-4261   Fax: (315) 859-4464
www.hamilton.edu/academics/departments?dept=Music
E-mail: gkolb@hamilton.edu

4 Year Institution

Chair: G. Roberts Kolb, 80A
Performing Arts Administrator: Michelle Reiser-Memmer, 80F

Lect	Balestra, Rick	M	70
Lect	Beevers, Suzanne	M	62C
Lect	Best, Stephen	B	66A,66G
Lect	Brown, Janet	M	61
Assoc Prof	Buchman, Heather	D	38,49,51,48,60B
Lect	Charbonneau, Paul	B	70
Lect	Cirmo, Michael	M	65
Lect	Garland, Jon	M	63B
Lect	Greene, Linda	B	64A,42
Lect	Gustafson, Eric	B	62B
Prof	Hamessley, Lydia	D	13C,12,14,20G,12A
Assoc Prof	Hopkins, Robert	D	13,12A,12,12F
Lect	Johns, Jim	M	65
Prof	Kolb, G. Roberts	D	60,12A,36,40
Lect	Kolb, Lauralyn	M	61
Lect	Kwasnicka, Ursula	M	62E
Lect	Larzelere, Raymond	M	61
Lect	Montalbano, Rick	B	66A
Lect	Pellman, Colleen	M	66A,66C
Prof	Pellman, Samuel	D	13,10B,10,34
Lect	Pritsker, Vladimir	M	62A
Lect	Quick, Gregory	M	64D
Lect	Rabin, Barbara	M	64C
Lect	Raschella, John	B	63A
	Renard-Payen, Florent	M	41
Lect	Rowe, Monk	B	64E
Lect	Sharp, Pat	M	64B
Lect	Sipher, John	M	63C,63D
Lect	Stockham, Jeff	M	63A
Lect	Strong, Sar-Shalom	M	66A
Lect	Valli, Ubaldo	M	62A
Prof	Woods, Michael	D	47,29

NY1400 Hartwick College
Department of Music
Anderson Ctr for the Arts 212
Oneonta, NY 13820
(607) 431-4800   Fax: (607) 431-4813
www.hartwick.edu
E-mail: paiged@hartwick.edu

4 Year Institution
Member of NASM

Chair & Dir., Undergraduate Studies: Diane M. Paige, 80A,80B,80F
Dir., Summer Programs: Jason Curley, 80G

Inst PT	Aldridge, Ben	M	63A
Inst PT	Arnold, Johana	M	61
Inst PT	Blake, Paul	M	63C,63D
Inst PT	Cumming, Christine	M	64E,32E
Asst Prof	Curley, Jason	D	60B,63B,37,49,32E
Inst PT	Davey, John	B	62D,29B,41
Inst PT	De Siro, David	M	65
Asst Prof	Deisler, Ann	D	32
Inst PT	Donaldson, Cynthia	M	61
Inst PT	Egan, Jered	M	62D
Inst PT	Forsha, Heather	M	13C,66A,66C,32E
Inst PT	Gonzalez, Ana Laura	D	64A,13A,13B
Inst PT	Hane, Daniel	M	64D
Inst PT	Horne, Timothy	M	66C
Inst PT	Huyge, Dana	M	62B
Assoc Prof	Kratochvil, Jirka	D	36,60A,40,61
Inst PT	LiCalzi, Gary	M	47
Inst PT	Lipari, Robert	B	65
Inst PT	Markuson, Stephen	D	14C,31A
PT	Mazarak, Eric	B	66F
Inst PT	Nanni, Steven	B	61,32D
Inst PT	Odell, Andrew	M	32E
Assoc Prof	Paige, Diane M.	D	12,29A,20,12A,20F
Inst PT	Paterson, Kim	M	66A,66H
Inst PT	Prins, Rene	M	64B
Inst PT	Ross, Mary Anne	M	61
Inst PT	Schneider, Charles	M	38,60B
Inst PT	Seletsky, Robin	M	64C
Inst PT	Speth, Uli	M	62A,41,51
Inst PT	Turechek, Dennis	M	70,29A
Inst PT	Vatalaro, Charles	M	64E
Inst PT	Whittenburg, Ben	B	62C

NY1450 Hebrew Union College

School of Sacred Music
1 W 4th St
New York, NY 10012-1105
(212) 674-5300   Fax: (212) 388-1720
www.huc.edu
E-mail: bruben@huc.edu

5 Year Institution of Sacred Music, Graduate School

Master of Sacred Music, Graduate Cantorial Investiture

Dean: Aaron D. Panken, 80A
Director: Bruce Ruben, 80A

	Abelson, Robert	B	31A
	Arian, Merri	B	60,32,70
	Edison, Andrew	B	31A
	Kligman, Mark L.	D	14
	Lefkowitz, David	B	31A
	Mendelson, Jacob	B	31A
	Novick, Martha	B	31A
	Rosenzweig, Joyce	M	14,66C,35E
	Schall, Noah	M	31A
	Schiller, Benjie-Ellen	M	31A
	Sever, Allan	M	66C

NY1550 Hobart & William Smith Colleges

Department of Music
4087 Scandling Center
Geneva, NY 14456
(315) 781-3347   Fax: (315) 781-3403
www.hws.edu/academics/music/
E-mail: cowles@hws.edu

4 Year Liberal Arts Institution

Chair: Robert Cowles, 80A

Inst PT	Barbuto, Robert C.	B	66A,47
Inst PT	Bass, Walden	M	62C
Prof	Berta, Joseph M.	M	11,12A,64
Inst PT	Calabrese, Angela Libertella	M	61
Inst PT	Calabrese, Anthony J.	D	50
Inst PT	Christiansen, Gregg S.	M	66A,13A,13B,13C
Prof	Cowles, Robert	D	13,36,60
Inst PT	Curry, Steven		65
Inst PT	Hamilton, MaryAnn	D	66G
Inst PT	Heaton, Meg Cognetta	B	66A
Asst Prof	Lofthouse, Charity	M	13,34B,34F,15,31A
Inst PT	Ma, Yunn-Shan	M	36
Inst PT	Mandel, Alan	M	64E
Inst PT	Meyer, Kenneth	D	11,70,41
Inst PT	Murphy, Suzanne	M	61
Prof	Myers, Patricia Ann	D	11,12,14,66H,20
Inst PT	Oberbrunner, John	M	64A,48
Asst Prof	Olivieri, Mark A.	PhD	10,13,20G,29,48

Inst PT	Ralston, Jeananne C.	M	66A
Inst PT	Sisbarro, Jennifer	M	61
Inst PT	Slocum, Troy	B	66A
Inst PT	Trowbridge, James	M	49,63D
Inst PT	Trowbridge, Wendra	M	61
Inst PT	Wachala, Greg	B	70,47
Inst PT	Zaplatynsky, Andrew	B	51,62A,62B

NY1600 Hofstra University

Department of Music
101 New Academic Bldg
106 Hofstra University
Hempstead, NY 11549
(516) 463-5490   Fax: (516) 463-6393
www.hofstra.edu/music
E-mail: nathalie.g.robinson@hofstra.edu

4 Year Institution, Graduate School

Master of Arts in Education, Master of Science in Education

Chair & Dir., Graduate Studies: Nathalie G. Robinson, 80A,80C
Dir., Graduate Studies: Cindy L. Bell, 80C
Assistant Chair: Philip S. Stoecker, 80H

Adj Prof	Abram, Blanche	B	41,66A,66D,66C
Adj Asst Prof	Alexander, Lisa M.	M	64D,42
Adj Asst Prof	Ballereau, Laurence	M	32,37,64
Adj Assoc Prof	Balson, Donna C.	M	61
Adj Inst	Behrens, Lisa	M	13,11
Assoc Prof	Bell, Cindy L.	D	32,11,36
Adj Asst Prof	Berardinelli, Paula	D	29,13A,13C,11,47
Prof	Boonshaft, Peter Loel	D	60B,32C,37
Adj Asst Prof	Callis, Cathy	D	13A,11
Prof	Carter, Chandler	D	13,10
Assoc Prof	Cassio, Francesca	D	12,12A,12C,20
Prof	Cinnamon, Howard	D	13
Adj Asst Prof	Dansker, Judith	M	64B
Prof Emeritus	Deutsch, Herbert A.	M	13,10,45,29A,35
Adj Asst Prof	Dragovich, James	M	65,63
Adj Asst Prof	Dragovich, Mindy	M	64
Adj Inst	Drucker, Naomi	B	48,64C,42
Adj Asst Prof	Dupont, Donald	M	32
Adj Prof	Estrin, Morton	B	66A,13A
Adj Inst	Etter, Troy L.	M	12,11
Adj Inst	Filadelfo, Gary A.	B	45,35C,35D
Adj Asst Prof	Friedman-Adler, Laurie	M	64C,42
Assoc Prof	Fryling, David N.	M	36,60A,60,32,13A
Adj Asst Prof	Grib, Sonia G.	M	41,66H
Adj Inst	Hatch, Montgomery	M	65,42,50
Adj Asst Prof	Hecht, Joshua	M	61
Adj Assoc Prof	Hensrud, Tammy J.	M	61
Adj Prof	Hettrick, Jane S.	D	12A,66G
Prof	Hettrick, William E.	D	12A,13,55,55B
Adj Asst Prof	Hiller, Brian	M	32
Adj Asst Prof	Hollander, Alan	M	64B,42
Adj Asst Prof	Hoover, Sarah	M	61
Adj Asst Prof	Jolles, Susan	B	62E
Adj Inst	Jones, Ryan C.	M	13C,13D,13A
Adj Asst Prof	Kenyon, Steven	M	64E,29
Prof	LaLama, David S.	M	47,66A,29
Assoc Prof	Lampl, Kenneth H.	D	35,10,64E,34,11
Adj Assoc Prof	Lehman, Marilyn J.	M	66A,66C,42
Adj Inst	Lehmann, Matthew	M	62A,51
Adj Inst	Low, Todd K.	M	62B
Adj Asst Prof	Mercer, Gregory S.	M	61
Adj Asst Prof	Milenski, Isabel	M	39,54
Adj Asst Prof	Morrongiello, Christopher	D	12A,12C
Adj Asst Prof	Noble, Jason	M	32,37
Adj Asst Prof	Park, Mary B.	M	62C
Adj Asst Prof	Petruzzi, Leon T.	D	63A,49
Adj Asst Prof	Raab-Pontecorvo, Luiza	M	63B,42,66A,66C
Asst Prof	Ramael, David R.	D	12,38,39,60B,51
Assoc Prof	Robinson, Nathalie G.	D	32,11
Adj Asst Prof	Ronis, David A.	M	61
Adj Inst	Ross, Holli W.	M	61,29
Adj Asst Prof	Rozenblatt, David I.	M	65,42,50
Adj Asst Prof	Salzman, Michael J.	M	63D,42
Adj Asst Prof	Sharpe, Alexander E.	D	62A,42,51
Adj Assoc Prof	Spencer, Patricia L.	M	64A,42,43
Adj Asst Prof	Stempel, Mark	M	32,37
Asst Prof	Stoecker, Philip S.	D	13
Adj Inst	Stone, Richard J.	B	70
Adj Asst Prof	Strauss, Gail	M	32,11
Adj Inst	Tedesco, Anthony C.	M	65
Adj Asst Prof	Terrigno, Loretta	M	13
Adj Inst	Verbsky, Franklin	M	62,62C,62D,11
Adj Asst Prof	Wind, Martin	M	62D,29
Adj Asst Prof	Wolff, Benjamin A.	M	62C
Adj Asst Prof	Zito, William F.	B	70,67G

NY1700 Houghton College

Greatbatch School of Music
One Willard Ave
Houghton, NY 14744
(585) 567-9400   Fax: (585) 567-9517
www.houghton.edu/greatbatch
E-mail: music@houghton.edu

4 Year Institution, Graduate School
Member of NASM

Master of Arts in Music, Master of Music in Composition, Master of Music in Performance, Master of Music in Conducting, Master of Music in Collaborative Performance

Director & Associate Dean: Ben R. King, 80A
Dir., Artist/Performance Series: Robert J. Galloway, 80F

Prof Emeritus	Allen, William T.	D	10
Inst PT	Alvarez, Euridice	M	64B
Inst PT	Black, Daniel	M	60A
Inst PT	Brown, Anne		32E
Prof Emeritus	Brown, Bruce C.	D	60,11,36,61,31A
Asst Prof	Casey, Brian	D	38,63B,60B,13C
Prof	Congdon, Judy A.	D	13,66G,66H,31A
Inst PT	Cox, Amanda K.	M	61
Inst PT	Crane, Kenneth	M	46,47
Asst Prof	Davies, David H.	D	13A,13C,13B,10,13
Prof	DeBoer, Paul	D	63,12A,49
	Farrington, Annette	M	64A
Prof	Galloway, Robert J.	M	12A,66A
Inst PT	Giambrone, Marcia		32C
Inst PT	Halberg, Virginia	B	66A,66D
Asst Prof	Hijleh, Kelley	M	61
Prof	Hijleh, Mark D.	D	10,13,31A
Assoc Prof	Johnson, Brandon P.	D	36,60A,61
Asst Prof PT	Johnson, Sharon L.	M	66C,66A,66D,31A
Prof	King, Ben R.	D	11,12A,61,39
Inst PT	Kuhl, Margaret		61
Inst PT	Lascell, Ernie	M	64C
Asst Prof	Lorenzo, Donna A.	M	62B,62A
Asst Prof PT	Machleder, Anton M.	D	70
Inst PT	Marling, Chisato Eda	M	64E
Inst PT	McBrearty, Angela S.	M	64A
Assoc Prof	Newbrough, William J.	D	66A,66B,13C,13E,66C
Prof Emeritus	Norton, Edgar	M	32,64C
Prof	Reigles, B. Jean	M	36,39,60A,61
Assoc Prof	Stith, Gary	M	32,37,60B,65
Asst Prof PT	Tiller, Jim	M	65
Inst PT	Wada, Rintaro	M	62C
Inst PT	Weiss, Abraham		64D
Prof Emeritus	Wilt, Lois J.	M	32,64A
Inst PT	Wong, Grace		62E

NY1800 Ithaca College

School of Music
3322 Whalen Ctr for Music
Ithaca, NY 14850-7000
(607) 274-3171   Fax: (607) 274-1727
www.ithaca.edu
E-mail: gwoodward@ithaca.edu

4 Year Institution, Graduate School
Member of NASM

Master of Music in Pedagogy, Master of Music in Composition, Master of Music in Performance, Master of Music in Conducting, Master of Science in Music Education, Master of Music in Music Education

Dean: Gregory S. Woodward, 80A
Dir., Undergraduate Studies: Craig Cummings, 80B
Dir., Undergraduate Studies: Kim Dunnick, 80B
Associate Dean & Dir., Undergraduate Studies: Keith A. Kaiser, 80B,80H
Dir., Undergraduate Studies: Deborah Martin, 80B
Dir., Graduate Studies & Summer Programs: Timothy A. Johnson, 80C,80G
Coord., Music Admissions: Thomas Kline, 80D
Senior Assistant: Christy Voytko, 80E,80F
Concert Manager: Erik Kibelsbeck, 80F

Lect	Alexander, Conrad	M	50,65
Assoc Prof	Avery, Susan J.	D	32
	Barbour, Cass	B	34B,34E
Assoc Prof	Birr, Diane	D	66A,66C,66D
Asst Prof	Black, Les	D	13
	Blakely, Doug	DIPL	72
Assoc Prof	Blooding, Randie	D	61
Prof	Campos, Frank G.	M	63A
Asst Prof	Cohen, Pablo	D	70
Lect	Covert, Kelly	M	64A
Prof	Cummings, Craig	D	13
Asst Prof	De Clercq, Trevor O.		
Asst Prof	DeMaris, Brian	M	39,54
Asst Prof	DiEugenio, Nicholas	D	62A
Assoc Prof	Dimaras, Charis	D	66A,66C
Prof	Doebler, Lawrence A.	M	60,36
	Dozoretz, Brian	B	35C,34D
Prof	Dunnick, Kim	D	63A
Assoc Prof	Faria, Richard Alan	D	64C
Prof	Fonder, Mark	D	60B,32,37
Prof	Galvan, Janet	D	60A,32,36
Prof	Galvan, Michael	M	64C
Prof	Goodhew, Lee	D	64D
Assoc Prof	Grossmann, Jorge V.	D	10A,10F
Asst Prof	Hayghe, Jennifer C.	D	66A
Assoc Prof	Haywood, Jennifer	M	32A,32B,32E
Asst Prof	Hess, Nathan A.	D	66A,66D,66C,66,66B
Asst Prof	Hougham, Bradley	M	61
Asst Prof	Isbell, Dan	D	32
Asst Prof	Jemian, Rebecca	D	13
Asst Prof Adj	Johengen, Carl	D	61
Assoc Prof	Johnson, Timothy A.	D	13
	Jordan, Rebecca	DIPL	16
Assoc Prof	Kaiser, Keith A.	D	32E,32G,49
Asst Prof	Kay, Jennifer	M	61
Asst Prof Adj	Lamb, Sally	D	13,10
Assoc Prof	Martin, Deborah	D	66A,66B,66D
Asst Prof	Mason, Emily J.	D	32A,32B,32C
Prof	Mauk, Steven	D	64E
Prof	McAmis, Carol	M	61
	McKechnie, Donald	DIPL	66F
Prof	Mehne, Wendy	D	64A
Prof	Mehta, Phiroze	D	66A
Asst Prof	Meyer, Jeffery David	D	38,66A,60B,43
Prof	Montgomery-Cove, Deborah	M	61
Prof	Moree, Debra	M	62B
Assoc Prof	Morgan, Paige	D	64B
Lect	Mygatt, Louise	D	12A,15
Lect	Nord, Merilee	M	13
Asst Prof	Nord, Timothy	D	13,34
Asst Prof	Pacun, David E.	D	13
Prof	Parks, David	D	61
Prof	Pastore, Patrice	M	61
Asst Prof	Perialas, Alexander	B	35C,13L
Assoc Prof	Peterson, Elizabeth	D	37,32E
Prof	Peterson, Stephen G.	M	60B,37
Lect	Pierce, Dawn	M	61
Lect	Radice, Jean	M	66G,66H
Prof	Radice, Mark A.	D	12A,12C
Asst Prof Adj	Reuning, Sanford	M	62A
Assoc Prof	Reynolds, Harold	D	63C
Asst Prof	Rifkin, Deborah	PhD	13
Prof	Rothbart, Peter	D	45,35C,35D
Asst Prof	Shuhan, Alexander G.	M	63B
Asst Prof	Silberman, Peter	D	13
Assoc Prof	Simkin, Elizabeth	M	62C
Prof	Stout, Gordon B.	M	50,65
Prof Emeritus	Swenson, Edward E.	D	12A,12
Asst Prof	Titlebaum, Michael	M	29,46,47
Assoc Prof	Unland, David	M	63D
Asst Prof	Walker, Nicholas	D	62D,67B,55B
Asst Prof	Waterbury, Susan	D	62A
Lect	Webster, Marc	M	61
Assoc Prof	White, John W.	D	13
Assoc Prof	Whitehead, Baruch	D	32B,32A,32C,20A
Prof	Wilson, Dana	D	10F,10A
Prof	Woodward, Gregory S.	D	10A,10F

NY1850 Jamestown Community College

Department of Music
525 Falconer St
Jamestown, NY 14701-1920
(716) 665-5220   Fax: (716) 665-9110
www.sunyjcc.edu/music
E-mail: MikeKelly@mail.sunyjcc.edu

2 Year Institution

Chair: Michael F. Kelly, 80A

	Bogey, Brian A.		36
	Buhite, Michelle		61
Inst	Eckstrom, William	M	47
	Gustafson, Steve		35
Prof	Kelly, Michael F.	M	36,61,66A,46,34
Inst	Rasmusson, Ralph	M	37,47,63,64,65
	Svensen-Smith, Carol		66A

NY1860 Jewish Theological Seminary
of America
College of Jewish Music
3080 Broadway
New York, NY 10027
(212) 678-8037   Fax: (212) 662-8989
www.jtsa.edu
E-mail: herosenblum@jtsa.edu

5 Year, Graduate Program in Jewish Music

Master of Arts in Sacred Music

Dean: Henry Rosenblum, 80A

Inst	Avery, Lawrence	M	61
Inst	Caplan, Joel	B	61
Asst Prof Adj	Cohen, Gerald	DMA	13A,13,10
Adj Prof	Davidson, Charles	D	31B
Inst	Fine, Perry	M	31B
Inst	Frieder, Raphael	B	61
Inst	Fuerstman, Marlena	M	31B,61,20F
Asst Prof Adj	Hyman, Adah	B	66
Inst	Kieval, Robert	B	61
Asst Prof	Levin, Neil	D	12C,12A,12
Asst Prof Adj	Mendelson, Jacob	B	61
Inst	Nadel, Richard	B	61
Inst	Novick, Martha	M	61
Asst Prof Adj	Rice, JoAnn	M	36,60
Inst	Rosenblum, Henry	M	31B,61,20F,13C
Inst	Steinsnyder, Faith	B	61
Asst Prof	Tarsi, Boaz	DMA	13,10,14
Asst Prof Adj	Tischler, Judith	D	13A,12A

NY1900 The Juilliard School
60 Lincoln Center Plz
New York, NY 10023-6500
(212) 799-5000   Fax: (212) 724-0263
www.juilliard.edu
E-mail: news@juilliard.edu

4 Year Institution, Graduate School

Graduate Diploma, DMA in Composition, DMA in Performance, Master of Music, Artist Diploma in Historical Performance, Artist Diploma in Jazz Studies, Artist Diploma in Music Performance, Artist Diploma in Opera Studies, Artist Diploma in String Quartet Studies

Dir., Graduate Studies: Laurie A. Carter, 80A,80C
Dean: Ara Guzelimian, 80A
President: Joseph W. Polisi, 80A
Dir., Graduate Studies: Virginia Allen, 80C
Dir., Graduate Studies: Noa Kageyama, 80C
Dir., Graduate Studies: Michael Musgrave, 80C
Dir., Graduate Studies: Wayne Oquin, 80C
Dir., Graduate Studies: Daniel P. Ott, 80C
Dir., Graduate Studies: Benjamin Sosland, 80C
Dir., Graduate Studies: Christoph Wolff, 80C
Associate Dean, Admissions: Lee Cioppa, 80D
Director of Diversity, Inclusion, and Outreach: Alison Scott-Williams, 80E
Vice President & Dean, Academic Affairs: Karen Wagner, 80H

	Aaron, Richard L.		62C
	Adkins, Darrett	D	62C
	Adler, Samuel	D	10
	Alessi, Joseph		63D,63C,49
	Allen, Carl	B	47,29
	Allen, Nancy	M	62E
	Allen, Virginia	D	60
	Amory, Misha	M	62B
	Appel, Toby		62B
	Arnon, Baruch	M	66D
	Ax, Emanuel	M	66A
	Axinn, Audrey	D	42
	Baer, Alan	M	63D
	Baker, William	D	60
	Barrett, Marianne		61
	Barron, Kenny		66A,29
	Bartlett, Eric		62C
	Beaser, Robert	D	10
	Berkeley, Edward		39
	Bers, Edith	M	61
	Bilous, Edward	D	13
	Birnbaum, Mary		61
	Blaha, Kyle	D	13C
	Blake, Ron		63A,29
	Blier, Steven	B	39
	Brevig, Per	D	49,63C
	Briggs, Kendall Durelle	D	32B,12A,29
	Brofsky, Natasha	M	62C,42
	Burton, James	M	42,29
	Cabaniss, Thomas	B	13
	Canin, Martin	M	66A
	Caporello-Szykman, Corradina		39
	Carter, Ron	M	29
	Castel, Nico	M	39
	Castleman, Heidi	M	62B
	Cataneo, Daniel O.	D	39
	Chan, David	B	62A
	Cho, Catherine	M	62A,42
	Chung, Kyung-Wha	B	62A
	Chung, Soon Bin	M	66B
	Ciacca, Antonio		29
	Clapp, Stephen	M	62A,42
	Cobb, Kevin	M	63A,49
	Cobb, Timothy	B	62D
	Copes, Ronald	M	62A,51
	Corigliano, John		10
	Cowart, Robert		39
	Cox, Mary A.	M	13
	Cunningham, Sarah		67A
	Davis, Xavier	B	47,29
	Dawe, Jonathan	D	10
	De Silva, Rohan	M	66C,41
	DePreist, James	D	60B,38
	DiBucci, Michelle	M	13
	Dicterow, Glenn	B	62A
	Douvas, Elaine		64B
	Dreyfus, Karen	M	62B
	Druckman, Daniel	M	65
	Drummond, Billy		29
	Drummond, Ray		29
	Dubal, David	D	12A
	Eddy, Timothy	M	62C
	Emelianoff, Andre	B	62C,41
	Enlow, David	M	66A
	Ewazen, Eric	D	13
	Eyerly, Scott	M	13
	Falcone, Mary Lou		61
	Farber, Andy		10,29
	Fehleisen, Fred	B	12A
	Feldman, Jonathan		66C
	Finckel, David		62C,42
	Garrett, Margo	M	66C
	Giampietro, John		61
	Gilbert, Albert	M	38,60
	Gilbert, Pia		12B
	Goldberg, Marc	M	48
	Gottlieb, Gordon	M	65
	Gottlieb, Jane	M	16,12C
	Gould, Mark		63A,49
	Griffel, L. Michael	D	12A,12
	Grubb, Thomas	M	61
	Haas, Arthur	M	67F
	Henderson, Eddie		63A,29
	Herwig, Conrad		63C,29
	Hoffmann, Cynthia	D	61
	Huang, Hsin-Yun		62B
	Huggett, Monica		67B
	Hughes, Nathan		64B
	Isbin, Sharon	M	70
	Iwazumi, Ray	D	62A
	Jacobs, Paul	M	66G
	Jaudes, Christian	M	29,63A
	Johansen, Dane		62C
	Jones, Rodney		47,29
	Kalichstein, Joseph	M	66A
	Kang, Choong Mo	D	66A
	Kang, Hyo		62A
	Kaplan, Lewis	M	51,62A
	Kaplinsky, Yoheved	D	66A
	Kavafian, Ida	M	62A,42
	Kawasaki, Masao		62A
	Kay, Alan R.	M	64C
	Kelley, R. J.		67E
	Khaner, Jeffrey	B	64A
	Kimbrough, Frank		29
	Kimura, Mari	D	35C
	Klorman, Edward	D	13,42
	Knowles, Gregory	D	29
	Kraft, Edith	M	66D
	Krosnick, Joel	B	51,62C
	Kurtz, James	D	12A
	LaBouff, Kathryn	D	39
	Landsman, Julie		63B
	Langevin, Robert		64A
	Laskowski, Kim		64D
	Lasser, Philip	D	13
	Laszlo, Albert	M	62D
	LeClair, Judith		64D
	Lev, Lara		42
	Levinson, Eugene		62D
	Levinson, Gina	M	39
	Levy, Sharon	D	
	Lin, Cho-Liang	B	62A
	Lin, Joseph	B	62A,42
	Lipkin, Seymour		66A
	Lowenthal, Jerome		66A
	Lustig, Raymond J.	D	13

Macomber, Curtis	D	51	
Magnarelli, Joe		29	
Mahoney, Shafer	D	10F	
Malas, Marlena Kleinman	B	61	
Mann, Nicholas	M	42	
Markey, James A.		63C	
Martin, Julian		66A	
Mase, Raymond	B	63A,49	
Masse, Denise		61	
McDonald, Robert	D	66A	
McGill, Anthony		64C	
Mealy, Robert		67	
Merrill, Kenneth	M	39	
Milarsky, Jeffrey	M	60B	
Miller, Sandra	B	67D	
Montone, Jennifer	B	63B	
Moody, David		39,61	
Morales, Ricardo		64C	
Morelli, Frank	D	64D	
Muller, John J. H.	M	12A	
Nairn, Robert	B	67B	
Neidich, Charles		64C,48	
Netz, Anthony R.	M	12A	
Neubauer, Paul	M	62B	
Nugent, Barli	D	29,64A	
O'Brien, Orin		62D	
O'Brien, Patrick		67G	
Oquin, Wayne	D	13C	
Oshima, Ayako		64C	
Ott, Daniel P.	D	13C	
Panner, Daniel	M	62B	
Paranosic, Milica	M	34	
Paul, David	B	61	
Penna, J.J.		61	
Pereira, Joseph	M	65	
Perlman, Itzhak		62A	
Pollard, Denson P.	D	63D,42	
Powell, Michael		63C,49	
Raekallio, Matti		66A	
Ralske, Erik	M	63B,42	
Ranjbaran, Behzad	D	13	
Rhodes, Samuel	M	51,41,62B	
Rhoten, Markus		65	
Richardson, Diane	M	39	
Roberts, Cynthia	M	67B	
Rogers, Patricia	B	64D	
Rojak, John D.	B	49,63C	
Rosenberg, Sylvia		62A	
Ross, James	M	60	
Rouse, Christopher	D	10	
Ruiz, Gonzalo		67D	
Sachs, Joel	D	12A,41,43	
Sandow, Greg	M	12	
Schaap, Phil		29A	
Schachter, Carl	D	13	
Schiff, Lauren	M		
Schulenberg, David	D		
Scott, Rebecca	M	13	
Shapiro, Eve		61	
Sheftel, Paul		66B	
Sherman, Robert	M	35A,29	
Sherry, Fred		62C	
Shinn, Michael A.	D	13,42	
Shrut, Arlene	D	39	
Slater, Jeanne	B	61	
Sosland, Benjamin	D	67	
Staples, Sheryl		62A	
Stelluto, George Edward	M	60B	
Stern, Nina		67C	
Stinson, Caroline	M	62C	
Stowe, Cameron		42	
Strommen, Linda	M	64B	
Sylvan, Sanford		61	
Takebe, Yoko		62A	
Tanaka, Naoko		62A	
Taylor, Stephen		48	
Temperley, Joe		64C,64E,29	
Tenenbom, Stephen		62B	
Teresi, Dominic	D	67D	
Thiessen, John		67E	
Thomas, Sally	M	62A	
Tree, Michael		62B	
Tritle, Kent	M	36	
Turre, Steve		29	
Verdrager, Martin	M	12A	
Vernon, Robert	B	62B	
Vinci, Mark		29	
Wadsworth, Stephen		39	
Wakefield, David	D	63B,49	
Wallace, David	M	32	
Washington, Kenny		29	
Wedow, Gary T.	M	39	
Weilerstein, Donald		62A	
Weilerstein, Vivian Hornik		66A	
Weiss, Kenneth	B	66H	
White, Michael	M	13	
White, Robert	M	61	
White, Robert C.	D	61	
Wiens, Edith	M	61	
Wilder, Joe		29	
Wilson, Steve		29	
Wincenc, Carol	M	64A,48	
Wolfe, Ben		29,62D	
Woodhouse, Reed	M	61	
Wunsch, Aaron M.	D	12,42	
Zeger, Brian	D	66C	
Zuber, Gregory	M	65	
Zyman, Samuel	D	13	

NY1950 Keuka College

Department of Music
Keuka Park, NY 14478
(315) 279-5303
www.keuka.edu
E-mail: jmdohert@keuka.edu

4 Year Institution

Music Contact: Jean Doherty, 80A
Chair, Humanities & Fine Arts: Alexis Haynes, 80A

Adj	Doherty, Jean	M	11,36
Adj	Stempien, Jeff	M	37

NY2050 Kingsborough Community College

Department of Comm & Perf Arts
2001 Oriental Blvd
Brooklyn, NY 11235-2333
(718) 368-5591   Fax: (718) 368-4879
www.kbcc.cuny.edu
E-mail: GNicosia@Kingsborough.edu

2 Year Institution

Chair: Gloria Nicosia, 80A

PT	Briggs, Monique	D	12A,13A
Prof	Cory, Eleanor	D	13,10,11,66A,66D
PT	Mangini, Mark	B	13A,13,11,36
PT	Paar, Sara		12A,13A
PT	Rathbun, Andrew	M	35C,35D,35G,10B,45
Assoc Prof	Rosner, Arnold	D	13A,13,11,14,66A
PT	Solomon, Joseph	M	47,53,29A
Lect	Williams, Marvin	M	10,11,12,13,20G

NY2100 Laguardia Community College

Department of Humanities-Prf Arts
31-10 Thomson Ave
Long Island City, NY 11101-3071
(718)482-5694   Fax: (718)482-5599
www.lagcc.cuny.edu
E-mail: jdavis@lagcc.cuny.edu

2 Year Institution, offering transfer Programs

Coordinator: John W. Williams, 80A

Asst Prof	Davis, John Henry	M	
Asst Prof	Hosten, Kevin	D	11,47,63,64,66D
Assoc Prof	Koolsbergen, William J.	D	
Asst Prof Adj	Moorman, Joyce Solomon	D	13,10,11,66A,66D
Asst Prof Adj	Moss, Suzan	D	52
Lect Adj	Suchow, Paul	M	70
Assoc Prof	Williams, John W.	M	13,11,36,61,54

NY2102 Long Island Univ-Brooklyn Campus

Department of Music
1 University Plaza
Brooklyn, NY 11201
(718) 488-1051   Fax: (718) 488-1372
www.liu.edu
E-mail: robert.aquino@liu.edu

4 Year Institution

Chair: Robert Aquino, 80A
Dean, Performing Arts: David Cohen, 80A

Prof	Aquino, Robert	M	13A,13,10,66A,66B
Adj	Barth, Bruce	M	29
Assoc Prof	Cooper, Gloria A.	D	13A,61,32C,36,47
Adj	Jemielita, James	B	66A,47

Adj	Keminski, Joe	D	20,14,12A,63A
Asst Prof	Newsome, Sam	B	29,20,64E
Prof Emeritus	Yellin, Peter	M	47,64E,46,29

NY2105 Long Island Univ-LIU Post Campus
Department of Music
FAC
720 Northern Blvd
Brookville, NY 11548-1300
(516) 299-2474   Fax: (516) 299-2884
www.liu.edu/svpa/music
E-mail: music@cwpost.liu.edu

4 Year Institution, Graduate School

Master of Science in Music Education, Master of Arts in History & Literature, Master of Arts in Music Theory-Composition

Chair: Jennifer Scott Miceli, 80A
Dean: Noel Zahler, 80A
Dir., Graduate Studies: Paul S. Kim, 80C
Dir., Summer Chamber Music Festival: Susan E. Deaver, 80G
Dir., Summer Chamber Music Festival: Maureen Hynes, 80G
Dir., Summer Chamber Music Festival: Dale Stuckenbruck, 80G

Adj Prof	Baer, Seth	M	64D
Adj	Becker, Harris	M	67G,70,41
Adj Prof	Behrens, Jeffrey	M	61
Adj Prof	Bianculli, Pasquale A.	M	70
Adj Prof	Blue, T. K.	M	47,29,29A,29B
Adj	Carroll, Gwendolyn J.	M	32
Adj Prof	Cassara, Frank	M	65,50
Adj Prof	Cassara, James	M	32
Prof	Chinn, Genevieve	D	13,11,12A,12
Adj Prof	Deaver, Susan E.	D	48,64A
Adj Prof	Dore, Christine	M	66C
Adj Prof	Dragonvich, James	M	65,32
Adj Prof	Erickson, James	M	11
Adj Prof	Feigin, Eugene	M	66D
Adj Prof	Fusco-Spera, Barbara	M	61
Adj Prof	Gates, Elaine	M	32
Adj Prof	Gellert, Karen	M	62D
Prof	Golden, Ruth E.	M	39,61,11
Adj Prof	Harrelson, Neal	M	61
Adj Prof	Holsberg, Lisa	M	61
Adj Prof	Holzman, David	M	12A,66D,13
Adj Prof	Hopkins, Christopher	M	13C
Adj Prof	Hynes, Maureen	M	38,67,62C,55,42
Adj Prof	Iacona, Richard	M	66
Adj Prof	Johnson, Jeffrey W.	M	61,12A,55D,12B
Adj Prof	Kang, Chun-Wei	M	66C
Adj Prof	Kim, Aeree	D	66A,66B
Adj Prof	Kim, Heawon	M	66A,66C
Adj Prof	Kim, Paul S.	D	66A,66B,12A
Adj Prof	Klein, Gary	M	66
Adj Prof	Kubey, Phyllis	M	61
Adj Prof	Lee, Rodger	M	63A,49
Adj	Madej, Andrew	M	63D,63
Adj Prof	Marino, Mark	M	70
Adj Prof	McRoy, Danielle M.	M	61
Prof	McRoy, James W.	D	60B,37,63,32E
Adj Prof	Meschi, John	M	10,34
Prof	Miceli, Jennifer Scott	D	32,36,60A
Adj Prof	Moe, Karla	M	64A,64
Adj Prof	Moe, Sharon	M	63B
Adj Prof	Mohar, Barbara	M	11
Adj Prof	Pergola, Joseph		32E
Adj Prof	Pulgram, Anthony	M	61
Adj Prof	Ray, John	M	62D
Adj Prof	Ruedeman, Timothy	D	64E
Adj Prof	Salas, Veronica	D	62B
Adj Prof	Sapadin, David	M	64C
Adj Prof	Schwartzman, Kenneth		32E
Prof	Shapiro, Mark L.	D	60A,36,40,13
Adj Prof	Siroky, Brad		63A
Adj Prof	Snyder, Mark	M	64B
Adj Prof	Sobel, Elise	M	32
Adj Prof	Spampinato, Robert		63
Adj Prof	Stanton, Ronald	M	63C,63
Adj Prof	Strommen, Carl	D	10,10F,10A
Adj Prof	Stuckenbruck, Dale	D	62A
Adj Prof	Sulzinski, Valerie	M	64B
Adj Prof	Vandegriff, Matthew	D	10,13C
Adj Prof	Waterman, Marla	M	11,61
Prof	Watt, Stephanie	M	13,66,66A,66B
Adj Prof	Williams, Earl	M	65
Adj Prof	Wirth, Jason	M	66C
Asst Prof	Wright, Vincent	M	11
Prof	Zahler, Noel	D	10,34

NY2150 Manhattan School of Music
120 Claremont Ave
New York, NY 10027-4003
(212) 749-2802   Fax: (212) 749-5471
www.msmnyc.edu
E-mail: mmerryman@msmnyc.edu

4 Year Institution, Graduate School

Master of Music in Composition, Master of Music in Performance, DMA in Composition, DMA in Performance, Master of Music in Jazz Studies

President: Robert Sirota, 80A
Dean of Students: Elsa Jean Davidson, 80D
Vice President, Instrumental Performance: David Geber, 80H
Vice President for Academics & Performance: Marjorie Merryman, 80H

	Aicher, Carol Ann	D	32E
	Anderson, Jay	B	29
	Andreacchi, Peter	D	13
	Archer, Gail	D	12
	Arnold, Craig S.	D	36
	Aronov, Arkady	D	66A
	Ascani, Argeo	M	12A
	Avshalomov, Daniel	M	62B
	Baer, Alan	B	63D
	Baker, Michelle	M	63B
	Barrett, Marianne	B	
	Baum, Jamie		29
	Bednar, Stanley	M	62A
	Beegle, Raymond	B	41
	Bers, Edith	M	61
	Biggs, William Hayes	D	13
	Black, Robert	M	62D
	Blake, John	B	29
	Bleckman, Theo	B	29,61
	Boccato, Rogerio	M	65
	Bonilla, Luis	M	29,63C
	Botti, Robert	M	64B
	Botti, Susan	M	10
	Brantley, Paul E.	M	60
	Breslaw, Irene		62B
	Brevig, Per	D	63C
	Bridgewater, Cecil		29
	Cahill, Catherine	M	35A
	Caplan, Joan	B	61
	Carney, Laurie	M	41,62A
	Chadabe, Joel		45
	Charlston, Erik	M	65
	Charney, Miriam	B	
	Chatterjee, Samir		29
	Chesis, Linda	B	64A
	Cilliers, Jeanne-Minette	M	61
	Cobb, Timothy	B	62D
	Cohen, Jeffrey L.	M	41,66A
	Cohen, Paul	D	48,64E
	Colby, Constance	M	
	Cooper, Kenneth	D	66H
	Crockett, Whitney	M	64D
	D'Angelo, Gerard		29
	Danielpour, Richard	D	10
	Delpriora, Mark	M	70
	DeMare, Anthony	M	66B
	DeRosa, Richard		29
	Dial, Garry	M	29
	DiCecco, Enrico	B	51
	DiCioccio, Justin	M	29
	Dicterow, Glenn	B	62A
	Dreyfus, Karen	B	62B
	Dubal, David		66D
	Dunn, Mignon		61
	Dutton, Lawrence		62B
	Eaton, Roy	M	29,35B
	Eisenbach, David	M	
	Eldridge, Peter	B	61,29
	Epstein, Daniel		41,66A
	Fader, Oren	M	70
	Feder, Donn Alexander	D	66A
	Feldman, Marion	M	41,62C
	Ferrari, John	D	65
	Finlayson, David	B	63C
	Fishbein, Zenon	M	66A
	Forconi, John	M	66C
	Frink, Laurie		29
	Fueting, Reiko	D	13,10
	Gale, Jack		29
	Gandara, Javier	B	63B
	Geber, David	M	62C
	Gilbert, David	M	60,38
	Gitler, Ira		29A
	Gordon, Wycliff	B	
	Gould, Mark	B	63A
	Grabois, Daniel	M	63B
	Green, Edward	D	12A,29
	Greenidge-Copprue, Delano	D	

Name		Codes
Greensmith, Clive	B	62C
Grossman, David	M	62D
Gursky, Isreal	D	61
Harris, Hilda		61
Heflin, Thomas	DMA	63,11
Heldrich, Claire	M	50,65,43
Herrington, Benjamin	M	63C
Hilse, Walter	D	66G
Hoffman, Deborah	M	62E
Hoffmann, Cynthia	M	61
Hsu, Yu-Pin	M	
Isenstead, Lisa	M	
Iyer, Vijay	D	
Janas, Mark		39
Jolles, Susan		62E
Jones, Rodney		29
Jones, Warren	M	66C
Kalinovsky, Grigory	M	62A
Kaplan, Burton	B	62A
Katz, Dick		29
Kawin, Phillip	M	66A
Kay, Alan	M	64C
Keever, Tom Dale	M	
Kelly, Jonathan	M	61
Kennedy, Karen	D	29,35A
Kiesler, Kenneth	M	60
Kim, Lisa	M	62A
Kircher, Bill		29A
Klibonoff, Jon	M	42
Koessel, Wolfram		62C
Kopec, Patinka	M	62A,62B
Kopelson, Robert		
Korman, Clifford	B	29A
Krakauer, David	M	64C
Kuuskmann, Martin	M	64D
Labouff, Kathryn	D	
Laclair, Jaqueline	D	64B
Lalama, David	M	29
Lamb, Christopher	B	65
Lamb, Virginia P.	M	66C
Langevin, Robert		64A
Langford, Jeffrey	D	12
Laskowski, Kim	M	64D
LeClair, Jacqueline	D	64B
Leisner, David	M	70
Leopold, Timothy	M	63A
Levine, Rhoda		39
Levy, Arthur		61
Lewin, Ann		
Lichten, Julia	M	62C
Liebman, David		29
Locke, Joe		65B
Lowenstein, Michael	D	64C
Macdonald, David	D	13
Macomber, Curtis	D	62A
Maki, Paul-Martin	D	66G
Malas, Marlena K.	B	61
Malas, Spiro	B	61
Malfitano, Catherine	B	61
Malkin, Isaac	DIPL	62A
Manahan, George	M	60
Manasia, Jeremy	M	29
Mann, Nicholas		62A
Mann, Robert		62A
Marano, Nancy	B	29
Marano-Murray, June	M	39
Markov, Albert	D	62A
Markowitz, Phil		29
Marlow, Carolyn	M	54
Martin, Marya	M	64A
Mason, Sonya G.	D	12A,66A,32
McCaslin, Donny		64E
McCoy, Jeremy		62D
McCrane, Barbara	B	
McKnight, Linda	B	62D
McNeely, James	B	29
Meader, Darmon	B	29
Merrill, Kenneth W.	M	66C
Merryman, Marjorie	D	10,13
Mikowsky, Solomon	D	66A
Milarsky, Jeffrey	M	65
Misslin, Patricia	M	61
Morelli, Frank	D	64D
Morton, Glenn		
Mosca, John	B	29
Muraco, Thomas	B	66C
Neidich, Charles	B	64C
Nelson, Jon	M	63A
Noon, David	D	12,10A,10,12A
Norrell, Stephen	M	63C
Nuccio, Mark		64C
Nye, Roger	B	64D
O'Brien, Orin	DIPL	62D
O'Connor, Tara	D	64A
O'Donohue, Deirdre	D	12A
Oldfather, Christopher	M	66A,66H
Olson, Marjean A.	D	67
Ostrowski, Gordon	M	39
Oswald, Mark	B	61
Overton, LeAnn		39
Pagano, John J.	D	
Papolos, Janice	B	35A
Parloff, Michael	B	64A
Parodi, Jorge	M	39
Patenaude-Yarnell, Joan		61
Patrelle, Francis	B	61
Patterson, Michael		29
Patton, Duncan	B	65
Pedatella, R. Anthony	D	
Pedatella, Stefan		
Penzarella, Vincent		63A
Peters, Maitland	M	61
Polk, Joanne	D	41,66A
Press, Daisy		
Putnam, Ashley	M	61
Radicheva, Maria	M	62A
Ralske, Erik C.	M	63B
Rednour, Scott		39
Reynolds, Todd	M	45
Rhee, Heasook	D	66C
Ridley, Larry	M	47,29A,62D,20A,20G
Riley, John	M	29
Rinehart, Robert		62B
Ritscher, Karen	M	62B
Robbins, Gerald	M	41
Robert, Lucie	M	41,62A
Robinson, McNeil	B	66G
Rodgers, Elizabeth	M	39
Rogers, Patricia	B	64D
Rosenberg, Christopher J.	M	47,29
Rosenberg, Sylvia		62A
Rosenshein, Neil		61
Rosenthal, Ted	M	29
Russo, Charles		64C
S., Harvie	B	29
Sanabria, Bobby	DIPL	47,29
Schag, Shane	M	61
Schick, Steven	M	65
Schub, Andre-Michel	DIPL	66A
Shelton, Lucy	M	61
Sherry, Fred		62C
Shrut, Arlene	D	
Silverman, Marc	D	41,66A
Sirguey, Gait	M	
Sirota, Nadia	M	62B
Sirota, Robert	D	39,10
Slagle, Steven	M	47,64E,29
Smith, Thomas		63A
Smukler, Lauri		62A
Soskin, Mark		29,66A
Soyer, David	DIPL	62C
Spanjer, R. Allen		63B
Sperry, Paul	B	
Stacy, Thomas	B	64B
Stambaugh, J. Mark	D	13
Stanescu, Christina	M	
Starobin, David	B	70
Stepansky, Alan	B	62C
Stewart, Jocelyn	D	66H
Stewart, Mark	DIPL	70
Stewart, Raymond	M	63
Stiles, Joan	M	29
Sussman, Richard	M	47,29
Svetlanova, Nina	DIPL	66A
Takebe, Yoko	DIPL	62A
Taylor, David	M	29
Taylor, Stephen	DIPL	64B
Temperley, Joe		29
Tracy, William		39
Tree, Michael	DIPL	62B
Tritle, Kent	M	36
Vassiliades, Christopher	M	13
Vaughn, Dona	M	39
Vigeland, Nils	D	13,10
Volckhausen, David	M	13
Wallenbrock, Nicole Beth	M	
Wang, Liang-yu	B	64B
Wendholt, Scott	B	29
Wilkins, Jack		29
Wilkins, Mariah	M	29
Willumstad, Jytte	M	
Wilson, Steven		29,64E
Wingreen, Harriet	B	66A
Winograd, Peter	M	62A
Wu, She-e	M	65
Yui, Lisa	B	67
Zlotkin, Frederick	D	62C
Zuckerman, Pinchas	D	62A,62B

NY2200 Manhattanville College
Department of Music
2900 Purchase St
Purchase, NY 10577
(914) 323-5260   Fax: (914) 323-5383
www.mville.edu
E-mail: francis.brancaleone@mville.edu

4 Year Institution, Graduate School

Master of Arts in Teaching

Chair: Francis P. Brancaleone, 80A

Rank	Name	Degree	Codes
Adj	Azzolina, Jay	M	70,29,47
Adj	Bettendorf, Carl	D	38,60
Prof	Brancaleone, Francis P.	D	13,66A,66D,66G,66C
Adj	Canova, Diana		61
Other	Cappon, Ronald	M	61
Artist in Res	Cherry, Mark	M	54,40,66C
Adj	Christie, Lyndon	D	62D
Prof	Comberiati, Carmelo	D	12,14
Adj	Cuk, John	M	36,39,54,40
Adj	Danby, Jen	D	54
Adj	Esham, Faith	M	61
Adj	Fluchaire, Olivier	M	32E,63A
Adj	Freas, Thomas	M	49,63A
Adj	Goldsmith, Jeremy	M	34
Adj	Guernsey, Diane	M	66C,61
Adj	Haiduck, Neal	M	64C,64E
Adj	Jones, Harold	B	64A,48
Adj	Kaczmarczyk, Mark	M	61
Assoc Prof	Kerlin, Jerry D.	PhD	32,20
Assoc Prof	Kidde, Geoffrey C.	D	10,13,34,45,32F
Adj	Kuan, Flora	D	13C,66A,42
Adj	Lionti, Victor C.	M	62B
Adj	Lorusso, James		70
Adj	Meade, Michael	M	62C
Adj	Meyer, Beverly	M	54,40,66C
Other	Rachlin, Harvey	M	35A,35D,35E
Adj	Reynolds, Terrance	M	46,49
Adj	Vincent, Ron	B	65,50,32E
Adj	Walker, Patricia	M	63B,32E
Adj	Yom, Jeongeun	M	66C

NY2250 Mannes College
The New School for Music
150 W 85th St
New York, NY 10024
(212) 580-0210   Fax: (212) 580-1738
www.mannes.newschool.edu
E-mail: mannesadmissions@newschool.edu

4 Year Institution, Graduate School

Master of Music in Composition, Master of Music in Music Theory, Master of Music in Performance, Master of Music in Orchestral Instruments, Master of Music in Vocal Accompanying, Professional Studies Diploma, Master of Music in Choral Conducting, Master of Music in Orchestral Conducting

Dean: Joel Lester, 80A
Dir., Admissions: Georgia Schmitt, 80D
Dir., Extension Division: Richard Russell, 80E
Dir., Preparatory Division: Kate Sheeran, 80E
Assistant Dean: Audrey Axinn, 80H
Associate Dean: George Fisher, 80H

Name	Degree	Codes
Aaron, Elizabeth	B	13
Abrams, Eugene		54
Alley, Laura		39
Alpern, Wayne	D	13
Arner, Lucia	M	61
Aronov, Arkady	D	66A
Baer, Alan		63D
Bagwell, Thomas		66C,39,40
Baker, James		50
Baker, Michelle	M	63B
Barrett, Marianne		61
Barrett, Richard	DIPL	61
Beilina, Nina	D	62A
Brevig, Per	D	49,63C
Burstein, Poundie	D	13
Burton, Amy	M	61
Caldwell, Susan		39
Champlin, Terry		41
Charry, Michael		38
Chen, Pei-Wen		61
Colaneri, Joseph	M	39
Cuckson, Robert	D	13,10
Cultice, Thomas	M	61
Dallesio, Richard	B	64B
Daniel, Anne Margaret		
Danilow, Marji	M	62D
Davidovsky, Mario	M	10
Diaz, Javier		65
Dokovska, Pavlina	M	66A
Douvas, Elaine	B	64B
Dreyfus, Karen		62B
Dueck, Jocelyn B.	D	66C,66A,61
Eddy, Timothy	M	41,62C
Edwards, Leo	M	13,10
Falcon, Ruth	M	61
Fehleisen, Fred	M	12A
Feltsman, Vladimir		66A
Fischbach, Garrett		62A
Fisher, George	D	13,66H
Frazier, Jordan	B	62D
Givens, Shirley	B	62A
Goldberg, Marc	M	64D,41
Goldsmith, Harris	M	41
Goode, Richard	DIPL	66A
Goren, Neal	B	39
Greene, Joshua		61
Groves, Marilyn		66D
Gunji, Maya		65
Haas, Arthur	M	66H
Halley, Sharon		54
Hamilton, Bonnie	B	61
Hand, Frederic	B	70
Hart, Bonny		
Hayes, David		60,38
Hindell, Leonard W.	M	41,64D
Hobbs, William	M	61
Huang, Hsin-Yun	M	62B,41
Hughes, Miriam Kartch	M	66D
Jolles, Susan	B	62E
Jolley, David	M	41,63B
Kahn, Sue Ann	M	41,64A
Kaplan, Lewis	M	62A
Khimm, Christina		62A
Kim, Chin	D	41,62A
Kim, Michelle		62A
Kim, Yuri	M	66A
Kling, Irene		61
Krakauer, David	M	41,64C
Laskowski, Kim		64D
Lateiner, Jacob		66A,41
Lavanne, Antonia		61
Lester, Joel	D	13,41
Levine, Rhoda		54
Levy, Arthur	B	61
Lewin, Ann		61
Loeb, David	M	13,10
Lutzke, Myron		55
Manoli, Anthony		61
Marek, Dan	M	61
Markey, James		63C
Marques, Alfredo		
McGaughey, Martha		
McGill, Anthony		64C,48
Mendenhall, Judith		64A,41
Meng, Mei-Mei	M	13,66D
Michell, Edna		41
Moravec, Paul		10
Morozova, Irina	M	66A
Morton, Glenn	M	66C,61
Myers, Philip		63B
Needelman, William	M	13
Neidich, Charles	DIPL	64C
Nelson, Susan		39
Nemhauser, Frank	B	13,60,61
Neubauer, Paul	M	62B
Newman, Michael	B	70,41
O'Brien, Orin	B	62D
Panner, Daniel	M	62B
Park, Christopher	D	13
Penzarella, Vincent	M	63A
Phillips, Daniel		41,62A
Phillips, Todd		41,62A
Ponthus, Marc		66A
Porterfield, Richard	M	13
Preiss, James	M	50,65
Prosser, Peter		41
Qian, Wen		62A
Ralske, Eric		63B
Raps, Gena		41,66A
Riccomini, Ray		63A
Robert, Lucie	M	62A
Roberts, Beth	M	61
Rosand, Aaron		62A
Rose, Jerome	M	66A
Rosen, Marcy	B	62C
Rosenbaum, Victor	D	66A
Santer, Renee	D	61
Sauer, Thomas	D	66A
Schachter, Carl	M	13,41
Setzer, Ann	D	41,62A
Seyfried, Sheridan		13
Shapiro, Madeleine	M	43

	Shapiro, Mark L.	DIPL	60A
	Sharp, Irene		62C
	Sherry, Fred		62C
	Siegel, Hedi		13
	Silverman, Faye-Ellen	D	12A
	Sivan, Noam		13
	Smith, Thomas		63A,41
	Smukler, Laurie		62A
	Song, JY	D	66A,41
	Sprott, Weston		63C
	Stanescu-Flagg, Cristina	D	66C,61
	Stein-Mallow, Barbara		62C
	Steinberg, Mark		62A
	Stewart, Aliza	D	54
	Stone, Christopher	M	13
	Svetlanova, Nina	D	66A
	Sylar, Sherry		64B
	Taylor, David	M	41,63C
	Taylor, Ted		39
	Tcimpidis, David	M	10
	Terrigno, Loretta	M	13
	Thomas, Sally	M	62A
	Tobias, Paul	M	62C
	Tompkins, Joseph		65
	Turner, Kyle		63D
	Underwood, Keith	M	64A
	Valjarevic, Vladimir	DMA	66A,66B
	Varney, John		
	Velez, Glen		65,65A
	Versage, Susan Woodruff		39
	Walsh, Diane	M	41,66A
	Watkins, Howard		61
	Weismann, Raymond	D	
	Weller, Ira		62B,41
	Wen, Eric	D	13
	Werner, Michael	B	65
	Williamson, Stephen		64C
	Willumstad, Jytte	M	
	Wilson, Nancy	M	55B
	Won, Allen	M	64E
	Yajima, Hiroko	DIPL	41,62A
	Zaretsky, Inessa	M	66A

NY2400 Mercy College

Music Program
555 Broadway
Dobbs Ferry, NY 10522-1134
(914) 674-7420   Fax: (914) 674-7488
www.mercy.edu
E-mail: jberrett@mercy.edu

4 Year Institution

Dean: Robert Arthurs, 80A
Chair: Joshua Berrett, 80A
Executive Director: Laura Calzolari, 80A

Adj	Adamy, Paul		70,29
	Arthurs, Robert		63A,29
Adj	Barton, Mary		62A,62B
Adj	Bell, Dennis		13A,13,10F
Asst Prof	Berle, Arnie		11,29A
Prof	Berrett, Joshua	D	13,11,29A,12,12B
Adj	Boder, Alexander		62A
Adj	Briskin, Efrem		66A
Adj	Caldwell, Frances Sherer		66A
	Calzolari, Laura		64A
Adj	Chase, Jennie Kao		61
Adj	Chase, Robert	D	13,12A,66H
Adj	Cultise, Theora		66C
Adj	Davidson, Doris		13
Adj	Dial, Frances		62C
Adj	Drelles, Andrew		64C
Adj	Finucan, David		64A
Adj	Frisch, Andrea		33
Adj	Gartner, Janet Sussman	B	66C
Adj	Giglid, Joseph		70,29
Adj	Gold, Michael		62D,29
Adj	Gorevic, Ronald	DIPL	62A,62B
Adj	Gottesman, Mila		66A
Adj	Harris, Alice Eaton		66A,66H
Adj	Harris, Ruth Berman		62E
Adj	Hijazi, Anne		66A
Adj	Hill, Margaret		62A
Adj	Hurley, Patricia		63A
Adj	Joffe, Lucy		39,61
Adj	Jonas, Dorothy		66A
Adj	Jones, Harold		64A
Adj	Khimm, Christina		62A
Adj	Kossodo, Verena		66C
Adj	Kostner, Douglas		11
Adj	Kresek, Emme	M	36
Adj	Krieger, David		62C,41
Adj	Kuo, Rita		66A
Adj	Landers, Karen		62A

Adj	Lanini, Phyllis		64B
Adj	Laskowitz, Lillian		66A
Adj	Lester, William		66A,66D,29
Adj	Lewis, Tim		66G
Adj	Lorusso, James		70
Adj	Lorusso, Mary Ann		67D,70
Adj	Magaziner, Elliot		60,41,62A
Adj	Magaziner, Sari		62B
Adj	Mangini, Nicholas		65
Adj	Maynard, Keith		13A,13,10F
Adj	Mazziotta, Laura		63A
Adj	McGlinn, Margaret		33
Adj	Miropolskaya, Mara		66A
Adj	Mohen, Gerald	D	13,11
Adj	Montello, Louise		33
Adj	Mueller, Ruth		32A
Adj	Pelekh, Anna		62A
Adj	Pierce, Joshua		66A
Adj	Poore, Mary Elizabeth		61
Asst Prof	Porter, Charles		13A,13,10,11,12A
Adj	Post, Julie Goodman		13
Adj	Prokop, Rick		47
Adj	Roane, Steve		10F
Adj	Roth, Michael		62B
Adj	Sandacata, Lisa		33
Adj	Sanders, David		35C,35D
Adj	Scarpa, Tony		33
Adj	Scharfstein, Tanya		66A
Adj	Schonthal, Ruth		13,10,66A
Adj	Shepley, Mary Ellen		64A,67B
Adj	Snyder, Fred		63C
Adj	Sophos, Anthony		62C
Adj	Starin, Stefani		64A,67B
Asst Prof	Steinman, Paul		35C,35D
Adj	Stephenson, Mary		62A
Adj	Sukonik, Inna		66A
Assoc Prof	Taylor, Betty Sue		13A,12,36,61,66
Adj	Thompson, Kenneth		61
Adj	Tompkins, Leslie		63B
Adj	Traficante, Marie		61
Adj	Weisenberg, Marvi		32A
Adj	Wessel, Kenneth		70,29
Adj	Wright, Joseph		11,29A
Adj	Yap, Kin		66A

NY2450 Molloy College

Department of Music
1000 Hempstead Ave
Rockville Centre, NY 11570-1100
(516) 678-5000 x 6192   Fax: (516) 255-4823
www.molloy.edu
E-mail: eselesky@molloy.edu

4 Year Institution

Master of Science in Music Therapy

Chair: Evelyn C. Selesky, 80A

Inst PT	Bayen, Diane	M	13C,61,36,60,32
Asst Prof PT	Berardinelli, George	M	63A
Asst Prof PT	Berardinelli, Paula	D	29A,13,66A
Inst PT	Breidenbach, Ruth	M	32
Inst PT	Carpente, John	D	33,70
Inst PT	Chung, Heejin	M	33
Inst PT	Goff, Terrence	M	61
Inst	Heller, Lora	M	33
Inst PT	Kim, Seung A.	D	33,66A
Inst PT	Kunins, Alan	M	62
Asst Prof Emeritus	Lenehan, Miriam C.	D	11,12A,32,66A,66D
Inst PT	Lozano, Denise	M	13A,11,64A
Inst PT	Lucente, Jill	M	33
Inst PT	Matthews, Britton	M	32,12,65
	McDannell, Karl	M	32B,32C,47,60
	McDonough, Lauren	M	33,66A
Asst Prof	McGann, Daniel	M	13A,13,12A,70
Inst PT	Montalbano, James	B	66A,66G
Inst PT	Ortiz, Gabriela	M	33
Inst PT	Rampal, Michelle	M	32
Inst PT	Rizzuto, Thomas	M	70,12A
Inst PT	Roof, Kimberly	M	64
Inst PT	Schwartz, Elizabeth	M	33
Asst Prof	Selesky, Evelyn C.	M	33,66A
	Sgouros, Michael	B	65
Asst Prof	Sorel, Suzanne	D	66A,33
Inst PT	Ventre, Madelaine	M	33
Inst PT	Viega, Michael	D	33
Assoc Prof PT	Yarrow, Anne	D	38,62A

NY2500 Monroe Community College
Department of Visual & Perf Arts
1000 E Henrietta Rd
Rochester, NY 14623
(585) 292-2000 x3350   Fax: (585) 427-2749
www.monroecc.edu
E-mail: kfragnoli@monroecc.edu

2 Year Institution

Chair: Kristen Fragnoli, 80A
Assistant Director, Student Activities: Thomas Priester, 80D,80H

Adj Inst	Brazofsky, Matthew	M	34D
Adj Inst	Brown, Don		61
Adj Inst	Dobbins, Evan	M	29A
Adj Inst	Falzano, Anthony		20G,35A
Prof	Fittipaldi, Thomas	M	36,66D,67,70,11
	Luk, Siu Yan	M	66C
Adj Inst	Machleder, Anton	D	70,53
Adj Inst	Mariano, Dennis		11
Adj Inst	Meeker, Christopher		13
Asst Prof	Nyerges, John	M	35C,47
Adj Inst	Robey, Matthew E.	D	66A,66C,66D,11,32E
Adj Inst	Ruby, Meg	M	32E
Assoc Prof	Shaw, David	D	13,10,11,12A
Adj Inst	Simmonds, Jim	M	11
Asst Prof	Wise, Herbert	D	63C,66A,66D,11,32E

NY2550 Nassau Community College
Department of Music
1 Education Dr
Garden City, NY 11530
(516) 572-7446/7   Fax: (516) 572-9791
www.ncc.edu
E-mail: musoff@ncc.edu

2 Year Institution
Member of NASM

Chair: T. Jeffrey Fox, 80A

Adj	Abbinanti, David A.	M	13A,35A
Adj	Arendsen, Benjamin D.	M	13A,13C
Adj	Baker, Meredith E.	M	13,66G,36
Adj	Becker, J. Harris	M	14C
Prof	Bouchard, George	M	11,46,47,66D,29
Adj	Camus, Amy E.	M	62C
Adj	Carubia, Michael R.		46,47
Adj	Castillo, Carlos		62D
Assoc Prof	Cavallo, Gail R.	M	32A,13A,66D
Adj	Coleman, Douglas		63A
Adj	Cooper, Stacey H.	M	35A
Adj	DeMilo, Bradford		63B
Adj	Devereaux, Deborah	D	66C
Adj	Dransite, Robert S.		64E,64C
Adj	Erickson, James M.	M	20G
Other	Ferraro, David C.	B	35C,35G
Adj	Ferrente, Joseph	B	66C
Adj	Fox, Marilyn F.	M	70,66D
Prof	Fox, T. Jeffrey	M	36,11,20G,14C
Adj	Gilley, Richard S.	M	11
Adj	Glickman, Eugene	D	13,12A
Assoc Prof	Golan, Jeanne K.	D	13B,13C,12A,66A,66D
Adj	Goodman, Jonathan M.		61
Adj	Grossman, George	D	20G,66D
Adj	Gustavson, Mark	D	10,64C,66D,10A,10F
Adj	Guttmann, Hadassah	D	32A,66D,66A
Adj	Guzman, Ronald P.	M	20G
Inst	Hughes, R. Daniel	M	36,13A,61
Adj	Jusino, Christopher		13A,72
Adj	Kapner, Harriet H.	M	70,13A,13B,13C
Adj	Karahalis, Dean	D	63C,63D
Adj	Kegerreis, Helen M.	M	32A,13C,66D
Asst Prof	Kelly, Kevin M.	B	34,35
Adj	Kim, Jisung	M	66A,66D
Adj	Koslovsky, Marc S.	M	70,10D
Adj	Laconti, Paul	M	35A
Adj	Lee, Rodger P.	M	14C
Adj	Lehr, Barry	B	62B
Adj	Leonard, Stephen		70
Inst	Marenstein, Harry	M	38,11,13A,13B
Adj	Moe, Karla		64A
Prof	Nachman, Myrna	D	66A,13A,12A,13C
Other	Napoli, Robert	B	35G
Inst	Neal, Nedra	M	13C,66D
Adj	Osborne, Robert M.		61
Adj	Osrowitz, Michael L.	M	50,65
Other	Ouellette, Garry		16,14C,72,34,35
Adj	Panacciulli, Louis M.		37
Adj	Rockwin, Howard	M	64D
Adj	Rowden, Charles H.	M	11,12A,66D
Adj	Rudoff, Patricia L.	B	62A,62B
Other	Schumaker, Alan	B	66F
Inst	Sheehan, Paul J.	D	13A,66D
Assoc Prof	Sobolewski, Susan F.	D	66D,13C,42,66A
Adj	Sulzinski, Valerie	M	64B
Adj	Weber, Kathleen F.	D	61
Adj	Wolinsky, Robert A.	M	66D,67F
Adj	Zatorski, Thomas	D	66D
Adj	Zito, William	B	70,41

NY2650 Nazareth College
Department of Music
4245 East Ave
Rochester, NY 14618-3790
(585) 389-2700   Fax: (585) 389-2939
www.naz.edu
E-mail: jdouthi2@naz.edu

4 Year Institution, Graduate School
Member of NASM

Master of Science in Music Education, Master of Science in Creative Arts Therapy Specialization in Music Therapy

Chair: James Russell Douthit, 80A
Dir., Preparatory Division: Gary Fisher, 80E

Lect PT	Aubin, Isabelle	M	66C
Lect PT	Bacon, Marcy D.	D	64C,48
Lect PT	Becker, Lauren	M	63B
Lect PT	Bellor, Jennifer K.	PhD	13
Collaborative Pianist	Bisbano, Tony	B	66C
Lect PT	Boianova, Linda	D	66A,13C,61,39,66C
Collaborative Pianist	Bowman, Jonathan	D	66C
Collaborative Pianist	Brennan, Mark	M	66C
Lect PT	Carlin, Eric	M	70
Assoc Prof	Carlson, Mary C.	PhD	32C,32
Asst Prof	Chase, Jared	D	37
Lect PT	Choi, Bonnie	D	66A,66D,66H
Lect PT	Cochrane, Amy L.	M	61
Lect PT	Cotroneo, Sue	M	61
Prof	Douthit, James Russell	DMA	66A,66B,66D
Lect PT	Driankova, Ivanka	D	13
Lect PT	Elliott, Mandy	B	33
Lect PT	Farrington, Annette	M	64A
Lect PT	Fava, Cristina	PhD	12A
Lect PT	Fisher, Gary	D	66A
Lect PT	Floriano, Joan	M	61
Lect PT	Folan, Andrea	M	61
Lect PT	Gold, Christopher A.	M	33
Lect PT	Granat, Bozena	M	13
Asst Prof	Granat, Zbigniew	D	12
Lect PT	Grigorov, Liisa Ambegaokar	M	64A,48
Lect PT	Halleran, Sandra	M	62C
	Hannigan Tabon, Katie	D	61
Lect PT	Hidlay, Rachel	M	66A
Lect	Hull, Barbara A.	D	63A,63,60
Lect PT	Hult, David W.	D	62A,62B,11,51
Prof	Hunter, Bryan C.	D	33
Lect PT	Hwang, Margery 'Mimi'	M	62C
Asst Prof	Keough, Laurie	M	33
Assoc Prof	Kim, Soo Yeon	D	61
Asst Prof	King, Betsey	D	33
Collaborative Pianist	Ko, EunMi	M	66C
Lect PT	Kodzas, Peter	D	70
Collaborative Pianist	Kong, Gary	M	66C
Lect	Koster, Keith	PhD	32
Lect	Kot, Don	M	66A,61,66D,66C,54
Lect PT	Leenhouts, Margaret A.	D	62A
Lect	Marling, Chisato Eda	D	64E,48
Asst Prof	Martinez, Mario E.		61
Lect PT	Massicot, Joshua	M	66D
Lect	Maynard-Christensen, Dianne	D	66G
Lect PT	McCarthy, David	M	13
Lect PT	McCormick, Gaelen	M	62D
Inst	McGuire, Kristen Shiner	M	50,65
Lect PT	Nitsch, Kevin	D	66A,13A,13C
Lect	Pratt, Alice	B	32
Lect PT	Preston, Brian	M	66A
Lect PT	Reed, Melissa	M	32
Lect PT	Rhee, Sarah	D	66C
Asst Prof	Roth, Marjorie	PhD	64A,12
Asst Prof	Sallmen, Mark	PhD	13
Lect PT	Schroeder, Kelly M.	M	32
Lect PT	Shatalov, Alexandra	M	64B
Lect PT	Smith, Derrick	M	61
Lect PT	Smith, Jeffrey	M	36
Prof	Smoker, Beverly A.	D	66A,66B,66D
Lect PT	Smoker, Paul	D	47
Lect PT	Stevens, Brian	M	36
Lect PT	Stoner, Jeremy	M	63D
Lect PT	Strauss, Robert	D	61,39
Lect PT	Strelau, Nancy	M	38,60B

Lect PT	Upcraft-Russ, Kimberly	M	61
Lect PT	VanBuren, Susan	M	64D
Lect PT	Vardanyan, Tigran	M	62A
Lect PT	Weingarten, Frederic	M	32
Lect PT	Wilke, Christopher	D	70
Lect PT	Willey, Jason	M	33
Assoc Prof	Zeigler, Mark C.	PhD	32D,36,40,60A
Lect PT	Zugelder, Steven	M	63D

NY2660 New School, The

for Jazz and Contemporary Music
55 W 13th St
5th Floor
New York, NY 10011
(212) 229-5896 x4589   Fax: (212) 229-8936
jazz.newschool.edu
E-mail: jazzadm@newschool.edu

4 Year Institution

Executive Director: Martin Mueller, 80A
Director of Admissions: Teri Lucas, 80D
Dir., Academics Affairs: Dan Greenblatt, 80H

Inst PT	Abdullah, Ahmed	M	47,63A
Inst PT	Arita, Junko	B	61,13B,13C
Inst PT	Bianchi, Jay	B	66
Prof	Bloom, Jane Ira	M	10,53,64,47
Inst PT	Boukas, Richard A.	B	61,70,20H,47
Inst PT	Brackeen, Joanne		10,66A,47,53
Inst PT	Bridgewater, Cecil	B	10,63A,53
Inst PT	Camelio, Brian	B	10,70,35C
Inst PT	Cardenas, Steve	B	47
Inst PT	Carney, Jeff	B	62D
Inst PT	Chambers, Joe	M	44,65,53
Inst PT	Cotton, Haim		66
Inst PT	Cyrille, Andrew	B	65,53
Inst PT	D'Angelo, Gerard	B	13A,13,13J
Inst PT	Donelian, Armen	B	13A,13C,10,66A,47
Inst PT	Escalera, Mario	M	64,53
Inst PT	Gallon, Ray		66A,47
Inst PT	Galper, Hal	B	66A,47
Inst PT	Garzone, George	B	64E,47
Inst PT	Glasser, David	M	64E,47
Prof	Greenblatt, Dan	D	64E,32E,47,29B
Inst PT	Hamilton, Chico	D	10,65,47
Inst PT	Hardy, Julie	M	61,47
Inst PT	Harper, Billy	B	64E,47
Inst PT	Harper, Richard	D	61,29B
Inst PT	Hemingway, Gerry	M	65,20,13
	Hoffman, Christopher		35C
Inst PT	Holzman, Adam		66A,47
Inst PT	Inoue, Satoshi	B	70,47
Inst PT	Juris, Vic		70,47
Inst PT	Karn, Michael	B	64E,47
Inst PT	Kettner, Scott	B	50
Inst PT	Kirchner, Bill	B	10,12,64,29
Inst PT	Kompanek, Rudolph (Sonny)	M	10
Inst PT	Lawson, Janet		61,47
Inst PT	Ledgerwood, Lee Ann		10,66A,47
Inst PT	Lohninger, Elisabeth	M	13C
Inst PT	London, Amy	B	61,47
Inst PT	Lopato, David	B	13,10,66A
Inst PT	Luthra, Arun	B	13,64E
Inst PT	MacEachen, Ed	B	70
Inst PT	Mance, Junior		47,66F
Inst PT	McKee, Andy		47,62D,53
Inst PT	Milne, Andy	B	66A,47
Inst PT	Morales-Matos, Rolando	M	50
Inst PT	Moser, Diane	B	47,10
Inst PT	Nurock, Kirk	M	10F,60,10,13J,29A
Inst PT	Owens, Jimmy	M	64E,35A,35B,35D,35E
Inst PT	Perla, Gene		62D
Inst PT	Persip, Charli		65,53
Inst PT	Petrides, Ron T.	D	10,29,70,13,12
Inst PT	Purdie, Bernard		47,65
Prof	Rapport, Evan	D	47
Inst PT	Sadin, Robert		60,10
Inst PT	Sanabria, Bobby	B	47,65
Inst PT	Schnitter, David	B	13,64E,47
Inst PT	Scott, Kenneth	B	61
Inst PT	Shachal, Harel		20B,64C,64E
Inst PT	Shemaria, Rich	M	60,10,66A
	Siegel, Jeff S.		65
Inst PT	Snidero, Jim		63B,64E
Inst PT	Stiles, Joan	D	66,13
Inst PT	Stuart, Rory		13,70,47
Inst PT	Tanksley, Francesca	M	13,66A,53
Inst PT	Tolliver, Charles		10,46,47,63A
Inst PT	Weidenmueller, Johannes	M	62D,13
Inst PT	Weiss, Doug	B	13,47
Inst PT	Wenninger, Karl	B	34
Prof	Workman, Reggie		10,47,62D,53
Inst PT	Z, Rachel	B	13B,29B,66A
Inst PT	Zak, Peter	B	47,66A,53
Inst PT	Ziv, Amir	B	47,65

NY2700 New York City Technical College

Program of Music
300 Jay St #A630
Brooklyn, NY 11201-1909
(718)260-5018   Fax: (718)260-5198
www.citytech.cuny.edu
E-mail: cporter@citytech.cuny.edu

4 Year Institution

Coordinator: Charles Porter, 80A

Adj	Lew, Howard	B	13A,12,66D
Prof	Porter, Charles	D	13A,11,12A,66D,29A
Adj	Schelfer, James	M	13A,20,29A
Adj	Smith, Michael Cedric	B	70,13A

NY2740 New York University

Department of Music
24 Waverly Pl/Rm 268
New York, NY 10003-6757
(212) 998-8300   Fax: (212) 995-4147
www.nyu.edu/gsas/dept/music
E-mail: ly332@nyu.edu

4 Year Institution, Graduate School

PhD in Music

Chair: Michael Beckerman, 80A
Dir., Undergraduate Studies: J. Martin Daughtry, 80B
Dir., Graduate Studies: Elizabeth D. Hoffman, 80C

Prof Emeritus	Bailey, Robert	D	13,12
Prof	Beckerman, Michael	D	12,14C
Prof	Boorman, Stanley H.	D	11,12A,12,55
Prof Emeritus	Burrows, David	D	11,12A,12,14
Prof Emeritus	Chusid, Martin	D	11,12A,12
Prof	Cusick, Suzanne G.	D	12A,12C,12D,15
Asst Prof	Daughtry, J. Martin	D	14A,14C,20B,20F,14D
Prof Emeritus	Fennelly, Brian	D	13,10,12A,45
Assoc Prof	Hoffman, Elizabeth D.	D	12D,13,10,45,34
Prof	Karchin, Louis S.	D	10F,60,10,36
Assoc Prof	Mahon, Maureen	D	14A,14E,14D,14F,15
Assoc Prof	Mueller, Rena Charnin	D	12,14C
Prof Emeritus	Roesner, Edward	D	11,12A,12,55
Assoc Prof	Samuels, David	D	14A,14C,14D,14F,20G
Asst Prof	Stanyek, Jason	D	34,12,14,20,12D

NY2750 New York University

Steinhardt School of Music & PA
35 W 4th St
Suite 1077
New York, NY 10012-1120
(212) 998-5424   Fax: (212) 995-4043
www.nyu.edu/education/music
E-mail: robert.rowe@nyu.edu

4 Year Institution, Graduate School

Master of Arts in Music Education, Master of Music in Composition, Master of Music in Performance, PhD in Composition, PhD in Music Education, PhD in Music Technology, PhD in Performance Practice, Master of Arts in Music Therapy, Master of Music in Scoring for Film and Multimedia, Master of Arts in Music Technology, Master of Arts in Music Business

Director: Robert Rowe, 80A
Director Emeritus: Lawrence Ferrara

	Aikawa, Atsundo	M	66F
Asst Prof	Alegria, Gabriel A.	D	29,47,63A
Adj Asst Prof	Alessi, Ralph P.	M	63A,47,10D
Inst	Anderer, Joseph T.		63B
Inst	Andjaparidze, Eteri	D	66A
Inst	Arjomand, Ramin Amir	D	10A,10F,13B,13C
Inst	Atorino, John J.	B	36
Adj Assoc Prof	Austin, Diane Snow	D	33
Inst	Aye, Jeremy K.		61
Asst Prof	Baer, Stephanie	M	62,42
Inst	Beaver, Martin P.		62A
Assoc Prof	Bello, Juan P.	D	34
Inst	Bengloff, Richard	M	35D

Title	Name	Col	Codes	Title	Name	Col	Codes
Inst	Bernstein, Peter A.	B	29,70,47	Clinical Asst Prof	Howard-Spink, Sam J.	D	35
Adj Assoc Prof	Bernstein, Seymour	B	66A	Inst	Hoyt, Thomas H.	D	63A
Adj Asst Prof	Besley, Megan C.	D	61	Inst	Hutchinson, Thomas		63C
Inst	Beyer, Tom	M	10,34	Adj Asst Prof	Iyer, Vijay S.	D	29,66,47
Inst	Bishai, Alf	M	13B,13C	Inst	Jacobsen, Eric	B	42,62C
Inst	Blakeman, Jennifer	B	35A	Adj Assoc Prof	Jampel, Peter F.	D	33
Adj Asst Prof	Bodner, Vicki Hope	M	64B	Adj Asst Prof	Johnston, Randy B.	B	29,70,47
Assoc Prof	Bongiorno, Joseph A.	M	62D,38,42,51	Inst	Kaplan, Chester	M	32
Adj Asst Prof	Bosco, Frank	M	33	Inst	Katz, Shmuel D.	M	42,62B
Adj Asst Prof	Bowen, William	B	34D,35G	Inst	Kerlin, Jerry	D	32
Vstng Prof	Bowman, Wayne	D	32,12C,12F,14	Inst	Kibbey, Bridget A.	M	62E
Inst	Boyar, Simon M.	M	65B,50	Inst	Kim, Mijin	D	33
Inst	Breaux, Michael L.	M	32B,32C,32E,32F	Inst	Koh, Jennifer	M	62A
Adj Asst Prof	Brescia, Tina M.	D	33	Adj Asst Prof	Kompanek, Rudolph W.	M	10C,10F
Inst	Bukvich-Nichols, Svetlana	M	34A	Inst	Kovacs, Anna	M	32D,36,60A
Inst	Bush, Christopher	M	64C,41,42,48	Adj Asst Prof	Kozinn, Allan	B	12B,12C
Assoc Prof	Bussert, Meg		54	Inst	Krakauer, David	B	64C
Inst	Canin, Martin	B	66A	Inst	Krantz, Wayne M.	B	29,70,49
Inst	Celentano, James	M	35A	Adj Asst Prof	Krause, Drew S.	D	13A,13B,13C,13D,13F
Adj Asst Prof	Chadabe, Joel A.	M	34	Inst	Krauss, David	M	49,63A
Adj Asst Prof	Chase, Stephanie	M	62A	Inst	Kwon, Hea-Kyung	D	33
	Church, Joseph	D	54,10A,10D	Inst	La Barbara, Joan	B	10A,10B
Inst	Cohen, Jean-Luc D.	M	34	Inst	Lalama, Ralph	M	29,47,64E
Adj Asst Prof	Cohen, Paul	D	64E	Assoc Prof	Lamneck, Esther	D	64C,43
Inst	Consoli, Marc-Antonio	D	13,10A	Inst	Lane, Brandie	B	34D
Inst	Crawford, Langdon C.	M	34D,34G	Inst	Langdon, Gillian S.	M	33
Inst	Cuffari, Gina Lynn		64D	Inst	Laurel, Edward	B	66C
Adj Asst Prof	Da Silva, Fabio Gardenal	D	66A,42,66C	Inst	Lawler, Daniel J.	M	61
Adj Asst Prof	Da Silva, Pedro Henriques	D	10D	Inst	Lee, Paul	D	32E
Other	Damast, Deborah G.	M	52	Inst	Lieberman, Bernard		32
Inst	Davis, Susan A.	D	32,51,62	Adj Assoc Prof	Lissemore, Richard	M	61
Inst	De Leo, Joseph A.	M	32,12A,13B,32C,32H	Adj Assoc Prof	Lovano, Joe S.	B	29,64E,47
Inst	De Mare, Anthony J.	M	66A,66C	Inst	Lucarelli, Humbert		64B
Adj Assoc Prof	Dello Joio, Justin N.	DMA	13B,13E,13F,10A,10F	Inst	MacFarlane, Thomas	D	13C,13D,13F,12A,12B
Inst	Diaz-Cassou, Isabel		34	Inst	Madden, Andrew	M	34D
Inst	Dick, Robert	M	64A,42,41	Inst	Mahadeen, Roger	M	62A
Adj Asst Prof	Didkovsky, Nick	M	34G	Vstng Inst	Marlowe, Sarah	M	13,13C,13D,13H,13I
Adj Asst Prof	DiPaolo, Daniel M.	M	13B,13C	Inst	Martinez-Forteza, Pascual	M	64C
Inst	Dobbis, Richard B.	B	35D	Inst	Mason, Elliot J.	B	63C
Adj Asst Prof	Doczi, Tom F.	M	34D,35G	Inst	Matthay, Christopher D.	D	13,14A,20D,20E,29A
Inst	Dodge, Leanne E.	D	12A,12,13A	Assoc Prof	Mavromatis, Panayotis	D	13B,13D,13F,13G,13K
Inst	Dos Santos, Adriano	M	47	Inst	McClure, Ron D.		62D,47
Inst	Drewes, William		29,47,64E	Inst	Meade, David B.	M	32E
Inst	Drummond, Billy R.	B	29,47,65	Adj Asst Prof	Mendez, Jose Ramon	D	66A
Prof	Elliott, David J.	D	32,12B,10A	Adj Asst Prof	Meyers, Joe	M	62C
Inst	Ellsworth, Ann	M	63B	Adj Asst Prof	Miller, Anton M.	M	62A,42
Inst	Eubanks, Robin	B	47,63C,29	Adj Asst Prof	Milne, Andy	B	29,47,66A
Asst Prof	Farbood, Morwaread Mary	D	34,10,66	Inst	Moon, Eileen	B	62C
Inst	Fastenow, William David	M	34	Assoc Prof	Moore, Catherine	D	35
Adj Asst Prof	Feiner, Susan	M	33	Inst	Moreno, Tony	B	47,29,65
Inst	Feldhusen, Roberta		32A,32B	Inst	Murphree, Scott	D	61
Inst	Feldman, Marion		62C,42	Inst	Murphy, Kevin M.		61
Inst	Ferber, Alan D.	M	63C	Inst	Naphtali, Dafna L.	M	34G,34H
Prof	Ferrara, Lawrence	D	13,12,32,66	Inst	Naranjo, Valerie D.	M	65B
Inst	Filadelfo, Gary A.	M	10,35C	Inst	Nesin, Richard	B	35A
Inst	Fleckenstein, Charles F.	M	35A	Inst	Nester, Kathleen M.	M	64A
Inst	Fried, Joshua	B	34A,34H	Inst	Newborn, Ira	B	10C
Inst	Friedman, Don E.		47,29,66A	Inst	Newsome, Leigh	B	34A
Inst	Frink, Laurie A.	M	63A	Asst Prof	Nonken, Marilyn C.	D	12,13,66A
Adj Asst Prof	Fulkerson, Gregory L.	D	62A	Adj Asst Prof	Oblak, Jerica	D	10A,10C
Inst	Galdston, Philip E.	B	10D	Adj Asst Prof	O'Donohue, Deirdre	D	66A
Inst	Garfein, Herschel	M	39,54	Inst	Oldham, Barbara	M	49,63B,48
Adj Asst Prof	Garner, Brad A.	D	64A	Inst	Paer, Lewis J.	B	42,62D
Adj Asst Prof	Gates, Elaine	M	36	Inst	Pardo-Tristan, Emiliano	D	70,10A
Asst Prof	Geluso, Paul		34D,35G	Inst	Park, Soo-Kyung	M	64A
Assoc Prof	Gilbert, John	D	10,32,34	Assoc Prof	Park, Tae Hong	D	10,34
Inst	Gilchrest, Suzanne M.		64A,48	Adj Asst Prof	Parodi, Jorge	M	40,61,66C
Asst Prof	Gill, Brian P.	D	61	Inst	Patterson, William M.	M	10D
Inst	Gill, Kimberly		61	Prof	Peacock, Kenneth J.	D	13,10,12,35,34
Inst	Glanz, James M.	B	35C,35G	Inst	Penzarella, Vincent	B	63A
Inst	Glaser, Susan J.	D	64A	Inst	Perry, Rich		64E
Inst	Glass, Susan	M	32	Adj Asst Prof	Pickett, Lenny B.	M	46,47,64E,29
Inst	Glunt, Patricia A.	M	32	Asst Prof	Pietro, David A.		64E,29,47
Inst	Goldin, Amy		32B	Inst	Pilc, Jean-Michel	B	29,66A,47
Inst	Goldstein, Gil B.	M	10D,47,66A,29	Inst	Pirard, Guillaume	M	62A,42
Inst	Gordon, Michael	M	10A	Inst	Porterfield, Richard R.		12,13,31A,55D
Inst	Gordon, Peter L.	M	41,49,63B	Inst	Potter, Christopher	M	46,47,64E,29
Inst	Gormley, Daniel	M	33	Inst	Pras, Amandine	D	34D
Inst	Gortler, Daniel	M	66A	Inst	Prieto, Dafnis		29,47,65
Adj Asst Prof	Green, Edward	D	12A	Inst	Quillen, Josh R.	M	50
Inst	Greenhut, Barry	M	10,34,13L	Clinical Asst Prof	Radbill, Catherine Fitterman	M	35
Inst	Greensmith, Clive S.	B	51,62C	Adj Asst Prof	Rayner, William S.	D	32E,70
Inst	Gress, Andrew D.	M	62D	Inst	Reimer, Christine E.	B	61
Inst	Griffin, J. Chris	B	34A	Inst	Ricciardone, Michael	M	36,54,66A
Inst	Guy, Larry L.	M	62,64C	Inst	Richmond, Mike	B	29,47,64D
Adj Asst Prof	Ha, Youngmi	D	10A,10E,13B,13C,13D	Inst	Ritscher, Karen	M	62B,42
Assoc Prof	Haas, Jonathan L.	M	50,65	Inst	Rodriguez, Michael J.	B	63A
Inst	Hadfield, John R.	B	29,47,65	Asst Prof	Roginska, Agnieska	D	34
Prof	Halim, Eduardus	M	66A	Inst	Rojak, John	B	63C
Inst	Hall, Jonathan B.	D	12A,13,31A,36,66G	Adj Asst Prof	Rojas, Marcus	B	63D
Inst	Harris, Brian T.	M	33	Adj Asst Prof	Rosenhaus, Steven L.	D	10,13F,10F,10A,10D
Adj Asst Prof	Harris, Esther L.	M	32	Inst	Rosenmeyer, David G.	M	36
Inst	Harris, Stefon	B	29,65B	Inst	Ross, Tyley	M	61
Asst Prof	Heldman, Dianna J.		61	Prof	Rowe, Robert	D	10,43,34,35C
Assoc Prof	Hesser, Barbara		33	Inst	Rubin-Bosco, Judi F.		33
Inst	Hindell, Leonard W.		64D	Inst	Ruiz, Kristen	M	61
Inst	Hirsch, Scott	M	34D	Assoc Prof	Sadoff, Ronald H.	D	13K,10A,10C,10D
Inst	Hoenig, Ari M.	B	65,29	Adj Asst Prof	Sadovnik, Nir	M	33
Inst	Holden, Jon	D	66C,66D	Adj Asst Prof	Sanders, Charles J.	M	35A
Inst	Hoppe, Jennifer R.	M	61	Inst	Saporito, James Frederick	B	65

Adj Asst Prof	Scheiby, Benedikte B.	M	33
Adj Asst Prof	Schocker, Gary M.	M	64A
Inst	Schoeppach, Brad W.	M	29,47
Assoc Prof	Schroeder, Dave	D	29,47,65,60B
Inst	Scofield, John L.	B	47,70
Adj Asst Prof	Scott-Moncrieff, Suzannah	M	33
Inst	Seidman, William		10D
Adj Asst Prof	Setzer, Ann	D	62A
Adj Asst Prof	Shankman, Ira	M	32,40,36,60
Adj Asst Prof	Shankman, Nancy Ellen	M	32,36,60
Adj Asst Prof	Shapiro, Noah	M	33
Inst	Sharpe, Alex E.	D	62A
Inst	Shaw, Giocille	M	32
Inst	Shelly, Daniel P.	M	64D
Inst	Shemaria, Rich S.	B	46,47,66A,29
Inst	Sherman, Joseph	M	38,32,62
Inst	Silverman, Alan	B	34D
Other	Simpkins, John	M	54
Inst	Smith, Matthew Shepard	M	61
Inst	Smylie, Dennis H.	M	64C
Inst	Sobol, Elise	M	32A,32B,32C
Inst	Song, MyungOk Julie	M	32,36,60,61
Inst	Soper, Lee H.	B	63A
Assoc Prof	Spear, David R.	B	10,10F,60,10C
Inst	Speiser, Paul	M	61
Inst	St. Onge, Sarah	M	32
Inst	Starnes, Timothy J.	M	34A,34D
Adj Asst Prof	Statser, Sean J.	M	42
Adj Asst Prof	Stein, George	JD	35
Adj	Subotnick, Morton	M	10A,10B
Asst Prof	Sullivan, Matt E.	M	64B
Inst	Suozzo, Mark John	M	10C,10F
Inst	Susman, Robert E.	M	32E
Inst	Swann, Jeffrey	D	66C
Inst	Sze, Eva	M	13B,13C,13F
Inst	Tanaka, Naoko	M	62A
Inst	Thomas, Sally	M	62A
Inst	Thornton, William C.	M	33
Inst	Timmerman, Mark	B	64D
Inst	Tint, Judith H.	M	35A
	Treuhaft, Ben		66F
Inst	Tucker, Allan	B	34D
Inst	Tucker, William S.	M	40,54
Inst	Turner, Mark F.	B	64E
Inst	Turry, Alan	M	33
Inst	Underwood, Keith W.	M	64A
Adj Prof	Underwood, Kent	D	12A,12C
Inst	Ury Greenberg, Linda	M	35A
Inst	Vento, Rosa B.	M	61
Inst	Vinao, Ezequiel P.	M	10A,10B
Inst	Von Oertzen, Alexandra 'Sasha'	M	34
Inst	Wagner, Chad A.	M	34G
Inst	Walker, Saul A.	B	35C
Inst	Wang, Liang	B	64B
Adj Asst Prof	Washington, Shirley A.	JD	35
Adj Asst Prof	Watson, Terry Gutterman	M	33
Asst Prof	Wenaus, Grant	D	39,61,66C,66
Inst	Werner, Kenny	M	47,66A
Asst Prof	Wesbrooks, William	B	54
Adj Asst Prof	White, Robert C.	D	61
	Wiencek, Joe R.	B	66F
Inst	Wind, Martin	M	29,47,62D
Inst	Winthrop, Anna	M	61
Inst	Wojcik, Leszek M.	M	34G
Asst Prof	Wolfe, Julia	D	10A
Inst	Wright, Chantel R.	B	36
Inst	Xiques, David	M	32,60A,61
Adj Asst Prof	Yen, Chianan	D	32F,34A,34B,34H
Adj Asst Prof	Zabin, Amy	D	33
Adj Assoc Prof	Zukerman, Eugenia	B	64A,42

NY2800 Niagara County Community College

Department of Music
3111 Saunders Settlement Rd
Sanborn, NY 14132
(716) 614-5965   Fax: (716) 614-6826
www.niagaracc.suny.edu
E-mail: hall@niagaracc.suny.edu

2 Year Institution

Coordinator: Lois Hall, 80A

Inst PT	Beaudreau, Jason	M	70
Prof	Hall, Lois	M	61,13C,42
Inst PT	Schultz, Marc	B	13A,20,13
Inst PT	Williams, Linda	M	11,42
Inst PT	Wingert, Bradley	B	61,36

NY2900 Nyack College

School of Music
1 South Blvd
Nyack, NY 10960
(845) 675-4687   Fax: (845) 348-8838
www.nyackcollege.edu
E-mail: glenn.koponen@nyack.edu

4 Year Institution
Member of NASM

Dean: Glenn Koponen, 80A

PT	Ahn, Jungeun	M	66A
PT	Allen, Barbara	M	62E
PT	August, David	M	66A
PT	Batchelor, Wayne	M	62D
PT	Bradley, Gwendolyn	B	61
PT	Cardillo, Michael	M	64E
PT	Carey, Mary	M	61
PT	Carillo, Dan	M	29A
PT	Christensen, Tom	M	64E
PT	Clapp, Stephen	M	62A
PT	Covey, Jason	M	60,32E
Inst	Fowler, Colin	M	36,13,12A,66A,66G
Assoc Prof	Frandsen, Lars	D	12A,13,70
PT	Harper, Sharmi	M	61
PT	Hinds, Esther	DIPL	61
PT	Hughes, Chris	M	65
Asst Prof	Jameson, Joel	M	36,61,60A
PT	Jameson, Shelley	M	61,39
Assoc Prof	Kenote, Marie Herseth	DMA	64A,12A,13B,13C,13D
PT	Kim, Chungsun	D	13,62C
Prof	Koponen, Glenn	D	60,37,41,63A,31A
PT	Kraus, Jeffrey	M	65
PT	Lenhart, Andrew Stevens	D	66A
PT	Li, Simon	M	66A,13A,13B,13C
Prof	Lum, Tammy K.	D	13,66A,66D,42
Asst Prof	Mallory, Joan	M	32
PT	Oehme, Jane	M	61
PT	Patterson, Mark	M	63C
PT	Rodriguez, Eleazer	M	70
PT	Scott, Jennifer	B	44
PT	Shen, Deborah	M	64A
PT	Sohn, Sungrai	M	62A,38
PT	Sparks, Glenn	M	70
PT	Speth, Uli	M	62A,38
Assoc Prof	Talley, Dana W.	PhD	61,12A,20,39,11
Assoc Prof	Talley, Sue	PhD	66A,12A,36,31A,31B
PT	Vollinger, William F.	M	10A,20
PT	Werking, Jon	M	66A
PT	Williams, Craig S.	M	66G

NY2950 Onondaga Community College

Department of Music
4585 W Seneca Turnpike
Syracuse, NY 13215
(315) 498-2256   Fax: (315) 498-2792
www.sunyocc.edu
E-mail: abramsd@sunyocc.edu

2 Year Institution

Chair: David Abrams, 80A

Prof	Abrams, David	D	13C,11,41,64C,12A
Adj	Bridge, Julie	M	63B
Prof	Bridge, Robert	D	65,37,50,20A
Adj	Brink-Button, Ilze	B	63B
Adj	Brown, David	M	70
Adj	Carello, Joseph	B	53,64E
Adj	Ciarelli, Katharine	M	66A,66D,11
Adj	Crocker, Susan	M	66A,66D
Adj	DeLuccia, Norma	M	66D
Adj	Dodd, Kit	M	62A
Adj	Emerson, Timothy	M	20A,11
Adj	Frank, Steven	M	47
Adj	Harris, William	M	63C,63D
Adj	Headlee, Will	M	66G
Prof	Loftus, Jean	M	39,61,54,13A,13B
Adj	Ludovico, Vincent		65
Prof	McCullough, Richard D.	M	13A,36,39,61,66D
Adj	Montcrieff, Kathy	B	61
Prof	Moore, Kevin	D	13,66A,66C,66D,10A
Prof	Moore, Selma	M	13,37,41,64A,66D
Adj	Osborne, Michelle M.	M	13A,11
Adj	Pugh, Darryl	M	62D
Adj	Schaffer, Richard	D	63A
Prof	Schmidt, Timothy	D	70,11,13C

NY3000 Orange County Community College
Department of Arts & Communication
115 South St
Middletown, NY 10940
(845) 341-4787   Fax: (845) 341-4775
www.sunyorange.edu
E-mail: mark.strunsky@sunyorange.edu

2 Year Institution

Chair: Jennifer Lehtinen, 80A
Assistant Chair: Linda Fedrizzi-Williams, 80H

Adj	Sicilia, Sheila	M	34,13A
Adj	Vacanti, Jennifer	M	65
Adj	Wogick, Jacqueline	D	62C,41
Adj	Zaplatynsky, Andrew	M	62A
Emeritus	Curtis, Stanley	M	11,13
Adj	Damaris, Christa	B	36,61,66D
Adj	Hey, Darryl	D	13
Adj	Kinney, Kaylyn	M	11,66D
Adj	Miele, David	M	47,14C,65
Adj	Moore, Hilarie Clark	D	38,41,63B
Prof	Parker, Christopher S.	M	47,66A,66D,53,29
Adj	Perna, Dana	M	11,35
Adj	Scott, Kevin	B	37
Assoc Prof	Strunsky, Mark	M	11,12A,70,14C

NY3100 Polytechnic University
Department of Humanities/SS
6 Metrotech Ctr
Brooklyn, NY 11201
(718) 260-3686
www.poly.edu
E-mail: mladerma@poly.edu

4 Year Institution

Music Contact: Michael Laderman, 80A

Chair: Richard E. Wener, 80A

Adj Asst Prof	Laderman, Michael	D	11,29,12A,14,20D

NY3250 Queensborough Community College
Department of Music
222-05 56th Ave
Bayside, NY 11364
(718) 631-6393   Fax: (718) 631-6041
www.qcc.cuny.edu
E-mail: kmontgomery@qcc.cuny.edu

2 Year Institution

Chair: Kip Montgomery, 80A

Lect	Anderson, Robert	M	11,34D,34H,35,13A
Asst Prof	Berkhout, Bjorn	D	10,62C,12A,13,14C
Asst Prof	Chang, Joanne	D	11,13,32,42,66
Asst Prof	Dahlke, Steven	D	11,13,36,60A,61
Assoc Prof	Hest, Jeff	M	11,29,35,37,47
Lect	Jackson, Ernie	B	34,35,70
Assoc Prof	Kashkin, Allan	M	34,40,61
Assoc Prof	Montgomery, Kip	D	11,12,13,64C
Prof	Nagler, Joseph	D	32,33,34
Assoc Prof	Sehman, Melanie	DMA	65,13A,20,11,13

NY3300 Rensselaer Polytechnic Institute
Department of the Arts
IEAR Studios
110 8th St
Troy, NY 12180-3590
(518) 276-4778   Fax: (518) 276-4370
www.arts.rpi.edu
E-mail: electronicarts@rpi.edu

Graduate School

MFA in Electronic Art, PhD in Electronic Art

Acting Head: Caren Canier, 80A
Dir., Graduate Studies: Tomie Hahn, 80C

Assoc Prof	Bahn, Curtis	D	43,13,10,12,45
Prof	Century, Michael	M	12,13,43,34H,66A
Assoc Prof	Hahn, Tomie	D	14,15,20,31G,34
Prof/Prac	Knowles, Eddie Ade	D	20,50
Prof/Prac	Oliveros, Pauline		12,13,10B,11
Prof	Rolnick, Neil B.	D	13,10,45,34

NY3350 Roberts Wesleyan College
Department of Music
2301 Westside Dr
Rochester, NY 14624-1997
(585) 594-6320   Fax: (585) 594-6534
www.roberts.edu/music
E-mail: kuhlman_kristyn@roberts.edu

4 Year Institution, Graduate School
Member of NASM

Master of Music in Music Education

Chair: Kristyn Kuhlman, 80A,80B,80E
Dean: Stanley C. Pelkey, 80A
Dir., Artist/Performance Series: David Dunn, 80F

Adj	Anderson, Marc	M	62B
Assoc Prof	Barta, Daniel	D	10,13,10A,10F
Adj Prof	Behr, Erik	D	64B
Prof	Berry, Paul	D	31A
Adj	Chin, David	M	36,60A
Prof	Cummings, Grace	D	32B,36,61,32C,32D
Adj Prof	Curlee, Alisa	D	66A
Adj	Espinoza, Dannel	M	64E,48
Assoc Prof	Fee, Constance	D	61,39
Adj Prof	Hamway, Jane	M	32E
Adj	Jones, Christopher	M	12A,11
Prof	Kuhlman, Kristyn	D	32B,32E,32G
Prof	Landrum, Michael	D	66A
Adj Prof	Maynard-Christensen, Dianne	D	66G
Adj	McCormick, Gaelen M.	M	62D
Assoc Prof	McGhee, Jeffrey	D	61,39
Adj Prof	Meyer, Alice	M	64C
Asst Prof	Nagle, Janice	M	66B,66A
Adj Prof	Ouyang, Angel	M	62A
Adj Prof	Palser, Caroline	B	62E
Adj Prof	Porter, Elizabeth	M	63B
Adj Prof	Pritchard, Jillian	M	65,50
Adj Prof	Richey, David	M	63C
Adj Prof	Runion, Julie	M	66A,66C
Adj	Scarbrough, Russell	D	46,29B
Prof	Shewan, Paul	D	60B,37,63A,32E,38
Adj Prof	Sholl, Martha	M	64B
Adj Prof	Smith, Diane	M	64A,48
Adj	Sutherland, Craig	M	63D
Asst Prof	VanAllen, Michael	M	29,66A,47
Adj	Ying, Keiko	D	62C

NY3400 Rockland Community College
Department of Music
145 College Rd
Suffern, NY 10901-3611
(845) 574-4000
www.sunyrockland.edu
E-mail: ptitland@sunyrockland.edu

Introduction Courses Only

Chair: Patricia Maloney-Titland, 80A

	Maloney-Titland, Patricia		

NY3450 Russell Sage College
Department of Music
45 Ferry St
Troy, NY 12180
(518) 244-2248
www.sage.edu
E-mail: musiam@sage.edu

4 Year Institution

Chair: Michael A. Musial, 80A

	Avitabile, Judy		61
Asst Prof	Musial, Michael A.	M	13A,11,12A,36,66A
	Woodbury, Elizabeth		66A

NY3475 St Bonaventure University
Department of Visual & Perf Arts
PO Box AU
Saint Bonaventure, NY 14778-2400
(716) 375-2320   Fax: (716) 375-7667
www.sbu.edu/music
E-mail: lsabina@sbu.edu

4 Year Institution

Chair: Leslie M. Sabina, 80A

Inst PT	Bellamy, Terry		41,70
Artist in Res	Black, Kathryn A.	M	61,36,40
Inst PT	Fox, Jason	B	37,49,63
Inst PT	Howden, Moses Mark	M	50,65
Lect	Peterson, Laura	M	11,12A,66A,20
Prof	Sabina, Leslie M.	D	29,10,34,13,47
Prof	Simone, Ed	D	54
Inst PT	Wada, Rintaro	M	51,62

NY3500 St Johns University
Department of Fine Arts-Music
8000 Utopia Pkwy
Jamaica, NY 11439
(718) 990-6250   Fax: (718) 990-2075
new.stjohns.edu/
E-mail: fabozzip@stjohns.edu

4 Year Catholic Institution

Chair: Paul F. Fabozzi, 80A
Dean: Jeffrey Fagan, 80A
Acting Dean: Mary Mulvihill, 80A
Dir., Summer Programs & Artist Series: Chieh-Mei Jamie Wu, 80F,80G

Asst Prof Adj	Cappillo, Frances	M	29A,11
Asst Prof Adj	Gelfand, Alexander Lyon	D	29A
Assoc Prof	LoBalbo, Anthony C.	D	13,29A,10C,12A,54
Assoc Prof Adj	Moser, Martin	M	13,12A,54,20G
Asst Prof Adj	Sergi, James	M	12A
Assoc Prof Adj	Tedesco, Anne C.	M	13,66A,54,29A,10
Asst Prof Adj	Wu, Chieh-Mei Jamie	D	11,13B,61,32D,36

NY3550 St Lawrence University
Department of Music
23 Romoda Dr
Canton, NY 13617
(315) 229-5166   Fax: (315) 229-7425
music.stlawu.edu
E-mail: dhen@stlawu.edu

4 Year Institution

Chair: David R. Henderson, 80A

Adj Inst	Boyette, Larry J.	M	70,12
Inst	DuBray, Terry E.	B	35
Assoc Prof	Farley, Michael	D	13,14,10,20
Assoc Prof	Henderson, David R.	D	14,20,12
Lect PT	Hosmer, Christian	B	62,51
Inst	Phillips-Farley, Barbara	D	66,13,12
Lect PT	Savage, Timothy L.	M	53
Inst	Torres, Barry A.	M	55,36,61
Asst Prof	Watts, Christopher M.	DMA	10B,34,34D,34H,10
Assoc Prof	Yoo, In-Sil	D	10,13,34A

NY3560 Sarah Lawrence College
Department of Music
1 Mead Way
Bronxville, NY 10708-5999
(914) 337-0700   Fax: (914) 395-2668
www.slc.edu

E-mail: jrudd@sarahlawrence.edu

4 Year Institution

Director: Chester Biscardi, 80A
Dir., Artist Series: John A. Yannelli, 80F

	Alexander, Glenn	M	41,47,70,29
	Anderson, William	M	41,70
	Biscardi, Chester	D	13,10F,10,11,12A
	Chung, Suna	M	13A,13,39,61,13C
	Davidoff, Judith	D	41,55B,67
	Goldray, Martin	D	13A,13,11,12A,66A
	Harris, Hilda	M	39,61
	King, Jonathan	D	13,10F,60,36,10
	Mort, Bari	M	66A
	Muchmore, Pat	D	13A,13
	Romano, Patrick	M	60,36,61
	Sanders, Wayne	M	39,61
	Schmidt, Carsten	D	13,11,12A,41,66A
	Sohn, Sung-Rai	M	60,38,41,51,62A
	Walzer, Barbara	M	16
	Wentworth, Jean	M	12A,41,66A
	Wohl, Daniel	M	10,10A,13,13F
	Yannelli, John A.	M	13,41,45,54,34
	Yates, Jonathan	M	38
	Young, Eddye Pierce	M	39,61
	Young, Thomas	M	39,61

NY3600 Schenectady County Comm College
School of Music
78 Washington Ave
Schenectady, NY 12305-2215
(518) 381-1232   Fax: (518) 381-1486
www.sunysccc.edu/academic/music
E-mail: mecklewa@sunysccc.edu

2 Year Institution
Member of NASM

Dean: William A. Meckley, 80A

Adj	Ahola, Mark	M	33
Adj	Aldi, Barbara	M	66D
Adj	Beer, Lucille	M	61
Adj	Bellino, Peter A.	D	63A
Adj	Brucker, Clifford	M	11,66D,29
Adj	Carucci, Brian	M	64C
Adj	Evans, Mark	M	66A,66B,66D
Adj	Gerbino, Thomas J.	M	64C,64E
Adj	Heilman, Annette	M	32
Adj	Hibberd, Gordon	B	66C
Assoc Prof	Hosmer, Karen E.	D	64B,13
Adj	Isachsen, Sten Y.	M	67D,41,70,34,29
Adj	Ivanov, Krassimir	M	64D
Adj	Janack, Andrew	M	65
Adj	Kassarova, Petia	M	62C
Asst Prof	Keyser, Allyson	D	63A,13,12A
Adj	Maekane, Nachiko	M	65
Prof	Meckley, William A.	D	47
Adj	Meidenbauer, Michael	M	63C,63D
Adj	Patneaude, Brian	B	64E,29,46
Adj	Phipps, Nathaniel J.	M	29
Adj	Pickreign, Christina	M	61
Adj	Pray, Keith	M	29
Adj	Sano, Anthony M.	M	70
Adj	Savoy, Deborah Ann	M	61
Adj	Savoy, Thomas	M	66C,66G
Adj	Schwartz, Ann Marie Barker	M	62A,62B
Adj	Strichman, Sherri	M	61
Adj	Thibodeau, Norman	M	64A
Prof	Wery, Brett L.	M	13,37,41,64C,64E
Adj	Wicks, Michael J.	M	62D
Adj	Wilding, Arla	B	66A,61
Adj	Wilson, James	B	70
Assoc Prof	Wu, Yiping	D	61,36

NY3650 Skidmore College
Department of Music
Arthur Zankel Music Center
815 N Broadway
Saratoga Springs, NY 12866
(518) 580-5320   Fax: (518) 580-5340
www.skidmore.edu/academics/music
E-mail: jbrown@skidmore.edu

4 Year Institution

Chair: Joel Brown, 80A

Senior Artist in Res	Baytelman, Pola	D	41,66A,66D,66E
Senior Artist in Res	Brown, Joel	M	70,42
Asst Prof	Bryant, Lei Ouyang	D	14,20C
Lect	Chandra, Veena V.	M	20E
Lect	Davidsen, Nancy Jo	B	61
Lect	Ellis, Randall	B	64B
Artist in Res	Emery, Michael	M	62A,62B,51

Lect	Foster, Mark H.	B	65
Vstng Lect	Gardiner, Katie	D	36,60A
Assoc Prof	Givan, Ben	D	13,14C
Lect	Grigsby, Brett	M	70
Lect	Hakim, Will J.	M	62B
Assoc Prof	Holland, Anthony G.	D	10A,60B,34,38,10B
Lect	Huntley, Elizabeth M.	M	62E
Lect	Kern, Gene Marie Callahan	B	61,36,13A,39
Lect	Kirk, John D.		62A,67H,20G
Lect	Latini, Eric J.	B	63A
Lect	Mack, Evan	D	66A
Lect	Malatestinic, Patrice A.	M	63B,49
Lect	Martula, Susan B.	M	64C
Lect	McGhee, Janet F.	M	36,13A,40,60A
	McLoughlin, Michelle F.	M	64D
	Meidenbauer, Michael	M	63C
Lect	Miller, Patricia M.	B	20G
Lect	Muscatello, George		29A,70
Senior Artist in Res	Nazarenko, John J.	M	47,66A,29
Lect	Parke, Nathaniel		62C
Lect	Rodriguez, Joshua A.	B	62A
Assoc Prof	Rohr, Deborah	D	13,11,12A
Lect	Silvagnoli, Michael F.	B	63D
Lect	Syracuse, Rich	B	62D
Prof	Thompson, Gordon R.	D	20D,20E,20F,14C,14B
Senior Artist in Res	Turner, Anne Z.	M	36,39,61
Senior Artist in Res	Vinci, Jan F.	D	41,64A
Lect	Vinci, Mark A.		47,64E,29

NY3680 Siena College

Department of Creative Arts
SH 321
515 Loudon Rd
Loudonville, NY 12211-1462
(518) 783-2325   Fax: (518) 782-6548
www.siena.edu
E-mail: rblasting@siena.edu

Catholic Liberal Arts College

Dean, Liberal Arts: Ralph Blasting, 80A

Lect	Burns, Ellen	PhD	12A,32E
Adj Inst	Grimm, Mark	M	35H
Asst Prof	Konye, Paul	PhD	13G,12A,38,10,12
Adj Inst	Schwartz, Anne-Marie	B	12A,62A
Adj Inst	Towse, Joanna		11,61

NY3700 State Univ of New York-Albany

Department of Music
PAC 310
1400 Washington Ave
Albany, NY 12222-0100
(518) 442-4187   Fax: (518) 442-4182
www.albany.edu/music
E-mail: musinfo@albany.edu

4 Year Institution

Chair: Reed J. Hoyt, 80A
Dean: Edelgard Wulfert, 80A

Lect PT	Albagli, Richard	M	65,50
Lect PT	Burns, Ellen J.	D	16,11
Lect PT	Champagne, Kevin	M	37
Assoc Prof Emeritus	Cockrell, Findlay	M	13A,13,11,66A
Lect PT	Conway, Nicholas	B	11
Assoc Prof	Cumming, Duncan J.	D	66A,13,11
Lect PT	Cumming, Hilary W.	M	62
Other	Ferlo, Patrick A.	M	35E
Assoc Prof	Gluck, Robert J.	M	10B,34D,31B,34,45
Assoc Prof Emeritus	Hartzell, K. Drew	D	11,12A,12
Lect PT	Hosley, David B.	M	47
Assoc Prof	Hoyt, Reed J.	D	13A,13,12A
Prof	Janower, David M.	D	13,60,12A,36
Prof	Lifchitz, Max	M	10,43,13A,13,10F
Prof Emeritus	Morris, James R.	D	13A,63A,13,11,49
Lect PT	Neubert, Christopher D.	M	38
Assoc Prof	Newman, Nancy	D	20F,20G,12
Asst Prof	von Arx, Victoria	M	66A,13,11
Lect PT	Wittman, Frances P.	M	61,20G
Prof	Zak, Albin J.	D	10

NY3705 State Univ of New York-Binghamton

Department of Music
PO Box 6000
Binghamton, NY 13902-6000
(607) 777-2592   Fax: (607) 777-4425
music.binghamton.edu
E-mail: tperry@binghamton.edu

4 Year Institution, Graduate School
Member of NASM

Master of Music in Composition, Master of Music in Performance, Master of Music in Conducting, Master of Music in History & Literature, Master of Music in Opera

Chair: Timothy B. Perry, 80A
Dir., Undergraduate Studies: Paul Schleuse, 80B
Dir., Graduate Studies: Bruce E. Borton, 80C

Lect PT	Aldridge, Benjamin L.	M	63A
Assoc Prof	Biggers, Jonathan E.	D	12A,66G,66H
Prof Emerita	Borroff, Edith	D	12A,12,12B
Assoc Prof	Borton, Bruce E.	D	60,36,61
Lect PT	Browne, Peter J.	M	36,13C
Assoc Prof	Burgess, Mary	B	39,61
Asst Prof	Burns, James	D	14,20
Assoc Prof Emeritus	Buttolph, David	M	60,36
Lect PT	Carbone, Michael	M	47,29A
Lect PT	Chandler, Sarah	M	64C
Prof Emeritus	Chianis, Sam	D	12A,12,14,20H
Lect PT	Choi, Janey	D	62A
Prof Emeritus	Clatworthy, David	M	61,39
Lect PT	Crawford, Roberta	M	41,62B,62A
	Di Costanzo, John		39
Lect PT	Fabricius, Daniel	M	50,65
Assoc Prof	Goldstaub, Paul R.	D	13A,13,10
Vstng Asst Prof	Goodheart, Thomas	M	61,39
Prof Emeritus	Hamme, Albert	M	47,64E,53,29A
Assoc Prof Emeritus	Hanson, John R.	D	13A,13
Prof Emeritus	Hibbitt, Peyton		39,61
Prof Emeritus	Jordan, Paul		66G,67B
Lect PT	Lalli, Marcus	M	11
Lect PT	Lathwell, John	M	64B
Lect PT	Lawson, William	M	61,66C
Lect PT	Lee, Jinah	D	66A
Prof Emeritus	Lincoln, Harry B.	D	11,12A,12,34
Lect PT	Lucas, April	M	64E
Lect PT	Mackiewicz-Wolfe, Ewa	M	66A
Lect PT	Maiolo, Georgetta	B	64A
Lect PT	Mallinson, Chai Kyou	M	66A,66C
Assoc Prof	Mitchell, Alice L.	M	11,12,13A
Prof	Perry, Timothy B.	D	60,37,38,64C
Lect PT	Reitz, Margaret A.	M	66C,66A
Assoc Prof PT	Richardson, Diane	M	39,61,66C
Lect PT	Robertson, Donald C.	M	49,63C,63D
Assoc Prof Emeritus	Rothgeb, John	D	13A,13
Lect PT	Salmirs, Michael		66A
Asst Prof	Schleuse, Paul	D	12
Prof Emerita	Schlosser, Roberta	D	39,61
Asst Prof Adj	Sicilian, Peter J.	D	39,61
Lect PT	Stalker, Stephen T.	M	62C,62D
Lect PT	Sternberg, Brian	M	63B
Lect PT	Weber, Martha	M	64D
Lect PT	Zank, Stephen	D	12

NY3717 State Univ of New York

College at Buffalo
Department of Music
1300 Elmwood Ave
Buffalo, NY 14222-1095
(716) 878-6401   Fax: (716) 878-6402
www.buffalostate.edu/music
E-mail: music@buffalostate.edu

4 Year Institution

Chair: Bradley J. Fuster, 80A

Lect PT	Aubin, Isabelle	M	66C
Lect PT	Barnum, Ellen M.	B	64D
Lect	Bewlay, Ho Eui Holly	D	61
Assoc Prof	Boyce, Emily W.	D	66D,66C,66A,66B
Lect PT	Branagan, Marcella E.	D	66A
Lect PT	Christie, Pamela	M	32E,62
Lect PT	Docenko, Gregory	M	62
Lect PT	Drummond, Evan E.	D	12A,13A,70
Lect PT	Ferington, Paul	M	38
Lect PT	Fleischman, John F.	M	32A,32B
Assoc Prof	Fleming, Ricky L.	D	60B,37,47,49,63C

Lect PT	Fradette, Amelie	M	62C,51
Asst Prof	Furby, Victoria J.	D	13C,15,32D
Assoc Prof	Fuster, Bradley J.		65,50
Lect PT	Galluzzo, Jacqueline	B	62A,51
Lect PT	Glidden, Amy	M	62A,51
Lect PT	Gormley, Lonna L.	B	63D
Asst Prof	Guzski, Carolyn	D	12A,14
Asst Prof	Henriques, J. Tomas	D	34,13
Lect PT	Hodges, Mark	M	65
Lect PT	Holzemer, Kate C.	B	62B,51
Lect PT	Hull, Robert A.	M	66A,66C
Lect PT	Jolley, Carolyn L.	M	61
Lect PT	King, Cheryl H.	B	61
Lect PT	Kostusiak, Thomas J.	B	35C,35D,35G
Lect PT	Maguda, John K.	M	63A
Lect PT	Maimine, Anna	M	66A,66B,66C
Prof	Mancuso, Charles	M	20G,29A,12E,14C
Lect PT	Mattix, Anna L.	M	64B
Lect PT	McAneny, Marc A.	M	13,10F
Lect PT	Nicely, Tiffany M.	M	20
Prof	Reinoso, Crystal Hearne	D	13B,48,64C,15
Lect PT	Schiavone, David C.	M	64E,48
Lect PT	Schuman, Susan	B	66A,66C
Lect PT	Spann, Joseph S.	D	61
Lect PT	Sweeley, Daniel	M	63B
Assoc Prof	Witakowski, Thomas E.	D	36,40,61,60A
Lect PT	Witnauer, Marlene P.	M	64A
Lect PT	Zapalowski, Paul	B	62D

NY3720 State Univ of New York-Cortland

Department of Performing Arts
PO Box 2000
Cortland, NY 13045-0900
(607) 753-2811   Fax: (607) 753-5728
www.cortland.edu
E-mail: david.neal@cortland.edu

4 Year Institution

Interim Dean: Bruce Mattingly, 80A
Chair: David E. Neal, 80A

Prof	Dudgeon, Ralph T.	D	12,67,14,38,63
Assoc Prof	Moore, Edward	M	20G,36,66A,11,29A
Prof	Neal, David E.	DMA	61,54,39,36
Prof	Wilson, Stephen B.	D	13,60,36,41,61
Assoc Prof	Zimmerman, Karen Bals	D	13,11,66A,66B,66C

NY3725 State Univ of New York-Fredonia

School of Music
Mason Hall
280 Central Ave
Fredonia, NY 14063
(716) 673-3151   Fax: (716) 673-3154
www.fredonia.edu/music
E-mail: music@fredonia.edu

4 Year Institution, Graduate School
Member of NASM

Master of Music in Performance, Master of Music in Music Education, Master of Music in Music Theory-Composition

irector: Karl Boelter, 80A
Assistant Director & Dir., Admissions: Barry M. Kilpatrick, 80D,80H
Associate Director: Patricia J. Corron, 80H

Adj	Bacon, John	B	65
Assoc Prof	Bernhard, H. Christian	D	32E,32
Vstng Prof	Beroukhim, Cyrus	D	62A
PT	Bingham, Tom		14C
Prof	Boelter, Karl	D	10
Adj	Bogey, Brian	M	66G
Prof Emeritus	Bohlen, Donald A.	D	10A,10F,13D,10
Adj	Brady, Judith L.	M	12
Adj	Brasch, Peter		32
Assoc Prof	Brinson, Barbara Ann	D	32,36
Prof Emeritus	Carpenter, Thomas H.	D	11,12A
Inst	Caruso, John A.		35C
Lect	Cobb, Mary Marden	M	66D,66A
Assoc Prof	Corron, Patricia J.	D	61
Prof	Davis, James A.	D	12A
Asst Prof	Deemer, Robert	D	10A,10C,43,10,60B
Adj	Dornberger, Laura	M	32
Adj	Doyle, Sean	M	13A,13B,13C
Adj	Drummond, Evan	M	70
Adj	Dubois, Mark		13,64B
Asst Prof	Duggan, Sean		66A
Prof Emeritus	East, James	M	64C
Prof Emeritus	East, Phyllis	M	66A
Assoc Prof Emeritus	Emilson, C. Rudolph	M	60,41,63D
Prof Emeritus	Evans, David F.	D	36,61
Assoc Prof Emeritus	Falcao, Mario	M	62E
Asst Prof	Farny, Natasha	D	62C
Adj	Fridmann, Dave		35C
Adj	Gestwicki, Tom		70
Adj	Giambrone, Marcia		32
Assoc Prof Emeritus	Gillette, John C.	D	13,64D,72
Assoc Prof	Gottinger, Bernd	M	35C
Assoc Prof	Gray, Gerald Thomas	M	61,36
Assoc Prof	Guy, Marc J.	D	13,63B
Asst Prof	Haas, Angela Dilkey	M	61
Assoc Prof	Hamilton, Sarah Jean	D	13,64B
Asst Prof	Harper, Joe Dan	M	61
Prof Emeritus	Hartley, Walter S.	D	10
Prof Emeritus	Hofmann, John T.	D	66G
Prof	Holcomb, Paula K.	D	37,60
Other	Howes, Graham	B	66F
Prof	Ihasz, Daniel	M	61
Assoc Prof	Jacobson, Harry P.	D	13,62D,35A
Lect	Johnstone, Bruce		29,47
Adj	Jokipii, Alex	D	63A
Prof Emeritus	Jordan, Robert	M	66A
Prof Emeritus	Joseph, Charles	M	60,62A,62B
Adj	Kayne, David	M	65
Adj	Kent, Peter		62
Prof	Kilpatrick, Barry M.	M	63C
Asst Prof	Koepke, Laura	M	64D
Prof	Lang, Donald P.	D	60,36
Prof Emeritus	Larson, Richard	D	60,32
Assoc Prof	Levy, Katherine M.	M	32
Adj	Lindblom, Peter	M	63A
Assoc Prof	MacDonald, J. Roderick	M	63A
Adj	Maguda, John	M	60B
Adj	Mancino, Kim		33
Asst Prof	Mann, Jonathan Edward	D	66A
Adj	Markham, I-Fei Chen	M	66C
Asst Prof	Markham, Michael	D	12
Prof	Mayo, Walter S.	D	60,32
Adj	Mazzio, Carl		63C,37
Lect	McMurtry, Lynne	M	61
Inst	Michki, Kevin	M	16
Assoc Prof	Milgram-Luterman, Joni F.	D	33
Assoc Prof	Murphy, Paul T.	D	13
Assoc Prof	Newell, Julie L.	M	39,61
Adj	Nicely, Tiffany	M	13,65
Prof Emeritus	Peterson, Keith L.	D	13,10,45
Prof	Phillips, Linda N.	D	12A,66D,29A
Prof	Piorkowski, James P.	M	70
Prof Emeritus	Regelski, Thomas A.	D	60,32
Assoc Prof Emeritus	Richardson, Lucille K.	M	66A
Adj	Ried, Michael	M	64E
Other	Rivers, Laurel R.	B	66F
Asst Prof	Root, Gordon	D	13
Adj	Rorick, Michael	M	35
Asst Prof	Rose, David	M	62B
Prof	Royal, Susan L.	D	64A
Assoc Prof	Rudge, David T.	D	38,62A
Prof Emeritus	Schoenbach, Peter Julian	D	12A
Adj	Seel, Nancy		32
Asst Prof	Seigel, Andrew	D	64C
Prof Emeritus	Sheil, Richard F.	D	61
Inst	Snow, Greg		34
Assoc Prof	Stewart, Raymond G.	M	63D
Assoc Prof	Stonefelt, Kay H.	D	50,65
Lect	Takagi, Shinobu		66C,66D
Adj	Tramuta, Laurie		61
Assoc Prof Emeritus	Willeford, Constance E.	M	33
Adj	Wilson, Matt	B	34A,34B
Adj	Witnauer, Marlene		64A
Prof Emeritus	Wyman, Laurence	D	64E
Adj	Yuen, Maureen	M	62A
Assoc Prof	Zumwalt, Wildy	M	64E,41

NY3730 State Univ of New York-Geneseo

School of the Arts-Music
One College Circle
Geneseo, NY 14454
(585) 245-5824   Fax: (585) 245-5826
sota.geneseo.edu
E-mail: gonder@geneseo.edu

4 Year Institution

Chair: Jonathan P. Gonder, 80A

Lect	Balkin, Laura M.	M	41,62A
Lect	Balkin, Richard A.	M	13A,41,62A
PT	Boianova, Linda	D	66C
Inst	Case, Alan L.		66C
PT	Dove-Pellito, Glennda M.	M	48,64A
Prof	Floriano, Gerard F.	D	60,36

PT	Floriano, Joan H.	M	61
PT	Gibson, David		63C,63D,47
Prof	Gonder, Jonathan P.	D	66A,66C,11,13A,13B
PT	Greenfield, Thomas A.	D	70
PT	Hunt, Mary H.	M	63B
Prof Emeritus	Isgro, Robert M.	D	
Assoc Prof PT	Johnston, Jack R.	M	13,66A,54,34
Lect	Kimball, James W.	M	13A,11,14,67E,70
Lect	Kirkwood, James H.	M	51,62C
PT	Kruger, Jonathan H.	D	47,63A,53
PT	Kurau, Pamela B.	D	61
Prof	Lancos, Jonette	MFA	52
PT	Lascell, Ernest D.	M	48,64C,64E
Emeritus	Leyerle, William	M	61
Vstng Asst Prof	Masci, Michael J.	D	11,13A,13B,13C,13D
PT	McCausland, Jacqueline J.		52
Assoc Prof Emeritus	Ray, Scott	MFA	52
Assoc Prof	Reynolds, Anne-Marie	D	11,12A,12
PT	Rodriguez, Samantha	M	62B,42
PT	Sholl, Martha P.	M	48,64A
Assoc Prof	Stanley, Amy A.	D	66A,66B
PT	Steltenpohl, Anna C.	M	64B,48
PT	Tiller, Jim A.	M	50,65
Prof	Walker, James A.	M	60,37,38,41
Prof Emeritus	Willey, James H.	D	13,10,11,66A

NY3760 State Univ of New York-New Paltz
Department of Music
1 Hawk Drive
New Paltz, NY 12561-2400
(845) 257-2700   Fax: (845) 257-3121
www.newpaltz.edu
E-mail: cowanc@newpaltz.edu

4 Year Institution, Graduate School
Member of NASM

Master of Science in Music Therapy

Chair: Carole Cowan, 80A
Dean, Fine & Performing Arts: Mary Hafeli, 80A
Dir., Institute/Festival/Workshop: Haewon Chung-Feltsman, 80F

Prof Emeritus	Boyle, Mary E.	D	70,33,66D
Adj	Buccelli, Sylvia	M	66D
Prof	Cowan, Carole	D	38,66D,62A,62B
Asst Prof	Dziuba, Mark	M	70,29A,47,35C
Asst Prof	Evans, Joel	D	37,64B,12A,13B,20
Prof	Feltsman, Vladimir	D	66A,66B,12A
Asst Prof	Gimeno, Montserrat	D	33
Vstng Lect	Hedges, John B.	M	13B,13D,13E,10
Assoc Prof	Lundergan, Edward	D	13A,13B,36,60,12A
Lect	Martucci, Vincent	M	29A,29B,66A,66D,47
Adj	Maryanova, Sofya	M	66D
Prof Emeritus	McCann, William J.	D	13A,13B,11
Adj	Menegon, John	M	12A,47,62D
Adj	Palmieri, Gary	M	66D
Assoc Prof	Ping, Jin	M	13,10,62A,20A,20B
Prof Emeritus	Pritchard, Lee H.	M	66D
Adj	Roiger, Teresa	B	12A,47,61
Adj	Schempf, Ruthanne	D	66A,66D,12A,13B
Lect	Seligman, Susan	M	13A,13C,11,41,62C
Adj	Siegel, Jeff S.	M	65,12A
Asst Prof	Smith, Kent	M	61

NY3765 State Univ of New York-Oneonta
Department of Music
115 Fine Art Bldg
108 Ravine Parkway
Oneonta, NY 13820
(607) 436-3415   Fax: (607) 436-2718
www.oneonta.edu
E-mail: legnamo@oneonta.edu

4 Year Institution

Chair: Orlando Legname, 80A

Lect	Aldridge, Ben	M	63A,60B,12A
Lect	Balins, Andris	B	35C,35D,35G,47,70
Prof	Barstow, Robert S.	D	12A,36,16,35
Asst Prof	Carter, Paul S.	D	13A,13B,66A
Lect	Falbush, Arthur	D	11,63,29A,46,41
Assoc Prof	Legname, Orlando	D	13A,13,10,35
Asst Prof	Licata, Julie M.	D	65,33,50,20,10B
Lect PT	Markuson, Steve H.	D	11,12A,61
Prof	Nepkie, Janet	D	13A,41,51,62C,35
Asst Prof	Newton, Timothy D.	D	60A,60B,66A,66C
Asst Prof	Pignato, Joseph M.	M	35,34,10,13
Assoc Prof	Prins, Rene	M	64B,37,13,41

Asst Prof	Roman, Robert	M	29,66A,20D,35A,46
Asst Prof	Scafide, Anthony	B	35,41,47
Lect	Thomas, Colby L.	M	39,60A,35F,61,54
Lect PT	Turechek, Dennis		70,29
Assoc Prof	Wall, Jeremy	M	34,35,36,47,66A

NY3770 State Univ of New York-Oswego
Department of Music
109 Tyler Hall
7060 State Route 104
Oswego, NY 13126
(315) 312-2130   Fax: (315) 312-5642
www.oswego.edu/music
E-mail: pamela.lavallee@oswego.edu

4 Year Institution
Member of NASM

Chair: Todd A. Graber, 80A
Dean, Communications, Media & the Arts: Fritz J. Messere, 80A

Inst PT	Allen, Robert J.	M	11
Assoc Prof	Auler, Robert M.	D	66A,66D,13A,40,35A
Inst PT	Balestra, Richard J.	M	41,70
Prof	Barach, Daniel P.	M	12A,62B,11
Inst PT	Caviness, Terrance E.	M	63
Inst PT	Dailey, Colleen M.	M	11
Inst PT	Darvill, Jackie	M	62A,62C
Assoc Prof	Graber, Todd A.	D	61,54,36,12A
Inst PT	Hollenbeck, Lisa	M	11
Inst PT	Horning, Rebecca	B	66A
Inst PT	Jorgensen, Kristen	M	11,48,64A,62A
Asst Prof	Jorgensen, Trevor	M	37,64,48,11
Inst PT	Kisselstein, Lisa A.	B	61
Assoc Prof	La Manna, Juan F.	D	38,66A,66D,11,39
Inst PT	McGrath, Thomas	M	65
Prof	Pretzat, Julie	D	13,60,36
Vstng Asst Prof	Price, Clayborn	D	13A,36
Other	Reece, A.	D	16,34
Inst PT	Richardson, W. Mack	D	11,35A
Assoc Prof	Schmitz, Eric B.	D	47,65,13B,13C,10A
Other	Senko, Robert	B	66F
Assoc Prof	Shallit, Jonathan O.	M	11,13A,62A
Prof	Smiley, Marilynn J.	D	12A,67C
Other	Wood, Dan	B	34,35C,35D,35G

NY3775 State Univ of New York-Plattsburgh
State University College
101 Broad St
Plattsburgh, NY 12901-2637
(518) 564-2180   Fax: (518) 564-2197
www.plattsburgh.edu
E-mail: daniel.gordon@plattsburgh.edu

4 Year Institution

Chair: Daniel J. Gordon, 80A

Lect	Balk, Malcolm	B	62C
Assoc Prof	Becker, Karen E.	D	66A,66C,13C,13A,36
Lect	Bjerke, Sophie	M	61
Lect	Cameron, Robin	M	41,64A
Lect	Chancler, Rose	D	66D
Prof	Davies, Richard	D	10,29,34,46,63D
Lect	Dionne, Louise M.	M	66D
Lect	Ellsworth, Ann	M	63B
Lect	Fratino, Michael A.	M	70,41
Assoc Prof	Gordon, Daniel J.	M	64E,11,37,48
Lect	Gorevic, Elizabeth	M	51,62A,62B
Lect	Jarrett, Gabriel	B	65,50
Lect	Kyle, Janice	B	64B
Lect	Matlock, Herman	M	63A,29A,49
Assoc Prof	Miano, Jo Ellen	M	13A,36,61,32I,40
Lect	Morningstar, Timothy P.	M	61,11
Assoc Prof	Pfaff, William P.	D	10,13,12A,13F,13I
Lect	Powell, Ellen		62D
Lect	Redmond, Daryle	M	65,50
Lect	Scherline, Janine	M	64C,48

NY3780 State Univ of New York-Potsdam

The Crane School of Music
44 Pierrepont Ave
Potsdam, NY 13676-2294
(315) 267-2775   Fax: (315) 267-2413
www.potsdam.edu/crane
E-mail: sittonmr@potsdam.edu

4 Year Institution, Graduate School

Master of Music in Composition, Master of Music in Performance, Master of Music in Music Education

Dean: Michael R. Sitton, 80A
Dir., Artist Series: Amy L. Flack, 80F
Dir., Summer Programs: Julianne Kirk-Doyle, 80G
Associate Dean & Dir., Admissions: David Heuser, 80H,80D,80C

Rank	Name	Deg	Areas
Prof	Andrews, Kenneth B.	M	41,64A,43
Assoc Prof	Baxter, Marsha L.	D	32,20H
Vstng Inst	Brabant, John-Paul	M	10,10B,10C,13
Inst	Britt, Carol H.	M	35
Adj Inst	Burchill, Kent S.	M	32
Prof	Busch, Gary D.	D	12A,66A,20G
Asst Prof	Campbell, Debra L.	D	32D,32B
Prof	Campbell, Mark Robin	D	32B
Prof	Case, Nelly Maude	D	12
Adj Inst	Cohen, Howard R.	M	32
Asst Prof	Collins, Caron L.	D	32E
Inst	Conley, Nancy S.	M	32E
Assoc Prof	Doyle, Brian K.	D	37,60B
Assoc Prof	Drifmeyer, Kelly B.	M	63B,41
Prof	Ellis, John R.	D	63A,41
Assoc Prof	Eyerly, Heather E.	D	32D
Other	Flack, Amy L.	M	35E
Asst Prof	Francom, Jeffery D.	D	36,32D
Other	Galo, Gary A.	M	13L,35G
Adj Inst	Geggie, John D.	M	62D
Assoc Prof	George, Donald	M	61
Prof	Gerber, Rebecca L.	D	12
Asst Prof	Germain, Francois	D	66A,66C
Adj Inst	Goodness, Donald R.	M	32
Prof	Graham, Carleen R.	D	39
Other	Grigel, Glen M.	M	72
Prof	Guy, Charles V.	D	63D,41
Adj Inst	Harea, Ioan	M	62A
Prof	Hartman, Mark S.	D	63C,41
Assoc Prof	Heinick, Carol	M	66D
Prof	Heinick, David G.	D	13,10A
Assoc Prof	Hendrickson, Anna	D	64B,11
Assoc Prof	Hersh, Sarah S.	D	62A,32E
Prof	Heuser, David	D	10A,10B,13,10F,10
Prof	Hosley, Robyn L.	D	32
Adj Inst	Hubbard, Kathy A.	M	32
Lect	Kessler, Jennifer	M	32B,32E
Assoc Prof	Kirk-Doyle, Julianne	D	64C,42,41
Librarian	Komara, Edward M.	M	16
Asst Prof	Lai, Ching-Chun	D	38,60B
Assoc Prof	Lanz, Christopher C.	D	55,60B
Adj Inst	LaVine, Scott	M	65
Prof	Lindsey, John R.	M	62A
Prof	Loushin, Boris M.	D	61
Assoc Prof	Lowe, Carol C.	D	64D,11
Prof	Madeja, James T.	D	32,63A,12C,49
Adj Inst	Martin-Atwood, Michelle R.	D	13
Assoc Prof	Massell, Deborah P.	D	61
Assoc Prof	McCoy, Peter M.	D	32E,32F,32C,32G,32B
Assoc Prof	McGinness, John R.	D	13
Adj Inst	Meunier, Catherine	D	65
Adj Inst	Miller, Julie Welsh	M	66C
Assoc Prof	Miller, Kathleen A.	D	61
Other	Miller, Lane E.	M	66F
Asst Prof	Mount, Andre	D	13
Other	Murdie, Lorelei T.	M	
Assoc Prof	Pearon, Jill R.	D	61
Prof	Petercsak, James J.	M	50,65
Assoc Prof	Pittman-Jennings, David	M	61
Assoc Prof	Reames, Rebecca	D	60A,32,36
Adj Inst	Redmond, Daryle J.	M	65
Adj Inst	Reeder, Jefferson	M	39
Adj Inst	Reifel, Edward	D	65
Prof	Rubio, Douglas	D	12A,41,70
Adj Inst	Rubio, Jill M.	M	64A
Assoc Prof	Sanders, Raphael P.	D	64C,41
Prof	Schaff, Michael P.	D	60B,37
Assoc Prof	Severtson, Kirk A.	D	61,66C,39
Asst Prof	Sherman, Kathryn D.	D	66D,66B
Prof	Siskind, Paul A.	D	13,10
Prof	Sitton, Michael R.	D	66A
Adj Inst	Solomon, Alan L.	D	33
Prof	Suchy-Pilalis, Jessica R.	D	13,62E,13H,13C,31A
Asst Prof	Sullivan, Lorraine Yaros	D	61
Asst Prof	Sullivan, Timothy R.	D	13,13A,13B,13C
Vstng Asst Prof	Suniga, Rosemarie	D	66D
Assoc Prof	Tramposh, Shelly	D	41,62B
Adj Inst	Tremblay, Dan	M	63A
Prof	Tsarov, Eugenia M.	M	66A
Assoc Prof	Tyre, Jess B.	D	12
Adj Inst	Vredenburg, Brenda	M	32
Adj Inst	Vredenburg, Jeffrey	M	32
Prof	Wanamaker, Gregory R.	D	13,10A
Adj Inst	Wanamaker, Tracy S.	M	33
Prof	Wexler, Mathias K.	D	41,62C
Asst Prof	Wheeler, Heather L.	M	66D
Asst Prof	Woods, Lonel	D	61
Assoc Prof	Wyse, Paul N.	D	66A
Vstng Asst Prof	Young, Robert	D	64E,41
Adj Inst	Zolner, Robert R.		35G
Prof	Zvacek, Bret R.	M	47,29

NY3785 State Univ of New York-Purchase

Conservatory of Music
735 Anderson Hill Rd
Purchase, NY 10577-1445
(914) 251-6700   Fax: (914) 251-6739
www.purchase.edu/music
E-mail: music@purchase.edu

4 Year Institution, Graduate School

Artist Diploma, Master of Music in Composition, Master of Music in Performance, Performer's Certificate

Interim Dean: Robert Thompson, 80A
Assistant Dean: Saul Spangenberg, 80H

Rank	Name	Deg	Areas
Inst PT	Abercrombie, John		70
Vstng Asst Prof	Adelson, Michael		60,38
Vstng Affiliate Artist	Albright, Timothy		63C
	Alexander, Eric		64E
Assoc Prof	Ashton, Graham		49,63A
Inst PT	Baird, Thomas		61
Collaborative Pianist	Bang, In-Sun		66A,66C
Asst Prof	Bellink, Allyson	M	10,10C,10A
Inst PT	Blenzig, Charles		10,66A,29,35B
Assoc Prof	Brookshire, Bradley	M	12A,12,55,66G,66H
Assoc Prof	Brown, Stephanie	M	66A
Inst PT	Buck, Stephen M.		13
Inst PT	Castellani, Daniel		10
Vstng Affiliate Artist	Clymer, Richard	M	63A
Inst PT	Cobb, Timothy B.		62D
Asst Prof	Coolman, Todd	D	47,62D,53,46,29
Inst PT	Corniel, Wilson 'Chembo'		65
Inst PT	Denenberg, Peter		34
Vstng Affiliate Artist	Diaz, Raymond		61
Artist in Res	Donato, Dominic		65,43
Inst PT	Driscoll, Kermit		62D,29
Inst PT	Du, Yun		10
Artist in Res	Faddis, Jon		47,63A,29
Asst Prof	Farrin, Suzanne		10
Inst PT	Fedchock, John		63C
	Ferry, Joe	D	10,29,35B,35D
Inst PT	Galper, Hal		66A,47
Lect	Gatti, Annmarie		10
Asst Prof	Gluck, David		10C,10D
Inst PT	Goodheart, Thomas		61
Lect	Gordon, Jon		64E
Inst PT	Hamilton, Bonnie		61
Inst PT	Hand, Frederic		70
Vstng Affiliate Artist	Hazeltine, David		66A
Lect	Hecht, Gerard		61,66C
Lect	Homsey, Ryan		10
Vstng Affiliate Artist	Ingliss, Robert	B	64B
Lect	Isacoff, Stuart M.		12
Vstng Affiliate Artist	Iverson, Cynde	M	64D
Lect	Jetter, Jonathan		35C
Inst PT	Johnston, Randy		70
Prof PT	Kaminsky, Laura		10
Collaborative Pianist	Kim, Mina		66A,66C
Inst PT	Koeppel, James		10C,10D
Inst PT	Krueger, Joan		61
Inst PT	Lalama, Ralph		64E
Lect	Lewitt, David		65
Inst PT	Lichten, Julia		62C,41
Lect	London, Frank		14
Assoc Prof	Lubin, Steven	D	13,12A,12,66A
Vstng Prof	Lucarelli, Humbert		64B
Asst Prof PT	Malinverni, Peter	M	13
Prof	McElwaine, James	M	41,47,20G,29,34
Inst PT	Morales, Richie		65,29
Assoc Prof	Munro, Douglas		47,29
Asst Prof	Murphy, Hugh		39,66C
Inst PT	Neidich, Ayako Oshima		64C,42
Asst Prof	O'Connor, Tara Helen	DMA	64A,42
Vstng Asst Prof	O'Farrill, Arturo		47,66A
Lect	Oge, Derin		66A
Artist in Res	Ostrovsky, Paul		41,66A
Inst PT	Overholt, Sherry		61
Inst PT	Piltzecker, Ted		13

Vstng Affiliate Artist	Pollard, Paul		63C
Lect	Recca, David		60,13
Vstng Affiliate Artist	Reit, Peter	B	63B
Vstng Affiliate Artist	Rieppi, Pablo		65
Inst PT	Riley, John		47
Inst PT	Rojas, Marcus		63D
Inst PT	Rotondi, Jim		63A,29
Vstng Affiliate Artist	Ruffels, David	M	62D
Inst PT	Ruo, Huang		10
Inst PT	Sato, Kaori		61
Collaborative Pianist	Shim, Jeong-Ja		66A,66C
Asst Prof	Smukler, Laurie		62A
Vstng Affiliate Artist	Sprott, Weston		63C
Vstng Affiliate Artist	Sussman, Richard	M	10
Asst Prof PT	Thome, Joel H.		13A,13
Assoc Prof	Trussel, Jacque		36,39,61
Vstng Affiliate Artist	Vinci, Mark		64E
Lect	Washington, Kenny		65
Inst PT	Weiss, Doug		62D
Assoc Prof	Weller, Ira	M	62B,42,51
Inst PT	Wendholt, Scott		63A
Asst Prof	Wiersma, Calvin		62A
Inst PT	Wilson, Steven		64E
Lect	Zori, Carmit		62A,42

NY3790 State Univ of New York-Stony Brook

Department of Music
3304 Staller Center
Stony Brook, NY 11794-5475
(631) 632-7330   Fax: (631) 632-7404
www.sunysb.edu/music
E-mail: judith.lochhead@stonybrook.edu

4 Year Institution, Graduate School

Master of Arts in Composition, Master of Arts in History & Theory of Music, Master of Music in Performance, PhD in History & Theory of Music, PhD in Composition, DMA in Performance

Chair: Judith Lochhead, 80A
Dir., Undergraduate Studies: Sheila Silver, 80B
Dir., Graduate Studies: Perry Goldstein, 80C
Dir., Community Music Programs: Michael F. Hershkowitz, 80E

Vstng Asst Prof	Adams, Margarethe A.	D	20A,20B,14
Prof	Anderson, Ray R.	B	46,47,53
Artist in Res	Bonazzi, Elaine	B	61
Assoc Prof	Calcagno, Mauro	D	12A,12D,12B,11
Prof	Carr, Colin	DIPL	41,62C
Artist in Res	Cobb, Kevin D.	M	63A,49,42
Artist in Res	Cords, Nicholas D.	B	62B
Assoc Prof	Dahl, Christina A.	M	41,66A,66C
Artist in Res	Deaver, Susan E.	M	38
Artist in Res	Diaz, Pedro	M	64B
Artist in Res	Drucker, Eugene S.	D	41,62A
Artist in Res	Dutton, Lawrence	M	41,62B
Artist in Res	Ellsworth, Ann	M	63B
Lect PT	Engel, Bruce E.	M	37
Artist in Res	Finckel, David	D	41,62C
Prof	Fuller, Sarah	D	11,12A,12,13
Assoc Prof	Goldstein, Perry	D	13A,13C,13E,10A,13F
Prof	Haas, Arthur S.	M	41,66H,67,55B
Artist in Res	Harris, Brenda	B	61
Artist in Res	Kaczorowska, Joanna Maria	D	62A,42
Prof	Kalish, Gilbert	B	41,66A,66C,43
Artist in Res	Kay, Alan B.	M	64C
Artist in Res	Kim, Soovin	M	62A
Prof	Lawton, David	D	60,12A,12,38,39
Assoc Prof	Leandro, Eduardo G.	M	65,50,43
Prof	Lochhead, Judith	D	13E,13F,12,13,12A
Assoc Prof	Long, Timothy G.	M	61,66C
Staff	Malenich, Thomas		66F
Assoc Prof	Minor, Ryan	D	12A,12D,12B,11,13E
Artist in Res	Morelli, Frank A.	D	64D,41
Artist in Res	Muroki, Kurt K.	B	62D
Staff	Nittoli, Andrew		35C,35D
Artist in Res	Panner, Daniel Z.	M	62B
Artist in Res	Powell, Michael E.	B	63C
Lect	Samuel, Jamuna	D	11,12A,13E,12B,13F
Artist in Res	Scarlata, Randall S.	M	61
Asst Prof	Schedel, Margaret	D	10A,10B,10C,10F
Assoc Prof	Semegen, Daria	M	13,10,45
Prof	Setzer, Philip E.	M	41,62A
Prof	Silver, Sheila	D	13B,13D,13E,10A,10F
Asst Prof	Steege, Benjamin A.	D	12A,12B,12C,13F,13
Assoc Prof	Weymouth, Daniel	D	13,10,45,34
Artist in Res	Willard, Jerry		67D,70
Artist in Res	Wincenc, Carol	M	64A
Prof	Winkler, Peter	M	13,10,20G,29A

NY4050 Suffolk County Comm College

Department of Music
533 College Rd
Selden, NY 11784-2851
(631) 451-4346   Fax: (631) 451-4426
www.sunysuffolk.edu
E-mail: boydc@sunysuffolk.edu

2 Year Institution

Chair: Craig E. Boyd, 80A

Adj	Belajonas, Michael	M	70
Prof	Boyd, Craig E.	M	60,11,47,70,29A
Adj	Brett, Douglas		66A
Inst	Bush, Eric W.	M	37,47,63A,13A,11
Asst Prof	Cavanaugh, Alice I.	D	36,12A,11
Adj	Francom, Jeffrey D.		66A
Adj	Greenberg, Russell	M	29A
Adj	Greene, Terry L.	D	29A
Adj	Hansen, Frank	M	11,38,62B
Adj	Jentsch, Christopher T.	M	11,29A
Adj	Kalson, Dorothy		66A,11
Adj	Karahalis, Dean	M	11,29,63C
Adj	Kohl, Jack	D	66A
Adj	Kosak, Johanna	M	66A
Adj	Lamendola, Gene	M	11
Adj	Li, Chihwei	M	66A
Asst Prof	Nohai-Seaman, Alexander	DMA	13,10,43
Adj	Preston, Byron L.	M	36
Adj	Smith, James	M	70,11
Adj	Vandegriff, Matthew M.	M	13
Adj	Wall, Sarah	M	64B,11
Assoc Prof	Williams, Ralph K.	M	13,11,61
Asst Prof	Wright, Richard	D	13,11,13C,66A,38
Inst	Zamek, Brian	M	11,37,47

NY4060 Suffolk County Comm College

Department of Arts & Humanities
Grant Campus
Crooked Hill Rd
Brentwood, NY 11717-1092
(631) 851-6585   Fax: (631) 851-6875
www.sunysuffolk.edu
E-mail: williar@sunysuffolk.edu

2 Year Institution

Academic Chair: Allen Keener, 80A

Adj Inst	Erickson, James M.	M	13,12A,11,70
Adj Asst Prof	Hanson, F.	M	13,12A,11,66A
Adj Inst	Jentsch, Christopher	D	13,12A,11,70
Adj Asst Prof	Karahalis, Dean	D	13,12A,11
Adj Inst	Kohl, Jack	D	13C,12A,11
Adj Inst	Lamendola, Gene	M	13,12A,11
Assoc Prof	Williams, Ralph K.	M	13,12A,11,61

NY4100 Syracuse University

Department of Art & Music Histories
Bowne Hall
Suite 308
Syracuse, NY 13244
(315) 443-4184   Fax: (315) 443-4186
www.syracuse.edu
E-mail: ljstraub@syr.edu

4 Year Institution

Chair: Amanda Eubanks Winkler, 80A
Dir., Undergraduate Studies: Stephen C. Meyer, 80B

Assoc Prof	Babiracki, Carol M.	PhD	12,12B,14,20B,20E
Asst Prof	Cateforis, Theodore P.	PhD	12,12D,20G,29A,14C
Asst Prof	Foster, Rodney W.	PhD	11,12,31A,34A,34F
Asst Prof	Hutchinson, Sydney	PhD	14,15
Inst	Kahler, Bette	M	11,12A,33,66A,66G
Assoc Prof	Meyer, Stephen C.	PhD	12,12A,12D,31A
Assoc Prof	Winkler, Amanda Eubanks	PhD	12,12A,15,31A,31G

NY4150 Syracuse University

Setnor School of Music
215 Crouse College
Syracuse, NY 13244-1010
(315) 443-5892   Fax: (315) 443-9713
vpa.syr.edu/music
E-mail: ammertz@syr.edu

4 Year Institution, Graduate School
Member of NASM

Master of Music in Composition, Master of Music in Performance, Master of Music in Conducting, Master of Science in Music Education, Master of Music in Music Education, PhD in Curriculum & Instruction (Music Education)

Director: Patrick Michael Jones, 80A
Coord., Recruiting & Admissions: Amy Mertz, 80D,80E
Coord., Academic Affairs: Janet E. Brown, 80H

Inst	Abbott, James S.	B	35C,35D,35G
PT	Blount, Alyssa	M	62A
PT	Bodley, Muriel M.	M	32E
PT	Brewster, Cornelia L.	M	64A
FT	Brown, Janet E.	M	61
PT	Bull, Michael W.	M	50,65
PT	Bunn, Deette	M	62E
PT	Caravan, Ronald L.	D	64C,64E
PT	Castilano, Edward P.	B	62D
PT	Choi, Bonnie L.	D	66A,66H,66D
PT	Coble, Deborah C.	M	64A
PT	Coggiola, Jill A.	D	32E,64C,64E
Assoc Prof	Coggiola, John C.	D	32,29,34,47,60B
Assoc Prof	Dekaney, Elisa M.	D	32,36,20H,60A
PT	Dekaney, Joshua A.	M	20H,65,32E
Asst Prof	DiCosimo, William J.	M	35,66A
PT	DiMartino, Gabriel V.	M	49,63A
Assoc Prof	Downing, Joseph	D	10,66G,13,13C,60
PT	English, Jonathan R.	M	61
PT	Enslin, Laura A.	M	61
Assoc Prof	Ethington, Bradley P.	D	60B,37,32E
PT	Ferre, Stephen G.	D	13,35
PT	Garland, Jon R.	B	63B
Prof	Godfrey, Daniel S.	D	13,10,12A
PT	Haddock, Kathleen	M	66A,66C
PT	Halligan, Robert S.		35A,35B,35D,35F
PT	Harris, William H.	M	63C,63D
PT	Harvey, Kathryn	M	35
FT	Hege, Daniel C.	M	43,60B
PT	Heyman, Amy G.	M	66D
Assoc Prof	Heyman, Steven M.	M	66A,66D,66C,66B
PT	James, Nancy B.	M	61
Assoc Prof	Johnson, Eric D.	M	61,39
Prof	Jones, Patrick Michael	D	32G,60B,32,12A,12E
Assoc Prof	Karpoff, Fred S.	D	42,66A,66C,66B
PT	Karpoff, Rebecca J.	D	61
PT	Kim, Adrienne	M	66A
Prof	Laverty, John M.	D	60B,37,32,63A
PT	Laverty, Mary	M	12C
Other	Lee, Robert W.		66F,72
PT	Liberatore, John	M	13
PT	McKinstry, Julia D.	M	61
Other	Mertz, Amy	M	
FT	Mertz, Justin J.	M	37,60B,32
PT	Meyer, Kenneth R.	D	70
PT	Miller, Donna Z.	M	61
PT	Montalbano, Rick C.		66A
PT	Moore, Kevin	D	35A
Asst Prof	Oesterle, Ulf	D	35A,35B,35D,35F
Asst Prof	Owolabi, Olukola P.	D	66G,13
PT	Panethiere, Darrell	D	35
PT	Pugh, Darryl L.	M	62D
PT	Quick, Gregory	B	64D
PT	Rezak, David M.		35A,35B,35D
Asst Prof	Rhodes, Harumi		62A
PT	Riposo, Joseph	M	47,46,32
Asst Prof	Roland-Silverstein, Kathleen		
PT	Rovit, Arvilla	M	62B
Asst Prof	Rovit, Peter M.	D	62A,67B
Assoc Prof	Sabol, Julianna M.	D	61
Assoc Prof	Scherzinger, Nicolas	D	13,10,34,64E
PT	Stearns, Anna Petersen	B	64B
PT	Stinson, Caroline S.	M	62C
PT	Tagg, Barbara M.	D	32,36,60A
Assoc Prof	Tapia, James R.	D	60B,38,32
PT	Thompson-Buechner, Patti	B	61
PT	Tili-Trebicka, Thomaidha	M	66A,66D,66C
Prof	Waggoner, Andrew B.	D	13,10,12A
Assoc Prof	Warren, John F.	D	36,32D,60A
PT	Weber, Carolyn R. T.	M	61
PT	Welcher, Jeffrey	M	36
Asst Prof	Welsch, James O.	M	13,49,39
PT	Wood, Gregory J.	B	62C

NY4200 Teachers College/Columbia Univ

Program in Music Education
525 W 120th St
Box 139
New York, NY 10027-6696
(212) 678-3283   Fax: (212) 678-4048
www.tc.edu/a&h/MusicEd
E-mail: dmanning@tc.edu

Graduate School

Master of Arts in Music Education, Master of Education in Music Education, Doctor of Education in Music Education, EDDCT in Music Education

Coordinator: Dwight C. Manning, 80A
Dir., Summer Programs: Harold F. Abeles, 80G
Dir., Summer Programs: Jeanne C. Goffi-Fynn, 80G

Prof	Abeles, Harold F.	D	32,13K,13L,12F
Asst Prof Adj	Allen, Virginia	D	60
Assoc Prof	Allsup, Randall Everett	D	43,32,13,12A,12B
Inst	Baldacchino, Laura Falzon	M	64A,32E,42,43
Inst	Barto, Mary B.	M	64A
Asst Prof Adj	Baxter, Marsha	D	12A,13
Inst	Beaudry, Paul	M	62D
Inst	Becker, Nicole M.	D	66A
Inst	Chen, Evelyn	D	66A
Asst Prof Adj	Cowin, Jasmin Bey	D	11,62E,12A,31B
Assoc Prof	Custodero, Lori A.	D	32A,32B,32G,12E,12C
Inst	Fossner, Alvin K.	D	64B,64C,64E
Assoc Prof Adj	Frankel, James Thomas		34,37,32,32F
Inst	Gavalchin, John E.	D	66A,12,13
Lect	Goffi-Fynn, Jeanne C.	D	40,61,13H,32B,32D
Inst	Greenfield, Hayes	M	64E
Inst	Henderson, Andrew Elliot	D	66G
Inst	Holsberg, Peter W.	D	63A
Assoc Prof Adj	Horowitz, Robert	D	32G
Inst	Jacobowski, Richard	D	70
Inst	Kim, Clara	D	62C
Asst Prof Adj	Lin, Victor	D	29,66A,62D
Lect	Manning, Dwight C.	D	64,42,32E,11,64B
Inst	Miranda, Angelo	D	65
Inst	Mongiardo, Josephine	M	61
Assoc Prof	Pogonowski, Lenore	D	53,32,12A,13
Inst	Robinson-Martin, Trineice	D	61
Inst	Santogade, Peter	D	61
Inst	Scialla, Peter	M	65
Inst	Sinsabaugh, Katherine Anne	D	62A,62B
Assoc Prof Adj	St. John, Patricia A.	D	32A,32B
Inst	Stewart, Jocelyn	D	66H
Inst	Thomas, Richard Pearson	D	66A,66C,10
Inst	Wolf, Eve	M	66A
Inst	Yoshizawa, Haruko	D	66A,29

NY4250 Tompkins-Cortland Comm College

Department of Music
170 North Rd/Box 139
Dryden, NY 13053
(607) 844-8211   Fax: (607) 844-9665
www.sunytccc.edu
E-mail: drakem@tc3.edu

2 Year Institution

Adj Inst	Drake, Melvyn		70,36
Adj Inst	Stremlin, Tatyana	D	13,11,61,66A,67C

NY4300 Ulster County Comm College/SUNYUlster

Department of Music
Stone Ridge, NY 12484
(845) 687-5066   Fax: (845) 687-5083
www.sunyulster.edu
E-mail: machelli@sunyulster.edu

2 Year Institution

Chair: Iain Machell, 80A

Inst PT	Dinger, Gregory	M	13,12A,70
Inst PT	Franks, Rebecca	M	29A,29B,46,47,34D
Inst PT	Izzo, Victor	M	37,38,13A
Inst PT	Leavitt, Edward	M	66A,66D
Inst PT	Stern, Margaret	M	36,40

NY4310 Union College

Department of Music
807 Union St
Schenectady, NY 12308
(518) 388-6785   Fax: (518) 388-6567
www.union.edu/music
E-mail: mcmulled@union.edu

4 Year Institution

Chair: Dianne M. McMullen, 80A

Lect	Cox, John	M	36,38,40,41,60
Asst Prof	Matsue, Jennifer	D	14,15,20C,20
Prof	McMullen, Dianne M.	D	13,12,66,31
Assoc Prof	Olsen, Timothy J.	D	13,10,47,63A,29
Prof	Tann, Hilary	D	13,10

NY4320 Univ at Buffalo (SUNY)

Department of Music
Box 604700/Baird Hall/Rm 220
Buffalo, NY 14260-4700
(716) 645-2765   Fax: (716) 645-3824
www.music.buffalo.edu
E-mail: ksausner@buffalo.edu

4 Year Institution, Graduate School

Master of Arts in Composition, Master of Arts in Music History, Master of Arts in Music Theory, Master of Music in Performance, PhD in Historical Musicology, PhD in Music Theory, PhD in Composition

Chair: Charles J. Smith, 80A
Associate Chair: Jeffrey Stadelman, 80H

Assoc Prof	Arnold, Tony	M	61
Adj Inst PT	Bacon, John	M	10
Adj Inst PT	Bassin, Daniel		38
Adj Inst PT	Castellani, Joanne C.	M	70
Prof Emeritus	Cipolla, Frank J.	M	37
Adj Asst Prof PT	Crawford, Barry J.	M	64A
Assoc Prof	Currie, James Robert	D	12
Prof Emerita	Dimiziani, Sylvia	M	61
Adj Inst PT	Fackelman, Harry	B	64E
Prof	Felder, David C.	D	10
Assoc Prof	Golove, Jonathan	D	10,62C
Prof	Grant, Kerry S.	D	12
Asst Prof	Huebner, Eric H.	M	66
Assoc Prof	Hyde, Martha M.	D	13,13J
Asst Prof	Kolor, Thomas P.	M	65
Prof	Kopperud, Jean K.	M	64C
Assoc Prof	Lippe, Cort	B	10,45,34
Adj Inst PT	Lombardo, Jonathan R.	B	63C
Assoc Prof	Long, Michael P.	D	12A,12,13J
Prof Emeritus	Manes, Stephen G.	M	66A,66C
Adj Inst PT	Martin, Roland E.	M	66G,66H,66C
Adj Inst PT	Mattix, Anna L.	M	64B
Assoc Prof Emeritus	Mols, Robert W.	D	
Assoc Prof	Nelson, Jon R.	B	37,47,63A
Prof Emeritus	Noble, Jeremy	M	
Adj Asst Prof	Nuzzo, Nancy B.		16
Adj Inst PT	Pendley, Daniel	M	62D
Asst Prof	Plotkin, Richard		13
Vstng Assoc Prof	Rosenbaum, Harold L.	M	36
Adj Inst PT	Schiavone, David C.	B	64C,64E,47
Prof Emeritus	Sigel, Allen R.	M	64C
Assoc Prof	Smith, Charles J.	D	13,13B,13I
Assoc Prof	Stadelman, Jeffrey	D	10,43
Assoc Prof Emeritus	Strainchamps, Edmond N.	M	12A,12
Adj Inst PT	Theriault, Kristen Moss		62E
Asst Prof	Vander Wel, Stephanie L.	D	12,14C
Adj Inst PT	Wagner, Michael F.		62D
Prof Emeritus	Williams, Jan G.	M	65
Adj Inst PT	Winter, Michael J.	B	63B
Adj Inst PT	Wooldridge, Jessica M.		64D
Adj Inst PT	Zabenova, Ainur		62A,62B

NY4350 Univ of Rochester

Department of Music
Todd 207/Box 270052
Rochester, NY 14627-0052
(585) 275-9397   Fax: (585) 273-5337
www.rochester.edu/college/MUR
E-mail: jcovach@mail.rochester.edu

4 Year Institution

Chair: John R. Covach, 80A
Administrator: Elaine M. Stroh, 80B
Manager, Music Performance: Josef M. Hanson, 80F

Assoc Prof	BaileyShea, Matthew L.	D	13,13E
Vstng Asst Prof	Bazler, Corbett D.	D	12A,12
Prof	Burgett, Paul	D	20G,11,29A,29D
Prof	Covach, John R.	D	13A,13,13J,10D
Prof	Frank, Bruce	DMA	66,13
Adj	Georgieva, Irina P.		40
	Hanson, Josef M.	M	13A,49
Prof	Harman, David	DMA	60,38,41,11
Prof	Kowalke, Kim	D	12A,12,39,54,20G
Adj	McAulliffe, Harold F.		10
Prof	Meconi, Honey	D	12A,12,15
Adj	Tiberio, William		47
Prof	Titus, Jason		13

NY4400 Utica College

Department of Perf & Fine Arts
1600 Burrstone Rd
Utica, NY 13502
(315) 792-3028   Fax: (315) 792-3831
www.utica.edu
E-mail: mhutchinson@utica.edu

4 Year Institution

Coordinator: Mary Anne Hutchinson, 80A

Adj	Beno, Charles W.	M	12A,11
Adj	DiMeo, Mike J.	M	37,11,47

NY4450 Vassar College

Department of Music
124 Raymond Ave
Poughkeepsie, NY 12604
(845) 437-7319   Fax: (845) 437-7114
music.vassar.edu
E-mail: kalibin@vassar.edu

4 Year Institution

Chair: Kathryn L. Libin, 80A

Adj Artist PT	Archer, Gail	D	66G,66H
Adj Artist PT	Bellino, Paul	M	63C
Adj Artist PT	Bishkoff, Cheryl	M	64B
Adj Artist PT	Cassara, Frank	M	65
Adj Artist PT	Champlin, Terry	B	70
Adj Artist PT	Charney, Miriam	B	66A,39
Prof	Chenette, Jonathan Lee	D	10,13,34,10A,10B
Prof	Crow, Todd	M	66A
Adj Artist PT	DeMicco, Mike	M	70
Adj Artist PT	Farina, Danielle	M	62B
Adj Artist PT	Files, Frederick	DMA	65
Adj Artist PT	Guy, Larry	M	64C
Asst Prof	Howlett, Christine R.	D	36,13C,61
Adj Artist PT	Jackson, Ashley	M	62E
Adj Artist PT	Lee, Jessica	M	62A
Assoc Prof	Libin, Kathryn L.	D	13,11,12A,12
Assoc Prof	Mann, Brian R.	D	11,12A,12,29A
Adj Inst PT	McCulloch, Peter	M	10B
Adj Asst Prof PT	Meltzer, Harold	D	10
Lect	Minter, Drew	B	61,40,39
Adj Artist PT	Mortensen, Dan	B	70
Lect	Navega, Eduardo	M	38,41,60
Adj Artist PT	Nessinger, Mary	B	61
Adj Artist PT	Osborn, James	M	47,63A,48
Adj Artist PT	Osborne, Robert	D	61
Adj Artist PT	Pappas, Louis	M	62D
Other	Patch, Justin	D	14,20
Prof	Pisani, Michael	D	11,12A,12,20G
Adj Artist PT	Polonsky, Anna	M	66A
Adj Artist PT	Quan, Linda	M	62A
Adj Artist PT	Reit, Peter	B	63B
Adj Artist PT	Romano, Elizabeth	B	64D

Adj Artist PT	Rosales, Rachel	M	61
Adj Artist PT	Ruff, James	M	61
Adj Artist PT	Shao, Sophie S.	M	62C
Adj Lect	Solum, John	B	64A
Adj Artist PT	Tomlinson, Peter	B	66A
Prof	Wilson, Richard E.	M	13,10A,10F
Adj Artist PT	Xiques, Ed	B	64E

NY4460 Villa Maria College of Buffalo

Department of Music
240 Pine Ridge Rd
Buffalo, NY 14225-3993
(716) 896-0700   Fax: (716) 891-9020
www.villa.edu
E-mail: amrozowicz@villa.edu

4 Year and 2 Year Institution

Chair: Mary Barbara Amrozowicz, 80A

	Amrozowicz, Mary Barbara	M	13A,13,66A,13C,13B
	Aquila, Carmen	M	35A,13A,35D,12A,10A
PT	Bacon, John	M	65,47
PT	Barone, Judith	M	66A,66G,13A,41
PT	Beaudreau, Jason	M	70
	Casuccio, Anthony	B	35D,35G
PT	Cooper, Barbara	M	61
	Crittenden, Eric	B	35A
PT	DeAngelo, Brian	M	20
PT	DelBello, Nicolas	B	63A
PT	Eckenrode, Bryan	M	62C,62A
PT	Flood, James	B	66A,66G
	Grmela, Sylvia	D	62B,20,13A,13C
PT	Hittle, Kevin	B	63D
PT	Hunt, Marc	M	35A
	Kurzdorfer, James	M	13,47,62D,53
PT	Piontek, Gregory	M	62D
PT	Powrie, Barbara	M	66A
PT	Rutkowski, Gary	M	50,65,11
PT	Schiavone, David	B	64
PT	Sparks, Jeremy	B	70
PT	Strauss, Richard	B	70
PT	Timmerman-Yorty, Carol	M	64C
PT	Tworek-Gryta, Adrienne	M	61,36

NY4500 Wagner College

Department of Music
One Campus Rd
Staten Island, NY 10301
(718) 390-3313   Fax: (718) 390-3392
www.wagner.edu/departments/music
E-mail: sbock@wagner.edu

4 Year Institution

Chair: David L. Schulenberg, 80A

Adj Asst Prof	Birgfeld, Kelly	D	61
Inst PT	Brown, Edward E.	M	70
Adj Asst Prof	Chung, Joyce	M	66A,66D
Inst PT	Clive, David	M	50,65
Inst PT	Corwin, Lucille H.	M	62A,62B
Prof	Cross, Ronald W.	D	13A,11,12A
Inst PT	Dornak, Alan W.	DIPL	61
Inst PT	Ionesco, Georgette	DIPL	64A
Adj Asst Prof	McClellan, Robinson	D	13B,13C
Inst PT	McCullough, Elizabeth L.	M	61
Inst PT	Ohrenstein, Dora	M	61
Inst PT	Pranschke, Janet	B	61
Inst PT	Rams, Robert	M	37
Prof	Schulenberg, David L.	D	11,12
Inst PT	Sergi, James	M	61
Inst PT	Sher, Ben	M	34,47,70
Inst PT	Turner, Anthony	M	61
Inst PT	Wesby, Barbara K.	B	10A
Assoc Prof	Wesby, Roger	D	11,29A,32D,36,40
Inst PT	Williams, Amy B.	M	61
Inst PT	Woodul, Lars V.	D	61

NY5000 Westchester Conservatory of Music

216 Central Ave
White Plains, NY 10606
(914) 761-3900   Fax: (914) 761-3984
www.musicconservatory.org
E-mail: jean@musiced.org

Community School, Degree and Credit Offered with NY2400

Chair: Jean Newton, 80A
Associate Chair: Sarah M. Wetherbee, 80H

	Arrucci, John	B	65
	Barnhill, Eric	M	11
	Bethel, Phyllis	M	33
	Brescia, Tina	D	33
	Briskin, Efrem	D	66A
	Briskin, Natalya	M	66A
	Broubechliev, Bojil	M	65A,65B
	Brown, Angeline	M	33
	Bunchman, Michael	M	66A
	Caldwell, Frances Sherer	B	66A
	Dempster, Loren	B	62C
	Devens, Richard	B	66A
	Draper, Frederick	B	70
	Feigin, Tatiana	M	62A
	Fidelibus, Joseph	D	33
	Flippin, Thomas	M	70,11
	Fong, Ming	M	66A
	Gerard, Eva	M	62A,62B
	Gopoian, Juliet	B	66A
	Gorokhovich, Svetlana	D	66A
	Hsu, Cindi	M	66A,10
	Hyun, June	M	62A
	Ishikawa, Chikae	B	11
	Jamerson, Celeste Emmons	D	61
	Jamerson, Thomas H.	M	61
	Jenner, Joanna	M	62A
	Jonas, Dorothy	B	66A
	Jones, Harold	DIPL	64A
	Kay, Min Soo	M	66A
	Khimm, Christina	B	62A
	Kozenko, Lisa A.	D	64B
	Krieger, David	M	62C
	Kwon, Su Jin	D	62A,62B
	Laskowitz, Lillian	B	66A
	Lewis, Tim	M	66G
	Li, Lin	M	66A
	Longo, Tatiana	M	62C
	Lorusso, James	DIPL	70
	Love, Shirley	B	61
	Magaziner, Elliot	B	62A,62B
	Mangini, Nick		65
	Maxon, James	M	33
	Micic, Alma	M	61
	Micic, Rale	B	70
	Mohen, Girard	D	64C,64E
	Neubert, Nils	D	61
	Newton, Jean	D	66H
	Pera, Adriana	M	62C
	Petite, Rachel Maria	D	62A
	Petursdottir, Ragga	B	62A
	Pierce, Joshua	M	66A
	Podgurski, Barbara	D	66A,11
	Poore, Mary Elizabeth	M	61
	Portenko, Irena	D	66A
	Prokop, Rick	B	66A
	Ranti, James	B	63A,63C
	Reit, Alyssa	M	62E
	Reit, Peter	B	63B
	Renino, Al	B	62D
	Rogizhyna, Maryna	M	66A,11
	Sandagata, Lisa	M	33
	Shentov, Lubima	M	62D
	Stanley, Justin	D	64C
	Starin, Stefani	M	64A
	Stephenson, Mary	M	62A
	Sukonik, Inna		66A
	Thomas, Taryn	M	33
	Tobey, Moira	B	62A
	Turner, Nakia		61
	Vilcci, Aldona	M	61
	Watson, Larry	M	62A,62B
	Wessel, Kenneth		70
	Wetherbee, Sarah M.	D	62A,62B
	Yamazaki, Hiroshi	B	66A
	Zeiger, Mikhail	D	66A

OH0050 Antioch College
Department of Music
150 ES South College St
Yellow Springs, OH 45387-1635
(937) 769-1028   Fax: (937) 767-6450
www.antioch-college.edu
E-mail: nfreeman@antiochcollege.org

4 Year Liberal Arts Institution

Head: John Rinehart, 80A

Inst	Johnston, James	M	62,38
Inst	Logan, Beverly	M	61
Inst	Mullhall, Kevin	M	70
Prof	Rinehart, John	D	13A,13,10F,10,12A

OH0100 Ashland University
Department of Music
Arts & Humanities Bldg
401 College Ave
Ashland, OH 44805
(419) 289-5100   Fax: (419) 289-5638
www.ashland.edu
E-mail: treed@ashland.edu

4 Year Liberal Arts Institution
Member of NASM

Chair: Thomas T. Reed, 80A
Dir., Artist/Performance Series: Elizabeth M. Pastor, 80F

Adj	Bekeny, Amanda K.	D	63A,49,11
Adj	Berkner, Jane	M	64A,48
Prof	Blackley, Rowland	D	60A,32D,36,40,55D
Adj	Brown, Lindsay	M	62C,62D,51
Assoc Prof	Butke, Marla A.	D	32,11,66D,36,60A
Adj	Cole, Dennis E.	D	14C,12A,11,20
Assoc Prof	Fuhrmann, Christina E.	D	13A,11,12,14
Assoc Prof	Garlock, Scott E.	D	29,47,63C,63D,46
Adj	Guenther, Timothy E.	DMA	66G,66H,66D
Adj	Hoy, Andria	M	64B
Adj	Hoy, Ian	M	64D
Adj	Leonard, Angela	M	37
Adj	Metcalf, Mary Louise	M	66D
Adj	Metcalf, Michael	M	63B,72,49
Adj	Milner Howell, Denise	M	61
Adj	Neitzke, Jeffrey	M	65,46,50
Adj	Parker Bennett, Dione	D	61
Prof	Pastor, Elizabeth M.	DIPL	
Adj	Peffley, Lynette	M	32A,11,66D
Adj	Poss, Nicholas	D	11,20
Adj	Reed, Jane	M	11,13A,62A,66D,62B
Prof	Reed, Thomas T.	D	10F,64C,64E,48
Assoc Prof	Salvo, Leonard P.	M	60B,32C,37,41,32E
Asst Prof	Sanchez-Behar, Alexander	D	13,10
Adj	Sarata, Adam	M	70
Prof	Sikora, Stephanie R.	M	36,39,61
Adj	Slade, Elizabeth	M	66D

OH0150 Athenaeum of Ohio
Department of Music
6616 Beechmont Ave
Cincinnati, OH 45230-5900
(513)231-2223   Fax: (513)231-3254
www.mtsm.org
E-mail: tdicello@mtsm.org

Roman Catholic Graduate School of Theology and Seminary

Master of Divinity in Worship Leadership

Director: Anthony J. DiCello, 80A

Asst Prof	DiCello, Anthony J.		36,61,66,31A,34

OH0200 Baldwin-Wallace College
Conservatory of Music
275 Eastland Rd
Berea, OH 44017-2088
(440) 826-2362   Fax: (440) 826-3239
www.bw.edu
E-mail: music@bw.edu

4 Year Liberal Arts College
Member of NASM

Assistant Dir., Preparatory Division & Outreach/Adult Ed & Summer Programs: Bryan L. Bowser, 80E,80G
Dir., Bach Institute/Festival: Melvin P. Unger, 80F
Assistant Dir., Academic Advising & Student Affairs: Nanette G. Canfield, 80H,80D
Assoc Dir., Conservatory Admissions: Anita S. Evans, 80H,80D

Lect	Amaral, Jorge A.	M	70
Lect	Banaszak, Greg J.	B	47,64E,29
Lect	Barber, Clarence	M	32E
Lect	Bowser, Bryan L.	B	35E
Lect	Brndiar, John J.	M	63A
Assoc Prof	Burns, Judith E.	D	60A,32D
Prof	Bussert, Victoria	M	54
Asst Prof	Canfield, Nanette G.	M	61
Other	Cary, Paul	M	16
Assoc Prof	Cleland, Kent D.	D	13,35E,34A
Lect	Co, Wei-Shu Wang	DIPL	62A
Lect	Conner, Jennifer A.	D	13,10
Lect	Czarnota, Benjamin D.	M	61
Assoc Prof	Dobrea-Grindahl, Mary	M	66A,66B,66C,32I,66D
Lect	Dorey, Christine S.	M	20
Prof	Eaglen, Jane	M	61
Lect	Ellison, Joan	M	61
Asst Prof	Fang, Man 'Mandy'	D	10
Asst Prof	Fralick, JR	D	61,39
Lect	Fuoco, Anthony	M	13
Lect	Fuoco, Christine M.	M	66D
Lect	Gabriel, Sean F.	M	64A
Lect	Gallagher, Lisa	M	33
Assoc Prof	Garner, Dirk A.	D	36,40,60A
Lect	Grady, Tracy R.	M	61
Other	Graham, Mark W.	B	66F
Lect	Guinn, Jody J.	M	62E
Lect	Hartzell, William H.	B	35G
Lect	Hirt, James A.	D	13,11,66A,10
Asst Prof	Hiser, Beth A.	D	13,10
Asst Prof	Joss, Laura L.	M	32,37,60
Lect	Kay, Lalene D.	M	33,70
Asst Prof	Kim, Sungeun	D	66A,66C
Lect	Kofsky, Allen	DIPL	63C,63D
Lect	Mackus, Boyd A.	M	61
Assoc Prof	Marshall, Herbert D.	D	32A,32B
Prof	Mayerovitch, Robert	D	66A
Lect	McCormick, Jesse D.	M	63B
Prof	McKelway, Daniel	M	64C
Lect	Meadows, Leslie	M	66D
Asst Prof	Metz, Andreas	ABD	13
Lect	Moyer, Jonathan W.	D	66G,66H
Prof	Mushabac, Regina M.	D	41,51
Prof	Mussard, Timothy S.	D	61
Lect	O'Connell, Cynthia	M	61
Prof	Oltman, Dwight	M	48,38
Lect	Peyrebrune, Henry L.	B	62D
Asst Prof	Plate, Scott F.	M	54
Lect	Pope, George S.	M	64A
Lect	Rathbun, Jeffrey J.	M	64B
Prof	Ross, Julian E.	D	41,62A
Asst Prof	Ryan, Josh T.	M	50,65
Lect	Scharf, Margaret R.	D	66G
Lect	Sherwin, Jonathan S.	M	64D
Assoc Prof	Smith, Benjamin W.	M	39
Asst Prof	Strasser, Michael C.	D	12A,20
Lect	Sugiyama, Yasuhito	B	63D
Lect	Sutte, Jack	M	63A
Prof	Unger, Melvin P.	D	16,12A,36
Lect	Uniatowski, Joanne M.	M	61
Lect	Upton, Gregory	M	11
Lect	Weagraff, Marc A.	D	61
Asst Prof	Willet, Gene K.	M	13B,13C,13D,13E
Lect	Winzenburger, Janet B.	M	55C
Lect	Zeitlin, Louise R.	M	62B

OH0250 Bluffton University
Department of Music
1 University Dr
Bluffton, OH 45817-2104
(419) 358-3347   Fax: (419) 358-3323
www.bluffton.edu/mus
E-mail: unraul@bluffton.edu

4 Year Institution
Member of NASM

Chair: Lucia Unrau, 80A
Dir., Artist/Performance Series: Adam Schattschneider, 80F

Inst PT	Baransy, Paul	M	63A,10F,60B,32E,37
Inst PT	Crites, Dennis	B	65,50
Inst PT	Diller, Alisa	B	63C
Inst PT	Edwards, Marilyn	M	63B
Inst PT	Glick, Nancy	M	62E
Inst PT	McDaniel, Carolyn	M	32A,32B,36
Inst PT	Miller, Tom	B	63D
Inst PT	Parnell, Scott	M	11,70,13
Asst Prof	Peterson, Jon C.	D	36,12A,44,11,54
Inst PT	Pinkney, Rachel	M	62C,62
Inst PT	Ringold, Allison	M	66A
Prof	Schattschneider, Adam	D	13,47,64A,64C,64E
Asst Prof	Sellers, Crystal Y.	D	61,11,12,31F
Inst PT	Skinner, Anita	B	62A,62B
Inst PT	Stembler-Smith, Anna	M	66A
Prof	Suderman, Mark	D	60A,32D,32B,36,61
Inst PT	Sycks, Linda	B	64B
Assoc Prof	Terry, Peter R.	D	34,10,13
Prof	Unrau, Lucia	D	66A,66B,66D,13C
Inst PT	Yost, Jennifer	M	64D

OH0300 Bowling Green State University
College of Musical Arts
1031 Moore Musical Arts Ctr
Bowling Green, OH 43403-0290
(419) 372-2181   Fax: (419) 372-2938
www.bgsu.edu/music
E-mail: lszych@bgsu.edu

4 Year Institution, Graduate School
Member of NASM

DMA in Contemporary Music, Master of Music in Composition, Master of Music in Music Theory, Master of Music in Performance, Master of Music in Music Education, Master of Music in Ethnomusicology, Master of Music in Music History

Dean: Jeffrey A. Showell, 80A
Associate Dean: Per F. Broman, 80H
Assistant Dean: Mary Natvig, 80H
Assistant Dean: Robert S. Satterlee, 80H
Assistant Dean: Kenneth Thompson, 80H

Inst PT	Ashmore, Lance	M	61
Inst	Attrep, Kara	D	14
Prof Emeritus	Baker, Walter W.	D	66A
Prof Emeritus	Beerman, Burton	D	10
Prof	Beluska, Vasile	M	62A
Prof Emeritus	Bentley, John E.	D	64B
Prof Emerita	Bentley, Judith C.	M	64A
Asst Prof	Bixler, David	M	64E,29
Prof Emerita	Bognar, Anna Belle	D	32
Assoc Prof	Broman, Per F.	D	13F,13C,13E,12B,13
Prof	Brown, Emily Freeman	D	60,38
Asst Prof PT	Bruggeman-Kurp, Jeanne	M	61
Asst Prof PT	Bunce, Mark Robert	M	34,35D,35G
Inst	Burger, Cole	D	66D
Prof	Buzzelli, Christopher	M	70
Asst Prof PT	Buzzelli, Julie	M	62E
Inst	Bylsma, Kevin	B	39,61
Assoc Prof PT	Carpenter, Lauraine	M	63A
Prof Emeritus	Cioffari, Richard J.	M	62D
Asst Prof	Cleveland, Susannah L.	M	16
Asst Prof PT	Cloeter, Chelsea	M	61
Asst Prof	Cloeter, Tim	M	36
Assoc Prof	Colprit, Elaine	D	32
Asst Prof PT	Cooper, Jennifer Goode	M	61
Asst Prof	Cooper, Sean	D	61
Asst Prof PT	Corrigan, Ann	D	61
Prof Emeritus	Corrigan, Vincent J.	D	12,66H
Inst PT	Darabie, Mohammed	M	32
Prof Emeritus	Dearborn, Keith	D	32
Asst Prof	Decker, Greg	D	13
Prof Emeritus	DePue, Wallace E.	D	10
Inst PT	Desmond, Robert	M	65
Asst Prof	Dietz, Christopher J.	D	13
Inst PT	Doles, Kurt	M	67H
Prof Emeritus	Dybdahl, Gene	D	39
Prof Emeritus	Eikum, Rex	M	61
Assoc Prof	Engebretsen, Nora A.	D	13
Inst PT	Fielder, Jonathan	M	34
Inst PT	Flegg, Lynne Mangan	M	64B
Inst PT	Fox, Clinton D.	M	13,66A,66D
Prof Emeritus	Glasmire, David	M	63C
Prof Emerita	Gromko, Joyce	D	32
Asst Prof	Gruenhagen, Lisa M.	D	32A,32B,32G,64A,32
Prof	Halsey, Jeff	M	29
Prof Emeritus	Hammond, Ivan	M	63D
Assoc Prof	Hayward, Carol M.	D	37
Prof Emeritus	Inglefield, Ken P.	D	13
Prof Emeritus	Jones, Wendell	M	65
Prof	Kantorski, Vincent J.	D	32
Prof Emeritus	Kelly, Mark	M	37
Prof Emeritus	Kennell, Richard P.	D	64E
Assoc Prof	Kruse, Penny Thompson	D	51,62A
Assoc Prof	Kuehn, Mikel	D	13,10F,10,45,43
Prof Emeritus	Lake, William E.	M	13
Inst PT	Lavender, Scott	D	60
Asst Prof	Lawrence, Sidra	D	14
Inst PT	Lee, Sujin	M	61
Assoc Prof	Lillios, Elainie	D	10B,10
Asst Prof	Liu, Solungga Fang-Tzu	D	66A
Prof Emerita	Lockard-Zimmerman, Barbara	D	61
Prof Emeritus	Marks, Ed	M	64C
Prof Emerita	Marks, Virginia	M	66A
Prof Emeritus	Mathey, Richard D.	M	36
Prof	Mathis, William B.	DMA	49,63C,47
Asst Prof	McBride Daline, Matthew	M	62B
Asst Prof	Meizel, Katherine L.	D	14
Prof	Melton, Laura	D	66A
Asst Prof	Menard, Elizabeth	PhD	32
Inst PT	Merrill, Allison	M	14
Prof	Merritt, Myra	M	61
Prof Emeritus	Moore, Robert	M	64D
Prof	Moss, Bruce B.	D	60,37
Assoc Prof	Munson, Mark	D	32,36
Prof	Natvig, Mary	D	12
Asst Prof	Nelson, Conor	D	64A
Asst Prof	Nelson, Susan J.	D	64D
Prof Emeritus	Novak, George	M	63A
Assoc Prof	Papanikolaou, Eftychia	D	12
Assoc Prof	Pelletier, Andrew J.	D	63B
Prof Emeritus	Pope, David	M	66A
Prof Emeritus	Poulimenos, Andreas	M	61
Inst	Rancier, Megan M.	D	14,11
Inst PT	Rathnaw, Dennis M.	D	14
Inst	Reece, Richard	M	32
Assoc Prof	Rodgers, Jane Schoonmaker	D	39,61
Asst Prof PT	Rohwer, Robert	M	62D
Asst Prof	Rosenkranz, Thomas H.	M	66A
Assoc Prof	Saenz, Charles	D	63A
Assoc Prof PT	Saltzman, David	M	63D
Prof	Sampen, John	D	64E
Inst PT	Sark, Brady	M	65
Assoc Prof	Satterlee, Robert S.	D	66A
Assoc Prof	Schempf, Kevin	M	64C
Assoc Prof	Scholl, Christopher	M	61
Asst Prof PT	Scholl, Ellen Strba	M	61
Prof	Schupp, Roger B.	D	65
Prof	Showell, Jeffrey A.	D	62B
Prof	Shrude, Marilyn	D	10
Assoc Prof PT	Simmons, Garth	M	63C
Prof	Smith, Alan M.	D	62C,42,38
Asst Prof	Spohr, Arne	D	12
Prof Emeritus	Starr, Virginia	M	61
Assoc Prof	Stegman, Sandra Frey	D	32,36
Asst Prof PT	Stephenson, Geoffrey	D	54,39
Inst PT	Stiegler, Morgen	M	47
Prof Emeritus	Tallarico, Pat	D	32
Prof Emeritus	Thayer, Robert W.	D	32
Assoc Prof	Thompson, Kenneth	D	37
Assoc Prof	Trantham, Gene S.	D	13,13A,13J
Assoc Prof PT	Wayland, Doug	M	61
Assoc Prof PT	Weed, Tad E.	M	66A
Prof Emeritus	Wilson, Donald	D	10
Inst PT	Wilson, Kathy	M	37
Prof Emeritus	Wolcott, Vernon	D	66G
Inst PT	Yeh, I-Chen	D	66A
Asst Prof	Zagorski, Marcus	D	12

OH0350 Capital University
Conservatory of Music
1 College & Main
Columbus, OH 43209-2394
(614) 236-6411   Fax: (614) 236-6935
www.capital.edu/music
E-mail: mlochsta@capital.edu

4 Year Institution, Graduate School
Member of NASM

Master of Music in Music Education Jazz Pedagogy Emphasis, Master of Music in Music Education Instrumental Emphasis, Master of Music in Music Education with Kodaly Emphasis

Chair: Mark L. Lochstampfor, 80A
Undergraduate Admissions: Heather Massey, 80B,80D
Graduate Admissions: Susanna Mayo, 80C,80D
Dir., Artist Series: Lou Fischer, 80F
Dir., Artist Series: Anthony Zilincik, 80F
Dir., Summer Programs: Lynn Roseberry, 80G

Adj	Adderley, Meisha N.	D	13B,13C,66D,66B
Adj	Aliyeva, Narmina	M	66A,66C
Adj	Anders, Nathan	B	65,50
Adj	Archambault, Ellen	D	13B,13C
Adj	Baker, Chad	B	66G,66D
Assoc Prof	Baker, Mark A.	M	61,39,54
Adj	Banion, Brian	M	61
Asst Prof	Barlow-Ware, Jackie	M	61
Adj	Barnard, Dene	M	66G
Adj	Beers, Heather	M	62D
Prof	Bennett, Sharon K.	M	61
Adj	Boggs, William	D	38,60,41,60B
Prof	Breithaupt, Robert	M	65,35A,35B,35E
Adj Inst	Burleson, Brett	B	70
Adj	Cordes, Jamie	M	61,47
Adj	Courtney, Craig	M	36
Prof	Cox, Michael W.	D	64E,29,48
Adj	Davis, Edward	M	20,60,65
Adj	Davis, Eillen	M	61
Adj	DesChamps, Elise	M	61
Adj	Dowdy, James	M	32E
Adj	Erken, Emily	M	14
Adj	Fink, Seymour	M	66A,66B,42
Prof	Fischer, Lou	D	47,29B,10F
Adj	Flugge, Mark	M	66A,66D,29B
Adj	Gilliland, Erin	M	62A
Adj	Groves, Matthew	M	34B
Adj	Hamilton, Ryan	B	63C,47,29B,53
Prof	Hasseler, Lynda	D	60A,36,40,32D
Adj	Herrmann, Tracy	M	32A,32B,32C
Adj	Hines, Roger	M	62D,11
Adj	Hutsko, Mark	M	32D
Assoc Prof	Jelle, Lisa A.	D	64A,48
Adj Inst	Keller, Jeffrey	D	32E,60B
Prof	Kopetz, Barry E.	D	60B,37
Adj	Kopetz, Gail	M	61
Assoc Prof	Lentsner, Dina	D	12A,13B,13C,13D,13E
Prof	Lochstampfor, Mark L.	PhD	13,10A,34A,34B,66A
Asst Prof	Loughrige, Chad	B	34,35C,10B,10D,45
Adj	Matsuda, Kenichiro	M	62B
Adj	McCann, Kimberly	M	63B
Prof Emerita	Moore, Nancy	M	33,13A,13B,13C
Adj	Mueller, Joseph	M	62C
Adj	Nagy, Russ	M	35A
Adj	Nienkirchen, Red	M	35A,70
Assoc Prof	Parton, Robert T.	M	63A,29,47,29A,53
Asst Prof	Paton, Eric	B	65,20A,20C,20H,47
Adj	Price, Matt	B	35C
Prof	Reuter, Rocky J.	D	10
Adj	Riley, Justin	B	34,35C,35D,35G,13G
Prof	Roseberry, Lynn	M	61,39,40,36
Asst Prof	Ryan, Thomas K.	D	64E,13B,13C,13D,13E
Adj	Sahr, Barbara	M	66D
Adj	Secan, Steve	M	64B
Adj	Shaw, Nathan	M	66D
Assoc Prof	Smith, Stan	B	70,10D
Adj	Stanojevic, Vera	D	13B,13C,13F
Adj	Stohrer, Sharon	M	61
Prof	Swearingen, James	M	10A,32E
Adj	Thomas, Steve	B	34A,34B,34D,35D
Adj	Townsend, Sid	M	32E
Adj	Voris, Dan J.	M	70,41
Assoc Prof	Wang, Tianshu	D	66A,66D,66C
Adj	Weait, Christopher	M	64D,48
Asst Prof	Zilincik, Anthony	M	63D,41,43,10F
Assoc Prof	Zugger, Gail Lehto	D	64C,48
Assoc Prof	Zugger, Thomas W.	D	63C,63D,49

OH0400 Case Western Reserve University
Department of Music
Haydn Hall
10900 Euclid Ave
Cleveland, OH 44106-7105
(216) 368-2400   Fax: (216) 368-6557
music.case.edu
E-mail: info@music.case.edu

4 Year Institution, Grad School, Joint Curricula with Cleveland Institute of Music
Member of NASM

Master of Arts in Music Education, Master of Arts in Music History, Master of Arts in Early Music, PhD in Music Education, PhD in Musicology, DMA in Early Music

Chair: Mary E. Davis, 80A

Asst Prof	Bennett, Peter	D	12A,55
Asst Prof	Brittan, Francesca	PhD	12A
Assoc Prof	Ciepluch, Gary	D	60,32,37,48
Prof	Cowart, Georgia	PhD	12A,12
Prof	Davis, Mary E.	PhD	12A,12,14
Prof	Duffin, Ross	D	12A,12,55
Inst	Egre, Bruce	M	35C,35D
Lect FT	Ferguson, Paul	M	47,29
Asst Prof	Garrett, Matthew L.	PhD	36,32D,60A
Assoc Prof	Goldmark, Daniel	D	12A,14C
Prof	Hefling, Stephen	PhD	12A,12
Assoc Prof	Horvath, Kathleen	PhD	32,51,62
Lect FT	Karpf, Nita	DMA	12,32
Asst Prof	Koops, Lisa	PhD	32,32A
Assoc Prof Emeritus	Quereau, Quentin W.	D	12A,12
Asst Prof	Rothenberg, David J.	PhD	12A
	Sieger, Crystal		

OH0450 Cedarville University
Department of Music and Worship
251 North Main St
Cedarville, OH 45314-0601
(937) 766-7728   Fax: (937) 766-7661
www.cedarville.edu
E-mail: porterb@cedarville.edu

4 Year Institution

Chair: Beth Cram Porter, 80A
Dean: Steven L. Winteregg, 80A

PT	Akins, Lori	M	64A
Asst Prof	Anderson, Connie	M	66A,66B,66D
Prof	Anderson, Lyle J.	D	60A,36,31A
PT	Bede, Judy	B	66B
Prof	Clevenger, Charles	D	66A,66B,66C,66D,12B
Prof	Curlette, Bruce	D	13,64C,10F
PT	Currie, Sheridan	M	62B
PT	Davis, Jackie	M	62E
Prof	DiCuirci, Michael P.	M	32B,32C,37,63D,46
PT	Filbrun, John	C	70
PT	Fitter, Todd	M	63B
PT	Grove, Lisa	M	64B
PT	Hutchison, Amy	M	66A
PT	Jenkins, Chester	M	64E
PT	LaMattina, Michael	M	65
PT	Millat, Andrew	M	63C
Assoc Prof	Mortensen, John J.	D	66A,66C,66D
Asst Prof	O'Neel, Roger	D	10A,31A,13A
PT	Padrichelli, Andra	M	62C
Prof	Pagnard, Charles	M	60B,32E,49,63A
PT	Pitzer, Lawrence	M	70
PT	Plemons, Susan	M	61
Assoc Prof	Porter, Beth Cram	M	36,61
Assoc Prof	Spencer, Mark	D	39,61
Asst Prof	Stabenow, Crystal	M	61
PT	Wilson, Peter Stafford	M	38
Prof	Winteregg, Steven L.	D	10,13
PT	Woolley, Stacey	M	62A
	Yang, Sandra S.	PhD	11,12

OH0500 Central State University
Department of Fine & Perf. Arts
1400 Brush Row Rd
PO Box 1004
Wilberforce, OH 45384
(937) 376-6403   Fax: (937) 376-6415
www.centralstate.edu
E-mail: wcaldwell@centralstate.edu

4 Year Institution, Historically Black College
Member of NASM

Chair, Fine & Performing Arts: William Caldwell, 80A
Dean: Lovette Chinwah, 80A
Dir., Preparatory Division: Jennifer Cruz, 80E

PT	Berg, Chris	M	13,10,62D
Prof	Caldwell, William	M	36,39,61,60
PT	Cashwell, Brian	M	66A,29
	Crockett-Hardin, Michelle	M	61
Assoc Prof	Cruz, Jennifer	D	66A,66B,66D
Assoc Prof	Denza, William M.	D	64A,48,64E,64C
PT	Duncan, Andrew	M	63C,63D
Asst Prof	Hoffman, Lee	M	39,61,66C,54
Assoc Prof	Joseph, Mervyn	D	32,63A
PT	Keates, Peter	M	39,61
Asst Prof	Key, Ramon	M	37,60B
PT	Knorr, Eric	M	63A,49
PT	Melia, Hal	M	29A,29B,48
Assoc Prof	Moses, Lennard	D	50,65,20A,20G
PT	Ralinovsky, John	B	66F
Prof	Smith, James E.	M	29,70,47,12A
Adj	Taylor, Sean	M	32D,10A

OH0550 Cincinnati Christian University
Department of Music & Worship
2700 Glenway Ave
Cincinnati, OH 45204-3200
(513) 244-8165   Fax: (513) 244-8140
www.ccuniversity.edu
E-mail: musicworship@ccuniversity.edu

4 Year Institution

Chair: Kenneth E. Read, 80A

Inst PT	Adamson, Jared	B	66D
Inst PT	Barrick, Christopher	M	65
Inst PT	Coffey, Matthew	M	70
Inst PT	Crissinger, Paula K.	B	66A
Other	Geans, Jeannine	B	16
Prof	Gregory, Gary J.	M	44,13,60,37,63C
Inst PT	Hickman, Melinda	D	11,66A,66B,66D
Prof	Lang, Brenda J.	M	36,60A,61,13A
Inst PT	Lawrence, Wesley	M	36,61
Inst PT	Read, Katie	M	61
Prof	Read, Kenneth E.	D	13E,31A,10A,10F,13B
Inst PT	Thornburg, Benjamin	B	34

OH0600 Cleveland Institute of Music
11021 East Blvd
Cleveland, OH 44106-1705
(216) 791-5000   Fax: (216) 707-4519
www.cim.edu
E-mail: adrian.daly@case.edu

4 Year Institution, Graduate School
Member of NASM

Performer Diploma, Master of Music in Collaborative Piano, Artist Diploma, Master of Music in Composition, Master of Music in Performance, DMA in Composition, DMA in Performance, Master of Music Suzuki Violin Pedagogy, Master of Music in Orchestral Conducting

Dean: Adrian Daly, 80A,80B,80C
President: Joel Smirnoff, 80A
Dir., Admissions: William Fay, 80D
Interim Dean, Preparatory and Continunig Ed: Sandra Shapiro, 80E

	Babayan, Sergei	DIPL	66A
	Bamberger, David	B	39
	Banaszak, Gregory	B	64E
	Bassett, Matthew	M	65
	Berg, Marla	M	61
	Better, Donald	B	70
	Billings, Judson	M	66A
	Billions, Clifford	M	61
	Bishop, Ronald	M	63D
	Bourne, Trina	M	42
	Boyko, Lisa	B	62B
	Brndiar, John	B	63A
	Brown, Kathryn	M	61,66A
	Callahan, Timothy		35D
	Camus, Elizabeth	B	48,64B
	Castellano, Ann	M	66A
	Ceaser, Janina Kuzma	M	66H
	Charnofsky, Eric	M	12A
	Clouser, John		64D,48
	Cohen, Franklin	B	64C,48
	Cole, Vinson	DIPL	61
	Connor, Jennifer	D	13
	Conrad, Robert	B	35H
	Cutler, Timothy S.	D	13
	D'Antonio, Peter	D	35C
	Davidson, Harry		39
	DeJongh, Katherine	B	64A
	DeMattia, Alan	M	63B
	DeMio, Elizabeth	M	66C
	DeMio, Mark	B	64D
	Dimoff, Maximilian	B	62D,60B
	Dixon, Scott	M	62D,51
	Doctor, Kirsten	B	51,62B
	Dumm, Bryan	M	62C
	Egre, Bruce	B	35C,35G
	Ferguson, Mary Kay		64A
	Ferguson, Paul	M	63C
	Fink, Mary Kay		64A
	Fitch, Keith	D	10
	Friscioni, Emanuela		66A
	Fullard-Rosenthal, Annie	M	51
	Geber, Stephen	B	62C
	Gilbert, Daniel		64C
	Gilson, David W.	M	32I,60A
	Griffith, Marshall	D	13
	Guinn, Caryl		62E
	Haddad, Jamey		20
	Heinlein, Kenneth		63D
	Hill, Christine	B	66C
	Hirt, James	D	13A,13B
	Horvath, Kathleen	D	62D
	Houghton, Monica		10,13
	Huang, Grace	D	66A,66D,66B
	Huss, Adeline	M	13,66G
	Irvine, Jeffrey K.	M	62B
	Jackobs, Mark	B	62B,51
	Jones, Joella	M	66A
	Jones, Linda	M	66C
	Kantor, Paul	M	62A
	King, Richard	B	63B,49,41
	Kohn, Steven Mark	M	10B,35D
	Kondonassis, Yolanda	M	62E
	Konopka, Stanley	DIPL	62B
	Kosower, Mark	M	62C
	Kraut, Melissa	D	62C
	Kwuon, Joan		62A
	LaRosa, Massimo		63C,49
	Lenti, Elizabeth	M	36,66G
	Mann, Erik	M	70
	Markovich, Lucia		66A
	Meier-Sims, Kimberly R.	M	62A
	Mercer, Ida K.		62C
	Miller, Michael		63A,49
	Nelson, Beth P.	D	13A
	Nelson, Richard B.	D	13
	Nereim, Linnea	B	64C
	Nishimura, Derek Rikio	M	66A
	Oh, Jung Eun	D	61
	Ostrander, Jeanette Davis	M	13
	Peckham, Merry	M	51,62C
	Pompa-Baldi, Antonio	B	66A
	Pontremoli, Anita	B	66C,66A
	Preucil, William	C	62A
	Quereau, Quentin	D	12A
	Radosavljevich, Olga	M	66A
	Rainsong, Lisa	D	13
	Ramsey, Lynne	M	62B
	Rathbun, Jeffrey	M	64B
	Reed, Kevin		53
	Renner, Jack L.	B	35C,35D
	Rose, Stephen		62A
	Rosenwein, Frank	M	64B,41
	Ruzicka, Carol	D	62A,12A
	Sachs, Michael	B	63A,49
	Salaff, Peter	M	41
	Sato, Mari	B	51
	Schenly, Paul	M	66A
	Schiller, Mary	D	61
	Schulze, Sean	D	66A,66B
	Selvaggio, Robert	M	53
	Shapiro, Daniel	D	66A
	Sherwin, Jonathan		64D
	Simmons, John	M	39,12A
	Sims, Stephen S.	M	62A
	Slusser, Anthony	B	32I

	Smirnoff, Joel	M	62A
	Smith, Joshua	DIPL	64A,48
	Solis, Richard	B	63B,41,49
	Speirs, Phyllis	B	61
	Stees, Barrick R.	M	64D,48
	Stout, Richard	B	63C,49
	Sweigart, Brian		32I
	Teissonniere, Gerardo	M	66A,66B
	Topilow, Carl	M	60,38
	Updegraff, David	M	62A
	Urista, Diane J.	D	13
	Vernon, Robert	B	62B
	Vieaux, Jason	B	70,41
	Warner, Carolyn Gadiel	M	41
	Watts, Donald	D	13
	Weckstrom, Virginia	M	66C
	Weilerstein, Alisa		62C
	Weiner, Richard	M	65
	Weiss, Richard	B	62C,51
	Wilson, Todd	M	66G
	Wohlschlager, Cynthia	M	61
	Yancich, Paul	B	65A,50

OH0650 Cleveland State University
Department of Music
2121 Euclid Ave
Cleveland, OH 44115-2403
(216) 687-5039   Fax: (216) 687-9279
www.csuohio.edu/music
E-mail: j.toerek@csuohio.edu

4 Year Institution, Graduate School
Member of NASM

Master of Music in Composition, Master of Music in Performance, Master of Music in Music Education

Chair: Birch P. Browning, 80A
Coord., Graduate Studies: Victor H. Liva, 80C
Dir., Admissions: Kate Bill, 80D
Dir., Center for the Arts & Innovation: Kay W. Shames, 80E
Coord., Cleveland Contemporary Players: Andrew P. Rindfleisch, 80F

Lect	Adams, Gary	M	63D
Prof Emeritus	Alexander, J. Heywood	D	
Lect	Bachmann, George	M	70
Lect	Bailey, Brian K.	D	36,61
Lect	Barber, Daniel R.	D	66A,13D,12A,66G
Vstng Asst Prof	Baumgartner, Michael	D	10,12A,11
Prof Emeritus	Blaser, Albert	M	32E,11
Lect	Blaser, Melanie		32B
Lect	Brockett, David	M	63B
Assoc Prof	Browning, Birch P.	PhD	32,41
Lect	Burgett, Gwendolyn	M	65B
Lect	Bush, Peter	M	61
Lect	Carleton, Charles	M	62D
Lect	Cassidy, Robert	D	66A
Prof	Chang, Angelin	D	66A
Lect	Cheshier, Treneere J.	M	63B
Assoc Prof	Chesko, Elizabeth Unis	B	61,39
Lect	Coach, Leo	M	20,14
Lect	Couch, Charles A.	M	63A
Assoc Prof	D'Alessio, Greg P.	D	13,10,45,43
Lect	DeMio, Mark	M	64D
Lect	Dixon, Scott	M	62D
Lect	Dumm, Bryan	M	62C
Prof Emerita	Eckelmeyer, Judith A.	D	
Lect	Fraser, Robert	B	70
Lect	Freer, Thomas	B	65
Lect	Fung-Dumm, Molly	B	62A
Lect	Gabriel, Sean	M	64A
Lect	Golden, Bruce	M	50,65
Lect	Gotera, Jose	M	61
Lect	Guinn, Caryl	M	62E
Lect	Hahnemann, Hanneberit	D	62A
Lect	Harrell, David Alan	M	62C
Lect	Hill, Christine F.	M	66A
Assoc Prof Emeritus	Hisey, Ernest	M	
Lect	Holmes, Glenn	B	62D,70
Lect	Israel, Shachar		63C
Staff	Kabat, Stephen	M	66F
Lect	Kay, Lalene D.	M	33
Lect	Klima, Arthur	M	62B
Lect	Layman, Deborah	M	33
Assoc Prof	Liva, Victor H.	D	38,62A
Prof Emeritus	London, Edwin	D	
Prof Emeritus	Martin, William R.	D	12
Lect	Mayhew, Rebecca S.	M	64B
Lect	McGuire, David O.	B	64B
Prof	Meeker, Howard G.	M	37,60
Lect	Moore, Eileen Marie	M	61
Lect	Otto, Peter	M	62A
Lect	Patterson, Joanna	M	62B
Lect	Paukert, Noriko F.	B	61

Assoc Prof	Perrine, John Mark	D	47,29A,64E
Lect	Pla, Maria	M	66A,66D
Lect	Ransom, William		65
Prof	Rindfleisch, Andrew P.	D	10,13,43
Lect	Scharf, Margaret	D	66G
Lect	Schaufele, Fritz	M	55
Lect	Shernit, George R.	M	64E
Lect	Sherwin, Jonathan	M	64D
Prof Emeritus	Smith, Howie		
Lect	Smith, Jason D.	M	63C
Lect	Sugiyama, Yasuhito	M	63D
Vstng Asst Prof	Watts, Sarah	D	32
Lect	Wehrmann, Rock	M	66A
Lect	Zadinsky, Derek A.	B	62D
Lect	Zadrozny, Edward A.	B	63C
Prof	Ziolek, Eric E.	D	13,10,11

OH0680 College of Mount St Joseph
Department of Music
5701 Delhi Rd
Cincinnati, OH 45233-1670
(513) 244-4863   Fax: (513) 244-4222
www.msj.edu
E-mail: philip_amalong@mail.msj.edu

4 Year Institution

Chair: Philip Amalong, 80A

Asst Prof	Amalong, Philip	M	66A,66C,13,11,42
Adj	Arnow, Chad A.	M	63C
Adj	Bierschenk, Kenny P.		37
Assoc Prof	Brinksmeier, Ulrike	M	12A,11,62E,14,20
Adj	Brown, Robert	M	70
Adj	Elliott, Richard	M	65,50,37,11,32E
Adj	Grantham, Jennifer	M	64E,29
Adj	Lovely, Brian	M	29,10C,10D,70,35
Adj	Lyke, Toby Russell	B	10F,47,29A
Adj	Magg, Susan A.	M	64A
Adj	Miller, Christian	M	61,36
Adj	O'Neill, SC, Alice Ann M.	D	32E,62C,41,62D
Adj	Owens, Tiffany	M	61,13C,40
	Poynter, Lynn	M	32
Adj	Sachs, Daniel	D	66A,66D
Adj	Wampler, Kris A.	M	63,32E
Adj	Waugh, Bob L.	B	62A

OH0700 College of Wooster, The
Department of Music
525 E University St
Wooster, OH 44691
(330) 263-2419   Fax: (330) 263-2051
www.wooster.edu/music
E-mail: twood@wooster.edu

4 Year Liberal Arts Institution
Member of NASM

Chair: Thomas G. Wood, 80A

PT	Albert, Heidi A.	M	62C
	Benjamin, Eric J.	M	38
	Brndiar, John	M	63A
Assoc Prof	Culver, Carrie	D	61,39
PT	Curtis, Michael	D	70
Prof	Ditmer, Nancy	M	32,37,60B
Prof	Duda, Theodor	D	13B,13C,12A,20G
PT	Dykstra, Brian	D	66A
Prof	Gallagher, Jack	D	63A,10,10F,13,12A
PT	Gardener, Karen Roll	D	64E
	Garlock, Scott	D	47,63C
PT	Kay, Lalene	M	70,33
Prof	Lindberg, Jeffrey	M	47,38,63C,29A
PT	Lueschen, David	M	63B,63D,49,11
PT	Maffett, Jon D.	B	58
PT	Mason, Joyce D.	B	36
Prof	Mowrey, Peter C.	D	10,66A,13,34
PT	Peersen, Hild	D	64C
PT	Roblee, Thomas	M	65,50
PT	Rotavera-Krain, Denise	M	64A
PT	Silverman, Laura	M	66A
PT	Slawson, Gregory	M	66A
PT	Steward, Jack L.	D	62D
PT	Stuneck, Julia	M	64D
PT	Thorson, Valerie	M	66G
PT	Timm, Cynthia L.	M	32
PT	Wallin, Susan	B	61
PT	Warren, Cynthia	B	64B
Prof	Wood, Thomas G.	D	62A,62B,12A,11
Prof	Wright, Josephine	D	12,20G
PT	Yarnell, Pamela	M	66A,66D
Inst	Yozviak, Lisa	M	36,32

OH0750 Cuyahoga Comm College-Metropolitn
Department of Music
2900 Community College Ave
Cleveland, OH 44115-3196
(216) 987-4256   Fax: (216) 987-4370
www.tri-c.edu
E-mail: stephen.enos@tri-c.edu

2 Year Institution

Chair: Steve Enos, 80A

Asst Prof	Enos, Steve	M	13,47,63A,29,46
Lect	Kozak, Brian	M	12B,20G,29,35
Inst PT	Steinmetz, Demetrius	M	62D,29
Inst PT	Sterner, Dave	M	13,47,70,29
Inst PT	Volkar, Carie	M	61
Inst PT	Warren, Jacquelyn	M	66,29

OH0755 Cuyahoga Comm College-West
Department of Music
11000 W Pleasant Valley Rd
Parma, OH 44130-5114
(216) 987-5279   Fax: (216) 987-5717
www.tri-c.edu
E-mail: kira.seaton@tri-c.edu

2 Year Institution

Dean, Liberal Arts: Mark Ludwig, 80A
Dir., Preparatory Division: Emanuela Friscioni, 80E
Dir., Summer Programs & Preparatory Division: Kira J. Seaton, 80G

PT	Betts, L. David	M	63,49
PT	Bonsignore, Joseph	M	70,43
PT	Castellana, Joseph	M	66D,66A,63A
PT	Csicsila, Mell	M	65,50,13A
PT	Kearney, Linda	M	64A
PT	Kwon, MiYoung	M	66A,66D
PT	Laycock, Rand	D	11,12A,32C,38,62D
PT	May, Theresa	M	29,63A
PT	Porter, Janine	M	61,39
PT	Riley, Edward	M	34,35
PT	Saito, Miki	M	61,39
PT	Scott, Christopher	B	47
Asst Prof	Scott, Gary	M	47,63A,20G,29,35B
Asst Prof	Seaton, Kira J.	M	13A,13,11,36,61
PT	Sidoti, Vincent	D	13,11,37,64C,64E
PT	Stiver, David Keith		61,13C
PT	Tolmacheka, Tatyana	M	66A

OH0850 Denison University
Department of Music
PO Box M
Granville, OH 43023
(740) 587-6220   Fax: (740) 587-6509
www.denison.edu
E-mail: carlson@denison.edu

4 Year Institution

Chair: Andrew Carlson, 80A
Dir., Artist/Performance Series: Lorraine Wales, 80F
Dir., Summer Programs: Patti Brown, 80G

Inst	Andrews-Smith, Belinda	D	61,36,39
Adj	Atria, Karen	M	64D
Asst Prof	Bruhn, Christopher	D	12,14
Adj	Burleson, Brett	M	70
Assoc Prof	Carlson, Andrew	D	62A,51,20G,38
Adj	Carpenter, Tim		36
Inst	Carroll, Tom		47,29,70
	Cheng, Wei	D	36
Adj	Clark, Antoine T.	D	12A,72,48,64,64C
Inst	Cook, Casey		70
Asst Prof	Harper, Nelson	D	66A
Adj	Henkle, Stephanie		61
Assoc Prof	Hu, Ching-chu	D	13,10,60
Adj	Hudson, Jed	M	63C,63D
Adj	Kuyvenhoven, Cora	D	62C
Asst Prof	Lee, HyeKyung	D	13,34
Inst	Lopez, Richard		47,66A
Adj	Maaser, Leslie G.	D	64A
Adj	Mahiet, Damien	D	38
Adj	Mills, Peter	M	64E,47,29
Adj	Nesmith, David	M	63B
Adj	Price, Debra	M	62B
Adj	Ramsey, Sarah E.	M	66A
Adj	Richeson, Doug		62D
Adj	Rogers, Seth	M	65,50
Adj	Rosenberg, Steven	M	64B
Adj	Tucker, Debra		60A
Inst	Wade, Mark Alan	D	63A,12A,11,32,60B
Adj	Wines, Kevin N.	M	61
Adj	Yan, Ni	M	62E

OH0950 Heidelberg College
Department of Music
310 E Market St
Tiffin, OH 44883-2434
(419) 448-2073   Fax: (419) 448-2124
www.heidelberg.edu
E-mail: dmcconne@heidelberg.edu

4 Year Institution
Member of NASM

Chair: Douglas W. McConnell, 80A

Inst PT	Akins, Lori B.	M	48,64A
Inst PT	Banfield-Taplin, Carrie	M	11,63B
Prof	Bevelander, Brian E.	D	66A,10A,10B,13E,13G
Inst PT	Bleyle, William B.	M	65,50,37
Inst PT	DiCuirci, Michael	M	63C,63D,37,32E
Inst PT	Dusdieker, Carol E.	M	61
Inst PT	Galu, Ioana	M	62A
Prof Emeritus	Gibson, Henry	M	66A,66G
Inst PT	Grobler, Pieter J.	D	11,66C
Asst Prof	Grobler, Sophia	M	66A,66C,66D,20
Inst PT	Hanson, David B.	M	62D,70
Inst PT	Kruse, Steven	D	62B
Prof Emeritus	Mann, Jay	D	61,36
Prof	McConnell, Douglas W.	D	13,10
Inst PT	McConnell, Joan	M	66C,66G,13C,66D,13B
Asst Prof PT	Norin-Kuehn, Deborah	D	61
Prof Emeritus	Ohl, Dorothy E.	DIPL	66C
Prof Emeritus	Ohl, Ferris E.		60,36,61
Prof	Ohl, Vicki	M	13,66A,66D
Prof	Owen, John E.	D	60B,37,47,63A
Prof Emeritus	Pepper, Ronald D.	M	62A,62B,12A
Asst Prof	Ramsdell, Gregory A.	D	37,55D,32B,32D,32C
Asst Prof	Schuetz, Jennifer Hilbish	D	61,39
PT	Sieberg, Michael		66F,72
Assoc Prof	Specht, Barbara	D	11,38,64C,64E,48
Prof Emerita	Thiedt, Catherine E.	D	13,12A,66A,66G,31A
Inst PT	Tosser, Michele	M	64B
Asst Prof	van der Westhuizen, Petrus	M	66A,66C,66D,13B,13C
Inst PT	Ziebold, Barbara	M	62A

OH1000 Hiram College
Department of Music
PO Box 67
Hiram, OH 44234
(330) 569-5294   Fax: (330) 569-6093
www.hiram.edu/music
E-mail: music@hiram.edu

4 Year Institution
Member of NASM

Chair: Randall J. Fusco, 80A

PT	Anderson, Leeann	M	11,32B,62E,32A,32C
PT	Babich, Christina		62C
PT	Dreisbach, Paul C.	M	64B,64D,64E,64C,48
Asst Prof	Dreisbach, Tina Spencer	PhD	12A,14,32H
PT	Duro, David A.	M	63A
Prof	Fusco, Randall J.	M	13B,38,66A,12A,11
PT	Gotera, Jose		61,39,54,36
Assoc Prof Emeritus	Kelly, Justin M.	D	61,32H
PT	Kennard, Bryan E.		64A
PT	Lacan, Dale		70
PT	Manns, Olugbala		50
PT	Matras, Stanley		63B
PT	Petric, Paul L.	M	70
PT	Pongracz, Andrew L.	M	50,65
Asst Prof	Sonntag, Dawn Lenore	DMA	36,61,66C,10A,10
PT	Stanziano, Stephen	D	13A,13B,13C,10,62D
PT	Staron, Timothy		62A,62C,38
PT	Tittle, Sandra	M	66A,66G,66H,66D

OH1050 John Carroll University

Music Performance Area-Fine Arts
20700 N Park Blvd
Cleveland, OH 44118
(216) 397-1609
www.jcu.edu
E-mail: ccaporella@jcu.edu

4 Year Liberal Arts Institution

	Caporella, Cynthia Anne	M	36,12A,66A,66C
	Hoehler, Martin R.	B	37,47

OH1100 Kent State University-Kent

Hugh A. Glauser School of Music
PO Box 5190
Kent, OH 44242-0001
(330) 672-2172   Fax: (330) 672-7837
www.kent.edu/music
E-mail: dseachri@kent.edu

4 Year Institution, Graduate School
Member of NASM

Master of Arts in Composition, Master of Arts in Music Theory, Master of Arts in Ethnomusicology, Master of Music in Performance, Master of Music in Conducting, Master of Music in Music Education, PhD in Music Education, PhD in Music Theory-Composition

Director: Denise A. Seachrist, 80A
Coord., Undergraduate Studies: Dana Brown, 80B,80D
Coord., Graduate Studies: Michael Chunn, 80C
Marketing Assistant: Richardo Sepulveda, 80F,80G
Assistant Director: Thomas Janson, 80H

Prof	Albrecht, Theodore	D	12
Asst Prof Adj	Bachmann, George	M	70,11
Assoc Prof	Baker, Charles	M	47,29
Asst Prof Adj	Bazan, Dale	M	32
Asst Prof Adj	Berg, Marla	M	61
Assoc Prof	Birch, Sebastian A.	DMA	13,10,34,13B,13A
Asst Prof	Brown, Dana	M	66D,66A
Prof	Chunn, Michael	M	41,63A
Asst Prof	Clark, Joe	M	16
Asst Prof Adj	Cosenza, Frank	M	37
Assoc Prof	Culver, Timothy	M	61
Prof	DeBolt, David	M	11,41,64D
Asst Prof Adj	DeMio, Mark	M	64D
Assoc Prof	Devore, Richard O.	D	13,34,10,20G,13F
Asst Prof Adj	DiCesare, John	B	63D
Asst Prof Adj	Donofrio, Anthony	D	13,11
Prof	Dressler, Jane	D	12A,61
	Evans, Amanda		16
Asst Prof Adj	Ferguson, Vivian	D	32
Asst Prof Adj	Foreman, Kelly	D	20
Asst Prof	Fucci, Melissa	M	11,20
Lect	Glann, Kerry	M	20,36,39
Asst Prof Adj	Grossman, Liza	M	38
Assoc Prof	Grutzmacher, Patricia Ann	D	32,41,64B,37,20
Asst Prof Adj	Heisler, Jeff A.	D	64E,42,37
Asst Prof Adj	Herrick, Matthew	D	32
Asst Prof Adj	Howard, Karen	D	32
Prof	Janson, Thomas	D	13,10A
Artist in Res	Jin, Yu	B	62B,42
Asst Prof Adj	Jones, Claire	D	38
Asst Prof Adj	Kolthammer, Stacy	D	32
Assoc Prof	Kramer, Kenneth	M	11,36,61
Asst Prof Adj	Kuntz, Tammy	D	32
Assoc Prof	Larmee, Kent	M	11,41,63B
Assoc Prof	Lee, Donna	D	66A,66B,66C,42
Asst Prof	Lee, Michael E.	M	11,32E
Asst Prof	Lisius, Peter	M	16
Assoc Prof	Lorenz, Ralph	D	13,34,10,13F,13D
Asst Prof Adj	Lukowicz, Thomas	M	63D
Assoc Prof	MacPherson, Scott A.	D	36
Asst Prof Adj	Martinovic, Nada	D	32
Assoc Prof	McCloskey, Diane L.	M	64A,41
Asst Prof	McPherson, Eve	D	11,20
Asst Prof Adj	Miller, Ethan	M	20,29
Asst Prof	Mitchell, David	M	63C
Asst Prof Adj	Moehle, Matthew	D	32
Prof	Mukuna, Kazadi Wa	D	14,20A,20B,11
Asst Prof Adj	Nanongkham, Priwan Keo	D	20,14
Asst Prof Adj	Neiman, Marcus	M	37,60B
Asst Prof Adj	Noh, Gerrey	M	13
Asst Prof Adj	Peterson, Amber Dahlen	D	32
Asst Prof Adj	Polanka, William Mark	D	13
Asst Prof Adj	Post, William	D	13
Assoc Prof	Quesada, Milagros	D	11,32,36
Asst Prof	Resta, Craig	M	32
Asst Prof Adj	Roberts, J. Christopher	D	32
Artist in Res	Robinson, Cathy Meng	M	62C,42
Artist in Res	Robinson, Keith	B	62C,42
Assoc Prof	Rounds, Theodore	M	50,65
Asst Prof Adj	Rounds, Tyler	M	11,20
	Schatt, Matthew D.	D	32
Asst Prof Adj	Schildt, Matthew	D	13
Assoc Prof	Seachrist, Denise A.	D	12C,14,20G
Asst Prof	Seeds, Laurel M.	M	66D,61
Asst Prof Adj	Selvaggio, Robert	M	47,29
Asst Prof	Shahriari, Andrew	D	11,20
Asst Prof Adj	Shank, Jennifer S.	D	32
Asst Prof Adj	Stoll, Joni L.	D	32
Asst Prof	Sundet, Danna	M	64B
	Tackett, Jeff	M	34
Asst Prof Adj	Teare, Racquel	M	66D
Inst Adj	Thomas, Bryan	B	62D
Asst Prof Adj	Tiffe, Janine	D	20
Asst Prof Adj	Troyer, Lara	D	61
Asst Prof	Vaccaro, Brandon C.	D	13,10,34,13B,13A
	Vardi, Amitai	M	64C,41
Asst Prof Adj	Venesile, Christopher J.	M	32
	Vesely, Blaine	B	66F
Prof	Walker, Linda B.	D	32,36
Asst Prof	White, Jay G.	D	61,67H
Asst Prof Adj	Wilding, James	D	13
Prof	Wiley, Frank	D	13,10,38,60B,43
Assoc Prof	Wong, Jerry	D	66A,66B,66C,42
Asst Prof	Yeh, I-Chen	D	66A,66C
Asst Prof Adj	Yoon, Sunmin	D	20,11

OH1110 Kent State University-Salem

Department of Music
2491 State Route 45 S
Salem, OH 44460-9421
(330) 332-0361   Fax: (330) 332-9256
www.salem.kent.edu
E-mail: mfucci@kent.edu

2 Year Regional Institution

Dean: Jeffrey L. Nolte, 80A
Music Contact: Melissa Fucci

Lect	Fucci, Melissa	M	11,36
Adj PT	Murray, Eric	M	14

OH1120 Kent State University-Tuscarawas

Department of Music
330 University Dr NE
New Philadelphia, OH 44663
(330) 339-3391   Fax: (330) 339-3321
www.tusc.kent.edu

2 Year Institution

Dean: Gregg L. Andrews, 80A

Asst Prof	Quesada Agostini, Milagros	D	14,32

OH1200 Kenyon College

Department of Music
Storer Hall
1 College Dr
Gambier, OH 43022
(740) 427-5197   Fax: (740) 427-5512
www.kenyon.edu/music.xml
E-mail: maloneyd@kenyon.edu

4 Year Institution

Coord., Applied Music Program: Donna J. Maloney, 80A
Chair: Reginald L. Sanders, 80A

Inst Adj	Biava, Luis Gabriel	M	62C,51
Prof	Buehrer, Theodore E.	D	13,10,29,63A,34
Prof Emerita	Cai, Camilla	D	11,12
Inst Adj	Clark, Antoine	D	64C,64E,48
Inst Adj	Cox, Robert D.		70
Inst Adj	Dachtyl, Cary	D	65,50
Inst Adj	Dachtyl, Linda D.	M	65
Inst Adj	Dingler, Diane	M	61
Asst Prof	Feller, Ross	D	13,15
Inst Adj	Hartman, Andrew	B	70
Prof	Heuchemer, Dane O.	D	11,12A,12,37,67

Prof	Locke, Benjamin R.	D	13A,60,36,38,61
Inst Adj	MacMullen, Jeffrey	M	61
Inst Adj	Mahaney, Cynthia	D	61
Inst Adj	Marcellana, Jennifer	M	61
Inst Adj	McCandless, Terry	M	66G,66H
Assoc Prof	Mendonca, Maria Alice	D	14F,20D,15
Inst Adj	Mentschukoff, Andrej		70
Inst Adj	Paescht, Matthew	B	62D,70
Inst Adj	Pelfrey, Patricia	B	66A,66C
Inst Adj	Poole, Jeff		70
Inst Adj	Rearick, Loretta A.	M	66A
Inst Adj	Redman, Carolyn	D	61
Inst Adj	Reed, Jim	B	63A
Inst Adj	Reitz, John	M	66A
Inst Adj	Ripley, Vanessa G.		62A,62B
Assoc Prof	Sanders, Reginald L.	D	11,12
Inst Adj	Seckel, Tamara J.	M	61
Inst Adj	Shonkwiler, Joel	D	63C,63D
Inst Adj	Sletner, Ariane	M	62A,62B
Inst Adj	Sorton, Bailey	M	64B,48
Inst Adj	Stimson, Ann	D	64A,41
Inst Adj	Thompson, Janet	B	62E,66A
Inst Adj	Wick, Heidi	D	63B,49

OH1250 Lake Erie College
Department of Fine Arts
Box 354/391 W Washington St
Painesville, OH 44077
(440) 352-3361
www.lec.edu
E-mail: pgothard@lec.edu

4 Year Institution

Director: Paul Gothard, 80A

Associate Dean: Maria De La Camara, 80H

Prof	Gothard, Paul		13A,13,10F,11,36

OH1300 Lorain County Community College
Department of Music
1005 Abbe Rd N
Elyria, OH 44035
(440) 366-7108   Fax: (440) 366-4663
www.lorainccc.edu
E-mail: rbecks@lorainccc.edu

2 Year Institution

Chair: Robert Beckstrom, 80A

PT	Adams, Daniel B.	D	11,70
PT	Archibald, Laurie		66A
Assoc Prof	Davis, Nancy	M	13A,11,36,47
Assoc Prof	Evans, Gerald	D	13,10,12A,14,66D
PT	Fuoco, Anthony	M	11,66A

OH1330 Lourdes College
Department of Music
6832 Convent Blvd
Sylvania, OH 43560-2853
(419) 885-3211   Fax: (419) 824-3513
www.lourdes.edu
E-mail: kbiscay@lourdes.edu

4 Year Liberal Arts Institution

Chair: Karen T. Biscay, 80A

PT	Barone, Ann Carmen	M	11,32A
FT	Biscay, Karen T.	M	13,11,12A,36,61
PT	Currie, Randolph	M	13,10,66G
PT	Dettinger, Mary Joyce	M	32A,32B,66A,31A
PT	Hetrick, Mark	M	11,61,66C
PT	Hummer, Ken	B	11,70
PT	Justice, Roberta	M	33
PT	Monachino, Paul	M	13,10A,66,60
PT	Ng, Michelle	B	66A

OH1350 Malone University
Department of Music
2600 Cleveland Ave NW
Canton, OH 44709
(330) 471-8476   Fax: (330) 471-8477
www.malone.edu/music
E-mail: ddonelson@malone.edu

4 Year Institution

Chair & Dir., Undergraduate Studies: David W. Donelson, 80A,80B

Prof	Ayers, Jesse M.	D	13,10,13C
Assoc Prof	Ballard, Jack	D	35,34A,34D,13L,34E
	Benson, Michael L.	D	66A,66B,12A,11,66
Adj	Carpenter, Tyler	M	65
Inst	Coen, Anne		11,31A
Adj	Cord, Adam	M	70
Adj	Curtis, Michael	D	70
Prof	Donelson, David W.	D	36,32D,60A
Adj	Georgieva-Smith, Ralitsa	M	66A
Adj	Grandmason, Nicole		66A
Adj	Houck, Alan	M	37
Adj	Kana, Dave	M	64E
Adj	Kroft, Pat	M	64D
Adj	Moore, Janice	M	62A,62B
Adj	Nauman, Sharon	B	62C
Assoc Prof	Nunez, Rachel	M	61,36,31A
Adj	Pylinski, Thomas	B	63C,63D
Adj	Rose, Angela	M	61,66D
Adj	Roshong, Janelle	M	32A,32B
Adj	Sarver, Julie	M	64A
Adj	Schroeder, Karen	M	13C
Adj	Schulz, Mark Alan	M	34D,35G,35D,62C,29B
Adj	Seymour, David	B	35D,35G
Adj	Spencer, Charles	M	61
Adj	Thewes, Mark	M	66G
Adj	Tryon, Colleen	M	64C
Adj	Willard, Michael L.	M	63A,49,63
Adj	Wohlschlager, Cynthia	M	61

OH1400 Marietta College
Edward MacTaggart Department of Music
215 5th St
Marietta, OH 45750
(740) 376-4696   Fax: (740) 376-4529
www.marietta.edu
E-mail: music@marietta.edu

4 Year Institution

Chair: Daniel G. Monek, 80A

Lect PT	Brannen, Randall	M	64C,64E
FT	Brasington, Merewyn	M	66C,66D,13C,66A
Prof Emeritus	Buelow, William L.	M	13A,13,10,66A,29
Lect PT	Coddington, Robert	M	70,41
Prof Emeritus	Cummings, Dean	D	12A,13,63C
Lect PT	Dearth, Christopher	M	63C
Lect PT	Goodman, Lindsey	M	64A
Lect PT	Herceg, Melissa	M	64A
Lect PT	Irvine, Jane	M	66A,32B
Assoc Prof	Kimball, Marshall C.	M	32,37,47,60B
Lect PT	Majoy, Jocelyn	M	64B,64D
Prof	Monek, Daniel G.	D	36,61,12A,60
Lect PT	Puls, Cyndi	M	11,62C,62D
Lect PT	Puls, David	M	11,62B
Prof Emeritus	Rader, Stephen M.	D	54
Lect PT	Tadlock, David	D	61,13C,54,39
Lect PT	Thacker, Elizabeth	M	61,32
Asst Prof	Yorgasen, Brent	D	13,10
Lect PT	Young, Karen	M	66A,66D,66B
	Zyla, Luke	M	63B

OH1450 Miami University

Department of Music
109 Presser Hall
501 S Patterson St
Oxford, OH 45056
(513) 529-3014   Fax: (513) 529-3027
www.muohio.edu/music
E-mail: bruce.murray@MiamiOH.edu

4 Year Institution, Graduate School
Member of NASM

Master of Music in Performance, Master of Music in Music Education

Dean: James P. Lentini, 80A
Chair: Bruce J. Murray, 80A
Dir., Graduate Studies Music Education: Kay L. Edwards, 80C
Dir., Graduate Studies: Brenda Mitchell, 80C
Dir., Artist/Performance Series: Patti Liberatore, 80F
Associate Chair: Christopher Tanner, 80H

Senior Lect	Acord, Alison	M	61
Prof	Albin, William R.	D	14,50,65
Vstng Inst	Andres, Rebecca	M	64A
Assoc Prof	Averbach, Ricardo Franco	D	11,38,60B
Prof	Bausano, William	D	60A,32C,36,61
Vstng Asst Prof	Beus, Stephen	D	66A
Asst Prof	Bloland, Per A.	D	34
Assoc Prof	Boge, Claire L.	D	13
Vstng Inst	Bowman, Randy	M	64A
Accompanist	Caldwell, Brad	M	66C
Assoc Prof	Chang, Pansy Y.	M	62C,51
Assoc Prof	Davis, Glen Roger	D	13,10
Vstng Inst	Davis, Jackie	M	62E
Assoc Prof	Edwards, Kay L.	D	32
Assoc Prof	Garcia, Thomas George Caracas	D	14,20H
Prof	Gingras, Michele	M	64C,42
Prof	Green, Richard D.	D	12A,12,12C
Prof	Harris, Mary	M	32,62B,51,42
Lect	Hoover, Elizabeth	D	12
Asst Prof	Jones, Jeremy D.	M	36,32D
Vstng Inst	Kelly, Michael	D	13A,13B,13C
Prof	Kernodle, Tammy L.	D	11,12,29A,29D
Vstng Inst	Kiradjieff, Amy	M	62A
Senior Inst	Lee, Robert E.	M	32,61
	Lentini, James P.	D	13,10,70,34
Vstng Prof	Lim, Tze Yean	D	62A
Asst Prof	Long, Jeremy A.	D	64E,47,42
Vstng Asst Prof	Luna, Audrey	M	61
Lect	Lytle, Stephen	D	37,48
Accompanist	MacPhail, Heather	M	66C,42
Assoc Prof	Mitchell, Brenda	D	32
Assoc Prof	Morales-Matos, Jaime	M	63C,63D,13C,42
Prof	Murray, Bruce J.	D	66A
Prof	Olcott, James L.	M	47,63A,49,42
Vstng Inst	Olt, Timothy J.	M	63D,49,72,67E
Assoc Prof	Opatz-Muni, Mari	M	39,61
Assoc Prof	Phillips, Gregory	M	49,63B,13A
Prof	Ridilla, Andrea	M	64B,48
Asst Prof	Schillinger, Christin M.	D	64D,13A
Vstng Asst Prof	Slagowski, Joshua	D	32E,32B,32C
Assoc Prof	Smolder, Benjamin W.	M	61,40
Inst	Sommerfeldt, Jerod	D	13,34
Prof	Speck, Gary A.	M	60,32C,48
Assoc Prof	Tan, Siok Lian	D	66A,66B,66D
Assoc Prof	Tanner, Christopher	D	14,50
Assoc Prof	Thurmer, Harvey	D	51,62A
Vstng Inst	Ullery, Steve	M	62D

OH1600 Mount Vernon Nazarene Univ

Department of Music
800 Martinsburg Rd
Mount Vernon, OH 43050-9509
(740) 392-6868   Fax: (740) 392-1689
www.mvnu.edu
E-mail: btocheff@mvnu.edu

4 Year Liberal Arts Institution

Dean, Arts & Humanities: Barney Cochran, 80A
Chair, Music: Robert Tocheff, 80A

Adj	Bishara, Aaron		65
Adj	Blaydes, Sharon		62A,62B,51
Adj	Brunetto, Rick		46
Asst Prof	Cameron, Virginia	M	60A,36,61,40,11
Adj	Cox, Robert		70
	Fry, Ben		62C
Adj	Hamilton, Ryan		63C
	Jantsch, Nancy	D	61
Prof	Koh-Baker, JoAnn Hwee Been	D	11,12A,66A,13A,13B
	Lain, Larry		61
Prof	Liles, B. David	D	61,31A,39
Adj	McCann, Kimberly		63B
Adj	Mentschukoff, Andrej		70
Adj	Myatt, Traci		66D,66C
Adj	Packard, Jennifer	M	64A,41
Asst Prof	Packard, John	D	37,49,63A,60B,10F
	Paetsch, Matt		62D,70
Adj	Pelfrey, Patricia		66A
Adj	Raker, Robert		64D
	Redman, Carolyn		61
Adj	Rosser, Geraldine	D	10A,66C
Adj	Sorton, Bailey		64B
Adj	Thompson, Janet		62E
Prof	Tocheff, Robert	D	60,11,32,36,66D
Adj	Tryon, Colleen	M	64C
Prof	Wood, Stanley D.	D	32,36,66D,13C,34

OH1650 Muskingum University

Department of Music
163 Stormont St
New Concord, OH 43762
(740) 826-8095   Fax: (740) 826-8109
www.muskingum.edu
E-mail: joycea@muskingum.edu

4 Year Institution, Graduate School
Member of NASM

Master of Arts in Education

Chair: Joyce L. Alesandrini, 80A

Assoc Prof	Abeyaratne, Harsha D.	D	66,13,13C
Prof	Alesandrini, Joyce L.	D	13,64D,66A
Adj	Bell, Jane H.	M	66A,66D
Adj	Bock, James D.	M	63D
Adj	Charles, Lewis O.	B	70,51
Adj	Charles, Nicole M.	D	64A,48
Adj	Dudack, Matthew J.	M	65,50
Adj	Flora, James	M	61
Adj	Gallant, Mark W.	D	66G,32
Asst Prof	Highben, Zebulon M.	D	36,40,61,32D
Prof	Jones, Robert Owen	M	36,61
Adj	Jones, Sheila L.	B	62A,62B
Adj	Kason, Don T.	M	63A,47
Adj	Perez, Olga	M	61,40,32B
Adj	Ruetz, Andrew	B	63C,63D
Inst PT	Schlacks, Mary M.	M	14,48,64C,11
Prof	Schumann, Laura E.	D	38,60,62A,12A,13A
Adj	Torres, Michael Rene	D	64E,48,10
Asst Prof	Turrill, David	D	37,32E,60,63A
Asst Prof	Wilcox-Jones, Carol	M	61,39,54

OH1700 Oberlin College

Conservatory of Music
77 West College St
Oberlin, OH 44074-1588
(440) 775-8200   Fax: (440) 775-8942
www.oberlin.edu/con
E-mail: conservatory@oberlin.edu

4 Year Institution, Graduate School
Member of NASM

Master of Music in Historical Performance, Master of Music in Conducting, Master of Music in Teaching, Master of Music in Opera

Dean: David H. Stull, 80A
Associate Dean: Andrea Kalyn, 80B,80E,80H
Associate Dean: Mary Kay Gray, 80H
Associate Dean: Gloria Kim, 80H
Associate Dean: Michael Lynn, 80H

Assoc Prof	Adkins, Darrett		62C
Prof	Alegant, Brian	D	13
Inst PT	Aron, Stephen	M	70
Assoc Prof	Ashby, Jay		29
Vstng Prof	Bartz, Gary		29
Prof	Bennett, Peggy D.	D	32
Prof	Bishop, Ronald	M	63D
Asst Prof	Bowlin, David Henderson		62A
Assoc Prof	Breitman, David	D	66,66E,66A
Prof	Cadwallader, Allen	D	13
Other	Campana, Deborah	D	16
Assoc Prof	Champagne, Salvatore C.	M	61
Inst PT	Chastain, Kathleen		64A
Assoc Prof	Cheng, Angela	M	66A

Assoc Prof	Chow, Alvin	M	66A
Prof	Christie, James David	D	66G
Prof	Coleman, Randolph E.	D	13,10
Asst Prof	Colton, Kendra	M	61
Assoc Prof	Cox, Arnie	PhD	13,12C
Prof	Darcy, Warren J.	D	13
Prof	DeSano, James	B	63C
Vstng Teacher	Dixon, Scott	M	62D
Prof	Dominguez, Peter	M	47,29
Prof	Duphil, Monique	DIPL	66A
Asst Prof	Eldan, Amir		62C
Prof	Erwin, Joanne	D	32,60
Assoc Prof	Eubanks, Robin		29
Assoc Prof	Ferrazza, Robert		29
Assoc Prof	Field, Jonathon	M	39
Asst Prof	Fraser, Jennifer	D	14
Prof	Fulkerson, Gregory	M	62A,41
Vstng Teacher	Gerk, Sarah		12
Vstng Asst Prof	Goeringer, Lyn		10,34
Prof	Haddad, Jamey		53
Asst Prof	Harris, Jason W.		60,36,61
Asst Prof	Hart, Billy		29
Asst Prof	Hartt, Jared C.	D	13
Assoc Prof	Hawkins, Richard	M	64C
Asst Prof	Heetderks, David	D	10A,13C,13E,60
Asst Prof	Heinzelmann, Sigrun B.	D	13
Prof	Highfill, Philip	M	66C,60B
Prof	Howsmon, James	M	66C
Assoc Prof	Jimenez, Raphael		60
Lect	Jones, Ralph Miles	M	14
Vstng Asst Prof	Jones, Sean		29
Lect	Kalyn, Andrea	D	12A,11
Assoc Prof	Kerchner, Jody L.	D	32,41
Asst Prof	Kondonassis, Yolanda	M	62E
Assoc Prof	LeFebvre, Timothy	M	61
Asst Prof	Levine, Josh	M	10
Assoc Prof	Leydon, Rebecca	D	13,13F,10C,10D
Assoc Prof	Lopez, Thomas Handman	D	10B,34,10,34A
Assoc Prof	Lubben, Joseph	D	13
	Lubin, Howard	M	66C,66A
Inst PT	Lynn, Kathie	M	67D,67C,64A
Prof	Lynn, Michael	B	67B,67E
Assoc Prof	Macdonald, Claudia	D	12
Prof	Mahy, Daune	D	61
Lect	Manderen, Michael		67D
Assoc Prof	Manz, Lorraine	M	61
Prof	Margolis, Sanford	M	66A
Asst Prof	McAlister, Andrea	D	66A,66C
Prof	McDonald, Marilyn	M	62A,67B
Assoc Prof	McGuire, Charles E.	D	12
Assoc Prof	Meints, Catharina	B	67A,67B
Asst Prof	Miyake, Jan	D	13
Asst Prof	Montoya, Kathryn	M	67C
Prof	Nielson, Lewis	PhD	10
Asst Prof	O'Leary, James		12A
Prof	Pandolfi, Roland		63B
Asst Prof	Pau, Andrew Yat-Ming	M	13
Prof	Plank, Steven E.	D	12A
Assoc Prof	Poper, Roy	M	63A,49,41
Vstng Teacher	Reynolds, Dennis		29,47
Prof	Rosen, Marlene Ralis	M	61
Prof	Rosen, Michael	M	50,65
Vstng Teacher	Rowell, Tracy		62D
Prof	Sakakeeny, George	B	64D,48,41
Vstng Teacher	Samuels, Paul		47
Prof	Shannon, Robert	M	66A
Prof	Slowik, Peter	M	62B,41
Assoc Prof	Song, Haewon	M	66A
Assoc Prof	Spano, Robert V.	M	60
Inst PT	Sperl, Thomas		62D
Assoc Prof	Still, Alexa	D	64A,20I
Assoc Prof	Strauss, Michael		62B,42
Asst Prof	Swendsen, Peter V.		34
Prof	Takacs, Peter	M	66A,41
Prof	Vitek, Milan	DIPL	62A
Assoc Prof	Wall, Daniel		29
Assoc Prof	Walters, Robert		64B
Assoc Prof	Weiss, Timothy	M	60,48
Assoc Prof	Wiggins, Webb	M	66H
Vstng Asst Prof	Wubbels, Eric		10

OH1750 Ohio Dominican College

Department of Music
1216 Sunbury Rd
Columbus, OH 43219-2086
(614) 251-4500   Fax: (614) 252-0776
www.ohiodominican.edu
E-mail: gibsonr2@ohiodominican.edu

4 Year Institution

Chair: Phillipa Burgess, 80A

Asst Prof	Burgess, Phillipa	D	36,55C,14C,12A,20
Adj	Mahaney, Cynthia	DMA	61

OH1800 Ohio Northern University

Department of Music
525 S Main St
Ada, OH 45810
(419) 772-2151   Fax: (419) 772-2488
www.onu.edu
E-mail: t-hunt.1@onu.edu

4 Year Institution
Member of NASM

Chair: Tom A. Hunt, 80A

Lect PT	Altstaetter, Dean E.	M	66A
Lect PT	Altstaetter, Lucinda J.	M	64A,48
Lect PT	Ashmore, Lance	M	61
Lect PT	Ashmore, Pamela J.	M	66A,66C
Prof	Bates, Charles N.	D	11,32E,37,47,60
Artist in Res	Butler, Lloyd S.	M	38,54
Asst Prof	Casey, Rebecca L.	D	66A,13,66D,66C
Prof	D'Arca, Denise	D	32,36,11,42
Lect PT	Eichelberger, Mary Jane	B	66A,66G
Lect PT	Gramm, Carol J.	M	61
Vstng Asst Prof	Kosmyna, David J.	D	63A,63B,49,47,29
Prof	Kratzer, Dennis L.	M	36,61,54,60A,40
Lect PT	Laukhuf, Dale		63C,63D,32E
Artist in Res	Osbun-Manley, Kirsten E.	M	39,61,54
Lect PT	Pinkney, Rachel	M	62C,62D
Lect PT	Russell, Thomas	B	35A
Lect PT	Stein, William	M	64C,32E
Lect PT	Sycks, Linda	B	64B
Lect PT	Waters, Sarah S.	D	13B,13C,12A
Lect PT	Yost, Jennifer	M	64D
Lect PT	Zank, Jeremy		51,62A,62B
Prof	Zank, MJ Sunny	D	13,20,10,12A,43
Lect PT	Zickafoose, Edward	M	66A,70

OH1850 Ohio State University-Columbus

School of Music
110 Weigel Hall
1866 College Rd
Columbus, OH 43210-1170
(614) 292-7664   Fax: (614) 292-1102
music.osu.edu
E-mail: reed.901@osu.edu

4 Year Institution, Graduate School
Member of NASM

Master of Arts in Music Education, Master of Arts in Music Theory, Master of Music in Composition, Master of Music in Performance, Master of Music in Conducting, PhD in Music Theory, PhD in Music Education, DMA in Composition, DMA in Conducting, DMA in Performance, PhD in Musicology, Master of Arts in Musicology

Director: Richard L. Blatti, 80A
Dir., Graduate Studies: C. Patrick Woliver, 80C,80H
Associate Director: Timothy Leasure, 80H,80B

Prof Emeritus	Adelson, Edward H.	M	62B
Assoc Prof	Ainger, Marc	D	10,34,35
Assoc Prof	Akins, James	M	63D
Prof Emeritus	Alch, Marion R.		61
Lect	Archambault, Ellen J.	D	13
Prof	Ashby, Arved M.	D	12A
Prof	Atkinson, Charles M.	PhD	12
Lect	Bak, Edward		61
Prof Emeritus	Baker, William		64B
Prof Emeritus	Battenberg, Thomas V.	M	47,63A,29
Lect	Beardslee, Thomas	B	14
Lect	Beaver, Dale		
Lect	Behan, Ryan J.	D	66C
Assoc Prof Emeritus	Benner, Charles		32
Lect	Bester, Matthew		12A
Prof	Blatti, Richard L.	M	60,37
Asst Prof	Bletstein, Beverly	D	32,36
Assoc Prof Emeritus	Blombach, Ann K.	D	13A,13,34,12F,12
Lect	Blosser, C. Andrew	B	61
Prof	Boone, Graeme M.		12
Assoc Prof	Bruenger, David	D	34
Prof Emeritus	Burkart, Richard	D	63A
Lect	Burleson, Brett	B	70
Prof Emeritus	Butler, David		13K,13C,13
Prof Emeritus	Casey, Maurice T.	M	60,36
Assoc Prof	Clampitt, David	D	13
Prof Emeritus	Conable, William E.	D	38,62C,32
Assoc Prof Emeritus	Cooper, Marianne G.	M	32,36
Prof Emeritus	Costanza, A. Peter	D	32,34

Lect	Cummiskey, Tim	M	70
Prof Emerita	Davis, Eileen	M	61
Asst Prof	Devaney, Johanna C.	D	13B,13E,13G,13K,13L
Assoc Prof Emeritus	Dobos, Lora Gingerich	D	13
Prof Emeritus	Droste, Paul E.	D	37,63D
Assoc Prof	Duchi, Joseph J.	M	63C
Lect	Ebright, Matthew		66C
Assoc Prof	Edwards, Jan	D	32
Prof	Ellis, Mark Carlton	D	32
Assoc Prof	Emoff, Ronald	D	14
	Erken, Emily	B	12
Lect	Essex, Malinda W.		32B,32C
Prof	Flowers, Patricia J.	D	32
Lect	Flugge, Mark	M	29,66A
Assoc Prof Emeritus	Forsythe, Jere L.	D	32
Asst Prof	Fosler-Lussier, Danielle		12A,12
Lect	Furlong, Allison		12A
Prof Emeritus	Gallagher, James S.	M	36
Assoc Prof Emeritus	Gano, Peter W.	D	12A,12
Asst Prof	Gawboy, Anna	D	13
Prof	Gerber, Timothy A.	D	32
Prof	Gillespie, Robert A.	D	32,62A
Prof	Glaser, Steven	M	
Assoc Prof	Green, Alan	M	16
Assoc Prof Emerita	Green, Burdette L.	D	13A,13,13J,12B
Prof Emeritus	Haddad, George		66A
Assoc Prof	Haddock, Marshall	M	60,38,64C
Lect	Hahn, Christina		66C
Prof Emeritus	Hare, Robert		13
Prof	Harris, Donald	M	
Lect	Harrison, Jane		12A
Assoc Prof	Hartig, Caroline A.	D	64C,42
Prof Emeritus	Held, Wilbur C.		66G,31A
Assoc Prof	Henniss, Bruce G.	M	63B
Prof Emeritus	Hightshoe, Robert B.		32
Assoc Prof	Hill, James S.	M	64E
Lect	Hoch, Christopher	B	32E
Assoc Prof	Hong, Caroline	D	11,66A,66C,66D
Assoc Prof Emeritus	Huff, Jay		13
Prof	Huron, David	D	13,12F
Lect	Johnson, Kris	M	29
Lect	Johnson, Nicholas		12A
Prof	Jones, Katherine Borst	M	64A
Assoc Prof	Jones, Scott A.	D	37,60B,32E
Lect	Keith, Kristopher D.		29
Asst Prof	Kinney, Daryl W.	D	32G,32E,62A
Lect	Krygier, Joe		29,65
Lect	Kung, Hsiong-Ning	M	14
Assoc Prof	Leasure, Timothy	M	63A,49
Prof Emeritus	LeBlanc, Robert L.	M	37,41,63D
Assoc Prof Emeritus	Lehr, Joan	D	32
Assoc Prof Emeritus	Levey, Joseph A.		13
Prof Emeritus	Lowder, Jerry E.	D	32,66D
Prof Emeritus	Maas, Martha C.	D	12A,12,55
Prof Emeritus	Main, Alexander	D	12A,12
Assoc Prof Emeritus	Major, James	M	32,36
Assoc Prof Emeritus	Marvin, Marajean M.		61
Lect	Masters, Jim		63C
Prof Emeritus	Mazo, Margarita L.	D	12,14
Prof Emeritus	McClure, Theron		62D,13
Prof	McCoy, Scott	D	61
Prof	McDaniel, William T.	D	20A,29,29A
Prof Emeritus	McGinnis, Donald E.		37
Prof	Mikkelson, Russel	D	37,60
Assoc Prof Emeritus	Moore, James L.	D	50,65
Lect	Morgan, John		70
Lect	Murray, Michael		12C
Lect	Norton, Jeanne	B	62E
Lect	Parry, A. Scott	M	61
Prof Emerita	Peeler, Karen	D	61
Lect	Pelletier, Christina	M	32B
Assoc Prof	Pierson, Karen	M	64D
Prof Emeritus	Platt, Rosemary D.	D	66A
Lect	Polonsky, Leonid	M	62A
Lect	Ponzner, Joseph	B	12
Lect	Poss, Nicholas		20A,20B
Assoc Prof	Powell, Susan K.	D	65
Lect	Powers, David		29
Assoc Prof Emeritus	Proctor, Gregory	D	13,10,34
Prof Emeritus	Pyne, James		48,64C
Prof	Radzynski, Jan	D	10
Lect	Regensburger, Tamara	M	61
Assoc Prof	Rice, John Robin	D	61
Assoc Prof	Robinson Woliver, Loretta	M	61
Prof Emeritus	Robinson, Paul G.	D	62D
Prof	Rosow, Lois	D	12A,12
Other	Rubinstein, Mark		35C,35D,34D,35G
Asst Prof	Rudoff, Mark	M	62C
Lect	Ruffin, Milton		32D
Lect	Rupp, Jim	B	29
Prof	Sanders, Paul	D	32,36
Lect	Scarbrough, Eric		72
Lect	Schnipke, Richard	DMA	32D,36
Lect	Schoeff, Kristin	M	66C
Asst Prof Emeritus	Sedonis, Robert D.		32,36
Prof Emerita	Sexton, A. Jeanette		32
Lect	Shellhammer, Jeff	M	32E
Lect	Singleton, Lynn	M	66D
Asst Prof	Skinner, Ryan	D	14
Lect	Smith, Michael	M	65,29,32E
Assoc Prof	Sorton, Robert	M	64B
Lect	Stablein, Maria		66C
Other	Staples, Mitch		66F
Lect	Stimson, Ann	D	13
Prof Emerita	Swank, Helen		61
Assoc Prof	Tan, Kia-Hui	D	62A,51,62B,13,42
Other	Tender, Peter	M	34,35C
Lect	Torpaga, Olivier		20A,20B
Assoc Prof	Tovey, David G.	D	32
Lect	Turner, Kevin P.		70
Lect	Utter, Hans		20
Asst Prof Emeritus	Von Gruenigan, Robert		32
Prof Emeritus	Waddell, Charles F.	M	48,63B
Assoc Prof	Wallace, Shawn	M	29,29A
Assoc Prof	Ward, Robert J.	D	60,36
Prof Emeritus	Weait, Christopher R.	M	64D
Prof	Wells, Thomas H.	D	10,45,34
Lect	Westfall, Casey		66C
Prof	White-Smith, Juliet	D	62B
Prof	Will, Udo	D	14
Assoc Prof	Williams, Kenneth T.	D	66A,66D,66B
Lect	Wohlwend, Karl	M	70
Assoc Prof	Woliver, C. Patrick	D	61
Prof Emeritus	Woods, Jon R.	D	32,37
Lect	Woodson, Andrew		29,62D
Asst Prof	Young, Margaret	D	32,66D

OH1860 Ohio State University-Lima Campus
Department of Music
4240 Campus Dr
Lima, OH 45804-3576
(419) 995-8289   Fax: (419) 995-8884
www.lima.ohio-state.edu
E-mail: bletstein.1@osu.edu

Regional Campus of OSU, 2 Year Institution

Coordinator: Bev R. Bletstein, 80A

Asst Prof	Bletstein, Bev R.	D	11,32,61,70
Lect	Sherrick, Richard	M	37
Asst Prof	Young, Margaret	D	11,32,66

OH1900 Ohio University
School of Music
440 R. Glidden Hall
Athens, OH 45701-2979
(740) 593-4244   Fax: (740) 593-1429
www.finearts.ohio.edu/music
E-mail: hayesc1@ohio.edu

4 Year Institution, Graduate School
Member of NASM

Master of Music in Collaborative Piano, Certificate, Master of Music in Composition, Master of Music in Music Theory, Master of Music in Performance, Master of Music in Conducting, Master of Music in Music Education, Master of Music in Music Therapy, Master of Music in History & Literature, Master of Music in Performance Pedagogy

Director: Christopher Hayes, 80A
Dir., Graduate Studies: Richard Wetzel, 80C
Dir., Community Music School: Elizabeth Braun, 80E
Associate Director: Matthew T. James, 80H
Assistant Director: Andrew J. Trachsel, 80H

Vstng Asst Prof	Antonellis, Evan	D	13
Assoc Prof	Barte, Paul T.	D	12A,11,66G,66H
Prof Emeritus	Bastin, Ernest	M	53
Prof Emerita	Berenson, Gail		66A,66B
Inst	Braun, Elizabeth	M	38,32
Prof	Braun, Roger	M	50,65
Assoc Prof	Bryant, Dorothy	D	32B,32A,11
Assoc Prof Emeritus	Butler, Milton	D	11,32B,32C
Assoc Prof	Carrera, Michael	D	62C,42
Vstng Asst Prof	Christiansen, Philip	D	61,39
Vstng Asst Prof	Cordell, Debra	M	33
Prof Emeritus PT	Eckes, Sylvia Reynolds	D	66A,66C
Asst Prof	Fiala, Michele	D	64B,41,13B,13C,64D
Asst Prof	Fisher, Christopher	D	66D,66A,66B
Assoc Prof	Geist, Kamile	M	33
Prof	Gribou, Andre	M	11,10,66A
Asst Prof	Hall, Daniel	D	60A,32C,36
Prof	Hayes, Christopher	D	
Inst	Horne, John	B	70,29,47
Assoc Prof	Huang, Steven	M	38,60B,43
Prof	James, Matthew T.	M	64E,47,53,46,29
Prof Emeritus	Jarjisian, Peter G.		36

Assoc Prof Emeritus PT	Kellogg, Michael	M	33
Asst Prof	Kim, You-Seong	M	61
Asst Prof	Kim, Youmee	D	66A,66C,66D
Inst	McDerment, Christopher	M	64E
Vstng Artist	McGann, Christina F.	M	62B
Asst Prof	Miahky, Stephen A.	D	62A,42
Inst	Millat, Andy	M	63C
Inst	Morris, Matthew B.	D	13,42,64D
Vstng Asst Prof	Osborn, Bradley T.	D	13
Vstng Asst Prof	Paradis, Sarah	M	63C,41
Prof	Parkinson, Wm. Michael	D	29,35G,47
Assoc Prof Emerita	Pease, Patricia	D	61
Prof	Phillips, Mark W.	D	43,10,45,34
Prof Emeritus	Reilly, Allyn D.	D	13
Prof Emeritus PT	Remonko, Guy	M	50,65
Inst	Rentz, Debra	M	61
Prof	Rischin, Rebecca M.	D	64C,41
Vstng Asst Prof	Rohrer, Katherine	M	61
Assoc Prof	Sayrs, Elizabeth P.	D	13
Prof	Schlabach, John	M	63A,41
Assoc Prof	Sincoff, Alison J. Brown	M	64A,41
Assoc Prof	Smith, C. Scott	M	13,63B,41
Prof	Smith, Jason R.	D	63D,13A,41
Inst	Spring, Erin	M	33
Assoc Prof Emerita	Steele, Anita Louise	M	33
Assoc Prof	Suk, Richard	D	32,37
Prof Emeritus	Syracuse, Richard D.	M	66A
Asst Prof	Trachsel, Andrew J.	D	37,43
Inst	VanHassel, Joseph	M	65
Inst	Wasserman, Garry P.	M	62D
Prof	Wetzel, Richard	D	12,29A
Prof	Wilson, Dora	D	12
Assoc Prof Emeritus	Young, Sylvester	D	32
Assoc Prof	Younge, Pascal Yao	D	20,32

OH1905 Ohio University-Lancaster
Department of Music
1570 Granville Pike
Lancaster, OH 43130-1037
(740) 654-6711   Fax: (740) 687-9497
www.lancaster.ohiou.edu
E-mail: John.Furlow.1@ohio.edu

4 Year Institution

Dean: John W. Furlow, 80A
Acting Associate Dean: Candice Thomas-Maddox, 80H

Inst PT	Wright, Debbie K.	M	36
Inst PT	Young, Paul G.	PhD	32

OH1910 Ohio University-Zanesville
Department of Music
1425 Newark Rd
Zanesville, OH 43701-2624
(740) 588-1482   Fax: (740) 453-6161
www.zanesville.ohiou.edu/
E-mail: christyw@ohiou.edu

2 and 4 Year Institution, Introductory Courses Only

Chair: William P. Christy, 80A
Dean: James W. Fonseca, 80A
Interim Associate Dean: John R. Kelbley, 80H

Asst Prof	Christy, William P.	M	13,12A,20G,29A,34
PT	Dodge, Steve W.	M	65
PT	Halvecka, Thomas	M	66D,66A,61
PT	Savage, Charles M.	M	13,12A,20G,36,61

OH2000 Ohio Wesleyan University
Department of Music
Sanborn Hall
61 S Sandusky St
Delaware, OH 43015
(740) 368-3700   Fax: (740) 368-3723
music.owu.edu
E-mail: musicd@owu.edu

4 Year Institution
Member of NASM

Chair: Timothy J. Roden, 80A

Inst PT	Burdett, Kimberly H.	D	50,65,32E
Inst PT	Burleson, Brett J.	M	70,32E
Inst PT	Damicone, Tiffany	M	32E
Asst Prof PT	Dickey, Timothy J.	D	11,12A,13E
Asst Prof	Edwards, Richard D.	D	37,32,60B,12F,32A
Asst Prof PT	Featherston, Mary	D	62C
Inst PT	Gaedeke-Riegel, Turid L.	M	32E
PT	Gagliardo, Don	M	66F
Prof	Gamso, Nancy M.	D	11,29A,48,64,32E
Prof	Griffin, Larry	D	60B,37,47,49,63A
Prof Emeritus PT	Griffith, Robert A.	M	66G
Asst Prof	Hiester, Jason A.	M	36,39,40,60A,61
Asst Prof	Jolley, Jennifer	D	10,13
Asst Prof PT	Kaneda, Mariko	D	66C,66A,66D,13B,13C
Emeritus	Lawrence, Robert C.	M	
Asst Prof PT	Mahamuti, Gulimina	D	66A,66D,66C,66B
Asst Prof PT	Malone, Michael J.	D	60B
Inst PT	McCann, Kimberly	M	63B
Prof PT	Nims, Marilyn		61,13C,32D
Emeritus	Nims, Robert D.	M	
Inst PT	Niwa, David	M	62A
Emeritus	Olson, Willis R.		
Inst PT	Pfeiffer, Karen	M	64B,11
Prof	Roden, Timothy J.	D	11,12A,20A,20D,20F
PT	Szabo, Peter	M	16
Emeritus	Wood, Darrell	D	

OH2050 Otterbein University
Department of Music
1 South Grove St
Westerville, OH 43081
(614) 823-1508   Fax: (614) 823-1118
www.otterbein.edu
E-mail: ddavenport@otterbein.edu

4 Year Institution
Member of NASM

Adj PT	Allen, Helen	M	61
Adj PT	Atria, Karen	D	64D
Adj PT	Barkhymer, Lyle	D	14,20C
Asst Prof	Bates, James	D	12A,20,32,38,62D
Adj PT	Berg, Christian	M	62B,47
Adj PT	Boskovich, Elizabeth	M	61
Adj PT	Boyce, Cody	B	70
Adj PT	Boyd, Kim	M	36,60A,32D,13C
Adj PT	Cheney, Brian	B	61
Prof	Chivington, Amy	D	32,36
Prof	Davenport, Dennis	D	54,10,13,36
Adj PT	Dunphy, Janice	M	66G
Assoc Prof	Eckenroth, Karen	D	39,61
Adj PT	Edge, David	M	41,62A
Adj PT	Gilliland, Erin	M	41,62A
Adj PT	Goodman, Kimberlee	D	64A,14,13A
Prof	Haberkorn, Michael	D	66A,20G,14C,11
Adj PT	Harvey, Lori Kay	B	61
Adj PT	Heim, Matthew	M	13
Adj PT	Huffman, Timothy	M	66A,13B,66B,66D,66C
Adj PT	Huntoon, Ben	M	63A
Adj PT	Jenny, Jack	D	13,10,50,65,43
Adj PT	Johnson, Catherine	D	39
Adj PT	Jones, Robert	M	64C
Adj PT	King, Dan	D	63A
Adj PT	Kuyvenhoven, Cora	D	62C
Adj PT	Locke, Douglas	M	62A
Adj PT	Lopez, Richard C.	D	66A,66D
Adj PT	McCann, Kimberly	M	63B
Asst Prof	Merkowitz, Jennifer Bernard	D	10,13,34
Adj PT	Miglia, Jay	M	29,64E,46,47
Adj PT	Mollenhauer, Jude	M	62E
Adj PT	Newcomb, Suzanne	D	66A,66D,66C
Adj PT	Nims, Robert	M	61
Adj PT	Phillips, Sheena	B	36
Adj PT	Price, David	M	61
Adj PT	Salido, Caroline	D	66A,66D
Adj PT	Sayre, Maya	B	39
Adj PT	Shonkwiler, Joel	D	63D
Adj PT	Stevens, Melissa	D	64B
Asst Prof	Underwood, Margaret	M	32E,37,60
Adj PT	Van Wagner, Eric	B	35G,35A,47
Prof	Walker, Gayle	D	13C,60,12A,36
Adj PT	Wedell, Steven	M	62B
Adj PT	Whitehead, Jennifer	M	61
Adj PT	Wilson, Peter	B	38
Senior Lect	Wohlwend, Karl	M	70,47
Asst Prof	Yonchak, Michael	D	34,37,32E,29,46

OH2100 Shawnee State University
Department of Music
Second St
Portsmouth, OH 45662
(740) 354-3205   Fax: (740) 355-2416
www.shawnee.edu
E-mail: eshabazz@shawnee.edu

4 Year Institution

Chair: Matthew Cram, 80A
Dir., Summer Programs: Shirley Evans Crothers-Marley, 80G

Asst Prof	Barnhart, Michael R.		
Assoc Prof	Crothers-Marley, Shirley Evans	M	12A,32,36,61

OH2120 Sinclair Community College
Department of Music
444 W 3rd St
Dayton, OH 45402-1421
(937) 512-2541   Fax: (937) 512-2054
www.sinclair.edu
E-mail: robert.ruckman@sinclair.edu

2 Year Institution

Chair: Robert Ruckman, 80A

Prof	Greene, Daniel B.	M	36,61
Prof	Kohlenberg, Kenneth	D	37,60B,12A,11,63A
Assoc Prof	Long, Nolan W.	M	36,32D,40,42
Assoc Prof	Parcell, John	D	13,66A,11,29,34C
Prof	Ruckman, Robert	D	66A,66D

OH2140 Terra State Comm College
Department of Music
2830 Napoleon Rd
Fremont, OH 43420
(419) 559-2378/2147   Fax: (419) 355-1248
www.terra.edu
E-mail: jcipiti@terra.edu

2 Year Institution, Community College

Dean: Nancy J. Sattler, 80A
Co-Dir., Musical Arts: Michael Shirtz, 80A
Dir., Artist Series: John Cipiti, 80F
Coord., Music Academy: Kris Perry, 80F

Inst	Barber, Keith	B	70,29
Inst	Beckley, Jane E.	M	66A,66C
Inst	Blanchard, Jeff L.	M	63A,47,49,29
Inst	Cavera, Chris S.	M	34,35,13,70,10
Inst	Cipiti, John	M	13,66A,10,14C
Inst	Eckermann, Joan E.	M	61,54
Inst	Forster, Marilyn	B	44,66D
Inst	Gahler, Jason R.	B	62D,29
Inst	Gregory, Monica	B	62B
Inst	Gruetter, Joy	B	61,32A
Inst	Kagy, Tamara K.	M	64A,48
Inst	Lester, David T.	B	70,35,45,42
Inst	Lupu, Virgil I.	M	62A,41,12A,11,34B
Inst	Magoto, Travis	B	63B
Inst	Michael, George	M	47,64E,29
Inst	Miller, Rodney L.	B	63D,63C
Inst	Piedra, Olman	B	65,50,43,29
Inst	Pochatko, Amanda R.	M	64B,42
Asst Prof	Shirtz, Michael	M	36,60,61,13,29
Inst	Wasserman, Lisa	B	64C,64D,42
Inst	Westgate, Karen	B	62E
Inst	Ziebold, Barbara M.	M	62,51

OH2150 Univ of Akron
School of Music
260 Guzzetta Hall
Akron, OH 44325-1002
(330) 972-7590   Fax: (330) 972-6409
www.uakron.edu/music
E-mail: ausher@uakron.edu

4 Year Institution, Graduate School
Member of NASM

Master of Music in Composition, Master of Music in Music Theory, Master of Music in Performance, Master of Music in Music Education, Master of Music in History & Literature, Master of Music in Accompanying, Master of Music in Music Technology, Master of Music in Conducting, Master of Music in Jazz Studies

Director: Ann L. Usher, 80A
Dir., Graduate, Undergraduate Studies & Admissions: Joseph Mincocchi, 80B,80C,80D
Dir., Graduate Studies: Brooks Toliver, 80C
Assistant Director: Robert Jorgensen, 80H

Prof Emeritus	Anderson, Alfred	M	39,54,61
Prof	Aron, Stephen	M	70
Artist in Res	Augustine, Joseph R.	B	66A
Lect PT	Berkner, Jane	M	48,64A
Prof Emeritus	Bernstein, David		
Prof Emeritus	Billions, Clifford		
Prof	Bodman, Alan	M	51,62A,62B
Assoc Prof	Bordo, Guy V.	D	38
Lect PT	Brndiar, Jack	M	63A
Lect FT	Brownlow, Robert J.	D	13,10
Lect FT	Cioffari, Cynthia A.	M	64D,48
Lect PT	Denman, Megan A.	M	66C
Lect PT	Dudack, Mark	M	65
Lect PT	Fraser, Robert W.	B	70
Lect PT	Gonder, Mark H.	M	65,29
Prof	Gordon, Samuel	D	60,12A,36,61,40
Lect PT	Graning, Gary Alan	D	66A,66D,66B
Prof Emeritus	Guegold, William K.	D	
Lect PT	Hammer, Levi	M	38,61
Lect PT	Harel, Jack	M	64B
Assoc Prof	Hicks, V. Douglas	M	34
Prof	Hoyt, William	M	49,63B
Lect FT	Jackman, Sean M.	D	32D,32F
Prof	Johnston, Scott	M	49,63A
Prof	Jolly, Tucker	D	49,63D
Prof	Jones, Kristina Belisle	D	64C
Prof	Jorgensen, Robert	M	37,60
Assoc Prof	Karriker, Galen	D	37,60
Lect PT	Karriker, Kendra	M	62A,11
Lect PT	Kear, Eleanor G.	M	66C
Lect PT	Kikuchi, Mayumi	D	66A
Prof	Lafferty, Laurie	D	32B,32C,63B
Lect PT	LaNasa, Patricia J.	M	61,11
Lect PT	Lange, Jesse	M	11
Assoc Prof	Lashbrook, Laurie E.	D	61
Lect PT	Locker, Fred	M	13,12
Assoc Prof Emerita	Lott, Marian J.	M	
Prof Emeritus	MacDonald, John A.	D	60,12A,12,36
Prof Emerita	MacGregor, Barbara J.	M	
Collaborative Pianist	Malyuk, Amy	M	66C
Lect PT	Marron, James	M	70
Vstng Lect	Mason, Justin	D	
Prof	McCarthy, Daniel	D	10,13
Vstng Lect	Milford, Gene F.	M	32
Emerita	Mills, Michele D.	D	13A,12A,66D
Lect PT	Nauman, Sharon	B	11
Lect PT	Neidlinger, Robert D.	M	11
Lect PT	Newton, Dean A.	M	70,47
Prof Emeritus	Paolucci, Roland	M	
Prof	Peeples, Georgia	D	12A,64D,15,48
Lect PT	Petrongelli, Amy	M	61
Lect PT	Polanka, William Mark	D	13,62A
Prof	Pope, George	M	48,64A
Lect PT	Powell, Timothy W.	B	62D
Prof	Resanovic, Nikola	D	13,10
Lect PT	Rosser, Christina	M	62C
Lect PT	Rowell, Tracy	M	62D
Assoc Prof	Schantz, Jack	M	29,46,47,63A
Prof Emerita	Schiller, Mary	D	
Assoc Prof	Shanklin, Richard L.	M	47,64E,29,35
Lect PT	Shimpo, Ryoji	M	66A,11
Prof Emeritus	Shirey, Richard		
Lect PT	Silverman, Laura	M	66C,66A
Lect PT	Smith, Cory	M	62A,62B
Prof	Snider, Larry D.	D	50,65
Assoc Prof	Thomson, Philip G.	M	66A
Lect PT	Thorson, Valerie	M	66G
Prof	Toliver, Brooks	D	11,12
Prof Emeritus	Turek, Ralph	D	
Prof	Usher, Ann L.	D	32,36,60A
Lect PT	Vardi, Amitai	M	64C
Lect PT	Veigel, Loren	M	32D
Asst Prof	Ward, Frank	D	61,39,54
Lect PT	Wehrmann, Rock	B	47,66A
Lect FT	Wilding, Jamie	M	13B,13C
Lect PT	Yekel, Amy L.	D	61
Lect PT	Yu, Jin	B	66C
Emeritus PT	Zadrozny, Edward A.	M	49,63C
Lect PT	Zollars, Robert P.	M	65

OH2200 Univ of Cincinnati

College Conservatory of Music
PO Box 210003
Cincinnati, OH 45221-0003
(513) 556-3737   Fax: (513) 556-3330
www.ccm.uc.edu
E-mail: whipplmy@ucmail.uc.edu

4 Year Institution, Graduate School
Member of NASM

Master of Music in Collaborative Piano, Artist Diploma, Master of Music in Composition, Master of Music in Music Theory, Master of Music in Performance, Master of Music in Conducting, Master of Music in Music Education, PhD in Music Theory, DMA in Composition, DMA in Conducting, DMA in Performance, PhD in Musicology, Master of Music in Music History

Interim Dean: Frank M. Weinstock, 80A
Dir., Graduate Studies: Steven J. Cahn, 80C
Assistant Dean & Dir., Admissions: Paul R. Hillner, 80D,80H
Dir., Preparatory Division: Amy F. Dennison, 80E
Interim Associate Dean: R. Terrell Finney, Jr., 80H

Rank	Name	Deg	Codes
Inst Adj	Adams, Clifford	B	11
Prof	Adams, David	M	61
Asst Prof	Anderson, Tim	M	63C
Asst Prof Adj	Aufmann, Ronald	B	64C
Assoc Prof	Baresel, Thomas	M	61
Assoc Prof	Belck, Scott	D	29
Asst Prof Adj	Belland, Douglas K.	D	11
Prof	Berg, Aubrey	D	54
Adj Inst	Berg, Christian R.	B	29
Assoc Prof	Berry, David Carson	D	13,13I,13D,13J
Adj Inst	Bowman, Randy C.	M	64A
Prof Emerita	Boyer, Rene	D	32
Asst Prof	Bunte, James	D	64E
Prof	Burge, Russell	M	50,65
Assoc Prof	Burke, Kevin F.	M	35H
Prof	Burnham, Michael		54
Assoc Prof	Cahn, Steven J.	D	13
Prof	Callahan, Clare	M	70
Prof Emeritus Adj	Campione, Carmine	B	64C
Asst Prof	Carberry, Deirdre		52
Assoc Prof	Carroll, Catharine L.	D	62B
Assoc Prof	Cash, Shellie B.	M	52
Inst Adj	Changchien, Wenting	M	62D,66C,62
Inst Adj	Chen, Ixi	M	64C
Assoc Prof	Chertock, Michael S.	M	66A
Adj Asst Prof	Collins, Phillip	M	63A
Prof	Conda, J. Michelle	D	66B,66D
Prof	Culley, James F.	M	50,65
Prof	Dal Vera, Rocco	M	54
Asst Prof Adj	Deaver, John	D	66G
Prof	DeGreg, Philip A.	M	29
Assoc Prof	Detwiler, Gwen	D	61
Prof Emeritus	Doan, Gerald R.	D	32
Adj Asst Prof	Dugger, Duane A.	M	63B
Assoc Prof	Fiday, Michael	D	10A
Inst Adj	Fields, Marc E.	B	29
Prof	Finney, R. Terrell	M	
Asst Prof	Fiol, Stefan	D	20
Prof	Fiser, Lee W.	B	62C
Asst Prof	Floyd, Eva	D	32,32D
Prof Emeritus	Foster, Donald H.	D	12A,12
Assoc Prof	Fox, Marjorie	M	35H
Prof Emeritus	Fraser, Malcolm	DIPL	39
Prof	Gage, James H.	M	54
Prof	Gardner, Randy C.	B	63B
Prof	Garner, Bradley A.	D	64A
Prof	Gary, Roberta S.	D	66G
Adj Prof	Gehl, Robin		12A,13,13F
Prof	Gibson, Mark I.	M	38,39
Inst Adj	Gise, Max E.	M	14
Assoc Prof	Goldstein, Steven	B	54,39
Inst Adj	Gore, Art	M	29
Asst Prof	Gottlieb, BettyAnne	M	32E,32G
Prof	Griffiths, Kenneth R.	M	66C
Assoc Prof	Grodsky, Roger	B	54
Adj Asst Prof	Grubb, William	D	41
Assoc Prof	Guarino, Robin	M	61
Inst Adj	Gwynne, William G.	B	29
Assoc Prof	Haines, Thomas	M	35H,35D
Asst Prof	Hamilton, Jean	M	35E
Prof	Hanani, Yuhuda	B	62C
Assoc Prof	Hatcher, Charles E.	M	35C
Asst Prof Adj	Hawley, Richard R.	B	64C
Prof	Helmuth, Mara M.	D	10,45,34
Prof	Hess, Richard E.	M	54
Prof	Hoffman, Joel H.	D	13,10
Prof Emerita	Honn, Barbara	M	61
Assoc Prof Adj	James, Martin E.	M	64D
Assoc Prof	Jiang, Qi M.	M	52
Assoc Prof	Joe, Jeongwon	D	12
Prof	Jones, K. Jennifer	M	54
Prof Adj	Kawasaki, Masao	B	62B
Assoc Prof	Kay, Michele A.	M	54
Inst Adj	Kelly, Michael A.	M	13
Prof	Knehans, Douglas	D	10
Asst Prof	Kregor, Jonathan	D	12
Asst Prof	Kronour, Dianne	M	32
Assoc Prof	Kvapil, Diane	DIPL	54
Prof	Lala, Diane	M	54
Assoc Prof	Laszlo, Albert	M	62D
Assoc Prof	Lefebvre, Marie-France	D	39
Inst Adj	Liao, Chien-Ju	M	62B
Assoc Prof	Linhart, Patricia M.	B	61,54
Prof	Loewy, Donna S.	M	66C
Assoc Prof	Losada, Cristina Catherine	D	13
Assoc Prof	Lusk, Terry	M	66C,39
Assoc Prof	Lykes, Karen S.	M	61
Assoc Prof	mcclung, bruce d.	D	12A,12
Prof	McGraw, William E.	M	61
Prof Emeritus	Metz, Donald E.	D	32
Assoc Prof	Milewski, Piotr	D	41,62A
Prof	Milligan, Terence G.	D	60,37,32
Prof	Mogle, Dean	M	39,54
Asst Prof Adj	Montgomery, Vivian	M	11,12A,55,66H,67F
Prof	Morrow, Mary Sue	D	12
Assoc Prof	Muni, Nicholas	B	39
Asst Prof	Ng, Samuel	D	13
Assoc Prof	Northcut, Timothy	M	49,63D
Inst Adj	Norton, Peter K.	B	63C
Prof Emeritus	Nowacki, Edward C.	D	12
Prof	Ostoich, Mark S.	D	64B
Prof	Otte, Allen C.	M	50,65
Assoc Prof	Owens, John W.	D	35H
Librarian	Palkovic, Mark	M	16
Inst Adj	Pappano, Annalisa		12
Assoc Prof	Paver, Barbara E.	D	61
Asst Prof	Peattie, Matthew	D	12
Asst Prof Adj	Pegis, Gabe	M	62A
Asst Prof	Pensyl, Kim C.	M	47
Adj Asst Prof	Piller, Paul R.	B	29
Prof	Plyler, Sylvia J.	M	66C
Assoc Prof	Porter, Ann M.	D	32,32E
Assoc Prof	Pratt, Awadagin K. A.	DIPL	66C
Prof	Pridonoff, Elizabeth A.	M	66A
Prof	Pridonoff, Eugene A.	M	66A
Prof	Rivers, Earl G.	D	60,36
Prof	Rivers, Sandra	M	66C
Prof	Roig-Francoli, Miguel A.	PhD	13,10
Asst Prof	Ruggaber, Brian J.	M	54
Prof	Sassmannshaus, Kurt	M	62A
Assoc Prof	Schlagel, Stephanie P.	D	12C,12,55,67
Asst Prof	Scott, L. Brett Cornish	D	60A,36
Assoc Prof Adj	Sella, Gillian Benet	D	62E
Assoc Prof	Shaw, Kenneth	M	61
Prof Emeritus	Shortt, Paul R.	M	
Prof	Siebert, Alan H.	M	63A
Adj Asst Prof	Smith, James E.	M	29
Inst Adj	Spangler, Julie M.	B	54
Prof	Stucky, Mary Henderson	M	61
Inst Adj	Stucky, Rodney D.	M	55
Assoc Prof	Tevlin, Michael J.	M	52
Prof	Tocco, James V.	DIPL	41,66A
Asst Prof	Tomaro, Annunziata	M	38,60B
Asst Prof	Truhart, Regina A.	M	54
Prof	Umfrid, Thomas C.	M	39,54
Prof Emeritus	VanMatre, Rick	M	47,64E,29
Inst Adj	Verbeck, Heather D.	M	64A
Inst Adj	Von Ohlen, John	B	47
Prof	Weinstock, Frank M.	M	
Prof	Wing, Lizabeth A.	D	32
Prof Adj	Winstead, William O.	M	64D
Prof	Winther, Rodney	M	37
Prof Emeritus	Wolfram, Manfred K.	D	35H
Prof	Yaffe, Alan	D	35E
Assoc Prof	Yim, Won-Bin	D	62A
Assoc Prof	Yurko, Kelly A.	B	54

OH2250 Univ of Dayton

Department of Music
300 College Park Ave
Dayton, OH 45469-0290
(937) 229-3936   Fax: (937) 229-3916
go.udayton.edu/music
E-mail: sgratto1@udayton.edu

4 Year Institution, Graduate School
Member of NASM

Master of Education with Concentration in Music Education

Chair: Sharon Davis Gratto, 80A
Dir., Graduate Program: Linda A. Hartley, 80C

Rank	Name	Deg	Codes
Prof Emeritus	Benedum, Richard P.	D	11,12A,66G
Artist in Res	Benjamin, John A.	M	66A,66C,66D

PT	Brant, Aaron	M	63B,49
PT	Brookshire, Eddie L.	B	47,70,62D
PT	Burkhead, Phillip	M	66A,29
PT	Charles, Nicole	D	64A,48
Prof	Chenoweth, Richard K.	D	63B,32E
Prof	Cox, Donna M.	D	20,36,32
Artist in Res	Daniel-Cox, Minnita D.	D	61,39
Asst Prof	Dorf, Samuel N.	D	12A,11,55A,55B,55C
Artist in Res	Farris, Phillip	M	66A,66C,66D,11
Assoc Prof	Gardstrom, Susan	D	33,12F,44
PT	Granthan, Daniel	M	63A,49
Prof	Gratto, Sharon Davis	D	36,20,32
Prof	Hartley, Linda A.	D	32E,37,64E,32G
Lect	Hiller, James	D	33,11
Asst Prof	Jones, Robert B.	D	60A,32C,36,32D
PT	Keener, Michael K.	D	63C,49,11,32E
PT	Keller Bick, Ingrid P.	D	66A
Lect	Kizer, Tremon B.	M	37,32E,11
PT	Kronour, Dianne	M	32A,32B
PT	Lardinios, John	M	62A,51
PT	Lardinois, Kara	M	62A,51
Artist in Res	Leslie, James M.	B	65,47,32B,37
Asst Prof	MacLachlan, Heather M.	D	12,20,14,20D
Prof	Magnuson, Phillip	D	13,10F,10A,62B
Artist in Res	McCutcheon, James R.	M	70,42
PT	McDonnell, David	D	10B,10F,34,64E,47
PT	McHugh, Larisa	M	33
Assoc Prof	Morris, Willie L.	D	37,47,64E,32
PT	Pascolini, Jon R.	M	62D
PT	Pepitone, Anthony F.	B	70,47
PT	Phillips, Dorie	M	33
PT	Reynolds, Heidi M.	B	33
Assoc Prof	Reynolds, Patrick A.	D	60,32E,37,38
PT	Richwine, Reginald L.	M	63A,47
Asst Prof	Rush, Toby	D	13,34C
Prof Emerita	Sandness, Marilyn I.	M	33,12F
Artist in Res	Sievers, David	D	61,39
PT	Smith, Kristen	M	64D,48
Prof	Snyder, Linda J.	D	39,61,11
PT	Sommerfeldt, Jerod	D	10F,34
Prof	Street, Eric	D	66A,66B,66C,11
PT	Vore, Wallis W.	M	64C,48
PT	Wagner, Shelbi	M	62C,51,32E
Artist in Res	Wells Chenoweth, Andrea	M	61,13A,13C
PT	Whalen, Eileen M.	M	64B
PT	Williams, James A.	D	61

OH2275 Univ of Findlay
Department of Music
1000 N Main St
Findlay, OH 45840-3653
(419) 434-4717   Fax: (419) 434-4822
www.findlay.edu
E-mail: anders@findlay.edu

4 Year Liberal Arts Institution, Graduate School

Chair: Micheal F. Anders, 80A

Lect PT	Abrams, Colleen	B	64C,64E
Prof	Anders, Micheal F.	D	12A,61,54,36
Lect PT	Ashmore, Lance	M	61
Lect PT	Balmer, Bill	B	72
Senior Lect PT	Bitz, Lori L.	B	63
Lect PT	Cable, Ron C.	M	37
Lect PT	Carey, Thomas C.	M	62A,62B,38,62C
Senior Lect PT	Damschroder, Norman L.	M	62D,13A,13B
Inst	Dettbarn-Slaughter, Vivian Robles	D	61,66A,11
Lect PT	Glick, Nancy	B	62E,66A
Asst Prof	Griffin, Gregory W.	M	54,35C,34
Lect PT	Hill-Kretzer, Kathleen	M	64A
Lect PT	Hoyt-Brackman, Brenda		52,54
	Hutton, Kelley		35E
Lect PT	Kretzer, Scott	B	37
Lect PT	Leaman, Jim	M	65
Lect PT	Lewis, Kelly	B	66C
Asst Prof Adj	Malloy, Michael	B	65,20G
Asst Prof	Matsos, Christopher	D	34
Inst	McClurkin, Vicki J.	B	54
Lect PT	McCoy, Eleanor K.	B	66C,66G
Lect PT	Neel, Douglas J.	M	70
Lect PT	Newell, Kathy	B	54
Lect PT	Reamsnyder, Richard	B	64B,64D
Lect PT	Reny, Alison	B	52
	Stimmel, Matthew D.	B	34,35C
Prof	Taylor, Jack M.	M	10,37,47,29
Lect PT	Vaas, Sharon	B	66C

OH2290 Univ of Mount Union
Department of Music
1972 Clark Ave
Alliance, OH 44601-3993
(330) 823-2180   Fax: (330) 823-2144
www.mountunion.edu/mu
E-mail: boehmp@mountunion.edu

4 Year Institution
Member of NASM

Chair: Patricia A. Boehm, 80A
Dean: Patricia Draves, 80A
Dir., Preparatory Division: Michelle Miller, 80E
Dir., Artist/Performance Series: Jerome P. Miskell, 80F

PT	Abbott, Amanda-Joyce	M	61,11
Prof	Anderson, Elaine M.	D	62C,13,38,41,42
PT	Benjamin, Eric	M	38,11
Assoc Prof	Boehm, Patricia A.	D	61,32,11
PT	Bracy, Katherine B.	M	62E
Assoc Prof	Cook, Grant W.	D	36,40,60,12
PT	Fesz, Maria	M	62C
	Howenstine, Nancy	B	66C
PT	Krauss, W. John	M	63D,32E
PT	Kroft, Patricia	M	64D
Assoc Prof	Liliestedt, Maira	D	12A,66A,66B
PT	Miller, Michelle	M	66A
Assoc Prof	Miskell, Jerome P.	D	34,62B,13A,11
PT	Mismas, James	M	61
PT	Mollenkopf, Jennifer	M	63B
Librarian	Moushey, Suzanne Z.	M	16
PT	Naragon, Jayne	M	64C
PT	Neitzke, Jeff	M	41,65,37
PT	Olsson, John A.	M	63C
PT	Olsson, Patricia	M	64E,20
Prof	Perone, James E.	D	11,13,12E,64C
PT	Reichenberger, Kathy	M	66C,66D
PT	Roberts, John	M	36
PT	Samu, Attila	M	61
PT	Sarata, Adam	M	70
PT	Schloneger, Brent	M	66C
PT	Shultz, Betty Sue	M	64B,42
PT	Steward, Jack	M	62D
PT	Subchak, Bohdan	M	62A,66C
PT	Tryon, Robin R.	M	41,64A
PT	Weber, Jessica	M	61
PT	Willard, Michael	M	63A,32E
Asst Prof	Willis, Jonathan	M	60B,32C,37,47,46

OH2300 Univ of Toledo
Department of Music
2801 W Bancroft St
Toledo, OH 43606-3390
(419) 530-2448   Fax: (419) 530-8483
www.utoledo.edu/cvpa/music
E-mail: timothy.brakel@utoledo.edu

4 Year Institution, Graduate School
Member of NASM

Master of Music in Performance, Master of Music in Music Education

Chair: Timothy D. Brakel, 80A
Assistant Chair: Michael Boyd, 80H

PT	Archer, Thaddeus	M	63A
Lect	Ballinger, Robert W.	M	39,66C,11,13A
PT	Black, Claude	M	29
Prof	Boyd, Michael	D	66A
Assoc Prof	Brakel, Timothy D.	D	32E,32,64E,13,60
PT	Campbell, Neal	M	63D
PT	Chang, Amy	M	62C
PT	Chidester, James	M	66G
Lect	Damschroder, Norman	M	62D,29A
PT	Harris, Daniel	D	63C
Prof	Hendricks, Jon	B	29,53
Assoc Prof	Heritage, Lee	D	13B,13C,29A,20G,10A
Prof	Hodge, Stephen	D	36,32C,61,32D,60A
Prof	Jex, David	D	13B,13C,13D,10,29
Assoc Prof	Johanson, Erik	M	61
PT	Johnson, Cecilia	M	32E,62A
PT	Lendrim, Nancy	M	62E
PT	Loch, Kim	M	64B
Prof	Marchionni, Raymond	D	66A,11,13
Lect	Mariasy, David	M	35C,34D
PT	McCage, Leslie	M	64A
Assoc Prof	Mossblad, Gunnar	M	64E,46,47,29B,29C
PT	Petersen, Alice V. Neff	D	55,67,11
PT	Piedra, Olman	M	50,65

PT	Reilly, Kevin	M	66D
Vstng Asst Prof	Rhodes, Andrew L.	M	37,32E,49
Asst Prof	Ritter-Bernardini, Denise	D	61,36
PT	Rudolph, Gladys	B	66C
PT	Sharp, Bradley	B	63A
PT	Smith, Linda	M	66D
Asst Prof	Stover, Pamela	D	32B,32C,32G,32H,32
Assoc Prof	Stumbo, Jason A.	D	37,32E
PT	Taplin, Alan	M	63B
PT	Tse, Joel	M	64A,48
Asst Prof	Weed, Tad	M	29
Lect	Weik, Jay C.	M	70
PT	Weiler, Joan	M	64D
Vstng Asst Prof	Williams, Christopher A.	D	12A,20,12C,11

OH2370 Walsh University

Humanities Division
2020 E Maple St NW
North Canton, OH 44720
(330) 499-7090   Fax: (330) 490-7165
www.walsh.edu
E-mail: dpalmer@walsh.edu

4 Year Comprehensive Institution

Chair, Humanities Division: Douglas B. Palmer, 80A
Dir., Performing Arts Series: Nancy Blackford, 80F

Asst Prof	Clark, Daniel	D	11,12A,13C
Asst Prof	Cooper, Britt	D	11,12A,14C,36,61

OH2400 Wilberforce University

Department of Music
PO Box 1001
Wilberforce, OH 45384
(937) 708-5526   Fax: (937) 708-5522
www.wilberforce.edu
E-mail: jwinston@wilberforce.edu

4 Year Institution, Historically Black College

Music Contact: Jeremy Winston, 80A

Vstng Prof	Graves, Tifton	M	39,61
Asst Prof	Jones, Everett N.	D	12A,66A,66B,66D
Vstng Prof	Kilby, Shelton	M	10A,11
Prof	Winston, Jeremy	M	36,61,47,13E,60A

OH2450 Wittenberg University

Department of Music
PO Box 720
Springfield, OH 45501-0720
(937) 327-7341   Fax: (937) 327-7347
www.wittenberg.edu/music
E-mail: dschubert@wittenberg.edu

4 Year Institution
Member of NASM

Chair: David T. Schubert, 80A

Inst Adj	Akins, Lori	M	48,64A
Inst Adj	Bear, Colvin	M	63B
Prof Emeritus	Busarow, Donald A.	D	13A,10A,66G,31A
Assoc Prof	Con, Adam Jonathan	D	36,32,11,60A,13C
Assoc Prof	Durrenberger, Chris	D	13A,11,66A,66F,12A
Prof Emerita	Faber, Trudy	M	12A,44,66G,66H,31A
Inst Adj	Fett, Basil	M	61,36
Inst Adj	Grogan, Charles L.	D	10A,13B
Inst Adj	Grove, Lisa	M	64B
Inst Adj	Hapner, David E.	M	66C,54
Inst Adj	Hapner, Lee Merrill	B	61
Inst Adj	Hesseman, Joseph	M	64D
Inst Adj	Hofeldt, Elizabeth	D	62A,62B,42
Assoc Prof	Jones, Brandon D.	D	37,38,32E,60
Prof	Kazez, Daniel	D	13A,11,20D,62C,62D
Inst Adj	McCord, Adam	D	64E,47
Inst Adj	Musselman, Susan	D	61,39
Inst Adj	Olt, Timothy	M	63D
Inst Adj	Pitzer, Lawrence	B	55B,67C,67D,70,67G
Asst Prof Emerita Adj	Scheffel, Gwendolyn W.	M	61
Prof	Schubert, David T.	D	61,11
Inst Adj	Seifried, Denver	M	63C
Prof Emerita	Siek, Stephen	D	12A,66A,66B,20G
Inst Adj	Slagle, Diane	M	66C
Inst Adj	Smarelli, Mark E.	M	65
Assoc Prof Emeritus	Wendel, Joyce	D	32,36,61,60A
Inst Adj	York, Richard	B	64C

OH2500 Wright State University

Department of Music
3640 Col Glenn Hwy
Dayton, OH 45435
(937) 775-2346   Fax: (937) 775-3786
www.wright.edu/music
E-mail: randall.paul@wright.edu

4 Year Institution, Graduate School
Member of NASM

Master of Music in Performance, Master of Music in Music Education, Master Humanities of Music

Chair: Randall S. Paul, 80A
Dir., Graduate Studies: Christopher Chaffee, 80C

PT	Aldredge, Steven	D	66A,66D
Prof Emeritus	Bland, Leland	D	13,34
Prof	Booth, David M.	D	60,37,63D,65
PT	Cashwell, Brian	M	29A
PT	Cataldi, Diana M.	M	61
Assoc Prof	Cha, In-Hong	D	60,38,62A
Assoc Prof	Chaffee, Christopher	D	64A,20,29A,11
Assoc Prof	Collins, Drew S.	D	32D,36
Asst Prof	Cox, Franklin	D	10,13
Prof	Dahlman, Hank	D	32,36,60
Inst	Davis, Vincent	M	61
PT	DeGruchy, Katherine	M	64B
Prof	Dregalla, Herbert E.	D	12,32,60,64C
Assoc Prof	Ellis, Brenda	D	20A,20G,32,36,66A
PT	Flamm, Ernest C.	M	32
PT	Hamilton, Margot E.	M	62D
Prof	Jagow, Shelley	D	64E,48,37
Librarian	Jenkins, Martin D.	M	16
Lect	Jobert, William	M	64D
Inst	Kurokawa, John K.	M	11,34,64C,32F
Prof Emeritus	Larkowski, Charles S.	D	12A,12,66H
Prof Emeritus	Laws, Francis	M	11,49,63C,63D
Prof	Leung, Jackson	D	66A,66D,66B,38
PT	Lindley, Debra	M	66A
Lect	Loranger, Dennis	D	12,12A
Lect	Lukowicz, Thomas	M	11,63D,13,13D,13E
PT	Markworth, Wayne	M	32E
Lect PT	McCutcheon, James	M	70
Inst	McNamara, Gretchen	D	63D,13B
PT	Minneman, Ginger	M	61
Prof Emerita	Nelson, Sharon	D	32B,66
PT	Noble, Gerald	B	65
Assoc Prof	Paul, Randall S.	D	64C,29,48,11
PT	Shilling, Scott	D	62B
PT	Sobieski, Thomas	M	62A
Inst	Thoms, Jonas	M	13,13C,63B,35
Assoc Prof	Tipps, James	D	32,36,66A,66D,60
Assoc Prof	Warrick, Kimberly	D	39,61
PT	Werner, J. Ritter	D	11,66G
Asst Prof	Zehringer, Daniel	M	63A,13A

OH2550 Xavier University

Department of Music
3800 Victory Parkway
Cincinnati, OH 45207-5511
(513) 745-3801   Fax: (513) 745-3343
www.xu.edu
E-mail: merrillt@xu.edu

4 Year Institution

Chair: Thomas G. Merrill, 80A

Adj	Anderson, Jim	M	62D
Adj	Andres, Rebecca	M	64A
Adj	Arnow, Charles	M	63C
Adj	Barone, Steve	B	70
Adj	Batchelor-Glader, Brian		66A
FT	Beebe, Harriet	B	39,61
Adj	Bell, Charles	M	63B
Adj	Bespalko, Polina	M	66A
Adj	Bolden, Christina	M	52
Adj	Bussell, Lon	D	64B
Adj	Campbell, Diane	B	52
Adj	Corrothers, Janette		66A
FT	Crawford, Glenda		36,32A,32C,32B,60
Adj	Davis, Jackie		62E
Adj	Ebert, Kevin	M	70,11
Adj	Grantham, Jennifer		29A,47
Adj	Harrison, Brady	M	65,50,11
Adj	Hart, James	B	34,45
Adj	Hart, Sasha	B	52
Adj	Hurst, Christon	D	52

Adj	Johns, Norman	M	62C
Adj	Kiradjieff, Chris	B	63A,49
FT	Kristiansen, Morten	D	12
Adj	Marquis, Eugene	M	64E,64C
Adj	Meinhart, Michelle	D	11
Assoc Prof	Merrill, Thomas G.	D	12,60,36,32
Adj	Phelps, Matthew		36
Adj	Piccirillo, Lauren		64D
Adj	Reynolds, Sonya Szabo	M	66A,66D
Prof	Roehrig, Helmut J.	D	66G
Adj	Roig-Francoli, Jennifer		33
Adj	Sherwood, Thomas W.	M	61
Prof	Skeirik, Kaleel	D	13,10F
Adj	Smith, Jewel Ann	D	11
Adj	Stinson, Jonathan		61
Adj	Templeman, Robert W.	M	11,20
Adj	Ventura, Maria	M	61
FT	Westgate, Matthew	D	37
Adj	White, Manami	B	62A,62B

OH2600 Youngstown State University

Dana School of Music
One University Plaza
Youngstown, OH 44555-0001
(330) 941-3636   Fax: (330) 941-1490
web.ysu.edu/fpa/music
E-mail: mrcrist@ysu.edu

4 Year Institution, Graduate School
Member of NASM

Master of Music in Music Education, Master of Music in Applied Music, Master of Music in Music Theory-Composition, Master of Music in Jazz Studies, Master of Music in Music History & Literature

Director: Michael Crist, 80A
Dir., Graduate Studies: Stephen Ausmann, 80CDir., Artist/Performance Series: Michael D. Gelfand, 80F
Assistant Director: Tedrow Perkins, 80H
Assistant Director: Steven Reale, 80H

Prof	Ausmann, Stephen	D	32,36
Asst Prof	Boczkowska, Eweline	D	12
Inst PT	Bush, Jeff	M	47
Inst PT	Byo, Donald W.	D	64D
Inst PT	Ciarniello, D. Jack	B	35G
Inst PT	Criazzo, Rocco	M	11
Prof	Crist, Michael	D	32E,63C,34
Inst PT	DeLamater, Elizabeth	M	65
Adj Inst	Edwards, Karen	M	32,66A
Assoc Prof	Engelhardt, Kent	D	64E,29,53,47
Asst Prof	Fowler, Francois	D	70
Inst PT	Gage, Stephanie	M	32A
Prof	Gage, Stephen	D	37,60
Prof	Gelfand, Michael D.	M	62C,11
Inst	Goldberg, Randall	M	12
Inst PT	Harris, Larry	M	66D
Inst PT	Hieronymus, Bryan	B	62D
Inst PT	Kana, David	M	47
Inst PT	Karsh, Ken	M	47
Inst PT	Kimbell, Sara	M	11
Asst Prof	Kiser, Brian D.	M	63D
Prof	Krummel, Christopher	D	49,63A
Inst PT	Laginya, Daniel	D	13A,13B,13C
Assoc Prof	Lee, Hae-Jong	D	36,61
Asst Prof	Louth, Joseph Paul	D	32
Inst PT	Manhollan, John W.	M	32F
Inst PT	Marchison, Matthew	M	63D
Assoc Prof	Morgan, David	D	62D,29,47,53
Assoc Prof	Mosher, Allan R.	D	39,61
Inst PT	Mosher, Jennifer Jones	M	61
Inst PT	Olsson, John	B	63C
Assoc Prof	Oltmanns, Caroline Marianne	D	66A
Inst PT	Pavloski, Rachael	M	61
Asst Prof	Payne, Brandt A.	D	37,60B
Prof	Perkins, Tedrow	D	13,64B
Asst Prof	Reale, Steven	D	13
Inst PT	Rollin, Gwen	D	13
Prof	Rollin, Robert	D	13,10,43
Asst Prof	Root, Jena	D	10,13
Inst PT	Rudnytsky, Susan	M	11
Assoc Prof	Schaft, Glenn	D	65,50
Inst PT	Scurich, Kelly	M	32D
Prof	Slocum, William	D	63B,38
Prof	Umble, James C.	D	64E,34
Asst Prof	Umble, Kathryn Thomas	D	64A
Inst PT	Van der Westhuizen, Sophia	M	66A
Inst PT	Vasimi, James	D	13
Asst Prof	Wang, Alice	D	64C
Assoc Prof	Wilcox, John	M	38,62A,62B,41
Inst	Wolfgang, Nancy Anderson	M	61
Inst PT	Yazvac, Diane	M	66A,66C,66D
Asst Prof	Yudha, Cicilia I.	DMA	66A
Assoc Prof	Yun, Misook	D	61
Inst PT	Zumpella, Clement	M	64C

OK0150 Cameron University

Department of Music
2800 W Gore Blvd
Lawton, OK 73505-6377
(580) 581-2440   Fax: (580) 581-5764
www.cameron.edu/music
E-mail: jlambert@cameron.edu

4 Year Institution
Member of NASM

Chair: James Lambert, 80A
Dean: Von E. Underwood, 80A

Adj	Anderson, David C.	B	66C
Adj	Chan-Spannagel, Yiu-Ka	M	66D,66C
Vstng Asst Prof	Compton, Michael	D	64,48,47,60B
Vstng Inst	Cornish, John	M	36,39,60A,61,13B
Asst Prof	Couch, Roy L.	D	37,63D,49,32E
Adj	Crabtree, Cecile	D	11,20G
Adj	Detweiler, Bruce	M	11,47,53
Adj	Diekman, Susan	M	64D
Assoc Prof	Duckett, Alfred	D	11,60
Adj	Duncan, David	M	32B
Adj	Henckel, Kristina	M	66C,11
Adj	Hickman, Kathryn	M	66C,11
Adj	Hill-Le, Holly	M	66C,13A
Prof	Hoepfner, Gregory	D	10A,32,61,10,11
Prof	Labe, Thomas A.	D	11,12A,66A,66B
Adj	Lambert, Doris	M	36,40,61,13C
Prof	Lambert, James	D	65,50,37,13,12D
Adj	Moots, John E.	M	32,49,63A,20G
Asst Prof	Underwood, Kirsten F.	M	62,38,11,62C,20
Prof	Whang, Hyunsoon	D	11,12A,66

OK0200 Carl Albert State College

Department of Music
1507 S McKenna St
Poteau, OK 74953-5207
(918) 647-1267   Fax: (918) 647-1266
www.carlalbert.edu
E-mail: ddinsmore@carlalbert.edu

2 Year Institution

Music Contact: Dana Dinsmore Davis, 80A
Chair, Communication & Fine Arts: Bob Hendricks, 80A

Curtis, Noma		66A
Davis, Dana Dinsmore		
Falkner, Dan		37
Hayes, Natlynn		61

OK0300 East Central University

Department of Music
1100 East 14th St
Ada, OK 74820
(580) 559-5474   Fax: (580) 559-5752
www.ecok.edu
E-mail: kalig@ecok.edu

4 Year Institution
Member of NASM

Music Coordinator: Kelley Alig, 80A
Dean, College of Liberal Arts: Mark Hollingsworth, 80A
Dir., School of Fine Arts: Brad Jessop, 80A

Assoc Prof	Alig, Kelley	D	32,61,11
Assoc Prof	Baggech, Melody A.	D	61,40,39
PT	Brady, Brandon D.	M	64
PT	Coale, Dean	M	32E,49,63C,63D
Asst Prof	Correll, Allen	M	37,32E,47,60B,63A
Asst Prof	Cox, Lauren J.		64C,64E,13,13C
PT	Craig, Genevieve	M	63B
Asst Prof	Finley, Benjamin	D	65,50
Asst Prof	Garcia, W. T. Skye	M	66A,66D,13B,13C,66B
Prof	Hibler, Starla	D	12A,66A,66C
Prof	Hollingsworth, Mark	DMA	20
PT	Lupinski, Rudy	B	66A,66D,13B,13C,66H
PT	Marshall, Allen	D	60A,61,13

PT	Morrison, Becky	M	61
PT	Overmier, Juliana	M	64A,48
PT	Rowe, Paul	B	66A,11,66D,66G
Prof	Walker, Steve	D	61,36,40,60A
PT	Whitmore, Michael R.	M	48,64C,64E
PT	Woolley, Susanne	B	62A

OK0350 Eastern Oklahoma State College
Department of Music
1301 W Main St
Wilburton, OK 74578-4901
(918) 465-1790   Fax: (918) 465-4470
www.eosc.edu
E-mail: pdenis@eosc.edu

2 Year Institution

Chair: Paul Enis, 80A

	Enis, Paul	M	13,36,37,61,63
Inst	Ford, Mary E.	M	11,13,36,66

OK0410 Hillsdale Free Will Baptist Coll
Department of Music
3701 S I 35 Service Rd
Moore, OK 73153
(405) 912-9000   Fax: (405) 912-9050
www.hc.edu
E-mail: kcarlton@hc.edu

4 Year Institution

Chair: Kathleen Carlton, 80A

Prof	Carlton, Kathleen	D	13,11,12A,61,31A

OK0450 Langston University
Department of Music
PO Box 1500
Langston, OK 73050-0392
(405) 466-2936   Fax: (405) 466-2990
www.langston.edu
E-mail: blfranklin@langston.edu

4 Year Institution, Historically Black College

Chair & Dir., Artist/Performance Series: Bonita Louise Franklin, 80A,80F

Adj PT	Attaway, Aiya	M	66A,66C,66D
Inst	Birden, Larry	M	13A,32E,10F,63,37
Inst	Brackeen, William	M	66A,66D,10A,13
Asst Prof	Franklin, Bonita Louise	M	32,36,60A,61
Adj PT	Gall, Sandra J.	D	61
Inst	Kennedy, Rajah B.	M	11,37,46,49,63
Adj PT	Langsam, Stuart	M	65,50
Adj PT	Thomas, Erica	M	61
Adj PT	Wade-Elkamely, Bobbie	M	51,62
Adj PT	Whitmore, Michael	M	32E,48,64

OK0500 Northeastern Oklahoma A&M College
Department of Fine Arts-Music
200 'I' St NE
Miami, OK 74354
(918) 540-6321   Fax: (918) 540-6490
www.neo.edu/Academics/AcademicSchools/LiberalArts/
    FineArts/Music/tabid/259/Default.aspx
E-mail: mswhaley@neo.edu

2 Year Institution

Chair, Fine Arts: Steven McCurley, 80A

Adj	Beard, Charles	M	64
Inst	Compton, Adam	M	13B,63,37,46,13
Adj	Dunn, Lisa	B	64A
Adj	Flannery, William	B	66G
Adj	Newman, Sean	M	63D
Adj	Rhoades, Vanessa	M	61,11
Adj	Roye, Nedra	D	66A,66D
Adj	Singleton, Ron	B	70
Adj	Swopes, Polly	B	62
Inst	Whaley, Mary Susan	M	11,36,61,54,13
Adj	Wheeler, Teresa	M	62E

OK0550 Northeastern State University
Department of Performing Arts
600 N Grand Ave
Tahlequah, OK 74464
(918) 444-2700   Fax: (918) 458-2348
www.nsumusic.com
E-mail: bighley@nsuok.edu

4 Year Institution

Chair: Mark Bighley, 80A

Asst Prof Emeritus	Bailey, Jane	M	
Prof Emeritus	Bailey, Robert E.	D	
Prof	Bighley, Mark	D	12A,66A,66G,66D
PT	Brown, Susie	M	64D
Prof	Chioldi, Ronald	D	13B,66A,66D,13D,13E
Inst	Combs, Mikel	M	62D
Assoc Prof	Daniel, Robert	D	13A,60,11,61,13C
Asst Prof	Dovel, Jason L.	D	63A,11,63B,10F
PT	Dovel, Suzanne	M	32B
Prof Emeritus	Foster, Gary A.	D	
PT	Hargrove, D'Ann	M	32B
Prof Emeritus	Lehman, Lowell	D	
Asst Prof	Lindroth, James	D	32,37
PT	Mayfield, Farren	M	11,66D
Asst Prof	Poole, Tommy A.	D	29,46,64E,10A
Assoc Prof Emeritus	Prechtl, Sylvanna	D	
PT	Reyes, William	M	70
Asst Prof	Roste, Vaughn	M	60,12A,36,61,20
PT	Smith, Roy	M	50,65
Prof Emeritus	Studebaker, Donald	D	20
PT	Surman, Patricia J.	DMA	64A
Asst Prof	Unger, Shannon M.	M	61,11,13C,39
PT	Wagoner, Lisa	M	64B
Asst Prof	Watson, Anne	D	64C,13A,13B,13C,20
Prof Emeritus	Whitworth, J. Ralph	D	
Asst Prof	Wika, Norman	D	60,37,63C,63D
PT	Young, Judy	M	32B

OK0600 Northwestern Oklahoma State Univ
Department of Fine Arts
709 Oklahoma Blvd
Alva, OK 73717
(580) 327-8692   Fax: (580) 327-8514
www.nwosu.edu/music
E-mail: irmessoloras@nwosu.edu

4 Year Institution, Graduate School

Master of Education

Chair: Irene Messoloras, 80A
Dir., Graduate Studies: Shawn Holliday, 80C

Asst Prof	Chan, Sarah S.	D	66A,66C,66D,13,11
PT	Gomez, Adrian	B	63
Asst Prof	Messoloras, Irene	D	36,12,60A,61,40
PT	Newell, Lawana	M	61,54
PT	Parker, Charla	M	66D,32B
PT	Ridgeway, Max A.	M	10,70,11,20,46
PT	Stephens, Wesley	M	65
Assoc Prof	Stone, Michael John	D	37,46,60B,63,32

OK0650 Oklahoma Baptist University
Division of Music
PO Box 61276
500 W University Ave
Shawnee, OK 74804-2590
(405) 878-2305   Fax: (405) 878-2328
www.okbu.edu
E-mail: kristen.todd@okbu.edu

4 Year Institution
Member of NASM

Division Chair: Kristen Stauffer Todd, 80A

Prof	Ballweg, D. Brent	D	36,60A
Assoc Prof Emerita	Bell, Carol Ann	D	66A,66D
Asst Prof	Dean, Michael	M	66
Asst Prof	Gerber, Casey	D	36,32
Asst Prof	Hansford, Conchita	M	32A,32B,61,66A,31A
Prof Emeritus	Hansford, James	D	38,32G,37,63D,41
Assoc Prof	Hinson, Lee	D	31A,11,36

Asst Prof	Johnson, Randolph B.	D	10,13
Asst Prof	Lilite, Louima	D	61,39
Asst Prof	McQuade, Jennifer H.	D	61,39
Asst Prof	McQuade, Mark A.	D	61,39
Assoc Prof	Meyer, Sandra G.	M	13B,13C,13E,66A,13
Assoc Prof Emerita	Partridge, Norma	M	39,61
Asst Prof	Pruiett, Kevin P.	M	47,63A,72,29A,49
Asst Prof	Purin, Peter	M	13,34
Asst Prof	Todd, Kristen Stauffer	D	12,14,20,11,55
Assoc Prof	Vernon, James R.	D	13,10,35C,11
Inst	Whitmore, Keith	D	66A,66H,66C,66D
Asst Prof	Wright, Lauren Denney	D	32E,37,64C,60B

OK0700 Oklahoma Christian University

Department of Music
PO Box 11000
Oklahoma City, OK 73136-1100
(405) 425-5530   Fax: (405) 425-5480
www.oc.edu/music
E-mail: music@oc.edu

4 Year Institution
Member of NASM

Chair: Kathy A. Thompson, 80A

Prof	Adams, Kenny L.	D	60,36,39,54,40
PT	Avrett, Martha	B	61
PT	Bruce, Gary	B	70,65,66F
PT	Clark, Wayne R.	D	63D,63C,63
PT	Coale, Laura	M	61
PT	Dvorak, Celeste	B	61
Prof Emeritus	Fletcher, Harold	D	13,12A
Prof	Fletcher, John M.	D	10F,60,37,13
PT	Grigg, Eric	B	66C
PT	Grimaldi, Regina	B	61
PT	Hindman, Helen	B	63A
Asst Prof	Hutton, Paula R.	M	13,12A,66A,11
Assoc Prof	Jones, Heath	D	64C,64E,47,72,34
PT	Kidwell, Jeff	B	63C
PT	Lee, Melvin	D	63B
PT	McCoy, June	M	62
PT	McLarry, Royce	B	62A,62B
PT	Palmer, Kirk	B	63A
PT	Rucker, Jennifer	B	64C
PT	Schimek, John	D	62D
PT	Steward, Nick	M	65
PT	Syring, Natalie	M	64A
PT	Tatge, Valorie	B	62C
Prof	Thompson, Kathy A.	D	13,32B,66A,66B,41
PT	Warlick, Gerald	B	64B
PT	Weger, Bill	B	61
PT	Wooden, Lori	D	64D

OK0750 Oklahoma City University

Petree College of Performing Arts
Wanda L Bass School of Music
2501 N Blackwelder Ave
Oklahoma City, OK 73106-1402
(405) 208-5474   Fax: (405) 208-5971
www.okcu.edu/music
E-mail: kkoehn@okcu.edu

4 Year Liberal Arts Institution, Graduate School
Member of NASM

Master of Music in Composition, Master of Music in Performance, Master of Music in Conducting, Master of Music in Opera, Master of Music in Musical Theatre, Master of Music in Vocal Coaching

Dean: Mark Edward Parker, 80A
Dir., Graduate Studies: David Steffens, 80C
Dir., Admissions: Amy McQuade, 80D
Associate Dean: Mark G. Belcik, 80H
Assistant Dean & Dir., Preparatory Division: JoBeth Moad, 80H,80E

PT	Allen, John	B	63C,46,49
Prof	Anderson, Michael P.	M	63A
PT	Arnold, John	M	62A,42
PT	Bardeguez, Lemuel	M	64E
PT	Barnard, Rachel	M	61
PT	Beck-Reed, Jonathan	B	54
Asst Prof	Behn, Bradford	M	64C,41
Asst Prof	Belcik, Mark G.	D	60B
Prof	Birdwell, Florence H.	M	61
Assoc Prof	Black, Lendell	M	10C,35D,34
PT	Cain, Donna	M	62B,42
PT	Carroll-Phelps, Claudia	M	66A
PT	Cheng, James	M	13
Prof	Christensen, William Nield	D	61
Asst Prof	Crouse, Courtney	M	61
Asst Prof	Easley, David B.	D	13,13J
PT	Flanagan, Leslie	D	61
PT	Fleming, Beth	D	16,12C
PT	Floan, Obed	M	61
PT	Fresonke, Michael	M	13A,70,14C,41
Assoc Prof	Gavito, Cory M.	D	12A
PT	Grimaldi, Regina	B	61
PT	Hamilton, Brian	B	61
PT	Harvey-Reed, Lisa	M	64B
PT	Hawkins, Candace	M	66A,66D
Assoc Prof	Heine, Erik	D	13,13B,10C,13E
Prof	Herendeen, David	D	39,54
Assoc Prof	Holleman, Brenda	M	61
Asst Prof	Holst, Kelly Margaret	D	61
PT	Johnson, Jake	M	20
PT	Jones, Warren Puffer	DMA	12A
Assoc Prof	Keller, Larry	M	61
Prof	Knight, Edward	D	10
PT	Koslowske, Charles T.	M	66C,61
Inst	Love, Lisa Reagan	M	61
Prof	Mailman, Matthew	D	60,37
PT	Maloy, Kris	D	10A
PT	McDaniel, Catherine	D	61
Assoc Prof	McDaniel, Jan	M	39,54,66C,12A,61
Assoc Prof	Miller, Karen Coe	M	54,39
Assoc Prof	Monteiro, Sergio	D	66A
PT	Nilles, Benjamin	M	38,10F
PT	O'Neal, Faith	M	62E
PT	Osborne, Brian	M	66C,61
PT	Owens, Parthena	M	48,64A,32E
PT	Parker, Rebekah Bruce	M	66C
PT	Payne, Peggy	M	66C
PT	Picon, Jeffrey	M	61
Asst Prof	Plamann, Melissa M.	D	66G,31A
Asst Prof	Pritchett, Kate	M	63B,42,13B,13C
Prof	Ragsdale, Frank	D	61
PT	Resnick, Anna	M	64D
PT	Robinson, Ryan	M	63D,49,32E
Asst Prof	Sarver, Sarah	D	13,13E
Prof	Schimek, John	M	32,62D
PT	Shackleton, Jean	M	66C
PT	Sholer, Jeannie	M	54
Prof	Steffens, David	D	50,65,32E
Prof	Von Ellefson, Randi	D	36,60A,40
Prof	Willoughby, Judith A.	M	36,60A,40,32
Inst	Zieba, Tomasz	M	62C,42

OK0770 Oklahoma Panhandle State Univ

Department of Humanities-Music
PO Box 430
Goodwell, OK 73939-0430
(580) 349-1483   Fax: (580) 349-2302
www.opsu.edu
E-mail: joel.garber@opsu.edu

4 Year Institution

Dean, Liberal Arts: Sara Jane Richter, 80A

Adj	Banks, Steven	B	46,70
Lect	Carrell-Coons, Mariah	M	66A,66C,66D,32E
Adj Inst	Coons, Kevin	M	65
Adj	Cross, Sandy	B	63,64
Inst	Garber, Joel	M	12A,61,14,36,60
Adj	Hugghins, Linda	M	11

OK0800 Oklahoma State University

Department of Music
132 Seretean Ctr Performing Arts
Stillwater, OK 74078-4077
(405) 744-6133   Fax: (405) 744-9324
music.okstate.edu
E-mail: brant.adams@okstate.edu

4 Year Institution, Graduate School
Member of NASM

Master of Music in Pedagogy & Performance

Head of Music: Brant Adams, 80A
Dir., Undergraduate Studies: Douglas Droste, 80B
Dir., Undergraduate Studies & Preparatory Division: Julia W. Haley, 80B,80E
Dir., Undergraduate Studies: Douglas S. Henderson, 80B
Coord., Graduate Studies: Allen Scott, 80C

Prof	Adams, Brant	D	13,10
Assoc Prof	Belter, Babette	M	32E,64C
Asst Prof	Blecha-Wells, Meredith	D	62C,11,42
Assoc Prof	Bovenschen, Wayne	M	65,37,50,32E
Asst Prof	Broffitt, Virginia	D	64A,42,11,32E
Adj PT	Brown, Susan	B	64D,32E
Assoc Prof	Compton, Lanette	M	63B,11,32E,42
Assoc Prof	Compton, Paul R.	M	63C,63D,47,49
Assoc Prof	Condacse, Anne Marie	D	61,39
Assoc Prof	Droste, Douglas	M	38,60B,32E
Prof Emeritus	Frank, Gerald	D	66G
Assoc Prof	Frehner, Celeste Johnson	M	64B,20,32E
Asst Prof	Gardner, Ryan B.	D	63A,49,46,42,47
Assoc Prof	Golliver, April	M	61,39
Assoc Prof	Haley, Julia W.	D	32
Asst Prof	Haygood, Christopher D.	M	36,32D
Asst Prof	Henderson, Douglas S.	D	37,32E
Vstng Asst Prof	Hoffman, Brian D.	D	13A,13B,13C,66D
Assoc Prof	Karaca, Igor	D	13,10,34
Adj PT	Kaurin-Karaca, Natasa	M	66D,13C,11,34B
Asst Prof	Kirkendoll, Michael	D	66A,66B,66D,42
Adj PT	Kunzer, Stephen	M	63D,11,29A
Adj PT	Langsam, Stuart	M	65,50,11
Adj PT	Lanners, Heather	M	66A,13C,66C
Prof	Lanners, Thomas	D	66A
Asst Prof	Loeffert, Jeffrey	D	64E,13
Vstng Asst Prof	Lorenzo, Benjamin	D	37,32E
Adj PT	Malicoate, Todd S.	M	53
Asst Prof	Malis, David H.	M	61,39
Prof	Missal, Joseph	D	37,60B,49
Assoc Prof	Scott, Allen	D	12
Assoc Prof	Speed, George M.	M	62D,11,42
Assoc Prof	Stroope, Z. Randall	D	36,60A,40,10A
Assoc Prof	Talbott, Laura	D	62A,62B,42
Adj PT	TeVelde, Rebecca	M	11
Adj PT	Williford-Avrett, Martha	B	61

OK0825 Oklahoma Wesleyan Univ
Music Program
2201 Silver Lake Rd
Bartlesville, OK 74006-6233
(918) 335-6200   Fax: (918) 335-6807
www.okwu.edu
E-mail: jstewart@okwu.edu

4 Year Liberal Arts Institution

Chair: Jonathan Stewart, 80A,80H

Adj	Barrett, Celeste	B	61
Adj	Cathey, Sheila Clagg	M	11,13C
Adj	Cunningham, Jennifer	M	12A,13
Adj	Daniel, Wade	M	66A
Adj	Elmore, Ashlee	M	32B,32C
Adj	Mueller, Susan	M	36
Adj	Pearson, Don	B	70
FT	Stewart, Jonathan	M	32B,11,13B,36,61
Adj	Thompson, Randy	D	64C,66G

OK0850 Oral Roberts University
Department of Music
7777 S Lewis Ave
Tulsa, OK 74171-0003
(918) 495-7500   Fax: (918) 495-7502
www.oru.edu
E-mail: music@oru.edu

4 Year Institution
Member of NASM

Chair: J. Randall Guthrie, 80A
Assistant Chair: Tim Waters, 80H

Inst Adj	Andrews, Christy	M	64C
Inst Adj	Barton, Lorelei	M	62E
Inst Adj	Benton, Leanne	D	53
Asst Prof	Bocanegra, Cheryl	D	13,66A,35D,47
Asst Prof	Bridgman, Joyce M.	M	66A,66H,66B,66C,66D
Inst	Brown, Christopher	M	70,51,53,47
Lect Adj	Brown, Susan	B	64D
Inst Adj	Chung, Young-Eun	M	66D
Lect Adj	Estes, Billy	B	65
Inst Adj	Fletcher, Douglas	M	63C
Prof	Guthrie, J. Randall	DMA	31A,60A,36,11,66G
Lect Adj	Guzik, Bernard	B	63D
Inst Adj	Haefner, Steven	B	63A
Inst Adj	Hamm, Steven	M	62A
Assoc Prof	Hatley, H. Jerome	DMA	10,61,34,13D
Asst Prof	Jin, Soohyun	DMA	61,36
Inst Adj	John, David	B	35B,34,35C
Inst Adj	Johnson, Michelle	B	63B
Inst Adj	Morales, Joshua	B	70,57
Inst	Pannill Raiford, Judith	M	61
Inst Adj	Parker, Erica	M	62C
Prof	Pierce, Edward A.	DMA	40,61,36
Asst Prof	Quant, Scott	PhD	11,32,61
Inst Adj	Rath, Richard	M	64,64B,64E
Inst Adj	Rush, John	M	64A
Inst Adj	Ryan, Donald	M	66A
Inst Adj	Scales-Neubauer, Sheri	M	62A
Inst Adj	Smith, Robin	M	62D
Lect Adj	Smith, Roy	B	50,65
Asst Prof	Stevenson, George	DMA	12A,14,36,61
Inst	Sutliff, Richard	M	39,61
Asst Prof	Walker, Vicki	M	13,66A,66D
Inst Adj	Waters, Tim	DMA	47,10,37
Inst Adj	Wheeler, Ron	B	38,60B,62B

OK1030 Redlands Community College
Department of Music
1300 S Country Club Rd
El Reno, OK 73036-5304
(405) 262-2552   Fax: (405) 422-1200
www.redlandscc.edu
E-mail: krittenbrinkj@redlandscc.edu

2 Year Institution

Chair: Juanita Krittenbrink, 80A

Adj Prof	Twyman, Nita	M	13A,11,61,66A

OK1050 Rose State College
Department of Music
6420 SE 15th St
Midwest, OK 73110
(405) 733-7380   Fax: (405) 736-0370
www.rose.edu
E-mail: eedwards@rose.edu

2 Year Institution

Chair: Elizabeth Edwards, 80A

	Clifton, Jeremy J.	D	35C,10,13,13K,13B
Prof	Gregg-Boothby, Tracey	M	36,61
Prof	Jones, Bernard	M	13,12A,61,11,64
Adj	Morris, Theodora	M	62
Adj	Roberts, Russ	M	70
Prof	Robinson, Emily	M	13,66
Adj	Thomas, Erica	M	61
Adj	Twyman, Venita	M	66
Prof	White, Chris	M	70,35,37

OK1100 St Gregorys University
Department of Music
1900 W MacArthur St
Shawnee, OK 74804
(405) 878-5461   Fax: (405) 878-5198
www.stgregorys.edu

4 Year Institution

Music Contact: Aaron Kellert, 80A

Inst FT	Kellert, Aaron	M	11,36,13A,54,61

OK1150 Southeastern Oklahoma State Univ
Department of Fine Arts
Box 4126/Station A
Durant, OK 74701-0609
(580) 745-2088   Fax: (580) 745-7482
www.se.edu
E-mail: sweger@se.edu

4 Year Institution
Member of NASM

Chair: Stacy Weger, 80A

Inst	Blackwood, Jeremy	M	61,39
Prof	Craige, Mary Ann	D	66A,66D
Prof	Emge, Steven	D	11,34
Prof	McFadden, Robert	D	12A,66A
Assoc Prof	Walker, Jeri	D	32,13C
Asst Prof	Wallace, Jacob E.	D	37,60B
Assoc Prof	Weger, Stacy	D	60A,32D,36
Prof	White, Marc M.	D	65,50

OK1200 Southern Nazarene University
School of Music
6729 NW 39th Expressway
Bethany, OK 73008
(405) 491-6345   Fax: (405) 717-6268
www.snu.edu
E-mail: sbetts@snu.edu

4 Year Institution
Member of NASM

Chair: Steven Betts, 80A

Adj	Adams, Margaret Ann	M	32B
Adj	Ambrosini, Jeffrey	M	61
Asst Prof	Ambrosini, Rebekah	M	39,61
Prof	Betts, Steven	D	66A,66B,66D,13,11
Adj	Bohn, William	B	63D
Adj	Brewer, James	M	64D
Adj	Buthman, Luke	B	70
Adj	Curtin, Jeff	B	63A
Adj	Denman, Matt	M	70
Adj	Fine, Joe	M	64E
Adj	Flick, DaLeesa J.	M	66A,12A
Asst Prof	Graves, Jim F.	M	36,32D,32B,60A,61
Asst Prof	Hanson, Andrea J.		61
Adj	Hutchins, Tony	M	63C
Assoc Prof	Lewis, Melissa	D	60,41,51,62A
Adj	Marek, Tim	M	66G
Adj	Moore, Harlan	B	47
Prof	Moore, Phil	D	37,49
Adj	Morren, Christian	D	61
Adj	Munday, Don	B	29B,62D
Prof	Reighard, Mark	D	13A,13,66A,11
Asst Prof	Rosfeld, Ken	B	34D,34E,35A,35C,35D
Adj	Rosfeld, Marilyn	D	66A
Adj	Rushing, Densi	B	62
Adj	Steward, Feodora	M	64A
Adj	Tatge, Valorie	M	62C
Adj	Walker, K. Dean	M	65,50
Adj	Warlick, Gerald	M	64B
Adj	Whitmore, Michael	M	64C

OK1250 Southwestern Oklahoma State Univ
Department of Music
100 Campus Dr
Weatherford, OK 73096
(580) 774-3708   Fax: (580) 774-3714
www.swosu.edu/music
E-mail: music@swosu.edu

4 Year Institution, Graduate School
Member of NASM

Master of Music in Performance, Master of Music in Music Education

Chair & Dir., Summer Programs: Keith M. Talley, 80A,80G
Dir., Graduate Studies: Dennis C. Widen, 80C

Inst PT	Bates, Elaine	M	32B,66A,13
Assoc Prof	Bessinger, David K.	M	13,50,65
Inst PT	Bessinger, Marti	M	32B
Prof	Chambers, Robert	D	38,63C,63D,13D,10F
Asst Prof	DiPaolo, Stacey	D	11,12A,64C
Inst PT	Dobrinski, Kathy	M	62C
Asst Prof	Farris, Daniel King	D	40,42,12,36,13
Inst PT	Fulmer, Fred	M	63D
Asst Prof	Griffeath, Kristin	D	12A,61,39,36
Asst Prof	Griffeath, Robin	D	11,61
Inst PT	Hughes, Amanda	M	61
Assoc Prof	Lee, Chihchen Sophia	D	33,32F,66A
Inst	Lin, Anthea	M	66A,66B
Inst	Mueller, Marc	M	37,63A,32E,60,34
Inst PT	Resnick, Anna	M	64B,64D
Inst PT	Robillard, David	M	62A,62B
Inst PT	Rogers, JoAnne	M	62D
Prof	South, James	D	37,63A
Inst	South, Janis	M	63B,11,12A,49,20
Inst PT	Surman, Patricia	D	64A,11
Assoc Prof	Talley, Keith M.	D	64E,32,48,34
Asst Prof	Tirk, Richard	D	47,63A,37
Assoc Prof	Widen, Dennis C.	D	66A,66D,13

OK1300 Tulsa Comm College-Southeast Campus
Department of Perf Arts
10300 East 81st St
Tulsa, OK 74133-7799
(918) 595-7752   Fax: (918) 595-7778
www.tulsacc.edu
E-mail: hrigert@tulsacc.edu

2 Year Institution

Music Contact: Heidi R. Burton, 80A
Dean, Performing Arts: Kelly Clark, 80A

Inst	Burton, Heidi R.	M	13A,13,11,66A,62A
Asst Prof	Engel, Tiffany	M	13,11,12A,66A
Inst	Katz, Robert S.	D	13,11,12A,12,62D
Inst	Mabrey, Paul	M	13,36,61
Inst	Vento, Steve	M	10,11,12,47,32E

OK1330 Univ of Central Oklahoma
School of Music
100 N University Dr
Box 179
Edmond, OK 73034-5207
(405) 974-5004   Fax: (405) 974-3891
www.uco.edu/cfad/academics/music/index.asp
E-mail: lwhite27@uco.edu

4 Year Institution, Graduate School
Member of NASM

Master of Music in Performance, Master of Music in Music Education, Master of Music in Jazz Performance, Master of Music in CD Production

Dean, College of Arts, Media & Design: John Clinton, 80A
Director: L. Keith White, 80A
Dir., Graduate Studies: Ted Honea, 80C

Lect	Bramlett, KaDee	M	64B
Asst Prof	Butterfield, Emily J.	D	64A
Asst Prof	Charoenwongse-Shaw, Chindarat	D	66A,66B,66D,66C
Adj	Chiang, Ju-Yu (Carol)	M	66D
Lect	Clark, Wayne	D	63C
Adj	Craig, Genevieve	M	63B
Lect	DeMaio Caprilli, Barbara J.	M	61,54,11
Lect	Deng, Lu	M	62A
Asst Prof	Eckard, Kevin L.	D	39,61
Assoc Prof	Eshelman, Darla	D	32A,32B,32D
Asst Prof	Forbat, David	D	66A,66B,66C,66D
Inst	Geib, Michael T.		62D
Asst Prof	Glaubitz, Robert	D	61
Lect	Gorrell, Brian	M	64E,46,34,47,29B
Assoc Prof	Govich, Marilyn S.	D	61
Lect	Hanan, David	M	37,60B,10F,34,63A
Inst	Hardman, David J.	M	50,65
Lect	Hefley, Earl	M	11,64C,64E
Asst Prof	Honea, Ted	D	12A,16,63B
Lect	Hurleigh, Shannon	M	54
Lect	Johnson, Scott	M	70
Lect	Kidwell, Jeff	M	47,63C,46,29
Asst Prof	Klages, James L.	D	63A
Artist in Res	Kuleshov, Valery	D	66A
Asst Prof	Lamb, Brian	D	60B,32,37
Asst Prof	Lindblade, Dawn Marie	D	64C
Prof	Magrill, Samuel	D	13,10A
Lect	McCullough, Thomas Eric	D	10,62C,13,38,10C
Lect	McLemore, Katherine		64B
Staff	Mitschell, P. Bryan	M	34D
Prof	Morris, Ralph	D	38,62A,62B,41,42
Lect	Morris, Theodora	M	62A,62B,67C,42
Asst Prof	Nelson, Karl		36,40
Lect	Owen, Linda	D	66A,66D
Assoc Prof	Remy-Schumacher, Tess	D	62C,41,42
Lect	Richman, Pamela L.		13C,13A,61
Lect	Rohr, Clint		29A,13A
Asst Prof	Rucker, Lee	M	37,47,63A,46,29
Lect	Smeltzer, Steven	B	54
Lect	Steward, Nicholas	M	65
Asst Prof	Streets, Barbara S.	D	32B,61
Lect	Syring, Natalie	M	13A,13B,13C
Asst Prof	Thompson, Sandra D.		11,32D
Lect	Vaughan, Danny	M	70
Inst	White, Greg	M	35A,54
Prof	White, L. Keith	D	10A,10B
Assoc Prof	Wooden, Lori L.	D	64D,41,38,42,48
Prof	Zhu, Hong	D	62A,41,42,51

OK1350 Univ of Oklahoma
School of Music
500 W Boyd St.
Room 138
Norman, OK 73019-2071
(405) 325-2081   Fax: (405) 325-7574
music.ou.edu
E-mail: oumusic@ou.edu

4 Year Institution, Graduate School
Member of NASM

Master of Music in Composition, Master of Music in Music Theory, Master of Music in Performance, Master of Music Education, PhD in Music Education, DMA in Composition, DMA in Performance, DMA in Choral Conducting, DMA in Instrumental Conducting

Director: Lawrence R. Mallett, 80A
Assistant Director & Coord., Undergraduate Studies: Brian Britt, 80B,80H
Assistant Director & Coord., Graduate Studies: Irvin Wagner, 80C,80H
Associate Director: Roland Barrett, 80H

Asst Prof	Ackmann, Rodney	M	64D,20G,41
Inst	Akarepi, Ekaterini	D	20
Vstng Asst Prof	Ambrosini, Armand	D	11
Inst	Anderson, Richard	M	61
Inst	Arana, Miranda	M	20
Asst Prof	Avery, Elizabeth	D	61,31
Assoc Prof	Barrett, Roland	M	13
Assoc Prof	Britt, Brian	M	37
Assoc Prof	Ciorba, Charles R.	D	32
Assoc Prof	Conlon, Paula J.	D	20G,20,14F,14
Vstng Asst Prof	Cox, Donna	M	61
Prof Emeritus	Curtis, Steven	D	32
Assoc Prof	Dell, Charlene	D	32E,32H,32,62,62A
Assoc Prof	Dobbins, Brian	M	63D
Assoc Prof	Drege, Lance	D	65
Assoc Prof	Ellis, Sarah	D	13
Prof	Enrico, Eugene	D	12A,12,55,67
Prof	Fast, Barbara	PhD	66A,66B,66D
Prof Emeritus	Faulconer, James	D	13,10,34,35
Assoc Prof	Ferrara, William	M	39
Vstng Asst Prof	Fowler, Bruce E.	M	61
Inst	Frazier, Damon	M	20A
Prof Emeritus	Gates, Edward	D	66A
Inst	Giacona, Christina	D	20
Inst	Goza, David	D	20
Asst Prof	Grossman, Hal	M	62A,41,51
Assoc Prof	Hall, Gail R.	D	11
Assoc Prof	Ham, Jeongwon	D	66A
Vstng Asst Prof	Hammett, Larry D.	M	70,29A
Prof	Josephson, Kim	M	61
Assoc Prof	Karathanasis, Konstantinos	D	34D,10A,10,35C,35G
Prof	Lamb, Marvin L.	D	10,43
Vstng Asst Prof	LeBlanc, Gaye F.	M	62E,11
Assoc Prof	Lee, Gregory	D	62A,41,51
Assoc Prof	Lee, Michael	D	12A,12,14,20G
Assoc Prof	Leffingwell, Dolores	D	61
Vstng Inst	Leon-Shames, Stephanie L.	M	66C,42
Inst	Lopez, Eduardo	M	20
Asst Prof	Lucas, Mark	D	60,32,36,41
Asst Prof	Lumsden, Rachel	D	13
Prof	Magrath, Jane	D	66B,66A,66D,66,66C
Prof	Mallett, Lawrence R.	D	
Prof	Matlick, Eldon	D	41,63B
Assoc Prof	Neill, William	M	61
Prof	Nelson, Joy	D	32A,32B
Assoc Prof	Neumann, Mark	D	62A,41,51
Assoc Prof	Pederson, Sanna	D	12A,20G,12
Assoc Prof	Raiber, Michael	D	32
Assoc Prof	Richstone, Lorne S.	M	61,31
Vstng Asst Prof	Riddick, Frank C.	D	13
Inst	Rideout, Roger R.	D	11
Asst Prof	Ruck, Jonathan C.	D	62C,41
Asst Prof	Saltzstein, Jennifer A.	D	12,12A
Inst	Schaeffer, Vicki J.	D	66G
Assoc Prof	Schwandt, John	D	66G,66H
Asst Prof	Schwartz, Daniel	D	64B,41
Assoc Prof	Shames, Jonathan	D	38,39
Assoc Prof	Sherinian, Zoe	D	14
Vstng Inst	Sievers, Beth	D	62A
Prof	Sievers, Karl H.	D	63A
Prof Emeritus	Smith, Jerry Neil	D	64C
Inst	Souza, Christine	D	65,20
Inst	Souza, Ricardo A.	D	20
Inst	Sproat, Joel	D	66G
Prof	Stephenson, Kenneth	D	13A,13
Assoc Prof	Stoops, Anthony	DMA	62D
Asst Prof	Tirk, Suzanne	M	64C
Asst Prof	Traficante, Debra	M	37,10F
Prof	Wagner, Irvin	D	49,63C,54
Prof	Wakefield, William	D	60,37,41
Prof	Watts, Valerie	D	64A,41
Vstng Asst Prof	Wilkinson, Jay	M	47,53,29
Assoc Prof	Zielinski, Richard	D	60,36,40

OK1400 Univ of Science & Arts of Oklahma
Department of Music
PO Box 82345
1727 W Alabama St
Chickasha, OK 73018-0001
(405) 574-1295   Fax: (405) 574-1220
www.usao.edu
E-mail: kbohannon@usao.edu

4 Year Institution
Member of NASM

Chair: Stephen Weber, 80A
Dir., Artist Series: Kenneth Bohannon, 80F

Adj PT	Barker, Kent	B	63
Assoc Prof	Bohannon, Kenneth	D	39,61,35A
Prof	Hanson, Dan L.	D	13,10,32C,47,37
Prof	Hanson, Jan	D	60,11,12A,32,36
Adj PT	Jech, Lori	B	64C
Adj PT	Johnson, Deborah	B	66C
Adj PT	Krieger, Angela	B	62
Adj PT	Morris, Gretchen	M	64
Adj PT	Settlemires, Joseph		47,70
Assoc Prof	Weber, Stephen	D	66A,34,66C,66D

OK1450 Univ of Tulsa
School of Music
800 S Tucker Dr
Tulsa, OK 74104
(918) 631-2262   Fax: (918) 631-3589
www.utulsa.edu
E-mail: teresa-reed@utulsa.edu

4 Year Institution
Member of NASM

Director: Teresa Shelton Reed, 80A

Adj Inst	Andrews, Christy D.	M	64C
Adj Inst	Barton, Lorelei	M	62E
Inst Adj	Bates, James I.	B	47,62D,70
Adj Inst	Bowers, Walt M.	B	34D
Adj Inst	Brown, Susan	B	64D
Asst Prof	Bucchianeri, Diane	M	11,12A,41,62C
Asst Prof	Childs, Kim J.	M	36,40,61
Staff	Clark, Tad	B	37
Inst	Deaver, Stuart T.	D	66A,66D,66B,13I,66
Adj Inst	Eskitch, Paulo S.		62B
Adj Inst	Fowler, Michael R.		70
Adj Inst	Glaser, Lise E.	B	64B
Asst Prof	Goldman-Moore, Susan J.	M	32,36,61
Asst Prof	Grass, Ken G.	M	37,64E,60B
Adj Inst	Gray, Sonny		66A
Adj Inst	Guzik, Bernie	B	63,49
Adj Inst	Harrington, Karen	M	66A
Asst Prof	Howard, Vernon D.	B	47,49,63C,63D,29
Adj Inst	Johnson, Brenda Seward	M	61
Adj Inst	Johnson, Michelle		63B
Adj Inst	Maher, Dana F.	M	66C
Adj Inst	McElligott, Brady R.		61
Adj Inst	McFadden, Tim J.	B	63A
Adj Inst	McKee, Lindsey L.	M	61
Adj Inst	Moore, David A.	D	10,13,11,36
Adj Inst	Moore, Michael D.	D	63A
Adj Inst	Morris, Kelley	M	66A,66D
Adj Inst	Morrow, Diane		61
Adj Inst	Newson, Jeffrey	M	66A,47
Prof	Norberg, Anna H.	M	66A,66C,66D,15
Inst	O'Boyle, Maureen E.	M	62A
Adj Inst	Pearson, Ronald	B	66G
Prof	Powell, John S.	D	11,12A,12,20
Adj Inst	Predl, Ronald E.	M	37,63A
Prof	Price, William Roger	D	10A,41,66A,10F
Assoc Prof	Reed, Teresa Shelton	D	13,12A
Assoc Prof	Rivers, Joseph L.	D	13,10A,10C,34D,34E
Adj Inst	Rush, John Phillip	M	64A,67D,12A,55C,56
Assoc Prof	Ryan, Francis J.	D	13,34,11
Adj Inst	Shadley, Jeffrey	B	34D,35C
Adj Inst	Smith, Roy S.	B	65
Assoc Prof	Strummer, Linda	B	39,61
Adj Inst	Thomas, Wendy E.		35E
Adj Inst	Wagner, Richard A.	M	38
Adj Inst	Yohe, Tony		65

OK1500 Western Oklahoma State College
Department of Music
2801 N Main St
Altus, OK 73521-1310
(580) 477-2000   Fax: (580) 477-7777
www.wosc.edu
E-mail: karla.shelby@wosc.edu

2 Year Institution

Chair: Karla Shelby, 80A

Inst	Gardner, Gary D.	M	11,62,63,37,47
Inst	Rowlett, Donn	M	13,11,66
	Shelby, Karla	M	10D,13A,60A,66A,36

OR0010 Blue Mountain Community College
Department of Music
PO Box 100
Pendleton, OR 97801-1000
(503)276-1260   Fax: (503)276-6119
www.bluecc.edu
E-mail: MMayer@Bluecc.edu

2 Year Institution

Executive Vice President: John Turner, 80A

Inst PT	Flagg, Lezlee	B	61
Inst	Lange, Daniel	M	12A,47,64,35
Inst	Miller, David	M	36,61,13,60
Inst PT	Reise, Adriene	M	66

OR0050 Clackamas Community College
Department of Music
19600 S Molalla Ave
Oregon City, OR 97045-8980
(503) 594-3337   Fax: (503) 650-6667
www.clackamas.edu
E-mail: wakelingt@clackamas.edu

2 Year Institution

Chair: Tom Wakeling, 80A

Inst	Cline, Lonnie		60,36,61
PT	Davis, Mike		70
	Deitz, Kevin	M	13,62D
PT	DenBeste, LeaAnne		61
Inst	Mills, David	M	13,10,12A,37,63A
Inst PT	Miyama, Yoko	D	66,13,12A,66C,66D
Emeritus	Nelson, Gary R.	M	
PT	Rose, Brian		34,35C,35D,35H
Inst	Wakeling, Tom	M	11,12A,47,29,35

OR0150 Concordia University
Music Program
2811 NE Holman St
Portland, OR 97211-6067
(503) 280-8511   Fax: (503) 280-8121
www.cu-portland.edu
E-mail: kberentsen@cu-portland.edu

4 Year Institution, Graduate School

Master of Arts Teaching Music Education

Chair, Performing & Visual Arts: Kurt Berentsen, 80A

Staff	Berentsen, Kurt	M	36,60,61,32A,40
Lect PT	Bozell, Casey	M	62A,62B,38,62C,51
Inst PT	Cox, John	M	63B
Inst PT	Homan, Jeff	M	64E
Inst PT	Iimori, Mitch	M	64B,64D
Inst PT	Jablonski, Darlyn	M	61
Inst PT	Jublonski, Anna	M	61
Lect PT	Krueger, Walter E.	D	13A,66A,12A,66G,66D
Staff	Kuhn, William	D	37,11,63C,60,13A
Inst PT	Kvach, Konstantin	M	61,39
Inst PT	Manuele, James	M	70

Inst PT	Mitchell, David	D	63A
Inst PT	Mooyman, Lisa	B	61
Lect PT	Neilson, Duncan	D	13A,13B,10,13C,13E
Inst PT	Oft, Mike	M	63D,63C
Inst PT	Schooler, Jason	B	62D
Lect PT	Schumacher, Judy	B	44
Inst PT	Sessa, Thomas	M	65
Inst PT	Tiedemann, Sarah	M	64A

OR0175 Corban University
Department of Music
5000 Deer Park Dr SE
Salem, OR 97317-9392
(503) 375-7019   Fax: (503) 315-2942
www.corban.edu
E-mail: music@corban.edu

4 Year Institution, Graduate School

Chair: Dan Shuholm, 80A

Asst Prof	Bartsch, John T.	M	13B,38,66,10F,10A
Prof	Cross, Virginia A.	D	31A,12A,66D,13A,66B
Adj	Dougherty, Peggy S.	M	66A,66D,13A,66B,13E
Adj	Gaither, Tiffany	B	32B
Adj	Griffiths, Brian	B	63D,46,37
Adj	Hawkins, Diane	M	64A
Adj	Johnson, Bonnie L.	M	61
Adj	Lipton, John	M	65
Adj	Noland, Brenda	B	66C
Asst Prof	Shuholm, Dan	M	37,46,31A
Assoc Prof	Strauser, Matthew L.	D	36,60,13C,32D
Adj	Such, Rich	M	47,64E
Adj	Thomas, Andy	M	66A
Adj	Weathers, Keith	B	60

OR0200 Eastern Oregon University
Department of Music
One University Blvd
La Grande, OR 97850-2899
(541) 962-3555   Fax: (541) 962-3596
www.eou.edu/music
E-mail: tfetz@eou.edu

4 Year Institution

Music Contact: Teun Fetz, 80A
Dean, Arts & Sciences: Steve Gammon, 80A

Inst PT	Boyer, Duane	B	70,51
Prof	Cooper, Matthew J.	DMA	13,47,66A,66D,29
Assoc Prof	Espinosa, Leandro	D	62C,62D,38,13A,11
Inst PT	Fetz, Katie	B	64,32E
Assoc Prof	Fetz, Teun	D	12A,65,48
Inst PT	Frasier, Michael	M	36,32D
Inst PT	Jacobson, Jaime	B	61
Inst PT	Johnson, Greg	B	64E
Prof	McKinnon, John A.	D	13,10,63,34,14
Inst PT	Paul, Lanetta	M	66G
Prof	Wordelman, Peter	D	60A,36,61,54

OR0250 George Fox University
Department of Fine Arts
414 N. Meridian
Newberg, OR 97132
(503) 554-2620   Fax: (503) 537-3902
www.georgefox.edu
E-mail: lwenz@georgefox.edu

4 Year Liberal Arts Institution
Member of NASM

Chair: Brent Weaver, 80A

	Athens, William		62D
	Bartels, Cindi		64C
	Brallier, Kathryn		64A
	Crane, David		63B
Adj	Daane, Maggie	M	61
Adj	Dougherty, Peggy	M	66A,13A
	Elliott, Richard		37,41
	Frame, Gary		36
	Glaros, Pam		61
Assoc Prof Emeritus	Howard, David	D	13,10,11,45,66G

	Huddleston, Debra		66C,66A,66G
Artist in Res	Hunt, William		38,62A,62B
	Iimori, Mitch		64B,64D
Assoc Prof	Lauinger, Robert		
Adj	Lawrence, Steve	M	65
Adj	Lowry, Gary	M	70
Adj	McGladrey, Cynthia	M	61
	Ollis, Ken		65
	Porter, Randy		29,66A
	Quinby, Jack		63C,63D
	Roberts, Sherill		62C
	Smith, Carol		63A
	Stewart, Barbara		66
	Tanner, Joel		46,64E
Asst Prof	Vandehey, Patrick	D	60,32,37,38,63C
Assoc Prof	Weaver, Brent	D	10,61,13,34,36
Prof	Willson, Kenneth F.	D	13,45,66A,66B,66C
Artist in Res	Zeller, Richard		

OR0350 Lane Community College

Department of Mus, Dance & Thtre
4000 E 30th Ave
Eugene, OR 97405-0640
(541) 463-5209   Fax: (541) 463-4172
www.lanecc.edu/perarts/
E-mail: mcmanuse@lanecc.edu

2 Year Institution

Lead Faculty: Edward McManus, 80A

Inst	Barbham, Vicki	M	36,66D
Inst	Bertucci, Ronald	M	37,13A,47,63C,13C
Inst	Denny, Mike	M	29A,13
Inst	Greenwood, James	M	13
Inst	Griffith, Glenn	M	13A
Inst	Gustafson, David	M	61,13A
Inst	McManus, Edward	M	63B,34A,35C,35G,13A
Inst	Michell, Ray	D	70
Inst	Myrick, Barbara	D	13,12A,66A,66D,64A
Inst	Noel, Debi	M	13A,36
Inst	Stark, Melissa	M	35G
Inst	Svoboda, Matt	M	36,40
Inst	Vik, Siri	M	61
Inst	Waddel, Nathan	M	20G,47
Inst	Watanabe, Hisao	M	13C,13D,13F,38,66D

OR0400 Lewis and Clark College

Department of Music
0615 SW Palatine Hill Rd
Portland, OR 97219
(503) 768-7460   Fax: (503) 768-7475
www.lclark.edu/dept/music
E-mail: gerhardt@lclark.edu

4 Year Institution

Chair: Dinah Dodds, 80A

PT	Balmer, Dan	B	70,47
PT	Banzi, Julia	D	20,14C,34B,14,10E
PT	Beck, Nathan	B	20
Prof	Beck, Nora	D	11,12A
Emeritus	Becker, David M.	M	60,32C,37,29,64
PT	Biel, Carol	M	66,66D
PT	Captein, Dave	B	62D
PT	Craig, Jennifer	M	62E
PT	DeLeon, Dorien	M	62C,42
PT	Dwyer, Jack	B	62
PT	English-Ward, Miriam	M	62B
PT	Eubanks, Mark	M	64D
PT	Evans, David	B	64E
PT	Ewer, Gregory	M	62A
PT	Feinberg, Joshua	M	20E
Asst Prof	FitzGibbon, Katherine L.	D	36,60,11
Prof Emeritus	Garrett, Lee R.	D	66G
PT	Haagenson, Anna	M	61
PT	Halverson, Carl	B	61
PT	Iimori, Mitch	M	64B
PT	Jennings, Dunja	M	64C
Asst Prof	Johanson, Michael	D	13,10
PT	Johnston, Mindy	M	20D
PT	Leonard, Jeff	M	70,10B,45
PT	Masterson, Rik	B	20E
PT	McBerry, Sue	M	61,54
PT	Mery, John	M	20H,62
PT	O'Banion, James	M	63A
PT	O'Connell, Tim	M	67H
PT	Pardew, Mike	B	70
PT	Paschal, Brett E. E.	D	65,13,11

Prof Emeritus	Pauly, Reinhard G.	D	12A
PT	Porter, Randy	M	66A
PT	Schooler, Jason	M	62D
Prof Emeritus	Seeley, Gilbert	D	60,12A,36,41
Asst Prof	Specht, Jeffrey	D	13,38,60,63D
PT	Stalnaker, Bill	B	63B
PT	Stirling, Michael	B	20E
PT	Teskey, Nancy	D	64A,32E
PT	Thompson, Stephanie	M	66,66C

OR0450 Linfield College

Department of Music
900 SE Baker St
McMinnville, OR 97128-6894
(503) 883-2275   Fax: (503) 883-2311
www.linfield.edu
E-mail: droot@linfield.edu

4 Year Institution
Member of NASM

Chair: Faun Tanenbaum Tiedge, 80A

Prof	Bourassa, Richard N.	D	13,10F,10A,11
Adj	Chen, Jay	M	60B,49,37,63A
Adj	Conzetti, Florian	D	65
Adj	Crocker, Emily	B	52
Adj	Engbretson, Chris	M	66A,66C
Adj	Ganske, Kathy	M	66C
Adj	Gilson, Tim	M	62D
Adj	Goldsmith, Pamela	B	70
Adj	Gunn, Natalie	M	61
Adj	Hettwer, Mike	M	63B
Adj	Huddleston, Debra	B	66C
Adj	Kravitz, Steve	M	64B,64E,64C,29,11
Adj	Lay, Jean	M	32B
Prof	Leonard, Gwenellyn	D	12A,61,39
Adj	Libonati, Dana	M	47
Prof Emeritus	Marsh, Lawrence B.	D	60,12A,32,36
Adj	McDaniel, Susan E.	M	66A
Adj	Newton, Jon	M	34D
Prof	Paddock, Joan Haaland	D	60,32,49,63A,37
Adj	Pederson, Robin	M	32D
Adj	Pich, Victoria	M	62A,62B
Adj	Roberts, Sherill	M	62C
Adj	Song, Anna	M	13C,36,55B,55A,40
Adj	Strand, Karen	M	64B
Prof	Tiedge, Faun Tanenbaum	D	11,13,12A,20,42
Prof	Timmons, Kathryn Jill	D	12A,66A,66H,66B,66C
Adj	Westby, Denise	B	64A

OR0500 Marylhurst University

Department of Music
PO Box 261
Marylhurst, OR 97036-0261
(503) 699-6263   Fax: (503) 636-9526
www.marylhurst.edu
E-mail: jpaul@marylhurst.edu

4 Year Institution
Member of NASM

Chair: John F. Paul, 80A

Adj PT	Balogh, Lajos	M	38,62A
Adj PT	Barnes, Michael	M	61
	Dazia, Mitzuki	B	67H
Adj	Elizabeth, Lori	M	11
Adj	Etlinger, David	D	34A,34D,34E
Adj PT	Evans, David		64E
Adj PT	Fabbro, Renato	D	66A,66D
Adj	Gardner, Brian	M	65
Asst Prof	Haek, Jonathan	M	34D,10A,13,66A
Adj PT	Hancock, Pollyanna	M	61
Adj PT	Harmon, Sally	M	66A,29B
Adj PT	Neuman, Gayle	B	12A
Adj PT	Neuman, Phil	B	12A,63C
Adj PT	Owen, Edward 'Ted'	M	33
Assoc Prof	Paul, John F.	D	10,13,34
Adj PT	Poris, Valerie Jill	M	14
Adj PT	Pritchard, Jerrold	D	64A
Adj	Putnam, Fay	M	11
Adj PT	Ross, Emily	M	33
Adj PT	Rousseau, Beth	M	33
Adj PT	Sandahl, Thomas	M	47,70,29B
Adj PT	Schmitt, James	B	61
Adj PT	Shakhman, Igor	D	64C
Asst Prof	Smith, Justin	D	36,11,60
Adj PT	Soltero, Jill	M	61
Adj PT	Still, Tamara G.	D	12A

Asst Prof	Story, Kirstin 'Maya'	M	33
Assoc Prof	West, Therese	D	33
Adj PT	Whitmore, Peter	M	13B,13C
Adj PT	Zisa, Peter	M	70

OR0550 Mount Hood Community College
Department of Music
26000 SE Stark St
Gresham, OR 97030-3300
(503) 491-6996   Fax: (503) 491-6013
www.mhcc.edu
E-mail: Marshall.Tuttle@mhcc.edu

2 Year Institution

Dean, Performing Arts: Wendy Schissel, 80A

Inst	Barduhn, David	M	13,10,47,29
Inst	Jones, Susie	M	13,37,47,29
Inst	Tuttle, Marshall	D	13,36,38

OR0600 Multnomah University
Department of Music
8435 NE Glisan St
Portland, OR 97220-5814
(503) 255-0332 x 390   Fax: (503) 251-5386
www.multnomah.edu
E-mail: music@multnomah.edu

4 Year Institution

Chair: Stanford Campbell, 80A

Inst	Campbell, Stanford	M	36,61,31A,60A
PT	Iula, Dave	M	70
PT	Johnson, Sidney	M	61
PT	Jones, Craig	M	66A,66D,60A
PT	Loomis, Melinda	M	61
PT	Moll, Benjamin	M	65,13A,13B,13C,10A
PT	Smith, Lonnie	B	64A
PT	Ward, Miriam English	D	62A,62B
PT	Yerden, Ruth	M	66A,66G

OR0700 Oregon State University
Department of Music
101 Benton Hall
Corvallis, OR 97331-2502
(541) 737-4061   Fax: (541) 737-4268
oregonstate.edu/cla/music
E-mail: music@oregonstate.edu

4 Year Institution, Graduate School

Master of Arts in Teaching, Master of Arts in Interdisciplinary Studies

Chair: Marlan Carlson, 80A

	Atchley, Elizabeth	M	61,66C
	Biesack, Ryan	M	65
	Boal, Nathan		64E
Asst Prof	Brudvig, Robert	D	65,13
Assoc Prof	Bull, Tina	D	32,36
Inst	Carlson, Angela	M	13
Prof	Carlson, Marlan	D	38,51
Asst Prof	Chapman, Christopher	D	32,37,46,63A,60B
	Chen, Jay	M	63A,49
	Christensen, Russ		36
Prof	Coolen, Michael T.	D	14,54,20,12A,35A
	Forry, Sharon R.		66A
Adj Inst	Goodwin, Julia	D	66A,66D,11,12A,66C
	Grabe, Ann	M	62C
	Grandstaff, Neil		70
	Grimes, Benjamin		20G,64A
	Hackett, Janet	M	61
	Hadley, Katie	M	32,32B,32C
	Hanson, Craig		66G
Adj	Henniger, Henry J.	M	63C,63D
Staff	Jeffers, Rebecca	M	13A,66B,66C,66D
	Johnson, Larry	M	63B,49
	Kincaid, Sam		34
	Korman, Fred		64B
	Kozak, Pete E.		70
	Kuhlmann, Evan	M	64D
	Lambert, Jessica I.		62A,62B
	Larson, Nicholas A.	D	61

	Looking Wolf, Jan Michael		20G,64A
Prof	McCabe, Rachelle	D	66A,66B,12A
	Meyn, Richard		62D
	Nine-Zielke, Nicola	M	61,66C
	Parsons, Jeffrey L.		
	Pauls, Jill	D	64A
Asst Prof	Poppino, Richard	M	61,39
	Reason, Dana		66D
	Robe, Carol M.		64C
	Sand, Megan	M	61
	Saul, Ken D.	M	63A
	Scollard, Dan T.		70
	Servias, David	M	66D
	Shaman, Sila		29B
	Spencer, Helena K.		64D
Inst	Townsend, Bradley G.	D	37,60B,32E
Asst Prof	Zielke, Steven M.	D	36,60,32D

OR0750 Pacific University Oregon
Department of Music
2043 College Way
Forest Grove, OR 97116-1756
(503) 352-2216   Fax: (503) 352-2910
www.pacificu.edu
E-mail: music@pacificu.edu

4 Year Institution
Member of NASM

Dean: John W. Hayes, 80A
Chair: Bryce M. Seliger, 80A,80B,80E
Dir., Artist/Performance Series: Paula Thatcher, 80F

Adj	Brown-Stephens, Kelli	M	66A
Prof	Burch-Pesses, Michael	D	60,32C,37,47,45
Adj	Campbell, Lars	M	63C
Adj	Coleman, Janet	M	66C
Adj	Conrow, Steve	M	63A
Adj	Curtis, Arlyn	B	62D
Adj	Galusha, Cessaries	M	66A,66D
Adj	Green, Les		61
Adj	Gross, John		47
Asst Prof	Ihas, Dijana		62B,11,32
Adj	Juza, Alan	M	64B
Adj	Kravitz, Steve	M	64A,64D,64E,41
Adj	Kvach, Konstantin	M	61
Adj	LaMotte, Adam		62A
Adj	McCallum, Laura		64A
Adj	McMickle, Doug	M	70,41
Adj	Niederloh, Angela	M	61,39
Adj	Parkhurst, Melissa	D	20,12
Adj	Peyton, Jeff		65A,65B
Adj	Reed, Anne	M	61,39
Adj	Rivas, David		66C
Adj	Seitz, Noah		62C
Assoc Prof	Seliger, Bryce M.	D	38,14A,13,12A
Prof	Stephens, Timothy	D	13,10F,10,12A
Adj	Still, Tamara	D	66G
Adj	Stowell, John	B	70,29
Assoc Prof	Tuomi, Scott	M	12A,12,14,61,55
Adj	Vreeland, Harold		64C
Adj	Walden, Kathy		62A,62B
Adj	Willette, Andrew	M	34
Adj	Zaik, Santha	B	63B,16

OR0800 Portland Community College
Department of Music
12000 SW 49th Ave
Portland, OR 97219-7132
(503) 977-4759   Fax: (503) 977-4874
www.pcc.edu
E-mail: jmery@pcc.edu

2 Year Institution

Director: John Christian Mery, 80A
Dean: Steve A. Ward, 80A

Inst PT	Addison, Don F.	D	20,14
Inst PT	Carr, Walter E.	D	12A,12,14,20G
Inst PT	Da Cunha, Cherise Ann	M	66
PT	Green, Dana S.	M	13A,11,66
Inst PT	Hedberg, Judy L.	M	12A,13A
PT	Izzett, Robert K.	M	37
Inst FT	Johnson, Julianne R.	B	36,40,29
PT	McCann, Jesse S.	M	70,13A,11
Inst FT	Mery, John Christian	M	13,10,41,70,34
PT	Schaal, Joelle E.	M	13,65,11

OR0850 Portland State University
Department of Music
PO Box 751
Portland, OR 97207-0751
(503) 725-3011 Fax: (503) 725-8215
www.fpa.pdx.edu/music.html
E-mail: music@pdx.edu

4 Year Institution, Graduate School
Member of NASM

Master of Arts in Music, Master of Music in Performance, Master of Music in Conducting, Master of Music in Jazz Studies, Master of Science in Music

Chair: Bryan Johanson, 80A
Assistant Chair & Dir., Graduate Studies: Joel Bluestone, 80C,80H

Assoc Prof	Babcock, Ronald	D	13,32E
Asst Prof	Bamonte, David	M	41,42,63A,49
PT	Belgique, Joel	B	62B
Prof	Bluestone, Joel	D	11,50,65,20G
Asst Prof	Carlson, Sydney R.	D	41,42,64A
Assoc Prof	Chan, Susan	D	66A,66B,66D,66C
Prof	Cheifetz, Hamilton		41,51,62C,20G,20F
PT	Dockendorf, Lyle		64A
PT	Franzen, David		70
PT	Fujikawa, Denise		62E
PT	Gildea, Dan		70,29
Asst Prof	Glaze, Debbie	M	32,36
Prof	Grant, Darrell	M	41,47,66A,66D,29
Prof	Gray, Charles	M	47,41,29
PT	Guggenheim, Janet		66A
PT	Hall, J. Scott		64E,29
PT	Halvorson, Carl		61
Prof	Hansen, Brad	D	13,29,10,34
Asst Prof	Heilmair, Barbara	D	12A,41,42,64C,48
Assoc Prof	Higgins, Edward	D	37,32E,60B
PT	Hinshaw, Susan		61
Prof Emeritus	Jimerson, David	M	32B,36,61
Prof	Johanson, Bryan	B	70,13,41,11,10
PT	Johnson, Jeffrey		62D
PT	Jones, Alan		47
Asst Prof	Kiyama, Wynn	D	12,20
PT	Kuhlmann, Evan		64D
PT	Lee, Julia		66A
PT	Marsh, Lisa		66A
Prof Emeritus	Martin, Stephen	D	14,12,20
PT	McCann, Jesse		70
Asst Prof	Meadows, Christine	M	39,61
PT	Medler, Ben	B	63C,47
Asst Prof	Miksch, Bonnie	D	10,13
PT	Moore, Glen		62D,29
PT	Newton, Farnell		63A,29
Inst	Newton, Jon	M	34,13A
PT	Niederloh, Angela		61
PT	Ollis, Ken		65,29
PT	Porter, Randy		66A,29
PT	Putterman, Jeff	M	70,29
Asst Prof	Robinson, Melissa Ann	D	41,42,49,63B
PT	Savaria, Suzanne	M	66A
Inst	Schneider, Doug	B	64E,66C
PT	Schulte, Dan	M	62D,47
Asst Prof	Selden, Ken	D	38,43,51,60B
Prof Emerita	Sheridan, Wilma F.	D	32B,12A
Prof Emerita	Shotola, Marilyn	D	13,64A,41,12A
PT	Simonovic Schiff, Jelena	M	13C,13B
Prof	Sindell, Carol A.	B	41,62A,42
Prof Emeritus	Solie, Gordon A.	M	60,32,37,64D
PT	South, Pam		61
Assoc Prof	Sperry, Ethan L.	D	36,60A
Prof Emeritus	Stalnaker, William P.	D	13,10,12A
Prof Emeritus	Stanford, Thomas S.	D	64C,12,48,41
Assoc Prof	Strand, Karen	M	64B,11
Prof Emeritus	Svoboda, Tomas	M	13,10
PT	Titterington, Connie	M	66A,66D
PT	Ward, Brian	M	66A,47
Prof Emeritus	Webster, Gerald	M	63A,12A
PT	Weiss, Ezra		66A,29
PT	Willette, Andrew C.	M	11,13A

OR0900 Reed College
Department of Music
3203 SE Woodstock Blvd
Portland, OR 97202
(503) 517-7734 Fax: (503) 777-7769
www.reed.edu
E-mail: burfordm@reed.edu

4 Year Institution

Chair: Mark Burford, 80A
Dir., Private Music Program: Denise VanLeuven, 80H

Asst Prof	Burford, Mark	D	12A,20G,14C,20H
Prof Emerita	Falk, Leila Birnbaum	B	11,12A,12B,41
Prof	Hancock, Virginia	D	13,12A,36
Asst Prof	Luker, Morgan James	D	14A,14C,14D,20H
Prof	Schiff, David	D	13,10A,20G,29,38

OR0950 Southern Oregon University
Department of Music
1250 Siskiyou Blvd
Ashland, OR 97520-5010
(541) 552-6101 Fax: (541) 552-6549
www.sou.edu/music
E-mail: KoranN@sou.edu

4 Year Institution, Graduate School
Member of NASM

Master of Music in Conducting

Chair: Terry Longshore, 80A
Associate Dean: Vicki T. Purslow, 80A
Dean, Arts & Sciences: Josie Wilson, 80A

Inst PT	Barton, Todd	M	10,45
Inst PT	Behnke, Martin	D	46,47,29A
Prof	Bender, Rhett	D	64E,13,52,64C
Inst PT	Berlet, Pat	M	62B
Inst PT	Brock, Andrew	M	13A,61
Inst PT	Cole, Scott	D	62A
Inst PT	Daly, Pat	M	11
Inst PT	Davidson, Steve	M	11
Lect PT	Dresser, Bruce	M	63A
Prof Emerita	Evans, Margaret R.	D	12A,66G
Inst PT	Foltz, Kristina	M	66A
Inst PT	French, Jodi		66D
Prof	French, Paul T.	D	11,12A,36,39,61
Assoc Prof	Grimland, Fredna H.	D	13A,32,61
Inst PT	Hunter, Laurie	M	61
Assoc Prof	Hutton, Cynthia	D	60,37,49,63B
Inst	Jacobs, Mark	D	63C
Lect PT	Kermode, Walker	M	64D
Lect PT	Kimball, Phebe	B	64A
Assoc Prof	Longshore, Terry	D	65,20,14,47,35A
Inst PT	Matthews, Don	M	61
Inst PT	McElrath, Katheryn	M	64A
Prof Emeritus	McKee, Max	M	60
Lect PT	Merusi, Rebecca	B	65
Lect PT	Miller, David	B	62D
Lect PT	Murray, Ellie	M	61
Assoc Prof	Purslow, Vicki T.	M	11,37,64E,29
Asst Prof	Richmond, Jeffrey W.	D	29
Lect PT	Rogers, David	M	70
Inst PT	Rubin, Lauren	M	20
Inst PT	Schmidt, Jody	M	63B
Inst PT	Scoggin, David	B	29A
Inst PT	Shaw, Kirby	D	40
Inst PT	Slawson, Wayne	D	10
Lect PT	Truelove, Lisa	M	62C
Inst PT	Truelove, Stephen	D	66A,66D
Prof	Tutunov, Alexander	D	13,66A,66D,66C
Inst PT	Vannice, Michael	M	13A,10,10F
Inst PT	Wight, Ed	D	12A

OR1000 Southwestern Oregon Comm College
Department of Music
1988 Newmark Ave
Coos Bay, OR 97420
(541) 888-7242
www.socc.edu
E-mail: mturner@socc.edu

2 Year Institution

Chair: Michael W. Turner, 80A

Inst	Aakre, Brett	M	40,61
Inst	Aakre, David		40
Inst	Allen, Mark		37,49,63A,63C,63B
Inst	Almich, Michael		64C,64E
Inst	Beckstrom, Tom		65
Inst	Kimball, Sarah		66A
Inst	Masters, Ken		46
Inst	McAndrews, Deb		64A
Inst	McLauchlin, Charlotte	M	13,66D,66A,67C,12A
Inst	Simonson, Jessica		62A,62B,62C
Prof	Turner, Michael W.	M	70,29,34,47

OR1010 Treasure Valley Comm College
Department of Perf Arts
650 College Blvd
Ontario, OR 97914-3423
(541) 881-5950   Fax: (541) 881-2770
www.tvcc.cc
E-mail: slaubach@tvcc.cc

2 Year Institution

Chair: Ted Fink, 80A

Adj	Armstrong, Robert	M	12A,63A,64C,64A
Adj	Baxter, Dawn		64A
Adj	Chavez, Arturo		62
Adj	Cox, Timothy	PhD	70
Inst	Denison, Mark	M	12A,29A,63C,46,60B
Adj	Gilman, Matt	M	64,60B
Adj	Hatvani, Robert	B	66A,66D
Adj	Jensen, DeNice		61
Adj	Poff, Sarah	B	60B
Inst	Replogle, Rebecca	M	36,61,13A,13C,40
Adj	Schmid, Ilo	M	66A,66G
Adj	Wheeler, Edwin	B	70

OR1020 Umpqua Community College
Department of Music
1140 College Rd
PO Box 967
Roseburg, OR 97470-0226
(503) 440-4693   Fax: (503) 677-3296
www.umpqua.edu
E-mail: jason.heald@umpqua.edu

2 Year Institution

Division Chair: Greg Fishwick, 80A
Chair: Jason A. Heald, 80A

Inst PT	Gronberg, John	M	63
Inst PT	Hall, Roberta	M	36,61
Inst PT	Hanson, Ross	M	70
Prof	Heald, Jason A.	D	13,10,47,36,38
Inst PT	Hinkle, Jean	M	11,13A,41,66A,66D
Inst PT	Palmer, Jason	M	66D,13,13C,29A,29B
Inst PT	Pecorilla, John	M	37,64,65
Inst PT	Riley, Kristin	B	62A,62B
Inst PT	Snyder, Dirk	B	46
Inst PT	Spicer, Donna	M	36,61,66A,66D
Inst PT	Ziebart, Hailey	M	66A,61

OR1050 Univ of Oregon
School of Music and Dance
1225 Univ of Oregon
Eugene, OR 97403-1225
(541) 346-3761   Fax: (541) 346-6101
music.uoregon.edu
E-mail: bfoley@uoregon.edu

4 Year Institution, Graduate School
Member of NASM

Master of Arts in Music Theory, Master of Music in Composition, Master of Music in Performance, Master of Music in Conducting, Master of Music in Music Education, PhD in Music Theory, PhD in Composition, PhD in Music Education, DMA in Composition, DMA in Performance, PhD in Musicology, Master of Arts in Musicology, Master of Music in Piano Pedagogy, Master of Music in Jazz Studies, Master of Music Intermedia Music Technology

Dean & Co-Dir., Chamber Music Series: Brad Foley, 80A,80F
Associate Dean & Dir., Undergraduate Studies: Phyllis M. Paul, 80B,80H
Associate Dean & Dir., Graduate Studies: Ann B. Tedards, 80C,80H
Assistant Dean & Dir., Admissions: Robert Ponto, 80D,80H
Dir., Preparatory Division: Leslie Straka, 80E
Dir., Preparatory Division: Lillie Wells, 80E
Co-Dir., Chamber Music Series: John Evans, 80F
Dir., Summer Programs: Jack Boss, 80G

Inst	Abbott, Tyler	M	62D,29,13
Inst	Baird, Barbara M.	D	66G,66H,67F,11
Asst Prof	Barth, Molly	M	64A,42,48,43
Assoc Prof	Boss, Jack	D	13,10A
Inst	Brown, Andiel	B	36,31F
Inst	Case, David	M	70,11
Asst Prof	Cheung, Pius	D	65,50
Assoc Prof	Crumb, David	D	10A,10F,13
Adj Inst	DeMartino, Louis	M	42,48,64C
Inst	Denny, Michael	M	70,47,29,29A
Asst Prof	Diaz, Frank M.	D	32,32G,13K
Assoc Prof	Dossin, Alexandre	D	66A
Inst	Esquivel, Karen L.	D	61,39
Prof	Foley, Brad	D	64E
Assoc Prof	Gearhart, Fritz	M	62A,42
Asst Prof	Grant, Roger Mathew	D	13
Adj Inst	Grasso, Eliot	D	11,20,14
Adj Inst	Gries, Peggy	D	12,55,67
Assoc Prof	Grose, Michael	D	11,63D,49,42
Inst	Hedgecoth, David	D	32,32E,37
Asst Prof	Henniger, Henry J.	M	49,63C
Adj Inst	Heyer, David	D	13
Adj Inst	Hobbs, Gary G.		29,65
Adj Inst	Ingram, Joe	M	32,32E
Asst Prof	Jacobs, David M.	D	38,60B
Adj Inst	Jantzi, John	D	66D
Adj Inst	Johnson, Teagan	M	32B
Asst Prof	Kajikawa, Loren	D	12A,14,20C,20G
Inst	Kerner, Winifred	M	66D
Assoc Prof	Koenigsberg, Tobias R.	M	29,47,66A
Assoc Prof	Kramer, Dean	D	66A
Assoc Prof	Kruckenberg, Lori	D	12A,12C,13J
Prof	Kyr, Robert	D	10A,10F,43,20D
Inst	Latarski, Donald	B	70,35G,41
Inst	Levy, Mark	D	20,14
Prof	Lucktenberg, Kathryn	B	62A,42
Prof Emerita	McLucas, Anne Dhu	D	12A,12C,20G,20F,14
Adj Inst	McQuilkin, Terry P.	D	10A
Assoc Prof	McWhorter, Brian J.	M	63A,49,43
Assoc Prof	Mentzel, Eric P.	M	61,67H,55,55D,55A
Adj Inst	Miller, Lance R.	A	35C,35G
Inst	Olin, Christopher S.	M	32D,36,60A
Prof	Owen, Stephen W.	M	46,47,53,29,64E
Inst	Pack, Tim S.	D	13
Assoc Prof	Paul, Phyllis M.	D	32A,32B,32C
Prof	Paul, Sharon J.	D	60A,36,40
Assoc Prof	Paul, Timothy A.	D	32E,37,60B
Asst Prof	Pena, Melissa	M	64B,11
Prof	Pologe, Steven	M	62C,42
Assoc Prof	Ponto, Robert	M	60B,37,41
Assoc Prof	Riley, David M.	D	66C,66A,42
Assoc Prof	Rodgers, Stephen	D	13
Adj Inst	Rogers, Michael	D	13
Adj Inst	Scheuerell, Doug	B	20D,65
Asst Prof	Shner, Idit	D	64E,42,47,29
Assoc Prof	Smith, Marian E.	D	12
Prof	Stolet, Jeffrey	D	13,45,10,34,10B
Prof	Straka, Leslie	D	42,62B
Prof	Tedards, Ann B.	D	61
Inst	Udell, Chester	D	10,10B,11,34,35
Prof	Vacchi, Steve	DMA	64D,42,48
Assoc Prof	Van Dreel, Lydia	M	63B,49,42
Assoc Prof	Vanscheeuwijck, Marc	D	55,12,67B
Prof	Vargas, Milagro	M	61
Assoc Prof	Wachter, Claire		66A,66B,66D
Inst	Wagoner, W. Sean	D	65,10F,50,37,11
Adj Inst	Wayte, Laura Decher	M	61
Adj Inst	Wayte, Lawrence A.	D	12,29
Inst	Wells, Lillie	M	32A,62A,32E
Assoc Prof	Wiltshire, Eric	D	37,32E,60B
Inst	Woideck, Carl	M	29A,20G,12
Adj Inst	Zaerr, Laura	M	62E,42

OR1100 Univ of Portland
Department of Fine & Perf Arts
5000 N Willamette Blvd
Portland, OR 97203-5743
(503) 943-7228   Fax: (503) 943-7805
college.up.edu/pfa
E-mail: connolly@up.edu

4 Year Institution
Member of NASM

Chair: Michael E. Connolly, 80A

Adj	Ashton, Jeff C.	B	70
Adj	Baker, Wade	M	61
Adj	Boelling, John F.	M	61
Adj	Briare, Maureen K.	M	31A
Adj	Campbell, Lars	M	63C
Prof	Connolly, Michael E.	D	36,12A,10A,61,13
Adj	Cox, John P.	M	63B
Asst Prof	De Lyser, David M.	D	13,10,38,41
Adj	Edson, Tracey D.	M	66A,66D,66C
Adj	Eubanks, Mark G.	B	64D
Adj	Fabbro, Renato S.	D	66A
Adj	Follett, Kathleen J.	M	62A
Adj	Homan, Jeff C.	B	64E
Adj	Iimori, Mitch S.	B	64B,64D
Prof	Kleszynski, Kenneth	D	13,32,38

Adj	Lee, Hwakyu (Julia)	M	66A
Asst Prof	Leupp Hanig, Nicole	D	61
Adj	Lindner, Jenny	B	62E
Adj	Logan, Hal	M	34
Adj	Mitchell, David W.	M	63A
Asst Prof	Murphy, Patrick C.	D	13B,37,32,41
Adj	Parker, David K.	M	47
Adj	Poris, Jill	M	61
Adj	Ratzlaff, Dieter	M	62C
Adj	Schooler, Jason G.	M	62D
Adj	Sessa, Thomas P.	M	65
Adj	Shakhman, Igor	C	64C
Adj	Soltero, Jill K.	D	61
Adj	Stokes, Tayler L.	M	63D
Adj	Stuber, Jon	D	66G
Adj	Wilson, Carla E.	M	64A

OR1150 Warner Pacific College
Department of Music
2219 SE 68th Ave
Portland, OR 97215-4026
(503) 517-1060   Fax: (503) 517-1350
www.warnerpacific.edu
E-mail: dplies@warnerpacific.edu

4 Year Institution

Chair: Dennis B. Plies, 80A

PT	Bolton, Chuck	M	32,37,49,63D
Asst Prof	Cameron, Jennifer	M	13,10F,64,60,51
PT	Davis, Michael	M	70
Prof Emeritus	Frolick, Jeanne	D	32
PT	Higgins, Lynn	M	31A
Prof	Miller, Thomas A.	D	60A,11,36,61,31A
Prof	Plies, Dennis B.	D	47,65B,66B,66D,13C
PT	Sanders, Debbie	M	61
PT	Yerden, Ruth	M	66A,66G,66D,66C

OR1210 Western Conserv Baptist Seminary
Department of Music
5511 SE Hawthorne Blvd
Portland, OR 97215-3367
(503) 233-8561   Fax: (503) 239-4216
www.westernseminary.edu

2 Year Institution

Adj	Borror, Gordon L.	M	31A

OR1250 Western Oregon University
Department of Music
345 Monmouth Ave N
Monmouth, OR 97361-1314
(503) 838-8275   Fax: (503) 838-8880
www.wou.edu/music
E-mail: baxterd@wou.edu

4 Year Institution, Graduate School
Member of NASM

Master of Music in Contemporary Music

Head, Music: Diane R. Baxter, 80A,80F,80G
Dir., Graduate Studies: Kevin Walczyk, 80C
Dir., Artist Series: Keller Coker, 80F

Inst PT	Amend, William	B	62D,47
Inst PT	Andrew, Isaac	M	63D
Inst PT	Bartels, Cindi	M	64C
Prof	Baxter, Diane R.	D	66,20,12A,14
Prof	Bergeron, Tom	D	13,64,47,35A
Inst PT	Bevington, Mike	M	63C
Inst PT	Brown, Mel	B	65
Inst PT	Chisholm, Amy B.	M	61
Prof	Coker, Keller	DMA	55,12A,63C,10D
Inst PT	Doan, John	B	70
Inst PT	Dulaney, John	M	32E,29A
Inst PT	Hall, Jamie	M	49,63A
Asst Prof	Harchanko, Joseph	D	10,13,62C
Assoc Prof	Helppie, Kevin	D	61,47,54,20G
Assoc Prof	Holmquist, Solveig	D	11,36,60,66G,69
Inst PT	Hsueh, Yvonne	M	62A,62B,67A,67B
Inst PT	Lee, Gordon	M	29,13A
Inst PT	Moore, Mike		35G
Inst PT	Morelli, Jackie	M	66A,66D
Asst Prof	Nail, James I. (Ike)	D	38,37,60B,32E
Inst PT	Palmer, Jason	M	65
Inst PT	Savage, John		64A
Prof	Walczyk, Kevin	D	13,45,63B,29,10
Inst PT	Whitley, William	M	13
Inst PT	Woitach, Christopher	B	70,47

OR1300 Willamette University
Department of Music
900 State St
Salem, OR 97301-3930
(503) 370-6255   Fax: (503) 370-6260
www.willamette.edu
E-mail: dtrevett@willamette.edu

4 Year Institution, Graduate School
Member of NASM

Master of Arts in Teaching

Chair & Dir., Artist/Performance Series: Anita King, 80A,80F

Inst PT	Baker, Wade	M	61,32D
Inst PT	Bartels, Cindi	M	64C,48
Prof	Behnke, Martin K.	D	60,37,66A,29
Inst PT	Bock, Stan	M	63C,63D,49
Inst PT	Boelling, John	M	61
Inst PT	Chen, Jay	M	37,63A,41
Prof	Coen, Jean-David	D	12A,66A,66C
Inst PT	Deitz, Kevin	B	62D
Prof	Denman, James L.	M	13,12A,66G,13F,13H
Asst Prof PT	Doan, John	M	70
Prof	Duerksen, Marva G.	D	13,12A
Asst Prof PT	Eikrem, Jeanne	B	64A,48
Inst PT	Elder, Christine Welch	M	36
Inst PT	Iimori, Mitch	B	64B
Inst PT	Ingram, David	M	66A,66C
Inst PT	Johnson, Janice	M	61,54
Inst PT	Kem, Randy		64E,42
Prof	King, Anita	D	13,66A,66C
Inst PT	King, Robert	D	66A
Inst PT	Klemme, Paul	D	36,66G
Prof	Long, Wallace H.	D	60,32C,36
Prof	McIntosh, Bruce	M	13,38,62C
Asst Prof	Miley, James	D	10,29,47,46,13
Inst PT	Murray, Warren	B	65,50
Asst Prof	Nord, Michael	D	32A,32B,34
Inst PT	Parsons, Jeffrey L.	M	62E
Comp_in_Res	Peel, John	D	10,12A
Prof	Rouslin, Daniel S.	D	11,38,41,62A,62B
Inst PT	Snelling, Ann		66C
Inst PT	Snow, Julian	B	66A
Inst PT	Swensen-Mitchell, Allison	M	61

PA0050 Albright College
Department of Music
PO Box 15234
Reading, PA 19612-5234
(610) 921-7872   Fax: (610) 921-7768
www.albright.edu
E-mail: abinger@alb.edu

4 Year Institution

Co-Chair: Adlai Binger, 80A
Co-Chair: Rebecca G. Butler, 80A

Inst	Binger, Adlai	M	36,61,66G,60A,66C
Prof	Butler, Rebecca G.	M	11,64A,37,34,13B
PT	Clark, Jesse	M	11,34D
PT	Cullen, David	B	70
PT	Earnest, JoAnne	M	66A,66D
PT	Eben, Michael	M	29A
Artist in Res	Lentz, Jeffrey	M	61,54
PT	Rodgers, Christopher	B	66A,66C,66G
Assoc Prof	Weary, Hal	ABD	35A,35D,35F

PA0100 Allegheny College
Department of Music
520 N Main St
PO Box 31
Meadville, PA 16335
(814) 332-3302 or 3356   Fax: (814) 337-3352
www.allegheny.edu
E-mail: achien@allegheny.edu

4 Year Institution

Chair: Alec F. Chien, 80A
Dir., Summer Programs & Artist/Performance Series: Timothy Cooper, 80G,80F

PT	Bond, Bronwell	B	64A,48
PT	Borthwick-Aiken, Rebecca A.	M	66G
PT	Branagan, Marcella	D	66A
Prof	Chien, Alec F.	D	11,42,66A,41
PT	Corsi, Stephen F.	M	65,50
Asst Prof	Dearden, Jennifer	D	63A,34,13A,13B,13C
PT	Froman, James	B	70,29
PT	Hepler, Julie E.	M	64B,64C,12A,64D,64E
Prof	Hepler, Lowell E.	D	12A,12C,37,66A,63D
PT	Jamison, Vicki	B	61,40
	Kalinowski, Diane	B	61
PT	Leech, Thomas		63B
PT	Niblock, Carol B.	M	61
Asst Prof	Niblock, James D.	D	36,61,60A,13A,13B
PT	Philipp, Hilary	M	64B
PT	Plyler, Wendy	M	66A
PT	Reash, Aimee	B	61
PT	Riley, Susanna	M	62C
PT	Rudolph, Robert A.	M	62A,62B,41,42,51
PT	Shellito, Kelli	M	66A,66D
PT	Showman, Deke	B	67H
PT	Stitt, Ronald	D	63C,47,29,46,34
PT	Symons, Kathy	M	61

PA0125 Arcadia University
Department of Music
450 S Easton Rd
Glenside, PA 19038
(215) 572-2900
www.arcadia.edu/
E-mail: frabizio@arcadia.edu

4 Year Institution

Chair: William V. Frabizio, 80A

Assoc Prof	Frabizio, William V.	D	13,11,12A,41
PT	Gaspero, Carmen	M	70,29
Assoc Prof PT	Haupt, Dorothy G.	D	12A,32B,36,66G
PT	Hellyar, Kathleen	M	12,66A
PT	Russo, John	M	64

PA0150 Baptist Bible College of Penn
Department of Music
538 Venard Rd
Clarks Summit, PA 18411-1250
(570) 586-2400   Fax: (570) 585-9607
www.bbc.edu
E-mail: lkauffman@bbc.edu

4 Year Institution

Chair: Larry D. Kauffman, 80A

Prof	Harris, David	D	36,61,31A,40,32D
Prof	Kauffman, Larry D.	D	12A,36,66A,31A
Inst	McGrew, David	M	10,13,66,31A,11
Inst	Truax, Jenean	B	13A,13C,32D,61,66A

PA0250 Bloomsburg University
Department of Mus, Theatre & Dance
400 E 2nd St
Bloomsburg, PA 17815-1301
(570) 389-4284   Fax: (570) 389-5010
www.bloomu.edu
E-mail: sclickar@bloomu.edu

4 Year Institution

Chair: Stephen D. Clickard, 80A
Interim Dean: Julie Kontos, 80A
Dir., Graduate Studies: Lawrence Fritz, 80C
Dir., Admissions: Christopher Keller, 80D
Dir., Artist/Performance Series: James Hollister, 80F
Dir., Summer Programs: Tom Fletcher, 80G

Prof	Anselm, Karen	M	54
Assoc Prof	Baker, Alan	D	60A,11,36,61,54
	Baldoria, Charisse J.	D	66A,66D,12A,11
Asst Prof	Campbell, Todd	M	34,11,65
Assoc Prof	Candlish, Bruce	M	54
Prof	Clickard, Stephen D.	D	37,63,47,60B
Assoc Prof	Howarth, Gifford	D	65,37
Asst Prof	Hower, Eileen	M	32,11,61
Prof	Jelinek, Mark R.	D	60B,11,38,62
Asst Prof	Kim, Kunyoung	D	66A,13E,11,66B
Asst Prof	Krupp, Ethan	M	54
Prof	Miller, Wendy L.	D	11,12A,36,61,54
Asst Prof	Petry, Julie	M	52
Asst Prof	Schmidt, Tracey	D	13,64A,11
Inst	Slotkin, Matthew C.	D	70

PA0350 Bucknell University
Department of Music
1 Dent Dr
Lewisburg, PA 17837-2029
(570) 577-1216   Fax: (570) 577-1215
www.bucknell.edu/music
E-mail: dana.olsen@bucknell.edu

4 Year Institution
Member of NASM

Chair: William Kenny, 80A
Dir., Artist/Performance Series: Kathryn L. Maguet, 80F

PT	Alico, Gregory	M	65
PT	Beckley, Susan	M	61
PT	Benjamin, Richard S.		63D
PT	Bixler, Ronald	M	64E
Asst Prof	Collier, Bethany	D	14,20,20D
PT	Cooper, Lawrence R.	M	63C,63D
PT	Cullen, Leslie		64A
Prof Emeritus	Duckworth, William	D	13,10
PT	Gallup, Trina	M	64D
Prof	Hannigan, Barry T.	D	13,66A
PT	Hartung, Colleen M.	D	64C
PT	Haynes, Philip	B	29A
Prof Emeritus	Hill, Jackson	D	10,12A,12,14,71
Prof	Kenny, William	D	60,11,37,63A,63B
Asst Prof	Long, Barry	DMA	29,47,13,63A,53
PT	Malone, Ryan M.	D	66G
PT	McCarty, Karena	B	64B
PT	Orris, Dale A.	M	63A
Assoc Prof	Para, Christopher	M	13,11,38,62A,62B
Assoc Prof	Payn, Catherine	D	32,39,61
Prof	Payn, William A.	D	36,44,66G,66H,31A
PT	Potter, Lou Ann	B	66A
PT	Rammon, Andrew	M	62C
Prof	Randall, Annie Janeiro	D	11,12A,12,12E
Asst Prof	Seskir, Sezi	D	12A,13A,66A,66C
PT	Smolensky, Marcus H.	D	62A,62B
PT	Stimpert, Elisabeth	M	64C
Prof Emerita	Svard, Lois	D	13,66A
PT	Umble, Jay	B	70
Asst Prof	Watts, Sarah	D	32A,32B,11

PA0400 Bucks County Community College
Department of Music
275 Swamp Rd
Newtown, PA 18940
(215) 968-8047

www.bucks.edu/academics/departments/arts/music/index.php
E-mail: bresnens@bucks.edu

2 Year Institution
Member of NASM

hair: Mark Benson, 80A

Inst PT	Apple, Marjorie	M	32A
Inst PT	Benson, Beth	B	64B
Prof	Benson, Mark	D	13,10,12,63,34
Assoc Prof	Bresnen, Steven M.	D	13,11,12A,66A,66D
Inst PT	Ferdinand, Edward	M	66A
Inst PT	Giammario, Matteo	D	13A,11,62A,62B

Inst PT	Goldenbaum, Cathy	M	11,61
Inst	Holcombe, Helen	B	13A,36,61,66D
Inst PT	Lawton, Thomas P.		66A,53
Prof	Nowak, Gerald C.	M	13,37,47,64
Inst PT	Pultorak, Mark	B	50,65
Inst PT	Racamato, Claire	M	64A
Inst PT	Schachter, Benjamin	M	64E,29
Inst PT	Sheridan, John	B	70,53,13A
Inst PT	Velosky, Ronald A.	B	62D,29

PA0450 Cabrini College

Department of Fine Arts
610 King of Prussia Rd
Radnor, PA 19087-3623
(610) 902-8380   Fax: (610) 902-8285
www.cabrini.edu
E-mail: adeline.bethany@cabrini.edu

4 Year Institution

Music Coordinator & Dir., Artist Series: Adeline M. Bethany, 80A,80F

Prof	Bethany, Adeline M.	D	11,20D,32A,32B,36
Lect	Brisbon, Perry	M	61
Lect	Canfield, Wanda	M	66A
Lect	D'Amico, John	M	29A
Lect	Napoli, Joseph	M	70
Lect	Schauer, Jerry	M	11

PA0500 Calif University of Pennsylvania

Department of Music
250 University Ave
California, PA 15419-1394
(724) 938-4242   Fax: (724) 938-4256
www.calu.edu
E-mail: gonano@calu.edu

4 Year Institution

Chair: Max A. Gonano, 80A

Inst PT	Davis, Greg	B	34A,34D,35C,35D,35G
Inst PT	Fung, Jan		50,65
Prof	Gonano, Max A.	M	11,12A,13A,29A,37
Inst PT	Guzzi, Ralph		10D
Prof	Ikach, Yugo Sava	D	61,38,11,13A,36
Inst PT	Karsh, Ken	M	70
Inst PT	Kovach Brovey, Lisa	M	61
Inst PT	Lonich, Nancy L.	M	32A,32B
Inst PT	Podroskey, Frank		63A,63B
Inst PT	Sacco, Kathy		66A
Inst PT	Schottman, Margret		62A,62B,62C
Prof	Sharer, Marty	D	11,37,12A,13A,13C
Inst PT	Shultz, Dane		64
Inst PT	Spang, Ron		63D,63C
Inst PT	Stahurski, Brian	M	70
Inst PT	Weaver, Joseph		70

PA0550 Carnegie Mellon University

School of Music
5000 Forbes Ave
Pittsburgh, PA 15213-3890
(412) 268-2372   Fax: (412) 268-1431
music.cmu.edu
E-mail: musicschool@andrew.cmu.edu

4 Year Institution, Graduate School
Member of NASM

Artist Diploma, Master of Music in Composition, Master of Music in Performance, Master of Music in Conducting, Master of Music in Music Education, Master of Science in Music & Technology

Dir., Recruitment/Enrollment: Michele McGregor, 80D
Dir., Special Music Programs: Daniel Barrett, 80E
Communiciations Manager: Kristi D. Ries, 80F
Assistant Head: Ross Garin, 80H
Associate Head: Natalie Ozeas, 80H
Dir., Student Services: Sharon L. Johnston

Assoc Prof	Ahlstedt, Douglas F.		61
Lect PT	Allen, Christopher		65
Lect PT	Almarza, Alberto		64A
Lect PT	Amato, Donna		66C
Prof	Balada, Leonardo	DIPL	13,10
Prof	Baxtresser, Jeanne	B	64A
Lect PT	Bell, Scott F.		64B
Lect PT	Berntsen, Neal		63A
Lect PT	Blackwell, Raymond		66C
Lect PT	Branson, Jeremy	M	65
Lect PT	Caballero, William		63B
Lect PT	Cagley, Judith L.		13C
Lect PT	Capizzi, Christopher		66A
Prof	Cardenas, Andres J.		62A
Lect	Carver, Mark		66C
Lect PT	Cherian, Rebecca S.		63C
Assoc Prof	Colwell, Denis R.	M	48
Asst Prof	Cowan, Richard D.		61
Lect PT	Crewe, Murray		63C
Lect PT	DeAlmeida, Cynthia K.		64B
Lect PT	DeFade, Eric		64E,47,29
Lect PT	Domencic, Mark L.		13A
Lect	Douglas, Thomas W.		47,60
Lect PT	Evans, Paul J.		65
Asst Prof	Fallon, Robert	D	12
Lect PT	Ferla, James		70
Prof	Forough, Cyrus	M	62A
Prof	Galbraith, Nancy	D	13,10
Lect PT	Gerlach, Paul D.		32
Lect PT	Goeres, Nancy E.		64D
Lect PT	Graf, Enrique		66A
Lect PT	Howard, Micah		62D
Lect	Irwin, Roseanna Lee		66C
Asst Prof	Ito, John Paul	D	13
Prof	Joseph, Annabelle	D	13,32I
Prof	Keeling, Kenneth	D	12
Lect PT	Kim, Sung-Im		66C
Lect PT	Knox, Craig		63D
Lect PT	Kostyniak, Stephen		63B
Lect	La Rocca, Carla		66A,66D
Lect PT	LaDuke, Lance		63D
Lect PT	Lawrence, Betsy		61
Prof	Lehane, Gregory J.		
Prof	Li, Hanna Wu		66A,66B,66D
Lect	Manriquez, Luz		66C
Lect PT	Marcinizyn, John		70
Assoc Prof	McKay, Anthony L.		
Lect PT	Neely, Stephen		32I
Lect PT	Ojeda, Rodrigo		66C
Lect PT	Opie, Benjamin		34
Prof	Ozeas, Natalie		32
Prof	Page, Robert		36,39
Lect PT	Pandolfi, Philip A.		64D
Lect PT	Posvar, Mildred Miller		61
Lect PT	Premo, David		62C
Asst Prof	Randall, Richard R.	D	13
Lect PT	Roethlisberger, Karen L.		66C
Lect PT	Rusinek, Michael		64C
Lect PT	Sargsyan, Vahan		66C
Assoc Prof	Schepkin, Sergey		66A
Lect PT	Schotting, MaryBeth Glasgow		62A
Lect	Schultz, Stephen		12,55B
Lect	Schulz, Riccardo		35C,35G
Lect PT	Steele, Terry	M	64E
Lect	Strouse, Lewis	D	60,32
Lect PT	Sullivan, Peter		63C
Prof	Thomas, Marilyn Taft	D	13,10
Lect	Thompson, Thomas		64C,64E
Lect PT	Totter, Stephen		61
Lect PT	Turner, Jeffrey		62D
Assoc Prof	Vali, M. Reza		13,34
Lect PT	Van Hoesen, Gretchen		62E
Asst Prof	Very, Laura Knoop		61
Lect PT	Vosburgh, George		63A
Lect PT	Whipple, R. James		13
Lect PT	Wilkins, Colette		13C
Lect PT	Wilkins, Donald G.	M	13,12A,66G
Lect PT	Williams, Anne Martindale		62C
Lect PT	Wilson, John		29,63A
Lect	Zahler, Clara		32,13C
Lect PT	Zelkowicz, Isaias	M	62B
Assoc Prof	Zollman, Ronald		38,60B

PA0600 Chatham University

Music Program
Woodland Rd
Pittsburgh, PA 15232
(412) 365-1679/1201   Fax: (412) 365-1720
www.chatham.edu
E-mail: mboyd@chatham.edu

4 Year Liberal Arts Institution

Music Contact: Michael Boyd, 80A
Chair, Arts & Design: Prajna Paramita Parasher, 80A
Dir., Artist Series: Pauline Rovkah, 80F

Asst Prof	Boyd, Michael	D	10A,10B,13,12
	Conner, Stacey	M	36,39,61

Adj	Garcia, Federico	D	10,12A,13,41
Adj	Lipman, Michael	M	62C,41
Adj	Lynch, Kelly	D	39,61,11,12A
Adj	Marcinizyn, John	D	13,10,70
Adj	Metil, Robert	D	14,29A,20G,70
Emerita	Ross Mehl, Margaret	D	36,39,61,11,12A
Artist in Res	Rovkah, Pauline	M	66A,41
Adj	Sisco, Paul	M	66A
Adj	Tretick, Stephanie	M	62A,62B
	Winkler, Chad	M	63A
Adj	Yoo, Peggy	M	64A

PA0650 Chestnut Hill College
Department of Music/Music Ed
9601 Germantown Ave
Philadelphia, PA 19118
(215) 248-7194 Fax: (215) 248-7155
www.chc.edu
E-mail: kmcclosk@chc.edu

4 Year Institution

Chair, Music/Music Education: Kathleen McCloskey, 80A

Lect PT	Castellanos, Juan	M	65
Prof	Glennon, Barbara	D	20G,13B,13C,64A,64C
Lect PT	King, Joan	M	62A,62B,62C,62D,31G
Assoc Prof PT	Kirchner, Joanne	D	66A
Lect PT	Kuczynski, Christopher	M	70
Lect PT	Lee, Hui Yu	M	62A
Asst Prof	McCloskey, Kathleen	M	11,12A,13A,66D
Lect PT	Mudry, Karen	M	34B
Lect PT	Naydan, William	M	40,60
Lect PT	Przybylowski, Michelle	M	32B
Asst Prof	Samson, David	D	47,13B,32C,63,60
Lect PT	Schmauk, Doris	B	36,61
Lect PT	Shockey, Mark	B	66A
Asst Prof	Strauman, Edward	D	10F,29A,13D,13B,35A

PA0675 Cheyney Univ of Pennsylvania
Department of Fine Arts
1837 University Circle
Cheyney, PA 19319-0200
(215) 399-2340 Fax: (215) 399-2270
www.cheyney.edu
E-mail: agardner@cheyney.edu

4 Year Institution

Chair: Lisa Schoenberg, 80A

	Barnes, Sebronette	D	61
	Dandridge, Damon H.	M	36
	Gardner, Allen D.	B	37

PA0700 Clarion Univ of Pennsylvania
Department of Music
840 Wood St
Clarion, PA 16214
(814) 393-2287 Fax: (814) 393-2723
www.clarion.edu/music
E-mail: stjohnson@clarion.edu

4 Year Institution
Member of NASM

Chair: Stephen R. Johnson, 80A

Assoc Prof	Alviani, Henry	D	36,40,60A,61
Prof	Amrod, Paula J.	D	66A,66D
Inst	Hepler, David	M	50,65,29A
Assoc Prof	Johnson, Stephen R.	D	10F,32D,13A,63D
Inst PT	Reefer, Russell	M	64C,64E
Prof	Register, P. Brent	D	12A,48,64A,64B,64D
Asst Prof	Teske, Casey C.	D	60B,13C,63B,11
Assoc Prof	Toney, Hubert	D	37,47,32E,63A
Asst Prof	Wardlaw, Jeffrey A.	D	63D,49,13,63C

PA0850 Curtis Institute of Music
1726 Locust St
Philadelphia, PA 19103-6107
(215) 893-5252 Fax: (215) 893-9065
www.curtis.edu
E-mail: paul.bryan@curtis.edu

4 Year Institution, Graduate School
Member of NASM

Diploma, Master of Music in Opera

President: Roberto Diaz, 80A
Chair, Liberal Arts: Jeanne McGinn, 80A

Allen, Virginia		M	60
Amory, Misha		M	62B
Ashbaker, Susan		M	39
Ashkenasi, Samuel		B	62A
Bilger, David		M	63A
Blatter, Alfred W.		D	13L
Bollinger, Blair		B	63C
Brey, Carter		M	51,62C
Caporello, Corradina		M	39
Carol, Norman		B	51
Coopersmith, Jonathan		D	13
Cuckson, Robert		D	13
Curnow, Jeffrey		M	49
Danchenko, Victor			62A
Danielpour, Richard		D	10
De Pasquale, Joseph		DIPL	62B
Deviney, Christopher		M	65,50
Diaz, Roberto		B	62B
Eliasen, Mikael			39
Fleisher, Leon			66A
Frank, Claude			66A
Frank, Pamela		B	41,62A
Garfield, Bernard		M	64D
Glandorf, Matthew		M	13
Graffman, Gary			66A
Hainen, Elizabeth		M	62E
Haroz, Nitzan			63C
Hayes, David		B	60,38
Hicks, Sarah Hatsuko		B	13,60
Higdon, Jennifer		D	13,10
Jantsch, Carol		B	63D
Kaderabek, Frank		DIPL	63A
Kavafian, Ida			62A
Keller, Lisa			39
Khaner, Jeffrey		B	64A
Krzywicki, Paul		M	63D
Lallerstedt, Ford		D	13,12
Lipkin, Seymour		B	66A
Liu, Meng-Chieh		B	41,66A
Liuzzi, Don		M	65
Loman, Judy			62E
Ludwig, David		M	13,10
Malas, Marlena		B	61
Matsukawa, Daniel		M	48,64D
McDonald, Robert		M	66A
Meng, Mei-Mei		B	13
Meyer, Edgar			62D
Meyer, Kenton		D	16
Montanaro, Donald		B	48,64C
Montone, Jennifer		M	63B
Moody, David		M	39
Morales, Ricardo			48
Morales-Matos, Rolando		M	65
Morrison, Alan		M	66G
Mueller, Otto Werner			60
Nowicki, Susan			39
Orlando, Danielle		M	39
Party, Lionel		D	66H
Patenaude-Yarnell, Joan			61
Petit, Annie		DIPL	66A
Robinson, Harold		DIPL	62D
Robinson, Scott		B	65
Rosand, Aaron			62A
Rowland, Robert		M	12A
Scott, Yumi Ninomiya			62A
Sessler, Eric S.		D	13
Silverstein, Joseph		B	41,62A
Sokoloff, Eleanor			66A
Solzhenitsyn, Ignat		B	66A
Soyer, David		DIPL	62C
St. Pierre, Donald			39
Steinhardt, Arnold			62A
Stokking, William		D	
Sung, Hugh		B	66C
Tenenbom, Steven			41
Tree, Michael		DIPL	62B
Van Sice, Robert		M	50,65B
Walker, Elizabeth		M	16
Wen, Eric		D	13,12A
Wiley, Peter		B	41,62C

Woodhams, Richard		B	48,64B
Zarzeczna, Marion		M	66A

PA0900 Delaware Valley College
Music Program
700 E Butler Ave
Doylestown, PA 18901-2607
(215) 345-1500   Fax: (215) 489-4950
www.delval.edu
E-mail: jack.schmidt@delval.edu

4 Year Institution, Intro Courses Only

Chair & Dir., Artist Series: Jack W. Schmidt, 80A,80F

Assoc Prof	Schmidt, Jack W.	PhD	11,12A,36,37,49
Inst	Tavianini, Marie A.	D	36,61
Inst	Tokar, David A.	PhD	12A,12C,70,12,11

PA0950 Dickinson College
Department of Music
PO Box 1773
Carlisle, PA 17013-2896
(717) 245-1568   Fax: (717) 245-1937
www.dickinson.edu/departments/music

4 Year Institution

Chair: Blanka Bednarz, 80A
Dean: Neil Weissman, 80A

Inst PT	Asmus, Elizabeth Etters		62E
Inst PT	Axsom, Ron	M	63C
Inst	Baik-Kim, Eun Ae	M	66A,66C,42
Assoc Prof	Bednarz, Blanka	D	13A,42,51,62A,62B
Assoc Prof	Blyth, Jennifer	D	66A,66B,66C,66D,13
Inst PT	Brye, Daniel	M	62A,62B,51
Inst PT	Cameron, Michael B.	M	62C,42
Inst PT	Clayville, Michael	M	37,47
Inst PT	Glasgow, David M.	M	66A,66C,13A
Inst PT	Hannigan, Mary	M	48,64A
Vstng Inst	Hays, Jonathan C.	M	61
Assoc Prof	Helding, Lynn E.	M	61,40,54
Inst PT	Henry, Eric	B	63D
Inst PT	Hontz, James	M	70,13A
Inst PT	James, Tim	B	66A,29B
Inst PT	Kelley, Kimberly Buchar	D	64D
Inst PT	King, Shirley S.	D	66G,66H
Inst PT	Marchione, Jill	M	64B
Inst PT	Ogilvie, Tyler	M	63B,42
Vstng Asst Prof	Parr, Sean M.	D	12A,55,11
Assoc Prof	Pound, Robert	D	13,10,11,38
Inst PT	Quigley, Fred	M	64E
PT	Sokol-Albert, Andrea C.	D	66A,66C
Inst PT	Stimpert, Elisabeth	M	64C,48
Inst PT	Strawley, Steven	M	63A
Assoc Prof	Wilson, Blake	D	12A,55,11
Asst Prof	Wlodarski, Amy	D	36,12
Inst PT	Zygmunt, David	B	65

PA1000 Drexel University
Department of Perf Arts
3141 Chestnut St 9-2018
Philadelphia, PA 19104
(215) 895-2451   Fax: (215) 895-2452
www.drexel.edu
E-mail: Perfarts@drexel.edu

4 Year Institution, Graduate School

Master of Science in Arts Administration

Chair & Dir., Graduate Program: Cecelia Fitzgibbon, 80A,80C

Inst	Abruzzo, Luke A.	M	70,10A,13,29
Inst	Bacon, Scott D.	B	11,14C,65
PT	Canfield, Wanda	M	66A,66D,53
Assoc Prof	Fitzgibbon, Cecelia	M	35E
Assoc Prof	Giguere, Miriam	M	52
PT	Kaminsky, Bruce	M	62D,12A,37,50
PT	Kelly, Darin	M	63A
Asst Prof	Klein, Jim	B	34,32F,45,13G,10C
PT	Lipscomb, Ronald		51,62C
PT	Mcneill, Karl		62D
Asst Prof	Moss, Myron D.	D	10,11,29,37,60

PT	Napoli, Joseph	B	70
PT	Oehlers, K. Rebecca	B	61
Asst Prof	Pollock, William	M	54
Assoc Prof	Powell, Steven S.	D	36,61,34,12A,32D
PT	Riley, Madeleine C.	B	11,45,64A,64E,29
PT	Ross, Gregory	B	36
PT	Shumate, Penny	M	61
Prof	Starks, George	D	20,14,47,64E,29
Asst Prof	Wagman, Marcy R.	D	35

PA1050 Duquesne University
Mary Pappert School of Music
600 Forbes Ave
Pittsburgh, PA 15282-1800
(412) 396-6082   Fax: (412) 396-1524
www.music.duq.edu
E-mail: kocher@duq.edu

4 Year Institution, Graduate School
Member of NASM

Artist Diploma, Master of Music in Performance, Master of Music in Music Theory-Composition, Master of Music in Sacred Music, Master of Music in Education, Master of Music in Music Technology

Dean: Edward W. Kocher, 80A
Dir., Undergraduate Studies: Kenneth Burky, 80B
Dir., Graduate Studies: Stephen J. Benham, 80C
Coord., Enrollment: Troy Centofanto, 80D

Asst Prof	Abbott, Elaine	D	33
PT	Allen, Christopher	B	65
Prof Emerita	Beck, Donna Marie	D	33
PT	Bell, Scott	B	64B,41
Assoc Prof	Benham, Stephen J.	D	32
PT	Benkovitz, Deborah		33
PT	Bickel, Ronald E.	M	66A
Asst Prof	Binder, Benjamin A.	D	12
Prof	Bowman, Judith A.	D	32,34
PT	Budway, Maureen	M	61
Asst Prof	Burke, Patrick	D	13,10,34
Prof	Burky, Kenneth	M	66A
PT	Burns, Patricia Donahue	M	61
PT	Bursill-Hall, Damian	B	64A
Prof	Cameron, Robert C.	D	60,32C,37
PT	Chapman, Michael	M	70
PT	Conner, Jennifer	B	64A
PT	Cornelius-Bates, Benjamin	M	31A,66G
PT	Crewe, Murray	B	63C
PT	Dallas, Joseph	B	46
Assoc Prof	Doerksen, Paul F.	D	32
PT	Dudt, Jay		34
PT	Gatch, Perry	B	32
PT	Gingras-Roy, Marylene	M	62B
PT	Gorton, James	B	64B
Assoc Prof	Guechev, Guenko	M	61,39
PT	Gunnell, Jonathan		32
Asst Prof	Hess, H. Carl	M	37,38,60,63A
Prof	Houlik, James	M	64E
PT	Howard, Micah	M	62D
PT	Howell, Jack	M	64C
PT	Hoydich, George	M	32
Prof Emeritus	Jenkins, Joseph W.	D	13,10F,10,12A
Assoc Prof	Jones, Sean	M	47,53,63A
Prof	Jordanoff, Christine E.	M	32F,32B,32C,32,36
PT	Karsh, Kenneth M.	M	70,29B
PT	Kenny, Rhian	B	64A
Asst Prof	Kikta, Thomas J.	B	70,34D,35C
PT	Knaub, Maribeth	D	11
PT	Knox, Craig	B	63D
PT	Koch, Mark	B	70
Prof	Kocher, Edward W.	D	32,63C,63D
PT	Kurth, Robert	M	60A
Prof	Labounsky, Ann	D	66G,31A
PT	LaDuke, Lance	B	63D
PT	Lauver, Eric	M	64E
PT	Lirette, Charles	B	63A
PT	Liu, Adam	M	62E
PT	Liu, Xiu-ru	M	39,61
PT	Mangone, Jeffrey	B	62D
PT	Moyer, John	M	39
PT	Mroziak, Jordan		11
Asst Prof	Nagy, Zvonimir	D	12
PT	Naus, Jesse	B	34
PT	Negri, Joseph H.		70
PT	Nova, James	M	63C
Asst Prof	Ozah, Marie Agatha	D	14
PT	Pandolfi, Philip		64D
PT	Pavlik, Charleen	D	33
PT	Pegher, Lisa	M	65
PT	Pinza, Claudia	DIPL	61
Assoc Prof	Purse, Lynn Emberg	M	10B,34,45
Prof	Purse, William E.	M	70,34

PT	Rael, Eliseo	M	65
Assoc Prof	Raevens, Jean M.	DIPL	13,11,12
PT	Reamer, Andrew	M	65
Prof	Riley, Carole	D	66A,66D
PT	Rodriguez, Francisco	B	35C
PT	Rogers, Leonard	M	65
PT	Rollett, Rebecca	M	67F
PT	Rounds, Joseph	B	63B
PT	Samuels, Ronald I.	B	64C
PT	Sanders, Linda	M	33
Prof Emeritus	Shankovich, Robert L.	D	12
Asst Prof	Sheehan, Joseph C.	D	13
PT	Smith, Bradley	M	34
PT	Smith, Zachary	B	63B
PT	Snitkovsky, Natasha	DIPL	66A,66D
PT	Stahurski, Brian	M	62D
Assoc Prof	Stegeman, Charles	M	62A
PT	Stegeman, Rachel	B	62A
PT	Stephan, Edward	M	65,65A
Prof Emeritus	Stock, David	M	60,43
PT	Sullivan, Peter	B	63C
PT	Sutton, Brigette	M	33
Assoc Prof	Tomaro, Michael	M	64E,47,53,29
PT	Turner, Jeffrey	B	62D
PT	Van Hoesen, Gretchen	M	62E
PT	Van Ouse, Philip	M	63D
PT	Vosburgh, George	B	63A
Prof	Wehr, David	M	66A
Asst Prof	Whitcomb, Rachel	D	32,32B,32A
Prof Emeritus	Wilson, John	D	29
Assoc Prof	Wiskus, Jessica	D	13J,12A,13E,13
PT	Zimmerman, Ronald J.	M	70

PA1100 East Stroudsburg University
Department of Music
Fine & Perf Arts Ctr
200 Prospect St
East Stroudsburg, PA 18301-2999
(570) 422-3759   Fax: (570) 422-3008
www.esu.edu
E-mail: bbuzzelli@po-box.esu.edu

4 Year Institution

Chair: Betsy Buzzelli-Clarke, 80A

Assoc Prof	Buzzelli-Clarke, Betsy	D	11,13A,12A,66A,66D
Inst	Collins, Jenny	M	11,13A,66A,66D,66C
Prof	Dorian, Patrick	M	10C,13B,29A,29C,29E
Assoc Prof	French, Otis C.	D	11,37,63,64,65
Assoc Prof	Maroney, James	D	11,36,61,13C,40

PA1150 Eastern University
Department of Music
1300 Eagle Rd
St. Davids, PA 19087
(610) 341-4397   Fax: (610) 341-1575
www.eastern.edu
E-mail: dbryant@eastern.edu

4 Year Institution

Chair: Ron Matthews, 80A

Adj	Best, Nneka	M	36
Inst PT	Bryant, David	M	66A,66D
Adj	Campetti, Cynthia	M	62A,62B
Inst PT	De Vault, Christine	M	61
Assoc Prof	Edgett, Bryan	D	63A,37
Inst PT	Fowler, Jeffrey	M	66G
Inst PT	Frost, Richard P.	M	31A
Inst PT	Greenland, John	M	35C,45
Inst PT	Kerrigan, William	M	65
Adj	Kim, Leah	M	62A,62B
Inst PT	Latimer, Carole	M	61
Inst PT	Lipscomb, Ronald	M	62C,62D
Assoc Prof	Maness, David	M	13,60,11,36,61
Inst PT	Manley, David	M	47,29,53,70
Prof	Matthews, Ron	D	13,10,12A,63A,66A
Inst PT	McIntire, Jean	M	32B
Adj	Mehrtens, Russell	M	63C
Assoc Prof	Nevola, Teresa	M	61,54,20G
Inst PT	Robinson, Scott	D	12,14,10
Inst PT	Smith, Joseph	M	64C
Inst PT	Stearns, Duncan	M	62E,66A
Adj	Stefano, Joseph	M	64D
Inst PT	Trolier, Kimberly	D	64A
Inst PT	Turley, Steve	M	70
Inst PT	Whitlow, Rebecca	M	61

PA1200 Edinboro Univ of Pennsylvania
Department of Music
Alexander Music Center
110 Kiltie Rd
Edinboro, PA 16444
(814) 732-2555   Fax: (814) 732-2559
www.edinboro.edu
E-mail: ggrant@edinboro.edu

4 Year Institution
Member of NASM

Chair: Gary S. Grant, 80A
Dir., Preparatory Division: LeAnne Wistrom, 80E

Inst PT	Amidon, Bradley	M	50,65
Inst PT	Black, Jacqueline	M	62C
Assoc Prof	Burdick, Daniel	D	63C,63D,49,11
Assoc Prof	Denton, David B.	D	13
Assoc Prof	Denton, Kristine West	D	66A,66C,66D
Prof	Grant, Gary S.	D	37,60,47
Prof	Howell, Allen C.	D	11,32,36
Asst Prof	Jones, Patrick R.	D	11,29,64,41
Inst PT	Lute, Charles	M	37
Inst PT	Lyon, Howard	B	62A,62B,41
Inst PT	Mann, Erik	M	70
Asst Prof	Ortega, Anne	D	39,61
Inst PT	Piatt, Kenneth H.	M	63A,63B
Inst PT	Priester, John Michael	M	62D
Inst PT	Regan, Patrick	M	67H
Inst	Snyder, Jean E.	D	11,12,20
Prof	van den Honert, Peter	D	60A,36,11,13A
Inst PT	Wistrom, LeAnne	M	64A

PA1250 Elizabethtown College
Department of Fine & Perf Arts
One Alpha Dr
Elizabethtown, PA 17022
(717) 361-1212   Fax: (717) 361-1187
www.etown.edu/fapa
E-mail: reynoldsa@etown.edu

4 Year Institution
Member of NASM

Chair: E. Douglas Bomberger, 80A
Dir., Admissions: Matthew P. Fritz, 80D
Dir., Preparatory Division & Summer Programs: Grant W. Moore, II, 80E,80G

Adj	Armstrong, James D.	M	65,50
Asst Prof	Badgerow, Justin A.	D	66A,66C,66D,13
Prof	Behrens, Gene Ann	D	33
Prof	Bomberger, E. Douglas	D	12,66A
Adj	Ciucci, Anthony A.	B	66G
Adj	Cosma, Tina	M	33
Artist in Res	Cullen, David T.	B	70
Asst Prof	Daughtrey, Sarah E.	D	61,11
Adj	Dinsmore, Ann	M	33
Adj	Drackley, Phyllis J.	M	61
Assoc Prof	Fritz, Matthew P.	D	36,60A,34,34E,60
Adj	Gingerich, Cheryl F.	M	66B,66A
Prof	Haines, James L.	D	13,10,33
Prof Emeritus	Harrison, John F.	D	12A,12,66A
Adj	Hillard, Leon H.	B	63A
Adj	Hinton, Jennifer	B	33
Adj	Howell, Devin	M	62D
Prof Emeritus	Kitchen, Otis D.	M	10F
Adj	Kohler-Ghiorzi, Elizabeth	B	33
Adj	Male, Sara	M	62C,51
Adj	Marchione, Jill M.	M	64B
Adj	McCullough, Stephanie	M	62A,62B
Adj	Mekeel, Alison R.	M	61
Adj	Moore, Grant W.	B	49,63D,47
Adj	Nelson, Paula C.	D	64A
Adj	Ober, Gail E.	B	64D
Adj	Phillips, Matt K.	M	33
Lect	Ronning, Debra D.	M	66A,66B,66D
Adj	Rowe, Victoria	M	33
Adj	Shiffer, Faith E.	M	64C,64E,41
Asst Prof	Shorner-Johnson, Kevin T.	D	32,20
Adj	Smith, Lauren	B	33
Asst Prof	Spence, J. Robert	D	37,38,32,60B
Adj	Staherski, Cheryl E.	B	63B
Adj	Stouffer, Janice W.	B	33
Adj	Walborn, Melanie	B	33
Adj	Winey, Richard	M	32E,62
Adj	Yoder-Frantz, Emily	M	33

PA1300 Franklin and Marshall College

Department of Music
PO Box 3003
Lancaster, PA 17604-3003
(717) 291-4346   Fax: (717) 358-7168
www.fandm.edu/music
E-mail: debra.joseph@fandm.edu

4 Year Institution

Chair: Matthew W. Butterfield, 80A
Coord., Concert Series: Doris J. Hall-Gulati, 80F
Department Coordinator: Debra A. Joseph

Asst Prof	Alajaji, Sylvia A.	D	14A,14C,11,12A,20
Adj Asst Prof	Banks, Rusty	M	70
Adj Asst Prof	Brown, Matthew	M	63D,63C
Asst Prof	Butterfield, Matthew W.	D	29,13,13B,29A,29B
Prof	Carbon, John J.	D	13A,13,10F,10
Adj Inst	Deemer, Geoffrey A.	B	64B
Artist in Res	Geyer, Gwynne	M	39,61
Artist in Res	Hall-Gulati, Doris J.	M	64C,42
Adj Asst Prof	Howell, Devin L.	M	62D
Senior Adj Asst Prof	Jamanis, Michael T.	D	62A
Senior Adj Inst	Keller, Elizabeth W.	B	66A
Adj Asst Prof	Kelley, Kimberly D. Buchar	D	64D
Adj Asst Prof	Laboranti, Jerry B.	M	64E,47
Adj Prof	Laudermilch, Kenneth	D	63A
Asst Prof	Leistra-Jones, Karen	D	11,12A,12
Adj Asst Prof	Male, Sara	M	62E
Adj Asst Prof	Mu, Ning	M	62B
Adj Asst Prof	Noel, Emily	M	61
	Norcross, Brian H.	D	60,37,38,60B
Adj Asst Prof	Pfaffle, Elizabeth L.	D	63B
Adj Asst Prof	Trolier, Kimberly A.	D	64A
	Wright, William B.	D	11,13,36,60
Adj Asst Prof	Yingling, Mark T.	D	65

PA1350 Geneva College

Department of Music
3200 College Ave
Beaver Falls, PA 15010-3557
(724) 847-6660   Fax: (724) 847-6687
www.geneva.edu
E-mail: dbk@geneva.edu

4 Year Liberal Arts Institution

Chair: Donald B. Kephart, 80A
Dir., Publicity: Ruth Vos, 80F

PT	Antonich, Mark	M	70
PT	Cochenour, Deborah	M	32B
Asst Prof	Copeland, Louise	M	36,61
PT	Donaldson, Kathryn	M	36,61
PT	Frantz, Jeremy	B	70
PT	Furlow, George	M	64E
PT	Hall, Elizabeth W.	B	44
Assoc Prof	Kephart, Donald B.	M	32C,37,63,46,60
Asst Prof	Kickasola, Matthew	D	12A,13C
Asst Prof	Luangkesorn, Sha	D	13,66
PT	Morrow, Daniel	B	65,50
Assoc Prof	Smith, David Kenneth	D	60A,61
PT	Tessmer, David	M	64A
PT	Troxler, Lorinda	B	51

PA1400 Gettysburg College

Sunderman Conservatory of Music
300 N Washington St
Gettysburg, PA 17325
(717) 337-6815   Fax: (717) 337-8558
www.gettysburg.edu/academics/conservatory/
E-mail: shoke@gettysburg.edu

4 Year Liberal Arts Institution

Director: S. Kay Hoke, 80A

Assoc Prof	Austerlitz, Paul	D	12,14,46
Adj Asst Prof	Ballard-Ayoub, Anna Claire	M	64D,42
Adj Asst Prof	Bell, Kenneth G.	M	63B,42
Adj Asst Prof	Botterbusch, Duane A.	D	62D,42
Adj Asst Prof	Bowers, Teresa M.	D	64A,64B,12A,36,42
Adj Asst Prof	Crowne, Scott	D	66C,66A,42
Asst Prof	Dorman, Avner	D	10A,10F,13,43
Adj Asst Prof	Eidson, Joseph M.	D	13B,13C
Adj Asst Prof	Fahnestock, Jeffrey L.	M	61
Adj Inst	Fieldhouse, Stephen M.	M	64E,29,42
Adj Inst	Hell, Felix	M	66G
Adj Inst	Henry, Rebecca	M	62B
Adj Inst	Hitz, Andrew	B	63D
Prof	Hoke, S. Kay	D	13,12A
Adj Asst Prof	Hontz, James R.	D	70
Adj Asst Prof	Howes, Sarah Marie	M	61,13C
Adj Inst	Jones, Gail	M	32E
Prof	Jones, John W.	D	13B,13C,13D,13E,10A
Asst Prof	Kahn, Alexander G.	D	38,12A,11,60B
Asst Prof	Kim, Yeon-Su	D	62A,42
Adj Asst Prof	Levitov, Daniel	D	62C,38,42,11
Vstng Asst Prof	Lindau, Elizabeth Ann	D	12,14C,20
Vstng Asst Prof	Mastrian, Stacey	DMA	61,39
Asst Prof	McCutcheon, Russell G.	D	37,32E,60,34,32C
Assoc Prof	Natter, Robert	D	34,36,61,60A
Adj Inst	Osifchin, Matthew	M	61
Adj Asst Prof	Pursell, John	D	63A
Assoc Prof	Robertson, Marta E.	D	12,14
Adj Inst	Schenck-Crowne, Leah Naomi	M	61
Adj Asst Prof	Scott, Aaron D.	M	64C,42
Adj Asst Prof	Sestrick, Timothy	M	16,65,50
Adj Asst Prof	Stanley, Ed L.	M	64B,42,13A,13C,11
Asst Prof	Swigger, Jocelyn A.	D	11,66A,66B,66C,66E
Inst	Talbot, Brent C.	M	32
Adj Asst Prof	Wise, Colin	M	63C

PA1450 Grove City College

Department of Music
100 Campus Dr
Grove City, PA 16127-2101
(724) 458-2084   Fax: (724) 458-2164
www.gcc.edu
E-mail: eparnold@gcc.edu

4 Year Institution

Chair: Edwin P. Arnold, 80A

Prof	Arnold, Edwin P.	D	32E,37,60B,48,49
Inst	Arnold, Ellen	M	32,37
Lect PT	Barron, Elizabeth	B	66D,64A
Prof	Browne, Douglas A.	D	13C,60A,36,61
Lect PT	Byo, Donald W.	M	64D
Prof	Carter, Beverly H.	D	11,12A,66A,66B
Lect PT	Churm, George W.	M	70
Lect PT	Colella, Lou M.	M	64C,64E
Asst Prof	Drake, Joshua F.	M	11,61
Lect PT	Dzugan, Eric	M	66A
Lect PT	Fennell, Drew	B	63A
Lect PT	Formeck, Michael C.	M	63D
Lect PT	Gershman, Laura	M	64B
Lect PT	Heid, R. J.	M	65
Lect PT	Kahn, David	M	62D
Lect PT	Kohanski, Elisa C.		62C
Prof	Konzen, Richard A.	D	38,51,66G,41,13B
Lect PT	Kubik, Paula A.	M	66A
Lect PT	May, Douglas L.	M	63C,49
Lect PT	McFarland, Joanne	B	61
Lect PT	Moser, Mary	M	62A,62B
Prof	Munson, Paul A.	D	12A,11
Asst Prof	Paparone, Stacy A.	M	32
Assoc Prof	Pisano, Joseph M.	D	47,45,53,46,34
Lect PT	Scanga, James V.	M	63B,49
Lect PT	Scott, Julia		62E
Lect PT	Sopher, Rebecca J.	M	66A
Lect PT	Tessmer, David P.	M	64A
Lect PT	Young, M. Susan		61,39

PA1500 Haverford College

Department of Music
370 Lancaster Ave
Haverford, PA 19041
(610) 896-1012   Fax: (610) 896-4902
www.haverford.edu/music
E-mail: rfreedma@haverford.edu

4 Year Institution

Chair: Richard Freedman, 80A

Assoc Prof	Arauco, Ingrid	D	13A,13,10
Inst PT	Cacioppo, Christine	M	66A
Prof	Cacioppo, Curt	D	13,10,20G,10F,66A
	Crandell, Adam	M	16
Prof	Freedman, Richard	D	11,12A,12,20D,29A
Assoc Prof PT	Jacob, Heidi	D	38,42,62C
Assoc Prof PT	Lloyd, Thomas	D	36,61

PA1550 Immaculata University
Department of Music
PO Box 703
Immaculata, PA 19345-0730
(610) 647-4400 x 3435   Fax: (610) 251-1668
www.immaculata.edu
E-mail: dbohn@immaculata.edu

4 Year Institution, Graduate School
Member of NASM

Master of Arts in Music Therapy

Chair & Dir., Undergraduate Studies: Donna M. Bohn, 80A,80B
Chair, Graduate Program: Anthony Meadows, 80C

PT	Ahlquist, Janet S.	M	66A
PT	Antonacci, Jarred M.	M	63C
Assoc Prof	Bohn, Donna M.	D	12A,13B,13C,65,60
PT	Borgia-Petro, Diana	M	61
PT	Bretzius, David	M	32B
PT	Campitelli, Stephen	M	66D,66A
Prof	Carr, William	D	13B,66D,66A,13D
PT	Cooper, Donna	M	62E
PT	Cullen, Danielle	M	64C
PT	Deemer, Geoffrey	B	64B
PT	DePasquale, Charles	M	51,62
Prof	Doutt, Kathleen C.	D	12A,32,13C,20
PT	Dragonetti, John	M	70,41
PT	Dugan, Leonardo	D	64E,47
Asst Prof	Eyre, Lillian	D	33
PT	Ferraro, Dolores	M	61
PT	Finegan, James	M	62A,62B
Assoc Prof	Foy, Regina	M	13B,10F,31A
PT	Gehring, Joseph	M	37,38,60,63
PT	Gordon, Regina	D	36,40
PT	Greenlee, Anita	M	66G
PT	Hall, David	M	61
PT	Hepler, Nathaniel	M	63A
PT	Iannone, Vincent	M	64,10A
PT	Jadus, John	M	64D
PT	Kadyk, Folkert	D	63C
PT	MacDonald, Scott	M	33
Assoc Prof	Meadows, Anthony	D	33
PT	Meashey, Kelly	M	61,33
PT	Muller, Bryan	D	70,34,33
PT	Nelson, Paula	D	64A,48
PT	Potter Faile, Erin	B	66A,33
PT	Potter, Sharon	M	32C
PT	Sorrentino, Ralph	M	65,50
PT	Veleta, Richard	D	66H
PT	Wetherill, David	B	63B

PA1600 Indiana Univ of Pennsylvania
Department of Music
Cogswell Hall Rm 103
422 S Eleventh St
Indiana, PA 15701-1070
(724) 357-2390   Fax: (724) 357-1324
www.iup.edu/music
E-mail: mkukula@iup.edu

4 Year Institution, Graduate School
Member of NASM

Master of Arts in Performance, Master of Arts in Music Education, Master of Arts in History & Literature, Master of Arts in Music Theory-Composition

Dean, College of Fine Arts: Michael J. Hood, 80A
Chair: John E. Stamp, 80A
Dir., Graduate Studies: Stephanie B. Caulder, 80C
Associate Chair: Kevin E. Eisensmith, 80H
Assistant Chair: John F. Scandrett, 80H

Asst Prof	Antonacos, Anastasia	D	66A,13,11,66C,66D
Assoc Prof	Baumer, Matthew R.	D	12A
Asst Prof	Baunoch, Joseph	D	61,32D
Prof Emeritus	Bird, Gary J.	D	63D
Assoc Prof	Caulder, Stephanie B.	D	12A,12D,48,64B,13C
Assoc Prof	Chepaitis, Stanley L.	D	41,62A,62B,51
Asst Prof	Clewell, Christine M.	D	66A,66G,66D,13
Asst Prof	Collins, Zachary	D	63D,12A,13B,49
Asst Prof	Dearing, James C.	M	36,40,12A
Inst	Dearing, Kristi Jo	M	61
Prof	Dickinson, Christian M.	D	13,49,63C,60B
Prof	Eisensmith, Kevin E.	D	47,49,63A
Assoc Prof PT	Ferguson, David A.	D	63A,32
Assoc Prof	Ferguson, Laura S.	D	32
Assoc Prof Emeritus	Fry, Edwin J.	M	11,66A,13
Assoc Prof	Hastings, Mary Logan	D	39,61,54
Asst Prof	Horner, Ronald G.	D	65,50
Assoc Prof	Jennings, Linda G.	D	62C,62D,13,51
Assoc Prof PT	Kauffman, Irvin C.		70,51
Assoc Prof	Kingan, Michael G.	D	50,65
Inst	Kuehn, Jacquelyn A.	M	66A
Prof	Kuehn, John W.	D	32,64C,48,72
Prof	Mantel, Sarah J.	D	39,61,54
Assoc Prof	Martynuik, David G.	D	37,13,32
Assoc Prof	Perlongo, Daniel J.	M	10,13,29
Prof Emeritus	Radell, Judith M.	D	13,66A,66D,66C
Prof	Rahkonen, Carl J.	D	16,14
Inst PT	Santos, Nathan H.	M	62D
Asst Prof Emeritus	Sartori, Nicolo A.	M	66A,66F
Assoc Prof	Scandrett, John F.	D	13,63B,34
	Scandrett, Lucy	M	62E
Asst Prof	Sommerville, David	PhD	13
Prof	Stamp, John E.	D	60,37,65
Prof Emeritus	Staples, James G.	D	13,66A
Assoc Prof	Wacker, Therese M.	D	64A,48,13
Prof	Wheatley, Susan E.	D	32,12C
Prof Emeritus	Wilson, Lorraine P.	D	32,66D,20G
Asst Prof	Wong Doe, Henry	D	66A,66,11,13,66D
Prof	Worzbyt, Jason W.	D	64D,13,37,48
Prof	Young, Keith R.	D	48,64E,47

PA1650 Juniata College
Department of Music
1700 Moore St
Huntingdon, PA 16652
(814) 641-3473   Fax: (814) 641-3472
www.juniata.edu
E-mail: shelley@juniata.edu

4 Year Institution

Chair: Russ Shelley, 80A

Lect PT	Berlin, Janet	M	64C
Lect PT	Bookhammer, Evelyn	M	62C
Lect PT	Butte, Jody	M	64D
Lect PT	Costa, Robyn Dixon	D	64B
Lect PT	Dingo, Matt	B	29B
Lect PT	Hamme, Nora Ruth	M	62A,62B
Lect PT	Herrera, Cathy	M	64A
Lect PT	Huhn, Kevin	B	62D
Assoc Prof	Latten, James E.	D	11,13A,37,50,65
Lect PT	McKinstry, Herb	M	63,49
Lect PT	Mianulli, Janice	M	61,40,36
Lect PT	Mullen, Stanley	B	70
Lect PT	Scafidi, Cathy	B	66A
Prof	Shelley, Russ	D	11,12B,36
Lect	Sheppard, Matthew	B	38
Lect PT	Smith, Christy	M	63B
Lect PT	Yoder, Dan	M	29

PA1700 Keystone Junior College
Department of Fine Arts
La Plume, PA 18440
(717) 945-5141
www.keystone.edu
E-mail: stacey.semenza@keystone.edu

2 Year Institution

Inst	Dower, Mary R.		11,36

PA1750 Kutztown University
Department of Music
PO Box 730
Kutztown, PA 19530
(610) 683-4550   Fax: (610) 683-1506
www.kutztown.edu/acad/music/
E-mail: rapp@kutztown.edu

4 Year Institution
Member of NASM

Chair: Willis M. Rapp, 80A
Associate Dean: Michelle Kiec, 80H
Assoicate Dean: Michelle Kiec, 80H

PT	Allen, JoAnna	M	32B
Assoc Prof Emeritus	Apple, A. Alan	D	13A,36,61,13C,40
Asst Prof	Asteriadou, Maria	D	11,66A,66B,41,42
PT	Bates, Joanne	B	62D

Prof	Cadieux, Marie-Aline	D	13,11,51,62C,42
PT	Cullen, David	B	70
Asst Prof	Goh, Soo	D	64C,41,11
Prof	Grapenthin, Ina	D	11,32B,66A,66G,66D
Asst Prof	Immel, Daniel	D	11,66A,66D
Assoc Prof	Justeson, Jeremy	D	64E,37,32E,43,11
	Kiec, Michelle	D	64,13,64C,64E,48
	Kiec, Michelle	D	64,13,64C,64E,11
Inst	Kirkwood, Neal	M	40,66A
Assoc Prof	Kjos, Kevin	D	11,47,63A,49
Inst	Kolker, Adam	M	64E
Assoc Prof	Kumor, Frank	D	50,65,13
PT	Lee, Carver Scott	M	62D
PT	Linares, Adriana	M	62B
Asst Prof	Loewy, Susanna L.	D	11,48,64A
Assoc Prof	Metcalf, John C.	D	34,10,11,49,63C
Asst Prof	Neuenschwander, Daniel	M	37,32,63C
Prof	Ogletree, Mary	D	13,11,62A,62B,51
Prof	Rapp, Willis M.	D	38,65
Asst Prof	Rober, R. Todd	D	11,12
Prof Emeritus	Running, Timothy	D	60,11,48,64A
PT	Ryan, Christine	M	32B
Asst Prof	Sabatino, T. M.	D	11,61,40
PT	Sunday, Shannon	M	32B
Asst Prof	Trollinger, Valerie L.	D	34,32,64D,11,32C
PT	Webster, Kim	B	64B
Assoc Prof	Williams, Dennis	D	54,36,61,60
PT	Williams, Todd D.	M	63B

PA1830 La Salle University

Department of FA/Music Div
1900 W Olney Ave
Philadelphia, PA 19141
(215) 951-1163
www.lasalle.edu
E-mail: valenti@lasalle.edu

4 Year Institution under auspices of the Christian Brothers

Chair: Julie R. Valenti, 80A

	Galvan, Gary	M	12,70,29A,34A
Adj Prof	Haffley, Robin L.	M	11,13A,29A,34D,14C
Adj Prof	McDonald, Susan M.	D	10A,10B,12A,15,34D
Adj Prof	Reese, Donald T.	M	11,12A,70,13A,14C

PA1850 Lafayette College

Department of Music
239 Williams Center
Easton, PA 18042-1768
(610) 330-5356   Fax: (610) 330-5058
music.lafayette.edu
E-mail: stocktoj@lafayette.edu

4 Year Institution

Chair: J. Larry Stockton, 80A
Operations Dir., Artist/Performance Series: Allison Quensen Blatt, 80F
Dir., Artist/Performance Series: Ellis Finger, 80F

Inst PT	Bell, Stephani	M	38,62A,62B
Inst PT	Brader, Kenneth E.	B	47,63A
Inst PT	Chamberlain, Rick E.	B	63C,63D
Inst PT	Charlton, Susan	M	41,64A
Prof	Cummings, Anthony M.	D	12
Inst PT	Davis, Glenn	B	65
Inst PT	Dicarlo, Tom V.	M	70,62D
Inst PT	Fisher, Alexis Z.	M	66A,66D
Inst PT	Flandorffer, Frank M.		70
Inst PT	Gairo, Tony P.	B	64E
Inst PT	Groat, Stephen P.	B	62D
Asst Prof	Kelly, Jennifer W.	D	60,36,61
Inst PT	Kitagawa, Nobuo	M	64B
Inst PT	Kozic, Tom		70
	Lewis, Darin		41
Inst PT	Marzullo, Anne Maria	M	66A
Inst PT	Mattock, David M.	B	66A
Inst PT	Oltman, Laura G.		70
Asst Prof	O'Riordan, Kirk	DMA	10,60B,13,64E
	Roadfeldt-O'Riordan, Holly K.	D	66A,12A,66C
Prof	Stockton, J. Larry	D	14,50,20,60
Inst PT	Tang, Betty		62C
Assoc Prof	Torres, George	D	12A,12,14,12D,20H
Inst PT	Van Hoven, Eric	M	61,66A
Assoc Prof	Wilkins, Skip	M	13,11,29

PA1900 Lebanon Valley College

Department of Music
101 N College Ave
Annville, PA 17003-1400
(717) 867-6275   Fax: (717) 867-6390
www.lvc.edu
E-mail: music@lvc.edu

4 Year Institution, Summer Graduate Program
Member of NASM

Master of Music in Music Education

Chair: Mark L. Mecham, 80A
Dir., Music Recording Technology: Barry R. Hill
Dir., Music Education: Mary L. Lemons
Dir., Music Business: Jeffrey S. Snyder

Assoc Prof PT	Barraclough, Michelle	M	64A
Assoc Prof PT	Butts, Beverly Ann K.	M	64C,48,64
Assoc Prof PT	Cadieux, Marie-Aline	D	62C
Asst Prof PT	Campbell, Cheryl Lynn	M	66A,66D
Assoc Prof PT	Campbell, Christopher	D	63A
Assoc Prof PT	Copenhaver, John E.	M	63A
Prof Emeritus	Curfman, George D.	D	
Prof	Dietrich, Johannes M.	D	60,38,62A,62B
	Dura, Marian T.	D	38,62,32,32B,62A
Prof	Eggert, Scott H.	D	13,10
Inst PT	Erdman, James A.		63C,63D
Assoc Prof PT	Fox, Suzanne D.	M	63B
Assoc Prof	Fung, Eric K.	D	13,66A,66D
Prof Emeritus	Hearson, Robert H.	D	
Asst Prof	Heffner, Christopher J.	D	32E,37,60,63
Prof	Hill, Barry R.	M	35G
Assoc Prof PT	Hsieh, Ai-Liu	D	13
Asst Prof PT	Hummel, Linda W.	M	11,32
Assoc Prof	Lemons, Mary L.	D	32
Inst PT	Lilarose, Robin	B	64A
Assoc Prof	Lister, Rebecca Crow	D	61
Asst Prof PT	Marchione, Jill	M	64B
Asst Prof PT	Marks, Randall J.	M	32B,32C,32D,32E
Prof	Mecham, Mark L.	D	32D,36,40,60A
Inst PT	Miller, James E.		62D,29
Assoc Prof PT	Mixon, Joseph D.	M	70,29
Prof	Moorman-Stahlman, Shelly	D	44,66A,66G,31A,66D
Prof Emeritus	Morgan, Philip G.	M	
Assoc Prof	Norris, Renee Lapp	D	14C,12A,20,12,13E
Assoc Prof PT	Nowak, Robert A.	M	11,65,29
Inst PT	Roberts, Andrew	B	29
Asst Prof	Rose, Victoria	M	61
Assoc Prof	Snyder, Jeffrey S.	M	35,34D,10B,32F,10D
Assoc Prof	Strohman, Thomas	M	47,64E,29
Prof	Sweigart, Dennis W.	D	13,66
Asst Prof PT	Tindall, Josh	M	66A,66D
Inst PT	Volpicelli, Thomas	B	35G
Assoc Prof PT	Wagner, Julia P.	M	64D
Assoc Prof PT	Wojkylak, Michael		36,61

PA1950 Lehigh University

Department of Music
420 E Packer Ave
Bethlehem, PA 18015
(610) 758-3839   Fax: (610) 758-6470
www.lehigh.edu/~inmsc
E-mail: inmsc@lehigh.edu

4 Year Institution

Chair: Nadine J. Sine, 80A
Admissions Coordinator: Linda C. Ganus, 80D

Assoc Prof	Albulescu, Eugene	M	11,66A,66C,41
Adj	Beedle, Helen E.	M	66A,66D
Lect	Diggs, David B.	M	13A,13B,37,64B,48
Prof/Prac	Lee, Sun Min	M	36,40,60,13C
Adj	Neumeyer, Albert J.	M	37
Adj	Perla, Gene	B	35A,35E,62D
Adj	Riekenberg, Dave	M	64E,47,29B
Prof	Salerni, Paul F.	D	13,10,43
Prof	Sametz, Steven P.	D	13,60,10,36
Prof/Prac	Schwarz, Timothy J.	D	62A,62B,51,41
Adj	Sessions, Timothy	M	63C,47
Prof	Sine, Nadine J.	D	11,12A,12
Assoc Prof	Warfield, William	M	47,63A,29

PA2000 Lincoln University
Department of Visual & Perf Arts
122 Ware Center
Lincoln University, PA 19352
(610) 932-1292   Fax: (610) 932-1213
www.lincoln.edu
E-mail: amos@lincoln.edu

4 Year Institution, Historically Black College

Chair: Alvin E. Amos, 80A

Prof	Amos, Alvin E.	D	29,13A,13C,48,64
Vstng Inst	Coleman, Edryn J.	M	61,36,60A,13B
Other	Green, Ronald	M	37,50,65
Vstng Inst	Jensen, Shane	M	34,32F
Vstng Inst	Johnson, H. Wade	M	37,63,11
Asst Prof	Kunkle, Kristen C.	D	61,39,11
Asst Prof	Limb, Christine M.	D	32,11,63
Other	Meacham, Helen M.	M	66A,66C,11,13A
Assoc Prof	Pettaway, Charles H.	M	13,11,12A,66,66G

PA2050 Lock Haven University
Department of Performing Arts
243 Sloan
401 N Fairview St
Lock Haven, PA 17745
(570) 893-2263   Fax: (570) 893-2819
www.lhup.edu/performing-arts/music.htm
E-mail: mgrass@lhup.edu

4 Year Institution

Chair: Mahlon O. Grass, 80A
Dean: Zac Hussain, 80A

Asst Prof	Becker, Melissa J.	M	10E,12,32,62
Assoc Prof	Curtin, David	D	66,13
Assoc Prof	Grass, Mahlon O.	D	12A,48,64B,64C,64E
Asst Prof	Miller, Ronald E.	M	13A,36,61
Inst	Mullen, Stan		29B,53,70,20G,20F
Asst Prof	Schmidt, John R.	M	60,14,50,65,37
Asst Prof	Severn, Eddie	M	32,29,46,47,63

PA2100 Lycoming College
Department of Music
700 College Place
Williamsport, PA 17701
(570) 321-4016   Fax: (570) 321-4090
www.lycoming.edu
E-mail: boerckel@lycoming.edu

4 Year Institution

Chair: Gary M. Boerckel, 80A

Inst	Adams, Richard	B	64E
Prof	Boerckel, Gary M.	D	11,12A,66A,20G,29
Inst	Breon, Timothy		34,35,62D,70
Inst	Campbell, Richard	B	64D
Asst Prof	Ciabattari, William S.	D	13,63D,32,37,47
Inst	Clark, Joan		52
Inst	Councill, Ruben	M	64A
Inst	Fisher, Don	B	65
Inst	Lakey, Richard	M	66A,66G
PT	Mianulli, Janice	M	61
Inst	Mitchell, Yvonne	B	66A
Inst	Muller, Riana	M	62
Inst	Orris, Dale A.	B	63A
Inst	Piastro-Tedford, Sasha	M	61
Inst	Rammon, Andrew	B	62C
Prof	Thayer, Fred M.	D	13,60,10,36
Inst	Whyman, Valerie	B	63B

PA2150 Mansfield University
Department of Music
18 Campus View Dr
Mansfield, PA 16933
(570) 662-4710   Fax: (570) 662-4114
music.mansfield.edu
E-mail: music@mansfield.edu

4 Year Institution, Graduate School
Member of NASM

Master of Arts in Music

Chair: Shellie Lynn Gregorich, 80A
Assistant Chair: Joseph M. Murphy, 80H

Inst PT	Alexander, Conrad	M	65
Prof	Boston, Nancy J.	D	66A,66B,66C,66D
Prof	Brennan, Adam	D	60B,37,50,65,10F
Prof	Dettwiler, Peggy	D	60,36,32C,61
Assoc Prof	Dodson-Webster, Rebecca	D	63B,13,12A,49
Inst PT	Filiano, Ken	M	62D
Prof	Galloway, Michael	D	47,63A,53,29
Assoc Prof	Gregorich, Shellie Lynn	D	13,66
PT	Hoferer, Kevin	D	29,10F
Asst Prof	Jacobsen, Jeffrey	D	38,32E,32C
Prof	Kim, Youngsuk	D	12A,39,61
Asst Prof	Laib, Susan	D	41,64B,64D
Asst Prof	McEuen, Stephen	M	11,63C,63D
Asst Prof	Monkelien, Sheryl	D	32,40
Asst Prof	Moritz, Benjamin	D	66A,66B,66C,66D
Inst	Moritz, Kristina	M	13A,13B,13C
Asst Prof	Moulton, Christine F.	D	64A,66A
Prof	Murphy, Joseph M.	D	48,64E,34A
Inst PT	Rammon, Philip A.	M	62C
Asst Prof	Ranney, Todd	D	61,39
Asst Prof	Rinnert, Nathan	D	60,37,32E
Asst Prof	Rose, Alissa	D	61
Prof	Sarch, Kenneth	D	51,62
Inst PT	Slotkin, Matthew	D	70
Asst Prof	Walters, Andrew B.	D	13,34D
Asst Prof	Wetzel, David B.	D	64C,35,34

PA2200 Marywood University
Department of Music/Theatre/Dance
2300 Adams Ave
Scranton, PA 18509-1514
(570) 348-6268   Fax: (570) 961-4721
www.marywood.edu/mtd
E-mail: dept.mtd@marywood.edu

4 Year Institution, Graduate School
Member of NASM

Master of Arts in Music Education, Master of Music Therapy

Chair: Joan McCusker, IHM, 80A

Prof	Appenheimer-Vaida, Christiane	M	62C,41,32E
Assoc Prof	Blackledge, Barbara	M	54
Lect	Carter, William	M	29A,66A
Lect	Cole, Joseph	B	62D
Assoc Prof	Cowgill, Jennifer Griffith	D	61
Asst Prof	Gadberry, Anita	D	33
Lect	Gallo, Paulette	M	62E
Lect	Grice, Wendy	M	61
Lect	Hamilton, Tom	M	64C,64E
Lect	Heinze, Thomas	M	64B,46,41
Asst Prof	Hoffenberg, Rick	D	36,40,60A,61
Lect	Hricko-Fay, Maria	M	33
Lect	Hrynkiw, Thomas T.	M	66A,66B
Lect	Hunter, Todd	M	63C
Lect	Ioanna, Philip	B	63D
Lect	Ivanov, Peter	M	63B
Asst Prof	Jumper, David	M	29,63A,32E,49
Lect	Koch, Patricia Schott	M	66B,66D
Lect	Laubach, Mark	M	31A,66G,66H
Lect	Lemire-Ross, Dominique	M	33
Lect	Mathiesen, Steven	M	10A,10F,50,65
Assoc Prof	McCusker, IHM, Joan	D	32A,32B,32C,32G
Lect	McDonald, Linn	M	52
Lect	Moran, Leslie Mason	B	61
Asst Prof	Parker, Nathaniel F.	D	38,60B,64,41
Lect	Paskert, IHM, Joan	M	66A
Lect	Roditski, William	B	34A,35G
Asst Prof	Romines, Fred David	D	37,60B,64E,32E
Lect	Rutkowski, Ellen	M	61,11
Asst Prof	Till, Sophie	M	62A,62B,13C,32E
Asst Prof	Truitt, D. Charles	M	70,13,41,13E,13B

Lect	Unice, Charles	M	61
Lect	Vaida, John	M	61,62A,62B
Lect	Wargo, Edward	M	64A

PA2250 Mercyhurst College

D'Angelo Department of Music
501 E 38th St
Erie, PA 16546-0002
(814) 824-2394   Fax: (814) 824-3332
music.mercyhurst.edu
E-mail: aglinsky@mercyhurst.edu

4 Year Institution

Chair: Louisa Jonason, 80A
Admissions Coordinator: Krista Lamb, 80D

PT	Amidon, Brad T.	M	65,32E
PT	Bischoff, Janet	M	20,66A
PT	Bommelje, Ann	M	66C
PT	Borland, Carolyn	M	64D
PT	Colantti, Stephen	M	38
PT	Dubois, Mark	M	64B
PT	Elberfeld, Sung Hui	M	66A
Prof	Glinsky, Albert	D	13,10,12A
PT	Howery, Lydia	M	
Asst Prof	Jonason, Louisa	M	39,61
PT	Kobler, Linda	M	11
PT	Lifshen, Faith	M	66C
Asst Prof	Meier, Scott Alan	D	47,53,64E,34,32E
PT	O'Connor, Martin	M	70
PT	Rapier, Christopher	M	63B
Asst Prof	Rotberg, Barton Samuel	D	62A,62B
Lect	Ryan, Rebecca	B	36,32C,60A
PT	Sydow, Holly	M	13C,48
Asst Prof	Tomlison, R. Scott	D	63A
PT	Tortolano, Jonathan	M	62C
PT	Tucker, Kent	B	63C
PT	Viebranz, Gary A.	D	63D
Asst Prof	Weber, Brent	M	61,32D,39,12A
Asst Prof	Yoo, Shirley S.	D	66
PT	Zurcher, Allen	M	29A

PA2300 Messiah College

Department of Music
Suite 3004
1 College Ave
Mechanicsburg, PA 17055
(717) 766-2511   Fax: (717) 691-2317
www.messiah.edu
E-mail: wstowman@messiah.edu

4 Year Institution, Graduate School
Member of NASM

Master of Music in Conducting

Chair: William Stowman, 80A
Assistant Chair: Timothy D. Dixon, 80H

PT	Asmus, Elizabeth	M	62E
PT	Carey, Larry		61
PT	Chang, Ya-ting	M	66A
PT	Clayville, Michael	M	63C
Assoc Prof	Cornacchio, Rachel	D	32
PT	Davis, Chris	B	34D
Assoc Prof	Dixon, Timothy D.	D	38,12A
PT	Durbin, Karen	D	31,44
Assoc Prof	Ewoldt, Patrice R.	D	66A,66C,66B,67F,42
Asst Prof	Genevro, Bradley	D	37,64C,64E,32E
PT	Gingrich, Shawn	M	66G,44
PT	Goranson, Jocelyn	M	64A,13A,13C,13B,42
Assoc Prof	Goranson, Todd A.	D	64E,64D,13A,47,42
Assoc Prof	Harcrow, Michael	D	63B,49,13
PT	Harker-Roth, Kerry	M	62B
PT	Haunstein, Jim	M	72
Senior Lect	Henderson, Elaine	M	39,61,54
PT	Henry, Eric	B	63D
Prof Emeritus	Higgins, William R.	D	32,64,72,34
PT	Hildebrand, Kirsta	B	32E,65
PT	Marchione, Jill	B	64B
PT	Meashey, Steven	B	62D
PT	Miller, Melanie	M	63A
Prof Emeritus	Miller, Ronald L.	D	12A,36,67B,31A,20G
PT	Reese, Kirk	B	29,66A
Prof	Roberson, Richard	D	66A,10A,10B
Senior Lect	Savarino, Damian	M	61,39
PT	Savarino, Tara	B	61
PT	Sirotin, Peter	M	62A,42
PT	Stimpert, Elisabeth	M	64C
Assoc Prof	Stowman, William	D	47,63A
Artist in Res	Tedford, Linda	M	60A,36,61
PT	Thompson, Fiona	M	62C,51
PT	Tilman, Ernest	B	31A
PT	Umble, Jay	B	70
PT	Warfield, Timothy	B	29
PT	Weaver, James	B	32E,65
PT	Yurko, Bruce	M	10,32E
PT	Yurko, Marcia	M	66A
Senior Lect	Zwally, Randall S.	M	11,70

PA2350 Millersville University

Department of Music
PO Box 1002
Millersville, PA 17551
(717) 872-3357   Fax: (717) 871-2304
www.millersville.edu/music
E-mail: micheal.houlahan@millersville.edu

4 Year Institution
Member of NASM

Chair: Michael Houlahan, 80A,80B,80D,80E,80F
Assistant Chair: Christy A. Banks, 80H

Asst Prof	Ardrey, Cathleen	D	32,36,61,66A
Asst Prof	Banks, Christy A.	D	35A,64C,64E
Inst PT	Behrens, Joel	M	12A,48,64A
Inst PT	Corley, Kirsten M.	D	66A,66C
Asst Prof	Darmiento, Madeleine	D	62A,62B
Inst PT	Ellison, Ross W.	D	66G
Inst PT	Englar, Marcia L.	M	70,29
Inst PT	Gordon, Kirstin	M	64B,64D
Adj	Grabowski, Donald	M	62D
Assoc Prof	Heslink, Daniel M.	D	11,14,37,65
Prof	Houlahan, Michael	D	13,12A
Asst Prof	Jester, Jennifer	D	35
Assoc Prof	Renfroe, Anita B.	D	66A,66D
Inst PT	Staherski, Cheryl	M	63B
Assoc Prof	Tacka, Philip V.	D	12,13,32
Adj	Volchansky, Vera	D	11,38
Assoc Prof	Wiley, N. Keith	D	32C,47,63A,29

PA2400 Montgomery County Comm College

Department of Music
340 DeKalb Pike Box 400
Blue Bell, PA 19422-0796
(215) 641-6505   Fax: (215) 641-6645
www.mc3.edu
E-mail: akoscies@mc3.edu

2 Year Institution

Coordinator: Andrew Kosciesza, 80A

Adj	Camacho, Loida	D	13,10,11
Adj	Goode, Gloria	D	11,20
Adj	Haffley, Robin	M	11,29,46
Adj	Herman, Matthew	D	10,11,13,34,35
Adj	Kosciesza, Andrew	M	11,12,20,36

PA2450 Moravian College

Department of Music
1200 Main St
Bethlehem, PA 18016
(610) 861-1650   Fax: (610) 861-1657
www.moravian.edu
E-mail: music@moravian.edu

4 Year Institution
Member of NASM

Chair: Hilde M. Binford, 80A

PT	Andrus, Deborah E.	D	64C,48,41
PT	Arnold, John	M	41,70
PT	Azzati, Eduardo	M	61,31A
PT	Baer, Sarah	M	64B,55B,12A,13E
Assoc Prof	Barnes, James E.	M	37,38,60,34,41
PT	Basta, JoAnna	M	62A
Assoc Prof	Binford, Hilde M.	D	13A,13,12A,12
PT	Birney, Allan	D	66H
PT	Bleiler-Conrad, Suzanne	M	64A
PT	Bortz, Jodi	B	64A

PT	Brodt, Ralph E.	B	63C
PT	Budlong, Trisha	M	39,61,32
PT	Checkeye, Jane	M	66A
PT	DeChellis, Dan	M	66A
PT	Demkee, Ronald	M	63D,32
PT	Diggs, David	M	64B
	Eyzerovich, Inna	M	62A
PT	Fix, Lou Carol	M	66G,69,31A,67B
	Gairo, Anthony	B	64E,29,47
PT	Ganus, Linda	B	64A
PT	Gaumer, Alan		47,63A
PT	Giasullo, Frank	M	66A,29B
PT	Gillespie, Alison	B	67H,62
PT	Goldina, Arianna	D	66A,66B
Vstng Inst	Hirokawa, Joy	M	32
PT	Huth, Lori	B	66A
PT	Jackson, Russell	M	66A,66G,66C
PT	Kani, Robin	M	41,48,64A
PT	Kistler, Linda	M	62A,62B
PT	Lanza, Lou	B	61,47,29,41
Prof Emeritus	Larson, Paul	D	32
Prof	Lipkis, Larry	D	13,10F,10,55,67
PT	Long, Jason	B	66A
PT	Mathiesen, Steven	M	50,65
PT	Mixon, Joseph D.	M	70
PT	Moulton, David	M	62C
PT	Nicholas, Lauren P.	M	64E,46,48
PT	Oaten, Gregory	M	60,61
PT	O'Brien, Tanya	M	61
PT	Rissmiller, Gary	C	65
PT	Robinson, Yvonne	D	61,54
PT	Rostock, Paul		47,62D,46,35A
PT	Roth, David	M	66A,29
PT	Saylor, Mary Ann	B	62A,62B
Prof Emerita	Schantz, Monica		12A
Prof Emeritus	Schantz, Richard		36
PT	Schrempel, Martha	M	66A,66C,66B
PT	Seifert, Kimberly		64D
PT	Simons, Audrey K.	M	62C
PT	Smyser, Peter		70
PT	Spieth, Donald	M	38
PT	Stockton, Larry	D	14
PT	Suggs, Nora	D	64A
PT	Terlaak Poot, Nancy	M	62A,62B
PT	Thompson, Barbara Tilden	M	66A,66B,13C,13,13A
PT	Torok, Debra	D	12A,13,38,66A,20G
Prof	Traupman-Carr, Carol A.	D	13A,13,12A,12,31A
PT	Walker, Scot	M	67E
Assoc Prof	Wetzel, Neil D.	D	47,64,29A,64E,46
PT	Wilkins, Skip	M	66A
PT	Williams, Todd	M	63B
PT	Wittchen, Andrea	M	41,62E
PT	Wright, Lawrence	M	37,41,49,63A
Assoc Prof	Zerkle, Paula R.	D	36,60,15,11,54

PA2500 Mount Aloysius College
Department of Music
7373 Admiral Peary Hwy
Cresson, PA 16630-1902
(814) 886-4131   Fax: (814) 886-2978
www.mtaloy.edu
E-mail: nway@mtaloy.edu

4 Year Institution

Chair: Thomas Coakley, 80A

Asst Prof	Rosensteel Way, Nancy	M	11,36

PA2550 Muhlenberg College
Department of Music
2400 Chew St
Allentown, PA 18104
(484) 664-3363   Fax: (484) 664-3633
www.muhlenberg.edu
E-mail: ovens@muhlenberg.edu

4 Year Institution

Chair: Douglas P. Ovens, 80A

Lect PT	Arnold, Robert D.		29,66A
Lect PT	Bara, Edward		61
Lect PT	Boring, Daniel		13,38,70
Lect PT	Chu, Brian Ming	M	61
Assoc Prof	Conner, Ted A.	D	11,12A,29A
Lect PT	Curnow, Lauren	M	61
Lect PT	Demkee, Ronald	M	63D
Lect PT	Fiore, Domenick J.		62D
Assoc Prof	Follet, Diane W.	D	13,15,42,13H
Lect PT	Gairo, Tony P.		64E
Lect PT	Gonen, Raya	D	61
Lect PT	Haley, Jill		64B
Lect PT	Hanegraaf, Margaret	D	61
Asst Prof	Helm, Patricia	M	
Asst Prof	Hiles, Karen	D	12A
Lect PT	Hughes, Donald L.		63A
Lect PT	Kennedy, John S.	M	61
Lect PT	Kozic, Thomas		70
Lect PT	Liebhaber, Barbara	D	13A,13B
Lect PT	Manus, Elizabeth A.	M	66A,66C
Lect PT	Martin, Elaine J.	B	64A
Emeritus	McClain, Charles	D	13,36,66G
Lect PT	Monaghan, Megan	M	61
Lect PT	Moulton, David	M	62C
Lect PT	Neumeyer, Albert J.	M	47,37
Lect PT	Oster, Andrew	D	12A
Prof	Ovens, Douglas P.	D	13,10,45,65
	Petit, Annie	DIPL	66A
Lect PT	Rissmiller, Gary		65
Emeritus	Schmidt, Henry L.	D	13,12A,63C,26,29A
Lect	Schnack, Michael B.	M	36,40,61
Lect PT	Seifert, Kim		
Lect PT	Simons, Anthony R.	M	64C,64E
Lect PT	Snow, Steven		61
Lect PT	Thoma, James E.		65
Lect PT	Thomas, June M.	M	61,29
Lect PT	Toth, Michael S.		66A
Lect PT	Trovato, Vincent		66A
Lect PT	Warda, Christa	B	61
Lect PT	Williams, Stephen C.	M	66G,39
Lect PT	Windt, Paul	B	62A,62B

PA2675 Penn College of Technology
Department of Music
1 College Ave
Williamsport, PA 17701-5778
(717)326-3761   Fax: (717)327-4503
www.pct.edu
E-mail: dkuhns@pct.edu

4 Year Institution

Director: Diana L. Kuhns, 80A

Inst PT	Dascher, Debra M.	M	11

PA2700 Penn State Univ-Abington
Department of Music
1600 Woodland Rd
Abington, PA 19001-3918
(215) 881-7300   Fax: (215) 881-7623
www.abington.psu.edu
E-mail: rlh48@psu.edu

4 Year Institution

Division Head: David E. Ruth, 80A
Dean: Karen W. Sandler, 80A
Acting Associate Dean: Samir Ouzomgi, 80H

Lect	DeLise, Louis	M	13A
Lect	Haffley, Robin L.	M	13A
Lect	Nocella, Peter S.	D	29A
Assoc Prof	Stace, Stephen	D	11,34
Lect	Weightman, Lindsay	D	14

PA2710 Penn State Univ-Altoona
Department of Intergrative Arts
Music - Misciagna Performing Art Ctr
Room 108
Altoona, PA 16601-3760
(814) 949-5607   Fax: (814) 949-5368
www.aa.psu.edu/

E-mail: kth2@psu.edu

4 Year Institution

Coordinator: KT Huckabee, 80A

Lect	Black, Christina		32B
Asst Prof	Cutsforth-Huber, Bonnie	D	61,36
Lect	Martin, Kent		37
Lect	McFee, Cathy		70

Lect	Melbinger, Timothy	D	12A,41,13B,13C,13E
Lect	Snyder, Jacob		13A,11
Asst Prof	Villani, A. David		34B,35G,29A
	Whetstone, Joni		20
Lect	White, James		11
Lect	Yon, John		36

PA2713 Penn State Univ-Beaver
Department of Music
100 University Dr
Monaca, PA 15061
(724) 773-3898
www.br.psu.edu
E-mail: jrh41@psu.edu

2 Year Institution, Branch Campus

PhD in Ethnomusicology, MFA in Music Theory

Assoc Prof	Rocco, Emma S.	PhD	13A,11,20F,36,54

PA2715 Penn State Univ-Erie
School of Humanities
Behrend College
4951 College Dr
Erie, PA 16563-1501
(814) 898-6108   Fax: (814) 898-6032
www.pserie.psu.edu/academic/hss/music/index.htm
E-mail: gav3@psu.edu

4 Year Institution

Dean: Donald L. Birx, 80A
Director, Humanities & Social Sciences: Steven V. Hick, 80A

Lect	Bishop, Jason	D	36
Senior Lect	Viebranz, Gary A.	DMA	12A,29A,32C

PA2720 Penn State Univ-McKeesport
Department of Music
4000 University Dr
Mc Keesport, PA 15132-7698
(412) 675-9177   Fax: (412) 675-9166
www.mk.psu.edu

E-mail: dxw39@psu.edu

2 Year Institution

Coordinator: Mary L. Romanek, 80A

Asst Prof	Romanek, Mary L.	D	12A,32A,32B,29A

PA2740 Penn State Univ-Schuylkill
Department of Hum. & Music
State Hwy
Schuylkill Haven, PA 17972
(570) 385-6000   Fax: (570) 385-6135
www.sl.psu.edu
E-mail: pwm3@psu.edu

4 Year Institution

Music Contact: Paul W. Miller, 80A

Lect PT	Evans, Chris	M	36,40,61
Asst Prof	Miller, Paul W.	D	10A,11,13A,29A,29B

PA2750 Penn State Univ-University Park
School of Music
233 Music Bldg
University Park, PA 16802-1901
(814) 865-0431   Fax: (814) 865-6785
www.music.psu.edu
E-mail: klw1@psu.edu

4 Year Institution, Graduate School
Member of NASM

Master of Arts in Music Theory & History, Master of Arts in Music Theory, Master of Education in Music Education, Master of Music in Performance, Master of Music in Conducting, PhD in Music Education, Master of Music in Music Theory-Composition, Master of Arts in Musicology, Master of Music in Voice Pedagogy & Performance, Master of Music in Piano Pedagogy & Performance, DMA in Music

Director: Sue E. Haug, 80A
Assistant Director: Daryl Durran, 80H
Assistant Director: Marisa S. Tacconi, 80H

Prof	Armstrong, Daniel C.	M	65
Assoc Prof Emerita	Armstrong, Eleanor Duncan	D	64A
Assoc Prof	Ballora, Mark E.	D	45
Assoc Prof	Barsom, Paul	D	10,45
Assoc Prof	Benitez, Vincent P.	D	13F,13D,13B,13J,13
Prof	Bontrager, Lisa Jane	M	63B
Prof	Brown, Velvet	M	63D
Prof	Bundy, O. Richard	D	32C,37
Prof	Carr, Maureen A.	D	13
Asst Prof	Christopher, Edward	M	61,39
Assoc Prof	Clements, Ann C.	D	32C
Inst	Cody, Thomas	M	13
Prof	Cook, Kim	M	62C
Asst Prof	Costa, Anthony J.	D	64C
Prof	Deighton, Timothy	D	62B
Prof	Drafall, Lynn	D	32C,36
Inst	Drane, Gregory		37
Prof	Durran, Daryl	M	64D
Assoc Prof	Edelstein, Gerardo	M	60,38
Prof	Fitzgerald, Langston	D	63A
Assoc Prof	Gardner, Robert	D	32E
Prof	Glocke, Dennis	M	60,37
Inst PT	Glocke, Jayne	M	36
Assoc Prof	Greer, Taylor A.	D	13
Asst Prof	Guzman, Christopher	M	66A
Prof	Haug, Sue E.	D	66A,66B,66C,66D
Asst Prof	Hopkins, Stephen O.	D	13
Inst PT	Howarth, Gifford W.	M	65B
Assoc Prof	Hurtz, Timothy	B	64B
Inst	Jenkins, Lisa Davenport	M	14
Prof	Kennedy, Richard R.	M	61
Assoc Prof	Kiver, Christopher A.	D	36
Prof	Leach, Anthony	D	32C,36
Prof	Lusk, Mark Lancaster	M	63C,63D
Prof	Lyon, James	M	62A
Assoc Prof	McKee, Eric John	D	13
Prof Emeritus	Merriman, Lyle C.	D	64C
Prof	Nairn, Robert	M	62D
Prof	Rutkowski, Joanne	D	32A,32B,32G
Asst Prof	Sage, Raymond	M	61,54
Prof	Saunders, Mary	M	61,54
Asst Prof	Seidman, Naomi K.	D	64A
Prof	Shafer, Timothy P.	D	66A,66B
Prof	Smith, Steven	D	66A
Prof	Spivey, Norman	D	61
Assoc Prof	Stambler, David B.	D	64E,29
Prof	Tacconi, Marisa S.	D	12
Assoc Prof	Thornton, Linda	D	32E
Asst Prof	Trost, Jennifer	M	61
Prof	Yoder, M. Dan	M	47,64E
Assoc Prof	Youmans, Charles D.	D	12
Asst Prof	Zorin, Max	M	62A

PA2775 Penn State Univ-Worthington
Department of Music
120 Ridge View Dr
Dunmore, PA 18512
(570) 963-2696   Fax: (570) 963-2535
www.sn.psu.edu
E-mail: sat11@psu.edu

2 & 4 Year Institution

Music Contact: Sharon Ann Toman, 80A

Inst	Toman, Sharon Ann	M	11,13A,29A,14C,36

PA2800 Philadelphia Biblical University
School of Music & Perf Arts
200 Manor Ave
Langhorne, PA 19047-2943
(215) 702-4329   Fax: (215) 702-4342
www.pbu.edu
E-mail: music@pbu.edu

4 Year Institution
Member of NASM

Dean: Paul R. Isensee, 80A

Inst Adj	Beale, Nancy	B	66A
Inst Adj	Belzer, Terry	B	64B
Adj	Black, Dorothy M.	M	12C
Asst Prof	Borrmann, Kenneth	M	66A,66B,66C,42,44
Inst Adj	Brown, Brian	M	63D
Asst Prof	Caminiti, Joseph D.	M	60,38,37,63B,32E
Inst Adj	Claudin, Margaret	M	64A,41
Inst Adj	Cocking, Roger	D	64
Adj	Condy, Steven	M	61,39
Inst Adj	Cooper, James	B	62C,42
Inst Adj	Correnti, James	M	66A
Inst Adj	Edgett, Bryan	D	63A
Inst Adj	Elliot, Thomas	M	63C
Inst Adj	Floyd, Ruth Naomi	B	61
Inst Adj	Frazier, John	M	64C
Inst Adj	Hesh, Joseph	M	47,42,66D
Prof	Hsu, Samuel	D	12A,66A,66B,13E
Prof	Isensee, Paul R.	D	31A,40
Adj	Kramer, David	M	63
Inst Adj	Kratz, Jay	M	70
Adj	Mariman, Devin	M	36
Inst Adj	Marino, Lori	M	64D
Inst Adj	Michelson, Bliss	B	62D
Inst Adj	Orlando, Hilary	M	66G
Adj	Petersons, Erik	B	62
Inst Adj	Priebe, William	M	65
Inst Adj	Ramsey, DonnaLee	M	61
Inst PT	Rudoi, Natalie	M	62A
Asst Prof	Shaw, Timothy B.	M	13B,13C,10A,13
Prof	Shockey, David M.	D	36,61,40
Inst Adj	Smith, Jacqueline H.	M	55
Inst Adj	Smith, Kile	M	10F
Inst Adj	Spicer, Jeffrey	M	70
Inst Adj	Taylor, Marshall	M	64E
Inst Adj	Thomas, Ronald B.	M	10
Adj	Watson, Scott	D	34
Prof	Wolf, Debbie Lynn	D	32,66A,66D,66B
Inst Adj	Zhou, Xiao-Fu	B	62A,62B

PA2900 Point Park University
Conservatory of Performing Arts
Music
201 Wood St
Pittsburgh, PA 15222
(412) 392-4786   Fax: (412) 392-6104
www.pointpark.edu
E-mail: rklein@pointpark.edu

4 Year Institution

MFA

Coord., Music & Core Curriculum Arts: Rochelle Z. Klein, 80A

Adj Inst	Ball, Alexandria	M	66C,66D,35E
Prof Emerita	Barasch, Shirley R.	D	61,32,54,10,35E
Adj Inst	Brovey-Kovach, Lisa	M	61
Adj Inst	Flora, James	M	61
Adj Inst	Frankenberry, Robert	M	61
Other	Greciano, Sandra	B	61,54
Adj Inst	Gruber, Sari	M	61
Other	Howell, Jane	M	66A,66C,13A,54,11
Adj Inst	Jenkins, Judith	M	61
Adj Inst	Jones, Richard	M	66C,11
Asst Prof	Klein, Rochelle Z.	M	32,35E,66A,11,13A
Adj Inst	Kurth, Robert	M	13C,61
Adj Inst	Marchukov, Sergey	B	66A,66D,66C,13A
Assoc Prof	McKelvey, Michael E.	D	35E,61,54,10
Adj Inst	Rainforth, Eva	M	61
Adj Inst	Steinhauer, Kimberly	D	61
Adj Inst	Tobia, Riccardo	B	61,36
Adj Inst	Williams, Katy Schakleton	B	61

PA2950 St Vincent College
Department of Fine Arts
300 Fraser Purchase Rd
Latrobe, PA 15650-2690
(724) 805-2107   Fax: (724) 537-4454
www.stvincent.edu
E-mail: nathan.cochran@email.stvincent.edu

4 Year Institution

Chair, Fine Arts: Nathan Cochran, OSB, 80A,80F

Adj	Auman, Richard	M	63C
Adj	Boulet, Michele	M	64A,48
Inst	Cochran, Nathan	M	11
Asst Prof	Concordia, Stephen	M	36,31A
Asst Prof	Constantine, Cyprian G.	D	66G,31A
Adj	Cottrill-Nelson, Lara Lynn	M	61
Adj	D'Abruzzo, Gabriel	M	66A
Adj	Frantz, Jeremy	B	70,41,47
Adj	Miller, Maureen	D	61
Adj	Molinaro, Lisa M.	M	64E
Inst	Octave, Thomas	M	61,36,39,40,11
Adj	Posey, Dawn	B	62A
Adj	Spang, Lisa	M	66A,66B
Asst Prof	Tiberio, Albert	D	11,12,13,10A,10F
Adj	Wygonik, David	M	63A,63B

PA3000 Seton Hill University
Department of Music
1 Seton Hill Dr
Greensburg, PA 15601
(724) 552-2900   Fax: (724) 830-1807
www.setonhill.edu
E-mail: scheib@setonhill.edu

4 Year Institution
Member of NASM

Chair: Curt A. Scheib, 80A
Dir., Community Music Division: Michelle L. Walters, 80E

PT	Alderson, Daphne	M	61,39
Assoc Prof	Campbell, Kathleen M.	M	60,37,38,48
Assoc Prof	DiSanti, Theodore A.	D	63A,47,49,13,10F
PT	Domencic, Joe	M	61
PT	Ferrell, Sarah	M	62C
PT	Glovier, Thomas	M	29,66A
PT	Gorinski, Nancy J.	M	66A
PT	Heid, Ronald J.	M	65
Asst Prof	Highberger, Edgar B.	M	12A,66G,31A
Assoc Prof	Huls, Marvin J.	M	13,36,44
Asst Prof	Huls, Shirley	M	13A,32A,32B,61
PT	Insko, Robert	B	29,62D
Assoc Prof	Jones, Laurie	M	33,61
PT	Kostilnik, Rise	B	64B
Asst Prof	Kuhn, Edward M.	M	66A
PT	Lintz, David	B	63B
PT	Lynch, Kelly Fiona	D	61
PT	Marcinizyn, John	D	10,70
PT	McManus, Keven M.	M	63C,46
PT	Mesare, Roi	M	64C
PT	Scandrett, Lucy	M	62E
Prof	Scheib, Curt A.	D	61,36,66C,60,60
PT	Shultis, Carol L.	M	33
PT	Sinclair, David W.	M	62A,62B
PT	Stryker, Crystal J.	M	32A,32B,61
PT	Touree, Marc	M	61
PT	Williams, Lynne	M	61
PT	Worzbty, Jason	D	37
PT	Zetts, Mary Jo F.	M	63D

PA3050 Shippensburg University
Department of Music & Theatre Arts
1871 Old Main Dr
Shippensburg, PA 17257
(717) 477-1638   Fax: (717) 477-4033
www.ship.edu/music_theater
E-mail: music@ship.edu

4 Year Institution

Chair: Trever R. Famulare, 80A
Dir., Artist/Performance Series: Margaret E. Lucia, 80F
Dir., Artist/Performance Series: Blaine F. Shover, 80F

Asst Prof	Dade, Fred S.	M	20,11,32B,36,66A
Asst Prof	Famulare, Trever R.	M	11,37,47,49,60
Asst Prof	Hartman, Mark L.	D	62,38,13,62A,29
Prof	Lucia, Margaret E.	D	13,11,12,66A
Prof	Ritz, Dennis W.	D	11
Prof	Shover, Blaine F.	D	11,12A,36,61,54

PA3100 Slippery Rock University
Department of Music
225 Swope Music Hall
Slippery Rock, PA 16057
(724) 738-2442   Fax: (724) 738-4469
academics.sru.edu/music/index.html
E-mail: david.glover@sru.edu

4 Year Institution
Member of NASM

Chair: David Glover, 80A
Dean: Eva Tsuquiashi-Daddesio, 80A
Dir., Summer Programs: Eliott G. Baker, 80G

Inst	Baker, Amy	B	64D
Asst Prof	Barr, Stephen A.	DMA	13,36,40,34
Asst Prof	Berry, James	M	11,37,60,32B,48
Inst	Douds, Nathan	M	11,50,65,66A
Assoc Prof	Glover, David	D	29,50,65,34,47
Assoc Prof	Gray, Colleen G.	D	61,39
Inst	Grubbs, Jeff	B	62D
Prof	Hadley, Susan J.	D	70,33,11,66D
Inst	Hahna, Nicole	M	32A,33,11
Prof	Hawk, Stephen L.	D	63A,47,29
Inst	Johnson, Heather	M	63B
Inst	Kiser, Candice C.	M	64C
Assoc Prof	Knaub, Maribeth J.	D	11,61,66D
Inst	Kush, Jason	D	64E,29,41,53,64C
Asst Prof	Meixner, Brian	D	12A,63C,49,11
Inst	Melago, Kathleen A.	D	32B,11,66D
Inst	Riggs, Paige	DMA	62C
Inst	Sakins, Renate	M	13,64,64B
Prof	Solomon, Nanette Kaplan	D	12A,66A,13C,15
Asst Prof	Steele, Stacey G.	M	32A,32B,48,64A
Prof	Utsch, Glenn R.	D	13C,66A,29A,66D

PA3150 Susquehanna University
Department of Music
514 University Ave
Selinsgrove, PA 17870-1001
(570) 372-4281   Fax: (570) 372-2789
www.susqu.edu/music
E-mail: musicdept@susqu.edu

4 Year Institution
Member of NASM

Head, Music: Patrick A. Long, 80A
Dean: Valerie G. Martin, 80A
Dir., Admissions & Summer Programs: Sara Adams, 80D,80G
Dir., Preparatory Program: Mary J. Lippert-Coleman, 80E

Lect PT	Alico, Gregory H.	M	50,65
Asst Prof	Armstrong, Colin	M	32D,36,13C
Lect PT	Ayoub, Anna Claire	M	64D,48
Asst Prof	Blinov, Ilya	D	66A,66C,11
Lect PT	Boris, Victor R.	B	66D,14C
Lect PT	Cullen, Leslie	M	64A,48
Asst Prof	Davis, Joshua	D	47,29,62D,13C,53
Lect PT	Fahnestock, Jeffrey	M	61
Asst Prof	Gadberry, David	D	32
Lect PT	Hartung, Colleen	D	64C,48
Lect PT	Hays, Jonathan C.	M	61
Lect PT	Henry, Eric L.	B	63D,49
Lect PT	Henry, Kevin	M	63C,49
Asst Prof	Hinton, Eric L.	D	37,60B,63A
Lect PT	Hooper, Kay	M	66A
Lect PT	Hunter, Ruth	B	62E
Asst Prof	Krieger, Marcos F.	D	13C,66H,66G,11,12A
Assoc Prof	Levinsky, Gail B.	D	48,64E,32E
Assoc Prof	Long, Patrick A.	D	13,10,34,12A,32E
Lect PT	Marchione, Jill	M	64B,41
Asst Prof	Niskala, Naomi	D	66A,66C,13
Lect PT	Ogilvie, Tyler	M	63B,49
Lect PT	Radspinner, Matthew	M	32E
Lect PT	Rammon, Andrew	M	62C,51
Lect PT	Scott, Diane	M	66D
Lect PT	Smith, Paul A.	B	32E
Lect PT	Smolensky, Marcus	D	62B
Assoc Prof	Steinau, David S.	D	61,39,12A
Asst Prof	Thorn, Julia	D	36,60A,61
Assoc Prof	Tober, Nina M.	D	61
Lect PT	Umble, Jay	B	70
Lect PT	White, Judith	B	61
Assoc Prof	Wiley, Jennifer Sacher	D	38,62A,32E

PA3200 Swarthmore College
Department of Music
500 College Ave
Swarthmore, PA 19081
(610) 328-8233   Fax: (610) 328-8551
www.swarthmore.edu/humanities/music
E-mail: music@swarthmore.edu

4 Year Institution

Chair: Michael Marissen, 80A

Assoc Prof	Alston, John	D	36
PT	Barone, Marcantonio	M	66
Asst Prof	DeVaron, Alexander	PhD	13
Librarian	Fournier, Donna	M	16
Prof Emeritus PT	Freeman, James	D	12,60
Assoc Prof	Hamer, Jan	D	13C
Asst Prof	Hauze, Andrew	M	38
PT	Johns, Michael	PhD	48,37,42
Asst Prof	Kochavi, Jonathan	D	13
Prof	Levinson, Gerald C.	PhD	13,10,20D
Prof	Ludemann, Hans	M	29
Prof	Marissen, Michael	PhD	11,12A,31
Asst Prof	Milewski, Barbara Ann	D	11,12
Inst	Sayre, Elizabeth	M	14,20
Asst Prof	Shanefield, Andrew	M	47,29A,29B
PT	Suadin, Nyoman		20D
Assoc Prof	Whitman, Thomas I.	PhD	13,20D,32

PA3250 Temple University
Boyer College of Music & Dance
2001 N 13th St
Philadelphia, PA 19122-6079
(215) 204-8301   Fax: (215) 204-4957
www.temple.edu/boyer
E-mail: music@temple.edu

4 Year Institution, Graduate School
Member of NASM

Master of Music in Composition, Master of Music in Music Theory, Master of Music in Performance, Master of Music in Conducting, Master of Music in Music Education, Master of Music in Music Therapy, PhD in Music Education, DMA in Composition, DMA in Performance, Master of Music in Piano Accompanying, Master of Music in Piano Pedagogy, Master of Music in String Pedagogy, Master of Music in Music History & Literature, PhD in Music Therapy

Dean: Robert Stroker, 80A
Associate Dean: Beth M. Bolton, 80H
Assistant Dean: David P. Brown, 80H
Associate Dean: Edward Flanagan, 80H
Associate Dean: Steven Kreinberg, 80H

Prof Adj	Abel, Alan D.	B	65
Prof	Abramovic, Charles	D	66A
Assoc Prof	Aigen, Kenneth	PhD	33
PT	Amoroso, Richard		62A
PT	An, Youngjoo		61
Assoc Prof	Andaya, Mitos	D	36,60A
PT	Anderson, Angela		64D
Assoc Prof	Anderson, Christine	D	61
PT	Arnold, David C.		
PT	Astafan, Marc A.		39,61
PT	Auerbach, Elise M.	M	61
PT	Bai, Millie		62A
PT	Bar-David, Ohad		62C
PT	Barnes, Mei Chen		62A
PT	Barth, Bruce D.	M	47,29
PT	Beiler, Jonathan		62A
Prof	Biava, Luis O.	M	38,62A
PT	Biederman, Bradley R.	M	33
PT	Bilger, David	M	63A
PT	Bishop, Julie		29,61
PT	Blumenfeld, Jonathan H.	B	64B
PT	Bollinger, Blair J.	B	63C
Assoc Prof	Bolton, Beth M.	D	32
PT	Boone, Michael E.	M	29,62D
PT	Booth, Davyd M.		62A
Assoc Prof	Brodhead, Richard C.	A	10
Assoc Prof	Brooks, Darlene M.	D	33
Asst Prof	Brunner, Matthew	D	37

PT	Bruno, Sophie		62E
Prof Emeritus	Bruscia, Kenneth E.	D	33
PT	Bryan, Paul	M	63C
Asst Prof	Buonviri, Nathan	D	32
PT	Camp, Laura		61
Assoc Prof	Cannata, David B.	D	12A
PT	Caviezel, Samuel R.		
PT	Chen, Che-Hung		62B
Prof Emeritus	Cho, Philip Y.	M	61
Prof Emeritus	Chodoroff, Arthur D.	M	37,47
PT	Chown, Andrew		39,61
Prof Emeritus	Colucci, Matthew J.	D	13,10
PT	Condran, Dena	M	33,61
PT	Conyers, Joseph		62D
PT	Cook, Carla		29,61
Prof Emeritus	Cornelius, Jeffrey M.	D	60,11,12A,36
PT	Cramer, David M.	B	64A
PT	Curnow, Jeffrey		63A
PT	Curtiss, Sidney		62B
PT	David, Norman		29
Prof Emeritus	Dean, Roger A.	D	32
PT	DeLise, Louis Anthony	B	29
PT	Demers, Paul	M	64C
Asst Prof	Deubner, Brett D.		62B
PT	deVaron, Alexander	M	13
PT	Deviney, Christopher		65
PT	Dibble, Benjamin		61
Prof	Dileo, Cheryl L.	PhD	33
Assoc Prof	Dilworth, Rollo A.	D	32
PT	Earley, Robert	M	63A
PT	Ebner, Craig	B	29,70
PT	Edwards, Renard		62B
Prof Emeritus	Epstein, Paul A.	M	13,10,55
PT	Fedchcok, John	M	29,63C
PT	Fidyk, Steve	M	29,65
Prof	Fiorillo, Alexander E.	M	66A
PT	Fisher, Kimberly		62A
Assoc Prof	Flanagan, Edward	D	29,35
Assoc Prof	Folio, Cynthia J.	D	13
Prof Emeritus	Frank, Arthur	D	32C,50
PT	Frank, Mike	M	47,66A,29
PT	Fre, Anna		39,61
PT	Giacabetti, Tom	CERT	29
Artist in Res	Gordon, Wycliffe		29,63C
Inst FT	Gratis, Lorie A.	D	61
PT	Gray, George A.		61
Prof	Greenbaum, Matthew J.	D	10
PT	Hainen, Elizabeth		62E
Prof Emeritus	Harler, Alan	M	36
PT	Haroz, Nitzan		63C
PT	Harrington, Roger J.	M	32
PT	Hood, John		62D
Asst Prof	Indik, Lawrence R.	D	61
PT	James, Sandy L.		34
PT	Jantsch, Carol		63
Prof	Johnson, John F.	M	13
Artist in Res	Jones, Paul		36
PT	Kerrigan, William	B	65
PT	Kesselman, Robert		62D
PT	Kettinger, Gregory S.	B	29
PT	Kirchner, Joann M.	PhD	66A
PT	Kirschen, Jeffry	B	63B
Assoc Prof	Klein, Michael L.	D	13,13F
PT	Knie, Robert	B	61
	Koen, John		62C
Inst FT	Krantz, Allen M.	M	70
PT	Kratz, Girard	D	10A,10B,13,10
Assoc Prof	Kreinberg, Steven	D	12A
Assoc Prof	Krush, Jay P.	M	63D
Prof	Krzywicki, Jan L.	M	13,66A
PT	Ku, Rachel		62B
Prof Emerita	Kwalwasser, Helen		62,62A
Prof Emeritus	Laird, Helen L.	M	39,61
PT	Lang, Jeffrey	M	63B
PT	Large, Duane	M	70
Assoc Prof	Latham, Edward D.	D	13
PT	Lawton, Tom P.		66A,29
PT	Levin, Dmitri		62A
PT	Lind, Loren N.	B	64A
Prof	Lindorff, Joyce Zankel	DMA	12A,12,66H,67C
Lect PT	Luise, Evelyn J.	B	62B
PT	Mack, Rodney		63A
PT	Marchione, Nick		29,63A
Lect	Marrazzo, Randi		61
PT	Masoudnia, Elizabeth		64B
Lect	Matsukawa, Daniel		64D
PT	Mayo, William M.	M	61
PT	Mazzeo, Frank		64E
PT	McCarrick-Dix, Patricia	D	33
PT	McClelland, Phillip	B	63C
PT	McClendon, Forrest		61
PT	Meehan, Jill		12A
Prof Emeritus	Meyer, Eve R.	D	13,12A,12
PT	Miceli, Anthony		65
Lect	Monaghan, Daniel		29B
PT	Monroe, Diane	B	62A
PT	Montone, Jennifer	M	63B
PT	Morales, Dara		62A
Lect	Morales, Ricado J.		64C
PT	Murphy, Kathy		32
PT	Natale, Michael A.	B	29
PT	Norris, Michael B.	M	66A
FT Asst Prof	Oatts, Dick		29,64E
Asst Prof	O'Banion, Philip R.		32
PT	Oka, Hirono		
Prof	Orkis, Lambert T.	M	66A,66C
PT	Parker, Charles H.	B	62A
Asst Prof	Pasbrig, David	D	66A
PT	Pascale, Joanna		29,61
PT	Patterson, Mark		29,63C
PT	Peterson, Anne L.		62D
PT	Picht-Read, Kathryn	M	62C
Prof Emerita	Poch, Gail B.	M	60,36
Assoc Prof	Rardin, Paul	D	60A
PT	Rast, Madison B.		29,62D
PT	Reeder, Deborah	M	62C
Assoc Prof	Reynolds, Alison M.	D	32,32A
PT	Richmond, Joshua		29,66A
PT	Rosen, Michelle		64D
PT	Rowe, Booker		62A
PT	Rowe, Kimberly	M	62E
PT	Ryan, Kerri		62B
Assoc Prof	Ryvkin, Valery	D	39
PT	Schleifer, Martha Furman	D	12
Prof	Schmieder, Eduard		62A
PT	Schweingruber, Eric J.	M	63A
PT	Scott, Yumi N.		62A
Prof	Sheldon, Deborah	D	32
Lect	Showers, Shelley		63B
PT	Sim, Hoejin	D	61
PT	Smith, Peter		64B
Prof	Solow, Jeffrey G.	B	62C
PT	Sonies, Barbara	M	62A
PT	St. Pierre, Donald		61
Prof	Stafford, Terell L.	M	29
Prof Emeritus	Steele, Glenn A.	M	50,65
Prof Emeritus	Stone, William	D	61,39
PT	Swana, John	B	29,63A
PT	Taubman, Dorothy		66A
Prof	Taylor, Maria C.	M	66A,66D
PT	Taylor, Marshall T.	M	64E
Assoc Prof	Threinen, Emily	D	37,60B
PT	Tokito, Kazuo	M	64A
PT	Tomasone, Adeline	B	64A
PT	Tryon, Denise		63B
PT	Tsinadze, Ana	M	66A
PT	Uhle, Grant	M	61
PT	Vaughan, Matthew	B	63C
	Vidiksis, Adam	M	
PT	Villafranca, Elio		29,66A
PT	Wade, James	B	66A
Prof Emeritus	Wagner, Lawrence R.	M	60,38,48,64C
Prof Emeritus	Walters, Darrel L.	D	32
PT	Warfield, Tim	B	29,64E
Prof Emeritus	Wedeen, Harvey D.	M	66A,66B
Assoc Prof	Weightman, Lindsay	D	32
PT	Weiskopf, Walter		29,64E
PT	Wiemken, Robert		67
Artist in Res	Williams, Buster		29,62D
PT	Williams, Daniel		63B
Assoc Prof	Willier, Stephen A.	D	12A
PT	Willwerth, Valissa		62A
PT	Wolf, Debbie	D	32
PT	Woodhams, Richard	B	64B
PT	Woods, Sheryl		39,61
PT	Wozniak, William		65
Prof	Wright, Maurice W.	D	10,34
Prof Emerita	Yamron, Janet M.	M	60,32,36
PT	Yurkovskaya, Irina	D	66A
Asst Prof	Zanders, Michael	PhD	33
PT	Zator-Nelson, Angela	M	65
PT	Zavadsky, Julia		36
PT	Zhou, Xiao-fu		62B
Prof	Zohn, Steven D.	D	12A

PA3260 Thiel College

Department of Music
75 College Ave
Greenville, PA 16125
(724) 589-2000   Fax: (724) 589-2010
www.thiel.edu
E-mail: mbray@thiel.edu

4 Year Institution

Chair: Michael R. Bray, 80A

Prof	Bray, Michael R.	D	60,61,11,36,12A
Adj	Erb, Andrew	M	63A,63C,37,47,49
Adj	Gant, Christina	M	62A,62B,62C
Adj	Gray, Kathryn A.	M	66A,66C,66G
Adj	Nold, Sherry		64A,64C,64E
Adj	Quinn, Brian	M	70
Adj	Tarantine, April A.	M	61

PA3330 Univ of the Arts

School of Music
320 S Broad St
Philadelphia, PA 19102-5022
(215) 717-6342   Fax: (215) 545-8056
www.uarts.edu
E-mail: mdicciani@uarts.edu

4 Year Institution, Graduate School
Member of NASM

Master of Arts in Teaching in Music Education, Master of Music in Jazz Studies, Graduate Diploma in Jazz Studies

Director: Marc Dicciani, 80A
Dir., Graduate Studies: Don Glanden, 80C
Dir., Summer Programs & Preparatory Program: Micah Jones, 80E,80G
Dir., Artist Series & Summer Programs: Randy Kapralick, 80F,80G

Senior Lect PT	Adkins, Paul	M	61
Senior Lect	Allen, Mark	M	64E
Lect	Allen, Virginia	D	37,38
Prof	Applebaum, Terry L.	D	65,35A,50
Senior Lect	Arbogast, Paul	M	63C
Senior Lect PT	Beskrone, Steve	B	62D,47
Senior Lect PT	Binek, Claire	B	61
Asst Prof	Binek, Justin	M	61,47
Asst Prof Adj	Blake, John	B	47,62A,29
Asst Prof Adj	Brosh, Robert	D	50,65,20G,14
Lect	Brown, Gerald	B	65
Senior Lect	Butler, Chuck	B	10,34
Senior Lect	Cappy, Matt	M	63A
Senior Lect	Cemprola, Michael	M	64E
Prof	Chittum, Donald	D	13,12A,12,14,12F
Senior Lect	Chuong, Jason	M	32E,65
Asst Prof PT	Clearfield, Andrea	D	66C,66D,10,12F
Asst Prof	David, Norman	D	64,47,10,29,13
Senior Lect	Davis, Matt	B	47,70
Senior Lect	DeCaumette, Patrick	D	39,10
Senior Lect	Desmond, Mary Ellen	B	61
Prof Adj	Dicciani, Marc	B	65,35,50
Prof	DiMedio, Annette	D	12A,12,66A,66D,11
Asst Prof Adj	Farr, Chris	M	47,64E,29
Asst Prof	Gallagher, Matt	M	47,63A,29
Asst Prof Adj	Germer, Mark	D	12
Asst Prof Adj	Giacabetti, Thomas	B	47,70,29
Prof	Glanden, Don	M	47,66A,13A,13,29
Senior Lect	Glover, Judy	B	66D,66C
Senior Lect PT	Goldberg, Marjorie	B	62,32
Asst Prof PT	Haddad, Orlando	B	47,50
Senior Lect	Hall, Rick		47,20
Senior Lect	Hanson, Kevin	B	70
Asst Prof	Hartl, David	B	47,66A,66D,34,29
Senior Lect	Heim, Charlie	B	65
Senior Lect	Hotchkiss, Richard	B	62C
Senior Lect	Johnson, Erik	B	29,65
Lect	Johnson, Michael	B	34
Asst Prof	Jones, Micah	M	47,62D,29,13,34
Senior Lect	Jost, Paul	M	61
Senior Lect PT	Kapralick, Randy	B	63C,20A,46
Senior Lect PT	Kennedy, Mike	M	70
Prof	Kerber, Ronald	B	47,64A,64E,29,41
Assoc Prof	Kern, Jeffrey	M	13A,36,44,61,66A
Adj Prof	Lawn, Richard J.	M	46,29
Senior Lect	Lawrence, Josh	B	63A
Senior Lect PT	Lawton, Thomas	M	66A
Senior Lect	Luttrell, Carol	B	61
Senior Lect PT	MacConnell, Kevin	B	47,62D,29
Senior Lect PT	Miceli, Tony	B	65B,29
Lect	Mitnick, Alex	B	70
Lect	Myers, Marcus	M	46,65
Asst Prof Adj	Nero, Joseph	DIPL	50,65
Lect	O'Neill, Ben	B	46
Senior Lect	Pindell, Reginald	M	36,39,61
Senior Lect	Pusey, Bill	B	47,63A
Senior Lect PT	Quaile, Michael	M	47,70
Senior Lect	Quaile, Robert	B	32,64B
Senior Lect	Rabbai, George		63A,47,49
Senior Lect	Richman, Josh	M	66
Senior Lect	Ross, Elizabeth	M	61
Asst Prof Adj	Rudolph, Thomas	D	34,32
Senior Lect	Ruttenberg, Samuel		65
Senior Lect PT	Salicandro, Anthony	B	64
Asst Prof Adj	Sciolla, Anne	M	39,47,61
Asst Prof	Sokolowski, Elizabeth	D	32
Prof	Solot, Evan	M	13,10F,10,47,46
Senior Lect PT	Stable, Arturo	M	20H,50
Lect PT	Swana, John	B	63A,53,47
Assoc Prof Adj	Thomas, Craig		47,62D,29
Asst Prof	Thomas, David	M	66D
Lect PT	Veasley, Gerald		62D,47
Lect PT	Wasko, Dennis	B	47,63A,49
Senior Lect	Welte, John	M	64C,64E
Asst Prof Adj	Worth, Mike	M	10,34

PA3350 Univ of Pennsylvania

Department of Music
201 S 34th St
Philadelphia, PA 19104
(215) 898-7544   Fax: (215) 573-2106
www.sas.upenn.edu/music
E-mail: malek@sas.upenn.edu

4 Year Institution, Graduate School

Master of Arts in Composition, PhD in Ethnomusicology, PhD in Composition, PhD in History & Music Theory

Chair: Jay Reise, 80A

Prof	Abbate, Carolyn	D	12A,12
Prof Emeritus	Bernstein, Lawrence F.	D	12A,12
Prof Emeritus	Connolly, Thomas H.	D	12A,12
Prof Emeritus	Crumb, George H.	D	13,10
Prof	Dillon, Emma	D	11,12A,12
Assoc Prof	Dolan, Emily I.	D	12A,12,11,12B
Prof	Kallberg, Jeffrey	D	12A,12,12D,15
Assoc Prof	Moreno, Jairo	D	13,13J,20H,29,12D
Prof	Muller, Carol A.	D	14,20A,20D,31F,31G
Prof Emeritus	Narmour, Eugene	D	13,12,38
Prof	Primosch, James	D	13,10,10B
Prof	Ramsey, Guthrie P.	D	12,35,20G,29,47
Prof	Reise, Jay	M	13,10F,10
Assoc Prof	Rommen, Timothy	D	14
Prof Emeritus	Smith, Norman E.	D	12A,12
Asst Prof	Waltham-Smith, Naomi	D	13
Prof	Weesner, Anna	D	13,10,11
Prof Emeritus	Wernick, Richard F.	M	13,60,10,41
Prof Emeritus	Zimmerman, Franklin B.	D	12A,12

PA3400 Univ of Pittsburgh-Bradford

Department of Music
300 Campus Dr
Bradford, PA 16701
(814) 362-7590   Fax: (814) 362-5037
www.upb.pitt.edu
E-mail: jclevey@pitt.edu

4 Year Institution

Chair, Communication & the Arts: Jeffrey Guterman, 80A

Adj	Baldwin, Catherine	D	61
Asst Prof	Levey, John C.	D	10,13,11,34,36
Adj	MacKown, Rosemary	M	66A
Adj	Myslewski, David	D	70
Adj	Tunstall, Julia	D	64A,11
Adj	Young, Frederick	D	62D,63D

PA3410 Univ of Pittsburgh-Johnstown

Department of Music
450 Schoolhouse Rd
Johnstown, PA 15904
(814) 269-7155   Fax: (814) 269-7196
www.upj.pitt.edu
E-mail: jeffwebb@pitt.edu

4 Year Institution

Chair, Humanities: Patty Derrick, 80A
Music Contact: Jeffrey L. Webb

Inst PT	Bodolosky, Michael		37,47,29A
Assoc Prof	Webb, Jeffrey L.	M	29A,36,13A,60,13

Directory of Institutions

PA3420 Univ of Pittsburgh
Department of Music
4337 5th Ave
Pittsburgh, PA 15260
(412) 624-4126   Fax: (412) 624-4186
www.music.pitt.edu
E-mail: musicdpt@pitt.edu

4 Year Institution, Graduate School

Master of Arts in Ethnomusicology, PhD in Ethnomusicology, PhD in Music Theory-Composition, PhD in Musicology, PhD in Jazz Studies, Master of Arts in Music Theory-Composition, Master of Arts in Musicology

Chair: Andrew Weintraub, 80A
Dir., Undergraduate Studies: John L. Goldsmith, 80B
Dir., Graduate Studies: Eric H. Moe, 80C
Dir., Graduate Admissions: Amy C. Williams, 80C

Asst Prof Adj	Cassaro, James P.	M	16,12C,15
Prof	Davis, Nathan T.	D	20G,47,64E,29
Prof Emeritus	Euba, Akin	D	
Prof Emeritus	Franklin, Don O.	D	
Senior Lect	Goldsmith, John L.	M	60A,36
Asst Prof	Helbig, Adriana	D	14A,14C,14D,20F,20H
Prof Emerita	Lewis, Mary S.	D	
Prof Emeritus	Lord, Robert S.	D	66G
Prof	Moe, Eric H.	PhD	13,10,45,10B
Asst Prof	Mundy, Rachel	D	12A
Asst Prof	Nisnevich, Anna V.	D	11,12A
Prof Emeritus	Nketia, Joseph K.	DIPL	20A,14
PT	Reiter, Burkhardt	D	10,13
Prof	Root, Deane L.	D	12A,12C,12,20G,12E
Prof	Rosenblum, Mathew	D	13,10F,10
Assoc Prof	Weintraub, Andrew	D	20D,14A,20G,14C,14D
Asst Prof	Williams, Amy C.	D	10,13
Prof Emeritus	Yung, Bell	D	
Lect	Zahab, Roger E.	M	38,13,10F,43,62A
Asst Prof	Zazulia, Emily	D	11,12A

PA3500 Univ of Scranton
College of Arts & Sciences
Dept of Performance Music
Houlihan McLean Center
Scranton, PA 18510
(570) 941-7624   Fax: (570) 941-7495
www.scranton.edu
E-mail: cheryl.boga@scranton.edu

4 Year Institution

Chair & Dir., Artist Series: Cheryl Boga, 80A,80F
Dean: Paul F. Fahey, 80A

	Boga, Cheryl	B	36,37,47,38,51
PT	Garofalo, Angelo	M	11,12A
	Lucas, M. Jayne	M	13,12A

PA3550 Ursinus College
Department of Music
PO Box 1000
Collegeville, PA 19426
(610) 409-3000 x 3227   Fax: (484) 762-4324
www.ursinus.edu
E-mail: jfrench@ursinus.edu

4 Year Institution

Chair: John French, 80A

PT	Ashby, Michael	M	61
PT	Doucette, Hannah	M	62
Prof	French, John	D	11,12,13,36
Asst Prof	Hope, Garrett E.	D	10,62D,13,34,51
Assoc Prof	Hubbs, Holly J.	D	11,37,47,29A,20
PT	Kenney, James	M	70
PT	Lee, Soh Yeong	D	66A
PT	Meany, Thomas	M	64A
PT	Metzler, Linda	M	62C
PT	Morrison, Alan	M	66G

PA3560 Valley Forge Christian College
Department of Music
1401 Charlestown Rd
Phoenixville, PA 19460
(610) 935-0450   Fax: (610) 935-9353
www.vfcc.edu
E-mail: djheadlee@vfcc.edu

4 Year Institution

Chair: William DeSanto, 80A

Asst Prof	Bilotta, Lee	M	60,32B,37,63,31A
Inst PT	Bilotta, Tony	B	64E
Inst PT	Carney, Sandy	M	61
Inst PT	Cho, Mison	M	66A,66D
Inst PT	DeSanto, Jennifer	M	66A,66D
Prof	DeSanto, William	D	36,66,31A,66C
Inst PT	Edgett, Bryan	D	63A
Inst PT	Jackson, Tom	M	62A
Inst PT	Kelly, Kimberly	D	64D
Inst PT	Mathews, Elisa	M	61
Prof	Richmond, C. Floyd	D	32,34,13
Inst PT	Riehman, Ken	M	65
Asst Prof	Smith, Kent M.	M	10,11,12A,31A

PA3580 Washington & Jefferson College
Department of Music
60 S Lincoln St
Washington, PA 15301-4801
(724) 223-6109   Fax: (724) 223-5271
www.washjeff.edu
E-mail: mswift@washjeff.edu

4 Year Institution

Chair: Mark D. Swift, 80A

Adj	Berry, Michael	B	65
Adj	Cottrill, Lara Lynn	M	61
Adj	DiAdamo, Richard	B	62A
Adj	Evans, Laurel S.	B	62C
Adj	Frost, Ryan	D	65
Adj	Grant, Courtney	M	65
Adj	Hartger, Susan	M	64A
Adj	Johnson, Curtis	M	64E
Adj	Johnson, Jeffry Blake	DMA	61
Adj	Lintz, David	M	63B
Assoc Prof	Medley, Susan	D	36,60A,40,11,13A
Adj	Murchison, Matthew	D	63C,63D
Adj	Ortiz, Carlos	M	63A
Adj	Ortner-Roberts, Susanne	M	64C
Adj	Rau, George	M	66G
Asst Prof	Simpson, Kyle	M	10,11,37,47
Assoc Prof	Swift, Mark D.	PhD	11,14A,14C,20
Adj	Williams, Katy	B	61
Prof	Woodard, Susan J.	DMA	11,12,66A,42
Adj	Yap, Juliana	D	66A

PA3600 West Chester University
School of Music -CVPA
Swope Music Bldg
817 S High St
West Chester, PA 19383
(610) 436-2739   Fax: (610) 436-2873
www.wcupa.edu/CVPA
E-mail: musicinfo@wcupa.edu

4 Year Institution, Graduate School
Member of NASM

Master of Music in Performance, Master of Music in Music Education, Master of Music in Music Theory-Composition, Master of Music in Piano Pedagogy, Master of Music in Music History

Dean: Timothy V. Blair, 80A
Coord., Undergraduate Studies: Allen Taylor, 80B
Coord., Graduate Studies: J. Bryan Burton, 80C
Associate Dean: John Villella, 80H

Prof	Ahramjian, Sylvia Davis	M	51,62A,62B
Asst Prof Emeritus	Albert, Kristen A.	M	32B
Inst PT	Avitsur, Haim	D	63C,49
Assoc Prof	Balthazar, Scott Leslie	D	13,12A
Prof	Bedford, Robert M.	D	66A,66B

Asst Prof PT	Briselli, Carol	M	62
Asst Prof	Bullock, Emily A.	D	61,39
Prof	Burton, J. Bryan	D	20G,20D,32
Assoc Prof Emeritus	Chilcote, Kathryn S.	D	39,61
Asst Prof	Craig, Vincent	D	66A,66D
Assoc Prof	Cranmer, Carl	D	66A,66C,66D
Inst PT	Cullen, David	M	70
Assoc Prof	Dannessa, Karen	D	64C,48
Prof	DeVenney, David P.	D	36,39,60A,61
Assoc Prof	Dobrzelewski, Jan	D	63A,49
Asst Prof PT	Fowler, Jonathon	D	63D,49
Inst PT	Gaarder, Jon	M	64E
Inst PT	Galante, Gloria	M	62E
Prof	Grabb, Henry	D	64B,48
Asst Prof	Greenlee, Anita	M	66G
Inst	Gross, Austin	D	13
Inst	Guerriero, Angela	M	32
Inst	Hagness, Jane	D	61
Asst Prof	Hanning, Chris	D	65
Inst	Hilowski-Fowler, Ann	D	11,12A
Assoc Prof	Jacoby, Marc Max	D	32,46,47
Inst	Kelly, Ryan	D	36,40,61,60A
Inst PT	Kim, Kyoungwoon Leah	M	62A
Asst Prof	Klinefelter, Theresa	D	66B
Asst Prof	Lee, In Young	D	61
Asst Prof	Lyons, Glenn	M	51,70
Prof	Maggio, Robert	D	13,10
Asst Prof	Marinescu, Ovidiu	D	38,62C,51
Asst Prof	Martin, Mark Gregory	D	37,32
Assoc Prof	McFarland, Ann L.	M	32
Inst PT	Nelson, David E.		65
Prof Emeritus	Nelson, Larry A.	D	13,10,45,34
Asst Prof	Ng, Stephen	D	61
Asst Prof	Oleson, Bradley	D	
Prof	Onderdonk, Julian	D	11,12A
Inst PT	Paulsen, Peter	M	62D
Asst Prof PT	Pfaffle, Elizabeth	D	63B
Asst Prof	Powell, Patricia	D	66,66D
Asst Prof	Purciello, Maria Anne	D	11,12A
Assoc Prof	Reighley, Kimberly	D	64A,48
Asst Prof PT	Resnianski, Igor	D	66,66D
Assoc Prof	Riley, Gregory E.	DMA	64E,46,48
Prof	Rimple, Mark T.	DMA	13,10
Assoc Prof	Rozin, Alexander	D	10,13
Asst Prof	Scarlata, Randall	M	61
Assoc Prof	Silverman, Adam B.	D	10,13
Asst Prof PT	Sorrentino, Ralph	M	65,50
Assoc Prof Emeritus	Sprenkle, David	D	36,41,61
Assoc Prof	Stiefel, Van	D	10,13
Inst PT	Swana, John	M	53
Asst Prof	Winters, Thomas D.	D	12A,12,29
Assoc Prof Emeritus	Wyss, Jane	D	36,61
Inst PT	Yokley, Darryl	M	64E
Assoc Prof	Yozviak, Andrew J.	D	37,60B

PA3650 Westminster College
Department of Music
319 S Market St
New Wilmington, PA 16172-0001
(724) 946-7270   Fax: (724) 946-6270
www.westminster.edu
E-mail: greigrt@westminster.edu

4 Year Institution
Member of NASM

Chair: R. Tad Greig, 80

A
PT	Ambert, William J.	B	61
PT	Antonich, Mark E.	M	70
PT	Antonucci, Robert	M	63D
Assoc Prof	Bentz, Anne Hagan	D	61,39
PT	Bremer, Jeff	B	47,53,62D
PT	Bruening, Anne	M	44
PT	Byo, William		64D
PT	Cole, Robert	M	34A,34B,49,63B,72
PT	Colella, Louis	M	64C,64E
Assoc Prof	DeSalvo, Nancy J.	D	13A,13B,66A,66B,13C
	Erb, Andrew	M	63A,47
PT	Flowers, Jim		64E
	Garman, Michelle	B	16
PT	Gatch, Perry	M	50,65
Assoc Prof	Greig, R. Tad	D	32E,37,47,60B,63C
PT	Groves, Edgar S.	M	14,32
PT	Harper, Kris	M	36,61
Vstng Lect	Howard, Jason	M	10,13
PT	Kane, Janet	M	31A,61
PT	Libal-Smith, Marie		66A
Assoc Prof	Lind, Robin A.	D	32C,36,40,61
PT	Mann, Victoria	M	32B
PT	Matchett, Robert		63C
PT	Miller, Kathryn	M	66A,66C,69
Asst Prof	Perttu, Daniel E.	D	10A,13
PT	Perttu, Melinda H. Crawford	M	38,62A,62B

Prof	Pitman, Grover A.	D	12A,29A
PT	Reynolds, Shawn	M	64B
PT	Tessmer, David	M	41,64A
PT	Valcu, Mihai	M	39
PT	Wachter, Jeffrey	M	66A,66C
PT	Wilson, Dean	M	32B

PA3680 Widener University
Department of Fine Arts
One University Pl
Chester, PA 19013-5792
(610) 499-4344   Fax: (610) 499-4605
www.widener.edu
E-mail: meparker@widener.edu

4 Year Institution

Music Contact: Mara Parker, 80A,80H

Adj	Frederick, John	M	36
Adj	Meehan, Jill	M	11,12A,13A
Prof	Parker, Mara	PhD	12A,11,41,51,62C
Lect	Vanore, John	B	60,10,47,49,63A

PA3700 Wilkes University
Division of Performing Arts
84 W. South St
Wilkes Barre, PA 18766
(570) 408-4420   Fax: (570) 408-7842
www.wilkes.edu/dpa
E-mail: maryellen.sloat@wilkes.edu

4 Year Institution

Chair, Performing Arts: Joseph C. Dawson, 80A
Coord.,Wilkes Community Conservatory: Lauren Gentilesco, 80E

Adj	D'Alessandro, Joseph	B	66F
Artist in Res	Degnan-Boonin, Kristin	M	52
Inst Adj	Driscoll, Nick	M	47,64E
Inst Adj	Gallo, Paulette M.	M	62E
Inst Adj	Insalaco, Vince	B	70
Inst Adj	Lindsey, A. Lish	M	64A
Inst Adj	Minsavage, Susan	M	61,39
Assoc Prof	Simon, Philip G.	D	11,37,41,51,63D
Inst Adj	Smallcomb, Matt	M	65
Inst Adj	Stabinsky, Ron	B	66A,66C
Assoc Prof	Thomas, Steven L.	D	36,61,40
Inst Adj	Unice, Charles	M	61
Inst Adj	Vaida, John M.	M	62A,62B
Accompanist	Waltich, Tsukasa	M	66C
Inst Adj	Zipay, Terry L.	D	13,35B,34A,13E,11

PA3710 York College of Pennsylvania
Division of Music
441 Country Club Rd
York, PA 17405-7199
(717) 815-1258   Fax: (717) 849-1602
www.ycp.edu
E-mail: fschrein@ycp.edu

4 Year Liberal Arts Institution

Division Head & Dir., Artist Series: Frederick Schreiner, 80A,80F

Lect	Beachley, Laine	B	66A,66C
Lect	Brown, Nina	M	61
Lect	Buchar-Kelley, Kimberly	D	64D
Lect	Cabott, Christopher	D	35A
Lect	Cresci, Jonathan		63A,32E
Asst Prof	Debes, Edward	M	35C,35D,35G,35H
Lect	Dekker, Gretchen	M	66A,66H,13C
Lect	Druck, William	B	70
Lect	Fogleman, Matthew	B	70
Lect	Gordon, Kirsten	M	64B
Lect	Herrera, Jennifer	M	62A,62B
Lect	Hilliker, Tom		62D
Lect	Kates, Christine	M	66A,66G
Lect	Kauffman, Rachel		62C
Lect	Kehler, Harry	M	32A,32B,32C
Lect	Knisely, Carole	M	35A,35B,35E,35F
Lect	Kosack, Alicia	D	64A,42,67D
Lect	Levi, Zachary	M	38,62
Lect	Loy, Susan	M	64C
Lect	Meckley, Rod		65
Lect	Moyer, Jon	M	49,63C,63D
Asst Prof	Muzzo, Grace	D	32,36,40,60A

Lect	Nielsen, Lois	M	66A
Asst Prof	Osowski, Kenneth	M	11,66A,66B
Lect	Protopapas, John	M	14
Asst Prof	Romer, Wayne Allen	D	13A,10F,60B,11,32
Assoc Prof	Schreiner, Frederick	D	11,12A,12,61,39
Lect	Stabley, Jeff	B	46,47,53,65,50
Lect	Valliant, James	M	61,66A,11
Lect	Woodfield, Randal	D	61,39,11

PR0100 Interamerican Univ of Puerto Rico

Department of Music
PO Box 5100
San German, PR 00683
(787) 264-1912 x 7378   Fax: (787) 264-0220
www.sg.inter.edu
E-mail: samuel_rosado_nazario@intersg.edu

4 Year Institution, Graduate School

Master of Arts in Music Education

Chair: Samuel Rosado-Nazario, 80A

Inst PT	Baez, Alberto	M	70
Inst PT	Barreto, Naitsabes	M	32E
Assoc Prof	Betancourt, Nilda	M	13,66A,66C,12A
Asst Prof	Cabrera, Ricardo	M	11,36,61,60,13A
Asst Prof	Centeno Martell, Ingrid	M	13,66A,66C,32
Asst Prof	Chellouf, Linda	M	70,13
Inst PT	Colon, Daisy	B	32
Prof	Landry, Jacques	D	47,70
Inst PT	Lopez, Hiram	B	62D
Assoc Prof	Montalvo, Raquel	D	36,61,13B
Prof	Morales, Gary A.	D	60,32,48,64C
Asst Prof	Moreno, Madja	M	39,61
Inst PT	Mulet, Mickael	D	34,35C
Inst PT	Nazario, Angel	B	70
Inst PT	Pagan, Leslie	B	64E
Inst PT	Rivera, Miguel	M	41,63D
Assoc Prof Emeritus	Rivera-Vega, Salvador	M	11,32,48,64E
Inst PT	Rodriguez, Ramon	B	32
Assoc Prof	Rosado-Nazario, Samuel	M	63,37,34
Inst FT	Santiago, Freddie	B	65
Inst PT	Tirado, Hector	M	62B
Inst PT	Toro, Cesar	B	66D
Inst FT	Valcarcel, Andres	M	62A,62B,51,38

PR0115 Puerto Rico Conservatory of Music

951 Ponce de Leon Ave
San Juan, PR 00907-3373
(787) 751-0160   Fax: (787) 766-1216
www.cmpr.edu
E-mail: mcgil@cmpr.pr.gov

4 Year Institution

Chancellor: Maria Del Carmen Gil, 80A
Dean, Academic Affairs: Melanie Santana-Santana, 80A
Dir., Admissions: Helen Gonzalez, 80D
Dean, Preparatory School: German A. Cespedes Diaz, 80E
Dir., Activities & Concerts: Wilma Colon, 80F

Asst Prof	Acevedo, Maria Teresa	M	66A,66D
Prof	Alicea, Jose R.	M	65,50
Adj PT	Alvarado Ortiz, Julio E.	B	63A
Adj PT	Amador Medina, Ruben J.	M	14C,29A
Inst	Barasorda, Antonio	D	61,39
Artist in Res	Barrueco, Manuel	B	70
Adj PT	Benjamin Figueroa, Haydee	M	32A
Asst Prof	Bermudez, Luis	M	13C,12A
Assoc Prof	Caban, Francisco J.	D	62A,41,42,51
Asst Prof	Carrillo, Carlos R.	D	13
Adj PT	Cartagena, Cynthia	M	41,42,64A
Asst Prof	Casillas-Rivera, Josue	M	64A
Inst	Ceide, Manuel J.	M	13F,10A,13A,13B,13E
Adj PT	Colon Carrion, Ismar	B	34
Asst Prof	Colon Jimenez, Frances	D	64B,41,42
Artist in Res	Colon, Emilio	M	62C
Adj PT	Corps, Wilfredo	M	41,64E,42
Adj PT	Davis, Kimberly	B	66C
Adj PT	De Lucas, Marina	B	66C
Artist in Res	Del Castillo, Jose Francisco		62A
Adj PT	Delannoy Pizzini, Jose R.	D	11
Adj PT	Diaz Torres, Jorge	B	63C
Artist in Res	Diaz, Justino		61
Adj PT	Dufrasne, J. Emmanuel	D	14C
Adj PT	Ferrer Brooks, Rafael	M	66C
Adj PT	Figueroa, Diana	M	66A,66B,66D
Adj PT	Flynn Cintron, Jorge A.	M	35
Asst Prof	Fred Carrasquillo, Luis	M	63C,49,41,42
Asst Prof	Fuentes, Alfonso	M	10,10F
Prof	Garcia, Marisa	M	66A,42
Artist in Res	Gomez, Edgar		62D,53
Adj PT	Gonzalez, Helen	M	60B
Adj PT	Guidobaldi Chittolina, Alberto	B	13,13C
Assoc Prof	Guzman, Ariel	M	32C,32B,32F
Adj PT	Havrilla, Adam A.	M	64D
Adj PT	Hernandez Candelas, Marta	M	33
Adj PT	Hernandez Guzman, Nestor	D	32G
Inst	Hernandez Mergal, Luis A.	M	12A,12B,14
Artist in Res	Hobson, Ian	D	66A
Adj PT	Hopkins, Brenda	D	66D
Assoc Prof	Irizarry, Rafael E.	M	37,12A,63B,42,49
Asst Prof	Jimenez, Pedro J.	M	66C
Prof Emeritus	Jones, Kathleen	M	64C,41,42
Prof	Julia, Luis Enrique	M	70
Adj PT	Laureano, Orlando	M	70
Asst Prof	Lazaro, Andrew A.	M	47,65,53
Inst	Lebron, Nelie	M	32A,32B
Prof	Lopez, Ilca	M	61,39
Assoc Prof	Lopez, Zoraida	M	61
Inst	Marin, Luis	B	29,66A,66D
Adj PT	Marquez-Reyes, John D.	B	11
Adj PT	Martinez Ortiz, Laura	M	11
Inst	Mattina, Fernando	B	29,70
Artist in Res	Mejias, Paoli		47
Assoc Prof	Melendez Dohnert, Victor	B	13A,13B,13C,66D
Artist in Res	Melendez, Jose		66A,66C
Adj PT	Menendez Abovici, Natalia E.	M	11
Inst	Morales, Fidel	B	29,65,53
Artist in Res	Morales, Leonel		66C
Adj PT	Navarro Romero, Emanuel	B	66D,47
Prof	Navarro, Gloria	M	13A,13C
Asst Prof	Olivieri, Emmanuel	M	62B,13E,13F
Adj PT	Ortiz Garcia, Norberto	M	64E
Asst Prof	Ortiz, Sheila	M	13A,13C
Adj PT	Ortiz, William	DMA	12A
Prof	Pabon, Roselin	M	60B,38
Adj PT	Perez Rivera, Pedro	B	62D,47
Adj PT	Ramirez Rios, Ruben J.	B	63D,41
Assoc Prof	Ramirez, Armando L.	M	10,13A,13B,13D,13F
Asst Prof	Ramirez, Roberto	B	63A,49
Adj PT	Ramos Asillo, Jorge	B	66C
Adj PT	Rijos, Ivan	M	70
Adj PT	Rios Escribano, Enrique B.	M	10C
Adj PT	Rivera Diaz, Almicar	D	32
Adj PT	Rivera Lassen, Carmen L.	M	11
Assoc Prof	Rivera Ortiz, William	M	13A,13C,36,60A
Adj PT	Rivera Ruiz, Alvaro M.	D	11
Adj PT	Rivera Trinidad, Miguel	B	63C
Adj PT	Rivera, Maricarmen	M	62D
Adj PT	Rivera-Guzman, Felix	D	66A
Prof	Rodriguez Alvira, Jose	M	13A,34,13B,13D,13G
Adj PT	Rodriguez Aponte, Dalia	M	66D
Adj PT	Rodriguez Curet, Marcos J.	B	29B,47
Asst Prof	Rodriguez, Alberto	M	70,41,42
Adj PT	Rodriguez, Sandra	M	32A,32D,32
Inst	Rodriguez-Hernandez, Gabriel	B	29,62D
Inst	Rojas, Luis Miguel	D	62C,41,42
Adj PT	Rosa Ramos, Luis S.	M	29,10F,47
Artist in Res	Sanchez, David		64E,46
Asst Prof	Santos, Elias	M	29A,47,29B,53
Adj PT	Sein Siaca, Maria P.	B	11
Adj PT	Sepulveda, Charles	B	29,63A,53
Asst Prof	Sueiras, Rafael	M	66C
Adj PT	Tiodang, Jasmin	M	66C
Adj PT	Torres Navarro, Pedro J.	M	11
Adj PT	Torres Perez, Elisa	M	62E
Adj PT	Torres Rivera, Alfredo	M	32E,32B,32C
Adj PT	Urdaz, Mayra E.	M	62A
Adj PT	Valdes Vivas, Eduardo	D	70,41
Adj PT	Valentin Pagan, Aldemar	M	62D,47,53
Inst	Velazquez, Omar	B	62A
Assoc Prof	Woodruff, William	M	61,54

PR0125 Univ Advent de Las Antillas

Department of Music
PO Box 118
Mayaguez, PR 00681-0118
(787) 834-9595   Fax: (787) 834-9597
www.uaa.edu
E-mail: admissions@uaa.edu

4 Year Institution, Graduate Program

Chair: Francise T. Restesan, 80A

Lect	Araujo, Ramon	M	13,10,37,64C
Asst Prof	Pedroza, Ricardo	M	13,60,36,66A,66D
Asst Prof	Restesan, Francise T.	M	13,60,12B,38,41
Lect	Seals, Debra	M	12A,61

PR0150 Univ de Puerto Rico
Facultad de Humanidades-Musica
PO Box 23335
San Juan, PR 00931-3335
(787) 764-0000 x-2612
www.uprrp.edu
E-mail: musica@uprrp.edu

4 Year Institution
Member of MSAC

Dean: Jose Luis Ramos Escobar, 80A
Chair/Dir., Summer Programs: Juan Sorroche, 80A,80G
Dir., Artist/Performance Series: Lianell Mirabal, 80F

Prof	Acevedo, Carmen	M	36,60A
Assoc Prof	Alonso, Ernesto	M	12A,11,62A,14A,55A
Prof	Alvarez, Luis M.	M	10A,11,13A,13B,14
Inst PT	Aponte, Maria P.	M	11,13C
Prof	Batista, Gustavo	M	11,12A,13A,13C,70
Assoc Prof	Cabrer, Carlos R.	D	10A,10F,11,13A,13B
Inst PT	Cartagena, Cynthia	M	64A
Adj	Castro, Margarita	B	11,39,61
	Colorado, Jose		
Inst	De La Torre, Javier	M	10A,10F,13A,13C
Inst PT	Garcia, Manuel	M	65
Inst PT	Guzman, Ariel	M	60B
Prof	Iguina, Jose R.	D	13A,13C,11,70
Inst PT	Laureano, Victor O.	B	70,51
Asst Prof	Li, Ping-Hui	D	13A,13C,14A,66A,66C
Prof	Mojica, Andres	M	11,66G
Inst PT	Morales, Samuel	B	47,46
Prof	Munoz, Nelida	D	11,13A,13C,44
Inst PT	Ortiz, Norberto	M	64C
Assoc Prof	Perez, Samuel	D	11,66A
Assoc Prof	Ponte, Nora	PhD	10A,13A,13B,13C,13D
Assoc Prof	Rivera, Felix	D	11,66A,66D
Inst PT	Rodriguez, Cristina	B	64E
Assoc Prof	Rosario, Harry	M	13A,13C,37,60B,64B
Assoc Prof	Sorroche, Juan	DIPL	13A,11,70,13C
Inst PT	Torres, Jose R.	M	61,54
Inst PT	Valdes, Eduardo	PhD	70,11
Prof	Vazquez, Carlos	D	10A,10B,10F,13A,13C

RI0050 Brown University
Department of Music
1 Young Orchard Ave/Box 1924
Providence, RI 02912-9045
(401) 863-3234   Fax: (401) 863-1256
www.brown.edu/music
E-mail: music@brown.edu

4 Year Institution, Graduate School

Master of Arts in Ethnomusicology, PhD in Ethnomusicology, Master of Arts in Electronic Music & Multimedia, PhD in Electronic Music & Multimedia

Chair: James Baker, 80A

Prof	Baker, James	D	13,13J,41
Prof	Bergeron, Katherine	D	12A,12D
Teach Assoc	Cole, Arlene	M	13A,13,66A
Assoc Prof	Gooley, Dana	D	12A,13B,12E,12D
Senior Lect	Jodry, Frederick	M	13,60,12A,36
Prof	Josephson, David	D	12A,12,55B,12E
Vstng Lect	Lehman, Frank M.		13,10C,12A
Senior Lect	McGarrell, Matthew	M	37,41,47,46
Assoc Prof	Miller, Kiri	D	14A,14C,14D,20G,31G
Assoc Prof	Perlman, Marc	D	14,20D,12E,13J,35D
Senior Lect	Phillips, Paul Schuyler	M	38,60,13,10,10F
Prof	Rovan, Joseph 'Butch'	D	10,45,34
Prof	Shapiro, Gerald	M	13,10,45,34
Prof	Steinberg, Michael	D	12A,12B,12C,12D
Prof	Titon, Jeff	D	20G,20F,14A
Asst Prof	Tucker, Joshua	D	14A,14C,14D,20H
Prof	Winkler, Todd	D	10,45,34

RI0100 Community College of Rhode Island
Flanagan Campus-Music
1762 Louisquisset Pike
Lincoln, RI 02865-4513
(401) 333-7213   Fax: (401) 333-7111
www.ccri.edu
E-mail: paforleo@ccri.edu

2 Year Institution

Inst PT	Greene, Thomas E.	M	29A
Inst PT	Kane, Marie A.	M	32A
Inst PT	Pratt, Dennis H.	M	29A
Inst PT	Santo, Amanda M.	M	61
Inst PT	Sobaje, Martha H.	D	11
Inst PT	Stott, Jacob T.	M	11,13A

RI0101 Community College of Rhode Island
Knight Campus-Perf. Arts Dept
400 East Ave
Warwick, RI 02886-1805
(401) 825-2168   Fax: (401) 825-2265
www.ccri.edu
E-mail: cmarkward@ccri.edu

2 Year Institution

Chair: Cheri D. Markward, 80A
Program Coordinator: Audrey K. Kaiser, 80H

Assoc Prof	Amante Y Zapata, Joseph J.	D	36,40,11,13A,13B
Inst PT	Bouvier, Monique	M	11
Prof Emerita	Carroll, Nancy M.		11
Inst PT	Dennewitz, John K.	M	70
Asst Prof	Gargrave, Eric	D	11,13A,29A,48,13B
Inst PT	Gregory, Thomas		29A,63D
Asst Prof	Kaiser, Audrey K.	D	66A,66D,13
Inst PT	Kane, Marie A.	M	32A
Prof	Lajoie, Stephen H.	D	47,66A,53,29,13A
Assoc Prof	Markward, Cheri D.	M	13,11,41,62,12A
Inst PT	Pratt, Dennis H.		29A,11,13A
Inst PT	Santo, Amanda M.	M	61,39,11
Inst PT	Sobaje, Martha H.	D	11,13A
Inst PT	Stott, Jacob	M	11,13
Inst PT	Stravato, James	A	34D

RI0102 Community College of Rhode Island
Newport Campus - Music
One John H Chaffe Blvd
Newport, RI 02840
(401) 852-2168   Fax: (401) 455-6047
www.ccri.edu/music
E-mail: paforleo@ccri.edu

2 Year Institution

Chair: Cheri Markward, 80A

Prof Emerita	Carroll, Nancy	M	11,10A
Inst PT	Dennewitz, John	M	13A
Inst PT	Gregory, Thomas	M	29A

RI0150 Providence College
Department of Music
1 Cunningham Square
Providence, RI 02918-4030
(401) 865-2183   Fax: (401) 865-2761
www.providence.edu/Music
E-mail: cgordon@providence.edu

4 Year Liberal Arts Institution
Member of NASM

Chair: Catherine Gordon-Seifert, 80A

Inst PT	Alfieri, Gabriel	M	61
Inst PT	Allmark, John		29,37
Lect	Benz, Fritz	M	32C,32E
Lect	Bill, Jennifer	M	32E,37
Inst PT	Chua, Rosalind Y.	M	66A
Asst Prof	Cichy, Patricia Wurst	D	32B,13C,64B,11,67D
Lect	Cichy, Roger	M	10A,10F
Inst PT	Cloutier, Randy		65B
Inst PT	Culpo, Susan	M	62B
Inst PT	Fishman, Guy	D	62C,55B
Inst PT	Gasper, Anne	M	64A
Prof	Gordon-Seifert, Catherine	D	13,12A,12C,55B,66H
Inst PT	Grace, Elizabeth		61
Lect	Harper, David R.	M	11,61,54,39,40
Asst Prof	Harper, T.J.	D	36,60,32C,32D,61
Assoc Prof	Himrod, Gail P.		12A,20,11
Inst PT	Kane, Kevin	M	63C,63D
Asst Prof	Kang, Sang Woo	D	13A,13B,66A
Asst Prof	Kelton, Christopher T.	D	47,64C,64E,29A
Lect	Kregler, Michael C.	M	66A,66C,47

Inst PT	Mamula, Stephen	M	12A,20
Inst PT	Martin, Klancy	M	63A
Inst PT	Martinez, David	M	66G,31A
Inst PT	Miele, William		47,62D
Inst PT	Monteiro, Shawnn		61
Inst PT	Nicholson, Hillary	M	61,39
Inst PT	Pagano, Vincent	B	65,65B
Inst PT	Porter, Eliot	B	62D
Lect	Riley, David	M	13,70
Inst PT	Roth, Kathryn	M	67D
Inst PT	Shabalin, Alexey	D	62A,51,38,32E
Inst PT	Tchantceva, Irena	D	66A
Inst PT	Tennenbaum, Judie	M	62E
Inst PT	Wood, Susan	M	64D
Inst PT	Zabinski, Marina		66A

RI0200 Rhode Island College

Department of Music, Theatre & Dan
600 Mount Pleasant Ave
Providence, RI 02908-1991
(401) 456-9883   Fax: (401) 456-9545
www.ric.edu/mtd
E-mail: rfranzblau@ric.edu

4 Year Institution, Graduate School
Member of NASM

Master of Music in Education

Chair: Jamie Taylor, 80A
Dir., Graduate Studies: Denise Guilbault, 80C
Dir., Artist /Performance Series: Judith L. Stillman, 80F
Assistant Chair: Robert Franzblau, 80H

Adj	Abate, Greg		29
Adj	Arsenauit, Greg		65
Adj	Beaudoin, Paul	D	10,13,12A,11
Adj	Bohn, James	D	13
Adj	Breindel, Christina	M	66C
Adj	Ceo, Joan	M	62E
Adj	Christensen, Eric	M	70
Assoc Prof	Coffman, Teresa S.	D	36,40,32D
Adj	Conlon, Kelly	M	32B
Adj	DeQuattro, Michael	M	50,65
Adj	Foley, Joseph	M	49,63A
Assoc Prof	Franzblau, Robert	D	32E,37
Adj	Gasper, Anne	M	64A
Adj	Gregory, Tom	M	63D
Asst Prof	Greitzer, Ian	M	64C,64E,48
Asst Prof	Guilbault, Denise	D	32
Asst Prof	Guzzio-Kregler, Mary Ellen	D	13C,64A,42
Adj	Hutchins, Georgette		61
Adj	Kane, Kevin	M	63C,63D
Adj	Kane, Lila	M	66C
Adj	Kolb, Barbara	M	10
Adj	Labonte, Celeste	M	32B
Adj	Leonard, George		70
Adj	Lund, Kara	M	61
Prof	Mack, George	M	10,13,34
Adj	Maker, Bill	M	42,70
Adj	Mamula, Stephen		14C
Adj	Mangeni, Andrew	M	20
Prof	Markward, Edward	D	38,61,60,39
Adj	Martorella, Philip	M	66A
Adj	Martorella, Stephen T.	M	12A,66A,66G,66H
Adj	Monteiro-Huelbig, Shawnn		61
Adj	Pezzullo, Louis	M	32B
Adj	Plaza-Martin, Denise	M	64B
Adj	Porter, Eliot	M	62D
Adj	Rodgers, Susan	M	61,39
Adj	Sanlikol, Mehmet	D	20
Adj	Scheff, Fredric S.	D	61
Adj	Seabra, James	M	65
Adj	Spiridopoulos, Sheffra		63B
Adj	St. Jean, Donald	M	61
Adj	St. Jean, Flo	M	61
Prof	Stillman, Judith L.	D	66A
Adj	Stott, Jacob	M	66D
Assoc Prof	Sumerlin, John	M	41,62A,62B
Adj	Torres, Stephanie	M	32B
Adj	Wardson, Greg		29
Adj	Wood, Susan	M	64D

RI0250 Salve Regina University

Department of Music
100 Ochre Point Ave
Newport, RI 02840-4192
(401) 847-6650 x 2945   Fax: (401) 341-2991
www.salve.edu
E-mail: davisp@salve.edu

4 Year Institution

Chair: Peter A. Davis, 80A

PT	Andrews, Julibeth	M	61
PT	Bernstein, Alan	M	62D
	Bishop, Roberta	M	61
PT	Bronner, Eric	M	61
PT	Brown, Frances A.	M	64C,32C
PT	Brown, Leland W.	M	32
PT	Ceo, Joseph	D	62
	D'Amico, David	B	66A
Artist in Res	Davis, Peter A.	M	13A,37,47,64
Prof	Day, Thomas Charles	D	13A,13,12
PT	Erickson, Stephen	M	66A,66D
	Hagerty, Matthew	M	70
PT	James, Deborah	M	64A
PT	Johnson, Michael		29
PT	Kane, Kevin	M	32
PT	Kane, Lila	B	66A
PT	Murray, Jane	M	64B
PT	Piltz, Peter	B	70
	Shadday, Craig	M	63A
Artist in Res	St. Jean, Donald	M	36,61
	Tiedemann, Patrice	M	61
	Totter, John	D	66G
PT	Wiant, William	M	66A,66G

RI0300 Univ of Rhode Island

Department of Music-FAC
105 Upper College Rd Ste 2
Kingston, RI 02881-0820
(401) 874-2431/5955   Fax: (401) 874-2772
www.uri.edu/artsci/mus
E-mail: music@etal.uri.edu

4 Year Institution, Graduate School
Member of NASM

Master of Music in Performance, Master of Music in Music Education

Chair: Ronald T. Lee, 80A
Dir., Graduate Studies: Eliane Aberdam, 80C
Dir., Graduate Studies: Manabu K. Takasawa, 80C
Coord., Preparatory Program: Jane Murray, 80E
Coordinator, Music Facilities: Gerard H. Heroux, 80G,80F
Associate Chair: John D. Dempsey, 80H

Asst Prof	Aberdam, Eliane	D	13,10F,10,12A,45
Inst PT	Acosta, Darren	M	49,63C
Inst PT	Beaton, K. Michelle	M	66C
Inst PT	Berney, Mark C.	M	29,47,63A
Inst PT	Buttery, Gary A.	M	11,47,49,63D,29A
Other	Calhoun, William	B	66F
Asst Prof	Cardany, Audrey	D	32
Lect	Cardany, Brian M.	D	32E,32G,37,60B
Inst PT	Carpenter, Jean	M	66C
Inst PT	Caufield, Stevi	M	64D
Inst PT	Ceo, Joan H.	M	62E
Assoc Prof	Conley, Mark	M	13,60,36,61,32D
Assoc Prof	Danis, Ann	M	60,38,11,62A,62B
Lect	De La Garza, Rene	M	39,41,61
Inst PT	Dean-Gates, Elizabeth	M	63B
Prof	Dempsey, John D.	M	13A,13,51,62A
Other	Devine, George M.	M	35C,35D,35G
Lect	Frazier, Margaret J.	M	11,61
Inst PT	Gendron, Mychal	M	70,42
Prof Emeritus	Gibbs, Geoffrey D.	D	10A,10F,13
Other	Heroux, Gerard H.	M	16,63B,11
Inst PT	Hofbauer, Eric	M	29,47,70
Inst PT	Howell, Andrew P.	M	36,66C,66G
Prof	Kent, George E.	M	11,49,63A,66G,66H
Other	Kim, David	M	41,62A
Prof	Ladewig, James L.	D	11,12A,12
Prof	Lee, Ronald T.	D	32,37,12B,12C
Prof Emerita	Livingston, Carolyn H.	D	32,36,66D,12C
Inst PT	Monllos, John	M	11,29A,70
Inst PT	Murray, Jane	M	38,41,48,64B
Inst PT	O'Connor, Kelli A.	M	48,64C
Assoc Prof	Parillo, Joseph M.		13,10,47,46,29
Inst PT	Platz, Eric	M	65,29,47
Prof	Pollart, Gene J.	D	60,32,37,29A

Inst PT	Porter, Eliot	M	62D
Inst PT	Sims, Jared N.	M	29,47,64E
Inst PT	Stabile, Ronald	M	32,41,50,65
Assoc Prof	Takasawa, Manabu K.	D	13A,66A,66B,66C,66D
Lect	Thomas, Susan H.	M	41,48,64A,34
Inst PT	Uricco, Grace E.	M	66C,66A
Inst PT	Zinno, David A.	B	47,62D,29

SC0050 Anderson University

College of Visual & Perf. Arts
316 Boulevard
Anderson, SC 29621-4002
(864) 231-2125   Fax: (864) 231-2083
www.andersonuniversity.edu
E-mail: rwilliamson@andersonuniversity.edu

4 Year Institution
Member of NASM

Dean: David Larson, 80A
Chair: Richard A. Williamson, 80A

PT	Bailey, Brandon	M	31A
PT	Burgess, William	M	34D,35G
Prof	Clark, James W.	D	13,66A,66D,66B
Asst Prof	Francis, Deirdre	M	61,40
PT	Golden, Lyman	M	10,51,70
Assoc Prof	Kim, Howard D.	D	66D,66D,13B,66C,11
PT	Lebo, Joanna	M	51,62A,62B
PT	Linkins, Jean Ellen	D	61
PT	Maher, Donna	D	64
PT	McDaniel, Rory	M	63B
PT	McGee, Ray	M	62D
PT	Norwine, Doug	M	13A,13B
Asst Prof	Perry, David L.	M	12A,13A,64C,32,20A
PT	Purtle, Jeff	M	63A
PT	Reed, John Perry	M	66A,66D
PT	Spainhour, Alex	M	38
Assoc Prof	Stern, David	D	37,63D,47,29A,60B
PT	Tarbutton, Butch	M	64E,42
PT	Varner, Kenneth	M	66A,66G
Assoc Prof	Watson, Tommy L.	D	11,61,39,12A,13A
PT	Whitt, Roger	B	65,50
Asst Prof	Williamson, Richard A.	D	13C,36,40,60A
PT	Wilson, Leah	M	48,64A
PT	Yates, Rebecca	M	61

SC0150 Benedict College

Department of Fine Arts
1600 Harden St
Columbia, SC 29204
(803) 705-4711   Fax: (803) 705-6599
www.benedict.edu
E-mail: brooksc@benedict.edu

4 Year Institution, Historically Black College

Chair, Fine Arts: Charles Brooks, 80A

Inst	Blalock, Angela	M	11,13A,13B,40,61
Assoc Prof	High, Ronald	D	11,12,31F,61,66
Inst	Jones, Herman	M	11,37,47,48,64
Assoc Prof	Kershaw, Linda L.	D	11,12,60,66A,36
Inst	Orlick, James	M	13,34,50
Asst Prof	Rojas, Nuria Mariela	D	11,12,13,34,66

SC0200 Bob Jones University

Division of Music
PO Box 34533
Greenville, SC 29614
(864) 242-5100 x 2710   Fax: (864) 467-9302
www.bju.edu
E-mail: edunbar@bju.edu

4 Year Institution, Graduate School

Master of Music in Performance, Master of Music in Church Music, Master of Music Education, Master of Music in Piano Pedagogy

Chair: Edward Dunbar, 80A
Dean & Dir., Artist/Performance Series: Darren P. Lawson, 80A,80F
Dir., Admissions: Gary Deedrick, 80D
Dir., Summer Programs: Paul Jantz, 80G

	Barrett, Amanda	M	64A
	Brundage, Laura	M	61
	Castle, Troy	M	60
	Chest, Robert	M	48,64B,64C,64D,64E
	Coleman, Fred	M	32,36,31A
	Coleman, Ruth	M	66A,66D
	Cook, Anne	M	66A
	Cook, Jean	M	66A,66B,66D
	Cook, Warren	D	13,60,36,31A,40
	Cox, Bruce	D	32C,49,63A
	Crawford, Donna	M	66A,66G,34
	Custer, Seth A.	D	13,64E,10A
	Davis, Peter	D	66A,66B,66D,34
	Dunbar, Edward	D	13,12A,66G,34
	Dunbar, Pamela	M	61
	Eby, Carole	M	16
	Eubank, Beth	D	32,64B
	Eubanks, Amber	M	62C
	Fields, Alex	M	48,64,72
	Figard, Kristin	M	62A
	Frederick, Mark	M	32,63B
	Greer, Jean	M	61
	Grimble, Thomas	M	66A,66D
	Grove, Rebecca	M	62A,62B
	Habegger, Christa	M	61
	Jantz, Paul	M	12A,49,63C,63D,34
	Kindall, Susan C.	D	66A,66B,35C,34
	Kirsop, Daniel	M	63A
	Lee, Christine	M	62C,60B
	Lehman, David	M	12A,66A,66B
	Lopez, Faye	M	13C,66A
	McCauley, William	D	12A,36,39,61
	McNeely, Heather	M	12A,12C,63A
	Moore, Deanna C.	D	66A,66B,12
	Moore, Michael W.	D	32C,32E,32G,37,13
	Overly, Paul	D	11,12,32,63C,63D
	Parker, David	D	61,34
	Parker, Joan	M	66A,66B,66D
	Parker, Mark	D	13A,32F,13B,13C,13G
	Pinkston, Joan	M	13,66A,34
	Pinner, Dianne	M	62A
	Quindag, Sue	D	32,62A,62B,34
	Rea, Edward	M	13,66A,66G,66F
	Rea, Judith	M	13,66A
	Ream, Duane	M	66A,66D,34
	Renfrow, Kenon	D	66A,66B,66D,34
	Schoolfield, Robnet	M	32,45,65,72
	Sprunger, Gina	M	66A
	Turcios, Lorri	M	66A,66B,66D
	Turner, Daniel	D	32B,32C,37,63D,34
	Waggoner, Emily	M	62E,12
	Wilson, Karen	D	12,66A,12C,20G,67
	Yanson, Eliezer G.	D	32D,13,60A,36,40

SC0275 Charleston Southern University

Horton School of Music
9200 Univ Blvd/PO Box 118087
Charleston, SC 29406-8087
(843) 863-7966   Fax: (843) 863-7042
www.csuniv.edu
E-mail: vbullock@csuniv.edu

4 Year Institution
Member of NASM

Chair: Valerie K. Bullock, 80A

Assoc Prof	Bordas, Ricard	M	36,61
PT	Brien, April Malone	M	33
Prof	Bullock, Valerie K.	D	60,32B,32C,36
Vstng Prof	Elshazly, Janet	D	66A,66C,66D
Assoc Prof	Forrester, Marshall	D	10,11,37,60
PT	Haldeman, Michael	D	11,37,65,50
PT	Hawkins, Randall	D	66C
Asst Prof	Hendricks, Allen	D	31,11
Asst Prof	Holland, Nicholas V.	D	11,37
PT	Jenkins, Kate	M	63C
PT	Kistler, Karen	D	64B
Asst Prof	Koester, Eugene	M	66A,66D
Assoc Prof	Lewis, Jill Terhaar	D	61
Prof	Luiken, Jennifer	D	61,39,54
PT	Malcher, Lindsay	M	61
PT	Matthews, Katherine	M	61
PT	Messersmith, Charles	M	64C,48
PT	Messersmith, Susan	B	63A,49
PT	Nichols, Brandon	B	63B
Asst Prof	Shaffer, Kris P.	D	13
PT	Shetler, Donald	D	62D
Asst Prof	Sterbank, Mark	M	64E,47,46,29
PT	Stoudenmire, Myungsook	M	66A,66D,66C
PT	Teves, Christopher	M	70,11
Prof	Whipple, Jennifer	D	33
PT	Wilson, Kathleen	M	62E
PT	Yost, Regina Helcher	M	64A,48

SC0300 The Citadel

Department of Music
171 Moultrie St
Charleston, SC 29409
(843) 953-6889 Fax: (843) 953-4993
www.citadel.edu
E-mail: mike.alverson@citadel.edu

4 Year Institution

Chair: J. Michael Alverson, 80A

	Alverson, J. Michael		13,37,60
	Dillahey, Samuel J.	M	20F,37
	Lefter, Nancy C.	M	36,66G,31A

SC0350 Claflin University

Department of Music
400 Magnolia St
Orangeburg, SC 29115
(803) 535-5193 Fax: (803) 535-5735
www.claflin.edu
E-mail: music@claflin.edu

4 Year Undergraduate Liberal Arts Institution
Member of NASM

Chair: Isaiah R. McGee, 80A

Asst Prof	Butler, Dorsey Mitchell	D	63C,60B,47,29
Asst Prof	Cho, Sujung	D	66A,66D,66C
Asst Prof	Fogle, Megan R.	D	13A,13B,13C,13E,13F
Asst Prof	Hicks, Lori C.	D	61,39,32D
Inst	Holliday, Stacey A.	M	66A,66C
Assoc Prof	House, Richard E.	D	37,63A,32E,60B
Adj Prof	Jones, Allison	M	61
Adj Prof	Kang, Hyun-Ku	M	11
Asst Prof	Keith, Laura J.	D	12A,66A,66D,32C,32D
Asst Prof	McGee, Isaiah R.	D	35,36,39,61,32D
Adj Prof	Murdaugh, Johnnie L.	D	64E,32C
Adj Prof	Reeves, Richard	M	65,50
Adj Prof	Sharrock, Barry R.	D	61
Asst Prof	Turner, Katherine L.	D	64C,12A,20,14A

SC0400 Clemson University

Department of Performing Arts
Box 341505/221 Brooks Ctr
Clemson, SC 29634-0525
(864) 656-3043 Fax: (864) 656-1013
www.clemson.edu/PerfArts/
E-mail: hartmad@clemson.edu

4 Year Institution

Chair: David Hartmann, 80A
Dir., Brooks Center, Performing Arts: Lillian U. Harder, 80F,80G

Asst Prof	Altstatt, Hamilton	B	34,35
Inst PT	Anderson, Matthew T.	B	63D,49
Lect	Bannister, Hazen Duane	B	66A
Inst PT	Baynard, Tim D.	B	65
Lect	Bleuel, John	D	64E
Lect	Bracchitta, Ian	M	62D
Assoc Prof	Buyer, Paul L.	D	65,50,14,20
Lect	Conley, David A.	M	60A
Lect	Craig, Monty S.	B	70,46,47,29B
Lect	Durham, Justin W.	D	36,60A
Assoc Prof	Dzuris, Linda	D	69,20G,66G,34
Lect	Goodloe, Cindy Roden	D	66A
Inst PT	Gourdin, Lori	M	66C
Prof	Harder, Lillian U.	M	66A,35E
Inst PT	Hosler, Cheryl L.	B	52
Assoc Prof	Hosler, Mark	D	11,20G
Lect	Hurlburt, Timothy R.	M	37,46,47,11
Lect	Jacobus, Rhea Beth	D	13,11
Inst PT	Kibler, Lea F.	M	64A,48
Lect	Lapin, Eric J.	M	64C,11
Assoc Prof	Levin, Andrew R.	D	11,41,38,13,42
Prof	Li-Bleuel, Linda	D	66C,11,32,12A,66
Lect	Odom, Lisa Sain	D	11,61,36
Lect	Parsons, Laurie N.	B	63B
Lect	Pyle, Laura	B	62C,42
Prof	Rash, Daniel R.	D	11,60A,54
Assoc Prof	Spede, Mark J.	D	37,60,12B
Inst PT	Stevenson, David E.	M	70
Inst PT	Warlick, Leslie Taylor	D	62A,62B
Inst PT	Warneck, Petrea	M	64B
Assoc Prof	Whisler, Bruce Allen	D	29A,41,35,34
Lect	Willey, Rich	M	63A

SC0420 Coastal Carolina University

Department of Music
PO Box 261954
Conway, SC 29528-6054
(843) 349-2515 Fax: (843) 349-4125
www.coastal.edu/music
E-mail: ppowell@coastal.edu

4 Year Institution, Graduate School

Master of Arts in Teaching Specialization Music

Chair: Philip M. Powell, 80A

PT	Althoff, Erin	B	62A,62B
Prof	Bankston, David	D	61,39
PT	Barbone, Anthony	M	32B
PT	Ben-Pazi, Tamar	B	62C
PT	Benson, Ann	D	61,39
PT	Chesanow, Marc	M	62D,11,10F,13B,35G
PT	Connelly, Chris	M	63C,63D,11,29
Assoc Prof	Edwards, Patti Yvonne	D	61,32D
PT	Evans, Charles	D	38
PT	Fowler, Andrew J.	D	13C,13A,11
Assoc Prof Emeritus	Hamilton, William R.	D	13,11
PT	Hull, Daniel	D	70,11
Prof	Johnson, Richard	D	32E,60B,13
Asst Prof	Jones, Jeffrey L.	D	61,39
PT	Miller, Jessica	M	64B
Lect	O'Reilly, Daniel	M	14C,64E,29A
Prof	Powell, Philip M.	D	66A,66B,66C,66D
Assoc Prof	Propst, Tonya	D	63B,32,32C
PT	Roper, Gretchen	B	64C
PT	Scrivner, Scott	B	64D
Lect	Shrewsbury, Matthew Monroe	M	37
Assoc Prof	Sinclair, Terri		36,61,32D,60A
Prof	Sloan, Donald S.	D	13,10A
Prof	Stegall, Gary Miles	D	66A,66D,13A,66C,66G
PT	Trinka, Jill L.	D	32A,20,32B
Asst Prof	Tully, Amy	D	64A,12A,41
Prof	Tully, James	D	37,32E,60B
Asst Prof	White, Matthew S.	D	63A,46,35,53
Asst Prof	Willis, Jesse	M	65,50,20,37

SC0450 Coker College

Department of Music
300 E College Ave
Hartsville, SC 29550
(843) 383-8065 Fax: (843) 383-8033
www.coker.edu
E-mail: gwood@coker.edu

4 Year Institution
Member of NASM

Chair & Dir., Artist/Performance Series: Phyllis Fields, 80A,80F
Dir., Admissions: Graham Wood, 80D

Assoc Prof	Carswell, William	D	31A,61,32,36,40
Lect FT	Hill, Serena	D	39,61
Lect PT	Holcombe, Candace	M	11,32B
Asst Prof	Matsuo, Jun	D	66A,66D,66B,66C,13
Assoc Prof	Wood, Graham	D	11,12,63B,54,20

SC0500 College of Charleston

School of the Arts - Music
66 George St
Charleston, SC 29424
(843) 953-5927 Fax: (843) 953-4914
music.cofc.edu
E-mail: music@cofc.edu

4 Year Institution

Master of Arts Teaching emphasis Choral Music

Dean: Valerie Bonita Morris, 80A
Chair: Steven E. Rosenberg, 80A

Prof	Ashley, Douglas D.	D	11,12A,66A
Artist in Res	Graf, Enrique G.	M	66A
Assoc Prof	Hart, Edward B.	D	10,11,13
Inst	Heywood, David John	M	11,37,64A,29,47
Assoc Prof	Khoma, Natalia	D	11,62C
Vstng Asst Prof	Lewis, Robert S. T.	M	11,47,64E
Prof	McBroom, Deanna H.	M	11,61
Prof	Regnier, Marc	M	11,70
Prof	Rosenberg, Steven E.	D	11,67C
Assoc Prof	Siow, Lee-Chin	M	11,62A
Asst Prof	Stevens, Blake	D	12,11
Assoc Prof	Taylor, Robert J.	D	11,36,61,60
Asst Prof	Templeton, David M.	M	61,39,11
Asst Prof	Vassilandonakis, Yiorgos	D	10,11,13,43
Lect	Zemp, William Robin	M	11,66A,66C,66D

SC0600 Columbia College

Music Program
1301 Columbia College Dr
Columbia, SC 29203
(803) 786-3810   Fax: (803) 786-3893
www.columbiasc.edu
E-mail: rjohnston@columbiasc.edu

4 Year Liberal Arts Institution
Member of NASM

Coordinator: Rebecca R. Johnston, 80A

Adj Inst	Brunson, Tomas	M	31,61
Prof Emerita	Gibson, Robyn	M	66A
Adj Inst	Grezeszak, Amanda	M	64E
Adj Inst	Hayes, Pamela	M	62
Adj Inst	Isenhour, Justin R.	M	63C
Adj Inst	Jacobs, Aletha	M	47
Asst Prof	Johnston, Rebecca R.	D	32,36,60,13C,61
Adj Inst	Jones, Matthew	B	65
Adj Inst	Knight, Alan	M	70,11,20
Adj Inst	Leadbitter, Robyn	B	64A
Prof	Love, Randolph D.	D	13,10,63,41,14C
Adj Inst	Lowry, David	D	66G
Prof Emerita	Palmer, Leila S.	M	61
	Preacher, Patrick Dale	M	64B
Adj Inst	Siemon, Brittnee	D	61
Adj Inst	Sturgeon, Laura	M	66B
Prof	Weinberg, Alan	D	11,66A,12A,66D

SC0620 Columbia International University

Department of Music
PO Box 3122
Columbia, SC 29230-3122
(803) 754-4100 x 3190   Fax: (803) 786-4209
www.ciu.edu/college/majors/music

4 Year Institution

PT	Duensing, Craig	M	36
PT	Duensing, Jane	M	61
PT	Hutchison, Lacey	M	66A
FT	Lewis, Rod	D	13,70,40
PT	Mandel, Jac	M	70
PT	Manoogian, Peggy Lee	M	66A
FT	Osterlund, David	D	60,14,32,66A

SC0650 Converse College

Petrie School of Music
580 E Main St
Spartanburg, SC 29302-1931
(864) 596-9021   Fax: (864) 596-9167
www.converse.edu
E-mail: patti.foy@converse.edu

4 Year Institution, Graduate School
Member of NASM

Master of Music in Performance, Master of Music in Music Education

Director: Patricia S. Foy, 80A
Dir., Community/Preparatory Division: Paula Morgan, 80E

Prof	Berry, S. David	D	10,13,34,35,12
Lect PT	Crisan, Patricia	M	66A,13C
Lect PT	Denbow, Anne	M	61
Lect PT	Flynn, Patrick	D	70
Prof	Foy, Patricia S.	D	32
Lect PT	Haecker, Arthur	M	63C
Prof	Hay, Beverly R.	D	61
Lect PT	Hicks, Sharalynn	M	66D
Lect PT	Hill, Karen	M	64C,64E
Assoc Prof	Hoffman, Miles	M	62B
Asst Prof	Holloway, John R.	D	63D,32,37,60B
Assoc Prof	Johnson, Sarah	B	62A
Prof	Jones, Keith	D	61,36,60
Lect PT	Larsen, Jens	M	63A
Assoc Prof	Lyle, Susan	D	61,40
Lect	MacPhail, Valerie	D	61
Lect PT	McDaniel, Adena	M	65
Lect PT	Mixter, Jan	B	62D
Lect PT	Pauly, Erica	M	66A
Lect PT	Poole, Mary Ada	M	32E
Lect PT	Popwell, Brooks	M	62C
Assoc Prof	Reichwald, Siegwart	D	12,38,60B
Prof	Robbins, Malcolm Scott	D	13,10,14C
Lect	Roche, Mildred A.	M	66C,13C
Asst Prof	Shultis, Carol	D	33
Lect PT	Szafron, Brennan	M	66G
Assoc Prof	Turner, Rebecca	M	61
Assoc Prof	Vaneman, Christopher	D	64A,12,42
Assoc Prof	Vaneman, Kelly McElrath	D	12A,64B,42,55,14
Lect PT	Waggoner, Emily	M	62E
Lect PT	Watson, Frank	M	32E,64D
Prof	Weeks, Douglas A.	D	66A
Prof	York, Elizabeth F.	D	33
Lect PT	Zuehlke, Anneka	M	63B

SC0700 Erskine College

Department of Music
PO Box 338
Due West, SC 29639
(864) 379-8709   Fax: (864) 379-2167
www.erskine.edu
E-mail: music@erskine.edu

4 Year Liberal Arts Institution and Seminary

Chair: James Brooks Kuykendall, 80A
Dir., Preparatory Division: Bradley Parker, 80E

Inst PT	Bolen, Patricia	B	63B
Inst PT	Brown, Shon	B	47,65
Inst PT	Collins, Susan	M	32
Inst PT	Diekhoff, Bill	M	61
Inst PT	Ellis, Thomas J.	M	61
Assoc Prof	Glick, Robert P.	M	66G,31A,11
Inst PT	Golden, Lyman	B	70
Inst PT	Gratton, Chris	M	62
Inst PT	Hilley, Byron	M	63
Emeritus	Koonts, Cortlandt	M	
Assoc Prof	Kuykendall, James Brooks	D	13,12,11,41,38
Inst PT	Maher, Donna	D	64
Asst Prof	Nabholz, Mark A.	D	36,60
Asst Prof	Parker, Bradley	D	66,13
Inst PT	Perry, Kathy	M	62,51,42
Inst PT	Svatanova, Lucie	M	61,39
Inst PT	Wilson, Leah	M	64A

SC0710 Francis Marion University

Department of Fine Arts
PO Box 100547
Florence, SC 29501
(843) 661-1385   Fax: (843) 661-1529
www.fmarion.edu/academics/finearts
E-mail: troberts@fmarion.edu

4 Year Institution

Chair: Lawrence P. Anderson, 80A

Inst PT	Fincher, James	M	11,61
Inst PT	Green, Feleighta	M	64
Asst Prof	Gualdi, Paolo Andre'	D	66A,11,13,66B,66C
Inst PT	Hull, Daniel	D	70
Inst	Jokisch, Kelly	M	11,32B
Inst PT	Matthews, Forrest	M	47,11
Assoc Prof	Orr, Sue Butler	M	11,36,61
Inst PT	Reeves, Shane	M	65,41
Asst Prof	Roberts, Terry	D	11,63,13C,35A,41
Inst PT	Thompson, Shaw	M	11,61
Prof Emeritus	Woods, Benjamin	D	

SC0750 Furman University

Department of Music
3300 Poinsett Hwy
Greenville, SC 29613
(864) 294-2176   Fax: (864) 294-2121
www.furman.edu/depts/music
E-mail: mark.britt@furman.edu

4 Year Institution
Member of NASM

Dean: John S. Beckford, 80A
Chair: Mark E. Britt, 80A
Coord., Fine Arts Admissions: Marta Lanier, 80D
Music Program Coordinator: Marcella Frese, 80G

Lect	Barksdale, Lisa Browne	M	61
Prof	Beckford, John S.	D	20
Lect	Bocook, Jay A.	M	37,10F
Prof Emeritus	Boda, Dan	D	
PT	Bracchitta, Ian	B	62D
Prof	Britt, Mark E.	D	63C,49,32E
PT	Burroughs-Price, Anita	M	62E
Asst Prof	Carmenates, Omar	D	65,50,20
Prof	Chesebro, Robert C.	D	12A,64,41
Lect	Cochran, Kathy	D	32B,32D
Assoc Prof	Colvin, Jennifer L.	M	16
PT	Davis, Keith		66A,46
PT	Easter, Timothy D.	B	62D
PT	Elkins, Phil	M	11,63A
PT	Eshelman, Karen	D	13,66D
Prof	Floyd, Hugh	D	61,60A,36,32D
Prof	Fuller, Trudy H.	D	61
Assoc Prof	Gross, David	D	66A,66C,66B,66D
PT	Guest, Ann	M	66B
Lect	Hamilton, Vivian	D	36,66C
Prof	Hicken, Leslie W.	D	60,37,32
PT	Hopkins, Cynthia	M	64A
Assoc Prof	Hutton, Christopher	D	62C,12A,51
PT	Hutton, Deirdre	M	62A,51
Lect	Joiner, Anna Barbrey	D	62B,42,32E
Prof	Joiner, Thomas	D	38,62A
Asst Prof	Kennedy, Laura E.	D	12
Prof	Kilstofte, Mark F.	D	10,13,43,13E
Prof	Koppelman, Daniel M.	D	66A,13,34,10
Prof Emeritus	Kyser, Ramon	D	
Prof	Malvern, Gary J.	D	63A,41,12A
Assoc Prof	Matthews, Tamara	M	61
Prof	Morgan, Ruby N.	D	66A,66B,66D
Vstng Lect	Moseley, Brian	M	13
PT	Moseley, Jessica Barnett	M	13,66C,66D
Lect	Neville, Ruth	D	66D,13
Assoc Prof	Olson, Matthew W.	D	64E,29,47,41,46
Prof	Parsons, Derek J.	D	13,66A,66B,66D
Vstng Prof	Preucil, William		62A
PT	Rhyne, Kathryn	M	11
PT	Riddle, Paula	M	11,63B
Prof	Schoonmaker, Bruce W.	D	39,61
Lect	Schoonmaker, Gail	M	61
Prof Emeritus	Smith, Charlotte R.	M	
Prof Emeritus	Smith, W. Lindsay	D	
PT	Taylor, Michael S.	M	63D
Vstng Prof	Tchivzhel, Edvard	D	60B
Prof	Thomas, William D.	D	40,61,31A
Lect	Tipton, Dewitt	D	66C
Prof	Tompkins, Charles B.	D	13,66G,66H,31A
Prof Emeritus	Vick, Bingham L.	D	
Lect	Walter, Steven	D	70,11,12A
PT	Warneck, Petrea	M	64B,11
Lect	Watson, J. Stephen	B	29A,70,46
PT	Wilson, Stephen	M	63C
PT	Yang, Amy	M	64D
	Grier, Jon Jeffrey	D	13
Inst	Parks, Karen	D	61
Inst	Ravnan, John	M	62B,42,13
	Robinson, Gary A.	D	63,64,65,38

SC0800 Lander University

Department of Music
320 Stanley Ave
Greenwood, SC 29649
(864) 388-8323   Fax: (864) 388-8144
www.lander.edu
E-mail: alawrence@lander.edu

4 Year Institution

Chair: Lila D. Noonkester, 80A

PT	Alter, Adam M.	M	64C,51
PT	Crenshaw, Sonja L.	M	63B
Prof Emeritus PT	Criswell, Paul D.	D	32
Asst Prof	Gallo, Reed P.	D	37,60B,32E,63A,49
Assoc Prof	Gardiner, Robert A.	M	11,29,47,32E,64E
PT	Gardner, Rebecca	B	64B
Asst Prof	Kelley, Robert T.	D	20,13,66A,66D,10
Prof	Lenti, Anthony A.	D	11,12A,66A
Assoc Prof	Neufeld, Charles W.	D	60A,61,36,32D
PT	Newell, Michael	B	70
Assoc Prof	Noonkester, Lila D.	D	13,39,61,11
PT	Pinner, Jay-Martin	M	62A
PT	Robinson, Dawn	M	64A
PT	Stern, David W.	D	63D
PT	Thieben, Jacob S.	D	50,65
PT	Thomas, Richard	D	62C

SC0850 Limestone College

Department of Music
1115 College Dr
Gaffney, SC 29340-3778
(864) 488-4509   Fax: (864) 487-8706
www.limestone.edu
E-mail: gpoovey@limestone.edu

4 Year Institution
Member of NASM

Music Executive: Gena E. Poovey, 80A
Dir., Artist/Performance Series: David B. Thompson, 80F

PT	Guzewicz, Rebecca	M	65A,65B
PT	Henson, Eric	M	63D
Prof	Hill, Harry H.	DMA	11,12A,64C,64E,48
PT	Hodges, David	M	63A,63C
PT	Parks, John	B	70,46,47
Prof	Poovey, Gena E.	DMA	36,61,60A,32D,40
Asst Prof	Presley, Douglas L.	PhD	37,50,32B,32C,65
PT	Siarris, Cathy Froneberger	M	61,11
Prof	Thompson, David B.	DMA	12A,13,66

SC0900 Newberry College

Department of Music
2100 College St
Newberry, SC 29108-2126
(803) 321-5633   Fax: (803) 321-5175
www.newberry.edu
E-mail: sally.cherrington@newberry.edu

4 Year Institution
Member of NASM

Chair: Sally Cherrington Beggs, 80A,80B,80F
Dir., Artist Series: Bill Long, 80F

Assoc Prof	Cherrington Beggs, Sally	D	13D,66,31A,12A
Inst PT	Driggers, Dawn		
Inst PT	Flowers, Kevin	B	65,50
Asst Prof	Haecker, Allyss	M	61,20,36,39
Inst PT	Larsen, Jens	M	10F,63A,49
Asst Prof	Larsen, Laurel	D	66A,66C,66B,13,66D
Assoc Prof	Long, Bill	M	37,47,65,60B,32E
Asst Prof	Long, Janet	M	62,32B,11,32A,32C
Assoc Prof	McGinnis, Barry E.	D	64,12A,29,48,29A
Inst PT	Neese, Wanda	M	66A,66C
Asst Prof	Sheppard, Chris	D	36,60A,61,40,34
Inst PT	Smith, Becky		66C
Inst PT	Smith, Matthew	B	70
Inst PT	Turnbough, Kimberlee	M	66A,66C
Inst PT	Valerio, John	D	29B,53,66A,10

SC0950 North Greenville University

Cline School of Music
PO Box 1892
Tigerville, SC 29688
(864) 977-7080   Fax: (864) 977-2193
www.ngu.edu
E-mail: jackie.griffin@ngu.edu

4 Year Institution

Dean & Dir., Undergraduate Studies: Jackie Griffin, 80A,80B

Prof	Combs, Barry	D	60,36,61,31A
Prof	Coppenbarger, Brent	D	13,11,64
Inst	Davis, Christopher A.	M	11,13,29,50,65
Prof	Greene, Cheryl	D	61

Prof	Griffin, Jackie	D	13,10,12A,66G,34
Prof	Holland, Marianne	D	32,66A
Assoc Prof	Lewis, Grant	D	39,34,61
Prof	Parrini, Fabio	DIPL	66A,66D,11,66C
Prof	Stoytcheva, Lilia S.	D	66A,66B,66C,66D
Asst Prof	Washington, Darian	D	37,49,63B
Assoc Prof	Weaver, Michael A.	D	12A,11,32,62A,62B

SC1000 Presbyterian College
Department of Music
503 S Broad St
Clinton, SC 29325
(864) 833-8470   Fax: (864) 833-8481
www.presby.edu/music
E-mail: pstokes@presby.edu

4 Year Institution

Interim Provost: Anita K. Gustafson, 80A
Chair & Dir., Undergraduate Studies: Porter Stokes, II, 80A,80B,80E,80F

Adj	Borgstedt, Bryson	M	64E,47,64C
Adj	Buckland, James P.	D	70,13
Assoc Prof	Buckland, Karen W.	D	66A,66C,66D
Adj	Condit, Sonja	M	64B,64D
Assoc Prof	Davis, Ron A.	D	13B,13C,31,66G,44
Asst Prof	Elser, Albert Christian	D	61,12A,34D,39
Adj	Fleury, Tacy S.	M	61
Adj	Fryml, Nathan	M	64C
Adj	Gearheart, Kerri	M	63B,32B
Adj	Haecker, Arthur	M	63D
Adj	Hipp, Gary O.	M	41
Assoc Prof	House, Richard	D	37,63A,32
Asst Prof	Howiler, Robert W.	D	34,10A,13G,10B
Adj	Jones, Matthew Craig	B	65
Adj	Kozak, Pawel K	D	51,62A,62B
Adj	Massey, Angela	M	64A
Asst Prof	Rudell, Alan M.	M	66A,66C
Prof	Stokes, Porter	D	36,61,60,32
Adj	Svatonova, Lucie Anna	M	61
Asst Prof	Thomas, Richard B.	D	62C,11,38,12A,62D

SC1050 South Carolina State University
Department of Visual & Perf Arts
300 College St NE
Orangeburg, SC 29117
(803) 536-7101   Fax: (803) 536-7192
www.scsu.edu
E-mail: rbeckford@scsu.edu

4 Year Institution, Historically Black College
Member of NASM

Music Coordinator: Richard E. Beckford, 80A

Assoc Prof	Beckford, Richard E.	D	13,60,11,36,66G
Inst	Celmer, Joey R.	C	63A,63B,63C,63D,47
Asst Prof	Clark, Jacob	D	66A,66D,12A
Asst Prof	Dingle, Rosetta	M	32,36,66D,13
Prof	Graham, Edward E.	D	66A,66C,66D,12A
Assoc Prof	Grenier, Robert M.	D	13,61,11
Inst	Johnson, Joel C.	M	13,10,20G,29A,34
Prof	Quick, Julia M.	D	11,38,41,51,62A
Inst	Ricks, Edward	M	65A,65B,37,50,13A
Inst	Ridges, Lameriel R.	M	13,66A,66C
Asst Prof	Sarjeant, Ronald	M	10F,60,37,64
Asst Prof	Simmons, Matthew	M	37,49,63C,63D

SC1080 Southern Wesleyan University
Department of Music
907 Wesleyan Dr
PO Box 1020
Central, SC 29630
(864) 644-5404   Fax: (864) 644-5912
www.swu.edu
E-mail: djachens@swu.edu

4 Year Institution

Chair, Fine Arts: Jane Dill, 80A
Coordinator, Music Studies: Darryl Jachens, 80A

Adj	Anderson, Matt	B	63C,63D
Adj	Buyer, Paul	D	65
Prof	Campbell, Don	D	13,60,36,61,12A
Assoc Prof	Day, Greg	M	13,10F,37,47,63
Prof	Dill, Jane	D	13,66A,66G,66C
Adj	Golden, Lyman	M	70
Adj	Harris, Kay	M	66C,66D
Prof	Jachens, Darryl	D	11,32,63C
Adj	Kibler, Lea	M	64A
Adj	Parson, Laurie	B	63B
Assoc Prof	Rowell, Melanie	D	12A,61,54,39
Adj	Skaar, Alice	M	62A
Adj	Spires, Henry Ray	B	64B,64C,64D,64E

SC1100 Univ of South Carolina Aiken
Department of Visual & Perf Arts
471 University Pkwy
Aiken, SC 29801-6309
(803) 641-3305   Fax: (803) 641-3691
www.usca.edu/visualandperformingarts/
E-mail: richardm@usca.edu

4 Year Institution

Chair: Jack Benjamin, 80A

PT	Courtney, Ken H.	M	11,66G,20
PT	Daniecki, John B.	M	61
PT	Dupee, Donald	M	32
PT	Field, Sandra T.	D	61
PT	Gangi, Jonathan	M	11,70
Lect	Hamilton, Anna	M	66
PT	Henderson, Matthew C.	M	63C
PT	Holmes, Isaac	M	20,61
PT	Losey, Mary	M	66A,66D
Prof	Maltz, Richard	D	13,10,65,12,14
PT	Massey, Robert	M	64C
Inst	Meccia, Lauren L.	M	37,41,47
PT	Ramsey, Laura	M	14,64D
PT	Redd, Ann	M	20
Asst Prof	Scraper, Joel	D	40,60A,32D,36,60
PT	Strong, Willie	M	12A,20
PT	Workman, Josh	M	63A
PT	Yonce, Tammy	D	64A
PT	Zakkary, Martha	M	61

SC1110 Univ of South Carolina-Columbia
School of Music
813 Assembly St
Columbia, SC 29208
(803) 777-4336   Fax: (803) 777-6508
www.music.sc.edu
E-mail: lgibson@mozart.sc.edu

4 Year Institution, Graduate School
Member of NASM

Master of Music in Opera-Music Theatre, Master of Music in Composition, Master of Music in Performance, Master of Music in Conducting, Master of Music in Music Education, PhD in Music Education, DMA in Composition, DMA in Conducting, DMA in Performance, Master of Music in Music History, Master of Music in Piano Pedagogy, Master of Music in Jazz Studies, DMA in Piano Pedagogy

Dean: C. Tayloe Harding, Jr., 80A
Associate Dean & Dir., Undergraduate Studies: Robert S. Pruzin, 80B,80H
Exec. Associate Dean & Dir., Graduate Studies: Andrew D. Gowan, 80C,80H
Dir., Admissions: Jennifer Jablonski, 80D
Dir., Preparatory Division: Gail V. Barnes, 80E
Dir., Preparatory Division: Constance Gee, 80E
Dir., Preparatory Division: Alena M. Pagal, 80E
Dir., Preparatory Division: Wendy Valerio, 80E
Assistant Dean: Rebecca S. Nagel, 80H

Assoc Prof	Ackley, James	M	49,63A
Assoc Prof Emeritus	Amstutz, A. Keith	D	63A
Prof	Bain, Reginald	D	13,10,34,45
Assoc Prof	Barnes, Gail V.	D	32,62B
Adj	Barton, Peter A.	M	61
Prof	Bates, William H.	D	12A,66G,31A
Prof	Berg, Christopher B.	M	55,70
Assoc Prof	Butterfield, Craig	M	62D,29,46,47
Adj	Casey, Neil	M	38,42
Prof Emeritus	Christie, Laury	M	39,61
Prof Emeritus	Copenhaver, James K.	M	32E,37
	Crenshaw, Timothy	B	71,72
Prof Emeritus	Curry, Jerry L.	D	13,66H,55,66E
	Cutler, David	D	13,10,12A
Assoc Prof	Cuttino, Walter E.	D	39,61
Prof	Davis, Ronald	M	11,49,63D
Prof	Douglas, Samuel O.	D	13,10,62D

Directory of Institutions   Page 345

Librarian	Dubnjakovic, Ana	M	16
Assoc Prof	Edwards, Bradley W.	D	63C,49
Assoc Prof	Eller, Joseph M.	M	64C,48
Inst FT	Fang, Man	D	10
Adj	Francis, Jeff	M	35C,35G
Prof	Fugo, Charles Leonard	D	66A,66C
Asst Prof	Gee, Constance	DMA	11,41,62B,42
Prof	Gowan, Andrew D.	D	60,32,37,64
Prof Emeritus	Graham, R. Douglas	M	47,64C,64E
Prof Emeritus	Gray, Donald N.	D	39,61
Prof Emeritus	Hall, James	D	65
Inst PT	Hara, Kunio	M	12
Prof	Harding, C. Tayloe	D	10,35E,43
Inst FT	Harley, Michael	M	13,42
Assoc Prof	Herring, David Scott	M	65
Asst Prof	Hopkins, Janet E.	M	61,39
Assoc Prof	Hubbert, Julie	D	12
Asst Prof	Hunter, Rebecca	D	62A
Asst Prof	Jenkins, John Daniel	D	13
Artist in Res	Jennings, Joseph	M	36
Prof	Jesselson, Robert M.	D	38,41,62C
Asst Prof	Johnson, Birgitta	PhD	14,20G
Assoc Prof	Kompass, Lynn R.	D	39,66C
Assoc Prof	Lane, Jeremy S.	D	32
Prof	Leaman, Clifford L.	D	64E
Prof	Ligon, Bert	M	46,47,66A,29,45
Assoc Prof	Lomazov, Marina	D	66A
Adj	McKeithen, Steve	M	32E
Prof	Nagel, Rebecca S.	D	11,64B,41
Adj	Pagal, Alena M.	M	66B,66D
Asst Prof	Parker-Harley, Jennifer	D	64A,48
Asst Prof	Phillips, Rebecca L.	D	32E,37,60B
Prof	Portnoy, Donald	D	60,38,62A
Prof	Price, Scott	D	66A,66B,66D
Prof	Pruzin, Robert S.	M	32C,49,63B
Asst Prof	Rackers, Joseph P.	D	66C
Assoc Prof	Rogers, John Fitz	D	10
Assoc Prof	Schlaefer, Ellen Douglas	M	39
Assoc Prof	Stallard, Tina Milhorn	D	39,61
Inst PT	Stuart, Gregory	M	12
Inst FT	Taylor, James W.	M	37,32E,60B
Prof	Terwilliger, William	D	62A,51,42
Adj	Valerio, John B.	M	29,11
Assoc Prof	Valerio, Wendy	D	32A,12
Artist in Res	Vizutti, Allen	D	29,63A
Asst Prof	Walker, Alicia W.	D	36,32D,60A
Assoc Prof	Will, Jacob	M	61,39
Assoc Prof Emeritus	Williams, John W.	M	66A
Asst Prof	Williams, Sarah F.	D	12A,14C,12,14,15
Prof	Wyatt, Larry D.	D	60,32,36

SC1200 Winthrop University
Department of Music
129 Conservatory of Music
Rock Hill, SC 29733-0001
(803) 323-2255   Fax: (803) 323-2343
www.winthrop.edu/cvpa/music/
E-mail: rogersd@winthrop.edu

4 Year Institution, Graduate School
Member of NASM

Master of Music in Performance, Master of Music in Conducting, Master of Music Education, Master of Arts in Teaching

Chair/Graduate Advisor: Donald M. Rogers, 80A,80C

Adj PT	Austin, Jennifer N.	M	66A,66D,66C,66B
Inst	Bradner, Janice B.	M	66D,66C,66A
Adj PT	Bronola-Dickert, Lannia N.	M	66A
Adj PT	Burns, Elizabeth D.	M	62C
Asst Prof	Bushman, Catharine Sinon	D	37,32E,42
Assoc Prof	Crochet, Lourinda S.	D	37,32E,42
Assoc Prof	Deguchi, Tomoko	D	13,66A,13F,13E,13A
Assoc Prof	Dickert, Lewis H.	D	70,53,29,13A,14
Adj PT	Dulin, Mark C.	D	63A,41
Adj PT	Fields, Donna	M	32B
Asst Prof	Fowler, John H.	D	61,39
	Giles, Kari	M	62A
Assoc Prof	Hale, Connie L.	D	32B,32H,32A
Prof Emeritus	Helton, Jerry L.	M	61,39
Adj PT	Hildreth, Thomas P.	M	62D,38
Adj PT	Hopper, Kerrin A.	M	32B
Adj PT	Hough, Jennifer C.	M	61
Prof	Hughes, William M.	D	13,49,63C,41
Adj PT	Imler, James R.	D	36,40
Adj PT	Irmiter, Kristopher	B	61
Assoc Prof	Kinsey, Katherine S.	D	32D,36,60A,40
Adj PT	Kulma, David T.	M	13
Assoc Prof	Lewis, Leonard Mark	D	10,13
Adj PT	Loomer, Deborah W.	D	64C
Prof Emeritus	Malambri, William F.	D	37
Prof	Manwarren, Matthew C.	D	66A,66B,12,41
Adj PT	Maxwell, Sarita J.	M	63D,41

Inst	McDaniel-Milliken, Jennifer L.	M	39,16
Adj PT	Miller, Joseph P.	M	34
Adj PT	Morris, Amy B.	M	66D
Adj PT	O'Neill, Jill L.	M	11,64A,48,14C,41
Assoc Prof	Parks, Ronald Keith	D	10,13,34,41
Prof	Pearson, Ian D.	D	12,55,41
Assoc Prof	Rogers, Donald M.	D	12C,32G
Adj PT	Rydel, Robert E.	B	63B
Adj PT	Snow, Adam M.	D	65
Adj PT	Stein, Daniel C.	M	61
Prof Emeritus	Thompson, Phil A.	D	47,64
Adj PT	Ulaky, Hollis B.	B	64B
Prof	Williams, Barry Michael	D	12A,50,65,20A,20B
Asst Prof	Wunderlich, Kristen A.	D	61
Adj PT	Yost, Hilary W.	M	64D,42

SD0050 Augustana College
Department of Perf. & Visual Arts-Music
2001 S Summit Ave
Sioux Falls, SD 57197
(605) 274-5451   Fax: (605) 274-5323
www.augie.edu/dept/music
E-mail: music@augie.edu

4 Year Institution
Member of NASM

Chair: Scott R. Johnson, 80A

Prof	Ammann, Bruce T.	D	60B,37,32E,64E
Inst PT	Andersen, Michael	M	63D
Inst PT	Anderson, Emily	B	48
Prof	Andrews, Rick	D	66A,66B,13
Prof PT	Barnard, Monty	D	61
	Carlson, Andrea		63B,49
Inst PT	Carter, Jeanne	M	61
	Casey, John		64D
Inst PT	Chiarello, Mario	D	62D
Assoc Prof	Grevlos, Lisa	D	39,61,32B,36,32D
Inst PT	Gunderson, Geoff	B	70
Inst PT	Hill, Christopher	M	64C
Inst PT	Hufnagle, Kathryn	M	62C
Inst PT	Isaackson, Mark	M	64E,47
Assoc Prof	Johnson, Scott R.	D	32,54,11
Inst	Joyce, Robert	M	10F,34
Inst PT	Koch, Cheryl	M	61
Inst PT	Larson, Angela	M	64C
Inst PT	Lutow, Justyna	M	62A
Inst PT	Masek, Patricia B.	M	64A
Inst PT	Melik-Stepanov, Karren	D	62C,51
Assoc Prof	Nesheim, Paul	D	36,32D
Inst PT	Olson, Scott	B	63A
Inst PT	Paul, Jeffrey		64B
Prof	Pennington, John C.	D	13A,65,50,10F
Inst PT	Reid, Debra		66C
Inst PT	Schempp, Marilyn	M	66G,66H
Asst Prof	Schilf, Paul R.	D	37,49,47,32E,29A
Inst PT	Schreck, Judith	B	61
Inst	Shoemaker, Vance	B	63C,63D,49
Assoc Prof	Stanichar, Christopher	D	38,60,12A
Inst PT	Steen, Solveig	M	66A
Inst PT	Svanoe, Kimberly Utke	D	66A,11
Asst Prof	Svenningsen, Russell	M	13,36,61
Inst PT	Tomkins, John	M	64D
Inst PT	Vorhes, Anna	M	62E
Inst PT	Zamora, Christian		62A

SD0100 Black Hills State University
Department of Music
1200 University St Unit 9097
Spearfish, SD 57799-9097
(605) 642-6241   Fax: (605) 642-6762
www.bhsu.edu
E-mail: randall.royer@bhsu.edu

4 Year Institution
Member of NASM

Chair: Randall D. Royer, 80A
Interim Dean: David Wolff, 80A

Asst Prof	Hahn, Christopher D.	M	63,37,60,11
Inst PT	Hubbard, Constance	M	66D
Inst PT	Martensen, Dave	M	64
Inst PT	Miller, Lori	M	66D
Asst Prof	Nero, Jonathan	D	36,32D,60
Assoc Prof Emeritus	Parker, Steven	M	36
Asst Prof	Roberts, Nancy	D	32,61
Prof	Royer, Randall D.	D	64,47,38,32E,70
Asst Prof	Waseen, Symeon	D	10A,10B,10F,13,66

SD0150 Dakota State University
Department of Music
820 N Washington St
Madison, SD 57042
(605) 256-5270   Fax: (605) 256-5021
www.dsu.edu
E-mail: sandra.champion@dsu.edu

4 Year Institution

Coordinator: Louis W. Pape, 80A
Dean, Liberal Arts: Eric Johnson

Inst PT	Hegg, Barbara	B	36,61,63B,60
Inst PT	Hegg, Dennis	M	37,47,63,64,65
Prof	Johnson, Eric	D	34,35E
Inst PT	Mortenson, Daniel	M	34,35C
Assoc Prof	Pape, Louis W.	M	13,10,11,32,66

SD0200 Dakota Wesleyan University
Department of Music
1200 W University Ave
Mitchell, SD 57301-4398
(605) 995-2658   Fax: (605) 995-2699
www.dwu.edu
E-mail: cldesmon@dwu.edu

4 Year Institution

Chair: Clinton J. Desmond, 80A

PT	Berens, Brad	M	37
FT	Desmond, Clinton J.	DMA	36,11,20,60,12
PT	Leffert, Kristine Lund	M	66,31
PT	Logan, Elizabeth	B	61
PT	Pekas, Joe F.	B	63,64

SD0300 Mount Marty College
Department of Music
1105 W 8th St
Yankton, SD 57078
(605) 668-1539   Fax: (605) 668-1607
www.mtmc.edu
E-mail: sean.vogt@mtmc.edu

4 Year Institution

Division Chair: James Simmons, 80A
Coordinator: Sean F. Vogt, 80A

Prof Emeritus	Klimisch, Mary J.	D	10,13J,66A,66G
Prof PT	Lillie, Erin	M	61
Asst Prof PT	Rettedal, Dean	M	37,60B,47,63,64
Adj	Toscano, Patricia	M	61,66A,66G,31A
Asst Prof	Vogt, Sean F.	D	60A,36,66G,32D,40

SD0400 Northern State University
Department of Music and Theatre
1200 S Jay St
Aberdeen, SD 57401
(605) 626-2497   Fax: (605) 626-2263
www.northern.edu/
E-mail: lafavea@northern.edu

4 Year Institution
Member of NASM

Dean: Alan LaFave, 80A
Chair: Boyd Perkins, 80A

Asst Prof	Beckler, Terry	D	65,50,37,46,11
Asst Prof	Bultema, Darci A.	D	11,61,39
Prof	Faflak, Marcela	D	66A,66B,66C
Asst Prof	Hemke, Frederic J. B.	M	47,48,64,29A
Prof	Jacobson, Allan	D	13,10A,66A,66G
Prof	LaFave, Alan	D	64C,60B
Prof	Manhart, Grant L.	D	49,63A,63B,11,46
Assoc Prof	Perkins, Boyd	D	63C,63D,37,60B,72
Inst	Skyles, Michael	M	61,54
Asst Prof	VanGent, Wendy	D	32,70
Assoc Prof	Vodnoy, Robert L.	D	12A,62,38,51,35E
Prof	Wieland, William	D	13,66D,66A,34,10
Assoc Prof	Woods, Timothy E.	D	60A,12A,36,61,40

SD0450 Sioux Falls Seminary
Department of Music
2100 S Summit Ave
Sioux Falls, SD 57105-2729
(605) 336-6588   Fax: (605) 335-9090
www.sfseminary.edu
E-mail: tfaszer@sfseminary.edu

Graduate Seminary

Master of Arts, Master of Divinity in Worship Leadership

Chair: Ted Faszer, 80A

Adj	Bill, Darlene	M	66G
Prof	Faszer, Ted	D	32,36,31A,34
Adj	Houts, Janice	M	66A

SD0500 South Dakota Schl of Mines & Tech
Division of Music
501 E Saint Joseph St
Rapid City, SD 57701-3995
(605) 394-2433   Fax: (605) 394-6124
music.sdsmt.edu
E-mail: james.feiszli@sdsmt.edu

4 Year Institution

Director: James D. Feiszli, 80A

Inst	Drobnak, Kenneth Paul	DMA	63D,37,11,47,49
Prof	Feiszli, James D.	D	12A,36,55D,61
Inst	Johnson, Christopher R.	M	70
Inst	MacInnes, James	M	66A
Inst	Schnittgrund, Tammy	M	51

SD0550 South Dakota State University
Department of Music
Lincoln Music Hall/Box 2212
Brookings, SD 57007
(605) 688-5187   Fax: (605) 688-4307
www.sdstate.edu/mus/
E-mail: paul.reynolds@sdstate.edu

4 Year Institution
Member of NASM

Dean: Dennis Papini, 80A
Chair: David Reynolds, 80A
Dir., Artist/Performance Series: John M. Walker, 80F

Inst PT	Beloncik, Anne	M	61
Assoc Prof	Brawand, John	D	11,12A,38,62
Inst	Coull, James	M	37,70,13
Prof	Crowe, Don R.	D	32,63C,72,35
Prof	Diddle, Laura D.	D	32B,32D,36
Asst Prof	Jorgensen, Nathan A.	D	47,64C,64D
Prof	Lis, Anthony	D	13,10F,10,66,20D
Inst PT	McCurdy, Robert	M	29A,47
Asst Prof	Peterson, Eric	D	63D,37,60B
Asst Prof	Ragsdale, Aaron	D	37,65,50
Prof	Reynolds, David	D	12C,63A,63B
Inst	Schantz, Cory Neal	D	61,36,60A
Assoc Prof	Toronto, Emily Wood	D	39,61,54
Assoc Prof	Walker, John M.	D	13,66A
Inst PT	Walker, Mary	M	66D
Asst Prof	Walsh, Michael	D	64C,12A,12C
Asst Prof	Yonce, Tammy Evans	D	11,12A,64A,20

SD0580 Univ of Sioux Falls
Department of Music
1101 W 22nd St
Sioux Falls, SD 57105-1600
(605) 331-6637   Fax: (605) 331-6615
www.usiouxfalls.edu
E-mail: Nancy.Wilcoxson@usiouxfalls.edu

4 Year Institution

Music Contact: Nancy Wilcoxson, 80A

Inst PT	Bearid, Rolyn	M	63D,63C
Inst PT	Casey, Marian	M	62D
Asst Prof	DeHoogh-Kliewer, David	M	60A,11,32D,36,40
Inst PT	Egan, Lora	B	65A,65B
Inst PT	Flower, Carol	M	66A,66C,66B
Inst PT	Goeller, Dan	B	34,32F
Inst PT	Harchanko, Lois	M	61
Inst PT	Hawkinson, Jennifer	M	64A
Inst PT	Larson, Angela	M	64C
Inst PT	McDowell, Robert	M	63B
Inst PT	Morris, Matt	M	63A
Inst PT	Morrison, Amy	M	61
Asst Prof	Neiderhiser, Jonathan	D	37,47,32E,13B,13C
Inst PT	Okins, Ann	M	32A,32B
Inst PT	Peters, Maria	M	62A,62B
Inst PT	Rygg, Beth	M	64B
Inst PT	Shotwell, Amanda	M	64E
Inst PT	Stehly, Theresa	M	61
Inst PT	Tomkins, John	M	64D
Inst PT	Vanderlinde, David	M	70
Inst PT	Vorhes, Anna	M	62E
Asst Prof	Wilcoxson, Nancy	M	13A,61,36,11,12A

SD0600 Univ of South Dakota
Department of Music
CFA114
414 E Clark St
Vermillion, SD 57069-2307
(605) 677-5274   Fax: (605) 677-5988
www.usd.edu/music
E-mail: Timothy.Farrell@usd.edu

4 Year Institution, Graduate School
Member of NASM

Master of Music in Performance, Master of Music in Music Education, Master of Music in History of Musical Instruments, Master of Music in Music History

Chair: Timothy P. Farrell, 80A
Dir., Graduate Studies: David V. Moskowitz, 80C
Dir., Summer Programs: Jonathan Alvis, 80G

Asst Prof	Alvis, Jonathan	D	63D,37,63C
Prof	Banks, Margaret	D	71
Inst PT	Farrell, Heidi	M	64B,48
Prof	Farrell, Timothy P.	D	47
Assoc Prof	Fett, Darlene L.	D	32
Asst Prof	Gagnon, Marie-Elaine	D	11,51,62C,41
Asst Prof	Gesteland, Tracelyn K.	D	61,39
Prof	Gray, Susan Keith	D	66A,66B,66C,66D
Asst Prof	Hendrickson, Brandon P.	M	61,39
Inst PT	Hilson, Mike	B	70
Asst Prof	Holdhusen, David	D	60A,36,61
Asst Prof	Kim, Eunho	D	62A,62B,51
Prof	Klauss, Sabine	D	71
Inst PT	Klinghammer, John	D	64C
Assoc Prof	Kocher, Christopher John	D	47,64E,53,46,29
Inst PT	Kocher, Stephanie	M	64A
Prof	Koster, John	B	71,72
Prof	Larson, Andre	D	71,16
Asst Prof	Lombardi, Paul	D	13A,13G,10F,10A,13B
Prof	Moskowitz, David V.	D	12A,20H,14C,12C,11
Assoc Prof	Olson, Rolf	D	37,47,49,63A,46
Assoc Prof	Reeves, Gary L.	D	60B,13G,37,63B
Prof	Rognstad, Richard	D	38,13A,62D,13C,11
Prof	Schou, Larry B.	D	66G,66H,20
Prof	Skyrm, Susanne L.	D	66A,66C,66D,66E
Inst PT	Thomas, Loretta	M	64D
Assoc Prof	Wadley, Darin J.	D	65,50,13A,13C,38
Assoc Prof Emeritus	Yarbrough, Stephen	D	13A,13G,10F,10A,13B

TN0050 Austin Peay State University
Department of Music
PO Box 4625
Clarksville, TN 37044
(931) 221-7818   Fax: (931) 221-7529
www.apsu.edu/music
E-mail: rosed@apsu.edu

4 Year Institution, Graduate School
Member of NASM

Master of Music in Performance, Master of Music in Conducting, Master of Music in Music Education

Chair: Douglas Rose, 80A

Asst Prof	Branscome, Eric	PhD	32,33
Adj	Breckling, Molly	M	11
Adj	Carver, Sylvia	B	11,66A
Adj	Conklin-Bishop, Lisa	M	61,39
Asst Prof	Crane, Emily Hanna	D	62A,62B
Adj	Dueker, Hollie	B	11,61
Adj	Esquillin, June		11
Asst Prof	Foster, Korre	D	36,60A
Prof Emeritus	Frank, Gloria	D	32,11
Prof	Glass, Anne	M	13A,66A,66G,66C
Adj	Guillen, Seth	M	70
Prof	Halbeck, Patricia	D	66A,66B,66C,66D
Adj	Horner, Brian	B	64E
Prof	King, Thomas R.	D	39,61
Asst Prof	Lara, Elizabeth K.	D	62C,13,62D,62B
Prof	Mabry, Sharon	D	61
Prof	Massinon, Francis	M	11,63B
Adj	Morrow, Lance	M	11
Staff	Padelford, Anne Marie	M	66C
Adj	Paull, Eric	M	11
Adj	Repass, Deidre	M	11
Adj	Ritter, Michael F.	M	11
Prof	Robinson-Oturu, Gail M.	D	61
Asst Prof	Schnettler, John	M	37
Adj	Scudder, Howard	M	11
Prof	Silverberg, Ann L.	D	12A,12,14,11
Adj	Smith, Susan	M	63C
Prof	Steffen, Richard	M	60B,49,63A,47,11
Prof	Steinquest, David	M	13,50,65
Adj	Vivio, Christopher J.	D	63D,11
Asst Prof	Wang, Mingzhe	M	64C,11
Assoc Prof	Wolynec, Gregory J.	D	37,38,10F
Prof	Wolynec, Lisa	D	11,64A
Prof	Wood, Jeffrey	D	13,10,66A,66D,20G
Prof	Yates, Stanley	D	70
Asst Prof	Zyko, Jeanette	D	11,64B,64D

TN0100 Belmont University
School of Music
1900 Belmont Blvd
Nashville, TN 37212-3757
(615) 460-6408   Fax: (615) 386-0239
www.belmont.edu/music
E-mail: cynthia.curtis@belmont.edu

4 Year Institution, Graduate School
Member of NASM

Master of Music in Composition, Master of Music in Performance, Master of Music in Church Music, Master of Music in Music Education, Master of Music in Pedagogy, Master of Music in Commercial Music

Dean: Cynthia R. Curtis, 80A
Dir., Graduate Studies: Kristie B. Elsberry, 80C
Associate Dir., Graduate Studies: Terry Klefstad, 80C
Assoc. Dean, Academic Studies: Madeline Bridges, 80H
Assoc. Dean, Performance Studies: Jeff Kirk, 80H

PT	Aber, Stephen	M	66A,66C
PT	Abrams, Paul E.	B	70
FT	Adlington, Stephanie	M	61
FT	Allen, Nancy	M	61,54
Assoc Prof	Ames, Jeffrey	D	36,60A
PT	Austin, Melissa	B	61
PT	Bela, Marcin	D	13
Assoc Prof	Belfiglio, Anthony	D	66A,13B
Inst FT	Bennett, Bruce	M	61
FT	Bennett, Elena	M	66A
FT	Beresford, Rick		35B
FT	Bond, Lawrence	D	61
PT	Booze, Leanna	D	64B
FT	Bridges, David	D	12F,31A
Prof	Bridges, Madeline	D	32,36
PT	Brown, Susan E.	M	66A,66C
FT	Bunn, Greg	D	66G
FT	Burks, Jo Lynn	M	61,54
FT	Byrd, Donald	M	13A
PT	Caldwell, William	D	36,60
PT	Casteel, Mike	B	63A
PT	Causey, Wayne	M	31A
PT	Chiavola, Kathy	M	61
PT	Cies-Muckala, Jennifer	D	12
PT	Clark, Bryan	D	10
Assoc Prof	Coleman, Jennifer	D	61
PT	Contreras, Billy	B	62A
PT	Cote, Sarah	M	62B
Prof	Curtis, Cynthia R.	D	32
PT	DaSilva, Mario	M	70
PT	Davidian, Joseph	M	66A
PT	Davis, Stephen	B	70,72
PT	Dickenson, Stephanie	M	62D
Asst Prof	Dudley, Bruce	M	66A,35B,53
Asst Prof	Dudley, Sandra	M	36,61,35B

Prof	Elsberry, Kristie B.	D	13,66A,66G
Asst Prof	Eng, Clare Sher Ling	D	13,13B,13D,63B,66A
Prof	Entsminger, Deen	D	13,10,32C,36,34
PT	Fey, Alan	M	13C
FT	Fisher, Jocelyn	B	61,35B
PT	Fogarty, Rachel	M	66A,66D
PT	Forester, Julie	M	61
PT	Frederick, Amy	M	66
PT	Fry, Laura	D	12
FT	George, Mary	M	61
FT	Gleckler, Megan	M	36,61
PT	Godwin, L. Mark	B	70
Prof Emeritus	Godwin, Paul M.	D	13,10F,10,34
PT	Goebel, Ellen Tift	M	61,35B
PT	Gooding, Alison	M	62A
Asst Prof	Graham, Alexander	D	64E,60B
Prof	Gregg, Robert B.	D	60,11,12A,38
PT	Haffner, Paula	M	62E
Assoc Prof	Halbert, Marjorie	M	61,54
Inst PT	Harmon, Linda	M	66A,66D
PT	Hartley, Dawn	M	64D
PT	Henderson, Paul	M	70
Prof	Hoffman, Richard	D	67C,13,55B
PT	Johnian, Paul	M	42
PT	Johnson, Elizabeth	B	36,61
FT	Kemp, Todd	M	65,13B
Prof Emeritus	Kimmel, Jim	M	36,60,32C
Assoc Prof	Kirk, Jeff	M	47,64E,35B
Asst Prof	Klefstad, Kristian I.	D	66A,66B,66D
Assoc Prof	Klefstad, Terry	D	12,14
Assoc Prof	Kraus, Barry N.	D	37,32E,60B
Asst Prof	Lamothe, Peter	D	12,14
FT	Lamothe, Virginia Christy	D	12A
Assoc Prof	Landes, Daniel	D	13A,13,66A,66D,31A
PT	Lassiter, Stan	M	70
PT	Lochrie, Daniel	D	64C,48
FT	London, Todd	M	65,35B
PT	MacCallum, Jeanette	M	13
PT	Madeira, David	M	13
Prof	Marler, Robert	D	66A,11,12A
Inst	Mason, Keith	M	34
PT	Mauldin, Steve	M	34
FT	McKay, David	M	66D
PT	McLain, Michael	B	70,53,35B
PT	Miller, Anna Maria	M	32E
Prof	Moore, Keith	D	61
PT	Nelson, Craig	B	62D
PT	Nelson, Paul	M	62C
PT	Nicholas, Keith	M	62C
PT	Nitti, Adam	B	62D
Prof	Norton, Christopher S.	D	50,65
PT	Oyen-Larsen, Valerie	M	61
PT	Palmer, Nicholas	M	70
Inst	Paradise, Kathryn L.	M	61,54
PT	Patton, David	B	35D
PT	Patton, Denise	B	35
Inst	Pell, John	B	70,35B
PT	Perry, Francis	M	70
PT	Petchulat, David	B	72
PT	Phillips, Jeffrey T.	M	63C
Assoc Prof	Pursell, William	D	10,12A,13,11,66G
PT	Ramsay, Susan	M	32
PT	Risinger, Andrew	M	66D,66G
PT	Roberts, Patricia	M	61
PT	Rogers King, Tammy	B	62A
PT	Rogers, Jefferson	M	62D
PT	Rusu, Radu	M	63B
PT	Shadinger, Marilyn	M	13C
Prof	Shadinger, Richard C.	D	12A,55,66A,31A,69
Assoc Prof	Shamburger, David	M	61,54
PT	Silverman, Tracy	B	62A
Asst Prof	Small, Elisabeth	M	41,62A,51
Inst	Smiley, Henry	M	61,54
PT	Spicher, Buddy	B	62
PT	Stanton, Zachary K.	DMA	10A,10F
PT	Thompson, Chester	B	65,35B,47
PT	Thompson, Robert	M	70,41
PT	Treybig, Carolyn	D	64A
Assoc Prof	Treybig, Joel	D	63A,13B
PT	Valeras, Michael	M	70
PT	Virelles, Amanda	D	66A
PT	Vivio, Chris	D	63D
FT	Vogt, Roy	M	70,53,35B
PT	Volker, Alyssa	M	61
Asst Prof	Volker, Mark D.	D	10,10A,10B,13C
PT	Wade, Patsy	M	29A
Assoc Prof	Warren, Jane	D	36,60A
PT	Watson, Derico	B	65
Assoc Prof	Whitten, Kristi	D	39,61,66
FT	Wigginton, James R.	B	61
PT	Willets, Steve	B	66A
Prof	Wylie, Ted	D	61,31A,54,39
PT	Yankeelov, Margie L.	M	13C
PT	Zoro,	B	65

TN0150 Bethel University

Division of Music
325 Cherry Ave
McKenzie, TN 38201
(731) 352-6416   Fax: (731) 352-6444
www.bethelu.edu
E-mail: everettb@bethelu.edu

4 Year Institution

Prof	Cross, Alan E.	D	11,12A,61,31A
Adj Inst	Grant, Tom	M	63A,63B
Asst Prof	Herris, Keith	D	66,13B
Adj Inst	Martin, Danny Ray	M	70,42,29,41
Adj Inst	McLemore, Jeff	M	64
Lect	Oakley, Tom	M	37,47,32H,10F
Adj Inst	Presson, Lucy	M	63D,63C
Asst Prof	Smith, Joshua D.	D	37,65,13A,50
Asst Prof	Smith, Tony L.	D	35A,35E,35F,10D

TN0200 Bryan College

Department of Music
721 Bryan Dr
Dayton, TN 37321
(423) 775-7289   Fax: (423) 775-7317
www.bryan.edu
E-mail: wilhoime@bryan.edu

4 Year Institution

Chair & Dir., Artist/Performance Series: Mel R. Wilhoit, 80A,80F
Dir., Institute/Festival/Workshop: David Luther, 80F

Prof	Keck, Kimberly	D	36,39,61,60A,13
Prof	Luther, David	D	60,36,61,31A,41
Prof	Luther, Sigrid	D	13,66A,66B,31A,66C
Prof	Wilhoit, Mel R.	D	10F,12A,32,49,63

TN0250 Carson-Newman College

Department of Music
CNC Box 72048
1620 Russell Ave
Jefferson City, TN 37760
(865) 471-3328   Fax: (865) 471-4849
www.cn.edu
E-mail: jbuckner@cn.edu

4 Year Institution
Member of NASM

Chair & Dir., Summer Programs: Jeremy Buckner, 80A,80G
Dir., Artist/Performance Series: Richard J. Scruggs, 80F

Inst PT	Benne, Steven	M	62D
Asst Prof	Bivens, Pat	M	11,47,63C,48,37
Inst PT	Brock, John	M	66G
Inst PT	Bryerton, Andrew	M	62C
Asst Prof	Buckner, Jeremy	D	32B,32C,66A,66D,11
Inst PT	Cloutier, Glenda L.	M	63A
Assoc Prof	Fogg, Ryan	D	66A,66D,66B,66C
Inst PT	Greene, Sean	M	63D
Inst PT	Harrell, Mark	M	63B
Assoc Prof	Holder, Angela	D	61,36,31,11
Assoc Prof	Hussung, Mark	D	66A,66D
Prof	Jones, Ann A.	M	36,61,60A
Prof	Measels, Clark	D	11,31A,20
Prof	Milligan, Thomas	D	13,12A,66A,34
Inst PT	Pulgar, Edward	M	62
	Pulgar, Mary		62
Assoc Prof	Scruggs, Richard J.	D	11,13B,41,48,64E
Inst PT	Scruggs, Tara A.	D	13A,64C
Inst PT	Stock, Jesse	M	36,61,60A,54
Inst PT	Swilley, Sue	D	64A
Prof	Thorsen, Eric	D	32,36,60
Inst PT	Weyer, Matthew	M	65,50
Librarian	Wright, Julie		16

TN0260 Chattanooga State Comm Coll
Department of Music
4501 Amnicola Hwy
Chattanooga, TN 37406-1018
(423) 697-3383   Fax: (423) 697-2444
www.chattanoogastate.edu
E-mail: ken.cardillo@chattanoogastate.edu

2 Year Institution

Chair, Fine Arts: Kenneth Cardillo, 80A

Adj	Anderson, Eric	M	64D
Asst Prof	Arbogast, Jennifer	D	11,13C,54,61,39
Prof	Cardillo, Kenneth	PhD	70,13,11,12B
Adj	Creel, David	M	11,62A
Adj	Feltner, Tiffany	M	63B
Adj	Hale, Adam	B	70
Adj	Hartline, Nicholas	M	64C,48
Adj	Hassevoort, Christine	M	61,11
Assoc Prof	Hassevoort, Darrin	M	36,61,47,60,54
Adj	Hyberger, Brett	M	61,11,39
Asst Prof	Hyberger, Sarah Amanda	D	11,13C,54,61,39
Adj	McDonald, Janelle	B	66A
Adj	Miller, Eric	M	63C
Prof	Nichols, Alan	D	66A,13A,11
Adj	Schwab, David	M	46,62D,66C
Adj	Solfest-Wallis, Cindy	M	11,64A
Adj	Vogler, Paul	M	34,65
Adj	Walters, David	M	29,66A
Adj	Wileman, Harv	M	11,61
Adj	Wilhoit, Mel	D	11

TN0300 Cleveland State Community College
Department of Music
PO Box 3570
Cleveland, TN 37320-3570
(423) 473-2311   Fax: (423) 478-6255
www.clevelandstatecc.edu
E-mail: wbenson@clevelandstatecc.edu

2 Year Institution

Chair & Dir., Artist/Performance Series: Will Benson, 80A,80F

Asst Prof	Benson, Will	M	11,13,34B,36,64
PT	Bindrim, Don	M	34,46
Assoc Prof	Dale, Karen M.	M	11,34B,36,54,61
PT	Michaels, Ben	B	70
PT	Randolph, Margaret Ann	M	66A,66C
PT	Royal, Jacquelyn A.	M	11,13,16,34B

TN0350 Columbia State Community College
Department of Music
PO Box 1315
Columbia, TN 38401
(931) 540-2722
www.columbiastate.edu/
E-mail: lee@columbiastate.edu

2 Year Institution

Adj	Adams, Marilyn		
Adj	Freeman, Dowyal		
Assoc Prof	Lee, Mark	D	37
Adj	Scheusner, Marsha		
Adj	Scheusner, Ronald		
Adj	Schulz, Maria		
Adj	Swiatek, Thomas		
Adj	Tucker, Laura		

TN0450 Dyersburg State Community College
Department of Music
1510 Lake Rd
Dyersburg, TN 38025-0648
(731) 285-6910 x 256   Fax: (731) 286-3333
www.dscc.edu
E-mail: cfeather@dscc.edu

2 Year Institution

PT	Cates, Mike		65,50
Prof	Feather, Carol Ann	D	13,11,38,63B
PT	Grunert, Judi	B	61
PT	Hernon, Bonnie	B	63A
PT	Hernon, Mike	D	63B
PT	Jones, Betty McLellan	B	66G
PT	King, Linda	M	66A
PT	Koons, Jessie	B	70
PT	Okpebhola, Dorthy White	M	62B
PT	Schlabach, Robert	M	64A,64B,64C,64E
PT	Speck, R. Floyd	M	36,46
PT	Vance, Howard		70
PT	Wilburn, Tricia	B	62A
PT	Willard, David	M	61

TN0500 East Tennessee State University
Department of Music
PO Box 70661
Johnson City, TN 37614
(423) 439-4270   Fax: (423) 439-4290
www.etsu.edu/music
E-mail: music@etsu.edu

4 Year Institution
Member of NASM

Chair: Frank J. Grzych, 80A

Assoc Prof	Blackman, Mary Dave	D	11,32C
Prof	Caton, Benjamin D.	D	13C,66A,66B
Prof	Champouillon, David	D	63A,46,29
Assoc Prof	Deadman, Alison Patricia	D	12A,64C
Prof	Grzych, Frank J.	D	60,32C
Asst Prof	Hu, Chih-Long	D	66A,66B
Prof Emeritus	Jenrette, Thomas S.	D	36,61,60
Asst Prof	Killmeyer, Heather N.	D	64B,12A,11,64D
Prof	Niederberger, Maria	D	13,10F,10
Asst Prof	Oh, Sun-Joo	D	61,39
Prof	Paluzzi, Rebecca Lile	M	48,64A
Assoc Prof	Sanderbeck, Rande	D	50,65
Asst Prof	Stevens, Alan E.	D	36,61
Assoc Prof	Zembower, Christian M.	D	63D,37,60B

TN0550 Fisk University
Department of Music
1000 17th Ave N
Nashville, TN 37208-3051
(615) 329-8702   Fax: (615) 329-8850
www.fisk.edu
E-mail: pautry@fisk.edu

4 Year Institution, Historically Black College
Member of NASM

Chair: Philip E. Autry, 80A
Dir., Humanities & Fine Arts: Lean'tin Bracks, 80A

Assoc Prof	Autry, Philip E.	D	66A,66B,66C,66D
	Davis, Garnett R.	M	63D
PT	Duke, Christopher A.	M	36
Lect	Kwami, Paul T.	M	20,36,66G,60A,66D
PT	Lassiter, Stan	M	70
Asst Prof	Mellins-Bumbulis, Valija	M	39,61
	Merideth, Sherry Francis	M	62
Assoc Prof	Nash, Gary Powell	D	10,13,47,64,10F
PT	Newby, Linda	M	61
PT	Pendergrast, Celine	M	64A
Asst Prof	Stofko, Diane L.	D	32,11,37,13A,60B
Assoc Prof	Williams, Anthony E.	D	66G

TN0580 Free Will Baptist Bible College
Department of Music
3606 West End Ave
Nashville, TN 37205
(615) 844-5000   Fax: (615) 269-6028
www.fwbbc.edu
E-mail: jstevens@fwbbc.edu

4 Year Institution

Chair: James M. Stevens, 80A

Adj Prof	Benton, Lisa	M	32,61
Adj Prof	Butler, Carol	M	66A,66B,66D
Inst	Fair, Carly	B	61

Adj Prof	Hahn, David	M	12A,34,35A,36,60
Adj Prof	Laarz, Bill	M	37,38,41,63
Inst	Martin, Jared	B	70,13A,31A
Adj Prof	Merrit, Doug	M	13C,62A,62B
Prof	Shipley, Linda P.	D	13,66A,66G
Prof	Stevens, James M.	D	10A,36,13E,13B

TN0600 Hiwassee College

Department of Music
225 Hiwassee College Dr
Madisonville, TN 37354
(423) 442-2001
www.hiwassee.edu
E-mail: eleazera@hiwassee.edu

2 Year Resident Liberal Arts Institution/Methodist Affiliated

Music Contact: Teresa McClellan, 80A

Asst Prof	Eleazer, Alan G.	M	36,40,11
Asst Prof	Jung, Eunsuk	D	13A,66A,66D,66G,13B
Lect	McClellan, Teresa	M	12A,61

TN0650 Johnson University

Department of Music
7900 Johnson Dr
Knoxville, TN 37998-0001
(865) 573-4517   Fax: (865) 251-2337
www.jbc.edu
E-mail: dtrent@johnsonu.edu

4 Year Institution

Chair: Donald R. Trentham, 80A

Prof	Chambers, Robert B.	D	60,61,31A,36,44
Inst PT	Moore, Sharon	M	66A
Prof	Trentham, Donald R.	M	11,12A,66A,31A,13
Asst Prof	Weaver, Brent	M	36,37,34,13

TN0700 Knoxville College

Department of Art/Music/Theatre
901 College St
Knoxville, TN 37921-4724
(423)524-6578   Fax: (423)524-6686
www.knoxvillecollege.edu/

4 Year Institution, Historically Black College

| PT | Coleman, Lilian | B | 36,66A |
| PT | Rule, Charles | M | 11,47,66A,29,35 |

TN0800 Lane College

Department of Music
545 Lane Ave
Jackson, TN 38301-4501
(901) 426-7543   Fax: (901) 427-3987
www.lanecollege.edu
E-mail: Mlewis@lanecollege.edu

4 Year Institution, Historically Black College

Chair: William B. Garcia, 80A

Assoc Prof	Dixon, Howard	M	13A,11,32B,63,64
Prof	Garcia, William B.	D	60,11,36,61,31A
Prof	Nelson, Allison	D	66A
Assoc Prof	Sampson, Kenneth C.	M	10F,32B,32C,37,63

TN0850 Lee University

School of Music
PO Box 3450
Cleveland, TN 37320-3450
(423) 614-8240   Fax: (423) 614-8242
www.leeuniversity.edu
E-mail: lholden@leeuniversity.edu

4 Year Institution, Graduate School
Member of NASM

Master of Music in Performance, Master of Music in Music Education, Master of Church Music

Chair & Dir., Undergraduate Studies: LuAnn Holden, 80A,80B
Dean: Stephen W. Plate, 80A
Chair & Dir., Undergraduate Studies: Phillip E. Thomas, 80A,80B
Dir., Graduate Studies: Ronald S. Brendel, 80C
Dir., Graduate Studies: Brad Moffett, 80C
Dir., Graduate Studies: Linda K. Thompson, 80C
Dir., Music Events & Special Projects: Nadine Goff, 80F
Dir., Instrumental Project: Winona Holsinger, 80G
Dean: William Green

Asst Prof	An, Ning	M	66A,66C
Assoc Prof	Bailey, Mark	D	13,32E,32C,37
Adj	Brendel, Cheryl M.	M	61,39
Asst Prof	Brendel, Ronald S.	DMA	61,39
Prof	Burns, Jim	D	11,61,31A
Asst Prof	Chien, Gloria	D	13C,13E,66A,66B
Assoc Prof	Deaton, Tony	M	61,39
Asst Prof	Dismukes, Andrea J.	D	61
Asst Prof	Frost, James	M	39,40,61
Asst Prof	Green, William	M	36,40,60A
Asst Prof	Holden, LuAnn	M	32,12A,36
Assoc Prof	Holsinger, David	D	60B,10,48
Asst Prof	Horton, Virginia	M	12A,61
Lect	Linton, Andrew	M	16,70
Asst Prof	Mauldin, Walter	D	60A,31A
Lect	Mears, Perry G.	M	66A,66C
Asst Prof	Moffett, Brad	D	36,31A,60A
Assoc Prof	Morehead, Phillip H.	M	13,41,63A,32E
Adj	Moye, Brenda	D	64E,41,34
Asst Prof	Patty, Austin T.	PhD	13A,13B,13C,13D
Prof	Plate, Stephen W.	D	38,60,32E,13B,13A
Asst Prof	Sheeks, Randy	M	66A,31A
Lect	Songer, Loralee	M	60A,36,61
Prof	Thomas, Phillip E.	D	13,12,38,66A
Asst Prof	Thompson, Linda K.	D	32A,32B,32C,32G
Adj	Ward, Michael	M	66A,13C
Asst Prof	Warner, Douglas G.	D	11,63D,13B,13C,63C
Inst	Wyatt, Alan	M	13,47,64E,35A,35B
Adj	Wyatt, Paula	B	47,66A
Asst Prof	Yu, Xiaoqing	M	62A,62B,41

TN0900 Lincoln Memorial University

Department of Fine Arts/Music
6965 Cumberland Gap Pkwy
Harrogate, TN 37752
(423) 869-3611   Fax: (423) 869-6426
www.lmunet.edu
E-mail: candace.armstrong@lmunet.edu

4 Year Institution

Chair: Sean Greene, 80A

Asst Prof	Armstrong, Candace	M	13C,36,60A,66A,11
Adj	Bray, Erin	M	64,42,11
Inst	Cook, Jeffrey	M	63B,12A,42,11
Adj	Disney, Dale	M	65
PT	Gilbert, David	B	66F
Asst Prof	Greene, Sean	D	63D,13,37,32,42
Adj	Hannah, Barry	M	70,42

TN0930 Lipscomb University

Department of Music
One University Park Dr
Nashville, TN 37204-3951
(615) 966-5932   Fax: (615) 966-7620
music.lipscomb.edu
E-mail: sally.reid@lipscomb.edu

4 Year Institution
Member of NASM

Chair: Sally Reid, 80A
Dir., Artist/Performance Series: Jerome A. Reed, 80F
Associate Chair: Marcia A. Hughes, 80H

Prof Emeritus	Griffith, Larry D.	D	60A,32C,36,61,32D
Adj Prof	Holeman, Janet	M	39,61
Prof	Hughes, Marcia A.	D	12A,32B,66A,66D
Inst	King, Donna Moore	M	11,66A,66D,69
Adj Prof	Magnuson, John	D	31
Adj Prof	Magyar, Paul R.	D	12,31
Adj Prof	Meadows, Erin	M	13A,13C
Adj Prof	Miller, Jean	M	61
Adj Prof	Newton, Jeanne	M	32,64
Adj Prof	Ramirez, Miguel	D	12
Prof	Reed, Jerome A.	D	10A,66A,66B,66C,43
Prof	Reid, Sally	D	10,13,64B,10C,34
Prof	Rhodes, Steve	D	60B,32E,37,47,63D
Adj Prof	Wan, Agnes	D	66
Prof	Wilson, Gary P.	D	60A,32C,36,61,32D

TN0950 Martin Methodist College
Department of Music
433 W Madison St
Pulaski, TN 38478-2716
(931) 363-7456   Fax: (931) 363-9818
www.martinmethodist.edu
E-mail: ahughes@martinmethodist.edu

2 Year Institution

Chair: Albert C. Hughes, 80A

Asst Prof	Engel, T. G.	D	70
Prof	Hughes, Albert C.	D	13,11,12A,36,61

TN1000 Maryville College
Department of Music
502 E Lamar Alexander Pkwy
Maryville, TN 37804-5907
(865) 981-8150   Fax: (865) 273-8873

www.maryvillecollege.edu/academics/divisions/finearts/index.asp
E-mail: bill.swann@maryvillecollege.edu

4 Year Liberal Arts College, Affiliated with Presbyterian Church (USA)
Member of NASM

Coordinator: Mark Hall, 80A
Chair: William E. Swann, 80A

Inst PT	Acuff, Rachel	M	64B
Inst PT	Burell, J. Ashley	M	66G,66H
Inst PT	Massie Legg, Alicia	M	61,12A
Assoc Prof	Matascik, Sheri L.	D	13,10,70,10B,13H
Inst PT	McCall, Gina	M	66A,66C
Inst PT	Nagge, Harold	M	70
Inst FT	Olander, Jennifer		66A,66B,66C
Inst PT	Robinson, Bill	M	38,62
Inst PT	Romines, Jeff	M	64E
Inst PT	Romines, Roann	M	64C
Inst FT	Rosevear, Burt L.	M	61,11
Inst PT	Schuetz, Shaun	M	65
Assoc Prof	Smithee, Larry G.	D	60,32,37,47,63
Assoc Prof	Swann, William E.	D	47,13,60B,29B,10D
Inst FT	Wilner, Stacey	M	12A,36,11,60A

TN1100 Middle Tennessee State University
School of Music
1301 E Main St
PO Box 47
Murfreesboro, TN 37132
(615) 898-2469   Fax: (615) 898-5037
www.mtsumusic.com
E-mail: griordan@mtsu.edu

4 Year Institution, Graduate School
Member of NASM

Master of Arts in Composition, Master of Arts in Performance, Master of Arts in Music Education, Master of Arts in Conducting, Master of Arts in Musicology, Master of Arts in Jazz Studies, Master of Arts Collaborative Piano/Instrumental or Vocal, Master of Arts in Composition for Contemporary Media

Director: George T. Riordan, 80A
Dir., Graduate Studies: Stephen Shearon, 80C
Assistant Director: Felicia M. Miyakawa, 80H

PT	Abrams, Paul E.	B	70
Prof	Aliquo, Don	M	29,64E,46,47
Prof Emerita	Allsbrook, Nancy Boone	D	32
Asst Prof	Arndt, Michael J.	D	63A,49
PT	Arndt, Sandra K.	M	66D
PT	Baratto, German	M	65
PT	Bartos, Titus	M	66D
PT	Baskin, Stanley	D	
Inst	Bela, Marcin	D	10,66A,66D
PT	Bell, Paula	B	66D
PT	Blooding, Karen	M	32B
PT	Briley, Crystal		61
PT	Brown, Robert W.		11
Librarian	Brown, Sarah	M	16
Prof	Bundage, Raphael	D	36,39,60A
Assoc Prof	Cancryn, Dina	M	61
PT	Castilla, Carlos	D	11
PT	Coil, Pat		66A,29,42
Asst Prof	Cornish, Craig S.	M	37
Assoc Prof	Davila, Gerardo	M	50,65
PT	Davila, Julia		65
Asst Prof	Dawson, Andrea	D	62A,51,11
Asst Prof	DeBoer, Angela	M	63B,49,13A,13B,13C
Asst Prof	Dent, Cedric	D	12A,10D,35A,13E
PT	Dunnavant, Jessica Guinn	D	64A,67D,11
PT	Feagans, David	M	11
PT	Ferguson, James W.	M	62D,47,41,61
PT	Ferris, Joe	B	62D
PT	Garretson, Paul	M	65
PT	Geib, Sally	M	11
PT	Gerlach, Brent	D	63C,11
PT	Gheith, Sarabeth	M	11,62
PT	Goodin, Glenda	M	13A,11
PT	Gross, Jeffrey	M	11
PT	Grove, Karla	M	11
PT	Harkness, Lisa	M	11
PT	Hudson, Roger	M	70
Prof	Isley-Farmer, Christine	D	61
PT	King, Amanda	M	11,61
Inst	Lambright, Spencer N.	D	10
PT	Lawson, Tonya	D	64C,64E,64B,11
Prof	Linton, Michael	D	13,10A
Asst Prof	Little, Deanna	M	64A,48
Prof	Loucky, David L.	D	63C,63D,49
PT	Lund, Matthew R.	M	70
PT	McCaffrey, Maureen	M	61
PT	McVey, Elyse Nicole	M	11
Assoc Prof	McWhirter, Jamila L.	D	32D,36,60A
PT	Middagh, Ryan	M	11,47
Assoc Prof	Miles, Benjamin E.	D	63D,34
PT	Milnar, Veronica Edwards	M	66D,66A
Assoc Prof	Miyakawa, Felicia M.	D	12A
Asst Prof	Nadgir, Arunesh N.	D	66A,66B,66C
Assoc Prof	Nies, Carol	D	38,60B
Asst Prof	Osterfield, Paul	D	13,10
PT	Paise, Michele	M	11
Prof Emeritus	Perkins, Jerry	D	66A,41
PT	Phillips, Derrek	M	65
Prof	Pigg, Dewayne	M	11
PT	Poythress, Christine	M	11
PT	Price, Thomas A.	M	11
Prof	Rice-See, Lynn	D	66A,66B,66C
Prof	Riordan, George T.	D	67D,11,64B
PT	Ross, Laura A.	M	48,64B
Assoc Prof	Shearon, Stephen	D	12
Asst Prof	Simmons, James	M	63A,47,46,29A,29B
Assoc Prof	Smith, Stephen	M	61
Assoc Prof	Thomas, Raymond D.	D	32E,37,60B
Inst	Tipps, Angela	M	66G,36,11
Inst	Vannatta-Hall, Jennifer E.	D	32
Assoc Prof	Waldecker, Todd	D	64C,48
PT	Walker, Joseph V.	M	66C
PT	Ward, Patricia	B	66C
Assoc Prof Emeritus	Wells, Paul F.		
PT	Whaley, Daniel M.	M	63A,11
PT	Williams, Christa	M	66D
Prof	Yelverton, William	D	70,42
PT	Zhang, Xiao-Fan	M	62C

TN1150 Milligan College
Music Program
PO Box 500
Milligan College, TN 37682
(423) 461-8723   Fax: (423) 461-8923
www.milligan.edu/music
E-mail: kbrown@milligan.edu

4 Year Institution

Chair: Kellie Dubel Brown, 80A

Asst Prof	Anderson, Charlotte	D	61,36
Assoc Prof	Brown, Kellie Dubel	D	62A,38,12A,60B,62B
Inst PT	Butler, Justin	M	70
Inst PT	Crawford, Tom	M	64C,64E,64A
Inst PT	Dalton, Ed	B	65
Asst Prof	DeLong, Noah	M	36,35C,60A,61
Asst Prof	Elliott, Anne	M	66A,66D,66B,66C,36
Inst PT	Ellison, Rachel	B	61
Inst PT	Fitzgerald, Cheryl	M	62C,62D
Inst PT	Grove-DeJarnett, Doug	M	60
Inst PT	Redman, Suzanne	M	32B
Prof	Runner, David C.	D	13,10F,66A,66G,10A
Assoc Prof	Simerly, Rick	M	63,29,49,47,32E

TN1200 Rhodes College

Department of Music
2000 N Parkway
Memphis, TN 38112-1624
(901) 843-3775   Fax: (901) 843-3789
www.rhodes.edu
E-mail: skoogw@rhodes.edu

4 Year Liberal Arts Institution

Chair: William M. Skoog, 80A
Dir., Artist Series: John Bass, III, 80F

Inst PT	Albert, Laurence	B	61
Inst PT	Assad, Mike	M	65,50,47
Inst PT	Bass, John	D	70,46,47,67G
Asst Prof	Blankenship, Carole	D	11,61
Assoc Prof	Bryant, Thomas E.	D	13,11,66A,66C,66H
Inst PT	Chiego, Sara	M	62D
Inst PT	Cornfoot, James	M	11,12E
Inst PT	Drannon, Andrew	M	34A,10
Inst PT	Feller, Rena	B	64C
Inst PT	Franks, Sandra	D	61
Inst PT	Garcia, Eric	D	65,50
Inst PT	Gilbert, Robert	B	63B
Inst PT	Harr, James	M	61
Assoc Prof	Harter, Courtenay L.	D	13,64B,41
Asst Prof	Kreitner, Mona B.	D	12A,36
Inst PT	Lay, David	B	70
Asst Prof	Montelione, Joseph	D	38,49,42
Inst PT	Neupert, Gina	M	62E,42
Inst PT	Ray, Brian	D	66A
Asst Prof	Rogers, Vanessa	D	12,55
Inst PT	Ross, John	M	70,67G,42
Inst PT	Schranze, Jane	M	62B
Inst PT	Skitch, Todd	B	64A
Assoc Prof	Skoog, William M.	D	36,61
Inst PT	Smith, Debbie	M	66A,66G,11
Inst PT	Stephens, Gerald	B	66A,47
Inst PT	Stimson, Kate	M	66A
Inst PT	Sunda, Robert		62D,47
Inst PT	Vail, Mark	B	63C,63D
Inst PT	Whitehead, Yukiko	D	66A
Inst PT	Whitney, Susanna	B	64D
Inst PT	Wolfe, Carl	B	64E
Inst PT	Yu, Wen-Yih	M	62A
Inst PT	Zombor, Iren	M	62C,42

TN1250 Roane State Community College

Department of Music
276 Patton Ln
Harriman, TN 37748-5011
(865) 882-4580   Fax: (865) 882-4558
www.roanestate.edu

2 Year Institution

Coordinator: Geol Greenlee, 80A

Inst PT	Atkisson, Lovelle	D	11
Inst PT	Barber, Charles	M	61,66A
Inst PT	Dunaway, Lourdes	M	11,66A,70
Inst PT	Eleazer, Alan	M	11
Inst PT	Goslee, Brenda	M	13A,13,11,66A,66G
Assoc Prof	Greenlee, Geol	D	13,66A,10F,10,11
Asst Prof	Luggie, Brenda	M	36,61,11
Inst PT	Nagge, Harold	M	70,53,47,29
Inst PT	Nemeth, Rudolph	M	66A,11
Inst PT	Vincent, Larry	M	11,70

TN1350 Southern Adventist University

School of Music
PO Box 370
Collegedale, TN 37315-0370
(423) 236-2880   Fax: (423) 236-1880
www.southern.edu
E-mail: sball@southern.edu

4 Year Institution
Member of NASM

Dean: W. Scott Ball, 80A
Dir., Artist/Performance Series: Bill Wohlers, 80F

PT	Ashton, J. Bruce	D	10A,31A,66A,10F,66C
Prof	Ball, W. Scott	D	11,12A,62D
Prof	Brown-Kibble, Gennevieve	D	11,36,60A,61
PT	Burks, Robert		64B
PT	Burroughs, John	M	63C,63D
PT	Cochrane, Jan	M	61
Prof	Cooper, Peter	D	13,66A
PT	Duscld, Patricia	M	64D
PT	Elder, Laura	M	62E
Prof	Glass, Judith	M	13,66G,66H,31A
PT	Hansel, Robert	M	70
PT	James, Gordon	M	63B,42
PT	Janzen, Elaine	M	66A,66D,13A
PT	Kile, Nora	M	64A,41
PT	Kuist, Bruce	M	64
PT	Olson, Adrienne	D	
Assoc Prof	Parsons, Kenneth	M	60B,49,37,46,34
Prof	Penner, Julie	D	11,61
Assoc Prof	Redmer Minner, Laurie K.	M	60B,38,51,32C,62B
PT	Reneau, Mark	M	62A,42
PT	Samaan, Sherilyn	M	32B,11,66A
PT	Schmitt, Clinton	M	64E,32E
PT	Silver, Patricia	M	63A,64C
PT	Stroud, James	D	62C
PT	Tejero, Nicolasa	M	64C

TN1380 Southwest Tennessee Comm College

Department of Music
737 Union Ave Room E223
Memphis, TN 38103
(901) 333-5208   Fax: (901) 333-5212
www.southwest.tn.edu
E-mail: mscott@southwest.tn.edu

2 Year Institution

Chair: Barbara Roseborough, 80A

Assoc Prof	Fuller, Lisa	M	61,11
Inst PT	Head, Stan	M	50,65
Prof	Katz, Steve	D	11,66A
Inst PT	Kramer, Kelly B.	M	
Inst PT	Lonardc, Tom	M	11,65
Inst PT	Pellay-Walker, Michelle T.	M	11
Assoc Prof	Pender, Charles	D	13,11,61,66A,60
Assoc Prof	Scott, Michael E.	M	11,47,53

TN1400 Tennessee State University

Department of Music
3500 John A Merritt Blvd
Nashville, TN 37209-1561
(615) 963-5341   Fax: (615) 963-5351
www.tnstate.edu/music
E-mail: relliott@tnstate.edu

4 Year Institution, Graduate School, Historically Black College
Member of NASM

Master of Science in Music Education

Head: Robert L. Elliott, 80A
Dir., Undergraduate Studies: Mark Crawford, 80B
Dir., Undergraduate Studies: Reginald McDonald, 80B
Dir., Undergraduate Studies: Darryl Nettles, 80B
Dir., Undergraduate Studies: Patricia Reeves, 80B
Dir., Preparatory Division: Roderic Bronaugh, 80E

Adj	Bowie, Audrey	M	61
Adj	Bowland, Jimmy	M	64E
Adj	Bronaugh, Roderic	M	11,36
Adj	Bunn, Gregg	D	66G

Adj	Button, James	M	64B
	Castilla, Carlos	D	13B,13C
Adj	Codreanu, Christian	M	11,41,63B
Assoc Prof	Crawford, Mark	D	35A,35B,45
Adj	Crimm, William	M	61
Adj	Crite, Kiera	M	66A
Adj	Crum, Martin	M	11,45
Asst Prof	Daniels, Sean	D	37,50,65
Adj	Davis, Garnett	M	63D
Asst Prof	Davis, Thomas L.	M	11
Adj	Davis, Victor	M	11,36,60
Adj	Deyo, Paul	M	41,63A
Adj	Doyle, Joseph	M	10D
Adj	Durham, Kevin	M	13A,66D,11
Prof	Elliott, Robert L.	D	13B,32,62D,11
Adj	Emerson, Deidre	M	62C,38,51
Adj	Fitzhugh, William	M	11,70
Assoc Prof	Graves, Edward	M	37,32
Adj	Gunter, Patricia	M	64D
Adj	Hackett, Hara	M	64C
Adj	Hallgren, Scott	B	35H,10C
Adj	Harris, Olga	D	10
Adj	Henderson, Paul	M	11,70
Adj	Hood, Jo Ann	M	32
Inst	Isaacs, David	M	70,11,35G,45
Adj	Jones, Maxine	M	66A,66D,11
Asst Prof	King, Vicki B.	D	66A,66D,12A
Adj	Laupp, Belinda	B	64A
Adj	Lohman, Gregg	M	65
Adj	McCaffrey, Maureen	M	11,61,32D,60A
Adj	McCoy, Pamela	M	11
Assoc Prof	McDonald, Reginald	D	32E,37,41,64E
Adj	Morton, Leonard	M	32
Assoc Prof	Nettles, Darryl	D	13B,32D,36,39,61
Assoc Prof	Perkey, Christine	D	13B,66A,13H
Adj	Petrescu, Stefan	M	51,62A
Adj	Rasmussen, Ljerka V.	D	20,14C,20F,35D,14
Assoc Prof	Reeves, Patricia	D	32
Adj	Santiago, Imer	M	63A,41
Staff	Sexton, James	M	37,46,63C
Adj	Spann, Thomas	M	65
Adj	Sparks, Phyllis	M	62E
Asst Prof	Todd, Richard	D	13E,13F,41,70
Adj	Utterstrum, Oscar	M	63C,63D
Adj	Van Goes, Paula	D	64E
Adj	Wires, Jonathan	M	62D

TN1450 Tennessee Tech University
Department of Music & Art
PO Box 5045
Cookeville, TN 38505-0001
(931) 372-3161   Fax: (931) 372-6279
www.tntech.edu/musicandart
E-mail: COsteen@tntech.edu

4 Year Institution, Comprehensive
Member of NASM

Chair & Dir., Artist/Performance Series: Arthur T. LaBar, 80A,80F
Dir., Summer Programs: Joshua Hauser, 80G

Assoc Prof	Allcott, Dan J.	M	38,60B,62C,11,42
Assoc Prof	Barham, Phillip	M	64E,41,13B
Adj	Benne, Steve	M	62D
Adj	Besser, Idalynn	M	62B
Other	Bledsoe, Lee		66F,71
Prof	Chang, Wei Tsun	DMA	11,32E,62A,41,62
Asst Prof	Clark, Michael	M	11
Prof	Danner, Greg	D	13,10
Prof	Decker, Charles	D	63A,41,63,49
Assoc Prof	Godes, Catherine	D	66A,66C,66D
Asst Prof	Hansen, Jeremy C.	D	63B,13C,42
Asst Prof	Harris, Eric	D	37,32E
Prof	Hauser, Joshua	D	63C,10F,13B,42
Adj	Hauser, Kristin	M	11
Prof	Hermann, Joseph W.	M	37,60B,32E
Prof	Kennedy, Frederick	D	39,61
Inst	Kim, Wonkak	M	64C,48,41
Prof	LaBar, Arthur T.	M	
Prof	Lotz, James	M	12A,64D,35G
Prof	Martin, Roger	D	64A,41,64
Prof	McCormick, Chris	M	47,29,32F
Prof	Morris, Winston	M	49,63D,41
Adj	Paick, Yoomi	D	11,13C,66C
Assoc Prof	Pulte, Diane	D	61
Adj	Stone, Kerry 'Doc'	M	70
Asst Prof	Sullivan, Judith	D	32B
Adj	Thurmond, Paul	M	66D,66C
Assoc Prof	Willie, Eric	D	50,65
Prof	Woodworth, William	M	64B,13B,13C,41,66G
Asst Prof	Zamer, Craig T.	D	36,60A,32D

TN1500 Tennessee Temple University
Department of Music
1815 Union Ave
Chattanooga, TN 37404
(423) 493-4351   Fax: (423) 493-4497
www.tntemple.edu
E-mail: knowlew@tntemple.edu

4 Year Institution

Chair: William A. Knowles, 80A

Adj Prof	Evans, Joseph D.	B	
Asst Prof	Knowles, William A.	D	
Adj Prof	Mays, Michael E.	M	

TN1550 Tennessee Wesleyan College
Department of Fine Arts
204 E College St
Athens, TN 37303
(423) 252-1121   Fax: (423) 744-9968
www.twcnet.edu
E-mail: dmanley@twcnet.edu

4 Year Institution

Chair: Douglas H. Manley, 80A

Asst Prof	Manley, Douglas H.	D	12,66,31,66G,12C
Asst Prof	Wheeler, W. Keith	M	36,61,13C,11
Asst Prof	Windt, Nathan J.	D	60A,61,11,32D,36

TN1600 Trevecca Nazarene University
Department of Music
333 Murfreesboro Rd
Nashville, TN 37210-2877
(615) 248-1288   Fax: (615) 248-1596
www.trevecca.edu/music
E-mail: ddiehl@trevecca.edu

4 Year Institution
Member of NASM

Chair: David J. Diehl, 80A

Adj Prof	Ablon, Judith		62B
Adj Prof	Aston, Janis	M	32A
Adj Prof	Bauer, Mike	M	70
Prof	Christianson, Paul A.	D	11,66A,66D
Prof	Cierpke, Timothy H.	D	10F,60,62,36,38
Adj Prof	Corey, Scott	B	65
Adj Prof	Cox, Jeff	M	70,13B
Adj Prof	Cox, Kellie	B	66A
Adj Prof	DaSilva, Mario	M	70
Assoc Prof	Diehl, David J.	D	12A,32C,36
Adj Prof	Fenn, Shiloah	M	61
Adj Prof	Hotchkiss, Shelia	M	32E
Adj Prof	Houchin, Blake	M	35C
Adj Prof	Huber, William	B	63C
Adj Prof	Johnson, David	B	62A
Adj Prof	Jones, Marvin	M	31A
Adj Prof	McLean, Kim	M	10D
Prof	Murdock, Matthew	D	13C,32E,29,37,47
Adj Prof	Neilan, Martin	B	63
Adj Prof	Nyetam, Rachel	M	61
Adj Prof	Oyen, Valerie	M	36,61
Adj Prof	Polk, Betty	B	64A
Prof	Ray, John	D	60A,61
Adj Prof	Sartor, David	M	10
Adj Prof	Shankle, Robert	B	64B,64C,64E
Adj Prof	Sturges, Tami	M	62A
Adj Prof	Torrans, Richard	M	66G
Prof	Wilson, Eric	D	13,34,10

TN1650 Tusculum College

Department of Music
PO Box 5081
Greeneville, TN 37743
(423) 636-7300   Fax: (423) 638-7166
www.tusculum.edu
E-mail: dhendricksen@tusculum.edu

4 Year Institution

Chair, Humanities: Ron McCallister, 80A

Adj Prof	Hendricksen, David Alan	D	36,61
Adj	Price, David	B	37
Adj	Tunstall, Charles	M	70
Adj	Winfree, James	B	66A,66G

TN1660 Union University

Department of Music
1050 Union Univ Dr
Jackson, TN 38305-3697
(731) 661-5345   Fax: (731) 661-5243
www.uu.edu/dept/music
E-mail: cmathews@uu.edu

4 Year Institution
Member of NASM

Chair: Christopher W. Mathews, 80A
Dir., Community Music Center: Betty Bedsole, 80E
Dir., Artist/Performance Series: Terry McRoberts, 80F

Prof	Bedsole, Betty	D	61,31A,32
Prof Emeritus	Boud, Ronald E.	D	66G
Inst Adj	Cepparulo, Kathie	M	66A
Prof	Dennis, David M.	D	13,66A,36
Inst Adj	Graves, Kim	M	66D,13C
Inst Adj	Hanson, Sarah Beth	M	64A
Inst Adj	Leach, Troy	M	70
Inst Adj	Luscombe, Greg	M	63C,49
Asst Prof	Mann, Michael	M	37,42,60B,65
Assoc Prof	Mathews, Christopher W.	D	36,13H,31A,60A,13C
Prof	McClune, David	D	47,64C,64E
Inst Adj	McClure, Carol	M	62E
Prof	McRoberts, Terry	D	66A,66C,66D,66B
Inst Adj	Miller, Esther	M	62A,42
Prof	Penny, Michael K.	D	39,61,31A
Inst Adj	Scott, Gina	M	66D
Inst Adj	Smith, Dennis	M	63A
Inst Adj	Thacker, Hope	D	61
Assoc Prof	Veltman, Joshua	M	11,12A,44
Prof	Warren, Stanley	D	61,39
Assoc Prof	Wellborn, Georgia G.	D	61

TN1680 Univ of Memphis

Rudi E. Scheidt School of Music
129 Music Bldg
Memphis, TN 38152-3160
(901) 678-2541   Fax: (901) 678-3096
music.memphis.edu
E-mail: music@memphis.edu

4 Year Institution, Graduate School
Member of NASM

Master of Music in Composition, Master of Music in Performance, Master of Music in Conducting, Master of Music in Music Education, Master of Music in Musicology, PhD in Music Education, DMA in Composition, DMA in Conducting, DMA in Performance, Master of Music in Jazz & Studio Music, PhD in Musicology, Master of Music in Orff Schulwerk, Master of Music in Pedagogy

Director: Randal J. Rushing, 80A
Assoc. Dir., Undergraduate Studies: John Chiego, 80B
Assistant Dir., Graduate Curriculum & Advising: Kenneth Kreitner, 80C
Assistant Dir., Graduate Admissions: Michelle Vigneau, 80C
Dir., Admissions: Kay B. Yager, 80D
Dir., Community Music School: Samuel Sidhom, 80E

Prof	Afshar, Lily	D	70
Assoc Prof	Altino, Leonardo	M	62C,42
Assoc Prof	Altino, Soh-Hyun Park	D	62A,42
Adj	Apple, Nancy K.		10D
Adj	Armour, Janet E.	B	32E
Adj	Assad, Michael	M	65
Assoc Prof	Asuncion, Victor S.	D	66A,66C
Adj	Barr, Evan	M	65
Adj	Bass, John	M	12A
Prof	Baur, John	D	13,10
Asst Prof	Butler, Esq., LL.M., Tonya D.	D	35A,35B,35F
Prof Emerita	Case-Stott, Angeline	M	66H
Prof	Chiego, John	M	62D
Adj	Clayton, Zedric K.		35A
Assoc Prof	Cline, Jeff	M	34,35C,35D
Adj	Cobb, Joyce	B	61
Assoc Prof	Cooper, Jack	D	29,64E,46
Librarian	DeBacco, Maria	M	16
Prof	Edwards, Lawrence	D	60,32,36
Assoc Prof	Ensley, Mark	M	39
Assoc Prof	Erskine, Bruce	M	48,64A
Prof	Evans, David	D	12A,20G,14
Adj	Franks, Sandra E.	D	61
Assoc Prof	Frazer, Jonathan	M	34,35C,35D
Assoc Prof	Gaston, Pamela	D	61
Prof	Gholson, James	D	48,64C
Prof Emerita	Gilbert, Joan	M	66A,66C
Adj	Gilmore, Susanna Perry	M	32E,62
Assoc Prof	Goodwin, Tim	M	29,62D
Adj	Henderson, Chip	M	70,29A,47
	Higgins, Scott		66F
Asst Prof	Holland, Nicholas V.	D	37,32E
Adj	Huddleston, Jeffrey L.	M	64E
Prof	Ince, Kamran	D	13,10,43
Prof	Jiang, Pu-Qi	D	60B,38
Asst Prof	Jones, Evan T.	M	61
Prof	Kreitner, Kenneth	D	12,67E,55
Adj	Kreitner, Mona B.	M	12A
Librarian	Lowry, Carol S.	B	16
Assoc Prof	Mueller, John T.	D	63C,63D,49
Adj	Murray, Edward	B	65
Librarian	Neal, Anna	M	16
Inst	Nguyen, Albert	D	37
Asst Prof	O'Sullivan, Laila K.	D	13,13C,29C
Asst Prof	Owen-Leinert, Susan	M	61
Assoc Prof	Page, Janet K.	D	12
Prof Emeritus	Peterson, John David	D	66G,31A,12A
Assoc Prof	Phillips, Daniel	M	63B
Prof Emeritus	Richens, James W.	M	13,10,45
Asst Prof	Richmond, Kevin D.	D	66A,66D,66B
Asst Prof	Rippe, Allen	M	48,64E,67C
Assoc Prof	Robinson, Nicole R.	D	32B,32C,32G,32H
Prof	Rushing, Randal J.	D	61
Asst Prof	Sanders, Kevin	D	49,63D
Assoc Prof	Schranze, Lenny	M	62B,42
Assoc Prof	Shaffer, Frank	D	65,50
Adj	Shaffer, Marian	M	62E
Assoc Prof	Shiu, Timothy	M	62A,42
Assoc Prof	Spencer, David	D	63A
Adj	Stephens, William G.	B	66D
Adj	Todd, Allen F.	M	36
Asst Prof	Vigneau, Michelle	D	64B,42,13
Assoc Prof	Viviano, Samuel	M	66A,66B
Assoc Prof	Washington, Lecolion	M	64D,42,11
Adj	Wilensky, Pamela B.	B	32E
Asst Prof	Woodruff, Copeland	M	39

TN1700 Univ of Tennessee-Chattanooga

Department of Music #1451
615 McCallie Ave
Chattanooga, TN 37403-2598
(423) 425-4601   Fax: (423) 425-4603
www.utc.edu/music
E-mail: lee-harris@utc.edu

4 Year Institution, Graduate School
Member of NASM

Master of Music in Performance, Master of Music in Music Education

Dean: Jeffery Elwell, 80A
Head & Dir., Artist Series: Lee Harris, 80A,80F
Dir., Preparatory Division: H. Paul Shurtz, 80E

Prof	Abril, Mario	D	13,10F,70
Prof	Ahn, Jooyong	M	38,60B
Prof	Benkert, Stuart M.	D	37,47,32E,60B
Prof	Carter, Roland M.	M	13,11,36,66A
Prof	Coulter, Monte	D	13A,11,50,65
Assoc Prof	Ford, Joseph Kevin	PhD	36,40,32D,60
Prof	Harris, Lee	D	32,13C,36
Prof	Lee, William R.	D	32,63D,11
Prof	McNair, Jonathan B.	D	10A,34D,13,10,34
Asst Prof	Schafer, Erika L.	D	63A,63,67E,37,46
Lect	Shurtz, H. Paul	D	12A,12C
Prof	St. Goar, Rebecca	D	61
Asst Prof	Tejero, Nikolasa	D	13,64C,41
Assoc Prof	Tsai, Sin-Hsing	D	66A,66B,66C
Asst Prof	Ward, Perry	M	61,39
Assoc Prof	Wilson, Kenyon	D	63D,13,41
Assoc Prof	Zimmer, Don	M	11,51,62A

TN1710 Univ of Tennessee-Knoxville

School of Music
2438 Dunford Hall
915 Volunteer Blvd
Knoxville, TN 37996-2600
(865) 974-3241   Fax: (865) 974-1941
www.music.utk.edu
E-mail: music@utk.edu

4 Year Institution, Graduate School
Member of NASM

Master of Music in Composition, Master of Music in Music Theory, Master of Music in Performance, Master of Music in Conducting, Master of Music in Music Education, Master of Music in Musicology, Master of Music in Jazz Studies, Master of Music in Pedagogy, Master of Music in Accompanying, Artist's Certificate

Director: Roger L. Stephens, 80A
Associate Dir., Undergraduate Studies: Barbara A. Murphy, 80B
Associate Dir., Graduate Studies: Angela L. Batey, 80C

Assoc Prof	Adams, Fay	M	66A,66C
Asst Prof	Baldwin, Wesley H. B.	D	62C
Assoc Prof	Batey, Angela L.	D	32,36
PT	Bible, Judith	D	66C
Assoc Prof	Binder, Shelley	D	64A
Assoc Prof	Boling, Mark E.	M	70,29
Prof	Brock, John	M	66G,66H,31A
Assoc Prof	Brown, Donald R.		47,66A,29A
Inst	Brown, Keith	B	47,67E
Assoc Prof	Brunell, David	D	66A,66C
Assoc Prof	Carter, Patricia	M	66D
Asst Prof	Class, Kevin	D	66C
Asst Prof	Cloutier, Daniel	M	49,63C
Prof PT	Coker, Jerry	M	47,29
Asst Prof	DiSimone, Lorraine	M	61
Lect FT	Douglass, Mark	M	50,65
Asst Prof	Fellenbaum, James	M	38,60B
Assoc Prof	Gay, Leslie C.	D	14,14A,14C,20,12
Assoc Prof	Golden, Rachel	D	12
Lect PT	Hart-Reilly, Kathy M.	B	62
Lect	Herndon, Hillary	M	62B
Inst	Holloway, Harold	B	62D
Assoc Prof	Hristov, Maria N.	D	16
Asst Prof	Hristov, Miroslav P.	D	51,62A
Prof	Jacobs, Kenneth A.	D	13,10,45
Inst PT	Ladd, Karen	D	12A
Prof	Leach, Catherine F.	D	13,63A
Lect PT	Lee, Ardyce	M	64
Prof	MacMorran, Sande	M	11,38,49,63D
Prof	McClelland, Keith	M	13,64D
Lect PT	McCollough, Sean	M	12,12A
Asst Prof	McConville, Brendan P.	D	13,13F,13I,62C
Prof	Moore, Marvelene C.	D	32A,32B,32I
Assoc Prof	Murphy, Barbara A.	D	13
Lect PT	Nall, Cecily	M	61
Prof	Northington, David B.	D	66A
Prof	Pederson, Donald	D	13
Lect PT	Peterson, Gene D.	M	32,36,40
Lect	Robbins, Allison	D	14C
Lect PT	Romines, Jay	M	64E
Assoc Prof	Royse, David M.	PhD	32E,32B,32C
Asst Prof	Ryder, Donald D.	D	37
Lect	Schuetz, Shaun Nicholas	M	50
Inst	Secrist, Phylis	M	64B
Asst Prof	Skoog, Andrew	M	61
Prof	Sousa, Gary D.	D	37,32
Assoc Prof	Sperl, Gary	M	64C,64E
Assoc Prof	Stephens, Marjorie	M	61
Prof	Stephens, Roger L.	D	39
Asst Prof	Stewart, Michael	D	37,65
Prof Emeritus	Stutzenberger, David R.	D	36
Asst Prof	Tardy, Gregory		64E
Lect PT	Thompson, Vance	M	63A,47
Lect PT	Vincent, Larry F.	M	70
Prof	Wentzel, Andrew	M	39,61
Lect PT	Werner, Wendel V.	M	29
Assoc Prof	Zelmanovich, Mark	M	51,62A

TN1720 Univ of Tennessee at Martin

Department of Music
314 Clement Hall
210 Hurt St
Martin, TN 38238
(731) 881-7402   Fax: (731) 881-7415
www.utm.edu/music
E-mail: music@utm.edu

4 Year Institution
Member of NASM

Chair: Elaine Atkins Harriss, 80A

Adj	Doss, Elwood	M	66F,11
Lect	Easley, Delana	B	66C
Adj	Frye, Christa J.	D	64C
Asst Prof	Frye, Joseph W.	D	63C,13A,13C,11,34
Assoc Prof	Gorman, Kurt	D	13A,34,63A,47
Prof	Harriss, Elaine Atkins	D	66A,66B,42,66D
Adj	Hernon, Bonnie	M	66D,11
Prof Emeritus	Hernon, Michael A.		
Assoc Prof	Hill, Julie	D	65,50
Assoc Prof	Mancusi, Roberto	D	39,61,60A,13C
Asst Prof	Oelrich, John A.	D	37,32E,60B
Asst Prof	Owens, Douglas A.	D	64B,64D,13
Prof	Roberts, David Scott	D	66G,13,10F
Assoc Prof	Simmons, Amy	D	42,64C,64E
Assoc Prof	Simmons, Mark	D	36,32D,60A
Inst	Stratton, Matthew	M	63D,11,34,37
Adj	Summers, Alvin	M	40
Adj	Swisher, Kristen		64A
Asst Prof	Thoman, Jessica	D	63B,12A,11
Asst Prof	Vest, Johnathan	D	32,66D
Assoc Prof	Yeung, Amy	D	61,39,13

TN1800 Univ of the South

Department of Music
735 University Ave
Sewanee, TN 37383
(931) 598-1874   Fax: (931) 598-1145
www.sewanee.edu
E-mail: smiller@sewanee.edu

4 Year Liberal Arts Institution

Chair: Stephen R. Miller, 80A

Vstng Asst Prof	Carlson, James	D	13A,13B,10A,10B,13C
Prof	Delcamp, Robert	D	13,12A,36,66G,31A
Vstng Inst	Duncan, Craig T.	M	62A
Vstng Inst	Lee, Joseph	M	60B
Inst	Lehman, Katherine	M	13A,62A
Vstng Asst Prof	Lo, Wei-Chun Bernadette	D	66A
Assoc Prof	Miller, Stephen R.	D	11,12A,12,14
Inst	Rupert, Susan	M	13A,61,54
Prof	Shrader, Steven	D	11,12A,12,66A,38
Vstng Inst	Wright, Prakash	M	47,29

TN1850 Vanderbilt University

Blair School of Music
2400 Blakemore Ave
Nashville, TN 37212-3499
(615) 322-7651   Fax: (615) 343-0324
blair.vanderbilt.edu
E-mail: pam.schneller@vanderbilt.edu

4 Year Institution
Member of NASM

Dean: Mark Wait, 80A,80B,80E
Assistant Dean & Dir., Admissions: Dwayne P. Sagen, 80B,80D,80H
Associate Provost: Cynthia Cyrus, 80H,80B,80E
Associate Dean: Melissa K. Rose, 80H,80B,80E
Associate Dean: Pamela Schneller, 80H,80B,80E

Senior Lect	Adair, William 'Billy'	B	29,46,47
Inst Adj	Ahima, Kwame		50
Lect PT	Ahner, Sally R.	M	32
Lect PT	Alley, Amy	M	32
Senior Artist Teacher Adj	Bartles, Martha	MFA	66A
Assoc Prof	Barz, Gregory F.	D	12,14,20,31,29A
Artist Teacher Adj	Biddlecombe, Mary	M	36
Assoc Prof	Biddlecombe, Thomas 'Tucker'	D	36,42,32D
Senior Lect	Bingham, Emelyne	M	13B,32E
Lect Adj	Blackmon, Odie	B	13F

Rank	Name	Degree	Areas
Artist Teacher Adj	Blackwell, Jessica	M	62A
Adj	Britain, Mat	B	50
Artist Teacher Adj	Brown, Alison	M	10E
Inst Adj	Buckingham, Steve	B	12A
Assoc Prof	Calico, Joy	D	12,20F
Assoc Prof	Cassel, David C.	D	32D
Artist Teacher Adj	Cassel-Greer, Kirsten	M	62C
Artist Teacher Adj	Chang, Seanad	M	62A,62B
Assoc Prof Adj	Chang, Wei-Tsun	M	62A
Prof Adj	Clarke, Karen	M	62A,62B,67B
Prof Emeritus	Cockrell, Dale	D	
Adj	Combs, Matt	B	62A
Senior Lect	Cooper, Peter	B	12
Artist Teacher Adj	Coplan, Lauren Jackson	B	66A
Prof Emerita	Cormier, Elizabeth	M	
Prof	Cox, Allan	M	63A,49,41
Prof	Cyrus, Cynthia	D	12,15,55,20F
Asst Prof Adj	Davis, Garnett R.	M	63D,49
Senior Lect	Deakin, Paul	D	13
Assoc Prof	Dikeman, Philip	M	64A,41,48
Assoc Prof	Dorfman, Amy	M	41,66A,66C
Adj	Dudley, Bruce J.	M	66A
Artist Teacher Adj	Eckert, Elizabeth	B	66A,66D
Senior Artist Teacher	Estill, Cynthia	M	64D
Inst Adj	Foote, Ed V.	B	66
Prof	Fountain, Robin	M	60,38,43
Senior Lect	Fry, Robert Webb	D	12
Artist Teacher Adj	Guerin, Constance Ely	B	36
Senior Lect	Gunderman, Jennifer	M	14C
Artist Teacher Adj	Hall, Erin	M	62A
Lect	Harris, Ben	M	66C
Asst Prof	Hauser, Jared E.	M	64B
Artist Teacher Adj	Hauser, Laura	M	64D
Prof	Heard, Cornelia	M	41,51,62A
Senior Lect	Hime, Michael	M	12A
Senior Lect	Holland, Michael	M	65A,65B
Artist Teacher Adj	Horner, Erin	M	63B
Assoc Prof	Huebl, Carolyn	D	62A,13G,32F,34,11
Senior Artist Teacher	Hwang, ChiHee	M	66A
Prof Adj	Iwasaki, Jun	M	62A
Assoc Prof	Jackson, Bil		64C,41,42
Senior Lect	Jarman, Amy	B	61,39,40
Assoc Prof	Johns, John	M	41,70,67G
Adj	Johnson, Elizabeth	B	29
Adj	Johnson, Sara	M	62A,32A
Prof Emerita	Katahn, Enid	M	
Assoc Prof Adj	Kimbrough, Jerome	B	70
Assoc Prof	Kirchner, Jane	M	
Assoc Prof	Kochanowski, John		41,51,62B,42
Assoc Prof	Kolkay, Peter	D	41,64D,48
Prof Adj	Korn, Mitchell	M	35C
Artist Teacher Adj	Koutsoukos, Sheree	M	66,66D
Assoc Prof	Krieger, Karen Ann	M	13,66A,66D,66B,68
Assoc Prof Adj	Kunkee, Patrick	M	63D
Assoc Prof	Kurek, Michael	D	13,10F,10
Artist Teacher Adj	Law, Zada	M	10C
Senior Artist Teacher	Lee, Cassandra	M	41,48,64C,42
Prof Emeritus	Lee, Douglas	D	
Assoc Prof	Link, Stan	D	12A,12,20G,14C,15
Adj Assoc Prof	Long, Gilbert	B	63D
Assoc Prof	Lovensheimer, James A.	M	12,14,20G,29
Assoc Prof	Lowe, Melanie D.	D	12A,12,20G,14C,15
Artist Teacher Adj	Madole, Craig	B	38
Asst Prof	Maiello, James V.	D	12A
Artist Teacher Adj	Mansell, Bradley	M	62C
Adj	May, Maureen	M	66D
Senior Lect	McGuire, Jennifer	M	66C
Senior Lect	McGuire, Joshua	M	13C
Assoc Prof Adj	Meyer, Edgar	B	41,62D
Senior Artist Teacher Adj	Middleton, Valerie	M	66A
Artist Teacher Adj	Miles, Sarah	DMA	64A
Lect PT	Montgomery, Cheri	M	61
Asst Prof Adj	Nelson, Craig E.	B	62D
Senior Artist Teacher Adj	Nies, Carol R.	D	60,38,13,32E
Assoc Prof	Nies, Craig	D	66A,41,66C
Assoc Prof	Norton, Leslie	B	41,48,63B,49
Assoc Prof Adj	Pearcy, Robert W.		20G
Lect	Perez, Erin	M	32
Asst Prof Adj	Phillips, Derrek C.	M	65
Senior Artist Teacher	Phillips, Joe Rea	M	41,70,33
Assoc Prof	Ploger, Marianne	D	13
Senior Artist Teacher	Plohman, Crystal	B	62A
Prof	Plummer, Kathryn	B	41,62A,62B,34
Adj Assoc Prof	Porter, Michael S.	M	
Asst Prof Adj	Prentice, Tracy	M	61
Artist Teacher Adj	Ramey, Lauren	M	13
Artist Teacher Adj	Ramsay, Susan	M	32
Senior Artist Teacher	Reagan, Jama	B	66A,32A
Assoc Prof Adj	Reinker, Daniel	M	62B
Assoc Prof Adj	Reist, Joel	M	62D
Assoc Prof	Retzlaff, Jonathan	DMA	61,39,40
Assoc Prof	Rose, Melissa K.	D	66C,41,40
Assoc Prof	Rose, Michael	D	13,10,12A,11,31
Adj	Rowe, Lee	B	10C
Prof Adj	Sagen, Dwayne P.	D	37
Prof Emeritus	Sawyer, John 'Del'	M	
Senior Lect	Schneller, Pamela	M	32C,32B,32D,60
Senior Artist Teacher	Schneller, Roland	M	66A,66C
Prof Adj	Shaffer, Marian	M	62E,41,42
Assoc Prof	Shay, Gayle D.	D	39,61
Asst Prof Adj	Simonett, Helena	D	12,14,20H
Assoc Prof	Slayton, Michael K.	D	13
Senior Lect	Smith, Carl	M	13,10A
Senior Artist Teacher	Smith, Carol F.	M	62A,32E,51
Lect	Smith, Gavin	M	32E,37
Adj	Solee, Denis		64E
Artist Teacher Adj	Spencer, Roger A.	B	29
Prof Adj	Steinquest, David E.	M	65B
Prof Emeritus	Taylor, Bobby G.	B	
Prof	Teal, Christian	M	41,51,62A
Senior Artist Teacher	Tuten, Celeste	M	62A
Assoc Prof Adj	Utley, Brian	D	64E
Asst Prof Adj	Vanosdale, Mary Kathryn	M	41,62A
Assoc Prof	Verrier, Thomas	D	37,60B,32C,32D,32
Artist Teacher Adj	Virelles, Amanda	D	66C
Artist Teacher Adj	Wade, Patsy B.	M	66A
Prof	Wait, Mark	D	66A
Artist Teacher Adj	Walker, Deanna	M	66A,10D
Assoc Prof	Wang, Felix	D	62C,41,51
Asst Prof Adj	Wanner, Glen	M	62D
Artist Teacher Adj	Warford, Allison	M	36
Assoc Prof Adj	Wiesmeyer, Roger	B	64B
Assoc Prof	Wiggins, William	M	41,50,65
Lect	Wilder, Matt		34
Senior Lect	Wiliams, David B.	M	13C,36
Senior Artist Teacher Adj	Williams, Anne	M	62A,62C
Assoc Prof	Wilson, Jeremy	D	63C

TN1900 Volunteer State Community College
Department of Music
1480 Nashville Pike
Gallatin, TN 37066
(615) 452-8600
www.volstate.edu/
E-mail: nancy.slaughter@volstate.edu

2 Year Institution

Associate Dean, Humanities: Dan Jewell

Rank	Name	Degree	Areas
Inst PT	Gibson, Melissa	M	61
Inst PT	Peterson, Lynn	B	70
Asst Prof	Slaughter, Nancy		61
Assoc Prof	Story, James W.		

TX0050 Abilene Christian University
Department of Music
WPAC ACU Box 28274
Abilene, TX 79699-8274
(325) 674-2199   Fax: (325) 674-2608
www.acu.edu/music
E-mail: matt.roberson@acu.edu

4 Year Institution
Member of NASM

Chair: Matt Roberson

Rank	Name	Degree	Areas
Assoc Prof	Bjorem, Pauline Kung	D	66,13C
Inst	Brown, Derek	M	29,13B,64E
Assoc Prof	Cook, Samuel	M	61,39
Staff	Lemmons, Cheryl T.	M	13C,66C
Lect	Missal, Jason	M	37,32E,63B
Inst	Mitchell, Dan	M	70
Prof Emeritus	Piersall, Paul	D	61
Asst Prof	Piersall, Rick	D	39,61,12A
Assoc Prof	Pruett, Julie	D	61
Assoc Prof	Roberson, Matt	D	12A
Prof	Scarbrough, Michael	D	36,61,60A
Assoc Prof	Straughn, Greg	D	12A
Prof	Teel, Allen J.	D	65,50,20,37
Inst	Teel, Susan	M	66A,32B,11,13C
Prof	Ward, Steven D.	D	60B,37,38
Prof	Williams, Kay	D	66A,66C,66D,13A,13B

TX0075 Alvin Community College
Department of Music
3110 Mustang Rd
Alvin, TX 77511-4898
(281) 756-3587   Fax: (281) 756-3880
www.alvincollege.edu
E-mail: kmoody@alvincollege.edu

2 Year Institution

Chair: Kevin M. Moody, 80A
Dean: Drew Nelson, 80A

Emeritus	Anderson, Andrew E.	M	29A,11
PT	Auer, Shelley	M	61,11
	Benoist, Debbie	M	13
PT	Calderon, John	B	70
PT	Gormly, Shane	B	65
FT	Griffith, David	M	11,37,46,63
PT	Harvey, James	M	11,70
PT	Holst, Carol	M	66A
FT	Moody, Kevin M.	M	54,61,11,36,40
PT	Salter, Tim	B	70
PT	Singletary, Pat	A	64,35D
PT	Termini, Steven	D	11,66A,13A
PT	Watson, Robyn	M	64D

TX0100 Amarillo College
Department of Music
PO Box 447
Amarillo, TX 79178-0001
(806) 371-5340   Fax: (806) 345-5570
www.actx.edu

2 Year Institution
Member of NASM

Chair: James Rauscher, 80A

Inst	Beckett, Scott	M	11,12,13,37,63
PT	Campos, Homero	B	70
Retired Prof	De La Bretonne, Beverly	M	13,38,41,62A,64A
PT	Easterday, Janice	B	61
PT	Gerald, Helen	M	62
Prof Emeritus PT	Gibson, Mila	M	39,61
PT	Gillespie, Robert C.	M	63D
Artist in Res	Johnson, Mary Jane	M	39,61
Prof	Laughlin, Jim	D	13A,12A,48,64C,64E
PT	McDonough, Raenell	M	66G
Inst	Nies, Camille Day	M	62A
PT	Rath, Eric	M	65
Prof	Rauscher, James	D	66
PT	Steadman, Russell	B	38,62C
PT	Teal, Kelly	M	61
Prof	Weber, Steven T.	D	36,41,61

TX0125 Angelina College
Department of Music and F. Arts
PO Box 1768
Lufkin, TX 75902
(936) 633-5233   Fax: (936) 633-5359
www.angelina.edu
E-mail: mhill@angelina.edu

2 Year Community College

Director, Fine Arts: Karen L. McBee, 80A

Inst	Compton, Beckie	M	66A,13,11,36,47
Inst	Greer, Larry	M	13,14C,29,46,70
	McBee, Karen L.	D	12A,11,66A,66C,66D

TX0150 Angelo State University
Department of Art & Music
Box 10906/ASU Station
San Angelo, TX 76909
(325) 942-2085   Fax: (325) 942-2152
www.angelo.edu/dept/artmusic/
E-mail: david.scott@angelo.edu

4 Year Institution
Member of NASM

Chair: David Scott, 80A
Interim Dean, College of Arts & Sciences: Paul Swets, 80A

Assoc Prof	Bonenfant, Timothy	D	64C,64E,47
Asst Prof	Elkins, Eleanor	D	66
Assoc Prof	Emmons, Stephen D.	D	13,10,10F,34
Prof	Irish, John E.	D	63A,63B,49,29A
Asst Prof	Kelley, Constance L.	D	37,32E,64A
Prof	Lambert, Kevin	D	11
Prof	Lee, Pamela	D	32,36,66A,60
Asst Prof	McCloud, Daniel	D	37,65
Assoc Prof	Raines, Scott	D	39,61,11
Prof	Scott, David	D	32,60
Asst Prof	Surface, Edward	D	11,63D
Asst Prof	Womack, Jeffrey	D	12A,64B,64D

TX0200 Arlington Baptist College
Department of Music
3001 W Division St
Arlington, TX 76012
(817) 461-8741   Fax: (817) 274-1138
www.arlingtonbaptistcollege.edu

4 Year Institution

Assoc Prof	Johnson, Carl	M	60,12A,32C,36,61
Lect PT	Mason, Vicki	M	13,32B

TX0250 Austin College
Department of Music
900 N Grand Ave
Sherman, TX 75090-4440
(903) 813-2251   Fax: (903) 813-2273
www.austincollegemusic.com
E-mail: wcrannell@austincollege.edu

4 Year Institution

Chair: Wayne T. Crannell, 80A
Dir., Artist/Performance Series: Joe Hicks, 80F

Inst PT	Archer, Robert	M	63D,37
Inst PT	Bush, Doug	M	65
Inst PT	Case, Barbara	D	66A
Assoc Prof	Crannell, Wayne T.	D	36,61,11,39,60
Inst PT	Cutler, Ann	M	66A,66D
Assoc Prof	Dominick, Daniel L.	D	66A,12,60B,38,60
Prof	Duhaime, Ricky	D	13,47,41,64,60B
Inst PT	Heffernan, Nancy	M	62D
Prof Emeritus	Isaac, Cecil	M	11,12
Inst PT	Johnson, Seth	M	63B
Inst PT	Narikawa, Masako	M	66C
Inst PT	Richardson, Cathy	M	62A,62B,51
Inst PT	Rivers, Sylvia	M	61,36
Inst PT	Russell, Cynthia	D	61,66A,66G,32B,32C
Prof Emeritus	Tappa, Richard J.	D	11,66G,69
Inst PT	Walker, Michael	M	63A

TX0300 Baylor University
School of Music
One Bear Place #97408
Waco, TX 76798-7408
(254) 710-1221   Fax: (254) 710-1191
www.baylor.edu/music
E-mail: william_may@baylor.edu

4 Year Institution, Graduate School
Member of NASM

Master of Music in Composition, Master of Music in Music Theory, Master of Music in Performance, Master of Music in Conducting, Master of Music in Church Music, Master of Music in Music Education, Master of Music in History & Literature, Master of Music in Pedagogy & Performance, Master of Music in Collaborative Piano

Dean: William V. May, 80A
Dir., Graduate Studies: Laurel E. Zeiss, 80C
Dir., Summer Programs: Alex Parker, 80G
Associate Dean: Georgia Green, 80H
Associate Dean: Michael Jacobson, 80H

Assoc Prof	Abbott-Kirk, Jane	M	66A
Assoc Prof	Alexander, Michael L.	D	32E,38
Asst Prof	Arnone, Francesca M.	D	64A,42,67D
Prof Emerita	Backus, Carolyn A.	D	61
Prof Emeritus	Bailey, Donald	D	60,36
Asst Prof	Bartlette, Christopher A.	D	13
Prof	Bennighof, James	D	13
Lect PT	Bennight, Brad	D	66H
Prof	Berg, Bruce	D	62A
Assoc Prof	Best, Robert L.	D	61
Senior Lect	Bolen, Bradley C.	D	66A,66D
Prof	Boyd, Jean A.	D	12A,20G,29A
Prof	Bradley, Randall	D	36,31A
Asst Prof	Cardenas, Octavio	M	39
Asst Prof	Cho, Soon	D	61
Senior Lect	Claybrook, Doug	D	13
Vstng Prof	Coldiron, Jack	M	61
Asst Prof	Colman, Alfredo C.	D	14,20H
Assoc Prof	Cosart, Jann	D	12A,55
Prof	Deloach, Doris	D	48,64B
Asst Prof	Demers, Isabelle	D	66G
Prof Emeritus	Elzinga, Harry	D	12A,12C
Asst Prof	Eshelman, Kent T.	D	63D
Lect	Espinosa, Ricardo	D	37
Prof	Gackle, Lynne	D	36,60A
Asst Prof	Gavin, Russell	D	32E
Assoc Prof	Gogichashvili, Eka Dalrymple	D	62A,42
Assoc Prof	Gordon, Jerry L.	D	61
Prof	Green, Georgia	D	32
Prof	Hardie, William Gary	D	62C,42
Assoc Prof	Henry, Michele L.	D	32D
Prof	Heyde, Stephen	M	38,60B
Lect	Hofmann, Cameron	D	66C
Assoc Prof Emerita	Horan, Leta	D	36,66A,66D
Asst Prof	Hosoda-Ayer, Kae	D	66C
Asst Prof	Hudson, Terry Lynn	D	66A,66D,66B
Lect	Hufty, Aaron	M	36,11
Prof	Jacobson, Michael	D	64E,34
Prof	Jordan, Krassimira	M	66A
Lect PT	Kelly, Patrick	M	70
Prof	Lai, Eric C.	D	13
Assoc Prof	Marks, Brian	D	66A
Asst Prof	Maxile, Horace J.	D	13
Prof	May, William V.	D	32D
Assoc Prof	McAllister, Lesley Ann	D	66A,66B,66D
Prof	McAllister, Scott	D	10
Prof	McKinney, Timothy R.	D	13
Asst Prof	Meehan, Todd	D	50,65
Senior Lect	Millar, Jana	D	13
Prof	Music, David W.	D	31A
Asst Prof	Odajima, Isaiah	D	37,60B
Asst Prof	Ostlund, Sandor	D	62D
Lect	Parker, Alex	M	29,47,46
Asst Prof	Peterson, Jeffrey Todd	D	39
Assoc Prof	Phillips, Brent	M	63C,49
Assoc Prof	Powers, Jeffrey S.	M	63B
Asst Prof	Qian, Jun	D	64C,48
Assoc Prof	Raines, Alan L.	D	36,60A,40
Prof	Rudd, Wortley F. 'Wiff'	M	63A
Assoc Prof	Scott, Daniel E.	D	61
Prof Emerita	Shanley, Helen A.	M	48,64A
Prof Emeritus	Shanley, Richard A.	D	48,64C
Asst Prof	Shoemaker, Ann H.	D	64D
Prof	Steely, Kathryn	D	62B
Senior Lect	Taylor, Edward J. F.	D	13
Assoc Prof	Umstead, Randall	D	61
Prof Emeritus	Van Cura, John	D	61
Prof	Wallace, Robin	D	12,11
Prof	Williams, James	D	66A
Assoc Prof	Williamson, Deborah K.	D	61
Assoc Prof	Wilson, J. Eric	D	37,60B
Lect PT	Woodson, Louisa Ellis	D	62E
Assoc Prof	Zeiss, Laurel E.	D	12A,12C,11,12

TX0340 Blinn College
Department of Music
Brenham, TX 77833
(979) 830-4261   Fax: (979) 830-4030
www.blinn.edu
E-mail: lcampbell@blinn.edu

2 Year Institution

Chair: Larry Campbell, 80A

	Blake, Harry D.		37
	Burke, Sarah M.	D	50,65
	Campbell, Larry	M	37,47,63B,63C,63D
	Dujka, John	M	66
	Garrett, Craig	M	36,47,63A
	Wise, Jennifer		61

TX0345 Blinn College
Department of Music
2423 Blinn Blvd.
Bryan, TX 77805
www.blinn.edu/
E-mail: lcampbell@blinn.edu

	Lim, Mi-Na	D	11,66A,66B
	Strong, Alan D.	D	11,32,66G

TX0350 Brazosport College
Department of Music
500 College Dr
Lake Jackson, TX 77566-3136
(979) 230-3272   Fax: (979) 230-3465
www.brazosport.edu
E-mail: richard.birk@brazosport.edu

2 Year Institution

Coordinator: Richard Birk, 80A

Inst PT	Becker, Jane	D	61
Assoc Prof	Birk, Richard	M	13,11,37,47,63
Inst PT	Fricker, Charles	M	65
Assoc Prof	Mason, Rodney	M	13,36,61,66A,66D

TX0370 Cedar Valley Coll-Dallas Comm Col
Department of Music
3030 N Dallas Ave
Lancaster, TX 75134-3705
(972) 860-8129
www.cedarvalleycollege.edu
E-mail: red3592@dcccd.edu

2 Year Institution

Division Dean: Jerry Cotton, 80A
Music Coordinator: Roger Dismore, 80A

Adj	Brown, Kathryn D.		11,35G
FT	Browne, Steve	B	34,35G
FT	Dismore, Roger	M	47,20G,29,35A,35G
FT	Germany, Sam	D	13,66D,35G
Adj	Harlas, Lou		35G,47
Adj	Hodan, Daniel		70,35G
Adj	Hurst, Michael Shane	D	61,40,35G
Adj	Irwin, Pamela		35G
FT	Jones, Arlington		13,10F,66A,35G
Adj	Kakouberi, Daredjan 'Baya'	D	66A,35G
Adj	McLure, Richard	B	35G,57,53,70
Adj	Richardson, Cathy	M	62A,35G
Adj	Scherschell, Rebecca	M	35G,62E
Adj	Smith, Ed	A	65B,35G
Adj	Spencer, Larry		35G,63A

TX0390 Cisco Junior College
Music Program
101 College Heights
Cisco, TX 76437-9803
(254) 442-2567   Fax: (254) 442-2546
www.cisco.edu/
E-mail: billy.smith@cisco.edu

2 Year Institution

Director: Billy Smith, 80A

Inst	Abel, Sandra	M	36,61,13A,13B,13C
	Martinez, Manuel		37
	Smith, Billy		36
Inst	Viertel, Kyle	B	37,63,64,65,46
Inst	Zell, Steven D.	M	13A,13B,13C,11,66A

TX0400 Concordia University-Austin
Department of Music
11400 Concordia University Dr
Austin, TX 78726-1887
(512) 486-2000   Fax: (512) 459-8517
www.concordia.edu
E-mail: patricia.burnham@concordia.edu

4 Year Institution

Dean: Alan Runge, 80A
Chair: Brian L. Trittin, 80A

Asst Prof	Eifert, Jonathan	M	36,60A,66G,31A
Prof Emeritus	Gastler, Bernard	D	
PT	Griggs-Burnham, Patricia	M	66A,11
PT	Gurgel, Denise	M	64A
PT	Hamelin, Karla M.	D	62
Adj Prof	Johnson, Ellen C.	D	64A,41
PT	Lawrie, Jim	B	70
Prof Emeritus	Rutz, Harold A.	M	
PT	Stone-Taborn, Susan	M	61
Assoc Prof	Trittin, Brian L.	D	12A,13,29,37,64E

TX0550 Del Mar College
Department of Music
101 Baldwin Blvd
Corpus Christi, TX 78404-3897
(361) 698-1211   Fax: (361) 698-1620
www.delmar.edu/music
E-mail: cbridges@delmar.edu

2 Year Institution
Member of NASM

Chair: Cynthia Bridges, 80A
Dir., Artist Series: David T. Sutanto, 80F
Dir., Summer Programs: Todd Ehle, 80G
Dir., Summer Programs: Abel Ramirez, 80G
Dir., Summer Programs: Dennis Richardson, 80G

Assoc Prof	Bissell, Paul	D	10B,34D,34E,35C,35D
Inst PT	Bowman, Paul A.	M	65
Asst Prof	Bridges, Cynthia	PhD	37,32H,60B,13C,32C
Inst PT	Burch, Alene	M	66A,66C,66D,66B
Asst Prof	Chen, Shao Shen	D	66A,66D,66B,66C
Assoc Prof	Ehle, Todd	M	62A,62B,38
Adj	Garcia, Glynn	M	20H
Inst PT	Hagarty, Mia	B	62A,32A,62B
Asst Prof	Hagarty, Scott	D	63A,13A,13C,49,41
Adj	Hansen, Steven	A	34D
Prof	Hii, Philip	M	41,70
Prof	Irving, David	M	47,70,46,29A,37
Adj	Justus, Keith	M	70,13C,14C,29B
Prof	Kairies, Joy E.	D	64A,34C,11,48
Assoc Prof	Kemm, Karl	M	63B,49,67E,14E,14F
Prof	Lipman, William	M	12A,64C,64E,11,48
Asst Prof	Longoria, Cynthia	M	40,61
Adj	McCarty, Evelyn	D	64B
Inst PT	Mellenbruch, Judy	M	66C
Adj	Perez, Michael	B	70
Asst Prof	Pinson, Donald L.	D	11,13A,63C,63D,49
Asst Prof	Rada, Raphael	D	61,11,13C,32B,36
Asst Prof	Ramirez, Abel	D	37,13A
Asst Prof	Richardson, Dennis	M	36,40,32B,66D,60A
Asst Prof	Richardson, Ouida	M	36,64A,32A
Asst Prof	Sisauyhoat, Neil	D	65,50,13A,13C
Prof	Struman, Susan Jean	M	51,62C,32A,11,62D
Asst Prof	Sutanto, David T.	M	66A,66D,66C,11,66B
Adj	Torres, Jose	M	20H
Adj	Weber, Linda	M	11,64A,66A,32,66D
Inst	Zamora, Gloria	B	70

TX0600 East Texas Baptist University
School of Fine Arts
One Tiger Dr
Marshall, TX 75670-1423
(903) 923-2158   Fax: (903) 934-8114
www.etbu.edu
E-mail: music@etbu.edu

4 Year Institution
Member of NASM

Dean: Thomas R. Webster, 80A

Prof	Boaz, Virginia Lile	D	12,61,39,12A
Asst Prof	Bugos, Kristen	D	32B,66D
Inst	Crim, Mark	M	37,32E,60B,44
Inst Adj	Denis, Andrea	M	63B
Asst Prof	Hodges, Justin	D	36,40,32D
Inst Adj	Hopkins, Ted	M	64
Prof	Lockard, Douglas T.	D	63A,37,47
Inst Adj	Robinson, Anthony	M	65,50
Prof	Sulton, Randall S.	D	66A,66C,13E,13B,13F
Asst Prof	Thomas, Eric S.	D	61,13C,13A,54
Inst Adj	Vinson, Danny	M	63D
Prof	Webster, Thomas R.	PhD	60A,49,48,13B
Inst Adj	Wright, Robert	M	66G

TX0700 Eastfield College
Department of Music
3737 Motley Dr
Mesquite, TX 75150-2033
(972) 860-7135   Fax: (972) 860-8342
www.eastfieldcollege.edu
E-mail: OscarPassley@dcccd.edu

2 Year Institution

Coordinator: Harrell C. Lucky, 80A

PT	Bowser, Teresa	M	
Inst	Bradshaw, Curt	M	13,29
PT	Drake, Mike	B	29
PT	Frajena, Roger	M	62D
PT	Greer, Clare	M	70
PT	Healy, Eddie	M	70,11
PT	Horlas, Lou	M	47,62D,29
PT	Lambert, Adam	M	63A
FT	Lercia, Louise	M	61
PT	Logozzo, Derrick	M	50
Inst	Lucky, Harrell C.	D	13,12A,36
Inst	Madriguera, Enric	D	62,70,11,12A
PT	Mcgill, Stan	M	36
Inst	Mouledous, Pierrette	M	66
PT	Nye, Randall	M	70,11
PT	Pangburn, Chuck	B	29
PT	Schultz, David	M	62A,62B
FT	Tavaglione, Eunice	M	

TX0750 Episcopal Theological Seminary
Department of Music
PO Box 2247
Austin, TX 78768-2247
(512) 472-4133
www.ssw.edu
E-mail: rschulz@ssw.edu

4 Year Institution

Assoc Prof Emeritus	Schulz, Russell E.	D	36,66G,31A

TX0850 Grayson County College
Department of Music
6101 Grayson Dr
Denison, TX 75020-8238
(903) 465-6030   Fax: (903) 463-5284
www.grayson.edu/music/index.htm
E-mail: blackst@grayson.edu

2 Year Institution

Director: James Dering, 80A

	Bays, Tatiana		66A
	Dering, James	M	36,47,13,13C,11
PT	Derix, Amye	M	61,13
	Tercero, David R.	B	70,63,13
	Whitfill, Jim		64,63,65

TX0900 Hardin-Simmons University
School of Music & Fine Arts
Box 16230
Abilene, TX 79698-6230
(325) 670-1426   Fax: (325) 670-5873
www.hsutx.edu/academics/music
E-mail: music@hsutx.edu

4 Year Institution, Graduate School
Member of NASM

Master of Music in Performance, Master of Music in Church Music, Master of Music in Music Education, Master of Music in Music Theory-Composition

Dean & Dir., Summer Programs: Lawson Hager, 80A,80G
Dir., Graduate Studies: Lynnette Chambers, 80C
Dir., Festivals: Peter R. Isaacson, 80F
Assistant Dean: Jaynne Middleton, 80H

Inst Adj	Anderson, Shirley	M	66D
Prof	Chambers, Lynnette	D	61
Asst Prof	Choi, Hye-Jean	ABD	66A,66G,66H,67C,13
Assoc Prof	Coltman, Charles	D	10F,41,64,35A
Asst Prof	Cottrell, Jeffrey	D	10A,63C,63D
Prof	Dorothy, Wayne F.	D	32C,32E,37,60B
Assoc Prof	Hager, Lawson	M	13,49,63B,41
Asst Prof	Hollingsworth, Christopher	D	61,39
Prof	Hunsaker, Leigh Anne	D	63A,32,49
Asst Prof	Isaacson, Kristin	D	13C,62C,62D
Assoc Prof	Isaacson, Peter R.	D	62A,38,41
Inst Adj	Lloyd, Keith	M	65
Prof	Middleton, Jaynne	D	61,12A,54
Inst Adj	Mitchell, Dan	M	70
Vstng Inst	Neubert, Peter	DMA	62B,62A,41
Inst Adj	Ordonez, Karla	D	64A
Assoc Prof	Puckett, Lauren J.	M	66A,66B
Prof	Puckett, Mark	D	66A
Asst Prof	Rich, Melody	D	61
Inst Adj	Rockett, Susetta	M	64B
Assoc Prof	Romines, Dee	D	32D,36
Assoc Prof	Scherr, Bernard	D	13,10,66D
Assoc Prof	Sickbert, Murl	D	16
Inst Adj	Straughn, Marcia	M	64A
Prof	Wolz, Larry	D	12A,20G,61,12C
Assoc Prof	Wright, Clell E.	D	31A,36,60

TX0910 Hill College
Department of Music
112 Lamar Dr
Hillsboro, TX 76645-0619
(254) 659-7882   Fax: (254) 582-7591
www.hillcollege.edu
E-mail: plowe@hillcollege.edu

2 Year Institution

Coordinator & Dir., Artist Series: Phillip Lowe, 80A,80F

Inst	Erickson, Shirley	M	11,13,36,61,66
Inst	Lowe, Phillip	M	13,12A,37,47,63
Inst	McCord, Larry	M	11,13B,14C,34B,66A

TX1000 Houston Baptist University
School of Music
7502 Fondren Rd
Houston, TX 77074-3204
(281) 649-3338   Fax: (281) 649-3313
www.hbu.edu
E-mail: music@hbu.edu

4 Year Institution

Director: John Yarrington, 80A

PT	Angerstein, Fred		63D
PT	Angerstein, Nancy		64E
PT	Blench, Karl E.	D	13
PT	Compson, Christy	M	61
Prof	Fiese, Richard K.	D	60B,32
Prof	Furr, Rhonda	D	12A,16,66G
PT	Garcia, Gregory	M	62D
Prof	Gebuhr, Ann K.	D	13,10,34
PT	Givens, Melissa	M	61
PT	Hesse, Shannon	D	66A
PT	Kenley, Nicole	M	61
Prof	Kramlich, Daniel L.	D	13,10F,66A
PT	Lester, Jason	D	61
PT	Lester, Laurie	D	61
PT	McLeland, James K.	D	62
PT	Royem, Dominique	D	13
PT	Shipman, Dan	M	63A
PT	Smith-Wright, Lovie	M	65
PT	Stinson, Carol	D	64C
PT	Wang, Yung-Chiu	D	66A
PT	Woodard, Eve		29,70
Prof	Yarrington, John	D	60A,36

TX1050 Howard College at Big Spring
Department of Music
1001 Birdwell Ln
Big Spring, TX 79720-3702
(432) 264-5145   Fax: (432) 264-5082
www.howardcollege.edu
E-mail: emcintosh@howardcollege.edu

2 Year Institution

Inst	McIntosh, Eulaine	M	52
Inst	Shirey, Julie	B	66
Inst	Vandewalker, Eddie R.		

TX1100 Howard Payne University
School of Music & Fine Arts
1000 Fisk Ave
Brownwood, TX 76801-2715
(325) 649-8500   Fax: (325) 649-8945
www.hputx.edu
E-mail: rtucker@hputx.edu

4 Year Institution
Member of NASM

Dean: Robert Tucker, 80A

Asst Prof	Ash, Corey	M	37,49,63A,32E,60B
Asst Prof	Beaumont, Lance	M	70
Asst Prof	Church, Celeste	D	61,39
Asst Prof	Church, Gregory E.	D	61,39
Assoc Prof	Garrett, Monte	M	60,36
Assoc Prof	Goacher, Stephen	M	60,48,64,47,29
PT	Greene, Elisabeth Mehl	D	10F,12A
PT	Ingram, Danny	M	63C,63D
PT	Neubert, Peter	D	51,62
Asst Prof	Owens, Diane	M	66A,66C,66D,32A,32B
Prof	Reed, Allen	D	13,44,66,31A
Prof	Wallace, Elizabeth	D	66A,66B,66C

TX1150 Huston-Tillotson University
Department of Music
900 Chicon St
Austin, TX 78702-2753
(512) 505-3113   Fax: (512) 505-3190
www.htu.edu
E-mail: glquinlan@htu.edu

4 Year Institution

Chair, Humanities & Performing Arts: Gloria H. Quinlan, 80A

Adj	Birdsong, Nikki S.	M	66A,66D
Prof	Burnaman, Stephen	DMA	13,66A,66G,66B,66C
Adj	Gilliam-Valls, Jessica	M	13A,62C,62D
Adj	Martin, Stephen	D	65
Prof	Quinlan, Gloria H.	DMA	32,36,61,66C,31A
Asst Prof	Stuppard, Javier	M	12,60B,63

TX1250 Jacksonville College
Department of Music
105 BJ Albritton Dr
Jacksonville, TX 75766-4746
(903) 586-2518   Fax: (903) 586-0743
www.jacksonville-college.edu
E-mail: shanna@jacksonville-college.edu

2 Year Liberal Arts Institution

Chair: Gerald Orr, 80A
Assistant Chair: Jason Millican, 80H

	Millican, Jason	M	13A,60,11,36,31A
	Orr, Gerald	M	13,11,36,37,66A

TX1300 Jarvis Christian College
Music Area
PO Box 1472
Hawkins, TX 75765-1470
(903) 769-5700   Fax: (903) 769-1282
www.jarvis.edu
E-mail: gbieritz@jarvis.edu

4 Year Institution, Historically Black College

Coord., Fine Arts: Gerald Bieritz, 80A
Division Chair: Gwendolyn Cudjoe, 80A

Assoc Prof	Bieritz, Gerald	D	12A,11,32A,36,60
Adj Inst	Davis, Hugh	M	36,11
Assoc Prof	Lee, Paul S.	D	66G,13B,11,60,66A
Prof	Smialek, William	D	34A,34B,35A,35B

TX1350 Kilgore College
Department of Music
1100 Broadway Blvd
Kilgore, TX 75662
(903) 984-8531   Fax: (903) 983-8124
www.kilgore.edu
E-mail: jeannej@kilgore.edu

2 Year Institution

Chair: Jeanne Johnson, 80A

PT	Denis, Andrea	M	63B
PT	Hector-Norwood, Diana	M	51,62
Inst	Johnson, Jeanne	M	13C,11,61
Inst	Kelley, Kevin	M	11,10,13,43
PT	Marshall, Alyssa	M	61
PT	Ogilvie, Kevin	M	46,63B
PT	Poteet, Sherry	M	61,11
Inst	Siler, Sandra K.	M	41,45,66A,66D
Inst	Sullivan, Melanie	B	12,61
Inst	Taylor, Jim	M	36,40,61
PT	Turpin, Mike H.	D	11,48,64
PT	Waggoner, Cathy	M	13A,66A
Inst	Wells, Glenn	M	37,11

TX1400 Lamar University
Mary M. Moore Department of Music
Box 10044
Beaumont, TX 77710-0044
(409) 880-8144   Fax: (409) 880-8143
www.lamar.edu/music
E-mail: robert.culbertson@lamar.edu

4 Year Institution, Graduate School
Member of NASM

Master of Music in Performance, Master of Music in Music Education

Interim Chair: Robert M. Culbertson, Jr., 80A
Dir., Graduate Studies: Charlotte P. Mizener, 80C

Adj Fac	Benson, Jack D.	M	11
Prof	Culbertson, Robert M.	D	11,32B,63B
Asst Prof	Deppe, Scott M.	M	37,60B,32G,32C
Prof	Dyess, J. Wayne	D	37,47,63C,49
Prof	Ellis, Kim S.	D	37,64C,64E,48
Adj Fac	Feldhausen, Scott	D	13A,13B,11
Asst Prof	Fife, Travis	M	65,50,32E
Adj Fac	Ganz, Isabelle	D	61
Adj Fac	Garvin, Marc	B	70
Assoc Prof	Gilman, Kurt	D	38,41,62A,62B,20
Inst	Greschner, Debra	M	61
Adj Fac	Haines, Yvonne Bonnie	M	64B,64D
Adj Fac	Hale, Nancy	M	32A,32B
Asst Prof	Han, Jong-Hoon 'James'	D	36,32D
Inst	Hines, Betsy Burleson	D	66D,66C
Vstng Asst Prof	Ilban, Serdar	D	61,39
Adj Fac	Isadore, Jennifer L.	M	64A
Adj Fac	Keele, Roger S.	D	39,66A,61
Assoc Prof	Mizener, Charlotte P.	D	32B,32G,32A
Adj Fac	Mizener, Gary	D	13
Adj Fac	Parks, Gary	M	65,70
Inst	Peirce, Dwight	M	66D
Inst	Pickering, Angela	M	61
Assoc Prof	Rissman, Maurice Nick	D	13,10F,10
Adj Fac	Schroeder, Thomas	M	62C
Asst Prof	Shook, Brian A.	D	63A,63D,32E
Inst	Smith, Ryan	M	63D,37
Adj Fac	Turner, Noel	M	61
Adj Fac	Zhang, Yi	D	66A

TX1425 Laredo Community College
Department of Performing Arts
1 W End Washington St
Laredo, TX 78040
(956) 721-5330   Fax: (956) 764-5924
www.laredo.edu
E-mail: jcrabtree@laredo.edu

2 Year Institution

Chair: Joseph C. Crabtree, 80A

Inst	Adams, Matthew	M	65,50,11,12
Inst	Bishop, Matthew	D	51,70,12A
Inst	Compean, Jose D.	M	13,32,47,63,64
Inst	Crabtree, Joseph C.	D	11,12,36,39
Inst	Gazdyszyn, Danuta U.	M	52,54
Inst	Gorecki, Maria De La Luz	M	52,54
Inst	Gorecki, Mikolaj P.	D	10,11,13,34,66A
Inst	Greco, Christine R.	B	52,54
Inst	Harsa, Sandra Y.	B	52,54
Inst	Hinojosa, Melissa S.	M	11,13,64A
Inst	Liu, Susan (Shao-Shan)	D	66A,66D,11,34
Inst	Mahtani, Lorena	B	52,54
Inst	McKinnis, Alicia V.	B	52,54
Inst	Ramo, Suzanne D.	M	61,11,36
Inst	Reimund, John	M	63D,63
Inst	Townsend, Brendan	M	10F,11,12A,13,62C
Inst	Vargas, Ruben	B	61,46,37,62,63

TX1450 Lee College
Department of Music
PO Box 818
Baytown, TX 77522-0818
(281) 425-6821   Fax: (832) 556-4005
www.lee.edu/vpa/music
E-mail: cmueller@lee.edu

2 Year Institution

Division Chair: Paul Lucke, 80A
Academic Dean: Donnetta Suchon, 80A

PT	Angerstein, Nancy	M	64C
PT	Beam, Joseph	M	65
PT	Black, Cassandra	D	61
Prof	Booker, Kenneth A.	D	37,46,47,60,13A
PT	Bradley, Nedra	M	66C
PT	Caporale, Matthew	M	66A,66D
PT	Cooper, Joseph	M	63A
PT	Eichler, Dennis	M	38
PT	Francis, Nancy	B	62C
PT	Hazelip, Richard	D	66A,66G
PT	Johnson, Alan	M	62A
PT	Keifer, John	M	70
PT	Klimaszewska, Alina	D	66A
PT	Langman, Shannon	M	61
PT	May, Brittany	M	64A
Inst	McKnight, Danny	A	70
Prof	Mueller, Charlotte G.	D	13,11,66A,66D
PT	Odell, Dennis	M	63B
PT	Rich, Kevin	M	63C
PT	Vaughn, Michael	M	61
Prof	Weinel, John	D	61,60,36,39,40

TX1510 Lon Morris College
Department of Music
800 College Ave
Jacksonville, TX 75766-2930
(903) 589-4000   Fax: (903) 586-8562
www.lonmorris.edu

2 Year Institution

Chair: Mary Tidwell, 80A

Asst Prof	Brooks, Jack	M	36,61,40,13C
Assoc Prof	Davis, Charles	M	11,63,64,37
Asst Prof	Eldridge, Ronda	M	11
Inst	Newman, Miranda	M	11,61
Assoc Prof	Tidwell, Mary	M	66A,66D,13B,13A
Adj	Burrell, Lisa M.	D	62A
Adj	Shibatani, Naomi	D	66A,66D,11

TX1550 Lubbock Christian University
Department of Comm/Fine Arts
5601 19th St
Lubbock, TX 79407-2031
(806) 720-7428   Fax: (806) 720-7255
www.lcu.edu
E-mail: laurie.doyle@lcu.edu

4 Year Liberal Arts Institution

Dean, Liberal Arts: Susan Blassingame, 80A
Chair: Laurie Doyle, 80A

Asst Prof	Babcock, Andrew	M	60B,63D,37,13,47
Inst PT	Babcock, Windy	M	32B
Asst Prof	Camp, Philip	PhD	36,61,13,32,40
Asst Prof	Doyle, Laurie	PhD	61,11,40,54
Inst PT	Fried, Melody	PhD	66A
Inst PT	Fruge, Jonathan	M	61
Inst PT	Grisanti, Susan	M	70
Inst PT	Henry, Anna	M	64A
Prof	Holmes, Ruth J.	PhD	12A,66A,66H,66B,13
Inst PT	Kelly, Brandon	DMA	63A
Inst PT	Patterson, Tracy	M	64C,64E
Lect	Smith, Allison	M	11,61
Inst PT	Young, Kevin	M	63D

TX1600 McLennan Community College
Department of Music
1400 College Dr
Waco, TX 76708-1402
(254) 299-8287   Fax: (254) 299-8242
www.mclennan.edu
E-mail: rpage@mclennan.edu

2 Year Institution

Chair: Robert S. Page, 80A
Dir., Artist Series: Richard Gimble, 80F

	Albrecht, Karen	D	61,54,40
	Balmos, Donald	D	36
	Cates, Tim	M	46
	Davis, William		13A
	Fox, Jon	M	70,53,13B
	Gimble, Richard	M	62D,70,53,35B
Adj	Green, Marsha	M	66A,66D
	Harris, Brian P.	D	37
	Haskett, William	D	49,63D,11
	Hooten, David M.	M	64C,11,48,64A
	Howard, Bill	M	10D,10,66A,35B,66D
Adj	Hudson, William Andrew	D	66A,11,66C,66D
	Jarianes, Stephen	B	66C
	Konzelman, Brian	M	35C,35D,35G
	Kutz, Jonathan	M	65A,65B,14C,50
Adj	McKee, Pat	M	70,53
Adj	Morrison, Mandy	M	11
	Nauert, Clark	M	70,53,13B,13C
	Pitts, Ruth	D	13,12A,66A
Adj	Thompson, Howard	M	11
	Uhl, Lise	M	39,61
	Ullman, Beth	M	61,60A
	Wade, Gail G.	M	13,39,66A,66D,66C

TX1650 McMurry University
Department of Music
McM Station Box 698
Abilene, TX 79697-0698
(325) 793-4888   Fax: (325) 793-4662
www.mcm.edu/newsite/web/academics/sal/
    music/index.htm
E-mail: wilson.christina@mcm.edu

4 Year Institution

Chair: Diana L. Ellis, 80A

Assoc Prof	Ellis, Diana L.	DMA	61,39,40
Asst Prof	Gomer, Wesley	DMA	13,66,69,12A,36
Inst	Lloyd, L. Keith	M	65,12A,14,12,50
Inst	Wilcox, Mark	M	13C,63A,49,29E,29C

TX1660 Midland College
Department of Music
3600 N Garfield St AFA
Midland, TX 79705-6329
(432) 685-4626   Fax: (432) 685-4769
www.midland.edu
E-mail: lula@midland.edu

2 Year Institution

Dean, Fine Arts & Communication: William Feeler, 80A

Asst Prof	Bewley, Rabon	M	11,12A,29,64E,13A
Inst	Bostic, Bert	B	36,47,66D
Adj Inst	Griffin, Ruth Ann	B	61,66D
Prof	Jordan, Michael D.	D	13A,13,11,39,61
Adj Inst	Miller, Mary		70
Adj Inst	Moss, Vivian		61
Adj Inst	Porter, Jacob		70
Adj Inst	Puga, Richy		65
Adj Inst	Pysh, Greg	M	61,12A
Adj Inst	Santorelli, Michael	M	63A
Adj Inst	Santorelli, Shari	M	13,66C
Adj Inst	Spain, Steve	B	66C

TX1700 Midwestern State University
Department of Music
3410 Taft Blvd
Wichita Falls, TX 76308-2095
(940) 397-4267   Fax: (940) 397-4502
www.mwsu.edu
E-mail: timothy.justus@mwsu.edu

4 Year Institution
Member of NASM

Chair: Timothy W. Justus, 80A

Assoc Prof	Archambo, Larry	D	60,32C,37,34,63C
Asst Prof	Black, Alan	M	11,37,47,50,65
Inst PT	Carafax, Bruce	M	70
Asst Prof	Crews, Norval	M	11,64C,64E,72
Inst PT	Diltz, Judy	M	61
Asst Prof	Harvey, Susan	D	63A,63B,66A,32B,32C
Assoc Prof	Justus, Timothy W.	D	10F,13
Assoc Prof	Lewis, Gary	M	11,66D
Prof	Maxwell, Don	D	61,39
Prof	Morrow, Ruth E.	D	66,12A,66A,13D,13E
Assoc Prof	Schuppener, James	D	36,61,32D

TX1725 Mountain View College
Department of Music
4849 W Illinois Ave
Dallas, TX 75211-6503
(214) 860-8671   Fax: (214) 860-8765
www.mvc.dcccd.edu
E-mail: vsoto@dcccd.edu

2 Year Institution

Director: Victor Soto-Medina, 80A

Prof	Armendarez, Christina	D	61
Prof	Franklin, Janice L.	M	11,66,54,34B
Adj	Garmon, Randy	M	37,46,47,63
Adj	Ginorio, Jorge	M	20H,50,65
Prof	Hettle, Mark	M	13,11,37,47,63A
Adj	Hooan, Dan	B	11,70
Adj	Imthurn, Melinda	M	11,36,61
Adj	Page, Gordon	M	11,13,36
Adj	Richardson, Cathy	M	11,62A
Adj	Schloss, David Lee	M	64,48
Prof	Soto-Medina, Victor	M	11,13,66,34B
Adj	Weiss, Linda	M	66G

TX1750 Navarro College
Department of Music
3200 W 7th Ave
Corsicana, TX 75110-4818
(903) 874-6501   Fax: (903) 874-4636
www.navarrocollege.edu/
E-mail: trina.jeffers@navarrocollege.edu

2 Year Institution

Chair: Mark Underwood, 80A
Academic Dean: Linda Timmerman

Inst	Herod, Sheila	M	13,12A,66A,66C,66D
PT	Kennedy, Rebecca		70
PT	Kuhl, Mary	M	48,64
Inst	Stubbs, James	M	46,32,13A,37,47
Inst	Timmerman, David	M	13A,13,36,41,61
PT	Van Schaik, Tom		65
PT	Vancura, Ken		61
PT	Vancura, Kim		61,66A

TX1775 North Central Texas College
Department of Music
1525 W California St
Gainesville, TX 76240-4636
(940) 668-7731   Fax: (940) 668-6049
www.nctc.edu
E-mail: mlinder@nctc.edu

2 Year Institution

Chair: J. Michael Linder, 80A

	Arnold, Stacy	M	70,11
	Dill, John	M	13A,11,66A,66G,12A
	Jennings, Tom	M	11,36,61
	Kobuck, Martin	M	13,63C,46,11
	Linder, J. Michael	D	13,36,61
	McMillan, Bart	M	11
	Studdard, Shane	M	66,66C,11
	Walter, Regina	M	61,54,11

TX1850 Odessa College
Department of Music
201 W University Blvd
Odessa, TX 79764-7105
(432) 335-6731   Fax: (432) 335-6730
www.odessa.edu/dept/music
E-mail: ebaker@odessa.edu

2 Year Institution
Member of NASM

Chair: Eric Baker, 80A

Inst	Baker, Eric		11,37,46,63A
Inst	Bizzell, Gayle	M	12A,66A,66C,66D
Adj	Carroll, John	M	65
Adj	Chance, Christopher	M	64C
Inst	Corman, David	M	39,36,40
Adj	Garcia, Gabriel	M	
Adj	Harris, Dennis	M	51,70
Inst	Lane, LuAnn	M	11,13,66A,66C,66D
Adj	Loudenback, Daniel	D	64E
Adj	Orta, Melissa	M	61
Adj	Walsh, Benjamin	M	63C

TX1900 Our Lady of the Lake University
Department of Music
411 SW 24th St
San Antonio, TX 78207-4617
(210) 434-6711 x 8137   Fax: (210) 431-4090
www.ollusa.edu
E-mail: fabrm@lake.ollusa.edu

4 Year Institution

Dean: Francine Danis, 80A

Lect	Alexander, Mark W.	D	66A,66C,66D
Lect	Carroll, John	D	63A,49,37,41,47
Lect	Girko, Elizabeth	B	62A
Lect	Loden, Larry	M	64C,64E,32E
Lect	Lyon, Leslie	B	70
Lect	Pape, Madlyn	M	36,61
Lect	Partlow, Mary Rita	M	66A,66D
Assoc Prof	Twomey, Michael P.	D	10A,13,10F,38,62

TX2000 Panola College
Department of Music
1109 W Panola St
Carthage, TX 75633-1149
(903) 693-2061   Fax: (903) 693-1149
www.panola.edu
E-mail: fmason@panola.edu

2 Year Institution

Chair, Fine Arts: Freddy Mason, 80A

	McGowan, Mike	M	11,37,49,13,29

TX2050 Paris Junior College
Department of Music
2400 Clarksville St
Paris, TX 75460-6258
(903) 782-0341   Fax: (903) 782-0370
www.parisjc.edu
E-mail: jvaughan@parisjc.edu

2 Year Institution

Assoc Dean, Communication & Fine Arts: Beth Shelton, 80A
Music Contact: Jennie Vaughan, 80A

Inst	Briggs, Philip	M	36,40,61,11
Inst	Vaughan, Jennie	M	13A,13B,13C,66A,11

TX2100 Prairie View A&M University
Department of Music & Theatre
PO Box 519 MS 2205
Prairie View, TX 77446-0519
(936) 261-3335   Fax: (936) 261-3331
www.pvamu.edu/pages/329.asp
E-mail: jlcornelius@pvamu.edu

4 Year Institution, Historically Black College

Interim Head: John L. Cornelius, II, 80A
Dean: Danny R. Kelley, 80A

Asst Prof	Bergin, Wendy I.	D	64A,48,13
Asst Prof	Cornelius, John L.	D	66C,66A,66D,13
Inst	Freeman, Jeffrey J.	M	11,63C,49,63D,34
Inst Adj	Gadgil, Sunil	D	64E,64C,11
Inst	Jones, Larry	M	13A,11,50,65
Inst Adj	McNeel, Mary	M	63B
Inst	McQueen, William F.	M	11,20A,49,63A
Inst	Moore, Christine E.	M	62,16
Inst Adj	Sanders, Robert	M	47,11
Assoc Prof	Seldon, Vicki A.	D	11,12A,66A,66C
Inst	Taylor, Arlecia Jan	M	11,36,32,66A
Inst	Turner, Leon P.	M	11,39,61

TX2150 Rice University
Shepherd School of Music
MS-532
6100 Main St
Houston, TX 77005-1892
(713) 348-4854   Fax: (713) 348-5317
music.rice.edu
E-mail: musi@rice.edu

4 Year Institution, Graduate School

DMA in Music, Master of Music

Dean: Robert Yekovich, 80A
Dir., Admissions: Geoffrey Scott, 80D
Dir., Preparatory Division: Julia Jalbert, 80E
Associate Dean: Gary A. Smith, 80H

Assoc Prof	Al-Zand, Karim	D	13,10
Prof	Atherholt, Robert	M	64B
Prof	Bado, Richard	M	39
Lect	Bailey, Nancy	D	12A
Assoc Prof	Bailey, Walter B.	D	11,12A,12
Assoc Prof	Barnett, Gregory	D	12A,12
Assoc Prof PT	Barnhill, Allen	M	63C,41,42
Assoc Prof	Brandt, Anthony K.	D	13,10
Prof	Brown, Richard	M	50,65,42
Lect	Buchman, Rachel	B	
Prof	Buyse, Leone	M	42,64A
Assoc Prof	Chen, Shih-Hui	D	13,10
Prof	Citron, Marcia J.	D	12
Artist in Res	Connelly, Brian	M	66A,66C,66E,42
Artist in Res PT	De Chambrier, Jan	M	39
Artist in Res PT	DerHovsepian, Joan	M	41
Artist in Res	Dickinson, Debra	M	39
Prof	Dunham, James	M	62B,42
Lect PT	Dunn, Susan L.	M	61
Prof	Ellison, Paul	M	42,62D
Assoc Prof	Ferris, David	D	12A,12
Artist in Res	Fischer, Jeanne Kierman	M	66A,66B,66D,42
Prof	Fischer, Norman	B	42,62C
Vstng Assoc Prof PT	Freeman, Phillip I.	B	63C
Artist in Res PT	French, Christopher J.		41
Prof	Goldsmith, Kenneth	M	42,62A
Prof	Gottschalk, Arthur	D	13,10,45
Artist in Res PT	Graf, Hans		38,60B
Lect	Gross, Robert W.	D	13B,13D,13E,13F,13I
Artist in Res PT	Halen, Eric J.	M	41
Prof	Hoebig, Desmond	M	62C,42
Prof Emeritus	Holloway, Clyde	D	66G
Prof	Jaber, Thomas I.	M	36,60A,66C
Prof	Jalbert, Pierre	D	13,10
Prof	Kamins, Benjamin		64D,42
Prof	Kaun, Kathleen	M	61
Prof	King, Stephen	D	61
Assoc Prof PT	Kirk, David E.	B	63D,42
Lect	Kloeckner, Phillip	D	66G,13C
Prof	Lavenda, Richard A.	D	13,10
Assoc Prof PT	LeGrand, Thomas	B	41
Prof	Lin, Cho-Liang	B	62A,42
Artist in Res	Loehnig, Grant A.	M	39
Asst Prof	Loewen, Peter V.	D	12A,12
Prof	Luca, Sergiu	DIPL	62A
Artist in Res PT	Macelaru, Cristian	M	38,60B
Emerita	Nance, Virginia	M	
Assoc Prof PT	Page, Paula	B	62E,42
Artist in Res	Park, Sohyoung	D	66A,66B,66D
Prof	Parker, Jon Kimura	D	66A,42
Prof	Pitts, Timothy	B	62D
Prof	Rachleff, Larry	M	60B,38
Artist in Res	Rarick, Janet	B	42
Prof	Roux, Robert	B	66A
Artist in Res	Shank, Dean	D	66B,66F
Assoc Prof PT	Smith, Brinton Averil	D	62C
Prof	Speziale, Marie	B	63A,41,42
Assoc Prof	Stallmann, Kurt D.	D	13,10,45,34
Lect Adj	Stasney, C. Richard	MD	61
Prof	Van der Werff, Ivo-Jan	B	62B,42
Prof	VerMeulen, William		63B,42
Lect PT	Watkins, Cornelia	M	
Prof PT	Webster, Michael	D	42,64C
Prof	Winkler, Kathleen	M	62A,42

TX2170 St Edwards University
Department of Music
3001 S Congress Ave
Austin, TX 78704-6425
(512)448-8670   Fax: (512)448-8492
www.stedwards.edu
E-mail: geraldm@admin.stedwards.edu

4 Year Catholic Liberal Arts Institution

Director: Gerald Muller, 80A

Adj	Bradford, Mary Pinkney	M	66A,66B,66D
Adj	Colarusso, Joey	M	64C,11
Adj	Jurcevic, S. Annette		
Adj	Layne, Darin		70
Assoc Prof	Muller, Gerald	M	13,11,12A,32,36
Adj	Rabago, Kathy		
Adj	Sadler, Cindy		61
Adj	Stevens, Morris		61

TX2200 St Marys University
Department of Music
1 Camino Santa Maria St
San Antonio, TX 78228-8562
(210) 436-3421   Fax: (210) 436-3640
www.stmarytx.edu/acad/music/
E-mail: jmoore@stmarytx.edu

4 Year Private Catholic
Member of NASM

Dean: Janet Dizinno, 80A
Chair: John Moore, 80A

PT	Boyd, Bonnie	M	62A
PT	Cantu, Jacob	B	61,39
PT	Carroll, John	M	63A
PT	Carter, Cecil		47,53
PT	Garza, Jeff	M	63B
Vstng Lect	Herbert, David		13A,64B,32,13B,13C
PT	Hipp, Lee		63D
PT	Johnson, Warren	B	65
PT	Kalson, James		62D
PT	King, Clarence M.	M	64E
PT	Kline, Peter	M	63C,63D
Vstng Asst Prof	Long, Daniel	M	36,61,60,11,13D
PT	Lyon, Leslie	B	11,70
PT	Menconi, Audra M.	M	65
PT	Mentzer, Larry E.	B	64C
PT	Mollenauer, David	B	62C
Assoc Prof	Moore, John	M	11,66A,66C,12A,66D
PT	Petkovich, Brian T.		64D
Assoc Prof	Rankin, John M.		11,47,63A,46
PT	Ross, William	M	66G
PT	Schultz, Dale	M	37,60,32C,63
Asst Prof	Sullivan, Michael	D	10,11,12A
PT	Vokes, Emmett	M	66A
PT	Wiehe, Beth A.	B	64A

TX2220 St Philips College
Department of Fine Arts
1801 Martin Luther King Dr
San Antonio, TX 78203-2098
(210) 531-3321   Fax: (210) 531-4768
www.alamo.edu/spc
E-mail: ggonzales@alamo.edu@alamo.edu

2 Year Institution

Chair: Gregory Gonzales, 80A
Dean: Gregory Hudspeth, 80A

Inst	Washington, Henry	B	36,11,66A,66G,66D

TX2250 Sam Houston State University
School of Music
PO Box 2208
Huntsville, TX 77341-2208
(936) 294-1360   Fax: (936) 294-3765
www.shsu.edu/~music
E-mail: music@shsu.edu

4 Year Institution, Graduate School
Member of NASM

Master of Music in Composition, Master of Music in Performance, Master of Music in Conducting, Master of Music in Music Education, Master of Music in Music Therapy, Master of Music in Musicology, Master of Music in Collaborative Piano/Chamber Music

Director: Scott D. Plugge, 80A
Associate Director: Kevin Clifton, 80H

Assoc Prof	Adams, Randal	M	63A
Assoc Prof	Barrett, Wayne	D	61,31
PT	Bronstein, Chase	M	65,50
Prof	Cannon, Rodney M.	D	65,29
Assoc Prof	Card, Patricia P.		64C
Vstng Asst Prof	Carrettin, Zachary	M	38,60B
PT	Cho, James	D	66D
Asst Prof	Clifton, Kevin		13
Emeritus	Corbin, Barbara	M	61
PT	Crabtree, John M.	D	13A,13B,13C
PT	Crosby, Alison		13
Assoc Prof	Daniel, Kathy	M	64A,32A,32B

PT	Daniel, Robert	M	63D
PT	Davis, Colin	M	13
Assoc Prof	DeMers, Peggy	D	63B,13
PT	Dunham, Deborah	M	62D
PT	Eaton, Denise	M	36,32D
PT	Englert, David	M	13A,13B,13C
PT	Esparza, Eric Peche	D	36,61
PT	Forbay, Bronwen	D	61
Asst Prof	Franklin, James C.	M	36,32D
PT	Franklin, Nicole	M	61
Asst Prof	Gibbs, Brian	M	37,32C
	Gjevre, Naomi	D	62A,42,12C
Asst Prof	Grimes, Rebecca	M	39,61
PT	Herrington, Brian P.	PhD	13A,13B,13C
PT	Heuer, Megan	M	64B
Prof	Howey, Henry E.	D	63D,63C
PT	Hunt, Robert	D	66C
Emeritus	Irvin, Virginia	M	32
PT	Johnson, James	M	70
PT	Keele, Roger	D	66C
Asst Prof	Kindred, Kyle	D	13A,13B,13C
Asst Prof	Koch, Nathan J.	D	64D,13C,12A
PT	Lake, Mary Kay	M	61,39
Assoc Prof	Lane, John W.	M	65
PT	Lee, Kaju	M	66C
Asst Prof	Lim, Hayoung Audrey	D	33
PT	McAdow, Seth	M	32E
PT	McCroskey, John	M	63C
Prof	McInturf, Matthew	M	32C,37,60B
Assoc Prof	Michel, Christopher	M	61
Assoc Prof	Miller, Karen Epps	M	33
Emeritus	Mills, Ralph L.	D	37
PT	Montiel, Alejandro	D	70
PT	Mott, Jammieca	D	61
Assoc Prof	Murphy-Manley, Sheryl K.	D	12
PT	Oliver, Sarah	M	62E
PT	Osborne, Robert B.	M	63C
Assoc Prof	Pinell, Javier	D	62A,42,51
Prof	Plugge, Scott D.	D	64E,20G,29,47
PT	Rawlins, Deborah	M	32A,32B
Assoc Prof	Ruiz, Sergio	D	66A,66B
Asst Prof	Rus-Edery, Ilonka Livia	D	66A,66C
PT	Saenz, Daniel	M	62C
PT	Salazar, Rene	M	62B
Asst Prof	Schneller, Aric	M	47,29,63C,61
Emeritus	Smith, Carol	D	38,51,60B,62,32E
PT	Valk, Alexis	D	62D
PT	Walsh, Michael	D	61
PT	Warkentin, Steve	M	63A

TX2260 San Antonio College

Department of Music
1300 San Pedro Ave
San Antonio, TX 78212-4299
(210) 733-2731   Fax: (210) 733-2985
www.alamo.edu/sac
E-mail: jhunt1@alamo.edu

2 Year Institution

Chair: Jeffrey Hunt, 80A
Dean: Conrad Krueger, 80A

Adj	Aguirre, Ruth		64C
Adj	Alexander, Mark	D	66A
Adj	Birt, Timothy		61
Inst	Blanchett, Madalyn	M	11,64A,66A,66D,67
Adj	Carey, Peter	M	11,29
Adj	Elizondo, Madeline		61
Adj	Ellis, Cynthia	M	66A,66D
Adj	Fabrique, Martha H.	D	64A
Adj	Gallego, Ignacio		62C
Inst	Gignac, Andrew	M	63A,13,10,11
Adj	Girko, Beth	M	62A
Adj	Girko, Stephen	M	64C
Adj	Gollihar, Stephen	D	
Adj	Gomez, Adalberto		
Asst Prof	Gomez, Alice	M	10,14,47,65,35A
Adj	Gonzalez, Ramon		31
Prof Emeritus	Gregory, George R.	M	62C,62E
Adj	Herbert, David P.	M	64B
Adj	Kalson, Jim		62D
Adj	King, Morgan	M	64E
Asst Prof	Kline, W. Peter	M	13A,11,37,49,63D
Adj	Morgan, Kerri		
Adj	Redzic, Zlatan		62D
Adj	Rogers, Mark	D	37
Asst Prof	Russell, Mary Lou	M	11,66A,66C,66D,29
Inst	Sanchez, Cynthia	M	36,61,64A,66A
Adj	Sprayberry, Tom		70
Adj	Swanson, Jenny		66G,66A
Adj	Torres, David		12A
Adj	Tracy, Janet M.	D	11
Adj	Van Gee, Jill		62B
Adj	Walker, Becky		

TX2295 San Jacinto College Central

Department of Music
PO Box 2007
Pasadena, TX 77501-2007
(281) 476-1831   Fax: (281) 542-2073
www.sjcd.edu
E-mail: eric.late@sjcd.edu

2 Year Institution

Interim Chair: Eric Late, 80A

Adj	Beaumont, Lance	M	70
Adj	Bielish, Aaron J.	M	62A,62B,41,11,13
Adj	Braswell, Martha	D	66A,66E,66G,11
Adj	Busselberg, Paul	M	61,36,13C
Adj	Busselberg, Rebecca Pyper	M	61
Adj	Crotts, Angela	B	35C,35G
Adj	Harris, Paul R.	M	64,11
Inst	Late, Eric		47,62D,11,34C
Inst	Marston, Karen L.	M	37,63C,11,13A,34C
Inst	Metcalfe, James L.	B	65,35C,35G,46
Inst	Mizma, Michael E.	M	50,65,35A,35C
Inst	Robbins, Janice B.	M	61
Adj	Rodriquez, Frank	B	70
Inst	Rowell, Chester D.	M	64C,64E,41
Adj	Saenz, Daniel	M	62C
Adj	Scoles, Philip	M	63A
Adj	Slezak, Lawrence L.	B	64E
Adj	Smith, Mike	M	63B
Inst	Spencer, Sarah	M	66A,66C,66D,12A
Adj	Valdez, Paul	B	35C
Adj	Warren, Alec	M	65
Adj	Wester, R. Glenn	M	61,66,11,13A
Inst	Williams, Lester C.	B	35D,35G

TX2300 San Jacinto College North

Department of Music
5800 Uvalde Rd
Houston, TX 77049-4513
(281) 458-4050 x 7228   Fax: (281) 459-7138
www.sanjac.edu
E-mail: randy.snyder@sjcd.edu

2 Year Institution

Chair, Fine Arts: Randy L. Snyder, 80A

PT	Au, Kingchi	D	66A
PT	Baca, Danny	M	64,11
PT	Hazelip, Richard	M	13B,66G,61,11
Inst FT	Moore, Edgar	M	11,36,61,12A
Inst FT	Morgan, Carol	M	63A,29,13B,11
PT	Muller, Carl	M	63B,63C,63D
Inst FT	Snyder, Randy L.	D	13A,13,11,47,63
PT	Warren, Alec	M	65

TX2310 San Jacinto College South

Department of Music
13735 Beamer Rd
Houston, TX 77089-6009
(281) 484-1900   Fax: (281) 922-3483
www.sanjac.edu
E-mail: lynne.brandt@sjcd.edu

2 Year Institution

Lead Faculty, Music: Lynne Brandt, 80A
Chair, Visual & Performing Arts: Christina Potts, 80A

PT	Benoist, Debbie	M	11,13A,34C,65,66
FT	Brandt, Lynne	M	13,64A,41,66A
FT	Garcia, Jeremy	M	70,11,41
PT	Kochen, Timothy	M	47
FT	Rader, Jana Elam	M	11,12A,34C,61
PT	Rawley, Joseph	M	11
PT	Richards, Julie	M	11,13A,62A,66C
PT	Roe, Gail	M	66A,11,66C
FT	Stevens, Cynthia C.	M	37,40,61
PT	Stuckey, John	M	37
PT	Wren, Bobby	M	37

TX2350 South Plains College

Department of Music
PO Box 52
Levelland, TX 79336-0054
(806) 894-9611 x 2261   Fax: (806) 894-5274
www.southplainscollege.edu/
E-mail: bkeeling@southplainscollege.edu

2 Year Institution

Chair: Bruce Keeling, 80A

PT	Aipperspach, Candice Lane	M	11
PT	Aipperspach, Ian B.	M	11
PT	Barfield, Sally	M	66A,66D
Prof	Gardner, Al	M	11,47,50,65
Inst	Gelber, Debbie	DMA	13A,13B,36,61,13C
Asst Prof	Ham, Donna	DMA	11,13A,66
PT	Henry, Anna W.	M	64A,48
Assoc Prof	Hudson, Gary	DMA	11,49,63A,63B
PT	Jenkins, Rosemary	M	66A,66D
Asst Prof	Ji, Hye-Gyung	DMA	66
Prof	Johnson, Jon S.	M	13,36,61,54,32D
Prof	Keeling, Bruce	DMA	11,12A,47,49,63D
Inst	Kennedy, John	D	14C,13A,46,49,32B
PT	Meineke, Robert	M	62A,62B,62C,62D,51
Asst Prof	Nazworth, Daniel	PhD	54
Asst Prof	Reid, John	B	11,10D,35B,62D
Prof	Reid, Lynda L.	M	13A,32B,37,48,64C
PT	Turner, Don	M	64C,64E
Asst Prof	Wheeler, Brent	M	70

TX2400 Southern Methodist University

Meadows School of the Arts-Music
PO Box 750356
Dallas, TX 75275-0356
(214) 768-1951   Fax: (214) 768-4669
www.meadows.smu.edu
E-mail: caroleh@mail.smu.edu

4 Year Institution, Graduate School
Member of NASM

Master of Music in Composition, Master of Music in Music Theory, Master of Music in Performance, Master of Music in Conducting, Master of Sacred Music, Master of Music in Music Education, Master of Music in Music Therapy, Master of Music in History & Literature, Master of Music in Piano Performance & Pedagogy, Master of Music in Instrumental Conducting, Performer Diploma

Dean: Jose A. Bowen, 80A
Director & Dir., Graduate Studies: Samuel S. Holland, 80A,80C,80H
Dir., Summer Programs: Julia K. Scott, 80G
Associate Dean: Martin Sweidel, 80H
Associate Director, Student Affairs: Alan Wagner, 80H

Prof	Achucarro, Joaquin		66A
Adj Assoc Prof	Adkins, Christopher	M	62C
Artist in Res	Albert, Matthew	M	42,62A
Asst Prof	Allen, Sarah	M	32E,37,32,60B,32B
Adj Asst Prof	Baron, Deborah		64A
Adj Lect	Bastable, Barbara	M	33
Adj Asst Prof	Bax, Alessio	M	66A
Lect	Booth, Thomas	M	63A
Adj Prof	Borok, Emanuel		62A
Prof	Bowen, Jose A.	D	47,12A,29,38,12
Adj Lect	Bryant, John		65
Adj Assoc Prof	Cherry, Kalman	DIPL	65A
Lect	Cherryholmes, Roy	B	35D
Adj Asst Prof	Corbet, Kim	M	53,29A
Adj Asst Prof	Dederich-Pejovich, Susan	B	62E
Prof	Delaney, Jack	D	60,37
Prof	Diaz, Andres	B	62C
Lect	Dietert, Dale	M	61
Prof	Dupuy, Virginia	M	61
Other	Emerson, Tara M.	M	66C
Adj Asst Prof	Fabian, Donald	M	64E
Adj Asst Prof	Feezell, Mark	D	13
Assoc Prof	Forbis, Clifton	M	61
Adj Assoc Prof	Foster, Gary	D	13
Assoc Prof	Frank, Robert J.	D	10,13
Adj Assoc Prof	Garner, Paul		64C
Lect	Gerhart, Martha	M	66C
Adj Assoc Prof	Good, Matt J.		63D
Vstng Asst Prof	Greenwood, Andrew	D	12
Adj Lect	Gunter, Kevin	M	66B
Adj Prof	Guthrie, Robert	B	70
Lect	Hammett, Hank	M	61,66C,39
Assoc Prof	Hanlon, Kevin	D	13,10F,10,43
Adj Assoc Prof	Hannigan, Erin	M	64B
Adj Asst Prof	Harder, Lane	D	13
Prof Emeritus	Hart, Kenneth W.		31A
Prof	Holland, Samuel S.	D	66A,66B,66D
Adj Lect	Hoops, Haley S.	M	63B
Adj Assoc Prof	Howard, Douglas	M	65
Assoc Prof	Huffman, Pamela G.	D	60A,36
Adj Prof	Hustis, Gregory	B	63B
Adj Lect	Jackson, Lynne A.	M	63
Prof	Karp, David	D	13,66A
Artist in Res	Kim, Chee-Yun	C	62A
Adj Asst Prof	Kitzman, Diane D.	B	62A
Adj Assoc Prof	Kitzman, John	B	63C
Lect	Kline, Matthew C.	M	66B,66D
Prof	Krout, Robert E.	D	33
Asst Prof	Kupfer, Peter A.	D	12
Adj Lect	Lang, Drew	B	65B
Adj Assoc Prof	Larson, Jean	M	64A
Adj Assoc Prof	Lederer, Thomas	B	62D
Adj Lect	Lee, Jon	M	50
Assoc Prof	Leone, Carol	D	41,66A
Lect	Lysinger, Catherine	D	66B,66D
Assoc Prof	Mancini, David	D	13
Adj Asst Prof	Merrill, Brian G.	M	32
Lect	Mohamed, Jamal		65
Prof	Moore, Barbara		61
Prof	Mouledous, Alfred	M	66A
Lect	Murray, Melissa M.	M	13
Prof Emeritus	Ode, James	D	32
Prof	Palmer, Larry	D	66G,66H
Adj Asst Prof	Perkins, Deborah	D	62
Prof	Phillips, Paul	D	60,38
Assoc Prof Emeritus	Powell, Ross	M	41,64C,43
Asst Prof	Ramos-Kittrell, Jesus	D	12,70
Adj Assoc Prof	Roberts, Wilfred A.	B	64D
Adj Assoc Prof	Rose, Ellen	M	62B
Prof	Sargon, Simon	M	13,10F
Adj Lect	Sato, Akira	M	46,47
Asst Prof	Scott, Julia K.	PhD	32
Adj Lect	Smith, Edward		65B
Lect	Smith, Jason B.	M	61
Adj Assoc Prof	Sudweeks, Barbara		62B
Assoc Prof	Sweidel, Martin	D	45,13
Prof	Tunks, Thomas W.	D	32,12F
Asst Prof	Wang, Xi	D	13

TX2550 Southwestern Adventist University

Department of Music
100 W Hillcrest
Keene, TX 76059
(817) 645-3921   Fax: (817) 556-4744
www.swau.edu
E-mail: davidra@swau.edu

4 Year Institution

Chair: John W. Boyd, 80A

Asst Prof	Anavitarte, David	M	36,61,66A,12A,32B
Inst PT	Boyd, John W.	D	49,11
Inst PT	Doroftei, Mugnr	D	13,38,62
Inst PT	Gilley, John	M	37,64
Inst PT	Scholl, Tim	M	13A,13E,32A,66,70

TX2570 Southwestern Assemblies of God Univ

Department of Music
1200 Sycamore
Waxahachie, TX 75165-2397
(972) 937-4010   Fax: (972) 923-8165
www.sagu.edu
E-mail: lrobins@sagu.edu

4 Year Institution

Chair: Linda Robins, 80A

Adj Inst	Block, Tyrone	M	32E,37,47,60B,63
Inst	Bridges, Jan	M	32A,32B,11
Inst	Chang, Donathan	M	31A,31B,61,60A,36
Adj Inst	Daugherty, Wendy	M	62A,62B,66A,32E
Adj Inst	Freeze, Marcus	B	62D
Lect	Guynes, Christi	B	66A,66D
Inst	Jones, Meredith	M	12A,31A,60A,61
Adj Inst	Jones, Nathan	B	70
Assoc Prof	Lee, Amanda	D	66A,13C,13B,13E,66B
Adj Inst	Lee, Won Yong	D	66A
Adj Inst	Perez, Jesus	B	65
Asst Prof	Robins, Linda	M	32B,36,66A,66B
Adj Inst	Solis, Kassi	M	61

TX2600 Southwestern Baptist Theo Sem
School of Church Music
PO Box 22390
Fort Worth, TX 76122-0390
(817) 923-1921   Fax: (817) 921-8762
www.swbts.edu
E-mail: scmusic@swbts.edu

Graduate School
Member of NASM

Master of Arts in Church Music, Master of Music in Church Music, DMA in Church Music, PhD in Church Music, Master of Arts in Worship

Dean: Stephen P. Johnson, 80A
Associate Dean, Undergraduate Studies: Tom Song, 80B
Associate Dean, Community Relations: John Simons, 80E,80H
Associate Dean, Performance: William Colson, 80H,80F
Senior Associate Dean, Academic & Graduate Studies: R. Allen Lott, 80H,80C

Adj	Aultman, Carol	M	61
Prof	Aultman, Gerald	D	13A,13,66A,66G
Adj	Burchill, Thomas	M	70,47
Assoc Prof	Cajas, Edgar	D	32A,32B,32C,12A
Prof	Cofer, Angela F.	D	61
Prof	Colson, William	D	13A,13,10F,10,13I
Adj Inst	Flauding, Richard (Ric) G.		10,34,10F,13
Assoc Prof	Hardin, Garry Joe	D	10A,13,29,38,46
Adj	Helbing, Stockton	B	47,65
Asst Prof	Hsieh, Fang-Lan	D	12A,16
Adj	Johnson, Michelle	D	66A,66B,66C,66D,66E
Assoc Prof	Johnson, Stephen P.	D	10,13,10F,60A,60
Assoc Prof	Lim, Yoon-Mi	M	66G,66A,13A
Prof	Lott, R. Allen	D	12A,12,14,12C
Adj	Montgomery, Ron	M	61
Adj	Park, Hana	D	66
Prof	Robinson, David	D	61
Adj	Runnels, Jason	D	12
Prof	Simons, John	D	31A
Prof	Smith, Robert C.	D	66
Assoc Prof	Song, Tom	D	36,60A,31A
Prof	Sprenger, Jill T.	D	66A,66B,66D
Adj	Sprenger, Kurt	D	62A,38,60B
Prof	Thye, David R.	D	60,32D,32E,36,38
Prof	Wyrtzen, Donald	M	10A,31A,66A

TX2650 Southwestern University
Department of Music
PO Box 770
Georgetown, TX 78627
(512) 863-1356   Fax: (512) 863-1422
www.southwestern.edu
E-mail: hoogerhj@southwestern.edu

4 Year Institution
Member of NASM

Chair: Jason Hoogerhyde, 80A

Asst Prof	Asbury, David	D	70,11,34,13C
Assoc Prof	Cain, Bruce A.	D	39,61
Asst Prof PT	Cannon, Robert V.	D	63A
Inst PT	Carney, Anna	M	64C,64E
Prof	Cooper, J. Michael	D	12A
Asst Prof PT	Creel, Randall Patrick	D	63B
Inst PT	Douglas, Susan	M	64B
Inst PT	Fedson, Delaine	M	62E
Prof	Ferrari, Lois	D	37,38,60B
Inst PT	Findlen, Kathryn	M	61
Asst Prof PT	Gilliam-Valls, Jessica	D	62D
Asst Prof PT	Guidi, David	D	47,64E
Assoc Prof	Hoogerhyde, Jason	DMA	13,10
Inst PT	Inglis, Adrienne	M	64A
Asst Prof PT	Kostelnik, Steve	D	70
Assoc Prof	Lam, Eri Lee	D	62A,32E,42
Asst Prof PT	Lam, Vincent	D	66A
Inst PT	Martysz, Erin	M	65
Inst PT	Miller, Eric	M	64D
Asst Prof PT	Polley, David	D	31,66G
Inst PT	Rossman, Pamela	M	66A,66D
Assoc Prof	Russell, Eileen Meyer	D	63D,13,13C,49,63C
Prof	Sheppard, Kenny	D	60A,36,32D
Inst PT	Simpson, Nicholas	D	61
Prof	Tamagawa, Kiyoshi	D	66A,13,66B
Inst PT	Utterback, David	M	66A,66D
Asst Prof PT	Warren, Robert	D	66A,66D
Inst PT	Washecka, Tim	M	62B,62A
Inst PT	Zenobi, Dana	M	61
Asst Prof PT	Zheng-Olefsky, Hai	M	62C,62D

TX2700 Stephen F Austin State University
School of Music
SFA Station Box 13043
Nacogdoches, TX 75962-3043
(936) 468-4602   Fax: (936) 468-5810
www.music.sfasu.edu
E-mail: sharris@sfasu.edu

4 Year Institution, Graduate School
Member of NASM

Master of Arts in Music Education (Distance Learning), Master of Arts in Music, Master of Arts in Music Education, Master of Music in Performance, Master of Music in Conducting

Director: Scott H. Harris, 80A
Dean, College of Fine Arts & Dir., Artist/Performance Series: A. C. 'Buddy' Himes, 80A,80F
Assistant Dir., Undergraduate Studies: Gary Wurtz, 80B
Assistant Dir., Graduate Studies: Stephen J. Lias, 80C

Assoc Prof	Ajero, Mario	D	66B,66C,66D
Prof	Allen, Fred J.	M	60B,32C,37,41
Prof	Anderson, Ronald E.	D	60A,11,12A,12C
Lect	Anglley, Tarney	D	60B,32C,37,41
Prof	Ayer, Christopher	D	64C
Lect	Berry, Debbie	M	61
Prof	Berry, Richard A.	D	61
Adj	Bruns, Jeremy	M	66G
Assoc Prof	Campo, David	D	32E,32C,37,60B
Asst Prof	Cotner, John S.	D	13
Assoc Prof	Dalmas, Jennifer	D	38,62A,62B,41
Assoc Prof	Dalton, Deborah	D	61
Adj	Davis, Charlotte	M	61
Adj	Fain, Jeremy	M	64D,11,13A,13B
Adj	Faucett, Jim	M	66B
Staff	Fung, Geneva	DMA	66C
Prof	Gavin, Charles	D	41,49,63B
Adj	Gaviria, Carlos	M	62D,11,13A,13B
Prof	Goodall, John W.	D	64B
Assoc Prof	Guenther, Christina	D	64A,20,41
Assoc Prof	Harris, Scott H.	D	50,65
Asst Prof	Howard, David L.	D	32C,36,60A
Lect	Hudson, Nita	M	11,61
Inst	Kelleher, Kevin	M	35C
Prof	King, Tim	D	60A,32C,36
Assoc Prof	LaGraff, Scott	D	61
Prof	Lias, Stephen J.	D	13,10F,10
Adj	McNellie, Myra	M	32A,32B
Lect	Midgley, Herbert	M	11,70,34,45
Adj	Mitchell, Emily	D	62E
Asst Prof	Moon, Gene H.	D	38,39,66,62A,62B
Assoc Prof	Nabb, Nathan	D	64E
Asst Prof	Nelson, Kristen	D	13
Prof	Parr, Andrew	D	66A,66D
Assoc Prof	Petti, Ronald T.	D	66C
Staff	Pitts, James L.	D	66C
Adj	Raychev, Evgeni	D	62C,41,11,62D
Adj	Roberts, Jean	M	66A,13B,13C
Prof	Roberts, John Noel	D	66A
Assoc Prof	Salas, Jorge Davi	D	63D,62D,42
Assoc Prof	Scott, Debra L.	D	47,63C,63D
Assoc Prof	Turner, Mark E.	D	32B,32A
Asst Prof	Weaver, Jamie G.	D	12
Prof	Wurtz, Gary	D	47,63A

TX2710 Sul Ross State University
Department of Fine Arts & Comm
Music/Box C43
Alpine, TX 79832
(432) 837-8218   Fax: (432) 837-8376
www.sulross.edu
E-mail: erumsey@sulross.edu

4 Year Institution, Senior Liberal Arts/Teacher Training

Chair: Esther Rumsey, 80A

Lect	Bennack, Steven	M	70,29A,66D
Adj	Ferguson, John	M	63D
Assoc Prof	Freed, Donald Callen	D	61,36,10A,13C,12A
Asst Prof	Lippard, Erin	D	61,13A,13B,40,54
Asst Prof	Lippard, Michael S.	D	13A,37,46,64,13B
Vstng Lect	Potts, Lana	M	66A
Lect	Steinmann, Ronald	B	65
Vstng Lect	Wallace, Carol	DIPL	66A
Prof Emeritus	Wilson, T. Rex	D	60,12A,32C,36,61

TX2750 Tarleton State University
Department of Fine Arts
Box T-0320
Stephenville, TX 76402
(254) 968-9245   Fax: (254) 968-9239
www.tarleton.edu/music
E-mail: davidian@tarleton.edu

4 Year Institution
Member of NASM

Master of Music in Music Education (Distance Learning)

Head of Music: Teresa Davidian, 80A
Dean, Liberal & Fine Arts: Dean Minix, 80A
Dir., Summer Programs: Heather Hawk, 80G

Asst Prof	Asakura, Iwao	D	61
Asst Prof	Ball, Greg L.	M	37,48,64,20G,29
Inst PT	Brudnak, Sondra	M	11
Inst	Chambers, Steve	M	13A,32B,66C
Inst PT	Cook, Justin	M	63D,63C
Inst PT	Crawford, Michael	M	65,50
Assoc Prof	Davidian, Teresa	D	13,10,12A,20
Inst PT	Eldridge, Ronda	M	11,20,48,64A
Vstng Asst Prof	Hagelstein, Kim Rooney	D	12A,13D,32E,63B
Inst PT	Hamilton, Heather	M	64B,66D
Asst Prof	Hawk, Heather	M	61,11
Inst PT	Johnson, Jeanine	M	64C
Inst PT	Johnson, Robert	M	11
Asst Prof	Johnson, Vicky V.	D	13,32B,14C,32,66B
Inst PT	Jones, Kate	M	11,62D
Asst Prof	Pursell, Anthony	D	37,41,48,60,63C
Prof	Rives, Charles L.	D	11,32C
Asst Prof	Robertson, Troy David	D	60,32C,36,61
Assoc Prof	Spotz, Leslie	D	13A,66A,66B,66D
Inst PT	Townson, Kevin	M	70,11
Inst PT	Tucker, John	M	61
Asst Prof	Walker, Brian	D	63A
Asst Prof	Westbrook, Gary W.	D	50,65,37,32E

TX2800 Temple College
Department of Performing Arts
2600 S 1st St
Temple, TX 76504-7499
(254) 298-8555   Fax: (254) 298-8549
www.templejc.edu
E-mail: colin.mason@templejc.edu

2 Year Institution

Dir., Division of Fine Arts: Thomas A. Fairlie, 80A
Chair: Colin M. Mason, 80A
Dir., Preparatory Division: Lois Reiter, 80E

PT	Atwood, Julie	B	61
Inst	Bergeron, Norm	M	65,50,10D,11,13A
PT	Bryce, Vincent	M	62D
PT	Carney, Anna	M	11,13A,14C,64C
Inst	Colwell, Brent	M	37,11,12A,63C,63D
PT	Fairlie, Mary	M	62A,62B,51,14C,38
Inst	Fairlie, Thomas A.	M	47
PT	Fiala, Keith	A	63A
PT	Goodnight, Sheryl	B	64A
Inst	Irom, Benjamin M.	D	29,29A,47,41,13
PT	Johnson, Michael E.	D	61
Inst	Johnson, Teri	M	61,11,39
PT	Liles, Reese	A	70
PT	Martin, Chris	M	62C
Inst	Mason, Colin M.	D	47,11,64E,29,48
PT	Miller, Eric	M	11
PT	Milne, Virginia E.	M	66A,66D
PT	Pinno, John	M	70
PT	Reiter, Lois	M	62A
PT	Santana, Priscilla	M	61,36,40
PT	Scharf, Deborah	M	63B

TX2850 Texarkana College
Performing Arts Division
2500 N Robinson Rd
Texarkana, TX 75599
(903) 823-3257   Fax: (903) 823-3451
www.texarkanacollege.edu
E-mail: crichard@texarkanacollege.edu

2 Year Institution

Program Coordinator: Michael Cooper, 80A
Chair, Humanities: Mary Ellen Young, 80A

Prof Emeritus	Alewine, Murry L.	D	
PT	Bennett, Laura	M	64
PT	Bennett, Steve	M	63,64
Asst Prof	Bougie, Marc-Andre	M	11,10,13,36
Asst Prof	Richardson, Celia	M	11,36,61,32B,13C
Inst PT	Richardson, Chuck	B	11,45,35C,35G
Asst Prof	Scott Goode, Mary	M	66A,11

TX2900 Texas A&M University-College Sta
Music Program
MS 4240 TAMU
College Station, TX 77843-4240
(979) 845-3355   Fax: (979) 862-2666
perf.tamu.edu/
E-mail: harris-m-berger@tamu.edu

4 Year Institution

Chair: Harris M. Berger, 80A

Asst Prof	Beaster-Jones, Jayson	D	14,20E
Prof	Berger, Harris M.	D	14,12B,29D,20G
Asst Prof	Bustos, Isaac	D	20,70
Lect PT	Gariazzo, Mariana Stratta	D	64A,12A,20,11
Prof	Hamera, Judith	D	
Assoc Prof	Houtchens, Alan	D	12A,12,63B
Lect PT	Hronek, Melissa	D	61
Lect PT	Imhoff, Andrea G.	M	13A,11,66C,66A
Lect PT	Kattari, Kim	D	14
Prof	Lieuwen, Peter	D	13,10,12A,29A
Lect	Marlow, Laurine	D	11,12A,66G,66A,66H
Lect PT	Mayfield, Nathaniel		63A
Lect PT	McManus, Emily	D	14
Asst Prof	Morris, Jeffrey M.	D	70,34,35G
Asst Prof	Regan, Martin	D	10,20C,13
Other	Rhea, Tim B.	D	10,37,64E
Lect PT	Rollins, Ian	D	65,12
Other	Wade, Jess E.	M	60,32C,61,66A
Lect PT	Wang, Yung-Chui	D	66
Assoc Prof	Wilborn, David F.	D	13,63C,63D,41,37

TX2930 Texas A&M University-Corpus Chris
Department of Music
6300 Ocean Dr Unit 5720
Corpus Christi, TX 78412-5720
(361) 825-2761   Fax: (361) 825-6097
www.tamucc.edu
E-mail: diana.sipes@tamucc.edu

4 Year Institution
Member of NASM

Chair: Diana Sipes, 80A

Assoc Prof	Anderson, Shane	D	13A,13B,13C,66A,66B
Asst Prof	Bernhardt, Ross C.	D	36,61
Adj	Brown, Robert	M	46,35C,34D
Adj	Faraone, John	M	11
Asst Prof	Flores, Jose G.	D	62A,62B,51,13C,42
Adj	Hii, Philip	M	70
Adj	Kemm, Karl	M	63B
Adj	Kisner, Brad	M	66D,39
Asst Prof	Lin, Hsin Yi	D	61
Adj	Long, Arlene	M	66A,66C,66D
Adj	McCarty, Evelyn	D	64B
Asst Prof	McClung, Matthew	D	65,12A,50
Adj	McDonald, Richard F.	D	10A
Adj	Moore, Michael	M	70
Adj	O'Brien, Richard	D	61,13A,13B,13C
Asst Prof	Pierce, Carrie	D	62C,62D,51,31A,13C
Adj	Pinson, Donald	D	63C
Adj	Reynolds, Marc	M	61,39,13C
Adj	Rogers, Mark	D	64D
Assoc Prof	Scott, Ronald	D	64C,64E,38,10F,60
Asst Prof	Shope, Bradley	D	14,20,12A
Asst Prof	Sipes, Danny T.	D	63D,35A,35C,35D,35G
Prof	Sipes, Diana	D	64A,12A,13E,42
Asst Prof	Smith, Shawn T.	M	63A,60B,37,32E
Asst Prof	Thornton, Mary	D	63A,29A,13B,13C

TX2955 Texas A&M University-Commerce
Department of Music
PO Box 3011
Commerce, TX 75429
(903) 886-5303   Fax: (903) 468-6010
www.tamu-commerce.edu/music
E-mail: christopher_white@tamu-commerce.edu

4 Year Institution, Graduate School
Member of NASM

Master of Music in Performance, Master of Music Education

Chair: Christopher Dale White, 80A

Inst	Baker, Jeff	M	63D
Inst	Beall, Stephen J.	M	62A,62B,51
Asst Prof	Bryant, Roger	M	61
Assoc Prof	Burkett, John	D	13,66A,66G,34,12C
Asst Prof	Clark, Jim	M	63C,49,63D
Inst	Clements, Phillip L.	M	60B,37,63D,13A,12A
Asst Prof	Druhan, Mary Alice	M	64C,41
Inst	Gorham, Dee Ann	M	61,39
Inst	Goynes, Tim	M	70
Prof	Hansen, Ted	D	13,10F,10A,66A
Asst Prof	Hooper, Randall	D	36,60A,32D,32B,40
Asst Prof	Kelly, Daniel	D	63A,47,13A,13B
Inst	Lagarenne, Cecile	M	64B
Lect	Meek, Darla	M	32A,32B,32H
Assoc Prof	Morrow, Michael	M	63B,63D,11
Asst Prof	Sanchez, Luis	D	66A,66C,66B
Inst	Sarte, Ysabel	M	12A
Assoc Prof	White, Christopher Dale	D	32D,36,40,60A,61
Asst Prof	Zator, Brian	D	50,65

TX2960 Texas A&M University-Kingsville
Department of Music
MSC 174
700 University Blvd
Kingsville, TX 78363
(361) 593-2803   Fax: (361) 593-2816
www.tamuk.edu
E-mail: paul.hageman@tamuk.edu

4 Year Institution, Graduate School

Master of Music in Music Education

Chair & Dir., Graduate Studies: Paul M. Hageman, 80A,80C
Dean: Scott Hughes, 80A
Dir., Graduate Studies: Judith W. Cole, 80C

Asst Prof	Benavidez, Justin		63D
Asst Prof	Brou, Melinda A.	D	61,39,54,13C
Prof	Cole, Judith W.	M	11,12A,32B
Lect	Converse, Andrew	D	63C
Asst Prof	Cord, John T.	D	63A,49
Lect	Dexter, Jonathan G.	M	62
Asst Prof	Diaz, Oscar	D	63C,49
Assoc Prof	Fluman, John R.	M	50,65
Asst Prof	Fronckowiak, Ann	DMA	64B,13
Lect	Garcia, Glynn A.	M	11
Lect	Guist, Anne P.	D	64D
Prof	Hageman, Paul M.	D	47,29
Asst Prof	Hoskisson, Darin T.	D	13,64D
Asst Prof	Janzen, Elizabeth A.	D	64A
Asst Prof	Kihle, Jason J.	D	11,37,50,65
Lect	Lee, Joohyun	D	66D,66C
Lect	Quijano, Kellie R.	M	64C
Asst Prof	Reinhuber, Joachim	D	66A,66D,66C
Prof	Sanders, Gregory L.	D	13,10F,10,34
Prof	Sanders, Nancy King	D	64C
Inst	Shelton, Brian M.	M	37,32,60
Assoc Prof	Sholtis, Jennifer Ratchford	D	63B
Lect	Stone, Jeff	M	11,32
Lect	Taylor, Bryce B.	M	32C,60
Lect	Ulmer, Allison C.	M	13
Assoc Prof	Warth, James R.	D	47,64E,64B
Assoc Prof	Williams, Kenneth D.	D	36,61,60A,40,39
Lect	Wood, T. Bennett	M	64C
Lect	Zaporta, Ouida I.	M	63D

TX3000 Texas Christian University
School of Music
TCU Box 297500
Fort Worth, TX 76129
(817) 257-7602   Fax: (817) 257-5818
www.music.tcu.edu
E-mail: music@tcu.edu

4 Year Institution, Graduate School
Member of NASM

Certificate, Artist Diploma, Master of Music in Performance, Master of Music in Conducting, Master of Music in Musicology, Master of Music Education, DMA in Composition, DMA in Conducting, DMA in Performance, Master of Music in Music Theory-Composition, Master of Music in Pedagogy, DMA in Piano Pedagogy

Director: Richard C. Gipson, 80A
Dir., Graduate Studies: H. Joseph Butler, 80C
Dir., Preparatory Division: Lori Christ, 80E
Assistant Director: Paul Cortese, 80H
Assistant Director: Kristen Queen, 80H

Inst	Adams, Pam	M	64A
Prof	Allen, Sheila M.	D	61
Asst Prof	Begnoche, David J.	M	63C
Asst Prof	Blessinger, Martin	D	10,13
Inst	Blumsack, Michelle	M	13
Assoc Prof	Brock, David	M	61
Inst	Burchill, Thomas	M	70,47
Assoc Prof	Burgess, Jon	D	63A
Prof	Butler, H. Joseph	D	66G,12,31
Inst	Carr, Jennifer	M	61
Inst	Carter, Joey	M	65,29A,29B,47
Assoc Prof	Castro-Balbi, Jesus	D	62C,41
Asst Prof	Cheney, Stuart G.	D	12
Inst	Christ, Chip	M	70
Inst	Cortese, Paul	M	34,11
Inst	Dean, Julie	M	13
Assoc Prof	Eckert, Joseph H.	M	64E,29,47
Inst	Elledge, Nancy	M	61
Assoc Prof	Estes, Richard A.	M	39,61
Artist in Res	Feghali, Jose	M	66A
Prof	Ferrandino, Blaise J.	D	10,62D,13
Prof	Francis, Bobby R.	M	37,60,32E
Prof	Gabel, Gerald R.	D	34,10,13,45
Assoc Prof	Galaganov, Misha	D	62C,41
Asst Prof	Gibbons, William J.	D	12,11
Assoc Prof	Giordano, John R.	D	60
Assoc Prof	Gipson, Ann M.	D	66B,66D,66A
Prof	Gipson, Richard C.	D	65,50,32G
Inst	Green, Kyp	M	62D
Inst	Gunter, Trey	M	13
Prof	Gutierrez, German A.	D	60,38
Inst	Hall, Charles	M	64D
Inst	Hall, David	M	65
Inst	Hames, Elizabeth	M	13
Vstng Prof	Harth-Bedoya, Miguel	M	38
Inst	Hodge, Jeffrey S.	M	65
Lect	Houston, Ronald	M	62A
Vstng Prof	Kaplinsky, Veda	D	66A
Assoc Prof	Kim, San-ky	D	61
Inst	Lin, Gloria	M	66A
Inst	Lin, Swang	M	62A
Inst	Logan, Laura	D	62E
Assoc Prof	Lu, Yuan Xiong	M	62D
Inst	Luperi, Victoria	B	64C
Prof	Martina, Harold	D	66A
Inst	Martinez, Guillermo	M	66D
Inst	Metcalf, Mark A.	M	39,61
Assoc Prof	Meyn, Till MacIvor	D	13,10
Inst	Murrow, Richard	B	63D
Inst	Musser, Amanda	B	32E
Assoc Prof	Neill, Sheri L.	D	32D,32B,32C,32G
Prof	Owings, John	M	66A
Assoc Prof	Pummill, Janet	M	66C
Inst	Queen, Kristen	M	64A
Vstng Prof	Shih, Michael	M	62A
Prof	Shrock, Dennis R.	D	60,36
Asst Prof	Simpson, R. Eric	D	32E,32F,32G
Inst	Stewart, Amy	D	60A
Inst	Stoughton, Zachariah	M	66A,12A,67F,11
Asst Prof	Strickland, Jeremy M.	M	37
Inst	Terbeek, Kathleen	M	61
Lect	Test, Heather	M	63B
Assoc Prof	Thompson, Curt	D	62A,41
Inst	Thompson, Ruth	M	11
Prof	Ungar, Tamas	M	66A
Inst	Ward, Allison	D	36
Asst Prof	Watkins, Timothy D.	D	12A,14,20,12
Prof	West, Brian	D	65,50
Inst	White, Brad	M	60A
Prof	Whitman, Gary	M	64C
Inst	Williams, Stewart	M	64B

Lect	Wilson, Angela Turner	M	61
Inst	Yeomans, David J.	D	12
Asst Prof	Youngblood, Brian	M	37,32E

TX3050 Texas College
Department of Music
2404 N Grand Ave
Tyler, TX 75702-1962
(903) 593-8311 x 235
www.texascollege.edu

4 Year Institution, Historically Black College

	Axtell, Les		66A,61
Assoc Prof	Heape, Mary Willis	DMA	32,61,13,12A
	Herbert, Jeffery		37
	Mitchell, William		36

TX3100 Texas Lutheran University
School of Music
1000 W Court St
Seguin, TX 78155-5999
(830) 372-6015   Fax: (830) 372-6832
www.tlu.edu
E-mail: dboyer@tlu.edu

4 Year Institution

Chair: Douglas R. Boyer, 80A
Arts & Entertainment Series: Susan Rinn, 80F

Inst PT	Bedell, Adam	M	50,65,32E
Inst PT	Bernard, Jennifer	M	64B
Assoc Prof	Boyer, Douglas R.	D	36,60,54,32D,13F
Asst Prof	Bronk, Mary Beth	M	32E,37,60,63A
Inst PT	Chambers, Carol	M	63A,13C,32E,10F,32A
Assoc Prof	Conoly, Shaaron	M	12A,39,61,54
Inst PT	Cooper, Joseph	M	63A,49
Inst PT	Corley, Paula	M	64C
Asst Prof	Daub, Eric	D	66A,13A,13B,13C,29A
Inst PT	Gnecco, Jeanne	M	64A
Inst PT	Grohovac, Janet	M	70,32E
Inst PT	Jenschke, Laura	M	36,61,32E
Inst PT	Jessop, Dustin	M	46,64E
Asst Prof PT	Lee, Elizabeth	D	62C
Inst PT	Lee, Patty	M	66A
Asst Prof	McElhaney, Carla	D	66C
Inst PT	Morris, Gayle	M	66G
Inst PT	Robinson, Keith	M	32B,63D
Inst PT	Rodriguez, Jill	M	63B,11
Asst Prof PT	Rogers, Mark	D	64D
Asst Prof	Thomason, Eliza	D	11,32E,62A,62B,51
Asst Prof PT	Warren, Robert	D	12A,66A,11
Asst Prof PT	Workman, K. Darren	D	63C,63D

TX3150 Texas Southern University
Department of Music
3100 Cleburne Ave
Houston, TX 77004-5413
(713) 313-7337   Fax: (713) 313-1869
www.tsu.edu
E-mail: Lee_RF@tsu.edu

4 Year Institution, Historically Black College

Master of Arts in Music

Interim Chair: Richard F. Lee, 80A
Dean: Danille Taylor, 80A

Prof	Adams, Daniel C.	D	10A,13D,13E,65,13
Assoc Prof	Butler, Benjamin	M	32,64
Inst	Gibson, Clarence	M	11,37,41,42
Prof	Harris, Howard	D	13A,10,37,47,39
Assoc Prof	Lee, Richard F.	M	37,63A
Inst	Lundy, Ann	M	51,62,38
Assoc Prof	Mack, Dianne	D	32,13C
Prof	Oby, Jason	D	36,39,61
Assoc Prof	Perkyns, Jane E.	D	66A,13,12A,66,66C
Inst	Singleton, Darryl	M	37,44,11
Prof	Thomas, Fennoyee	D	66A,66G

TX3175 Texas State University-San Marcos
School of Music
601 University Dr
San Marcos, TX 78666-4616
(512) 245-2651   Fax: (512) 245-8181
www.music.txstate.edu
E-mail: music@txstate.edu

4 Year Institution, Graduate School

Master of Music in Music Education, Master of Music

Director: Thomas S. Clark, 80A
Dir., Graduate Studies: Mary Ellen Cavitt, 80C
Associate Director: Joey Martin, 80H

Lect	Asbell, Stephanie Ames	D	62B,32E
Assoc Prof	Babcock, Jonathan	D	36,61,32D
Lect	Bartz, Ezra	M	66D
Asst Prof	Beatty, Caroline	M	37,32E,60B
Lect	Bellini, Brigitte	M	61
Lect	Bird, Paula E.	D	62A,51
Assoc Prof	Brinckmeyer, Lynn	D	32D,36
Assoc Prof Emeritus	Brunner, Peggy G.	M	61
Lect PT	Carnes, Glenda	M	32B
Prof	Cavitt, Mary Ellen	D	32E
Prof	Clark, Thomas S.	D	10,13,10B
Lect PT	Corley, Alton L.	D	37,32E
Lect	Cruz, Mark A.	M	70,51
Prof	Davidson, Ian	D	11,64B,41
Lect	Dawson, David J.	B	32D,62D
Lect	DeBow, Faith	M	66C,66D
Lect PT	Dierolf, Wallace	M	32E
Senior Lect	Ditto, Charles J.	D	13,10
Lect	Eaton, Rebecca M. Doran	D	13
Lect PT	Elliott, Barbara	D	32B
Assoc Prof	Erickson, Mark	B	35C,35D,35G
Senior Lect	Fleming, Pat W.	M	32B,32D,13A
Assoc Prof	Garcia, Washington	D	66A,42
Assoc Prof	Gonzales, Cynthia I.	D	13
Prof	Gonzalez, Genaro	M	50,65
Lect	Gorina, Alena	M	66D
Prof	Hager, H. Stephen	M	13A,13,49,63B
Senior Lect	Haight, Russell P.	D	29,41,64E
Senior Lect	Hale, Daris Word	M	64D,11
Senior Lect	Hall, Richard D.	M	11,10B,34
Senior Lect	Hehmsoth, Henry	M	35C,35D,35G,66A
Lect	Henry, William R.	M	35C,35D,35G
Lect PT	Hickinbotham, Gary		35C,35D,35G
Lect	Hill, Phillip	M	61
Assoc Prof	Hudiburg, Howard B.	D	32E,38,60B
Prof	Hurt, Charles R.	M	49,63C
Prof	Jones, Adah T.	D	48,64A
Senior Lect	Jones, Gordon	M	11,20
Senior Lect	Klier, Kari	M	65,50
Assoc Prof	Kwak, Jason	D	66A,42
Prof	Laumer, Jack C.	M	49,63A
Assoc Prof	Ledbetter, Lynn F.	D	62A,62B,42,51
Lect	Lee, Kyung-Ae	D	13,66B
Lect	Lipton, Kay	D	12A
Assoc Prof	Lopez, John A.	M	37,65
Lect	Lopez, Robert	M	65,50
Prof	Martin, Joey	D	36,32D,60A
Senior Lect	Mazak, Grant	B	70,51
Asst Prof	McCain, Martin G.	D	63C,29,46,49
Senior Lect	Mendoza, Freddie	M	29,47,63C
Assoc Prof	Michaels, Cary	M	61
Lect	Miles, Butch	M	65,29,46
Asst Prof	Mooney, Kevin E.	D	12A
Asst Prof	Mungo, Samuel	D	61,39
Senior Lect	Nelms, Morris H.	M	11
Lect	Ninov, Dimitar	D	13
Asst Prof	Oxford, Todd	D	64E,48
Senior Lect	Parrish, Cheryl A.	M	61
Asst Prof	Pedroza, Ludim R.	D	12A,20H,66D
Prof	Pino, David J.	D	64C
Lect PT	Quintero, Michelle A.	M	61
Prof	Riepe, Russell C.	D	13,10,45
Assoc Prof	Rodriguez, Raul I.	M	49,63D
Lect	Scanlon, Russell J.	B	69
Prof	Schmidt, John C.	D	13,12A,66G
Assoc Prof	Schueller, Rodney C.	D	13A,32E,60B
Prof	Schuler, Nico S.	D	13,12C,34B,13F
Asst Prof	Simmons, Amy L.	D	32E
Asst Prof	Stein, Robin	M	32
Lect PT	Summer, Stephen O.	M	35,12A
Lect PT	Tangarov, Vanguel G.	M	64C,48
Prof	Thomas, Naymond	D	11
Lect	Tower, Mollie	M	32B
Asst Prof	Ulen, Ronald	D	61
Prof	Winking, Keith R.	D	47,63A,29
Assoc Prof	Wood, Juli	M	61
Senior Lect	Worthington, Oliver W.	D	61

TX3200 Texas Tech University

School of Music
PO Box 42033
Lubbock, TX 79409-2033
(806) 742-2270   Fax: (806) 742-2294
www.depts.ttu.edu/music
E-mail: michael.stoune@ttu.edu

4 Year Institution, Graduate School
Member of NASM

Master of Music in Music Theory, Master of Music in Performance, Master of Music in Music Education, Master of Music in History & Literature, DMA in Composition, DMA in Conducting, DMA in Performance, PhD in Fine Arts, DMA in Piano Pedagogy

Director: William Ballenger, 80A
Associate Dir., Graduate Studies: Michael Stoune, 80C
Associate Director & Assoc. Dir., Undergraduate Studies: Alan Shinn, 80H,80B

Assoc Prof	Anderson, Amy B.	M	11,64B
Asst Prof	Anderson, Christopher M.	M	37,32E
Assoc Prof	Arnold, Clara S.	M	61
Prof	Ballenger, William	M	10A,32E,37,63A
Prof	Barber, Gail G.	M	13,62E
Inst	Berg, Jason	M	12A,29
Asst Prof	Berry, Michael	M	13
Prof	Bjella, Richard L.	M	36,40
Asst Prof	Boyle, Annie Chalex	M	62A
Asst Prof	Brumfield, Susan Hendrix	D	32
Asst Prof	Cash, Carla Davis	D	66B,66D,29B,66A,66
Asst Prof	Cimarusti, Thomas M.		12A,13E,20,12C,68
Asst Prof	Cruse, Carolyn S.		36,40,32D,32G
Assoc Prof	Deahl, Lora	D	66A,66C,66B,12A
Asst Prof	Decker, James	M	63C
Assoc Prof	Dees, David	M	47,64E,29
Adj Prof	Dees, Jennifer		32A,32B
Prof	Dent, Karl D.	M	61
Assoc Prof	Dolter, Gerald	M	39,61,54
Prof	Dye, Keith G.	M	60B,37,32C,32E
Asst Prof	Fischer, Peter H.	D	13,10A,10B
Assoc Prof	Fried, Eric	D	60,11
Asst Prof	George, Andrew	D	38,60B,39,32E
Assoc Prof	Gilbert, John Haspel	D	12A,62A
Prof	Henry, Robert	D	32
Prof	Hobbs, Wayne C.	D	13,12E,35E,20G
Asst Prof	Hollins, John S.	D	60,36,41
Asst Prof	Hughes, Thomas	D	66G,34,35C
Asst Prof	Jocoy, Stacey	M	12G,12E,12C,31A,11
Asst Prof	Jones, Stephen W.	M	46,47
Inst	Kalhous, David		66A,66B
Prof	Killian, Janice N.	D	32
Asst Prof	Lastrapes, Jeffrey Noel	M	62C,42,51,11,32E
Asst Prof	Lin, Mei-Fang	D	10A,13A,13I,13L,10F
Asst Prof	Mariani, Angela	M	12A
Asst Prof	Martens, Peter A.	D	13
Assoc Prof	McKoin, Sarah	D	60B,37
Asst Prof	McNeil, Kathy J.	M	61
Prof	Meek, Richard	M	13,64D
Asst Prof	Meidell, Katrin	M	62B
Inst	Meixner, Micah L.		61
Adj Inst	Ogaard, Sigurd	D	66C
Assoc Prof	Rogers, Lisa	D	50,65
Assoc Prof	Santa, Lisa Garner	D	64A
Assoc Prof	Santa, Matthew	D	13,10
Assoc Prof	Shea, David L.	D	34,41,64A,64C,64E
Prof	Shinn, Alan	M	50,65,47,29
Asst Prof	Skerik, Renee		62B
Assoc Prof	Smith, Christopher J.	M	12A,12,14
Assoc Prof	Smith, Christopher M.	D	63B
Prof	Stoune, Michael	D	13,64A
Assoc Prof	Streider, Will E.	M	37,49,63A
Prof Emerita	Van Appledorn, Mary Jeanne	D	13,10
Asst Prof	Wass, Kevin	M	63D
Prof	Westney, William F.	D	66A
Assoc Prof	Wilson, Jane Ann H.	D	66A,66D,66C
Assoc Prof	Wood, Bruce	PhD	32E,62
Asst Prof	Yon, Kirsten A.	M	62A,42

TX3250 Texas Wesleyan University

Department of Music
1201 Wesleyan St
Fort Worth, TX 76105-1536
(817) 531-4992   Fax: (817) 531-6583
txwes.edu/academics/artsLetters/music.aspx
E-mail: jfisher@txwes.edu

4 Year Institution
Member of NASM

Chair: John Fisher, 80A

Asst Prof	Araujo, Ilka Vasconcelos	D	66A,11,12A,20G
Asst Prof	Beason, Christine F.	M	37,48,63B,32,10F
Assoc Prof	Bierschenk, Jerome Michael	D	36,37,32D,61,63A
Prof	Fisher, John	PhD	13A,13B,10A,15,66A
Assoc Prof	McCoy, Julie	M	61,39

TX3300 Texas Woman's University

Department of Music & Drama
PO Box 425768
Denton, TX 76204-5768
(940) 898-2500   Fax: (940) 898-2494
www.twu.edu
E-mail: pyoungblood@twu.edu

4 Year Institution, Graduate School
Member of NASM

Master of Arts in Performance, Master of Arts in Music Education, Master of Arts in Pedagogy, Master of Arts in Music Therapy

Chair: James Chenevert, 80A

Inst PT	Allen, Roy	M	64E
Asst Prof	Baker, Vicki	D	32
Prof	Benge, Sharon J.	M	54
Inst PT	Bowles, Suzanne	M	61
Inst PT	Boyle, Holly	M	61
Inst PT	Brannock, Robert D.	M	65
Prof	Brown, Thomas K.	D	66G
Asst Prof	Bynane, Patrick	D	54
Prof	Chenevert, James	D	10,13
Prof	Cohen, Nicki S.	D	61,33,20
Asst Prof	Evans, Garry W.	D	64C,37,12A,41,60B
Asst Prof	Gorman, Rhonda	M	54
Prof	Hadsell, Nancy A.	D	33,70
Asst Prof	Haefner, Jaymee	D	62E
Asst Prof	Hobbs, James D.	D	64B
Asst Prof	Hoch, Beverly	M	61
Asst Prof	Jensen, Joni L.	D	13C,36,61,32D,60A
Assoc Prof	Lee, Soojeong	D	61,39
Inst PT	Matney, William	M	65
Asst Prof	Pezzimenti, Carlo	M	70
Asst Prof	Pinson, Joseph Warren	M	33
Asst Prof	Raschen, Gudrun E.	M	62D,62C,67B,51
Assoc Prof	Shuster, Richard J.	D	66
Vstng Asst Prof	Stoupy, Etienne	D	49,63A,63B
Inst PT	Wallace, Noel	M	63D,47
Inst PT	Winter, Angela	M	63B
Asst Prof	Young, Steven	M	54
Prof	Youngblood, Pamela J.	D	41,64A,13A,13B,15

TX3360 Trinity Valley Community College

Department of Music
100 Cardinal Dr
Athens, TX 75751
(903) 675-6230   Fax: (903) 675-6280
www.tvcc.edu
E-mail: bmcgilvray@tvcc.edu

2 Year Institution

Chair, Fine Arts Division: Kelly Driskell, 80A
Chair, Music: Byron McGilvray, 80A
Coordinator, Music: Mary Tidwell, 80H

Inst	Crutchfield, Robert	M	50,65
Inst	Hudson, Milton	D	11,37
Inst	Matchael, Michael	M	37,48,64
Inst	McGilvray, Byron	D	61,36,40
Inst	Miller, Peter	M	66C,61,64C,66G
Inst	Overmoe, Kirk	M	66A,66D
Inst	Tidwell, Mary		13,11
Inst	Wright, Marylyn	M	13A,66A,66C,66D,66G

TX3370 Tyler Junior College
Department of Music
PO Box 9020
Tyler, TX 75711-9020
(903) 510-2483   Fax: (903) 510-2800
www.tjc.edu
E-mail: jbai@tjc.edu

2 Year Institution

Director: Larry W. Marta, 80A

Inst	Baham, Kerry M.	M	13B,66A,11,66C,12A
PT	Cooper, Kelli	M	66A
PT	Ford, Jeffrey	M	66A,66C
Inst	Guenette, Maria Mika	D	66A,66D,66C
PT	Hale, Cheryl	B	64C,64A
PT	Ivey, Carol	B	63B
Inst	Kimlicko, Franklin	M	70,34,35C
Inst	Marta, Larry W.	M	13A,13,66A,66G
PT	McCoy, Molly	D	61
Inst	McGowan, Thomas	M	37,41,50,65
Inst	Mensch, Thomas	B	37,41,63C,49,48
Inst	Mensh, Heather	M	37,41,46,48,63D
PT	Morrow, Ruth	M	66A,66B
Inst	Myers, Adam	M	48,64C,64E
PT	Norwood, Diana	M	62A,62B
PT	Oglesby, Michael	M	63A
Inst	Oxler, Cora Jean	M	61,11,13C
PT	Rumbley, Phil	B	62D
Inst	Russell, Nathan	M	36,11,61,13C
PT	Schodowski, Timothy	B	63A
Inst	Trent, Andrea	M	11,61
PT	Vinson, Danny S.	M	63B

TX3400 Univ of Houston
Moores School of Music
120 School of Music Bldg
Houston, TX 77204-4017
(713) 743-3009   Fax: (713) 743-3166
www.music.uh.edu
E-mail: musicinfo@uh.edu

4 Year Institution, Graduate School
Member of NASM

Master of Music in Composition, Master of Music in Music Theory, Master of Music in Music Education, DMA in Composition, DMA in Conducting, DMA in Performance, DMA in Music Education, Master of Music in Applied Music, Master of Music in Music Literature, Master of Music in Performance & Pedagogy, Master of Music in Accompanying & Chamber Music

Director: David A. White, 80A
Dir., Graduate Studies: Andrew Davis, 80C
Dir., Preparatory Division: Toni Capra, 80E
Dir., Artist Series & Summer Programs: Alan Austin, 80F,80G
Associate Director: Lynn B. Lamkin, 80H

Artist in Res	Barton, Mark	B	41,63D
Assoc Prof	Bates, Robert F.	D	66G
Lect	Benzer, John	M	32E
Assoc Prof	Bertagnolli, Paul A.	D	12A
Assoc Prof	Bertman, David	M	32C,37
Lect	Brink, Rhona	M	32A,32B
Artist in Res	Brooks, Wayne	DIPL	62B
Artist in Res	Chase, George	M	63A
Vstng Asst Prof	Ciscon, Katherine	M	66C
Asst Prof	Clayton, Cynthia	M	61
Assoc Prof	Davis, Andrew	D	13
Assoc Prof	Dirst, Matthew	D	12A,55,67C
Artist in Res	Dorough, Aralee	B	64A
Asst Prof	Durrani, Aahminah	M	13
Prof	Evans, Joseph	M	61
Artist in Res	Freeman, Phillip	B	63C
Artist in Res	Fulgham, Joel		47,65
Lect	Gabbart, Ryan	M	29A
Artist in Res	Gelok, Daniel	M	64E
Prof	Grabiec, Andrzej	M	41,62A
Artist in Res	Gregory, Lee	M	61
Artist in Res	Griffin, Randall	M	64C
Prof	Hausmann, Charles S.	D	36,61
Assoc Prof	Hester, Timothy	M	66A,66B,66C
Artist in Res	Hough, Robin Z.	D	64B
Artist in Res	Huang, Frank	B	62A
Artist in Res	Huddleston, Cheryl	M	64D
Artist in Res	Hulten, Thomas	M	63C
Lect	Humphries, Terri	M	32
Assoc Prof	Jones, Timothy A.	D	65,61
Lect	Kangas, Ryan R.	D	12C
Artist in Res	Kauk, Brian	M	63C
Artist in Res	Keeney, Jennifer	M	64A
Artist in Res	Klingensmith, David	M	47,62D
Assoc Prof	Koozin, Timothy	D	13
Prof	Krager, Franz Anton	M	60,38
Vstng Assoc Prof	Lamkin, Lynn B.		11
Assoc Prof	Lange, Rose	D	14
Artist in Res	Leek, Anne		64B
Vstng Assoc Prof	Lowe, Nina Kay	D	61
Assoc Prof	Marmolejo, Noe	M	47,29
Asst Prof	Maroney, Marcus K.	D	10
Assoc Prof	Mayes, Robert	M	60,32C,37
Artist in Res	McKnight, Lynda Keith	M	61
Asst Prof	Morgulis, Tali	D	66A
Prof Emeritus	Nelson, Robert S.	D	13A,13,10F,10
Artist in Res	Page, Paula	M	62E
Prof	Pollack, Howard	D	12A,12,14,20G
Artist in Res	Reed, Gavin		63B
Asst Prof	Reifinger, James L.	D	32B,32C
Artist in Res	Robinson, Jeff	M	64D
Prof	Ross, Buck		39,54
Artist in Res	Rowell, Chester		64C
Artist in Res	Russell, Peggy	M	64A
Lect	Russell, Tracy	M	20,14C
Prof	Saradjian, Vagram	D	62C
Inst	Shaw, Betty		32,66B,66D
Artist in Res	Shirley, Alicia	M	66A
Prof	Simon, Abbey	DIPL	66A
Assoc Prof	Smith, Robert Thomas	D	13A,13,10,43
Prof	Snyder, John L.	D	13,11,12
Assoc Prof	Sonnenberg, Melanie	M	61
Assoc Prof	Sposato, Jeffrey S.	D	12,36
Artist in Res	Stanton, Philip		63B
Artist in Res	Suhr, Melissa	M	64A
Vstng Assoc Prof	Suits, Brian	M	66C
Asst Prof	Turner, Kelly J.	D	36
Artist in Res	Vasquez, Hector		61
Artist in Res	Vassallo, James	M	41,63A
Vstng Assoc Prof	Wang, Yung-Hsiang	D	62A,12A,38,11
Artist in Res	Warren, Alec	M	65,50
Prof	Weber, Betsy Cook	D	32C,36
Prof	Weems, Nancy	M	66A
Lect	Welch, Chapman	D	32F
Assoc Prof	Wheeler, Lawrence	B	11
Artist in Res	Wheeler, Mike	B	47,70
Artist in Res	White, Brad K.	M	63C
Prof	White, David A.	D	13,10,31A
Artist in Res	Whittaker, Dennis	M	62D
Assoc Prof	Wilkins, Blake	D	65,50
Artist in Res	Witt, Woody W.	D	47,64E,29

TX3410 Univ of the Incarnate Word
Department of Music
4301 Broadway St
San Antonio, TX 78209-6318
(210) 829-3848   Fax: (210) 829-3880
www.uiw.edu/music
E-mail: gokelman@uiwtx.edu

4 Year Institution

Dean, College of Arts & Science: Bob J. Connelly, 80A
Chair: William Gokelman, 80A

Prof	Bussineau-King, D. E.	M	61,15,39
Lect PT	Carroll, John	D	63A
Lect PT	Cortez, Brooke D.	M	33
Assoc Prof	Dvorkin, Janice	D	33
Lect PT	Ferris, Rachel	M	62E
Lect PT	Frazor, Terance	M	38
Lect PT	Gnecco, Jeanne E.	M	64A
Lect PT	Godoy, John E.	M	65
Prof	Gokelman, William	M	60,36,66A,66C,31A
Lect PT	Gonzalez, Joe	M	70
Lect PT	Ha, Jaehyuk	D	66G
Lect PT	Hill, Mark	M	63C
Lect PT	Kilmer, Richard L.	M	62A
Lect PT	Kobialka, Daniel	D	62A
Lect PT	Loden, Larry D.	M	64E
Lect PT	Lopez, Joel H.	M	63B
Lect PT	Lynn, Sarah B.	M	33
Prof	Metz, Ken	D	13,10,29,29A
Lect PT	Pomerantz, Mark	M	13
Lect PT	Ridgway, Meredith K.	M	66A,66D
Lect PT	Ridgway, Zachary M.	M	66A
Asst Prof	Salfen, Kevin	D	11,12,13A,20
Lect PT	Syler, James	D	10
Lect PT	Tamez, Ray	M	70
Inst FT	Vollmar, Ferdinand	M	37,32E
Lect FT	Waller, Jim	M	35G,10C,29B,47,35A

Directory of Institutions

TX3415 Univ of Mary Hardin-Baylor
CVPA-Music Department
UMHB Box 8012
900 College St
Belton, TX 76513
(254) 295-4678   Fax: (254) 295-4158
www.umhb.edu/music
E-mail: mhumphrey@umhb.edu

4 Year Institution

Chair: Mark Aaron Humphrey, 80A
Dir., Preparatory Division: Jonathan Gary, 80E

Assoc Prof	Clement, Lisa	M	61
Prof	Crawford, Stephen J.	D	37,12A,50,65
Asst Prof	Crosby, Matthew	M	36,13A,13B
PT	Goodnight, Cheryl	M	64A
Asst Prof	Hogan, George	M	61,39,54
Inst	Hogan, Penny	M	61,39,54
Assoc Prof	Humphrey, Mark Aaron	D	10,13
Assoc Prof	Jones, Deborah	D	32,13A,13C
Inst	Landsberg, Nils F.	M	37,60B,46
Prof	Roueche, Michelle	D	60,36,66C
Assoc Prof	Schumann, Michelle	D	66
Prof	Stansbury, George	D	60,31A,44
PT	Steinbauer, Robert	D	12A,66A
Inst	Whitis, James	M	37,63D
Assoc Prof	Whitis, Jessye	M	66,13
Assoc Prof	Wilson, Guy	D	61

TX3420 Univ of North Texas
College of Music
1155 Union Cir #311367
Denton, TX 76203-5017
(940) 565-2791   Fax: (940) 565-2002
www.music.unt.edu
E-mail: james.scott@unt.edu

4 Year Institution, Graduate School
Member of NASM

Master of Arts in Music, Master of Music in Composition, Master of Music in Music Theory, Master of Music in Performance, Master of Music in Music Education, Master of Music in Musicology, PhD in Music Theory, PhD in Music Education, DMA in Composition, DMA in Conducting, DMA in Performance, PhD in Musicology, Master of Music in Jazz Studies

Dean: James C. Scott, 80A
Dir., Undergraduate Studies: Jaymee Haefner, 80B
Dir., Graduate Studies: Graham H. Phipps, 80C
Senior Associate Dean: Warren Henry, 80H,80B
Associate Dean: Jon C. Nelson, 80H
Assistant Chair: Eric M. Nestler, 80H
Associate Dean: John C. Scott, 80H

Asst Prof	Alonso-Minutti, Ana R.	D	11,12
Assoc Prof	Alorwoyie, Gideon F.		20,65,31F,50,52
Adj Prof	Aponte, Jose Porentud	M	50,65,46
Assoc Prof	Austin, Stephen F.	D	61
Assoc Prof	Baker, Tony E.	M	63C,29
Prof	Banowetz, Joseph M.	M	66A
Senior Lect	Beckman, Bradley J.	D	66A,66B
Adj Prof	Bennight, Bradley J.	D	66H
Asst Prof	Bithell, David	D	10
Lect	Booth, Rodney	M	63A,29
Adj Prof	Borok, Emanuel	M	62A,62
Prof	Bowman, Brian	D	63D
Prof	Bradetich, Jeff	M	62D
Asst Prof	Brand, Benjamin D.	D	12A,12
Adj Prof	Brooks, Debbie	M	35
Assoc Prof	Bush, Deanna D.	D	12A,12
Assoc Prof	Bushkova, Julia	DIPL	62A
Assoc Prof	Chesky, Kris	D	32
Principal Lect	Chisholm, Rose Marie	M	61
Prof	Cho, Gene	D	13,20D
Prof	Clardy, Mary Karen	D	41,48,64A
Adj Prof	Clay, William	M	62D
Adj Prof	Cloutier, David	D	39,66C
Adj Prof	Coad, Daryl L.	M	64C
Adj Prof	Collins, C. Keith	D	67D
Adj Prof	Cooper, Justin L.	B	72
Prof	Corporon, Eugene Migliaro	M	60B,37
Senior Lect	Couturiaux, Clay	D	60B,38,62C
Prof	Croft, Richard	M	61
Adj Prof	De Villiers, Liesl-Ann	M	62B
Assoc Prof	Deane, Christopher	M	65A,65B
Assoc Prof	DeRosa, Richard J.	M	29
Prof	Di Fiore, Linda	D	61
Adj Prof	Drake, Michael	M	65
Assoc Prof	Dubberly, Stephen	D	39
Prof	Dubois, Susan L.	D	62B
Prof	Dworak, Paul E.	D	13,34
Adj Prof	Eckert, Rosana C.	M	47,61
Assoc Prof	Emmanuel, Donna T.	D	32B,32G,20D,20H,35A
Prof	Eschbach, Jesse	D	66G
Adj Prof	Fabian, Deborah U.	M	64C
Prof	Fisher, Dennis W.	M	60B,32C,37
Adj Prof	Fisher, Jonathan	B	29,62D
Prof	Ford, Mark	M	65,50
Prof	Friedson, Steven	D	11,14,65
Adj Prof	Gibbons, Henry	M	32D
Prof	Gillespie, James E.	D	41,64C
Adj Prof	Gordon, Adam	M	67E,55B
Assoc Prof	Groom, Joan	D	13
Senior Lect	Haefner, Jaymee	M	62E,62
Adj Prof	Haerle, Dan	M	66A,34B,29
Prof	Hamilton, Frederick	M	47,70,53,29
Assoc Prof	Hammer, Christoph	DIPL	66E,66G,67F
Prof	Harlos, Steven C.	D	66A,66C
Prof	Heidlberger, Frank	D	13J,12A,12,13
Adj Prof	Helbing, Stockton T.	B	35A,35B
Prof	Henry, Warren	D	32B,32
Assoc Prof	Holt, John	M	63A
Prof	Homer, Paula	M	39
Assoc Prof	Illari, Bernardo	M	12,20H
Prof	Itkin, David C.	M	38,60B
Prof	Jackson, Timothy L.	D	13,13I
Prof	Johnson, J. Keith	M	63A
Principal Lect	Johnson, Karrell	M	32,51,62B
Asst Prof	Johnson, Thomas M.	M	70
Adj Prof	Johnston, Noel H.	M	70,53,29
Adj Prof	Kagarice, Jan M.	M	63C
Prof	Kagarice, Vern L.	D	41,49,63C,63D
Adj Prof	Kang, Heejung	D	66A
Prof	Karlsson, Stefan	M	29B,29C,47,66A
Lect	Kennedy, Laura E.	D	12
Prof	Kern, R. Fred	D	13A,66B,66D
Adj Prof	King, Pamela	M	61
Adj Prof	Kinnett, Randy	D	12
Adj Prof	Klein, Heidi	M	61
Prof	Klein, Joseph	D	10F,10A
Asst Prof	Kruse, Nathan B.	D	32,32E
Assoc Prof	Lane, Jennifer R.	D	61
Adj Prof	Lattimore, Lee	D	64A,67E
Asst Prof	Leali, Brad	M	29,47,64E
Adj Prof	LeBlanc, Paul	D	70
Prof	Leenhouts, Paul T.	M	55B,67C
Prof	Lewis, Philip J.	M	41,62A
Adj Prof	Liikala, Blair	M	35G
Prof	Little, Donald C.	M	41,49,63D
Adj Prof	MacMillan, Ann E.	M	72
Librarian	Martin, Morris	M	16
Assoc Prof	May, Andrew D.	D	10A,10B,10F,34A,34D
Assoc Prof	McClung, Alan C.	D	32C,32D,32G,60A,13C
Prof	McCoy, Jerry	D	60A,36
Adj Prof	McGinney, William L.	D	12
Adj Prof	McGuire, Christopher	M	47
Adj Prof	McKnight, Mark	D	16,12
Adj Prof	McLure, Richard	M	70
Senior Lect	McNutt, Elizabeth	D	64A,43
Prof	McTee, Cindy K.	D	10A
	Mitchell, Rachel E.	M	13
Asst Prof	Morscheck, Stephen M.	D	61
Prof	Murphy, John P.	D	29,14,47,64E
Prof	Nelson, Jon C.	D	10A,10B,10F,34
Prof	Nestler, Eric M.	D	41,64E
Assoc Prof	Notley, Margaret	D	12
Lect	Odnoposoff, Berthe Huberman	DIPL	66A
Adj Prof	Okstel, Henry J.	B	65
Assoc Prof	Olschofka, Felix	D	62A
Adj Prof	O'Rear, Susan A.	M	32B
Assoc Prof	Osadchy, Eugene	M	62C
Adj Prof	Papich, George	D	42,62B
Prof	Paul, Pamela Mia	D	66A
Adj Prof	Perry, Brian N.	M	62D
Prof	Phipps, Graham H.	D	13,13J
Adj Prof	Prado, Danny	M	32
Assoc Prof	Puccinelli, Elvia	D	66C
Prof	Ramsey, Darhyl S.	D	32
Principal Lect	Rennick, Paul	M	65,50
Assoc Prof	Reynolds, Kathleen	M	41,64D
Adj Prof	Reynolds, Terence	M	63B
Principal Lect	Roberts, Cynthia	M	55B,62A
Prof	Rohwer, Debbie A.	PhD	32C,32B,64A
Assoc Prof	Romero, Gustavo	M	66A,42
Asst Prof	Ruzevic, Nikola	D	42,62C
Adj Prof	Sato, Akira	M	29,63A,47,60A
Principal Lect	Saunders, John Jay	M	47,63A,29,46
Prof	Scharnberg, William	D	41,49,63B
Adj Prof	Schietroma, Robert J.	D	65
Asst Prof	Schulze, Hendrik	D	12
Assoc Prof	Schwarz, David	D	13
Prof	Scott, James C.	D	64A
Prof	Scott, John C.	D	41,64C
Adj Prof	Scott, P. Mark	B	66G
Assoc Prof	Seaton, Lynn	D	62D,29
Adj Prof	Serrin, Bret E.	M	66A
Assoc Prof	Slottow, Stephen	D	13I,13D,13F,13

Adj Prof	Smith, Ed		65
Assoc Prof	Snider, Jeffrey	D	61
Prof	Soph, Ed	B	65,29
Prof	Sovik, Thomas	D	13,31A,14C,13J,34
Adj Prof	Sparks, Richard	D	60A,36,55D
Adj Prof	Sriji, Poovalur		65,50
Prof	Steinel, Michael L.	M	53,29
Prof	Stout, David L.	M	34
Assoc Prof	Sundberg, Terri	M	41,64A
Adj Prof	Sundquist, David	B	61
Asst Prof	Taylor, Donald M.	D	32,32B
Prof	Veazey, Charles	D	41,64B
Prof	Viardo, Vladimir	DIPL	66A
Vstng Prof	Wallach, Joelle	D	10
Adj Prof	Wermuth, Bruce M.	M	29,61
Adj Prof	Whear, P. Allen	D	67B,67A,55B
Assoc Prof	Wiest, Steve	M	10,29,47,63C
Asst Prof	Williams, Nicholas	M	60B,37
Prof	Wodnicki, Adam	M	66A
Adj Prof	Worlton, James T.	D	10
Adj Prof	Yoshioka, Masataka	D	12

TX3450 Univ of St. Thomas
Department of Music
3800 Montrose Blvd
Houston, TX 77006-4626
(713) 525-3159   Fax: (713) 942-5912
www.stthom.edu
E-mail: garridog@stthom.edu

4 Year Institution

Chair: Glenn Garrido, 80A
Dean: Joseph Pilsner, CSB, 80A
Dir., Preparatory Division: Paul Krystofiak, 80E

PT	Angerstein, Fred	M	63D,37
PT	Austin, Alan S.	B	62A
PT	Brewer, Robert S.	M	66H,66G
PT	Carrettin, Zachary	M	62A,38
PT	Daniell-Knapp, Courtney	M	60A,32
PT	Eisenstein-Baker, Paula	M	41,62C
PT	Fairbanks, Ann K.	D	13A,12A,41,64A
Assoc Prof	Garrido, Glenn	D	60B,32E,20H,37
PT	Gaschen, Terry	M	70
PT	Hatem, Jasmine	M	66A,66B,66C
PT	Klingensmith, David C.	M	62D
Asst Prof	Knapp, Brady	D	39,40,36
PT	Krystofiak, Paul	M	66A
PT	Leslie, Evan A.	M	62C
PT	Lowe, Edward	M	63C
PT	Martin, Noel	B	41
PT	Nunemaker, Richard	M	64C,48
PT	Ochoa, Reynaldo	D	63A,49,13
Asst Prof	Rector, Malcolm W.	D	13,10,29,47
PT	Russell-Dickson, Marion	M	61
PT	Smith-Wright, Lovie	M	50,65
PT	Wheeler, Michael	B	70,29

TX3500 Univ of Texas-Arlington
Department of Music
Box 19105
Arlington, TX 76019
(817) 272-3471   Fax: (817) 272-3434
www.uta.edu/music
E-mail: music@uta.edu

4 Year Institution, Graduate School
Member of NASM

Graduate Certificate in Performance, Master of Music in Performance, Master of Music in Music Education

Chair: John R. Burton, 80A
Dir., Graduate Studies: Clifton J. Evans, 80C
Associate Chair: Rick G. Bogard, 80H

Asst Prof	Atkinson, Sean E.	D	11,12A,13
Assoc Prof	Bogard, Rick G.	D	63A,49
Senior Lect	Bubert, Dennis	M	63C
Prof	Burton, John R.	D	62C,42
Asst Prof	Cavanagh, Daniel	D	47,29,46
Assoc Prof	Chave, George B.	PhD	13,10
Asst Prof	Cho, Young-Hyun	D	66A,41,66C,66B,12A
Assoc Prof	Espinosa, Sergio	DMA	32,11,62A
Asst Prof	Evans, Clifton J.	DMA	38,60B,11
Asst Prof	Frisof, Sarah A.	D	41,64A
Asst Prof	Grogan, David C.	D	61,32D,36,39,40
Vstng Asst Prof	Hayes, Micah	M	34,35

Assoc Prof	Hunt, Graham G.	D	13,12,10F,11,12A
Assoc Prof	Ishii, Timothy	M	29,46,47,64E
Assoc Prof	Jessup, Carol A.	D	48,64C
Assoc Prof	Kenaston-French, Karen	D	36,61,32D,40,60A
Assoc Prof	Kim, Soo Hong	D	61,39
Assoc Prof	Lange, Diane	D	32
Asst Prof	Luttrell, Matthew	D	37,32
Prof	Morrow, Elizabeth N.	D	62C,51,11
	Pool, Scott	D	64D,13,48,11,64E
Prof	Powell, Linton	D	12,66G,66H
Lect	Savko, Carolyn	M	66D,66A
Assoc Prof	Solomons, John	D	66A,41,66C
Assoc Prof	Stotter, Douglas	D	37,41,60B
Prof	Tam, Jing Ling	M	36,61,60A
Assoc Prof	Varner, Michael	D	50,65,14,20
Asst Prof	Walvoord, Martha J.	D	62A,51
Inst	Yakas, James	M	65,50,20

TX3510 Univ of Texas-Austin
Butler School of Music
2406 Robert Dedman Dr
Stop E3100
Austin, TX 78712-1555
(512) 471-7764   Fax: (512) 471-2333
www.music.utexas.edu
E-mail: generalinfo@mail.music.utexas.edu

4 Year Institution, Graduate School
Member of NASM

Master of Music in Composition, Master of Music in Music Theory, Master of Music in Performance, Master of Music in Musicology, PhD in Ethnomusicology, PhD in Music Theory, DMA in Composition, DMA in Performance, PhD in Musicology, Master of Music in Literature & Pedagogy, Master of Music in Music & Human Learning, DMA in Music & Human Learning, PhD in Music & Human Learning, Artist Diploma

Director: Glenn Richter, 80A
Dir., Undergraduate Studies: Steven Bryant, 80B
Dir., Graduate Studies: Byron Paul Almen, 80C
Dir., Admissions: Suzanne M. Pence, 80D
Associate Director: Robert A. DeSimone, 80H,80F,80G,80C
Associate Director: Jeffrey Hellmer, 80H
Associate Director: Winton Reynolds, 80H
Dir., Graduate Studies: Eugenia Costa-Giomi

Lect	Albert, Donnie Ray	M	61
Prof	Allen, Gregory	M	66A
Assoc Prof	Almen, Byron Paul	D	13,13H
Prof	Antokoletz, Elliott M.	D	11,12A,12
Specialist	Barrera, J. J.		20H
Prof	Brickens, Nathaniel O.	DMA	63C,49
Assoc Prof	Bryant, Steven	M	49,63D
Assoc Prof	Buhler, James	D	13
Assoc Prof	Burritt, Thomas		65
Assoc Prof	Candelaria, Lorenzo		11,12A,12
Assoc Prof	Carnochan, Robert M.	D	37,48,32
Asst Prof	Carson, Charles	PhD	12
Lect	Castro, Zeke		20H,14C
Prof	Chandler, B. Glenn	D	13
Senior Lect	Ching, Daniel	M	62A,42
Prof	Costa-Giomi, Eugenia	D	32,32A
Lect	Davis, Scott		31A,66G
Prof	Dell'Antonio, Andrew	D	11,12A,12
Prof	DeSimone, Robert A.	D	39
Lect	Dillard, Chuck	M	66C
Specialist	Dotson, Dennis W.		63A,29
Assoc Prof	Drott, Eric	D	13
Prof	Duke, Robert A.	D	32
Specialist	Edwards, Tony		65
Prof	Epperson, Anne	M	66C
Prof	Erlmann, Veit	D	14
Lect	Fair, Ed	MSW	35A
Senior Lect	Fedkenheuer, William	M	62A,51
Senior Lect	Fedson, Delaine		62E
Prof	Freeman, Robert S.	D	12
Assoc Prof	Fremgen, John	M	62D,29,47,46
Prof	Garrett, Nancy B.	M	66A
Prof	Gedigian, Marianne	B	64A
Assoc Prof	Gilmson, Sophia	DIPL	66B
Senior Lect	Gindele, Joshua	M	62C,42
Prof	Grantham, Donald	D	13,10F,10
Assoc Prof	Gratovich, Eugene	D	41,62A
Specialist	Guzman, Joel J.		20H
Senior Lect	Hancock, Judith E.	D	66G,31A
Lect	Hanna, Scott S.	D	60,37
Prof	Hatten, Robert S.	PhD	13
Prof	Hellmer, Jeffrey	M	29,35A,35B,46
Prof	Henderson, Rebecca	M	64B
Asst Prof	Henninger, Jacqueline	D	32,32E
Prof	Hilley, Martha F.	M	66D
Prof	Holzman, Adam	M	70

Assoc Prof	Hughes, Patrick	M	63B
Senior Lect	Hunter, David	D	12,12C
Prof	Jellison, Judith A.	D	32,33
Prof	Jensen, Kristin	M	41,64D
Prof	Junkin, Jerry	M	60,37
Lect	Kattari, Kim	D	12
Lect	Kuo, Kelly	M	39,60A
Senior Lect	Largess, John		62B,42
Prof	Lewis, Brian D.	M	62A,42
Prof	Lewis, William	B	39,61
Lect	Luperi, Victoria	B	64C
Prof	March, Hunter	D	32,32B
Lect	Marinello, Anthony	M	60B,37
Lect	Masters, Richard J.	D	66C,39
Assoc Prof	Mills, John	D	64E,29,47,46
Prof	Moore, Robin D.	D	14,31F,14C,14F,20H
Lect	Morrow, Cindy	D	61
Assoc Prof	Morrow, James	D	60,36
Prof	Myers, Roger	M	62B,42
Assoc Prof	Nardini, Luisa	D	12,12A
Prof	Nel, Anton	M	66A,41
Prof	Neumeyer, David	D	13,10
Lect	Olivieri, Guido	D	12A,12,67B
Asst Prof	O'Meara, Caroline	D	12,20G
Assoc Prof	Pearsall, Edward	D	13
Assoc Prof	Pence, Suzanne M.	D	32,36
Prof	Pennycook, Bruce	D	45
Prof	Pinkston, Russell F.	D	10,45,34
Prof	Pittel, Harvey	M	64E
Senior Lect	Powell, Gary		35
Assoc Prof	Renner, David	M	66A
Lect	Reynolds, Winton	D	13
Prof	Richter, Glenn	M	60,37,35A
Senior Lect	Rowley, Rick E.		66A,66C
Specialist	Salzmann, Wayne W.	M	65
Prof	Sasaki, Ray	M	63A
Lect	Saunders, Bruce		70,47
Assoc Prof	Scott, Laurie	D	32,62
Asst Prof	Seeman, Sonia T.	D	20A,20B,14A
Asst Prof	Sharlat, Yevgeniy	M	10
Prof	Slawek, Stephen M.	D	20D,14A
Assoc Prof	Small, David	M	61,39
Assoc Prof	Storojev, Nikita	DIPL	61,39
Lect	Swenson, Ruth Ann	M	61
Assoc Prof	Tsang, Bion	D	62C,42
Asst Prof	Turci-Escobar, John	D	13
Prof	Tusa, Michael C.	D	11,12A,12
Lect	Valentine, Colette	D	66C,66A
Senior Lect	Villarrubia, Charles	M	63D,41
Prof	Welcher, Dan E.		10,43
Assoc Prof	Wheeldon, Marianne	D	13,13C
Prof	Wiley, Darlene	M	61,39
Assoc Prof	Williams, Nathan L.	D	64C
Senior Lect	Yamamoto, Sandy	M	62A,42
Asst Prof	Zhang, DaXun	B	62D
Prof	Zimmermann, Gerhardt	M	38,60B

TX3515 Univ of Texas-Brownsville

Department of Music
80 Fort Brown St
Brownsville, TX 78520-4956
(956) 882-8247   Fax: (956) 882-3808
www.utb.edu
E-mail: sue.z.urbis@utb.edu

4 Year Institution, Graduate School

Master of Music in Music Education

Dean, Liberal Arts: Javier Martinez, 80A
Chair: Sue Zanne Williamson Urbis, 80A
Dir., Graduate Studies: Kenneth N. Saxon, 80C
Dir., Music Academy: Rocio Molina, 80E
Dir., Artist/Performance Series: Richard Urbis, 80F

Asst Prof	Andrade, Juan Pablo	D	13,66B,66C
Asst Prof	Asel, Nicole	M	61
Adj Prof	Balboa, Javier	M	32B
Asst Prof	Ballatori, Cristina	D	64A,11,42,13
Assoc Prof	Briseno, Antonio	M	11,20H,41
Prof	Brownlow, James A.	D	11,12A,49,63A,20
Adj Prof	Brumley, Dianne	M	36,32D,60A
Adj Prof	Capistran, Raul W.	D	66C,66D
Assoc Prof	Clark, Allen	M	32C,37,63D
Adj Prof	Cruhm, Robert	M	66C
Asst Prof	de Ghize, Susan K.	D	13
Asst Prof	Geeseman, Katherine	D	11,62C,62D
Adj Prof	Goodwin, Sydney	M	13
Asst Prof	Guist, Jonathan B.	D	64C,32,42
Asst Prof	Hunter-Holly, Daniel	D	13,61,42
Asst Prof	Hurley-Glowa, Susan M.	D	12A,14
Adj Prof	Lopez-Trujillo, David	M	11,50,65
Assoc Prof	McNabb, Carol	D	13B,13C,64D,67C,64B
Adj Prof	Molina, Rocio	M	66C,66D
Asst Prof	Nevill, Tom	D	65,13A,13C,50,37
Lect	Placeres, Martha	M	62A,38,13A,13C
Assoc Prof	Quantz, Michael	D	11,41,62,20H
Adj Prof	Ramirez, Pamela	M	32B
Adj Prof	Sachs, Carol	M	39,61
Assoc Prof	Saxon, Kenneth N.	D	66B,66C
Asst Prof	Shoop, Stephen S.	PhD	32,41,60B,63D
Prof	Tomlin, Terry	M	47,64E,29,34,32F
Lect	Trenfield, Sally	M	32A,32B,66C,66D
Prof	Urbis, Richard		10F,66A,66C
Assoc Prof	Urbis, Sue Zanne Williamson	D	32,66C
Adj Prof	Wade, Elaine San Juan	D	66D

TX3520 Univ of Texas-El Paso

Department of Music
500 W University Ave
El Paso, TX 79968-8900
(915) 747-5606   Fax: (915) 747-5023
academics.utep.edu/music
E-mail: music@utep.edu

4 Year Institution, Graduate School
Member of NASM

Master of Music in Performance, Master of Music in Music Education, Master of Music in Music Theory-Composition

Chair: Lowell Graham, 80A
Dir., Graduate Studies: David Ross, 80C
Assistant Chair: William McMillan, 80H

Senior Lect	Bailey, Zuill	M	62C
Assoc Prof	Colgin-Abeln, Melissa	D	12A,64A
Asst Prof	Dousa, Dominic	D	13
Asst Prof	Eylon, Orit	D	39
Prof	Fountain, Marcia	D	13,16
Prof	Graham, Lowell	D	13,60
PT	Gunnarson, Eike	M	61
Lect	Guttierez, Ruben	M	10,35B,35C
Senior Lect	Haddad, Steve	B	63D,34,35
Prof	Hufstader, Ron	D	60,37,38
Asst Prof	Jones, Dena Kay	D	66,32,20F,14F,15
PT	Lambrecht, Richard	M	12A,49,63B
Assoc Prof	Leinberger, Charles	D	13
Senior Lect	Luffey, Gregory	M	64E,11
Staff	M. de Oca, Patricia	M	66D,66C,54
Prof	Macchioni, Oscar E.	D	66A,66B,66D,66,14
Assoc Prof	McMillan, William	D	36,61,60
Assoc Prof	Meyers, Stephanie	D	62A,62B
Prof Emeritus	Paul, Arryl S.	D	66A
Prof	Ross, David	D	12A,64C
Vstng Assoc Prof	Schuppener, Mark	D	62A,62B,11
Asst Prof	Siqueiros, John	M	70
Senior Lect	Taylor, Nancy		63A,49
Assoc Prof	Tredway, Curtis B.	D	37,32
Asst Prof	Unsworth, Erik	M	62D
Lect	Walker, Carmen Diaz		61
Assoc Prof	Warren, J. Curt	M	70,53,29
Prof	White, James L.		50,65
Assoc Prof	Wilkinson, Donald G.	D	64B,64D,64E,46,32H
Staff	Wilkinson, Judi	B	66,54
PT	Williams, Demetrius	B	65,50
Asst Prof	Wilson, Elisa	D	61,54,47,39
PT	Wilson, Ellen M.	M	61,54,39,12
Assoc Prof	Wilson, Steve	D	63D,29A,37

TX3525 Univ of Texas-Pan American

Department of Music
1201 W University Dr
Edinburg, TX 78539-2999
(956) 381-3471   Fax: (956) 381-3472
www.utpa.edu/dept/music
E-mail: martinezp@utpa.edu

4 Year Institution

Chair: Pedro Martinez, 80A

Lect FT	Amorim, George J.	M	62D,13,51
Lect PT	Butts, Leon	D	70,11,41
Assoc Prof	Canty, Dean R.	D	60,37,63A,63B,11
Lect FT	Cellon, Cheryl		66C,66A
Lect PT	Coleman, Malcolm J.		64A
Asst Prof	Crews, Ruth	M	61,11
Asst Prof	Cripps, Cynthia L.	D	64E,64D
Assoc Prof	Dabrowski, Peter	D	60,10F
Lect FT	Daussat, David	M	63D,49
Asst Prof	Davis, Virginia Wayman	D	32
Prof	Davis, Wendell R.	D	61,11

Assoc Prof	Grossman, Morley K.	D	11,66A,66C,66D
Lect FT	Hoffer, Heike	M	64B,11,32
Lect FT	Kapps, Sarah	M	62C
Lect FT	Lee, So Yoon	D	66A
Lect FT	Loera, Francisco	M	11,20H
Asst Prof	Martinez, Kurt	D	11,70,41
Asst Prof	Martinez, Pedro	D	63D,63C
Prof	Munn, Albert Christopher	D	13,12A,36,67,55B
Assoc Prof	Munn, Vivian C.	D	13,32C,36,61
Prof	O'Neil, Lorne W.	D	11,41,48,64
Asst Prof	Pagan, Joel G.	D	62B,62A
Prof	Raimo, John B.	D	11,12A,66A,66C,66D
Asst Prof	Ramirez, Mark Joseph	D	65,50
Lect PT	Varlamova, Liudmila	D	66D,66A
Asst Prof	Walker, Michael	D	13

TX3527 Univ of Texas-Permian Basin
Department of Fine Arts-Humanities
4901 E University Blvd
Odessa, TX 79762
(432) 552-4292   Fax: (432) 552-3280
cas.utpb.edu/academic-departments/visual-and-performing-arts-department/music-program/
E-mail: keast_d@utpb.edu

4 Year Institution

Coordinator, Music: Dan A. Keast, 80A
Chair, Visual & Performing Arts: Shawn Watson, 80A

Asst Prof	Alexander, Cory T.	D	36,32D,61,32,40
Adj	Basney, Nyela	M	61,66,36,38,60
Adj	Butler, Debbie D.	B	66A,66C,66D
Adj	Chance, Chris	M	64C
Adj	De La Garza, Luis	M	64D
Adj	DeLavan, Bill	M	62D
Adj	Harden, Bill	M	64D,37,38
Adj	Harris, Dennis	M	70
Adj	Hohstadt, Tom	D	38,41,56,60
Adj	Huzjak, Amy	M	62C
Assoc Prof	Keast, Dan A.	PhD	32,34B,34F,32G,32C
Adj	Keast, Michelle	M	11,32,32A
Adj	Lotspeich, Melissa	M	64A
Adj	Madrid, Albert	B	42
Adj	Madura, John	M	62A
Adj	Madura, Melissa	M	62B
Adj	McAfee, Karen	M	38
Adj	Olague, Jimmy	B	65
Adj	Puga, John	B	46,47
Adj	Pysh, Gregory	M	10,13,61,60A,36
Adj	Rasura, Ricky	B	62E
Adj	Santorelli, Michael	M	63A
Adj	Spires, Rozanne	M	66A,66C,66D
Adj	Viverette, Connie	M	66C
Adj	Young, Kevin	M	63D,49,11

TX3530 Univ of Texas-San Antonio
Department of Music
One UTSA Circle
San Antonio, TX 78249
(210) 458-4354   Fax: (210) 458-4381
music.utsa.edu
E-mail: steven.hill@utsa.edu

4 Year Institution, Graduate School
Member of NASM

Master of Music in Performance, Master of Music in Conducting, Master of Music in Music Education, Master of Music in Piano Pedagogy & Performance

Chair: R. J. David Frego, 80A
Dir., Institute for Music Research: Susan Dill Bruenger, 80F
Associate Chair: Stacey Davis, 80H

Lect	Acevedo, Michael	M	20H
Assoc Prof	Allan, Diana	D	61
Prof	Balentine, James S.	D	13,10,47,29A
Lect	Beavers, Jennifer	M	13
Lect	Brewer, Robert	M	66C
Asst Prof	Brill, Mark	D	12
Assoc Prof	Bruenger, Susan Dill	D	32B,32C,32D
Lect	Bryant, Jordan	M	61
Lect	Buchanan, Laurie	B	62E
Lect	Cline, Christopher	B	34
Asst Prof	Crappell, Courtney Joseph	D	66B,66A
Assoc Prof	Davis, Stacey	D	13,13K,12F
Lect	Dawkins, Allyson	M	62B
Lect	Debus, Christine	M	66C
Lect	Debus, David	M	64E
Lect	Donald, Larry Scott	D	66A
Assoc Prof	Dowdy, Eugene	D	38
Lect	Downey, Sherri	M	66D
Asst Prof	Dunne, Matthew R.	D	70,29,47,35
Lect	Eaton, David D.	D	66G,13,66H,67F
Lect	El-Farrah, Rami	D	64E
Lect	Ellis, Ron	M	37
Lect	Francis, Graeme	D	65
Prof	Frego, R. J. David	D	32,32I
Lect	Freudigman, Ken	M	62C
Lect	Frommeyer, Heinz	B	66A
Lect	Frost, Randi	M	52
Lect	Goree, Mary Ellen	M	62A
Lect	Hamrick, Utah	D	47
Lect	Hayes, Kristin Delia	D	64A
Lect	Herbert, David	M	13,64B
Assoc Prof	Keeling, Kasandra Kenneda	D	66A
Lect	Kelly, Laura L.	D	13
Lect	King, Morgan	M	13,11
Lect	Krause, Stephen	M	34D,34E
Lect	Kuentz, Charles	M	32E
Lect	Leonhardt, Angela J.	B	32
Assoc Prof	Linard, Rita A.	D	13,64A
Asst Prof	Linial, Christine A.	D	13
Assoc Prof	Mabry, Gary L.	D	36,61
Assoc Prof	McCrary, William	D	39,61
Lect	Mentzer, Larry E.	M	64C
Asst Prof	Miller, Donald K.	D	37,60
Asst Prof	Millican, Si	D	32E,37,10F,35B
Lect	Nix, Catherine	D	61
Assoc Prof	Nix, John Paul	M	61,13L,32D
Asst Prof	Olson, Susan	DMA	61
Lect	Parker, Steven C.	D	63C
Asst Prof	Pellegrino, Kristen	D	32E
Lect	Pietri, Michelle M.	M	54,52
Prof	Poetschke, Linda	M	61
Lect	Richter, Michael	M	70
Lect	Rodriguez, Javier	M	64D
Lect	Roller, Jan D.	B	63A
Lect	Rubins, Peter	M	63B
Lect	Rubins, Sherry D.	M	65
Lect	Saliers, James R.	M	63D
Lect	Sherrill, William	D	11
Lect	Shterenberg, Ilya F.	M	64E
Prof	Silantien, John J.	D	60,36
Assoc Prof	Stephen, J. Drew	D	12A,63B,67E,12
Lect	Syler, James	M	20G,29,35,10
Lect	Thrower, Daniel N.	D	63A
Lect	Tirado, Jonathan	M	65
Lect	Twehues, Mark A.	M	64,32E
Lect	Westney, Stephanie Teply	D	62A
Asst Prof	Wickman, Ethan F.	DMA	10A,13,36,10
Lect	Williams, Megan	M	52
Lect	Zeserman, Steven B.	B	62D
Lect	Zollars, Dan	M	62C

TX3535 Univ of Texas at Tyler
School of Performing Arts
3900 University Blvd
Tyler, TX 75799
(903) 566-7450   Fax: (903) 566-7483
www.uttyler.edu/music
E-mail: music@uttyler.edu

4 Year Institution, Graduate School

Master of Arts in Interdisciplinary Studies

Dir., School of Performing Arts: Michael Thrasher, 80A

PT	Bonnett, Kurt	M	49,63A,63B
PT	Bugg, Sue	M	64A,32
PT	Campagna, Alison	M	61
Senior Lect	Conway, Vicki J.	M	66A,66B,66D
PT	Crutchfield, Robert	M	65
Assoc Prof	Emge, Jeffrey D.	D	32,37,60,64B
PT	Fain, Jeremy	M	64D
PT	Grinnell, Michael	M	62A,62B,38
PT	Guenette, Maria	D	66
Asst Prof	Gullings, Kyle	D	10,13,13F,10A
Assoc Prof	Johnson, Molly	D	61,54,39
PT	Millett, Michael J.	D	13,10
PT	Newman, Miranda	M	61
PT	Ogilvie, Jessica	M	32
PT	Roebke, Catherine	M	62C
Asst Prof	Rose, Cameron J.	D	36,32D,11,10
PT	Sherrod, Ron	D	70,11
Assoc Prof	Thrasher, Michael	D	64C,12A,12C
PT	Vinson, Danny	M	63C,63D
Prof	Webb, John	D	20,47,64E

TX3540 Vernon College
Department of Music
4400 College Dr
Vernon, TX 76384-4005
(940) 552-6291   Fax: (940) 552-9229
www.vernoncollege.edu
E-mail: iyeung@vernoncollege.edu

2 Year Institution

Dean: Gary Don Harkey, 80A
Chair: Joe Johnston, 80A

Adj	Hawkey, Walter	M	11
Adj	Mikalunas, Robin	M	11,13A
Adj	Tanner, Greg	M	11
Inst	Yeung, Ian	D	36,60A,40,31A,38

TX3600 Victoria College
Department of Music
2200 E Red River
Victoria, TX 77901
(361) 573-3291   Fax: (361) 572-3850
www.victoriacollege.edu
E-mail: marylynn.fletcher@victoriacollege.edu

2 Year Institution

Coordinator, Fine Arts: Jonathan Anderson, 80A
Dean, Arts, Humanities and Social Science: Cindy Buchholz, 80A
Academic Vice President: Patricia Vandervoort, 80H

Asst Prof	Anderson, Jonathan	M	13,47,64E
PT	Balmer, Patricia	M	61
Prof	Fletcher, Marylynn L.	D	34C,36,11,66A,12A
PT	Fuhrman, Eugenie	M	61
PT	Johannsen, Ann	M	13
PT	McCullough, Daryl	M	63,70
PT	McFarland, James	D	11,13,66D,66G

TX3650 Wayland Baptist University
School of Music
1900 W 7th St #1286
Plainview, TX 79072
(806) 291-1076   Fax: (806) 291-1967
www.wbu.edu/music
E-mail: stutesa@wbu.edu

4 Year Institution

Dean: Ann B. Stutes, 80A,80E
Dir., Admissions: Joe Berry, 80D

Prof	Belshaw, Gary D.	D	10F,10,66,34
Asst Prof	Brown, Kimberly	D	61
Asst Prof	Chae, Hyung Sek	D	36,31A,44,60,32D
Assoc Prof	Flournoy-Buford, Debbie	D	32B,32D,34,66C,66A
Asst Prof	Fountain, Richard	D	66
Assoc Prof	Kelley, Timothy S.	M	60,37,49,63,41
Asst Prof	Kuhnert, Brian	M	61,39,54,40
Prof	Mosteller, Sandra M.	D	64,32E,48,20,31B
Prof	Stutes, Ann B.	PhD	13
Asst Prof	Vandiver, Joseph	M	29,63,46,47,34

TX3700 Weatherford College
Department of Music
225 College Park Dr
Weatherford, TX 76086
(817) 598-6233
www.wc.edu
E-mail: clewiston@wc.edu

2 Year Institution

Chair, Fine Arts & Communications: Cal Lewiston, 80A

	Laney, Robert	M	11,13,36
	Lewiston, Cal	D	13,47,11
Artist in Res	Song, Hyeyoung	D	66A

TX3750 West Texas A&M University
Department of Music
WTAMU Box 60879
Canyon, TX 79016
(806) 651-2840   Fax: (806) 651-2958
www.wtamu.edu
E-mail: ekahler@wtamu.edu

4 Year Institution, Graduate School
Member of NASM

Master of Arts in Music, Master of Music in Performance

Interim Head, Music: Robert Krause, 80A

Inst PT	Anderson, Kay	M	32B
Asst Prof	Bartley, Mark	M	36,38,60,60B
Asst Prof	Brooks, BJ	D	13,10A
Assoc Prof	Cansler, Joe Ella	D	61
Prof	Carpenter, Tina	D	64D,13,11,34C
Lect PT	Cotik, Tomas	M	62A
Prof	DuBois, Ted	D	11,12A,34C
Asst Prof	Hall, Daniel	D	36,60A
Prof	Hansen, Robert	D	61,54
Assoc Prof	Kahler, Edward P.	D	33,32A
Prof	Krause, Robert	D	64B,13,55C
Assoc Prof	Kuhnert, Cloyce	D	61,39
Assoc Prof	Lefevre, Donald	M	37,64E,48
Inst	Lemon, Ronald	M	63B,11
Inst	Lewis, Jeremy	M	63D,49
Lect PT	Lopez, Emmanuel	M	62C
Asst Prof	Morales, Raimundo	D	63C,37,49
Asst Prof	Nam, Choong-ha	D	66A,66D
Asst Prof	Parr-Scanlin, Denise	D	66A,66B,66C
Lect PT	Redpath, Keith	D	62A
Inst	Scales, Nicholas	M	13,62D,11
Lect PT	Snyder, Jennifer	M	62B
Assoc Prof	Storey, Douglas	M	64C
Asst Prof	Takacs, William	D	63A,11
Prof	Tariq, Susan Martin	D	65,50
Asst Prof	Teweleit, Russell D.	D	32,46,37
Inst	Wiegard, William James	M	63B,49,11

TX3800 Western Texas College
Department of Music
6200 S College Ave
Snyder, TX 79549-6105
(915) 573-8511   Fax: (915) 573-9321
www.wtc.edu
E-mail: gcorkran@wtc.edu

2 Year Institution

Chair, Fine Arts: Ty Brunson, 80A

Inst PT	Garner, Jerald	M	44
Inst PT	Lyon, William	M	66A
Inst PT	McFaul, Cathi	B	63
Asst Prof	Palomaki, Jonathan	M	60,12A,36,61,70
Inst PT	Smith, Melanie	M	61
PT	Wilson, George	B	66C

TX3850 Wharton County Junior College
Department of Music
911 E Boling Hwy
Wharton, TX 77488-3252
(979) 532-4560   Fax: (979) 532-6587
www.wcjc.edu
E-mail: waldropj@wcjc.edu

2 Year Institution

Music Contact: Joseph Waldrop, 80A

PT	Lemson, Deborah	M	66A,66G,66C,66D
	Lemson, Lee	M	13A,11,36,61
	Lester, Jason	D	11,12A,13F,29A
	Waldrop, Joseph	M	13A,32B,37,13B,64

UT0050 Brigham Young University

School of Music
C-550 Harris Fine Arts Center
Provo, UT 84602-6410
(801) 422-8903   Fax: (801) 422-0533
music.byu.edu
E-mail: music@byu.edu

4 Year Institution, Graduate School
Member of NASM

Master of Arts in Music Education, Master of Music in Composition, Master of Music in Performance, Master of Music in Conducting, Master of Music in Music Education, Master of Arts in Musicology

Director: Kory L. Katseanes, 80A
Assoc Dir., Undergraduate Studies: Geralyn Giovannetti, 80B
Assoc. Dir., Graduate Studies: Thomas L. Durham, 80C
Assistant Dir., Admissions & Scholarships: Mark Ammons, 80D,80H
Associate Dir., Performance: Don L. Peterson, 80H

PT	Allen, Travis	B	34D
Inst	Ammons, Mark	M	47,29
PT	Anderson, Anamae	M	41
Assoc Prof	Anderson, Richard P.	D	66A,66B,66C,66D
PT	Applonie, Jean	M	32
Assoc Prof	Asplund, Christian	D	10A,10B,13,34
Asst Prof	Babidge, Darrell	D	61
Assoc Prof	Belknap, Monte	M	62A,41
Assoc Prof	Bigelow, Claudine	M	62B
PT	Bloomfield, Tara	M	61
Assoc Prof	Boothe, Randall W.	M	61,54,20G,35
PT	Bounous, Barry	M	61
PT	Bounous, Debra	B	61
PT	Bradford, Daron	M	64C,64E
PT	Brady, Nicole B.	D	62E
Assoc Prof	Broomhead, Paul	D	32,36
Prof	Brough, Ronald P.	D	60,32C,37,65,72
Assoc Prof	Brown, David C.	M	63A,49
PT	Brown, Kayson	M	62C
Prof	Bush, Douglas E.	D	12,55,66G,67,31A
PT	Call, Monica	B	62C
Prof	Call, R. Steven	D	47,63D,46,29
Inst	Christensen, Janielle	B	12A,36,39,54,35
PT	Christensen, Ruth M.	B	61
Assoc Prof	Clayton, April	D	63A,48
PT	Colton, Kathy	M	63B
Assoc Prof	Cook, Don	D	66G,69,31A
PT	Crabb, Amanda	M	61
Prof	Dabczynski, Andrew	D	32,62
PT	Duke, Richard	B	34D
Prof	Dunn, Robert	D	32C,32G,32D
Prof	Durham, Thomas L.	D	13,10F,10
PT	Geslison, Mark	B	20G
Prof	Giovannetti, Geralyn	D	13,48,64B
PT	Green, Larry	M	70
Asst Prof	Grimshaw, Jeremy	D	14A,14D,20D
Assoc Prof	Hall, Rosalind	M	60,36
PT	Hancock, Robin	D	66C
Assoc Prof	Hansen, Eric	D	62D,38,51
Assoc Prof	Harker, Brian	D	63A
Prof	Hicks, Michael D.	D	13,43
PT	Hillam, Barry	D	63A
Assoc Prof	Hinckley, Jaren S.	D	64C,11,48
Prof	Hopkin, J. Arden	D	39,61,54
Assoc Prof	Jaccard, Jerry L.	D	32B
PT	Johnson, Kerilyn	B	61
PT	Johnson, Shauna	M	32B
Prof	Johnson, Steven P.	D	12A,12,14,12F
Prof	Katseanes, Kory L.	D	38,60,62A
Assoc Prof	Kenney, Susan H.	M	32A,32B
PT	Kimball, Hillary	M	64A
Assoc Prof	Kimball, Will	D	41,63C
PT	Latu, Kalotini	M	66A
PT	Lawrence, Jay	M	65
Prof	Lindeman, Stephan	D	13,29
Assoc Prof	Lockwood, Gayle	M	39,61,54,20G,35
Prof	Lowe, Laurence	D	63B
Inst	McInnis, Fred	M	37
PT	McKinney, Russell	B	63C
PT	Morgan, LeeAnn	M	62A,62B
PT	Orton, Korianne	B	61
Prof	Peery Fox, Irene	D	66A
Assoc Prof	Peterson, Don L.	D	13,12A,13J,63B
Asst Prof	Reich, Diane T.	D	61
PT	Rich, Harvey	B	66A
Assoc Prof	Ricks, Steven L.	D	10A,10B,13A,34
PT	Rosborough-Bowman, Monika	M	62C
Prof	Saville, Kirt	D	37,60B,64C,32E,32C
PT	Schaerrer, Bart	B	34D
PT	Scott, Michele	M	61
Prof	Shumway, Jeffrey	D	66A,66B,66C
Inst	Simpson, Ron	B	35A,35B,35D,35E,35F
PT	Skidmore, Jon	D	33
Prof	Smith, C. Raymond	D	47,64,53,46,29
Assoc Prof	Smith, Christian B.	D	64D
Prof	Staheli, Ronald	D	60,36,41,61,66A
PT	Stevens, James	B	40
PT	Thorne, Cecilia	M	66A
Prof	Vincent, Lawrence P.	D	39,61
PT	Warren, Jessica	B	62E
PT	Williams, Barbara	B	62A,42
PT	Winters, Jill	M	60A
Vstng Asst Prof	Woods, Alexander G.	M	62A,41
PT	Wright, Nathan	M	60A

UT0150 Dixie State College of Utah

Department of Fine Arts
225 S 700 E
St George, UT 84770-3875
(435) 652-7790   Fax: (435) 656-4129
www.dixie.edu
E-mail: webbg@dixie.edu

4 Year Institution

Dean, Fine Arts: Don Hinton, 80A
Chair: Glenn Webb, 80A
Associate Dean, Fine Arts: Brent Hanson, 80H

Asst Prof	Abegg, Paul	D	62A,38,51,54,62B
Asst Prof	Allred, Nancy C.	D	66A,66B,66D,66C
Adj Inst	Andrus, Victoria	M	62A,62B
Lect	Brickey, James	M	63D,32
Asst Prof	Briggs, Robert	D	36,61,12A,60A
Assoc Prof	Caldwell, Gary	M	13,60,37,63A
Adj Inst	Crowley, Lisle	B	70,41
Adj Inst	Dean, Lynn	D	11,66A,66B
Adj Inst	Gardner, Jessica	B	61
Prof Emeritus	Garner, Ronald L.	D	13,11,12A,63B
Adj Inst	Graf, Kendra	B	63B
Inst	Hardy, James	M	62C,11,41
Adj Inst	Hilton, Randalin	B	66A
Adj Inst	Jennings, Caroline	M	66A,66D
Adj Inst	Johnston, Greg	M	64C
Adj Inst	Myers, Geoffrey	M	66G
Adj Inst	Paterson, Amy	B	63A
Assoc Prof	Peterson, Ken	D	36,39,40,61
Adj Inst	Porter, Ami	A	64A
Adj Inst	Rhodes, Rhonda L.	M	64B,64E
Adj Inst	Riddle-Jackson, Jackie	B	61
Assoc Prof	Roberts, Shannon B.	D	13,41,49,63C,10
Adj Prof	Seegmiller, Lisa	B	61
Adj Inst	Smith, Jennifer	M	61
Adj Inst	Stevenson, Sandra	B	61
Asst Prof	Webb, Glenn	M	37,41,47,50,65
Inst	Webb, Merrilee	M	36,66D,66A
Adj Inst	Ziegler, Shanda	B	61

UT0190 Snow College

Horne School of Music
150 E College Ave
Ephraim, UT 84627
(801) 283-7472   Fax: (801) 283-7479
www.snow.edu/music
E-mail: steve.meredith@snow.edu

2 Year Institution

Chair: Steven Meredith, 80A
Dir., Summer Programs: Vance Larsen, 80G

Adj	Allred, Jody		61,11
Assoc Prof	Applewhite, Willie	M	66,20,29,63C
Adj	Ashton, Alice	M	62A,62B
Adj	Ashton, Jack	M	62A,62B
Adj	Blackinton, David	D	63A
Adj	Boothe, Greg		70
Adj	Bosshardt, Heather	M	29,66
Inst	Dixon, Rich	B	70,47,34,35
Adj	Ellefsen, Roy	D	13,11,36
Adj	Gunnell, Sarah	M	62A
Adj	Hansen, Kathleen	B	36,66A
Adj	Hicks, Roger		64D
Adj	Hinckley, Edwin	B	34,35
Adj	James, Laurel	M	61
Asst Prof	Johnson, Madeline	D	13,11,34,64C
Adj	Jorgensen, Elaine	D	11,41,48,64A
	Kidder, Tim		29,64E
Assoc Prof	Larsen, Vance	M	60,37,49,32
Adj	Lawrence, Jay	B	65,47
Assoc Prof	Liao, Amber Yiu-Hsuan	D	66,13
Adj	Litteral, Ron		11
Adj	McKinney, Russell	B	63C,63D

Asst Prof	Meredith, Steven	D	13,36,61,34
Adj	Nelson, Lizzy		64B
Adj	Rasmussen, Josh		29
Adj	Seamons, Nathan		37
Asst Prof	Smith, Brent	D	39,62C,13,12A,51
Adj	Smith, Marcie	B	66A,66D,13C,11
	Wang, Han Yuan	B	62A,66A
Adj	Woodward, Bruce		63B

UT0200 Southern Utah University
Department of Music
351 W Center St
Cedar City, UT 84720
(435) 586-7890   Fax: (435) 865-8288
www.suu.edu/pva/music
E-mail: mcintyre@suu.edu

4 Year Institution
Member of NASM

Chair: Keith M. Bradshaw, 80A

Inst PT	Andersen, LeGrand	D	61,66D,13C,13B
Inst PT	Andersen, Mary Ann	M	66
Inst PT	Barraclough, D. J.	M	63A
Inst PT	Bohnenstengel, Christian	D	66A,66C,13A,13B,13C
Assoc Prof	Bradshaw, Keith M.	D	10A,10F,13,36
Inst PT	Bradshaw, Tracey	B	66C,66D
Inst PT	Brown, LuAnn	M	62A
Inst PT	Gliadkovsky, Anna	D	66A,66B
Asst Prof	Gliadkovsky, Kirill	D	66A,12A
Asst Prof	Herb, Thomas	D	13C,34,47,32C,32D
Inst PT	Jackson, Jackie	M	61
Asst Prof	Johnson, Lawrence	M	11,13C,61
Inst PT	Johnson, Nathaniel	M	12A,61
Inst PT	Johnston, Greg	M	64C
Inst PT	Linder, Susan	M	63B
Prof	Modesitt, Carol Ann	M	39,61
Inst PT	Rhodes, Rhonda	M	64E
Asst Prof	Stickney, Mark A.	D	37,63D,41,49,63
Prof	Stitt, Virginia K.	D	11,32B,64B,64D,12A
Assoc Prof	Sun, Xun	M	60,38,62A
Inst PT	Tebbs, Mckay	M	70
Asst Prof	Vartan, Lynn	D	65,41,20
Inst PT	Yu, Ling	M	62B

UT0250 Univ of Utah
School of Music
1375 E Presidents Circle
Room 204
Salt Lake City, UT 84112-0030
(801) 581-6762   Fax: (801) 581-5683
www.music.utah.edu
E-mail: Jas.Gardner@utah.edu

4 Year Institution, Graduate School
Member of NASM

Master of Music in Composition, Master of Music in Music Theory, Master of Music in Performance, Master of Music in Conducting, Master of Music in Music Education, PhD in Composition, PhD in Music Education, DMA in Conducting, DMA in Performance, Master of Arts in Musicology, Master of Music in Music History, Master of Music in Jazz Studies, Doctorate of Musical Arts

Director: James E. Gardner, 80A
Dir., Undergraduate Studies: David Power, 80B
Dir., Graduate Studies: Robert L. Baldwin, 80C
Dir., Preparatory Division: Gretchen Tanner, 80E

Adj PT	Allred, Carol Ann	D	61
Adj PT	Angulo, Denson	M	62D,70
Prof	Baldwin, Robert L.	D	38,60B
Lect	Basinger, BettieJo	D	12
Adj PT	Booth, Brian	M	10,47
Assoc Prof	Borup, Hasse		62A
Adj PT	Braus, Leonard P.	B	62A
Prof	Breault, Robert	D	39,61
Adj PT	Brown, George		65
Adj PT	Brown, Lenora N.	M	66A
Adj PT	Bybee, Ariel		61
Adj PT	Byrnes, Lisa B.		64A
Asst Prof	Cathey, Tully J.	D	13,70
Adj PT	Cheney, Elliott	D	62C,11
Asst Prof	Chikinda, Michael	PhD	13
Prof	Chuaqui, Miguel Basim	PhD	13,10
Lect	Clayton, Cathryn	D	62E,20,12A
Assoc Prof	Conner, Heather	D	66A,66D
Prof Emeritus	Cooksey, John M.	D	36,32C,32D
Lect	Costa, John V.	D	13,11
Lect	Cottle, David M.	D	13,34
Adj PT	Dorgan, Paul	D	39
Adj PT	Dresher, Mary Ann	M	61
Prof	Duehlmeier, Susan	D	66A,66D
Adj PT	Eckstein, John B.	M	62C
Adj PT	Elias, Gerald A.	M	62A
Prof	Ely, Mark	D	32C,37,64E
Adj PT	Emerson, Stephen	M	62C
Adj PT	Englund, John		62A,62B
Prof	Gardner, James E.	D	62A,12,31,31A
Adj PT	Gee, Larry	M	66A
Prof Emeritus	Goodfellow, Susan S.	M	64A
Adj PT	Gornik, Holly	M	64B
Prof Emeritus	Gritton, Bonnie	D	66A
Assoc Prof	Gunlogson, Kirsten	M	61
Assoc Prof	Hagen, Scott	M	37,32E,60B
Adj PT	Halliday, David		64E
Adj PT	Johansen, Keven W.		70,29,11
Lect	Jones, Pamela Palmer	D	66D,13C
Adj PT	Keen, Stephen		66A
Adj PT	Lawrence, Jay		65
Assoc Prof	Lien, Joelle L.	PhD	32
Adj PT	Lu, Jie	D	66A
Assoc Prof	Lu, Ning	D	66A
Prof Emeritus	Mann, Janet	D	66A
Adj PT	Margetts, Linda	PhD	66G
Adj PT	Margulies, Peter	M	63A
Adj PT	Matson, Ralph	M	62A
Asst Prof	Mayes, Catherine	D	12A,12B,12C
Adj PT	McBeth, Christopher		
Adj PT	Miller, Geoffrey	B	70
Prof Emeritus	Miller, Roger L.	D	12A,12
Assoc Prof	Napoles, Jessica	D	32
Prof	Nardo, Rachel L.	D	32,32B,34,32A,32D
Asst Prof	Neimoyer, Susan	D	12A,14C,10A,12
Adj PT	Norton, Nick M.	M	63A
Adj PT	Ofenloch, Gary	B	63D
Adj PT	Ownbey, Shru De Li	M	62E
Adj PT	Park, David H.	M	62A
Adj PT	Patterson, Myron	D	66G
Assoc Prof	Pope, Kathy	M	64C
Assoc Prof	Power, David	D	61
Lect	Price, Jeffrey L.	B	66A
Adj PT	Proser, Stephen	M	63B
Lect	Quaglia, Bruce	D	13
Assoc Prof	Roens, Steven	D	13,10
Assoc Prof	Rorke, Margaret A.	D	12A,12
Prof	Rosenzweig, Morris	D	13,10F,10
Assoc Prof	Schaefer, Donn	D	63C
Assoc Prof	Schmidt, Russell	M	66A,29,47
Adj PT	Scowcroft, Barbara Ann	B	62A
Adj PT	Sedgley, Tiffany	M	64C
Adj PT	Shore, Melanie	M	66A
Lect	Sproul, Brian	D	37
Adj PT	Stephenson, Robert J.	DIPL	64E
Adj PT	Stewart, Lynnette	DIPL	62A
Adj PT	Subotic, Vedrana	D	66A
Adj PT	Tanner, Gretchen	M	66B
Adj PT	Terry, Patrick L.		70
Prof Emeritus	Thompson, Edgar	D	36
Adj PT	Udy, Kenneth L.	D	66G
Adj PT	Waldis, Daniel		66A
Adj PT	Wallis, Kelly		65
Adj PT	Watanabe, Vera		66A
Prof Emeritus	Watts, Ardean W.	M	13,39
Adj PT	Whang, Pegsoon		62C
Adj PT	Wike, Lori J.	M	64D
Adj PT	Wilberg, Mack		60
Prof	Wolf, Douglas J.	M	37,65
Prof Emeritus	Wolking, Henry C.	M	13,10F,47,46,29
Adj PT	Woodbury, Todd K.		70
Prof	Wright-Costa, Julie	M	61
Adj PT	Yavornitzky, David W.	B	62D
Adj PT	Zalkind, Larry	M	63C
Adj PT	Zalkind, Roberta S.		62A

UT0300 Utah State University
Department of Music
4015 Old Main Hill
Logan, UT 84322-4015
(435) 797-3000   Fax: (435) 797-1862
music.usu.edu
E-mail: music@usu.edu

4 Year Institution, Graduate School
Member of NASM

Master of Music in Piano Performance

Department Head: Cynthia Dewey, 80A
Dean, College of the Arts: Craig D. Jessop, 80A
Assistant Department Head: Gary Amano, 80H
Assistant Department Head: Dennis Hirst, 80H
Assistant Chair: Nicholas Morrison, 80H
Assistant Department Head: Leslie Timmons, 80H

Rank	Name		Areas
Prof	Amano, Gary	M	13,66A,66B,66C
Prof	Ballam, Michael	D	39,54
	Bankhead, James M.	D	60
Asst Prof Emeritus	Beecher, Betty	M	66A,66D
Assoc Prof	Bernal, Sergio	M	38,13C
Prof Emeritus	Burton, Warren L.	D	11,32A,32B,62C
Vstng Asst Prof	Christiansen, Corey	M	70
Prof	Christiansen, Michael	M	70
Assoc Prof	Dewey, Cynthia	D	61,54,39,13A
Assoc Prof	Emile, Mark A.	D	10F,60B,62A,62B
Asst Prof	Evans, Cory	D	32D,36,40
Prof	Fallis, Todd	D	32C,63C,63D,47,41
Assoc Prof Emeritus	Fifield, Glen	D	13A,32A,32B,49,63A
Lect	Francis, Anne	M	62C
Prof Emeritus	Griffin, Dennis	D	50,34,65,13G,41
Assoc Prof	Gudmundson, Jon K.	D	29,64E,47,41
Asst Prof	Hearns, Maureen	M	33
Assoc Prof	Hirst, Dennis	M	66A,66B,66C,66D
Vstng Asst Prof	Huff, Michael D.	D	60,60A,60B
Lect	Hugo, Chilali	M	62E
	Jemison-Keisker, Lynn C.	D	39,54
Assoc Prof Emeritus	Johnson, Mildred	D	13,12A,12,62B
Prof Emeritus	Madsen, Farrell D.	D	13,10,12A
Lect	McFaul, Rebecca	M	62A
Prof	Morrison, Nicholas	D	37,64C,48,41
Asst Prof	Nicholson, Jason	D	65,50,41
Asst Prof	Olson, Kevin R.	PhD	66,66A,66B
Lect	Ottesen, Bradley		62A
Assoc Prof	Rohrer, Thomas	D	37,32
Assoc Prof	Saperston, Bruce M.	D	33
Asst Prof	Scheer, Christopher	D	12
Prof Emeritus	Smith, Larry G.	D	13,29,47,64E,46
Assoc Prof	Timmons, Leslie	M	32A,32B,64A,48,41
Vstng Inst	Vaclavik, Jude	D	13,13A,13B,13D
Prof Emeritus	Wardle, Alvin	D	32C,63B,63C,63D
Prof	Zattiero, Joanna R.		12A,64E

UT0305 Utah State University
College of Eastern Utah
Department of Music
451 E 400 N
Price, UT 84501
(435) 613-5000   Fax: (435) 613-5422
eastern.usu.edu
E-mail: greg.benson@usu.edu

2 Year Institution

Vice Chancellor & Music Contact: Gregory V. Benson, 80A

Assoc Prof	Benson, Gregory V.	D	37
Adj	Thrower, Daniel	D	11
Adj	Tuttle, Elise	B	66
Assoc Prof	Wilson, Russell G.	M	11,13,36,61

UT0325 Utah Valley University
Department of Music
800 W University Pkwy #165
Orem, UT 84058
(801) 222-8347   Fax: (801) 764-7344
www.uvu.edu/music/
E-mail: erickswa@uvsc.edu

2 and 4 Year Institution

Chair: Bryce Rytting, 80A

Adj	Andrews, Anita		66A
Adj	Angulo, Denson		62D
Adj	Barney, Kara		61
Adj	Benish, Serena Kanig		61
Adj	Blalock, Karen		62A,62B
Adj	Bryce, Daniel		63D
Adj	Call, Monica		62C
Artist in Res	Cardon, Sam		34
Asst Prof	Colonna, Jim	D	63A,32,37
Asst Prof	Criddle, Reed		36,61
	Demske, Hilary	M	66A,13
Adj	Drummond, Jayne		64B
Asst Prof	Fairbanks, Donna		51,62,38
Adj	Ferguson, Daniel		20
Adj	Harlow, Leslie		62B,42
Adj	Hicks, Brian		64D
Adj	Hunter, Steven		63C
Adj	Jensen, Constance		61,36
Prof	Johnson, G. Larry	M	36,60A,13A,13B,13C
Adj	Johnson, Shauna	M	32B,61
Adj	Layton, Myrna		20
Adj	Lee, Mitch		65
Adj	Lee, Russell		70
Adj	Leslie, Justin		70
Adj	Margetts, David		62A,62B
Asst Prof	Nelson, Mattew		13,64
Adj	Oshida, Joanna		66A
Adj	Pinnell-Jackson, Nicole		62C
Adj	Richards, Cynthia		62A
Adj	Richards, Mary		64A
Asst Prof	Rytting, Bryce	D	12,13,38,60
Adj	Rytting, Lysa		62E
Adj	Stephens, Berin		64E
Adj	Wallace, Elizabeth Kuefler		62B
Asst Prof	Wallace, Jeb		49

UT0350 Weber State University
Department of Performing Arts
1905 University Cir
Ogden, UT 84408-1905
(801) 626-6437   Fax: (801) 626-6811
www.weber.edu
E-mail: tpriest@weber.edu

4 Year Institution
Member of NASM

Chair: Thomas L. Priest, 80A

Adj	Basinger, Bettie Jo	D	12
Prof	Brookens, Karen	D	61,39
Asst Prof	Campbell, Carey	D	12,11,63
Adj	Campbell, Susan	M	11,31
Adj	Christiansen, Rulon	B	66G
Adj	Cox, Ann	B	62B
Adj	Duffin, Greg	M	11
Prof	Feller, David E.	D	11,12A,48,64,31
Adj	Gutierrez, Martha	M	61
Adj	Hamblin, Michael	D	32B
Adj	Harris, Evelyn	M	61
Adj	Henderson, Benjamin	M	62D
Adj	Henderson, Cindy	B	64A
Prof	Henderson, Mark A.	D	60,10,11,36,32D
Adj	Johnson, Gordon	D	20,11
Adj	Johnson, Kendra	M	64B
Prof	Keipp, Donald K.	D	13A,11,65,29,47
Adj	LeCheminant, Reed	B	63A
Adj	Maxson, Carrie	M	62A,32E
Adj	Maxson, Mark D.	B	34,70
Adj	Nelson, Kent	M	63C,63D,63
Prof	Palumbo, Michael A.	D	38,62B,32E,60,41
Prof	Priest, Thomas L.	D	32,64D,11
Prof	Root, Thomas R.	D	13,10,37,41
Adj	Sorenson, Gary	M	61
Adj	Steiner, Sean	M	66A
Adj	Tall, Malinda	M	13A,13B,13C,66A,66C
Adj	Tarbox, Maurie	B	13,61
Assoc Prof	Uzur, Viktor	D	13,10F,51,62C,42
Assoc Prof	Van der Beek, Ralph	D	66A,13
Adj	Vickerman, Louise	M	62E
Prof	Wang, Shi-Hwa	D	62A,13
Adj	Wiemer, Gerta	M	66,13
Adj	Woodbury, Todd	M	70,41
Prof	Yang, Yu-Jane	D	66A,66B,66C,66D

UT0400 Westminster College
Department of Music
1840 South 1300 East
Salt Lake City, UT 84105
(801) 832-2435   Fax: (801) 832-3102
www.westminstercollege.edu/music
E-mail: kbond@westminstercollege.edu

4 Year Institution

Chair: Karlyn Bond, 80A

Applied Artist	Adams-McMillan, Aubrey	M	61
	Applonie, Brent	M	41
Assoc Prof	Bond, Karlyn	D	11,12A,12B
Asst Prof	Chipman, Michael	M	61,39
	Derfler, Brandon		66A,10
Applied Artist	Dresher, Mary Ann	M	61
Adj	Halliday, David		64E,47
Applied Artist	Hart, Cheryl		61
Adj PT	Holder, Hope	M	66D

Adj PT	Humphreys, Sally	M	64A
Adj	Kawashima, Kimi		20,66A
Applied Artist	Keen, Stephen	B	66A
Applied Artist	Livengood, Lee		64C
Applied Artist	MacQueen, Yuki	M	62A
Applied Artist	Mark, Julie		70
Applied Artist	Porter, David		62B
Assoc Prof	Quinn, Christopher	D	13,36
Applied Artist	Ray, Willy		65
Applied Artist	Rowe, Alex	M	70
Applied Artist	Stucki, Brian		61
Applied Artist	Subotic, Vedrana	D	66
Applied Artist	Swidnicki, Susan		64B
Adj	Thorpe, Austin		36
Applied Artist	Wallis, Kelly		65
Applied Artist	Whang, Pegsoon	M	62C
Applied Artist	Wike, Lori	M	64D
Adj PT	Woodbury, Todd	C	70
Adj	Zabriskie, David		34
Applied Artist	Zera, Tom	M	62D

VA0050 Bluefield College
Department of Music
3000 College Dr
Bluefield, VA 24605-1737
(276) 326-4248   Fax: (276) 326-4288
www.bluefield.edu
E-mail: bmoxley@bluefield.edu

4 Year Institution

Chair, Division Fine Arts: Walter Shroyer, 80A
Music Contact: Bryant Moxley

Adj Inst	Allen, Susan	M	13C,11,66A,66D
Adj Inst	Book, Ryan		70
Adj Inst	Hedrick, Teresa		64
Asst Prof	Hudson, Barbara	D	61,36,12A
Adj Inst	Johnson, Chrisa		66A,13B,13C,11
Adj Inst	Keeny, Jonan		65
Asst Prof	Moxley, Bryant	M	13,66A,60A,31A,36
Adj Inst	Moxley, Lisa	M	66A,66D,31A,13A,11
Asst Prof	Necessary, Andrew	D	12A,32B,37,46,63C
Adj Inst	Oyenard, Geronimo		62

VA0100 Bridgewater College
Department of Music
402 E College St
Bridgewater, VA 22812
(540) 828-5303   Fax: (540) 828-5637
www.bridgewater.edu
E-mail: ltaylor@bridgewater.edu

4 Year Institution

Chair & Dir., Artist/Performance Series: Jesse E. Hopkins, 80A,80F
Dir., Summer Programs: Arthur Hessler, 80G

Prof	Adams, K. Gary	D	11,12A,12,66A
Inst PT	Adams, Mary Kay	M	64A
Inst PT	Adams, Richard C.	M	70
Prof Emeritus	Barr, John	D	13,10,66A,31A
Inst PT	Flory, Mary Beth	M	66A
Inst PT	Foster, Marlon	M	65A,65B
Prof	Hopkins, Jesse E.	D	32,36,61,44,60A
Inst PT	Miller, Sharon	M	62A
Inst PT	Quesenberry, Karen	M	64E
Inst PT	Stees, Rhonda L.	M	64B,62
Asst Prof	Taylor, Larry Clark	D	66A,66G,13B,13D,13E
Inst PT	Wead, Joyce A.	M	61
Asst Prof	Weir, Timothy	D	32C,32E,37,47,42

VA0150 Christopher Newport University
Department of Music
1 University Place
Newport News, VA 23606
(757) 594-7074   Fax: (757) 594-7591
music.cnu.edu
E-mail: reimer@cnu.edu

4 Year Institution

Chair: Mark U. Reimer, 80A

Adj	Boyles, John	M	70
Prof Emeritus	Brockett, Clyde W.	D	12C
Adj	Carlson, Patti		64C
Inst	Cook, Christopher E.	D	34,13
Adj	Corbett, George	M	64B
Inst	Falvey, Joseph	D	63B,37,34G,32E,49
Assoc Prof	Fowler-Calisto, Lauren	D	36,60A
Adj	Greydanus, Peter	B	62C
Adj	Hammel, Alice M.	D	32
Asst Prof	Holland, Rachel J.	D	61,39
Adj	Kim, Bonnie		64A,48
Adj	Leverenz, Chris	M	62D
Adj	Martell, Rodney	B	63C,63D
Inst	Mooney, Chris	M	61,39
Inst	Musselwhite, Eric	M	47,64E
Prof	Reimer, Mark U.	D	13C,60B,37
Adj	Richmond, James	M	64E,48
Adj	Rossum, Kelly	D	63A,29,67E,47
Asst Prof	Sadlier, David	D	61,40,39
Inst	Sadlier, Lelia	D	66D,66A
Adj	Savige, David	M	64D
Adj	Shepherd, Michael		65
Inst	Stevens, Annie J.	M	65,37,50,34
Adj	Sully, Eldon	B	47
Adj	Thompson, J. Lynn	M	38
Adj	Tomassetti, Beth	M	66A,66D
Asst Prof	Ward-Griffin, Danielle	D	12,20,14
Adj	Zhang, Yun	B	62A,62B

VA0250 College of William and Mary
Department of Music
PO Box 8795
Williamsburg, VA 23187-8795
(757) 221-1071   Fax: (757) 221-3171
www.wm.edu/music
E-mail: eacova@wm.edu

4 Year Institution

Chair: Thomas B. Payne, 80A
Director, Applied Music: Judith Zwerdling Zwelling, 80A

Lect	Aguirre, Sherrie Lake	B	64B
Assoc Prof	Armstrong, James I.	DMA	36,12A,60,12C
Asst Prof	Bartlett, Jamie	D	36
Lect	Beckner, Woody	AD	70,29
Asst Prof	Bhasin, Paul K.	D	37,63A,38,42,41
Lect	Bland, Sarah	M	66A
Asst Prof	Bowers, Greg J.	D	13,10,10A
Lect	Brydges, Christopher		62D
Lect	Carlson, Patti	M	48,64C
Lect	Cary, Neal	M	51,62C
Lect	Connolly, Martha	M	61
Lect	Dole, Frederick	M	62D
Lect	DuBeau, Peter	M	63D,49
Lect	Fletcher, Mary Eason	B	61
Lect	Fletcher, Ryan	B	61,39
Lect	Gilman, Grant	M	38,60
Lect	Glosson, Sarah	B	67A
Assoc Prof Adj	Griffioen, Ruth	D	67D,55,12A
Assoc Prof	Hulse, Brian	D	13
Lect	Jellison, Anastasia	M	62E
Lect	Johnson, Tripp		41
Lect	Jones, Brian		65,29
Lect	Katz, Max	M	14
Lect	Kijanowska, Anna	D	66A
Lect	Lawson, Jennifer	B	64A
Lect	Leisring, Laura	M	48,64E,64D,41,64C
Lect	Lindberg, John		65,50
Lect	Lyttle, Eric	M	13A,13C,66A
Lect	Marshall, Thomas	M	66A,66G,66H,66D
Lect	Martell, Rodney		63C
Lect	Mauthe, Timothy		13,10
Lect	Mott, Jonathan		62A,62B
Asst Prof	Murchison, Gayle	D	12A,12,20G,12C
Lect	Nakasian O'Brian, Stephanie		61,29
Lect	Nesbit, James B.	B	64E,48,29
Lect	Niehaus, Christine J.	M	66A,66D
Lect	Olbrych, Timothy	M	67B,67G,70,41
Assoc Prof	Payne, Thomas B.	D	12A,12,12C
Prof	Preston, Katherine K.	D	12A,12,20G,12C
Lect	Ransom, Robert		29,63A
Assoc Prof	Rasmussen, Anne K.	D	14,20G,31,41,12C
Assoc Prof	Serghi, Sophia	D	13,10F,10,43,10A
Lect	Simon, Harris W.		29A,66A,47,29
Lect	Sparr, Kimberly		62B
Lect	Via, Susan	B	62A
Lect	Vonderheide, David E.	B	63A
Lect	Wick, David	M	63B
Lect	Yefimova, Maria	D	66A
Lect	Zwelling, Judith Zwerdling	M	66A

VA0300 Eastern Mennonite University
Department of Music
1200 Park Rd
Harrisonburg, VA 22802
(540) 432-4225 Fax: (540) 432-4622
www.emu.edu
E-mail: mathewsl@emu.edu

4 Year Institution

Chair: Joan Griffing, 80A
Dir., Preparatory Music: Sharon Miller, 80E
Dir., Festival & Artist Series: Mary Kay Adams, 80F

Senior Lect	Adams, Mary Kay	M	13,12A
Asst Prof	Fast, John W.	M	13,66A,66G
Prof	Griffing, Joan	D	62A,38,41,60B,62B
Assoc Prof	Mackey, Lynne A.	D	66A,66B,66C,66D,13
Asst Prof	Miller, Sharon	M	32B,62A,32C,32E
Prof	Nafziger, Kenneth J.	D	60,36,31A,38,11
Asst Prof	Richardson, James K.	M	61,11,36,54,39

VA0350 Emory & Henry College
Department of Music
PO Box 947
Emory, VA 24327
(276) 944-4121 Fax: (276) 944-6259
www.ehc.edu
E-mail: lwithers@ehc.edu

4 Year Institution

Chair: Lisa Ann Withers, 80A
Dir., Artist Series: Anita Coulthard, 80F

Inst Adj	Clay, Shea	M	32A,32B
Inst Adj	Coulthard, Anita	M	66G,32A,32B,31A
Inst Adj	Crawford, Thomas	M	64A,64C,64E
Inst Adj	Frazer, Liz	M	61,11,39
Asst Prof	Frederick, Matthew D.	D	63A,12A,41,60B,32E
Inst Adj	Hole, Kristopher	M	70
Asst Prof	Roll, Christianne		61,32A,13C
Inst Adj	Sieck, Stephen	D	36,61,60A,32D
Adj Prof	Tompkins, Daniel	B	70
Asst Prof	Withers, Lisa Ann	D	66A,66C,13B,13C,13F

VA0400 Ferrum College
School of Arts & Humanities
215 Ferrum Mountain Rd
Ferrum, VA 24088-2612
(540) 365-4321 Fax: (540) 365-4203
www.ferrum.edu
E-mail: jburton@ferrum.edu

4 Year Institution

Coordinator: Susan M. Spataro, 80A

Prof	Evans, Gary	D	13A,13B,13C,11,12A
Inst PT	Johnson, Velshera	B	61,36,40,66A
Inst	Spataro, Susan M.	M	64A,47,11,32A,32B

VA0450 George Mason University
School of Music
417 Performing Arts Bldg
4400 Univ Dr. MSN 3E3
Fairfax, VA 22030-4444
(703) 993-1380 Fax: (703) 993-1394
www.gmu.edu/departments/music
E-mail: music@gmu.edu

4 Year Institution, Graduate School
Member of NASM

Master of Music in Pedagogy, Master of Music in Composition, Master of Music in Performance, Master of Music in Conducting, Master of Music in Music Education

Interim Director: Mark D. Camphouse, 80A
Dir., Graduate Studies: Lisa A. Billingham, 80C
Dir., Potomac Academy: Elizabeth A. Curtis, 80E
Dir., Artist/Performance Series: Tom Reynolds, 80F
Associate Director: Linda Apple Monson, 80H

Prof	Balakerskaia, Anna	D	66A,66C
Asst Prof Adj	Beach, Wade		66A,29B
Prof Adj	Beckwith, Hubert	D	13A,13,12
Prof Adj	Behrend, Roger L.	M	63D,41
Asst Prof Adj	Berger, Lisa		61
Inst Adj	Bergman, Mark	M	11
Assoc Prof	Bergman, Rachel	D	13
Asst Prof Adj	Berkshire-Brown, Lorrie	M	64B
Assoc Prof	Billingham, Lisa A.	D	32D,36,60A
Adj Asst Prof	Bogachek, Zinoviy	M	62A
Assoc Prof Adj	Bonds, Samuel		61
Asst Prof Adj	Bonneau, Sharon J.	M	64C
Prof	Camphouse, Mark D.	M	10,60B,37
Prof	Carroll, James R.		47,64E,29,46
Assoc Prof	Casagrande, John E.	M	37,32C,32E,32G
Asst Prof Adj	Chalifoux, Jeanne		62E
Adj Assoc Prof	Chao, Philippe	M	62B
Prof Adj	Colon, Frank		66C,39
Asst Prof Adj	Crabill, Michael	M	66C
Asst Prof Adj	Curtis, Stanley	D	63A
Adj Inst	Delaney, Carrie Ann		11
Prof Adj	Dewey, Glenn A.	M	62D
Inst Adj	East, Mary Ann H.	M	32C
Prof Adj	Edelbrock, Dennis E.	D	63A
Prof	Engebretson, Stan P.	D	36,60A,60,40
Prof Emeritus	Gabriel, Arnald D.	D	
Asst Prof Adj	Gerber, Stephen K.	D	12C,16
Assoc Prof Emeritus	Giles, Martha M.	D	
Asst Prof	Guessford, Jesse	D	11,13A,34
Prof Adj	Haase, Peter	M	62A,42
Prof Adj	Harbison, Kenneth C.		65
Prof Adj	Haroutounian, Joanne	D	66A,66B
Asst Prof Adj	Healey, John	D	66D
Prof	Hearden, Kathryn	D	61
Assoc Prof Emeritus	Hill, Thomas H.	D	
Prof	Johonnott, Edwin		62A,62B,42
Prof Adj	Jones, Brian	D	64C
Assoc Prof Emeritus	Kanyan, Joseph M.	D	
Assoc Prof	Ker-Hackleman, Kelly	D	66,13C,11
Adj Asst Prof	Kilkenny, John	M	65
Prof	Lapple, Judith A.	M	64A,41
Prof	Layendecker, Dennis M.	D	60,38,41
Prof	Maiello, Anthony J.	M	60,37,38,41
Asst Prof Adj	McCarthy, Glen	M	70,32C
Prof	Miller, Patricia A.	M	39,61,54
Prof	Monson, Linda Apple	D	13C,66A
Asst Prof Adj	Moore, Eric	M	63B
Asst Prof Adj	Nam, Seong	D	61
Asst Prof Adj	Neff, Matthew	M	63C
Prof Adj	Neil, William W.	M	66G
Asst Prof	Nickens, Michael W.	D	37,13C,11
Asst Prof	Novak, Richard A.	M	61,39
Asst Prof Adj	Okamoto, Kyoko M.		20D
Asst Prof Adj	Owens, Margaret B.	M	11,12A,64
Assoc Prof	Owens, Thomas C.	D	11,12
Prof Adj	Parker, Patricia	D	66A,66C
Asst Prof Adj	Parrell, Richard N.	M	42,64E
Assoc Prof	Rendler-McQueeney, Elaine J.	D	13
Adj Asst Prof	Rittenhouse, Kenneth	M	63A
Adj Assoc Prof	Roberts, Timothy	D	64E
Asst Prof	Robinson, Gregory J.	D	11,12,14,20H
Prof	Smith, Glenn E.	D	13,10,45,34,42
Prof Adj	Snitzler, Larry J.		70
Asst Prof Adj	Stephansky, Joyce	M	32B
Adj Prof	Sternbach, David J.	M	32G,63B
Adj Asst Prof	Summey, Harold		65
Adj Assoc Prof	Taylor, Wayne	M	32
Adj Assoc Prof	Teie, David	M	62C
Assoc Prof Adj	Thayer, Edwin C.		63B
Adj Assoc Prof	Watters, Harry	M	63C
Asst Prof Adj	Wenner, Debby	M	61
Adj Asst Prof	Whitehead, Richard		70
Adj Asst Prof	Yang, Mira	D	61

VA0500 Hampton University
Department of Music
Armstrong Hall
Room 137
Hampton, VA 23668
(757) 727-5237/637-2242 Fax: (757) 728-6572
www.hamptonu.edu
E-mail: sheila.maye@hamptonu.edu

4 Year Institution
Member of NASM

Dean: Mamie Locke, 80A
Chair: Shelia J. Maye, 80A

Directory of Institutions

Asst Prof	Bell, Lorriane	B	11,61,35A
Asst Prof	Bracey, Jerry A.	M	37,38,47,62,29
Asst Prof	Davis, Alfred L.	M	32E,32F,32B,32C,10F
Asst Prof	Dillard, Royzell L.	M	36,61
Asst Prof	Eccles, Elizabeth		32,61,66A
Inst	Hall, Teddy		13A,13B,13C,32C,11
Prof	Harris, Carl G.	D	60,12A,66,69
Inst	Holmes, Rasan		63C,37,34
Asst Prof	Maye, Shelia J.	D	11,61,32
Librarian	Reiff, Eric	B	16
Inst	Shipley, Lori R.	M	48,12A,13A,64A,41
Prof	Stokes, Harvey J.	D	13,10,64B,34
Asst Prof	Tomassetti, Benjamin	D	35G,10B,34D,35C,64E

VA0550 Hollins University

Department of Music
PO Box 9643
Roanoke, VA 24020
(540) 362-6511   Fax: (540) 362-6648
www.hollins.edu
E-mail: jcline@hollins.edu

4 Year Institution

Chair, Music & Dir., Artist Series: Judith A. Cline, 80A,80F
Dir., Undergraduate Studies & Artist Series: William Craig Krause, 80B,80F

Prof	Cline, Judith A.	D	39,61,54,20G,11
PT	Dobyns, Whitney		62E
PT	Eggleston, Mary	B	61
PT	Espinosa, Vladimir		67H
PT	Garber, Melia	M	66A,66D
PT	Hedrick, Teresa	M	64C,64E,64A,64B
Asst Prof	Krause, William Craig	D	70,11,12A,20H,35E
PT	Kresge, Jeff	M	63A
Lect	Mackin, Barbara J.	M	66A,13
PT	Milam, Michael R.	M	32
PT	Morgiewicz, Kerry L.	M	66A,66B,54
PT	Rudolph, Richard		62A,38,62B,62C,65B
	Wahl, Shelbie L.	M	13C,36

VA0600 James Madison University

School of Music
MSC 7301
880 S Main St
Harrisonburg, VA 22807
(540) 568-6197   Fax: (540) 568-7819
www.jmu.edu/music
E-mail: wampledk@jmu.edu

4 Year Institution, Graduate School
Member of NASM

Master of Music in Performance, Master of Music in Conducting, Master of Music in Music Education, DMA in Conducting, DMA in Performance, Master of Music in Music Theory-Composition

Director: Jeffrey E. Bush, 80A
Dir., Graduate Studies: Mary Jean Speare, 80C
Dir., Admissions: Michele B. Kirkdorffer, 80D

Asst Prof	Aponte, Pedro R.	D	12A
Inst PT	Axtell, Katherine L.	D	11
Asst Prof	Azikiwe, Amadi	M	62B
Assoc Prof	Barber, Susan N.	DMA	64D,42
Prof	Bolstad, Stephen P.	D	37,60B
Prof PT	Brady, Patricia L.	D	66B,66D
Prof	Bush, Jeffrey E.	D	32
Inst PT	Carr, Thomas	B	35G
Inst PT	Carrillo, Christine Ennis	D	63A,13B
Asst Prof	Carrillo, Christopher J.	D	63A,29
Assoc Prof	Chandler, Beth E.	D	64A,42,35E
Inst PT	Chapdelaine, Karine	M	62D
Assoc Prof	Cockburn, Brian	M	16,12C
Assoc Prof	Connell, Andrew M.	D	14,29A
Prof	Cottrell, David	D	35
Prof PT	Cross, Samuel G.	M	62D
Asst Prof	Curry, Vicki L.	D	13,11
Asst Prof	Dabback, William M.	D	32
Inst PT	Deloney, Rick	B	37
Assoc Prof	Dobner, Gabriel	D	66A,66C
Assoc Prof	Donakowski, Carl		62C
Prof	Dotas, Charles J.	D	46,29
Inst PT	Foster, Marlon A.	M	65
Inst PT	Gant, Edward	D	13C
Assoc Prof	Gibson, Jonathan B.	D	11,12A,55
Inst PT	Glago, Mikael	B	35
Asst Prof	Hallahan, Robert	B	29
Assoc Prof	Haney, Jason	D	13,10
Asst Prof	Hayes, William Bryce	D	32D,36
Inst PT	Heitsch, Paul	B	35G
Prof	Hilliard, John S.	D	13,10
Inst PT	Hook, Terry	B	66F
Assoc Prof	Huang, Wanchi	D	62A
Inst PT	Hyden, Derek	B	37
Inst PT	Kirby, Brett	M	29
Assoc Prof	Kirkdorffer, Michele B.	D	64B
Assoc Prof	Lankford, Andrew	D	63C
Prof	Little, John A.	D	61
Assoc Prof	Maddison, Dorothy E.	D	61
Asst Prof	Maynard, Lisa M.	D	32
Prof	McCashin, Robert D.	D	60,38
Asst Prof	McMillan, Kevin	M	61
Assoc Prof	Minor, Janice L.	D	64C
Inst PT	Newman, David A.	D	61
Assoc Prof PT	Norton, Michael	D	11
Inst PT	Overfield-Zook, Kathleen	M	13C
Inst PT	Overman, Michael M.	D	65,65B,50
Asst Prof	Piitz, Lori E.	D	66A
Assoc Prof	Pope, David J.	M	64E,47
Inst PT	Posey, William	B	37
Inst PT	Rabinovitsj, Max	M	62A
Prof	Rice, C. William	M	50,65
Assoc Prof	Rierson, Don G.	D	39,11
Inst	Rikkers, Scott D.	M	37
Prof	Ritcher, Gary	D	32
Prof	Ruple, Eric K.	D	66A
Inst PT	Smith, Scott Z.	M	61
Assoc Prof	Speare, Mary Jean	D	12A
Prof	Stees, Kevin J.	M	49,63D
Asst Prof	Steinberg, Paulo	D	66A
Assoc Prof	Stevens, Carrie L.	D	61
Inst PT	Stevens, Keith	M	70,57
Asst Prof	Stringham, David A.	M	32
Inst PT	Stuckey, Bridgett	B	62E
Asst Prof	Taylor, Joseph	M	35
Asst Prof	Van der Vat-Chromy, Jo-Anne	D	32
Inst PT	Voigt, Steve	M	10,11,13
Asst Prof	Wheaton, J. Randall	D	13B,13D,13A,13I,13F
Inst PT	Witmer, Brenda K.	M	61
Asst Prof	Zook, Ian R.	M	63B

VA0650 Liberty University

Department of Music & Humanities
1971 University Blvd
Lynchburg, VA 24502-2269
(434) 582-2318   Fax: (434) 582-2891

www.liberty.edu/academics/arts-sciences/musicandhumanities/
E-mail: jwhugo@liberty.edu

4 Year Institution

Chair, Music & Humanities: John William Hugo, 80A
Dean: Roger Schultz, 80A

Prof	Babcock, Michael	D	66A,11
Assoc Prof	Beavers, Sean M.	D	12A,13A,13B,13C,41
Assoc Prof	Chiarizzio, R. Kevin	D	63,32B,32C,32F
Prof	Crider, Joe	D	11,12A
Prof	Ehrman, David	M	66A,66B,66D
Assoc Prof	Foley, Ruth	D	32,61
Assoc Prof	Granger, Linda	M	61,66C
Prof	Hugo, John William	D	36,61,12A,60A
Assoc Prof	Kerr, Stephen P.	D	63,37,60B,48
Asst Prof	Kim, Taeseong	D	66A,66B,13C
Prof	Kompelien, Wayne	D	40,61,60A
Asst Prof	Mills, Robert P.	M	11,13B,13C
Assoc Prof	Super, Kevin	D	65,50,37
Assoc Prof	Suzano, L. Armenio	D	20F,11,13C,41,64
Asst Prof	Trombetta, Adelaide Muir	AD	61
Prof	Wellman, Samuel	D	66A,66D,10,13A,13B

VA0700 Longwood University

Department of Music
201 High St
Farmville, VA 23909
(434) 395-2504
www.longwood.edu/music
E-mail: music@longwood.edu

4 Year Institution, Graduate School
Member of NASM

Master of Science in Curriculum & Instruction/Music

Chair & Dir., Artist Series: Charles E. Kinzer, 80A,80F
Dir., Graduate Studies: Patricia D. Lust, 80C

Inst PT	Brightbill, Elizabeth	M	64A,48
Inst PT	Britton, Rex	M	62
Inst PT	Brock, Andrew	M	47,64E,32H
Asst Prof	Capaldo, Jennifer R.	M	61,13C,12A
Inst PT	Gassler, Christopher J.	D	63D,20
Accompanist	Harper, Carole	B	66C
Inst PT	Karnatz, Roland	D	11,14C
Inst PT	Kidd, Teri D.	M	32H
Prof	Kinzer, Charles E.	D	12A,47,64E
Assoc Prof	Kinzer, Lisa B.	D	66
Inst PT	Kjorness, Christopher	M	20,14C
Prof	Lust, Patricia D.	D	61,32
Asst Prof	McDermott, Pamela D. J.	D	61,60,36,13C
Inst PT	Neithamer, David	M	29A,64C,32E
Prof	Ring, Gordon L.	D	13,10,37,34
Assoc Prof	Swanson, Christopher	D	13C,61,12A,11,39
Inst PT	Thomas, John	M	50,65
Inst PT	Tuckwiller, George	M	63A,63B

VA0750 Lynchburg College

School of Comm & Arts
1501 Lakeside Dr
Lynchburg, VA 24501-3199
(434) 544-8344   Fax: (434) 544-8810
www.lynchburg.edu
E-mail: hatcher@lynchburg.edu

4 Year Institution, Graduate School

Master of Arts in Conducting

Coordinator & Dir., Undergraduate Studies: Oeida M. Hatcher, 80A,80B
Coord., Graduate Studies: Jong H. Kim, 80C

Inst Adj	Bouknight, Tara	M	61
Inst Adj	Campbell, John	M	63A,49
Inst Adj	Creasy, Catherine	M	63B
Inst Adj	Farmer, Harry	M	64E,47,42,43
Inst Adj	Folger, Bill	B	63D
Inst Adj	Gatti, Pat	M	64C
Inst Adj	Habitzruther, Bruce E.	M	38,62C
Inst Adj	Habitzruther, Ellen M.	M	62A
Inst Adj	Hale, Kris	M	70
Assoc Prof	Hatcher, Oeida M.	D	32,37,41,38,11
Inst Adj	Hugo, Alycia	M	64A
Inst	James, Pamela A.	D	32A,61,13C,66D,32B
Assoc Prof	Kim, Jong H.	D	36,13,61,60A,40
Inst Adj	Otto, Noemi	M	66A,66D
Inst Adj	Parrish, Bill	M	64B
Asst Prof	Ramsey, Cynthia B.	D	66A,12A,66C,13E,42
Inst Adj	Roberts, Elizabeth	M	64D
Inst	Scott, F. Johnson	M	34,13B,13A,66G,66C
Inst Adj	Smith, Brian	M	50,65

VA0800 Mary Baldwin College

Department of Music
318 Prospect St
Staunton, VA 24402
(540) 887-7193   Fax: (540) 887-7139
www.mbc.edu
E-mail: lkeiter@mbc.edu

4 Year Womens' Liberal Arts Institution

Chair: Lise Keiter, 80A

Assoc Prof	Allen, Robert T.	D	11,12A,29A,60A
Inst Adj	Blake, Elise A.	M	62A,62B,42
Asst Prof Adj	Brightbill, Elizabeth	D	64A,42,11
Asst Prof Adj	Cantrell, Elizabeth K.	D	62C,62D
Inst Adj	Hill, Leah	M	61
Inst Adj	Johnson, Lacey	M	66A,66C
Assoc Prof	Keiter, Lise	D	13,11,66A,12A,15
Asst Prof Adj	Kornicke, Eloise	D	66A,13A
Inst Adj	Quagliariello, Rachel M.	M	61,40
Inst Adj	Sales, Humberto O.	B	70
Inst Adj	Sumner, Melissa M.	M	61,11,40
Inst Adj	Tate, David L.	M	32,36

VA0900 New River Community College

Department of Music
PO Box 1127
Dublin, VA 24084-1127
(540) 674-3600   Fax: (540) 674-3642
www.nr.edu/billaud
E-mail: lbillaud@nr.edu

2 Year Institution

Dean: Carol Hurst, 80A

Assoc Prof	Billaud, Louise	M	11,12A,13A

VA0950 Norfolk State University

Department of Music
700 Park Ave
Norfolk, VA 23504
(757) 823-8544   Fax: (757) 823-2605
www.nsu.edu
E-mail: sbdorsey@nsu.edu

4 Year Institution, Graduate School, Historically Black College
Member of NASM

Master of Music in Performance, Master of Music in Music Education, Master of Music in Music Theory-Composition

Chair: Sam Brian Dorsey, 80A
Dir., Summer Programs: Marjorie S. Johnson, 80G

Assoc Prof	Adams, Paul	M	63D,12A,37
Asst Prof	Amos, Gloria	M	13A,11,61
Asst Prof	Bethea, William	M	65,11,37,50
Inst	Boone, Geraldine T.	M	10A,32,11,13D,13F
Prof	Brown, Ernest	D	14,66A
Asst Prof	Brown, Rogers	M	10F,37,47,63D,29
Inst	Butler, Terry	M	13C,32D,66A,66G
Inst	Crawford, Eric	M	13B,66
Prof	Dorsey, Sam Brian	D	12A,70
Prof	Haywood, Carl	D	13,60,41,66G
Prof	Johnson, Marjorie S.	D	13,66A,66B,66D,34
Inst	Nixon, Patricia	M	36,46,13C,61
Prof	Ross-Hammond, Amelia	D	13,13J,36,66
Asst Prof	Sanders, Stephanie	M	37,64
Assoc Prof	Sanford, O'Neil	M	37,14A,63A
Inst	Timmey, Zachery	D	63A,11,37

VA0975 Northern Virginia Comm College

Department of Music
8333 Little River Tpke
Annandale, VA 22003-3743
(703) 323-3114   Fax: (703) 323-4248
www.nvcc.edu/annandale/la/music
E-mail: jfay@nvcc.edu

2 Year Institution

Chair: Bruce Mann, 80A

Prof	Fay, James	D	13,12A,64C
Asst Prof	Smith, Herbert	M	53,29,47
Assoc Prof	Webb, Robert	M	11,36,13

VA1000 Old Dominion University

Department of Music
4810 Elkhorn Ave
Norfolk, VA 23529-0202
(757) 683-4061   Fax: (757) 683-5056
al.odu.edu/music
E-mail: JToomey@odu.edu

4 Year Institution, Graduate School
Member of NASM

Master of Music Education

Chair: Douglas T. Owens, 80A
Chair: John F. Toomey, 80A
Coord., Graduate Program: Nancy K. Klein, 80C
Dir., Community Music Division: Sally Wright, 80E
Assistant Dean for the Arts: Fred S. Bayersdorfer, 80H

Adj Prof	Acosta, Anibal A.	D	70
Asst Prof Adj	Aguirre, Sherrie Lake	B	64B
Adj Prof	Armstrong, Vahn R.	M	62A
Assoc Prof Adj	Bennett, Hye-Yun Chung	M	62E,66A
Assoc Prof Adj	Carlson, Patti F.	M	48,64C
Adj Prof	Carlson, Stephen R.	D	63A
Adj Assoc Prof	Coxe, Stephen	D	13A,13B,13D,10
Asst Prof Adj	Cross, Debra W.	B	64A
Adj Asst Prof	DeDominick, Jeanne D.	M	62A
Asst Prof Adj	Dubeau, Peter C.	M	63D
Adj Asst Prof	Ford, Marlene	M	63B
Asst Prof Adj	Forman, Marilyn T.	M	66A,66D
Adj Asst Prof	Frittelli, Leslie	M	62C,51,41
Lect	Fuller, Agnes M.	M	61
Prof	Hailstork, Aldolphus C.	D	10,10F
Asst Prof	Hall, Michael	D	63D,49,63C
Adj Assoc Prof	Halstead, Amanda R.	D	66A
Assoc Prof	Kasparov, Andrey R.	D	13,66A,10,43
Inst	Kim, Bonnie	M	64A
Assoc Prof	Klein, Nancy K.	D	36,60A,32A,32B,32C
Prof	Kosnik, James W.	D	12A,66G
Lect	Latham, Louis S.	M	13A,34,35A,35C,35D
Adj Prof	Lutsyshyn, Oksana	D	13A,13B,66A,66C
Asst Prof	Manning, Lucy	D	38,62A,32E,41,51
Adj Asst Prof	Migliozzi, Anastasia E.	M	62B
Adj Inst	Muth, Roy	B	63A
Asst Prof	Nedvin, Brian A.	D	61,39
Adj Asst Prof	Nesbit, James B.	B	64E
Assoc Prof	Owens, Douglas T.	D	32,47,60B,29
Vstng Lect	Peterson, Jason P.	D	13A,13B,20
Adj Assoc Prof	Philbrick, Keith E.	M	46,47
Prof Adj	Protsman, Harold S.	M	66A,66C,41
Lect	Samarzea, Kelly J.	D	61
Adj Assoc Prof	Savige, David	M	64D
Assoc Prof Adj	Teply, Lee	D	13,55,66G,66H
Prof	Toomey, John F.	M	66A,29,47
Asst Prof	Trevino, Alexander R.	D	37
Lect	Walker, David L.	M	50,65,60B,11,13A
Adj Asst Prof	Watters, Patti	M	64A
Adj Assoc Prof	White, Christopher B.	M	62D
Adj Inst	Willoughby, Vicki	M	32B
Adj Asst Prof	Wright, Robert	M	34,35A,35C,35D,35G
Adj Asst Prof	Wright, Sally	M	66A,11
Prof	Zeisler, Dennis J.	M	11,37,64C,48

VA1030 Piedmont Virginia Comm College

Department of Humts,FA and SS
501 College Dr
Charlottesville, VA 22902-9806
(804) 977-3900   Fax: (804) 296-8395
www.pvcc.edu
E-mail: kbethea@pvcc.edu

2 Year Institution

Chair: Clifford Haury, 80A

Prof	Bethea, Kay	D	13,11,12A,66A,66D

VA1100 Radford University

Department of Music
801 East Main St
PO Box 6968
Radford, VA 24142
(540) 831-5177   Fax: (540) 831-6133
music.asp.radford.edu
E-mail: awojtera@radford.edu

4 Year Institution, Graduate School
Member of NASM

Master of Arts in Music, Master of Science in Music Therapy

Interim Dean: Margaret Devaney, 80A
Chair: Allen F. Wojtera, 80A
Interim Provost: Joseph P. Scartelli

PT	Allen, David R.	M	64C,64E
Prof	Borling, James E.	M	33
Assoc Prof	Castonguay, David O.	M	60,36,61
PT	Castonguay, Lois	B	32D
Inst	Channell, Timothy L.	M	35A,35G
PT	Copeland-Burns, Carla	M	66A
PT	Devlin, Michelle P.	M	63C,63D
PT	Duke, Barbara	B	64D
Assoc Prof	Gallops, R. Wayne	D	13A,32C,32E,29,37
Asst Prof	Glarner, Robert L.	D	13,10,32I,66G,12
PT	Hagwood, Angela	M	32B
PT	Hale, Kristopher	M	70
PT	Hall, Donald L.	B	62D
Prof	James, Clarity	M	39,61
Assoc Prof	Kats, Nitza	M	66A,13C
PT	Kennelly, Patrick	M	63
PT	Kresge, Jeff	M	63
PT	Kromin, Vladimir	M	62A,62B,51
Prof	Mahin, Bruce P.	D	10,34,13,35C
Inst	Riebe, Jenice	M	61
Prof	Scartelli, Joseph P.	D	33
Prof	Trent, Robert S.	D	70,67G,41,57
Asst Prof	White, Christopher K.	M	29,64E,32E,64,12B
Inst	Williams, Brenda	M	66A,66C,66D
Prof	Wojtera, Allen F.	M	50,65,29
PT	Wyatt, Benjamin H.		62C,67B,12,13I,12B
Assoc Prof	Zuschin, David	D	13,12A,61

VA1125 Randolph College

Department of Music
2500 Rivermont Ave
Lynchburg, VA 24503-1526
(434) 947-8530   Fax: (434) 947-8536
www.randolphcollege.edu
E-mail: echua@randolphcollege.edu

4 Year Institution

Chair & Dir., Artist Series: Emily Yap Chua, 80A,80F

Inst PT	Bouknight, Tara	M	61
Assoc Prof	Chua, Emily Yap	D	13B,15,42,66A
Inst PT	Fosnaugh, Christopher	M	65
Inst PT	Gabbert, Andrew	M	62C
Inst PT	Hendricks, Hermina	M	29A,14C
Inst PT	Hugo, Alycia	M	64A
Inst PT	Moore, Nora	M	61
Inst PT	Parrish, Bill	M	64B,64C
Prof	Raessler, Daniel	D	11,12,13B,13F,13A
Inst PT	Ross, Jana	M	62A
Inst PT	Scarfullery, Rafael	D	70
Inst PT	Seipp, Larry	M	63A
Assoc Prof	Speer, Randall	D	61,36,60A,40

VA1150 Randolph-Macon College

Department of Arts-Music
200 College Ave
Ashland, VA 23005
(804) 752-7298   Fax: (804) 752-7231
www.rmc.edu
E-mail: jmattys@rmc.edu

4 Year Institution

Chair: Joe Mattys, 80A

Adj	Brill, Jodie	B	66A
Assoc Prof	Doering, James M.	D	13,11,12A,66A,66G
Adj	Eschen, Elizabeth D.	M	61
Adj	Flowe, Barry	M	37
Adj	Forry, James	B	62C
Adj	Fox, Kim	M	66A,66C
Adj	Harding, Kevin	M	20,29
Adj	Henderson, V. Douglas	B	66C,66F
Adj	Horn, Fred	M	61
Adj	Karnatz, Roland	D	35G,64C
Adj	McEntire, Jeremy	M	64A
Adj	McEvoy, Andrew	B	70
Asst Prof	Ryder, Christopher O.	D	34,61,32,13,40
Adj	Schwoebel, David	M	10
Adj	Stanley, Christine	M	61
Adj	Stevens, Thomas	B	62A

VA1250 Roanoke College

Department of Music
Olin Hall
221 College Ln
Salem, VA 24153
(540) 375-2374   Fax: (540) 375-2559
www.roanoke.edu
E-mail: partin@roanoke.edu

4 Year Institution

Chair: Bruce Partin, 80A
Dir., Artist/Performance Series: George N. Arthur, 80F

Adj	Bachelder, Elizabeth Y.	D	66A,66B
Assoc Prof	Blaha, Joseph L.	D	46,10,12A,48,63C
PT	Galyen, Tom	M	65
Artist in Res	Goodfriend, Benedict N.		62A
PT	Hedrick, Steve		63A
PT	Hedrick, Teresa		64E
PT	Hickcox, Julee	M	64A
Assoc Prof	Marsh, Gordon E.	D	10,66,13,10A,66A
PT	Purcell, William		65
PT	Quigley, Roger N.	B	64C
Prof	Sandborg, Jeff R.	D	60,11,12A,36,61
Adj	Sandborg, Marianne	M	61
PT	Smith, John P.	M	62D
PT	Weinstein, Alan	M	41,62C,62D,70

VA1300 St Pauls College

Department of English & Humanities
115 College Dr
Lawrenceville, VA 23868
(434) 848-6460
www.saintpauls.edu

4 Year Institution

Inst	Baugh, Kim C.	M	13A,37

VA1350 Shenandoah Conservatory

1460 University Dr
Winchester, VA 22601-5100
(540) 665-4600   Fax: (540) 665-5402
www.su.edu
E-mail: mstepnia@su.edu

4 Year Institution, Graduate School
Member of NASM

Master of Music in Collaborative Piano, Certificate, Artist Diploma, Master of Music in Composition, Master of Music in Performance, Master of Music in Conducting, Master of Music in Church Music, Master of Music in Music Therapy, Master of Music Education, DMA in Performance, DMA in Music Education, Master of Music Therapy, Master of Science in Music w/Teacher Licensure, DMA in Vocal Pedagogy, MFA, Master of Science in Arts Administration, Master of Music in Pedagogy, Master of Music in Dance Accompanying

Dean: Michael Stepniak, 80A
Associate Dean, Undergraduate Studies: Aime Sposato, 80B,80H
Associate Dean, Graduate Studies: Karen Walker, 80C,80H

Assoc Prof	Adams, Jennifer	M	54
Asst Prof	Aiosa, Charlotte	M	61
Assoc Prof	Albert, Thomas	D	13,10,54
Adj Inst	Anderson, Sally	B	54
Asst Prof	Arnett, Alan	M	52
Prof Emerita	Averitt, Frances Lapp	D	48,64A,41
Prof Emeritus	Averitt, William E.	D	13,10
Adj Asst Prof	Ayau, Joel T.	D	61
Adj Asst Prof	Barley, Marsha	M	32
Adj Asst Prof	Baylock, Alan	M	29
Prof	Black, Donald	M	13,60
Adj Asst Prof	Bly, Carl	M	32
Prof Emerita	Boyd, Sue Marston	D	66A,66H,66C,66D
Prof	Bozman, William M.	M	54
Adj Asst Prof	Brooks, Margaret	B	61
Adj Asst Prof	Brooks, Thomas	B	54
Adj Assoc Prof	Bunn, Michael	M	63D
Adj Inst	Caborn, Peter	M	35E
Prof	Caluda, Elizabeth	D	66A,66D
Prof	Caluda, Glenn	D	70
Adj Asst Prof	Carmichael, Matthew J.	M	64E
Adj Asst Prof	Chavez, David E.	D	13C
Assoc Prof	Chen, Ting Yu	M	52
Adj Asst Prof	Cho, Grace	D	61
Prof	Collins, Charlotte A.	D	13,32
Adj Prof	Collins, Irma H.	D	32
Prof Emeritus	Collins, Verne E.	D	35E
Adj Asst Prof	Connelly Bush, Judith	M	32
Prof	Cooksey, Steven	D	12A,36,66G,31A
Adj Asst Prof	Correll, Larry	M	32
Adj Assoc Prof	Correll, Sue	M	32
Adj Asst Prof	Coulson-Grigsby, Carolyn	D	54
Inst	DeBord, Kathryn	B	52
Adj Inst	DiFranco, Paul		35C,35D
Adj Asst Prof	Dransfield, Lee Ann	M	66D
Asst Prof	Edelman, David	M	35E
Asst Prof	Edwards, Matthew C.	M	61
Prof Emerita	Evans, Eugenia H.	M	66A,66B
Asst Prof	Flom, Jonathan	M	54
Lect	Follett, Karen	M	52
Assoc Prof	Forest, Michael	M	61
Adj Assoc Prof	Fraedrich, Craig	M	63A,29
Asst Prof	Fraga, Maurice	M	52
Asst Prof	Fransen, Wade	D	54
Inst	Furr, Ricky		35C,35D
Asst Prof	Gibson, Elijah	B	52
Adj Inst	Goshorn, Jereme		52
Prof	Green, Kathryn	D	61
Adj Prof	Gullstrand, Donna	M	61
Adj Asst Prof	Hall, Kenneth	M	70
Adj Asst Prof	Ham, Christopher M.	M	52
Assoc Prof	Helm, Erica	M	52
Prof Emeritus	Herman, Harold	B	54
Prof Emerita	Herman, Linde		54
Adj Assoc Prof	Herman, Matthew James	D	10,13,13F
Adj Asst Prof	Hoyt, Lucy Owen	D	61
Assoc Prof	Ingham, William	M	54
Prof Emeritus	Johnston, Stephen K.	D	37,48,64C
Asst Prof	Jones, Byron A.	D	61,39
Prof	Keating, Karen	D	66A,36
Adj Asst Prof	Kim, Eun Hee	D	61
Assoc Prof	Larson, Robert	M	66A
Prof Emeritus	Laster, James	D	60,36,66G,31A
Assoc Prof	Lederer, Doris M.		62B,62A,42
Adj Asst Prof	Leonard, Linda	B	61
Adj Assoc Prof	Linney, William E.	M	64E
Adj Assoc Prof	Lipe, Anne	D	33
Asst Prof	Little, David	D	10
Adj Asst Prof	Maher, Michael	M	66A
Adj Asst Prof	Marion, Ricki	M	35E
Assoc Prof	Marlatt, Jeffrey	D	32,61
Asst Prof	McManus, Laurie	D	12A
Assoc Prof	Meyer, David	D	61
Adj Lect	Miller, Linda		52
Adj Assoc Prof	Mitts, Thomas	D	13
Adj Assoc Prof	Murphy, Michael D.	D	70
Adj Inst	Murray, Amy	M	61
Prof	Nelson, Scott	M	48,46,63A,37
Adj Assoc Prof	Niess, Matt	M	47
Artist in Res	O'Conor, John	B	66
Prof Emerita	Ogg, Janette	D	61
Asst Prof	Ohriner, Mitchell S.	PhD	13,13K,13E
Asst Prof	Olson, Adam	M	35A,35B
Assoc Prof	O'Neill, Golder	B	29,35A,35B
Assoc Prof	Pierson, William	M	54
Adj Assoc Prof	Roberts, Timothy	D	64E
Adj Asst Prof	Romano, Charlene	M	64A,13
Asst Prof	Romine, Ryan D.	DMA	64D,13
Adj Asst Prof	Rowe, Carl	M	63A
Assoc Prof	Ruhadze, Medea Namoradze	D	61
Asst Prof	Ruscella, J. J.	M	54
Adj Asst Prof	Ruth, Christopher	M	12A
Adj Asst Prof	Rylatko, Oleg	M	62A
Asst Prof	Salley, Keith P.	M	13
Assoc Prof	Sargent, Philip	D	61
Adj Asst Prof	Schroth, Robyn	M	52
Prof	Shafer, Robert	M	60,36
Prof	Shaw, Clyde Thomas	M	62C,42,12A,41
Prof Emeritus	Sheats, Jackson	B	39,61
Adj Asst Prof	Shores, Daniel	B	35A,35B
Adj Inst	Shumway, Angelina	M	61
Prof	Snowden, Jonathan	B	64A
Adj Inst	Sokol, Mike		35C,35D

Prof	Sposato, Aime	D	61
Asst Prof	Standerfer, Stephanie	D	32A,32B,32C
Prof	Stepniak, Michael	M	12,38,31A,41,32
Assoc Prof	Stokes, Donovan	D	62D
Adj Asst Prof	Strain, Robert L.	D	66A
Adj Assoc Prof	Stuckey, Bridgett	B	62E
Prof Emerita	Sung, Marion	M	33
Asst Prof	Tague, Daniel	D	33
Assoc Prof	Takayama, Akemi	M	62A
Assoc Prof	Talley, Damon S.	D	37
Prof	Temple, Elizabeth A.	M	66A
Assoc Prof	Trump, Kirsten	M	54
Assoc Prof	Wagner, Jan	M	60B,38
Assoc Prof	Walker, Karen	D	66D,66C
Adj Asst Prof	Weekly, Edrie Means	M	61
Assoc Prof	Wells, Wayne W.	D	49,63C,41
Adj Asst Prof	White, Diana	M	66A,66D
Adj Asst Prof	Whitehead, Richard	B	70,29
Adj Asst Prof	Wright, Elaine	M	66A,66D
Adj Inst	Wyrick, Inez	B	62D
Assoc Prof	Yancey, Cheryl	M	54
Adj Asst Prof	Young, Alphonso	M	67
Assoc Prof	Yowell, Earl R.	M	65
Prof	Zerull, David	D	32,37
Asst Prof	Zoeter, Garrick A.	M	64C

VA1400 Sweet Briar College
Department of Music
Sweet Briar, VA 24595
(434) 381-6100   Fax: (434) 381-6489
www.sbc.edu
E-mail: nross@sbc.edu

4 Year Institution

Chair: Nicholas Piers Ross, 80A

Inst PT	Billias, Anna	M	66C,66A
Adj Inst	Bolling-May, Joan		61
Adj Inst	Creasy, Catherine S.	M	63B
Adj Inst	Gabbert, Andrew		62C
Inst PT	Hugo, Alycia	M	64A
Vstng Asst Prof	Ingber, Jeffrey	M	20,11
Prof	McCord, Rebecca	D	13,66A,66C
Inst PT	Parrish, William	B	64E
Inst PT	Ross, Jana	M	62A,62B
Asst Prof	Ross, Nicholas Piers	D	13,66A,66C,12
Inst PT	Scarfullery, Rafael	D	70
Adj Inst	Schweninger, Virginia	B	62E
Inst PT	Thom, Marcia	B	61,39

VA1475 Univ of Mary Washington
Department of Music
1301 College Ave
Fredericksburg, VA 22401-5300
(540) 654-1012   Fax: (540) 654-1966
www.umw.edu/music
E-mail: dlong@umw.edu

4 Year Institution
Member of NASM

Chair: Gregg Stull, 80A

Inst PT	Ahearn, Kathryn	M	61,39
Asst Prof	Bartram, Kevin P.	D	37,60B,38,32E
Inst PT	Beaver, Johanna L.	D	62A,62B,51
Inst PT	Bollino, Damien	M	63B
Inst PT	Carper, Gary E.	B	63D
Inst PT	Chalifoux, Jeanne D.	M	62E
Prof	Fickett, Martha V.	D	11,12A,12E,66A
Inst PT	Ford, Jim S.	B	63A
Inst PT	Forry, James L.	B	62C
Senior Lect	Gately, Doug T.	M	47,48,29,64
Asst Prof	Greenan, April	D	11,12A,12B,12F,20
Inst PT	Henry, Paul S.	B	62D
Inst PT	Hichborn, Kathryn D.	B	66D
Prof	Long, David J.	D	13,10A,10F
Inst PT	Maley, Marshall E.	M	65
Inst PT	McCoy, William F.	M	66G
Inst PT	McMurray, Heather A.	M	61
Inst PT	Middle, Bruce H.	B	70
Inst PT	Roach, Donna Kay	M	12A
Asst Prof	Snyder, Mark L.	D	13,10B,10F,34
Asst Prof	Tavernier, Jane	D	61,36,39,40
Inst PT	Whitmore, Judith B.	M	66A

VA1500 Univ of Richmond
Department of Music
Booker Hall
Richmond, VA 23173
(804) 289-8277   Fax: (804) 287-6814
music.richmond.edu
E-mail: bmelton@richmond.edu

4 Year Institution

Chair: Gene Anderson, 80A
Executive Dir., Modlin Center Concert Series: Deborah Sommers, 80F

Prof	Anderson, Gene	D	13,11
Inst PT	Arthur, Charles	M	70
Inst PT	Baedke, Ron	M	63C
Inst PT	Bajekal, Nirmal	M	67H
Assoc Prof	Becker, Richard	M	10A,66A
Other	Bennett, Mary Beth	D	66C
Inst PT	Blake, Cory	M	70
Other	Breakall, Raymond	B	66F
Assoc Prof	Broening, Benjamin	D	10,34,13,35C,35D
Prof Emerita	Bunting, Suzanne Kidd	M	
Assoc Prof	Cable, Jennifer A.	D	11,61
Prof	Davison, Michael A.	D	11,29,46,47,49
Vstng Asst Prof	Duvall, Matthew		43,65
Prof Emeritus	Erb, James B.	D	
Inst PT	Esleck, David	D	11,29
Librarian	Fairtile, Linda B.	D	16
Asst Prof	Fillerup, Jessie	D	12
Inst PT	Friedman, Jonathan I.	M	64D
Inst PT	Frook, Sarah	M	61
Inst PT	Guthmiller, Anne	M	61,42
Inst PT	Hanson, Paul	D	66A,42
Inst PT	Harding, Kevin	B	70
Inst PT	Highstein, Gustav	M	64B
Inst PT	Jellison, Anastasia	M	62E,42
Inst PT	Jones, Brian	B	65
Vstng Asst Prof	Kaplan, Lisa		43,66A
Prof Emerita	Kirby, Catharine C.	B	
Other	Kong, Joanne	D	66A,66H,66C,55
Inst PT	Kordzaia, Alexander	M	38,42
Vstng Asst Prof	Lam, Michelle	M	62A,62B,43
Inst PT	Lawson, Jennifer	M	64A
Vstng Asst Prof	Maccafferri, Michael		43,64C
Inst PT	McComb, Jason B.	M	62C
Inst PT	McEntire, Jeremy R.	M	64A
Asst Prof	McGraw, Andrew	D	14,20I
Inst PT	Niethamer, David B.	M	64C,37
Inst PT	Pedersen, David	M	36
Inst PT	Pharr, Randall		62D
Vstng Asst Prof	Photinos, Nicholas		43,62C
Inst PT	Puig, Martha	M	66A,66D
Assoc Prof	Riehl, Jeffrey S.	D	11,36,61,60
Prof Emeritus	Rudolf, Homer	D	
Inst PT	Sanchez, Joseph W.	B	65
Inst PT	Scott, Jason B.	M	64E
Inst PT	Smith, James		61
Inst PT	Stevens, Bruce	M	66G
Inst PT	Stevens, Thomas		62A,62B
Inst PT	Velvikis, Rachel N.	M	63B
Inst PT	Weaver, James	M	61
Inst PT	Ycaza, Stephanie	M	63D
Inst PT	Yim, Susy	M	62A
Vstng Asst Prof	Yoon, Paul	D	11,14,20C

VA1550 Univ of Virginia
McIntire Department of Music
112 Old Cabell Hall
Charlottesville, VA 22903
(434) 924-3052   Fax: (434) 924-6033
www.virginia.edu/music/index.html
E-mail: music-web@virginia.edu

4 Year Institution, Graduate School

PhD in Composition, PhD Critical & Comparative Studies Music

Chair: Richard Will, 80A
Dir., Undergraduate Studies: Michael James Puri, 80B
Dir., Graduate Studies: Fred Everett Maus, 80C

Lect PT	Balija, Ayn	M	62B,51,42
Lect PT	Barolsky, Ruth	D	66A
Lect PT	Beasley, Pamela	M	61
Asst Prof	Burtner, Matthew	DMA	10,34,35C,12F
Lect PT	Carter, Adam C.	DMA	62C,51
Asst Prof	Coffey, Ted	D	10B,10,34,35C,35G
Lect PT	Colwell, David A.	DMA	62A,51,42
Lect PT	Cook, Seth		63D
Lect PT	D'earth, John E.		20G,47,63A,53

Lect PT	Decker, Jeffrey C.	M	64E,42,47
Assoc Prof	DeVeaux, Scott K.	D	13,12A,12,14,29
Lect PT	Dishman, Nathan	M	63C
Lect PT	Eversole, Bridgid	D	61
Lect PT	Fang, I-Jen	DMA	50,65
Lect PT	Fritts, Susan L.	M	63B
Lect PT	Gross, Kelly	M	66A
Lect PT	Hanley, Wells	M	66A
Lect PT	Hill, Aaron S.	M	64B
Prof	Holsinger, Bruce	D	12,31A
Lect PT	Howard, Greg		62
Lect PT	Hsieh, Lily	M	61
Lect PT	Jellison, Anastasia I.		62E
Lect PT	Jospe, Robert D.		65
Lect PT	Kelly, Angela	B	64A
Assoc Prof	Kisliuk, Michelle	D	14,20A
Asst Prof	Koch, Andrew	M	37,63
Lect PT	Larrabee, Adam	M	
Assoc Prof	Maus, Fred Everett	D	13,12B,15,12D,14C
	Mayhood, Erin L.	M	16
Lect PT	Mayhood, John		66A
Prof Emerita	McClymonds, Marita P.	D	12A,12
Lect PT	Moore, Barbara	M	66A,66G
Lect PT	Nakasian, Stephanie	M	61
Lect PT	Neebe, Paul M.	DMA	63A,49,13C,13A
Lect PT	Owens, Chris		61
Assoc Prof	Pease, William	M	37
Assoc Prof	Puri, Michael James	D	13,12
Lect PT	Roberts, Elizabeth 'Ibby'	M	64D,48
Lect PT	Rosensky, Michael	M	70,42,47
Asst Prof	Rubin, Joel E.	D	14A,14C,64C,41,31B
Lect PT	Sariti, David J.	DMA	62A,67B,51,42
Prof	Shatin, Judith	D	10B,10A,10F,10,13
Asst Prof	Slon, Michael	M	36,39,60
Lect PT	Spaar, Peter	M	62D,42,47
Prof	Tamarkin, Kate	DMA	38,60B,12A,43
Lect PT	Taylor, James	M	61
Lect PT	Thompson, Dawn		61
Lect PT	Tripathi, Nitin		65
Lect PT	Tung, Mimi	M	66A,42
Lect PT	Warren, Tasha	DMA	64C,48
Assoc Prof	Will, Richard	D	12A,12,20G,14C

VA1580 Univ of Virginia-College at Wise

Department of Visual & Perf Arts
1 College Ave
Wise, VA 24293
(276) 376-0271
www.uvawise.edu
E-mail: music@uvawise.edu

4 Year Institution

Chair: Suzanne Adams-Ramsey, 80A
Coordinator: David Paul Volk, 80A

Adj	Barker, David	M	13A,32B
Adj	Cox, Michael	B	36,61,32D,60A
Inst	Galyean, Richard D.	M	37,60B,49,63D,32E
Adj	Masters, Suzanna	M	64C,11,13A,64E,48
Other	Sorah, Donald	M	34,63A,29,14C,20
Assoc Prof	Volk, David Paul	D	13,36,12A,66A,10

VA1600 Virginia Commonwealth Univ

Department of Music
922 Park Ave
Richmond, VA 23284-2004
(804) 828-1166   Fax: (804) 827-0230
www.vcumusic.org
E-mail: music@vcu.edu

4 Year Institution, Graduate School
Member of NASM

Master of Music in Music Education

Interim Chair: Darryl Harper, 80A
Assistant Chair: John Patykula, 80H
Assistant Director: James Wiznerowicz, 80H

Inst PT	Ali, Kelly S.	M	62D
Inst PT	Ashby, Steven	M	70,13B,13C
Prof	Austin, Terry	D	32,37,60
Inst PT	BeVille, Jesse	M	36
Inst PT	Carlin, Patrick	D	12
Inst PT	Davis, Susan	M	64A
Asst Prof	Day, Melanie	M	39,61
Inst PT	Dole, Frederick	M	62D
Assoc Prof	Donnell, Cynthia S.	M	61
Inst PT	Dvoskin, Victor	DIPL	62D,29
Asst Prof	Easley, Tabatha	D	64A
Inst PT	Ellithorpe, Robert	M	63C,32E
Inst PT	Ess, Michael	B	70,29,47
Inst PT	Gailes, George		47,64E,29B
Assoc Prof	Garcia, Antonio	M	29,47,63C,35,46
Inst PT	Gebo, Kevin	D	63A
Asst Prof	Greennagel, David J.	D	32
Inst PT	Gulick, Michelle	B	39,61
Inst PT	Guthmiller, Anne	M	61
Inst PT	Hammel, Alice	D	13B,13C
Assoc Prof	Hammel, Bruce R.	D	13,64D
Inst PT	Hanley, Wells	M	29,66A
Asst Prof	Harper, Darryl	D	29,10,14
Inst PT	Hooten, Bryan	M	13B,13C,63C
Inst PT	Jacobson, James	D	65A
Inst PT	Jones, Brian	B	65
Asst Prof	Klein, Susanna	M	62A,42,32E
Inst PT	Kuhl, J. C.	B	64E
Inst PT	LaPointe, Simon	M	62A
Inst PT	Larrabee, Adam	M	70
Prof PT	Lohuis, Ardyth J.	D	66G,12A,12C
Asst Prof	Martin, Peter J.	M	65
Inst PT	Martucci, Anthony		65,47
Inst PT	McComb, Dana	M	62C
Inst PT	Messerschmidt, William H.	B	65
Inst PT	Moeser, Charles	B	70
Asst Prof	Myssyk, Daniel	M	38,60
Inst PT	Niethamer, David	M	64C
Inst PT	Oyan, Sheri	D	64E
Assoc Prof	Patykula, John	M	70
Inst PT	Pharr, Randall	B	62D
Inst PT	Puig, Marta	M	66A
Inst PT	Regni, Albert	M	64E
Prof	Richards, Douglas	M	12A,29A,29B
Assoc Prof	Richardson, Edward 'Rex'	D	63A,29,49
Inst PT	Robinson, David	M	70
Inst PT	Schmidt, Stephen	M	62A,62B
Inst PT	Sharp, Molly	M	62A
Inst PT	Simpson, Michael	B	36
Inst PT	Smedina-Starke, Ruta	M	66A
Inst PT	Smith, James	M	61
Assoc Prof	Smith, Patrick G.	PhD	12A,63B
Inst PT	Staples, Charles	D	66A
Inst PT	Strawley, Brian	M	63A
Inst PT	Taylor, James	M	61
Inst PT	Toussaint, David	M	70
Asst Prof	Tyree, Rebecca	M	36,32
Prof	Vlahcevic, Sonia K.	D	13,66A
Assoc Prof	Walter, Ross A.	D	63C,63D,34,49
Inst PT	Welk, Shawn	M	64B
Prof	West, Charles W.	DMA	48,64C,60
Inst PT	White, Laura	B	66A,66D
Inst PT	Wilson, Russell	M	66A,11
Assoc Prof	Wiznerowicz, James	D	10A,10F,13,13H,10
Asst Prof	Wood, Kenneth E.	D	61,39
Inst PT	Ycaza, Stephanie	M	20
Asst Prof	Zheng, Yin	D	66

VA1650 Virginia Intermont College

Department of Music
1013 Moore St
VIC Box 249
Bristol, VA 24203
(276) 669-6101   Fax: (276) 466-7963
www.vic.edu
E-mail: crhineh@vic.edu

4 Year Institution

Dir., Artist/Performance Series: Linda Creasey, 80F

Alonzo, Deborah	M	61
Oblinger, Amy	M	36
Smith, Trevor	D	61,66A

VA1700 Virginia Polytech Inst & St Univ

Department of Music
241 Squires Student Ctr (0240)
Blacksburg, VA 24061
(540) 231-5685   Fax: (540) 231-5034
www.music.vt.edu
E-mail: music@vt.edu

4 Year Institution

Adj Inst	Ball, David	D	11
Asst Prof	Bigler, Dwight	D	36,60A
Asst Prof	Bukvic, Ivica Ico	D	10,34,10A,13L,10C
Prof	Burnsed, C. Vernon	D	32

Vstng Asst Prof	Chafin, Robert	M	13C,39,34,61
Assoc Prof	Cole, Richard C.	M	11,12A,20G
Assoc Prof	Cowden, Tracy E.	DMA	66C,66A,66D,13C
Asst Prof	Crafton, Jason A.	DMA	63A,46,47
Senior Inst	Crone, Elizabeth	M	64A,34C
Asst Prof	Cross, Travis J.	M	32E,37,60
Senior Inst	Dunston, Michael	B	34
Assoc Prof	Easter, Wallace E.	M	37,63B,13
Assoc Prof	Floyd, John M.	D	50,65
Assoc Prof	Glazebrook, James	M	60,38,62A,62B
Prof	Holliday, K. A.	D	13,66A
Assoc Prof	Howell, John	M	36,67,35,55
Assoc Prof	Husser, John S.	M	64D,64E,34
Assoc Prof	Jacobsen, David C.	D	64A,64E
Vstng Prof	King, Steve E.	D	32E,32G,37
Adj Inst	Langosch, Paul	DIPL	20H,29,35D,46,47
Senior Inst	McKee, David	M	37
Inst	McNeill, George	DIPL	37
Asst Prof	Middleton, Polly K.	D	32E,32G,37,41
Asst Prof	Parkes, Kelly Anne	D	32B
Prof	Sochinski, James	D	13,37,63C,63D,34
Adj Inst	Turner, Patrick	M	11,29,34D,34H,35C
Asst Prof	Walker, John L.	D	64B,13,14,20H
Asst Prof	Weinstein, Alan	M	62C,62D,12B
Prof	Widder, David R.	D	12A,37,48,64C
Adj Inst	Williamson, Scott	D	36,39,40,60,61
Asst Prof	Wyatt, Ariana	M	61

VA1750 Virginia State University

Department of Mus, Art & Design
PO Box 9007
Petersburg, VA 23806
(804) 524-5311   Fax: (804) 524-6862
www.vsu.edu
E-mail: mphillips@vsu.edu

4 Year Institution
Member of NASM

Interim Dean: Andrew J. Kanu, 80A
Chair: Mark W. Phillips, 80A

Assoc Prof	Burrs, Lisa Edwards	PhD	11,13A,36,61
Asst Prof	Edmonds, Johnnella	M	60,32B,32C,36,61
Assoc Prof	Floyd-Savage, Karen	PhD	11,13A,36,61
Assoc Prof	Haughton, Ethel Norris	PhD	13,12A,12,20G,66C
Inst	Holden, James	M	13,20G,37,64E,46
Assoc Prof	Larose, Thomas	D	
Prof	Phillips, Mark W.	PhD	32C,37,49,63C,63D
Prof	Schwartz, Richard I.	D	13,48,64C,10
Prof	Shaffer-Gottschalk, David D.	D	13,66A,66C
Asst Prof	Tuckwiller, George	M	60,11,41,49,63A

VA1800 Virginia Union University

Department of Music
1500 N Lombardy St
Richmond, VA 23220-1711
(804) 257-5665   Fax: (804) 354-5929
www.vuu.edu
E-mail: VWest@vuu.edu

4 Year Institution

Music Coordinator: Shelia D. Tate, 80A
Chair: John Ware, 80A

Asst Prof	Carson, Virginia	M	13,10,66A
Assoc Prof	Esleck, David	D	11,66A,29,34,35
Inst PT	McCallum, Gregory	M	37,64C,64E
Asst Prof	Savage, Karen	M	39,61
Inst Adj	Strother, Martin	B	39,61
Asst Prof	Tate, Shelia D.	M	11,32,16,36
Inst Adj	Teasley, Kevin	B	47,29
Assoc Prof	Ware, John	D	13,10,12,66

VA1830 Virginia Wesleyan College

Department of Music
1584 Wesleyan Dr
Norfolk, VA 23502-5512
(804) 455-3200   Fax: (804) 461-5025
www.vwc.edu/music/
E-mail: ljordananders@vwc.edu

4 Year Institution

Coordinator: Lee Jordan-Anders, 80A

	Billy, Sandra S.	D	31A
Adj	Carr, Deborah		66G,60A
Assoc Prof	Jordan-Anders, Lee	M	13,11,41,66A
Asst Prof	Trotta, Michael J.	D	32D,12A,36,40

VA1840 Virginia Western Comm College

Department of Music
PO Box 14007
Roanoke, VA 24038-4007
(540) 857-7958
www.virginiawestern.edu/
E-mail: ldurham@virginiawestern.edu

2 Year Institution

Chair: Linda Eileen Durham, 80A

Prof	Durham, Linda Eileen	PhD	12A

VA1850 Washington & Lee University

Department of Music
Wilson Hall
204 W Washington St
Lexington, VA 24450
(540) 458-8852   Fax: (540) 458-8104
www.wlu.edu
E-mail: alexanderd@wlu.edu

4 Year Institution

Interim Chair: Timothy R. Gaylard, 80A

Inst PT	Artwick, Thomas	B	64E,53
Inst PT	Bunts, Joseph	M	62D
Inst PT	Clark, Judith	M	66C
Inst PT	Del Vecchio, Peter H.	M	63,49,47
Inst PT	Gaylard, Catharine P.	B	61
Prof	Gaylard, Timothy R.	D	11,12A,66A,20G
Inst PT	Goudimova, Julia	M	62C
Inst PT	Jellison, Anastasia	M	62E
Assoc Prof	Kolman, Barry	D	13,37,38,64C,60
Inst PT	Leath, Nate R.	B	62A,70
Inst PT	Letourneau, Jaime H.	M	62A
Asst Prof	Lynch, Shane	D	36,40,61
Inst PT	McCorkle, William	M	66G,66H,66A
Inst PT	Overman, Michael	D	65
Inst PT	Penne, Cynthia S.	M	62A,62B,41
Inst PT	Petty, Byron W.	B	64A,13
Inst	Petty, Shuko Watanabe	D	66A,66C,13C
Inst PT	Pomeroy, Loren	M	70
Inst	Spice, Graham	M	34
Assoc Prof	Vosbein, Terry	D	10,13,29A,47,29
Inst PT	Widney, Jason	M	61

VI0050 Univ of the Virgin Islands

Department of Music
#2 John Brewer's Bay
Saint Thomas, USVI 00802-9990
(340) 693-1192   Fax: (340) 693-1195
www.uvi.edu
E-mail: avenzen@uvi.edu

4 Year Institution, Historically Black College

Chair: Lorna C. Young-Wright, 80A

Asst Prof	Green, Elvira O.	M	13C,36,61
Adj Prof	James, Jo-Sandra	M	66A,66B,66D
Asst Prof	Lamkin, Martin J.	M	11,12A,32A,47,60B
Assoc Prof	Venzen, Austin A.	M	10F,11,32B,37,42
Prof	Young-Wright, Lorna C.	D	13,66,60A

VT0050 Bennington College
Department of Music
One College Dr
Bennington, VT 05201
(802) 440-4510   Fax: (802) 440-4511
www.bennington.edu
E-mail: stjones@bennington.edu

4 Year Institution, Graduate School

MFA

Coordinator, Music: Suzanne Jones, 80A

Inst	Bisio, Michael	B	62D,53,29
Faculty	Bogdan, Thomas	B	36,61,31,40
Inst	Botts, Nathan	M	11,29,49,63,67E
Faculty	Brazelton, Kitty	D	13,10F,10,11,53
Faculty	Brooke, Nicholas	D	13,10,20,34
Inst	Hand, Frederic	B	70
Faculty	Ibarra, Susie	B	20,29,50,47,53
Inst	Kirk, John		20G
Faculty	Last, Julie		34D,35D,35G
Faculty	Lehrer, Scott	B	34C,35D,35G
Inst	Lewis, Christopher	B	66A,66B,66C,66D
Faculty	Neal, Randall	MFA	12,36,45
Inst	Parke, Nathaniel	MFA	62C
Faculty	Rosales, Rachel A.	M	61,66H
Faculty	Shawn, Allen	M	13,10,66A
Comp_in_Res	Stewart, Jeremy	B	13A,13B,13C
Inst	Van der Linde, Polly	M	66A,66B,66C
Inst	Washiyama, Kaori	M	62A,62B
Faculty	Williamson, Bruce	M	64C,64E,66A,67,47
Faculty	Wimberly, Michael	M	10,20,29,35,65

VT0100 Castleton State College
Department of Music-FAC
45 Alumni Dr
Castleton, VT 05735
(802) 468-1261   Fax: (802) 468-1440
www.castleton.edu/music/index.htm
E-mail: glenn.giles@castleton.edu

4 Year Institution

Chair: Glenn Giles, 80A
Dean: Tony Peffer, 80A

Adj Lect	Baker, Kent	M	66A,66D,46,13,10F
Asst Prof	Blodget, Sherril	D	40,36,60,61,11
Adj Lect	Cassarino, James	M	66G,66H
Adj Lect	Coolidge, Tiffany	M	64D
Prof Emeritus	Diehl, Richard C.	D	13,60,47,10,37
Adj Lect	Etzler, David		63A
Adj Prof	Gettel, Court		64A,13,20
Prof	Giles, Glenn	M	63C,63D,60,37,46
Asst Prof	Grove, Marna		66A
Adj Lect	Grycel, Gail	M	64B
Adj Lect	Harding, Mark		62D,70
Adj Lect	James, Karen		66A,66D
Adj Lect	Keck, Bill	M	63D
	Lamey, Phil		65
Adj Lect	Lenox, Michael		64E
Adj Lect	Madsen, Charles A.	D	66A,12,11,66C
Adj Prof	Matteson, Vicki	M	64C,32
Assoc Prof	McEnerny, Harry	M	54
Adj Lect	Mercier, William		61
Adj Lect	Merrill, Suzanne Kantorski		61
Adj Lect	Miller, Peter	M	62,32,51
Adj Lect	Roth, Robert	M	65
Adj Prof	Shapiro, Jarred	M	62C,11,20
Asst Prof	Smith, Matthew K.	D	37,32,11,63B,60
Adj Lect	Sowards, James	M	62D
Adj Lect	Tennenbaum, Lucy		61
Adj Prof	Ullman, Richard	M	70,67D,13C
Adj Lect	Zsoldos, Michael	M	64E

VT0125 Community College of Vermont
Department of Music
32 College St
Montpelier, VT 05602
(802) 828-4060
www.ccv.edu/locations/montpelier/index.html

4 Year Institution

Assoc Prof	Webb, Brian P.	M	13A,13,11,12A,36

VT0150 Goddard College
Interdisciplinary Arts Department
123 Pitkin Rd
Plainfield, VT 05667
(802) 454-8311   Fax: (802) 454-1451
www.goddard.edu
E-mail: admissions@goddard.edu

Low-residency Adult Education

Master of Arts in Education

Contact: Danielle Boutet, 80A

Boutet, Danielle	M	
Fleming, Susan	D	
Garthwaite, Lucinda	M	

VT0200 Green Mountain College
Department of Visual & Perf. Arts
Music - 1 College Circle
Poultney, VT 05764
(802) 287-8249   Fax: (802) 287-8009
www.greenmtn.edu
E-mail: cassarinoj@greenmtn.edu

4 Year Institution

Chair: James P. Cassarino, 80A

Adj	Bloch, Gus	B	64C,64E
Prof	Cassarino, James P.	M	12,14,20,36,37
Adj	DeNicola, Alan	B	62A,62B,62C
Adj	Gibson, Alan	M	11,12A
Adj	Goodman, Donald	B	46,70
Adj	Grove, Marna	B	66A
Adj	MacKenzie, David	B	63A
Adj	Meitrott, Gary	B	20A,20B
Adj	Opel, Paul E.	B	66A,70
Adj	Tenenbaum, Lucy	B	61

VT0250 Johnson State College
Department of Music
337 College Hill
Johnson, VT 05656
(802) 635-1310   Fax: (802) 635-1248
www.jsc.vsc.edu
E-mail: Stephen.Blair@jsc.edu

4 Year Institution

Co-Chair: Steve Blair, 80A

Lect PT	Austin, Mary Jane	M	66A
Asst Prof	Blair, Steve	M	10,47,70
Lect PT	Capps, Joe	B	70,34,35A
Lect PT	Church, Alan	M	62
Lect PT	Cleary, Tom	M	66A
Lect PT	Geraci, Anthony	M	
Lect PT	Gibson, Mary	M	62
Lect PT	Gillies, Lee	M	64E
Lect PT	Hendon, Sally	M	62A
Asst Prof	Huling, Diane	M	13,66A,66B,66D
Lect PT	Ingalls, Glendon	M	63
Prof	Jablow, Lisa	D	60,12A,36,41,61
Lect PT	Moore, Celina	M	61
Lect PT	Rivers, John	M	63
Lect PT	Salisbury, Jeff	B	50,65
Lect PT	Sorrell, Martha	M	32
Lect PT	Stats, Clyde	M	53,20A,20G

VT0300 Lyndon State College
Department of Fine & Perf Arts
1001 College Rd
Lyndonville, VT 05851
(802) 626-6255
www.lyndonstate.edu
E-mail: elizabeth.norris@lyndonstate.edu

4 Year Institution

Chair: Elizabeth Norris, 80A

Adj Prof	Brown, Philip	B	11,13A,36,44,47
Adj Prof	Charles, Jean	B	11,70
Adj Prof	Cotte, William	B	11,13H,36,61,66
Adj Prof	Moore, Britt	M	13L,34D,35,61,34E
Adj Prof	Moulton, William	M	13A,29C,33,34B,35A
Asst Prof	Norris, Elizabeth	D	11,13A,20,61,36

VT0350 Middlebury College
Department of Music
Center for the Arts-307
Middlebury, VT 05753
(802) 443-5221   Fax: (802) 443-2057
www.middlebury.edu/academics/music
E-mail: phamlin@middlebury.edu

4 Year Private Institution

Chair: Peter S. Hamlin, 80A
Coord., Arts Center: Deborah Young

Assoc Prof	Buettner, Jeff	D	13A,36,40,13B,13C
Artist in Res	Clemmons, Francois		31
	Forman, Dick		47,29,66C
Assoc Prof	Hamberlin, Larry D.		10A,12A,29A,13A,13C
Prof	Hamlin, Peter S.	D	10A,10B,10F,13A,13B
Asst Prof	Kafumbe, Damascus	D	14A,14C,10E,20,31F
Artist in Res	Massey, Andrew J.	M	38
Prof	Tan, Su Lian	D	10,13,64A,42
Prof	Vitercik, Greg	D	13,12A,12,66C

VT0400 St Michaels College
Department of Fine Arts
Winooski Park
Colchester, VT 05439
(802) 654-2000   Fax: (802) 645-2679
www.smcvt.edu/academics/music/
E-mail: jviens@smcvt.edu

4 Year Institution

Chair: Peter Harrigan, 80A

Inst	Belford, Rick		70
Inst	Jarrett, Gabriel		65
Inst	Klimowski, Steve		64C,64E
Prof	LeClair, Paul	D	13,12A,48,37,64E
Assoc Prof	Lew, Nathaniel G.	D	12A,13,36,40
Inst	Monachino, Jerome		70
Lect	Price, Josselyne		14,20,50
Inst	Spoelstra, Annemieke		66A,66C
Prof	Summerfield, Susan	D	13,11,41,66
Inst	Voyer, Jessica		61

VT0450 Univ of Vermont
Department of Music
Redstone Campus
Burlington, VT 05405-0145
(802) 656-3040   Fax: (802) 656-0759
www.uvm.edu/music
E-mail: music@uvm.edu

4 Year Institution

Interim Dean: Joel Goldberg, 80A
Chair: D. Thomas Toner, 80A

Artist Teacher	Asbell, Paul	B	70
Artist Teacher	Capps, Joseph	B	70
Artist Teacher	Carpenter, Nadine	B	64B
Artist Teacher	Cleary, Thomas	B	66A,47,66D
Artist Teacher	Davies, Rick A.	D	63C
Artist Teacher	DeLaurentis, Amber	B	61
Artist Teacher	Elliott, Rachael	M	64D
Artist Teacher	Ferraris, Steve	B	65
Asst Prof	Feurzeig, David K.	D	13,10
Artist Teacher	Janson, Anne	M	64A
Assoc Prof	Julien, Patricia A.	D	13,12,10D,29
Artist Teacher	Klimowski, Stephen	M	64C,64E
Asst Prof	Kono, Yutaka		63D,34,38,60
Artist Teacher	Kwanza, Evelyn		61
Artist Teacher	Mantegna, John	M	70
Prof	Neiweem, David	D	36,61
Artist Teacher	Orgel, Paul	M	66A
Lect	Parker, Sylvia	M	13,66A,66D,66B
Lect	Parshley, Alan O.	M	63B,13A,66D
Artist Teacher	Polk, Suzanne	B	62C
Artist Teacher	Read, Evelyn	M	62A,62B,16,42
Prof Emeritus	Read, Thomas L.	D	13,10
Assoc Prof	Riley, Patricia E.	D	32
Artist Teacher	Rivers, John	B	62D
Artist Teacher	Salisbury, Jeff M.		65
Assoc Prof	Schneider, Wayne J.	D	12,11
Artist Teacher	Soons, Heidi	M	62E
Lect	Stats, Clyde	M	29A
Assoc Prof	Stewart, Alexander	D	14,53,20,29,47
Artist Teacher	Tilley, William T.	B	62D
Prof	Toner, D. Thomas	D	65,20,37,50,60
Lect	Vega, Ray	B	29,47,63A
Artist Teacher	Wigness, Robert Clyde	D	63C
Artist Teacher	Zsoldos, Michael	M	64E

WA0030 Bellevue Community College
Department of Music
3000 Landerholm Cir SE
Bellevue, WA 98007-6406
(425) 564-2686   Fax: (425) 563-2690
bellevuecollege.edu/ArtsHum/music.asp
E-mail: lyneen.patnoe@bellevuecollege.edu

2 Year Institution

Chair: Thomas Almli, 80A
Performing Arts Coordinator: Lyneen Patnoe, 80A

Adj	Adams, Bob		20,14
Adj	Baglio, Brennan		66D
Adj	Kunz, Kelly		35D,13
PT	Sherman, Hal	M	47
FT	Wilson, Ken	M	11,36,61
Adj	Wilson, Mark		70,12A

WA0050 Central Washington University
Department of Music
400 E University Way
Ellensburg, WA 98926-7458
(509) 963-1216   Fax: (509) 963-1239
www.cwu.edu/music
E-mail: shivert@cwu.edu

4 Year Institution, Graduate School
Member of NASM

Master of Music in Composition, Master of Music in Performance, Master of Music in Conducting, Master of Music in Music Education, Master of Music in Performance & Pedagogy

Chair: Todd Shiver, 80A
Assistant Chair & Dir., Graduate Studies: Chris Bruya, 80C,80H
Dir., Preparatory Division: Bret Smith, 80E

Lect PT	Betts, Timothy	M	62B,42,11
Asst Prof	Blaisdell, Gayla Bauer	D	61,39
Lect PT	Blaisdell, Tor	M	61
Lect PT	Boldt-Neurohr, Kirsten	D	13A,13B,13C,13F
Prof	Brooks, Joseph H.	M	41,48,64B,64C,64E
Prof	Bruya, Chris	M	46,47,29,13
Assoc Prof	Caoile, Nikolas	D	38
Lect	Dillenbeck, Denise	M	62A,42
Lect PT	Durkee, James	B	70
Lect	Flory, Neil	D	10,13
Assoc Prof	Goodenberger, Mark	M	65,50
Prof	Gookin, Larry D.	M	60,37,49,63C
Lect PT	Hages, Brent	B	64B
Lect PT	Hamar, Jon	M	62D
Assoc Prof	Harbaugh, John	M	29A,53,49,63A
Assoc Prof	Lane, Mark	M	37,32
Assoc Prof	Lipori, Daniel	D	11,64D,12A,12C
Prof	Michel, John	M	11,41,51,62C
Lect PT	Nesselroad, Sidney	D	61
Asst Prof	Neurohr, John	D	63C
Prof	Ott, Hal J.	D	12A,41,48,64A,67D
Lect PT	Peacock, Curtis	M	11,49,63D
Lect PT	Peterson, Scott R.	D	36
Lect PT	Pickett, Barbara	M	66C,66D,66A
Prof	Pickett, John	D	13,11,12A,66A,66B
Prof	Rehkopf-Michel, Carrie	M	41,51,62A,62B
Lect	Roditeleva-Wibe, Maria I.	D	14A,12A,20F,66A,66G
Lect PT	Rothenberg, Florie		64C
Lect PT	Schiel, Melissa		61
Prof	Shiver, Todd	D	63C,32,37,47,49
Prof	Singh, Vijay	M	47,60,36,61,35A
Assoc Prof	Smith, Bret	D	11,32,12F
Prof	Snedeker, Jeffrey	D	12,49,63B

Lect	Spencer, Mia	M	13A,13B,13C,61
Lect PT	Wallen, Norm	M	10
Assoc Prof	Weidenaar, Gary	D	36

WA0100 Centralia College
Department of Music
600 W Locust St
Centralia, WA 98531-4035
(206) 736-9391   Fax: (206) 753-3404
www.centralia.edu/

2 Year Institution

Chair: Donna M. Huffman, 80A

Adj	Harwood, Baxter	D	13,13C
	Huffman, Donna M.	D	13,13J,36,47,49
Adj	Woodcock, Ruth	M	11,12A,20,13A,13G

WA0150 Columbia Basin College
Department of Music
2600 N 20th Ave
Pasco, WA 99301
(509) 547-0511 x 2331   Fax: (509) 546-0401
www.columbiabasin.edu
E-mail: bill.mckay@columbiabasin.edu

2 Year Institution

Dean, Arts & Humanities: William McKay, 80A

Inst	Burroughs, D. Robert	M	13,11,62A,53,38
Inst	Cazier, David	M	36,61,29A,40
Inst	Hubbs, Randall	M	13,37,47,63A,29A

WA0200 Cornish College of the Arts
Department of Music
1000 Lenora St
Seattle, WA 98121
(206) 726-5030   Fax: (206) 726-5183
www.cornish.edu
E-mail: music@cornish.edu

4 Year Institution

Chair: Kent Devereaux, 80A
Music Coordinator: Mandy Bowker, 80B

Inst	Anang, Kofi		50
Inst	Banks, Eric	M	13C
Inst	Boeckman, Vicki	M	67C
Inst	Carmona, Marcos		70
Inst	Clement, Dawn	B	13A,66A,66D,29
Inst	Cunningham, Tekla	M	67B,55B
Prof	Deardorf, Chuck		62D,53,29,35
Inst	DeLaurenti, Christopher	B	34
Assoc Prof	Delos, Michael	B	61,39
Inst	DeLuca, Laura	B	64C
Prof	Devereaux, Kent	M	10,12D
Assoc Prof	Doolittle, Emily L.	D	10A,13,13D
Inst	Dupree, Jillon Stoppels	M	66H
Inst	Duran, Becca		61
Inst	Duykers, John	D	61
Inst	Eilander, Maxine	B	62E
Inst	Emerich, Justin	M	63A
Inst	Gearman, Mara	M	62B
Prof	Giteck, Janice	M	13A,13,10,12A
Inst	Goodhew, Denney B.		47
Inst	Gordon, Valerie Muzzolini	M	62E
Prof	Halberstadt, Randy	B	13,66A,66D,53,29
Inst	Harland, Kelly		61,29
Inst	Harley, Gretta	B	13C
Inst	Hauck, Ross	M	61
Inst	Hay, Jeff		63C,29
Inst	Horvitz, Wayne B.	B	10,34
Inst	Ivester, Mark	B	65,29
Inst	Kaufman, Joe	M	62D
Prof	Kendrick, Johnaye	B	61,47,29
Inst	Kenney, Jessika	B	61
Prof	Knapp, James	M	10,47,63A,53,29
Inst	Kocmieroski, Matthew		50
Inst	Krimsky, Seth	M	64D
Inst	Kwapis, Kris	M	67E
Inst	Lee, Janet	B	67D
Prof	Lerch, Natalie	D	61,39
Inst	Lerner, Paige Stockley	M	62C
Inst	Lim, Michael	M	62B
Prof	Mack, Peter	D	66A,41,13C
Inst	Matthews, Ingrid	M	67B
Prof	Nelson, Roger	M	60,36,66A
Inst	Nicolella, Michael		70
Asst Prof	Peterson, David		47,70,29
Assoc Prof	Pos, Margie	B	29,62D,66A,13
Prof	Powell, Jarrad	M	13A,10,20D,45,34
Prof	Priester, Julian		10,47,63C,63D,29
Inst	Ritt, David		63C
Inst	Robbins, Mark	M	63B
Inst	Sanders, Murl Allen	M	68
Assoc Prof	Santos-Neto, Jovino	B	47,66A,66D
Inst	Schenkman, Byron	M	66H
Inst	Sieden, Cyndia	M	61
Inst	Stern, Adam	M	10,60
Inst	Stewart, Chris	B	13G
Inst	Stubbs, Stephen	M	67G,55B
Prof	Taub, Paul	M	41,64A,35
Inst	Teuber, Hans		64E
Inst	Thomas, Ben	D	65B
Inst	Thomas, Jay	B	64
Inst	Tindemans, Margriet	B	67A
Inst	Valdes, Cristina	M	66A
Inst	Varner, Tom	B	63B,47
Inst	Waterfall, Linda	B	10D
Inst	Weld, Kathryn		61
Inst	Whitaker, Nathan	D	67B
Asst Prof	Winter, Beth	B	61,53,29
Inst	Zylstra, Nancy	M	61

WA0250 Eastern Washington University
Department of Music
119 Music Building
Cheney, WA 99004-2434
(509) 359-2241   Fax: (509) 359-7028
www.ewu.edu/music
E-mail: jmiddleton@ewu.edu

4 Year Institution, Graduate School
Member of NASM

Master of Arts in Music

Chair: Jonathan N. Middleton, 80A
Dir., Graduate Studies: Jane Ellsworth, 80C
Dir., Artist Series: Phillip Doyle, 80F

Adj	Ahrend, Janet	D	66G
Adj	Baldwin, Karen	M	32B
Adj	Bodden, Bruce	B	64A,34C
Lect PT	Brockman, Luke	M	29,46,66A
Adj	Cotter, Daniel	M	64C
Lect	Doyle, Phillip	M	64E,47,48
Assoc Prof	Ellsworth, Jane	D	12A,12
Senior Lect	Feeney, Kendall	M	66A,43,66C
Adj	Feller-Marshall, Lynne	D	64D
Inst PT	Foster, Erin	M	13
Asst Prof	Gomez-Giraldo, Julian	M	38,60B,13C
Lect	Goodwin, Don	M	13,66A,37,46
Assoc Prof	Graves, Jody C.	D	66A,66B,66C
Adj	Helseth, Daniel	M	63D
Adj	Holcombe, Ross	M	63C,46,49
Adj	Honn, Linda	M	32B
Adj	Joham, Kristin		63B
Adj	Kimura, Tomoko	M	66A
Prof	Marshall, John	D	62C,70,32E,41,32F
	McCoy, Alan		66F
Prof	Middleton, Jonathan N.	D	13,10,35C,34,35
Adj	Millham, Michael	M	70
Lect	Mortier, Steve	M	61
Prof	Noble, Karen	D	11
Senior Lect	Plamondon, Andrew	M	63A,46,47
Adj	Plewniak, Kim	M	63D
Assoc Prof	Ploeger, Kristina	M	32,36,60A
Adj	Robertson, Ben	M	10B,45,35G,34D
Inst	Salerno, Julia	D	62A,62B,41
Adj	Schoeff, Bethany	M	64B
Adj	Steed, Scott	B	62D,47
Lect PT	Van Winkle, Brian	M	13
Assoc Prof	Wagner, Randel	D	36,40,61,54,60A
Assoc Prof	Waldrop, Michael	D	50,65
Adj	Ward, Brian	M	66A
Adj	Windham, Susan	M	61
Prof	Winters, Patrick	M	37,32E
Assoc Prof	Woodward, Sheila C.	PhD	32
Prof Emeritus	Zyskowski, Martin	M	50,65,60B

WA0300 Everett Community College
Department of Music
2000 Tower St
Everett, WA 98201
(425) 388-9456   Fax: (425) 388-9129
www.everettcc.edu
E-mail: rwaldron@everettcc.edu

2 Year Institution

Dean, Arts & Learning: Jeanne Leader, 80A

	Goff, Kathleen	M	61
Inst PT	Hines, Terry		
Inst PT	Mathews, Lee	M	36,60A
	Moidel, Jeffrey		
Inst PT	Osborne, Tam		
Inst PT	Strunk, Michael	M	20,34C
Inst	Waldron, Richard	M	11,13A,13H,13K,13C

WA0350 Evergreen State College
Dept of Expressive Arts
COM 301
Olympia, WA 98505
(360) 866-6000   Fax: (360) 866-6663
www.evergreen.edu
E-mail: williams@evergreen.edu

4 Year Institution

Performance Arts Manager: Christopher Yates, 80A
Dir., Institute/Festival/Workshops: Sean Williams, 80F

Adj	Black, Cary	B	62D,53,29,35,47
	Chandra, Arun	D	10A,10B,43,34D,11
Adj	Farrell, Scott	B	61,66,54
	Randlette, Peter	B	34
	Setter, Terry A.	M	10F,10,12B,45,35C
	Williams, Sean	D	11,12,14,20G,70

WA0400 Gonzaga University
Department of Music
AD Box 79
502 E Boone Ave
Spokane, WA 99258
(509) 313-6733   Fax: (509) 313-5950
www.gonzaga.edu/music
E-mail: music@gonzaga.edu

4 Year Institution

Chair: Gary Uhlenkott, S. J., 80A

Prof Adj	Abeid, Mellad	B	70,42
Prof Adj	Ahrend, Janet	D	66G,13C,66D
Prof Adj	Aldridge, Rachel		61
Prof Adj	Brummett, Jennifer	M	63B
Prof Adj	Carper, Nick	M	62A,62B
Prof Adj	Cook, Christopher	M	63A,11
Prof Adj	Cox, Daniel	B	65,50
Inst	Fague, David	M	29,46,47
Prof Adj	Foster, Erin	B	64D
Prof Adj	Goodwin, Donald	M	66A
Prof Adj	Grove, Paul	D	70,13A,13B,13C
Prof Adj	Halvorson, Marjory		61
Assoc Prof	Hekmatpanah, Kevin	D	11,12A,38,51,62C
Prof Adj	Holcombe, Ross		63C,63D
Prof Adj	Howard-Phillips, Amanda		62A
Prof Adj	Hunter, Colleen	D	66A,66D
Prof Adj	Jacobson, Sheri	M	64A
Prof Adj	McCann, Brian		62D
Prof Adj	Millham, Michael	B	70,57
Prof Adj	Moody, Erica	M	62E
Prof Adj	Parkin, Christopher	M	64E
Prof Adj	Phillips, Chip	M	64C
Prof Adj	Plewniak, Kim	M	62D
Prof Adj	Plowman, Gary	M	64B
Prof Adj	Presley, Greg	D	66A
Prof Adj	Preston, Darnelle		61
Assoc Prof	Spittal, Robert	D	37,11,42,48,60B
Assoc Prof	Uhlenkott, Gary	M	13A,66A,13B,35H,47
Prof	Waters, J. Kevin	D	10
Prof Adj	Webster, Margee		66A
Asst Prof	Westerhaus, Timothy P.	M	11,60A,61

WA0450 Grays Harbor College
Department of Music
1620 Edward P. Smith Dr
Aberdeen, WA 98520
(360) 538-4188   Fax: (360) 532-6716
www.ghc.edu
E-mail: bdyer@ghc.edu

2 Year Institution

Chair: Robert C. Richardson, 80A

PT	Boyer, Laura	B	66
PT	Jenson, Don	M	62
	Logan, Shelly	M	36,61
	Neisinger, Robert	M	61,65
	Richardson, Robert C.	M	13,11,37,38,47
PT	Stensager, Eugene	M	64
PT	Wellington, Craig	M	63

WA0460 Highline Community College
Department of Music
2400 S. 240th St.
PO Box 98000
Seattle, WA 98198
(206) 878-3710 x3445
flightline.highline.edu/music/index.php
E-mail: bthomas@highline.edu

Chair: Benjamin Thomas, 80A

	Akaka, Sheryl		
	Glover, Sandra	D	61
	Stegall, Sydney Wallace	D	13,14,10B,14F,10
	Thomas, Benjamin	D	65
	Zimberg, Todd		

WA0480 Lower Columbia College
Department of Music
1600 Maple St
Longview, WA 98632-0310
(360) 442-2680   Fax: (360) 442-2609
www.lowercolumbia.edu
E-mail: kharbaugh@lowercolumbia.edu

2 Year Institution

Chair: Gary B. Nyberg, 80A
Dean: Fran Zarubick, 80A

Inst	Groff, Dale	B	34D,34G,34C,34F,29B
Inst	Harbaugh, Kurt	B	50
Inst	Heller, Ryan	M	36,39,61
Inst	Heredia, Joel	M	47,63A,46,29,35A
Inst	Hinshaw, Susan	B	39,61
	Nyberg, Gary B.	D	13,10,37,63D,54
Inst	Sherry, Martin	D	13,11,12A,14,64A

WA0550 Northwest University
Department of Music
5520 108th Ave NE Box 579
Kirkland, WA 98083-0579
(425) 889-5255   Fax: (425) 889-7815
www.northwestu.edu
E-mail: bill.owen@northwestu.edu

4 Year Institution

Chair: William E. Owen, 80A

Adj Prof	Berteig, Laurence	B	10F
Adj Prof	Boone, Kathleen	M	64B,64C,70,32E,13C
Adj Prof	Castro, Edward	D	63A,32E
Adj	Erickson, Sheryl	B	32
Asst Prof	Fells, Mizue	M	66A,66D,13C,11,20
Adj	Fleming, Diana M.	M	66A
Adj Prof	Hall, Heidi	M	61
Adj Prof	Hamar, Jon	M	29,62C,62D,32E,51
Adj Prof	Korn, Steven	B	65,32E
Adj Prof	Kwiram, Bernie	B	61
Adj Prof	Measel, Jane	M	64A
Assoc Prof	Owen, William E.	M	36,60,12A,40,31A

Assoc Prof	Prettyman, Ken	M	10A,13A,13B,46,47
Inst	Rasmussen, Brenda	B	11,31A,36,13A
Adj Prof	Tjoelker, Joy	B	66A
Adj Prof	Voulgaris, Virginia	D	61
Adj	Wight, Doug	B	70

WA0600 Olympic College
Department of Music
1600 Chester Ave
Bremerton, WA 98337-1699
(360) 475-7117   Fax: (360) 475-7689
www.olympic.edu
E-mail: tfraser@olympic.edu

2 Year Institution

Chair, & Dir., Jazz Classic: Teresa L. Fraser, 80A,80F

PT	Dell, Craig	B	70
PT	Demmert, Wade C.	B	63D
PT	Ferguson, Roger L.	B	70
Inst	Fraser, Teresa L.	M	36,47,13A,40
PT	Hooker, Tracy	B	63A,63B,63
PT	Ivester, Mark D.	B	65
PT	Knoop, Tracy V.	B	64C,64E
PT	Ohls, Ray	B	66A,66
PT	Paxson, Joyce M.	B	61
PT	Ryker, Pamela R.	M	64A
PT	Stoican, Michael	B	70
PT	Trainer, Robert F.	D	61,11
PT	Trainer, Susan	B	39,61
PT	Welle, Talman J.	M	66A,66D
Inst	White, Rick	D	11,29A,20,37,46

WA0650 Pacific Lutheran University
School of Arts & Communication
1010 122 St South
Tacoma, WA 98447-0003
(253) 535-7150   Fax: (253) 536-5063
www.plu.edu/music
E-mail: music@plu.edu

4 Year Institution
Member of NASM

Dean: Cameron Bennett, 80A
Chair: David P. Robbins, 80A

Lect PT	Agent, Betty	M	62B
Lect PT	Anderson, Clipper		62D
Lect PT	Bell Hanson, Jeffrey	D	38
Prof	Bennett, Cameron	D	66A
Lect PT	Bowman, Jennifer	M	66A
Senior Lect PT	Brown, Elizabeth	B	70
Asst Prof	Brown, James L.	D	61,39
Lect PT	Buchanan, Marlette	M	61
Lect PT	Burns, Noelle	M	64B
Senior Lect PT	Campos, LeeAnne	B	61
Lect	Castro, Ed	D	63A
Lect PT	Clubb, Maurice		62D
Senior Lect PT	Daverso, Denise	M	61
Assoc Prof	Deacon-Joyner, David	D	47,29
Lect PT	English, Aaron	B	10C,10D
Lect PT	Evans, Paul	B	63D
Asst Prof	Ezhokina, Oksana	D	66A,66B,66C,66
Asst Prof	Galante, Brian Edward		36,10,60A,32D
Lect PT	Gilliam, Jason	M	63D
Asst Prof	Gillie, Gina	M	13C,63B
Lect PT	Guhr, Glen	D	61
Lect PT	Habedank, Kathryn	B	41,67C
Senior Lect PT	Harty, Jane	D	66A
Senior Lect PT	Houston, Janeanne	M	61
Lect PT	Howland, Stephen	D	70
Senior Lect PT	Johnson, Barry	M	61
Lect PT	Joyner, Maria	B	65
Lect PT	Knudson, Donna	M	32B
Lect PT	Kramlich, Daniel	B	66A
Lect PT	Leisawitz, Jeffrey	B	10C,10D,10F
Asst Prof	Lyman, Zachary	M	13,63A
Lect PT	Manning, Mary	B	62A
Lect PT	Milanese, Jessica	B	61
Assoc Prof	Nance, Richard	D	60,36
Vstng Inst	Nole, Nancy	M	32,32B
Lect PT	Peterson, Francine	M	64D
Lect PT	Pettit, Joseph	B	66G
Lect PT	Plagemann, Melissa	M	61
Asst Prof	Poppe, Donna	M	62D
Asst Prof	Powell, Edwin C.	D	37,41,32E,60B
Lect PT	Reid, Clement	M	10
Senior Lect PT	Rhyne, Jennifer	D	64A
Lect PT	Rine, Craig	B	64C
Prof	Robbins, David P.	M	13,50,65
Asst Prof	Ronning, Svend John	D	62A
Lect PT	Sieden, Cyndia	B	61
Lect PT	Steighner, Erik	D	64E
Lect PT	Stephens, Charles R.	B	61
Lect PT	Strong, Timothy	M	66A
Lect PT	Takekawa, Miho	M	65
Assoc Prof	Tegels, Paul	D	66G
Lect PT	Treat, Richard	M	62C
Senior Lect PT	Walker, Diana	M	66A
Lect PT	Wetherington, John M.	B	32E
Lect PT	Winkle, Keith	M	63C
Lect PT	Wooster, Pat	B	62E
Prof	Youtz, Gregory	D	10,13,14,43
Lect PT	Zylstra, Nancy	M	61

WA0700 Peninsula College
Department of Music
1502 E Lauridsen Blvd
Port Angeles, WA 98362-6660
(360) 452-9277 x 6437   Fax: (360) 457-8100
www.pc.ctc.edu
E-mail: djones@pencol.edu

2 Year Institution

Adj PT	Grier, George	M	11,13,32D,47,65
	Jones, David P.	M	13,10F,10
Adj PT	Livingston, Jaie	M	61
Adj PT	McClain, Denise		61
Prof Adj	Rambeau, Deborah	D	66A,66B,66C,66D
Prof	Thompson, Fred	D	41
Adj PT	Williams, Jay	M	46,47

WA0750 Pierce College
Department of Music
9401 Farwest Dr SW
Lakewood, WA 98498-1919
(253) 964-6220   Fax: (253) 840-8388
www.pierce.ctc.edu
E-mail: jknudtse@pierce.ctc.edu

2 Year Institution

Chair: Jere Knudtsen, 80A

PT	Connie, Meredith	M	70,11,41
PT	Davidson, Heidi	M	61,66A,11,13A
	Jasinski, Mark	M	62A,38,32
PT	Jones, Peter	B	34D
PT	Kandi, Kareem	B	47,64E
Inst	Knudtsen, Jere	D	11,37,47,64A,29A
PT	Lambert, Evin R.	M	11,36,66A,61,13A
PT	Litch, Randy	B	70
Inst	Owen, Kenneth L.	M	11,61,36,66A,13A

WA0800 Seattle Pacific University
School of Music
3307 Third Ave W
Seattle, WA 98119-1997
(206) 281-2205   Fax: (206) 281-2430
www.spu.edu
E-mail: ramonaho@spu.edu

4 Year Institution
Member of NASM

Chair: Ramona A. Holmes, 80A

PT	Adams, Dan	M	65
PT	Alvarez, Ian M.		32E
Asst Prof	Anderson, David	M	36,20G
PT	Brennand, Meg	B	62C
Assoc Prof	Brown, Carlene J.	D	12A,13,33
PT	Burnett, Rodger	M	63B
PT	Capp, Myrna	D	66A,66B,32I,20A
PT	Catford, Julian	B	70
PT	De Barros, Paul	B	29
PT	Doiron, Michelle E.	B	65B
PT	Gowers, Todd B.	B	62D
PT	Gresso, Selina	B	64B
PT	Haight, Catherine M.	B	61
PT	Haight, Ronald S.	B	34,35C,35D
PT	Halm, Jack L.	M	32D

Prof	Hanson, Eric A.	D	60,12A,38,10,64C
Prof	Holmes, Ramona A.	D	14,32,38,62
PT	Hussong, Suzi R.	B	62E
Prof	Johnson, Wayne D.	D	11,12A,66A,66C
PT	Kantor, Mary L.	B	64C
PT	Koreski, Jacinta T.	M	61,39
PT	Kramlich, Dan P.	M	36,66A
PT	Kwiram, Bernie R.	M	61
PT	Lieurance, Neil W.	M	36
Inst	Marsh, Gerry Jon	M	34,35C,37,10
PT	Martin, Les K.	M	66G,66H
Assoc Prof	Newby, Stephen M.	D	10,36
Asst Prof	Okun, Matthew J.		
PT	Park, William B.		47,63C
Assoc Prof	Parks, Andrew	D	61,31A,12A,36
PT	Pendergrass, Ken E.	M	36
PT	Peterson, Francine G.	M	64D
PT	Schneider, Matt	B	64E
PT	Sigars, Julie Kae	M	61
PT	Swan, Robert	D	66A
PT	Talvi, Ilkka	C	62A
PT	Zabelle, Kim A.	M	62A,62B,67A,51

WA0850 Seattle University
Department of Fine Arts
901 12th Ave Box 222000
Seattle, WA 98122-4338
(206) 296-5360   Fax: (206) 296-5433
www.seattleu.edu/artsci/finearts/
E-mail: talleys@seattleu.edu

4 Year Institution

Chair: Josef Venker, SJ, 80A

Inst	Kouratachvili, Tinatin	M	32C,32E
Inst	Morris, Quinton	A	41
Asst Prof	Sherman, Joy	D	11,36,40,61
Inst	Wopat, Ann	M	61,32I,32A,32B,32C

WA0860 Shoreline Community College
Department of Music
16101 Greenwood Ave N
Shoreline, WA 98133-5667
(206) 546-4687   Fax: (206) 546-5881
www.shore.ctc.edu
E-mail: jjunkins@shoreline.edu

2 Year Institution, Programs & Degrees

Dean: Norma Goldstein, 80A
Co-Chair: Jeff Junkinsmith, 80A
Co-Chair: Bruce Spitz, 80A

Inst	Azevedo, Helena	M	66A,66D
Inst	Byington, Jensina	M	13,66A,66D
Inst	Dolacky, Susan	M	11,39,61,66D,54
Inst	Ehrlich, Barry	M	13,11,37,63C,63D
	Enlow, Charles	D	66D,40,54,39
	Ennis, Sue	M	35,10C
	Fordham, Matthew	B	35A,35B,35C,35D,35G
	Friedman, Tamara	M	66A
	Groom, Cody		34
	Junkinsmith, Jeff	D	13,66A,10
	Kim, Steve		62D,47,53
Inst	Lokken, Fred	B	61
Inst	Malott, Steve	B	35A,35B,35C,35D
Inst	Matesky, Nancy	M	13,66A,66D
	Mitchell, Erin	M	52
	Moran, Tom		
Inst	Noreen, Ken	M	37
	Peterson, Rai		34
Inst	Reid, Doug	M	47,64E,53,46,29
	Richard, Sarah	M	61,52
Inst	Spitz, Bruce	M	66,34,35,13L
	Stecker-Thorsen, Meg	M	61
	Vaicekonis, Dainius	D	66A

WA0900 Skagit Valley College
Department of Music
2405 College Way
Mount Vernon, WA 98273
(360) 416-7655   Fax: (360) 416-7698
www.skagit.edu
E-mail: diane.johnson@skagit.edu

2 Year Institution

Chair: Diane Johnson, 80A

PT	Atterbury, Rick		65
PT	Bethea, Stephanie	M	13,10,64A
PT	Brossard, Marilyn	M	66A,66D,66B
PT	Fejeran, Vince		47,63C,37,46
Prof	Johnson, Diane	D	36,61,54,11,20
PT	Savage, John		66A,70

WA0940 Spokane Community College
Department of Music
1810 N Greene St # MS-2011
Spokane, WA 99207-5320
(509)533-7381   Fax: (509)533-8059
www.scc.spokane.edu/

2 Year Institution

Chair: Mary Ann Gilpin, 80A

	Gilpin, Mary Ann	M	11,32

WA0950 Spokane Falls Community College
Department of Music-MS 3150
3410 W Fort George Wright Dr
Spokane, WA 99224-5288
(509) 533-3720   Fax: (509) 533-3528
www.spokanefalls.edu
E-mail: geraldk@spokanefalls.edu

2 Year Institution

Chair: Gerald A. Krumbholz, 80A

Inst PT	Amend, Holly	M	63C,63D
Inst PT	Butler, Louise		62C
Inst PT	Cotter, Daniel	M	38,64C,13B,13C
PT	Drumm, Melissa Percy	M	61,40
Inst	Edighoffer, Gary B.	M	64A,64E,35D
Inst	Gamberoni, Steve		35C,35G
Inst	Guerrero, Rosi E.	D	66A,66D,13A,13B,13D
Emeritus	Halversen, Paul J.	M	
Inst	Krumbholz, Gerald A.	D	13A,13B,13C,13D,10C
Inst	Lansing, Nathan	M	36,40,13B,13C,13A
Inst PT	McCollim, Danny		45,66A,35D,47,35A
Inst PT	Meyer, Pam		35C
Inst PT	Potter, Shelley		51,62A,20,13A,13D
Inst PT	Shields, John Paul		70
Inst PT	Westrick, Rick		65
Inst PT	Yang, Zhao	D	66C,13A,13B,13C,13D
Inst PT	Zyskowski, Marty	M	65,50,37

WA0960 Tacoma Community College
Department of Music
6501 S 19th St
Tacoma, WA 98466-6139
(253) 460-4374   Fax: (253) 460-4378
www.tacoma.ctc.edu
E-mail: jfalskow@tacomacc.edu

2 Year Institution

Division Chair: David Endicott, 80A
Music Chair: John Falskow, 80A,80H

PT	Buser, Charles	B	70
FT	Falskow, John	D	37,63A,38,11,13
PT	Fulton, Carolyn J.	PhD	20
PT	Renander, Cindy	D	64C,11
PT	Stevens, Eric	B	46

WA0980 Trinity Lutheran College
Department of Music & Worship
2802 Wetmore Ave
Everett, WA 98201
(425) 249-4763   Fax: (425) 392-0404
www.tlc.edu
E-mail: michael.miller@TLC.edu

4 Year Institution

Dean: Jeff Mallinson, 80A
Chair: Michael Miller, 80A

	Aamodt-Nelson, Norma	M	31A
	Bendickson, Sean	B	10D,70
	Larsen, Karin	B	66B
	Mathews, Lee	M	36,60A
	Miller, Michael	M	32D,36,60A
	Thomas, Vicky	M	20

WA1000 Univ of Puget Sound
School of Music #1076
1500 N Warner St
Tacoma, WA 98416-1076
(253) 879-3700   Fax: (253) 879-2906
www.pugetsound.edu
E-mail: kward@pugetsound.edu

4 Year Institution
Member of NASM

Director: Keith C. Ward, 80A

Adj	Adam, Joseph J.	D	66G,66H
Prof	Block, Geoffrey	D	12A
Asst Prof	Brown, Gwynne Kuhner	M	12A,29A,13C,20,12B
Adj	Burnett, Rodger	M	49,63B
Adj	Christie, Tim	M	62A
Adj	Delos, Michael	B	61
Adj	Edwards, Huw	M	38
Adj	Flygare, Karla	M	48,64A
Adj	Folsom, Gunnar	M	65,32E
Adj	Harris, Paul K.	D	12A,11,13B
Prof	Hulbert, Duane	D	66A,13C
Assoc Prof	Hutchinson, Robert G.	D	13,10A
Adj	Knoop, Tracy	B	46
Adj	Kowalski, Christina	M	61
Prof	Krueger, Pat	D	32
Adj	Lehmann, Kathryn	M	61
Adj	Lyman, Anne E.	D	36,13C
Asst Prof	Morris, Gerard	M	37,60B,11
Adj	Nelson, Jennifer	M	48,64C
Asst Prof	Padula, Dawn M.	D	61,39
Adj	Rafanelli, Paul	M	64D
Adj	Ramee, Joyce	B	62B,32E
Artist in Res	Requiro, David	M	62C,41,42
Adj	Rice, Douglas	M	70
Assoc Prof	Sampen, Maria	D	62A,13C,42
Adj	Schermer, Stephen	M	62D,32E
Adj	Schultz, Ryan	D	63D
Adj	Scott, Judson	M	63A,49
Prof	Stambuk, Tanya	D	66A,66C,66D
Prof	Ward, Keith C.	D	11,35A
Adj	Williams, Dan	M	64B
Adj	Williams, Mark	M	63C
Adj	Winkler, Fred	M	64E,41,32E
Adj	Wooster, Pat	M	62E
Asst Prof	Zophi, Steven	D	36,60A,61

A1050 Univ of Washington
School of Music
Box 353450
Seattle, WA 98195-3450
(206) 543-1201   Fax: (206) 685-9499
www.music.washington.edu
E-mail: karpen@u.washington.edu

4 Year Institution, Graduate School

Master of Arts in Music Education, Master of Arts in Music History, Master of Arts in Music Theory, Master of Arts in Ethnomusicology, Master of Music in Composition, PhD in Ethnomusicology, PhD in Music Theory, PhD in Music Education, DMA in Composition, PhD in Music History, DMA in Choral Conducting, Master of Music in Choral Conducting, Master of Music in Brass Performance, Master of Music in Harp Performance, Master of Music in Harpischord Performance, Master of Music in Jazz Studies & Improv Music, Master of Music in Percussion Performance, Master of Music in Organ Performance, Master of Music in String Performance, Master of Music in Woodwind Performance, DMA in Brass Performance, DMA in Harp Performance, DMA in Harpsichord Performance, DMA in Percussion Performance, DMA in Piano Performance, DMA in Organ Performance, DMA in String Performance, DMA in Vocal Performance, DMA in Woodwind Performance, DMA in Instrumental Conducting, Master of Music in Instrumental Conducting, Master of Music in Piano Performance, Master of Music in Vocal Performance

Director: Richard Karpen, 80A
Dir., Graduate Studies: JoAnn Taricani, 80C
Associate Director: Joel F. Durand, 80H

Assoc Prof Emeritus	Benshoof, Kenneth W.	M	13,10,54
Artist in Res PT	Bergman, Luke	B	29
Prof	Bernard, Jonathan	D	13
Assoc Prof	Boers, Geoffrey	D	60,36,38
Prof	Bozarth, George	D	12A,12
Artist in Res PT	Brockman, Michael	M	64E
Artist in Res PT	Byrdwell, Phyllis	M	31A,47
Other	Cady-Willanger, Susan		66F
Prof	Campbell, Patricia Shehan	D	32A,20A,12C,32B,20D
Prof Emeritus	Carlsen, James	D	34,12B,12F,12,12C
Assoc Prof	Collier, Thomas	M	47,65,20G
Artist in Res PT	Crusoe, Michael	B	65
Prof	Demorest, Steven M.	PhD	32B,32C,36
Prof Emeritus	Dempster, Stuart R.	M	63C,43
Assoc Prof	Dudley, Shannon	D	20D
Prof	Durand, Joel F.	D	13,10,34
Prof Emeritus	Ellingson, Ter	D	20D
Prof Emeritus	Eros, Peter	DIPL	60,39
Artist in Res PT	Fair, Jeffrey	M	63B
Artist in Res PT	Gordon, David	DIPL	63A
Artist in Res PT	Gordon, Valerie Muzzolini	B	62E
Prof Emeritus	Grossman, Arthur	DIPL	41,64D
Assoc Prof	Harper, Thomas	M	61
Asst Prof	Heneghan, Aine	D	13
Prof Emeritus	Hokanson, Randolph		66A
Assoc Prof Emeritus	Jussila, Clyde	M	32,62,64
Prof Emeritus	Kaplan, Abraham	DIPL	60,36,38
Prof Emeritus	Kappy, David	M	13A,41,48,63B
Prof	Karpen, Richard	D	13,10,34
Prof Emeritus	Kechley, Gerald	M	13,10,36
Artist in Res PT	Kelsey, Philip	M	39
Artist in Res PT	Kline, Rhonda	B	66C
Artist in Res PT	Korn, Steve	M	29A
Artist in Res PT	Krimsky, Seth	M	64D
Artist in Res PT	Lieberman, Barry	DIPL	62D
Prof Emeritus	Lundquist, Barbara Reeder	D	32,12E
Prof	McCabe, Robin	D	41,66A
Prof Emeritus	McColl, William	DIPL	41,64C
Assoc Prof Emeritus	Michaelian, Patricia	DIPL	41,66A,66B
Prof	Morrison, Steven J.	D	32
Artist in Res PT	Nelson, Jennifer	M	64C
Artist in Res PT	Olka, Christopher	M	63D
Assoc Prof	Pampin, Juan	D	10,34
Artist in Res PT	Partington, Michael	B	67D
Lect PT	Pasternack, Jonathan R.	D	38,39,12A,60B
Prof	Patterson, Ronald	DIPL	41,62A
Lect PT	Radke, Fred		29,63A
Lect PT	Radke, Gina Funes		61
Lect FT	Ragan, Kari	D	61
Prof Emeritus	Rahn, John	D	13,10,34
Assoc Prof Emeritus	Rosinbum, Ralph R.	M	39
Assoc Prof	Rumph, Stephen	D	12,12A
Prof	Saks, Toby	M	41,62C
Prof	Salzman, Timothy	M	60,37,49,63D
Assoc Prof Emeritus	Schuyler, Philip	D	20A,20D
Prof	Seales, Marc	B	66A,29
Prof	Sheppard, Craig D.	M	66A
Asst Prof	Shin, Donna	M	64A
Prof Emeritus	Siki, Bela	DIPL	66A
Prof Emeritus	Smith, William O.	M	13,10,43
Artist in Res PT	Spicciati, Shannon	B	64B
Prof	Starr, Lawrence	D	12A,12,20G
Prof Emeritus	Staryk, Steven S.	DIPL	41,62A
Prof Emeritus	Storch, Laila	B	41,64B
Asst Prof	Sunardi, Christina	D	20D
Assoc Prof	Taricani, JoAnn	D	12A,12
Prof	Terry, Carole	D	66G,66H,67E
Prof Emerita	Thome, Diane	D	13,10
Librarian	Tsou, Judy	M	16
Emerita	Vokolek, Pamela	M	62E,41
Assoc Prof	Vu, Cuong	B	29,63A
Assoc Prof	Watras, Melia	D	62B
Other	Wood, Douglas	B	66F
Asst Prof	Wyers, Giselle Eleanor	D	36,61
Artist in Res PT	Yamamoto, Ko-Ichiro	M	63C

WA1100 Walla Walla University
Department of Music
204 S College Ave
College Place, WA 99324-1198
(509) 527-2561   Fax: (509) 527-2177
music.wallawalla.edu
E-mail: karin.thompson@wallawalla.edu

4 Year Institution
Member of NASM

Chair: Karin E. Thompson, 80A

Adj	Agidius, Michael	M	47
Assoc Prof	Beck, Brandon	M	37,63,60B,38,32C
Adj	Berry, William	B	63A
Adj	Coleman, Ron	B	64C
Adj	Cree, Christopher	M	65
Adj	Diamond, Shirley A.	D	64E,64C,32E
Adj	Foster, Erin	M	64D
Adj	Gish, Benjamin	M	62C,62D
Adj	Gourley, Sonja	B	61
Adj	Irland, Jeremy	M	61,11
Adj	Izquierdo, Pablo	M	64B
Adj	Janis, Christine	D	61
Adj	Kinne, Wafia	M	66A
Adj	Kravig, Dean	M	63B
Adj	LeFevre, Michael	B	70
Adj	Lineberger, Rhonda	M	32B
Adj	Lynch, Phil	B	70
Adj	Pih, Kevin	M	63D
Prof	Richter, Leonard	D	66A,66B,13A,13B
Prof	Ritz, Lyn	D	62A,62B,42,13,10F
Prof	Scott, Kraig	D	36,31A,66G,66H,60A
Adj	Spence, Chelsea	M	62E
Adj	Stilson, Alicia	B	64A
Adj	Takemoto, Maya	B	62A
Assoc Prof	Thompson, Karin E.	D	62C,20,12A,42,13C
Adj	Vining-Stauffer, Kristin	B	66A

WA1150 Washington State University
School of Music
PO Box 645300
Pullman, WA 99164-5300
(509) 335-3898   Fax: (509) 335-4245
libarts.wsu.edu/music
E-mail: music@wsu.edu

4 Year Institution, Graduate School
Member of NASM

Master of Arts in Music

Director: Greg Yasinitsky, 80A
Dir., Undergraduate Studies: Richard Kriehn, 80B
Coord., Graduate Studies: Julie Wieck, 80C

Prof Emeritus	Argersinger, Charles	D	13,10,66A
Assoc Prof	Arksey, Meredith	DMA	13,62A,62B
Asst Prof	Aubin, Matthew	DMA	63B,38
Prof	Berthiaume, Gerald B.	DMA	66A
	Bjur, David	B	35C,35D,35G
Inst	Blasco, Scott	DMA	13,10A,10B
Asst Prof	Boden-Luethi, Ruth	DMA	62C,62D,13,51,42
Inst	Carter, Brian	DMA	61
Clinical Assoc Prof	Converse, Sheila K.	D	61,15
Inst	Dickey, Christopher J.	M	13C,11,63D
Inst	Edwards, Brent	M	37
Inst	Hagelganz, David	M	47,64E,29,53
Assoc Prof	Hare, Ryan	DMA	13,64D,10A,10B
Clinical Assoc Prof	Hower, Don	M	37,63C
Inst	Hungerford, Del	DMA	32A,32B,32C,11
Prof	Jarvis, David	M	10,47,50,65,14C
Inst	Kriehn, Richard	M	11,70,62A,34
Asst Prof	Luethi, Dean A.	M	36,47,61,32D
Assoc Prof	McCarthy, Keri E.	D	64B,12A,13,11,12C
Inst	Mielke, Michelle	M	66A,66B
	Payne, William	DMA	16
Asst Prof	Pham, Danh	DMA	32D,60B,48
Asst Prof	Savage, Jeffrey R.	DMA	66A,66B,66C,13C
Asst Prof	Savage, Karen Hsiao	DMA	66A,66C
Inst	Schneider, Jill L.	DMA	66G
Inst	Scott, Shannon	D	64C,12A
	Severance, David	B	66F
Inst	Snider, Dave	M	62D,47
Inst	Snider, Denise G.	M	29A,11
Assoc Prof	Turnbull, David	DMA	49,63A,67E,37
Inst	Ward, Brian	M	66A,10D,13C,14C,29A
Assoc Prof	Wieck, Julie	DMA	39,61,54
Prof	Wiest, Lori J.	D	36,55B,61,60A

Clinical Prof	Yasinitsky, Ann	M	48,64A
Prof	Yasinitsky, Greg	DMA	47,64E,29,10F,10A

WA1200 Wenatchee Valley College
Department of Music
1300 5th St
Wenatchee, WA 98801-1741
(509) 664-2565   Fax: (509) 664-2552
www.wvc.edu
E-mail: jiwaasa@wvc.edu

2 Year Institution

Dean, Transfer Education: Robert C. Branch, 80D

Inst	Caulkins, Tamara		
		M	70,13A,13B,13C,13D
PT	Cortez, Juan		43
PT	Crowe, Nancy	M	61
Inst	Hibbett, Michael	D	11,36
	Iwaasa, Juel	M	10
PT	Rappe, Terri	M	66C,66D,66A
PT	Vandivort, Roger	M	47

WA1250 Western Washington University
Department of Music
516 High St PAC 273
Bellingham, WA 98225-9107
(360) 650-3130   Fax: (360) 650-7538
www.wwu.edu/music/
E-mail: lesley.sommer@wwu.edu

4 Year Institution, Graduate School
Member of NASM

Master of Arts in Music Theory, Master of Music in Composition, Master of Music in Performance, Master of Music in Conducting, Master of Music in Music Education, Master of Music in History & Literature

Chair: Lesley Sommer, 80A

Asst Prof	Bianco, Christopher	M	37,38
Inst PT	Bone, Amber Sudduth		61
Prof	Briggs, Roger	D	43,10F,10,66A
Inst	Cook, Edward		61
Inst PT	Cox, Gregory A.	M	63C
Asst Prof	Donnellan, Grant	M	41,42
Assoc Prof	Feingold, David W.	M	11,70,13
Asst Prof	Fitzpatrick, Tim	M	61
Assoc Prof	Friesen, John	D	13,51,62C
Assoc Prof	Gilliam, Jeffrey	M	66A,66C
Inst PT	Green, Vincent	M	63A,13
Assoc Prof	Guelker-Cone, Leslie	D	36,39,61
Asst Prof	Hamilton, Bruce	M	10A,10B,13
Asst Prof	Jovanovic, Milica Jelaca	D	66A,66B
Inst PT	Kean, Eric	M	62B
Inst PT	McCarthy, Lisa	B	64A
Inst PT	Musa, Ben	M	63D
Inst PT	Peterson, Francine G.	M	64D
Inst	Pitzer, Robert M.	M	32,32B,32C,32H
Inst PT	Reed, Richard	M	63B
Inst PT	Roozendaal, Jay		61
Prof	Rutschman, Carla J.	D	12A,12,32,63D
Assoc Prof	Rutschman, Edward R.	D	13A,13,11,12A,12
Assoc Prof	Schwede, Walter	M	51,62,62A
Inst PT	Shaw, Arthur E.		60B
Asst Prof	Sommer, Lesley	M	13,10,45
Inst PT	Steege, David J.	B	66F
Emeritus	Terey-Smith, Mary	D	
Inst PT	Tucker, Rob	M	65
Prof	Van Boer, Bertil H.	D	13E,12,55,12A
Emeritus	Wallace, David	D	
Inst PT	Whitman, Jill		62E
Inst PT	Widrig, Judith	D	66C
Prof	Zoro, Eugene S.	M	48,64

WA1300 Whitman College
Department of Music
345 Boyer Ave
Walla Walla, WA 99362
(509) 527-5232   Fax: (509) 527-4925
www.whitman.edu
E-mail: waggonbi@whitman.edu

4 Year Institution

Chair: Lee D. Thompson, 80A

Adj	Baglio, Genevieve	M	61
Adj	Berry, William		63A
Senior Lect	Crawford, Peter	M	34,48,37,66A
Adj	Curtis, Laura	M	66A
Assoc Prof	Dixon, Edward E.	D	38,62C,13C,62D
Adj	Dodds, Amy	M	62A,62B,13
Adj	Earnest, John David		10
Prof	Glenn, David B.	M	10,47,63D,29
Adj	Lynch, Phil		70
Adj	Martin, Spencer	M	65
Adj	Newton, Robyn		61
Adj	Parnicky, Lori M.		64A
Prof	Pickett, Susan	D	13A,13,12A,51,62A
Adj	Potts, Leo W.		64C,64E
Adj	Scott, Kraig		66G
Adj	St. Hilaire, Jon		70
Adj	Takemoto, Maya	B	62A
Prof	Thompson, Lee D.	D	12A,39,66A,66C
Adj	Vining-Stauffer, Kristin	B	66A
Senior Lect	Wood, Jackie Coe		66A
Adj	Zizzi, Karen	M	61

WA1350 Whitworth University
Department of Music
W 300 Hawthorne Rd
Spokane, WA 99251-1701
(509) 777-3280   Fax: (509) 777-3739
www.whitworth.edu
E-mail: dhansen@whitworth.edu

4 Year Institution
Member of NASM

Chair: Deborah Hansen, 80A

Adj	Asplin, David	D	10A
Adj	Baldwin, Karen	M	32B
Assoc Prof	Baldwin, Philip R.	D	62A,41,38,60B
Adj	Bodinger, John	D	66G
Adj	Bogue, Bryan	M	13G,10F
Adj	Bottelli, Roberta	M	62C
Adj	Brewster, David	M	66A,66D
Assoc Prof	Brody, Ben	D	31A,60,11,12A
Adj	Brummett, Jennifer	M	63B
Adj	Dutton, David	B	64B
Assoc Prof	Edstrom, Brent	M	10,66A,34,47,13
Adj	Fague, Kyla	M	37,60
Adj	Feller, Lynne	D	64D
Adj	Fennessy, Ann	M	61
Adj	Grove, Paul	D	70
Prof	Hafso, Marc A.	D	60,36,10A,32D,61
Assoc Prof	Hansen, Deborah	D	60,36,13B
Adj	Hungerford, Del	D	64C,51
Adj	Jablonsky, Eugene	B	62D
Adj	Jacobson, Sheri	M	64A
Prof	Keberle, Daniel	D	47,63A,29,29A
Adj	McNally, Patrick	M	62D
Asst Prof	Miller, Scott D.	DMA	61,39
Adj	Moe, Eric	M	63A
Adj	Moody, Earecka	M	62E
Lect	Parkin, Chris	M	64E,46,47
Lect	Porter, Amy		61
Adj	Raymond, Paul	M	65
Adj	Rhodes, Beverly	M	66A,66C
Prof	Schoepflin, Judith	D	66A,66D,16,66B
Adj	Shook, Lee	M	32E
Lect	Shook, Thomas M.	D	29,13B,13C
Prof	Strauch, Richard	D	37,63D,60B,41,12A
Adj	Wakeley, David A.	M	29A
Adj	Wee-Yang, Jeannette	M	62B
Adj	Westrick, Rick	B	65
Adj	Windham, Susan	M	61
Adj	Zimmerman, Charles R.	M	61

WA1400 Yakima Valley College
Department of Music
PO Box 22520
Yakima, WA 98907-2520
(509) 574-4839   Fax: (509) 574-6860
www2.yvcc.edu/music/
E-mail: speterson@yvcc.edu

2 Year Institution

Dean, Arts & Sciences: Judith Kjellman, 80A
Dir., Artist/Performance Series: Kelly Robbins, 80F

Inst	Blink, David	M	47,13,63A,29
Adj	Durkee, Jim	M	70
Adj	Krueger, Karen Merola	M	66D
Adj	Price, Larry	B	29
Adj	Schilperoort, Anne	M	66A

WI0050 Alverno College
Department of Music
3400 South 43rd St
Milwaukee, WI 53234-3922
(414) 382-6162   Fax: (414) 382-6354
www.alverno.edu
E-mail: peter.roller@alverno.edu

4 Year Institution
Member of NASM

Chair: Peter Roller, 80A
Dir., Artist/Performance Series: David Ravel, 80F

Inst PT	Dexter-Schabow, Nancy	M	33
Prof Emerita	Hueller, Mary	D	66G
Inst PT	Jirovec, Mary	M	64C
Asst Prof	Kamenski, Michael	M	60,13,34
Assoc Prof	Knight, Diane	M	33
Inst PT	Lockett, Wendelyn	M	61
Emerita	Matts, Kathleen	B	61
Inst PT	Nielsen, Linda	D	64A
Asst Prof	Pufall, Molly	M	36
Asst Prof	Roller, Peter	M	20G,70,20H
Inst PT	Schecher, Mary	M	
Inst PT	Short, Charlie	M	65
Assoc Prof Emerita	Shurr, Janet	M	55B,62,67
Emeritus	Stornido, Carl	M	63
Inst PT	Stryck, Mary	M	33

WI0100 Beloit College
Department of Music
700 College St
Beloit, WI 53511
(608) 363-2366   Fax: (608) 363-2718
wwW.beloit.edu
E-mail: pohlb@beloit.edu

4 Year Institution

Acting Chair: Susan Rice, 80A

Prof	Anderson, David	M	66A,38,66C,13E,42
Prof	Barolsky, Daniel G.	D	13,12
Inst PT	Cramer, Christopher		70,41
Inst PT	Dolphin, Amber	M	62A,62B
Inst PT	Dunegan, Martha	M	62C
Inst PT	Farina, Jack		65
Inst PT	Geoffrey, Suzanne		64B
Inst PT	Jursik, Katherine		62D
Inst PT	Marshall, Elizabeth	D	64A,48
Inst PT	Meyers, John		63A,47
Inst PT	Newman, David		66A,66D,41
Inst PT	Nie, Emily		67C
Assoc Prof	Nie, James Ian	D	66A,66C,35D,35C
Inst PT	Pemberton, Rick		70
Inst PT	Pickart, John		62C
Prof	Premezzi, Renato	M	66A,41
Asst Prof	Rice, Susan	DMA	40,36,13A
Inst PT	Roberdeau, Dan		64C
Inst PT	Rosing, Carol A.		64D
Inst PT	Sams, Jennifer		61
Prof Emeritus	Shepherd, Eudora	B	61
Inst PT	Siler, Christine		61
Prof	Slominski, Tes	D	14,15
Inst PT	Suarez, Jeff		63B

Directory of Institutions

Inst PT	Svanoe, Anders		64E,41
Prof	Tomaro, Robert		29A
Inst PT	Wilfong, Glen		37,63A
Inst PT	Wilson, Jordan	M	61
Inst PT	Yi, Young		62A,62B
Prof Emeritus	Yount, Max	D	66G,66H

WI0150 Cardinal Stritch University

Department of Music
6801 N Yates Rd
Milwaukee, WI 53217-3985
(414) 410-4349   Fax: (414) 410-4111
www.stritch.edu
E-mail: dwking@stritch.edu

4 Year Institution

Chair: Dennis W. King, 80A

Adj	Baime, Peter	B	70,43
Adj	Batcho, Michael J.	M	60A
Adj	Belich, Kay	M	39,61,32B
Adj	Carlton, David	M	49,62C,62D
Adj	Davis, Mark	B	47,29,53
Adj	Frank, Jolita	M	66A
Adj	Greif, Carol	M	61,39
Adj	Jirovec, Mary	M	64C
Assoc Prof	King, Dennis W.	D	60,11,32,13
Adj	Klabunde, Timothy A.	B	62A
Adj	Korducki, Linda Nielsen	M	64A
Assoc Prof	Kwak, Eun-Joo	D	66A,66B,66C,42,12A
Adj	Maske, Dan	D	10,34
Adj	Mihopulos, Michael	B	66F
Adj	Norden, James C.	D	66A
Adj	Tuhuilka, Olga	B	62B
Adj	Verhaalen, Marion	D	66D
Inst	Wenzel, Scott	M	14,65,55,50,20A
Adj	Zitoun, Adrien	M	62C

WI0200 Carroll College

Department of Music
100 N East Ave
Waukesha, WI 53186-3103
(262) 524-7188   Fax: (262) 524-7181
www.carrollu.edu/music
E-mail: lharper@carrollu.edu

4 Year Institution

Director of Bands: Larry D. Harper, 80A
Dir., Artist/Performance Series: Hugo J. Hartig, 80F

Assoc Prof	Boerger, Kristina G.	D	36
Adj	Carpenter, Keith A.		
Asst Prof	Couch, Leon		
Adj	Courtier, Jessica M.		
Lect PT	Daya, Shanti Rajaratnam	M	66D
Adj	Doepke, Kari J.		
Prof	Harper, Larry D.	D	60,37,41,63B
Prof	Hartig, Hugo J.	D	13,10F,10,12A
Adj	Kashino, Motoaki		
PT	Kirby, Rick B.	M	47
Adj	Lange, Peter V.		
Adj	Matthys, Joel W.		
Adj	Moore, Carol A.		11,32B
Adj	O'Meally, Christine		
Adj	Schreiber, David R.		
Lect PT	Solfest-Wallis, Cindy L.	D	64A

WI0250 Carthage College

Department of Music
2001 Alford Park Dr
Kenosha, WI 53140-1994
(262) 511-2159   Fax: (262) 551-5868
www.carthage.edu/music
E-mail: cness@carthage.edu

4 Year Institution
Member of NASM

Chair: Peter D. Dennee, 80A
Dir., Artist Series: Jane Livingston, 80F

Asst Prof	Berg, Gregory	M	11,61,39
Adj	Boresi, Matthew	M	54,39
Adj	Butler, Jocelyn	M	62C,42
PT	Cardamone, Melissa	M	66C
PT	Carmichael, Steve R.	M	47,11,29
Assoc Prof	Dennee, Peter D.	D	32C,32D,36,60,40
Assoc Prof	Garcia-Novelli, Eduardo	D	36,40,32D,13C,60
Adj	Georg, Klaus	M	61
Adj	Gorke, Sarah	M	61
Asst Prof	Haines, Amy	M	11,61
Adj	Hall, Crystal	M	64B
Assoc Prof	Hodges, Woodrow	D	13,13E,32E,64D
PT	Hoskins, Richard	D	66G,31A
PT	Hull, Allison	D	61
PT	James, Steve		72
Adj	Kozakis, Michael		65
Asst Prof	Livingston, Jane	M	66A,66D,66B
PT	Marks, Adam	M	66A,42
PT	Masloski, Deborah	D	66A
Adj	Miller, Matthew		70,41
Adj	Morse-Hambrock, Anne		62E
Adj	Murphey, Maura	M	32B
Asst Prof	Ness, Corinne	M	61,54,32B,39
Asst Prof	Petering, Mark D.	D	10,13,34
Assoc Prof	Ripley, James	D	37,41,32E,60B,38
PT	Rivest, Darlene	M	62B,32E,38,62A,41
	Schwaber, Lorian Stein	B	61
PT	Seigfried, Karl E.	D	70,62D,11
Asst Prof	Shapovalov, Dimitri	D	12A,66D,36,66A
PT	Snoza, Melissa	M	64A,41
PT	Suarez, Karen		63B,41
PT	Tegge, Scott	M	63D
PT	Tillman-Kemp, Gloria		
Adj	Todd, Colette	M	32D,36,47
PT	Tracy, Shawn	M	64C
PT	Von Hoff, Paul	M	63C,63D
PT	Wood, Kevin	M	63A
Adj	Woodrum, Jennifer		64C

WI0300 Concordia University Wisconsin

Department of Music
12800 N Lake Shore Dr
Mequon, WI 53097-2418
(262) 243-5700   Fax: (262) 243-4351
www.cuw.edu
E-mail: louis.menchaca@cuw.edu

4 Year Institution, Graduate School

Master of Arts

Chair: Louis A. Menchaca, 80A

PT	Atwater, Jennifer	M	63A
PT	Babinec, Lori	B	64D
PT	Baker, Brian	M	62D
Prof	Behnke, John A.	D	10,44,66G,31A
PT	Betz, Michael	M	62
PT	Cohen, Bonnie	B	
Asst Prof	Freese, James	M	66G
PT	Hibler, John	M	64E
PT	Hoelscher, Mark		
PT	Kachelmeier, Diane		66C
Prof	Kosche, Kenneth	D	13,60,10,36,31A
PT	Lane, Diane	M	61
Asst Prof	Little, Lynn	M	34,13
PT	Lundin, Paul	M	62A
Prof	Menchaca, Louis A.	D	13A,13,60,37,29
PT	Otto, Clark	B	70
PT	Roberdeaux, Dan	B	
PT	Sander, Marie	M	64A
PT	Smirl, Terry	M	65
PT	Stephens, Mary Ann	B	
PT	Thiele, Michael	D	66A,66D
PT	Weis, Patricia	B	12A,61
PT	Williams, Kimberly	B	44

WI0350 Lawrence University
Conservatory of Music SPC 14
711 East Boldt Way
Appleton, WI 54911-5690
(920) 832-6614   Fax: (920) 832-6633
www.lawrence.edu/conservatory
E-mail: ellen.m.mitala@lawrence.edu

4 Year Institution
Member of NASM

Dean: Brian G. Pertl, 80A
Dean, Admissions: Ken Anselment, 80D
Dir., Preparatory Division: Karen Bruno, 80E

Lect	Adnyana, I Dewa Ketut Alit		20D
Prof	Anthony, Janet	M	12A,41,62C,51
Lect PT	Baruth, Philip A.	B	70
Asst Prof	Bates, Ian	PhD	13
Assoc Prof	Bell, David	M	41,64C
Inst	Benson, John Halvor		13,10
Assoc Prof	Biringer, Gene D.	D	13,10
Inst	Bozeman, Joanne H.	B	61
Prof	Bozeman, Kenneth W.	M	61
Lect PT	Buchman, Nell J.	M	66D
Lect PT	Carpenter, Kelley K.	M	32E
Lect PT	Carrothers, Bill	B	29,66A
Vstng Asst Prof	Ceballos, Sara Gross	PhD	12
Assoc Prof	Daniel, John	M	63A,42
Inst	Darling, Patricia A.	B	46
Assoc Prof	Decorsey, James H.	M	12A,41,63B
Lect	DiBella, Donna J.	B	13
Inst	Dochnahl, Jesse	M	64E,41
Other	Downing, Sonja Lynn	PhD	14,15,20D,64A,32
Artist in Res	Duesing, Dale L.	B	61
Inst	Encarnacion, Jose	D	29,64E
Inst	Erickson, Marty		63D,42
Vstng Asst Prof	Gates, John T.	D	61
Assoc Prof	George, Samantha	D	62A,41,51
Asst Prof	Gu, Wen-Lei	M	62A,41
Lect PT	Handford, Kathrine	M	66G,66H
Vstng Asst Prof	Helvering, David A.	M	13
Prof	Jordheim, Steven	M	41,64E
Lect PT	Jordheim, Suzanne	M	64A
Prof	Kautsky, Catherine C.	D	66A,66C,66E,41
Assoc Prof	Keelan, Nick	M	32,49,63C,63D
Inst	Kind, Sara	M	13
Asst Prof	Koestner, Bonnie	M	39,61
Inst	Kohlbeck-Boeckman, Anne	M	13,66A,66D,13A
Asst Prof	Lesser, Erin	M	64A
Asst Prof	Mast, Andrew	D	37,41,42,60
Inst	McCardell, Stephen	M	13,10
Lect PT	McCardell, Susan L.	B	32E
Asst Prof	McQuinn, Julie	M	12
Assoc Prof	Metcalf, Joanne	M	10A,13D,13F,12A,31G
Lect PT	Michelic, Leslie O.	B	32E
Assoc Prof	Michelic, Matthew C.	B	41,62B
Assoc Prof	Miller, Brigetta F.	M	32
Asst Prof	Mizrahi, Michael	D	66A,41
Assoc Prof	Moss, Kirk D.	D	11,32E,38,51,62
Prof	Niblock, Howard	M	13,10F,12B,41,64B
Assoc Prof	Padilla, Anthony	M	66A,66C,41,42
Lect PT	Peplin, Steve	B	70
Prof	Pertl, Brian G.	M	14
Lect PT	Planet, Janet		61
Lect PT	Post, Bryan	B	61
Assoc Prof	Post, Karen Leigh	D	61,39
Inst	Rath, Carl	M	64D,42,14C
Prof	Richeson, Dane M.	M	50,65
Vstng Prof	Salzer, Rebecca		52
Inst	Seidl, Teresa	DIPL	61
Asst Prof	Sieck, Steven	D	36,60A
Asst Prof	Spears, Steven	M	61
Asst Prof	Srinivasan, Asha	M	13,10
Assoc Prof	Stannard, Jeffrey	D	63A
Prof	Sturm, Fred	M	10,29,46,47
Assoc Prof	Swan, Phillip A.	M	36,60,61,32D,60A
Lect	Turner, Matthew	M	53
Asst Prof	Urness, Mark	M	62D,29A
Inst	Van DeLoo, Mary F.	M	66A,66B,66D
Lect PT	Walby, Catherine	M	66D
Lect PT	Wysock, Nathan	D	70
	Ziesemer, Bruce		66F

WI0400 Marian University of Fond Du Lac
Department of Music
45 S National Ave
Fond Du Lac, WI 54935-4621
(920) 926-2116   Fax: (920) 923-8751
www.marianuniversity.edu
E-mail: David.Thompson@marianuniversity.edu

4 Year Institution

Chair: David Thompson, 80A

PT	Chaudoir, Marianne	M	11,66A,66D,13A
PT	Hein, David	M	40,61
Asst Prof	Lydeen, Brian	M	64,47,37,42,64E
Prof	Thompson, David	D	13,11,14,66A,35

WI0425 Marquette Unversity
Department of Performing Arts
PO Box 1881 AMU 121
Milwaukee, WI 53201
(414) 288-7125   Fax: (414) 288-3111
www.marquette.edu
E-mail: erik.janners@marquette.edu

4 Year Institution

Chair, Performing Arts: Stephen Hudson-Mairet, 80A
Director of Music: Erik N. Janners, 80A

Lect	Carpenter, Gregory	M	36,11
Lect	Eubanks, Nathaniel	B	36
Lect	Janners, Erik N.	D	37,47,60,12,13
Lect	Konewko, Mark	M	11,35A,34,69
Lect	Laddy, Jason	D	38,37

WI0450 Milwaukee Area Technical College
Department of Music
700 W State St
Milwaukee, WI 53233-1443
(414) 297-7378   Fax: (414) 297-6935
www.matc.edu
E-mail: heighwar@matc.edu

2 Year Institution

LAS Dean: Dan Burrell, 80A
Coord., Music Program: Robbi A. Heighway, 80A

PT	Berdnikova, Natalya L.	B	11,66D
PT	Brandenburg, Julie A.	B	10D,36,61,66D
PT	Hans, Ben J.	B	11,35A,50,65
FT	Heighway, Robbi A.	M	11,13C,13D,66B,66D
PT	Klecker, Deb J.	B	11,66D
PT	Lewis, Don R.	B	11
PT	McGirr, Tom A.	B	47,62D,53
FT	Miller, Harold L.	M	10,13A,13G,20,47
FT	Peplin, Steve W.	B	10A,11,13B,47,70
PT	Smirl, Terry W.	B	53,66A,66D
PT	Taylor, Jeffrey B.	B	34D,35A,35D,35C
PT	Williams, Gary R.		47,70,53

WI0500 Mount Mary College
Department of Music
2900 N Menomonee River Pkwy
Milwaukee, WI 53222-4545
(414) 258-4810 ext. 389   Fax: (414) 256-1224
www.mtmary.edu
E-mail: duffd@mtmary.edu

4 Year Institution

Chair: Margaret V. Otwell, 80A

Inst PT	Caceres, Abraham	D	20
Inst PT	Cruz, Samantha	M	32A,32B,32C,11
Inst PT	Mitchell, James	B	70
Asst Prof	Otwell, Margaret V.	D	66A,66C,66D,66B,12A
Inst PT	Vascan, Ligia	M	40,61,36,54,29

WI0600 Northland College
Department of Music
1411 Ellis Ave
Ashland, WI 54806
(715) 682-1304   Fax: (715) 682-1308
www.northland.edu
E-mail: jglickman@northland.edu

4 Year Institution

Coordinator, Performing Arts: Joel Glickman, 80A

Asst Prof	Anderson, Jared L.	D	36,61,66A,13,12A
Prof	Glickman, Joel	M	60,32,37,38,47

WI0700 Ripon College
Department of Music
PO Box 248
Ripon, WI 54971-0248
(920) 748-8791   Fax: (920) 748-8181
www.ripon.edu
E-mail: brownle@ripon.edu

4 Year Liberal Arts Institution

Chair: Leslie Ellen Brown, 80A
Dir., Artist Series: Kurt R. Dietrich, 80F

Prof	Brown, Leslie Ellen	D	12A,13
Inst PT	Cox, Eleanor Christman	M	62C,62D,60B
Prof	Dietrich, Kurt R.	D	13,32,37,47,29
Inst PT	Dietrich, Maria K.	B	66A,66B
Inst	Graham, Seong-Kyung	M	61,32D,36,60A
Inst PT	Hardt, Adam C.	B	65
Inst PT	Hines, Edith	D	62A,62B
Prof	Kraaz, Sarah Mahler	D	12A,55,66,11,67C
Inst PT	Lawler, Dawn	D	64A
Inst PT	McMahon, Kevin	D	38
Inst PT	Nelson, William A.	M	64C,64E
Inst PT	Polcyn, Sandra	M	64D,64B,32E
Prof Emeritus	Stahura, Raymond	D	

WI0750 St Norbert College
Department of Music
100 Grant St
De Pere, WI 54115-2099
(920) 403-3112   Fax: (920) 403-4442
www.snc.edu/music
E-mail: holly.huntley@snc.edu

4 Year Institution

Director: Sarah S. Parks, 80A

Asst Prof	Cook, Linda Klein	D	63A,12,13,63B,10F
Adj Inst	Feldmann, Linda	M	61,39
Adj Inst	Gross-Hixon, Andrea	D	64B
Adj Inst	Hennessy, Michael	M	62D
Asst Prof	Henson, Blake R.		13
Asst Prof	High, Eric	M	63C,47,13,12,49
Adj Asst Prof	James, Kortney	M	64A,32,48
Asst Prof	Knight, Michael D.	D	37,60B,32E,64C,64E
Adj Inst	Liedtke, Kris	M	62
Adj Inst	Moss, Elaine	M	66C,66D,66B,66A,32A
Adj Inst	Nimmer, Rebecca		32
Asst Prof	Niu, Elaine	D	61,39,36,60A,13C
Asst Prof	Parks, Sarah S.	M	36,32D,60A,61
Adj Inst	Paulsen, Kent D.	D	36,32D,61,60,13C
Adj Inst	Robl, James	M	65
Assoc Prof	Rosewall, Michael	D	36,61,12A,13A,13B
Adj Inst	Stefiuk, Karen		64C
Adj Inst	Thier, Bethany	M	61,66,47
Adj Inst	Verkuilen, Jeffrey	B	66G

WI0770 Silver Lake College of The Holy Family
Department of Music
2406 S Alverno Rd
Manitowoc, WI 54220-9340
(920) 686-6173   Fax: (920) 684-7082
www.sl.edu
E-mail: mwagner@silver.sl.edu

4 Year Liberal Arts Institution, Graduate School
Member of NASM

Master of Music in Music Education with Kodaly Emphasis

Chair & Dir., Undergraduate Studies: Marella Wagner, 80A,80B,80F
Dir., Summer Programs & Graduate Studies: Lorna Zemke, 80C,80E,80G

Asst Prof	Carlson, Damon J.	M	60A,61,40,36
Inst	Eis, Jeremiah	M	34,48,47,60B,63
Adj	Eithun, Sandra	B	44
Adj	Pierce, Ted		63A
Adj	Shebesta, Bob	B	70
Inst	Steede, Marcus	M	62
Prof	Wagner, Marella	M	12A,13J,20
Assoc Prof	White, Perry D.	D	36,40
Prof	Zemke, Lorna	D	32,14A,29,20G

WI0800 Univ of Wisconsin-Baraboo
Department of Music
1006 Connie Rd
Baraboo, WI 53913
(608) 355-5200   Fax: (608) 356-4074
www.baraboo.uwc.edu
E-mail: claude.cailliet@uwc.edu

2 Year Institution

Chair: Claude Cailliet, 80A

Prof	Cailliet, Claude		11,13,63,37,47
Lect	Frederiksen, Clifford		70
Lect	Horjus-Lang, Deanna		36,61,11
Lect	Kallian, Sandra		66
Lect	Stich, Gerald		37

WI0801 Univ of Wisconsin-Barron County
Department of Music
1800 College Dr
Rice Lake, WI 54868
(715) 234-8176 x 5480   Fax: (715) 234-1975
www.barron.uwc.edu
E-mail: benjamin.schoening@uwc.edu

2 Year Institution

Administrator: Benjamin S. Schoening, 80A

Adj Inst	Hurst, James	M	65
Adj Inst	Johnson, Pamela	M	66D,66A,64
Adj Inst	Joosten, Mike	M	37
Adj Inst	Midboe, David J.	M	61
Adj Inst	Radley, Dan	M	63D
Asst Prof	Schoening, Benjamin S.	DMA	11,13,36,61,63
Senior Lect	Wiesner, Terry	M	54

WI0803 Univ of Wisconsin-Eau Claire
Department of Music & Theatre Art
156 Haas Fine Arts
121 Water St
Eau Claire, WI 54702-4004
(715) 836-4954   Fax: (715) 836-3952
www.uwec.edu
E-mail: murphyvb@uwec.edu

4 Year Institution
Member of NASM

Chair: Vanissa B. Murphy, 80A
Dir., Fine Arts Programming: Jennifer Lynn Brockpahler, 80F

Adj	Anderson, Robert P.	M	62D
Prof	Baca, Robert J.	M	47,63A,29
Assoc Prof	Crowell, Jeffrey W.	D	47,65
Adj	Cruciani, Lori L.	M	66A,66D
Assoc Prof	Dickerson, Randy C.	D	60,32C,37
Assoc Prof	Don, Gary W.	D	13,10F,10A
Asst Prof	Fox, Julie C.	M	52
Assoc Prof	Garvey, Christa N.	D	13B,13C,64B
Asst Prof	Jones, Ryan Patrick	D	11,12A,13,29A
Assoc Prof	Kim, Namji C.	D	66A,66D
Asst Prof	Koprowski, Melissa	D	64C,48
Prof	Lane, Timothy	D	14,48,64A
Asst Prof	Lovell, Owen C.	D	66A,66D
Adj	Moses, Richard	M	36
Asst Prof	Mowry, Mark R.	D	39,61
Prof	Murphy, Vanissa B.	D	32B,20G
Adj	O'Connor, Douglas	M	64E,47
Adj	Ormsby, Verle A.	D	63B
Adj	Ostrander, Allison	M	62B
Assoc Prof	Ostrander, Phillip A.	D	37,63C
Prof	Patterson, Donald L.	D	66A,66B,66D,66H
Adj	Pereira, Kenneth	D	61
Assoc Prof	Peters, Gretchen	D	11,12A,14
Adj	Petillot, Elizabeth A.	D	61
Asst Prof	Phillips, Nicholas S.	D	66A,66D
Assoc Prof	Rasar, Lee Anna	M	33,20G
Assoc Prof	Rieck, Alan J.	D	32C,36
Asst Prof	Rondon, Tulio J.	D	62C,32E
Assoc Prof	Sadeghpour, Mitra M.	D	61,39
Prof	Schwartzhoff, Gary R.	D	60,36
Adj	Smith, Paula M.	M	62E
Asst Prof	Wilson, Jacqueline M.	D	64D,48,13B,13C
Asst Prof	Yasuda, Nobuyoshi	M	38,62A,51
Adj	Young, Barbara G.	D	13A,32B
Prof	Young, Jerry A.	D	11,32C,63D

WI0804 Univ of Wisconsin-Fond Du Lac

Department of Music
400 University Dr
Fond Du Lac, WI 54935
(920) 929-1100   Fax: (920) 929-7640
www.fdl.uwc.edu
E-mail: patricia.eby@uwc.edu

2 Year Institution

Dean: Daniel Blankenship, 80A
Chair: Patricia Eby, 80A
Dir., Summer Programs: LeeAnn Doyle, 80G

	Combe, Charles	M	70
	Eby, Patricia	M	13,11,36,60A,47
	Elford, Scott	M	65
	Gibson, John	D	62D
	Jones, Grace	M	61
	Lydeen, Brian	M	37,64
	Rager, Dan	M	37,13,46
	Schani, Steve	M	62B
	Schrankler, Helene	B	66A
	Thompson, David	D	38

WI0806 Univ of Wisconsin-Fox Valley

Department of Music
1478 Midway Rd
Menasha, WI 54952
(920) 832-2688   Fax: (920) 832-2674
www.uwfox.uwc.edu
E-mail: lynda.zimmerman@uwc.edu

2 Year Institution

Dean: James Perry, 80A
Department Representative: Lynda Zimmerman, 80A

Lect	Davis, Cara	M	36,61,29A,11
Lect	Juhl, Aaron	M	29A
Asst Prof	Sackman, Marc L.	D	13B,37,64A,47,11
Asst Prof	Zimmerman, Lynda	M	13A,66A,66D,11

WI0808 Univ of Wisconsin-Green Bay

Department of Music
2420 Nicolet Dr
Green Bay, WI 54311-7003
(920) 465-2348   Fax: (920) 465-2890
www.uwgb.edu/music
E-mail: salernoj@uwgb.edu

4 Year Institution
Member of NASM

Dean: Scott Furlons, 80A
Chair: John Salerno, 80A

Assoc Prof	Collins, Kevin	M	37,63D
Lect PT	Collins, Nancy	M	48,64A,41
Asst Prof	Gaines, Adam W.	D	63,47,37,63A,29
Assoc Prof	Grosso, Cheryl	D	50,65,43,14,13C
Lect PT	Hall, Stefan	D	70
Lect PT	Hanke, Craig	D	62D
Asst Prof	Hansen, Eric	M	64C,37,13,32E
Assoc Prof	Kiehn, Mark T.	D	32A,66D,70,63A,32B
Lect PT	Krubsack, Kathy	M	63B
Asst Prof	Meder, Randall A.	D	60,11,36,40,32D
Assoc Prof	Meredith, Sarah A.	D	39,61,54,15
Lect PT	O'Grady, Judy	B	66C
Prof	O'Grady, Terence J.	D	13,12A,12,14,55
Lect PT	Osterbers, Janet	B	66C,66D
Lect	Parins, Linda	M	61
Lect PT	Salerno, Christine	M	40,47,66,61
Assoc Prof	Salerno, John	D	13,10,47,48,29
Asst Prof	Severtson, David		66A,13,66D,12A,66C
Lect PT	Weaver, Daniel	B	70

WI0810 Univ of Wisconsin-La Crosse

Department of Music
1725 State St
La Crosse, WI 54601
(608) 785-8409   Fax: (608) 785-6749
www.uwlax.edu/music
E-mail: cfrye@uwlax.edu

4 Year Institution
Member of NASM

Chair: Christopher B. Frye, 80A

Prof	Balfany, Gregory J.	D	47,64C,46,29
Lect	Bean, Scott	M	63D,12A,11,49
Adj	Brown, Tom	M	11,41,49,63A,63B
Adj	Clark, Derek	M	62C
Prof Emeritus	Estes, William V.	D	
Asst Prof	Fisher, Tammy M.	D	60,37,65,32,11
Prof	Frye, Christopher B.	D	13,10F,10,34
Emeritus	Grill, Joyce	M	
Prof Emeritus	Hayes, Truman	D	
Adj	Hindson, Harry	D	64
Assoc Prof	Kelly, Terence	D	11,61,54
Adj	Krause, Kristi		64B
Adj	MacDonald, Ben		70
Assoc Prof Emeritus	Mewaldt, David	M	
Lect	Moran, Kathryn	M	36,61
Lect	Quinn, Karyn	M	47,62D,46,29,13A
Lect	Richardson, David	M	36
Asst Prof	Ritterling, Soojin Kim	D	32B,32C,11,61,32A
Asst Prof Emeritus	Roggenbuck, Therese	M	
Assoc Prof	Tollefson, Mary J.	D	11,66A,66D,66B
Adj	Tristano, Barbara	M	64A
Prof	Walth, Gary Kent	D	60,11,32C,36,54
Prof Emeritus	Weekley, Dallas	D	
Assoc Prof Emeritus	Wessler, Robert	D	

WI0815 Univ of Wisconsin-Madison
School of Music
455 N Park St
Madison, WI 53706-1483
(608) 263-1900   Fax: (608) 262-8876
www.music.wisc.edu
E-mail: music@music.wisc.edu

4 Year Institution, Graduate School
Member of NASM

Master of Music in Collaborative Piano, Master of Arts in Music Theory, Master of Arts in Ethnomusicology, Master of Music in Composition, Master of Music in Performance, Master of Music in Music Education, PhD in Ethnomusicology, PhD in Music Theory, DMA in Composition, DMA in Performance, PhD in Music History, DMA in Choral Conducting, PhD in Musicology, Master of Arts in Musicology, Master of Music in String Development, PhD in Curriculum & Instruction (Music Education), Artist's Certificate

Director: John Stevens, 80A
Associate Director & Dir., Undergraduate Studies: Janet L. Jensen, 80B,80H
Dir., Graduate Studies: Todd G. Welbourne, 80C
Dir., Summer Programs & Artist Series: Chelcy L. Bowles, 80F,80G

Prof	Aley, John	M	63A
Artist in Res	Anderson, Lyle	M	69
Lect	Atz, Karen	M	62E
Prof	Bartley, Linda L.	D	64C
Artist in Res	Beia, Suzanne		62A
Prof	Blasius, Leslie	D	13
Prof PT	Bowles, Chelcy L.	D	55,67
Prof	Calderon, Javier	D	70,51
Prof	Chisholm, Sally	M	62B
Prof	Crook, David	D	12
Prof	Davis, Richard	B	39,61
Prof	Dembski, Stephen	D	10F,10
Assoc Prof	Di Sanza, Anthony E.	D	65
Prof	Dill, Charles	D	12
Asst Prof	Dobbs, Teryl L.	D	32E,32
Prof	Doing, James	M	61
Prof	Earp, Lawrence	D	11,12A,12
Prof	Farlow, William	M	39,61
Asst Prof	Faulkner, Julia	M	61
Prof	Fink, Marc	M	48,64B
Assoc Prof	Fischer, Martha	M	66A,66C,39,41
Prof	Fulmer, Mimmi	M	61
Lect	Gladstone, Bruce	M	60A,36
Asst Prof	Grabois, Daniel	M	32,49,63A
Prof	Greive, Tyrone	D	62A
Assoc Prof	Hetzler, Mark	M	63C,49
Prof	Hyer, Brian	D	13,13I
Prof	Jensen, Janet L.	D	32,62A,38,51
Assoc Prof	Johnson, Jessica G.	D	66A,66B
Prof	Jutt, Stephanie	M	64A
Prof	Karp, Parry	M	51,62C
Artist in Res	Kimball, Linda	M	63B
Prof	Koza, Julia Eklund	D	32,32D
Prof	Leckrone, Michael E.	M	60,37,20G
Prof	Moye, Felicia K.		62A
Prof	Perry, David	M	11,62A
Prof	Potter, Pamela	D	12,12C
Prof	Radano, Ronald	D	20G
Prof	Rowe, Paul	M	61
Prof	Schaffer, John D.	D	63D,49
Prof	Schwendinger, Laura Elise	D	10,43
Prof	Smith, James	M	38,51,62,60B
Prof	Stevens, John	D	63D,60B,35,10,13
Lect	Stolarik, Justin R.	D	37,60B,32E,65,10F
Prof	Stowe, J. Chappell	D	66G,55
Prof	Sutton, R. Anderson	D	11,12A,20D,14A
Prof	Swack, Jeanne	D	12A,12,67,55,67D
Prof	Taylor, Beverly	M	60,36
Prof	Taylor, Christopher		66A
Assoc Prof	Teeple, Scott	M	37,60B
Prof	Thimmig, Les	D	10,47,64E,29
Assoc Prof	Vallon, Marc	PP	64D
Prof	Vardi, Uri	M	62C
Prof	Welbourne, Todd G.	D	66A,34A,34D,43

WI0817 Univ of Wisconsin-Manitowoc
Department of Music
705 Viebahn St
Manitowoc, WI 54220-6699
(920) 683-4688   Fax: (920) 683-4776
www.uwmanitowoc.uwc.edu
E-mail: paul.thompson@uwc.edu

2 Year Transfer Institution

Dean: Martin Rupp, 80A

Chair: Paul Thompson, 80A

Prof	Arendt, Michael J.	M	37,47
Lect	Thompson, Paul	M	36,13B,13C,11

WI0825 Univ of Wisconsin-Milwaukee
Peck School of the Arts-Music
PO Box 413
Milwaukee, WI 53201-0413
(414) 229-4393   Fax: (414) 229-2776
www.uwm.edu/PSOA
E-mail: jonw@uwm.edu

4 Year Institution, Graduate School
Member of NASM

Master of Music in Collaborative Piano, Master of Music in Performance, Master of Music in Conducting, Master of Music in Music Education, Master of Music in History & Literature, Master of Music in Music Librarianship, Master of Music in Chamber Music, Master of Music in Accompanying, Master of Music in Music Theory-Composition

Chair: Jon Welstead, 80A
Dir., Institute Chamber Music: Stefan Kartman, 80F

Lect	Abend, Elena	M	66A,41
Lect	Baime, Peter	B	70
Senior Lect	Belfer, Beverly	D	13A,70
Lect	Billmann, Peter	B	70
Prof	Boico, Efim	DIPL	62A
Adj Prof	Borghesani, Dean	M	65
Lect	Brauner, Mitchell	D	12A,12,12C,11
Prof Emeritus	Burda, Pavel	M	13A,60,50,65
Lect	Burmeister, James R.	M	13A,13C
Asst Prof	Burns, Christopher	D	10,13,34,43,45
Senior Lect	Chekan, Elina	M	70
Prof	Climer, John	D	60,37,43
Lect	Colburn, Steve	M	64B
Lect	Cook, Scott A.	M	62C,51,41
Prof Emeritus	Cook, Wayne E.	M	49,63A
Lect	Corley, Scott R.	D	37
Lect	Cucunato, Lou	M	10
Prof	Deutsch, Margery	M	60,38
Prof Emeritus	Downey, John W.	D	13,10F,10,45,43
Senior Lect	Drexler, Darcy	M	62A,62B
Prof Emeritus	Duvall, William	M	39,61
Prof Emeritus	Dvorak, Thomas	M	60,37
Prof	Emmons, Scott	D	32,32C,32E
Adj Prof	Erickson, Martin	M	63D
Assoc Prof	Errante, Valerie	D	61,39
Prof	Evans, Ralph	D	62A
Asst Prof	Feay-Shaw, Sheila J.	D	32,20
Asst Prof	Flint, Gregory	B	63B
Lect	Garthee, Jeffrey A.	M	32
Lect	Gettel, Jennifer	M	61
Adj Prof	Giacobassi, Beth		64D
Prof Emeritus	Goodberg, Robert	M	41,48,64A
Lect	Haas, Connie	D	61
Lect	Hanrahan, Curt	M	47
Lect	Hansen, Gloria	M	36
Prof	Hansen, Sharon A.	D	60,36
Prof	Hartman, Kevin	M	49,63A
Assoc Prof	Heinrichs, William C.	D	13,10,34
Adj Prof	Hoelscher, Mark	M	63C
Prof Emeritus	Hollander, Jeffrey	D	66A,66D
Prof Emeritus	Horner, Jerry	M	41,62B
Inst	Hulbert, David	B	66F
Asst Prof	Izquierdo, Rene	DIPL	70,41
Prof	Jaimes, Judit		41,66A,66B,66C,42
Assoc Prof	Kartman, Stefan	D	62C,42,51,41
Prof Emeritus	Kramer, Paul	M	
Lect	Krueger, Leslie	M	66A,66D
Senior Lect	Kuhn, Judith	D	12A,14
Prof Emeritus	Laufer, Wolfgang	DIPL	62C
Assoc Prof Emeritus	Lavonis, William	D	61,39
Adj Prof	Levy, Todd		64C
Lect	Linke, David	B	70,29,47
Adj Prof	Lobotzke, Ann	M	62E
Prof Emeritus	Miller, Franklin	M	12A,12
Lect PT	Moberg, Jonathan		66F
Lect	Monhardt, Jonathan	D	10,13
Prof Emeritus	Nelson, Daniel	M	39,61
Senior Lect	Nelson-Raney, Steven	M	13A,13,29B
Lect	Noonan, Timothy	D	12A,12,11
Lect	Nunley, David	B	36
Lect	Ollmann, Kurt	M	61,39
Lect	Otwell, Margaret	D	66
Adj Prof	Padilla, Margaret	M	64,48
Assoc Prof	Peterson, Jeffry F.	M	66A,66C,66D
Senior Lect	Phillabaum, Katja	DIPL	66A,66C
Asst Prof	Rodger, Gillian	D	12A,12C,20G,20D,14
Lect	Rosenblum, Martin J.	D	12A

Adj Prof	Rosove, Lewis E.	M	62B
Lect	Ruck, Tanya Kruse	M	61,39
Inst	Schlei, Kevin	M	34
Prof Emeritus	Schmid, William	D	20G,32C,70
Prof Emeritus	Snavely, Jack	M	41,64C,64E
Adj Prof	Snyder, Laura		62D
Adj Prof	Soluri, Theodore	M	64D
Inst	Stevenson, Patricia	B	66F
Lect	Storniolo, Carl	M	65
Other	Stropes, John	B	70
Assoc Lect	Thompson, Paul	D	60,36
Prof Emeritus	Thompson, Robert	B	11,41,48,64D
Prof	Welstead, Jon	D	10,13,34,43,45
Adj Prof	Wetzel, Thomas	M	65,50
Prof Emeritus	Yannay, Yehuda	D	13,10,45,43
Assoc Prof	Zinck, Bernard F.	D	62A

WI0830 Univ of Wisconsin-Oshkosh
Department of Music
800 Algoma Blvd
Oshkosh, WI 54901-3686
(920) 424-4224   Fax: (920) 424-1266
www.uwosh.edu/music
E-mail: music@uwosh.edu

4 Year Institution
Member of NASM

Chair: Robert McWilliams, 80A
Dir., Artist Series: Bruce W. Atwell, 80F

Prof	Andrews, Joyce	M	61
Assoc Prof	Astolfi, Jeri-Mae G.	D	66D,13C
Prof	Atwell, Bruce W.	D	63B,13,11
Prof	Bahcall, Klara	M	41,62A,62B
Lect	Barnum, Eric	M	36
Lect PT	Brumbelow, Rosemary	M	64C
Lect	Brusky, Paula	D	64D,35A
Asst Prof	Chmura-Moore, Dylan Thomas	D	63C,38,11
Lect	Chybowski, Julia J.	D	12,11
Lect	Dies, David	D	13,10A
Lect	Fee, Daniel	M	32
Lect PT	Gross-Hixon, Andrea	D	64B
Lect PT	Imobersteg, John	C	72,66F
Assoc Prof	Kalman, Eli	D	66A,66D
Lect PT	Kind, Sara	M	64C
Asst Prof	Krueger, Nathan E.	D	61
Lect PT	Lethco, Leigh-Ann M.	D	32E,37,63A,32
Assoc Prof	Liske, Kenneth L.	D	32,32C,32F,32B,32D
Assoc Prof	Martin, Edward P.	D	13,10B
Lect PT	McWilliams, Heather	D	32,11,63D
Prof	McWilliams, Robert	D	37,32,29A,60B
Lect	Messner, Walter	M	35C,35D
Lect PT	Miller, Matthew	D	70
Asst Prof	Pereksta, Linda H.	D	64A
Assoc Prof	Robinson, Marty	D	63A,29A,47
Lect PT	Sachen, Andrew	M	62D
Assoc Prof	Shaw, Alison	D	65,50
Lect PT	Stephan, Charles	M	62C

WI0835 Univ of Wisconsin-Parkside
Department of Music
PO Box 2000
Kenosha, WI 53141-2000
(262) 595-2457   Fax: (262) 595-2271
www.uwp.edu
E-mail: karen.sorensen@uwp.edu

4 Year Institution

Chair: Alvaro Garcia, 80A

Adj	Bayles, David S.	B	65,50
Prof Emeritus	Bedford, Frances M.	M	66H
Assoc Prof Emeritus	Bell, Timothy R.	M	47,64C,64E,29,48
Adj	Bjorkman, Jan	M	64A
Adj	Bohn, David M.	D	20
Asst Prof	Bouterse, Ami K.	M	61,39
Adj	Bruss, Jillian	M	61
Asst Prof	Crowley, James F.	D	13,10F,10
Adj	Dissmore, Randy L.	M	62C
Assoc Prof	Eichner, Mark J.	M	60,32C,37,63A,32A
Adj	Frank, Jolita Y.	M	66D,13A
Assoc Prof	Garcia, Alvaro	M	38,62B,60,51
Adj	Geoffrey, Suzanne L.	M	64B
Adj	Gudbaur, Michael A.	B	62D
Adj	Hodges, Woodrow J.	D	64D
Adj	Hoelscher, Mark A.	M	63C,63D,49
Adj	Hull, Allison R.	D	61
Asst Prof	Johnson, Russell	M	47,29

Prof	Kinchen, James B.	D	60,36,32C
Adj	Kosmala, Diane	B	64C
Adj	Lindquist, George C.	M	41,70
Adj	Mandl, Alexander	D	62A
Prof	McKeever, James I.	D	12A,66A,66C,66B
Adj	McKeever, Susan M.	M	66A
Adj	Morse-Hambrock, Anne	B	62E
Prof Emeritus	Mueller, Frank	D	13,12
Adj	Nielsen, Linda	D	64A
Adj	Nishikiori, Fumi	M	66D,13A
Adj	Sodke, James W.	D	13A,29,35A
Asst Prof	Whitaker, Nancy L.	D	32

WI0840 Univ of Wisconsin-Platteville
Department of Fine Arts
1 University Plz
Platteville, WI 53818-3012
(608) 342-1143   Fax: (608) 342-1039
www.uwplatt.edu
E-mail: fairchig@uwplatt.edu

4 Year Institution
Member of NASM

Chair: G. Daniel Fairchild, 80A

Assoc Prof	Alcalay, Eugene C.	D	66A,66B,66C
Asst Prof	Cooper, David	D	47,49,63A,11,29A
Lect	Cordingley, Allen	M	11,64E,37,47
Lect	Cornils, Margaret A.	M	64A,11,48,66D
Lect	Day, Susan	D	61,39
Lect	Demaree, Rebekah	M	61
Prof	Demaree, Robert K.	D	12A,36
Prof	Ellis, Barry L.	D	60,37,64D,64E,32
Prof	Fairchild, G. Daniel	M	10F,11,32,63B
Lect	Fairchild, Nancy	M	32B,32A
Asst Prof	Forbes, Michael I.	D	63D,13,34
Lect	Gregg, Matthew D.		37,13
Lect	Klockow, Stephanie	D	36,32
Lect	Lienert, Keith	M	65
Lect	Marco, John	M	11,13,64C
Lect	Medisky, Laura M.	M	64B
Lect	Price-Brenner, Kevin		11,38
Lect	Price-Brenner, Paul Alan	M	11,62A,62B,34
Lect	Savage Day, Susan	D	61,54
Lect	Townsend, Bradley	M	11

WI0842 Univ of Wisconsin-Richland
Department of Music
1200 Highway 14 W
Richland Center, WI 53581
(608) 647-6186   Fax: (608) 647-2275
www.richland.uwc.edu
E-mail: james.aagaard@uwc.edu

2 Year Institution

Chair: J. Kjersgaard Aagaard, 80A
Dean: Patrick Hagen, 80A

Asst Prof	Aagaard, J. Kjersgaard	M	13,11,36,37,49
Lect	Behrens, Jeff	B	65
Lect	Berns, Kathleen	B	66A
Lect	Laubmeir, George	M	66
Lect	Miklik, Carlie	M	61
Lect	Spicer, Luke	B	64

WI0845 Univ of Wisconsin-River Falls
Department of Music
410 S 3rd St
River Falls, WI 54022-5001
(715) 425-3183   Fax: (715) 425-0668
www.uwrf.edu/music
E-mail: music@uwrf.edu

4 Year Institution
Member of NASM

Dean, College of Arts & Sciences: Terry Brown, 80A
Chair: David Milne, 80A

Assoc Prof	Barnett, Thomas	D	63A,37,13
Lect	Bjorlie, Carol	M	11,62C
Prof	Britton, Carolyn	D	11,66A,66H
Lect	Edman, Laura	M	66G

Lect	Gaynor, Rick	M	63C,49,11
Lect	Graham, Eric	M	62D
Lect	Hagedorn, Joseph	M	70
Asst Prof	Hamilton, Hilree J.	D	11,20,32A,32B,66D
Lect	Hara, Craig	M	35G,11
Lect	Hillyer, Giselle	D	62A,62B,51
	Jacobsen, Lesa L.	D	61,32C,32D,60A,36
Lect	King, Stanley	M	64B
Assoc Prof	McVey, Roger D.	D	12A,66A,66B,66C,66D
Prof	Milne, David	D	29A,47,48,64E
Lect	O'Keefe, Patrick	D	64C,48
Lect	Palmquist, Krista	D	61
Assoc Prof	Park, Jong-Won	D	36,40,61,60A
Lect	Parks, Andrew	M	63B
Prof	Roy, J. Michael	M	13,10A,10F
Lect	Scheib, Joy	M	39,61
Lect	Smith, Carole Mason	B	64D
Assoc Prof	Tjornehoj, Kris	D	38,11,60B,37,32E
Lect	Watson, Michael	M	62D
Lect	Wazanowski, Charles	M	63D

WI0847 Univ of Wisconsin-Rock County
Department of Music
2909 Kellogg Ave
Janesville, WI 53546-5606
(608) 758-6554   Fax: (608) 758-6560
rock.uwc.edu
E-mail: jsuarez@uwc.edu

2 Year Institution

Coordinator: Jeff Suarez, 80A

Prof Emeritus	Holt, Robert	M	29A
Assoc Lect	Ramsey, David		66A
Asst Prof	Suarez, Jeff	M	10,13,29,42,20G

WI0848 Univ of Wisconsin-Sheboygan
Department of Music
1 University Dr
Sheboygan, WI 53081-4760
(920) 459-6618   Fax: (920) 459-6602
sheboygan.uwc.edu
E-mail: paul.sucherman@uwc.edu

2 Year Institution

	Brunette, Jessica		
	Brusse, Allan		
	Hanes, Jill		
	Pedersen, Kathy		
	Sucherman, Paul		47
	Talbott, Christy		61
Inst PT	Vander Linden, Dan	D	36,61,66
	Zeinemann, Glenn		

WI0850 Univ of Wisconsin-Stevens Point
Department of Music
NFAC 254
1800 Portage St
Stevens Point, WI 54481
(715) 346-3107   Fax: (715) 346-3163
www.uwsp.edu/music
E-mail: pholland@uwsp.edu

4 Year Institution, Graduate School
Member of NASM

Master of Music in Music Education

Chair: Patricia C. Holland, 80A
Dean, College of Fine Arts & Dir., Artist/Performance Series: Jeff Morin, 80A,80F
Dir., Aber Suzuki Center: Patricia D'Ercole, 80F

Assoc Prof	Bender, Susan Maria	M	61,39,40
Assoc Prof	Berk, Stacey J.	M	13A,13B,64B,41,10F
Assoc Prof	Besalyan, Raffi	D	66A,66D
Prof	Bjella, Steven A.	M	41,62A,32E
Prof	Bond, Judith	D	32,32A,32B,32C
Prof	Buchman, Matthew	M	47,53,66A
Asst Prof	Caldwell, Brendan	M	37,32E,60B
Asst Prof	Connors, Sean	D	50,65
Lect	D'Ercole, Patricia	M	32
Prof	Hastings, David M.	M	64E,42,13A,13B,13C
Prof	Holland, Patricia C.	D	64D,12A,42
Staff	Hulbert, David	B	66F
Lect	James, Kortney	D	64A
Lect	Korb, Ryan		29A,65,47
Asst Prof	Lawrence, Patrick	D	63C,63D,37,32E
Assoc Prof	Leviton, Lawrence	D	11,62C
Assoc Prof	Markham, Matthew E.	D	61,39,40
Lect	Martz, Dee	B	62B
Lect	McComb, Thomas	B	70
Prof	Miles, Patrick	D	49,63B,38
Assoc Prof	Roseman, Molly J.	D	66,66A,66B,66D,66C
Prof	Splittberger-Rosen, Andrea	D	48,64C
Asst Prof	Story, David	M	62D,53,51,13A,13B
Prof	Thayer, Lucinda J.	M	60A,36,32D
Asst Prof	Turney, Brent	M	47,29A,63A
Prof	Young, Charles R.	D	13,10F,35C,10A

WI0855 Univ of Wisconsin-Stout
Department of Theatre & Music
721 3rd St East
Menomonie, WI 54751
(715) 232-2308   Fax: (715) 232-1468
www.uwstout.edu
E-mail: stauffacherp@uwstout.edu

4 Year Institution

Interim Dean: Raymond Hayes, 80A
Chair: Paul Stauffacher, 80A
Dir., Artist/Performance Series: Darrin Witucki, 80F
Dir., Summer Programs: Claudia Smith, 80G

Asst Prof	Durst, Aaron M.	D	11,37,47,64E
Prof	Liebergen, Patrick	D	11,36,61
Assoc Prof	Nelson, Margaret	D	11,32A,32B
Lect	Schmidt, Juliana	M	11,20,29A

WI0860 Univ of Wisconsin-Superior
Department of Music
Holden FAC 1100
PO Box 2000
Superior, WI 54880-2873
(715) 394-8115   Fax: (715) 394-8578
www.uwsuper.edu/music
E-mail: bgilbert@uwsuper.edu

4 Year Institution
Member of NASM

Chair: E. Beth Gilbert, 80A
Chancellor: Renee Wachter, 80A
Dir., Artist Series: Erin Aldridge, 80F

PT	Aerie, Josh	M	62C
Assoc Prof	Aldridge, Erin	D	38,62A,13C,51,60B
PT	Berryhill, Dennis	B	66F
PT	Bombardier, Brad	M	10F,64D
PT	Bustos, Nixon	M	62D
Assoc Prof	Bustos, Pamela B.	D	32E,37,48,60B,64C
Prof	Faerber, Matthew L.	D	60A,36,32D,40,13C
Asst Prof	Fingalson, Vicki	D	61,39
PT	Gibbens, Tracey	M	63C,63D,49
Prof	Gilbert, E. Beth	D	66C,66A,66B,13B
Asst Prof	Guderian, Lois Veenhoven	D	11,32
PT	Hoberg, Gwen	M	63B
PT	Hoeschen, Kevin	M	62B,20
Assoc Prof	Jones, Brett	D	65,20,50
PT	Kaiser, Tyler	B	10A,70
PT	Lawrence, Sarah	M	61
PT	Lemire, Janell	B	62E
PT	Madison, Jeffrey W.	D	61
Prof	Moore, Gregory	D	13C,47,64E,29,10A
PT	Salemink, Earl	M	63A
PT	Sandor, Alexander		66A,66D
PT	Sever, Melanie M.	M	64A
Prof	Stevlingson, Norma	D	13B,12A,66G,13E,13D
PT	Van Brunt, Laurie	M	64B

WI0862 Univ of Wisconsin-Washington Ctny
Department of Music
400 University Dr
West Bend, WI 53095
(414) 335-5200   Fax: (414) 335-5220
washington.uwc.edu
E-mail: pgibeau@uwc.edu

2 Year Institution

Chair: Peter Gibeau, 80A

Lect PT	Ackley, Dan	M	11,37,64E
Assoc Prof Emeritus	Asch, Arthur	M	13,12A,37,48
Assoc Prof	Gibeau, Peter	D	13,36,41,62D,66A
Assoc Lect	Hart, Cherie	M	66D,64A

I0865 Univ of Wisconsin-Whitewater
Department of Music
800 W Main St
Whitewater, WI 53190
(262) 472-1310   Fax: (262) 472-2808
academics.uww.edu/music
E-mail: music@uww.edu

4 Year Institution
Member of NASM

Chair: J. Michael Allsen, 80A
Dean: Mark L. McPhail, 80A
Dir., Artist/Performance Series: Sarah A. Altermatt, 80F
Dir., Summer Programs & Institutes/Festival/Workshops: Eric G. Field, 80G,80F

Prof	Allsen, J. Michael	D	11,12,14,20
Adj	Athas, James	M	66G
Lect	Boe, Karen	M	66A,66B,66C,66D
Adj	Bziukiewicz-Kulig, Brygida	M	61
Lect	Chandler, Susan	M	32E,38,62
Prof	Chung, Myung-Hee	D	66A,66B,66C
Asst Prof	Cross, Julie A.	D	61
Asst Prof	Dugan, Michael D.	D	11,47,49,63C
Prof	Ellenwood, Christian K.	D	13,64C,41
Prof	Fellows, Robin B.	D	13A,11,41,64A
Prof	Ferencz, George J.	D	13,10
Assoc Prof	Ferencz, Jane Riegel	D	67,11,12,15
Asst Prof	Gehrenbeck, Robert	D	36,40,39,60A
Adj	Geoffrey, Suzanne	M	64B
Prof	Hanson, Frank E.	D	11,49,63A
Prof	Hayes, Glenn C.	D	60,32,37
Assoc Prof	Herriott, Jeffrey	D	10,11,43,35E
Asst Prof	Holmes, Alena	D	20,32
Adj	Kimball, Linda	M	63B
Adj	League, Leanne	M	62A,62B
Lect	Leeper, Brian K.	M	61,39,54
Adj	Lindquist, George	M	70
Adj	Paulson, Jennifer Clare	D	62A,62B
Lect	Rindt, Steven	M	38
Adj	Rosing, Carol A.	M	64D
Lect	Rubinstein, Matan	D	11,29,32B,47
Lect	Scheffield, Eric	B	16
Lect	Severing, Richard	M	36,40,54,61
Assoc Prof	Sintchak, Matthew A.	D	64E,29,43,47,48
Adj	Townsend, Bradley	M	62D
Lect	Tuinstra, John	D	11,37,63D
Assoc Prof	Whitcomb, Benjamin	D	62C,13C,13E,13K,13
Lect	Wilkinson, Tobie L.	M	65,50

WI0920 Univ of Wisconsin-Marinette
Department of Music
750 W Bay Shore St
Marinette, WI 54143
(715) 735-4316   Fax: (715) 735-4307
www.marinette.uwc.edu
E-mail: dgiebler@uwc.edu

2 Year Institution

Steering Chair: Albert Bugaj, 80A

Assoc Prof	Giebler, David	M	13,11,36,41,66A

WI0922 Univ of Wisconsin-Marshfield
Department of Music-Wood Cnty
2000 W 5th St
Marshfield, WI 54449-3310
(715) 389-6542   Fax: (715) 389-6517
www.marshfield.uwc.edu
E-mail: david.delyser@uwc.edu

2 Year Institution

Asst Prof	Brunson, Richard		36
Assoc Lect	Plautz, Gigi		66A
Lect	Schubert, Linda		12A

WI0925 Univ of Wisconsin-Marathon County
Department of Music
518 S Seventh Ave
Wausau, WI 54401-5362
(715) 261-6100   Fax: (715) 261-6333
www.uwmc.uwc.edu
E-mail: russell.thorngate@uwc.edu

2 Year Institution

Music Contact: Russell Thorngate, 80A

Lect PT	Applegate, Ann	M	66D,13A,13B,66A
Lect FT	Erickson, Jeff	M	47,13C,29A,13B
Assoc Lect	Korb, Ryan		29A,65,47
Lect PT	Premeau, Chad	M	37,63
Asst Prof	Thorngate, Russell	D	11,13A,36,40,61

WI0960 Univ of Wisconsin-Waukesha
Department of Music
1500 University Dr
Waukesha, WI 53186
(262) 521-5447   Fax: (262) 521-5528
www.waukesha.uwc.edu
E-mail: craig.hurst@uwc.edu

2 Year Institution

Chair: Craig W. Hurst, 80A
Dean: Harry Muir, 80A

Prof	Hurst, Craig W.	D	11,37,47,41,63A
Lect	Patterson, Thomas	M	29A,36,11,63C
Assoc Lect	Van Brunt, Jennifer	M	61,66A,66C,66D
Asst Prof	Van Brunt, Nancy	D	13A,13B,13C,66D,40

WI1100 Viterbo University
Department of Music
900 Viterbo Dr
La Crosse, WI 54601-4777
(608) 796-3760   Fax: (608) 796-3736
www.viterbo.edu/music
E-mail: dfoust@viterbo.edu

4 Year Institution
Member of NASM

Chair: Diane Foust, 80A
Dean, Fine Arts: Timothy B. Schorr, 80A

Assoc Prof	Allen, Nancy	M	60A,32,36,54
Prof	Foust, Diane	D	36,61,13A,40,13B
Adj	Fox, Elizabeth	M	13A,13B,13C,11
Assoc Prof	Haupert, Mary Ellen	D	12A,13,34,66H
Prof	Johnson-Wilmot, Daniel	M	39,61
Adj	Kelly, Pamela	D	66D
Adj	Luckner, Brian	D	66G,31A
Adj	Rhodes, Carol	D	11
Inst	Richardson, David	M	39,66C,61
Assoc Prof	Saladino, Jean	M	61,36,13C
Asst Prof	Schoenecker, Ann Elise	D	61,36
Assoc Prof	Schorr, Timothy B.	D	66A,12A,13E,66C
Adj	Skemp-Moran, Kathryn	M	61
Inst	Stafslien, Judy	B	66C,36,61

WI1150 Wisconsin Conservatory of Music

1584 N Prospect Ave
Milwaukee, WI 53202
(414) 276-5760   Fax: (414) 276-6076
www.wcmusic.org
E-mail: info@wcmusic.org

Community Music School
Member of NASM, NGCSA

Diploma

President/CEO: Karen Deschere, 80A
Registrar: Eric Meyer, 80D
Executive Assistant: Rachel Fritz
Library Manager: Raymond Mueller

PT	Adedapo, Adekola		61,29
PT	Arndt, Kevin		35
PT	Ayers, Steven	M	66A
PT	Babbitt, John	M	62D
PT	Baime, Peter		70
PT	Baker, Mark	M	61
PT	Barczak, Bonnie Jean	B	33
PT	Bayles, David	B	65,47
PT	Bergey, Matthew	M	66A
PT	Bermudez, Ana Ruth	B	62C
PT	Brandes, Jan	M	33
PT	Breiwick, Jamie		63A
PT	Christmas, Pam	B	33
PT	Cline, Nancy		63D
PT	Clippert, Thomas	M	70
PT	Cole, Melissa	B	33
PT	Cook, Wayne	M	63A
PT	Cotton, Maurice		61,66A
PT	Craney-Welch, Karen	B	33
PT	Darga, Karen	B	33
PT	Davis, Mark	B	66A,29
PT	Day, Maxon	M	63C
PT	De Souza, Michele	B	33
PT	DeGreiff-Beisser, Andrea	M	66A
PT	Drews, Teresa	M	66A
PT	Erlandson, Elise	B	
PT	Figueroa, Robert		
PT	Finlayson, Jahmes Anthony	B	14,65
PT	Flanagan-Zitoun, Braden	M	62C
PT	Foshager, John	B	63C,66A
PT	Fritz, Rachel	M	66A
PT	Fudge, Berkeley		47,64E,53,64A,29
PT	Garcia, Elisa Mon	M	62A
PT	Gardner, Aaron	B	64E,64A
PT	Gettel, Jennifer	M	61
PT	Grimm, Stephen	B	70
PT	Grossman, Phillip	B	62A
PT	Gullickson, Sigrid	B	62A
PT	Hamann, Jeff		62D,29,47
PT	Hammers, Eric	B	33
PT	Harjung, Dan		45
PT	Henkel, Kayme	M	66A
PT	Henry, Barbara	M	66D,66
PT	Henry, Leslie	M	33
PT	Hershaft, Lisa	M	32A
PT	Jacob, Stefanie	M	13A,66A
PT	Jones, Linda	M	64C
PT	Kaiser, Pat	M	33
PT	Kammin, Benjamin	B	70
PT	Ketchum, Joseph		62A
PT	Kirkpatrick, Daniel		65
PT	Klabunde, Timothy		62A
PT	Klein, Korinthia	B	62B
PT	Larsen, Karli	B	64B,63B
PT	Lee, Jordan		35G
PT	Lesbines, Tele	B	50,65
PT	Lindquist, George	M	41,70
PT	Litvin, Michail	M	
PT	Lopez, Catherine	M	33,64C
PT	Lucernoni Haasler, JoAnn		62A
PT	Mandl, Alexander B.	M	62A
PT	Mangi, Mary		33
PT	Manno, John		
PT	Matts, Kathleen	M	39,61
PT	Medford, Sue		66A
PT	Meves, Carol	B	64A
PT	Meyer, Eric	B	35F
PT	Migliaccio, Tatiana		62A
PT	Monahan, Katie	B	33
PT	Morris, Tahlia	M	62E
PT	Mueller, Raymond	B	70,16
PT	Nishikiori, Fumi	M	66A
PT	O'Brien, Colin		70
PT	O'Brien, Linda	M	66A
PT	Oosterwaal, Amber	M	64D
PT	Paolo, James	B	62D
PT	Pardo, Danielle	M	62A,62B
PT	Pearl, Phillip	M	61
PT	Plog-Benavides, Bony	M	65
PT	Pluer, Robin		61
PT	Rambo, Kathryn	B	33
PT	Ramirez, Anthony		65
PT	Ramthum, Kerry	M	33
PT	Roginske, Lynn		13A,13
PT	Rooney, Laura G.	M	62A,62B
PT	Sabo, Marlee	M	39,61
PT	Sadler, Trevor		35G
PT	Schroeder, Matthew	B	70
PT	Seitz, Jeanette		33
PT	Sewrey, Jacques		35G
PT	Sherman, Joshua	B	65
PT	Silbergleit, Paul	B	70,47,29
PT	Song, J. Z.	M	66A
PT	Sonnentag, Kathleen		61
PT	Spethmann, Molly	B	32A
PT	Stotlar, Curtis	M	66A
PT	Terrien, Paul	B	70
PT	Thiele, Michael	M	66A
PT	Tice, Joshua	B	32A
PT	Tisdel, Scott	M	62C
PT	Tremarello, Richard	M	63B
PT	Watkins, Lenora		33
PT	Wiggin, Christine	B	33
PT	Wilson, Jack Forbes		
PT	Wirth, Mary Jo	M	33
PT	Woodall, Jeanne		61
PT	Wunsch, Doreen		64B
PT	Wysock, Nathan		70

WI1155 Wisconsin Lutheran College

Department of Music
8800 W Bluemound Rd
Milwaukee, WI 53226-4626
(414) 443-8800   Fax: (414) 443-8600
www.wlc.edu
E-mail: james.nowack@wlc.edu

4 Year Liberal Arts Institution

Chair: James Nowack, 80A

Assoc Prof	Becker, Juanita	D	66A,13,66B,66C,66D
Prof	Braun, William	D	13,10,12,55B,34
	Floeter, Valerie	M	66G,31A
PT	Fons, Carolyn	B	61,36
PT	Franke, Jerome	D	62A
PT	Haack, Donald	B	63C,63D
PT	Hibler, John	M	64A,64E,64C
PT	Hirschmann, Craig	M	10A,44,66G
PT	Krubsack, Kathryn	M	63B
PT	Najoom, Dennis	M	63A
Assoc Prof	Nowack, James	D	60,36,13C
PT	Swery, James	M	65
PT	Tamburello, John	M	70,20A,20B
PT	Topolovec, David	B	62B,62C,62D
Inst	Treuden, Terry	M	37,47,32,10F
PT	Wunch, Doreen	M	64B
PT	Zitoun, Adrien	M	62C

WV0050 Alderson-Broaddus College

Department of Music
101 College Hill Dr
PO Box 2126
Philippi, WV 26416
(304) 457-6200   Fax: (304) 457-6239
www.ab.edu
E-mail: lindseylm@ab.edu

4 Year Institution

Chair: Lauren Lindsey, 80A

Assoc Prof	Boey, Hooi Yin	D	66A,66D,20,66B,66C
Prof	Bracey, Judson F.	D	13,10
PT	Chiado, Joshua	B	65
PT	Cottrill, Heather	M	61,32A,32B
Prof	DeWitt, Timothy L.	D	49,63A,13E,63B,63C
Asst Prof	Gould, Valerie	M	32E,34,37,41,60B
Asst Prof	Hall, Lewis R.	M	32,40,54,61
Asst Prof	Lindsey, Lauren	D	12A,36,40,61
PT	Lindsey, Logan	B	29A,41,49,63D
Assoc Prof	Long, Lillian F.	M	61,66C,66G,39,44
PT	Vaughan, John	M	70

WV0100 Bethany College
Department of Vis. & Perf. Arts - Music
Steinman Hall
Main St
Bethany, WV 26032
(304) 829-7329 Fax: (304) 829-7528
www.bethanywv.edu
E-mail: drudari@bethanywv.edu

4 Year, Private, Non-Profit, Liberal Arts Institution

Music Contact & Dir., Artist Series: David J. Rudari, 80A,80F

Lect	Carey, Aaron L.	B	41,62,70
Asst Prof	Collaros, Pandel Lee	M	70,62,66A,46
Lect	Irwin, Jeffrey	M	62
Lect	Lee, Sun Jung	M	66A,66C,66D
Asst Prof	Rudari, David J.	M	61,36,12A,32B,54
Lect	White, Joseph M.	B	65,50,37,63,64

WV0200 Concord College
Department of Music
PO Box 1000
Athens, WV 24712
(304) 384-5275 Fax: (304) 384-3384
www.concord.edu
E-mail: mainlandt@concord.edu

4 Year Institution

Chair: Jack Sheffler, 80A
Dir., Artist Series: Timothy L. Mainland, 80F

	Baldwin, Nathan Taylor	M	66C,61
	Cangelosi, Casey	M	61,65,29,34
Prof	Mainland, Timothy L.	D	13,10,70,10F,62
Asst Prof	Miller, Josh	M	36,61,32D,11,60A
	Peak, Linda	M	32
Assoc Prof	Smith, J. W.	DMA	11,12A,66A,66B,66D
Prof	Turner, Dean W.	D	48,64
Adj	Wyatt, Ariana	M	11,61
Asst Prof	Zamzow, Laura	D	11,63D,60B,32,37

WV0250 Davis & Elkins College
Department of Fine & Perf. Arts
100 Campus Dr
Elkins, WV 26241
(304) 637-1212 Fax: (304) 637-1287
www.dewv.edu
E-mail: darasa@dewv.edu

4 Year Liberal Arts Institution

Chair, Fine and Performing Arts: April L. Daras, 80A

Lect PT	Marshall, Elizabeth	M	61,36,40
Lect PT	Masten, Rob	M	29,63,65,47,46
Adj Lect	Maynard, Seth	B	70
Lect PT	Stalnaker, Donna	M	11,12A,32B,66A,66H

WV0300 Fairmont State University
School of Fine Arts
Wallman Hall
1201 Locust Ave Rm 304
Fairmont, WV 26554
(304) 367-4219 Fax: (304) 367-4248
www.fairmontstate.edu
E-mail: plach@fairmontstate.edu

4 Year Institution

Dean, Fine Arts: Peter Lach, 80A
Dir., Music Preparatory Division: J. Patrick Joyce, 80E
Associate Dean, Fine Arts: Constance Edwards, 80H

PT	Ashton, John H.	M	38,63A,63B
Assoc Prof	Bennett, Mary Lynne	D	66B,66A,66D,66,66C
Assoc Prof	Edwards, Constance	D	64D,12,11,12A,10F
Asst Prof	Eichenbaum, Daniel	D	13,10,11
PT	Hall, W. Randall	M	64B,64C,64E,48
Assoc Prof	Huffman, Valarie A.	D	37,32,63D,32E,49
PT	Joyce, J. Patrick	D	70,12,42
PT	Morrison, John	M	62,66C
Prof	Patterson, Anne L.	PhD	11,12A,32A
Prof Emeritus	Poland, Jeffrey T.	D	32D,36,61,60
Prof Emeritus	Schooley, John	M	13,49,63D,62D
PT	Schoonmaker, Matt	M	65,50
PT	Skidmore, Dorothy L.	M	64A
Asst Prof	Spears, Samuel B.	D	32D,36,61,60A

WV0350 Glenville State College
Department of Music
200 High St
Glenville, WV 26351-1292
(304) 462-7361 x 7340 Fax: (304) 462-4407
www.glenville.edu
E-mail: Sheri.Skidmore@glenville.edu

4 Year Institution

Coordinator & Dir., Undergraduate Studies: Lloyd E. Bone, Jr., 80A,80B

Asst Prof	Bone, Lloyd E.	M	12A,49,63,37,11
Inst	Brenner, Liza	M	
Asst Prof	Chapman, Duane	M	
Asst Prof	Dody, Teresa D.	D	61,13C,13K,32B,32D
Inst	Griffin, Buddy	M	62,34,35
Asst Prof	Lewis, David P.	D	64,37,41,12A,32E
Assoc Prof	McKinney, John S.	M	50,65,34,60B,41
Adj	White, Anita		66

WV0400 Marshall University
Department of Music
One John Marshall Dr
Huntington, WV 25755-2232
(304) 696-3117 Fax: (304) 696-4379
www.marshall.edu/cofa/music
E-mail: castlebe@marshall.edu

4 Year Institution, Graduate School
Member of NASM

Master of Arts in Performance, Master of Arts in Music Education, Master of Arts in Teaching in Music Education, Master of Arts in History & Literature, Master of Arts in Music Theory-Composition

Interim Director: David Castleberry, 80A
Dir., Graduate Studies: Michael Stroeher, 80C
Dir., Admissions: Jennifer R. Parsons, 80D
Dir., Insitute/Festival/Workshop: Steven Barnett, 80F
Dir., Insitute/Festival/Workshop: W. Edwin Bingham, 80F
Dir., Artist/Performance Series: Solen Dikener, 80F

Asst Prof	Alves, Julio	M	70,13
Assoc Prof	Barnett, Steven	M	10F,32E,37,60
Asst Prof	Bingham, Ann Marie	D	12A,64B,64C,32E
Prof	Bingham, W. Edwin	D	47,64E,64D,29
Prof	Castleberry, David	D	60,12A,36,61
Inst PT	Cushing, Alanna B.	M	66A,66C
Inst PT	Daniel, Jane	D	12A,11
	Dempsey, Paul E.	B	66F
Assoc Prof	Dikener, Solen	D	11,12A,62C,62D
Prof	Dobbs, Linda M.	M	39,61
Prof	Dobbs, Wendell B.	D	11,13,41,48,64A
Assoc Prof	Hall, Steven	M	14,47,50,65
Inst PT	Hatfield, Grover 'Clancy'	M	70
Inst PT	Holbrook-Bratka, Branita A.	M	61
Inst PT	Johnson, Pamela A.	M	32
Inst PT	Lawson, Kay	M	32,64D
Prof	Lawson, Stephen J.	D	13,63B,29,49,37
Inst PT	Markun, Mila M.	M	32A,66A,66C,66D
Prof	Miller, Ben F.	D	11,50,65,35A,37
Inst PT	Palton, George A.	B	63D
Inst PT	Pappas, Joan H.	M	11
Asst Prof	Parsons, Sean	D	29,46,47,66A
Prof	Petteys, Leslie	D	66,66A,66B,66C,12
Inst PT	Rous, Bruce	M	13,66D
Assoc Prof	Saunders, Martin	M	63A,53,49,47,34
Prof	Smith, Elizabeth Reed	D	38,41,51,62A,62B
Prof	Stickler, Larry W.	D	36,32B,32C,61,32D
Prof	Stroeher, Michael	D	63D,49,63C,32,29
Asst Prof	Stroeher, Vicki P.		11,12,13,14
Asst Prof	Vauth, Henning	D	66A,66C,66D,13C
Inst PT	Williams, Don A.	D	64C,64E
Inst PT	Wolfe, Jeffrey L.	M	34,29A,47
Asst Prof	Wray, Robert	M	32,60,61
Inst PT	Zabel, Albert	M	44,66G,31A,10,66C
Assoc Prof	Zanter, Mark J.	D	13,29,10,70,34

WV0440 Ohio Valley University
Department of Music
1 Campus View Dr
Vienna, WV 26105-8000
(877) 466-8668
www.ovu.edu
E-mail: steve.hardy@ovu.edu

4 Year Institution

Dean: Steven Hardy, 80A

Asst Prof	Berry, James	D	11,12,13,33,61
Inst	Clark, Courtney	B	40
Inst	Cornell, Ernest	B	47
Lect	Hamm, Laura	B	32,36,66A,66D,66C

WV0500 Potomac State College of WV Univ
Department of Music
101 Fort Ave
Keyser, WV 26726
(304) 788-6965   Fax: (304) 788-6847
www.potomacstatecollege.edu
E-mail: jahawkins@mail.wvu.edu

2 Year Institution

Music Contact: John A. Hawkins, 80A

Prof Emeritus	Davis, Richard A.	M	13,60,12A,36,61
Prof	Hawkins, John A.	D	13A,13,11,36,66
PT	Kesner, Fred	M	37,47

WV0550 Shepherd University
Department of Music
Frank Creative Arts Center
PO Box 5000
Shepherdstown, WV 25443
(304) 876-5555   Fax: (304) 876-0955
www.shepherd.edu/musicweb
E-mail: mmccoy@shepherd.edu

Limited Graduate School
Member of NASM

Master of Music Education

Chair: Robert W. Tudor, 80A
Dir., Preparatory Division: Lisa Oswald, 80E

Asst Prof	Adams, Kurtis B.	D	47,46,13
PT	Austin-Stone, Heather	M	62A,62B,11
Prof	Beard, Robert Scott	D	66,13C,13A,66B,66C
PT	Booth, Adam	M	11
PT	Botterbusch, Duane A.	M	62D
PT	Cameron, Wayne	M	63A
PT	Carpenter, Susan	M	66A
PT	Carter, Daniel	M	63B
Asst Prof	Cook, Mark Andrew	D	13,29B,47,46,10
PT	Czarkowski, Stephen	M	62C,11,51
PT	Drosinos, David	B	64C
PT	Duane, Carol Rose	M	66A
PT	Evers, Brooke E.	M	61
PT	Feasly, William	M	70,13C
Assoc Prof	Gonzol, David J.	D	32,12A
PT	Humphreys, Michelle	B	65
Asst Prof	Jones, Erik Reid	D	36,39,40,60A,61
PT	King, Mark	M	66G,66H
PT	Koch, Jeremy	M	64E
PT	Kuhn, Lois	M	32
PT	Lincoln-DeCusatis, Nathan J.	D	10,13,34
PT	Marsh, David		62D,53
PT	Miller, Daniel J.	B	66A
PT	Mullenax, Gary	M	66A,11,66D
PT	Munro, Anne	B	64A,48,38,51
PT	Polonchak, Richard	M	64D
PT	Quade, Christopher	M	63D
PT	Regan, Joseph	M	61
Assoc Prof	Renninger, Laura Ann	D	11,12A,12F,14
PT	Rumpf, Randy	M	32E
PT	Ryon, Jim	M	63C
PT	Shaw, Ronnie		65
PT	Shook, Gregory	B	64B
PT	Shrader, Mary Kathryn	M	62
	Tudor, Robert W.	D	61,39,54
PT	Turchi, Elizabeth	M	61

WV0560 Univ of Charleston
Department of Music
2300 MacCorkle Ave SE
Charleston, WV 25304-1045
(304) 357-4905   Fax: (304) 357-4715
www.ucwv.edu
E-mail: jjanisch@ucwv.edu

4 Year Institution

Chair: Joseph Janisch, 80A

Adj	Brightbill, Janet	B	66C,66A
Asst Prof	Janisch, Joseph	D	36,60,32,13A,32B
Adj	Kirkpatrick, Mary Beth	M	62A,62B,62C,62D
Adj	Lange, James	M	70
Adj	Van Dalsom-Boggs, Mariel	M	61
Assoc Prof	Wright, Barbara	D	13A,13,12A,12,66G

WV0600 West Liberty University
Music Division
CSC 125
208 University Dr
West Liberty, WV 26074-1082
(304) 336-8006   Fax: (304) 336-8056
www.westliberty.edu
E-mail: rbrown@westliberty.edu

4 Year Institution
Member of NASM

Interim Chair, Arts & Communication: Richard L. Brown, 80A
Interim Chair: Matthew D. Harder, 80A

Prof	Baldauff, Brian	M	65,37
Asst Prof	Barrick, Christopher	D	64,11,41,34,47
Adj	Billock, Becky	D	66A
Prof	Brown, Richard L.	D	32,63D,72,11
Asst Prof	Cowan, Linda	D	61
Adj Prof	Day, Angela	D	61
Assoc Prof	De Jaager, Alfred R.	M	36,32D,60,11
Adj	Driscoll, Robin		64B
Adj	Elliott, Scott	M	70
Assoc Prof	Harder, Matthew D.	D	65,34B,34D,10A,10B
Assoc Prof	Inkster, Matthew	D	63A,63B,37,47,49
Adj	Keeling, Ryan		61
Adj Inst	Kumer, Wendy	M	64A
Assoc Prof	Lee, Gerald K.	D	66A,66B,66C,66D
Adj	Peck, Jamie		34
Adj	Robinson, Evan		63C
Asst Prof	Stephan-Robinson, Anna K.	M	13B,13C,13F
Adj	Tignor, Scott	D	63D

WV0650 West Virginia Inst of Technology
Department of Music
405 Fayette Pike
Montgomery, WV 25136
(304)442-3192   Fax: (304)442-3059
www.wvutech.edu
E-mail: tech-admissions@mail.wvu.edu

4 Year Institution

Chair: Frederick Meyer, 80A

Assoc Prof	Baker, Guy O.	M	60,36,61
Prof	Martyn, Charles F.	D	37,47,64A,64C,64E
Prof	Meyer, Frederick	D	13,32,48,64B
PT	Morris, Hamilton		63A

WV0700 West Virginia State University
Department of Music
CB4
PO Box 1000
Institute, WV 25112-5100
(304) 766-3196   Fax: (304) 766-5100
www.wvstateu.edu
E-mail: swoodar1@wvstateu.edu

4 Year Institution

Chair: Brenda M. Vanderford, 80A

Asst Prof	Johnson, Dirk	D	36
Adj	Lawson, David		64
PT	Porter, David	B	63A,34
Inst	Ross, John	M	13,64A,11
Assoc Prof	Vanderford, Brenda M.	M	13A,13,11,66G,31A
Asst Prof	Waltner, Anne	D	66A
PT	Washington, Phil	M	11,29B,70
PT	Wood, Jennifer	M	62A
Asst Prof	Woodard, Scott	M	37,47,32C,63,49

WV0750 West Virginia University
CAC-School of Music
PO Box 6111
Morgantown, WV 26506-6111
(304) 293-5511   Fax: (304) 293-7491
music.wvu.edu
E-mail: keith.jackson@mail.wvu.edu

4 Year Institution, Graduate School
Member of NASM

Master of Music in Composition, Master of Music in Music Theory, Master of Music in Performance, Master of Music in Music Education, Master of Music in History & Literature, PhD in Music Education, DMA in Composition, DMA in Performance, Master of Music in Collaborative Piano

Chair: Keith Jackson, 80A
Dean: Paul K. Kreider, 80A
Dir., Graduate Studies: Cynthia Anderson, 80C

Prof	Amstutz, Peter	D	66A,66C
Assoc Prof	Anderson, Cynthia	M	13,48,64B
Assoc Prof	Arnold, Mitchell A.	D	38,60B
Prof	Beall, John	D	13,10F,10,43
Assoc Prof	Bess, David	D	32
Vstng Asst Prof	Campbell, Timothy	D	36
Assoc Prof Emeritus	Catalfano, Joyce A.	M	48,64A
Assoc Prof	Crotty, John E.	D	13A,13
Asst Prof	Drury, Jay	M	37
Lect PT	Elliott, Scott	M	70,47
Prof Emeritus	Faini, Philip J.	M	20A,65
Assoc Prof	Ferer, Mary T.	D	11,12A,12
Prof	Haller, William P.	D	13,12A,66G,31A
Assoc Prof	Hendricks, John	M	32,37
Asst Prof	Hileman, Lynn	D	64D,13C,13B,13A,13D
Asst Prof	Houde, Andrea	D	13C,32,41,42,62B
Prof Emeritus	Hudson, Barton	D	12A,12,66H
Asst Prof	Ibrahim, Michael	M	64E,32E,48
Prof	Jackson, Keith	M	47,49,63C,63D
Assoc Prof Emeritus	Johnson, Curtis	M	64E,29
Prof	Kefferstan, Christine	D	66A,66B,66C,66D
Lect PT	Kisner, Janna	M	32A,32B
Assoc Prof	Koehler, Hope E.	D	61
Lect PT	Koehler, William D.	D	61,39
Assoc Prof	Kohn, Andrew	D	62D
Lect PT	Love, Diana	D	32B,32C
Assoc Prof	Mauro, Lucy	D	66A,66C,66B
Lect PT	McCollum, David	M	63D
Assoc Prof	McTeer, Mikylah Myers	D	62A,32E,41,42
Prof	Miltenberger, James E.	D	12A,66A,66B,29
Lect	Nichter, Christopher	M	32E,37,60B
Prof Emeritus	Paglialunga, Augusto N.	M	61
Assoc Prof Emerita	Peri, Janis-Rozena	M	61
Asst Prof	Perna, Nicholas K.	D	61
Lect	Plitnik, Brian	M	63C,49
Asst Prof	Redding, Jeffery	D	36,60A
Prof	Robbins, Janet	D	32
Assoc Prof	Scea, Paul	M	64E,29,47
Assoc Prof	Schwartz, Sandra M.	D	32D,32G
Assoc Prof	Shannon, Kathleen	D	36,32,60
Prof	Skidmore, William	M	13,41,62C
Lect PT	Spivak, Mandy A.	D	61
Prof Emerita	Sturm, Connie Arrau	D	66A,66B,66D
Prof	Taddie, David	D	13,10,45
Prof	Thieme, Robert	M	39,66A,66C
Prof	Thompson, Virginia M.	D	49,63B
Asst Prof	Vercelli, Michael B.	D	20,14,31F,41,42
Prof	Weaver, Molly A.	PhD	32,32E,32G,34
Prof	Weigand, John	D	48,64C
Prof Emeritus	Wilcox, Don G.	M	60,37
Prof	Wilkinson, Christopher	D	13,11,12A,12
Assoc Prof	Willis, George R.		10D,11,32B,52,65
Prof	Wilson, Cecil B.	D	10F,60,12A,12
Prof	Winkler, John	D	49,63A
Lect	Wrublesky, Albert	M	65
Lect PT	Wyatt, Renee	M	32B,32C

WV0760 West Virginia Univ-Parkersburg
Department of Music
300 Campus Dr
Parkersburg, WV 26104-8647
(304) 424-8248   Fax: (304) 424-8354
www.wvup.edu
E-mail: hg.young@mail.wvu.edu

4 Year Institution

Chair & Dir., Artist/Performance Series: H. G. Young, III, 80A,80F

Adj	Coddington, Robert	B	70
Adj	Evans, Laura	M	61
Adj	Smith, Jan	M	66
Prof	Young, H. G.	D	13,11,12A,36,54

WV0800 West Virginia Wesleyan College
Department of Music
59 College Ave
Buckhannon, WV 26201
(304) 473-8805   Fax: (304) 473-8888
www.wvwc.edu
E-mail: meadows@wvwc.edu

4 Year Institution
Member of NASM

Chair: Melody Meadows, 80A

PT	Baden, Robert		50,65
PT	Bostonia, Marguerite	M	66A,13F
PT	Carr, Sarah	M	36,60A
PT	DeFade, Eric		64E,64D
PT	Dody, Teresa	D	61
PT	Green, Scott	D	10F
	Hamilton, Anne	M	62
PT	Hamrick, Mark		70
PT	Mallory, Marie	M	66A
PT	Manspeaker, Rick		62D
Prof	Meadows, Melody	DMA	13,12A,66G,34,35A
PT	Miller, Brett	D	16
Asst Prof	Moore, James H.	M	37,47,29A,11
Prof	Parsons, Larry R.	DMA	36,61,31A
Prof	Sabak, Linda	DMA	12A,66,11
Asst Prof	Spivak, Mandy		61,39
PT	Turizziani, Robert	M	64C,60B,48
PT	Wagner, Linda	M	32B
PT	Wolfersheim, Linda	M	64A

WY0050 Casper College
Department of Music
125 College Dr
Casper, WY 82601-4612
(307) 268-2606   Fax: (307) 268-3023
www.caspercollege.edu
E-mail: dbull@caspercollege.edu

2 Year Institution
Member of NASM

Music Coordinator: Douglas Bull, 80A
Dean: Eric W. Unruh, 80A
Dir., Kinser Jazz Festival: Patrick Patton, 80F
Dir., Kinser Jazz Festival: Tracy Pfau, 80F
Assistant Coordinator: Jennifer Cowell, 80H
Exec. Director, Kinser Jazz Festival: Jerome Fleg

Inst	Baker, Nathan A.	M	13,11
Inst	Bull, Douglas	B	37,63,11,32E
Inst PT	Burger, Larry		34D
Inst	Cowell, Jennifer	M	38,41,66D,62A
Inst PT	DePaolo, Gary	B	62B
Inst PT	Dunbar, Christine	M	62C
Emeritus	Fenner, Roger	M	
Inst	Fleg, Jerome	D	64C,29,47,64E
Inst	Gunderson, Terry	D	65,34,29,13,12E
Inst	Lenth, Kristen	M	61
Inst PT	McIntire, Donna	B	66A,66G
Inst	Olm, James	M	54,61,13A
Inst	Patton, Patrick	D	36,61,40
Inst	Pfau, Tracy	B	47,70,53
Inst PT	Thornton, Delores	B	48,64A
Inst	Tichenor, Jean-Marie	M	61,40,12A
Inst PT	Turner, Richard	M	64D,67C,11
Inst PT	Wallace, Connie	M	62E

WY0060 Central Wyoming College
Department of Music
2660 Peck Ave
Riverton, WY 82501-2215
(307) 855-2213   Fax: (307) 855-2090
www.cwc.edu
E-mail: rhussa@cwc.edu

2 Year Institution

Chair: Mark Nordeen, 80A
Dir., Summer Programs: Mohammed Waheed, 80G

Inst	Dalton, Sharon	B	13,44,61,66
Prof	Hussa, Robert	M	11,12A,35C,36,61
Inst	Traylor, Steve	M	13,46,47

WY0100 Eastern Wyoming College
Department of Music
3200 West C St
Torrington, WY 82240-1603
(307) 532-8283   Fax: (307) 532-8229
ewc.wy.edu
E-mail: janet.howard@ewc.wy.edu

2 Year Institution

PT	Howard, Janet	M	66A
	Kreiger, Donna	M	34

WY0115 Laramie County Community College
Department of Music
1400 E College Dr
Cheyenne, WY 82007-3204
(307) 778-1272/1160   Fax: (307) 778-1177
www.lccc.wy.edu
E-mail: jransom@lccc.wy.edu

2 Year Institution

Co-Coordinator: Gary Hall, 80A
Co-Coordinator: Judy L. Ransom, 80A
Dean: Kathleen Urban, 80A

Adj Inst	Askvig, Jamie		64C
Adj Inst	Barker, Stephanie		64B,64D
Adj Inst	Bowell, Jeffrey T.		63C
Adj Inst	Coelho-Foust, Jenny		62E
Adj Inst	Frazee, Nickolas		64E
Adj Inst	Green, Sheila		61,66A
Inst	Hall, Gary	M	11,12A,13B,13C,47
Adj Inst	Harrison, Leslie Anne		13C
Adj Inst	Kilpatrick, Terry		35C
	Maytum, Jeremiah		65,50
Adj Inst	Miller, Jane		64A
Adj Inst	Miller, Steve		63D
Adj Inst	Novotny, Edward		70
Inst	Ransom, Judy L.	DMA	13B,13F,36,40,66D
Adj Inst	Reynolds, Lindsey Bird	D	64B
Adj Inst	Schmid, Lucinda		63B
Adj Inst	Shaul, David		62E
Adj Inst	Smith, Kara		61,66A
Adj Inst	Stolz, Patrick		61,70
Adj Inst	Swanson, Isaac	B	63A
Adj Inst	Wagner, Lorraine		62A,62B,62C,62D,51

WY0130 Northwest College
Department of Music
231 W 6th St
Powell, WY 82435-1898
(307) 754-6425   Fax: (307) 754-6245
area.northwestcollege.edu/area/music
E-mail: neil.hansen@northwestcollege.edu

2 Year Institution
Member of NASM

Chair, Visual & Performing Arts: Neil E. Hansen, 80A

Coordinator, Music: Robert C. Rumbolz, 80H

PT	Akin, Maurine	B	62A,62B
PT	Bibbey, Marianne	B	64C
PT	Bree, Karen		66A,66D
PT	Cook, Ed		70
PT	Frescoln, Austin	B	64A
PT	Grover, Morgan	M	11
Prof	Hansen, Neil E.	M	37,47,63A,32,49
Asst Prof	Kliewer, Jan Michael	M	13,36,61,62D,38
PT	Martin, Spencer	M	65
PT	McSwain, Jenna		66A
PT	Murray, Linda	B	62C
PT	Olson, Craig	M	64E,48,64A,40,46
PT	Parmer, Pat	B	63B
PT	Parmer, Richard	M	63C,63D,60,49
PT	Retzlaff, Dustin	M	62D
Assoc Prof	Rumbolz, Robert C.	PhD	13,35C,35D,34,20A
Inst	Schoessler, Tim	B	66A,66D,13,12A
PT	Scott, Geri	B	64B
PT	Streeter, Vicki	B	61

WY0150 Sheridan College
Department of Music
3059 Coffeen Ave
Sheridan, WY 82801
(307) 674-6446   Fax: (307) 672-6157
www.sheridan.edu
E-mail: cerickson@sheridan.edu

2 Year Institution

Music Contact: Christian Erickson, 80A

Adj Inst	Ashear, Aaron	B	70
Inst	Erickson, Christian	D	10,11,13,34,35
Inst	Flynn, Michael P.	D	11,37,41,47,63
Adj Inst	Johnson, DeeDee	M	66A
Adj Inst	Moline, Garth	B	64C,64E
Inst	Sager, Gene	M	36,40,61,11
Adj Inst	Viren, Leslie	B	64A
Adj Inst	Wirth, Jordan	M	65

WY0200 Univ of Wyoming
Department of Music #3037
1000 E University Ave
Laramie, WY 82071-3037
(307) 766-5242   Fax: (307) 766-5326
www.uwyo.edu/music
E-mail: musicdpt@uwyo.edu

4 Year Institution, Graduate School
Member of NASM

Master of Music in Performance, Master of Music in Music Education

Chair: Theresa L. Bogard, 80A
Dir., Undergraduate Studies: Jennifer Turpen, 80B
Dir., Graduate Studies: David J. Brinkman, 80C

Prof	Barnhart, Stephen L.	D	65,50,32E
Prof	Belser, Robert S.	D	37,63D,11
Inst PT	Berlinsky, Elena		66A
Inst PT	Boddicker, Maureen	M	61
Prof	Bogard, Theresa L.	D	13C,66
Inst PT	Breazeale, Edward	M	47
Prof	Brinkman, David J.	D	32
Assoc Prof	Fadial, John	D	62A,41,55B
Prof	Garnett, Rodney A.	M	64A,20,67H
Prof	Griffith, Michael Ted	D	60,38,42
Assoc Prof	Guzzo, Anne M.	D	13,10,12A,13F,15
Inst FT	Hart, Kevin S.	M	70
Prof	Hensel, Larry L.	DMA	39,61
Inst PT	Hoffman, Steven	D	66G,13D
Inst PT	Johnston, Jason	M	63B,49,12A
Asst Prof	Lamartine, Nicole C.		36,60A,32D
Inst PT	Latchininsky, Alla	M	66A
Inst PT	Markley, Ben D.	D	66A,47
Asst Prof	McGee, Blake Anthony	PhD	12,64C,48
Lect	McKeage, Kathleen M.	D	11,62D,13C,32
Asst Prof	Meredith, Scott	D	63A,67E,12,32E,49
Prof	Przygocki, James T.	M	62B,51,32E
Inst PT	Reynolds, Lindsey	D	64B
Inst PT	Riner, Nicole	D	64A,14C,32G,48
Inst PT	Schefter, Hillary	M	62E
Lect	Sinift, Sherry	M	62A
Inst PT	Soueidi, Mark	M	63C
Inst PT	Strampe, Gregory	M	66A
Lect	Turpen, Jennifer	D	13A,13B,48
Prof	Turpen, Scott	D	64E,47,29,60B
Inst PT	Uno-Jack, Kaori	M	64D
Asst Prof	Vanderborgh, Beth	D	41,62C,55B
Lect	Williamson, Brad	D	37,63C
Assoc Prof	Wu, Chi-Chen	D	66A,66C,66B
Prof	Zook, Katrina J.	D	11,61

Index by Area of Music Specialization

Contents of the Areas of Music Specialization Index

Music Composition
Composition (All Areas) . . . 415
Traditional Compositional Practices . . . 422
Electroacoustic Music . . . 423
Film, Television, and Radio Music . . . 424
Popular Music . . . 425
World Folk Music . . . 425
Orchestration . . . 425

Music in General Studies/Music Appreciation
Music in General Studies/Music Appreciation . . . 427

Scholarship and Research
Musicology (All Areas) . . . 444
History of Music . . . 449
Aesthetics of Music . . . 459
Research and Methodology . . . 460
Critical Theory . . . 460
Sociomusicology . . . 461
Psychomusicology . . . 461
Musical Iconography . . . 461

Music Theory (All Areas) . . . 461
Rudiments . . . 477
Harmony . . . 483
Eartraining/Sightsinging/Solfege . . . 485
Counterpoint . . . 490
Formal Analysis . . . 490
20th Century Music Theory . . . 491
Computer Applications . . . 491
Music Theory Pedagogy . . . 492
Schenkerian Analysis . . . 492
History of Music Theory . . . 492
Perception/Cognition . . . 492
Acoustics . . . 493

Ethnomusicology (All Areas) . . . 493
Research and Methodology . . . 495
Organology . . . 495
Popular Music . . . 495
Critical Theory . . . 496
Archaeology . . . 496
Anthropology . . . 496

Gender Studies . . . 497
Music Librarian . . . 497

World Musics
World Musics (All Areas) . . . 498
Sub-Saharan Africa . . . 500
Western and Central Asia/North Africa . . . 501
East Asia . . . 501
Southeast Asia . . . 501
South Asia . . . 502
Europe . . . 502
North America . . . 502
Central and South America, Mexico, and the Caribbean . . . 503
Oceania and Australia . . . 504

Jazz Studies (All Areas) . . . 504
History of Jazz . . . 511
Jazz Theory . . . 513
Analysis of Jazz . . . 513
Sociology of Jazz . . . 513
Jazz Critical Theory . . . 513

Music and Practice in Religious Life
Music in Religious Life (All Areas) . . . 513
Music in Christianity . . . 514
Music in Judaism . . . 515
Music in Islam . . . 515
Music in Buddhism . . . 515
Music in Hinduism . . . 515
Music in African and African-Derived Religions . . . 516
Music of Diverse Religious and Ritual Systems . . . 516

Music Education
Music Education (All Areas) . . . 516
Early Childhood Education . . . 522
Elementary General Music . . . 523
Secondary General Music . . . 525
Choral Music . . . 527
Instrumental Music . . . 529
Computer Applications . . . 532
Research and Assessment . . . 532
Interdisciplinary . . . 533
Dalcroze Eurhythmics . . . 533

Music Therapy
Music Therapy . . . 533

Music and Technology
Music and Technology (All Areas) . . . 535
Multimedia . . . 539
Web-based Music Instruction . . . 539
Distance Learning . . . 540
Digital Audio . . . 540
Digital Video . . . 541
Curriculum and Standards . . . 541
Software Development . . . 541
New Media . . . 541

Music Business and Industry
Music Business and Industry (All Areas) . . . 541
Music Business . . . 543
Commercial Business . . . 544
Sound Technology . . . 544
Recording Industry . . . 546
Arts Administration . . . 546
Talent Management . . . 547
Recording Technology . . . 547
Radio/Television . . . 548

Conductors and Directors of Performance Organizations
Choral . . . 548
Band . . . 558
Orchestra . . . 565
Opera . . . 569
Vocal Chamber Ensemble . . . 574
Instrumental Chamber Ensemble . . . 576
Chamber Ensemble Coaching . . . 582
New Music Ensemble . . . 586
Bell Choir . . . 587
Electronic Music Ensemble . . . 587
Jazz/Stage Band . . . 588
Jazz Ensemble . . . 590
Woodwind Ensemble . . . 598
Brass Ensemble . . . 601
Percussion Ensemble . . . 604
String Ensemble . . . 606
Dance/Ballet Troupe . . . 608
Improvisation Ensemble . . . 609
Theatre Music . . . 610
Early Music Ensemble (all) . . . 613
Medieval Ensemble . . . 613
Baroque Ensemble . . . 613
Renaissance Ensemble . . . 614
Early Music Vocal Ensemble . . . 614
Baroque Orchestra . . . 614
Guitar Ensemble . . . 614
Bagpipe Corps . . . 614
DJ Techniques . . . 614

Performance Instruction
Conducting (All Areas) . . . 614
Choral and Vocal . . . 618
Instrumental . . . 621
Voice . . . 623
Strings (All Areas) . . . 645
Violin . . . 646
Viola . . . 653
Cello . . . 657
Bass . . . 661
Harp . . . 665
Brass (All Areas) . . . 666
Trumpet . . . 668
Horn . . . 673
Trombone . . . 676
Low Brass . . . 680
Woodwinds (All Areas) . . . 684
Flute . . . 685
Oboe . . . 690
Clarinet . . . 693
Bassoon . . . 697
Saxophone . . . 700
Percussion (All Areas) . . . 705
Timpani . . . 711
Mallet . . . 712
Keyboard (All Areas) . . . 712
Piano . . . 714
Piano Pedagogy . . . 732
Accompanying and Collaborative Piano . . . 735
Group Piano . . . 742
Fortepiano . . . 748
Piano Technician . . . 748
Organ . . . 748
Harpsichord . . . 752
Early Instruments (All Areas) . . . 753
Viols . . . 753
Baroque Strings . . . 753
Recorders . . . 754
Baroque Winds . . . 754
Brass . . . 754
Keyboard . . . 754
Lute . . . 755
Other . . . 755
Accordion . . . 755
Carillon . . . 755
Guitar . . . 755
Music Instrument Curator . . . 763
Music Instrument Repair . . . 764

Composition (All Areas)

Name	Code	Areas
Aaberg, David E.	MO1790	47,29,10
Aberdam, Eliane	RI0300	13,10F,10,12A,45
Accurso, Joseph	NJ0030	13A,13,60,10,35B
Adams, Brant	OK0800	13,10
Adams, Byron	CA5040	13,10F,10,12
Adams, Richard	MI2250	10,49,13L,13,10F
Adashi, Judah E.	MD0650	13,10
Adkins, Don	CA0300	13,10F,10,12A,62D
Adler, Christopher A.	CA5200	10,14,13,10A,20D
Adler, Samuel	NY1900	10
Ainger, Marc	OH1850	10,34,35
Al-Zand, Karim	TX2150	13,10
Albert, Thomas	VA1350	13,10,54
Alburger, Mark	CA1560	10,13,38
Albury, Robert T.	AZ0350	13,10
Aldrich, Jon	MA0260	10
Aldridge, Robert	NJ1130	13,10
Alexander, Eric	CO0950	13B,13C,10,13
Alexander, Joe L.	LA0250	10,13,63D,10A,49
Alexander, Kathryn J.	CT0900	13,10,34,43
Alhaddad, Frederick I.	MI1200	13,10,66
Allemeier, John	NC2420	13,10,34
Allen, William T.	NY1700	10
Allik, Kristi A.	AG0250	10,45,34,32F
Alves, William	CA2175	10,14,45,34
Amlin, Martin	MA0400	13,10
Anderman, Mark	CA4460	13,34,10,70,13A
Anderson, Douglas K.	NY0270	13,10F,60,10,38
Anderson, Jonathan	MI2200	10,13
Anderson, Stephen	NC2410	10,29
Andres, Hoyt	CO0550	13,10
Anhalt, Istvan	AG0250	13,10
Annicchiarico, Michael	NH0350	13B,13C,13E,10
Applebaum, Mark S.	CA4900	13,10,20G
Applin, Richard	MA0260	10
Aquino, Robert	NY2102	13A,13,10,66A,66B
Arauco, Ingrid	PA1500	13A,13,10
Araujo, Ramon	PR0125	13,10,37,64C
Archer, Kimberly K.	IL2910	10,13,32E,10A,10F
Argento, Dominick J.	MN1623	13,10F,10,12A
Argersinger, Charles	WA1150	13,10,66A
Armer, Elinor	CA4150	10
Armstrong, John	AG0400	13,10F,10
Arnold, Larry	NC2435	10,29A,13,34A,62D
Arrell, Christopher A.	MA0700	10,13,34A,34D
Ashley, Richard	IL2250	13,10,29
Asia, Daniel I.	AZ0500	13,10,43
Ator, James	IN0905	13,10,48,64E,29
Austin, Kevin	AI0070	13,10F,10,34,35C
Austin, Michael	MO0850	34,35C,13,35,10
Averitt, William E.	VA1350	13,10
Ayers, Jesse M.	OH1350	13,10,13C
Babbitt, Milton	NJ0900	13,10
Baber, Joseph W.	KY1450	13,10
Bacon, John	NY4320	10
Bahn, Curtis	NY3300	43,13,10,12,45
Bahr, Jason	FL0680	10,13,31A,13C,13B
Bain, Reginald	SC1110	13,10,34,45
Baker, W. Claude	IN0900	10
Balada, Leonardo	PA0550	13,10
Baldini, Christian	CA5010	38,10,13,39
Balentine, James S.	TX3530	13,10,47,29A
Bales, Kenton W.	NE0610	13,10,43,34
Baley, Virko	NV0050	10,13
Ball, Leonard V.	GA2100	13,10,45,34
Balter, Marcos	IL0720	10,13
Bancks, Jacob	IL0100	10,10F,43,13,12A
Barasch, Shirley R.	PA2900	61,32,54,10,35E
Barata, Antonio G.	CA0600	10,34D,35D,35G
Barduhn, David	OR0550	13,10,47,29
Barker, Jennifer M.	DE0150	10
Barlow, Carla	NM0450	13,10,34
Barnes, James	KS1350	10F,10,12A
Barnes, Larry J.	KY1350	13,10,29A,34,14C
Barnett, Carol	MN0050	10
Barr, John	VA0100	13,10,66,31A
Barsom, Paul	PA2750	10,45
Barta, Daniel	NY3350	10,13,10A,10F
Barton, Todd	OR0950	10,45
Bartus Broberg, Kirsten A.	MN1625	13,10
Bashaw, Howard	AA0100	10,13
Bashwiner, David M.	NM0450	13,10
Bass, Eddie	NC0910	10
Bass, Eddie C.	NC2430	13,10
Batzner, Jay C.	MI0400	13,10,34,10A,13F
Bauer, Ross	CA5010	13,10,43,29
Bauman, Marcia	CA4700	10,14C,34,35
Baumgartner, Michael	OH0650	10,12A,11
Baur, John	TN1680	13,10
Bavicchi, John	MA0260	10
Baxter, David	AG0130	10
Beall, John	WV0750	13,10F,10,43
Beaser, Robert	NY1900	10
Beaudoin, Paul	RI0200	10,13,12A,11
Beaudoin, Richard A.	MA1050	13,12D,10
Beck, Stephen David	LA0200	10,45,34
Becker, Daniel	CA4150	10,12A
Beckwith, John	AG0450	10,20G
Becos, Pelarin	IL3310	10,13,13C
Bedrossian, Franck	CA5000	10,13
Beerman, Burton	OH0300	10
Behnke, John A.	WI0300	10,44,66G,31A
Behrens, Jack	AG0500	13,10,20G
Bejerano, Martin	FL1900	29,10,66A,53
Beken, Munir N.	CA5031	13,10
Bela, Marcin	TN1100	10,66A,66D
Belden, George R.	AK0100	13,12,10,34
Belet, Brian	CA4400	10,13B,13C,13E,13F
Bell, Allan	AA0150	13,10,20G,10F
Bell, Larry	MA0260	10
Bell, Malcolm E.	AA0080	10,13,47,65
Bell, Peter J.	MA2030	10,13,31A,34
Bell, Vicki	KY0100	13,10,36
Bellink, Allyson	NY3785	10,10C,10A
Belshaw, Gary D.	TX3650	10F,10,66,34
Ben-Amots, Ofer	CO0200	13,10F,10,11,34
Benadon, Fernando Raul	DC0010	13,34,10
Benjamin, William E.	AB0100	13,10
Bennett, Bruce Christian	CA4200	10,13,34,10A,10B
Benshoof, Kenneth W.	WA1050	13,10,54
Benson, John Halvor	WI0350	13,10
Benson, Mark	PA0400	13,10,12,63,34
Berg, Chris	OH0500	13,10,62D
Berg, Kenneth	AL0800	10
Berg, Reinhard	AA0020	13,10,12A,66A,66G
Berger, Jonathan	CA4900	13,10,45,34
Bergs, Roger	AG0450	10
Berkhout, Bjorn	NY3250	10,62C,12A,13,14C
Berners, John	IN1650	10,13
Berry, S. David	SC0650	10,13,34,35,12
Bethea, Stephanie	WA0900	13,10,64A
Betinis, Abbie	MN0610	10
Bettison, Oscar	MD0650	10
Betts, Donald	MN0950	66A,10
Beyer, Tom	NY2750	10,34
Bhagwati, Sandeep	AI0070	10
Bielawa, Herbert	CA4200	13A,13,10F,10,45
Bierman, Benjamin	NY0630	63A,10,13,34,35
Binckes, Fred B.	MT0350	13,10,11,66G
Birch, Sebastian A.	OH1100	13,10,34,13B,13A
Biringer, Gene D.	WI0350	13,10
Biscardi, Chester	NY3560	13,10F,10,11,12A
Bitensky, Laurence S.	KY0450	13,10
Bithell, David	TX3420	10
Blaha, Joseph L.	VA1250	46,10,12A,48,63C
Blair, Steve	VT0250	10,47,70
Blais, Jerome	AF0100	10,13
Blanchard, Terence	FL1900	63A,10,47
Blenzig, Charles	NY3785	10,66A,29,35B
Blessinger, Martin	TX3000	10,13
Bloom, Jane Ira	NY2660	10,53,64,47
Blumberg, Stephen F.	CA0840	13,10
Blumberg, Stephen	CA0150	10
Blume, Philipp G.	IL3300	13,10,10A,10F
Blumhofer, Jonathan	MA0650	10,12
Boehm, Norman	AR0350	13,10,12A,66A,11
Boelter, Karl	NY3725	10
Bogdan, Valentin Mihai	LA0100	66A,10,35A
Bohlen, Donald A.	NY3725	10A,10F,13D,10
Boisvert, Claude	AI0220	10
Bolcom, William E.	MI2100	10
Bonacci, Andrew	MA2100	10,13,10A,10F
Bondari, Brian	TX3350	10,13,34,10A,10B
Bonde, Allen R.	MA1350	10
Booker, Charles L.	AR0730	10,32E,13,60B
Boon, Rolf J.	AA0200	13,34,10,35
Boone, Benjamin V.	CA0810	13,10,29
Booth, Brian	UT0250	10,47
Boozer, Pat	NC2350	10,32B,66A,13A,13B
Borwick, Susan Harden	NC2500	13,12,31,10,15
Botly, George	AG0130	10
Botti, Susan	NY2150	10
Boubel, Karen A.	MN1000	13,10,34,13C,10A
Bougie, Marc-Andre	TX2850	11,10,13,36
Bouliane, Denys	AI0150	10
Bourland, Roger	CA5030	13,10
Boury, Robert	AR0750	13,10,11
Bowen, Nathan	CA3100	13,11,10,34
Bowers, Greg J.	VA0250	13,10,10A
Bowlby, Timothy	IL1520	13,10
Boyce, Douglas J.	DC0100	13,10
Boyd, Michael	MS0360	70,62D,41,10,11
Boyer, Peter	CA1050	10,60,35
Boykan, Martin	MA0500	13,10,12A,10A,13A
Boyle, Benjamin C. S.	NJ1350	10,64A,13
Brabant, John-Paul	NY3780	10,10B,10C,13
Bracey, Judson F.	WV0050	13,10
Brackeen, Joanne	NY2660	10,66A,47,53
Bradbury, William	CA0847	13,10,11,34,20G
Brandt, Anthony K.	TX2150	13,10
Bratt, Wallis	ID0050	13,10
Braun, William	WI1155	13,10,12,55B,34
Braxton, Anthony	CT0750	10,20G,29
Brazelton, Kitty	VT0050	13,10F,10,11,53
Breedon, Daniel	MN0600	13,10,12A,54
Brellochs, Christopher	NY1050	47,10,13,12,64E
Bremer, Carolyn	CA0825	13,10
Bresnick, Martin I.	CT0850	10,43
Bridgewater, Cecil	NY2660	10,63A,53
Briggs, Nancy L.	CA4580	29,10,66,53,20
Briggs, Roger	WA1250	43,10F,10,66A
Brindell, Sarah	MA0260	10
Brodhead, Richard C.	PA3250	10
Brody, Martin	MA2050	13,10,12A
Broening, Benjamin	VA1500	10,34,13,35C,35D
Brooke, Nicholas	VT0050	13,10,20,34
Brotman, Justin	AZ0490	62D,10,32E
Brown, Frank Burch	IN0300	12A,66A,12B,10
Brown, J. Bruce	MI2000	13,10,11,34,51
Brown, Stephen	AB0210	10,13A,13B,13C,13D
Brown, Uzee	GA1450	13,10,61,11
Browning, Zack D.	IL3300	13,10,43
Brownlow, Robert J.	OH2150	13,10
Brunk, Jeremy	IL1750	13,12,65,10
Brunner, David L.	FL1800	60,36,32D,10
Brunner, Roy	MA0950	13,10,66G,66H,31A
Brust, Paul W.	MA1175	10,13,43
Buchwald, Peter	CO0150	64E,35C,35D,10
Buczynski, Walter	AG0450	13,10F,10,66A
Buehrer, Theodore E.	OH1200	13,10,29,63A,34
Buelow, William L.	OH1400	13A,13,10,66A,29
Buhr, Glenn	AG0600	10,53
Bukvic, Ivica Ico	VA1700	10,34,10A,13L,10C
Bukvich, Daniel J.	ID0250	13,10,47,50,65
Bulow, Harry T.	IN1300	10,13,34,13A
Bunk, Louis	NH0110	34,10,11,13,43
Burchard, Richard	KY0250	10,13,20,34,35
Burdick, David H.	IL1750	10,13,34,70,35
Burge, John	AG0250	13,10,10F,13I
Burke, Patrick	PA1050	13,10,34
Burns, Christopher	WI0825	10,13,34,43,45
Burns, Patrick J.	NJ0800	13A,13,10
Burry, Dean	AG0300	10
Burtner, Matthew	VA1550	10,34,35C,12F
Buskey, Sherry	MA2000	10,11
Butler, Chuck	PA3330	10,34
Butler, Gregory G.	AB0100	13,10,12A,12
Butler, Steve	CA5550	10,13,34,10A,13E
Butterfield, Christopher	AB0150	13,10,43
Byrne, Madelyn	CA3460	10,11,34
Cable, Howard	AA0200	10,11,35,47,60
Cacioppo, Curt	PA1500	13,10,20G,10F,66A
Caldwell, James M.	IL3500	13,10,45
Callahan, David	MA0260	10
Callender, Clifton D.	FL0850	10
Camacho, Loida	PA2400	13,10,11
Camelio, Brian	NY2660	10,70,35C
Campbell, Arthur	MN1450	10,13
Campbell, William G.	IA1300	10,13,20,34
Camphouse, Mark D.	VA0450	10,60B,37
Caniato, Michele	MA0930	10,38,29,13,47
Carastathis, Aris	AG0170	13,10,43
Carbon, John J.	PA1300	13A,13,10F,10
Carillo, Dan	NY0550	47,13,46,10,29

Name	Code	Areas
Carl, Robert B.	CT0650	13,10,45
Carlsen, Philip	ME0410	13,10,29A,38,34
Carlson, Mark	CA5030	10,13
Carlson, Mark	CA4450	13,10
Carney, Horace R.	AL0010	13,60,10,36
Carrabre, T. Patrick	AC0050	13,10,43,20G,35
Carroll, Gregory D.	NC2430	13,10,11
Carroll, Kevin	GA1600	10,64,60B,11,13
Carruthers, Ian	AA0050	10,13
Carson, Benjamin Leeds	CA5070	13K,10
Carson, Virginia	VA1800	13,10,66A
Carter, Chandler	NY1600	13,10
Carter, Greg	AF0150	64E,29,10
Casinghino, Justin	MA0400	13,10
Castellani, Daniel	NY3785	10
Castillo, Ramon	MA0260	10
Catan, Daniel	CA1265	13A,13,10,11,12A
Catlin-Smith, Linda	AG0600	10
Cattaneo, Susan K.	MA0260	10
Cavera, Chris S.	OH2140	34,35,13,70,10
Celona, John	AB0150	13,10,43
Chafe, Chris	CA4900	10,45,34,13L
Chagas, Paulo	CA5040	10
Chamberlain, Donald J.	IA0400	13,10F,10,11,47
Chamberlin, Robert	MO1950	13,10F,10,45
Chambers, Evan	MI2100	10,45
Chang, Dorothy	AB0100	10A,10F,10
Chaplin, Clay	CA0510	10,34,35G
Chapman, Joe C.	GA1500	13,66A,10
Chappell, Jeffrey	MD0400	47,66A,29,29B,10
Charke, Derek	AF0050	13D,13E,10,13
Chase, Jon	MA0260	10,35C,35G
Chatman, Stephen G.	AB0100	13,10,43
Chaudhuri, Swapan	CA0050	13A,10,12A,65
Chave, George B.	TX3500	13,10
Chemay, Frank	LA0700	10,63D,10F,11,49
Chen, Shih-Hui	TX2150	13,10
Chen, Yi	MO1810	10
Chenette, Jonathan Lee	NY4450	10,13,34,10A,10B
Chenevert, James	TX3300	10,13
Chenoweth, Gerald	NJ1130	13,10
Cherney, Brian	AI0150	13,10,12A
Chestnut, Louise	MD0060	10,62B
Chihara, Paul	CA5030	10,13
Child, Peter	MA1200	13,10
Childs, Adrian P.	GA2100	10,13,43
Choi, Kyong Mee	IL0550	10,13,66G
Chou, Godwin	IL2775	10A,13,66A,66,10
Chou, Sarana	AL0800	13,10,34
Chowning, John M.	CA4900	10,45,34,13L
Christensen, James	CA1425	10
Christopher, Paul	LA0550	10,13,51,62C,62D
Chuaqui, Miguel Basim	UT0250	13,10
Ciach, Brian	KY0950	10,13
Ciamaga, Gustav	AG0450	13,10,45,34
Cipiti, John	OH2140	13,66A,10,14C
Cipullo, Tom	NY0280	13A,13,10,36,61
Clark, Bryan	TN0100	10
Clark, Thomas S.	TX3175	10,13,10B
Clarke, Garry E.	MD1100	13,10F,10,12A
Clearfield, Andrea	PA3330	66C,66D,10,12F
Clements, Peter J.	AG0500	13,10,45
Clifton, Jeremy J.	OK1050	35C,10,13,13K,13B
Cobb, Gary W.	CA3600	13,10,12,66G,66B
Coburn, Robert	CA5350	13,10,45
Coffey, Ted	VA1550	10B,10,34,35C,35G
Cogan, Robert	MA1400	13,10
Coghlan, Michael	AG0650	13,10,29,34,43
Cohen, Alla Elana	MA0260	10
Cohen, Allen L.	NJ0400	13,10,54,39,36
Cohen, Douglas H.	NY0500	13,10,11,34
Cohen, Fred S.	GA0550	10,13
Cohen, Gerald	NY1860	13A,13,10
Coleman, Ian D.	MO2000	13,10,34
Coleman, Michael	FL1500	13,10,11,66A,34
Coleman, Randolph E.	OH1700	13,10
Coleman, Todd	NC0750	10,34,62D,35G,45
Colleen, Jeffrey	IL1550	13,10,36,66A,31A
Collins, Dana L.	IN1560	10,12A,34,35C,13
Collins, Philip M.	CA0400	10
Colquhoun, Michael	NY0400	10,20
Colson, David J.	MI2250	10,65,60
Colson, William	TX2600	13A,13,10F,10,13I
Colucci, Matthew J.	PA3250	13,10
Comotto, Brian	MD0175	10,35C,35D,35G,66A
Conner, Jennifer A.	OH0200	13,10
Constantinides, Dinos	LA0200	10
Conte, David	CA4150	10,12A,36
Cook, Mark Andrew	WV0550	13,29B,47,46,10
Cooper, John H.	ME0270	10,29,13,64E,10F
Cope, David H.	CA5070	13,10,12A
Corbett, Ian	KS0590	10,34,35D,35G,13G
Corigliano, John	NY0600	10F,10
Corigliano, John	NY0635	10F,10,11,54
Corigliano, John	NY1900	10
Corina, John H.	GA2100	13,10,64B
Corkey, Jim	ID0070	10
Cornejo, Robert Joseph	CA5510	13,11,34C,10,12A
Cornell, Richard	MA0400	13,10
Cornicello, Anthony	CT0150	10,34,13,34D,13F
Cortese, Michael	NY0450	10,11,20,34,47
Corwin, Mark	AI0070	10F,10,45,34,35C
Cory, Eleanor	NY2050	13,10,11,66A,66D
Coutts, Greg A.	IL2650	13,10,34
Couvillon, Thomas M.	KY0550	13,10B,10A,10,13F
Cowart, Steed D.	CA2950	10,13,43
Cox, Cindy	CA5000	10,13
Cox, Franklin	OH2500	10,13
Cox, Robin V.	CA0825	13,10
Coxe, Stephen	VA1000	13A,13B,13D,10
Crespo, Fabra Desamparados	NJ0825	10,13,34
Crist, Timothy D.	AR0110	13,45,10,70
Crockett, C. Edgar	IL0300	13,10,47,35,63A
Crockett, Donald	CA5300	13,10F,10
Crowley, James F.	WI0835	13,10F,10
Crozier, Daniel G.	FL1550	13,10,12A
Crumb, George H.	PA3350	13,10
Csapo, Gyula	AJ0150	13,10,45,10F
Cuckson, Robert	NY2250	13,10
Cucunato, Lou	WI0825	10
Currie, Randolph	OH1330	13,10,66G
Curtis-Smith, Curtis O.	MI2250	10,14,66A,20G
Custer, Beth	CA2950	10
Cutler, David	SC1110	13,10,12A
Czernowin, Chaya	MA1050	10
Dahn, Luke	IA0500	10
Dal Farra, Ricardo	AI0070	10
Dal Porto, Mark	NM0100	10,13,66A,34,13A
D'Alessio, Greg P.	OH0650	13,10,45,43
D'Ambrosio, Michael	KY0950	13,10
Danby, Judd	IN1310	10,13,29B,10A,13F
Danek, Leonard P.	MN1280	13,10,66G
Dangerfield, Joseph Allen	IA0300	10,13,66A,38,43
Daniel, Omar	AG0500	13,10,10F,34,35C
Danielpour, Richard	NY2150	13
Danielpour, Richard	PA0850	10
Danner, Greg	TN1450	13,10
Daugherty, Michael	MI2100	10
Davenport, Dennis	OH2050	54,10,13,36
David, James M.	CO0250	13,10,10F,63C
David, Norman	PA3330	64,47,10,29,13
Davidian, Teresa	TX2750	13,10,12A,20
Davidovsky, Mario	NY2250	10
Davies, David H.	NY1700	13A,13C,13B,10,13
Davies, Paul	CA1800	13,11,13A,66A,10
Davies, Richard	NY3775	10,29,34,46,63D
Davis, Anthony	CA5050	20G,66A,10,53
Davis, Daniel	NC0600	10,14,15,20A
Davis, Glen Roger	OH1450	13,10
Davis, Joel Scott	CA2810	10,13D
Davis, Joel	AL0800	10,13,34
Davis, John Douglas	CA0650	13,10,47,29
Davis, Richard	MA0260	10
Dawe, Jonathan	NY1900	10
De Lyser, David M.	OR1100	13,10,38,41
de Murga, Manuel	FL1750	10,10F,13E,34,43
Deadman, Randall	IL0850	63A,10
DeCaumette, Patrick	PA3330	39,10
Decker, Bradley	IL0800	13,10
Deemer, Robert	NY3725	10A,10C,43,10,60B
Del Aguila, Miguel	CA5360	10,66A,13A,11
Del Tredici, David	NY0550	60,10
Del Tredici, David	NY0600	10F,10
Delin, Diane	IL0720	29,62A,10
DeLio, Thomas	MD1010	13,10
Demars, James R.	AZ0100	13,10F,10
Dembski, Stephen	WI0815	10F,10
Demos, Nickitas J.	GA1050	10,43
Denham, Robert	CA0350	13,10,34,43
Denisch, Beth	MA0260	13,10F,10,15
DePue, Wallace E.	OH0300	10
Derfler, Brandon	UT0400	66A,10
Derry, Lisa	ID0070	13,10,34,66A,66B
Dessen, Michael J.	CA5020	10,12D,29E
Deutsch, Herbert A.	NY1600	13,10,45,29A,35
DeVasto, David	IL0850	10,13,32E,66
Devereaux, Kent	WA0200	10,12D
Devore, Richard O.	OH1100	13,34,10,20G,13F
Dickerson, Roger	LA0720	10F,10,12A,36,29
Dickinson, Paul J.	AR0850	10,13,43,34
Dickow, Robert H.	ID0250	13,10,63B,34
Diehl, Richard C.	VT0100	13,60,47,10,37
Diemer, Emma Lou	CA5060	13,10F,10
Dillon, James	MN1623	10
Dillon, Lawrence M.	NC1650	13A,13,10,43
Dilthey, Michael R.	MA1185	10,13,34
Dimitrov, Georges	AI0070	10
Dinda, Robin	MA0930	10,11,13,29,66G
Dippre, Keith	NC1350	13,11,10,47,34
Dirksen, Dale B. H.	AJ0030	10,13,32,61,66
Ditto, Charles J.	TX3175	13,10
Dobrian, Christopher	CA5020	10
Dodson, John	MI0050	10,12,38
Donelian, Armen	NY2660	13A,13C,10,66A,47
Dong, Kui	NH0100	13,10,20D,45,43
Doran, David Stephen	KY1460	13A,13,10,11,12A
Dougherty, William P.	IA0550	13,10F,10,34
Douglas, Samuel O.	SC1110	13,10,62D
Douyon, Marcaisse	FL1310	13,10,34
Downey, John W.	WI0825	13,10F,10,45,43
Downing, Joseph	NY4150	10,66G,13,13C,60
Drannon, Andrew	TN1200	34A,10
Drummond, Dean J.	NJ0800	13,43,10
Du, Yun	NY3785	10
Dubiel, Joseph	NY0750	10,11,13
Duckworth, William	PA0350	13,10
Dunbar, Brian	MN0620	10,13,36,34,60A
Dunker, Amy	IA0250	13,10,63A,41,49
Durand, Joel F.	WA1050	13,10,34
Durant, David Z.	AL1300	13,10,34,10A,10B
Durant, Douglas F.	MA1450	13,10,11,12A
Durham, Thomas L.	UT0050	13,10F,10
Durland, James	CA0400	10,34
Dusman, Linda J.	MD1000	10,13
Dutton, Brent	CA4100	13,10F,10,49,63D
Dvorin, David	CA0800	13,10,35G,45
Dye, Kenneth W.	IN1700	10,37
Dzubay, David	IN0900	10,43
Eagle, David	AA0150	13,10F,10,34,43
Earnest, John David	WA1300	10
Eckardt, Jason K.	NY0500	10,10F,13
Eckardt, Jason	NY0600	10
Edstrom, Brent	WA1350	10,66A,34,47,13
Edwards, George H.	NY0750	13,10,11
Edwards, Jason R.	IA0900	64,13,10,32E
Edwards, Leo	NY2250	13,10
Eggert, John	MN0610	10,13,31A,66G
Eggert, Scott H.	PA1900	13,10
Ehle, Robert	CO0950	13,10,13L
Eichenberg, Daniel	WV0300	13,10,11
Eigenfeldt, Arne	AB0080	10,45,34,35,12F
Elezovic, Ivan	FL1850	10,13,34
Elgart, Matthew	CA0830	70,10,13
Elliott, Bill	MA0260	10,35C,35G
Elwood, Paul	CO0950	10,13
Emmons, Stephen D.	TX0150	13,10,10F,34
Engebretson, Mark	NC2430	10
Engelmann, Marcus W.	CA0100	13,10,12A,45,20G
Enns, Leonard J.	AG0470	13,60,10,36
Entsminger, Deen	TN0100	13,10,32C,36,34
Epstein, Marti J.	MA0260	10
Epstein, Paul A.	PA3250	13,10,55
Erickson, Christian	WY0150	10,11,13,34,35
Errante, Steven	NC2440	13,10F,60,10,38
Esler, Robert	AZ0490	50,14C,35C,10
Evans, Gerald	OH1300	13,10,12A,14,66D
Everett, Steve	GA0750	60,10,41,45,34
Eychaner, Frank	CO0150	10,32,13,47,60
Eylar, Leo B.	CA0840	10,12A,38
Fandrich, Rita E.	FL0800	13,66A,66B,10
Fang, Man 'Mandy'	OH0200	10
Fang, Man	SC1110	10
Farber, Andy	NY1900	10,29
Farbood, Morwaread Mary	NY2750	34,10,66
Farley, Michael	NY3550	13,14,10,20
Farrell, David E.	CO0550	10,13

Index by Area of Teaching Interest

Name	Code	Areas
Farrin, Suzanne	NY3785	10
Faulconer, James	OK1350	13,10,34,35
Faust, Randall E.	IL3500	63B,10,63,13,49
Feder, Janet	CO0560	10,70,12A,13A,53
Feigin, Joel	CA5060	10,10A,10F,13D
Feinberg, Henry A.	MI1700	12A,10
Felder, David C.	NY4320	10
Feldman, Bernardo	CA1265	13A,13,10F,10,11
Felice, Frank	IN0250	10,10B,10D,34D,13D
Fennelly, Brian	NY2740	13,10,12A,45
Ferencz, George J.	WI0865	13,10
Ferguson, Charles Alan	CA1250	10,70
Ferguson, Sean	AI0150	10,45
Ferneyhough, Brian	CA4900	10
Fernisse, Glenn	GA0400	10,63D,34,32E
Ferrandino, Blaise J.	TX3000	10,62D,13
Ferry, Joe	NY3785	10,29,35B,35D
Fessler, Scott	MA0260	10
Festinger, Richard	CA4200	13,10,45,34
Fetler, Paul	MN1623	13,10F,10
Feurzeig, David K.	VT0450	13,10
Filadelfo, Gary A.	NY2750	10,35C
Fink, Michael Jon	CA0510	12A,12,35,10
First, Craig P.	AL1170	13,10,45,34
Fisher, Alfred	AG0250	13,10
Fitch, Keith	OH0600	10
Fitzell, Gordon D.	AC0100	10,34,43
Flaherty, Thomas E.	CA1050	10
Flaherty, Thomas E.	CA3650	13,10,12A,45
Flauding, Richard (Ric) G.	TX2600	10,34,10F,13
Fleisher, Robert J.	IL2200	13,10
Flores, Carlos	MI0250	13,10,35,34,10F
Flory, Neil	WA0050	10,13
Foltz, Roger	NE0610	13,10
Fonville, John	CA5050	13,10,64A,53,43
Forrester, Marshall	SC0275	10,11,37,60
Forsyth, Malcolm	AA0100	13,10F,10,38
Foster, Robert	GA0250	13,10,11,47,48
Frangipane, Ron	NJ0760	13,10F,60,10,12A
Frank, Andrew D.	CA5010	13,10,11
Frank, Robert J.	TX2400	10,13
Franklin, Cary J.	MN0950	10,37,38,42,60B
Frazelle, Kenneth	NC1650	13,10F,10
Free, Scott	MA0260	10,29
Freeman, Alexander	MN0300	10,13,11
Frehner, Paul	AG0500	13,10
Freund, Don	IN0900	10
Freund, Stefan	MO1800	13,10
Friedman, Arnold J.	MA0260	10,62C,13
Friedman, Jeffrey A.	MA0260	10,29
Friedman, Stanley Arnold	MS0700	10
Friedmann, Michael	CT0900	10,13,66A
Friesen-Carper, Dennis	IN1750	60,10,41,38
Fritze, Gregory P.	MA0260	10
Froelich, Kenneth D.	CA0810	10,34,43
Fruehwald, Robert D.	MO1500	13,10,45,64A
Fry, James	MD1010	13,10F,10
Frye, Christopher B.	WI0810	13,10F,10,34
Fuchs, Kenneth	CT0600	10
Fuentes, Alfonso	PR0115	10,10F
Fuentes, David	MI0350	13,10F,10
Fueting, Reiko	NY2150	13,10
Fuller, Wesley M.	MA0650	13,10,34
Funkhouser, James	KS0050	63B,10
Furlow, Shaw	MS0200	13,11,10,37,47
Furman, Pablo	CA4400	13,10,34,35C
Fussell, Charles	NJ1130	13,10
Futterer, Kenneth	AR0200	10,48,64B,64D,64E
Gabel, Gerald R.	TX3000	34,10,13,45
Gable, Christopher	ND0500	13,10
Gabriel, Todd A.	LA0050	10,13,38
Gabrielsen, Dag	NY0625	10,11
Galante, Brian Edward	WA0650	36,10,60A,32D
Galbraith, Nancy	PA0550	13,10
Gallagher, Jack	OH0700	63A,10,10F,13,12A
Galvan, Alex	CA1000	10,13,37,60
Gamer, Carlton	CO0200	13,10,11,20D,34
Gandolfi, Michael	MA1400	10
Garbutt, Don	AG0130	34,10
Garcia, Federico	PA0600	10,12A,13,41
Garcia, Orlando Jacinto	FL0700	10,34A
Garner, David	CA4150	13,10
Garnett, Guy E.	IL3300	10,34,13
Garrop, Stacy	IL0550	10,13
Garton, Bradford	NY0750	10,11,45,34
Gates, Gerald	MA0260	13,10
Gatti, Annmarie	NY3785	10
Gebuhr, Ann K.	TX1000	13,10,34
Gellman, Steven	AG0400	13,10F,10
Gendelman, Martin	GA0950	10,13,70,34A
Genovese, John	MA0400	13,10
Geraci, Paul	IN1350	13,10,29,63A,32B
Gerhold, John	CA0270	13,10,66D,13A
Gerlach, Bruce	MO0200	13,10,11,54,66G
Gibson, Mara	MO1810	10
Gibson, Richard L.	AE0100	13,10F,10,37,63
Gibson, Robert L.	MD1010	13,10,45,43
Gifford, Troy S.	FL2120	11,13,46,70,10
Gignac, Andrew	TX2260	63A,13,10,11
Gilbert, Jan M.	MN0950	13A,13C,10
Gilbert, John	NY2750	10,32,34
Gilbert, Peter A.	NM0450	10,13
Gillingham, David R.	MI0400	13A,13,10F,10
Gilmore, Bernard H.	CA5020	10,13
Gilmour, F. Matthew	MO0850	13,10,11,12A,34
Ginader, Gerhard	AC0050	13,10,45,62A
Ginther, Kathleen C.	IL2900	13,10
Giron, Arsenio	AG0500	13,10
Giteck, Janice	WA0200	13A,13,10,12A
Glarner, Robert L.	VA1100	13,10,321,66G,12
Glazer, Stuart	FL0650	13,10,64
Glenn, David B.	WA1300	10,47,63D,29
Glinsky, Albert	PA2250	13,10,12A
Godfrey, Daniel S.	NY4150	13,10,12A
Godwin, Paul M.	TN0100	13,10F,10,34
Goeringer, Lyn	OH1700	10,34
Golden, Lyman	SC0050	10,51,70
Goldstaub, Paul R.	NY3705	13A,13,10
Golijov, Osvaldo	MA0700	20G,13,10,11,12A
Golove, Jonathan	NY4320	10,62C
Gomez, Alice	TX2260	10,14,47,65,35A
Gompper, David	IA1550	13,10
Gooch, Warren P.	MO1780	10,13,10A
Goodman, David	CA4450	13,10,34
Gorbos, Stephen	DC0050	10
Gordon, David M.	IL3550	13,10
Gorecki, Mikolaj P.	TX1425	10,11,13,34,66A
Gotfrit, Martin	AB0080	10,45,34,35,12F
Gottlieb, David	NJ0750	10,13A,13B,34D,64E
Gottschalk, Arthur	TX2150	13,10,45
Graham, Alta Elizabeth	CO0350	13,10,12A
Gran, Charles	MO1780	11,13,34,10
Grantham, Donald	TX3510	13,10F,10
Grasse, Jonathan B.	CA0805	34D,13,20,14C,10
Gratz, Reed	CA5100	13,10,14C,29,11
Greco, Christopher J.	KS0100	13,10,64,64E,13F
Greenbaum, Matthew J.	PA3250	10
Greenberg, Laura	NY0630	13,10,66A,66D,11
Greenberg, Lionel	CA2700	13,10,66A
Greenhut, Barry	NY2750	10,34,13L
Greenlee, Geol	TN1250	13,66A,10F,10,11
Greeson, James R.	AR0700	13,10,70,47
Gribou, Andre	OH1900	11,10,66A
Griebling, Karen	AR0350	13,10,38,62B,14
Griffin, Jackie	SC0950	13,10,12A,66G,34
Griffin, John C.	MI2250	10,13,13C,66C
Griffith, Joan E.	MN0950	47,70,29,10,62D
Grimes, Calvin B.	GA1450	13,10,12,20G,31A
Gross, Murray	MI0150	38,13,60B,10,20
Grudzinski, Richard	MA0260	10,10B
Gryc, Stephen Michael	CT0650	13,10F,10
Gullings, Kyle	TX3535	10,13,13F,10A
Gustavson, Mark	NY2550	10,64C,66D,10A,10F
Guthrie, James M.	NC0400	13,10,34,66G,66H
Guttierez, Ruben	TX3520	10,35B,35C
Guzzo, Anne M.	WY0200	13,10,12A,13F,15
Gwiazda, Henry	MN1120	13,10
Haarhues, Charles D.	CO0100	10,13,29,70,11
Habib, Kenneth S.	CA0600	14,10,13,20B,14C
Hackbarth, Glenn A.	AZ0100	13,10F,10,43
Hailstork, Aldolphus C.	VA1000	10,10F
Haimo, Ethan	IN1700	13,10,10F
Haines, James L.	PA1250	13,10,33
Haladyna, Jeremy	CA5060	10,43
Hallstrom, Jonathan F.	ME0250	13,60,10,38,45
Halper, Matthew R.	NJ0700	10,13,34
Hamel, Keith A.	AB0100	13,10,34
Hamilton, Chico	NY2660	10,65,47
Haney, Jason	VA0600	13,10
Hanks, N. Lincoln	CA3600	55D,13,10,34,12A
Hanlon, Kevin	TX2400	13,10F,10,43
Hanna, Frederick	NE0160	13,37,38,10
Hansen, Brad	OR0850	13,29,10,34
Hanson, Dan L.	OK1400	13,10,32C,47,37
Hanson, Eric A.	WA0800	60,12A,38,10,64C
Hanzelin, Fred	IL2775	13,34,11,10
Harbison, John H.	MA1200	13,10,12A
Harbold, Mark A.	IL0850	13,10F,10,16,12A
Harchanko, Joseph	OR1250	10,13,62C
Harding, C. Tayloe	SC1110	10,35E,43
Harlan, Paul	FL1740	66A,10,34,35C
Harman, Chris	AI0150	10
Harper, Darryl	VA1600	29,10,14
Harrington, E. Michael	MA0260	35,10,20,14
Harris, Howard	TX3150	13A,10,37,47,39
Harris, Olga	TN1400	10
Hart, Edward B.	SC0500	10,11,13
Hartig, Hugo J.	WI0200	13,10F,10,12A
Hartke, Stephen	CA5300	13,10
Hartley, Walter S.	NY3725	10
Hartway, James	MI2200	13A,10,10F,66D,13B
Hartwell, Hugh	AG0200	13,10,11,29
Hasenpflug, Thom	ID0100	65,13,20,10,50
Hasty, Christopher	MA1050	13,10,12A,13J
Hatch, Peter	AG0600	13,10
Hatley, H. Jerome	OK0850	10,61,34,13D
Hatmaker, J. E.	IL2200	13,10
Hatzis, Christos	AG0450	10,35H,34,35C,13L
He, Jianjun	FL1000	13,34,10
Headrick, Samuel P.	MA0400	13,10,45
Heald, Jason A.	OR1020	13,10,47,36,38
Heap, Matthew	DC0010	13,10,13F
Heard, Alan	AG0500	13,10F,10
Hedges, John B.	NY3760	13B,13D,13E,10
Heinemann, Steven	IL0400	13,10,64C
Heinrichs, William C.	WI0825	13,10,34
Heiss, John C.	MA1400	10,12A,41,43
Helmuth, Mara M.	OH2200	10,45,34
Hemmel, Ronald A.	NJ1350	13,10,34D,13L
Henderson, Mark A.	UT0350	60,10,11,36,32D
Herman, Martin	CA0825	10F,13,10,34
Herman, Matthew	PA2400	10,11,13,34,35
Herman, Matthew James	VA1350	10,13,13F
Hernandez, Bernardo	MA0260	10,35G,35C
Hernandez, Rafael	CA0807	10,13,34
Herriott, Jeffrey	WI0865	10,11,43,35E
Hersch, Michael	MD0650	10
Hetu, Jacques	AI0210	10
Heukeshoven, Eric	MN1400	63C,63D,34,10
Heuser, David	NY3780	10A,10B,13,10F,10
Hevia, Lonnie	MD0850	13,13E,13C,10
Higdon, Jennifer	PA0850	13,10
Hijleh, Mark D.	NY1700	10,13,31A
Hill, Bill	CO0900	10
Hill, Jackson	PA0350	10,12A,12,14,71
Hilliard, John S.	VA0600	13,10
Hilliard, Quincy C.	LA0760	13,10,32C
Hilmy, Steven C.	DC0100	10,45,34
Hirsch, Michael	NJ0825	10,54
Hirt, Beth A.	OH0200	13,11,66A,10
Hiser, Beth A.	OH0200	13,10
Ho, Hubert	MA1450	10,13,13K,11
Ho, Ting	NJ0800	13,10,45,43
Hodge, Cheryl	AB0070	10,36,61,53,35H
Hoepfner, Gregory	OK0150	10A,32,61,10,11
Hoffman, Elizabeth D.	NY2740	12D,13,10,45,34
Hoffman, Joel H.	OH2200	13,10
Holland, Jonathan Bailey	MA0260	10A,10F,13A,10
Holman, Derek	AG0450	13,10
Holmes, Jeffrey W.	MA2000	10,47,46,29
Holober, Michael	NY0550	66A,29,10,46,47
Holsinger, David	TN0850	60B,10,48
Holz, Ronald	KY0100	12,38,41,49,10
Homsey, Ryan	NY3785	10
Homzy, Andrew	AI0070	10,47,29,29A,34
Honour, Eric C.	MO1790	10,34,13,13F,35C
Hoogerhyde, Jason	TX2650	13,10
Hooper, John	AA0015	60A,13,10
Hope, Garrett E.	PA3550	10,62D,13,34,51
Hopkins, Christopher	IA0850	13,10B,34,10,67A
Hopkins, Gregory	MA0260	10,29
Hoppmann, Kenneth	IN0005	10,16,20F,35A,66
Horst, Martha C.	IL1150	13,10
Horvitz, Wayne B.	WA0200	10,34
Houchins, Andrew	KS0300	13,10,34D
Houghton, Monica	OH0600	10,13

417

Name	Code	Areas
Houlihan, Patrick	AR0500	13,10
Howard, Bill	TX1600	10D,10,66A,35B,66D
Howard, David	OR0250	13,10,11,45,66G
Howard, David R.	MA0260	10,35C
Howard, Jason	PA3650	10,13
Howland, John L.	NJ1140	10,12,20,29,29A
Hsu, Cindi	NY5000	66A,10
Hu, Ching-chu	OH0850	13,10,60
Hughes, Curtis K.	MA0350	10
Hui, Melissa	AI0150	10
Hulen, Peter Lucas	IN1850	13,10,34,34A,41
Humphrey, Mark Aaron	TX3415	10,13
Hunkins, Arthur B.	NC2430	13,10,45,34
Hurst, Derek	MA0260	10
Hurtado, Jose-Luis	NM0450	10,13,32B
Hutcheson, Jere T.	MI1400	10
Hyde, John	AA0050	10,13,62D
Hyla, Lee	IL2250	10
Iannaccone, Anthony J.	MI0600	10A,38,13,10,12A
Ince, Kamran	TN1680	13,10,43
Isaacs, Kevin	CT0800	13,60,10,12B,36
Isele, David	FL2050	10F,10,36,61,66G
Italiano, Richard	CO0300	13,10,11,66A,66D
Ivanova, Vera	CA0960	10A,10B,10F,10,66A
Iwaasa, Juel	WA1200	10
Iwanusa, Charles	MI0450	13,10,11,47,29
Jackson, Gregory	AL0050	65,13,20,10,36
Jackson, Isaiah	MA0260	10
Jacobs, Kenneth A.	TN1710	13,10,45
Jaffe, Stephen	NC0600	13,10F,10
Jalbert, Pierre	TX2150	13,10
Jang, Jae Hyeok	IL1850	13,10,31A
Jarvis, David	WA1150	10,47,50,65,14C
Jazwinski, Barbara M.	LA0750	13,10,43
Jenkins, Joseph W.	PA1050	13,10F,10,12A
Jenks, Alden	CA4150	10,45
Jenny, Jack	OH2050	13,10,50,65,43
Jex, David	OH2300	13B,13C,13D,10,29
Johanson, Bryan	OR0850	70,13,41,11,10
Johanson, Michael	OR0400	13,10
Johnson, Barry	KY0750	13,10F,10,11
Johnson, Cory	CA1900	10,47,66A
Johnson, David H.	GA0850	13,10,10B,10C
Johnson, Jeffrey	CT0550	10,11,12,13
Johnson, Jenny O.	MA2050	10,13
Johnson, Joel C.	SC1050	13,10,20G,29A,34
Johnson, Keith	CA2975	10,20,34,35,13B
Johnson, Lee E.	GA1200	10,35B,35A
Johnson, Marvin	AL1170	13,10,45
Johnson, Paul	IN1700	13,10,34
Johnson, Randolph B.	OK0650	10,13
Johnson, Shersten	MN1625	13,10
Johnson, Stephen P.	TX2600	10,13,10F,60A,60
Johnson, William T.	CA4700	13,10,11,43,12A
Johnston, Ben	NC1750	13,10
Jolley, Jennifer	OH2000	10,13
Jones, Christopher	IL0750	10,13
Jones, David P.	WA0700	13,10F,10
Jones, David Evan	CA5070	13,10
Jones, Hilton Kean	FL2000	10,35,13,45,66G
Jones, Judy	NM0450	10
Jordan, Jeff	KS0350	37,32E,60B,63B,10
Jordan, William S.	AA0150	13,10,10F
Josselyn-Cranson, Heather	IA1200	66A,31A,10,20
Joyce, Brooke	IA0950	10,13,34,12
Juncker, Arthur	CA1950	13,10,12A,41,34
Junkinsmith, Jeff	WA0860	13,66A,10
Jurcisin, Mark	NJ0750	10,13A,13B,13C,11
Kachulis, James A.	MA0260	10
Kaiser, Tyler	MN0450	70,10,13
Kallstrom, Michael	KY1550	13,10
Kalogeras, Alexandros	MA0260	10
Kam, Dennis	FL1900	13,10
Kaminsky, Laura	NY3785	10
Kaplan, Amelia S.	IN0150	10,13
Kapuscinski, Jaroslaw	CA4900	10,20C
Karaca, Igor	OK0800	13,10,34
Karathanasis, Konstantinos	OK1350	34D,10A,10,35C,35G
Karchin, Louis S.	NY2740	10F,60,10,36
Karpen, Richard	WA1050	13,10,34
Kasparov, Andrey R.	VA1000	13,66A,10,43
Kavasch, Deborah H.	CA0850	10A,13,61,10,10F
Keane, David R.	AG0250	13,10
Keberle, David S.	NY0644	10,10B,64C,42,13A
Kechley, Gerald	WA1050	13,10,36
Kelley, Kevin	TX1350	11,10,13,43
Kelley, Robert T.	SC0800	20,13,66A,66D,10
Kenins, Talivaldis	AG0450	10
Kennedy, John M.	CA0830	10,13F,43,10F,13
Kennedy, Martin P.	MO1900	10,13
Kennison, Kendall	MD0400	13,10
Kernis, Aaron Jay	CT0850	10
Kershner, Brian	CT0050	10,13,64D
Kesselman, Lee R.	IL0630	13,10,36,54,60
Keys, Scarlet	MA0260	10,10D
Khan, Ali Akbar	CA0050	13A,10,11,12A,62
Khan, Pranesh	CA0050	13A,10,65
Kidde, Geoffrey C.	NY2200	10,13,34,45,32F
Kies, Christopher	NH0350	13B,10,66A,13F
Kilstofte, Mark F.	SC0750	10,13,43,13E
Kim, Hi Kyung	CA5070	13,10
Kim-Quathamer, Chan Ji	FL0150	10,11,13,34
King, Brian	CA5300	10,35H,35
King, Jonathan	NY3560	13,10F,60,36,10
King, Mary J.	CA0450	10,13
Kinney, Michael	NY0350	13,10,11
Kirby, Wayne J.	NC2400	10,45,34,35,62D
Kirchner, Bill	NY2660	10,12,64,29
Kirk, Jonathon J.	IL2050	13,10,20,34
Klein, Wendy L.	MA0260	10,35C
Kleinsasser, William	MD0850	10,43
Klement, David A.	NM0310	10,36
Klimisch, Mary J.	SD0300	10,13J,66A,66G
Klingbeil, Michael	CT0900	10,13
Kluball, Jeff L.	GA0625	37,63,29,13,10
Knapp, James	WA0200	10,47,63A,53,29
Knapp, Peter J.	CA2550	13,10,12A
Knechtges, Eric T.	KY1000	10,13
Knehans, Douglas	OH2200	10
Knight, Edward	OK0750	10
Knox, Charles C.	GA1050	10
Knutson, John R.	CA1510	36,13,10
Kocandrle, Mirek	MA0260	10,35C
Kohn, Karl G.	CA3650	13,10,11,12A
Kohrs, Jonathan A.	IL0730	10,36,11,31A,34
Kolb, Barbara	RI0200	10
Kompanek, Rudolph (Sonny)	NY2660	10
Konye, Paul	NY3680	13G,12A,38,10,12
Koonce, Paul C.	FL1850	13,10
Koplow, Philip	KY1000	13,10
Kopp, David	MA0400	13,10
Koppel, Mary Montgomery	MA0400	10
Koppelman, Daniel M.	SC0750	66A,13,34,10
Kopplin, David F.	CA0630	10,20,29,14C,46
Koprowski, Peter P.	AG0500	13,10
Korde, Shirish	MA0700	13,10,14,20,29
Korneitchouk, Igor	CA4050	13A,10,11,12A,34
Kosche, Kenneth	WI0300	13,60,10,36,31A
Kothman, Keith K.	IN0150	10B,10,34,13,35C
Kovacovic, Paul	IA0200	10,12A,66A,66C
Kowalkowski, Jeffrey F.	IL0750	10,11
Kozel, Paul	NY0550	10,45,35
Kramer, Ernest Joachim	MO0950	13,10,11,66A,66H
Kratz, Girard	PA3250	10A,10B,13,10
Kreiger, Arthur V.	CT0100	13,35C,10,45,34
Kreuze, Brandon R.	GA0600	10,34,13,12C
Krieger, Ulrich	CA0510	10,34D,12A,45,64E
Krouse, Ian	CA5030	13,10
Krouseup, Jack	CA3520	10,13B,13A,13F,47
Krusemark, Ruth E.	KS0100	13,10,66A,66G,66D
Kubik, Ladislav	FL0850	10
Kuchera-Morin, JoAnn	CA5060	13,10F,10,45,13L
Kuehn, Mikel	OH0300	13,10F,10,45,43
Kuivila, Ronald	CT0750	10,45
Kulenovic, Vuk	MA0260	10
Kulesha, Gary	AG0450	10,63C,29
Kurek, Michael	TN1850	13,10F,10
Kuss, Mark	CT0450	13,10,45,66A,34
Kuster, Kristin P.	MI2100	10
La Rocca, Frank J.	CA0807	13,10F,10
Labenske, Victor	CA3640	66A,66D,12A,10
Labor, Tim A.	CA5040	10,10A,10B,10C
Lackman, Susan Cohn	FL1550	13,10,12A,35
Laderman, Ezra	CT0850	10
Laganella, David	DE0200	10,13,34,14C,12A
Lalonde, Alain	AI0200	10,13C
Lamarche, Andre	AI0210	10
Lamb, Marvin L.	OK1350	10,43
Lamb, Sally	NY1800	13,10
Lambright, Spencer N.	TN1100	10
Lampl, Kenneth H.	NY1600	35,10,64E,34,11
Landgrave, Phillip	KY1200	10,35C,31A
Lang, David	CT0850	10
Langley, Jeff	CA4700	10,14C
Lansky, Paul	NJ0900	13,10,45,34
Lapin, Lawrence	FL1900	13,10,36,47,29
Larocque, Jacques	AI0220	10,41,48,64E,34
Lauridsen, Morten	CA5300	13,10
Lavenda, Richard A.	TX2150	13,10
Lawler, Douglas	MD0175	10,54
Lawson, Robert	CA1265	10,38,41,66A,66D
Lawson, Robert	CA5360	13,10,11,66D,12A
LeBaron, Anne	CA0510	10,12,62E
Leclair, Francois-Hugues	AI0200	10
Leclaire, Dennis	MA0260	10,63B
Ledgerwood, Lee Ann	NY2660	10,66A,47
Lee, Brent	AG0550	13,10,45,43,53
Lee, Owen J.	CA1560	13,10
Lee, Richard A.	HI0200	13,10,12A,64E,64A
Lee, Thomas Oboe	MA0330	13,10,29B
Lee-Keller, Derek	CA1500	10,10B
Lefkowitz, David S.	CA5030	13,10
Leger, James K.	NM0150	10,60,12,14,38
Legname, Orlando	NY3765	13A,13,10,35
Leiter, Cherise D.	CO0550	11,13,10
Lemay, Robert	AG0150	13,10,12A
Lennon, John A.	GA0750	13,10
Lentini, James P.	OH1450	13,10,70,34
Leon, Tania	NY0500	10,38,41,60
Leon, Tania	NY0600	10,60
Leone, Gustavo	IL1615	10,13
Leong, Daphne	CO0800	13,10
Lerdahl, Fred	NY0750	10,12F,11
Lerner, Peter	IL0720	29,70,10
Leroux, Philippe	AI0150	10
Lesage, Jean	AI0150	10
Lesemann, Frederick	CA5300	13,10F,10,45
Leshnoff, Jonathan	MD0850	13,10
Lesser, George	NJ0550	32E,63,10,32C,32F
LeVelle, Teresa	CA6000	13,10,44,42
Levey, John C.	PA3400	10,13,11,34,36
Levine, Josh	OH1700	10
LeVines, T. Allen	MA0260	10
Levinson, Gerald C.	PA3200	13,10,20D
Levinson, Ilya	IL0720	13,10
Levy, Ben	AZ0100	10,13
Lewis, Bernice	MA2250	10,40
Lewis, James E.	FL2000	13,10F,10,43
Lewis, Leonard Mark	SC1200	10,13
Lewis, Roger	KS0210	13,10,37,47,53
Liang, Lei	CA5050	10,13B,13D,10A,10B
Lias, Stephen J.	TX2700	13,10F,10
Lidov, David	AG0650	10
Lieuwen, Peter	TX2900	13,10,12A,29A
Lifchitz, Max	NY3700	10,43,13A,13,10F
Lillios, Elainie	OH0300	10B,10
Limbert, Thom	IN0910	10,13,20
Lincoln-DeCusatis, Nathan J.	WV0550	10,13,34
Link, John	NJ1400	13,10F,10,34
Lipkis, Larry	PA2450	13,10F,10,55,67
Lippe, Cort	NY4320	10,45,34
Lippens, Nancy Cobb	IN0800	10,13,36
Liptak, David	NY1100	10
Lis, Anthony	SD0550	13,10F,10,66,20D
List, Andrew	MA0260	10
Lister, Rodney	MA0400	10,13
Little, David	VA1350	10
Liu-Rosenbaum, Aaron	AI0190	10,34,35G,13,14C
Lloyd, Gerald J.	MA2030	10,13,10A
Locklair, Dan	NC2500	13,10,11,31A,66G
Loeb, David	NY2250	13,10
Loeb, John	NV0050	29,10,47
Lofstrom, Douglas	IL0720	60B,10
Logan, Kenneth	MI0250	66G,34,10,10F,31A
Lombardi, Paul	NM0450	10,13
Long, Patrick A.	PA3150	13,10,34,12A,32E
Longtin, Michel	AI0200	10,13E
Lopato, David	NY2660	13,10,66A
Lopez, Barbara	CA0400	61,66A,10
Lopez, Thomas Handman	OH1700	10B,34,10,34A
Lorenz, Ralph	OH1100	13,34,10,13F,13D
Lorenz, Ricardo	MI1400	10
Love, Randolph D.	SC0600	13,10,63,41,14C
Lowell, Richard L.	MA0260	10,29
Lowenstein, Marc	CA0510	13,10,60,39,43
Lowrey, Norman E.	NJ0300	13A,13,10,45,34

Index by Area of Teaching Interest

Name	Code	Areas
Lubet, Alex	MN1623	13,10
Lucas, Elena	MA0260	10
Lucier, Alvin	CT0750	10,45,34
Ludwig, David	PA0850	13,10
Lund, Erik R.	IL3300	13,10,43
Luzko, Daniel	CA2390	13,10F,10,34
Lynch, Brian	FL1900	63A,10,47,46,29B
Lynch, Timothy	CA1290	13,10,11,14
Macbride, David	CT0650	13,10
Macchia, Salvatore	MA2000	10,62D
MacDonald, Andrew	AI0050	13,10F,10,45,70
MacDonald, Don	AB0070	10,61,62A,64E,35A
MacIntyre, David K.	AB0080	13,10,39,43
Mack, George	RI0200	10,13,34
MacKay, James S.	LA0300	13,10
Mackey, Steven	NJ0900	13,10F,10,11,41
Macomber, Jeffrey R.	MO0800	10,11,12A,32E,63D
Macy, Carleton	MN0950	13,10,67,55,47
Madsen, Farrell D.	UT0300	13,10,12A
Madsen, Pamela	CA0815	13A,13,10
Maggio, Robert	PA3600	13,10
Mahin, Bruce P.	VA1100	10,34,13,35C
Mahoney, Shafer	NY0625	13A,13,10
Mahr, Timothy	MN1450	60B,37,10
Mainland, Timothy L.	WV0200	13,10,70,10F,62
Makan, Keeril	MA1200	10,10F,34,13
Makela, Steven L.	MN0600	10A,10B,13,10,34D
Makris, Kristina	AZ0440	10,13,35A,29A,61
Mallia, John	MA1400	10B,10,34
Malloy, Chris	CO0900	10,13
Malsky, Matthew	MA0650	10A,10B,34,13,10
Maltz, Richard	SC1100	13,10,65,12,14
Mamey, Norman	CA1000	66A,10,12A,13,35A
Mandrell, Nelson E.	IL2150	13,10,45,34
Mann, Rochelle	CO0350	10,11,32,64
Manoury, Philippe	CA5050	10
Marcinizyn, John	PA0600	13,10,70
Marcinizyn, John	PA3000	10,70
Marcus, David	GA0490	10,11,12A,13A,29A
Marcus, Edward	MN0800	10
Mardirosian, Haig L.	DC0010	13,10,66G,11
Marinescu, Liviu	CA0835	10A,13E,13F,10
Maroney, Marcus K.	TX3400	10
Marsh, Gerry Jon	WA0800	34,35C,37,10
Marsh, Gordon E.	VA1250	10,66,13,10A,66A
Marshall, Christopher J.	FL1800	10
Marshall, Ingram	CT0850	10
Martin, Henry	NJ1140	13,10,12,29,29A
Marvin, John W.	CA0850	10
Maske, Dan	WI0150	10,34
Matascik, Sheri L.	TN1000	13,10,70,10B,13H
Matejka, Merle	AJ0030	10,12A,31A,13,29
Mathes, James	FL0850	13,10
Matheson, Jennifer	AF0120	10,66D,66A
Matthews, Bill	ME0150	13,10,29,34
Matthews, Justus F.	CA0825	13,10,43,34
Matthews, Michael	AC0100	10
Matthews, Ron	PA1150	13,10,12A,63A,66A
Matthusen, Paula A.	CT0750	34,45,10
Mauceri, Frank	ME0340	10,13,12B
Maurtua, Jose Luis	MI0400	13A,13,10F,60,10
Mauthe, Timothy	VA0250	13,10
Mayrose, John S.	IN0910	10,13
Mays, Walter A.	KS1450	13,10
Maz, Andrew	CA1900	34,10
McAllister, Margaret	MA0260	10,13,34H,10A,34
McAllister, Scott	TX0300	10
McArthur-Brown, Gail	MA0260	10,35C,35G
McAuliffe, Harold F.	NY4350	10
McBride, Michael S.	IL2100	10,34,13,31,12A
McCabe, Matthew	GA0550	34,13,10
McCardell, Stephen	WI0350	13,10
McCarthy, Daniel	OH2150	10,13
McConnell, Douglas W.	OH0950	13,10
McCray, James	CO0250	10,32C,12A
McCullough, Thomas Eric	OK1330	10,62C,13,38,10C
McDonald, John	MA1900	13A,10,12A,43,13
McDonnell, Donald	MA0260	10
McFatter, Larry E.	CA0845	13,10F,10,66A
McFerron, Mike	IL1520	13A,13,10F,34,10
McGah, Thomas J.	MA0260	10
McGee, William James	CA3400	13,10F,10,66A,34
McGowan, James	AG0200	10,11
McGrew, David	PA0150	10,13,66,31A,11
McGuinness, Peter	NJ1400	13,10,29,41
McGuire, David	NY1250	13,10,12A,13A,47
McIntyre, Eric L.	IA0700	10,38,60,12A,13
McIntyre, John	IN1400	13,34,12A,36,10
McIntyre, John	IN1350	13,10,60,36
McKay, Frances	DC0170	13,10
McKay, Neil	HI0210	10,13
McKelvey, Michael E.	PA2900	35E,61,54,10
McKenna, Fr. Edward	IN0005	10,62A,16,31A,11
McKenney, W. Thomas	MO1800	13,10,34D
McKinnon, John A.	OR0200	13,10,63,34,14
McLean, Greg	GA0940	13,11,29,10
McNair, Jonathan B.	TN1700	10A,34D,13,10,34
McWain, Andrew J.	MA2020	29,10,13B
Meckler, David C.	CA0855	11,20,12A,10,13A
Meister, Scott R.	NC0050	10,65,43,50
Meltzer, Harold	NY4450	10
Menoche, Charles Paul	CT0050	10,12,13,34
Mensah, Sowah	MN0950	12A,20A,10
Menton, Allen W.	CA0845	10,13
Merkowitz, Jennifer Bernard	OH2050	10,13,34
Merriman, Margarita L.	MA0250	13,10,66A
Merritt, Justin W.	MN1450	10,13,43,13A,34
Merryman, Marjorie	NY2150	10,13
Mery, John Christian	OR0800	13,10,41,70,34
Meschi, John	NY2105	10,34
Metcalf, John C.	PA1750	34,10,11,49,63C
Metz, Ken	TX3410	13,10,29,29A
Meyer, Donald C.	IL1400	13,12A,10,34
Meyn, Till MacIvor	TX3000	13,10
Middleton, Jonathan N.	WA0250	13,10,35C,34,35
Miksch, Bonnie	OR0850	10,13
Miles, Stephen T.	FL1360	13,10,43
Miley, James	OR1300	10,29,47,46,13
Miller, Dennis H.	MA1450	13,10,45,34
Miller, Harold L.	WI0450	10,13A,13G,20,47
Miller, Jeffrey L.	CA0807	13,10
Millett, Michael J.	TX3535	13,10
Mills, David	OR0050	13,10,12A,37,63A
Mitchell, Darleen C.	NE0590	10,10,15,43,12B
Mitchell, Jennifer	GA1150	13B,13C,11,10
Mitchell, Roscoe	CA2950	10,29,53
Miura, Hiroya	ME0150	10,13,38
Moe, Eric H.	PA3420	13,10,45,10B
Mok, April H.	LA0900	10,66G
Mollicone, Henry	CA1950	10,12A
Monhardt, Jonathan	WI0825	10,13
Monseur, George	MA0260	10,60
Montalto, Richard Michael	MS0550	13,12A,35,10,13F
Moore, David A.	OK1450	10,13,11,36
Moore, F. Richard	CA5050	10,45,34,35C,13L
Moore, James Walter	KY0400	34,13,10,70
Moore, Robert S.	CA5300	13,10
Moorman, Joyce Solomon	NY2100	13,10,11,66A,66D
Moral, Carmen	MA0260	10
Moravec, Paul	NY2250	10
Moravec, Paul	NY0050	13,10
Morawetz, Oskar	AG0450	10
Morehead, Patricia	IL0720	10F,10,64B
Moretti, Daniel D.	MA0260	10
Morrill, Dexter G.	NY0650	10,45,29A,34
Morris, Robert D.	NY1100	10,12,13,20E,31E
Morrison, John H.	MA1175	10,13
Moser, Diane	NY2660	47,10
Moses, Leonard	MD0060	10
Moss, Lawrence	MD1010	10,13,10F
Moss, Myron D.	PA1000	10,11,29,37,60
Mott, David	AG0650	13A,10
Mountain, Rosemary	AI0070	13,10F,10,45,34
Mountford, Fritz	NE0300	32C,36,60A,10,20
Mowitz, Ira	NJ0750	10,13A,13B,41,66A
Mowrey, Peter C.	OH0700	10,66A,13,34
Moyer, J. Harold	KS0200	10
Mozetich, Marjan	AG0250	10
Mueller, Robert K.	AR0700	10,13
Muhl, Erica	CA5300	13,10
Mulvey, Bob	MA0260	10,35
Mumford, Larry	CA0350	10
Mumford, Lawrence R.	CA5355	10,12,13,10F
Munger, Philip	AK0100	10,13A,33
Muniz, Jorge	IN0910	10A,13,10B,10,43
Munn, Zae	IN1450	13,10F,10,43
Murail, Tristan C.	NY0750	10,34,13L,12F,10F
Murphy, Joanna	FL0200	10,13
Murray, Michael F.	MO0775	10,13
Musgrave, Thea	NY0642	10
Myska, David	AG0500	13,10,45,34,35C
Nagel, Jody	IN0150	13,10,45,35C
Nangle, Richard	MA0400	10,70
Narducci, Kenneth	CA2420	10,37,32E,46,13
Nash, Gary Powell	TN0550	10,13,47,64,10F
Nauert, Paul	CA5070	13,10
Navari, Jude Joseph	CA4625	10,11,13,36,61
Neidhoefer, Christoph	AI0150	13,10
Neilson, Duncan	OR0150	13A,13B,10,13C,13E
Nelson, David W.	CA0859	13,13A,10F,10,38
Nelson, Larry A.	PA3600	13,10,45,34
Nelson, Richard	ME0340	10,34,13,29,47
Nelson, Robert S.	TX3400	13A,13,10F,10
Neumeyer, David	TX3510	13,10
Nevin, Jeff	CA4850	63A,20H,10
Newby, Stephen M.	WA0800	10,36
Newton, James	CA5031	29,10
Nez, Catherine Ketty	MA0400	10,66A,10A
Nichols, Charles Sabin	MT0400	10A,10B,10,45,34
Nichols, Jeff W.	NY0642	10,10F,13
Nichols, Samuel S.	CA5010	13,10,70,10B
Niederberger, Maria	TN0500	13,10F,10
Nielsen, Robert	CA1850	10,11
Nielson, Lewis	OH1700	10
Nieske, Robert	MA0500	10,47,62D,53,46
Nin, Chan Ka	AG0450	13A,13,10,10F
Nixon, Roger A.	CA4200	10
Nohai-Seaman, Alexander	NY4050	13,10,43
Noon, David	NY2150	12,10A,10,12A
Notareschi, Loretta K.	CO0650	10,11,13
Noya, Francisco	MA0260	10
Nurock, Kirk	NY2660	10F,60,10,13J,29A
Nyberg, Gary B.	WA0480	13,10,37,63D,54
Obermueller, Karola	NM0450	10,13
O'Brien, Eugene	IN0900	10
O'Donnell, Shaugn	NY0550	13,10,12
Ogdon, Will L.	CA5050	13,10F,10,12A
OGrady, Douglas M.	CT0800	13,34,35G,10
Oh, Seung-Ah	IL0750	10,13,13F,10A
Okpebholo, Shawn E.	IL3550	13,10
Olan, David M.	NY0250	13,10,11
Olan, David	NY0600	10F,10,10B
Oliver, Harold	NJ1050	13,10F,10,41,53
Oliverio, James C.	FL1850	10,34
Oliveros, Pauline	CA2950	10,15
Olivieri, Mark A.	NY1550	10,13,20G,29,48
Olsen, Timothy J.	NY4310	13,10,47,63A,29
Onofrio, Marshall	NJ1350	13,10,29,34,32E
Oravitz, Michael	IN0150	13,10
Orfe, John	IL0400	10,13
O'Riordan, Kirk	PA1850	10,60B,13,64E
Orpen, Rick	MN0750	13,70,34,10
Ortiz, Pablo	CA5010	13,10,45,29,34
Osterfield, Paul	TN1100	13,10
Ovens, Douglas P.	PA2550	13,10,45,65
Overmier, Douglas R.	MO0950	60B,60A,37,47,10
Owen, Charles (Chuck) R.	FL2000	47,29,10
Owens, Theodore	NV0125	10,11,12A,61,54
Paccione, Paul	IL3500	13,10,43,20G
Pace, Matthew	MO1950	10,13
Packales, Joseph	ME0500	13,10F,10
Palej, Norbert	AG0450	10,13
Palestrant, Christopher	NC0700	13,10
Pampin, Juan	WA1050	10,34
Pann, Carter N.	CO0800	13,10
Paoli, Kenneth N.	IL0630	13,10,11,35,34
Pape, Louis W.	SD0150	13,10,11,32,66
Paraskevas, Apostolos	MA0260	10
Parillo, Joseph M.	RI0300	13,10,47,46,29
Park, Sang Eui	IN0005	10,60,12,13,31A
Park, Tae Hong	NY2750	10,34
Parke, Steve	IL2450	10,47,63A,29A,35A
Parker, Philip	AR0200	13,10F,10,65,50
Parker, Val	GA0490	10,11,13A,34D,29A
Parks, Ronald Keith	SC1200	10,13,34,41
Pascuzzi, Greg	MD0060	10,63A
Pashkin, Elissa Brill	MA1100	13,10
Patitucci, John	NY0550	10,46,47,51,50
Patterson, David N.	MA2010	13,10,11,20G,34
Patterson, Michael R.	IA1350	12A,32B,66A,13,10
Patton, Jeb	NY1275	10,13B,29B,29C,66A
Paul, John F.	OR0500	10,13,34
Payne, Tony L.	IL3550	10,34
Peacock, Kenneth J.	NY2750	13,10,12,35,34
Pedneault-Deslauriers, Julie	AG0400	13,10
Peel, John	OR1300	10,12A

419

Index by Area of Teaching Interest

Name	Code	Areas
Pejrolo, Andrea	MA0260	34,10C,10,35C,35G
Pellman, Samuel	NY1350	13,10B,10,34
Pelo, Mika	CA5010	10,11,13,43
Perkins, Scott	IN0350	10,13
Perlongo, Daniel J.	PA1600	10,13,29
Perricone, Jack	MA0260	10
Perrotte, Jean-Paul	NV0100	10,13B,13F,13G,13E
Petering, Mark D.	WI0250	10,13,34
Peterson, Keith L.	NY3725	13,10,45
Peterson, Wayne T.	CA4200	13,10F,10,12A,66A
Peterson, William F.	FL0850	10,29
Pethel, Stan	GA0300	13,60,10,63C,10F
Petrides, Ron T.	NY2660	10,29,70,13,12
Peyton, Malcolm C.	MA1400	10
Pfaff, William P.	NY3775	10,13,12A,13F,13I
Phan, P. Q.	IN0900	10
Phelps, James	IL2200	10,45,34
Phillips, Joel	NJ1350	13,10,34
Phillips, Mark W.	OH1900	43,10,45,34
Phillips, Paul Schuyler	RI0050	38,60,13,10F
Piccone, James	NJ1050	13,10,34
Pierce, Forrest D.	KS1350	13,10,43
Pieslak, Jonathan	NY0550	10,13
Pignato, Joseph M.	NY3765	35,34,10,13
Pilkington, Robert	MA0260	10,29
Ping, Jin	NY3760	13,10,62A,20A,20B
Pinkston, Dan	CA4600	13,12A,14,10,20
Pinkston, Russell F.	TX3510	10,45,34
Piper, Deirdre	AG0100	13,10,12A
Pisaro, Michael J.	CA0510	13,10,12D
Plash, Duane	AL1195	13,10,66A,40
Polansky, Larry	NH0100	13,10,45,34
Poniatowski, Mark	MA0260	10,35C,35G
Popeney, Mark	CA5300	10,13
Porter, Charles	NY2400	13A,13,10,11,12A
Portnoy, Kim	MO1950	10F,10,29
Post, J. Brian	CA2250	34,35,13,10
Potes, Cesar I.	MI1200	13,10,11,34
Poulsen, James	IA1350	13,66A,66C,10
Pound, Robert	PA0950	13,10,11,38
Pounds, Michael S.	IN0150	10,34D,13,45,34
Powell, Jarrad	WA0200	13A,10,20D,45,34
Powers, Daniel	IN0800	10
Prescott, John S.	MO0775	13,10,20
Price, William M.	AL1150	13,10
Priester, Julian	WA0200	10,47,63C,63D,29
Primosch, James	PA3350	13,10,10B
Prince, Curtis L.	IN0005	10,12,20G,65,47
Pritchard, Bob	AB0100	13,10,34
Proctor, Gregory	OH1850	13,10,34
Prouty, Patrick	MI2120	47,13,43,10
Ptaszynska, Marta	IL3250	13,10,10F
Pullig, Kenneth	MA0260	10,29
Pursell, William	TN0100	10,12A,13,11,66G
Pusztai, Tibor J.	MA0260	10
Puts, Kevin M.	MD0650	10
Pysh, Gregory	TX3527	10,13,61,60A,36
Qualliotine, Armand Guy	MA0260	10
Quathamer, Mark	FL0150	10,13,34
Quist, Pamela	CA4425	13,10,66A,12
Radford, Laurie	AA0150	10,10F,13,43
Radzynski, Jan	OH1850	10
Rahn, John	WA1050	13,10,34
Rakowski, David	MA1400	10
Rakowski, David	MA0500	13,10,12A
Ramirez, Armando L.	PR0115	10,13A,13B,13D,13F
Ran, Shulamit	IL3250	10
Randall, James K.	NJ0900	13,10
Raskin, Jon	CA2950	10,64E
Raynovich, William Jason	IL0600	13,10,34
Rea, John	AI0150	13,10
Read, Thomas L.	VT0450	13,10
Reasoner, Eric	MA0260	10
Rector, Malcolm W.	TX3450	13,10,29,47
Reed, S. Alexander	FL1850	13,10
Reeves, Matthew	MA0400	10
Regan, Martin	TX2900	10,20C,13
Reid, Clement	WA0650	10
Reid, Darlene Chepil	AG0170	13F,13I,10
Reid, Sally	TN0930	10,13,64B,10C,34
Reid, Wendy	CA2950	10
Reiprich, Bruce J.	AZ0450	13,10,34
Reise, Jay	PA3350	13,10F,10
Reiter, Burkhardt	PA3420	10,13
Reller, Paul	FL2000	10,34
Remele, Rebecca	AL0300	10,34
Repar, Patricia Ann	NM0450	10,45
Resanovic, Nikola	OH2150	13,10
Reuter, Rocky J.	OH0350	10
Reyes, James E.	MA0260	10
Reynolds, Roger L.	CA5050	13,10F,10,20G,34
Rhea, Tim B.	TX2900	10,37,64E
Rhodes, Phillip	MN0300	13A,13,10,11
Richards, Paul	FL1850	13,10
Richardson, Danene	AZ0440	13,10
Richens, James W.	TN1680	13,10,45
Richmond, Thomas	MN0600	13,10,11,12A
Rickard, Jeffrey H.	CA5150	10,60,36,31A
Ridgeway, Max A.	OK0600	10,70,11,20,46
Riepe, Russell C.	TX3175	13,10,45
Rigler, Jane	CO0810	64A,10B,34D,10
Riley, Steve	KS0050	65,50,10
Rimple, Mark T.	PA3600	13,10
Rindfleisch, Andrew P.	OH0650	10,13,43
Rinehart, John	OH0050	13A,13,10F,10,12A
Ring, Gordon L.	VA0700	13,10,37,34
Rinzler, Paul	CA0600	13,10,47,66A,29
Rissman, Maurice Nick	TX1400	13,10F,10
Rivers, James	KS1400	11,66A,66C,10
Rizzer, Gerald	IL2750	66A,13,10
Robbins, Malcolm Scott	SC0650	13,10,14C
Roberts, Sara	CA0510	10,34
Roberts, Shannon B.	UT0150	13,41,49,63C,10
Robertson, Eric	AG0450	10,13
Robinson, Scott	PA1150	12,14,10
Rochon, Gaston	AI0210	10
Rockmaker, Jody D.	AZ0100	13A,13,10,12A,43
Rodgers, Lloyd A.	CA0815	13,10,43
Roens, Steven	UT0250	13,10
Rogalsky, Matt	AG0250	10,45,34,32F
Rogers, John E.	NH0350	13B,10,13D,13E,13G
Rogers, John Fitz	SC1110	10
Rogers, Rodney	AZ0100	13,10F,10
Rohde, Kurt E.	CA5010	13,10,11,43
Rohlig, Harald	AL0450	10,66G,31A
Roig-Francoli, Miguel A.	OH2200	13,10
Rolfe, James	AG0450	10,13
Rollin, Robert	OH2600	13,10,43
Rolls, Timothy	KS0350	10,13,34,35C,35G
Rolnick, Neil B.	NY3300	13,10,45,34
Romig, James	IL3500	13,13F,10A,10
Rommereim, John Christian	IA0700	60,10,36,61
Root, Jena	OH2600	10,13
Root, Thomas R.	UT0350	13,10,37,41
Rose, Cameron J.	TX3535	36,32D,11,10
Rose, Francois	CA5350	13,10
Rose, Michael	TN1850	13,10,12A,11,31
Rosenblum, Mathew	PA3420	13,10F,10
Rosenboom, David	CA0510	10,43,66A
Rosenhaus, Steven L.	NY2750	10,13F,10F,10A,10D
Rosenzweig, Morris	UT0250	13,10F,10
Ross, Clark	AD0050	13,10
Ross, John C.	KS1050	13,10,10F
Roter, Bruce	NY0700	10,13,12A,64C
Roubal, Peter	IL2350	13,10,34B,47
Rouse, Christopher	NY1900	10
Rouse, Steve	KY1500	10
Roush, Dean	KS1450	13,10F,10,34
Rovan, Joseph 'Butch'	RI0050	10,45,34
Rowe, Robert	NY2750	10,43,34,35C
Roze, Chris	CA5300	13,10
Rozin, Alexander	PA3600	10,13
Rubin, Anna I.	MD1000	10,34
Rubin, Justin H.	MN1600	13,34,66G,10,66A
Ruehr, Elena	MA1200	13,10,34
Ruggiero, Charles	MI1400	13,10
Ruiz, Otmaro	CA5300	66A,10
Ruo, Huang	NY3785	10
Rusche, Marjorie M.	IN0910	10,13
Russell, Armand	HI0210	10,13
Rutty, Alejandro	NC2430	10
Ryan, William E.	MI0900	10,43
Sabina, Leslie M.	NY3475	29,10,34,13,47
Sachdev, Salil	MA0510	10,13A,20A,50,13B
Sadin, Robert	NY2660	60,10
Sain, James Paul	FL1850	13,10,34
Salerni, Paul F.	PA1950	13,10,43
Salerno, John	WI0808	13,10,47,48,29
Sametz, Steven P.	PA1950	13,60,10,36
San Martin, Laurie A.	CA5010	10,13,43,35E
Sanchez-Behar, Alexander	OH0100	13,10
Sanchez-Gutierrez, Carlos	NY1100	10
Sander, Kurt L.	KY1000	10,13
Sanders, Gregory L.	TX2960	13,10F,10,34
Sandred, Orjan	AC0100	10,13,34
Sandroff, Howard	IL3250	10,45,34,13L
Sanford, David	MA1350	13,10,29A
Santa, Matthew	TX3200	13,10
Santore, Jonathan C.	NH0250	13,10
Santos, Erik	MI2100	10,34A,45
Sapieyevski, Jerzy	DC0010	13,10,45,11,34
Sartor, John E.	TN1600	10
Satterwhite, Marc	KY1500	13,10
Sauerwein, Andrew Mark	MS0100	13,10,29B,43,64B
Sawyer, Eric	MA0100	10,13,34,43
Saylor, Bruce	NY0600	10F,10
Saylor, Bruce S.	NY0642	13,10F,10
Sayre, Charles L.	GA1700	10
Scearce, J. Mark	NC1700	13,10
Schane-Lydon, Cathy	MA1850	10,36,66
Schelle, Michael	IN0250	13,10,43,10F
Scherr, Bernard	TX0900	13,10,66D
Scherzinger, Nicolas	NY4150	13,10,34,64E
Schildt, Matthew C.	CO0050	13,10,10D,13E,34
Schindler, Karl W.	AZ0470	10,13,34,12A
Schirmer, Timothy	IL2350	13,10,34B,54
Schleiffer, Marlene J.	IN0700	10,64B
Schmidt, Fred	MA0260	10,35
Schmitz, Alan W.	IA1600	13,10
Schober, David	NY0642	13,10A,66A,10
Schoendorff, Matthew	MI2200	10
Schoenfield, Paul	MI2100	10
Schonthal, Ruth	NY2400	13,10,66A
Schrader, Barry	CA0510	13,10,12A,34
Schreiber, Paul	MS0560	10,13,34,10B,10A
Schroeder, Phillip J.	AR0300	13,10
Schultz, Arlan N.	AA0200	10,34,13,12B
Schultz, Eric	CA0900	10,13,34
Schultz, Willis Jackson	MA0260	10,29
Schulze, Otto	IN0005	62A,67,10,13,36
Schumaker, Adam T.	MI2250	10,11
Schurger, Phillip	IN0700	70,10
Schwabe, Jonathan C.	IA1600	13,10,29
Schwartz, Elliott S.	ME0200	10F,10,11,12A,41
Schwartz, Richard I.	VA1750	13,48,64C,10
Schwendinger, Laura Elise	WI0815	10
Schwoebel, David	VA1150	10,43
Schyman, Garry	CA5300	10
Scism, William	MA0260	10,29
Sclater, James	MS0400	13E,10F,10,13C
Scott, Stephen	CO0200	10,11,45,43,29
Sekhon, Baljinder S.	FL2000	10,65,13,34
Semegen, Daria	NY3790	13,10,45
Serghi, Sophia	VA0250	13,10F,10,43,10A
Setter, Terry A.	WA0350	10F,10,12B,45,35C
Setziol, Paul	CA1550	13,10
Sevilla, Tiffany	IL0720	10,34
Shabani, Afrim	IL2510	11,10,13,34B,13C
Shackleton, Phil	CA0250	13,10,34
Shapiro, Gerald	RI0050	13,10,45,34
Sharlat, Yevgeniy	TX3510	10
Sharpe, Carlyle	MO0350	13,10F,10
Shatin, Judith	VA1550	10B,10A,10F,10,13
Shaw, David	NY2500	13,10,11,12A
Shawn, Allen	VT0050	13,10,66A
Shemaria, Rich	NY2660	60,10,66A
Shende, Vineet	ME0200	10,13,20C,20E,31E
Sheng, Bright	MI2100	13,10
Shepard, Brian K.	CA5300	34,10,13,34C,65
Sherr, Laurence E.	GA1150	13,12A,10
Shockley, Alan	CA0825	13,10
Shrude, Marilyn	OH0300	10
Shultis, Christopher	NM0450	12,12B,10
Sichel, John	NJ0975	13,10,11,12A,36
Sidoti, Vincent	ND0600	10,13B
Silverman, Adam B.	PA3600	10,13
Simoncic, Max	CA4300	13,10,11
Simos, Mark	MA0260	10,10D
Simpson, Andrew Earle	DC0050	10,10F,13,66A,43
Simpson, Kyle	PA3580	10,11,37,47
Sink, Damon W.	NC2600	10,13,34,34B,13I
Sirota, Robert	NY2150	39,10
Siskind, Paul A.	NY3780	13,10
Slavin, Peter	IN0005	10,13,66,66A,11
Slawson, A. Wayne	CA5010	13,10,34
Slawson, Wayne	OR0950	10

Index by Area of Teaching Interest

Name	Code	Areas
Sleeper, Thomas M.	FL1900	10F,60,10,38
Smaldone, Edward	NY0642	13,10,10F,11
Smart, Gary	FL1950	13,10F,10,66A,53
Smith, Douglas	AB0050	13A,13,10,13C,12
Smith, Glenn E.	VA0450	13,10,45,34,42
Smith, James Russell	MA0260	10
Smith, Joel Larue	MA1900	29,47,10,53,13A
Smith, Joseph	MA0260	10
Smith, Kent M.	PA3560	10,11,12A,31A
Smith, Larry Alan	CT0650	10
Smith, Leland C.	CA4900	13,10,12A,34
Smith, Robert Thomas	TX3400	13A,13,10,43
Smith, Stuart Saunders	MD1000	13,10
Smith, Wadada Leo	CA0510	63A,29,10,45,53
Smith, William O.	WA1050	13,10,43
Smolenski, Scott	FL1675	66A,10,11,13,20
Sollberger, Harvey	CA5050	10F,60,10,64A,43
Solomon, Jason Wyatt	GA0050	10,13
Solot, Evan	PA3330	13,10F,10,47,46
Solum, Stephen	MN1050	13,20G,10,35G,34
Sommer, Lesley	WA1250	13,10,45
Sommerville, Daniel A.	IL3550	38,10,60B
Sonenberg, Daniel M.	ME0500	10A,13F,13C,10,13
Sonntag, Dawn Lenore	OH1000	36,61,66C,10A,10
Soper, Kate	MA1750	10,10B
Spaneas, Demetrius	NY1275	10,29,46,64E,10F
Spaniola, Joseph T.	FL2100	47,46,63D,11,10
Sparks, David	CA1100	16,10,66A
Spear, David R.	NY2750	10,10F,60,10C
Speck, Frederick A.	KY1500	10,37,43
Spies, Claudio	NJ0900	13,60,10,39
Spraggins, Mark	CA0550	13,10,34
Sproul Pulatie, Leah	MO0050	10,13
Squires, David	AB0090	10,12A
Srinivasan, Asha	WI0350	13,10
Stadelman, Jeffrey	NY4320	10,43
Stahlke, Jonathan E.	IL0730	13,10,38,10F
Stallings, Jim	GA0940	10
Stallings, Kendall	MO1950	13,10
Stallmann, Kurt D.	TX2150	13,10,45,34
Stalnaker, William P.	OR0850	13,10,12A
Stamps, Jack W.	NJ1160	10,34
Staniland, Andrew	AD0050	34,10
Stano, Richey	FL1675	70,10
Stanton, Geoffrey	MI1300	13,10,45,34
Stanziano, Stephen	OH1000	13A,13B,13C,10,62D
Stasack, Jennifer	NC0550	10,20,31G
Stearns, Loudon	MA0260	10,35C,35G
Steen, Kenneth	CT0650	10,13,45
Stegall, Sydney Wallace	WA0460	13,14,10B,14F,10
Steiger, Rand	CA5050	13,10,34
Steinbach, Richard	IA0100	13,10,66,34
Stemper, Frank L.	IL2900	13,10,43
Stephens, Michael	NE0050	10,29,46,13,64
Stephens, Timothy	OR0750	13,10F,10,12A
Stern, Adam	WA0200	10,60
Stevens, John	WI0815	63D,60B,35,10,13
Stevens, John L.	MA0260	10
Stevenson, Janis	CA1800	13A,10,70
Stewart, Louis	MA0260	10
Stiefel, Van	PA3600	10,13
Stinnett, Jim	MA0260	10,35C
Stokes, Harvey J.	VA0500	13,10,64B,34
Stolet, Jeffrey	OR1050	13,45,10,34,10B
Stolte, Charles	AA0035	64E,13A,13,10,43
Strommen, Carl	NY2105	10,10F,10A
Stucky, Steven	NY0900	10,13B,13D,13F,43
Studinger, Bob	CO0625	11,10,13
Sturm, Fred	WI0350	10,29,46,47
Suarez, Jeff	WI0847	10,13,29,42,20G
Suber, Stephen C.	LA0650	13,10,11
Sullivan, Mark	MI1400	10,12B,34
Sullivan, Michael	TX2200	10,11,12A
Susa, Conrad	CA4150	10,13D
Sussman, Richard	NY3785	10
Suter, Anthony	CA5150	13D,13E,10
Svoboda, Tomas	OR0850	13,10
Swilley, Daniel	IL1200	10,13,34,13A,13B
Swist, Christopher	NH0150	50,65,13,10
Sykes, Jerilyn	MA0260	10,35C
Syler, James	TX3530	20G,29,35,10
Syler, James	TX3410	10
Sylvern, Craig	NH0150	64E,34,32F,10,48
Syswerda, Todd	IN1025	13A,13,10,11,10F
Tabor, Jerry N.	MD0800	13,10,29B,47,11
Taddie, David	WV0750	13,10,45
Taggart, Mark Alan	NC0650	13,10
Talaga, Steve	MI1050	66A,29A,29B,29C,10
Talpash, Andriy	AA0100	10,13
Tan, Su Lian	VT0350	10,13,64A,42
Tann, Hilary	NY4310	13,10
Tanner, Robert	GA1450	10,12A,11,65,34
Tapia-Carreto, Veronica	AA0050	10,13
Taranto, Vernon	FL1650	10,11,13B,36,13C
Tarsi, Boaz	NY1860	13,10,14
Taube, Heinrich K.	IL3300	13,10,34
Taylor, Jack M.	OH2275	10,37,47,29
Taylor, Priscilla	MA2010	13,10,62C,41
Taylor, Stephen A.	IL3300	13,10
Taylor, Valerie	MA0260	10
Tcimpidis, David	NY2250	10
Tedesco, Anne C.	NY3500	13,66A,54,29A,10
Teichler, Robert Christopher	IL3150	47,10,38
Terry, Peter R.	OH0250	34,10,13
Thayer, Fred M.	PA2100	13,60,10,36
Theisen, Alan	NC1250	13,10,34,35G,64E
Theodore, Michael	CO0800	45,34,10
Theofanidis, Christopher	CT0850	10
Thimmig, Les	WI0815	10,47,64E,29
Thomalla, Hans Christian	IL2250	10
Thomas, Marilyn Taft	PA0550	13,10
Thomas, Richard Pearson	NY4200	66A,66C,10
Thomas, Robert E.	NY0700	10,13A,13B,13C,13D
Thomas, Ronald B.	PA2800	10
Thome, Diane	WA1050	13,10
Thompson, Christopher K.	AR0950	13A,13,10F,10,66A
Thompson, Douglas S.	NJ0500	13,10,12A,34
Thompson, John	GA0950	34,10
Thompson, Timothy D.	FL1450	10,13,34,64E
Thorman, Marc	NY0500	10,13,12A,20,14C
Ticheli, Frank	CA5300	13,10
Tipei, Sever	IL3300	13,10,34
Toensing, Richard E.	CO0800	13,10,45
Tolley, David	DE0050	10,34,35
Tolliver, Charles	NY2660	10,46,47,63A
Torres, Michael Rene	OH1650	64E,48,10
Toutant, William P.	CA0835	10,11
Tower, Joan	NY0150	10,43
Travers, Aaron	IN0900	10
Trawick, Eleanor	IN0150	10,13,13F,13H,13L
Trayle, Mark	CA0510	10,34,45
Trester, Francine G.	MA0260	10
Truax, Barry D.	AB0080	10,45,34,35C,13L
Trueman, Daniel	NJ0900	13,10B,10
Tsontakis, George	NY0150	10
Tuck, Patrick M.	KY1425	10,13,49,63A,63B
Turner, George	ID0150	10,13,60B,63C,63D
Turrin, Joseph	NJ0700	10,10C
Tutschku, Hans	MA1050	10,10B
Twombly, Kristian	MN1300	10B,34H,12B,10,11
Udell, Chester	OR1050	10,10B,11,34,35
Ueno, Ken	CA5000	10,13,34A,34D
Ulman, Erik	CA4900	10,13,12B,62A
Ulrich, Jerry	GA0900	10,36,32,32D,60A
Umezaki, Kojiro	CA5020	10,13,34
Underhill, Owen	AB0080	13,60,10,12,43
Ung, Chinary	CA5050	10,20D,64
Vaccaro, Brandon C.	OH1100	13,10,34,13B,13A
Vaglio, Anthony J.	NC1300	13,10,32,34
Valerio, John	SC0900	29B,53,66A,10
Van Appledorn, Mary Jeanne	TX3200	13,10
Van Buren, Harvey	DC0350	13A,13,10F,10,66G
Vandegriff, Matthew	NY2105	10,13C
Vannice, Michael	OR0950	13A,10,10F
Vanore, John	PA3680	60,10,47,49,63A
Variego, Jorge	ND0600	10,13B,48,64C,64B
Vassilandonakis, Yiorgos	SC0500	10,11,13,43
Vayo, David J.	IL1200	10F,10,10D,10B,10A
Veenker, Jonathan	MN0250	13,10F,10
Vehar, Persis Parshall	NY0400	10,66A
Velazquez, Ileana Perez	MA2250	10,13,34D
Vento, Steve	OK1300	10,11,12,47,32E
Vercoe, Barry	MA1200	13,10,45,34
Vernon, James R.	OK0650	13,10,35C,11
Vigeland, Nils	NY2150	13,10
Vogel, Roger C.	GA2100	13,10
Voigt, Steve	VA0600	10,11,13
Volk, David Paul	VA1580	13,36,12A,66A,10
Volker, Mark D.	TN0100	10,10A,10B,13C
Vollrath, Carl P.	AL1050	10,11
Von Kampen, David	NE0150	10
Von Schweinitz, Wolfgang	CA0510	10,12
Vores, Andy	MA0350	10,13B
Vosbein, Terry	VA1850	10,13,29A,47,29
Waggoner, Andrew B.	NY4150	13,10,12A
Walczyk, Kevin	OR1250	13,45,63B,29,10
Walicki, Kenneth J.	CA0815	10,13,34
Walker, Christopher	CA3150	13,10,31A
Walker, Gregory	MN0350	13,10,45,34
Wallace, John H.	MA0400	10,13
Wallace, William	AG0200	13,10F,10
Wallach, Joelle	TX3420	10
Wallen, Norm	WA0050	10
Walsh, Craig T.	AZ0500	10,10B,13,10A
Wannamaker, Robert	CA0510	13,10
Ward-Steinman, David	IN0900	10,11
Ware, John	VA1800	13,10,12,66
Warren, Ron	MD0150	10F,10,66C
Warshaw, Dalit Hadass	MA0350	10,13,66A,10F,13E
Waschka, Rodney A.	NC1700	10,12A,13F,10B,13
Waters, J. Kevin	WA0400	10
Waters, Joseph	CA4100	10,45,34,35C
Waters, Renee	MO1550	13,10,66A,34,11
Waters, Tim	OK0850	47,10,37
Watson, William E.	MD0175	10,47,14C,20
Watts, Christopher M.	NY3550	10B,34,34D,34H,10
Watts, Mike	CA0350	10
Weaver, Brent	OR0250	10,61,13,34,36
Weaver, Carol Ann	AG0470	13,10,12,20A,29A
Weesner, Anna	PA3350	13,10,11
Weinberg, Henry	NY0642	10,13
Weinstein, Michael	MA0260	10
Weinzweig, John	AG0450	10
Weise, Christopher	NC1000	13,10,34,35
Weisert, Lee	NC2410	13,10
Welcher, Dan E.	TX3510	10,43
Wellman, Samuel	VA0650	66A,66D,10,13A,13B
Wells, Thomas H.	OH1850	10,45,34
Welstead, Jon	WI0825	10,13,34,43,45
Welwood, Arthur	MA0260	10
Wernick, Richard F.	PA3350	13,60,10,41
Werntz, Julia	MA1400	10
Werren, Philip	AG0650	10F,10,45
Westcott, William W.	AG0650	10
Westerberg, Kurt H.	IL0750	13,10,11
Westergaard, Peter	NJ0900	13,60,10,39
Weston, Trevor L.	NJ0300	11,20B,13,10
Weymouth, Daniel	NY3790	13,10,45,34
Wheeler, Candace	FL0200	66,11,32,10,66A
Wheeler, George	CA0825	10,13
Wheeler, Scott	MA0850	13,60,10,54,43
Wheelock, Donald	MA1750	10
Whitaker, Howard	IL3550	13,10F,10,64C
White, Barbara A.	NJ0900	13A,10,13,10F,43
White, David A.	TX3400	13,10,31A
White, Kevin	MO0750	13,10F,10,63A,53
White, Tyler G.	NE0600	10,38
Whitfield, James M. (Matt)	NC0850	10A,13,37,10F,10
Whitworth, Albin C.	KY0150	13A,13,10,36,66
Wickman, Ethan F.	TX3530	10A,13,36,10
Wieland, William	SD0400	13,66D,66A,34,10
Wiest, Steve	TX3420	10,29,47,63C
Wild, Jonathan	AI0150	10,13
Wiley, Amy C.	OH1100	13,10,38,60B,43
Willey, James H.	NY3730	13,10,11,66A
Williams, Amy C.	PA3420	10,13
Williams, Julius P.	MA0260	10
Williams, Marvin	NY2050	10,11,12,13,20G
Williams, Natalie	GA2100	10,13
Williams, Patrick C.	MT0400	10A,13,13C,13D,10
Willis, A. Rexford	FL1745	13,10,70,13A
Wills, Christopher	CA0350	10,13
Wilson, Brian S.	CA4700	10,37,13,43,60
Wilson, Donald	OH0300	10
Wilson, Eric	TN1600	13,34,10
Wilson, Mark	MD1010	13,10F,10
Wilson, Olly W.	CA5000	10,20G,29
Wilson, Steve	CA0400	13,10
Wimberly, Michael	VT0050	10,20,29,35,65
Wingate, Mark	FL0850	10,34
Winkler, Peter	NY3790	13,10,20G,29A
Winkler, Todd	RI0050	10,45,34
Winn, James	NV0100	66,13,10
Winslow, Richard	CT0750	13A,13,10
Wintergg, Steven L.	OH0450	10,13
Wirt, Ronald	GA0550	13,48,64D,10

Name	Code	Areas
Witmyer, Clyde	MA0260	10
Wittgraf, Michael A.	ND0500	10,13,34,10A,10B
Wiznerowicz, James	VA1600	10A,10F,13,13H,10
Wohl, Daniel	NY3560	10,10A,13,13F
Wold, Wayne L.	MD0500	13,66G,66H,10
Womack, Donald Reid	HI0210	10,13,13E,10A,10F
Wood, Jeffrey	TN0050	13,10,66A,66D,20G
Woodward, James E.	AL0500	13,10
Workman, Reggie	NY2660	10,47,62D,53
Worley, Daniel T.	KY1500	10,10F
Worlton, James T.	TX3420	10
Worth, Mike	PA3330	10,34
Wright, Geoffrey	MD0400	10,34
Wright, James	AG0100	13,10
Wright, Maurice W.	PA3250	10,34
Wright, Steve	MN0750	47,63A,35,46,10
Wubbels, Eric	OH1700	10
Wyatt, Scott A.	IL3300	13,10,34,45
Wyner, Yehudi	MA0500	10F,10,41
Yannay, Yehuda	WI0825	13,10,45,43
Yarmolinsky, Benjamin	NY0280	13A,13,10,45,70
Yim, Jay Alan	IL2250	13,10
Yoo, In-Sil	NY3550	10,13,34A
Yorgasen, Brent	OH1400	13,10
Young, Stefan	NJ1350	13,10
Youtz, Gregory	WA0650	10,13,14,43
Yuasa, Joji	CA5050	10,20D,35H,34,35C
Yurko, Bruce	PA2300	10,32E
Yurko, Bruce	NJ1050	10
Zabel, Albert	WV0400	44,66G,31A,10,66C
Zahler, Noel	NY2105	10,34
Zaimont, Judith Lang	MN1623	10
Zak, Albin J.	NY3700	10
Zaki, Mark	NJ1100	10,34,10B,34D,10A
Zaninelli, Luigi	MS0750	10
Zank, MJ Sunny	OH1800	13,20,10,12A,43
Zanter, Mark J.	WV0400	13,29,10,70,34
Zhou, Long	MO1810	10
Zimmerman, Robert R.	NC0600	10,13
Ziolek, Eric E.	OH0650	13,10,11
Ziporyn, Evan	MA1200	13,10,20D,64C,29
Zocchi, Michael	MN1625	13,10
Zoffer, David	MA0260	10,35C,35G
Zohn, Andrew	GA0550	70,10
Zohn-Muldoon, Ricardo	NY1100	10,20H
Zork, Stephen	MI0250	36,61,60,10,39
Zupko, Mischa	IL3100	10,66A
Zwilich, Ellen T.	FL0850	10

Traditional Compositional Practices

Name	Code	Areas
Abruzzo, Luke A.	PA1000	70,10A,13,29
Adams, Daniel C.	TX3150	10A,13D,13E,65,13
Adler, Christopher A.	CA5200	10,14,13,10A,20D
Admiral, Roger	AA0110	13B,13C,10A,42
Ahn, Jean	CA5350	10A
Alexander, Joe L.	LA0250	10,13,63D,10A,49
Alvarez, Luis M.	PR0150	10A,11,13A,13B,14
Amundson, Steven	MN1450	13,60B,38,10A
Anderson, Allen L.	NC2410	10A,13B,13D,13E,13F
Anderson-Himmelspach, Neil	MD0475	13,13,14C,34,62D
Aquila, Carmen	NY4460	35A,13A,35D,12A,10A
Archer, Kimberly K.	IL2910	10,13,32E,10A,10F
Arjomand, Ramin Amir	NY2750	10A,10F,13B,13C
Ashton, J. Bruce	TN1350	10A,31A,66A,10F,66C
Asplin, David	WA1350	10A
Asplund, Christian	UT0050	10A,10B,13,34
Atteberry, Ron	MO0100	10F,36,61,10A
Aylward, John J.	MA0650	10A,10B,13
Ball, Karen	IL2300	10A,66A,66B,13B,13C
Ballenger, William	TX3200	10A,32E,37,63A
Barlow, Clarence	CA5060	10A,10B,13G
Barta, Daniel	NY3350	10,13,10A,10F
Bartsch, John T.	OR0175	13B,38,66,10F,10A
Batzner, Jay C.	MI0400	13,10,34,10A,13F
Becker, Richard	VA1500	10A,66A
Belkin, Alan	AI0200	13,10A
Bellink, Allyson	NY3785	10,10C,10A
Bennett, Bruce Christian	CA4200	10,13,34,10A,10B
Bevelander, Brian E.	OH0950	66A,10A,10B,13E,13G
Biro, Daniel Peter	AB0150	13B,13C,13E,13F,10A
Blasco, Scott	WA1150	13,10A,10B
Blume, Philipp G.	IL3300	13,10,10A,10F
Bohlen, Donald A.	NY3725	10A,10F,13D,10
Bolles, Marita	IL0750	10A
Bonacci, Andrew	MA2100	10,13,10A,10F
Bondari, Brian	TX3350	10,13,34,10A,10B
Boone, Geraldine T.	VA0950	10A,32,11,13D,13F
Booth, Todd	AG0130	10A,10D,10F,11,13
Boquiren, Sidney M.	NY0050	10A,13A,20D,31A,10F
Boss, Jack	OR1050	13,10A
Boubel, Karen A.	MN1000	13,10,34,13C,10A
Bourassa, Richard N.	OR0450	13,10F,10A,11
Bourcier, Tom	IA0950	47,10A
Bowen, Robert E.	CA3200	13,10A,29A,34
Bower, John E.	DC0050	10A,13C,10F
Bowers, Greg J.	VA0250	13,10,10A
Boyd, Michael	PA0600	10A,10B,13,12
Boyer, Justin	MD0550	13B,13C,10A
Boykan, Martin	MA0500	13,10,12A,10A,13A
Brackeen, William	OK0450	66A,66D,10A,13
Bradshaw, Keith M.	UT0200	10A,10F,13,36
Bradshaw, Robert J.	MA1650	10A,10C,10F,35A,35G
Broad-Ginsberg, Elaine	NH0150	13,31B,10A,36
Brock, Gordon R.	FL1950	37,48,64E,60B,10A
Brooks, BJ	TX3750	13,10A
Brooks, Jonathan E.	IN0100	13,10A
Brown, Chris	CA2950	10B,10A,20,13,14
Brown, Whitman P.	MA0500	10A,13A,13B
Bryden, Kristy	IA0850	13,10A,10F,34A,34H
Bukvic, Ivica Ico	VA1700	10,34,10A,13L,10C
Bunch, James D.	IL3300	10A
Busarow, Donald A.	OH2450	13A,10A,66G,31A
Butler, Steve	CA5550	10,13,34,10A,13E
Byrd, Joshua	GA2130	37,10A,13G,48,10F
Cabrer, Carlos R.	PR0150	10A,10F,11,13A,13B
Cado, Michael	AG0650	10A,32,47,70
Cameron, Tristan	AA0020	10A,10C,10D,70
Campbell, Brian G.	MN0350	13,10A,20,12B,10F
Campi-Walters, Lisa	CO0350	13,12A,66,10A
Cantwell, Richard E.	KS1300	13,60,10A,37,38
Carlson, James	TN1800	13A,13B,10A,10B,13C
Carrell, Scott	AR0250	10A,13,34,66A,66B
Carroll, Nancy	RI0102	11,10A
Castelli, James A.	NJ1050	10A
Castonguay, Roger	AE0100	12,10A,13A
Ceide, Manuel J.	PR0115	13F,10A,13A,13B,13E
Chandra, Arun	WA0350	10A,10B,43,34D,11
Chang, Dorothy	AB0100	10A,10F,10
Chang, Yu-Hui	MA0500	10A,10F,13B,13D,13F
Chasalow, Eric	MA0500	13,10A,10B,11,29A
Chauls, Robert	CA2750	11,38,66A,10A,39
Chen, Yao	IL3300	10A
Chenette, Jonathan Lee	NY4450	10,13,34,10A,10B
Chin, Pablo	IL2650	10A,13
Chou, Godwin	IL2775	10A,13,66A,66,10
Church, Joseph	NY2750	54,10A,10D
Cichy, Roger	RI0150	10A,10F
Connolly, Michael E.	OR1100	36,12A,10A,61,13
Consoli, Marc-Antonio	NY2750	13,10A
Cottrell, Jeffrey	TX0900	10A,63C,63D
Couvillon, Thomas M.	KY0550	13,10B,10A,10,13F
Crumb, David	OR1050	10A,10F,13
Cubbage, John	MT0370	13,12A,66A,10A
Custer, Seth A.	SC0200	13,64E,10A
Danby, Judd	IN1310	10,13,29B,10A,13F
De La Torre, Javier	PR0150	10F,10A,13A,13C
Decker, Van A.	CA2300	11,13A,34D,47,10A
Deemer, Robert	NY3725	10A,10C,43,10,60B
Dello Joio, Justin N.	NY2750	13B,13E,13F,10A,10F
Di Vittorio, Salvatore	NY0050	10A,38
Dicke, Ian	CA5040	10A,10B,10C
Dicke, Ian	CA5040	10A,10B,10C
Dies, David	WI0830	13,10A
Dobbins, William	NY1100	29B,29C,10A,10F,46
Dobry, John T.	LA0750	10A,13B,47
Don, Gary W.	WI0803	13,10F,10A
Doolittle, Emily L.	WA0200	10A,13,13D
Dorman, Avner	PA1400	10A,10F,13,43
Dorsa, James	CA0835	66H,10A,67F,13C,12A
Dubois, Laura	NJ0760	10A,11,32E,66
Duff, Robert P.	NH0100	36,60,10A,40,13C
Durant, David Z.	AL1300	13,10,34,10A,10B
Eckert, Michael	IA1550	13,10A
Elliott, David J.	NY2750	32,12B,10A
Erickson, Gary	IL1050	34B,10A,13G,31A,35D
Ernste, Kevin	NY0900	10B,10A,34
Evangelista, Jose	AI0200	10A,20D
Feigin, Joel	CA5060	10,10A,10F,13D
Fiday, Michael	OH2200	10A
Fineberg, Joshua	MA0400	10B,10A
Finn, Neal	NC0800	10A,10F,29A,47,63C
Fischer, Peter H.	TX3200	13,10A,10B
Fisher, John	TX3250	13A,13B,10A,15,66A
Flynn, Timothy	MI1800	10A,12,36,39,13
Forrester, Sheila	FL1675	10A,13,66D,13D,13E
Freed, Donald Callen	TX2710	61,36,10A,13C,12A
Friedman, Joel Phillip	CA4425	13B,10A,10D,12A
Frith, Fred	CA2950	10A,10B,53,43,11
Fritschel, James E.	CA0550	10A,36
Froom, David	MD0750	13,10A,10B,10F
Funk, Eric	MT0200	10A,10F,60,29,13
Garcia, Jose Manuel	GA2050	66A,66D,11,10A
Geers, Douglas E.	NY0500	10A,10B,10F
Geller, Ian R.	IN0005	61,10A,60,36
Gibbs, Geoffrey D.	RI0300	10A,10F,13
Gilligan, Heather M.	NH0150	13,10A
Goldman, Edward 'Ted'	NY1100	13K,13C,13B,10A,10F
Goldstein, Perry	NY3790	13A,13C,13E,10A,13F
Gooch, Warren P.	MO1780	10,13,10A
Gordon, Michael	NY2750	10A
Gougeon, Denis	AI0200	10A
Grogan, Charles L.	OH2450	10A,13B
Grossmann, Jorge V.	NY1800	10A,10F
Gullings, Kyle	TX3535	10,13,13F,10A
Gustavson, Mark	NY2550	10,64C,66D,10A,10F
Ha, Youngmi	NY2750	10A,10E,13B,13C,13D
Haakenson, Matthew A.	FL1750	10A,66G,13,13D,13J
Haebich, Kenneth	IL0850	62D,10A,10F
Haek, Jonathan	OR0500	34D,10A,13,66A
Hafso, Marc A.	WA1350	60,36,10A,32D,61
Hamberlin, Larry D.	VT0350	10A,12A,29A,13A,13C
Hamilton, Bruce	WA1250	10A,10B,13
Hamlin, Peter S.	VT0350	10A,10B,10F,13A,13B
Hannesson, Mark	AA0100	10B,10A
Hansen, Ted	TX2955	13,10F,10A,66A
Hanson, David	CO0900	66A,29,35B,10A,10C
Harder, Matthew D.	WV0600	65,34B,34D,10A,10B
Hardin, Garry Joe	TX2600	10A,13,29,38,46
Harding, Scott R.	MI0400	10A,13C,29A,65,13A
Hare, Ryan	WA1150	13,64D,10A,10B
Harlen, Benjamin	LA0400	10A,31A,13B,13C,13D
Harley, James I.	AG0350	10B,10A,34
Heetderks, David	OH1700	10A,13C,13E,60
Hegarty, James	IL2400	10A,29A,34D,47,13A
Heifetz, Robin J.	CA0200	11,20,10A,43,12
Heinick, David G.	NY3780	13,10A
Henderson, Jean	NE0450	13A,13B,13C,13D,10A
Heritage, Lee	OH2300	13B,13C,29A,20G,10A
Heuermann, Beryl Lee	MT0400	10A
Heuser, David	NY3780	10A,10B,13,10F,10
Highman, Daniel R.	CA0807	10A,12A
Hindman, Dorothy Elliston	FL1900	10A,10F,13
Hirschmann, Craig	WI1155	10A,44,66G
Hodkinson, Sydney P.	FL1750	10A
Hoepfner, Gregory	OK0150	10A,32,61,10,11
Holland, Anthony G.	NY3650	10A,60B,34,38,10B
Holland, Jonathan Bailey	MA0260	10A,10F,13A,10
Hollingsworth, Devon	IN0005	10A,12,13,32,66G
Holm-Hudson, Kevin	KY1450	13F,13,10A,13E,13H
Horel, Charles	GA0950	10A,70,13A,13C
Howiler, Robert W.	SC1000	34,10A,13G,10B
Hulling, Cliff	CA0350	13,47,50,10A
Humphreys, Paul W.	CA2800	14A,13A,13B,29A,10A
Hundemer, Thomas	LA0050	63B,16,10A
Hundley, Marion S.	FL0100	10A,66A,66C,13
Husa, Karel	NY0900	10F,60,10A
Hutchinson, Robert G.	WA1000	13,10A
Hutter, Greg J.	IL0750	13C,13D,10A,11
Iannaccone, Anthony J.	MI0600	10A,38,13,10,12A
Iannone, Vincent	PA1550	64,10A
Itoh, Takuma	HI0210	10A,13A,13B,13C,13D
Ivanova, Vera	CA0960	10A,10B,10F,10,66A
Jablonsky, Stephen	NY0550	11,63A,10A,10F,13
Jacobs, Edward	NC0650	10A,10B,13,43
Jacobson, Allan	SD0400	10,10A,66A,66G
Janson, Thomas	OH1100	13,10A
Jaskot, Matthew	MD0550	10A
Johansen-Werner, Bonnie	IL3370	10A,13
Johnson, Aaron E.	MO1250	10A,34D,13,70
Jones, John W.	PA1400	13B,13C,13D,13E,10A
Jordan, Paul	IN0005	10A,61,13,20F,31A
Junokas, Michael	IL0850	10A,10B,13,34
Kaiser, Tyler	WI0860	10A,70
Kanda, Sanae	MA1650	10A,42,66A,66C,66D

Index by Area of Teaching Interest

Name	Code	Areas
Karathanasis, Konstantinos	OK1350	34D,10A,10,35C,35G
Kavasch, Deborah H.	CA0850	10A,13,61,10,10F
Kearney, Joseph B.	CA1265	10A,29,13B,70
Kechley, David S.	MA2250	10A,10F,13A,13B,13D
Keever, Howard	MS0850	10A,10D,13A,13B,13D
Keller, Daniel	CA2650	13,10A
Kelley, Anthony M.	NC0600	11,13,29,10A,10C
Kellogg, Daniel	CO0800	10A,10F
Kerr, Daniel	ID0060	10A,13,66G,10F
Kershaw, Yvonne	AE0120	64A,64D,10A,11,13A
Kilby, Shelton	OH2400	10A,11
Kirchoff, Leanna	CO0900	10A
Klein, Joseph	TX3420	10F,10A
Kramer, Timothy	IL1100	13,10F,10A,10B
Kratz, Girard	PA3250	10A,10B,13,10
Krause, Melissa M.	MN1300	13,64A,10A,10F
Kudo, Takeo	HI0210	10A,10F,13,20D
Kyr, Robert	OR1050	10A,10F,43,20D
La Barbara, Joan	NY2750	10A,10B
Labe, Paul E.	MD0475	13,10A
Labor, Tim A.	CA5040	10,10A,10B,10C
Landers, Joseph	AL1200	10A,10F,13B,13C,13E
Landey, Peter	AG0050	12B,13J,10A,10B,10F
Langer, Kenneth P.	MA1500	10A,10B,13,34D,11
Leathwood, Jonathan	CO0900	70,41,13D,10A,13E
Lee, Abe	MA0260	10A,10D,35C,35G
Lee, Damon Thomas	NE0600	10A,10B,10C,10F,34A
Leggatt, Jacqueline	AB0200	13,10A
Leibinger, Douglas J.	CA4700	47,29B,63C,10A
Levin, Rami Y.	IL1400	13,11,38,10A
Levy, Fabien	NY0750	10A,10F,13E,13F
Lewis, George E.	NY0750	10A,10B,12E,29E,34H
Liang, Lei	CA5050	10,13B,13D,10A,10B
Liaropoulos, Panagiotis	MA0260	10A,10F
Lin, Mei-Fang	TX3200	10A,13A,13I,13L,10F
Lindroth, Scott A.	NC0600	13,34D,34H,10A,10B
Linton, Michael	TN1100	13,10A
Lloyd, Gerald J.	MA2030	10,13,10A
Lochstampfor, Mark L.	OH0350	13,10A,34A,34B,66A
Lohr, Tom L.	NC1300	66A,10A
Lombardi, Paul	SD0600	13A,13G,10F,10A,13B
Long, David J.	VA1475	13,10A,10F
Lothringer, Peter	MN1500	70,10A,13
Lovelace, Jason R.	DC0050	10A,13C,10F
Lowry, Douglas	NY1100	37,38,10A,10B,10C
Lyndon-Gee, Christopher	NY0050	10A,14A,38,39,42
MacLean, Alasdair	AE0050	10A,34,13
Magnuson, Phillip	OH2250	13,10F,10A,62B
Magrill, Samuel	OK1330	13,10A
Makela, Steven L.	MN0600	10A,10B,13,10,34D
Maloy, Kris	OK0750	10A
Malsky, Matthew	MA0650	10A,10B,34,13,10
Marinescu, Liviu	CA0835	10A,13E,13F,10
Marsh, Gordon E.	VA1250	10,66,13,10A,66A
Mason, Charles Norman	FL1900	10A,10B,10F,34D
Mathiesen, Steven	PA2200	10A,10F,50,65
Mauleon-Santana, Rebeca	CA1020	66D,20H,10A
May, Andrew D.	TX3420	10A,10B,10F,34A,34D
McAllister, James	KS0440	37,10A,63,60B,32C
McAllister, Margaret	MA0260	10,13,34H,10A,34
McAneny, Marc	MA0500	13B,13E,13F,10A
McDonald, Richard F.	TX2930	10A
McDonald, Susan M.	PA1830	10A,10B,12A,15,34D
McKinley, Thomas L.	FL1125	13,10A,12A,34F
McLoskey, Lansing D.	FL1900	10A,10F,13,55D
McMahan, Robert Y.	NJ0175	13B,13C,13F,10B,10A
McNair, Jonathan B.	TN1700	10A,34D,13,10,34
McQuilkin, Terry P.	OR1050	10A
McTee, Cindy K.	TX3420	10A
Metcalf, Joanne	WI0350	10A,13D,13F,12A,31G
Meyer, Elizabeth C.	MI1450	38,62A,62B,10A
Michaud, Pierre	AI0200	10A,10B
Miller, Paul W.	PA2740	10A,11,13A,29A,29B
Miller, Scott L.	MN1300	13,10A,10B,10C,34
Miller-Thorn, Jill	NY1275	10A,10F,13,66D,12C
Miyakovs, Kurt	IL2800	13,10A,34,10C
Mobberley, James C.	MO1810	10A,10B,10F
Moll, Benjamin	OR0600	65,13A,13B,13C,10A
Mollicone, Henry	CA3270	10A,12A,39,54,60
Monachino, Paul	OH1330	13,10A,66,60
Moore, Gregory	WI0860	13C,47,64E,29,10A
Moore, Kevin	NY2950	13,66A,66C,66D,10A
Moreland, Michael	KS0570	10A,10B,34D
Muniz, Jorge	MO0100	10A,10F
Muniz, Jorge	IN0910	10A,13,10B,10,43
Myers, Andre K.	CA3300	10A,10B,10F,13
Neimoyer, Susan	UT0250	12A,14C,10A,12
Nelson, Jon C.	TX3420	10A,10B,10F,34
Nestor, Leo Cornelius	DC0050	10A,31A,36,40,60A
Nez, Catherine Ketty	MA0400	10,66A,10A
Nicholeris, Carol A.	MA0510	10A,13D,13A,36,13
Nichols, Charles Sabin	MT0400	10A,10B,10,45,34
Nichols, Jeff	NY0600	10A,13E,10F
Noon, David	NY2150	12,10A,10,12A
Novak, Christina D.	AZ0490	11,13,66A,10A,66D
Nozny, Brian	ND0100	13,10A,10F,34A,34B
Oblak, Jerica	NY2750	10A,10C
O'Connor, Thomas	AR0110	13,32,47,10A,10F
Oh, Seung-Ah	IL0750	10,13,13F,10A
O'Neel, Roger	OH0450	10A,31A,13A
Osborne, Thomas	HI0210	10A,10F,13,43
O'Shea, Patrick	MN1400	60,12A,36,61,10A
Panneton, Isabelle	AI0200	13,10A
Pardo-Tristan, Emiliano	NY2750	70,10A
Pelusi, Mario J.	IL1200	10A,10F,13,43,29B
Peplin, Steve W.	WI0450	10A,11,13B,47,70
Perkins, Andrew	NC0450	10A,13A,20G,46,11
Perla, James 'Jack'	CA4425	10A,10B,66A
Perron, Alain	AJ0100	10A,10B,10C,43,10F
Perttu, Daniel E.	PA3650	10A,13
Petersen, Lynn	MT0075	10A,11,13A,66A,47
Polay, Bruce	IL1350	10A,10F,12A,13B,60B
Polcari, Jeanne	NH0300	66A,66B,10A
Polot, Barton L.	MI1900	10A,10B,10F,12,13
Ponte, Nora	PR0150	10A,13A,13B,13C,13D
Poole, Tommy A.	OK0550	29,46,64E,10A
Porter, Thomas	ND0400	36,13B,10A,32D,31A
Post, William Dean	AK0150	13,12A,10A
Prettyman, Ken	WA0550	10A,13A,13B,46,47
Price, William Roger	OK1450	10A,41,66A,10F
Read, Kenneth E.	OH0550	13E,31A,10A,10F,13B
Reed, Jerome A.	TN0930	10A,66A,66B,66C,43
Reese, Randall	GA0200	10F,47,64E,10A,13,D
Reinhart, Robert	IL0720	10A
Rhein, Robert	IN0200	10A,66A,11,12A,13
Richards, Eric	NE0600	47,10A,10D,13G
Richards, Eric J.	NE0400	63C,37,10A,13B,47
Richardson, Mark Douglas	NC0650	13,10A
Ricks, Steven L.	UT0050	10A,10B,13A,34
Rivers, Joseph L.	OK1450	13,10A,10C,34D,34E
Roberson, Richard	PA2300	66A,10A,10B,A
Rocco, Robert	NJ0700	11,13,13B,10A
Roman, Dan	CT0500	34,70,10A,10F,13
Romig, James	IL3500	13,13F,10A,10
Rosenhaus, Steven L.	NY2750	10,13F,10F,10A,10D
Rosser, Geraldine	OH1600	10A,66C
Roy, J. Michael	WI0845	13,10A,10F
Rudy, Paul	MO1810	10A,10B,10C,10F
Runner, David C.	TN1150	13,10F,66A,66G,10A
Sadoff, Ronald H.	NY2750	13K,10A,10C,10D
Santo, Joseph A.	DC0050	10A,10F,13B,13H,13C
Saul, Walter B.	CA1860	10A,66A,13,20,10F
Saya, Mark	CA2800	13B,10A,13D,13E,13F
Schedel, Margaret	NY3790	10A,10B,10C,10F
Schiff, David	OR0900	13,10A,20G,29,38
Schimmel, Carl W.	IL1150	10A,13
Schindler, Allan	NY1100	10A,10B,10C,34H
Schmitz, Eric B.	NY3770	47,65,13B,13C,10A
Schnauber, Thomas	MA0900	10A,10C,13A,11,10F
Schober, David	NY0642	13,10A,66A,10
Schreiber, Paul	MS0560	10,13,34,10B,10A
Schulze, Theodora	IN0005	61,10A,13,50,51
Schumaker, Adam	MI1150	10A,10B,10C,10D,70
Seo, Ju Ri	IL3300	10A
Serghi, Sophia	VA0250	13,10F,10,43,10A
Shapero, Harold S.	MA0500	10A,13A,10B,13B,13G
Sharp, Michael D.	LA0400	66A,66B,31A,34,10A
Shatin, Judith	VA1550	10B,10A,10F,10,13
Shaw, Timothy B.	PA2800	13B,13C,10A,13
Shearer, Allen R.	CA0807	61,10A
Sieg, Jerry	LA0800	10A,10F,13,12A
Sierra, Roberto	NY0900	10A,10F,13B,13F
Silver, Sheila	NY3790	13B,13D,13E,10A,10F
Sir, Neil	NH0350	10A,13
Skoumal, Zdenek	AB0060	10A,13
Sloan, Donald S.	SC0420	13,10A
Smallwood, Scott	AA0100	10A,10B
Smith, Carl	TN1850	13,10A
Smith, Douglas	AB0200	13,10F,10A
Smith, Kevin	MN0625	36,60,40,10A
Smith, Roy C.	IN0005	61,11,10A,60,36
Sokolovic, Ana	AI0200	10A
Sonenberg, Daniel M.	ME0500	10A,13F,13C,10,13
Sonntag, Dawn Lenore	OH1000	36,61,66C,10A,10
Stanton, Zachary K.	TN0100	10A,10F
Sternfeld-Dunn, Aleksander	KS1450	10A
Stevens, James M.	TN0580	10A,36,13E,13B
Stinson, Scott	FL1900	10A,10F,13D,13F
Strommen, Carl	NY2105	10,10F,10A
Stroope, Z. Randall	OK0800	36,60A,40,10A
Subotnick, Morton	NY2750	10A,10B
Supko, John	NC0600	10A,13,13C,13D,10B
Swanson, Philip	MA1650	63C,10A,13B,13C,13F
Swearingen, James	OH0350	10A,32E
Taylor, Sean	OH0500	32D,10A
Tedder, Teresa C.	KY1150	10A,10C,10F,66A,11
Thompson, Robert Scott	GA1050	10A,10B,10C,45,34
Tiberio, Albert	PA2950	11,12,13,10A,10F
Tollefson, Tim	MN0200	13,10A,34
Trosvig, Michael	MN1100	10A,13
Twomey, Michael P.	TX1900	10A,13,10F,38,62
Vander Gheynst, John R.	IN0907	29A,10A,63,34D,35A
Vanderwoude, Matt	AG0130	10A,11,13,29,34
Vayo, David J.	IL1200	10F,10,10D,10B,10A
Vazquez, Carlos	PR0150	10A,10B,10F,13A,13C
Vinao, Ezequiel P.	NY2750	10A,10B
Volker, Mark D.	TN0100	10,10A,10B,13C
Vollinger, William F.	NY2900	10A,20
Wallis, David N.	MO0650	36,10A,11,13,32D
Walsh, Craig T.	AZ0500	10,10B,13,10A
Wanamaker, Gregory R.	NY3780	13,10A
Warner, Daniel C.	MA1000	13,10A,10B,12D,34
Waseen, Symeon	SD0100	10A,10B,10F,13,66
Waters, Becky	AL1160	10A,11,13C
Webber, Allen L.	FL1470	13,11,61,10A,66A
Wesby, Barbara K.	NY4500	10A
Weston, Craig A.	KS0650	10A,10B,13,34
White, L. Keith	OK1330	10A,10B
Whitfield, James M. (Matt)	NC0850	10A,13,37,10F,10
Wickman, Ethan F.	TX3530	10A,13,36,10
Wiemann, Beth	ME0440	10F,64C,34,10A,13D
Wilken, David M.	NC2400	63C,46,47,10A
Williams, Patrick C.	MT0400	10A,13,13C,13D,10
Willis, Sharon J.	GA0490	10A,11,12,61,13A
Wilson, Dana	NY1800	10F,10A
Wilson, Eugene N.	AB0100	10A,13
Wilson, Richard E.	NY4450	13,10A,10F
Wilt, Kevin	MI1260	10A,10C,10F,34
Wittgraf, Michael A.	ND0500	10,13,34,10A,10B
Wiznerowicz, James	VA1600	10A,10F,13,13H,10
Wohl, Daniel	NY3560	10,10A,13,13F
Wolfe, Julia	NY2750	10A
Womack, Donald Reid	HI0210	10,13,13E,10A,10F
Wood, Eric	CA5350	10A,11,20,13A,13E
Woodward, Gregory S.	NY1800	10A,10F
Worley, Dan	KY0450	70,10A,10B,10C,34B
Wraggett, Wes	AB0210	10A,10B,13B,13L
Wramage, Gregg	NJ0050	10A,10F,11
Wyrtzen, Donald	TX2600	10A,31A,66A
Yang, Fengshi	IL0720	10A,13
Yarbrough, Stephen	SD0600	13A,13G,10F,10A,13B
Yasinitsky, Greg	WA1150	47,64E,29,10F,10A
Yasui, Byron K.	HI0210	70,10A,10F,13,20B
Young, Charles R.	WI0850	13,10F,35C,10A
Young, Ovid	IL2300	66A,66C,10A
Zaki, Mark	NJ1100	10,34,10B,34D,10A

Electroacoustic Music

Name	Code	Areas
Abbati, Joseph S.	FL1900	10B,34A,35C,45,34E
Aspland, Christian	UT0050	10A,10B,13,34
Aylward, John J.	MA0650	10A,10B,13
Barlow, Clarence	CA5060	10A,10B,13G
Bedard, Martin	AI0200	10B
Bennett, Bruce Christian	CA4200	10,13,34,10A,10B
Bevelander, Brian E.	OH0950	66A,10A,10B,13E,13G
Bischoff, John	CA2950	45,10B,12A,13B,20F
Bissell, Paul	TX0550	10B,34D,34E,35C,35D
Blasco, Scott	WA1150	13,10A,10B
Bondari, Brian	TX3350	10,13,34,10A,10B
Boyd, Michael	PA0600	10A,10B,13,12
Boyle, McGregor	MD0650	10B,34
Brabant, John-Paul	NY3780	10,10B,10C,13
Brandon, Mack	NJ0950	10B,31F,36,41
Brickman, Scott T.	ME0420	14C,13,32B,10B,66D

Index by Area of Teaching Interest

Name	Code	Areas
Brown, Chris	CA2950	10B,10A,20,13,14
Brunner, George	NY0500	34,35C,10B
Carlson, James	TN1800	13A,13B,10A,10B,13C
Casal, David Plans	NH0100	10B,10F,34,13,35
Casey, Michael	NH0100	10B,10F,34,13,35
Chandra, Arun	WA0350	10A,10B,43,34D,11
Chasalow, Eric	MA0500	13,10A,10B,11,29A
Chattah, Juan	FL1900	13,10B,10C
Chenette, Jonathan Lee	NY4450	10,13,34,10A,10B
Clark, Thomas S.	TX3175	10,13,10B
Coffey, Ted	VA1550	10B,10,34,35C,35G
Coulter, Ronald E.	IL2900	65,10B,50
Couvillon, Thomas M.	KY0550	13,10B,10A,10,13F
Dicke, Ian	CA5040	10A,10B,10C
Dicke, Ian	CA5040	10A,10B,10C
Driessen, Peter	AB0150	10B,35C,35D
Dunston, Douglas E.	NM0350	10B,36,38,47,54
Durant, David Z.	AL1300	13,10,34,10A,10B
Eisel, Gunnar	CA1000	10B,12A,13A,14C,29A
Ernste, Kevin	NY0900	10B,10A,34
Fei, James	CA2950	10B,34A
Felice, Frank	IN0250	10,10B,10D,34D,13D
Fields, Kenneth	AA0150	10B,34
Fineberg, Joshua	MA0400	10B,10A
Fischer, Peter H.	TX3200	13,10A,10B
Forehan, Jeff	CA5510	10B,13A,34D,35G,35D
Forget, Georges	AI0200	10B
Frengel, Mike	MA1450	10B,34,35
Frith, Fred	CA2950	10A,10B,53,43,11
Froom, David	MD0750	13,10A,10B,10F
Gauthier, Thierry	AI0200	10B
Geers, Douglas E.	NY0500	10A,10B,10F
Gibson, John	IN0900	10B
Gluck, Robert J.	NY3700	10B,34D,31B,34,45
Grudzinski, Richard	MA0260	10,10B
Haaheim, Bryan Kip	KS1350	10B
Hall, Richard D.	TX3175	11,10B,34
Hamilton, Bruce	WA1250	10A,10B,13
Hamlin, Peter S.	VT0350	10A,10B,10F,13A,13B
Hannesson, Mark	AA0100	10B,10A
Harder, Matthew D.	WV0600	65,34B,34D,10A,10B
Hare, Ryan	WA1150	13,64D,10A,10B
Harley, James I.	AG0350	10B,10A,34
Harris, Roger	IN0005	10B,13,29,47,66A
Hass, Jeffrey E.	IN0900	10B
Hatfield, Bradley	MA1450	35A,10B
Head, Russell	KS0750	10B,10D,34,35,45
Heller, Brian	MN1050	10B,34,12A,35B,35G
Heuser, David	NY3780	10A,10B,13,10F,10
Hisama, Ellie M.	NY0750	15,13E,12A,10B,13F
Hiscocks, Mike	CA2650	11,13A,61,45,10B
Holland, Anthony G.	NY3650	10A,60B,34,38,10B
Hopkins, Christopher	IA0850	13,10B,34,10,67A
Howe, Hubert S.	NY0600	13,10B
Howiler, Robert W.	SC1000	34,10A,13G,10B
Ianni, Davide	MA0400	10B
Ivanova, Vera	CA0960	10A,10B,10F,10,66A
Jacobs, Edward	NC0650	10A,10B,13,43
Johnson, David H.	GA0850	13,10,10B,10C
Judson, Tohm	NC2700	10B,62D,70,34,35
Junokas, Michael	IL0850	10A,10B,13,34
Kamerin, Kim	CA2400	10B,35A,36,61
Keberle, David S.	NY0644	10,10B,64C,42,13A
Kizer, Kay	IN0910	10B
Knoles, Amy	CA0510	65,50,13A,10B
Kohn, Steven Mark	OH0600	10B,35D
Kothman, Keith K.	IN0150	10B,10,34,13,35C
Kramer, Timothy	IL1100	13,10F,10A,10B
Kratz, Girard	PA3250	10A,10B,13,10
La Barbara, Joan	NY2750	10A,10B
Labor, Tim A.	CA5040	10,10A,10B,10C
Lackey, William J.	MO1800	10B,34
Landey, Peter	AG0050	12B,13J,10A,10B,10F
Langer, Kenneth P.	MA1500	10A,10B,13,34D,11
Lee, Damon Thomas	NE0600	10A,10B,10C,10F,34A
Lee-Keller, Derek	CA1500	10,10B
Leider, Colby N.	FL1900	34A,35C,10B,34D,35G
Leonard, Jeff	OR0400	70,10B,45
Lewis, George E.	NY0750	10A,10B,12E,29E,34H
Liang, Lei	CA5050	10,13B,13D,10A,10B
Licata, Julie M.	NY3765	65,33,50,20,10B
Lillios, Elainie	OH0300	10B,10
Lindroth, Scott A.	NC0600	13,34D,34H,10A,10B
Logan, Jennifer	CA3300	10B,13A,13B,13C,35C
Lopez, Thomas Handman	OH1700	10B,34,10,34A
Loughrige, Chad	OH0350	34,35C,10B,10D,45
Lowry, Douglas	NY1100	37,38,10A,10B,10C
MacCallum, John	CA5000	10B
MacCallum, John	MA1450	10B,34
Makela, Steven L.	MN0600	10A,10B,13,10,34D
Mallia, John	MA1400	10B,10,34
Malsky, Matthew	MA0650	10A,10B,34,13,10
Martin, Edward P.	WI0830	13,10B
Mason, Charles Norman	FL1900	10A,10B,10F,34D
Matascik, Sheri L.	TN1000	13,10,70,10B,13H
Matthews, Mark	FL1650	10B,13A,34B,35A,70
May, Andrew D.	TX3420	10A,10B,10F,34A,34D
McCulloch, Peter	NY4450	10B
McDonald, Susan M.	PA1830	10A,10B,12A,15,34D
McDonnell, David	OH2250	10B,10F,34,64E,47
McGarity, Kristin A.	MT0200	10B,34,64B
McMahan, Robert Y.	NJ0175	13B,13C,13F,10B,10A
McNally, Kirk	AB0150	10B,34D,34E,35C,35D
Michaud, Pierre	AI0200	10A,10B
Miller, Scott L.	MN1300	13,10A,10B,10C,34
Mobberley, James C.	MO1810	13,10,45,10F
Moe, Eric H.	PA3420	13,10,45,10B
Moreland, Michael	KS0570	10A,10B,34D
Morin, Eric	AI0190	10B,10F
Muniz, Jorge	IN0910	10A,13,10B,10,43
Myers, Andre K.	CA3300	10A,10B,10F,13
Nakra, Teresa Marrin	NJ0175	13,34,10B
Naylor, Stephen	AF0050	34,10B
Nelson, Jon C.	TX3420	10A,10B,10F,34
Nichols, Charles Sabin	MT0400	10A,10B,10,45,34
Nichols, Samuel S.	CA5010	13,10,70,10B
Normandeau, Robert	AI0200	10B
Nottingham, Douglas	AZ0350	65,50,45,10B,35
Olan, David	NY0600	10F,10,10B
Oliveros, Pauline	NY3300	12,13,10B,11
Olvera, Victor	KS0570	10B,34D
Pastrana, Jorge	CA4850	47,46,45,35D,10B
Payne, Maggi	CA2950	10B,35D,35C,35G
Pedde, David	MN1250	66A,10B,14C,31A
Pellman, Samuel	NY1350	13,10B,10,34
Perla, James 'Jack'	CA4425	10A,10B,66A
Perron, Alain	AJ0100	10A,10B,10C,43,10F
Perry, Jeffery S.	MA0260	10B,34
Pfenninger, Rik C.	NH0250	64E,29,35,32E,10B
Piche, Jean	AI0200	10B
Polot, Barton L.	MI1900	10A,10B,10F,12,13
Popham, Phillip F.	MI2000	64B,10B,13C
Primosch, James	PA3350	13,10,10B
Purse, Lynn Emberg	PA1050	10B,34,45
Rathbun, Andrew	NY2050	35C,35D,35G,10B,45
Reba, Christopher H.	CT0700	34D,10B,35G,62D,13
Resnick, David	IA0250	10B,10F,13A,37,48
Ricks, Steven L.	UT0050	10A,10B,13A,34
Rigler, Jane	CO0810	64A,10B,34D,10
Ritz, John	KY1500	10B,53
Roads, Curtis	CA5060	10B
Roberson, Richard	PA2300	66A,10A,10B
Robertson, Ben	WA0250	10B,45,35G,34D
Robinson, Stephanie	MA1750	10B
Rudy, Paul	MO1810	10A,10B,10C,10F
Sabino, Robert	CA5010	10B
Schedel, Margaret	NY3790	10A,10B,10C,10F
Schindler, Allan	NY1100	10A,10B,10C,34H
Schloss, Andrew	AB0150	10B,34,14,20H,13L
Schreiber, Paul	MS0560	10,13,34,10B,10A
Schumaker, Adam	MI1150	10A,10B,10C,10D,70
Secco, Leonardo	AI0200	10B
Settel, Zack	AI0200	10B
Shapero, Harold S.	MA0500	10A,13A,10B,13B,13G
Shatin, Judith	VA1550	10B,10A,10F,10,13
Smallwood, Scott	AA0100	10A,10B
Smiley, William C.	NC1550	10B,35C,35G,45
Snyder, Jeffrey S.	PA1900	35,34D,10B,32F,10D
Snyder, Mark L.	VA1475	13,10B,10F,34
Sonami, Laetitia	CA2950	10B
Soper, Kate	MA1750	10,10B
Stegall, Sydney Wallace	WA0460	13,14,10B,14F,10
Stewart, D. Andrew	AA0200	34D,10B,45,35A
Stolet, Jeffrey	OR1050	13,45,10,34,10B
Stuck, Les	CA2950	10B,34A,13G,35C,10C
Subotnick, Morton	NY2750	10A,10B
Supko, John	NC0600	10A,13B,13C,13D,10B
Thompson, Robert Scott	GA1050	10A,10B,10C,45,34
Tidaback, Darrell	IN0910	62D,10B,47
Tomassetti, Benjamin	VA0500	35G,10B,34D,35C,64E
Topel, Spencer	NH0100	10B,10F,34,13,35
Trueman, Daniel	NJ0900	13,10B,10
Tsabary, Eldad	AI0070	10B,12A,13C
Tutschku, Hans	MA1050	10B
Twombly, Kristian	MN1300	10B,34H,12B,10,11
Udell, Chester	OR1050	10,10B,11,34,35
Van Buskirk, Jeremy	MA1175	10B
Vayo, David J.	IL1200	10F,10,10D,10B,10A
Vazquez, Carlos	PR0150	10A,10B,10F,13A,13C
Vinao, Ezequiel P.	NY2750	10A,10B
Volker, Mark D.	TN0100	10,10A,10B,13C
Walsh, Craig T.	AZ0500	10,10B,13,10A
Warner, Daniel C.	MA1000	13,10A,10B,12D,34
Warren, Alicyn	IN0900	10B
Waschka, Rodney A.	NC1700	10,12A,13F,10B,13
Waseen, Symeon	SD0100	10A,10B,10F,13,66
Watts, Christopher M.	NY3550	10B,34,34D,34H,10
Weston, Craig A.	KS0650	10A,10B,13,34
White, L. Keith	OK1330	10A,10B
Willey, Robert K.	LA0760	13,34,35,10B,45
Wittgraf, Michael A.	ND0500	10,13,34,10A,10B
Wolek, Krzysztof	KY1500	10B
Worley, Dan	KY0450	70,10A,10B,10C,34B
Wraggett, Wes	AB0210	10A,10B,13B,13L
Wright, Geoffrey	MD0650	45,34,10B
Zaki, Mark	NJ1100	10,34,10B,34D,10A

Film, Television, and Radio Music

Name	Code	Areas
Argiro, James	MA2100	35C,35H,46,10C
Beckett, Hal	AB0100	10C
Bellink, Allyson	NY3785	10,10C,10A
Bjorck, Andreas	MA0260	10C
Black, Lendell	OK0750	10C,35D,34
Boardman, Christopher	FL1900	10C,35
Bostrom, Sandra	CA0835	66A,10C,12A,34,65A
Brabant, John-Paul	NY3780	10,10B,10C,13
Bradshaw, Robert J.	MA1650	10A,10C,10F,35A,35G
Brown, Royal	NY0600	10C
Bukvic, Ivica Ico	VA1700	10,34,10A,13L,10C
Burlingame, Jon	CA5300	35H,10C
Cameron, Tristan	AA0020	10A,10C,10D,70
Carlin, Dan	MA0260	10C
Chang, Gary	IL0720	10C
Chattah, Juan	FL1900	13,10B,10C
Coppola, Thomas	NC2400	66A,66D,10C,29
Daversa, John	CA0835	10C,29,63A
Deemer, Robert	NY3725	10A,10C,43,10,60B
Dicke, Ian	CA5040	10A,10B,10C
Dicke, Ian	CA5040	10A,10B,10C
DiPippo, Angelo	NY1275	10C,10D,68
Dorian, Patrick	PA1100	10C,13B,29A,29C,29E
Dougall, Sean	CA5300	10C
English, Aaron	WA0650	10C,10D
Ennis, Sue	WA0860	35,10C
Francavilla, Nadia	AE0120	10C,62A
Frazier, Bruce H.	NC2600	10C,10F,35
Freeman, Jack	MA0260	10C
Glasgow, Scott	CA0835	10C
Gluck, David	NY3785	10C,10D
Grey, Benoit	CA0835	10C
Grubbs, David	NY0500	10C,12,34
Hallgren, Scott	TN1400	35H,10C
Hanson, David	CO0900	66A,29,35B,10A,10C
Heine, Erik	OK0750	13,13B,10C,13E
Johnson, David H.	GA0850	13,10,10B,10C
Kelley, Anthony M.	NC0600	11,13,29,10A,10C
Kirst, Patrick	CA5300	10C
Klee, David A.	IA0150	10C,29A,34D,35A,47
Klein, Jim	PA1000	34,32F,45,13G,10C
Kleinsasser, Jerome S.	CA0650	11,12A,12,10C
Koeppel, James	NY3785	10C,10D
Kompanek, Rudolph W.	NY2750	10C,10F
Krumbholz, Gerald A.	WA0950	13A,13B,13C,13D,10C
Labor, Tim A.	CA5040	10,10A,10B,10C
LaMarca, Perry	CA0825	10C
Lavoie, Mathieu	AI0200	34,10C
Law, Zada	TN1850	10C
Lee, Damon Thomas	NE0600	10A,10B,10C,10F,34A
Lehman, Frank M.	RI0050	13,10C,12A
Leisawitz, Jeffrey	WA0650	10C,10D,10F
Levinson, Ross	CA0830	35,34A,10C,10D
Leydon, Rebecca	OH1700	13,13F,10C,10D
LoBalbo, Anthony C.	NY3500	13,29A,10C,12A,54
Louchouarn, Bruno E.	CA3300	10C,34H

Index by Area of Teaching Interest

Lovely, Brian	OH0680	29,10C,10D,70,35
Lowry, Douglas	NY1100	37,38,10A,10B,10C
Mann, Hummie	IL0720	10C
McCullough, Thomas Eric	OK1330	10,62C,13,38,10C
McHugh, David	IL0720	10C
McNeely, Joel	CA5300	10C
Miller, Scott L.	MN1300	13,10A,10B,10C,34
Miyashiro, Kurt	IL2800	13,10A,34,10C
Moshier, Josh	IL3550	29,10C,47
Murciano, Raul	FL1900	35,20H,10C
Ndaliko, Cherie Rivers	NC2410	10C,12,14
Neidhart, Gregory	MN1700	35A,35E,10C
Neill, Roger	CA0630	10C
Newborn, Ira	NY2750	10C
Oblak, Jerica	NY2750	10A,10C
Pejrolo, Andrea	MA0260	34,10C,10,35C,35G
Perron, Alain	AJ0100	10A,10B,10C,43,10F
Plante, Alison	MA0260	10C
Pontbriand, Roget	FL1450	45,46,35,10D,10C
Ragazzi, Claudio	MA0260	10C
Randolph, Anthony W.	DC0150	10C,11
Reid, Sally	TN0930	10,13,64B,10C,34
Rheault, Pierre-Daniel	AI0200	10C,34
Rios Escribano, Enrique B.	PR0115	10C
Rivers, Joseph L.	OK1450	13,10A,10C,34D,34E
Rowe, Lee	TN1850	10C
Rudy, Paul	MO1810	10A,10B,10C,10F
Sadoff, Ronald H.	NY2750	13K,10A,10C,10D
Schedel, Margaret	NY3790	10A,10B,10C,10F
Schindler, Allan	NY1100	10A,10B,10C,34H
Schmidt, Eric	CA5300	10C
Schnauber, Thomas	MA0900	10A,10C,13A,11,10F
Schumaker, Adam	MI1150	10A,10B,10C,10D,70
Sellers, Elizabeth A.	CA0835	10C,46,60B
Sever, Ivan	MA0260	35C,35D,10C
Sharp, Thom	CA0960	10C
Sharp, Thomas	CA0815	10C,10F
Shoopman, Chad	FL1550	10C
Spear, David R.	NY2750	10,10F,60,10C
Stuck, Les	CA2950	10B,34A,13G,35C,10C
Suozzo, Mark John	NY2750	10C,10F
Sweet, Michael	MA0260	10C
Tedder, Teresa C.	KY1150	10A,10C,10F,66A,11
Thompson, Robert Scott	GA1050	10A,10B,10C,45,34
Turrin, Joseph	NJ0700	10,10C
Turrin, Joseph E.	NJ0800	11,13,10C
Waller, Jim	TX3410	35G,10C,29B,47,35A
Wight, Steve	CA0830	35,34A,10C,10D,10F
Wilt, Kevin	MI1260	10A,10C,10F,34
Winer, Arthur H.	CA0630	10D,34D,35G,35,10C
Worley, Dan	KY0450	70,10A,10B,10C,34B

Popular Music

Abad, Andy	CA5300	10D,14C
Albano, John	CA2900	10D,29,47,70
Alessi, Ralph P.	NY2750	63A,47,10D
Allen, Jeffrey L.	CA5300	10D,14C
Anderson, Robert J.	CA5300	10D,14C
Apple, Nancy K.	TN1680	10D
Archibald, Becky H.	IN0100	10D
Barber, Deborah L.	AR0200	34,32B,10D,70,32C
Bendickson, Sean	WA0980	10D,70
Bergeron, Norm	TX2800	65,50,10D,11,13A
Booth, Todd	AG0130	10A,10D,10F,11,13
Brandenburg, Julie A.	WI0450	10D,36,61,66D
Byrd, Joseph	CA1280	14C,10D,12A,13A
Cameron, Tristan	AA0020	10A,10C,10D,70
Casas, Jorge	IL1050	62D,47,10D
Church, Joseph	NY2750	54,10A,10D
Clark, John W.	CA4410	13,11,12A,10D
Coe, Judith A.	CO0830	61,10D,34,14C,12C
Coker, Keller	OR1250	55,12A,63C,10D
Cole, Daniel	CA3500	10D,35
Coluzzi, Seth	MA0500	10D,11,13A,12A,12C
Covach, John	NY1100	13,13A,13J,10D
Covach, John R.	NY4350	13A,13,13J,10D
Cullison, Jonathan	CO0625	62D,10D
Da Silva, Pedro Henriques	NY2750	10D
Delto, Clare E.	CA1960	10D,54,11,47
Dent, Cedric	TN1100	12A,10D,35A,13E
DiPippo, Angelo	NY1275	10C,10D,68
Dohr, Richard William	CA5300	10D,14C
Doiel, Mark	CA2900	10D,11,12A,13,37
Doyle, Joseph	TN1400	10D
Dozier, Lamont	CA5300	10D,14C
Drake, Erwin	NY1275	10D
English, Aaron	WA0650	10C,10D
Faris, Marc R.	NC0650	13,10D,11
Felice, Frank	IN0250	10,10B,10D,34D,13D
Franklin, Jeshua	IL1612	61,66D,10D
Friedman, Joel Phillip	CA4425	13B,10A,10D,12A
Galdston, Philip E.	NY2750	10D
Gauthier, Michael	AI0050	70,29A,47,10D
Gleason, Stephen	NY1275	10D,12A,13B,14C,34D
Gluck, David	NY3785	10C,10D
Goldstein, Gil B.	NY2750	10D,47,66A,29
Guzzi, Ralph	PA0500	10D
Hackel, Erin H.	CO0830	36,13,11,10D
Hampton, Bradley	CA0845	10D,40
Head, Russell	KS0750	10B,10D,34,35,45
Holland, Deborah	CA0830	35,10D
Howard, Bill	TX1600	10D,10,66A,35B,66D
Inserto, Ayn	MA1175	10D
Jones, Kelly	CA0630	10D
Joyce, David	CA3500	61,10D
Julien, Patricia A.	VT0450	13,12,10D,29
Keever, Howard	MS0850	10A,10D,13A,13B,13D
Keys, Scarlet	MA0260	10D
Koeppel, James	NY3785	10C,10D
Kortz, Owen	CO0830	61,10D
Koslovsky, Marc S.	NY2550	70,10D
Krikun, Andrew	NJ0020	35A,10D,47,14,20
Krumrei, Randall	CA0200	10D
Kupka, Craig	CA1960	10D,46
Lee, Abe	MA0260	10A,10D,35C,35G
Leisawitz, Jeffrey	WA0650	10D,10F
Levinson, Ross	CA0830	35,34A,10C,10D
Leydon, Rebecca	OH1700	13,13F,10C,10D
Livingston, Edwin U.	CA5300	10D,14C
Loughrige, Chad	OH0350	34,35C,10B,10D,45
Lovely, Brian	OH0680	29,10C,10D,70,35
McLane, Brian	AZ0460	10D
McLean, Kim	TN1600	10D
Nelson, Curt	CA2900	10D,36,40,54
O'Mahoney, Terrence	AF0150	50,65,29,10D,66A
Patterson, William M.	NY2750	10D

Pinnock, Rob	AE0120	10D
Pontbriand, Roget	FL1450	45,46,35,10D,10C
Potaczek, Amanda Lee	IN0100	10D,35A
Reid, John	TX2350	11,10D,35B,62D
Richards, Eric	NE0600	47,10A,10D,13G
Richards, Scott D.	NJ0800	10D,13B,13C,54
Robbins, Daniel C.	CA2050	11,13A,10D
Roberts, Gene	CO0830	61,10D
Roberts, Tim	CA3320	46,14C,10D,13
Rosenhaus, Steven L.	NY2750	10,13F,10F,10A,10D
Rushen, Patrice Louise	CA5300	10D,14C
Ryan, Michael	CA5100	70,42,10D
Sadoff, Ronald H.	NY2750	13K,10A,10C,10D
Sanchez, Rey	FL1900	10D,34C,35A,20G,43
Schildt, Matthew C.	CO0050	13,10,10D,13E,34
Schumaker, Adam	MI1150	10A,10B,10C,10D,70
Seidman, William	NY2750	10D
Shelby, Karla	OK1500	10D,13A,60A,66A,36
Simos, Mark	MA0260	10,10D
Smith, Stan	OH0350	70,10D
Smith, Tony L.	TN0150	35A,35E,35F,10D
Smolik, Vicky	IL2970	11,63A,10D,35D
Snyder, Jeffrey S.	PA1900	35,34D,10B,32F,10D
Soich, Leslie	CO0830	36,13,11,10D
Sorce, Richard P.	NJ0950	10D,13,34D
Stolpe, Andrea Kay	CA5300	10D,14C
Sushel, Michael	CA1000	10D,66A,66B,11,29A
Swann, William E.	TN1000	47,13,60B,29B,10D
Thomas, Gates	MA0260	10D
Toft, Robert	AG0500	10D,12A,12C,13J
Vayo, David J.	IL1200	10F,10,10D,10B,10A
Viswanathan, Sundar	AG0650	29,64E,10D,61
Walker, Deanna	TN1850	66A,10D
Walley, Steve	IN0905	13G,34,10D
Ward, Brian	WA1150	66A,10D,13C,14C,29A
Waterfall, Linda	WA0200	10D
Wight, Steve	CA0830	35,34A,10C,10D,10F
Willis, George R.	WV0750	10D,11,32B,52,65
Winer, Arthur H.	CA0630	10D,34D,35G,35,10C
Yeston, Maury	NY1275	10D,54

World Folk Music

Alcorn, Allison A.	IL3150	10E,11,12A,20,31A
Banzi, Julia	OR0400	20,14C,34B,14,10E
Becker, Melissa J.	PA2050	10E,12,32,62
Broscious, Timothy L.	MN1600	10E,65
Brown, Alison	TN1850	10E
Ha, Youngmi	NY2750	10A,10E,13B,13C,13D
Junker, Tercio	IN0300	60A,36,31A,32D,10E
Kafumbe, Damascus	VT0350	14A,14C,10E,20,31F
Larner, James M.	IN1100	12A,48,10E,64A,29A
Schmidt, Daniel	CA2950	72,10E,20D
Sidhu, Inderjeet	IL1085	10E
Tate, Elda Ann	MI1600	13,10E,41,64A
Tewari, Laxmi	CA4700	14,13A,61,10E,31D

Orchestration

Aberdam, Eliane	RI0300	13,10F,10,12A,45
Abril, Mario	TN1700	13,10F,70
Adams, Byron	CA5040	13,10F,10,12
Adams, Richard	MI2250	10,49,13L,13,10F
Adkins, Don	CA0300	13,10F,10,12A,62D
Alsobrook, Joseph	MO0650	10F,32E,37,34F,35A
Anderson, Douglas K.	NY0270	13,10F,60,10,38
Aquilanti, Giancarlo	CA4900	13,10F,60,37,49
Archer, Kimberly K.	IL2910	10,13,32E,10A,10F
Argento, Dominick J.	MN1623	13,10F,10,12A
Arjomand, Ramin Amir	NY2750	10A,10F,13B,13C
Armstrong, John	AG0400	13,10F,10
Arrowsmith, Brenda	AG0070	48,64,10F,13A,13B
Ashton, J. Bruce	TN1350	10A,31A,66A,10F,66C
Atteberry, Ron	MO0100	10F,36,61,10A
Austin, Kevin	AI0070	13,10F,10,34,35C
Avramov, Bogidar	CA2800	38,51,11,10F,60B
Baker, Kent	VT0100	66A,66D,46,13,10F
Bancks, Jacob	IL0100	10,10F,43,13,12A
Baransy, Paul	OH0250	63A,10F,60B,32E,37
Barnes, Arthur P.	CA4900	13,10F,37
Barnes, James	KS1350	10F,10,12A
Barnett, Steven	WV0400	10F,32E,37,60
Barta, Daniel	NY3350	10,13,10A,10F
Bartsch, John T.	OR0175	13B,38,66,10F,10A
Bauer, William R.	NY0644	10F,12A,12C,13
Bauman, Jeffrey Milo	GA2300	36,61,54,10F,60A
Beall, John	WV0750	13,10F,10,43
Beason, Christine F.	TX3250	37,48,63B,32,10F
Beckman, Linda L.	AR0400	66A,11,10F,34,66C
Belfield, Roy L.	NC2700	66G,36,60A,10F,12A
Bell, Allan	AA0150	13,10,20G,10F
Bell, Dennis	NY2400	13A,13,10F
Belshaw, Gary D.	TX3650	10F,10,66,34
Ben-Amots, Ofer	CO0200	13,10F,10,11,34
Benoit, John	IA1350	13,11,63C,10F,55
Berk, Stacey J.	WI0850	13A,13B,64B,41,10F
Berteig, Laurence	WA0550	10F
Bielawa, Herbert	CA4200	13A,13,10F,10,45
Birden, Larry	OK0450	13A,32E,10F,63,37
Biscardi, Chester	NY3560	13,10F,10,11,12A
Blackwood, Easley R.	IL3250	10F,13L
Block, Steven	NM0450	13A,13,10F
Blume, Philipp G.	IL3300	13,10,10A,10F
Bocook, Jay A.	SC0750	37,10F
Bogue, Bryan	WA1350	13G,10F
Bohlen, Donald A.	NY3725	10A,10F,13D,10
Bombardier, Brad	WI0860	10F,64D
Bonacci, Andrew	MA2100	10,13,10A,10F
Booth, Todd	AG0130	10A,10D,10F,11,13
Boquiren, Sidney M.	NY0050	10A,13A,20D,31A,10F
Bourassa, Richard N.	OR0450	13,10F,10A,11
Bower, John E.	DC0050	10A,13C,10F
Boysen, Andrew A.	NH0350	37,60B,10F
Bradshaw, Keith M.	UT0200	10A,10F,13,36
Bradshaw, Robert J.	MA1650	10A,10C,10F,35A,35G
Brandes, David E.	NH0110	13,10F,60,36,66G
Brazelton, Kitty	VT0050	13,10F,10,11,53
Brennan, Adam	PA2150	60B,37,50,65,10F
Briggs, Roger	WA1250	43,10F,10,66A
Brink, Daniel	CO0200	13A,13,10F,11,66A
Brown, Rogers	VA0950	10F,37,47,63D,29
Bryant, Curtis	GA1050	13A,10F
Bryden, Kristy	IA0850	13,10,10F,34A,34H
Buczynski, Walter	AG0450	13,10F,10,66A
Burge, John	AG0250	13,10,10F,13I
Byrd, Joshua	GA2130	37,10A,13G,48,10F

Index by Area of Teaching Interest

Name	Code	Areas
Cabrer, Carlos R.	PR0150	10A,10F,11,13A,13B
Cacioppo, Curt	PA1500	13,10,20G,10F,66A
Cameron, Jennifer	OR1150	13,10F,64,60,51
Campbell, Brian G.	MN0350	13,10A,20,12B,10F
Campbell, Roy	MA0510	11,10F,38,46,47
Carbon, John J.	PA1300	13A,13,10F,10
Carter, Allen L.	MN1120	13,10F,65,47
Casal, David Plans	NH0100	10B,10F,34,13,35
Casey, J. Warren	AR0250	10F,11,32,47,64C
Casey, Michael	NH0100	10B,10F,34,13,35
Cass, Howard	MI0600	42,10F
Chamberlain, Donald J.	IA0400	13,10F,10,11,47
Chamberlin, Robert	MO1950	13,10F,10,45
Chambers, Carol	TX3100	63A,13C,32E,10F,32A
Chambers, Robert	OK1250	38,63C,63D,13D,10F
Chang, Dorothy	AB0100	10A,10F,10
Chang, Yu-Hui	MA0500	10A,10F,13B,13D,13F
Chemay, Frank	LA0700	10,63D,10F,11,49
Chesanow, Marc	SC0420	62D,11,10F,13B,35G
Chrisman, Richard	NJ1130	13,10F,13J
Cichy, Roger	RI0150	10A,10F
Cierpke, Timothy H.	TN1600	10F,60,62,36,38
Clarke, Garry E.	MD1100	13,10F,10,12A
Clegg, Neill M.	NC0900	10F,12A,64,53,29A
Clemmons, Bill	CA3640	13,34,10F
Colson, William	TX2600	13A,13,10F,10,13I
Coltman, Charles	TX0900	10F,41,64,35A
Cook, Linda Klein	WI0750	63A,12,13,63B,10F
Cooper, John H.	ME0270	10,29,13,64E,10F
Corigliano, John	NY0600	10F,10
Corigliano, John	NY0635	10F,10,11,54
Corkern, David	MO0500	46,63A,37,47,10F
Corwin, Mark	AI0070	10F,10,45,34,35C
Crockett, Donald	CA5300	13,10F,10
Crowley, James F.	WI0835	13,10F,10
Crumb, David	OR1050	10A,10F,13
Csapo, Gyula	AJ0150	13,10,45,10F
Culver, Eric	MA0700	11,60,10F,38,41
Curlette, Bruce	OH0450	13,64C,10F
Dabrowski, Peter	TX3525	60,10F
Daniel, Omar	AG0500	13,10,10F,34,35C
David, James M.	CO0250	13,10,10F,63C
Davis, Alfred L.	VA0500	32E,32F,32B,32C,10F
Day, Greg	SC1080	13,10F,37,47,63
De La Torre, Javier	PR0150	10A,10F,13A,13C
de Murga, Manuel	FL1750	10,10F,13E,34,43
Del Tredici, David	NY0600	10F,10
Dello Joio, Justin N.	NY2750	13B,13E,13F,10A,10F
Demars, James R.	AZ0100	13,10F,10
Dembski, Stephen	WI0815	10F,10
Denisch, Beth	MA0260	13,10F,10,15
Desby, Neal	CA5300	13,10F
DiBlasio, Denis	NJ1050	10F,47,64E,53,29
Dickerson, Roger	LA0720	10F,10,12A,36,29
Diemer, Emma Lou	CA5060	13,10F,10
DiSanti, Theodore A.	PA3000	63A,47,49,13,10F
Dobbins, William	NY1100	29B,29C,10A,10F,46
Don, Gary W.	WI0803	13,10F,10A
Dorman, Avner	PA1400	10A,10F,13,43
Dougherty, William P.	IA0550	13,10F,10,34
Dovel, Jason L.	OK0550	63A,11,63B,10F
Downey, John W.	WI0825	13,10F,10,45,43
Dubbiosi, Stelio	NJ0825	13,10F,66A,66G
Dudley, Sherwood	CA5070	13,10F,12A,39
Durham, Thomas L.	UT0050	13,10F,10
Dutton, Brent	CA4100	13,10F,10,49,63D
Eagle, David	AA0150	13,10F,10,34,43
Eckardt, Jason K.	NY0500	10,10F,13
Edwards, Constance	WV0300	64D,12,11,12A,10F
Emile, Mark A.	UT0300	10F,60B,62A,62B
Emmons, Stephen D.	TX0150	13,10,10F,34
Errante, Steven	NC2440	13,10F,60,10,38
Fairchild, G. Daniel	WI0840	10F,11,32,63B
Fannin, John E.	KY0950	32,37,10F
Feigin, Joel	CA5060	10,10A,10F,13D
Feinstein, Allen G.	MA1450	13,10F,60,37,48
Feldman, Bernardo	CA1265	13A,13,10F,10,11
Fetler, Paul	MN1623	13,10F,10
Finn, Neal	NC0800	10A,10F,29A,47,63C
Fischer, Lou	OH0350	47,29B,10F
Flauding, Richard (Ric) G.	TX2600	10,34,10F,13
Fletcher, John M.	OK0700	10F,60,37,13
Flores, Carlos	MI0250	13,10,35,34,10F
Forsyth, Malcolm	AA0100	13,10F,10,38
Fosheim, Karen	MS0250	66A,13B,50,20A,10F
Fox, Jeremy	IA1400	13,10F,37,50,34
Foy, Regina	PA1550	13B,10F,31A
Frangipane, Ron	NJ0760	13,10F,60,10,12A
Frazelle, Kenneth	NC1650	13,10F,10
Frazier, Bruce H.	NC2600	10C,10F,35
Froom, David	MD0750	13,10A,10B,10F
Fry, James	MD1010	13,10F,10
Frye, Christopher B.	WI0810	13,10F,10,34
Fuentes, Alfonso	PR0115	10,10F
Fuentes, David	MI0350	13,10F,10
Funk, Eric	MT0200	10A,10F,60,29,13
Gallagher, Jack	OH0700	63A,10,10F,13,12A
Ge, Tao	GA0550	10F,13C
Geers, Douglas E.	NY0500	10A,10B,10F
Gellman, Steven	AG0400	13,10F,10
Gerdes, John	MO0700	10F,29A,63
Getzov, Israel	AR0850	38,10F
Gibbs, Geoffrey D.	RI0300	10A,10F,13
Gibson, Richard L.	AE0100	13,10F,10,37,63
Gillingham, David R.	MI0400	13A,13,10F,10
Gilroy, Gary P.	CA0810	13C,10F,60B,37
Girtmon, Paxton	MS0100	37,47,64E,10F,60
Glancey, Gregory T.	CA5355	10F,13,34,35
Godwin, Paul M.	TN0100	13,10F,10,34
Goldman, Edward 'Ted'	NY1100	13K,13C,13B,10A,10F
Goldstein, Howard A.	AL0200	10F,62A,11,12A,38
Gonzalez, Claudio	MI0250	38,60B,10F,20,12A
Gordon, William	AC0050	10F,12A,63B
Gothard, Paul	OH1250	13A,13,10F,11,36
Grantham, Donald	TX3510	13,10F,10
Green, Scott	WV0800	10F
Greene, Elisabeth Mehl	TX1100	10F,12A
Greene, Roger W.	MA0150	13,34,66A,13A,10F
Greenlee, Geol	TN1250	13,66A,10F,10,11
Greenough, Forest G.	CO0250	47,62D,10F,34
Grossmann, Jorge V.	NY1800	10A,10F
Gryc, Stephen Michael	CT0650	13,10F,10
Guerra, Stephen J.	FL1900	10F,29A,29B,47
Gustafson, Kirk	CO0225	13,10F,60,62C
Gustavson, Mark	NY2550	10,64C,66D,10A,10F
Hackbarth, Glenn A.	AZ0100	13,10F,10,43
Haebich, Kenneth	IL0850	62D,10A,10F
Hailstork, Aldolphus C.	VA1000	10,10F
Haimo, Ethan	IN1700	13,10,10F
Hall, Robert	AG0150	13,60,36,61,10F
Hamlin, Peter S.	VT0350	10A,10B,10F,13A,13B
Hanan, David	OK1330	37,60B,10F,34,63A
Hanlon, Kevin	TX2400	13,10F,10,43
Hansen, Ted	TX2955	13,10F,10A,66A
Harbold, Mark A.	IL0850	13,10F,10,16,12A
Hardaway, Travis	MD0650	13,10F
Hartig, Hugo J.	WI0200	13,10F,10,12A
Hartway, James	MI2200	13A,10,10F,66D,13B
Hauser, Joshua	TN1450	63C,10F,13B,42
Heard, Alan	AG0500	13,10F,10
Hehr, Milton G.	MO1810	13,10F,12A
Heidenreich, Christopher	MI2120	37,49,11,10F
Held, Jeffrey	CA1425	11,12A,37,32E,10F
Henry, James	MO1830	36,40,60A,32D,10F
Herman, Martin	CA0825	10F,13,10,34
Hersey, Joanna R.	NC2435	10F,63C,63D,12A
Heuser, David	NY3780	10A,10B,13,10F,10
Hindman, Dorothy Elliston	FL1900	10A,10F,13
Hoehne, Bill	CA1000	10F,12C,64A,13,29
Hoferer, Kevin	PA2150	29,10F
Holland, Jonathan Bailey	MA0260	10A,10F,13A,10
Horton, Dennis	MI0400	10F,63A
Houze, Reginald M.	MA0150	10F,36,37,60,63D
Hunt, Graham G.	TX3500	13,12,10F,11,12A
Husa, Karel	NY0900	10F,60,10A
Isele, David	FL2050	10F,10,36,61,66G
Ivanova, Vera	CA0960	10A,10B,10F,10,66A
Jablonsky, Stephen	NY0550	11,63A,10A,10F,13
Jaffe, Stephen	NC0600	13,10F,10
Jefcoat, Priscilla	GA0350	13A,66A,10F,12A,13D
Jeffreys, Harold L.	NC2150	10F,32,64C,65,46
Jenkins, Joseph W.	PA1050	13,10F,10,12A
Johnson, Barry	KY0750	13,10F,10,11
Johnson, Campbell	AR0700	10F,66G
Johnson, Stephen P.	TX2600	10,13,10F,60A,60
Johnson, Stephen R.	PA0700	10F,32D,13A,63D
Johnston, Gary	KY1000	10F,11,34
Jones, Arlington	TX0370	13,10F,66A,35G
Jones, David P.	WA0700	13,10F,10
Jordan, William S.	AA0150	13,10,10F
Joyce, Robert	SD0050	10F,34
Jureit-Beamish, Marie	IL2400	38,64A,66A,10F,11
Justus, Timothy W.	TX1700	10F,13
Kahn, Richard	CA2750	10F,13A,66A
Kammerer, David	HI0050	10F,37,35B,63A,13C
Karchin, Louis S.	NY2740	10F,60,10,36
Kavasch, Deborah H.	CA0850	10A,13,61,10,10F
Kechley, David S.	MA2250	10A,10F,13A,13B,13D
Kellogg, Daniel	CO0800	10A,10F
Kennedy, John M.	CA0830	10,13F,43,10F,13
Kern, Philip	IN1100	13,10F,36,54,66A
Kerr, Daniel	ID0060	10A,13,66G,10F
King, Jonathan	NY3560	13,10F,60,36,10
Kiser, Daniel W.	NC1100	13A,10F,60B,37,63A
Kitchen, Otis D.	PA1250	10F
Klein, Joseph	TX3420	10F,10A
Kompanek, Rudolph W.	NY2750	10C,10F
Kramer, Timothy	IL1100	13,10F,10A,10B
Kramlich, Daniel L.	TX1000	13,10F,66A
Krause, Melissa M.	MN1300	13,64A,10A,10F
Kresky, Jeffrey	NJ1400	13,10F,11,66D
Kubis, Thomas M.	CA2050	10F,13A,29B,46,47
Kuchera-Morin, JoAnn	CA5060	13,10F,10,45,13L
Kudo, Takeo	HI0210	10A,10F,13,20D
Kuehn, Mikel	OH0300	13,10F,10,45,43
Kunda, Keith	IN1560	13B,13C,10F
Kurek, Michael	TN1850	13,10F,10
Kyr, Robert	OR1050	10A,10F,43,20D
La Rocca, Frank J.	CA0807	13,10F,10
LaChance, Marc	NE0300	63C,63D,13,10F,29
Lambert, Nathan T.	CO0350	10F,11,14C,42,51
Lamkin, John R.	MD1020	10F,37,47,63
Landers, Joseph	AL1200	10A,10F,13B,13C,13E
Landey, Peter	AG0050	12B,13J,10A,10B,10F
Larsen, Jens	SC0900	10F,63A,49
Latta, Jonathan R.	CO0350	10F,47,50,65,20
Lee, Charles	CO0650	62C,41,51,10F,60
Lee, Damon Thomas	NE0600	10A,10B,10C,10F,34A
Leisawitz, Jeffrey	WA0650	10C,10D,10F
Lesemann, Frederick	CA5300	13,10F,10,45
Levy, Fabien	NY0750	10A,10F,13E,13F
Lewis, H. M.	KY0610	10F,11,12A,49,63A
Lewis, James E.	FL2000	13,10F,10,43
Liaropoulos, Panagiotis	MA0260	10A,10F
Lias, Stephen J.	TX2700	13,10F,10
Lifchitz, Max	NY3700	10,43,13A,13,10F
Lin, Mei-Fang	TX3200	10A,13A,13I,13L,10F
Link, John	NJ1400	13,10F,10,34
Linn, Don	KS0650	37,32E,10F
Lipkis, Larry	PA2450	13,10F,10,55,67
Lis, Anthony	SD0550	13,10F,10,66,20D
Logan, Kenneth	MI0250	66G,34,10,10F,31A
Lombardi, Paul	SD0600	13A,13G,10F,10A,13B
Long, David J.	VA1475	13,10A,10F
Lovelace, Jason R.	DC0050	10A,13C,10F
Lubaroff, Scott C.	MO1790	37,32E,10F,60
Lundberg, Kim	AG0500	13,10F
Lutch, Mitchell B.	IA0200	10F,32E,37,60
Luzko, Daniel	CA2390	13,10F,10,34
Lyke, Toby Russell	OH0680	10F,47,29A
MacDonald, Andrew	AI0050	13,10F,10,45,70
Mackey, Steven	NJ0900	13,10F,10,11,41
Magnuson, Phillip	OH2250	13,10F,10A,62B
Magruder, Michael	NC2700	10F,37,64C
Mahoney, Shafer	NY1900	10F
Mainland, Timothy L.	WV0200	13,10,70,10F,62
Makan, Keeril	MA1200	10,10F,34,13
Markou, Kypros L.	MI2200	10F,38,62A
Mason, Charles Norman	FL1900	10A,10B,10F,34D
Mathiesen, Steven	PA2200	10A,10F,50,65
Matthews, Michael K.	MO0850	13A,13,10F,47,63C
Maurtua, Jose Luis	MI0400	13A,13,10F,60,10
May, Andrew D.	TX3420	10A,10B,10F,34A,34D
Maynard, Keith	NY2400	13A,13,10F
McAllister, Michael	NC1750	13,10F,60,11,47
McAneny, Marc A.	NY3717	13,10F
McBride, M. Scott	KY0900	60B,32,10F,63C,37
McDonnell, David	OH2250	10B,10F,34,64E,47
McFatter, Larry E.	CA0845	13,10F,10,66A
McFerron, Mike	IL1520	13A,13,10F,34,10
McGee, William James	CA3400	13,10F,10,66A,34
McIlhagga, Samuel D.	MI0100	10F,37,14C,32E
McKinney, Kevin	GA1900	13A,10F,11
McLoskey, Lansing D.	FL1900	10A,10F,13,55D
McMullen, George	CA2650	47,46,10F
Mendelson, Ruth J.	MA0260	10F

Index by Area of Teaching Interest

Name	Code	Areas
Milarsky, Jeffrey F.	NY0750	38,10F,60
Miller-Thorn, Jill	NY1275	10A,10F,13,66D,12C
Millican, Si	TX3530	32E,37,10F,35B
Mirowitz, Sheldon P.	MA0260	10F
Mishra, Michael	IL2910	10F,60,38
Mitchell, Jon	MA2010	10F,60,32,38
Mobberley, James C.	MO1810	10A,10B,10F
Moffett, C. Mondre	NC1550	63A,10F,29A,47,31F
Moore, Anthony	NC1450	10F,13G,13E
Morehead, Patricia	IL0720	10F,10,64B
Morin, Eric	AI0190	10B,10F
Moss, Lawrence	MD1010	10,13,10F
Mountain, Rosemary	AI0070	13,10F,10,45,34
Mueller, Paul F.	NY0625	10F,60,11,12A,36
Muller, David J.	CA6000	10F,11,12A,60B,64D
Mumford, Lawrence R.	CA5355	10,12,13,10F
Muniz, Jorge	MO0100	10A,10F
Munn, Zae	IN1450	13,10F,10,43
Murail, Tristan C.	NY0750	10,34,13L,12F,10F
Myers, Andre K.	CA3300	10A,10B,10F,13
Nash, Gary Powell	TN0550	10,13,47,64,10F
Nelson, David W.	CA0859	13,13A,10F,10,38
Nelson, Jon C.	TX3420	10A,10B,10F,34
Nelson, Robert S.	TX3400	13A,13,10F,10
Nelson, Timothy	IL2300	13,10F,66A,66G
Niblock, Howard	WI0350	13,10F,12B,41,64B
Nichols, Jeff	NY0600	10A,13E,10F
Nichols, Jeff W.	NY0642	10,10F,13
Niederberger, Maria	TN0500	13,10F,10
Nilles, Benjamin	OK0750	38,10F
Nin, Chan Ka	AG0450	13A,13,10,10F
Nix, Brad K.	KS1250	66B,66A,66C,10F,66D
Norris, Philip E.	MN1280	10F,11,32E,63A,31A
Nozny, Brian	ND0100	13,10A,10F,34A,34B
Nurock, Kirk	NY2660	10F,60,10,13J,29A
Oakley, Tom	TN0150	37,47,32H,10F
O'Connor, Thomas	AR0110	13,32,47,10A,10F
Ogdon, Will L.	CA5050	13,10F,10,12A
Olan, David	NY0600	10F,10,10B
Oliver, Harold	NJ1050	13,10F,10,41,53
Osborne, Thomas	HI0210	10A,10F,13,43
Packales, Joseph	ME0500	13,10F,10
Packard, John	OH1600	37,49,63A,60B,10F
Painter, Noel	FL1750	13,10F
Parenteau, Gilles	AB0070	10F,45,66,35H
Parker, Philip	AR0200	13,10F,10,65,50
Pelusi, Mario J.	IL1200	10A,10F,13,43,29B
Pennington, John C.	SD0050	13A,65,50,10F
Perron, Alain	AJ0100	10A,10B,10C,43,10F
Peterson, Wayne T.	CA4200	13,10F,10,12A,66A
Pethel, Stan	GA0300	13,60,10,63C,10F
Phillips, Paul Schuyler	RI0050	38,60,13,10,10F
Pickett, Glen	CA0450	10F,66A,66C
Piippo, Richard	MI1050	38,41,51,62C,10F
Polay, Bruce	IL1350	10A,10F,12A,13B,60B
Polot, Barton L.	MI1900	10A,10B,10F,12,13
Portnoy, Kim	MO1950	10F,10,29
Pozdnyakov, Aleksandr	AI0200	10F
Price, William Roger	OK1450	10A,41,66A,10F
Ptaszynska, Marta	IL3250	13,10,10F
Purves-Smith, Michael	AG0600	60,37,55,10F
Raboy, Asher	CA3400	37,13D,10F,13E,11
Radford, Laurie	AA0150	10,10F,13,43
Ratliff, Phillip	AL0650	13,12A,10F,34
Read, Kenneth E.	OH0550	13E,31A,10A,10F,13B
Reed, Thomas T.	OH0100	10F,64C,64E,48
Reese, Randall	GA0200	10F,47,64E,10A,13D
Reise, Jay	PA3350	13,10F,10
Resnick, David	IA0250	10B,10F,13A,37,48
Reynolds, Roger L.	CA5050	13,10F,10,20G,34
Ricci, Robert	MI2250	13,10F,12B,29
Richards, James	MO1830	10F,60,38
Rinehart, John	OH0050	13A,13,10F,10,12A
Rissman, Maurice Nick	TX1400	13,10F,10
Ritz, Lyn	WA1100	62A,62B,42,13,10F
Rivard, Gene	MN0625	13,10F,49,63A,31A
Roane, Steve	NY2400	10F
Roberts, David Scott	TN1720	66G,13,10F
Rogers, Rodney	AZ0100	13,10F,10
Roller, Jonathan	KY0100	11,10F
Roman, Dan	CT0500	34,70,10A,10F,13
Romer, Wayne Allen	PA3710	13A,10F,60B,11,32
Rosa Ramos, Luis S.	PR0115	29,10F,47
Rosenblum, Mathew	PA3420	13,10F,10
Rosenhaus, Steven L.	NY2750	10,13F,10F,10A,10D
Rosenzweig, Morris	UT0250	13,10F,10
Ross, John C.	KS1050	13,10,10F
Roush, Dean	KS1450	13,10F,10,34
Rox, David	MA0950	10F,60,32,37,41
Roy, J. Michael	WI0845	13,10A,10F
Rudy, Paul	MO1810	10A,10B,10C,10F
Ruff, Willie H.	CT0850	35,10F,13
Runner, David C.	TN1150	13,10F,66A,66G,10A
Runyan, William E.	CO0250	10F,12C,12A
Ruocco, Phyllis	AR0550	13A,13,11,66A,10F
Sampson, Kenneth C.	TN0800	10F,32B,32C,37,63
Sanders, Gregory L.	TX2960	13,10F,10,34
Santo, Joseph A.	DC0050	10A,10F,13B,13H,13C
Sargon, Simon	TX2400	13,10F
Sarjeant, Ronald	SC1050	10F,60,37,64
Saul, Walter B.	CA1860	10A,66A,13,20,10F
Saylor, Bruce	NY0600	10F,10
Saylor, Bruce S.	NY0642	13,10F,10
Schaeffer, Greg	AZ0400	10F
Schedel, Margaret	NY3790	10A,10B,10C,10F
Schelle, Michael	IN0250	13,10,43,10F
Schnauber, Thomas	MA0900	10A,10C,13A,11,10F
Schoen, Theodore A.	MN1600	64C,64E,41,10F
Schuttenheim, Tom	CT0650	10F,13F
Schwartz, Elliott S.	ME0200	10F,10,11,12A,41
Sclater, James	MS0400	13E,10F,10,13C
Scott, Ronald	TX2930	64C,64E,38,10F,60
Serghi, Sophia	VA0250	13,10F,10,43,10A
Setter, Terry A.	WA0350	10F,10,12B,45,35C
Shafer, Sharon Guertin	DC0250	10F,12A,39,61
Sharp, Thomas	CA0815	10C,10F
Sharpe, Carlyle	MO0350	10F,10
Shatin, Judith	VA1550	10B,10A,10F,10,13
Shaw, Gary R.	IL1750	10F,60,37,63C
Shufro, Joseph L.	IA1100	10F,13E,34,38,62C
Sieg, Jerry	LA0800	10A,10F,13,12A
Sierra, Roberto	NY0900	10A,10F,13B,13F
Silver, Sheila	NY3790	13B,13D,13E,10A,10F
Simpson, Andrew Earle	DC0050	10,10F,13,66A,43
Sizer, Todd	CO0275	63D,10F,34,42
Skeirik, Kaleel	OH2550	13,10F
Sleeper, Thomas M.	FL1900	10F,60,10,38
Smaldone, Edward	NY0642	13,10,10F,11
Smart, Gary	FL1950	13,10F,10,66A,53
Smith, Douglas	AB0200	13,10F,10A
Smith, Kile	PA2800	10F
Snyder, Mark L.	VA1475	13,10F,10F,34
Sobaskie, James William	MS0500	13,13E,10F,13I,12
Sollberger, Harvey	CA5050	10F,60,10,64A,43
Solot, Evan	PA3330	13,10F,10,47,46
Sommerfeldt, Jerod	OH2250	10F,34
Spaneas, Demetrius	NY1275	10,29,46,64E,10F
Spear, David R.	NY2750	10,10F,60,10C
Stahlke, Jonathan E.	IL0730	13,10,38,10F
Stanton, Zachary K.	TN0100	10A,10F
Stephens, Timothy	OR0750	13,10F,10,12A
Stinson, Scott	FL1900	10A,10F,13D,13F
Stolarik, Justin R.	WI0815	37,60B,32E,65,10F
Stolberg, Tom	MO0060	10F,34,31A,32B,60
Strauman, Edward	PA0650	10F,29A,13D,13B,35A
Strommen, Carl	NY2105	10,10F,10A
Suozzo, Mark John	NY2750	10C,10F
Syswerda, Todd	IN1025	13A,13,10,11,10F
Talbott, Doug	KS0150	10F,32E,37,47,49
Tedder, Teresa C.	KY1150	10A,10C,10F,66A,11
Tharp, Reynold	IL3300	10F
Thiel, Robb G.	IN1350	10F,60B,32,37,65
Thompson, Christopher K.	AR0950	13A,13,10F,10,66A
Tiana, Mayo	IL2150	29,46,47,10F
Tiberio, John	PA2950	11,12,13,10A,10F
Topel, Spencer	NH0100	10B,10F,34,13,35
Townsend, Brendan	TX1425	10F,11,12A,13,62C
Traficante, Debra	OK1350	37,10F
Treuden, Terry	WI1155	37,47,32,10F
Turner, Timothy R.	LA0900	13G,10F,32E,34,37
Twomey, Michael P.	TX1900	10A,13,10F,38,62
Urbis, Richard	TX3515	10F,66A,66C
Uzur, Viktor	UT0350	13,10F,51,62C,42
Valdivia, Hector	MN0300	10F,60,11,38,41
Van Buren, Harvey	DC0350	13A,13,10F,10,66G
Vannice, Michael	OR0950	13A,10,10F
Vayo, David J.	IL1200	10F,10,10D,10B,10A
Vazquez, Carlos	PR0150	10A,10B,10F,13A,13C
Veenker, Jonathan	MN0250	13,10F,10
Venzen, Austin A.	VI0050	10F,11,32B,37,42
Vezinho, Ed	NJ1050	10F
Waggoner, Dori	MO0100	13E,10F,64A,37,13C
Wagoner, W. Sean	OR1050	65,10F,50,37,11
Wallace, William	AG0200	13,10F,10
Wang, Richard A.	IL3310	10F,12A,47,53,29
Warren, Ron	MD0150	10F,10,66C
Warshaw, Dalit Hadass	MA0350	10,13,66A,10F,13E
Waseen, Symeon	SD0100	10A,10B,10F,13,66
Weimann, Viljar P.	AL1250	62A,62B,38,10F
Werren, Philip	AG0650	10F,10,45
Whitaker, Howard	IL3550	13,10F,10,64C
White, Barbara A.	NJ0900	13A,10,13,10F,43
White, Kevin	MO0750	13,10F,10,63A,53
Whitfield, James M. (Matt)	NC0850	10A,13,37,10F,10
Wiemann, Beth	ME0440	10F,64C,34,10A,13D
Wight, Kevin	CA0830	35,34A,10C,10D,10F
Wilhoit, Mel R.	TN0200	10F,12A,32,49,63
Wilson, Cecil B.	WV0750	10F,60,12A,12
Wilson, Dana	NY1800	10F,10A
Wilson, Geoffrey	IA1800	12A,13,66A,10F
Wilson, Mark	MD1010	13,10F,10
Wilson, Richard E.	NY4450	13,10A,10F
Wilt, Kevin	MI1260	10A,10C,10F,34
Wiznerowicz, James	VA1600	10A,10F,13,13H,10
Wolf, Donald	AL1195	10F,37,46,47,63A
Wolfe, Anne Marie	IN0150	63D,64,32E,10F,60B
Wolking, Henry C.	UT0250	13,10F,47,46,29
Wolynec, Gregory J.	TN0050	37,38,10F
Womack, Donald Reid	HI0210	10,13,13E,10A,10F
Woods, Chris P.	IL1050	13A,10F,13C,49,63
Woodward, Gregory S.	NY1800	10A,10F
Worley, Daniel T.	KY1500	10,10F
Wramage, Gregg	NJ0050	10A,10F,11
Wyner, Yehudi	MA0500	10F,10,41
Yarbrough, Stephen	SD0600	13A,13G,10F,10A,13B
Yasinitsky, Greg	WA1150	47,64E,29,10F,10A
Yasui, Byron K.	HI0210	70,10A,10F,13,20B
Young, Charles R.	WI0850	13,10F,35C,10A
Zahab, Roger E.	PA3420	38,13,10F,43,62A
Zilincik, Anthony	OH0350	63D,41,43,10F

Music in General Studies/Music Appreciation

Name	Code	Areas
Aagaard, J. Kjersgaard	WI0842	13,11,36,37,49
Aamodt, Rucci R.	HI0150	32,11,66A,66D
Abbot, Louis	FL0200	11
Abbott, Amanda-Joyce	OH2290	61,11
Abraham, Daniel E.	DC0010	11,12,14C,36,60
Abrams, David	NY2950	13C,11,41,64C,12A
Aceto, Jonathan D.	GA0950	51,62A,11,62B,13E
Acker-Mills, Barbara E.	AL0200	11
Ackley, Dan	WI0862	11,37,64E
Acosta, Tim	CA4650	11,63,29A
Acsadi, Daniel	MA0510	70,11
Adam, Mark	AF0050	11,13C,46,47,65
Adams, Andrew	NC2600	66C,11,66A,66D
Adams, Ann M.	FL1750	64B,11,32C
Adams, Clifford	OH2200	11
Adams, Daniel B.	OH1300	11,70
Adams, J. Robert	GA0490	61,14,11,39,40
Adams, K. Gary	VA0100	11,12A,12,66A
Adams, Matthew	TX1425	65,50,11,12
Adams, Robert C.	GA0875	11
Adams, Robert L.	MO0700	11,12A,12,66A
Adan, Jose	FL1300	11,70,13A
Adan, Jose	FL0050	70,13,13C,11,29A
Adkins, Kathy	AL0750	11,36,61,66A
Aduonum, Ama Oforiwaa Konadu	IL1150	20,11
Agee, Richard J.	CO0200	13,11,12,66H,67D
Aho, Kyle	MO0775	11,66A,47
Ahuvia, Saar	NJ0700	66C,11
Ailshie, Tyson	CO0100	11,13,62D,70,29
Aipperspach, Candice Lane	TX2350	11
Aipperspach, Ian B.	TX2350	11
Akers, Ruth	FL0850	11
Alajaji, Sylvia A.	PA1300	14A,14C,11,12A,20
Albo, Francisco Javier	GA1050	11
Albrecht, Ronald	IA1350	13A,13,66A,11
Albrecht, Tamara	GA0750	11,12A,32A
Albrecht, Timothy	GA0750	11,12A,66A,31A
Albulescu, Eugene	PA1950	11,66A,66C,41
Alcorn, Allison A.	IL3150	10E,11,12A,20,31A
Alderson, Erin	IL1800	11,13A,32E,37,64
Alesi-Pazian, Melody	NJ0800	11
Alig, Kelley	OK0300	32,61,11

Index by Area of Teaching Interest

Name	Code	Areas
Allcott, Dan J.	TN1450	38,60B,62C,11,42
Allen, James O.	MS0550	11,12A,16,66A,66C
Allen, Ray	NY0500	11,20G,29A,20H
Allen, Robert J.	NY3770	11
Allen, Robert T.	VA0800	11,12A,29A,60A
Allen, Stephen Arthur	NJ1000	13,11,12A,12,20
Allen, Susan	VA0050	13C,11,66A,66D
Alley, Rob	AR0110	11
Allison, Edward	NC0050	11,32E
Allison, Joseph	KY0550	11
Allred, Jody	UT0190	61,11
Allsen, J. Michael	WI0865	11,12,14,20
Allsup, Neal	KS0550	11,12A,36,60,61
Alm, Gina	CA5355	11,66A,66B,66C,66D
Aloisio, Gerard S.	MN1000	11,49,63C
Alonso, Ernesto	PR0150	12A,11,62A,14A,55A
Alonso-Minutti, Ana R.	TX3420	11,12
Alstat, Sara	IL2500	11,13A,13C,36,61
Althouse, Paul L.	CT0100	11,60A,12A,36
Altman, I. H.	GA1300	11,66A
Alvarez, Franklin	AZ0300	11,51,62,38,13C
Alvarez, Luis M.	PR0150	10A,11,13A,13B,14
Alviso, Ric	CA0835	11,50
Alviso, Ric	CA4450	11
Amalong, Philip	OH0680	66A,66C,13,11,42
Amante Y Zapata, Joseph J.	RI0101	36,40,11,13A,13B
Amati-Camperi, Alexandra	CA5353	12A,11,12C,13A,12
Ambrosini, Armand	OK1350	11
Amico, Stephen	NJ0020	11,14
Amos, Gloria	VA0950	13A,11,61
Amrein, Emilie	IL1400	36,12A,13C,60,11
An, Won-Hee	MA1450	11,60B,66
Anastasia, Stephen	CA3200	61,11
Anderson, Amy B.	TX3200	11,64B
Anderson, Andrew E.	TX0075	29A,11
Anderson, Eric	MN0040	11,41
Anderson, Gene	VA1500	13,11
Anderson, Jared	MI1450	36,40,11,12A
Anderson, John	CA3050	13,11,37,64A
Anderson, Juliet V.	GA0490	11,39,61
Anderson, Leeann	OH1000	11,32B,62E,32A,32C
Anderson, Robert	NY3250	11,34D,34H,35,13A
Anderson, Ronald E.	TX2700	60A,11,12A,12C
Andrade, Ken	CA1760	13A,11
Andraso, Margaret B.	KY1100	11,36,61,63A
Andrews, Paul	AL0400	11
Annoni, Maria T.	MN0900	11,13A,13B,70,14C
Anthony, James	MD0850	11,12,16
Anthony, John P.	CT0100	13A,11,12A,66D,66G
Antokoletz, Elliott M.	TX3510	11,12A,12
Antonacos, Anastasia	PA1600	66A,13,11,66C,66D
Aponte, Maria P.	PR0150	11,13C
Appell, Glen	CA1560	11,29,46,47
Apple, Ryan	MI0910	13,12,70,11
Araujo, Ilka Vasconcelos	TX3250	66A,11,12A,20G
Arbogast, Jennifer	TN0260	11,13C,54,61,39
Arcaro, Peter	FL1100	13B,11,29A,47
Archbold, Lawrence	MN0300	11,12A,66G,15,12D
Archetto, Maria	GA0755	11,12A,12B,13A,20
Ard, Sharon	AR0600	11,13A
Armstrong, Candace	TN0900	13C,36,60A,66A,11
Armstrong, Jeff	NY1050	11
Armstrong, Robin E.	MD0520	11,14,29A,12,12A
Arnett, Nathan D.	IL1240	11,13C,32A,36,40
Arnold, Alison E.	NC1700	11,20,20E,14
Arnold, Mark	NY1250	13A,11,70
Arnold, Stacy	TX1775	70,11
Arrigotti, Stephanie	NV0150	13A,11,66A,66B,66D
Asbury, David	TX2650	70,11,34,13C
Ashe, Jennifer	MA0700	11,61,55D,40
Ashe, Jennifer	CT0150	11
Ashley, Douglas D.	SC0500	11,61
Ashmore, Michel	MO0250	11,12A,66A
Asteriadou, Maria	PA1750	11,66A,13A
Aston, Spencer	MA0510	11,66A,66B,41,42
Atapine, Dmitri	NV0100	63A,11
Atkinson, Sean E.	TX3500	62C,42,11
Atkisson, Lovelle	TN1250	11,12A,13
Atwell, Bruce W.	WI0830	11
Aubrey, Robert	MS0700	63B,13,11
Aubuchon, Ann Marie	CA2700	32B,11
AuBuchon, Elaine	MO1780	11,66
Auer, Shelley	TX0075	64B,64D,11
Augenblick, John	FL0700	61,11
Austin-Stone, Heather	WV0550	60A,36,11
Avdeeff, Melissa	AA0110	62A,62B,11
Averbach, Ricardo Franco	OH1450	11,12,14C
Avidon, Scott	NJ0700	11,38,60B
Aviguetero, Anthony	CA2800	11
Avramov, Bogidar	CA2800	38,51,11,10F,60B
Axtell, Katherine L.	VA0600	11
Ayesh, Kevin	NC0220	13,11,12A,66A,66D
Ayres, Carol	IA0800	11,37,47,64,29A
Babcock, Michael	VA0650	66A,11
Baca, Danny	TX2300	64,11
Bachmann, George	OH1100	70,11
Back, Douglas	AL0345	11,70
Bacon, Scott D.	PA1000	11,14C,65
Badami, Charles A.	MO0950	66C,66A,66D,11
Bade, Christopher	IN1560	11,38,48,64,12A
Baham, Kerry M.	TX3370	13B,66A,11,66C,12A
Bailey, Candace L.	NC1600	12,29D,15,11,12A
Bailey, Darrell	IN0907	11
Bailey, Jon D.	CA3650	60,12A,36,11
Bailey, Mary Lindsey	CO0225	64B,11
Bailey, Scott	MA2100	66C,66D,11
Bailey, Walter B.	TX2150	11,12A,12
Baird, Barbara M.	OR1050	66G,66H,67F,11
Baker, Alan	PA0250	60A,11,36,61,54
Baker, Eric	TX1850	11,37,46,63A
Baker, Jan Berry	GA1050	64E,11,13E
Baker, Nathan A.	WY0050	13,11
Baker, Ron	MI1180	11
Baker, Ruth	GA0300	11,61
Baker, Sidney	IA0790	11,62
Baker, Wilbur	NJ0825	11,32
Baldoria, Charisse J.	PA0250	66A,66D,12A,11
Balensuela, Matthew	IN0350	11,12A
Balian, Muriel G.	CA1700	13A,11
Balian, Muriel	CA1960	11,66A,66D,36,55D
Ball, David	VA1700	11
Ball, W. Scott	TN1350	11,12A,62D
Ballard, Alice	MS0300	66A,66G,66D,11
Ballard-Ayoub, Anne Claire	MD0300	11,64D
Ballatori, Cristina	TX3515	64A,11,42,13
Ballengee, Chris	FL1675	11,20
Ballinger, Robert W.	OH2300	39,66C,11,13A
Banagale, Ryan	CO0200	11,12,29,34
Banfield-Taplin, Carrie	OH0950	11,63B
Bangle, Jerry	NC2640	13,11,38,53,29
Banister, Linda	GA0250	11,39,61
Banks, Timothy	AL0800	11
Barach, Daniel P.	NY3770	12A,62B,11
Barkley, Elizabeth F.	CA1800	11,12A,66A,66C,66D
Barland, Charles J.	IA1450	13,11,31A,66A,36
Barlar, Nancy	FL0670	64C,32B,32C,32E,11
Barnes, Jonathan	NJ1050	11
Barnhill, Eric	NY5000	11
Barone, Ann Carmen	OH1330	11,32A
Barr, Dustin	CA3200	37,11
Barraca, Rudy	AL0335	11,63,65
Barrett, Robert H.	CO1050	11,47,64,34,29
Barrick, Christopher	WV0600	64,11,41,34,47
Barrientos, Paul	NM0350	11,36,61
Barte, Paul T.	OH1900	12A,11,66G,66H
Bartlett, Jacob Kenneth	NE0500	36,61,11
Barton, Stephen	MI0850	36,40,11,12A,61
Bartow, James	NY0270	11,20A,20G,29A,70
Basinger, Rhonda	IL1245	13,11,66
Basini, Laura	CA0840	11,12
Baskin, Jason	MO0850	11,65,34
Bass, Michael	MS0580	11,49,37,63
Bastian, William	MN0450	39,61,11
Bates, Charles N.	OH1800	11,32E,37,47,60
Bates, Vincent C.	MO0950	63B,32B,32C,11
Batista, Gustavo	PR0150	11,12A,13A,13C,70
Battipaglia, Diana M.	NY0635	11,32,36,66A,38
Baum, Joshua	IL0150	61,11,39,12
Baumgartner, Michael	OH0650	10,12A,11
Baur, Christine	AF0100	11,12A,12D,12E,14C
Bazinet, Ryan	MA0280	11,20
Beach, Sue Odem	IA0420	64,13,11
Beams, Mahala	MA1560	11,12A,66A,13A
Bean, Scott	WI0810	63D,12A,11,49
Beard, Christine E.	NE0610	64A,48,11,13
Bearden, Gregory	GA0250	11
Beaudoin, Paul	RI0200	10,13,12A,11
Beavers, Doug	CA2775	11
Beck, Nora	OR0400	11,12A
Becker, Jeral Blaine	MO1250	61,36,11,60,39
Becker, Paul	AR0800	66A,66B,66C,66D,11
Beckett, Scott	TX0100	11,12,13,37,63
Beckford, Richard	LA0700	11,36,66G,13
Beckford, Richard E.	SC1050	13,60,11,36,66G
Beckler, Terry	SD0400	65,50,37,46,11
Beckman, Gary D.	NC1700	12A,67G,11,35A,35B
Beckman, Linda L.	AR0400	66A,11,10F,34,66C
Beecher, Randy	CA2100	66A,11
Beert, Michael	IL2560	11,12A,13,38,20
Beery, John	MI1650	32,37,47,63,11
Behling, John F.	IL0750	11
Behrens, Lisa	NY1600	13,11
Behroozi, Bahram	CA4350	13A,11,12A,14,70
Bekeny, Amanda K.	OH0100	63A,49,11
Belcher, Debbie	KY1550	11
Belfy, Jeanne M.	ID0050	11,12,64B
Bell, Cindy L.	NY1600	32,11,36
Bell, Lorriane	VA0500	11,61,35A
Bellamy, Amy J.	NY0450	11,29A,36,61
Belland, Douglas	KY1000	11,14C
Belland, Douglas K.	OH2200	11
Bellassai, Marc C.	AZ0250	11,12A,66A,66F,66G
Beller-McKenna, Daniel	NH0350	12A,12C,11,14C
Bellisario, Kristen	IN0900	11
Belser, Robert S.	WY0200	37,63D,11
Bempechat, Paul-Andre	NJ1000	11,12A
Ben-Amots, Ofer	CO0200	13,10F,10,11,34
Bender, Sharla A.	AL0345	11,61,66A
Benedum, Richard P.	OH2250	11,12A,66G
Benjamin, Eric	OH2290	38,11
Benkman, Noel	CA1950	11,20
Benkman, Noel	CA0900	11,20,66
Bennett, Barbara A.	CA5040	13B,13,11,45,34
Bennett, Lawrence E.	IN1850	11,12A,12,13A
Beno, Charles W.	NY4400	12A,11
Benoist, Debbie	TX2310	11,13A,34C,65,66
Benoit, John	IA1350	13,11,63C,10F,55
Benson, Jack D.	TX1400	11
Benson, Mark F.	AL0210	13,12A,11,65,20
Benson, Michael L.	OH1350	66A,66B,12A,11,66
Benson, Will	TN0300	11,13,34B,36,64
Bent, Ian	NY0750	11,12A,12,13J
Benya, Susan	IA1140	37,13,11
Berard, Jesus Manuel	DC0010	38,60,13,11
Berardinelli, Paula	NY1600	29,13A,13C,11,47
Berdnikova, Natalya L.	WI0450	11,66D
Berg Oram, Stephanie	CO0625	11,12A,61,34B
Berg, Gregory	WI0250	11,61,39
Bergeron, Norm	TX2800	65,50,10D,11,13A
Bergman, James	CA4450	13A,11
Bergman, Mark	VA0450	11
Bergseth, Heather	MI0900	11,12
Berle, Arnie	NY2400	11,29A
Bernier, Lucas	ND0400	65,50,11,34
Bernstein, Harry	CA1020	13A,11
Bernstein, Jane A.	MA1900	11,12A,12,12C
Berrett, Joshua	NY2400	13,11,29A,12,12B
Berry, James	WV0440	11,12,13,33,61
Berry, James	PA3100	11,37,60,32B,48
Berry, Rodney	NC0050	47,11
Bersin, Michael D.	MO1790	11,12A,62C,62D
Berta, Joseph M.	NY1550	11,12A,64
Bertrand, Lynn Wood	GA0750	13,11,12A,12
Besharse, Kari	LA0650	11,13C
Bethany, Adeline M.	PA0450	11,20D,32A,32B,36
Bethea, Kay	VA1030	13,11,12A,66A,66D
Bethea, William	VA0950	65,11,37,50
Betts, Steven	OK1200	66A,66B,66D,13,11
Betts, Timothy	WA0050	62B,42,11
Betz, Brian	NJ1050	11
Beuche, William A.	CA3950	11
Bewley, Rabon	TX1660	11,12A,29,64E,13A
Beyer, George	CA1520	47,13A,11,20G
Beyer, Loretta	MI0200	13,66A,32B,11
Beyt, Christopher	IL2510	11
Bianchi, Eric	NY1300	11,12A,12G,13J,31
Biebesheimer, Arlene	AR0850	11
Bielish, Aaron J.	TX2295	62A,62B,41,11,13
Bieritz, Gerald	TX1300	12A,11,32A,36,60
Bigelow, Ira	CO0625	11,34B
Bigelow, Ira	CO0830	11
Biggs, Charlene	AG0070	11,66A,66B,66C
Bilderback, Barry T.	ID0250	11,12A,20B,12C,14A
Billaud, Louise	VA0900	11,12A,13A
Billingslea, Sandra	NY0646	11
Binckes, Fred B.	MT0350	13,10,11,66G

Index by Area of Teaching Interest

Name	Code	Areas
Bingham, Steve	FL1675	11,13A,20,29,64
Binkley, Lindabeth	MI0400	64B,41,48,11
Birk, Richard	TX0350	13,11,37,47,63
Birkemeier, Richard	CA0825	11,63A,49
Biscardi, Chester	NY3560	13,10F,10,11,12A
Biscay, Karen T.	OH1330	13,11,12A,36,61
Bishop, Darcie	MS0350	11,41,49,63A
Bivens, Pat	TN0250	11,47,63C,48,37
Bizinkauskas, Maryte	MA0510	61,11
Bjorlie, Carol	WI0845	11,62C
Black, Alan	TX1700	11,37,47,50,65
Black, Amy King	GA0500	11
Black, Elizabeth P.	NC0805	11,29A,20G
Blackburn, Bradford	FL2050	13,11
Blackburn, Ruth	MA1175	11
Blackman, Mary Dave	TN0500	11,32C
Blackshear, Alan	AL0831	37,13,11,29
Blackshear, Glinda	AL0831	60,11,36,39,61
Blackwell, Manley	AL1350	11,12A,66A
Blaine, Robert	MS0350	11,38,32E,63C,60B
Blake, C. Marc	CA2600	13,11,34,45,35B
Blake, Daniel	NY0500	11,13
Blakeman, Lee	KY1550	63C,13C,11,41
Blalock, Angela	SC0150	11,13A,13B,40,61
Blanchard, Gerald J.	MI1160	11,36,13,60A,61
Blanchett, Madalyn	TX2260	11,64A,66A,66D,67
Blankenbaker, Scott E.	MN1290	11,13,61,36
Blankenship, Carole	TN1200	11,61
Blankenship, William	NV0150	11
Blaser, Albert	OH0650	32E,11
Blecha-Wells, Meredith	OK0800	62C,11,42
Bleiler, Loueda	NY0950	11,12A,13A,13B,36
Bletstein, Bev R.	OH1860	11,32,61,70
Blinov, Ilya	PA3150	66A,66C,11
Bloch, Robert S.	CA5010	13,11,41,62A,62B
Blodget, Sherril	VT0100	40,36,60,61,11
Bloomfield, Ruta	CA2810	66H,11
Bloomquist, Paul	IA0790	11,63,60B,13,37
Bloxam, Jennifer	MA2250	11,15,12
Bluestone, Joel	OR0850	11,50,65,20G
Blundell, Reuben E.	NY0625	38,11
Board, Ryan A.	CA3600	11,32C,36,31A,60A
Bobbitt, Kayleen	MI0750	11,66,13,40
Bobetsky, Victor V.	NY0625	11,12A,62E
Boehm, Norman	AR0350	13,10,12A,66A,11
Boehm, Patricia A.	OH2290	61,32,11
Boerckel, Gary M.	PA2100	11,12A,66A,20G,29
Bogojevic, Natasha	IL0750	11
Bohn, James	MA0510	11,34
Bohnert, David A.	NE0700	63A,60B,37,11,32E
Bohnet, Keith	AL1300	11
Boldin, James E.	LA0770	63B,12A,11
Bolin, Daniel	IN0250	32,11
Bolton, Bryan	KY0050	11,13A,32,36,61
Bombardier, Bradley A.	MN1600	64C,64E,11
Bomer, Delain	MI1180	11,63B
Bomgardner, Stephen D.	MO0350	61,39,12A,11
Bonacci, Mary Brown	MA2100	61,11,13A
Bond, Karlyn	UT0400	11,12A,12B
Bonds, Mark Evan	NC2410	11,12
Bone, Lloyd E.	WV0350	12A,49,63,37,11
Bookout, Melanie	IN0905	11,12A,12,55,67A
Boone, Geraldine T.	VA0950	10A,32,11,13D,13F
Boorman, Stanley H.	NY2740	11,12A,12,55
Booth, Adam	WV0550	11
Booth, Todd	AG0130	10A,10D,10F,11,13
Borg, Paul	IL1150	13A,13,11,12A,12
Bostick, D. Jane	NC0100	66A,11
Bostock, Matthew	MA2100	13A,11,12A
Bostwick, Stacey	IA0420	11,65
Boswell, Ronald L.	AR0750	13,11,29A
Botelho, Mauro	NC0550	13,11,20H
Botts, Nathan	VT0050	11,29,49,63,67E
Bouchard, George	NY2550	11,46,47,66D,29
Boucher, Leslie H.	GA0700	12,20,13,62,11
Bouffard, Sophie	AJ0100	12A,61,11,13C
Bougie, Marc-Andre	TX2850	11,10,13,36
Boullion, Linda	NE0460	13,11,40,36,61
Bounds, Kevin S.	AL1160	12A,11,13A
Bourassa, Richard N.	OR0450	13,10F,10A,11
Bourgois, Louis	KY0750	11,12A,49,63D,34
Boury, Robert	AR0750	13,10,11
Bouvier, Monique	RI0101	11
Bowden, Derek	MD0800	11,66D,66A
Bowen, Nathan	CA3100	13,11,10,34
Bowen, Richard L.	IN1850	36,12,12A,11,12B
Bowers, Kathryn Smith	MO1950	11
Bowker, Barbara E.	IL1085	13,11,13B,13C,12A
Bowman, J. D.	KS0900	12A,11
Boyd, Craig E.	NY4050	60,11,47,70,29A
Boyd, Fern Glass	MT0400	12A,51,62C,11
Boyd, Jesse	LA0080	11,13,29,62,70
Boyd, John W.	TX2550	49,11
Boyd, Michael	MS0360	70,62D,41,10,11
Boyer, Charles G.	CO0050	32,11,32E,37
Boyer, D. Royce	AL1160	11,12A,36,61,31A
Boynton, Susan	NY0750	11,12A,12,12B
Bradbury, William	CA0847	13,10,11,34,20G
Bradley-Kramer, Deborah	NY0750	11,12A,41
Bradshaw, Murray C.	CA5032	13,11,12A,13J
Brammeier, Meredith	CA0600	13,11
Brandes, Christine	CA4200	11,13C,32D,39,61
Brantley, Mitch	MS0370	11,41,70
Braswell, Martha	TX2295	66A,66E,66G,11
Brauner, Mitchell	WI0825	12A,12,12C,11
Brawand, John	SD0550	11,12A,38,62
Bray, Erin	TN0900	64,42,11
Bray, Michael R.	PA3260	60,61,11,36,12A
Brazelton, Kitty	VT0050	13,10F,10,11,53
Breckenridge, Carol Lei	IA0200	11,66A,66B,66C,66H
Breckling, Molly	TN0050	11
Breneman, Marianne Leitch	KY1000	11,64C,32E,64B
Bresnen, Steven M.	PA0400	13,11,12A,66A,66D
Brewer, Johnny	AL0620	13A,13B,11,46,13C
Brewer, Paul	AZ0490	11,13,29,32E,47
Brian, Aric J.	FL2000	11
Bridges, Jan	TX2570	32A,32B,11
Briggs, Kurt	NY0270	11,62A
Briggs, Philip	TX2050	36,40,61,11
Briggs, Ray	CA3500	20,11,29
Brightbill, Elizabeth	VA0800	64A,42,11
Brings, Allen	NY0642	13,11
Brink, Daniel	CO0200	13A,13,10F,11,66A
Brinksmeier, Ulrike	OH0680	12A,11,62E,14,20
Brinner, Benjamin	CA5000	13K,14,20B,20D,11
Briones, Marella	MO0650	61,11,36,32B,39
Briseno, Antonio	TX3515	11,20H,41
Bristol, Caterina	AL0050	11,12A,64E
Bristol, Cynthia	MI0850	11,66A,20
Britt, Carol	LA0450	13,11,12A,66D
Britto, Richard	MA2020	64E,11,46
Britton, Carolyn	WI0845	11,66A,66H
Broderick, Daniela	IL1250	11,66A,66D,20G,54
Broderick, Daniela C.	IL1890	11,66A,66D
Brody, Ben	WA1350	31A,60,11,12A
Brody, James	CO0800	11,64B
Broffitt, Virginia	OK0800	64A,42,11,32E
Bronaugh, Roderic	TN1400	11,36
Brook, Sharon D.	CA4400	11,66A,66C,66D
Brooks, Melinda K.	AL0850	11,13,66A,66D
Brosius, Amy T.	NJ1000	11,12,13,20,12A
Brostoff, Neal	CA2700	11,13
Brothers, Grey	CA5550	13,36,61,11,12A
Brothers, Lester D.	MO1790	11,12A,12C
Brown, Andrea E.	GA0900	37,38,11
Brown, Beverly	NC1400	11,29A,47,37,64C
Brown, Bruce C.	NY1700	60,11,36,61,31A
Brown, Christine A.	IN1010	11,66A,13,66B
Brown, Debra	KS0570	11,34B
Brown, J. Bruce	MI2000	13,10,11,34,51
Brown, J. F. Mark	AL0831	61,35,36,11
Brown, James	FL1300	11,12A,38,64C
Brown, Jeffrey C.	IN1750	47,50,65,11
Brown, Joseph	IL3500	11
Brown, Kathryn D.	TX0370	11,35G
Brown, L. Joel	IA0900	13,12A,14,66,11
Brown, Leonard	MA1450	11,14,64E,29A,12E
Brown, Melba	AL1195	32,61,11,39
Brown, Michael R.	MS0500	11
Brown, Philip	VT0300	11,13A,36,44,47
Brown, Richard L.	WV0600	32,63D,72,11
Brown, Robert W.	TN1100	11
Brown, Tom	WI0810	11,41,49,63A,63B
Brown, Uzee	GA1450	13,10,61,11
Brown-Kibble, Gennevieve	TN1350	11,36,60A,61
Brownlee, Jordan	CA1550	70,11
Brownlow, James A.	TX3515	11,12A,49,63A,20
Brucker, Clifford	NY3600	11,66D,29
Bruckner, Susan	CA0400	66A,11
Brudnak, Sondra	TX2750	11
Bruner, G. Edward	CA5040	11,36
Bruno, Zachary	CA4625	11,32,37,47,41
Bryan, Alan	MN1625	11,39,61,54
Bryan, Karen M.	AR0750	12A,11
Bryan, Dorothy	OH1900	32B,32A,11
Bryant, John	GA2300	11,13C,63A,20
Bryant, Thomas E.	TN1200	13,11,66A,66C,66H
Bucchianeri, Diane	OK1450	11,12A,41,62C
Buchierre, Alisa	MA1500	11,13C,36
Buckholz, Christopher John	IA1600	63C,29,41,11
Buckner, Jeremy	TN0250	32B,32C,66A,66D,11
Budds, Cain	LA0250	70,11,13A,13B,13C
Budds, Michael J.	MO1800	12A,11,29
Budke, Tiffany	KS0300	66A,66C,11
Buis, Johann S.	IL3550	12,20,11
Bull, Douglas	WY0050	37,63,11,32E
Bullock, Kathy	KY0300	11,20A,36,13A,13C
Bulow, Ellen	IN1300	11
Bultema, Darci A.	SD0400	11,61,39
Bumcrot, Charles	NJ0700	63A,49,11
Bunk, Louis	NH0110	34,10,11,13,43
Burdick, Daniel	PA1200	63C,63D,49,11
Burgett, Paul	NY4350	20G,11,29A,29D
Burkart, Rebecca L.	IN0150	11
Burke, Richard N.	NY0625	11,12A,12,20G
Burns, Ellen J.	NY3700	16,11
Burns, Jim	TN0850	11,61,31A
Burns, Pamela T.	AL0050	11,32,61
Burns, Susan M.	CA0630	13A,11,39,61,54
Burrack, Frederick	KS0650	32,12B,11,32,37
Burroughs, D. Robert	WA0150	13,11,62A,53,38
Burrows, David	NY2740	11,12A,12,14
Burrs, Lisa Edwards	VA1750	11,13A,36,61
Burton, Heidi R.	OK1300	13A,13,11,66A,62A
Burton, Sean Michael	IA0100	36,61,41,11,13D
Burton, Warren L.	UT0300	11,32A,32B,62C
Busch, Gregg	MO0200	11,13A,31A,36,61
Bush, Eric W.	NY4050	37,47,63A,13A,11
Buskey, Sherry	MA2000	10,11
Buss, Gary	CO0830	11
Bustamante, Linda	FL1300	11,38,51,62C,62D
Bustamante, Tamara A.	KY1100	36,11,13,66C,66A
Butke, Marla A.	OH0100	32,11,66D,36,60A
Butler, Milton	OH1900	11,32B,32C
Butler, Rebecca G.	PA0050	11,64A,37,34,13B
Buttery, Gary A.	RI0300	11,47,49,63D,29A
Butts, Leon	TX3525	70,11,41
Butts, Robert W.	NJ0800	11
Butturi, Renato	IN1600	70,11,67G,47,29
Buzzelli-Clarke, Betsy	PA1100	11,13A,12A,66A,66D
Byrket, Patrick S.	IN0907	11
Byrne, Madelyn	CA3460	10,11,34
Byun, John	CA3800	61,36,11
Cable, Howard	AA0200	10,11,35,47,60
Cable, Jennifer A.	VA1500	11,61
Cabrer, Carlos R.	PR0150	10A,10F,11,13A,13B
Cabrera, Ricardo	PR0100	11,36,61,60,13A
Cabrini, Michele	NY0625	12B,12A,13B,11,12
Cadieux, Marie-Aline	PA1750	13,11,51,62C,42
Cahow, Matthew	CA3200	11,20G
Cahueque, David A.	CA0630	11,13A,70
Cahueque, David	CA3200	11,13A,13B,13C,70
Cai, Camilla	OH1200	11,12
Cailliet, Claude	WI0800	11,13,63,37,47
Cain, Sarah	GA1400	11
Calcagno, Mauro	NY3790	12A,12D,12B,11
Calderone, Kathleen	NJ0700	11
Caldwell, Ann	GA0850	66A,66D,66G,11
Calhoun, Valerie J.	GA1070	11
Calissi, Jeff L.	CT0150	37,65B,11
Calkin, Joshua	NE0700	63D,37,11,49,63C
Calkins, Katherine Charlton	CA3200	11,12A,20G
Callis, Cathy	NY1600	13A,11
Calvo, Francisco	CA0960	11
Camacho, Loida	PA2400	13,10,11
Cameron, Virginia	OH1600	60A,36,61,40,11
Cameron, Wes	MS0850	11,63,64,65,34
Campana, Alessandra	MA1900	12,12A,11
Campbell, Carey	UT0350	12,11,63
Campbell, Dianna	FL1700	61,36,40,11,32D
Campbell, Jefferson	MN1600	11,64D,34
Campbell, Jennifer L.	MI0400	11,12,20
Campbell, John W.	KY0610	60,11,32,61,36
Campbell, Michael J.	GA2300	60B,47,64E,32E,11
Campbell, Roy	MA0510	11,10F,38,46,47
Campbell, Susan	UT0350	11,31

429

Name	Code	Areas
Campbell, Todd	PA0250	34,11,65
Campiglia, Paul	GA2150	65,29,71,50,11
Cancio-Bello, Susan	NH0050	11,54,61,36,33
Candee, Jan	ND0400	66A,66D,66G,32B,11
Candelaria, Lorenzo	TX3510	11,12A,12
Canfield, Jennifer K.	AL0450	11,32A,32D,66D,32B
Cangro, Richard	IL3500	32E,11
Cannava, Ruth	NH0300	11
Cannon, Jimmie	CA2300	11,13A,46
Canty, Dean R.	TX3525	60,37,63A,63B,11
Caplan, Stephen	NV0050	64B,42,11
Cappillo, Frances	NY3500	29A,11
Card, Catherine	CA1960	13A,61,11
Cardillo, Kenneth	TN0260	70,13,11,12B
Carey, Charles	NE0050	11,13A,70
Carey, Peter	TX2260	11,29
Carlin, Pete	IL0300	11
Carlisle, David	MS0700	11
Carlisle, Kris	GA0300	11,66A,13
Carlson, Dan	MN1100	11,35A,37,46,63
Carlson, Mark	MD0610	63,11,12,13,37
Carlson, Tammi	IL1890	13F,11,64A
Carlton, Kathleen	OK0410	13,11,12A,61,31A
Carmichael, Steve R.	WI0250	47,11,29
Carney, Anna	TX2800	11,13A,14C,64C
Carney, Peter	IL2650	11,29
Carney, Robert D.	MO1550	66A,66B,66C,11,13C
Carney, Timothy F.	HI0060	36,11,13A,54,61
Carnine, Albert J.	MO0800	11,61
Carpenter, Alexander	AA0110	12,13C,13B,11,13E
Carpenter, Gregory	WI0425	36,11
Carpenter, Thomas H.	NY3725	11,12A
Carpenter, Tina	TX3750	64D,13,11,34C
Carr, Julie Anne	MI2120	61,11
Carr, Tracy A.	NM0100	64B,12A,41,64D,11
Carrell, Cynthia T.	AR0250	11,13,32E,37,63A
Carroll, Don	CA3200	11,14,29A,20G
Carroll, Gregory D.	NC2430	13,10,11
Carroll, Kevin	GA1600	10,64,60B,11,13
Carroll, Nancy M.	RI0101	11
Carroll, Nancy	RI0102	11,10A
Carroll, Roy W.	IA0940	66,13,12,11,31A
Carson, Caroline	LA0800	11,36,32D,60A
Carter, Beverly H.	PA1450	11,12A,66A,66B
Carter, Christina	FL1550	60A,61,11
Carter, David	MN1450	11,41,62C,42
Carter, David	AR0730	64C,64E,48,11
Carter, Henrietta McKee	CA2050	11,61,13A
Carter, John R.	CA1375	11,12A,36,61,13C
Carter, Roland M.	TN1700	13,11,36,66A
Carter, Shannon	AG0350	11,12,13A
Carter, Stewart	NC2500	13,11,12A,55,67
Carucci, Christine	MN1300	32C,11
Carver, Sylvia	TN0050	11,66A
Cary, Jane G.	NY0400	11,12A,66H
Caschetta, Todd	CA4850	20G,11,12,14,50
Case, David	OR1050	70,11
Casey, J. Warren	AR0250	10F,11,32,47,64C
Cass, Patrick	MS0320	13,11,47,64,70
Castilla, Carlos	TN1100	11
Castilla, Kathy	MS0650	11,36,61
Castro, Margarita	PR0150	11,39,61
Castro, Miguel	GA1400	50,65,11,47
Catan, Daniel	CA1265	13A,13,10,11,12A
Cathey, Sheila Clagg	OK0825	11,13C
Cavanaugh, Alice I.	NY4050	36,12A,11
Cech, Jessica	MI2120	64A,11,12A
Cee, Vincent	AK0150	32,29,38,34B,11
Cerabona, Linda M.	IL3400	11,13A,20A,31A,32D
Cervantes, Elizabeth	CA0270	11,13A
Chabora, Robert J.	MN0600	66A,66B,66D,11,13
Chacholiades, Linda P.	MN0610	11,20,12A
Chafe, Eric	MA0500	13A,11,12A,12,13J
Chaffee, Christopher	OH2500	64A,20,29A,11
Chafin, Gerald	KY0860	60A,11,32,36,44
Chagnon, Richard	CA4050	11,12A,36,61
Chamberlain, Donald J.	IA0400	13,10F,10,11,47
Chamberlain, Julie Rhyne	NC0350	66A,66B,66C,66D,11
Chan, Sarah S.	OK0600	66A,66C,66D,13,11
Chandler, Chris	GA0200	11
Chandler, Gulya	LA0030	66A,66C,66D,11,12A
Chandra, Arun	WA0350	10A,10B,43,34D,11
Chang, Anita L.	CA2650	66A,13A,11
Chang, Joanne	NY3250	11,13,32,42,66
Chang, Peter M.	IL2150	11,14,12,42
Chang, Wei Tsun	TN1450	11,32E,62A,41,62
Chapman, David	CA3000	11,70,20
Chapman, David F.	NJ1130	11,12A
Chapman, Susannah	NJ0700	62C,42,11
Charles, Jean	VT0300	11,70
Charloff, Ruth	CA5040	60,11,36,38
Charsky, Thomas	NJ0050	32B,11
Charsky, Thomas	NJ1400	32B,11
Chasalow, Eric	MA0500	13,10A,10B,11,29A
Chaudoir, Marianne	WI0400	11,66A,66D,13A
Chauls, Robert	CA2750	11,38,66A,10A,39
Cheatham-Stricklin, Teresa	AL0500	13A,11,61,54
Cheek, John	NC1100	13,11,66A,20G
Cheetham, Andrew	IL0800	63A,47,66A,11
Chemay, Frank	LA0700	10,63D,10F,11,49
Chen, Ting-Lan	NE0590	11,13B,62A,62B,13C
Chen, Xiaolun	FL1500	11,36,61
Cheney, Elliott	UT0250	62C,11
Cheney, Kathryn	GA0250	63A,13A,11
Cheng, Marietta	NY0650	13,60,11,36,38
Chenoweth, Jonathan N.	IA1600	11,41,62C
Cherry, Amy K.	NC2600	11
Chesanow, Marc	SC0420	62D,11,10F,13B,35G
Chevalier, Angelis	CA3200	11,66A
Chevan, David	CT0450	11,12A,47,53,29
Chien, Alec F.	PA0100	11,42,66A,41
Chinn, Genevieve	NY2105	13,11,12A,12
Chmura-Moore, Dylan Thomas	WI0830	63C,38,11
Choe, EJ	IN0907	13,11,32A,32B,66
Christensen, Brandon J.	MO1500	62A,62B,42,11
Christensen, James	AL0210	13A,11
Christensen, Linda	NE0700	66A,66D,34,66B,11
Christianson, Paul A.	TN1600	11,66A,66D
Christopher, Casey R.	ID0150	11,29B,34,35,37
Christopher, Un Chong	MO0060	11,12A,13,66A,66C
Chusid, Martin	NY2740	11,12A,12
Chybowski, Julia J.	WI0830	12,11
Ciarelli, Katharine	NY2950	66A,66D,11
Cichy, Patricia Wurst	RI0150	32B,13C,64B,11,67D
Cienniwa, Paul D.	MA2020	12A,12,11,34B
Cifelli, Cheryl L.	MO0800	64C,64D,12A,11,13E
Ciucci, Alessandra	NY0750	11,14,15,14C,20B
Clancy, Todd A.	MA1650	47,11,70
Clark, Alice V.	LA0300	12A,11,31A,12
Clark, Brenda J.	IN1650	32,11,37
Clark, Daniel	OH2370	11,12A,13C
Clark, Jesse	PA0050	11,34D
Clark, John	CT0100	11,13,29
Clark, John W.	CA4410	13,11,12A,10D
Clark, Jonathan	MA0150	11,49,63A
Clark, Maribeth	FL1360	11,12,14,15
Clark, Mark Ross	LA0770	39,54,61,11
Clark, Michael	TN1450	11
Clark, Norman Alan	GA1400	11,37,49,64
Clark, Rich	IL0300	11
Clemente, Peter	MA0200	11,13A,13,70,20
Clency, Cleveland	IL0650	11,66,40,36
Cleveland, Lisa A.	NH0310	13,11,29A,66
Clifton, Keith E.	MI0400	12,11,20
Climis, Sarah	IN0900	11
Cline, James E.	CO0400	70,11
Cline, Judith A.	VA0550	39,61,54,20G,11
Cloer, John	NC2420	11
Coats, Syble M.	AL0831	66A,66D,11,13A
Cobb, James	NC0915	11,36,66G
Cobbs, Jerry	AL0330	61,36,11
Cobert, Claude	MA2020	64A,11,12A
Cochran, Martin	AL1150	63,11
Cochran, Matthew	GA0625	11,70
Cochran, Nathan	PA2950	11
Cockle, Katherine G.	IL3550	11
Cockrell, Findlay	NY3700	13A,13,11,66A
Coco, Joseph W.	NJ0800	11
Codreanu, Christian	TN1400	11,41,63B
Coen, Anne	OH1350	11,31A
Cogdell, Jerry	MS0320	13,11,50,63,54
Cohen, Douglas H.	NY0500	13,10,11,34
Cohen, Fredric T.	MA2000	11,38,64B
Cohen, Lynne	NJ0700	64B,11
Cohen, Richard Scott	MI0650	11,37,38
Colarusso, Joey	TX2170	64C,11
Cole, Darlyn	NC1950	61,66D,60A,11,13
Cole, Dennis R.	OH0100	14C,12A,11,20
Cole, Judith E.	GA1150	11,13C,13A,66C
Cole, Judith W.	TX2960	11,12A,32B
Cole, Malcolm S.	CA5032	11,12A,12,66G,31A
Cole, Richard C.	VA1700	11,12A,20G
Cole, Roger	ID0250	11,64C
Coleman, Michael	FL1500	13,10,11,66A,34
Colla, Ginger	CA3000	11
Collins, Jenny	PA1100	11,13A,66A,66D,66C
Collins, Shelley	MS0250	11,64A,12A,48
Collison, Craig	AR0110	11,41,50,65
Colunga, Richard	CA2300	66D,11
Colwell, Brent	TX2800	37,11,12A,63C,63D
Combs, Julia C.	MO0775	64B,13B,12A,11,13C
Comeaux, Garrick	MN0050	11
Compton, Beckie	TX0125	66A,13,11,36,47
Compton, Lanette	OK0800	63B,11,32E,42
Comstock, Allan D.	KS0300	11,64B,64D,12A
Con, Adam Jonathan	OH2450	36,32,11,60A,13C
Condon, Clay	IL2150	65,50,11
Congo, John R.	CT0250	11
Conklin, Michael	NJ0175	11,29A
Connelly, Chris	SC0420	63C,63D,11,29
Conner, Ted A.	PA2550	11,12A,29A
Connie, Meredith	WA0750	70,11,41
Connors, Thomas	NJ0700	37,11,32E,60B
Conrad, Robert	CA4625	13,11,12A,61
Conway, Nicholas	NY3700	11
Cook Glen, Constance	IN0900	11
Cook, Andrew	AL0345	60B,63,11,47,64
Cook, Bruce	CA1560	66,14,11,20
Cook, Christopher	WA0400	63A,11
Cook, Gloria	FL1550	66A,66B,13C,11,66C
Cook, James	NE0590	11,66A,66D
Cook, Jeffrey	TN0900	63B,12A,42,11
Cook, Jenni	NH0350	61,11
Cook, Lisa M.	CO0550	11,12A,20G,31A,14
Cook, Stephen	CA6000	66A,35A,34,36,11
Cooper, Britt	OH2370	11,12A,14C,36,61
Cooper, David	WI0840	47,49,63A,11,29A
Cooper, Kevin	CA1850	11,70,13A
Cooper, Marva W.	DC0350	11,12A,66A,66B,66C
Copenhaver, Lee R.	MI0900	13,11,12A,38,62C
Coppenbarger, Brent	SC0950	13,11,64
Coppola, Catherine	NY0625	11,12A
Corcoran, James R.	KY1425	65,34,11,50
Cordingley, Allen	WI0840	11,64E,37,47
Corey, Horace E.	NV0100	13A,11,41,70
Corigliano, John	NY0635	10F,10,11,54
Corin, Amy R.	CA3100	14,11,13C,12A
Cornejo, Robert Joseph	CA5510	13,11,34C,10,12A
Cornelius, Jeffrey M.	PA3250	60,11,12A,36
Cornfoot, James	TN1200	11,12E
Cornils, Margaret A.	WI0840	64A,11,48,66D
Cornish, Glenn S.	FL0500	13,11,66A
Cortese, Michael	NY0450	10,11,20,34,47
Cortese, Paul	TX3000	34,11
Corvino, William	NJ0750	11,70
Cory, Craig	CA1290	11
Cory, Eleanor	NY2050	13,10,11,66A,66D
Costa, John V.	UT0250	13,11
Costanzo, Samuel R.	CT0250	13,11,29A
Cotte, William	VT0300	11,13H,36,61,66
Cottle, W. Andrew	DE0150	11
Coulter, Chris	CA1960	11,13A
Coulter, Chris	CA1700	11
Coulter, Monte	TN1700	13A,11,50,65
Courtney, Ken H.	SC1100	11,66G,20
Coutsouridis, Peter	MA2100	65,41,29A,11,13B
Couture, Marie	NH0300	11,16
Cowan, Kathryn Jean	IL2150	61,11
Cowan, Scott M.	MI2250	11,47,63,29
Cowin, Jasmin Bey	NY4200	11,62,12A,31B
Cox, Daniel R.	ID0140	50,65,53,11
Cox, Melissa	GA0750	11,12,13
Cox, Patricia J.	AR0250	11,32,34C,38,62B
Crabtree, Cecile	OK0150	11,20G
Crabtree, Joseph C.	TX1425	11,12,36,39
Crain, Timothy M.	MA2030	12,20,29A,11
Craioveanu, Mihai	MI1050	11,62A,41
Crane, Teresa Ann	IL1500	66C,61,66,66A,11
Crannell, Wayne T.	TX0250	36,61,11,39,60
Crawford, Jeremy	AL0050	11,63D
Crawley-Mertins, Marilee	IA0425	11,66A,66D,34
Creel, David	TN0260	11,62A
Crews, Norval	TX1700	11,64C,64E,72
Crews, Ruth	TX3525	61,11
Criazzo, Rocco	OH2600	11

Index by Area of Teaching Interest

Name	Code	Areas
Crider, Joe	VA0650	11,12A
Crocker, Ronald	NE0590	11,38,65
Crosby, Luanne M.	NY0100	11,36,61,54
Crosby, Tracy	MS0300	63C,11,13
Cross, Alan E.	TN0150	11,12A,61,31A
Cross, Ronald W.	NY4500	13A,11,12A
Crossland, Carolyn M.	NC1075	13A,11,32A,36,32B
Crull, Terry	KS0350	11,36,40,60A
Crum, Martin	TN1400	11,45
Crummer, Larry D.	CA1760	20,13,11,14,66A
Crump, Jason	NC2700	11
Cruz, Samantha	WI0500	32A,32B,32C,11
Cubek, David	CA2175	38,11,13,60
Cubek, David	CA4500	38,11,60,13
Cubek, David	CA3620	38,11,13,60
Cubek, David	CA1060	38,11,13,60
Cuffari, Gina	CT0800	64D,48,11
Culbertson, Robert M.	TX1400	11,32B,63B
Culver, Eric	MA0700	11,60,10F,38,41
Cumming, Danielle	MD0800	70,11,41
Cumming, Duncan J.	NY3700	66A,13,11
Cunningham, James E.	FL0650	14,20,32,11,12A
Curinga, Nick	CA1700	11
Curry, Jeffrey P.	NE0040	11,13C,32,37,49
Curry, Nick	FL1950	62C,12,11
Curry, Vicki L.	VA0600	13,11
Curtis, Peter	CA3800	11,70,14,20,29
Curtis, Stanley	NY3000	11,13
Cushing, Diane	NH0150	36,61,54,11
Cutsforth-Huber, Bonnie	MD0095	13A,13,11,12A,13B
Cutting, W. Scott	MI1550	13,11,66A,66D,34D
Czarkowski, Stephen	WV0550	62C,11,51
Dade, Fred S.	PA3050	20,11,32B,36,66A
Dahl Saville, Lara R.	GA1050	11,64B
Dahlke, Steven	NY3250	11,13,36,60A,61
Dailey, Colleen M.	NY3770	11
Dakin, Deborah	IL0100	11,62B,62A
Dale, Karen M.	TN0300	11,34B,36,54,61
Dalton, Grant B.	AL0800	65,11,32E,47,50
Dalton, Lester	KS0590	11
Daly, Kathleen	NJ0700	62A,32E,11
Daly, Pat	OR0950	11
Daly, Rachel	MA0510	63B,11
Dana, Julie R.	CA1850	36,61,11
Daniel, Jane	WV0400	12A,11
Daniel, Robert	OK0550	13A,60,11,61,13C
Daniel, Thomas	AL0335	13,11,47
Danis, Ann	RI0300	60,38,11,62A,62B
D'Arca, Denise	OH1800	32,36,11,42
Darnell, Debra Jean	FL0680	61,11,39
Dascher, Debra M.	PA2675	11
Dashevskaya, Olga	CO0625	11,13A,66A,13B
Dauer, Robin	AR0110	13,11,63B
Daughtrey, Sarah E.	PA1250	61,11
David, Myrtle	LA0700	11,66A,66B,66C,66D
Davidovich, Theodore C.	MA2100	60A,11,36
Davidovici, Robert	FL0700	62A,62B,11
Davidson, Harry L.	NC0600	38,11
Davidson, Heidi	WA0750	61,66A,11,13A
Davidson, Ian	TX3175	11,64B,41
Davidson, Steve	OR0950	11
Davies, Daniel E.	CA0850	62C,13A,11,13B
Davies, James	CA5000	11,12A,12E,20A,66A
Davies, Paul	CA1800	13,11,13A,66A,10
Davila, William	CA3450	13A,11,12A,66A,67D
Davis, Cara	WI0806	36,61,29A,11
Davis, Charles	TX1510	11,63,64,37
Davis, Christopher A.	SC0950	11,13,29,50,65
Davis, Clarissa	MS0300	11,61
Davis, D. Edward	NY0500	11,13
Davis, Daniel	NM0450	11
Davis, Hope	CA2300	13A,12,11,37,13B
Davis, Hugh	TX1300	36,11
Davis, John E.	GA0300	60,11,37,64A,64E
Davis, Karen	MS0320	11,36
Davis, Kevin	AL1300	11,66G,13C
Davis, Mike	MI1650	11
Davis, Nancy	OH1300	13A,11,36,47
Davis, Ronald	SC1110	11,49,63D
Davis, Thomas L.	TN1400	11
Davis, Victor	TN1400	11,36,60
Davis, Wendell R.	TX3525	61,11
Davis, William	NV0150	11
Davison, Michael A.	VA1500	11,29,46,47,49
Dawson, Andrea	TN1100	62A,51,11
Day, John	KY0600	11
Day, Michael	NC1550	11,32E,32F,63A,63B
De Dobay, Thomas	CA0950	11,12A,61,66D
de Graaf, Melissa J.	FL1900	12,12A,11
De Jaager, Alfred R.	WV0600	36,32D,60,11
De Pasquale, Lawrence	NJ1050	11,12A
Dean, Lynn	UT0150	11,66A,66B
Dean, Myron	KY1000	11
Dean, Terry Lynn	IN0800	11,12A,13
Deaville, James A.	AG0200	11,12A,12,41,12C
DeBoer, Jack	MI0900	11,13A,12A
DeBolt, David	OH1100	11,41,64D
Decker, Van A.	CA2300	11,13A,34D,47,10A
Declue, Gary L.	IL1245	12A,13A,11,61,36
DeCoro, Helena	CA1520	61,66A,11,12A,39
Decorso, Theodore	FL2050	11,64
Decuir, Michael	GA0150	11,20,29,37,47
Dees, Pamela Youngdahl	MO1250	66A,66B,66C,11,12A
Deeter, Gary	CA1850	11
DeFord, Ruth	NY0625	11,12A,12,12C
DeFrain, Debbie	NE0500	66A,11,32B
DeGoti, Mark D.	AL0200	63A,49,11
DeHoogh-Kliewer, David	SD0580	60A,11,32D,36,40
DeJournett, William	MS0700	37,12B,11
Del Aguila, Miguel	CA5360	10,66A,13A,11
Delaney, Carrie Ann	VA0450	11
Delaney, Douglas	CA1150	13,11,37,47,64
Delannoy Pizzini, Jose R.	PR0115	11
DeLaRosa, Lou	CA5510	13A,13C,12A,11,34C
Delgado-Pelton, Celeste	CO0600	13,11,34,36,47
Dell'Antonio, Andrew	TX3510	11,12A,12
Delony, Willis	LA0200	47,11
Delto, Clare E.	CA1960	10D,54,11,47
DeLuca, Mike	CO0275	13,64C,11,32
DeMaio Caprilli, Barbara J.	OK1330	61,54,11
DeMichele, Anna	CA0859	36,61,13A,38,11
Demmond, Edward C.	CA3100	13A,11
Dempsey, Harry J.	MI0650	11,35
Demsey, Karen B.	NJ1400	64A,48,12,11,12A
Denmon, Alan	GA2300	11,13A,13B,32C,32E
Denson, Keith	NC0860	11,29,12A
DeQuattro, Anthony	CT0250	11,12A
Derechailo, Melissa	NE0700	63B,11,35
Dering, James	TX0850	36,47,13,13C,11
DeRusha, Stanley	IN0250	32E,11,60B
Desmond, Clinton J.	SD0200	36,11,20,60,12
DeSpain, Geoff	AZ0300	37,63,46,47,11
Dettbarn-Slaughter, Vivian Robles	OH2275	61,66A,11
Detweiler, Bruce	OK0150	11,47,53
Deveau, David	MA1200	11,41,66A
Devine, Dave	CO0830	11
D'Haiti, Maxine	AZ0150	66D,11
Di Grazia, Donna M.	CA3650	60,11,12A,36
DiCenso, Daniel J.	MA0700	11,12
DiChiacchio, Josh	CA1760	11
Dickenson, Andrew	MD0175	11,70
Dicker, Michael H.	IL1150	11,48,64D
Dickerson, Shane	AL0200	11,64E,64D
Dickey, Christopher J.	WA1150	13C,11,63D
Dickey, Timothy J.	OH2000	11,12A,13E
Dickson, Douglas R.	CT0250	11
Dikener, Solen	WV0400	11,12A,62C,62D
Dill, John	TX1775	13A,11,66A,66G,12A
Dillon, Emma	PA3350	11,12A,12
Dillon, Rhonda	CA0859	61,11
DiMedio, Annette	PA3330	12A,12,66A,66D,11
DiMeo, Mike J.	NY4400	37,11,47
Dinda, Robin	MA0930	10,11,13,29,66G
DiOrio, Andrea R.	IL2050	64C,11,42,43
DiPaolo, Stacey	OK1250	11,12A,64C
Dippre, Keith	NC1350	13,11,10,47,34
Dixon, Howard	TN0800	13A,11,32B,63,64
Dobbins, Lori E.	NH0350	13B,11
Dobbs, Wendell B.	WV0400	11,13,41,48,64A
Doebler, Jeffrey S.	IN1750	11,32,37
Doering, James M.	VA1150	13,11,12A,66A,66G
Doherty, Jean	NY1950	11,36
Doiel, Mark	CA2900	10D,11,12A,13,37
Dolacky, Susan	WA0860	11,39,61,66D,54
Dolan, Drew	GA1150	11
Dolan, Emily I.	PA3350	12A,12,11,12B
Dolatowski, David	AZ0510	66A,36,11
Donofrio, Anthony	OH1100	13,11
Doo, Lina J.	HI0150	11,61,36,54,20
Dooly, Louann	AR0730	64D,11
Doran, David Stephen	KY1460	13A,13,10,11,12A
Dorf, Samuel N.	OH2250	12A,11,55A,55B,55C
Dorough, Prince	IL1090	11
Dorris, Jennifer	CO0625	11,34B
Doss, Elwood	TN1720	66F,11
Dotson, Ronald	CA5510	11,34C,66D,14C,12A
Douds, Nathan	PA3100	11,50,65,66A
Doughty, Ryan	KY1550	11
Douglas, Bill	CO0560	13,11,12A,36,66A
Douglass, Mark	MI2120	11
Douthit, LaTika	NC2700	11,37,64A
Dovel, Jason L.	OK0550	63A,11,63B,10F
Dower, Mary R.	PA1700	11,36
Downes, Suzanne	IL2310	66D,47,11,37,65
Doyle, Alicia M.	CA0825	11,14,20
Doyle, Laurie	TX1550	61,11,40,54
Doyle, William	CA1750	11,37,38,63,60
Draayer, Suzanne Collier	MN1700	39,61,11
Drake, Joshua F.	PA1450	11,61
Drayton, Keith	MI1100	13,11,36,32,61
Drennan, Jennifer	IL2970	11,14C,20
Dressler, John C.	KY0950	12A,63B,11,12C
Drews, Michael R.	IN0907	13A,13,13C,13E,11
Driggers, Doris	CA2400	11
Drobnak, Kenneth Paul	SD0500	63D,37,11,47,49
Dubiel, Joseph	NY0750	10,11,13
Dubois, Laura	NJ0760	10A,11,32E,66
DuBois, May	CA5500	11,13A,66A
DuBois, Ted	TX3750	11,12A,34C
DuBose, E. L.	AL0210	11
Dubowchik, Rosemary	CT0450	11,12A
Duckett, Alfred	OK0150	11,60
Dueker, Hollie	TN0050	11,61
Duerden, Darren	HI0050	32E,65,50,47,11
Duerden, Jennifer	HI0050	11,66A,66C,66D
Duffer, Rodger	CA3800	61,11
Duffin, Greg	UT0350	11
Duffy, Kathryn Ann Pohlmann	IA0650	11,12,13,36,60
Dugan, Michael D.	WI0865	11,47,49,63C
Duggan, Sean B.	LA0600	11,12A,36,66,31A
Dumm, Mary Elizabeth	MD0700	13A,13,11,66A
Dunaway, Lourdes	TN1250	11,66A,70
Duncan, Steven	IL3200	11,63C
Duncan, Warren L.	AL1100	13,11,47,65
Dunn, Christopher	MS0570	11,35,70
Dunnavant, Jessica Guinn	TN1100	64A,67D,11
Dunnell, Rebecca	MO0950	64A,12A,14,11,20
Duquaine, Kenneth	MI0450	11,29A
Durant, Douglas F.	MA1450	13,10,11,12A
Durham, Kevin	TN1400	13A,66D,11
Durrenberger, Chris	OH2450	13A,11,66A,66F,12A
Durst, Aaron M.	WI0855	11,37,47,64E
Durst, Dean	IL2560	11
Duso, Lorraine C.	AR0850	64B,64D,11
Dutton, Douglas	CA2600	13A,13,11,66A
Dykema, Dan H.	AR0600	13B,11,66A,66D,13C
Eagle, Keith	NC0860	11
Eanes, Edward	GA1150	12A,11,12C,20G
Earle, Diane K.	KY0800	11,66
Earp, Lawrence	WI0815	11,12A,12
Ebert, Kevin	OH2550	70,11
Ebert, Shari E.	IL1330	11,20
Eby, John D.	AI0050	11,12A,12C,20G,31A
Eby, Patricia	WI0804	13,11,36,60A,47
Eddins, Judy	FL1500	11,61
Edel, Theodore	IL3310	11,66A,12A
Edgar, Scott N.	IL1400	37,32,11,13A
Edgerton, Sara A.	MO1500	11,12A,38,62D,62C
Edwards, Constance	WV0300	64D,12,11,12A,10F
Edwards, Eric F.	KS1450	20F,11
Edwards, Geoff	IL0150	11
Edwards, George L.	DC0350	11,32C,48,64A,64C
Edwards, George H.	NY0750	13,10,11
Edwards, Stacey	IN0150	11
Edwards, Steven C.	LA0080	11,12,36,40,61
Egan, John B.	IN1350	13,66,66G,11
Ehrlich, Barry	WA0860	13,11,37,63,63D
Ehrlich, Janina	IL0100	11,12,41,62C
Eichenbaum, Daniel	WV0300	13,10,11
Eide, Christina	AZ0350	11,66A,66D
Eikner, Steven	GA2200	12A,66A,66C,66D,11
Eischeid, Susan	GA2150	64B,11,48,42
Eisman, Lawrence W.	NY0642	11,32
Eissenberg, Judith	MA0500	41,62A,11
Eldridge, Ronda	TX2750	11,20,48,64A
Eldridge, Ronda	TX1510	11

Name	Code	Areas
Eleazer, Alan G.	TN0600	36,40,11
Eleazer, Alan	TN1250	11
Elfline, Robert	IL0100	66A,11,13
Elias, Cathy A.	IL0750	11,12A,12C
Elizabeth, Lori	OR0500	11
Elkins, Phil	SC0750	11,63A
Ellefsen, Roy	UT0190	13,11,36
Ellins, Rachael Starr	CO0250	62E,11
Elliott, Richard	OH0680	65,50,37,11,32E
Elliott, Robert L.	TN1400	13B,32,62D,11
Ellis, Lloyd	CA2400	11,46,47
Ellis, Margaret J.	IL0100	13C,11,63A
Ellison, Glenn	IL2775	11,65
Ellison, Sue	CO0550	11
Embretson, Deborah	MN1100	61,66D,11,20,66C
Emerson, Timothy	NY2950	20A,11
Emge, Steven	OK1150	11,34
Enciso, Franz J.	CA1020	13C,66D,11
Engberg, Kristina L.	IL2350	66D,11,13,34B
Engel, Tiffany	OK1300	13,11,12A,66A
Engelhart, Robert	MI1600	39,61,36,11
Engelson, Robert A.	IA0050	13,60,11,36,54
Engle, Martha Ramm	CA2050	12A,11,54
English, Christopher	MD0800	11
Engstrom, Greg	KY0550	11
Enloe, Luther D.	GA0300	70,11
Entzi, Karen	NC1450	62,11,41
Epperson, Dean	AK0100	11,12A,66A,66D,66B
Epstein, Joan O.	FL0450	13,11,12A,53,63A
Erdmann, Thomas R.	NC0750	11,38,13E,13F,63A
Erhard, Paul	CO0800	11,62D
Erickson, Christian	WY0150	10,11,13,34,35
Erickson, James M.	NY4060	13,12A,11,70
Erickson, James	NY2105	11
Erickson, Kurt	CA1500	66,11,13C
Erickson, Shirley	TX0910	11,13,36,61,66
Ernest, David J.	MN1300	13A,11,64B
Eshbach, Robert	NH0350	11,62A,41
Esleck, David	VA1500	11,29
Esleck, David	VA1800	11,66A,29,34,35
Espinosa, Leandro	OR0200	62C,62D,38,13A,11
Espinosa, Sergio	TX3500	32,11,62A
Espinosa, Teresita	CA3150	11,12A,32,61,20G
Esquillin, June	TN0050	11
Estes, Linda	GA0200	11
Etcheto, Sally A.	CA0805	11,36,61,54
Etheridge, Kay	CA5200	11,32B,66A,66B,66C
Ethridge, William J.	GA1450	11,66A
Etienne, David	AR0300	11,20,32E
Etter, Troy L.	NY1600	12,11
Ettinger, Karl Erik	FL1700	66A,11,12A
Etzel, Laurel	IL1090	11,63B
Evans, Clifton J.	TX3500	38,60B,11
Evans, David H.	AR0300	13,11,12A,32,48
Evans, Gary	VA0400	13A,13B,13C,11,12A
Evans, Mathew J.	CO0275	63B,11,13C,42
Fahrion, Stacy	CO0300	11,66A,66D
Fain, Jeremy	TX2700	64D,11,13A,13B
Fair, Gary	CA3000	11,37
Fairchild, G. Daniel	WI0840	10F,11,32,63B
Fairfield, John	IL2200	11,63B
Fairfield, Patrick K.	MI1850	11,15,20,70
Falbush, Arthur	NY3765	11,63,29A,46,41
Falck, Robert A.	AG0450	11,12A,12
Falk, Leila Birnbaum	OR0900	11,12A,12B,41
Falk, Marc	IA0300	36,11,12A,60A,40
Falkenstein, Richard	NY0400	11,12A,70
Falskow, John	WA0960	37,63A,38,11,13
Faltstrom, Gloria V.	HI0300	13A,11,66D,61,36
Famulare, Trever R.	PA3050	11,37,47,49,60
Fannin, Karen M.	AR0350	29,11,13A,47,37
Faraone, John	TX2930	11
Farina, Geoff	IL0750	11
Faris, Marc R.	NC0650	13,10D,11
Farrell, Diane	NJ0800	11
Farris, Phillip	OH2250	66A,66C,66D,11
Farzinpour, Peyman	MA2020	11,12A,13B
Fassett, Charles K.	MA2150	60,11,12A,36
Fast, Susan	AG0200	13A,11,12A,12,55
Faux, Tom	IL1150	11,20
Favreau, Janet	CA2650	66A,66D,13A,11
Fawcett-Yeske, Maxine	CO0750	11,12,14,16,20
Feagans, David	TN1100	11
Feather, Carol Ann	TN0450	13,11,38,63B
Feingold, David W.	WA1250	11,70,13
Feldhausen, Scott	TX1400	13A,13B,11
Feldman, Bernardo	CA1265	13A,13,10F,10,11
Feldman, Martha	IL3250	11,12A,12,15
Feldman, Stephen B.	AR0850	11,41,62C
Feller, David E.	UT0350	11,12A,48,64,31
Feller, Robert	CA0350	11,37,49,63,60
Fellows, Robin B.	WI0865	13A,11,41,64A
Fells, Mizue	WA0550	66A,66D,13C,11,20
Feltman, Joshua	NY0500	11,13,43
Fenderson, Mark W.	MT0175	11,37,63A,63B
Fenimore, Ross	NC0550	11,12,14C,14D
Fenley, J. Franklin	MO1790	11,12A,64A
Fenwick, Jerry	CA4000	11,66A,54,29,35
Ferencz, Jane Riegel	WI0865	67,11,12,15
Ferer, Mary T.	WV0750	11,12A,12
Ferguson, James	CA1760	13A,11,70
Ferguson, Linda C.	IN1750	12A,20G,11
Fern, Terry L.	NC0850	11,39,61,54,69
Ferrara, Lawrence	CA1020	11,70,34C
Ferrari, John	NJ1400	13A,11,50,65
Fiala, Joy	AR0110	13,11,32
Fickett, Martha V.	VA1475	11,12A,12E,66A
Fiddmont, Keith	CA4450	11,29,13A,46,47
Fields, Tami	NC0915	11,36
Finch, Scott	AJ0030	60A,31A,12A,13A,11
Fincher, James	SC0710	11,61
Finegold, Michael G.	MA1500	13,11,29
Fink, Katherine	NY0646	11,12
Fink, Simon B.	MO0850	11
Finson, Jon W.	NC2410	11,12
Fisher, Tammy M.	WI0810	60,37,65,32,11
Fisher, Will J.	AZ0510	36,11,66D
Fishman, Guy	MA0510	11,62C
Fiske, Jane	MA0930	11,15,32,66
Fiske, Richard Allen	CA4550	11,38,66A,63
Fittipaldi, Thomas	NY2500	36,66D,67,70,11
FitzGibbon, Katherine L.	OR0400	36,60,11
Fitzhugh, William	TN1400	11,70
Flack, Michael	IL0550	11,66,13,29,32B
Flanigan, Glen	KY0100	11,32C,41,47,63D
Flannery, Katie	CO0550	11
Fleitz, Patrick	FL0800	66A,11
Fleming, Gail H.	IL2970	11,36,66A,40,20
Fleming, Kyle J.	CO0150	36,11,31A,60A
Fletcher, Marylynn L.	TX3600	34C,36,11,66A,12A
Fletcher, Seth	NE0590	63D,63C,13B,13C,11
Flippin, Jay	KY0900	11
Flippin, Thomas	NY5000	70,11
Floden, Andrea	MI0450	11,66D
Flom, James H.	MN1300	13A,11
Flood, John	CA4100	20A,13A,11,65,50
Florez, Anthony	IL1080	11,34,65,70,13
Florine, Jane Lynn	IL0600	11,12A,12,20A,64A
Flowers, Alan	AL1250	11,12A
Floyd, Rosalyn	GA0250	13A,13,11,66A,66C
Floyd-Savage, Karen	VA1750	11,13A,36,61
Fluchaire, Olivier	NY0644	62A,62B,11,13A,42
Flyger, Paul	MI1180	66A,66D,11
Flynn, Michael P.	WY0150	11,37,41,47,63
Flythe, Bernard	GA1150	32E,63D,41,11
Foley, Megan J.	CA1700	11,13A
Follingstad, Karen J.	CA4100	11,66A,66C,66D
Fooster, Harold	AR0810	60,11,37,50,65
Ford, Mary E.	OK0350	11,13,36,66
Ford, Ronnal	NC2700	64,64B,11,64D,62A
Forney, Kristine	CA0825	12A,67,11
Forrester, Marshall	SC0275	10,11,37,60
Forsythe, Jada P.	MS0570	11,64C,64E,37,48
Fortney, Julie T.	NC1250	11,61,34C
Fossa, Matthew A.	FL1500	11,66B
Foster, Robert	GA0250	13,10,11,47,48
Foster, Rodney W.	NY4100	11,12,31A,34A,34F
Fowler, Andrew J.	SC0420	13C,13A,11
Fowler, Kurt	IN0800	62C,11,12A,51
Fox, David E.	NC0900	66A,12A,66D,43,11
Fox, Elizabeth	WI1100	13A,13B,13C,11
Fox, Rebecca	AL1195	13,11,32,66A
Fox, T. Jeffrey	NY2550	36,11,20G,14C
Foy, Randolph M.	NC1700	11,12A,38
Frabizio, William V.	PA0125	13,11,12A,41
Francis, Lorie	MO0825	11,12A,13,36,66A
Franco-Summer, Mariana	CA5360	11,13A,66
Frank, Andrew D.	CA5010	13,10,11
Frank, Gloria	TN0050	32,11
Frank, Mary Lou	IN1010	11,13A
Franklin, Janice L.	TX1725	11,66,54,34B
Frary, Peter Kun	HI0160	13,11,12A,70,34
Frazer, Liz	VA0350	61,11,39
Frazier, Margaret J.	RI0300	11,61
Fredenburgh, Lisa M.	IL0150	36,11,40,60A
Fredrick, Samuel	AL1050	11
Freedman, Deborah	NE0590	11,12A,38,63B
Freedman, Richard	PA1500	11,12A,12,20D,29A
Freeman, Alexander	MN0300	10,13,11
Freeman, Janean	KY1100	61,11
Freeman, Jeffrey J.	TX2100	11,63C,49,63D,34
Frelly, Robert	CA0960	11,32
French, John	PA3550	11,12,13,36
French, Otis C.	PA1100	11,37,63,64,65
French, Paul T.	OR0950	11,12A,36,39,61
Frey, Kevin T.	CA4350	13,11,14,63,53
Fried, Eric	TX3200	60,11
Friedley, Geoffrey A.	ID0100	61,11,12A
Friedrichs, Charles	CA4100	11,37,63C,13A,32
Friedson, Steven	TX3420	11,14,65
Friesen, Milton	CA1860	11,36,70
Frisch, Miranora O.	NC2420	62C,11
Frisch, Walter	NY0750	11,12A,12
Frith, Fred	CA2950	10A,10B,53,43,11
Fritz, Benno P.	DC0100	37,49,60,11
Frogley, Jane	CT0600	11
Fruehauf, Tina	NY0500	11,12
Fry, Edwin J.	PA1600	11,66A,13
Frye, Joseph W.	TN1720	63C,13A,13C,11,34
Fucci, Melissa	OH1100	11,20
Fucci, Melissa	OH1110	11,36
Fudge, James	IA1300	62A,11
Fudge, James	IL0300	11,62
Fuhrmann, Christina E.	OH0100	13A,11,12,14
Fukuda, Joni	CA5355	11,13A,32D,36,61
Fulgham, Marc S.	MO1500	11,49,63A,63B
Fuller, Lisa	TN1380	61,11
Fuller, Sarah	NY3790	11,12A,12,13
Fuller, Stephen	MN1300	60A,11,20D,31A
Fullerton, Kevin T.	KS1400	14C,12A,29A,63D,11
Fulmer, Daniel	FL0570	11
Fuoco, Anthony	OH1300	11,66A
Furlow, Shaw	MS0200	13,11,10,37,47
Furman, Lisa J.	MI1800	37,60B,11,13,32
Furry, Stephanie	GA0950	63B,49,33,11
Fusco, Randall J.	OH1000	13B,38,66A,12A,11
Fuzesy, Brianne	ND0050	11,63,42
Gable, David D.	GA0490	11,12A,12B,13A,16
Gabrielsen, Dag	NY0625	10,11
Gach, Peter F.	CA3460	66,11,13
Gackstatter, Gary	MO1120	37,11,38
Gadgil, Sunil	TX2100	64E,64C,11
Gaetano, Mario A.	NC2600	50,65,11
Gagnon, Marie-Elaine	SD0600	11,51,62C,41
Galasso, Mathew	CA1900	11,12A,66A,13
Galen, Ronald	CA1450	11,70
Gallon, Ray	NY0550	29,11
Gambetta, Charles	NC2700	11,12E
Gamer, Carlton	CO0200	13,10,11,20D,34
Gamso, Nancy M.	OH2000	11,29A,48,64,32E
Gandy, V. Gay	KY1400	36,61,13A,13C,11
Gangi, Jonathan	SC1100	11,70
Garber, Ron	KS0210	11,12A,36,41,61
Garcia, Eduardo	CA0847	20H,11,70
Garcia, Glynn A.	TX2960	11
Garcia, Jeremy	TX2310	70,11,41
Garcia, Jose Manuel	GA2050	66A,66D,11,10A
Garcia, William B.	TN0800	60,11,36,61,31A
Garcia-Leon, Jose M.	CT0700	11,12A,13,66A,66D
Gardiner, Robert A.	SC0800	11,29,47,32E,64E
Gardner, Al	TX2350	11,47,50,65
Gardner, Gary D.	OK1500	11,62,63,37,47
Gardner, Kara	CA5353	12,11
Gardner, Richard	IL1240	11,66D
Gargrave, Eric	RI0101	11,13A,29A,48,13B
Gariazzo, Mariana Stratta	TX2900	64A,12A,20,11
Garner, Ronald L.	UT0150	13,11,12A,63B
Garner, Rusty	FL0900	60,11,61,54,64D
Garnica, Kevin	CA0350	11,66A,39
Garofalo, Angelo	PA3500	11,12A
Garrett, Glen R.	CA0835	29A,11
Garrison, Karen H.	AL0200	11,64A,48
Garritano, Andrea	KS0300	11,61
Garry, Kevin M.	CO0400	70,13A,11,12A,14C
Garton, Bradford	NY0750	10,11,45,34
Gass, Glenn	IN0900	20G,11

Index by Area of Teaching Interest

Name	Code	Areas
Gaston, Greg	MN0150	34,11
Gates, Charles R.	MS0700	63A,11
Gaub, Eugene	IA0700	13,12A,66A,11
Gauvin, Marcelle	MA2020	61,13A,11
Gaviria, Carlos	TX2700	62D,11,13A,13B
Gawlick, Ralf	MA0330	13A,13,11
Gaylard, Timothy R.	VA1850	11,12A,66A,20G
Gaynor, Rick	WI0845	63C,49,11
Gee, Constance	SC1110	11,41,62B,42
Gee, Patricia	CA5150	61,11
Geeseman, Katherine	TX3515	11,62C,62D
Geeting, Daniel	CA0550	64E,64C,38,11,60B
Geib, Sally	TN1100	11
Gelfand, Michael D.	OH2600	62C,11
Gelineau, Phyllis	CT0450	13A,11
Gemmill, Matthew	IL3550	11
Gennaro, Joe	FL1800	11,12A,20
George, Kevin	LA0080	11,13,34,35
George, Rosemary	NY0270	66A,61,12A,11
Gerber, Alan E.	FL2120	11,55,61,36
Gerber, Thomas E.	IN1650	11,66H,55B,12A
Gerbino, Giuseppe	NY0750	11,12A,12
Gerlach, Brent	TN1100	63C,11
Gerlach, Bruce	MO0200	13,10,11,54,66G
Gerrish, June	IL1890	66A,11
Gerritson, Sasha L.	IL2150	11,13C,39,13A
Getter, Joseph	CT0450	11,14
Gewirtz, Jonathan	MI1800	47,64E,64C,11,29
Gheith, Sarabeth	TN1100	11,62
Giammario, Matteo	PA0400	13A,11,62A,62B
Gibbons, William J.	TX3000	12,11
Gibbs, Lawrence	LA0250	11,29A,37,47,64C
Gibson, Alan	VT0200	11,12A
Gibson, Christopher A.	MO0950	11,64B,64C,64D,64E
Gibson, Clarence	TX3150	11,37,41,42
Gibson, David	KY1550	11,61
Gibson, Jeannette	FL1500	11
Gibson, Jonathan B.	VA0600	11,12A,55
Gibson, Marilyn	LA0770	11,63A,49
Gibson, Robbie L.	AL0345	11,70
Giebler, David	WI0920	13,11,36,41,66A
Gifford, Amy L.	FL1550	61,11,54
Gifford, Tell	NV0125	11,12A,13,66A
Gifford, Troy S.	FL2120	11,13,46,70,10
Gignac, Andrew	TX2260	63A,13,10,11
Giles, Leonard	GA0810	11,32,37,47,63
Gillan, Michael	MI0850	11,37,63C,63D,47
Gilleland, Katharine	NC2525	66G,11,13A,29A,36
Gillespie, Luke O.	IN0900	11,29
Gillette, Michael	NJ0760	11,62,32E
Gilley, Richard S.	NY2550	11
Gilliam, Bryan	NC0600	11,12A,12B,12C,12D
Gillick, Amy	CA1425	64D,11
Gillis, Ron	CA2100	11,13
Gilmore, Robert	AL1300	11,63D
Gilmour, F. Matthew	MO0850	13,10,11,12A,34
Gilpin, Mary Ann	WA0940	11,32
Ginwala, Cyrus	CA4200	38,13B,11,60B
Gipson, Crystal	AL0050	11
Girdham, Jane C.	MI1850	11,12A,13B,13C,13E
Glasman, Ilan David	CA1550	36,40,61,11
Glassman, Bill	CA1900	11
Glenn, James H.	NC2000	36,61,60A,11,12A
Glick, Robert P.	SC0700	66G,31A,11
Glyde, Judith	CO0800	11,51,62C
Goeke, Matthew	NY0270	11,62C
Goforth, Stephen C.	KY1300	11,36,60A,61,12A
Goh, Soo	PA1750	64C,41,11
Goldberg, Merryl	CA0847	64E,32,11
Golden, Joseph	GA0550	39,66G,11,12
Golden, Ruth E.	NY2105	39,61,11
Goldenbaum, Cathy	PA0400	11,61
Goldman, Lawrence	MS0560	66A,66D,66,11,66C
Goldray, Martin	NY3560	13A,13,11,12A,66A
Goldsmith, Maryll	CA3850	11,66A
Goldsmith, Michael	MO0750	11,13,66A
Goldstein, Howard A.	AL0200	10F,62A,11,12A,38
Goldstein, Joanna	IN1010	13,66A,66C,38,11
Goldstein, Louis	NC2500	11,66A
Golijov, Osvaldo	MA0700	20G,13,10,11,12A
Gomez-Imbert, Luis	FL0700	62D,43,11
Gonano, Max A.	PA0500	11,12A,13A,29A,37
Gonder, Jonathan P.	NY3730	66A,66C,11,13A,13B
Gonzalez, Fr. George	IN0005	11,14,20,66G,32
Gonzalez, Roberto-Juan	CA3250	11,29A
Gonzalez, Susan	NY0625	11,61,54
Goode, Gloria	PA2400	11,20
Goodin, Glenda	TN1100	13A,11
Goodwin, Julia	OR0700	66A,66D,11,12A,66C
Gordon, Barbara N.	NJ0500	11,36,60A,66D,61
Gordon, Daniel J.	NY3775	64E,11,37,48
Gordon, Joshua	MA0500	11,41,42,62,62C
Gordon, Patricia	MI0900	11,32B
Gordon, Tony A.	MS0050	66A,66D,66B,66C,11
Gorecki, Mikolaj P.	TX1425	10,11,13,34,66A
Gorgichuk, Carmen	AA0025	11,13,66
Goslee, Brenda	TN1250	13A,13,11,66A,66G
Gothard, Paul	OH1250	13A,13,10F,11,36
Goulet, Marie-Maude	AI0190	11
Grabowski, Robert	FL0700	29A,11
Grace, Michael	CO0200	11,12A,12,55
Graf, Greg	MO0750	36,40,60,11
Graham, Dave	CA5400	47,13A,11,46,29A
Gran, Charles	MO1780	11,13,34,10
Granat, Zbigniew	MA0280	13A,13,11
Grapenthin, Ina	PA1750	11,32B,66A,66G,66D
Grasso, Eliot	OR1050	11,20,14
Gratz, Reed	CA5100	13,10,14C,29,11
Grau-Schmidt, Anna K.	IL0750	11,12A
Grave, Floyd	NJ1130	11,12A,12,13J
Graves, Daniel H.	IN0400	11,12A,36,60,41
Gray, Laura J.	AG0470	11,12A,12,14,20
Graziano, Amy	CA0960	11,12A,12F
Green, Dana S.	OR0800	13A,11,66
Green, Maria	NJ0825	11,32
Green, Martin	CA1000	11,13H,32D,36,39
Greenan, April	VA1475	11,12A,12B,12F,20
Greenberg, Laura	NY0630	13,10,66A,66D,11
Greene, Doug	IA1400	11
Greene, Richard C.	GA0850	70,13C,11,13E,12A
Greenlee, Geol	TN1250	13,66A,10F,10,11
Greenwood, Matthew	AL1300	65,11
Gregg, Nan F.	NC0850	11,61
Gregg, Robert B.	TN0100	60,11,12A,38
Grenier, Robert M.	SC1050	13,61,11
Gresham, David Allen	NC0250	61,11,34,13
Grew, Melody A.	MD0050	11,32,36,61,66A
Grey, Meg	MO0600	11,12A,32,66A,66G
Gribbroek, Michael	NJ1400	11
Gribou, Andre	OH1900	11,10,66A
Grieb, Scott	IN0900	11
Grier, George	WA0700	11,13,32D,47,65
Griesheimer, James	IA0950	12,11,13
Griffeath, Robin	OK1250	11,61
Griffin, Jennifer J.	IL2200	11,61
Griffin, Robert	KY0750	13A,11,50,65
Griffin, Stephen W.	AL0332	11,36,37,47,64
Griffin-Seal, Mary	FL0500	66A,11,66D,13C
Griffith, David	TX0075	11,37,46,63
Griffith, Joan	MN1625	11,70,29
Griffiths, Amy	GA0550	64E,32E,11,47
Griggs-Burnham, Patricia	TX0400	66A,11
Grimpo, Elizabeth	NE0150	11,13,66A
Grinnell, Justin	CA2100	11
Griswold, Randall L.	CA0847	20,11
Grobler, Pieter J.	OH0950	11,66C
Grodrian, Ericka	IN1750	11,13C,49,63B
Groesbeck, Rolf A.	AR0750	11,12,14,66A,20
Grose, Michael	OR1050	11,63D,49,42
Gross, Allen	CA3300	11,38,60B,42
Gross, Anne	DE0150	11,12A
Gross, Jeffrey	TN1100	11
Grossman, Andrea	IN1010	11,66A,13A,66D
Grossman, Morley K.	TX3525	11,66A,66C,66D
Grove, Karla	TN1100	11
Grover, Morgan	WY0130	11
Groves, Robert W.	ND0350	11,12A,66A,20G,66H
Grubb, Steve	CA3000	11,66D,66G,66H
Grymes, James A.	NC2420	12,12A,11
Gualdi, Paolo Andre'	SC0710	66A,11,13,66B,66C
Guberman, Daniel	NC0650	11,13
Gubrud, Darcy Lease	MN1285	13,11,36,61,40
Guderian, Lois Veenhoven	WI0860	11,32
Gudmundson, Paula	MN1600	11,13B,64A
Guenoit, Eric	LA0450	60B,11,37,65,50
Guenther, Roy J.	DC0100	13E,13F,11,12A
Guessford, Jesse	VA0450	11,13A,34
Guilbault, Jocelyne	CA5000	11,14,20H
Guiles, Kay	MS0360	11,66A,66D,66G
Guntren, Alissa	IN0900	11
Gustafson, Karen	AK0150	37,63A,41,11,60B
Guthrie, J. Randall	OK0850	31A,60A,36,11,66G
Guy, Todd	IN1025	36,31A,61,60A,11
Haarhues, Charles D.	CO0100	10,13,29,70,11
Haas, David	GA2100	11,12
Haberkorn, Michael	OH2050	66A,20G,14C,11
Hache, Reginald	FL0570	11,66A
Hackel, Erin H.	CO0830	36,13,11,10D
Hadley, Susan J.	PA3100	70,33,11,66D
Hadlock, Heather L.	CA4900	11,12A,12
Haffley, Robin	PA2400	11,29,46
Haffley, Robin L.	PA1830	11,13A,29A,34D,14C
Haftecek, Pierre	NJ0700	11,46,47
Hager, Nancy M.	NY0500	13,11,12A,12
Hagerott, Dawn	ND0050	40,61,11
Haglund, Richard	IL0350	11,13
Hagy, David	NC2500	11,38,51
Hahn, Christopher D.	SD0100	63,37,60,11
Hahna, Nicole	PA3100	32A,33,11
Haines, Amy	WI0250	11,61
Hainsworth, Jason D.	FL0200	11,29,46,47,64E
Hair, Harriet	GA2100	11,32,34,12F
Hakken, Lynda S.	IA0400	66G,13,66C,66A,11
Haldeman, Michael	SC0275	11,37,65,50
Haldey, Olga	MD1010	12,12A,11,14
Hale, Daris Word	TX3175	64D,11
Haley, Timothy R.	NC2210	11,13A,46,34C,34A
Hall, Doris S.	AL0010	11,48,64A,64E
Hall, Frederick A.	AG0200	11,12A,12,20G
Hall, Gail R.	OK1350	11
Hall, Gary	WY0115	11,12A,13B,13C,47
Hall, Richard D.	TX3175	11,10B,34
Hall, Teddy	VA0500	13A,13B,13C,32C,11
Hall, Van-Anthoney	NC1550	11,12D,40,42,61
Halle, John	NY0150	13,11
Halliday, Anna Rebecca	AL1200	11,32A,32B
Halsell, George K.	ID0075	13,37,63,11,71
Halsey, Glynn	GA0490	11,36,40,60A
Ham, Donna	TX2350	11,13A,66
Hamersma, Carol	NJ1160	11,14C,29A,70
Hamilton, Hilree J.	WI0845	11,20,32A,32B,66D
Hamilton, Janet	IN1010	11,66G
Hamilton, William R.	SC0420	13,11
Hamm, Bruce	CA0050	13A,11,12A
Hamman, James	LA0800	11,12A,13A,55B,66G
Hammond, Gary	NY0625	11,66A,66D
Hampton, Anitra C.	AL0650	12A,32,32G,11
Han, Sang-In	IA0250	61,11
Hanawalt, Anita	CA5100	13A,11
Hand, Angela R.	IL0100	61,11
Haneline, Stacie	IA0910	66A,11
Haney, Joel C.	CA0650	11,12A,41
Hanks, Kenneth B.	FL0930	66,13,11
Hanning, Barbara Russano	NY0550	13A,11,12A,12
Hans, Ben J.	WI0450	11,35A,50,65
Hansen, Frank	NY4050	11,38,62B
Hansen, Kristen S.	GA0550	13,11,32E
Hansen, Mark R.	ID0050	66A,13E,11,66G
Hanson, Brian L.	LA0650	11
Hanson, F.	NY4060	13,12A,11,66A
Hanson, Frank E.	WI0865	11,49,63A
Hanson, Jan	OK1400	60,11,12A,32,36
Hanzelin, Fred	IL2775	13,34,11,10
Hara, Craig	WI0845	35G,11
Harden, Patricia A.	NC2050	11
Harden, Shirley	MI1900	11
Harder, Melissa	AJ0030	61,11,60A
Hardin, Larry E.	AL0500	11
Hardy, Bruce	CA5360	11,29A,14C
Hardy, James	UT0150	62C,11,41
Haringer, Andrew	MA2250	12,11
Haritun, Rosalie	IN0905	11
Harkness, Lisa	TN1100	11
Harman, David	NY4350	60,38,41,11
Harms, Janet	CA0630	13A,11,66
Harms, Lawrence	IL1090	11,47,64C,64E,29A
Harper, David R.	RI0150	11,61,54,39,40
Harrington, Richard	CA0050	13A,11,12A
Harriott, Janette	NE0590	32A,32B,11
Harris, B. Joan	MS0200	11,12A,66
Harris, Ellen T.	MA1200	13,11,12A,12
Harris, Paul K.	WA1000	12A,11,13B
Harris, Paul R.	TX2295	64,11
Harris, Rachel	LA0200	11
Harris, Ray	MS0570	11,36,66,54
Harris, Robert	GA0200	12A,60,61,11,32D

Name	Code	Areas
Harris, Rod D.	CA1375	13A,11,64E,29B,34
Harris, Timothy	CA0900	37,11,12A,32E
Harris, Ward	MD0550	11,14C,12A
Harris-Warrick, Rebecca	NY0900	11,12,52
Harrison, Brady	OH2550	65,50,11
Harrison, Joy	IA0420	11,61
Hart, Edward B.	SC0500	10,11,13
Hart, Michael D.	LA0030	37,63A,11,13,47
Hartman, Jane	IL1610	13,11,66A,46,47
Hartwell, Hugh	AG0200	13,10,11,29
Hartzell, K. Drew	NY3700	11,12A,12
Harvey, Brent	NC2700	11,63D
Harvey, James	TX0075	11,70
Harvey, Mark	MA1200	11,29
Harwood, Gregory	GA0950	11,12
Haskett, William	TX1600	49,63D,11
Haskins, Jodi	AL1150	62A,62B,11
Hassevoort, Christine	TN0260	61,11
Hastings, Todd J.	KS1050	63A,29,11,41,42
Hasty, Robert	CA1700	11
Hatcher, George	NC2300	11,12A
Hatcher, Oeida M.	VA0750	32,37,41,38,11
Hauger, Karin	CO0830	11,13,36
Hauser, Kristin	TN1450	11
Hausey, Collette J.	CA2050	11,37,41,65
Hawk, Heather	TX2750	61,11
Hawkey, Walter	TX3540	11
Hawkins, John A.	WV0500	13A,13,11,36,66
Hawkins, Phillip	CA2975	11,20H,34,50
Hawley, Lucrecia	AL0010	11,32,66D
Haworth, Laurie	AL0530	11
Hay, Dennis	AR0050	13A,13B,11,66A,66C
Hay, James	MA0510	11,12A,66A,66B
Hayes, Beth Tura	LA0800	34A,34B,32,11
Hayes, Casey J.	IN0500	36,32,11
Hayes, Tyrone	AL0050	61,11
Hayner, Joy	GA1650	11,13,66
Hayner, Phillip A.	GA1650	11,12,66A,66C,66D
Haynes, Juliana	LA0900	63A,11
Hays, Sorrel	GA2130	11
Hazelip, Richard	TX2300	13B,66G,61,11
Healy, Eddie	TX0700	70,11
Hearn, Priscilla	KS0550	66A,11,12,66D,13C
Hearn, William	GA0500	11,41,70,20
Hearnsberger, Keith	AR0750	11,32
Heath, Guy	FL1430	11,36,35A
Heath, Malissa	KY1540	11,66D,32B,13,12A
Heavner, Tabitha	CT0050	11,13A
Hedges, Don P.	IL3150	13,31A,11,39
Heffernan, Michele	NJ1100	11,13C,29,33,66A
Hefley, Earl	OK1330	11,64C,64E
Heflin, Thomas	NY2150	63,11
Heidenreich, Christopher	MI2120	37,49,11,10F
Heifetz, Robin J.	CA0200	11,20,10A,43,12
Heighway, Robbi A.	WI0450	11,13C,13D,66B,66D
Heil, Teri	NE0250	66A,13,11
Heimbecker, Sara	CO0950	12A,11,13A,14C
Heinz-Thompson, Leslie	MO0850	61,11
Heinzen, Craig	LA0700	11,63A,63B
Heitzman, Jill M.	IA0450	61,64A,66A,11
Hekmatpanah, Kevin	WA0400	11,12A,38,51,62C
Held, Jeffrey	CA1425	11,12A,37,32E,10F
Helfter, Susan	CA5300	11,63B
Helman, Michael	ID0100	63B,11
Hemenway, Langston	IL2050	11,32E,37,41
Henckel, Kristina	OK0150	66C,11
Henderson, Mark A.	UT0350	60,10,11,36,32D
Henderson, Matthew	GA0250	11,63C,63D
Henderson, Paul	TN1400	11,70
Hendricks, Allen	SC0275	31,11
Hendrickson, Anna	NY3780	64B,11
Hendrickson, Daniel	MI1180	11,12A,36,37,61
Henkel, Karl		11
Henry, Joseph W.	MN0610	11
Hensley, David L.	CA3700	11,36
Henson, Karen A.	NY0750	11,15,39,12A,12B
Hepworth, Elise M.	NE0700	32D,61,32B,32C,11
Herald, Terry	MI1750	35G,35C,11
Herman, Matthew	PA2400	10,11,13,34,35
Hernon, Bonnie	TN1720	66D,11
Heroux, Gerard H.	RI0300	16,63B,11
Herrington, Carolyn	AA0200	66C,11
Herriott, Jeffrey	WI0865	10,11,43,35E
Herron, Teri A.	MS0250	61,11
Heslink, Daniel M.	PA2350	11,14,37,65
Hess, Fred	CO0550	11,13,29
Hess, Jeffrey	MN1200	61,34,32,11
Hesse, Robert	AR0500	37,11
Hest, Jeff	NY3250	11,29,35,37,47
Hetrick, Mark	OH1330	11,61,66C
Hettle, Mark	TX1725	13,11,37,47,63A
Heuchemer, Dane O.	OH1200	11,12A,12,37,67
Heukeshoven, Janet	MN1400	37,32,60,11,41
Hewell, Rob	AR0500	31A,44,11
Heydenburg, Audrejean	MI2000	11,12A,66A,66B,66C
Heywood, David John	SC0500	11,37,64A,29,47
Hibbard, Dave	IL0650	11,47,46
Hibbard, Jason	FL1950	11,66D
Hibbard, Sarah	IL2150	11
Hibbett, Michael	WA1200	11,36
Hickman, Kathryn	OK0150	66C,11
Hickman, Melinda	OH0550	11,66A,66B,66D
Hickman, Roger	CA0825	11,12A,38
Hicks, Martha K.	MO1550	31A,11,60,13C,32B
Higdon, Paul	MO1100	13,66A,66B,11,66D
High, Ronald	SC0150	11,12,31F,61,66
Hildreth, John W.	IL0100	11,14,20
Hill, Camille	KY0600	13A,11,36,61,66D
Hill, George R.	NY0250	11,12A,12,16
Hill, Harry H.	SC0850	11,12A,64C,64E,48
Hill, John	MI0450	11,29A,62D
Hill, Kyle W.	MS0580	13B,11,37,50,65
Hill, Matthew	IN0550	66A,66B,11,12A
Hillard, Claire Fox	GA0625	11,62A,62B,66D,62
Hiller, James	OH2250	33,11
Hillyer, Dirk M.	MA1650	63B,11,12A,13E,13F
Hilowski-Fowler, Ann	PA3600	11,12A
Hilton, Suzanne	MD0550	11,13A,34C
Himrod, Gail P.	RI0150	12A,20,11
Hinckley, Jaren S.	UT0050	64C,11,48
Hines, Roger	OH0350	62D,11
Hinkle, Jean	OR1020	11,13A,41,66A,66D
Hinojosa, Melissa S.	TX1425	11,13,64A
Hinson, Lee	OK0650	31A,11,36
Hiranpradist, Barbara	MI1200	11,32B,20
Hirsch, Marjorie	MA2250	11,12,15,20G
Hirt, James A.	OH0200	13,11,66A,10
Hiscock, Fred	NC0860	11,29
Hiscocks, Mike	CA2650	11,13A,61,45,10B
Ho, Hubert	MA1450	10,13,13K,11
Ho, Stephanie	NJ0700	66A,66C,11
Hoag, Bret	MI1750	70,41,11
Hobbins, William	GA0250	32,36,61,11
Hobson, David	LA0050	36,11,31A,12A
Hodge, R. Matthew	KY0400	11,13A
Hodges, Betsi	ID0050	11
Hodges, Brian D.	ID0050	62C,11,42
Hodgson, Ken	MN1620	36,61,34D,11,60A
Hodson, Steven R.	CA5550	11,36,60,66A
Hoeckner, Berthold	IL3250	11,12,12A
Hoefle, Andrew	IL2775	11,37,47,63D,29
Hoepfner, Gregory	OK0150	10A,32,61,10,11
Hoffer, Heike	TX3525	64B,11,32
Hoffman, Adrian	AF0100	11
Hoffman, Edward C. 'Ted'	AL1200	11,32C,32E,60B
Hoffman, Patrick	DE0050	63A,63B,13,11,49
Hoffmann, Shulamit	CA1250	66A,11
Hogan, Lisa	NJ0800	11
Hogue, Harry	MD0360	70,12A,63D,13,11
Hoifeldt, Steven	IA0425	61,11,40
Hokin, Harlan B.	AZ0480	11
Holcombe, Candace	SC0450	11,32B
Holder, Angela	TN0250	61,36,31,11
Holder, Brian	FL1675	11,20,13A,65,50
Holland, Nicholas V.	SC0275	11,37
Hollander, Jeffrey M.	IN1750	12A,15,11,12
Holleman, James A.	MI1000	60,11,36,38
Hollenbeck, Lisa	NY3770	11
Hollerbach, Peter	NY0270	13A,11,14,47,70
Hollinden, Andrew J.	IN0900	11,29
Hollinger, Deborah	IL3550	66A,11,66D
Hollinger, Lowell	MS0350	11,13A,32C,48,64E
Hollingsworth, Dina L.	CO0275	64A,64E,29,41,11
Hollis, Brenda	KY1540	32B,20,11
Holliston, Robert	AB0210	66C,12A,11,39,66A
Holly, Janice	MD0300	13B,11
Holm, Thomas	IA1200	12A,36,11,60,61
Holmes, Christopher	IN0100	12A,12C,20,11
Holmes, Isaac	GA1600	60A,11,36,61,39
Holmquist, Solveig	OR1250	11,36,60,66G,69
Holoman, D. Kern	CA5010	60,11,12A,12
Holroyd, Megan Calgren	MN0050	11,35
Holzer, Linda	AR0750	66A,66B,42,15,11
Hong, Caroline	OH1850	11,66A,66C,66D
Hong, Xiangtang	IL1850	60A,31A,36,44,11
Hooan, Dan	TX1725	11,70
Hoogenstyn, Don	MI1550	11,12A
Hooten, David M.	TX1600	64C,11,48,64A
Hopkins, William T.	CA4200	11,12A,12,12F
Horan, Sara	GA1000	32,11,61
Horgan, Maureen A.	GA0850	63D,11,49,63C,29A
Horjus-Lang, Deanna	WI0800	36,61,11
Horn, Lawrence C.	MS0560	11,32A,48,64
Horton, Christian	GA1260	20A,11
Horvath, Maria	IL1610	66A,66C,13,66D,11
Hosler, Mark	SC0400	11,20G
Hosten, Kevin	NY2100	11,47,63,64,66D
Hotle, Dana	MO0700	11,64C
Hotle, Dana	MO1120	11
Howard, David	OR0250	13,10,11,45,66G
Howard, Jacqueline	GA1450	11
Howell, Allen C.	PA1200	11,32,36
Howell, Jane	PA2900	66A,66C,13A,54,11
Hower, Eileen	PA0250	32,11,61
Howland, Pamela	NC2500	11
Huang, Rachel Vetter	CA4500	62A,11,13A,42
Hubbs, Holly J.	PA3550	11,37,47,29A,20
Hucke, Adam	IL2970	11,13A,29A,63A,47
Huckleberry, Heather	IA0250	11,64B
Hudson, Gary	TX2350	11,49,63A,63B
Hudson, Mark E.	CO0275	11,32,60B
Hudson, Milton	TX3360	11,37
Hudson, Nita	TX2700	11,61
Hudson, S.	KY0350	11,13,36
Hudson, Stephen	NJ0975	66A,66B,66C,11
Hudson, Virginia	AR0730	64A,11
Hudson, William Andrew	TX1600	66A,11,66C,66D
Huebl, Carolyn	TN1850	62A,13G,32F,34,11
Huff, Christina	IN1025	32A,32B,32C,11,36
Huff, Douglas M.	IL3500	64D,12A,11,48
Huff, Dwayne	MO0200	11,66A,66B,66C,66D
Huff, Lori	CA0630	13A,11,48,64E,32
Hufft, Bradley	CA0810	14C,13,11
Hufty, Aaron	TX0300	36,11
Hugghins, Linda	OK0770	11
Huggins, Mark	AZ0350	11,12A
Hughes, Albert C.	TN0950	13,11,12A,36,61
Hughes, Andrew	AG0450	11,12,13J,12G
Hughes, Brian L.	IA0940	60,11,32,37,47
Hughes, Evelyn	GA0940	11,12A,61
Hughes, Julayne	MI1830	11,13A
Hull, Daniel	SC0420	70,11
Hull, Kenneth	AG0470	11,12A,31A,36
Hulse, Mark	CA0300	13,11,32B,32C,61
Hult, David W.	NY2650	62A,62B,11,51
Hultgren, Craig	AL1150	11,62C
Human, Richard	MS0500	63C,11
Humble, Dina M.	CA3800	61,36,11,34,29
Humes, Scot A.	LA0770	64C,64E,11
Hummel, Linda W.	PA1900	11,32
Hummer, Ken	OH1330	11,70
Hund, Jennifer L.	IN1300	12,66A,12A,11
Hungerford, Del	WA1150	32A,32B,32C,11
Hunnicutt, Heather Winter	KY0610	61,32,11
Hunt, Emily	GA2130	11
Hunt, Graham G.	TX3500	13,12,10F,11,12A
Hunt, Keena Redding	GA0350	11
Hunt, Trevor	MS0580	11,70,13C,13G
Hunter, Mary K.	ME0200	13A,13,11,12A,12
Hurd, James L.	CA1750	11,66A,66G
Hurlburt, Timothy R.	SC0400	37,46,47,11
Hurst, Craig W.	WI0960	11,37,47,41,63A
Husarik, Stephen	AR0730	11,69,12A
Huseynova, Aida N.	IN0900	11
Hussa, Robert	WY0060	11,12A,35C,36,61
Hussey, Peter	IL1500	65,20,11,50,12A
Hussung, Lisa	KY1550	61,11
Huston, Spencer	KS0590	11,66A
Hutchings, James	IL0420	11,13B,12A,61,13A
Hutchins, Tony	IA1100	11,29A,63B,63C,32E
Hutchinson, Chad	IA1200	11,38,51
Hutchinson, Raymond	IL1900	66A,63A,63B,11
Hutter, Greg J.	IL0750	13C,13D,10A,11
Hutton, Paula R.	OK0700	13,12A,66A,11
Hwang, Christine	IL1615	11,66D
Hwang, Okon	CT0150	14,66,11,12,13

Index by Area of Teaching Interest

Name	Code	Areas
Hyberger, Brett	TN0260	61,11,39
Hyberger, Sarah Amanda	TN0260	11,13C,54,61,39
Hyland, Judy	IA1300	13A,66C,11
Idenden, John	NJ0100	13A,11,12A,61,66A
Iguina, Jose R.	PR0150	13A,13C,11,70
Ihas, Dijana	OR0750	62B,11,32
Ikach, Yugo Sava	PA0500	61,38,11,13A,36
Ikner, W. Joseph	AL0200	70,11
Imhoff, Andrea G.	TX2900	13A,11,66C,66A
Immel, Daniel	PA1750	11,66A,66D
Imperio, Roy	MA0250	66A,66B,41,66C,11
Imsand, Patrick K.	AL1300	70,11,51
Imthurn, Melinda	TX1725	11,36,61
Infusino, Patrick	IL0275	11,64E,13C
Ingber, Jeffrey	VA1400	20,11
Ingersoll, Orbie D.	CA3100	13A,11
Ingwerson, John	MS0300	70,11
Irland, Jeremy	WA1100	61,11
Irving, Marcy	CA1510	11
Isaac, Cecil	TX0250	11,12
Isaacs, David	TN1400	70,11,35G,45
Isenhour, Justin	AR0500	63C,63D,11,13C
Ishigaki, Miles M.	CA0810	48,64C,41,11,14C
Ishikawa, Chikae	NY5000	11
Italiano, Richard	CO0300	13,10,11,66A,66D
Iwanusa, Charles	MI0450	13,10,11,47,29
Jablonsky, Stephen	NY0550	11,63A,10A,10F,13
Jachens, Darryl	SC1080	11,32,63C
Jackson, Albert	IL2775	13A,11,36,61
Jackson, Gregory	AL0345	11,65
Jackson, L. Max	KY0200	13,11,36,66A
Jackson, Milton	AR0810	13,11,49,63,70
Jackson, Stephen	IL0420	48,11,20,41,47
Jacob, Jeffrey	IN1450	11,66A,66B
Jacobs, Ed	IL2970	63D,11,13A,37,46
Jacobson, Daniel C.	MI2250	11,12A,12,34
Jacobson, Joshua R.	MA1450	11,12A,36,13,31B
Jacobson, Marin	CA1425	36,12A,61,11
Jacobus, Rhea Beth	SC0400	13,11
Jakubiec, Aaron F.	IL0800	11,64B,13B
James, Candace	KY0550	11
James, Judy A. G.	LA0700	11,32,32I,66D
James, Richard	FL1700	11
Jander, Owen	MA2050	11,12A,12
Janson, Peter	MA2010	70,29,11,20,47
Jarvis, Jeffery W.	AR0850	63D,11,12A
Jeffery, Peter	NJ0900	11,12A,12,31A
Jeffries, Curt	NE0700	11
Jelinek, Mark R.	PA0250	60B,11,38,62
Jenkins, Ellie	GA0610	11
Jenkins, John A.	MA2000	11,37
Jenkins, Miriam R.	MA2000	11
Jenner, Bryan	NJ0760	11,37
Jennings, Arthur	FL1850	11,63C,63D
Jennings, David J.	IL0650	11,65,13
Jennings, Tom	TX1775	11,36,61
Jensen, Andrew	AR0050	60A,36,11,61,13C
Jensen, Karen	AC0100	61,11
Jensen-Moulton, Stephanie	NY0500	11,12,12E
Jentsch, Christopher	NY4060	13,12A,11,70
Jentsch, Christopher T.	NY4050	11,29A
Jernigan, Richard	FL1500	11,64
Jerosch, Sebastian	ME0340	63C,11
Jewell, Vickie L.	AL0345	11,37,63B,66A
Jocoy, Stacey	TX3200	12G,12E,12C,31A,11
Johansen, David A.	LA0650	63C,11,63D,49
Johansen, Judy	CA3800	11,66C
Johansen, Keven W.	UT0250	70,29,11
Johanson, Bryan	OR0850	70,13,41,11,10
Johns, Amy	GA1070	66A,66D,11
Johns, Kristen	GA2150	63B,11,42,49
Johns, Lana Kay	MS0500	13A,11,64A
Johns, Stephen	FL1745	11
Johnson, Barry	KY0750	13,10F,10,11
Johnson, Brad	MS0200	60,11,36,44,61
Johnson, Carly	AL0345	11,63A
Johnson, Chrisa	VA0050	66A,13B,13C,11
Johnson, Clifford	CT0450	11
Johnson, Cornelius	IL0450	13A,66A,11,36,20
Johnson, Craig	CA3640	61,39,11
Johnson, Deborah S.	NE0300	13A,11,48,64A,13B
Johnson, Diane	WA0900	36,61,54,11,20
Johnson, Dylan	CA1510	11,70
Johnson, Gordon	UT0350	20,11
Johnson, H. Wade	PA2000	37,63,11
Johnson, Herbert	MN0250	11,66A,66B,66C
Johnson, James R.	MN1300	13,11,12
Johnson, Jeanne	TX1350	13C,11,61
Johnson, Jeffrey	CT0550	10,11,12,13
Johnson, Kerry	CO0300	61,11
Johnson, Kevin P.	GA1900	60,11,32A,32B,34
Johnson, Lawrence	UT0200	11,13C,61
Johnson, Lynne	HI0210	11,12A
Johnson, Madeline	UT0190	13,11,34,64C
Johnson, Melody	MN1280	11
Johnson, Nikki	MS0360	11,61,54,36
Johnson, Patricia	KY1550	11,13C
Johnson, Randall	GU0500	11,36,47,61,64E
Johnson, Robert	TX2750	11
Johnson, Scott R.	SD0050	32,54,11
Johnson, Teri	TX2800	61,11,39
Johnson, Victoria	MS0360	11,66A,66D
Johnson, Wayne D.	WA0800	11,12A,66A,66C
Johnson, William T.	CA4700	13,10,11,43,12A
Johnston, Gary	KY1000	10F,11,34
Johnston, Gregory	AG0450	11,12A,12,31A
Johnston, Jesse A.	MI2110	11,12A,29A
Jokisch, Kelly	SC0710	11,32B
Jones, Bernard	OK1050	13,12A,61,11,64
Jones, Christine	MO1100	11,66
Jones, Christopher	NY3350	12A,11
Jones, Colby	ID0075	11
Jones, Colette	KY0300	32B,11,66A,66D
Jones, Dani R.	AL0500	11,61
Jones, Emily	FL0040	11,12A,13C,41,70
Jones, Gordon	TX3175	11,20
Jones, Gregory R.	MO1780	11,63A,49
Jones, Herman	SC0150	11,37,47,48,64
Jones, Jeff	CA3200	13A,11
Jones, Joshua	IL1300	61,11,39,54
Jones, Kate	TX2750	11,62D
Jones, Larry	TX2100	13A,11,50,65
Jones, Leslie I.	MO1500	61,39,11,54
Jones, Martin David	GA0250	11,66A,66H,66B,13
Jones, Maxine	TN1400	66A,66D,11
Jones, Melvin	GA1450	11,37,29,63A
Jones, Pamela	MS0580	11,61,13C
Jones, Patrick R.	PA1200	11,29,64,41
Jones, Rebecca	GA1650	11
Jones, Richard	PA2900	66C,11
Jones, Ryan Patrick	WI0803	11,12A,13,29A
Jones, T. Marshall	GA0150	11,29,47,53
Jones, Tony	IL1090	37,63,13A,11
Jones, William	DC0350	11,36,61,66A,66G
Jones-Bamman, Richard	CT0150	11,14,32,20
Jordahl, Patricia	AZ0300	36,54,66D,61,11
Jordan, Christopher	AL0010	11,61
Jordan, Edward	LA0720	11,20G,37,47,64
Jordan, John M.	IN1600	12A,11,31A,20
Jordan, L. Thomas	KY1000	11,34
Jordan, Michael D.	TX1660	13A,13,11,39,61
Jordan, Rachel	MS0350	62A,11,13A,13B,42
Jordan, Rachel	LA0720	11,62A
Jordan-Anders, Lee	VA1830	13,11,41,66A
Jorgensen, Elaine	UT0190	11,41,48,64A
Jorgensen, Kristen	NY3770	11,48,64A,62A
Jorgensen, Michael	MN0750	61,11,32D,14C
Jorgensen, Trevor	NY3770	37,64,48,11
Joseph, Jane	MS0300	11,66A
Joseph, Richard	MN0040	11,61
Joy, Nancy	NM0310	63B,49,13A,11
Joyce, John J.	LA0750	11,12,29
Joyner, Rochelle	NC0200	11,66A,66D
Julian, Suzanne	CA1700	66A,11
Julian, Suzanne	CA3100	11,66A,66D
Jumpeter, Joseph A.	PA1750	11,29A,20,36,66G
Jung, Eun-Young	CA5050	11,12D,14,20C
Jurcisin, Mark	NJ0750	10,13A,13B,13C,11
Jureit-Beamish, Marie	IL2400	38,64A,66A,10F,11
Justeson, Jeremy	PA1750	64E,37,32E,43,11
Kachian, Christopher	MN1625	11,70,20
Kadetsky, Mark	NJ0550	62D,51,11
Kagin, Roberta S.	MN0050	33,11
Kahler, Bette	NY4100	11,12A,33,66A,66G
Kahn, Alexander G.	PA1400	38,12A,11,60B
Kairies, Joy E.	TX0550	64A,34C,11,48
Kairoff, Peter	NC2500	11,66A
Kaizer, Edward	IL0400	11,12A,66A,66B
Kalson, Dorothy	NY4050	66A,11
Kalyn, Andrea	OH1700	12A,11
Kam, Genna	IN0910	11,66D
Kamatani, Pamela M.	CA1020	11,13B,13C
Kamatani, Pamela	CA5353	12A,11,12C,13
Kameria, Kim	CA1290	11,32D,35A,35B,35C
Kamien, Roger	NY0642	11,13
Kamm, Charles W.	CA2175	36,11,12,60
Kamm, Charles W.	CA1060	36,11,12,60
Kamm, Charles W.	CA3620	36,11,12,60
Kang, Haysun	IL1615	11,66A,66D
Kang, Hyun-Ku	SC0350	11
Kaplan, Allan Richard	NM0310	11,63C,53
Karahalis, Dean	NY4050	11,29,63C
Karahalis, Dean	NY4060	13,12A,11
Karass, Alan M.	MA0700	11,16
Karnatz, Roland	VA0700	11,14C
Karriker, Kendra	OH2150	62A,11
Kashap, Philip	AJ0150	11,62A
Kasunic, David M.	CA3300	12A,12B,12D,11
Katz, Robert S.	OK1300	13,11,12A,12,62D
Katz, Steve	TN1380	11,66A
Kaufhold, Jessica	AL0530	36,11,13A,13B,13C
Kaurin-Karaca, Natasa	OK0800	66D,13C,11,34B
Kazez, Daniel	OH2450	13A,11,20D,62C,62D
Keast, Michelle	TX3527	11,32,32A
Keberle, Ryan	NY0625	29,47,11,13,63
Keck, Vail	CA3100	36,60,11,13A,61
Kee, Soyoung	IL0850	66A,11
Keebaugh, Aaron	FL1675	11,20,13A,63
Keef, Ardith A.	ME0500	13A,11,64D
Keehn, Samantha	IL0100	63C,63D,11
Keeler, Elden L.	IL0650	11,65,13
Keeling, Bruce	TX2350	11,12A,47,49,63D
Keenan, Larry W.	KY0900	11,66A,66G,66D,66H
Keenan, Maureen	NY0270	11,13,64A
Keener, Michael K.	OH2250	63C,49,11,32E
Kehle, Robert G.	KS1050	11,47,29,63C
Kehler, David T.	GA1150	37,60B,11
Keiler, Allan R.	MA0500	11,12A,12D,13E,13J
Keipp, Donald K.	UT0350	13A,11,65,29,47
Keiter, Lise	VA0800	13,11,66A,12A,15
Kellan, Ross	IL0850	60,32,37,11,13
Keller, Daniel B.	CA3000	11,36,60
Keller, Dennis L.	CA3320	36,61,20,11,40
Kellert, Aaron	OK1100	11,36,13A,54,61
Kelley, Anthony M.	NC0600	11,13,29,10A,10C
Kelley, Kevin	TX1350	11,10,13,43
Kelly, Elizabeth	MA0600	11,61
Kelly, Frankie J.	LA0800	66C,40,41,42,11
Kelly, Terence	WI0810	11,61,54
Kelly, Thomas Forrest	MA1050	11,12A,12,13J
Kempster, James	CA3400	11,12A,36,61,31A
Kendrick, Robert L.	IL3250	11,31,12,14
Kennedy, Charles	AL0630	11,70,66A,61
Kennedy, Daniel J.	CA0840	11,65
Kennedy, Nancy	KS0570	11,61
Kennedy, Rajah B.	OK0450	11,37,46,49,63
Kennedy, T. Frank	MA0330	11,12,31A,20H
Kenneson, Claude E.	AA0100	13A,11
Kenney, James	CA3375	13A,11,14C,66D
Kenny, William	PA0350	60,11,37,63A,63B
Kent, George E.	RI0300	11,49,63A,66G,66H
Ker-Hackleman, Kelly	VA0450	66,13C,11
Kerber, Patrick C.	LA0650	70,11
Kernodle, Tammy L.	OH1450	11,12,29A,29D
Kershaw, Linda L.	SC0150	11,12,60,66A,36
Kershaw, Yvonne	AE0120	64A,64D,10A,11,13A
Keyl, Stephen M.	AZ0500	11
Keys, John M.	IL2250	11
Keyser, Dorothy	ND0500	11,12A,14
Khan, Ali Akbar	CA0050	13A,10,11,12A,62
Khoma, Natalia	SC0500	11,62C
Kidd, Christine	NM0400	13A,61,11
Kidula, Jean	GA2100	14,20,11,31,12
Kiec, Michelle	PA1750	64,13,64C,64E,11
Kihle, Jason J.	TX2960	11,37,50,65
Kilby, Shelton	OH2400	10A,11
Killmeyer, Heather N.	TN0500	64B,12A,11,64D
Kilstofte, Anne C.	AZ0350	11,29A,20
Kim, Ariana	IN1650	62A,11,38,32E
Kim, Howard D.	SC0050	66A,66D,13B,66C,11
Kim, Hyesook	MI0350	66A,66B,11,42
Kim, Jean	NY0270	11,13,66A,66C
Kim, Kunyoung	PA0250	66A,13E,11,66B
Kim, Rebecca Y.	MA1450	11,13F
Kim, Seung-Ah	NC2435	11,66D,66C
Kim-Quathamer, Chan Ji	FL0150	10,11,13,34

Name	Code	Areas	Name	Code	Areas
Kimball, James W.	NY3730	13A,11,14,67E,70	Lambert, Evin R.	WA0750	11,36,66A,61,13A
Kimbell, Sara	OH2600	11	Lambert, Kevin	TX0150	11
King, Amanda	TN1100	11,61	Lambert, Nathan T.	CO0350	10F,11,14C,42,51
King, Ben R.	NY1700	11,12A,61,39	Lambert, Philip	NY0250	13A,13,11,12A
King, Bryan T.	AL0200	11,66	Lambrecht, Cynthia A.	IL0100	64B,11
King, Dennis W.	WI0150	60,11,32,13	Lamendola, Gene	NY4050	11
King, Donna Moore	TN0930	11,66A,66D,69	Lamendola, Gene	NY4060	13,12A,11
King, Morgan	TX3530	13,11	Lamkin, Kathleen J.	CA5100	12A,11,12,62A,66A
King, Richard G.	MD1010	11,12A,12,20G,12C	Lamkin, Lynn B.	TX3400	11
KinKennon, Heather Marie	CA0200	11,60,66,66D	Lamkin, Martin J.	VI0050	11,12A,32A,47,60B
Kinney, Kaylyn	NY3000	11,66D	Lammers, Ed	KS0040	46,37,65,63,11
Kinney, Michael	NY0350	13,10,11	Lampl, Kenneth H.	NY1600	35,10,64E,34,11
Kinsley, Eric B.	CA0550	11,66A,66H,66D	LaNasa, Patricia J.	OH2150	61,11
Kireilis, Ramon J.	CO0900	11	Lancaster, Michael	CO0830	11
Kirk, Caroline	MN1400	11,66A,66B,66D	Land, W. Reese	KY0400	11,13A,41
Kirk, Elizabeth	NC0860	11,20G	Landgrebe, Junauro	MA1450	11,14C,41
Kirk, Erin	CA5400	11,13A	Landis, Stella Baty	LA0750	12A,11
Kirkeby, Gary	MD0700	12A,11,61	Lane, LuAnn	TX1850	11,13,66A,66C,66D
Kirkland, Anthony B.	MS0500	63A,42,49,67E,11	Laney, Robert	TX3700	11,13,36
Kirschstein, Natalie	CO0650	11,20,13A	Lange, Jesse	OH2150	11
Kiss, Boglarka	CA3500	11,12A,64A	Langer, Kenneth P.	MA1500	10A,10B,13,34D,11
Kitson, Jeffrey	NE0040	11,13,36,40,61	Langford, Bruce	CA1000	11,12A,32D,36,39
Kizer, Tremon B.	OH2250	37,32E,11	Langsam, Stuart	OK0800	65,50,11
Kjos, Kevin	PA1750	11,47,63A,49	Langsford, Christopher M.	KS0750	36,32,11,12,13
Klaus, Kenneth S.	LA0450	60A,11,36,61,40	Lanier Miller, Pamela	AL0330	61,11,66A
Klecker, Deb J.	WI0450	11,66D	Lanning, Rebecca	GA1260	11,36,61
Klee, Michael	NE0460	65,11	Lanter, Mark W.	AL1150	11
Klein, Jon	ID0060	11,63B	Lantz, Lisa E.	NY0100	11,38,51,62,13A
Klein, Lonnie	NM0310	11,38,41,60	Lapin, Eric J.	SC0400	64C,11
Klein, Rochelle Z.	PA2900	32,35E,66A,11,13A	Lapka, Christine	IL3500	32,11,12C
Kleinsasser, Jerome S.	CA0650	11,12A,12,10C	Lapp, Beverly K.	IN0550	66B,66A,11,66C
Kline, W. Peter	TX2260	13A,11,37,49,63D	Large, Karen McLaughlin	KS0650	13,11,64A,13A,48
Klipp, Barbara A.	IL0650	13A,11,64A	Larison, Adam	FL0350	70,11
Kloppers, Jacobus	AA0035	11,12A,12,66G,31A	Larmee, Kent	OH1100	11,41,63B
Klugherz, Laura	NY0650	13,11,41,62A,62B	Larson, Philip	CA5050	13A,11,12A,36,61
Knaub, Maribeth	PA1050	11	LaRue, Peter	KY0610	60,11,32,37,63D
Knaub, Maribeth J.	PA3100	11,61,66D	Lastrapes, Jeffrey Noel	TX3200	62C,42,51,11,32E
Knauth, Dorcinda	NY1050	11,66	Late, Eric	TX2295	47,62D,11,34C
Knecht, Melissa Gerber	MI1000	11,32,42,62A,62B	Latten, James E.	PA1650	11,13A,37,50,65
Knelman, Jennifer	AG0350	13A,11	Lau, Jennifer	NM0450	64A,11
Knibbs, Lester A.	NC0800	11,66C	Laubenthal, Jennifer	NM0100	64C,11,13A
Knier, Lawrence	MD0800	37,13C,63,13K,11	Lauderdale, Rod	LA0350	11,63B
Knight, Alan	SC0600	70,11,20	Laudon, Robert	MN1623	11,12A,12,66H
Knight, Joshua	AR0730	65,50,11	Lauer, Eileen	IL1900	61,11,20
Knoeloch, Glenn	IL2970	11	Lautar, Rebecca	FL0650	11,41,51,62A,62B
Knop, Robert	CA0845	32E,29,64E,11	Lawrence, Robert J.	MO1790	32,36,11,47
Knowles, Debbie	IL1400	65,11	Laws, Francis	OH2500	11,49,63C,63D
Knox, Daniel	AL0750	11,70,63,64,13A	Lawson, Dianne	IA0910	66A,11
Knudsen, Joel	KS0210	13,11,66	Lawson, Robert	CA5360	13,10,11,66D,12A
Knudtsen, Jere	WA0750	11,37,47,64A,29A	Lawson, Ronald S.	IA0910	63C,65,11,50
Ko, EunMi	NY1250	11,66A	Lawson, Tonya	TN1100	64C,64E,64B,11
Kobernik, Lynnette	CA3800	64B,11	Lawthers, Carol	CA4000	11,32B,61,66A
Kobler, Linda	PA2250	11	Lawton, Richard	AI0150	11,12,63
Kobuck, Martin	TX1775	13,63C,46,11	Laycock, Rand	OH0755	11,12A,32C,38,62D
Koch, Danielle	MO0350	11	Laymon, Michael	IL1080	11,13,35,63C
Kochis, Jane	MN1285	66A,66C,11	Layne, R. Dennis	MN1300	11
Koehler, Elisa C.	MD0400	38,63A,60,11,13A	Leach, Brenda	MD0850	38,11,66G
Koehner, Leon	IA1170	66,11	Leafstedt, Carl S.	TX3350	11,12A,14,20
Koenig, Chris	NH0300	11	Leahy, Eugene J.	IN1700	11,12A,12
Koenigberg, Rebecca Anne	CO0650	61,11,54	Leaptrott, Ben	GA0350	11,13,39,66A,66B
Koh-Baker, JoAnn Hwee Been	OH1600	11,12A,66A,13A,13B	Lease, Gus	CA4400	11
Kohl, Jack	NY4060	13C,12A,11	Lease, Nancy	IA0250	12A,66,11
Kohlenberg, Kenneth	OH2120	37,60B,12A,11,63A	Leathersich, Stacey	CA0150	11,61
Kohn, Karl G.	CA3650	13,10,11,12A	Leatherwood, John G.	FL1430	61,11
Kohrs, Jonathan A.	IL0730	10,36,11,31A,34	LeBlanc, Gaye F.	OK1350	62E,11
Kolbeck, Karl F.	NE0700	12A,72,48,64,11	Ledeen, Lydia Hailparn	NJ0300	11,12A,15,12C
Kolwinska, Jeremy	MN1280	63C,63D,11,63B	Lee, April	IL0800	36,11
Konewko, Mark	WI0425	11,35A,34,69	Lee, Brian	IL1850	66A,11
Konoval, Brandon	AB0100	11	Lee, Jaeryoung	CA4050	32E,13A,11
Kopfstein-Penk, Alicia	DC0010	70,12,13C,11	Lee, James	AZ0200	12A,11,29
Korbitz, Ronald S.	IL3450	11	Lee, Marian Y.	IA1300	66A,66B,66C,13C,11
Korneitchouk, Igor	CA4050	13A,10,11,12A,34	Lee, Michael E.	OH1100	11,32E
Kosciesza, Andrew	PA2400	11,12,20,36	Lee, Paul S.	TX1300	66G,13B,11,60,66A
Kostner, Douglas	NY2400	11	Lee, Sang-Hie	FL2000	11,12C
Kowalkowski, Jeffrey F.	IL2150	11	Lee, William R.	TN1700	32,63D,11
Kowalkowski, Jeffrey F.	IL0750	10,11	Lefferts, Peter M.	NE0600	11,12A,12
Koza, John	CA2150	11	Legette, Lee David	NC2700	11,32B,37,47,64E
Kozlova, Yulia	CA4450	11,13,41,66	Lehman, Stephanie	NY0270	65,11,13
Kraaz, Sarah Mahler	WI0700	12A,55,66,11,67C	Lehninger, Marcia	NH0150	11,20H,62A,62B
Kramer, Elizabeth A.	GA2130	12A,14,11,13A,62A	Leistra-Jones, Karen	PA1300	11,12A,12
Kramer, Ernest Joachim	MO0950	13,10,11,66A,66H	Leiter, Cherise D.	CO0550	11,13,10
Kramer, Jonathan C.	NC1700	11,12A,20D,20A,62C	Lemon, Ronald	TX3750	63B,11
Kramer, Kenneth	OH1100	11,36,61	Lemons, Chris H.	IL0750	11
Kramme, Joel I.	MO0825	11,36,55,67,12A	Lemons, Robert M.	CT0150	11,60,32,63A
Krause, Douglas	CO0830	13A,11,35A,35B,35C	Lemson, Lee	TX3850	13A,11,36,61
Krause, William Craig	VA0550	70,11,12A,20H,35E	Lenehan, Miriam C.	NY2450	11,12A,32,66A,66D
Kravchak, Richard	CA0805	11,64,38,37,32	Lenney, James	NJ0700	11,32
Kravitz, Steve	OR0450	64B,64E,64C,29,11	Lenti, Anthony A.	SC0800	11,12A,66A
Krebill, Kerry	DC0350	60,11	Leonardo, Manuel	CA1400	11,12A,36,61
Krebs, Jesse D.	MO1780	11,64C,13D,48	Leone, Gary	FL0500	65,11
Krebs, John A.	AR0350	66A,66C,39,11,13	Leppert-Largent, Anna	MI1850	11,66A
Kreft, Anne	IL0275	64A,11	Lerdahl, Fred	NY0750	10,12F,11
Kreider, David G.	MD0520	11,66A,66G,66B,66D	Lerner, Neil	NC0550	11,12,34H,66H
Kreiling, Jean L.	MA0510	13A,11,12A,12,66D	Lesbines, Melissa	NC0050	11,66A,66C
Kremer, Kelly	MO0550	11	Lester, Jason	TX3850	11,12A,13F,29A
Kresky, Jeffrey	NJ1400	13,10F,11,66D	Levey, John C.	PA3400	10,13,11,34,36
Krieger, Marcos F.	PA3150	13C,66H,66G,11,12A	Levin, Andrew R.	SC0400	11,41,38,13,42
Kriehn, Richard	WA1150	11,70,62A,34	Levin, Rami Y.	IL1400	13,11,38,10A
Krishnaswami, Donald	MA0510	11,12A,62A,62B,51	Levine, Barry	NJ0550	11,64C,64E,29A
Kroll, Mark	MA1450	11,66H	Levine, Dena	NJ1160	11,66D,66A
Krueger, Timothy	CO0550	11	Levine, Victoria Lindsay	CO0200	11,20E
Kruja, Mira	AL0010	66A,66B,13,11	Leviton, Lawrence	WI0850	11,62C
Krusemark, William	KS1375	36,39,61,54,11	Levitov, Daniel	PA1400	62C,38,42,11
Kubiak, Paul	CA0859	13A,11	Levy, David B.	NC2500	13,11,12A
Kuchar, Evan	IL0600	13,11	Levy, Kenneth	NJ0900	11,12A,12
Kudlawiec, Nancy A.	AL1350	11,32,66A,12A,13	Lewis, Alexandra M.	NY0500	11,12,13C,66D
Kuhn, Michael	AZ0480	29,11,46	Lewis, Andrew	MD0175	11,66A,66C
Kuhn, Stephanie	NC0450	64C,11	Lewis, Daniel	MD0175	11,13,66D,70
Kuhn, William	OR0150	37,11,63C,60,13A	Lewis, Don R.	WI0450	11
Kukec, Catherine	IL1900	11,41,47,50,48	Lewis, Gary	TX1700	11,66D
Kulpa, John	NJ0750	11,13A,13B,13C	Lewis, H. M.	KY0610	10F,11,12A,49,63A
Kunderna, Jerry	CA1560	11	Lewis, Ian	CA2750	11,13A
Kunkle, Kristen C.	PA2000	61,39,11	Lewis, Katherine J.	IL1150	11,62B
Kunzer, Stephen	OK0800	63D,11,29A	Lewis, Nora A.	KS0650	64B,12A,11
Kurokawa, John K.	OH2500	11,34,64C,32F	Lewis, Robert S. T.	SC0500	11,47,64E
Kuykendall, James Brooks	SC0700	13,12,11,41,38	Lewis, Robert J.	KY0300	13B,11,66A,66B,66D
La Manna, Juan F.	NY3770	38,66A,66D,11,39	Lewis, Ryan C.	AR0500	65,32,62A,11
Labe, Thomas A.	OK0150	11,12A,66A,66B	Lewiston, Cal	TX3700	13,47,11
Labonville, Marie E.	IL1150	11,12A,12,20D	L'Hommedieu, Randi L.	MI0400	32,11
Laderman, Michael	NY3100	11,29,12A,14,20D	Li, Lei	IL0650	13A,11,66A,66D
Ladewig, James L.	RI0300	11,12A,12	Li-Bleuel, Linda	SC0400	66C,11,32,12A,66
Laflen, Betty Jo	KS0400	11,13C,32B,37,64	Liaropoulos, Panagiotis	MA2010	66,11
LaGruth, Anthony	NJ0550	11	Libin, Kathryn L.	NY4450	13,11,12A,12
LaGuardia, Frank	CA0550	11	Lidge, Kenneth	MO1810	13,11
Lai, Juliet	MA0510	11,64C	Liebergen, Patrick	WI0855	11,36,61
Laird, Tracey	GA0050	12,14,11,29A	Liebowitz, Marian L.	CA4100	11,41,48,64C,35B
Lalli, Marcus	NY3705	11	Liesch, Barry	CA0350	11,34,31A
Lamb, William	NM0250	13,11,37,47,63	Lim, Benedict M.	CA1020	20C,20D,11,66D

Index by Area of Teaching Interest

Name	Code	Areas
Lim, Mi-Na	TX0345	11,66A,66B
Limb, Christine M.	PA2000	32,11,63
Linahon, Jim	CA1900	11,63A
Lincoln, Harry B.	NY3705	11,12A,12,34
Lindahl, Susan	MI0400	11
Lindekugel, Denise	MD0550	11,13A
Lindenfelser, Kathryn	MN0040	11,20,33
Lindholm, Eric C.	CA3650	13A,60,11,38,41
Lindsay, Julia	MI0250	11,61,54,39
Lindsey, Roberta	IN0907	11,13A,34C,34B,14A
Lington, Victoria	CA4400	11,66D
Link, Dorothea	GA2100	11,12
Linnenbom, Harriett	MD0700	13A,11,66A,66D
Lipman, William	TX0550	12A,64C,64E,11,48
Lipori, Daniel	WA0050	11,64D,12A,12C
Lippoldt-Mack, Valerie	KS0210	11,36,61,32I,52
Lisek, Carol A.	CA3500	11
Liston, Robin	KS0050	32A,32B,12A,11
Litera, Ina	NY0270	11,62
Litteral, Ron	UT0190	11
Littler, William	AG0300	11
Liu, Kexi	MO0800	11,51,62A,62B
Liu, Susan (Shao-Shan)	TX1425	66A,66D,11,34
Llewellyn, Cherrie	CA3000	11,61,54,39
Lloyd, Charles	LA0700	13,39,11,66D
Lloyd, Joe	AZ0400	32C,37,63A,11,60
Lobitz, Beverly	AR0800	13E,11,12A,61,13C
Locke, Brian	IL3500	11,20F,12
Locke, David	MA1900	11,14,20A
Locke, Scott A.	KY0950	64C,11,20
Locklair, Dan	NC2500	13,10,11,31A,66G
Loehrke, John	NJ0975	11,62D,47,29B
Loera, Francisco	TX3525	11,20H
Loewy, Susanna L.	PA1750	11,48,64A
Lofgren, Ronald R.	NE0700	11,32D,36,60A,61
Logan, Cameron	CT0600	11
Lohr, Tom L.	NC1750	11
Lonardo, Tom	TN1380	11,65
London, Lawrence	CA3320	13A,11
Long, Daniel	TX2200	36,61,60,11,13D
Long, Janet	SC0900	62,32B,11,32A,32C
Loos, James C.	IA0420	11,61,66A
Loparits, Elizabeth	NC2440	66C,11
Lopez, Christine Sotomayor	CA0859	36,66A,66D,11,66B
Lopez, Michael	NC0450	11,63C,63D
Lopez-Trujillo, David	TX3515	11,50,65
LoPiccolo, John	ID0100	11
Lorch, Kimberly	GA0500	11,64B
Lordo, Jacqueline L.	MO0100	11,63D
Lorenzetti, Kristen	NJ0700	11,32
Lorenzo, Elizabeth	CT0300	11
Lorenzo, Elizabeth	CT0050	12,11,15,12A
Lott, Peter Tell	AL0010	11,63A
Loubriel, Luis E.	IL0275	11,13A,34,63,35
Lovallo, Lee T.	CA3258	11,34B,67F,12A
Lowe, Carol C.	NY3780	64D,11
Lowi, Ralph	CA4410	12A,11,62D
Lozano, Denise	NY2450	13A,11,64A
Lucas, Ann E.	MA0500	14,11,20,20B,12A
Lucas, Ann D.	CA0100	11,12A,20
Lucas, James A.	IL2150	11
Luchsinger, Brenda	AL0050	11,63B,13A
Lucia, Margaret E.	PA3050	13,11,12,66A
Luck, Kyle	CA3500	37,47,11
Ludwig, Mary	NC0450	11
Lueschen, David	OH0700	63B,63D,49,11
Luffey, Gregory	TX3520	64E,11
Luggie, Brenda	TN1250	36,61,11
Lugo, Edward	FL0930	70,11
Lukowicz, Thomas	OH2500	11,63D,13,13D,13E
Lundak, Gayle	IA0420	11
Lundblad, Genevieve	MD0450	32A,11,33
Lundy, Alexis	GA1070	11
Lupu, Virgil I.	OH2140	62A,41,12A,11,34B
Lyashenko, Natalia E.	IL2250	11
Lynch, Christopher	IN0350	11,12A
Lynch, Kelly	PA0600	39,61,11,12A
Lynch, Timothy	CA1290	13,10,11,14
Lyon, Leslie	TX2200	11,70
Lyons, James H.	MD0350	11,20,32B
Lyons, Lyndel	AL0530	11
Mabary, Judith A.	MO1800	12A,20,11
Macdonald, David	AG0150	11,13A
MacDonald, Laurence E.	MI0450	11,12A,66A,66D
Mach, Elyse J.	IL2150	11,66D,66B
MacInnis, John	IA0500	12,13A,13B,11
Mack-Bervin, Linda	CO0350	11,32D,36,60A
Mackey, Steven	NJ0900	13,10F,10,11,41
MacMorran, Sande	TN1710	11,38,49,63D
MacMullen, Michael J.	FL1470	13A,11,36,61,54
Macomber, Jeffrey R.	MO0800	10,11,12A,32E,63D
MacPherson, William A.	MA2150	11,12,66G,66H
Maddox, Timothy	NC1075	11,13A,13B,13C,13D
Madriguera, Enric	TX0700	62,70,11,12A
Madsen, Charles A.	VT0100	66A,12,11,66C
Maes, James	MA1100	66A,66G,66C,66D,11
Mair, Jim	KS0590	11,47,53,46
Maisonpierre, Elizabeth	NC2435	11,13,66A,66B,66D
Maisonpierre, Jonathan	NC2435	11,66A
Major, Michael	MI0050	11,39,61
Majors, Gayle	KY1425	32,66,11
Maki, Daniel H.	IL0840	13,11,37,64A,66D
Maki, Erik	CA3000	37,11,63,64,65
Makubuya, James	IN1850	13A,13C,11,14,20
Malamut, Myra Lewinter	NJ0550	11,64A,67B,20G,13A
Maldonado, Anna Maria	CA0950	20,11
Malkiewicz, Martha	NY0400	11,64D
Maloney, Patrick H.	IN1700	11,61
Malpede, William V.	CA0835	11,46
Maltese, John	AL0500	11,38,62A
Manchester, John	MS0300	13,34,11
Manduca, Mark W.	ME0500	63C,11
Maness, David	PA1150	13,60,11,36,61
Mangels, Jeffrey W.	MD0550	13A,34C,11,13C,34D
Mangini, Mark	NY2050	13A,13,11,36
Manhart, Grant L.	SD0400	49,63A,63B,11,46
Maniates, Maria R.	AG0450	11,12A,12,12B
Mann, Brian R.	NY4450	11,12A,12,29A
Mann, George	AR0730	11
Mann, Rochelle	CO0350	10,11,32,64
Mannell, David	IN0907	11,61,36,32B
Manning, Dwight C.	NY4200	64,42,32E,11,64B
Marble, Jamie	IL2970	20,11
Marcel, Linda A.	NJ0020	12B,66A,66D,32,11
Marchionni, Raymond	OH2300	66A,11,13
Marciniak, Alex B.	MI0700	13A,37,66A,13,11
Marco, John	WI0840	11,13,64C
Marcus, David	GA0490	10,11,12A,13A,29A
Mardirosian, Haig L.	DC0010	13,10,66G,11
Marenstein, Harry	NY2550	38,11,13A,13B
Margaglione, Louis A.	IL2450	64,13A,13C,11
Mariano, Dennis	NY2500	11
Marissen, Michael	PA3200	11,12A,31
Markiw, Victor R.	CT0700	66,13,12A,66A,11
Marks, Martin	MA1200	11,12A,54
Markuson, Steve H.	NY3765	11,12A,61
Markward, Cheri D.	RI0101	13,11,41,62,12A
Marler, Robert	TN0100	66A,11,12A
Marlow, Laurine	TX2900	11,12A,66G,66A,66H
Maroney, James	PA1100	11,36,61,13C,40
Marquez-Reyes, John D.	PR0115	11
Marschner, Joseph A.	MD0450	11,45,70,34
Marsh, John	GA1150	66D,11
Marshall, Jean V.	KS1400	11
Marshall-McClure, Clara	IN0907	11
Marston, Karen L.	TX2295	37,63C,11,13A,34C
Martin, Andree	GA0550	64A,11,43,12
Martin, Anne L.	CA3000	11,62,38
Martin, Bradley	NC2600	11,66A
Martin, Flora	MD0700	11,36,61
Martin, James	CA4450	13A,13,11
Martin, James	MO1950	11,37,47,63D
Martin, Jennifer	CA1510	32E,11,13,48,63C
Martin, John	KY1550	70,11,34B,34G,41
Martin, Joshua	FL0350	13,11,66A,66D
Martin, Kyle	MA2300	13A,13,11,66,35B
Martin, Margo	CA3200	11,14
Martin, Michael D.	GA0150	11,12A,13C,32,49
Martin, Michelle Denise	GA0150	11,65,66D,60B
Martin, William	NC2600	61,11
Martinez Ortiz, Laura	PR0115	11
Martinez, Kurt	TX3525	11,70,41
Masci, Michael J.	NY3730	11,13A,13B,13C,13D
Mason, Adam	AA0200	13A,11,65
Mason, Alan	FL0050	11,12,31B,66A,66C
Mason, Colin M.	TX2800	47,11,64E,29,48
Massinon, Francis	TN0050	11,63B
Masters, Suzanna	VA1580	64C,11,13A,64E,48
Mathes, Gerard	ID0140	13,11,13J,62A,34
Mathew, Nicholas	CA5000	11,12
Mathews, Peter	FL1950	11,12
Mathieson, Carol Fisher	MO0300	12A,39,61,31A,11
Matsushita, Hidemi	CO0100	66A,11,12,15,13
Matthews, Forrest	SC0710	47,11
Matthews, Robin L.	CA2050	11,35H
Mattison, Travis	IL2970	70,11
Mattison, Travis	IL1500	70,11,13A
Mattix, Daniel J.	IL1850	11
Mattox, Amanda M.	MS0570	64,13,11
Mattson, Sheri	MO1790	11,64B,64D
Maturani, Marilyn Muns	KY0550	11
Mautner, Roselida	FL0200	40,61,11
Maxedon, Lisa M.	LA0250	61,11,39
Maxwell, Steven	KS0650	63D,11,41
May, Eldonna	MI2200	11,12
May, Juliana	CT0450	11,13
Maye, Shelia J.	VA0500	11,61,32
Mayes, Kathleen	NJ1050	11
Mayfield, Farren	OK0550	11,66D
Mayse, Susie	CA3800	11
McAllister, Michael	NC1750	13,10F,60,11,47
McBain, Jeremy	IL0800	11
McBain, Katherine C.	IL0800	63B,41,11
McBee, Karen L.	TX0125	12A,11,66A,66C,66D
McBroom, Deanna H.	SC0500	11,61
McCabe, Brent Poe	MT0450	37,11,32E,70
McCaffrey, Maureen	TN1400	11,61,32D,60A
McCann, Jesse S.	OR0800	70,13A,11
McCann, John	MA1900	13A,11,37
McCann, William J.	NY3760	13A,13B,11
McCargar, Barbara Witham	MI0300	11,61,39
McCarrey, Scott	HI0050	66A,66B,13E,12A,11
McCarthy, Keri E.	WA1150	64B,12A,13,11,12C
McCartney, Lynn R.	NH0300	61,11
McCarty, Patrick	MO0050	11,32E,37,65,50
McClary, Michael	GA0940	11,37,47,63
McCleery, Mark	LA0770	11,41,62C,62D
McCloskey, Kathleen	PA0650	11,12A,13A,66D
McCollum, Jonathan	MD1100	63C,63D,11,12,20
McConnell, Miles	IA0250	11,70
McConnell, Roger	IN0150	11
McCord, Larry	TX0910	11,13B,14C,34B,66A
McCoy, Pamela	TN1400	11
McCready, Matthew A.	MO0550	11,12A,63,13A,20
McCullough, Michael	CA0200	13A,11
McDermid, Aaron	ND0150	36,60A,61,11,32
McDermott, Sheila	LA0080	11,13,61,66D
McDonald, Timothy L.	MO1010	11,12A,36,20G
McEuen, Christopher	PA2150	11,63C,63D
McFarland, James	TX3600	11,13,66D,66G
McFarland, Kay Dawn	KY1425	11,66A,66C,66D
McFarland, Timothy	MA2010	13,11,66A
McGahan, Christopher	MA2030	11,13A,36
McGhee, Michael	GA2200	13,11,12A,66G,66H
McGinnis, Beth	AL0800	66D,11,12A
McGowan, James	AG0200	10,11
McGowan, Mike	TX2000	11,37,49,13,29
McGrann, Jeremiah	MA0330	11,12,20G
McGregor, Cynthia	CA4850	13,11,34
McGrew, David	PA0150	10,13,66,31A,11
McGuire, John	CO0250	63B,11
McGuire, K. Christian	MN0050	11,47
McIntosh, Jim	NV0050	11
McKamie, Shirley	MO1780	11,66D,66H
McKeage, Kathleen M.	WY0200	11,62D,13C,32
McKeithen, Steven	LA0550	11,32,37
McKellip, Hope	MS0580	11,66
McKenna, Fr. Edward	IN0005	10,62A,16,31A,11
McKenzie-Stubbs, Mary E.	NJ0700	61,11
McKinney, Kevin	GA1900	13A,10F,11
McLean, Greg	GA0940	13,11,29,10
McManus, James M.	CA3320	13,45,29A,12A,11
McMillan, Bart	TX1775	11
McMurray, William	MO0850	12A,11
McNair, Linda	MO0550	62A,11
McNeela, Rico	MO0850	38,11,62A,62B,60
McPherson, Eve	OH1100	11,20
McQueen, William F.	TX2100	11,20A,49,63A
McTyre, Robert A.	GA1400	11,13,61
McVey, Elyse Nicole	TN1100	11
McWilliams, Heather	WI0830	32,11,63D
Meacham, Helen M.	PA2000	66A,66C,11,13A
Meade, Karen	MO0500	32,11,66A,66G
Means, Matthew L.	KS0350	11,62A,62B,41,42
Measels, Clark	TN0250	11,31A,20
Mecham, Jessica	ID0060	11,20

Name	Code	Areas
Meckler, David C.	CA0855	11,20,12A,10,13A
Meder, Randall A.	WI0808	60,11,36,40,32D
Medley, Susan	PA3580	36,60A,40,11,13A
Medwin, Marc	DC0010	11,29,12,20
Meehan, Jill	PA3680	11,12A,13A
Meggison, Shelly	AL1170	64B,11
Meier, Margaret	CA3200	13A,11,66D
Meier, Steven	GA1500	11,12A,29
Meinhart, Michelle	OH2550	11
Meixner, Brian	PA3100	12A,63C,49,11
Melago, Kathleen A.	PA3100	32B,11,66D
Melkonyan, Magdalina	MD0700	66A,11
Mello, Christopher	CA1750	11,70
Meltzer, Howard S.	NY0270	11,13,12,66A,63
Mendoza, Cristina	LA0450	63,46,49,11,41
Menendez Abovici, Natalia E.	PR0115	11
Merriman, John C.	AL0500	11,49,63A,70
Mertens, Michael	CA2750	13B,11,63,64,37
Messing, Scott	MI0150	11,12A,66A,16,13A
Metcalf, John C.	PA1750	34,10,11,49,63C
Metzler, James	MI0900	11,36
Meyer, Jeffrey	MN0600	12A,13,11,14,20
Meyer, Kenneth	NY1550	11,70,41
Meyers, Angela	CT0300	66A,11
Michael, Louis	IL1500	29,66A,13,11,34A
Michel, John	WA0050	11,41,51,62C
Mickey, Patricia A.	MO1780	63B,11,13D
Mickey, Sarah	AR0600	37,48,64C,11
Middagh, Ryan	TN1100	11,47
Middleton, R. Hugh	NC0500	11,66A,66C
Middleton, Robert M.	NJ0050	47,29,64,13,11
Midgley, Herbert	TX2700	11,70,34,45
Mikalunas, Robin	TX3540	11,13A
Miles, Charles F.	MS0700	11
Milewski, Barbara Ann	PA3200	11,12
Milham, Edwin M.	MA0510	11,61
Millar, Robert R.	CA4625	13A,13,11,12A,66
Miller, Allan	CA6050	11,12,37,47,63
Miller, Ben F.	WV0400	11,50,65,35A,37
Miller, Eric	TX2800	11
Miller, Everett F.	KS0225	11,36,34,70,20
Miller, Joan	MN1300	20D,11,32B
Miller, Josh	WV0200	36,61,32D,11,60A
Miller, Karla	MN1260	13A,11,36,61,66A
Miller, Leta	CA5070	11,12A,12,64A,67E
Miller, Paul W.	PA2740	10A,11,13A,29A,29B
Miller, Peter	IN1025	61,11
Miller, Stephen R.	TN1800	11,12A,12,14
Miller, Tess Anissa	MI0150	64A,11,41
Miller, Thomas A.	OR1150	60A,11,36,61,31A
Miller, Wendy L.	PA0250	11,12A,36,61,54
Millcan, Brady	MA0800	13,11,12A,66A,66C
Millican, Jason	TX1250	13A,60,11,36,31A
Mills, Robert P.	VA0650	11,13B,13C
Milstein, Amir	MA0510	11,20H
Milton, Kenneth	MS0560	11,47,49,63A,63B
Minard, Juliet	IL0300	11
Minasian, Linda	CA5400	11,66D,66A
Minasian, Mark	HI0160	11,12A,29,34,35
Mindell, Pamela Getnick	MA0700	11,36,40
Minor, Ryan	NY3790	12A,12D,12B,11,13E
Miranda, Charles	IA0420	11,62A,62B
Miranda, Charles	IA0650	62A,62B,11
Miranda, Michael A.	CA2800	11,67G,70,12A,41
Misenheimer, Aaron L.	NC0850	32E,34,11,63,49
Miskell, Jerome P.	OH2290	34,62B,13A,11
Mitchell, Adrian	MS0350	11,63A,37,32C,49
Mitchell, Alice L.	NY3705	11,12,13A
Mitchell, Andrew	AG0200	11
Mitchell, Bryan P.	MS0570	11,37,46,65,50
Mitchell, Dan	CA1550	11,34
Mitchell, Ian	AZ0150	11
Mitchell, Jennifer	GA1150	13B,13C,11,10
Mitchell, Linda	CA2440	36,60A,11,12A,13A
Mitchell, Michael A.	MI1750	60A,36,11
Mixon, John	MS0575	37,11,63
Mizicko, Shane J.	MO1500	11,50,65A,65B,65
Mocny, Timothy S.	MI0400	11
Moder, Jennifer	KS0590	11,13A
Moege, Gary R.	MO1790	11,63B,70,71,12A
Moegle, Mary Steele A.	LA0250	11,66A,66C,66D
Mohar, Barbara	NY2105	11
Mohen, Gerald	NY2400	13,11
Mojica, Andres	PR0150	11,66G
Molloy, Steve	MO0850	63A,11
Monical, Dwight	IN1300	13,11
Monllos, John	RI0300	11,29A,70
Monroe, Marc	KY0600	11
Monroe, Martha Frances	MS0570	11
Montague, Matthew G.	KS1050	32,36,60A,11
Montford, Kimberlyn	TX3350	11,12A,12
Montgomery, Kip	NY3250	11,12,13,64C
Montgomery, Vivian	OH2200	11,12A,55,66H,67F
Moody, Kevin M.	TX0075	54,61,11,36,40
Moon, Brian A.	AZ0500	11
Moon, Hosun	NY1275	11,66,13B,32D,36
Moore, Albert L.	MN1300	49,63B,63A,11
Moore, Carol A.	WI0200	11,32B
Moore, Christine	AL0050	11,32B
Moore, David A.	OK1450	10,13,11,36
Moore, Edgar	TX2300	11,36,61,12A
Moore, Edward	NY3720	20G,36,66A,11,29A
Moore, James H.	WV0800	37,47,29A,11
Moore, John	TX2200	11,66A,66C,12A,66D
Moore, Kevin	AL0890	11,31
Moore, Rick	AZ0200	13,11,37,46,49
Moore, Vicki	CA0270	12A,11
Moore-Mitchell, Teresa A.	NC2700	11,61
Moore-Mitchell, Teresa	NC1150	61,11
Moorman, Joyce Solomon	NY2100	13,10,11,66A,66D
Moorman, Joyce E.	NY0270	11,13,20A,34D,66
Moorman, Wilson	NY0270	11,20,65,29
Morales, David	CA2910	13A,11,36,61,66
Morden, James	GA2000	13,11,12A,63A
Moreau, Barton	ID0050	13,11,66C,66D,66A
Morehouse, Katherine	GA1150	11,20
Moreland, Irina	CO0830	66A,11,12A
Morelock, Donald	MI1900	13,11,12A,66A,66B
Moresi, Matthew S.	MI0650	11,46,66
Morey, Carl	AG0450	11,12A,12,20G
Morgan, Carol	TX2300	63A,29,13B,11
Morgan, Philip	NC2500	37,47,50,11
Mori, Akira	IA0550	38,51,11
Morningstar, Timothy P.	NY3775	61,11
Moroney, Davitt	CA5000	11,12,55B,56
Morreale, Michael	NY0644	11,63A,29A,47,13A
Morris, Gerard	WA1000	37,60B,11
Morris, Gregory	MO0400	11,66A,66B,13
Morris, James R.	NY3700	13A,63A,13,11,49
Morrison, Linda	KY1460	11,32,36,66A,66G
Morrison, Mable R.	DE0050	11,12A,66A,66D
Morrison, Mandy	TX1600	11
Morrison, Simon	NJ0900	13,12A,12,11
Morrow, David E.	GA1450	60,11,36,61,66A
Morrow, Elizabeth N.	TX3500	62C,51,11
Morrow, Jo L.	LA0650	11,66D
Morrow, Lance	TN0050	11
Morrow, Michael	TX2955	63B,63D,11
Mosenbichler-Bryant, Verena	NC0600	37,11
Moses, Dee	FL2000	11,62D
Moses, Oral	GA1150	11,36,61
Moshier, Steve	CA3750	13,11,12A,34,43
Moskowitz, David V.	SD0600	12A,20H,14C,12C,11
Moss, Frances	AL0330	11
Moss, Kirk D.	WI0350	11,32E,38,51,62
Moss, Myron D.	PA1000	10,11,29,37,60
Moss, Patricia J.	AL0650	12A,11
Mosteller, Paul W.	AL1150	61,11
Mouffe, Jerome	MA0510	70,11
Moulton, Elizabeth	NJ0700	11
Moulton, Paul F.	ID0070	11,12A,32,14
Mount, Lorna	HI0120	13A,11,12A,70,36
Moxley, Lisa	VA0050	66A,66D,31A,13A,11
Mroziak, Jordan	PA1050	11
Mruzek, David M.	IN0650	11,37,38,47
Muchnick, Amy Faye	MO0775	11,12A,62B,41
Muehlenbeck Pfotenhauer, Thomas R.	MN1600	63A,47,29,11,11
Mueller, Charlotte G.	TX1450	13,11,66A,66D
Mueller, Paul F.	NY0625	10F,60,11,12A,36
Mukuna, Kazadi Wa	OH1100	14,20A,20B,11
Mulder, Erin	GA1070	11
Mulford, Ruth Stomne	DE0175	13,11,12A,62A,20G
Mulholland, James Q.	IN0250	11,61
Mullenax, Gary	WV0550	66A,11,66D
Muller, David J.	CA6000	10F,11,12A,60B,64D
Muller, Gerald	TX2170	13,11,12A,32,36
Mullins, Steve	CO0400	70,11
Mundy, John	MN1700	13A,11
Munoz, Nelida	PR0150	11,13A,13C,44
Munson, Paul A.	PA1450	12A,11
Murasugi, Sachiho	MD0800	62A,62B,11,13A,51
Murawski, Marianne	NJ0990	14,11,20
Muresan, Branden A.	CA2100	11,62A
Murray, David	IN0250	62D,11
Murray, Kris A.	IL2730	36,70,11,51
Murray, Monica	MN0610	11,13A,61
Murray, Renardo	MS0350	37,11,32C,49,63D
Musgrove, Abby R.	IL1100	36,40,11,32C,32D
Musial, Robert A.	NY3450	13A,11,12A,36,66A
Myers, Gerald C.	MO1120	11,36,40,54,13
Myers, Jeff	MS0320	11,66,13
Myers, Patricia Ann	NY1550	11,12,14,66H,20
Myers, Patricia	GA0250	12A,61,11
Myers-Tegeder, Christine	NJ0550	11,60
Myintoo, Sylvia C.	IL2150	62A,11
Nabb, David	NE0590	64,11,12A,48
Nachef, Joanna	CA1750	60,11,36,61
Naegele, Elizabeth M.	IL1850	13A,13,66A,66G,11
Nafziger, Kenneth J.	VA0300	60,36,31A,38,11
Nagatani, Chie	CA1700	66A,13,11
Nagel, Rebecca S.	SC1110	11,64B,41
Nash, Robert	LA0650	62D,11
Nathanson, Robert	NC2440	70,11,13A
Nauman, Sharon	OH2150	11
Navari, Jude Joseph	CA4625	10,11,13,36,61
Near, John R.	IL2400	11,12A,12C,66G
Neeley, Henrietta	IL1085	62A,11,42,62B
Neff, Lyle	DE0150	11
Neff, Teresa M.	MA1200	13,11
Neidlinger, Robert D.	OH2150	11
Neisler, Joseph	IL1150	11,63B
Nelms, Morris H.	TX3175	11
Nelsen, Jack	ID0075	11,32B
Nelson, Jocelyn C.	NC0650	70,12A,67H,11
Nelson, Jon	CA4460	12A,11
Nelson, Margaret	WI0855	11,32A,32B
Nemeth, Rudolph	TN1250	66A,11
Nemko, Deborah G.	MA0510	66A,66C,66D,11
Ness, David J.	IL0650	70,11,13
Ness, Marjorie S.	MA0930	11,20,32,36,66G
Neuharth, Randall	NE0460	11,37,47,63
Newell, Meri	MS0360	11,32,64,37,48
Newlin, Georgia A.	NY0050	11,12A,13C,32,36
Newman, Miranda	TX1510	11,61
Newton, Barry	CA5360	62D,11
Newton, Gregory	CA1960	70,13A,11
Newton, Gregory	CA2600	70,11
Nguyen, Quynh	NY0625	11,66A
Nichols, Alan	TN0260	66A,13A,11
Nichols, Edward	MD0800	65A,65B,11,34A,34B
Nichols, Lois J.	CA4600	66,32,44,67B,11
Nichols, Sandra	IL1612	11,32E,66A
Nickens, Michael W.	VA0450	37,13C,11
Niebur, Louis	NV0100	12,20,14,11
Nielsen, Robert	CA1850	10,11
Nieuwenhuis, Bruce	MI0450	11
Nieuwenhuis, Mary	MI0450	13A,11,36,61
Nigro, Christie	MA2300	13A,11,12A,36,62A
Nilsson, Donna	GA0525	11,32
Niren, Ann Glazer	IN1010	11,12A
Nishibun, Tiffany	AL0345	11,61
Nisnevich, Anna V.	PA3420	11,12A
Nissen, James C.	MI2110	11,12A
Nisula, David	MI1850	11,55,67
Nitschke, Brad	IN0005	11,12,13,60,63
Nivans, David	CA2050	11,13A,20,29A
Nivans, David	CA0805	14C,29A,20,13,11
Noble, Jason L.	NJ0700	11
Noble, Karen	WA0250	11
Noel, John M.	NC1800	11
Nolan, Denise G.	NH0110	48,64A,11,13C
Noonan, Timothy	WI0825	12A,12,11
Noone, Elizabeth	MA0150	66A,66D,11,13A,20B
Noone, Michael J.	MA0330	11,12,31
Noonkester, Lila D.	SC0800	13,39,61,11
Norberg, Rebecca	MN1250	61,54,12A,11
Nordstrom, Erland	NJ1400	32E,11
Noriega, Scott	NY0625	11
Norman, John L.	CA1270	11,13A
Norris, Elizabeth	VT0300	11,13A,20,61,36
Norris, Philip E.	MN1280	10F,11,32E,63A,31A
Norton, John	IL1890	64C,11
Norton, Michael	VA0600	11
Notareschi, Loretta K.	CO0650	10,11,13
Novak, Christina D.	AZ0490	11,13,66A,10A,66D
Nowak, Robert A.	PA1900	11,65,29

Index by Area of Teaching Interest

Name	Code	Areas
Nuccio, David A.	IL1250	11,29A,34,54,66A
Nuccio, David	IL2650	11
Nuss, Patricia	GA1400	11
Nye, Randall	TX0700	70,11
Oakley, Paul E.	NC0350	36,40,61,11
Oberle, Curtis P.	MO1000	11,70
O'Connor, Margaret	NJ1400	11,32
O'Connor, Michael B.	FL1450	12A,11,20,55
Octave, Thomas	PA2950	61,36,39,40,11
O'Dell, Debra	ID0140	66A,66C,11,66D,12A
Odello, Denise	MN1620	11,12,64B,14,20
Odom, David H.	AL0200	64C,11
Odom, Donald R.	MS0850	36,13C,11,32D,60A
Odom, Lisa Sain	SC0400	11,61,36
Oelschlaeger-Fischer, Curtis	IL0300	11
Offard, Felton	IL0600	13A,11,47,70,29A
Ogletree, Mary	PA1750	13,11,62A,62B,51
Oh, Annette	IL1090	11,61,36,13B,13C
Oh, Yoojin	NY0644	11,42,66
Olan, David M.	NY0250	13,10,11
Oldham, Ryan P.	MO1810	11
O'Leary, Jed	NE0700	11
Oleskiewicz, Mary	MA2010	11,12A,12,14B,64A
Olin, Elinor	IL2000	11,12A,12,64A
Olinyk, George Yuri	CA0150	11,66A,13A
Oliver, Brenda	NH0300	11,32
Oliver, Murray	CO0250	11
Oliveros, Pauline	NY3300	12,13,10B,11
Olsen, Lance	NJ0990	13A,13,11,34
Olson, Anthony	MO0950	11,66A,66G,66D
Olson, Jennifer	CA3500	11
Olthafer, Rebecca	IL2100	11
Onalbayeva, Kadisha	FL1500	11,66
Onderdonk, Julian	PA3600	11,12A
O'Neal, Melinda P.	NH0100	60,11,36
O'Neal, Thomas	MO1800	11
O'Neil, Lorne W.	TX3525	11,41,48,64
O'Neill, Jill L.	SC1200	11,64A,48,14C,41
Ongaro, Giulio M.	CA5350	11,12
Oppelt, Maren	ID0075	11
Ordaz, Joseph	CA2975	11,66A,66D,38
Orenstein, Arbie	NY0642	13A,13,11,12A
Organ, Wayne	CA1450	11,13A,13B,13C,34
Orr, Gerald	TX1250	13,11,36,37,66A
Orr, Sue Butler	SC0710	11,36,61
Ortiguera, Joseph	AL1200	11,12A,13B
Orzolek, Douglas	MN1625	11,32,37,60
Osborne, Michelle M.	NY2950	13A,11
Osowski, Kenneth	PA3710	11,66A,66B
Osteen, Kim	AZ0200	11
Osten, Mark	CA4460	11
Otal, Monica D.	MD0175	36,61,11
Otto, Steven	AG0650	11,14,13L
Overly, Paul	SC0200	11,12,32,63C,63D
Owen, John Edward	AR0110	60,11,63D
Owen, Kenneth L.	WA0750	11,61,36,66A,13A
Owens, Janet	FL1450	66D,13,11
Owens, Jeremy	IA0100	11,12A,66
Owens, Margaret B.	VA0450	11,12A,64
Owens, Robert	NC0800	11,66D,66G
Owens, Rose Mary	MO0775	11
Owens, Theodore	NV0125	10,11,12A,61,54
Owens, Thomas C.	VA0450	11,12
Owren, Betty Ann	CA1760	36,61,13C,13A,11
Oxler, Cora Jean	TX3370	61,11,13C
Padgham Albrecht, Carol	ID0250	11,12A,64B,32E,41
Page, Gordon	TX1725	11,13,36
Paick, Yoomi	TN1450	11,13C,66C
Paige-Green, Jacqueline	LA0700	61,39,11
Paise, Michele	TN1100	11
Palecek, Brian	ND0400	11
Palmer, Bradley E.	GA0550	63C,11,34,32F,41
Palmier, Darice	IL2970	66A,66D,11,13A,66C
Palmquist, Jane E.	NY0500	32,11
Pane, Steven	ME0410	12A,66A,12,12B,11
Pang, Wilma C.	CA1020	66D,11,13A
Paoli, Kenneth N.	IL0630	13,10,11,35,34
Pape, Louis W.	SD0150	13,10,11,32,66
Papillon, Andre	AI0190	11,41,64A
Pappas, J.	MO0550	65,11,34
Pappas, Joan H.	WV0400	11
Para, Christopher	PA0350	13,11,38,62A,62B
Parakilas, James P.	ME0150	13,11,42,12
Parcell, John	OH2120	13,66A,11,29,34C
Park, Clara	GA0250	66A,11
Park, In-Sook	AL1160	11
Park-Song, Sophia	CO0830	11,13,66A
Parker, Clinton R.	NC0050	11,61
Parker, Grant	CA1500	13,11,12A,49,37
Parker, Linda	NC0200	11,32,44,13,64
Parker, Mara	PA3680	12A,11,41,51,62C
Parker, Mary Ann	AG0450	11,12A,12
Parker, Nancy	MN0610	11,20,32D
Parker, Patricia G.	AL0500	11,66A,66D
Parker, Salli	CA2440	66A,13A,11
Parker, Val	GA0490	10,11,13A,34D,29A
Parker, Wesley	AR0250	65,11,20,37
Parkhurst, Raymond	IL2350	11
Parmer, Dillon	AG0400	11,12,12B,12C
Parnell, Dennis	CA2700	11,36,61
Parnell, Scott	OH0250	11,70,13
Parr, Sean M.	PA0950	12A,55,11
Parr, Sharon M.	IN1650	11,66A,66D,12A
Parran, John D.	NY0270	11,13,20,29,64
Parrini, Fabio	SC0950	66A,66D,11,66C
Parrish, Eric	MN1175	11,13,36,61
Parrish, Susan K.	CA0400	11
Parsche, Paula	FL0800	13,66A,66C,11
Parsons, Laura E.	AL0950	63A,63,12A,13A,11
Partain, Gregory L.	KY1350	11,41,66A,66B,12A
Parton-Stanard, Susan	IL1500	61,40,36,11,32D
Party, Daniel	IN1450	14C,12A,11,20H
Paschal, Brett E. E.	OR0400	65,13,11
Pasler, Jann C.	CA5050	11,12A,12,12B,12E
Pasqua, Ferdinand A.	CT0250	11
Pastorello, Cristian	IL0150	66A,66B,66C,11,13
Patman, Rebecca	NM0200	11,66A
Patterson, Anne L.	WV0300	11,12A,32A
Patterson, David N.	MA2010	13,10,11,20G,34
Patterson, Thomas	WI0960	29A,36,11,63C
Pattila, Michael	MS0500	11
Pattishall, Teresa	FL1700	11,37
Paul, Randall S.	OH2500	64C,29,48,11
Pauley, John-Bede	MN0350	61,13,11
Paull, Eric	TN0050	11
Pauly, Elizabeth	MN1050	61,60A,11,36,13A
Pawlak, Keith V.	AZ0500	11,16
Pawlicki, Michael	CA2700	11,66A,66D
Payne, Benjamin	FL0670	11,34,13,66A,66D
Payne, James	NE0590	11,63A,63B,46,35A
Payton, Chad	MS0250	11,13C,61
Peacock, Curtis	WA0050	11,49,63D
Pearson, Holly	NJ0700	11
Pecherek, Michael J.	IL1175	13,60,11,38,62C
Pedersen, Keith	CA3640	36,11,60A
Peeples, Terrance P.	IL1520	65,14C,11,50
Peffley, Lynette	OH0100	32A,11,66D
Pelischek, Jeff	KS0550	11,37,48,64C,64E
Pellay-Walker, Michelle T.	TN1380	11
Pellegrino, Larry	NV0050	11
Pelo, Mika	CA5010	10,11,13,43
Peloza, Cavid	CA5400	62,11,13A,66D
Pena, Melissa	OR1050	64B,11
Pender, Charles	TN1380	13,11,61,66A,60
Pendowski, Michael	AL0200	64E,46,47,11
Penner, Julie	TN1350	11,61
Penniman, G. Victor	MO1010	55,12A,62,11,36
Peplin, Steve W.	WI0450	10A,11,13B,47,70
Perconti, William J.	ID0130	13,11,47,64
Perera, Selina	CA3500	11,20,14C
Peretz, Marc	MI1850	11,32,66D,34
Perez, Miguel	MA0510	11,62A,51
Perez, Samuel	PR0150	11,66A
Perkins, Andrew	NC0450	10A,13A,20G,46,11
Perkins, Leeman L.	NY0750	11,12,31A,36
Perna, Dana	NY3000	11,35
Perone, James E.	OH2290	11,13,12E,64C
Perry, David	WI0815	11,62A
Peterman, Lewis E.	CA4100	14A,41,55,11
Peters, Gretchen	WI0803	11,12A,14
Peters, Mark	IL3100	11,20,13E,12
Petersen, Alice V. Neff	OH2300	55,67,11
Petersen, Lynn	MT0075	10A,11,13A,66A,47
Peterson, Douglas	NV0050	11
Peterson, Douglas A.	FL0400	11,37,38,64C
Peterson, Jon C.	OH0250	36,12A,44,11,54
Peterson, Kirsten	CT0450	11
Peterson, Larry	IL0100	66A,66C,11
Peterson, Laura	NY3475	11,12A,66A,20
Peterson, Vince	NY0500	36,60A,32D,13,11
Peterson, William J.	CA3650	11,12A,66G,66H
Petillot, Aurelien	IL2900	62B,62A,42,11,12A
Pettaway, Charles H.	PA2000	13,11,12A,66,66G
Petters, Robert B.	NC1700	60,11
Petzet, John M.	LA0200	11,36
Pfaltzgraff, Philip	NE0700	66C,11,42,12A
Pfeiffer, Karen	OH2000	64B,11
Pfutzenreuter, Leslie D.	CA2840	11,36,38,39,61
Pherigo, Johnny L.	FL1800	11,41,49,48,63B
Phifer, Larry	IL2500	11
Philipsen, Michael D.	IA0750	13,11,36,61,66A
Phillips, Gerald	MD0850	11,61
Phillips, Katrina	AL0050	11,64C
Phillips, Katrina R.	AL0050	11,12A,64E
Phillips, Sheila A.	MO0950	36,11
Phillipus, Donna	AL0500	11
Phoenix-Neal, Diane	IA0200	62,11,12,51
Pickering, Matthew	MS0360	63,37,11,49,60B
Pickett, John	WA0050	13,11,12A,66A,66B
Pierce, Michael	LA0720	37,41,64A,11
Pierson, Steve	IL3550	63,11
Pigg, Dewayne	TN1100	11
Pike, Lisa	NJ0700	63B,11
Pilkington, Jonathan	GA1650	61,39,11
Piltz, Hans-Karl	AB0100	11,62
Pilzer, Joshua	NY0750	11,14,20C
Pimentel, Bret R.	MS0250	64,29,64B,11,64C
Pinckney, Warren R.	CA0800	11,20G,29A,13
Pinson, Donald L.	TX0550	11,13A,63C,63D,49
Pisani, Michael	NY4450	11,12A,12,20G
Pisano, Kristin	KS0350	11,64C,64E,12A,14C
Pitt-Kaye, Melinda	IL1610	61,11
Pittman, Daniel	GA0950	11
Pituch, David A.	IL0750	64E,11,12A
Platoff, John	CT0500	13,11,14C,12,12F
Platt, Heather	IN0150	11,12,12A
Plum, Sarah A.	IA0550	62A,62B,11,42
Podgurski, Barbara	NY5000	66A,11
Poff, Megan	AL1160	61,11
Pohly, Linda L.	IN0150	11,12,14,12A
Polk, Ben	KY1550	11
Polk, Keith	NH0350	11,12A,12C,63B
Pollard, Shawn	AZ0150	13A,37,11,63D
Polman, Bert	MI0350	31,11,20
Pomerantz, James	CA0050	13A,11,12A
Ponce, Adriana	IL1200	12A,11,20
Ponce, Julie	IL0650	11
Pool, Scott	TX3500	64D,13,48,11,64E
Poole, Elissa	AB0150	11
Pope, Jerry	KS0590	13,66A,11
Porter, Charles	NY2700	13A,11,12A,66D,29A
Porter, Charles	NY2400	13A,13,10,11,12A
Porter, Judith	NC0860	11,20G
Porterfield-Pyatt, Chaumonde	CA1290	11,66A,66G,66D
Posch, Carl	AZ0150	13,11,37,47,63D
Poss, Nicholas	OH0100	11,20
Poteet, Sherry	TX1350	61,11
Potes, Cesar I.	MI1200	13,10,11,34
Potratz, Robert C.	MN1030	11,12A,66G,13A
Pound, Robert	PA0950	13,10,11,38
Powe, Holly	AL0330	61,13,11,60,47
Powell, Daniel	FL0350	11,13,47,63,64
Powell, John S.	OK1450	11,12A,12,20
Powers, Ollie	CA5360	35G,35C,11,12A,34
Poythress, Christine	TN1100	11
Pratt, Dennis H.	RI0101	29A,11,13A
Prescott, Steve C.	IN1400	32E,11,60B,64,37
Price, Jeffrey	MI2120	64E,11
Price, Thomas A.	TN1100	11
Price-Brenner, Kevin	WI0840	11,38
Price-Brenner, Paul Alan	WI0840	11,62A,62B,34
Priest, Thomas L.	UT0350	32,64D,11
Primatic, Stephen P.	GA0200	65,13,29,11,47
Procopio, Mary J.	MI0450	11,20,37,64
Pugh, Joel	ND0500	63C,63D,11
Puller, Shawn I.	GA0150	11,61,12A,32A,39
Puls, Cyndi	OH1400	11,62C,62D
Puls, David	OH1400	11,62B
Purciello, Maria Anne	PA3600	11,12A
Purnell, Tom F.	IL0650	11,66A
Pursell, William	TN0100	10,12A,13,11,66G
Purslow, Vicki T.	OR0950	11,37,64E,29
Putnam, Fay	OR0500	11
Pyle, Daniel S.	GA0500	11,66G
Pyle, Jane	FL1300	13,11,12A,66A,66B
Quant, Scott	OK0850	11,32,61

Name	Code	Areas
Quantz, Michael	TX3515	11,41,62,20H
Quesada, Milagros	OH1100	11,32,36
Quick, Julia M.	SC1050	11,38,41,51,62A
Quinn, Kelly	MO1120	11
Rabe, Gigi 'Gee'	CA0835	11,50
Raboy, Asher	CA3400	37,13D,10F,13E,11
Rachor, David J.	IA1600	11,64D,64E,72
Rackipov, Errol	FL0700	29A,65B,11
Rackley, David	CA0100	11
Rackley, David	CA1510	11,13
Rada, Raphael	TX0550	61,11,13C,32B,36
Rader, Jana Elam	TX2310	11,12A,34C,61
Radomski, James V.	CA0845	11,12A,12,14
Raessler, Daniel	VA1125	11,12,13B,13F,13A
Raevens, Jean M.	PA1050	13,11,12
Rafal, Jeremy	NJ0050	11,20
Ragsdale, C. David	AL1160	37,60,11,64E
Raickovich, Milos	NY0644	11,13A,20
Raimo, John B.	TX3525	11,12A,66A,66C,66D
Raines, Jean	NC1900	12A,11,66A,32
Raines, Scott	TX0150	39,61,11
Raisor, Steve C.	NC0500	11,13,37,47,70
Ramo, Suzanne D.	TX1425	61,11,36
Ramsey, Laura	GA0250	11,64D
Rancier, Megan M.	OH0300	14,11
Randall, Annie Janeiro	PA0350	11,12A,12,12E
Randall, James	MT0400	12,14,20,11
Randolph, Anthony W.	DC0150	10C,11
Rankin, John M.	TX2200	11,47,63A,46
Ransom, Adriana LaRosa	IL1150	11,62C
Rapoport, Paul	AG0200	13,11,12A,12
Rash, Daniel R.	SC0400	11,60A,54
Rasmussen, Brenda	WA0550	11,31A,36,13A
Ratelle, Dan	CA4050	11,12A
Ratliff, Phillip W.	AL1150	11
Raval, Shanti	NY0270	64C,11,20
Rawley, Joseph	TX2310	11
Rawls, J. Archie	MS0580	13,11,64,46,48
Ray, Mary Ruth	MA0500	41,62B,11
Ray, W. Irwin	GA1550	60,11,41,36,40
Rayapati, Sangeetha	IL0100	11,61
Raychev, Evgeni	TX2700	62C,41,11,62D
Reagan, Ann B.	CO0750	11,12A,12,41,66A
Real-D'Arbelles, Giselle	FL0200	11
Reams, John D.	GA0200	64C,11
Reams, Lisa	GA0200	11
Redding, Eric	AK0050	11,36,66A,70,53
Redfern, Nancy	MI1600	66,11,66D,66B,66G
Redfield, Clayborn	CA0840	11,32E,37
Rediger, JoAnn K.	IN1560	36,31A,60A,11,40
Redmond, Michael	IN0907	11
Reed, James	FL0570	11
Reed, Jane	OH0100	11,13A,62A,66D,62B
Reed-Lunn, Rebecca	KY1550	62B,11
Reese, Donald T.	PA1830	11,12A,70,13A,14C
Reese, Jodi	KS0265	36,11,13C,61,60A
Reeves, Bethany	NY0270	11,36,39,60A,61
Reeves, M. Bryan	AL0050	37,32E,11,49,60
Regnier, Marc	SC0500	11,70
Rehberg, Jeanette	ND0050	11,64,42
Reid, James	ID0250	11,41,70
Reid, John	TX2350	11,10D,35B,62D
Reid, Susanne M.	CA5355	11,12A,20,31A
Reid, Todd	CO0830	11,20,29,65
Reifsnyder, Robert	IL1890	11
Reighard, Mark	OK1200	13A,13,66A,11
Reigler, Susan	IN1010	11
Reimer, David	MI0350	11,32E,42,62A,41
Reisch, Carla	CA2390	11,14,34
Renander, Cindy	WA0960	64C,11
Rene, Benjamin	AI0190	11
Renfroe, Dennis C.	NC1025	11,12A,32,36,63
Renninger, Laura Ann	WV0550	11,12A,12F,14
Renter, David	MI0900	11,13,29
Repass, Deidre	TN0050	11
Reul, Barbara M.	AJ0100	11,12A,12C,12D
Reynerson, Rodney T.	NC0050	66A,66C,66D,11,41
Reynolds, Anne-Marie	NY3730	11,12A,12
Reynolds, Christopher A.	CA5010	12,11
Reynolds, Robert	KY0860	13A,13,11,66A,20G
Rhein, Robert	IN0200	10A,66A,11,12A,13
Rhinehart, James	IN0150	11
Rhoades, Vanessa	OK0500	61,11
Rhoads, Mark	MN0250	11,32,31A
Rhodebeck, Jacob	NY0270	66A,66C,11,13
Rhodes, Ann G.	KY0300	11,12A,61,32D,29A
Rhodes, Carol	WI1100	11
Rhodes, Phillip	MN0300	13A,13,10,11
Rhyne, Kathryn	SC0750	11
Rhyneer, Barbara	MI1600	60,38,41,62,11
Ribchinsky, Julie C.	CT0050	13A,13C,62C,11,38
Ricci-Rogel, Susan	MD0700	11,66A,66C
Rice, Marc	MO1780	11,12A,14C
Richards, Julie	TX2310	11,13A,62A,66C
Richardson, Cathy	TX1725	11,62A
Richardson, Celia	TX2850	11,36,61,32B,13C
Richardson, Chuck	TX2850	11,45,35C,35G
Richardson, Donald G.	CA4450	11,12A,61
Richardson, Holly	MI0450	11,66A
Richardson, James K.	VA0300	61,11,36,54,39
Richardson, Neal	MO1950	11,13C
Richardson, Robert C.	WA0450	13,11,37,38,47
Richardson, W. Mack	NY3770	11,35A
Richardson, William	MO0950	47,63A,11
Richeson, David T.	AR0750	63A,11,35A
Richmond, Thomas	MN0600	13,10,11,12A
Rickey, Shirley	AL0400	11
Riddle, Paula	SC0750	11,63B
Rideout, Roger R.	OK1350	11
Ridgeway, Max A.	OK0600	10,70,11,20,46
Riehl, Jeffrey S.	VA1500	11,36,61,60
Rieppel, Daniel	MN1500	66A,11,38,66C,12
Rierson, Don G.	NC0550	39,11
Rife, Jerry E.	NJ1000	13,11,12A,12,37
Riley, Madeleine C.	PA1000	11,45,64A,64E,29
Riley, William	MA2020	70,11,13C
Riordan, George T.	TN1100	67D,11,64B
Ritchey, Mary Lynn	MA0150	61,36,60A,40,11
Ritter, Michael F.	TN0050	11
Ritterling, Soojin Kim	WI0810	32B,32C,11,61,32A
Ritz, Dennis W.	PA3050	11
Rivera Lassen, Carmen L.	PR0115	11
Rivera Ruiz, Alvaro M.	PR0115	11
Rivera, Felix	PR0150	11,66A,66D
Rivera, Lino	CA3920	11,41
Rivera-Vega, Salvador	PR0100	11,32,48,64E
Rivers, James	KS1400	11,66A,66C,10
Rives, Charles L.	TX2750	11,32C
Rizzer, Gerald M.	IL0750	11
Rizzo, Stephen	AL0260	11,63
Robbins, Daniel C.	CA2050	11,13A,10D
Rober, R. Todd	PA1750	11,12
Roberson, Heather D.	CO1050	61,36,11,60A,32D
Robert, James	NC0750	65,11,50
Roberts, Kate	IA0910	61,11
Roberts, Shawn M.	NC0050	11,65
Roberts, Tamara	CA5000	11,14C,14D,20G
Roberts, Terry	SC0710	11,63,13C,35A,41
Robertson, Anne Walters	IL3250	11,12A,12
Robertson, Elizabeth A.	IN1600	64B,11,41
Robertson, Jemmie	IL0800	63,11
Robertson, Paul	NJ0825	65,11
Robey, Matthew E.	NY2500	66A,66C,66D,11,32E
Robinson, Brian	MA1450	11,12A
Robinson, Elizabeth	KS0650	11
Robinson, Gregory J.	VA0450	11,12,14,20H
Robinson, Kathleen E.	MN1280	31A,11,12A,13C
Robinson, Nathalie G.	NY1600	32,11
Robinson, Rick	NY0270	11,13,65,32
Robinson-Martin, Trineice	NJ0750	11,12A,29,61
Robock, Alison	IL0400	64B,11
Rocco, Emma S.	PA2713	13A,11,20F,36,54
Rocco, Robert	NJ0700	11,13A,13B,10A
Rochford, Stephen M.	CA2390	37,38,11
Rockwell, Joti	CA3650	13,14C,11
Rockwell, Owen P.	MS0350	11,32C,37,65A,65B
Roden, Stella D.	MO1790	61,11
Roden, Timothy J.	OH2000	11,12A,20A,20D,20F
Rodgers, Kenneth	KS0500	66G,66A,66D,66C,11
Rodriguez, Elvin	CA2420	11,66A,35G,35C
Rodriguez, Jill	TX3100	63B,11
Roe, Gail	TX2310	66A,11,66C
Roed, Tom	MO0750	13,11,66A
Roelofs, Laura Leigh	MI2200	62A,32E,41,11
Roesner, Edward	NY2740	11,12A,12,55
Rogers, Timothy	NH0150	66D,11
Rogizhyna, Maryna	NY5000	66A,11
Rognstad, Richard	SD0600	38,13A,62D,13C,11
Rohde, Kurt E.	CA5010	13,10,11,43
Rohr, Deborah	NY3650	13,11,12A
Rojas, Nuria Mariela	SC0150	11,12,13,34,66
Rojek, Justin J.	AL0345	11,66,13
Rokeach, Martin	CA3920	13A,13,11,12A,41
Rolle, Nina	CO0560	11,35H
Roller, Jonathan	KY0100	11,10F
Romano, Darlene	CA1270	36,61,11,13A,40
Romeo, James	CA4050	11,37,47,48,29
Romer, Wayne Allen	PA3710	13A,10F,60B,11,32
Rosa, Gerard	CT0050	11,62A,12A
Rosado, Ana Maria	NJ0825	70,41,11,12A
Rose, Cameron J.	TX3535	36,32D,11,10
Rose, Michael	TN1850	13,10,12A,11,31
Rose, Richard F.	FL1300	11,32B,32C,62D,29
Rosenfeld, Andrew	MD0610	11,12,13,20F,36
Rosenholtz-Witt, Jason	CO0250	11
Rosenshein, Ingrid	FL1675	11,13A,61,66D,54
Rosensteel Way, Nancy	PA2500	11,36
Rosevear, Burt L.	TN1000	61,11
Rosner, Arnold	NY2050	13A,13,11,14,66A
Ross Mehl, Margaret	PA0600	36,39,61,11,12A
Ross, Daniel F.	AR0110	11,41,64B,64D,72
Ross, John	WV0700	13,64A,11
Ross, Laura	MO1120	11
Rossomando, Fred E.	CT0250	36,11
Roth, Jonathan D.	IN0910	11
Rothshteyn, Eleonora	NY0270	66C,11
Rotola, Albert	MO1250	11,12A
Rottenberg, Helene	MI1260	70,11
Rounds, Tyler	OH1100	11,20
Roush, Clark	NE0720	11,12A,13A,32C,32B
Rouslin, Daniel S.	OR1300	11,38,41,62A,62B
Routen, I. J.	AR0750	11
Rowan, Kami	NC0910	70,11,51,12E
Rowden, Charles H.	NY2550	11,12A,66D
Rowe, Paul	OK0300	66A,11,66D,66G
Rowlett, Donn	OK1500	13,11,66
Rowlett, Michael T.	MS0700	64C,11,41
Rownd, Gary	IL1850	13A,66A,66D,11
Royal, Jacquelyn A.	TN0300	11,13,16,34B
Royal, Matthew	AG0050	13,11,12B
Royse, Dennis	CA0250	13,12A,32C,11
Rubinstein, Matan	WI0865	11,29,32B,47
Ruckert, George	MA1200	13A,11,20G,20D,20F
Rudd, Stephen W.	CA0950	11
Rudnytsky, Susan	OH2600	11
Rudolph, Jon	ND0600	11,13A,70
Ruffin, W. Floyd	GA1450	66A,11
Rule, Charles	TN0700	11,47,66A,29,35
Rule, Tom	GA1260	66A,11
Rundlett, Jennifer	MD0300	64A,11,41
Runefors, Bjorn	AE0120	36,37,13,11,64A
Runnels, Brent	GA1550	66A,11,29,47,13A
Running, Donald	MA0510	37,38,46,47,11
Running, Timothy	PA1750	60,11,48,64A
Ruocco, Phyllis	AR0550	13A,13,11,66A,10F
Russell, Carlton T.	MA2150	11,12A,66G,31A
Russell, Craig H.	CA0600	11,12A,12,67B,70
Russell, Mary Lou	TX2260	11,66A,66C,66D,29
Russell, Nathan	TX3370	36,11,61,13C
Russell, Tilden	CT0450	11,12A,12,41
Rutkowski, Ellen	PA2200	61,11
Rutkowski, Gary	NY4460	50,65,11
Rutschman, Edward R.	WA1250	13A,13,11,12A,12
Ryan, Francis J.	OK1450	13,34,11
Ryan, Kathreen A.	IL0800	11
Ryder, Carol	CA2250	61,36,11
Ryder, William H.	LA0700	11,32,64,13
Ryner, Jayson	IA1170	32C,36,61,11,13C
Sabak, Linda	WV0800	12A,66,11
Sabatino, T. M.	PA1750	11,61,40
Sabo, Vyki	FL0950	61,11
Sackman, Marc L.	WI0806	13B,37,64A,47,11
Sadak, John	NC2420	64C,11
Saelzer, Pablo	MD0550	11,13A,13C,38,62A
Saeverud, Trond	ME0430	11,13A,41,36
Sager, Anne	WY0150	36,40,61,11
Saginario, Donald	FL1100	11,32A
Sahagian, Robert	MA2300	11,12A
Salfen, Kevin	TX3410	11,12,13A,20
Saliba, Raphael	FL0570	11
Saloman, Ora Frishberg	NY0250	11,12A,12
Salucka, Ray	IA0930	13,36,60,11,47
Salvo, Joel	MN0040	62C,11
Salwen, Barry	NC2440	11,66A,66B,66D
Samaan, Sherilyn	TN1350	32B,11,66A

Index by Area of Teaching Interest

Name	Code	Areas
Samball, Michael L.	ID0050	11,12A,29A,35A
Samuel, Jamuna	NY3790	11,12A,13E,12B,13F
Sanborn, Pamela	NH0050	11
Sanborne, Deborah	IA1300	12,66G,66C,11
Sanchez, Theresa	MS0360	11,66
Sandberg, Scott	ND0400	64,13B,13C,11,48
Sandborg, Jeff R.	VA1250	60,11,12A,36,61
Sandefur, Lynn	FL1675	11,13A,36,40,61
Sanders, Carolyn I.	AL1160	13A,11,63A
Sanders, Reginald L.	OH1200	11,12
Sanders, Robert	TX2100	47,11
Sandness, Dorothy	MN0850	11,20G
Santiago, Nephtali	GA2150	70,29,11
Santo, Amanda M.	RI0101	61,39,11
Sapieyevski, Jerzy	DC0010	13,10,45,11,34
Sargent, Joseph	AL1200	11,12A,13B,13C
Satterfield, Sarah	FL0365	12A,64A,11,42,48
Saunders, Harris S.	IL3310	11,12A,12
Saunders, Steven E.	ME0250	11,12A,12,66H
Sausser, Darrell	CA3800	11
Saya, Virginia	CA2800	12A,39,12C,11
Scaffidi, Susan	CA0270	1
Scales, Nicholas	TX3750	13,62D,11
Scarnati, Blase S.	AZ0450	11,12,14
Scelba, Anthony	NJ0700	12A,13E,11,62D
Schaal, Joelle E.	OR0800	13,65,11
Schaffer, William R.	AL0200	13,11,63B,49
Schantz, Allen P.	CO0150	11,12B,13,68
Schauer, Jerry	PA0450	11
Schauert, Paul W.	MI1750	20,11
Scheffler, Jeff	IA0910	70,11
Schenbeck, Lawrence A.	GA1900	11,12A,12C
Schenk, Kathryn E.	MN0610	11,66A,66H
Scherling, John	KS0210	11
Scherperel, Loretta	FL0200	13,11,66G
Schick, Steven	CA5050	11,50,65,43,29
Schisler, Charles	GA0750	11,12
Schlabach, Eugene	IL3200	11,12A,66A
Schlacks, Mary M.	OH1650	14,48,64C,11
Schlatter, Carolyn	FL1430	66A,13,11
Schlesinger, Scott L.	NC2525	66G,11,13A,29A,36
Schloneger, Matthew	KS0500	61,54,11
Schmann, Phillip M.	KY0550	11,63B
Schmid, Alice	GA0950	11,63A
Schmidt, Carl B.	MD0850	11,12
Schmidt, Carsten	NY3560	13,11,12A,41,66A
Schmidt, Charles	IL0100	11,66A,13
Schmidt, Jack W.	PA0900	11,12A,36,37,49
Schmidt, James	NC0450	66A,29A,66D,47,11
Schmidt, Juliana	WI0855	11,20,29A
Schmidt, Timothy	NY2950	70,11,13C
Schmidt, Tracey	PA0250	13,64A,11
Schnauber, Thomas	MA0900	10A,10C,13A,11,10F
Schneider, Lisa A.	AL1160	11,64B,41
Schneider, Wayne J.	VT0450	12,11
Schoening, Benjamin S.	WI0801	11,13,36,61,63
Scholl, Gerald	KS1450	65,50,11
Schoyen, Jeffrey G.	MD0800	62C,38,13A,11,62D
Schraer-Joiner, Lyn	NJ0700	32,11,13A,60
Schreckengost, John	IN1750	63B,49,11
Schreier, Kathleen	IA0790	13,11,36,54
Schreiner, Frederick	PA3710	11,12A,12,61,39
Schubert, David T.	OH2450	61,11
Schubert, John	MI0200	11,47,13C
Schulenberg, David L.	NY4500	11,12
Schultz, Margaret	NE0460	13C,66A,66C,11,32B
Schumaker, Adam T.	MI2250	10,11
Schuppener, Mark	TX3520	62A,62B,11
Schuttenhelm, Thomas	CT0050	11,13,70,34
Schwanda, Grace	MI0850	11
Schwantes, Melody	NC0050	33,11
Schwarm-Glesner, Elizabeth	CO0550	11
Schwartz, Elliott S.	ME0200	10F,10,11,12A,41
Schwartz, Richard A.	LA0650	29,47,64E,11,46
Schwarze, Penny	MN0450	12A,11,38,62A,67A
Schweitzer, Kenneth	MD1100	20,29,34,35,11
Scialla, Carmen J.	NJ0760	11
Scott Goode, Mary	TX2850	66A,11
Scott, Michael E.	TN1380	11,47,53
Scott, Rosemary	GA0250	32A,32B,32C,11
Scott, Stanley	CT0450	11,14
Scott, Stephen	CO0200	10,11,45,43,29
Scroggins, Sterling Edward	DC0010	61,16,11
Scruggs, Richard J.	TN0250	11,13B,41,48,64E
Scudder, Howard	TN0050	11
Scully, Francis	LA0560	13A,12A,11
Scully, Joseph D.	IL0450	13A,11,36,20
Seaton, Kira J.	OH0755	13A,13,11,36,61
Seay, Sandra	AR0110	11,61,32
Seebacher, Robert	AL1300	11,38,51
Seeley, Jeffery	NY1150	11,20,36
Seeman, Rebecca	CA5353	13A,11,36,38,61
Seeman, Sharon	NJ0750	64A,64B,64C,64D,11
Sehman, Melanie	NY3250	65,13A,20,11,13
Seigfried, Karl E.	WI0250	70,62D,11
Sein Siaca, Maria P.	PR0115	11
Seitz, Carole J.	NE0160	39,61,11
Seitz, Christine	IN0910	11
Seitz, Christine	MO1800	39,11
Seldess, Zachary	NY0500	11,13
Seldon, Vicki A.	TX2100	11,12A,66A,66C
Seligman, Susan	NY3760	13A,13C,11,41,62C
Sellers, Crystal Y.	OH0250	61,11,12,31F
Senn, Geoff	MN0040	29,63A,34,41,11
Sessoms, Sydney	NC1150	13E,32E,37,60B,11
Seto, Mark	CT0100	11,12,13A,13C,38
Seward, Owen	FL1450	65,11
Shabani, Afrim	IL2510	11,10,13,34B,13C
Shaheen, Ronald T.	CA5200	11,12A,13A,61
Shahriari, Andrew	OH1100	11,20
Shallit, Jonathan O.	NY3770	11,13A,62A
Shane, Lynn	MA1650	11,61,32B,32D,36
Shank, Kevin	KY0600	11,37
Shannon, Pamela	MO0950	11,61
Shapiro, Jarred	VT0100	62C,11,20
Sharer, Marty	PA0500	11,37,12A,13A,13C
Sharp, David	IA0750	13,11,47,64
Shaw, A. Herndon	GA1600	11
Shaw, David	NY2500	13,10,11,12A
Shea, Joy	NC2600	20D,11
Shearer, James E.	NM0310	63D,12A,11
Shearin, Arthur Lloyd	AR0250	11,36,61
Sheinbaum, John J.	CO0900	12,13E,11,12A
Shelley, Russ	PA1650	11,12B,36
Shelton, Adam	MO0775	11,64E
Shelton, Frank	CO0200	11,66G
Shepard, Hilary	KS0350	64,11,20
Shepherd, William	IA1600	11,32C,37
Sheridan, Daniel	MN1700	64C,60,32C,13A,11
Sherman, Joy	WA0850	11,36,40,61
Sherrill, William	TX3530	11
Sherrod, Ron	TX3535	70,11
Sherry, Martin	WA0480	13,11,12A,14,64A
Sherwin, Ronald G.	MA0150	11,31A,60A,36,32
Shevitz, Matthew	IL1080	11,13,29,47,46
Shibatani, Naomi	TX1520	66A,66D,11
Shimpo, Ryoji	OH2150	66A,11
Shively, Joseph L.	MI1750	32G,34,11,32,32C
Shoemaker, Michelle N.	MA1175	12A,64,11,64C
Shotwell, Clayton	GA0250	12,20,34,11,13A
Shover, Blaine F.	PA3050	11,12A,36,61,54
Shrader, Steven	TN1800	11,12A,12,66A,38
Shumway, Angelina	MD0700	11,66D,61,13A
Siarris, Cathy Froneberger	SC0850	61,11
Sichel, John	NJ0975	13,10,11,12A,36
Sidoti, Vincent	OH0755	13,11,37,64C,64E
Sieben, Patrick	KS0225	37,20,13,46,11
Sifferman, James P.	MO1500	11,66A,66D
Silva, Linda	CA0630	11,64C
Silva, Ulisses C.	GA1700	62B,11
Silver, Phillip A.	ME0440	12A,66C,66A,11
Silverberg, Ann L.	TN0050	12A,12,14,11
Silverberg, Laura Gail	NY0750	11,12
Simi, David R.	CA4400	11,66G
Simmonds, Jim	NY2500	11
Simon, Philip G.	PA3700	11,37,41,51,63D
Simoncic, Max	CA4300	13,10,11
Simons, Carolyn	CA2810	11,20,60A,12
Simons, Dennis	ND0250	11,13,20,38
Simpson, Alexander T.	KY0250	11,12A,36,44,60A
Simpson, Kyle	PA3580	10,11,37,47
Simpson, Scott	NJ1400	11
Sine, Nadine J.	PA1950	11,12A,12
Singer, David	NJ0800	41,48,64C,11
Singleton, Darryl	TX3150	37,44,11
Singley, H. E.	IL1850	66A,66G,11,36,31A
Siow, Lee-Chin	SC0500	11,62A
Sipley, Kenneth L.	MS0575	11,12A,13A
Sisbarro, Jennifer L.	NY1250	13A,11,61
Sisman, Elaine	NY0750	12,11,12A,12B
Sitterly, James	CA2650	11
Skoglund, Frances	FL0675	66A,66D,13A,11
Skornia, Dale E.	MI0650	11,32B,37,64
Skroch, Diana	ND0600	11,66D
Slater, Sheri	MO0400	11,48,64C
Slavin, Dennis	NY0250	11,12
Slavin, Peter	IN0005	10,13,66,66A,11
Slotterback, Floyd	MI1600	60,36,11
Slowik, Gregory	MA1700	13,11,12A,66A,66C
Smaldone, Edward	NY0642	13,10,10F,11
Smalley, Charles	AZ0150	13C,11,36,61,20G
Smart, David	KS0590	11
Smart, Marilyn	FL1950	11,39,61
Smart, Mary Ann	CA5000	11,12,15
Smith, Allison	TX1550	11,61
Smith, Angie	NC2370	11,36
Smith, Bret	WA0050	11,32,12F
Smith, Carey	MS0370	63,64,65,11,13
Smith, David K.	KS0950	36,11,61,13,66A
Smith, David J.	AL0300	61,11
Smith, Debbie	TN1200	66A,66G,11
Smith, Derek T.	MO0600	11,13,29
Smith, Geoff	NY1250	47,11,35A,35B,35C
Smith, Glenda G.	CA1700	13A,11
Smith, Hope Munro	CA0800	14,20H,11,12A,12C
Smith, J. W.	WV0200	11,12A,66A,66B,66D
Smith, James	NY4050	70,11
Smith, James W.	AL1050	63D,32E,11
Smith, Jewel Ann	OH2550	11
Smith, Joseph R.	NJ0800	11
Smith, Justin	OR0500	36,11,60
Smith, Kathleen	NC1400	11,13A
Smith, Kent M.	PA3560	10,11,12A,31A
Smith, Lee	CA4950	11,41,62
Smith, Linda S.	KS1400	11
Smith, Marcie	UT0190	66A,66D,13C,11
Smith, Matthew K.	VT0100	37,32,11,63B,60
Smith, Robert	NC1100	11,13,66G
Smith, Ross	LA0050	11,66A,13A,13B,13C
Smith, Roy C.	IN0005	61,11,10A,60,36
Smith, Timothy C.	AK0100	11,66A,66B,66C
Smith, Vernon L.	FL1300	11,36,61
Smith, William D.	NC1350	70,11
Smithey, David B.	LA0350	11,61
Smolenski, Scott	FL1675	66A,10,11,13,20
Smolik, Vicky	IL2970	11,63A,10D,35D
Snider, Denise G.	WA1150	29A,11
Snider, Karl William	CA2800	13A,11,61,40
Snyder, Colleen	CA2400	11,29A,37,66D,60
Snyder, David	CT0450	11,13
Snyder, Jacob	PA2710	13A,11
Snyder, Jean E.	PA1200	11,12,20
Snyder, John L.	TX3400	13,11,12
Snyder, Linda J.	OH2250	39,61,11
Snyder, Mark S.	CT0800	64B,48,11
Snyder, Randy L.	TX2300	13A,13,11,47,63
Sobaje, Martha H.	RI0100	11
Sobaje, Martha H.	RI0101	11,13A
Soehnlen, Edward J.	MI1850	11,66A,66G
Soich, Leslie	CO0830	36,13,11,10D
Solfest-Wallis, Cindy	TN0260	11,64A
Soll, Beverly A.	MA1650	11,66A,66C
Solomonson, Terry	IL3500	11,63D,35C,35D,35G
Song, James J.	CA3100	60,11,12,38,13
Sorenson, Allin	MO0350	60,11,36,61
Sorroche, Juan	PR0150	13A,11,70,13C
Soto-Medina, Victor	TX1725	11,13,66,34B
South, Janis	OK1250	63B,11,12A,49,20
Southard, Robert G.	MI1050	37,60B,41,11
Southard, Sarah	MI1050	64B,11
Sowers, Jodi L.	IN1650	64A,11
Sowers, Jodi L.	IN0907	11,64A,41
Spangler, Pamela	CA2550	11,66A
Spaniola, Joseph T.	FL2100	47,46,63D,11,10
Spann, Joseph	AL0890	11,13,70,34A,34D
Spataro, Susan M.	VA0400	64A,47,11,32A,32B
Speake, Constance J.	IL2150	11,32
Specht, Barbara	OH0950	11,38,64C,64E,48
Speed, George M.	OK0800	62D,11,42
Spelius, Susan M.	ID0075	11,66D,13B,13C
Spell, Cindy	NC0450	70,11
Spence, Stephen	NC0220	11
Spicer, Mark J.	NY1150	13,11,64A,66A,20G
Spicer-Lane, Anita	MD0170	11,61
Spiller, W. Terrence	CA0600	66,11
Spittal, Robert	WA0400	37,11,42,48,60B

441

Name	Code	Areas
Spitzer, David Martin	NC2435	37,11,64E
Sprayberry, Shane	MS0300	37,11
Squatrito, Fred	CA0400	13,11,66A
St. Clair, Collette	CO0550	11
Stace, Stephen	PA2700	11,34
Stafford, John	KS0590	36,40,47,11,13A
Stafford, Timothy	IL1850	60A,11
Stagg, David L.	MO1790	11,37,63C
Stallings, Joe	FL1500	13,11,70,34
Stalnaker, Donna	WV0250	11,12A,32B,66A,66H
Stamps, Justin	ID0050	63A,11
Stancu, Letitia G.	NJ0800	11
Stanley, Ed L.	PA1400	64B,42,13A,13C,11
Stanley, Glenn	CT0600	11,12A,12,12B
Staples, Thomas	AA0200	60,11,49,63
Stapleton, Chip	IN0907	29A,64E,14C,11
Stark, Deborah	GA0700	12A,54,11,61,40
Staron, Michael	IL3200	13,11,29,62D
Staron, Michael	IL0750	11
Starr, Jeremy A.	KS0300	38,62A,62B,11
Stauch, Thomas J.	IL1085	36,40,61,32D,11
Steed, Brad B.	CA3500	13A,11,16
Steele, Timothy	MI0350	11,12
Steffen, Richard	TN0050	60B,49,63A,47,11
Steib, Murray	IN0150	11,12,12A
Stein, Ken J.	IL2560	11,13B,20,47,64E
Steinhaus, Barbara	GA0350	61,11,39
Stella, Martin	MI1250	13,11
Stencel, Paul L.	NY1210	13A,11,12A,41,47
Stephens, Loren	NE0050	11,64A
Stepner, Daniel	MA0500	41,62A,11
Stern, Kalai	HI0110	11,36,40,13A,13C
Stern, Theodore	CA1960	11,12A,54,13A
Sternfeld, Barbara	CA5400	11,38,62
Steva, Elizabeth Ryland	KY1000	62,11,12
Stevens, Blake	SC0500	12,11
Stevens, Jane	CA5050	11,12A,12
Stewart, Jonathan	OK0825	32D,11,13B,36,61
Stewart, Leslie	CO0250	62A,62B,38,11
Stewart, Shirley	LA0720	11,36,61,31A,32
Stewart, Stanley W.	MS0200	11,37,47,49,48
Stibler, Robert	NH0350	11,63A,67C,49,67E
Stier, Greg	CA3200	11
Stillwell, Roy	IL1500	66G,66A,11
Stilwell, Jama Liane	IA0400	11,12,20G,13,64A
Stinson, Russell	AR0425	13,11,12A,12,66
Stitt, Virginia K.	UT0200	11,32B,64B,64D,12A
Stofko, Diane L.	TN0550	32,11,37,13A,60B
Stokes, Jennifer	IN0907	66A,66B,66D,11,66C
Stokes, Jordan	NY0625	11
Stone, Jeff	TX2960	11,32
Stone, Michael	KY0550	11
Stott, Jacob T.	RI0100	11,13A
Stott, Jacob	RI0101	11,13
Stoughton, Zachariah	TX3000	66A,12A,67F,11
Stowe, Samuel P.	NC0850	11,48,64A
Strahl, Margaret A.	GA2100	11,66A
Strain, James A.	MI1600	65,13,41,11
Strand, Julie	MA1450	20A,20D,11
Strand, Karen	OR0850	64B,11
Strandberg, Kristen	IN1850	11,12,13A
Strattan, Ken	FL0200	11
Stratton, Matthew	TN1720	63D,11,34,37
Strauss, Gail	NY1600	32,11
Street, Eric	OH2250	66A,66B,66C,11
Stremlin, Tatyana	NY4250	13,11,61,66A,67C
Stringer, Sandra	AA0200	61,36,11
Stripling, Allen	GA0810	11,36,66,32,40
Stroeher, Vicki P.	WV0400	11,12,13,14
Strong, Alan D.	TX0345	11,32,66G
Strong, Bent	MA0510	70,11
Strong, James Anthony	NJ0975	13,12A,66,11,54
Stroud, Stephen	CA3000	11,12A
Strouf, Linda Kay	MI1050	11,66D
Struman, Susan Jean	TX0550	51,62C,32A,11,62D
Strunsky, Mark	NY3000	11,12A,70,14C
Stuart, David H.	IA0850	63D,42,34A,34C,11
Stubbe, Joan	CA4400	11,66D
Stubbs, Frederick	MA2010	11,14
Studdard, Shane	TX1775	66,66C,11
Studinger, Bob	CO0625	11,10,13
Stukart, Lynne	IL0300	64A,11
Sturm, Jonathan	IA0850	12A,11,20G,20
Sturman, Janet L.	AZ0500	14,11
Suber, Stephen C.	LA0650	13,10,11
Suda, Carolyn	IL1800	11,12A,62C,38,42
Suda, Carolyn W.	IL1350	11,42,51,62C
Sullivan, Keith	AL0850	70,11
Sullivan, Michael	TX2200	10,11,12A
Sullivan, Todd E.	AZ0450	11,12,14,20
Summerfield, Susan	VT0400	13,11,41,66
Sumner, Melissa M.	VA0800	61,11,40
Surface, Edward	TX0150	11,63D
Surman, Patricia	OK1250	64A,11
Sushel, Michael	CA1000	10D,66A,66B,11,29A
Sutanto, David T.	TX0550	66A,66D,66C,11,66B
Sutton, R. Anderson	WI0815	11,12A,20D,14A
Suzano, L. Armenio	VA0650	20F,11,13C,41,64
Suzuki, Dean P.	CA4200	11,12,20G
Svanoe, Kimberly Utke	SD0050	66A,11
Svorinich, Victor	NJ0700	11
Swanson, Christopher	VA0700	13C,61,12A,11,39
Swantek, Paul	MI0900	11
Swartz, Anne	NY0250	11,12A,12
Swears, Marilyn	AL0345	11,54,66A
Sweet, Bridget Mary	IL3300	32,11,60A
Swenson, Sonya	CA4950	11
Swift, Mark D.	PA3580	11,14A,14C,20
Swift, Robert F.	NH0250	11,32,36
Swigger, Jocelyn A.	PA1400	11,66A,66B,66C,66E
Switzer, Mark	FL0930	11,70
Syswerda, Todd	IN1025	13A,13,10,11,10F
Szurek, Jaroslaw P.	AL0800	11,16
Tabor, Angela	CA3800	11,65
Tabor, Jerry N.	MD0800	13,10,29B,47,11
Tacke, Tom	AZ0150	11
Taggart, Charlotte A.	KS1400	11
Tahere, David	GA0600	11,54,61
Tait, Alicia Cordoba	IL0275	20,12A,15,35,11
Tait, Kristen N.	MI1750	11,35A
Takacs, William	TX3750	63A,11
Talbert, Rebecca	MO2050	61,66A,13,12A,11
Taliaferro-Jones, Gene	NC0450	11,37
Tallant, Audrey	IL2910	11,35
Talley, Dana W.	NY2900	61,12A,20,39,11
Tallman, Thomas J.	IL0630	13,11,47,63,29
Tam, TinShi	IA0850	69,66G,11,34B,66D
Tang, Patricia	MA1200	20,11,13
Tanner, Greg	TX3540	11
Tanner, Robert	GA1450	10,12A,11,65,34
Tapanes-Inojosa, Adriana	IL1080	11,20,36,12,66
Tappa, Richard J.	TX0250	11,66G,69
Taranto, Vernon	FL1650	10,11,13B,36,13C
Tarrant, Fredrick A.	GA1800	11,12,14,20,55
Taruskin, Richard	CA5000	11,12
Tashjian, B. Charmian	IL0750	11
Tate, Brian	MO1800	11,34
Tate, Galen	CT0300	11,35
Tate, Shelia D.	VA1800	11,32,16,36
Taylor, Arlecia Jan	TX2100	11,36,32,66A
Taylor, Dowell	MS0350	11,13C,34
Taylor, Greg	AR0750	11
Taylor, James	NC1050	41,36,61,31A,11
Taylor, Jeffrey J.	NY0500	12,11,29A
Taylor, Robert J.	SC0500	11,36,61,60
Taylor, Rowan S.	CA2700	13,11
Taylor, Steve M.	GA2150	62C,11
Taylor, Una D.	NE0050	36,61,32B,11,40
Teager, Michael	MI2000	11,20
Teal, Terri	KS0570	11,40,61,36
Tebbets, Gary	KS0040	12A,11,36,54,62
Tedder, Teresa C.	KY1150	10A,10C,10F,66A,11
Teel, Susan	TX0050	66A,32B,11,13C
Teichmer, Shawn	MI2000	32,60,64,12A,11
Templeman, Robert W.	OH2550	11,20
Templeton, David M.	SC0500	61,39,11
Tenison-Willis, MaryJo	AR0750	11
Termini, Steven	TX0075	11,66A,13A
Terrell, Maurice	FL1700	11,29,37,47,60B
Teruel, Hugo	IL2150	11
Tesch, John	MN1120	32E,37,63C,11
Teske, Casey C.	PA0700	60B,13C,63B,11
Teter, Francis	CA1750	11,37,38,48,64
TeVelde, Rebecca	OK0800	11
Teves, Christopher	SC0275	70,11
Thevenot, Maxine R.	NM0450	11,36
Thibodeaux, David	AZ0350	11
Thoman, Jessica	TN1720	63B,12A,11
Thomas, Edwin	IN0005	65,11,12,32,60
Thomas, Joel Wayne	KS0265	11,13,29,66
Thomas, Kenneth B.	AL0340	11
Thomas, Margaret E.	CT0100	13,11,12C
Thomas, Matthew	CA3500	11
Thomas, Michael	AL0530	11
Thomas, Naymond	TX3175	11
Thomas, Richard B.	SC1000	62C,11,38,12A,62D
Thomas, Susan R.	GA2100	11,12,14,20H,34A
Thomason, Eliza	TX3100	11,32E,62A,62B,51
Thomen, Willard	IL3370	61,11
Thompson, Christopher	LA0770	41,62A,62B,11
Thompson, David	WI0400	13,11,14,66A,35
Thompson, Howard	TX1600	11
Thompson, Jonathan	AB0090	11,36,12A,60,38
Thompson, Paul	WI0817	36,13B,13C,11
Thompson, Paul	MO1500	11,41,64A,29A,55C
Thompson, Robert	WI0825	11,41,48,64D
Thompson, Ruth	TX3000	11
Thompson, Sandra D.	OK1330	11,32D
Thompson, Shannon	NC2600	64C,11
Thompson, Shaw	SC0710	11,61
Thompson, Steven D.	CA0150	37,38,63C,11,13A
Thomsen, John David	CA1550	66A,11
Thomsen, Kathy	MN0800	66A,66D,11
Thorn, Becky	MO1950	11
Thorngate, Russell	WI0925	11,13A,36,40,61
Thorp, Steven	NM0250	13,11,36,61,40
Threlkeld, David M.	KY1425	11,12A,47,48,64
Thrower, Daniel	UT0305	11
Thurber, Donald W.	CA2420	11,32
Thwaites, Mary Evelyn Clark	AL1300	11
Tibbs, Elizabeth J.	AZ0150	66A,11,66D
Tiberio, Albert	PA2950	11,12,13,10A,10F
Tice, Loren C.	KY1350	11,66A,66H,66C,66G
Tichgraeber, Heidi	KS0210	11,61
Tidwell, Mary	TX3360	13,11
Tiedge, Faun Tanenbaum	OR0450	11,13,12A,20,42
Tigges, Kristie M.	MN1295	61,11
Tilley, Janette M.	NY0635	12A,11,12
Tillman, Joshua	NC2700	63A,11
Timmey, Zachery	VA0950	63A,11,37
Timothy, Sarah O.	AL0890	61,11,36,13,32
Tindall, Danny H.	FL1740	36,37,65,11
Tiner, Kris	CA0270	47,29A,11
Tinsley, David	AL0400	11,36,61
Tipps, Angela	TN1100	66G,36,11
Titmus, Jon	CA5360	63,11,13A
Titus, Julia	IA0300	11,66A,66D
Tjornehoj, Kris	WI0845	38,11,60B,37,32E
Tocheff, Robert	OH1600	60,11,32,36,66D
Todd, Charles E.	GA2150	11
Todd, Kenneth W.	CO1050	11,38,51,62
Todd, Kristen Stauffer	OK0650	12,14,20,11,55
Todorov, Jassen	CA4200	62A,35,11
Tokar, David A.	PA0900	12A,12C,70,12,11
Tolar, Ron	AL0400	13,11,66A,66G
Toliver, Brooks	OH2150	11,12
Toliver, Nicki Bakko	MN0040	11,13,40,61
Tollefson, Mary J.	WI0810	11,66A,66D,66B
Toman, Sharon Ann	PA2775	11,13A,29A,14C,36
Tomasello, Andrew	NY0250	11,12,14,29A,35
Tomlin, Laura A.	GA0250	62A,11,13A
Toops, Gary	CA3200	13,11,66G
Torkelson, Suzanne	IA1800	11,66A,66B,66C
Torosian, Brian L.	IL2150	70,11,13H
Torres Navarro, Pedro J.	PR0115	11
Torres, Adam A.	CO0250	11
Torres, Gregory J.	LA0450	60B,11,37,34B,32B
Touliatos-Miles, Diane	MO1830	11,12A,12,29A
Toutant, William P.	CA0835	10,11
Townsend, Bradley	WI0840	11
Townsend, Brendan	TX1425	10F,11,12A,13,62C
Townsend, Norma	CA3800	66D,11
Townson, Kevin	TX2750	70,11
Towse, Joanna	NY3680	11,61
Trabold, William E.	CA4450	61,11,13A,12
Tracy, Janet M.	TX2260	11
Trainer, Robert F.	WA0600	61,11
Tramiel, Leonard	MS0560	60,11,37,63C,63D
Trauth, Vincent	IL2350	66D,11
Trautwein, Mark	MO0550	11
Trent, Andrea	TX3370	11,61
Trentham, Donald R.	TN0650	11,12A,66A,31A,13
Tresler, Matthew T.	CA2390	36,61,11
Trimborn, Thomas J.	MO1780	60,11,32
Trollinger, Valerie L.	PA1750	34,32,64D,11,32C
Tsai, Shang-Ying	CA5400	13A,11,20G

Index by Area of Teaching Interest

Name	Code	Areas
Tsai, Tammy	CA0859	13A,11,62A
Tuckwiller, George	VA1750	60,11,41,49,63A
Tuinstra, John	WI0865	11,37,63D
Tumino, Joe	IL1890	63D,11
Tunstall, Julia	PA3400	64A,11
Turino, Thomas R.	IL3300	11,20A,20H,14
Turley, Edward L.	MN0350	11,66A,66B,66C
Turner, J. Frank	CA4450	13A,11,12A,54,13B
Turner, Leon P.	TX2100	11,39,61
Turner, Leon	LA0700	11,61
Turner, Patrick	VA1700	11,29,34D,34H,35C
Turner, Randy	LA0150	11
Turner, Richard	WY0050	64D,67C,11
Turner, Tammy	KY1540	29A,11,32B
Turner, Tammy	KY0950	11,12
Turnquist-Steed, Melody	KS0150	11,13C,31,44,66G
Turon, Charles T.	FL1745	11,13,66A,66D
Turpin, Mike H.	TX1350	11,48,64
Turrin, Joseph E.	NJ0800	11,13,10C
Tusa, Michael C.	TX3510	11,12A,12
Twombly, Kristian	MN1300	10B,34H,12B,10,11
Twyman, Nita	OK1030	13A,11,61,66A
Tymas, Byron	NC1600	11,46,70,47,41
Tyson, LaDona	MS0580	11,40,36,61
Tyson, Liana	AR0350	64A,11,48
Udell, Chester	OR1050	10,10B,11,34,35
Udland, Matt	KS0210	11,36,43,61
Ulffers, Christopher	NC0650	12A,64D,11
Ulreich, Douglas	IL2775	11
Underwood, Kirsten F.	OK0150	62,38,11,62C,20
Unger, Ruth Shelly	GA0750	64D,11
Unger, Shannon M.	OK0550	61,11,13C,39
Unrath, Wendy	IL0850	66A,66D,12A,11
Upton, Gregory	OH0200	11
Urban, Guy	MA2150	13,60,11,66A
Vail, Eleanore	IN0400	11,12A,66A
Valdes, Eduardo	PR0150	70,11
Valdivia, Hector	MN0300	10F,60,11,38,41
Valerio, John B.	SC1110	29,11
Valliant, James	PA3710	61,66A,11
Van Cleave, Brad	CA0050	13A,11,12A
van den Honert, Peter	PA1200	60A,36,11,13A
Van Orden, Katherine	CA5000	11,12A,12D,55,67
Van Regenmorter, Paula	LA0450	64,12A,11,48,20
Van Wyck, Helen J.	IL3100	13,60A,11,36,32D
Vanderbeck, Sue Ann	MI1300	11,12A,66A,66B,66D
Vanderford, Brenda M.	WV0700	13A,13,11,66G,31A
Vanderwoude, Matt	AG0130	10A,11,13,29,34
Vangelisti, Claire	LA0770	61,11
Vascotto, Norma	AG0600	12A,11,20
Vasquez, Hector	FL1300	13,11,12A,66A
Vassilandonakis, Yiorgos	SC0500	10,11,13,43
Vaughan, Jennie	TX2050	13A,13B,13C,66A,11
Vaughn, Beverly Joyce	NJ0990	36,11,13A,20G,61
Veal, Larry	NH0350	11,62C,13A,41
Veenstra, Kimberly	MI0990	11,12,13
Vega, Rebecca	NJ0050	32,37,11,64A,60B
Veltman, Joshua	TN1660	11,12A,44
Vento, Steve	OK1300	10,11,12,47,32E
Venzen, Austin A.	VI0050	10F,11,32B,37,42
Verbsky, Franklin	NY1600	62,62C,62D,11
Vernon, James R.	OK0650	13,10,35C,11
Verzosa, Noel	MD0500	12,11
Vetter, Roger R.	IA0700	11,14
Vickers, Jeffrey E.	AR0600	64,11,64E,64A,12A
Viemeister, Jane Stave	CA4580	66A,11
Villa, Tara Towson	NC0550	11,38,60B
Villines, Roger	FL1500	63A,47,11
Vincent, Larry	TN1250	11,70
Vines, Lisa	AL0530	11
Vinson, Nancy	AL0200	11
Violett, Martha Watson	CO1050	11,12,66
Virgoe, Betty	CA1520	66,11,13A,20G
Visentin, Peter	AA0200	12A,62A,67B,11
Vivio, Christopher J.	TN0050	63D,11
Vliek, Pamela	CA3800	64A,11
Vogan, Nancy F.	AE0050	11,32
Vogel, Dorothy	MI1650	66D,11
Vogt, Nancy	NE0450	63C,63D,11
Voigt, Steve	VA0600	10,11,13
Volchansky, Vera	PA2350	11,38
Vollmer, Jeffrey	IN0900	11
Vollrath, Carl P.	AL1050	10,11
von Arx, Victoria	NY3700	66A,13,11
Von Villas, Muriel	DC0100	11,39,54
Vranna, Jeff	ND0100	11
Wachsmuth, Karen	IA1140	13,11,12A,66A
Wacker, Lori	NC0650	13,11
Waddell, Mike	NC2440	64B,64C,64D,11,32
Waddell, Rachel Lynn	MI1000	11,12,32E,42,64A
Wade, Bonnie C.	CA5000	11,14,20C,20E,12G
Wade, Mark Alan	OH0850	63A,12A,11,32,60B
Wadsworth, Amanda	LA0080	11,66A,66D
Waeber, Jacqueline	NC0600	11,12A,12B
Wagoner, W. Sean	OR1050	65,10F,50,37,11
Wakeling, Tom	OR0050	11,12A,47,29,35
Walden, Sandra	IA1600	39,11,61
Walden, Valerie	CA1290	11
Waldoff, Jessica	MA0700	11,12
Waldron, Richard	WA0300	11,13A,13H,13K,13C
Walker, Abigail	AL0345	11,64D
Walker, Abigail	FL1500	11,64D,66D
Walker, Cherilee	KS0590	36,13,11,61,29A
Walker, Christopher G.	GA0150	11,32,64,48
Walker, David L.	VA1000	50,65,60B,11,13A
Walker, Gregory T. S.	CO0830	11,62A,20G,62B,46
Walker, James E.	IL1090	11
Walker, Michael	CA1510	66A,11
Wall, Sarah	NY4050	64B,11
Wallace, James A.	GA1070	36,13C,40,11
Wallace, Robin	TX0300	12,11
Wallin, Nicholas L.	IL1400	38,13,11,20
Wallis, David N.	MO0650	36,10A,11,13,32D
Walrath, Brian	MI2000	11,12A,65,31,34
Walston, Patricia	MS0400	11,66A,66B
Walter, Elaine R.	DC0050	11,12A,39
Walter, Regina	TX1775	61,54,11
Walter, Steven	SC0750	70,11,12A
Walters, Corinne	LA0080	11
Walters, Mark A.	CO0350	60,11,48,37,64
Walters, Teresa	NJ0200	13,60,11,12A,36
Walth, Gary Kent	WI0810	60,11,32C,36,54
Waltz, Sarah Clemmens	CA5350	11,12
Wang, Esther	MN0750	66A,66C,11
Wang, Mingzhe	TN0050	64C,11
Wang, Yung-Hsiang	TX3400	62A,12A,38,11
Wanner, Dan	CA2600	13,11,35A,66A
Ward, Keith C.	WA1000	11,35A
Ward, Larry F.	IL0630	11,20,14
Ward, Robert J.	MA1450	70,11,13,20G
Ward, Tom R.	IL3300	11,12
Ward-Steinman, David	IN0900	10,11
Ware, David N.	MS0350	63A,34C,47,11,13B
Ware, John Earl	LA0900	11,36,39,41,61
Warfield, Scott A.	FL1800	12,20,11
Warneck, Petrea	SC0750	64B,11
Warner, Douglas G.	TN0850	11,63D,13B,13C,63C
Warren, James	CA2700	11,61,66A
Warren, Jeff	MN1280	11
Warren, John	IL1900	36,11,12A,13B,13C
Warren, Maredia D. L.	NJ0825	13,11,32
Warren, Robert	TX3100	12A,66A,11
Washington, Henry	TX2220	36,11,66A,66G,66D
Washington, Lecolion	TN1680	64D,42,11
Washington, Phil	WV0700	11,29B,70
Waterman, Marla	NY2105	11,61
Waters, Becky	AL1160	10A,11,13C
Waters, Renee	MO1550	13,10,66A,34,11
Watson, Jed	MI0900	11
Watson, Marva	IL1240	66A,66B,66C,11,12A
Watson, Scott C.	KS1350	11,49,63D
Watson, Tommy L.	SC0050	11,61,39,12A,13A
Watts, Joel	CA4850	11,66D
Watts, Sarah	PA0350	32A,32B,11
Waynick, Mark	AR0730	11
Weatherford, Benjamin	AL0500	70,11
Weaver, Lane	KS0350	11,63D,37,49
Weaver, Michael A.	SC0950	12A,11,32,62A,62B
Webb, Brian P.	VT0125	13A,13,11,12A,36
Webb, Mark	MI0300	63,32C,32D,32E,11
Webb, Robert	VA0975	11,36,13
Webber, Allen L.	FL1470	13,11,61,10A,66A
Webber, Danny R.	MD0450	11,70,13
Webber, Kelly Marie	KS0560	11,13A,12A,61,60A
Weber, Angela	IL2150	11
Weber, Linda	TX0550	11,64A,66A,32,66D
Weber, Mary	MO1250	63A,13,11
Wechesler, David J.	NY0644	11,13A,29A,41,64A
Weddle, John W.	CA0850	32C,32B,20G,64C,11
Weeda, Linn	AK0100	11,36,49,63,63A
Weesner, Anna	PA3350	13,10,11
Wegman, Rob	NJ0900	11,12A,12,20G
Weinberg, Alan	SC0600	11,66A,12A,66D
Weiner-Jamison, Sarah	FL0200	61,11
Weinstein, Michael	MA2200	13A,11,12A,49
Weiss, Lisa G.	MD0400	13A,11,42,66A,66C
Wells, Glenn	TX1350	37,11
Wells, Jesse R.	KY0900	11,53,62A,70
Wells, Prince	IL2910	13,11,29,35
Wen, Andy	AR0750	11,13,64,64E
Weng, Pamela	CO0830	13,11,12A,66A
Wenger, Alan J.	MO1790	11,63A
Werner, J. Ritter	OH2500	11,66G
Wesby, Roger	NY4500	11,29A,32D,36,40
Wesche, Nancy	KS0210	36,61,11
Wesley, Arthur B.	AL0010	11,37,47,65
Wesley, Charles E.	MS0050	36,61,12A,11
West, Lara L.	KS0100	40,11,66D,66G,20
Westbrook, Randy	KY0550	66C,12,11
Wester, R. Glenn	TX2295	61,66,11,13A
Westerberg, Kurt H.	IL0750	13,10,11
Westerhaus, Timothy P.	WA0400	11,60A,61
Weston, Trevor L.	NJ0300	11,20B,13,10
Westra, Mitzi	IN1650	61,13A,11,44
Whalen, Margaret F.	NC2000	11,12A,20B,29A
Whaley, Daniel M.	TN1100	63A,11
Whaley, Mary Susan	OK0500	11,36,61,54,13
Whang, Hyunsoon	OK0150	11,12A,66
Wheeler, Candace	FL0200	66,11,32,10,66A
Wheeler, John	GA0940	11
Wheeler, Lawrence	TX3400	11,12A,20G
Wheeler, Mark	NC0915	11,12A,20G
Wheeler, W. Keith	TN1550	36,61,13C,11
Whitaker, Jane	FL0950	54,11
Whitaker-Auvil, Melissa	MI1985	11,61
White, Coralie	LA0770	11,66A,66D
White, Frank	LA0700	13,39,66A,11,60
White, James	PA2710	11
White, Janice	CA5500	11,13A,36,61,66A
White, Katherine	AR0730	61,11
White, Phyllis	MI1750	11,13A
White, Rick	WA0600	11,29A,20,37,46
White, William	MO1710	11,37,47,65,63
Whitehead, Corey	CA0810	70,11,14C
Whitford, Trudy	IN1025	64A,11
Whitlock, Christina	IN1560	11
Whittall, Geoffrey	AA0025	14,65,20,13,11
Whitten, Douglas	KS1050	37,63D,32E,11,49
Wiebe, Laura	IA0300	36,11
Wieck, Anatole	ME0440	38,62A,62B,11
Wiegard, William James	TX3750	63B,49,11
Wiggins, Tracy Richard	NC2435	65,11,37,50
Wilbourne, Emily	NY0750	11,12,15,20F
Wilcken, Geoff	KS0570	11
Wilcoxson, Nancy	SD0580	13A,61,36,11,12A
Wilder, Ralph	IL2100	64C,32E,64E,11,42
Wileman, Harv	TN0260	11,61
Wilhelm, Philip	IL1740	64D,32,40,11
Wilhoit, Mel	TN0260	11
Wilkes, Jamey	GA2000	11,16
Wilkins, Skip	PA1850	13,11,29
Wilkinson, Christopher	WV0750	13,11,12A,12
Wilkinson, Leslie	MI0900	11
Willette, Andrew C.	OR0850	11,13A
Willey, James H.	NY3730	13,10,11,66A
Williams, Bonnie Blu	MS0400	11,32
Williams, Christopher A.	OH2300	12A,20,12C,11
Williams, John W.	NY2100	13,11,36,61,54
Williams, Linda	NY2800	11,42
Williams, Marvin	NY2050	10,11,12,13,20G
Williams, Milton H.	CA4625	11,61,29,34
Williams, Milton H.	CA1250	11,66A
Williams, Nancy	CA0950	66D,16,11
Williams, Oscar	LA0700	12A,64,11,29A
Williams, Ralph K.	NY4060	13,12A,11,61
Williams, Ralph K.	NY4050	13,11,61
Williams, Robert	NC0800	11,12A,36,61
Williams, Sean	WA0350	11,12,14,20G,70
Williams, Shane	MO0650	11,13,32E,38,41
Williams, Steven	NC2550	11,54,39,66G
Williamson, Amber	IL2500	11
Willis, George R.	WV0750	10D,11,32B,52,65
Willis, Sharon J.	GA0490	10A,11,12,61,13A
Willson, Brian S.	NY0500	65,11
Wilner, Stacey	TN1000	12A,36,11,60A
Wilson, Blake	PA0950	12A,55,11

443

Name	Code	Areas
Wilson, Chris	AR0110	49,32E,11
Wilson, Frances	NC2210	13A,36,61,11
Wilson, Grover	NC1600	11,36,66A,66C,66D
Wilson, Joyce	IN0800	11,64A
Wilson, Ken	WA0030	11,36,61
Wilson, Russell	VA1600	66A,11
Wilson, Russell G.	UT0305	11,13,36,61
Wimberly, Larry	MS0150	11,13A,31A,34E,46
Windham, Mark	AR0800	11,63,32E,32F,37
Windt, Nathan J.	TN1550	60A,61,11,32D,36
Wingate, Owen K.	FL0675	13,11,12A,61,36
Winslow, Robert J.	FL0930	66A,46,13,34D,11
Winstead, Elizabeth	NC0100	61,11
Winter, Robert	MD0175	70,11
Wise, Herbert	NY2500	63C,66A,66D,11,32E
Witt, James	CA4050	13A,11,12A,47,62D
Witt, James	CA4000	13A,11,35
Witter, Tim	CA0050	13A,11,12A
Wittstadt, Kurt	MD0175	11,42,63B
Woger, Scott	IL1600	13,11,66A,47
Wojcik, Richard J.	IL3400	11,12A,36,61,31A
Woldu, Gail Hilson	CT0500	11,14C,12A,15
Wolek, Nathan	FL1750	34,11,45
Wolf, Scott	CA3460	70,11
Wolfe, Jennifer	MI1050	13C,66C,12A,11
Wolinski, Mary E.	KY1550	12A,11
Wollman, Elizabeth L.	NY0250	11,14C,14,15,20
Wollner, William	MI1850	11,13B,37,63B,60B
Wolters-Fredlund, Benita	MI0350	13,11,12A
Wolynec, Lisa	TN0050	11,64A
Wong Doe, Henry	PA1600	66A,66,11,13,66D
Wong, Yau-Sun	NM0200	11,60,13B,36,37
Wood, Eric	CA5350	10A,11,20,13A,13E
Wood, Graham	SC0450	11,12,63B,54,20
Wood, Jodi	AL1300	11,63B
Wood, Pamela	MA1200	13A,11
Wood, Rose Ann	CA2050	13A,13B,13C,11,66D
Wood, Thomas G.	OH0700	62A,62B,12A,11
Woodard, Susan J.	PA3580	11,12,66A,42
Woodcock, Ruth	WA0100	11,12A,20,13A,13G
Wooderson, Joseph	MO1550	11,61
Woodfield, Randal	PA3710	61,39,11
Woodruff, Ernest	MO0950	11,32E,63D
Woodruff, Louis	NJ0750	60,11,37
Woodruff, Sidney	GA0250	70,11
Woodward, Todd	KY1550	11
Woodworth, Jessica A.	MO0500	11,34,13,66A
Woody, John	AZ0150	11
Woolley, Clara	IN0010	13,11,32,66A,66G
Worsley, Margaret	CA3200	11
Wotring, Linda	MI1900	11,32A,32B,66A,66B
Wramage, Gregg	NJ0050	10A,10F,11
Wright, Craig M.	CT0900	11,12A,12
Wright, J. Clay	KS0440	11,13,36,40,61
Wright, Joseph	NY2400	11,29A
Wright, Joseph	MI2120	64C,11
Wright, Lesley A.	HI0210	11,12
Wright, Richard	NY4050	13,11,13C,66A,38
Wright, Sally	VA1000	66A,11
Wright, Trudi Ann	CO0830	11
Wright, Trudi Ann	CO0550	11
Wright, Vincent	NY2105	11
Wright, William B.	PA1300	11,13,36,60
Wu, Chieh-Mei Jamie	NY3500	11,13B,61,32D,36
Wubbena, Jan Helmut	AR0400	13,66G,12A,11
Wurgler, Norman F.	KY1540	11,36,20G,61,54
Wyatt, Ariana	WV0200	11,61
Yamamoto, Travis S.	CO0830	66A,11,13C
Yancey, Patty	CA5400	11,61,36
Yancho, Mari	MI0450	11,70,41
Yang, Sandra S.	OH0450	11,12
Yanovskiy, Leonid	FL2100	62A,62B,38,11,41
Yates, Derrick	AL0010	11,37,47,63A
Yates, Peter	CA0630	11,51,70,13A
Yau, Eugenia Oi Yan	NY0270	11,36,61,40,60A
Yeager, Katherine	CO0250	11
Yearsley, David	NY0900	12,13,11,66H,66G
Yeung, Alwen	GA1000	11,66C,13C,66D
Yon, Franklin	MI0450	63,47,29A,11
Yonce, Tammy Evans	SD0550	11,12A,64A,20
Yoon, Paul	VA1500	11,14,20C
Yoon, Sunmin	OH1100	20,11
Yoselevich, Gerald	NJ0700	11
You, Yali	MN0800	38,41,62C,11,12A
Youens-Wexler, Laura	DC0100	11,12
Young, Ann	CA4450	13,67B,11
Young, H. G.	WV0760	13,11,12A,36,54
Young, Jerry A.	WI0803	11,32C,63D
Young, Karen L.	AL1160	61,11,39
Young, Kevin	TX3527	63D,49,11
Young, Louis G.	AR0850	11
Young, Margaret	OH1860	11,32,66
Young, Phillip D.	CA3500	11,66A,66D
Young, Shawn David	GA0500	14C,35A,31A,35,11
Young, Steven	MA0510	36,11,55,66A,20G
Younge, J. Sophia	IL0450	13A,66A,11,36
Yount, Matthew W.	MO1500	11,66C
Yourke, Peter	NY0644	11
Yu, Ka-Wai	IL0800	62C,11,13B
Zabriskie, Alan N.	MO1790	11,40,36,60A
Zacharella, Alexandra	AR0730	63C,63D,11,49,37
Zackery, Harlan H.	MS0350	11,66A,66B,66C,66D
Zamek, Brian	NY4050	11,37,47
Zamzow, Laura	WV0200	11,63D,60B,32,37
Zavadsky, Julia	NJ1100	11,13A,36,60A
Zazulia, Emily	PA3420	11,12A
Zec, John	NJ0550	12A,31,66G,13,11
Zeidel, Scott	CA3200	13A,11,70
Zeidel, Scott	CA1520	70,11
Zeisler, Dennis J.	VA1000	11,37,64C,48
Zeiss, Laurel E.	TX0300	12A,12C,11,12
Zell, Steven D.	TX0390	13A,13B,13C,11,66A
Zemp, William Robin	SC0500	11,66A,66C,66D
Zerkle, Paula R.	PA2450	36,60,15,11,54
Zilber, Michael	CA2775	11,64E,12A,20G,29
Zimmer, Don	TN1700	11,51,62A
Zimmer, Susan	MD0800	66A,66C,11,66G
Zimmerman, Karen Bals	NY3720	13,11,66A,66B,66C
Zimmerman, Lynda	WI0806	13A,66A,66D,11
Zimmerman, R. Edward	IL3550	11,66G,66H,31A
Zinn, Daniel L.	CA0807	47,64E,41,29A,11
Ziolek, Eric E.	OH0650	13,10,11
Zipay, Terry L.	PA3700	13,35B,34A,13E,11
Zook, Katrina J.	WY0200	11,61
Zuluaga, Daniel	CA1960	11,70
Zupko, Mischa	IL0750	11
Zusman, Shanon P.	CA4450	67A,12,11
Zwally, Randall S.	PA2300	11,70
Zyko, Jeanette	TN0050	11,64B,64D

Musicology (All Areas)

Name	Code	Areas
Abbate, Carolyn	PA3350	12A,12
Abraham, Daniel E.	DC0010	11,12,14C,36,60
Adams, Byron	CA5040	13,10F,10,12
Adams, K. Gary	VA0100	11,12A,12,66A
Adams, Matthew	TX1425	65,50,11,12
Adams, Robert L.	MO0700	11,12A,12,66A
Agawu, V. Kofi	NJ0900	12
Agee, Richard J.	CO0200	13,11,12,66H,67D
Ahlquist, Karen	DC0100	12,14
Ahn, Suhnne	MD0650	12
Ake, David	NV0100	12,20,29A,14,66A
Albrecht, Theodore	OH1100	12
Alden, Jane	CT0750	12,55
Alexander, Lois L.	MI2120	63D,49,12,32
Allaire, Jean-Sebastien	AG0100	12,13,36,60A
Allen, Aaron S.	NC2430	12
Allen, Stephen Arthur	NJ1000	13,11,12A,12,20
Allison, Adrian	MN1295	12,20
Allsen, J. Michael	WI0865	11,12,14,20
Alonso-Minutti, Ana R.	TX3420	11,12
Altstatt, Alison	IA1600	12
Amati-Camperi, Alexandra	CA5353	12A,11,12C,13A,12
Amos, C. Nelson	MI0600	12A,12,67D,70
Anderson, Michael Alan	NY1100	12,12A,14F
Ansari, Emily	AG0500	12
Anthony, James	MD0850	11,12,16
Antokoletz, Elliott M.	TX3510	11,12A,12
Apple, Ryan	MI0910	13,12,70,11
Archer, Gail	NY2150	12
Archibald, Elizabeth	MD0650	12
Armstrong, Robin E.	MD0520	11,14,29A,12,12A
Arnold, Ben	KY1450	12,12A
Asai, Rika	IN0900	12
Atkinson, Charles M.	OH1850	12
Atlas, Allan W.	NY0600	12A,12
Atlas, Allan	NY0500	13,12A,12
Austerlitz, Paul	PA1400	12,14,46
Austern, Linda	IL2250	12
Avdeeff, Melissa	AA0110	11,12,14C
Averill, Gage	AB0100	12,14
Baber, Katherine	CA5150	12
Babiracki, Carol M.	NY4100	12,12B,14,20B,20E
Bahn, Curtis	NY3300	43,13,10,12,45
Bailey, Candace L.	NC1600	12,29D,15,11,12A
Bailey, Robert	NY2740	13,12
Bailey, Terence	AG0500	12,12C
Bailey, Walter B.	TX2150	11,12A,12
Bakan, Jonathon E.	AG0500	12
Baker, William	IN0005	12,13,60,36,39
Bakkum, Nathan	IL0720	20,12
Balzano, Gerald	CA5050	13A,34,13L,12F,12
Banagale, Ryan	CO0200	11,12,29,34
Banducci, Antonia L.	CO0900	12A,12,12C
Barg, Lisa	AI0150	12
Barnett, Gregory	TX2150	12A,12
Barolsky, Daniel G.	WI0100	13,12
Baron, John H.	LA0750	12A,12,20F,20G,31B
Barone, Anthony	NV0050	12,12A,12C
Barz, Gregory F.	TN1850	12,14,20,31,29A
Basinger, Bettie Jo	UT0350	12
Basinger, BettieJo	UT0250	12
Basini, Laura	CA0840	11,12
Bauer, Glen	MO1950	13,12,12A
Baum, Joshua	IL0150	61,11,39,12
Bauman, Thomas	IL2250	12
Bazler, Corbett	NY1100	12
Bazler, Corbett D.	NY4350	12A,12
Beal, Amy C.	CA5070	12A,12,43,20G
Becker, Melissa J.	PA2050	10E,12,32,62
Beckerman, Michael	NY2740	12,14C
Beckett, Scott	TX0100	11,12,13,37,63
Beckwith, Hubert	VA0450	13A,13,12
Beckwith, Sterling	AG0650	12,36,61,12F
Beecher, Randy	CA4050	66A,66B,66C,66D,12
Beghin, Tom	AI0150	66E,12
Belden, George R.	AK0100	13,12,10,34
Belfy, Jeanne M.	ID0050	11,12,64B
Bellman, Jonathan	CO0950	12
Benamou, Marc	IN0400	14,12,20,20D,12B
Bennett, Lawrence E.	IN1850	11,12A,12,13A
Benoit-Otis, Marie-Helene	AI0200	12
Benson, Jeremy L.	AL0500	64A,64B,12
Benson, Mark	PA0400	13,10,12,63,34
Bent, Ian	NY0750	11,12A,12,13J
Berger, Karol	CA4900	12A,12,13J,12B
Bergseth, Heather	MI0900	11,12
Berna, Linda	IL0550	13,12
Bernstein, Jane A.	MA1900	11,12A,12,12C
Bernstein, Lawrence F.	PA3350	12A,12
Berrett, Joshua	NY2400	13,11,29A,12,12B
Berry, James	WV0440	11,12,13,33,61
Berry, S. David	SC0650	10,13,34,35,12
Bertrand, Lynn Wood	GA0750	13,11,12A,12
Bick, Sally M.	AG0550	12
Biermann, Joanna Cobb	AL1170	12
Billings, Carolyn A.	NC0850	13,12,66A,66B
Binder, Benjamin A.	PA1050	12
Binford, Hilde M.	PA2450	13A,13,12A,12
Bittmann, Antonius O.	NJ1130	12,66G
Blachly, Alexander	IN1700	60,12,36,55,12A
Black, Brian	AA0200	12,66C,13E
Bloechl, Olivia A.	CA5032	12,12A,12D,20G,31A
Blombach, Ann K.	OH1850	13A,13,34,12F,12
Bloom, Peter A.	MA1750	12A,12
Bloxam, Jennifer	MA2250	11,15,12
Blum, Stephen	NY0600	12,14
Blumhofer, Jonathan	MA0650	10,12
Blunsom, Laurie	MN1120	12
Boaz, Virginia Lile	TX0600	12,61,39,12A
Bobak, Jacqueline	CA0510	12,42,61,32G
Boczkowska, Eweline	OH2600	12
Bomberger, E. Douglas	PA1250	12,66A
Bonds, Mark Evan	NC2410	11,12
Bonus, Alexander	NC0600	55,12
Bookout, Melanie	IN0905	11,12A,12,55,67A
Boone, Graeme M.	OH1850	12
Boorman, Stanley H.	NY2740	11,12A,12,55
Booth, John D.	MO0500	12,44,61,31A,70
Borders, James M.	MI2100	12,14B,71
Borg, Paul	IL1150	13A,13,11,12A,12
Borroff, Edith	NY3705	12A,12,12B
Borwick, Susan Harden	NC2500	13,12,31,10,15
Bostock, Matthew	MA1100	12,13A

Name	Code	Areas
Boucher, Leslie H.	GA0700	12,20,13,62,11
Boulanger, Richard	AE0100	12A,12,66A
Bourion, Sylveline	AI0200	12
Boutwell, Brett N.	LA0200	12
Bowen, Jose A.	TX2400	47,12A,29,38,12
Bowen, Richard L.	IN1850	36,12,12A,11,12B
Bower, Calvin	IN1700	12A,12
Boyd, Melinda J.	IA1600	12
Boyd, Michael	PA0600	10A,10B,13,12
Boyette, Larry J.	NY3550	70,12
Boynton, Susan	NY0750	11,12A,12,12B
Bozarth, George	WA1050	12A,12
Brackett, David	AI0150	12,14C
Brady, Judith L.	NY3725	12
Brand, Benjamin D.	TX3420	12A,12
Braun, William	WI1155	13,10,12,55B,34
Brauner, Mitchell	WI0825	12A,12,12C,11
Braus, Ira	CT0650	12A,12
Breckbill, David	NE0200	12,66C
Brellochs, Christopher	NY1050	47,10,13,12,64E
Brewer, Charles E.	FL0850	12A,12
Brill, Mark	TX3530	12
Briscoe, James R.	IN0250	12A,14,12C,12
Brobeck, John T.	AZ0500	12,55
Brodbeck, David	CA5020	12
Brodsky, Seth	CT0900	12
Brookshire, Bradley	NY3785	12A,12,55,66G,66H
Brosius, Amy T.	NJ1000	11,12,13,20,12A
Brown, Jennifer Williams	IA0700	12,55,67,66H
Brown, Julie Hedges	AZ0450	12
Brown, Rae Linda	CA5020	12,29A
Brown, Richard	CA0835	12
Broyles, Michael	FL0850	12
Bruhn, Christopher	OH0850	12,14
Brunk, Jeremy	IL1750	13,12,65,10
Brunner, Lance	KY1450	12A,12
Buchanan, Donna A.	IL3300	20F,12,14
Budasz, Rogerio	CA5040	12,20H
Buis, Johann S.	IL3550	12,20,11
Bunbury, Richard R.	MA0400	12,66G,32H,31A,32
Bunch, Ryan	NJ1100	12
Burdette, Glenn E.	MI2200	12,66A,66H
Burke, Kevin R.	IN0500	12,13,20,42,63B
Burke, Richard N.	NY0625	11,12A,12,20G
Burke, Richard	NY0600	12
Burkholder, J. Peter	IN0900	12
Burnett, Henry	NY0642	12,14
Burnett, Henry	NY0600	12,14
Burns, Deb S.	IN0907	33,12
Burrows, David	NY2740	11,12A,12,14
Burton, Justin D.	NJ1000	12
Bush, Deanna D.	TX3420	12A,12
Bush, Douglas E.	UT0050	12,55,66G,67,31A
Bushard, Anthony J.	NE0600	12,29A
Busse Berger, Anna Maria	CA5010	12A,12
Butler, Gregory G.	AB0100	13,10,12A,12
Butler, H. Joseph	TX3000	66G,12,31
Butler, Margaret R.	FL1850	12
Caballero, Carlo	CO0800	12
Cabrini, Michele	NY0625	12B,12A,13B,11,12
Cai, Camilla	OH1200	11,12
Cain, Jerry	AI0150	12
Cain, M. Celia	AG0450	12,20G
Calico, Joy	TN1850	12,20F
Calvo, Francisco	CA1900	36,32,12
Campana, Alessandra	MA1900	12,12A,11
Campbell, Carey	UT0350	12,11,63
Campbell, Jennifer L.	MI0400	11,12,20
Candelaria, Lorenzo	TX3510	11,12A,12
Carlin, Patrick	VA1600	12
Carlsen, James	WA1050	34,12B,12F,12,12C
Carlson, Mark	MD0610	63,11,12,13,37
Caron, Sylvain	AI0200	13,31A,12
Carpenter, Alexander	AA0110	12,13C,13B,11,13E
Carr, Walter E.	OR0800	12A,12,14,20G
Carroll, Roy W.	IA0940	66,13,12,11,31A
Carslake, Louise	CA2950	12,55,64A,67
Carson, Charles	TX3510	12
Carter, Marva G.	GA1050	12,20G,20,20A
Carter, Shannon	AG0350	11,12,13A
Carter, Timothy	NC2410	12,13
Caschetta, Todd	CA4850	20G,11,12,14,50
Case, Nelly Maude	NY3780	12
Cassarino, James P.	VT0200	12,14,20,36,37
Cassio, Francesca	NY1600	12,12A,12C,20
Castonguay, Gerald	MA0650	12A,12
Castro, Christi-Anne Salazar	MI2100	12
Catefforis, Theodore P.	NY4100	12,12D,20G,29A,14C
Ceballos, Sara Gross	WI0350	12
Celotto, Albert Gerard	CT0700	13,12,66A
Century, Michael	NY3300	12,13,43,34H,66A
Chafe, Eric	MA0500	13A,11,12A,12,13J
Chang, Peter M.	IL2150	11,14,12,42
Chapman, Dale E.	ME0150	12,13,29
Charles, Sydney R.	CA5010	12A,12
Cheney, Stuart G.	TX3000	12
Chianis, Sam	NY3705	12A,12,14,20H
Chiasson, Rachelle	AI0150	12
Chinn, Genevieve	NY2105	13,11,12A,12
Chittum, Donald	PA3330	13,12A,12,14,12F
Christensen, Jean M.	KY1500	12,29A
Christiansen, Paul V.	ME0500	12
Chusid, Martin	NY2740	11,12A,12
Chybowski, Julia J.	WI0830	12,11
Cienniwa, Paul D.	MA2020	12A,12,11,34B
Cies-Muckala, Jennifer	TN0100	12
Cinquegrani, David	CT0350	31A,36,41,12
Citron, Marcia J.	TX2150	12
Clague, Mark A.	MI2100	12
Clark, Alice V.	LA0300	12A,11,31A,12
Clark, Caryl L.	AG0450	12A,12
Clark, Maribeth	FL1360	11,12,14,15
Clark, Walter A.	CA5040	12,20H
Clarkson, Austin	AG0650	12,32
Clifton, Keith E.	MI0400	12,11,20
Cobb, Gary W.	CA3600	13,10,12,66G,66B
Cochran, Timothy	NJ1350	12
Coehlo, Victor	MA0400	12
Cohen, Albert	CA4900	12A,12,13J,20G
Cohen, Flynn	NH0150	13,12
Cole, Malcolm S.	CA5032	11,12A,12,66G,31A
Cole, Ronald F.	ME0500	12A,12,66A
Colin, Marie-Alexis	AI0200	12
Collins, Willa	FL1900	12,14C
Colton, Glenn	AG0170	12,20G,14C,14D
Comberiati, Carmelo	NY2200	12,14
Condaris, Christine	MA1185	12,14,36
Connolly, Thomas H.	PA3350	12A,12
Cook, Grant W.	OH2290	36,40,60,12
Cook, Linda Klein	WI0750	63A,12,13,63B,10F
Cooper, Frank E.	FL1900	12,66A,66H,67
Cooper, Peter	TN1850	12
Corrigan, Vincent J.	OH0300	12,66H
Cowart, Georgia	OH0400	12A,12
Cowger, Kelsey	AF0100	12
Cox, Melissa	GA0750	11,12,13
Crabtree, Joseph C.	TX1425	11,12,36,39
Crain, Timothy M.	MA2030	12,20,29A,11
Crist, Stephen A.	GA0750	12
Crook, David	WI0815	12
Crooks, Mack	CA4650	13,12,66A,34
Crookshank, Esther R.	KY1200	12,14,62
Crowell, Gregory	MI0900	13,12,66G,66H
Cruz, Gabriela G.	MI2100	12
Cryderman-Weber, Molly	MI1200	12,20,13B,13,65
Culver, Daniel	IL0100	13,60B,12,38
Cumming, Julie	AI0150	12
Cummings, Anthony M.	PA1850	12
Cummins, Linda P.	AL1170	12
Currie, Gabriela	MN1623	12
Currie, James Robert	NY4320	12
Curry, Nick	FL1950	62C,12,11
Cutting, Linda	MA1175	12
Cypess, Rebecca	NJ1130	12,66E,66H,56
Cyrus, Cynthia	TN1850	12,15,55,20F
D'Accone, Frank A.	CA5032	12A,12,13J
Dahlenburg, Jane	AR0850	12
Dailey, Jeff	NY1275	12,32
Dalby, Bruce	NM0450	32C,47,12
Dalton, Dana	MA1400	66A,12A,12,66C
Darby, Joseph E.	NH0150	12
Davenport, Mark	CO0650	12,55,67C,29A,14C
Davies-Wilson, Dennis	NM0450	12
Davis, Hope	CA2300	13A,12,11,37,13B
Davis, Mary E.	OH0400	12A,12,14
Day, Thomas Charles	RI0250	13A,13,12
Day-O'Connell, Sarah K.	IL1350	12,14,66A,66E
de Graaf, Melissa J.	FL1900	12,12A,11
De Medicis, Francois	AI0200	12
De More, Christine	CA5300	12
De Stefano, Reno	AI0200	29,12
De Val, Dorothy	AG0650	12
Deaville, James	AG0100	12,29,35
Deaville, James A.	AG0200	11,12A,12,41,12C
Decker, Todd R.	MO1900	12,12A
DeFord, Ruth	NY0625	11,12A,12,12C
DeFord, Ruth	NY0600	12
DelDonna, Anthony R.	DC0075	12,12A,12B,12C,12D
Dell'Antonio, Andrew	TX3510	11,12A,12
DeLong, Kenneth	AA0150	12,13J
Demsey, Karen B.	NJ1400	64A,48,12,11,12A
Desmond, Clinton J.	SD0200	36,11,20,60,12
DeVeaux, Scott K.	VA1550	13,12A,12,14,29
Deville, Mary	LA0550	66G,12
DeWitt, Debora	MI0850	66,12
DiCenso, Daniel J.	MA0700	11,12
Dickensheets, Janice	CO0950	12,34A,14,12B,12A
Dill, Charles	WI0815	12
Dillon, Emma	PA3350	11,12A,12
Dilthey, Michael R.	MA2250	12
DiMedio, Annette	PA3330	12A,12,66A,66D,11
Dineen, P. Murray	AG0400	13,12
Dobbins, Francis	AI0200	12
Dodds, Michael R.	NC1650	12
Dodge, Leanne E.	NY2750	12A,12,13A
Dodson, John	MI0050	10,12,38
Dohoney, Ryan	KS1350	12
Dolan, Emily I.	PA3350	12A,12,11,12B
Dolata, David	FL0700	12,67G,55,56,67H
Dolp, Laura A.	NJ0800	12
Dominick, Daniel L.	TX0250	66A,12,60B,38,60
dos Santos, Silvio J.	FL1850	12
Doukhan, Lilianne	MI0250	12A,12,14,31A,12C
Downs, Philip	AG0500	12,13J
Dregalla, Herbert E.	OH2500	12,32,60,64C
Drury, Stephen	MA1400	66A,43,12
Duchesneau, Michel	AI0200	12
Dudas, Michael	MA1175	12
Dudgeon, Ralph T.	NY3720	12,67,14,38,63
Duffin, Ross	OH0400	12A,12,55
Duffy, Kathryn Ann Pohlmann	IA0650	11,12,13,36,60
DuPree, Mary	ID0250	12A,12,43,14C
Dzapo, Kyle J.	IL0400	12A,12,64A
Earp, Lawrence	WI0815	11,12A,12
Echard, William	AG0100	12,20,29,34,35
Edwards, Constance	WV0300	64D,12,11,12A,10F
Edwards, Steven C.	LA0080	11,12,36,40,61
Edwards, T. Matthew	MD0060	66A,13,66C,12,36
Ehrlich, Janina	IL0100	11,12,41,62C
Eidsheim, Nina	CA5032	12A,12,13
Elliott, Robin W.	AG0450	12,12A,20G
Ellison, Paul	CA4200	12,31,55
Ellsworth, Jane	WA0250	12A,12
Engelhardt, Jeffers	MA0100	20,33,12
Enrico, Eugene	OK1350	12A,12,55,67
Erken, Emily	OH1850	12
Etter, Troy L.	NY1600	12,11
Eyerly, Sarah J.	IN0250	12,13A,14A,15
Fader, Don	AL1170	55C,67C,12
Falck, Robert A.	AG0450	11,12A,12
Fallon, Robert	PA0550	12
Farris, Daniel King	OK1250	40,42,12,36,13
Fast, Susan	AG0200	13A,11,12A,12,55
Fauser, Annegret	NC2410	12,15
Fawcett-Yeske, Maxine	CO0750	11,12,14,16,20
Feisst, Sabine M.	AZ0100	12
Feldman, Martha	IL3250	11,12A,12,15
Fenimore, Ross	NC0550	11,12,14C,14D
Ferencz, Jane Riegel	WI0865	67,11,12,15
Ferer, Mary T.	WV0750	11,12A,12
Ferrara, Lawrence	NY2750	13,12,32,66
Ferris, David	TX2150	12A,12
Fillerup, Jessie	VA1500	12
Fillion, Michelle	AB0150	12
Fink, Katherine	NY0646	11,12
Fink, Michael Jon	CA0510	12A,12,35,10
Fink, Robert W.	CA5032	13,12,34,20G
Finson, Jon W.	NC2410	11,12
Fischer Faw, Victoria	NC0750	12,66A,66B,41
Fisher, Alexander	AB0100	12,55,67D
Florea, Luminita D.	IL0800	12
Floreen, John E.	NJ1140	12,36,66G
Florine, Jane Lynn	IL0600	11,12,12A,20A,64A
Flynn, Timothy	MI1800	10A,12,36,39,13
Fontijn, Claire	MA2050	12A,12
Ford, Kelly	IN1350	36,61,60A,12,64E

445

Name	Code	Areas
Ford, Philip	IN0900	12
Foreman, George C.	GA2100	12
Fosler-Lussier, Danielle	OH1850	12A,12
Foster, Donald H.	OH2200	12A,12
Foster, Rodney W.	NY4100	11,12,31A,34A,34F
Francis, Kimberly	AG0350	15,13,12
Frandsen, Mary E.	IN1700	12A,12
Frantz, Charles	NJ1350	12
Freedman, Richard	PA1500	11,12A,12,20D,29A
Freeman, James	PA3200	12,60
Freeman, Robert S.	TX3510	12
Freeze, Timothy	IN0900	12
French, John	PA3550	11,12,13,36
Frisch, Walter	NY0750	11,12A,12
Frogley, Alain	CT0600	12
Fruehauf, Tina	NY0500	11,12
Fry, Laura	TN0100	12
Fry, Robert Webb	TN1850	12
Fuhrmann, Christina E.	OH0100	13A,11,12,14
Fulcher, Jane	MI2100	12,12A
Fuller, Sarah	NY3790	11,12A,12,13
Gable, Frederick K.	CA5040	12A,12,31A
Gall, Jeffrey C.	NJ0800	55,61,12A,12,39
Gallagher, Sean	MA0400	12
Galvan, Gary	PA1830	12,70,29A,34A
Gano, Peter W.	OH1850	12A,12
Garcia, David F.	NC2410	12,14,20
Gardner, David	AG0100	12A,12
Gardner, James E.	UT0250	62A,12,31,31A
Gardner, Kara	CA5353	12,11
Garlington, Aubrey S.	NC2430	12,12A
Garrett, Charles	MI2100	12
Garrison, Leonard	ID0250	64A,13,12,13B,13C
Gavalchin, John E.	NY4200	66A,12,13
Gay, Leslie C.	TN1710	14,14A,14C,20,12
Geary, Jason D.	MI2100	12
Gerber, Rebecca L.	NY3780	12
Gerbino, Giuseppe	NY0750	11,12A,12
Gerk, Sarah	OH1700	12
Germer, Mark	PA3330	12
Gertig, Suzanne	CO0900	62E,16,12
Getz, Christine S.	IA1550	12A,12
Ghuman, Nalini G.	CA2950	13,12A,12C,12
Giarusso, Richard	MD0650	12
Gibbons, William J.	TX3000	12,11
Gibbs, Christopher	NY0150	12
Gibson, Maya	MO1800	12
Gier, Christina B.	AA0100	12A,12D,12B,12,15
Giger, Andreas	LA0200	12
Gillingham, Bryan	AG0100	12A,12,36
Gingerich, John M.	MD0650	12
Ginter, Anthony F.	CA5040	12,38
Girard, Sharon	CA4200	12A,12,14
Glarner, Robert L.	VA1100	13,10,321,66G,12
Glixon, Beth	KY1450	12
Glixon, Jonathan	KY1450	12,55
Godwin, Joscelyn	NY0650	12A,12
Goertzen, Christopher	MS0750	12
Goertzen, Valerie Woodring	LA0300	12
Goldberg, Halina	IN0900	12
Goldberg, Randall	OH2600	12
Golden, Joseph	GA0550	39,66G,11,12
Golden, Rachel	TN1700	12
Goldman, Jonathan	AB0150	12,13
Gollner, Marie L.	CA5032	12A,12,13J
Gossett, Philip	IL3250	12A,12
Grace, Michael	CO0200	11,12A,12,55
Gradone, Richard	NJ0250	13,12A,12,47,63A
Gramit, David	AA0100	12
Granat, Zbigniew	NY2650	12
Grant, Joyce	NY1210	12,13A,36
Grant, Kerry S.	NY4320	12
Grapes, Dawn	CO0250	12
Grave, Floyd	NJ1130	11,12A,12,13J
Gray, Laura J.	AG0470	11,12A,12,14,20
Grayson, David	MN1623	12
Greco, Eugene A.	FL1300	36,12A,67F,12,67
Green, Richard D.	OH1450	12A,12,12C
Greene, Oliver N.	GA1050	12,20H
Greenlee, Robert K.	ME0200	60,36,12A,12,55
Greenspan, Bertram	NJ1050	62A,51,12A,12
Greenwald, Helen	MA1400	12
Greenwood, Andrew	TX2400	12
Greenwood, Joanna E.	MD0400	12,20
Gregory, David	KY1200	61,16,12
Grey, Thomas S.	CA4900	13,12A,12
Grier, James	AG0500	12,13J
Gries, Peggy	OR1050	12,55,67
Griesheimer, James	IA0950	12,11,13
Griffel, L. Michael	NY1900	12A,12
Grimes, Calvin B.	GA1450	13,10,12,20G,31A
Grimes, Robert R.	NY1300	12,14,20
Groesbeck, Rolf A.	AR0750	11,12,14,66A,20
Groos, Arthur	NY0900	12
Grubbs, David	NY0500	10C,12,34
Gruhn, Charles	CA1700	12,12A
Grymes, James A.	NC2420	12,12A,11
Guertin, Ghyslaine	AI0200	12
Guertin, Marcelle	AI0200	13,12
Guinn, John R.	MI2200	12
Haas, David	GA2100	11,12
Hadlock, Heather L.	CA4900	11,12A,12
Hafer, Edward	MS0750	12,12A
Hager, Nancy M.	NY0500	13,11,12A,12
Haggh-Huglo, Barbara	MD1010	12A,12
Haines, John D.	AG0450	12A,12,20F
Haldey, Olga	MD1010	12,12A,11,14
Hall, Barbara L.	KY0450	13,12A,12,36,60
Hall, Frederick A.	AG0200	11,12A,12,20G
Hallman, Diana R.	KY1450	12,20A
Hallmark, Rufus	NJ1130	12,12A
Halmo, Joan	AJ0150	12
Hamessley, Lydia	NY1350	13C,12,14,20G,12A
Hanning, Barbara	NY0600	12A,12
Hanning, Barbara Russano	NY0550	13A,11,12A,12
Hara, Kunio	SC1110	12
Haramaki, Gordon	CA4400	12
Harbec, Jacinthe	AI0200	12,11
Haringer, Andrew	MA2250	12,11
Harley, Anne	CA4500	61,39,12
Harness, Kelley	MN1623	12,14
Harris, Donald	AJ0150	32,63,12
Harris, Ellen T.	MA1200	13,11,12A,12
Harris-Warrick, Rebecca	NY0900	11,12,52
Harrison, John F.	PA1250	12A,12,66A
Hart, Brian J.	IL2200	12A,12
Hartzell, K. Drew	NY3700	11,12A,12
Harwood, Craig	CT0900	12,14
Harwood, Gregory	GA0950	11,12
Haughton, Ethel Norris	VA1750	13,12A,12,20G,66C
Hawkshaw, Paul	CT0850	12
Hayner, Phillip A.	GA1650	11,12,66A,66C,66D
Hays, Elizabeth	IA0700	12,55,66H
Hearn, Priscilla	KS0550	66A,11,12,66D,13C
Hedden, Laura	NJ1000	12
Hefling, Stephen	OH0400	12A,12
Heidlberger, Frank	TX3420	13J,12A,12,13
Heifetz, Robin J.	CA0200	11,20,10A,43,12
Heimarck, Brita Renee	MA0400	12
Heller, Wendy B.	NJ0900	12A,12,39,14A
Hellyar, Kathleen	PA0125	12,66A
Henderson, David R.	NY3550	14,20,12
Hepokoski, James	CT0900	12
Herl, Joseph	NE0150	12,13,31A
Hess, Carol A.	CA5010	12,20H
Heuchemer, Dane O.	OH1200	11,12A,12,37,67
High, Eric	WI0750	63C,47,13,12,49
High, Ronald	SC0150	11,12,31F,61,66
Hildebrand, David K.	MD0650	12
Hill, George R.	NY0250	11,12A,12,16
Hill, Jackson	PA0350	10,12A,12,14,71
Hinterbichler, Karl	NM0450	12A,12,63C,63D
Hinton, Stephen W.	CA4900	12A,12
Hirsch, Marjorie	MA2250	11,12,15,20G
Hix, Michael T.	NM0450	61,13A,12A,12
Ho, Allan	IL2910	13,12A,12
Ho, Meilu	MI2100	12
Hobbs, Wayne C.	TX3200	13,12,35E,20G
Hodgson, Jay	AG0500	14,29,35C,35D,12
Hoeckner, Berthold	IL3250	11,12,12A
Hoefnagels, Anna	AG0100	12,20
Hollander, Jeffrey M.	IN1750	12A,15,11,12
Hollingsworth, Devon	IN0005	10A,12,13,32,66G
Holoman, D. Kern	CA5010	60,11,12A,12
Holsinger, Bruce	VA1550	12,31A
Holst, Robert I.	IL1520	12A,12,61
Holz, Ronald	KY0100	12,38,41,49,10
Honisch, Erika	MO1810	12
Hoover, Elizabeth	OH1450	12
Hopkins, Robert	NY1350	13,12A,12,12F
Hopkins, William T.	CA4200	11,12A,12,12F
Houghton, Edward F.	CA5070	12A,12
House, LeAnn	MN0450	13,12,66
Houser, Steven	MO0600	13,12A,12,64
Houtchens, Alan	TX2900	12A,12,63B
Howland, John L.	NJ1140	10,12,20,29,29A
Hsu, Dolores M.	CA5060	12A,12,20D,14A,14B
Hsu, Pattie	CA5353	12,20
Huang, Hao	CA4500	66A,12,20C,20G,29
Hubbert, Julie	SC1110	12
Hubner, Carla	DC0110	12A,12,66A,35E
Hudson, Barton	WV0750	12A,12,66H
Hudson, Richard	CA5032	12A,12
Huebner, Steven	AI0150	12
Hughes, Andrew	AG0450	11,12,13J,12G
Hund, Jennifer L.	IN1300	12,66A,12A,11
Hung, Eric Hing-tao	NJ1350	12,14
Hunt, Graham G.	TX3500	13,12,10F,11,12A
Hunter, David	TX3510	12,12C
Hunter, Mary K.	ME0200	13A,13,11,12A,12
Huovinen, Erkki	MN1623	12
Hurley, David R.	KS1050	12,20,64B
Hwang, Okon	CT0150	14,66,11,12,13
Illari, Bernardo	TX3420	12,20H
Ingraham, Mary	AA0100	12
Isaac, Cecil	TX0250	11,12
Isacoff, Stuart M.	NY3785	12
Jackson, Barbara G.	AR0700	13,12A,12,55B,67A
Jackson, Roland	CA1050	13,12
Jackson, Roland	CA2710	13,12A,12
Jacobson, Daniel C.	MI2250	11,12A,12,34
Jander, Owen	MA2050	11,12A,12
Janners, Erik N.	WI0425	37,47,60,12,13
Jaquez, Candida	CA4500	14,20,12,41
Jarjour, Tala	IN1700	12,20
Jaros, Marc	MN1200	12,36,20,40
Jeffery, Peter	NJ0900	11,12A,12,31A
Jenkins, Chadwick	NY0600	12
Jensen-Moulton, Stephanie	NY0500	11,12,12E
Joe, Jeongwon	OH2200	12
Johns, Donald C.	CA5040	12,29
Johnson, Douglas	NJ1130	12A,12
Johnson, James R.	MN1300	13,11,12
Johnson, Jeffrey	CT0550	10,11,12,13
Johnson, Lindsay	CA4500	12
Johnson, Mildred	UT0300	13,12A,12,62B
Johnson, Roger O.	NJ0950	12,14C,35A
Johnson, Steven P.	UT0050	12A,12,14,12F
Johnston, Gregory	AG0450	11,12A,12,31A
Josephson, David	RI0050	12A,12,55B,12E
Joubert, Estelle	AF0100	12
Joyce, Brooke	IA0950	10,13,34,12
Joyce, J. Patrick	WV0300	70,12,42
Joyce, John J.	LA0750	11,12,29
Julien, Patricia A.	VT0450	13,12,10D,29
Kagan, Alan L.	MN1623	12A,12,14
Kallberg, Jeffrey	PA3350	12A,12,12D,15
Kallick, Jenny L.	MA0100	13,12A,39,41,12
Kaloyanides, Michael G.	CT0700	12,13,14,20,34
Kamm, Charles W.	CA3620	36,11,12,60
Kamm, Charles W.	CA1060	36,11,12,60
Kamm, Charles W.	CA2175	36,11,12,60
Kamm, Charles W.	CA4500	36,12,40,60
Kang, YouYoung	CA4500	13,12,20C,20G
Karnes, Kevin C.	GA0750	12,12C
Karpf, Nita	OH0400	12,32
Karr, John F.	CA0810	12,14C
Kattari, Kim	TX3510	12
Katz, Dolores	CA5060	12A,12
Katz, Mark	NC2410	12,14,20,34
Katz, Robert S.	OK1300	13,11,12A,12,62D
Keathley, Elizabeth L.	NC2430	12A,12
Keeling, Kenneth	PA0550	12
Keenan-Takagi, Kathleen D.	NY0400	32,36,12
Kehrberg, Kevin	NC2550	12,14C,20,60A,62D
Keillor, Elaine	AG0100	12A,12,14,66A,20G
Keister, Jay	CO0800	12
Keller, Karlton	CA3400	13,47,48,49,12
Kelly, Kevin	GA2100	16,12
Kelly, Thomas Forrest	MA1050	11,12A,12,13J
Kendrick, Robert L.	IL3250	11,31,12,14
Kennedy, Laura E.	TX3420	12
Kennedy, Laura E.	SC0750	12
Kennedy, T. Frank	MA0330	11,12,31A,20H
Kenworthy, Dan	NJ1000	12
Kernodle, Tammy L.	OH1450	11,12,29A,29D

Index by Area of Teaching Interest

Name	Code	Areas
Kerr, Hugh	FL0050	12
Kershaw, Linda L.	SC0150	11,12,60,66A,36
Kidula, Jean	GA2100	14,20,11,31,12
Kim, Min	NJ0825	13,12,66A,66B,41
Kinderman, William A.	IL3300	12
King, Richard G.	MD1010	11,12A,12,20G,12C
King, Valeria G.	LA0720	13,60,12A,12,20G
Kinnett, Randy	TX3420	12
Kirchner, Bill	NY2660	10,12,64,29
Kiyama, Wynn	OR0850	12,20
Klefstad, Terry	TN0100	12,14
Kleinsasser, Jerome S.	CA0650	11,12A,12,10C
Klemp, Merilee I.	MN0050	12A,12,64B,48,40
Kloppers, Jacobus	AA0035	11,12A,12,66G,31A
Klumpenhouwer, Henry	AA0100	13,12
Knapp, Raymond L.	CA5032	12A,12
Koegel, John	CA0815	12,14
Kok, Roe-Min	AI0150	12,14
Kolt, Robert P.	AR0500	12,12A,60
Konye, Paul	NY3680	13G,12A,38,10,12
Kopfstein-Penk, Alicia	DC0010	70,12,13C,11
Kosciesza, Andrew	PA2400	11,12,20,36
Kowalke, Kim	NY4350	12A,12,39,54,20G
Kraft, Leo	NY0642	12,13
Kramer, Lawrence	NY1300	12
Kramer, Richard	NY0600	12A,12
Krasner, Orly	NY0550	12
Kregor, Jonathan	OH2200	12
Kreider, J. Evan	AB0100	12
Kreiling, Jean L.	MA0510	13A,11,12A,12,66D
Kreitner, Kenneth	TN1680	12,67E,55
Kreuzer, Gundula	CT0900	12
Kreyszig, Walter	AJ0150	12A,12,20G,55
Kristiansen, Morten	OH2550	12
Kroll, Mark	MA0400	66H,66E,12,67F,13
Kronengold, Charles	CA4900	12,20
Kulp, Jonathan	LA0760	12A,12
Kupfer, Peter A.	TX2400	12
Kurtzman, Jeffrey	MO1900	12A,12
Kushner, David Z.	FL1850	12,12A,12B,12E,20G
Kuykendall, James Brooks	SC0700	13,12,11,41,38
Kwon, Donna L.	KY1450	12,20
Labonville, Marie E.	IL1150	11,12A,12,20D
Ladewig, James L.	RI0300	11,12A,12
Laing, Laurence 'Corky'	AG0500	12
Laird, Paul R.	KS1350	12A,12,55B,55C
Laird, Tracey	GA0050	12,14,11,29A
Lallerstedt, Ford	PA0850	13,12
Lamb, Robert E.	FL0150	36,13,12,60A
Lambert, Sterling	MD0750	12,13B
Lamkin, Kathleen J.	CA5100	12A,11,12,62A,66A
Lamothe, Peter	TN0100	12,14
Lang, Zoe	FL2000	12
Langford, Jeffrey	NY2150	12
Langsford, Christopher M.	KS0750	36,32,11,12,13
Lanza, Alcides	AI0150	12
Largey, Michael	MI1400	12,14,20
Larkowski, Charles S.	OH2500	12A,12,66H
Laudon, Robert	MN1623	11,12A,12,66H
Laurance, Emily R.	CA4150	12
Laurent, Linda	CT0050	13,12,66A,66D,42
Lawrence, Deborah	MD0750	12,20
Lawson, Sonya R.	MA2100	12A,62B,29A,12,20
Lawton, David	NY3790	60,12A,12,38,39
Lawton, Richard	AI0150	11,12,63
Le Guin, Elisabeth C.	CA5032	12A,12,62C,67B,15
Leahy, Eugene J.	IN1700	11,12A,12
LeBaron, Anne	CA0510	10,12,62E
L'Ecuyer, Sylvia	AI0200	12
Lee, Katherine In-Young	CA5010	14,12,20C,12D
Lee, Michael	OK1350	12A,12,14,20G
Lefebvre, Marie-Therese	AI0200	12,20G
Lefferts, Peter M.	NE0600	11,12A,12
Leger, James K.	NM0150	10,60,12,14,38
Lein, Melinda	NC2650	61,12
Leistra-Jones, Karen	PA1300	11,12A,12
Lerner, Edward	NY0642	12
Lerner, Neil	NC0550	11,12,34H,66H
Levin, Neil	NY1860	12C,12A,12
Levitz, Tamara	CA5032	12A,12,13
Levy, Kenneth	NJ0900	11,12A,12
Lew, Howard	NY2700	13A,12,66D
Lewis, Alexandra M.	NY0500	11,12,13C,66D
Lewis-Hammond, Susan	AB0150	12
Libin, Kathryn L.	NY4450	13,11,12A,12
Lieberman, Fredric	CA5070	12,14
Lih, Lars	AI0150	12
Lincoln, Harry B.	NY3705	11,12A,12,34
Lindau, Elizabeth Ann	PA1400	12,14C,20
Lindorff, Joyce Zankel	PA3250	12A,12,66H,67C
Link, Dorothea	GA2100	11,12
Link, Stan	TN1850	12A,12,20G,14C,15
Litterick, Louise	MA1350	13,12A,12
Lloyd, L. Keith	TX1650	65,12A,14,12,50
Lochhead, Judith	NY3790	13E,13F,12,13,12A
Locke, Brian	IL3500	11,20F,12
Locker, Fred	OH2150	13,12
Loewen, Peter V.	TX2150	12A,12
Lohman, Laura Ann	CA0815	12,14,14C
Long, Michael	IN0900	12
Long, Michael P.	NY4320	12A,12,13J
Lopez-Gonzalez, Monica	MD0650	12
Loranger, Dennis	OH2500	12,12A
Lorenzo, Elizabeth	CT0050	12,11,15,12A
Lott, R. Allen	TX2600	12A,12,14,12C
Lovensheimer, James A.	TN1850	12,14,20G,29
Lowe, Melanie D.	TN1850	12A,12,20G,14C,15
Lubin, Steven	NY3785	13,12A,12,66A
Lucia, Margaret E.	PA3050	13,11,12,66A
Luko, Alexis	AG0100	12
Luu, Bing	CA4050	20,12
Maas, Martha C.	OH1850	12A,12,55
Macdonald, Claudia	OH1700	12
MacDonald, John A.	OH2150	60,12A,12,36
MacDonald, Michael	AA0100	12,14
MacInnis, John	IA0500	12,13A,13B,11
MacIntyre, Bruce C.	NY0600	12
MacIntyre, Bruce C.	NY0500	12A,12,36
Mackenzie, Barbara Dobbs	NY0600	12,34
Macklin, Christopher B.	GA1300	12
MacLachlan, Heather M.	OH2250	12,20,14,20D
MacNeil, Anne E.	NC2410	12,15
MacPherson, William A.	MA2150	11,12,66G,66H
Macy, Elizabeth	CA0960	12
Madsen, Charles A.	VT0100	66A,12,11,66C
Magee, Jeffrey	IL3300	12,20G,29A
Magyar, Paul R.	TN0930	12,31
Mahon, Brad	AA0150	12,14
Maier, Ralph	AA0150	70,41,12,14
Main, Alexander	OH1850	12A,12
Malin, Yonatan	CO0800	13,12
Maloy, Rebecca	CO0800	12
Maltz, Richard	SC1100	13,10,65,12,14
Malvinni, David J.	CA4410	12,20
Malyshko, Olga	AG0250	12A,12,71,55
Manabe, Noriko	NJ0900	12
Mangsen, Sandra	AG0500	12,66H
Maniates, Maria R.	AG0450	11,12A,12,12B
Manley, Douglas H.	TN1550	12,66,31,66G,12C
Mann, Brian R.	NY4450	11,12A,12,29A
Mansure, Victor N.	NC0050	12
Manwarren, Matthew C.	SC1200	66A,66B,12,41
Markham, Michael	NY3725	12
Markstrom, Kurt	AC0100	12
Marosek, Scott	NC1350	12,66A,66B
Marsh, Carol	NC2430	12A,12,55,67
Marsh, Peter K.	CA0807	14,12,20B,20
Marshall, Robert L.	MA0500	12
Martin, Andree	GA0550	64A,11,43,12
Martin, Henry	NJ1140	13,10,12,29,29A
Martin, Stephen	OR0850	14,12,20
Martin, William R.	OH0650	12
Martinez, Adriana	AZ0470	12
Marvin, Clara	AG0250	12A,12,12E
Mason, Alan	FL0050	11,12,31B,66A,66C
Mathew, Nicholas	CA5000	11,12
Mathews, Peter	FL1950	11,12
Matsushita, Hidemi	CO0100	66A,11,12,15,13
Matthews, Britton	NY2450	32,12,65
May, Eldonna	MI2200	11,12
May, Ernest D.	MA2000	12A,12,66G
Mayo, John	AG0450	12A,12
Mazo, Margarita L.	OH1850	12,14
Mazullo, Mark	MN0950	12,66
mcclung, bruce d.	OH2200	12A,12
McClymonds, Marita P.	VA1550	12A,12
McCollough, Sean	TN1710	12,12A
McCollum, Jonathan	MD1100	63C,63D,11,12,20
McCollum, Jonathan Ray	MD0060	12,13,20,55,63C
McCormack, Jessica D.	IN0910	61,39,12,15,67H
McCrickard, Eleanor	NC2430	12
McFarland, Alison	LA0200	12
McGee, Blake Anthony	WY0200	12,64C,48
McGee, Timothy J.	AG0450	12A,12,55
McGinney, William L.	TX3420	12
McGrann, Jeremiah	MA0330	11,12,20G
McGuire, Charles E.	OH1700	12
McKnight, Mark	TX3420	16,12
McLamore, Alyson	CA0600	12A,12,32,16,20G
McLaren, Malena	LA0550	12,64C,64E,47
McLean, Hugh J.	AG0500	12,14A,66G,31A
McManus, Lanny	AL0550	32D,36,12,13E,40
McMullen, Dianne M.	NY4310	13,12,66,31
McMullen, Tracy	ME0200	29,15,12,53,14A
McQuinn, Julie	WI0350	12
Meconi, Honey	NY1100	12A,12,55
Meconi, Honey	NY4350	12A,12,15
Medwin, Marc	DC0010	11,29,12,20
Melamed, Daniel R.	IN0900	12
Meltzer, Howard S.	NY0270	11,13,12,66A,63
Mengozzi, Stefano	MI2100	12
Menoche, Charles Paul	CT0050	10,12,13,34
Mercer-Taylor, Peter	MN1623	12
Meredith, Scott	WY0200	63A,67E,12,32E,49
Meredith, William	CA4400	12
Merkley, Paul	AG0400	12
Merrill, Thomas G.	OH2550	12,60,36,32
Messoloras, Irene	OK0600	36,12,60A,61,40
Metcalfe, Scott	MA0400	12
Meyer, Eve R.	PA3250	13,12A,12
Meyer, Stephen C.	NY4100	12,12A,12D,31A
Micznik, Vera G.	AB0100	12,12B,12A
Milewski, Barbara Ann	PA3200	11,12
Miljkovic, Katarina	MA1400	13C,13B,12A,12
Miller, Allan	CA6050	11,12,37,47,63
Miller, Franklin	WI0825	12A,12
Miller, Gabriel	LA0150	12
Miller, Leta	CA5070	11,12A,12,64A,67E
Miller, Roger L.	UT0250	12A,12
Miller, Stephen R.	TN1800	11,12A,12,14
Minorgan, Bruce	AI0150	12A,12
Mirchandani, Sharon	NJ1350	13,12
Mitchell, Alice L.	NY3705	11,12,13A
Moersch, Charlotte Mattax	IL3300	67F,66H,12A,55C,12
Moll, Kevin N.	NC0650	12,55,67A,12A,12B
Monchick, Alexandra	CA0835	12
Monson, Craig	MO1900	12A,12
Monson, Dale E.	GA2100	12
Monson, Ingrid	MA1050	14,12,29
Montagnier, Jean-Paul	AI0150	12
Montford, Kimberlyn	TX3350	11,12A,12
Montgomery, Kip	NY3250	11,12,13,64C
Monts, Lester P.	MI2100	12
Moore, Deanna C.	SC0200	66A,66B,12
Morey, Carl	AG0450	11,12A,12,20G
Morin, Joseph C.	MD1000	12
Moroney, Davitt	CA5000	11,12,55B,56
Morris, Mitchell B.	CA5032	12A,12,20G,15
Morris, Robert D.	NY1100	10,12,13,20E,31E
Morris, Stephen	GA0050	12
Morrison, Simon	NJ0900	13,12A,12,11
Morrow, Mary Sue	OH2200	12
Moseley, Roger S.	NY0900	12,13,14D,34H
Moser, Bruce	NC0400	12,66A,66B,13,66D
Mueller, Frank	WI0835	13,12
Mueller, Rena Charnin	NY2740	12,14C
Mumford, Lawrence R.	CA5355	10,12,13,10F
Murata, Margaret K.	CA5020	12A,12
Murchison, Gayle	VA0250	12A,12,20G,12C
Murphy-Manley, Sheryl K.	TX2250	12
Musmann, Lois S.	CA3270	12,39,60,66H
Muxfeldt, Kristina	IN0900	12
Myers, Patricia Ann	NY1550	11,12,14,66H,20
Nadas, John L.	NC2410	12
Nagy, Zvonimir	PA1050	12
Nardini, Luisa	TX3510	12,12A
Narmour, Eugene	PA3350	13,12,38
Naroditskaya, Inna	IL2250	12
Nattiez, Jean-Jacques	AI0200	12
Natvig, Mary	OH0300	12
Ndaliko, Cherie Rivers	NC2410	10C,12,14
Neal, Randall	VT0050	12,36,45
Nedbal, Martin	AR0700	12
Neimoyer, Susan	UT0250	12A,14C,10A,12
Neville, Donald	AG0500	12A,12,12B
Newcomb, Anthony A.	CA5000	12A,12

447

Index by Area of Teaching Interest

Name	Code	Areas
Newman, Nancy	NY3700	20F,20G,12
Newsom, Mary Ellen	IN0005	12,14,32,61,62
Niebur, Louis	NV0100	12,20,14,11
Nitschke, Brad	IN0005	11,12,13,60,63
Nonken, Marilyn C.	NY2750	12,13,66A
Noon, David	NY2150	12,10A,10,12A
Noonan, Timothy	WI0825	12A,12,11
Noone, Michael J.	MA0330	11,12,31
Norman-Sojourner, Elizabeth	IL0600	61,39,12
Norris, James Weldon	DC0150	12A,12,36
Norris, Renee Lapp	PA1900	14C,12A,20,12,13E
Norton, Kay	AZ0100	12
Notley, Margaret	TX3420	12
Nott, Kenneth	CT0650	12A,12,66G
Nowacki, Edward C.	OH2200	12
Nutter, David A.	CA5010	12A,12,55
Oates, Jennifer Lynn	NY0600	12,16,12A,12C
Odello, Denise	MN1620	11,12,64B,14,20
O'Donnell, Shaugn	NY0550	13,10,12
O'Grady, Terence J.	WI0808	13,12A,12,14,55
Oja, Carol J.	MA1050	12,12A
Oldani, Robert	AZ0100	12A,12
Oleskiewicz, Mary	MA2010	11,12A,12,14B,64A
Olin, Elinor	IL2000	11,12A,12,64A
Oliveros, Pauline	NY3300	12,13,10B,11
Olivieri, Guido	TX3510	12A,12,67B
O'Meara, Caroline	TX3510	12,20G
Ong, Seow-Chin	KY1500	12
Ongaro, Giulio M.	CA5350	11,12
Ossi, Massimo M.	IN0900	12
Overly, Paul	SC0200	11,12,32,63C,63D
Owens, Thomas C.	VA0450	11,12
Page, Janet K.	TN1680	12
Paige, Diane M.	NY1400	12,29A,20,12A,20F
Painter, Karen	MN1623	12
Palmer, John	CA4700	12,13
Pane, Steven	ME0410	12A,66A,12,12B,11
Papanikolaou, Eftychia	OH0300	12
Pappano, Annalisa	OH2200	12
Paquette-Abt, Mary	MI2200	12
Parakilas, James P.	ME0150	13,11,42,12
Park, Sang Eui	IN0005	10,60,12,13,31A
Parker, Craig B.	KS0650	12A,63A,12
Parker, Mary Ann	AG0450	11,12A,12
Parkhurst, Melissa	OR0750	20,12
Parmentier, Edward L.	MI2100	12A,12,66H
Parmer, Dillon	AG0400	11,12,12B,12C
Parr, Sean M.	NH0310	12
Parsons, James B.	MO0775	12
Pasler, Jann C.	CA5050	11,12A,12,12B,12E
Paul, David	CA5060	12A,12,13B
Paul, Helene	AI0210	12
Payne, Thomas B.	VA0250	12A,12,12C
Peacock, Kenneth J.	NY2750	13,10,12,35,34
Pearson, Ian D.	SC1200	12,55,41
Peattie, Matthew	OH2200	12
Peattie, Thomas A.	MA0400	12
Pederson, Sanna	OK1350	12A,20G,12
Pen, Ronald	KY1450	20G,29A,12A,12
Pennington, Stephen	MA1900	12D,29A,29E,15,12
Perkins, Leeman L.	NY0750	11,12,31A,36
Perry, Mark E.	GA1500	20,12
Pesce, Dolores	MO1900	12A,12,13J
Peters, G. David	IN0907	34,12C,12,35C,35A
Peters, Mark	IL3100	11,20,13E,12
Petrides, Ron T.	NY2660	10,29,70,13,12
Petteys, Leslie	WV0400	66,66A,66B,66C,12
Phillips, Moses	NY0640	12,13A,13B,13C,64A
Phillips, Timothy S.	AL1050	64C,12,48
Phillips-Farley, Barbara	NY3550	66,13,12
Phoenix-Neal, Diane	IA0200	62,11,12,51
Pisani, Michael	NY4450	11,12A,12,20G
Pisaro, Kathryn G.	CA0510	12
Plack, Rebecca	CA4150	12,61
Planer, John H.	IN1050	20,12,13,14,61
Platoff, John	CT0500	13,11,14C,12,12F
Platt, Heather	IN0150	11,12,12A
Pohly, Linda L.	IN0150	11,12,14,12A
Pollack, Howard	TX3400	12A,12,14,20G
Polot, Barton L.	MI1900	10A,10B,10F,12,13
Ponzner, Joseph	OH1850	12
Porter, Lewis R.	NJ1140	13,12,29,29A
Porterfield, Richard R.	NY2750	12,13,31A,55D
Potter, Pamela	WI0815	12,12C
Powell, John S.	OK1450	11,12A,12,20
Powell, Linton	TX3500	12,66G,66H
Preston, Katherine K.	VA0250	12A,12,20G,12C
Pridmore, Craig	CA5400	37,49,12
Prince, Curtis L.	IN0005	10,12,20G,65,47
Prindle, Daniel	MA2250	12
Prizer, William	CA5060	12A,12
Prouty, Kenneth E.	MI1400	12,14,29
Provine, Robert C.	MD1010	12,14
Pruiksma, Rose	NH0350	12
Puri, Michael James	VA1550	13,12
Quereau, Quentin W.	OH0400	12A,12
Quist, Pamela	CA4425	13,10,66A,12
Radomski, James V.	CA0845	11,12A,12,14
Raessler, Daniel	VA1125	11,12,13B,13F,13A
Raevens, Jean M.	PA1050	13,11,12
Rahn, Jay	AG0650	13,12
Raifsnider, Christoper J.	MD0060	12,13,64C
Ramael, David R.	NY1600	12,38,39,60B,51
Ramirez, Miguel	TN0930	12
Ramos, Rene	CA2420	13A,13,12A,12,66A
Ramos-Kittrell, Jesus	TX2400	12,70
Ramsey, Guthrie P.	PA3350	12,35,20G,29,47
Randall, Annie Janeiro	PA0350	11,12A,12,12E
Randall, James	MT0400	12,14,20,11
Randel, Julia	MI1050	12,20
Rapoport, Paul	AG0200	13,11,12A,12
Rawlins, Nancy	NJ1050	66D,66G,13,12
Rawlins, Robert	NJ1050	13,12
Reagan, Ann B.	CO0750	11,12A,12,41,66A
Reardon, Colleen A.	CA5020	12
Redman, Will	MD0850	12,13
Rees, Fred J.	IN0907	34,12C,35C,32,12
Reichwald, Siegwart	SC0650	12,38,60B
Reitz, Christina L.	NC2600	12,66A,12A
Revuluri, Sindhumathi	MA1050	12,12A,12C,14C,20D
Reynolds, Anne-Marie	NY3730	11,12A,12
Reynolds, Christopher A.	CA5010	12,11
Rice, Eric N.	CT0600	55,12,1A,13A,12
Richards, Annette	NY0900	12,13A,13B,66G
Rieppel, Daniel	MN1500	66A,11,38,66C,12
Rife, Jerry E.	NJ1000	13,11,12A,12,37
Rifkin, Joshua	MA0400	12
Riis, Thomas L.	CO0800	12,20G
Rischar, Richard A.	MI2110	12,29,40,14,20
Rober, R. Todd	PA1750	11,12
Roberge, Marc-Andre	AI0190	12A,12
Roberson, Matt	AL0345	12,61
Roberts, John H.	CA5000	12,16
Roberts, Wesley	KY0400	12,14,31,66
Robertson, Anne Walters	IL3250	11,12A,12
Robertson, Marta E.	PA1400	12,14
Robinson, Gregory J.	VA0450	11,12,14,20H
Robinson, Jason	MA0100	12,13,14,34
Robinson, Scott	PA1150	12,14,10
Robison, John O.	FL2000	13,12A,12,67
Rodin, Jesse	CA4900	12
Roesner, Edward	NY2740	11,12A,12,55
Rogers, Vanessa	TN1200	12,55
Rojas, Nuria Mariela	SC0150	11,12,13,34,66
Rollins, Ian	TX2900	65,12
Root, Deane L.	PA3420	12A,12C,12,20G,12E
Rorke, Margaret A.	UT0250	12A,12
Rosand, Ellen	CT0900	12A,12
Rosenberg, Jesse	IL2250	12
Rosenblatt, Jay M.	AZ0500	12
Rosenfeld, Andrew	MD0610	11,12,13,20F,36
Rosow, Lois	OH1850	12A,12
Ross, John G.	NC1100	12,60
Ross, Nicholas Piers	VA1400	13,66A,66C,12
Ross, Ryan M.	MS0500	12
Roth, Marjorie	NY2650	64A,12
Roust, Colin	IL0550	12
Row, Peter	MA1400	14,12,13
Rubinoff, Kailan	NC2430	67D,14,12
Rumph, Stephen	WA1050	12,12A
Runnels, Jason	TX2600	12
Russell, Craig H.	CA0600	11,12A,12,67B,70
Russell, Joan	AI0100	32B,32C,12,12C
Russell, Tilden	CT0450	11,12A,12,41
Rutschman, Carla J.	WA1250	12A,12,32,63D
Rutschman, Edward R.	WA1250	13A,13,11,12A,12
Rytting, Bryce	UT0325	12,13,38,60
Saavedra, Leonora	CA5040	12,20H
Salfen, Kevin	TX3410	11,12,13A,20
Sallis, Friedemann	AA0150	12,13
Saloman, Ora Frishberg	NY0250	11,12A,12
Saloman, Ora Frishberg	NY0600	12A,12
Saltzstein, Jennifer A.	OK1350	12
Sanborne, Deborah	IA1300	12,66G,66C,11
Sanden, Paul	AA0200	12,12A
Sanders, Reginald L.	OH1200	11,12
Sandow, Greg	NY1900	12
Sands, Rosita M.	IL0720	14,12,20
Saunders, Harris S.	IL3310	11,12A,12
Saunders, Steven E.	ME0250	11,12A,12,66H
Scarnati, Blase S.	AZ0450	11,12,14
Scharfenberger, Paul E.	NH0110	12,67C,43,55,15
Scheer, Christopher	UT0300	12
Schisler, Charles	GA0750	11,12
Schlagel, Stephanie P.	OH2200	12C,12,55,67
Schleifer, Martha Furman	PA3250	12
Schleuse, Paul	NY3705	12
Schmalenberger, Sarah	MN1625	12A,63B,12,67E,14
Schmelz, Peter	MO1900	12,12A
Schmidt, Carl B.	MD0850	11,12
Schneider, David E.	MA0100	12,64C,43,13,41
Schneider, Wayne J.	VT0450	11,12
Schrader, David D.	IL0550	12,51
Schreibman, Janice	IN0907	12,33
Schreiner, Frederick	PA3710	11,12A,12,61,39
Schroeder, David	AF0100	13,12A,12,12E,12C
Schulenberg, David L.	NY4500	11,12
Schultz, Stephen	PA0550	12,55B
Schulze, Hendrik	TX3420	12
Schwartz, Robert	CA4625	12,66
Schwartz, Roberta Freund	KS1350	12
Schwartz-Kates, Deborah	FL1900	12,20H,14
Scott, Allen	OK0800	12
Scripp, Lawrence	MA1400	12
Scrivner, Matthew	MO0050	61,12,13
Seaton, Douglass	FL0850	12A,12D,12C,12
Seitz, Elizabeth	MA0350	12
Sellers, Crystal Y.	OH0250	61,11,12,31F
Semmens, Richard	AG0500	12,13J,55,67B,13L
Seter, Ronit	MD0650	12
Seto, Mark	CT0100	11,12,13A,13C,38
Seybert, John M.	FL1740	60,66A,32,64E,12
Shankovich, Robert L.	PA1050	12
Shay, Robert	MO1800	12
Shearon, Stephen	TN1100	12
Sheinbaum, John J.	CO0900	12,13E,11,12A
Sheldon, Vanessa R.	CA3265	12,13C,13A,62E,66A
Shelemay, Kay K.	MA1050	12,14
Sherr, Richard J.	MA1750	12A,12
Sheveloff, Joel L.	MA0400	12A,12
Sholes, Jacquelyn	MA0400	12
Shotwell, Clayton	GA0250	12,20,34,11,13A
Shrader, Steven	TN1800	11,12A,12,66A,38
Shreffler, Anne C.	MA1050	12,12A
Shulstad, Reeves	NC0050	12,14,20
Shultis, Christopher	NM0450	12,12B,10
Silverberg, Ann L.	TN0050	12A,12,14,11
Silverberg, Laura Gail	NY0750	11,12
Simms, Bryan R.	CA5300	12A,12
Simonett, Helena	TN1850	12,14,20H
Simons, Carolyn	CA2810	11,20,60A,12
Sine, Nadine J.	PA1950	11,12A,12
Sisman, Elaine	NY0750	12,11,12A,12B
Skinner, Josh	ID0060	12,13A,13B,13C,62D
Skinner, Kate	ID0060	12,13A,13B,13C,61
Slavin, Dennis	NY0250	11,12
Slavin, Dennis	NY0600	12A,12
Slim, H. Colin	CA5020	12
Slobin, Mark	CT0750	12,14
Smart, Mary Ann	CA5000	11,12,15
Smigel, Eric	CA4100	12
Smith, Ayana	IN0900	12
Smith, Christopher J.	TX3200	12A,12,14
Smith, Douglas	AB0050	13A,13,10,13C,12
Smith, Gordon E.	AG0250	12,14,20G,12C
Smith, Jeremy L.	CO0800	12
Smith, Marian E.	OR1050	12
Smith, Norman E.	PA3350	12A,12
Snedeker, Jeffrey	WA0050	12,49,63B
Snyder, Jean E.	PA1200	11,12,20
Snyder, John L.	TX3400	13,11,12
Sobaskie, James William	MS0500	13,13E,10F,13I,12
Solis, Gabriel	IL3300	12,20G
Song, James J.	CA3100	60,11,12,38,13
Spilker, John D.	NE0450	12
Spiller, Henry	CA5010	14,12,15,20D,12D

Name	Code	Areas
Spitzer, John	CA4150	12
Spohr, Arne	OH0300	12
Sposato, Jeffrey S.	TX3400	12,36
Sprout, Leslie A.	NJ0300	12A,12C,13A,12
Stanbridge, Alan	AG0450	12
Stanford, Thomas S.	OR0850	64C,12,48,41
Stanley, Glenn	CT0600	11,12A,12,12B
Stanyek, Jason	NY2740	34,12,14,20,12D
Starr, Lawrence	WA1050	12A,12,20G
Starr, Pamela	NE0600	12A,12
Steel, Matthew	MI2250	12A,12,14,55
Steele, Timothy	MI0350	11,12
Stefaniak, Alexander	MO1900	12,12A
Steib, Murray	IN0150	11,12,12A
Stein, Beverly	CA0830	12,14
Stein, Louise K.	MI2100	12
Steiner, Ruth	DC0050	12A,12,14A
Stempel, Larry	NY1300	13,12,54,29
Stephen, J. Drew	TX3530	12A,63B,67E,12
Stepniak, Michael	VA1350	12,38,31A,41,32
Steva, Elizabeth Ryland	KY1000	62,11,12
Stevance, Sophie	AI0200	12
Stevens, Blake	SC0500	12,11
Stevens, Jane	CA5050	11,12A,12
Stevenson, Robert M.	CA5032	12,14,20G,20H
Stilwell, Jama Liane	IA0400	11,12,20G,13,64A
Stilwell, Robyn	DC0075	12,14
Stimeling, Travis D.	IL1750	12,63D,12D,14
Stinson, Russell	AR0425	13,11,12A,12,66
Stohrer, Baptist	IL0780	12A,12,61
Stokes, Jeffrey	AG0500	12,62D
Stokes, Katarina Markovic	MA1400	12
Stone, Anne	NY0600	12A,12
Stone, Anne	NY0642	12
Stowe, Daniel	IN1700	12,36,38
Strainchamps, Edmond N.	NY4320	12A,12
Strandberg, Kristen	IN1850	11,12,13A
Stroeher, Vicki P.	WV0400	11,12,13,14
Struss, Jane	MA1175	12
Stuart, Gregory	SC1110	12
Stubley, Eleanor	AI0150	12,32
Stuppard, Javier	TX1150	12,60B,63
Sullivan, Melanie	TX1350	12,61
Sullivan, Todd E.	AZ0450	11,12,14,20
Summers, William J.	NH0100	12A,12,67C
Sumner Lott, Marie	GA1050	12
Sun, Cecilia	CA5020	12
Suzuki, Dean P.	CA4200	11,12,20G
Swack, Jeanne	WI0815	12A,12,67,55,67D
Swartz, Anne	NY0250	11,12A,12
Swartz, Anne	NY0600	12A,12
Swayne, Steven R.	NH0100	12A,12,39,54
Swenson, Edward E.	NY1800	12A,12
Tacconi, Marisa S.	PA2750	12
Tacka, Philip V.	PA2350	12,13,32
Talle, Andrew	MD0650	12
Tapanes-Inojosa, Adriana	IL1080	11,20,36,12,66
Taricani, JoAnn	WA1050	12A,12
Tarrant, Fredrick A.	GA1800	11,12,14,20,55
Taruskin, Richard	CA5000	11,12
Taylor, Betty Sue	NY2400	13A,12,36,61,66
Taylor, Jeffrey J.	NY0500	12,11,29A
Taylor, Timothy D.	CA5031	12,14,34
Tcharos, Stefanie	CA5060	12A,12
Teal, Kimberly Hannon	NY1100	12,14C
Teeters, Donald	MA1400	12
TellerRatner, Sabina	AI0200	12
Thomas, Edwin	IN0005	65,11,12,32,60
Thomas, Jennifer	FL1850	12
Thomas, Phillip E.	TN0850	13,12,38,66A
Thomas, Susan R.	GA2100	11,12,14,20H,34A
Thursby, Stephen	MD0650	12
Tiberio, Albert	PA2950	11,12,13,10A,10F
Tick, Judith	MA1450	12,20G
Tilley, Janette M.	NY0635	12A,11,12
Titus, Jamie	MO0050	64A,12,13,48
Titus, Joan M.	NC2430	12
Todd, Kristen Stauffer	OK0650	12,14,20,11,55
Tokar, David A.	PA0900	12A,12C,70,12,11
Toliver, Brooks	OH2150	11,12
Tomasello, Andrew	NY0250	11,12,14,29A,35
Tomasello, Andrew	NY0600	12,14,29A
Torre, Robert Anthony	GA0050	12,14
Torres, George	PA1850	12A,12,14,12D,20H
Touliatos-Miles, Diane	MO1830	11,12A,12,29A
Trabold, William E.	CA4450	61,11,13A,12
Traficante, Frank	CA1050	13,12A,12
Traupman-Carr, Carol A.	PA2450	13A,13,12A,12,31A
Treadwell, Nina	CA5300	12
Trinkle, Karen M.	MO1950	12,15,12A
Tucker, Gary	AE0050	13A,13,12
Tuomi, Scott	OR0750	12A,12,14,61,55
Turner, Charles	CT0650	12A,12,67
Turner, Tammy	KY0950	11,12
Tusa, Michael C.	TX3510	11,12A,12
Tyre, Jess B.	NY3780	12
Underhill, Owen	AB0080	13,60,10,12,43
Upton, Elizabeth R.	CA5032	12A,12,13J
Uribe, Patrick Wood	MA0400	12
Valdez, Stephen	GA2100	29,12
Valerio, Wendy	SC1110	32A,12
Van Boer, Bertil H.	WA1250	13E,12,55,12A
Van der Bliek, Rob	AG0650	12,14C,29
Vander Wel, Stephanie L.	NY4320	12,14C
Vaneman, Christopher	SC0650	64A,12,42
Vanscheeuwijck, Marc	OR1050	55,12,67B
Vaughn, Michael	IL2000	12A,12,32A,66A
Veenstra, Kimberly	MI0900	11,12,13
Vento, Steve	OK1300	10,11,12,47,32E
Vercoe, Elizabeth	MA1600	12
Verzosa, Noel	MD0500	12,11
Violett, Martha Watson	CO1050	11,12,66
Vitercik, Greg	VT0350	13,12A,12,66C
Von Glahn, Denise	FL0850	12A,12
Von Schweinitz, Wolfgang	CA0510	10,12
Waddell, Rachel Lynn	MI1000	11,12,32E,42,64A
Waggoner, Emily	SC0200	62E,12
Wagstaff, Grayson	DC0050	12A,12,12C
Waldoff, Jessica	MA0700	11,12
Walker, Alan	AG0200	13,12A,12
Walker, Erin	KY1450	12,20,50,65
Wallace, Robin	TX0300	12,11
Waltz, Sarah Clemmens	CA5530	11,12
Ward, Tom R.	IL3300	11,12
Ward-Griffin, Danielle	VA0150	12,20,14
Ware, John	VA1800	13,10,12,66
Warfield, Patrick R.	MD1010	12
Warfield, Scott A.	FL1800	12,20,11
Watkins, Timothy D.	TX3000	12A,14,20,12
Wayte, Lawrence A.	OR1050	12,29
Weaver, Andrew H.	DC0050	12A,12,12C,62B
Weaver, Carol Ann	AG0470	13,10,12,20A,29A
Weaver, Jamie G.	TX2700	12
Webster, James	NY0900	12,13B,13D,13I
Wegman, Rob	NJ0900	11,12A,12,20G
Weidner, Raymond	MD0060	12,13,36
Weiss, Susan F.	MD0650	12A,12
Wells, Elizabeth A.	AE0050	12A,12,14,20G
Westbrook, Randy	KY0550	66C,12,11
Wetzel, Don Louis	CA5300	12
Wetzel, Richard	OH1900	12,29A
Wexler, Richard	MD1010	12A,12,55,29A
Whitesell, Lloyd	AI0150	12
Whiting, Steven M.	MI2100	12
Wicke, Peter	AG0100	12,35,12F
Wilbourne, Emily	NY0750	11,12,15,20F
Wilkinson, Christopher	WV0750	13,11,12A,12
Will, Richard	VA1550	12A,12,20G,14C
Williams, Marvin	NY2050	10,11,12,13,20G
Williams, Peter F.	NC0600	12A,12,14B
Williams, Sarah F.	SC1110	12A,14C,12,14,15
Williams, Sean	WA0350	11,12,14,20G,70
Willis, Sharon J.	GA0490	10A,11,12,61,13A
Wilson Kimber, Marian	IA1550	12
Wilson, Cecil B.	WV0750	10F,60,12A,12
Wilson, Dora	OH1900	12
Wilson, Ellen M.	TX3520	61,54,39,12
Wilson, Karen	SC0200	12,66A,12C,20G,67
Winkler, Amanda Eubanks	NY4100	12,12A,15,31A,31G
Winograd, Barry	IL0720	29,12
Winterfeldt, Chad	MN0750	66G,44,12
Winters, Thomas D.	PA3600	12A,12,29
Wischusen, Mary A.	MI2200	12A,12,14C
Wlodarski, Amy	PA0950	36,12
Woideck, Carl	OR1050	29A,20G,12
Wolf, Richard	MA1050	12,14
Wolff, Christoph	MA1050	12A,12,12C
Wood, Graham	SC0450	11,12,63B,54,20
Wood, Robert	AG0500	32C,34,12F,12,12C
Woodard, Susan J.	PA3580	11,12,66A,42
Worster, Larry	CO0550	12
Wrazen, Louise	AG0650	12,14
Wright, Barbara	WV0560	13A,13,12A,12,66G
Wright, Craig M.	CT0900	11,12A,12
Wright, Jeffrey	IN0910	12
Wright, Josephine	OH0700	12,20G
Wright, Lesley A.	HI0210	11,12
Wunsch, Aaron M.	NY1900	12,42
Wyatt, Benjamin H.	VA1100	62C,67B,12,13I,12B
Yaffe, Carl	DC0170	13,12
Yang, Mina	CA5300	12
Yang, Sandra S.	OH0450	11,12
Yaraman, Sevin H.	NY1300	13,14,12
Yardley, Anne B.	NJ0300	12,14,31,55
Yearsley, David	NY0900	12,13,11,66H,66G
Yeomans, David J.	TX3000	12
Yoshioka, Masataka	TX3420	12
Youens, Susan	IN1700	12A,12
Youens-Wexler, Laura	DC0100	11,12
Youmans, Charles D.	PA2750	12
Yubovich, Benjamin	IN0005	60,16,12,13,14
Yudkin, Jeremy	MA0400	12
Yuzefovich, Victor	MD0150	12A,12,62B,32I
Zagorski, Marcus	OH0300	12
Zamzow, Beth Ann	IA0930	13,41,42,37,12
Zank, Stephen	NY3705	12
Zanovello, Giovanni	IN0900	12
Zaslaw, Neal	NY0900	12,55B
Zeiss, Laurel E.	TX0300	12A,12C,11,12
Zheng, Su	CT0750	12,14
Zimmerman, Franklin B.	PA3350	12A,12
Zobel, Elizabeth W.	IL0350	12,13,36,60,61
Zusman, Shanon P.	CA4450	67A,12,11

History of Music

Name	Code	Areas
Abbate, Carolyn	PA3350	12A,12
Abbate, Elizabeth	MA0350	12A
Abbott, David	MI0100	12A,66A,42
Aberdam, Eliane	RI0300	13,10F,10,12A,45
Abrams, David	NY2950	13C,11,41,64C,12A
Ackerly, Olga	MO1810	12A
Adams, K. Gary	VA0100	11,12A,12,66A
Adams, Liselyn	AI0070	13,12A,41,64A,43
Adams, Mary Kay	VA0300	13,12A
Adams, Nell	MS0400	61,12A
Adams, Paul	VA0950	63D,12A,37
Adams, Robert L.	MO0700	11,12A,12,66A
Adkins, Cathy L.	NC1250	12A,66G
Adkins, Don	CA0300	13,10F,10,12A,62D
Aks, David M.	CA0835	12A,13C,39,60B,62C
Alajaji, Sylvia A.	PA1300	14A,14C,11,12A,20
Albrecht, Tamara	GA0750	11,12A,32A
Albrecht, Timothy	GA0750	11,12A,66G,31A
Alcorn, Allison A.	IL3150	10E,11,12A,20,31A
Aldana, Milton	MD0600	63C,13,12A
Aldridge, Ben	NY3765	63A,60B,12A
Aleksander, Elizabeth	NE0400	64C,12A
Alexander, Marina	NY0644	36,12A,12C,60A
Alexander, Michael	GA1150	38,60B,12A,35A
Alexander, Travis	NC1550	12A,36,40,66
Allen, Ivalah	KS0350	61,39,12A,20F
Allen, James O.	MS0550	11,12A,16,66A,66C
Allen, Robert T.	VA0800	11,12A,29A,60A
Allen, Stephen Arthur	NJ1000	13,11,12A,12,20
Allison, James	IL1550	12A,61
Allison, Rees	MN0800	12A,66A,66H
Allsup, Neal	KS0550	11,12A,36,60,61
Allsup, Randall Everett	NY4200	43,32,13,12A,12B
Almond, Frank W.	CA4100	60,12A,36
Alms, Anthony	MA0350	12A
Alms, Anthony	NJ0175	12A
Alonso, Ernesto	PR0150	12A,11,62A,14A,55A
Althouse, Paul L.	CT0100	11,60A,12A,36
Amati-Camperi, Alexandra	CA5353	12A,11,12C,13A,12
Amos, C. Nelson	MI0600	12A,12,67D,70
Amos, Shaun	GA0500	60,36,13B,13C,12A
Amrein, Emilie	IL1400	36,12A,13C,60,11
Anavitarte, David	TX2550	36,61,66A,12A,32B
Anders, Micheal F.	OH2275	12A,61,54,36
Anderson, Gary L.	KY1350	60A,12A,36
Anderson, H. Gerald	IL2300	66A,66C,66D,12A
Anderson, James N.	GA0200	12A,32,37
Anderson, Jared	MI1450	36,40,11,12A
Anderson, Jared L.	WI0600	36,61,66A,13,12A

Name	Code	Areas
Anderson, Michael Alan	NY1100	12,12A,14F
Anderson, Ronald E.	TX2700	60A,11,12A,12C
Anthony, Janet	WI0350	12A,41,62C,51
Anthony, John P.	CT0100	13A,11,12A,66D,66G
Antokoletz, Elliott M.	TX3510	11,12A,12
Aponte, Pedro R.	VA0600	12A
Appello, Patrick	NJ0550	70,67G,13B,13A,12A
Aquila, Carmen	NY4460	35A,13A,35D,12A,10A
Araujo, Ilka Vasconcelos	TX3250	66A,11,12A,20G
Archbold, Lawrence	MN0300	11,12A,66G,15,12D
Archer, Gail	NY0200	36,12A
Archeto, Maria	GA0755	11,12A,12B,13A,20
Ardovino, Lori	AL1200	12A,48,64C,64E,67C
Argento, Dominick J.	MN1623	13,10F,10,12A
Arlen, Walter	CA2800	12A
Armstrong, Alan	NC1500	12A,14B,13,62C,66A
Armstrong, James I.	VA0250	36,12A,60,12C
Armstrong, Richard	AL0500	12A,12C,61
Armstrong, Robert	OR1010	12A,63A,64C,64A
Armstrong, Robin E.	MD0520	11,14,29A,12,12A
Arnold, Ben	KY1450	12,12A
Arshagouni, Michael H.	CA2750	13B,13C,12A,66A,36
Artesani, Laura	ME0440	12A,66C,15,32B,32C
Ascani, Argeo	NY2150	12A
Asch, Arthur	WI0862	13,12A,37,48
Ashby, Arved M.	OH1850	12A
Ashley, Douglas D.	SC0500	11,12A,66A
Ashworth, John	KY1500	12A,55,66H,67
Asti, Martha S.	NC2650	12A
Atkinson, Sean E.	TX3500	11,12A,13
Atlas, Allan W.	NY0600	12A,12
Atlas, Allan	NY0500	13,12A,12
Ayesh, Kevin	NC0220	13,11,12A,66A,66D
Ayllon, Robert	MO1950	12A
Bach, Timothy	CA4150	12A,41,66C
Bachmann, Nancy	CA2775	13A,13B,12A,66A,66B
Bacon, Joel	CO0250	66G,12A,66H
Bade, Christopher	IN1560	11,38,48,64,12A
Baer, Sarah	PA2450	64B,55B,12A,13E
Baham, Kerry M.	TX3370	13B,66A,11,66C,12A
Bailey, Candace L.	NC1600	12,29D,15,11,12A
Bailey, John R.	NE0600	64A,42,12A
Bailey, Jon D.	CA3650	60,12A,36,11
Bailey, Nancy	TX2150	12A
Bailey, Walter B.	TX2150	11,12A,12
Baird, Julianne C.	NJ1100	12A,12C,40,61,67E
Baker, Nicole	CA0815	12A,36
Baldoria, Charisse J.	PA0250	66A,66D,12A,11
Balensuela, Matthew	IN0350	11,12A
Ball, W. Scott	TN1350	11,12A,62D
Ballard, Marcus	LA0900	64,12A
Balthazar, Scott Leslie	PA3600	13,12A
Bancks, Jacob	IL0100	10,10F,43,13,12A
Banducci, Antonia L.	CO0900	12A,12,12C
Barach, Daniel P.	NY3770	12A,62B,11
Barber, Daniel R.	OH0650	66A,13D,12A,66G
Barber, Julie	IN1560	66A,61,40,12A
Barkley, Elizabeth F.	CA1800	11,12A,66A,66C,66D
Barlar, Douglas	FL0670	12A,63D,49,32E
Barnes, James	KS1350	10F,10,12A
Barnett, Gregory	TX2150	12A,12
Barnum, Ellen M.	NY0400	12A,64D,15
Baron, John H.	LA0750	12A,12,20F,20G,31B
Barone, Anthony	NV0050	12,12A,12C
Barr, Cyrilla	DC0050	12A,12C
Barry, Barbara R.	FL1125	12A,12C
Barstow, Robert S.	NY3765	12A,36,16,35
Barta, Michael	IL2900	12A,62A,62B
Barte, Paul T.	OH1900	12A,11,66G,66H
Bartee, Neale	AR0110	60,12A,49,63C
Bartig, Kevin	MI1400	12A
Barton, Karl S.	GA1990	64,47,12A,34
Barton, Stephen	MI0850	36,40,11,12A,61
Bashford, Christina	IL3300	12A,12C,12D,42,51
Bass, John	TN1680	12A
Batchvarova, Madlen T.	IN0650	60A,36,61,66A,12A
Bates, James	OH2050	12A,20,32,38,62D
Bates, Mason W.	CA4150	12A
Bates, Michael J.	AR0810	36,13,60,12A,66A
Bates, Pamela	IL0900	12A,13,66A,66C,66D
Bates, William H.	SC1110	12A,66G,31A
Batista, Gustavo	PR0150	11,12A,13A,13C,70
Bauer, Glen	MO1950	13,12,12A
Bauer, William R.	NY0600	12A,29A
Bauer, William R.	NY0644	10F,12A,12C,13
Baumer, Matthew R.	PA1600	12A
Baumgartner, Michael	OH0650	10,12A,11
Baur, Steven	AF0100	11,12A,12D,12E,14C
Baxter, Diane R.	OR1250	66,20,12A,14
Baxter, Marsha	NY4200	12A,13
Bazler, Corbett D.	NY4350	12A,12
Beal, Amy C.	CA5070	12A,12,43,20G
Beams, Mahala	MA1560	11,12A,66A,13A
Bean, Scott	WI0810	63D,12A,11,49
Beaudoin, Paul	RI0200	10,13,12A,11
Beavers, Sean M.	VA0650	12A,13A,13B,13C,41
Beck, Nora	OR0400	11,12A
Becker, Daniel	CA4150	10,12A
Becker, Michael	IL3450	14,12A
Beckman, Gary D.	NC1700	12A,67G,11,35A,35B
Beeks, Graydon F.	CA3650	60,12A,37,16,54
Beert, Michael	IL2560	11,12A,13,38,20
Behrens, Joel	PA2350	12A,48,64A
Behroozi, Bahram	CA4350	13A,11,12A,14,70
Belfield, Roy L.	NC2700	66G,36,60A,10F,12A
Bellassai, Marc C.	AZ0250	11,12A,66A,66F,66G
Beller-McKenna, Daniel	NH0350	12A,12C,11,14C
Bemberg, Stephanie	MO1110	12A,66A
Bempechat, Paul-Andre	NJ1000	11,12A
Benavides, Raul	NY0625	12A
Benedum, Richard P.	OH2250	11,12A,66G
Bennett, Lawrence E.	IN1850	11,12A,12,13A
Bennett, Peter	OH0400	12A,55
Bennett, Rebecca K.	IL2250	12A
Beno, Charles W.	NY4400	12A,11
Benson, Mark F.	AL0210	13,12A,11,65,20
Benson, Michael L.	OH1350	66A,66B,12A,11,66
Bent, Ian	NY0750	11,12A,12,13J
Bentley, Joe	MI1830	12A,32D,60,36
Bentley, Julia	IL2100	12A,12C
Berg Oram, Stephanie	CO0625	11,12A,61,34B
Berg, Jason	TX3200	12A,29
Berg, Reinhard	AA0020	13,10,12A,66A,66G
Berg, Wesley P.	AA0100	12A,20G
Berger, Karol	CA4900	12A,12,13J,12B
Bergeron, Chuck	FL1900	62D,47,29A,46,12A
Bergeron, Katherine	RI0050	12A,12D
Bergstrom, Melissa	MN0040	36,40,12A,38,61
Berkhout, Bjorn	NY3250	10,62C,12A,13,14C
Berkolds, Paul	CA0510	61,39,40,12A,68
Bermudez, Luis	PR0115	13C,12A
Bernard, Gilles	NJ0825	13,12A,49,63C,63D
Bernstein, David	CA2950	13,12A,13J
Bernstein, Jane A.	MA1900	11,12,12,12C
Bernstein, Lawrence F.	PA3350	12A,12
Bersin, Michael D.	MO1790	11,12A,62C,62D
Berta, Joseph M.	NY1550	11,12A,64
Bertagnolli, Paul A.	TX3400	12A
Bertrand, Lynn Wood	GA0750	13,11,12A,12
Bester, Matthew	OH1850	12A
Betancourt, Nilda	PR0100	13,66A,66C,12A
Bethea, Kay	VA1030	13,11,12A,66A,66D
Bewley, Rabon	TX1660	11,12A,29,64E,13A
Bianchi, Eric	NY1300	11,12A,12G,13J,31
Bible, Kierstin Michelle	MO0260	36,61,12A,13A,54
Bicigo, James Michael	AK0150	12A,32,37,41,63D
Bieritz, Gerald	TX1300	12A,11,32A,36,60
Biggers, Jennifer E.	NY3705	12A,66G,66H
Bighley, Mark	OK0550	12A,66A,66G,66D
Bilderback, Barry T.	ID0250	11,12A,20B,12C,14A
Billaud, Louise	VA0900	11,12A,13A
Billingsley, Michael	NJ0060	13,12A
Binford, Hilde M.	PA2450	13A,13,12A,12
Bingham, Ann Marie	WV0400	12A,64B,64C,32E
Biscardi, Chester	NY3560	13,10F,10,11,12A
Biscay, Karen T.	OH1330	13,11,12A,36,61
Bischoff, John	CA2950	45,10B,12A,13B,20F
Biser, Larry	MI0300	34B,12A,40,66G
Bishop, James	FL0150	12A,37,38,47,64E
Bishop, Matthew	TX1425	51,70,12A
Bizzell, Gayle	TX1850	12A,66A,66C,66D
Blachly, Alexander	IN1700	60,12,36,55,12A
Blackwell, Manley	AL1350	11,12A,66A
Blaha, Joseph L.	VA1250	46,10,12A,48,63C
Blair, Suanne Hower	KY0900	12A,62C,62D,62E
Blancq, Charles C.	LA0800	29A,12A
Bleiler, Loueda	NY0950	11,12A,13A,13B,36
Block, Geoffrey	WA1000	12A
Bloechl, Olivia A.	CA5032	12,12A,12D,20G,31A
Bloom, Peter A.	MA1750	12A,12
Boaz, Virginia Lile	TX0600	12,61,39,12A
Bobetsky, Victor V.	NY0625	11,12A,62E
Boehm, Norman	AR0350	13,10,12A,66A,11
Boepple, Hans C.	CA4425	13,12A,66A,66B,66C
Boerckel, Gary M.	PA2100	11,12A,66A,20G,29
Boettcher, Bonna	NY0900	16,12A,12C
Bogas, Roy	CA2200	60,12A,38,66A,66B
Bohn, Donna M.	PA1550	12A,13B,13C,65,60
Bohnet, Andra	AL1300	12A,41,64A,62E,35A
Boldin, James E.	LA0770	63B,12A,11
Bolton, Thomas W.	KY1200	61,31A,36,12A
Bomgardner, Stephen D.	MO0350	61,39,12A,11
Bond, Karlyn	UT0400	11,12A,12B
Bond, Kori	ID0100	12A,66A,66B,66C
Bone, Lloyd E.	WV0350	12A,49,63,37,11
Book, A. Ryan	NC2210	70,12A,13,41
Bookout, Melanie	IN0905	11,12A,12,55,67A
Boorman, Stanley H.	NY2740	11,12A,12,55
Borg, Paul	IL1150	13A,13,11,12A,12
Borgerding, Todd Michael	ME0250	13,12A,55B
Borja, Jonathan	MO1810	12A
Borroff, Edith	NY3705	12A,12,12B
Bosse, Joanna	MI1400	12A,14
Bostic, Ronald D.	NC2650	60,12A
Bostock, Matthew	MA2100	13A,11,12A
Bostrom, Sandra	CA0835	66A,10C,12A,34,65A
Boswell, Michael	IN1400	39,61,12A
Boudreaux, Margaret A.	MD0520	60,12A,32D,36
Bouffard, Sophie	AJ0100	12A,61,11,13C
Boulanger, Richard	AE0100	12A,12,66A
Bounds, Kevin S.	AL1160	12A,11,13A
Bourgois, Louis	KY0750	11,12A,49,63D,34
Bowen, Jose A.	TX2400	47,12A,29,38,12
Bowen, Richard L.	IN1850	36,12,12A,11,12B
Bowen, William	AG0450	12A
Bower, Calvin	IN1700	12A,12
Bowers, Teresa M.	PA1400	64A,64B,12A,36,42
Bowker, Barbara E.	IL1085	13,11,13B,13C,12A
Bowman, J. D.	KS0900	12A,11
Boyd, Fern Glass	MT0400	12A,51,62C,11
Boyd, Jean A.	TX0300	12A,20G,29A
Boyer, D. Royce	AL1160	11,12A,36,61,31A
Boykan, Martin	MA0500	13,10,12A,10A,13A
Boynton, Susan	NY0750	11,12A,12,12B
Bozarth, George	WA1050	12A,12
Bradley-Kramer, Deborah	NY0750	11,12A,41
Bradshaw, Murray C.	CA5032	13,11,12A,13J
Branch, Stephen F.	CA3975	12A,61,31A,36,40
Brand, Angela	CA0450	66A,12A
Brand, Benjamin D.	TX3420	12A,12
Brannon, Patrick V.	IL3370	14,12A,36,60A,40
Brauner, Mitchell	WI0825	12A,12,12C,11
Braus, Ira	CT0650	12A,12
Bravo, Fabiana	DC0050	61,12A
Brawand, John	SD0550	11,12A,38,62
Bray, Michael R.	PA3260	60,61,11,36,12A
Brazzel, Russel	IL1100	70,12A
Breckenridge, Stan	CA2390	12A,13A,14
Breedon, Daniel	MN0600	13,10,12A,14
Bresnen, Steven M.	PA0400	13,11,12A,66A,66D
Brewer, Charles E.	FL0850	12A,12
Briggs, Kendall Durelle	NY1900	32B,12A,29
Briggs, Monique	NY2050	12A,13A
Briggs, Robert	UT0150	36,61,12A,60A
Brinksmeier, Ulrike	OH0680	12A,11,62E,14,20
Briscoe, James R.	IN0250	12A,14,12C,12
Bristol, Caterina	AL0050	11,12A,64E
Britt, Carol	LA0450	13,11,12A,66D
Brittan, Francesca	OH0400	12A
Britton, Jason	IA0950	13,12A,70,13I
Brody, Ben	WA1350	31A,60,11,12A
Brody, Martin	MA2050	13,10,12A
Brooks, Erin	CA1075	12A
Brooks-Lyle, Alma B.	AL0050	13,64A,12B,12A
Brookshire, Bradley	NY3785	12A,12,55,66G,66H
Brosius, Amy T.	NJ1000	11,12,13,20,12A
Brothers, Grey	CA5550	13,36,61,11,12A
Brothers, Lester D.	MO1790	11,12A,12C
Brothers, Thomas	NC0600	12A,12C,12E,29
Brown, Breighan M.	MI1985	12A
Brown, Bruce W.	CA5300	12A
Brown, Carlene J.	WA0800	12A,13,33
Brown, Frank Burch	IN0300	12A,66A,12B,10
Brown, Gwynne Kuhner	WA1000	12A,29A,13C,20,12B
Brown, James	FL1300	11,12A,38,64C
Brown, Jennie S.	IL3550	64A,12A,13C,42

Index by Area of Teaching Interest

Name	Code	Areas
Brown, Kellie Dubel	TN1150	62A,38,12A,60B,62B
Brown, Kristi A.	CA1075	12A
Brown, L. Joel	IA0900	13,12A,14,66,11
Brown, Leslie Ellen	WI0700	12A,13
Browne, Kimasi L.	CA0250	12A,14,20
Brownlow, James A.	TX3515	11,12A,49,63A,20
Bruce, Cynthia	AF0050	13C,33,66D,12A
Bruce, Neely	CT0750	12A,36,20G
Brunelli, Stephanie	KS0150	66A,12A,13,13B
Brunner, Lance	KY1450	12A,12
Bryan, Karen M.	AR0750	12A,11
Bucchianeri, Diane	OK1450	11,12A,41,62C
Buckingham, Steve	TN1850	12A
Budds, Michael J.	MO1800	12A,11,29
Bulen, Jay C.	MO1780	12C,12A,63C
Burford, Mark	OR0900	12A,20G,11,14C,20H
Burgess, Phillipa	OH1750	36,55C,14C,12A,20
Burke, Richard N.	NY0625	11,12A,12,20G
Burleson, Geoffrey	NY0625	66A,13,12A,66,42
Burnett, Marty Wheeler	NE0100	12A,13,66A,36,66G
Burnham, Scott	NJ0900	13,12A
Burnham, Stuart	NC1500	12A,13C,66A,20
Burns, Brian E.	IA0250	36,12A,32C,32D,60
Burns, Ellen	NY3680	12A,32E
Burnside, Joanna	MS0420	13,12A,66
Burrows, David	NY2740	11,12A,12,14
Busch, Gary D.	NY3780	12A,66A,20G
Bush, Deanna D.	TX3420	12A,12
Bushong, Claire B.	NE0400	12A,13B,13C,66A,66G
Busse Berger, Anna Maria	CA5010	12A,12
Butler, Gregory G.	AB0100	13,10,12A,12
Buzzelli-Clarke, Betsy	PA1100	11,13A,12A,66A,66D
Bynum, Leroy E.	GA0150	12A,39,61
Byrd, Joseph	CA1280	14C,10D,12A,13A
Byrne, David	AC0100	13,12A
Cabrini, Michele	NY0625	12B,12A,13B,11,12
Cahill, Sarah	CA4150	12A
Cajas, Edgar	TX2600	32A,32B,32C,12A
Calcagno, Mauro	NY3790	12A,12D,12B,11
Calkins, Katherine Charlton	CA3200	11,12A,20G
Callaghan, Marjorie S.	CT0800	12A,13,63B
Callaway, Patricia	GA1200	61,12A,41
Callon, Gordon J.	AF0050	12A,13D
Campana, Alessandra	MA1900	12,12A,11
Campbell, Don	SC1080	13,60,36,61,12A
Campi-Walters, Lisa	CO0350	13,12A,66,10A
Candelaria, Lorenzo	TX3510	11,12A,12
Cannata, David B.	PA3250	12A
Capaldo, Jennifer R.	VA0700	61,13C,12A
Caporella, Cynthia Anne	OH1050	36,12A,66A,66C
Caputo, John	NJ0200	12A,14,37,64,20G
Caputo, Michael	NJ0250	12A,14,37,48,64
Carlton, Kathleen	OK0410	13,11,12A,61,31A
Carpenter, Thomas H.	NY3725	11,12A
Carr, Tracy A.	NM0100	64B,12A,41,64F,11
Carr, Walter E.	OR0800	12A,12,14,20G
Carroll, Don	CA0859	12A
Carson, William S.	IA0300	60B,37,12A,32E,64C
Carter, Beverly H.	PA1450	11,12A,66A,66B
Carter, John R.	CA1375	11,12A,36,61,13C
Carter, Stewart	NC2500	13,11,12A,55,67
Cary, Jane G.	NY0400	11,12A,66H
Case, Del W.	CA3400	66G,44,13,12A,36
Cason, Tony	CA3600	41,32E,60B,38,12A
Cassio, Francesca	NY1600	12,12A,12C,20
Castleberry, David	WV0400	60,12A,36,61
Castonguay, Gerald	MA0650	12A,12
Castonguay, Roger	AE0100	12A,10A,13A
Catan, Daniel	CA1265	13A,13,10,11,12A
Catsalis, Marie-Louise	CA4425	12A,66A
Caulder, Stephanie B.	PA1600	12A,12D,48,64B,13C
Cavanaugh, Alice I.	NY4050	36,12A,11
Cech, Jessica	MI2120	64A,11,12A
Celenza, Anna H.	DC0075	12A,12B,12C,12G
Cerny, William J.	IN1700	12A,41,66A,66C
Chacholiades, Linda P.	MN0610	11,20,12A
Chafe, Eric	MA0500	13A,11,12A,12,13J
Chagnon, Richard	CA0450	11,12A,36,61
Chandler, Gulya	LA0030	66A,66C,66D,11,12A
Chapman, David F.	NJ1130	11,12A
Chapman, Norman	MS0600	13A,13,12A,66A
Charles, Sydney R.	CA5010	12A,12
Charnofsky, Eric	OH0600	12A
Charter, Ian R.	AA0010	12A,13A,31A,32E,60
Chase, David A.	CA3460	13A,13,12A,36,60
Chase, Robert	NY2400	13,12A,66H
Chaudhuri, Swapan	CA0050	13A,10,12A,65
Cherney, Brian	AI0150	13,10,12A
Cherrington Beggs, Sally	SC0900	13D,66,31A,12A
Chesebro, Robert C.	SC0750	12A,64,41
Chessa, Luciano	CA4150	12A
Chevan, David	CT0450	11,12A,47,53,29
Chianis, Sam	NY3705	12A,12,14,20H
Chiaravalloti, Charissa	CO0350	36,40,60,12A,32D
Childs, David T.	MN0600	13,12A
Chilingarian, Samvel	CA1700	12A,38,62
Chinn, Genevieve	NY2105	13,11,12A,12
Chittum, Donald	PA3330	13,12A,12,14,12F
Cho, Young-Hyun	TX3500	66A,41,66C,66B,12A
Chou, Mei-En	LA0150	66A,66B,66C,12A
Christensen, Janielle	UT0050	12A,36,39,54,35
Christeson, Jane	FL1750	61,12A,39,36
Christopher, Un Chong	MO0060	11,12A,13,66A,66C
Christy, William P.	OH1910	13,12A,20G,29A,34
Chuah, Cheong	CA2775	12A,13A,34
Chusid, Martin	NY2740	11,12A,12
Cienniwa, Paul D.	MA2020	12A,12,11,34B
Cifelli, Cheryl L.	MO0800	64C,64D,12A,11,13E
Cimarusti, Thomas M.	TX3200	12A,13E,20,12C,68
Clark, Alice V.	LA0300	12A,11,31A,12
Clark, Antoine T.	OH0850	12A,72,48,64,64C
Clark, Caryl L.	AG0450	12A,12
Clark, Daniel	OH2370	11,12A,13C
Clark, Jacob	SC1050	66A,66D,12A
Clark, John W.	CA4410	13,11,12A,10D
Clark, Michael	FL1570	13,12A,36,66,54
Clark, Wallace	FL0600	12A,32C,37
Clarke, Garry E.	MD1100	13,10F,10,12A
Clayton, Cathryn	UT0250	62E,20,12A
Clegg, Neill M.	NC0900	10F,12A,64,53,29A
Clements, Phillip L.	TX2955	60B,37,63D,13A,12A
Clenman, David	AB0150	13,12A,13A,13B,13C
Climie, Stanley	AA0050	12A,48,64C
Coates, Norma	AG0500	12A,12D,15,35A
Cobert, Claude	MA2020	64A,11,12A
Cochran, Alfred W.	KS0650	12A,13A,13B,13E
Cochrane, Keith A.	NM0400	60,12A,32B,37,47
Cockburn, Neil	AA0050	66G,67F,12A
Cockey, Linda E.	MD0800	12A,66A,66B,13E
Coen, Jean-David	OR1300	12A,66A,66C
Cohen, Albert	CA4900	12A,12,13J,20G
Cohen, David E.	NY0750	13,12A,13J
Coker, Keller	OR1250	55,12A,63C,10D
Cole, Dennis E.	OH0100	14C,12A,11,20
Cole, Judith W.	TX2960	11,12A,32B
Cole, Malcolm S.	CA5032	11,12A,12,66G,31A
Cole, Richard C.	VA1700	11,12A,20G
Cole, Ronald F.	ME0500	12A,12,66A
Colgin-Abeln, Melissa	TX3520	12A,64A
Coll, Peter	NJ1400	12A
Collins, Dana L.	IN1560	10,12A,34,35C,13
Collins, Shelley	MS0250	11,64A,12A,48
Collins, Zachary	PA1600	63D,12A,13B,49
Coluzzi, Seth	MA0500	10D,11,13A,12A,12C
Colwell, Brent	TX2800	37,11,12A,63C,63D
Combs, Julia C.	MO0775	64B,13B,12A,11,13C
Comstock, Allan D.	KS0300	11,64B,64D,12A
Conner, Ted A.	PA2550	11,12A,29A
Connolly, Michael E.	OR1100	36,12A,10A,61,13
Connolly, Thomas H.	PA3350	12A,12
Conoly, Shaaron	TX3100	12A,39,61,54
Conrad, Robert	CA4625	13,11,12A,61
Conroy, Thomas	CA4150	12A,13
Conte, David	CA4150	10,12A,36
Conway, Robert	MI2200	66A,66B,66D,12A
Cook, Jeffrey	TN0900	63B,12A,42,11
Cook, Lisa M.	CO0550	11,12A,20G,31A,14
Cook, Thomas	MI1250	13,12A,38,63C
Cooksey, Steven	VA1350	12A,36,66G,31A
Coolen, Michael T.	OR0700	14,54,20,12A,35A
Cooper, Britt	OH2370	11,12A,14C,36,61
Cooper, J. Michael	TX2650	12A
Cooper, Marva W.	DC0350	11,12A,66A,66B,66C
Cooper, Rex	CA5350	66A,12A
Cope, David H.	CA5070	13,10,12A
Copenhaver, Lee R.	MI0900	13,11,12A,38,62C
Coppola, Catherine	NY0625	11,12A
Corcoran, Kathleen	AA0110	12A,61,39
Cordell, Tim	NC2000	12A
Corin, Amy R.	CA3100	14,11,13C,12A
Cornejo, Robert Joseph	CA5510	13,11,34C,10,12A
Cornelius, Jeffrey M.	PA3250	60,11,12A,36
Cornett-Murtada, Vanessa	MN1625	66A,13,12A,66B
Cortese, Federico	MA1050	38,12A,12B
Cosart, Jann	TX0300	12A,55
Cowart, Georgia	OH0400	12A,12
Cowin, Jasmin Bey	NY4200	11,62E,12A,31B
Cox, Buford	FL0040	13A,12A,66A,66C
Cox, Dennis K.	ME0440	60A,12A,36
Cramer, Alfred W.	CA3650	13,12A,12B
Cramer, Craig	IN1700	12A,66G
Cratty, William	CA4050	13A,13,12A,14,32
Crawford, Stephen J.	TX3415	37,12A,50,65
Crider, Joe	VA0650	11,12A
Cromley, Dorothea	MT0175	12A,66A,66B
Crookall, Christine	GA0250	13A,13,62C,12A,41
Crosby, Richard A.	KY0550	66A,66D,12A
Cross, Alan E.	TN0150	11,12A,61,31A
Cross, Ronald W.	NY4500	13A,11,12A
Cross, Virginia A.	OR0175	31A,12A,66D,13A,66B
Crothers-Marley, Shirley Evans	OH2100	12A,32,36,61
Crozier, Daniel G.	FL1550	13,10,12A
Cubbage, John	MT0370	13,12A,66A,10A
Culloton, Michael	MN0600	36,12A
Culverhouse, William	IN0400	36,12A,60
Cummings, Dean	OH1400	12A,13,63C
Cunningham, James E.	FL0650	14,20,32,11,12A
Cunningham, Jennifer	OK0825	12A,13
Currie, Neil	AJ0150	12A
Cusick, Suzanne G.	NY2740	12A,12C,12D,15
Cutler, David	SC1110	13,10,12A
Cutsforth-Huber, Bonnie	MD0095	13A,13,11,12A,13B
D'Accone, Frank A.	CA5032	12A,12,13J
Dacus, Edward	MS0400	12A,61
Dalen, Brenda	AA0100	12A
Dalton, Dana	MA1400	66A,12A,12,66C
Damuth, Laura	NE0600	12A
Daniel, Jane	WV0400	12A,11
Davidian, Teresa	TX2750	13,10,12A,20
Davies, Drew Edward	IL2250	12A
Davies, James	CA5000	11,12A,12E,20A,66A
Davila, William	CA3450	13A,11,12A,66A,67D
Davis, James A.	NY3725	12A
Davis, Mary E.	OH0400	12A,12,14
Davis, Rachelle Berthelsen	CA3400	62A,12A,38
Davis, Richard A.	WV0500	13,60,12A,36,61
Day, Gary	AJ0150	12A
De Dobay, Thomas	CA0950	11,12A,61,66D
de Graaf, Melissa J.	FL1900	12,12A,11
De Launay, Anne M.	MO1810	61,12A
De Leo, Joseph A.	NY2750	32,12A,13B,32C,32H
De Pasquale, Lawrence	NJ1050	11,12A
Deadman, Alison Patricia	TN0500	12A,64C
Deahl, Lora	TX3200	66A,66C,66B,12A
Dean, Terry Lynn	IN0800	11,12A,13
Dearing, James C.	PA1600	36,40,12A
Deaville, James A.	AG0200	11,12A,12,41,12C
Debly, Patricia	AG0050	12A,12C
DeBoer, Jack	MI0900	11,13A,12A
DeBoer, Paul	NY1700	63,12A,49
Decker, Todd R.	MO1900	12,12A
Declue, Gary L.	IL1245	12A,13A,11,61,36
DeCoro, Helena	CA1520	61,66A,11,12A,39
Decorsey, James H.	WI0350	12A,41,63B
Dees, Pamela Youngdahl	MO1250	66A,66B,66C,11,12A
DeFord, Ruth	NY0625	11,12A,12,12C
DeLamater, Elizabeth L.	AZ0490	20,29A,12A,65
DeLaRosa, Lou	CA5510	13A,13C,12A,11,34C
Delcamp, Robert	TN1800	13,12A,36,66G,31A
DelDonna, Anthony R.	DC0075	12,12A,12B,12C,12D
Dell'Antonio, Andrew	TX3510	11,12A,12
Demaree, Robert K.	WI0840	12A,36
Demsey, Karen B.	NJ1400	64A,48,12,11,12A
Denison, Mark	OR1010	12A,29A,63C,46,60B
Denman, James L.	OR1300	13,12A,66G,13F,13H
Dennis, Thomas A.	MI1700	12A,66A,46
Denson, William	NC0860	11,29,12A
Dent, Cedric	TN1100	12A,10D,35A,13E
DeQuattro, Anthony	CT0250	11,12A
DeVeaux, Scott K.	VA1550	13,12A,12,14,29
Di Bacco, Giuliano	IN0900	12A,13J
Di Grazia, Donna M.	CA3650	60,11,12A,36
Diamond, Douglas	MN0050	60B,38,51,12A
Dickensheets, Janice	CO0950	12,34A,14,12B,12A
Dickerson, Roger	LA0720	10F,10,12A,36,29
Dickey, Timothy J.	OH2000	11,12A,13E

Index by Area of Teaching Interest

Name	Code	Areas
Diehl, David J.	TN1600	12A,32C,36
Dikener, Solen	WV0400	11,12A,62C,62D
Dill, John	TX1775	13A,11,66A,66G,12A
Dillenger, Robert	CA2775	12A,13A
Dillon, Emma	PA3350	11,12A,12
DiMedio, Annette	PA3330	12A,12,66A,66D,11
Dinger, Gregory	NY4300	13,12A,70
DiPalma, Maria	IA1350	12A,39,61
DiPaolo, Stacey	OK1250	11,12A,64C
Dirst, Matthew	TX3400	12A,55,67C
Dixon, Timothy D.	PA2300	38,12A
Dodge, Leanne E.	NY2750	12A,12,13A
Dodson-Webster, Rebecca	PA2150	63B,13,12A,49
Doering, James M.	VA1150	13,11,12A,66A,66G
Doggett, Cynthia Krenzel	IA0200	12A,20,48,64C,64E
Doiel, Mark	CA2900	10D,11,12A,13,37
Dolan, Emily I.	PA3350	12A,12,11,12B
Doran, David Stephen	KY1460	13A,13,10,11,12A
Dorf, Samuel N.	OH2250	12A,11,55A,55B,55C
Dorsa, James	CA0835	66H,10A,67F,13C,12A
Dorsey, Sam Brian	VA0950	12A,70
Dotson, Ronald	CA5510	11,34C,66D,14C,12A
Douglas, Bill	CO0560	13,11,12A,36,66A
Doukhan, Lilianne	MI0250	12A,12,14,31A,12C
Doutt, Kathleen C.	PA1550	12A,32,13C,20
Dreisbach, Tina Spencer	OH1000	12A,14,32H
Dressler, Jane	OH1100	12A,61
Dressler, John C.	KY0950	12A,63B,11,12C
Drummond, Evan E.	NY3717	12A,13A,70
Dubal, David	NY1900	12A
DuBois, Ted	TX3750	11,12A,34C
Dubowchik, Rosemary	CT0450	11,12A
Duda, Theodor	OH0700	13B,13C,12A,20G
Dudley, Sherwood	CA5070	13,10F,12A,39
Duerksen, Marva G.	OR1300	13,12A
Duffin, Ross	OH0400	12A,12,55
Duggan, Sean B.	LA0600	11,12A,36,66A,31A
Dunbar, Edward	SC0200	13,12A,66G,34
Dunevant, David L.	KY1000	12A,63C
Dunnell, Rebecca	MO0950	64A,12A,14,11,20
DuPree, Mary	ID0250	12A,12,43,14C
Durant, Douglas F.	MA1450	13,10,11,12A
Durham, Carol S.	MS0400	66G,66A,66C,66H,12A
Durham, Linda Eileen	VA1840	12A
Durrenberger, Chris	OH2450	13A,11,66A,66F,12A
Dussault, Michel J.	AI0220	12A,66A,66B
Dzapo, Kyle J.	IL0400	12A,12,64A
Eanes, Edward	GA1150	12A,11,12C,20G
Earp, Lawrence	WI0815	11,12A,12
Eby, John D.	AI0050	11,12A,12C,20G,31A
Echols, Charles	MN1300	66H,12A,66A,66G
Eckert, William H.	DC0110	13,12A,32A,66G
Edel, Theodore	IL3310	11,66A,12A
Edgerton, Sara A.	MO1500	11,12A,38,62D,62C
Ediger, Thomas L.	NE0500	12A,32,36,66
Edwards, Constance	WV0300	64D,12,11,12A,10F
Edwards, Julie	IN0800	13,12A
Egler, Steven	MI0400	12A,66H,66G,31A
Eidsheim, Nina	CA5032	12A,12,13
Eikner, Edward	GA2200	12A,66A,66C,66D,11
Eisel, Gunnar	CA1000	10B,12A,13A,14C,29A
Eisenstein, Robert	MA2000	12A,55B,67
Elias, Cathy A.	IL0750	11,12A,12C
Elliott, Robin W.	AG0450	12,12A,20G
Ellsworth, Jane	WA0250	12A,12
Elser, Albert Christian	SC1000	61,12A,34D,39
Elzinga, Harry	TX0300	12A,12C
Engel, Tiffany	OK1300	13,11,12A,66A
Engelmann, Marcus W.	CA0100	13,10,12A,45,20G
Engle, Martha Ramm	CA2050	12A,11,54
Enman, Thomas	MA1175	66C,12A,54,66A,61
Enns, Ruth	AB0200	12A
Ennulat, Egbert M.	GA2100	12A,66G,66H
Enrico, Eugene	OK1350	12A,12,55,67
Ensor, Robert	MO0260	12A,47,66A,66C,54
Entwistle, Erik	MA1175	12A,12C
Epperson, Dean	AK0100	11,12A,66A,66D,66B
Epstein, Joan O.	FL0450	13,11,12A,53,63A
Erickson, James M.	NY4060	13,12A,11,70
Esch, Michael	AG0300	66A,12A
Espinosa, Teresita	CA3150	11,12A,32,61,20G
Esse, Melina	NY1100	12A,12B,12D,14C,15
Ettinger, Karl Erik	FL1700	66A,11,12A
Evans, David H.	AR0300	13,11,12A,32,48
Evans, David	TN1680	12A,20G,14
Evans, Garry W.	TX3300	64C,37,12A,41,60B
Evans, Gary	VA0400	13A,13B,13C,11,12A
Evans, Gerald	OH1300	13,10,12A,14,66D
Evans, Joel	NY3760	37,64B,12A,13B,20
Evans, Margaret R.	OR0950	12A,66G
Everett, William A.	MO1810	12A
Ewing, Rosella	GA0600	12A,61
Eylar, Leo B.	CA0840	10,12A,38
Ezoe, Magdalena	MI1950	66A,13,12B,12A,41
Faber, Trudy	OH2450	12A,44,66G,66H,31A
Fairbanks, Ann K.	TX3450	13A,12A,41,64A
Falck, Robert A.	AG0450	11,12A,12
Falk, Leila Birnbaum	OR0900	11,12A,12B,41
Falk, Marc	IA0300	36,11,12A,60A,40
Falkenstein, Richard	NY0400	11,12A,70
Fallis, David	AG0450	12A
Farrell, Peter S.	CA5050	13,12A,62C,67A
Farzinpour, Peyman	MA2020	11,12A,13B
Fassett, Charles K.	MA2150	60,11,12A,36
Fassnacht, Therese	CA3150	13B,13C,20H,12A
Fast, Susan	AG0200	13A,11,12A,12,55
Fava, Cristina	NY2650	12A
Fay, James	VA0975	13,12A,64C
Feder, Janet	CO0560	10,70,12A,13A,53
Fedoruk, Claire	CA0250	12A
Fehleisen, Fred	NY1900	12A
Fehleisen, Fred	NY2250	12A
Feinberg, Henry A.	MI1700	12A,10
Feiszli, James D.	SD0500	12A,36,55D,61
Feldman, Martha	IL3250	11,12A,12,15
Feldman, Susan M.	CA5300	62A,67B,12A
Feller, David E.	UT0350	11,12A,48,64,31
Feltsman, Vladimir	NY3760	66A,66B,12A
Fenley, J. Franklin	MO1790	11,12A,64A
Fennelly, Brian	NY2740	13,10,12A,45
Ferer, Mary T.	WV0750	11,12A,12
Ferguson, Linda C.	IN1750	12A,20G,11
Ferris, David	TX2150	12A,12
Fetz, Teun	OR0200	12A,65,48
Feurzeig, Lisa	MI0900	12C,12A,20
Fickett, Martha V.	VA1475	11,12A,12E,66A
Finch, Scott	AJ0030	60A,31A,12A,13A,11
Fine, R. Samuel	MD0850	12A
Fink, Michael Jon	CA0510	12A,12,35,10
Finney, John W.	KY0700	13,12A,36,61,66A
Finnsson, Karen	AJ0100	12A,64E,64
Fisher, Stan F.	AF0050	32E,12A
Fisk, Charles	MA2050	13A,13,12A,66A
Fithian, Bruce S.	ME0500	39,12A,61
Flaherty, Thomas E.	CA3650	13,10,12A,45
Flandreau, Tara	CA1150	12A,13,38,41,62
Fleming, Nancy P.	AR0350	12A,36,60A
Fletcher, Harold	OK0700	13,12A
Fletcher, Marylynn L.	TX3600	34C,36,11,66A,12A
Fletcher, Terry W.	MS0300	36,61,12A
Flick, DaLeesa J.	OK1200	66A,12A
Florine, Jane Lynn	IL0600	11,12A,12,20A,64A
Flory, Andrew	MN0300	12A,29A
Flowers, Alan	AL1250	11,12A
Foley, Christopher	AG0300	12A
Fontijn, Claire	MA2050	12A,12
Forney, Kristine	CA0825	12A,67,11
Fosler-Lussier, Danielle	OH1850	12A,12
Foster, Donald H.	OH2200	12A,12
Fowler, Colin	NY2900	36,13,12A,66A,66G
Fowler, Kurt	IN0800	62C,11,12A,51
Fox, David E.	NC0900	66A,12A,66D,43,11
Fox, Rachelle	CA5300	12A
Foy, Randolph M.	NC1700	11,12A,38
Frabizio, William V.	PA0125	13,11,12A,41
Fralin, Sandra L.	KY1200	12A
Francis, Lorie	MO0825	11,12A,13,36,66A
Frandsen, Lars	NY2900	12A,13,70
Frandsen, Mary E.	IN1700	12A,12
Frangipane, Ron	NJ0760	13,10F,60,10,12A
Frary, Peter Kun	HI0160	13,11,12A,70,34
Frederick, Matthew D.	VA0350	63A,12A,41,60B,32E
Freed, Donald Callen	TX2710	61,36,10A,13C,12A
Freedman, Deborah	NE0590	11,12A,38,63B
Freedman, Richard	PA1500	11,12A,12,20D,29A
Freeman, Graham	AG0450	12A
Freitas, Roger	NY1100	12A,12C,12D,15
French, Paul T.	OR0950	11,12A,36,39,61
Frey, Loryn E.	LA0150	12A,39,61
Friedley, Geoffrey A.	ID0100	61,11,12A
Friedman, Eve A.	NJ1050	12A
Friedman, Joel Phillip	CA4425	13B,10A,10D,12A
Frisch, Walter	NY0750	11,12A,12
Froelich, Andrew I.	ND0350	13,12A,66A,66H
Fryns, Jennifer	FL0365	20,12A
Fulcher, Jane	MI2100	12,12A
Fuller, Sarah	NY3790	11,12A,12,13
Fullerton, Kevin T.	KS1400	14C,12A,29A,63D,11
Furlong, Allison	OH1850	12A
Furr, Barbara	NC2440	12A,66A,66D
Furr, Rhonda	TX1000	12A,16,66G
Fusco, Randall J.	OH1000	13B,38,66A,12A,11
Futterer, Karen	AR0200	12A,48,64A
Gable, David D.	GA0490	11,12A,12B,13A,16
Gable, Frederick K.	CA5040	12A,12,31A
Gabrielse, Kenneth J.	LA0400	60,36,31A,12A
Galasso, Mathew	CA1900	11,12A,66A,13
Gall, Jeffrey C.	NJ0800	55,61,12A,12,39
Gallagher, Jack	OH0700	63A,10,10F,13,12A
Gallagher, Mark	MD0350	64C,48,13,12A
Galloway, Robert J.	NY1700	12A,66A
Gano, Peter W.	OH1850	12A,12
Ganus, Clifton L.	AR0250	12A,31A,36,60A
Garber, Joel	OK0770	12A,61,14,36,60
Garber, Ron	KS0210	11,12A,36,41,61
Garcia, Federico	PA0600	10,12A,13,41
Garcia-Leon, Jose M.	CT0700	11,12A,13,66A,66D
Gardner, David	AG0100	12A,12
Gardner, Kara	CA4150	12A
Gardner, Stefanie	AZ0350	12A
Gariazzo, Mariana Stratta	TX2900	64A,12A,20,11
Garlington, Aubrey S.	NC2430	12,12A
Garner, Ronald L.	UT0150	13,11,12A,63B
Garofalo, Angelo	PA3500	11,12A
Garry, Kevin M.	CO0400	70,13A,11,12A,14C
Gaspar, Carole	MO1950	12A,61
Gaub, Eugene	IA0700	13,12A,66A,11
Gavito, Cory M.	OK0750	12A
Gaylard, Timothy R.	VA1850	11,12A,66A,20G
Gehl, Robin	OH2200	12A,13,13F
Geihsler, Rebecca	MS0100	61,12A,14C
Gelbart, Matthew	NY1300	12A,13J,14A,14D,20F
Gemme, Terese	CT0450	13A,12A,36,66G
Gennaro, Joe	FL1800	11,12A,20
Gentry, Philip	DE0150	12A
George, Rosemary	NY0270	66A,61,12A,11
Gerber, Thomas E.	IN1650	11,66H,55B,12A
Gerber, Thomas	IN1100	12A,66A
Gerbino, Giuseppe	NY0750	11,12A,12
Getz, Christine S.	IA1550	12A,12
Ghuman, Nalini G.	CA2950	13,12A,12C,12
Gianforte, Matthew P.	KY0950	66A,66D,66B,66,12A
Gibson, Alan	VT0200	11,12A
Gibson, Joice Waterhouse	CO0550	34B,34C,12A,12C,13A
Gibson, Jonathan B.	VA0600	11,12A,55
Gier, Christina B.	AA0100	12A,12D,12B,12,15
Gifford, Tell	NV0125	11,12A,13,66A
Gilbert, Adam	CA5300	12A
Gilbert, John Haspel	TX3200	12A,62A
Gilbert, Rotem	CA5300	12A
Gilliam, Bryan	NC0600	11,12A,12B,12C,12D
Gillingham, Bryan	AG0100	12A,12,36
Gilmour, F. Matthew	MO0850	13,10,11,12A,34
Girard, Sharon	CA4200	12A,12,14
Girdham, Jane C.	MI1850	11,12A,13B,13C,13E
Giteck, Janice	WA0200	13,13,10,12A
Gitz, Raymond	LA0560	12A,66A,31A
Gleason, Stephen	NY1275	10D,12A,13B,14C,34D
Glenn, James H.	NC2000	36,61,60A,11,12A
Gliadkovsky, Kirill	UT0200	66A,12A
Glickman, Eugene	NY2550	13,12A
Glinsky, Albert	PA2250	13,10,12A
Glofcheskie, John	AB0050	13A,13,12A
Godfrey, Daniel S.	NY4150	13,10,12A
Godwin, Joscelyn	NY0650	12A,12
Goehring, Edmund J.	AG0500	12A,12E
Goforth, Stephen C.	KY1300	11,36,60A,61,12A
Golan, Jeanne K.	NY2550	13B,13C,12A,66A,66D
Goldmark, Daniel	OH0400	12A,14C
Goldray, Martin	NY3560	13A,13,11,12A,66A
Goldstein, Howard A.	AL0200	10F,62A,11,12A,38
Golightly, John Wesley	KY0650	12A,31A,66,34,13D
Golijov, Osvaldo	MA0700	20G,13,10,11,12A
Gollner, Marie L.	CA5032	12A,12,13J
Gomer, Wesley	TX1650	13,66,69,12A,36
Gomez, Routa Kroumovitch	FL1750	12A,62A,62B

Index by Area of Teaching Interest

Name	Code	Areas
Gonano, Max A.	PA0500	11,12A,13A,29A,37
Gonzalez, Claudio	MI0250	38,60B,10F,20,12A
Gonzol, David J.	WV0550	32,12A
Goodman, Glenda	CA1075	12A
Goodwin, Julia	OR0700	66A,66D,11,12A,66C
Goold, William C.	KY0150	60,12A,36,61,31A
Gooley, Dana	RI0050	12A,13B,12E,12D
Gordon, Samuel	OH2150	60,12A,36,61,40
Gordon, Stewart	CA5300	12A,66A
Gordon, Thomas	AD0050	12A
Gordon, William	AC0050	10F,12A,63B
Gordon-Seifert, Catherine	RI0150	13,12A,12C,55B,66H
Gorman, Sharon L.	AR0900	12A,66G
Gosine, C. Jane	AD0050	12A
Gossett, Philip	IL3250	12A,12
Gould, Brian	CA3350	12A,66A
Graber, Todd A.	NY3770	61,54,36,12A
Grace, Michael	CO0200	11,12A,12,55
Gradone, Richard	NJ0250	13,12A,12,47,63A
Graham, Alta Elizabeth	CO0350	13,10,12A
Graham, Edward E.	SC1050	66A,66C,66D,12A
Granade, S. Andrew	MO1810	12A
Grass, Mahlon O.	PA2050	12A,48,64B,64C,64E
Grau-Schmidt, Anna K.	IL0750	11,12A
Grave, Floyd	NJ1130	11,12A,12,13J
Graves, Daniel H.	IN0400	11,12A,36,60,41
Gray, D'Arcy	AF0150	12A
Gray, Laura J.	AG0470	11,12A,12,14,20
Graziano, Amy	CA0960	11,12A,12F
Greco, Eugene A.	FL1300	36,12A,67F,12,67
Green, Edward	NY2750	12A
Green, Edward	NY2150	12A,29
Green, Richard D.	OH1450	12A,12,12C
Greenan, April	VA1475	11,12A,12B,12F,20
Greene, Elisabeth Mehl	TX1100	10F,12A
Greene, Gordon K.	AG0600	12A
Greene, Kimberly	CA0815	12A
Greene, Richard C.	GA0850	70,13C,11,13E,12A
Greenlee, Robert K.	ME0200	60,36,12A,12,55
Greenspan, Bertram	NJ1050	62,51,12A,12
Gregg, Robert B.	TN0100	60,11,12A,38
Grenfell, Mary-Jo	MA1650	12A,32,38,41,42
Grey, Meg	MO0600	11,12A,32,66A,66G
Grey, Thomas S.	CA4900	13,12A,12
Griffeath, Kristin	OK1250	12A,61,39,36
Griffel, L. Michael	NY1900	12A,12
Griffin, Jackie	SC0950	13,10,12A,66G,34
Griffioen, Ruth	VA0250	67D,55,12A
Grolman, Ellen K.	MD0350	12A,62C
Grooms, Pamela	MO0650	12A,20,32D,60,66
Gross, Anne	DE0150	11,12A
Gross, Ernest H.	IL1300	37,49,60B,63D,12A
Groves, Robert W.	ND0350	11,12A,66A,20G,66H
Grugin, Stephen	MI1600	37,63D,12A,32C,32E
Gruhn, Charles	CA1700	12,12A
Grymes, James A.	NC2420	12,12A,11
Gudmundson, Paula	MN0040	64A,64,12A,14
Guenther, Roy J.	DC0100	13E,13F,11,12A
Gutshall, Christi	AZ0400	66A,66B,66D,12A
Guzski, Carolyn	NY3717	12A,14
Guzzo, Anne M.	WY0200	13,10,12A,13F,15
Hadlock, Heather L.	CA4900	11,12A,12
Hafer, Edward	MS0750	12,12A
Hagelstein, Kim Rooney	TX2750	12A,13D,32E,63B
Hager, Nancy M.	NY0500	13,11,12A,12
Haggh-Huglo, Barbara	MD1010	12A,12
Hahn, David	TN0580	12A,34,35A,36,60
Hahn, Richard	ID0250	64A,12A
Haines, John D.	AG0450	12A,12,20F
Haldey, Olga	MD1010	12,12A,11,14
Hall, Barbara L.	KY0450	13,12A,12,36,60
Hall, Cory	FL1650	66D,66A,12A
Hall, Frederick A.	AG0200	11,12A,12,20G
Hall, Gary	WY0115	11,12A,13B,13C,47
Hall, Jonathan B.	NY2750	12A,13,31A,36,66G
Haller, William P.	WV0750	13,12A,66G,31A
Hallmark, Anne Vaughan	MA1400	12A
Hallmark, Rufus	NJ1130	12,12A
Hamberlin, Larry D.	VT0350	10A,12A,29A,13A,13C
Hamessley, Lydia	NY1350	13C,12,14,20G,12A
Hamilton, David	MN0600	61,12A
Hamm, Bruce	CA0050	13A,11,12A
Hamm, Samuel J.	MT0350	12A,13,63D
Hamman, James	LA0800	11,12A,13A,55B,66G
Hammond, June C.	FL1600	12A,36,61,66A,37
Hammond, L. Curtis	KY0900	63B,12A
Hampton, Anitra C.	AL0650	12A,32,32G,11
Hancock, Virginia	OR0900	13,12A,36
Handel, Thomas	MA1400	12A,13B
Haney, Joel C.	CA0650	11,12A,41
Hanks, N. Lincoln	CA3600	55D,13,10,34,12A
Hanning, Barbara	NY0600	12A,12
Hanning, Barbara Russano	NY0550	13A,11,12A,12
Hansbrough, Yvonne	NY0700	64A,67D,12A,42
Hansen, Richard K.	MN1300	60B,37,20G,12A
Hanserd, Mary	AL0550	13,12A
Hanson, Alice	MN1450	12A
Hanson, Ellen	GA2200	12A,61,39
Hanson, Eric A.	WA0800	60,12A,38,10,64C
Hanson, F.	NY4060	13,12A,11,66A
Hanson, Jan	OK1400	60,11,12A,32,36
Harbison, John H.	MA1200	13,10,12A
Harbold, Mark A.	IL0850	13,10F,10,16,12A
Hardeman, Anita	IL3500	66G,12A,66A
Harrington, Richard	CA0050	13A,11,12A
Harris, B. Joan	MS0200	11,12A,66
Harris, Carl G.	VA0500	60,12A,66,69
Harris, Duane	MO0350	32,36,61,12A
Harris, Ellen T.	MA1200	13,11,12A,12
Harris, Kim	KY0250	12A,62B,62C
Harris, Paul K.	WA1000	12A,11,13B
Harris, Robert	GA0200	12A,60,61,11,32D
Harris, Timothy	CA0900	37,11,12A,32E
Harris, Ward	MD0550	11,14C,12A
Harrison, Jane	OH1850	12A
Harrison, John F.	PA1250	12A,12,66A
Hart, Brian J.	IL2200	12A,12
Hart, Thomas J.	IA0600	60,36,12A
Hartig, Hugo J.	WI0200	13,10F,10,12A
Hartwell, Robert	CA1800	66D,20G,12A
Hartzell, K. Drew	NY3700	11,12A,12
Harvey, Peter J.	CT0240	13,12A,36,54,20G
Harvey, Susan	CA4150	12A
Haskins, Robert	NH0350	12A
Hasty, Christopher	MA1050	13,10,12A,13J
Hatcher, George	NC2300	11,12A
Hathaway, Janet J.	IL2200	12A,55,67,12C
Haughton, Ethel Norris	VA1750	13,12A,12,20G,66C
Haupert, Mary Ellen	WI1100	12A,13,34,66H
Haupt, Dorothy G.	PA0125	12A,32B,36,66G
Hausmann, John P.	KY1500	12A
Hay, James	MA0510	11,12A,66A,66B
Haynes, Kimberly	FL0100	12A,39,61
Heape, Mary Willis	TX3050	32,61,13,12A
Heath, Malissa	KY1540	11,66D,32B,13,12A
Hedberg, Judy L.	OR0800	12A,13A
Hefling, Stephen	OH0400	12A,12
Hehr, Milton G.	MO1810	13,10F,12A
Heidlberger, Frank	TX3420	13J,12A,12,13
Heidner, Eric C.	CA4410	37,47,13,29,12A
Heilmair, Barbara	OR0850	12A,41,42,64C,48
Heiman, Lawrence F.	IN1350	12A,13A
Heimbecker, Sara	CO0950	12A,11,13A,14C
Heisler, Wayne H.	NJ0175	12A,14,20
Heiss, John C.	MA1400	10,12A,41,43
Hekmatpanah, Kevin	WA0400	11,12A,38,51,62C
Held, Jeffrey	CA1425	11,12A,37,32E,10F
Heller, Brian	MN1050	10B,34,12A,35B,35G
Heller, Wendy B.	NJ0900	12A,12,39,14A
Hellmann, Mary	NC0700	66A,66D,12A
Helm, Jon E.	AA0040	13A,13,12A,63,49
Henderson, Peter	MO0700	12A,13,42,66A
Hendrickson, Daniel	MI1180	11,12A,36,37,61
Hennessey, Patrick D.	HI0110	37,47,29A,12A,63C
Henry, Joseph D.	IL0900	12A,20G,36,40,32C
Henson, Karen A.	NY0750	11,15,39,12A,12B
Hepler, Julie E.	PA0100	64B,64C,12A,64D,64E
Hepler, Lowell E.	PA0100	12A,12C,37,66A,63D
Hermiston, Nancy	AB0100	12A,39,61
Hernandez Mergal, Luis A.	PR0115	12A,12B,14
Herod, Sheila	TX1750	13,12A,66A,66C,66D
Hersey, Joanna R.	NC2435	10F,63C,63D,12A
Hersh, Paul	CA4150	12A,42,62B,66A
Hess, Debra L.	FL0680	12A
Hettrick, Jane S.	NY1600	12A,66G
Hettrick, William E.	NY1600	12A,13,55,55B
Heuchemer, Dane O.	OH1200	11,12A,12,37,67
Heydenburg, Audrejean	MI2000	11,12A,66A,66B,66C
Hibler, Starla	OK0300	12A,66A,66C
Hickman, Roger	CA0825	11,12A,38
Hicks, Andrew	NY0900	12A,13J
Highberger, Edgar B.	PA3000	12A,66G,31A
Highman, Daniel R.	CA0807	10A,12A
Higney, John	AG0100	12A
Hilburn, Aaron Ichiro	FL1550	12A
Hiles, Karen	PA2550	12A
Hill, George R.	NY0250	11,12A,12,16
Hill, Harry H.	SC0850	11,12A,64C,64E,48
Hill, Jackson	PA0350	10,12A,12,14,71
Hill, Matthew	IN0550	66A,66B,11,12A
Hillyer, Dirk M.	MA1650	63B,11,12A,13E,13F
Hilowski-Fowler, Ann	PA3600	11,12A
Hime, Michael	TN1850	12A
Himrod, Gail P.	RI0150	12A,20,11
Hinson, G. Maurice	KY1200	12A,66A,31A,66B,66C
Hinterbichler, Karl	NM0450	12A,12,63C,63D
Hinton, Stephen W.	CA4900	12A,12
Hirota, Yoko	AG0150	66,13B,12A,66A,12B
Hisama, Ellie M.	NY0750	15,13E,12A,10B,13F
Hix, Michael T.	NM0450	61,13A,12A,12
Ho, Allan	IL2910	13,12A,12
Hobson, David	LA0050	36,11,31A,12A
Hoeckner, Berthold	IL3250	11,12,12A
Hoekstra, Gerald	MN1450	12A,55,29A
Hogue, Harry	MD0360	70,12A,63D,13,11
Hoke, S. Kay	PA1400	13,12A
Holden, LuAnn	TN0850	32,12A,36
Holland, Patricia C.	WI0850	64D,12A,42
Hollander, Jeffrey M.	IN1750	12A,15,11,12
Holliston, Robert	AB0210	66C,12A,11,39,66A
Holm, Thomas	IA1200	12A,36,11,60,61
Holman, Colin	IL1615	38,12A
Holman, Colin	IL2100	12A
Holmes, Christopher	IN0100	12A,12C,20,11
Holmes, Michael	MD0850	12A
Holmes, Ruth J.	TX1550	12A,66A,66H,66B,13
Holoman, D. Kern	CA5010	60,11,12A,12
Holst, Robert I.	IL1520	12A,12,61
Holzer, Robert R.	CT0850	12A
Holzman, David	NY2105	12A,66D,13
Honea, Ted	OK1330	12A,16,63B
Honnold, Adrianne	MO0700	12A,64E
Hontos, Margaret Ellen	CA4410	13,13A,12A,20
Hoogenstyn, Don	MI1550	11,12A
Hopkins, Robert	NY1350	13,12A,12,12F
Hopkins, William T.	CA4200	11,12A,12,12F
Hoppmann, Ken J.	NE0525	66A,66B,20,66C,12A
Hornsby, Richard	AE0120	64C,12A,29A,34,60
Horsley, Paul J.	MO1000	12A,66A
Horton, Virginia	TN0850	12A,61
Houghton, Edward F.	CA5070	12A,12
Houlahan, Michael	PA2350	12A
Houle, George L.	CA4900	12A,55,67B
Houser, Steven	MO0600	13,12A,12,64
Houtchens, Alan	TX2900	12A,12,63B
Howe, Blake	LA0200	12A
Howe, Donald	CA3520	12A,29A,14C,63C
Howey, Robert J.	AA0025	12A,13B,37,46,64
Hoyt, Reed J.	NY3700	13A,13,12A
Hsieh, Fang-Lan	TX2600	12A,16
Hsu, Dolores M.	CA5060	12A,12,20D,14A,14B
Hsu, Samuel	PA2800	12A,66A,66B,13E
Hubner, Carla	DC0110	12A,12,66A,35E
Hudgens, Helen	IL2100	13,31,12A
Hudson, Barbara	VA0050	61,36,12A
Hudson, Barton	WV0750	12A,12,66H
Hudson, Richard	CA5032	12A,12
Huff, Douglas M.	IL3500	64D,12A,11,48
Huff, Kelly A.	KS1400	12A
Huggins, Mark	AZ0350	11,12A
Hughes, Albert C.	TN0950	13,11,12A,36,61
Hughes, Evelyn	GA0940	11,12A,61
Hughes, Marcia A.	TN0930	12A,32B,66A,66D
Hughes, Robert L.	MO1250	12A,29,13,29A,29E
Hughes, Walden D.	ID0150	12A,41,42,66
Huglo, Michel	MD1010	12A
Hugo, John William	VA0650	36,61,12A,60A
Hull, Kenneth	AG0470	11,12A,31A,36
Hulme, Lance	NC1600	13,12A
Hund, Jennifer L.	IN1300	12,66A,12A,11
Hunt, Graham G.	TX3500	13,12,10F,11,12A
Hunt, Paul B.	KS0650	63C,12A,29A
Hunter, Mary K.	ME0200	13A,13,11,12A,12
Hurley-Glowa, Susan M.	TX3515	12A,14
Hurt, Phyllis A.	IL2150	12A,61,54
Husarik, Stephen	AR0730	11,69,12A

Name	Code	Areas
Hussa, Robert	WY0060	11,12A,35C,36,61
Hussey, Peter	IL1500	65,20,11,50,12A
Hutchings, James	IL0420	11,13B,12A,61,13A
Hutchinson, Jean Leslie	KY1500	12A
Hutson, Danny J.	AL0010	12A,13E,60,63C
Hutton, Christopher	SC0750	62C,12A,51
Hutton, Paula R.	OK0700	13,12A,66A,11
Iannaccone, Anthony J.	MI0600	10A,38,13,10,12A
Idenden, John	NJ0100	13A,11,12A,61,66A
Irizarry, Rafael E.	PR0115	37,12A,63B,42,49
Irving, Howard L.	AL1150	12A
Isenor, Ted	AA0080	12A
Izdebski, Christy	MD0100	12A,32,66A,66D,36
Jablow, Lisa	VT0250	60,12A,36,41,61
Jackson, Barbara G.	AR0700	13,12A,12,55B,67A
Jackson, Roland	CA2710	13,12A,12
Jacobson, Daniel C.	MI2250	11,12A,12,34
Jacobson, Joshua R.	MA1450	11,12A,36,13,31B
Jacobson, Marin	CA1425	36,12A,61,11
Jacobson, Mikael	CA1270	12A
Jakelski, Lisa	NY1100	12A,12E,12B,12C,14F
Jamason, Corey	CA4150	66H,66E,12A,55B
Jander, Owen	MA2050	11,12A,12
Janower, David M.	NY3700	13,60,12A,36
Jantz, Paul	SC0200	12A,49,63C,63D,34
Janzen, Wesley	AB0090	60,12A,36,31A
Jarvis, Jeffery W.	AR0850	63D,11,12A
Jefcoat, Priscilla	GA0350	13A,66A,10F,12A,13D
Jeffery, Peter	NJ0900	11,12A,12,31A
Jenkins, Jennifer R.	IL2250	12A
Jenkins, Joseph W.	PA1050	13,10F,10,12A
Jennings, Vance	FL2000	12A,14A
Jensen, Byron W.	NE0300	13B,38,12A,62,32C
Jentsch, Christopher	NY4060	13,12A,11,70
Jerosch, Anita	ME0340	32,12A,13A
Jimenez, Lissette	FL0700	61,12A,13C
Jodry, Frederick	RI0050	13,60,12A,36
Joella, Benjamin R.	FL0650	12A
Joella, Laura	FL0650	38,12A,62D,60B
Johnson, Ben S.	NC2350	61,12A,31
Johnson, Bryan	FL2130	12A,34
Johnson, Calvert	GA0050	66G,15,31,66H,12A
Johnson, Carl	TX0200	60,12A,32C,36,61
Johnson, Daniel	FL1700	12A,13,65
Johnson, Douglas	NJ1130	12A,12
Johnson, Edmond	CA3300	12A
Johnson, Herbert	MN1250	12A,13,31A,66B,66C
Johnson, Jeffrey W.	NY2105	61,12A,55D,12B
Johnson, Kenneth W.	IN0905	13B,12A
Johnson, Lynne	HI0210	11,12A
Johnson, Mildred	UT0300	13,12A,12,62B
Johnson, Nathaniel	UT0200	12A,61
Johnson, Nicholas	OH1850	12A
Johnson, Steven P.	UT0050	12A,12,14,12F
Johnson, Todd Alan	CA0845	65,12A,14,50,29A
Johnson, Wayne D.	WA0800	11,12A,66A,66C
Johnson, William T.	CA4700	13,10,11,43,12A
Johnston, Gregory	AG0450	11,12A,12,31A
Johnston, Jason	WY0200	63B,49,12A
Johnston, Jesse A.	MI2110	11,12A,29A
Jones, Bernard	OK1050	13,12A,61,11,64
Jones, Christopher	NY3350	12A,11
Jones, Emily	FL0040	11,12A,13C,41,70
Jones, Everett N.	OH2400	12A,66A,66B,66D
Jones, Lawrence	AC0050	66A,12A
Jones, Meredith	TX2570	12A,31A,60A,61
Jones, Patrick Michael	NY4150	32G,60B,32,12A,12E
Jones, Rufus	DC0075	38,12A
Jones, Ryan Patrick	WI0803	11,12A,13,29A
Jones, Timothy	NV0050	65,12A
Jones, Warren Puffer	OK0750	12A
Jonsson, Johan	MT0200	62A,12A
Jordan, John M.	IN1600	12A,11,31A,20
Jordan, Patrick	AG0300	12A
Josephson, David	RI0050	12A,12,55B,12E
Juncker, Arthur	CA1950	13,10,12A,41,34
Jurkowski, Edward	AA0200	13,12A,34
Kagan, Alan L.	MN1623	12A,12,14
Kahan, Sylvia	NY0600	66A,12A
Kahan, Sylvia	NY0644	12A,12C,66,13A,13C
Kahler, Bette	NY4100	11,12A,33,66A,66G
Kahn, Alexander G.	PA1400	38,12A,11,60B
Kaizer, Edward	IL0400	11,12A,66A,66B
Kajikawa, Loren	OR1050	12A,14,20C,20G
Kallberg, Jeffrey	PA3350	12A,12,12D,15
Kallick, Jenny L.	MA0100	13,12A,39,41,12
Kallstrom, Wayne	NE0100	66A,66G,12A
Kalyn, Andrea	OH1700	12A,11
Kamatani, Pamela	CA5353	12A,11,12C,13
Kaminsky, Bruce	PA1000	62D,12A,37,50
Kantack, Jerri Lamar	MS0150	60,36,61,12A,32
Kaplan, William	IL3310	13,12A,64D
Karahalis, Dean	NY4060	13,12A,11
Karis, Aleck	CA5050	13,12A,66A,66H,43
Kasling, Kim R.	MN0350	12A,66G,31A,66A
Kasunic, David M.	CA3300	12A,12B,12D,11
Katz, Derek	CA5060	12A,12
Katz, Joel	AG0300	61,12A
Katz, Robert S.	OK1300	13,11,12A,12,62D
Kauffman, Deborah	CO0950	12A,12C
Kauffman, Larry D.	PA0150	12A,36,66A,31A
Kays, Mark	IN1485	12A,13B,37,47,60B
Keathley, Elizabeth L.	NC2430	12A,12
Keaton, Kenneth D.	FL0650	60,12A,41,67D,70
Keays, James	CA5150	12A,49,63B
Keeling, Bruce	TX2350	11,12A,47,49,63D
Keiler, Allan R.	MA0500	11,12A,12D,13E,13J
Keillor, Elaine	AG0100	12A,12,14,66A,20G
Keiter, Lise	VA0800	13,11,66A,12A,15
Keith, Laura J.	SC0350	12A,66A,66D,32C,32D
Kelly, Aileen	CA0150	62E,12A,66A
Kelly, James J.	NJ0750	12A,13,29A,47,70
Kelly, Stephen K.	MN0300	12A,55,29A
Kelly, Thomas Forrest	MA1050	11,12A,12,13J
Keminski, Joe	NY2102	20,14,12A,63A
Kempster, James	CA3400	11,12A,36,61,31A
Kennedy, P. Kevin	CO0625	61,60,12A,66A,66
Kenote, Marie Herseth	NY2900	64A,12A,13B,13C,13D
Keyser, Allyson	NY3600	63A,13,12A
Keyser, Dorothy	ND0500	11,12A,14
Khan, Ali Akbar	CA0050	13A,10,11,12A,62
Kickasola, Matthew	PA1350	12A,13C
Kidger, David M.	MI1750	12A
Killmeyer, Heather N.	TN0500	64B,12A,11,64D
Kim, Paul S.	NY2105	66A,66B,12A
Kim, Soovin	MD0650	12A
Kim, Youngsuk	PA2150	12A,39,61
Kim-Infiesto, Marilyn Liu	HI0160	36,61,12A,32,13A
Kimball, Carol	NV0050	12A,61
Kinchen, Lucy C.	CA2450	12A,36,61,66A
King, Ben R.	NY1700	11,12A,61,39
King, Richard G.	MD1010	11,12A,12,20G,12C
King, Valeria G.	LA0720	13,60,12A,12,20G
King, Vicki B.	TN1400	66A,66D,12A
Kinzer, Charles E.	VA0700	12A,47,64E
Kippen, James R.	AG0450	12A,14
Kirby, David S.	NC1900	12A,64C,64E,64D,41
Kirkeby, Gary	MD0700	12A,11,61
Kirkell, Lorie	CA2100	32,12A
Kiss, Boglarka	CA3500	11,12A,64A
Kleinsasser, Jerome S.	CA0650	11,12A,12,10C
Klemp, Merilee I.	MN0050	12A,12,64B,48,40
Klingenstein, Beth Gigante	ND0600	12A,66B,66D
Klopfenstein, Reginald	IN0200	13,12A,47,50,65
Kloppers, Jacobus	AA0035	11,12A,12,66G,31A
Kluksdahl, Scott	FL2000	12A,62C
Knapp, Karl D.	AK0150	12A,62C
Knapp, Peter J.	CA2550	13,10,12A
Knapp, Raymond L.	CA5032	12A,12
Knepp, Richard	GA2300	70,41,12A
Knight, Jonathan	CA2775	12A,13A,60B,63
Knupps, Terri L.	MO1550	12A,20,63C,63D,42
Knyt, Erinn	MA2000	12A
Koblyakov, Lev	IL2350	13,12A,34B
Koch, Nathan J.	TX2250	64D,13C,12A
Koch, Thomas	NC1700	13,12A
Koehler, Andrew	MI1150	60,38,62A,62B,12A
Koh-Baker, JoAnn Hwee Been	OH1600	11,12A,66A,13A,13B
Kohl, Jack	NY4060	13C,12A,11
Kohlenberg, Kenneth	OH2120	37,60B,12A,11,63A
Kohn, Karl G.	CA3650	13,10,11,12A
Kolb, G. Roberts	NY1350	60,12A,36,40
Kolbeck, Karl F.	NE0700	12A,72,48,64,11
Kolt, Robert P.	AR0500	12,12A,60
Konye, Paul	NY3680	13G,12A,38,10,12
Korneitchouk, Igor	CA4050	13A,10,11,12A,34
Korstvedt, Benjamin M.	MA0650	12A,12B,12C,12D
Kosnik, James W.	VA1000	12A,66G
Koukios, Ann Marie	MI2200	36,12A,66D
Kovacovic, Paul	IA0200	10,12A,66A,66C
Kowalke, Kim H.	NY1100	12A,12B,12C,12D,15
Kowalke, Kim	NY4350	12A,12,39,54,20G
Kozlovsky, Danielle Godbout	AI0220	12A
Kraaz, Sarah Mahler	WI0700	12A,55,66,11,67C
Kramer, Elizabeth A.	GA2130	12A,14,11,13A,62A
Kramer, Jonathan C.	NC1700	11,12A,20D,20A,62C
Kramer, Richard	NY0600	12A,12
Kramme, Joel I.	MO0825	11,36,55,67,12A
Krause, William Craig	VA0550	70,11,12A,20H,35E
Kreiling, Jean L.	MA0510	13A,11,12A,12,66D
Kreinberg, Steven	PA3250	12A
Kreitner, Mona B.	TN1680	12A
Kreitner, Mona B.	TN1200	12A,36
Kresnicka, Judith	MN0200	12A,66G,55C
Kreyszig, Walter	AJ0150	12A,12,20G,55
Krieger, Marcos F.	PA3150	13C,66H,66G,11,12A
Krieger, Ulrich	CA0510	10,34D,12A,45,64E
Krishnaswami, Donald	MA0510	11,12A,62A,62B,51
Kruckenberg, Lori	OR1050	12A,12C,13J
Krueger, Walter E.	OR0150	13A,66A,12A,66G,66D
Kudlawiec, Nancy A.	AL1350	11,32,66A,12A,13
Kuhn, Judith	WI0825	12A,14
Kukec, Paul E.	IL1900	13A,13,12A,36,66A
Kulp, Jonathan	LA0760	12A,12
Kurtz, James	NY1900	12A
Kurtzman, Jeffrey	MO1900	12A,12
Kushner, David Z.	FL1850	12,12A,12B,12E,20G
Kwak, Eun-Joo	WI0150	66A,66B,66C,42,12A
Kwan, Eva	IN1560	12A,32,44,20
Labaree, Robert	MA1400	12A
Labe, Thomas A.	OK0150	11,12A,66A,66B
Labenske, Victor	CA3640	66A,66D,12A,10
Labonville, Marie E.	IL1150	11,12A,12,20D
Lackman, Susan Cohn	FL1550	13,10,12A,35
LaCosse, Steven R.	NC1650	39,12A
Lacoste, Debra	AG0600	12A
Ladd, Karen	TN1710	12A
Laderman, Michael	NY3100	11,29,12A,14,20D
Ladewig, James L.	RI0300	11,12A,12
Laganella, David	DE0200	10,13,34,14C,12A
Laird, Paul R.	KS1350	12A,12,55B,55C
Lamb, Earnest	NC0800	12A,32C,51,62
Lambert, Philip	NY0250	13A,13,11,12A
Lamberton, Elizabeth	AB0060	12A
Lambrecht, Richard	TX3520	12A,49,63B
Lamendola, Gene	NY4060	13,12A,11
Lamkin, Kathleen J.	CA5100	12A,11,12,62A,66A
Lamkin, Martin J.	VI0050	11,12A,32A,47,60B
Lamothe, Donat	MA0200	12A,67C,20G,20H
Lamothe, Virginia Christy	TN0100	12A
Lamott, Bruce	CA4150	12A
Landis, Stella Baty	LA0750	12A,11
Lane, Laura L.	IL1350	12A,60,36,40,61
Lange, Daniel	OR0010	12A,47,64,35
Langford, Bruce	CA1000	11,12A,32D,36,39
Larkowski, Charles S.	OH2500	12A,12,66H
Larner, James M.	IN1100	12A,48,10E,64A,29A
Larsen, Arved	IL1150	13,12A,63C
Larsen, Robert L.	IA1350	12A,36,39,66A,66C
Larson, Allen C.	MO1950	13,60,12A,38
Larson, Nancy	MD0850	12A
Larson, Philip	CA5050	13A,11,12A,36,61
Lau, Daniel	MD0150	66A,66B,66C,12A
Lauderdale, Lynne A.	FL2100	12A,66A,66G,66D,66B
Laudon, Robert	MN1623	11,12A,12,66H
Laughlin, Jim	TX0100	13A,12A,48,64C,64E
Laughlin, Mark	GA1000	66A,13,12A,66D,13B
Laughrey, Gary	KY0800	64,32F,12A,13
Lawrence-White, Stephanie	NC0200	12A,66A,12C,20F,66B
Lawson, Robert	CA5360	13,10,11,66D,12A
Lawson, Sonya R.	MA2100	12A,62B,29A,12,20
Lawton, David	NY3790	60,12A,12,38,39
Laycock, Rand	OH0755	11,12A,32C,38,62D
Le Guin, Elisabeth C.	CA5032	12A,12,62C,67B,15
Leafstedt, Carl S.	TX3350	11,12A,14,20
Leahy, Eugene J.	IN1700	11,12A,12
Leary-Warsaw, Jacqueline J.	AL0300	61,12A
Lease, Nancy	IA0250	12A,66,11
LeClair, Paul	VT0400	13,12A,48,37,64E
Ledbetter, Steven	MA1400	12A
Ledeen, Lydia Hailparn	NJ0300	11,12A,15,12C
Lee, Donzell	MS0050	12A,32,66A
Lee, Hayoung Heidi	CA4150	12A
Lee, James	AZ0200	12A,11,29
Lee, Michael	OK1350	12A,12,14,20G
Lee, Richard A.	HI0200	13,10,12A,64E,64A

Index by Area of Teaching Interest

Name	Code	Areas
Lefferts, Peter M.	NE0600	11,12A,12
Lehman, David	SC0200	12A,66A,66B
Lehman, Frank M.	RI0050	13,10C,12A
Leikin, Anatole	CA5070	13,12A,66A
Leistra-Jones, Karen	PA1300	11,12A,12
Lemay, Robert	AG0150	13,10,12A
Lenehan, Miriam C.	NY2450	11,12A,32,66A,66D
Lenti, Anthony A.	SC0800	11,12A,66A
Lentsner, Dina	OH0350	12A,13B,13C,13D,13E
Leonard, Charlotte	AG0150	12A,63D,63C,15,63B
Leonard, Gwenellyn	OR0450	12A,61,39
Leonardo, Manuel	CA1400	11,12A,36,61
Lesiuk, Teresa L.	FL1900	33,12A
Lester, Jason	TX3850	11,12A,13F,29A
Leve, James	AZ0450	12A,12C
Levin, Neil	NY1860	12C,12A,12
Levine, Iris S.	CA0630	12A,32,36,60
Levitz, Tamara	CA5032	12A,12,13
Levy, Beth E.	CA5010	12A,12B,12C,20G
Levy, David B.	NC2500	13,11,12A
Levy, Kenneth	NJ0900	11,12A,12
Levy, Sharon G.	MD0650	13,12A
Lew, Nathaniel G.	VT0400	12A,13,36,40
Lewis, David P.	WV0350	64,37,41,12A,32E
Lewis, Eric	CT0800	12A,62B,51,62A,12B
Lewis, H. M.	KY0610	10F,11,12A,49,63A
Lewis, Nora A.	KS0650	64B,12A,11
Lewis, Ryan C.	AR0500	65,32E,12A,11
Li-Bleuel, Linda	SC0400	66C,11,32,12A,66
Libin, Kathryn L.	NY4450	13,11,12A,12
Lieberman, Carol	MA0700	62A,13,12A,67,62
Lieuwen, Peter	TX2900	13,10,12A,29A
Ligate, Linda	MO0400	12A,6A,31A
Liley, Thomas	IL1250	13,12A,64
Liliestedt, Maira	OH2290	12A,6A,66B
Lin, Jolie	MD0650	13,12A
Lincoln, Harry B.	NY3705	11,12A,12,34
Lindberg, John E.	MN1000	12A,12C,48,64D,72
Lindeman, Timothy H.	NC0910	13,12A,66A,20
Lindgren, Lowell	MA1200	12A,20G
Lindorff, Joyce Zankel	PA3250	12A,12,66H,67C
Lindsey, Lauren	WV0050	12A,36,40,61
Link, Nathan	KY0450	12A,14C
Link, Stan	TN1850	12A,12,20G,14C,15
Linney, Lloyd	FL1750	13,61,12A
Lipman, William	TX0550	12A,64C,64E,11,48
Lipori, Daniel	WA0050	11,64D,12A,12C
Lipton, Jeffrey S.	NY1275	12A,13B,32C,36,61
Lipton, Kay	TX3175	12A
Liston, Robin	KS0050	32A,32B,12A,11
Litterick, Louise	MA1350	13,12A,12
Lloyd, L. Keith	MN0200	12A,37,38,47,62
Lo, Adrian	TX1650	65,12A,14,12,50
LoBalbo, Anthony C.	NY3500	13,29A,10C,12A,54
Lobitz, Beverly	AR0800	13E,11,12A,61,13C
Lochhead, Judith	NY3790	13E,13F,12,13,12A
Locke, Ralph P.	NY1100	12A,12B,12C,12D
Loewen, Peter V.	TX2150	12A,12
Logan, Joseph C.	NC0050	12A,32,36,61
Lohuis, Ardyth J.	VA1600	66G,12A,12C
Lombard, Becky	LA0400	13,12A,66A,66G,12C
Lombard, Becky	GA2050	66A,13B,13C,12A,66C
London, Justin	MN0300	13,12B,12F,20G,12A
Long, Michael P.	NY4320	12A,12,13J
Long, Patrick A.	PA3150	13,10,34,12A,32E
Looker, Wendy	NC0910	60,36,70,12A,13A
Lopinski, Janet	AG0300	12A
Loranger, Dennis	OH2500	12,12A
Lord, Suzanne	IL2900	64A,12A
Lorenz, James	FL0680	12A
Lorenzo, Elizabeth	CT0050	12,11,15,12A
Lott, R. Allen	TX2600	12A,12,14,12C
Lotz, James	TN1450	12A,64D,35G
Lovallo, Lee T.	CA3258	11,34B,67F,12A
Low, David G.	NE0610	12A,62C
Lowe, Melanie D.	TN1850	12A,12,20G,14C,15
Lowe, Phillip	TX0910	13,12A,37,47,63
Lowi, Ralph	CA4410	12A,11,62D
Lubin, Steven	NY3785	13,12A,12,66A
Lucas, Ann E.	MA0500	14,11,20,20B,12A
Lucas, Ann D.	CA0100	11,12A,20
Lucas, M. Jayne	PA3500	13,12A
Lucky, Harrell C.	TX0700	13,12A,36
Lundeen, Douglas	NJ1130	12A,63B
Lundergan, Edward	NY3760	13A,13B,36,60,12A
Lupu, Virgil I.	OH2140	62A,41,12A,11,34B
Lutter, Lisa	NJ0950	36,61,54,12A
Lyman, Kent M.	NC1300	66A,66B,12A
Lynch, Christopher	IN0350	11,12A
Lynch, Kelly	PA0600	39,61,11,12A
Maas, Martha C.	OH1850	12A,12,55
Mabary, Judith A.	MO1800	12A,20,11
Macan, Ed	CA1280	66A,13A,13B,13C,12A
MacDonald, John A.	OH2150	60,12A,12,36
MacDonald, Laurence E.	MI0450	11,12A,66A,66D
MacDonald, Robert M.	FL0800	66A,12A,35A,35E,35F
Macey, Patrick	NY1100	12A,12C,55D
MacFarlane, Thomas	NY2750	13C,13D,13F,12A,12B
Machlin, Paul S.	ME0250	12A,36,20G,29A
MacIntyre, Bruce C.	NY0500	12A,12,36
Mackey, Melissa A.	IL2900	64D,12A
Macomber, Jeffrey R.	MO0800	10,11,12A,32E,63D
Madriguera, Enric	TX0700	62,70,11,12A
Madsen, Farrell D.	UT0300	13,10,12A
Magaldi, Cristina	MD0850	14C,12A,14,20G,20H
Magee, Gayle Sherwood	IL3300	12A
Magee, Robert G.	AR0950	12A,60,36,61,31A
Mager, Guillermo E.	CT0700	13,12A,34,35,32
Mahe, Darren	AB0070	13,47,70,53,12A
Maher, John	IN1025	13,12A,66G,16,34
Mahrt, William P.	CA4900	12A,55,67E,31A
Maiello, James V.	TN1850	12A
Main, Alexander	OH1850	12A,12
Malley, Nicole	IL1350	12A,20,47,29,31F
Maltester, Diane	CA2775	12A,64,41,13C
Malvern, Gary J.	SC0750	63,41,12A
Malyshko, Olga	AG0250	12A,12,71,55
Mamey, Norman	CA1000	66A,10,12A,13,35A
Mammon, Marielaine	NJ0250	12A,32,36,41,61
Mamula, Stephen	RI0150	12A,20
Mangrum, Leslie	KS0700	61,36,39,12A
Maniates, Maria R.	AG0450	11,12A,12,12B
Mann, Brian R.	NY4450	11,12A,12,29A
Mann, Jenny L.	AL1170	64D,12A,13A
Marcades, Michael	AL0900	12A,12B,13,32,36
March, James J.	IA1100	66A,66B,66C,12A
Marchand, Rebecca G.	MA1175	12A,31A,12E
Marchand, Rebecca	MA0350	12A
Marcus, David	GA0490	10,11,12A,13A,29A
Margetts, James A.	NE0050	66,12A,13,32A
Mariani, Angela	TX3200	12A
Marissen, Michael	PA3200	11,12A,31
Markiw, Victor R.	CT0700	66,13,12A,66A,11
Markow, Andrew	AG0300	12A,66B
Marks, Martin	MA1200	11,12A,54
Markuson, Steve H.	NY3765	11,12A,61
Markward, Cheri D.	RI0101	13,11,41,62,12A
Marler, Robert	TN0100	66A,11,12A
Marlow, Laurine	TX2900	11,12A,66G,66A,66H
Marple, Olive	MA0800	13,12A,66A
Marrs, Stuart	ME0440	12A,65,50,34
Marsch, Debra	IL1050	12A,61
Marsh, Carol	NC2430	12A,12,55,67
Marsh, Lawrence B.	OR0450	60,12A,32,36
Martell, Vanessa	MN1270	61,12A,36
Martin, Gayle H.	AE0050	60A,66G,36,12A,55D
Martin, Margot	CA1750	12A,12B,20,66H,12E
Martin, Michael D.	GA0150	11,12A,13C,32,49
Martin, Sherrill	NC2440	12A,66A,66B,20G
Martin, Stephanie	AG0650	12A,55,60
Martinez, Jeordano S.	IL2050	12A,36,39,54,38
Martorella, Stephen T.	RI0200	12A,6A,66G,66H
Marvin, Clara	AG0250	12A,12,12E
Mason, Sonya G.	NY2150	12A,6A,32
Masonson, Norman	CA1150	13A,12A
Massie Legg, Alicia	TN1000	61,12A
Masterson, Stephanie C.	FL1570	12A,61,54
Matejka, Merle	AJ0030	10,12A,31A,13,29
Mathieson, Carol Fisher	MO0300	12A,39,61,31A,11
Matthews, Ron	PA1150	13,10,12A,63A,66A
Matych-Hager, Susan	MI1950	12A,32,36,61
May, Ernest D.	MA2000	12A,12,66G
Mayer, Anne B.	MN0300	13A,41,66A,12A
Mayes, Catherine	UT0250	12A,12B,12C
Mayo, John	AG0450	12A,12
Mazzaferro, Anthony	CA1900	13,63,37,12A
McAllister, Elizabeth	NC1750	12A,41,48,64C,64E
McArthur, Lisa R.	KY0400	13,48,64A,12A,12F
McBee, Karen L.	TX0125	12A,11,66A,66C,66D
McBride, Michael S.	IL2100	10,34,13,31,12A
McCabe, Rachelle	OR0700	66A,66B,12A
McCachren, Renee	NC0350	13,12A,66A,13E,13J
McCarrey, Scott	HI0050	66A,66B,13E,12A,11
McCarthy, Keri E.	WA1150	64B,12A,13,11,12C
McCarthy, Kerry R.	NC0600	12A,12C,31A,55
McCauley, William	SC0200	12A,36,39,61
McClellan, Teresa	TN0600	12A,61
McCloskey, Kathleen	PA0650	11,12A,13A,66D
mcclung, bruce d.	OH2200	12A,12
McClung, Matthew	TX2930	65,12A,50
McClymonds, Marita P.	VA1550	12A,12
McCollough, Sean	TN1710	12,12A
McCollough, Teresa	CA4425	13,12A,66A,66B,66C
McCoy, Darcy	IN0350	66A,66C,12A,66B
McCoy, Marilyn L.	MA1400	12A
McCray, James	CO0250	10,32C,12A
McCready, Matthew A.	MO0550	11,12A,63,13A,20
McDaniel, Jan	OK0750	39,54,66C,12A,61
McDonald, John	MA1900	13A,10,12A,43,13
McDonald, Steven	KS1000	66,38,60B,12A,41
McDonald, Susan M.	PA1830	10A,10B,12A,15,34D
McDonald, Timothy L.	MO1010	11,12A,36,20G
McDowell, Laura	NC0250	12C,12A,66D,67C
McFadden, Robert	OK1150	12A,66A
McFarland, Thomas J.	KY1400	60,12A,32E,49,63
McGann, Daniel	NY2450	13A,13,12A,70
McGee, Timothy J.	AG0450	12A,12,55
McGhee, Michael	GA2200	13,11,12A,66G,66H
McGinnis, Barry E.	SC0900	64,12A,29,48,29A
McGinnis, Beth	AL0800	66D,11,12A
McGrath, Edward J.	MA0260	12A
McGuire, David	NY1250	13,10,12A,13A,47
McIntosh, W. Legare	AL0500	12A,13,66A,66G
McIntyre, Eric L.	IA0700	10,38,60,12A,13
McIntyre, John	IN1400	13,34,12A,36,10
McKamie, David W.	MO1780	13,12A,66A
McKee, Richard	NC0300	12A,66A
McKeever, James I.	WI0835	12A,66A,66C,66B
McKinley, Thomas L.	FL1125	13,10A,12A,34F
McKinney, Roger W.	NJ0175	64C,12A,48
McKnight, Charles M.	NC2400	13,12A
McLamore, Alyson	CA0600	12A,12,32,16,20G
McLauchlin, Charlotte	OR1000	13A,66D,66A,67C,12A
McLucas, Anne Dhu	OR1050	12C,12C,20G,20F,14
McManus, James M.	CA3320	13,45,29A,12A,11
McManus, Laurie	VA1350	12A
McMillin, Timothy A.	IA1350	60,36,61,32D,12A
McMullen, William W.	NE0600	13,12A,64B
McMurray, William	MO0850	12A,11
McNeely, Heather	SC0200	12A,12C,63A
McNiven, Lisa	ID0060	12A,62B
McQuiston, Kate	HI0210	12A,12B,12C
McVey, Roger D.	WI0845	12A,66A,66B,66C,66D
Meadows, Melody	WV0800	13,12A,66G,34,35A
Meckler, David C.	CA0855	11,20,12A,10,13A
Meconi, Honey	NY1100	12A,12,55
Meconi, Honey	NY4350	12A,12,15
Meehan, Jill	PA3680	11,12A,13A
Meehan, Jill	PA3250	12A
Meeks, Joseph D.	GA1150	13,12A,66,66B
Meffert-Nelson, Karrin	MN0750	64C,37,48,32E,12A
Meier, Steven	GA1500	11,12A,29
Meixner, Brian	PA3100	12A,63C,49,11
Melbinger, Timothy	PA2710	12A,41,13B,13C,13E
Menard, Aileen	AG0500	12A
Menegon, John	NY3760	12A,47,62D
Mensah, Sowah	MN0950	12A,20A,10
Menth, Christelle	CO0150	66,12A,20
Merchant, Tanya H.	CA5070	20B,15,12A
Messing, Scott	MI0150	11,12A,66A,16,13A
Metcalf, Joanne	WI0350	10A,13D,13F,12A,31G
Meyer, Donald C.	IL1400	13,12A,10,34
Meyer, Eve R.	PA3250	13,12A,12
Meyer, Jeffrey	MN0600	12A,13,11,14,20
Meyer, Stephen C.	NY4100	12,12A,12D,31A
Michaelsen, Garrett	MA2030	12A,13
Micucki, Vera G.	AB0100	12,12B,12A
Middleton, Jaynne	TX0900	61,12A,54
Mikhalevsky, Nina	DC0110	12A,12B
Miljkovic, Katarina	MA1400	13C,13B,12A,12
Millar, Robert R.	CA4625	13A,13,11,12A,66
Miller, Ann Elizabeth	CA5350	62A,42,12A,41
Miller, Dan	IN1800	12A,36,44,61
Miller, Franklin	WI0825	12A,12
Miller, Kenny	AZ0470	13C,12A,36,40,61
Miller, Leta	CA5070	11,12A,12,64A,67E

455

Name	Code	Areas
Miller, Lisa	IN1800	32,61,54,12A
Miller, Roger L.	UT0250	12A,12
Miller, Ronald L.	PA2300	12A,36,67B,31A,20G
Miller, Stephen R.	TN1800	11,12A,12,14
Miller, Wendy L.	PA0250	11,12A,36,61,54
Millican, Brady	MA0800	13,11,12A,66A,66C
Milligan, Thomas	TN0250	13,12A,66A,34
Mills, David	OR0050	13,10,12A,37,63A
Mills, Michele D.	OH2150	13A,12A,66D
Miltenberger, James E.	WV0750	12A,66A,66B,29
Minasian, Mark	HI0160	11,12A,29,34,35
Mindock, Rebecca A.	AL1300	64B,64D,12A,34,42
Minevich, Pauline M.	AJ0100	12A,64C,12C,12D
Minor, Ryan	NY3790	12A,12D,12B,11,13E
Minorgan, Bruce	AI0150	12A,12
Minter, Karen	KS0100	12A,39,61
Miranda, Michael A.	CA2800	11,67G,70,12A,41
Mitchell, Linda	CA2440	36,60A,11,12A,13A
Miyakawa, Felicia M.	TN1100	12A
Miyama, Yoko	OR0050	66,13,12A,66C,66D
Moege, Gary R.	MO1790	11,63B,70,71,12A
Moehlman, Carl B.	IA0900	13,12A,44,66G,31A
Moersch, Charlotte Mattax	IL3300	67F,66H,12A,55C,12
Molina, Linda	MD0475	62A,12A,20
Moll, Kevin N.	NC0650	12,55,67A,12A,12B
Mollicone, Henry	CA1950	10,12A
Mollicone, Henry	CA3270	10A,12A,39,54,60
Monek, Daniel G.	OH1400	36,61,12A,60
Monson, Craig	MO1900	12A,12
Montalto, Richard Michael	MS0550	13,12A,35,10,13F
Montford, Kimberlyn	TX3350	11,12A,12
Montgomery, Vivian	OH2200	11,12A,55,66H,67F
Montiel, Brenda F.	CA3460	12A,55,66A,67B,67C
Mooney, Kevin E.	TX3175	12A
Moore, Christopher	AG0400	12A,12B,12D
Moore, Edgar	TX2300	11,36,61,12A
Moore, John	TX2200	11,66A,66C,12A,66D
Moore, Vicki	CA0270	12A,11
Moran, John	MD0650	67A,12A
Morden, James	GA2000	13,11,12A,63A
Moreland, Irina	CO0830	66A,11,12A
Morelock, Donald	MI1900	13,11,12A,66A,66B
Morey, Carl	AG0450	11,12A,12,20G
Morris, Martha M.	IL2650	12A,32,64A
Morris, Mitchell B.	CA5032	12A,12,20G,15
Morrison, Leah A.	CA5300	31A,13J,12A,12D
Morrison, Mable R.	DE0050	11,12A,66A,66D
Morrison, Simon	NJ0900	13,12A,12,11
Morrongiello, Christopher	NY1600	12A,12C
Morrow, Matthew	NY1100	12A,12B,12D
Morrow, Ruth E.	TX1700	66,12A,66A,13D,13E
Morrow-King, Janet	CO0250	61,39,12A
Moschenross, Ian	IL1800	12A,13E,20,66A,66G
Moseley, William	ME0340	12A,47,64A,35C,29
Moser, Martin	NY3500	13,12A,54,20G
Moshell, Gerald	CT0500	60,12A,54
Moshier, Steve	CA3750	13,11,12A,34,43
Moskowitz, David V.	SD0600	12A,20H,14C,12C,11
Moss, Patricia J.	AL0650	12A,11
Moulton, Paul F.	ID0070	11,12A,32,14
Mount, Lorna	HI0120	13A,11,12A,70,36
Muchnick, Amy Faye	MO0775	11,12A,62B,41
Muehlenbeck, Bettina	MN1600	12A
Mueller, Paul F.	NY0625	10F,60,11,12A,36
Mueller, Todd D.		65,12A
Mulder, Geoffrey	CA0850	34,35C,35D,12A,62A
Mulford, Ruth Stomne	DE0175	13,11,12A,62A,20G
Mulhall, Sean	KY1500	12A
Muller, David J.	CA6000	10F,11,12A,60B,64D
Muller, Gerald	TX2170	13,11,12A,32,36
Muller, John J. H.	NY1900	12A
Mumma, Gordon	CA5070	12A,45
Mundy, Rachel	PA3420	12A
Munn, Albert Christopher	TX3525	13,12A,36,67,55B
Munson, Paul A.	PA1450	12A,11
Murata, Margaret K.	CA5020	12A,12
Murchison, Gayle	VA0250	12A,12,20G,12C
Murphy, Bill S.	MD0475	12A
Murphy, Michael	ID0250	36,40,32D,12A,32C
Murray, Russell E.	DE0150	12A,15,55,67D,67B
Musial, Michael A.	NY3450	13A,11,12A,36,66A
Myers, Patricia	GA0250	12A,61,11
Mygatt, Louise	NY1800	12A,15
Myrick, Barbara	OR0350	13,12A,66A,66D,64A
Nabb, David	NE0590	64,11,12A,48
Nachman, Myrna	NY2550	66A,13A,12A,13C
Nardini, Luisa	TX3510	12,12A
Near, John R.	IL2400	11,12A,12C,66G
Necessary, Andrew	VA0050	12A,32B,37,46,63C
Nehre, Heather	MO1950	12A
Neimoyer, Susan	UT0250	12A,14C,10A,12
Nelson, Jocelyn C.	NC0650	70,12A,67H,11
Nelson, Jon	CA4460	12A,11
Netz, Anthony R.	NY1900	12A
Neuman, Gayle	OR0500	12A
Neuman, Phil	OR0500	12A,63C
Neville, Donald	AG0500	12A,12,12B
Newcomb, Anthony A.	CA5000	12A,12
Newlin, Georgia A.	NY0050	11,12A,13C,32,36
Ng, Tian Hui	MA1350	38,60,12A
Nichols, Eugene C.	ME0430	13,36,37,46,12A
Nigrelli, Christopher	NC1100	12A,47,44,63C,63D
Nigro, Christie	MA2300	13A,11,12A,36,62A
Niren, Ann Glazer	IN1010	11,12A
Nisbett, Robert	CO0250	13,12A,66C
Nisnevich, Anna V.	PA3420	11,12A
Nissen, James C.	MI2110	11,12A
Noble, Steve L.	KY1500	12A
Noon, David	NY2150	12,10A,10,12A
Noonan, Jeffrey	MO1500	12A,14,67D,70,20G
Noonan, Timothy	WI0825	12A,12,11
Norberg, Rebecca	MN1250	61,54,12A,11
Norris, James Weldon	DC0150	12A,12,36
Norris, Mike	FL1790	36,12A
Norris, Renee Lapp	PA1900	14C,12A,20,12,13E
Nott, Kenneth	CT0650	12A,12,66G
Nutter, David A.	CA5010	12A,12,55
Oates, Jennifer Lynn	NY0600	12,16,12A,12C
Obrecht, Guy	AA0050	12A,13,47
O'Connor, Michael B.	FL1450	12A,11,20,55
O'Dell, Debra	ID0140	66A,66C,11,66D,12A
O'Donohue, Deirdre	NY2150	12A
Oft, Eryn	AL0500	64B,64D,12A,12C
Ogdon, Will L.	CA5050	13,10F,10,12A
Oglesby, Donald T.	FL1900	60,12A,36
O'Grady, Terence J.	WI0808	13,12A,12,14,55
Oja, Carol J.	MA1050	12,12A
Oldani, Robert	AZ0100	12A,12
O'Leary, James	OH1700	12A
Oleskiewicz, Mary	MA2010	11,12A,12,14B,64A
Olin, Elinor	IL2000	11,12A,12,64A
Olivares, Walter G.	AK0100	12A,51,62
Oliver, Sylvester	MS0600	12A,20G,37,46
Olivieri, Guido	TX3510	12A,12,67B
Onderdonk, Julian	PA3600	11,12A
O'Neal, Whitney	AL1250	12A,13A
Orchard, Joseph T.	NJ0050	12A
Orenstein, Arbie	NY0600	12A
Orenstein, Arbie	NY0642	13A,13,11,12A
Orlando, John	CA0400	12A,66A
Orozco, Eduardo	ND0350	12A
Ortiguera, Joseph	AL1200	11,12A,13B
Ortiz, William	PR0115	12A
O'Shea, Patrick	MN1400	60,12A,36,61,10A
Oster, Andrew	PA2550	12A
Oswalt, Lewis	MS0400	12A,13,31A
Ott, Daniel	NY1300	12A,29A,54,13B,13C
Ott, Hal J.	WA0050	12A,41,48,64A,67D
Otwell, Margaret V.	WI0500	66A,66C,66D,66B,12A
Owen, William E.	WA0550	36,60,12A,40,31A
Owens, Jeremy	IA0100	11,12A,66
Owens, Jessie Ann	CA5010	12A,13J,15
Owens, Margaret B.	VA0450	11,12A,64
Owens, Theodore	NV0125	10,11,12A,61,54
Paar, Sara	NY2050	12A,13A
Pace, Roberto J.	NJ1050	12A
Padgham Albrecht, Carol	ID0250	11,12A,64B,32E,41
Pahel, Timothy	IL1800	32,36,61,12A
Paige, Diane M.	NY1400	12,29A,20,12A,20F
Palomaki, Jonathan	IL0300	12A,32B,36,70,61
Palomaki, Jonathan	TX3800	60,12A,36,61,70
Palter, Morris	AK0150	12A,29A,42,43,14C
Pane, Steven	ME0410	12A,66A,12,12B,11
Pankratz, Timothy	AZ0480	12A
Parker, Craig B.	KS0650	12A,63A,12
Parker, Grant	CA1500	13,11,12A,49,37
Parker, Mara	PA3680	12A,11,41,51,62C
Parker, Mary Ann	AG0450	11,12A,12
Parks, Andrew	WA0800	61,31A,12A,36
Parmentier, Edward L.	MI2100	12A,12,66H
Parr, Sean M.	PA0950	12A,55,11
Parr, Sharon M.	IN1650	11,66A,66D,12A
Parsons, Laura E.	AL0950	63A,63,12A,13A,11
Partain, Gregory L.	KY1350	11,41,66A,66B,12A
Party, Daniel	IN1450	14C,12A,11,20H
Pasler, Jann C.	CA5050	11,12A,12,12B,12E
Pasternack, Jonathan R.	WA1050	38,39,12A,60B
Patterson, Anne L.	WV0300	11,12A,32A
Patterson, Michael R.	IA1350	12A,32B,66A,13,10
Pattison, C. Pat	MA0260	12A
Paul, David	CA5060	12A,12,13B
Pauly, Reinhard G.	OR0400	12A
Payette, Jessica	MI1750	12A,12C
Payne, Thomas B.	VA0250	12A,12,12C
Peck, David	ID0060	12A,12B,12C,61
Pederson, Sanna	OK1350	12A,20G,12
Pedroza, Ludim R.	TX3175	12A,20H,66D
Peel, John	OR1300	10,12A
Peeples, Georgia	OH2150	12A,64D,15,48
Pen, Ronald	KY1450	20G,29A,12A,12
Penniman, G. Victor	MO1010	55,12A,62,11,36
Pepetone, Gregory	GA0850	12A,32,66A,66B,66D
Pepper, Ronald D.	OH0950	62A,62B,12A
Peraino, Judith A.	NY0900	12A,12D,15
Perkins, Daniel R.	NH0250	36,61,12A,32D,60A
Perkins, John D.	MO0100	63A,63B,12A,42,49
Perkyns, Jane E.	TX3150	66A,13,12A,66,66C
Perlove, Nina	KY1000	64A,12A
Perry, David L.	SC0050	12A,13A,64C,32,20A
Pershing, Drora	NY0642	13,12A
Pesce, Dolores	MO1900	12A,12,13J
Peters, Gretchen	WI0803	11,12A,14
Petersen, Marian F.	MO1810	13,12A
Peterson, Don L.	UT0050	13,12A,13J,63B
Peterson, Floyd	ID0250	13,12A
Peterson, Jay	IL1650	13,12A,14,66A,66G
Peterson, John David	TN1680	66G,31A,12A
Peterson, Jon C.	OH0250	36,12A,44,11,54
Peterson, Laura	NY3475	11,12A,66A,20
Peterson, Wayne T.	CA4200	13,10F,10,12A,66A
Peterson, William J.	CA3650	11,12A,66G,66H
Petillot, Aurelien	IL2900	62B,62A,42,11,12A
Petricic, Marko	IN1650	12A,66G
Pettaway, Charles H.	PA2000	13,11,12A,66,66G
Pfaff, William P.	NY3775	10,13,12A,13F,13I
Pfaltzgraff, Philip	NE0700	66C,11,42,12A
Pfau, Marianne Richert	CA5200	12A,67D
Pfeiffer, Ruth Imperial	HI0160	13A,12A,32,36,66
Phillips, Katrina R.	AL0050	11,12A,64E
Phillips, Linda N.	NY3725	12A,66D,29A
Phipps, Danny K.	MI0900	64D,12A,12C,13E
Pickering, David C.	KS0650	66A,66G,66H,13,12A
Pickett, John	WA0050	13,11,12A,66A,66B
Pickett, Susan	WA1300	13A,13,12A,51,62A
Piekut, Benjamin	NY0900	12A,12D,12E
Pierce, David M.	MI0600	12A,64D
Piersall, Rick	TX0050	39,61,12A
Pinkerton, Louise	ND0500	61,12A
Pinkston, Dan	CA4600	13,12A,14,10,20
Piontek, Gregory	NY1210	12A,47,29
Piper, Deirdre	AG0100	13,10,12A
Pisani, Michael	NY4450	11,12A,12,20G
Pisano, Kristin	KS0350	11,64C,64E,12A,14C
Pitman, Grover A.	PA3650	12A,29A
Pitts, Ruth	TX1600	13,12A,66A
Pituch, David A.	IL0750	64E,11,12A
Place, Logan B.	LA0650	63A,37,12A
Placilla, Christina D.	NC2700	12A,20,38,62A,62B
Plank, Steven E.	OH1700	12A
Plantamura, Carol	CA5050	12A,55,61,54,43
Platt, Heather	IN0150	11,12,12A
Poellnitz, Michael	AL0310	12A,47,63,35B
Pogonowski, Lenore	NY4200	53,32,12A,13
Pohly, Linda L.	IN0150	11,12,14,12A
Poissant, Michael	MD0850	12A
Polay, Bruce	IL1350	10A,10F,12A,13B,60B
Polk, Keith	NH0350	11,12A,12C,63B
Pollack, Howard	TX3400	12A,12,14,20G
Pomerantz, James	CA0050	13A,11,12A
Ponce, Adriana	IL1200	12A,11,20
Popp, Harold	KS1450	12A,12C
Poriss, Hilary	MA1450	12A
Porter, Charles	NY2700	13A,11,12A,66D,29A
Porter, Charles	NY2400	13A,13,10,11,12A
Post, Olaf	MA1050	12A,12B
Post, William Dean	AK0150	13,12A,10A

Index by Area of Teaching Interest

Name	Code	Areas
Potratz, Robert C.	MN1030	11,12A,66G,13A
Powell, John S.	OK1450	11,12A,12,20
Powell, Steven S.	PA1000	36,61,34,12A,32D
Power, Brian E.	AG0050	62A,67,12A,12C,13G
Powers, Ollie	CA5360	35G,35C,11,12A,34
Pranno, Arthur J.	FL0800	62A,38,51,62B,12A
Prebys, Marylee A.	ND0400	66A,66B,12A
Press, Stephen D.	IL1200	12A,12E
Preston, Katherine K.	VA0250	12A,12,20G,12C
Price, Henry P.	CA3600	61,39,12A
Prichard, Laura D.	MA2030	12A
Prigge, Sarah	ND0350	12A,66D
Pritchard, Gary	CA0859	20G,29A,20H,12A
Prizer, William	CA5060	12A,12
Prowse, Robert W.	NJ0825	36,40,61,12A
Pruiksma, Rose A.	MA1400	12A
Puchala, Mark	MI1650	12A,36,61,34,41
Puller, Shawn I.	GA0150	11,61,12A,32A,39
Purciello, Maria Anne	PA3600	11,12A
Purciello, Maria Anne	DE0150	12A
Pursell, William	TN0100	10,12A,13,11,66G
Pyle, Jane	FL1300	13,11,12A,66A,66B
Pysh, Greg	TX1660	61,12A
Quantz, Don E.	AA0010	12A,32D,36,40,41
Quereau, Quentin W.	OH0400	12A,12
Quereau, Quentin	OH0600	12A
Rader, Jana Elam	TX2310	11,12A,34C,61
Radice, Mark A.	NY1800	12A,12C
Radomski, James V.	CA0845	11,12A,12,14
Ragogini, Ernest	MD0100	13,12A,66A,12C
Raimo, John B.	TX3525	11,12A,66A,66C,66D
Raines, Jean	NC1900	12A,11,66A,32
Rakowski, David	MA0500	13,10,12A
Raley, Lynn	MS0385	66A,12A,29
Ramach, Michael E.	KY1500	54,12A
Ramos, Rene	CA2420	13A,13,12A,12,66A
Ramsey, Cynthia B.	VA0750	66A,12A,66C,13E,42
Randall, Annie Janeiro	PA0350	11,12A,12,12E
Rapoport, Paul	AG0200	13,11,12A,12
Rappoport, Katharine	AG0300	12A
Ratelle, Dan	CA4050	11,12A
Ratliff, Phillip	AL0650	13,12A,10F,34
Ray, Marcie	MI1400	12A,15
Reagan, Ann B.	CO0750	11,12A,12,41,66A
Reager, John	CA2450	36,66A,61,12A
Reed, Teresa Shelton	OK1450	13,12A
Reese, Donald T.	PA1830	11,12A,70,13A,14C
Register, P. Brent	PA0700	12A,48,64A,64B,64D
Rehding, Alexander	MA1050	13,12A,12B,12C,12G
Rehwoldt, Lisa	MD0100	13,12A,66A
Reid, Susanne M.	CA5355	11,12A,20,31A
Reish, Gregory N.	IL0550	12A
Reitz, Christina L.	NC2600	12,66A,12A
Renfroe, Dennis C.	NC1025	11,12A,32,36,63
Renner-Hughes, Marty	MO1110	12A,36,54
Renninger, Laura Ann	WV0550	11,12A,12F,14
Restesan, Frank	NE0550	38,13C,62A,51,12A
Retif, T. N.	GA0400	13E,12A,61,44
Reul, Barbara M.	AJ0100	11,12A,12C,12D
Reuter, Ted A.	IA1800	12A,66A
Revuluri, Sindhumathi	MA1050	12,12A,12C,14C,20D
Reynolds, Anne-Marie	NY3730	11,12A,12
Rhein, Robert	IN0200	10A,66A,11,12A,13
Rhodes, Ann G.	KY0300	11,12A,61,32D,29A
Rhodes, Debra	NE0300	12A,64,48
Rice, Eric N.	CT0600	55,12A,13A,12
Rice, Marc	MO1780	11,12A,14C
Rice, Paul	AD0050	12A
Richards, Douglas	VA1600	12A,29A,29B
Richards, Mark C.	AA0200	13,12A
Richardson, Donald G.	CA4450	11,12A,61
Richmond, Thomas	MN0600	13,10,11,12A
Rickman, Michael	FL1750	66A,12A,66B,66D
Rife, Jerry E.	NJ1000	13,11,12A,12,37
Riggs, Robert D.	MS0700	12A,12B,41,62A,62B
Rigler, Ann Marie	MO2000	66A,66G,31A,12A,12C
Riley, William	NY0050	12A
Rinehart, John	OH0050	13A,13,10F,10,12A
Rizzuto, Thomas	NY2450	70,12A
Roach, Donna Kay	VA1475	12A
Roadfeldt-O'Riordan, Holly K.	PA1850	66A,12A,66C
Roberge, Marc-Andre	AI0190	12A,12
Roberson, Matt	TX0050	12A
Roberts, Adam	AZ0350	12A,64E,29A
Roberts, James E.	AL0500	60,12A,49,63C
Robertson, Anne Walters	IL3250	11,12A,12
Robinson, Brian	MA1450	11,12A
Robinson, Florence	FL0600	12A,66A,66,66D
Robinson, Kathleen E.	MN1280	31A,11,12A,13C
Robinson, N. Scott	MD0850	12A,14C,50
Robinson-Martin, Trineice	NJ0750	11,12A,29,61
Robison, John O.	FL2000	13,12A,12,67
Rockmaker, Jody D.	AZ0100	13A,13,10,12A,43
Roden, Timothy J.	OH2000	11,12A,20A,20D,20F
Rodger, Gillian	WI0825	12A,12C,20G,20D,14
Roditeleva-Wibe, Maria I.	WA0050	14A,12A,20F,66A,66G
Rodriguez, Linda M.	FL2050	12A,66A
Roesner, Edward	NY2740	11,12A,12,55
Rogosin, David	AE0050	66A,12A,66C
Rohr, Deborah	NY3650	13,11,12A
Roiger, Teresa	NY3760	12A,47,61
Rokeach, Martin	CA3920	13A,13,11,12A,41
Romanek, Mary L.	PA2720	12A,32A,32B,29A
Root, Deane L.	PA3420	12A,12C,12,20G,12E
Rorke, Margaret A.	UT0250	12A,12
Rosa, Gerard	CT0050	11,62A,12A
Rosado, Ana Maria	NJ0825	70,41,11,12A
Rosand, Ellen	CT0900	12A,12
Rose, Michael	TN1850	13,10,12A,11,31
Roseman, Jacob	KY0900	12A
Rosen, David	NY0900	12A,12B,12C
Rosenblum, Martin J.	WI0825	12A
Rosewall, Michael	WI0750	36,61,12A,13A,13B
Rosow, Lois	OH1850	12A,12
Ross Mehl, Margaret	PA0600	36,39,61,11,12A
Ross, David	TX3520	12A,64C
Roste, Vaughn	OK0550	60,12A,36,61,20
Roter, Bruce	NY0700	10,13,12A,64C
Rothenberg, David J.	OH0400	12A
Rothstein, William	NY0600	12A
Rotola, Albert	MO1250	11,12A
Roush, Clark	NE0720	11,12A,13A,32C,32B
Rowden, Charles H.	NY2550	11,12A,66D
Rowell, Melanie	SC1080	12A,61,54,39
Rowland, Robert	PA0850	12A
Royse, Dennis	CA0250	13,12A,32C,11
Rubio, Douglas	NY3780	12A,41,70
Rudari, David J.	WV0100	61,36,12A,32B,54
Rumph, Stephen	WA1050	12,12A
Runyan, William E.	CO0250	10F,12C,12A
Rupprecht, Philip	NC0600	12A,12D,13E,13F
Rush, John Phillip	OK1450	64A,67D,12A,55C,56
Rushton, Christianne	AF0050	12A,15,32D,61
Russell, Carlton T.	MA2150	11,12A,66G,31A
Russell, Craig H.	CA0600	11,12A,12,67B,70
Russell, Robert J.	ME0500	12A,36,60
Russell, Tilden	CT0450	11,12A,12,41
Ruth, Christopher	VA1350	12A
Rutschman, Carla J.	WA1250	12A,12,32,63D
Rutschman, Edward R.	WA1250	13A,13,11,12A,12
Ruymann, Karen	MA0350	12A
Ruzicka, Carol	OH0600	62A,12A
Ryberg, J. Stanley	IL1085	13B,13C,12A,63C,63D
Sabak, Linda	WV0800	12A,66,11
Sabin, Paula	CA0825	12A
Sachs, Joel	NY1900	12A,41,43
Sage, Robert	CA0250	66A,12A
Sagues, Marie	CA1650	12A
Sahagian, Robert	MA2300	11,12A
Sajnovsky, Cynthia B.	GU0500	13A,12A,20C,66D,67C
Saker, Marilyn	MI0600	13,12A
Saloman, Ora Frishberg	NY0250	11,12A,12
Saloman, Ora Frishberg	NY0600	12A,12
Saltzstein, Jennifer A.	OK1350	12A,12A
Salyer, Douglas W.	CT0200	13,34,12A,36,66
Samball, Michael L.	ID0050	11,12A,29A,35A
Samuel, Jamuna	NY3790	11,12A,13E,12B,13F
Sandborg, Jeff R.	VA1250	60,11,12A,36,61
Sanden, Paul	AA0200	12,12A
Sanders, Donald C.	AL0800	12A,66A
Santosuosso, Alma	AG0600	12A
Sargent, Joseph	AL1200	11,12A,13B,13C
Sarte, Ysabel	TX2955	12A
Satterfield, Sarah	FL0365	12A,64A,11,42,48
Saucier, Catherine	AZ0100	12A
Sauer-Ferrand, Deborah	CA1860	12A,61,31A,54
Saulter, Gerry	NY1275	12A,13C,70,42,41
Saunders, David R.	ID0050	63B,60B,13E,12A
Saunders, Harris S.	IL3310	11,12A,12
Saunders, Steven E.	ME0250	11,12A,12,66H
Savage, Charles M.	OH1910	13,12A,20G,36,61
Sawyer, John E.	AB0100	55,67A,12A
Saya, Virginia	CA2800	12A,39,12C,11
Saylor, Eric A.	IA0550	20,12A
Saylor, Jonathan	IL3550	12A,64D,41
Scelba, Anthony	NJ0700	12A,13E,11,62D
Schachter, Carl	NY0642	13,12A
Schantz, Monica	PA2450	12A
Schechter, Dorothy E.	CA0550	12A,66A,66B,66D
Scheide, Kathleen	NJ1350	66G,12A,67F,66H
Schempf, Ruthanne	NY3760	66A,66D,12A,13B
Schenbeck, Lawrence A.	GA1900	11,12A,12C
Schenkel, Steve	MO1950	12A,31,45,29,35
Schiavo, Joseph C.	NJ1100	13B,13D,12A,13F,13
Schimpf, Peter	CO0550	12A
Schindler, Karl W.	AZ0470	10,13,34,12A
Schlabach, Eugene	IL3200	11,12A,66A
Schlabaugh, Karen Bauman	KS0200	13,66A,66B,66C,12A
Schmalenberger, Sarah	MN1625	12A,63B,12,67E,14
Schmalfeldt, Janet	MA1900	13,12A,13J,13L
Schmelz, Peter	MO1900	12,12A
Schmidt, Alan G.	NY1220	13A,12A,47,20G,29A
Schmidt, Carsten	NY3560	13,11,12A,41,66A
Schmidt, Henry L.	PA2550	13,12A,63C,26,29A
Schmidt, Jack W.	PA0900	11,12A,36,37,49
Schmidt, John C.	TX3175	13,12A,66G
Schmitz, Michael	CA3270	66A,12A,13,20,41
Schoenbach, Peter Julian	NY3725	12A
Schoenhals, Joel	MI0600	12A,66A
Schoessler, Tim	WY0130	66A,66D,13,12A
Schorr, Timothy B.	WI1100	66A,12A,13E,66C
Schrader, Barry	CA0510	13,10,12A,34
Schreiner, Frederick	PA3710	11,12A,12,61,39
Schroeder, David	AF0100	13,12A,12,12E,12C
Schubert, Linda	WI0922	12A
Schulze, Hendrik	IL3300	12A
Schumann, Laura E.	OH1650	38,60,62A,12A,13A
Schuster-Craig, John	MI0900	13E,12A,13F,13B
Schwartz, Anne-Marie	NY3680	12A,62A
Schwartz, Elliott S.	ME0200	10F,10,11,12A,41
Schwarze, Penny	MN0450	12A,11,38,62A,67A
Scott, David R.	LA0350	12A,49,63A
Scott, Shannon	WA1150	64C,12A
Scully, Francis	LA0560	13A,12A,11
Scully, Lawrence L.	GA2150	66,12A
Seals, Debra	PR0125	12A,61
Sears, E. Ann	MA2150	12A,66A,29A,20G
Seaton, Douglass	FL0850	12A,12D,12C,12
Seeley, Gilbert	OR0400	60,12A,36,41
Seldon, Vicki A.	TX2100	11,12A,66A,66C
Self, Stephen	MN0250	12A,66A,66G
Seliger, Bryce M.	OR0750	38,14A,13,12A
Serebryany, Vadim	AL0450	66A,12A,13B
Sergi, James	NY3500	12A
Seskir, Sezi	PA0350	12A,13A,66A,66C
Severtson, David	WI0808	66A,13,66D,12A,66C
Shadinger, Richard C.	TN0100	12A,55,66A,31A,69
Shadle, Douglas W.	KY1500	12A
Shadle-Peters, Jennifer	CO0275	12A,20,32,36,67
Shafer, Sharon Guertin	DC0250	13,10F,12A,39,61
Shaffer, Rebecca Boehm	IA0950	63B,49,12A,32E,13C
Shaheen, Ronald T.	CA5200	11,12A,13A,61
Shanahan, Ellen Cooper	MA0280	13,12A,36,54,29A
Shapovalov, Dimitri	WI0250	12A,66D,36,66A
Sharer, Marty	PA0500	11,37,12A,13A,13C
Sharnetzka, Charles S.	MD0475	37,12A,63A
Shatzkin, Merton T.	MO1810	13,12A,62A
Shaw, Clyde Thomas	VA1350	62C,42,12A,41
Shaw, David	NY2500	13,10,11,12A
Shearer, James E.	NM0310	63D,12A,11
Sheinbaum, John J.	CO0900	12,13E,11,12A
Sheppard, W. Anthony	MA2250	12A,20C,14C,12D,20G
Sheridan, Wilma F.	OR0850	32B,12A
Sherman, Paul	CA5300	12A
Sherr, Laurence E.	GA1150	13,12A,10
Sherr, Richard J.	MA1750	12A,12
Sherry, Mark	WA0480	13,11,12A,14,64A
Sheveloff, Joel L.	MA0400	12A,12
Shipley, Lori R.	VA0500	48,12A,13A,64A,41
Shively, Victoria	MI1750	13B,13C,12A
Shkoda, Natalya	CA0800	66,13,13A,13B,12A
Shoemaker, Michelle N.	MA1175	12A,64,11,64C
Shope, Bradley	TX2930	14,20,12A
Shorter, Lloyd	DE0150	48,64B,12A
Shotola, Marilyn	OR0850	13,64A,41,12A
Shover, Blaine F.	PA3050	11,12A,36,61,54

Name	Code	Areas
Shrader, James A.	GA2150	60,12A,61,36,39
Shrader, Steven	TN1800	11,12A,12,66A,38
Shreffler, Anne C.	MA1050	12,12A
Shurtz, H. Paul	TN1700	12A,12C
Sichel, John	NJ0975	13,10,11,12A,36
Sieg, Jerry	LA0800	10A,10F,13,12A
Siegel, Jeff S.	NY3760	65,12,A
Siek, Stephen	OH2450	12A,66A,66B,20G
Silbiger, Alexander	NC0600	12A,12B,12C,13J
Silver, Phillip A.	ME0440	12A,66C,66A,11
Silverberg, Ann L.	TN0050	12A,12,14,11
Silverman, Faye-Ellen	NY2250	12A
Simmons, John	OH0600	39,12A
Simms, Bryan R.	CA5300	12A,12
Simonot, Colette	AC0050	12A
Simpson, Alexander T.	KY0250	11,12A,36,44,60A
Sine, Nadine J.	PA1950	11,12A,12
Sipes, Diana	TX2930	64A,12A,13E,42
Sipley, Kenneth L.	MS0575	11,12A,13A
Sirbaugh, Nora	NJ0750	12A,39,61
Sisk, Lawrence T.	IL1520	38,12A,36,31A
Sisman, Elaine	NY0750	12,11,12A,12B
Slavich, Richard	CO0900	12A,51,62C,41
Slavin, Dennis	NY0600	12A,12
Slawson, John G.	IL0840	60,12A,36,38,54
Sledge, Larry	FL0800	60,12A,31A,36,13
Slowik, Gregory	MA1700	13,11,12A,66A,66C
Smiley, Marilynn J.	NY3770	12A,67C
Smith, Brent	UT0190	39,62C,13,12A,51
Smith, Christopher J.	TX3200	12A,12,14
Smith, Hope Munro	CA0800	14,20H,11,12A,12C
Smith, J. W.	WV0200	11,12A,66A,66B,66D
Smith, James E.	OH0500	29,70,47,12A
Smith, Kent M.	PA3560	10,11,12A,31A
Smith, Leland C.	CA4900	13,10,12A,34
Smith, Marion	FL0450	13,12A,36
Smith, Nicholas	KS1450	63B,49,12A
Smith, Norman E.	PA3350	12A,12
Smith, Patrick G.	VA1600	12A,63B
Smith, Paul	CA1150	12A,66A,66C,66D,54
Smith, Ronald	NC1950	37,32,63,12A
Smith, Susan	MO0400	16,61,12A
Smith, Timothy	AR0200	13,12A,66A,66C
Snyder, Timothy	FL1000	36,40,12A,32D,60A
Soderlund, Sandra	CA2950	66G,66H,12A
Sokasits, Jonathan F.	NE0300	66A,66D,66B,42,12A
Solis, Ted	AZ0100	12A,20G,14
Solomon, Nanette Kaplan	PA3100	12A,66A,13C,15
South, Janis	OK1250	63B,11,12A,49,20
Southard, Bruce	ND0100	36,60A,12A,61,60
Sparks, Michael	AL1450	12A,36,66A,31A,34
Speare, Mary Jean	VA0600	12A
Spencer, Sarah	TX2295	66A,66C,66D,12A
Spicknall, John P.	IN0800	12A,47,64C
Sprenkle, Elam Ray	MD0650	13,12A
Spring, Howard	AG0350	14,70,29,12A,13D
Sprout, Leslie A.	NJ0300	12A,12C,13A,12
Sprowles, Michael David	KY1500	12A
Squires, David	AB0090	10,12A
Stallsmith, John	AL0260	12A,36,47,66,31A
Stalnaker, Donna	WV0250	11,12A,32B,66A,66H
Stalnaker, William P.	OR0850	13,10,12A
Stanichar, Christopher	SD0050	38,60,12A
Stanley, Glenn	CT0600	11,12A,12,12B
Stark, Deborah	GA0700	12A,54,11,61,40
Starr, Lawrence	WA1050	12A,12,20G
Starr, Pamela	NE0600	12A,12
Stauffer, George B.	NJ1130	12A,66G
Steege, Benjamin A.	NY3790	12A,12B,12C,13F,13
Steel, Matthew	MI2250	12A,12,14,55
Steele, Edward L.	LA0400	12A,13A,13B,13C,61
Stefaniak, Alexander	MO1900	12,12A
Steib, Murray	IN0150	11,12,12A
Steinau, David S.	PA3150	61,39,12A
Steinbauer, Robert	TX3415	12A,66A
Steinberg, A. Jay	KS0150	64C,12A
Steinberg, Michael	RI0050	12A,12B,12C,12D
Steiner, Ruth	DC0050	12A,12,14A
Stencel, Paul L.	NY1210	13A,11,12A,41,47
Stephen, J. Drew	TX3530	12A,63B,67F,12
Stephens, Timothy	OR0750	13,10F,10,12A
Stern, Theodore	CA1960	11,12A,54,13A
Sternfeld, Jessica	CA0960	12A
Stevens, Jane	CA5050	11,12A,12
Stevenson, George	OK0850	12A,14,36,61
Stevlingson, Norma	WI0860	13B,12A,66G,13E,13D
Steward, Gail	AL0500	12A,66A,66D
Still, Tamara G.	OR0500	12A
Stinson, Russell	AR0425	13,11,12A,12,66
Stitt, Virginia K.	UT0200	11,32B,64B,64D,12A
Stohrer, Baptist	IL0780	12A,12,61
Stone, Anne	NY0600	12A,12
Stopa, Alex	NV0050	12A,65
Stoughton, Zachariah	TX3000	66A,12A,67F,11
Strainchamps, Edmond N.	NY4320	12A,12
Strandt, Terry W.	IL1850	12A,61,29
Strasser, Michael C.	OH0200	12A,20
Strauch, Richard	WA1350	37,63D,60B,41,12A
Straughn, Greg	TX0050	12A
Strawn, Lee	CA3270	12A,39
Strimple, Nick	CA5300	12A,60A
Strong, James Anthony	NJ0975	13,12A,66,11,54
Strong, Willie	SC1100	12A,20
Stroud, Stephen	CA3000	11,12A
Strunsky, Mark	NY3000	11,12A,70,14C
Stupin, Mary	CA1270	12A,41
Sturm, Jonathan	IA0850	12A,11,20G,20
Suda, Carolyn	IL1800	11,12A,62C,38,42
Sudano, Gary R.	IN1300	12A
Sullivan, Michael	TX2200	10,11,12A
Summer, Stephen O.	TX3175	35,12,A
Summers, William J.	NH0100	12A,12,67C
Survilla, Maria Paula	IA1800	13,12A,14
Sutton, R. Anderson	WI0815	11,12A,20D,14A
Svistoonoff, Katherine	FL0800	66A,13,12A
Svoboda, George	CA4050	70,12A
Swack, Jeanne	WI0815	12A,12,67,55,67D
Swafford, Jan	MA0350	12A
Swanson, Brent	FL0700	12A,14,20
Swanson, Christopher	VA0700	13C,61,12A,11,39
Swartz, Anne	NY0250	11,12A,12
Swartz, Anne	NY0600	12A,12
Swayne, Steven R.	NH0100	12A,12,39,54
Sweeney, Joyce	CA5500	12A,13,35A,61
Swenson, Edward E.	NY1800	12A,12
Swingle, Ira	AL0310	12A,66A
Sylvester, Lisa M.	CA5300	61,12,A
Szego, Kati	AD0050	12A,14,20
Tabaka, Jim	MN1500	70,20,12A
Taddie, Daniel L.	AR0900	12A,36,61
Tait, Alicia Cordoba	IL0275	20,12A,15,35,11
Talbert, Rebecca	MO2050	61,66A,13,12A,11
Talley, Dana W.	NY2900	61,12A,20,39,11
Talley, Sue	NY2900	66A,12A,36,31A,31B
Tamarkin, Kate	VA1550	38,60B,12A,43
Tanner, Robert	GA1450	10,12A,11,65,34
Taranto, Cheryl	NV0050	16,12A,12C
Taricani, JoAnn	WA1050	12A,12
Tate, Henry Augustine	MA0260	12A
Tayerle, Loren	CA1550	12A,38,41
Taylor, Kristin Jonina	IA1750	12A,20,66A,66D,66
Taylor, Sue	MO1900	12A
Taylor-Gibson, Cristina	DC0050	12A
Tcharos, Stefanie	CA5060	12A,12
Tebay, John	CA1900	36,61,66D,66A,12A
Tebbets, Gary	KS0040	12A,11,36,54,62
Teichmer, Shawn	MI2000	32,60,64,12A,11
Ten Brink, Jonathan	MN0625	12A,61
Thesen, Anita	MD0600	64A,12A
Thibodeaux, Tatiana	CA4500	66A,12A,13C,66C
Thiedt, Catherine E.	OH0950	13,12A,66A,66G,31A
Thoman, Jessica	TN1720	63B,12A,11
Thomas, Jeffrey	CA5010	60,36,12A
Thomas, Matthew	CA0815	12A
Thomas, Richard B.	SC1000	62C,11,38,12A,62D
Thompson, David B.	SC0850	12A,13,66
Thompson, Douglas S.	NJ0500	13,10,12A,34
Thompson, Gregory T.	NC1000	66A,66C,12A,31A
Thompson, Jonathan	AB0090	11,36,12A,60,38
Thompson, Karin E.	WA1100	62C,20,12A,42,13C
Thompson, Lee D.	WA1300	12A,39,66A,66C
Thompson, Timothy F.	AR0700	12A,63B
Thoms, Jason A.	NY0850	36,32D,61,55D,12A
Thorman, Marc	NY0500	10,13,12A,20,14C
Thrasher, Michael	TX3535	64C,12A,12C
Threlkeld, David M.	KY1425	11,12A,47,48,64
Thym, Jurgen	NY1100	12A,12B,12C
Tichenor, Jean-Marie	WY0050	61,40,12A
Tickner, French A.	AB0100	12A,39,61
Tiedge, Faun Tanenbaum	OR0450	11,13,12A,20,42
Tiefenbach, Peter	AG0300	12A,66C
Tilley, Janette M.	NY0635	12A,11,12
Tilney, Colin	AB0150	12A,66E
Timmons, Kathryn Jill	OR0450	12A,66A,66H,66B,66C
Tischler, Judith	NY1860	13A,12A
Todd, R. Larry	NC0600	12A,13J,12C,13E,13I
Toft, Robert	AG0500	10D,12,12C,13J
Tokar, David A.	PA0900	12A,12C,70,12,11
Torok, Debra	PA2450	12A,13,38,66A,20G
Torres, David	TX2260	12A
Torres, George	PA1850	12A,12,14,12D,20H
Touliatos-Miles, Diane	MO1830	11,12A,12,29A
Towne, Gary	ND0500	12A,55,12C
Townsend, Brendan	TX1425	10F,11,12A,13,62C
Traficante, Frank	CA1050	13,12A,12
Trail, Julian	DC0170	12A,13,66A
Tranquilino, Armando	FL0700	13A,13B,13C,34B,12A
Traupman-Carr, Carol A.	PA2450	13A,13,12A,12,31A
Treadwell, Nina K.	CA5070	12A,67G,55
Trentham, Donald R.	TN0650	11,12A,66A,31A,13
Trinkle, Karen M.	MO1950	12,15,12A
Tripold, David	NJ0760	13,12A,32,31A,33
Trittin, Brian L.	TX0400	12A,13,29,37,64E
Trotta, Michael J.	VA1830	32D,12A,36,40
Troxtel, Diane C.	MI1700	12A
Tsabary, Eldad	AI0070	10B,12A,13C
Tully, Amy	SC0420	64A,12A,41
Tung, Leslie Thomas	MI1150	12A,66A,66C,66E,13
Tuomi, Scott	OR0750	12A,12,14,61,55
Turetzky, Bertram	CA5050	12A,41,62D,43,29
Turner, Charles	CT0650	12A,12,67
Turner, J. Frank	CA4450	13A,11,12A,54,13B
Turner, Katherine L.	SC0350	64C,12A,20,14A
Turner, Kristen	NC1800	12A
Turner, Kristin Meyers	NC1700	12A
Tusa, Michael C.	TX3510	11,12A,12
Tweed, Randall L.	CA2100	38,36,12A
Tyrrell, Sarah	MO1810	12A,20
Ulffers, Christopher	NC0650	12A,64D,11
Underwood, Kent	NY2750	12A,12C
Unger, Melvin P.	OH0200	16,12A,36
Unrath, Wendy	IL0850	66A,66D,12A,11
Upton, Elizabeth R.	CA5032	12A,12,13J
Urquhart, Peter W.	NH0350	12C,13B,12A
Utterback, Joe	CT0300	12A,20G,29A
Vail, Eleanore	IN0400	11,12A,66A
Vaillancourt, Scott J.	ME0500	13A,12A
Valente, Liana	FL1550	61,38,13E,39,12A
Van Boer, Bertil H.	WA1250	13E,12,55,12A
Van Cleave, Brad	CA0050	13A,11,12A
Van Deusen, Nancy	CA1050	12A,12B,12C,14
Van Evera, Angeline Smith	MD0850	12A,12C
Van Orden, Katherine	CA5000	11,12A,12D,55,67
Van Regenmorter, Paula	LA0450	64,12,11,41,48,20
Vance, Paul	MN1700	12A,62D,38,51,62C
Vanderbeck, Sue Ann	MI1300	12A,11,66A,66B,66D
VanDessel, Joan	MI0520	12A,13D,37,64C,48
Vaneman, Kelly McElrath	SC0650	12A,64B,42,55,14
VanNordstrand, Shelby	IA0910	12A,13,61
Vascotto, Norma	AG0600	12A,11,20
Vasquez, Hector	FL1300	13,11,12A,66A
Vaughn, Michael	IL2000	12A,12,32A,66A
Veltman, Joshua	TN1660	11,12A,44
Verdrager, Martin	NY1900	12A
Vickers, Jeffrey E.	AR0600	64,11,64E,64A,12A
Viebranz, Gary A.	PA2715	12A,29A,32C
Visentin, Peter	AA0200	12A,62A,67B,11
Vitercik, Greg	VT0350	13,12A,12,66C
Vodnoy, Robert L.	SD0400	12A,62,38,51,35E
Vogel, Allan	CA0510	12A,55B,64B,13C
Volk, David Paul	VA1580	13,36,12A,66A,10
Von Glahn, Denise	FL0850	12A,12
Vorwerk, Paul	CA0510	60,13C,12A
Vowan, Ruth A.	AR0225	61,12A,36,39
Wachsmuth, Karen	IA1140	13,11,12A,66A
Wade, Mark Alan	OH0850	63A,12A,11,32,60B
Waeber, Jacqueline	NC0600	11,12A,12B
Waggener, Joshua A.	NC2350	12A,38,13E
Waggoner, Andrew B.	NY4150	13,10,12A
Wagner, David O.	MI1260	12A,13B,13C,35,66G
Wagner, Marella	WI0770	12A,13J,20
Wagstaff, Grayson	DC0050	12A,12,12C
Wait, Patricia	AG0650	41,64C,13A,12A
Wakeling, Tom	OR0050	11,12A,47,29,35
Walentine, Richard L.	ND0150	61,54,13A,39,12A
Walker, Alan	AG0200	13,12A,12

Name	Code	Areas
Walker, Gayle	OH2050	13C,60,12A,36
Walker, Margaret Edith	AG0250	14,12G,13K,20E,12A
Walker, Tammie Leigh	IL3500	66D,66A,12A
Walrath, Brian	MI2000	11,12A,65,31,34
Walsh, Michael	SD0550	64C,12A,12C
Walter, Elaine R.	DC0050	11,12A,39
Walter, Steven	SC0750	70,11,12A
Walters, Teresa	NJ0200	13,60,11,12A,36
Wang, Richard A.	IL3310	10F,12A,47,53,29
Wang, Yung-Hsiang	TX3400	62A,12A,38,11
Wanken, Matthew	IL0420	12A,13A,13B,13C
Wanner, Dan	CA3150	12A
Warren, John	IL1900	36,11,12A,13B,13C
Warren, Robert	TX3100	12A,66A,11
Warwick, Jacqueline	AF0100	12A,12D,14C,15,29A
Waschka, Rodney A.	NC1700	10,12A,13F,10B,13
Watchorn, Peter G.	MA0350	12A
Waters, Sarah S.	OH1800	13B,13C,12A
Watkins, Holly	NY1100	12A,12B,12D,13J,14C
Watkins, Timothy D.	TX3000	12A,14,20,12
Watson, Marva	IL1240	66A,66B,66C,11,12A
Watson, Tommy L.	SC0050	11,61,39,12A,13A
Weaver, Andrew H.	DC0050	12A,12,12C,62B
Weaver, Michael A.	SC0950	12A,11,32,62A,62B
Webb, Brian P.	VT0125	13A,13,11,12A,36
Webber, Kelly Marie	KS0560	11,13A,12A,61,60A
Webber, Sophie C.	IL1400	62C,20,12A
Weber, Brent	PA2250	61,32D,39,12A
Webster, Gerald	OR0850	63A,12A
Wegman, Rob	NJ0900	11,12A,12,20G
Weinberg, Alan	SC0600	11,66A,12A,66D
Weinstein, Michael	MA2200	13A,11,12A,49
Weis, Patricia	WI0300	12A,61
Weiss, Susan F.	MD0650	12A,12
Weller, Ellen	CA3460	12A,55,20,29A,60
Wells, Elizabeth A.	AE0050	12A,12,14,20G
Wen, Eric	PA0850	13,12A
Wenderoth, Valeria	HI0210	12A
Weng, Pamela	CO0830	13,11,12A,66A
Wente, Steven F.	IL0730	13,66G,12A,31A
Wentworth, Jean	NY3560	12A,41,66A
Wesley, Charles E.	MS0050	36,61,12A,11
West, Jean	FL1750	12A,64A
Wexler, Richard	MD1010	12A,12,55,29A
Whalen, Margaret F.	NC2000	11,12A,20B,29A
Whang, Hyunsoon	OK0150	11,12A,66
Wheeler, Mark	NC0915	11,12A,20G
Wheelock, Gretchen A.	NY1100	12A,12B,12C,12D,15
White, Christopher T.	KY1500	12A,34D
Whitney, Nadine C.	GA2200	12A,36,61,40,39
Wiberg, Janice	MT0300	13,12A,32,36,66
Widder, David R.	VA1700	12A,37,48,64C
Wight, Ed	OR0950	12A
Wilbourne, Emily	NY0642	12A,12E
Wilcoxson, Nancy	SD0580	13A,61,36,11,12A
Wiley, Roland J.	MI2100	12A
Wilhoit, Mel R.	TN0200	10F,12A,32,49,63
Wilkins, Donald G.	PA0550	13,12A,66G
Wilkinson, Christopher	WV0750	13,11,12A,12
Will, Richard	VA1550	12A,12,20G,14C
Williams, Barry Michael	SC1200	12A,50,65,20A,20B
Williams, Christopher A.	OH2300	12A,20,12C,11
Williams, Ellen	NC1300	12A,39,61
Williams, Michael	CA2775	70,12A
Williams, Oscar	LA0700	12A,64,11,29A
Williams, Peter F.	NC0600	12A,12,14B
Williams, Ralph K.	NY4060	13,12A,11,61
Williams, Robert	NC0800	11,12A,36,61
Williams, Sarah F.	SC1110	12A,14C,12,14,15
Williams, Yolanda	MN1050	12A,20,47,29A,41
Willier, Stephen A.	PA3250	12A
Willoughby, Angela	MS0400	12A,66A,66B
Wilner, Stacey	TN1000	12A,36,11,60A
Wilson, Blake	PA0950	12A,55,11
Wilson, Cecil B.	WV0750	10F,60,12A,12
Wilson, Geoffrey	IA1800	12A,13,66A,10F
Wilson, James Dale	CT0100	14,20C,12A,12E,29B
Wilson, Mark	WA0030	70,12A
Wilson, T. Rex	TX2710	60,12A,32C,36,61
Wingate, Owen K.	FL0675	13,11,12A,61,36
Winkler, Amanda Eubanks	NY4100	12,12A,15,31A,31G
Winstead, Elizabeth	NC1350	61,12A
Winters, Donald Eugene	MS0850	61,31A,12A,60A
Winters, Thomas D.	PA3600	12A,12,29
Wischusen, Mary A.	MI2200	12A,12,14C
Wiskus, Jessica	PA1050	13J,12A,13E,13
Witmer, Ruth	FL1550	12A,14,20
Witt, James	CA4050	13A,11,12A,47,62D
Witten, David	NJ0800	13B,12A,66A,66B,66C
Witter, Tim	CA0050	13A,11,12A
Wojcik, Richard J.	IL3400	11,12A,36,61,31A
Wojnar, William A.	ND0150	12A,66A,66G,31B,31A
Wolbers, Mark	AK0100	60,12A,32C,64C,48
Woldu, Gail Hilson	CT0500	11,14C,12A,15
Wolfe, Jennifer	MI1050	13C,66C,12A,11
Wolfe-Ralph, Carol	MD1050	66A,66G,66B,66C,12A
Wolff, Christoph	MA1050	12A,12,12C
Wolgast, Brett	IA0300	66A,66G,13,12A
Wolinski, Mary E.	KY1550	12A,11
Wolters-Fredlund, Benita	MI0350	13,11,12A
Wolz, Larry	TX0900	12A,20G,61,12C
Womack, Jeffrey	TX0150	12A,64B,64D
Woo, Betty	CA2200	13,12A,66A
Wood, Charles E.	AL1200	61,39,12A
Wood, Thomas G.	OH0700	62A,62B,12A,11
Woodcock, Ruth	WA0100	11,12A,20,13A,13G
Woodruff, Neal	IL2300	60,36,38,61,12A
Woods, Timothy E.	SD0400	60A,12A,36,61,40
Woody, Gilbert P.	CA3850	12A
Woolly, Kimberly A.	MS0750	64D,12A,41,48,72
Worthen, Douglas	IL2900	12A,64A
Wright, Barbara	WV0560	13A,13,12A,12,66G
Wright, Craig M.	CT0900	11,12A,12
Wubbena, Jan Helmut	AR0400	13,66G,12A,11
Wulfhorst, Dieter	CA1860	62C,62D,12A,12C,41
Yeh, Ying	CA0800	39,61,12A
Yoes, Milas	AZ0470	12A,29,37,46,63C
Yonce, Tammy Evans	SD0550	11,12A,64A,20
Yost, Laurel	MT0200	66A,66B,66C,12A
You, Yali	MN0800	38,41,62C,11,12A
Youens, Susan	IN1700	12A,12
Young, Eileen M.	NC2500	64C,64E,41,64,12A
Young, H. G.	WV0760	13,11,12A,36,54
Youngdahl, Janet Ann	AA0200	36,12A,61
Ypma, Nancy S.	IL1740	12A,36,66G
Yri, Kirsten	AG0600	12A
Yuzefovich, Victor	MD0150	12A,12,62B,32I
Zamparas, Grigorios	FL2050	66A,66H,12A
Zank, MJ Sunny	OH1800	13,20,10,12A,43
Zappulla, Robert	CA1050	12A,12C,13,66H
Zattiero, Joanna R.	UT0300	12A,64E
Zazulia, Emily	PA3420	11,12A
Zbikowski, Lawrence	IL3250	13,12A,13J,29C
Zec, John	NJ0550	12A,31,66G,13,11
Zeiss, Laurel E.	TX0300	12A,12C,11,12
Zeller, Kurt-Alexander	GA0500	61,39,12A
Zhou, Tianxu	MA2020	36,61,12A
Zigler, Amy E.	NC2205	12A,15
Zilber, Michael	CA2775	11,64E,12A,20G,29
Zimmerman, Daniel	MD1010	12A
Zimmerman, Franklin B.	PA3350	12A,12
Zogleman, Deanne	KS0980	12A,13,20G,36,40
Zohn, Steven D.	PA3250	12A
Zuschin, David	VA1100	13,12A,61

Aesthetics of Music

Name	Code	Areas
Allsup, Randall Everett	NY4200	43,32,13,12A,12B
Archetto, Maria	GA0755	11,12A,12B,13A,20
Babiracki, Carol M.	NY4100	12,12B,14,20B,20E
Bakriges, Christopher	MA1550	29,14D,12B,20,31G
Benamou, Marc	IN0400	14,12,20,20D,12B
Berger, Harris M.	TX2900	14,12B,29D,20G
Berger, Karol	CA4900	12A,12,13J,12B
Berrett, Joshua	NY2400	13,11,29A,12,12B
Blair, Deborah V.	MI1750	32B,32C,12B,12F,32D
Bond, Karlyn	UT0400	11,12A,12B
Borroff, Edith	NY3705	12A,12,12B
Bowen, Richard L.	IN1850	36,12,12A,11,12B
Boynton, Susan	NY0750	11,12A,12,12B
Broman, Per F.	OH0300	13F,13C,13E,12B,13
Brooks-Lyle, Alma B.	AL0050	13,64A,12B,12A
Brown, Frank Burch	IN0300	12A,66A,12B,10
Brown, Gwynne Kuhner	WA1000	12A,29A,13C,20,12B
Burrack, Frederick	KS0650	32,12B,11,32,37
Cabrini, Michele	NY0625	12B,12A,13B,11,12
Calcagno, Mauro	NY3790	12A,12D,12B,11
Campbell, Brian G.	MN0350	13,10A,20,12B,10F
Cardillo, Kenneth	TN0260	70,13,11,12B
Carlsen, James	WA1050	34,12B,12F,12,12C
Celenza, Anna H.	DC0075	12A,12B,12C,12G
Cha, Jee-Weon	IA0700	13,12B
Cheng, Gloria	CA5030	12C,12B
Clevenger, Charles	OH0450	66A,66B,66C,66D,12B
Collins, Leo W.	MA2200	12B,31A,20G
Cortese, Federico	MA1050	38,12A,12B
Cramer, Alfred W.	CA3650	13,12A,12B
DeJournett, William	MS0700	37,12B,11
DelDonna, Anthony R.	DC0075	12,12A,12B,12C,12D
Dickensheets, Janice	CO0950	12,34A,14,12B,12A
Dolan, Emily I.	PA3350	12A,12,11,12B
Elliott, David J.	NY2750	32,12B,10A
Engle, Marilyn	AA0150	41,66A,66B,66C,12B
Esse, Melina	NY1100	12A,12B,12D,14C,15
Ezoe, Magdalena	MI1950	66A,13,12B,12A,41
Falk, Leila Birnbaum	OR0900	11,12A,12B,41
Gable, David D.	GA0490	11,12A,12B,13A,16
Gier, Christina B.	AA0100	12A,12D,12B,12,15
Gilbert, Pia	NY1900	12B
Giles, Jennifer	AG0100	13,12B,14A
Gilliam, Bryan	NC0600	11,12A,12B,12C,12D
Green, Burdette L.	OH1850	13A,13,13J,12B
Green, J. Paul	AG0500	60,12B,32,12C
Greenan, April	VA1475	11,12A,12B,12F,20
Henson, Karen A.	NY0750	11,15,39,12A,12B
Hernandez Mergal, Luis A.	PR0115	12A,12B,14
Hirota, Yoko	AG0150	66,13B,12A,66A,12B
Isaacs, Kevin	CT0800	13,60,10,12B,36
Jakelski, Lisa	NY1100	12A,12E,12B,12C,14F
Johnson, Jeffrey W.	NY2105	61,12A,55D,12B
Judkins, Jennifer	CA5030	12B,12C
Kaminsky, Peter	CT0600	13,13J,12B
Kasunic, David M.	CA3300	12A,12B,12D,11
Korstvedt, Benjamin M.	MA0650	12A,12B,12C,12D
Kowalke, Kim H.	NY1100	12A,12B,12C,12D,15
Kozak, Brian	OH0750	12B,20G,29,35
Kozinn, Allan	NY2750	12B,12C
Kushner, David Z.	FL1850	12,12A,12B,12E,20G
Landey, Peter	AG0050	12B,13J,10A,10B,10F
Lee, Ronald T.	RI0300	32,37,12B,12C
Levy, Beth E.	CA5010	12A,12B,12C,20G
Lewis, Eric	CT0800	12A,62B,51,62A,12B
Locke, Ralph P.	NY1100	12A,12B,12C,12D
London, Justin	MN0300	13,12B,12F,20G,12A
MacFarlane, Thomas	NY2750	13C,13D,13F,12A,12B
Maniates, Maria R.	AG0450	11,12A,12,12B
Marcades, Michael	AL0900	12A,12B,13,32,36
Marcel, Linda A.	NJ0020	12B,66A,66D,32,11
Martin, Margot	CA1750	12A,12B,20,66H,12E
Mattingly, Jacqueline	NE0600	63B,12B
Mauceri, Frank	ME0340	10,13,12B
Maus, Fred Everett	VA1550	13,12B,15,12D,14C
Mayes, Catherine	UT0250	12A,12B,12C
McQuiston, Kate	HI0210	12A,12B,12C
Micznik, Vera G.	AB0100	12,12B,12A
Mikhalevsky, Nina	DC0110	12A,12B
Minor, Ryan	NY3790	12A,12D,12B,11,13E
Mitchell, Darleen C.	NE0590	13,10,15,43,12B
Moeser, James	NC2410	12B
Moll, Kevin N.	NC0650	12,55,67A,12A,12B
Moore, Christopher	AG0400	12A,12B,12D
Morrow, Matthew	NY1100	12A,12B,12D
Mortyakova, Julia V.	MS0550	66A,66D,66B,66C,12B
Neville, Donald	AG0500	12A,12,12B
Niblock, Howard	WI0350	13,10F,12B,41,64B
Pane, Steven	ME0410	12A,66A,12,12B,11
Parmer, Dillon	AG0400	11,12,12B,12C
Pasler, Jann C.	CA5050	11,12A,12,12B,12E
Peck, Donald	ID0060	12A,12B,12C,61
Post, Olaf	MA1050	12A,12B
Rehding, Alexander	MA1050	13,12A,12B,12C,12G
Restesan, Francise T.	PR0125	13,60,12B,38,41
Ricci, John	MI2250	13,10F,12B,29
Riggs, Robert D.	MS0700	12A,12B,41,62A,62B
Rosen, David	NY0900	12A,12B,12C
Royal, Matthew	AG0050	13,11,12B
Samuel, Jamuna	NY3790	11,12A,13E,12B,13F
Savage, Roger W. H.	CA5031	12B,12E
Schantz, Allen P.	CO0150	11,12B,13,68
Schultz, Arlan N.	AA0200	10,34,13,12B
Setter, Terry A.	WA0350	10F,10,12B,45,35C
Shelley, Russ	PA1650	11,12B,36
Shepherd, John	AG0100	12B,35B,12E,12C
Shultis, Christopher	NM0450	12,12B,10
Silbiger, Alexander	NC0600	12A,12B,12C,13J

Index by Area of Teaching Interest

Sisman, Elaine	NY0750	12,11,12A,12B
Spede, Mark J.	SC0400	37,60,12B
Stanley, Glenn	CT0600	11,12A,12,12B
Steege, Benjamin A.	NY3790	12A,12B,12C,13F,13
Steinberg, Michael	RI0050	12A,12B,12C,12D
Sullivan, Mark	MI1400	10,12B,34
Swain, Joseph P.	NY0650	13,12B,12F,12C
Syer, Katherine R.	IL3300	12B
Thym, Jurgen	NY1100	12A,12B,12C
Twombly, Kristian	MN1300	10B,34H,12B,10,11
Ulman, Erik	CA4900	10,13,12B,62A
Van Deusen, Nancy	CA1050	12A,12B,12C,14
Waeber, Jacqueline	NC0600	11,12A,12B
Warren, Jeff	AB0090	12B,13F,47,62D
Watkins, Holly	NY1100	12A,12B,12D,13J,14C
Weinstein, Alan	VA1700	62C,62D,12B
Wheelock, Gretchen A.	NY1100	12A,12B,12C,12D,15
White, Christopher K.	VA1100	29,64E,32E,64,12B
Woodford, Paul	AG0500	60,12B,32,37,63
Wyatt, Benjamin H.	VA1100	62C,67B,12,13I,12B

Research and Methodology

Alexander, Marina	NY0644	36,12A,12C,60A
Alves, William	CA1050	12C,35C,34D
Amati-Camperi, Alexandra	CA5353	12A,11,12C,13A,12
Anderson, Ronald E.	TX2700	60A,11,12A,12C
Armstrong, James I.	VA0250	36,12A,60,12C
Armstrong, Richard	AL0500	12A,12C,61
Bailey, Terence	AG0500	12,12C
Baird, Julianne C.	NJ1100	12A,12C,40,61,67E
Banducci, Antonia L.	CO0900	12A,12,12C
Barone, Anthony	NV0050	12,12A,12C
Barr, Cyrilla	DC0050	12A,12C
Barry, Barbara R.	FL1125	12A,12C
Barry, JoAnne	LA0650	12C
Bashford, Christina	IL3300	12A,12C,12D,42,51
Bauer, William R.	NY0644	10F,12A,12C,13
Beckett, Christine	AI0070	13,12C,32C,38,62A
Beller-McKenna, Daniel	NH0350	12A,12C,11,14C
Bentley, Julia	IL2100	12A,12C
Bernstein, Jane A.	MA1900	11,12A,12,12C
Bilderback, Barry T.	ID0250	11,12A,20B,12C,14A
Black, Dorothy M.	PA2800	12C
Boettcher, Bonna	NY0900	16,12A,12C
Bowman, Wayne	NY2750	32,12C,12F,14
Bradley, Mark	KY0400	12C,32G,36,39,61
Brauner, Mitchell	WI0825	12A,12,12C,11
Briscoe, James R.	IN0250	12A,14,12C,12
Brockett, Clyde W.	VA0150	12C
Brothers, Lester D.	MO1790	11,12A,12C
Brothers, Thomas	NC0600	12A,12C,12E,29
Bulen, Jay C.	MO1780	12C,12A,63C
Burkett, John	TX2955	13,66A,66G,34,12C
Campbell, Patricia Shehan	WA1050	32A,20A,12C,32B,20D
Carlsen, James	WA1050	34,12B,12F,12,12C
Cassaro, James P.	PA3420	16,12C,15
Cassio, Francesca	NY1600	12,12A,12C,20
Celenza, Anna H.	DC0075	12A,12B,12C,12G
Cheng, Gloria	CA5030	12C,12B
Christensen, Dieter	NY0750	14,14A,12C
Cimarusti, Thomas M.	TX3200	12A,13E,20,12C,68
Cockburn, Brian	VA0600	16,12C
Coe, Judith A.	CO0830	61,10D,34,14C,12C
Coluzzi, Seth	MA0500	10D,11,13A,12A,12C
Cook, Kenneth	NY1275	12C,13,29A
Cox, Arnie	OH1700	13,12C
Cusick, Suzanne G.	NY2740	12A,12C,12D,15
Custodero, Lori A.	NY4200	32A,32B,32G,12E,12C
Davis, William B.	CO0250	33,12C
Deaville, James A.	AG0200	11,12A,12,41,12C
Debly, Patricia	AG0050	12A,12C
DeFord, Ruth	NY0625	11,12A,12,12C
DelDonna, Anthony R.	DC0075	12,12A,12B,12C,12D
Doukhan, Lilianne	MI0250	12A,12,14,31A,12C
Dressler, John C.	KY0950	12A,63B,11,12C
Eanes, Edward	GA1150	12A,11,12C,20G
Eby, John D.	AI0050	11,12A,12C,20G,31A
Elias, Cathy A.	IL0750	11,12A,12C
Elzinga, Harry	TX0300	12A,12C
Entwistle, Erik	MA1175	12A,12C
Evans, Lorraine	CO0830	12C
Feurzeig, Lisa	MI0900	12C,12A,20
Finn, Geraldine	AG0100	12E,12C
Fitch, Frances	MA1175	12C
Fleming, Beth	OK0750	16,12C
Freitas, Roger	NY1100	12A,12C,12D,15
Fullerton, J. Graeme	AB0100	12C
Gerber, Stephen K.	VA0450	12C,16
Ghuman, Nalini G.	CA2950	13,12A,12C,12
Gibson, Joice Waterhouse	CO0550	34B,34C,12A,12C,13A
Gilliam, Bryan	NC0600	11,12A,12B,12C,12D
Gjevre, Naomi	TX2250	62A,42,12C
Gordon-Seifert, Catherine	RI0150	13,12A,12C,55B,66H
Gottlieb, Jane	NY1900	16,12C
Green, J. Paul	AG0500	60,12B,32,12C
Green, Richard D.	OH1450	12A,12,12C
Gregoire, Carole	AI0190	12C
Guralnick, Elissa	CO0800	12C
Hathaway, Janet J.	IL2200	12A,55,67,12C
Helsen, Katherine E.	AG0500	12C
Hepler, Lowell E.	PA0100	12A,12C,37,66A,63D
Hoehne, Bill	CA1000	10F,12C,64A,13,29
Holly, Janice E.	MD1010	12C
Holmes, Christopher	IN0100	12A,12C,20,11
Hunter, David	TX3510	12,12C
Jakelski, Lisa	NY1100	12A,12E,12B,12C,14F
Jocoy, Stacey	TX3200	12G,12E,12C,31A,11
Johnston, Dennis	NY0700	32E,12C,49,63A,60B
Judkins, Jennifer	CA5030	12B,12C
Kahan, Sylvia	NY0644	12A,12C,66,13A,13C
Kamatani, Pamela	CA5353	12A,11,12C,13
Kangas, Ryan R.	TX3400	12C
Karnes, Kevin C.	GA0750	12,12C
Kauffman, Deborah	CO0950	12A,12C
Kendall, Roger A.	CA5031	32,13L,12F,12C
King, Richard G.	MD1010	11,12A,12,20G,12C
Kleppinger, Stanley V.	NE0600	13,63A,37,12C
Korstvedt, Benjamin M.	MA0650	12A,12B,12C,12D
Kowalke, Kim H.	NY1100	12A,12B,12C,12D,15
Kozinn, Allan	NY2750	12B,12C
Krause, Philip	IL2100	39,12C
Kreuze, Brandon R.	GA0600	10,34,13,12C
Kruckenberg, Lori	OR1050	12A,12C,13J
Lammers, Mark E.	MN0750	12C
Lapka, Christine	IL3500	32,11,12C
Laverty, Mary	NY4150	12C
Lawrence-White, Stephanie	NC0200	12A,66A,12C,20F,66B
Ledeen, Lydia Hailparn	NJ0300	11,12A,15,12C
Lee, Ronald T.	RI0300	32,37,12B,12C
Lee, Sang-Hie	FL2000	11,12C
Leve, James	AZ0450	12A,12C
Levin, Neil	NY1860	12C,12A,12
Levy, Beth E.	CA5010	12A,12B,12C,20G
Lewis, Barbara E.	ND0500	12F,12C,32A,32B
Lindberg, John E.	MN1000	12A,12C,48,64D,72
Lipori, Daniel	WA0050	11,64D,12A,12C
Livingston, Carolyn H.	RI0300	32,36,66D,12C
Locke, Ralph P.	NY1100	12A,12B,12C,12D
Lohuis, Ardyth J.	VA1600	66G,12A,12C
Lombard, Becky	LA0400	13,12A,66A,66G,12C
Lott, R. Allen	TX2600	12A,12,14,12C
Luttmann, Stephen	CO0950	16,12C
MacAyeal, Gregory	IL2100	12C
Macey, Patrick	NY1100	12A,12C,55D
Madeja, James T.	NY3780	32,63A,12C,49
Madsen, Clifford K.	FL0850	32,33,12C
Manley, Douglas H.	TN1550	12,66,31,66G,12C
Martin, Cathy	AI0150	12C,16
Mayes, Catherine	UT0250	12A,12B,12C
McCarthy, Keri E.	WA1150	64B,12A,13,11,12C
McCarthy, Kerry R.	NC0600	12A,12C,31A,55
McDowell, Laura	NC0250	12C,12A,66D,67C
McLucas, Anne Dhu	OR1050	12A,12C,20G,20F,14
McMillan, Brian	AI0150	12C,16
McNeely, Heather	SC0200	12A,12C,63A
McQuiston, Kate	HI0210	12A,12B,12C
Miller-Thorn, Jill	NY1275	10A,10F,13,66D,12C
Minevich, Pauline M.	AJ0100	12A,64C,12C,12D
Mooney, Kevin	AG0500	13,13J,12C
Morrongiello, Christopher	NY1600	12A,12C
Moskowitz, David V.	SD0600	12A,20H,14C,12C,11
Murchison, Gayle	VA0250	12A,12,20G,12C
Murray, Michael	OH1850	12C
Near, John R.	IL2400	11,12A,12C,66G
Oates, Jennifer Lynn	NY0600	12,16,12A,12C
Oft, Eryn	AL0500	64B,64D,12A,12C
O'Neill, Darren D.	NJ0800	70,12C
Orlofsky, Diane	AL1050	32,12C,36
Ottervik, Jennifer	MD0650	12C
Parmer, Dillon	AG0400	11,12,12B,12C
Payette, Jessica	MI1750	12A,12C
Payne, Thomas B.	VA0250	12A,12,12C
Peck, David	ID0060	12A,12B,12C,61
Peters, G. David	IN0907	34,12C,12,35C,35A
Phipps, Danny K.	MI0900	64D,12A,12C,13E
Polk, Keith	NH0350	11,12A,12C,63B
Popp, Harold	KS1450	12A,12C
Potter, Pamela	WI0815	12,12C
Power, Brian E.	AG0050	62A,67,12A,12C,13G
Preston, Katherine K.	VA0250	12A,12,20G,12C
Puckette, Miller	CA5050	34,12C
Radice, Mark A.	NY1800	12A,12C
Ragogini, Ernest	MD0100	13,12A,66A,12C
Rasmussen, Anne K.	VA0250	14,20G,31,41,12C
Rees, Fred J.	IN0907	34,12C,35C,32,12
Rehding, Alexander	MA1050	13,12A,12B,12C,12G
Reul, Barbara M.	AJ0100	11,12A,12C,12D
Revuluri, Sindhumathi	MA1050	12,12A,12C,14C,20D
Reynolds, David	SD0550	12C,63A,63B
Rigler, Ann Marie	MO2000	66A,66G,31A,12A,12C
Rodger, Gillian	WI0825	12A,12C,20G,20D,14
Rogers, Donald M.	SC1200	12C,32G
Root, Deane L.	PA3420	12A,12C,12,20G,12E
Rosen, David	NY0900	12A,12B,12C
Rosenthal, Roseanne K.	IL3450	12C
Runyan, William E.	CO0250	10F,12C,12A
Russell, Joan	AI0100	32B,32C,12,12C
Saya, Virginia	CA2800	12A,39,12C,11
Schenbeck, Lawrence A.	GA1900	11,12A,12C
Schlagel, Stephanie P.	OH2200	12C,12,55,67
Schroeder, David	AF0100	13,12A,12,12E,12C
Schuler, Nico S.	TX3175	13,12C,34B,13F
Seachrist, Denise A.	OH1100	12C,14,20G
Seaton, Douglass	FL0850	12A,12D,12C,12
Shepherd, John	AG0100	12B,35B,12E,12C
Shurtz, H. Paul	TN1700	12A,12C
Silbiger, Alexander	NC0600	12A,12B,12C,13J
Smith, Gordon E.	AG0250	12,14,20G,12C
Smith, Hope Munro	CA0800	14,20H,11,12A,12C
Sprout, Leslie A.	NJ0300	12A,12C,13A,12
Steege, Benjamin A.	NY3790	12A,12B,12C,13F,13
Steinberg, Michael	RI0050	12A,12B,12C,12D
Steinmetz, John	CA5030	64D,12C
Steinmetz, John	CA1000	64D,12C
Stulberg, Neal	CA5030	38,12C
Swain, Joseph P.	NY0650	13,12B,12F,12C
Taranto, Cheryl	NV0050	16,12A,12C
Thomas, Margaret E.	CT0100	13,11,12C
Thrasher, Michael	TX3535	64C,12A,12C
Thym, Jurgen	NY1100	12A,12B,12C
Tietjen, Linda	CO0830	12C
Todd, R. Larry	NC0600	12A,13J,12C,13E,13I
Toft, Robert	AG0500	10D,12A,12C,13J
Tokar, David A.	PA0900	12A,12C,70,12,11
Towne, Gary	ND0500	12A,55,12C
Underwood, Kent	NY2750	12A,12C
Urquhart, Peter W.	NH0350	12C,13B,12A
Van Deusen, Nancy	CA1050	12A,12B,12C,14
Van Evera, Angeline Smith	MD0850	12A,12C
Wagstaff, Grayson	DC0050	12A,12,12C
Walsh, Michael	SD0550	64C,12A,12C
Wang, Cecilia	KY1450	32,12C
Weaver, Andrew H.	DC0050	12A,12,12C,62B
Westervelt, Todd G.	FL0100	32,12C,63A
Wheatley, Susan E.	PA1600	32,12C
Wheelock, Gretchen A.	NY1100	12A,12B,12C,12D,15
Wiggins, Donna	NC2700	12C,32,32G
Williams, Christopher A.	OH2300	12A,20,12C,11
Wilson, Karen	SC0200	12,66A,12C,20G,67
Winter, Robert	CA5030	12C
Wolff, Christoph	MA1050	12A,12,12C
Wolz, Larry	TX0900	12A,20G,61,12C
Wood, Robert	AG0500	32C,34,12F,12,12C
Wulfhorst, Dieter	CA1860	62C,62D,12A,12C,41
Zager, Daniel	NY1100	16,12C
Zappulla, Robert	CA1050	12A,12C,13,66H
Zdzinski, Stephen	FL1900	32,32G,32H,12C,13K
Zeiss, Laurel E.	TX0300	12A,12C,11,12

Critical Theory

Archbold, Lawrence	MN0300	11,12A,66G,15,12D
Bashford, Christina	IL3300	12A,12C,12D,42,51

Index by Area of Teaching Interest

Bauer, Amy M.	CA5020	13,13F,12D		Davis, Stacey	TX3530	13,13K,12F
Baur, Steven	AF0100	11,12A,12D,12E,14C		Edwards, Richard D.	OH2000	37,32,60B,12F,32A
Beaudoin, Richard A.	MA1050	13,12D,10		Eigenfeldt, Arne	AB0080	10,45,34,35,12F
Bergeron, Katherine	RI0050	12A,12D		Fiske, Harold	AG0500	32,12F
Bloechl, Olivia A.	CA5032	12,12A,12D,20G,31A		Gardstrom, Susan	OH2250	33,12F,44
Burr, Anthony	CA5050	64C,43,13D,14C,12D		Gotfrit, Martin	AB0080	10,45,34,35,12F
Calcagno, Mauro	NY3790	12A,12D,12B,11		Graham, Richard M.	GA2100	33,12F
Cateforis, Theodore P.	NY4100	12,12D,20G,29A,14C		Gray, Lori F.	MT0400	32,12F
Caulder, Stephanie B.	PA1600	12A,12D,48,64B,13C		Graziano, Amy	CA0960	11,12A,12F
Christensen, Thomas	IL3250	13,13J,12D		Greenan, April	VA1475	11,12A,12B,12F,20
Clark, Suzannah	MA1050	13,12D		Hair, Harriet	GA2100	11,32,34,12F
Coates, Norma	AG0500	12A,12D,15,35A		Heller, Jack J.	FL2000	32,12F
Cusick, Suzanne G.	NY2740	12A,12C,12D,15		Hopkins, Robert	NY1350	13,12A,12,12F
DelDonna, Anthony R.	DC0075	12,12A,12B,12C,12D		Hopkins, William T.	CA4200	11,12A,12,12F
Demers, Joanna	CA5300	12D		Huron, David	OH1850	13,12F
Dessen, Michael J.	CA5020	10,12D,29E		Jackson, Isaiah	MA1175	12F
Devereaux, Kent	WA0200	10,12D		Johnson, Steven P.	UT0050	12A,12,14,12F
Esse, Melina	NY1100	12A,12B,12D,14C,15		Kendall, Roger A.	CA5031	32,13L,12F,12C
Freitas, Roger	NY1100	12A,12C,12D,15		Lapidis, Rachael	CA0960	12F
Gier, Christina B.	AA0100	12A,12D,12B,12,15		Lauzon, Paul	AF0050	33,12F
Gilliam, Bryan	NC0600	11,12A,12B,12C,12D		Lerdahl, Fred	NY0750	10,12F,11
Gooley, Dana	RI0050	12A,13B,12E,12D		Lewis, Barbara E.	ND0500	12F,12C,32A,32B
Hall, Van-Anthoney	NC1550	11,12D,40,42,61		London, Justin	MN0300	13,12B,12F,20G,12A
Hoffman, Elizabeth D.	NY2740	12D,13,10,45,34		McArthur, Lisa R.	KY0400	13,48,64A,12A,12F
Jung, Eun-Young	CA5050	11,12D,14,20C		McKay, James R.	AG0500	37,38,41,64D,12F
Kallberg, Jeffrey	PA3350	12A,12,12D,15		Murail, Tristan C.	NY0750	10,34,13L,12F,10F
Kasunic, David M.	CA3300	12A,12B,12D,11		Platoff, John	CT0500	13,11,14C,12,12F
Keiler, Allan R.	MA0500	11,12A,12D,13E,13J		Renninger, Laura Ann	WV0550	11,12A,12F,14
Korstvedt, Benjamin M.	MA0650	12A,12B,12C,12D		Sandness, Marilyn I.	OH2250	33,12F
Kowalke, Kim H.	NY1100	12A,12B,12C,12D,15		Smith, Bret	WA0050	11,32,12F
Lambert, James	OK0150	65,50,37,13,12D		Smith, Kenneth H.	MI2250	32,34,12F
Lee, Katherine In-Young	CA5010	14,12,20C,12D		Swain, Joseph P.	NY0650	13,12B,12F,12C
Locke, Ralph P.	NY1100	12A,12B,12C,12D		Takesue, Sumy A.	CA4450	13A,66,12F,13B,13C
Maus, Fred Everett	VA1550	13,12B,15,12D,14C		Tan, Siu-Lan	MI1150	12F
Meyer, Stephen C.	NY4100	12,12A,12D,31A		Thaut, Michael H.	CO0250	12F,33
Minevich, Pauline M.	AJ0100	12A,64C,12C,12D		Tunks, Thomas W.	TX2400	32,12F
Minor, Ryan	NY3790	12A,12D,12B,11,13E		Waddington, Alan	CA1000	12F,14,29,46,47
Moore, Christopher	AG0400	12A,12B,12D		Wessel, David	CA5000	12F,13G,13K,13L
Moreno, Jairo	PA3350	13,13J,20H,29,12D		Wicke, Peter	AG0100	12,35,12F
Morrison, Leah A.	CA5300	31A,13J,12A,12D		Wiggins, Jacqueline H.	MI1750	12F,32B,32G
Morrow, Matthew	NY1100	12A,12B,12D		Wood, Robert	AG0500	32C,34,12F,12,12C
Page, Tim	CA5300	12D		Woody, Robert H.	NE0600	32B,12F
Pennington, Stephen	MA1900	12D,29A,29E,15,12		Zavac, Nancy C.	FL1900	16,12F
Peraino, Judith A.	NY0900	12A,12D,15				
Piekut, Benjamin	NY0900	12A,12D,12E		**Musical Iconography**		
Pisaro, Michael J.	CA0510	13,10,12D		Bianchi, Eric	NY1300	11,12A,12G,13J,31
Ratliff, Richard J.	IN1650	13,66A,12D		Blazekovic, Zdravko	NY0600	12G
Reul, Barbara M.	AJ0100	11,12A,12C,12D		Brown, Jeremy S.	AA0150	37,64E,29,12G,48
Rodman, Ronald	MN0300	13,37,63C,63D,12D		Celenza, Anna H.	DC0075	12,12B,12C,12G
Rupprecht, Philip	NC0600	12A,12D,13E,13F		Chodacki-Ford, Roberta	GA0550	16,12G
Seaton, Douglass	FL0850	12A,12D,12C,12		Hughes, Andrew	AG0450	11,12,13J,12G
Sheppard, W. Anthony	MA2250	12A,20C,14C,12D,20G		Jocoy, Stacey	TX3200	12G,12E,12C,31A,11
Spiller, Henry	CA5010	14,12,15,20D,12D		Rehding, Alexander	MA1050	13,12A,12B,12C,12G
Stanyek, Jason	NY2740	34,12,14,20,12D		Wade, Bonnie C.	CA5000	11,14,20C,20E,12G
Steinberg, Michael	RI0050	12A,12B,12C,12D		Walker, Margaret Edith	AG0250	14,12G,13K,20E,12A
Stimeling, Travis D.	IL1750	12,63D,12D,14				
Torres, George	PA1850	12A,12,14,12D,20H		**Music Theory (All Areas)**		
Van Orden, Katherine	CA5000	11,12A,12D,55,67		Aagaard, J. Kjersgaard	WI0842	13,11,36,37,49
Warner, Daniel C.	MA1000	13,10A,10B,12D,34		Aaron, Elizabeth	NY2250	13
Warwick, Jacqueline	AF0100	12A,12D,14C,15,29A		Abbott, Tyler	OR1050	62D,29,13
Watkins, Holly	NY1100	12A,12B,12D,13J,14C		Abbott, Wesley	CA2600	36,61,35B,13
Wheelock, Gretchen A.	NY1100	12A,12B,12C,12D,15		Aberdam, Eliane	RI0300	13,10F,10,12A,45
				Abeyaratne, Harsha D.	OH1650	66,13,13C
Sociomusicology				Abigana, Brett	MA0400	13
Abril, Carlos	FL1900	32,12E		Abril, Mario	TN1700	13,10F,70
Baur, Steven	AF0100	11,12A,12D,12E,14C		Abruzzo, Luke A.	PA1000	70,10A,13,29
Brothers, Thomas	NC0600	12A,12C,12E,29		Accurso, Joseph	NJ0030	13A,13,60,10,35B
Brown, Leonard	MA1450	11,14,64E,29A,12E		Adams, Brant	OK0800	13,10
Cornfoot, James	TN1200	11,12E		Adams, Byron	CA5040	13,10F,10,12
Custodero, Lori A.	NY4200	32A,32B,32G,12E,12C		Adams, Daniel C.	TX3150	10A,13D,13E,65,13
Davies, James	CA5000	11,12A,12E,20A,66A		Adams, Kristine	MA0260	13A,13
Fickett, Martha V.	VA1475	11,12A,12E,66A		Adams, Kurtis B.	WV0550	47,46,13
Finn, Geraldine	AG0100	12E,12C		Adams, Kyle	IN0900	13
Fox, Aaron A.	NY0750	14,20G,12E		Adams, Liselyn	AI0070	13,12A,41,64A,43
Gambetta, Charles	NC2700	11,12E		Adams, Mark	NY0646	13,66
Goehring, Edmund J.	AG0500	12A,12E		Adams, Mary Kay	VA0300	13,12A
Gooley, Dana	RI0050	12A,13B,12E,12D		Adams, Richard	MI2250	10,49,13L,13,10F
Gunderson, Terry	WY0050	65,34,29,13,12E		Adan, Jose	FL0050	70,13,13C,11,29A
Jakelski, Lisa	NY1100	12A,12E,12B,12C,14F		Adashi, Judah E.	MD0650	13,10
Jensen-Moulton, Stephanie	NY0500	11,12,12E		Addamson, Paul	NC1050	66A,66C,66D,13A,13
Jocoy, Stacey	TX3200	12G,12E,12C,31A,11		Adkins, Don	CA0300	13,10F,10,12A,62D
Jones, Patrick Michael	NY4150	32G,60B,32,12A,12E		Adler, Christopher A.	CA5200	10,14,13,10A,20D
Josephson, David	RI0050	12A,12,55B,12E		Agee, Richard J.	CO0200	13,11,12,66H,67D
Kennedy, Matthew	CA4150	12E		Aghababian, Vartan	MA0400	13
Kushner, David Z.	FL1850	12,12A,12B,12E,20G		Ailshie, Tyson	CO0100	11,13,62D,70,29
Lewis, George E.	NY0750	10A,10B,12E,29E,34H		Al-Zand, Karim	TX2150	13,10
Lundquist, Barbara Reeder	WA1050	32,12E		Albert, Thomas	VA1350	13,10,54
Manabe, Noriko	NY0500	14,12E,20		Albrecht, Ronald	IA1350	13A,13,66A,11
Mancuso, Charles	NY3717	20G,29A,12E,14C		Alburger, Mark	CA1560	10,13,38
Marchand, Rebecca G.	MA1175	12A,31A,12E		Albury, Robert T.	AZ0350	13,10
Martin, Margot	CA1750	12A,12B,20,66H,12E		Aldana, Milton	MD0600	63C,13,12A
Marvin, Clara	AG0250	12A,12,12E		Aldins, Peter	MA1175	13
Mezzadri, Danilo	MS0750	64A,12E,48		Aldridge, Robert	NJ1130	13,10
Pasler, Jann C.	CA5050	11,12A,12,12B,12E		Alegant, Brian	OH1700	13
Perlman, Marc	RI0050	14,20D,12E,13J,35D		Alesandrini, Joyce L.	OH1650	13,64D,66A
Perone, James E.	OH2290	11,13,12E,64C		Alexander, Eric	CO0950	13B,13C,10,13
Piekut, Benjamin	NY0900	12A,12D,12E		Alexander, Joe L.	LA0250	10,13,63D,10A,49
Press, Stephen D.	IL1200	12A,12E		Alexander, Kathryn J.	CT0900	13,10,34,43
Puterbaugh, Parke	NC0910	12E		Alhaddad, Frederick I.	MI1200	13,10,66
Randall, Annie Janeiro	PA0350	11,12A,12,12E		Allaire, Jean-Sebastien	AG0100	12,13,36,60A
Root, Deane L.	PA3420	12A,12C,12,20G,12E		Allemeier, John	NC2420	13,10,34
Rowan, Kami	NC0910	70,11,51,12E		Allen, Stephen Arthur	NJ1000	13,11,12A,12,20
Russell, Ralph Anthony	NJ0175	13,29A,12E		Allman, Garrett N.	IL1100	13,66C,38,66A,60B
Savage, Roger W. H.	CA5031	12B,12E		Allsup, Randall Everett	NY4200	43,32,13,12A,12B
Schroeder, David	AF0100	13,12A,12,12E,12C		Almen, Byron Paul	TX3510	13,13H
Shepherd, John	AG0100	12B,35B,12E,12C		Alpern, Wayne	NY2250	13
Trottier, Danick	AI0200	12E		Alverson, J. Michael	SC0300	13,37,60
Watson, Nessim	MA1850	12E		Alves, Julio	WV0400	70,13
Wilbourne, Emily	NY0642	12A,12E		Amalong, Philip	OH0680	66A,66C,13,11,42
Wilson, James Dale	CT0100	14,20C,12A,12E,29B		Amano, Gary	UT0300	13,66A,66B,66C
				Amlin, Martin	MA0400	13,10
Psychomusicology				Amorim, George J.	TX3525	62D,13,51
Abeles, Harold F.	NY4200	32,13K,13L,12F		Amrozowicz, Mary Barbara	NY4460	13A,13,66A,13C,13B
Asmus, Edward P.	FL1900	32,12F		Amundson, Steven	MN1450	13,60B,38,10A
Balzano, Gerald	CA5050	13A,34,13L,12F,12		Anderman, Mark	CA4460	13,34,10,70,13A
Beckwith, Sterling	AG0650	12,36,61,12F		Anderson, Carl H. C.	AL0500	13,48,64A,64C
Blair, Deborah V.	MI1750	32B,32C,12B,12F,32D		Anderson, Cheryl M.	CA0400	13,36,39
Blombach, Ann K.	OH1850	13A,13,34,12F,12		Anderson, Cynthia	WV0750	13,48,64B
Bowman, Wayne	NY2750	32,12C,12F,14		Anderson, Dennis	CA3200	13
Bridges, David	TN0100	12F,31A		Anderson, Dianna M.	ND0250	13,66
Burtner, Matthew	VA1550	10,34,35C,12F		Anderson, Douglas K.	NY0270	13,10F,60,10,38
Carlsen, James	WA1050	34,12B,12F,12,12C		Anderson, Elaine M.	OH2290	62C,13,38,41,42
Chittum, Donald	PA3330	13,12A,12,14,12F		Anderson, Erik	ND0250	62D,62C,13,51,29
Clearfield, Andrea	PA3330	66C,66D,10,12F		Anderson, Gene	VA1500	13,11

Name	Code	Areas
Anderson, Jared L.	WI0600	36,61,66A,13,12A
Anderson, John	CA3050	13,11,37,64A
Anderson, Jonathan	TX3600	13,47,64E
Anderson, Jonathan	MI2200	10,13
Anderson-Himmelspach, Neil	MD0475	10A,13,14C,34,62D
Andrade, Juan Pablo	TX3515	13,66B,66C
Andreacchi, Peter	NY2150	13
Andres, Hoyt	CO0550	13,10
Andrews, Dwight D.	GA0750	13,14,31A,29
Andrews, Rick	SD0050	66A,66B,13
Anhalt, Istvan	AG0250	13,10
Anson-Cartwright, Mark	NY0600	13
Anson-Cartwright, Mark	NY0642	13
Anthony, Carl	AR0850	13,66A
Antonacos, Anastasia	PA1600	66A,13,11,66C,66D
Antonelli, Amy	DC0050	13
Antonellis, Evan	OH1900	13
Apple, Ryan	MI0910	13,12,70,11
Applebaum, Mark S.	CA4900	13,10,20G
Aquilanti, Giancarlo	CA4900	13,10F,60,37,49
Aquina, Carmen	NY0400	13
Aquino, Robert	NY2102	13A,13,10,66A,66B
Arauco, Ingrid	PA1500	13A,13,10
Araujo, Ramon	PR0125	13,10,37,64C
Archambault, Ellen J.	OH1850	13
Archer, Kimberly K.	IL2910	10,13,32E,10A,10F
Archer, Naida	AJ0150	13A,13,66A,66D
Argento, Dominick J.	MN1623	13,10F,10,12A
Argersinger, Charles	WA1150	13,10,66A
Arksey, Meredith	WA1150	13,62A,62B
Armfield, Terri E.	NC2600	64B,13
Armstrong, Alan	NC1500	12A,14B,13,62C,66A
Armstrong, John	AG0400	13,10F,10
Armstrong, Kathy	AG0100	13,20A
Arndt, Matthew J.	IA1550	13
Arnold, Larry	NC2435	10,29A,13,34A,62D
Arrell, Christopher A.	MA0700	10,13,34A,34D
Arrivee, David	CA0600	38,13,41,13A,13C
Arvin, Tammy J.	IL1090	13,64C
Asch, Arthur	WI0862	13,12A,37,48
Ashley, Richard	IL2250	13,10,29
Asia, Daniel I.	AZ0500	13,10,43
Asplund, Christian	UT0050	10A,10B,13,34
Atkinson, Sean E.	TX3500	11,12A,13
Atlas, Allan	NY0500	13,12A,12
Atlas, Raphael	MA1750	13A,13,13F,13D
Ator, James	IN0905	13,10,48,64E,29
Atwell, Bruce W.	WI0830	63B,13,11
Au, Hiu-Wah	NC0050	13
Auerbach, Brent	MA2000	13
Aultman, Gerald	TX2600	13A,13,66A,66G
Auner, Edith	MA1900	13A,13,42
Austin, Kenneth L.	IL3100	13,32C,37,49,46
Austin, Kevin	AI0070	13,10F,10,34,35C
Austin, Michael	MO0850	34,35C,13,35,10
Averitt, William E.	VA1350	13,10
Ayers, Jesse M.	OH1350	13,10,13C
Ayesh, Kevin	NC0220	13,11,12A,66A,66D
Aylward, John J.	MA0650	10A,10B,13
Babbitt, Milton	NJ0900	13,10
Babcock, Andrew	TX1550	60B,63D,37,13,47
Babcock, Mark A.	IA0200	36,40,66,13
Babcock, Ronald	OR0850	13,32E
Baber, Joseph W.	KY1450	13,10
Backlin, William	IA1170	13,66
Bacon, Boyd	NE0450	13,36,61,40
Badgerow, Justin A.	PA1250	66A,66C,66D,13
Bahn, Curtis	NY3300	43,13,10,12,45
Bahr, Jason	FL0680	10,13,31A,13C,13B
Bailey, Kathryn	AG0500	13
Bailey, Mark	TN0850	13,32E,32C,37
Bailey, Robert	NY2740	13,12
BaileyShea, Matthew L.	NY4350	13,13E
Bain, Jennifer	AF0100	13E,13F,13B,13J,13
Bain, Reginald	SC1110	13,10,34,45
Baker, James	RI0050	13,13J,41
Baker, Kent	VT0100	66A,66D,46,13,10F
Baker, Meredith E.	NY2550	13,66G,36
Baker, Michael	KY1450	13,13C,13E,13G,13I
Baker, Nathan A.	WY0050	13,11
Baker, Steve	CA2100	66A,13,29
Baker, William	IN0005	12,13,60,36,39
Bakos, Daniel F.	GA2130	13,47,29
Balada, Leonardo	PA0550	13,10
Balagurchik, James	NM0450	13
Baldini, Christian	CA5010	38,10,13,39
Baldwin, John	ID0050	13,50,65
Balentine, James S.	TX3530	13,10,47,29A
Bales, Kenton W.	NE0610	13,10,43,34
Baley, Virko	NV0050	10,13
Ball, Leonard V.	GA2100	13,10,45,34
Ballatori, Cristina	TX3515	64A,11,42,13
Balter, Marcos	IL0720	10,13
Balthazar, Scott Leslie	PA3600	13,12A
Bamberger, Jeanne	MA1200	13H,13K,13G,32F,13
Bancks, Jacob	IL0100	10,10F,43,13,12A
Bangle, Jerry	NC2640	13,11,38,53,29
Barber, Gail G.	TX3200	13,62E
Barber, June	CA0300	13A,13,61
Barduhn, David	OR0550	13,10,47,29
Barland, Charles J.	IA1450	13,11,31A,66A,36
Barlar, Rebecca	FL0670	13,66A,66B,66C
Barlow, Carla	NM0450	13,10,34
Barnes, Arthur P.	CA4900	13,10F,37
Barnes, Larry J.	KY1350	13,10,29A,34,14C
Barnett, Thomas	WI0845	63A,37,13
Barolsky, Daniel G.	WI0100	13,12
Barr, John	VA0100	13,10,66,31A
Barr, Stephen A.	PA3100	13,36,40,34
Barrett, Roland	OK1350	13
Barrow, Lee G.	GA1500	13,60,34
Barta, Daniel	NY3350	10,13,10A,10F
Barth, George	CA4900	13,66A,67C
Bartholomew, Douglas	MT0200	13
Bartle, Barton	NJ1350	13,34
Bartlette, Christopher A.	TX0300	13
Bartus Broberg, Kirsten A.	MN1625	13,10
Bashaw, Howard	AA0100	10,13
Bashwiner, David M.	NM0450	13,10
Basinger, Rhonda	IL1245	13,11,66
Basler, Paul	FL1850	13,63B,34
Bass, Eddie C.	NC2430	13,10
Bass, Richard	CT0600	13
Bates, Elaine	OK1250	32B,66A,13
Bates, Ian	WI0350	13
Bates, Michael J.	AR0810	36,13,60,12A,66A
Bates, Pamela	IL0900	12A,13,66A,66C,66D
Batzner, Jay C.	MI0400	13,10,34,10A,13F
Bauer, Amy M.	CA5020	13,13F,12D
Bauer, Glen	MO1950	13,12,12A
Bauer, Ross	CA5010	13,10,43,29
Bauer, William R.	NY0644	10F,12A,12C,13
Bauman, Carol	AG0600	13,65
Baur, John	TN1680	13,10
Baxter, Marsha	NY4200	12A,13
Bayer, Joshua	DC0010	29,20,13,62D,70
Bazayev, Inessa	LA0200	13
Beach, Sue Odem	IA0420	64,13,11
Beall, John	WV0750	13,10F,10,43
Beaman, M. Teresa	CA0810	13A,13,48,64A,34
Bean, Robert G.	AL1450	13,37,47,63,29
Beard, Christine E.	NE0610	64A,48,11,13
Beard, R. Daniel	MS0750	13
Beaudoin, Paul	RI0200	10,13,12A,11
Beaudoin, Richard A.	MA1050	13,12D,10
Beavers, Jennifer	TX3530	13
Bebe, David M.	NY0700	38,13,42,62C
Beck, Lynn	NC0750	13,63B
Becker, Juanita	WI1155	66A,13,66B,66C,66D
Becker, Thomas R.	KS0050	70,13
Beckett, Christine	AI0070	13,12C,32C,38,62A
Beckett, Scott	TX0100	11,12,13,37,63
Beckford, Richard	LA0700	11,36,66G,13
Beckford, Richard E.	SC1050	13,60,11,36,66G
Beckwith, Hubert	VA0450	13A,13,12
Becos, Pelarin	IL3310	10,13,13C
Bedrossian, Franck	CA5000	10,13
Beebe, Jon P.	NC0050	13,48,64D,32E,42
Beert, Michael	IL2560	11,12A,13,38,20
Behrens, Jack	AG0500	13,10,20G
Behrens, Lisa	NY1600	13,11
Beken, Munir N.	CA5031	13,10
Bela, Marcin	TN0100	13
Belden, George R.	AK0100	13,12,10,34
Belkin, Alan	AI0200	13,10A
Bell, Allan	AA0150	13,10,20G,10F
Bell, Dennis	NY2400	13A,13,10F
Bell, Malcolm E.	AA0080	10,13,47,65
Bell, Peter J.	MA2030	10,13,31A,34
Bell, Richard	GA0500	32E,13,38,60B,62D
Bell, Vicki	KY0100	13,10,36
Bellor, Jennifer K.	NY2650	13
Ben-Amots, Ofer	CO0200	13,10F,10,11,34
Benadon, Fernando Raul	DC0010	13,34,10
Bender, Rhett	OR0950	64E,13,52,64C
Benitez, Vincent P.	PA2750	13F,13D,13B,13J,13
Benjamin, Thomas	MD0650	13
Benjamin, William E.	AB0100	13,10
Bennett, Barbara A.	CA5040	13B,13,11,45,34
Bennett, Bruce Christian	CA4200	10,13,34,10A,10B
Bennighof, James	TX0300	13
Benoist, Debbie	TX0075	13
Benoit, John	IA1350	13,11,63C,10F,55
Benshoof, Kenneth W.	WA1050	13,10,54
Benson, John Halvor	WI0350	13,10
Benson, Mark	PA0400	13,10,12,63,34
Benson, Mark F.	AL0210	13,12A,11,65,20
Benson, Will	TN0300	11,13,34B,36,64
Benya, Susan	IA1140	37,13,11
Berard, Jesus Manuel	DC0010	38,60,13,11
Berardinelli, Paula	NY2450	29A,13,66A
Berg, Chris	OH0500	13,10,62D
Berg, Reinhard	AA0020	13,10,12A,66A,66G
Berger, Jonathan	CA4900	13,10,45,34
Berger, Talya	CA4900	13,13A,13B,13C
Bergeron, Tom	OR1250	13,64,47,35A
Bergin, Wendy I.	TX2100	64A,48,13
Bergman, Rachel	VA0450	13
Berkhout, Bjorn	NY3250	10,62C,12A,13,14C
Berna, Linda	IL0550	13,12
Bernard, Gilles	NJ0825	13,12A,49,63C,63D
Bernard, Jonathan	WA1050	13
Bernard-Stevens, Sarah	KS0700	37,38,13,64D
Bernatis, William	NV0050	13A,13,49,63B
Berners, John	IN1650	10,13
Bernstein, David	CA2950	13,12A,13J
Bernthal, John P.	IN1750	13,66G
Berrett, Joshua	NY2400	13,11,29A,12,12B
Berry, David Carson	OH2200	13,13I,13D,13J
Berry, James	WV0440	11,12,13,33,61
Berry, Michael	TX3200	13
Berry, S. David	SC0650	10,13,34,35,12
Berry, Whitney	ND0500	13
Bertrand, Lynn Wood	GA0750	13,11,12A,12
Bessinger, David K.	OK1250	13,50,65
Betancourt, Nilda	PR0100	13,66A,66C,12A
Beteta, Xavier	CA4100	13
Bethea, Kay	VA1030	13,11,12A,66A,66D
Bethea, Stephanie	WA0900	13,10,64A
Betts, James E.	IL1800	13,20,29A,63,34
Betts, Steven	OK1200	66A,66B,66D,13,11
Beyer, Loretta	MI0200	13,66A,32B,11
Biamonte, Nicole	AI0150	13
Bianchi, Douglas	MI2200	37,13,60B
Bielawa, Herbert	CA4200	13A,13,10F,10,45
Bielish, Aaron J.	TX2295	62A,62B,41,11,13
Bierman, Benjamin	NY0630	63A,10,13,34,35
Biggs, William Hayes	NY2150	13
Billings, Carolyn A.	NC0850	13,12,66A,66B
Billingsley, Michael	NJ0060	13,12A
Bilous, Edward	NY1900	13
Binckes, Fred B.	MT0350	13,10,11,66G
Binford, Hilde M.	PA2450	13A,13,12A,12
Birch, Sebastian A.	OH1100	13,10,34,13B,13A
Biringer, Gene D.	WI0350	13,10
Birk, Richard	TX0350	13,11,37,47,63
Biscardi, Chester	NY3560	13,10F,10,11,12A
Biscay, Karen T.	OH1330	13,11,12A,36,61
Bishop, Bruce W.	AZ0300	34,36,61,13,60A
Bitensky, Laurence S.	KY0450	13,10
Black, Donald	VA1350	13,60
Black, Les	NY1800	13
Blackburn, Bradford	FL2050	13,11
Blackie, Ruth	AF0120	64C,13
Blackshear, Alan	AL0831	37,13,11,29
Blais, Jerome	AF0100	10,13
Blake, C. Marc	CA2600	13,11,34,45,35B
Blake, Daniel	NY0500	11,13
Blanchard, Gerald J.	MI1160	13,36,13,60A,61
Bland, Leland	OH2500	13,34
Blankenbaker, Scott E.	MN1290	11,13,61,36
Blasco, Scott	WA1150	10A,10B
Blasius, Leslie	WI0815	13
Blench, Karl E.	TX1000	13
Blersch, Jeffrey	NE0150	13,36,66G
Blessinger, Martin	TX3000	10,13

Index by Area of Teaching Interest

Name	Code	Areas
Blink, David	WA1400	47,13,63A,29
Bloch, Robert S.	CA5010	13,11,41,62A,62B
Block, Steven	NM0450	13A,13,10F
Blombach, Ann K.	OH1850	13A,13,34,12F,12
Blomquist, Jane K.	CA2600	36,61,13
Bloomquist, Paul	IA0790	11,63,60B,13,37
Blumberg, Stephen F.	CA0840	13,10
Blume, Philipp G.	IL3300	13,10,10A,10F
Blumsack, Michelle	TX3000	13
Blyth, Jennifer	PA0950	66A,66B,66C,66D,13
Bobbitt, Kayleen	MI0750	11,66,13,40
Bocanegra, Cheryl	OK0850	13,66A,35D,47
Boden-Luethi, Ruth	WA1150	62C,62D,13,51,42
Bodine, Gerald B.	IN1300	13
Boehm, Norman	AR0350	13,10,12A,66A,11
Boepple, Hans C.	CA4425	13,12A,66A,66B,66C
Boge, Claire L.	OH1450	13
Bognar, Joseph A.	IN1750	66A,13,66H,66G
Bohn, James	RI0200	13
Bolduan, Kathleen	MO1900	13A,13
Bonacci, Andrew	MA2100	10,13,10A,10F
Bondari, Brian	TX3350	10,13,34,10A,10B
Book, A. Ryan	NC2210	70,12A,13,41
Booker, Charles L.	AR0730	10,32E,13,60B
Boon, Rolf J.	AA0200	13,34,10,35
Boone, Benjamin V.	CA0810	13,10,29
Boone, Christine	IN0800	13
Boos, Kenneth G.	FL1310	13,60,36,41,61
Booth, Todd	AG0130	10A,10D,10F,11,13
Bor, Mustafa	AA0100	13
Borah, Bernard	IL0800	13,64D
Borchert, Laroy	NM0310	13,32,64C
Borg, Paul	IL1150	13A,13,11,12A,12
Borgerding, Todd Michael	ME0250	13,12A,55B
Boring, Daniel	PA2550	13,38,70
Bortolussi, Paolo	AB0060	64A,48,13
Borwick, Susan Harden	NC2500	13,12,31,10,15
Boss, Jack	OR1050	13,10A
Boswell, Ronald L.	AR0750	13,11,29A
Botelho, Mauro	NC0550	13,11,20H
Bottge, Karen	KY1450	13
Boubel, Karen A.	MN1000	13,10,34,13C,10A
Boucher, Leslie H.	GA0700	12,20,13,62,11
Bougie, Marc-Andre	TX2850	11,10,13,36
Boullion, Linda	NE0460	13,11,40,36,61
Boumpani, Neil M.	GA1070	13,37
Bourassa, Richard N.	OR0450	13,10F,10A,11
Bourland, Roger	CA5030	13,10
Boury, Robert	AR0750	13,10,11
Bowen, K. Scott	CA4300	13,36
Bowen, Meredith Y.	MI1200	36,20,13
Bowen, Nathan	CA3100	13,11,10,34
Bowen, Robert E.	CA3200	13,10A,29A,34
Bowers, Greg J.	VA0250	13,10,10A
Bowker, Barbara E.	IL1085	13,11,13B,13C,12A
Bowlby, Timothy	IL1520	13,10
Boyce, Douglas J.	DC0100	13,10
Boyd, Jesse	LA0080	11,13,29,62,70
Boyd, Michael	PA0600	10A,10B,13,12
Boykan, Martin	MA0500	13,10,12A,10A,13A
Boyle, Benjamin C. S.	NJ1350	10,64A,13
Brabant, John-Paul	NY3780	10,10B,10C,13
Bracey, Judson F.	WV0050	13,10
Brackeen, William	OK0450	66A,66D,10A,13
Brackett, John	NC2410	13,14C
Bradbury, William	CA0847	13,10,11,34,20G
Bradfield, David	CA0805	13,34,66A
Bradshaw, Curt	TX0700	13,29
Bradshaw, Dean	AF0120	13,66A
Bradshaw, Keith M.	UT0200	10A,10F,13,36
Bradshaw, Murray C.	CA5032	13,11,12A,13J
Brakel, Timothy D.	OH2300	32E,32,64E,13,60
Brammeier, Meredith	CA0600	13,11
Brancaleone, Francis P.	NY2200	13,66A,66D,66G,66C
Brandes, David E.	NH0110	13,10F,60,36,66G
Brandes, Lambert	MA0800	13,66G,13L
Brandt, Anthony K.	TX2150	13,10
Brandt, Lynne	TX2310	13,64A,41,66A
Brasky, Jill T.	FL2000	13,13B,13C,62A
Bratt, Wallis	ID0050	13,10
Braun, William	WI1155	13,10,12,55B,34
Braunlich, Helmut	DC0050	13
Braunschweig, Karl	MI2200	13
Brazelton, Kitty	VT0050	13,10F,10,11,53
Breedon, Daniel	MN0600	13,10,12A,14
Breland, Barron	NE0160	13,36
Brellochs, Christopher	NY1050	47,10,13,12,64E
Bremer, Carolyn	CA0825	13,10
Bresnen, Steven M.	PA0400	13,11,12A,66A,66D
Brewer, Paul	AZ0490	11,13,29,32E,47
Bribitzer-Stull, Matthew	MN1623	13
Brickman, Scott T.	ME0420	14C,13,32B,10B,66D
Briggs, Amy	IL3250	41,13
Briggs, Margery S.	CA3650	13,61
Brings, Allen	NY0642	13,11
Brink, Daniel	CO0200	13A,13,10F,11,66A
Bristol, Doug S.	AL0050	13,29,63C,47
Britt, Carol	LA0450	13,11,12A,66D
Britton, Jason	IA0950	13,12A,70,13I
Broad-Ginsberg, Elaine	NH0150	13,31B,10A,36
Broderick, James	FL1300	13,63A,53,34
Brody, Martin	MA2050	13,10,12A
Broening, Benjamin	VA1500	10,34,13,35C,35D
Broman, Per F.	OH0300	3F,13C,13E,12B,13
Brooke, Nicholas	VT0050	13,10,20,34
Brooks, BJ	TX3750	13,10A
Brooks, Jonathan E.	IN0100	13,10A
Brooks, Melinda K.	AL0850	11,13,66A,66D
Brooks, Susan G.	MA0950	13,39,61
Brooks-Lyle, Alma B.	AL0050	13,64A,12B,12A
Brosius, Amy T.	NJ1000	11,12,13,20,12A
Brostoff, Neal	CA2700	11,13
Brothers, Grey	CA5550	13,36,61,11,12A
Brown, Carlene J.	WA0800	12A,13,33
Brown, Chris	CA2950	10B,10A,20,13,14
Brown, Christine A.	IN1010	11,66A,13,66B
Brown, Ellen	AZ0470	66,13
Brown, J. Bruce	MI2000	13,10,11,34,51
Brown, L. Joel	IA0900	13,12A,14,66,11
Brown, Leslie Ellen	WI0700	12A,13
Brown, Ray	CA0400	13,29
Brown, Stephen C.	AZ0450	13
Brown, Uzee	GA1450	13,10,61,11
Browning, Zack D.	IL3300	13,10,43
Brownlow, Robert J.	OH2150	13,10
Brubacher, Scott	AG0500	13
Brubeck, Dave W.	FL1300	13,37,47,63C,49
Bruck, Douglas	CA4050	13A,13,66A,60
Brudvig, Robert	OR0700	65,13
Bruk, Elfrida	IN0005	66A,13,31B,66C,66H
Brumbeloe, Joseph	MS0750	13
Brunelli, Stephanie	KS0150	66A,12A,13,13B
Brunk, Jeremy	IL1750	13,12,65,10
Brunner, Roy	MA0950	13,10,66G,66H,31A
Bruns, Steven	CO0800	13
Brust, Paul W.	MA1175	10,13,43
Bruya, Chris	WA0050	46,47,29,13
Bryant, Thomas E.	TN1200	13,11,66A,66C,66H
Bryden, Kristy	IA0850	13,10A,10F,34A,34H
Buchanan, Douglas	MD0850	13
Buchler, Michael	FL0850	13
Buck, Stephen M.	NY3785	13
Buckland, James P.	SC1000	70,13
Buczynski, Walter	AG0450	13,10F,10,66A
Budde, Paul J.	MN1625	13
Buehrer, Theodore E.	OH1200	13,10,29,63A,34
Buelow, William L.	OH1400	13A,13,10,66A,29
Bugbee, Fred	NM0310	65,13
Buhaiciuc, Mihaela	AL1195	39,13,61
Buhler, James	TX3510	13
Bukvich, Daniel J.	ID0250	13,10,47,50,65
Bulow, Harry T.	IN1300	10,13,34,13A
Bump, Delbert	CA4650	13A,13,36,53
Bunk, Louis	NH0110	34,10,11,13,43
Burchard, Marcia Earle	CA1650	66A,13
Burchard, Richard	KY0250	10,13,20,34,35
Burdick, David H.	IL1750	10,13,34,70,35
Burdick, Paul	MA1400	13G,13,34,32
Burge, John	AG0250	13,10,10F,13I
Burke, Kevin R.	IN0500	12,13,20,42,63B
Burke, Patrick	PA1050	13,10,34
Burkett, John	TX2955	13,66A,66G,34,12C
Burkhardt, Rebecca L.	IA1600	13,38,60
Burkhart, Charles L.	NY0642	13A,13,66A
Burleson, Geoffrey	NY0625	66A,13,12A,66,42
Burnaman, Stephen	TX1150	13,66A,66G,66B,66C
Burnett, Marty Wheeler	NE0100	12A,13,66A,36,66G
Burnette, Sonny	KY0610	13,47,64E,34
Burnham, Scott	NJ0900	13,12A
Burns, Christopher	WI0825	10,13,34,43,45
Burns, Lori	AG0400	13,14C
Burns, Patrick J.	NJ0800	13A,13,10
Burnside, Joanna	MS0420	13,12A,66
Burroughs, D. Robert	WA0150	13,11,62A,53,38
Burstein, L. Poundie	NY0600	13
Burstein, L. Poundie	NY0625	13A,13
Burstein, Poundie	NY2250	13
Burton, Deborah	MA0400	13
Burton, Heidi R.	OK1300	13A,13,11,66A,62A
Bussiere, Michael	AG0100	13A,13,45,34
Bustamante, Tamara A.	KY1100	36,11,13,66C,66A
Butler, David	OH1850	13K,13C,13
Butler, Gregory G.	AB0100	13,10,12A,12
Butler, Mark J.	IL2250	13
Butler, Steve	CA5550	10,13,34,10A,13E
Butterfield, Christopher	AB0150	13,10,43
Butterfield, Matthew W.	PA1300	29,13,13B,29A,29B
Buys, Douglas	MA1400	13
Byerly, Douglas	MD0060	13,36,39
Byington, Jensina	WA0860	13,66A,66D
Byrd, Richard W.	KY0550	13,63A
Byrne, David	AC0100	13,12A
Byros, Vasili	IL2250	13
Cabaniss, Thomas	NY1900	13
Cacioppo, Curt	PA1500	13,10,20G,10F,66A
Cademcian, Gerard	IN0005	66A,31A,31B,67F,13
Cadieux, Marie-Aline	PA1750	13,11,51,62C,42
Cadwallader, Allen	OH1700	13
Cahn, Steven J.	OH2200	13
Cailliet, Claude	WI0800	11,13,63,37,47
Cairns, Zachary	MO1830	13
Caldwell, Gary	UT0150	13,60,37,63A
Caldwell, Glenn G.	MD0520	13,29B
Caldwell, James M.	IL3500	13,10,45
Callaghan, Marjorie S.	CT0800	12A,13,63B
Callahan, Michael R.	MI1400	13
Camacho, Loida	PA2400	13,10,11
Camacho-Zavaleta, Martin	AL0050	66,13
Cameron, Jennifer	OR1150	13,10F,64,60,51
Camp, Philip	TX1550	36,61,13,32,40
Campbell, Arthur	MN1450	10,13
Campbell, Arthur J.	MI0900	64C,64E,13
Campbell, Brian G.	MN0350	13,10A,20,12B,10F
Campbell, Don	SC1080	13,60,36,61,12A
Campbell, Helen E.	AL0310	13A,13,36,61,66
Campbell, William G.	IA1300	10,13,20,34
Campi-Walters, Lisa	CO0350	13,12A,66,10A
Campion, Edmund	CA5000	20,13,34,35G
Caniato, Michele	MA0930	10,38,29,13,47
Cantwell, Richard E.	KS1300	13,60,10A,37,38
Cantwell, Terry	GA1260	13A,13,70,51
Caplin, William	AI0150	13
Capuzzo, Guy	NC2430	13
Carastathis, Aris	AG0170	13,10,43
Carbon, John J.	PA1300	13A,13,10F,10
Cardillo, Kenneth	TN0260	70,13,11,12B
Carey, Christian B.	NJ1350	13
Carey, Norman	NY0600	13,42
Carillo, Dan	NY0550	47,13,46,10,29
Carl, Robert B.	CT0650	13,10,45
Carlisle, Kris	GA0300	11,66A,13
Carlsen, Philip	ME0410	13,10,29A,38,34
Carlson, Angela	OR0700	13
Carlson, Mark	MD0610	63,11,12,13,37
Carlson, Mark	CA5030	10,13
Carlson, Mark	CA4450	13,10
Carlton, Kathleen	OK0410	13,11,12A,61,31A
Carney, Horace R.	AL0010	13,60,10,36
Caron, Jocelyn	AI0200	13,31A,12
Carpenter, Ellon D.	AZ0100	13,13J
Carpenter, Tina	TX3750	64D,13,11,34C
Carr, Maureen A.	PA2750	13
Carr-Richardson, Amy	NC0650	13
Carrabre, T. Patrick	AC0050	13,10,43,20G,35
Carrell, Cynthia T.	AR0250	11,13,32E,37,63A
Carrell, Scott	AR0250	10A,13,34A,66A,66B
Carrillo, Carlos R.	PR0115	13
Carroll, Gregory D.	NC2430	13,10,11
Carroll, Kevin	GA1600	10,64,60B,11,13
Carroll, Roy W.	IA0940	66,13,12,11,31A
Carruthers, Ian	AA0050	10,13
Carson, Virginia	VA1800	13,10,66A
Carter, Allen L.	MN1120	13,10F,65,47
Carter, Chandler	NY1600	13,10
Carter, Roland M.	TN1700	13,11,36,66A
Carter, Stewart	NC2500	13,11,12A,55,67

Name	Code	Areas
Carter, Timothy	NC2410	12,13
Casal, David Plans	NH0100	10B,10F,34,13,35
Case, Del W.	CA3400	66G,44,13,12A,36
Casey, Lisa R.	MO0775	13,63B
Casey, Michael	NH0100	10B,10F,34,13,35
Casey, Rebecca L.	OH1800	66A,13,66D,66C
Casinghino, Justin	MA0400	13,10
Cass, Patrick	MS0320	13,11,47,64,70
Cassara, Charles	MA0260	13A,13
Castiglione, Anita	FL1450	66C,13
Castro, David R.	MN1450	13
Catan, Daniel	CA1265	13A,13,10,11,12A
Cathey, Tully J.	UT0250	13,70
Cavanaugh, Jennifer Gookin	MT0400	64B,64D,13
Cavera, Chris S.	OH2140	34,35,13,70,10
Celona, John	AB0150	13,10,43
Celotto, Albert Gerard	CT0700	13,12,66A
Centeno Martell, Ingrid	PR0100	13,66A,66C,32
Century, Michael	NY3300	12,13,43,34H,66A
Cepeda, Manny	CA2100	20H,13
Cerqua, Joe	IL0720	13,13C
Cha, Jee-Weon	IA0700	13,12B
Chabora, Robert J.	MN0600	66A,66B,66D,11,13
Chamberlain, Donald J.	IA0400	13,10F,10,11,47
Chamberlin, Robert	MO1950	13,10F,10,45
Chan, Sarah S.	OK0600	66A,66C,66D,13,11
Chan, See Tsai	IL0350	66A,66G,13
Chandler, B. Glenn	TX3510	13
Chang, Joanne	NY3250	11,13,32,42,66
Chang, Melody Jun Yao	CO0100	35,66A,13
Chang, Phillip	CO0800	13
Chapman, Dale E.	ME0150	12,13,29
Chapman, Joe C.	GA1500	13,66A,10
Chapman, Norman	MS0600	13A,13,12A,66A
Chappell, Jeffrey	DC0170	13,29,66A
Charke, Derek	AF0050	13D,13E,10,13
Chasalow, Eric	MA0500	13,10A,10B,11,29A
Chase, Corinne Sloan	MA0260	13A,13
Chase, David A.	CA3460	13A,13,12A,36,60
Chase, Robert	NY2400	13,12A,66H
Chatman, Stephen G.	AB0100	13,10,43
Chattah, Juan	FL1900	13,10B,10C
Chave, George B.	TX3500	13,10
Check, John D.	MO1790	13
Cheek, John	NC1100	13,11,66A,20G
Chellouf, Linda	PR0100	70,13
Chen, Donald	IL0550	60B,13
Chen, Shih-Hui	TX2150	13,10
Chenette, Jonathan Lee	NY4450	10,13,34,10A,10B
Chenette, Timothy	MA2000	13
Chenevert, James	TX3300	10,13
Cheng, James	OK0750	13
Cheng, Marietta	NY0650	13,60,11,36,38
Chenoweth, Gerald	NJ1130	13,10
Cherlin, Michael	MN1623	13,13J
Cherney, Brian	AI0150	13,10,12A
Chesman, Jeremy A.	MO0775	13,66G,69
Chi, Jacob	CO0275	13,38,60B
Chiao, Faye	MD0850	13
Chihara, Paul	CA5030	10,13
Chikinda, Michael	UT0250	13
Child, Peter	MA1200	13,10
Childress Orchard, Nan	NJ0050	66,13,54
Childs, Adrian P.	GA2100	10,13,43
Childs, David T.	MN0600	13,12A
Chin, Pablo	IL2650	10A,13
Chinn, Genevieve	NY2105	13,11,12A,12
Chittum, Donald	PA3330	13,12A,12,14,12F
Cho, Gene	TX3420	13,20D
Cho, Peter	LA0080	13,34,35,47,66A
Chobaz, Raymond	FL1850	13,60,38
Choe, EJ	IN0907	13,11,32A,32B,66
Choi, Hye-Jean	TX0900	66A,66G,66H,67C,13
Choi, Kyong Mee	IL0550	10,13,66G
Chou, Godwin	IL2775	10A,13,66A,66,10
Chou, Sarana	AL0800	13,10,34
Chrisman, Richard	NJ1130	13,10F,13J
Christensen, Carl J.	CA2150	13,38,37,34G,13A
Christensen, Thomas	IL3250	13,13J,12D
Christofferson, Carol	AZ0480	64C,13
Christopher, Paul	LA0550	10,13,51,62C,62D
Christopher, Un Chong	MO0060	11,12A,13,66A,66C
Christy, William P.	OH1910	13,12A,20G,29A,34
Chu, George	MN0800	13,36,61
Chuaqui, Miguel Basim	UT0250	13,10
Chung, Hyunjung Rachel	GA1900	66A,13,66C
Chung, Mia	MA0950	13,66A,66B
Chung, Suna	NY3560	13A,13,39,61,13C
Ciabattari, William S.	PA2100	13,63D,32,37,47
Ciach, Brian	KY0950	10,13
Ciamaga, Gustav	AG0450	13,10,45,34
Cinnamon, Howard	NY1600	13
Cipiti, John	OH2140	13,66A,10,14C
Cipullo, Tom	NY0280	13A,13,10,36,61
Claar, Elizabeth	MI1050	13
Clampitt, David	OH1850	13
Clark, James W.	SC0050	13,66A,66D,66B
Clark, John	CT0100	11,13,29
Clark, John W.	CA4410	13,11,12A,10D
Clark, Mark	KS1250	36,32D,13,40
Clark, Michael	FL1570	13,12A,36,66,54
Clark, Suzannah	MA1050	13,12D
Clark, Suzanne M.	MA0260	13A,13
Clark, Thomas S.	TX3175	10,13,10B
Clark, William F.	CO0830	47,63D,13,49,29
Clarke, Garry E.	MD1100	13,10F,10,12A
Claybrook, Doug	TX0300	13
Cleland, Kent D.	OH0200	13,35E,34A
Clemente, Peter	MA0200	11,13A,13,70,20
Clements, Peter J.	AG0500	13,10,45
Clemmons, Bill	CA3640	13,34,10F
Clemons, Gregory G.	IL1085	37,63A,41,13
Clendinning, Jane Piper	FL0850	13
Clenman, David	AB0150	13,12A,13A,13B,13C
Cleveland, Lisa A.	NH0310	13,11,29A,66
Clewell, Christine M.	PA1600	66A,66G,66D,13
Clifft, Al	CA0250	36,60,13
Clifft, Al	CA0450	13,36,37
Clifton, Jeremy J.	OK1050	35C,10,13,13K,13B
Clifton, Kevin	TX2250	13
Coan, Darryl	IL2910	13,32,62E,67
Cobb, Gary W.	CA3600	13,10,12,66G,66B
Coburn, Robert	CA5350	13,10,45
Cockrell, Findlay	NY3700	13A,13,11,66A
Code, David Loberg	MI2250	13
Cody, Thomas	PA2750	13
Coelho, Benjamin A.	IA1550	64D,13
Cogan, Robert	MA1400	13,10
Cogdell, Jerry	MS0320	13,11,50,63,54
Coghlan, Michael	AG0650	13,10,29,34,43
Cohen, Allen L.	NJ0400	13,10,54,39,36
Cohen, David	AI0150	13
Cohen, David E.	NY0750	13,12A,13J
Cohen, Douglas H.	NY0500	13,10,11,34
Cohen, Flynn	NH0150	13,12
Cohen, Fred S.	GA0550	10,13
Cohen, Gerald	NY1860	13A,13,10
Cohn, Richard L.	CT0900	13
Coker, Timothy C.	MS0385	13,60,32,36,66A
Cole, Arlene	RI0050	13A,13,66A
Cole, Darlyn	NC1950	61,66D,60A,11,13
Coleman, Ian D.	MO2000	13,10,34
Coleman, Michael	FL1500	13,10,11,66A,34
Coleman, Randolph E.	OH1700	13,10
Coletta, Michelle	CA1900	13,64
Collaros, Rebecca L.	DC0170	13,64A
Colleen, Jeffrey	IL1550	13,10,36,66A,31A
Colletti, Carla	MO1950	13
Collins, Charlotte A.	VA1350	13,32
Collins, Dana L.	IN1560	10,12A,34,35C,13
Colson, William	TX2600	13A,13,10F,10,13I
Colucci, Matthew J.	PA3250	13,10
Combs, Ronald	IN0005	61,13
Comeau, Gilles	AG0400	32,13
Compean, Jose D.	TX1425	13,32,47,63,64
Compton, Adam	OK0500	13B,63,37,46,13
Compton, Beckie	TX0125	66A,13,11,36,47
Congdon, Judy A.	NY1700	13,66G,66H,31A
Conley, Mark	RI0300	13,60,36,61,32D
Connell, Robin	MI0300	66A,13
Conner, Jennifer A.	OH0200	13,10
Connolly, Michael E.	OR1100	36,12A,10A,61,13
Connor, Jennifer	OH0600	13
Connor, Mark	MO0700	13,20,41,47
Connor, Mark	IL1740	13
Conrad, Robert	CA4625	13,11,12A,61
Conroy, Thomas	CA4150	12A,13
Consoli, Marc-Antonio	NY2750	13,10A
Conway, Eric	MD0600	13,66A
Cook, Christopher E.	VA0150	34,13
Cook, Kenneth	NY1275	12C,13,29A
Cook, Linda Klein	WI0750	63A,12,13,63B,10F
Cook, Mark Andrew	WV0550	13,29B,47,46,10
Cook, Robert C.	IA1550	13
Cook, Thomas	MI1250	13,12A,38,63C
Cook, Warren	SC0200	13,60,36,31A,40
Cooper, John H.	ME0270	10,29,13,64E,10F
Cooper, Matthew J.	OR0200	13,47,66A,66D,29
Cooper, Nancy Joyce	MT0400	13,66G,66H,69
Cooper, Peter	TN1350	13,66A
Coopersmith, Jonathan	PA0850	13
Cope, David H.	CA5070	13,10,12A
Copenhaver, Lee R.	MI0900	13,11,12A,38,62C
Coppenbarger, Brent	SC0950	13,11,64
Coreil, Kristine	LA0550	63B,13,41
Corina, John H.	GA2100	13,10,64B
Cornejo, Robert Joseph	CA5510	13,11,34C,10,12A
Cornelius, John L.	TX2100	66C,66A,66D,13
Cornell, Richard	MA0400	13,10
Cornett-Murtada, Vanessa	MN1625	66A,13,12A,66B
Cornicello, Anthony	CT0150	10,34,13,34D,13F
Cornish, Glenn S.	FL0500	13,11,66A
Cornwall, Lonieta	NC2300	13,60,36,66D
Cory, Eleanor	NY2050	13,10,11,66A,66D
Costa, John V.	UT0250	13,11
Costanzo, Samuel R.	CT0250	13,11,29A
Cotner, John S.	TX2700	13
Cotroneo, P. J.	NJ0950	29,70,13
Cottle, David M.	UT0250	13,34
Coull, James	SD0550	37,70,13
Coutts, Greg A.	IL2650	13,10,34
Couvillon, Thomas M.	KY0550	13,10B,10A,10,13F
Covach, John	NY1100	13,13A,13J,10D
Covach, John R.	NY4350	13A,13,13J,10D
Cowart, Steed D.	CA2950	10,13,43
Cowles, Robert	NY1550	13,36,60
Cox, Arnie	OH1700	13,12C
Cox, David	CA5000	13,10
Cox, Franklin	OH2500	10,13
Cox, Lauren J.	OK0300	64C,64E,13,13C
Cox, Mary A.	NY1900	13
Cox, Melissa	GA0750	11,12,13
Cox, Robin V.	CA0825	13,10
Cox, Thomas E.	AR0750	13,47,66A,66D
Cramer, Alfred W.	CA3650	13,12A,12B
Cratty, William	CA2960	13,66
Cratty, William	CA4050	13A,13,12A,14,32
Crawford, Jenn	AJ0030	66A,66B,66C,13
Crawford, Lawrence E.	MD0850	13,66A
Crespo, Fabra Desamparados	NJ0825	10,13,34
Crist, Timothy D.	AR0110	13,45,10,70
Crockett, C. Edgar	IL0300	13,10,47,35,63A
Crockett, Donald	CA5300	13,10F,10
Crook, Harold	MA0260	13A,13
Crook, Keith R.	ME0500	13,70
Crookall, Christine	GA0250	13A,13,62C,12A,41
Crooks, Mack	CA4650	13,12,66A,34
Crosby, Alison	TX2250	13
Crosby, Tracy	MS0300	63C,11,13
Crotty, John E.	WV0750	13A,13
Crowell, Gregory	MI0900	13,12,66G,66H
Crowley, James F.	WI0835	13,10F,10
Crozier, Daniel G.	FL1550	13,10,12A
Crumb, David	OR1050	10A,10F,13
Crumb, George H.	PA3350	13,10
Crummer, Larry D.	CA1760	20,13,11,14,66A
Cryderman-Weber, Molly	MI1200	12,20,13B,13,65
Csapo, Gyula	AJ0150	13,10,45,10F
Cubbage, John	MT0370	13,12A,66A,10A
Cubek, David	CA3620	38,11,13,60
Cubek, David	CA2175	38,11,13,60
Cubek, David	CA4500	38,11,60,13
Cubek, David	CA1060	38,11,13,60
Cuciurean, John D.	AG0500	13
Cuckson, Robert	NY2250	13,10
Cuckson, Robert	PA0850	13
Cullison, Jon	CO0830	13,45
Culver, Daniel	IL0100	13,60B,12,38
Cumming, Duncan J.	NY3700	66A,13,11
Cummings, Craig	NY1800	13
Cummings, Dean	OH1400	12A,13,63C
Cunningham, Jennifer	OK0825	12A,13
Curlette, Bruce	OH0450	13,64C,10F
Currie, Randolph	OH1330	13,10,66G
Curry, Jerry L.	SC1110	13,66H,55,66E
Curry, Vicki L.	VA0600	13,11

Index by Area of Teaching Interest

Name	Code	Areas
Curtin, David	PA2050	66,13
Curtis, Stanley	NY3000	11,13
Cushman, Cathy	NY1250	66A,13A,13
Custer, Gerald	MI2200	36,60A,13
Custer, Seth A.	SC0200	13,64E,10A
Cutler, David	SC1110	13,10,12A
Cutler, Timothy S.	OH0600	13
Cutsforth-Huber, Bonnie	MD0095	13A,13,11,12A,13B
Cutting, W. Scott	MI1550	13,11,66A,66D,34D
Cvetkov, Vasil	LA0650	66D,13
D'Addio, Daniel F.	CT0050	13,32,37,49,63A
Dahlke, Steven	NY3250	11,13,36,60A,61
Dal Porto, Mark	NM0100	10,13,66A,34,13A
Dale, Stephen	MA0260	13A,13
D'Alessio, Greg P.	OH0650	13,10,45,43
Dalton, Sharon	WY0060	13,44,61,66
D'Ambrosio, Michael	KY0950	13,10
Damschroder, David	MN1623	13,13J
Danby, Judd	IN1310	10,13,29B,10A,13F
Danek, Leonard P.	MN1280	13,10,66G
D'Angelo, Gerard	NY2660	13A,13,13J
Dangerfield, Joseph Allen	IA0300	10,13,66A,38,43
Daniel, Omar	AG0500	13,10,10F,34,35C
Daniel, Thomas	AL0335	13,11,47
Daniels, John	FL0600	13,32C,64A,64C
Danner, Greg	TN1450	13,10
Darcy, Warren J.	OH1700	13
Darling, John A.	ND0050	37,60B,47,13,41
Dauer, Robin	AR0110	13,11,63B
Davenport, Dennis	OH2050	54,10,13,36
David, James M.	CO0250	13,10,10F,63C
David, Norman	PA3330	64,47,10,29,13
Davidian, Teresa	TX2750	13,10,12A,20
Davidson, Doris	NY2400	13
Davidson, Lyle	MA1400	13,32
Davies, David H.	NY1700	13A,13C,13B,10,13
Davies, Paul	CA1800	13,11,13A,66A,10
Davies, Susan Azaret	CA0600	13,66A,66C
Davies, Thomas H.	CA0600	13,60,36,61
D'Avignon, India	CA0600	66A,13
Davis, Andrew	TX3400	13
Davis, Christopher A.	SC0950	11,13,29,50,65
Davis, Colin	TX2250	13
Davis, D. Edward	NY0500	11,13
Davis, Glen Roger	OH1450	13,10
Davis, Joel	AL0800	10,13,34
Davis, John Douglas	CA0650	13,10,47,29
Davis, Jolene	GA2100	13,66G,31A
Davis, Randy	AL1195	37,38,60,13,48
Davis, Richard A.	WV0500	13,60,12A,36,61
Davis, Stacey	TX3530	13,13K,12F
Davis, William	GA2100	13,64D
Dawe, Jill A.	MN0050	13,66A,66B,66D
Dawson, Robert B.	CA1700	13A,35,13,53
Day, Greg	SC1080	13,10F,37,47,63
Day, Thomas Charles	RI0250	13A,13,12
Day-O'Connell, Jeremy	IL1350	13
de Ghize, Susan K.	TX3515	13
De La Bretonne, Beverly	TX0100	13,38,41,62A,64A
De Lyser, David M.	OR1100	13,10,38,41
De Sousa, Beth Ann	AG0600	13,39,66C
Deagan, Gail	IN1300	13,20
Deakin, Paul	TN1850	13
Dean, Brandon	MN0750	36,13,20,32D,34B
Dean, Julie	TX3000	13
Dean, Terry Lynn	IN0800	11,12A,13
Decker, Bradley	IL0800	13,10
Decker, Greg	OH0300	13
Decker, Pamela A.	AZ0500	66G,13
Deguchi, Tomoko	SC1200	13,66A,13F,13E,13A
Deitz, Kevin	OR0050	13,62D
Del Nero, Paul	MA0260	13A,13
Delaney, Douglas	CA1150	13,11,37,47,64
Delcamp, Robert	TN1800	13,12A,36,66G,31A
Delgado-Pelton, Celeste	CO0600	13,11,34,36,47
DeLio, Thomas	MD1010	13,10
DeLuca, Mike	CO0275	13,64C,11,32
Demars, James R.	AZ0100	13,10F,10
DeMers, Peggy	TX2250	63B,13
DeMotta, David	NY0625	13
Dempsey, John D.	RI0300	13A,13,51,62A
Dempsey, O. S.	AL0500	66A,66B,13
Demske, Hilary	UT0325	66A,13
Denham, Robert	CA0350	13,10,34,43
Denisch, Beth	MA0260	13,10F,10,15
Denman, James L.	OR1300	13,12A,66G,13F,13H
Dennis, David M.	TN1660	13,66A,36
Denny, Mike	OR0350	29A,13
Denton, David B.	PA1200	13
DeOgburn, Scott	MA0260	13A,13
D'Ercole, Kendra	AZ0470	13
Dering, James	TX0850	36,47,13,13C,11
Derix, Amye	TX0850	61,13
Derry, Lisa	ID0070	13,10,34,66A,66B
Desby, Neal	CA5300	13,10F
Desjardins, Jacques	CA4150	43,60B,13
Deuson, Nicolas	GA0050	13,34A,34D,35G,70
Deutsch, Herbert A.	NY1600	13,10,45,29A,35
DeVaron, Alexander	PA3200	13
deVaron, Alexander	PA3250	13
DeVasto, David	IL0850	10,13,32E,66
DeVeaux, Scott K.	VA1550	13,12A,12,14,29
Devore, Richard O.	OH1100	13,13,34,10,20G,13F
DeZeeuw, Anne Marie	KY1500	13
DiBella, Donna J.	WI0350	13
DiBlassio, Brian	MI2120	47,13,43
DiBucci, Michelle	NY1900	13
Dickinson, Christian M.	PA1600	13,49,63C,60B
Dickinson, Paul J.	AR0850	10,13,43,34
Dickinson, Stefanie C.	AR0850	66A,13
Dickow, Robert H.	ID0250	13,10,63B,34
Diden, Benjamin	GA0900	37,13
Diehl, Richard C.	VT0100	13,60,47,10,37
Diemer, Emma Lou	CA5060	13,10F,10
Dies, David	WI0830	13,10A
Dietrich, Kurt R.	WI0700	13,32,37,47,29
Dietz, Christopher J.	OH0300	13
Dill, Jane	SC1080	13,66A,66G,66C
Dillon, Christopher	MD0850	13
Dillon, Lawrence M.	NC1650	13A,13,10,43
Dilthey, Michael R.	MA1185	10,13,34
Dilworth, Gary	CA0840	13,63A,20G
Dimond, Raymond R.	AR0300	47,65,53,13,32E
DiMuzio, Richard J.	MA0260	13A,13
Dinda, Robin	MA0930	10,11,13,29,66G
Dineen, P. Murray	AG0400	13,12
Dinger, Gregory	NY4300	13,12A,70
Dingle, Rosetta	SC1050	32,36,66D,13
Dippre, Keith	NC1350	13,11,10,47,34
Dirksen, Dale B. H.	AJ0030	10,13,32,61,66
DiSanti, Theodore A.	PA3000	63A,47,49,13,10F
Ditto, Charles J.	TX3175	13,10
Dixon, Gail S.	AG0500	13
Dobbs, Wendell B.	WV0400	11,13,41,48,64A
Dobos, Lora Gingerich	OH1850	13
Dodds, Amy	WA1300	62A,62B,13
Dodson, Alan	AB0100	13
Dodson-Webster, Rebecca	PA2150	63B,13,12A,49
Doering, James M.	VA1150	13,11,12A,66A,66G
Doiel, Mark	CA2900	10D,11,12A,13,37
Doll, Christopher	NJ1130	13
Domek, Richard C.	KY1450	13,13J
Don, Gary W.	WI0803	13,10F,10A
Doneski, Sandra	MA0950	32,36,13
Dong, Kui	NH0100	13,10,20D,45,43
Donofrio, Anthony	OH1100	13,11
Doolittle, Emily L.	WA0200	10A,13,13D
Doran, David Stephen	KY1460	13A,13,10,11,12A
Dorhauer, John	IL0850	20A,13,63A
Dorin, Ryan	NY0644	13
Dorman, Avner	PA1400	10A,10F,13,43
Doroftei, Mugnr	TX2550	13,38,62
Dougherty, William P.	IA0550	13,10F,10,34
Douglas, Bill	CO0560	13,11,12A,36,66A
Douglas, Samuel O.	SC1110	13,10,62D
Douglass, Ronald L.	MI1100	13,37,41,63,29
Dousa, Dominic	TX3520	13
Douyon, Marcaisse	FL1310	13,10,34
Downey, John W.	WI0825	13,10F,10,45,43
Downing, Joseph	NY4150	10,66G,13,13C,60
Draskovic, Ines	NY1250	66A,13A,13C,13
Drayton, Keith	MI1100	13,11,36,32,61
Driankova, Ivanka	NY2650	13
Dries, Eric	CA0815	13,13E,13D,29A,66
Drott, Eric	TX3510	13
Drummond, Dean J.	NJ0800	13,43,10
Dubbiosi, Stelio	NJ0825	13,10F,66A,66G
Dubiel, Joseph	NY0750	10,11,13
Dubois, Mark	NY3725	13,64B
Duce, Geoffrey	IN0910	13,66A,66C,66D
Duckett, Linda B.	MN1000	13,66G,66H
Duckworth, William	PA0350	13,10
Dudley, Sherwood	CA5070	13,10F,12A,39
Duerksen, Marva G.	OR1300	13,12A
Duffy, Kathryn Ann Pohlmann	IA0650	16,11,12,13,36,60
Duffy, Thomas	CT0850	13,37,47
Duhaime, Ricky	TX0250	13,47,41,64,60B
Dumm, Mary Elizabeth	MD0700	13A,13,11,66A
Dunbar, Brian	MN0620	10,13,36,34,60A
Dunbar, Edward	SC0200	13,12A,66G,34
Duncan, Ellen	MI1300	13A,13,60,36,40
Duncan, Warren L.	AL1100	13,11,47,65
Dunker, Amy	IA0250	13,10,63A,41,49
Dunker, Joel F.	WA1050	10,34
Durant, David Z.	AL1300	13,10,34,10A,10B
Durant, Doug	AZ0440	13,61
Durant, Douglas F.	MA1450	13,10,11,12A
Durham, Thomas L.	UT0050	13,10F,10
Durrani, Aahminah	TX3400	13
Dusman, Linda J.	MD1000	10,13
Dutton, Brent	CA4100	13,10F,10,49,63D
Dutton, Douglas	CA2600	13A,13,11,66A
Dvorin, David	CA0800	13,10,35G,45
Dworak, Paul E.	TX3420	13,34
Eagle, David	AA0150	13,10F,10,34,43
Earles, Randy A.	ID0100	13,20G
Easley, David B.	OK0750	13,13J
Easter, Wallace E.	VA1700	37,63B,13
Eaton, David D.	TX3530	66G,13,66H,67F
Eaton, Rebecca M. Doran	TX3175	13
Eby, Kristen	IA1450	44,61,40,36,13
Eby, Patricia	WI0804	13,11,36,60A,47
Eckardt, Jason K.	NY0500	10,10F,13
Eckert, Michael	IA1550	13,10A
Eckert, Stefan	IL0800	13,13J,13E
Eckert, William H.	DC0110	13,12A,32A,66G
Ediger, Thomas L.	NE0500	13,12A,32,36,66
Edstrom, Brent	WA1350	10,66A,34,47,13
Edwards, Denise	IL1610	13,66A
Edwards, George H.	NY0750	13,10,11
Edwards, Jason R.	IA0900	64,13,10,32E
Edwards, Julie	IN0800	13,12A
Edwards, Leo	NY2250	13,10
Edwards, Matthew	MO0850	66A,66B,66C,66D,13
Edwards, T. Matthew	MD0060	66A,13,66C,12,36
Edwards, Timothy D.	IL0720	13,34D
Edwards-Henry, Jacqueline	MS0500	13,66A,66B,66C
Egan, John B.	IN1350	13,66,66G,11
Eggert, John	MN0610	10,13,31A,66G
Eggert, Scott H.	PA1900	13,10
Ehle, Robert	CO0950	13,10,13L
Ehrlich, Barry	WA0860	13,11,37,63C,63D
Eichenbaum, Daniel	WV0300	13,10,11
Eidsheim, Nina	CA5032	12A,12,13
Eklund, Jason	GA0750	13
Elezovic, Ivan	FL1850	10,13,34
Elfline, Robert	IL0100	66A,11,13
Elgart, Matthew	CA0830	70,10,13
Ellefsen, Roy	UT0190	13,11,36
Ellenwood, Christian K.	WI0865	13,64C,41
Ellias, Rod	AI0070	13,47,70,53,29
Ellis, Sarah	OK1350	13
Ellzey, Michael R.	NM0100	63A,13,32E
Elsberry, Kristie B.	TN0100	13,66A,66G
Elwood, Paul	CO0950	10,13
Emmons, Stephen D.	TX0150	13,10,10F,34
Eng, Clare Sher Ling	TN0100	13,13B,13D,63B,66A
Engberg, Kristina L.	IL2350	66D,11,13,34B
Engberg, Michael	CO0100	13,70,41,35,47
Engebretsen, Nora A.	OH0300	13
Engel, Tiffany	OK1300	13,11,12A,66A
Engelmann, Marcus W.	CA0100	13,10,12A,45,20G
Engelsdorfer, Amy L.	IA0950	13,13D
Engelson, Robert A.	IA0050	13,60,11,36,54
Enis, Paul	OK0350	13,36,37,61,63
Enns, Leonard J.	AG0470	13,60,10,36
Enos, Steve	OH0750	13,47,63A,29,46
Entsminger, Deen	TN0100	13,10,32C,36,34
Epstein, Joan O.	FL0450	13,11,12A,53,63A
Epstein, Paul A.	PA3250	13,10,55
Erickson, Christian	WY0150	10,11,13,34,35
Erickson, James M.	NY4060	13,12A,11,70
Erickson, Kim	AG0170	13,36,20,39
Erickson, Shirley	TX0910	11,13,36,61,66
Ernst, John	NJ1000	13,13C
Errante, Steven	NC2440	13,10F,60,10,38

465

Index by Area of Teaching Interest

Name	Code	Areas
Escot, Pozzi	MA1400	13
Eshelman, Karen	SC0750	13,66D
Eskey, Kathryn F.	NC2430	13,66G
Evans, David H.	AR0300	13,11,12A,32,48
Evans, Gerald	OH1300	13,10,12A,14,66D
Evans, Peter J.	MA1175	13
Everett, Walter T.	MI2100	13
Everett, Yayoi Uno	GA0750	13
Everitt, Allison	FL1430	13,36,61,55
Ewazen, Eric	NY1900	13
Ewell, Philip	NY0625	13,13F,13I,62C
Ewell, Terry B.	MD0850	64D,13,64E
Eychaner, Frank	CO0150	10,32,13,47,60
Eyerly, Scott	NY1900	13
Ezoe, Magdalena	MI1950	66A,13,12B,12A,41
Falby, Vern C.	MD0650	13
Falskow, John	WA0960	37,63A,38,11,13
Fandrich, Rita E.	FL0800	13,66A,66B,10
Fankhauser, Gabe	NC0050	13
Fankhauser, James L.	AB0100	13,36,55,61
Faris, Marc R.	NC0650	13,10D,11
Farley, Michael	NY3550	13,14,10,20
Farquharson, Michael	MA0260	13
Farrell, David E.	CO0550	10,13
Farrell, Peter S.	CA5050	13,12A,62C,67A
Farris, Daniel King	OK1250	40,42,12,36,13
Fast, John W.	VA0300	13,66A,66G
Fatone, Gina Andrea	ME0150	13,14,20,20D
Faulconer, James	OK1350	13,10,34,35
Faust, Randall E.	IL3500	63B,10,63,13,49
Fay, James	VA0975	13,12A,64C
Feather, Carol Ann	TN0450	13,11,38,63B
Feezell, Mark	TX2400	13
Feingold, David W.	WA1250	11,70,13
Feinstein, Allen G.	MA1450	13,10F,60,37,48
Feldkamp, Timothy L.	IA0930	13,41,47,64
Feldman, Bernardo	CA1265	13A,13,10F,10,11
Feller, Ross	OH1200	13,15
Feltman, Joshua	NY0500	11,13,43
Felts, Randolph C.	MA0260	13A,13
Fennelly, Brian	NY2740	13,10,12A,45
Ferenc, Anna	AG0600	13,13F
Ferencz, George J.	WI0865	13,10
Ferguson, Danise J.	AE0050	13,41,62C
Ferguson, Dianne S.	NE0200	13,66A,66C,66D
Ferrandino, Blaise J.	TX3000	10,62D,13
Ferrantelli, Sal	CA3050	13,36,61
Ferrara, Lawrence	NY2750	13,12,32,66
Ferre, Stephen G.	NY4150	13,35
Ferreira, Copper	CO0250	13
Ferri, John P.	NC1650	13
Festinger, Richard	CA4200	13,10,45,34
Fetler, Paul	MN1623	13,10F,10
Feurzeig, David K.	VT0450	13,10
Fiala, Joy	AR0110	13,11,32
Fieldman, Hali	MO1810	13
Finegold, Michael G.	MA1500	13,11,29
Fink, Robert W.	CA5032	13,12A,34,20G
Finney, John W.	KY0700	13,12A,36,61,66A
First, Craig P.	AL1170	13,10,45,34
Fischer, Peter H.	TX3200	13,10A,10B
Fisher, Alfred	AG0250	13,10
Fisher, George	NY2250	13,66H
Fisk, Charles	MA2050	13A,13,12A,66A
Fitzgearld, Gayl	NM0310	13
Fitzgerald, Chris	KY1500	29B,13
Flack, Michael	IL0650	11,66,13,29,32B
Flaherty, Thomas E.	CA3650	13,10,12A,45
Flanagan, Sean	MA1400	13
Flandreau, Tara	CA1150	12A,13,38,41,62
Flauding, Richard (Ric) G.	TX2600	10,34,10F,13
Fleisher, Robert J.	IL2200	13,10
Fleming, Drew	NY0625	13
Fletcher, Harold	OK0700	13,12A
Fletcher, John M.	OK0700	10F,60,37,13
Flick, Daniel K.	FL1550	70,13,42
Flora, Sim	AR0500	32,37,47,63,13
Flores, Carlos	MI0250	13,10,35,34,10F
Florez, Anthony	IL1080	11,34,65,70,13
Flory, Neil	WA0050	10,13
Floyd, Rosalyn	GA0250	13A,13,11,66A,66C
Flynn, Timothy	MI1800	10A,12,36,39,13
Fogg, Matthew	ME0340	66A,13
Foglesong, Scott	CA4150	13
Foley, Gretchen C.	NE0600	13
Foley, Mark	KS1450	62D,29,13
Folio, Cynthia J.	PA3250	13
Follet, Diane W.	PA2550	13,15,42,13H
Folse, Stuart J.	IL0550	13
Foltz, Roger	NE0610	13,10
Fonville, John	CA5050	13,10,64A,53,43
Forbes, Michael I.	WI0840	63D,13,34
Ford, Barry M.	NE0610	13,20
Ford, Mary E.	OK0350	11,13,36,66
Ford, Peter	MI0050	13
Forrester, Sheila	FL1675	10A,13,66D,13D,13E
Forsberg, Charles	MN1450	13
Forsyth, Malcolm	AA0100	13,10F,10,38
Foster, Erin	WA0250	13
Foster, Gary	TX2400	13
Foster, Robert	GA0250	13,10,11,47,48
Foulkes-Levy, Laurdella	MS0700	13
Fountain, Marcia	TX3520	13,16
Fournier, Karen J.	MI2100	13
Fowler, Colin	NY2900	36,13,12A,66A,66G
Fox, Clinton D.	OH0300	13,66A,66D
Fox, Jeremy	IA1400	13,10F,37,50,34
Fox, Rebecca	AL1195	13,11,32,66A
Frabizio, William V.	PA0125	13,11,12A,41
Francis, Kimberly	AG0350	15,13,12
Francis, Lorie	MO0825	11,12A,13,36,66A
Franck, Peter	AG0500	13
Frandsen, Lars	NY2900	12A,13,70
Frangipane, Ron	NJ0760	13,10F,60,10,12A
Frank, Andrew D.	CA5010	13,10,11
Frank, Bruce	NY4350	66,13
Frank, Robert J.	TX2400	10,13
Franks, Carol	AL1050	13,64A,48
Frary, Peter Kun	HI0160	13,11,12A,70,34
Frazelle, Kenneth	NC1650	13,10F,10
Freeman, Alexander	MN0300	10,13,11
Frehner, Paul	AG0500	13,10
French, John	PA3550	11,12,13,36
Frengel, Michael	MA0350	13
Freund, Stefan	MO1800	13,10
Frey, Kevin T.	CA4350	13,11,14,63,53
Friedman, Arnold J.	MA0260	10,62C,13
Friedmann, Michael	CT0900	10,13,66A
Friedmann, Michael L.	CT0850	13
Friesen, John	WA1250	13,51,62C
Fritts, Lawrence	IA1550	13
Froelich, Andrew I.	ND0350	13,12A,66A,66H
Fronckowiak, Ann	TX2960	64B,13
Froom, David	MD0750	13,10A,10B,10F
Fruehwald, Robert D.	MO1500	13,10,45,64A
Fry, Edwin J.	PA1600	11,66A,13
Fry, James	MD1010	13,10F,10
Frye, Christopher B.	WI0810	13,10F,10,34
Fuelberth, Brett J.	IA0800	13,36,47,44
Fuentes, David	MI0350	13,10F,10
Fueting, Reiko	NY2150	13,10
Fuller, Sarah	NY3790	11,12A,12,13
Fuller, Wesley M.	MA0650	13,10,34
Fulton, Ruby	MD0650	13
Fung, Eric K.	PA1900	13,66A,66D
Funk, Curtis H.	IL3550	13,32
Funk, Eric	MT0200	10A,10F,60,29,13
Fuoco, Anthony	OH0200	13
Furlow, Shaw	MS0200	13,11,10,37,47
Furman, Lisa J.	MI1800	37,60B,11,13,32
Furman, Pablo	CA4400	13,10,34,35C
Fussell, Charles	NJ1130	13,10
Gabel, Gerald R.	TX3000	34,10,13,45
Gable, Christopher	ND0500	13,10
Gabriel, Todd A.	LA0050	10,13,38
Gach, Peter F.	CA3460	66,11,13
Gaff, Isaac	IL1550	34,13G,13,35C,35G
Gage, Darren J.	NJ1400	13
Gagne, David	NY0642	13
Galand, Joel	FL0700	13J,13
Galasso, Mathew	CA1900	11,12A,66A,13
Galbraith, Nancy	PA0550	13,10
Galindo, Jeffrey A.	MA0260	13A,13
Gallagher, Jack	OH0700	63A,10,10F,13,12A
Gallagher, Mark	MD0350	64C,48,13,12A
Gallas, Heidi	AG0600	13
Gallet, Coralie	NY0200	61,13
Galvan, Alex	CA1000	10,13,37,60
Gambetta, Charles L.	NC0900	38,60B,13,62D
Gamer, Carlton	CO0200	13,10,11,20D,34
Garcia, Federico	PA0600	10,12A,13,41
Garcia-Leon, Jose M.	CT0700	11,12A,13,66A,66D
Gardiner, Ronald	FL1740	13,62,60B,51,38
Gardner, Mike	AA0050	13,47,64E
Garner, David	CA4150	13,10
Garner, Ronald L.	UT0150	13,11,12A,63B
Garnett, Guy E.	IL3300	10,34,13
Garrison, Leonard	ID0250	64A,13,12,13B,13C
Garrop, Stacy	IL0550	10,13
Gates, Gerald	MA0260	13,10
Gates, Steven	CA3500	13
Gaub, Eugene	IA0700	13,12A,66A,11
Gaughan, Warren J.	NC2550	47,13,66A,46,29
Gavalchin, John E.	NY4200	66A,12,13
Gawboy, Anna	OH1850	13
Gawlick, Ralf	MA0330	13A,13,11
Gebuhr, Ann K.	TX1000	13,10,34
Gehl, Robin	OH2200	12A,13,13F
Geisler, Herbert G.	CA1425	14,32,44,13,31
Gellman, Steven	AG0400	13,10F,10
Gendelman, Martin	GA0950	10,13,70,34A
Genge, Anthony	AF0150	13,66A,20G,29
Genovese, John	MA0400	13,10
Gentry, Sarah	IL1150	13,62A,62B
George, Arnold E.	NC1600	47,45,64,34,13
George, Kevin	LA0080	11,13,34,35
Geraci, Paul	IN1350	13,10,29,63A,32B
Gerber, Tom	IN0250	13,66H
Gerhold, John	CA0270	13,10,66D,13A
Gerlach, Bruce	MO0200	13,10,11,54,66G
Germain, Anthony	MA0260	13A,13
Germany, Sam	TX0370	13,66D,35G
Gertsch, Emily	GA2100	13
Gettel, Court	VT0100	64A,13,20
Ghuman, Nalini G.	CA2950	13,12A,12C,12
Gibbons, Helen	IL1750	13,61
Gibbs, Brett	IL2500	61,13
Gibbs, Geoffrey D.	RI0300	10A,10F,13
Gibeau, Peter	WI0862	13,36,41,62D,66A
Gibson, David	LA0770	13,64B,64D,29A
Gibson, Don	FL0850	13
Gibson, Richard L.	AE0100	13,10F,10,37,63
Gibson, Robert L.	MD1010	13,10,45,43
Giebler, David	WI0920	13,11,36,41,66A
Gifford, Tell	NV0125	11,12A,13,66A
Gifford, Troy S.	FL2120	11,13,46,70,10
Gignac, Andrew	TX2260	63A,13,10,11
Gil, Gustavo	CA0950	36,13,46
Gilbert, Peter A.	NM0450	10,13
Giles, Jennifer	AG0100	13,12B,14A
Gillespie, Jeffrey L.	IN0250	13
Gillette, John C.	NY3725	13,64D,72
Gilligan, Heather M.	NH0150	10,13A
Gillingham, David R.	MI0400	13A,13,10F,10
Gillis, Ron	CA2100	11,13
Gilman, Joe	CA0150	13,66A,53,29
Gilmore, Bernard H.	CA5020	10,13
Gilmour, F. Matthew	MO0850	13,10,11,12A,34
Ginader, Gerhard	AC0050	13,10,45,62A
Ginenthal, Robin	MA0260	13A,13
Ginocchio, John	MN1500	37,13,47,32E,60B
Ginther, Kathleen C.	IL2900	13,10
Giovannetti, Geralyn	UT0050	13,48,64B
Giron, Arsenio	AG0500	13,10
Girton, Irene	CA3300	13,34B,34G
Giteck, Janice	WA0200	13A,13,10,12A
Gittins, John	AG0650	29,13,47
Givan, Ben	NY3650	13,14C
Gjerdingen, Robert	IL2250	13,13J,20G
Gladysheva, Alla	CA4150	13,16
Glancey, Gregory T.	CA5355	10F,13,34,35
Glanden, Don	PA3330	47,66A,13A,13,29
Glandorf, Matthew	PA0850	13
Glarner, Robert L.	VA1100	13,10,32I,66G,12
Glass, Judith	TN1350	13,66G,66H,31A
Glazer, Stuart	FL0650	13,10,64
Glencross, Laurie A.	IL1750	13,41,64A
Glickman, Eugene	NY2550	13,12A
Glinsky, Albert	PA2250	13,10,12A
Glofcheskie, John	AB0050	13A,13,12A
Godfrey, Daniel S.	NY4150	13,10,12A
Godin, Jon-Thomas	AG0400	13
Godwin, Paul M.	TN0100	13,10F,10,34
Goldman, Jonathan	AB0150	12,13
Goldray, Martin	NY3560	13A,13,11,12A,66A
Goldsmith, Michael	MO0750	11,13,66A

Index by Area of Teaching Interest

Name	Code	Areas
Goldstaub, Paul R.	NY3705	13A,13,10
Goldstein, Joanna	IN1010	13,66A,66C,38,11
Goldston, Chris	IL0720	66,13
Golijov, Osvaldo	MA0700	20G,13,10,11,12A
Gollin, Ed	MA2250	13
Gomer, Wesley	TX1650	13,66,69,12A,36
Gompper, David	IA1550	13,10
Gonzales, Cynthia I.	TX3175	13
Gooch, Warren P.	MO1780	10,13,10A
Goode, Elizabeth	GA2150	64A,48,13
Goodman, David	CA4450	13,10,34
Goodman, Joseph	NY0642	13
Goodwin, Don	WA0250	13,66A,37,46
Goodwin, Mark A.	GA0700	13,32,37,64
Goodwin, Sydney	TX3515	13
Gopinath, Sumanth	MN1623	13
Gordon, Daniel	FL1740	13,32,60A,36
Gordon, David M.	IL3550	13,10
Gordon, Douglas L.	AL0500	13,34
Gordon-Seifert, Catherine	RI0150	13,12A,12C,55B,66H
Gorecki, Mikolaj P.	TX1425	10,11,13,34,66A
Gorgichuk, Carmen	AA0025	11,13,66
Gorman, John	NJ0250	13,66A
Goslee, Brenda	TN1250	13A,13,11,66A,66G
Gosman, Alan	MI2100	13
Goter, Arlene	MN1295	66A,66B,13,66D
Gothard, Paul	OH1250	13A,13,10F,11,36
Gottschalk, Arthur	TX2150	13,10,45
Gove, John	CA2450	13,47,29A
Gracia-Nuthmann, Andre	NM0150	13,60,36,55,61
Gradone, Richard	NJ0250	13,12A,12,47,63A
Graef, Sara Carina	CA0830	13
Graham, Alta Elizabeth	CO0350	13,10,12A
Graham, Lowell	TX3520	13,60
Gran, Charles	MO1780	11,13,34,10
Granat, Bozena	NY2650	13
Granat, Zbigniew	MA0280	13A,13,11
Grant, David	IL0720	13
Grant, Donald R.	MI1600	64B,64C,64D,64E,13
Grant, Margaret	KY1000	13,64B
Grant, Roger Mathew	OR1050	13
Grantham, Donald	TX3510	13,10F,10
Grasse, Jonathan B.	CA0805	34D,13,20,14C,10
Gratz, Reed	CA5100	13,10,14C,29,11
Graveline, Michelle	MA0200	15,13,36
Graves, Paul	KS0980	13,61
Gray, John	KS0250	36,13,61
Gray, Steven	CA3460	13,66A,66G,66H
Graybill, Roger	MA1400	13
Greco, Christopher J.	KS0100	13,10,64,64E,13F
Green, Burdette L.	OH1850	13A,13,13J,12B
Green, Vincent	WA1250	63A,13
Greenberg, Laura	NY0630	13,10,66A,66D,11
Greenberg, Lionel	CA2700	13,10,66A
Greene, Roger W.	MA0150	13,34,66A,13A,10F
Greene, Sean	TN0900	63D,13,37,32,42
Greenlee, Geol	TN1250	13,66A,10F,10,11
Greenspan, Stuart	IL0720	13,35G
Greenwood, James	OR0350	13
Greer, Larry	TX0125	13,14C,29,46,70
Greer, Taylor A.	PA2750	13
Greeson, James R.	AR0700	13,10,70,47
Gregg, Matthew D.	WI0840	37,13
Gregorich, Shellie Lynn	PA2150	13,66
Gregory, Gary J.	OH0550	44,13,60,37,63C
Grenier, Robert M.	SC1050	13,61,11
Gresham, David Allen	NC0250	61,11,34,13
Gretz, Ronald	MD0175	13A,13,66A,66C,54
Grey, Thomas S.	CA4900	13,12A,12
Griebling, Karen	AR0350	13,10,38,62B,14
Grier, George	WA0700	11,13,32D,47,65
Grier, Jon Jeffrey	SC0765	13
Griesheimer, James	IA0950	12,11,13
Griffin, Jackie	SC0950	13,10,12A,66G,34
Griffin, John C.	MI2250	10,13,13C,66C
Griffin, Rose	IL3550	13
Griffith, Marshall	OH0600	13
Grimes, Calvin B.	GA1450	13,10,12,20G,31A
Grimpo, Elizabeth	NE0150	11,13,66A
Gronemann, Robert	MN1200	66A,13
Groom, Joan	TX3420	13
Groskreutz, Shannon	FL1750	13
Gross, Austin	PA3600	13
Gross, Murray	MI0150	38,13,60B,10,20
Grover, Elaine	MI1300	13A,13,66A,66G,31A
Grover, Steve	ME0340	47,65,66A,29,13
Gryc, Stephen Michael	CT0650	13,10F,10
Gualdi, Paolo Andre'	SC0710	66A,11,13,66B,66C
Guberman, Daniel	NC0650	11,13
Gubrud, Darcy Lease	MN1285	13,11,36,61,40
Guck, Marion A.	MI2100	13
Guertin, Marcelle	AI0200	13,12
Guidobaldi Chittolina, Alberto	PR0115	13,13C
Guild, Jane E.	LA0750	13A,13,61
Gullings, Kyle	TX3535	10,13,13F,10A
Gunderson, Terry	WY0050	65,34,29,13,12E
Gunn, Nancy E.	ME0500	13
Gunter, Trey	TX3000	13
Gustafson, Kirk	CO0225	13,10F,60,62C
Guthrie, James M.	NC0400	13,10,34,66G,66H
Guy, Marc J.	NY3725	13,63B
Guzzo, Anne M.	WY0200	13,10,12A,13F,15
Gwiazda, Henry	MN1120	13,10
Haakenson, Matthew A.	FL1750	10A,66G,13,13D,13J
Haarhues, Charles D.	CO0100	10,13,29,70,11
Habib, Kenneth S.	CA0600	14,10,13,20B,14C
Hackbarth, Glenn A.	AZ0100	13,10F,10,43
Hackel, Erin H.	CO0830	36,13,11,10D
Haek, Jonathan	OR0500	34D,10A,13,66A
Hager, H. Stephen	TX3175	13A,13,49,63B
Hager, Lawson	TX0900	13,49,63B,41
Hager, Nancy M.	NY0500	13,11,12A,12
Haglund, Richard	IL0350	11,13
Haimo, Ethan	IN1700	13,10,10F
Haines, James L.	PA1250	13,10,33
Hakken, Lynda S.	IA0400	66G,13,66C,66A,11
Halberstadt, Randy	WA0200	13,66A,66D,53,29
Hall, Barbara L.	KY0450	13,12A,12,36,60
Hall, Jonathan B.	NY2750	12A,13,31A,36,66G
Hall, Patricia	MI2100	13
Hall, Randall	IL0100	64E,13
Hall, Robert	AG0150	13,60,36,61,10F
Halle, John	NY0150	13,11
Haller, William P.	WV0750	13,12A,66G,31A
Hallstrom, Jonathan F.	ME0250	13,60,10,38,45
Halper, Matthew R.	NJ0700	10,13,34
Halsell, George K.	ID0075	13,37,63,11,71
Hamel, Keith A.	AB0100	13,10,34
Hames, Elizabeth	TX3000	13
Hamilton, Bruce	WA1250	10A,10B,13
Hamilton, Margaret J.	MI2250	63B,32,13,35E
Hamilton, Sarah Jean	NY3725	13,64B
Hamilton, William R.	SC0420	13,11
Hamm, Samuel J.	MT0350	12A,13,63D
Hammel, Bruce R.	VA1600	13,64D
Hampton, Edwin Kevin	GA0200	13,66
Han, Jiyon	DC0170	13,66A
Hancock, Virginia	OR0900	13,12A,36
Haney, Jason	VA0600	13,10
Hanks, Kenneth B.	FL0930	66,13,11
Hanks, N. Lincoln	CA3600	55D,13,10,34,12A
Hanlon, Kevin	TX2400	13,10F,10,43
Hanna, Cassandra	FL1310	13,66A,66D,36
Hanna, Frederick	NE0160	13,37,38,10
Hannigan, Barry T.	PA0350	13,66A
Hanninen, Dora A.	MD1010	13
Hansen, Bente	AA0200	66A,13
Hansen, Brad	OR0850	13,29,10,34
Hansen, Eric	WI0808	64C,37,13,32E
Hansen, Jack	IN0005	66A,13,61
Hansen, Kathleen	MT0175	13,20
Hansen, Kristen S.	GA0550	13,11,32E
Hansen, Ted	TX2955	13,10F,10A,66A
Hanserd, Mary	AL0550	13,12A
Hanson, Dan L.	OK1400	13,10,32C,47,37
Hanson, F.	NY4060	13,12A,11,66A
Hanson, John R.	NY3705	13A,13
Hanson, Melanie	MN0150	62A,13
Hanzelin, Fred	IL2775	13,34,11,10
Harbinson, William G.	NC0050	13,34
Harbison, John H.	MA1200	13,10,12A
Harbold, Mark A.	IL0850	13,10F,10,16,12A
Harchanko, Joseph	OR1250	10,13,62C
Harcrow, Michael	PA2300	63B,49,13
Hardaway, Travis	MD0650	13,10F
Harder, Lane	TX2400	13
Hardin, Garry Joe	TX2600	10A,13,29,38,46
Hare, Robert	OH1850	13
Hare, Ryan	WA1150	13,64D,10A,10B
Harkins, Edwin	CA5050	13A,13,63A,54,43
Harley, Michael	SC1110	13,42
Harper, Steven A.	GA1050	13
Harrelson, Lee	MO0850	13,63D
Harrington, Danny	MA0260	13A,13
Harris, Ellen T.	MA1200	13,11,12A,12
Harris, Roger	IN0005	10B,13,29,47,66A
Harris, Scott	ME0500	13
Harrison, Daniel	CT0900	13
Harrison, Joanne K.	NC1150	13,66G,31A,66A
Harrison, Judy	FL0900	13,36,60A,66
Hart, Edward B.	SC0500	10,11,13
Hart, Kevin	IL1150	13,66A
Hart, Michael D.	LA0030	37,63A,11,13,47
Harter, Courtenay L.	TN1200	13,64B,41
Hartig, Hugo J.	WI0200	13,10F,10,12A
Hartke, Stephen	CA5300	13,10
Hartman, Jane	IL1610	13,11,66A,46,47
Hartman, Mark L.	PA3050	62,38,13,62A,29
Hartt, Jared C.	OH1700	13
Hartwell, Hugh	AG0200	13,10,11,29
Harvey, Julie	AZ0400	66A,13
Harvey, Peter J.	CT0240	13,12A,36,54,20G
Harwood, Baxter	WA0100	13,13C
Hasegawa, Robert	AI0150	13
Hasenpflug, Thom	ID0100	65,13,20,10,50
Hasty, Christopher	MA1050	13,10,12A,13J
Hatch, Peter	AG0600	13,10
Hatfield, Gaye Tolan	MA0260	13A,13
Hatmaker, J. E.	IL2200	13,10
Hatten, Robert S.	TX3510	13
Hauger, Karin	CO0830	11,13,36
Haughton, Ethel Norris	VA1750	13,12A,12,20G,66C
Haupers, James Mitch	MA0260	13A,13
Haupert, Mary Ellen	WI1100	12A,13,34,66H
Hawkins, Anne	FL2000	13
Hawkins, John A.	WV0500	13A,13,11,36,66
Hayner, Joy	GA1650	11,13,66
Hays, Timothy O.	IL0850	13,62D,45,34,35
Haywood, Carl	VA0950	13,60,41,66G
He, Jianjun	FL1000	13,34,10
Head, Brian	CA5300	13,70
Headrick, Samuel P.	MA0400	13,10,45
Heald, Jason A.	OR1020	13,10,47,36,38
Heap, Matthew	DC0010	13,10,13F
Heape, Mary Willis	TX3050	32,61,13,12A
Heard, Alan	AG0500	13,10F,10
Heath, Malissa	KY1540	11,66D,32B,13,12A
Hebert, Sandra M.	MA0330	13A,13,66A,66B
Hedges, Don P.	IL3150	13,31A,11,39
Hehr, Milton G.	MO1810	13,10F,12A
Heidlberger, Frank	TX3420	13J,12A,12,13
Heidner, Eric C.	CA4410	37,47,13,29,12A
Heil, Teri	NE0250	66A,13,11
Heim, Matthew	OH2050	13
Heim, Sean	CA0960	13,20
Heine, Erik	OK0750	13,13B,10C,13E
Heinemann, Steven	IL0400	13,10,64C
Heinick, David G.	NY3780	13,10A
Heinrichs, William C.	WI0825	13,10,34
Heinzelmann, Sigrun B.	OH1700	13
Heller, James	TX3350	13,66G,66H,31A
Helm, Jon E.	AA0040	13A,13,12A,63,49
Helvering, David A.	WI0350	13
Helvering, R. Douglas	NJ1350	13
Helvey, Emily	AZ0470	66A,13
Hemingway, Gerry	NY2660	65,20,13
Hemmel, Ronald A.	NJ1350	13,10,34D,13L
Henderson, Peter	MO0700	12A,13,42,66A
Hendrickson, Peter A.	MN0050	60,36,13,66G
Heneghan, Aine	WA1050	13
Hennel, Daniel	IL0850	13,66A
Henriques, J. Tomas	NY3717	34,13
Henry, John P.	NC1550	13,63D
Henry, Paul	IN0005	70,13
Henson, Blake R.	WI0750	13
Herbert, David	TX3530	13,64B
Herl, Joseph	NE0150	12,13,31A
Herman, Martin	CA0825	10F,13,10,34
Herman, Matthew	PA2400	10,11,13,34,35
Herman, Matthew James	VA1350	10,13,13F
Herman, Richard	NM0450	13A,13
Hernandez, Rafael	CA0807	10,13,34
Herod, Sheila	TX1750	13,12A,66A,66C,66D
Hess, Fred	CO0550	11,13,29
Hesse, Ted	IL1750	13,36,61
Hettle, Mark	TX1725	13,11,37,47,63A

Name	Code	Areas	Name	Code	Areas
Hettrick, William E.	NY1600	12A,13,55,55B	Hwang, Okon	CT0150	14,66,11,12,13
Heuser, David	NY3780	10A,10B,13,10F,10	Hyatt, Jack	NY0635	13,63A
Hevia, Lonnie	MD0850	13,13E,13C,10	Hyde, John	AA0050	10,13,62D
Hey, Darryl	NY3000	13	Hyde, Martha M.	NY4320	13,13J
Heyer, David	OR1050	13	Hyer, Brian	WI0815	13,13I
Hicks, Michael D.	UT0050	13,43	Hynes, Tom	CA1000	13,29,47,53,70
Hicks, Sarah Hatsuko	PA0850	13,60	Iannaccone, Anthony J.	MI0600	10A,38,13,10,12A
Hickson, Carolyn R.	AR0700	13,66A	Imara, Mtafiti	CA0847	13,14,64,47,29
Hiebert, Thomas N.	CA0810	13,63B	Ince, Kamran	TN1680	13,10,43
Higdon, Jennifer	PA0850	13,10	Inglefield, Ken P.	OH0300	13
Higdon, Paul	MO1100	13,66A,66B,11,66D	Irish, Michael J.	MI1450	13,47,45,53,29
High, Eric	WI0750	63C,47,13,12,49	Irom, Benjamin M.	TX2800	29,29A,47,41,13
Hijleh, Mark D.	NY1700	10,13,31A	Isaacs, Kevin	CT0800	13,60,10,12B,36
Hildebrandt, Darcy	AJ0030	66A,66B,66C,13	Isaacson, Eric J.	IN0900	13,34
Hilliard, John S.	VA0600	13,10	Italiano, Richard	CO0300	13,10,11,66A,66D
Hilliard, Quincy C.	LA0760	13,10,32C	Ito, John Paul	PA0550	13
Hills, Ernie M.	CA0840	13,63C	Ivanovitch, Roman M.	IN0900	13
Hinderlie, Sanford E.	LA0300	13	Iverson, Jennifer	IA1550	13
Hindman, Dorothy Elliston	FL1900	10A,10F,13	Iwanusa, Charles	MI0450	13,10,11,47,29
Hinkeldey, Jeanette	IA0150	13,64B,64D,66	Jablonsky, Stephen	NY0550	11,63A,10A,10F,13
Hinojosa, Melissa S.	TX1425	11,13,64A	Jackson, Barbara G.	AR0700	13,12A,12,55B,67A
Hirshfield, L. Russell	CT0800	16,13,66,66B,66A	Jackson, Gregory	AL0050	65,13,20,10,36
Hirt, James A.	OH0200	13,11,66A,10	Jackson, Jane	CA1250	13,66A
Hiser, Beth A.	OH0200	13,10	Jackson, L. Max	KY0200	13,11,36,66A
Hlasny, Susan	AA0050	66A,13	Jackson, Milton	AR0810	13,11,49,63,70
Ho, Allan	IL2910	13,12A,12	Jackson, Roland	CA2710	13,12A,12
Ho, Hubert	MA1450	10,13,13K,11	Jackson, Roland	CA1050	13,12
Ho, Ting	NJ0800	13,10,45,43	Jackson, Timothy L.	TX3420	13,13I
Hobbs, Sandy	IN1350	13	Jacobi, Bonnie S.	CO0250	32B,66A,13,32I,32
Hobbs, Wayne C.	TX3200	13,12,35E,20G	Jacobs, Edward	NC0650	10A,10B,13,43
Hodges, Woodrow	WI0250	13,13E,32E,64D	Jacobs, Kenneth A.	TN1710	13,10,45
Hodson, Robert	MI1050	13,29B,47	Jacobson, Allan	SD0400	13,10A,66A,66G
Hoehne, Bill	CA1000	10F,12C,64A,13,29	Jacobson, Harry P.	NY3725	13,62D,35A
Hoffman, Elizabeth D.	NY2740	12D,13,10,45,34	Jacobson, Joshua R.	MA1450	11,12A,36,13,31B
Hoffman, Joel H.	OH2200	13,10	Jacobus, Rhea Beth	SC0400	13,11
Hoffman, Patrick	DE0050	63A,63B,13,11,49	Jaffe, Stephen	NC0600	13,10F,10
Hoffman, Richard	TN0100	67C,13,55B	Jalbert, Pierre	TX2150	13,10
Hogue, Harry	MD0360	70,12A,63D,13,11	James, Jeffrey R.	NE0250	13,60,32,37,63
Hohlstein, Marjorie Rahima	MA0280	66,13,66A	James, Kimberly Gratland	MT0400	61,40,13
Hoke, S. Kay	PA1400	13,12A	Janello, Mark	MD0650	13
Holbrook, Amy K.	AZ0100	13,13J	Jang, Jae Hyeok	IL1850	13,10,31A
Holden, James	VA1750	13,20G,37,64E,46	Janners, Erik N.	WI0425	37,47,60,12,13
Holland, Linda L.	CA4410	13,13A,13C	Janower, David M.	NY3700	13,60,12A,36
Holliday, James T.	DC0150	13A,13,61	Janson, Thomas	OH1100	13,10A
Holliday, K. A.	VA1700	13,66A	Janssen, Brett	KS0215	66,13
Hollingsworth, Devon	IN0005	10A,12,13,32,66G	Janz, Tim	AA0050	13
Hollis, C. Kimm	IN0650	13,66A	Jarrell, Boyd	CA1150	13,36,40
Holm-Hudson, Kevin	KY1450	13F,13,10A,13E,13H	Jarrell, Erinn	CA5355	13,66A,66B,66C,66D
Holman, Derek	AG0450	13,10	Jazwinski, Barbara M.	LA0750	13,10,43
Holmes, Jeffrey	CA0960	13	Jemian, Rebecca	NY1800	13
Holmes, Ruth J.	TX1550	12A,66A,66H,66B,13	Jenkins, John Daniel	SC1110	13
Holstedt, Lucile	MA0260	13	Jenkins, Joseph W.	PA1050	13,10F,10,12A
Holzman, David	NY2105	12A,66D,13	Jennings, David J.	IL0650	11,65,13
Honda, Lorence	CA1850	13,48,64,29	Jennings, Linda G.	PA1600	62C,62D,13,51
Hong, Hye Jung	MO0775	13,66A	Jenny, Jack	OH2050	13,10,50,65,43
Honour, Eric C.	MO1790	10,34,13,13F,35C	Jensen-Abbott, Lia	MI0100	13,66A
Hontos, Margaret Ellen	CA4410	13,13A,12A,20	Jentsch, Christopher	NY4060	13,12A,11,70
Hoogerhyde, Jason	TX2650	13,10	Jermihov, Peter	IL3200	36,13
Hook, Julian L.	IN0900	13	Jetter, Katherine	CO0350	38,62C,62D,13,51
Hooper, Jason	MA2000	13	Jinright, John W.	AL1050	13,64D,34,64B,66A
Hooper, John	AA0015	60A,13,10	Jodry, Frederick	RI0050	13,60,12A,36
Hope, Garrett E.	PA3550	10,62D,13,34,51	Johannsen, Ann	TX3600	13
Hopkins, Christopher	IA0850	13,10B,34,10,67A	Johansen-Werner, Bonnie	IL3370	10A,13
Hopkins, Robert	NY1350	13,12A,12,12F	Johanson, Bryan	OR0850	70,13,41,11,10
Hopkins, Stephen O.	PA2750	13	Johanson, Michael	OR0400	13,10
Horlacher, Gretchen G.	IN0900	13	Johnson, Aaron E.	MO1250	10A,34D,13,70
Horn, Goffery C.	FL0600	13A,13	Johnson, Barry	KY0750	13,10F,10,11
Horne, William P.	LA0300	13	Johnson, Daniel	FL1700	12A,13,65
Horst, Amy S.	HI0200	36,13	Johnson, David H.	GA0850	13,10,10B,10C
Horst, Martha C.	IL1150	13,10	Johnson, David	MA0260	13A,13
Horvath, Maria	IL1610	66A,66C,13,66D,11	Johnson, Derek Martin	IN0150	13
Hoskisson, Darin T.	TX2960	13,64D	Johnson, Gary V.	IL2730	13,13C,29,34
Hosmer, Karen E.	NY3600	64B,13	Johnson, Herbert	MN1250	12A,13,31A,66B,66C
Hostetter, Elizabeth	AL0550	66A,66D,66C,13,66	Johnson, James R.	MN1300	13,11,12
Houchins, Andrew	KS0300	13,10,34D	Johnson, Jeffrey	CT0550	10,11,12,13
Houghton, Monica	OH0600	10,13	Johnson, Jenny O.	MA2050	10,13
Houlahan, Michael	PA2350	13,12A	Johnson, Joel C.	SC1050	13,10,20G,29A,34
Houlihan, Patrick	AR0500	13,10	Johnson, John F.	PA3250	13
House, LeAnn	MN0450	13,12,66	Johnson, Jon S.	TX2350	13,36,61,54,32D
Houser, Steven	MO0600	13,12A,12,64	Johnson, Joyce F.	GA1900	13,66
Howard, Beverly A.	CA0450	13,34A,66G,66A,66H	Johnson, Kari M.	MO0050	66A,66B,13
Howard, David	OR0250	13,10,11,45,66G	Johnson, Madeline	UT0190	13,11,34,64C
Howard, Jason	PA3650	10,13	Johnson, Marjorie S.	VA0950	13,66A,66B,66D,34
Howe, Hubert S.	NY0642	13,45,34	Johnson, Marvin	AL1170	13,10,45
Howe, Hubert S.	NY0600	13,10B	Johnson, Mildred	UT0300	13,12A,12,62B
Howland, Patricia L.	NJ1130	13	Johnson, Paul	IN1700	13,10,34
Hoyt, Reed J.	NY3700	13A,13,12A	Johnson, Peggy J.	MN0600	13
Hsieh, Ai-Liu	PA1900	13	Johnson, Randolph B.	OK0650	10,13
Hu, Ching-chu	OH0850	13,10,60	Johnson, Richard	SC0420	32E,60B,13
Hubbs, Randall	WA0150	13,37,47,63A,29A	Johnson, Shersten	MN1625	13,10
Huber, John	KS0350	13,66A,66D	Johnson, Stephen P.	TX2600	10,13,10F,60A,60
Huber, Wayne	CA1860	37,49,63A,67C,13	Johnson, Timothy A.	NY1800	13
Hudgens, Helen	IL2100	13,31,12A	Johnson, Vicky V.	TX2750	13,32B,14C,32,66B
Hudson, S.	KY0350	11,13,36	Johnson, William T.	CA4700	13,10,11,43,12A
Huener, Thomas J.	NC0650	13,63A,55B	Johnston, Ben	NC1750	13,10
Huey, Daniel J.	GA1800	13,66G	Johnston, Blair	IN0900	13
Huff, Jay	OH1850	13	Johnston, Jack R.	NY3730	13,66A,54,34
Huffman, Donna M.	WA0100	13,13J,36,47,49	Jolley, Jennifer	OH2000	10,13
Hufft, Bradley	CA0810	14C,13,11	Jones, Arlington	TX0370	13,10F,66A,35G
Hughes, Albert C.	TN0950	13,11,12A,36,61	Jones, Arnold	NJ0950	13,20G
Hughes, Bryn	FL1900	13	Jones, Bernard	OK1050	13,12A,61,11,64
Hughes, Robert L.	MO1250	12A,29,13,29A,29E	Jones, Boyd M.	FL1750	13,66G
Hughes, William M.	SC1200	13,49,63C,41	Jones, Christopher	IL0750	10,13
Hukill, Cynthia L.	AR0200	66A,13	Jones, David P.	WA0700	13,10F,10
Hulen, Peter Lucas	IN1850	13,10,34,34A,41	Jones, David Evan	CA5070	13,10
Hulin, Charles J.	FL1740	13,66D,66A,66G	Jones, Evan	FL0850	13
Huling, Diane	VT0050	13,66A,66B,66D	Jones, Hilton Kean	FL2000	10,35,13,45,66G
Hulling, Cliff	CA0350	13,47,50,10A	Jones, Martin David	GA0250	11,66A,66H,66B,13
Hulme, Lance	NC1600	13,12A	Jones, Melvin Rusty	IN0250	13
Huls, Marvin J.	PA3000	13,36,44	Jones, Micah	PA3330	47,62D,29,13,34
Hulse, Brian	VA0250	13	Jones, Michael C.	KS1200	47,63A,63B,63C,13
Hulse, Mark	CA0300	13,11,32B,32C,61	Jones, Ryan Patrick	WI0803	11,12A,13,29A
Humiston, Robert G.	MI2250	13	Jones, Susie	OR0550	13,37,47,29
Humphrey, Mark Aaron	TX3415	10,13	Jordan, James	NJ1350	66G,36,13,60
Hundley, Marion S.	FL0100	10A,66A,66C,13	Jordan, Michael D.	TX1660	13A,13,11,39,61
Hunkins, Arthur B.	NC2430	13,10,45,34	Jordan, Paul	IN0005	10A,61,13,20F,31A
Hunnicutt, Bradley C.	NC2300	13,66,34,13A,13E	Jordan, William S.	AA0150	13,10,10F
Hunt, Graham G.	TX3500	13,12,10F,11,12A	Jordan-Anders, Lee	VA1830	13,11,41,66A
Hunter, Mary K.	ME0200	13A,13,11,12A,12	Joseph, Annabelle	PA0550	13,32I
Hunter, Rosemary Herlong	AL0400	13,66A	Joyce, Brooke	IA0950	10,13,34,12
Hunter-Holly, Daniel	TX3515	13,61,42	Judy, Ned	MD0700	13,29,66,34,47
Huron, David	OH1850	13,12F	Julien, Patricia A.	VT0450	13,12,10D,29
Hurtado, Jose-Luis	NM0450	10,13,32B	Juncker, Arthur	CA1950	13,10,12A,41,34
Huss, Adeline	OH0600	13,66G	Jung, Hyesook	AL0950	66A,66B,66C,13
Hussey, William G.	IL0550	13	Junkinsmith, Jeff	WA0860	13,66A,10
Hutchinson, Robert G.	WA1000	13,10A	Junokas, Michael	IL0850	10A,10B,13,34
Hutton, Judy F.	NC2650	13,66A,66B,66C,66D	Jurkowski, Edward	AA0200	13,12A,34
Hutton, Paula R.	OK0700	13,12A,66A,11	Justus, Timothy W.	TX1700	10F,13

Index by Area of Teaching Interest

Name	Code	Areas
Kaiser, Audrey K.	RI0101	66A,66D,13
Kaiser, Tyler	MN0450	70,10,13
Kalib, Sylvan	MI0600	13
Kallick, Jenny L.	MA0100	13,12A,39,41,12
Kallstrom, Michael	KY1550	13,10
Kaloyanides, Michael G.	CT0700	12,13,14,20,34
Kam, Dennis	FL1900	13,10
Kamatani, Pamela	CA5353	12A,11,12C,13
Kamenski, Michael	WI0050	60,13,34
Kamien, Roger	NY0642	11,13
Kaminsky, Peter	CT0600	13,13J,12B
Kang, Cecilia	ND0350	64C,13
Kang, Sooyoung	NC2150	66A,13
Kang, YouYoung	CA4500	13,12,20C,20G
Kania, Robert P.	IL1300	66A,13
Kaplan, Amelia S.	IN0150	10,13
Kaplan, William	IL3310	13,12A,64D
Karaca, Igor	OK0800	13,10,34
Karahalis, Dean	NY4060	13,12A,11
Karis, Aleck	CA5050	13,12A,66A,66H,43
Karp, David	TX2400	13,66A
Karpen, Richard	WA1050	13,10,34
Karpinski, Gary S.	MA2000	13,13J
Kaschub, Alan R.	ME0500	13
Kasparov, Andrey R.	VA1000	13,66A,10,43
Kassel, Philip	ID0070	13
Kastner, Kathleen	IL3550	13A,13,50,65,20
Katz, Bruce	MA0260	13A,13
Katz, Darrell	MA0260	13A,13
Katz, Robert S.	OK1300	13,11,12A,12,62D
Kauffman, Bradley	KS0500	13,36,37
Kavasch, Deborah H.	CA0850	10A,13,61,10,10F
Kawarsky, Jay A.	NJ1350	13
Kean, Kristen	KY0550	64A,13A,13,42,48
Keane, David R.	AG0250	13,10
Kearney, Joe	CA0200	13,70,35
Keberle, Ryan	NY0625	29,47,11,13,63
Kechley, Gerald	WA1050	13,10,36
Keck, Kimberly	TN0200	36,39,61,60A,13
Keeler, Elden L.	IL0650	11,65,13
Keenan, Maureen	NY0270	11,13,64A
Kehn, Conrad	CO0900	13,43
Keiter, Lise	VA0800	13,11,66A,12A,15
Kellan, Ross	IL0850	60,32,37,11,13
Keller, Daniel	CA2650	13,10A
Keller, Karlton	CA3400	13,47,48,49,12
Keller, Merry	MO1950	31A,32D,13
Kelley, Anthony M.	NC0600	11,13,29,10A,10C
Kelley, Cheryl K.	MN1280	13,32,48,64D
Kelley, Kevin	TX1350	11,10,13,43
Kelley, Robert T.	SC0800	20,13,66A,66D,10
Kelly, James J.	NJ0750	12A,13,29A,47,70
Kelly, Kevin J.	CA2600	13
Kelly, Laura L.	TX3530	13
Kelly, Michael A.	OH2200	13
Kennedy, John M.	CA0830	10,13F,43,10F,13
Kennedy, Martin P.	MO1900	10,13
Kennison, Kendall	MD0400	13,10
Kent, Libbie	AZ0400	13
Kern, Philip	IN1100	13,10F,36,54,66A
Kerr, Daniel	ID0060	10A,13,66G,10F
Kershner, Brian	CT0050	10,13,64D
Kersten, Joanne	MN1250	13,66A,32B
Kesselman, Lee R.	IL0630	13,10,36,54,60
Keyser, Allyson	NY3600	63A,13,12A
Khadavi, Linda	KS0570	13,66A
Khannanov, Ildar	MD0650	13
Kidde, Geoffrey C.	NY2200	10,13,34,45,32F
Kiec, Michelle	PA1750	64,13,64C,64E,11
Kiec, Michelle	PA1750	64,13,64C,64E,48
Kielian-Gilbert, Marianne	IN0900	13
Kilburn, Ke-Yin	IN0005	33,66A,66B,13
Kilp, Brian T.	IN0800	63B,13
Kilstofte, Mark F.	SC0750	10,13,43,13E
Kim, Chungsun	NY2900	13,62C
Kim, Hi Kyung	CA5070	13,10
Kim, Jean	NY0270	11,13,66A,66C
Kim, Jong H.	VA0750	36,13,61,60A,40
Kim, Min	NJ0825	13,12,66A,66B,41
Kim, Misook	IL3550	13
Kim, Myung Whan	KY1200	13
Kim-Quathamer, Chan Ji	FL0150	10,11,13,34
Kind, Sara	WI0350	13
Kindred, Janis B.	FL1750	13
King, Adam	AL1195	66A,13,66D,66C
King, Anita	OR1300	13,66A,66C
King, Curtis R.	FL0600	13A,13,32,61,62
King, Dennis W.	WI0150	60,11,32,13
King, Jonathan	NY3560	13,10F,60,36,10
King, Mary J.	CA0450	10,13
King, Morgan	TX3530	13,11
King, Valeria G.	LA0720	13,60,12A,12,20G
Kinney, Michael	NY0350	13,10,11
Kirilov, Kalin	MD0850	13
Kirk, Jeremy	KS0250	37,13,20A,50,65
Kirk, Jonathon J.	IL2050	13,10,20,34
Kirk, Kenneth P.	GA2150	63A,49,13,39
Kirov, Milen	CA0960	13
Kirov, Milen	CA0835	13
Kitchen, Jennifer	MI0400	13
Kitson, Jeffrey	NE0040	11,13,36,40,61
Klassen, Carolyn	KS0440	66,34,13,20F
Klein, Michael L.	PA3250	13,13F
Kleppinger, Stanley V.	NE0600	13,63A,37,12C
Kleszynski, Kenneth	OR1100	13,32,38
Kliewer, Jan Michael	WY0130	13,36,61,62D,38
Klimko, Ronald	ID0250	13,64D
Klingbeil, Michael	CT0900	10,13
Klonoski, Edward	IL2200	13
Klorman, Edward	NY1900	13,42
Kluball, Jeff L.	GA0625	37,63,29,13,10
Klugherz, Laura	NY0650	13,11,41,62A,62B
Klumpenhouwer, Henry	AA0100	13,12
Knable, Robert	CA3850	13,38,34
Knapp, Peter J.	CA2550	13,10,12A
Knechtges, Eric T.	KY1000	10,13
Knipschild, Ann	AL0200	13,48,64B,64E
Knoepfel, Justin	MN0750	62B,62A,38,42,13
Knudsen, Joel	KS0210	13,11,66
Knutson, John R.	CA1510	36,13,10
Koblyakov, Lev	IL2350	13,12A,34B
Kobuck, Martin	TX1775	13,63C,46,11
Koch, Thomas	NC1700	13,12A
Kochavi, Jonathan	PA3200	13
Kohlbeck-Boeckman, Anne	WI0350	13,66A,66D,13A
Kohn, Karl G.	CA3650	13,10,11,12A
Kolek, Adam J.	MA1100	13
Kolman, Barry	VA1850	13,37,38,64C,60

Name	Code	Areas
Kominami, Miko	IA0950	66A,13
Konecky, Larry	MS0050	13,62,70,34
Koonce, Paul C.	FL1850	13,10
Koozin, Timothy	TX3400	13
Koplow, Philip	KY1000	13,10
Kopp, David	MA0400	13,10
Koppelman, Daniel M.	SC0750	66A,13,34,10
Koprowski, Peter P.	AG0500	13,10
Korde, Shirish	MA0700	13,10,14,20,29
Korey, Judith A.	DC0350	13A,13,66A,29,34
Kornfield, Jono	CA4200	13
Kornick, Rebecca	IL1615	13
Korsyn, Kevin E.	MI2100	13
Korzun, Jonathan	MI1985	32E,37,47,13
Kosar, Anthony	NJ1350	13
Kosche, Kenneth	WI0300	13,60,10,36,31A
Kothman, Keith K.	IN0150	10B,10,34,13,35C
Kowalkowski, Paula	IL0720	13
Kozlova, Yulia	CA4450	11,13,41,66
Kraft, Leo	NY0642	12,13
Kramer, Ernest Joachim	MO0950	13,10,11,66A,66H
Kramer, Keith A.	CT0050	13,34
Kramer, Timothy	IL1100	13,10F,10A,10B
Kramlich, Daniel L.	TX1000	13,10F,66A
Kratz, Girard	PA3250	10A,10B,13,10
Kraus, Joseph C.	FL0850	13
Krausas, Veronika	CA5300	13
Krause, Melissa M.	MN1300	13,64A,10A,10F
Krause, Robert	TX3750	64B,13,55C
Krebs, Harald M.	AB0150	13,66C
Krebs, John A.	AR0350	66A,66C,39,11,13
Kreiger, Arthur V.	CT0100	13,35C,10,45,34
Kresky, Jeffrey	NJ1400	13,10F,11,66D
Kress, Richard	MA0260	13A,13
Kreuze, Brandon R.	GA0600	10,34,13,12C
Krieger, Karen Ann	TN1850	13,66A,66D,66B,68
Kroetsch, Terence	AG0600	13,66D,66A
Kroll, Mark	MA0400	66H,66E,12,67F,13
Krouse, Ian	CA5030	13,10
Kruja, Mira	AL0010	66A,66B,13,11
Krupa, Mary Ann	IL3450	13,54,66A
Krusemark, Ruth E.	KS0100	13,10,66A,66G,66D
Kruspe, John	AG0450	13
Krzywicki, Jan L.	PA3250	13,66A
Kubin, Brian	MO1780	62C,13,51,62D
Kuchar, Evan	IL0600	13,11
Kuchera-Morin, JoAnn	CA5060	13,10F,10,45,13L
Kudlawiec, Nancy A.	AL1350	11,32,66A,12A,13
Kudo, Takeo	HI0210	10A,10F,13,20D
Kuehn, Mikel	OH0300	13,10F,10,45,43
Kugler, Roger T.	KS1000	32E,63,13,37
Kukec, Paul E.	IL1900	13A,13,12A,36,66A
Kulma, David T.	SC1200	13
Kumor, Frank	PA1750	50,65,13
Kunda, Keith	IN0250	13
Kunz, Kelly	WA0030	35D,13
Kurek, Michael	TN1850	13,10F,10
Kurokawa, Paul	CA2100	13,47,63,64
Kurth, Richard	AB0100	13
Kurzdorfer, James	NY4460	13,47,62D,53
Kuss, Mark	CT0450	13,10,45,66A,34
Kuykendall, James Brooks	SC0700	13,12,11,41,38
Kuzmenko, Larysa	AG0450	13A,13,66A
La Rocca, Frank J.	CA0807	13,10F,10
Labe, Paul E.	MD0475	13,10A
LaChance, Marc	NE0300	63C,63D,13,10F,29
Lackey, Mark A.	MD0850	13
Lackman, Susan Cohn	FL1550	13,10,12A,35
Laganella, David	DE0200	10,13,34,14C,12A
Lai, Eric C.	TX0300	13
Lake, William E.	OH0300	13
Lallerstedt, Ford	PA0850	13,12
Lamar, Linda Kline	ID0050	13,62B,41
Lamb, Robert E.	FL0150	36,13,12,60A
Lamb, Sally	NY1800	13,10
Lamb, William	NM0250	13,11,37,47,63
Lambert, James	OK0150	65,50,37,13,12D
Lambert, Philip	NY0600	13,13F
Lambert, Philip	NY0250	13A,13,11,12A
Lamendola, Gene	NY4060	13,12A,11
Landes, Daniel	TN0100	13A,13,66A,66D,31A
Lane, LuAnn	TX1850	11,13,66A,66C,66D
Laney, Robert	TX3700	11,13,36
Langer, Kenneth P.	MA1500	10A,10B,13,34D,11
Langsford, Christopher M.	KS0750	36,32,11,12,13
Lansky, Paul	NJ0900	13,10,45,34
Lapin, Lawrence	FL1900	13,10,36,47,29
Lara, Elizabeth K.	TN0050	62C,13,62D,62B
Large, Karen McLaughlin	KS0650	13,11,64A,13A,48
Larsen, Arved	IL1150	13,12A,63C
Larsen, Laurel	SC0900	66A,66C,66B,13,66D
Larson, Allen C.	MO1950	13,60,12A,38
Lasser, Philip	NY1900	13
Latartara, John	MS0700	13,34
Latham, Edward D.	PA3250	13
Lauber, Anne	AI0210	13
Lauffer, Peter	NJ1000	13,13C
Laughlin, Mark	GA1000	66A,13,12A,66D,13B
Laughrey, Gary	KY0800	64,32F,12A,13
Laurent, Linda	CT0050	13,12,66A,66D,42
Lauridsen, Morten	CA5300	13,10
Lavenda, Richard A.	TX2150	13,10
Lawson, Charles E.	CO0250	13,64C,41
Lawson, Robert	CA5360	13,10,11,66D,12A
Lawson, Stephen J.	WV0400	13,63B,29,49,37
Laymon, Michael	IL1080	11,13,35,63C
Layton, Richard Douglas	MD1010	13
Leach, Catherine F.	TN1710	13,63A
Leaptrott, Ben	GA0350	11,13,39,66A,66B
LeClair, Paul	VT0400	13,12A,48,37,64E
Lecuyer, Michael P.	MA1500	13,47,34
Leduc, Yolande	AI0210	13
Lee, Brent	AG0550	13,10,45,43,53
Lee, Genevieve Feiwen	CA3650	66A,13
Lee, HyeKyung	OH0850	13,34
Lee, Kyung-Ae	TX3175	13,66B
Lee, Owen J.	CA1560	13,10
Lee, Richard A.	HI0200	13,10,12A,64E,66A
Lee, Thomas Oboe	MA0330	13,10,29B
Lefkowitz, David S.	CA5030	13,10
Leggatt, Jacqueline	AB0200	13,10A
Legname, Orlando	NY3765	13A,13,10,35
Lehman, Frank M.	RI0050	13,10C,12A
Lehman, Stephanie	NY0270	65,11,13
Lehmann, Jay	CA2450	60,13,64,63
Leibensperger, Peter	NY0625	13
Leikin, Anatole	CA5070	13,12A,66A
Leinberger, Charles	TX3520	13

469

Name	Code	Areas
Leiter, Cherise D.	CO0550	11,13,10
Lemay, Robert	AG0150	13,10,12A
Lennon, John A.	GA0750	13,10
Lentini, James P.	OH1450	13,10,70,34
Lenz, Andrea	NV0100	13,64B,66C
Lenz, Eric	IL2900	13,62C
Leone, Gustavo	IL1615	10,13
Leong, Daphne	CO0800	13,10
Lesemann, Frederick	CA5300	13,10F,10,45
Leshnoff, Jonathan	MD0850	13,10
Lester, Joel	NY2250	13,41
Leupold, John K.	MD1100	13
LeVelle, Teresa	CA6000	13,10,44,42
Levesque, Craig	NJ1130	13
Levey, John C.	PA3400	10,13,11,34,36
Levey, Joseph A.	OH1850	13
Levi, Michael	NY0700	36,29B,13,60A,32D
Levin, Andrew R.	SC0400	11,41,38,13,42
Levin, Rami Y.	IL1400	13,11,38,10A
Levine, Art D.	AG0650	13
Levinson, Gerald C.	PA3200	13,10,20D
Levinson, Ilya	IL0720	13,10
Levitz, Tamara	CA5032	12A,12,13
Levy, Ben	AZ0100	10,13
Levy, David B.	NC2500	13,11,12A
Levy, Sharon G.	MD0650	13,12A
Lew, Nathaniel G.	VT0400	12A,13,36,40
Lewis, Brian	MA0260	13A,13
Lewis, Daniel	MD0175	11,13,66D,70
Lewis, Gail D.	IN0250	63B,13
Lewis, James E.	FL2000	13,10F,10,43
Lewis, Leonard Mark	SC1200	10,13
Lewis, Rod	SC0620	13,70,40
Lewis, Roger	KS0210	13,10,37,47,53
Lewiston, Cal	TX3700	13,47,11
Leydon, Rebecca	OH1700	13,13F,10C,10D
Liao, Amber Yiu-Hsuan	UT0190	66,13
Lias, Stephen J.	TX2700	13,10F,10
Libby, Cynthia Green	MO0775	13,64B,64D,20,48
Liberatore, John	NY4150	13
Libin, Kathryn L.	NY4450	13,11,12A,12
Licata, Thomas V.	NC0050	13
Lidge, Kenneth	MO1810	13,11
Lieberman, Carol	MA0700	62A,13,12A,67,62
Lieuwen, Peter	TX2900	13,10,12A,29A
Lifchitz, Max	NY3700	10,43,13A,13,10F
Liley, Thomas	IL1250	13,12A,64
Limbert, Thom	IN0910	10,13,20
Lin, Jolie	MD0650	13,12A
Lin, Ruth	MN0750	38,13
Linard, Rita A.	TX3530	13,64A
Lincoln-DeCusatis, Nathan J.	WV0550	10,13,34
Lindeman, Stephan	UT0050	13,29
Lindeman, Timothy H.	NC0910	13,12A,66A,20
Linder, J. Michael	TX1775	13,36,61
Lindroth, Scott A.	NC0600	13,34D,34H,10A,10B
Lindstrom, G. Mikael	AR0900	13,36
Linial, Christine A.	TX3530	13
Link, Jeffrey	MA0280	13,34,47
Link, John	NJ1400	13,10F,10,34
Linney, Lloyd	FL1750	13,61,12A
Linton, Michael	TN1100	13,10A
Lipkis, Larry	PA2450	13,10F,10,55,67
Lippens, Nancy Cobb	IN0800	10,13,36
Lis, Anthony	SD0550	13,10F,10,66,20D
Lissance, Alizon J.	MA0260	13A,13
Lister, Michael C.	NY0700	32D,32C,55D,36,13
Lister, Rodney	MA0400	10,13
Litke, David	AG0550	13
Litke, Sheila	KS1300	66,13,66A,66B,13A
Litterick, Louise	MA1350	13,12A,12
Little, Julie Evans	MI2250	13
Little, Lynn	WI0300	34,13
Liu-Rosenbaum, Aaron	AI0190	10,34,35G,13,14C
Lloyd, Charles	LA0700	13,39,11,66D
Lloyd, Gerald J.	MA2030	10,13,10A
LoBalbo, Anthony C.	NY3500	13,29A,10C,12A,54
Lochhead, Judith	NY3790	13E,13F,12,13,12A
Lochstampfor, Mark L.	OH0350	13,10A,34A,34B,66A
Locker, Fred	OH2150	13,12
Locklair, Dan	NC2500	13,10,11,31A,66G
Loeb, David	NY2250	13,10
Loeffert, Jeffrey	OK0800	64E,13
Loewy, Andrea Kapell	LA0760	13,64A
Lofthouse, Charity	NY1550	13,34B,34F,15,31A
Lombard, Becky	LA0400	13,12A,66A,66G,12C
Lombardi, Paul	NM0450	10,13
London, Justin	MN0300	13,12B,12F,20G,12A
Long, Barry	PA0350	29,47,13,63A,53
Long, David J.	VA1475	13,10A,10F
Long, Kevin	IL1750	54,13
Long, Louanne J.	CA5150	13,66A,66B,66C
Long, Patrick A.	PA3150	13,10,34,12A,32E
Longfield, Richard O.	AZ0510	13,60,37,38,47
Lopato, David	NY2660	13,10,66A
Lord, Roger	AE0100	13,66A,66D
Lorek, Mary Jo	MO1810	13
Lorenz, Michael L.	MI1950	13,47,63,29,34
Lorenz, Ralph	OH1100	13,34,10,13F,13D
Losada, Cristina Catherine	OH2200	13
Lothringer, Peter	MN1500	70,10A,13
Love, Randolph D.	SC0600	13,10,63,41,14C
Lowe, Phillip	TX0910	13,12A,37,47,63
Lowe, Shannon R.	GA2150	64D,48,13
Lowenstein, Marc	CA0510	13,10,60,39,43
Lowery, Daryl	MA0260	13
Lowrey, Norman E.	NJ0300	13A,13,10,45,34
Luangkesorn, Sha	PA1350	13,66
Lubben, Joseph	OH1700	13
Lubet, Alex	MN1623	13,10
Lubin, Steven	NY3785	13,12A,12,66A
Lucas, Adonna	NC1950	13,36,64A,66,31A
Lucas, M. Jayne	PA3500	13,12A
Luchese, Diane	MD0850	13
Lucia, Margaret E.	PA3050	13,11,12,66A
Lucky, Harrell C.	TX0700	13,12A,36
Ludwig, David	PA0850	13,10
Lukowicz, Thomas	OH2500	11,63D,13,13D,13E
Lum, Tammy K.	NY2900	13,66A,66D,42
Lumsden, Rachel	OK1350	13
Lund, Erik R.	IL3300	13,10,43
Lundberg, Kim	AG0500	13,10F
Lunn, Robert A.	MI1180	13,70
Lustig, Andrea	NJ1050	13
Lustig, Raymond J.	NY1900	13
Luther, Sigrid	TN0200	13,66A,66B,31A,66C
Luthra, Arun	NY2660	13,64E
Luxner, Michael	IL1750	13,38
Luzko, Daniel	CA2390	13,10F,10,34
Lyerla, Trilla R.	KS0050	13,66A,66B,20
Lyman, Zachary	WA0650	13,63A
Lynch, Timothy	CA1290	13,10,11,14
Lynn, Robert	IN0700	13,37,38,62C,63D
Mabrey, Paul	OK1300	13,36,61
Macbride, David	CT0650	13,10
MacCallum, Jeanette	TN0100	13
MacDonald, Andrew	AI0050	13,10F,10,45,70
Macdonald, David	NY2150	13
MacDonald, James M.	IL0720	13
MacIntyre, David K.	AB0080	13,10,39,43
Mack, George	RI0200	10,13,34
MacKay, James S.	LA0300	13,10
Mackey, Lynne A.	VA0300	66A,66B,66C,66D,13
Mackey, Steven	NJ0900	13,10F,10,11,41
Mackin, Barbara J.	VA0550	66A,13
MacLean, Alasdair	AE0050	10A,34,13
Macrae, Craig	MA0260	13
Macy, Carleton	MN0950	13,10,67,55,47
Madeira, David	TN0100	13
Madsen, Farrell D.	UT0300	13,10,12A
Madsen, Pamela	CA0815	13A,13,10
Mager, Guillermo E.	CT0700	13,12A,34,35,32
Maggio, Robert	PA3600	13,10
Magnuson, Phillip	OH2250	13,10F,10A,62B
Magrill, Samuel	OK1330	13,10A
Mahe, Darren	AB0070	13,47,70,53,12A
Maher, John	IN1025	13,12A,66G,16,34
Mahin, Bruce P.	VA1100	10,34,13,35C
Mahoney, Shafer	NY0625	13A,13,10
Mahonske, Adam	MD0600	13
Mainland, Timothy L.	WV0200	13,10,70,10F,62
Maisonpierre, Elizabeth	NC2435	11,13,66A,66B,66D
Makan, Keeril	MA1200	10,10F,34,13
Makas, George	IL1085	13,62A
Makela, Steven L.	MN0600	10A,10B,13,10,34D
Maki, Daniel H.	IL0840	13,11,37,64A,66D
Maki, David J.	IL2200	13
Makris, Kristina	AZ0440	10,13,35A,29A,61
Malin, Yonatan	CO0800	13,12
Malinverni, Peter	NY3785	13
Mallak, Augustine	IL0275	13
Malloy, Chris	CO0900	10,13
Maloff, Nikolai	AB0100	13
Malone, Patrick R.	FL0040	13,66G
Malsky, Matthew	MA0650	10A,10B,34,13,10
Maltz, Richard	SC1100	13,10,65,12,14
Mamey, Norman	CA1000	66A,10,12A,13,35A
Manchester, John	MS0300	13,34,11
Mancini, David	TX2400	13
Mandat, Eric P.	IL2900	13,64C,64E
Mandelbaum, Joel	NY0642	13,60
Mandle, William Dee	DC0350	13A,13,32B,66A,66D
Mandrell, Nelson E.	IL2150	13,10,45,34
Maness, David	PA1150	13,60,11,36,61
Mangini, Mark	NY2050	13A,13,11,36
Manik, Rich	MN1300	13
Manzo, Erica	MO1800	13,64C
Marcades, Michael	AL0900	12A,12B,13,32,36
Marchionni, Raymond	OH2300	66A,11,13
Marciniak, Alex B.	MI0700	13A,37,66A,13,11
Marcinizyn, John	PA0600	13,10,70
Marco, John	WI0840	11,13,64C
Marco, Margaret	KS1350	64B,13
Marcozzi, Rudy T.	IL0550	13A,13,13J
Mardirosian, Haig L.	DC0010	13,10,66G,11
Margetts, James A.	NE0050	66,12A,13,32A
Margulis, Elizabeth	AR0700	13
Mariner, Justin	AI0150	13
Marinic, Boro	IA0850	13,62A,62B
Markiw, Victor R.	CT0700	66,13,12A,66A,11
Marks, Christopher	NE0600	66G,66H,13
Markward, Cheri D.	RI0101	13,11,41,62,12A
Marlowe, Sarah	NY2750	13,13C,13D,13H,13I
Marple, Olive	MA0800	13,12A,66A
Marr, John	CA0859	13
Marsh, Gordon E.	VA1250	10,66,13,10A,66A
Marshall, Allen	OK0300	60A,61,13
Marta, Larry W.	TX3370	13A,13,66A,66G
Martens, Peter A.	TX3200	13
Martin, Edward P.	WI0830	13,10B
Martin, Henry	NJ1140	13,10,12,29,29A
Martin, James	IA0400	13,66A,66B,20G
Martin, James	CA4450	13A,13,11
Martin, Jennifer	CA1510	32E,11,13,48,63C
Martin, Joshua	FL0350	13,11,66A,66D
Martin, Kyle	MA2300	13A,13,11,66,35B
Martin, Linda	IA0950	36,13,32B
Martin-Atwood, Michelle R.	NY3780	13
Martinez, Jesus E.	CA1700	13,29A,37,46
Martynuik, David G.	PA1600	37,13,32
Masaki, Megumi	AC0050	13,66A,66C,43,66B
Mason, Rodney	TX0350	13,36,61,66A,66D
Mason, Vicki	TX0200	13,32B
Masterson, Daniel J.	KS0150	13,41,66A,66B,42
Matascik, Sheri L.	TN1000	13,10,70,10B,13H
Mateiescu, Carmen	NJ1350	13
Mateiescu, Carmen	NJ1000	13,13C
Matejka, Merle	AJ0030	10,12A,31A,13,29
Matesky, Nancy	WA0860	13,66A,66D
Mathes, Gerard	ID0140	13,11,13J,62A,34
Mathes, James	FL0850	13,10
Mathews, Paul	MD0650	13
Mathews, Robert P.	CA6050	13,64,48,70
Matsuo, Jun	SC0450	66A,66D,66B,66C,13
Matsuoka, Yumiko	MA0260	13A,13
Matsushita, Hidemi	CO0100	66A,11,12,15,13
Matthay, Christopher D.	NY2750	13,14A,20D,20E,29A
Matthews, Bill	ME0150	13,10,29,34
Matthews, Justus F.	CA0825	13,10,43,34
Matthews, Michael K.	MO0850	13A,13,10F,47,63C
Matthews, Ron	PA1150	13,10,12A,63A,66A
Mattingly, Alan F.	NE0600	63B,13,42
Mattingly, Douglas	MD0060	13,29,35,70
Mattox, Amanda M.	MS0570	64,13,11
Mauceri, Frank	ME0340	10,13,12B
Maurtua, Jose Luis	MI0400	13A,13,10F,60,10
Maus, Fred Everett	VA1550	13,12B,15,12D,14C
Mauthe, Timothy	VA0250	13,10
Maxile, Horace J.	TX0300	13
May, Joanne	IL0850	13,38,42
May, Juliana	CT0450	11,13
Maynard, Keith	NY2400	13A,13,10F
Mayrose, John S.	IN0910	10,13
Mays, Walter A.	KS1450	13,10
Mazzaferro, Anthony	CA1900	13,63,37,12A
Mazzola, Guerino	MN1623	13

Index by Area of Teaching Interest

Name	Code	Areas
McAdoo, Susan	NJ1140	13,61,36
McAllister, Margaret	MA0260	10,13,34H,10A,34
McAllister, Michael	NC1750	13,10F,60,11,47
McAneny, Marc	MA0350	13
McAneny, Marc A.	NY3717	13,10F
McArthur, Lisa R.	KY0400	13,48,64A,12A,12F
McBride, Michael S.	IL2100	10,34,13,31,12A
McCabe, Matthew	GA0550	34,13,10
McCachren, Renee	NC2450	13,12A,66A,13E,13J
McCardell, Stephen	WI0350	13,10
McCarthy, Daniel	OH2150	10,13
McCarthy, David	NY2650	13
McCarthy, Keri E.	WA1150	64B,12A,13,11,12C
McClain, Charles	PA2550	13,36,66G
McClelland, Keith	TN1710	13,64D
McClelland, Ryan	AG0450	13
McClung, Sam W.	FL0365	60B,37,13,47,46
McClure, Sam	MO1780	13,38,62A,62B
McClure, Theron	OH1850	62D,13
McColley, Stacey	FL0800	64C,48,13
McCollough, Teresa	CA4425	13,12A,66A,66B,66C
McCollum, Jonathan Ray	MD0060	12,13,20,55,63C
McComas, Inez S.	FL1450	64E,13
McConnell, Douglas W.	OH0950	13,10
McConville, Brendan P.	TN1710	13,13F,13I,62C
McCord, Rebecca	VA1400	13,66A,66C
McCray, Jeffrey	NE0600	64D,13
McCreless, Patrick	CT0900	13
McCullam, Audrey	MD0600	13,32B,32C,66A,66D
McCullough, Allen	GA1300	13
McCullough, Thomas Eric	OK1330	10,62C,13,38,10C
McDermott, Dennette Derby	LA0550	13,64A
McDermott, Sheila	LA0080	11,13,61,66D
McDonald, John	MA1900	13A,10,12A,43,13
McDonald, Matthew	MA1450	13
McFarland, James	TX3600	11,13,66D,66G
McFarland, Mark J.	GA1050	13
McFarland, Timothy	MA2010	13,11,66A
McFatter, Larry E.	CA0845	13,10F,10,66A
McFerron, Mike	IL1520	13A,13,10F,34,10
McGann, Daniel	NY2450	13A,13,12A,70
McGee, Deron	KS1350	13,34
McGee, William James	CA3400	13,10F,10,66A,34
McGhee, Michael	GA2200	13,11,12A,66G,66H
McGinness, John R.	NY3780	13
McGowan, Mike	TX2000	11,37,49,13,29
McGregor, Cynthia	CA4850	13,11,34
McGrew, David	PA0150	10,13,66,31A,11
McGuinness, Peter	NJ1400	13,10,29,41
McGuire, David	NY1250	13,10,12A,13A,47
McIntosh, Bruce	OR1300	13,38,62C
McIntosh, John S.	AG0500	13,66G,66C,31A
McIntosh, W. Legare	AL0500	12A,13,66A,66G
McIntyre, Eric L.	IA0700	10,38,60,12A,13
McIntyre, John	IN1400	13,34,12A,36,10
McIntyre, John	IN1350	13,10,60,36
McKamie, David W.	MO1780	13,12A,66A
McKay, Frances	DC0170	13,10
McKay, Janis	NV0050	13,41,55,64D
McKay, Neil	HI0210	10,13
McKee, Eric John	PA2750	13
McKenney, W. Thomas	MO1800	13,10,34D
McKinley, Thomas L.	FL1125	13,10A,12A,34F
McKinney, David	KS0265	13,37,63D,64,29
McKinney, Timothy R.	TX0300	13
McKinnon, John A.	OR0200	13,10,63,34,14
McKittrick, Cam	AG0600	13
McKnight, Charles M.	NC2400	13,12A
McLean, Greg	GA0940	13,11,29,10
McLoskey, Lansing D.	FL1900	10A,10F,13,55D
McManus, James M.	CA3320	13,45,29A,12A,11
McMullen, Dianne M.	NY4310	13,12,66,31
McMullen, William W.	NE0600	13,12A,64B
McNair, Jonathan B.	TN1700	10A,34D,13,10,34
McQuere, Gordon	KS1400	13
McReynolds, Clifton	IL0720	13
McSpadden, George	AL0350	13,36,49,66A,66G
McTyre, Robert A.	GA1400	11,13,61
McVay, Vicki	KY1450	66D,13,66B,13C
Mead, Andrew W.	MI2100	13A,13
Meador, Rebecca	KS1400	13,64A
Meadows, Melody	WV0800	13,12A,66G,34,35A
Meek, Richard	TX3200	13,64D
Meeker, Christopher	NY2500	13
Meeks, Joseph D.	GA1150	13,12A,66,66B
Meissner, Marla	NJ0800	13A,13,20G
Melloni, Romeo	NH0250	13
Meltzer, Howard S.	NY0270	11,13,12,66A,63
Menchaca, Louis A.	WI0300	13A,13,60,37,29
Mendel, Traci R.	AL1050	13
Meng, Mei-Mei	PA0850	13
Meng, Mei-Mei	NY2250	13,66D
Menhart, Donna	CT0650	13
Menoche, Charles Paul	CT0050	10,12,13,34
Menton, Allen W.	CA0845	10,13
Mercer, Scott A.	IN1800	13A,13,47,61,53
Meredith, Steven	UT0190	13,36,61,34
Merkowitz, Jennifer Bernard	OH2050	10,13,34
Merriman, Margarita L.	MA0250	13,10,66A
Merritt, Justin W.	MN1450	10,13,43,13A,34
Merryman, Marjorie	NY2150	10,13
Mery, John Christian	OR0800	13,10,41,70,34
Metcalfe, Evelyn	FL2130	13,66
Metz, Andreas	OH0200	13
Metz, Ken	TX3410	13,10,29,29A
Metz, Paul W.	CO0250	13
Metzer, David	AB0100	13,29A,15
Meyer, Donald C.	IL1400	13,12A,10,34
Meyer, Eve R.	PA3250	13,12A,12
Meyer, Frederick	WV0650	13,32,48,64B
Meyer, Jeffrey	MN0600	12A,13,11,14,20
Meyer, Sandra G.	OK0650	13B,13C,13E,66A,13
Meyn, Till MacIvor	TX3000	13,10
Michael, Louis	IL1500	29,66A,13,11,34A
Michaelsen, Garrett	MA2030	12A,13
Middleton, Jonathan N.	WA0250	13,10,35C,34,35
Middleton, Robert M.	NJ0050	47,29,64,13,11
Mietz, Joshua	NM0400	64C,64E,13,38
Miksch, Bonnie	OR0850	10,13
Milam, Brent	GA1050	13
Miles, Stephen T.	FL1360	13,10,43
Miles, Tammy	MS0370	13,66A,66C,36
Miley, James	OR1300	10,29,47,46,13
Millan, Luis	MT0400	38,70,60B,13
Millar, Jana	TX0300	13
Millar, Robert R.	CA4625	13A,13,11,12A,66
Miller, Bruce	CA1900	13,66
Miller, David	OR0010	36,61,13,60
Miller, David	MS0050	13,47,46,29
Miller, Dennis H.	MA1450	13,10,45,34
Miller, Jeffrey L.	CA0807	13,10
Miller, John	ND0350	13,34
Miller, Michael	MI2250	13,48,64B
Miller, Patrick	CT0650	13
Miller, Paul V.	CO0800	13
Miller, Scott L.	MN1300	13,10A,10B,10C,34
Miller, Sue	ID0075	13,32B,66
Miller-Thorn, Jill	NY1275	10A,10F,13,66D,12C
Millett, Michael J.	TX3535	13,10
Millican, Brady	MA0800	13,11,12A,66A,66C
Milligan, Thomas	TN0250	13,12A,66A,34
Mills, David	OR0050	13,10,12A,37,63A
Mills, Joan G.	CA4450	13,66
Mills, Robert	AZ0440	13,66A,66C
Minturn, Neil	MO1800	13
Mirchandani, Sharon	NJ1350	13,12
Mitchell, Carol	GA0940	13,66A,66G,66C,66D
Mitchell, Darleen C.	NE0590	13,10,15,43,12B
Mitchell, Rachel E.	TX3420	13
Mitchell, Robert	MO0600	13,32,36
Mitts, Thomas	VA1350	13
Miura, Hiroya	ME0150	10,13,38
Miyake, Jan	OH1700	13
Miyama, Yoko	OR0050	66,13,12A,66C,66D
Miyamoto, Peter M.	MO1800	66,13,42
Miyashiro, Kurt	IL2800	13,10A,34,10C
Mizener, Gary	TX1400	13
Mobley, Mel	LA0770	65,13
Moe, Eric H.	PA3420	13,10,45,10B
Moehlen, Carl B.	IA0900	13,12A,44,66G,31A
Mohen, Gerald	NY2400	13,11
Molberg, Keith	AJ0030	66A,34D,13,66C,13A
Moltoni, Giovanni	MA0260	13
Monachino, Paul	OH1330	13,10A,66,60
Monhardt, Jonathan	WI0825	10,13
Monical, Dwight	IN1300	13,11
Monier, Shelly	MO1100	13
Montague, Eugene	DC0100	13,34A
Montalto, Richard Michael	MS0550	13,12A,35,10,13F
Montgomery, Kip	NY3250	11,12,13,64C
Moody, Gary E.	CO0250	64B,13,41,64D
Mooney, Kevin	AG0500	13,13J,12C
Moore, David A.	OK1450	10,13,11,36
Moore, James Walter	KY0400	34,13,10,70
Moore, Julianna	MO1780	13,48,64A
Moore, Kevin	NY2950	13,66A,66C,66D,10A
Moore, Michael W.	SC0200	32C,32E,32G,37,13
Moore, Rick	AZ0200	13,11,37,46,49
Moore, Robert S.	CA5300	13,10
Moore, Selma	NY2950	13,37,41,64A,66D
Moorman, Joyce Solomon	NY2100	13,10,11,66A,66D
Moorman, Joyce E.	NY0270	11,13,20A,34D,66
Moravec, Paul	NY0050	13,10
Morden, James	GA2000	13,11,12A,63A
Moreau, Barton	ID0050	13,11,66C,66D,66A
Morehead, Phillip H.	TN0850	13,41,63A,32E
Morelock, Donald	MI1900	13,11,12A,66A,66B
Moreno, Jairo	PA3350	13,13J,20H,29,12D
Mori, Akane	CT0650	13
Morris, Brian	MI0850	70,13,34D
Morris, Gregory	MO0400	11,66A,66B,13
Morris, J. David	GA2150	65,34,13,50
Morris, James R.	NY3700	13A,63A,13,11,49
Morris, Matthew B.	OH1900	13,42,64D
Morris, Robert D.	NY1100	10,12,13,20E,31E
Morrison, Charles D.	AG0600	13
Morrison, John H.	MA1175	10,13
Morrison, Kenneth	AB0100	13
Morrison, Simon	NJ0900	13,12A,12,11
Moseley, Brian	SC0750	13
Moseley, Jessica Barnett	SC0750	13,66C,66D
Moseley, Roger S.	NY0900	12,13,14D,34H
Moser, Bruce	NC0400	12,66A,66B,13,66D
Moser, Martin	NY3500	13,12A,54,20G
Moshier, Steve	CA3750	13,11,12A,34,43
Moss, Lawrence	MD1010	13,10,10F
Moss, Orlando	MS0560	13,60,36,61
Mount, Andre	NY3780	13
Mountain, Rosemary	AI0070	13,10F,10,45,34
Mowrey, Peter C.	OH0700	10,66A,13,34
Moxley, Bryant	VA0050	13,66A,60A,31A,36
Moyer, Cynthia M.	CA2250	13,41,62A,62B
Muchmore, Pat	NY3560	13A,13
Mudge, Ashley	FL1700	13,64A
Muegel, Glenn	NC0050	13,41,62A,62B
Mueller, Charlotte G.	TX1450	13,11,66A,66D
Mueller, Frank	WI0835	13,12
Mueller, Robert K.	AR0700	10,13
Muhl, Erica	CA5300	13,10
Mulford, Ruth Stomne	DE0175	13,11,12A,62A,20G
Mulholland, Joseph	MA0260	13A,13
Muller, Gerald	TX2170	13,11,12A,32,36
Mumford, Lawrence R.	CA5355	10,12,13,10F
Muniz, Michelle	IN0910	10A,13,10B,10,43
Munn, Albert Christopher	TX3525	13,12A,36,67,55B
Munn, Vivian C.	TX3525	13,32C,36,61
Munn, Zae	IN1450	13,10F,10,43
Murphree, John	MA0350	13
Murphy, Barbara A.	TN1710	13
Murphy, Cynthia	NE0300	16,66A,66D,13
Murphy, Edward W.	AZ0500	13,13J
Murphy, James L.	ID0250	13
Murphy, Joanna	FL0200	10,13
Murphy, Paul T.	NY3725	13
Murphy, Scott	KS1350	13
Murray, Janice	NC0250	66A,66C,66D,13
Murray, Melissa M.	TX2400	13
Murray, Michael F.	MO0775	10,13
Murray, Michael A.	MO0775	13,51,62C
Murray, Stephen	MA0280	13
Myers, Andre K.	CA3300	10A,10B,10F,13
Myers, Gerald C.	MO1120	11,36,40,54,13
Myers, Jeff	MS0320	11,66,13
Myers, Ty	IA0200	13,38
Myrick, Barbara	OR0350	13,12A,66A,66D,64A
Myska, David	AG0500	13,10,45,34,35C
Naegele, Elizabeth M.	IL1850	13A,13,66A,66G,11
Naeve, Denise	IA0790	61,66A,13
Nagatani, Chie	CA1700	66A,13,11
Nagel, Jody	IN0150	13,10,45,35C
Naidoo, Shaun	CA0960	13
Nakra, Teresa Marrin	NJ0175	13,34,10B
Narducci, Kenneth	CA2420	10,37,32E,46,13
Narmour, Eugene	PA3350	13,12,38
Narum, Jessica	MN0600	13
Nash, Gary Powell	TN0550	10,13,47,64,10F

Name	Code	Areas
Nauert, Paul	CA5070	13,10
Navari, Jude Joseph	CA4625	10,11,13,36,61
Neal, Jocelyn	NC2410	13,20G,34,14C
Neblett, Sonja	CA4150	13,60
Needelman, William	NY2250	13
Needleman, Gail	CA2200	13
Neff, Severine	NC2410	13
Neff, Teresa M.	MA1200	13,11
Negrete, Merida	NC2410	32,13
Neidhoefer, Christoph	AI0150	13,10
Neil, Mary	IL0100	13,66A,66C,66B
Nelson, David W.	CA0859	13,13A,10F,10,38
Nelson, David L.	NC2430	13,60,37
Nelson, Kristen	TX2700	13
Nelson, Larry A.	PA3600	13,10,45,34
Nelson, Mark	AZ0480	37,13,63D,34
Nelson, Mattew	UT0325	13,64
Nelson, Richard	ME0340	10,34,13,29,47
Nelson, Richard B.	OH0600	13
Nelson, Robert S.	TX3400	13A,13,10F,10
Nelson, Timothy	IL2300	13,10F,66A,66G
Nelson-Raney, Steven	WI0825	13A,13,29B
Nemhauser, Frank	NY2250	13,60,61
Ness, David J.	IL0650	70,11,13
Neumeyer, David	TX3510	13,10
Neville, Ruth	SC0750	66D,13
New, Laura	KS0570	13
Newlin, Yvonne	IL1612	13,60,37,66,47
Newman, Ronald	MI1400	13
Ng, Samuel	OH2200	13
Niblock, Howard	WI0350	13,10F,12B,41,64B
Nicely, Tiffany	NY3725	13,65
Nicholeris, Carol A.	MA0510	10A,13D,13A,36,13
Nicholl, Matthew J.	MA0260	13
Nichols, Eugene C.	ME0430	13,36,37,46,12A
Nichols, Jeff W.	NY0642	10,10F,13
Nichols, Kenneth	AC0050	66A,13
Nichols, Samuel S.	CA5010	13,10,70,10B
Nicholson, Tina	IL1750	13,64B
Niederberger, Maria	TN0500	13,10F,10
Nies, Carol R.	TN1850	60,38,13,32E
Nin, Chan Ka	AG0450	13A,13,10,10F
Ninov, Dimitar	TX3175	13
Nisbett, Robert	CO0250	13,12A,66C
Niskala, Naomi	PA3150	66A,66C,13
Nissen, James	MI1900	13A,13,37,34
Nitschke, Brad	IN0005	11,12,13,60,63
Nivans, David	CA0805	14C,29A,20,13,11
Noh, Gerrey	OH1100	13
Nohai-Seaman, Alexander	NY4050	13,10,43
Nolan, Catherine	AG0500	13,13J
Nonken, Marilyn C.	NY2750	12,13,66A
Noonkester, Lila D.	SC0800	13,39,61,11
Nord, Merilee	NY1800	13
Nord, Timothy	NY1800	13,34
Nordgren, Jon	CA0400	13,37,46,47,60
Norris, Joshua L.	KS0900	36,60,13,32
Notareschi, Loretta K.	CO0650	10,11,13
Novak, Christina D.	AZ0490	11,13,66A,10A,66D
Novak, John K.	IL2200	13
Nowak, Gerald C.	PA0400	13,37,47,64
Nozny, Brian	ND0100	13,10A,10F,34A,34B
Nuss, Steven R.	ME0250	13,14
Nyberg, Gary B.	WA0480	13,10,37,63D,54
Obermueller, Karola	NM0450	10,13
Obrecht, Guy	AA0050	12A,13,47
Ochoa, Reynaldo	TX3450	63A,49,13
O'Connor, Thomas	AR0110	13,32,47,10A,10F
Odom, Leslie S.	FL1850	13,64B
O'Donnell, Shaugn	NY0550	13,10,12
Ogdon, Will L.	CA5050	13,10F,10,12A
Ogletree, Mary	PA1750	13,11,62A,62B,51
OGrady, Douglas M.	CT0800	13,34,35G,10
O'Grady, Terence J.	WI0808	13,12A,12,14,55
Oh, Seung-Ah	IL0750	10,13,13F,10A
Ohia, Chinyerem	DC0150	13
Ohl, Vicki	OH0950	13,66A,66D
Ohriner, Mitchell S.	VA1350	13,13K,13E
Okpebholo, Shawn E.	IL3550	13,10
Okumura, Lydie	MA0260	13A,13
Olah, John J.	FL1900	13,49,63D
Olan, David M.	NY0250	13,10,11
Oliver, Harold	NJ1050	13,10F,10,41,53
Oliveros, Pauline	NY3300	12,13,10B,11
Olivier, Thomas	KS0980	70,13
Olivieri, Mark A.	NY1550	10,13,20G,29,48
Ollen, Joy	AB0050	13
Olsen, Lance	NJ0990	13A,13,11,34
Olsen, Timothy J.	NY4310	13,10,47,63A,29
Olson, Mia	MA0260	13A,13
Onofrio, Marshall	NJ1350	13,10,29,34,32E
Oravitz, Michael	IN0150	13,10
Orenstein, Arbie	NY0642	13A,13,11,12A
Orfe, John	IL0400	10,13
O'Riordan, Kirk	PA1850	10,60B,13,64E
Orlick, James	SC0150	13,34,50
Orpen, Rick	MN0750	13,70,34,10
Orr, Gerald	TX1250	13,11,36,37,66A
Orr, Kevin Robert	FL1850	66A,66B,66D,13A,13
Ortiz, Pablo	CA5010	13,10,45,29,34
Osborn, Bradley T.	OH1900	13
Osborne, Thomas	HI0210	10A,10F,13,43
Osmun, Ross	AI0050	13,41,42,66A,66B
Osten, Mark	CA3250	13
Osterfield, Paul	TN1100	13,10
Ostrander, Jeanette Davis	OH0600	13
O'Sullivan, Laila K.	TN1680	13,13C,29C
Oswalt, Lewis	MS0400	12A,13,31A
Outland, Joyanne	IN0905	13,66A,66D,66B
Ovens, Douglas P.	PA2550	13,10,45,65
Owens, Douglas A.	TN1720	64B,64D,13
Owens, Janet	FL1450	66D,13,11
Owolabi, Olukola P.	NY4150	66G,13
Oyen, David W.	KY0900	13,48,64D
Paccione, Paul	IL3500	13,10,43,20G
Pace, Matthew	MO1950	10,13
Pack, Tim S.	OR1050	13
Packales, Joseph	ME0500	13,10F,10
Pacun, David E.	NY1800	13
Page, Gordon	TX1725	11,13,36
Page, Sandra	AA0050	13A,13,66A
Painter, Noel	FL1750	13,10F
Palej, Norbert	AG0450	10,13
Palestrant, Christopher	NC0700	13,10
Palmer, Edit	FL1750	13,66A
Palmer, Jason	OR1020	66D,13,13C,29A,29B
Palmer, John	CA4700	12,13
Panetti, Joan	CT0850	13
Pann, Carter N.	CO0800	13,10
Panneton, Isabelle	AI0200	13,10A
Paoli, Kenneth N.	IL0630	13,10,11,35,34
Pape, Louis W.	SD0150	13,10,11,32,66
Pappas, Mark	MI0600	13,29
Para, Christopher	PA0350	13,11,38,62A,62B
Parakilas, James P.	ME0150	13,11,42,12
Parcell, John	OH2120	13,66A,11,29,34C
Parchman, Thomas	ME0500	13A,13,64C
Parillo, Joseph M.	RI0300	13,10,47,46,29
Paris, John	IL0720	13
Park, Christopher	NY2250	13
Park, Sang Eui	IN0005	10,60,12,13,31A
Park-Song, Sophia	CO0830	11,13,66A
Parker, Bradley	SC0700	66,13
Parker, Don	NC0800	13,50,65,29
Parker, Grant	CA1500	13,11,12A,49,37
Parker, Linda	NC0200	11,32,44,13,64
Parker, Philip	AR0200	13,10F,10,65,50
Parker, Sylvia	VT0450	13,66A,66D,66B
Parks, Richard S.	AG0500	13
Parks, Ronald Keith	SC1200	10,13,34,41
Parnell, Scott	OH0250	11,70,13
Parran, John D.	NY0270	11,13,20,29,64
Parrish, Eric	MN1175	11,13,36,61
Parsche, Paula	FL0800	13,66A,66C,11
Parsons, Derek J.	SC0750	13,66A,66B,66D
Paschal, Brett E. E.	OR0400	65,13,11
Pashkin, Elissa Brill	MA1100	13,10
Paslawski, Gordon	AB0100	13
Pastorello, Cristian	IL0150	66A,66B,66C,11,13
Patrick, Dennis M.	AG0450	13,45,13L,34,35C
Patterson, David N.	MA2010	13,10,11,20G,34
Patterson, Michael R.	IA1350	12A,32B,66A,13,10
Patton, Robert	MA0260	13A,13
Pau, Andrew Yat-Ming	OH1700	13
Paul, John F.	OR0500	10,13,34
Paul, Philip	NC0050	13,36,63B
Pauley, John-Bede	MN0350	61,13,11
Payne, Benjamin	FL0670	11,34,13,66A,66D
Peacock, Kenneth J.	NY2750	13,10,12,35,34
Pearsall, Edward	TX3510	13
Pecherek, Michael J.	IL1175	13,60,11,38,62C
Peck, Robert W.	LA0200	13
Pederson, Donald	TN1710	13
Pedneault-Deslauriers, Julie	AG0400	13,10
Pedroza, Ricardo	PR0125	13,60,36,66A,66D
Peebles, Crystal	AZ0450	13,34
Peles, Stephen	AL1170	13
Pellegrin, Richard S.	MO1800	13
Pellman, Samuel	NY1350	13,10B,10,34
Pelo, Mika	CA5010	10,11,13,43
Pelto, William L.	NC0050	13
Pelusi, Mario J.	IL1200	10A,10F,13,43,29B
Pender, Charles	TN1380	13,11,61,66A,60
Pennington, Curt	IN0800	13,66D
Perconti, William J.	ID0130	13,11,47,64
Perkins, Richard	MN0040	13
Perkins, Scott	IN0350	10,13
Perkins, Tedrow	OH2600	13,64B
Perkyns, Jane E.	TX3150	66A,13,12A,66,66C
Perlongo, Daniel J.	PA1600	10,13,29
Perone, James E.	OH2290	11,13,12E,64C
Perry, Jeffrey	LA0200	13
Perry, Tiffany	DC0170	13,64C
Pershing, Drora	NY0642	13,12A
Perttu, Daniel E.	PA3650	10A,13
Petering, Mark D.	WI0250	10,13,34
Peters, Lorna G.	CA0840	66A,66H,13
Petersen, Marian F.	MO1810	13,12A
Peterson, Don L.	UT0050	13,12A,13J,63B
Peterson, Floyd	ID0250	13,12A
Peterson, Jay	IL1650	13,12A,14,66A,66G
Peterson, Keith L.	NY3725	13,10,45
Peterson, Vince	NY0500	36,60A,32D,13,11
Peterson, Wayne T.	CA4200	13,10F,10,12A,66A
Pethel, Stan	GA0300	13,60,10,63C,10F
Petrides, Ron T.	NY2660	10,29,70,13,12
Pettaway, Charles H.	PA2000	13,11,12A,66,66G
Petty, Byron W.	VA1850	64A,13
Petty, Judith V.	MI2100	13
Petty, Wayne C.	MI2100	13A,13
Pfaff, William P.	NY3775	10,13,12A,13F,13I
Pflueger, Bethany	CA1960	13,41
Philipsen, Michael D.	IA0750	13,11,36,61,66A
Phillips, Joel	NJ1350	13,10,34
Phillips, Paul Schuyler	RI0050	38,60,13,10,10F
Phillips-Farley, Barbara	NY3550	66,13,12
Phipps, Graham H.	TX3420	13,13J
Piagentini, Susan M.	IL2250	13C,13H,13K,13
Piccone, James	NJ1050	13,10,34
Pickering, David C.	KS0650	66A,66G,66H,13,12A
Pickett, John	WA0050	13,11,12A,66A,66B
Pickett, Susan	WA1300	13A,13,12A,51,62A
Pierce, Forrest D.	KS1350	13,10,43
Pieslak, Jonathan	NY0550	10,13
Pignato, Joseph M.	NY3765	35,34,10,13
Piltzecker, Ted	NY3785	13
Pinckney, Warren R.	CA0800	11,20G,29A,13
Ping, Jin	NY3760	13,10,62A,20A,20B
Pinkston, Dan	CA4600	13,12A,14,10,20
Pinkston, Joan	SC0200	13,66A,34
Piper, Deirdre	AG0100	13,10,12A
Pisano, James	KS0200	64C,64E,47,53,13
Pisaro, Michael J.	CA0510	13,10,12D
Pitts, Ruth	TX1600	13,12A,66A
Planer, John H.	IN1050	20,12,13,14,61
Plash, Duane	AL1195	13,10,66A,40
Platoff, John	CT0500	13,11,14C,12,12F
Platt, Nathan	KY1200	13,60,61,31A
Plazak, Joseph S.	IL1200	13
Ploger, Marianne	TN1850	13
Plotkin, Richard	NY4320	13
Plude, Patricia	CA4425	13
Pogonowski, Lenore	NY4200	53,32,12A,13
Poklewski, Annamarie	CA1550	13,66A
Polanka, William Mark	OH1100	13
Polanka, William Mark	OH2150	13,62A
Polansky, Larry	NH0100	13,10,45,34
Polett, Thomas C.	MO0300	63,47,32,13,20
Polot, Barton L.	MI1900	10A,10B,10F,12,13
Pomerantz, Mark	TX3410	13
Pomeroy, David Boyd	AZ0500	13
Pool, Scott	TX3500	64D,13,48,11,64E
Poole, Eric	NC2150	13,60,20G,36,41
Pope, Jerry	KS0590	13,66A,11
Popeney, Mark	CA5300	10,13
Popoff-Parks, Linette A.	MI1260	13,66A,66B,66C

Index by Area of Teaching Interest

Name	Code	Areas
Porter, Charles	NY2400	13A,13,10,11,12A
Porter, Lewis R.	NJ1140	13,12,29,29A
Porterfield, Richard R.	NY2750	12,13,31A,55D
Porterfield, Richard	NY2250	13
Pos, Margie	WA0200	29,62D,66A,13
Posch, Carl	AZ0150	13,11,37,47,63D
Poshek, Joe	CA3350	13,70
Post, J. Brian	CA2250	34,35,13,10
Post, Julie Goodman	NY2400	13
Post, William	OH1100	13
Post, William Dean	AK0150	13,12A,10A
Potes, Cesar I.	MI1200	13,10,11,34
Poudrier, Eve	CT0900	13,13I,13F,13K,13J
Poulsen, James	IA1350	13,66A,66C,10
Pound, Robert	PA0950	13,10,11,38
Pounds, Michael S.	IN0150	10,34D,13,45,34
Powe, Holly	AL0330	61,13,11,60,47
Powell, Curtis Everett	GA0490	36,13,32,32D
Powell, Daniel	FL0350	11,13,47,63,64
Presar, Jennifer	IL2900	63B,13B,13C,13
Prescott, John S.	MO0775	13,10,20
Pretzat, Julie	NY3770	13,60,36
Prevost, Roxane	AG0400	13
Price, Berkeley	CA0200	13,37,48,64
Price, Hannah E.	NC0050	13
Price, William M.	AL1150	13,10
Priest, Charles	KY1200	13
Primatic, Stephen P.	GA0200	65,13,29,11,47
Primosch, James	PA3350	13,10,10B
Prince, J. Whitney	MI0600	13
Prins, Rene	NY3765	64B,37,13,41
Priore, Irna	NC2430	13,13I
Pritchard, Bob	AB0100	13,10,34
Proctor, Freda	KS1375	66,64A,13,37,41
Proctor, Gregory	OH1850	13,10,34
Proksch, Bryan	LA0350	13
Prosser, Steve	MA0260	13A,13
Prouten, William	AA0032	13,47,64,53,29A
Prouty, Patrick	MI2120	47,13,43,10
Ptaszynska, Marta	IL3250	13,10,10F
Puckett, Joel W.	MD0650	13
Puri, Michael James	VA1550	13,12
Purin, Peter	OK0650	13,34
Pursell, William	TN0100	10,12A,13,11,66G
Pyle, Jane	FL1300	13,11,12A,66A,66B
Pysh, Gregory	TX3527	10,13,61,60A,36
Quaglia, Bruce	UT0250	13
Quathamer, Mark	FL0150	10,13,34
Quinn, Christopher	UT0400	13,36
Quinn, Ian	CT0900	13
Quist, Pamela	CA4425	13,10,66A,12
Rackley, David	CA1510	11,13
Radell, Judith M.	PA1600	13,66A,66D,66C
Radford, Laurie	AA0150	10,10F,13,43
Radley, Roberta	MA0260	13A,13
Rae, Wendy	AA0050	13,32A,66A
Raevens, Jean M.	PA1050	13,11,12
Rager, Dan	WI0804	37,13,46
Ragogini, Ernest	MD0100	13,12A,66A,12C
Rahn, Jay	AG0650	13,12
Rahn, John	WA1050	13,10,34
Raifsnider, Christoper J.	MD0060	12,13,64C
Rainsong, Lisa	OH0600	13
Raisor, Steve C.	NC0500	11,13,37,47,70
Rakowski, David	MA0500	13,10,12A
Ramey, Lauren	TN1850	13
Ramos, Rene	CA2420	13A,13,12A,12,66A
Ramstrum, Momilani	CA4050	13
Randall, James K.	NJ0900	13,10
Randall, Richard R.	PA0550	13
Ranjbaran, Behzad	NY1900	13
Ransom, McCoy	LA0100	13,66A,66G,66C
Rao, Nancy	NJ1130	13
Rapoport, Alexander	AG0450	13
Rapoport, Paul	AG0200	13,11,12A,12
Ratliff, Phillip	AL0650	13,12A,10F,34
Ratliff, Richard J.	IN1650	13,66A,12D
Ravenscroft, Brenda	AG0250	13,13F,13A
Ravnan, John	SC0765	62B,42,13
Rawlins, Nancy	NJ1050	66D,66G,13,12
Rawlins, Robert	NJ1050	13,12
Rawls, J. Archie	MS0580	13,11,64,46,48
Raynovich, William Jason	IL0600	13,10,34
Rea, Edward	SC0200	13,66A,66G,66F
Rea, John	AI0150	13,10
Rea, Judith	SC0200	13,66A
Rea, Stephanie	KY0950	64A,13
Read, Thomas L.	VT0450	13,10
Reale, Steven	OH2600	13
Reams, John	GA1800	13,38,41,64
Reba, Christopher H.	CT0700	34D,10B,35G,62D,13
Recca, David	NY3785	60,13
Rector, Malcolm W.	TX3450	13,10,29,47
Reddick, Carissa	CO0950	13
Redman, Will	MD0850	12,13
Redwood, Andre	IN1700	13
Reed, Allen	TX1100	13,44,66,31A
Reed, S. Alexander	FL1850	13,10
Reed, Teresa Shelton	OK1450	13,12A
Reeves, Scott	NY0550	13,47,53,29
Regan, Martin	TX2900	10,20C,13
Rehding, Alexander	MA1050	13,12A,12B,12C,12G
Rehwoldt, Lisa	MD0100	13,12A,66A
Reid, Sally	TN0930	10,13,64B,10C,34
Reid, Steven	IN0005	63A,36,37,38,13
Reighard, Mark	OK1200	13A,13,66A,11
Reilly, Allyn D.	OH1900	13
Reiprich, Bruce J.	AZ0450	13,10,34
Reise, Jay	PA3350	13,10F,10
Reiter, Burkhardt	PA3420	10,13
Rendleman, Ruth	NJ0800	13,66A,66B
Rendler-McQueeney, Elaine J.	VA0450	13
Renter, David	MI0900	11,13,29
Rentz, David Joseph	CA4500	13
Renwick, William J. M.	AG0200	13,60,13J
Resanovic, Nikola	OH2150	13,10
Restesan, Francise T.	PR0125	13,60,12B,38,41
Rewoldt, Todd	CA4100	13,29,64E
Rey, Mario	NC0650	14,13,20H
Reynolds, Robert	KY0860	13A,13,11,66A,20G
Reynolds, Roger L.	CA5050	13,10F,10,20G,34
Reynolds, Winton	TX3510	13
Rhein, Robert	IN0200	10A,66A,11,12A,13
Rhodebeck, Jacob	NY0270	66A,66C,11,13
Rhodes, Phillip	MN0300	13A,13,10,11
Ribando, Jeremy S.	FL1430	61,13
Ricci, Adam	NC2430	13
Ricci, Robert	MI2250	13,10F,12B,29
Richards, Mark C.	AA0200	13,12A
Richards, Paul	FL1850	13,10
Richards, Richard	MN1620	13
Richardson, Abby	AG0450	13
Richardson, Danene	AZ0440	13,10
Richardson, Mark Douglas	NC0650	13,10A
Richardson, Robert C.	WA0450	13,11,37,38,47
Richens, James W.	TN1680	13,10,45
Richmond, C. Floyd	PA3560	32,34,13
Richmond, Thomas	MN0600	13,10,11,12A
Richter, Tiffany	AL1450	13,36,40,61
Riddick, Frank C.	OK1350	13
Ridges, Lameriel R.	SC1050	13,66A,66C
Riepe, Russell C.	TX3175	13,10,45
Rieth, Dale	FL0950	13,36,47,61,66A
Rife, Jerry E.	NJ1000	13,11,12A,12,37
Rifkin, Deborah	NY1800	13
Riley, David	RI0150	13,70
Riley, Denise	MS0200	13,36,61
Riley, Raymond G.	MI0150	66A,13,34,34H
Rimple, Mark T.	PA3600	13,10
Rindfleisch, Andrew P.	OH0650	10,13,43
Rinehart, John	OH0050	13A,13,10F,10,12A
Ring, Gordon L.	VA0700	13,10,37,34
Rings, Steven M.	IL3250	13
Rinzler, Paul	CA0600	13,10,47,66A,29
Riseling, Robert A.	AG0500	13,37,38,41,64C
Rissman, Maurice Nick	TX1400	13,10F,10
Ritz, Lyn	WA1100	62A,62B,42,13,10F
Rivard, Gene	MN0625	13,10F,49,63,31A
Rivers, Joseph L.	OK1450	13,10A,10C,34D,34E
Rizzer, Gerald	IL2750	66A,13,10
Robbins, David P.	WA0650	13,50,65
Robbins, Malcolm Scott	SC0650	13,10,14C
Roberts, David Scott	TN1720	66G,13,10F
Roberts, Shannon B.	UT0150	13,41,49,63C,10
Roberts, Tim	CA3320	46,14C,10D,13
Robertson, Eric	AG0450	10,13
Robertson, James D.	MT0175	13,60B,63C,63D,47
Robertson, Kaestner	MA0250	66A,13,36,66B,66C
Robertson, Masson	IN0905	13,66A,66B,66C
Robinson, Curtis	IN0005	13,16,29,34,35
Robinson, Emily	OK1050	13,66
Robinson, Jason	MA0100	12,13,14,34
Robinson, Rick	NY0270	11,13,65,32
Robinson, Schuyler	KY1450	13,66G,66H,31A
Robinson, Thomas	AL1170	13
Robison, John O.	FL2000	13,12A,12,67
Rocco, Robert P.	NC1650	66C,13
Roche-Wallace, Catherine	LA0760	13,63B
Rochinski, Stephen	MA0260	13A,13
Rockmaker, Jody D.	AZ0100	13A,13,10,12A,43
Rockwell, Joti	CA3650	13,14C,11
Rodgers, Joseph W.	MN1000	38,62C,13,62D
Rodgers, Lloyd A.	CA0815	13,10,43
Rodgers, Stephen	OR1050	13
Rodland, Catherine	MN1450	13,66G
Rodman, Ronald	MN0300	13,37,63C,63D,12D
Rodriguez-Salazar, Martha	CA1250	13,64A
Roed, Tom	MO0750	13,11,66A
Roeder, John B.	AB0100	13
Roens, Steven	UT0250	13,10
Rogers, Lynne	NJ1400	13
Rogers, Martha	MA0350	13,32I
Rogers, Michael	OR1050	13
Rogers, Nancy Marie	FL0850	13B,13H,13K,13C,13
Rogers, Rodney	AZ0100	13,10F,10
Roginske, Lynn	WI1150	13A,13
Rohde, Kurt E.	CA5010	13,10,11,43
Rohr, Deborah	NY3650	13,11,12A
Roig-Francoli, Miguel A.	OH2200	13,10
Roitman, Tatiana	AR0750	66A,66D,13
Rojahn, Karolina	MA0350	13
Rojas, Nuria Mariela	SC0150	11,12,13,34,66
Rojek, Justin J.	AL0345	11,66,13
Rokeach, Martin	CA3920	13A,13,11,12A,41
Rolfe, James	AG0450	10,13
Rollin, Gwen	OH2600	13
Rollin, Robert	OH2600	13,10,43
Rolls, Timothy	KS0350	10,13,34,35C,35G
Rolnick, Neil B.	NY3300	13,10,45,34
Roman, Dan	CT0500	34,70,10A,10F,13
Romano, Charlene	VA1350	64A,13
Romig, James	IL3500	13,13F,10A,10
Romine, Ryan D.	VA1350	64D,13
Root, Gordon	NY3725	13
Root, Jena	OH2600	10,13
Root, Thomas R.	UT0350	13,10,37,41
Rose, Francois	CA5350	13,10
Rose, Gwendolyn	MI2250	13,48,64D
Rose, Michael	TN1850	13,10,12A,11,31
Rose, William G.	LA0350	13,49,34,63D,63C
Roseland, Chad	IN0800	13,64D
Rosenberg, Aaron H.	MA2030	13,66D
Rosenblum, Mathew	PA3420	13,10F,10
Rosenfeld, Andrew	MD0610	11,12,13,20F,36
Rosenzweig, Morris	UT0250	13,10F,10
Rosner, Arnold	NY2050	13A,13,11,14,66A
Ross, Clark	AD0050	13,10
Ross, Jared	KS0060	13,60,31A,36,61
Ross, John C.	KS1050	13,10,10F
Ross, John	WV0700	13,64A,11
Ross, Nicholas Piers	VA1400	13,66A,66C,12
Ross-Hammond, Amelia	VA0950	13,13J,36,66
Roter, Bruce	NY0700	10,13,12A,64C
Rothfarb, Lee	CA5060	13J,13I,13B,13E,13
Rothgeb, John	NY3705	13A,13
Rothstein, William	NY0642	13
Roubal, Peter	IL2350	13,10,34B,47
Rous, Bruce	WV0400	13,66D
Roush, Dean	KS1450	13,10F,10,34
Row, Peter	MA1400	14,12,13
Rowlett, Donn	OK1500	13,11,66
Roy, J. Michael	WI0845	13,10A,10F
Royal, Jacquelyn A.	TN0300	11,13,16,34B
Royal, Matthew	AG0050	13,11,12B
Roye, Tobin	CA0800	70,13
Royem, Dominique	TX1000	13
Royse, Dennis	CA0250	13,12A,32C,11
Roze, Chris	CA5300	13,10
Rozin, Alexander	PA3600	10,13
Rozman, Jure	FL0200	66A,13,41
Rubin, Justin H.	MN1600	13,34,66G,10,66A
Ruehr, Elena	MA1200	13,10,34
Ruff, Willie H.	CT0850	35,10F,13
Ruggiero, Charles	MI1400	13,10
Rumbolz, Robert C.	WY0130	13,35C,35D,34,20A
Rumney, Jon	ND0250	13,38,41,62A,62B

Name	Code	Areas
Runefors, Bjorn	AE0120	36,37,13,11,64A
Runner, David C.	TN1150	13,10F,66A,66G,10A
Ruocco, Phyllis	AR0550	13A,13,11,66A,10F
Rusch, Rene	AI0150	13
Rusche, Marjorie M.	IN0910	10,13
Rush, Toby	OH2250	13,34C
Rushton, David	AB0090	13,60,32C,31A
Russell, Armand	HI0210	10,13
Russell, Eileen Meyer	TX2650	63D,13,13C,49,63C
Russell, Jennifer	AZ0450	13
Russell, Ralph Anthony	NJ0175	13,29A,12E
Rust, Douglas	MS0750	13
Rutkowski, Chris	IN0905	13,34D
Rutschman, Edward R.	WA1250	13A,13,11,12A,12
Ryan, Francis J.	OK1450	13,34,11
Ryan, Sarah E.	MO1800	13,66D
Ryder, Christopher O.	VA1150	34,61,32,13,40
Ryder, William H.	LA0700	11,32,64,13
Rytting, Bryce	UT0325	12,13,38,60
Sabatella, Marc	CO0900	13,29B
Sabina, Leslie M.	NY3475	29,10,34,13,47
Sabourin, Carmen	AI0150	13
Sabre, Alejandro	CA3000	13,66A
Sain, James Paul	FL1850	13,10,34
Saker, Marilyn	MI0600	13,12A
Sakins, Renate	PA3100	13,64,64B
Salazar, Jason	MO0400	34,13,35,43,47
Salerni, Paul F.	PA1950	13,10,43
Salerno, John	WI0808	13,10,47,48,29
Salley, Keith P.	VA1350	13
Sallis, Friedemann	AA0150	12,13
Sallmen, Mark	NY2650	13
Salucka, Ray	IA0930	13,36,60,11,47
Salyer, Douglas W.	CT0200	13,34,12A,36,66
Samarotto, Frank	IN0900	13
Sametz, Steven P.	PA1950	13,60,10,36
Samson, Louise	AI0210	13
Samuelson, Linda	MN1270	13,20,37,46,64
San Martin, Laurie A.	CA5010	10,13,43,35E
Sanborn, Timothy	IN0250	13
Sanchez-Behar, Alexander	OH0100	13,10
Sander, Kurt L.	KY1000	10,13
Sanders, Gregory L.	TX2960	13,10F,10,34
Sandler, Felicia A.	MA1400	13
Sandred, Orjan	AC0100	10,13,34
Sanford, David	MA1350	13,10,29A
Santa, Matthew	TX3200	13,10
Santore, Jonathan C.	NH0250	13,10
Santorelli, Shari	TX1660	13,66C
Santos, Denis Almeida	KY0400	64A,13
Sapieyevski, Jerzy	DC0010	13,10,45,11,34
Sargon, Simon	TX2400	13,10F
Sarver, Sarah	OK0750	13,13E
Saslaw, Janna K.	LA0300	13
Satre, Paul J.	IL3150	36,66A,66G,60,13
Satterwhite, Marc	KY1500	13,10
Satyendra, Ramon	MI2100	13
Sauerwein, Andrew Mark	MS0100	13,10,29B,43,64B
Saul, Walter B.	CA1860	10A,66A,13,20,10F
Savage, Charles M.	OH1910	13,12A,20G,36,61
Sawyer, Eric	MA0100	10,13,34,43
Sawyer, Lisa Lee	MN0600	13,61,66A
Saylor, Bruce S.	NY0642	13,10F,10
Sayrs, Elizabeth P.	OH1900	13
Scales, Nicholas	TX3750	13,62D,11
Scandrett, John F.	PA1600	13,63B,34
Scarnati, Rebecca Kemper	AZ0450	64B,13,41
Scearce, J. Mark	NC1700	13,10
Schaal, Joelle E.	OR0800	13,65,11
Schachter, Carl	NY2250	13,41
Schachter, Carl	NY0642	13,12A
Schachter, Carl	NY1900	13
Schaffer, William R.	AL0200	13,11,63B,49
Schantz, Allen P.	CO0150	11,12B,13,68
Scharf, Scott L.	IL2100	13
Schattschneider, Adam	OH0250	13,47,64A,64C,64E
Schechter, John M.	CA5070	13,14,20H
Schelle, Michael	IN0250	13,10,43,10F
Scherperel, Loretta	FL0200	13,11,66G
Scherr, Bernard	TX0900	13,66D
Scherzinger, Nicolas	NY4150	13,10,34,64E
Schiano, Michael	CT0650	13,13J,20G,34
Schiavo, Joseph C.	NJ1100	13B,13D,12A,13F,13
Schiff, David	OR0900	13,10A,20G,29,38
Schildt, Matthew	OH1100	13
Schildt, Matthew C.	CO0050	13,10,10D,13E,34
Schimmel, Carl W.	IL1150	10A,13
Schindler, Karl W.	AZ0470	10,13,34,12A
Schipull, Larry D.	MA1350	13,66G,66H
Schirmer, Timothy	IL2350	13,10,34B,54
Schlabaugh, Karen Bauman	KS0200	13,66A,66B,66C,12A
Schlatter, Carolyn	FL1430	66A,13,11
Schlicht, Ursel	NJ0950	13,14,15,53
Schmalfeldt, Janet	MA1900	13,12A,13J,13L
Schmidt, Carsten	NY3560	13,11,12A,41,66A
Schmidt, Charles	IL0100	11,66A,13
Schmidt, Henry L.	PA2550	13,12A,63C,26,29A
Schmidt, John C.	TX3175	13,12A,66G
Schmidt, Tracey	PA0250	13,64A,11
Schmitz, Alan W.	IA1600	13,10
Schmitz, Michael	CA3270	66A,12A,13,20,41
Schneider, David E.	MA0100	12,64C,43,13,41
Schneider, David	KY1000	13,13E
Schneider, M. Christine	IA0550	13
Schnitter, David	NY2660	13,64E,47
Schober, David	NY0642	13,10A,66A,10
Schoening, Benjamin S.	WI0801	11,13,36,61,63
Schoessler, Tim	WY0130	66A,66D,13,12A
Schonthal, Ruth	NY2400	13,10,66A
Schooley, John	WV0300	13,49,63D,62D
Schrader, Barry	CA0510	13,10,12A,34
Schreiber, Paul	MS0560	10,13,34,10B,10A
Schreier, Kathleen	IA0790	13,11,36,54
Schroeder, David	AF0100	13,12A,12,12E,12C
Schroeder, Michael	CA4150	13,38
Schroeder, Phillip J.	AR0300	13,10
Schuberg, Margaret	MT0400	13,48,64A
Schubert, Peter	AI0150	13,13J,36
Schuessler, Philip T.	LA0650	13
Schuler, Nico S.	TX3175	13,12C,34B,13F
Schultz, Arlan N.	AA0200	10,34,13,12B
Schultz, Eric	CA0900	10,13,34
Schultz, Marc	NY2800	13A,20,13
Schultz, Paul	DC0150	63C,13
Schultz, Robert D.	MA2000	13
Schulz, Patrick	CA1750	13,38
Schulze, Otto	IN0005	62A,67,10,13,36
Schulze, Theodora	IN0005	61,10A,13,50,51
Schuttenhelm, Thomas	CT0050	11,13,70,34
Schwabe, Jonathan C.	IA1600	13,10,29
Schwartz, Richard I.	VA1750	13,48,64C,10
Schwarz, David	TX3420	13
Schwendener, Ben	MA1175	13
Scott, Michael	MA0260	13A,13
Scott, Rebecca	NY1900	13
Scott, Tatiana	CA0150	66A,13
Scotto, Ciro G.	FL2000	13
Scrivner, Matthew	MO0050	61,12,13
Scully, Mathew	CA3950	36,61,13
Seaton, Kira J.	OH0755	13A,13,11,36,61
Segall, Christopher	AL1170	13
Segger, Joachim	AA0035	13,13J,66A,66B,43
Sehman, Melanie	NY3250	65,13A,20,11,13
Seidman, Mitch	MA0260	13
Seifert, James	AZ0440	61,13
Seitz, Christine L.	IN0550	13,66C,34
Sekhon, Baljinder S.	FL2000	10,65,13,34
Seldess, Zachary	NY0500	11,13
Seliger, Bryce M.	OR0750	38,14A,13,12A
Semegen, Daria	NY3790	13,10,45
Sepulveda, Sonja	NC2205	36,47,13,60
Serghi, Sophia	VA0250	13,10F,10,43,10A
Sessler, Eric S.	PA0850	13
Setziol, Paul	CA1550	13,10
Severtson, David	WI0808	66A,13,66D,12A,66C
Seward, Philip	IL0720	13,13B,13C,13E
Seyfried, Sheridan	NY2250	13
Shabani, Afrim	IL2510	11,10,13,34B,13C
Shackleton, Phil	CA0250	13,10,34
Shafer, Sharon Guertin	DC0250	13,10F,12A,39,61
Shaffer, Kris P.	SC0275	13
Shaffer-Gottschalk, David D.	VA1750	13,66A,66C
Shaftel, Matthew R.	FL0850	13
Shanahan, Ellen Cooper	MA0280	13,12A,36,54,29A
Shapiro, Gerald	RI0050	13,10,45,34
Shapiro, Mark L.	NY2105	60A,36,40,13
Sharp, David	IA0750	13,11,47,64
Sharpe, Carlyle	MO0350	13,10F,10
Shatin, Judith	VA1550	10B,10A,10F,10,13
Shatzkin, Merton T.	MO1810	13,12A,62A
Shaw, David	NY2500	13,10,11,12A
Shaw, Timothy B.	PA2800	13B,13C,10A,13
Shawn, Allen	VT0050	13,10,66A
Sheehan, Joseph C.	PA1050	13
Shende, Vineet	ME0200	10,13,20C,20E,31E
Sheng, Bright	MI2100	13,10
Shepard, Brian K.	CA5300	34,10,13,34C,65
Sherr, Laurence E.	GA1150	13,12A,10
Sherry, Martin	WA0480	13,11,12A,14,64A
Shevitz, Matthew	IL1080	11,13,29,47,46
Shields, Lisa	MT0100	13,36,37,64E
Shilansky, Mark	MA0260	13A,13
Shimron, Omri D.	NC0750	13,66A,66D
Shinn, Michael A.	NY1900	13,42
Shipley, Linda P.	TN0580	13,66A,66G
Shirtz, Michael	OH2140	36,60,61,13,29
Shkoda, Natalya	CA0800	66,13,13A,13B,12A
Shockley, Alan	CA0825	13,10
Shook, Timothy	KS1200	66A,66B,66D,13
Shotola, Marilyn	OR0850	13,64A,41,12A
Sichel, John	NJ0975	13,10,11,12A,36
Sidoti, Vincent	OH0755	13,11,37,64C,64E
Sieben, Patrick	KS0225	37,20,13,46,11
Sieg, Jerry	LA0800	10A,10F,13,12A
Siegel, Hedi	NY2250	13
Sigmon, Susan McEwen	GA0940	13,36,66A,66G,40
Silberman, Peter	NY1800	13
Silverman, Adam B.	PA3600	10,13
Simon, Dennis	IA0790	66A,13
Simoncic, Max	CA4300	13,10,11
Simons, Dennis	ND0250	11,13,20,38
Simpson, Andrew Earle	DC0050	10,10F,13,66A,43
Simpson, Peter	KY1450	13,64D,41
Simpson, Reynold	MO1810	13
Simpson-Litke, Rebecca	GA2100	13,14C,20H
Sink, Damon W.	NC2600	10,13,34,34B,13I
Sir, Neil	NH0350	10A,13
Siskind, Paul A.	NY3780	13,10
Sivan, Noam	NY2250	13
Skeirik, Kaleel	OH2550	13,10F
Skidmore, William	WV0750	13,41,62C
Skogen, Meaghan	NC0750	62C,13,41
Skoumal, Zdenek	AB0060	10A,13
Slavin, Peter	IN0005	10,13,66,66A,11
Slawson, A. Wayne	CA5010	13,10,34
Slayton, Michael K.	TN1850	13
Sledge, Larry	FL0800	60,12A,31A,36,13
Sloan, Donald S.	SC0420	13,10A
Slottow, Stephen	TX3420	13I,13D,13F,13
Slowik, Gregory	MA1700	13,11,12A,66A,66C
Sly, Gordon C.	MI1400	13
Smaldone, Edward	NY0642	13,10,10F,11
Smart, Gary	FL1950	13,10F,10,66A,53
Smith, Andrew	MA0400	13
Smith, Brent	UT0190	39,62C,13,12A,51
Smith, C. Scott	OH1900	13,63B,41
Smith, Carey	MS0370	63,64,65,11,13
Smith, Carl	TN1850	13,10A
Smith, Charles J.	NY4320	13,13B,13I
Smith, Curtis F.	CO0810	13,34D,36,66A
Smith, Daniel Ian	MA0260	13A,13
Smith, David K.	KS0950	36,11,61,13,66A
Smith, David	CT0800	13,50,65,34
Smith, Derek T.	MO0600	11,13,29
Smith, Douglas	AB0050	13A,13,10,13C,12
Smith, Douglas	AB0200	13,10F,10A
Smith, Elizabeth Lena	IL1150	13
Smith, Fran	CA2200	13
Smith, G. D.	KY1200	13,60,38,63A
Smith, Gene	AF0150	13,47,49,63C,29
Smith, Glenn E.	VA0450	13,10,45,34,42
Smith, James E.	CA4450	13,60,36,38
Smith, Jason	IA1400	13,36,61,60A
Smith, Kandie K.	FL1950	61,13
Smith, Larry G.	UT0300	13,29,47,64E,46
Smith, Leland C.	CA4900	13,10,12A,34
Smith, Marion	FL0450	13,12A,36
Smith, Neal	IL1750	32E,37,32C,13
Smith, Peter H.	IN1700	13
Smith, Randall A.	MO1780	13,64E
Smith, Robert Thomas	TX3400	13A,13,10,43
Smith, Robert	NC1100	11,13,66G
Smith, Stuart	MA2030	13,29B,35C
Smith, Stuart Saunders	MD1000	13,10
Smith, Susan A.	MS0360	61,40,13,36,13B
Smith, Timothy	AR0200	13,12A,66A,66C

Index by Area of Teaching Interest

Name	Code	Areas
Smith, Timothy A.	AZ0450	13,34
Smith, William O.	WA1050	13,10,43
Smolenski, Scott	FL1675	66A,10,11,13,20
Smooke, David	MD0650	13
Smucker, Peter	IN1750	13
Smyth, David H.	LA0200	13
Snarrenberg, Robert	MO1900	13,13J
Snodgrass, Jennifer Sterling	NC0050	13,13F,13C,13H,13G
Snodgrass, Laura	CA2250	64A,13,35A
Snukst, Penny	IN0005	33,13,31A
Snyder, David	CT0450	11,13
Snyder, John L.	TX3400	13,11,12
Snyder, Mark L.	VA1475	13,10B,10F,34
Snyder, Randy L.	TX2300	13A,13,11,47,63
Snyder, Steven D.	KY0900	13,47,66A,29
Sobaskie, James William	MS0500	13,13E,10F,13I,12
Sochinski, James	VA1700	13,37,63C,63D,34
Soich, Leslie	CO0830	36,13,11,10D
Solomon, Jason Wyatt	GA0050	10,13
Solot, Evan	PA3330	13,10F,10,47,46
Solum, Stephen	MN1050	13,20G,10,35G,34
Sommer, Lesley	WA1250	13,10,45
Sommerfeldt, Jerod	OH1450	13,34
Sommerville, David	PA1600	13
Sonenberg, Daniel M.	ME0500	10A,13F,13C,10,13
Song, James J.	CA3100	60,11,12,38,13
Sorce, Richard P.	NJ0950	10D,13,34D
Sorensen, Julie	ID0100	13
Sorensen, Randall J.	LA0250	63A,63B,13,13B,13A
Soroka, Solomia	IN0550	13,62A,41
Soto-Medina, Victor	TX1725	11,13,66,34B
Southall, John K.	FL0950	13,63A,60B,37,32E
Sovik, Thomas	TX3420	13,31A,14C,13J,34
Spann, Joseph	AL0890	11,13,70,34A,34D
Sparti, Patricia C.	NC0850	13,60,38,63D
Specht, Jeffrey	OR0400	13,38,60,63D
Spedden, Patricia R.	IN0700	66A,66B,13,66C,66D
Spicer, Mark J.	NY1150	13,11,64A,66A,20G
Spicer, Mark	NY0625	13A,13
Spicer, Mark	NY0600	13,14C
Spiegelberg, Scott C.	IN0350	13
Spies, Claudio	NJ0900	13,60,10,39
Spraggins, Mark	CA0550	13,10,34
Sprenkle, Elam Ray	MD0650	13,12A
Sproul Pulatie, Leah	MO0050	10,13
Squatrito, Fred	CA0400	13,11,66A
Squibbs, Ronald J.	CT0600	13
Srinivasan, Asha	WI0350	13,10
St. Clair, Eniko	CA0250	13
Stackhouse, Eunice Wonderly	NC1450	13,66A,66B,66D,66C
Stahlke, Jonathan E.	IL0730	13,10,38,10F
Stallings, Joe	FL1500	13,11,70,34
Stallings, Kendall	MO1950	13,10
Stallmann, Kurt D.	TX2150	13,10,45,34
Stalnaker, William P.	OR0850	13,10,12A
Stambaugh, J. Mark	NY2150	13
Stanley, Bill J.	CO0800	13A,13,63C
Stanton, Geoffrey	MI1300	13,10,45,34
Staples, James G.	PA1600	13,66A
Staron, Michael	IL3200	13,11,29,62D
Stearns, Roland H.	AK0100	13,70,51
Steege, Benjamin A.	NY3790	12A,12B,12C,13F,13
Steen, Kenneth	CT0650	10,13,45
Steffen, Cecil	IL0780	13,66A,66D
Steffen, Christina	AZ0440	64A,41,13
Stegall, Sydney Wallace	WA0460	13,14,10B,14F,10
Steidel, Mark	CA1560	13,35,34
Steiger, Rand	CA5050	13,10,34
Stein, Deborah	MA1400	13
Steinbach, Richard	IA0100	13,10,66,34
Steinbeck, Paul	MO1900	13
Steinquest, David	TN0050	13,50,65
Stella, Martin	MI1250	13,11
Stempel, Larry	NY1300	13,12,54,29
Stemper, Frank L.	IL2900	13,10,43
Stephens, John	DC0350	13,60
Stephens, Michael	NE0050	10,29,46,13,64
Stephens, Timothy	OR0750	13,10F,10,12A
Stephenson, Kenneth	OK1350	13A,13
Sterner, Dave	OH0750	13,47,70,29
Stevens, John	WI0815	63D,60B,35,10,13
Stewart, Jon	CO0560	13
Stewart, Lawrence	NJ1050	13,64D
Stiefel, Van	PA3600	10,13
Stiles, Joan	NY2660	66,13
Stilwell, Jama Liane	IA0400	11,12,20G,13,64A
Stimson, Ann	OH1850	13
Stinner, Rita	NE0710	13,36,20G
Stinson, Russell	AR0425	13,11,12A,12,66
Stoecker, Philip S.	NY1600	13
Stokes, Harvey J.	VA0500	13,10,64B,34
Stolet, Jeffrey	OR1050	13,45,10,34,10B
Stolte, Charles	AA0035	64E,13A,13,10,43
Stone, Christopher	NY2250	13
Stone, George J.	CA1510	13,47,34,66A,35D
Stone, Stephen C.	MD0650	13
Stone, Susan E.	IL0100	13,62A
Storochuk, Allison M.	MO0775	64C,13,48
Stott, Jacob	RI0101	11,13
Stoune, Michael	TX3200	13,64A
Strain, James A.	MI1600	65,13,41,11
Straus, Joseph N.	NY0600	13
Streder, Mark	IL0850	13,66A,53,34,45
Street, D. Alan	KS1350	13
Stremlin, Tatyana	NY4250	13,11,61,66A,67C
Strid-Chadwick, Karen	AK0100	13,47,66A,66D,29
Stroeher, Vicki P.	WV0400	11,12,13,14
Strong, James Anthony	NJ0975	13,12A,66,11,54
Stuart, Rory	NY2660	13,70,47
Studinger, Bob	CO0625	11,10,13
Stumpf, Robert	IL3370	36,13
Sturm, Julie	IA0850	13
Stutes, Ann B.	TX3650	13
Suarez, Jeff	WI0847	10,13,29,42,20G
Suber, Stephen C.	LA0650	13,10,11
Suchy-Pilalis, Jessica R.	NY3780	13,62E,13H,13C,31A
Sudduth, Steven	KY1425	13,32E,37,60B,63C
Sudeith, Mark A.	IL0600	13,66A,66G,66C
Sullivan, Timothy R.	NY3780	13,13A,13B,13C
Sult, Michael	CA1800	13,70,29,13A
Summerfield, Susan	VT0400	13,11,41,66
Summers, George	AZ0440	70,13
Survilla, Maria Paula	IA1800	13,12A,14
Svard, Lois	PA0350	13,66A
Svenningsen, Russell	SD0050	13,36,61
Svistoonoff, Katherine	FL0800	66A,13,12A
Svoboda, Tomas	OR0850	13,10
Swain, Joseph P.	NY0650	13,12B,12F,12C
Swann, William E.	TN1000	47,13,60B,29B,10D
Sweeney, Joyce	CA5500	12A,13,35A,61
Sweidel, Martin	TX2400	45,13
Sweigart, Dennis W.	PA1900	13,66
Swilley, Daniel	IL1200	10,13,34,13A,13B
Swinden, Kevin J.	AG0600	13,13B,13C
Swist, Christopher	NH0150	50,65,13,10
Sykes, Robert	DC0170	13,66A,29
Syswerda, Kristin	IN1025	13A,13,10,11,10F
Taavola, Kristin	CO0900	13,13H,13C
Tabor, Jerry N.	MD0800	13,10,29B,47,11
Tacka, Philip V.	PA2350	12,13,32
Taddie, David	WV0750	13,10,45
Taft, Burns	CA5360	13,60,36,66A,38
Taggart, Bruce F.	MI1400	13,34
Taggart, Mark Alan	NC0650	13,10
Talbert, Rebecca	MO2050	61,66A,13,12A,11
Tallman, Thomas J.	IL0630	13,11,47,63,29
Talpash, Andriy	AA0100	10,13
Tamagawa, Kiyoshi	TX2650	66A,13,66B
Tan, Kia-Hui	OH1850	62A,51,62B,13,42
Tan, Su Lian	VT0350	10,13,64A,42
Tang, Jenny	MA2050	66A,66C,13
Tang, Patricia	MA1200	20,11,13
Taniguchi, Naoki	CA5510	13,66D
Tanksley, Francesca	NY2660	13,66A,53
Tann, Hilary	NY4310	13,10
Tanosaki, Kazuko	MD1000	13,20C
Tapia-Carreto, Veronica	AA0050	10,13
Tarbox, Maurie	UT0350	13,61
Tarsi, Boaz	NY1860	13,10,14
Tate, Elda Ann	MI1600	13,10E,41,64A
Taube, Heinrich K.	IL3300	13,10,34
Taylor, Clifton	MS0420	13,47,49,63C,37
Taylor, Edward J. F.	TX0300	13
Taylor, Paul	DC0050	13
Taylor, Priscilla	MA2010	13,10,62C,41
Taylor, Rhonda	NM0310	64E,13
Taylor, Rowan S.	CA2700	13,11
Taylor, Stephen A.	IL3300	13,10
Tedesco, Anne C.	NY3500	13,66A,54,29A,10
Tejero, Nikolasa	TN1700	13,64C,41
Telesco, Paula	MA2030	13,13H,13C
Teply, Lee	VA1000	13,55,66G,66H
Tercero, David R.	TX0850	70,63,13
Terrigno, Loretta	NY2250	13
Terrigno, Loretta	NY1600	13
Terrigno, Loretta	NY0625	13
Terry, Peter R.	OH0250	34,10,13
Thayer, Fred M.	PA2100	13,60,10,36
Theisen, Alan	NC1250	13,10,34,35G,64E
Theisen, Kathleen Ann	CT0800	13,66
Thiedt, Catherine E.	OH0950	13,12A,66A,66G,31A
Thomas, Joel Wayne	KS0265	11,13,29,66
Thomas, Margaret E.	CT0100	13,11,12C
Thomas, Marilyn Taft	PA0550	13,10
Thomas, Omar	MA0260	13
Thomas, Phillip E.	TN0850	13,12,38,66A
Thomas, Robert	NJ1400	13
Thomas, Russell	MS0350	47,64E,29,13
Thome, Diane	WA1050	13,10
Thome, Joel H.	NY3785	13A,13
Thompson, Barbara Tilden	PA2450	66A,66B,13C,13,13A
Thompson, Bruce A.	NC1000	36,13,66A,61
Thompson, Christopher K.	AR0950	13A,13,10F,10,66A
Thompson, David B.	SC0850	12A,13,66
Thompson, David	WI0400	13,11,14,66A,35
Thompson, Douglas S.	NJ0500	13,10,12A,34
Thompson, Jewel	NY0625	13A,13
Thompson, Kathy A.	OK0700	13,32B,66A,66B,41
Thompson, Timothy D.	FL1450	10,13,34,64E
Thoms, Jonas	OH2500	13,13C,63B,35
Thomson, Jacqueline	IA1400	13,36,61,60A
Thomson, Susan N.	GA0950	13B,13E,66A,13
Thorman, Marc	NY0500	10,13,12A,20,14C
Thornburg, Scott	MI2250	13A,13,49,63A
Thorp, Steven	NM0250	13,11,36,61,40
Thorpe, Allan	AB0090	13,48,64D,13A,37
Thurgood, George	AG0300	13,29
Thurmaier, David P.	FL0680	13,13C,13B,13E,13F
Tiberio, Albert	PA2950	11,12,13,10A,10F
Ticheli, Frank	CA5300	13,10
Tidwell, Mary	TX3360	13,11
Tiedge, Faun Tanenbaum	OR0450	11,13,12A,20,42
Tillotson, J. Robert	IL1085	37,13,41,64C
Timmerman, David	TX1750	13A,13,36,41,61
Timothy, Sarah O.	AL0890	61,11,36,13,32
Tipei, Sever	IL3300	13,10,34
Titus, Jamie	MO0050	64A,12,13,48
Titus, Jason	NY4350	13
Tobey, Forrest	IN0400	38,47,13,34
Todorovski, Catherine	AI0200	13
Toensing, Richard E.	CO0800	13,10,45
Tolar, Ron	AL0400	13,11,66A,66G
Toliver, Nicki Bakko	MN0040	11,13,40,61
Tollefson, Tim	MN0200	13,10A,34
Tomassi, Edward	MA0260	13A,13
Tompkins, Charles B.	SC0750	13,66G,66H,31A
Toops, Gary	CA3200	13,11,66G
Topel, Spencer	NH0100	10B,10F,34,13,35
Torok, Debra	PA2450	12A,13,38,66A,20G
Tot, Zvonimir	IL3310	29,13,13C,70,47
Town, Stephen	MO0950	13,61,36
Towne, Lora Rost	AZ0440	39,61,54,13
Townsend, Brendan	TX1425	10F,11,12A,13,62C
Traficante, Frank	CA1050	13,12A,12
Trail, Julian	DC0170	12A,13,66A
Trantham, Gene S.	OH0300	13,13A,13J
Traupman-Carr, Carol A.	PA2450	13A,13,12A,12,31A
Traut, Donald G.	AZ0500	13
Trawick, Eleanor	IN0150	10,13,13F,13H,13L
Traylor, Steve	WY0060	13,46,47
Trentham, Donald R.	TN0650	11,12A,66A,31A,13
Tripold, David	NJ0760	13,12A,32,31A,33
Trittin, Brian L.	TX0400	12A,13,29,37,64E
Trosvig, Michael	MN1100	10A,13
Trueman, Daniel	NJ0900	13,10B,10
Truitt, D. Charles	PA2200	70,13,41,13E,13B
Truniger, Matthias	MA1400	13
Tuck, Patrick M.	KY1425	10,13,49,63A,63B
Tucker, Gary	AE0050	13A,13,12
Tung, Leslie Thomas	MI1150	12A,66A,66C,66E,13
Turci-Escobar, John	TX3510	13
Turner, Aaron	CO0275	50,65A,65B,13,41
Turner, George	ID0150	10,13,60B,63C,63D
Turner, Gregory E.	KS0400	13,38,36,60,61
Turner, Ronald A.	KY1200	13,61
Turon, Charles T.	FL1745	11,13,66A,66D

475

Index by Area of Teaching Interest

Name	Code	Areas
Turrin, Joseph E.	NJ0800	11,13,10C
Tuttle, Julie	AZ0470	13,66
Tuttle, Marshall	OR0550	13,36,38
Tutunov, Alexander	OR0950	13,66A,66D,66C
Twomey, Michael P.	TX1900	10A,13,10F,38,62
Tymoczko, Dmitri	NJ0900	13
Uchida, Rika	IA0550	13,66A,66C,66D
Ueno, Ken	CA5000	10,13,34A,34D
Uitermarkt, Cynthia D.	IL1850	13A,13,66A,31A
Ulman, Erik	CA4900	10,13,12B,62A
Ulmer, Allison C.	TX2960	13
Umezaki, Kojiro	CA5020	10,13,34
Unal, Fureya	CA0815	13
Underhill, Owen	AB0080	13,60,10,12,43
Underwood, Michael P.	AR0750	13,37,63
Urban, Guy	MA2150	13,60,11,66A
Urban, Timothy	NJ1350	13
Urista, Diane J.	OH0600	13
Uzur, Viktor	UT0350	13,10F,51,62C,42
Vaccaro, Brandon C.	OH1100	13,10,34,13B,13A
Vaclavik, Jude	UT0300	13,13A,13B,13D
Vaglio, Anthony J.	NC1300	13,10,32,34
Vali, M. Reza	PA0550	13,34
Van Appledorn, Mary Jeanne	TX3200	13,10
Van Buren, Harvey	DC0350	13A,13,10F,10,66G
Van Den Toorn, Pieter	CA5060	13,13F,13I
Van der Beek, Ralph	UT0350	66A,13
Van Herck, Bert	IA1550	13
Van Kooten, Jan	MI0350	13
Van Oyen, Lawrence G.	IL2050	13,64E,37
Van Winkle, Brian	WA0250	13
Van Wyck, Helen J.	IL3100	13,60A,11,36,32D
Vance, Virginia L.	NC1800	13,66G
Vandegriff, Matthew M.	NY4050	13
Vander Weg, John D.	MI2200	13B,13F,13E,13
Vanderford, Brenda M.	WV0700	13A,13,11,66G,31A
Vanderheyden, Joel	MO0550	64E,46,47,29,13
Vanderwoude, Matt	AG0130	10A,11,13,29,34
VanHandel, Leigh A.	MI1400	13,13K,13G
VanNordstrand, Shelby	IA0910	12A,13,61
VanRandwyk, Carol A.	MI0850	13,13C,66A,13D
Vasimi, James	OH2600	13
Vasquez, Hector	FL1300	13,11,12A,66A
Vassilandonakis, Yiorgos	SC0500	10,11,13,43
Vassiliades, Christopher	NY2150	13
Veenker, Jonathan	MN0250	13,10F,10
Veenstra, Kim	MI1050	13
Veenstra, Kimberly	MI0900	11,12,13
Veeraraghauen, Lee	AG0600	13
Velazquez, Ileana Perez	MA2250	10,13,34D
Vercoe, Barry	MA1200	13,10,45,34
Verdie' de Vas-Romero, Adriana	CA0825	13
Vernon, James R.	OK0650	13,10,35C,11
Vigeland, Nils	NY2150	13,10
Vigil, Ryan H.	NH0350	13
Vigneau, Kevin	NM0450	64B,13A,13
Vigneau, Michelle	TN1680	64B,42,13
Villeneuve, Andre	AI0210	13
Viragh, Gabor	CT0650	13
Vitercik, Greg	VT0350	13,12A,12,66C
Viton, John	KY0900	13,64B
Vlahcevic, Sonia K.	VA1600	13,66A
Vogel, Roger C.	GA2100	13,10
Voigt, Steve	VA0600	10,11,13
Vojcic, Aleksandra	MI2100	13
Volckhausen, David	NY2150	13
Volk, David Paul	VA1580	13,36,12A,66A,10
von Arx, Victoria	NY3700	66A,13,11
Von Foerster, Richard	CO0900	13
Vosbein, Terry	VA1850	10,13,29A,47,29
Vuori, Ruston	AA0080	66D,13
Wachmann, Eric	IA1800	13,64C,48
Wachsmuth, Karen	IA1140	13,11,12A,66A
Wacker, Lori	NC0650	13,11
Wacker, Therese M.	PA1600	64A,48,13
Wade, Gail G.	TX1600	13,39,66A,66D,66C
Wade, Thomas	NJ1050	13,66D
Wadsworth, Benjamin K.	GA1150	13
Waggoner, Andrew B.	NY4150	13,10,12A
Wagler, Trevor	AG0600	13
Walczyk, Kevin	OR1250	13,45,63B,29,10
Walicki, Kenneth J.	CA0815	10,13,34
Walker, Alan	AG0200	13,12A,12
Walker, Cherilee	KS0590	36,13,11,61,29A
Walker, Christopher	CA3150	13,10,31A
Walker, Gregory	MN0350	13,10,45,34
Walker, John L.	VA1700	64B,13,14,20H
Walker, John M.	SD0550	13,66A
Walker, Michael	TX3525	13
Walker, Vicki	OK0850	13,66A,66D
Wallace, John H.	MA0400	10,13
Wallace, William	AG0200	13,10F,10
Wallin, Nicholas L.	IL1400	38,13,11,20
Wallis, David N.	MO0650	36,10A,11,13,32D
Walsh, Craig T.	AZ0500	10,10B,13,10A
Walsh, Eileen	AF0120	64C,13
Walsh, James	LA0300	13
Walters, Andrew B.	PA2150	13,34D
Walters, David	AL0500	13,37,63,60
Walters, Teresa	NJ0200	13,60,11,12A,36
Walters, Timothy	FL0650	13,41,63A,29
Waltham-Smith, Naomi	PA3350	13
Wanamaker, Gregory R.	NY3780	13,10A
Wang, Shi-Hwa	UT0350	62A,13
Wang, Xi	TX2400	13
Wannamaker, Robert	CA0510	13,10
Wanner, Dan	CA2600	13,11,35A,66A
Ward, Robert J.	MA1450	70,11,13,20G
Wardlaw, Jeffrey A.	PA0700	63D,49,13,63C
Wardlaw-Bailey, Freya	AK0100	13
Wardzinski, Anthony J.	CA3100	13A,13
Ware, John	VA1800	13,10,12,66
Wark, Stephen	MA0260	13A,13
Warkentien, Vicky	IN0200	13,66,41,51,38
Warner, Daniel C.	MA1000	13,10A,10B,12D,34
Warren, Maredia D. L.	NJ0825	13,11,32
Warsaw, Benjamin	GA0940	66A,13
Warshaw, Dalit Hadass	MA0350	10,13,66A,10F,13E
Wartchow, Brett	MN1300	13
Wartofsky, Michael	MA0260	13A,13
Waschka, Rodney A.	NC1700	10,12A,13F,10B,13
Waseen, Symeon	SD0100	10A,10B,10F,13,66
Washut, Robert	IA1600	13,47,29
Waters, Keith	CO0800	13
Waters, Renee	MO1550	13,10,66A,34,11
Watt, Stephanie	NY2105	13,66,66A,66B
Watters, August	MA0260	13A,13
Watts, Ardean W.	UT0250	13,39
Watts, Donald	OH0600	13
Weale, Gerald	MA0400	13
Weast, Wade P.	NC1650	13
Weaver, Brent	TN0650	36,37,34,13
Weaver, Brent	OR0250	10,61,13,34,36
Weaver, Carol Ann	AG0470	13,10,12,20A,29A
Weaver, Zac	GA0750	13
Webb, Brian P.	VT0125	13A,13,11,12A,36
Webb, Jeffrey L.	PA3410	29A,36,13A,60,13
Webb, Robert	VA0975	11,36,13
Webber, Allen L.	FL1470	13,11,61,10A,66A
Webber, Danny R.	MD0450	11,70,13
Weber, Mary	MO1250	63A,13,11
Weesner, Anna	PA3350	13,10,11
Weidenmueller, Johannes	NY2660	62D,13
Weidman-Winter, Becky	CO1050	64A,41,13
Weidner, Raymond	MD0060	12,13,36
Weigt, Steven	MA0400	13
Weinberg, Henry	NY0642	10,13
Weisberg, David	NJ1400	13
Weise, Christopher	NC1000	13,10,34,35
Weiser, Mark L.	CA5300	13
Weisert, Lee	NC2410	13,10
Weiss, Daniel	IN1300	29A,13
Weiss, Doug	NY2660	13,47
Welling, Joelle	AA0150	13,61
Wells, Prince	IL2910	13,11,29,35
Wells, Ryan	NE0550	13,66A,66B,66C
Welsch, James O.	NY4150	13,49,39
Welstead, Jon	WI0825	10,13,34,43,45
Wen, Andy	AR0750	11,13,64,64E
Wen, Eric	NY2250	13
Wen, Eric	PA0850	13,12A
Wendland, Kristin	GA0750	13,66A
Weng, Pamela	CO0830	13,11,12A,66A
Wennerstrom, Mary H.	IN0900	13
Wente, Steven F.	IL0730	13,66G,12A,31A
Werkema, Jason R.	MI0750	70,13,29,34
Wernick, Richard F.	PA3350	13,60,10,41
Wery, Brett L.	NY3600	13,37,41,64C,64E
West, William	IL1200	13,64A,64E,41,67E
Westerberg, Kurt H.	IL0750	13,10,11
Westergaard, Peter	NJ0900	13,60,10,39
Western, Daniel	AL0650	64,47,35D,13,29A
Westgate, Phillip Todd	AL0950	13,36,66A,66G,66C
Weston, Craig A.	KS0650	10A,10B,13,34
Weston, Trevor L.	NJ0300	11,20B,13,10
Weymouth, Daniel	NY3790	13,10,45,34
Whaley, Mary Susan	OK0500	11,36,61,54,13
Whang, Un-Young	IL1850	13,66A,66B
Wharton, William	ID0250	13,41,62C,62D
Wheatley, Greg	IL3550	13
Wheeldon, Marianne	TX3510	13,13C
Wheeler, Charles Lynn	CA3400	66A,66B,66D,13
Wheeler, George	CA0825	10,13
Wheeler, Scott	MA0850	13,60,10,54,43
Whipple, R. James	PA0550	13
Whitaker, Howard	IL3550	13,10F,10,64C
Whitcomb, Benjamin	WI0865	62C,13C,13E,13K,13
White, Barbara A.	NJ0900	13A,10,13,10F,43
White, Cindy	MO1710	64,13,36,61,66A
White, David A.	TX3400	13,10,31A
White, Edward C.	AR0730	61,39,13
White, Frank	LA0700	13,39,66A,11,60
White, John W.	NY1800	13
White, Kevin	MO0750	13,10F,10,63A,53
White, Michael	NY1900	13
Whitfield, James M. (Matt)	NC0850	10A,13,37,10F,10
Whitis, Jessye	TX3415	66,13
Whitley, H. Moran	NC0300	32,31A,13
Whitley, William	OR1250	13
Whitman, Thomas I.	PA3200	13,20D,32
Whittall, Geoffrey	AA0025	14,65,20,13,11
Whitworth, Albin C.	KY0150	13A,13,10,36,66
Wiberg, Janice	MT0300	13,12A,32,36,66
Wickman, Ethan F.	TX3530	10A,13,36,10
Widen, Dennis C.	OK1250	66A,66D,13
Wieland, William	SD0400	13,66B,66A,34,10
Wiemer, Gerta	UT0350	66,13
Wilborn, David F.	TX2900	13,63C,63D,41,37
Wild, Jonathan	AI0150	10,13
Wilding, James	OH1100	13
Wile, Kip D.	MD0650	13
Wiley, Frank	OH1100	13,10,38,60B,43
Wilkins, Donald G.	PA0550	13,12A,66G
Wilkins, Skip	PA1850	13,11,29
Wilkinson, Carlton J.	NJ0175	13
Wilkinson, Christopher	WV0750	13,11,12A,12
Willett, Jim R.	KY0550	13,63D
Willey, James H.	NY3730	13,10,11,66A
Willey, Mark	MD0150	13,66G
Willey, Robert K.	LA0760	13,34,35,10B,45
Williams, Amy C.	PA3420	10,13
Williams, J. Kent	NC2430	13,34
Williams, John W.	NY2100	13,11,36,61,54
Williams, Leland Page	CA2600	13A,13,66A
Williams, Mark D.	CA2440	13,36,61,38,34
Williams, Marvin	NY2050	10,11,12,13,20G
Williams, Natalie	GA2100	10,13
Williams, Patrick C.	MT0400	10A,13,13C,13D,10
Williams, Ralph K.	NY4050	13,11,61
Williams, Ralph K.	NY4060	13,12A,11,61
Williams, Shane	MO0650	11,13,32E,38,41
Williamson, Melissa	KS1200	64A,48,13
Willis, A. Rexford	FL1745	13,10,70,13A
Wills, Christopher	CA0350	10,13
Willson, Kenneth F.	OR0250	13,45,66A,66B,66C
Willy, Alan	IN0005	66A,66G,70,13
Wilson, Brian S.	CA4700	10,37,13,43,60
Wilson, Eric	TN1600	13,34,10
Wilson, Eugene N.	AB0100	10A,13
Wilson, Geoffrey	IA1800	12A,13,66A,10F
Wilson, Kenyon	TN1700	63D,13,41
Wilson, Larry K.	CA3975	60,32C,13,66A,36
Wilson, Mark	MD1010	13,10F,10
Wilson, Richard E.	NY4450	13,10A,10F
Wilson, Russell G.	UT0305	11,13,36,61
Wilson, Stephen B.	NY3720	13,60,36,41,61
Wilson, Steve	CA0400	13,10
Wingate, Owen K.	FL0675	13,11,12A,61,36
Winkelman, David	NC1650	13
Winkler, Peter	NY3790	13,10,20G,29A
Winn, James	NV0100	66,13,10
Winslow, Richard	CT0750	13A,13,10
Winslow, Robert J.	FL0930	66A,46,13,34D,11
Winteregg, Steven L.	OH0450	10,13
Wirt, Ronald	GA0550	13,48,64D,10
Wise, Sherwood W.	NY0700	64B,48,13,64D,42

Index by Area of Teaching Interest

Name	Code	Areas
Wiskus, Jessica	PA1050	13J,12A,13E,13
Wittgraf, Michael A.	ND0500	10,13,34,10A,10B
Wiznerowicz, James	VA1600	10A,10F,13,13H,10
Woger, Scott	IL1600	13,11,66A,47
Wohl, Daniel	NY3560	10,10A,13,13F
Wold, Wayne L.	MD0500	13,66G,66H,10
Wolf, Matthew	MI0500	48,13,60,32H
Wolfe-Ralph, Carol	MD0400	13,66A
Wolgast, Brett	IA0300	66A,66G,13,12A
Wolking, Henry C.	UT0250	13,10F,47,46,29
Woll, Greg	CA1900	13,49,63,43
Wolters-Fredlund, Benita	MI0350	13,11,12A
Womack, Donald Reid	HI0210	10,13,13E,10A,10F
Wong Doe, Henry	PA1600	66A,66,11,13,66D
Woo, Betty	CA2200	13,12A,66A
Wood, Catherine M.	AC0050	64C,13
Wood, Jeffrey	TN0050	13,10,66A,66D,20G
Wood, Peter J.	AL1300	63A,13,49,41
Woodruff, Christopher J.	CA0600	37,13,63A
Woodruff, Jennifer A.	ME0150	13,14
Woods, Alyssa	AG0400	13
Woodward, James E.	AL0500	13,10
Woodward-Cooper, Marlene	FL1450	13,66A,66B,66C
Woodworth, Jessica A.	MO0500	11,34,13,66A
Wooldridge, Marc	IN1025	13
Woolley, Clara	IN0010	13,11,32,66A,66G
Work, George P.	IA0850	51,62C,62D,13
Woronecki, Stuart	CT0600	13
Worzbyt, Jason W.	PA1600	64D,13,37,48
Wray, Ron E.	AL1160	64C,37,13,60
Wright, Barbara	WV0560	13A,13,12A,12,66G
Wright, J. Clay	KS0440	11,13,36,40,61
Wright, James	AG0100	13,10
Wright, Richard	NY4050	13,11,13C,66A,38
Wright, William B.	PA1300	11,13,36,60
Wright, William	AG0450	13,66G
Wubbena, Jan Helmut	AR0400	13,66G,12A,11
Wubbena, Teresa R.	AR0400	13,32,41,16,64
Wyatt, Alan	TN0850	13,47,64E,35A,35B
Wyatt, Scott A.	IL3300	13,10,34,45
Wynkoop, Rodney A.	NC0600	13,60,36
YaDeau, William Ronald	IL1750	13,66A,66D
Yaffe, Carl	DC0170	13,12
Yandell, Ruth	AZ0440	66A,66G,13
Yang, Ben Hoh	LA0150	13,66A,66C
Yang, Clara	NC2410	66A,66B,13
Yang, Fengshi	IL0720	10A,13
Yannay, Yehuda	WI0825	13,10,45,43
Yannelli, John A.	NY3560	13,41,45,54,34
Yanson, Eliezer G.	SC0200	32D,13,60A,36,40
Yaraman, Sevin H.	NY1300	13,14,12
Yarmolinsky, Benjamin	NY0280	13A,13,10,45,70
Yasui, Byron K.	HI0210	70,10A,10F,13,20B
Yearsley, David	NY0900	12,13,11,66H,66G
Yeary, Mark	IN0900	13
Yeung, Amy	TN1720	61,39,13
Yeung, Angela C.	CA5200	13,38,41,42,62C
Yih, Annie	CA5060	13,13I,13C
Yim, Jay Alan	IL2250	13,10
Yoelin, Shelley	IL3200	13A,13,37,47,64E
Yoo, In-Sil	NY3550	10,13,34A
Yoon, Choon Sil	CA3950	13
Yorgasen, Brent	OH1400	13,10
Yost, Jacqueline	NC2420	13,66G
You, JaeSong	NY0625	13
Young, Ann	CA4450	13,67B,11
Young, Charles R.	WI0850	13,10F,35C,10A
Young, Gregory D.	MT0200	13,64C
Young, H. G.	WV0760	13,11,12A,36,54
Young, Stefan	NJ1350	13,10
Young-Wright, Lorna C.	VI0050	13,66,60A
Youtz, Gregory	WA0650	10,13,14,43
Yubovich, Benjamin	IN0005	60,16,12,13,14
Yust, Jason	MA0400	13
Zahab, Roger E.	PA3420	38,13,10F,43,62A
Zamzow, Beth Ann	IA0930	13,41,42,37,12
Zank, MJ Sunny	OH1800	13,20,10,12A,43
Zanter, Mark J.	WV0400	13,29,10,70,34
Zappulla, Robert	CA1050	12A,12C,13,66H
Zaritzky, Gerald	MA1400	13
Zbikowski, Lawrence	IL3250	13,12A,13J,29C
Zec, John	NJ0550	12A,31,66G,13,11
Zhao, Grace Xia	CA5100	66,14,13,66A,66C
Zimmerman, John	IL3550	13,66A
Zimmerman, Karen Bals	NY3720	13,11,66A,66B,66C
Zimmerman, Robert R.	NC0600	10,13
Ziolek, Eric E.	OH0650	13,10,11
Zipay, Terry L.	PA3700	13,35B,34A,13E,11
Ziporyn, Evan	MA1200	13,10,20D,64C,29
Zirk, Willard	MI0600	13,49,63B
Zirnitis, Anda	MO0300	13,66A,66C,66D
Zito, Vincent	FL0730	13A,13
Zobel, Elizabeth W.	IL0350	12,13,36,60,61
Zocchi, Michael	MN1625	13,10
Zogleman, Deanne	KS0980	12A,13,20G,36,40
Zolper, Stephen T.	MD0850	13
Zubow, Zachariah	IA0700	13
Zuschin, David	VA1100	13,12A,61
Zwerneman, Jane	CA2100	13
Zyman, Samuel	NY1900	13

Rudiments

Name	Code	Areas
Abbinanti, David A.	NY2550	13A,35A
Abel, Sandra	TX0390	36,61,13A,13B,13C
Abigana, Brett K.	MA1400	13A,13C
Accurso, Joseph	NJ0030	13A,13,60,10,35B
Adams, Kristine	MA0260	13A,13
Adan, Jose	FL1300	11,70,13A
Addamson, Paul	NC1050	66A,66C,66D,13A,13
Aikin, Diane	NE0300	66G,13A
Albrecht, Ronald	IA1350	13A,13,66A,11
Alderson, Erin	IL1800	11,13A,32E,37,64
Allen, Frances	MD0170	13A,66A
Alstat, Sara	IL2500	11,13A,13C,36,61
Alvarez, Luis M.	PR0150	10A,11,13A,13B,14
Amante Y Zapata, Joseph J.	RI0101	36,40,11,13A,13B
Amati-Camperi, Alexandra	CA5353	12A,11,12C,13A,12
Amos, Alvin E.	PA2000	29,13A,13C,48,64
Amos, Gloria	VA0950	13A,11,61
Amrozowicz, Mary Barbara	NY4460	13,13,66A,13C,13B
Anderman, Mark	CA4460	13,34,10,70,13A
Anderson, Matthew	NJ0500	13A
Anderson, Michael J.	IL3310	13A,60,36
Anderson, Robert	NY3250	11,34D,34H,35,13A
Anderson, Shane	TX2930	13A,13B,13C,66A,66B
Andrade, Ken	CA1760	13A,11
Annoni, Maria T.	MN0900	11,13A,13B,70,14C
Anthony, John P.	CT0100	13A,11,12A,66D,66G
Antolini, Anthony	ME0200	36,13A,66D
Appello, Patrick	NJ0550	70,67G,13B,13A,12A
Apple, A. Alan	PA1750	13A,36,61,13C,40
Applegate, Ann	WI0925	66D,13A,13B,66A
Aquila, Carmen	NY4460	35A,13A,35D,12A,10A
Aquino, Robert	NY2102	13A,13,10,66A,66B
Aranda, Patrick	CA0950	13A,37,47,63C,29A
Arauco, Ingrid	PA1500	13A,13,10
Archer, Esther	CA5510	66A,13A
Archer, Kelly	MO1650	13A,66A
Archer, Naida	AJ0150	13A,13,66A,66D
Archeto, Maria	GA0755	11,12A,12B,13A,20
Ard, Sharon	AR0600	11,13A
Arendsen, Benjamin D.	NY2550	13A,13C
Armstrong, James E.	NC2700	63A,13A,37,46,49
Arnold, Mark	NY1250	13A,11,70
Arrigotti, Stephanie	NV0150	13A,11,66A,66B,66D
Arrivee, David	CA0600	38,13,41,13A,13C
Arrowsmith, Brenda	AG0070	48,64,10F,13A,13B
Arrowsmith, Jamie	AG0070	38,60B,62,13A,13B
Ashmore, Michel	MO0250	11,66A,13A
Atlas, Raphael	MA1750	13A,13,13F,13D
Auler, Robert M.	NY3770	66A,66D,13A,40,35A
Aultman, Gerald	TX2600	13A,13,66A,66G
Auner, Edith	MA1900	13A,13,42
Axelrod, Lawrence	IL0720	13A
Bachmann, Nancy	CA2775	13A,13B,12A,66A,66B
Bailey, Ronda J.	KS0400	13A
Bales, Bruce	CA2050	40,61,67,13A,36
Balian, Muriel G.	CA1700	13A,11
Balkin, Richard A.	NY3730	13A,41,62A
Ball, Sheridan J.	CA1520	36,41,61,13A
Ballinger, Robert W.	OH2300	39,66C,11,13A
Ballmaier, Robert	IL0720	13A,13C
Balzano, Gerald	CA5050	13A,34,13L,12F,12
Barbee, Larry	NJ0975	13A,47,70,29
Barber, June	CA0300	13A,13,61
Barclay, Timothy R.	IL0650	13A,64E,46,47
Bares, William	MA0260	13A,13B
Barker, David	VA1580	13A,32B
Barnfather, Samantha	FL1675	13A
Barone, Judith	NY4460	66A,66G,13A,41
Barron, Jason	AA0200	13A
Basiletti, Sarah	CA2400	13A,66D
Bassler, Samantha Elizabeth	NJ1400	13A,13B
Batista, Gustavo	PR0150	11,12A,13A,13C,70
Bauer, David T.	MN1030	13A,34,66A,66G
Baugh, Kim C.	VA1300	13A,37
Beaman, M. Teresa	CA0810	13A,13,48,64A,34
Beams, Mahala	MA1560	11,12A,66A,13A
Bean, Robert D.	IN0905	13A,66A,66B,66C,66D
Bean, Shirley Ann	MO1810	13A,13B,13C,13D,13E
Beard, Robert Scott	WV0550	66,13C,13A,66B,66C
Beavers, Sean M.	VA0650	12A,13A,13B,13C,41
Becker, Karen E.	NY3775	66A,66C,13C,13A,36
Beckwith, Hubert	VA0450	13A,13,12
Bednarz, Blanka	PA0950	13A,42,51,62A,62B
Beghtol, Jason W.	MS0570	37,13A,46,63,49
Behroozi, Bahram	CA4350	13A,11,12A,14,70
Belfer, Beverly	WI0825	13A,70
Bell, Dennis	NY2400	13A,13,10F
Benham, Helen	NJ0030	13A,66A,66H,66B,66C
Bennet, Pratt H.T.	MA0260	13A
Bennett, Lawrence E.	IN1850	11,12A,12,13A
Bennett, Marie Micol	IL2050	64A,48,41,13A,42
Benoist, Debbie	TX2310	11,13A,34C,65,66
Berardinelli, Paula	NY1600	29,13A,13C,11,47
Beres, Karen E.	NC1650	13A,66D
Berger, Talya	CA4900	13,13A,13B,13C
Bergeron, Andrew	MI0850	70,13A,13D
Bergeron, Norm	TX2800	65,50,10D,11,13A
Bergman, James	CA4450	13A,11
Berk, Stacey J.	WI0850	13A,13B,64B,41,10F
Bernatis, William	NV0050	13A,13,49,63B
Bernstein, Harry	CA1020	13A,11
Bersaglia, G. Scott	KY0400	13A,60,37
Bertucci, Ronald	OR0350	37,13A,47,63C,13C
Bewley, Rabon	TX1660	11,12A,29,64E,13A
Beyer, George	CA1520	47,13A,11,20G
Bible, Kierstin Michelle	MO0260	36,61,12A,13A,54
Bielawa, Herbert	CA4200	13A,13,10F,10,45
Billaud, Louise	VA0900	11,12A,13A
Binford, Hilde M.	PA2450	13A,13,12A,12
Bingham, Steve	FL1675	11,13A,20,29,64
Birch, Sebastian A.	OH1100	13,10,34,13B,13A
Birden, Larry	OK0450	13A,32E,10F,63,37
Bishop, Saundra	MS0575	13A,36,66A,66D,13B
Blake, Michael	ND0500	13A,50,53,65
Blalock, Angela	SC0150	11,13A,13B,40,61
Blazar, Sally	MA0260	13A
Bleiler, Loueda	NY0950	11,12A,13A,13B,36
Block, Steven	NM0450	13A,13,10F
Blombach, Ann K.	OH1850	13A,13,34,12F,12
Bohm, Keith	CA0840	13A,64E
Bohnenstengel, Christian	UT0200	66A,66C,13A,13B,13C
Boldt-Neurohr, Kirsten	WA0050	13A,13B,13C,13F
Bolduan, Kathleen	MO1900	13A,13
Bolton, Bryan	KY0050	11,13A,32,36,61
Bonacci, Mary Brown	MA2100	61,11,13A
Bonkowski, Anita	AB0150	29A,29B,13A,13B,13D
Booker, Kenneth A.	TX1450	37,46,47,60,13A
Boozer, Pat	NC2350	10,32B,66A,13A,13B
Boquiren, Sidney M.	NY0050	10A,13A,20D,31A,10F
Boren, Mark	ND0250	63A,63B,13A,41
Borg, Paul	IL1150	13A,13,11,12A,12
Bostic-Brown, Tiffany	AL1250	39,61,54,13A
Bostock, Matthew	MA1100	12,13A
Bostock, Matthew	MA2100	13A,11,12A
Boudreault, Mary	NC2700	63B,13A,13D,13E,13B
Bounds, Kevin S.	AL1160	12A,11,13A
Boyer, Allen	CA3000	13A,47,61,20G
Boykan, Martin	MA0500	13,10,12A,10A,13A
Bozina, Robert	CA4425	20H,70,13A,14F,14C
Bozina, Robert P.	CA1020	13A,70
Breckenridge, Stan	CA2390	12A,13A,14
Bresler, Ross	MA0260	13
Brewer, Johnny	AL0620	13A,13B,11,46,13C
Briggs, Monique	NY2050	12A,13A
Brinegar, Donald L.	CA3500	13A,36,61,60
Brink, Daniel	CO0200	13A,13,10F,11,66A
Brisson, Eric	MN1700	13A,13B,13C,13E,66C
Britt, Joshua	KS0650	13A
Brock, Andrew	OR0950	13A,61
Brown, Helen F.	IN1300	13A
Brown, Philip	VT0300	11,13A,36,44,47
Brown, Stephen	AB0210	10,13A,13B,13C,13D

Name	Code	Areas
Brown, Whitman P.	MA0500	10A,13A,13B
Bruck, Douglas	CA4050	13A,13A,66A,60
Bryant, Curtis	GA1050	13A,10F
Budds, Cain	LA0250	70,11,13A,13B,13C
Budginas, Rudolfas	CA1510	13A,29A
Buelow, William L.	OH1400	13A,13,10,66A,29
Buettner, Jeff	VT0350	13A,36,40,13B,13C
Bullock, Karen	NC2350	66A,13A,66C
Bullock, Kathy	KY0300	11,20A,36,13A,13C
Bulow, Harry T.	IN1300	10,13,34,13A
Bump, Delbert	CA4650	13A,13,36,53
Burch, Steve	CA3100	13A
Burda, Pavel	WI0825	13A,60,50,65
Burkhart, Charles L.	NY0642	13A,13,66A
Burmeister, James R.	WI0825	13A,13C
Burnett, Lawrence E.	MN0300	36,40,31F,61,13A
Burns, Patrick J.	NJ0800	13A,13,10
Burns, Susan M.	CA0630	13A,11,39,61,54
Burrs, Lisa Edwards	VA1750	11,13A,36,61
Burstein, L. Poundie	NY0625	13A,13
Burt, Patricia A.	IL1200	13A,66A,66D,13B,13C
Burton, Heidi R.	OK1300	13A,13,11,66A,62A
Busarow, Donald A.	OH2450	13A,10A,66G,31A
Busch, Gregg	MO0200	11,13A,31A,36,61
Bush, Eric W.	NY4050	37,47,63A,13A,11
Bussiere, Michael	AG0100	13A,13,45,34
Buzzelli-Clarke, Betsy	PA1100	11,13A,12A,66A,66D
Byers, Eric	MA0260	13A
Bynum, Josh L.	GA2100	63C,63D,13A
Byrd, Donald	TN0100	13A
Byrd, Joseph	CA1280	14C,10D,12A,13A
Cabrer, Carlos R.	PR0150	10A,10F,11,13A,13B
Cabrera, Ricardo	PR0100	11,36,61,60,13A
Cahueque, David A.	CA0630	11,13A,70
Cahueque, David	CA3200	11,13A,13B,13C,70
Callis, Cathy	NY1600	13A,11
Cameron, Janet	IL0720	13A
Campbell, Helen E.	AL0310	13A,13,36,61,66
Cannon, Jimmie	CA2300	11,13A,46
Cantwell, Guy	CA0400	13A,70
Cantwell, Terry	GA1260	13A,13,70,51
Capezza, June	FL0200	61,13A,13B,13C
Carbon, John J.	PA1300	13A,13,10F,10
Card, Catherine	CA1960	13A,61,11
Carey, Charles	NE0050	11,13A,70
Carlson, James	TN1800	13A,13B,10A,10B,13C
Carney, Anna	TX2800	11,13A,14C,64C
Carney, Timothy F.	HI0060	36,11,13A,54,61
Carreira, Jonathan	IL0720	13A
Carter, Henrietta McKee	CA2050	11,61,13A
Carter, Jeffrey Richard	MO1950	60A,36,61,13A
Carter, Paul S.	NY3765	13A,13B,66A
Carter, Shannon	AG0350	11,12,13A
Casano, Steven	HI0210	13A,13B,13C,13D
Cassara, Charles	MA0260	13A,13
Castonguay, Roger	AE0100	12A,10A,13A
Castro, Chris	CA1510	13A
Catan, Daniel	CA1265	13A,13,10,11,12A
Caulkins, Tamara	WA1200	70,13A,13B,13C,13D
Cavallo, Gail R.	NY2550	32A,13A,66D
Cedeno, Eduardo	NC1400	62A,13A
Ceide, Manuel J.	PR0115	13F,10A,13A,13B,13E
Cerabona, Linda M.	IL3400	11,13A,20A,31A,32D
Cervantes, Elizabeth	CA0270	11,13A
Chafe, Eric	MA0500	13A,11,12A,12,13J
Chambers, James Alan	IN1050	61,13A,36
Chambers, Steve	TX2750	13A,32B,66C
Chang, Anita L.	CA2650	66A,13A,11
Chang, Soo-Yeon Park	CA0650	66,42,13A,13C
Chapman, Norman	MS0600	13A,13,12A,66A
Charter, Ian R.	AA0010	12A,13A,31A,32E,60
Chase, Corinne Sloan	MA0260	13A,13
Chase, David A.	CA3460	13A,13,12A,36,60
Chaudhuri, Swapan	CA0050	13A,10,12A,65
Chaudoir, Marianne	WI0400	11,66A,66D,13A
Cheatham-Stricklin, Teresa	AL0500	13A,11,61,54
Cheney, Kathryn	GA0250	63A,13A,11
Chevalier, Jason	CA3200	13A,37,20G
Chipman, Paula	MD0300	61,13A,13C
Christensen, Carl J.	CA2150	13,38,37,34G,13A
Christensen, James	AL0210	13A,11
Christiansen, Gregg S.	NY1550	66A,13A,13B,13C
Chuah, Cheong	CA2775	12A,13A,34
Chui, Eddie	CA1020	66D,13A
Chung, Suna	NY3560	13A,13,39,61,13C
Cifarelli, Joan	CA2775	66A,29,13A
Cipullo, Tom	NY0280	13A,13,10,36,61
Clark, Suzanne M.	MA0260	13A,13
Clarke, Penelope	AG0170	13A,64C
Clement, Dawn	WA0200	13A,66A,66D,29
Clemente, Peter	MA0200	11,13A,13,70,20
Clements, Phillip L.	TX2955	60B,37,63D,13A,12A
Clenman, David	AB0150	13,12A,13A,13B,13C
Coats, Syble M.	AL0831	66A,66D,11,13A
Cochran, Alfred W.	KS0650	12A,13A,13B,13E
Cockrell, Findlay	NY3700	13A,13,11,66A
Cogen, Ellen	MA1100	61,40,36,13A,54
Cohen, Gerald	NY1860	13A,13,10
Coker, Warren	NJ1000	13A
Cole, Arlene	RI0050	13A,13,66A
Cole, Judith E.	GA1150	11,13C,13A,66C
Cole, Kathryn	MO0400	61,13A,13C
Collerd, Gene J.	IL3310	13A,60,37,64C
Collins, Jenny	PA1100	11,13A,66A,66D,66C
Collinsworth, Andy	CA4700	13A,32,37,41,69B
Colson, William	TX2600	13A,13,10F,10,13I
Coluzzi, Seth	MA0500	10D,11,13A,12A,12C
Conatser, Brian	AR0200	13A,66A,13B,13C,66C
Connors, Maureen	MA0150	13A,66A,66C
Conti, Michael	NJ0500	13A,13C
Contrino, Joseph L.	MO1500	65,29A,13A,13C
Cooper, Gloria A.	NY2102	13A,61,32C,36,47
Cooper, Kevin	CA1850	11,70,13A
Corey, Horace E.	NV0100	13A,11,41,70
Cormier, Eugene	AF0050	13A,34,70
Coroniti, Joseph	MA0260	13A
Coulter, Chris	CA1960	11,13A
Coulter, Monte	TN1700	13A,11,50,65
Covach, John	NY1100	13,13A,13J,10D
Covach, John R.	NY4350	13A,13,13J,10D
Cox, Buford	FL0040	13A,12A,66A,66C
Coxe, Stephen	VA1000	13A,13B,13D,10
Crabiel, Jon	IN0250	65,13A
Crabtree, John M.	TX2250	13A,13B,13C
Cratty, William	CA4050	13A,13,12A,14,32
Crook, Harold	MA0260	13A,13
Crookall, Christine	GA0250	13A,13,62C,12A,41
Crosby, Matthew	TX3415	36,13A,13B
Cross, Ronald W.	NY4500	13A,11,12A
Cross, Virginia A.	OR0175	31A,12A,66D,13A,66B
Crossland, Carolyn M.	NC1075	13A,11,32A,36,32B
Crotty, John E.	WV0750	13A,13
Csicsila, Mell	OH0755	65,50,13A
Cunneff, Philip B.	MD0475	13A,65,29A,14C
Cunningham, Geoffrey A.	MA1100	13A,37
Curlee, J. Matthew	NY1100	13A,13B,13C,13D,13K
Curtis, Charles	CA5050	13A,41,62C
Cushman, Cathy	NY1250	66A,13A,13
Cutsforth-Huber, Bonnie	MD0095	13A,13,11,12A,13B
Czarkowski, Stephen	MD0550	38,62C,13A
Da Silva, Paul	CA0859	13A,66D,66A
Dal Porto, Mark	NM0100	10,13,66A,34,13A
Dale, Stephen	MA0260	13A,13
Daley, Caron	AF0100	13A,13C,36
Dallinger, Carol	IN1600	62A,13A,62B,51
Damschroder, Norman L.	OH2275	62D,13A,13B
Dana, Christy L.	CA5000	13A,13C,29B,47,29C
D'Angelo, Gerard	NY2660	13A,13,13J
Daniel, Robert	OK0550	13A,60,11,61,13C
Dashevskaya, Olga	CO0625	11,13A,66A,13B
Daub, Eric	TX3100	66A,13A,13B,13C,29A
Davidson, Heidi	WA0750	61,66A,11,13A
Davidson, Thomas	AI0150	13C,66A,13A
Davies, Daniel E.	CA0850	62C,13A,11,13B
Davies, David H.	NY1700	13A,13C,13B,10,13
Davies, Paul	CA1800	13,11,13A,66A,10
Davila, William	CA3450	13A,11,12A,66A,67D
Davis, Hope	CA2300	13A,12,11,37,13B
Davis, Nancy	OH1300	13A,11,36,47
Davis, Peter A.	RI0250	13A,37,47,64
Davis, William	TX1600	13A
Davison, Dorothy	CA4460	13A
Dawe, Karla	AC0100	13A,13J,13C
Dawson, Robert B.	CA1700	13A,35,13,53
Day, Thomas Charles	RI0250	13A,13,12
De La Torre, Javier	PR0150	10A,10F,13A,13C
Deakins, Mark	KY0650	13A,60,36,31A,40
Dearden, Jennifer	PA0100	63A,34,13A,13B,13C
DeBoer, Angela	TN1100	63B,49,13A,13B,13C
DeBoer, Jack	MI0900	11,13A,12A
Decker, Van A.	CA2300	11,13A,34D,47,10A
Declue, Gary L.	IL1245	12A,13A,11,61,36
Deffner, David	CA0150	66G,13A
Deguchi, Tomoko	SC1200	13,66A,13F,13E,13A
DeHoog, David	FL1100	13A,29A
Del Aguila, Miguel	CA5360	10,66A,13A,11
Del Nero, Paul	MA0260	13A,13
DeLaRosa, Lou	CA5510	13A,13C,12A,11,34C
DeLise, Louis	PA2700	13A
Delto, Byron	CA1960	34,70,13A
DeMichele, Anna	CA0859	36,61,13A,38,11
Demmond, Edward C.	CA3100	13A,11
Dempsey, John D.	RI0300	13A,13,51,62A
Denmon, Alan	GA2300	11,13A,13B,32C,32E
Dennewitz, John	RI0102	13A
DeOgburn, Scott	MA0260	13A,13
DeSalvo, Nancy J.	PA3650	13A,13B,66A,66B,13C
Dewey, Cynthia	UT0300	61,54,39,13A
Dickens, Pierce	GA0400	13A,13B,13C,13E,66A
Dickert, Lewis H.	SC1200	70,53,29,13A,14
Dickinson, Marci	IN1010	66A,13A
Diggs, David B.	PA1950	13A,13B,37,64B,48
Dill, John	TX1775	13A,11,66A,66G,12A
Dillenger, Robert	CA2775	12A,13A
Dillon, Lawrence M.	NC1650	13A,13,10,43
Dimitrov, Georges	AI0200	13A,13E
DiMuzio, Richard J.	MA0260	13A,13
Dixon, Howard	TN0800	13A,11,32B,63,64
Dixon, Kara	AC0050	13C
Dixon, Walter	NY0646	13A,72
Dodge, Leanne E.	NY2750	12A,12,13A
Domencic, Mark L.	PA0550	13A
Domingues, Cameron	CA3200	13A
Donelian, Armen	NY2660	13A,13C,10,66A,47
Donovick, Jeffery	FL1650	66D,13A,13B,13C,34C
Doran, David Stephen	KY1460	13A,13,10,11,12A
Dougherty, Peggy S.	OR0175	66A,66D,13A,66B,13E
Dougherty, Peggy	OR0250	66A,13A
Doyle, Sean	NY3725	13A,13B,13C
Draskovic, Ines	NY1250	66A,13A,13C,13
Drews, Michael R.	IN0907	13A,13B,13C,13E,11
Droke, Marilyn	MO0200	13A,32B,44
Drummond, Evan E.	NY3717	12A,13A,70
DuBois, May	CA5500	11,13A,66A
Dumm, Mary Elizabeth	MD0700	13A,13,11,66A
Duncan, Ellen	MI1300	13A,13,60,36,40
Dunn, Alexander	AB0150	70,13A
Durham, Kevin	TN1400	13A,66D,11
Durham-Lozaw, Susan	NC2350	13A,13B,13C,61
Durrenberger, Chris	OH2450	13A,11,66A,66F,12A
Dutton, Douglas	CA2600	13A,13,11,66A
Eastman, George	MA0260	13A
Eastman, Patricia	MO1950	13A,13B,13C,66A
Eastwood, Deb A.	KY0900	13A,13B,13C,63A
Eckhart, Michael	NJ0975	13A,34,70
Edberg, C. Eric	IN0350	41,62C,13A
Edgar, Scott N.	IL1400	37,32,11,13A
Eisel, Gunnar	CA1000	10B,12A,13A,14C,29A
Elswick, Beth L.	MO1810	13A,13B,13C,13D
Emery, Marian L.	IN0910	13A
Englert, David	TX2250	13A,13B,13C
Engstrom, Dale	CA1850	13A,37,49
Erjavec, Donald L.	CA0859	13A,47,29,20G
Ernest, David J.	MN1300	13A,11,64B
Espinosa, Leandro	OR0200	62C,62D,38,13A,11
Estrin, Morton	NY1600	66A,13A
Etters, Stephen C.	NC0350	60,32,37,63D,13A
Eubanks, Erdie	CA1900	13A,66A
Evans, Darryl	AR0810	32E,47,63D,13A,13B
Evans, Gary	VA0400	13A,13B,13C,11,12A
Eyerly, Sarah J.	IN0250	12,13A,14A,15
Fain, Jeremy	TX2700	64D,11,13A,13B
Fairbanks, Ann K.	TX3450	13A,12A,41,64A
Faltstrom, Gloria V.	HI0300	13A,11,66D,61,36
Fannin, Karen M.	AR0350	29,11,13A,47,37
Fast, Susan	AG0200	13A,11,12A,12,55
Favreau, Janet	CA2650	66A,66D,13A,11
Fears, Angela	CA3520	13A,13C,64D,16
Feder, Janet	CO0560	10,70,12A,13A,53
Feldhausen, Scott	TX1400	13A,13B,11
Feldman, Bernardo	CA1265	13A,13,10F,10,11
Fellows, Robin B.	WI0865	13A,11,41,64A
Felton, Jukube	IL0600	13A,29
Felts, Randolph C.	MA0260	13A,13
Fergus, Brian S.	CA1020	34,13A
Ferguson, James	CA1760	13A,11,70

Index by Area of Teaching Interest

Name	Code	Areas
Ferrari, John	NJ1400	13A,11,50,65
Ferrington, Darryl	LA0400	13A,36,32,31A
Festinger, Kurt	CA5500	13A,29,47
Fiddmont, Keith	CA4450	11,29,13A,46,47
Fields, Melinda	CT0600	13A
Fifield, Glen	UT0300	13A,32A,32B,49,63A
Finch, Scott	AJ0030	60A,31A,12A,13A,11
Fisher, John	TX3250	13A,13B,10A,15,66A
Fisk, Charles	MA2050	13A,13,12A,66A
Fleming, Pat W.	TX3175	32B,32D,13A
Flom, James H.	MN1300	13A,11
Flood, John	CA4100	20A,13A,11,65,50
Flores, Rick	CA0900	13A,70
Floyd, Rosalyn	GA0250	13A,13,11,66A,66C
Floyd-Savage, Karen	VA1750	11,13A,36,61
Fluchaire, Olivier	NY0644	62A,62B,11,13A,42
Fogle, Megan R.	SC0350	13A,13B,13C,13E,13F
Foley, Megan J.	CA1700	11,13A
Forehan, Jeff	CA5510	10B,13A,34D,35G,35D
Foreman, Karen C.	CA0100	66D,13A
Foster, Christopher	NY0100	36,63,13A,47,41
Foster, Stephen Wolf	MA0260	13A
Foust, Diane	WI1100	36,61,13A,40,13B
Fowler, Andrew J.	SC0420	13C,13A,11
Fox, Elizabeth	WI1100	13A,13B,13C,11
Franco-Summer, Mariana	CA5360	11,13A,66
Frank, Jolita Y.	WI0835	66D,13A
Frank, Mary Lou	IN1010	11,13A
Franklin, Virgil	IN1800	34D,13A,34
Franzetti-Brewster, Allison	NJ0700	66C,41,13A,13B,13C
Fraser, Teresa L.	WA0600	36,47,13A,40
Freeman, Christine L.	IN0905	13A,66C,66A
Freemyer, Janice	CA1960	13A
Fresonke, Michael	OK0750	13A,70,14C,41
Friedrichs, Charles	CA4100	11,37,63C,13A,32
Frye, Joseph W.	TN1720	63C,13A,13C,11,34
Fryling, David N.	NY1600	36,60A,60,32,13A
Fuhrmann, Christina E.	OH0100	13A,11,12,14
Fukuda, Joni	CA5355	11,13A,32D,36,61
Fuschetto, W.	AB0040	13A,13B
Gable, David D.	GA0490	11,12A,12B,13A,16
Galindo, Jeffrey A.	MA0260	13A,13
Gallops, R. Wayne	VA1100	13A,32C,32E,29,37
Gandy, V. Gay	KY1400	36,61,13A,13C,11
Gannon, Thomas	MA2100	13A,63B
Gardner, Peter S.	MA0260	13A
Gargrave, Eric	RI0101	11,13A,29A,48,13B
Garry, Kevin M.	CO0400	70,13A,11,12A,14C
Gauvin, Marcelle	MA2020	61,13A,11
Gaviria, Carlos	TX2700	62D,11,13A,13B
Gavrilova, Julia	AI0150	66A,13A
Gawlick, Ralf	MA0330	13A,13,11
Gelber, Debbie	TX2350	13A,13B,36,61,13C
Gelineau, Phyllis	CT0450	13A,11
Gemme, Terese	CT0450	13A,12A,36,66G
Gengaro, Christine Lee	CA2600	13A,32A,61
George, Elizabeth	AZ0450	13A,13B,66D
Gerhold, John	CA0270	13,10,66D,13A
Germain, Anthony	MA0260	13A,13
Gerritson, Sasha L.	IL2150	11,13C,39,13A
Gertsenzon, Galina	MA2100	66A,66D,13A
Giammario, Matteo	PA0400	13A,11,62A,62B
Gibson, Joice Waterhouse	CO0550	34B,34C,12A,12C,13A
Gifford, Gene	AL1250	13A,61,13E
Gilbert, Jan M.	MN0950	13A,13C,10
Gilleland, Katharine	NC2525	66G,11,13A,29A,36
Gilliam-Valls, Jessica	TX1150	13A,62C,62D
Gillingham, David R.	MI0400	13A,13,10F,10
Ginenthal, Robin	MA0260	13A,13
Giteck, Janice	WA0200	13A,13,10,12A
Glanden, Don	PA3330	47,66A,13A,13,29
Glasgow, David M.	PA0950	66A,66C,13A
Glass, Anne	TN0050	13A,66A,66G,66C
Glidwell, Delrae	MO1550	32B,32C,13A
Glofcheskie, John	AB0050	13A,13,12A
Gnandt, Edwin E.	AA0010	13A,66A,42,13B,66D
Goff, Carolyn	GA1300	13A,66C,66A
Goldblatt, David Nathan	FL1675	13A
Goldray, Martin	NY3560	13A,13,11,12A,66A
Goldstaub, Paul R.	NY3705	13A,13,10
Goldstein, Perry	NY3790	13A,13C,13E,10A,13F
Gonano, Max A.	PA0500	11,12A,13A,29A,37
Gonder, Jonathan P.	NY3730	66A,66C,11,13A,13B
Gonzalez, Ana Laura	NY1400	64A,13A,13B
Gonzalez-Matos, Adonis	AL0050	66,13A
Goodin, Glenda	TN1100	13A,11
Goodman, Kimberlee	OH2050	64A,14,13A
Goranson, Jocelyn	PA2300	64A,13A,13C,13B,42
Goranson, Todd A.	PA2300	64E,64D,13A,47,42
Gorman, Kurt	TN1720	13A,34,63A,47
Goslee, Brenda	TN1250	13A,13,11,66A,66G
Gothard, Paul	OH1250	13A,13,10F,11,36
Gottlieb, David	NJ0750	10,13A,13B,34D,64E
Graef, Becky	IN1750	66A,66D,13A
Graham, Brenda J.	IN1250	13A,32,37,62,31A
Graham, Dave	CA5400	47,13A,11,46,29A
Graham, Patricia S.	MD0650	13A,66D
Granat, Zbigniew	MA0280	13A,13,11
Grant, Joyce	NY1200	13A,20G,29A
Grant, Joyce	NY1210	12,13A,36
Grant, Kristin	AR0500	64A,13A,13B,13C
Grasmick, David M.	CA0630	13A,34,63A,29
Gray, Serap Bastepe	MD0300	70,13A
Green, Burdette L.	OH1850	13A,13,13J,12B
Green, Dana S.	OR0800	13A,11,66
Green, Peter	CA1960	13A,66A,36,40
Greene, Janet E.	MN0800	32E,13A,37,64C
Greene, Roger W.	MA0150	13,34,66A,13A,10F
Greene, Ted	AB0060	13A,34
Gretz, Ronald	MD0175	13A,13,66A,66C,54
Griffin, Joel	MO0400	64E,46,47,13A,13B
Griffin, Robert	KY0750	13A,11,50,65
Griffin, William	FL0680	61,13A
Griffith, Dorothy S.	CA1900	13A,66A,66H
Griffith, Glenn	OR0350	13A
Grile, Kathy	IN1560	66A,66B,13A
Grimland, Fredna H.	OR0950	13A,32,61
Grinwis, Brandan	MI0850	65,50,13A
Grmela, Sylvia	NY4460	62B,20,13A,13C
Grossman, Andrea	IN1010	11,66A,13A,66D
Grove, Paul	WA0400	70,13A,13B,13C
Grover, Elaine	MI1300	13A,13,66A,66G,31A
Guerrero, Rosi E.	WA0950	66,66D,13A,13B,13D
Guessford, Jesse	VA0450	11,13A,34
Guha-Thakurta, Sonya	AA0150	13A
Guild, Jane E.	LA0750	13A,13,61
Gumm, Alan	MI0400	13A,32
Gurin, Shelley Foster	IL2150	13A,32E
Gustafson, David	OR0350	61,13A
Hackett, Patricia	CA4200	13A,32
Haddock, Lynette	CA3200	13A
Haffley, Robin L.	PA1830	11,13A,29A,34D,14C
Haffley, Robin L.	PA2700	13A
Hagarty, Scott	TX0550	63A,13A,13C,49,41
Hagedorn, David	MN1450	13A,65,50,47,13B
Hager, H. Stephen	TX3175	13A,13,49,63B
Haines, Janice	CA0950	13A,13C,66D
Hajda, John M.	CA5060	13K,13L,13A,13B,14A
Haley, Timothy R.	NC2210	11,13A,46,34C,34A
Hall, Teddy	VA0500	13A,13B,13C,32C,11
Ham, Donna	TX2350	11,13A,66
Hamberlin, Larry D.	VT0350	10A,12A,29A,13A,13C
Hamlin, Peter S.	VT0350	10A,10B,10F,13A,13B
Hamm, Bruce	CA0050	13A,11,12A
Hamman, James	LA0800	11,12A,13A,55B,66G
Hanawalt, Anita	CA5100	13A,11
Hanning, Barbara Russano	NY0550	13A,11,12A,12
Hanson, John R.	NY3705	13A,13
Hanson, Josef M.	NY4350	13A,49
Harding, Scott R.	MI0400	10A,13C,29A,65,13A
Harkins, Edwin	CA5050	13A,13,63A,54,43
Harms, Janet	CA0630	13A,11,66
Harrington, Danny	MA0260	13A,13
Harrington, Richard	CA0050	13A,11,12A
Harris, Carole J.	NY0400	13A,13B,13C,13D
Harris, Howard	TX3150	13A,10,37,47,39
Harris, Rod D.	CA1375	13A,11,64E,29B,34
Hartman, Lee	MO1790	13A
Hartway, James	MI2200	13A,10,10F,66D,13B
Hastings, David M.	WI0850	64E,42,13A,13B,13C
Hasty, Barbara P.	CA1700	13A,61,66A,36
Hatfield, Gaye Tolan	MA0260	13A,13
Haupers, James Mitch	MA0260	13A,13
Hawkins, John A.	WV0500	13A,13,11,36,66
Hawkins, William	CA3460	13A,32A,49,63,29
Hay, Dennis	AR0050	13A,13B,11,66A,66C
Hearn, Carmelita	AF0120	13A,66A,66D
Heavner, Tabitha	CT0050	11,13A
Hebert, Sandra M.	MA0330	13A,13,66A,66B
Hedberg, Judy L.	OR0800	12A,13A
Hegarty, James	IL2400	10A,29A,34D,47,13A
Heimbecker, Sara	CO0950	12A,11,13A,14C
Helm, Jon E.	AA0040	13A,13,12A,63,49
Helms, Elizabeth	CA5360	66C,13A,13C,36,39
Henderson, Jean	NE0450	13A,13B,13C,13D,10A
Hendricks, James	IL0600	13A,47,66A,66D,29
Henson, Mitchell	GA1700	64E,47,13A
Herbert, David	TX2200	13A,64B,32,13B,13C
Hermann, Richard	NM0450	13A,13
Hernandez, Richard	CA4450	13A
Herrington, Brian P.	TX2250	13A,13B,13C
Hickey, Katherine M.	CA5150	32,13A,13C,36,40
Hicks, Gail	CA4625	66A,13A
Hiebert, Lenore	CA0810	66A,13A
Hileman, Lynn	WV0750	64D,13C,13B,13A,13D
Hill, Camille	KY0600	13A,11,36,61,66D
Hill-Le, Holly	OK0150	66C,13A
Hilton, Suzanne	MD0550	11,13A,34C
Hines, Billy C.	NC0700	13A,36,61
Hinkle, Jean	OR1020	11,13A,41,66A,66D
Hirt, James	OH0600	13A,13B
Hiscocks, Mike	CA2650	11,13A,61,45,10B
Hix, Michael T.	NM0450	61,13A,12A,12
Hodge, R. Matthew	KY0400	11,13A
Hoegberg, Elisabeth Honn	IN1650	61,13A,13B
Hoffman, Brian D.	OK0800	13A,13B,13C,66D
Holcombe, Helen	PA0400	13A,36,61,66D
Holder, Brian	FL1675	11,20,13A,65,50
Holland, Jonathan Bailey	MA0260	10A,10F,13A,10
Holland, Linda L.	CA4410	13,13A,13C
Hollerbach, Peter	NY0270	13A,11,14,47,70
Holliday, James T.	DC0150	13A,13,61
Hollinger, Lowell	MS0350	11,13A,32C,48,64E
Hollinger, Trent A.	MO0300	64,37,13C,13A,60B
Holt, Drew	CA4450	13A
Hontos, Margaret Ellen	CA4410	13,13A,12A,20
Hontz, James	PA0950	70,13A
Horel, Charles	GA0950	10A,70,13A,13C
Horn, Goffery C.	FL0600	13A,13
Howe, Ryan	IA1400	13A,13B,13C
Howell, Jane	PA2900	66A,66C,13A,54,11
Hoyt, Reed J.	NY3700	13A,13,12A
Huang, Hai Tao	IL3310	13A,63A
Huang, Rachel Vetter	CA4500	62A,11,13A,42
Hubbell, Judy	CA1020	61,66D,13A
Hucke, Adam	IL2970	11,13A,29A,63A,47
Hudspeth, Charles M.	CA1020	36,13A,66D
Huff, Lori	CA0630	13A,11,48,64E,32
Hughes, Julayne	MI1830	11,13A
Hughes, R. Daniel	NY2550	36,13A,61
Huls, Shirley	PA3000	13A,32A,32B,61
Humbert, William	AZ0350	37,64,63,13A,60
Humphreys, Paul W.	CA2800	14A,13A,13B,29A,10A
Humphries, Stephen	GA0600	13A,20,50,65
Hunnicutt, Bradley C.	NC2300	13,66,34,13A,13E
Hunter, Mary K.	ME0200	13A,13,11,12A,12
Hurd, Mary	MI0300	66A,66B,66C,66D,13A
Hurst, Chloe	AB0200	13A,13B,13C
Hurst, Twyla	MS0370	13A,36,61,66D
Hutchings, James	IL0420	11,13B,12A,61,13A
Hyland, Judy	IA1300	13A,66C,11
Hylton, Doris	MO1830	32B,13A,13C
Idenden, John	NJ0100	13A,11,12A,61,66A
Iguina, Jose R.	PR0150	13A,13C,11,70
Ikach, Yugo Sava	PA0500	61,38,11,13A,36
Imhoff, Andrea G.	TX2900	13A,11,66C,66A
Ingersoll, Orbie D.	CA3100	13A,11
Inkman, Joanne	NC2500	66A,66C,66D,13A
Itoh, Takuma	HI0210	10A,13A,13B,13C,13D
Izzo, Victor	NY4300	37,38,13A
Jackson, Albert	IL2775	13A,11,36,61
Jacob, Stefanie	WI1150	13A,66A
Jacobs, Ed	IL2970	63D,11,13A,37,46
Janisch, Joseph	WV0560	36,60,32,13A,32B
Janzen, Elaine	TN1350	66A,66D,13A
Jasinski, Nathan David	KY0550	62C,32E,38,42,13A
Jefcoat, Priscilla	GA0350	13A,66A,10F,12A,13D
Jeffers, Rebecca	OR0700	13A,66B,66C,66D
Jensen, Joan F.	LA0750	66A,66D,13A
Jerosch, Anita	ME0340	32,12A,13A
Jin, Jungwon	CA1960	66D,13A
Johansen, Ken	MD0650	13A,66D
Johns, Christopher	NC2440	62C,13A
Johns, Lana Kay	MS0500	13A,11,64A
Johnson, Byron	MS0050	13A,13B,13C,61,39
Johnson, Cornelius	IL0450	13A,66A,11,36,20

Index by Area of Teaching Interest

Name	Code	Areas
Johnson, David	CA0510	13A,65,50
Johnson, David	MA0260	13A,13
Johnson, David	ID0070	13A,41,62B,42,51
Johnson, Deborah S.	NE0300	13A,11,48,64A,13B
Johnson, G. Larry	UT0325	36,60A,13A,13B,13C
Johnson, Lura	MD0650	13A,66D
Johnson, Ruth	CA5360	13A,66A,66D
Johnson, Shirley M.	FL0600	13A,61,66A,66D
Johnson, Stephen R.	PA0700	10F,32D,13A,63D
Jones, Deborah	TX3415	32,13A,13C
Jones, Jeff	CA3200	13A,11
Jones, Joel C.	AL0050	66,36,13A
Jones, Larry	TX2100	13A,11,50,65
Jones, Ryan C.	NY1600	13C,13D,13A
Jones, Tony	IL1090	37,63,13A,13C
Jones, Zebedee	MS0600	13A,32,36,66A
Jordan, Michael D.	TX1660	13A,13,11,39,61
Jordan, Rachel	MS0350	62A,11,13A,13B,42
Joy, Nancy	NM0310	63B,49,13A,11
Jung, Eunsuk	TN0600	13A,66A,66D,66G,13B
Jurcisin, Mark	NJ0750	10,13A,13B,13C,11
Jusino, Christopher	NY2550	13A,72
Kacos, Lisa	MI0850	13A,13C
Kahan, Sylvia	NY0644	12A,12C,66,13A,13C
Kambeitz, Gus	CA5510	46,37,47,29,13A
Kang, Sang Woo	RI0150	13A,13B,66A
Kaplan, Sara	IL2775	63B,13A
Kapner, Harriet H.	NY2550	70,13A,13B,13C
Kappy, David	WA1050	13A,41,48,63B
Kastner, Kathleen	IL3550	13A,13,50,65,20
Katz, Bruce	MA0260	13A,13
Katz, Darrell	MA0260	13A,13
Kaufhold, Jessica	AL0530	36,11,13A,13B,13C
Kazez, Daniel	OH2450	13A,11,20D,62C,62D
Kean, Kristen	KY0550	64A,13A,13,42,48
Keberle, David S.	NY0644	10,10B,64C,42,13A
Kechley, David S.	MA2250	10A,10F,13A,13B,13D
Keck, Vail	CA3100	36,60,11,13A,61
Kee, Edna Gayles	NY1200	13A,36
Keebaugh, Aaron	FL1675	11,20,13A,63
Keef, Ardith A.	ME0500	13A,11,64D
Keene, Theresa	CA0150	13A,66A
Keever, Howard	MS0850	10A,10D,13A,13B,13D
Keipp, Donald K.	UT0350	13A,11,65,29,47
Kellert, Aaron	OK1100	11,36,13A,54,61
Kelly, Daniel	TX2955	63A,47,13A,13B
Kelly, Michael	OH1450	13A,13B,13C
Kennedy, John	TX2350	14C,13A,46,49,32B
Kennedy, Nathan	MN0610	13A,13B,13C,13D,13F
Kenneson, Claude E.	AA0100	13A,11
Kenney, James	CA3375	13A,11,14C,66D
Kern, Gene Marie Callahan	NY3650	61,36,13A,39
Kern, Jeffrey	PA3330	13A,36,44,61,66A
Kern, R. Fred	TX3420	13A,66B,66D
Kershaw, Yvonne	AE0120	64A,64D,10A,11,13A
Kerstetter, Tod	KS0650	13A,48,64C,13B
Khan, Ali Akbar	CA0050	13A,10,11,12A,62
Khan, Pranesh	CA0050	13A,10,65
Kidd, Christine	NM0400	13A,61,11
Kim, Gloria	CA1265	61,13A,66A
Kim, Irene	CA2600	13A,61,36
Kim, Jung Eun	CA4450	66,13A
Kim-Infiesto, Marilyn Liu	HI0160	36,61,12A,32,13A
Kimball, James W.	NY3730	13A,11,14,67E,70
Kimmel, Pamela J.	IL0550	13A,70
Kindred, Kyle	TX2250	13A,13B,13C
King, Curtis R.	FL0600	13A,13,32,61,62
Kirchoff, Leanna	CO0550	66D,13A
Kirk, Erin	CA5400	11,13A
Kirschstein, Natalie	CO0650	11,20,13A
Kiser, Daniel W.	NC1100	13A,10F,60B,37,63A
Klakowich, Robert	AA0020	13A,13B,13C,13D,13E
Klein, Rochelle Z.	PA2900	32,35E,66A,11,13A
Kline, W. Peter	TX2260	13A,11,37,49,63D
Klipp, Barbara A.	IL0650	13A,11,64A
Klopfenstein, Reginald	IN0200	13A,12A,47,50,65
Klotzbach, Susan	IL1200	66C,13A,13B,13C
Knelman, Jennifer	AG0350	13A,11
Knight, Jonathan	CA2775	12A,13A,60B,63
Knoles, Amy	CA0510	65,50,13A,10B
Knox, Daniel	AL0750	11,70,63,64,13A
Koehler, Elisa C.	MD0400	38,63A,60,11,13A
Koh-Baker, JoAnn Hwee Been	OH1600	11,12A,66A,13A,13B
Kohlbeck-Boeckman, Anne	WI0350	13,66A,66D,13A
Koop, Ruth B.	AJ0030	13A,31A,35A,35E,61
Korey, Judith A.	DC0350	13A,13,66A,29,34
Korneitchouk, Igor	CA4050	13A,10,11,12A,34
Kornicke, Eloise	VA0800	66A,13A
Koza, Matt	NY0646	13A,64C,64E
Kozubek, Michael	CA0250	70,13A
Kramer, Elizabeth A.	GA2130	12A,14,11,13A,62A
Kraus, James	MI1180	66G,13A,66A
Krause, Douglas	CO0830	13A,11,35A,35B,35C
Krause, Drew S.	NY2750	13A,13B,13C,13D,13F
Kreiling, Jean L.	MA0510	13A,11,12A,12,66D
Kress, Richard	MA0260	13A,13
Krouseup, Jack	CA3520	10,13B,13A,13F,47
Krueger, Walter E.	OR0150	13A,66A,12A,66G,66D
Krumbholz, Gerald A.	WA0950	13A,13B,13C,13D,10C
Kubiak, Paul	CA0859	13A,11
Kubis, Thomas M.	CA2050	10F,13A,29B,46,47
Kuhn, William	OR0150	37,11,63C,60,13A
Kukec, Paul E.	IL1900	13A,13,12A,36,66A
Kulpa, John	NJ0750	11,13A,13B,13C
Kushnir, Regina	CO0100	13A,66A
Kuzmenko, Larysa	AG0450	13A,13,66A
Kvetko, Peter J.	MA1650	14,13A,14C,20E,41
Lach, Malgorzata	MA1350	70,13A
LaCreta, Joseph	MA1100	70,13A
Laginya, Daniel	OH2600	13A,13B,13C
Lajoie, Stephen H.	RI0101	47,66A,53,29,13A
Lambert, Evin R.	WA0750	11,36,66A,61,13A
Lambert, Philip	NY0250	13A,13,11,12A
Lamprey, Audrey	CA0630	13A,49,63B
Lamprey, Audrey	CA5040	13A,63B
Land, W. Reese	KY0400	11,13A,41
Landes, Daniel	TN0100	13A,13,66A,66D,31A
Landsberg, Paul	AB0070	13A,70,53,47,29
Lane, Mathew	MD0400	13A,13C,66A,66C
Lang, Brenda J.	OH0550	36,60A,61,13A
Lanham, Barbara	IL1610	13A,36,66A,66D
Lansing, Nathan	WA0950	36,40,13B,13C,13A
Lantz, Lisa E.	NY0100	11,38,51,62,13A
Large, Karen McLaughlin	KS0650	13,11,64A,13A,48
Larson, Philip	CA5050	13A,11,12A,36,61
Latham, Louis S.	VA1000	13A,34,35A,35C,35D
Latten, James E.	PA1650	11,13A,37,50,65
Laubenthal, Jennifer	NM0100	64C,11,13A
Laughlin, Jim	TX0100	13A,12A,48,64C,64E
Lawson, Matthew	KY0250	13A,63A
Lee, Christopher	MA2030	13A,13B,13C
Lee, Gordon	OR1250	29,13A
Lee, Jaeryoung	CA4050	32E,13A,11
Lee, Sung Ae	CA0859	13A,66A,66D
Legname, Orlando	NY3765	13A,13,10,35
Lehman, Katherine	TN1800	13A,62A
Lemson, Lee	TX3850	13A,11,36,61
Lew, Howard	NY2700	13A,12,66D
Lewis, Brian	MA0260	13A,13
Lewis, Ian	CA2750	11,13A
Li, Lei	IL0650	13A,11,66A,66D
Li, Ping-Hui	PR0150	13A,13C,14A,66A,66C
Li, Simon	NY2900	66A,13A,13B,13C
Liebhaber, Barbara	PA2550	13A,13B
Lifchitz, Max	NY3700	10,43,13A,13,10F
Lim, Yoon-Mi	TX2600	66G,66A,13A
Lin, I-Bei	HI0210	62C,41,42,13A
Lin, James	CA5510	13A,13B,42,13C,13D
Lin, Mei-Fang	TX3200	10A,13A,13I,13L,10F
Linch-Parker, Sheryl	NC0800	13A,32B,32C,49,63C
Lindekugel, Denise	MD0550	11,13A
Lindeman, Carolynn A.	CA4200	13A,32,66D,34
Lindholm, Eric C.	CA3650	13A,60,11,38,41
Lindsey, Roberta	IN0907	11,13A,34C,34B,14A
Linnenbom, Harriett	MD0700	13A,11,66A,66D
Lippard, Erin	TX2710	61,13A,13B,40,54
Lippard, Michael S.	TX2710	13A,37,46,64,13B
Lipton, Jamie	AR0300	63D,49,13A
Lissance, Alizon J.	MA0260	13A,13
Litke, Sheila	KS1300	66,13,66A,66B,13A
Littrell, David	KS0650	38,41,62C,62D,13A
Livingston-Hakes, Beth	AZ0490	61,54,13A
Locke, Benjamin R.	OH1200	13A,60,36,38,61
Loeb, Jaemi	KY0450	38,13A,41,42,60B
Loftus, Jean	NY2950	39,61,54,13A,13B
Logan, Jennifer	CA3300	10B,13A,13B,13C,35C
Lombardi, Paul	SD0600	13A,13G,10F,10A,13B
London, Lawrence	CA3320	13A,11
Long, Rebecca A.	GA1050	13A,64C,64E
Long, Rebecca	NC1250	13A,13B,13C
Looker, Wendy	NC0910	60,36,70,12A,13A
Lopez Yanez, Ruth	CA3460	13A,60,66,66C
Loubriel, Luis E.	IL0275	11,13A,34,63,35
Lowrey, Norman E.	NJ0300	13A,13,10,45,34
Lozano, Denise	NY2450	13A,11,64A
Luchansky, Andrew	CA0840	13A,51,62C
Luchsinger, Brenda	AL0050	11,63B,13A
Luke, Nadine	ID0060	13A,13B,13C,64A
Lundergan, Edward	NY3760	13A,13B,36,60,12A
Lunte, Sandra K.	LA0770	13A,64A,48
Lurie, Kenneth P.	NC0050	62C,42
Lutsyshyn, Oksana	VA1000	13A,13B,66A,66C
Luttinger, Elizabeth	CA0960	13A
Lutz, Nina	GA2150	62A,13A
Lyttle, Eric	VA0250	13A,13C,66A
Macan, Ed	CA1280	66A,13A,13B,13C,12A
Macdonald, David	AG0150	11,13A
MacInnis, John	IA0500	12,13A,13B,11
MacMullen, Michael J.	FL1470	13A,11,36,61,54
MacNeil, Robert	CA1000	13A,39,61
Maddox, Timothy	NC1075	11,13A,13B,13C,13D
Maddren, Chauncey	CA2750	13A,13B
Madsen, Pamela	CA0815	13A,13,10
Mahoney, Shafer	NY0625	13A,13,10
Makeever, Gerald	MT0200	13A,42,63A
Makubuya, James	IN1850	13A,13C,11,14,20
Malamut, Myra Lewinter	NJ0550	11,64A,67B,20G,13A
Maldonado, Ana Marie	CA0630	13A,62C,20H
Mallarino, Larry	CA2440	29,63,13A
Mandle, William Dee	DC0350	13A,13,32B,66A,66D
Mangels, Jeffrey W.	MD0550	13A,34C,11,13C,34D
Mangini, Mark	NY2050	13A,13,11,36
Mann, Jenny L.	AL1170	64D,12A,13A
Marchukov, Sergey	PA2900	66A,66D,66C,13A
Marciniak, Alex B.	MI0700	13A,37,66A,13,11
Marcozzi, Rudy T.	IL0550	13A,13,13J
Marcus, David	GA0490	10,11,12A,13A,29A
Marenstein, Harry	NY2550	38,11,13A,13B
Margaglione, Louis A.	IL2450	64,13A,13C,11
Marrs, Leslie	IA0550	64A,48,13A
Marrs, Margie V.	IA0300	61,13A,13C
Marshall, Jonathan	MI0850	13A,70
Marston, Karen L.	TX2295	37,63C,11,13A,34C
Marta, Larry W.	TX3370	13A,13,66A,66G
Martin, James	CA4450	13A,13,11
Martin, Jared	TN0580	70,13A,31A
Martin, Kyle	MA2300	13A,13,11,66,35B
Marvin, Elizabeth W.	NY1100	13A,13C,13F,13G,13K
Marvin, William	NY1100	13A,13B,13C,13H,13I
Masci, Michael J.	NY3730	11,13A,13B,13C,13D
Mason, Adam	AA0200	13A,11,65
Masonson, Norman	CA1150	13A,12A
Mast, Anthony	CT0050	13A
Masters, Suzanna	VA1580	64C,11,13A,64E,48
Matalon, Leon	CA0200	13A,47,53,48
Mather, Pierrette	AI0150	13A,13C
Matsuoka, Yumiko	MA0260	13A,13
Matthews, Andrea	NH0150	13A,32
Matthews, Mark	FL1650	10B,13A,34B,35A,70
Matthews, Michael K.	MO0850	13A,13,10F,47,63C
Mattison, Travis	IL1500	70,11,13A
Mauldin, Mark K.	DC0150	13A,13B,32,63C
Maurtua, Jose Luis	MI0400	13A,13,10F,60,10
Maxwell, Susan	KS0650	13A,13B,64D
Mayer, Anne B.	MN0300	13A,41,66A,12A
Maynard, Keith	NY2400	13A,13,10F
Mayor, Jeff	CA3350	13A
Mazer, Susan	CT0300	13A,13B,13C
McCann, Jesse S.	OR0800	70,13A,11
McCann, John	MA1900	13A,11,37
McCann, William J.	NY3760	13A,13B,11
McCloskey, Kathleen	PA0650	11,12A,13A,66D
McCosh, Ruth	AA0050	13A,66A
McCready, Matthew A.	MO0550	11,12A,63,13A,20
McCreary, Teresa J.	HI0110	37,13A,13C,38,47
McCulloch, Doug	HI0210	13A,13B,13C,13D
McCullough, Michael	CA0200	13A,11
McCullough, Richard D.	NY2950	13A,36,39,61,66D
McDermott, Tom	CA2800	13A
McDonald, Mike	MA1900	13A,10,12A,43,13
McDonald, Nan	CA4100	13A,32
McFerron, Mike	IL1520	13A,13,10F,34,10
McGahan, Christopher	MA2030	11,13A,36
McGann, Daniel	NY2450	13A,13,12A,70
McGhee, Janet F.	NY3650	36,13A,40,60A
McGlone, Jeff	AZ0400	70,13A

Name	Code	Areas
McGowan, Sean C.	CO0830	13A,13B,13C,13E,29B
McGuire, David	NY1250	13,10,12A,13A,47
McKinney, Kevin	GA1900	13A,10F,11
McLauchlin, Charlotte	OR1000	13A,66D,66A,67C,12A
McManus, Edward	OR0350	63B,34A,35C,35G,13A
Meacham, Helen M.	PA2000	66A,66C,11,13A
Mead, Andrew W.	MI2100	13A,13
Meadows, Erin	TN0930	13A,13C
Meckler, David C.	CA0855	11,20,12A,10,13A
Medley, Susan	PA3580	36,60A,40,11,13A
Meehan, Jill	PA3680	11,12A,13A
Mehaffey, Matthew W.	MN1623	36,13A
Meier, Margaret	CA3200	13A,11,66D
Meissner, Marla	NJ0800	13A,13,20G
Melendez Dohnert, Victor	PR0115	13A,13B,13C,66D
Melson, Christine	CT0500	13A,13C,36,66C
Menchaca, Louis A.	WI0300	13A,13,60,37,29
Mercer, Scott A.	IN1800	13A,13,47,61,53
Merritt, Justin W.	MN1450	10,13,43,13A,34
Messing, Scott	MI0150	11,12A,66A,16,13A
Mezei, Margaret	AA0200	13A,64C,64E
Miano, Jo Ellen	NY3775	13A,36,61,32I,40
Mietus, Raymond	NC2700	13A,37,50,65
Mikalunas, Robin	TX3540	11,13A
Millar, Cameron	MD0300	13A,34B,35C,13C,34D
Millar, Robert R.	CA4625	13A,13,11,12A,66
Miller, Elaine	NC2000	13C,66A,66C,66B,13A
Miller, Harold L.	WI0450	10,13A,13G,20,47
Miller, Heather	IL1740	66,13A
Miller, Karla	MN1260	13A,11,36,61,66A
Miller, Leigh	GA2300	13A,13B,64C
Miller, Mark	CO0560	29,13A,41,47,64A
Miller, Paul W.	PA2740	10A,11,13A,29A,29B
Miller, Rebecca S.	MA1000	14,13A,20F,31B,35H
Miller, Ronald E.	PA2050	13A,36,61
Millican, Jason	TX1250	13A,60,11,36,31A
Mills, Michele D.	OH2150	13A,12A,66D
Miskell, Jerome P.	OH2290	34,62B,13A,11
Mitchell, Alice L.	NY3705	11,12,13A
Mitchell, Linda	CA2440	36,60A,11,12A,13A
Moder, Jennifer	KS0590	11,13A
Moebus-Bergeron, Susanne	MA0260	13A
Molberg, Keith	AJ0030	66A,34D,13,66C,13A
Moldenhauer, Kermit G.	MN1030	13A,36,66G,31A,60A
Molinaro, Anthony G.	IL1615	66A,29,13A,13B,13D
Moll, Benjamin	OR0600	65,13A,13B,13C,10A
Moore, Nancy	OH0350	33,13A,13B,13C
Morales, David	CA2910	13A,11,36,61,66
Moreau, Leslie M.	ID0050	64C,13A,13B,48
Morgan, Charles	IL1250	13A,60B,37,47,63
Moritz, Kristina	PA2150	13A,13B,13C
Morreale, Michael	NY0644	11,63A,29A,47,13A
Morris, James R.	NY3700	13A,63A,13,11,49
Morris, Scott	CA2650	70,13A
Mortenson, Kristin	KS0650	13A,13B
Mott, David	AG0650	13A,10
Moulton, William	VT0300	13A,29C,33,34B,35A
Mount, Lorna	HI0120	13A,11,12A,70,36
Mowitz, Ira	NJ0750	10,13A,13B,41,66A
Moxley, Lisa	VA0050	66A,66D,31A,13A,11
Moxness, Paul	MN1000	13A,32,64E
Muchmore, Pat	NY3560	13A,13
Mulholland, Joseph	MA0260	13A,13
Mundy, John	MN1700	13A,11
Munger, Philip	AK0100	10,13A,33
Munoz, Nelida	PR0150	11,13A,13C,44
Munson, Jordan	IN0907	45,53,13A
Murasugi, Sachiho	MD0800	62A,62B,11,13A,51
Murray, John	AA0025	61,36,13A,13C
Murray, Michele C.	IN0100	13A,13B,13C,66D
Murray, Monica	MN0610	11,13A,61
Murray, Renardo	MS0050	37,32,63,13A
Musial, Michael A.	NY3450	13A,11,12A,36,66A
Musso, Paul J.	CO0830	70,47,53,13A
Myers-McKenzie, Laurl	CA3200	64A,13A
Nachman, Myrna	NY2550	66A,13A,12A,13C
Naegele, Elizabeth M.	IL1850	13A,13,66A,66G,11
Nathanson, Robert	NC2440	70,11,13A
Navarro, Gloria	PR0115	13A,13C
Neal, Mary Elizabeth	AL0300	13A,13B,13C,13D
Neebe, Paul M.	VA1550	63A,49,13C,13A
Neilson, Duncan	OR0150	13A,13B,10,13C,13E
Nelson, Beth P.	OH0600	13A
Nelson, David W.	CA0859	13,13A,10F,10,38
Nelson, Margaret	NJ0975	13A,66C,66D
Nelson, Robert S.	TX3400	13A,13,10F,10
Nelson-Raney, Steven	WI0825	13A,13,29B
Nepkie, Janet	NY3765	13A,41,51,62C,35
Nevill, Tom	TX3515	65,13A,13C,50,37
Newton, Gregory	CA1960	70,13A,11
Newton, Jon	OR0850	34,13A
Niblock, James D.	PA0100	36,61,60A,13A,13B
Nicholeris, Carol A.	MA0510	10A,13D,13A,36,13
Nichols, Alan	TN0260	66A,13A,11
Nicholson, David	CA5360	13A,64C
Nieuwenhuis, Mary	MI0450	13A,11,36,61
Nigro, Christie	MA2300	13A,11,12A,36,62A
Nin, Chan Ka	AG0450	13A,13,10,10F
Nishibun, Tiffany	AL0450	13A,61
Nishikiori, Fumi	WI0835	66D,13A
Nissen, James	MI1900	13A,13,37,34
Nitsch, Kevin	NY2650	66A,13A,13C
Nitzberg, Roy J.	NY0642	13A,13B,13C,13D
Nivans, David	CA2050	11,13A,20,29A
Noel, Debi	OR0350	13A,36
Nolte, John P.	MN1030	13A,32D
Noone, Elizabeth	MA0150	66A,66D,11,13A,20B
Norman, John L.	CA1270	11,13A
Norris, Elizabeth	VT0300	11,13A,20,61,36
Northrop, Jonathan	CT0050	13A,13B,13C,13E
Norwine, Doug	SC0050	13A,13B
Nunez, John	CA1700	13
O'Brien, Richard	TX2930	61,13A,13B,13C
Offard, Felton	IL0600	13A,11,47,70,29A
Ogle, Deborah A.	GA1200	36,13A,60,40,61
Okumura, Lydie	MA0260	13A,13
Olinyk, George Yuri	CA0150	11,66A,13A
Oliver, Holly E.	NH0250	32B,32C,13A
Olm, James	WY0050	54,61,13A
Olsen, Eric	NJ0800	13A,13B,13C,66D
Olsen, Lance	NJ0990	13A,13,11,34
Olson, Mia	MA0260	13A,13
O'Neal, Whitney	AL1250	12A,13A
O'Neel, Roger	OH0450	10A,31A,13A
Orenstein, Arbie	NY0642	13A,13,11,12A
Organ, Wayne	CA1450	11,13A,13B,13C,34
Orland, Michael	CA5000	13A,66D,66A,13C
Orr, Kevin Robert	FL1850	66A,66B,66D,13A,13
Ortiz, Sheila	PR0115	13A,13C
Osborne, Michelle M.	NY2950	13A,11
Owen, Kenneth L.	WA0750	11,61,36,66A,13A
Owren, Betty Ann	CA1760	36,61,13C,13A,11
Paar, Sara	NY2050	12A,13A
Page, Sandra	AA0050	13A,13,66A
Paglialonga, Phillip O.	FL0100	64C,41,48,13A,13B
Palchak, Mary	CA2390	64A,13A
Palmer, David	NC1900	13A,66A,13B,13C,66G
Palmer, Robert	NC0250	13A,13B,13C
Palmier, Darice	IL2970	66A,66D,11,13A,66C
Paney, Andrew S.	MS0700	32B,13A,66A,32A
Pang, Wilma C.	CA1020	66D,11,13A
Papador, Nicholas G.	AG0550	13A,13B,13D,65,32E
Parchman, Thomas	ME0500	13A,13,64C
Pardue, Jane	NC1400	36,66A,66D,13A,13B
Park, Christine	CA2600	66A,13A,13B,13C,41
Parker, Laura M.	IL2400	13A,41,42,62A,66A
Parker, Mark	SC0200	13A,32F,13B,13C,13G
Parker, Salli	CA2440	66A,13A,11
Parker, Val	GA0490	10,11,13A,34D,29A
Parkins, Robert	NC0600	66G,13A,13B,13C
Parshley, Alan O.	VT0450	63B,13A,66D
Parsons, Laura E.	AL0950	63A,63,12A,13A,11
Patton, Robert	MA0260	13A,13
Patty, Austin T.	TN0850	13A,13B,13C,13D
Pauly, Elizabeth	MN1050	61,60A,11,36,13A
Peloza, Susan	CA5400	62,11,13A,66D
Pennington, John C.	SD0050	13A,65,50,10F
Perkins, Andrew	NC0450	10A,13A,20G,46,11
Perry, David L.	SC0050	12A,13A,64C,32,20A
Petersen, Lynn	MT0075	10A,11,13A,66A,47
Peterson, Jason P.	VA1000	13A,13B,20
Petrik, Rebecca	ND0250	32,13A,61,70,36
Petrowska-Quilico, Christina	AG0650	13A,41,66A,66B
Petty, Wayne C.	MI2100	13A,13
Pfeiffer, Ruth Imperial	HI0160	13A,12A,32,36,66
Phillips, Gregory	OH1450	49,63B,13A
Phillips, Moses	NY0640	12,13A,13B,13C,64A
Pickett, Susan	WA1300	13A,13,12A,51,62A
Pinson, Donald L.	TX0550	11,13A,63C,63D,49
Placeres, Martha	TX3515	62A,38,13A,13C
Plate, Stephen W.	TN0850	38,60,32E,13B,13A
Plummer, William	KY0250	13A
Polk, Kristin	KY1550	64B,64D,32E,13A,13B
Pollard, Shawn	AZ0150	13A,37,11,63D
Pomerantz, James	CA0050	13A,11,12A
Ponte, Nora	PR0150	10A,13A,13B,13C,13D
Porter, Charles	NY2400	13A,13,10,11,12A
Porter, Charles	NY2700	13A,11,12A,66D,29A
Potratz, Robert C.	MN1030	11,12A,66G,13A
Potter, Shelley	WA0950	51,62A,20,13A,13D
Powell, Aaron	IA0650	70,13A
Powell, Jarrad	WA0200	13A,10,20D,45,34
Pratt, Dennis H.	RI0101	29A,11,13A
Presler, Anna H.	CA0840	13A,51
Prettyman, Ken	WA0550	10A,13A,13B,46,47
Price, Clayborn	NY3770	13A,36
Prosser, Steve	MA0260	13A,13
Prudchenko, Slava	GA0940	37,13A,13B,13C
Pullman, Marlene	AJ0030	13A,66A,66B,66D
Puschendorf, Gunther F.	CA1100	13A,36,38,66A
Quinn, Karyn	WI0810	47,62D,46,29,13A
Raby, Lee Worley	CA2801	47,64E,13A,13B,64
Radley, Roberta	MA0260	13A,13
Raessler, Daniel	VA1125	11,12,13B,13F,13A
Raickovich, Milos	NY0644	11,13A,20
Ramey, Richard C.	AR0700	13A,64D
Ramirez, Abel	TX0550	37,13A
Ramirez, Armando L.	PR0115	10,13A,13B,13D,13F
Ramirez, Catherine	MN1450	13A,64A,48,42,13B
Ramos, Rene	CA2420	13A,13,12A,12,66A
Raschiatore, Lisa C.	MI0050	13A
Rasmussen, Brenda	WA0550	11,31A,36,13A
Ravenscroft, Brenda	AG0250	13,13F,13A
Ray, Eric J.	CA2720	13A,70
Reddick, Don	IL2300	32E,46,34,13A
Reddish, Debbie	CA0200	13A,66A
Reed, Jane	OH0100	11,13A,62A,66D,62B
Reese, Donald T.	PA1830	11,12A,70,13A,14C
Reich, Amy J.	NJ0800	13A,13B,13C
Reid, Lynda L.	TX2350	13A,32B,37,48,64C
Reighard, Mark	OK1200	13A,13,66A,11
Reinhart, Robert A.	IL2250	13A
Replogle, Rebecca	OR1010	36,61,13A,13C,40
Resnick, David	IA0250	10B,10F,13A,37,48
Reuter-Riddle, Pat	IA1800	13A,66A
Reynolds, Robert	KY0860	13A,13,11,66A,20G
Rhodes, Phillip	MN0300	13A,13,10,11
Ribchinsky, Julie C.	CT0050	13A,13C,62C,11,38
Rice, Eric N.	CT0600	55,12A,13A,12
Rice, Susan	WI0100	40,36,13A
Richards, Annette	NY0900	12,13A,13B,66G
Richards, Julie	TX2310	11,13A,62A,66C
Richman, Pamela L.	OK1330	13C,13A,61
Richter, Kimberlie J.	IL2050	13A,61,64E,29
Richter, Leonard	WA1100	66A,66B,13A,13B
Ricks, Edward	SC1050	65A,65B,37,50,13A
Ricks, Steven L.	UT0050	10A,10B,13A,34
Rinehart, John	OH0050	13A,13,10F,10,12A
Rivera Ortiz, William	PR0115	13A,13C,36,60A
Robbins, Daniel C.	CA2050	11,13A,10D
Rocco, Emma S.	PA2713	13A,11,20F,36,54
Rocco, Robert	NJ0700	11,13A,13B,10A
Rochinski, Stephen	MA0260	13A,13
Rockmaker, Jody D.	AZ2100	13A,13,10,12A,43
Rodriguez Alvira, Jose	PR0115	13A,34,13B,13D,13G
Rogers, Sharon	AC0050	13A,13C
Roginske, Lynn	WI1150	13A,13
Rognstad, Richard	SD0600	38,13A,62D,13C,11
Rogoff, Noah T.	NE0590	62C,62D,13A,13B
Rohr, Clint	OK1330	29A,13A
Rokeach, Martin	CA3920	13A,13,11,12A,41
Rold, Julie	MA0260	13A
Romano, Darlene	CA1270	36,61,11,13A,40
Romer, Wayne Allen	PA3710	13A,10F,60B,11,32
Rosado, Sara	MD0550	66A,13A
Rosario, Harry	PR0150	13A,13C,37,60B,64B
Rose, Brent	LA0800	64C,29A,13A,13B,13C
Rose, Gil B.	MA1450	60,38,41,13A
Rosenak, Karen	CA5000	13A,13C,43
Rosenshein, Ingrid	FL1675	11,13A,61,66D,54
Rosewall, Michael	WI0750	36,61,12A,13A,13B
Rosner, Arnold	NY2050	13A,13,11,14,66A
Ross, Elaine M.	CA1075	13A,13B,13C
Rossow, Stacie	FL0650	61,36,13A
Roth, Lisa	IA1400	53,61,46,13A,13B
Rothgeb, John	NY3705	13A,13

Name	Code	Areas	Name	Code	Areas
Roush, Clark	NE0720	11,12A,13A,32C,32B	Steigerwalt, Gary	MA1350	66A,13A
Rownd, Gary	IL1850	13A,66A,66D,11	Steinke, David	FL0950	13C,13A,13B
Royle, Frances	AF0120	13A,66A	Stencel, Paul L.	NY1210	13A,11,12A,41,47
Ruckert, George	MA1200	13A,11,20G,20D,20F	Stephenson, Kenneth	OK1350	13A,13
Rudman, Jessica	NY0600	13A	Stern, Kalai	HI0110	11,36,40,13A,13C
Rudolph, Jon	ND0600	11,13A,70	Stern, Theodore	CA1960	11,12A,54,13A
Runnels, Brent	GA1550	66A,11,29,47,13A	Stevenson, Janis	CA1800	13A,10,70
Ruocco, Phyllis	AR0550	13A,13,11,66A,10F	Stevenson, Roxanne	IL0600	13A,20G,32,37,64
Rupert, Susan	TN1800	13A,61,54	Stewart, Jeremy	VT0050	13A,13B,13C
Rush, Tobias	CO0950	13B,13C,13A	Stewart, Tobin E.	FL0680	51,13A,13C
Rutschman, Edward R.	WA1250	13A,13,11,12A,12	Stich, Adam	AZ0490	36,60A,61,40,13A
Rydell, Claire	CA2750	13A	Stiller, Paul	MA0260	13A
Ryder, Raymond T.	AZ0480	66A,13A,66D	Stofko, Diane L.	TN0550	32,11,37,13A,60B
Sabine, David	AA0032	35,13A,13C,37,65	Stolte, Charles	AA0035	64E,13A,13,10,43
Sachdev, Salil	MA0510	10,13A,20A,50,13B	Story, David	WI0850	62D,53,51,13A,13B
Saelzer, Pablo	MD0550	11,13A,13C,38,62A	Stott, Jacob T.	RI0100	11,13A
Saeverud, Trond	ME0430	11,13A,41,36	Stovall, Jeremy	AL0500	13A,37,41,54
Sajnovsky, Cynthia B.	GU0500	13A,12A,20C,66D,67C	Stovall, Leah	NM0400	13A
Sala, Karen	IL1240	13A,13B,13E,13F,61	Stover, Pamela J.	IL2900	32,13A
Salem, Ernest	CA0815	13A,41,62A,62B	Strandberg, Kristen	IN1850	11,12,13A
Salfen, Kevin	TX3410	11,12,13A,20	Struyk, Pieter	MA0150	13A,65A,65B
Sandefur, Lynn	FL1675	11,13A,36,40,61	Stubbs, James	TX1750	46,32,13A,37,47
Sanders, Carolyn I.	AL1160	13A,11,63A	Sullivan, Timothy R.	NY3780	13,13A,13B,13C
Sanders, Trevor	AA0110	13A,70,13B,13C	Sult, Andrew	CA1800	13,70,29,13A
Schaefer, Elaine	CA1300	13A,36,54,61,40	Swanson-Ellis, Kathryn	CT0650	13A
Schefer, James	NY2700	13A,20,29A	Swenson, Thomas S.	NC2205	13A,66B,35C,34,32
Schillinger, Christin M.	OH1450	64D,13A	Swilley, Daniel	IL1200	10,13,34,13A,13B
Schlesinger, Scott L.	NC2525	66G,11,13A,29A,36	Syring, Natalie	OK1330	13A,13B,13C
Schmidt, Alan G.	NY1220	13A,12A,47,20G,29A	Syswerda, Todd	IN1025	13A,13,10,11,10F
Schmidt, Doris D.	NY1220	13A	Tak, Young-Ah	FL1740	66A,60,13A,13B,41
Schnauber, Thomas	MA0900	10A,10C,13A,11,10F	Takasawa, Manabu K.	RI0300	13A,66A,66B,66C,66D
Scholl, Tim	TX2550	13A,13E,32A,66,70	Takesue, Sumy A.	CA4450	13A,66,12F,13B,13C
Schowalter, Elise Anne	KY1000	13A,13B	Tall, Malinda	UT0350	13A,13B,13C,66A,66C
Schoyen, Jeffrey G.	MD0800	62C,38,13A,11,62D	Tancredi, Dominick	NY0644	13A,29A
Schraer-Joiner, Lyn	NJ0700	32,11,13A,60	Tashjian, Charmian	IL1085	13A,13B,13C
Schroeder, Joy A.	MI1500	32B,13A,13C	Taylor, Betty Sue	NY2400	13A,12,36,61,66
Schueller, Rodney C.	TX3175	13A,32E,60B	Teed, Pamela	AG0070	13A,61
Schultz, Marc	NY2800	13A,20,13	Termini, Steven	TX0075	11,66A,13A
Schumann, Laura E.	OH1650	38,60,62A,12A,13A	Tewari, Laxmi	CA4700	14,13A,61,10E,31D
Scott, F. Johnson	VA0750	34,13B,13A,66G,66C	Thomas, Eric S.	TX0600	61,13C,13A,54
Scott, Laurie	MN1600	13A,13C,64A	Thomas, Nicholas	IL1890	60A,66D,13A,36,61
Scott, Michael	MA0260	13A,13	Thomas, Robert E.	NY0700	10,13A,13B,13C,13D
Scruggs, Tara A.	TN0250	13A,64C	Thome, Joel H.	NY3785	13A,13
Scully, Francis	LA0560	13A,12A,11	Thompson, Barbara Tilden	PA2450	66A,66B,13C,13,13A
Scully, Joseph D.	IL0450	13A,11,36,20	Thompson, Christopher K.	AR0950	13A,13,10F,10,66A
Seal, Mary Griffin	FL0680	13A,13C	Thompson, Jewel	NY0625	13A,13
Sears, Peggy	CA0650	13A,39,61	Thompson, Steven D.	CA0150	37,38,63C,11,13A
Seaton, Kira J.	OH0755	13A,13,11,36,61	Thompson, William C.	MA0260	13A
Seaward, Jeffery A.	CA1290	13A,36,41,61,54	Thornburg, Scott	MI2250	13A,13,49,63A
Sedloff, Michael	FL0800	13A,62D	Thorngate, Russell	WI0925	11,13A,36,40,61
Seeman, Rebecca	CA5353	13A,11,36,38,61	Thornton, Robert	FL1800	13C,13A
Segrest, Linda H.	MS0550	13A,13B,66A,66D,13C	Thorpe, Allan	AB0090	13,48,64D,13A,37
Sehman, Melanie	NY3250	65,13A,20,11,13	Tidwell, Mary	TX1510	66A,66D,13B,13A
Seiler, Richard D.	LA0770	66A,66C,13A,13D	Timmerman, David	TX1750	13A,13,36,41,61
Seitz, Paul T.	MO1800	13A,13B,13C	Tischler, Judith	NY1860	13A,12A
Seligman, Susan	NY3760	13A,13C,11,41,62C	Titmus, Jon	CA4450	13A,20F
Seppanen, Keith C.	CA0800	13A,35A,35C,35D	Titmus, Jon	CA5360	63,11,13A
Seskir, Sezi	PA0350	12A,13A,66A,66C	Toman, Sharon Ann	PA2775	11,13A,29A,14C,36
Seto, Mark	CT0100	11,12,13A,13C,38	Tomassi, Edward	MA0260	13A,13
Shahani, Michael M.	CA1020	39,54,13A	Tomlin, Laura A.	GA0250	62A,11,13A
Shaheen, Ronald T.	CA5200	11,12A,13A,61	Trabold, William E.	CA4450	61,11,13A,12
Shallit, Jonathan O.	NY3770	11,13A,62A	Tranquilino, Armando	FL0700	13A,13B,13C,34B,12A
Shannon, William	CA0900	13A,13B,34,63B,35	Trantham, Gene S.	OH0300	13,13A,13J
Shapero, Harold S.	MA0500	10A,13A,10B,13B,13G	Traupman-Carr, Carol A.	PA2450	13A,13,12A,12,31A
Sharer, Marty	PA0500	11,37,12A,13A,13C	Triest, Amelia	CA5010	13A,13C,66D
Sheehan, Paul J.	NY2550	13A,66D	Trinkle, Steven W.	NV0050	63A,41,42,38,13A
Shelby, Karla	OK1500	10D,13A,60A,66A,36	Troxler, Rebecca	NC0600	13A,64A,42,67D
Sheldon, Vanessa R.	CA3265	12,13C,13A,62E,66A	Truax, Jenean	PA0150	13A,13C,32D,61,66A
Sheridan, Daniel	MN1700	64C,60,32C,13A,11	Trumbore, Lisa	KY0200	13A,32B
Sheridan, John	PA0400	70,53,13A	Tsai, Shang-Ying	CA5400	13A,11,20G
Shew, Jamie	CA1900	53,60,13A,13B,66D	Tsai, Tammy	CA0859	13A,11,62A
Shilansky, Mark	MA0260	13A,13	Tsong, Mayron K.	MD1010	13A,66A,66
Shinn, Barbara A.	AL0800	13C,13B,13A,66D	Tucker, Gary	AE0050	13A,13,12
Shipley, Lori R.	VA0500	48,12A,13A,64A,41	Tucker, Scott	NY0900	60,36,40,13A,20A
Shkoda, Natalya	CA0800	66,13,13A,13B,12A	Turner, J. Frank	CA4450	13A,11,12A,54,13B
Shotwell, Clayton	GA0250	12,20,34,11,13A	Turner, Mitchell	GA1200	13A,13B,13C,13F,13G
Shumway, Angelina	MD0700	11,66D,61,13A	Turner, Veronica R.	CO0350	61,13A,13B,13C,13D
Sicilia, Sheila	NY2950	34,13A	Turpen, Jennifer	WY0200	13A,13B,48
Sipley, Kenneth L.	MS0575	11,12A,13A	Tusing, Susan	GA0500	66A,66B,13A,13B
Sisauyhoat, Neil	TX0550	65,50,13A,13C	Twyman, Nita	OK1030	13A,11,61,66A
Sisbarro, Jennifer L.	NY1250	13A,11,61	Uhlenkott, Gary	WA0400	13A,66A,13B,35H,47
Skinner, Josh	ID0060	12,13A,13B,13C,62D	Uitermarkt, Cynthia D.	IL1850	13A,13,66A,31A
Skinner, Kate	ID0060	12,13A,13B,13C,61	Vaccaro, Brandon C.	OH1100	13,10,34,13B,13A
Skoglund, Frances	FL0675	66A,66D,13A,11	Vaclavik, Jude	UT0300	13,13A,13B,13D
Sloane, Marcia	CA2840	13A	Vaillancourt, Scott J.	ME0500	13A,12A
Smaga, Svitlana	CA1300	13A,66A	Van Brunt, Nancy	WI0960	13A,13B,13C,66D,40
Smith, Daniel Ian	MA0260	13A,13	Van Buren, Harvey	DC0350	13A,13,10F,10,66G
Smith, Douglas	AB0050	13A,13,10,13C,12	Van Cleave, Brad	CA0050	13A,11,12A
Smith, Glenda G.	CA1700	13A,11	van den Honert, Peter	PA1200	60A,36,11,13A
Smith, Jason R.	OH1900	63D,13A,41	Vanderford, Brenda M.	WV0700	13A,13,11,66G,31A
Smith, Joel Larue	MA1900	29,47,10,53,13A	Vannice, Michael	OR0950	13A,10,10F
Smith, John Robert	MI0600	13A	Vasallo, Nicholas R.	CA0807	34D,13A
Smith, Joshua D.	TN0150	37,65,13A,50	Vaughan, Jennie	TX2050	13A,13B,13C,66A,11
Smith, Kathleen	NC1400	11,13A	Vaughn, Beverly Joyce	NJ0990	36,11,13A,20G,61
Smith, Kimo	CA2420	66,13A	Vazquez, Carlos	PR0150	10A,10B,10F,13A,13C
Smith, Mark	IL0600	13A,50,65,29,20G	Veal, Larry	NH0350	11,62C,13A,41
Smith, Michael Cedric	NY2700	70,13A	Vigneau, Kevin	NM0450	64E,13A,13
Smith, Michael	CO0950	13A,32,32H	Virgoe, Betty	CA1520	66,11,13A,20G
Smith, Robert Thomas	TX3400	13A,13,10,43	Voelker, Dale	IL1300	13A,13B,60A,36,66G
Smith, Ross	LA0050	11,66A,13A,13B,13C	Voronietsky, Baycka	ME0440	66A,66B,66C,13A
Smith, Ruth	CA2300	13A	Vose, David	MA0260	13A
Snider, Karl William	CA2800	13A,11,61,40	Wadley, Darin J.	SD0600	65,50,13A,13C,38
Snodgrass, Ann A.	MA0260	13A	Waggoner, Cathy	TX1350	13A,66A
Snyder, Jacob	PA2710	13A,11	Wagner, Wayne L.	MN1030	13A,32,36,66G,66D
Snyder, Randy L.	TX2300	13A,13,11,47,63	Wait, Patricia	AG0650	41,64C,13A,12A
Sobaje, Martha H.	RI0101	11,13A	Waldron, Richard	WA0300	11,13A,13H,13K,13C
Sodke, James W.	WI0835	13A,29,35A	Waldrop, Joseph	TX3850	13A,32B,37,13B,64
Sokol, Casey	AG0650	13A,66A,53,43	Walentine, Richard L.	ND0150	61,54,13A,39,12A
Solomon, Evan	MD0550	13A,13B	Walker, David L.	VA1000	50,65,60B,11,13A
Solomon, Larry J.	AZ0480	13A	Walker, Jesse	GA0150	13A,63C,63D,13B,13C
Sorensen, Randall J.	LA0250	63A,63B,13,13B,13A	Wanken, Matthew	IL0420	12A,13A,13B,13C
Sorroche, Juan	PR0150	13A,11,70,13C	Wardzinski, Anthony J.	CA3100	13A,13
Spencer, Mia	WA0050	13A,13B,13C,61	Wark, Stephen	MA0260	13A,13
Spicer, Mark	NY0625	13A,13	Wartofsky, Michael	MA0260	13A,13
Spielman, Mark	AB0070	13A,47,62D,20G	Waterbury, Elizabeth	CA4550	36,61,40,13A,39
Spotz, Leslie	TX2750	13A,66A,66B,66D	Watson, Anne	OK0550	64C,13A,13B,13C,20
Sprout, Leslie A.	NJ0300	12A,12C,13A,12	Watson, Tommy L.	SC0050	11,61,39,12A,13A
Stafford, John	KS0590	36,40,47,11,13A	Watters, August	MA0260	13A,13
Stanley, Bill J.	CO0800	13A,13,63C	Webb, Brian P.	VT0125	13A,13,11,12A,36
Stanley, Ed L.	PA1400	64B,42,13A,13C,11	Webb, Jeffrey L.	PA3410	29,36,13A,60,13
Stanziano, Stephen	OH1000	13A,13B,13C,10,62D	Webber, Kelly Marie	KS0560	11,13A,12A,61,60A
Star, Allison	AC0050	13A,13C	Weber, Deanna F.	GA0150	13A,13B,13C,13D,61
Starner, Robert	CA0200	13A	Wechesler, David J.	NY0644	11,13A,29A,41,64A
Steed, Brad B.	CA3500	13A,11,16	Weilbaecher, Daniel	LA0750	66A,13A
Steele, Daniel L.	MI0400	13A,32	Weinstein, Michael	MA2200	13A,11,12A,49
Steele, Edward L.	LA0400	12A,13A,13B,13C,61	Weiss, Lisa G.	MD0400	13A,11,42,66A,66C
Steele, Janet	NY0550	13A,55,61,66A,36	Weiss, Louise	IL1050	13A,32B,48,64A,66C
Stegall, Gary Miles	SC0420	66A,66D,13A,66C,66G	Wellman, Samuel	VA0650	66A,66D,10,13A,13B

Index by Area of Teaching Interest

Name	Code	Areas
Wells Chenoweth, Andrea	OH2250	61,13A,13C
Wells, Rebecca Schaffer	KY1300	13A,13B,13C,13D,13E
West, Margaret	CA1760	13A,66A,66D
Wester, R. Glenn	TX2295	61,66,11,13A
Westra, Mitzi	IN1650	61,13A,11,44
Wheaton, J. Randall	VA0600	13B,13D,13A,13I,13F
White, Barbara A.	NJ0900	13A,10,13,10F,43
White, Janice	CA5500	11,13A,36,61,66A
White, Molly E.	CA2720	66A,13A
White, Phyllis	MI1750	11,13A
Whitworth, Albin C.	KY0150	13A,13,10,36,66
Wichael, Scott	KS0590	13A,61
Wiksyk, Crystal	AB0210	13A,13B,13C,13H
Wilcoxson, Nancy	SD0580	13A,61,36,11,12A
Wilder, Mary Ann	KY0100	66A,66C,66D,13A,13B
Wilkerson, Steve	CA3200	13A,29A
Willette, Andrew C.	OR0850	11,13A
Williams, Kay	TX0050	66A,66C,66D,13A,13B
Williams, Leland Page	CA2600	13A,13,66A
Willis, A. Rexford	FL1745	13,10,70,13A
Willis, Sharon J.	GA0490	10A,11,12,61,13A
Wilson, Frances	NC2210	13A,36,61,11
Wilson, Mark	NJ0760	61,13A
Wimberly, Larry	MS0150	11,13A,31A,34E,46
Winslow, Richard	CT0750	13A,13,10
Witt, James	CA4000	13A,11,35
Witt, James	CA4050	13A,11,12A,47,62D
Witter, Tim	CA0050	13A,11,12A
Wolfe, Chris	MD0175	13A,60,37,64C,64E
Wood, Eric	CA5350	10A,11,20,13A,13E
Wood, Gary F.	MA1650	36,61,60,13A
Wood, Matthew P.	AL0200	63D,13A
Wood, Pamela	MA1200	13A,11
Wood, Rose Ann	CA2050	13A,13B,13C,11,66D
Woodcock, Ruth	WA0100	11,12A,20,13A,13G
Woods, Chris P.	IL1050	13A,10F,13C,49,63
Wright, Barbara	WV0560	13A,13,12A,12,66G
Wright, Marylyn	TX3360	13A,66A,66C,66D,66G
Wurster, Miles B.	MN1030	37,13A,64,65
Wytko, Anna Marie	KS0650	64E,13A,48
Xiques, David	CA4200	13A,13C,36
Yang, Zhao	WA0950	66C,13A,13B,13C,13D
Yarbrough, Stephen	SD0600	13A,13G,10F,10A,13B
Yarmolinsky, Benjamin	NY0280	13A,13,10,45,70
Yates, Peter	CA0630	11,51,70,13A
Yoelin, Shelley	IL3200	13A,13,37,47,64E
Yoshikawa, Christine	FL0350	66A,13A
Young, Barbara G.	WI0803	13A,32B
Youngblood, Pamela J.	TX3300	41,64A,13A,13B,15
Younge, J. Sophia	IL0450	13A,66A,11,36
Yun, Francis Y.	NJ0800	13A,13B,13C
Zavadsky, Julia	NJ1100	11,13A,36,60A
Zawilak, Alexander	AZ0490	70,13A,42,41
Zehringer, Daniel	OH2500	63A,13A
Zeidel, Scott	CA3200	13A,11,70
Zell, Steven D.	TX0390	13A,13B,13C,11,66A
Zimmerman, Lynda	WI0806	13A,66A,66D,11
Zito, Vincent	FL0730	13A,13

Harmony

Name	Code	Areas
Abel, Sandra	TX0390	36,61,13A,13B,13C
Abel, Sean	CA1300	13B,13C,20G,29A,34C
Adam, Nathaniel	CT0050	13B,13C
Adderley, Meisha N.	OH0350	13B,13C,66D,66B
Admiral, Roger	AA0110	13B,13C,10A,42
Alexander, Eric	CO0950	13B,13C,10,13
Alvarez, Heidi Pintner	KY1550	64A,13B,41
Alvarez, Luis M.	PR0150	10A,11,13A,13B,14
Amante Y Zapata, Joseph J.	RI0101	36,40,11,13A,13B
Amos, Shaun	GA0500	60,36,13B,13C,12A
Amrozowicz, Mary Barbara	NY4460	13A,13,66A,13C,13B
Andersen, LeGrand	UT0200	61,66D,13C,13B
Anderson, Allen L.	NC2410	10A,13B,13D,13E,13F
Anderson, Matthew M.	GA1700	70,13B
Anderson, Shane	TX2930	13A,13B,13C,66A,66B
Annicchiarico, Michael	NH0350	13B,13C,13E,10
Annoni, Maria T.	MN0900	11,13A,13B,70,14C
Appello, Patrick	NJ0550	70,67G,13B,13A,12A
Applegate, Ann	WI0925	66D,13A,13B,66A
Arcaro, Peter	FL1100	13B,11,29A,47
Archambault, Ellen	OH0350	13B,13C
Arenson, Michael	DE0150	13B,34B
Arita, Junko	NY2660	61,13B,13C
Arjomand, Ramin Amir	NY2750	10A,10F,13B,13C
Armstrong, Heather M.	IA0950	13B,64B,32E
Arrowsmith, Brenda	AG0070	48,64,10F,13A,13B
Arrowsmith, Jamie	AG0070	38,60B,62,13A,13B
Arshagouni, Michael H.	CA2750	13B,13C,12A,66A,36
Ashby, Steven	VA1600	70,13B,13C
Bachmann, Nancy	CA2775	13A,13B,12A,66A,66B
Badolato, James V.	MD0550	13B
Baham, Kerry M.	TX3370	13B,66A,11,66C,12A
Bahr, Jason	FL0680	10,13,31A,13C,13B
BaileyShea, Matthew	NY1100	13B,13E,13F,13I
Bain, Jennifer	AF0100	13E,13F,13B,13J,13
Bakenhus, Douglas	LA0550	13B,38,60B,64D
Ball, Karen	IL2300	10A,66A,66B,13B,13C
Bares, William	MA0260	13A,13B
Barham, Phillip	TN1450	64E,41,13B
Bartsch, John T.	OR0175	13B,38,66,10F,10A
Baruth, Lori E.	KY0900	13B,13C,64C
Bassler, Samantha Elizabeth	NJ1400	13A,13B
Bean, Shirley Ann	MO1810	13A,13B,13C,13D,13E
Beaudet, Luce	AI0200	13B,13C,13E
Beavers, Sean M.	VA0650	12A,13A,13B,13C,41
Belet, Brian	CA4400	10,13B,13C,13E,13F
Belfiglio, Anthony	TN0100	66A,13B
Benitez, Vincent P.	PA2750	13F,13D,13B,13J,13
Bennett, Barbara A.	CA5040	13B,13,11,45,34
Bennett, Travis	NC2600	63B,13B,13C
Berger, Talya	CA4900	13,13A,13B,13C
Berk, Stacey J.	WI0850	13A,13B,64B,41,10F
Biber, Sarah J.	MT0200	13B,41,62C
Bingham, Emelyne	TN1850	13B,32E
Birch, Sebastian A.	OH1100	13,10,34,13B,13A
Biro, Daniel Peter	AB0150	13B,13C,13E,13F,10A
Bischoff, John	CA2950	45,10B,12A,13B,20F
Bishai, Alf	NY2750	13B,13C
Bishop, Saundra	MS0575	13A,36,66A,66D,13B
Blalock, Angela	SC0150	11,13A,13B,40,61
Bleiler, Loueda	NY0950	11,12A,13A,13B,36
Bohn, Donna M.	PA1550	12,13B,13C,65,60
Bohnenstengel, Christian	UT0200	66A,13C,66C,13A,13B,13C
Boldt-Neurohr, Kirsten	WA0050	13A,13B,13C,13F
Bonkowski, Anita	AB0150	29A,29B,13A,13B,13D
Boozer, Pat	NC2350	10,32B,66A,13A,13B

Name	Code	Areas
Boren, Benjamin J.	CA0850	66A,66B,66C,66D,13B
Boudreault, Mary	NC2700	63B,13A,13D,13E,13B
Bowker, Barbara E.	IL1085	13,11,13B,13C,12A
Boyer, Justin	MD0550	13B,13C,10A
Brasky, Jill T.	FL2000	13,13B,13C,62A
Brewer, Johnny	AL0620	13A,13B,11,46,13C
Brisson, Eric	MN1700	13A,13B,13C,13E,66C
Brown, Derek	TX0050	29,13B,64E
Brown, Matthew	NY1100	13B,13D,13I,13J
Brown, Stephen	AB0210	10,13A,13B,13C,13D
Brown, Whitman P.	MA0500	10A,13A,13B
Brunelli, Stephanie	KS0150	66A,12A,13,13B
Buckner, Nathan	NE0590	66A,66C,66D,13B,13C
Budds, Cain	LA0250	70,11,13A,13B,13C
Buettner, Jeff	VT0350	13A,36,40,13B,13C
Burchard, Marcia	CA4460	66A,13B
Burt, Patricia A.	IL1200	13A,66A,66D,13B,13C
Busch, Michael	CA1425	36,60,13B,32D
Bushong, Claire B.	NE0400	12A,13B,13C,66A,66G
Butler, Charles Mark	MS0250	63B,32B,13B,13E,13B,66G
Butler, Rebecca G.	PA0050	11,64A,37,34,13B
Butterfield, Matthew W.	PA1300	29,13,13B,29A,29B
Cabrer, Carlos R.	PR0150	10A,10F,11,13A,13B
Cabrini, Michele	NY0625	12B,12A,13B,11,12
Cahueque, David	CA3200	11,13A,13B,13C,70
Capezza, June	FL0200	61,13A,13B,13C
Carlson, James	TN1800	13A,13B,10A,10B,13C
Carpenter, Alexander	AA0110	12,13C,13B,11,13E
Carr, William	PA1550	13B,66D,66A,13D
Carrillo, Christine Ennis	VA0600	63A,13B
Carter, Paul S.	NY3765	13A,13B,66A
Casano, Steven	HI0210	13A,13B,13C,13D
Castilla, Carlos	TN1400	13B,13C
Caulkins, Tamara	WA1200	70,13A,13B,13C,13D
Cavanagh, Lynn	AJ0100	13B,13E,13F,13J,13I
Ceide, Manuel J.	PR0115	13F,10A,13A,13B,13E
Chang, Yu-Hui	MA0500	10A,10F,13B,13D,13F
Chao, Joanna K.	NJ0175	66A,13C,13B
Chen, Ting-Lan	NE0590	11,13B,62A,62B,13C
Cheramy, Michelle	AD0050	64A,13B
Chesanow, Marc	SC0420	62D,11,10F,13B,35G
Chioldi, Ronald	OK0550	13B,66A,66D,13D,13E
Christianson, Gregg S.	NY1550	66A,13A,13B,13C
Chua, Emily Yap	VA1125	13B,15,42,66A
Clenman, David	AB0150	13,12A,13A,13B,13C
Clifton, Jeremy J.	OK1050	35C,10,13,13K,13B
Cobo, Ricardo	NV0050	70,13B
Cochran, Alfred W.	KS0650	12A,13A,13B,13E
Coleman, Edryn J.	PA2000	61,36,60A,13B
Collins, Zachary	PA1600	63D,12A,13B,49
Combest, Chris	IL2900	63D,13B
Combs, Julia C.	MO0775	64B,13B,12A,11,13C
Compton, Adam	OK0500	13B,63,37,46,13
Conatser, Brian	AR0200	13A,66A,13B,13C,66C
Cornish, John	OK0150	36,39,60A,61,13B
Cotter, Daniel	WA0950	38,64C,13B,13C
Coutsouridis, Peter	MA2100	65,41,29A,11,13B
Cox, Jeff	TN1600	70,13B
Coxe, Stephen	VA1000	13A,13B,13D,10
Crabtree, John M.	TX2250	13A,13B,13C
Crawford, Eric	VA0950	13B,66
Crawford, Richard	FL0200	13B,13C
Crosby, Matthew	TX3415	36,13A,13B
Crouse, David L.	AR0600	66A,13C,61,66G,13B
Cryderman-Weber, Molly	MI1200	12,20,13B,13,65
Curlee, J. Matthew	NY1100	13A,13B,13C,13D,13K
Cutsforth-Huber, Bonnie	MD0095	13A,13,11,12A,13B
Dahlgren, Winnie	MA0260	13B
Dahn, Luke	IA1200	66A,13B,13C,13D,13E
Daigle, Paulin	AI0190	13B,13D,13E
Dalton, James	MA0350	13B,13C,20
Damschroder, Norman L.	OH2275	62D,13A,13B
Dashevskaya, Olga	CO0625	11,13A,66A,13B
Daub, Eric	TX3100	66A,13A,13B,13C,29A
Davidson, Tom	AG0250	13B,66A,66D
Davies, Daniel E.	CA0850	62C,13A,11,13B
Davies, David H.	NY1700	13A,13C,13B,10,13
Davis, Hope	CA2300	13A,12,11,37,13B
Davis, Ron A.	SC1000	13B,13C,31,66G,44
De Leo, Joseph A.	NY2750	32,12A,13B,13C,32H
Dearden, Jennifer	PA0100	63A,34,13A,13B,13C
DeBoer, Angela	TN1100	63B,49,13A,13B,13C
Dello Joio, Justin N.	NY2750	13B,13E,13F,10A,10F
Denmon, Alan	GA2300	11,13A,13B,13C,32E
DeSalvo, Nancy J.	PA3650	13A,13B,66A,66B,13C
Devaney, Johanna C.	OH1850	13B,13E,13G,13K,13L
Dickens, Pierce	GA0400	13A,13B,13C,13E,66A
Diggs, David B.	PA1950	13A,13B,37,64B,48
DiPaolo, Daniel M.	NY2750	13B,13C
Dobbins, Lori E.	NH0350	13B,11
Dobry, John T.	LA0750	10A,13B,47
Donovick, Jeffery	FL1650	66D,13A,13B,13C,34C
Dorian, Patrick	PA1100	10C,13B,29A,29C,29E
Doyle, Sean	NY3725	13A,13B,13C
Drews, Michael R.	IN0907	13A,13B,13C,13E,11
Duda, Theodor	OH0700	13B,13C,12A,20G
Duker, Philip	DE0150	13B,13C
Dunn, John	LA0550	13B
Durham-Lozaw, Susan	NC2350	13A,13B,13C,61
Dykema, Dan H.	AR0600	13B,11,66A,66D,13C
Eastman, Patricia	MO1950	13A,13B,13C,66A
Eastwood, Deb A.	KY0900	13A,13B,13C,63A
Ehrlich, Martin L.	MA1000	29,13B,13C
Eidson, Joseph M.	PA1400	13B,13C
Elliott, Robert L.	TN1400	13B,32,62D,11
Elsey, Eddie L.	AL1250	49,13B,63C,63D
Elswick, Beth L.	MO1810	13A,13B,13C,13D
Eng, Clare Sher Ling	TN0100	13,13B,13D,63B,66A
Englert, David	TX2250	13A,13B,13C
Erickson, Jeff	WI0925	47,13C,29A,13B
Ericson, Michael	IL3500	13B,13C,6A,48
Escalante, Roosevelt	KY0900	13B,13C,32D,36
Evans, Darryl	AR0810	32E,47,63D,13A,13B
Evans, Gary	VA0400	13A,13B,13C,11,12A
Evans, Joel	NY3760	37,64B,12A,13B,20
Fain, Jeremy	TX2700	64D,11,13A,13B
Farzinpour, Peyman	MA2020	11,12A,13B
Fassler-Kerstetter, Jacqueline	KS0650	63B,13E,13B
Fassnacht, Therese	CA3150	13B,13C,20H,12A
Feldhausen, Scott	TX1400	13A,13B,11
Fiala, Michele	OH1900	64B,41,13B,13C,64D
Fiedler, Anne	IN1600	13B,13C,66A
Fisher, John	TX3250	13A,13B,10A,15,66A
Flaniken, Jeffrey Z.	AL0800	62A,13B,32E
Fleck, Allyson	GA1150	62B,42,13B
Fletcher, Seth	NE0590	63D,63C,13B,13C,11
Flores, Yasmin A.	AL1250	64C,64E,64D,48,13B
Fogle, Megan R.	SC0350	13A,13B,13C,13E,13F

Index by Area of Teaching Interest

Name	Code	Areas
Fosheim, Karen	MS0250	66A,13B,50,20A,10F
Foust, Diane	WI1100	36,61,13A,40,13B
Fox, Elizabeth	WI1100	13A,13B,13C,11
Fox, Jon	TX1600	70,53,13B
Foy, Regina	PA1550	13B,10F,31A
Francis, Kelly A.	GA1150	13B,13C
Frank, Bruce	NY1100	13B,13C,13D,13H,13I
Franzetti-Brewster, Allison	NJ0700	66C,41,13A,13B,13C
Friedman, Joel Phillip	CA4425	13B,10A,10D,12A
Fuschetto, W.	AB0040	13A,13B
Fusco, Randall J.	OH1000	13B,38,66A,12A,11
Galieva-Szokolay, Julia	AG0300	13B,13C
Garcia, W. T. Skye	OK0300	66A,66D,13B,13C,66B
Gargrave, Eric	RI0101	11,13A,29A,48,13B
Garrison, Leonard	ID0250	64A,13,12,13B,13C
Garvey, Christa N.	WI0803	13B,13C,64B
Gaviria, Carlos	TX2700	62D,11,13A,13B
Gelber, Debbie	TX2350	13A,13B,36,61,13C
George, Elizabeth	AZ0450	13A,13B,66D
Gilbert, E. Beth	WI0860	66C,66A,66B,13B
Ginwala, Cyrus	CA4200	38,13B,11,60B
Girdham, Jane C.	MI1850	11,12A,13B,13C,13E
Gleason, Stephen	NY1275	10D,12A,13B,14C,34D
Glennon, Barbara	PA0650	20G,13B,13C,64A,64C
Gnandt, Edwin E.	AA0010	13A,66A,42,13B,66D
Golan, Jeanne K.	NY2550	13B,13C,12A,66A,66D
Goldman, Edward 'Ted'	NY1100	13K,13C,13B,10A,10F
Goldspiel, Alan	AL1200	70,13C,13B,51
Gonder, Jonathan P.	NY3730	66A,66C,11,13A,13B
Gonzalez, Ana Laura	NY1400	64A,13A,13B
Gooley, Dana	RI0050	12A,13B,12E,12D
Goranson, Jocelyn	PA2300	64A,13A,13C,13B,42
Gottlieb, David	NJ0750	10,13A,13B,34D,64E
Grant, Kristin	AR0500	64A,13A,13B,13C
Griffin, Joel	MO0400	64E,46,47,13A,13B
Grogan, Charles L.	OH2450	10A,13B
Gross, Robert W.	TX2150	13B,13D,13E,13F,13I
Groulx, Timothy J.	IN1600	13B,13C,32
Grove, Paul	WA0400	70,13A,13B,13C
Gudmundson, Paula	MN1600	11,13B,64A
Guerrero, Jean	NY1100	13B,13E,13F,13J
Guerrero, Rosi E.	WA0950	66A,66D,13A,13B,13D
Gunlogson, Elizabeth	NH0350	64C,13B
Gurin, Vladimir	MA0350	13B
Gustafson, Steven	KS0900	61,66G,40,13B,36
Ha, Youngmi	NY2750	10A,10E,13B,13C,13D
Hagedorn, David	MN1450	13A,65,50,47,13B
Hagen, Sara L.	ND0600	13B,32B,32C,35A
Hajda, John M.	CA5060	13K,13L,13A,13B,14A
Hall, Gary	WY0115	11,12A,13B,13C,47
Hall, Teddy	VA0500	13A,13B,13C,32C,11
Halloran, Stephen	MA0350	13B,13C
Hamlin, Peter S.	VT0350	10A,10B,10F,13A,13B
Hammel, Alice	VA1600	13B,13C
Handel, Thomas	MA1400	12A,13B
Hanlon, Kenneth	NV0050	13B,13D
Hansen, Deborah	WA1350	60,36,13B
Harlen, Benjamin	LA0400	10A,31A,13B,13C,13D
Harris, Alonzo	MA0260	13B
Harris, Carole J.	NY0400	13A,13B,13C,13D
Harris, David	MA0260	13B
Harris, Paul K.	WA1000	12A,11,13B
Harshenin, Leon A.	IN1560	66A,13B
Hart, Michael	CA0550	37,13B,13C,63C,63D
Hartway, James	MI2200	13A,10,10F,66D,13B
Hastings, David M.	WI0850	64E,42,13A,13B,13C
Hastings, Stella	KS1050	38,13B,13C,66D
Hauser, Joshua	TN1450	63C,10F,13B,42
Hay, Dennis	AR0050	13A,13B,11,66A,66C
Hayes, Jane	AB0060	66A,66D,13B,42,66B
Hazelip, Richard	TX2300	13B,66G,61,11
Hedges, John B.	NY3760	13B,13D,13E,10
Heine, Erik	OK0750	13,13B,10C,13E
Henderson, Jean	NE0450	13A,13B,13C,13D,10A
Herbert, David	TX2200	13A,64B,32,13B,13C
Heritage, Lee	OH2300	13B,13C,29A,20G,10A
Herrington, Brian P.	TX2250	13A,13B,13C
Herris, Keith	TN0150	66,13B
Hileman, Lynn	WV0750	64D,13C,13B,13A,13D
Hill, Kyle W.	MS0580	13B,11,37,50,65
Hirota, Yoko	AG0150	66,13B,12A,66A,12B
Hirt, James	OH0600	13A,13B
Hoag, Melissa E.	MI1750	13B,13C,13D,13E,13F
Hoegberg, Elisabeth Honn	IN1650	61,13A,13B
Hoffman, Brian D.	OK0800	13A,13B,13C,66D
Hojnacki, Thomas W.	MA0260	13B
Holly, Janice	MD0300	13B,11
Hooten, Bryan	VA1600	13B,13C,63C
Howard, Timothy P.	CA0835	13B,13C,66G
Howe, Ryan	IA1400	13A,13B,13C
Howey, Robert J.	AA0025	12A,13B,37,46,64
Huffman, Timothy	OH2050	66A,13B,66B,66D,66C
Humphreys, Paul W.	CA2800	14A,13A,13B,29A,10A
Hurst, Chloe	AB0200	13A,13B,13C
Hutchings, James	IL0420	11,13B,12A,61,13A
Inserto, Ayn	MA0260	13B
Itoh, Takuma	HI0210	10A,13A,13B,13C,13D
Ivy, Julie	NV0050	13C,13B
Jakubiec, Aaron F.	IL0800	11,64B,13B
James, Woodrow	CA2750	47,13B,13C
Jensen, Byron W.	NE0300	13B,38,12A,62,32C
Jensen, Jocelyn	NV0050	36,13B,13C
Jeon, Hey Rim	MA0260	66A,13B
Jex, David	OH2300	13B,13C,13D,10,29
Johnson, Byron	MS0050	13A,13B,13C,61,39
Johnson, Chrisa	VA0050	66A,13B,13C,11
Johnson, Deborah S.	NE0300	13A,11,48,64A,13B
Johnson, G. Larry	UT0325	36,60A,13A,13B,13C
Johnson, Keith	CA2975	10,20,34,35,13B
Johnson, Kenneth W.	IN0905	13B,12A
Jones, John W.	PA1400	13B,13C,13D,13E,10A
Jones, Melinda	MO1550	66A,66D,66B,13B,13C
Jordan, Rachel	MS0350	62A,11,13A,13B,42
Josenhans, Thomas	IN1600	64C,13B,13C,64E,41
Jung, Eunsuk	TN0600	13A,66A,66D,66G,13B
Jurcisin, Mark	NJ0750	10,13A,13B,13C,11
Kahn, Richard	CA2750	10F,13B,34,66A
Kamatani, Pamela M.	CA1020	11,13B,13C
Kamstra, Darin	CO0225	65,29,13B,47,50
Kaneda, Mariko	OH2000	66C,66A,66D,13B,13C
Kang, Ann Teresa	DC0010	13B,13I
Kang, Sang Woo	RI0150	13A,13B,66A
Kapner, Harriet H.	NY2550	70,13A,13B,13C
Kaufhold, Jessica	AL0530	36,11,13A,13B,13C
Kays, Darryl	IN1485	12A,13B,37,47,60B
Kearney, Joseph B.	CA1265	10A,29,13B,70
Kechley, David S.	MA2250	10A,10F,13A,13B,13D
Keever, Howard	MS0850	10A,10D,13A,13B,13D
Kelly, Daniel	TX2955	63A,47,13A,13B
Kelly, Michael	OH1450	13A,13B,13C
Kemp, Todd	TN0100	65,13B
Kennedy, Nathan	MN0610	13A,13B,13C,13D,13F
Kenote, Marie Herseth	NY2900	64A,12A,13B,13C,13D
Kerstetter, Tod	KS0650	13A,48,64C,13B
Keyne, Lori V.	AZ0250	13B,13C,36,66D
Khosrowpour, Iman	CA2390	62A,62B,13B
Kiel, Dyke	MO0250	13B,13C,64
Kies, Christopher	NH0350	13B,10,66A,13F
Kim, Howard D.	SC0050	66A,66D,13B,66C,11
Kim, Young	NY0700	13B,13C,66A,66D
Kindred, Kyle	TX2250	13A,13B,13C
Kirby, Steven	MA0260	13B
Klakowich, Robert	AA0020	13A,13B,13C,13D,13E
Klotzbach, Susan	IL1200	66C,13A,13B,13C
Knier, Veronica T.	MD1020	13B,13E,66
Knupp, Robert	MS0400	66G,13I,13B,66A
Koh-Baker, JoAnn Hwee Been	OH1600	11,12A,66A,13A,13B
Konzen, Richard A.	PA1450	38,51,66G,41,13B
Kraakevik, Kari	CO0550	13B
Krause, Drew S.	NY2750	13A,13B,13C,13D,13F
Krouseup, Jack	CA3520	10,13B,13A,13F,47
Krumbholz, Gerald A.	WA0950	13A,13B,13C,13D,10C
Kulpa, John	NJ0750	11,13A,13B,13C
Kunda, Keith	IN1560	13B,13C,10F
Kunz, Jean-Willy	AI0200	13B,13E
Laginya, Daniel	OH2600	13A,13B,13C
Laitz, Steven	NY1100	13B,13C,13H,13I
Lambert, Sterling	MD0750	12,13B
Lan, Catherine	FL0200	13B,13C,66D
Landers, Joseph	AL1200	10A,10F,13B,13C,13E
Lansing, Nathan	WA0950	36,40,13B,13C,13A
Larragoity, Ingrid	AR0300	37,32E,13B,48
Laughlin, Mark	GA1000	66A,13,12A,66D,13B
Leduc, Pierre	AI0200	66A,13B,47
Lee, Amanda	TX2570	66A,13C,13B,13E,66B
Lee, Christopher	MA2030	13A,13B,13C
Lee, Paul S.	TX1300	66G,13B,11,60,66A
Lemons, Nancy	IL1300	66A,13B
Lentsner, Dina	OH0350	12A,13B,13C,13D,13E
Lewis, Robert J.	KY0300	13B,11,66A,66B,66D
Li, Simon	NY2900	66A,13A,13B,13C
Liang, Lei	CA5050	10,13B,13D,10A,10B
Lidral, Karel	ME0440	13B,47,64E,29B
Liebhaber, Barbara	PA2550	13A,13B
Lim, Rachel	AL0800	13B
Lin, James	CA5510	13A,13B,42,13C,13D
Lind, Stephanie	AG0250	13B,13D,13E,13F
Lippard, Erin	TX2710	61,13A,13B,40,54
Lippard, Michael S.	TX2710	13A,37,46,64,13B
Lipton, Jeffrey S.	NY1275	12A,13B,32C,36,61
Loftus, Jean	NY2950	39,61,54,13A,13B
Logan, Jennifer	CA3300	10B,13A,13B,13C,35C
Lombard, Becky	GA2050	66A,13B,13C,12A,66C
Lombardi, Paul	SD0600	13A,13G,10F,10A,13B
Long, Rebecca	NC1250	13A,13B,13C
Lovell, Stephanie	CA5150	13B
Luke, Nadine	ID0060	13A,13B,13C,64A
Lundergan, Edward	NY3760	13A,13B,36,60,12A
Lupica, Anthony J.	CA1700	36,38,13B,70,61
Lupinica, Rudy	OK0300	66A,66D,13B,13C,66H
Lutsyshyn, Oksana	VA1000	13A,13B,66A,66C
Macan, Ed	CA1280	66A,13A,13B,13C,12A
MacInnis, John	IA0500	12,13A,13B,11
Maddox, Timothy	NC1075	11,13A,13B,13C,13D
Maddren, Chauncey	CA2750	13A,13B
Marenstein, Harry	NY2550	38,11,13A,13B
Martins, Jose Oliveira	NY1100	13B,13E,13F
Marvin, William	NY1100	13A,13B,13C,13H,13I
Masci, Michael J.	NY3730	11,13A,13B,13C,13D
Mason, Scott	IL0550	13B,13C,53,29
Matters, Helene	CA2200	66A,13B,13C
Maugans, Stacy	IN1750	48,64E,13B
Mauldin, Mark K.	DC0150	13A,13B,32,63C
Mavromatis, Panayotis	NY2750	13B,13D,13F,13G,13K
Maxwell, Susan	KS0650	13A,13B,64D
Mazer, Susan	CT0300	13A,13B,13C
McAneny, Marc	MA0500	13B,13E,13F,10A
McCann, William J.	NY3760	13A,13B,11
McClellan, Robinson	NY4500	13B,13C
McConnell, Joan	OH0950	66C,66G,13C,66D,13B
McCord, Larry	TX0910	11,13B,14C,34B,66A
McCulloch, Doug	HI0210	13A,13B,13C,13I
McGowan, Sean C.	CO0830	13A,13B,13C,13E,29B
McKinney, Jane Grant	NC0900	32C,13B,32D,39
McMahan, Robert Y.	NJ0175	13B,13C,13F,10B,10A
McMullian, Neal	IL2300	13B,32E,64D,60,37
McNabb, Carol	TX3515	13B,13C,64D,67C,64B
McNamara, Gretchen	OH2500	63D,13B
McWain, Andrew J.	MA2020	29,10,13B
Melbinger, Timothy	PA2710	12A,41,13B,13C,13E
Melendez Dohnert, Victor	PR0115	13A,13B,13C,66D
Mertens, Michael	CA2750	13B,11,63,64,37
Meyer, Sandra G.	OK0650	13B,13C,13E,66A,13
Miljkovich, Katarina	MA1400	13C,13B,12A,12
Millard, Joshua P.	MA2030	13B,13C,41,47
Miller, Leigh	GA2300	13A,13B,64C
Miller, Thomas E.	CA5400	13B,13C,36,39,54
Mills, Robert P.	VA0650	11,13B,13C
Mitchell, Jennifer	GA1150	13B,13C,11,10
Mohr, Deanne	MN1700	66A,66C,66B,13B,13C
Molinaro, Anthony G.	IL1615	66A,29,13A,13B,13D
Moll, Benjamin	OR0600	65,13A,13B,13C,10A
Monahan, Seth	NY1100	13B,13C,13D,13E
Montalvo, Raquel	PR0100	36,61,13B
Moon, Hosun	NY1275	11,66,13B,32D,36
Moore, Kathy Bundock	CO0950	62E,13B,13C,13E
Moore, Nancy	OH0350	33,13A,13B,13I
Moreau, Leslie M.	ID0050	64C,13A,13B,48
Morgan, Carol	TX2300	63A,29,13B,13
Moritz, Kristina	PA2150	13A,13B,13C
Mortenson, Kristin	KS0650	13A,13B
Mowitz, Ira	NJ0750	10,13A,13B,41,66A
Mueller, Gerald A.	CA1020	13B
Murphy, Patrick C.	OR1100	13B,37,32,41
Murray, Kathy	MO0775	13B,13C
Murray, Michele C.	IN0100	13A,13B,13C,66D
Nalesnik, David A.	MO1950	13B,13C
Nangle, Richard P.	MA2030	13B,13C,13D,13E,13F
Nauert, Clark	TX1600	70,53,13B,13C
Naylor, Susan E.	GA1700	13B,66A,13C
Neal, Mary Elizabeth	AL0300	13A,13B,13C,13D
Neiderhiser, Jonathan	SD0580	37,47,32E,13B,13C
Neilson, Duncan	OR0150	13A,13B,10,13C,13E
Nettles, Darryl	TN1400	13B,32D,36,39,61
Niblock, James D.	PA0100	36,61,60A,13A,13B
Niedermaier, Edward G.	IL0550	13B,13C,13E

Index by Area of Teaching Interest

Name	Code	Areas
Nitzberg, Roy J.	NY0642	13A,13B,13C,13D
North, Geoffrey	IN0905	13B,13C
Northrop, Jonathan	CT0050	13A,13B,13C,13E
Norwine, Doug	SC0050	13A,13B
Oba, Junko	MA1000	13B,13C,20C
O'Brien, Kevin	DC0050	36,13B,60A,40
O'Brien, Richard	TX2930	61,13A,13B,13C
Oh, Annette	IL1090	11,61,36,13B,13C
Olsen, Eric	NJ0800	13A,13B,13C,66D
Organ, Wayne	CA1450	11,13A,13B,13C,34
Ortiguera, Joseph	AL1200	11,12A,13B
Ott, Daniel	NY1300	12A,29A,54,13B,13C
Paglialonga, Phillip O.	FL0100	64C,41,48,13A,13B
Palmer, David	NC1900	13A,66A,13B,13C,66G
Palmer, Robert	NC0250	13A,13B,13C
Papador, Nicholas G.	AG0550	13A,13B,13D,65,32E
Pardue, Jane	NC1400	36,66A,66D,13A,13B
Park, Christine	CA2600	66A,13A,13B,13C,41
Parker, Mark	SC0200	13A,32F,13B,13C,13G
Parkins, Robert	NC0600	66G,13A,13B,13C
Patton, Jeb	NY1275	10,13B,29B,29C,66A
Patty, Austin T.	TN0850	13A,13B,13C,13D
Paul, David	CA5060	12A,12,13B
Peplin, Steve W.	WI0450	10A,11,13B,47,70
Pereira, David	CA5000	13B,13H
Perkey, Christine	TN1400	13B,66A,13H
Perrotte, Jean-Paul	NV0100	10,13B,13F,13G,13E
Peterson, Jason P.	VA1000	13A,13B,20
Phillips, Moses	NY0640	12,13A,13B,13C,64A
Plate, Stephen W.	TN0850	38,60,32E,13B,13A
Polay, Bruce	IL1350	10A,10F,12A,13B,60B
Polk, Kristin	KY1550	64B,64D,32E,13A,13B
Ponte, Nora	PR0150	10A,13A,13B,13C,13D
Porter, Thomas	ND0400	36,13B,10A,32D,31A
Presar, Jennifer	IL2900	63B,13B,13C,13
Prettyman, Ken	WA0550	10A,13A,13B,46,47
Pritchett, Kate	OK0750	63B,42,13B,13C
Prudchenko, Slava	GA0940	37,13A,13B,13C
Raby, Lee Worley	CA2801	47,64E,13A,13B,64
Raessler, Daniel	VA1125	11,12,13B,13F,13A
Ramirez, Armando L.	PR0115	10,13A,13B,13D,13F
Ramirez, Catherine	MN1450	13A,64A,48,42,13B
Randall, Jean	MI1830	66A,13D,13E,13B
Ransom, Judy L.	WY0115	13B,13F,36,40,66D
Read, Kenneth E.	OH0550	13E,31A,10A,10F,13B
Reich, Amy J.	NJ0800	13A,13B,13C
Reinoso, Crystal Hearne	NY3717	13B,48,64C,15
Richards, Annette	NY0900	12,13A,13B,66G
Richards, Eric J.	NE0400	63C,37,10A,13B,47
Richards, Scott D.	NJ0800	10D,13B,13C,54
Richter, Leonard	WA1100	66A,66B,13A,13B
Roberts, Jean	TX2700	66A,13B,13C
Rocco, Robert	NJ0700	11,13A,13B,10A
Rodriguez Alvira, Jose	PR0115	13A,34,13B,13D,13G
Rogers, John E.	NH0350	13B,10,13D,13E,13G
Rogers, Nancy Marie	FL0850	13B,13H,13K,13C,13
Rogoff, Noah T.	NE0590	62C,62D,13A,13B
Rojahn, Rudolf	MA0350	13B,13C
Rolf, Marie	NY1100	13B,13F,13H
Rose, Brent	LA0800	64C,29A,13A,13B,13C
Rosewall, Michael	WI0750	36,61,12A,13A,13B
Ross, Elaine M.	CA1075	13A,13B,13C
Roth, Lisa	IA1400	53,61,46,13A,13B
Rothfarb, Lee	CA5060	13J,13I,13B,13E,13
Rush, Tobias	CO0950	13B,13C,13A
Russell, Scott	IN1450	63B,13B,13C
Ryan, Thomas K.	OH0350	64E,13B,13C,13D,13E
Ryberg, J. Stanley	IL1085	13B,13C,12A,63C,63D
Sachdev, Salil	MA0510	10,13A,20A,50,13B
Sackman, Marc L.	WI0806	13B,37,64A,47,11
Sala, Karen	IL1240	13A,13B,13E,13F,61
Samson, David	PA0650	47,13B,32C,63,60
Sandberg, Scott	ND0400	64,13B,13C,11,48
Sanders, Trevor	AA0110	13A,70,13B,13C
Santo, Joseph A.	DC0050	10A,10F,13B,13H,13C
Sargent, Joseph	AL1200	11,12A,13B,13C
Saya, Mark	CA2800	13B,10A,13D,13E,13F
Schempf, Ruthanne	NY3760	66A,66D,12A,13B
Schiavo, Joseph C.	NJ1100	13B,13C,12A,13F,13
Schmidt, Timothy R.	IA1750	13B,31A,66A,66H
Schmitz, Eric B.	NY3770	47,65,13B,13C,10A
Schowalter, Elise Anne	KY1000	13A,13B
Schuster-Craig, John	MI0900	13E,12A,13F,13B
Scott, F. Johnson	VA0750	34,13B,13A,66G,66C
Scruggs, Richard J.	TN0250	11,13B,41,48,64E
Segrest, Linda H.	MS0550	13A,13B,66A,66D,13C
Seitz, Paul T.	MO1800	13A,13B,13C
Serebryany, Vadim	AL0450	66A,12A,13B
Seward, Philip	IL0720	13,13B,13C,13E
Shannon, William	CA0900	13A,13B,34,63B,35
Shapero, Harold S.	MA0500	10A,13A,10B,13B,13G
Shaw, Timothy B.	PA2800	13B,13C,10A,13
Shew, Jamie	CA1900	53,60,13A,13B,13C
Shin, Jung-Won	MS0250	66A,66D,66B,66C,13B
Shinn, Barbara A.	AL0800	13C,13B,13A,66D
Shinn, Ronald R.	AL0800	66A,66C,13B
Shively, Victoria	MI1750	13B,13C,12A
Shkoda, Natalya	CA0800	66,13,13A,13B,12A
Shook, Thomas M.	WA1350	29,13B,13C
Sidoti, Vincent	ND0600	10,13B
Sierra, Roberto	NY0900	10A,10F,13B,13F
Silver, Sheila	NY3790	13B,13D,13E,10A,10F
Silvio, Will	MA0260	13B
Simonovic Schiff, Jelena	OR0850	13C,13B
Skinner, Josh	ID0060	12,13A,13B,13C,62D
Skinner, Kate	ID0060	12,13A,13B,13C,61
Slominski, Johnandrew	NY1100	13B,13C,13E,13H
Smith, Charles J.	NY4320	13,13B,13I
Smith, Ross	LA0050	11,66A,13A,13B,13C
Smith, Susan A.	MS0360	61,40,13,36,13B
Solomon, Evan	MD0550	13A,13B
Sorensen, Randall J.	LA0250	63A,63B,13,13A,13B,13A
Soroka, Michele R.	MI1750	13B,13C
Spelius, Susan M.	ID0075	11,66D,13B,13C
Spencer, Mia	WA0050	13A,13B,13C,61
Spitler, Carolyn	IN1250	64A,66A,13B,13C,66G
St. Julien, Marcus	LA0300	13B,13C,61,66G
Stainigner, Lynn L.	MD0300	36,66A,13B,40,61
Stanek, Mark	IN0100	70,13B,13C,41
Stanojevic, Vera	OH0350	13B,13C,13F
Stanziano, Stephen	OH1000	13A,13B,13C,10,62D
Stark-Williams, Turia	AL0450	61,13B
Steele, Edward L.	LA0400	12A,13A,13B,13C,61
Stein, John	MA0260	13B
Stein, Ken J.	IL2560	11,13B,20,47,64E
Steinke, David	FL0950	13C,13A,13B
Stephan-Robinson, Anna K.	WV0600	13B,13C,13F
Stevens, Daniel B.	DE0150	13B,13C
Stevens, James M.	TN0580	10A,36,13E,13B
Stevlingson, Norma	WI0860	13B,12A,66G,13E,13D
Stewart, Jeremy	VT0050	13A,13B,13C
Stewart, Jonathan	OK0825	32D,11,13B,36,61
Stiles, Allen	AB0060	13B,66A,66D
Stockdale, Michael	MI0520	70,53,13B
Story, David	WI0850	62D,53,51,13A,13B
Strauman, Edward	PA0650	10F,29A,13D,13B,35A
Stucky, Steven	NY0900	10,13B,13D,13F,43
Sullivan, Timothy R.	NY3780	13,13A,13B,13C
Sulton, Randall S.	TX0600	66A,66C,13E,13B,13F
Supko, John	NC0600	10A,13B,13C,13D,10B
Swanson, Philip	MA1650	63C,10A,13B,13C,13F
Swiatkowski, Chet	CA3150	13B,13C,13E,66A
Swilley, Daniel	IL1200	10,13,34,13A,13B
Swinden, Kevin J.	AG0600	13,13B,13C
Syring, Natalie	OK1330	13A,13B,13C
Sze, Eva	NY2750	13B,13C,13F
Tak, Young-Ah	FL1740	66A,60,13A,13B,41
Takesue, Sumy A.	CA4450	13A,66,12F,13B,13C
Tall, Malinda	UT0350	13A,13B,13C,66A,66C
Taranto, Vernon	FL1650	10,11,13B,36,13C
Tashjian, Charmian	IL1085	13A,13B,13C
Taylor, Janet	MS0400	13B,13C,66A
Taylor, Larry Clark	VA0100	66A,66G,13B,13D,13E
Temperley, David	NY1100	13B,13G,13K
Terefenko, Dariusz	NY1100	13B,13D,13B,13H,29
Thimmesch, Richard	IA0650	13B,13C,32E,37,47
Thomas, John	MO1950	13B,13C,63B
Thomas, Robert E.	NY0700	10,13A,13B,13C,13D
Thompson, Paul	WI0817	36,13,13C,11
Thomson, Susan N.	GA0950	13B,13E,66A,13
Thornton, Mary	TX2930	63A,29A,13B,13C
Thurmaier, David P.	FL0680	13,13C,13B,13E,13F
Tidwell, Mary	TX1510	66A,66D,13B,13A
Tonnu, Tuyen	IL1150	66A,66B,13B,13C
Tranquilino, Armando	FL0700	13A,13B,13C,34B,12A
Treybig, Joel	TN0100	63A,13B
Trubow, Valentina	IN1560	61,13C,13B
Truitt, D. Charles	PA2200	70,13,41,13E,13B
Tsao-Lim, May	AR0300	66A,66C,66D,66B,13B
Tunnell, Meme	KY0250	13B,66A,66B,66D
Turner, J. Frank	CA4450	13A,11,12A,54,13B
Turner, Mitchell	GA1200	13A,13B,13C,13F,13G
Turner, Veronica R.	CO0350	61,13A,13B,13C,13D
Turpen, Jennifer	WY0200	13A,13B,48
Tusing, Susan	GA0500	66A,66B,13A,13B
Uhlenkott, Gary	WA0400	13A,66A,13B,35H,47
Urquhart, Peter W.	NH0350	12C,13B,12A
Vaccaro, Brandon C.	OH1100	13,10,34,13B,13A
Vaclavik, Jude	UT0300	13,13A,13B,13D
Van Brunt, Nancy	WI0960	13A,13B,13C,66D,40
van der Westhuizen, Petrus	OH0950	66A,66C,66D,13B,13C
Vander Weg, John D.	MI2200	13B,13F,13E,13
VanDyke, Susanne	MS0575	36,61,13B,13C
Variego, Jorge	ND0600	10,13B,48,64C,64B
Vaughan, Jennie	TX2050	13A,13B,13C,66A,11
Voelker, Dale	IL1300	13A,13B,60A,36,66G
Vores, Andy	MA0350	10,13B
Wagner, David O.	MI1260	12A,13B,13C,35,66G
Waldrop, Joseph	TX3850	13A,32B,37,13B,64
Walker, Jesse	GA0150	13A,62C,63D,13B,13C
Wang, Jing	MA2020	34,13B,13E,13F
Wanken, Matthew	IL0420	12A,13A,13B,13C
Ware, David N.	MS0350	63A,34C,47,11,13B
Warner, Douglas G.	TN0850	11,63D,13B,13C,63C
Warren, John	IL1900	36,11,12A,13B,13C
Wason, Robert W.	NY1100	13B,13D,13F,13J,29C
Waters, Jeffery L.	MO1550	13B,47,64
Waters, Sarah S.	OH1800	13B,13C,12A
Watson, Anne	OK0550	64C,13A,13B,13C,20
Weber, Deanna F.	GA0150	13A,13B,13C,13D,61
Webster, James	NY0900	12,13B,13D,13I
Webster, Thomas R.	TX0600	60A,49,48,13B
Wegge, Glen T.	IA1750	13C,13B,13G,64C
Wellman, Samuel	VA0650	66A,66D,10,13A,13B
Wells, Rebecca Schaffer	KY1300	13A,13B,13C,13D,13E
Whatley, Jay K.		13B,13C,66D,66C,66G
Wheaton, J. Randall	VA0600	13B,13D,13A,13I,13F
Whitmore, Peter	OR0500	13B,13C
Wiksyk, Crystal	AB0210	13A,13B,13C,13H
Wilder, Mary Ann	KY0100	66A,66C,66D,13A,13B
Wilding, Jamie	OH2150	13B,13C
Willet, Gene K.	OH0200	13B,13C,13D,13E
Williams, Eddy	AL0450	65,13B,32C,37,60B
Williams, Kay	TX0050	66A,66C,66D,13A,13B
Williams, Richard	GA0550	13B,13C
Wilson, Jacqueline M.	WI0803	64D,48,13B,13C
Wise, Wilson	IA1100	64C,13B,32E,37,60B
Withers, Lisa Ann	VA0350	66A,66C,13B,13C,13F
Witten, David	NJ0800	13B,12A,66A,66B,66C
Wollner, William	MI1850	11,13B,37,63B,60B
Wong, Yau-Sun	NM0200	11,60,13B,36,37
Wood, Rose Ann	CA2050	13A,13B,13C,11,66D
Woodard, Peter	CT0650	13B,47,66A,29
Woodworth, William	TN1450	64B,13B,13C,41,66G
Worthen, Mary	AR0500	61,13B,13C
Wraggett, Wes	AB0210	10A,10B,13B,13L
Wu, Chieh-Mei Jamie	NY3500	11,13B,61,32D,36
Yang, Zhao	WA0950	66C,13A,13B,13C,13D
Yarbrough, Stephen	SD0600	13A,13G,10F,10A,13B
Yih, Annie	CA3600	13B,13C
Youngblood, Pamela J.	TX3300	41,64A,13A,13B,15
Yu, Ka-Wai	IL0800	62C,11,13B
Yun, Francis Y.	NJ0800	13A,13B,13C
Z, Rachel	NY2660	13B,29B,66A
Zell, Steven D.	TX0390	13A,13B,13C,11,66A

Eartraining/Sightsinging/Solfege

Name	Code	Areas
Abel, Sandra	TX0390	36,61,13A,13B,13C
Abel, Sean	CA1300	13B,13C,20G,29A,34C
Abeyaratne, Harsha D.	OH1650	66,13,13C
Abigana, Brett K.	MA1400	13A,13C
Abrams, David	NY2950	13C,11,41,64C,12A
Adam, Jennifer	KY1550	32D,13C,36
Adam, Mark	AF0050	11,13C,46,47,65
Adam, Nathaniel	CT0050	13B,13C
Adams, Clinton	MD0650	13C
Adams, Michelle	ID0100	66D,13C
Adamson, Philip I.	AG0550	66A,66B,66D,13C,66C
Adan, Jose	FL0050	70,13,13C,11,29A
Adderley, Meisha N.	OH0350	13B,13C,66D,66B
Admiral, Roger	AA0110	13B,13C,10A,42
Afonso, Daniel R.	CA0850	36,40,13C,32D,60A
Ahn, Christina H.	CA5350	13C
Ahrend, Janet	WA0400	66G,13C,66D

Index by Area of Teaching Interest

Name	Code	Areas
Aks, David M.	CA0835	12A,13C,39,60B,62C
Aldridge, Erin	WI0860	38,62A,13C,51,60B
Alexander, Eric	CO0950	13B,13C,10,13
Allen, Susan	VA0050	13C,11,66A,66D
Allesee, Eric	NJ0750	66A,13C
Almquist, Bradley L.	KY0950	60,32,36,13C
Alstat, Sara	IL2500	11,13A,13C,36,61
Alvarez, Franklin	AZ0300	11,51,62,38,13C
Amos, Alvin E.	PA2000	29,13A,13C,48,64
Amos, Shaun	GA0500	60,36,13B,13C,12A
Amrein, Emilie	IL1400	36,12A,13C,60,11
Amrozowicz, Mary Barbara	NY4460	13A,13,66A,13C,13B
Andersen, LeGrand	UT0200	61,66D,13C,13B
Anderson, Jon	ID0250	13C,47,66A,66E
Anderson, Matt	GA1500	70,13C
Anderson, Shane	TX2930	13A,13B,13C,66A,66B
Annicchiarico, Michael	NH0350	13B,13C,13E,10
Aponte, Maria P.	PR0150	11,13C
Apple, A. Alan	PA1750	13A,36,61,13C,40
Appleman, Tom	MA0260	13C
Aquino, Diane	CT0050	61,13C
Arbogast, Jennifer	TN0260	11,13C,54,61,39
Archambault, Ellen	OH0350	13B,13C
Arendsen, Benjamin D.	NY2550	13A,13C
Arita, Junko	NY2660	61,13B,13C
Arjomand, Ramin Amir	NY2750	10A,10F,13B,13C
Armstrong, Candace	TN0900	13C,36,60A,66A,11
Armstrong, Colin	PA3150	32D,36,13C
Arnett, Nathan D.	IL1240	11,13C,32A,36,40
Arrivee, David	CA0600	38,13,41,13A,13C
Arshagouni, Michael H.	CA2750	13B,13C,12A,66A,36
Asbury, David	TX2650	70,11,34,13C
Ashby, Steven	VA1600	70,13B,13C
Ashworth, Teresa	MN1100	61,36,40,20,13C
Asly, Monica	AI0150	13C
Astolfi, Jeri-Mae G.	WI0830	66D,13C
Aucoin, Amy	KY0950	32,36,60A,13C
Ayers, Jesse M.	OH1350	13,10,13C
Bahr, Jason	FL0680	10,13,31A,13C,13B
Bailey, Don	AR0730	13C,29A,29B,46,64E
Baker, Michael	KY1450	13,13C,13E,13G,13I
Balke, Maureen	MI0100	13C,39,61
Ball, Karen	IL2300	10A,66A,66B,13B,13C
Ball, Wesley A.	CT0800	32,32B,13C
Ballmaier, Robert	IL0720	13A,13C
Banister, Suzanne	AR0850	13C
Banks, Eric	WA0200	13C
Bansal, Juhi	CA3500	13C
Baruth, Lori E.	KY0900	13B,13C,64C
Batista, Gustavo	PR0150	11,12A,13A,13C,70
Bayen, Diane	NY2450	13C,61,36,60,32
Bean, Shirley Ann	MO1810	13A,13B,13C,13D,13E
Beard, Robert Scott	WV0550	66,13C,13A,66B,66C
Beaudet, Luce	AI0200	13B,13C,13E
Beavers, Sean M.	VA0650	12A,13A,13B,13C,41
Becker, Karen A.	NE0600	62C,42,13C
Becker, Karen E.	NY3775	66A,66C,13C,13A,36
Becos, Pelarin	IL3310	10,13,13C
Belet, Brian	CA4400	10,13B,13C,13E,13F
Bennett, Travis	NC2600	63B,13B,13C
Bent, Catherine	MA0260	13C,62C
Benton, Carol W.	GA0200	13C,13K,32B,32D,32G
Berardinelli, Paula	NY1600	29,13A,13C,11,47
Berger, Talya	CA4900	13,13A,13B,13C
Bergeron, Andrew	MI0900	13C
Bergman, Catherine	KS0300	64A,13C
Bermudez, Luis	PR0115	13C,12A
Bernal, Sergio	UT0300	38,13C
Bertucci, Ronald	OR0350	37,13A,47,63C,13C
Besharse, Kari	LA0650	11,13C
Biro, Daniel Peter	AB0150	13B,13C,13E,13F,10A
Bishai, Alf	NY2750	13B,13C
Bjorem, Pauline Kung	TX0050	66,13C
Black, Karen	IA1800	13C,31A,36,66G
Blaha, Kyle	NY1900	13C
Blakeman, Lee	KY1550	63C,13C,11,41
Blanchard, Scott	MA2100	13C
Blankenburg, Gayle R.	CA3650	66A,13C
Bleuel, John	GA2130	13C,60,64E,64B,64D
Bogard, Theresa L.	WY0200	13C,66
Bohn, Donna M.	PA1550	12A,13B,13C,65,60
Bohnenstengel, Christian	UT0200	66A,66C,13A,13B,13C
Boianova, Linda	NY2650	66A,13C,61,39,66C
Boldt-Neurohr, Kirsten	WA0050	13A,13B,13C,13F
Bondar, Liudmila E.	MI1200	66D,13C
Booker, Sally	MN1600	13C,66A
Boone, Kathleen	WA0550	64B,64C,70,32E,13C
Boozer, Mark	GA0490	13C,66A,66B,66D
Bosscher, Scott	MI0850	61,13C
Boubel, Karen A.	MN1000	13,10,34,13C,10A
Bouffard, Sophie	AJ0100	12A,61,11,13C
Bower, John E.	DC0050	10A,13C,10F
Bowker, Barbara E.	IL1085	13,11,13B,13C,12A
Boyd, Kim	OH2050	36,60A,32D,13C
Boyer, Justin	MD0550	13B,13C,10A
Boyer, Maurice C.	IL0730	13C,36,38,44
Braamse, Shudong	FL1740	61,13C
Braaten, Brenda	AB0210	13C
Bradley, Annette	AA0080	66A,32B,13C,66D,42
Brandes, Christine	CA4200	11,13C,32D,39,61
Brasington, Merewyn	OH1400	66C,66D,13C,66A
Brasky, Jill T.	FL2000	13,13B,13C,62A
Brauer, Vincent	AI0190	13C,66D
Breton, Jean-Francois	AG0170	65,13C,50
Brewer, Johnny	AL0620	13A,13B,11,46,13C
Bridges, Cynthia	TX0550	37,32H,60B,13C,32C
Brisson, Eric	MN1700	13A,13B,13C,13E,66C
Brockmann, Nicole M.	IN0350	62B,32I,13C
Broman, Per F.	OH0300	13F,13C,13E,12B,13
Brooks, Jack	TX1510	36,61,40,13C
Brotherton, Jonathan P.	NC0900	36,13C,32D
Brou, Melinda A.	TX2960	61,39,54,13C
Brower, Nori	ID0060	13C,36
Brown, Gwynne Kuhner	WA1000	12A,29A,13C,20,12B
Brown, Jennie S.	IL3550	64A,12A,13C,42
Brown, Stephen	AB0210	10,13A,13B,13C,13D
Browne, Douglas A.	PA1450	13C,60A,36,61
Browne, Peter J.	NY3705	36,13C
Bruce, Cynthia	AF0050	13C,33,66D,12A
Bryan, David	LA0650	13G,13C,70
Bryant, Edward	FL1740	13C,36,61,39,40
Bryant, John	GA2300	11,13C,63A,20
Buchierre, Alisa	MA1500	11,13C,36
Buckner, Nathan	NE0590	66A,66C,66D,13B,13C
Budds, Cain	LA0250	70,11,13A,13B,13C
Buettner, Jeff	VT0350	13A,36,40,13B,13C
Bullock, Kathy	KY0300	11,20A,36,13A,13C
Burmeister, James R.	WI0825	13A,13C
Burnham, Stuart	NC1500	12A,13C,66A,20
Burroughs, Mary	NC0650	42,63B,13C
Burt, Jack W.	ME0440	13C,49,63A
Burt, Patricia A.	IL1200	13A,66A,66D,13B,13C
Bushong, Claire B.	NE0400	12A,13B,13C,66A,66G
Busselberg, Paul	TX2295	61,36,13C
Butler, David	OH1850	13K,13C,13
Butler, Terry	VA0950	13C,32D,66A,66G
Buzza, Scott	KY1000	13C
Cagley, Judith L.	PA0550	13C
Cahueque, David	CA3200	11,13A,13B,13C,70
Cairns, Whitney	MO1830	13C
Calloway, Edwin S.	GA2300	13C,35C
Campbell, Andy	MO1550	36,61,13C
Campbell, Betty	AL0550	61,13C
Capaldo, Jennifer R.	VA0700	61,13C,12A
Capezza, June	FL0200	61,13A,13B,13C
Carew, David	MI1985	36,61,40,32D,13C
Carlson, James	TN1800	13A,13B,10A,10B,13C
Carney, Robert D.	MO1550	66A,66B,66C,11,13C
Carpenter, Alexander	AA0110	12,13C,13B,11,13E
Carter, John R.	CA1375	11,12A,36,61,13C
Casano, Steven	HI0210	13A,13B,13C,13D
Casey, Brian	NY1700	38,63B,60B,13C
Castilla, Carlos	TN1400	13B,13C
Cathey, Sheila Clagg	OK0825	11,13C
Caton, Benjamin D.	TN0500	13C,66A,66B
Caulder, Stephanie B.	PA1600	12A,12D,48,64B,13C
Caulkins, Tamara	WA1200	70,13A,13B,13C,13D
Cella, Lisa M.	MD1000	64A,13C,41
Cerqua, Joe	IL0720	13,13C
Cetto, Edward	CA5350	36,32D,13C
Chafin, Robert	VA1700	13C,39,34,61
Chambers, Carol	TX3100	63A,13C,32E,10F,32A
Chang, Soo-Yeon Park	CA0650	66,42,13A,13C
Chao, Joanna K.	NJ0175	66A,13C,13B
Chase, Allan	MA0260	13C
Chavez, David E.	VA1350	13C
Chen, Moh Wei	CA5100	66A,66D,13C
Chen, Ting-Lan	NE0590	11,13B,62A,62B,13C
Chien, Gloria	TN0850	13C,13E,66A,66B
Chipman, Paula	MD0300	61,13A,13C
Christiansen, Gregg S.	NY1550	66A,13A,13B,13C
Chung, Suna	NY3560	13A,13,39,61,13C
Cichy, Patricia Wurst	RI0150	32B,13C,64B,11,67D
Clark, Daniel	OH2370	11,12A,13C
Clark, Joseph	IL0750	13C
Clary, Philip	KY1000	13C
Clements, Jon	AR0200	61,39,13C
Clenman, David	AB0150	13,12A,13A,13B,13C
Clifft, Joel	CA0250	66,13C
Cole, Judith E.	GA1150	11,13C,13A,66C
Cole, Kathryn	MO0400	61,13A,13C
Coleman, Earl	GA0550	61,13C
Collins, Allison	CA0900	61,13C
Combs, Julia C.	MO0775	64B,13B,12A,11,13C
Con, Adam Jonathan	OH2450	36,32,11,60A,13C
Conatser, Brian	AR0200	13A,66A,13B,13C,66C
Conrad, Jon Alan	DE0150	13C
Conti, Michael	NJ0500	13A,13C
Contrino, Joseph L.	MO1500	65,29A,13A,13C
Cook, Gloria	FL1550	66A,66B,13C,11,66C
Corin, Amy R.	CA3100	14,11,13C,12A
Corrie, John H.	ME0150	13C,36,61,66G,66H
Cotter, Daniel	WA0950	38,64C,13B,13C
Cowden, Tracy E.	VA1700	66C,66A,66D,13C
Cox, Lauren J.	OK0300	64C,64E,13,13C
Crabtree, John M.	TX2250	13A,13B,13C
Craig, Phebe	CA5010	13C,56,66H
Cranford, Dennis	MS0100	13C
Crawford, Richard	FL0200	13B,13C
Cresci, Jonathan	MD0550	63A,34D,13C,34C,14C
Crisan, Patricia	SC0650	66A,13C
Crouse, David L.	AR0600	66A,13C,61,66G,13B
Culver, Jerry	MI1700	36,13C,60
Curlee, J. Matthew	NY1100	13A,13B,13C,13D,13K
Curry, Jeffrey P.	NE0040	11,13C,32,37,49
Cushman, Kevin	MI1260	60,13C
Dahn, Luke	IA1200	66A,13B,13C,13D,13E
Daley, Caron	AF0100	13A,13C,36
Dalton, James	MA0350	13B,13C,20
Dana, Christy L.	CA5000	13A,13C,29B,47,29C
Daniel, Robert	OK0550	13A,60,11,61,13C
Daub, Eric	TX3100	66A,13A,13B,13C,29A
Davidson, Thomas	AI0150	13C,66A,13A
Davies, David H.	NY1700	13A,13C,13B,10,13
Davies, Josh	AA0200	63A,47,29A,13C
Davis, Caroline	IL2250	13C
Davis, Gene	AL0450	61,36,13C
Davis, Joshua	PA3150	47,29,62D,13C,53
Davis, Kevin	AL1300	11,66G,13C
Davis, Ron A.	SC1000	13B,13C,31,66G,44
Dawe, Brenda M.	NY0350	13C,61
Dawe, Karla	AC0100	13A,13J,13C
De Castro, Margaret	AI0150	13C
De La Torre, Javier	PR0150	10A,10F,13A,13C
Dearden, Jennifer	PA0100	63A,34,13A,13B,13C
DeBoer, Angela	TN1100	63B,49,13A,13B,13C
Dekker, Gretchen	PA3710	66A,66H,13C
DeLaRosa, Lou	CA5510	13A,13C,12A,11,34C
DeMol, Karen	IA0500	64C,13C
Dering, James	TX0850	36,47,13,13C,11
DeRosa, Julia	MI1800	61,39,13C
DeSalvo, Nancy J.	PA3650	13A,13B,66A,66B,13C
DeWitt, Mark F.	LA0760	14,29A,13C,20G
Dickens, Pierce	GA0400	13A,13B,13C,13E,66A
Dickey, Christopher J.	WA1150	13C,11,63D
DiPaolo, Daniel M.	NY2750	13B,13C
DiPinto, Mark	MD0150	66A,66B,66C,13C
Dix, Ted	MD0520	66G,13C
Dixon, Edward E.	WA1300	38,62C,13C,62D
Dixon, Kara	AC0050	13A,13C
Dobreff, Kevin J.	MI0850	20F,61,67C,55D,13C
Dody, Teresa D.	WV0350	61,13C,13K,32B,32D
Donaldson, Doree	MO0400	66A,13C
Donelian, Armen	NY2660	13A,13C,10,66A,47
Donovick, Jeffery	FL1650	66D,13A,13B,13C,34C
Dorsa, James	CA0835	66H,10A,67F,13C,12A
Doutt, Kathleen C.	PA1550	12A,32,13C,20
Dowling, Eugene	AB0150	42,13C,63C,63D
Downing, Joseph	NY4150	10,66G,13,13C,60
Doyle, Sean	NY3725	13A,13B,13C
Draskovic, Ines	NY1250	66A,13A,13C,13
Drews, Michael R.	IN0907	13A,13B,13C,13E,11
Duda, Theodor	OH0700	13B,13C,12A,20G
Duff, Robert P.	NH0100	36,60,10A,40,13C
Duker, Philip	DE0150	13B,13C
Duncan, Norah	MI2200	36,13C,66G

Index by Area of Teaching Interest

Name	Code	Areas
Durham-Lozaw, Susan	NC2350	13A,13B,13C,61
Dykema, Dan H.	AR0600	13B,11,66A,66D,13C
Eastman, Patricia	MO1950	13A,13B,13C,66A
Eastwood, Deb A.	KY0900	13A,13B,13C,63A
Effler, Charles E.	LA0650	66C,39,13C
Ehrke, David	NV0100	13C,64C,64E,41
Ehrlich, Martin L.	MA1000	29,13B,13C
Eichhorst, Diane	ND0050	13C,66
Eidson, Joseph M.	PA1400	13B,13C
Ellingson, Peter	CO0830	66,13C,29
Ellis, Margaret J.	IL0100	13C,11,63A
Elswick, Beth L.	MO1810	13A,13B,13C,13D
Enciso, Franz J.	CA1020	13C,66D,11
Englert, David	TX2250	13A,13B,13C
Epstein, Nomi R.	IL0750	13C
Erickson, Jeff	WI0925	47,13C,29A,13B
Erickson, Kurt	CA1500	66,11,13C
Ericson, Michael	IL3500	13B,13C,64B,48
Ernst, John	NJ1000	13,13C
Escalante, Roosevelt	KY0900	13B,13C,32D,36
Eshleman, Elizabeth	CA2950	61,13C
Evans, Gary	VA0400	13A,13B,13C,11,12A
Evans, Mathew J.	CO0275	13A,13B,13C,42
Everett, Micah P.	MS0700	63C,63D,13C,41,49
Faerber, Matthew L.	WI0860	60A,36,32D,40,13C
Falconbridge, Vaida	CA3250	61,13C
Fassnacht, Therese	CA3150	13B,13C,20H,12A
Fears, Angela	CA3520	13A,13C,64D,16
Feasly, William	WV0550	70,13C
Fells, Mizue	WA0550	66A,66D,13C,11,20
Ferrier, Robert	MA1100	70,53,29,13C
Fey, Alan	TN0100	13C
Fiala, Michele	OH1900	64B,41,13B,13C,64D
Fiedler, Anne	IN1600	13B,13C,66A
Fletcher, Seth	NE0590	63D,63C,13B,13C,11
Flores, Jose G.	TX2930	62A,62B,51,13C,42
Fogle, Megan R.	SC0350	13A,13B,13C,13E,13F
Forquer, Ty	MI1800	65,50,13C
Forsha, Heather	NY1400	13C,66A,66C,32E
Fowler, Andrew J.	SC0420	13C,13A,11
Fox, Elizabeth	WI1100	13A,13B,13C,11
Francis, Kelly A.	GA1150	13B,13C
Frank, Bruce	NY1100	13B,13C,13D,13H,13I
Franzetti-Brewster, Allison	NJ0700	66C,41,13A,13B,13C
Fraser, Amy	NE0720	13C
Fredrickson, Ann	MN0200	61,36,39,54,13C
Freed, Donald Callen	TX2710	61,36,10A,13C,12A
Freeman, Wendy	AA0200	37,13C
Frisbie, Jodi	KS0150	61,36,39,13C
Frye, Joseph W.	TN1720	63C,13A,13C,11,34
Fuller, John A.	NC1700	37,13C
Furby, Victoria J.	NY3717	13C,15,32D
Gabriel, Charles M.	MA2030	62D,13C,47
Galieva-Szokolay, Julia	AG0300	13B,13C
Gandy, V. Gay	KY1400	36,61,13A,13C,11
Gant, Edward	VA0600	13C
Garcia, W. T. Skye	OK0300	66A,66D,13B,13C,66B
Garcia-Novelli, Eduardo	WI0250	36,40,32D,13C,60
Garrison, Leonard	ID0250	64A,13,12,13B,13C
Garvey, Christa N.	WI0803	13B,13C,64B
Gaub, Nancy McFarland	IA0700	62A,13C,41
Gaudette, Fannie	AI0050	13C,66C
Ge, Tao	GA0550	10F,13C
Gelber, Debbie	TX2350	13A,13B,36,61,13C
Gerritson, Sasha L.	IL2150	11,13C,39,13A
Gilbert, Jan M.	MN0950	13A,13C,10
Gillie, Gina	WA0650	13C,63B
Gillies, Peter	AL1160	13C
Gilroy, Gary P.	CA0810	13C,10F,60B,37
Girdham, Jane C.	MI1850	11,12A,13B,13C,13E
Glennon, Barbara	PA0650	20G,13B,13C,64A,64C
Golan, Jeanne K.	NY2550	13B,13C,12A,66A,66D
Goldman, Edward 'Ted'	NY1100	13K,13C,13B,10A,10F
Goldspiel, Alan	AL1200	70,13C,13B,51
Goldstein, Perry	NY3790	13A,13C,13E,10A,13F
Gomez-Giraldo, Julian	WA0250	38,60B,13C
Goranson, Jocelyn	PA2300	64A,13A,13C,13B,42
Gordon, Heidi Cohenour	AR0810	61,13C,66D,36
Gosswiller, Julie	MT0200	13C,66D,66A
Grant, David	IL0750	13C
Grant, David	IL2050	13C
Grant, Kristin	AR0500	64A,13A,13B,13C
Graves, Kim	TN1660	66D,13C
Green, Elvira O.	VI0050	13C,36,61
Greenblatt, Richard	MA0260	13C
Greene, Richard C.	GA0850	70,13C,11,13E,12A
Greenwald, Laura	NJ0050	36,13C,61,39
Greitzer, Mary	NY1100	13C,13D,13E,13F,13H
Griffin, Christopher	NC2650	63B,13C
Griffin, John C.	MI2250	10,13,13C,66C
Griffin-Seal, Mary	FL0500	66A,11,66D,13C
Grmela, Sylvia	NY4460	62B,20,13A,13C
Grodrian, Ericka	IN1750	11,13C,49,63B
Grosso, Cheryl	WI0808	50,65,43,14,13C
Groulx, Timothy J.	IN1600	13B,13C,32
Grove, Paul	WA0400	70,13A,13B,13C
Guidobaldi Chittolina, Alberto	PR0115	13,13C
Guzzio-Kregler, Mary Ellen	RI0200	13C,64A,42
Ha, Youngmi	NY2750	10A,10E,13B,13C,13D
Hagarty, Scott	TX0550	63A,13A,13C,49,41
Haines, Janice	CA0950	13A,13C,66D
Hall, Elena	FL0500	66A,66D,13C
Hall, Gary	WY0115	11,12A,13B,13C,47
Hall, Lois	NY2800	61,13C,42
Hall, Teddy	VA0500	13A,13B,13C,32C,11
Halloran, Stephen	MA0350	13B,13C
Hamberlin, Larry D.	VT0350	10A,12A,29A,13A,13C
Hamer, Jan	PA3200	13C
Hamessley, Lydia	NY1350	13C,12,14,20G,12A
Hammel, Alice	VA1600	13B,13C
Hansen, Jeremy C.	TN1450	63B,13C,42
Harding, Scott R.	MI0400	10A,13C,29A,65,13A
Harlen, Benjamin	LA0400	10A,31A,13B,13C,13D
Harley, Gretta	WA0200	13C
Harrington, Elisabeth	CA2250	39,61,13C
Harris, Carole J.	NY0400	13A,13B,13C,13D
Harris, Lee	TN1700	32,13C,36
Harrison, Leslie Anne	WY0115	13C
Hart, Michael	CA0550	37,13B,13C,63C,63D
Harwood, Baxter	WA0100	13,13C
Hastings, David M.	WI0850	64E,42,13A,13B,13C
Hastings, Stella	KS1050	38,13B,13C,66D
Hearn, Priscilla	KS0550	66A,11,12,66D,13C
Hebert, Ryan	FL2050	60,36,13C,66G
Heetderks, David	OH1700	10A,13C,13E,60
Heffernan, Michele	NJ1100	11,13C,29,33,66A
Heighway, Robbi A.	WI0450	11,13C,13D,66B,66D
Heinen, Julia M.	CA0835	64C,42,13C
Helman, Shandra K.	ID0100	64C,13C,48,20,64E
Helms, Elizabeth	CA5360	66C,13A,13C,36,39
Henderson, Jean	NE0450	13A,13B,13C,13D,10A
Henjum, Katherine	ND0400	61,40,13C
Henson, Bill	MI1800	61,39,13C
Herb, Thomas	UT0200	13C,34,47,32C,32D
Herbert, David	TX2200	13A,64B,32,13B,13C
Heritage, Lee	OH2300	13B,13C,29A,20G,10A
Herrington, Brian P.	TX2250	13A,13B,13C
Hevia, Lonnie	MD0850	13,13E,13C,10
Hickey, Katherine M.	CA5150	32,13A,13C,36,40
Hicks, Martha K.	MO1550	31A,11,60,13C,32B
Higgins, William L.	AR0300	39,61,60A,13C
Hileman, Lynn	WV0750	64D,13C,13B,13A,13D
Hixson, Mary	GA2000	13C,20,40,43
Hoag, Melissa E.	MI1750	13B,13C,13D,13E,13F
Hoffart, Danica	AA0080	36,61,54,13C
Hoffman, Brian D.	OK0800	13A,13B,13C,66D
Hoffman, Matt	CO0550	13C
Holland, Linda L.	CA4410	13,13A,13C
Hollinger, Trent A.	MO0300	64,37,13C,13A,60B
Hooten, Bryan	VA1600	13B,13C,63C
Hopkins, Christopher	NY2105	13C
Horel, Charles	GA0950	10A,70,13A,13C
Hornbach, Christina M.	MI1050	32,13C
Horvath, Janos	AA0150	32B,32D,36,42,13C
Houde, Andrea	WV0750	13C,32,41,42,62B
Howard, Timothy P.	CA0835	13B,13C,66G
Howe, Ryan	IA1400	13A,13B,13C
Howes, Sarah Marie	PA1400	61,13C
Howlett, Christine R.	NY4450	36,13C,61
Hulbert, Duane	WA1000	66A,13C
Hung, Yu-Sui	IL3450	66A,66D,13C
Hunt, Trevor	MS0580	11,70,13C,13G
Hurst, Chloe	AB0200	13A,13B,13C
Hurty, Sonja	IL0100	36,61,13C
Hutter, Greg J.	IL0750	13C,13D,10A,11
Hyberger, Sarah Amanda	TN0260	11,13C,54,61,39
Hylton, Doris	MO1830	32B,13A,13C
Iguina, Jose R.	PR0150	13A,13C,11,70
Infusino, Patrick	IL0275	11,64E,13C
Isaacson, Kristin	TX0900	13C,62C,62D
Isenhour, Justin	AR0500	63C,63D,11,13C
Itoh, Takuma	HI0210	10A,13A,13B,13C,13D
Ivey, Bobby	GA0350	32,36,13C,40
Ivry, Jessica	CA1150	51,42,62,13C,38
Ivy, Julie	NV0050	13C,13B
James, Pamela A.	VA0750	32A,61,13C,66D,32B
James, Woodrow	CA2750	47,13B,13C
Jensen, Andrew	AR0050	60A,36,11,61,13C
Jensen, Jocelyn	NV0050	36,13B,13C
Jensen, Joni L.	TX3300	13C,36,61,32D,60A
Jex, David	OH2300	13B,13C,13D,10,29
Jimenez, Lissette	FL0700	61,12A,13C
Johnson, Byron	MS0050	13A,13B,13C,61,39
Johnson, Chrisa	VA0050	66A,13B,13C,11
Johnson, Craig R.	IL2100	13C
Johnson, G. Larry	UT0325	36,60A,13A,13B,13C
Johnson, Gary V.	IL2730	13,13C,29,34
Johnson, Jeanne	TX1350	13C,11,61
Johnson, Lawrence	UT0200	11,13C,61
Johnson, Patricia	KY1550	11,13C
Johnson, Tracey	MO2000	66A,66D,13C
Johnson, Will	CA4460	13C
Johnston, Rebecca R.	SC0600	32,36,60,13C,61
Jolley, David	NY0642	13C,63
Jones, Deborah	TX3415	32,13A,13C
Jones, Emily	FL0040	11,12A,13C,41,70
Jones, Henry S.	LA0650	66A,66B,66D,13C
Jones, John W.	PA1400	13B,13C,13D,13E,10A
Jones, Melinda	MO1550	66A,66D,66B,13B,13C
Jones, Pamela Palmer	UT0250	66D,13C
Jones, Pamela	MS0580	11,61,13C
Jones, Ryan C.	NY1600	13C,13D,13A
Jones, Sue	IL1550	42,66A,66C,66D,13C
Josenhans, Thomas	IN1600	64C,13B,13C,64E,41
Juhn, Hee-Kyung	AR0300	66A,13C,66G,66C,66B
Julian, Michael	CA2750	35D,35C,35G,13C,13D
Jurcisin, Mark	NJ0750	10,13A,13B,13C,11
Justus, Keith	TX0550	70,13C,14C,29B
Kacos, Lisa	MI0850	13A,13C
Kahan, Sylvia	NY0644	12A,12C,66,13A,13C
Kamatani, Pamela M.	CA1020	11,13B,13C
Kammerer, David	HI0050	10F,37,35B,63A,13C
Kaneda, Mariko	OH2000	66C,66A,66D,13B,13C
Kang, Juyeon	IA1200	66A,66D,66C,13C
Kantar, Ned D.	MN0050	13C,35
Kapner, Harriet H.	NY2550	70,13A,13B,13C
Kasper, Kathryn	KS0200	39,61,54,13C
Katona, Brian	NJ1130	13C
Kats, Nitza	VA1100	66A,13C
Kaufhold, Jessica	AL0530	36,11,13A,13B,13C
Kaurin-Karaca, Natasa	OK0800	66D,13C,11,34B
Kegerreis, Helen M.	NY2550	32A,13C,66D
Kelly, Kathryn	MA0260	13C
Kelly, Michael	OH1450	13A,13B,13C
Kennedy, Nathan	MN0610	13A,13B,13C,13D,13F
Kennedy, Patricia E.	IN0905	13C,32D
Kenote, Marie Herseth	NY2900	64A,12A,13B,13C,13D
Ker-Hackleman, Kelly	VA0450	66,13C,11
Keyne, Lori V.	AZ0250	13B,13C,36,66D
Kickasola, Matthew	PA1350	12A,13C
Kiel, Dyke	MO0250	13B,13C,64
Kilgore Wood, Janice	MD1050	13C,66A,36,66B,31A
Kim, Taeseong	VA0650	66A,66B,13C
Kim, Young	NY0700	13B,13C,66A,66D
Kindred, Kyle	TX2250	13A,13B,13C
Klakowich, Robert	AA0020	13A,13B,13C,13D,13E
Kloeckner, Phillip	TX2150	66G,13C
Klotzbach, Susan	IL1200	66C,13A,13B,13C
Knier, Lawrence	MD0800	37,13C,63,13K,11
Koch, Nathan J.	TX2250	64D,13C,12A
Kocyan, Wojciech	CA2800	66A,13C
Kohl, Jack	NY4060	13C,12A,11
Kopfstein-Penk, Alicia	DC0010	70,12,13C,11
Kovacs, Jolan	AI0150	13C
Kozak, Kevin J.	AL0800	63B,13C,41
Kraakevik, Kari	CO0550	13B,13C
Kramer, Atossa	KY0300	13C,48,64C,66A,67C
Krause, Drew S.	NY2750	13A,13B,13C,13D,13F
Krieger, Marcos F.	PA3150	13C,66H,66G,11,12A
Krueger, Carol J.	KS0300	13C,60,36,32D
Krumbholz, Gerald A.	WA0950	13A,13B,13C,13D,10C
Kuan, Flora	NY2200	13C,66A,42
Kulpa, John	NJ0750	11,13A,13B,13C
Kunda, Keith	IN1560	13B,13C,10F
Kurth, Robert	PA2900	13C,61
Kwok, Sarita	CT0900	13C

Name	Code	Areas
Laflen, Betty Jo	KS0400	11,13C,32B,37,64
Laginya, Daniel	OH2600	13A,13B,13C
Laitz, Steven	NY1100	13B,13C,13H,13I
Lalonde, Alain	AI0200	10,13C
Lambert, Doris	OK0150	36,40,61,13C
Lambert, Jean-Francois	AI0190	47,13C
Lambrecht, James M.	IL0100	37,49,63A,60B,13C
Lan, Catherine	FL0200	13B,13C,66D
Land, Michael	ND0400	13C,66A
Landers, Joseph	AL1200	10A,10F,13B,13C,13E
Lane, Mathew	MD0400	13A,13C,66A,66C
Lanners, Heather	OK0800	66A,13C,66C
Lansing, Nathan	WA0950	36,40,13B,13C,13A
Laprade, Paul	IL2560	13C,36,61,66D,32
Laufer, Milton R.	NC1800	66A,13C
Lauffer, Peter	NJ1000	13,13C
LaVoie, Karen R.	MA2100	13C,60B,37,63A
Lawrence, Edwin	MA2250	13C,66A,66G,66H,66C
Leblanc, Mario	AI0200	13C,13D
Lee, Amanda	TX2570	66A,13C,13B,13E,66B
Lee, Christopher	MA2030	13A,13B,13C
Lee, Marian Y.	IA1300	66A,66B,66C,13C,11
Lee, Rosey	MA0260	13C
Lee, Sun Min	PA1950	36,40,60,13C
Lemmons, Cheryl T.	TX0050	13C,66C
Lentsner, Dina	OH0350	12A,13B,13C,13D,13E
Lewis, Alexandra M.	NY0500	11,12,13C,66D
Li, Ping-Hui	PR0150	13A,13C,14A,66A,66C
Li, Simon	NY2900	66A,13A,13B,13C
Lin, James	CA5510	13A,13B,42,13C,13D
Lindholm, Eric	CA1050	13C,38,60B
Linton, Deborah	AG0050	61,13C
Lobitz, Beverly	AR0800	13E,11,12A,61,13C
Logan, Jennifer	CA3300	10B,13A,13B,13C,35C
Lohninger, Elisabeth	NY2660	13C
Lombard, Becky	GA2050	66A,13B,13C,12A,66C
Long, Rebecca	NC1250	13A,13B,13C
Lopez, Faye	SC0200	13C,66A
Lovelace, Jason R.	DC0050	10A,13C,10F
Loy, David	MD0300	13C,61
Luke, Nadine	ID0060	13A,13B,13C,64A
Lupinski, Rudy	OK0300	66A,66D,13B,13C,66H
Lyman, Anne E.	WA1000	36,13C
Lyttle, Eric	VA0250	13A,13C,66A
Macan, Ed	CA1280	66A,13A,13B,13C,12A
MacFarlane, Thomas	NY2750	13C,13D,13F,12A,12B
Mack, Dianne	TX3150	32,13C
Mack, Peter	WA0200	66A,41,13C
Maddox, Timothy	NC1075	11,13A,13B,13C,13D
Magnussen, John P.	CA0835	65,13C
Makubuya, James	IN1850	13A,13C,11,14,20
Mallin, Claire	AF0050	13C,40,61,60A
Mallory, Jason	IA0300	61,13C
Maltester, Diane	CA2775	12A,64,41,13C
Mancusi, Roberto	TN1720	39,61,60A,13C
Mangels, Jeffrey W.	MD0550	13A,34C,11,13C,34D
March, Kathryn Lucas	IA1100	13C,66A,66D,66C
Margaglione, Louis A.	IL2450	64,13A,13C,11
Marlowe, Sarah	NY2750	13,13C,13D,13H,13I
Maroney, James	PA1100	11,36,61,13C,40
Marrs, Margie V.	IA0300	61,13A,13C
Martin, Blair	KS1250	13C,37,46,41,32
Martin, Michael D.	GA0150	11,12A,13C,32,49
Marvin, Elizabeth W.	NY1100	13A,13C,13F,13G,13K
Marvin, William	NY1100	13A,13B,13C,13H,13I
Masci, Michael J.	NY3730	11,13A,13B,13C,13D
Mason, Scott	IL0550	13B,13C,53,29
Mateiescu, Carmen	NJ1000	13,13C
Mather, Pierrette	AI0150	13A,13C
Mathews, Christopher W.	TN1660	36,13H,31A,60A,13C
Matters, Helene	CA2200	66A,13B,13C
Mazer, Susan	CT0300	13A,13B,13C
McCarthy, Marta	AG0350	60,36,13C
McClellan, Robinson	NY4500	13B,13C
McClung, Alan C.	TX3420	32C,32D,32G,60A,13C
McConnell, Joan	OH0950	66C,66G,13C,66D,13B
McCord, G. Dawn Harmon	GA2130	32B,32C,32A,13C,66D
McCreary, Teresa J.	HI0110	37,13A,13C,38,47
McCulloch, Doug	HI0210	13A,13B,13C,13D
McDaniel, Carol	CA1425	32B,13C,31A,66G
McDermott, Pamela D. J.	VA0700	61,60,36,13C
McGowan, Sean C.	CO0830	13A,13B,13C,13E,29B
McGuire, Joshua	TN1850	13C
McKeage, Kathleen M.	WY0200	11,62D,13C,32
McKelvey, Berke	MA0260	13C
McMahan, Robert Y.	NJ0175	13B,13C,13F,10B,10A
McNabb, Carol	TX3515	13B,13C,64D,67C,64B
McVay, Vicki	KY1450	66D,13,66B,13C
Meadows, Erin	TN0930	13A,13C
Melbinger, Timothy	PA2710	12A,41,13B,13C,13E
Melendez Dohnert, Victor	PR0115	13A,13B,13C,66D
Melson, Christine	CT0500	13A,13C,36,66C
Merrit, Doug	TN0580	13C,62A,62B
Meyer, Sandra G.	OK0650	13B,13C,13E,66A,13
Mieses, Nermis	KY1450	64B,13C,41
Miljkovic, Katarina	MA1400	13C,13B,12A,12
Millar, Cameron	MD0300	13A,34B,35C,13C,34D
Millar, Tania	AG0070	66A,66D,13C
Millard, Joshua P.	MA2030	13B,13C,41,47
Miller, Andrew	ND0050	36,60A,40,13C
Miller, Elaine	NC2000	13C,66A,66C,66B,13A
Miller, Kenny	AZ0470	13C,12A,36,40,61
Miller, Thomas E.	CA5400	13B,13C,36,39,54
Mills, Robert P.	VA0650	11,13B,13C
Milovanovic, Biljana	NJ0700	66A,66H,13C
Miotke, David	CA3520	66A,66H,66C,13C
Mitchell, Jennifer	GA1150	13B,13C,11,10
Modica, Joseph	CA5150	13C,36
Mohr, Deanne	MN1700	66A,66C,66B,13B,13C
Moll, Benjamin	OR0600	65,13A,13B,13C,10A
Molumby, Nicole L.	ID0050	64A,32E,32I,13C
Monahan, Seth	NY1100	13B,13C,13D,13E
Monson, Linda Apple	VA0450	13C,66A
Moore, Gregory	WI0860	13C,47,64E,29,10A
Moore, Kathy Bundock	CO0950	62E,13B,13C,13E
Moore, Nancy	OH0350	33,13A,13B,13C
Moore, Stephen F.	CA0805	13C,29,47,60,66
Morales-Matos, Jaime	OH1450	63C,63D,13C,42
Moreno, Maria Teresa	AI0190	13C
Morgan, Tom T.	KS1400	50,65,13C
Morita, Lina	LA0350	13C,41,66A,66C,66D
Moritz, Kristina	PA2150	13A,13B,13C
Morris, Eric	CA3270	13C,39
Moss, Gary	IA0950	61,13C
Motter, Catherine	CO0150	66A,13C
Muniz, Jennifer	MO0100	66A,66D,13C,13E
Munoz, Nelida	PR0150	11,13A,13C,44
Murdock, Matthew	TN1600	13C,32E,29,37,47
Murray, John	AA0025	61,36,13A,13C
Murray, Kathy	MO0775	13B,13C
Murray, Michele C.	IN0100	13A,13B,13C,66D
Nachman, Myrna	NY2550	66A,13A,12A,13C
Nagel, Douglas	MT0175	61,36,60A,13C
Nair, Garyth	NJ0300	36,38,61,60,13C
Nalesnik, David A.	MO1950	13B,13C
Namminga, Jaime	ND0600	13C,66C,66A
Nangle, Richard P.	MA2030	13B,13C,13D,13E,13F
Nauert, Clark	TX1600	70,53,13B,13C
Navarro, Gloria	PR0115	13A,13C
Naylor, Earl	MO1950	13C
Naylor, Susan E.	GA1700	13B,66A,13C
Neal, Mary Elizabeth	AL0300	13A,13B,13C,13D
Neal, Nedra	NY2550	13C,66D
Neebe, Paul M.	VA1550	63A,49,13C,13A
Neiderhiser, Jonathan	SD0580	37,47,32E,13B,13C
Neilson, Duncan	OR0150	13A,13B,10,13C,13E
Netsky, Hankus H.	MA1400	29,13C,47,53,20F
Nevill, Tom	TX3515	65,13A,13C,50,37
New, Laura L.	MO1810	13C
Newbrough, William J.	NY1700	66A,66B,13C,13E,66C
Newby, David L.	CA0200	13C,36,38,39
Newlin, Georgia A.	NY0050	11,12A,13C,32,36
Newsome, Bo	NC0650	64B,13C
Nickens, Michael W.	VA0450	37,13C,11
Niedermaier, Edward G.	IL0550	13B,13C,13E
Niezen, Richard S.	CO0150	62C,62D,13C,13G
Nims, Marilyn	OH2000	61,13C,32D
Nitsch, Kevin	NY2650	66A,13A,13C
Nitzberg, Roy J.	NY0642	13A,13B,13C,13D
Niu, Elaine	WI0750	61,39,36,60A,13C
Nixon, Patricia	VA0950	36,46,13C,61
Nolan, Denise G.	NH0110	48,64A,11,13C
Nordlund, Moya L.	AL0800	32,13C
North, Geoffrey	IN0905	13B,13C
Northrop, Jonathan	CT0050	13A,13B,13C,13E
Nowack, James	WI1155	60,36,13C
Nozny, Rachel	ND0100	64A,13C
Oba, Junko	MA1000	13B,13C,20C
O'Brien, Richard	TX2930	61,13A,13B,13C
Odom, Donald R.	MS0850	36,13C,11,32D,60A
Oh, Annette	IL1090	11,61,36,13B,13C
Olsen, Eric	NJ0800	13A,13B,13C,66D
Oquin, Wayne	NY1900	13C
Organ, Wayne	CA1450	11,13A,13B,13C,34
Orland, Michael	CA5000	13A,66D,66A,13C
Orlando, Courtney Sian	MD0650	13C
Orovich, Nicholas	NH0350	13C,37,63C,63D
Ortiz, Sheila	PR0115	13A,13C
Oshima-Ryan, Yumiko	MN0750	66A,66B,13C
O'Sullivan, Laila K.	TN1680	13,13C,29C
Ott, Daniel P.	NY1900	13C
Ott, Daniel	NY1300	12A,29A,54,13B,13C
Overfield-Zook, Kathleen	VA0600	13C
Overy, Charles	AI0200	13C
Owens, Tiffany	OH0680	61,13C,40
Owren, Betty Ann	CA1760	36,61,13C,13A,11
Oxler, Cora Jean	TX3370	61,11,13C
Oye, Deanna	AA0200	66A,66C,66,13A,13C,66B
Pagano, Stephen	NY1275	13C,61
Paick, Yoomi	TN1450	11,13C,66C
Palmer, David	NC1900	13A,66A,13B,13C,66G
Palmer, David	AG0550	66A,66G,31A,13C,66H
Palmer, Jason	OR1020	66D,13,13C,29A,29B
Palmer, Robert	NC0250	13A,13B,13C
Park, Christine	CA2600	66A,13A,13B,13C,41
Parker, Mark	SC0200	13A,32F,13B,13C,13G
Parkins, Robert	NC0600	66G,13A,13B,13C
Patty, Austin T.	TN0850	13A,13B,13C,13D
Paulsen, Kent D.	WI0750	36,32D,61,60,13C
Payton, Chad	MS0250	11,13C,61
Peabody, Martha	MA1450	61,33,13C
Perriment, Andrew	AB0200	13D,13C
Perry, Eileen	AZ0480	66A,13C,66D
Perry, Margaret	CA5350	66B,66D,66C,13C
Person, Philip	MA0260	13C
Petitto, Jacqueline	CA1075	13C
Petty, Shuko Watanabe	VA1850	66A,66C,13C
Phillips, Moses	NY0640	12,13A,13B,13C,64A
Piagentini, Susan M.	IL2250	13C,13H,13K,13
Pierce, Carrie	TX2930	62C,62D,51,31A,13C
Pifer, Joshua K.	AL0200	13C
Pitts, Larry	CA2250	66A,66C,66D,13C
Placeres, Martha	TX3515	62A,38,13A,13C
Plies, Dennis B.	OR1150	47,65B,66B,66D,13C
Ponte, Nora	PR0150	10A,13A,13B,13C,13D
Popham, Phillip F.	MI2000	64B,10B,13C
Potter, Jane	MA0260	13C
Potter, Kenney	NC2650	36,13C,60A
Pozzi, Dave A.	CA0835	13C,14C
Presar, Jennifer	IL2900	63B,13B,13C,13
Pritchett, Kate	OK0750	63B,42,13B,13C
Prudchenko, Slava	GA0940	37,13A,13B,13C
Quong, Meijane	AB0060	66A,66D,13C
Rada, Raphael	TX0550	61,11,13C,32B,36
Rainwater, Brian	FL0670	60,37,13C,63C,47
Rasmussen, G. Rosalie	CA3400	32,44,66B,66D,13C
Raths, P. Nicholas	MN0350	70,13C
Reed, Kathryn	IA0950	13C,55,66H
Reese, Jodi	KS0265	36,11,13C,61,60A
Reich, Amy J.	NJ0800	13A,13B,13C
Reimer, Mark U.	VA0150	13C,60B,37
Reisman, Leana	CT0650	52,13C
Replogle, Rebecca	OR1010	36,61,13A,13C,40
Restesan, Frank	NE0550	38,13C,62A,51,12A
Reynolds, Jeremy W.	CO0900	64C,33,13C,13H
Reynolds, Marc	TX2930	61,39,13C
Ribchinsky, Julie C.	CT0050	13A,13C,62C,11,38
Richards, Scott D.	NJ0800	10D,13B,13C,54
Richardson, Celia	TX2850	11,36,61,32B,13C
Richardson, Neal	MO1950	11,13C
Richman, Pamela L.	OK1330	13C,13A,61
Ries, Ardelle	AA0110	13C,36,60A
Riley, William	MA2020	70,11,13C
Ring, Eric	MO1950	64D,48,13C
Rivera Ortiz, William	PR0115	13A,13C,36,60A
Roberts, Jean	TX2700	66A,13B,13C
Roberts, Terry	SC0710	11,63,13C,35A,41
Robinson, Kathleen E.	MN1280	31A,11,12A,13C
Roche, Mildred A.	SC0650	66C,13C
Rogers, Nancy Marie	FL0850	13B,13H,13K,13C,13
Rogers, Sharon	AC0050	13A,13C
Rogine, Peter	NY1275	13C,29,47,70
Rognstad, Richard	SD0600	38,13A,62D,13C,11
Roitstein, David	CA0510	13C,47,29,66A
Rojahn, Rudolf	MA0350	13B,13C
Roll, Christianne	VA0350	61,32A,13C

Index by Area of Teaching Interest

Name	Code	Areas
Roop, Cynthia M.	NC1250	64A,32A,32E,13C,41
Rosario, Harry	PR0150	13A,13C,37,60B,64B
Rose, Brent	LA0800	64C,29A,13A,13B,13C
Rosenak, Karen	CA5000	13A,13C,43
Rosenblum, Henry	NY1860	31B,61,20F,13C
Ross, Elaine M.	CA1075	13A,13B,13C
Rush, Tobias	CO0950	13B,13C,13A
Russell, Eileen Meyer	TX2650	63D,13,13C,49,63C
Russell, Nathan	TX3370	36,11,61,13C
Russell, Scott	IN1450	63B,13B,13C
Ryan, Thomas K.	OH0350	64E,13B,13C,13D,13E
Ryberg, J. Stanley	IL1085	13B,13C,12A,63C,63D
Ryner, Jayson	IA1170	32C,36,61,11,13C
Sabine, David	AA0032	35,13A,13C,37,65
Saelzer, Pablo	MD0550	11,13A,13C,38,62A
Saladino, Jean	WI1100	61,36,13C
Salanki, Hedi	FL2100	13C,13E,66A,66H,41
Saltzman, James A.	NJ0300	64E,29,13C
Samolesky, Jeremy	AL0200	66A,66D,13C
Sampen, Maria	WA1000	62A,13C,42
Sandberg, Scott	ND0400	64,13B,13C,11,48
Sanders, Trevor	AA0110	13A,70,13B,13C
Santo, Joseph A.	DC0050	10A,10F,13B,13H,13C
Sargent, Joseph	AL1200	11,12A,13B,13C
Saulter, Gerry	NY1275	12A,13C,70,42,41
Savage, Jeffrey R.	WA1150	66A,66B,66C,13C
Schachnick, Gilson	MA0260	13C
Schmidt, Timothy	NY2950	70,11,13C
Schmitz, Eric B.	NY3770	47,65,13B,13C,10A
Schroeder, Joy A.	MI1500	32B,13A,13C
Schroeder, Karen	OH1350	13C
Schultz, Margaret	NE0460	13C,66A,66C,11,32B
Schutt, Jackie T.	IL2050	32,13C,36
Schwindt, Dan	CO0830	13C,70
Sclater, James	MS0400	13E,10F,10,13C
Scoles, Shannon	MI2250	13C
Scott, Chris	IL0100	36,61,13C
Scott, Laurie	MN1600	13A,13C,64A
Seal, Mary Griffin	FL0680	13A,13C
Segrest, Linda H.	MS0550	13A,13B,66A,66D,13C
Seitz, Paul T.	MO1800	13A,13B,13C
Seligman, Susan	NY3760	13A,13C,11,41,62C
Seto, Mark	CT0100	11,12,13A,13C,38
Seward, Philip	IL0720	13,13B,13C,13E
Shabani, Afrim	IL2510	11,10,13,34B,13C
Shade, Timothy	KS0200	63D,38,37,13C,32E
Shadinger, Marilyn	TN0100	13C
Shaffer, Rebecca Boehm	IA0950	63B,49,12A,32E,13C
Sharer, Marty	PA0500	11,37,12A,13A,13C
Sharples, Pamela	NJ0750	13C,36,66A,66C
Shaw, Timothy B.	PA2800	13B,13C,10A,13
Sheldon, Vanessa R.	CA3265	12,13C,13A,62E,66A
Shen, Yang	FL1125	66C,66D,13C
Shin, MinKyoo	IL3100	13C,66A,66D,66G
Shinn, Barbara A.	AL0800	13C,13B,13A,66D
Shively, Victoria	MI1750	13B,13C,12A
Shook, Thomas M.	WA1350	29,13B,13C
Silver, Noreen	ME0440	42,32E,13C,62C
Simonovic Schiff, Jelena	OR0850	13C,13B
Sisauyhoat, Neil	TX0550	65,50,13A,13C
Skinner, Josh	ID0060	12,13A,13B,13C,62D
Skinner, Kate	ID0060	12,13A,13B,13C,61
Slominski, Johnandrew	NY1100	13B,13C,13E,13H
Smale, Marcelyn	MN1300	32A,13C,66D,32B,32D
Smalley, Charles	AZ0150	13C,11,36,61,20G
Smith, Douglas	AB0050	13A,13,10,13C,12
Smith, Elizabeth	IN0700	13C,62A
Smith, Marcie	UT0190	66A,66D,13C,11
Smith, Ross	LA0050	11,66A,13A,13B,13C
Smith, Susan K.	MO0800	61,13C
Snodgrass, Jennifer Sterling	NC0050	13,13F,13C,13H,13G
Soares, Luciana	LA0450	66A,66C,13F,51,13C
Sobolewski, Susan F.	NY2550	66D,13C,42,66A
Solomon, Marisa	ME0440	13C
Solomon, Nanette Kaplan	PA3100	12A,66A,13C,15
Sonenberg, Daniel M.	ME0500	10A,13F,13C,10,13
Song, Anna	OR0450	13C,36,55B,55A,40
Soroka, Michele R.	MI1750	13B,13C
Sorroche, Juan	PR0150	13A,11,70,13C
Spelius, Susan M.	ID0075	11,66D,13B,13C
Spencer, Mia	WA0050	13A,13B,13C,61
Spitler, Carolyn	IN1250	64A,66A,13B,13C,66G
St. Julien, Marcus	LA0300	13B,13C,61,66G
Stanek, Mark	IN0100	70,13B,13C,41
Stanley, Ed L.	PA1400	64B,42,13A,13C,11
Stanojevic, Vera	OH0350	13B,13C,13F
Stanziano, Stephen	OH1000	13A,13B,13C,10,62D
Stapleson, Donald	MD0750	46,47,64E,13C
Star, Allison	AC0050	13A,13C
Steele, Edward L.	LA0400	12A,13A,13B,13C,61
Steinke, David	FL0950	13C,13A,13B
Stellrecht, Eric	NC0650	66A,66C,13C
Stephan-Robinson, Anna K.	WV0600	13B,13C,13F
Stern, Kalai	HI0110	11,36,40,13A,13C
Stevens, Daniel B.	DE0150	13B,13C
Stewart, Jeremy	VT0050	13A,13B,13C
Stewart, Tobin E.	FL0680	51,13A,13C
Stiver, David Keith	OH0755	61,13C
Strauser, Matthew L.	OR0175	36,60,13C,32D
Strauss, Virginia F.	IA0950	62A,13C,13D
Streator, Carol	IN1050	61,13C
Suchy-Pilalis, Jessica R.	NY3780	13,62E,13H,13C,31A
Sullivan, Nick A.	AA0200	63D,63C,13C
Sullivan, Timothy R.	NY3780	13,13A,13B,13C
Supko, John	NC0600	10A,13B,13C,13D,10B
Suzano, L. Armenio	VA0650	20F,11,13C,41,64
Swanson, Christopher	VA0700	13C,61,12A,11,39
Swanson, Philip	MA1650	63C,10A,13B,13C,13F
Swiatkowski, Chet	CA3150	13B,13C,13E,66A
Swinden, Kevin J.	AG0600	13,13B,13C
Sydow, Holly	PA2250	13C,48
Syring, Natalie	OK1330	13A,13B,13C
Sze, Eva	NY2750	13B,13C,13F
Taavola, Kristin	CO0900	13,13H,13C
Tadlock, David	OH1400	61,13C,54,39
Takesue, Sumy A.	CA4450	13A,66,12F,13B,13C
Tall, Malinda	UT0350	13A,13B,13C,66A,66C
Tanaka, Rieko	MA2020	66C,13C,66A,66D
Taranto, Vernon	FL1650	10,11,13B,36,13C
Tashjian, Charmian	IL1085	13A,13B,13C
Taylor, Dowell	MS0350	11,13C,34
Taylor, Janet	MS0400	13B,13C,66A
Taylor, Steven	CO0150	39,61,31A,44,13C
Tchougounov, Evgueni	AG0170	66,66A,13C
Teel, Susan	TX0050	66A,32B,11,13C
Telesco, Paula	MA2030	13,13H,13C
Terenzi, Mark J.	NJ0700	36,40,60A,13C
Teske, Casey C.	PA0700	60B,13C,63B,11
Thaller, Gregg	IN0550	65,32,13C,38
Thayer, Heather	AR0500	63B,13C
Therrien, Gabrielle	AI0200	13C
Thibodeaux, Tatiana	CA4500	66,12A,13C,66C
Thimmesch, Richard	IA0650	13B,13C,32E,37,47
Thomas, Eric S.	TX0600	61,13C,13A,54
Thomas, John	MO1950	13B,13C,63B
Thomas, Robert E.	NY0700	10,13A,13B,13C,13D
Thompson, Barbara Tilden	PA2450	66A,66B,13C,13,13A
Thompson, Karin E.	WA1100	62C,20,12A,42,13C
Thompson, Paul	WI0817	36,13B,13C,11
Thoms, Jonas	OH2500	13,13C,63B,35
Thornton, Mary	TX2930	63A,29A,13B,13C
Thornton, Robert	FL1800	13C,13A
Threadgill, Gwen J.	AL1050	32B,13C,66A,66D
Thurmaier, David P.	FL0680	13,13C,13B,13E,13F
Till, Sophie	PA2200	62A,62B,13C,32E
Tonnu, Tuyen	IL1150	66A,66B,13B,13C
Toren-Immerman, Limor	CA0810	62A,62B,13C
Tormann, Cynthia	AG0250	66A,13C,66D
Tot, Zvonimir	IL3310	29,13,13C,70,47
Tranquilino, Armando	FL0700	13A,13B,13C,34B,12A
Triest, Amelia	CA5010	13A,13C,66D
Tripp, Scott	FL0700	13C
Truax, Jenean	PA0150	13A,13C,32D,61,66A
Trubow, Valentina	IN1560	61,13C,13B
Tsabary, Eldad	AI0070	10B,12A,13C
Turgeon, Melanie E.	AA0035	60,36,42,13C,32D
Turner, Mitchell	GA1200	13A,13B,13C,13F,13G
Turner, Veronica R.	CO0350	61,13A,13B,13C,13D
Turnquist-Steed, Melody	KS0150	11,13C,31,44,66G
Ullman, Richard	VT0100	70,67D,13C
Unger, Shannon M.	OK0550	61,11,13C,39
Unrau, Lucia	OH0250	66A,66B,66D,13C
Urban, Tim	NJ1130	13C
Utsch, Glenn R.	PA3100	13C,66A,29A,66D
Vaillancourt, Paul	GA0550	65,50,13C,43
Van Brunt, Nancy	WI0960	13A,13B,13C,66D,40
van der Westhuizen, Petrus	OH0950	66A,66C,66D,13B,13C
Vandegriff, Matthew	NY2105	10,13C
Vanderkooy, Christine	AJ0100	66A,66B,66C,13C
VanDessel, Peter	MI0520	13C,66A,66D,13E
VanDyke, Susanne	MS0575	36,61,13B,13C
Vangjel, Matthew S.	AR0730	63A,46,13C
VanRandwyk, Carol A.	MI0850	13,13C,66A,13D
Vaughan, Jennie	TX2050	13A,13B,13C,66A,11
Vauth, Henning	WV0400	66A,66C,66D,13C
Vazquez, Carlos	PR0150	10A,10B,10F,13A,13C
Viliunas, Brian	AL0800	64C,38,13C,32E,60B
Vogel, Allan	CA0510	12A,55B,64B,13C
Volker, Mark D.	TN0100	10,10A,10B,13C
Vorwerk, Paul	CA0510	60,13C,12A
Wadley, Darin J.	SD0600	65,50,13A,13C,38
Waggoner, Dori	MO0100	13E,10F,64A,37,13C
Wagner, David O.	MI1260	12A,13B,13C,35,66G
Wahl, Shelbie L.	VA0550	13C,36
Waldron, Richard	WA0300	11,13A,13H,13K,13C
Walker, Gayle	OH2050	13C,60,12A,36
Walker, Jeri	OK1150	32,13C
Walker, Jesse	GA0150	13A,63C,63D,13B,13C
Wallace, James A.	GA1070	36,13C,40,11
Wanken, Matthew	IL0420	12A,13A,13B,13C
Ward, Brian	WA1150	66A,10D,13C,14C,29A
Ward, Michael	TN0850	66A,13C
Warner, Douglas G.	TN0850	11,63D,13B,13C,63C
Warren, John	IL1900	36,11,12A,13B,13C
Watanabe, Hisao	OR0350	13C,13D,13F,38,66D
Waters, Becky	AL1160	10A,11,13C
Waters, Sarah S.	OH1800	13B,13C,12A
Watson, Anne	OK0550	64C,13A,13B,13C,20
Wayne, Nicholas	MN0200	61,13C
Weber, Deanna F.	GA0150	13A,13B,13C,13D,61
Wegge, Glen T.	IA1750	13C,13B,13G,64C
Wells Chenoweth, Andrea	OH2250	61,13A,13C
Wells, Bradley C.	MA2250	13C,36,40,60A,61
Wells, Rebecca Schaffer	KY1300	13A,13B,13C,13D,13E
Whatley, Jay K.		13B,13C,66D,66C,66G
Wheeldon, Marianne	TX3510	13,13C
Wheeler, W. Keith	TN1550	36,61,13C,11
Whitcomb, Benjamin	WI0865	62C,13C,13E,13K,13
Whitmore, Peter	OR0500	13B,13C
Wickelgren, John	MD0300	66A,13C,66C,66D
Wiens, Paul W.	IL3550	13C,60A,36
Wiksyk, Crystal	AB0210	13A,13B,13C,13H
Wilcox, Mark	TX1650	13C,63A,49,29E,29C
Wilding, Jamie	OH2150	13B,13C
Wiliams, David B.	TN1850	13C,36
Wilkins, Colette	PA0550	13C
Willet, Gene K.	OH0200	13B,13C,13D,13E
Williams, Catherine	MI0300	66A,13C
Williams, Patrick C.	MT0400	10A,13,13C,13D,10
Williams, Richard	GA0550	13B,13C
Williamson, Richard A.	SC0050	13C,36,40,60A
Wilson, Darcel	MA0260	13C
Wilson, Jacqueline M.	WI0803	64D,48,13B,13C
Wilson, Jill	IA1100	63B,36,32B,60,13C
Wilson, Miranda	ID0250	13C,41,42,62D,62C
Withers, Lisa Ann	VA0350	66A,66C,13B,13C,13F
Wolfe, Jennifer	MI1050	13C,66C,12A,11
Wolff, Lisa	NV0100	36,40,61,13C
Wood, Rose Ann	CA2050	13A,13B,13C,11,66D
Wood, Stanley D.	OH1600	32,36,66D,13C,34
Wood, Zeno D.	NY0500	66F,13C
Woods, Chris P.	IL1050	13A,10F,13C,49,63
Woodworth, William	TN1450	64B,13B,13C,41,66G
Worthen, Mary	AR0500	61,13B,13C
Wright, Richard	NY4050	13,11,13C,66A,38
Wright-FitzGerald, Jesse	CA0960	13C
Wright-FitzGerald, Jesse	CA3500	13C
Xiques, David	CA4200	13A,13C,36
Yamamoto, Travis S.	CO0830	66A,11,13C
Yang, Zhao	WA0950	66C,13A,13B,13C,13D
Yanish, Dorothy	NH0110	61,13C
Yankeelov, Margie L.	TN0100	13C
Yee, Thomas	HI0210	13C,66A,66C,66B
Yeung, Alwen	GA1000	11,66C,13C,66D
Yih, Annie	CA3600	13B,13C
Yih, Annie	CA5060	13,13I,13C
Young, Sam	CO0550	13C
Young, Susan	AB0150	61,36,13C,39
Yun, Francis Y.	NJ0800	13A,13B,13C
Zahler, Clara	PA0550	32,13C
Zell, Steven D.	TX0390	13A,13B,13C,11,66A
Zezelj-Gualdi, Danijela	NC2440	62A,62B,13C
Zoolalian, Linda A.	CA3650	66A,66C,13C

Counterpoint

Adams, Daniel C.	TX3150	10A,13D,13E,65,13
Anderson, Allen L.	NC2410	10A,13B,13D,13E,13F
Atlas, Raphael	MA1750	13A,13,13F,13D
Barber, Daniel R.	OH0650	66A,13D,12A,66G
Bean, Shirley Ann	MO1810	13A,13B,13C,13D,13E
Benitez, Vincent P.	PA2750	13F,13D,13B,13J,13
Bergeron, Andrew	MI0850	70,13A,13D
Berry, David Carson	OH2200	13,13I,13D,13J
Bohlen, Donald A.	NY3725	10A,10F,13D,10
Bonkowski, Anita	AB0150	29A,29B,13A,13B,13D
Boone, Geraldine T.	VA0950	10A,32,11,13D,13F
Boudreault, Mary	NC2700	63B,13A,13D,13E,13B
Bradshaw, Daniel	HI0050	13D,42,41
Brown, Jenine	MI1260	13D,13E
Brown, Matthew	NY1100	13B,13D,13I,13J
Brown, Stephen	AB0210	10,13A,13B,13C,13D
Burr, Anthony	CA5050	64C,43,13D,14C,12D
Burton, Sean Michael	IA0100	36,61,41,11,13D
Callon, Gordon J.	AF0050	12A,13D
Carr, William	PA1550	13B,66D,66A,13D
Casano, Steven	HI0210	13A,13B,13C,13D
Caulkins, Tamara	WA1200	70,13A,13B,13C,13D
Chambers, Robert	OK1250	38,63C,63D,13D,10F
Chang, Yu-Hui	MA0500	10A,10F,13B,13D,13F
Charke, Derek	AF0050	13D,13E,10,13
Cherrington Beggs, Sally	SC0900	13D,66,31A,12A
Chioldi, Ronald	OK0550	13B,66A,66D,13D,13E
Connell, Robin L.	MI0850	13D
Coxe, Stephen	VA1000	13A,13B,13D,10
Curlee, J. Matthew	NY1100	13A,13B,13C,13D,13K
Dahn, Luke	IA1200	66A,13B,13C,13D,13E
Daigle, Paulin	AI0190	13B,13D,13E
Davis, Joel Scott	CA2810	10,13D
Doolittle, Emily L.	WA0200	10A,13,13D
Dries, Eric	CA0815	13,13E,13D,29A,66
Elswick, Beth L.	MO1810	13A,13B,13C,13D
Eng, Clare Sher Ling	TN0100	13,13B,13D,63B,66A
Engelsdorfer, Amy L.	IA0950	13,13D
Feigin, Joel	CA5060	10,10A,10F,13D
Felice, Frank	IN0250	10,10B,10D,34D,13D
Forrester, Sheila	FL1675	10A,13,66D,13D,13E
Frank, Bruce	NY1100	13B,13C,13D,13H,13I
Golightly, John Wesley	KY0650	12A,31A,66,34,13D
Greitzer, Mary	NY1100	13C,13D,13E,13F,13H
Gross, Robert W.	TX2150	13B,13D,13E,13F,13I
Guerrero, Rosi E.	WA0950	66A,66D,13A,13B,13D
Ha, Youngmi	NY2750	10A,10E,13B,13C,13D
Haakenson, Matthew A.	FL1750	10A,66G,13,13D,13J
Hagelstein, Kim Rooney	TX2750	12A,13D,32E,63B
Hanlon, Kenneth	NV0050	13B,13D
Harlen, Benjamin	LA0400	10A,31A,13B,13C,13D
Harris, Carole J.	NY0400	13A,13B,13C,13D
Hatley, H. Jerome	OK0850	10,61,34,13D
Hedges, John B.	NY3760	13B,13D,13E,10
Heighway, Robbi A.	WI0450	11,13C,13D,66B,66D
Henderson, Jean	NE0450	13A,13B,13C,13D,10A
Hennessy, Jeff	AF0050	13D,13E
Hileman, Lynn	WV0750	64D,13C,13B,13A,13D
Hoag, Melissa E.	MI1750	13B,13C,13D,13E,13F
Hoffman, Steven	WY0200	66G,13D
Horton, Charles T.	AC0100	66A,13D,13E,13F
Hutter, Greg J.	IL0750	13C,13D,10A,11
Itoh, Takuma	HI0210	10A,13A,13B,13C,13D
James, Matthew H.	LA0770	61,13D,39,54,60A
Jefcoat, Priscilla	GA0350	13A,66A,10F,12A,13D
Jex, David	OH2300	13B,13C,13D,10,29
Jones, John W.	PA1400	13B,13C,13D,13E,10A
Jones, Ryan C.	NY1600	13C,13D,13A
Julian, Michael	CA2750	35D,35C,35G,13C,13D
Kechley, David S.	MA2250	10A,10F,13A,13B,13D
Keever, Howard	MS0850	10A,10D,13A,13B,13D
Kennedy, Nathan	MN0610	13A,13B,13C,13D,13F
Kenote, Marie Herseth	NY2900	64A,12A,13B,13C,13D
Klakowich, Robert	AA0020	13A,13B,13C,13D,13E
Krause, Drew S.	NY2750	13A,13B,13C,13D,13F
Krebs, Jesse D.	MO1780	11,64C,13D,48
Krumbholz, Gerald A.	WA0950	13A,13B,13C,13D,10C
Leathwood, Jonathan	CO0900	70,41,13D,10A,13E
Leblanc, Mario	AI0200	13C,13D
Lentsner, Dina	OH0350	12A,13B,13C,13D,13E
Lewis, Huw R.	MI1050	13D,66G,66H,31A
Liang, Lei	CA5050	10,13B,13D,10A,10B
Lin, James	CA5510	13A,13B,42,13C,13D
Lind, Stephanie	AG0250	13B,13D,13E,13F
Long, Daniel	TX2200	36,61,60,11,13D
Lorenz, Ralph	OH1100	13,34,10,13F,13D
Lukowicz, Thomas	OH2500	11,63D,13,13D,13E
MacFarlane, Thomas	NY2750	13C,13D,13F,12A,12B
Maddox, Timothy	NC1075	11,13A,13B,13C,13D
Mann, Ted	NH0150	70,14C,13D
Marlowe, Sarah	NY2750	13,13C,13D,13H,13I
Masci, Michael J.	NY3730	11,13A,13B,13C,13D
Mavromatis, Panayotis	NY2750	13B,13D,13F,13G,13K
McCulloch, Doug	HI0210	13A,13B,13C,13D
Metcalf, Joanne	WI0350	10A,13D,13F,12A,31G
Mickey, Patricia A.	MO1780	63B,11,13D
Miller, Bruce E.	CA1075	13D,13E,13F
Molinaro, Anthony G.	IL1615	66A,29,13A,13B,13D
Monahan, Seth	NY1100	13B,13C,13D,13E
Morrow, Ruth E.	TX1700	66,12A,66A,13D,13E
Nangle, Richard P.	MA2030	13B,13C,13D,13E,13F
Neal, Mary Elizabeth	AL0300	13A,13B,13C,13D
Neske, Joe	MO1950	13D,13E
Nicholeris, Carol A.	MA0510	10A,13D,13A,36,13
Nitzberg, Roy J.	NY0642	13A,13B,13C,13D
Papador, Nicholas G.	AG0550	13A,13B,13D,65,32E
Patty, Austin T.	TN0850	13A,13B,13C,13D
Perriment, Andrew	AB0200	13D,13C
Ponte, Nora	PR0150	10A,13A,13B,13C,13D
Potter, Shelley	WA0950	51,62A,20,13A,13D
Raboy, Asher	CA3400	37,13D,10F,13E,11
Ramirez, Armando L.	PR0115	10,13A,13B,13D,13F
Randall, Jean	MI1830	66A,13D,13E,13B
Reed, Douglas	IN1600	66G,66H,13D,31A
Reese, Randall	GA0200	10F,47,64E,10A,13D
Rodriguez Alvira, Jose	PR0115	13A,34,13B,13D,13G
Rogers, John E.	NH0350	13B,10,13D,13E,13G
Ryan, Thomas K.	OH0350	64E,13B,13C,13D,13E
Saya, Mark	CA2800	13B,10A,13D,13E,13F
Schiavo, Joseph C.	NJ1100	13B,13D,12A,13F,13
Seiler, Richard D.	LA0770	66A,66C,13A,13D
Shchegolev, Aleksey	AI0200	13D
Silver, Sheila	NY3790	13B,13D,13E,10A,10F
Slottow, Stephen	TX3420	13I,13D,13F,13
Spring, Howard	AG0350	14,70,29,12A,13D
Stevlingson, Norma	WI0860	13B,12A,66G,13E,13D
Stinson, Scott	FL1900	10A,10F,13D,13F
Strauman, Edward	PA0650	10F,29A,13D,13B,35A
Strauss, Virginia F.	IA0950	62A,13C,13D
Stucky, Steven	NY0900	10,13B,13D,13F,43
Supko, John	NC0600	10A,13B,13C,13D,10B
Susa, Conrad	CA4150	10,13D
Suter, Anthony	CA5150	13D,13E,10
Taylor, Larry Clark	VA0100	66A,66G,13B,13D,13E
Terefenko, Dariusz	NY1100	13B,13D,13E,13H,29
Thomas, Robert E.	NY0700	10,13A,13B,13C,13D
Turner, Veronica R.	CO0350	61,13A,13B,13C,13D
Vaclavik, Jude	UT0300	13,13A,13B,13D
VanDessel, Joan	MI0520	12A,13D,37,64C,48
VanRandwyk, Carol A.	MI0850	13,13C,66A,13D
Wason, Robert W.	NY1100	13B,13D,13F,13J,29C
Watanabe, Hisao	OR0350	13C,13D,13F,38,66D
Weber, Deanna F.	GA0150	13A,13B,13C,13D,61
Webster, James	NY0900	12,13B,13D,13I
Wells, Rebecca Schaffer	KY1300	13A,13B,13C,13D,13E
Wheaton, J. Randall	VA0600	13B,13D,13A,13I,13F
Wiemann, Beth	ME0440	10F,64C,34,10A,13D
Willet, Gene K.	OH0200	13B,13C,13D,13E
Williams, Patrick C.	MT0400	10A,13,13C,13D,10
Yang, Zhao	WA0950	66C,13A,13B,13C,13D

Formal Analysis

Aceto, Jonathan D.	GA0950	51,62A,11,62B,13E
Adams, Daniel C.	TX3150	10A,13D,13E,65,13
Anderson, Allen L.	NC2410	10A,13B,13D,13E,13F
Anderson, David	WI0100	66A,38,66C,13E,42
Annicchiarico, Michael	NH0350	13B,13C,13E,10
Baer, Sarah	PA2450	64B,55B,12A,13E
BaileyShea, Matthew	NY1100	13B,13E,13F,13I
BaileyShea, Matthew L.	NY4350	13,13E
Bain, Jennifer	AF0100	13E,13F,13B,13J,13
Baker, Jan Berry	GA1050	64E,11,13E
Baker, Michael	KY1450	13,13C,13E,13G,13I
Barrett, Dan	ME0440	13E,63C
Beach, David	AG0450	13E,13I,13J
Bean, Shirley Ann	MO1810	13A,13B,13C,13D,13E
Beaudet, Luce	AI0200	13B,13C,13E
Belet, Brian	CA4400	10,13B,13C,13E,13F
Bevelander, Brian E.	OH0950	66A,10A,10B,13E,13G
Biro, Daniel Peter	AB0150	13B,13C,13E,13F,10A
Black, Brian	AA0200	12,66C,13E
Boudreault, Mary	NC2700	63B,13A,13D,13E,13B
Brisson, Eric	MN1700	13A,13B,13C,13E,66C
Broman, Per F.	OH0300	13F,13C,13E,12B,13
Brown, Jenine	MI1260	13D,13E
Butler, Charles Mark	MS0250	63B,32B,13E,13B,66G
Butler, Steve	CA5550	10,13,34,10A,13E
Carpenter, Alexander	AA0110	12,13C,13B,11,13E
Cavanagh, Lynn	AJ0100	13B,13E,13F,13J,13I
Ceide, Manuel J.	PR0115	13F,10A,13A,13B,13E
Charke, Derek	AF0050	13D,13E,10,13
Chien, Gloria	TN0850	13C,13E,66A,66B
Chioldi, Ronald	OK0550	13B,66A,66D,13D,13E
Cifelli, Cheryl L.	MO0800	64C,64D,12A,11,13E
Cimarusti, Thomas M.	TX3200	12A,13E,20,12C,68
Cochran, Alfred W.	KS0650	12A,13A,13B,13E
Cockey, Linda E.	MD0800	12A,66A,66B,13E
Dahn, Luke	IA1200	66A,13B,13C,13D,13E
Daigle, Paulin	AI0190	13B,13D,13E
de Murga, Manuel	FL1750	10,10F,13E,34,43
Deguchi, Tomoko	SC1200	13,66A,13F,13E,13A
Dell Aquila, Paul	KY1500	13E
Dello Joio, Justin N.	NY2750	13B,13E,13F,10A,10F
Dent, Cedric	TN1100	12A,10D,35A,13E
Devaney, Johanna C.	OH1850	13B,13E,13G,13K,13L
DeWitt, Timothy L.	WV0050	49,63A,13E,63B,63C
Dickens, Pierce	GA0400	13A,13B,13C,13E,66A
Dickey, Timothy J.	OH2000	11,12A,13E
Dimitrov, Georges	AI0200	13A,13E
Dougherty, Peggy S.	OR0175	66A,66D,13A,66B,13E
Drews, Michael R.	IN0907	13A,13B,13C,13E,11
Dries, Eric	CA0815	13,13E,13D,29A,66
Duquaine, Kenneth	MI2120	64,13E
Eckert, Stefan	IL0800	13,13J,13E
Erdmann, Thomas R.	NC0750	11,38,13E,13F,63A
Fassler-Kerstetter, Jacqueline	KS0650	63B,13E,13B
Fogle, Megan R.	SC0350	13A,13B,13C,13E,13F
Forrester, Sheila	FL1675	10A,13,66D,13D,13E
Gifford, Gene	AL1250	13A,61,13E
Girdham, Jane C.	MI1850	11,12A,13B,13C,13E
Goldstein, Perry	NY3790	13A,13C,13E,10A,13F
Greene, Richard C.	GA0850	70,13C,11,13E,12A
Greitzer, Mary	NY1100	13C,13D,13E,13F,13H
Gross, Robert W.	TX2150	13B,13D,13E,13F,13I
Guenther, Roy J.	DC0100	13E,13F,11,12A
Guerrero, Jean	NY1100	13B,13E,13F,13J
Hansen, Mark R.	ID0050	66A,13E,11,66G
Hedges, John B.	NY3760	13B,13D,13E,10
Heetderks, David	OH1700	10A,13C,13E,60
Heine, Erik	OK0750	13,13B,10C,13E
Hennessy, Jeff	AF0050	13D,13E
Hevia, Lonnie	MD0850	13,13E,13C,10
Hillyer, Dirk M.	MA1650	63B,11,12A,13E,13F
Hisama, Ellie M.	NY0750	15,13E,12A,10B,13F
Hoag, Melissa E.	MI1750	13B,13C,13D,13E,13F
Hodges, Woodrow	WI0250	13,13E,32E,64D
Holm-Hudson, Kevin	KY1450	13F,13,10A,13E,13H
Horton, Charles T.	AC0100	66A,13D,13E,13F
Hsu, Samuel	PA2800	12A,66A,66B,13E
Hunnicutt, Bradley C.	NC2300	13,66,34,13A,13E
Hutson, Danny J.	AL0010	12A,13E,60,63C
Jenkins, Pamela	ME0340	64A,64C,64E,32,13E
Johnson, Ken	IN1025	13E,70
Jones, John W.	PA1400	13B,13C,13D,13E,10A
Keiler, Allan R.	MA0500	11,12A,12D,13E,13J
Kilstofte, Mark F.	SC0750	10,13,43,13E
Kim, Kunyoung	PA0250	66A,13E,11,66B
Klakowich, Robert	AA0020	13A,13B,13C,13D,13E
Knier, Veronica T.	MD1020	13B,13E,66
Kunz, Jean-Willy	AI0200	13B,13E
Landers, Joseph	AL1200	10A,10F,13B,13C,13E
Leathwood, Jonathan	CO0900	70,41,13D,10A,13E
Lee, Amanda	TX2570	66A,13C,13B,13E,66B
Lentsner, Dina	OH0350	12A,13B,13C,13D,13E
Levy, Fabien	NY0750	10A,10F,13E,13F
Lind, Stephanie	AG0250	13B,13D,13E,13F
Lobitz, Beverly	AR0800	13E,11,12A,61,13C
Lochhead, Judith	NY3790	13E,13F,12,13,12A
Longtin, Michel	AI0200	10,13E
Lukowicz, Thomas	OH2500	11,63D,13,13D,13E
Marinescu, Liviu	CA0835	10A,13E,13F,10
Martins, Jose Oliveira	NY1100	13B,13E,13F

Index by Area of Teaching Interest 491

McAneny, Marc	MA0500	13B,13E,13F,10A
McCachren, Renee	NC0350	13,12A,66A,13E,13J
McCarrey, Scott	HI0050	66A,66B,13E,12A,11
McGowan, Sean C.	CO0830	13A,13B,13C,13E,29B
McIntire, Dennis K.	GA1700	36,13E
McManus, Lanny	AL0550	32D,36,12,13E,40
Melbinger, Timothy	PA2710	12A,41,13B,13C,13E
Meyer, Sandra G.	OK0650	13B,13C,13E,66A,13
Miller, Bruce E.	CA1075	13D,13E,13F
Miller, DaVaughn	NC1150	36,13E,20B,60
Minor, Ryan	NY3790	12A,12D,12B,11,13E
Monahan, Seth	NY1100	13B,13C,13D,13E
Moore, Anthony	NC1450	10F,13G,13E
Moore, Kathy Bundock	CO0950	62E,13B,13C,13E
Morrow, Ruth E.	TX1700	66,12A,66A,13D,13E
Moschenross, Ian	IL1800	12A,13E,20,66A,66G
Moylan, William D.	MA2030	35C,13E
Muniz, Jennifer	MO0100	66A,66D,13C,13E
Nangle, Richard P.	MA2030	13B,13C,13D,13E,13F
Neilson, Duncan	OR0150	13A,13B,10,13C,13E
Neske, Joe	MO1950	13D,13E
Newbrough, William J.	NY1700	66A,66B,13C,13E,66C
Nichols, Jeff	NY0600	10A,13E,10F
Niedermaier, Edward G.	IL0550	13B,13C,13E
Norris, Renee Lapp	PA1900	14C,12A,20,12,13E
Northrop, Jonathan	CT0050	13A,13B,13C,13E
Ohriner, Mitchell S.	VA1350	13,13K,13E
Olivieri, Emmanuel	PR0115	62B,13E,13F
Perrotte, Jean-Paul	NV0100	10,13B,13F,13G,13E
Peters, Mark	IL3100	11,20,13E,12
Phipps, Danny K.	MI0900	64D,12A,12C,13E
Powell, William E.	CA0510	48,64C,42,13E
Raboy, Asher	CA3400	37,13D,10F,13E,11
Ramsey, Cynthia B.	VA0750	66A,12A,66C,13E,42
Randall, Jean	MI1830	66A,13D,13E,13B
Read, Kenneth E.	OH0550	13E,31A,10A,10F,13B
Retif, T. N.	GA0400	13E,12A,61,44
Rogers, John E.	NH0350	13B,10,13D,13E,13G
Rothfarb, Lee	CA5060	13J,13I,13B,13E,13
Roy, Joseph	AG0170	70,13E
Rupprecht, Philip	NC0600	12A,12D,13E,13F
Ryan, Thomas K.	OH0350	64E,13B,13C,13D,13E
Sala, Karen	IL1240	13A,13B,13E,13F,61
Salanki, Hedi	FL2100	13C,13E,66A,66H,41
Samuel, Jamuna	NY3790	11,12A,13E,12B,13F
Sarver, Sarah	OK0750	13,13E
Saunders, David E.	ID0050	63B,60B,13E,12A
Saya, Mark	CA2800	13B,10A,13D,13E,13F
Scelba, Anthony	NJ0700	12A,13E,11,62D
Schildt, Matthew C.	CO0050	13,10,10D,13E,34
Schneider, David	KY1000	13,13E
Scholl, Tim	TX2550	13A,13E,32A,66,70
Schorr, Timothy B.	WI1100	66A,12A,13E,66C
Schuster-Craig, John	MI0900	13E,12A,13F,13B
Sclater, James	MS0400	13E,10F,10,13C
Sessoms, Sydney	NC1150	13E,32E,37,60B,11
Seward, Philip	IL0720	13,13B,13C,13E
Sheinbaum, John J.	CO0900	12,13E,11,12A
Shufro, Joseph L.	IA1100	10F,13E,34,38,62C
Silver, Sheila	NY3790	13B,13D,13E,10A,10F
Sipes, Diana	TX2930	64A,12A,13E,42
Slominski, Johnandrew	NY1100	13B,13C,13E,13H
Sobaskie, James William	MS0500	13,13E,10F,13I,12
Stevens, James M.	TN0580	10A,36,13E,13B
Stevlingson, Norma	WI0860	13B,12A,66G,13E,13D
Sulton, Randall S.	TX0600	66A,66C,13E,13B,13F
Suter, Anthony	CA5150	13D,13E,10
Swiatkowski, Chet	CA3150	13B,13C,13E,66A
Taylor, Allan	MA2100	13E,66G,36
Taylor, Larry Clark	VA0100	66A,66G,13B,13D,13E
Terefenko, Dariusz	NY1100	13B,13D,13E,13H,29
Thomson, Susan N.	GA0950	13B,13E,66A,13
Thurmaier, David P.	FL0680	13,13C,13B,13E,13F
Todd, R. Larry	NC0600	12A,13J,12C,13E,13I
Todd, Richard	TN1400	13E,13F,41,70
Truitt, D. Charles	PA2200	70,13,41,13E,13B
Valente, Liana	FL1550	61,38,13E,39,12A
Van Boer, Bertil H.	WA1250	13E,12,55,12A
Vander Weg, John D.	MI2200	13B,13F,13E,13
VanDessel, Peter	MI0520	13C,66A,66D,13E
Waggener, Joshua A.	NC2350	12A,38,13E
Waggoner, Dori	MO0100	13E,10F,64A,37,13C
Wang, Jing	MA2020	34,13B,13E,13F
Warshaw, Dalit Hadass	MA0350	10,13,66A,10F,13E
Wells, Rebecca Schaffer	KY1300	13A,13B,13C,13D,13E
Whitcomb, Benjamin	WI0865	62C,13C,13E,13K,13
Willet, Gene K.	OH0200	13B,13C,13D,13E
Winston, Jeremy	OH2400	36,61,47,13E,60A
Wiskus, Jessica	PA1050	13J,12A,13E,13
Womack, Donald Reid	HI0210	10,13,13E,10A,10F
Wood, Eric	CA5350	10A,11,20,13A,13E
Zent, Donald	KY0100	13E,66B,66A,66C,66D
Zipay, Terry L.	PA3700	13,35B,34A,13E,11
Zuidema, Jeannie	MT0175	13E,66D

20th Century Music Theory

Anderson, Allen L.	NC2410	10A,13B,13D,13E,13F
Atlas, Raphael	MA1750	13A,13,13F,13D
BaileyShea, Matthew	NY1100	13B,13E,13F,13I
Bain, Jennifer	AF0100	13E,13F,13B,13J,13
Batzner, Jay C.	MI0400	13,10,34,10A,13F
Bauer, Amy M.	CA5020	13,13F,12D
Belet, Brian	CA4400	10,13B,13C,13E,13F
Benitez, Vincent P.	PA2750	13F,13D,13B,13J,13
Biro, Daniel Peter	AB0150	13B,13C,13E,13F,10A
Blackmon, Odie	TN1850	13F
Boldt-Neurohr, Kirsten	WA0050	13A,13B,13C,13F
Boone, Geraldine T.	VA0950	10A,32,11,13D,13F
Bostonia, Marguerite	WV0800	66A,13F
Both, Christoph	AF0050	13F,62,34
Boyer, Douglas R.	TX3100	36,60,54,32D,13F
Broman, Per F.	OH0300	13F,13C,13E,12B,13
Carlson, Tammi	IL1890	13F,11,64A
Cavanagh, Lynn	AJ0100	13B,13E,13F,13J,13I
Ceide, Manuel J.	PR0115	13F,10A,13A,13B,13E
Chang, Yu-Hui	MA0500	10A,10F,13B,13D,13F
Cornicello, Anthony	CT0150	10,34,13,34D,13F
Couvillon, Thomas M.	KY0550	13,10B,10A,10,13F
Danby, Judd	IN1310	10,13,29B,10A,13F
Deguchi, Tomoko	SC1200	13,66A,13F,13E,13A
Dello Joio, Justin N.	NY2750	13B,13E,13F,10A,10F
Denman, James L.	OR1300	13,12A,66G,13F,13H
Devore, Richard O.	OH1100	13,34,10,20G,13F
Dunsby, Jonathan	NY1100	13F,13I,13K
Edwards, Carla Grace	IN0350	66G,13F
Erdmann, Thomas R.	NC0750	11,38,13E,13F,63A
Ewell, Philip	NY0625	13,13F,13I,62C
Ferenc, Anna	AG0600	13,13F
Fogle, Megan R.	SC0350	13A,13B,13C,13E,13F
Gehl, Robin	OH2200	12A,13,13F
Goldstein, Perry	NY3790	13A,13C,13E,10A,13F
Greco, Christopher J.	KS0100	13,10,64,64E,13F
Greitzer, Mary	NY1100	13C,13D,13E,13F,13H
Gross, Robert W.	TX2150	13B,13D,13E,13F,13I
Guenther, Roy J.	DC0100	13E,13F,11,12A
Guerrero, Jean	NY1100	13B,13E,13F,13J
Gullings, Kyle	TX3535	10,13,13F,10A
Guzzo, Anne M.	WY0200	13,10,12A,13F,15
Headlam, David	NY1100	13F,13G,13L,34A,34B
Heap, Matthew	DC0010	13,10,13F
Herman, Matthew James	VA1350	10,13,13F
Hilley, Dirk M.	MA1650	63B,11,12A,13E,13F
Hisama, Ellie M.	NY0750	15,13E,12A,10B,13F
Hoag, Melissa E.	MI1750	13B,13C,13D,13E,13F
Holm-Hudson, Kevin	KY1450	13F,13,10A,13E,13H
Honour, Eric C.	MO1790	10,34,13,13F,35C
Horton, Charles T.	AC0100	66A,13D,13E,13F
Kennedy, John M.	CA0830	10,13F,43,10F,13
Kennedy, Nathan	MN0610	13A,13B,13C,13D,13F
Kies, Christopher	NH0350	13B,10,66A,13F
Kim, Rebecca Y.	MA1450	11,13F
Klein, Michael L.	PA3250	13,13F
Krause, Drew S.	NY2750	13A,13B,13C,13D,13F
Krouseup, Jack	CA3520	10,13B,13A,13F,47
Lambert, Philip	NY0600	13,13F
Lester, Jason	TX3850	11,12A,13F,29A
Levy, Fabien	NY0750	10A,10F,13E,13F
Leydon, Rebecca	OH1700	13,13F,10C,10D
Lind, Stephanie	AG0250	13B,13D,13E,13F
Lochhead, Judith	NY3790	13E,13F,12,13,12A
Lorenz, Ralph	OH1100	13,34,10,13F,13D
MacFarlane, Thomas	NY2750	13C,13D,13F,12A,12B
Marinescu, Liviu	CA0835	10A,13E,13F,10
Martins, Jose Oliveira	NY1100	13B,13E,13F
Marvin, Elizabeth W.	NY1100	13A,13C,13F,13G,13K
Mavromatis, Panayotis	NY2750	13B,13D,13F,13G,13K
McAneny, Marc	MA0500	13B,13E,13F,10A
McConville, Brendan P.	TN1710	13,13F,13I,62C
McMahan, Robert Y.	NJ0175	13B,13C,13F,10B,10A
Metcalf, Joanne	WI0350	10A,13D,13F,12A,31G
Miller, Bruce E.	CA1075	13D,13E,13F
Montalto, Richard Michael	MS0550	13,12A,35,10,13F
Nangle, Richard P.	MA2030	13B,13C,13D,13E,13F
O'Donnell, Shaugn	NY0600	13F,14C
Oh, Seung-Ah	IL0750	10,13,13F,10A
Olivieri, Emmanuel	PR0115	62B,13E,13F
Perrotte, Jean-Paul	NV0100	10,13B,13F,13G,13E
Pfaff, William P.	NY3775	10,13,12A,13F,13I
Pieslak, Jonathan	NY0600	13F
Poudrier, Eve	CT0900	13,13I,13F,13K,13J
Raessler, Daniel	VA1125	11,12,13B,13F,13A
Ramirez, Armando L.	PR0115	10,13A,13B,13D,13F
Ransom, Judy L.	WY0115	13B,13F,36,40,66D
Ravenscroft, Brenda	AG0250	13,13F,13A
Reeves, Nicholas	NJ1000	13F
Reid, Darlene Chepil	AG0170	13F,13I,10
Rolf, Marie	NY1100	13B,13F,13H
Romig, James	IL3500	13,13F,10A,10
Rosenhaus, Steven L.	NY2750	10,13F,10F,10A,10D
Rupprecht, Philip	NC0600	12A,12D,13E,13F
Sala, Karen	IL1240	13A,13B,13E,13F,61
Samuel, Jamuna	NY3790	11,12A,13E,12B,13F
Saya, Mark	CA2800	13B,10A,13D,13E,13F
Schiavo, Joseph C.	NJ1100	13B,13D,12A,13F,13
Schuler, Nico S.	TX3175	13,12C,34B,13F
Schuster-Craig, John	MI0900	13E,12A,13F,13B
Schuttenheim, Tom	CT0650	10F,13F
Seigel, Lester C.	AL0300	60,36,39,66C,13F
Sierra, Roberto	NY0900	10A,10F,13B,13F
Slottow, Stephen	TX3420	13I,13D,13F,13
Snodgrass, Jennifer Sterling	NC0050	13,13F,13C,13H,13G
Soares, Luciana	LA0450	66A,66C,13F,51,13C
Sonenberg, Daniel M.	ME0500	10A,13F,13C,10,13
Stanojevic, Vera	OH0350	13B,13C,13F
Steege, Benjamin A.	NY3790	12A,12B,12C,13F,13
Stephan-Robinson, Anna K.	WV0600	13B,13C,13F
Stinson, Scott	FL1900	10A,10F,13D,13F
Stucky, Steven	NY0900	10,13B,13D,13F,43
Sulton, Randall S.	TX0600	66A,66C,13E,13B,13F
Swanson, Philip	MA1650	63C,10A,13B,13C,13F
Sze, Eva	NY2750	13B,13C,13F
Thurmaier, David P.	FL0680	13,13C,13B,13E,13F
Todd, Richard	TN1400	13E,13F,41,70
Trawick, Eleanor	IN0150	10,13,13F,13H,13L
Turner, Mitchell	GA1200	13A,13B,13C,13F,13G
Van Den Toorn, Pieter	CA5060	13,13F,13I
Vander Weg, John D.	MI2200	13B,13F,13E,13
Wang, Jing	MA2020	34,13B,13E,13F
Warren, Jeff	AB0090	12B,13F,47,62D
Waschka, Rodney A.	NC1700	10,12A,13F,10B,13
Wason, Robert W.	NY1100	13B,13D,13F,13J,29C
Watanabe, Hisao	OR0350	13C,13D,13F,38,66D
Wettstein Sadler, Shannon Leigh	MN0050	66A,66C,13F
Wheaton, J. Randall	VA0600	13B,13D,13A,13I,13F
White, Chris	IL2050	66A,13F,29A,29B,29C
Withers, Lisa Ann	VA0350	66A,66C,13B,13C,13F
Wlosok, Pavel	NC2600	47,13F,29,66A
Wohl, Daniel	NY3560	10,10A,13,13F

Computer Applications

Baker, Michael	KY1450	13,13C,13E,13G,13I
Bamberger, Jeanne	MA1200	13H,13K,13G,32F,13
Barlow, Clarence	CA5060	10A,10B,13G
Bevelander, Brian E.	OH0950	66A,10A,10B,13E,13G
Bogue, Bryan	WA1350	13G,10F
Bryan, David	LA0650	13G,13C,70
Burdick, Paul	MA1400	13G,13,34,32
Byrd, Joshua	GA2130	37,10A,13G,48,10F
Corbett, Ian	KS0590	10,34,35D,35G,13G
Devaney, Johanna C.	OH1850	13B,13E,13G,13K,13L
Erickson, Gary	IL1050	34B,10A,13G,31A,35D
Gaff, Isaac	IL1550	34,13G,13,35C,35G
Garcia, Tim	MO1950	13G
Griffin, Dennis	UT0300	50,34,65,13G,41
Headlam, David	NY1100	13F,13G,13L,34A,34B
Howiler, Robert W.	SC1000	34,10A,13G,10B
Huebl, Carolyn	TN1850	62A,13G,32F,34,11
Hunt, Trevor	MS0580	11,70,13C,13G
Johnson, Richard	KS0590	13G,32F,34D,35C,35D
Klein, Jim	PA1000	34,32F,45,13G,10C
Konye, Paul	NY3680	13G,12A,38,10,12
Lombardi, Paul	SD0600	13A,13G,10F,10A,13B

Name	Code	Areas
MacNaughton, Roger	MI0300	66A,13G,32F
Marvin, Elizabeth W.	NY1100	13A,13C,13F,13G,13K
Mavromatis, Panayotis	NY2750	13B,13D,13F,13G,13K
McAdams, Stephen	AI0150	13G,13K,34
Miller, Harold L.	WI0450	10,13A,13G,20,47
Moore, Anthony	NC1450	10F,13G,13E
Myers, Michael	NC1450	64,13G
Najar, Michael	CA3270	13G,36,40
Niezen, Richard S.	CO0150	62C,62D,13C,13G
Parker, Mark	SC0200	13A,32F,13B,13C,13G
Peck, Gordon	NM0400	70,13G
Perrotte, Jean-Paul	NV0100	10,13B,13F,13G,13E
Power, Brian E.	AG0050	62A,67,12A,12C,13G
Reeves, Gary L.	SD0600	60B,13G,37,63B
Richards, Eric	NE0600	47,10A,10D,13G
Riedel, Kimberly	NJ1130	13G,34
Riley, Justin	OH0350	34,35C,35D,35G,13G
Rodriguez Alvira, Jose	PR0115	13A,34,13B,13D,13G
Rogers, John E.	NH0350	13B,10,13D,13E,13G
Schubert, John	MI0200	11,47,13G
Shapero, Harold S.	MA0500	10A,13A,10B,13B,13G
Smith, Scott	CA1270	54,13G
Snodgrass, Jennifer Sterling	NC0050	13,13F,13C,13H,13G
Stewart, Chris	WA0200	13G
Stuck, Les	CA2950	10B,34A,13G,35C,10C
Temperley, David	NY1100	13B,13G,13K
Turner, Mitchell	GA1200	13A,13B,13C,13F,13G
Turner, Timothy R.	LA0900	13G,10F,32E,34,37
Valcarcel, David Shawn	CA3265	45,65,35C,13G,66A
Valcarcel, David	CA3950	45,65,35C,13G,66A
VanHandel, Leigh A.	MI1400	13,13K,13G
Walley, Steve	IN0905	13G,34,10D
Wegge, Glen T.	IA1750	13C,13B,13G,64C
Wessel, David	CA5000	12F,13G,13K,13L
Woodcock, Ruth	WA0100	11,12A,20,13A,13G
Yarbrough, Stephen	SD0600	13A,13G,10F,10A,13B

Music Theory Pedagogy

Name	Code	Areas
Almen, Byron Paul	TX3510	13,13H
Bamberger, Jeanne	MA1200	13H,13K,13G,32F,13
Cotte, William	VT0300	11,13H,36,61,66
Denman, James L.	OR1300	13,12A,66G,13F,13H
Follet, Diane W.	PA2550	13,15,42,13H
Frank, Bruce	NY1100	13B,13C,13D,13H,13I
Goffi-Fynn, Jeanne C.	NY4200	40,61,13H,32B,32D
Green, Martin	CA1000	11,13H,32D,36,39
Greitzer, Mary	NY1100	13C,13D,13E,13F,13H
Holm-Hudson, Kevin	KY1450	13F,13,10A,13E,13H
Laitz, Steven	NY1100	13B,13C,13H,13I
Marlowe, Sarah	NY2750	13,13C,13D,13H,13I
Marvin, William	NY1100	13A,13B,13C,13H,13I
Matascik, Sheri L.	TN1000	13,10,70,10B,13H
Mathews, Christopher W.	TN1660	36,13H,31A,60A,13C
Pereira, David	CA5000	13B,13H
Perkey, Christine	TN1400	13B,66A,13H
Piagentini, Susan M.	IL2250	13C,13H,13K,13
Reynolds, Jeremy W.	CO0900	64C,33,13C,13H
Rogers, Nancy Marie	FL0850	13B,13H,13K,13C,13
Roff, Marie	NY1100	13B,13F,13H
Santo, Joseph A.	DC0050	10A,10F,13B,13H,13C
Slominski, Johnandrew	NY1100	13B,13C,13E,13H
Snodgrass, Jennifer Sterling	NC0050	13,13F,13C,13H,13G
Sperrazza, Rose U.	IL2150	64C,48,13H
Suchy-Pilalis, Jessica R.	NY3780	13,62E,13H,13C,31A
Taavola, Kristin	CO0900	13,13H,13C
Telesco, Paula	MA2030	13,13H,13C
Terefenko, Dariusz	NY1100	13B,13D,13E,13H,29
Torosian, Brian L.	IL2150	70,11,13H
Trawick, Eleanor	IN0150	10,13,13F,13H,13L
Waldron, Richard	WA0300	11,13A,13H,13K,13C
Wiksyk, Crystal	AB0210	13A,13B,13C,13H
Wiznerowicz, James	VA1600	10A,10F,13,13H,10

Schenkerian Analysis

Name	Code	Areas
BaileyShea, Matthew	NY1100	13B,13E,13F,13I
Baker, Michael	KY1450	13,13C,13E,13G,13I
Beach, David	AG0450	13E,13I,13J
Beach, David	AG0300	13I
Berry, David Carson	OH2200	13,13I,13D,13J
Britton, Jason	IA0950	13,12A,70,13I
Brown, Matthew	NY1100	13B,13D,13I,13J
Burge, John	AG0250	13,10,10F,13I
Cavanagh, Lynn	AJ0100	13B,13E,13F,13J,13I
Colson, William	TX2600	13A,13,10F,10,13I
Deaver, Stuart T.	OK1450	66A,66D,66B,13I,66
Dunsby, Jonathan	NY1100	13F,13I,13K
Ewell, Philip	NY0625	13,13F,13I,62C
Frank, Bruce	NY1100	13B,13C,13D,13H,13I
Gross, Robert W.	TX2150	13B,13D,13E,13F,13I
Hyer, Brian	WI0815	13,13I
Jackson, Timothy L.	TX3420	13,13I
Kang, Ann Teresa	DC0010	13B,13I
Knupp, Robert	MS0400	66G,13I,13B,66A
Laitz, Steven	NY1100	13B,13C,13H,13I
Lin, Mei-Fang	TX3200	10A,13A,13I,13L,10F
Marlowe, Sarah	NY2750	13,13C,13D,13H,13I
Marvin, William	NY1100	13A,13B,13C,13H,13I
McConville, Brendan P.	TN1710	13,13F,13I,62C
Pfaff, William P.	NY3775	10,13,12A,13F,13I
Poudrier, Eve	CT0900	13,13I,13F,13K,13J
Priore, Irna	NC2430	13,13I
Reid, Darlene Chepil	AG0170	13F,13I,10
Rothfarb, Lee	CA5060	13J,13I,13B,13E,13
Sink, Damon W.	NC2600	10,13,34,34B,13I
Slottow, Stephen	TX3420	13I,13D,13F,13
Smith, Charles J.	NY4320	13,13B,13I
Sobaskie, James William	MS0500	13,13E,10F,13I,12
Stoddard, David	MN1100	70,13I
Todd, R. Larry	NC0600	12A,13J,12C,13E,13I
Van Den Toorn, Pieter	CA5060	13,13F,13I
Webster, James	NY0900	12,13B,13D,13I
Wheaton, J. Randall	VA0600	13B,13D,13A,13I,13F
Wyatt, Benjamin H.	VA1100	62C,67B,12,13I,12B
Yih, Annie	CA5060	13,13I,13C

History of Music Theory

Name	Code	Areas
Bain, Jennifer	AF0100	13E,13F,13B,13J,13
Baker, James	RI0050	13,13J,41
Beach, David	AG0450	13E,13I,13J
Benitez, Vincent P.	PA2750	13F,13D,13B,13J,13
Bent, Ian	NY0750	11,12A,12,13J
Berger, Karol	CA4900	12A,12,13J,12B
Bernstein, David	CA2950	13,12A,13J
Berry, David Carson	OH2200	13,13I,13D,13J
Bianchi, Eric	NY1300	11,12A,12G,13J,31
Bradshaw, Murray C.	CA5032	13,11,12A,13J
Brown, Matthew	NY1100	13B,13D,13I,13J
Carpenter, Ellon D.	AZ0100	13,13J
Cavanagh, Lynn	AJ0100	13B,13E,13F,13J,13I
Chafe, Eric	MA0500	13A,11,12A,12,13J
Cherlin, Michael	MN1623	13,13J
Chrisman, Richard	NJ1130	13,10F,13J
Christensen, Thomas	IL3250	13,13J,12D
Cohen, Albert	CA4900	12A,12,13J,20G
Cohen, David E.	NY0750	13,12A,13J
Covach, John	NY1100	13,13A,13J,10D
Covach, John R.	NY4350	13A,13,13J,10D
Cox, Bradley	MO1000	13J,66A
D'Accone, Frank A.	CA5032	12A,12,13J
Damschroder, David	MN1623	13,13J
D'Angelo, Gerard	NY2660	13A,13,13J
Dawe, Karla	AC0100	13A,13J,13C
DeLong, Kenneth	AA0150	12,13J
Di Bacco, Giuliano	IN0900	12A,13J
Domek, Richard C.	KY1450	13,13J
Downs, Philip	AG0500	12,13J
Easley, David B.	OK0750	13,13J
Eckert, Stefan	IL0800	13,13J,13E
Galand, Joel	FL0700	13J,13
Gelbart, Matthew	NY1300	12A,13J,14A,14D,20F
Gjerdingen, Robert	IL2250	13,13J,20G
Gollner, Marie L.	CA5032	12A,12,13J
Grave, Floyd	NJ1130	11,12A,12,13J
Green, Burdette L.	OH1850	13A,13,13J,12B
Grier, James	AG0500	12,13J
Guerrero, Jean	NY1100	13B,13E,13F,13J
Haakenson, Matthew A.	FL1750	10A,66G,13,13D,13J
Hall, Sarah	AC0050	13J,61
Hasty, Christopher	MA1050	13,10,12A,13J
Heidlberger, Frank	TX3420	13J,12A,12,13
Hicks, Andrew	NY0900	12A,13J
Holbrook, Amy K.	AZ0100	13,13J
Huffman, Donna M.	WA0100	13,13J,36,47,49
Hughes, Andrew	AG0450	11,12,13J,12G
Hyde, Martha M.	NY4320	13,13J
Kaminsky, Peter	CT0600	13,13J,12B
Karpinski, Gary S.	MA2000	13,13J
Keiler, Allan R.	MA0500	11,12A,12,13,13J
Kelly, Thomas Forrest	MA1050	11,12A,12,13J
Klimisch, Mary J.	SD0300	10,13J,66A,66G
Kruckenberg, Lori	OR1050	12A,12C,13J
Landey, Peter	AG0050	12B,13J,10A,10B,10F
Long, Michael P.	NY4320	12A,12,13J
Marcozzi, Rudy T.	IL0550	13A,13,13J
Mathes, Gerard	ID0140	13,11,13J,62A,34
McCachren, Renee	NC0350	13,12A,66A,13E,13J
Mooney, Kevin	AG0500	13,13J,12C
Moreno, Jairo	PA3350	13,13J,20H,29,12D
Morrison, Leah A.	CA5300	31A,13J,12A,12D
Moshaver, Maryam A.	AA0100	13J
Murphy, Edward W.	AZ0500	13,13J
Nolan, Catherine	AG0500	13,13J
Nurock, Kirk	NY2660	10F,60,10,13J,29A
Owens, Jessie Ann	CA5010	12A,13J,15
Packman, Jeffrey L.	AG0450	13J
Perlman, Marc	RI0050	14,20D,12E,13J,35D
Pesce, Dolores	MO1900	12A,12,13J
Peterson, Don L.	UT0050	13,12A,13J,63B
Phipps, Graham H.	TX3420	13,13J
Poudrier, Eve	CT0900	13,13I,13F,13K,13J
Renwick, William J. M.	AG0200	13,60,13J
Ross-Hammond, Amelia	VA0950	13,13J,36,66
Rothfarb, Lee	CA5060	13J,13I,13B,13E,13
Schiano, Michael	CT0650	13,13J,20G,34
Schmalfeldt, Janet	MA1900	13,12A,13J,13L
Schubert, Peter	AI0150	13,13J,36
Segger, Joachim	AA0035	13,13J,66A,66B,43
Semmens, Richard	AG0500	12,13J,55,67B,13L
Silbiger, Alexander	NC0600	12A,12B,12C,13J
Snarrenberg, Robert	MO1900	13,13J
Sovik, Thomas	TX3420	13A,14C,13J,34
Todd, R. Larry	NC0600	12A,13J,12C,13E,13I
Toft, Robert	AG0500	10D,12A,12C,13J
Trantham, Gene S.	OH0300	13,13A,13J
Upton, Elizabeth R.	CA5032	12A,12,13J
Viragh, Katalin	CT0650	13J
Wagner, Marella	WI0770	12A,13J,20
Wason, Robert W.	NY1100	13B,13D,13F,13J,29C
Watkins, Holly	NY1100	12A,12B,12D,13J,14C
Wiskus, Jessica	PA1050	13J,12A,13E,13
Zbikowski, Lawrence	IL3250	13,12A,13J,29C

Perception/Cognition

Name	Code	Areas
Abeles, Harold F.	NY4200	32,13K,13L,12F
Bamberger, Jeanne	MA1200	13H,13K,13G,32F,13
Benton, Carol W.	GA0200	13C,13K,32B,32D,32G
Brinner, Benjamin	CA5000	13K,14,20B,20D,11
Butler, David	OH1850	13K,13C,13
Carson, Benjamin Leeds	CA5070	13K,10
Clifton, Jeremy J.	OK1050	35C,10,13,13K,13B
Curlee, J. Matthew	NY1100	13A,13B,13C,13D,13K
Davis, Stacey	TX3530	13,13K,12F
Devaney, Johanna C.	OH1850	13B,13E,13G,13K,13L
Diaz, Frank M.	OR1050	32,32G,13K
Dody, Teresa D.	WV0350	61,13C,13K,32B,32D
Dunsby, Jonathan	NY1100	13F,13I,13K
Fujioka, Takako	CA4900	34,13K
Goldman, Edward 'Ted'	NY1100	13K,13C,13B,10A,10F
Gosselin, Nathalie	AI0200	13K
Hajda, John M.	CA5060	13K,13L,13A,13B,14A
Ho, Hubert	MA1450	10,13,13K,11
Knier, Lawrence	MD0800	37,13C,63,13K,11
Levitin, Daniel	AI0150	13K
Marvin, Elizabeth W.	NY1100	13A,13C,13F,13G,13K
Mavromatis, Panayotis	NY2750	13B,13D,13F,13G,13K
McAdams, Stephen	AI0150	13G,13K,34
Ohriner, Mitchell S.	VA1350	13,13K,13E
Palmer, Caroline	AI0150	13K
Piagentini, Susan M.	IL2250	13C,13H,13K,13
Poudrier, Eve	CT0900	13,13I,13F,13K,13J
Rogers, Nancy Marie	FL0850	13B,13H,13K,13C,13
Rogers, Susan	MA0260	35C,13K,13L
Sadoff, Ronald H.	NY2750	13K,10A,10C,10D
Temperley, David	NY1100	13B,13G,13K
VanHandel, Leigh A.	MI1400	13,13K,13G
Waldron, Richard	WA0300	11,13A,13H,13K,13C
Walker, Margaret Edith	AG0250	14,12G,13K,20E,12A
Wessel, David	CA5000	12F,13G,13K,13L
Whitcomb, Benjamin	WI0865	62C,13C,13E,13K,13

Zdzinski, Stephen　　　FL1900　　　32,32G,32H,12C,13K

Acoustics

Abeles, Harold F.	NY4200	32,13K,13L,12F
Adams, Richard	MI2250	10,49,13L,13,10F
Andrews, Bradford	CA5150	35C,13L
Ballard, Jack	OH1350	35,34A,34D,13L,34E
Balzano, Gerald	CA5050	13A,34,13L,12F,12
Blackwood, Easley R.	IL3250	10F,13L
Blatter, Alfred W.	PA0850	13L
Brandes, Lambert	MA0800	13,66G,13L
Bukvic, Ivica Ico	VA1700	10,34,10A,13L,10C
Burleigh, Ian G.	AA0200	13L,34
Case, Alexander	MA2030	35C,47,13L
Chafe, Chris	CA4900	10,45,34,13L
Chowning, John M.	CA4900	10,45,34,13L
Devaney, Johanna C.	OH1850	13B,13E,13G,13K,13L
Ehle, Robert	CO0950	13,10,13L
Fishell, John C.	IN0150	13L,34D
Galo, Gary A.	NY3780	13L,35G
Goomas, Steve	CA2650	35C,35G,13L
Greenhut, Barry	NY2750	10,34,13L
Groene, Robert W.	MO1810	33,13L
Hajda, John M.	CA5060	13K,13L,13A,13B,14A
Hatzis, Christos	AG0450	10,35H,34,35C,13L
Headlam, David	NY1100	13F,13G,13L,34A,34B
Hemmel, Ronald A.	NJ1350	13,10,34D,13L
Kendall, Roger A.	CA5031	32,13L,12F,12C
Kuchera-Morin, JoAnn	CA5060	13,10F,10,45,13L
Kurtz, Justin	CT0650	35C,13L
Lin, Mei-Fang	TX3200	10A,13A,13I,13L,10F
Marvit, Betsy	CA4150	13L
Middleton, Peter	IL2200	45,64A,34,35C,13L
Moore, Britt	VT0300	13L,34D,35,61,34E
Moore, F. Richard	CA5050	10,45,34,35C,13L
Murail, Tristan C.	NY0750	10,34,13L,12F,10F
Nix, John Paul	TX3530	61,13L,32D
Otto, Steven	AG0650	11,14,13L
Patrick, Dennis M.	AG0450	13,45,13L,34,35C
Perialas, Alexander	NY1800	35C,13L
Perrault, Paul	AI0220	45,34,35C,35E,13L
Rogers, Susan	MA0260	35C,13K,13L
Sandroff, Howard	IL3250	10,45,34,13L
Schloss, Andrew	AB0150	10B,34,14,20H,13L
Schmalfeldt, Janet	MA1900	13,12A,13J,13L
Semmens, Richard	AG0500	12,13J,55,67B,13L
Simonson, Donald R.	IA0850	39,61,13L,34C,34D
Smith, Julius O.	CA4900	34,13L
Spitz, Bruce	WA0860	66,34,35,13L
Traube, Caroline	AI0200	13L,35C,34
Trawick, Eleanor	IN0150	10,13,13F,13H,13L
Truax, Barry D.	AB0080	10,45,34,35C,13L
Valera, Philip	NC0100	34D,35G,35C,35D,13L
Vance, Scott	CA0845	35B,35C,35D,13L
Verfaille, Vincent	AI0200	13L,14B
Wang, Ge	CA4900	34,35,13L
Watkinson, Christopher L.	ME0200	13L,34D,35D,35G
Wessel, David	CA5000	12F,13G,13K,13L
Wraggett, Wes	AB0210	10A,10B,13B,13L

Ethnomusicology (All Areas)

Abbott, Thomas	MN1300	14,61
Abe, Marie	MA0400	14
Adams, Bob	WA0030	20,14
Adams, J. Robert	GA0490	61,14,11,39,40
Adams, Margarethe A.	NY3790	20A,20B,14
Addison, Don F.	OR0800	20,14
Adler, Christopher A.	CA5200	10,14,13,10A,20D
Ahlquist, Karen	DC0100	12,14
Ake, David	NV0100	12,20,29A,14,66A
Albin, William R.	OH1450	14,50,65
Allen, Matthew H.	MA2150	14C,20E,20H,31,14
Allsen, J. Michael	WI0865	11,12,14,20
Alvarez, Luis M.	PR0150	10A,11,13A,13B,14
Alves, William	CA2175	10,14,45,34
Amico, Stephen	NJ0020	11,14
Andrews, Dwight D.	GA0750	13,14,31A,29
Armstrong, Robin E.	MD0520	11,14,29A,12,12A
Arnold, Alison E.	NC1700	11,20,20E,14
Asai, Susan M.	MA1450	14,20D,20H
Attrep, Kara	OH0300	14
Austerlitz, Paul	PA1400	12,14,46
Averill, Gage	AB0100	12,14
Babiracki, Carol M.	NY4100	12,12B,14,20B,20E
Bakan, Michael	FL0850	14,20D,20G
Banzi, Julia	OR0400	20,14C,34B,14,10E
Barkhymer, Lyle	OH2050	14,20C
Barz, Gregory F.	TN1850	12,14,20,31,29A
Barzel, Tamar	MA2050	14
Baxter, Diane R.	OR1250	66,20,12A,14
Beal, Elmer	ME0270	14
Beardslee, Thomas	QH1850	14
Beaster-Jones, Jayson	TX2900	14,20E
Beaudry, Nicole	AI0210	14
Becker, Michael	IL3450	14,12A
Behroozi, Bahram	CA4350	13A,11,12A,14,70
Benamou, Marc	IN0400	14,12,20,20D,12B
Berger, Harris M.	TX2900	14,12B,29D,20G
Birenbaum Quintero, Michael	ME0200	14,20H,31F
Blum, Stephen	NY0600	12,14
Bohlman, Philip V.	IL3250	14,20G
Borgo, David R.	CA5050	64E,14,29,47
Bosse, Joanna	MI1400	12A,14
Bowman, Rob	AG0650	14,20G,29A
Bowman, Wayne	NY2750	32,12C,12F,14
Brannon, Patrick V.	IL3370	14,12A,36,60A,40
Breckenridge, Stan	CA2390	12A,13A,14
Breedon, Daniel	MN0600	13,10,12A,14
Briggs, Ray A.	CA0825	14,29,46,47
Brinksmeier, Ulrike	OH0680	12A,11,62E,14,20
Brinner, Benjamin	CA5000	13K,14,20B,20D,11
Briscoe, James R.	IN0250	12A,14,12C,12
Brosh, Robert	PA3330	50,65,20G,14
Brown, Chris	CA2950	10B,10A,20,13,14
Brown, Ernest	VA0950	14,66A
Brown, L. Joel	IA0900	13,12A,14,66,11
Brown, Leonard	MA1450	11,14,64E,29A,12E
Browne, Kimasi L.	CA0250	12A,14,20
Bruhn, Christopher	OH0850	12,14
Bryant, Lei Ouyang	NY3650	14,20C
Bryant, Wanda	CA0510	14
Buchanan, Donna A.	IL3300	20F,12,14
Burke, Patrick L.	MO1900	14
Burleson, Richard F.	AC0100	14,55,67G

Burnett, Henry	NY0642	12,14
Burnett, Henry	NY0600	12,14
Burns, Carolyn	ND0100	32,20,14,55B
Burns, James	NY3705	14,20
Burrows, David	NY2740	11,12A,12,14
Butler, Melvin L.	IL3250	14,20
Buyer, Paul L.	SC0400	65,50,14,20
Caputo, Michael	NJ0200	12A,14,37,64,20G
Caputo, Michael	NJ0250	12A,14,37,48,64
Carr, James H.	NC2430	14
Carr, Walter E.	OR0800	12A,12,14,20G
Carrasco, Jacqui	NC2500	62A,62B,51,41,14
Carroll, Don	CA3200	11,14,29A,20G
Caschetta, Todd	CA4850	20G,11,12,14,50
Cassarino, James P.	VT0200	12,14,20,36,37
Catalano, Roberto F.	CA3950	14,20
Catalano, Roberto	CA5100	14,20
Catlin, Amy	CA5031	14,20C,20D,20E
Chang, Peter M.	IL2150	11,14,12,42
Charles, David	MT0200	14,20,47
Charry, Eric	CT0750	14
Chianis, Sam	NY3705	12A,12,14,20H
Chittum, Donald	PA3330	13,12A,12,14,12F
Chopyak, James D.	CA0840	14
Christensen, Dieter	NY0750	14,14A,12C
Ciucci, Alessandra	NY0750	11,14,15,14C,20B
Clark, Maribeth	FL1360	11,12,14,15
Coach, Leo	OH0650	20,14
Collier, Bethany	PA0350	14,20,20D
Colman, Alfredo C.	TX0300	14,20H
Comberiati, Carmelo	NY2200	12,14
Condaris, Christine	MA1185	12,14,36
Conlon, Paula J.	OK1350	20G,20,14F,14
Connell, Andrew M.	VA0600	14,29A
Cook, Bruce	CA1560	66,14,11,20
Cook, Lisa M.	CO0550	11,12A,20G,31A,14
Coolen, Michael T.	OR0700	14,54,20,12A,35A
Corin, Amy R.	CA3100	14,11,13C,12A
Cratty, William	CA4050	13A,13,12A,14,32
Crook, Larry	FL1850	14,50,20H
Crookshank, Esther R.	KY1200	12,14,62
Crummer, Larry D.	CA1760	20,13,11,14,66A
Cunningham, James E.	FL0650	14,20,32,11,12A
Currie, Scott	MN1623	14
Curtis, Peter	CA3800	11,70,14,20,29
Curtis-Smith, Curtis O.	MI2250	10,14,66A,20G
Damberg, John	AK0100	14,50,65
Davis, Art	IL2050	63A,14,29A,29B
Davis, Daniel	NC0600	10,14,15,20A
Davis, Mary E.	OH0400	12A,12,14
Day-O'Connell, Sarah K.	IL1350	12,14,66A,66E
De Castro, Paul	CA0830	14,29,20H,66A
Delgado, Kevin M.	CA4100	14,20H
Desroches, Monique	AI0200	14
DeVeaux, Scott K.	VA1550	13,12A,12,14,29
DeWitt, Mark F.	LA0760	14,29A,13C,20G
Diamond, Beverley	AD0050	14
Diamond, Jody	NH0100	14,53,43
Dickensheets, Janice	CO0950	12,34A,14,12B,12A
Dickert, Lewis H.	SC1200	70,53,29,13A,14
Dinnerstein, Noe	NY0630	14
Dor, George	MS0700	14,20
Dosunmu, Oyebade A.	MA2250	14,20
Douglas, Gavin D.	NC2430	14,20D
Doukhan, Lilianne	MI0250	12A,12,14,31A,12C
Downing, Sonja Lynn	WI0350	14,15,20D,64A,32
Doyle, Alicia M.	CA0825	11,14,20
Dreisbach, Tina Spencer	OH1000	12A,14,32H
Duchan, Joshua S.	MI2200	14
Dudgeon, Ralph T.	NY3720	12,67,14,38,63
Dunn, Ron	CA1550	70,14
Dunnell, Rebecca	MO0950	64A,12A,14,11,20
Emoff, Ronald	OH1850	14
Erken, Emily	OH0350	14
Erlmann, Veit	TX3510	14
Evans, David	TN1680	12A,20G,14
Evans, Gerald	OH1300	13,10,12A,14,66D
Farley, Michael	NY3550	13,14,10,20
Fatone, Gina Andrea	ME0150	13,14,20,20D
Fawcett-Yeske, Maxine	CO0750	11,12,14,16,20
Fernando, Nathalie	AI0200	14
Fikentscher, Kai	NJ0950	14,20,45
Finlayson, Jahmes Anthony	WI1150	14,65
Fish, David Lee	NC0350	35,14,34,20C,29
Foreman, Kelly	MI2200	14
Fox, Aaron A.	NY0750	14,20G,12E
Fraser, Jennifer	OH1700	14
Frey, Kevin T.	CA4350	13,11,14,63,53
Friedson, Steven	TX3420	11,14,65
Frishkopf, Michael	AA0100	20A,20F,14,31C
Fuhrmann, Christina E.	OH0100	13A,11,12,14
Gallo, Tony	AB0090	64E,14
Galm, Eric A.	CT0500	14,20,20H,50,65
Garber, Joel	OK0770	12A,61,14,36,60
Garcia, David F.	NC2410	12,14,20
Garcia, Thomas George Caracas	OH1450	14,20H
Gay, Leslie C.	TN1710	14,14A,14C,20,12
Geisler, Herbert G.	CA1425	14,32,44,13,31
Getter, Joseph	CT0050	14
Getter, Joseph	CT0450	11,14
Gill-Gurtan, Denise	MO1900	14
Girard, Sharon	CA4200	12A,12,14
Gise, Max E.	OH2200	14
Gomez, Alice	TX2260	10,14,47,65,35A
Gonzalez, Fr. George	IN0005	11,14,20,66G,32
Goodman, Kimberlee	OH2050	64A,14,13A
Graham, Sandra J.	MA0255	14,20A,20G,31F
Granite, Bonita	NJ1050	14,20D,61
Grasso, Eliot	OR1050	11,20,14
Gray, Laura J.	AG0470	11,12A,12,14,20
Greene, Kenneth H.	TX3350	14,38,62B,51
Griebling, Karen	AR0350	13,10,38,62B,14
Grimes, Judith	IL0850	60,14,32,37
Grimes, Robert R.	NY1300	12,14,20
Groesbeck, Rolf A.	AR0750	11,12,14,66A,20
Grosso, Cheryl	WI0808	50,65,43,14,13C
Groves, Edgar S.	PA3650	14,32
Gudmundson, Paula	MN0040	64A,64,12A,14
Guilbault, Jocelyne	CA5000	11,14,20H
Gunderson, Frank	FL0850	14,20A,20B
Guy, Nancy	CA5050	14,20D
Guzman, Juan-Tony	IA0950	32,47,14,29,20
Guzski, Carolyn	NY3717	12A,14
Habib, Kenneth S.	CA0600	14,10,13,20B,14C
Hagedorn, Katherine J.	CA3650	14,20H,20A
Hahn, Tomie	NY3300	14,15,20,31G,34
Haldey, Olga	MD1010	12,12A,11,14
Hall, Dana	IL0750	14,29

Index by Area of Teaching Interest

Name	Code	Numbers
Hall, Steven	WV0400	14,47,50,65
Hamessley, Lydia	NY1350	13C,12,14,20G,12A
Hamill, Chad	AZ0450	14,20
Hampton, Barbara L.	NY0625	14,20G,29A
Hampton, Barbara	NY0600	14
Hansen, Julia	CA4625	14,66A,20
Harbert, Benjamin J.	DC0075	14
Harness, Kelley	MN1623	12,14
Harnish, David D.	CA5200	14,20,31,41
Harper, Darryl	VA1600	29,10,14
Harrington, E. Michael	MA0260	35,10,20,14
Harris Walsh, Kristen	AD0050	14
Hartigan, Royal	MA2020	14,20
Harvey, Trevor	IA1550	14
Harwood, Craig	CT0900	12,14
Hatch, Martin	NY0900	14,20B,20D,20E
Hayes, Eileen M.	MD0850	14
Heisler, Wayne H.	NJ0175	12A,14,20
Henderson, David R.	NY3550	14,20,12
Henriques, Donald A.	CA0810	14,20H
Hernandez Mergal, Luis A.	PR0115	12A,12B,14
Heslink, Daniel M.	PA2350	11,14,37,65
Hesselink, Nathan	AB0100	14
Hildreth, John W.	IL0100	11,14,20
Hildreth, Todd	KY0250	14,34,47,66A
Hill, Jackson	PA0350	10,12A,12,14,71
Hodgson, Jay	AG0500	14,29,35C,35D,12
Hollerbach, Peter D.	NY0600	14
Hollerbach, Peter	NY0270	13A,11,14,47,70
Holley, Timothy	NC1600	14,62,62C,20G
Holmes, Ramona A.	WA0800	14,32,38,62
Hung, Eric Hing-tao	NJ1350	12,14
Hurley-Glowa, Susan M.	TX3515	12A,14
Hutchinson, Sydney	NY4100	14,15
Hwang, Okon	CT0150	14,66,11,12,13
Imara, Mtafiti	CA0847	13,14,64,47,29
Jackson, Travis A.	IL3250	29,20,29D,29E,14
Jankowsky, Rich	MA1900	14,31C,20B,14F
Jaquez, Candida	CA4500	14,20,12,41
Jenkins, Lisa Davenport	PA2750	14
Johnson, Birgitta	SC1110	14,20G
Johnson, Maria V.	IL2900	14
Johnson, Steven P.	UT0050	12A,12,14,12F
Johnson, Todd Alan	CA0845	65,12A,14,50,29A
Jones, Ralph Miles	OH1700	14
Jones, Robert J.	ND0350	39,61,54,14
Jones-Bamman, Richard	CT0150	11,14,32,20
Jung, Eun-Young	CA5050	11,12D,14,20C
Kagan, Alan L.	MN1623	12,12,14
Kajikawa, Loren	OR1050	12A,14,20C,20G
Kaloyanides, Michael G.	CT0700	12,13,14,20,34
Kattari, Kim	TX2900	14
Katz, Mark	NC2410	12,14,20,34
Katz, Max	VA0250	14
Kearney Guigne, Anna	AD0050	14
Keillor, Elaine	AG0100	12A,12,14,66A,20G
Keminski, Joe	NY2102	20,14,12A,63A
Kendrick, Robert L.	IL3250	11,31,12,14
Keyser, Dorothy	ND0500	11,12A,14
Kidula, Jean	GA2100	14,20,11,31,12
Kimball, James W.	NY3730	13A,11,14,67E,70
Kippen, James R.	AG0450	12A,14
Kishiuk, Michelle	VA1550	14,20A
Klefstad, Terry	TN0100	12,14
Kligman, Mark L.	NY1450	14
Koegel, John	CA0815	12,14
Koen, Benjamin D.	FL0850	14,20B
Kok, Roe-Min	AI0150	12,14
Koontz, Jason	KY0550	50,65,14,34B
Korde, Shirish	MA0700	13,10,14,20,29
Koskoff, Ellen	NY1100	14,15,20G,20D,31
Kramer, Elizabeth A.	GA2130	12A,14,11,13A,62A
Krikun, Andrew	NJ0020	35A,10D,47,14,20
Kuhn, Judith	WI0825	12A,14
Kung, Hsiong-Ning	OH1850	14
Kvetko, Peter J.	MA1650	14,13A,14C,20E,41
Kyker, Jennifer	NY1100	14,14C,20,20A
Laderman, Michael	NY3100	11,29,12A,14,20D
Laird, Tracey	GA0050	12,14,11,29A
Lam, Joseph S. C.	MI2100	14
Lamothe, Peter	TN0100	12,14
Lane, Timothy	WI0803	14,48,64A
Lange, Rose	TX3400	14
Lapidus, Benjamin	NY0630	14,70,20H
Largey, Michael	MI1400	12,14,20
Lawrence, Sidra	OH0300	14
Leafstedt, Carl S.	TX3350	11,12A,14,20
Lee, Katherine In-Young	CA5010	14,12,20C,12D
Lee, Michael	OK1350	12A,12,14,20G
Lee, Tong Soon	GA0750	14,20C,20D,14D,14F
Leger, James K.	NM0150	10,60,12,14,38
Leon, Javier F.	IN0900	14,20H
Leotar, Frederic	AI0100	14
Levin, Theodore C.	NH0100	14
Levy, Mark	OR1050	20,14
Lieberman, Fredric	CA5070	12,14
Lipp, Carolyn	MI0500	14,66A,66H,66B
Lloyd, L. Keith	TX1650	65,12A,14,12,50
Locke, David	MA1900	11,14,20A
Lohman, Laura Ann	CA0815	12,14,14C
London, Frank	NY3785	14
Longshore, Terry	OR0950	65,20,14,47,35A
LoPiccolo, Joseph	CA3200	14,70
Lorenz, Shanna	CA3300	14,20G,20H
Lornell, Christopher 'Kip'	DC0100	29A,14
Lott, R. Allen	TX2600	12A,12,14,12C
Lovensheimer, James A.	TN1850	12,14,20G,29
Lowery, Christopher	IL1520	14
Lozano, Danilo	CA6000	47,64A,20,29A,14
Lucas, Ann E.	MA0500	14,11,20,20B,12A
Lynch, Timothy	CA1290	13,10,11,14
Lysloff, Rene T.A.	CA5040	14,20,20D,20G
Macchioni, Oscar E.	TX3520	66A,66B,66D,66,14
MacDonald, Michael	AA0100	12,14
MacLachlan, Heather M.	OH2250	12,20,14,20D
Magaldi, Cristina	MD0850	14C,12A,14,20G,20H
Mahon, Brad	AA0150	12,14
Maier, Ralph	AA0150	70,41,12,14
Makubuya, James	IN1850	13A,13C,11,14,20
Maltz, Richard	SC1100	13,10,65,12,14
Manabe, Noriko	NY0500	14,12E,20
Manuel, Peter	NY0630	14
Manuel, Peter G.	NY0600	14,20C,20H
Marcus, Scott	CA5060	14,20B,20E
Marcuzzi, Michael	AG0650	32,20H,14
Markoff, Irene	AG0650	14,20
Marsh, Peter K.	CA0807	14,12,20B,20
Martin, Margo	CA3200	11,14
Martin, Stephen	OR0850	14,12,20
Mason, Kaley R.	IL3250	14,20
Matsue, Jennifer	NY4310	14,15,20C,20
Mazo, Margarita L.	OH1850	12,14
McGraw, Andrew	VA1500	14,20I
McKinley, Kathy	AG0100	14
McKinnon, John A.	OR0200	13,10,63,34,14
McLucas, Anne Dhu	OR1050	12A,12C,20G,20F,14
McManus, Emily	TX2900	14
McNeil, Albert J.	CA5010	60,14,32,36
Meizel, Katherine L.	OH0300	14
Merrill, Allison	OH0300	14
Metil, Robert	PA0600	14,29A,20G,70
Meyer, Jeffrey	MN0600	12A,13,11,14,20
Miller, Rebecca S.	MA1000	14,13A,20F,31B,35H
Miller, Stephen R.	TN1800	11,12A,12,14
Modirzadeh, Hafez	CA4200	14,20,64E
Monson, Ingrid	MA1050	14,12,29
Moonert, Judy	MI2250	14,50,65
Moore, Robin D.	TX3510	14,31F,14C,14F,20H
Morelli, Sarah	CO0900	14
Moulton, Paul F.	ID0070	11,12A,32,14
Mukuna, Kazadi Wa	OH1100	14,20A,20B,11
Muller, Carol A.	PA3350	14,20A,20D,31F,31G
Murawski, Marianne	NJ0990	14,11,20
Murphy, John P.	TX3420	29,14,47,64E
Murray, Eric	OH1110	14
Myers, Patricia Ann	NY1550	11,12,14,66H,20
Nanongkham, Priwan Keo	OH1100	20,14
Naylor, Michael L.	MI2200	14
Ndaliko, Cherie Rivers	NC2410	10C,12,14
Nettl, Bruno	IL3300	14,20G
Newsom, Mary Ellen	IN0005	12,14,32,61,62
Niebur, Louis	NV0100	12,20,14,11
Ninoshvili, Lauren	NY0200	14,66A
Nketia, Joseph K.	PA3420	20A,14
Noonan, Jeffrey	MO1500	12A,14,67D,70,20G
Norfleet, Dawn	CA0630	14
Novotney, Eugene D.	CA2250	14,50,65,20
Nuss, Steven R.	ME0250	13,14
Odello, Denise	MN1620	11,12,64B,14,20
O'Grady, Terence J.	WI0808	13,12A,12,14,55
Okigbo, Austin	CO0800	31F,20,14
Omojola, Olabode	MA1350	14,20
Omoumi, Hossein	CA5020	14
Osterland, David	SC0620	60,14,32,66A
Otto, Steven	AG0650	11,14,13L
Ozah, Marie Agatha	PA1050	14
, Panaiotis	FL1750	14
Patch, Justin	NY4450	14,20
Perlman, Marc	RI0050	14,20D,12E,13J,35D
Perman, Anthony	IA0700	14,20
Pertl, Brian G.	WI0350	14
Peters, Gretchen	WI0803	11,12A,14
Peterson, Jay	IL1650	13,12A,14,66A,66G
Pier, David G.	CA4425	14,46
Pilzer, Joshua	AG0450	14
Pilzer, Joshua	NY0750	11,14,20C
Pinkston, Dan	CA4600	13,12A,14,10,20
Planer, John H.	IN1050	20,12,13,14,61
Pohly, Linda L.	IN0150	11,12,14,12A
Pollack, Howard	TX3400	12A,12,14,20G
Pond, Steven	NY0900	14,29
Poris, Valerie Jill	OR0500	14
Price, Andrea M.	GA1650	61,39,14
Price, Emmett G.	MA1450	14,29,66A,47
Price, Josselyne	VT0400	14,20,50
Protopapas, John	PA3710	14
Prouty, Kenneth E.	MI1400	12,14,29
Provine, Robert C.	MD1010	12,14
Quesada Agostini, Milagros	OH1120	14,32
Qureshi, Regula	AA0100	14
Radomski, James V.	CA0845	11,12A,12,14
Rahaim, Matthew	MN1623	14
Rahkonen, Carl J.	PA1600	16,14
Ramsey, Laura	SC1100	14,64D
Rancier, Megan M.	OH0300	14,11
Randall, James	MT0400	12,14,20,11
Rasmussen, Anne K.	VA0250	14,20G,31,41,12C
Rasmussen, Ljerka V.	TN1400	20,14C,20F,35D,14
Rathnaw, Dennis M.	OH0300	14
Reisch, Carla	CA2390	11,14,34
Renninger, Laura Ann	WV0550	11,12A,12F,14
Rey, Mario	NC0650	14,13,20H
Rischar, Richard A.	MI2110	12,29,40,14,20
Ritter, Jonathan	CA5040	14,20,20H
Rivera, Francesca M.	CA5353	14,20H,41
Roberts, Wesley	KY0400	12,14,31,66
Robertson, Marta E.	PA1400	12,14
Robinson, Gregory J.	VA0450	11,12,14,20H
Robinson, Jason	MA0100	12,13,14,34
Robinson, Scott	PA1150	12,14,10
Rodger, Gillian	WI0825	12A,12C,20G,20D,14
Romero, Brenda M.	CO0800	14
Rommen, Timothy	PA3350	14
Rosenberg, Ruth Emily	IL3310	20F,15,14
Rosenzweig, Joyce	NY1450	14,66C,35E
Rosner, Arnold	NY2050	13A,13,11,14,66A
Row, Peter	MA1400	14,12,13
Roy, Bruno	AI0210	14
Rubinoff, Kailan	NC2430	67D,14,12
Russell, Melinda	MN0300	14
Sands, Rosita M.	IL0720	14,12,20
Sandstrom, Boden	MD1010	14,15
Sarkissian, Margaret	MA1750	14,20D
Sayre, Elizabeth	PA3200	14,20
Scarnati, Blase S.	AZ0450	11,12,14
Schechter, John M.	CA5070	13,14,20H
Schlacks, Mary M.	OH1650	14,48,64C,11
Schlicht, Ursel	NJ0950	13,14,15,53
Schloss, Andrew	AB0150	10B,34,14,20H,13L
Schmalenberger, Sarah	MN1625	12A,63B,12,67E,14
Schmidt, Catherine M.	MN1700	32B,14,32,A
Schmidt, John R.	PA2050	60,14,50,65,37
SchoederDorn, Jill	CO0300	14
Schreffler, Gibb	CA3650	14,20B,20G
Schwartz-Kates, Deborah	FL1900	12,20H,14
Scott, Stanley	CT0450	11,14
Seachrist, Denise A.	OH1100	12C,14,20G
Searles, Julie	MA2150	14,14C,20H,20G
Semmes, Laurie R.	NC0050	14,20
Shabazz, Hafiz F.	NH0100	14,50
Shelemay, Kay K.	MA1050	12,14
Sherinian, Zoe	OK1350	14
Sherry, Martin	WA0480	13,11,12A,14,64A
Shonekan, Stephanie	MO1800	14,20
Shope, Bradley	TX2930	14,20,12A
Shulstad, Reeves	NC0050	12,14,20

Index by Area of Teaching Interest

Name	Code	Areas
Silverberg, Ann L.	TN0050	12A,12,14,11
Simms, Rob	AG0650	20,14
Simonett, Helena	TN1850	12,14,20H
Skelton, William	NY0650	14,20D,38,64D
Skinner, Ryan	OH1850	14
Slobin, Mark	CT0750	14,15
Slominski, Tes	WI0100	14,15
Smith, Barbara B.	HI0210	20I,20C,14
Smith, Christina	AD0050	14
Smith, Christopher J.	TX3200	12A,12,14
Smith, Gordon E.	AG0250	12,14,20G,12C
Smith, Hope Munro	CA0800	14,20H,11,12A,12C
Solis, Ted	AZ0100	12A,20G,14
Soto, Amanda C.	ID0250	14,20H,32B,32G,32H
Spiller, Henry	CA5010	14,12,15,20D,12D
Spinetti, Frederico	AA0100	14,20B
Spring, Howard	AG0350	14,70,29,12A,13D
Stanyek, Jason	NY2740	34,12,14,20,12D
Starks, George	PA1000	20,14,47,64E,29
Steel, David	MS0700	14,66H,55,66G
Steel, Matthew	MI2250	12A,12,14,55
Stegall, Sydney Wallace	WA0460	13,14,10B,14F,10
Stein, Beverly	CA0830	12,14
Stevenson, George	OK0850	12A,14,36,61
Stevenson, Robert M.	CA5032	12,14,20G,20H
Stewart, Alexander	VT0450	14,53,20,29,47
Stilwell, Robyn	DC0075	12,14
Stimeling, Travis D.	IL1750	12,63D,12D,14
Stockton, J. Larry	PA1850	14,50,20,60
Stockton, Larry	PA2450	14
Stroeher, Vicki P.	WV0400	11,12,13,14
Stubbs, Frederick	MA2010	11,14
Sturman, Janet L.	AZ0500	14,11
Sugarman, Jane	NY0600	14
Sullivan, Todd E.	AZ0450	11,12,14,20
Sunkett, Mark E.	AZ0100	50,65,29A,14
Survilla, Maria Paula	IA1800	13,12A,14
Swanson, Brent	FL0700	12A,14,20
Szego, Kati	AD0050	12A,14,20
Tanner, Christopher	OH1450	14,50
Tarrant, Fredrick A.	GA1800	11,12,14,20,55
Tarsi, Boaz	NY1860	13,10,14
Taylor, Timothy D.	CA5031	12,14,34
Taylor, Timothy D.	CA5032	14,20,34
Tenzer, Michael	AB0100	20D,14
Tewari, Laxmi	CA4700	14,13A,61,10E,31D
Thomas, Susan R.	GA2100	11,12,14,20H,34A
Thompson, David	WI0400	13,11,14,66A,35
Thrasher, Alan R.	AB0100	20D,14
Todd, Kristen Stauffer	OK0650	12,14,20,11,55
Tolbert, Elizabeth D.	MD0650	14
Tomasello, Andrew	NY0600	12,14,29A
Tomasello, Andrew	NY0250	11,12,14,29A,35
Tonelli, Chris	AD0050	14
Torre, Robert Anthony	GA0050	12,14
Torres, George	PA1850	12A,12,14,12D,20H
Treer, Leonid P.	FL0650	14,66A,66B,42
Tuomi, Scott	OR0750	12A,12,14,61,55
Turino, Thomas R.	IL3300	11,20A,20H,14
Tyler, Paul	IL2000	14,20
Van Deusen, Nancy	CA1050	12A,12B,12C,14
Vandermeer, Philip R.	NC2410	14,16
Vaneman, Kelly McElrath	SC0650	12A,64B,42,55,14
Varner, Michael	TX3500	50,65,14,20
Veal, Michael E.	CT0900	14,20A,20G
Vercelli, Michael B.	WV0750	20,14,31F,41,42
Vetter, Roger R.	IA0700	11,14
Vosen, Elyse Carter	MN0450	14,15
Waddington, Alan	CA1000	12F,14,29,46,47
Wade, Bonnie C.	CA5000	11,14,20C,20E,12G
Walker, John L.	VA1700	64B,13,14,20H
Walker, Margaret Edith	AG0250	14,12G,13K,20E,12A
Ward, Larry F.	IL0630	11,20,14
Ward-Griffin, Danielle	VA0150	12,20,14
Washburne, Christopher	NY0750	14,29,47
Waterman, Ellen F.	AD0050	64A,14
Watkins, Timothy D.	TX3000	12A,14,20,12
Weightman, Lindsay	PA2700	14
Weiss, Sarah	CT0900	14,20
Wells, Elizabeth A.	AE0050	12A,12,14,20G
Wenzel, Scott	WI0150	14,65,55,50,20A
Whittall, Geoffrey	AA0025	14,65,20,13,11
Will, Udo	OH1850	14
Williams, Maria	NM0450	14,20H,20G
Williams, Sarah F.	SC1110	12A,14C,12,14,15
Williams, Sean	WA0350	11,12,14,20G,70
Wilson, James Dale	CT0100	14,20C,12A,12E,29B
Witmer, Robert	AG0650	14,20G,29
Witmer, Ruth	FL1550	12A,14,20
Witzleben, J. Lawrence	MD1010	14,20,20C
Wolf, Richard	MA1050	12,14
Wollman, Elizabeth L.	NY0250	11,14C,14,15,20
Wong, Deborah	CA5040	14,20,20D,20G,31D
Wong, Ketty	KS1350	14
Woodruff, Jennifer A.	ME0150	13,14
Wrazen, Louise	AG0650	12,14
Yaraman, Sevin H.	NY1300	13,14,12
Yardley, Anne B.	NJ0300	12,14,31,55
Yoon, Paul	VA1500	11,14,20C
Youtz, Gregory	WA0650	10,13,14,43
Yu, Hongmei	AA0150	14
Yubovich, Benjamin	IN0005	60,16,12,13,14
Zhao, Grace Xia	CA5100	66,14,13,66A,66C
Zheng, Su	CT0750	12,14
Zlabinger, Tom	NY0646	62D,29,14,20,47

Research and Methodology

Name	Code	Areas
Alajaji, Sylvia A.	PA1300	14A,14C,11,12A,20
Alonso, Ernesto	PR0150	12A,11,62A,14A,55A
Berliner, Paul F.	NC0600	20A,14A,14F,14B,31F
Bilderback, Barry T.	ID0250	11,12A,20B,12C,14A
Browner, Tara C.	CA5031	20G,14A
Brucher, Katherine	IL0750	14A,20
Christensen, Dieter	NY0750	14,14A,12C
Cooley, Timothy J.	CA5060	20F,20G,14A,14C,14D
Daughtry, J. Martin	NY2740	14A,14C,20B,20F,14D
Dent, Geoffrey	CA2800	14A
DjeDje, Jacqueline Cogdell	CA5031	20A,20G,14A
Eyerly, Susan J.	IN0250	12,13A,14A,15
Gay, Leslie C.	TN1710	14,14A,14C,20,12
Gelbart, Matthew	NY1300	12A,13J,14A,14D,20F
Giles, Jennifer	AG0100	13,12B,14A
Gleason, Bruce	MN1625	32,14A
Gray, Ellen	NY0750	14A,14E,15,20F,14D
Grimshaw, Jeremy	UT0050	14A,14D,20D
Hagedorn, Katherine	CA1050	20A,20G,14A

Hajda, John M.	CA5060	13K,13L,13A,13B,14A
Helbig, Adriana	PA3420	14A,14C,14D,20F,20H
Heller, Wendy B.	NJ0900	12A,12,39,14A
Hsu, Dolores M.	CA5060	12A,12,20D,14A,14B
Humphreys, Paul W.	CA2800	14A,13A,13B,29A,10A
Jennings, Vance	FL2000	12A,14A
Kafumbe, Damascus	VT0350	14A,14C,10E,20,31F
Keyes, Cheryl L.	CA5031	20G,14A
Lau, Frederick C.	HI0210	14A,38,43,64D,20C
Lee, Byong Won	HI0210	20A,20D,14A
Li, Ping-Hui	PR0150	13A,13C,14A,66A,66C
Lindsey, Roberta	IN0907	11,13A,34C,34B,14A
Loza, Steven	CA5031	14A,20H,20G
Luker, Morgan James	OR0900	14A,14C,14D,20H
Lyndon-Gee, Christopher	NY0050	10A,14A,38,39,42
Mahon, Maureen	NY2740	14A,14E,14D,14F,15
Matthay, Christopher D.	NY2750	13,14A,20D,20E,29A
McLean, Hugh J.	AG0500	12,14A,66G,31A
McMillan, Glenn	NY0640	14A,14B
McMullen, Tracy	ME0200	29,15,12,53,14A
Meintjes, Louise	NC0600	20A,14A,14C,14D,14F
Miller, Kiri	RI0050	14A,14C,14D,20G,31G
Moulin, Jane	HI0210	20D,14A,55,67A
Neuman, Daniel M.	CA5031	20E,14A
Novak, David	CA5060	14A,14C,14D,20C
Peterman, Lewis E.	CA4100	14A,41,55,11
Petrovic, Ankica	CA5031	20F,14A,31
Racy, A. J.	CA5031	20B,14A,14B
Rees, Helen	CA5031	20C,20D,20E,14A
Rice, Timothy	CA5031	20E,14A
Roditeleva-Wibe, Maria I.	WA0050	14A,12A,20F,66A,66G
Rubin, Joel E.	VA1550	14A,14C,64C,41,31B
Sakata, Lorraine	CA5031	20B,14A,20E
Sala, Aaron J.	HI0210	14A
Samuels, David	NY2740	14A,14C,14D,14F,20G
Sanford, O'Neil	VA0950	37,14A,63A
Seeger, Anthony	CA5031	20H,14A,20G,35A,35D
Seeman, Sonia T.	TX3510	20A,20B,14A
Seliger, Bryce M.	OR0750	38,14A,13,12A
Slawek, Stephen M.	TX3510	20D,14A
Steiner, Ruth	DC0050	12A,12,14A
Summit, Jeffrey	MA1900	20F,31B,14A,14D
Sutton, R. Anderson	WI0815	11,12A,20D,14A
Swift, Mark D.	PA3580	11,14A,14C,20
Talusan Lacanlale, Mary	CA2800	14A
Titon, Jeff	RI0050	20G,20F,14A
Trimillos, Ricardo D.	HI0210	20D,20I,14D,14A,14F
Tucker, Joshua	RI0050	14A,14C,14D,20H
Turner, Katherine L.	SC0350	64C,12A,20,14A
Weintraub, Andrew	PA3420	20D,14A,20G,14C,14D
Zemke, Lorna	WI0770	32,14A,29,20G

Organology

Name	Code	Areas
Armstrong, Alan	NC1500	12A,14B,13,62C,66A
Berliner, Paul F.	NC0600	20A,14A,14F,14B,31F
Borders, James M.	MI2100	12,14B,71
Hsu, Dolores M.	CA5060	12A,12,20D,14A,14B
McMillan, Glenn	NY0640	14A,14B
Oleskiewicz, Mary	MA2010	11,12A,12,14B,64A
Racy, A. J.	CA5031	20B,14A,14B
Thompson, Gordon R.	NY3650	20D,20E,20F,14C,14B
Verfaille, Vincent	AI0200	13L,14B
Williams, Peter F.	NC0600	12A,12,14B

Popular Music

Name	Code	Areas
Abad, Andy	CA5300	10D,14C
Abraham, Daniel E.	DC0010	11,12,14C,36,60
Aglinskas, Peter	IL1085	70,14C
Alajaji, Sylvia A.	PA1300	14A,14C,11,12A,20
Aldag, Daniel	CA2250	63D,29,14C,63C,47
Allen, Jeffrey L.	CA5300	10D,14C
Allen, Matthew H.	MA2150	14C,20E,20H,31,14
Amador Medina, Ruben J.	PR0115	14C,29A
Anderson, Robert J.	CA5300	10D,14C
Anderson-Himmelspach, Neil	MD0475	10A,13,14C,34,62D
Annoni, Maria T.	MN0900	11,13A,13B,70,14C
Avdeeff, Melissa	AA0110	11,12,14C
Babb, Douglas	IN1100	14C
Bacon, Scott D.	PA1000	11,14C,65
Baker, Hill	CO0625	14C,20,65,34B
Banzi, Julia	OR0400	20,14C,34B,14,10E
Barnes, Larry J.	KY1350	13,10,29A,34,14C
Bauman, Marcia	CA4700	10,14C,34,35
Baur, Steven	AF0100	11,12A,12D,12E,14C
Becker, J. Harris	NY2550	14C
Beckerman, Michael	NY2740	12,14C
Belland, Douglas	KY1000	11,14C
Beller-McKenna, Daniel	NH0350	12A,12C,11,14C
Benedick, Kristi	MO1120	14C
Berkhout, Bjorn	NY3250	10,62C,12A,13,14C
Bingham, Tom	NY3725	14C
Boedges, Bob	MO1120	46,14C
Boris, Victor R.	PA3150	66D,14C
Bozina, Robert	CA4425	20H,70,13A,14F,14C
Brackett, David	AI0150	12,14C
Brackett, John	NC2410	13,14C
Brandt, Jeffrey	MT0400	14C
Bretz, Jeffrey	CA0200	14C
Brickman, Scott T.	ME0420	14C,13,32B,10B,66D
Burford, Mark	OR0900	12A,20G,14C,20H
Burgess, Phillipa	OH1750	36,55C,14C,12A,20
Burns, Lori	AG0400	13,14C
Burr, Anthony	CA5050	64C,43,13D,14C,12D
Byrd, Joseph	CA1280	14C,10D,12A,13A
Carney, Anna	TX2800	11,13A,14C,64C
Castro, Zeke	TX3510	20H,14C
Catefonis, Theodore P.	NY4100	12,12D,20G,29A,14C
Cipiti, John	OH2140	13,66A,10,14C
Ciucci, Alessandra	MA1450	14C,14F,20B,20H
Ciucci, Alessandra	NY0750	11,14,15,14C,20B
Coe, Judith A.	CO0830	61,10D,34,14C,12C
Cohen, Stanley	NY1275	14C,32,46,47,64
Cole, Dennis E.	OH0100	14C,12A,11,20
Collins, Willa	FL1900	12,14C
Colton, Glenn	AG0170	12,20G,14C,14D
Cooley, Timothy J.	CA5060	20F,20G,14A,14C,14D
Cooper, Britt	OH2370	11,12A,14C,36,61
Cote, Gerald	AI0190	14C
Cresci, Jonathan	MD0550	63A,34D,13C,34C,14C
Cunneff, Philip B.	MD0475	13A,65,29A,14C
Curry, Paul	IN1010	14C
Darling, Matthew H.	CA0810	50,65,14C
Daughtry, J. Martin	NY2740	14A,14C,20B,20F,14D
Davenport, Mark	CO0650	12,55,67C,29A,14C

Name	Code	Areas
Dillon, Nathan	CA0200	35,14C
Dobra, William R.	AZ0470	63A,14C
Dohr, Richard William	CA5300	10D,14C
Dotson, Ronald	CA5510	11,34C,66D,14C,12A
Dozier, Lamont	CA5300	10D,14C
Drennan, Jennifer	IL2970	11,14C,20
Duff, Jim	AD0050	14C
Dufrasne, J. Emmanuel	PR0115	14C
DuPree, Mary	ID0250	12A,12,43,14C
Eccleston, Colleen	AB0150	14C
Eisel, Gunnar	CA1000	10B,12A,13A,14C,29A
Esler, Robert	AZ0470	14C
Esler, Robert	AZ0490	50,14C,35C,10
Esse, Melina	NY1100	12A,12B,12D,14C,15
Fairlie, Mary	TX2800	62A,62B,51,14C,38
Fenimore, Ross	NC0550	11,12,14C,14D
Fox, T. Jeffrey	NY2550	36,11,20G,14C
Fresonke, Michael	OK0750	13A,70,14C,41
Fullerton, Kevin T.	KS1400	14C,12A,29A,63D,11
Garry, Kevin M.	CO0400	70,13A,11,12A,14C
Gay, Leslie C.	TN1710	14,14A,14C,20,12
Geihsler, Rebecca	MS0100	61,12A,14C
Gibson, Christina Taylor	MD0550	14C
Givan, Ben	NY3650	13,14C
Gleason, Stephen	NY1275	10D,12A,13B,14C,34D
Goldmark, Daniel	OH0400	12A,14C
Grandy, Larry	CA4550	37,47,64C,29,14C
Grasse, Jonathan B.	CA0805	34D,13,20,14C,10
Gratz, Reed	CA5100	13,10,14C,29,11
Greer, Larry	TX0125	13,14C,29,46,70
Grubb, Jay	NJ0750	14C,35A
Gunderman, Jennifer	TN1850	14C
Haberkorn, Michael	OH2050	66A,20G,14C,11
Habib, Kenneth S.	CA0600	14,10,13,20B,14C
Haffley, Robin L.	PA1830	11,13A,29A,34D,14C
Hamant, Alan D.	DE0150	14C
Hamersma, Carol	NJ1160	11,14C,29A,70
Hardy, Bruce	CA5360	11,29A,14C
Harris, Ward	MD0550	11,14C,12A
Hawkins, Wes	AZ0470	14C,65,50,29A
Heimbecker, Sara	CO0950	12A,11,13A,14C
Helbig, Adriana	PA3420	14A,14C,14D,20F,20H
Hendricks, Hermina	VA1125	29A,14C
Hentges, Londa	MN1250	14C
Honnold, Adrianne	MO1120	14C
Howe, Donald	CA3520	12A,29A,14C,63C
Hufft, Bradley	CA0810	14C,13,11
Ishigaki, Miles M.	CA0810	48,64C,41,11,14C
Jackson, Kymberly	CA4625	14C,29,35
Jacobson, Mary Ann	MT0200	64C,14C,41
Jarvis, David	WA1150	10,47,50,65,14C
Johnson, Roger O.	NJ0950	12,14C,35A
Johnson, Vicky V.	TX2750	13,32B,14C,32,66B
Jorgensen, Michael	MN0750	61,11,32D,14C
Justus, Keith	TX0550	70,13C,14C,29B
Kafumbe, Damascus	VT0350	14A,14C,10E,20,31F
Karnatz, Roland	VA0700	11,14C
Karr, John	CA0810	12,14C
Kehrberg, Kevin	NC2550	12,14C,20,60A,62D
Kennedy, John	TX2350	14C,13A,46,49,32B
Kenney, James	CA3375	13A,11,14C,66D
Kjorness, Christopher	VA0700	20,14C
Kopplin, David F.	CA0630	10,20,29,14C,46
Kutz, Jonathan	TX1600	65A,65B,14C,50
Kvetko, Peter J.	MA1650	14,13A,14C,20E,41
Kyker, Jennifer	NY1100	14,14C,20,20A
Lacasse, Serge	AI0190	14C,14D
Laganella, David	DE0200	10,13,34,14C,12A
Lambert, Nathan T.	CO0350	10F,11,14C,42,51
Landgrebe, Junauro	MA1450	11,14C,41
Langley, Jeff	CA4700	10,14C
Ledbetter, Robert	MT0400	37,50,65,20H,14C
Lee, Rodger P.	NY2550	14C
Lindau, Elizabeth Ann	PA1400	12,14C,20
Link, Nathan	KY0450	12A,14C
Link, Stan	TN1850	12A,12,20G,14C,15
Liu-Rosenbaum, Aaron	AI0190	10,34,35G,13,14C
Livingston, Edwin U.	CA5300	10D,14C
Lohman, Laura Ann	CA0815	12,14,14C
Love, Randolph D.	SC0600	13,10,63,41,14C
Lowe, Melanie D.	TN1850	12A,12,20G,14C,15
Luker, Morgan James	OR0900	14A,14C,14D,20H
Magaldi, Cristina	MD0850	14C,12A,14,20G,20H
Mamula, Stephen	RI0200	14C
Mancuso, Charles	NY3717	20G,29A,12E,14C
Mann, Ted	NH0150	70,14C,13D
Markuson, Stephen	NY1400	14C,31A
Martinez, Robby	CA0270	14C
Maus, Fred Everett	VA1550	13,12B,15,12D,14C
McCool, Jason	MD0550	14C
McCord, Larry	TX0910	11,13B,14C,34B,66A
McCully, Michael	CA0200	35,14C
McIlhagga, Samuel D.	MI0100	10F,37,14C,32E
Meintjes, Louise	NC0600	20A,14A,14C,14D,14F
Miele, David	NY3000	47,14C,65
Miller, Fred	IL2775	70,47,14C
Miller, Kiri	RI0050	14A,14C,14D,20G,31G
Mook, Richard W.	AZ0100	14C
Moore, D. Scott	MN0750	49,14C
Moore, Robin D.	TX3510	14,31F,14C,14F,20H
Moskowitz, David V.	SD0600	12A,20H,14C,12C,11
Moulder, John	IL0275	14C,29,70
Mountain, Toby	MA0700	34,14C
Mueller, Rena Charnin	NY2740	12,14C
Neal, Jocelyn	NC2410	13,20G,34,14C
Neimoyer, Susan	UT0250	12A,14C,10A,12
Nelson, Ron	AG0650	14C
Nivans, David	CA0805	14C,29A,20,13,11
Norris, Renee Lapp	PA1900	14C,12A,20,12,13E
Novak, David	CA5060	14A,14C,14D,20C
O'Donnell, Shaugn	NY0600	13F,14C
O'Neill, Jill L.	SC1200	11,64A,48,14C,41
O'Reilly, Daniel	SC0420	14C,64E,29A
Ouellette, Garry	NY2550	16,14C,72,34,35
Palter, Morris	AK0150	12A,29A,42,43,14C
Parsons, Donna S.	IA1550	14C
Party, Daniel	IN1450	14C,12A,11,20H
Pedde, David	MN1250	66A,10B,14C,31A
Peeples, Terrance P.	IL1520	65,14C,11,50
Pegley, Kip	AG0250	14C,15,32E
Perera, Selina	CA3500	11,20,14C
Pisano, Kristin	KS0350	11,64C,64E,12A,14C
Pittman, Dwight	MO1120	14C
Platoff, John	CT0500	13,11,14C,12,12F
Pozzi, Dave A.	CA0835	13C,14C
Rasmussen, Ljerka V.	TN1400	20,14C,20F,35D,14
Rath, Carl	WI0350	64D,42,14C
Reese, Donald T.	PA1830	11,12A,70,13A,14C
Revuluri, Sindhumathi	MA1050	12,12A,12C,14C,20D
Rice, Marc	MO1780	11,12A,14C
Riner, Nicole	WY0200	64A,14C,32G,48
Robbins, Allison	TN1710	14C
Robbins, Malcolm Scott	SC0650	13,10,14C
Roberts, Tamara	CA5000	11,14C,14D,20G
Roberts, Tim	CA3320	46,14C,10D,13
Robinson, N. Scott	MD0850	12A,14C,50
Rockwell, Joti	CA3650	13,14C,11
Romeo, Arthur	NY1275	14C,29A
Roper, Scott	AZ0490	14C
Rose, Bernard	NY1275	14C,29A,32E
Rubin, Joel E.	VA1550	14A,14C,64C,41,31B
Rushen, Patrice Louise	CA5300	10D,14C
Russell, Benjamin A.	MD0475	47,64E,14C
Russell, Tracy	TX3400	20,14C
Ruth, Byron	AZ0470	14C,29A,64E
Samuels, David	NY2740	14A,14C,14D,14F,20G
Schaefer, G. W. Sandy	NE0050	14C,46,65,29,35
Schweitzer, Kenneth	DE0150	14C
Searles, Julie	MA2150	14,14C,20H,20G
Shellans, Michael	AZ0100	14C
Sheppard, W. Anthony	MA2250	12A,20C,14C,12D,20G
Shipley, John	NV0150	66A,34,14C
Simpson-Litke, Rebecca	GA2100	13,14C,20H
Snyder, Randall	NE0500	14C
Sorah, Donald	VA1580	34,63A,29,14C,20
Sovik, Thomas	TX3420	13,31A,14C,13J,34
Spencer, Theresa Forrester	MO0250	36,40,61,14C
Spicer, Mark	NY0600	13,14C
Stapleton, Chip	IN0907	29A,64E,14C,11
Stolpe, Andrea Kay	CA5300	10D,14C
Strunsky, Mark	NY3000	11,12A,70,14C
Swift, Mark D.	PA3580	11,14A,14C,20
Teal, Kimberly Hannon	NY1100	12,14C
Thompson, Gordon R.	NY3650	20D,20E,20F,14C,14B
Thorman, Marc	NY0500	10,13,12A,20,14C
Tolson, Gerald H.	KY1500	32,47,29,14C
Toman, Sharon Ann	PA2775	11,13A,29A,14C,36
Trask, Alvin	MD0550	63A,53,29A,14C,47
Tucker, Joshua	RI0050	14A,14C,14D,20H
Vacca, Anthony	AZ0490	29A,14C
Vaccaro, Brian	MO1120	47,14C
Vallee, Mickey	AA0100	14C
Van der Bliek, Rob	AG0650	12,14C,29
Vander Wel, Stephanie L.	NY4320	12,14C
VanderWoude, Matthew	AG0650	14C
Versaevel, Stephen	MT0200	65,50,14C
VonBerg, Craig	CA0810	29,47,14C
Waksman, Steve M.	MA1750	29A,14C
Ward, Brian	WA1150	66A,10D,13C,14C,29A
Warwick, Jacqueline	AF0100	12A,12D,14C,15,29A
Watkins, Holly	NY1100	12A,12B,12D,13J,14C
Watson, Richard	ND0250	14C,20G
Watson, William E.	MD0175	10,47,14C,20
Weintraub, Andrew	PA3420	20D,14A,20G,14C,14D
Whitehead, Corey	CA0810	70,11,14C
Will, Richard	VA1550	12A,12,20G,14C
Williams, Ray	AG0650	14C
Williams, Sarah F.	SC1110	12A,14C,12,14,15
Wischusen, Mary A.	MI2200	12A,12,14C
Woldu, Gail Hilson	CT0500	11,14C,12A,15
Wollman, Elizabeth L.	NY0250	11,14C,14,15,20
Woods, Bret	AL1050	14C,20,34
Wright, Trey	GA1150	70,47,29A,29B,14C
Yanez, Raul	AZ0490	66A,47,14C,29A
Young, Shawn David	GA0500	14C,35A,31A,35,11

Critical Theory

Name	Code	Areas
Bakriges, Christopher	MA1550	29,14D,12B,20,31G
Colton, Glenn	AG0170	12,20G,14C,14D
Cooley, Timothy J.	CA5060	20F,20G,14A,14C,14D
Daughtry, J. Martin	NY2740	14A,14C,20B,20F,14D
Fenimore, Ross	NC0550	11,12,14C,14D
Gelbart, Matthew	NY1300	12A,13J,14A,14D,20F
Gray, Ellen	NY0750	14A,14E,15,20F,14D
Grimshaw, Jeremy	UT0050	14A,14D,20D
Helbig, Adriana	PA3420	14A,14C,14D,20F,20H
Lacasse, Serge	AI0190	14C,14D
Lee, Tong Soon	GA0750	14,20C,20D,14D,14F
Luker, Morgan James	OR0900	14A,14C,14D,20H
Mahon, Maureen	NY2740	14A,14E,14D,14F,15
Meintjes, Louise	NC0600	20A,14A,14C,14D,14F
Miller, Christopher J.	NY0900	20D,14D
Miller, Kiri	RI0050	14A,14C,14D,20G,31G
Moseley, Roger S.	NY0900	12,13,14D,34H
Novak, David	CA5060	14A,14C,14D,20C
Roberts, Tamara	CA5000	11,14C,14D,20G
Samuels, David	NY2740	14A,14C,14D,14F,20G
Summit, Jeffrey	MA1900	20F,31B,14A,14D
Trimillos, Ricardo D.	HI0210	20D,20I,14D,14A,14F
Tucker, Joshua	RI0050	14A,14C,14D,20H
Weintraub, Andrew	PA3420	20D,14A,20G,14C,14D

Archaeology

Name	Code	Areas
Gray, Ellen	NY0750	14A,14E,15,20F,14D
Kemm, Karl	TX0550	63B,49,67E,14E,14F
London, Robert	AZ0470	35,14E
Mahon, Maureen	NY2740	14A,14E,14D,14F,15

Anthropology

Name	Code	Areas
Anderson, Michael Alan	NY1100	12,12A,14F
Berliner, Paul F.	NC0600	20A,14A,14F,14B,31F
Bozina, Robert	CA4425	20H,70,13A,14F,14C
Ciucci, Alessandra	MA1450	14C,14F,20B,20H
Conlon, Paula J.	OK1350	20G,20,14F,14
Jakelski, Lisa	NY1100	12A,12E,12B,12C,14F
Jankowsky, Rich	MA1900	14,31C,20B,14F
Jones, Dena Kay	TX3520	66,32,20F,14F,15
Kemm, Karl	TX0550	63B,49,67E,14E,14F
Lee, Tong Soon	GA0750	14,20C,20D,14D,14F
Mahon, Maureen	NY2740	14A,14E,14D,14F,15
Meintjes, Louise	NC0600	20A,14A,14C,14D,14F
Mendonca, Maria Alice	OH1200	14F,20,15
Moore, Robin D.	TX3510	14,31F,14C,14F,20H
Neuman, Dard A.	CA5070	20E,14F
Samuels, David	NY2740	14A,14C,14D,14F,20G
Stegall, Sydney Wallace	WA0460	13,14,10B,14F,10
Trimillos, Ricardo D.	HI0210	20D,20I,14D,14A,14F

Index by Area of Teaching Interest

Gender Studies

Archbold, Lawrence	MN0300	11,12A,66G,15,12D
Artesani, Laura	ME0440	12A,66C,15,32B,32C
Bailey, Candace L.	NC1600	12,29D,15,11,12A
Barnum, Ellen M.	NY0400	12A,64D,15
Bloxam, Jennifer	MA2250	11,15,12
Borwick, Susan Harden	NC2500	13,12,31,10,15
Brown, Cristy Lynn	NC2205	61,15,54
Bryson, Amity H.	MO0050	36,61,60A,15,32D
Bussineau-King, D. E.	TX3410	61,15,39
Cassaro, James P.	PA3420	16,12C,15
Chua, Emily Yap	VA1125	13B,15,42,66A
Ciucci, Alessandra	NY0750	11,14,15,14C,20B
Clark, Maribeth	FL1360	11,12,14,15
Coates, Norma	AG0500	12A,12D,15,35A
Coker, Cheryl W.	MS0385	15,61
Colatosti, Camille	MA0260	15
Converse, Sheila K.	WA1150	61,15
Cusick, Suzanne G.	NY2740	12A,12C,12D,15
Cyrus, Cynthia	TN1850	12,15,55,20F
Davis, Daniel	NC0600	10,14,15,20A
Denisch, Beth	MA0260	13,10F,10,15
Downing, Sonja Lynn	WI0350	14,15,20D,64A,32
Dunn, Cherry W.	MS0550	61,39,15
Esse, Melina	NY1100	12A,12B,12D,14C,15
Eyerly, Sarah J.	IN0250	12,13A,14A,15
Fairfield, Patrick K.	MI1850	11,15,20,70
Fauser, Annegret	NC2410	12,15
Feldman, Martha	IL3250	11,12A,12,15
Feller, Ross	OH1200	13,15
Ferencz, Jane Riegel	WI0865	67,11,12,15
Fisher, John	TX3250	13A,13B,10A,15,66A
Fiske, Jane	MA0930	11,15,32,66
Flory, Jennifer Morgan	GA0850	36,32D,15,60A,61
Follet, Diane W.	PA2550	13,15,42,13H
Foulk, Lin	MI2250	63B,15,41,48,49
Francis, Kimberly	AG0350	15,13,12
Freitas, Roger	NY1100	12A,12C,12D,15
Furby, Victoria J.	NY3717	13C,15,32D
Gier, Christina B.	AA0100	12A,12D,12B,12,15
Graveline, Michelle	MA0200	15,13,36
Gray, Ellen	NY0750	14A,14E,15,20F,14D
Guzzo, Anne M.	WY0200	13,10,12A,13F,15
Hahn, Tomie	NY3300	14,15,20,31G,34
Harbach, Barbara	MO1830	66G,67F,15,66H,34A
Henson, Karen A.	NY0750	11,15,39,12A,12B
Hirsch, Marjorie	MA2250	11,12,15,20G
Hisama, Ellie M.	NY0750	15,13E,12A,10B,13F
Hollander, Jeffrey M.	IN1750	12A,15,11,12
Holloway, Peggy A.	NE0610	61,32B,15,36,40
Holzer, Linda	AR0750	66A,66B,42,15,11
Hutchinson, Sydney	NY4100	14,15
Johnson, Calvert	GA0050	66G,15,31,66H,12A
Jones, Dena Kay	TX3520	66,32,20F,14F,15
Kallberg, Jeffrey	PA3350	12A,12,12D,15
Keiter, Lise	VA0800	13,11,66A,12A,15
Koskoff, Ellen	NY1100	14,15,20G,20D,31
Kowalke, Kim H.	NY1100	12A,12B,12C,12D,15
Lamb, Roberta	AG0250	32,15,67C
Le Guin, Elisabeth C.	CA5032	12A,12,62C,67B,15
Ledeen, Lydia Hailparn	NJ0300	11,12A,15,12C
Leonard, Charlotte	AG0150	12A,63D,63C,15,63B
Link, Stan	TN1850	12A,12,20G,14C,15
Lofthouse, Charity	NY1550	13,34B,34F,15,31A
Lorenzo, Elizabeth	CT0050	12,11,15,12A
Lowe, Melanie D.	TN1850	12A,12,20G,14C,15
MacNeil, Anne E.	NC2410	12,15
Mahon, Maureen	NY2740	14A,14E,14D,14F,15
Matsue, Jennifer	NY4310	14,15,20C,20
Matsushita, Hidemi	CO0100	66A,11,12,15,13
Maus, Fred Everett	VA1550	13,12B,15,12D,14C
McCormack, Jessica D.	IN0910	61,39,12,15,67H
McDonald, Susan M.	PA1830	10A,10B,12A,15,34D
McMullen, Tracy	ME0200	29,15,12,53,14A
Meconi, Honey	NY4350	12A,12,15
Mendonca, Maria Alice	OH1200	14F,20D,15
Merchant, Tanya H.	CA5070	20B,15,12A
Meredith, Sarah A.	WI0808	39,61,54,15
Metzer, David	AB0100	13,29A,15
Mitchell, Darleen C.	NE0590	13,10,15,43,12B
Morris, Mitchell B.	CA5032	12A,12,20G,15
Murchison, Pamela	MD0350	64A,48,20,15
Murray, Russell E.	DE0150	12A,15,55,67D,67B
Mygatt, Louise	NY1800	12A,15
Norberg, Anna H.	OK1450	66A,66C,66D,15
Oliveros, Pauline	CA2950	10,15
Owens, Jessie Ann	CA5010	12A,13J,15
Peeples, Georgia	OH2150	12A,64D,15,48
Pegley, Kip	AG0250	14C,15,32E
Pennington, Stephen	MA1900	12D,29A,29E,15,12
Peraino, Judith A.	NY0900	12A,12D,15
Ray, Marcie	MI1400	12A,15
Reinoso, Crystal Hearne	NY3717	13B,48,64C,15
Rosenberg, Ruth Emily	IL3310	20F,15,14
Rushton, Christianne	AF0050	12A,15,32D,61
Sandstrom, Boden	MD1010	14,15
Scharfenberger, Paul E.	NH0110	12,67C,43,55,15
Schlicht, Ursel	NJ0950	13,14,15,53
Slominski, Tes	WI0100	14,15
Smart, Mary Ann	CA5000	11,12,15
Soebbing, Steven	MD0350	61,20,15
Solomon, Nanette Kaplan	PA3100	12A,66A,13C,15
Spiller, Henry	CA5010	14,12,15,20D,12D
Tait, Alicia Cordoba	IL0275	20,12A,15,35,11
Trejo, Kyndell	IL2750	15
Trinkle, Karen M.	MO1950	12,15,12A
Vosen, Elyse Carter	MN0450	14,15
Warwick, Jacqueline	AF0100	12A,12D,14C,15,29A
Wheelock, Gretchen A.	NY1100	12A,12B,12C,12D,15
Wilbourne, Emily	NY0750	11,12,15,20F
Williams, Sarah F.	SC1110	12A,14C,12,14,15
Winkler, Amanda Eubanks	NY4100	12,12A,15,31A,31G
Woldu, Gail Hilson	CT0500	11,14C,12A,15
Wollman, Elizabeth L.	NY0250	11,14C,14,15,20
Youngblood, Pamela J.	TX3300	41,64A,13A,13B,15
Zerkle, Paula R.	PA2450	36,60,15,11,54
Zigler, Amy E.	NC2205	12A,15

Music Librarian

Adkins, Richard C.	IA0300	16,71,66F
Allen, James O.	MS0550	11,12A,16,66A,66C
Anthony, James	MD0850	11,12,16
Axworthy, Tamra	CO0275	16
Barstow, Robert S.	NY3765	12A,36,16,35
Beeks, Graydon F.	CA3650	60,12A,37,16,54
Biondo, Steven A.	CA5100	34,16,20A
Boettcher, Bonna	NY0900	16,12A,12C
Boye, Gary	NC0050	16
Breckbill, Anita	NE0600	16
Bristah, Pamela	MA2050	16
Brooks, Victoria	FL0100	16
Brown, Sarah	TN1100	16
Burns, Ellen J.	NY3700	16,11
Campana, Deborah	OH1700	16
Carbone, Kathy	CA0510	16
Cary, Paul	OH0200	16
Cassaro, James P.	PA3420	16,12C,15
Castles, JoAnn	AL1450	16,34C
Cherkaoui, Tsukasa	FL1125	16
Chodacki-Ford, Roberta	GA0550	16,12G
Christensen, Beth	MN1450	16
Chyun, Mi-Hye	NJ1350	16
Clark, Dan	FL0850	16
Clark, Joe	OH1100	16
Cleveland, Susannah L.	OH0300	16
Clifton, Felecia	ND0500	16
Clinkscales, Joyce	GA0750	16
Cockburn, Brian	VA0600	16,12C
Cohen, Sarah Hess	FL0850	16
Colvin, Jennifer L.	SC0750	16
Coscarelli, William F.	GA2100	16
Couture, Marie	NH0300	11,16
Crandell, Adam	PA1500	16
Crane, Rachel L.	KS1450	16
Daegling, Sharon	CA4300	16
Davis, Elizabeth	NY0750	16
DeBacco, Maria	TN1680	16
DeLand, Robert	IL3450	16
Delvin, Robert	IL1200	16
Dempf, Linda	NJ0175	16
Dovel, Teresa	CA5355	16
Dubnjakovic, Ana	SC1110	16
Eby, Carole	SC0200	16
Edington-Hogg, Lynn	CA4100	16
Ericson, Margaret D.	ME0250	16
Evans, Amanda	OH1100	16
Fairtile, Linda B.	VA1500	16
Faison, Vernice	NC1600	16
Fawcett-Yeske, Maxine	CO0750	11,12,14,16,20
Fears, Angela	CA3520	13A,13C,64D,16
Fisken, Patricia B.	NH0100	16
Fitzgerald, Gregory	MI2250	16
Fleming, Beth	OK0750	16,12C
Fountain, Marcia	TX3520	13,16
Fournier, Donna	PA3200	16
Fuertges, Dan H.	IL0400	16
Furr, Rhonda	TX1000	12A,16,66G
Gable, David D.	GA0490	11,12A,12B,13A,16
Garman, Michelle	PA3650	16
Geans, Jeannine	OH0550	16
Gerber, Stephen K.	VA0450	12C,16
Gertig, Suzanne	CO0900	62E,16,12
Gibbs, George E.	KS1350	16
Gladysheva, Alla	CA4150	13,16
Gottlieb, Jane	NY1900	16,12C
Green, Alan	OH1850	16
Gregory, David	KY1200	61,16,12
Haefliger, Kathleen	IL0600	16
Hansen, Alicia S.	LA0300	16
Harbold, Mark A.	IL0850	13,10F,10,16,12A
Hardin, Dan	FL0700	16,66G
Hatch, Ken	AR0110	41,64C,64E,16
Hawthorne, Leroy	LA0100	70,20G,16,47
Herdan, Eric S.	CA3500	16
Heroux, Gerard H.	RI0300	16,63B,11
Hill, George R.	NY0250	11,12A,12,16
Hirshfield, L. Russell	CT0800	16,13,66,66B,66A
Honea, Ted	OK1330	12A,16,63B
Hoppe, Frank	CA3500	16
Hoppmann, Kenneth	IN0005	10,16,20F,35A,66
Hoyer, John	MI1050	16
Hristov, Maria N.	TN1710	16
Hsieh, Fang-Lan	TX2600	12A,16
Hundemer, Thomas	LA0050	63B,16,10A
Jenkins, Martin D.	OH2500	16
Jordan, Rebecca	NY1800	16
Juengling, Pamela K.	MA2000	16
Kamtman, Leslie E.		16
Karass, Alan M.	MA0700	11,16
Kasling, Tess	MN0350	16
Kelly, Kevin	GA2100	16,12
Klice, Joseph A.	CA3500	66A,16
Klinebriel, Jill	IA0250	16,54
Komara, Edward M.	NY3780	16
Kubesheski, Cindy	IA0250	16
Larson, Andre	SD0600	71,16
Leive, Cynthia	AI0150	16
Linton, Andrew	TN0850	16,70
Lipartito, Robert	NJ1050	16
Lisius, Peter	OH1100	16
Lowry, Carol S.	TN1680	16
Luttmann, Stephen	CO0950	16,12C
Lybarger, Lowell H.	AR0200	20,16
Maher, John	IN1025	13,12A,66G,16,34
Maloney, Timothy	MN1623	16
Maring, Marvel A.	NE0610	16
Martin, Cathy	AI0150	12C,16
Martin, Morris	TX3420	16
Mayhood, Erin L.	VA1550	16
McCoy, Jane O.	NC2550	61,16,40
McDaniel-Milliken, Jennifer L.	SC1200	39,16
McKenna, Fr. Edward	IN0005	10,62A,16,31A,11
McKnight, Mark	TX3420	16,12
McLamore, Alyson	CA0600	12A,12,32,16,20G
McLane, Alec	CT0750	16
McLaughlin, Kevin	CA4150	16
McMillan, Brian	AI0150	12C,16
McMorrow, Kathleen	AG0450	16
Messing, Scott	MI0150	11,12A,66A,16,13A
Meyer, Kenton	PA0850	16
Meyers Sawa, Suzanne	AG0450	16
Michki, Kevin	NY3725	16
Miller, Brett	WV0800	16
Miller, Cynthia F.	AL1170	16
Moore, Christine E.	TX2100	62,16
Morris, Marjorie	NJ1050	16
Moushey, Suzanne Z.	OH2290	16
Mueller, Raymond	WI1150	70,16
Murphy, Cynthia	NE0300	16,66A,66D,13
Neal, Anna	TN1680	16
Nuzzo, Nancy B.	NY4320	16
Oates, Jennifer Lynn	NY0600	12,16,12A,12C
Ouellette, Garry	NY2550	16,14C,72,34,35

Name	Code	Areas
Palkovic, Mark	OH2200	16
Pawlak, Keith V.	AZ0500	11,16
Payne, William	WA1150	16
Rahkonen, Carl J.	PA1600	16,14
Raphael, Honora	NY0500	16
Read, Evelyn	VT0450	62A,62B,16,42
Reece, A.	NY3770	16,34
Reiff, Eric	VA0500	16
Roberts, John H.	CA5000	12,16
Robinson, Curtis	IN0005	13,16,29,34,35
Rogan, Michael J.	MA1900	16
Rorick, William	NY0642	16
Rothrock, Donna K.	NC2205	16,32E,63D
Royal, Jacquelyn A.	TN0300	11,13,16,34B
Rudolph, Roy	MA1175	16
Ryder, Virginia	CA2250	64,16
Sampsel, Laurie	CO0800	16
Scheffield, Eric	WI0865	16
Schoepflin, Judith	WA1350	66A,66D,16,66B
Scott, Sarah	CA5355	16,66D
Scroggins, Sterling Edward	DC0010	61,16,11
Sestrick, Timothy	PA1400	16,65,50
Sharpe, Rod L.	IL3500	16
Sheldon, Janene	NE0450	61,32B,36,40,16
Sickbert, Murl	TX0900	16
Smith, Deborah	CA1075	16
Smith, James A.	KS1350	16
Smith, Susan	MO0400	16,61,12A
Snyder, Laura	AA0100	16
Sparks, David	CA1100	16,10,66A
Steed, Brad B.	CA3500	13A,11,16
Stevens, Daryll	CO0200	64C,16
Szabo, Peter	OH2000	16
Szurek, Jaroslaw P.	AL0800	11,16
Taranto, Cheryl	NV0050	16,12A,12C
Tate, Shelia D.	VA1800	11,32,16,36
Tsou, Judy	WA1050	16
Unger, Melvin P.	OH0200	16,12A,36
Vandermeer, Philip R.	NC2410	14,16
Wald, Jean P.	FL1750	16
Walker, Elizabeth	PA0850	16
Walzer, Barbara	NY3560	16
Weil, Susan	CA1520	16
Weisbrod, Liza	AL0200	16,66
Whitehouse, Jackie	CA3320	16
Wilkes, Jamey	GA2000	11,16
Williams, Johnny	FL0600	16
Williams, Laura	NC0600	16
Williams, Nancy	CA0950	66D,16,11
Wright, Julie	TN0250	16
Wubbena, Teresa R.	AR0400	13,32,41,16,64
Yubovich, Benjamin	IN0005	60,16,12,13,14
Zager, Daniel	NY1100	16,12C
Zaik, Santha	OR0750	63B,16
Zavac, Nancy C.	FL1900	16,12F

World Musics (All Areas)

Name	Code	Areas
Acker, Gregory	IN1010	20
Adams, Bob	WA0030	20,14
Addison, Don F.	OR0800	20,14
Aduonum, Ama Oforiwaa Konadu	IL1150	20,11
Akarepi, Ekaterini	OK1350	20
Ake, David	NV0100	12,20,29A,14,66A
Aksoy, Ozan	NY0625	20
Alajaji, Sylvia A.	PA1300	14A,14C,11,12A,20
Alcorn, Allison A.	IL3150	10E,11,12A,20,31A
Allen, Stephen Arthur	NJ1000	13,11,12A,12,20
Allison, Adrian	MN1295	12,20
Allsen, J. Michael	WI0865	11,12,14,20
Alorwoyie, Gideon F.	TX3420	20,65,31F,50,52
Amox, Jennifer	AR0300	64A,20
Applewhite, Willie	UT0190	66,20,29,63C
Arana, Miranda	GA0755	11,12A,12B,13A,20
Archetto, Maria	NC1700	11,20,20E,14
Arnold, Alison E.	MI0650	20,36,66
Arroe, Cate	MN1100	61,36,40,20,13C
Ashworth, Teresa	MD0550	20,42,62C
Avery, Dawn	CO0625	14C,20,65,34B
Baker, Hill	IL0720	20,12
Bakkum, Nathan	MA1550	29,14D,12B,20,31G
Bakriges, Christopher	FL1675	11,20
Ballengee, Chris	OR0400	20,14C,34B,14,10E
Banzi, Julia	TN1850	12,14,20,31,29A
Barz, Gregory F.	OH2050	12A,20,32,38,62D
Bates, James	OR1250	66,20,12A,14
Baxter, Diane R.	DC0010	29,20,13,62D,70
Bayer, Joshua	MA0280	11,20
Bazinet, Ryan	OR0400	20
Beck, Nathan	IL2650	20
Becker, Michael	SC0750	20
Beckford, John S.	IL2560	11,12A,13,38,20
Beert, Michael	MO0775	20
Beisswenger, Donald A.	IN0400	14,12,20,20D,12B
Benamou, Marc	MN1280	20
Benham, John	CA1950	11,20
Benkman, Noel	CA0900	11,20,66
Benkman, Noel	AL0210	13,12A,11,65,20
Benson, Mark F.	MN0040	20,32,37,41,47
Bergstrom, Samuel	IL1800	13,20,29A,63,34
Betts, James E.	FL1675	11,13A,20,29,64
Bingham, Steve	PA2250	20,66A
Bischoff, Janet	WV0050	66A,66D,20,66B,66C
Boey, Hooi Yin	MA2100	20,64C
Boggs, Isabelle	MA1100	20,64C,62A,62B
Boggs, Isabelle	WI0835	20
Bohn, David M.	CA5353	47,20
Bokar Thiam, Pascal	IL2970	65,20
Bolen, Jerry	AR0110	48,64A,20
Bonner, Joe	NC2350	60,20,36,31,61
Boozer, John E.	GA0700	12,20,13,62,11
Boucher, Leslie H.	MI1200	36,20,13
Bowen, Meredith Y.	CA4580	29,10,66,53,20
Briggs, Nancy L.	CA3500	20,11,29
Briggs, Ray	OH0680	12A,11,62E,14,20
Brinksmeier, Ulrike	MI0850	11,66A,20
Bristol, Cynthia	VT0050	13,10,20,34
Brooke, Nicholas	NJ1000	11,12,13,20,12A
Brosius, Amy T.	CA2950	10B,10A,20,13,14
Brown, Chris	WA1000	12A,29A,13C,20,12B
Brown, Gwynne Kuhner	CA0250	12,14,20
Browne, Kimasi L.	TX3515	11,12A,49,63A,20
Brownlow, James A.	IN0550	39,61,36,31A,20
Brubaker, Debra	IL0750	14A,20
Brucher, Katherine	GA2300	11,13C,63A,20
Bryant, John	MN0950	20
Bryant, Lei Ouyang		

Name	Code	Areas
Buis, Johann S.	IL3550	12,20,11
Burchard, Richard	KY0250	10,13,20,34,35
Burgess, Phillipa	OH1750	36,55C,14C,12A,20
Burke, Kevin R.	IN0500	12,13,20,42,63B
Burnham, Stuart	NC1500	12A,13C,66A,20
Burns, Carolyn	ND0100	32,20,14,55B
Burns, James	NY3705	14,20
Bustos, Isaac	TX2900	20,70
Butler, Melvin L.	IL3250	14,20
Buyer, Paul L.	SC0400	65,50,14,20
Byl, Julia S.	MN1450	20
Caceres, Abraham	WI0500	20
Cain, Michael D.	MA1400	29,66A,34,31,20
Camino, Suzanne	MI0500	20
Campbell, Brian G.	MN0350	13,10A,20,12B,10F
Campbell, Jennifer L.	MI0400	11,12,20
Campbell, William G.	IA1300	10,13,20,34
Campion, Edmund	CA5000	20,13,34,35G
Canon, Sherri D.	CA2720	20,29A,66A
Carmenates, Omar	SC0750	65,50,20
Carney, Michael	CA0825	65,29,20,50
Carper, Ken	FL0680	20
Carter, Marva G.	GA1050	12,20G,20,20A
Cassarino, James P.	VT0200	12,14,20,36,37
Cassio, Francesca	NY1600	12,12A,12C,20
Catalano, Roberto F.	CA3950	14,20
Catalano, Roberto	CA0630	20
Catalano, Roberto	CA5100	14,20
Chacholiades, Linda P.	MN0610	11,20,12A
Chaffee, Christopher	OH2500	64A,20,29A,11
Chapman, David	CA3000	11,70,20
Charles, David	MT0200	14,20,47
Childs-Helton, Sally	IN0250	20
Cimarusti, Thomas M.	TX3200	12A,13E,20,12C,68
Clayton, Cathryn	UT0250	62E,20,12A
Clemente, Peter	MA0200	11,13A,13,70,20
Clifton, Keith E.	MI0400	12,11,20
Coach, Leo	OH0650	20,14
Cohen, Judith	AG0650	20,55C,55A,32E
Cohen, Nicki S.	TX3300	61,33,20
Cole, Dennis E.	OH0100	14C,12A,11,20
Collier, Bethany	PA0350	14,20,20D
Colquhoun, Michael	NY0400	10,20
Colson, Steve	NJ0800	20,66D
Conlon, Paula J.	OK1350	20G,20,14F,14
Connor, Mark	MO0700	13,20,41,47
Cook, Bruce	CA1560	66,14,11,20
Coolen, Michael T.	OR0700	14,54,20,12A,35A
Corbin, Dwayne	CA4550	38,20
Cortese, Michael	NY0450	10,11,20,34,47
Coughran, Steven J.	CA1500	47,20,29A,70
Courtney, Ken H.	SC1100	11,66G,20
Cox, Donna M.	OH2250	20,36,32
Crain, Michael R.	CA0840	20,34
Crain, Timothy M.	MA2030	12,20,29A,11
Crawford, Michael	MI0850	62D,20
Craycraft, Jeremy	MN0450	20,50,34,65
Cronk, M. Sam	CA4500	20
Croskery, Virginia	IA1350	61,20
Crummer, Larry D.	CA1760	20,13,11,14,66A
Cryderman-Weber, Molly	MI1200	12,20,13B,13,65
Cunningham, James E.	FL0650	14,20,32,11,12A
Curtis, Peter	CA3800	11,70,14,20,29
Dade, Fred S.	PA3050	20,11,32B,36,66A
Dalton, James	CA4400	20
Dameron, Beth	TX2750	13,10,12A,20
Davidian, Teresa	OH0350	20,60,65
Davis, Edward	IN1300	13,20
Deagan, Gail	MN0750	36,13,20,32D,34B
Dean, Brandon	NY4460	20
DeAngelo, Brian	GA0150	11,20,29,37,47
Decuir, Michael	AZ0490	20,29A,12A,65
DeLamater, Elizabeth L.	SD0200	36,11,20,60,12
Desmond, Clinton J.	KS1400	66A,66B,66D,20
Ding, Xiaoli	IA0200	12A,20,48,64C,64E
Doggett, Cynthia Krenzel	HI0150	11,61,36,54,20
Doo, Lina J.	MS0700	14,20
Dor, George	OH0200	20
Dorey, Christine S.	MA2250	14,20
Dosunmu, Oyebade A.	PA1550	12A,32,13C,20
Doutt, Kathleen C.	CA0825	11,14,20
Doyle, Alicia M.	IL2970	11,14C,20
Drennan, Jennifer	NY0625	20
Dumbauld, Benjamin	MO0950	64A,12A,14,11,20
Dunnell, Rebecca	CT0050	20
Eagleson, Ian	IL1330	11,20
Ebert, Shari E.	AG0100	12,20,29,34,35
Echard, William	TX2750	11,20,48,64A
Eldridge, Ronda	MN1100	61,66D,11,20,66C
Embretson, Deborah	MA0100	20,33,12
Engelhardt, Jeffers	NV0100	47,20,64E
Epstein, Peter	IA0600	20,31A,38,66A
Ergo, Jack	AG0170	13,36,20,39
Erickson, Kim	AR0300	11,20,32E
Etienne, David	NY3760	37,64B,12A,13B,20
Evans, Joel	MI1850	11,15,20,70
Fairfield, Patrick K.	NY3550	13,14,10,20
Farley, Michael	ME0150	13,14,20,20D
Fatone, Gina Andrea	IL1150	11,20
Faux, Tom	IL1740	61,20
Favazza, Kathleen	CO0750	11,12,14,16,20
Fawcett-Yeske, Maxine	WI0825	32,20
Feay-Shaw, Sheila J.	WA0550	66A,66D,13C,11,20
Fellis, Mizue	UT0325	20
Ferguson, Daniel	CA0960	20
Fernandez, Robert	MI0900	12C,12A,20
Feurzeig, Lisa	NJ0950	14,20,45
Fikentscher, Kai	OH2200	20
Fiol, Stefan	IL2970	11,36,66A,40,20
Fleming, Gail H.	NE0610	13,20
Ford, Barry M.	OH1100	20
Foreman, Kelly	NY0850	61,20
Foss, Treva M.	NC0250	50,65,20,32E
Franklin, Laura L.	KS0300	65,50,20,34D
Freeze, Tracy	OK0800	64B,20,32E
Frehner, Celeste Johnson	FL0365	20,12A
Fryns, Jennifer	OH1100	11,20
Fucci, Melissa	WA0960	20
Fulton, Carolyn J.	MO1790	20,64C,64E
Gai, James R.	CT0500	14,20,20H,50,65
Galm, Eric A.	NC2410	12,14,20
Garcia, David F.	TX2900	64A,12A,20,11
Gariazzo, Mariana Stratta	WY0200	64A,20,67H
Garnett, Rodney A.	NY0625	20
Garvey, Bradford	VA0700	63D,20
Gassler, Christopher J.	TN1710	14,14A,14C,20,12
Gay, Leslie C.	FL1800	11,12A,20
Gennaro, Joe		

Index by Area of Teaching Interest

Name	Code	Areas
Gerberg, Miriam	MN0800	20
Gerstin, Julian	NH0150	20
Gettel, Court	VT0100	64A,13,20
Giacona, Christina	OK1350	20
Giampietro, Matilda	CT0800	20
Gilman, Kurt	TX1400	38,41,62A,62B,20
Glann, Kerry	OH1100	20,36,39
Goering, John	KS1450	29,20,66A
Gonzalez, Claudio	MI0250	38,60B,10F,20,12A
Gonzalez, Fr. George	IN0005	11,14,20,66G,32
Goode, Gloria	PA2400	11,20
Goslin, Gerald H.	MI1700	61,66A,20
Gould, Brooke	IA0420	20
Goza, David	OK1350	20
Grasse, Jonathan B.	CA0805	34D,13,20,14C,10
Grasso, Eliot	OR1050	11,20,14
Gratto, Sharon Davis	OH2250	36,20,32
Gray, Laura J.	AG0470	11,12A,12,14,20
Greenan, April	VA1475	11,12A,12B,12F,20
Greenwood, Joanna E.	MD0400	12,20
Grimes, Robert R.	NY1300	12,14,20
Grippo, James	CA5360	20
Griswold, Randall L.	CA0847	20,11
Grmela, Sylvia	NY4460	62B,20,13A,13C
Grobler, Sophia	OH0950	66A,66C,66D,20
Groesbeck, Rolf A.	AR0750	11,12,14,66A,20
Grooms, Pamela	MO0650	12A,20,32D,60,66
Gross, Murray	MI0150	38,13,60B,10,20
Grutzmacher, Patricia Ann	OH1100	32,41,64B,37,20
Guenther, Christina	TX2700	64A,20,41
Guzman, Juan-Tony	IA0950	32,47,14,29,20
Haddad, Jamey	MA1400	29,20,65
Haddad, Jamey	OH0600	20
Haecker, Allyss	SC0900	61,20,36,39
Hahn, Tomie	NY3300	14,15,20,31G,34
Hall, Rick	PA3330	47,20
Hamill, Chad	AZ0450	14,20
Hamilton, Hilree J.	WI0845	11,20,32A,32B,66D
Hansen, Julia	CA4625	14,66A,20
Hansen, Kathleen	MT0175	13,20
Harding, Kevin	VA1150	20,29
Harnish, David D.	CA5200	14,20,31,41
Harrington, E. Michael	MA0260	35,10,20,14
Hartenberger, Aurelia	MO1830	20,32
Hartigan, Royal	MA2020	14,20
Hasenpflug, Thom	ID0100	65,13,20,10,50
Hearn, William	GA0500	11,41,70,20
Heifetz, Robin J.	CA0200	11,20,10A,43,12
Heim, Sean	CA0960	13,20
Heisler, Wayne H.	NJ0175	12A,14,20
Helman, Shandra K.	ID0100	64C,13C,48,20,64E
Hemingway, Gerry	NY2660	65,20,13
Henderson, David R.	NY3550	14,20,12
Henning, Mary	KY0350	20,44,32,36
Hernly, Patrick	FL2050	20,65
Hildreth, John W.	IL0100	11,14,20
Hill-Kretzer, Kelly	MI0050	20,64A
Himrod, Gail P.	RI0150	12A,20,11
Hiranpradist, Barbara	MI1200	11,32B,20
Hixson, Mary	GA2000	13C,20,40,43
Hoag, Bret	MI1830	70,20
Hodges, William Robert	CA3700	20
Hoefnagels, Anna	AG0100	12,20
Hoeschen, Kevin	WI0860	62B,20
Holder, Brian	FL1675	11,20,13A,65,50
Hollingsworth, Mark	OK0300	20
Hollis, Brenda	KY1540	32B,20,11
Holmes, Alena	WI0865	20,32
Holmes, Christopher	IN0100	12A,12C,20,11
Holmes, Isaac	SC1100	20,61
Hontos, Margaret Ellen	CA4410	13,13A,12A,20
Hoppmann, Ken J.	NE0525	66A,66B,20,66C,12A
Horner, Ronald	MD0350	65,20,50
Howland, John L.	NJ1140	10,12,20,29,29A
Hsu, Pattie	CA5353	12,20
Hubbs, Holly J.	PA3550	11,37,47,29A,20
Hughes, Matthew	IL3500	62D,20,29
Humphries, Stephen	GA0600	13A,20,50,65
Hurley, David R.	KS1050	12,20,64B
Hussey, Peter	IL1500	65,20,11,50,12A
Ibarra, Susie	VT0050	20,29,50,47,53
Ingber, Jeffrey	VA1400	20,11
Jackson, Gregory	AL0050	65,13,20,10,36
Jackson, Stephen	IL0420	48,11,20,41,47
Jackson, Travis A.	IL3250	29,20,29D,29E,14
Jamieson, Jake	CA5031	20,32
Janson, Peter	MA2010	70,29,11,20,47
Jaquez, Candida	CA4500	14,20,12,41
Jarjour, Tala	IN1700	12,20
Jaros, Marc	MN1200	12,36,20,40
Johnson, Cornelius	IL0450	13A,66A,11,36,20
Johnson, Diane	WA0900	36,61,54,11,20
Johnson, Gordon	UT0350	20,11
Johnson, Jake	OK0750	20
Johnson, Keith	CA2975	10,20,34,35,13B
Johnson, Sherry A.	AG0650	20
Jones, Brett	WI0860	65,20,50
Jones, Gordon	TX3175	11,20
Jones-Bamman, Richard	CT0150	11,14,32,20
Jordan, John M.	IN1600	12A,11,31A,20
Josselyn-Cranson, Heather	IA1200	66A,31A,10,20
Jumpeter, Joseph A.		11,29A,20,36,66G
Kachian, Christopher	MN1625	11,70,20
Kafumbe, Damascus	VT0350	14A,14C,10E,20,31F
Kakish, Wael	CA3500	20
Kaloyanides, Michael G.	CT0700	12,13,14,20,34
Kastner, Kathleen	IL3550	13A,13,50,65,20
Katz, Mark	NC2410	12,14,20,34
Kaufman, Howard	CA2250	65,20,50
Kawashima, Kimi	UT0400	20,66A
Keebaugh, Aaron	FL1675	11,20,13A,63
Kehrberg, Kevin	NC2550	12,14C,20,60A,62D
Keller, Dennis L.	CA3320	36,61,20,11,40
Kelley, Robert T.	SC0800	20,13,66A,66D,10
Keminski, Joe	NY2102	20,14,12A,63A
Kendall, Michael	IN0200	60,37,32,20,34
Kerlin, Jerry D.	NY2200	32,20
Khan, Aashish	CA0510	20
Kidula, Jean	GA2100	14,20,11,31,12
Kilstofte, Anne C.	AZ0350	11,29A,20
Kirk, Jonathon J.	IL2050	13,10,20,34
Kirschstein, Natalie	CO0650	11,20,13A
Kiyama, Wynn	OR0850	12,20
Kjorness, Christopher	VA0700	20,14C
Knight, Alan	SC0600	70,11,20
Knowles, Eddie Ade	NY3300	20,50
Knupps, Terri L.	MO1550	12A,20,63C,63D,42
Koeller, David	IL2100	20
Kopplin, David F.	CA0630	10,20,29,14C,46
Korde, Shirish	MA0700	13,10,14,20,29
Kornelis, Benjamin	IA0500	20,32D,36,60A,40
Kosciesza, Andrew	PA2400	11,12,20,36
Krikun, Andrew	NJ0020	35A,10D,47,14,20
Kronengold, Charles	CA4900	12,20
Kurasz, Rick	IL3500	65,20
Kwami, Paul T.	TN0550	20,36,66G,60A,66D
Kwan, Eva	IN1560	12A,32,44,20
Kwon, Donna L.	KY1450	12,20
Kyker, Jennifer	NY1100	14,14C,20,20A
Ladzekpo, Alfred K.	CA0510	20
Largey, Michael	MI1400	12,14,20
Lasmawan, I. Made	CO0800	20
Latta, Jonathan R.	CO0350	10F,47,50,65,20
Lauer, Eileen	IL1900	61,11,20
Launius, Michael	GA0550	20
Lawluvi, Beatrice	CA0510	20
Lawrence, Deborah	MD0750	12,20
Lawson, Sonya R.	MA2100	12A,62B,29A,12,20
Layton, Myrna	UT0325	20
Leafstedt, Carl S.	TX3350	11,12A,14,20
Leech, Alan B.	MT0200	64D,64E,20,64,42
Leonard, Katy E.	AL0300	20
Levy, Mark	OR1050	20,14
Lew, Jackie Chooi-Theng	MD0800	32A,32B,20,32C,66
Libby, Cynthia Green	MO0775	13,64B,64D,20,48
Licata, Julie M.	NY3765	65,33,50,20,10B
Lim, Benedict	CA1250	20
Limbert, Thom	IN0910	10,13,20
Lindau, Elizabeth Ann	PA1400	12,14C,20
Lindeman, Timothy H.	NC0910	13,12A,66A,20
Lindenfelser, Kathryn	MN0040	11,20,33
Locke, Scott A.	KY0950	64C,11,20
Longshore, Terry	OR0950	65,20,14,47,35A
Lopez, Eduardo	OK1350	20
Lozano, Danilo	CA6000	47,64A,20,29A,14
Lucas, Ann E.	MA0500	14,11,20,20B,12A
Lucas, Ann D.	CA0100	11,12A,20
Luu, Bing	CA4050	20,12
Lybarger, Lowell H.	AR0200	20,16
Lyerla, Trilla R.	KS0050	13,66A,66B,20
Lyons, James H.	MD0350	11,20,32B
Lysloff, Rene T.A.	CA5040	14,20,20D,20G
Mabary, Judith A.	MO1800	12A,20,11
MacLachlan, Heather M.	OH2250	12,20,14,20D
Macy, Elizabeth	CA5031	20
Maddox, Eric	GA0550	32E,20
Mahinka, Janice	NY0625	20
Makubuya, James	IN1850	13A,13C,11,14,20
Maldonado, Anna Maria	CA0950	20,11
Malley, Nicole	IL1350	12A,20,47,29,31F
Malone, Thomas	MA2030	20,32D,60A
Malone, William	CO0810	64E,64C,64A,29A,20
Malvinni, David J.	CA4410	12,20
Mamula, Stephen	RI0150	12A,20
Manabe, Noriko	NY0500	14,12E,20
Mangeni, Andrew	RI0200	20
Marble, Jamie	IL2970	20,11
Markoff, Irene	AG0650	14,20
Marquez-Barrios, Victor	MI0900	29A,20
Marr, John	CA2390	20
Marsh, Peter K.	CA0807	14,12,20B,20
Martin, Margot	CA1750	12A,12B,20,66H,12E
Martin, Stephen	OR0850	14,12,20
Mason, Kaley R.	IL3250	14,20
Matsue, Jennifer	NY4310	14,15,20C,20
McCollum, Jonathan Ray	MD0060	12,13,20,55,63C
McCollum, Jonathan	MD1100	63C,63D,11,12,20
McCready, Matthew A.	MO0550	11,12A,63,13A,20
McPherson, Eve	OH1100	11,20
Measels, Clark	TN0250	11,31A,20
Mecham, Jessica	ID0060	11,20
Meckler, David C.	CA0855	11,20,12A,10,13A
Medwin, Marc	DC0010	11,29,12,20
Meints, Kenneth	NE0500	63,20,65,35A,32
Mensah, Sowah	MN1625	20
Menth, Christelle	CO0150	66,12A,20
Meyer, Jeffrey	MN0600	12A,13,11,14,20
Milenkovic, Vladan	MN0050	29,20
Miller, Ethan	OH1100	20,29
Miller, Everett F.	KS0225	11,36,34,70,20
Miller, Harold L.	WI0450	10,13A,13G,20,47
Mills, Susan W.	NC0050	20,32B,32C,61,36
Mina, Niloofar	NJ0825	20
Modirzadeh, Hafez	CA4200	14,20,64E
Molina, Linda	MD0475	62A,12A,20
Mollenhauer, Shawn	CO0550	20
Moorman, Wilson	NY0270	11,20,65,29
Morehouse, Katherine	GA1150	11,20
Moschenross, Ian	IL1800	12A,13E,20,66A,66G
Mosteller, Sandra M.	TX3650	64,32E,48,20,31B
Mountford, Fritz	NE0300	32C,36,60A,10,20
Murawski, Marianne	NJ0990	14,11,20
Murchison, Pamela	MD0350	64A,48,20,15
Myers, Patricia Ann	NY1550	11,12,14,66H,20
Nanongkham, Priwan Keo	OH1100	20,14
Ness, Marjorie S.	MA0930	11,20,32,36,66G
Newsome, Sam	NY2102	29,20,64E
Nicely, Tiffany M.	NY3717	20
Nichols, Kevin A.	IL3500	65,20
Niebur, Louis	NV0100	12,20,14,11
Nivans, David	CA2050	11,13A,20,29A
Nivans, David	CA0805	14C,29A,20,13,11
Norris, Elizabeth	VT0300	11,13A,20,61,36
Norris, Renee Lapp	PA1900	14C,12A,20,12,13E
Novotney, Eugene D.	CA2250	14,50,65,20
O'Connor, Michael B.	FL1450	12A,11,20,55
Odello, Denise	MN1620	11,12,64B,14,20
Odem, Susan	IA0650	64D,20,64B,64E
Okigbo, Austin	CO0800	31F,20,14
Olsson, Patricia	OH2290	64E,20
Omojola, Olabode	MA1350	14,20
Orgill, Edward	MA2100	20,64E
Paige, Diane M.	NY1400	12,29A,20,12A,20F
Parker, Nancy	MN0610	11,20,32D
Parker, Wesley	AR0250	65,11,20,37
Parkhurst, Melissa	OR0750	20,12
Parran, John D.	NY0270	11,13,20,29,64
Patch, Justin	NY4450	14,20
Perera, Selina	CA3500	11,20,14C
Perman, Anthony	IA0700	14,20
Perry, Mark E.	GA1500	20,12
Peters, Mark	IL3100	11,20,13E,12
Peterson, Jason P.	VA1000	13A,13B,20
Peterson, Laura	NY3475	11,12A,66A,20
Peterson, Leroy	CA3400	20,62A
Phillips, Gary J.	MD0350	20

499

Name	Code	Areas
Pias, Ed	NM0310	65,20
Pillich, G. Simeon	CA3300	20,29
Pinkston, Dan	CA4600	13,12A,14,10,20
Placilla, Christina D.	NC2700	12A,20,38,62A,62B
Planer, John H.	IN1050	20,12,13,14,61
Polett, Thomas C.	MO0300	63,47,32,13,20
Polman, Bert	MI0350	31,11,20
Ponce, Adriana	IL1200	12A,11,20
Poss, Nicholas	OH0100	11,20
Potter, Shelley	WA0950	51,62A,20,13A,13D
Powell, John S.	OK1450	11,12A,12,20
Pratt, Holly	KY1000	20
Prescott, John S.	MO0775	13,10,20
Price, Josselyne	VT0400	14,20,50
Procopio, Mary J.	MI0450	11,20,37,64
Prossaird, Didier	MD0550	66A,20
Rafal, Jeremy	NJ0050	11,20
Raickovich, Milos	NY0644	11,13A,20
Randall, James	MT0400	12,14,20,11
Randel, Julia	MI1050	12,20
Rapport, Evan	NY0644	20
Rasmussen, Ljerka V.	TN1400	20,14C,20F,35D,14
Raval, Shanti	NY0270	64C,11,20
Redd, Ann	SC1100	20
Reid, Susanne M.	CA5355	11,12A,20,31A
Reid, Todd	CO0830	11,20,29,65
Rhyne-Bray, Constance	NC2000	39,61,20
Richardson, Lisa	CA4450	20
Ridgeway, Max A.	OK0600	10,70,11,20,46
Rischar, Richard A.	MI2110	12,29,40,14,20
Ritter, Jonathan	CA5040	14,20,20H
Rivera, Luis C.	AL1300	20,32E,41,65,50
Roland, Tomm	NE0610	65,20,34H,50
Roste, Vaughn	OK0550	60,12A,34,36,61,20
Rounds, Tyler	OH1100	11,20
Rubin, Lauren	OR0950	20
Russell, Tracy	TX3400	20,14C
Salazar, Lauryn C.	CA5031	20
Salfen, Kevin	TX3410	11,12,13A,20
Samuelson, Linda	MN1270	13,20,37,46,64
Sands, Rosita M.	IL0720	14,12,20
Sanlikol, Mehmet	RI0200	20
Santos, John	CA1250	20,65
Saul, Walter B.	CA1860	10A,66A,13,20,10F
Saylor, Eric A.	IA0550	20,12A
Sayre, Elizabeth	PA3200	14,20
Schauert, Paul W.	MI1750	20,11
Schelfer, James	NY2700	13A,20,29A
Schmidt, Juliana	WI0855	11,20,29A
Schmitz, Michael	CA3270	66A,12A,13,20,41
Schou, Larry B.	SD0600	66G,66H,20
Schultz, Kirsten M.	AG0500	20
Schultz, Marc	NY2800	13A,20,13
Schweitzer, Kenneth	MD1100	20,29,34,35,11
Scully, Joseph D.	IL0450	13A,11,36,20
Seeley, Jeffery	NY1150	11,20,36
Sehman, Melanie	NY3250	65,13A,20,11,13
Semmes, Laurie R.	NC0050	14,20
Shadle-Peters, Jennifer	CO0275	12A,20,32,36,67
Shahriari, Andrew	OH1100	11,20
Shapiro, Jarred	VT0100	62C,11,20
Sharp, Charles	CA0815	29A,20
Shepard, Hilary	KS0350	64A,11,20
Shonekan, Stephanie	MO1800	14,20
Shope, Bradley	TX2930	14,20,12A
Shorley, Ken	AF0050	20
Shorner-Johnson, Kevin T.	PA1250	32,20
Shotwell, Clayton	GA0250	12,20,34,11,13A
Shulstad, Reeves	NC0050	12,14,20
Sieben, Patrick	KS0225	37,20,13,46,11
Simms, Rob	AG0650	20,14
Simons, Carolyn	CA2810	11,20,60A,12
Simons, Dennis	ND0250	11,13,20,38
Sirotta, Michael	NY0644	20
Smolenski, Scott	FL1675	66A,10,11,13,20
Snodgrass, William G.	MO0800	20
Snow, Lydia F.	IL2150	32B,20
Snyder, Jean E.	PA1200	11,12,20
Soebbing, Steven	MD0350	61,20,15
Sorah, Donald	VA1580	34,63A,29,14C,20
South, Janis	OK1250	63B,11,12A,49,20
Souza, Christine	OK1350	65,20
Souza, Ricardo A.	OK1350	20
Spencer, Philip	IL1250	20,61,66A,36,60A
Squance, Rod Thomas	AA0150	20,50,65
Stanyek, Jason	NY2740	34,12,14,20,12D
Starks, George	PA1000	20,14,47,64E,29
Stasack, Jennifer	NC0550	10,20,31G
Stein, Ken J.	IL2560	11,13B,20,47,64E
Stevens, Deborah	IA1450	20
Stewart, Alexander	VT0450	14,53,20,29,47
Stockton, J. Larry	PA1850	14,50,20,60
Stone, Mark	MI1750	20,50
Strasser, Michael C.	OH0200	12A,20
Strawbridge, Nathan	FL2050	20,65
Strong, Willie	SC1100	12A,20
Strunk, Michael	WA0300	20,34C
Strunk, Michael J.	CA0400	65,20,20H,50
Studebaker, Donald	OK0550	20
Sturm, Jonathan	IA0850	12A,11,20G,20
Sullivan, Todd E.	AZ0450	11,12,14,20
Suvada, Steve	IL0850	70,41,20
Swanson, Brent	FL0700	12A,14,20
Swift, Mark D.	PA3580	11,14A,14C,20
Szego, Kati	AD0050	12A,14,20
Tabaka, Jim	MN1500	70,20,12A
Tait, Alicia Cordoba	IL0275	20,12A,15,35,11
Talley, Dana W.	NY2900	61,12A,20,39,11
Tang, Patricia	MA1200	20,11,13
Tapanes-Inojosa, Adriana	IL1080	11,20,36,12,66
Tarrant, Fredrick A.	GA1800	11,12,14,20,55
Taylor, Kristin Jonina	IA1750	12A,20,66A,66D,66
Taylor, Mitchell	IL1500	20,61,34B
Taylor, Timothy D.	CA5032	14,20,34
Teager, Michael	MI2000	11,20
Teel, Allen J.	TX0050	65,50,20,37
Templeman, Robert W.	OH2550	11,20
Thomas, Vicky	WA0980	20
Thompson, Karin E.	WA1100	62C,20,12A,42,13C
Thorman, Marc	NY0500	10,13,12A,20,14C
Tiedge, Faun Tanenbaum	OR0450	11,13,12A,20,42
Tiffe, Janine	OH1100	20
Tinnin, Randall C.	FL1950	63A,49,37,32E,20
Todd, Kristen Stauffer	OK0650	12,14,20,11,55
Toner, D. Thomas	VT0450	65,20,37,50,60
Tones, Daniel	AB0060	20,50,65
Tremura, Welson Alves	FL1850	70,20
Trinka, Jill L.	SC0420	32A,20,32B
Turner, Katherine L.	SC0350	64C,12A,20,14A
Tyler, Paul	IL2000	14,20
Tyrrell, Sarah	MO1810	12A,20
Underwood, Kirsten F.	OK0150	62,38,11,62C,20
Utter, Hans	OH1850	20
Valiente, Jessica L.	NJ0800	20
Van Regenmorter, Paula	LA0450	64,12A,11,48,20
Vanselow, Jason	MN0040	20,70
Varner, Michael	TX3500	50,65,14,20
Vartan, Lynn	UT0200	65,41,20
Vascotto, Norma	AG0600	12A,11,20
Velykis, Theodore	NJ1100	20,70
Vercelli, Michael B.	WV0750	20,14,31F,41,42
Vollinger, William F.	NY2900	10A,20
Wagner, Marella	WI0770	12A,13J,20
Walker, Erin	KY1450	12,20,50,65
Wallin, Nicholas L.	IL1400	38,13,11,20
Wang, Jui-Ching	IL2200	32,20
Ward, Larry F.	IL0630	11,20,14
Ward-Griffin, Danielle	VA0150	12,20,14
Warfield, Scott A.	FL1800	12,20,11
Warne, David	MI1650	50,65,20
Warren, Ron	MD0550	20
Watanabe, Mihoko	IN0150	64A,20
Watkins, Timothy D.	TX3000	12A,14,20,12
Watson, Anne	OK0550	64C,13A,13B,13C,20
Watson, William E.	MD0175	10,47,14C,20
Webb, John	TX3535	20,47,64E
Webber, Sophie C.	IL1400	62C,20,12A
Weber, Brent M.	MD0350	64E,64D,29,47,20
Weiss, Sarah	CT0900	14,20
Weller, Ellen	CA3460	12A,55,20,29A,60
Wells, Yelena	MI0850	66A,66D,20
West, Lara L.	KS0100	40,11,66D,66G,20
Westervelt, Dirck	CT0800	20
Wetherill, Linda Marie	NY0050	64A,20
Whetstone, Joni	PA2710	20
White, Rick	WA0600	11,29A,20,37,46
Whittall, Geoffrey	AA0025	14,65,20,13,11
Williams, Alan	MA2030	35C,35A,20
Williams, Brent	GA2150	62A,20
Williams, Christopher A.	OH2300	12A,20,12C,11
Williams, Kenyon C.	MN1120	65,50,20
Williams, Yolanda	MN0050	29A,20
Williams, Yolanda	MN1050	12A,20,47,29A,41
Williamson, Emily	NY0625	20
Willis, Jesse	SC0420	65,50,20,37
Wimberly, Michael	VT0050	10,20,29,35,65
Wint, Suzanne	IL2250	20
Witmer, Ruth	FL1550	12A,14,20
Witzleben, J. Lawrence	MD1010	14,20,20C
Wollman, Elizabeth L.	NY0250	11,14C,14,15,20
Wong, Deborah	CA5040	14,20,20D,20G,31D
Wood, Eric	CA5350	10A,11,20,13A,13E
Wood, Graham	SC0450	11,12,63B,54,20
Woodcock, Ruth	WA0100	11,12A,20,13A,13G
Woods, Bret	AL1050	14C,20,34
Yacoub, Allison	MD0600	64C,32E,20
Yakas, James	TX3500	65,50,20
Ycaza, Stephanie	VA1600	20
Yonce, Tammy Evans	SD0550	11,12A,64A,20
Yoon, Sunmin	OH1100	20,11
Younge, Pascal Yao	OH1900	20,32
Zank, MJ Sunny	OH1800	13,20,10,12A,43
Zlabinger, Tom	NY0646	62D,29,14,20,47

Sub-Saharan Africa

Name	Code	Areas
Adams, Margarethe A.	NY3790	20A,20B,14
Adzenyah, Abraham	CT0750	20A
Armstrong, Kathy	AG0100	13,20A
Awe, Francis P.	CA3500	20A
Bartow, James	NY0270	11,20A,20G,29A,70
Bartow, James	NY0625	20A,20G,70
Berliner, Paul F.	NC0600	20A,14A,14F,14B,31F
Biondo, Steven A.	CA5100	34,16,20A
Boyle, Patrick	AB0150	20A,29B,47,53
Bridge, Robert	NY2950	65,37,50,20A
Bullock, Kathy	KY0300	11,20A,36,13A,13C
Calloway, John	CA4200	20A
Campbell, Patricia Shehan	WA1050	32A,20A,12C,32B,20D
Capp, Myrna	WA0800	66A,66B,32I,20A
Carter, Marva G.	GA1050	12,20G,20,20A
Cerabona, Linda M.	IL3400	11,13A,20A,31A,32D
Conde, Moussa	IL3300	20A
Daddy, S. Kwaku	CA1020	20A
Davies, James	CA5000	11,12A,12E,20A,66A
Davis, Daniel	NC0600	10,14,15,20A
Diallo, YaYa	KY0250	20A,65
DjeDje, Jacqueline Cogdell	CA5031	20A,20G,14A
Dorhauer, John	IL0850	20A,13,63A
Dunyo, Fred	AG0450	20A
Edwards, Mahiri	MD1010	20A,20B
Ellis, Brenda	OH2500	20A,20G,32,36,66A
Emerson, Timothy	NY2950	20A,11
Faini, Philip J.	WV0750	20A,65
Flood, John	CA4100	20A,13A,11,65,50
Florine, Jane Lynn	IL0600	11,12A,12,20A,64A
Fosheim, Karen	MS0250	66A,13B,50,20A,10F
Frazier, Damon	OK1350	20A
Frishkopf, Michael	AA0100	20A,20F,14,31C
Graham, Sandra J.	MA0255	14,20A,20G,31F
Green, Verna	NY0640	20A,20H,32D,32E,36
Grueschow, Andrew	CA0510	20A
Gunderson, Frank	FL0850	14,20A,20B
Hagedorn, Katherine J.	CA3650	14,20H,20A
Hagedorn, Katherine	CA1050	20A,20G,14A
Hallman, Diana R.	KY1450	12,20A
Hanson, Jordan	AB0150	20A,20B
Haworth, Janice	MN0150	32A,32C,32B,36,20A
Horton, Christian	GA1260	20A,11
Kabir, Chaitanya Mahmud	CO0560	20A,31C,20B,20C,20E
Kapralick, Randy	PA3330	63C,20A,46
Kirk, Jeremy	KS0250	37,13,20A,50,65
Kisliuk, Michelle	VA1550	14,20A
Kramer, Jonathan C.	NC1700	11,12A,20D,20A,62C
Kyker, Jennifer	NY1100	14,14C,20,20A
Ladzekpo, C. K.	CA5000	20A
Ladzekpo, C. K.	CA2950	20A,20B,50
Ladzekpo, Kobla	CA5031	20A,65
Leake, Jerry	MA1400	20A,20E,47,65
Lee, Byong Won	HI0210	20A,20D,14A
Locke, David	MA1900	11,14,20A
McDaniel, William T.	OH1850	20A,29,29A
McKoy, Constance L.	NC2430	32B,32A,20A,32
McQueen, William F.	TX2100	11,20A,49,63A
Meintjes, Louise	NC0600	20A,14A,14C,14D,14F

Index by Area of Teaching Interest

Meitrott, Gary	VT0200	20A,20B
Mensah, Sowah	MN0950	12A,20A,10
Moorman, Joyce E.	NY0270	11,13,20A,34D,66
Moses, Lennard	OH0500	50,65,20A,20G
Mukuna, Kazadi Wa	OH1100	14,20A,20B,11
Muller, Carol A.	PA3350	14,20A,20D,31F,31G
Muparutsa, Tendai	MA2250	20A,20B
Nketia, Joseph K.	PA3420	20A,14
Paton, Eric	OH0350	65,20A,20C,20H,47
Payton, Denise	NC0800	20A,36,39,60A,61
Perry, David L.	SC0050	12A,13A,64C,32,20A
Ping, Jin	NY3760	13,10,62A,20A,20B
Poss, Nicholas	OH1850	20A,20B
Randruut, Avo	IL0750	20A
Ridley, Larry	NY2150	47,29A,62D,20A,20G
Roden, Timothy J.	OH2000	11,12A,20A,20D,20F
Rumbolz, Robert C.	WY0130	13,35C,35D,34,20A
Sachdev, Salil	MA0510	10,13A,20A,50,13B
Schuyler, Philip	WA1050	20A,20D
Seeman, Sonia T.	TX3510	20A,20B,14A
Stats, Clyde	VT0250	53,20A,20G
Stephens, Robert W.	CT0600	32,20A,20G
Strand, Julie	MA1450	20A,20D,11
Tamburello, John	WI1155	70,20A,20B
Torpaga, Olivier	OH1850	20A,20B
Tucker, Scott	NY0900	60,36,40,13A,20A
Turino, Thomas R.	IL3300	11,20A,20H,14
Veal, Michael E.	CT0900	14,20A,20G
Weaver, Carol Ann	AG0470	13,10,12,20A,29A
Wenzel, Scott	WI0150	14,65,55,50,20A
West, Glenn A.	NY1100	20A
Whitehead, Baruch	NY1800	32B,32A,32C,20A
Williams, Barry Michael	SC1200	12A,50,65,20A,20B

Western and Central Asia/North Africa

Adams, Margarethe A.	NY3790	20A,20B,14
Akrong, Isaac	AG0650	20B
Babiracki, Carol M.	NY4100	12,12B,14,20B,20E
Bilderback, Barry T.	ID0250	11,12A,20B,12C,14A
Boateng, Kwabena	MA2020	20B
Brinner, Benjamin	CA5000	13K,14,20B,20D,11
Chappell, Robert	IL2200	20B,29
Ciucci, Alessandra	NY0750	11,14,15,14C,20B
Ciucci, Alessandra	MA1450	14C,14F,20B,20H
Daughtry, J. Martin	NY2740	14A,14C,20B,20F,14D
Dunyo, Kwasi	AG0650	20B
Edwards, Mahiri	MD1010	20A,20B
Fuson, Tim Abdellah	CA5000	20B
Graves, Larry	AG0650	20B
Gunderson, Frank	FL0850	14,20A,20B
Habib, Kenneth S.	CA0600	14,10,13,20B,14C
Hanson, Jordan	AB0150	20A,20B
Hatch, Martin	NY0900	14,20B,20D,20E
Jankowsky, Rich	MA1900	14,31C,20B,14F
Kabir, Chaitanya Mahmud	CO0560	20A,31C,20B,20C,20E
Kean, Ronald M.	CA0270	36,20B,20H
Koen, Benjamin D.	FL0850	14,20B
Kpogo, Robert	AA0100	20B
Ladzekpo, C. K.	CA2950	20A,20B,50
LaPerna, Eric	ME0150	20B
Libby, Amos	ME0150	20E,20B
Lucas, Ann E.	MA0500	14,11,20,20B,12A
Marcus, Scott	CA5060	14,20B,20E
Marsh, Peter K.	CA0807	14,12,20B,20
Meitrott, Gary	VT0200	20A,20B
Melnikoff, Anna	AG0650	20B
Merchant, Tanya H.	CA5070	20B,15,12A
Miller, DaVaughn	NC1150	36,13E,20B,60
Mukuna, Kazadi Wa	OH1100	14,20A,20B,11
Muparutsa, Tendai	MA2250	20A,20B
Noone, Elizabeth	MA0150	66A,66D,11,13A,20B
Ping, Jin	NY3760	13,10,62A,20A,20B
Poss, Nicholas	OH1850	20A,20B
Pourmehdi, Houman	CA0510	65,50,20B
Racy, A. J.	CA5031	20B,14A,14B
Sakata, Lorraine	CA5031	20B,14A,20E
Schreffler, Gibb	CA3650	14,20B,20G
Seeman, Sonia T.	TX3510	20A,20B,14A
Shachal, Harel	NY2660	20B,64C,64E
Sims, Lamar	MO1000	20B,66A
Spinetti, Frederico	AA0100	14,20B
Tamburello, John	WI1155	70,20A,20B
Torpaga, Olivier	OH1850	20A,20B
Verrilli, Catherine J.	MN1300	61,20B
Weston, Trevor L.	NJ0300	11,20B,13,10
Whalen, Margaret F.	NC2000	11,12A,20B,29A
Williams, Barry Michael	SC1200	12A,50,65,20A,20B
Yasui, Byron K.	HI0210	70,10A,10F,13,20B

East Asia

Anno, Mariko	IL1400	20C,64A
Barkhymer, Lyle	OH2050	14,20C
Bryant, Lei Ouyang	NY3650	14,20C
Caplan, Linda	AG0650	20C
Catlin, Amy	CA5031	14,20C,20D,20E
Chan, Patty	AG0650	20C
Fish, David Lee	NC0350	35,14,34,20C,29
Heitzenrater, John	NC1600	64D,20C,20D,20E
Hong, Charles	AG0650	20C
Hong, Gao	MN0300	20C,20E
Huang, Hao	CA4500	66A,12,20C,20G,29
Jung, Eun-Young	CA5050	11,12D,14,20C
Kabir, Chaitanya Mahmud	CO0560	20A,31C,20B,20C,20E
Kajikawa, Loren	OR1050	12A,14,20C,20G
Kang, YouYoung	CA4500	13,12,20C,20G
Kapuscinski, Jaroslaw	CA4900	10,20C
Keister, Mami Itasaka	CO0800	20C
Kim, Dong Suk	CA5031	20C,62,65
Kurai, Tom	CA5040	20C,65
Lau, Frederick C.	HI0210	14A,38,43,64A,20C
Lee, Katherine In-Young	CA5010	14,12,20C,12D
Lee, Tong Soon	GA0750	14,20C,20D,14D,14F
Li, Chi	CA5031	20C,62,64,65
Lim, Benedict M.	CA1020	20C,20D,11,66D
Manuel, Peter G.	NY0600	14,20C,20H
Matsue, Jennifer	NY4310	14,15,20C,20
Miyashiro, Darin	HI0210	20C
Novak, David	CA5060	14A,14C,14D,20C
Oba, Junko	MA1000	13B,13C,20C
Okamoto, Kyoko	MD1010	20C
Paton, Eric	OH0350	65,20A,20C,20H,47
Pilzer, Joshua	NY0750	11,14,20C
Rees, Helen	CA5031	20C,20D,20E,14A
Regan, Martin	TX2900	10,20C,13
Sajnovsky, Cynthia B.	GU0500	13A,12A,20C,66D,67C
Sano, Stephen M.	CA4900	60,36,20C,20I
Shahouk, Bassam	AG0650	20C
Shende, Vineet	ME0200	10,13,20C,20E,31E
Sheppard, W. Anthony	MA2250	12A,20C,14C,12D,20G
Smith, Barbara B.	HI0210	20I,20C,14
Sue, Phig Choy	AG0650	20C
Tanosaki, Kazuko	MD1000	13,20C
Wade, Bonnie C.	CA5000	11,14,20C,20E,12G
Wilson, James Dale	CT0100	14,20C,12A,12E,29B
Witzleben, J. Lawrence	MD1010	14,20,20C
Xia, Vivian	AG0650	20C
Yoon, Paul	VA1500	11,14,20C
Yun, Gerard	AG0650	20C
Zhao, Wen	AG0650	20C

Southeast Asia

Adler, Christopher A.	CA5200	10,14,13,10A,20D
Adnyana, I Dewa Ketut Alit	WI0350	20D
Asai, Susan M.	MA1450	14,20D,20H
Asnawa, I Ketut Gede	IL3300	20D
Bakan, Michael	FL0850	14,20D,20G
Bandem, I Made	MA0700	20D
Beck, Gina C.	MD1000	20D
Benamou, Marc	IN0400	14,12,20,20D,12B
Bethany, Adeline M.	PA0450	11,20D,32A,32B,36
Boquiren, Sidney M.	NY0050	10A,13A,20D,31A,10F
Brinner, Benjamin	CA5000	13K,14,20B,20D,11
Burman-Hall, Linda C.	CA5070	55B,20D,20F,66H,67C
Burton, J. Bryan	PA3600	20G,20D,32
Campbell, Patricia Shehan	WA1050	32A,20A,12C,32B,20D
Catlin, Amy	CA5031	14,20C,20D,20E
Chaudhuri, Swapan	CA0510	20D
Chew, Sherlyn	CA2450	20D,38
Cho, Gene	TX3420	13,20D
Collier, Bethany	PA0350	14,20,20D
De Leon, Tagumpay	CA5040	20D,51
Dong, Kui	NH0100	13,10,20D,45,43
Douglas, Gavin D.	NC2430	14,20D
Downing, Sonja Lynn	WI0350	14,15,20D,64A,32
Drummond, Barry	MA1900	20D
Dudley, Shannon	WA1050	20D
Ellingson, Ter	WA1050	20D
Emmanuel, Donna T.	TX3420	32B,32G,20D,20H,35A
Evangelista, Jose	AI0200	10A,20D
Fatone, Gina Andrea	ME0150	13,14,20,20D
Freedman, Richard	PA1500	11,12A,12,20D,29A
Fuller, Stephen	MN1300	60A,11,20D,31A
Fung, C. Victor	FL2000	32G,32,20D
Gamer, Carlton	CO0200	13,10,11,20D,34
Gloss, Randy	CA0510	65,20D,50
Gold, Lisa R.	CA5000	20D
Granite, Bonita	NJ1050	14,20D,61
Grimshaw, Jeremy	UT0050	14A,14D,20D
Guy, Nancy	CA5050	14,20D
Harjito, I. M.	MA2020	20D
Harjito, I.	CT0750	20D
Hatch, Martin	NY0900	14,20B,20D,20E
Heitzenrater, John	NC1600	64D,20C,20D,20E
Hossain, Hamid	MD1000	20D
Hsiang, Cynthia H.	CA3500	20D
Hsu, Dolores M.	CA5060	12A,12,20D,14A,14B
Johnston, Mindy	OR0400	20D
Kalanduyan, Danongan	CA4625	20D
Kane, Dreena	HI0160	20D
Kaneshiro, Norman	HI0210	20D
Kazez, Daniel	OH2450	13A,11,20D,62C,62D
Koskoff, Ellen	NY1100	14,15,20G,20D,31
Kramer, Jonathan C.	NC1700	11,12A,20D,20A,62C
Kudo, Takeo	HI0210	10A,10F,13,20D
Kyr, Robert	OR1050	10A,10F,43,20D
Labonville, Marie E.	IL1150	11,12A,12,20D
Laderman, Michael	NY3100	11,29,12A,14,20D
Lasmawan, I. Made	CO0200	20D
Lee, Byong Won	HI0210	20A,20D,14A
Lee, Tong Soon	GA0750	14,20C,20D,14D,14F
Levinson, Gerald C.	PA3200	13,10,20D
Lim, Benedict M.	CA1020	20C,20D,11,66D
Lis, Anthony	SD0550	13,10F,10,66,20D
Lysloff, Rene T.A.	CA5040	14,20,20D,20G
MacLachlan, Heather M.	OH2250	12,20,14,20D
Matthay, Christopher D.	NY2750	13,14A,20D,20E,29A
Mendonca, Maria Alice	OH1200	14F,20D,15
, Midiyanto	CA5000	20D
Miller, Christopher J.	NY0900	20D,14D
Miller, Joan	MN1300	20D,11,32B
Moulin, Jane	HI0210	20D,14A,55,67A
Muley, Nandkishor	FL1750	20D
Muller, Carol A.	PA3350	14,20A,20D,31F,31G
Nagata, Gary	AG0450	20D,65
Okamoto, Kyoko M.	VA0450	20D
Peebles, William L.	NC2600	64D,20D
Perlman, Marc	RI0050	14,20D,12E,13J,35D
Powell, Jarrad	WA0200	13A,10,20D,45,34
Prescott, Anne	IL3300	20D
Rees, Helen	CA5031	20C,20D,20E,14A
Revuluri, Sindhumathi	MA1050	12,12A,12C,14C,20D
Roden, Timothy J.	OH2000	11,12A,20A,20D,20F
Rodger, Gillian	WI0825	12A,12C,20G,20D,14
Roman, Robert	NY3765	29,66A,20D,35A,46
Ruckert, George	MA1200	13A,11,20G,20D,20F
Sanger, Annette	AG0450	20D
Sankaran, Trichy	AG0650	20D
Sarkissian, Margaret	MA1750	14,20D
Scheuerell, Doug	OR1050	20D,65
Schmidt, Daniel	CA2950	72,10E,20D
Schuyler, Philip	WA1050	20A,20D
Shamoto, Masatoshi	HI0210	20D
Shea, Joy	NC2600	20D,11
Skelton, William	NY0650	14,20D,38,64D
Slawek, Stephen M.	TX3510	20D,14A
Spiller, Henry	CA5010	14,12,15,20D,12D
Strand, Julie	MA1450	20A,20D,11
Suadin, I. Ketut	NY1100	20D
Suadin, Nyoman	PA3200	20D
Sumarna, Undang	CA5070	20D
Sumarsam,	CT0750	20D
Sunardi, Christina	WA1050	20D
Suparta, I Dewa Made	AI0200	20D
Sutton, R. Anderson	WI0815	11,12A,20D,14A
Tenzer, Michael	AB0100	20D,14
Thompson, Gordon R.	NY3650	20D,20E,20F,14C,14B
Thrasher, Alan R.	AB0100	20D,14
Trimillos, Ricardo D.	HI0210	20D,20I,14D,14A,14F
Ung, Chinary	CA5050	10,20D,64
Vetter, Valerie	IA0700	20D

Name	Code	Areas
Walujo, Djoko	CA4100	20D
Walujo, Djoko	CA0510	20D
Weintraub, Andrew	PA3420	20D,14A,20G,14C,14D
Wenten, I. Nyoman	CA5031	20D
Wenten, I. Nyoman	CA0510	20D
Wenten, Nanik	CA0510	20D
Wenten, Nyoman	CA3650	20D
Whetstone, David	MN0300	20D
Whetstone, David S.	MN0950	20D
Whitman, Thomas I.	PA3200	13,20D,32
Wong, Deborah	CA5040	14,20,20D,20G,31D
Yampolsky, Philip	IL3300	20D
Yuasa, Joji	CA5050	10,20D,35H,34,35C
Ziporyn, Evan	MA1200	13,10,20D,64C,29

South Asia

Name	Code	Areas
Allen, Matthew H.	MA2150	14C,20E,20H,31,14
Arnold, Alison E.	NC1700	11,20,20E,14
Babiracki, Carol M.	NY4100	12,12B,14,20B,20E
Balasubrahmaniyan, B.	CT0750	20E
Beaster-Jones, Jayson	TX2900	14,20E
Bhattacharya, Subrata	IL3300	20E
Catlin, Amy	CA5031	14,20C,20D,20E
Chandra, Veena V.	NY3650	20E
Feinberg, Joshua	OR0400	20E
Hatch, Martin	NY0900	14,20B,20D,20E
Heitzenrater, John	NC1600	64D,20C,20D,20E
Hong, Gao	MN0300	20C,20E
Kabir, Chaitanya Mahmud	CO0560	20A,31C,20B,20C,20E
Kapur, Ajay	CA0510	34,20E,45
Kaur, Kamaljeet	AA0100	61,20E
Kaushal, Abhiman	CA5040	20E,65
Kaushal, Abhiman	CA5031	20E
Khan, Shujaat Husain	CA5031	20E,62,61
Kvetko, Peter J.	MA1650	14,13A,14C,20E,41
Leake, Jerry	MA1400	20A,20E,47,65
Levine, Victoria Lindsay	CO0200	11,20E
Libby, Amos	ME0150	20E,20B
Made Suparta, I Dewa	AI0200	50,20E
Marcus, Scott	CA5060	14,20B,20E
Masterson, Rik	OR0400	20E
Mathur, Sharmila	AA0100	20E,62
Matthay, Christopher D.	NY2750	13,14A,20D,20E,29A
Morris, Robert D.	NY1100	10,12,13,20E,31E
Naimpally, Ravi	AG0650	20E
Nelson, David	CT0750	20E
Neuman, Daniel M.	CA5031	20E,14A
Neuman, Dard A.	CA5070	20E,14F
Pontbriand, David	ME0150	20E
Ranganathan, Lakshmi	AG0250	20E
Rao, Nikhail	AA0100	20E,65
Rees, Helen	CA5031	20C,20D,20E,14A
Rice, Timothy	CA5031	20E,14A
Sakata, Lorraine	CA5031	20B,14A,20E
Schultz, Anna	CA4900	20E,20G,20F
Shende, Vineet	ME0200	10,13,20C,20E,31E
Stirling, Michael	OR0400	20E
Thompson, Gordon R.	NY3650	20D,20E,20F,14C,14B
Tsabar, David	AB0100	20E
Wade, Bonnie C.	CA5000	11,14,20C,20E,12G
Walker, Margaret Edith	AG0250	14,12G,13K,20E,12A
You, Daisy	CA4900	67H,20E

Europe

Name	Code	Areas
Allen, Ivalah	KS0350	61,39,12A,20F
Baron, John H.	LA0750	12A,12,20F,20G,31B
Bischoff, John	CA2950	45,10B,12A,13B,20F
Boire, Paula L.	KS0350	61,20F
Bolger, Jean	CO0200	20F
Buchanan, Donna A.	IL3300	20F,12,14
Bulwinkle, Belle	CA2950	66A,66C,20F
Burman-Hall, Linda C.	CA5070	55B,20D,20F,66H,67C
Calico, Joy	TN1850	12,20F
Cheifetz, Hamilton	OR0850	41,51,62C,20G,20F
Connolly, Damien	CT0300	20F
Cooley, Timothy J.	CA5060	20F,20G,14A,14C,14D
Cowdery, James R.	NY0600	20F
Cyrus, Cynthia	TN1850	12,15,55,20F
Daughtry, J. Martin	NY2740	14A,14C,20B,20F,14D
Dillahey, Samuel J.	SC0300	20F,37
Dobreff, Kevin J.	MI0850	20F,61,67C,55D,13C
Dodson, Brent A.	CA4450	20F
Edwards, Eric F.	KS1450	20F,11
Frishkopf, Michael	AA0100	20A,20F,14,31C
Fuerstman, Marlena	NY1860	31B,61,20F
Gelbart, Matthew	NY1300	12A,13J,14A,14D,20F
Gray, Ellen	NY0750	14A,14E,15,20F,14D
Haines, John D.	AG0450	12A,12,20F
Helbig, Adriana	PA3420	14A,14C,14D,20F,20H
Hoppmann, Kenneth	IN0005	10,16,20F,35A,66
Janeczko, Jeffrey M.	CA5031	20F,20G,20H
Jones, Dena Kay	TX3520	66,32,20F,14F,15
Jordan, Paul	IN0005	10A,61,13,20F,31A
Klassen, Carolyn	KS0440	66,34,13,20F
Krogol, D.J.	MI1000	20F,67E
Lawrence-White, Stephanie	NC0200	12A,66A,12C,20F,66B
Locke, Brian	IL3500	11,20F,12
McLucas, Anne Dhu	OR1050	12A,12C,20G,20F,14
Miller, Rebecca S.	MA1000	14,13A,20F,31B,35H
Mullen, Stan	PA2050	29B,53,70,20G,20F
Negyesy, Janos	CA5050	20F,41,62A,43,34
Netsky, Hankus H.	MA1400	29,13C,47,53,20F
Neuman, Rahul	CA5031	20F,62
Newman, Nancy	NY3700	20F,20G,12
Paige, Diane M.	NY1400	12,29A,20,12A,20F
Petrovic, Ankica	CA5031	20F,14A,31
Piza, Antoni	NY0600	20F
Powell, Jason	IN0300	20F,20H,31A,66A,66G
Rasmussen, Ljerka V.	TN1400	20,14C,20F,35D,14
Rocco, Emma S.	PA2713	13A,11,20F,36,54
Roden, Timothy J.	OH2000	11,12A,20A,20D,20F
Roditeleva-Wibe, Maria I.	WA0050	14A,12A,20F,66A,66G
Rosenberg, Ruth Emily	IL3310	20F,15,14
Rosenblum, Henry	NY1860	31B,61,20F,13C
Rosenfeld, Andrew	MD0610	11,12,13,20F,36
Ruckert, George	MA1200	13A,11,20G,20D,20F
Scanlan, Mary	MI0850	66A,66H,66C,66D,20F
Schultz, Anna	CA4900	20E,20G,20F
Summit, Jeffrey	MA1900	20F,31B,14A,14D
Suzano, L. Armenio	VA0650	20F,11,13C,41,64
Tadic, Miroslav	CA0510	70,47,20F
Thompson, Gordon R.	NY3650	20D,20E,20F,14C,14B
Titmus, Jon	CA4450	13A,20F
Titon, Jeff	RI0050	20G,20F,14A
Varimezov, Ivan S.	CA5031	20F,64
Varimezova, Tzvetanka	CA5031	20F,61
Waters, Robert F.	NJ1160	20F
Wilbourne, Emily	NY0750	11,12,15,20F

North America

Name	Code	Areas
Abel, Sean	CA1300	13B,13C,20G,29A,34C
Ackmann, Rodney	OK1350	64D,20G,41
Albright, Bruce Randall	IN0907	20G
Allen, Lisa M.	GA1100	20G,32,36,31A
Allen, Ray	NY0600	20G
Allen, Ray	NY0500	11,20G,29A,20H
Anderson, David	WA0800	36,20G
Andrews, Nancy	ME0270	35B,35C,35F,45,20G
Angelillo, Vic	AI0210	20G
Applebaum, Mark S.	CA4900	13,10,20G
Araujo, Ilka Vasconcelos	TX3250	66A,11,12A,20G
Bakan, Michael	FL0850	14,20D,20G
Ball, Greg L.	TX2750	37,48,64,20G,29
Balough, Teresa	CT0150	20G
Baron, John H.	LA0750	12A,12,20F,20G,31B
Bartow, James	NY0270	11,20A,20G,29A,70
Bartow, James	NY0625	20A,20G,70
Beal, Amy C.	CA5070	12A,12,43,20G
Beckley-Roberts, Lisa	FL1790	20G,29
Beckwith, John	AG0450	10,20G
Behrens, Jack	AG0500	13,10,20G
Bell, Allan	AA0150	13,10,20G,10F
Berg, Wesley P.	AA0100	12A,20G
Berger, Harris M.	TX2900	14,12B,29D,20G
Beyer, George	CA1520	47,13A,11,20G
Black, Elizabeth P.	NC0805	11,29A,20G
Bloechl, Olivia A.	CA5032	12,12A,12D,20G,31A
Bluestone, Joel	OR0850	11,50,65,20G
Boardman, Gregory	ME0150	20G,62A
Boerckel, Gary M.	PA2100	11,12A,66A,20G,29
Bohlman, Philip V.	IL3250	14,20G
Boivin, Luc	AI0210	20G
Boothe, Randall W.	UT0050	61,54,20G,35
Bowman, Rob	AG0650	14,20G,29A
Boyd, Jean A.	TX0300	12A,20G,29A
Boyer, Allen	CA3000	13A,47,61,20G
Bradbury, William	CA0847	13,10,11,34,20G
Braxton, Anthony	CT0750	10,20G,29
Broderick, Daniela	IL1250	11,66A,66D,20G,54
Brosh, Robert	PA3330	50,65,20G,14
Brown, Leonard	MA2200	20G,20H,29
Brown, T. Dennis	MA2000	32,20G,29A,34
Browner, Tara C.	CA5031	20G,14A
Bruce, Neely	CT0750	12A,36,20G
Bumpers, Wayne	FL1300	36,66A,66D,20G,66B
Burford, Mark	OR0900	12A,20G,14C,20H
Burgett, Paul	NY4350	20G,11,29A,29D
Burke, Richard N.	NY0625	11,12A,12,20G
Burton, J. Bryan	PA3600	20G,20D,32
Busch, Gary D.	NY3780	12A,66A,20G
Cacioppo, Curt	PA1500	13,10,20G,10F,66A
Cahow, Matthew	CA3200	11,20G
Cain, M. Celia	AG0450	12,20G
Caldwell, Hansonia	CA0805	20G,36
Calkins, Katherine Charlton	CA3200	11,12A,20G
Caputo, Michael	NJ0200	12A,14,37,64,20G
Carlson, Andrew	OH0850	62A,51,20G,38
Carr, Walter E.	OR0800	12A,12,14,20G
Carrabre, T. Patrick	AC0050	13,10,43,20G,35
Carroll, Don	CA3200	11,14,29A,20G
Carter, Joseph	CT0300	70,29A,20G,20H,47
Carter, Marva G.	GA1050	12,20G,20,20A
Caschetta, Todd	CA4850	20G,11,12,14,50
Cateforis, Theodore P.	NY4100	12,12D,20G,29A,14C
Cheek, John	NC1100	13,11,66A,20G
Cheifetz, Hamilton	OR0850	41,51,62C,20G,20F
Chevalier, Jason	CA3200	13A,37,20G
Christy, William P.	OH1910	13,12A,20G,29A,34
Cline, Judith A.	VA0550	39,61,54,20G,11
Cohen, Albert	CA4900	12A,12,13J,20G
Cole, Richard C.	VA1700	11,12A,20G
Collier, Thomas	WA1050	47,65,20G
Collins, Leo W.	MA2200	12B,31A,20G
Colton, Glenn	AG0170	12,20G,14C,14D
Conlon, Paula J.	OK1350	20G,20,14F,14
Cook, Lisa M.	CO0550	11,12A,20G,31A,14
Cooley, Timothy J.	CA5060	20F,20G,14A,14C,14D
Cox, Terrance	AG0050	20G,29A
Crabtree, Cecile	OK0150	11,20G
Curtis-Smith, Curtis O.	MI2250	10,14,66A,20G
Davis, Anthony	CA5050	20G,66A,10,53
Davis, Bob	CA1020	70,20G
Davis, Nathan T.	PA3420	20G,47,64E,29
D'earth, John E.	VA1550	20G,47,63A,53
Devore, Richard O.	OH1100	13,34,10,20G,13F
DeWitt, Mark F.	LA0760	14,29A,13C,20G
Dilworth, Gary	CA0840	13,63A,20G
Dismore, Roger	TX0370	47,20G,29,35A,35G
DjeDje, Jacqueline Cogdell	CA5031	20A,20G,14A
Dorrite, Frank	CA2775	20G,35,34
Druckman, Joel	CA4450	20G
Duda, Theodor	OH0700	13B,13C,12A,20G
Dzuris, Linda	SC0400	69,20G,66G,34
Eanes, Edward	GA1150	12A,11,12C,20G
Earles, Randy A.	ID0100	13,20G
Eby, John D.	AI0050	11,12A,12C,20G,31A
Elliott, Robin W.	AG0450	12,12A,20G
Ellis, Brenda	OH2500	20A,20G,32,36,66A
Engelmann, Marcus W.	CA0100	13,10,12A,45,20G
Ersben, Wayne	NC2550	20G,70
Erickson, James M.	NY2550	20G
Erjavec, Donald L.	CA0859	13A,47,29,20G
Espinosa, Teresita	CA3150	11,12A,32,61,20G
Evans, David	TN1680	12A,20G,14
Falzano, Anthony	NY2500	20G,35A
Ferguson, Linda C.	IN1750	12A,20G,11
Fink, Robert W.	CA5032	13,12,34,20G
Fleischmann, Rob	FL1790	20G
Foreman, Charles	AA0150	66A,66B,66C,20G,41
Fox, Aaron A.	NY0750	14,20G,12E
Fox, T. Jeffrey	NY2550	36,11,20G,14C
Gass, Glenn	IN0900	20G,11
Gaylard, Timothy R.	VA1850	11,12A,66A,20G
Genge, Anthony	AF0150	13,66A,20G,29
Geslison, Mark	UT0050	20G
Gjerdingen, Robert	IL2250	13,13J,20G
Glennon, Barbara	PA0650	20G,13B,13C,64A,64C
Golijov, Osvaldo	MA0700	20G,13,10,11,12A
Graham, Sandra J.	MA0255	14,20A,20G,31F
Grant, Joyce	NY1200	13A,20G,29A

Index by Area of Teaching Interest

Name	Code	Areas
Grimes, Benjamin	OR0700	20G,64A
Grimes, Calvin B.	GA1450	13,10,12,20G,31A
Grossman, George	NY2550	20G,66D
Groves, Robert W.	ND0350	11,12A,66A,20G,66H
Guzman, Ronald P.	NY2550	20G
Haberkorn, Michael	OH2050	66A,20G,14C,11
Hagedorn, Katherine	CA1050	20A,20G,14A
Hall, Frederick A.	AG0200	11,12A,12,20G
Hamessley, Lydia	NY1350	13C,12,14,20G,12A
Hampton, Barbara L.	NY0625	14,20G,29A
Hansen, Richard K.	MN1300	60B,37,20G,12A
Hartwell, Robert	CA1800	66D,20G,12A
Harvey, Peter J.	CT0240	13,12A,36,54,20G
Haughton, Ethel Norris	VA1750	13,12A,12,20G,66C
Hawthorne, Leroy	LA0100	70,20G,16,47
Heard, Richard	NC2500	61,20G
Hebert, Pierre	AI0210	20G
Helppie, Kevin	OR1250	61,47,54,20G
Henderson, Luther L.	CA2600	20G,38,62,45
Henry, Joseph D.	IL0900	12A,20G,36,40,32C
Heritage, Lee	OH2300	13B,13C,29A,20G,10A
Hirsch, Marjorie	MA2250	11,12,15,20G
Hobbs, Wayne C.	TX3200	13,12,35E,20G
Hoggard, Jay	CT0750	20G,29
Holden, James	VA1750	13,20G,37,64E,46
Holley, Timothy	NC1600	14,62,62C,20G
Hosler, Mark	SC0400	11,20G
Huang, Hao	CA4500	66A,12,20C,20G,29
Jamison, Phil A.	NC2550	72,70,20G
Janeczko, Jeffrey M.	CA5031	20F,20G,20H
Johnson, Birgitta	SC1110	14,20G
Johnson, Joel C.	SC1050	13,10,20G,29A,34
Jones, Arnold	NJ0950	13,20G
Jones, M. Douglas	KY1460	20G,67D,70
Jones, Stephen	MI2250	49,63A,20G
Jordan, Edward	LA0720	11,20G,37,47,64
Julian, Tijuana	MO0350	63A,49,20G
Junker, Jay	HI0210	20G
Kajikawa, Loren	OR1050	12A,14,20C,20G
Kallmann, Helmut	AG0100	20G
Kang, YouYoung	CA4500	13,12,20C,20G
Keillor, Elaine	AG0100	12A,12,14,66A,20G
Keyes, Cheryl L.	CA5031	20G,14A
King, Fredericka	MA0850	20G,20H
King, Richard G.	MD1010	11,12A,12,20G,12C
King, Valeria G.	LA0720	13,60,12A,12,20G
Kirk, Elizabeth	NC0860	11,20G
Kirk, John D.	NY3650	62A,67H,20G
Kirk, John	VT0050	20G
Koshinski, Eugene	MN1600	47,65,29,20G,35
Koskoff, Ellen	NY1100	14,15,20G,20D,31
Kowalke, Kim	NY4350	12A,12,39,54,20G
Kozak, Brian	OH0750	12B,20G,29,35
Kreitzer, Mark	MN0300	20G
Kreyszig, Walter	AJ0150	12A,12,20G,55
Kushner, David Z.	FL1850	12,12A,12B,12E,20G
Lamothe, Donat	MA0200	12A,67C,20G,20H
Leckrone, Michael E.	WI0815	60,37,20G
Lee, Michael	OK1350	12A,12,14,20G
Lefebvre, Marie-Therese	AI0200	12,20G
Levy, Beth E.	CA5010	12A,12B,12C,20G
Lindgren, Lowell	MA1200	12A,20G
Link, Stan	TN1850	12A,12,20G,14C,15
Lockwood, Gayle	UT0050	39,61,54,20G,35
London, Justin	MN0300	13,12B,12F,20G,12A
Looking Wolf, Jan Michael	OR0700	20G,64A
Lorenz, Shanna	CA3300	14,20G,20H
Lovensheimer, James A.	TN1850	12,14,20G,29
Lowe, Melanie D.	TN1850	12A,12,20G,14C,15
Loza, Steven	CA5031	14A,20H,20G
Lysloff, Rene T.A.	CA5040	14,20,20D,20G
Lytle, Cecil W.	CA5050	66A,29,20G
Lytle, Gwendolyn L.	CA3650	61,20G
Mabrey, Charlotte	FL1950	50,65,43,20G
Machlin, Paul S.	ME0250	12A,36,20G,29A
Magaldi, Cristina	MD0850	14C,12A,14,20G,20H
Magee, Jeffrey	IL3300	12,20G,29A
Malamut, Myra Lewinter	NJ0550	11,64A,67B,20G,13A
Malloy, Michael	OH2275	65,20G
Mancuso, Charles	NY3717	20G,29A,12E,14C
Martin, James	IA0400	13,66A,66B,20G
Martin, Sherrill	NC2440	12A,66A,66B,20G
McCormick, Scott	MA0260	29B,32F,32H,20G,34G
McCormick, Thomas	FL1300	64E,20G,29
McDonald, Timothy L.	MO1010	11,12A,36,20G
McElwaine, James	NY3785	41,47,20G,29,34
McGrann, Jeremiah	MA0330	11,12,20G
McLamore, Alyson	CA0600	12A,12,32,16,20G
McLucas, Anne Dhu	OR1050	12A,12C,20G,20F,14
McRoberts, Gary	CA1900	32,36,66A,20G
Meissner, Marla	NJ0800	13A,13,20G
Metil, Robert	PA0600	14,29A,20G,70
Miller, Kiri	RI0050	14A,14C,14D,20G,31G
Miller, Patricia M.	NY3650	20G
Miller, Ronald L.	PA2300	12A,36,67B,31A,20G
Moham, Carren D.	IL1200	20G,61
Moore, Edward	NY3720	20G,36,66A,11,29A
Moots, John E.	OK0150	32,49,63A,20G
Morey, Carl	AG0450	11,12A,12,20G
Morris, Mitchell B.	CA5032	12A,12,20G,15
Moser, Martin	NY3500	13,12A,54,20G
Moses, Lennard	OH0500	50,65,20A,20G
Mulford, Ruth Stomne	DE0175	13,11,12A,62A,20G
Mullen, Stan	PA2050	29B,53,70,20G,20F
Murchison, Gayle	VA0250	12A,12,20G,12C
Murphy, Vanissa B.	WI0803	32B,20G
Neal, Jocelyn	NC2410	13,20G,34,14C
Nettl, Bruno	IL3300	14,20G
Neves, Joel	MI1450	38,39,42,20G
Nevola, Teresa	PA1150	61,54,20G
Newman, Nancy	NY3700	20F,20G,12
Noonan, Jeffrey	MO1500	12A,14,67D,70,20G
Oliver, Sylvester	MS0600	12A,20G,37,46
Olivieri, Mark A.	NY1550	10,13,20G,29,48
O'Meara, Caroline	TX3510	12,20G
Owens, Craig	KS1450	47,70,53,29A,20G
Paccione, Paul	IL3500	13,10,43,20G
Parish, Steven	AB0070	65,20G,34,35C
Parman, David L.	IN1800	41,62C,62D,70,20G
Patterson, David N.	MA2010	13,10,11,20G,34
Pearcy, Robert W.	TN1850	20G
Pederson, Sanna	OK1350	12A,20G,12
Pen, Ronald	KY1450	20G,29A,12A,12
Perkins, Andrew	NC0450	10A,13A,20G,46,11
Perlis, Vivian M.	CT0850	20G
Pinckney, Warren R.	CA0800	11,20G,29A,13
Pisani, Michael	NY4450	11,12A,12,20G
Pittman, Deborah M.	CA0840	64C,20G
Plugge, Scott D.	TX2250	64E,20G,29,47
Pollack, Howard	TX3400	12A,12,14,20G
Poole, Eric	NC2150	13,60,20G,36,41
Porter, Judith	NC0860	11,20G
Poston, Ken	CA0825	20G,35B,29A
Preston, Katherine K.	VA0250	12A,12,20G,12C
Prince, Curtis L.	IN0005	10,12,20G,65,47
Pritchard, Gary	CA0859	20G,29A,20H,12A
Radano, Ronald	WI0815	20G
Ramsey, Guthrie P.	PA3350	12,35,20G,29,47
Rasar, Lee Anna	WI0803	33,20G
Rasmussen, Anne K.	VA0250	14,20G,31,41,12C
Ray, Robert	MO1830	20G,36,66A
Reed, Joel F.	NC1250	20G,60A,36,61,31A
Reis, Marzo	CT0300	20G,20H
Reynolds, Robert	KY0860	13A,13,11,66A,20G
Reynolds, Roger L.	CA5050	13,10F,10,20G,34
Rhoades, Connie A.	KY0550	64C,64E,20G
Richards, Walter	FL1790	20G
Ridley, Larry	NY2150	47,29A,62D,20A,20G
Riis, Thomas L.	CO0800	12,20G
Ring, Richard	AI0210	20G
Roach, Hildred E.	DC0350	20G,66A,66B,66C,66D
Roberson, James	CA5031	20G,61
Roberts, Tamara	CA5000	11,14C,14D,20G
Rodger, Gillian	WI0825	12A,12C,20G,20D,14
Roller, Peter	WI0050	20G,70,20H
Root, Deane L.	PA3420	12A,12C,12,20G,12E
Rozie, Edward Rick	CT0650	20G,47,62D,29
Ruckert, George	MA1200	13A,11,20G,20D,20F
Samuels, David	NY2740	14A,14C,14D,14F,20G
Sanchez, Rey	FL1900	10D,34C,35A,20G,43
Sandness, Dorothy	MN0850	11,20G
Savage, Charles M.	OH1910	13,12A,20G,36,61
Schiano, Michael	CT0650	13,13J,20G,34
Schiff, David	OR0900	13,10A,20G,29,38
Schleeter, Bob	CA1150	20G,29A,34D
Schmid, William	WI0825	20G,32C,70
Schmidt, Alan G.	NY1220	13A,12A,47,20G,29A
Schreffler, Gibb	CA3650	14,20B,20G
Schultz, Anna	CA4900	20E,20G,20F
Scott, Gary	OH0755	47,63A,20G,29,35B
Seachrist, Denise A.	OH1100	12C,14,20G
Searles, Julie	MA2150	14,14C,20H,20G
Sears, E. Ann	MA2150	12A,66A,29A,20G
Seeger, Anthony	CA5031	20H,14A,20G,35A,35D
Shaw, Roger	CA3200	20G
Sheppard, W. Anthony	MA2250	12A,20C,14C,12D,20G
Shostak, Anthony	ME0150	20G
Siek, Stephen	OH2450	12A,66A,66B,20G
Smalley, Charles	AZ0150	13C,11,36,61,20G
Smith, Gordon E.	AG0250	12,14,20G,12C
Smith, Mark	IL0600	13A,50,65,29,20G
Solis, Gabriel	IL3300	12,20G
Solis, Ted	AZ0100	12A,20G,14
Solum, Stephen	MN1050	13,20G,10,35G,34
Spence, Larry	NC1250	70,20G
Spencer, Dianthe M.	CA4200	66A,66D,20G,29
Spicer, Mark J.	NY1150	13,11,64A,66A,20G
Spielman, Mark	AB0070	13A,47,62D,20G
Spoor, Aaron	CA3200	20G
Starr, Lawrence	WA1050	12A,12,20G
Stats, Clyde	VT0250	53,20A,20G
Stephens, Robert W.	CT0600	32,20A,20G
Stevenson, Robert M.	CA5032	12,14,20G,20H
Stevenson, Roxanne	IL0600	13A,20G,32,37,64
Stilwell, Jama Liane	IA0400	11,12,20G,13,64A
Stinner, Rita	NE0710	13,36,20G
Sturm, Jonathan	IA0850	12A,11,20G,20
Suarez, Jeff	WI0847	10,13,29,42,20G
Suzuki, Dean P.	CA4200	11,12,20G
Syler, James	TX3530	20G,29,35,10
Tick, Judith	MA1450	12,20G
Titon, Jeff	RI0050	20G,20F,14A
Torok, Debra	PA2450	12A,13,38,66A,20G
Tsai, Shang-Ying	CA5400	13A,11,20G
Ullman, Michael	MA1900	20G,29A
Unsworth, Arthur E.	NC0050	20G,35
Utterback, Joe	CT0300	12A,20G,29A
Vaughn, Beverly Joyce	NJ0990	36,11,13A,20G,61
Veal, Michael E.	CT0900	14,20A,20G
Virgoe, Betty	CA1520	66,11,13A,20G
Waddel, Nathan	OR0350	20G,47
Waites, Althea	CA0825	66A,66D,20G
Walker, Gregory T. S.	CO0830	11,62A,20G,62B,46
Ward, Robert J.	MA1450	70,11,13,20G
Watson, Richard	ND0250	14C,20G
Weddle, John W.	CA0850	32C,32B,20G,64C,11
Wegman, Rob	NJ0900	11,12A,12,20G
Weintraub, Andrew	PA3420	20D,14A,20G,14C,14D
Wells, Elizabeth A.	AE0050	12A,12,14,20G
Wheeler, Mark	NC0915	11,12A,20G
Will, Richard	VA1550	12A,12,20G,14C
Williams, Maria	NM0450	14,20H,20G
Williams, Marvin	NY2050	10,11,12,13,20G
Williams, Sean	WA0350	11,12,14,20G,70
Wilson, Karen	SC0200	12,66A,12C,20G,67
Wilson, Lorraine P.	PA1600	32,66D,20G
Wilson, Olly W.	CA5000	10,20G,29
Winkler, Peter	NY3790	13,10,20G,29A
Winslow, Richard D.	CA0800	49,63A,63B,29A,20G
Witmer, Robert	AG0650	14,20G,29
Wittman, Frances P.	NY3700	61,20G
Woideck, Carl	OR1050	29A,20G,12
Wolz, Larry	TX0900	12A,20G,61,12C
Wong, Deborah	CA5040	14,20,20D,20G,31D
Wood, Jeffrey	TN0050	13,10,66A,66D,20G
Wright, Josephine	OH0700	12,20G
Wurgler, Norman F.	KY1540	11,36,20G,61,54
Young, Steven	MA0510	36,11,55,66A,20G
Zachow, Barbara	IL2350	36,20G
Zemke, Lorna	WI0770	32,14A,29,20G
Zilber, Michael	CA2775	11,64E,12A,20G,29
Zogleman, Deanne	KS0980	12A,13,20G,36,40
Zucker, Laurel	CA0840	64A,20G

Central and South America, Mexico, and the Caribbean

Name	Code	Areas
Acevedo, Michael	TX3530	20H
Addington, Joe	CA3300	20H
Allen, Matthew H.	MA2150	14C,20E,20H,31,14
Allen, Ray	NY0500	11,20G,29A,20H
Asai, Susan M.	MA1450	14,20D,20H
Barilari, Elbio Rodriguez	IL3310	20H
Barrera, J. J.	TX3510	20H
Baxter, Marsha L.	NY3780	32,20H
Berrocal, Esperanza	DC0050	20H

Name	Code	Areas
Birenbaum Quintero, Michael	ME0200	14,20H,31F
Botelho, Mauro	NC0550	13,11,20H
Boukas, Richard A.	NY2660	61,70,20H,47
Bozina, Robert	CA4425	20H,70,13A,14F,14C
Branchal, Nick	CO0050	20H
Briseno, Antonio	TX3515	11,20H,41
Brown, Leonard	MA2200	20G,20H,29
Budasz, Rogerio	CA5040	12,20H
Burford, Mark	OR0900	12A,20G,14C,20H
Burgess, Gareth	AG0650	20H
Burgess, Lindy	AG0650	20H
Butler, Erica E.	ME0150	20H
Carter, Joseph	CT0300	70,29A,20G,20H,47
Castro, Cesar	CA3300	20H
Castro, Zeke	TX3510	20H,14C
Cepeda, Manny	CA2100	20H,13
Chavez, Robert	CA1700	20H
Chianis, Sam	NY3705	12A,12,14,20H
Ciucci, Alessandra	MA1450	14C,14F,20B,20H
Clark, Jonathan	CA4900	20H
Clark, Walter A.	CA5040	12,20H
Colman, Alfredo C.	TX0300	14,20H
Crook, Larry	FL1850	14,50,20H,29
Dasilva, Mario	KY1460	47,70,20H,29
De Castro, Paul	CA0830	14,29,20H,66A
Dekaney, Elisa M.	NY4150	32,36,20H,60A
Dekaney, Joshua A.	NY4150	20H,65,32E
Delgado, Kevin M.	CA4100	14,20H
Dixon, Patricia	NC2500	70,20H
Emmanuel, Donna T.	TX3420	32B,32G,20D,20H,35A
Esguerra, Ruben	AG0650	20H
Estoque, Kevin S.	LA0650	65,50,46,20H
Fassnacht, Therese	CA3150	13B,13C,20H,12A
Fogelquist, Mark	CA4100	20H
Galm, Eric A.	CT0500	14,20,20H,50,65
Garcia, Eduardo	CA0847	20H,11,70
Garcia, Glynn	TX0550	20H
Garcia, Peter J.	CA0835	20H
Garcia, Thomas George Caracas	OH1450	14,20H
Garrido, Glenn	TX3450	60B,32E,20H,37
Gartner, Kurt	KS0650	65,20H,47,50
Gerhart, David	CA0825	65,20H,37,50
Ginorio, Jorge	TX1725	20H,50,65
Green, Verna	NY0640	20A,20H,32D,32E,36
Greene, Oliver N.	GA1050	12,20H
Guilbault, Jocelyne	CA5000	11,14,20H
Guzman, Jesus	CA5031	20H
Guzman, Joel J.	TX3510	20H
Hagedorn, Katherine J.	CA3650	14,20H,20A
Hawkins, Phillip	CA2975	11,20H,34,50
Helbig, Adriana	PA3420	14A,14C,14D,20F,20H
Henriques, Donald A.	CA0810	14,20H
Hernandez, Edgar	CA0830	20H
Hess, Carol A.	CA5010	12,20H
Illari, Bernardo	TX3420	12,20H
Janeczko, Jeffrey M.	CA5031	20F,20G,20H
Jensen, Espen	IN0900	20H
Kean, Ronald M.	CA0270	36,20B,20H
Kennedy, T. Frank	MA0330	11,12,31A,20H
King, Fredericka	MA0850	20G,20H
Krause, William Craig	VA0550	70,11,12A,20H,35E
Lamothe, Donat	MA0200	12A,67C,20G,20H
Landau, Gregory P.	CA1020	20H
Langosch, Paul	VA1700	20H,29,35D,46,47
Lapidus, Benjamin	NY0630	14,70,20H
Larson, Leon	FL1675	20H,65
Lazar, Richard	AG0650	20H
Ledbetter, Robert	MT0400	37,50,65,20H,14C
Lehninger, Marcia	NH0150	11,20H,62A,62B
Leon, Javier F.	IN0900	14,20H
Lezcano, Jose	NH0150	41,70,20H
Loera, Francisco	TX3525	11,20H
Lorenz, Shanna	CA3300	14,20G,20H
Loza, Steven	CA5031	14A,20H,20G
Lozano, Danilo	CA0830	20H
Luker, Morgan James	OR0900	14A,14C,14D,20H
Magaldi, Cristina	MD0850	14C,12A,14,20G,20H
Maldonado, Ana Marie	CA0630	13A,62C,20H
Manuel, Peter G.	NY0600	14,20C,20H
Marcuzzi, Michael	AG0650	32,20H,14
Mauleon-Santana, Rebeca	CA1020	66D,20H,10A
Mery, John	OR0400	20H,62
Milstein, Amir	MA0510	11,20H
Moore, Robin D.	TX3510	14,31F,14C,14F,20H
Moreno, Jairo	PA3350	13,13J,20H,29,12D
Moskowitz, David V.	SD0600	12A,20H,14C,12C,11
Murciano, Raul	FL1900	35,20H,10C
Nevin, Jeff	CA4850	63A,20H,10
Ormandy, Paul	AG0650	20H
Party, Daniel	IN1450	14C,12A,11,20H
Paton, Eric	OH0350	65,20A,20C,20H,47
Pedroza, Ludim R.	TX3175	12A,20H,66D
Picard, Paul	AI0200	65,20H
Powell, Jason	IN0300	20F,20H,31A,66A,66G
Pritchard, Gary	CA0859	20G,29A,20H,12A
Quantz, Michael	TX3515	11,41,62,20H
Ramirez, George	CA1850	20H
Reis, Marzo	CT0300	20G,20H
Rey, Mario	NC0650	14,13,20H
Rios, Fernando	MD1010	20H
Rios, Fernando	IL3300	20H
Rios, Juan	CA5040	20H,52
Ritter, Jonathan	CA5040	14,20,20H
Rivera, Francesca M.	CA5353	14,20H,41
Robinson, Gregory J.	VA0450	11,12,14,20H
Roller, Peter	WI0050	20G,70,20H
Saavedra, Leonora	CA5040	12,20H
Schechter, John M.	CA5070	13,14,20H
Schloss, Andrew	AB0150	10B,34,14,20H,13L
Schwartz-Kates, Deborah	FL1900	12,20H,14
Searles, Julie	MA2150	14,14C,20H,20G
Seeger, Anthony	CA5031	20H,14A,20G,35A,35D
Simonett, Helena	TN1850	12,14,20H
Simpson-Litke, Rebecca	GA2100	13,14C,20H
Smart, Carlos	CA2910	20H
Smith, Hope Munro	CA0800	14,20H,11,12A,12C
Sobrino, Laura	CA5040	20H,51
Soto, Amanda C.	ID0250	14,20H,32B,32G,32H
Stable, Arturo	PA3330	20H,50
Stevenson, Robert M.	CA5032	12,14,20G,20H
Strunk, Michael J.	CA0400	65,20,20H,50
Teague, Liam	IL2200	20H
Thomas, Susan R.	GA2100	11,12,14,20H,34A
Torres, George	PA1850	12A,12,14,12D,20H
Torres, Jose	TX0550	20H
Tucker, Joshua	RI0050	14A,14C,14D,20H
Turino, Thomas R.	IL3300	11,20A,20H,14
Vasconcellos, Renato	KY1500	20H,34C
Velez, Gilbert Y.	AZ0500	20H
Walker, John L.	VA1700	64B,13,14,20H
Washington, Kera M.	MA2050	20H
Williams, Maria	NM0450	14,20H,20G
Yi, Ann	CA0855	66A,66D,20H
Young, Donald	CA3850	20H,34,35
Zohn-Muldoon, Ricardo	NY1100	10,20H

Oceania and Australia

Name	Code	Areas
McGraw, Andrew	VA1500	14,20I
Medeiros, Peter	HI0210	20I
Nahulu, Nola A.	HI0210	36,20I
Sano, Stephen M.	CA4900	60,36,20C,20I
Smith, Barbara B.	HI0210	20I,20C,14
Still, Alexa	OH1700	64A,20I
Suadin, I. Ketut	MD1010	20I
Takamine, Victoria	HI0210	20I
Trimillos, Ricardo D.	HI0210	20D,20I,14D,14A,14F
Zuttermeister, Noenoelani	HI0210	20I

Jazz Studies (All Areas)

Name	Code	Areas
Aaberg, David E.	MO1790	47,29,10
Abadey, Nasar	MD0650	29
Abate, Greg	RI0200	29
Abbott, Tyler	OR1050	62D,29,13
Abdul Al-Khabyyr, Muhammad	AI0150	63C,29
Abruzzo, Luke A.	PA1000	70,10A,13,29
Adair, William 'Billy'	TN1850	29,46,47
Adams, Kris	MA2050	29,61
Adamy, Paul	NY2400	70,29
Adedapo, Adekola	WI1150	61,29
Ailshie, Tyson	CO0100	11,13,62D,70,29
Akagi, Kei	CA5020	53,29,47
Akin, Willie	MO1950	29
Alamo, Juan	NC2410	29,65,50
Alarie, Frederic	AI0200	62D,29
Albano, John	CA2900	10D,29,47,70
Albaugh, John	IA0550	29,70
Aldag, Daniel	CA2250	63D,29,14C,63C,47
Alegria, Gabriel A.	NY2750	29,47,63A
Alexander, Glenn	NY3560	41,47,70,29
Aliquo, Don	TN1100	29,64E,46,47
Allen, Carl	NY1900	47,29
Allen, Eddie	NY0500	63A,29
Allen, Geri	MI2100	29
Allen, Jeremy	IN0900	62D,29
Allison, Robert	IL2900	63A,29
Allmark, John	RI0150	29,37
Almario, Justo	CA5031	29,64
Alper, Garth	LA0760	66A,29,35
Amirault, Greg	AI0150	70,29
Amirault, Steve	AI0150	66A,29
Ammons, Mark	UT0050	47,29
Amos, Alvin E.	PA2000	29,13A,13C,48,64
Anderson, Dan	IL0720	62D,63D,29
Anderson, Erik	ND0250	62D,62C,13,51,29
Anderson, Jay	NY2150	29
Anderson, Jeff	IN1560	47,29
Anderson, Leon	FL0850	47,65,29,46
Anderson, Stephen	NC2410	10,29
Andrews, Dwight D.	GA0750	13,14,31A,29
Appell, Glen	CA1560	11,29,46,47
Applegate, Erik	CO0950	29,47
Applewhite, Willie	UT0190	66,20,29,63C
Archard, Chuck	FL1550	47,62D,53,29
Ard, Kenneth	CA2100	66,29
Arnay, David	CA5300	66A,29
Arnold, Horacee	NJ1400	29
Arnold, Robert D.	PA2550	29,66A
Arthurs, Robert	NY2400	63A,29
Ashby, Jay	OH1700	29
Ashley, Richard	IL2250	13,10,29
Askren, David	CA0830	29
Ator, James	IN0905	13,10,48,64E,29
AuBuchon, Tim	MO1780	29,46,47
Azzolina, Jay	NY2200	70,29,47
Baca, Robert J.	WI0803	47,63A,29
Bachman, Jerome	NY0350	29,47
Baker, Charles	OH1100	47,29
Baker, David N.	IN0900	47,29
Baker, Malcolm Lynn	CO0900	47,53,46,29
Baker, Steve	CA2100	66A,13,29
Baker, Tony E.	TX3420	63C,29
Bakos, Daniel F.	GA2130	13,47,29
Bakriges, Christopher	MA1550	29,14D,12B,20,31G
Bales, Kevin	GA1050	29
Balfany, Gregory J.	WI0810	47,64C,46,29
Ball, Greg L.	TX2750	37,48,64,20G,29
Ballou, David L.	MD0850	29,53,63A,29A,36
Bambrick, Heather	AG0450	61,29
Banagale, Ryan	CO0200	11,12,29,34
Banaszak, Greg J.	OH0200	47,64E,29
Bangle, Jerry	NC2640	13,11,38,53,29
Banks, Ansyn P.	KY1500	63A,29
Barbee, Larry	NJ0975	13A,47,70,29
Barber, Keith	OH2140	70,29
Barbuto, Robert	NY1250	66A,29
Barduhn, David	OR0550	13,10,47,29
Barnard, William	MN1600	70,29,42
Barnhart, William	FL0850	29,63A
Barrett, Robert H.	CO1050	11,47,64,34,29
Barron, Kenny	NY1900	66A,29
Barry, Rebecca	AL1195	29,64E
Barth, Bruce D.	PA3250	47,29
Barth, Bruce	NY2102	29
Bartlett, Anthony	AZ0440	63C,29
Bartz, Gary	OH1700	29
Bastian, William M.	MI1200	66A,29
Batchelor, Daryl	KS0550	47,63A,29,29A
Batiste, Alvin	LA0700	64A,64C,29,47,35A
Battenberg, Thomas V.	OH1850	47,63A,29
Battistone, Christopher	DC0170	63A,29
Bauer, Ross	CA5010	13,10,43,29
Baum, Jamie	NY2150	29
Bayer, Joshua	DC0100	29,20,13,62D,70
Baylock, Alan	VA1350	29
Bazan, Michael	IL3550	64E,29
Beach, Douglas	IL0850	47,53,71,29,35
Bean, Robert G.	AL1450	13,37,47,63,29
Beaugrand, Luc	AI0200	53,66A,29
Becker, David M.	OR0400	60,32C,37,29,64
Beckley-Roberts, Lisa	FL1790	20G,29
Beckner, Woody	VA0250	70,29
Begian, Jamie	CT0800	41,70,53,47,29

Index by Area of Teaching Interest

Name	Code	Areas
Behnke, Martin K.	OR1300	60,37,66A,29
Bejerano, Martin	FL1900	29,10,66A,53
Belck, Scott	OH2200	29
Bell, Timothy R.	WI0835	47,64C,64E,29,48
Benedetti, Fred	CA2100	70,53,35B,29
Benedict, Jeffrey W.	CA0830	29,47,64E,41
Benson, George	MI2200	29,64E
Berardinelli, Paula	NY1600	29,13A,13C,11,47
Berg, Christian R.	OH2200	29
Berg, Jason	TX3200	12A,29
Berg, Shelton G.	FL1900	66A,66C,29,46,47
Bergman, Luke	WA1050	29
Bergonzi, Jerry	MA1400	29,64E,47
Berkman, David	NY0642	29,66A
Berman, Ronald M.	CA3500	70,29
Berney, Mark C.	RI0300	29,47,63A
Bernstein, Peter A.	NY2750	29,70,47
Bertoncini, Gene	NJ1400	29
Bewley, Rabon	TX1660	11,12A,29,64E,13A
Bilden, Jeff	CA1290	37,47,29,63,64
Billington, Ryan	AF0150	36,40,29,61
Billington, Ryan	AF0120	61,29,36
Bingham, Steve	FL1675	11,13A,20,29,64
Bingham, W. Edwin	WV0400	47,64E,64D,29
Bishop, Andrew	MI2100	29
Bishop, Julie	PA3250	29,61
Bisio, Michael	VT0050	62D,53,29
Bixler, David	OH0300	64E,29
Black, Cary	WA0350	62D,53,29,35,47
Black, Claude	OH2300	29
Black, David	MO1950	29,70
Blackshear, Alan	AL0831	37,13,11,29
Blake, John	NY2150	29
Blake, John	PA3330	47,62A,29
Blake, Ran	MA1400	29,66A,53
Blake, Ron	NY1900	63A,29
Blanchard, Jeff L.	OH2140	63A,47,49,29
Bland, Ron	CO0150	29,62D
Bleckman, Theo	NY2150	29,61
Blenzig, Charles	NY3785	10,66A,29,35B
Blink, David	WA1400	47,13,63A,29
Blue, T. K.	NY2105	47,29,29A,29B
Boerckel, Gary M.	PA2100	11,12A,66A,20G,29
Bohanon, George	CA5031	63C,29
Bolduc, Remi	AI0150	64E,29
Boling, Mark E.	TN1710	70,29
Bollenback, Paul	MD0650	29
Bongiorno, Frank	NC2440	47,64E,29
Bonilla, Luis	NY2150	29,63C
Booker, Adam	MN1600	29,41,46,62D
Boone, Benjamin V.	CA0810	13,10,29
Boone, Michael E.	PA3250	29,62D
Booth, Doug	CA2100	70,29
Booth, Rodney	TX3420	63A,29
Borgo, David R.	CA5050	64E,14,29,47
Boris, William	IL0720	70,29
Borla, Janice	IL2050	53,29,29A,29B
Bosshardt, Heather	UT0190	29,66
Botts, Nathan	VT0050	11,29,49,63,67E
Bouchard, George	NY2550	11,46,47,66D,29
Bovinette, James	IA0850	47,63A,29
Bowen, Jose A.	TX2400	47,12A,29,38,12
Bowen, Ralph	NJ1130	47,64E,29
Bowman, Bob	MO1810	29,62D
Bowyer, Don	AR0110	63C,63D,29,35C,47
Boyd, Jesse	LA0080	11,13,29,62,70
Boyd, Lance	MT0400	47,63C,63D,53,29
Boykin-Settles, Jessica	DC0150	29
Bracey, Jerry A.	VA0500	37,38,47,62,29
Bradfield, Ann	NM0100	29,46,47,64A,64E
Bradfield, Geoffrey	IL2200	64E,29
Bradshaw, Curt	TX0700	13,29
Braid, David	AG0450	29,66A
Branker, Anthony D.J.	NJ0900	47,29,46
Braxton, Anthony	CT0750	10,20G,29
Brewer, Paul	AZ0490	11,13,29,32E,47
Brewer, Paul S.	MI0300	60B,37,32E,29,63C
Brewer, Paul	AZ0440	29
Bridgewater, Cecil	NY2150	29
Bridgewater, Ronald S.	IL3300	47,64E,29
Briggs, Kendall Durelle	NY1900	32B,12A,29
Briggs, Nancy L.	CA4580	29,10,66,53,20
Briggs, Ray	CA3500	20,11,29
Briggs, Ray A.	CA0825	14,29,46,47
Bristol, Doug S.	AL0050	13,29,63C,47
Brochu, Paul	AI0200	65,29
Brockman, Luke	WA0250	29,46,66A
Brothers, Thomas	NC0600	12A,12C,12E,29
Brown, Ari	IL3310	64E,29
Brown, Derek	TX0050	29,13B,64E
Brown, Jeremy S.	AA0150	37,64E,29,12G,48
Brown, Jeri	AI0070	36,47,61,29
Brown, Leonard	MA2200	20G,20H,29
Brown, Philip	IL2900	62D,29,35
Brown, Ray	CA0400	13,29
Brown, Rogers	VA0950	10F,37,47,63D,29
Brucker, Clifford	NY3600	11,66D,29
Brunkhorst, Kevin	AF0150	70,34,29
Bruya, Chris	WA0050	46,47,29,13
Buckholz, Christopher John	IA1600	63C,29,41,11
Buckingham, Katisse	CA0835	29
Buckmaster, Matthew	NC0750	63D,29,63C,49,32
Buda, Frederick	MA1400	65,29
Budds, Michael J.	MO1800	12A,11,29
Buehrer, Theodore E.	OH1200	13,10,29,63A,34
Buelow, William L.	OH1400	13A,13,10,66A,29
Burkhead, Phillip	KY1000	29
Burkhead, Phillip	OH2250	66A,29
Burrell, Kenneth	CA5031	29
Burton, James	NY1900	42,29
Buselli, Mark	IN0150	63A,29,47
Butler, Dorsey Mitchell	SC0350	63C,60B,47,29
Butterfield, Craig	SC1110	62D,29,46,47
Butterfield, Matthew W.	PA1300	29,13,13B,29A,29B
Butturi, Renato	IN1600	70,11,67G,47,29
Byrd, Eric B.	MD0520	36,66A,29
Byrne, Tom	MO1950	29,70
Caffey, H. David	CO0950	29
Cain, Joren R.	GA2150	29,64E
Cain, Michael	AC0050	29,47,66A
Cain, Michael	NJ1100	29
Cain, Michael D.	MA1400	29,66A,34,31,20
Call, R. Steven	UT0050	47,63D,46,29
Cameron, Clayton	CA5031	29,65
Campbell, Gary	FL0700	64E,29,53,47
Campiglia, Paul	GA0625	47,29,53,65
Campiglia, Paul	GA2150	65,29,71,50,11
Cangelosi, Casey	WV0200	61,65,29,34
Caniato, Michele	MA0930	10,38,29,13,47
Cannon, Derek	CA2100	29,63A,47
Cannon, Rodney M.	TX2250	65,29
Carere, Anthony	GA1500	29
Carey, Peter	TX2260	11,29
Carillo, Dan	NY0550	47,13,46,10,29
Carmichael, Steve R.	WI0250	47,11,29
Carney, Michael	CA0825	65,29,20,50
Carney, Peter	IL2650	11,29
Carrillo, Christopher J.	VA0600	63A,29
Carroll, James R.	VA0450	47,64E,29,46
Carroll, Kenneth D.	AR0110	29,64E,37,46
Carroll, Tom	OH0850	47,29,70
Carrothers, Bill	WI0350	29,66A
Carryer, Steven J.	MI2200	70,29
Carter, Greg	AF0150	64E,29,10
Carter, Kenyon W.	AL0500	64E,29
Carter, Kenyon	GA1500	64E,29
Carter, Ron	NY1900	29
Carter, Ronald	IL2200	47,29
Cashwell, Brian	OH0500	66A,29
Cassino, Peter	MA1175	47,29
Castellanos, Gilbert	CA5300	29,63A
Cavanagh, Daniel	TX3500	47,29,46
Cee, Vincent	AK0150	32,29,38,34B,11
Chaffee, Gary	MA1400	29,65
Chambers, Joseph	NC2440	29
Champouillon, David	TN0500	63A,46,29
Chancler, Ndugu	CA5300	29,65
Chapman, Dale E.	ME0150	12,13,29
Chappell, Jeffrey	MD0400	47,66A,29,29B,10
Chappell, Jeffrey	DC0170	13,29,66A
Chappell, Robert	IL2200	20B,29
Charles, Etienne	MI1400	29,63A,47
Chase, Allan S.	MA1400	47,29,53,64E
Chatterjee, Samir	NY2150	29
Chevan, David	CT0450	11,12A,47,53,29
Christiansen, Corey M.	IN0900	70,29
Ciacca, Antonio	NY1900	29
Cifarelli, Joan	CA2775	66A,29,13A
Clancy, Eric	IN0700	47,29,53
Clark, John	CT0100	11,13,29
Clark, William F.	CO0830	47,63D,13,49,29
Clarke, Terry	AG0450	65,29
Classen, Andrew B.	IA0550	47,49,63A,29
Claussen, Tina	MO0350	47,64E,46,29
Clayton, Greg	AI0150	47,70,29
Clayton, Jay	MD0650	29
Clement, Dawn	WA0200	13A,66A,66D,29
Cline, Gilbert D.	CA2250	63A,49,29,67E,63B
Clothier, Stephen	CA0630	29,46
Cochrane, Michael	NJ1140	66A,29
Coffman, Timothy J.	IL0750	29,63C
Coggiola, John C.	NY4150	32,29,34,47,60B
Coghlan, Michael	AG0650	13,10,29,34,43
Coil, Pat	TN1100	66A,29,42
Coker, Jerry	TN1710	47,29
Cole, Monty	GA1300	29,32E,46,64C,64E
Coleman, Anthony	MA1400	53,29
Connelly, Chris	SC0420	63C,63D,11,29
Converse, Ralph D.	NM0500	64,41,38,48,29
Coogan, Chris	CT0550	29,66,47
Cook, Carla	PA3250	29,61
Cooke, India	CA2950	62A,29
Coolman, Todd	NY3785	47,62D,53,46,29
Cooper, Jack	TN1680	29,64E,46
Cooper, John	IL3500	29,63A
Cooper, John H.	ME0270	10,29,13,64E,10F
Cooper, Matthew J.	OR0200	13,47,66A,66D,29
Coppola, Thomas	NC2400	66A,66D,10C,29
Corbin, Dwayne V.	CA4600	37,38,65,29
Cotroneo, P. J.	NJ0950	29,70,13
Couture, Jocelyn	AI0150	63A,29
Covington, Charles	DC0150	29
Cowan, Scott M.	MI2250	11,47,63,29
Cox, Michael W.	OH0350	64E,29,48
Coye, Gene	CA0835	29,65
Coyle, Brian	MI1050	47,29,53
Craig, Sean	AI0150	29,47
Crouch, Jay	MI1985	63A,29
Cunliffe, William H.	CA0815	29,47,41
Curtis, Peter	CA3800	11,70,14,20,29
Dagradi, Anthony	LA0300	64,64E,29
Dailey, Raleigh K.	KY1450	29,46
Dana, Michael	CA1850	29,47,35A,34
D'Angelo, David	GA2100	29,53
D'Angelo, Gerard	NY2150	29
Danielsson, Per	FL1800	29,66A
Dashiell, Carroll V.	NC0650	47,62D,29
Dasilva, Mario	KY1460	47,70,20H,29
Daversa, John	CA0835	10C,29,63A
David, Norman	PA3250	29
David, Norman	PA3330	64,47,10,29,13
Davies, Richard	NY3775	10,29,34,46,63D
Davis, Art	IL2200	63A,29
Davis, Christopher A.	SC0950	11,13,29,50,65
Davis, Duane Shields	MI2250	29,61
Davis, John Douglas	CA0650	13,10,47,29
Davis, John S.	CO0800	47,29,29A,63A
Davis, Joshua	PA3150	47,29,62D,13C,53
Davis, Kenneth	NJ1130	62D,29
Davis, Mark	WI1150	66A,29
Davis, Mark	WI0150	47,29,53
Davis, Nathan T.	PA3420	20G,47,64E,29
Davis, Quincy	AC0100	29,65,47
Davis, Steve	CT0650	29
Davis, Xavier	NY1900	47,29
Davison, Michael A.	VA1500	11,29,46,47,49
Dawson, Bradley J.	KS0350	47,49,63A,29
De Barros, Paul	WA0800	29
De Boeck, Garry	AA0050	47,65,29,35B
De Castro, Paul	CA0830	14,29,20H,66A
De Stefano, Reno	AI0200	29,12
Deacon-Joyner, David	WA0650	47,29
Dean, Kevin	AI0150	63A,29
Deardorf, Chuck	WA0200	62D,53,29,35
Dease, Michael	MI1400	29,63C
Deaville, James	AG0100	12,29,35
Decuir, Michael	GA0150	11,20,29,37,47
Dees, David	TX3200	47,64E,29
DeFade, Eric	PA0550	64E,47,29
DeGreg, Philip A.	OH2200	29
Delin, Diane	IL0720	29,62A,10
DeLise, Louis Anthony	PA3250	29
DeMarinis, Paul	MO1950	64E,53,29
Demsey, David	NJ1400	64E,29
Denny, Michael	OR1050	70,47,29,29A
Denson, Keith	NC0860	11,29,12A

505

Index by Area of Teaching Interest

Name	Code	Areas
DeRosa, Richard J.	TX3420	29
DeRosa, Richard	NY2150	29
DeVeaux, Scott K.	VA1550	13,12A,12,14,29
Dial, Garry	NY2150	29
DiBlasio, Denis	NJ1050	10F,47,64E,53,29
DiCioccio, Justin	NY2150	29
Dickerson, Roger	LA0720	10F,10,12A,36,29
Dickert, Lewis H.	SC1200	70,53,29,13A,14
Dickman, Marcus	FL1950	63D,53,29
Dickson, Robert	GA1050	29
Diehl, Bruce P.	MA0100	29,64E,47,46
Dietrich, Kurt R.	WI0700	13,32,37,47,29
DiLauro, Ron	AI0150	63A,29,47
Dinda, Robin	MA0930	10,11,13,29,66G
Dismore, Roger	TX0370	47,20G,29,35A,35G
Dobbins, Sean	MI1750	47,65,29
Dobbins, Sean	MI2200	29
Dominguez, Peter	OH1700	47,29
Donelian, Armen	NJ1400	29
Dotas, Charles J.	VA0600	46,29
Dotson, Dennis W.	TX3510	63A,29
Douglass, Ronald L.	MI1100	13,37,41,63,29
Downing, Andrew	AG0450	29
Doxas, Chet	AI0150	64E,29
Doxas, Jim	AI0150	29,65
Drake, Mike	TX0700	29
Drayton, Leslie	CA4450	29
Drennon, Eddie	DC0170	62A,29
Dresel, Bernie	NV0050	29
Dresser, Mark	CA5050	62D,29
Drewes, William	NY2750	29,47,64E
Drexler, Richard	FL1800	29
Driscoll, Kermit	NY3785	62D,29
Drost, Michael	MI0900	46,47,29
Drumheller, John	CO0800	29
Drummond, Billy R.	NY2750	29,47,65
Drummond, Billy	NY1900	29
Drummond, Ray	NY1900	29
Duncan, Christine	AG0450	29
Dunne, Matthew R.	TX3530	70,29,47,35
Durst, Alan Edward	CA0810	64E,29,32,46,47
Dvoskin, Victor	VA1600	62D,29
Eade, Dominique	MA1400	61,53,47,29
Eaton, Roy	NY2150	29,35B
Eberhardt, Allan	CO0275	47,63A,46,49,29
Ebner, Craig	PA3250	29,70
Eby, Chad	NC2430	46,47,29
Echard, William	AG0100	12,20,29,34,35
Eckard, Steven C.	MD0520	47,62D,29
Eckert, Joseph H.	TX3000	64E,29,47
Ehrlich, Martin L.	MA1000	29,13B,13C
Eifertsen, Dyne	CA0150	29,63C,46,47
Eldridge, Peter	NY2150	61,29
Ellias, Rod	AI0070	13,47,70,53,29
Ellingson, Peter	CO0830	66,13C,29
Ellison, Charles	AI0070	47,63A,53,46,29
Ellwood, Jeff	CA0815	64E,29
Elmes, Barry	AG0650	47,29
Embrey, Danny	MO1810	29
Emerzian, Jimmy	CA0825	29
Emmons, Tim	CA0830	62D,29
Encarnacion, Jose	WI0350	29,64E
Encke, William	IA1450	70,46,47,29
Engelhardt, Kent	OH2600	64E,29,53,47
Enghauser, Christopher M.	AL0500	62D,29
Englar, Marcia L.	PA2350	70,29
Enos, Steve	OH0750	13,47,63A,29,46
Eriksson, Johan	MT0400	64E,29
Erjavec, Donald L.	CA0859	13A,47,29,20G
Erskine, Peter C.	CA5300	29,65
Eschete, Ron	CA0815	29,70
Esleck, David	VA1800	11,66A,29,34,35
Esleck, David	VA1500	11,29
Espinosa, Gabriel	IA0200	47,53,29,40
Ess, Michael	VA1600	70,29,47
Estabrook, Peter	CA4460	29
Eubanks, Robin	NY2750	47,63C,29
Eubanks, Robin	OH1700	29
Eulau, Andrew	NJ0825	29,62D
Evoskevich, Paul	NY0700	47,64E,53,29,42
Faddis, Jon	NY3785	47,63A,29
Fagaly, Sam W.	IL0800	64E,47,29,48
Fague, David	WA0400	29,46,47
Fannin, Karen M.	AR0350	29,11,13A,47,37
Farber, Andy	NY1900	10,29
Farnsworth, Anne	CA5300	61,29
Farr, Chris	PA3330	47,64E,29
Fazecash, Robert	AG0550	46,47,63A,29
Fedchcok, John	PA3250	29,63C
Felton, Jukube	IL0600	13A,29
Fenwick, Jerry	CA4000	11,66A,54,29,35
Ferber, Alan	MD0650	29
Ferguson, Paul	OH0400	47,29
Ferrante, Russell K.	CA5300	29
Ferrazza, Robert	OH1700	29
Ferrier, Robert	MA1100	70,53,29,13C
Ferry, Joe	NY3785	10,29,35B,35D
Festinger, Kurt	CA5500	13A,29,47
Fiddmont, Keith	CA4450	11,29,13A,46,47
Fidyk, Steve	PA3250	29,65
Fieldhouse, Stephen M.	PA1400	64E,29,42
Fields, Marc E.	OH2200	29
Figueroa, Angel	CA5300	65,29
Finegold, Michael G.	MA1500	13,11,29
Finet, Christopher	AZ0450	29,47,62D
Fish, David Lee	NC0350	35,14,34,20C,29
Fisher, Chad	AL1150	29
Fisher, Jonathan	TX3420	29,62D
Flack, Michael	IL0650	11,66,13,29,32B
Flanagan, Edward	PA3250	29,35
Fleg, Jerome	WY0050	64C,29,47,64E
Flugge, Mark	OH1850	29,66A
Foley, Mark	KS1450	62D,29,13
Ford, James	CA0830	63A,29
Forman, Dick	VT0350	47,29,66C
Formanek, Michael	MD0650	29,46
Fournier, Gilles	AC0050	62D,29
Foy, Leonard C.	IN0350	63A,49,29
Fradette, Gilbert	AI0200	65,29
Fraedrich, Craig	VA1350	63A,29
Fraize, Peter W.	DC0100	47,53,64E,29
Frane, Ryan	MN1600	29,47,66A,46
Frank, Mike	PA3250	47,66A,29
Free, Scott	MA0260	10,29
Fremgen, John	TX3510	62D,29,47,46
Friedman, Bennett	CA4460	29,53,47
Friedman, Don E.	NY2750	47,29,66A
Friedman, Jeffrey A.	MA0260	10,29
Frink, Laurie	NY2150	29
Froman, James	PA0100	70,29
Froncek, Tim	MI0900	29,65,29A,47,46
Fudge, Berkeley	WI1150	47,64E,53,64A,29
Fuller, Matthew	CO0950	29
Funk, Eric	MT0200	10A,10F,60,29,13
Fusco, Andrew	NJ0700	64E,47,29,46
Gahler, Jason R.	OH2140	62D,29
Gailey, Dan J.	KS1350	47,29
Gaines, Adam W.	WI0808	63,47,37,63A,29
Gairo, Anthony	PA2450	64E,29,47
Gale, Jack	NY2150	29
Gallagher, Matt	PA3330	47,63A,29
Gallo, Joseph	CA1520	35,34,66A,29,53
Gallon, Ray	NY0550	29,11
Gallops, R. Wayne	VA1100	13A,32C,32E,29,37
Galloway, Michael	PA2150	47,63A,53,29
Garcia, Antonio	VA1600	29,47,63C,35,46
Gardiner, Robert A.	SC0800	11,29,47,32E,64E
Garling, Tom	IL2200	29,63C
Garlock, Scott E.	OH0100	29,47,63C,63D,46
Garzone, George	MA1400	47,29,64E
Gaspero, Carmen	PA0125	70,29
Gast, Kim	MN1300	47,64E,29
Gately, Doug T.	VA1475	47,48,29,64
Gaughan, Warren J.	NC2550	47,13,66A,46,29
Gauthier, Michael	AI0150	70,29
Gauthier, Tommy	AI0200	62A,29
Gearey, Jon	AI0150	29,70
Gekker, Chris	MD1010	70,29
Gelispie, Randle	MI1400	29,65
Gemberling, John	MT0370	47,29,63
Genge, Anthony	AF0150	13,66A,20G,29
Geraci, Paul	IN1350	13,10,29,63A,32B
Gessner, Dave	IL0600	66A,29
Gewirtz, Jonathan	MI1800	47,64E,64C,11,29
Giacabetti, Thomas	PA3330	47,70,29
Giacabetti, Tom	PA3250	29
Gibble, David L.	FL1470	29,47,37,53,49
Giglid, Joseph	NY2400	70,29
Gildea, Dan	OR0850	70,29
Gillespie, Luke O.	IN0900	11,29
Gilman, Joe	CA0150	13,66A,53,29
Gilman, Joseph	CA0840	66A,29
Ginn, Glenn A.	KY0900	29,70
Gittins, John	AG0650	29,13,47
Glanden, Don	PA3330	47,66A,13A,13,29
Glaser, Michael P.	AL1150	29
Glenn, David B.	WA1300	10,47,63D,29
Glover, David	PA3100	29,50,65,34,47
Glovier, Thomas	PA3000	29,66A
Goacher, Stephen	TX1100	60,48,64,47,29
Goble, Daniel P.	CT0800	47,64E,53,29,41
Goering, John	KS1450	29,20,66A
Goins, Wayne	KS0650	46,47,70,29
Gold, Michael	NY2400	62D,29
Goldman, Jason	CA5300	29
Goldstein, Gil B.	NY2750	10D,47,66A,29
Goldstein, Richard	CT0650	70,29
Gonder, Mark H.	OH2150	65,29
Gonzalez, Pepe	DC0170	29,62D
Goodwin, Tim	TN1680	29,62D
Gordon, Wycliffe	PA3250	29,63C
Gore, Art	OH2200	29
Gossage, Dave	AI0150	29,64A
Grandy, Larry	CA4550	37,47,64,29,14C
Grant, Darrell	OR0850	41,47,66A,66D,29
Grantham, Jennifer	OH0680	64E,29
Grasmick, David M.	CA0630	13A,34,63A,29
Gratz, Reed	CA5100	13,10,14C,29,11
Gray, Charles	OR0850	47,41,29
Gray, Lawrence	IL3300	29,62C,62D
Green, Bunky	FL1950	64E,53,29
Green, Edward	NY2150	12A,29
Green, Stuart	CA5150	29,70
Greene, Barry	FL1950	47,70,29
Greene, James S.	CT0800	29,64E,46
Greer, Larry	TX0125	13,14C,29,46,70
Gregg, Gary	CA0200	63C,29,35
Griffin, T. Joel	MO0400	29,31A,47,64E
Griffith, Joan E.	MN0950	47,70,29,10,62D
Griffith, Joan	MN1625	11,70,29
Grimes, William F.	LA0200	47,29
Grismore, Steven D.	IA1550	29
Gross, Mark	NJ1130	64E,29,29A
Grott, Dave	AI0150	29
Grover, Steve	ME0340	47,65,66A,29,13
Gudmundson, Jon K.	UT0300	29,64E,47,41
Gunderson, Terry	WY0050	65,34,29,13,12E
Gunnson, Eric	CO0900	29,66A
Gunther, John	CO0800	29,45
Guzman, Juan-Tony	IA0950	32,47,14,29,20
Gwynne, William G.	OH2200	29
Haar, Paul	NE0600	29,64E
Haarhues, Charles D.	CO0100	10,13,29,70,11
Haddad, Jamey	MA1400	29,20,65
Hadfield, John R.	NY2750	29,47,65
Haerle, Dan	TX3420	66A,34B,29
Haffley, Robin	PA2400	11,29,46
Hagelganz, David	WA1150	47,64E,29,53
Hageman, Paul M.	TX2960	47,29
Haight, Russell P.	TX3175	29,41,64E
Haines, Steve J.	NC2430	29,62D
Hainsworth, Jason D.	FL0200	11,29,46,47,64E
Haist, Dean	NE0450	47,63A,29
Halberstadt, Randy	WA0200	13,66A,66D,53,29
Hall, Alan M.	CA0807	65,29
Hall, Dana	IL0750	14,29
Hall, J. Scott	OR0850	64E,29
Hall, Keith	MI2250	29,65
Hall, Tom	IL0720	29,46,47
Hallahan, Robert	VA0600	29
Halsey, Jeff	OH0300	29
Ham, Lawrence	NY1050	53,29
Hamann, Jeff	WI1150	62D,29,47
Hamar, Jon	WA0550	29,62C,62D,32E,51
Hamel, Gabriel	AI0190	47,29,70
Hamilton, Frederick	TX3420	47,70,53,29
Hamm, Randall P.	MO0775	47,64E,29
Hanley, Wells	VA1600	29,66A
Hanlon, Jake	AF0150	29,70
Hanseler, Ryan	NC0650	29,66A
Hansen, Brad	OR0850	13,29,10,34
Hanson, David	CO0900	66A,29,35B,10A,10C
Haque, Fareed	IL2200	70,53,29
Harbison, Patrick L.	IN0900	47,29
Hardin, Garry Joe	TX2600	10A,13,29,38,46
Harding, Kevin	VA1150	20,29

Index by Area of Teaching Interest

Name	Code	Areas
Harlan, Evan	MA1400	29
Harland, Kelly	WA0200	61,29
Harper, Darryl	VA1600	29,10,14
Harris, Anton	GA0050	29,64E
Harris, Jarrard	IL2750	29
Harris, Karin	CA5300	29
Harris, Roger	IN0005	10B,13,29,47,66A
Harris, Stefon	NY2750	29,65B
Harrison, Charley	CA5031	29,47
Hart, Antonio	NY0642	29,64E
Hart, Billy	MA1400	29,65
Hart, Billy	OH1700	29
Hartl, David	PA3330	47,66A,66D,34,29
Hartman, Mark L.	PA3050	62,38,13,62A,29
Hartwell, Hugh	AG0200	13,10,11,29
Harvey, Mark	MA1200	11,29
Haskell, Jeffrey R.	AZ0500	47,46,29,35
Hastings, Todd J.	KS1050	63A,29,11,41,42
Hawk, Stephen L.	PA3100	63A,47,29
Hawkins, William	CA3460	13A,32A,49,63,29
Hay, Jeff	WA2600	63C,29
Hayden, Marion	MI2100	29,62D
Haydon, Rick	IL2910	70,29,35G,53,47
Hayward, Andre	MA1400	63C,29
Heath, James	NY0642	29
Heffernan, Michele	NJ1100	11,13C,29,33,66A
Heidner, Eric C.	CA4410	37,47,13,29,12A
Hellmer, Jeffrey	TX3510	29,35A,35B,46
Hendelman, Tamir	CA5031	29,66A
Henderson, Alan E.	AG0650	47,29,46
Henderson, Eddie	NY1900	63A,29
Hendricks, James	IL0600	13A,47,66A,66D,29
Hendricks, Jon	OH2300	29,53
Heredia, Joel	WA0480	47,63A,46,29,35A
Herring, Vincent	NJ1400	64E,29,47
Herwig, Conrad	NY1900	63C,29
Herwig, Conrad	NJ1130	29,63C
Hess, Fred	CO0550	11,13,29
Hest, Jeff	NY3250	11,29,35,37,47
Hester, Karlton E.	CA5070	29
Heywood, David John	SC0500	11,37,64A,29,47
Hickey, Joan B.	IL3300	47,66B,29
Hicks, Calvin	MA1175	29
Hill, Dennis	FL0500	37,47,64A,64E,29
Hill, Willie L.	MA2000	32,29
Hines, Clarence	FL1950	63C,29
Hipskind, Tom	IL0720	29
Hiscock, Fred	NC0860	11,29
Hobbs, Gary G.	OR1050	29,65
Hodgson, Jay	AG0500	14,29,35C,35D,12
Hoefle, Andrew	IL2775	11,37,47,63D,29
Hoehne, Bill	CA1000	10F,12C,64A,13,29
Hoenig, Ari M.	NY2750	65,29
Hofbauer, Eric	RI0300	29,47,70
Hoferer, Kevin	PA2150	29,10F
Hogg, William	KY1000	29,64E
Hoggard, Jay	CT0750	20G,29
Holland, Dave	MA1400	62D,47,29
Hollinden, Andrew J.	IN0900	11,29
Hollingsworth, Dina L.	CO0275	64A,64E,29,41,11
Hollins, Fraser	AI0150	29,62D
Holly, Richard	IL2200	50,65,29
Holmes, Jeffrey W.	MA2000	10,47,46,29
Holober, Michael	NY0550	66A,29,10,46,47
Homan, Steven	CA0840	29,70
Homzy, Andrew	AI0070	10,47,29,29A,34
Honda, Lorence	CA1850	13,48,64,29
Hood, Alan	CO0900	63A,29
Hopkins, Gregory	MA0260	10,29
Horlas, Lou	TX0700	47,62D,29
Horne, John	OH1900	70,29,47
Horner, Tim	NJ0825	29,65
Horton, Ron	AR0110	29
Houghton, Stacey	GA0500	47,29,64E,64C
Howard, Vernon D.	OK1450	47,49,63C,63D,29
Howland, John L.	NJ1140	10,12,20,29,29A
Huang, Hao	CA4500	66A,12,20C,20G,29
Hudson, Stephen	NJ1350	29,66D
Hughes, Luther	CA0815	29,62D
Hughes, Matthew	IL3500	62D,20,29
Hughes, Robert L.	MO1250	12A,29,13,29A,29E
Humble, Dina M.	CA3800	61,36,11,34,29
Hungerford, Jay	MO1950	62D,29
Hunter, Michael	MI1650	47,63C,29,64E
Hurley, Brian	AI0150	62D,29
Hurst, Robert	MI2100	29
Hynes, Tom	CA1000	13,29,47,53,70
Hyslop, Greg	NC0910	70,29
Ibarra, Susie	VT0050	20,29,50,47,53
Imara, Mtafiti	CA0847	13,14,64,47,29
Insko, Robert	PA3000	29,62D
Irish, Michael J.	MI1450	13,47,45,53,29
Irom, Benjamin M.	TX2800	29,29A,47,41,13
Isachsen, Sten Y.	NY3600	67D,41,70,34,29
Ishii, Timothy	TX3500	29,46,47,64E
Ivester, Mark	WA0200	65,29
Iwanusa, Charles	MI0450	13,10,11,47,29
Iyer, Vijay S.	NY2750	29,66,47
Jackson, D. D.	NY0625	29,47
Jackson, Herman	LA0700	65,29,50
Jackson, Kymberly	CA4625	14C,29,35
Jackson, Travis A.	IL3250	29,20,29D,29E,14
Jacobsen, Chad	IA0550	29,35G
Jaffe, Andy W.	MA2250	29,46,47
James, Matthew T.	OH1900	64E,47,53,46,29
Janson, Peter	MA2010	70,29,11,20,47
Jarczyk, Jan	AI0150	29,63C,66A
Jarvis, Jeffrey S.	CA0825	63A,29
Jaudes, Christian	NY1900	29,63A
Jefferson, Kelly	AG0650	29,64E
Jeffrey, Paul H.	NC0600	47,29
Jekabson, Erik	CA0807	63A,29
Jekabson, Erik	CA0900	63B,29
Jemmott, Thomas	FL2050	29,70
Jenkins, Jeff C.	CO0800	29
Jennings, Joseph W.	GA1900	47,64C,29,64E
Jensen, Christine	AI0150	29,64E
Jensen-Hole, Catherine	MA2000	47,61,29
Jewell, Joe	CA1900	47,70,29
Jex, David	OH2300	13B,13C,13D,10,29
Jimenez, Carlos	AI0150	70,29
Johansen, Keven W.	UT0250	70,29,11
Johns, Donald C.	CA5040	12,29
Johnson, Alphonso	CA5300	29
Johnson, Curtis	WV0750	64E,29
Johnson, Elizabeth	TN1850	29
Johnson, Erik	PA3330	29,65
Johnson, Gary V.	IL2730	13,13C,29,34
Johnson, Julianne R.	OR0800	36,40,29
Johnson, Kris	OH1850	29
Johnson, Michael	MO0600	32,29
Johnson, Michael	RI0250	29
Johnson, Russell	WI0835	47,29
Johnston, Jeffrey	AI0150	66A,29
Johnston, Noel H.	TX3420	70,53,29
Johnston, Paul R.	IL0800	46,29,53
Johnston, Randy B.	NY2750	29,70,47
Johnstone, Bruce	NY3725	29,47
Jones, Brian	VA0250	65,29
Jones, Calvin	DC0350	47,62D,63C,63D,29
Jones, Melvin	GA1450	11,37,29,63A
Jones, Micah	PA3330	47,62D,29,13,34
Jones, Patrick R.	PA1200	11,29,64,41
Jones, Rodney	NY1900	47,29
Jones, Rodney	NY2150	29
Jones, Sean	OH1700	29
Jones, Susie	OR0550	13,37,47,29
Jones, T. Marshall	GA0150	11,29,47,53
Jones, Terry	ID0140	37,47,49,63A,29
Jordan, Rodney	FL0850	47,62D,29
Joyce, John J.	LA0750	11,12,29
Judy, Ned	MD0700	13,29,66,34,47
Julien, Patricia A.	VT0450	13,12,10D,29
Jumper, David	PA2200	29,63A,32E,49
Juris, Vic	NJ1130	70,29
Kamalidiin, Sais	DC0150	64A,29
Kambeitz, Gus	CA5510	46,37,47,29,13A
Kamstra, Darin	CO0225	65,29,13B,47,50
Karahalis, Dean	NY4050	11,29,63C
Karloff, Michael	AG0550	29,46,66A
Karloff, Michael	MI2200	47,46,29,66A
Karpowicz, Mike	MO1950	29,41
Katz, Dick	NY2150	29
Kearney, Joseph B.	CA1265	10A,29,13B,70
Keberle, Daniel	WA1350	47,63A,29,29A
Keberle, Ryan	NY0625	29,47,11,13,63
Kehle, Robert G.	KS1050	11,47,29,63C
Keipp, Donald K.	UT0350	13A,11,65,29,47
Keith, Kristopher D.	OH1850	29
Keller, Gary W.	FL1900	64E,29,47
Kelley, Anthony M.	NC0600	11,13,29,10A,10C
Kelly, Keith	CA0850	29,47,46,41
Kendrick, Johnaye	WA0200	61,47,29
Kennedy, Donny	AI0150	29,64E,47
Kennedy, Karen	NY2150	29,35A
Kennedy, William	FL0850	47,29,64E
Kenyon, Steven	NY1600	64E,29
Kerber, Ronald	PA3330	47,64A,64E,29,41
Ketch, James E.	NC2410	47,63A,46,29
Kettinger, Gregory S.	PA3250	29
Kidder, Tim	UT0190	29,64E
Kidwell, Jeff	OK1330	47,63C,46,29
Kimbrough, Frank	NY1900	29
Kirby, Brett	VA0600	29
Kirby, Steve	AC0100	29,47,62D
Kirchner, Bill	NY2660	10,12,64,29
Kischuk, Ronald K.	MI2200	63C,29
Kluball, Jeff L.	GA0625	37,63,29,13,10
Klugh, Vaughn	AG0550	70,29,46,61
Knapp, James	WA0200	10,47,63A,53,29
Knepp, Marty	MD0060	29,47
Knific, Thomas	MI2250	47,51,62D,46,29
Knop, Robert	CA0845	32E,29,64E,11
Knowles, Gregory	NY1900	29
Kobayashi, Ron	CA0350	29
Kobza, Tim	CA5300	70,29
Kocher, Christopher John	SD0600	47,64E,53,46,29
Koeble, Robert	FL1800	29
Koehler, Raymund	IL3200	29,66
Koenigsberg, Tobias R.	OR1050	29,47,66A
Kopplin, David F.	CA0630	10,20,29,14C,46
Korb, Kristin	CA5300	62D,29
Korde, Shirish	MA0700	13,10,14,20,29
Korey, Judith A.	DC0350	13A,13,66A,29,34
Koshinski, Eugene	MN1600	47,65,29,20G,35
Kosmyna, David J.	OH1800	63A,63B,49,47,29
Kostur, Glenn	NM0450	47,29
Kovalcheck, Steve	CO0950	29
Kozak, Brian	OH0750	12B,20G,29,35
Kozak, Christopher M.	AL1170	29,62D
Krajewski, Michael J.	MN1120	70,47,29
Krantz, Wayne M.	NY2750	29,70,49
Kravitz, Steve	OR0450	64B,64E,64C,29,11
Kreibich, Paul	CA0815	29,65
Krygier, Joe	OH1850	29,65
Kuhn, Michael	AZ0480	29,11,46
Kulesha, Gary	AG0450	10,63C,29
Kunkel, Jeffrey	NJ0800	32,47,29,53,46
Kush, Jason	PA3100	64E,29,41,53,64C
Kyle, Scott	CA4100	29
Kynaston, Trent	MI2250	47,64E,46,29
LaBrosse, Denis	AI0200	62D,29
LaChance, Marc	NE0300	63C,63D,13,10F,29
Laderman, Michael	NY3100	11,29,12A,14,20D
Laing, David	AI0150	65,29
Lajoie, Stephen H.	RI0101	47,66A,53,29,13A
LaLama, David S.	NY1600	47,66A,29
Lalama, David	NY2150	29
Lalama, Ralph	NY2750	29,47,64E
Lambert, David D.	AL0500	63C,29
Lambert, Michel	AI0150	65,29
Lammers, Paula	MN0610	29,61
Landry, Dana	CO0950	29,66A,47
Landsberg, Paul	AB0070	13A,70,53,47,29
Langham, Patrick	CA5350	46,47,29,53
Langosch, Paul	VA1700	20H,29,35D,46,47
Lanza, Lou	PA2450	61,47,29,41
Lapin, Lawrence	FL1900	13,10,36,47,29
Lark, Robert J.	IL0750	29,63A,47
Laronga, Barbara	CA2600	63A,29,47,63
LaSpina, Steven	NJ1400	29A,47,62D,29
Laverne, Andrew	CT0650	29
Law, Bill R.	ND0350	62D,29
Lawn, Richard J.	PA3330	46,29
Lawson, Stephen J.	WV0400	13,63B,29,49,37
Lawton, Tom P.	PA3250	66A,29
Leali, Brad	TX3420	29,47,64E
Leasure, Michael	FL0150	29,70
Lee, Gordon	OR1250	29,13A
Lee, James	AZ0200	12A,11,29
Lee, Ranee	AI0190	29,61
Lee, Ranee	AI0150	61,29
Lenihan, William	MO1900	70,29
Lennon, Debby	MO1950	36,61,29,47
Lerner, Peter	IL0720	29,70,10
Leroux, Andre	AI0150	29,64E

Index by Area of Teaching Interest

Name	Code	Areas
Lessard, Daniel	AI0150	62D,29
Lester, William	NY2400	66A,66D,29
Lewis, Jeffrey	CA4400	29,63A
Lewis, Jim	AG0450	29,47
Lewis, Victor	NJ1130	65,29
Liebman, David	NY2150	29
Ligon, Bert	SC1110	46,47,66A,29,45
Lin, Victor	NY4200	29,66A,62D
Lindahl, Robert	MI0400	49,63C,29
Lindeman, Stephan	UT0050	13,29
Lindsay, Gary M.	FL1900	47,64E,29
Lington, Aaron	CA4400	29,46,63,29B
Linke, David	WI0825	70,29,47
Livermore, Allen	MA0280	47,64E,29
Lobenstein, David	NY0050	29,47
Lockwood, John	MA1400	62D,29
Loeb, David	NV0050	29,10,47
Long, Barry	PA0350	29,47,13,63A,53
Long, Bob	MO0850	29,64E,47
Lorenz, Michael L.	MI1950	13,47,63,29,34
Lotter, Rich	CA0840	29
Lovano, Joe S.	NY2750	29,64E,47
Lovely, Brian	OH0680	29,10C,10D,70,35
Lovensheimer, James A.	TN1850	12,14,20G,29
Lowell, Richard L.	MA0260	10,29
Lowenthal, Richard	NJ0825	63A,53,46,29
Lozano, Frank	AI0150	29,64E
Luciani, Dante T.	FL1900	47,63C,29
Luckey, Robert	LA0760	47,64E,29
Ludemann, Hans	PA3200	29
Luer, Thomas D.	CA0630	29,46
Lukiwski, Terry	AG0450	29,63C
Lyons, Lisanne E.	FL1900	61,29,53,47
Lytle, Cecil W.	CA5050	66A,29,20G
Mabern, Harold	NJ1400	29
Macar, Robert	FL2050	29,66A
MacConnell, Kevin	PA3330	47,62D,29
MacDonald, Earl M.	CT0600	29,47,46
MacDonald, Kirk	AG0450	29
Mack, Kyle	ND0350	60,37,47,63C,29
Madsen, Peter C.	NE0610	63C,47,29,49
Magee, Chris	TX3350	63A,46,29,47,53
Magnarelli, Joe	NY1900	29
Magnarelli, Joe A.	NJ1130	63A,29
Magnarelli, Joe	NJ0825	29,63A
Mahar, Bill	AI0150	63A,29
Mahoney, John A.	LA0300	29
Mallarino, Larry	CA2440	29,63,13A
Malley, Nicole	IL1350	12A,20,47,29,31F
Manasia, Jeremy	NY2150	29
Mancini, Nick	CA0835	29,65B
Manley, David	PA1150	47,29,53,70
Marano, Nancy	NJ1400	61,29
Marano, Nancy	NY2150	29
Marchione, Nick	PA3250	29,63A
Marin, Luis	PR0115	29,66A,66D
Marko, Thomas	IL1150	47,29
Markowitz, Phil	NY2150	29
Marlier, Mike	CO0900	65B,53,29
Marmolejo, Noe	TX3400	47,29
Marsalis, Ellis	LA0300	35A,29
Marsh, Kerry	CA0840	29,36,47
Marshall, Wolf	CA5031	29,70
Martel, Helene	AI0200	61,29
Martin, Danny Ray	TN0150	70,42,29,41
Martin, Henry	NJ1140	13,10,12,29,29A
Martinelli, Lisa	AG0450	29,61,47
Mason, Colin M.	TX2800	47,11,64E,29,48
Mason, Scott	IL0550	13B,13C,53,29
Mason, Thom	CA5300	47,29
Masten, Rob	WV0250	29,63,65,47,46
Matejka, Merle	AJ0030	10,12A,31A,13,29
Matta, Thomas	IL0750	63C,29
Matthews, Bill	ME0150	13,10,29,34
Matthews, Zachary P.	CA3500	62D,29,34
Mattina, Fernando	PR0115	29,70
Mattingly, Douglas	MD0060	13,29,35,70
Maureau, Wayne	LA0300	29
May, Theresa	OH0755	29,63A
Mayes, Frank	LA0300	29
McBee, Cecil	MA1400	29,47,62D
McCain, Martin G.	TX3175	63C,29,46,49
McCann, Chris	AI0150	65,29
McCormick, Chris	TN1450	47,29,32F
McCormick, Thomas	FL1300	64E,20G,29
McCourry, Christopher C.	MI1000	29,42,63A
McCurdy, Ronald	CA5300	29
McCurdy, Roy	CA5300	65,29
McDaniel, William T.	OH1850	20A,29,29A
McElwaine, James	NY3785	41,47,20G,29,34
McGinnis, Barry E.	SC0900	64,12A,29,48,29A
McGowan, Mike	TX2000	11,37,49,13,29
McGuinness, Peter	NJ1400	13,10,29,41
McGuire, Dennis	MN1400	70,50,29
McKee, Paul	FL0850	29,63C
McKinney, David	KS0265	13,37,63D,64,29
McLaren, Robert	AG0450	65,29
McLaurine, Marcus	NJ1400	29
McLean, Allan	AI0150	47,29
McLean, Greg	GA0940	13,11,29,10
McLean, John T.	IL2050	70,29,53
McLean, John	IL0550	47,70,29
McLean, Rene	CT0650	29,29A
McMullen, Michael	CA0840	29
McMullen, Tracy	ME0200	29,15,12,53,14A
McNeely, James	NY2150	29
McNeil, John	MA1400	29,47,63A
McNeill, Charles	IL3300	29
McNeill, Dean	AJ0150	63A,29,46,47
McWain, Andrew J.	MA2020	29,10,13B
McWilliams, Larry	IN0150	47,29
Meader, Darmon	NY2150	29
Medwin, Marc	DC0010	11,29,12,20
Meggs, Gary L.	AR0800	60B,64,47,46,29
Meier, Steven	GA1500	11,12A,29
Meister, Blake	MD0650	29
Melford, Myra J.	CA5000	29,47,53
Menchaca, Louis A.	WI0300	13A,13,60,37,29
Mendoza, Freddie	TX3175	29,47,63C
Mendoza, Vince	CA5300	29
Merz, Christopher Linn	IA1600	64E,47,29
Metz, Ken	TX3410	13,10,29,29A
Metzger, Jon	NC0750	65,29,47,50,53
Meyers, Paul	NJ0825	70,29
Meyers, Paul	NJ1400	70,29
Miceli, Tony	PA3330	65B,29
Michael, George	OH2140	47,64E,29
Michael, Louis	IL1500	29,66A,13,11,34A
Michaels, Matthew	MI2200	47,66A,29
Middleton, Robert M.	NJ0050	47,29,64,13,11
Miedema, Harry F.	IN1650	47,64E,29,53
Miglia, Jay	OH2050	29,64E,46,47
Milenkovic, Vladan	MA0510	29,66A,66D
Milenkovic, Vladan	MN0050	29,20
Miles, Butch	TX3175	65,29,46
Miles, Ron	CO0550	47,63A,29
Miley, James	OR1300	10,29,47,46,13
Miller, Connaitre	DC0150	29
Miller, David	MS0050	13,47,46,29
Miller, Ethan	OH1100	20,29
Miller, James E.	PA1900	62D,29
Miller, Joel	AI0150	29,64E
Miller, Mark	CO0560	29,13A,41,47,64A
Miller, Mulgrew	NJ1400	29
Miller, Russell	MI2200	29,64
Miller, Stewart	IL3310	62D,29
Mills, John	TX3510	64E,29,47,46
Mills, Peter	OH0850	64E,47,29
Milne, Andy	NY2750	29,47,66A
Miltenberger, James E.	WV0750	12A,66A,66B,29
Minasian, Mark	HI0160	11,12A,29,34,35
Mindeman, John	IL3500	63D,63C,49,29
Mintzer, Bob	CA5300	29
Miranda, Roberto	CA5031	29,62D
Mitchell, Nicole	IL3310	29,29A,64A
Mitchell, Roscoe	CA2950	10,29,53
Mixon, Joseph D.	PA1900	70,29
Moe, Aaron	MN1200	29,47
Moio, Dom	AZ0100	29
Molinaro, Anthony G.	IL1615	66A,29,13A,13B,13D
Monaghan, Michael	MA0700	47,64A,64E,53,29
Monear, Clifford E.	MI2200	29,66A
Monson, Ingrid	MA1050	14,12,29
Monteiro, Shawn	CT0650	29
Moore, Glen	OR0850	62D,29
Moore, Gregory	WI0860	13C,47,64E,29,10A
Moore, Rich	IL2200	64E,29
Moore, Stephen F.	CA0805	13C,29,47,60,66
Moorman, Wilson	NY0270	11,20,65,29
Morales, Fidel	PR0115	29,65,53
Morales, Richie	NY3785	65,29
Morell, Martin	FL1800	29
Moreno, Jairo	PA3350	13,13J,20H,29,12D
Moreno, Tony	NY2750	47,29,65
Morgan, Carol	TX2300	63A,29,13B,11
Morgan, David	OH2600	62D,29,47,53
Morris, Joe	MA1400	29,47,70
Morrison, Audrey	IL0720	29,63C
Morrison, Barbara	CA5031	61,29
Morton, James	CA2100	29,65
Mosca, John	NJ1400	29
Mosca, John	NY2150	29
Moseley, William	ME0340	12A,47,64A,35C,29
Moses, Robert	MA1400	47,65,29
Moshier, Josh	IL3550	29,10C,47
Moss, Myron D.	PA1000	10,11,29,37,60
Mossman, Michael	NY0642	29,35B,63A
Motley, Gary D.	GA0750	29,46,47
Moulder, John	IL0275	14C,29,70
Moulder, John P.	IL2250	29,70
Muehlenbeck Pfotenhauer, Thomas R.	MN1600	63A,47,29,11,11
Munro, Douglas	NY3785	47,29
Murdock, Matthew	TN1600	13C,32E,29,37,47
Murley, Michael	AG0450	64E,29
Murphy, Daniel	CA5150	34,35,29
Murphy, John P.	TX3420	29,14,47,64E
Murphy, Paul R.	CA5150	29,70
Murphy, Timothy	MD0850	29,66A,66H
Murphy, Timothy	MD0650	29,47
Murray, Mark S.	IN0100	29,63A,34,35
Myers, Allen	MO2000	35A,66A,29
Nadel, James	CA4900	41,29
Nagge, Harold	TN1250	70,53,47,29
Nakasian O'Brian, Stephanie	VA0250	61,29
Natale, Michael A.	PA3250	29
Nazarenko, John J.	NY3650	47,66A,29
Neault, Sylvain	AI0190	29,62
Neill, Dave	AG0450	29
Nelson, Josh	CA0835	29
Nelson, Larry	KY0550	64E,53,29,47,29A
Nelson, Richard	ME0340	10,34,13,29,47
Nesbit, James B.	VA0250	64E,48,29
Netsky, Hankus H.	MA1400	29,13C,47,53,20F
Nevela, Andrew	AL0500	29,35A,35C
Newsome, Charles	MI2200	29,46,47,70
Newsome, Sam	NY2102	29,20,64E
Newton, Farnell	OR0850	63A,29
Newton, James	CA5031	29,10
Newton, Joseph	NC0750	70,53,29
Nichol, John	MI0400	47,48,64E,29
Nicholas, Julie	CA1650	29,61,47
Nielsen, Ryan	ID0060	29,46,47,63A
Nieske, Robert	MA1400	29,47
Nimmons, Phil	AG0450	32,47,29
Normandeau, Dale	AC0050	29,70
Norris, Alexander	MD0650	29,47
Norton, Kevin	NJ1400	29
Nowak, Robert A.	PA1900	11,65,29
Nugent, Barli	NY1900	29,64A
Nurullah, Shahida	AG0550	29,46,61
Oatts, Dick	PA3250	29,64E
Oberholtzer, Christopher W.	ME0500	29,47,63C
Occhipinti, David	AG0450	70,29
O'Connell, William	NJ1130	29
O'Dell, Timothy J.	ME0500	29,64E
Oleszkiewicz, Dariusz	CA5300	29
Olivieri, Mark A.	NY1550	10,13,20G,29,48
Ollis, Ken	OR0850	65,29
Olsen, Timothy J.	NY4310	13,10,47,63A,29
Olson, Matthew W.	SC0750	64E,29,47,41,46
O'Mahoney, Terrence	AF0150	50,65,29,10D,66A
O'Neal, Kevin	CA4450	29
O'Neill, Golder	VA1350	29,35A,35B
Onofrio, Marshall	NJ1350	13,10,29,34,32E
Optiz, Robert	GA1700	29,63A
Ortiz, Pablo	CA5010	13,10,45,29,34
Osland, Miles	KY1450	47,64E,29,53,48
Owen, Charles (Chuck) R.	FL2000	47,29,10
Owen, Stephen W.	OR1050	46,47,53,29,64E
Owens, Charles	CA5031	29,47,64
Owens, Douglas T.	VA1000	32,47,60B,29
Owens, Priscilla	NY0625	47,29
Paat, Joel	CA3800	66,29
Pack, Lester	AR0800	65,46,47,29,70
Page, Richard L.	NH0110	47,64E,29
Palacio, Jon	CA0900	29,46,47,66A

Name	Code	Areas
Palance, Thomas M.	MA1650	29,46,47,63A
Panella, Lawrence	MS0750	29,64E,47
Pangburn, Chuck	TX0700	29
Pantoja, Rique	CA0350	29,31A
Pappas, Mark	MI0600	13,29
Parcell, John	OH2120	13,66A,11,29,34C
Pardo, Brian	CA0807	70,29
Parillo, Joseph M.	RI0300	13,10,47,46,29
Parker, Alex	TX0300	29,47,46
Parker, Christopher S.	NY3000	47,66A,66D,53,29
Parker, Don	NC0800	13,50,65,29
Parker, Gene	MI2200	29
Parkinson, Wm. Michael	OH1900	29,35G,47
Parr, J. D.	KS0050	37,47,48,64,29
Parran, John D.	NY0270	11,13,20,29,64
Parsons, Longineu	FL0600	47,63A,29
Parsons, Sean	WV0400	29,46,47,66A
Parton, Robert T.	OH0350	63A,29,47,29A,53
Pascale, Joanna	PA3250	29,61
Pasqua, Alan	CA5300	47,29
Pastin, John R.	NJ1050	37,60,29,46,48
Patneaude, Brian	NY3600	64E,29,46
Patnode, Matthew A.	ND0350	64E,64A,29,48,47
Patterson, Ann	CA1750	29,64B,64E
Patterson, James H.	GA0490	29,32,46,63,47
Patterson, Mark	PA3250	29,63C
Patterson, Michael	NY2150	29
Patterson, Roy	AG0450	29
Paul, Randall S.	OH2500	64C,29,48,11
Paulson, John C.	MN1400	47,64,29,34,35
Peffer, Ed	CA2390	47,29,53
Pepin, Pierre	AI0150	62D,29
Perez, Danilo	MA1400	29
Perez, Frank	IA0600	37,47,32,29,63C
Perlongo, Daniel J.	PA1600	10,13,29
Peterson, David	WA0200	47,70,29
Peterson, William F.	FL0850	10,29
Petrides, Ron T.	NY2660	10,29,70,13,12
Pfenninger, Rik C.	NH0250	64E,29,35,32E,10B
Phillips, Damani	IA0700	29,47
Phipps, Nathaniel J.	NY3600	29
Pickens, Willie	IL2200	66A,29
Pickett, Lenny B.	NY2750	46,47,64E,29
Piedra, Olman	OH2140	65,50,43,29
Pietro, David A.	NY2750	64E,29,47
Pilc, Jean-Michel	NY2750	29,66A,47
Pilkington, Robert	MA0260	10,29
Piller, Paul R.	OH2200	29
Pillich, G. Simeon	CA3300	20,29
Pimentel, Bret R.	MS0250	64,29,64B,11,64C
Pincock, Christian P.	NM0450	29
Pineda, Gerry	CA5350	29
Pineda, Gerry	CA0840	29
Pino, Carlos E.	AL1150	29
Piontek, Gregory	NY1210	12A,47,29
Pipho, Robert S.	MI2200	47,29,66A
Pittson, Suzanne	NY0550	29,61
Pivec, Matthew	IN0250	29,64E
Plainfield, Kim	MA0260	65,29
Platz, Eric	RI0300	65,29,47
Platz, Eric	AC0050	46,47,29
Pliskow, Dan J.	MI2200	62D,29
Plugge, Scott D.	TX2250	64E,20G,29,47
Polischuk, Derek Kealii	MI1400	66A,66B,66D,38,29
Pond, Steven	NY0900	14,29
Poole, Tommy A.	OK0550	29,46,64E,10A
Porter, Lewis R.	NJ1140	13,12,29,29A
Porter, Randy	OR0850	66A,29
Porter, Randy	OR0250	29,66A
Portnoy, Kim	MO1950	10F,10,29
Pos, Margie	WA0200	29,62D,66A,13
Potenza, Frank	CA5300	70,29
Potter, Christopher	NY2750	46,47,64E,29
Powers, David	OH1850	29
Pray, Keith	NY3600	29
Price, Emmett G.	MA1450	14,29,66A,47
Price, Jeffrey	AG0550	64E,29,46
Price, Larry	WA1400	29
Price, Ruth	CA5031	29,61
Priester, Julian	WA0200	10,47,63C,63D,29
Prieto, Dafnis	NY2750	29,47,65
Primatic, Stephen P.	GA0200	65,13,29,11,47
Promane, Terry	AG0450	29,47
Prouty, Kenneth E.	MI1400	12,14,29
Proznick, Jodi	AB0060	29
Pullig, Kenneth	MA0260	10,29
Purslow, Vicki T.	OR0950	11,37,64E,29
Putterman, Jeff	OR0850	70,29
Quinn, Karyn	WI0810	47,62D,46,29,13A
Radke, Fred	WA1050	29,63A
Rager, Josh	AI0150	29,66A
Raley, Lynn	MS0385	66A,12A,29
Ramsey, Guthrie P.	PA3350	12,35,20G,29,47
Ransom, Robert	VA0250	29,63A
Rask, Perry J.	IL1750	47,64E,29
Rasmussen, Josh	UT0190	29
Rast, Madison B.	PA3250	29,62D
Read, Paul	AG0450	47,29
Rector, Malcolm W.	TX3450	13,10,29,47
Reese, Kirk	PA2300	29,66A
Reeves, Nat	CT0650	29
Reeves, Scott	NY0550	13,47,53,29
Reid, Doug	WA0860	47,64E,53,46,29
Reid, Todd	CO0830	11,20,29,65
Renter, David	MI0900	11,13,29
Restivo, Dave	AG0450	66A,29
Rewoldt, Todd	CA4100	13,29,64E
Reyman, Randall	IL1750	47,63A,53,29
Reynolds, Dennis	OH1700	29,47
Ricci, John	FL1000	64E,47,29
Ricci, Robert	MI2250	13,10F,12B,29
Richard, Charles	CA3800	47,64E,29,34,42
Richardson, Edward 'Rex'	VA1600	63A,29,49
Richmond, Jeffrey W.	OR0950	29
Richmond, Joshua	PA3250	29,66A
Richmond, Mike	NY2750	29,47,64D
Richter, Kimberlie J.	IL2050	13A,61,64E,29
Ries, Tim	AG0450	29
Riley, John	NY2150	29
Riley, Madeleine C.	PA1000	11,45,64A,64E,29
Rimmington, Rob	FL0650	62D,29
Rinzler, Paul	CA0600	13,10,47,66A,29
Rischar, Richard A.	MI2110	12,29,40,14,20
Rivera, Diego	MI1400	29,64E,53
Roach, Seth	KS0750	65,66,29,70,50
Roach, Stephen W.	CA0840	47,29
Roberts, Andrew	PA1900	29
Roberts, Marcus	FL0850	29,66A
Roberts, Steven	AL1150	29,63A,47
Robinson, Curtis	IN0005	13,16,29,34,35
Robinson, Marty	FL0600	47,45,63A,29
Robinson, Thomas S.	NH0250	66A,46,47,29
Robinson-Martin, Trineice	NJ0750	11,12A,29,61
Rodgers, Ernest E.	MI2200	64E,29,47
Rodriguez, Bobby	CA5031	29,63A
Rodriguez-Hernandez, Gabriel	PR0115	29,62D
Rogers, Dave	NJ1400	29,63A
Rogine, Peter	NY1275	13C,29,47,70
Roitstein, David	CA0510	13C,47,29,66A
Romain, James P.	IA0550	64E,29A,35A,29,47
Roman, Robert	NY3765	29,66A,20D,35A,46
Romeo, James	CA4050	11,37,47,48,29
Roney, John	AI0150	29,66A
Rosa Ramos, Luis S.	PR0115	29,10F,47
Rose, Richard F.	FL1300	11,32B,32C,62D,29
Rosenberg, Christopher J.	NY2150	47,29
Rosenn, Jamie	CA0835	29,70
Rosenthal, Ted	NY2150	29
Ross, Holli W.	NY1600	61,29
Rossmiller, Adam	MN0610	29,47
Rossum, Kelly	VA0150	63A,29,67E,47
Roth, David	PA2450	66A,29
Rotondi, Jim	NY3785	63A,29
Routenberg, Scott	IN0150	29,66A
Rowe, Ellen H.	MI2100	47,29,66A
Rowe, Simon B.	CA5350	29
Royal, Guericke	DC0150	29,35
Rozie, Edward Rick	CT0650	20G,47,62D,29
Rubinstein, Matan	WI0865	11,29,32B,47
Rucker, Lee	OK1330	37,47,63A,46,29
Rucker, Steve P.	FL1900	65,47,29
Rudkin, Ronald	NC1650	47,29,53
Rule, Charles	TN0700	11,47,66A,29,35
Runnels, Brent	GA1550	66A,11,29,47,13A
Rupert, Jeffrey M.	FL1800	29,46
Rupp, Jim	OH1850	29
Russell, George	MA0260	29
Russell, Mary Lou	TX2260	11,66A,66C,66D,29
Russell, Robert A.	NC2440	70,29
Ryan, James	MI2200	65,29
Ryga, Campbell	AB0060	29,46,47,64E
S., Harvie	NY2150	29
Sabina, Leslie M.	NY3475	29,10,34,13,47
Salerno, John	WI0808	13,10,47,48,29
Salerno, Steven	NY0050	29,47,70
Salman, Randy Keith	IN0350	47,64C,64E,29
Saltzman, James A.	NJ0300	64E,29,13C
Samuels, David	MA1400	29
Sanabria, Bobby	NY2150	47,29
Sanborn, Chase	AG0450	63A,29
Sandy, Brent	IA1550	29
Santiago, Nephtali	GA2150	70,29,11
Sarath, Ed	MI2100	46,29
Sarjeant, Lindsey B.	FL0600	47,49,53,46,29
Sato, Akira	TX3420	29,63A,47,60A
Saunders, John Jay	TX3420	47,63A,29,46
Sawyer, Scott	NC0650	29,70
Saxe, Peter	IL0720	29,66,53
Scea, Paul	WV0750	64E,29,47
Schachter, Benjamin	PA0400	64E,29
Schaefer, G. W. Sandy	NE0050	14C,46,65,29,35
Schantz, Jack	OH2150	29,46,47,63A
Schaphorst, Kenneth	MA1400	29
Schenkel, Steve	MO1950	12A,31,45,29,35
Schick, Steven	CA5050	11,50,65,43,29
Schiff, David	OR0900	13,10A,20G,29,38
Schirm, Ronald	AG0600	47,29
Schmid, William	GA0950	63A,46,29,49,47
Schmid, Carol	MO1950	66A,29
Schmidt, Russell	UT0250	66A,29,47
Schneller, Aric	TX2250	47,29,63C,61
Schoeppach, Brad W.	NY2750	29,47
Scholz, Steve	CA1560	29,66
Schroeder, Dave	NY2750	29,47,65,60B
Schultz, Andrew J.	NE0150	29,37,60B,63A
Schultz, Willis Jackson	MA0260	10,29
Schwabe, Jonathan C.	IA1600	13,10,29
Schwartz, Richard A.	LA0650	29,47,64E,11,46
Schweitzer, Kenneth	MD1100	20,29,34,35,11
Schwendener, Benjamin	MA1400	29
Scism, William	MA0260	10,29
Scott, Gary	OH0755	47,63A,20G,29,35B
Scott, Marshall	KY1550	41,47,63A,29
Scott, Stephen	CO0200	10,11,45,43,29
Seales, Marc	WA1050	66A,29
Seaton, Lynn	TX3420	62D,29
Secor, Robert	CA4300	29
Selvaggio, Robert	OH1100	47,29
Sepulveda, Charles	PR0115	29,63A,53
Serfaty, Aaron	CA5300	29
Severn, Eddie	PA2050	32,29,46,47,63
Shanklin, Richard L.	OH2150	47,64E,29,35
Shaw, George W.	CA2550	47,29,34,35
Shemaria, Rich S.	NY2750	46,47,66A,29
Sheppard, Robert	CA5300	64E,29
Sherman, Robert	NY1900	35A,29
Sherry, James Wallace	IA1450	29,63A
Shevitz, Matthew	IL1080	11,13,29,47,46
Shinn, Alan	TX3200	50,65,47,29
Shirtz, Michael	OH2140	36,60,61,13,29
Shner, Idit	OR1050	64E,42,47,29
Shook, Thomas M.	WA1350	29,13B,13C
Shynett, Jerald	NC2440	29,63C
Sidener, Whitney F.	FL1900	47,64E,29
Siegel, Jeff S.	CT0800	53,41,65,29
Sielert, Vern	ID0250	47,63A,29
Silbergleit, Paul	WI1150	70,47,29
Sill, Kelly	IL2200	62D,29
Simerly, Rick	TN1150	63,29,49,47,32E
Simon, Harris W.	VA0250	29A,66A,47,29
Sims, Jared N.	RI0300	29,47,64E
Sintchak, Matthew A.	WI0865	64E,29,43,47,48
Skelton, Sam	GA1150	64E,47,29
Slagle, Steven	NY2150	47,64E,29
Smith, C. Raymond	UT0050	47,64,53,46,29
Smith, Chuck	ID0050	29,66A
Smith, Derek T.	MO0600	11,13,29
Smith, Gene	AF0150	13,47,49,63C,29
Smith, Herbert	VA0975	53,29,47
Smith, James E.	OH0500	29,70,47,12A
Smith, James E.	OH2200	29
Smith, Joel L.	MA1450	47,29
Smith, Joel Larue	MA1900	29,47,10,53,13A
Smith, Larry G.	UT0300	13,29,47,64E,46
Smith, Mark	IL0600	13A,50,65,29,20G
Smith, Michael	OH1850	65,29,32E

Index by Area of Teaching Interest

Name	Code	Areas
Smith, Mike	IL0550	64E,29
Smith, Raymond H.	AL1050	47,37,34,64E,29
Smith, Wadada Leo	CA0510	63A,29,10,45,53
Snapp, Doug R.	MN1000	46,47,63A,29
Sneider, Robert	NY1100	29,70
Snow, Thomas	ME0150	29,47,46,66A
Snyder, Craig	NY1250	70,29
Snyder, Rory	CA1560	29,46,47
Snyder, Steven D.	KY0900	13,47,66A,29
Sodke, James W.	WI0835	13A,29,35A
Soph, Ed	TX3420	65,29
Sorah, Donald	VA1580	34,63A,29,14C,20
Soskin, Mark	NY2150	29,66A
Spaneas, Demetrius	NY1275	10,29,46,64E,10F
Speight, Andrew	CA4200	29,64E,46,47
Spencer, Dianthe M.	CA4200	66A,66D,20G,29
Spencer, Roger A.	TN1850	29
Spring, Howard	AG0350	14,70,29,12A,13D
Springfield, David	GA2150	29,35G,63C
Spurr, Kenneth	IL1085	66A,53,29,47
Stacke, Robert J.	MN0050	37,47,29
Stafford, Terell L.	PA3250	29
Stagnaro, Oscar	MA1400	29
Stambler, David B.	PA2750	64E,29
Starks, George	PA1000	20,14,47,64E,29
Starling, Gary	FL1000	70,29
Staron, Michael	IL3200	13,11,29,62D
Steinel, Michael L.	TX3420	53,29
Steinmetz, Demetrius	OH0750	62D,29
Stempel, Larry	NY1300	13,12,54,29
Stephens, John C.	IL3300	29,46,47
Stephens, Michael	NE0050	10,29,46,13,64
Sterbank, Mark	SC0275	64E,47,46,29
Sterner, Dave	OH0750	13,47,70,29
Stevenson, Francois	AI0150	29,65B
Stewart, Alexander	VT0450	14,53,20,29,47
Stiles, Joan	NY2150	29
Stinson, Ron	KS0570	29,37,41,46,47
Stitt, Ronald	PA0100	63C,47,29,46,34
Stowell, John	OR0750	70,29
Strait, Tom	MN1120	63A,29,63B,47
Strandt, Terry W.	IL1850	12A,61,29
Strid-Chadwick, Karen	AK0100	13,47,66A,66D,29
Stride, Frederick	AB0100	47,29
Stroeher, Michael	WV0400	63D,49,63C,32,29
Strohman, Thomas	PA1900	47,64E,29
Stryker, Michael S.	IL3500	66A,29
Sturm, Fred	WI0350	10,29,46,47
Suarez, Jeff	WI0847	10,13,29,42,20G
Suh-Rager, Min-Jung	AI0150	66A,29
Sullivan, Joe	AI0150	63A,29,47
Sult, Michael	CA1800	13,70,29,13A
Sumares, Frank	CA4400	63,29
Sussman, Richard	NY2150	47,29
Swana, John	PA3250	29,63A
Swindler, Wil J.	CO0250	29,47,64E
Sykes, Robert	DC0170	13,66A,29
Syler, James	TX3530	20G,29,35,10
Tallman, Thomas J.	IL0630	13,11,47,63,29
Tanouye, Nathan	NV0050	29,63C,47
Tapper, Robert	MT0400	29,63C,46,47
Taylor, David	NY2150	29
Taylor, David B.	MI2200	29,65
Taylor, Jack M.	OH2275	10,37,47,29
Taylor, Jeffrey	NY0600	29
Teasley, Kevin	VA1800	47,29
Temperley, Joe	NY2150	29
Temperley, Joe	NY1900	64C,64E,29
Terefenko, Dariusz	NY1100	13B,13D,13E,13H,29
Terrell, Maurice	FL1700	11,29,37,47,60B
Terry, Lesa	CA4450	29
Thimmig, Les	WI0815	10,47,64E,29
Thomas, Craig	PA3330	47,62D,29
Thomas, Gary	MD0650	47,29
Thomas, Joel Wayne	KS0265	11,13,29,66
Thomas, John	CA5300	47,29
Thomas, June M.	PA2550	61,29
Thomas, Reginald	MI1400	29,66A,53
Thomas, Russell	MS0350	47,64E,29,13
Thurgood, George	AG0300	13,29
Tiana, Mayo	IL2150	29,46,47,10F
Tidmore, Natasha	AL0850	36,29
Tini, Dennis J.	MI2200	60,36,29,35
Titlebaum, Michael	NY1800	29,46,47
Tolson, Gerald H.	KY1500	32,47,29,14C
Tomaro, Michael	PA1050	64E,47,53,29
Tomasello, Randal S.	FL1300	29
Tomlin, Terry	TX3515	47,64E,29,34,32F
Toomey, John F.	VA1000	66A,29,47
Tot, Zvonimir	IL3310	29,13,13C,70,47
Towell, Gordon L.	KY0900	47,64E,53,29
Travers, Martha	MI2100	29
Trittin, Brian L.	TX0400	12A,13,29,37,64E
Trottier, Jean-Nicolas	AI0200	63C,29
Trottier, Jean-Nicolas	AI0150	29,63C
True, Carolbeth	MO1950	66A,29
Tulga, Philip	CA0840	29,63C
Tumlinson, Charles	CA0815	47,41,29
Turechek, Dennis	NY3765	70,29
Turetzky, Bertram	CA5050	12A,41,62D,43,29
Turner, Dave	AI0150	29,64E
Turner, George	IL3500	29,70
Turner, Michael W.	OR1000	70,29,34,47
Turner, Patrick	VA1700	11,29,34D,34H,35C
Turpen, Scott	WY0200	64E,47,29,60B
Turre, Steve	NY1900	29
Tynan, Paul	AF0150	37,63A,29
Vadala, Christopher	MD1010	47,64E,53,29
Valdez, Stephen	GA2100	29,12
Valerio, John B.	SC1110	29,11
Van der Bliek, Rob	AG0650	12,14C,29
VanAllen, Michael	NY3350	29,66A,47
Vanderheyden, Joel	MO0550	64E,46,47,29,13
Vandermeer, Aaron D.	NC2435	29,35,47
Vanderwoude, Matt	AG0130	10A,11,13,29,34
Vandiver, Joseph	TX3650	29,63,46,47,34
VanMatre, Rick	OH2200	47,64E,29
Varnes, Justin	GA1050	65,29
Vascan, Ligia	WI0500	40,61,36,54,29
Vega, Ray	VT0450	29,47,63A
Velosky, Ronald A.	PA0400	62D,29
Vernick, Gordon Jay	GA1050	47,46,29
Villafranca, Elio	PA3250	29,66A
Villanueva, Rodrigo	IL0200	29,47
Vinci, Mark A.	NY3650	47,64E,29
Vinci, Mark	NY1900	29
Viswanathan, Sundar	AG0650	29,64E,10D,61
Vitro-Wickliffe, Roseanne	NJ0825	29,61
Vivian, Jim	AG0450	62D,29
Vizutti, Allen	SC1110	29,63A
Von Hombracht, Willem	MO1950	29,62D
VonBerg, Craig	CA0810	29,47,14C
Vosbein, Terry	VA1850	10,13,29A,47,29
Voyement, Jacques	CA5300	29
Vu, Cuong	WA1050	29,63A
Wacker, Jonathan D.	NC0650	50,65,29
Waddington, Alan	CA1000	12F,14,29,46,47
Wakeling, Tom	OR0050	11,12A,47,29,35
Walburn, Jacob A.	IL3300	63A,29
Walczyk, Kevin	OR1250	13,45,63B,29,10
Walker, Kenneth	CO0900	62D,29
Walkington, Alec	AI0150	29,29C,62D
Wall, Daniel	OH1700	29
Wallace, Shawn	OH1850	29,29A
Wallarab, Brent K.	IN0900	29,47
Walters, David	TN0260	29,66A
Walters, Timothy	FL0650	13,41,63A,29
Wang, Richard A.	IL3310	10F,12A,47,53,29
Ward-Steinman, Patrice Madura	IN0900	32G,32D,32,29,47
Wardson, Greg	RI0200	29
Warfield, Tim	PA3250	29,64E
Warfield, Timothy	PA2300	29
Warfield, William	PA1950	47,63A,29
Warnock, Matthew	IL0350	29,70
Warren, J. Curt	TX3520	70,53,29
Warren, Jacquelyn	OH0750	66,29
Warrington, Thomas	NV0050	62D,47,29
Washburne, Christopher	NY0750	14,29,47
Washington, Kenny	NY1900	29
Washington, Salim	NY0500	47,46,29,29B
Washut, Robert	IA1600	13,47,29
Watrous, Bill	CA5300	29
Watters, Ken G.	AL1160	29
Wayte, Lawrence A.	OR1050	12,29
Weber, Brent M.	MD0350	64E,64D,29,47,20
Weed, Tad	OH2300	29
Weed, Tad	MI1750	66A,29,47
Weidman, James	NJ1400	29,66A
Weir, Michele	CA5031	61,29
Weir, Tim	ME0340	47,63A,29,32E
Weiskopf, Walter	PA3250	29,64E
Weiss, Ezra	OR0850	66A,29
Weisz, Deborah	CT0800	29,63C
Wells, Prince	IL2910	13,11,29,35
Wendholt, Scott	NY2150	29
Werkema, Jason R.	MI0750	70,13,29,34
Wermuth, Bruce M.	TX3420	29,61
Werner, Wendel V.	TN1710	29
Wertico, Paul	IL0550	65,29
Wessel, Kenneth	NY2400	70,29
Wheaton, Michael	MI2250	29
Wheeler, Michael	TX3450	70,29
Whitaker, Rodney	MI1400	47,29,62D
White, Andre	AI0150	65,66A,29A,29
White, Christopher K.	VA1100	29,64E,32E,64,12B
White, Darryl A.	NE0600	63A,29
White, James	CO0950	29,47,65
White, William	MI1750	63A,29
Whitehead, Glen	CO0810	63A,47,29,45
Whitehead, Richard	VA1350	70,29
Whitted, Pharez	IL0600	63A,29,47,49
Whittington, Andy	NC2440	66A,29
Wickham, Donna	CO0900	29,61
Wiest, Steve	TX3420	10,29,47,63C
Wiggins, Ira T.	NC1600	47,64A,64E,29,46
Wilder, Joe	NY1900	29
Wiley, Mathew S.	AL1150	29
Wiley, N. Keith	PA2350	32C,47,63A,29
Wilkerson, Andrea	CA3500	47,61,29,46,53
Wilkins, Ashby	FL2000	47,29
Wilkins, Jack	NY2150	29
Wilkins, Mariah	NY2150	29
Wilkins, Skip	PA1850	13,11,29
Wilkinson, Jay	OK1350	47,53,29
Wilkinson, Todd R.	KS1000	47,64E,29,32E
Williams, Anthony N.	ND0400	29,47,63C,63D
Williams, Brad	IL3550	29
Williams, Buster	PA3250	29,62D
Williams, Milton H.	CA4625	11,61,29,34
Wilson, Dennis E.	MI2100	63C,29,47
Wilson, John	PA1050	29
Wilson, John	PA0550	29,63A
Wilson, Olly W.	CA5000	10,20G,29
Wilson, Scott	FL1850	29
Wilson, Stephen K.	NC0250	47,29,63
Wilson, Steve	NY1900	29
Wilson, Steven	NY2150	29,64E
Wimberly, Michael	VT0050	10,20,29,35,65
Wind, Martin	NY1600	62D,29
Wind, Martin	NY2750	29,47,62D
Winking, Keith R.	TX3175	47,63A,29
Winograd, Barry	IL0720	29,12
Winslow, Michael Rocky	CA0800	29,47,63A
Winter, Beth	WA0200	61,53,29
Winters, Ellen	IL0720	29,61
Winters, Thomas D.	PA3600	12A,12,29
Wise, Phillip C.	MO0800	29,32
Witmer, Robert	AG0650	14,20G,29
Witt, Woody W.	TX3400	47,64E,29
Wittman, Jesse C.	IN1650	29
Wlosok, Pavel	NC2600	47,13F,29,66A
Wojtera, Allen F.	VA1100	50,65,29
Wolfe, Ben	NY1900	29,62D
Wolfe, Thomas	AL1170	47,70,29,35B
Wolking, Henry C.	UT0250	13,10F,47,46,29
Woodard, Eve	TX1000	29,70
Woodard, Peter	CT0650	13B,47,66A,29
Woods, Michael	NY1350	47,29
Woodson, Andrew	OH1850	29,62D
Worman, James	TX3350	32,37,47,29,64E
Wright, Prakash	TN1800	47,29
Wright, Todd T.	NC0050	29,47
Yandell, Scott	AZ0440	29,35C,35D
Yasinitsky, Greg	WA1150	47,64E,29,10F,10A
Yeager, Bill	CA4100	47,63C,29
Yellin, Peter	NY2102	47,64E,46,29
Yoder, Dan	PA1650	29
Yoes, Milas	AZ0470	12A,29,37,46,63C
Yonchak, Michael	OH2050	34,37,32E,29,46
Yonely, Jo Belle	NV0050	61,29
Yoshizawa, Haruko	NY4200	66A,29
Zanter, Mark J.	WV0400	13,29,10,70,34
Zemke, Lorna	WI0770	32,14A,29,20G
Zilber, Michael	CA2775	11,64E,12A,20G,29
Zimmerman, Brian	AC0050	29,70
Zinn, Dann	CA0900	64E,29

Index by Area of Teaching Interest

Zinno, David A.	RI0300	47,62D,29
Ziporyn, Evan	MA1200	13,10,20D,64C,29
Zlabinger, Tom	NY0646	62D,29,14,20,47
Zocher, Norman M. E.	MA1400	29
Zvacek, Bret R.	NY3780	47,29

History of Jazz

Abel, Sean	CA1300	13B,13C,20G,29A,34C
Acosta, Tim	CA4650	11,63,29A
Adan, Jose	FL0050	70,13,13C,11,29A
Ake, David	NV0100	12,20,29A,14,66A
Allen, Kristopher	CT0500	47,29A
Allen, Ray	NY0500	11,20G,29A,20H
Allen, Robert T.	VA0800	11,12A,29A,60A
Amador Medina, Ruben J.	PR0115	14C,29A
Anderson, Andrew E.	TX0075	29A,11
Aranda, Patrick	CA0950	13A,37,47,63C,29A
Arcaro, Peter	FL1100	13B,11,29A,47
Armstrong, Robin E.	MD0520	11,14,29A,12,12A
Arnold, Larry	NC2435	10,29A,13,34A,62D
Atherton, Timothy	MA2100	63C,63D,29A
Averhoff, Carlos	FL0700	64E,29A
Ayres, Carol	IA0800	11,37,47,64,29A
Bailey, Don	AR0730	13C,29A,29B,46,64E
Bair, Jeffery J.	NC0650	64E,42,29A
Baldini, Donald	NH0150	38,47,62D,29A
Balentine, James S.	TX3530	13,10,47,29A
Ball, James	MI0100	29A,38,47,63D,60B
Ballou, David L.	MD0850	29,53,63A,29A,36
Barnes, Larry J.	KY1350	13,10,29A,34,14C
Bartow, James	NY0270	11,20A,20G,29A,70
Barz, Gregory F.	TN1850	12,14,20,31,29A
Batchelor, Daryl	KS0550	47,63A,29,29A
Bauer, William R.	NY0600	12A,29A
Becraft, Steven C.	AR0300	64C,29A,64E,48,32E
Behnke, Martin	OR0950	46,47,29A
Bellamy, Amy J.	NY0450	11,29A,36,61
Bennack, Steven	TX2710	70,29A,66D
Berardinelli, Paula	NY2450	29A,13,66A
Bergeron, Chuck	FL1900	62D,47,29A,46,12A
Berle, Arnie	NY2400	11,29A
Bernhardt, Barry W.	FL0700	37,47,63A,29A
Berrett, Joshua	NY2400	13,11,29A,12,12B
Berry, Fredrick J.	CA4900	47,29A
Betts, James E.	IL1800	13,20,29A,63,34
Biggs, Gunnar	CA3460	60B,47,29A
Black, Elizabeth P.	NC0805	11,29A,20G
Blancq, Charles C.	LA0800	29A,12A
Blue, T. K.	NY2105	47,29,29A,29B
Bodolosky, Michael	PA3410	37,47,29A
Bonkowski, Anita	AB0150	29A,29B,13A,13B,13D
Borla, Janice	IL2050	53,29,29A,29B
Boswell, Ronald L.	AR0750	13,11,29A
Bourquin, Cindy	CA4450	40,29A
Bowen, Robert E.	CA3200	13,10A,29A,34
Bowman, Rob	AG0650	14,20G,29A
Boyd, Craig E.	NY4050	60,11,47,70,29A
Boyd, Jean A.	TX0300	12A,20G,29A
Bradford, Bobby L.	CA3650	47,29A
Broussard, George L.	NC1400	42,63C,29A
Brown, Beverly	NC1400	11,29A,47,37,64C
Brown, Donald R.	TN1710	47,66A,29A
Brown, Gwynne Kuhner	WA1000	12A,29A,13C,20,12B
Brown, John V.	NC0600	62D,47,29A,29B,29C
Brown, Leonard	MA1450	11,14,64E,29A,12E
Brown, Miles	MI1750	62D,47,29A,29B,46
Brown, Rae Linda	CA5020	12,29A
Brown, T. Dennis	MA2000	32,20G,29A,34
Budginas, Rudolfas	CA1510	13A,29A
Burgett, Paul	NY4350	20G,11,29A,29D
Burke, Larry	FL0800	32B,63D,29A,49,35A
Bush, Nathan	CA2550	29A
Bushard, Anthony J.	NE0600	12,29A
Butler, Hunt	KY0750	47,48,64,53,29A
Butterfield, Matthew W.	PA1300	29,13,13B,29A,29B
Buttery, Gary A.	RI0300	11,47,49,63D,29A
Campbell, Jeff	NY1100	29A,29B,29C,62D,47
Canon, Sherri	CA2660	66A,29A
Canon, Sherri D.	CA2720	20,29A,66A
Cappillo, Frances	NY3500	29A,11
Carbone, Michael	NY3705	47,29A
Carillo, Dan	NY2900	29A
Carlon, Paul	NY0644	29A,64E
Carlsen, Philip	ME0410	13,10,29A,38,34
Carlson, Lennis Jay	CA1020	70,46,29A
Carroll, Don	CA3200	11,14,29A,20G
Carter, Joey	TX3000	65,29A,29B,47
Carter, Joseph	CT0300	70,29A,20G,20H,47
Carter, William	PA2200	29A,66A
Cashwell, Brian	OH2500	29A
Cateforis, Theodore P.	NY4100	12,12D,20G,29A,14C
Cazier, David	WA0150	36,61,29A,40
Chaffee, Christopher	OH2500	64A,20,29A,11
Chasalow, Eric	MA0500	13,10A,10B,11,29A
Christensen, Jean M.	KY1500	12,29A
Christy, William P.	OH1910	13,12A,20G,29A,34
Clegg, Neill M.	NC0900	10F,12A,64,53,29A
Cleveland, Lisa A.	NH0310	13,11,29A,66
Collins, Christopher	MI2200	47,64E,29A,35
Conklin, Michael	NJ0175	11,29A
Connell, Andrew M.	VA0600	14,29A
Conner, Ted A.	PA2550	11,12A,29A
Contrino, Joseph L.	MO1500	65,29A,13A,13C
Cook, Kenneth	NY1275	12C,13,29A
Cooper, David	WI0840	47,49,63A,11,29A
Corbet, Kim	TX2400	53,29A
Corbus, Dave	CO0800	29A
Costanzo, Samuel R.	CT0250	13,11,29A
Coughran, Steven J.	CA1500	47,20,29A,70
Coutsouridis, Peter	MA2100	65,41,29A,11,13B
Cox, Terrance	AG0050	20G,29A
Crain, Timothy M.	MA2030	12,20,29A,11
Crews, Joel	MO1110	29A
Crofts, Tim	AF0100	29A
Cunneff, Philip B.	MD0475	13A,65,29A,14C
D'Amico, John	PA0450	29A
Damschroder, Norman	OH2300	62D,29A
Daniels, Chris	CO0830	35,29A
Danko, Harold	NY1100	29A,29B,29C,66A,47
Daub, Eric	TX3100	66,13A,13B,13C,29A
Davenport, Mark	CO0650	12,55,67C,29A,14C
Davies, Josh	AA0200	63A,47,29A,13C
Davis, Art	IL2050	63A,14,29A,29B
Davis, Cara	WI0806	36,61,29A,11
Davis, John S.	CO0800	47,29,29A,63A
Davis, Scott	IA0420	29A,47,63A
De Wetter-Smith, Brooks	NC2410	64A,29A
DeHoog, David	FL1100	13A,29A
DeLamater, Elizabeth L.	AZ0490	20,29A,12A,65
Demarinis, Paul	MO1900	29A
Denison, Mark	OR1010	12A,29A,63C,46,60B
Denny, Michael	OR1050	70,47,29,29A
Denny, Mike	OR0350	29A,13
DeQuattro, Anthony	CT0550	29A
Deutsch, Herbert A.	NY1600	13,10,45,29A,35
DeWitt, Mark F.	LA0760	14,29A,13C,20G
Dobbins, Evan	NY2500	29A
Dolske, Christopher C.	FL1550	63A,49,29A
Dorian, Patrick	PA1100	10C,13B,29A,29C,29E
Dries, Eric	CA0815	13,13E,13D,29A,66
Dubberly, James	CA0850	63C,63D,29A,41
Dulaney, John	OR1250	32E,29A
Dunlap, Phil	MO1830	29A
Duquaine, Kenneth	MI0450	11,29A
Dziuba, Mark	NY3760	70,29A,47,35C
Eben, Michael	PA0050	29A
Eckroth, Rachel	AZ0470	66A,29B,29A
Eisel, Gunnar	CA1000	10B,12A,13A,14C,29A
Erickson, Jeff	WI0925	47,13C,29A,13B
Evans, Thomas	MI1150	37,47,63C,29A,32
Falbush, Arthur	NY3765	11,63,29A,46,41
Farnham, Allen	NJ0825	29A,29B
Farrington, Robert	CA1550	41,47,63,64,29A
Fettig, Mary	CA4150	29A
Fienberg, Gary	NJ0175	63A,29A,47,49
Finn, Neal	NC0800	10A,10F,29A,47,63C
Fischer, Stewart R.	CA1265	46,29A
Flaherty, Mark	MI1600	47,63A,29A,34,63B
Flory, Andrew	MN0300	12A,29A
Forney, Fred	AZ0440	63A,46,29A
Frackenpohl, David J.	GA1050	29A
Franks, Rebecca	NY4300	29A,29B,46,47,34D
Freedman, Richard	PA1500	11,12A,12,20D,29A
Frohrip, Kenton R.	MN1300	29A,35,63A
Froncek, Tim	MI0900	29,65,29A,47,46
Fullerton, Kevin T.	KS1400	14C,12A,29A,63D,11
Gabbart, Ryan	TX3400	29A
Galvan, Gary	PA1830	12,70,29A,34A
Gamso, Nancy M.	OH2000	11,29A,48,64,32E
Gardner, Derrick	AC0100	63A,29A,46,47
Gareau, Larry	CT0050	63,29A
Gargrave, Eric	RI0101	11,13A,29A,48,13B
Garrett, Glen R.	CA0835	29A,11
Gatien, Gregory	AC0050	64E,29A,47
Gauthier, Michael	AI0050	70,29A,47,10D
Gelfand, Alexander Lyon	NY3500	29A
Gerdes, John	MO0700	10F,29A,63
Gewirtz, Jonathon D.	MI1200	47,64E,29A
Gibbs, Lawrence	LA0250	11,29A,37,47,64C
Gibson, David	LA0770	13,64B,64D,29A
Gilleland, Katharine	NC2525	66G,11,13A,29A,36
Gitler, Ira	NY2150	29A
Gonano, Max A.	PA0500	11,12A,13A,29A,37
Gonzalez, Roberto-Juan	CA3250	11,29A
Goode, Bradley	CO0800	63A,29A,29B
Goss, Kim	MI1500	29A
Gove, John	CA2450	13,47,29A
Grabowski, Robert	FL0700	29A,11
Graham, Dave	CA5400	47,13A,11,46,29A
Grant, Joyce	NY1200	13A,20G,29A
Grantham, Jennifer	OH2550	29A,47
Greenberg, Russell	NY4050	29A
Greene, Terry L.	NY4050	29A
Greene, Thomas E.	RI0100	29A
Gregory, Thomas	RI0101	29A,63D
Gregory, Thomas	RI0102	29A
Gross, Mark	NJ1130	64E,29,29A
Guerra, Stephen J.	FL1900	10F,29A,29B,47
Haas, Frederick L.	NH0100	64E,66A,29A,29B,47
Haffley, Robin L.	PA1830	11,13A,29A,34D,14C
Hamada, Brian	CA0810	47,65,29A
Hamberlin, Larry D.	VT0350	10A,12A,29A,13A,13C
Hamersma, Carol	NJ1160	11,14C,29A,70
Hamme, Albert	NY3705	47,64E,53,29A
Hammett, Larry D.	OK1350	70,29A
Hampton, Barbara L.	NY0625	14,20G,29A
Harbaugh, John	WA0050	29A,53,49,63A
Hardiman, David A.	CA1020	46,29,29B
Harding, Scott R.	MI0400	10A,13C,29A,65,13A
Hardy, Bruce	CA5360	11,29A,14C
Harms, Lawrence	IL1090	11,47,64C,64E,29A
Hawkins, Wes	AZ0470	14C,65,50,29A
Hayes, Andrew	NC0910	29A,47
Haynes, Philip	PA0350	29A
Hegarty, James	IL2400	10A,29A,34D,47,13A
Hemke, Frederick J. B.	SD0400	47,48,64,29A
Henderson, Chip	TN1680	70,29A,47
Hendricks, Hermina	VA1125	29A,14C
Hennessey, Patrick D.	HI0110	37,47,29A,12A,63C
Hepler, David	PA0700	50,65,29A
Heritage, Lee	OH2300	13B,13C,29A,20G,10A
Herrick, Dennis R.	AL0450	60,63,34,29A,32C
Hill, John	MI0450	11,29A,62D
Hoekstra, Gerald	MN1450	12A,55,29A
Hofbauer, Eric	MA0850	29A
Hofmockel, Jeff	CA2100	29A
Holt, Robert	WI0847	29A
Homzy, Andrew	AI0070	10,47,29,29A,34
Horgan, Maureen A.	GA0850	63D,11,49,63C,29A
Hornsby, Richard	AE0120	64C,12A,29A,34,60
Howe, Donald	CA3520	12A,29A,14C,63C
Howland, John L.	NJ1140	10,12,20,29,29A
Hubbs, Holly J.	PA3550	11,37,47,29A,20
Hubbs, Randall	WA0150	13,37,47,63A,29A
Hucke, Adam	IL2970	11,13A,29A,63A,47
Hughes, Robert L.	MO1250	12A,29,13,29A,29E
Humphreys, Paul W.	CA2800	14A,13A,13B,29A,10A
Hunt, Paul B.	KS0650	63C,12A,29A
Hunter, Robert	AZ0440	32E,63A,37,46,29A
Hutchins, Tony	IA1100	11,29A,63B,63C,32E
Inserto, Ayn	MA1400	29A
Irish, John E.	TX0150	63A,63B,49,29A
Irom, Benjamin M.	TX2800	29,29A,47,41,13
Irving, David	TX0550	47,70,46,29A,37
Jensen, Brent	ID0075	29A
Jentsch, Christopher T.	NY4050	11,29A
Johnson, Joel C.	SC1050	13,10,20G,29A,34
Johnson, Todd Alan	CA0845	65,12A,14,50,29A
Johnston, Jesse A.	MI2110	11,12A,29A
Jones, Ryan Patrick	WI0803	11,12A,13,29A
Juhl, Aaron	WI0806	29A
Jumpeter, Joseph A.		11,29A,20,36,66G
Justison, Brian	IL1750	29A,50,65
Keberle, Daniel	WA1350	47,63A,29,29A

Index by Area of Teaching Interest

Name	Code	Areas
Keller, Justin	NY0644	29A
Kelly, James J.	NJ0750	12A,13,29A,47,70
Kelly, Stephen K.	MN0300	12A,55,29A
Kelton, Christopher T.	RI0150	47,64C,64E,29A
Kernodle, Tammy L.	OH1450	11,12,29A,29D
Kilstofte, Anne C.	AZ0350	11,29A,20
Kircher, Bill	NY2150	29A
Kirchner, William	NJ0825	29A
Klee, David A.	IA0150	10C,29A,34D,35A,47
Klich, Chris	CA2100	29A
Knox, Carl	CT0050	64E,29A,46,47
Knudtsen, Jere	WA0750	11,37,47,64A,29A
Korb, Ryan	WI0850	29A,65,47
Korb, Ryan	WI0925	29A,65,47
Korman, Clifford	NY2150	29A
Korn, Steve	WA1050	29A
Kotan, Emrah	GA0050	65,29A,47
Kunzer, Stephen	OK0800	63D,11,29A
LaBarbera, Joe	CA0510	65,29A,47
Lagana, Tom	MD0850	70,29A,51
Laird, Tracey	GA0050	12,14,11,29A
Lampert, Steven	NY0050	29A,29B
Langford, R. Gary	FL1850	37,47,29A
LaPierre, Art	CA0150	36,47,29A,61
Larner, James M.	IN1100	12A,48,10E,64A,29A
Larson, Tom	NE0600	29A
LaSpina, Steven	NJ1400	29A,47,62D,29
Lawing, William D.	NC0550	29A,47,63A,34D,49
Lawson, Sonya R.	MA2100	12A,62B,29A,12,20
LeBlanc, Eric	AB0210	29A
Lester, Jason	TX3850	11,12A,13F,29A
Levine, Barry	NJ0550	11,64C,64E,29A
Levine, Theodore	MA1100	64E,29A
Levine, Theodore	MA2100	64E,46,29A
Lieuwen, Peter	TX2900	13,10,12A,29A
Lindberg, Jeffrey	OH0700	47,38,63C,29A
Lindsey, Logan	WV0050	29A,41,49,63D
LoBalbo, Anthony C.	NY3500	13,29A,10C,12A,54
Lopato, David	NJ0800	29A
Lornell, Christopher 'Kip'	DC0100	29A,14
Lozano, Danilo	CA6000	47,64A,20,29A,14
Lyke, Toby Russell	OH0680	10F,47,29A
Machlin, Paul S.	ME0250	12A,36,20G,29A
Mackie, Henry	LA0800	70,29A,29B,47
Magee, Jeffrey	IL3300	12,20G,29A
Magnani, Victor A.	NY0644	29A
Makris, Kristina	AZ0440	10,13,35A,29A,61
Malone, William	CO0810	64E,64C,64A,29A,20
Mancuso, Charles	NY3717	20G,29A,12E,14C
Manji, K. C.	CA1265	60,38,49,41,29A
Mann, Brian R.	NY4450	11,12A,12,29A
Marcus, David	GA0490	10,11,12A,13A,29A
Marks, Dennis J.	FL1950	62D,66A,47,29A
Marquez-Barrios, Victor	MI0900	29A,20
Martin, Henry	NJ1140	13,10,12,29,29A
Martinez, Jesus E.	CA1700	13,29A,37,46
Martucci, Vincent	NY3760	29A,29B,66A,66D,47
Matlock, Herman	NY3775	63A,29A,49
Matthay, Christopher D.	NY2750	13,14A,20D,20E,29A
Mazzatenta, Mark	NC0915	29A
McCord, Kimberly A.	IL1150	32B,32C,32F,29A,32A
McCord, Vicki	IL0420	29A,29B
McCurdy, Robert	SD0550	29A,47
McDaniel, William T.	OH1850	20A,29,29A
McFalls, James	MD0850	63C,29A,46
McGarvey, Timothy	IA1200	37,60,32E,41,29A
McGinnis, Barry E.	SC0900	64,12A,29,48,29A
McLean, Rene	CT0650	29,29A
McManus, James M.	CA3320	13,45,29A,12A,11
McWilliams, Robert	WI0830	37,32,29A,60B
Melia, Hal	OH0500	29A,29B,48
Metcalf, Lee	CT0800	29A,70
Metil, Robert	PA0600	14,29A,20G,70
Metz, Ken	TX3410	13,10,29,29A
Metzer, David	AB0100	13,29A,15
Millar, Michael W.	CA0630	63C,35E,29A,35A
Miller, Paul W.	PA2740	10A,11,13A,29A,29B
Milne, David	WI0845	29A,47,48,64E
Mitchell, Nicole	IL3310	29,29A,64A
Mitchell, Roman	NY0640	29A,29B,66A,66B
Moder, Jennifer	IL1090	29A
Moffett, C. Mondre	NC1550	63A,10F,29A,47,31F
Monllos, John	RI0300	11,29A,70
Moore, Edward	NY3720	20G,36,66A,11,29A
Moore, James H.	WV0800	37,47,29A,11
Moore, Joel	IL1520	64E,29A
Morreale, Michael	NY0644	11,63A,29A,47,13A
Morrill, Dexter G.	NY0650	10,45,29A,34
Mouse, Eugene	IL2050	53,47,29A,29B
Muscatello, George	NY3650	29A,70
Neithamer, David	VA0700	29A,64C,32E
Nelson, Larry	KY0550	64E,53,29,47,29A
Newman, Timothy	NJ1400	47,63,29A
Nivans, David	CA2050	11,13A,20,29A
Nivans, David	CA0805	14C,29A,20,13,11
Nocella, Peter S.	PA2700	29A
Nolen, Paul	IL1150	64E,29A
Nuccio, David A.	IL1250	11,29A,34,54,66A
Nurock, Kirk	NY2660	10F,60,10,13J,29A
Offard, Felton	IL0600	13A,11,47,70,29A
O'Reilly, Daniel	SC0420	14C,64E,29A
Orta, Michael	FL0700	66A,29A,29B,47
Ott, Daniel	NY1300	12A,29A,54,13B,13C
Ott, Joseph	IL0100	53,47,29A
Owens, Craig	KS1450	47,70,53,29A,20G
Page, Andy	NC0050	29A,29B,70
Paige, Diane M.	NY1400	12,29A,20,12A,20F
Paliga, Mitch L.	IL2050	64E,29A,41,47,48
Paliga, Mitchell L.	IL1400	64E,47,29A
Palmer, Jason	OR1020	66D,13,13C,29A,29B
Palter, Morris	AK0150	12A,29A,42,43,14C
Parke, Steve	IL2450	10,47,63A,29A,35A
Parker, Val	GA0490	10,11,13A,34D,29A
Parton, Robert T.	OH0350	63A,29,47,29A,53
Patterson, Ann E.	CA2650	29A,29D,47
Patterson, Thomas	WI0960	29A,36,11,63C
Pen, Ronald	KY1450	20G,29A,12A,12
Pennington, Stephen	MA1900	12D,29A,29E,15,12
Peppo, Bret	CA1560	36,29A,60
Perrine, John Mark	OH0650	47,29A,64E
Phillips, Linda N.	NY3725	12A,66D,29A
Pinckney, Warren R.	CA0800	11,20G,29A,13
Pisciotta, Eva Mae	AZ0200	36,61,29A
Pitchford, Timothy	IL1200	63C,29A,46,47,53
Pitman, Grover A.	PA3650	12A,29A
Polack, Eric	NJ1100	29A
Pollart, Gene J.	RI0300	60,32,37,29A
Porter, Charles	NY2700	13A,11,12A,66D,29A
Porter, Lewis R.	NJ1140	13,12,29,29A
Postle, Matthew W.	NC2000	47,29A
Poston, Ken	CA0825	20G,35B,29A
Pratt, Dennis H.	RI0101	29A,11,13A
Pratt, Dennis H.	RI0100	29A
Pritchard, Gary	CA0859	20G,29A,20H,12A
Prouten, William	AA0032	13,47,64,53,29A
Provost, Sarah	MA0650	29A
Pruiett, Kevin P.	OK0650	47,63A,72,29A,49
Psurny, Robert D.	MT0075	29A,36,40,54,61
Quinn, Kelly	MO1110	29A
Rack, John	NC2440	32,65,29A
Rackipov, Errol	FL0700	29A,65B,11
Reid, John	AA0150	29A
Reynolds, Jeffrey L.	AG0450	49,63A,37,29A
Rhodes, Ann G.	KY0300	11,12A,61,32D,29A
Richards, Douglas	VA1600	12A,29A,29B
Ridley, Larry	NY2150	47,29A,62D,20A,20G
Roberts, Adam	AZ0350	12A,64E,29A
Robinson, Marty	WI0830	63A,29A,47
Rohr, Clint	OK1330	29A,13A
Romain, James P.	IA0550	64E,29A,35A,29,47
Romanek, Mary L.	PA2720	12A,32A,32B,29A
Romeo, Arthur	NY1275	14C,29A
Rose, Bernard	NY1275	14C,29A,32E
Rose, Brent	LA0800	64C,29A,13A,13B,13C
Russell, Ralph Anthony	NJ0175	13,29A,12E
Ruth, Byron	AZ0470	14C,29A,64E
Salmon, John C.	NC2430	66A,66C,29A
Samball, Michael L.	ID0050	11,12A,29A,35A
Sandim, Carmen	CO0550	29A,66D
Sanford, David	MA1350	13,10,29A
Santos, Elias	PR0115	29A,47,29B,53
Schaap, Phil	NY1900	29A
Schelfer, James	NY2700	13A,20,29A
Schilf, Paul R.	SD0050	37,49,47,32E,29A
Schleeter, Bob	CA1150	20G,29A,34D
Schlesinger, Scott L.	NC2525	66G,11,13A,29A,36
Schmidt, Alan G.	NY1220	13A,12A,47,20G,29A
Schmidt, Henry L.	PA2550	13,12A,63C,26,29A
Schmidt, James	NC0450	66A,29A,66D,47,11
Schmidt, Juliana	WI0855	11,20,29A
Scoggin, David	OR0950	29A
Scott, Dave	CA4700	63A,29A
Scott, J. B.	FL1950	63A,53,47,29A
Sears, E. Ann	MA2150	12A,66A,29A,20G
Senn, Geoff	MN0040	29A,63A,34,41,11
Seybold, Donald	IN1300	29A
Shanahan, Ellen Cooper	MA0280	13,12A,36,54,29A
Shanefield, Andrew	PA3200	47,29A,29B
Sharp, Charles	CA0815	29A,20
Silberschlag, Jeffrey	MD0750	29A,35A,60,38,63A
Simmons, James	CA2550	29A
Simmons, James	TN1100	63A,47,46,29A,29B
Simon, Harris W.	VA0250	29A,66A,47,29
Smith, Arnold	NJ0825	29A
Smith, Donald S.	AZ0350	29A,63A,49
Smith, Robbie Malcolm	MI0400	47,29A
Snider, Denise G.	WA1150	29A,11
Snowden, Donald	FL1500	37,47,63D,29A
Snyder, Colleen	CA2400	11,29A,37,66D,60
Sole, Meryl	NY0050	29A,29B
Solomon, Joseph	NY2050	47,53,29A
Stapleton, Chip	IN0907	29A,64E,14C,11
Stats, Clyde	VT0450	29A
Stern, David	SC0050	37,63D,47,29A,60B
Strathman, Marc	MO1100	29A
Strauman, Edward	PA0650	10F,29A,13D,13B,35A
Sunkett, Mark E.	AZ0100	50,65,29A,14
Sushel, Michael	CA1000	10D,66A,66B,11,29A
Talaga, Steve	MI1050	66A,29A,29B,29C,10
Tancredi, Dominick	NY0644	13A,29A
Tatum, Mark	NM0450	62D,29A
Taylor, Jeffrey J.	NY0500	12,11,29A
Tedesco, Anne C.	NY3500	13,66A,54,29A,10
Thompson, Paul	MO1500	11,41,64A,29A,55C
Thompson, Richard O.	CA4100	47,66A,29A
Thornton, Mary	TX2930	63A,29A,13A,13C
Tiner, Kris	CA0270	47,29A,11
Toman, Sharon Ann	PA2775	11,13A,29A,14C,36
Tomaro, Robert	WI0100	29A
Tomasello, Andrew	NY0250	11,12,14,29A,35
Tomasello, Andrew	NY0600	12,14,29A
Touliatos-Miles, Diane	MO1830	11,12A,12,29A
Trask, Alvin	MD0550	63A,53,29A,14C,47
Trowers, Robert	NC1600	63C,63D,46,29A
Turechek, Dennis	NY1400	70,29A
Turner, Tammy	KY1540	29A,11,32B
Turney, Brent	WI0850	47,29A,63A
Ullman, Michael	MA1900	20G,29A
Urness, Mark	WI0350	62D,29A
Utsch, Glenn R.	PA3100	13C,66A,29A,66D
Utterback, Joe	CT0300	12A,20G,29A
Vacca, Anthony	AZ0490	29A,14C
Vana, John G.	IL3500	64E,29A
Vander Gheynst, John R.	IN0907	29A,10A,63,34D,35A
Viebranz, Gary A.	PA2715	12A,29A,32C
Villani, A. David	PA2710	34B,35G,29A
Vosbein, Terry	VA1850	10,13,29A,47,29
Wade, Patsy	TN0100	29A
Wakeley, David A.	WA1350	29A
Waksman, Steve M.	MA1750	29A,14C
Walker, Cherilee	KS0590	36,13,11,61,29A
Wallace, Shawn	OH1850	29,29A
Walsh, Allan	AG0150	64E,47,46,29A,29B
Walton, Scott	CA3460	29A
Ward, Brian	WA1150	66A,10D,13C,14C,29A
Warwick, Jacqueline	AF0100	12A,12D,14C,15,29A
Watson, J. Stephen	SC0750	29A,70,46
Watson, Robert M.	MO1810	29A,29B,29C,47,64E
Weaver, Carol Ann	AG0470	13,10,12,20A,29A
Webb, Jeffrey L.	PA3410	29A,36,13A,60,13
Wechesler, David J.	NY0644	11,13A,29A,41,64A
Weiss, Daniel	IN1300	29A,13
Weller, Ellen	CA3460	12A,55,20,29A,60
Wesby, Roger	NY4500	11,29A,32D,36,40
West, George	FL1750	47,29A,53
Western, Daniel	AL0650	64,47,35D,13,29A
Wetzel, Neil D.	PA2450	47,64,29A,64E,46
Wetzel, Richard	OH1900	12,29A
Wexler, Richard	MD1010	12A,12,55,29A
Whalen, Margaret F.	NC2000	11,12A,20B,29A
Whisler, Bruce Allen	SC0400	29A,41,35,34
White, Andre	AI0150	65,6A,29A,29
White, Chris	IL2050	66A,13F,29A,29B,29C
White, Rick	WA0600	11,29A,20,37,46
Wilkerson, Steve	CA3200	13A,29A
William, Jacob	MA2020	29A,34

Index by Area of Teaching Interest

Williams, Bradley	IL0750	29A
Williams, Oscar	LA0700	12A,64,11,29A
Williams, Yolanda	MN0050	29A,20
Williams, Yolanda	MN1050	12A,20,47,29A,41
Wilson, Steve	TX3520	63D,29A,37
Winkler, Peter	NY3790	13,10,20G,29A
Winslow, Richard D.	CA0800	49,63A,63B,29A,20G
Woideck, Carl	OR1050	29A,20G,12
Wolf, Aaron	CA1510	29A
Wolfe, Jeffrey L.	WV0400	34,29A,47
Wolfinbarger, Steve	MI2250	49,63C,29A
Wood, Charles H.	CA4410	29A
Wright, Joseph	NY2400	11,29A
Wright, Trey	GA1150	70,47,29A,29B,14C
Yanez, Raul	AZ0490	66A,47,14C,29A
Yon, Franklin	MI0450	63,47,29A,11
Zappa, John	KY1000	29A
Zifer, Timothy	IN1600	47,63A,29A,49
Zinn, Daniel L.	CA0807	47,64E,41,29A,11
Zurcher, Allen	PA2250	29A

Jazz Theory

Arriale, Lynne	FL1950	66A,29B,46
Atkins, Victor	LA0800	29B,46,47,66A
Bagg, Joseph	CA1000	29B,66A
Bailey, Don	AR0730	13C,29A,29B,46,64E
Beach, Wade	VA0450	66A,29B
Beeson, D. Allen	MO1830	29B
Blue, T. K.	NY2105	47,29,29A,29B
Bonkowski, Anita	AB0150	29A,29B,13A,13B,13D
Bonness, Will	AC0100	29B,47,66A
Borla, Janice	IL2050	53,29,29A,29B
Boyle, Patrick	AB0150	20A,29B,47,53
Brown, John V.	NC0600	62D,47,29A,29B,29C
Brown, Miles	MI1750	62D,47,29A,29B,46
Burks, Ricky	AL1450	48,64,46,29B,37
Butcher, Paul	FL0800	29B,47,35A,63A
Butterfield, Matthew W.	PA1300	29,13,13B,29A,29B
Caldwell, Glenn G.	MD0520	13,29B
Campbell, Jeff	NY1100	29A,29B,29C,62D,47
Carter, Joey	TX3000	65,29A,29B,47
Cash, Carla Davis	TX3200	66B,66D,29B,66A,66
Chappell, Jeffrey	MD0400	47,66A,29,29B,10
Christopher, Casey R.	ID0150	11,29B,34,35,37
Clark, Dave	KY0250	29B,47,53,64E
Clements, Gordon	AB0210	46,47,29B,64E,64C
Cook, Mark Andrew	WV0550	13,29B,47,46,10
Craig, Monty S.	SC0400	70,46,47,29B
Dana, Christy L.	CA5000	13A,13C,29B,47,29C
Danby, Judd	IN1310	10,13,29B,10A,13F
Danko, Harold	NY1100	29A,29B,29C,66A,47
Davey, John	NY1400	62D,29B,41
Davis, Art	IL2050	63A,14,29A,29B
Dingo, Matt	PA1650	29B
Dobbins, William	NY1100	29B,29C,10A,10F,46
Drayton, Leslie	CA5360	46,47,29B
Eckroth, Rachel	AZ0470	66A,29B,29A
Ellwood, Jeffrey	CA3200	29B
Farnham, Allen	NJ0825	29A,29B
Fernandez, David D.	FL0700	29B
Fischer, Lou	OH0350	47,29B,10F
Fitzgerald, Chris	KY1500	29B,13
Flugge, Mark	OH0350	66A,66D,29B
Franks, Rebecca	NY4300	29A,29B,46,47,34D
Fryer, Nicholas	CA5350	47,29B
Gailes, George	VA1600	47,64E,29B
Gantt, William	CA3250	47,29B,60B
Garling, Tom	IL0550	29B,63C
Giasullo, Frank	PA2450	66A,29B
Goode, Bradley	CO0800	63A,29A,29B
Gorrell, Brian	OK1330	64E,46,34,47,29B
Greenblatt, Dan	NY2660	64E,32E,47,29B
Groff, Dale	WA0480	34D,34G,34C,34F,29B
Guerra, Stephen J.	FL1900	10F,29A,29B,47
Haas, Frederick L.	NH0100	64E,66A,29A,29B,47
Hall, Jeff	MI1850	47,64C,64E,66A,29B
Halt, Hans	NV0100	29B,62D,66A
Hamilton, Ryan	OH0350	63C,47,29B,53
Hardiman, David A.	CA1020	46,29A,29B
Harmon, Sally	OR0500	66A,29B
Harper, Richard	NY2660	61,29B
Harris, Rod D.	CA1375	13A,11,64E,29B,34
Hart, Kevin M.	IL1350	29B,53,66A,47,65
Haydon, Geoffrey Jennings	GA1050	66A,66F,29B
Helzer, Richard A.	CA4100	29B,29C,66A,47,53
Hodson, Robert	MI1500	13,29B,47
Hunan, Steve	CA1500	47,29B,70
Huntington, Lawrence	MI1250	47,29B
Jackson, Tyrone	GA1150	66A,29B,66D,53
James, Tim	PA0950	66A,29B
Jenkins, Clay	NY1100	29B,29C,63A,47
Jenkins, E. Morgan	MD0450	64A,64E,70,29B
Johnson, Doug	MA2050	66A,29B
Jones, Hugh	MO1830	29B
Justus, Keith	TX0550	70,13C,14C,29B
Karlsson, Stefan	TX3420	29B,29C,47,66A
Karsh, Kenneth M.	PA1050	70,29B
Kubis, Thomas M.	CA2050	10F,13A,29B,46,47
Lampert, Steven	NY0050	29A,29B
Lee, Thomas Oboe	MA0330	13,10,29B
Leibinger, Douglas J.	CA4700	47,29B,63C,10A
Levi, Michael	NY0700	36,29B,13,60A,32D
Levy, James D.	DC0100	47,66A,29B
Lidral, Karel	ME0440	13B,47,64E,29B
Lington, Aaron	CA4400	29,46,63,29B
Loehrke, John	NJ0975	11,62D,47,29B
Lynch, Brian	FL1900	63A,10,47,46,29B
Mackie, Henry	LA0800	70,29,29B,47
Martucci, Vincent	NY3760	29A,29B,66A,66D,47
Masakowski, Steve	LA0800	70,35B,35C,29B,47
Matzke, Rex	CO0200	64E,29B
McCarley, Ron	CA1510	47,29B
McCord, Vicki	IL0420	29A,29B
McCormick, Scott	MA0260	29B,32F,32H,20G,34G
McGowan, Sean C.	CO0830	13A,13B,13C,13E,29B
McNeely, James	NJ1400	29B
Melia, Hal	OH0500	29A,29B,48
Merrill, Paul	NY0900	46,47,29B,29C,63A
Miller, Paul W.	PA2740	10A,11,13A,29A,29B
Mitchell, Roman	NY0640	29A,29B,66A,66B
Monaghan, Daniel	PA3250	29B
Mossblad, Gunnar	OH2300	64E,46,47,29B,29C
Mouse, Eugene	IL2050	53,47,29A,29B
Mullen, Stan	PA2050	29B,53,70,20G,20F
Mullett, Scott	NH0150	53,47,29B
Munday, Don	OK1200	29B,62D
Nelson-Raney, Steven	WI0825	13A,13,29B
Novros, Paul	CA0510	64E,47,29B
Orta, Michael	FL0700	66A,29A,29B,47
Page, Andy	NC0050	29A,29B,70
Palmer, Jason	OR1020	66D,13,13C,29A,29B
Patton, Jeb	NY1275	10,13B,29B,29C,66A
Pelusi, Mario J.	IL1200	10A,10F,13,43,29B
Peterson, Edward	LA0800	47,64C,29B
Posey, Dale	FL0950	62D,29B
Richards, Douglas	VA1600	12A,29A,29B
Riekenberg, Dave	PA1950	64E,47,29B
Rodriguez Curet, Marcos J.	PR0115	29B,47
Rose, Brent	LA0080	29B,64
Sabatella, Marc	CO0900	13,29B
Sandahl, Thomas	OR0500	47,70,29B
Santos, Elias	PR0115	29A,47,29B,53
Sauerwein, Andrew Mark	MS0100	13,10,29B,43,64B
Scarbrough, Russell	NY3350	46,29B
Scherer, Paul	IL1520	29B,66A
Schulz, Mark Alan	OH1350	34D,35G,35D,62C,29B
Shaman, Sila	OR0700	29B
Shanefield, Andrew	PA3200	47,29A,29B
Sifford, Jason	IA1550	66B,66D,66,29B,66A
Simmons, James	TN1100	63A,47,46,29A,29B
Smith, Joey	AB0210	29B,29C,47
Smith, Stuart	MA2030	13,29B,35C
Sole, Meryl	NY0050	29A,29B
Sunderland, Paul	IL1050	29B,31A,43,70
Swann, William E.	TN1000	47,13,60B,29B,10D
Tabor, Jerry N.	MD0800	13,10,29B,47,11
Talaga, Steve	MI1050	66A,29A,29B,29C,10
Taylor, Keith A.	AL1160	66A,29B,46
Taylor, Tom	CO0200	70,29B,46,47
Valerio, John	SC0900	29B,53,66A,10
Waller, Jim	TX3410	35G,10C,29B,47,35A
Walsh, Allan	AG0150	64E,47,46,29A,29B
Washington, Phil	WV0700	11,29B,70
Washington, Salim	NY0500	47,46,29,29B
Watson, Robert M.	MO1810	29A,29B,29C,47,64E
White, Arthur	MO1800	47,64C,29B
White, Chris	IL2050	66A,13F,29A,29B,29C
Widner, James	MO1830	46,29B,29C,47
Wilkinson, Michael	FL1800	63C,47,29B
Wilson, James Dale	CT0100	14,20C,12A,12E,29B
Wright, Trey	GA1150	70,47,29A,29B,14C
Z, Rachel	NY2660	13B,29B,66A

Analysis of Jazz

Brown, John V.	NC0600	62D,47,29A,29B,29C
Campbell, Jeff	NY1100	29A,29B,29C,62D,47
Dana, Christy L.	CA5000	13A,13C,29B,47,29C
Danko, Harold	NY1100	29A,29B,29C,66A,47
Dobbins, William	NY1100	29B,29C,10A,10F,46
Dorian, Patrick	PA1100	10C,13B,29A,29C,29E
Hart, Billy W.	NJ0800	65,29C
Helzer, Richard A.	CA4100	29B,29C,66A,47,53
Jenkins, Clay	NY1100	29B,29C,63A,47
Karlsson, Stefan	TX3420	29B,29C,47,66A
Merrill, Paul	NY0900	46,47,29B,29C,63A
Mossblad, Gunnar	OH2300	64E,46,47,29B,29C
Moulton, William	VT0300	13A,29C,33,34B,35A
O'Sullivan, Laila K.	TN1680	13,13C,29C
Patton, Jeb	NY1275	10,13B,29B,29C,66A
Smith, Joey	AB0210	29B,29C,47
Talaga, Steve	MI1050	66A,29A,29B,29C,10
Walkington, Alec	AI0150	29,29C,62D
Wason, Robert W.	NY1100	13B,13D,13F,13J,29C
Watson, Robert M.	MO1810	29A,29B,29C,47,64E
Wesolowski, Brian	GA2100	32E,32G,29C
White, Chris	IL2050	66A,13F,29A,29B,29C
Widner, James	MO1830	46,29B,29C,47
Wilcox, Mark	TX1650	13C,63A,49,29E,29C
Zbikowski, Lawrence	IL3250	13,12A,13J,29C

Sociology of Jazz

Bailey, Candace L.	NC1600	12,29D,15,11,12A
Berger, Harris M.	TX2900	14,12B,29D,20G
Burgett, Paul	NY4350	20G,11,29A,29D
Jackson, Travis A.	IL3250	29,20,29D,29E,14
Kernodle, Tammy L.	OH1450	11,12,29A,29D
Patterson, Ann E.	CA2650	29A,29D,47

Jazz Critical Theory

Dessen, Michael J.	CA5020	10,12D,29E
Dorian, Patrick	PA1100	10C,13B,29A,29C,29E
Hughes, Robert L.	MO1250	12A,29,13,29A,29E
Jackson, Travis A.	IL3250	29,20,29D,29E,14
Lewis, George E.	NY0750	10A,10B,12E,29E,34H
Norgaard, Martin	GA1050	32E,32F,62A,29E,32
Pennington, Stephen	MA1900	12D,29A,29E,15,12
Wilcox, Mark	TX1650	13C,63A,49,29E,29C

Music in Religious Life (All Areas)

Allen, Matthew H.	MA2150	14C,20E,20H,31,14
Avery, Elizabeth	OK1350	61,31
Barrett, Wayne	TX2250	61,31
Barz, Gregory F.	TN1850	12,14,20,31,29A
Bianchi, Eric	NY1300	11,12A,12G,13J,31
Bogdan, Thomas	VT0050	36,61,31,40
Boozer, John E.	NC2350	60,20,36,31,61
Borwick, Susan Harden	NC2500	13,12,31,10,15
Brunson, Tomas	SC0600	31,61
Burkett, Phil L.	IN0700	31
Butler, H. Joseph	TX3000	66G,12,31
Cain, Michael D.	MA1400	29,66A,34,31,20
Campbell, Susan	UT0350	11,31
Castilla, Willenham	MS0350	36,31,32D,61
Caston, Ben	GA0400	44,61,31
Clemmons, Francois	VT0350	31
Davis, Ron A.	SC1000	13B,13C,31,66G,44
Durbin, Karen	PA2300	31,44
Ellis, Laura	FL1850	66G,69,66H,31
Ellison, Paul	CA4200	12,31,55
Feller, David E.	UT0350	11,12A,48,64,31
Gardner, James E.	UT0250	62A,12,31,31A
Geisler, Herbert G.	CA1425	14,32,44,13,31
Godwin, Nannette Minor	NC2350	31,66A,66G,32B
Gonzalez, Ramon	TX2260	31
Harnish, David D.	CA5200	14,20,31,41
Hendricks, Allen	SC0275	31,11
Holder, Angela	TN0250	61,36,31,11

Name	Code	Areas
Hudgens, Helen	IL2100	13,31,12A
Johnson, Ben S.	NC2350	61,12A,31
Johnson, Calvert	GA0050	66G,15,31,66H,12A
Kendrick, Robert L.	IL3250	11,31,12,14
Kidula, Jean	GA2100	14,20,11,31,12
Koskoff, Ellen	NY1100	14,15,20G,20D,31
Kotowich, Bruce J. G.	IA0940	61,36,31
Leffert, Kristine Lund	SD0200	66,31
Magnuson, John	TN0930	31
Magyar, Paul R.	TN0930	12,31
Manley, Douglas H.	TN1550	12,66,31,66G,12C
Marissen, Michael	PA3200	11,12A,31
Martinez, Taione	NJ1350	31,36
Matrone, Tom	MO0400	31
McBride, Michael S.	IL2100	10,34,13,31,12A
McMullen, Dianne M.	NY4310	13,12,66,31
Moore, Kevin	AL0890	11,31
Neely-Chandler, Thomasina	GA1450	31,66D
Noone, Michael J.	MA0330	11,12,31
Petrovic, Ankica	CA5031	20F,14A,31
Pfautz, John S.	IL0100	39,61,31
Polley, David	TX2650	31,66G
Polman, Bert	MI0350	31,11,20
Rasmussen, Anne K.	VA0250	14,20G,31,41,12C
Richstone, Lorne S.	OK1350	61,31
Roberts, Wesley	KY0400	12,14,31,66
Rose, Michael	TN1850	13,10,12A,11,31
Sanchez, Pete	AL1195	31,43
Scanlon, Andrew	NC0650	66G,31
Schenkel, Steve	MO1950	12A,31,45,29,35
Shelton, Tom	NJ1350	31,32,36,60A
Swanson, Barry	ID0150	31,36,40
Thurmond, Gloria J.	NJ1160	61,31
Turnquist-Steed, Melody	KS0150	11,13C,31,44,66G
Walrath, Brian	MI2000	11,12A,65,31,34
White, Kayla	AR0400	31,40,61
Yardley, Anne B.	NJ0300	12,14,31,55
Zambito, Pete I.	MO0600	65,31
Zec, John	NJ0550	12A,31,66G,13,11

Music in Christianity

Name	Code	Areas
Aamodt-Nelson, Norma	WA0980	31A
Abelson, Robert	NY1450	31A
Albrecht, Timothy	GA0750	11,12A,66G,31A
Alcorn, Allison A.	IL3150	10E,11,12A,20,31A
Allen, Lisa M.	GA1100	20G,32,36,31A
Anderson, Lyle J.	OH0450	60A,36,31A
Andrews, Dwight D.	GA0750	13,14,31A,29
Ashton, J. Bruce	TN1350	10A,31A,66A,10F,66C
Askew, Jeff	CA0350	31A,70
Azzati, Eduardo	PA2450	61,31A
Bahr, Jason	FL0680	10,13,31A,13C,13B
Bailey, Brandon	SC0050	31A
Bain, Clare	IN1100	36,31A
Barland, Charles J.	IA1450	13,11,31A,66A,36
Barr, John	VA0100	13,10,66,31A
Bates, William H.	SC1110	12A,66G,31A
Bauchspies, Cindy	MD0900	31A,36
Bauer, Michael J.	KS1350	36,66G,66H,31A
Bedsole, Betty	TN1660	61,31A,32
Behnke, John A.	WI0300	10,44,66G,31A
Bell, Joby	NC0050	66G,66H,36,31A
Bell, Peter J.	MA2030	10,13,31A,34
Berry, Paul	NY3350	31A
Billy, Sandra S.	VA1830	31A
Bilotta, Lee	PA3560	60,32B,37,63,31A
Black, Karen	IA1800	13C,31A,36,66G
Bloechl, Olivia A.	CA5032	12,12A,12D,20G,31A
Board, Ryan A.	CA3600	11,32C,36,31A,60A
Bolton, Thomas W.	KY1200	61,31A,36,12A
Booth, John D.	MO0500	12,44,61,31A,70
Boquiren, Sidney M.	NY0050	10A,13A,20D,31A,10F
Borror, Gordon L.	OR1210	31A
Boyer, D. Royce	AL1160	11,12A,36,61,31A
Bradley, Randall	TX0300	36,31A
Branch, Stephen F.	CA3975	12A,61,31A,36,40
Brewton, Greg	KY1200	31A
Briare, Maureen K.	OR1100	31A
Bridges, David	TN0100	12F,31A
Brister Rachwal, Wanda	FL0850	61,31A
Brock, John	TN1710	66G,66H,31A
Brody, Ben	WA1350	31A,60,11,12A
Brown, Aaron	MN1625	36,31A
Brown, Bruce C.	NY1700	60,11,36,61,31A
Brown, Samuel B.	AL0500	39,61,31A
Brubaker, Debra	IN0550	39,61,36,31A,20
Brugh, Lorraine S.	IN1750	36,31A,66G
Brunner, Roy	MA0950	13,10,66G,66H,31A
Bunbury, Richard R.	MA0400	12,66G,32H,31A,32
Burns, Jim	TN0850	11,61,31A
Busarow, Donald A.	OH2450	13A,10A,66G,31A
Busch, Gregg	MO0200	11,13A,31A,36,61
Bush, Douglas E.	UT0050	12,55,66G,67,31A
Byrdwell, Phyllis	WA1050	31A,47
Cademcian, Gerard	IN0005	66A,31A,31B,67F,13
Callahan, Anne	KS1375	31A
Campbell, Jayne E.	CA1960	36,55,61,31A
Campbell, Stanford	OR0600	36,61,31A,60A
Carlton, Kathleen	OK0410	13,11,12A,61,31A
Caron, Sylvain	AI0200	13,31A,12
Carroll, Roy W.	IA0940	66,13,12,11,31A
Carswell, William	SC0450	31A,61,32,36,40
Causey, Wayne	TN0100	31A
Cerabona, Linda M.	IL3400	11,13A,20A,31A,32D
Chae, Hyung Sek	TX3650	36,31A,44,60,32D
Chambers, Robert B.	TN0650	60,61,31A,36,44
Chang, Donathan	TX2570	31A,31B,61,60A,36
Charter, Ian R.	AA0010	12A,13A,31A,32E,60
Cherrington Beggs, Sally	SC0900	13D,66,31A,12A
Christiansen, David	IL0850	66G,31A
Christie, James David	MA0700	66G,66H,31A
Cinquegrani, David	CT0350	31A,36,41,12
Clark, Alice V.	LA0300	12A,11,31A,12
Coen, Anne	OH1350	11,31A
Cole, Malcolm S.	CA5032	11,12A,12,66G,31A
Coleman, Fred	SC0200	32,36,31A
Colleen, Jeffrey	IL1550	13,10,36,66A,31A
Collins, David	MN1250	31,61,36,46
Collins, Leo W.	MA2200	12B,31A,20G
Combs, Barry	SC0950	60,36,61,31A
Concordia, Stephen	PA2950	36,31A
Congdon, Judy A.	NY1700	13,66G,66H,31A
Constantine, Cyprian G.	PA2950	66G,31A
Coogan, W. Jack	CA1050	31A
Cook, Don	UT0050	66G,69,31A
Cook, Lisa M.	CO0550	11,12A,20G,31A,14

Name	Code	Areas
Cook, Warren	SC0200	13,60,36,31A,40
Cooksey, Steven	VA1350	12A,36,66G,31A
Cornelius-Bates, Benjamin	PA1050	31A,66G
Coulthard, Anita	VA0350	66G,32A,32B,31A
Council, Thomas	GA2000	31A,61,36,60,40
Cross, Alan E.	TN0150	11,12A,61,31A
Cross, Virginia A.	OR0175	31A,12A,66D,13A,66B
Cunha, Alcingstone DeOliveira	KY0400	31A,36
Davis, Jolene	GA2100	13,66G,31A
Davis, Mindy	ID0060	31A
Davis, Scott	TX3510	31A,66G
Day, Mary	IA0100	41,61,67,31A,39
Deakins, Mark	KY0650	13A,60,36,31A,40
DeGarmeaux, Mark	MN0200	31A
Delcamp, Robert	TN1800	13,12A,36,66G,31A
DeSanto, William	PA3560	36,66,31A,66C
Dettinger, Mary Joyce	OH1330	32A,32B,66A,31A
DiCello, Anthony J.	OH0150	36,61,66,31A,34
Ditto, John A.	MO1810	66G,31A
Dixon, Joan DeVee	MD0350	66,31A,35
Doukhan, Lilianne	MI0250	12,12,14,31A,12C
Duggan, Sean B.	LA0600	11,12A,36,66,31A
Eby, John D.	AI0050	11,12A,12C,20G,31A
Edison, Andrew	NY1450	31A
Eggert, John	MN0610	10,13,31A,66G
Egler, Steven	MI0400	12A,66H,66G,31A
Eifert, Jonathan	TX0400	36,60,66G,31A
Ergo, Jack	IA0600	20,31A,38,66A
Erickson, Gary	IL1050	34B,10A,13G,31A,35D
Etter, David D.	KY1425	36,61,31A,60
Etter, Paul J.	NC0850	60A,36,44,60,31A
Faber, Trudy	OH2450	12A,44,66G,66H,31A
Faszer, Ted	SD0450	32,36,31A,34
Ferguson, John	MN1450	36,66G,31A
Ferrington, Darryl	LA0400	13A,36,32,31A
Finch, Scott	AJ0030	60A,31A,12A,13A,11
Finley, William	CT0300	61,31A
Fix, Lou Carol	PA2450	66G,69,31A,67B
Fleming, Kyle J.	CO0150	36,11,31A,60A
Floeter, Valerie	WI1155	66G,31A
Foster, Rodney W.	NY4100	11,12,31A,34A,34F
Foy, Regina	PA1550	13B,10F,31A
Fragomeni, Richard	IN1350	31A
Frost, Richard P.	PA1150	31A
Fuller, Stephen	MN1300	60A,11,20D,31A
Gable, Frederick K.	CA5040	12,12,31A
Gabrielse, Kenneth J.	LA0400	60,36,31A,12A
Ganus, Clifton L.	AR0250	12A,31A,36,60A
Garcia, William B.	TN0800	60,11,36,61,31A
Gardner, Charles	IN1100	31A
Gardner, James E.	UT0250	62A,12,31,31A
Gitz, Raymond	LA0560	12A,66A,31A
Glass, Judith	TN1350	13,66G,66H,31A
Glick, Robert P.	SC0700	66G,31A,11
Gokelman, William	TX3410	60,36,66A,66C,31A
Golightly, John Wesley	KY0650	12A,13A,66,34,13D
Goold, William C.	KY0150	60,12A,36,61,31A
Gorham, Fr. Daniel	IN0005	31A,33,61
Graham, Brenda J.	IN1250	13A,32,37,62,31A
Griffin, T. Joel	MO0400	29,31A,47,64E
Grimes, Calvin B.	GA1450	13,10,12,20G,31A
Grover, Elaine	MI1300	13A,13,66A,66G,31A
Guthrie, J. Randall	OK0850	31A,60A,36,11,66G
Guy, Todd	IN1025	36,31A,61,60A,11
Hagel, Clint	AA0020	31A,36,61,66C
Hall, Jonathan B.	NY2750	12A,13,31A,36,66G
Haller, William P.	WV0750	13,12A,66G,31A
Hancock, Judith E.	TX3510	66G,31A
Hansford, Conchita	OK0650	32A,32B,61,66A,31A
Harlen, Benjamin	LA0400	10A,13A,13B,13C,13D
Harrell, Paula D.	NC1600	32,66A,66G,66D,31A
Harrington, William	CA3520	32,38,41,63B,31A
Harris, David	PA0150	36,61,31A,40,32D
Harrison, Joanne K.	NC1150	13,66G,31A,66A
Hart, Kenneth W.	TX2400	31A
Hedges, Don P.	IL3150	13,31A,11,39
Heiman, Lawrence F.	IN1350	12A,31A
Held, Wilbur C.	OH1850	66G,31A
Heller, David	TX3350	13,66G,66H,31A
Herl, Joseph	NE0150	12,13,31A
Hetrick, Esther A.	MI0910	61,60,31A,36,32B
Hewell, John	AR0500	31A,44,11
Hicks, Martha K.	MO1550	31A,11,60,13C,32B
Higdon, James M.	KS1350	66G,66H,31A
Higgins, Lynn	OR1150	31A
Highberger, Edgar B.	PA3000	12A,66G,31A
Hijleh, Mark D.	NY1700	10,13,31A
Hinson, G. Maurice	KY1200	12A,66A,31A,66B,66C
Hinson, Lee	OK0650	31A,11,36
Hobson, David	LA0050	36,11,31A,12A
Holsinger, Bruce	VA1550	12,31A
Hong, Xiangtang	IL1850	60A,31A,36,44,11
Hood, Heather	MN1280	31A
Hoskins, Richard	WI0250	66G,31A
Hughes, Patricia	IN1350	31A
Hull, Kenneth	AG0470	11,12A,31A,36
Intintoli, Helen	CA4650	36,61,66A,31A,54
Isensee, Paul R.	PA2800	31A,40
Jackson, Dan	CA3640	31A,36
Janco, Martin	IN1350	31A
Jang, Jae Hyeok	IL1850	13,10,31A
Janzen, Wesley	AB0090	60,12A,36,31A
Jeffery, Peter	NJ0900	11,12,12,31A
Jenkins, David	MN1625	66G,31A
Jewett, Dennis A.	KY0800	61,31A,32,36
Jocoy, Stacey	TX3200	12G,12E,12C,31A,11
Johnson, Herbert	MN1250	12A,13,31A,66B,66C
Johnson, Sharon L.	NY1700	66C,66A,66D,31A
Johnston, Gregory	AG0450	11,12A,12,31A
Jones, Dani S.	AL0650	61,39,31A,60
Jones, Marvin	TN1600	31A
Jones, Meredith	TX2570	12A,31A,60A,61
Jordan, John M.	IN1600	12A,11,31A,20
Jordan, Paul	IN0005	10A,61,13,20F,31A
Jordening, Jon	CA1425	31A
Josselyn-Cranson, Heather	IA1200	66A,31A,10,20
Judge, Joseph	NC1900	36,61,31A,40
Junker, Tercio	IN0300	60A,36,31A,32D,10E
Kane, Janet	PA3650	31A,61
Kasling, Kim R.	MN0350	12A,66G,31A,66A
Kauffman, Larry D.	PA0150	12A,36,66A,31A
Keller, Merry	MO1950	31A,32D,13
Kemper, Margaret M.	IL2250	66G,31A
Kempster, James	CA3400	11,12A,36,61,31A
Kennedy, T. Frank	MA0330	11,12,31A,20H
Kilgore Wood, Janice	MD1050	13C,66A,36,66B,31A
Killion, Jamie	CA0450	61,32,31A
King, Sandi	CA3520	36,61,31A

Name	Code	Areas
Kloppers, Jacobus	AA0035	11,12A,12,66G,31A
Kohrs, Jonathan A.	IL0730	10,36,11,31A,34
Koop, Ruth B.	AJ0030	13A,31A,35A,35E,61
Koponen, Glenn	NY2900	60,37,41,63A,31A
Koriath, Kirby L.	IN0150	66G,66H,31A,34
Kosche, Kenneth	WI0300	13,60,10,36,31A
Labounsky, Ann	PA1050	66G,31A
Landes, Daniel	TN0100	13A,13,66A,66D,31A
Landgrave, Phillip	KY1200	10,35C,31A
Laster, James	VA1350	60,36,66G,31A
Laubach, Mark	PA2200	31A,66G,66H
Lefkowitz, David	NY1450	31A
Lefter, Nancy C.	SC0300	36,66G,31A
Lewis, Huw R.	MI1050	13D,66G,66H,31A
Liesch, Barry	CA0350	11,34,31A
Ligate, Linda	MO0400	12A,66A,31A
Liles, B. David	OH1600	61,31A,39
Lock, William R.	CA0350	60,36,61,31A
Locklair, Dan	NC2500	13,10,11,31A,66G
Lofthouse, Charity	NY1550	13,34B,34F,15,31A
Logan, Kenneth	MI0250	66G,34,10,10F,31A
Longhin, Daniel	MI0750	31A
Louis, Kenneth	DC0350	36,61,31A
Lowe, Donald R.	GA2100	32,31A
Lucas, Adonna	NC1950	13,36,64A,66,31A
Luckner, Brian	WI1100	66G,31A
Luther, David	TN0200	60,36,61,31A,41
Luther, Sigrid	TN0200	13,66A,66B,31A,66C
Lynerd, Betty Ann	IL1850	31A,44,36
Magee, Robert G.	AR0950	12A,60,36,61,31A
Mahrt, William P.	CA4900	12A,55,67E,31A
Malfatti, Dennis	IN1600	36,40,31A
Marchand, Rebecca G.	MA1175	12A,31A,12E
Markuson, Stephen	NY1400	14C,31A
Martin, Jared	TN0580	70,13A,31A
Martinez, David	RI0150	66G,31A
Marzolf, Dennis	MN0200	60,36,31A,61,54
Matejka, Merle	AJ0030	10,12A,31A,13,29
Mathews, Christopher W.	TN1660	36,13H,31A,60A,13C
Mathieson, Carol Fisher	MO0300	12A,39,61,31A,11
Mathis, Eric L.	AL0800	31A
Matzke, Laura	MN0200	66A,66G,66C,68,31A
Mauldin, Walter	TN0850	60A,31A
Maxwell, Monte	MD0900	66G,38,36,31A,51
McCardle, Dennis	KY0150	31A
McCarthy, Kerry R.	NC0600	12A,12C,31A,55
McClure, Ryan	NE0250	31A
McDaniel, Carol	CA1425	32B,13C,31A,66G
McGrew, David	PA0150	10,13,66,31A,11
McIntosh, John S.	AG0500	13,66G,66C,31A
McKenna, Fr. Edward	IN0005	10,62A,16,31A,11
McKissick, Marvin L.	CA0250	31A
McLean, Hugh J.	AG0500	12,14A,66G,31A
Measels, Clark	TN0250	11,31A,20
Melton, James L.	CA5355	60,36,31A,32D,35E
Mendelson, Jacob	NY1450	31A
Mennicke, David	MN0610	31A,32,60,61
Meyer, Stephen C.	NY4100	12,12A,12D,31A
Miller, Ronald L.	PA2300	12A,36,67B,31A,20G
Miller, Thomas A.	OR1150	60A,11,36,61,31A
Millican, Jason	TX1250	13A,60,11,36,31A
Mims, Lloyd	FL1450	61,31A,38
Moehlman, Carl B.	IA0900	13,12A,44,66G,31A
Moffett, Brad	TN0850	36,31A,60A
Moldenhauer, Kermit G.	MN1030	13A,36,66G,31A,60A
Moorman-Stahlman, Shelly	PA1900	44,66A,66G,31A,66D
Morrison, Chuck	AZ0400	31A
Morrison, Leah A.	CA5300	31A,13J,12A,12D
Morrow, Phil J.	NC0300	60,36,31A,61
Moxley, Bryant	VA0050	13,66A,60A,31A,36
Moxley, Lisa	VA0050	66A,66D,31A,13A,11
Music, David W.	TX0300	31A
Nafziger, Kenneth J.	VA0300	60,36,31A,38,11
Nelson, David P.	NC2350	31A
Nestor, Leo Cornelius	DC0050	10A,31A,36,40,60A
Norris, Philip E.	MN1280	10F,11,32E,63A,31A
Novick, Martha	NY1450	31A
Nunez, Rachel	OH1350	61,36,31A
Oakley, Paul E.	KY0800	61,31A,36
Olsen, Timothy	NC2205	66G,31A,66H,42,56
O'Neel, Roger	OH0450	10A,31A,13A
Oswalt, Lewis	MS0400	12A,13,31A
Owen, William E.	WA0550	36,60,12A,40,31A
Palmer, David	AG0550	66A,66G,31A,13C,66H
Pantoja, Rique	CA0350	29,31A
Park, Sang Eui	IN0005	10,60,12,13,31A
Parks, Andrew	WA0800	61,31A,12A,36
Parsons, Larry R.	WV0800	36,61,31A
Payn, William A.	PA0350	36,44,66G,66H,31A
Pedde, David	MN1250	66A,10B,14C,31A
Penny, Michael K.	TN1660	39,61,31A
Perkins, Leeman L.	NY0750	11,12,31A,36
Peterson, Gregory M.	IA0950	44,66G,31A
Peterson, John David	TN1680	66G,31A,12A
Pierce, Carrie	TX2930	62C,62D,51,31A,13C
Pilkington, Steve	NJ1350	36,31A
Plamann, Melissa M.	OK0750	66G,31A
Platt, Nathan	KY1200	13,60,61,31A
Plew, Paul T.	CA2810	60,36,61,31A
Porter, Thomas	ND0400	36,13B,10A,32D,31A
Porterfield, Richard R.	NY2750	12,13,31A,55D
Powell, Jason	IN0300	20F,20H,31A,66A,66G
Prochnow, Peter	NE0150	31A,35G
Profitt, Tommee	MI0750	34,31A
Quinlan, Gloria H.	TX1150	32,36,61,66C,31A
Rasmussen, Brenda	WA0550	11,31A,36,13A
Read, Kenneth E.	OH0550	13E,31A,10A,10F,13B
Rediger, JoAnn K.	IN1560	36,31A,60A,11,40
Reed, Allen	TX1100	13,44,66,31A
Reed, Douglas	IN1600	66G,66H,13D,31A
Reed, Joel F.	NC1250	20G,60A,36,61,31A
Reid, Susanne M.	CA5355	11,12A,20,31A
Reiss, Deborah	NY0850	44,40,31A,66C
Rhoads, Mark	MN0250	11,32,31A
Richardson, Paul A.	AL0800	61,31A
Rickard, Jeffrey H.	CA5150	10,60,36,31A
Rigler, Ann Marie	MO2000	66A,66G,31A,12A,12C
Rivard, Gene	MN0625	13,10F,49,63,31A
Rivers, Cynthia	GA1100	66A,66G,66C,31A,36
Roberts, Stanley L.	GA1300	60A,36,31A
Robinson, Kathleen E.	MN1280	31A,11,12A,13C
Robinson, Schuyler	KY1450	13,66G,66H,31A
Rohlig, Harald	AL0450	10,66,31A
Rose, John	CT0500	36,66G,69,31A
Ross, Jared	KS0060	13,60,31A,36,61
Rowell, Michael	GA0700	31A,60A,47,36
Rushton, David	AB0090	13,60,32C,31A
Russell, Carlton T.	MA2150	11,12A,66G,31A

Name	Code	Areas
Sauer-Ferrand, Deborah	CA1860	12A,61,31A,54
Schall, Noah	NY1450	31A
Schell, Mark	KY0100	44,66G,31A
Schiller, Benjie-Ellen	NY1450	31A
Schmidt, Timothy R.	IA1750	13B,31A,66A,66H
Schulz, Russell E.	TX0750	36,66G,31A
Scinta, Frank	NY0400	61,31A,32C,36
Scott, Karla	MD0900	36,31A
Scott, Kraig	WA1100	36,31A,66G,66H,60A
Shadinger, Richard C.	TN0100	12A,55,66A,31A,69
Sharp, Michael D.	LA0400	66A,66B,31A,34,10A
Shasberger, Michael	CA5550	36,31A,38,60,61
Sheeks, Randy	TN0850	66A,31A
Shelt, Christopher A.	MS0100	60A,36,31A,61,40
Sherwin, Ronald G.	MA0150	11,31A,60A,36,32
Shuholm, Dan	OR0175	37,46,31A
Simons, John	TX2600	31A
Singleton, H. Craig	CA1650	36,61,31A
Singley, H. E.	IL1850	66A,66G,11,36,31A
Sisk, Lawrence T.	IL1520	38,12A,36,31A
Skeris, Robert	DC0050	31A,36
Sledge, Larry	FL0800	60,12A,31A,36,13
Smith, Aaron	MD0900	31A,36,54,40
Smith, Kent M.	PA3560	10,11,12A,31A
Snukst, Penny	IN0005	33,13,31A
Song, Tom	TX2600	36,60A,31A
Sovik, Thomas	TX3420	13,31A,14C,13J,34
Sparks, Michael	AL1450	12A,36,66A,31A,34
Spicer, Nan	IN0005	61,60A,66A,66G,31A
Sprow, Margaret	MS0100	31A
Stallsmith, John	AL0260	12A,36,47,66,31A
Stam, Carl L.	KY1200	36,31A
Stansbury, George	TX3415	60,31A,44
Stepniak, Michael	VA1350	12,38,31A,41,32
Stewart, Shirley	LA0720	11,36,61,31A,32
Stolberg, Tom	MO0060	10F,34,31A,32B,60
Suchy-Pilalis, Jessica R.	NY3780	13,62E,13H,13C,31A
Sunderland, Paul	IL1050	29B,31A,43,70
Sutton, John	CA0250	60,31A,36
Swanson, Carl B.	CA0550	66G,31A
Talley, Sue	NY2900	66A,12A,36,31A,31B
Taylor, James	NC1050	41,36,61,31A,11
Taylor, Steven	CO0150	39,61,31A,44,13C
Taylor, Terry D.	AL0800	31A
Tel, Martin	NJ0850	36,66G,31A
Thiedt, Catherine E.	OH0950	13,12A,66A,66G,31A
Thogersen, Chris	IN0550	66A,66G,32B,31A
Thomas, William D.	SC0750	40,61,31A
Thompson, Gregory T.	NC1000	66A,66C,12A,31A
Tilman, Ernest	PA2300	31A
Tompkins, Charles B.	SC0750	13,66G,66H,31A
Toscano, Patricia	SD0300	61,66A,66G,31A
Traupman-Carr, Carol A.	PA2450	13A,13,12A,12,31A
Trentham, Donald R.	TN0650	11,12A,66A,31A,13
Tripold, David	NJ0760	13,12A,32,31A,33
Tuttle, John	AG0450	36,31A
Uitermarkt, Cynthia D.	IL1850	13A,13,66,66A,31A
Vanderford, Brenda M.	WV0700	13A,13,11,66G,31A
Vogel, Bradley D.	KS1300	60,32B,36,61,31A
Walker, Christopher	CA3150	13,10,31A
Wente, Steven F.	IL0730	13,66G,12A,31A
Westermeyer, Paul	MN1450	31A
White, David A.	TX3400	13,10,31A
Whitley, H. Moran	NC0300	32,31A,13
Wilds, Timothy	NC1450	61,31A,36,40
Wilson, Jeffrey S.	IL1050	60,36,61,40,31A
Wimberly, Larry	MS0150	11,13A,31A,34E,46
Wingard, Alan B.	GA1800	31A
Winkler, Amanda Eubanks	NY4100	12,12A,15,31A,31G
Winters, Donald Eugene	MS0850	61,31A,12A,60A
Witvliet, John	MI0350	36,31A
Wojcik, Richard J.	IL3400	11,12A,36,61,31A
Wojnar, William A.	ND0150	12A,66A,66G,31B,31A
Wright, Clell E.	TX0900	31A,36,60
Wright, Jeffrey E.	IN0100	31A,32G
Wylie, Ted	TN0100	61,31A,54,39
Wyrtzen, Donald	TX2600	10A,31A,66A
Yeung, Ian	TX3540	36,60A,40,31A,38
Yoder, Tim	IN1025	31A
Yoon, Sujin	MO1350	36,66G,66H,31A,60A
Young, Shawn David	GA0500	14C,35A,31A,35,11
Zabel, Albert	WV0400	44,66G,31A,10,66C
Zielke, Gregory D.	NE0250	60,32C,36,61,31A
Zimmerman, R. Edward	IL3550	11,66G,66H,31A

Music in Judaism

Name	Code	Areas
Baron, John H.	LA0750	12A,12,20F,20G,31B
Broad-Ginsberg, Elaine	NH0150	13,31B,10A,36
Bruk, Elfrida	IN0005	66A,13,31B,66C,66H
Cademcian, Gerard	IN0005	66A,31A,31B,67F,13
Chang, Donathan	TX2570	31A,31B,61,60A,36
Cowin, Jasmin Bey	NY4200	11,62E,12A,31B
Davidson, Charles	NY1860	31B
Fine, Perry	NY1860	31B
Fuerstman, Marlena	NY1860	31B,61,20F
Gluck, Robert J.	NY3700	10B,34D,31B,34,45
Jacobson, Joshua R.	MA1450	11,12A,36,13,31B
Mason, Alan	FL0050	11,12,31B,66A,66C
Miller, Rebecca S.	MA1000	14,13A,20F,31B,35H
Mosteller, Sandra M.	TX3650	64,32E,48,20,31B
Rosenblum, Henry	NY1860	31B,61,20F,13C
Rubin, Joel E.	VA1550	14A,14C,64C,41,31B
Summit, Jeffrey	MA1900	20F,31B,14A,14D
Tadmor, Tali	CA0510	66A,66C,31B
Talley, Sue	NY2900	66A,12A,36,31A,31B
Wojnar, William A.	ND0150	12A,66A,66G,31B,31A

Music in Islam

Name	Code	Areas
Frishkopf, Michael	AA0100	20A,20F,14,31C
Jankowsky, Rich	MA1900	14,31C,20B,14F
Kabir, Chaitanya Mahmud	CO0560	20A,31C,20B,20C,20E
Rauch, Benjamin	CT0650	61,31C

Music in Buddhism

Name	Code	Areas
Tewari, Laxmi	CA4700	14,13A,61,10E,31D
Wong, Deborah	CA5040	14,20,20D,20G,31D

Music in Hinduism

Name	Code	Areas
Morris, Robert D.	NY1100	10,12,13,20E,31E
Shende, Vineet	ME0200	10,13,20C,20E,31E

Music in African and African-Derived Religions

Alorwoyie, Gideon F.	TX3420	20,65,31F,50,52
Berliner, Paul F.	NC0600	20A,14A,14F,14B,31F
Birenbaum Quintero, Michael	ME0200	14,20H,31F
Brandon, Mack	NJ0950	10B,31F,36,41
Brown, Andiel	OR1050	36,31F
Burnett, Lawrence E.	MN0300	36,40,31F,61,13A
Graham, Sandra J.	MA0255	14,20A,20G,31F
High, Ronald	SC0150	11,12,31F,61,66
Kafumbe, Damascus	VT0350	14A,14C,10E,20,31F
Malley, Nicole	IL1350	12A,20,47,29,31F
Moffett, C. Mondre	NC1550	63A,10F,29A,47,31F
Moore, Robin D.	TX3510	14,31F,14C,14F,20H
Muller, Carol A.	PA3350	14,20A,20D,31F,31G
Okigbo, Austin	CO0800	31F,20,14
Sellers, Crystal Y.	OH0250	61,11,12,31F
Sledge, Sylstea	DC0010	31F,60A
Vercelli, Michael B.	WV0750	20,14,31F,41,42

Music of Diverse Religious and Ritual Systems

Bakriges, Christopher	MA1550	29,14D,12B,20,31G
Hahn, Tomie	NY3300	14,15,20,31G,34
King, Joan	PA0650	62A,62B,62C,62D,31G
McHugh, Ernestine	NY1100	31G
Metcalf, Joanne	WI0350	10A,13D,13F,12A,31G
Miller, Kiri	RI0050	14A,14C,14D,20G,31G
Muller, Carol A.	PA3350	14,20A,20D,31F,31G
Stasack, Jennifer	NC0550	10,20,31G
Winkler, Amanda Eubanks	NY4100	12,12A,15,31A,31G

Music Education (All Areas)

Aamodt, Rucci R.	HI0150	32,11,66A,66D
Aamodt, Rucci R.	HI0210	32,66
Abeles, Harold F.	NY4200	32,13K,13L,12F
Abrahams, Ellen M.	NJ1350	32
Abrahams, Frank E.	NJ1350	32
Abramo, Joseph M.	CT0600	32,64E
Abril, Carlos	FL1900	32,12E
Adams, Bobby L.	FL1750	32,37,60B
Addo, Akosua O.	MN1623	32
Aguilar, Carla E.	CO0550	32
Ahner, Sally R.	TN1850	32
Akinskas, Joseph	NJ1100	32,63
Alexander, Cory T.	TX3527	36,32D,61,32,40
Alexander, Lois L.	MI2120	63D,49,12,32
Alig, Kelley	OK0300	32,61,11
Allen, Lisa M.	GA1100	20G,32,36,31A
Allen, Nancy	WI1100	60A,32,36,54
Allen, Sarah	TX2400	32E,37,32,60B,32B
Alley, Amy	TN1850	32
Allison, Elizabeth Catherine	MA0260	32
Allsbrook, Nancy Boone	TN1100	32
Allsup, Randall Everett	NY4200	43,32,13,12A,12B
Almquist, Bradley L.	KY0950	60,32,36,13C
Altman, Timothy	NC2435	60,32,37,63A,63B
Ambush, June	MA1560	32
Amundson, Bret	MN0450	32,36,60A
Anderson, James N.	GA0200	12A,32,37
Andrews, Adrianna	IL3500	32
Andrews, Jane E.	IA1800	32,36
Anthony, Robert	CA0350	32
Applegate, Janice	IN1300	32
Applonie, Jean	UT0050	32
Ardrey, Cathleen	PA2350	32,36,61,66A
Arian, Merri	NY1450	60,32,70
Arnold, Ellen	PA1450	32,37
Asmus, Edward P.	FL1900	32,12F
Atherton, Susan	IN0150	32
Aucoin, Amy	KY0950	32,36,60A,13C
Ausmann, Stephen	OH2600	32,36
Austin, James R.	CO0800	32
Austin, Stephanie	CA1450	36,61,66,40,32
Austin, Terry	VA1600	32,37,60
Austin, Valerie A.	NC2435	32,55
Avery, Susan J.	NY1800	32
Axelson, Shelley	NJ0800	32,64
Baccus, Jessica	MD0150	32
Baker, Katherine Ramos	CA0835	32,36
Baker, Kevin L.	MO0300	36,32D,61,60,32
Baker, Vicki	TX3300	32
Baker, Wilbur	NJ0825	11,32
Ball, Wesley A.	CT0800	32,32B,13C
Ballard, Dennis L.	IN0800	32
Ballereau, Laurence	NY1600	32,37,64
Balog, George	NJ0175	37,32
Barasch, Shirley R.	PA2900	61,32,54,10,35E
Barley, Marsha	VA1350	32
Barnes, Gail V.	SC1110	32,62B
Barrett, Janet R.	IL2250	32
Barron, Fran	MD0060	32
Bartel, Lee R.	AG0450	32
Bartolome, Sarah J.	LA0200	32
Basilio, Edwin L.	CA5200	60A,32
Bates, James	OH2050	12A,20,32,38,62D
Batey, Angela L.	TN1710	32,36
Battipaglia, Diana M.	NY0635	11,32,36,66A,38
Bauer, William I.	FL1850	32,34
Baxter, Marsha L.	NY3780	32,20H
Bayen, Diane	NY2450	13C,61,36,60,32
Bazan, Dale	OH1100	32
Beason, Christine F.	TX3250	37,48,63B,32,10F
Bechen, Gene	IA1300	37,32E,60,32
Becker, Melissa J.	PA2050	10E,12,32,62
Bedsole, Betty	TN1660	61,31A,32
Beery, John	MI1650	32,37,47,63,11
Bell, Cindy L.	NY1600	32,11,36
Bell, John	IL2910	32,32C,37,60B
Bell, John	MO0850	32,38,63B
Benedict, Cathy L.	FL0700	32
Benham, Stephen J.	PA1050	32
Benner, Charles	OH1850	32
Bennett, Peggy D.	OH1700	32
Benton, Lisa	TN0580	32,61
Berg, Margaret Haefner	CO0800	32
Bergee, Martin	KS1350	32
Berger, Linda	MN1450	32
Bergstrom, Samuel	MN0040	20,32,37,41,47
Bernard, Rhoda J.	MA0350	32
Bernhard, H. Christian	NY3725	32E,32
Berz, William L.	NJ1130	32,37
Bess, David	WV0750	32
Bicigo, James Michael	AK0150	12A,32,37,41,63D
Bletstein, Bev R.	OH1860	11,32,61,70
Bletstein, Beverly	OH1850	32,36

Blose, Dennis	NJ0175	37,32
Bly, Carl	VA1350	32
Boehm, Patricia A.	OH2290	61,32,11
Bognar, Anna Belle	OH0300	32
Bolin, Daniel	IN0250	32,11
Bolton, Beth M.	PA3250	32
Bolton, Bryan	KY0050	11,13A,32,36,61
Bolton, Chuck	OR1150	32,37,49,63D
Bond, Judith	WI0850	32,32A,32B,32C
Bondurant-Koehler, Shela	IL1200	32
Boone, Geraldine T.	VA0950	10A,32,11,13D,13F
Borchert, Laroy	NM0310	13,32,64C
Bose, Judith	MA1175	32
Bott, Darryl J.	NJ1130	32,37
Bowers, Judy	FL0850	32,36
Bowman, Judith A.	PA1050	32,34
Bowman, Wayne	NY2750	32,12C,12F,14
Boyer, Charles G.	CO0050	32,11,32E,37
Boyer, Rene	OH2200	32
Boyle, Audrey	CA0650	64A,32
Bradley, Deborah	AG0450	32,66
Brakel, Timothy D.	OH2300	32E,32,64E,13,60
Branscome, Eric	TN0050	32,33
Brasch, Peter	NY3725	32
Brasco, Richard	GA0250	32
Brashier, Joe H.	GA2150	32,37,60
Braun, Elizabeth	OH1900	38,32
Braunstein, Riki	NY0500	32
Breidenbach, Ruth	NY2450	32
Bresler, Liora	IL3300	32
Brewer, Jane	IN1650	32
Brickey, James	UT0150	63D,32
Bridges, Madeline	TN0100	32,36
Brimmer, Timothy	IN0250	60,32,36,34
Brinkman, David J.	WY0200	32
Brinson, Barbara Ann	NY3725	32,36
Brittin, Ruth	CA5350	32
Brizzi, Paul D.	IA0550	32
Broeker, Jay	MN1625	32
Bromley, Tanya M.	KY0900	32
Broomhead, Paul	UT0050	32,36
Brophy, Timothy S.	FL1850	32
Brown, Charles P.	IL0730	36,60,32
Brown, Leland W.	RI0250	32
Brown, Linda	CA5300	32
Brown, Melba	AL1195	32,61,11,39
Brown, Richard L.	WV0600	32,63D,72,11
Brown, Susan	CA0400	41,51,62,32
Brown, T. Dennis	MA2000	32,20G,29A,34
Brownell, John	AG0450	32,65
Browning, Birch P.	OH0650	32,41
Browning, Doug	MS0550	32,40,42,47,60
Brumfield, Susan Hendrix	TX3200	32
Bruno, Zachary	CA4625	11,32,37,47,41
Buck, Michael W.	MN0050	32
Buckmaster, Matthew	NC0750	63D,29,63C,49,32
Budlong, Trisha	PA2450	39,61,32
Bugg, Sue	TX3535	64A,32
Bugos, Jennifer A.	FL2000	32
Bull, Tina	OR0700	32,36
Bunbury, Richard R.	MA0400	12,66G,32H,31A,32
Bundra, Judy Iwata	IL0750	32
Buonviri, Nathan	PA3250	32
Burchill, Kent S.	NY3780	32
Burdick, Paul	MA1400	13G,13,34,32
Burke, Karen M.	AG0650	61,60A,36,32
Burkett, Eugenie I.	NV0050	32,32E,32G
Burns, Carolyn	ND0100	32,20,14,55B
Burns, Pamela T.	AL0050	11,32,61
Burnsed, C. Vernon	VA1700	32
Burrack, Frederick	KS0650	32,12B,11,32,37
Burton, J. Bryan	PA3600	20G,20D,32
Burwasser, Daniel	NY0625	32
Busch, Stephen E.	CO0250	32,44,66D
Bush, Jeffrey E.	VA0600	32
Butke, Marla A.	OH0100	32,11,66D,36,60A
Butler, Abigail	MI2200	32
Butler, Benjamin	TX3150	32,64
Byo, James L.	LA0200	32
Byrnes, Jason	CO0950	63D,32
Cado, Michael	AG0650	10A,32,47,70
Callahan, Gary L.	NC1150	48,64,32,46
Calvo, Francisco	CA1900	36,32,12
Camilli, Theresa Chardos	IA1600	66B,32
Camp, Marjorie	CO0550	32
Camp, Philip	TX1550	36,61,13,32,40
Campbell, John W.	KY0610	60,11,32,61,36
Cape, Janet	NJ1350	32,34
Cardany, Audrey	MD0650	32
Cardany, Audrey	RI0300	32
Carlow, Regina	NM0450	32
Carlson, Mary C.	NY2650	32C,32
Carlton, Elizabeth	NC0350	32,66A,66B,66D
Carnochan, Robert M.	TX3510	37,48,32
Carroll, Gwendolyn J.	NY2105	32
Carswell, William	SC0450	31A,61,32,36,40
Carucci, Christine	KY0550	64D,32
Casey, Donald E.	IL0750	32
Casey, J. Warren	AR0250	10F,11,32,47,64C
Casey-Nelson, Colleen Mary	CT0050	32
Cassara, James	NY2105	32
Cavanar, Mary	NH0300	32
Cee, Vincent	AK0150	32,29,38,34B,11
Centeno Martell, Ingrid	PR0100	13,66A,66C,32
Cervantes, Ernest	CA0650	65,32
Chadwick, Sheelagh	AC0050	32,32C
Chafin, Gerald	KY0860	60A,11,32,36,44
Chandler, Kyle	AR0110	32,36,47,32D,32G
Chang, Joanne	NY3250	11,13,32,42,66
Chapman, Christopher	OR0700	32,37,46,63A,60B
Chen-Hafteck, Lily	NJ0700	32
Chesebrough, James C.	NH0150	37,60,32,63D,32E
Chesky, Kris	TX3420	32
Cheyne, Donald R.	GA1700	32,72
Chivington, Amy	OH2050	32,36
Ciabattari, William S.	PA2100	13,63D,32,37,47
Ciepluch, Gary	OH0400	60,32,37,48
Ciorba, Charles R.	OK1350	32
Clair, Alicia A.	KS1350	32,33
Clark, Brenda J.	IN1650	32,11,37
Clark, William D.	NM0310	32,37
Clarkson, Austin	AG0650	12,32
Clausen, Brett	CA0650	64B,32
Coan, Darryl	IL2910	13,32,62E,67
Cofer, R. Shayne	IL2150	32,37,49
Coggiola, John C.	NY4150	32,29,34,47,60B
Cohen, Howard R.	NY3780	32
Cohen, Joanne	MN0600	32,51,62A,62B

Index by Area of Teaching Interest

Name	Code	Areas
Cohen, Mary L.	IA1550	32
Cohen, Stanley	NY1275	14C,32,46,47,64
Coker, Timothy C.	MS0385	13,60,32,36,66A
Cole, David C.	FL0680	38,51,39,62A,32
Cole, Mark R.	NC0850	32
Cole, Thomas	CA0815	32
Coleman, Fred	SC0200	32,36,31A
Coleman, Matthew	AZ0350	32,65
Collett, Jacqueline L.	MO1780	32,36,61,39
Collins, Charlotte A.	VA1350	13,32
Collins, Irma H.	VA1350	32
Collins, Susan	SC0700	32
Collinsworth, Andy	CA4700	13A,32,37,41,60B
Colon, Daisy	PR0100	32
Colonna, Jim	UT0325	63A,32,37
Colprit, Elaine	OH0300	32
Colwell, Cynthia	KS1350	32
Comeau, Gilles	AG0400	32,13
Compean, Jose D.	TX1425	13,32,47,63,64
Con, Adam Jonathan	OH2450	36,32,11,60A,13C
Conable, William E.	OH1850	38,62C,32
Connelly Bush, Judith	VA1350	32
Connelly, Marianne	MN0450	37,32,47,64,60B
Conway, Colleen	MI0050	32,63B
Conway, Colleen	MI2100	32
Cooper, Marianne G.	OH1850	32,36
Cooper, Shelly	AZ0500	32,32A,32B,32G,32H
Corbin, Lynn Ann	GA2150	32,61,60A
Cornacchio, Rachel	PA2300	32
Correll, Larry	VA1350	32
Correll, Sue	VA1350	32
Cosenza, Glenda L.	IL2200	32
Cossette, Isabelle	AI0150	32
Costa-Giomi, Eugenia	TX3510	32,32A
Costanza, A. Peter	OH1850	32,34
Cox, Donna M.	OH2250	20,36,32
Cox, Patricia J.	AR0250	11,32,34C,38,62B
Craig, Mary Ann	NJ0800	32,37,63D,49
Cratty, William	CA4050	13A,13,12A,14,32
Criswell, Paul D.	SC0800	32
Crosson, Gail	IL0850	32,64C
Crothers-Marley, Shirley Evans	OH2100	12A,32,36,61
Crowe, Don R.	SD0550	32,63C,72,35
Culver, Robert L.	MI2100	32,62B
Cummings, Paul C.	CA2250	32,37,38,64C
Cunningham, James E.	FL0650	14,20,32,11,12A
Curry, Jeffrey P.	NE0040	11,13C,32,37,49
Curtis, Cynthia R.	TN0100	32
Curtis, Steven	OK1350	32
Dabback, William M.	VA0600	32
Dabczynski, Andrew	UT0050	32,62
D'Addio, Daniel F.	CT0050	13,32,37,49,63A
Dahlman, Hank	OH2500	32,36,60
Dailey, Jeff	NY1275	12,32
Dakon, Jacob M.	KS1350	32,33
Dally, John	CA3640	37,32
Damm, Robert J.	MS0500	32
Dammers, Richard J.	NJ1050	32,32E,32F
Daniell-Knapp, Courtney	TX3450	60A,32
Darabie, Mohammed	OH0300	32
D'Arca, Denise	OH1800	32,36,11,42
Darr, Steven L.	FL2130	60,32,36,61
Daugherty, James F.	KS1350	32,36
Dauphin, Claude	AI0210	32
Davidson, Lyle	MA1400	13,32
Davis, Lapointe M.	DE0050	32,48,64
Davis, Susan A.	NY2750	32,51,62
Davis, Virginia Wayman	TX3525	32
De Leo, Joseph A.	NY2750	32,12A,13B,32C,32H
de Quadros, Andre F.	MA0400	32
Deal, John J.	NC2430	32,34
DeAlbuquerque, Joan	CA0825	32,37
Dean, Roger A.	PA3250	32
Dearborn, Keith	OH0300	32
DeBoer, James	MI1050	32
Deisler, Ann	NY1400	32
Dekaney, Elisa M.	NY4150	32,36,20H,60A
DeLaO, Armalyn	CA0845	32
Dell, Charlene	OK1350	32E,32H,32,62,62A
Dell, Kay	CA0835	32
Delorenzo, Lisa	NJ0800	32,66D
DeLuca, Mike	CO0275	13,64C,11,32
Demitry, E. Hope	NJ0175	32
Demkee, Ronald	PA2450	63D,32
DeNardo, Gregory F.	IL3300	32
D'Ercole, Patricia	WI0850	32
Diaz, Frank M.	OR1050	32,32G,13K
Dickey, Marc R.	CA0815	32,37,64
Dietrich, Kurt R.	WI0700	13,32,37,47,29
Dilworth, Rollo A.	PA3250	32
Dimmick, Penny	IN0250	32,65,34
Dingle, Rosetta	SC1050	32,36,66D,13
Dion, David	CT0600	32
Dirksen, Dale B. H.	AJ0030	10,13,32,61,66
Ditmer, Nancy	OH0700	32,37,60B
Doan, Gerald R.	OH2200	32
Doane, Christopher	KY1500	32
Dobbs, Teryl L.	WI0815	32E,32
Dobroski, Bernard J.	IL2250	32H,63D,32,60,35E
Doebler, Jeffrey S.	IN1750	11,32,37
Doerksen, Paul F.	PA1050	32
Doherty, Mary Lynn	IL2200	32
Doneski, Sandra	MA0950	32,36,13
Dornberger, Laura	NY3725	32
Douglas, Kenneth	IN0910	32,37,60B
Doutt, Kathleen C.	PA1550	12A,32,13C,20
Dowling, Thomas	AG0450	32,64C
Downing, Sonja Lynn	WI0350	14,15,20D,64A,32
Doyle, Jennifer	MD1010	32
Doyle, Tracy A.	CO0050	64A,32,32B
Dragonvich, James	NY2105	65,32
Drayton, Keith	MI1100	13,11,36,32,61
Dregalla, Herbert E.	OH2500	12,32,60,64C
Droe, Kevin	IA1600	32
Dubikovsky, Nadya	IN1300	32
Dubois, Chantal	AI0210	32
Duerksen, George L.	KS1350	32,33
Duke, Robert A.	TX3510	32
Dunafin, Cathy A.	IL2050	32
Dupee, Donald	SC1100	32
Dupont, Donald	NY1600	32
Dura, Marian T.	PA1900	38,62,32,32B,62A
Durst, Alan Edward	CA0810	64E,29,32,46,47
Eccles, Elizabeth	VA0500	32,61,66A
Eckroth-Riley, Joan	ND0050	32
Edgar, Scott N.	IL1400	37,32,11,13A
Ediger, Thomas L.	NE0500	13,12A,32,36,66
Edmund, Carina	MN1600	32
Edmund, David	MN1600	32
Edwards, Jan	OH1850	32
Edwards, Karen	OH2600	32,66A
Edwards, Kay L.	OH1450	32
Edwards, Lawrence	TN1680	60,32,36
Edwards, Malcolm V.	AA0150	32,36,60A
Edwards, Richard D.	OH2000	37,32,60B,12F,32A
Eisman, Lawrence W.	NY0642	11,32
Elliott, David J.	NY2750	32,12B,10A
Elliott, David J.	NJ1130	32
Elliott, Robert L.	TN1400	13B,32,62D,11
Ellis, Barry L.	WI0840	60,37,64D,64E,32
Ellis, Brenda	OH2500	20A,20G,32,36,66A
Ellis, Mark Carlton	OH1850	32
Ellsworth, E. Victor	AR0750	32,62,38
Emge, Jeffrey D.	TX3535	32,37,60,64B
Emmons, Scott	WI0825	32,32C,32E
Erb, Jack	CA4100	32
Erickson, Sheryl	WA0550	32
Eros, John	CA0807	32,32E,32B
Erwin, Joanne	OH1700	32,60
Espinosa, Sergio	TX3500	32,11,62A
Espinosa, Teresita	CA3150	11,12A,32,61,20G
Ester, Don P.	IN0150	32
Etters, Stephen C.	NC0350	60,32,37,63D,13A
Eubank, Beth	SC0200	32,64B
Evans, David H.	AR0300	13,11,12A,32,48
Evans, Thomas	MI1150	37,47,63C,29A,32
Ewashko, Laurence J.	AG0400	32,36
Eychaner, Frank	CO0150	10,32,13,47,60
Eyler, David	MN0600	32,50,65,42
Fairchild, G. Daniel	WI0840	10F,11,32,63B
Falk Romaine, Diane	NJ1400	32
Fannin, John E.	KY0950	32,37,10F
Farmer, Dawn	ID0050	32
Fashun, Christopher H.	IN0550	38,65,32,47,62B
Faszer, Ted	SD0450	32,36,31A,34
Feay-Shaw, Sheila J.	WI0825	32,20
Fee, Daniel	WI0830	32
Fennell, Mitchell	CA0815	60,32,37
Fenton, Kevin	FL0850	60,32,36
Ferguson, David A.	PA1600	63A,32
Ferguson, Laura S.	PA1600	32
Ferguson, Vivian	OH1100	32
Ferneding, Mary Jo	IL0550	32
Ferrara, Dominick J.	MA0260	32
Ferrara, Lawrence	NY2750	13,12,32,66
Ferrington, Darryl	LA0400	13A,36,32,31A
Fett, Darlene L.	SD0600	32
Fiala, Joy	AR0110	13,11,32
Fiese, Richard K.	TX1000	60B,32
Fisher, Tammy M.	WI0810	60,37,65,32,11
Fiske, Harold	AG0500	32,12F
Fiske, Jane	MA0930	11,15,32,66
Fitzpatrick, Kate R.	MI2100	32
Flamm, Ernest C.	OH2500	32
Flanigan, Nina	MI1750	32
Flora, Sim	AR0500	32,37,47,63,13
Flowers, Patricia J.	OH1850	32
Floyd, Eva	OH2200	32,32D
Foley, Ruth	VA0650	32,61
Fonder, Mark	NY1800	60B,32,37
Foote, Jack E.	CA0840	32,64E
Forbes, Guy	IL1750	32,36
Fordice, William	IA0950	32,60A
Forsythe, Jere L.	OH1850	32
Fox, Rebecca	AL1195	13,11,32,66A
Foy, Patricia S.	SC0650	32
Frank, Gloria	TN0050	32,11
Frankel, James Thomas	NY4200	34,37,32,32F
Franklin, Bonita Louise	OK0450	32,36,60A,61
Fraser, Jo-Anne	AI0190	32
Frederick, Mark	SC0200	32,63B
Frederickson, Karen	AG0250	32,36,60A
Fredrickson, William E.	FL0850	32G,32E,32
Fredstrom, Tim	IL1150	32D,36,60A,32
Freeman, Peter	AI0150	64E,32
Frego, R. J. David	TX3530	32,32I
Frelly, Robert	CA0960	11,32
Friedrichs, Charles	CA4100	11,37,63C,13A,32
Frierson-Campbell, Carol	NJ1400	32,63B,60
Fritts, C. Nelson	MD0850	32
Frolick, Jeanne	OR1150	32
Fryling, David N.	NY1600	36,60A,60,32,13A
Fung, C. Victor	FL2000	32G,32,20D
Funk, Curtis H.	IL3550	13,32
Furman, Lisa J.	MI1800	37,60B,11,13,32
Gadberry, David	PA3150	32
Gaddis, J. Robert	KY0400	60,32,51,63D,38
Gainey, Denise A.	AL1150	64C,32
Gallahan, Carla A.	AL1050	32,63B
Gallant, Mark W.	OH1650	66G,32
Galvan, Janet	NY1800	60A,32,36
Galyen, S. Daniel	IA1600	37,41,32E,60B,32
Gamble, Sue G.	MI0400	32B,32C,32H,32
Garard-Brewer, Gay	MT0450	66A,32
Garthee, Jeffrey A.	WI0825	32
Gassi, Gloria	AG0500	36,32
Gatch, Brent M.	PA1050	32
Gates, Elaine	NY2105	32
Gault, Brent M.	IN0900	32
Gauthier, Delores	MI2250	32
Geisler, Herbert G.	CA1425	14,32,44,13,31
Gerber, Casey	OK0650	36,32
Gerber, Timothy A.	OH1850	32
Gerlach, Paul D.	PA0550	32
Gerrity, Kevin W.	IN0150	32
Giambrone, Marcia	NY3725	32
Gibbs, Beth	MI0900	32
Gibson, Robert	AI0150	37,32
Giersch, Sandra	CA0810	32
Gilbert, John	NY2750	10,32,34
Giles, Leonard	GA0810	11,32,37,47,63
Gillespie, Robert A.	OH1850	32,62A
Gilpin, Mary Ann	WA0940	11,32
Gindin, Suzanne B.	IN1050	32,37,38,41,63B
Glass, Susan	NY2750	32
Glaze, Debbie	OR0850	32,36
Glaze, Richard T.	FL2100	60,32,37,48,64
Gleason, Bruce	MN1625	32,14A
Glickman, Joel	WI0600	60,32,37,38,47
Glunt, Patricia A.	NY2750	32
Goldberg, Marjorie	PA3330	62,32
Goldberg, Merryl	CA0847	64E,32,11
Goldman-Moore, Susan J.	OK1450	32,36,61
Golemo, Michael	IA0850	37,60,64E,32
Gonzalez, Fr. George	IN0005	11,14,20,66G,32
Gonzol, David J.	WV0550	32,12A

Index by Area of Teaching Interest

Name	Code	Areas
Good, Jonathan E.	NV0050	60B,32,37,32E
Goodness, Donald R.	NY3780	32
Goodwin, Mark A.	GA0700	13,32,37,64
Gordon, Daniel	FL1740	13,32,60A,36
Gosselin, Karen	AL0550	32,60,36,40,44
Gould, Elizabeth	AG0450	32
Gowan, Andrew D.	SC1110	60,32,37,64
Grabois, Daniel	WI0815	32,49,63A
Graham, Brenda J.	IN1250	13A,32,37,62,31A
Granberry, Marsha	KS1200	32
Grant, Joe W.	IL3300	60,32,36
Grashel, John W.	IL3300	32
Gratto, Sharon Davis	OH2250	36,20,32
Graves, Edward	TN1400	37,32
Gray, Donavon D.	CA0250	37,44,49,32,48
Gray, Lori F.	MT0400	32,12F
Grechesky, Robert	IN0250	60,32
Green, Georgia	TX0300	32
Green, J. Paul	AG0500	60,12B,32,12C
Green, Maria	NJ0825	11,32
Green, Sharon	MI1600	32,61,70
Green, Stuart	CA0845	32,70
Greenberg, Marvin	HI0210	32
Greene, Gary A.	IL0850	32
Greene, Sean	TN0900	63D,13,37,32,42
Greennagel, David J.	VA1600	32
Greher, Gena R.	MA2030	32,32H,34A
Grenfell, Mary-Jo	MA1650	12A,32,38,41,42
Grew, Melody A.	MD0050	11,32,36,61,66A
Grey, Meg	MO0600	11,12A,32,66A,66G
Griffin, Peter J.	IL0850	32,37,60B,63C,63D
Grimes, Judith	IL0850	60,14,32,37
Grimland, Fredna H.	OR0950	13A,32,61
Groeling, Charles	IL3200	32,37
Gromko, Joyce	OH0300	32
Groom, Mitzi	KY1550	32,69,66G
Groulx, Timothy J.	IN1600	13B,13C,32
Groves, Edgar S.	PA3650	14,32
Gruenhagen, Lisa M.	OH0300	32A,32B,32G,64A,32
Grutzmacher, Patricia Ann	OH1100	32,41,64B,37,20
Guastavino, Catherine	AI0150	32
Guderian, Lois Veenhoven	WI0860	11,32
Guerriero, Angela	PA3600	32
Guerrini, Susan C.	NJ0175	32
Guilbault, Denise	RI0200	32
Guist, Jonathan B.	TX3515	64C,32,42
Gumm, Alan	MI0400	13A,32
Gunn, Katherine	IN0800	64B,32
Gunnell, Jonathan	PA1050	32
Guzman, Juan-Tony	IA0950	32,47,14,29,20
Haack, Paul	MN1623	32
Haas, Janet	MA0260	32
Hackett, Patricia	CA4200	13A,32
Hackworth, Rhonda S.	NJ1130	32B,32C,32A,36,32
Hadley, Katie	OR0700	32,32B,32C
Hagen, Julie	MN0600	32,36
Hagon, John	MA0260	32
Hair, Harriet	GA2100	11,32,34,12F
Hakoda, Ken	KS0700	36,38,32
Haley, Julia W.	OK0800	32
Hall, Amy	MI2120	32
Hall, Doreen	AG0450	32
Hall, Lewis R.	WV0050	32,40,54,61
Hall, Louis O.	ME0440	60,32,64B,64E
Hamann, Donald L.	AZ0500	32,62,32E,32G
Hamann, Keitha Lucas	MN1623	32
Hamilton, Alexander W.	MO1810	32
Hamilton, Margaret J.	MI2250	63B,32,13,35E
Hamm, Laura	WV0440	32,36,66A,66D,66C
Hammel, Alice M.	VA0150	32
Hammond, Tony	MT0350	37,47,32
Hampton, Anitra C.	AL0650	12A,32,32G,11
Hancock, Carl B.	AL1170	32G,32,34
Handel, Greg	LA0550	32
Hanna, Wendell	CA4200	32B,64D,32
Hansen, Neil E.	WY0130	37,47,63A,32,49
Hanson, Jan	OK1400	60,11,12A,32,36
Harney, Kristin	MT0200	32
Harrell, Paula D.	NC1600	32,66A,66G,66D,31A
Harrington, Roger J.	PA3250	32
Harrington, William	CA3520	32,38,41,63B,31A
Harris, Donald	AJ0150	32,63,12
Harris, Duane	MO0350	32,36,61,12A
Harris, Esther L.	NY2750	32
Harris, Lee	TN1700	32,13C,36
Harris, Mary	OH1450	32,62B,51,42
Hartenberger, Aurelia	MO1830	20,32
Harwood, Eve E.	IL3300	32
Hash, Phillip M.	MI0350	32
Haskett, Brandon L.	GA1500	32
Hatcher, Oeida M.	VA0750	32,37,41,38,11
Hawkins, Ben	KY1350	60B,32,37,38,63B
Hawkins, Jemmie Peevy	AL0650	32,66C
Hawley, Lucrecia	AL0010	11,32,66D
Hayes, Beth Tura	LA0800	34A,34B,32,11
Hayes, Casey J.	IN0500	36,32,11
Hayes, Glenn C.	WI0865	60,32,37
Haygood, James	LA0760	32,36
Heape, Mary Willis	TX3050	32,61,13,12A
Hearn, Elizabeth	IN1100	32
Hearn, Sidney T.	IN1100	32,32E,34,37,63A
Hearnsberger, Keith	AR0750	11,32
Hebert, Joseph G.	LA0300	32,37,46,35
Hedden, Debra Gordon	KS1350	32
Hedgecoth, David	OR1050	32,32E,37
Hedrick, David	KY0400	61,32
Heilman, Annette	NY3600	32
Heller, Jack J.	FL2000	32,12F
Hellman, Daniel S.	MO0775	32
Henderson, Jenny	AR0250	66A,32
Hendricks, John	WV0750	32,37
Hendricks, Steven	MO1500	32,37,34,36
Henning, Mary	KY0350	20,44,32,36
Henninger, Jacqueline	TX3510	32,32E
Henry, Robert	TX3520	32
Henry, Warren	TX3420	32B,32
Herbert, David	TX2200	13A,64B,32,13B,13C
Herrick, Matthew	OH1100	32
Hess, Jeffrey	MN1200	61,34,32,11
Hetzel, Lori	KY1450	32,36,32D
Heukeshoven, Janet	MN1400	37,32,60,11,41
Heuser, Frank	CA5030	32
Hewitt, Michael P.	MD1010	60,32,38
Hicken, Leslie W.	SC0750	60,37,32
Hickey, Katherine M.	CA5150	32,13A,13C,36,40
Hickey, Maud	IL2250	32
Hicks, Ann M.	IN0150	32
Higgins, William R.	PA2300	32,64,72,34
High, Linda	NC0650	32
Hightshoe, Robert B.	OH1850	32
Hill, Cheryl Frazes	IL0550	32,36,60A
Hill, Monty K.	NM0310	37,32
Hill, Willie L.	MA2000	32,29
Hiller, Brian	NY1600	32
Hirokawa, Joy	PA2450	32
Hobbins, William	GA0250	32,36,61,11
Hodges, Don	NC2430	32
Hodgman, Thomas	MI0050	32,36,40
Hoepfner, Gregory	OK0150	10A,32,61,10,11
Hofer, Calvin	CO0225	32,37,49,63A,60B
Hoffer, Charles	FL1850	32
Hoffer, Heike	TX3525	64B,11,32
Hoffman, Julia	NM0450	32
Holcomb, Al	NJ1350	32,36,60A
Holden, LuAnn	TN0850	32,12A,36
Holland, Katherine N.	GA1300	64D,32,64
Holland, Margaret	NJ0175	32
Holland, Marianne	SC0950	32,66A
Hollinger, Diana	CA4400	32,60
Hollingsworth, Devon	IN0005	10A,12,13,32,66G
Holloway, John R.	SC0650	63D,32,37,60B
Holmes, Alena	WI0865	20,32
Holmes, Ramona A.	WA0800	14,32,38,62
Holt, Dennis	FL1950	32
Homburg, Andrew H.	MO0775	32
Hood, Jo Ann	TN1400	32
Hoover, Lloyd W.	DC0350	32,37
Hopkins, Jesse E.	VA0100	32,36,61,44,60A
Hopkins, Michael	MI2100	32
Horan, Sara	GA1000	32,11,61
Hornbach, Christina M.	MI1050	32,13C
Horvath, Kathleen	OH0400	32,51,62
Hosley, Robyn L.	NY3780	32
Houde, Andrea	WV0750	13C,32,41,42,62B
Hourigan, Amy	IN0150	32
Hourigan, Ryan M.	IN0150	32
House, Richard	SC1000	37,63A,32
Howard, Karen	OH1100	32
Howard, Sandra	NH0150	32,36,40
Howell, Allen C.	PA1200	11,32,36
Hower, Eileen	PA0250	32,11,61
Hoydich, George	PA1050	32
Hubbard, Kathy A.	NY3780	32
Hudson, Mark E.	CO0275	11,32,60B
Hudson, Michael	KY1450	32
Huff, Daniel M.	NC2410	32,36
Huff, Lori	CA0630	13A,11,48,64,64E,32
Huffman, Valarie A.	WV0300	37,32,63D,32E,49
Hughes, Brian L.	IA0940	60,11,32,37,47
Hughes, Robert	AG0500	32,50,65
Hughes, Winston	NJ0175	32
Hummel, Linda W.	PA1900	11,32
Humphreys, Jere T.	AZ0100	32,32G,32E
Humphries, Terri	TX3400	32
Hunnicutt, Heather Winter	KY0610	61,32,11
Hunsaker, Leigh Anne	TX0900	63A,32,49
Hunter, Andrew	LA0150	37,65,32
Huntley, Lawrence	NC0250	32
Hurley, Gregory	NC0650	32
Ihas, Dijana	OR0750	62B,11,32
Immel, Dean	CA5300	32
Ingram, Joe	OR1050	32,32E
Irvin, Virginia	TX2250	32
Irwin, Donna	KY0400	32
Isbell, Dan	NY1800	32
Ivey, Bobby	GA0350	32,36,13C,40
Izdebski, Christy	MD0100	12A,32,66A,66D,36
Jachens, Darryl	SC1080	11,32,63C
Jacobi, Bonnie S.	CO0250	32B,66A,13,32I,32
Jacoby, Marc Max	PA3600	32,46,47
Jaeschke, Rick	IL0100	32,37,34
James, Jeffrey R.	NE0250	13,60,32,37,63
James, Judy A. G.	LA0700	11,32,32I,66D
James, Kortney	WI0750	64A,32,48
Jamieson, Jake	CA5031	20,32
Janisch, Joseph	WV0560	36,60,32,13A,32B
Jarjisian, Catherine	CT0600	32
Jasinski, Mark	WA0750	62A,38,32
Jeffreys, Harold L.	NC2150	10F,32,64C,65,46
Jellison, Judith A.	TX3510	32,33
Jenkins, Jeffry	CA4850	32,66D
Jenkins, Pamela	ME0340	64A,64C,64E,32,13E
Jensen, Janet L.	WI0815	32,62A,38,51
Jensen, Michelle	CA0250	32,36,55
Jerosch, Anita	ME0340	32,12A,13A
Jetton, Caroline K.	IN0350	32
Jewett, Dennis A.	KY0800	61,31A,32,36
John, Bina	AG0450	32
Johnson, Christopher	KS1350	32
Johnson, Daniel C.	NC2440	32,63D,34,32B,63C
Johnson, David A.	IA0900	60,32,37,47,65
Johnson, Erik A.	CO0250	32,32E
Johnson, John Paul	KS1450	32,36
Johnson, Karrell	TX3420	32,51,62B
Johnson, Michael	MO0600	32,29
Johnson, Pamela A.	WV0400	32
Johnson, Scott R.	SD0050	32,54,11
Johnson, Vicky V.	TX2750	13,32B,14C,32,66B
Johnson, Yvonne P.	DE0050	32,66D,62
Johnston, Rebecca R.	SC0600	32,36,60,13C,61
Jones, Deborah	NJ1400	32
Jones, Dena Kay	TX3415	32,13A,13C
Jones, Douglas	TX3520	66,32,20F,14F,15
Jones, Eddie	KY1500	32
Jones, Patrick Michael	AR0700	32,36
Jones, Russell L.	NY4150	32G,60B,32,12A,12E
Jones, Zebedee	KS1050	32,64D
Jones-Bamman, Richard	MS0600	13A,32,36,66A
Jordan, Grace	CT0150	11,14,32,20
Jordanoff, Christine E.	FL1800	32
Jorgensen, Estelle R.	PA1050	32D,32B,32C,32,36
Joseph, Mervyn	IN0900	32
Joss, Laura L.	OH0500	32,63A
Jothen, Michael	OH0200	32,37,60
Joy, Sharon	MD0850	32
Junda, Mary Ellen	LA0550	32A,32B,32H,32G,32
Jussila, Clyde	CT0600	32,36
Kane, Kevin	WA1050	32,62,64
Kantack, Jerri Lamar	RI0250	32
Kantorski, Vincent J.	MS0150	60,36,61,12A,32
Kaplan, Chester	OH0300	32
Karpf, Nita	NY2750	32
Kaschub, Michele E.	OH0400	12,32
Katz, Brian	ME0500	32
Keast, Dan A.	AG0450	32
	TX3527	32,34B,34F,32G,32C

Name	Code	Areas
Keast, Michelle	TX3527	11,32,32A
Keelan, Nick	WI0350	32,49,63C,63D
Keeler, Paula	IA0150	32,36,39,41,61
Keenan-Takagi, Kathleen D.	NY0400	32,36,12
Kehrberg, Donald A.	KS0200	64B,37,32
Keiser, Douglas	IN0800	37,32
Kellan, Ross	IL0850	60,32,37,11,13
Kelley, Cheryl K.	MN1280	13,32,48,64D
Kelly, Steven N.	FL0850	32,37
Kelly, Todd	IL0400	32,47,63A,35
Kelly-McHale, Jacqueline	IL0750	32
Kelton, Anne	MA0350	32
Kendall, Michael	IN0200	60,37,32,20,34
Kendall, Roger A.	CA5031	32,13L,12F,12C
Kerchner, Jody L.	OH1700	32,41
Kerlin, Jerry	NY2750	32
Kerlin, Jerry D.	NY2200	32,20
Kerstetter, Kathleen	NC1500	32,49,34,64A
Kidd-Szymczak, Deanna	MA0260	32
Killian, George W.	IN0700	60A,32,36
Killian, Janice N.	TX3200	32
Killion, Jamie	CA0450	61,32,31A
Kim-Infiesto, Marilyn Liu	HI0160	36,61,12A,32,13A
Kimball, Marshall C.	OH1400	32,37,47,60B
King, Curtis R.	FL0600	13A,13,32,61,62
King, Dennis W.	WI0150	60,11,32,13
King, Gerald	AB0150	32,37,60B
Kirkell, Lorie	CA2100	32,12A
Kish, David	CO0550	37,32E,60B,32
Klein, Rochelle Z.	PA2900	32,35E,66A,11,13A
Kleinknecht, Daniel E.	IA1140	60,32,36,61
Kleszynski, Kenneth	OR1100	13,32,38
Klockow, Stephanie	WI0840	36,32
Knecht, Melissa Gerber	MI1000	11,32,42,62A,62B
Knight, Gerald R.	NC0750	36,60,61,32
Knight, Gloria J.	NC0700	32,36,61
Kocher, Edward W.	PA1050	32,63C,63D
Kohlenberg, Randy	NC2430	32,63C
Kolthammer, Stacy	OH1100	32
Koops, Alexander	CA0250	37,32
Koops, Lisa	OH0400	32,32A
Kos, Ronald P.	MA0400	32
Koster, Keith	NY2650	32
Koza, Julia Eklund	WI0815	32,32D
Kratus, John	MI1400	32
Kravchak, Richard	CA0805	11,64,38,37,32
Kritzmire, Judith A.	MN1600	32
Kronour, Dianne	OH2200	32
Krueger, Pat	WA1000	32
Kruse, Nathan B.	TX3420	32,32E
Kudlawiec, Nancy A.	AL1350	11,32,66A,12A,13
Kuehn, John W.	PA1600	32,64C,48,72
Kuehne, Jane M.	AL0200	32,32D,32F
Kuhn, Lois	WV0550	32
Kunkel, Jeffrey	NJ0800	32,47,29,53,46
Kuntz, Tammy	OH1100	32
Kvam, Nancy E.	CA0400	32
Kvet, Edward J.	LA0300	32
Kwan, Eva	IN1560	12A,32,44,20
Labuta, Joseph	MI2200	60,32
Lamb, Brian	OK1330	60B,32,37
Lamb, Roberta	AG0250	32,15,67C
Land, Mary	GA2300	37,32
Lane, Jeremy S.	SC1110	32
Lane, Mark	WA0050	37,32
Lange, Diane	TX3500	32
Langner, Gerald	AJ0150	32,36
Langol, Stefani	MA0260	32
Langsford, Christopher M.	KS0750	36,32,11,12,13
Lapka, Christine	IL3500	32,11,12C
Laprade, Paul	IL2560	13C,36,61,66D,32
Larose, Christine	AI0190	32
Larsen, Vance	UT0190	60,37,49,32
Larson, Paul	PA2450	32
Larson, Richard	NY3725	60,32
LaRue, Peter	KY0610	60,11,32,37,63D
Lautzenheiser, Tim N.	IN0150	32
Lautzenheiser, Tim	IN0905	32
Laverty, John M.	NY4150	60B,37,32,63A
Lawrence, Lisa	FL0100	32,54,61
Lawrence, Robert J.	MO1790	32,36,11,47
Lawson, Kay	WV0400	32,64D
Lebon, Rachel L.	FL1900	47,61,32,35A,54
Leck, Henry	IN0250	60,36,32
LeCroy, Hoyt F.	GA1650	65,32
Lee, Donzell	MS0050	12A,32,66A
Lee, Pamela	TX0150	32,36,66A,60
Lee, Robert E.	OH1450	32,61
Lee, Ronald T.	RI0300	32,37,12B,12C
Lee, William R.	TN1700	32,63D,11
Legette, Roy M.	GA2100	32
Leglar, Mary A.	GA2100	32
Legutki, Allen R.	IL0275	37,38,32
Lehr, Joan	OH1850	32
Lemieux, Christiane	AI0190	32
Lemke, Jeffrey J.	LA0350	32,37,60
Lemons, Mary L.	PA1900	32
Lemons, Robert M.	CT0150	11,60,32,63A
Lenehan, Miriam C.	NY2450	11,12A,32,66A,66D
Lenney, James	NJ0700	11,32
Leonhardt, Angela J.	TX3530	32
Lessard, Brigitte-Louise	AI0190	32
Lessly, Chris Ann	IN1025	32,41,48,64C,64E
Lethco, Leigh-Ann M.	WI0830	32E,37,63A,32
Levine, Iris S.	CA0630	12A,32,36,60
Levinowitz, Lili	NJ1050	32,32A,32B
Levy, Katherine M.	NY3725	32
L'Hommedieu, Randi L.	MI0400	32,11
Li-Bleuel, Linda	SC0400	66C,11,32,12A,66
Lieberman, Bernard	NY2750	32
Lien, Joelle L.	UT0250	32
Limb, Christine M.	PA2000	32,11,63
Lind, Vicki R.	AR0750	32
Lindeman, Carolynn A.	CA4200	13A,32,66D,34
Lindroth, James	OK0550	32,37
Lipscomb, Scott D.	MN1623	32
Liske, Kenneth L.	WI0830	32,32C,32F,32B,32D
Livingston, Carolyn H.	RI0300	32,36,66D,12C
Logan, Joseph C.	NC0050	12A,32,36,61
Logsdon, Anthony	AL0500	60,32,64E
Loong, ChetYeng	HI0210	32
Lorenzetti, Kristen	NJ0700	11,32
Lorenzino, Lisa	AI0150	32
Louth, Joseph Paul	OH2600	32
Lowder, Jerry E.	OH1850	32,66D
Lowe, Donald R.	GA2100	32,31A
Lucas, Mark	OK1350	60,32,36,41
Luebke, Linda M.	IN0800	32
Luedders, Jerry D.	CA0835	32,64E
Lueth, Faith	MA0260	32
Lundquist, Barbara Reeder	WA1050	32,12E
Lust, Patricia D.	VA0700	61,32
Luttrell, Matthew	TX3500	37,32
Lychner, John	MI2250	32,37
Lyman, Kristin M.	GA0500	32,65
Mack, Dianne	TX3150	32,13C
MacLeod, Rebecca	NC2430	32
MacMullin, Dennis	NJ0175	64D,32
Madden, John	MI1400	37,32
Madeja, James T.	NY3780	32,63A,12C,49
Madison, Vicki	KY0950	32
Madsen, Clifford K.	FL0850	32,33,12C
Mager, Guillermo E.	CT0700	13,12A,34,35,32
Maher, James	NJ1350	32
Maimonis, Nina	IL0850	32
Mains, Ronda	AR0700	64A,32B,32
Major, James	OH1850	32,36
Majors, Gayle	KY1425	32,66,11
Maldonado, Ana Maria	CA0845	32,62C,51
Mallory, Joan	NY2900	32
Maltais, Helene	AI0200	32,32B
Maltas, Carla Jo	MO1790	32,32B
Mammon, Marielaine	NJ0250	12A,32,36,41,61
Manfredo, Joseph	IL1150	32E,60B,37,32
Mann, Rochelle	CO0350	10,11,32,64
Mann, Sylvia Lee	CA0805	32,62,38
Mantie, Roger	MA0400	32
Marcades, Michael	AL0900	12A,12B,13,32,36
Marcel, Linda A.	NJ0020	12B,66A,66D,32,11
March, Hunter	TX3510	32,32B
Marcuzzi, Michael	AG0650	32,20H,14
Marks, Martin	MI0050	37,46,32
Marlatt, Jeffrey	VA1350	32,61
Marlett, Judy	ID0150	32,36,39,54,60A
Marsh, Lawrence B.	OR0450	60,12A,32,36
Martin, Barry	MI0900	60,37,32
Martin, Blair	KS1250	13C,37,46,41,32
Martin, Jeffrey A.	AE0050	32,35
Martin, Mark Gregory	PA3600	37,32
Martin, Michael D.	NC1350	32,36
Martin, Michael D.	GA0150	11,12A,13C,32,49
Martinovic, Nada	OH1100	32
Martynuik, David G.	PA1600	37,13,32
Mason, Sonya G.	NY2150	12A,66A,32
Mativetsky, Shawn	AI0150	32,65
Matteson, Vicki	VT0100	64C,32
Matthews, Andrea	NH0150	13A,32
Matthews, Britton	NY2450	32,12,65
Matthews, Wendy K.	MI2200	32,32E
Matych-Hager, Susan	MI1950	12A,32,36,61
Mauldin, Mark K.	DC0150	13A,13B,32,63C
May, Lissa F.	IN0900	32
Maye, Shelia J.	VA0500	11,61,32
Maynard, Lisa M.	VA0600	32
Mayo, Walter S.	NY3725	60,32
Maytan, Sandra	MI0900	32
McAllister, Peter A.	AZ0500	32
McBride, M. Scott	KY0900	60B,32,10F,63C,37
McBride, Nick	NJ1350	32
McCabe, Melissa	MD0850	32
McCallum, Wendy M.	AC0050	64E,32E,37,60B,32
McCarthy, Marie F.	MI2100	32
McCarty, Diane	KS0300	32
McCauley, Thomas E.	NJ0800	37,60B,32
McConkie, Dawn	KS0300	32,64C,64E
McCoy, Matthew T.	KS0650	32
McCullough, David	IN0250	37,32
McDermid, Aaron	ND0150	36,60A,61,11,32
McDonald, Nan	CA4100	13A,32
McDonnell, John	NJ0175	36,32
McFarland, Ann L.	PA3600	32
McGuire, Kenneth	AL1170	32
McKeage, Kathleen M.	WY0200	11,62D,13C,32
McKeithen, Steven	LA0550	11,32,37
McKellar, Donald A.	AG0500	60,32
McKenzie, Art	NJ1350	32,54
McKoy, Constance L.	NC2430	32B,32A,20A,32
McLain, Barbara	HI0210	32
McLamore, Alyson	CA0600	12A,12,32,16,20G
McMosley, William F.	KS0700	46,32
McNeil, Albert J.	CA5010	60,14,32,36
McQuarrie, Sarah	MA0510	32
McRoberts, Gary	CA1900	32,36,66A,20G
McWilliams, Heather	WI0830	32,11,63D
McWilliams, Robert	WI0830	37,32,29A,60B
Meade, Karen	MO0500	32,11,66A,66G
Mehling, Gordon	CA0650	32
Meints, Kenneth	NE0500	63,20,65,35A,32
Melville, Alison	AG0450	32,67B
Menard, Elizabeth	OH0300	32
Menghini, Charles T.	IL3450	60,37,32
Mennicke, Patricia	MN0610	31A,32,60,61
Meredith, Henry M.	AG0500	32,63A,63B,67E
Meredith, Victoria	AG0500	60,32,36,41
Merrill, Brian G.	TX2400	32
Merrill, Thomas G.	OH2550	12,60,36,32
Merritt, Frank	NC1100	63A,63B,32
Mertz, Justin J.	NY4150	37,60B,32
Methe, Daniel	CA0815	32
Metz, Donald E.	OH2200	32
Meyer, Frederick	WV0650	13,32,48,64B
Meyer, Lisa M.	MI2200	32
Miceli, Jennifer Scott	NY2105	32,36,60A
Mielcarz, Kelly	IL2050	32,32D
Miksza, Peter J.	IN0900	32
Milam, Michael R.	VA0550	32
Milford, Gene F.	OH2150	32
Miller, Brigetta F.	WI0350	32
Miller, James Patrick	MA2000	37,32,60B
Miller, Kelly A.	FL1800	32,36
Miller, Kenneth E.	MO1830	32
Miller, Kevin D.	MI0600	60,32,38
Miller, Lisa	IN1800	32,61,54,12A
Miller, Peter	VT0100	62,32,51
Milligan, Terence G.	OH2200	60,37,32
Mills, Charlotte	CO0950	32,66D
Minear, Carolyn	MO1950	32
Miranda, Martina	CO0800	32
Misenhelter, Dale D.	AR0700	32
Mishra, Jennifer	MO1830	32
Mitchell, Alan	MI0250	60,32,37,49,48
Mitchell, Brenda	OH1450	32
Mitchell, Deborah H.	CA0825	32
Mitchell, Jon	MA2010	10F,60,32,38
Mitchell, Joseph	CA0805	32,65
Mitchell, Robert	MO0600	13,32,36

Name	Code	Areas
Mixon, Laura	AL1050	36,32
Moe, Judy	IL0550	32
Moehle, Matthew	OH1100	32
Momand, Elizabeth B.	AR0730	39,61,32
Monkelien, Sheryl	PA2150	32,40
Montague, Matthew G.	KS1050	32,36,60A,11
Montano, David R.	CO0900	66A,66B,66D,32
Montemayor, Mark	CO0950	32
Montgomery, David L.	MI2250	32,37
Montgomery, Janet	MD1010	32,32A,32B
Moore, Brian	NE0600	32,34
Moots, John E.	OK0150	32,49,63A,20G
Morales, Gary A.	PR0100	60,32,48,64C
Morgan, Angela L.	GA0250	32,38,51,62A
Morris, Martha M.	IL2650	12A,32,64A
Morris, Willie L.	OH2250	37,47,64E,32
Morrison, Linda	KY1460	11,32,36,66A,66G
Morrison, Steven J.	WA1050	32
Morrow, Sharon	NJ1350	32
Morton, Leonard	TN1400	32
Moser, Janet	IL0850	66A,66D,32A,32
Moslak, Judy	MI1260	32,66A
Moss, Emily A.	NY0500	32,48,64D,60B
Moulton, Paul F.	ID0070	11,12A,32,14
Mowrer, Tony	CA0810	32D,32,32C
Moxness, Paul	MN1000	13A,32,64E
Mueller, Alicia K.	MD0850	32
Muller, Gerald	TX2170	13,11,12A,32,36
Munson, Mark	OH0300	32,36
Muntefering, Scott	IA1800	32,63A,49
Murphy, Kathy	PA3250	32
Murphy, Patrick C.	OR1100	13B,37,32,41
Murray, Renardo	MS0050	37,32,63,13A
Muzzo, Grace	PA3710	32,36,40,60A
Myers, David E.	MN1623	32
Myrick, John	AL1195	32,62A,62B,41,51
Nagle, Donna	MA2030	32
Nagler, Joseph	NY3250	32,33,34
Napoles, Jessica	UT0250	32
Nardo, Rachel L.	UT0250	32,32B,34,32A,32D
Neely, Linda Page	CT0600	32
Negrete, Merida	NC2410	32,13
Nelson, Troy	MI1300	32
Ness, Marjorie S.	MA0930	11,20,32,36,66G
Neuenschwander, Daniel	PA1750	37,32,63C
Neufeld, Gerald	AG0500	36,55D,60,32
Newell, Meri	MS0360	11,32,64,37,48
Newlin, Georgia A.	NY0050	11,12A,13C,32,36
Newsom, Daniel	MA0260	32
Newsom, Mary Ellen	IN0005	12,14,32,61,62
Newton, Jeanne	TN0930	32,64
Nichols, Lois J.	CA4600	66,32,44,67B,11
Nicolucci, Sandra	MA0400	32
Nielsen, John	IA0650	61,32
Nielsen, John	IA0200	44,32
Nierman, Glenn E.	NE0600	32
Nilsson, Donna	GA0525	11,32
Nimmer, Rebecca	WI0750	32
Nimmons, Phil	AG0450	32,47,29
Noble, James	MI1800	32
Noble, Jason	NY1600	32,37
Nole, Nancy	WA0650	32,32B
Nordlund, Moya L.	AL0800	32,13C
Norgaard, Martin	GA1050	32E,32F,62A,29E,32
Norris, Joshua L.	KS0900	36,60,13,32
Norton, Edgar	NY1700	32,64C
O'Banion, Philip R.	PA3250	32
O'Connell, Debora S.	NC2700	32
O'Connor, Margaret	NJ1400	11,32
O'Connor, Thomas	AR0110	13,32,47,10A,10F
Ode, James	TX2400	32
Ogilvie, Jessica	TX3535	32
Olander, Virginia	LA0300	32
Oliver, Brenda	NH0300	11,32
Oliver, Timothy	AR0110	37,32
Olsen, Ryan	CO0250	36,32
O'Neill, Susan	AG0500	32
Onofrio, Susan	NJ1350	32
Opfer, Stephen R.	CA2810	32,37,38,60B,47
Orlofsky, Diane	AL1050	32,12C,36
Orman, Evelyn	LA0200	32
Orzolek, Douglas	MN1625	11,32,37,60
Osterlund, David	SC0620	60,14,32,66A
Overland, Corin T.	FL1900	40,32,60A
Overly, Paul	SC0200	11,12,32,63C,63D
Owens, Douglas T.	VA1000	32,47,60B,29
Ozeas, Natalie	PA0550	32
Paddock, Joan Haaland	OR0450	60,32,49,63A,37
Page, Fran M.	NC1300	36,32
Pahel, Timothy	IL1800	32,36,61,12A
Palac, Judith A.	MI1400	32
Palese, Richard	IL3450	32,34
Palmer, Anthony J.	MA0400	32
Palmquist, Jane E.	NY0500	32,11
Panelli, Sal	CA0650	63A,32
Pannell, Larry J.	LA0100	64,34,35C,37,32
Paparone, Stacy A.	PA1450	32
Pape, Louis W.	SD0150	13,10,11,32,66
Pare', Craig T.	IN0350	32,37,65,60
Park, Angela	CA0350	32
Parker, Harlan D.	MD0650	60,32
Parker, Laura J.	MD0650	32
Parker, Linda	NC0200	11,32,44,13,64
Parker, Olin G.	GA2100	32
Parker-Brass, Myran	MA1175	32
Parnell, Janine	NC0700	62A,32
Parrish, Regina T.	AL1170	32
Patrick, Louise R.	FL0680	32
Patterson, James H.	GA0490	29,32,46,63,47
Patterson, Trent A.	MO1950	60A,61,32,36,39
Pavasaris, Walter	MA0350	32
Payn, Catherine	PA0350	32,39,61
Payne, Phillip	KS0650	32
Peak, Linda	WV0200	32
Pence, Suzanne M.	TX3510	32,36
Pennington, Lynn	AR0950	32,66A,66D
Peot, Deborah L.	IL0750	32
Pepetone, Gregory	GA0850	12A,32,66A,66B,66D
Peretz, Marc	MI1850	11,32,66D,34
Perez, Erin	TN1850	32
Perez, Frank	IA0600	37,47,32,29,63C
Perry, David L.	SC0050	12A,13A,64C,32,20A
Persellin, Diane C.	TX3350	32,44
Peterson, Amber Dahlen	OH1100	32
Peterson, Gene D.	TN1710	32,36,40
Petrik, Rebecca	ND0250	32,13A,61,70,36
Pfeiffer, Ruth Imperial	HI0160	13A,12A,32,36,66
Phillips, Kenneth	FL1450	32
Phillips, Kenneth H.	MA0950	32
Pitzer, Robert M.	WA1250	32,32B,32C,32H
Placek, Robert W.	GA2100	32,34
Platt, Melvin C.	MO1800	32
Platter, Donald R.	MI2200	37,32
Ploeger, Kristina	WA0250	32,36,60A
Pogonowski, Lenore	NY4200	53,32,12A,13
Polancich, Ronald	IL0550	32
Polett, Thomas C.	MO0300	63,47,32,13,20
Pollard, Catherine	NV0100	32
Pollart, Gene J.	RI0300	60,32,37,29A
Poloz, Zimfira	AG0450	32
Porter, Ann M.	OH2200	32,32E
Posegate, Stephen C.	IL3150	32,37,49,34
Posey, Benjamin C.	AL0300	32,37,60B,63A
Poulter, Patricia S.	IL0800	32
Powell, Clay	KY1550	32
Powell, Curtis Everett	GA0490	36,13,32,32D
Powell, Sean	GA0550	32
Poynter, Lynn	OH0680	32
Prado, Danny	TX3420	32
Pratt, Alice	NY2650	32
Price, Harry E.	GA1150	32
Prickett, Carol A.	AL1170	32,33
Priest, Thomas L.	UT0350	32,64D,11
Prince, Penny	NY0635	32,66A,66B,66C
Propst, Tonya	SC0420	63B,32,32C
Provencio, Robert	CA0650	60,32,36
Quaile, Robert	PA3330	32,64B
Quant, Sharon	OK0850	11,32,61
Quesada Agostini, Milagros	OH1120	14,32
Quesada, Milagros	OH1100	11,32,36
Quindag, Sue	SC0200	32,62A,62B,34
Quinlan, Gloria H.	TX1150	32,36,61,66C,31A
Rack, John	NC2440	32,65,29A
Raiber, Michael	OK1350	32
Raines, Jean	NC1900	12A,11,66A,32
Rampal, Michelle	NY2450	32
Ramsay, Susan	TN1850	32
Ramsay, Susan	TN0100	32
Ramsey, Darhyl S.	TX3420	32
Rankin, Charles	FL1950	32,37
Rao, Doreen	AG0450	32,36,60,61
Rasmussen, G. Rosalie	CA3400	32,44,66B,66D,13C
Rasmussen, Warren	CA4200	32
Ray, Julia J.	CA0835	32
Reames, Rebecca	NY3780	60A,32,36
Recktenwald, Karl	NJ0175	32
Reece, Richard	OH0300	32
Reed, Melissa	NY2650	32
Reedy, Hillary	IL1612	32,65
Rees, Fred J.	IN0907	34,12C,35C,32,12
Reeves, Patricia	TN1400	32
Regelski, Thomas A.	NY3725	60,32
Reichling, Mary	LA0760	32,66D
Reimer, Robert	NJ0175	32
Renfroe, Dennis C.	NC1025	11,12A,32,36,63
Resta, Craig	OH1100	32
Reynolds, Alison M.	PA3250	32,32A
Rhoads, Mark	MN0250	11,32,31A
Rhodes, Ruth	IL3450	48,64C,32
Richard, Monique M.	AE0100	32,36,40,60A
Richards, Wade	NY1100	32
Richmond, C. Floyd	PA3560	32,34,13
Richmond, John W.	NE0600	32D,32G,36,32
Riley, Martha C.	IN1300	32
Riley, Patricia E.	VT0450	32
Rimington, James	IL0400	32,61
Ringwall, Lauren	GA1650	32,60,36
Rios, Giselle Elgarresta	FL0050	61,36,60,32,41
Riposo, Joseph	NY4150	47,46,32
Ritcher, Gary	VA0600	32
Rivera Diaz, Almicar	PR0115	32
Rivera, Jose	NC2435	32,36,61,60
Rivera-Vega, Salvador	PR0100	11,32,48,64E
Rizzo, Jacques	NJ1400	32
Robbins, Janet	WV0750	32
Roberts, J. Christopher	OH1100	32
Roberts, Nancy	SD0100	32,61
Robinson, Greg	CA0805	32,63D
Robinson, Mitchell	MI1400	32
Robinson, Nathalie G.	NY1600	32,11
Robinson, Rick	NY0270	11,13,65,32
Robinson, Russell	FL1850	32,36
Rodriguez, Carlos Xavier	MI2100	32
Rodriguez, Ramon	PR0100	32
Rodriguez, Sandra	PR0115	32A,32D,32
Roebuck, Nikole D.	LA0100	32,64C
Rogers, Dennis G.	MO0850	32,65
Rogers, George L.	MA2100	32
Rohrer, Thomas	UT0300	37,32
Romer, Wayne Allen	PA3710	13A,10F,60B,11,32
Rose, Sarah Elizabeth	NC0050	32,33
Rotella, Gloria	NJ0760	32,66A,66D
Rox, David	MA0950	60,32,37,41
Rudolph, Thomas	PA3330	10F,60,32,37,41
Runions, Greg	AG0250	34,32
Ruthmann, Alex	MA2030	47,50,32,65
Rutschman, Carla J.	WA1250	32,34A
Ryan, Charlene	MA0260	12A,12,32,63D
Ryder, Christopher O.	VA1150	32
Ryder, William H.	LA0700	34,61,32,13,40
Salvador, Karen	MI2120	11,32,64,13
Sanders, Paul	OH1850	32
Sapegin, Judy	CO0550	32,36
Schabas, Ezra	AG0450	32
Schaefer, Carl	CA0815	32
Schafer, Carl	CA0450	32
Schatt, Matthew D.	OH1100	32,48,64
Scheib, John W.	IN0150	32
Schimek, John	OK0750	32,32E
Schlegel, Amanda L.	MS0750	32,62D
Schliff, Mary A.	CA0835	32
Schmidt, Margaret	AZ0100	32
Schmidt, Michael P.	MN0950	32
Schmidt, Patrick	FL0700	61,64D,32
Schneider, Benjamin D.	ND0150	32
Schneider, Brandt	CT0550	37,38,60B,64,32
Schoolfield, Robnet	SC0200	32
Schraer-Joiner, Lyn	NJ0700	32,45,65,72
Schroeder, Kelly M.	NY2650	32,11,13A,60
Schuette, Rebecca C.	IL0800	32
Schutt, Jackie T.	IL2050	32,13C,36
Sciarrotta, Jo-Ann	NJ0175	32
Scott, David	TX0150	32,60
Scott, Julia K.	TX2400	32
Scott, Laurie	TX3510	32,62
Scott, Sheila	AC0050	32,32B

Index by Area of Teaching Interest

Name	Code	Areas
Seay, Sandra	AR0110	11,61,32
Sedonis, Robert D.	OH1850	32,36
Seel, Nancy	NY3725	32
Sehmann, Karin M.	KY0550	32
Senders, Warren	MA1400	32
Severn, Eddie	PA2050	32,29,46,47,63
Sexton, A. Jeanette	OH1850	32
Seybert, John M.	FL1740	60,66A,32,64E,12
Sfraga, Debbie	NJ1160	32,37,47,64
Shadle-Peters, Jennifer	CO0275	12A,20,32,36,67
Shank, Jennifer S.	OH1100	32
Shankman, Ira	NY2750	32,40,36,60
Shankman, Nancy Ellen	NY2750	32,36,60
Shanley, Steven	IA0300	32,46,47,53
Shannon, Kathleen	WV0750	36,32,60
Shaw, Betty	TX3400	32,66B,66D
Shaw, Giocille	NY2750	32
Sheldon, Deborah	PA3250	32
Shelton, Brian M.	TX2960	37,32,60
Shelton, Tom	NJ1350	31,32,36,60A
Sherbon, James W.	NC2430	32
Sherman, Joseph	NY2750	38,32,62
Sherwin, Ronald G.	MA0150	11,31A,60A,36,32
Shields, Larry	AG0450	32,63C
Shively, Joseph L.	MI1750	32G,34,11,32,32C
Shiver, Todd	WA0050	63A,32,37,47,49
Shoop, Stephen S.	TX3515	32,41,60B,63D
Shorner-Johnson, Kevin T.	PA1250	32,20
Silverman, Marissa	NY0500	32
Silvester, William	NJ0175	60B,32,37
Sinclair, John V.	FL1550	60,32,36,41,38
Sinclair, Robert L.	IL3450	36,32,60A
Sinclair, Terrol	AG0650	32
Sink, Patricia E.	NC2430	32
Skadsem, Julie A.	MI2100	32D,32
Sletto, Thomas A.	IA0550	32
Small, Ann R.	FL1750	32,36
Smith, Bret	WA0050	11,32,12F
Smith, David S.	MI2250	32
Smith, Deborah	IL2910	32,32I
Smith, Kenneth H.	MI2250	32,34,12F
Smith, Lisa Kingston	CA5300	32
Smith, Matthew K.	VT0100	37,32,11,63B,60
Smith, Michael V.	DC0050	60,32,32B,32C,32D
Smith, Michael	CO0950	13A,32,32H
Smith, Ronald	NC1950	37,32,63,12A
Smith, Tawnya D.	IN0150	32
Smithee, Larry G.	TN1000	60,32,37,47,63
Smoak, Jeff C.	KY1425	32,36,61,40,43
Snyder, David W.	IL1150	32,37
Sobel, Elise	NY2105	32
Sobke, Catherine	CA4850	32
Sogin, David	KY1450	32
Sokolowski, Elizabeth	PA3330	32
Solie, Gordon A.	OR0850	60,32,37,64D
Song, MyungOk Julie	NY2750	32,36,60,61
Sorrell, Martha	VT0250	32
Sousa, Gary D.	TN1710	37,32
Souza, Thomas	MA0500	60B,64C,37,32,46
Spano, Fred P.	NC2420	32B,32D,32G,32
Speake, Constance J.	IL2150	11,32
Spence, J. Robert	PA1250	37,38,32,60B
Spencer, William G.	NC0050	60,32,64D,65
Spurgeon, Alan L.	MS0700	32
St. Juliana, Linda	MO0500	32
St. Onge, Sarah	NY2750	32
Stabile, Ronald	RI0300	32,41,50,65
Stallsmith, Becki	AL0260	32,38,50,61,66C
Stamer, Rick A.	AZ0450	32
Stanley, John	CA4700	32
Stauffer, Sandra L.	AZ0100	32
Steele, Daniel L.	MI0400	13A,32
Steele, Nalora L.	MA0260	32
Steele, Natalie	IA0850	32
Steele, Stephen K.	IL1150	60,32,37
Stegman, Sandra Frey	OH0300	32,36
Stein, Robin	TX3175	32
Stempel, Mark	NY1600	32,37
Stephens, Robert W.	CT0600	32,20A,20G
Stepniak, Michael	VA1350	12,38,31A,41,32
Stevenson, Roxanne	IL0600	13A,20G,32,37,64
Stewart, Shawna	CA0350	60,36,32
Stewart, Shirley	LA0720	11,36,61,31A,32
Stith, Gary	NY1700	32,37,60B,65
Stofko, Diane L.	TN0550	32,11,37,13A,60B
Stokes, Porter	SC1000	36,61,60,32
Stoll, Joni L.	OH1100	32
Stone, Jeff	TX2960	11,32
Stone, Michael John	OK0600	37,46,60B,63,32
Stone, Michael D.	CA0650	32
Stover, Pamela J.	IL2900	32,13A
Stover, Pamela	OH2300	32B,32C,32G,32H,32
Strauss, Gail	NY1600	32,11
Stringham, David A.	VA0600	32
Stripling, Allen	GA0810	11,36,66,32,40
Stroeher, Michael	WV0400	63D,49,63C,32,29
Strong, Alan D.	TX0345	11,32,66G
Strouse, Lewis	PA0550	60,32
Stubbs, James	TX1750	46,32,13A,37,47
Stubley, Eleanor	AI0150	12,32
Studt-Shoemaker, Lauren	MN0750	32
Stufft, David	GA2000	37,41,47,32,60B
Suabedissen, Gary	NJ0175	32
Suk, Richard	OH1900	32,37
Sullivan, Jill	AZ0100	32
Summers, C. Oland	NC0850	32,63C,64D,65,72
Sutton, Leslie	IN1300	32
Swanson, Michelle	IA1600	32
Swanzy, David	LA0300	32
Sweeney, Christopher R.	AK0100	32,63D,63C,32E,32B
Sweet, Bridget Mary	IL3300	32,11,60A
Swenson, Thomas S.	NC2205	13A,66B,35C,34,32
Swift, Robert F.	NH0250	11,32,36
Swinyar, Carol	MA0250	32
Tacka, Philip V.	PA2350	12,13,32
Tagg, Barbara M.	NY4150	32,36,60A
Taggart, Cynthia Crump	MI1400	32
Takacs, Miklos	AI0210	32,36
Talbot, Brent C.	PA1400	32
Tallarico, Pat	OH0300	32
Talley, Keith M.	OK1250	64E,32,48,34
Talmadge, Samantha	CT0100	61,32
Tapia, James R.	NY4150	60B,38,32
Tate, David L.	VA0800	32,36
Tate, Philip	NJ0175	38,60B,32
Tate, Shelia D.	VA1800	11,32,16,36
Taylor, Arlecia Jan	TX2100	11,36,32,66A
Taylor, Clint 'Skip'	GA2100	32
Taylor, Donald M.	TX3420	32,32B
Taylor, Wayne	VA0450	32
Teachout, David J.	NC2430	32
Teichmer, Shawn	MI2000	32,60,64,12A,11
Tendall, Rosita	IL0100	32
Tevis, Royce	CA0800	32,37,63A,60
Teweleit, Russell D.	TX3750	32,46,37
Thacker, Elizabeth	OH1400	61,32
Thaller, Gregg	IN0550	65,32,13C,38
Thayer, Robert W.	OH0300	32
Thiel, Robb G.	IN1350	10F,60B,32,37,65
Thielen-Gaffey, Tina	MN1600	36,61,40,32
Thomas, Andre J.	FL0850	60A,32,36
Thomas, Edwin	IN0005	65,11,12,32,60
Thompson, Anne	MI0900	32
Thomson, John	IL0550	32
Thorson, Eric	TN0250	32,36,60
Thurber, Donald W.	CA2420	11,32
Timm, Cynthia L.	OH0700	32
Timothy, Sarah O.	AL0890	61,11,36,13,32
Tipps, James	OH2500	32,36,66A,66D,60
Tocheff, Robert	OH1600	60,11,32,36,66D
Tolbert, Patti	GA0850	32,65,50
Tolson, Gerald H.	KY1500	32,47,29,14C
Tovey, David G.	OH1850	32
Trapp, Ken	CT0550	32
Traster, Jeff	FL2050	37,49,63D,32
Tredway, Curtis B.	TX3520	37,32
Treuden, Terry	WI1155	37,47,32,10F
Trimborn, Thomas J.	MO1780	60,11,32
Tripold, David	NJ0760	13,12A,32,31A,33
Trollinger, Valerie L.	PA1750	34,32,64D,11,32C
Tunks, Thomas W.	TX2400	32,12F
Tuohey, Terese M.	MI2200	32,32E
Turner, Charles	KY0300	32,37,63,47,41
Turpin, Douglas	MO1830	32
Tyree, Rebecca	VA1600	36,32
Ulrich, Jerry	GA0900	10,36,32,32D,60A
Urbis, Sue Zanne Williamson	TX3515	32,66C
Usher, Ann L.	OH2150	32,36,60A
Usher, Jon	CA0845	64C,32
Vaglio, Anthony J.	NC1300	13,10,32,34
Vaillancourt, Josee	AI0190	32,36
Vallentine, John	IA1600	32,37,64C
Vallieres, Claude	AI0220	32
Vallo, Victor	GA0850	32,37,60B
Van der Vat-Chromy, Jo-Anne	VA0600	32
Vandehey, Patrick	OR0250	60,32,37,38,63C
Vandelict, Roy D. 'Skip'	MO0100	32,37,60B,64A,47
VanGent, Wendy	SD0400	32,70
Vannatta-Hall, Jennifer E.	TN1100	32
VanWeelden, Kimberly	FL0850	60,32,36
Vartanian, Tina M.	CA5300	32
Vega, Rebecca	NJ0050	32,37,11,64A,60B
Venesile, Christopher J.	OH1100	32
Verdicchio, Linda	NJ1400	32
Veres, Fran A.	AZ0500	32
Verrier, Thomas	TN1850	37,60B,32C,32D,32
Vest, Johnathan	TN1720	32,66D
Vincent, Dennis	FL1000	32,34
Vincent, Jennifer J.	IN0800	32
Vogan, Nancy F.	AE0050	11,32
Von Gruenigan, Robert	OH1850	32
Von Kampen, Kurt E.	NE0150	36,60A,32
Vote, Larry	MD0750	60,32,36,61
Vredenburg, Brenda	NY3780	32
Vredenburg, Jeffrey	NY3780	32
Vroman, David	IL0400	60,32,37,63B
Waddell, Mike	NC2440	64B,64C,64D,11,32
Wade, Mark Alan	OH0850	63A,12A,11,32,60B
Waggoner, David	AZ0500	32
Wagner, Wayne L.	MN1030	13A,32,36,66G,66D
Waldon, Stanley H.	MI2200	32,66D
Waldron, Janice Lynn	AG0550	32
Walker, Christopher G.	GA0150	11,32,64,48
Walker, Jeri	OK1150	32,13C
Walker, Kerry E.	CT0800	32,48,64A
Walker, Linda B.	OH1100	32,36
Wallace, David	NY1900	32
Walls, Kimberly C.	AL0200	32,34C,32F,32G
Walter, Cameron	AG0450	32,63C,63D,37,44
Walters, Darrel L.	PA3250	32
Walters, Kerry E.	IL0400	61,32,39
Wang, Cecilia	KY1450	32,12C
Wang, Jui-Ching	IL2200	32,20
Wapnick, Joel	AI0150	32
Ward, Wayne	MA0260	32
Ward-Steinman, Patrice Madura	IN0900	32G,32D,32,29,47
Warren, Maredia D. L.	NJ0825	13,11,32
Washington-Harris, Kara E.	AL0050	32
Wasiak, Ed	AA0200	32,37,63A
Watkins, Wilbert O.	IL0275	36,40,32
Watts, Sarah	OH0650	32
Wayman, John B.	GA2300	32,36,61
Weaver, Michael A.	SC0950	12A,11,32,62A,62B
Weaver, Molly A.	WV0750	32,32E,32G,34
Weber, Linda	TX0550	11,64A,66A,32,66D
Webster, Peter R.	IL2250	32
Weightman, Lindsay	PA3250	32
Weingarten, Frederic	NY2650	32
Weldon-Stephens, Amber	GA1150	32,33
Wells, Larry	NC1350	32,63A
Wendel, Joyce	OH2450	32,36,61,60A
West, Cheryl	IN0250	40,32
Westervelt, Todd G.	FL0100	32,12C,63A
Whale, Mark	AG0450	32
Wheatley, Susan E.	PA1600	32,12C
Wheeler, Candace	FL0200	66,11,32,10,66A
Wheeler, Kathy	MI0400	32
Whitaker, Nancy L.	WI0835	32
Whitcomb, Rachel	PA1050	32,32B,32A
Whitener, John L.	CA5300	32
Whitley, H. Moran	NC0300	32,31A,13
Whitlock, Mark	MN1600	32,37,49,63C,63D
Whitman, Thomas I.	PA3200	13,20D,32
Wiberg, Janice	MT0300	13,12A,32,36,66
Wiggins, Donna	NC2700	12C,32,32G
Wiles, John L.	IA1600	36,60A,61,32
Wilhelm, Philip	IL1740	64D,32,40,11
Wilhoit, Mel R.	TN0200	10F,12A,32,49,63
Wilkins, Sharon	MO0400	32,36,66A
Williams, Bonnie Blu	MS0400	11,32
Willingham, Lee	AG0600	32,36
Willman, Fred	MO1830	32,34
Willoughby, Judith A.	OK0750	36,60A,40,32
Wilson, Lorraine P.	PA1600	32,66D,20G
Wilt, Lois J.	NY1700	32,64A
Wine, Thomas	KS1450	32,36,60A

Name	Code	Areas
Wing, Lizabeth A.	OH2200	32
Winkle, Carola	ID0050	64C,32
Wise, Phillip C.	MO0800	29,32
Witt, Anne C.	AL1170	62,32
Wolf, Debbie	PA3250	32
Wolf, Debbie Lynn	PA2800	32,66A,66D,66B
Wood, Stanley D.	OH1600	32,36,66D,13C,34
Woodford, Paul	AG0500	60,12B,32,37,63
Woods, Jon R.	OH1850	32,37
Woodward, Sheila C.	WA0250	32
Woolley, Clara	IN0010	13,11,32,66A,66G
Wooten, Ronnie	IL2200	32,37
Workman, Darin D.	KS1110	60,32,37,47,64
Worman, James	TX3350	32,37,47,29,64E
Wray, Robert	WV0400	32,60,61
Wright, Helen	NY0642	32
Wright, Ruth	AG0500	32
Wubbena, Teresa R.	AR0400	13,32,41,16,64
Wurgler, Pamela S.	KY0950	32
Wyatt, Larry D.	SC1110	60,32,36
Xiques, David	NY2750	32,60A,61
Yamron, Janet M.	PA3250	60,32,36
Yontz, Timothy	IL3550	32E,37,63A,32
Yoshioka, Airi	MD1000	32,41,51,62A
Young, Margaret	OH1850	32,66D
Young, Margaret	OH1860	11,32,66
Young, Paul G.	OH1905	32
Young, Sylvester	OH1900	32
Younge, Pascal Yao	OH1900	20,32
Younker, Betty Anne	AG0500	32
Yozviak, Lisa	OH0700	36,32
Zahler, Clara	PA0550	32,13C
Zahn, George	MN0350	32
Zalantis, Helen	NY0625	32
Zamzow, Laura	WV0200	11,63D,60B,32,37
Zanutto, Daniel R.	CA0825	32,60
Zdzinski, Stephen	FL1900	32,32G,32H,12C,13K
Zemek, Michael D.	IL0100	32,36,60A
Zemke, Lorna	WI0770	32,14A,29,20G
Zerull, David	VA1350	32,37
Zielinski, Mark D.	NH0350	32

Early Childhood Education

Name	Code	Areas
Albrecht, Tamara	GA0750	11,12A,32A
Almeida, Artie	FL1800	32A
Amchin, Robert A.	KY1500	32B,32H,32A
Anderson, Leeann	OH1000	11,32B,62E,32A,32C
Andrews, Laura J.	KS0350	32B,32C,32A,32G,32H
Apple, Marjorie	PA0400	32A
Arnett, Nathan D.	IL1240	11,13C,32A,36,40
Asbo, Kayleen	CA4150	32A
Aston, Janis	TN1600	32A
Babb, Tim	NC1250	32A
Baker, Jessica	IL2750	32A
Barfield, Susan	MT0175	32A,32B,32C
Barksdale, Alicia	MD0850	32A
Barone, Ann Carmen	OH1330	11,32A
Bartley, Peter	AG0500	32A,62A
Bath, Joanne	NC0650	62A,32A
Bauer, Elizabeth	IL3550	32A,32B,32C
Becerra, Janelle	MO0850	32A,32B
Beck, Laurel D.	CA3500	32A
Benjamin Figueroa, Haydee	PR0115	32A
Berentsen, Kurt	OR0150	36,60,61,32A,40
Berke, Melissa	NE0610	32A,32B
Bernstorf, Elaine D.	KS1450	32A,32B
Bethany, Adeline M.	PA0450	11,20D,32A,32B,36
Bieritz, Gerald	TX1300	12A,11,32A,36,60
Bond, Judith	WI0850	32,32A,32B,32C
Boner, Jan	GA1150	32A
Boucher, Helene	AI0150	32A
Brannen, Malcolm	MI0850	62A,62B,38,32A
Bridges, Jan	TX2570	32A,32B,11
Brink, Rhona	TX3400	32A,32B
Brooks-Smith, Emma	MS0350	32A,32B,32C,32G
Brown, Charlene	AA0110	61,32A
Bryant, Dorothy	OH1900	32B,32A,11
Buck, Barbara	KY0750	32A,32B,32C,32D,61
Buffington, Blair	IA1750	61,36,40,32A,60A
Burton, Warren L.	UT0300	11,32A,32B,62C
Cajas, Edgar	TX2600	32A,32B,32C,12A
Campbell, Patricia Shehan	WA1050	32A,20A,12C,32B,20D
Canfield, Jennifer K.	AL0450	11,32A,32D,66D,32B
Cavallo, Gail R.	NY2550	32A,13A,66D
Chambers, Carol	TX3100	63A,13C,32E,10F,32A
Choe, EJ	IN0907	13,11,32A,32B,66
Clarke, Leland	MA2200	32A,32B,66A,66B
Clay, Shea	VA0350	32A,32B
Cook, Sophia	DC0170	32A
Cooper, Shelly	AZ0500	32,32A,32B,32G,32H
Costa-Giomi, Eugenia	TX3510	32,32A
Cottrill, Heather	WV0050	61,32A,32B
Coulthard, Anita	VA0350	66G,32A,32B,31A
Crawford, Glenda	OH2550	36,32A,32C,32B,60
Creasy, Kathleen	GA1150	32A
Cross, Sandra	IL2750	32A,61
Crossland, Carolyn M.	NC1075	13A,11,32A,36,32B
Cruz, Samantha	WI0500	32A,32B,32C,11
Custodero, Lori A.	NY4200	32A,32B,32G,12E,12C
Dale, Monica	DC0170	32A,66A
D'Ambrosio, Kara Ireland	CA4400	32A,32B
Daniel, Kathy	TX2250	64A,32A,32B
Davis, Beth A.	AL1160	32A,32B
Dees, Jennifer	TX3200	32A,32B
Dettinger, Mary Joyce	OH1330	32A,32B,66A,31A
Diepeveen, Susan	AF0120	66A,32A
Dolloff, Lori-Anne	AG0450	32A,32B,60,36,66C
Domenico, Tony	MD0450	32A,47
Dornian, Kathy	AA0050	66A,66C,32A
Drayson, Susan	AA0050	32A
Dubois, Chantal	AI0190	32A,32B
Durlam, Zachary D.	CA1860	36,60,32A,32B,40
Dzuik, Youlee	DC0170	32A
Eberenz, Gina	KY0250	32A,32B,32C
Eckert, William H.	DC0110	13,12A,32A,66G
Edwards, Richard D.	OH2000	37,32,60B,12F,32A
Eichner, Mark J.	WI0835	60,32C,37,63A,32A
Eppink, Joseph A.	NY0700	32B,66G,66H,32C,32A
Eshelman, Darla	OK1330	32A,32B,32D
Fairchild, Nancy	WI0840	32B,32A
Feierabend, John	CT0650	32A,32B
Feldhusen, Roberta	NY2750	32A,32B
Feria, Marissa	AA0050	32A,66A
Fifield, Glen	UT0300	13A,32A,32B,49,63A
Finch, Abraham L.	MA1650	32A,50,65A,65B
Finkelstein, Marc	NJ0550	32A,32B,66A,70
Fisher, Anna	DC0170	66A,32A
Fleischman, John F.	NY3717	32A,32B
Flores, Lisa	IL2750	32A
Fox, Donna Brink	NY1100	32A,32B,32C,32G
Frakes, Louise	IA0900	32A,32B
Fresne, Jeannette	AL1300	32A,32B,32C,32D,32I
Frizzell, Patricia	AA0050	32A
Gage, Stephanie	OH2600	32A
Gengaro, Christine Lee	CA2600	13A,32A,61
Gravel, Manon	AI0220	32B,32A,66B
Grayburn, Margaret	GA1150	32A
Grice, June	KY0900	32A,32B,32C,32G,32H
Griffen, Jane	MO0500	60A,32A,32B,36,61
Grigoriu, Katrina	AA0050	32A,62A,62B
Gruenhagen, Lisa M.	OH0300	32A,32B,32G,64A,32
Gruetter, Joy	OH2140	61,32A
Guttmann, Hadassah	NY2550	32A,66D,66A
Haager, Julia	AA0050	32A,66C
Hackworth, Rhonda S.	NJ1130	32B,32C,32A,36,32
Hagarty, Mia	TX0550	62A,32A,62B
Hahna, Nicole	PA3100	32A,33,11
Hale, Connie L.	SC1200	32B,32H,32A
Hale, Nancy	TX1400	32A,32B
Hall, Nadine	CA3500	32A
Halliday, Anna Rebecca	AL1200	11,32A,32B
Hamilton, Hilree J.	WI0845	11,20,32A,32B,66D
Hansen, Demaris	CT0650	32A,32B,32G,32H
Hansford, Conchita	OK0650	32A,32B,61,66A,31A
Harriott, Janette	NE0590	32A,32B,11
Harris, Brenda	IL1612	66,32A
Hawkins, Michelle Kennedy	AA0110	32A,61,66A
Hawkins, William	CA3460	13A,32A,49,63,29
Haworth, Janice	MN0150	32A,32C,32B,36,20A
Haywood, Jennifer	NY1800	32A,32B,32E
Herrmann, Tracy	OH0350	32A,32B,32C
Hershaft, Lisa	WI1150	32A
Hitsky, Seth	IL2750	32A
Horn, Lawrence C.	MS0560	11,32A,48,64
Huck, Patricia	AA0050	32A,66A
Huff, Christina	IN1025	32A,32B,32C,11,36
Huls, Shirley	PA3000	13A,32A,32B,61
Hungerford, Del	WA1150	32A,32B,32C,11
Hunt, Catherine	KS1400	32A,32B,32C
Jalilian, Zeinab	AA0050	32A
James, Pamela A.	VA0750	32A,61,13C,66D,32B
Jensen, Gary J.	IL0800	32A,32B,32H,32C
Johnson, Daniel	IL1200	32A,32B,32C,32D,32E
Johnson, Kevin P.	GA1900	60,11,32A,32B,34
Johnson, Sara	TN1850	62A,32A
Johnston, Susan	DC0170	32A
Joy, Sharon	LA0550	32A,32B,32H,32G,32
Jurchuk, Tobi	AA0050	32A,62A
Kahler, Edward P.	TX3750	33,32A
Kane, Marie A.	RI0100	32A
Kane, Marie A.	RI0101	32A
Keast, Michelle	TX3527	11,32,32A
Kegerreis, Helen M.	NY2550	32A,13C,66D
Kehler, Harry	PA3710	32A,32B,32C
Kempter, Susan	NM0450	62,32A,32B,32C
Kenney, Susan H.	UT0050	32A,32B
Kent, James	MN1590	32A
Khalsa, Gurjeet	DC0170	32A
Kiehn, Mark T.	WI0808	32A,66D,70,63A,32B
Kilchyk, Olena	AA0050	32A,62C
Kisner, Janna	WV0750	32A,32B
Klein, Nancy K.	VA1000	36,60A,32A,32B,32C
Koops, Lisa	OH0400	32,32A
Kretchner, Darlene	CA0830	32B,32A,32E,32F,32G
Kronour, Dianne	OH2250	32A,32B
Kuller, Ronnie	IL2750	32A
Lamkin, Martin J.	VI0050	11,12A,32A,47,60B
Lancaster, Linda K.	KY1200	32A,32B
Laskey, Anne	CA2200	32A,32B
Lebron, Nelie	PR0115	32A,32B
Lee, Pamela Perec	DC0170	32A
Levinowitz, Lili	NJ1050	32,32A,32B
Lew, Jackie Chooi-Theng	MD0800	32A,32B,20,32C,66
Lewis, Barbara E.	ND0500	12F,12C,32A,32B
Linklater, Joan	AC0100	32A
Liston, Robin	KS0050	32A,32B,12A,11
Long, Janet	SC0900	62,32B,11,32A,32C
Lonich, Nancy L.	PA0500	32A,32B
Lundblad, Genevieve	MD0450	32A,11,33
Malone, Mark H.	MS0850	32A,32B,32C,32D
Margetts, James A.	NE0050	66,12A,13,32A
Maring, Eric	DC0170	32A
Markovich, Kimberly	CA3250	32A
Markun, Mila M.	WV0400	32A,66A,66C,66D
Marshall, Herbert D.	OH0200	32A,32B
Mason, Emily J.	NY1800	32A,32B,32C
Mauthe, Holger	AA0050	32A
McConkey, Michelle	CA0800	32A,32B,32C
McCord, G. Dawn Harmon	GA2130	32B,32C,32A,13C,66D
McCord, Kimberly A.	IL1150	32B,32C,32F,29A,32A
McCusker, IHM, Joan	PA2200	32A,32B,32C,32G
McDaniel, Carolyn	OH0250	32A,32B,36
McHugh, Barbara	IL1500	32A,36
McKee, Angela	GA1150	32A,32B,32G
McKee, Richard	GA1150	32A
McKoy, Constance L.	NC2430	32B,32A,20A,32
McNellie, Myra	TX2700	32A,32B
Meek, Darla	TX2955	32A,32B,32H
Michalek, Thomas	NE0300	32B,32A
Milenkovic, Michelle	AA0020	32A,61
Miller, Marie C.	KS0300	32A,32B,66A
Mims, Mary	MO1500	32A,32B
Mizener, Charlotte P.	TX1400	32B,32G,32A
Montgomery, Glen	AA0050	66A,32A
Montgomery, Janet	MD1010	32,32A,32B
Moore, Marvelene C.	TN1710	32A,32B,32I
Morin, Carmen	AA0050	32A,66A
Moser, Janet	IL0850	66A,66D,32A,32
Moss, Elaine	WI0750	66C,66D,66B,66A,32A
Mueller, Ruth	NY2400	32A
Mueller, Susan	NV0050	32A,32B
Nardo, Rachel L.	UT0250	32,32B,34,32A,32D
Nelson, Joy	OK1350	32A,32B
Nelson, Joy	AJ0150	32A,32B
Nelson, Margaret	WI0855	11,32A,32B
Nelson, Marie	MA2020	32A,32B,32C,66D
Nord, Michael	OR1300	32A,32B,34
Okins, Ann	SD0580	32A,32B
Otero, Erica	NM0450	32A,32B
Owens, Diane	TX1100	66A,66C,66D,32A,32B
Paney, Andrew S.	MS0700	32B,13A,66A,32A
Parker, Elizabeth	GA0550	32A,32B,32C,32D
Parr, Carlotta	CT0050	32A,32B,32C,36,32G
Patterson, Anne L.	WV0300	11,12A,32A

Paul, Phyllis M.	OR1050	32A,32B,32C
Peffley, Lynette	OH0100	32A,11,66D
Perlau, Anita	AA0050	36,32A
Phillips, Paula	AF0120	61,32A
Piersall, Janie	IL1612	32A,32B,66A
Popowich, Jamie	AA0050	32A,36
Puller, Shawn I.	GA0150	11,61,12A,32A,39
Rae, Wendy	AA0050	13,32A,66A
Rampp, Rose K.	DC0170	32A
Rawlins, Deborah	TX2250	32A,32B
Reagan, Jama	TN1850	66A,32A
Regester, Kristen	IL2750	32A,65
Reynolds, Alison M.	PA3250	32,32A
Richardson, Ouida	TX0550	36,64A,32A
Ritterling, Soojin Kim	WI0810	32B,32C,11,61,32A
Riveire, Janine	CA0630	32A,32B,32C
Rodriguez, Sandra	PR0115	32A,32D,32
Roll, Christianne	VA0350	61,32A,13C
Rolsten, Kathy	MN1120	32A,32B,32D,36,61
Romanek, Mary L.	PA2720	12A,32A,32B,29A
Roop, Cynthia M.	NC1250	64A,32A,32E,13C,41
Roshong, Janelle	OH1350	32A,32B
Rubens, Beth	DC0170	32A
Russell, Teresa P.	CA4850	60,36,61,54,32A
Rutkowski, Joanne	PA2750	32A,32B,32G
Sacalamitao, Melonie	CA4850	32A,32B,32C,66D,36
Saginario, Donald	FL1100	11,32A
Sands-Pertel, Judith	CA1500	32A,32B,66
Scheidker, Barbara	CA4850	32A,32B
Schmidt, Catherine M.	MN1700	32B,14,32A
Scholl, Tim	TX2550	13A,13E,32A,66,70
Scott, Rosemary	GA0250	32A,32B,32C,11
Scriggins, Elizabeth	AA0050	32A,62A
Sexton, Lucinda	DC0170	32A
Simpson, Brennetta	NC1600	32B,32A,32D
Sims, Wendy L.	MO1800	32A,32B,32G
Smale, Marcelyn	MN1300	32A,13C,66D,32B,32D
Smith, Marilyn	MS0420	36,32A,32B
Sobol, Elise	NY2750	32A,32B,32C
Spataro, Susan M.	VA0400	64A,47,11,32A,32B
Spethmann, Molly	WI1150	32A
St. John, Patricia A.	NY4200	32A,32B
Stambaugh, Laura	GA0950	32A,32B,32C,32E,32G
Standerfer, Stephanie	VA1350	32A,32B,32C
Standley, Jayne	FL0850	32A,33
Stanley, Lynnette	AR0850	66C,32A
Steele, Stacey G.	PA3100	32A,32B,48,64A
Struman, Susan Jean	TX0550	51,62C,32A,11,62D
Stryker, Crystal J.	PA3000	32A,32B,61
Supeene, Susan	AA0040	32A,61,36
Swaim, Doris	NC2640	32A,36,61,66D
Swanson, Robyn	KY1550	32A,32B,32G,32H
Szanto, Judit	AA0050	32A
Talley, Terri	GA1150	32A
Taylor-Bilenki, Jan	AA0050	32A
Teresi, Cindy	CA0150	32A
Thiele, Margaret	MI0600	32A,32B
Thompson, Linda K.	TN0850	32A,32B,32C,32G
Tice, Joshua	WI1150	32A
Timmons, Leslie	UT0300	32A,32B,64A,48,41
Trenfield, Sally	TX3515	32A,32B,66C,66D
Trinka, Jill L.	SC0420	32A,20,32B
Tu, Ming	IL1750	32A,32B
Turner, Corinne	DC0170	32A
Turner, Mark E.	TX2700	32B,32A
Valerio, Wendy	SC1110	32A,12
Vasey, Monika	DC0170	32A
Vaughn, Michael	IL2000	12A,12,32A,66A
Veblen, Kari	AG0500	32A,32B
Watts, Sarah	PA0350	32A,32B,11
Waymire, Mark D.	MS0750	32A,32B,32C
Weisenberg, Marvi	NY2400	32A
Welborn, Daniel C.	GA1050	32A
Wells, Lillie	OR1050	32A,62A,32E
Whitcomb, Rachel	PA1050	32,32B,32A
White, Kim	MN0610	32A,32B
Whitehead, Baruch	NY1800	32B,32A,32C,20A
Willcox, Carolyn	AA0110	32A,66A
Williams, Barbara	CA5350	32A,32B
Wohlgemuth, J. Leigh	MN0625	32A
Wopat, Ann	WA0850	61,32I,32A,32B,32C
Wotring, Linda	MI1900	11,32A,32B,66A,66B
Zanjani, Azadeh	AA0050	32A,66A
Zavzavadjian, Sylvia	AA0050	32A,66A,66C
Zilli, Carol	CA3320	32A,32B

Elementary General Music

Adams, Julie R.	MN1120	61,32B
Adams, Margaret Ann	OK1200	32B
Ahern, Patty	KS0265	32B
Albert, Kristen A.	PA3600	32B
Allen, JoAnna	PA1750	32B
Allen, Sarah	TX2400	32E,37,32,60B,32B
Allen, Tom	MO1710	70,32B
Amchin, Robert A.	KY1500	32B,32H,32A
Amendola, James	NC2435	32B
Anavitarte, David	TX2550	36,61,66A,12A,32B
Anderson, Diana	CO0200	32B,66A,66G
Anderson, Kay	TX3750	32B
Anderson, Leeann	OH1000	11,32B,62E,32A,32C
Andrews, Laura J.	KS0350	32B,32C,32A,32G,32H
Anthon, Gina	LA0650	32B
Artesani, Laura	ME0440	12A,66C,15,32B,32C
Aubrey, Robert	MS0700	32B,11
Babcock, Windy	TX1550	32B
Bailey, Shad	MT0730	32B
Balboa, Javier	TX3515	32B
Baldwin, Karen	WA0250	32B
Baldwin, Karen	WA1350	32B
Ball, Wesley A.	CT0800	32,32B,13C
Baptiste, Renee L.	AL0500	32B,32C,32D,32G,36
Barber, Deborah L.	AR0200	34,32B,10D,70,32C
Barbone, Anthony	SC0420	32B
Barfield, Susan	MT0175	32A,32B,32C
Barker, David	VA1580	13A,32B
Barlar, Nancy	FL0670	64C,32B,32C,32E,11
Bates, Elaine	OK1250	32B,66A,13
Bates, Vincent C.	MO0950	63B,32B,32C,11
Battersby, Sharyn L.	DC0050	32B,32C,66D,32D,32H
Bauer, Elizabeth	IL3550	32A,32B,32C
Becerra, Janelle	MO0850	32A,32B
Belich, Kay	WI0150	39,61,32B
Bell, MaryLynn	KS0150	32B
Bennett, Cindy	IL3370	63,32B
Benton, Carol W.	GA0200	13C,13K,32B,32D,32G
Berke, Melissa	NE0610	32A,32B
Bernstorf, Elaine D.	KS1450	32A,32B
Berry, James	PA3100	11,37,60,32B,48
Bessinger, Marti	OK1250	32B
Bethany, Adeline M.	PA0450	11,20D,32A,32B,36
Beyer, Loretta	MI0200	13,66A,32B,11
Bilotta, Lee	PA3560	60,32B,37,63,31A
Black, Christina	PA2710	32B
Blair, Deborah V.	MI1750	32B,32C,12B,12F,32D
Blaser, Melanie	OH0650	32B
Blooding, Karen	TN1100	32B
Bond, Judith	WI0850	32,32A,32B,32C
Boozer, Pat	NC2350	10,32B,66A,13A,13B
Bottorf, Deane	CA5355	32B
Bradley, Annette	AA0080	66A,32B,13C,66D,42
Brandon, Joan Lynette	IN0100	32B,36,32C,32D
Brandon, Mark	AL0500	32B,32C,64C
Breaux, Michael L.	NY2750	32B,32C,32E,32F
Bretzius, David	PA1550	32B
Brickman, Scott T.	ME0420	14C,13,32B,10B,66D
Bridges, Jan	TX2570	32A,32B,11
Briggs, Kendall Durelle	NY1900	32B,12A,29
Brink, Rhona	TX3400	32A,32B
Briones, Marella	MO0650	61,11,36,32B,39
Britts, Judy	CA0840	32B
Brooks-Smith, Emma	MS0350	32A,32B,32C,32G
Brown, Alise	CO0950	32B
Brown, Kathy	MO1550	32B,61
Bruenger, Susan Dill	TX3530	32B,32C,32D
Bryant, Deanne	IL1200	32B,32C,32D,32E
Bryant, Dorothy	OH1900	32B,32A,11
Buck, Barbara	KY0750	32A,32B,32C,32D,61
Buckner, Jeremy	TN0250	32B,32C,66A,66D,11
Bugos, Kristen	TX0600	32B,66D
Bullock, Valerie K.	SC0275	60,32B,32C,36
Burke, Larry	FL0800	32B,63D,29A,49,35A
Burke, Martha	DE0150	32B
Burton, Warren L.	UT0300	11,32A,32B,62C
Butler, Charles Mark	MS0250	63B,32B,13E,13B,66G
Butler, Milton	OH1900	11,32B,32C
Cajas, Edgar	TX2600	32A,32B,32C,12A
Campbell, Debra L.	NY3780	32D,32B
Campbell, Mark Robin	NY3780	32B
Campbell, Patricia Shehan	WA1050	32A,20A,12C,32B,20D
Candee, Jan	ND0400	66A,66D,66G,32B,11
Canfield, Jennifer K.	AL0450	11,32A,32D,66D,32B
Carlisle, Katie	GA1050	32B,32C
Carnes, Glenda	TX3175	32B
Carr, Johnny	GA0250	32B
Catallo, Jennifer Kincer	MI1750	32B
Chambers, Steve	TX2750	13A,32B,66C
Charsky, Thomas	NJ0050	32B,11
Charsky, Thomas	NJ1400	32B,11
Chiarizzio, R. Kevin	VA0650	63,32B,32C,32F
Choe, EJ	IN0907	13,11,32A,32B,66
Cichy, Patricia Wurst	RI0150	32B,13C,64B,11,67D
Clarke, Leland	MA2200	32A,32B,66A,66B
Clay, Shea	VA0350	32A,32B
Cochenour, Deborah	PA1350	32B
Cochran, Kathy	SC0750	32B,32D
Cochrane, Keith A.	NM0400	60,12A,32B,37,47
Cole, Judith W.	TX2960	11,12A,32B
Collins, Myrtice J.	AL0500	32B,66D,36
Colvin, Maura	NC2600	32B
Colwitz, Erin E.	AL1160	32B,61,60A,36,32C
Conlon, Kelly	RI0200	32B
Connors, David	CA0830	32B,32C,61
Cooper, Shelly	AZ0500	32,32A,32B,32G,32H
Cottrill, Heather	WV0050	61,32A,32B
Coulthard, Anita	VA0350	66G,32A,32B,31A
Cowell, Kimberly S.	MO1830	32B
Cox, Kris	IL1100	32B,32C
Craig, Susan	CA0350	32B
Crawford, Glenda	OH2550	36,32A,32C,32B,60
Crawford, Ted	AJ0030	65,32B,32C
Crossland, Carolyn M.	NC1075	13A,11,32A,36,32B
Cruz, Samantha	WI0500	32A,32B,32C,11
Culbertson, Robert M.	TX1400	11,32B,63B
Cummings, Grace	NY3350	32B,36,61,32C,32D
Custodero, Lori A.	NY4200	32A,32B,32G,12E,12C
Dade, Fred S.	PA3050	20,11,32B,36,66A
D'Ambrosio, Kara Ireland	CA4400	32A,32B
Daniel, Kathy	TX2250	64A,32A,32B
Daniels, William B.	KY1100	32B,37,47,49,63
Davis, Alfred L.	VA0500	32E,32F,32B,32C,10F
Davis, Beth A.	AL1160	32A,32B
Deats, Carol	KS1050	32B,63B
Dees, Jennifer	TX3200	32A,32B
DeFrain, Debbie	NE0500	66A,11,32B
Demorest, Steven M.	WA1050	32B,32C,36
Derrickson, Keith W.	MD0850	32B
Dettinger, Mary Joyce	OH1330	32A,32B,66A,31A
DiCuirci, Michael P.	OH0450	32B,32C,37,63D,46
Diddle, Laura D.	SD0550	32B,32D,36
Dixon, Howard	TN0800	13A,11,32B,63,64
Dockery, Darryl D.	KY1550	32B
Dody, Teresa D.	WV0350	61,13C,13K,32B,32D
Dolloff, Lori-Anne	AG0450	32A,32B,60,36,66C
Dovel, Suzanne	OK0550	32B
Doyle, Tracy A.	CO0050	64A,32,32B
Droke, Marilyn	MO0200	13A,32B,44
Dubois, Chantal	AI0190	32A,32B
Dufault, Jenny E.	MN1120	32B,39,61
Duncan, David	OK0150	32B
Dura, Marian T.	PA1900	38,62,32,32B,62A
Durlam, Zachary D.	CA1860	36,60,32A,32B,40
Eberenz, Gina	KY0250	32A,32B,32C
Edmonds, Johnnella	VA1750	60,32B,32C,36,61
Elliott, Barbara	TX3175	32B
Elmore, Ashlee	OK0825	32B,32C
Elmore, Doug	KY1500	32B,32C
Embree, Marc A.	IL0750	61,32B
Emmanuel, Donna T.	TX3420	32B,32G,20D,20H,35A
Endris, Robert R.	IN1400	60,32B,36
Eppink, Joseph A.	NY0700	32B,66G,66H,32C,32A
Eros, John	CA0807	32,32E,32B
Eshelman, Darla	OK1330	32A,32B,32D
Essex, Malinda W.	OH1850	32B,32C
Etheridge, Kay	CA5200	11,32B,66A,66B,66C
Fairchild, Nancy	WI0840	32B,32A
Faiver, Rosemary T.	MI1200	32B,66D
Falkner, Dianne	MS0700	32B
Feierabend, John	CT0650	32A,32B
Feldhusen, Roberta	NY2750	32A,32B
Ferrebee, Sarah	CT0050	32B,32C,32D
Ferrell, Rene	CA0650	32B,32C,60A,32D
Fields, Donna	SC1200	32B
Fifield, Glen	UT0300	13A,32A,32B,49,63A
Fillingim, Debra K.	MO1810	32B

Index by Area of Teaching Interest

Name	Code	Areas
Finkelstein, Marc	NJ0550	32A,32B,66A,70
Flack, Michael	IL0650	11,66,13,29,32B
Fleischman, John F.	NY3717	32A,32B
Fleming, Gail	MO1830	32B,32C
Fleming, Pat W.	TX3175	32B,32D,13A
Flournoy-Buford, Debbie	TX3650	32B,32D,34,66C,66A
Foughty, Sharon	IA1200	32B
Fox, Donna Brink	NY1100	32A,32B,32C,32G
Frakes, Louise	IA0900	32A,32B
Fresne, Jeannette	AL1300	32A,32B,32C,32D,32I
Fulton, Judy	IL1100	32B,32C
Gagnon, Yvaine	AI0190	32B
Gaither, Tiffany	OR0175	32B
Gamble, Sue G.	MI0400	32B,32C,32H,32
Gearheart, Kerri	SC1000	63B,32B
Georges, Julia	AL0800	32B
Geraci, Paul	IN1350	13,10,29,63A,32B
Gibson, Chris	MI1180	64A,32B
Giessow, David	MA2010	36,39,61,32B,32C
Glen, Nancy L.	CO0950	63B,32B
Glidwell, Delrae	MO1550	32B,32C,13A
Godwin, Nannette Minor	NC2350	31,66A,66G,32B
Goffi-Fynn, Jeanne C.	NY4200	40,61,13H,32B,32D
Goldin, Amy	NY2750	32B
Goodman, James A.	ID0050	32B,32C,32D,32F
Gordon, Patricia	MI0900	11,32B
Grapenthin, Ina	PA1750	11,32B,66A,66G,66D
Gravel, Manon	AI0220	32B,32A,66B
Graves, Jim F.	OK1200	36,32D,32B,60A,61
Graves, Paul	AR0500	32B
Grevlos, Lisa	SD0050	39,61,32B,36,32D
Grice, June	KY0900	32A,32B,32C,32G,32H
Griffen, Jane	MO0500	60A,32A,32B,36,61
Gruenhagen, Lisa M.	OH0300	32A,32B,32G,64A,32
Guzman, Ariel	PR0115	32C,32B,32F
Hackworth, Rhonda S.	NJ1130	32B,32C,32A,36,32
Hadley, Katie	OR0700	32,32B,32C
Hagen, Sara L.	ND0600	13B,32B,32C,35A
Hagwood, Angela	VA1100	32B
Hale, Connie L.	SC1200	32B,32H,32A
Hale, Nancy	TX1400	32A,32B
Hallberg, Carol	IA0500	32B
Halliday, Anna Rebecca	AL1200	11,32A,32B
Halverson, Janelle C.	MN1120	32B
Hamblin, Michael	UT0350	32B
Hamilton, Hilree J.	WI0845	11,20,32A,32B,66D
Hammond, Barbara	GA1150	32B
Hanagan, Joyce	CO0200	32B
Hanna, Wendell	CA4200	32A,64D,32
Hansen, Demaris	CT0650	32A,32B,32G,32H
Hansford, Conchita	OK0650	32A,32B,61,66A,31A
Hanson, Sylva	MN1400	32B,64C
Hargrove, D'Ann	OK0550	32B
Harrel, Shawn	MO1810	32B
Harriott, Janette	NE0590	32A,32B,11
Harris, Mitzi	IA1300	32B
Harrison, Joy	IA0650	32B,61
Hartenberger, Aurelia	MO1950	32B,32C,32G,32H
Hartwig, Judy	NE0250	32B
Hartwig, Judy	NE0610	32B
Harvey, Susan	TX1700	63A,63B,66A,32B,32C
Hastings, Gena M.	IN0905	32B
Hathaway, Cheryl	MN0625	32B
Haupt, Dorothy G.	PA0125	12A,32B,36,66G
Haworth, Janice	MN0150	32A,32C,32B,36,20A
Hayden, Paulina	IN1450	32B
Haywood, Jennifer	NY1800	32A,32B,32E
Heath, Malissa	KY1540	11,66D,32B,13,12A
Henry, Warren	TX3420	32B,32
Hepworth, Elise M.	NE0700	32D,61,32B,32C,11
Herrmann, Tracy	OH0350	32A,32B,32C
Hetrick, Esther A.	MI0910	61,60,31A,36,32B
Hicks, Jarrett	IL2750	32B,32C,32E,65
Hicks, Martha K.	MO1550	31A,11,60,13C,32B
Hinson, Amalie	NC1100	32D,32B
Hiranpradist, Barbara	MI1200	11,32B,20
Holcombe, Candace	SC0450	11,32B
Hollis, Brenda	KY1540	32B,20,11
Holloway, Peggy A.	NE0610	61,32B,15,36,40
Holz, Beatrice	KY0100	32B,36,39,61,32D
Honn, Linda	WA0250	32B
Hood, Marcia Mitchell	GA0150	66A,60A,32B,36,40
Hooper, Randall	TX2955	36,60A,32D,32B,40
Hope, Colleen	CO0150	32B
Hopper, Kerrin A.	SC1200	32B
Horvath, Janos	AA0150	32B,32D,36,42,13C
Huff, Christina	IN1025	32A,32B,32C,11,36
Hughes, Marcia A.	TN0930	12A,32B,66A,66D
Huls, Shirley	PA3000	13A,32A,32B,61
Hulse, Mark	CA0300	13,11,32B,32C,61
Hungerford, Del	WA1150	32A,32B,32C,11
Hungerford, Delores	ID0250	32B,64C
Hunt, Catherine	KS1400	32A,32B,32C
Hurtado, Jose-Luis	NM0450	10,13,32B
Hylton, Doris	MO1830	32B,13A,13C
Inks, Kimberly	IN0150	32B
Irvine, Jane	OH1400	66A,32B
Jaccard, Jerry L.	UT0050	32B
Jacobi, Bonnie S.	CO0250	32B,66A,13,32I,32
James, Pamela A.	VA0750	32A,61,13C,66D,32B
Janisch, Joseph	WV0560	36,60,32,13A,32B
Jennings, Jori Johnson	IL1850	61,32B
Jensen, Gary J.	IL0800	32A,32B,32H,32C
Jimerson, David	OR0850	32B,36,61
Johnson, Daniel C.	NC2440	32,63D,34,32B,63C
Johnson, Daniel	IL1200	32A,32B,32C,32D,32E
Johnson, Kevin P.	GA1900	60,11,32A,32B,34
Johnson, Shauna	UT0050	32B
Johnson, Shauna	UT0325	32B,61
Johnson, Teagan	OR1050	32B
Johnson, Vicky V.	TX2750	13,32B,14C,32,66B
Jokisch, Kelly	SC0710	11,32B
Jones, Colette	KY0300	32B,11,66A,66D
Jordanoff, Christine E.	PA1050	32D,32B,32C,32,36
Joy, Sharon	LA0550	32A,32B,32H,32G,32
Julian, Ester	KY1540	32B
Kehler, Harry	PA3710	32A,32B,32C
Kempter, Susan	NM0450	62,32A,32B,32C
Kennedy, John	TX2350	14C,13A,46,49,32B
Kenney, Susan H.	UT0050	32A,32B
Kersten, Joanne	MN1250	13,66A,32B
Kessler, Jennifer	NY3780	32B,32E
Khan, Lori Conlon	ID0050	32B
Kiehn, Mark T.	WI0808	32,66D,70,63A,32B
Kisner, Janna	WV0750	32A,32B
Klein, Nancy K.	VA1000	36,60,32A,32B,32C
Knudson, Donna	WA0650	32B
Koehler, William	IL1150	32B,32C,62D
Koepsel, Keith	CO1050	32B
Koerselman, Herbert L.	KY1500	63A,32B
Kolbeck, Brandi	NE0700	32B
Krenek, Catherine	MI1300	32B,32C
Kretchner, Darlene	CA0830	32B,32A,32E,32F,32G
Kronour, Dianne	OH2250	32A,32B
Kuhlman, Kristyn	NY3350	32B,32E,32G
Kumme, Karl	CT0050	32B,32E
Labonte, Celeste	RI0200	32B
Lafferty, Laurie	OH2150	32B,32C,63B
Laflen, Betty Jo	KS0400	11,13C,32B,37,64
Lancaster, Linda K.	KY1200	32A,32B
Lane, Roger	NC0900	32B,32F
Laskey, Anne	CA2200	32A,32B
Lathrum, Linda	FL0700	32B
Latta, Matthew	IN1800	61,32B,36,54
Laursen, Amy	AR0300	63B,32B
Lawrence, Kenya L.	LA0650	36,32B
Lawthers, Carol	CA4000	11,32B,61,66A
Lay, Jean	OR0450	32B
Lebron, Nelie	PR0115	32A,32B
Ledressay, Joanne	AB0090	64C,32B
Legette, Lee David	NC2700	11,32B,37,47,64E
Lehmberg, Lisa J.	MA2000	32B
Leslie, James M.	OH2250	65,47,32B,37
Leslie, Tracy	KY1540	32B
Levinowitz, Lili	NJ1050	32,32A,32C,66
Lew, Jackie Chooi-Theng	MD0800	32A,32B,20,32C,66
Lewis, Barbara E.	ND0500	12F,12C,32A,32B
Linch-Parker, Sheryl	NC0800	13A,32B,32C,49,63C
Lineberger, Rhonda	WA1100	32B
Liske, Kenneth L.	WI0830	32,32C,32F,32B,32D
Liston, Robin	KS0050	32A,32B,12A,11
Llewellyn, Raymond	CA0815	32B,37,65
Lloyd, Leslie	KY1550	32B
Long, Janet	SC0900	62,32B,11,32A,32C
Lonich, Nancy L.	PA0500	32A,32B
Love, Diana	WV0750	32B,32C
Lyons, James H.	MD0350	11,20,32B
Mains, Ronda	AR0700	64A,32B,32
Malone, Mark H.	MS0850	32A,32B,32C,32D
Maltas, Carla Jo	MO1790	32,32B
Mandle, William Dee	DC0350	13A,13,32B,66A,66D
Mann, Victoria	PA3650	32B
Mannell, David	IN0907	11,61,36,32B
Mansfield, Cynthia	CT0800	32B
Manternach, LaDonna	IA0250	61,32B
March, Hunter	TX3510	32,32B
Marks, Randall J.	PA1900	32B,32C,32D,32E
Marshall, Herbert D.	OH0200	32A,32B
Martin, Linda	IA0950	36,13,32B
Mason, Emily J.	NY1800	32A,32B,32C
Mason, Vicki	TX0200	13,32B
Mattson-Hill, Jodi	MT0075	32B
McAllister, DeeAnn	AZ0400	32B
McConkey, Michelle	CA0800	32A,32B,32C
McCord, G. Dawn Harmon	GA2130	32B,32C,32A,13C,66D
McCord, Kimberly A.	IL1150	32B,32C,32F,29A,32A
McCoy, Peter M.	NY3780	32E,32F,32C,32G,32B
McCullam, Audrey	MD0600	13,32B,32C,66A,66D
McCullough, David M.	AL1250	32B,63B,32C,32E
McCusker, IHM, Joan	PA2200	32A,32B,32C,32G
McDaniel, Carol	CA1425	32B,13C,31A,66G
McDaniel, Carolyn	OH0250	32A,32B,36
McDannell, Karl	NY2450	32B,32C,47,60
McIntire, Jean	PA1150	32B
McKee, Angela	GA1150	32A,32B,32G
McKoy, Constance L.	NC2430	32B,32A,20A,32
McMahan, Cassandra	NE0150	32B
McNeil, Carol	MI0520	32B
McNellie, Myra	TX2700	32A,32B
Meek, Darla	TX2955	32A,32B,32H
Melago, Kathleen A.	PA3100	32B,11,66D
Merchlewitz, Brenda	MN1700	32B
Metz, Sue	CA0840	32B
Michalek, Thomas	NE0300	32B,32A
Micheletti, Joan	MT0350	32B
Miles, Stacey	MS0750	32B
Miller, Becky	IL1612	36,32B,32C
Miller, Joan	MN1300	20D,11,32B
Miller, June Entwisle	IL3100	36,32B
Miller, Marie C.	KS0300	32A,32B,66A
Miller, Sharon	VA0300	32B,62A,32C,32E
Miller, Sue	ID0075	13,32B,66
Mills, Susan W.	NC0050	20,32B,32C,61,36
Mims, Mary	MO1500	32A,32B
Mitchell, Charlene	MO0600	32B,66A,66C,66D
Mizener, Charlotte P.	TX1400	32B,32G,32A
Moe, Charlette	ND0350	32B,32D,36
Montgomery, Janet	MD1010	32,32A,32B
Moon, Kathleen	CA3150	32B,32C
Moore, Carol A.	WI0200	11,32B
Moore, Christine	AL0050	11,32B
Moore, Janet L. S.	FL2000	32B
Moore, Marvelene C.	TN1710	32A,32B,32I
Moxness, Diana	MN1000	32B,61
Mueller, Susan	NV0050	32A,32B
Mullins, Devoyne	NE0400	32B
Murphey, Maura	WI0250	32B
Murphy, Kathleen	IN1600	33,32B,66D
Murphy, Vanissa B.	WI0803	32B,20G
Musselman, Diana	CO0225	63B,32B
Nardo, Rachel L.	UT0250	32,32B,34,32A,32D
Necessary, Andrew	VA0050	12A,32B,37,46,63C
Neill, Sheri L.	TX3000	32D,32B,32C,32G
Nelsen, Jack	ID0075	11,32B
Nelson, Joy	OK1350	32A,32B
Nelson, Joy	AJ0150	32A,32B
Nelson, Margaret	WI0855	11,32A,32B
Nelson, Marie	MA2020	32A,32B,32C,66D
Nelson, Sharon	OH2500	32B,66
Ness, Corinne	WI0250	61,54,32B,39
Neumann, Ben	AA0050	32B,38,51,62A
Nicolosi, Ida	CA3600	61,32B
Nole, Nancy	WA0650	32,32B
Nord, Michael	OR1300	32A,32B,34
Noseworthy, Susan	NH0350	32B
Oare, Steven	KS1450	32E,32B,32C
Ohlman, Kathleen	NE0200	32B,32C,32D,32E
Okins, Ann	SD0580	32A,32B
Oliver, Holly E.	NH0250	32B,32C,13A
Oliver, Jon	KY1400	32B
O'Rear, Susan L.	TX3420	32B
Otero, Erica	NM0450	32A,32B
Owens, Diane	TX1100	66A,66C,66D,32A,32B
Palomaki, Jonathan	IL0300	12A,32B,36,70,61
Paney, Andrew S.	MS0700	32B,13A,66A,32A
Parker, Charla	OK0600	66D,32B

Name	Code	Areas
Parker, Elizabeth	GA0550	32A,32B,32C,32D
Parker, Nancy	MN1300	32B
Parkes, Kelly Anne	VA1700	32B
Parr, Carlotta	CT0050	32A,32B,32C,36,32G
Patterson, Michael R.	IA1350	12A,32B,66A,13,10
Paugh, Rob	KY1550	32B
Paul, Phyllis M.	OR1050	32A,32B,32C
Pelletier, Christina	OH1850	32B
Perez, Olga	OH1650	61,40,32B
Perry, Pamela J.	CT0050	32B,32C,36,32D,60A
Pezzullo, Louis	RI0200	32B
Piersall, Janie	IL1612	32A,32B,66A
Pitzer, Robert M.	WA1250	32,32B,32C,32H
Poniros, Risa	NC1500	32B,40,36,61
Portis, Vicki	AL0800	32B
Presley, Douglas L.	SC0850	37,50,32B,32C,65
Provencio, Linda	CA0650	32B
Przybylowski, Michelle	PA0650	32B
Rada, Raphael	TX0550	61,11,13C,32B,36
Ramirez, Pamela	TX3515	32B
Ramsdell, Gregory A.	OH0950	37,55D,32B,32D,32C
Rawlins, Deborah	TX2250	32A,32B
Raymond, Diane	MI1260	32B
Redman, Suzanne	TN1150	32B
Reid, Lynda L.	TX2350	13A,32B,37,48,64C
Reifinger, James L.	TX3400	32B,32C
Resch, Barbara	IN0905	32B,32C
Reynolds, Geoffrey	CT0650	32B,32C,32D,32F,32G
Reznicek, Steven	MN0150	36,32B,32C
Richardson, Celia	TX2850	11,36,61,32B,13C
Richardson, Dennis	TX0550	36,40,32B,66D,60A
Risser, Martha	MO2000	32B
Ritterling, Soojin Kim	WI0810	32B,32C,11,61,32A
Riveire, Janine	CA0630	32A,32B,32C
Robins, Linda	TX2570	32B,36,66A,66B
Robinson, Keith	TX3100	32B,63D
Robinson, Nicole R.	TN1680	32B,32C,32G,32H
Rodewald, Marion	CA2100	66A,32B
Rohwer, Debbie A.	TX3420	32C,32B,64A
Rolsten, Kathy	MN1120	32A,32B,32D,36,61
Romanek, Mary L.	PA2720	12A,32A,32B,29A
Rose, Leslie Paige	AR0850	32B,34,32E
Rose, Richard F.	FL1300	11,32B,32C,62D,29
Roshong, Janelle	OH1350	32A,32B
Roush, Clark	NE0720	11,12A,13A,32C,32B
Rowley, Terra	IN0700	32B
Royse, David M.	TN1710	32E,32B,32C
Rubinstein, Matan	WI0865	11,29,32B,47
Rudari, David J.	WV0100	61,36,12A,32B,54
Runner, Lisa	NC0050	32B
Russell, Cynthia	TX0250	61,66A,66G,32B,32C
Russell, Joan	AI0100	32B,32C,12,12C
Rutkowski, Joanne	PA2750	32A,32B,32G
Ryan, Christine	PA1750	32B
Sacalamitao, Melonie	CA4850	32A,32B,32C,66D,36
Samaan, Sherilyn	TN1350	32B,11,66A
Sampson, Kenneth C.	TN0800	10F,32B,32C,37,63
Sands-Pertel, Judith	CA1500	32A,32B,66
Sapegin, Judith	CO0950	32B
Scheidker, Barbara	CA4850	32A,32B
Schernikau, Burt	NE0450	32B,61
Schmidt, Catherine M.	MN1700	32B,14,32A
Schneller, Pamela	TN1850	32C,32B,32D,60
Schroeder, Joy A.	MI1500	32B,13A,13C
Schultz, Margaret	NE0460	13C,66A,66C,11,32B
Scott, Jan	LA0350	32B,48,64B,64D,64C
Scott, Rosemary	GA0250	32A,32B,32C,11
Scott, Sheila	AC0050	32,32B
Scott, Vicky	MO0775	32B,32C
Seis, Catherine	GA2300	32B
Shane, Lynn	MA1650	11,61,32B,32D,36
Sheldon, Janene	NE0450	61,32B,36,40,16
Sheridan, Wilma F.	OR0850	32B,12A
Shirey, Kim F.	AR0600	32B
Siebenaler, Dennis	CA0815	32B
Siivola, Carolyn	MI1200	32B
Simoneau, Brigitte	AI0220	32B
Simpson, Brennetta	NC1600	32B,32A,32D
Sims, Wendy L.	MO1800	32A,32B,32G
Skornia, Dale E.	MI0650	11,32B,37,64
Slagowski, Joshua	OH1450	32E,32B,32C
Smale, Marcelyn	MN1300	32A,13C,66D,32B,32D
Smathers, Robin H.	NC1250	32B
Smith, Ada	NC1100	32B
Smith, Carl H.	KY0750	60,32B,32C,36
Smith, Janice P.	NY0642	32B,32F
Smith, Marilyn	MS0420	36,32A,32B
Smith, Michael V.	DC0050	60,32,32B,32C,32D
Snodgrass, Debra D.	MO0800	32B
Snow, Lydia F.	IL2150	32B,20
Sobol, Elise	NY2750	32A,32B,32C
Somma, Sal	NY1275	32B,32C
Soto, Amanda C.	ID0250	14,20H,32B,32G,32H
Spano, Fred P.	NC2420	32B,32D,32G,32
Spataro, Susan M.	VA0400	64A,47,11,32A,32B
Spencer, Stacia C.	IL2250	32B,62A,62B
St. John, Patricia A.	NY4200	32A,32B
Stalnaker, Donna	WV0250	11,12A,32B,66A,66H
Stambaugh, Laura	GA0950	32A,32B,32C,32E,32G
Stamer, Linda	AZ0450	32B
Standerfer, Stephanie	VA1350	32A,32B,32C
Stanley, Ann Marie	NY1100	32B,32G,32H
Steele, Stacey G.	PA3100	32A,32B,48,64A
Stegall, Pat	AL1250	32B,32C
Stephansky, Joyce	VA0450	32B
Steuer, Jeff	IL1300	32B
Stevens, Lynn	CA0840	32B
Stickler, Larry W.	WV0400	36,32B,32C,61,32D
Stitt, Virginia K.	UT0200	11,32B,64B,64D,12A
Stolberg, Tom	MO0060	10F,34,31A,32B,60
Stover, Pamela	OH2300	32B,32C,32G,32H,32
Strand, Katherine D.	IN0900	32B,32C,32H,32G
Streets, Barbara S.	OK1330	32B,61
Stryker, Crystal J.	PA3000	32A,32B,61
Suderman, Mark	OH0250	60A,32D,32B,36,61
Sullivan, Judith	TN1450	32B
Sumner, Daniel	LA0770	32B,32C,32D,32G
Sunday, Shannon	PA1750	32B
Svengalis, Judy	IA0420	32B,66A
Swanson, Robyn	KY1550	32A,32B,32G,32H
Sweeney, Christopher R.	AK0100	32,63D,63C,32E,32B
Taylor, Donald M.	TX3420	32,32B
Taylor, Una D.	NE0050	36,61,32B,11,40
Teel, Susan	TX0050	66A,32B,11,13C
Tempas, Fred	CA2250	63D,32B
Thiele, Margaret	MI0600	32A,32B
Thogersen, Chris	IN0550	66A,66G,32B,31A
Thomas-Lee, Paula	GA1700	66A,66B,32B
Thompson, Kathy A.	OK0700	13,32B,66A,66B,41
Thompson, Linda K.	TN0850	32A,32B,32C,32G
Threadgill, Gwen J.	AL1050	32B,13C,66A,66D
Timmons, Leslie	UT0300	32A,32B,64A,48,41
Tiner, Kris	CA0650	47,32B
Tomlinson, Rebecca	CA0845	64A,32B
Torres Rivera, Alfredo	PR0115	32E,32B,32C
Torres, Gregory J.	LA0450	60B,11,37,34B,32B
Torres, Stephanie	RI0200	32B
Tower, Mollie	TX3175	32B
Trenfield, Sally	TX3515	32A,32B,66C,66D
Trinka, Jill L.	SC0420	32A,20,32B
Trumbore, Lisa	KY0200	13,32B
Tu, Ming	IL1750	32A,32B
Turner, Daniel	SC0200	32B,32C,37,63D,34
Turner, Mark E.	TX2700	32B,32A
Turner, Tammy	KY1540	29A,11,32B
Valeria, Anna	FL1310	32B,66D
Varner, Ed	MT0370	32B,37,65
Vazquez-Ramos, Angel M.	CA0960	60A,36,32D,32B
Veblen, Kari	AG0500	32A,32B
Venzen, Austin A.	VI0050	10F,11,32B,37,42
Vogel, Bradley D.	KS1300	60,32B,36,61,31A
Vondra, Nancy	NE0610	32B
Wagner, Linda	WV0800	32B
Waldrop, Joseph	TX3850	13,32B,37,13B,64
Watts, Sarah	PA0350	32A,32B,11
Waymire, Mark D.	MS0750	32A,32B,32C
Weddle, John W.	CA0850	32C,32B,20G,64C,11
Wehr, Erin	IA1550	32B,32C,32E
Weiss, Louise	IL1050	13A,32B,48,64A,66C
Wesley, Dee	IL1612	66,32B
Westfall, Claude R.	MO0100	32B,32D,32B,36,60A,70
Whitcomb, Rachel	PA1050	32,32B,32A
White, Karin	MI1260	32B,32E,32D
White, Kim	MN0610	32A,32B
Whitehead, Baruch	NY1800	32B,32A,32C,20A
Wiggins, David	KS0150	32B
Wiggins, Jacqueline H.	MI1750	12F,32B,32G
Williams, Barbara	CA5350	32A,32B
Willis, George R.	WV0750	10D,11,32B,52,65
Willoughby, Vicki	VA1000	32B
Wilson, Dean	PA3650	32B
Wilson, Jill	IA1100	63B,36,32B,60,13C
Winn, Jack	MI0520	32B
Wolverton, Peggy	KY1000	32B
Womack, Sara	AL1150	32B
Woody, Robert H.	NE0600	32B,12F
Wopat, Ann	WA0850	61,32I,32A,32B,32C
Wotring, Linda	MI1900	11,32A,32B,66A,66B
Wyatt, Renee	WV0750	32B,32C
Wyrick, Ginger	NC2650	36,32B
Young, Barbara G.	WI0803	13A,32B
Young, Judy	OK0550	32B
Ziek, Terrisa A.	KS0300	32B,63B
Zilli, Carol	CA3320	32A,32B

Secondary General Music

Name	Code	Areas
Adams, Ann M.	FL1750	64B,11,32C
Allen, Fred J.	TX2700	60B,32C,37,41
Anderson, Christopher	AR0200	60,32C,37
Anderson, Leeann	OH1000	11,32B,62E,32A,32C
Andrews, Laura J.	KS0350	32B,32C,32A,32G,32H
Angliey, Tamey	TX2700	60B,32C,37,41
Anthony, Johnny	MS0350	32C,37,49,63
Archambo, Larry	TX1700	60,32C,37,34,63C
Artesani, Laura	ME0440	12A,66C,15,32B,32C
Atkinson, Monte	CO0225	60,32C,36,61,66A
Austin, Kenneth L.	IL3100	13,32C,37,49,46
Bailey, Mark	TN0850	13,32E,32C,37
Ballif, Adam	ID0060	32C,32E,64C
Baptiste, Renee L.	AL0500	32B,32C,32D,32G,36
Barber, Deborah L.	AR0200	34,32B,10D,70,32C
Barfield, Susan	MT0175	32A,32B,32C
Barlar, Nancy	FL0670	64C,32B,32C,32E,11
Bates, Vincent C.	MO0950	63B,32B,32C,11
Battersby, Sharyn L.	DC0050	32B,32C,66D,32D,32H
Bauer, Elizabeth	IL3550	32A,32B,32C
Bausano, William	OH1450	60A,32C,36,61
Bayless, Robert R.	AZ0500	32C,32E,37,60B
Beard, Michael R.	NE0590	37,32C
Beck, Brandon	WA1100	37,63,60B,38,32C
Becker, David M.	OR0400	60,32C,37,29,64
Beckett, Christine	AI0070	13,12C,32C,38,62A
Bell, John	IL2910	32,32C,37,60B
Benz, Fritz	RI0150	32C,32E
Bertman, David	TX3400	32C,37
Bimm, Greg L.	IL0750	32C
Bing, Charles S.	FL0600	32C,37,63C,63D
Blackman, Mary Dave	TN0500	11,32C
Blair, Deborah V.	MI1750	32B,32C,12B,12F,32D
Board, Ryan A.	CA3600	11,32C,36,31A,60A
Bond, Judith	WI0850	32,32A,32B,32C
Bonds, Eric	AL0200	32C
Boonshaft, Peter Loel	NY1600	60B,32C,37
Bowles, Kenneth E.	ND0250	36,61,39,60,32C
Brandon, Joan Lynette	IN0100	32B,36,32C,32D
Brandon, Mark	AL0500	32B,32C,64C
Breaux, Michael L.	NY2750	32B,32C,32E,32F
Brewer, Robert G.	CO0250	32C,63D,49
Bridges, Cynthia	TX0550	37,32H,60B,13C,32C
Brooks-Smith, Emma	MS0350	32A,32B,32C,32G
Brough, Ronald P.	UT0050	60,32C,37,65,72
Brown, Frances A.	RI0250	64C,32C
Brownwell, John	AG0200	32C,65
Bruenger, Susan Dill	TX3530	32B,32C,32D
Bryant, Deanne	IL1200	32B,32C,32D,32E
Buck, Barbara	KY0750	32A,32B,32C,32D,61
Buckner, Jeremy	TN0250	32B,32C,66A,66D,11
Budde, Paul	MN1300	32C
Budde, Paul J.	MN0750	63D,49,32C
Bullock, Valerie K.	SC0275	60,32B,32C,36
Bundy, O. Richard	PA2750	32C,37
Burch-Pesses, Michael	OR0750	60,32C,37,47,45
Burns, Brian E.	IA0250	36,12A,32C,32D,60
Burton, Suzanne L.	DE0150	32C
Butler, Milton	OH1900	11,32B,32C
Cajas, Edgar	TX2600	32A,32B,32C,12A
Cameron, Robert C.	PA1050	60,32C,37
Campo, David	TX2700	32E,32C,37,60B
Camwell, David J.	IA1350	32C,46,47,64E,48
Carlisle, Katie	GA1050	32B,32C
Carlson, Mary C.	NY2650	32C,32
Carucci, Christine	MN1300	32C,11
Casagrande, John E.	VA0450	37,32C,32E,32G
Chadwick, Sheelagh	AC0050	32,32C

Name	Code	Areas
Chiarizzio, R. Kevin	VA0650	63,32B,32C,32F
Chipman, Shelby R.	FL0600	60,32C,37,63A
Clark, Allen	TX3515	32C,37,63D
Clark, Wallace	FL0600	12A,32C,37
Clements, Ann C.	PA2750	32C
Colwitz, Erin E.	AL1160	32B,61,60A,36,32C
Conger, Robert B.	MO1500	60B,32C,63C,63D
Conkling, Susan W.	MA0400	32D,36,32C,32F,32G
Connors, David	CA0830	32B,32C,61
Cooksey, John M.	UT0250	36,32C,32D
Cooper, Gloria A.	NY2102	13A,61,32C,36,47
Corley, Sheila	AZ0400	32C,36,39,61
Cox, Bruce	SC0200	32C,49,63A
Cox, Kris	IL1100	32B,32C
Craig, Ed	CA0350	32C,32E
Crawford, Glenda	OH2550	36,32A,32C,32B,60
Crawford, Ted	AJ0030	65,32B,32C
Cruz, Samantha	WI0500	32A,32B,32C,11
Culvahouse, John N.	GA1150	37,32C,32E,60B
Cummings, Grace	NY3350	32B,36,61,32C,32D
Dalby, Bruce	NM0450	32C,47,12
Daniels, John	FL0600	13,32C,64A,64C
Davis, Alfred L.	VA0500	32E,32F,32B,32C,10F
De Leo, Joseph A.	NY2750	32,12A,13B,32C,32H
De Melo, Dorvalino	AI0220	60,32C,37,47,64E
Dearden, Katherine Norman	ND0500	32C
DeGraffenreid, George	CA0830	32C,32E,32G
Demorest, Steven M.	WA1050	32B,32C,36
Denmon, Alan	GA2300	11,13A,13B,32C,32E
Dennee, Peter D.	WI0250	32C,32D,36,60,40
Deppe, Scott M.	TX1400	37,60B,32G,32C
Dettwiler, Peggy	PA2150	60,36,32C,61
DeTurk, Mark	NH0350	32C,32E,32G
Dickerson, Randy C.	WI0803	60,32C,37
DiCuirci, Michael P.	OH0450	32B,32C,37,63D,46
Diehl, David J.	TN1600	12A,32C,36
Dohrmann, Diana	NJ0550	32C,32D
Dorothy, Wayne F.	TX0900	32C,32E,37,60B
Drafall, Lynn	PA2750	32C,36
Dunn, Robert	UT0050	32C,32G,32D
Dunnigan, Patrick	FL0850	32C,37,60B
Dye, Keith G.	TX3200	60B,37,32C,32E
East, Mary Ann H.	VA0450	32C
Eberenz, Gina	KY0250	32A,32B,32C
Eckerty, Michael	IA1350	64D,32C,37,60,48
Edmonds, Johnnella	VA1750	60,32B,32C,36,61
Edwards, George L.	DC0350	11,32C,48,64A,64C
Eichner, Mark J.	WI0835	60,32C,37,63A,32A
Elias, Carlos	CO0225	32C,38,62A,62B,51
Elmore, Ashlee	OK0825	32B,32C
Elmore, Doug	KY1500	32B,32C
Ely, Mark	UT0250	32C,37,64E
Emmons, Scott	WI0825	32,32C,32E
Enloe, Loraine D.	ID0250	32E,64,37,64C,32C
Entsminger, Deen	TN0100	13,10,32C,36,34
Epley, Arnold	MO2000	60A,32C,36,61,40
Eppink, Joseph A.	NY0700	32B,66G,66H,32C,32A
Essex, Malinda W.	OH1850	32B,32C
Ewing, Randy	IA1200	32C
Fallis, Todd	UT0300	32C,63C,63D,47,41
Fernisse, Susan	GA0400	32C
Ferrebee, Sarah	CT0050	32B,32C,32D
Ferrell, Rene	CA0650	32B,32C,60A,32D
Fisher, Dennis W.	TX3420	60B,32C,37
Flanigan, Glen	KY0100	11,32C,41,47,63D
Fleming, Gail	MO1830	32B,32C
Fox, Donna Brink	NY1100	32A,32B,32C,32G
Frank, Arthur	PA3250	32C,50
Frechou, Paul A.	LA0650	64C,37,32C,32E
Freer, Patrick K.	GA1050	32D,32C,32G,36,60A
Fresne, Jeannette	AL1300	32A,32B,32C,32D,32I
Frye, Danny	NC0930	65,50,37,65B,32C
Fulton, Judy	IL1100	32B,32C
Gallo, Franklin J.	IL0750	32C,32D
Gallops, R. Wayne	VA1100	13A,32C,32E,29,37
Gamble, Sue G.	MI0400	32B,32C,32H,32
Gervais, Jean	AI0190	32C
Geston, Mary K.	MN1280	40,32D,60A,32C,36
Giambrone, Marcia	NY1700	32C
Gibbs, Brian	TX2250	37,32C
Giessow, David	MA2010	36,39,61,32B,32C
Gillis, Glen	AJ0150	60,32C,37,48,64E
Glidwell, Delrae	MO1550	32B,32C,13A
Goodman, James A.	ID0050	32B,32C,32D,32F
Grice, June	KY0900	32A,32B,32C,32G,32H
Griffith, Larry D.	TN0930	60A,32C,36,61,32D
Grugin, Stephen	MI1600	37,63D,12A,32C,32E
Grzych, Frank J.	TN0500	60,32C
Guzman, Ariel	PR0115	32C,32B,32F
Hackworth, Rhonda S.	NJ1130	32B,32C,32A,36,32
Hadley, Katie	OR0700	32,32B,32C
Hagen, Sara L.	ND0600	13B,32B,32C,35A
Hall, Daniel	OH1900	60A,32C,36
Hall, Teddy	VA0500	13A,13B,13C,32C,11
Hanson, Dan L.	OK1400	13,10,32C,47,37
Harper, T.J.	RI0150	36,60,32C,32D,61
Hartenberger, Aurelia	MO1950	32B,32C,32G,32H
Harvey, Susan	TX1700	63A,63B,66A,32B,32C
Hawkins, Allan	MN0625	61,32C,32D
Haworth, Janice	MN0150	32A,32C,32B,36,20A
Hemberger, Glen J.	LA0650	60B,32C,37,63C,47
Henry, Joseph D.	IL0900	12A,20G,36,40,32C
Hepworth, Elise M.	NE0700	32D,61,32B,32C,11
Herb, Thomas	UT0200	13C,34,47,32C,32D
Herrick, Dennis R.	AL0450	60,63,34,29A,32C
Herrmann, Tracy	OH0350	32A,32B,32C
Hibbard, Kevin	GA2130	36,32D,61,60,32C
Hicks, Jarrett	IL2750	32B,32C,32E,65
Hill, Douglas M.	GA1300	60B,32C,37,49,63A
Hilliard, Quincy C.	LA0760	13,10,32C
Hinton, Jeffrey	MO0850	60,32C,37,64E
Hochkeppel, William J.	LA0760	37,32C
Hodge, Stephen	OH2300	36,32C,61,32D,60A
Hoffman, Edward C. 'Ted'	AL1200	11,32C,32E,60B
Hollinger, Lowell	MS0350	11,13A,32C,48,64E
Holmes, Brad	IL1750	60,32C,36
Holquist, Robert A.	NC2600	32C,36,55D,32D
Hopkins, Mark E.	AF0050	37,32E,32C,60,60B
Howard, David L.	TX2700	32C,36,60A
Huff, Christina	IN1025	32A,32B,32C,11,36
Hulse, Mark	CA0300	13,11,32B,32C,61
Hungerford, Del	WA1150	32A,32B,32C,11
Hunt, Catherine	KS1400	32A,32B,32C
Jacobsen, Jeffrey	PA2150	38,32,32C
Jacobsen, Lesa L.	WI0845	61,32C,32D,60A,36
James, Shaylor L.	FL0600	32C,50,65
Janzen, Eldon A.	AR0700	60,32C,37
Jensen, Byron W.	NE0300	13B,38,12A,62,32C
Jensen, Gary J.	IL0800	32A,32B,32H,32C
Johnson, Carl	TX0200	60,12A,32C,36,61
Johnson, Daniel	IL1200	32A,32B,32C,32D,32E
Johnston, Margaret	IL0750	32C,32E
Jones, Robert B.	OH2250	60A,32C,36,32D
Jones, Trevor	IL0750	32C,32D
Jones, William Darryl	LA0350	32C,36
Jordanoff, Christine E.	PA1050	32D,32B,32C,32,36
Jossim, J.	FL0800	64B,37,32C
Keast, Dan A.	TX3527	32,34B,34F,32G,32C
Kehler, Harry	PA3710	32A,32B,32C
Keith, Laura J.	SC0350	12A,66A,66D,32C,32D
Kellert, Carolyn	IL1350	32C,32D,61
Kempster, William G.	NH0350	36,32C
Kempter, Susan	NM0450	62,32A,32B,32C
Kephart, Donald B.	PA1350	32C,37,63,46,60
Kimmel, Jim	TN0100	36,60,32C
Kinchen, James B.	WI0835	60,36,32C
King, Tim	TX2700	60A,32C,36
Kjelland, James	IL2250	60,32C,38,62
Klein, Nancy K.	VA1000	36,60A,32A,32B,32C
Knighten, Janet W.	AR0700	32C,32E
Knotts, Clara	FL1750	32C,32E
Koehler, William	IL1150	32B,32C,62D
Kouratachvili, Tinatin	WA0850	32C,32E
Krenek, Catherine	MI1300	32B,32C
Kristjanson, William	AC0100	32C
Kula, Jeff	AC0100	32C
Lafferty, Laurie	OH2150	32B,32C,63B
Lamb, Earnest	NC0800	12A,32C,51,62
Laux, Charles	GA1150	32E,34C,38,62,32C
Laycock, Rand	OH0755	11,12A,32C,38,62D
Leach, Anthony	PA2750	32C,36
Lesser, Jeffrey	NJ0550	32E,63,10,32C,32F
Lew, Jackie Chooi-Theng	MD0800	32B,32C,20,32C,66
Linch-Parker, Sheryl	NC0800	13A,32B,32C,49,63C
Lind, Robin A.	PA3650	32C,36,40,61
Lipton, Jeffrey S.	NY1275	12A,13B,32C,36,61
Liske, Kenneth L.	WI0830	32,32C,32F,32B,32D
Lister, Michael C.	NY0700	32D,32C,55D,36,13
Lloyd, Joe	AZ0400	32C,37,63A,11,60
Locke, John R.	NC2430	60,32C,37
Long, Janet	SC0900	62,32B,11,32A,32C
Long, Wallace H.	OR1300	60,32C,36
Love, Diana	WV0750	32B,32C
Lynn, Daniel	NE0550	60A,61,36,32C,32D
Mack, William G.	MO0850	60,32C,37,49,63A
Malone, Mark H.	MS0850	32A,32B,32C,32D
Mann, Alison	GA1150	40,60A,32C,32D
Marks, Laurence L.	NC2420	37,64C,32C,41*
Marks, Randall J.	PA1900	32B,32C,32D,32E
Martin, Peter J.	ME0500	60,32C,37
Mason, Emily J.	NY1800	32A,32B,32C
Mathews, Jeffrey	LA0550	37,32C
Mayes, Robert	TX3400	60,32C,37
McAllister, James	KS0440	37,10A,63,60B,32C
McCarthy, Glen	VA0450	70,32C
McCaskill, Janet L.	MI2200	63D,32E,60B,32C
McClung, Alan C.	TX3420	32C,32D,32G,60A,13C
McConkey, Michelle	CA0800	32A,32B,32C
McCord, G. Dawn Harmon	GA2130	32B,32C,32A,13C,66D
McCord, Kimberly A.	IL1150	32B,32C,32F,29A,32A
McCoy, Peter M.	NY3780	32E,32F,32C,32G,32B
McCray, James	CO0250	10,32C,12A
McCullam, Audrey	MD0600	13,32B,32C,66A,66D
McCullough, David M.	AL1250	32B,63B,32C,32E
McCusker, IHM, Joan	PA2200	32A,32B,32C,32G
McCutcheon, Russell G.	PA1400	37,32E,60,34,32C
McDannell, Karl	NY2450	32B,32C,47,60
McGilvray, Byron	CA4200	60,32C,36
McGrannahan, A. Graydon	NV0100	37,32C,41,63C,63D
McInturf, Matthew	TX2250	32C,37,60B
McKinney, Jane Grant	NC0900	32C,13B,32D,39
Mercer, James	CA3400	32C,61,35C
Messenger, Richard	CA5355	32C,36
Miller, Becky	IL1612	36,32B,32C
Miller, Sharon	VA0300	32B,62A,32C,32E
Mills, David	CT0600	32C,37,49
Mills, Susan W.	NC0050	20,32B,32C,61,36
Mitchell, Adrian	MS0350	11,63A,37,32C,49
Miyamura, Henry	HI0210	32C,38,64C
Montzka Smelser, Ann	IL3550	32C,62
Moon, Kathleen	CA3150	32B,32C
Moore, Michael W.	SC0200	32C,32E,32G,37,13
Moser, Steven R.	MS0750	60,32C
Mountford, Fritz	NE0300	32C,36,60A,10,20
Mowrer, Tony	CA0810	32D,32,32C
Munn, Vivian C.	TX3525	13,32C,36,61
Murdaugh, Johnnie L.	SC0350	64E,32C
Murphy, Michael	ID0250	36,40,32D,12A,32C
Murray, Renardo	MS0350	37,11,32C,49,63D
Musgrove, Abby R.	IL1100	36,40,11,32C,32D
Neill, Sheri L.	TX3000	32D,32B,32C,32G
Nelson, Marie	MA2020	32A,32B,32C,66D
Nimmo, Douglas	MN0750	60B,32C,32E
Oare, Steven	KS1450	32E,32B,32C
Ohlman, Kathleen	NE0200	32B,32C,32D,32E
Okamura, Grant K.	HI0210	60,32C,37,63A
Olfert, Warren	ND0350	60,32C,37,63C
Oliver, Holly E.	NH0250	32B,32C,13A
Ozzello, Kenneth B.	AL1170	60B,32C,37
Parker, Elizabeth	GA0550	32A,32B,32C,32D
Parr, Carlotta	CT0050	32A,32B,32C,36,32G
Paul, Phyllis M.	OR1050	32A,32B,32C
Paulk, Jason	NM0100	60A,32C,36
Peck, Thomas	MI0520	32C,32E
Perry, Pamela J.	CT0050	32B,32C,36,32D,60A
Peters, Valerie	AI0190	32C
Phillips, Mark W.	VA1750	32C,37,49,63C,63D
Phipps, Dennis	IN1450	32C
Pierard, George	IL3370	32C,32E
Pitzer, Robert M.	WA1250	32,32B,32C,32H
Potter, Sharon	PA1550	32C
Presley, Douglas L.	SC0850	37,50,32B,32C,65
Propst, Tonya	SC0420	63B,32,32C
Pruzin, Robert S.	SC1110	32C,49,63B
Ragland, Janice	MO0850	61,36,32C
Ramsdell, Gregory A.	OH0950	37,55D,32B,32D,32C
Rand, Catherine	MS0750	60,32C,37
Randles, Clinton A.	FL2000	32C,32G,32E
Redmer Minner, Laurie K.	TN1350	60B,38,51,32C,62B
Reed, Jonathan I.	MI1400	60A,32C,36
Reifinger, James L.	TX3400	32B,32C
Resch, Barbara	IN0905	32B,32C
Reynolds, Geoffrey	CT0650	32B,32C,32D,32F,32G
Reznicek, Steven	MN0150	36,32B,32C
Rickels, David A.	CO0800	32C,32E,32F,32G,32H
Rieck, Alan J.	WI0803	32C,36

Index by Area of Teaching Interest

Name	Code	Areas
Ritterling, Soojin Kim	WI0810	32B,32C,11,61,32A
Riveire, Janine	CA0630	32A,32B,32C
Rives, Charles L.	TX2750	11,32C
Roach, L. Leroy	CA4200	32C,49,63,37
Robbins, Catherine	AC0100	32D,32C,60A
Robertson, Troy David	TX2750	60,32C,36,61
Robinson, Nicole R.	TN1680	32B,32C,32G,32H
Roby, Lloyd	CA0800	32C,49,63D
Rockwell, Owen P.	MS0350	11,32C,37,65A,65B
Rohwer, Debbie A.	TX3420	32C,32B,64A
Roman, Joe	IL0400	32C
Rombach-Kendall, Eric	NM0450	32C,37
Rose, Richard F.	FL1300	11,32B,32C,62D,29
Rothlisberger, Dana	MD0850	32C,37
Roush, Clark	NE0720	11,12A,13A,32C,32B
Rowsey, Les	MI0520	32C,32D
Royse, David M.	TN1710	32E,32B,32C
Royse, Dennis	CA0250	13,12A,32C,11
Rushton, David	AB0090	13,60,32C,31A
Russell, Cynthia	TX0250	61,66A,66G,32B,32C
Russell, Joan	AI0100	32B,32C,12,12C
Ryan, Rebecca	PA2250	36,32C,60A
Ryner, Jayson	IA1170	32C,36,61,11,13C
Sacalamitao, Melonie	CA4850	32A,32B,32C,66D,36
Salvo, Leonard P.	OH0100	60B,32C,37,41,32E
Sampson, Kenneth C.	TN0800	10F,32B,32C,37,63
Samson, David	PA0650	47,13B,32C,63,60
Sang, Richard C.	NY0642	32C,37
Sarver, Heidi	DE0150	32C,37
Saville, Kirt	UT0050	37,60B,64C,32E,32C
Schmid, William	WI0825	20G,32C,70
Schneller, Pamela	TN1850	32C,32B,32D,60
Scholz, David M.	CA0800	36,61,32C,60
Schultz, Dale	TX2200	37,60,32C,63
Scinta, Frank	NY0400	61,31A,32C,36
Scott, Rosemary	GA0250	32A,32B,32C,11
Scott, Vicky	MO0775	32B,32C
Shand, Patricia	AG0450	32C,51,62A,62B
Sheinberg, Art	NM0450	62D,32C
Shepherd, William	IA1600	11,32C,37
Sheridan, Daniel	MN1700	64C,60,32C,13A,11
Shetler, Timothy	MA0800	60,32C,36,61
Shively, Joseph L.	MI1750	32G,34,11,32,32C
Slagowski, Joshua	OH1450	32E,32B,32C
Smith, Carl H.	KY0750	60,32B,32C,36
Smith, Eddie	CA5150	60,32C,37,64E
Smith, Michael V.	DC0050	60,32,32B,32C,32D
Smith, Neal	IL1750	32E,37,32C,13
Snell, Alden	DE0150	32C,32E
Sobol, Elise	NY2750	32A,32B,32C
Somma, Sal	NY1275	32B,32C
Speck, Gary A.	OH1450	60,32C,48
Spurgeon, Debra L.	MS0700	32C,36
Stambaugh, Laura	GA0950	32A,32B,32C,32E,32G
Standerfer, Stephanie	VA1350	32A,32B,32C
Stegall, Pat	AL1250	32B,32C
Stickler, Larry W.	WV0400	36,32B,32C,61,32D
Stites, Joseph	KY1550	32C,37
Stoffel, Lawrence F.	CA0835	32C,37
Stover, Pamela	OH2300	32B,32C,32G,32H,32
Strand, Katherine D.	IN0900	32B,32C,32H,32G
Sumner, Daniel	LA0770	32B,32C,32D,32G
Taylor, Brian S.	LA0760	37,32C,60
Taylor, Bryce B.	TX2960	32C,60
Taylor, Charles L.	LA0800	37,60B,64C,32C,32E
Thibeault, Matthew	IL3300	32C,32F
Thompson, Laura	LA0250	32C,32D,36,60A,61
Thompson, Linda K.	TN0850	32A,32B,32C,32G
Tobias, Evan	AZ0100	32C,32F,32G,32H
Torres Rivera, Alfredo	PR0115	32E,32B,32C
Trollinger, Valerie L.	PA1750	34,32,64D,11,32C
Turner, Connie	AC0100	32C
Turner, Daniel	SC0200	32B,32C,37,63D,34
Vance, Jeanne	KS1450	32C
Verrier, Thomas	TN1850	37,60B,32C,32D,32
Viebranz, Gary A.	PA2715	12A,29A,32C
Voldman, Yakov	LA0650	60,32C,38,51,62
Wade, Jess E.	TX2900	60,32C,61,66A
Wagoner, Cynthia L.	NC0650	32E,32C
Walth, Gary Kent	WI0810	60,11,32C,36,54
Walton, Madalyn	FL2130	61,32C
Wardle, Alvin	UT0300	32C,63B,63C,63D
Waymire, Mark D.	MS0750	32A,32B,32C
Webb, Mark	MI0300	63,32C,32D,32E,11
Weber, Betsy Cook	TX3400	32C,36
Weddle, John W.	CA0850	32C,32B,20G,64C,11
Wehr, Erin	IA1550	32B,32C,32E
Weir, Timothy	VA0100	32C,32E,37,47,42
White, Dennine	FL0600	32C,37,64A
White, Julian E.	FL0600	60,32C,37,64A,64B
Whitehead, Baruch	NY1800	32B,32A,32C,20A
Wiley, N. Keith	PA2350	32C,47,63A,29
Williams, Deborah	IL0600	32C,36,61,32D
Williams, Eddy	AL0450	65,13B,32C,37,60B
Willis, Jonathan	OH2290	60B,32C,37,47,46
Wilson, Bruce	MD0150	63C,63D,49,37,32C
Wilson, Gary P.	TN0930	60A,32C,36,61,32D
Wilson, Larry K.	CA3975	60,32C,13,66A,36
Wilson, T. Rex	TX2710	60,12A,32C,36,61
Woike, David O.	MI0600	37,32E,32C
Wolbers, Mark	AK0100	60,12A,32C,64C,48
Wood, Robert	AG0500	32C,34,12F,12,12C
Woodard, Scott	WV0700	37,47,32C,63,49
Wopat, Ann	WA0850	61,32I,32A,32B,32C
Worthy, Michael D.	MS0700	32C,32E,32G,47
Wyatt, Renee	WV0750	32B,32C
Young, Jerry A.	WI0803	11,32C,63D
Zerbe, David	MI0150	65,37,50,32C,32E
Zielke, Gregory D.	NE0250	60,32C,36,61,31A

Choral Music

Name	Code	Areas
Aamot, Kirk C.	MT0200	36,40,32D,60A
Abbott, Patricia	AI0150	32D,60A
Adam, Jennifer	KY1550	32D,13C,36
Adams, Jacquelyn	AL1050	32D
Afonso, Daniel R.	CA0850	36,40,13C,32D,60A
Alexander, Cory T.	TX3527	36,32D,61,32,40
Amonson, Christina	AL1050	60A,32D,39
Anderson, Jeff	KS1000	36,32D,60A
Antal, Tom	CA0825	32D
Apfelstadt, Hilary	AG0450	32D
Archibeque, Charlene	CA4400	36,40,60A,32D
Armstrong, Colin	PA3150	32D,36,13C
Ashby, Eda	ID0060	36,61,32D
Aspaas, Christopher	MN1450	36,61,60A,32D
Aune, Gregory	MN0750	60A,36,32D
Babcock, Jonathan	TX3175	36,61,32D
Baker, Kevin L.	MO0300	36,32D,61,60,32
Baker, Wade	OR1300	61,32D
Baptiste, Renee L.	AL0500	32B,32C,32D,32G,36
Barham, Terry	MO1810	32D
Bassett, Jon	FL0670	36,61,51,38,32D
Battersby, Sharyn L.	DC0050	32B,32C,66D,32D,32H
Bauer, David	NE0590	36,61,60A,32D
Baunoch, Joseph	PA1600	61,32D
Belgiovane, Alicia	CO1050	32D
Bentley, Joe	MI1830	12A,32D,60,36
Benton, Carol W.	GA0200	13C,13K,32B,32D,32G
Biddlecombe, Thomas 'Tucker'	TN1850	36,42,32D
Bierschenk, Jerome Michael	TX3250	36,37,32D,61,63A
Billingham, Lisa A.	VA0450	32D,36,60A
Blackley, Rowland	OH0100	60A,32D,36,40,55D
Blair, Deborah V.	MI1750	32B,32C,12B,12F,32D
Bolster, Stephen C.	KY0300	60,32D,36,40,61
Boudreaux, Margaret A.	MD0520	60,12A,32D,36
Boyd, Bob	IL2250	32D
Boyd, Kim	OH2050	36,60A,32D,13C
Boyd, Robert	IL3550	32D
Boyer, Douglas R.	TX3100	36,60,54,32D,13F
Brandes, Christine	CA4200	11,13C,32D,39,61
Brandon, Joan Lynette	IN0100	32B,36,32C,32D
Breden, Mary C.	CA2800	60A,36,32D
Brinckmeyer, Lynn	TX3175	32D,36
Bronfman, Joshua	ND0500	36,40,32D,60A
Brotherton, Jonathan P.	NC0900	36,13C,32D
Brower, Kevin	ID0060	36,61,32D
Bruenger, Susan Dill	TX3530	32B,32C,32D
Brumley, Dianne	TX3515	36,32D,60A
Brunner, David L.	FL1800	60,36,32D,10
Bryant, Deanne	IL1200	32B,32C,32D,32E
Bryson, Amity H.	MO0050	36,61,60A,15,32D
Buchanan, Heather J.	NJ0800	32D,36,40,60A
Buck, Barbara	KY0750	32A,32B,32C,32D,61
Burleson, Jill	CO0950	60A,36,32D
Burnett, J.D.	NJ0800	32D,60A
Burns, Brian E.	IA0250	36,12A,32C,32D,60
Burns, Judith E.	OH0200	60A,32D
Busch, Michael	CA1425	36,60,13B,32D
Butler, Terry	VA0950	13C,32D,66A,66G
Campbell, Debra L.	NY3780	32D,32B
Campbell, Dianna	FL1700	61,36,40,11,32D
Canfield, Jennifer K.	AL0450	11,32A,32D,66D,32B
Carew, David	MI1985	36,61,40,32D,13C
Carson, Caroline	LA0800	11,36,32D,60A
Cassel, David C.	TN1850	32D
Castilla, Willenham	MS0350	36,31,32D,61
Castonguay, Lois	VA1100	32D
Cerabona, Linda M.	IL3400	11,13A,20A,31A,32D
Cetto, Edward	CA5350	36,32D,13C
Chae, Hyung Sek	TX3650	36,31A,44,60,32D
Chandler, Kyle	AR0110	32,36,47,32D,32G
Chiaravalloti, Charissa	CO0350	36,40,60,12A,32D
Clark, Mark	KS1250	36,32D,13,40
Clary, Carol	CA2550	32D
Clements, Allen	AL0345	32D,36,60A,40,61
Cochran, Kathy	SC0750	32B,32D
Coffman, Teresa S.	RI0200	36,40,32D
Collins, Cherie	ND0250	61,36,32D,64B
Collins, Drew S.	OH2500	32D,36
Conkling, Susan W.	MA0400	32D,36,32C,32F,32G
Conley, Mark	RI0300	13,60,36,61,32D
Cooksey, John M.	UT0250	36,32C,32D
Corbin, Patricia	AL0500	60A,32D,61,55D,60
Correlli, Christopher	MD0850	32D
Cottrell, Duane	DE0150	36,32D
Cox, Michael	VA1580	36,61,32D,60A
Cruse, Carolyn S.	TX3200	36,40,32D,32G
Cummings, Grace	NY3350	32B,36,61,32C,32D
Cummins, Nicholaus B.	MS0250	36,60A,32D,40
Cunningham, Chuck	NM0500	66A,66G,32D,36,40
Darrough, Galen P.	CO0950	60A,36,32D
Dawson, David J.	TX3175	32D,62D
De Jaager, Alfred R.	WV0600	36,32D,60,11
De Jager, Ron	AJ0030	60A,36,52,61,32D
Dean, Brandon	MN0750	36,13,20,32D,34B
DeHoogh-Kliewer, David	SD0580	60A,11,32D,36,40
Dennee, Peter D.	WI0250	32C,32D,36,60,40
Dennison, Jessica	GA0850	61,32D
Diddle, Laura D.	SD0550	32B,32D,36
Dody, Teresa D.	WV0350	61,13C,13K,32B,32D
Dohrmann, Diana	NJ0550	32C,32D
Donelson, David W.	OH1350	36,32D,60A
Dunn, Robert	UT0050	32C,32G,32D
Durow, Peter J.	MO1500	36,32D,60A
Eaton, Denise	TX2250	36,32D
Edwards, Patti Yvonne	SC0420	61,32D
Eklund, Peter A.	NE0600	60,32D,36
Elpus, Kenneth	MD1010	32D,32G,36
Escalante, Roosevelt	KY0900	13B,13C,32D,36
Eshelman, Darla	OK1330	32A,32B,32D
Evans, Cory	UT0300	32D,36,40
Everett, Beth	MI0600	36,60,32D
Eyerly, Heather E.	NY3780	32D
Faerber, Matthew L.	WI0860	60A,36,32D,40,13C
Ferrebee, Sarah	CT0050	32B,32C,32D
Ferreebee, Sarah	CT0650	32D
Ferrell, Rene	CA0650	32B,32C,60A,32D
Fields-Moffitt, Rebecca	IA0300	32D
Fisher, Ryan A.	AR0850	32D,36
Fleet, Ken	AG0500	32D
Fleming, Pat W.	TX3175	32B,32E,32D,13A
Flores, Carolina	CT0650	32D
Flory, Jennifer Morgan	GA0850	36,32D,15,60A,61
Flournoy-Buford, Debbie	TX3650	32B,32D,34,66C,66A
Floyd, Eva	OH2200	32,32D
Floyd, Hugh	SC0750	61,60A,36,32D
Ford, Joseph Kevin	TN1700	36,40,32D,60
Fox, Ryan H	AR0300	36,60A,32D,40
Francom, Jeffery D.	NY3780	36,32D
Franklin, James C.	TX2250	36,32D
Frasier, Michael	OR0200	36,32D
Fredstrom, Tim	IL1150	32D,36,60A,32
Freer, Patrick K.	GA1050	32D,32C,32D,36,60A
Fresne, Jeannette	AL1300	32A,32B,32C,32D,32I
Friesen, Elroy	AC0100	36,60A,32D
Fuelberth, Rhonda J.	NE0600	32D,36
Fukuda, Joni	CA5355	11,13A,32D,36,61
Furby, Victoria J.	NY3717	13C,15,32D
Futrell, Stephen A.	NC0750	36,32D,60,35C,40
Galante, Brian Edward	WA0650	36,10,60A,32D
Gallo, Franklin J.	IL0750	32C,32D
Garcia-Novelli, Eduardo	WI0250	36,40,32D,13C,60
Garrett, Matthew L.	OH0400	36,32D,60A
Gemmell, Jeffrey S.	CO0800	36,32D,60A

Name	Code	Areas
Gerber, Gary G.	AR0500	36,61,32D,60A
Geston, Mary K.	MN1280	40,32D,60A,32C,36
Gibbons, Henry	TX3420	32D
Goffi-Fynn, Jeanne C.	NY4200	40,61,13H,32B,32D
Goodman, James A.	ID0050	32B,32C,32D,32F
Goodwin, Casey S.	NH0350	37,32D,47,60B
Graham, Seong-Kyung	WI0700	61,32D,36,60A
Graves, Jim F.	OK1200	36,32D,32B,60A,61
Green, Martin	CA1000	11,13H,32D,36,39
Green, Verna	NY0640	20A,20H,32D,32E,36
Grevlos, Lisa	SD0050	39,61,32B,36,32D
Grier, George	WA0700	11,13,32D,47,65
Griffith, Larry D.	TN0930	60A,32C,36,61,32D
Grogan, David C.	TX3500	61,32D,36,39,40
Grooms, Pamela	MO0650	12A,20,32D,60,66
Guter, Christine	CA0825	47,61,32D
Haan, Keith A.	IA1300	60,36,32D,61,40
Haberlen, John B.	GA1050	60,32D,36
Hafso, Marc A.	WA1350	60,36,10A,32D,61
Hahn, Mari	AK0100	61,39,54,32D
Haldeman, Randy	NC2420	36,32D
Halm, Jack L.	WA0800	32D
Ham, Robert	IN0200	32D,36,40
Han, Jong-Hoon 'James'	TX1400	36,32D
Harden, Matthew C.	NE0610	36,60A,32D,40
Harper, T.J.	RI0150	36,60,32C,32D,61
Harris, David	PA0150	36,61,31A,40,32D
Harris, Robert	GA0200	12A,60,61,11,32D
Hart, Steven R.	MT0350	36,61,32D
Hasseler, Lynda	OH0350	60A,36,40,32D
Hawkins, Allan	MN0625	61,32C,32D
Hayes, William Bryce	VA0600	32D,36
Haygood, Christopher D.	OK0800	36,32D
Heil, Leila T.	CO0800	32D
Henderson, Mark A.	UT0350	60,10,11,36,32D
Henry, James	MO1830	36,40,60A,32D,10F
Henry, Michele L.	TX0300	32D
Hensley, Hunter C.	KY0550	36,61,60A,55,32D
Hepworth, Elise M.	NE0700	32D,61,32B,32C,11
Herb, Thomas	UT0200	13C,34,47,32C,32D
Hetzel, Lori	KY1450	32,36,32D
Hibbard, Kevin	GA2130	36,32D,61,60,32C
Hicks, Lori C.	SC0350	61,39,32D
Highben, Zebulon M.	OH1650	36,40,61,32D
Hightower, Allen	IA0950	36,32D,60
Hinson, Amalie	NC1100	32D,32B
Hodge, Stephen	OH2300	36,32C,61,32D,60A
Hodges, Justin	TX0600	36,40,32D
Holder, Ryan	AZ0450	32D,36,60A
Holquist, Robert A.	NC2600	32C,36,55D,32D
Holz, Beatrice	KY0100	32B,36,39,61,32D
Hondorp, Paul	KY1550	36,60A,32D,61,40
Hooper, Randall	TX2955	36,60A,32D,32B,40
Hopkins, Stephen M.	NC0050	36,60A,32D
Horvath, Janos	AA0150	32B,32D,36,42,13C
Hutsko, Mark	OH0350	32D
Hylton, John B.	MO1830	32D
Jackman, Sean M.	OH2150	32D,32F
Jacobsen, Lesa L.	WI0845	61,32C,32D,60A,36
James, Buddy	CA0807	36,32D,61,60A
Jeffreys, Shannon	GA0950	36,32D
Jensen, Joni L.	TX3300	13C,36,61,32D,60A
Jesse, Lynda	MO0200	32D,36,54,60,61
Jirak, James	ID0050	36,32D,60A
Johnson, Daniel	IL1200	32A,32B,32C,32D,32E
Johnson, Jon S.	TX2350	13,36,61,54,32D
Johnson, Stephen R.	PA0700	10F,32D,13A,63D
Jones, Jeremy D.	OH1450	36,32D
Jones, Robert B.	OH2250	60A,32C,36,32D
Jones, Trevor	IL0750	32C,32D
Jordanoff, Christine E.	PA1050	32D,32B,32C,32,36
Jorgensen, Michael	MN0750	61,11,32D,14C
Judisch, David	IA0950	39,61,32D
Junker, Tercio	IN0300	60A,36,31A,32D,10E
Kameria, Kim	CA1290	11,32D,35A,35B,35C
Keith, Laura J.	SC0350	12A,66A,66D,32C,32D
Keller, Merry	MO1950	31A,32D,13
Kellert, Carolyn	IL1350	32C,32D,61
Kenaston-French, Karen	TX3500	36,61,32D,40,60A
Kennedy, Patricia E.	IN0905	13C,32D
Kinsey, Katherine S.	SC1200	32D,36,60A,40
Kornelis, Benjamin	IA0500	20,32D,36,60A,40
Kovacs, Anna	NY2750	32D,36,60A
Koza, Julia Eklund	WI0815	32,32D
Krueger, Carol J.	KS0300	13C,60,36,32D
Kuehne, Jane M.	AL0200	32,32D,32F
Lamartine, Nicole C.	WY0200	36,60A,32D
Lancaster, Michael	NC2600	60A,55D,61,36,32D
Langford, Bruce	CA1000	11,12A,32D,36,39
Lanier, Brian	MO0950	32D,36,60A,61
Latimer, Marvin E.	AL1170	32D,36,60A
Lee, Nancy	MN1450	32D
Levi, Michael	NY0700	36,29B,13,60A,32D
Lewis-Hale, Phyllis	MS0350	61,39,32D
Li, Tai-Wai	AK0100	32D,40
Linford, Jon	ID0060	39,61,32D
Liske, Kenneth L.	WI0830	32,32C,32F,32B,32D
Lister, Michael C.	NY0700	32D,32C,55D,36,13
Livesay, Charles	MI2000	60,32D,36,40,61
Lofgren, Ronald R.	NE0700	11,32D,36,60A,61
Logan, P. Bradley	MN0150	60A,36,32D,40
Long, Nolan W.	OH2120	36,32D,40,42
Loo, Janet	AG0500	61,32D
Luethi, Dean A.	WA1150	36,47,61,32D
Lynn, Daniel	NE0550	60A,61,36,32C,32D
Mack-Bervin, Linda	CO0350	11,32D,36,60A
Maglione, Anthony	MO2000	36,32D,60
Major, James E.	IL1150	36,40,32D
Major, Marci L.	MO1800	32D,60A
Malone, Mark H.	MS0850	32A,32B,32C,32D
Malone, Thomas	MA2030	20,32D,60A
Mann, Alison	GA1150	40,60A,32C,32D
Marks, Randall J.	PA1900	32B,32C,32D,32E
Martin, Joey	TX3175	36,32D,60A
May, William V.	TX0300	32D
McCaffrey, Maureen	TN1400	11,61,32D,60A
McClung, Alan C.	TX3420	32C,32D,32G,60A,13C
McGee, Isaiah R.	SC0350	35,36,39,61,32D
McIntyre, Sarah Elizabeth	IL2750	32D
McKinney, Jane Grant	NC0900	32C,13B,32D,39
McManus, Lanny	AL0550	32D,36,12,13E,40
McMillin, Timothy A.	IA1350	60,36,61,32D,12A
McWhirter, Jamila L.	TN1100	32D,36,60A
Mecham, Mark L.	PA1900	32D,36,40,60A
Mechell, Harry A.	MN1700	60,36,32D,61,54
Meder, Randall A.	WI0808	60,11,36,40,32D
Melton, James L.	CA5355	60,36,31A,32D,35E
Melton, Michael D.	IL2150	36,40,32D,61,60A
Mendoza, Michael D.	NJ0175	60A,32D,36
Mielcarz, Kelly	IL2050	32,32D
Miller, Josh	WV0200	36,61,32D,11,60A
Miller, Michael	WA0980	32D,36,60A
Mitchell, Aaron Paul	IN0905	32D,36,40,60A
Moe, Charlette	ND0350	32B,32D,36
Moon, Hosun	NY1275	11,66,13B,32D,36
Mooy, Mary Annaleen	HI0050	60A,32D,36
Mowrer, Tony	CA0810	32D,32,32C
Murphy, Michael	ID0250	36,40,32D,12A,32C
Murphy, Sheila C.	FL2100	61,39,32D
Musgrove, Abby R.	IL1100	36,40,11,32C,32D
Nanni, Steven	NY1400	61,32D
Nardo, Rachel L.	UT0250	32,32B,34,32A,32D
Neill, Kelly	AR0250	32D,36,40,61
Neill, Sheri L.	TX3000	32D,32B,32C,32G
Nelson, Sheri	CA0630	32D
Nero, Jonathan	SD0100	36,32D,60
Nesheim, Paul	SD0050	36,32D
Nettles, Darryl	TN1400	13B,32D,36,39,61
Neufeld, Charles W.	SC0800	60A,61,36,32D
Nims, Marilyn	OH2000	61,13C,32D
Nix, John Paul	TX3530	61,13L,32D
Nolker, D. Brett	NC2430	32D
Nolte, John P.	MN1030	13A,32D
Norris, Charles	MI0900	32D,32G,36
O'Connell, Brian	MA2030	32D,60A
Odom, Donald R.	MS0850	36,13C,11,32D,60A
Ohlman, Kathleen	NE0200	32B,32C,32D,32E
Olesen, Bradley C.	LA0200	32D
Olin, Christopher S.	OR1050	32D,36,60A
Oliver, Ronald D.	MI2250	36,60A,32D
Olsen, David	ID0060	32D,39,61
Oppenheim, Joshua	KS0650	32D,36
Ottley, Jerold	HI0050	32D,36,60A
Owen, Christopher S.	IL2150	36,32D
Paparo, Stephen A.	MA2000	32D
Parker, Elizabeth	GA0550	32A,32B,32C,32D
Parker, Gregory B.	NC0400	36,61,60A,40,32D
Parker, Nancy	MN0610	11,20,32D
Parker, Webster	MS0750	32D
Parks, Sarah S.	WI0750	36,32D,60A,61
Parr, Clayton G.	MI0100	36,40,60A,32D
Parton-Stanard, Susan	IL1500	61,40,36,11,32D
Paulsen, Kent D.	WI0750	36,32D,61,60,13C
Pederson, Robin	OR0450	32D
Pehlivanian, Elisabeth	CA0825	61,32D
Perkins, Daniel R.	NH0250	36,61,12A,32D,60A
Perry, Pamela J.	CT0050	32B,32C,36,32D,60A
Peterson, Christopher	CA0815	32D,36
Peterson, Dean	MT0400	60A,32D,36,40
Peterson, Vince	NY0500	36,60A,32D,13,11
Pham, Danh	WA1150	32D,60B,48
Plummer, Mark W.	IL0150	36,32D,40
Poland, Jeffrey T.	WV0300	32D,36,61,60
Pool, Ellen	MI0900	32D,36,60A
Poovey, Gena E.	SC0850	36,61,60A,32D,40
Porter, Michael	NC0250	36,40,60,61,32D
Porter, Thomas	ND0400	36,13B,10A,32D,31A
Potterton, Matthew	KS0050	60,36,32D
Powell, Curtis Everett	GA0490	36,13,32,32D
Powell, Steven S.	PA1000	36,61,34,12A,32D
Prickett, Todd O.	AR0700	36,32D
Quantz, Don E.	AA0010	12A,32D,36,40,41
Quintana, Ariel	CA0845	36,32D
Quist, Amanda R.	NJ1350	32D,36,60
Ramsdell, Gregory A.	OH0950	37,55D,32B,32D,32C
Reid, Ted	CA0825	32D
Reynolds, Geoffrey	CT0650	32B,32C,32D,32F,32G
Rhodes, Ann G.	KY0300	11,12A,61,32D,29A
Richards, E. Earl	CA2420	32D,36,60A
Richmond, John W.	NE0600	32D,32G,36,32
Robbins, Catherine	AC0100	32D,32C,60A
Roberson, Heather D.	CO1050	61,36,11,60A,32D
Robertson, Patricia	IN1560	39,61,32D
Robinson, Charles R.	MO1810	36,32D,32H
Rodde, James	IA0850	36,60,32D
Rodriguez, Sandra	PR0115	32A,32D,32
Rolsten, Kathy	MN1120	32A,32B,32D,36,61
Romines, Dee	TX0900	32D,36
Rose, Cameron J.	TX3535	36,32D,11,10
Rothlisberger, Rodney	MN1120	32D,36,66G
Rowsey, Les	MI0520	32C,32D
Royo, Johanna	GA2100	32D
Rozukalns, Thelma	NC1100	32D
Ruffin, Milton	OH1850	32D
Runestad, Kurt	NE0200	36,32D,60A,47
Runyan, Donald	IL1612	36,32D,61
Rushton, Christianne	AF0050	12A,15,32D,61
Russell, John	CA0845	36,40,32D,60A
Russell, John K.	CA1520	32D,36,40,60A
Schauer, Elizabeth	AZ0500	36,32D,61
Schmidt, Nolan	NE0200	32D
Schneller, Pamela	TN1850	32C,32B,32D,60
Schnipke, Richard	OH1850	32D,36
Schreuder, Joel T.	NE0050	60A,36,61,40,32D
Schuppener, James	TX1700	36,61,32D
Schwartz, Sandra M.	WV0750	32D,32G
Scott, Sandra C.	GA1600	36,40,60A,32D,66A
Scraper, Joel	SC1100	40,60A,32D,36,60
Scurich, Kelly	OH2600	32D
Settle, David	KS1250	61,32D
Shane, Lynn	MA1650	11,61,32B,32D,36
Shanklin, Bart	IL3500	61,60A,36,32D
Shaw, Martha	GA1700	36,32D,60A
Sheppard, Kenny	TX2650	60A,36,32D
Sieck, Stephen	VA0350	36,61,60A,32D
Silvey, Philip E.	NY1100	32D,32G
Simmons, Mark	TN1720	36,32D,60A
Simons, Kevin	MI1850	61,36,32D,60A
Simpson, Brennetta	NC1600	32B,32A,32D
Sinclair, Terri	SC0420	36,61,32D,60A
Skadsem, Julie A.	MI2100	32D,32
Smale, Marcelyn	MN1300	32A,13C,66D,32B,32D
Smith, Michael V.	DC0050	60,32,32B,32C,32D
Snow, Sandra	MI1400	32D,36
Snyder, Timothy	FL1000	36,40,12A,32D,60A
Soderberg, Karen	MD0350	61,36,40,32D,60A
Sowers, Richard L.	IN0100	60A,36,32D
Spano, Fred P.	NC2420	32B,32D,32G,32
Spears, Samuel B.	WV0300	32D,36,61,60A
Stauch, Thomas J.	IL1085	36,40,61,32D,11
Stegall, James C.	IL3500	36,32D,60A
Stegner, John M.	KY1425	32D,61
Stephen, Anne	NV0050	32D
Stewart, Jonathan	OK0825	32D,11,13B,36,61
Stickler, Larry W.	WV0400	36,32B,32C,61,32D
Stornetta, Catherine	MA0850	60A,32D,36

Strauser, Matthew L.	OR0175	36,60,13C,32D
Suderman, Mark	OH0250	60A,32D,32B,36,61
Sumner, Daniel	LA0770	32B,32C,32D,32G
Swan, Phillip A.	WI0350	36,60,61,32D,60A
Taylor, Sean	OH0500	32D,10A
Thayer, Lucinda J.	WI0850	60A,36,32D
Theimer, Axel K.	MN0350	60A,36,61,32D
Thompson, Laura	LA0250	32C,32D,36,60A,61
Thompson, Sandra D.	OK1330	11,32D
Thoms, Jason A.	NY0850	36,32D,61,55D,12A
Thye, David R.	TX2600	60,32D,32E,36,38
Todd, Colette	WI0250	32D,36,47
Trotta, Michael J.	VA1830	32D,12A,36,40
Truax, Jenean	PA0150	13A,13C,32D,61,66A
Turgeon, Melanie E.	AA0035	60,36,42,13C,32D
Ulrich, Jerry	GA0900	10,36,32,32D,60A
Van Wyck, Helen J.	IL3100	13,60A,11,36,32D
Vazquez-Ramos, Angel M.	CA0960	60A,36,32D,32B
Veigel, Loren	OH2150	32D
Verrier, Thomas	TN1850	37,60B,32C,32D,32
Vogt, Sean F.	SD0300	60A,36,66G,32D,40
Walker, Alicia W.	SC1110	36,32D,60A
Wallis, David N.	MO0650	36,10A,11,13,32D
Ward, Jeffrey	NC0650	32D,36
Ward-Steinman, Patrice Madura	IN0900	32G,32D,32,29,47
Warren, John F.	NY4150	36,32D,60A
Waters, Richard	KY0550	36,60A,32D,40
Watson, Tim M.	IA1100	32D,47,36,60A
Webb, Mark	MI0300	63,32C,32D,32E,11
Weber, Brent	PA2250	61,32D,39,12A
Weger, Stacy	OK1150	60A,32D,36
Weiller, David B.	NV0050	60A,32D,36
Wesby, Roger	NY4500	11,29A,32D,36,40
West, Cheryl E.	IN1650	32D
Westfall, Claude R.	MO0100	32B,32D,36,60A,70
White, Christopher Dale	TX2955	32D,36,40,60A,61
White, Karin	MI1260	32B,32E,32D
Williams, Deborah	IL0600	32C,36,61,32D
Wilson, Gary P.	TN0930	60A,32C,36,61,32D
Windt, Nathan J.	TN1550	60A,61,11,32D,36
Wis, Ramona M.	IL2050	60A,42,32D,36
Wolff, David	DC0170	32D
Wolverton, Vance D.	KY1000	32D
Wu, Chieh-Mei Jamie	NY3500	11,13B,61,32D,36
Yanson, Eliezer G.	SC0200	32D,13,60A,36,40
Young, Susan	IL2250	32D
Younse, Stuart	CT0650	32D
Yu-Oppenheim, Julie	KS0650	32D,36,60A
Zamer, Craig T.	TN1450	36,60A,32D
Zeigler, Mark C.	NY2650	32D,36,40,60A
Zielke, Steven M.	OR0700	36,60,32D

Instrumental Music

Acklin, Amy	KY1500	32E,37,60B
Adderley, Cecil L.	MA0260	32E,32F,32G,62A,64C
Aicher, Carol Ann	NY2150	32E
Alderson, Erin	IL1800	11,13A,32E,37,64
Aldrich, Mark L.	MA1650	37,32E,32F,34D,60B
Alexander, Michael L.	TX0300	32E,38
Allen, Greg	IL1740	32E
Allen, Sarah	TX2400	32E,37,32,60B,32B
Alley, Gregory	MI0300	63A,32E
Allison, Edward	NC0050	11,32E
Alsobrook, Joseph	MO0650	10F,32E,37,34F,35A
Alvarez, Ian M.	WA0800	32E
Ambrose, Robert J.	GA1050	37,32E,60B
Amidon, Brad T.	PA2250	65,32E
Ammann, Bruce T.	SD0050	60B,37,32E,64E
Anderson, Christopher M.	TX3200	37,32E
Angeles, L. Dean	LA0300	38,32E,60B
Appenheimer-Vaida, Christiane	PA2200	62C,41,32E
Archer, Kimberly K.	IL2910	10,13,32E,10A,10F
Armour, Janet E.	TN1680	32E
Armstrong, Heather M.	IA0950	13B,64B,32E
Arnold, Edwin P.	PA1450	32E,37,60B,48,49
Asbell, Stephanie Ames	TX3175	62B,32E
Asbill, M. Miller	NC0250	37,32E
Ash, Corey	TX1100	37,49,63A,32E,60B
Ashton, Ted	ID0060	41,62A,32E
Azzara, Christopher D.	NY1100	32E,32G
Babcock, Ronald	OR0850	13,32E
Bailey, Kalomo	KY0750	37,32E
Bailey, Mark	TN0850	13,32E,32C,37
Baldacchino, Laura Falzon	NY4200	64A,32E,42,43
Ballenger, William	TX3200	10A,32E,37,63A
Ballif, Adam	ID0060	32C,32E,64C
Baransy, Paul	OH0250	63A,10F,60B,32E,37
Barber, Clarence	OH0200	32E
Barczyk, Cecylia	MD0850	41,62C,32E,51
Barlar, Douglas	FL0670	12A,63D,49,32E
Barlar, Nancy	FL0670	64C,32B,32C,32E,11
Barnett, Steven	WV0400	10F,32E,37,60
Barnhart, Stephen L.	WY0200	65,50,32E
Barreto, Naitsabes	PR0100	32E
Barrier, Gray	CO0950	50,65,32E
Barton, David	ID0060	32E
Bartram, Kevin P.	VA1475	37,60B,38,32E
Bates, Charles N.	OH1800	11,32E,37,47,60
Bayless, Robert R.	AZ0500	32C,32E,37,60B
Bazan, Dale E.	NE0600	32E,32F,32G,32H,34
Beatty, Caroline	TX3175	37,32E,60B
Bechen, Gene	IA1300	37,32E,60,32
Becraft, Steven C.	AR0300	64C,29,64E,48,32E
Bedell, Adam	TX3100	50,65,32E
Beebe, Jon P.	NC0050	13,48,64D,32E,42
Beeson, Robert	DC0050	32E,64E
Bell, Richard	GA0500	32E,13,38,60B,62D
Belter, Babette	OK0800	32E,64C
Benkert, Stuart M.	TN1700	37,47,32E,60B
Bennett, Larry	MO0100	32E,63D,63C,41
Benz, Fritz	RI0150	32C,32E
Benzer, John	TX3400	32E
Bergonzi, Louis	IL3300	32E,38,62,32G,60B
Bernhard, H. Christian	NY3725	32E,32
Betancourt, David	CA0859	37,46,38,32E,60B
Bettencourt, Blair	MA2030	32E
Biggs, Dana M.	CO0800	37,32E
Bill, Jennifer	RI0150	32E,37
Bingham, Ann Marie	WV0400	12A,64B,64C,32E
Bingham, Emelyne	TN1850	13B,32E
Bingham, Thomas	HI0210	32E,37,60
Birden, Larry	OK0450	13A,32E,10F,63,37
Bitticks, Meret	IL0750	32E
Bjella, Steven A.	WI0850	41,62A,32E
Blaine, Robert	MS0350	11,38,32E,63C,60B
Blair, Starla	MO0400	32E

Blakemore, Linda	MI0300	32E
Blaser, Albert	OH0650	32E,11
Blocher, Larry	AL1050	32E,37
Block, Tyrone	TX2570	32E,37,47,60B,63
Bodley, Muriel M.	NY4150	32E
Boggs, David G.	IL1740	37,32E,60B
Bohnert, David A.	NE0700	63A,60B,37,11,32E
Booker, Charles L.	AR0730	10,32E,13,60B
Boone, Kathleen	WA0550	64B,64C,70,32E,13C
Bossuat, Judy	CA0840	32E,62
Boulden, George	KY1450	37,60,32E
Bovenschen, Wayne	OK0800	65,37,50,32E
Bovenzi, Michael	FL1950	34,32E,64E
Boyd, Bruce	KS1250	62A,62B,70,32E,62C
Boyer, Charles G.	CO0050	32,11,32E,37
Bradshaw, Eric E.	GA2150	63D,32E,37,60
Brakel, Timothy D.	OH2300	32E,32,64E,13,60
Brandes, Gary W.	MO1830	37,60,32E
Breaux, Michael L.	NY2750	32B,32C,32E,32F
Breneman, Marianne Leitch	KY1000	11,64C,32E,64B
Brenner, Brenda L.	IN0900	62A,32E
Brewer, Paul	AZ0490	11,13,29,32E,47
Brewer, Paul S.	MI0300	60B,37,32E,29,63C
Brewer, Wesley D.	IL0550	32E,32F
Bright, Jeff R.	KY1550	37,32E,34
Britt, Mark E.	SC0750	63C,49,32E
Broffitt, Virginia	OK0800	64A,42,11,32E
Bronk, Mary Beth	TX3100	32E,37,60,63A
Brotman, Justin	AZ0490	62D,10,32E
Brown, Al	CA0850	32E,65,50
Brown, Anne	NY1700	32E
Brown, Darrell	ID0060	32E,65,50
Brown, Eric	GA2300	65,32E
Brown, Susan	OK0800	64D,32E
Bruno, Anthony	IL0750	32E
Bryant, Deanne	IL1200	32B,32C,32D,32E
Buck, Lynn	IL1200	32E
Buckles, Michael	LA0350	32E,62A
Buckner, James R.	AR0300	49,63A,32E
Bull, Douglas	WY0050	37,63,11,32E
Burdett, John	CA0630	32E,37,60B
Burdett, Kimberly H.	OH2000	50,65,32E
Burkett, Eugenie I.	NV0050	32,32E,32G
Burleson, Brett J.	OH2000	70,32E
Burns, Ellen	NY3680	12A,32E
Burns, Lauren	GA2150	62B,32E,51
Bush, Doug W.	NE0600	32E,37
Bushman, Catharine Sinon	SC1200	37,32E,42
Bustos, Pamela B.	WI0860	32E,37,48,60B,64C
Butrico, Michael	NC0400	32E,37,46,60B,63
Cabalo, Eric	CA4700	70,32E,41
Caldwell, Brendan	WI0850	37,32E,60B
Caminiti, Joseph D.	PA2800	60,38,37,63B,32E
Campbell, Michael J.	GA2300	60B,47,64E,32E,11
Campo, David	TX2700	32E,32C,37,60B
Cangro, Richard	IL3500	32E,11
Caravan, Lisa	AL0200	62C,62D,32E
Cardany, Brian M.	RI0300	32E,32G,37,60B
Carpenter, Kelley K.	WI0350	32E
Carrell, Cynthia T.	AR0250	11,13,32E,37,63A
Carrell-Coons, Mariah	OK0770	66A,66C,66D,32E
Carson, William S.	IA0300	60B,37,12A,32E,64C
Carter, Robert Scott	NC0650	60B,37,41,32E
Casagrande, John E.	VA0450	37,32C,32E,32G
Cason, Tony	CA3600	41,32E,60B,38,12A
Castro, Edward	WA0550	63A,32E
Cavitt, Mary Ellen	TX3175	32E
Chambers, Carol	TX3100	63A,13C,32E,10F,32A
Champney, Morgen	NC2420	32E
Chance, Mike	AR0250	32E,37,38,63C,63D
Chandler, Susan	WI0865	32E,38,62
Chang, Wei Tsun	TN1450	11,32E,62A,41,62
Chapman, Alicia	NC0050	55C,64B,32E
Charter, Ian R.	AA0010	12A,13A,31A,32E,60
Cheeseman, Andrea L.	NC0050	64C,32E
Chenoweth, Richard K.	OH2250	63B,32E
Chesebrough, James C.	NH0150	37,60,32,63D,32E
Chesher, Michael	IA0950	32E,42,64C,64E
Chesnutt, Rod M.	FL0680	37,38,60,32E,32F
Christensen, Donald	NY0500	32E,64C,64
Christie, Pamela	NY3717	32E,62
Chuong, Jason	PA3330	32E,65
Clarke, W. Harry	KY1450	60,32E
Coale, Dean	OK0300	32E,49,63C,63D
Coffman, Don D.	FL1900	32E,32G
Coggiola, Jill A.	NY4150	32E,64C,64E
Cohen, Judith	AG0650	20,55C,55A,32E
Cole, Carol	FL1125	62A,42,32E
Cole, Monty	GA1300	29,32E,46,64C,64E
Coleman, Randall	AL1170	37,60B,32E
Colenbrander, Caroline	AG0650	32E
Collins, Caron L.	NY3780	32E
Compton, Lanette	OK0800	63B,11,32E,42
Conley, Nancy S.	NY3780	32E
Connors, Thomas	NJ0700	37,11,32E,60B
Copenhaver, James K.	SC1110	32E,37
Corcoran, Gary J.	NH0250	37,60B,63A,32E
Corley, Alton L.	TX3175	37,32E
Cornwell, Tina	AR0200	32E
Correll, Allen	OK0300	37,32E,47,60B,63A
Couch, Roy L.	OK0150	37,63D,49,32E
Covey, Jason	NY2900	60,32E
Cox, Gregory	AG0550	32E
Craig, Ed	CA0350	32C,32E
Craig, Mark	MD0850	32E,65
Crawford, Pete	NC0900	32E,65
Creasap, Susan D.	KY0900	32E,37
Cresci, Jonathan	PA3710	63A,32E
Crim, Mark	TX0600	37,32E,60B,44
Crist, Michael	OH2600	32E,63C,34
Crochet, Lourinda S.	SC1200	37,32E,42
Cross, Travis J.	VA1700	32E,37,60
Cudd, Patti	MN0350	65,32E,50
Culvahouse, John N.	GA1150	37,32C,32E,60B
Cumming, Christine	NY1400	64E,32E
Curley, Jason	NY1400	60B,63B,37,49,32E
Dalby, Kathy	NE0200	32E
Dalton, Grant B.	AL0800	65,11,32E,47,50
Daly, Kathleen	NJ0700	62A,32E,11
Damicone, Tiffany	OH2000	32E
Dammers, Richard J.	NJ1050	32,32E,32F
Dansereau, Diana R.	MA0400	32G
Daughtery, Wendy	TX2570	62A,62B,66A,32E
Davis, Alfred L.	VA0500	32E,32F,32B,32C,10F
Davis, Jan	MO1830	32E
Davis, Paul G.	MO1950	60B,37,38,32E
Day, James G.	NJ0175	32E
Day, Michael	NC1550	11,32E,32F,63A,63B

Index by Area of Teaching Interest

Name	Code	Areas
DeBenedetto, Patricia	CA1860	32E,37,64E,64C,48
DeGraffenreid, George	CA0830	32C,32E,32G
DeGroff, Jason	CT0700	32E,37,46
Dekaney, Joshua A.	NY4150	20H,65,32E
del Grazia, Nicolas M.	AR0200	32E,41,48,64C
Dell, Charlene	OK1350	32E,32H,32,62,62A
Denmon, Alan	GA2300	11,13A,13B,32C,32E
DeRusha, Stanley	IN0250	32E,11,60B
DeTurk, Mark	NH0350	32C,32E,32G
DeVasto, David	IL0850	10,13,32E,66
Diamond, Shirley A.	WA1100	64E,64C,32E
Dickey, Nathaniel H.	MN0600	37,63C,63D,32E,49
DiCuirci, Michael	OH0950	63C,63D,37,32E
Dierolf, Wallace	TX3175	32E
Dimond, Raymond R.	AR0300	47,65,53,13,32E
Dobbs, Teryl L.	WI0815	32E,32
Dorfman, Jay	MA0400	32E,32G
Dorothy, Wayne F.	TX0900	32C,32E,37,60B
Dowdy, James	OH0350	32E
Droste, Douglas	OK0800	38,60B,32E
Dubois, Laura	NJ0760	10A,11,32E,66
Duerden, Darren	HI0050	32E,65,50,47,11
Dufford, Gregory	CO0550	64C,32E
Dugger, Clay	IL1740	32E
Duitman, Henry E.	MI0900	51,38,32E,41
Dulaney, John	OR1250	32E,29A
Dunham, Robert W.	GA0950	32E,37
Durbin, Timothy T.	KY1500	32E
Dye, Keith G.	TX3200	60B,37,32C,32E
Eccles, David F.	IL3450	51,32E,38
Edelberg, Joe	CA4700	32E,38,42,62A,62B
Edwards, Jason R.	IA0900	64,13,10,32E
Elliott, Richard	OH0680	65,50,37,11,32E
Ellithorpe, Robert	VA1600	63C,32E
Ellzey, Michael R.	NM0100	63A,13,32E
Emmons, Scott	WI0825	32,32C,32E
Engle, Tiffany J.	MI0350	64E,60B,37,32E
Enloe, Loraine D.	ID0250	32E,64,37,64C,32C
Ensel, Amy	KY1500	32E
Erdahl, Rolf	IA0950	62D,32E
Eros, John	CA0807	32,32E,32B
Ethington, Bradley P.	NY4150	60B,37,32E
Etienne, David	AR0300	11,20,32E
Evans, Darryl	AR0810	32E,47,63D,13A,13B
Fahy, Alison	MN0610	32E,51
Fallin, Nicky G.	GA0250	37,32E,63A,49,60B
Falvey, Joseph	VA0150	63B,37,34G,32E,49
Fansler, Michael J.	IL3500	37,60B,32E
Farnham, Curvin G.	ME0440	60B,32E,37
Fernisse, Glenn	GA0400	10,63D,34,32E
Fetter, John	NY1100	32E
Fetz, Katie	OR0200	64,32E
Fife, Travis	TX1400	65,50,32E
Filipovich, Natalie	MN1700	62A,62B,32E
Fisher, Stan F.	AF0050	32E,12A
Flaniken, Jeffrey Z.	AL0800	62A,13B,32E
Flegg, Mark	MI2200	63A,32E
Fluchaire, Olivier	NY2200	32E,63A
Flythe, Bernard	GA1150	32E,63D,41,11
Folsom, Gunnar	WA1000	65,32E
Foor, Morris	GA0550	32
Forsha, Heather	NY1400	13C,66A,66C,32E
Foster, Adam	AL1050	32E
Foster, Mark	CO0550	50,65,32E
Foster, Robert E.	KS1350	32E
Francis, Bobby R.	TX3000	37,60,32E
Franklin, Laura L.	NC0250	50,65,20,32E
Franzblau, Robert	RI0200	32E,37
Fraschillo, Tom	GA1700	37,60B,32E
Frechou, Paul A.	LA0650	64C,37,32C,32E
Frederick, Matthew D.	VA0350	63A,12A,41,60B,32E
Fredrickson, Matthew	MO0650	63D,32E,49,63C
Fredrickson, William E.	FL0850	32G,32E,32
Frehner, Celeste Johnson	OK0800	64B,20,32E
French, Todd M.	IL0800	63D,32E
Frutkoff, Peter	NY0050	32E,63,64
Fuchs, Craig	KS1050	60B,37,32E
Fuchs, Jeffrey W.	NC2410	32E,37
Gaedeke-Riegel, Turid L.	OH2000	32E
Gallo, Reed P.	SC0800	37,60B,32E,63A,49
Gallops, R. Wayne	VA1100	13A,32C,32E,29,37
Galyean, Richard D.	VA1580	37,60B,49,63D,32E
Galyen, S. Daniel	IA1600	37,41,32E,60B,32
Gamerl, Darci	NE0160	64B,32E,67H
Gamso, Nancy M.	OH2000	11,29A,48,64,32E
Gardiner, Robert A.	SC0800	11,29,47,32E,64E
Gardner, Robert	PA2750	32E
Garofalo, Robert	DC0050	32E,37,60B
Garrido, Glenn	TX3450	60B,32E,20H,37
Gavin, Russell	TX0300	32E
Geary, Michael	IA0950	65,50,32E
Genevro, Bradley	PA2300	37,64C,64E,32E
George, Andrew	TX3200	38,60B,39,32E
Gephardt, Donald L.	NJ1050	64C,32E,32G
Gillette, Michael	NJ0760	11,62,32E
Gilmore, Susanna Perry	TN1680	32E,62
Ginocchio, John	MN1500	37,13,47,32E,60B
Goll-Wilson, Kathleen	IL2250	32E
Good, Jonathan E.	NV0050	60B,32,37,32E
Good, Kevin	MI0900	32E
Goodrich, Andrew M.	MA0400	32E,32G
Gottlieb, BettyAnne	OH2200	32E,32G
Gould, Valerie	WV0050	32E,34,37,41,60B
Green, Verna	NY0640	20A,20H,32D,32E,36
Greenblatt, Dan	NY2660	64E,32E,47,29B
Greene, Janet E.	MN0800	32E,13A,37,64C
Gregory, M. David	GA1700	32E,37,32F,60B
Greig, R. Tad	PA3650	32E,37,47,60B,63C
Griffiths, Amy	GA0550	64E,32E,11,47
Griggs, Kevin D.	MT0400	37,60B,32E
Grise', Monte	MN1120	64E,32E,47,37,60B
Grohovac, Janet	TX3100	70,32E
Grugin, Stephen	MI1600	37,63D,12A,32C,32E
Gruner, Greg	AL1300	37,63D,60B,32E,35
Grunow, Richard F.	NY1100	32E,32G
Gurin, Shelley Foster	IL2150	13A,32E
Haberman, Peter J.	MN0600	37,32E
Hagelstein, Kim Rooney	TX2750	12A,13D,32E,63B
Hagen, Scott	UT0250	37,32E,60B
Hall, Crystal	IL0750	32E
Hamann, Donald L.	AZ0500	32,62,32E,32G
Hamar, Jon	WA0550	29,62C,62D,32E,51
Hammer, Eric	CA5350	60B,37,32E
Hamway, Jane	NY3350	32
Hankins, Paul	MS0250	63A,41,47,32E
Hanman, Theodore	KS0100	65,60B,47,37,32E
Hansbrough, Robert S.	NY0700	32E,42,37,65
Hansen, Dallin	ID0060	62A,32E
Hansen, Eric	WI0808	64C,37,13,32E
Hansen, Kristen S.	GA0550	13,11,32E
Harris, Eric	TN1450	37,32E
Harris, Timothy	CA0900	37,11,12A,32E
Harrison, Albert D.	IN1560	60B,37,47,63D,32E
Harrison, David E.	GA1700	32E
Hartley, Linda A.	OH2250	32E,37,64E,32G
Haston, Warren	CT0650	32E,37,32G
Hayslett, Dennis J.	FL1450	37,32E
Haywood, Jennifer	NY1800	32A,32B,32E
Hearn, Sidney T.	IN1100	32,32E,34,37,63A
Heavner, Tracy	AL1300	32E,64E,47,53
Hedgecoth, David	OR1050	32,32E,37
Heffner, Christopher J.	PA1900	32E,37,60,63
Held, Jeffrey	CA1425	11,12A,37,32E,10F
Heller, Lauren B.	CT0050	37,32E,60B,64A
Hemenway, Langston	IL2050	11,32E,37,41
Henderson, Douglas S.	OK0800	37,32E
Hendricks, Karin S.	IN0150	32E
Henninger, Jacqueline	TX3510	32,32E
Heppner-Harjo, Tianna	NV0050	62B,32E,42
Hermann, Joseph W.	TN1450	37,60B,32E
Hersh, Mark S.	NY3780	62A,32E
Hess, Susan M.	ID0250	64D,32E,41
Hester, Carol	IA0950	64A,32E
Hettenhausen, Amy	IL1740	32E
Hicks, Jarrett	IL2750	32B,32C,32E,65
Higgins, Edward	OR0850	37,32E,60B
Higgins, Lee D.	MA0400	32E,32G
Hildebrand, Kirsta	PA2300	32E,65
Hinkie, William H.	CO0950	32E
Hinkle, Laura	IL1300	62,32E
Hoch, Christopher	OH1850	32E
Hodges, Woodrow	WI0250	13,13E,32E,64D
Hoffman, Edward C. 'Ted'	AL1200	11,32C,32E,60B
Holland, Nicholas V.	TN1680	37,32E
Hopkins, Mark E.	AF0050	37,32E,32C,60,60B
Hopwood, Brian	MO1550	32E,37,38,63
Horneff, Donald C.	MD0520	66F,66C,66D,66H,32E
Hotchkiss, Shelia	TN1600	32E
House, Richard E.	SC0350	37,63A,32E,60B
Hudiburg, Howard B.	TX3175	32E,38,60B
Huff, Sharon	IL1750	63D,32E
Huffman, Valarie A.	WV0300	37,32,63D,32E,49
Hughes, Christopher A.	NM0310	37,60B,32E,63A,38
Hulihan, Charles	AZ0350	70,41,32E,32F
Hume, John	IL1100	32E,63A,63B
Humphreys, Jere T.	AZ0100	32,32G,32E
Hunter, Robert	AZ0440	32E,63A,37,46,29A
Hutchins, Tony	IA1100	11,29A,63B,63C,32E
Hynson, Bernard	MD0850	32E
Ibrahim, Michael	WV0750	64E,32E,48
Ingram, Joe	OR1050	32,32E
Isakson, Aaron	MN0610	32E,37,50,60B,65
Jackson, James	AL1250	32E
Jackson, Jay Craig	NC0050	60,32E
Jacobsen, Jeffrey	PA2150	38,32E,32C
James, Joshua	MI1260	32E,47
James, Matthew C.	IN1650	32E
James, Ray	KS0050	37,63D,32E,49
Jasinski, Nathan David	KY0550	62C,32E,38,42,13A
Jenschke, Laura	TX3100	36,61,32E
Jessop, Dustin	TX3350	32E,64E
Jessup, Nancy	CA1425	44,32E
Johnson, Cecilia	OH2300	32E,62A
Johnson, Daniel	IL1200	32A,32B,32C,32D,32E
Johnson, Erik A.	CO0250	32,32E
Johnson, Mark	GA0200	32E,37,60B,63C
Johnson, Richard	SC0420	32E,60B,13
Johnston, Dennis	NY0700	32E,12C,49,63A,60B
Johnston, Margaret	IL0750	32C,32E
Joiner, Anna Barbrey	SC0750	62B,42,32E
Jones, Brandon D.	OH2450	37,38,32E,60
Jones, Eric W.	MI1000	32E,37,50,65
Jones, Gail	PA1400	32E
Jones, Lloyd	AL1250	64,37,47,32E,34A
Jones, Scott A.	OH1850	37,60B,32E
Jones, Troy V.	FL0680	32E,37,65
Jordan, Jeff	KS0350	37,32E,60B,63B,10
Juchniewicz, Jay	NC0650	32E
Jumper, David	PA2200	29,63A,32E,49
Justeson, Jeremy	PA1750	64E,37,32E,43,11
Kaiser, Keith A.	NY1800	32E,32G,49
Kallestad, Scott	NC0050	32E,64E
Karahalis, Dean	NY1275	32E,37
Karrick, Brant	KY1000	37,60B,32E
Kawaller, Meaghan	IL0750	32E
Keener, Michael K.	OH2250	63C,49,11,32E
Keller, Jeffrey	OH0350	32E,60B
Kelley, Constance L.	TX0150	37,32E,64A
Keroack, Marc	MA2030	32E
Kessler, Jennifer	NY3780	32B,32E
Kim, Ariana	IN1650	62A,11,38,32E
King, Steve E.	VA1700	32E,32G,37
Kinney, Daryl W.	OH1850	32G,32E,62A
Kish, David	CO0550	37,32E,60B,32
Kizer, Tremon B.	OH2250	37,32E,11
Kleiman, Carey D.	FL0200	34,35A,64,35,32E
Klein, Susanna	VA1600	62A,42,32E
Klickman, Philip	MD0350	63B,37,32E,60B
Klickman, William	IN0905	38,32E
Knight, Michael D.	WI0750	37,60B,32E,64C,64E
Knight, Steven M.	AR0300	37,32E
Knighten, Christopher	AR0700	32E,37
Knighten, Janet W.	AR0700	32C,32E
Knop, Robert	CA0845	32E,29,64E,11
Knopps, Amy	MI0600	32E,37
Knotts, Clara	FL1750	32C,32E
Korn, Jonathan	WA0550	65,32E
Korzun, Jonathan	MI1985	32E,37,47,13
Kouratachvili, Tinatin	WA0850	32C,32E
Kraus, Barry N.	TN0100	37,32E,60B
Krauss, W. John	OH2290	63D,32E
Kretchner, Darlene	CA0830	32B,32A,32E,32F,32G
Kruse, Nathan B.	TX3420	32,32E
Kuehner, Denise	IN1450	32E
Kuentz, Charles	TX3530	32E
Kugler, Roger T.	KS1000	32E,63,13,37
Kuhlman, Kristyn	NY3350	32B,32E,32G
Kull, James A.	IL0840	32E
Kumme, Karl	CT0050	32B,32E
Kutz, Eric A.	IA0950	62C,32E,42
LaBounty, Anthony	NV0050	37,32E
Lam, Eri Lee	TX2650	62A,32E,42
Lamb, William	NM0500	61,63,32E
Lambert, Adam E.	NE0050	32E,37,60B,63,49
Langenberg, Kelly	IL0750	32E
Larragoity, Ingrid	AR0300	37,32E,13B,48

Index by Area of Teaching Interest

Name	Code	Areas
Larson, Danelle	IL0800	32E,37
Larson, Stacey L.	IL3450	32E,37,60B
Lastrapes, Jeffrey Noel	TX3200	62C,42,51,11,32E
Laughlin, Tina	IL0750	32E
Laukhuf, Dale	OH1800	63C,63D,32E
Laux, Charles	GA1150	32E,34C,38,62,32C
Lawing, Hollie	GA1150	32E
Lawrence, Patrick	WI0850	63C,63D,37,32E
Lee, Jaeryoung	CA4050	32E,13A,11
Lee, Matt	IL0750	63A,32E
Lee, Michael E.	OH1100	11,32E
Lee, Paul	NY2750	32E
Lesser, Jeffrey	NJ0550	32E,63,10,32C,32F
Lethco, Leigh-Ann M.	WI0830	32E,37,63A,32
Levinsky, Gail B.	PA3150	48,64E,32E
Lewis, David P.	WV0350	64,37,41,12A,32E
Lewis, Ryan C.	AR0500	65,32E,12A,11
Leyva, Jesse	IL3300	60B,37,32E
Linklater, Fraser	AC0100	63A,32E,37,48,60B
Linn, Don	KS0650	37,32E,10F
Liperote, Kathy	NY1100	32E,32G
Locke, John G.	MD0650	65,32E
Loden, Larry	TX1900	64C,64E,32E
Loeffler, Rodney J.	MN1280	32E
Long, Bill	SC0900	37,47,65,60B,32E
Long, Derle R.	LA0770	60,32E,37
Long, Patrick A.	PA3150	13,10,34,12A,32E
Lorenzo, Benjamin	OK0800	37,32E
Lortz, Mark E.	MD0520	32E
Loughran, Robert	NJ1350	62,32E
Lovejoy, Donald G.	MN1700	37,63A,41,60,32E
Lubaroff, Scott C.	MO1790	37,32E,10F,60
Lundin, Claudia	GA0850	32E
Lutch, Mitchell B.	IA0200	10F,32E,37,60
Lyons, Greg	LA0250	32E,65,50
MacDonald, R. Richard	MN1700	47,50,65,32E
Macomber, Jeffrey R.	MO0800	10,11,12A,32E,63D
Maddox, Eric	GA0550	32E,20
Magney, Lucia	MN0350	62C,62D,32E,42
Manfredo, Joseph	IL1150	32E,60B,37,32
Manning, Dwight C.	NY4200	64,42,32E,11,64B
Manning, Lucy	VA1000	38,62A,32E,41,51
Manning, Sheri	NV0050	32E
Markiewicz, Larry	NJ0800	32E
Marks, Randall J.	PA1900	32B,32C,32D,32E
Markworth, Wayne	OH2500	32E
Marshall, John	WA0250	62C,70,32E,41,32F
Marshall, Ruth	IL0750	32E
Martin, Freddie	GA1700	37,32E
Martin, Gregg	DC0050	32E
Martin, Jennifer	CA1510	32E,11,13,48,63C
Martin, Peter H.	IL2250	32E
Matchim, David	MD0650	32E
Mathie, David	ID0050	63C,32E,63D,49
Mathis, Carolynne	MN0610	32E,44,65
Matthews, Brandon Stephen	CO0550	38,42,32E
Matthews, Wendy K.	MI2200	32,32E
Maxson, Carrie	UT0350	62A,32E
May-Patterson, Eleanor	IA1100	32E,62A,62B
Mayne, Richard	CO0950	32E,37
McAdow, Seth	TX2250	32E
McCabe, Brent Poe	MT0450	37,11,32E,70
McCallum, Wendy M.	AC0050	64E,32E,37,60B,32
McCandless, Marty	IL1100	64C,64E,32E,47,41
McCardell, Susan L.	WI0350	32E
McCarty, Patrick	MO0050	11,32E,37,65,50
McCaskill, Janet L.	MI2200	63D,32E,60B,32C
McClard Kirk, Jennifer	KS1250	32E,64A,64C
McCoy, Peter M.	NY3780	32E,32F,32C,32G,32B
McCullough, David M.	AL1250	32B,63B,32C,32E
McCutcheon, Russell G.	PA1400	37,32E,60,34,32C
McDonald, Reginald	TN1400	32E,37,41,64E
McEnaney, Rick	NV0050	32E
McFarland, Thomas J.	KY1400	60,12A,32E,49,63
McGarvey, Timothy	IA1200	37,60,32E,41,29A
McIlhagga, Samuel D.	MI0100	10F,37,14C,32E
McKeithen, Steve	SC1110	32E
McMullian, Neal	IL2300	13B,32E,64D,60,37
McMunn, Ben	IL0750	32E
McNeal, Steve W.	CO0250	38,32E
McNeill, Marvin	CT0600	37,32E
McRoy, James W.	NY2105	60B,37,63,32E
McTeer, Mikylah Myers	WV0750	62A,32E,41,42
Meade, David B.	NY2750	32E
Mecham, Bryce	ID0060	63C,41,32E
Meffert-Nelson, Karrin	MN0750	64C,37,48,32E,12A
Meier, Scott Alan	PA2250	47,53,64E,34,32E
Meredith, Scott	WY0200	63A,67F,12,32E,49
Metlicka, Scott D.	IL0840	32E
Meunier, Robert W.	IA0550	60B,37,65,32E
Michelic, Leslie O.	WI0350	32E
Middleton, Polly K.	VA1700	32E,32G,37,41
Miedema, Bradley	IA0500	32E,37,38,60B
Milicevic, Zeljko	MI1750	32E
Miller, Anna Maria	TN0100	32E
Miller, Sharon	VA0300	32B,62A,32C,32E
Miller, Ward	AL1300	37,63D,41,32E,60B
Millican, Si	TX3530	32E,37,10F,35B
Mills, Alan W.	CO0275	37,66A,63A,32E,60B
Minichiello, Molly J.	NJ0800	32E
Misenheimer, Aaron L.	NC0850	32E,34,11,63,49
Missal, Jason	TX0050	37,32E,63B
Moes, Brook	CA5350	32E
Molumby, Nicole L.	ID0050	64A,32E,32I,13C
Montgomery, Annette	MI2250	32E
Moore, J. Steven	MO1790	37,32E,60B
Moore, Joe D.	MS0250	37,32E,60B
Moore, Michael W.	SC0200	32C,32E,32G,37,13
Mora, Richard	CA4450	32E
Morehead, Phillip H.	TN0850	13,41,63A,32E
Moss, Kirk D.	WI0350	11,32E,38,51,62
Mosteller, Sandra M.	TX3650	64,32E,48,20,31B
Moyer, Iain	AL1250	65,32E
Mueller, Marc	OK1250	37,63A,32E,60,34
Mumm, Daniel C.	NJ0800	32E
Murdock, Matthew	TN1600	13C,32E,29,37,47
Musser, Amanda	TX3000	32E
Nail, James I. (Ike)	OR1250	38,37,60B,32E
Nam, Jason	CA0845	32E
Narducci, Kenneth	CA2420	10,37,32E,46,13
Neiderhiser, Jonathan	SD0580	37,47,32E,13B,13C
Neidlinger, Erica	IL0750	36,32E
Neithamer, David	VA0700	29A,64C,32E
Nichols, Sandra	IL1612	11,32E,66A
Nicholson, Chad	DE0150	37,32E
Nicholson, Daniel	IL0750	32E
Nichter, Christopher	WV0750	32E,37,60B
Nies, Carol R.	TN1850	60,38,13,32E
Nimmo, Douglas	MN0750	60B,37,32C,32E
Nolan, Julia	AB0100	64E,32E,42
Nordlund, Caroline	AL0800	62A,32E
Nordman, Robert W.	MO1830	32E
Nordstrom, Erland	NJ1400	32E,11
Norgaard, Martin	GA1050	32E,32F,62A,29E,32
Norris, Philip E.	MN1280	10F,11,32E,63A,31A
Oare, Steven	KS1450	32E,32B,32C
Odell, Andrew	NY1400	32E
Oelrich, John A.	TN1720	37,32E,60B
Ohlman, Kathleen	NE0200	32B,32C,32D,32E
O'Neill, SC, Alice Ann M.	OH0680	32E,62C,41,62D
Onofrio, Marshall	NJ1350	13,10,29,34,32E
Owens, Parthena	OK0750	48,64A,32E
Padgham Albrecht, Carol	ID0250	11,12A,64B,32E,41
Pagnard, Charles	OH0450	60B,32E,49,63A
Palumbo, Michael A.	UT0350	38,62B,32E,60,41
Papador, Nicholas G.	AG0550	13A,13B,13D,65,32E
Parisi, Joseph	MO1810	32E,32F,37
Paul, Timothy A.	OR1050	32E,37,60B
Peck, Thomas	MI0520	32C,32E
Pegley, Kip	AG0250	14C,15,32E
Pellegrino, Kristen	TX3530	32E
Pergola, Joseph	NY2105	32E
Perry, Dawn A.	NC2650	63C,32E,37,47,60B
Petersen, William	AL1300	32E,37,63D,60B,49
Peterson, Elizabeth	NY1800	37,32E
Pfenninger, Rik C.	NH0250	64E,29,35,32E,10B
Phillips, Rebecca L.	SC1110	32E,37,60B
Pickney, Linda M.	NC2420	63B,32E,38
Pierard, George	IL3370	32C,32E
Pilato, Nikk	CA0825	63,37,38,32E,60B
Plate, Stephen W.	TN0850	38,60,32E,13B,13A
Polcyn, Sandra	WI0700	64D,64B,32E
Polk, Kristin	KY1550	64B,64D,32E,13A,13B
Poole, Mary Ada	SC0650	32E
Poor, Andrew F.	GA0550	32E
Popejoy, James R.	ND0500	37,60B,32E
Porter, Ann M.	OH2200	32,32E
Posnock, Jason	NC0250	62A,62B,32E
Powell, Edwin C.	WA0650	37,41,32E,60B
Prescott, Steve C.	IN1400	32E,11,60B,64,37
Przygocki, James T.	WY0200	62B,51,32E
Radspinner, Matthew	PA3150	32E
Ramee, Joyce	WA1000	62B,32E
Randles, Clinton A.	FL2000	32C,32G,32E
Ratti, Linda	KY1500	32E
Rayner, William S.	NY2750	32E,70
Reddick, Don	IL2300	32E,46,34,13A
Redfield, Clayborn	CA0840	11,32E,37
Redmon, Steve	MI0300	32E,51
Reed, John	GA0400	32E
Reeves, M. Bryan	AL0050	37,32E,11,49,60
Reimer, David	MI0350	11,32E,42,62A,41
Reynolds, Martin C.	MO1500	37,63C,41,47,32E
Reynolds, Patrick A.	OH2250	60,32E,37,38
Reznicow, Joshua	IA0300	32E
Rhodes, Andrew L.	OH2300	37,32E,49
Rhodes, Steve	TN0930	60B,32E,37,47,63D
Richards, Erik W.	IA0850	37,32E
Richardson, Colleen	AG0500	60B,37,32E,41,42
Richardson, Kevin	NC0050	37,32E
Richardson, Vernal	GA2300	32E
Rickels, David A.	CO0800	32C,32E,32F,32G,32H
Rinnert, Nathan	PA2150	60,37,32E
Ripley, James	WI0250	37,41,32E,60B,38
Rippy, Sylvia	NC0050	32E,66D
Risinger, Ed	IL1200	63D,32E,37
Rittenhouse, Kerry	GA2300	32E
Rivera, Luis C.	AL1300	20,32E,41,65,50
Rivest, Darlene	WI0250	62B,32E,38,62A,41
Robblee, Timothy	IL2250	37,47,32E
Robey, Matthew E.	NY2500	66A,66C,66D,11,32E
Robinson, Michael C.	NC1250	32E,60B,37
Robinson, Michael C.	GA2100	37,60,32E,60B
Robinson, Ryan	OK0750	63D,49,32E
Roeder, Matthew J.	CO0800	37,32E,60B
Roelofs, Laura Leigh	MI2200	62A,32E,41,11
Romines, Fred David	PA2200	37,60B,64E,32E
Rondon, Tulio J.	WI0803	62C,32E
Roop, Cynthia M.	NC1250	64A,32A,32E,13C,41
Rose, Bernard	NY1275	14C,29A,32E
Rose, Leslie Paige	AR0850	32B,34,32E
Ross, John Stanley	NC0050	37,32E
Rothrock, Donna K.	NC2205	16,32E,63D
Royer, Randall D.	SD0100	64,47,38,32E,70
Royse, David M.	TN1710	32E,32B,32C
Ruby, Meg	NY2500	32E
Rumpf, Randy	WV0550	32E
Rzasa, Karl	IL0750	32E
Saker, James	NE0610	32E,37,60B
Salvo, Leonard P.	OH0100	60B,32C,37,41,32E
Samuels, Sue	AL1150	37,32E,60B
Saville, Kirt	UT0050	37,60B,64C,32E,32C
Schallock, Michael G.	NC2600	32E,63D,60B
Scheffel, Rich	IA1800	63D,32E
Scheib, John W.	IN0150	32,32E
Schermer, Stephen	WA1000	62D,32E
Schilf, Paul R.	SD0050	37,49,47,32E,29A
Schimming, Paul	MN0610	32E,64E,64C
Schmitt, Clinton	TN1350	64E,32E
Schneeloch-Bingham, Nancy	NC0050	64A,48,32E
Schoon, Marcus	MI1750	32E,64D
Schueller, Rodney C.	TX3175	13A,32E,60B
Schuman, Mohamad	MS0750	37,32E
Schwartzman, Kenneth	NY2105	32E
Secor, Greg	MI1050	50,65,32E
Seifert, Dustin	NM0100	37,63C,63D,60B,32E
Self, Cale	GA2130	37,63C,63D,32E,49
Seligman, Jonathan D.	MD0520	50,65,32E
Sessoms, Sydney	NC1150	13E,32E,37,60B,11
Shabalin, Alexey	RI0150	62A,51,38,32E
Shade, Timothy	KS0200	63D,38,37,13C,32E
Shaffer, Rebecca Boehm	IA0950	63B,49,12A,32E,13C
Shaver, Cynthia L.	IN0100	32E
Shellhammer, Jeff	OH1850	32E
Sherman, Steve	AA0080	32E,37,63A,46,35
Shewan, Paul	NY3350	60B,37,63A,32E,38
Shires, Brent A.	AR0850	63B,32E,42,49
Shook, Brian A.	TX1400	63A,63D,32E
Shook, Lee	WA1350	32E
Sidon, Ashley Sandor	IA0550	62C,32E,41
Silver, Noreen	ME0440	42,32E,13C,62C
Silvey, Brian A.	MO1800	32E,60B
Simerly, Rick	TN1150	63,29,49,47,32E
Simmons, Amy L.	TX3175	32E
Simpson, R. Eric	TX3000	32E,32F,32G
Sindberg, Laura K.	MN1623	32E

531

Name	Code	Areas
Skidgel, Wesley	IL0850	63A,32E
Slagowski, Joshua	OH1450	32E,32B,32C
Smar, Benedict J.	MA2000	32E,32G
Smart, James	MT0400	37,63A,32E,60B
Smisek, James J.	AL0800	60B,37,32E
Smith, Carol	TX2250	38,51,60B,62,32E
Smith, Carol F.	TN1850	62A,32E,51
Smith, Gavin	TN1850	32E,37
Smith, James W.	AL1050	63D,32E,11
Smith, Jeff	CT0800	32E
Smith, Judith	CT0800	62C,32E,41
Smith, Michael	OH1850	65,29,32E
Smith, Neal	IL1750	32E,37,32C,13
Smith, Paul A.	PA3150	32E
Smith, Shawn T.	TX2930	63A,60B,37,32E
Snell, Alden	DE0150	32C,32E
Southall, John K.	FL0950	13,63A,60B,37,32E
Sparrow, James	NC1250	63D,32E,41,63C,63
Spaulding, Sue	CT0650	32E
Stambaugh, Laura	GA0950	32A,32B,32C,32E,32G
Standland, James	MS0750	37,32E
Staskevicius, Algis	AR0300	62A,62B,32E
Staub, William D.	NC0650	37,32E
Steffens, David	OK0750	50,65,32E
Stein, William	OH1800	64C,32E
Stoffan, George C.	MI1750	64C,48,42,32E
Stolarik, Justin R.	WI0815	37,60B,32E,65,10F
Streng, Richard	MI0300	32E
Strom, Jeffrey	MN1700	32E
Stumbo, Jason A.	OH2300	37,32E
Sudduth, Steven	KY1425	13,32E,37,60B,63C
Susman, Robert E.	NY2750	32E
Svanoe, Erika K.	MN0150	64C,60B,37,32E,45
Swearingen, James	OH0350	10A,32E
Sweeney, Christopher R.	AK0100	32,63D,63C,32E,32B
Tackitt, Elliott	AZ0450	37,32E
Talbot, Brent	IL3300	32E
Talbott, Doug	KS0150	10F,32E,37,47,49
Taylor, Caroline	AR0500	48,64,32E
Taylor, Charles L.	LA0800	37,60B,64C,32C,32E
Taylor, James W.	SC1110	37,32E,60B
Taylor, Susan Lynnette	IN0100	32E,37,48,60B
Tejada, Rob	IL2250	32E
Tembras, Dan	IN0905	32E,37,60B
Tesch, John	MN1120	32E,37,63C,11
Teskey, Nancy	OR0400	64A,32E
Thimmesch, Richard	IA0650	13B,13C,32E,37,47
Thoma, August	MI1830	32E,37,64C
Thomas, Raymond D.	TN1100	32E,37,60B
Thomason, Eliza	TX3100	11,32E,62A,62B,51
Thompson, Steven	MN0250	37,60B,63A,32E,49
Thornton, Linda	PA2750	32E
Thye, David R.	TX2600	60,32D,32E,36,38
Tiffin, Corey	IL0750	32E
Till, Sophie	PA2200	62A,62B,13C,32E
Tinnell, Jennifer L.	KY0400	37,63C,32E,47
Tinnin, Randall C.	FL1950	63A,49,37,32E,20
Tjornehoj, Kris	WI0845	38,11,60B,37,32E
Tobias, Scott C.	FL1800	37,32E,60
Toney, Hubert	PA0700	37,47,32E,63A
Torosian, Brian	IL3550	70,32E
Torres Rivera, Alfredo	PR0115	32E,32B,32C
Towner, Cliff	GA0850	32E,37,47,60B
Townsend, Bradley G.	OR0700	37,60B,32E
Townsend, Sid	OH0350	32E
Tracz, Frank	KS0650	60B,37,32E
Tully, James	SC0420	37,32E,60B
Tuohey, Terese M.	MI2200	32,32E
Turner, Timothy R.	LA0900	13G,10F,32E,34,37
Turrill, David	OH1650	37,32E,60,63A
Tutt, Kevin	MI0900	37,32E,32G
Twehues, Mark A.	TX3530	64,32E
Underwood, Margaret	OH2050	32E,37,60
Vento, Steve	OK1300	10,11,12,47,32E
Viliunas, Brian	AL0800	64C,38,13C,32E,60B
Vincent, Ron	NY2200	65,50,32E
Vollmar, Ferdinand	TX3410	37,32E
Wacker, John M.	CO1050	60,63,37,49,32E
Waddell, Rachel Lynn	MI1000	11,12,32E,42,64A
Waddelow, Jim M.	NC1300	41,62,38,32E
Waggoner, Robert	MO1950	32E
Wagner, Shelbi	OH2250	62C,51,32E
Wagoner, Cynthia L.	NC0650	32C,32C
Walker, Garry	ID0250	32E,32G
Walker, Patricia	NY2200	63B,32E
Walter, Jennifer Stewart	NC2430	32E,37
Wampler, Kris A.	OH0680	63,32E
Wanken, Matthew	IL0400	32E
Warren, John	GA1150	64C,32E,42
Warren, W. Dale	AR0700	60B,32E,37
Washburn, Rodney	IL1740	32E
Watson, Frank	SC0650	32E,64D
Weaver, James	PA2300	32E,65
Weaver, Molly A.	WV0750	32,32E,32G,34
Webb, John C.	AR0800	41,32E,37,60B,63
Webb, Mark	MI0300	63,32C,32D,32E,11
Webb, Richard	MA2000	32E
Webber, David	KY1000	32E
Wehr, Erin	IA1550	32B,32C,32E
Weir, Tim	ME0340	47,63A,29,32E
Weir, Timothy	VA0100	32C,32E,37,47,42
Wells, Donovan V.	FL0100	37,32E
Wells, Greg	MI0300	32E
Wells, Lillie	OR1050	32A,62A,32E
Wesolowski, Brian	GA2100	32E,32G,29C
West, John T.	NC2600	32E,37,60B
West, Julie A.	CA0835	32E
Westbrook, Gary W.	TX2750	50,65,37,32E
Wetherington, John M.	WA0650	32E
Whitaker, Jennifer A.	NC2420	32E,37
White, Christopher G.	ME0440	37,60,32E
White, Christopher K.	VA1100	29,64E,32E,64,12B
White, Dale A.	MN0350	60B,37,41,32E,63
White, Karin	MI1260	32B,32E,32D
Whitener, Edward	NC0050	32E
Whitmore, Michael	OK0450	32E,48,64
Whitten, Douglas	KS1050	37,63D,32E,11,49
Wilder, Ralph	IL2100	64C,32E,64E,11,42
Wilensky, Pamela B.	TN1680	32E
Wiley, Jennifer Sacher	PA3150	38,62A,32E
Wilkinson, Todd R.	KS1000	47,64E,29,32E
Willard, Michael	OH2290	63A,32E
Williams, David A.	FL2000	32E,32G
Williams, Lindsey R.	MO1810	32E,60,32H,32G,63C
Williams, Shane	MO0650	11,13,32E,38,41
Wilsey, Jennifer	CA4700	65,50,32E
Wilson, Chris	AR0110	49,32E,11
Wilson, J. P.	AR0600	37,63D,63C,32E,60B
Wilson, Ruth	CA4700	32E,42,49,63B
Wiltshire, Eric	OR1050	37,32E,60B
Windham, Mark	AR0800	11,63,32E,32F,37
Winey, Richard	PA1250	32E,62
Winkler, Fred	WA1000	64E,41,32E
Winters, Patrick	WA0250	37,32E
Wise, Herbert	NY2500	63C,66A,66D,11,32E
Wise, Wilson	IA1100	64C,13B,32E,37,60B
Witcher, William	NC0050	32E
Woike, David O.	MI0600	37,32E,32C
Wolfe, Anne Marie	IN0150	63D,64,32E,10F,60B
Wood, Bruce	TX3200	32E,62
Wood, Michael	MI1000	32E,63B
Woodruff, Ernest	MO0950	11,32E,63D
Worthy, Michael D.	MS0700	32C,32E,32G,47
Wright, Lauren Denney	OK0650	32E,37,64C,60B
Wright, Randy	AZ0150	32E
Xydas, Spiros	MI1750	32E
Yacoub, Allison	MD0600	64C,32E,20
Yehuda, Guy	FL1950	64C,60B,41,32E
Yonchak, Michael	OH2050	34,37,32E,29,46
Yontz, Timothy	IL3550	32E,37,63A,32
York, Kevin	ID0100	37,47,34,32E
Young, David	NE0450	32E
Youngblood, Brian	TX3000	37,32E
Yurko, Bruce	PA2300	10,32E
Zerbe, David	MI0150	65,37,50,32C,32E
Zitek, Sam	NE0450	37,64E,60B,32E

Computer Applications

Name	Code	Areas
Adderley, Cecil L.	MA0260	32E,32F,32G,62A,64C
Aldrich, Mark L.	MA1650	37,32E,32F,34D,60B
Allik, Kristi A.	AG0250	10,45,34,32F
Bamberger, Jeanne	MA1200	13H,13K,13G,32F,13
Bascom, Brandon R.	ID0060	32F,66A,66C
Baumgarnder, Brad	KS0590	34D,32F,35C,35D
Bazan, Dale E.	NE0600	32E,32F,32G,32H,34
Brandeburg, Michael	CA4460	32F
Breaux, Michael L.	NY2750	32B,32C,32E,32F
Brewer, Wesley D.	IL0550	32E,32F
Brooks, Beth	IN0907	32F
Chesnutt, Rod M.	FL0680	37,38,60,32E,32F
Chiarizzio, R. Kevin	VA0650	63,32B,32C,32F
Chittum, John	KS0590	34D,32F,35C,35D
Conkling, Susan W.	MA0400	32D,36,32C,32F,32G
Dammers, Richard J.	NJ1050	32,32E,32F
Davis, Alfred L.	VA0500	32E,32F,32B,32C,10F
Day, Michael	NC1550	11,32E,32F,63A,63B
Espar, Michael	NY0646	32F,34,35
Frankel, James Thomas	NY4200	34,37,32,32F
Gallo, Donna	IL0750	32F
Gammon, Richard	KS0590	32F,34D
Goeller, Dan	SD0580	34,32F
Goodman, James A.	ID0050	32B,32C,32D,32F
Gregory, M. David	GA1700	32E,37,32F,60B
Guzman, Ariel	PR0115	32C,32B,32F
Harris, Ben	FL0100	34,35C,35G,32F
Huebl, Carolyn	TN1850	62A,13G,32F,34,11
Hulihan, Charles	AZ0350	70,41,32E,32F
Jackman, Sean M.	OH2150	32D,32F
Jensen, Shane	PA2000	34,32F
Johnson, Jason	AR0730	32F
Johnson, Richard	KS0590	13G,32F,34D,35C,35D
Khamda, Mazdak	CA3250	66A,66D,32F,35C
Kidde, Geoffrey C.	NY2200	10,13,34,45,32F
Klein, Jim	PA1000	34,32F,45,13G,10C
Kretchner, Darlene	CA0830	32B,32A,32E,32F,32G
Kuehne, Jane M.	AL0200	32,32D,32F
Kurokawa, John K.	OH2500	11,34,64C,32F
Lane, Roger	NC0900	32B,32F
Laughrey, Gary	KY0800	64,32F,12A,13
Lee, Chihchen Sophia	OK1250	33,32F,66A
Lesser, Jeffrey	NJ0550	32E,63,10,32C,32F
Liske, Kenneth L.	WI0830	32,32C,32F,32B,32D
MacNaughton, Roger	MI0300	66A,13G,32F
Manhollan, John W.	OH2600	32F
Marshall, John	WA0250	62C,70,32E,41,32F
McCord, Kimberly A.	IL1150	32B,32C,32F,29A,32A
McCormick, Chris	TN1450	47,29,32F
McCormick, Scott	MA0260	29B,32F,32H,20G,34G
McCoy, Peter M.	NY3780	32E,32F,32C,32G,32B
McNally, Blair	AG0070	32F,34D,63D
Miller-Brown, Donna	KS0590	34D,32F,35C,35D
Norgaard, Martin	GA1050	32E,32F,62A,29E,32
Palmer, Bradley E.	GA0550	63C,11,34,32F,41
Parisi, Joseph	MO1810	32E,32F,37
Parker, Mark	SC0200	13A,32F,13B,13C,13G
Pejril, Veronica	IN0350	32F
Phillips, Scott L.	AL1150	32F,34,45
Pixton, Clayton	KS0590	34D,32F,35C,35D
Poitier, James	FL0100	37,49,63,32F,41
Reynolds, Geoffrey	CT0650	32B,32C,32D,32F,32G
Rickels, David A.	CO0800	32C,32E,32F,32G,32H
Rogalsky, Matt	AG0250	10,45,34,32F
Simpson, R. Eric	TX3000	32E,32F,32G
Smith, Janice P.	NY0642	32B,32F
Snyder, Jeffrey S.	PA1900	35,34D,10B,32F,10D
Solomon, William	CT0050	32F
Sylvern, Craig	NH0150	64E,34,32F,10,48
Thibeault, Matthew	IL3300	32C,32F
Thomas, William	AG0650	32F,37,38
Tobias, Evan	AZ0100	32C,32F,32G,32H
Tomlin, Terry	TX3515	47,64E,29,34,32F
VanWick, Brad	KS0590	34D,32F,35C,35D
Walls, Kimberly C.	AL0200	32,34C,32F,32G
Welch, Chapman	TX3400	32F
Windham, Mark	AR0800	11,63,32E,32F,37
Yen, Chianan	NY2750	32F,34A,34B,34H

Research and Assessment

Name	Code	Areas
Adderley, Cecil L.	MA0260	32E,32F,32G,62A,64C
Andrews, Laura J.	KS0350	32B,32C,32A,32G,32H
Azzara, Christopher D.	NY1100	32E,32G
Baptiste, Renee L.	AL0500	32B,32C,32D,32G,36
Bazan, Dale E.	NE0600	32E,32F,32G,32H,34
Benton, Carol W.	GA0200	13C,13K,32B,32D,32G
Bergonzi, Louis	IL3300	32E,38,62,32G,60B
Bobak, Jacqueline	CA0510	12,42,61,32G
Bradley, Mark	KY0400	12C,32G,36,39,61
Brooks-Smith, Emma	MS0350	32A,32B,32C,32G
Burkett, Eugenie I.	NV0050	32,32E,32G
Cardany, Brian M.	RI0300	32E,32G,37,60B
Casagrande, John E.	VA0450	37,32C,32E,32G
Chandler, Kyle	AR0110	32,36,47,32D,32G

Coffman, Don D.	FL1900	32E,32G
Conkling, Susan W.	MA0400	32D,36,32C,32F,32G
Cooper, Shelly	AZ0500	32,32A,32B,32G,32H
Cruse, Carolyn S.	TX3200	36,40,32D,32G
Custodero, Lori A.	NY4200	32A,32B,32G,12E,12C
Dansereau, Diana R.	MA0400	32E,32G
DeGraffenreid, George	CA0830	32C,32E,32G
Deppe, Scott M.	TX1400	37,60B,32G,32C
DeTurk, Mark	NH0350	32C,32E,32G
Diaz, Frank M.	OR1050	32,32G,13K
Dorfman, Jay	MA0400	32E,32G
Draves, Tami	AZ0500	32G,32H
Duke, Robert	CA1075	32G
Dunn, Robert	UT0050	32C,32G,32D
Elpus, Kenneth	MD1010	32D,32G,36
Emmanuel, Donna T.	TX3420	32B,32G,20D,20H,35A
Fox, Donna Brink	NY1100	32A,32B,32C,32G
Fredrickson, William E.	FL0850	32G,32E,32
Freer, Patrick K.	GA1050	32D,32C,32G,36,60A
Fung, C. Victor	FL2000	32G,32G,20D
Gephardt, Donald L.	NJ1050	64C,32E,32G
Gipson, Richard C.	TX3000	65,50,32G
Goodrich, Andrew M.	MA0400	32E,32G
Gottlieb, BettyAnne	OH2200	32E,32G
Gray, Patricia	NC2430	32G
Grice, June	KY0900	32A,32B,32C,32G,32H
Gruenhagen, Lisa M.	OH0300	32A,32B,32G,64A,32
Grunow, Richard F.	NY1100	32E,32G
Hamann, Donald L.	AZ0500	32,62,32E,32G
Hampton, Anitra C.	AL0650	12A,32,32G,11
Hancock, Carl B.	AL1170	32G,32,34
Hansen, Demaris	CT0650	32A,32B,32G,32H
Hansford, James	OK0650	38,32G,37,63D,41
Hartenberger, Aurelia	MO1950	32B,32C,32G,32H
Hartley, Linda A.	OH2250	32E,37,64E,32G
Haston, Warren	CT0650	32E,37,32G
Hendricks, Karin S.	IL3300	32G
Hernandez Guzman, Nestor	PR0115	32G
Higgins, Lee D.	MA0400	32E,32G
Horowitz, Robert	NY4200	32G
Humphreys, Jere T.	AZ0100	32,32G,32E
Jones, Patrick Michael	NY4150	32G,60B,32,12A,12E
Joy, Sharon	LA0550	32A,32B,32H,32G,32
Jutras, Peter J.	GA2100	66A,66B,66D,32G
Kaiser, Keith A.	NY1800	32E,32G,49
Keast, Dan A.	TX3527	32,34B,34F,32G,32C
King, Steve E.	VA1700	32E,32G,37
Kinney, Daryl W.	OH1850	32G,32E,62A
Kretchner, Darlene	CA0830	32B,32A,32E,32F,32G
Kuhlman, Kristyn	NY3350	32B,32E,32G
Liperote, Kathy	NY1100	32E,32G
Mathieu, Louise	AI0190	32G,32I
McClung, Alan C.	TX3420	32C,32D,32G,60A,13C
McCoy, Peter M.	NY3780	32E,32F,32C,32G,32B
McCusker, IHM, Joan	PA2200	32A,32B,32C,32G
McKee, Angela	GA1150	32A,32B,32G
Middleton, Polly K.	VA1700	32E,32G,37,41
Mizener, Charlotte P.	TX1400	32B,32G,32A
Moore, Michael W.	SC0200	32C,32E,32G,37,13
Neill, Sheri L.	TX3000	32D,32B,32C,32G
Norris, Charles	MI0900	32D,32G,36
Parr, Carlotta	CT0050	32A,32B,32C,36,32G
Randles, Clinton A.	FL2000	32C,32G,32E
Reynolds, Geoffrey	CT0650	32B,32C,32D,32F,32G
Richmond, John W.	NE0600	32D,32G,36,32
Rickels, David A.	CO0800	32C,32E,32F,32G,32H
Riner, Nicole	WY0200	64A,14C,32G,48
Robinson, Nicole R.	TN0150	32B,32C,32G,32H
Rogers, Donald M.	SC1200	12C,32G
Rutkowski, Joanne	PA2750	32A,32B,32G
Schwartz, Sandra M.	WV0750	32D,32G
Shively, Joseph L.	MI1750	32G,34,11,32,32C
Silvey, Philip E.	NY1100	32D,32G
Simpson, R. Eric	TX3000	32E,32F,32G
Sims, Wendy L.	MO1800	32A,32B,32G
Smar, Benedict J.	MA2000	32E,32G
Soto, Amanda C.	ID0250	14,20H,32B,32G,32H
Spano, Fred P.	NC2420	32B,32D,32G,32
Stambaugh, Laura	GA0950	32A,32B,32C,32E,32G
Stanley, Ann Marie	NY1100	32B,32G,32H
Sternbach, David J.	VA0450	32G,63B
Stover, Pamela	OH2300	32B,32C,32G,32H,32
Strand, Katherine D.	IN0900	32B,32C,32H,32G
Sumner, Daniel	LA0770	32B,32C,32D,32G
Swanson, Robyn	KY1550	32A,32B,32G,32H
Thompson, Linda K.	TN0850	32A,32B,32C,32G
Tobias, Evan	AZ0100	32C,32F,32G,32H
Tutt, Kevin	MI0900	37,32E,32G
Walker, Garry	ID0250	32E,32G
Walls, Kimberly C.	AL0200	32,34C,32F,32G
Ward-Steinman, Patrice Madura	IN0900	32G,32D,32,29,47
Weaver, Molly A.	WV0750	32,32E,32G,34
Wesolowski, Brian	GA2100	32E,32G,29C
Wiggins, Donna	NC2700	12C,32,32G
Wiggins, Jacqueline H.	MI1750	12F,32B,32G
Williams, David A.	FL2000	32E,32G
Williams, Lindsey R.	MO1810	32E,60,32H,32G,63C
Worthy, Michael D.	MS0700	32C,32E,32G,47
Wright, Jeffrey E.	IN0100	31A,32G
Zdzinski, Stephen	FL1900	32,32G,32H,12C,13K

Interdisciplinary

Abrams, Brian	NY0500	32H
Amchin, Robert A.	KY1500	32B,32H,32A
Andrews, Laura J.	KS0350	32B,32C,32A,32G,32H
Battersby, Sharyn L.	DC0050	32B,32C,66D,32D,32H
Bazan, Dale E.	NE0600	32E,32F,32G,32H,34
Beard, Christine	MS0850	32H
Bridges, Cynthia	TX0550	37,32H,60B,13C,32C
Brock, Andrew	VA0700	47,64E,32H
Brozak, George A.	IL2900	37,32H
Bunbury, Richard R.	MA0400	12,66G,32H,31A,32
Cooper, Shelly	AZ0500	32,32A,32B,32G,32H
De Leo, Joseph A.	NY2750	32,12A,13B,32C,32H
Dell, Charlene	OK1350	32E,32H,32,62,62A
Dobroski, Bernard J.	IL2250	32H,63D,32,60,35E
Draves, Tami	AZ0500	32G,32H
Dreisbach, Tina Spencer	OH1000	12A,14,32H
Gamble, Sue G.	MI0400	32B,32C,32H,32
Greher, Gena R.	MA2030	32,32H,34A
Grice, June	KY0900	32A,32B,32C,32G,32H
Hale, Connie L.	SC1200	32B,32H,32A
Hansen, Demaris	CT0650	32A,32B,32G,32H
Hartenberger, Aurelia	MO1950	32B,32C,32G,32H
Jensen, Gary J.	IL0800	32A,32B,32H,32C
Joy, Sharon	LA0550	32A,32B,32H,32G,32
Kelly, Justin M.	OH1000	61,32H
Kidd, Teri D.	VA0700	32H
McCormick, Scott	MA0260	29B,32F,32H,20G,34G
Meek, Darla	TX2955	32A,32B,32H
Oakley, Tom	TN0150	37,47,32H,10F
Pitzer, Robert M.	WA1250	32,32B,32C,32H
Rickels, David A.	CO0800	32C,32E,32F,32G,32H
Robinson, Charles R.	MO1810	36,32D,32H
Robinson, Nicole R.	TN1680	32B,32C,32G,32H
Smith, Michael	CO0950	13A,32,32H
Soto, Amanda C.	ID0250	14,20H,32B,32G,32H
Stanley, Ann Marie	NY1100	32B,32G,32H
Stover, Pamela	OH2300	32B,32C,32G,32H,32
Strand, Katherine D.	IN0900	32B,32C,32H,32G
Swanson, Robyn	KY1550	32A,32B,32G,32H
Titterington, Beth	MO1810	32H
Tobias, Evan	AZ0100	32C,32F,32G,32H
Wilkinson, Donald G.	TX3520	64B,64D,64E,46,32H
Williams, Lindsey R.	MO1810	32E,60,32H,32G,63C
Wolf, Matthew	MI0500	48,13,60,32H
Zdzinski, Stephen	FL1900	32,32G,32H,12C,13K

Dalcroze Eurhythmics

Aschbrenner, Charles C.	MI1050	66A,32I
Ausch, Adriana	MA1175	32I
Brockmann, Nicole M.	IN0350	62B,32I,13C
Brown, Isabelle	AI0190	32I
Caldwell, J. Timothy	MI0400	61,32I
Capp, Myrna	WA0800	66A,66B,32I,20A
Cardone, Alissa	MA1175	32I
Dobrea-Grindahl, Mary	OH0200	66A,66B,66C,32I,66D
Fraser, Jo-Anne	AI0210	32I
Frego, R. J. David	TX3530	32,32I
Fresne, Jeannette	AL1300	32A,32B,32C,32D,32I
Gilson, David W.	OH0600	32I,60A
Glarner, Robert L.	VA1100	13,10,32I,66G,12
Ishizuka, Eiko	MA1175	32I
Jacobi, Bonnie S.	CO0250	32B,66A,13,32I,32
James, Judy A. G.	LA0700	11,32,32I,66D
Joseph, Annabelle	PA0550	13,32I
Latts, Ginny	MA1175	32I
Lippoldt-Mack, Valerie	KS0210	11,36,61,32I,52
Mathieu, Louise	AI0190	32G,32I
Miano, Jo Ellen	NY3775	13A,36,61,32I,40
Molumby, Nicole L.	ID0050	64A,32E,32I,13C
Moore, Marvelene C.	TN1710	32A,32B,32I
Neely, Stephen	PA0550	32I
Parente, Thomas	NJ1350	66A,66D,32I
Parker, Lisa	MA1175	32I
Richman, Yoriko	CA4150	32I
Rittenhouse, Virginia Gene	MD0150	38,62A,66A,32I
Rogers, Martha	MA0350	13,32I
Rudzik, Sarina Rommedahl	AA0050	32I
Slusser, Anthony	OH0600	32I
Smith, Deborah	IL2910	32,32I
Sweigart, Brian	OH0600	32I
Tucker, Melissa	MA1175	32I
Wopat, Ann	WA0850	61,32I,32A,32B,32C
Yuzefovich, Victor	MD0150	12A,12,62B,32I

Music Therapy

Abbott, Elaine	PA1050	33
Abrams, Brian	NJ0800	33
Adamek, Mary	IA1550	33
Agen, Kristine	IN0905	33
Ahola, Mark	NY3600	33
Ahonen-Erikainen, Heidi	AG0600	33
Aigen, Kenneth	PA3250	33
Amato, Beatrice	MO0700	33
Arnason, Carolyn	AG0600	33
Austin, Diane Snow	NY2750	33
Barczak, Bonnie Jean	WI1150	33
Bastable, Barbara	TX2400	33
Beck, Donna Marie	PA1050	33
Behrens, Gene Ann	PA1250	33
Belgrave, Melita	MO1810	33
Benkovitz, Deborah	PA1050	33
Berry, James	WV0440	11,12,13,33,61
Bethel, Phyllis	NY5000	33
Biederman, Bradley R.	PA3250	33
Bock, Susan V.	IL1150	33
Borczon, Ronald M.	CA0835	70,33
Borling, James E.	VA1100	33
Bosco, Frank	NY2750	33
Bowles, Shannon	KY1500	33
Boyle, Mary E.	NY3760	70,33,66D
Boyle, Sharon	IN1400	33,70
Brandes, Jan	WI1150	33
Branscome, Eric	TN0050	32,33
Brescia, Tina	NY5000	33
Brescia, Tina M.	NY2750	33
Brien, April Malone	SC0275	33
Briggs, Cynthia	MO0700	33
Brooks, Darlene M.	PA3250	33
Brown, Angeline	NY5000	33
Brown, Carlene J.	WA0800	12A,13,33
Brown, Laura E.	IL3500	33
Bruce, Cynthia	AF0050	13C,33,66D,12A
Bruscia, Kenneth E.	PA3250	33
Burns, Deb S.	IN0907	33,12
Cancio-Bello, Susan	NH0050	11,54,61,36,33
Carpente, John	NY2450	33,70
Carroll, Debbie	AI0210	33
Cassity, Michael	MO0350	33
Cevasco, Andrea	AL1170	33
Chadwick, Donna	MA0260	33
Chen, Chia-Chi	IN0005	33
Chong, John	AG0300	33
Christmas, Pam	WI1150	33
Chung, Heejin	NY2450	33
Chung, Hsieh	IN0005	33
Chung, Miri	IN0907	62A,62B,33,51
Clair, Alicia A.	KS1350	32,33
Clarkson, Amy LYN	NJ0800	33
Clements-Cortes, Amy	AG0550	33
Codding, Peggy	MA0260	33
Cohen, Nicki S.	TX3300	61,33,20
Cole, Melissa	WI1150	33
Condran, Dena	PA3250	33,61
Cordell, Debra	OH1900	33
Cortez, Brooke D.	TX3410	33
Cosma, Tina	PA1250	33
Cotten, Paul	MS0850	33
Craney-Welch, Karen	WI1150	33

Index by Area of Teaching Interest

Name	Code	Areas
Crimmins, Andrea	IL1150	33
Crowe, Barbara	AZ0100	33
Dakon, Jacob M.	KS1350	32,33
Darga, Karen	WI1150	33
Darrow, Alice-Ann	FL0850	33
Davis, William B.	CO0250	33,12C
De L'Etoile, Shannon K.	FL1900	33
De Souza, Michele	WI1150	33
Decuir, Anthony	LA0300	61,33
Dexter-Schabow, Nancy	WI0050	33
Dileo, Cheryl L.	PA3250	33
Dinsmore, Ann	PA1250	33
Doak, Bridget A.	MN0050	33
Dolas, Helen G.	CA0835	33
Duerksen, George L.	KS1350	32,33
Dvorkin, Janice	TX3410	33
Ellias, Marjorie K.	NJ0800	33
Elliott, Mandy	NY2650	33
Engelhardt, Jeffers	MA0100	20,33,12
Engen, Rebecca	NC2000	33
Eyre, Lillian	PA1550	33
Falkenberger, Kristen	AG0600	33
Farlow, Peggy	IN0905	33
Feiner, Susan	NY2750	33
Fidelibus, Joseph	NY5000	33
Finnerty, Rachel	AG0600	33
Frisch, Andrea	NY2400	33
Furry, Stephanie	GA0950	63B,49,33,11
Gadberry, Anita	PA2200	33
Gallagher, Lisa	OH0200	33
Gardstrom, Susan	OH2250	33,12F,44
Geist, Kamile	OH1900	33
Gfeller, Kate	IA1550	33
Gimeno, Montserrat	NY3760	33
Gold, Christopher A.	NY2650	33
Gooding, Lori	KY1450	33
Goodman, Karen D.	NJ0800	33
Gorham, Fr. Daniel	IN0005	31A,33,61
Gormley, Daniel	NY2750	33
Graham, Richard M.	GA2100	33,12F
Grant, Roy	GA2100	33
Greenidge, Evelyn	AG0600	33
Gregory, Dianne	FL0850	33
Groene, Robert W.	MO1810	33,13L
Hadley, Susan J.	PA3100	70,33,11,66D
Hadsell, Nancy A.	TX3300	33,70
Hahna, Nicole	PA3100	32A,33,11
Haines, James L.	PA1250	13,10,33
Hairston, Michelle P.	NC0650	33
Hammers, Eric	WI1150	33
Hanser, Suzanne	MA0260	33
Hanson-Abromeit, Deanna	MO1810	33
Harms, Melanie	IA1800	33
Harris, Brian T.	NY2750	33
Harris, Rob	AG0600	33
Hearns, Maureen	UT0300	33
Heffernan, Michele	NJ1100	11,13C,29,33,66A
Heller, Lora	NY2450	33
Henry, Leslie	WI1150	33
Hernandez Candelas, Marta	PR0115	33
Hesser, Barbara	NY2750	33
Hiller, James	OH2250	33,11
Hinsey, Jackie	IN0905	33
Hinton, Jennifer	PA1250	33
Holmberg, Teri	KS0650	33
Houde, Marc	AG0600	33
Howland, Kathleen	MA0260	33
Hricko-Fay, Maria	PA2200	33
Hsaio, Fei-Lin	CA5350	33
Hunter, Bryan C.	NY2650	33
Ibershoff, Emily	KY1500	33
Ichikawa, Andrew	AA0200	33
Isenberg-Grzeda, Connie	AI0210	33
Jackson, Nancy	IN0905	33
Jacobs, Nicole	NE0150	33
Jampel, Peter F.	NY2750	33
Jarred, Jennifer	FL0950	33
Jellison, Judith A.	TX3510	32,33
Jenkins, Jack	MO0700	33,36,60
Ji, Ming Sheng	IN0005	33
Johnson, Meg	NC2000	33,44
Johnson, Sarah	CO0250	33
Jones, Jennifer D.	IL3500	33
Jones, Laurie	PA3000	33,61
Justice, Roberta	MI0600	33
Justice, Roberta	OH1330	33
Kagin, Roberta S.	MN0050	33,11
Kahler, Bette	NY4100	11,12A,33,66A,66G
Kahler, Edward P.	TX3750	33,32A
Kaiser, Pat	WI1150	33
Kay, Lalene D.	OH0200	33,70
Kay, Lalene	OH0700	70,33
Kay, Lalene D.	OH0650	33
Keith, Douglas	GA0850	33
Kellogg, Michael	OH1900	33
Kenehan, Garrett	MA0260	33
Kennedy, Roy	GA2100	33
Keough, Laurie	NY2650	33
Khare, Kimberly	MA0260	33
Kilburn, Ke-Yin	IN0005	33,66A,66B,13
Kim, Chi Gook	MA0260	33
Kim, Mijin	NY2750	33
Kim, Seung A.	NY2450	33,66A
King, Betsey	NY2650	33
Knight, Andrew	ND0500	33
Knight, Diane	WI0050	33
Kohler-Ghiorzi, Elizabeth	PA1250	33
Krout, Robert E.	TX2400	33
Kwon, Hea-Kyung	NY2750	33
Kwoun, Soo Jin	MO0700	33,61,66A
Lagasse, Blythe	CO0250	33
Langdon, Gillian S.	NY2750	33
Lathom-Radocy, Wanda	MO1810	33
Lauzon, Paul	AF0050	33,12F
Layman, Deborah	OH0650	33
Lee, Chihchen Sophia	OK1250	33,32F,66A
Lee, Colin	AG0600	53,33
Lefebvre, Claire	AI0210	33
Leist, Christine	NC0050	33
LeMessurier, Susan	AG0600	33
Lemire-Ross, Dominique	PA2200	33
Lesiuk, Teresa L.	FL1900	33,12A
Licata, Julie M.	NY3765	65,33,50,20,10B
Lim, Hayoung Audrey	TX2250	33
Lin, Chen-Chi	IN0005	33
Lindenfelser, Kathryn	MN0040	11,20,33
Lipe, Anne	VA1350	33
Liu, Hsien-Ping	IN0005	33
Lopez, Catherine	WI1150	33,64C
Lucente, Jill	NY2450	33
Lundblad, Genevieve	MD0450	32A,11,33
Lynn, Sarah B.	TX3410	33
MacDonald, Mary Carla	MA0150	33
MacDonald, Scott	PA1550	33
Madsen, Clifford K.	FL0850	32,33,12C
Mancino, Kim	NY3725	33
Mangi, Mary	WI1150	33
Masko, Meganne	ND0500	33
Maxon, James	NY5000	33
McBay, Brian	AG0600	33
McCarrick-Dix, Patricia	PA3250	33
McClain, Frances	NC2000	33,44
McDonough, Lauren	NY2450	33,66A
McGlinn, Margaret	NY2400	33
McHugh, Larisa	OH2250	33
McKinney, Cathy	NC0050	33
McKinnon, Taryn	AG0600	33
McPhee, Rosemary	AF0050	33,40
Meadows, Anthony	PA1550	33
Measthey, Kelly	PA1550	61,33
Memmott, Jenny	MO0050	66A,66C,33
Memory, Barbara	NC0650	33
Mercado, Chesley	GA0850	33
Merrill, Theresa R.	MI0600	33
Meyer, Peter	MN0050	33
Milgram-Luterman, Joni F.	NY3725	33
Miller, Karen Epps	TX2250	33
Mitchell, Elizabeth	AG0600	33
Monahan, Katie	WI1150	33
Moniz, Michael	MA0260	33
Montello, Louise	NY2400	33
Moore, Nancy	OH0350	33,13A,13B,13C
Mosko, Beth	CO0250	33
Moulton, William	VT0300	13A,29C,33,34B,35A
Muller, Bryan	PA1550	70,34,33
Munger, Philip	AK0100	10,13A,33
Murillo, Julie	AZ0100	33
Murphy, Kathleen	IN1600	33,32B,66D
Nagler, Joseph	NY3250	32,33,34
Ortiz, Gabriela	NY2450	33
Osburn, Carmen E.	MS0550	33
Owen, Edward 'Ted'	OR0500	33
Pasiali, Varvara	NC2000	33,53
Pavlik, Charleen	PA1050	33
Peabody, Martha	MA1450	61,33,13C
Phillips, Dorie	OH2250	33
Phillips, Joe Rea	TN1850	41,70,33
Phillips, Matt K.	PA1250	33
Pierce, James	MS0850	33
Pinson, Joseph Warren	TX3300	33
Plaskett, Anna	AF0050	33
Potter Faile, Erin	PA1550	66A,33
Prickett, Carol A.	AL1170	32,33
Purcell, Julia	KY1500	33
Rambo, Kathryn	WI1150	33
Ramthum, Kerry	WI1150	33
Rasar, Lee Anna	WI0803	33,20G
Register, Dena M.	KS1350	33
Reynolds, Heidi M.	OH2250	33
Reynolds, Jeremy W.	CO0900	64C,33,13C,13H
Richardson, Tracy	IL1612	33
Richardson, Tracy	IN1400	33
Rio, Robin	AZ0100	33
Ritchey, Doris Ellen	GA2100	33,61
Rivera, Nicole	IL0750	33
Robinson, Vicky	GA0850	33
Roig-Francoli, Jennifer	OH2550	33
Ropp, Cindy	IL1150	33
Rose, Sarah Elizabeth	NC0050	32,33
Ross, Emily	OR0500	33
Roth, Edward	MI2250	33
Rousseau, Beth	OR0500	33
Routhier, Christine	MA1650	33
Rowe, Victoria	PA1250	33
Rubin-Bosco, Judi F.	NY2750	33
Sadovnik, Nir	NY2750	33
Sandacata, Lisa	NY2400	33
Sandagata, Lisa	NY5000	33
Sanders, Linda	PA1050	33
Sandness, Marilyn I.	OH2250	33,12F
Saperston, Bruce M.	UT0300	33
Scarpa, Tony	NY2400	33
Scartelli, Joseph P.	VA1100	33
Scheiby, Benedikte B.	NY2750	33
Schreibman, Janice	IN0907	12,33
Schwaberow, Denise	IN0905	33
Schwantes, Melody	NC0050	33,11
Schwartz, Elizabeth	NY2450	33
Schwartzberg, Edward	MN1623	33
Scott-Moncrieff, Suzannah	NY2750	33
Seabrook, Deborah	AG0600	33
Seitz, Jeanette	WI1150	33
Selesky, Evelyn C.	NY2450	33,66A
Shapiro, Noah	NY2750	33
Shultis, Carol	SC0650	33
Shultis, Carol L.	PA3000	33
Silverman, Michael	MN1623	33
Skidmore, Jon	UT0050	33
Sletta, Lauren	CO0250	33
Smith, Lauren	PA1250	33
Snukst, Penny	IN0005	33,13,31A
Solomon, Alan L.	NY3780	33
Sorel, Suzanne	NY2450	66A,33
Spring, Erin	OH1900	33
Standley, Jayne	FL0850	32A,33
Steele, Anita Louise	OH1900	33
Story, Kirstin 'Maya'	OR0500	33
Stouffer, Janice W.	PA1250	33
Stryck, Mary	WI0050	33
Summer, Lisa	MA0150	33
Summers, Debora	MO0700	33
Sung, Marion	VA1350	33
Sutton, Brigette	PA1050	33
Tague, Daniel	VA1350	33
Thaut, Michael H.	CO0250	12F,33
Thomas, Caryl Beth	MA1450	33
Thomas, Taryn	NY5000	33
Thornton, William C.	NY2750	33
Tripold, David	NJ0760	13,12A,32,31A,33
Turry, Alan	NY2750	33
Vega, Victoria P.	LA0300	33
Ventre, Madelaine	NY2450	33
Viega, Michael	NY2450	33
Wacks, Karen S.	MA0260	33
Walborn, Melanie	PA1250	33
Waldon, Eric	CA5350	33

Name	Code	Areas
Walker, Joey	IA1550	33
Walworth, Darcy DeLoach	FL0850	33
Walworth, Darcy	FL0950	33
Wanamaker, Tracy S.	NY3780	33
Washington, Donna	DC0150	33
Watkins, Lenora	WI1150	33
Watson, Terry Gutterman	NY2750	33
Webb, William	MN0050	33
Weber, Susan	MO0700	33
Weldon-Stephens, Amber	GA1150	32,33
West, Therese	OR0500	33
Whipple, Jennifer	SC0275	33
Wiggin, Christine	WI1150	33
Willeford, Constance E.	NY3725	33
Willey, Jason	NY2650	33
Wilshusen, Nicole	CO0250	33
Wilson, Brian	MI2250	33
Wirth, Mary Jo	WI1150	33
Wong, Wing Ho	IN0005	33
Wright-Bower, Linda	IN0905	33
Wylie, Mary Ellen	IN1600	33
Yang, Hao	IN0005	33
Yinger, Olivia	KY1450	33
Yoder-Frantz, Emily	PA1250	33
York, Elizabeth F.	SC0650	33
Zabin, Amy	NY2750	33
Zanders, Michael	PA3250	33
Zigo, Julie Buras	MA0260	33

Music and Technology (All Areas)

Name	Code	Areas
Abel, Jonathan	CA4900	34
Ainger, Marc	OH1850	10,34,35
Alexander, Kathryn J.	CT0900	13,10,34,43
Alexander, Prince Charles	MA0260	34,35C,35G
Allemeier, John	NC2420	13,10,34
Allen, Burt	LA0550	36,60A,60,34,61
Allen, David	IL3300	34
Allen, Nancy	CA2550	34,35B,35C,35D
Allik, Kristi A.	AG0250	10,45,34,32F
Altstatt, Hamilton	SC0400	34,35
Alves, William	CA2175	10,14,45,34
Amaya, Jennifer	CA0630	34
Anderman, Mark	CA4460	13,34,10,70,13A
Anderson, Mark	CA1800	34,35A,35B,45,35C
Anderson, Thad	FL1800	65,50,34
Anderson-Himmelspach, Neil	MD0475	10A,13,14C,34,62D
Apel, Ted R.	ID0050	34
Archambo, Larry	TX1700	60,32C,37,34,63C
Arnold, Roger	CT0700	34
Asbury, Herb	TX2650	70,11,34,13C
Asplund, Christian	UT0050	10A,10B,13,34
Auman, Kevin	NC1450	34,35
Austin, Kevin	AI0070	13,10F,10,34,35C
Austin, Michael	MO0850	34,35C,13,35,10
Baddorf, Donald	IL3550	34,35C
Bailey, Richard H.	AR0810	34,35C,35G,63A
Bain, Reginald	SC1110	13,10,34,45
Bales, Kenton W.	NE0610	13,10,43,34
Ball, Leonard V.	GA2100	13,10,45,34
Balzano, Gerald	CA5050	13A,34,13L,12F,12
Banagale, Ryan	CO0200	11,12,29,34
Barber, Deborah L.	AR0200	34,32B,10D,70,32C
Barkan, Paul Michael	NY1275	34
Barlow, Carla	NM0450	13,10,34
Barnes, James E.	PA2450	37,38,60,34,41
Barnes, Larry J.	KY1350	13,10,29A,34,14C
Barr, Stephen A.	PA3100	13,36,40,34
Barrett, Robert H.	CO1050	11,47,64,34,29
Barrick, Christopher	WV0600	64,11,41,34,47
Barrow, Lee G.	GA1500	13,60,34
Bartle, Barton	NJ1350	13,34
Barton, Karl S.	GA1990	64,47,12A,34
Baskin, Jason	MO0850	11,65,34
Basler, Paul	FL1850	13,63B,34
Batzner, Jay C.	MI0400	13,10,34,10A,13F
Bauer, David T.	MN1030	13A,34,66A,66G
Bauer, William I.	FL1850	32,34
Bauman, Marcia	CA4700	10,14C,34,35
Baust, Jeffrey P.	MA0260	34
Bazan, Dale E.	NE0600	32E,32F,32G,32H,34
Beaman, M. Teresa	CA0810	13A,13,48,64A,34
Bech, Soren	AI0150	34,35G
Beck, Stephen David	LA0200	10,45,34
Beckman, Linda L.	AR0400	66A,11,10F,34,66C
Begault, Durand	AI0150	34,35G
Belanger, Olivier	AI0200	34
Belden, George R.	AK0100	13,12,10,34
Bell, Peter J.	MA2030	10,13,31A,34
Bello, Juan P.	NY2750	34
Belshaw, Gary D.	TX3650	10F,10,66,34
Ben-Amots, Ofer	CO0200	13,10F,10,11,34
Benadon, Fernando Raul	DC0010	13,34,10
Bennett, Barbara A.	CA5040	13B,13,11,45,34
Bennett, Bruce Christian	CA4200	10,13,34,10A,10B
Benson, Mark	PA0400	13,10,12,63,34
Berger, Brad	MA0260	34,35C,35G
Berger, Jonathan	CA4900	13,10,45,34
Berners, David P.	CA4900	34
Bernier, Lucas	ND0400	65,50,11,34
Berry, S. David	SC0650	10,13,34,35,12
Betts, James E.	IL1800	13,20,29A,63,34
Beyer, Tom	NY2750	10,34
Bierman, Benjamin	NY0630	63A,10,13,34,35
Bindrim, Don	TN0300	34,46
Biondo, Steven A.	CA5100	34,16,20A
Birch, Sebastian A.	OH1100	13,10,34,13B,13A
Bishop, Bruce W.	AZ0300	34,36,61,13,60A
Black, Lendell	OK0750	10C,35D,34
Blake, C. Marc	CA2600	13,11,34,45,35B
Bland, Leland	OH2500	13,34
Bledsoe, Joshua	AR0850	63C,34
Bliton, Nathaniel	MI0900	72,34
Bloland, Per A.	OH1450	34
Blombach, Ann K.	OH1850	13A,13,34,12F,12
Bobrowski, Christine	CA1250	45,34,35C
Bohn, James	MA0510	11,34
Bondari, Brian	TX3350	10,13,34,10A,10B
Bonnefond, James L.	CT0700	34
Boon, Rolf J.	AA0200	13,34,10,35
Borgers, Ken	CA2550	34,35H
Bosi-Goldberg, Marina	CA4900	34
Bostrom, Sandra	CA0835	66A,10C,12A,34,65A
Botelho, Paul J.	LA0300	34
Both, Christoph	AF0050	13F,62,34
Boubel, Karen A.	MN1000	13,10,34,13C,10A
Bourgois, Louis	KY0750	11,12A,49,63D,34
Bovenzi, Michael	FL1950	34,32E,64E
Bowen, Nathan	CA3100	13,11,10,34
Bowen, Robert E.	CA3200	13,10A,29A,34
Bowers, Michael	NC0750	34,35
Bowman, Judith A.	PA1050	32,34
Boyle, McGregor	MD0650	10B,34
Braasch, Jonas	AI0150	34,35G
Bradbury, William	CA0847	13,10,11,34,20G
Bradfield, David	CA0805	13,34,66A
Brame, Robert	FL1750	34
Branch, Robert	NM0500	34,70
Brashear, Wayne	CA2550	34,35B
Braun, William	WI1155	13,10,12,55B,34
Breon, Timothy	PA2100	34,35,62D,70
Breuleux, Yan	AI0200	34
Bright, Jeff R.	KY1550	37,32E,34
Brimmer, Timothy	IN0250	60,32,36,34
Brink, Brian S.	FL0800	63C,49,34
Broderick, James	FL1300	13,63A,53,34
Broening, Benjamin	VA1500	10,34,13,35C,35D
Brooke, Nicholas	VT0050	13,10,20,34
Brown, J. Bruce	MI2000	13,10,11,34,51
Brown, T. Dennis	MA2000	32,20G,29A,34
Browne, Steve	TX0370	34,35G
Bruenger, David	OH1850	34
Brunkhorst, Kevin	AF0150	70,34,29
Brunner, George	NY0500	34,35C,10B
Buehrer, Theodore E.	OH1200	13,10,29,63A,34
Bukvic, Ivica Ico	VA1700	10,34,10A,13L,10C
Bullock, Robert	AL1050	34,35
Bulow, Harry T.	IN1300	10,13,34,13A
Bunce, Mark Robert	OH0300	34,35D,35G
Bunk, Louis	NH0110	34,10,11,13,43
Burchard, Richard	KY0250	10,13,20,34,35
Burdick, David H.	IL1750	10,13,34,70,35
Burdick, Paul	MA1400	13G,13,34,32
Burgess, Scott	MI0400	34,34D
Burke, Patrick	PA1050	13,10,34
Burkett, John	TX2955	13,66A,66G,34,12C
Burleigh, Ian G.	AA0200	13L,34
Burnette, Sonny	KY0610	13,47,64E,34
Burns, Christopher	WI0825	10,13,34,43,45
Burtner, Matthew	VA1550	10,34,35C,12F
Bussiere, Michael	AG0100	13A,13,45,34
Butler, Chuck	PA3330	10,34
Butler, Rebecca G.	PA0050	11,64A,37,34,13B
Butler, Steve	CA5550	10,13,34,10A,13E
Byrne, Madelyn	CA3460	10,11,34
Cain, Michael D.	MA1400	29,66A,34,31,20
Caldwell, Robert	AB0050	45,65,34,46,41
Camardella, Dominic P.	CA4410	34
Cameron, Wes	MS0850	11,63,64,65,34
Campbell, Jefferson	MN1600	11,64D,34
Campbell, Todd	PA0250	34,11,65
Campbell, William G.	IA1300	10,13,20,34
Campion, Edmund	CA5000	20,13,34,35G
Cangelosi, Casey	WV0200	61,65,29,34
Cape, Janet	NJ1350	32,34
Capps, Joe	VT0250	70,34,35A
Cardon, Sam	UT0325	34
Carenbauer, Michael	AR0750	45,51,70,34
Carlsen, James	WA1050	34,12B,12F,12,12C
Carlsen, Philip	ME0410	13,10,29A,38,34
Casal, David Plans	NH0100	10B,10F,34,13,35
Casey, Michael	NH0100	10B,10F,34,13,35
Cavera, Chris S.	OH2140	34,35,13,70,10
Chadabe, Joel A.	NY2750	34
Chafe, Chris	CA4900	10,45,34,13L
Chafin, Robert	VA1700	13C,39,34,61
Chaney, Carol	MI2120	34
Chaplin, Clay	CA0510	10,34,35G
Cheesman, Robert	MS0300	63,46,34
Chenette, Jonathan Lee	NY4450	10,13,34,10A,10B
Cho, Peter	LA0080	13,34,35,47,66A
Chordia, Parag	GA0900	34
Chou, Sarana	AL0800	13,10,34
Chowning, John M.	CA4900	10,45,34,13L
Christensen, Linda	NE0700	66A,66D,34,66B,11
Christopher, Casey R.	ID0150	11,29B,34,35,37
Christy, William P.	OH1910	13,12A,20G,29A,34
Chuah, Cheong	CA2775	12A,13A,34
Ciamaga, Gustav	AG0450	13,10,45,34
Clark, Frank L.	GA0900	34
Clemmons, Bill	CA3640	13,34,10F
Cline, Christopher	TX3530	34
Cline, Jeff	TN1680	34,35C,35D
Cloutier, Jean	AI0190	34
Cockerham, Scott	FL0150	41,70,34
Coe, Judith A.	CO0830	61,10D,34,14C,12C
Coffey, Ted	VA1550	10B,10,34,35C,35G
Cogan, Jeff	CA0960	70,34
Coggiola, John C.	NY4150	32,29,34,47,60B
Coghlan, Michael	AG0650	13,10,29,34,43
Cohen, Douglas H.	NY0500	13,10,11,34
Cohen, Jean-Luc D.	NY2750	34
Coleman, Ian D.	MO2000	13,10,34
Coleman, Michael	FL1500	13,10,11,66A,34
Coleman, Todd	NC0750	10,34,62D,35G,45
Collins, Dana L.	IN1560	10,12A,34,35C,13
Colon Carrion, Ismar	PR0115	34
Cook, Christopher E.	VA0150	34,13
Cook, Peter	AI0150	34,35G
Cook, Stephen	CA6000	66A,35A,34,36,11
Corbett, Ian	KS0590	10,34,35D,35G,13G
Corcoran, James R.	KY1425	65,34,11,50
Corey, Jason	MI2100	34
Cormier, Eugene	AF0050	13A,34,70
Cornicello, Anthony	CT0150	10,34,13,34D,13F
Cortese, Michael	NY0450	10,11,20,34,47
Cortese, Paul	TX3000	34,11
Corwin, Michael	AI0070	10F,10,45,34,35C
Costanza, A. Peter	OH1850	32,34
Cottle, David M.	UT0250	13,34
Coulas, Ben	AB0040	34,35D,35G,34D
Court, Tom	MI2200	34
Coutts, Greg A.	IL2650	13,10,34
Crain, Michael R.	CA0840	20,34
Crain, Michael	CA0150	34
Crawford, Donna	SC0200	66A,66G,34
Crawford, Peter	WA1300	34,48,37,66A
Crawley-Mertins, Marilee	IA0425	11,66A,66D,34
Craycraft, Jeremy	MN0450	20,50,34,65
Crespo, Fabra Desamparados	NJ0825	10,13,34
Crist, Michael	OH2600	32E,63C,34
Cronk, Daniel L.	MI0650	34,35
Crooks, Mack	CA4650	13,12,66A,34
Croson, James M.	FL1550	34
Dahl, Stanley E.	IA0200	50,65,34,65A,65B

Index by Area of Teaching Interest

Name	Code	Areas
Dal Porto, Mark	NM0100	10,13,66A,34,13A
Dana, Michael	CA1850	29,47,35A,34
Daniel, Omar	AG0500	13,10,10F,34,35C
Davies, Richard	NY3775	10,29,34,46,63D
Davis, Dennis	KY0550	70,45,34
Davis, Joel	AL0800	10,13,34
Davis, Peter	SC0200	66A,66B,66D,34
De Francisco, Martha	AI0150	34,35G
de Murga, Manuel	FL1750	10,10F,13E,34,43
De Ritis, Anthony	MA1450	35,62B,34,45
Deal, John J.	NC2430	32,34
Deal, W. Scott	IN0907	34,65
Dearden, Jennifer	PA0100	63A,34,13A,13B,13C
DeLaurenti, Christopher	WA0200	34
Delgado-Pelton, Celeste	CO0600	13,11,34,36,47
Delto, Byron	CA1960	34,70,13A
Denenberg, Peter	NY3785	34
Denham, Robert	CA0350	13,10,34,43
Depalle, Philippe	AI0150	34
Derry, Lisa	ID0070	13,10,34,66A,66B
Dethlefson, James	CA0650	34
Dethlefson, John	CA0270	34
Devore, Richard O.	OH1100	13,34,10,20G,13F
Diaz-Cassou, Isabel	NY2750	34
DiCello, Anthony J.	OH0150	36,61,66,31A,34
Dickau, David C.	MN1000	60,36,45,34
Dickinson, Paul J.	AR0850	10,13,43,34
Dickow, Robert H.	ID0250	13,10,63B,34
DiGiallonardo, Richard L.	IN0150	34
Dilthey, Michael R.	MA1185	10,13,34
Dimmick, Penny	IN0250	32,65,34
Dippre, Keith	NC1350	13,11,10,47,34
Dixon, Rich	UT0190	70,47,34,35
Doms, David	MA0260	34
Dorritie, Frank	CA2775	20G,35,34
Dougherty, William P.	IA0550	13,10F,10,34
Douyon, Marcaisse	FL1310	13,10,34
Dow, David Charles	CA3000	45,66D,34
Dubnov, Shlomo	CA5050	34,34B
Ducharme, Jay	MA2100	34
Dudt, Jay	PA1050	34
Dunbar, Brian	MN0620	10,13,36,34,60A
Dunbar, Edward	SC0200	13,12A,66G,34
Dunston, Michael	VA1700	34
Durand, Joel F.	WA1050	13,10,34
Durant, David Z.	AL1300	13,10,34,10A,10B
Durland, James	CA0400	10,34
Dworak, Paul E.	TX3420	13,34
Dzuris, Linda	SC0400	69,20G,66G,34
Eagle, David	AA0150	13,10F,10,34,43
Echard, William	AG0100	12,20,29,34,35
Eckhart, Michael	NJ0975	13A,34,70
Edstrom, Brent	WA1350	10,66A,34,47,13
Eigenfeldt, Arne	AB0080	10,45,34,35,12F
Eis, Jeremiah	WI0770	34,48,47,60B,63
Elezovic, Ivan	FL1850	10,13,34
Ellinger, John	MN0300	41,34,70
Elliott, John	CA4050	34,35C
Emge, Steven	OK1150	11,34
Emmons, Stephen D.	TX0150	13,10,10F,34
England, Peter	AJ0150	34
Entsminger, Deen	TN0100	13,10,32C,36,34
Epstein, Joshua	AI0150	35G,34
Erickson, Christian	WY0150	10,11,13,34,35
Ernste, Kevin	NY0900	10B,10A,34
Erskine, John K.	MI1050	35C,35D,34
Esleck, David	VA1800	11,66A,29,34,35
Esler, Robert	AZ0350	34,35
Espar, Michael	NY0646	32F,34,35
Essl, Georg	MI2100	34
Evans, William	MD1010	34
Everett, Steve	GA0750	60,10,41,45,34
Fantova, Marketa	NY0100	34
Farbood, Morwaread Mary	NY2750	34,10,66
Farrell, Frankie	CA2420	34,35
Farwell, Douglas G.	GA2150	63C,49,34,35C,35D
Fastenow, William David	NY2750	34
Faszer, Ted	SD0450	32,36,31A,34
Faulconer, James	OK1350	13,10,34,35
Fay, Edmund	NJ1400	65,34
Fergus, Brian S.	CA1020	34,13A
Fernisse, Glenn	GA0400	10,63D,34,32E
Festinger, Richard	CA4200	13,10,45,34
Fielder, Jonathan	OH0300	34
Fields, Kenneth	AA0150	10B,34
Fink, Robert W.	CA5032	13,12,34,20G
First, Craig P.	AL1170	13,10,45,34
Fish, David Lee	NC0350	35,14,34,20C,29
Fitzell, Gordon D.	AC0100	10,34,43
Flaherty, Mark	MI1600	47,63A,29A,34,63B
Flauding, Richard (Ric) G.	TX2600	10,34,10F,13
Flores, Carlos	MI0250	13,10,35,34,10F
Florez, Anthony	IL1080	11,34,65,70,13
Flournoy-Buford, Debbie	TX3650	32B,32D,34,66C,66A
Forbes, Douglas	CA1265	34
Forbes, Michael I.	WI0840	63D,13,34
Fox, Jeremy	IA1400	13,10F,37,50,34
Frankel, James Thomas	NY4200	34,37,32,32F
Franklin, Virgil	IN1800	34B,13A,34
Frary, Peter Kun	HI0160	13,11,12A,70,34
Frazer, Jonathan	TN1680	34,35C,35D
Freeman, Jason A.	GA0900	34
Freeman, Jeffrey J.	TX2100	11,63C,49,63D,34
Frengel, Mike	MA1450	10B,34,35
Fritz, Matthew P.	PA1250	36,60A,34,34E,60
Froelich, Kenneth D.	CA0810	10,34,43
Frye, Christopher B.	WI0810	13,10F,10,34
Frye, Joseph W.	TN1720	63C,13A,13C,11,34
Fujinaga, Ichiro	AI0150	34
Fujioka, Takako	CA4900	34,13K
Fuller, Wesley M.	MA0650	13,10,34
Furman, Pablo	CA4400	13,10,34,35C
Gabel, Gerald R.	TX3000	34,10,13,45
Gable, Laura Beth	AL0800	66D,34
Gaff, Isaac	IL1550	34,13G,13,35C,35G
Gage, Darren J.	NJ1130	34
Galindo, Guillermo	CA1250	45,34,35C
Gallo, Joseph	CA1520	35,34,66A,29,53
Gamer, Carlton	CO0200	13,10,11,20D,34
Garbutt, Don	AG0130	34,10
Garcia, Tim	MO0700	34
Garnett, Guy E.	IL3300	10,34,13
Garton, Bradford	NY0750	10,11,45,34
Gaston, Greg	MN0150	34,11
Gay, Kirk	FL1800	50,65,34
Gebuhr, Ann K.	TX1000	13,10,34
George, Arnold E.	NC1600	47,45,64,34,13
George, Kevin	LA0080	11,13,34,35
Gerber, Heidi	DC0170	34
Geringer, John M.	FL0850	34
Gibbson, Jef	AB0090	34
Gibson, Thomas S.	GA1150	63C,34,41
Gilbert, John	NY2750	10,32,34
Gilmour, F. Matthew	MO0850	13,10,11,12A,34
Gitt, Michael	MA0260	34,35,35C,35G
Glancey, Gregory T.	CA5355	10F,13,34,35
Glover, David	PA3100	29,50,65,34,47
Gluck, Robert J.	NY3700	10B,34D,31B,34,45
Godwin, Paul M.	TN0100	13,10F,10,34
Goeller, Dan	SD0580	34,32F
Goeringer, Lyn	OH1700	10,34
Goldsmith, Jeremy	NY2200	34
Golightly, John Wesley	KY0650	12A,31A,66,34,13D
Goodman, David	CA4450	13,10,34
Gorbachow, Yuri	AG0130	34
Gordon, Douglas L.	AL0500	13,34
Gorecki, Mikolaj P.	TX1425	10,11,13,34,66A
Gorman, Kurt	TN1720	13A,34,63A,47
Gorrell, Brian	OK1330	64E,46,34,47,29B
Gotfrit, Martin	AB0080	10,45,34,35,12F
Gould, Valerie	WV0050	32E,34,37,41,60B
Gran, Charles	MO1780	11,13,34,10
Granet, Peter	CA0550	34
Grasmick, David M.	CA0630	13A,34,63A,29
Greaves, Robert	NY0350	34
Greene, Roger W.	MA0150	13,34,66A,13A,10F
Greene, Ted	AB0060	13A,34
Greenhut, Barry	NY2750	10,34,13L
Greenough, Forest G.	CO0250	47,62D,10F,34
Gresham, David Allen	NC0250	61,11,34,13
Griffin, Buddy	WV0350	62,34,35
Griffin, Dennis	UT0300	50,34,65,13G,41
Griffin, Gregory W.	OH2275	54,35C,34
Griffin, Jackie	SC0950	13,10,12A,66G,34
Groom, Cody	WA0860	34
Grubbs, David	NY0500	10C,12,34
Guessford, Jesse	VA0450	11,13A,34
Guiterrez, Charles	CA2550	39,53,46,35B,34
Gunderson, Terry	WY0050	65,34,29,13,12E
Gurevich, Michael	MI2100	34
Guter, Gerhard	CA3800	34
Guthrie, James M.	NC0400	13,10,34,66G,66H
Gutierrez, Charles	CA0859	34
Haddad, Steve	TX3520	63D,34,35
Hahn, David	TN0580	12A,34,35A,36,60
Hahn, Tomie	NY3300	14,15,20,31G,34
Haight, Ronald S.	WA0800	34,35C,35D
Hair, Harriet	GA2100	11,32,34,12F
Hall, Richard D.	TX3175	11,10B,34
Halper, Matthew R.	NJ0700	10,13,34
Hamel, Keith A.	AB0100	13,10,34
Hanan, David	OK1330	37,60B,10F,34,63A
Hancock, Carl B.	AL1170	32G,32,34
Hanks, N. Lincoln	CA3600	55D,13,10,34,12A
Hansen, Brad	OR0850	13,29,10,34
Hansen, Peter	NY1275	34
Hanzelin, Fred	IL2775	13,34,11,10
Harbinson, William G.	NC0050	13,34
Harlan, Paul	FL1740	66A,10,34,35C
Harley, James I.	AG0350	10B,10A,34
Harris, Ben	FL0100	34,35C,35G,32F
Harris, Rod D.	CA1375	13A,11,64E,29B,34
Hart, James	OH2550	34,45
Hartl, David	PA3330	47,66A,66D,34,29
Hatley, H. Jerome	OK0850	10,61,34,13D
Hatzis, Christos	AG0450	10,35H,34,35C,13L
Haupert, Mary Ellen	WI1100	12A,13,34,66A
Hawkins, Phillip	CA2975	11,20H,34,50
Hayes, Micah	TX3500	34,35
Hays, Timothy O.	IL0850	13,62D,45,34,35
He, Jianjun	FL1000	13,34,10
Head, Russell	KS0750	10B,10D,34,35,45
Hearn, Sidney T.	IN1100	32,32E,34,37,63A
Heinrichs, William C.	WI0825	13,10,34
Heller, Brian	MN1050	10B,34,12A,35B,35G
Helmuth, Mara M.	OH2200	10,45,34
Hendricks, Steven	MO1500	32,37,34,36
Henriques, J. Tomas	NY3717	34,13
Henry, James	CA4850	34,35A,35B,35C,35D
Herb, Thomas	UT0200	13C,34,47,32C,32D
Herman, Martin	CA0825	10F,13,10,34
Herman, Matthew	PA2400	10,11,13,34,35
Hernandez, Rafael	CA0807	10,13,34
Herrick, Dennis R.	AL0450	60,63,34,29A,32C
Hess, Jeffrey	MN1200	61,34,32,11
Heukeshoven, Eric	MN1400	63C,63D,34,10
Hewlett, Walter	CA4900	34
Hicks, V. Douglas	OH2150	34
Higgins, William R.	PA2300	32,64,72,34
Hildreth, Todd	KY0250	14,34,47,66A
Hilmy, Steven C.	DC0100	10,45,34
Hinckley, Edwin	UT0190	34,35
Hoffman, Elizabeth D.	NY2740	12D,13,10,45,34
Holland, Anthony G.	NY3650	10A,60B,34,38,10B
Holmes, Rasan	VA0500	63C,37,34
Homzy, Andrew	AI0070	10,47,29,29A,34
Honour, Eric C.	MO1790	10,34,13,13F,35C
Hope, Garrett E.	PA3550	10,62D,13,34,51
Hopkins, Christopher	IA0850	13,10B,34,10,67A
Hornsby, Richard	AE0120	64C,12A,29A,34,60
Horvitz, Wayne B.	WA0200	10,34
Howe, Hubert S.	NY0642	13,45,34
Howiler, Robert W.	SC1000	34,10A,13G,10B
Hueblein, Carolyn	TN1850	62A,13G,32F,34,11
Hughes, Thomas	TX3200	66G,34,35C
Hulen, Peter Lucas	IN1850	13,10,34,34A,41
Humble, Dina M.	CA3800	61,36,11,34,29
Humphrey, AnDrue R.	NE0610	34
Hunkins, Arthur B.	NC2430	13,10,45,34
Hunnicutt, Bradley C.	NC2300	13,66,34,13A,13E
Husser, John S.	VA1700	64D,64E,34
Isaacson, Eric J.	IN0900	13,34
Isachsen, Sten Y.	NY3600	67D,41,70,34,29
Jackson, Ernie	NY3250	34,35,70
Jackson, Ryan D.	MN1120	34,35C,35D
Jacobson, Daniel C.	MI2250	11,12A,12,34
Jacobson, Michael	TX0300	64E,34
Jaeschke, Rick	IL0100	32,37,34
James, Robert R.	KY0550	35,34
James, Sandy L.	PA3250	34
Janikian, Leon C.	MA1450	35,34,64C
Janke, Tom J.	IN0907	34,62D
Jantz, Paul	SC0200	12A,49,63C,63D,34
Jaroszewicz, Martin	CA0835	34
Jensen, Shane	PA2000	34,32F
Jinright, John W.	AL1050	13,64D,34,64B,66A

Index by Area of Teaching Interest

Name	Code	Areas
Johanningsmeier, Scott	IN1010	34
John, David	OK0850	35B,34,35C
Johnson, Alfred	NY0640	34,35
Johnson, Bryan	FL2130	12A,34
Johnson, Daniel C.	NC2440	32,63D,34,32B,63C
Johnson, Eric	SD0150	34,35E
Johnson, Gary V.	IL2730	13,13C,29,34
Johnson, Joel C.	SC1050	13,10,20G,29A,34
Johnson, Keith	CA2975	10,20,34,35,13B
Johnson, Kevin P.	GA1900	60,11,32A,32B,34
Johnson, Madeline	UT0190	13,11,34,64C
Johnson, Marjorie S.	VA0950	13,66A,66B,66D,34
Johnson, Michael	PA3330	34
Johnson, Paul	IN1700	13,10,34
Johnson, Timothy	KY0100	34
Johnston, Gary	KY1000	10F,11,34
Johnston, Jack R.	NY3730	13,66A,54,34
Jones, Heath	OK0700	64C,64E,47,72,34
Jones, Micah	PA3330	47,62D,29,13,34
Jones, Richard	NE0450	50,65,34,70
Jones, Robert D.	FL1470	66A,66G,66C,66D,34
Jordan, L. Thomas	KY1000	11,34
Joyce, Brooke	IA0950	10,13,34,12
Joyce, Robert	SD0050	10F,34
Judson, Tohm	NC2700	10B,62D,70,34,35
Judy, Ned	MD0700	13,29,66,34,47
Julian, Michael	CA1700	34
Juncker, Arthur	CA1950	13,10,12A,41,34
Junokas, Michael	IL0850	10A,10B,13,34
Jurkowski, Edward	AA0200	13,12A,34
Kahn, Richard	CA2600	34
Kahn, Richard	CA2750	10F,13B,34,66A
Kallay, Aron	CA0960	34
Kaloyanides, Michael G.	CT0700	12,13,14,20,34
Kamenski, Michael	WI0050	60,13,34
Kamprath, Richard	CA1560	34,35
Kapur, Ajay	CA0510	34,20E,45
Karaca, Igor	OK0800	13,10,34
Karpen, Richard	WA1050	13,10,34
Kashkin, Allan	NY3250	34,40,61
Katz, Mark	NC2410	12,14,20,34
Kelly, Gary	NY0700	35,34,62D,43
Kelly, Kevin M.	NY2550	34,35
Kelly, Michael F.	NY1850	36,61,66A,46,34
Kendall, Michael	IN0200	60,37,32,20,34
Kerr, William	CA1000	34
Kerstetter, Kathleen	NC1500	32,49,34,64A
Kidde, Geoffrey C.	NY2200	10,13,34,45,32F
Kilianski, Harold	AI0150	34,35G
Kim, Hyun Kyung	MD0400	34
Kim-Boyle, David	MD1000	34,35C,35G
Kim-Quathamer, Chan Ji	FL0150	10,11,13,34
Kimlicko, Franklin	TX3370	70,34,35C
Kincaid, Sam	OR0700	34
Kindall, Susan C.	SC0200	66A,66B,35C,34
King, Richard	AI0150	34,35G
Kirby, Wayne J.	NC2400	10,45,34,35,62D
Kirk, Jonathon J.	IL2050	13,10,20,34
Kirshner, Andrew	MI2100	34
Klassen, Carolyn	KS0440	66,34,13,20F
Kleiman, Carey D.	FL0200	34,35A,64,35,32E
Klein, Benjamin	CT0050	34
Klein, Jim	PA1000	34,32F,45,13G,10C
Knable, Robert	CA3850	13,38,34
Koenig, Mark	IN0907	34,63A
Kohrs, Jonathan A.	IL0730	10,36,11,31A,34
Kolstad, Michael L.	MO0400	49,63C,63D,47,34
Konecky, Larry	MS0050	13,62,70,34
Konewko, Mark	WI0425	11,35A,34,69
Kono, Yutaka	VT0450	63D,34,38,60
Koppelman, Daniel M.	SC0750	66A,13,34,10
Korey, Judith A.	DC0350	13A,13,66A,29,34
Koriath, Kirby L.	IN0150	66G,66H,31A,34
Korneitchouk, Igor	CA4050	13A,10,11,12A,34
Kostlan, Robert	CA0847	34
Kothman, Keith K.	IN0150	10B,10,34,13,35C
Kramer, Keith A.	CT0050	13,34
Krawezyk, Shelly	CA2550	34,35A,35B
Kreiger, Arthur V.	CT0100	13,35C,10,45,34
Kreiger, Donna	WY0100	34
Kreuze, Brandon R.	GA0600	10,34,13,12C
Krewitsky, Michael	CA2100	34
Kriehn, Richard	WA1150	11,70,62A,34
Krugman, Murray	CT0700	35,34
Kurokawa, John K.	OH2500	11,34,64C,32F
Kuss, Mark	CT0450	13,10,45,66A,34
Lackey, William J.	MO1800	10B,34
LaCroix, John	CA0200	34,35
Laganella, David	DE0200	10,13,34,14C,12A
Laird, Scott	NC1800	60,34
Lampl, Kenneth H.	NY1600	35,10,64E,34,11
Lansky, Paul	NJ0900	13,10,45,34
Larish, Charles	IA0910	34
Larocque, Jacques	AI0220	10,41,48,64E,34
Larson, John	IL0400	34
Latartara, John	MS0700	13,34
Latham, Louis S.	VA1000	13A,34,35A,35C,35D
Lavoie, Mathieu	AI0200	34,10C
Lecuyer, Michael P.	MA1500	13,47,34
Lee, HyeKyung	OH0850	13,34
Lee, Michael	CA0250	34
Lehrman, Paul D.	MA1900	35C,34,35B,45,45
Lentini, James P.	OH1450	13,10,70,34
Levey, John C.	PA3400	10,13,11,34,36
Lewis, Grant	SC0950	39,34,61
Liesch, Barry	CA0350	11,34,31A
Lincoln, Harry B.	NY3705	11,12A,12,34
Lincoln-DeCusatis, Nathan J.	WV0550	10,13,34
Lindeman, Carolyn A.	CA4200	13A,32,66D,34
Link, Jeffrey	MA0280	13,34,47
Link, John	NJ1400	13,10F,10,34
Lippe, Cort	NY4320	10,45,34
Little, Lynn	WI0300	34,13
Liu, Susan (Shao-Shan)	TX1425	66A,66D,11,34
Liu-Rosenbaum, Aaron	AI0190	10,34,35G,13,14C
Logan, Hal	OR1100	34
Logan, Kenneth	MI0250	66G,34,10,10F,31A
Long, Patrick A.	PA3150	13,10,34,12A,32E
Lopez, Thomas Handman	OH1700	10B,34,10,34A
Lorenz, Michael L.	MI1950	13,47,63,29,34
Lorenz, Ralph	OH1100	13,34,10,13F,13D
Loubriel, Luis E.	IL0275	11,13A,34,63,35
Loughrige, Chad	OH0350	34,35C,10B,10D,45
Love, Maurice	CA2550	46,34,35B
Lowrey, Norman E.	NJ0300	13A,13,10,45,34
Luca, Nancy	CA2550	34,35B,35C,35D
Lucier, Alvin	CT0750	10,45,34
Luzko, Daniel	CA2390	13,10F,10,34
MacCallum, John	MA1450	10B,34
Mack, George	RI0200	10,13,34
Mackenzie, Barbara Dobbs	NY0600	12,34
Mackey, Ryan	KS0215	34
MacLean, Alasdair	AE0050	10A,34,13
MacLean, Stephen	MA0260	34,35C
Maddox, Craig	FL1750	34,61
Mager, Guillermo E.	CT0700	13,12A,34,35,32
Maher, John	IN1025	13,12A,66G,16,34
Mahin, Bruce P.	VA1100	10,34,13,35C
Makan, Keeril	MA1200	10,10F,34,13
Mallard, Manley	IL1750	41,70,34
Mallia, John	MA1400	10B,10,34
Malsky, Matthew	MA0650	10A,10B,34,13,10
Manchester, John	MS0300	13,34,11
Mandrell, Nelson E.	IL2150	13,10,45,34
Manson, David	FL1650	47,63C,63D,53,34
Manzo, V.J.	NJ0800	34
Mapp, Douglas	NJ1050	62D,47,53,34
Markovich, Frank	CA4625	70,34
Marrs, Stuart	ME0440	12A,65,50,34
Marschall, Ron	AZ0490	34,35
Marschner, Joseph A.	MD0450	11,45,70,34
Marsh, Gerry Jon	WA0800	34,35C,37,10
Marshack, Rose	IL1150	34,35A
Martens, William	AI0150	34,35G
Martin, Greg	CA2550	34,35A,35B
Maske, Dan	WI0150	10,34
Mason, Keith	TN0100	34
Massenburg, George	AI0150	34,35G
Mathes, Gerard	ID0140	13,11,13J,62A,34
Matsos, Christopher	OH2275	34
Matthews, Bill	ME0150	13,10,29,34
Matthews, Justus F.	CA0825	13,10,43,34
Matthews, Zachary P.	CA3500	62D,29,34
Matthusen, Paula A.	CT0750	34,45,10
Mauldin, Steve	TN0100	34
Maxson, Mark D.	UT0350	34,70
Maz, Andrew	CA1900	34,10
McAdams, Stephen	AI0150	13G,13K,34
McAllister, Margaret	MA0260	10,13,34H,10A,34
McBride, Michael S.	IL2100	10,34,13,31,12A
McCabe, Matthew	GA0550	34,13,10
McClement, Doug	AG0130	34
McCutcheon, Russell G.	PA1400	37,32E,60,34,32C
McDonnell, David	OH2250	10B,10F,34,64E,47
McElwaine, James	NY3785	41,47,20G,29,34
McFerron, Mike	IL1520	13A,13,10F,34,10
McGarity, Kristin A.	MT0200	10B,34,64B
McGee, Deron	KS1350	13,34
McGee, William James	CA3400	13,10F,10,66A,34
McGregor, Cynthia	CA4850	13,11,34
McIntire, David D.	MO1790	34,35A
McIntyre, Chris	AA0025	70,34
McIntyre, John	IN1400	13,34,12A,36,10
McKinney, John S.	WV0350	50,65,34,60B,41
McKinnon, John A.	OR0200	13,10,63,34,14
McKittrick, Cam	AG0350	34
McLay, Mark	AG0130	34
McMahan, Andrew	CA0600	60,37,63A,54,34
McNair, Jonathan B.	TN1700	10A,34D,13,10,34
Meadows, Melody	WV0800	13,12A,66G,34,35A
Meeker, Jared	CA0200	70,34
Megas, Alexander	CA3800	34
Meier, Scott Alan	PA2250	47,53,64E,34,32E
Menoche, Charles Paul	CT0050	10,12,13,34
Meredith, Steven	UT0190	13,36,61,34
Merkowitz, Jennifer Bernard	OH2050	10,13,34
Merritt, Justin W.	MN1450	10,13,43,13A,34
Mery, John Christian	OR0800	13,10,41,70,34
Meschi, John	NY2105	10,34
Messer, Benjamin	AZ0470	34
Metcalf, John C.	PA1750	34,10,11,49,63C
Meyer, Donald C.	IL1400	13,12A,10,34
Michael, Doug	CA1560	34,35
Middleton, Jonathan N.	WA0250	13,10,35C,34,35
Middleton, Peter	IL2200	45,64A,34,35C,13L
Midgley, Herbert	TX2700	11,70,34,45
Miles, Benjamin E.	TN1100	63D,34
Miller, Dennis H.	MA1450	13,10,45,34
Miller, Everett F.	KS0225	11,36,34,70,20
Miller, John	ND0350	13,34
Miller, Joseph P.	SC1200	34
Miller, Randy	MI0520	34
Miller, Robert F.	CT0600	34,34D
Miller, Scott L.	MN1300	13,10A,10B,10C,34
Milligan, Thomas	TN0250	13,12A,66A,34
Minasian, Mark	HI0160	11,12A,29,34,35
Mindock, Rebecca A.	AL1300	64B,64D,12A,34,42
Misenheimer, Aaron L.	NC0850	32E,34,11,63,49
Miskell, Jerome P.	OH2290	34,62B,13A,11
Mitchell, Dan	CA1550	11,34
Mitchell, Geoffrey	AI0150	34,35D
Miyashiro, Kurt	IL2800	13,10A,34,10C
Molina, Jose	CA1520	34,45
Moon, Brian C.	AL1150	34
Moore, Brian	NE0600	32,34
Moore, F. Richard	CA5050	10,45,34,35C,13L
Moore, James Walter	KY0400	34,13,10,70
Moore, Matthew	ID0060	34,41,63D
Moore, Matthew	MO0400	34
Mooy, James D.	CA4410	45,35C,34,46,64
Moran, Kenny	AG0130	34
Morrill, Dexter G.	NY0650	10,45,29A,34
Morris, J. David	GA2150	65,34,13,50
Morris, Jeffrey M.	TX2900	70,34,35G
Mortenson, Daniel	SD0150	34,35C
Moshier, Steve	CA3750	13,11,12A,34,43
Mountain, Rosemary	AI0070	13,10F,10,45,34
Mountain, Toby	MA0700	34,14C
Mowrey, Peter C.	OH0700	10,66A,13,34
Moye, Brenda	TN0850	64E,41,34
Mueller, Marc	OK1250	37,63A,32E,60,34
Mulder, Axel	AI0150	34
Mulder, Geoffrey	CA0850	34,35C,35D,12A,62A
Mulet, Mickael	PR0100	34,35C
Muller, Bryan	PA1550	70,34,33
Murail, Tristan C.	NY0750	10,34,13L,12F,10F
Murphy, Daniel	CA5150	34,35,29
Murray, Mark S.	IN0100	29,63A,34,35
Myska, Robert	AG0500	13,10,45,34,35C
Nagler, Joseph	NY3250	32,33,34
Nakra, Teresa Marrin	NJ0175	13,34,10B
Nardo, Rachel L.	UT0250	32,32B,34,32A,32D
Natter, Robert	PA1400	34,36,61,60A
Naus, Jesse	PA1050	34
Naylor, Stephen	AF0050	34,10B
Neal, Jocelyn	NC2410	13,20G,34,14C

Index by Area of Teaching Interest

Name	Code	Areas
Neal, Mark	AL1450	65,47,34,35
Negyesy, Janos	CA5050	20F,41,62A,43,34
Nelson, Jon C.	TX3420	10A,10B,10F,34
Nelson, Larry A.	PA3600	13,10,45,34
Nelson, Mark	AZ0480	37,13,63D,34
Nelson, Mary Anne	NY0700	34,35
Nelson, Richard	ME0340	10,34,13,29,47
Neumann, Kyle	KY0250	34
Newton, Jon	OR0850	34,13A
Nichols, Charles Sabin	MT0400	10A,10B,10,45,34
Nissen, James	MI1900	13A,13,37,34
Nord, Michael	OR1300	32A,32B,34
Nord, Timothy	NY1800	13,34
Noyes, Christopher R.	MA0260	34
Nuccio, David A.	IL1250	11,29A,34,54,66A
Ochs, Hunter	CA0960	34
O'Connell, Jason	CA4150	34
OGrady, Douglas M.	CT0800	13,34,35G,10
Oliverio, James C.	FL1850	10,34
Olsen, Lance	NJ0990	13A,13,11,34
O'Modhrain, Sile	MI2100	34
Onofrio, Marshall	NJ1350	13,10,29,34,32E
Opie, Benjamin	PA0550	34
Organ, Wayne	CA1450	11,13A,13B,13C,34
Orlick, James	SC0150	13,34,50
Orpen, Rick	MN0750	13,70,34,10
Ortiz, Pablo	CA5010	13,10,45,29,34
Ouellette, Garry	NY2550	16,14C,72,34,35
Paduck, Ted	MA0260	34,35C,35G
Palese, Richard	IL3450	32,34
Palmer, Bradley E.	GA0550	63C,11,34,32F,41
Pampin, Juan	WA1050	10,34
Panion, Henry	AL1150	34
Pannell, Larry J.	LA0100	64,34,35C,37,32
Paoli, Kenneth N.	IL0630	13,10,11,35,34
Pappas, J.	MO0550	65,11,34
Paranosic, Milica	NY1900	34
Parish, Steven	AB0070	65,20G,34,35C
Park, Tae Hong	NY2750	10,34
Parker, David	SC0200	61,34
Parks, Ronald Keith	SC1200	10,13,34,41
Parrish, Robert E.	NJ0175	54,34
Parsons, Kenneth	TN1350	60B,49,37,46,34
Patrick, Dennis M.	AG0450	13,45,13L,34,35C
Patterson, David N.	MA2010	13,10,11,20G,34
Paul, John F.	OR0500	10,13,34
Paulson, John C.	MN1400	47,64,29,34,35
Payne, Benjamin	FL0670	11,34,13,66A,66D
Payne, Tony L.	IL3550	10,34
Peacock, Kenneth J.	NY2750	13,10,12,35,34
Peck, Jamie	WV0600	34
Peebles, Crystal	AZ0450	13,34
Pejrolo, Andrea	MA0260	34,10C,10,35C,35G
Pellman, Samuel	NY1350	13,10B,10,34
Peretz, Marc	MI1850	11,32,66D,34
Perrault, Paul	AI0220	45,34,35C,35E,13L
Perry, Jeffery S.	MA0260	10B,34
Petering, Mark D.	WI0250	10,13,34
Peters, G. David	IN0907	34,12C,12,35C,35A
Peterson, Rai	WA0860	34
Phelps, James	IL2200	10,45,34
Phillips, Joel	NJ1350	13,10,34
Phillips, Mark W.	OH1900	43,10,45,34
Phillips, Scott L.	AL1150	32F,34,45
Piccone, James	NJ1050	13,10,34
Pignato, Joseph M.	NY3765	35,34,10,13
Pilchner, Martin	AG0130	34
Pinkston, Joan	SC0200	13,66A,34
Pinkston, Russell F.	TX3510	10,45,34
Pisano, Joseph M.	PA1450	47,45,53,46,34
Placek, Robert W.	GA2100	32,34
Plummer, Kathryn	TN1850	41,62A,62B,34
Polansky, Larry	NH0100	13,10,45,34
Polk, Sylvester	FL0100	34,63A,35A,35D,35G
Porter, David	WV0700	63A,34
Posegate, Stephen C.	IL3150	32,37,49,34
Post, J. Brian	CA2250	34,35,13,10
Potes, Cesar I.	MI1200	13,10,11,34
Pounds, Michael S.	IN0150	10,34D,13,45,34
Powell, Jarrad	WA0200	13A,10,20D,45,34
Powell, Steven S.	PA1000	36,61,34,12A,32D
Powers, Ollie	CA5360	35G,35C,11,12A,34
Price-Brenner, Paul Alan	WI0840	11,62A,62B,34
Pritchard, Bob	AB0100	13,10,34
Proctor, Gregory	OH1850	13,10,34
Profitt, Tommee	MI0750	34,31A
Puchala, Mark	MI1650	12A,36,61,34,41
Puckette, Miller	CA5050	34,12C
Purin, Peter	OK0650	13,34
Purse, Lynn Emberg	PA1050	10B,34,45
Purse, William E.	PA1050	70,34
Quathamer, Mark	FL0150	10,13,34
Quindag, Sue	SC0200	32,62A,62B,34
Rahn, John	WA1050	13,10,34
Randlette, Peter	WA0350	34
Ratliff, Phillip	AL0650	13,12A,10F,34
Raynovich, William Jason	IL0600	13,10,34
Ream, Duane	SC0200	66A,66D,34
Reddick, Don	IL2300	32E,46,34,13A
Redmond, James Ryan	AZ0200	34
Reece, A.	NY3770	16,34
Rees, Fred J.	IN0907	34,12C,35C,32,12
Reid, Sally	TN0930	10,13,64B,10C,34
Reiprich, Bruce J.	AZ0450	13,10,34
Reisch, Carla	CA2390	11,14,34
Reller, Paul	FL2000	10,34
Remele, Rebecca	AL0300	10,34
Renfrow, Kenon	SC0200	66A,66B,66D,34
Reuter, Eric Lehman	MA0260	34,35C,35D
Reynolds, Roger L.	CA5050	13,10F,10,20G,34
Rhea, Thomas L.	MA0260	34
Rheault, Pierre-Daniel	AI0200	10C,34
Richard, Charles	CA3800	47,64E,29,34,42
Richardson, Jack	AG0130	34
Richmond, C. Floyd	PA3560	32,34,13
Ricks, Steven L.	UT0050	10A,10B,13A,34
Riddle, Donald	MO2000	34,35C
Riedel, Kimberly	NJ1130	13G,34
Riley, Edward	OH0755	34,35
Riley, Justin	OH0350	34,35C,35D,35G,13G
Riley, Raymond G.	MI0150	66A,13,34,34H
Ring, Gordon L.	VA0700	13,10,37,34
Rivard, Michele M.	CA0400	61,34
Roberts, Sara	CA0510	10,34
Robinson, Curtis	IN0005	13,16,29,34,35
Robinson, Jason	MA0100	12,13,14,34
Roche, Deryck	AG0130	34
Rodriguez Alvira, Jose	PR0115	13A,34,13B,13D,13G
Rodriguez, Alex	MA0260	34,35C,35G
Rogalsky, Matt	AG0250	10,45,34,32F
Rogers, Tom	AG0130	34
Roginska, Agnieska	NY2750	34
Rojas, Nuria Mariela	SC0150	11,12,13,34,66
Rolls, Timothy	KS0350	10,13,34,35C,35G
Rolnick, Neil B.	NY3300	13,10,45,34
Roman, Dan	CT0500	34,70,10A,10F,13
Romero, Frank	NM0310	63A,47,72,34
Ronkin, Bruce	MA1450	64E,34,35
Rosado-Nazario, Samuel	PR0100	63,37,34
Rose, Brian	OR0050	34,35C,35D,35H
Rose, Leslie Paige	AR0850	32B,34,32E
Rose, Lloyd	MA0280	34
Rose, William G.	LA0350	13,49,34,63D,63C
Roston, John	AI0150	34,35G
Roth, John	MN0610	34,40,41,70
Roush, Dean	KS1450	13,10F,10,34
Rovan, Joseph 'Butch'	RI0050	10,45,34
Rowe, Robert	NY2750	10,43,34,35C
Rubel, Mark B.	IL0800	34
Rubin, Anna I.	MD1000	10,34
Rubin, Justin H.	MN1600	13,34,66G,10,66A
Rudolph, Thomas	PA3330	34,32
Ruehr, Elena	MA1200	13,10,34
Rumbolz, Robert C.	WY0130	13,35C,35D,34,20A
Russo, Tadd	MD0600	34
Rust, Ty	CA2420	67,35C,34
Ryan, Francis J.	OK1450	13,34,11
Ryder, Christopher O.	VA1150	34,61,32,13,40
Sabina, Leslie M.	NY3475	29,10,34,13,47
Sain, James Paul	FL1850	13,10,34
Salazar, Jason	MO0400	34,13,35,43,47
Salyer, Douglas W.	CT0200	13,34,12A,36,66
Sanders, Gregory L.	TX2960	13,10F,10,34
Sandred, Orjan	AC0100	10,13,34
Sandroff, Howard	IL3250	10,45,34,13L
Sapieyevski, Jerzy	DC0010	13,10,45,11,34
Saunders, Martin	WV0400	63A,53,49,47,34
Savage, Steve	CA2775	35,34
Sawyer, Eric	MA0100	10,13,34,43
Sawyer, Tony	NC0750	37,65,34
Scandrett, John F.	PA1600	13,63B,34
Scavone, Gary	AI0150	34
Schaller, Thilo	AA0200	34,35
Scherzinger, Nicolas	NY4150	13,10,34,64E
Schiano, Michael	CT0650	13,13J,20G,34
Schildt, Matthew C.	CO0050	13,10,10D,13E,34
Schindler, Karl W.	AZ0470	10,13,34,12A
Schlei, Kevin	WI0825	34
Schloss, Andrew	AB0150	10B,34,14,20H,13L
Schmunk, Richard	CA5300	34,35
Schmutte, Peter J.	IN1650	36,45,35C,35G,34
Schneider, John	CA2700	41,45,70,34
Schrader, Barry	CA0510	13,10,12A,34
Schreiber, Paul	MS0560	10,13,34,10B,10A
Schultz, Arlan N.	AA0200	10,34,13,12B
Schultz, Eric	CA0900	10,13,34
Schuttenhelm, Thomas	CT0050	11,13,70,34
Schweitzer, Kenneth	MD1100	20,29,34,35,11
Scott, F. Johnson	VA0750	34,13B,13A,66G,66C
Scott, Jennifer	CO0300	62A,34
Seitz, Christine L.	IN0550	13,66C,34
Sekhon, Baljinder S.	FL2000	10,65,13,34
Selfridge-Field, Eleanor	CA4900	34
Senn, Geoff	MN0040	29A,63A,34,41,11
Sevilla, Tiffany	IL0720	10,34
Shackleton, Phil	CA0250	13,10,34
Shannon, William	CA0900	13A,13B,34,63B,35
Shapiro, Gerald	RI0050	13,10,45,34
Sharp, Michael D.	LA0400	66A,66B,31A,34,10A
Shaw, George W.	CA2550	47,29,34,35
Shea, David L.	TX3200	34,41,64A,64C,64E
Shepard, Brian K.	CA5300	34,10,13,34C,65
Sheppard, Chris	SC0900	36,60A,61,40,34
Sher, Ben	NY4500	34,47,70
Shiner, Richard	CA2775	35,34
Shipley, John	NV0150	66A,34,14C
Shively, Joseph L.	MI1750	32G,34,11,32,32C
Shotwell, Clayton	GA0250	12,20,34,11,13A
Shufro, Joseph L.	IA1100	10F,13E,34,38,62C
Sicilia, Sheila	NY2950	34,13A
Simmons, Jim	CA0859	34
Sink, Damon W.	NC2600	10,13,34,34B,13I
Sizer, Todd	CO0275	63D,10F,34,42
Slaney, Malcolm	CA4900	34
Slawson, A. Wayne	CA5010	13,10,34
Smith, Bradley	PA1050	34
Smith, David	CT0800	13,50,65,34
Smith, Glenn E.	VA0450	13,10,45,34,42
Smith, Julius O.	CA4900	34,13L
Smith, Kenneth H.	MI2250	32,34,12F
Smith, Leland C.	CA4900	13,10,12A,34
Smith, Matthew	IL1150	34
Smith, Raymond H.	AL1050	47,37,34,64E,29
Smith, Robert W.	AL1050	35,34
Smith, Ronald B.	MA1450	34
Smith, Timothy A.	AZ0450	13,34
Snow, Greg	NY3725	34
Snyder, Mark L.	VA1475	13,10B,10F,34
Sochinski, James	VA1700	13,37,63C,63D,34
Solum, Stephen	MN1050	13,20G,10,35G,34
Sommerfeldt, Jerod	OH2250	10F,34
Sommerfeldt, Jerod	OH1450	13,34
Sorah, Donald	VA1580	34,63A,29,14C,20
Sovik, Thomas	TX3420	13,31A,14C,13J,34
Sparks, Michael	AL1450	12A,36,66A,31A,34
Spice, Graham	VA1850	34
Spitler, Justin	IN0700	34
Spitz, Bruce	WA0860	66,34,35,13L
Spraggins, Mark	CA0550	13,10,34
Stace, Stephen	PA2700	11,34
Stallings, Joe	FL1500	13,11,70,34
Stallmann, Kurt D.	TX2150	13,10,45,34
Stamps, Jack W.	NJ1160	10,34
Staniland, Andrew	AD0050	34,10
Stanton, Geoffrey	MI1300	13,10,45,34
Stanyek, Jason	NY2740	34,12,14,20,12D
Steidel, Mark	CA1560	13,35,34
Steiger, Rand	CA5050	13,10,34
Steinbach, Richard	IA0100	13,10,66,34
Stevens, Annie J.	VA0150	65,37,50,34
Stewart, James	CA0400	34
Stimmel, Matthew D.	OH2275	34,35C
Stitt, Ronald	PA0100	63C,47,29,46,34
Stokes, Harvey J.	VA0500	13,10,64B,34
Stolberg, Tom	MO0060	10F,34,31A,32B,60
Stolet, Jeffrey	OR1050	13,45,10,34,10B

Index by Area of Teaching Interest

Name	Code	Numbers
Stone, George J.	CA1510	13,47,34,66A,35D
Stout, David L.	TX3420	34
Stratton, Matthew	TN1720	63D,11,34,37
Streder, Mark	IL0850	13,66A,53,34,45
Sudol, Jacob David	FL0700	34,35,45
Sullivan, Mark	MI1400	10,12B,34
Sullivan, Shawn	CA2050	34
Suvada, Steven	IL1085	70,34,35
Swendsen, Peter V.	OH1700	34
Swenson, Thomas S.	NC2205	13A,66B,35C,34,32
Swilley, Daniel	IL1200	10,13,34,13A,13B
Sylvern, Craig	NH0150	64E,34,32F,10,48
Tackett, Jeff	OH1100	34
Taggart, Bruce F.	MI1400	13,34
Talley, Keith M.	OK1250	64E,32,48,34
Tanner, Robert	GA1450	10,12A,11,65,34
Tapia, Doug	CO0625	34,34A,34D,34B
Tate, Brian	MO1800	11,34
Taube, Heinrich K.	IL3300	13,10,34
Taylor, Dowell	MS0350	11,13C,34
Taylor, Timothy D.	CA5031	12,14,34
Taylor, Timothy D.	CA5032	14,20,34
Tender, Peter	OH1850	34,35C
Terry, Peter R.	OH0250	34,10,13
Testa, Michael	MA1650	34,34D
Theisen, Alan	NC1250	13,10,34,35G,64E
Theodore, Michael	CO0800	45,34,10
Therrian, Dennis	MI1200	66A,34
Thomas, Susan H.	RI0300	41,48,64A,34
Thompson, Douglas S.	NJ0500	13,10,12A,34
Thompson, John	GA0950	34,10
Thompson, Robert Scott	GA1050	10A,10B,10C,45,34
Thompson, Timothy D.	FL1450	10,13,34,64E
Thornburg, Benjamin	OH0550	34
Tim, Raotana	CA2550	34,35A,35B
Tingen, Jolie	NC2500	34
Tipei, Sever	IL3300	13,10,34
Tobey, Forrest	IN0400	38,47,13,34
Tollefson, Tim	MN0200	13,10A,34
Tolley, David	DE0050	10,34,35
Tomlin, Terry	TX3515	47,64E,29,34,32F
Topel, Spencer	NH0100	10B,10F,34,13,35
Towner, John	IL1085	34,35
Towner, John	IL0850	45,34
Traub, Thomas	NJ1050	34
Traube, Caroline	AI0200	13L,35C,34
Trayle, Mark	CA0510	10,34,45
Trollinger, Valerie L.	PA1750	34,32,64D,11,32C
Truax, Barry D.	AB0080	10,45,34,35C,13L
Turnbull, Kai	MA0260	34
Turner, Daniel	SC0200	32B,32C,37,63D,34
Turner, Michael W.	OR1000	70,29,34,47
Turner, Timothy R.	LA0900	13G,10F,32E,34,37
Udell, Chester	OR1050	10,10B,11,34,35
Umble, James C.	OH2600	64E,34
Umezaki, Kojiro	CA5020	10,13,34
Ungar, Leanne	MA0260	34,35C,35G
Vaccaro, Brandon C.	OH1100	13,10,34,13B,13A
Vaglio, Anthony J.	NC1300	13,10,32,34
Vali, M. Reza	PA0550	13,34
Van Regenmorter, Merlyn	CA0150	34,35B
Vanderwoude, Matt	AG0130	10A,11,13,29,34
Vandiver, Joseph	TX3650	29,63,46,47,34
Vees, Jack	CT0850	34
Vercoe, Barry	MA1200	13,10,45,34
Verge, Marc-Pierre	AI0150	34
Verplank, William	CA4900	34
Villec, John	CA4300	34
Vincent, Dennis	FL1000	32,34
Vogler, Paul	TN0260	34,65
Von Oertzen, Alexandra 'Sasha'	NY2750	34
Waldrep, Mark	CA0805	34,35C,35D
Walicki, Kenneth J.	CA0815	10,13,34
Walker, Elaine	AZ0490	34
Walker, Gregory	MN0350	13,10,45,34
Walker, Tim	CA1450	34
Walker, Timm	CA2775	34
Wall, Jeremy	NY3765	34,35,36,47,66A
Walley, Steve	IN0905	13G,34,10D
Walrath, Brian	MI2000	11,12A,65,31,34
Walter, Ross A.	VA1600	63C,63D,34,49
Waltl, Herbert	AI0150	34,35G
Wanderley, Marcelo	AI0150	34
Wang, Ge	CA4900	34,35,13L
Wang, Jing	MA2020	34,13B,13E,13F
Warner, Daniel C.	MA1000	13,10A,10B,12D,34
Waters, Joseph	CA4100	10,45,34,35C
Waters, Renee	MO1550	13,10,66A,34,11
Watson, Scott	PA2800	34
Watts, Christopher M.	NY3550	10B,34,34D,34H,10
Weaver, Brent	TN0650	36,37,34,13
Weaver, Brent	OR0250	10,61,13,34,36
Weaver, Molly A.	WV0750	32,32E,32G,34
Weber, Stephen	OK1400	66A,34,66C,66D
Wegner, Rob	AZ0490	34,35A,35C
Weinberg, Gil	GA0900	34
Weise, Christopher	NC1000	13,10,34,35
Wells, Thomas H.	OH1850	10,45,34
Welstead, Jon	WI0825	10,13,34,43,45
Wenninger, Karl	NY2660	34
Werkema, Jason R.	MI0750	70,13,29,34
Weston, Craig A.	KS0650	10A,10B,13,34
Wetzel, David B.	PA2150	64C,35,34
Weymouth, Daniel	NY3790	13,10,45,34
Wheaton, Dana	CA3350	37,63C,34,53
Wheeler, George	CA1520	34,45
Whisler, Bruce Allen	SC0400	29,A,41,35,34
White, Michael	AG0300	34
White, Timothy J.	CA1560	34,35
Wieland, William	SD0400	13,66D,66A,34,10
Wiemann, Beth	ME0440	10F,64C,34,10A,13D
Wilder, Matt	TN1850	34
Willette, Andrew	OR0750	34
Willey, Robert K.	LA0760	13,34,35,10B,45
William, Jacob	MA2020	29A,34
Williams, J. Kent	NC2430	13,34
Williams, Jeff	MA0260	34,35C
Williams, Mark D.	CA2440	13,36,61,38,34
Williams, Milton H.	CA4625	11,61,29,34
Willman, Fred	MO1830	32,34
Wilsey, Darren	CA2390	34
Wilson, Edward	AG0650	34,35
Wilson, Eric	TN1600	13,34,10
Wilt, Kevin	MI1260	10A,10C,10F,34
Windeyer, Richard	AG0600	34
Wingate, Mark	FL0850	10,34
Winkler, Todd	RI0050	10,45,34
Wittgraf, Michael A.	ND0500	10,13,34,10A,10B
Wolek, Nathan	FL1750	34,11,45
Wolfe, Jeffrey L.	WV0400	34,29A,47
Wolter, Bill	CA1560	34,35
Wood, Dan	NY3770	34,35C,35D,35G
Wood, Robert	AG0500	32C,34,12F,12,12C
Wood, Stanley D.	OH1600	32,36,66D,13C,34
Woods, Bret	AL1050	14C,20,34
Woodworth, Jessica A.	MO0500	11,34,13,66A
Worth, Mike	PA3330	10,34
Woszczyk, Wieslaw	AI0150	34,35G
Wright, Geoffrey	MD0400	10,34
Wright, Geoffrey	MD0650	45,34,10B
Wright, Maurice W.	PA3250	10,34
Wright, Robert	VA1000	34,35A,35C,35D,35G
Wurzbach, George	NJ0760	34,35
Wyatt, Scott A.	IL3300	13,10,34,45
Wyner, Jonathan	MA0260	34,35C,35G
Yannelli, John A.	NY3560	13,41,45,54,34
Yerkins, Gary	IL0720	34
Yonchak, Michael	OH2050	34,37,32E,29,46
York, Kevin	ID0100	37,47,34,32E
Young, Donald	CA3850	20H,34,35
Yuasa, Joji	CA5050	10,20D,35H,34,35C
Zabriskie, David	UT0400	34
Zacharias, Andrew	CA1520	34,45,70
Zager, Michael	FL0650	34,35
Zahler, Noel	NY2105	10,34
Zaki, Mark	NJ1100	10,34,10B,34D,10A
Zanter, Mark J.	WV0400	13,29,10,70,34
Zbyszynski, Michael F.	CA5353	34,43
Zwartjes, Martijn	CA0510	34

Multimedia

Name	Code	Numbers
Abbati, Joseph S.	FL1900	10B,34A,35C,45,34E
Armstrong, Stephen	AG0130	34A
Arnarson, Stefan Orn	NJ1100	34A,34D,35C,62,38
Arnold, Larry	NC2435	10,29A,13,34A,62D
Arrell, Christopher A.	MA0700	10,13,34A,34D
Ballard, Jack	OH1350	35,34A,34D,13L,34E
Bryden, Kristy	IA0850	13,10A,10F,34A,34H
Bukvich-Nichols, Svetlana	NY2750	34A
Buonamassa, John	CA0835	34A,34B,46
Carrell, Scott	AR0250	10A,13,34A,66A,66B
Clark, Colleen	MD0800	34A,34D
Cleland, Kent D.	OH0200	13,35E,34A
Cole, Robert	PA3650	34A,34B,49,63B,72
Crawford, Jeff D.	CA5350	35G,34A,34D
Davis, Greg	PA0500	34A,34D,35C,35D,35G
Deuson, Nicolas	GA0050	13,34A,34D,35G,70
Dickensheets, Janice	CO0950	12,34A,14,12B,12A
Drannon, Andrew	TN1200	34A,10
Eisenstein, Robert	MA1350	67,34A
Etlinger, David	OR0500	34A,34D,34E
Fei, James	CA2950	10B,34A
Foster, Rodney W.	NY4100	11,12,31A,34A,34F
Fried, Joshua	NY2750	34A,34H
Galvan, Gary	PA1830	12,70,29A,34A
Garcia, Orlando Jacinto	FL0700	10,34A
Gendelman, Martin	GA0950	10,13,70,34A
Gionfriddo, Mark	MA1350	66A,47,34A
Greher, Gena R.	MA2030	32,32H,34A
Griffin, J. Chris	NY2750	34A
Haley, Timothy R.	NC2210	11,13A,46,34C,34A
Harbach, Barbara	MO1830	66G,67F,15,66H,34A
Hayes, Beth Tura	LA0800	34A,34B,32,11
Headlam, David	NY1100	13F,13G,13L,34A,34B
Howard, Beverly A.	CA0450	13,34A,66G,66A,66H
Hulen, Peter Lucas	IN1850	13,10,34,34A,41
Hyland, Greg	AG0130	34A
Jones, Lloyd	AL1250	64,37,47,32E,34A
Lee, Damon Thomas	NE0600	10A,10B,10C,10F,34A
Leider, Colby N.	FL1900	34A,35C,10B,34D,35G
Levinson, Ross	CA0830	35,34A,10C,10D
Lochstampfor, Mark L.	OH0350	13,10A,34A,34B,66A
Lopez, Thomas Handman	OH1700	10B,34,10,34A
May, Andrew D.	TX3420	10A,10B,10F,34A,34D
McManus, Edward	OR0350	63B,34A,35C,35G,13A
Meng, Chuiyuan	IN0907	34A,66A,34G
Mercer, Christopher A.	IL2250	34A,34D
Michael, Louis	IL1500	29,66A,13,11,34A
Milam, Timothy A.	FL0100	34A,34B,34D,34E
Miller, R J	CO0550	34A
Montague, Eugene	DC0100	13,34A
Murphy, Joseph M.	PA2150	48,64E,34A
Newsome, Leigh	NY2750	34A
Nichols, Edward	MD0800	65A,65B,11,34A,34B
Nozny, Brian	ND0100	13,10A,10F,34A,34B
Pirkle, William C.	FL1900	34A,34D,34G,35C,35G
Roditski, William	PA2200	34A,35G
Rush, Stephen J.	MI2100	52,34A
Ruthmann, Alex	MA2030	32,34A
Santos, Erik	MI2100	10,34A,45
Smialek, William	TX1300	34A,34B,35A,35B
Spann, Joseph	AL0890	11,13,70,34A,34D
Starnes, Timothy J.	NY2750	34A,34D
Stuart, David H.	IA0850	63D,42,34A,34C,11
Stuck, Les	CA2950	10B,34A,13G,35C,10C
Tapia, Doug	CO0625	34,34A,34D,34B
Thomas, Steve	OH0350	34A,34B,34D,35D
Thomas, Susan R.	GA2100	11,12,14,20H,34A
Ueno, Ken	CA5000	10,13,34A,34D
Walker, Richard L.	IN0907	65,35,34A,50,37
Welbourne, Todd G.	WI0815	66A,34A,34D,43
Wight, Steve	CA0830	35,34A,10C,10D,10F
Wilson, Matt	NY3725	34A,34B
Winters, Gregg	CT0800	34A,34B
Yen, Chianan	NY2750	32F,34A,34B,34H
Yoo, In-Sil	NY3550	10,13,34A
Zipay, Terry L.	PA3700	13,35B,34A,13E,11

Web-based Music Instruction

Name	Code	Numbers
Arenson, Michael	DE0150	13B,34B
Baker, Hill	CO0625	14C,20,65,34B
Banzi, Julia	OR0400	20,14C,34B,14,10E
Barbour, Cass	NY1800	34B,34E
Benson, Will	TN0300	11,13,34B,36,64
Berg Oram, Stephanie	CO0625	11,12A,61,34B
Bigelow, Ira	CO0625	11,34B
Biser, Larry	MI0300	34B,12A,40,66G
Brown, Debra	KS0570	11,34B
Buonamassa, John	CA0835	34A,34B,46
Cee, Vincent	AK0150	32,29,38,34B,11
Cienniwa, Paul D.	MA2020	12A,12,11,34B
Cole, Robert	PA3650	34A,34B,49,63B,72

Index by Area of Teaching Interest

Name	Code	Areas
Dale, Karen M.	TN0300	11,34B,36,54,61
Dean, Brandon	MN0750	36,13,20,32D,34B
Dorris, Jennifer	CO0625	11,34B
Dubnov, Shlomo	CA5050	34,34B
Engberg, Kristina L.	IL2350	66D,11,13,34B
Erickson, Gary	IL1050	34B,10A,13G,31A,35D
Franklin, Janice L.	TX1725	11,66,54,34B
Gibson, Joice Waterhouse	CO0550	34B,34C,12A,12C,13A
Girton, Irene	CA3300	13,34B,34G
Groves, Matthew	OH0350	34B
Haerle, Dan	TX3420	66A,34B,29
Harder, Matthew D.	WV0600	65,34B,34D,10A,10B
Hayes, Beth Tura	LA0800	34A,34B,32,11
Headlam, David	NY1100	13F,13G,13L,34A,34B
Johnson, Charles	CA5350	34B
Kaurin-Karaca, Natasa	OK0800	66D,13C,11,34B
Keast, Dan A.	TX3527	32,34B,34F,32G,32C
Koblyakov, Lev	IL2350	13,12A,34B
Koontz, Jason	KY0550	50,65,14,34B
Lindsey, Roberta	IN0907	11,13A,34C,34B,14A
Lochstampfor, Mark L.	OH0350	13,10A,34A,34B,66A
Lofthouse, Charity	NY1550	13,34B,34F,15,31A
Lovallo, Lee T.	CA3258	11,34B,67F,12A
Lupu, Virgil I.	OH2140	62A,41,12A,11,34B
Martin, John	KY1550	70,11,34B,34G,41
Matthews, Mark	FL1650	10B,13A,34B,35A,70
McCord, Larry	TX0910	11,13B,14C,34B,66A
Milam, Timothy A.	FL0100	34A,34B,34D,34E
Millar, Cameron	MD0300	13A,34B,35C,13C,34D
Moulton, William	VT0300	13A,29C,33,34B,35A
Mudry, Karen	PA0650	34B
Nichols, Edward	MD0800	65A,65B,11,34A,34B
Nozny, Brian	ND0100	13,10A,10F,34A,34B
Porter, Mark	MO0400	34B
Roubal, Peter	IL2350	13,10,34B,47
Royal, Jacquelyn A.	TN0300	11,13,16,34B
Schirmer, Timothy	IL2350	13,10,34B,54
Schuler, Nico S.	TX3175	13,12C,34B,13F
Shabani, Afrim	IL2510	11,10,13,34B,13C
Sink, Damon W.	NC2600	10,13,34,34B,13I
Smialek, William	TX1300	34A,34B,35A,35B
Soto-Medina, Victor	TX1725	11,13,66,34B
Tam, TinShi	IA0850	69,66G,11,34B,66D
Tapia, Doug	CO0625	34,34A,34D,34B
Taylor, Mitchell	IL1500	20,61,34B
Thomas, Steve	OH0350	34A,34B,34D,35D
Torres, Gregory J.	LA0450	60B,11,37,34B,32B
Tranquilino, Armando	FL0700	13A,13B,13C,34B,12A
Villani, A. David	PA2710	34B,35G,29A
Wilson, Matt	NY3725	34A,34B
Winters, Gregg	CT0800	34A,34B
Worley, Dan	KY0450	70,10A,10B,10C,34B
Yen, Chianan	NY2750	32F,34A,34B,34H

Distance Learning

Name	Code	Areas
Abel, Sean	CA1300	13B,13C,20G,29A,34C
Benoist, Debbie	TX2310	11,13A,34C,65,66
Bodden, Bruce	WA0250	64A,34C
Carpenter, Tina	TX3750	64D,13,11,34C
Castles, JoAnn	AL1450	16,34C
Cornejo, Robert Joseph	CA5510	13,11,34C,10,12A
Cox, Patricia J.	AR0250	11,32,34C,38,62B
Cresci, Jonathan	MD0550	63A,34D,13C,34C,14C
Crone, Elizabeth	VA1700	64A,34C
DeLaRosa, Lou	CA5510	13A,13C,12A,11,34C
Donovick, Jeffery	FL1650	66D,13A,13B,13C,34C
Dotson, Ronald	CA5510	11,34C,66D,14C,12A
DuBois, Ted	TX3750	11,12A,34C
Ferrara, Lawrence	CA1020	11,70,34C
Fletcher, Marylynn L.	TX3600	34C,36,11,66A,12A
Fortney, Julie T.	NC1250	11,61,34C
Gibson, Joice Waterhouse	CO0550	34B,34C,12A,12C,13A
Gottlieb, Daniel	FL1950	65,46,34C
Groff, Dale	WA0480	34D,34G,34C,34F,29B
Haley, Timothy R.	NC2210	11,13A,46,34C,34A
Hilton, Suzanne	MD0550	11,13A,34C
Hosmer, Christopher D.	AL0500	63B,34C
Kairies, Joy E.	TX0550	64A,34C,11,48
Late, Eric	TX2295	47,62D,11,34C
Laux, Charles	GA1150	32E,34C,38,62,32C
Lehrer, Scott	VT0050	34C,35D,35G
Lindsey, Roberta	IN0907	11,13A,34C,34B,14A
Mangels, Jeffrey W.	MD0550	13A,34C,11,13C,34D
Marston, Karen L.	TX2295	37,63C,11,13A,34C
Mullins, Debra	IN0907	66A,34C
Parcell, John	OH2120	13,66A,11,29,34C
Rader, Jana Elam	TX2310	11,12A,34C,61
Rush, Toby	OH2250	13,34C
Sanchez, Rey	FL1900	10D,34C,35A,20G,43
Shepard, Brian K.	CA5300	34,10,13,34C,65
Simonson, Donald R.	IA0850	39,61,13L,34C,34D
Smith, Stewart	AC0100	63D,34C
Strunk, Michael	WA0300	20,34C
Stuart, David H.	IA0850	63D,42,34A,34C,11
Vasconcellos, Renato	KY1500	20H,34C
Walker, Elizabeth	KS0750	39,61,54,35,34C
Walls, Kimberly C.	AL0200	32,34C,32F,32G
Ware, David N.	MS0350	63A,34C,47,11,13B

Digital Audio

Name	Code	Areas
Aguilar, Gustavo	ME0410	53,34D
Aldrich, Mark L.	MA1650	37,32E,32F,34D,60B
Allen, Travis	UT0050	34D
Alves, William	CA1050	12C,35C,34D
Anderson, Dennis W.	CA3350	34D
Anderson, James	MA1450	34D,35
Anderson, Robert	NY3250	11,34D,34H,35,13A
Arnason, Stefan Orn	NJ1100	34A,34D,35C,62,38
Arrell, Christopher A.	MA0700	10,13,34A,34D
Ballard, Jack	OH1350	35,34A,34D,13L,34E
Barata, Antonio G.	CA0600	10,34D,35D,35G
Barnes, Rich	IL0720	34D
Baumgarnder, Brad	KS0590	34D,32F,35C,35D
Beardslee, Tony	NE0460	35C,35D,35G,34D,34E
Bennett, Christopher	FL1900	34D,34G,34H
Benson, Robert	IA0300	34D,35G
Bissell, Paul	TX0550	10B,34D,34E,35C,35D
Borja, Eric	IL0720	34D
Bowen, William	NY2750	34D,35G
Bowers, Walt M.	OK1450	34D
Brazofsky, Matthew	NY2500	34D
Brown, Robert	TX2930	46,35C,34D
Burger, Larry	WY0050	34D
Burgess, Scott	MI0400	34D
Burgess, William	SC0050	34D,35G
Campbell, Todd A.	NC0700	35G,34D,35D,65,35C
Carney, David	CA4100	34D,35C,35G,72
Chandra, Arun	WA0350	10A,10B,43,34D,11
Chittum, John	KS0590	34D,32F,35C,35D
Clark, Colleen	MD0800	34A,34D
Clark, Jesse	PA0050	11,34D
Cohen, Alan	NJ0950	34D,35G
Coobatis, Christy	CA2960	35,34D
Corinthian, Randy	FL0200	34D,37
Cornicello, Anthony	CT0150	10,34,13,34D,13F
Coulas, Ben	AB0040	34,35D,35G,34D
Crawford, Jeff D.	CA5350	35G,34A,34D
Crawford, Langdon C.	NY2750	34D,34G
Cresci, Jonathan	MD0550	63A,34D,13C,34C,14C
Cutting, W. Scott	MI1550	13,11,66A,66D,34D
Czink, Andrew	AB0040	35D,35G,34D
Davis, Chris	PA2300	34D
Davis, Greg	PA0500	34A,34D,35C,35D,35G
Decker, Van A.	CA2300	11,13A,34D,47,10A
Deuson, Nicolas	GA0050	13,34A,34D,35G,70
Doczi, Tom F.	NY2750	34D,35G
Dozoretz, Brian	NY1800	35C,34D
Drown, Steve	ME0340	35G,34D
Duke, Richard	UT0050	34D
Edwards, Timothy D.	IL0720	13,34D
Elser, Albert Christian	SC1000	61,12A,34D,39
Etlinger, David	OR0500	34A,34D,34E
Feindell, S.	AB0040	35D,35G,34D
Felice, Frank	IN0250	10,10B,10D,34D,13D
Fishell, John C.	IN0150	13L,34D
Fisher, Daniel	IN0905	34D
Forehan, Jeff	CA5510	10B,13A,34D,35G,35D
Franklin, Virgil	IN1800	34D,13A,34
Franks, Rebecca	NY4300	29A,29B,46,47,34D
Freeze, Tracy	KS0300	65,50,20,34D
Gammon, Richard	KS0590	32F,34D
Geluso, Paul	NY2750	34D,35G
Gleason, Stephen	NY1275	10D,12A,13B,14C,34D
Gluck, Robert J.	NY3700	10B,34D,31B,34,45
Gorrie, Gregg	AB0040	34D
Gottlieb, David	NJ0750	10,13A,13B,34D,64E
Grasse, Jonathan B.	CA0805	34D,13,20,14C,10
Groff, Dale	WA0480	34D,34G,34C,34F,29B
Haek, Jonathan	OR0500	34D,10A,13,66A
Haffley, Robin L.	PA1830	11,13A,29A,34D,14C
Hansen, Steven	TX0550	34D
Harder, Matthew D.	WV0600	65,34B,34D,10A,10B
Harrison, Thomas	FL1000	34D,35,35A,35B,35F
Hartman, Tony	AZ0470	35,34D
Hegarty, James	IL2400	10A,29A,34D,47,13A
Heldt, Tim	MI0850	34D,35D,35G
Hemmel, Ronald A.	NJ1350	13,10,34D,13L
Hirsch, Scott	NY2750	34D
Hodgson, Ken	MN1620	36,61,34D,11,60A
Homan, Jim W.	NE0610	34D
Houchins, Andrew	KS0300	13,10,34D
Houlihan, Mickey	CO0560	34D,35G
Jaskowiak, Jeffrey	IL3370	34H,34D,34G
Johnson, Aaron E.	MO1250	10A,34D,13,70
Johnson, Richard	KS0590	13G,32F,34D,35C,35D
Jones, Peter	WA0750	34D
Karathanasis, Konstantinos	OK1350	34D,10A,10,35C,35G
Kasun, Scott	AZ0480	34D
Kelly, Alex	CA1150	34D
Kikta, Thomas J.	PA1050	70,34D,35C
Klee, David A.	IA0150	10C,29A,34D,35A,47
Krause, Stephen	TX3530	34D,34E
Krieger, Ulrich	CA0510	10,34D,12A,45,64E
Kubis, Jon-Michael	CA2050	34D
Lane, Brandie	NY2750	34D
Langer, Kenneth P.	MA1500	10A,10B,13,34D,11
Laranja, Ricardo	IN0907	34D,35C
Last, Julie	VT0050	34D,35D,35G
Lawing, William D.	NC0550	29,47,63A,34D,49
Leider, Colby N.	FL1900	34A,35C,10B,34D,35G
Lewis, Jeremy	IN1800	34D,34H
Lindroth, Scott A.	NC0600	13,34D,34H,10A,10B
Lippstrew, Lee	CO0600	46,34D,35G,35A
Madden, Andrew	NY2750	34D
Makela, Steven L.	MN0600	10A,10B,13,10,34D
Mangels, Jeffrey W.	MD0550	13A,34C,11,13C,34D
Mariasy, David	OH2300	35C,34D
Mason, Charles Norman	FL1900	10A,10B,10F,34D
Matheson, Bryan	CA0900	34D,35
May, Andrew D.	TX3420	10A,10B,10F,34A,34D
McDonald, Susan M.	PA1830	10A,10B,12A,15,34D
McKenney, W. Thomas	MO1800	13,10,34D
McKinney, Matthew	AL1200	34D,34H,35C,35G
McLowry, Sean	NY0700	34D,35G,34E,34F,34H
McNair, Jonathan B.	TN1700	10A,34D,13,10,34
McNally, Blair	AG0070	32F,34D,63D
McNally, Kirk	AB0150	10B,34D,34E,35C,35D
Mehrmann, Dan	IL2970	34D,35H
Mercer, Christopher A.	IL2250	34A,34D
Milam, Timothy A.	FL0100	34A,34B,34D,34E
Millar, Cameron	MD0300	13A,34B,35C,13C,34D
Miller, Robert F.	CT0600	34,34D
Miller, Tim	NE0460	35C,35D,35G,34D,34E
Miller-Brown, Donna	KS0590	34D,32F,35C,35D
Mitschell, P. Bryan	OK1330	34D
Molberg, Keith	AJ0030	66A,34D,13,66C,13A
Moore, Britt	VT0300	13L,34D,35,61,34E
Moorman, Joyce E.	NY0270	11,13,20A,34D,66
Moreland, Michael	KS0570	10A,10B,34D
Morris, Brian	MI0850	70,13,34D
Mosher, Jimm	NC0350	35D,35G,34D
Newton, Jon	OR0450	34D
Olvera, Victor	KS0570	10B,34D
Parker, Val	GA0490	10,11,13A,34D,29A
Pierce, Bradley	MA0150	34D,35D,35G
Pirkle, William C.	FL1900	34A,34D,34G,35C,35G
Pixton, Clayton	KS0590	34D,32F,35C,35D
Pounds, Michael S.	IN0150	10,34D,13,45,34
Pras, Amandine	NY2750	34D
Ray, James	FL1550	66D,34D,60A,35C
Reba, Christopher H.	CT0700	34D,10B,35G,62D,13
Reynolds, Steve	LA0800	34D,35C,35D,35G
Rigler, Jane	CO0810	64A,10B,34D,10
Rivers, Joseph L.	OK1450	13,10A,10C,34D,34E
Robertson, Ben	WA0250	10B,45,35G,34D
Rosfeld, Ken	OK1200	34D,34E,35A,35C,35D
Rubinstein, Mark	OH1850	35C,35D,34D,35G
Rutkowski, Chris	IN0905	13,34D
Scarano, Robert	CA3265	34D,35G,70
Schaerrer, Bart	UT0050	34D
Schermerhorn, David	NC1450	34D,34E,35C
Schleeter, Bob	CA1150	20G,29A,34D

Name	Code	Areas
Schmidt, David	AZ0350	47,53,35D,34D
Scholwin, Richard M.	NE0590	35C,35G,34D
Schulz, Mark Alan	OH1350	34D,35G,35D,62C,29B
Scull, Erik	IN0907	34D
Seagrave, Charles	CA3250	35C,34D
Shadley, Jeffrey	OK1450	34D,35C
Shpachenko, Nadia	CA0630	66A,66C,66B,66,34D
Siegel, Dan	CA2960	35C,35D,34D,35G
Silverman, Alan	NY2750	34D
Simonson, Donald R.	IA0850	39,61,13L,34C,34D
Smith, Curtis F.	CO0810	13,34D,36,66A
Snyder, Jeffrey S.	PA1900	35,34D,10B,32F,10D
Sorce, Richard P.	NJ0950	10D,13,34D
Spann, Joseph	AL0890	11,13,70,34A,34D
Starnes, Timothy J.	NY2750	34A,34D
Stewart, D. Andrew	AA0200	34D,10B,45,35A
Stravato, James	RI0101	34D
Suchy, John	MD0175	35C,34D
Tapia, Doug	CO0625	34,34A,34D,34B
Taylor, Jeffrey B.	WI0450	34D,35A,35D,35C
Testa, Michael	MA1650	34,34D
Thomas, Steve	OH0350	34A,34B,34D,35D
Tomassetti, Benjamin	VA0500	35G,10B,34D,35C,64E
Tucker, Allan	NY2750	34D
Turner, Patrick	VA1700	11,29,34D,34H,35C
Ueno, Ken	CA5000	10,13,34A,34D
Valera, Philip	NC0100	34D,35G,35C,35D,13L
Van Dijk, G. Hage	CA4400	34D
Vander Gheynst, John R.	IN0907	29A,10A,63,34D,35A
VanWick, Brad	KS0590	34D,32F,35C,35D
Vasallo, Nicholas R.	CA0807	34D,13A
Velazquez, Ileana Perez	MA2250	10,13,34D
VonBerg, Craig	CA1850	34D
Wallace, Roy	MI0850	34D
Walters, Andrew B.	PA2150	13,34D
Watkinson, Christopher L.	ME0200	13L,34D,35D,35G
Watts, Christopher M.	NY3550	10B,34,34D,34H,10
Weddle, Jamison	AZ0470	35,34D
Welbourne, Todd G.	WI0815	66A,34A,34D,43
White, Christopher T.	KY1500	12A,34D
Winer, Arthur H.	CA0630	10D,34D,35G,35,10C
Winslow, Robert J.	FL0930	66A,46,13,34D,11
Wolzinger, Renah	CA2050	34D
Wonneberger, Alan A.	MD1000	34D
Young, Jeff	AB0040	34D,35D,35E,35F,35G
Zaki, Mark	NJ1100	10,34,10B,34D,10A

Digital Video

Name	Code	Areas
Abbati, Joseph S.	FL1900	10B,34A,35C,45,34E
Ballard, Jack	OH1350	35,34,34A,34D,13L,34E
Barbour, Cass	NY1800	34B,34E
Beardslee, Tony	NE0460	35C,35D,35A,34D,34E
Bissell, Paul	TX0550	10B,34D,34E,35C,35D
Etlinger, David	OR0500	34A,34D,34E
Fritz, Matthew P.	PA1250	36,60A,34,34E,60
Gabour, James	LA0300	34E
Krause, Stephen	TX3530	34D,34E
McLowry, Sean	NY0700	34D,35G,34E,34F,34H
McNally, Kirk	AB0150	10B,34D,34E,35C,35D
Milam, Timothy A.	FL0100	34A,34B,34D,34E
Miller, Tim	NE0460	35C,35D,35G,34D,34E
Moore, Britt	VT0300	13L,34D,35,61,34E
Rivers, Joseph L.	OK1450	13,10A,10C,34D,34E
Rosfeld, Ken	OK1200	34D,34E,35A,35C,35D
Schermerhorn, David	NC1450	34D,34E,35C
Skogstoe, John	NE0460	35H,34E
Wimberly, Larry	MS0150	11,13A,31A,34E,46

Curriculum and Standards

Name	Code	Areas
Alsobrook, Joseph	MO0650	10F,32E,37,34F,35A
Foster, Rodney W.	NY4100	11,12,31A,34A,34F
Groff, Dale	WA0480	34D,34G,34C,34F,29B
Keast, Dan A.	TX3527	32,34B,34F,32G,32C
Lofthouse, Charity	NY1550	13,34B,34F,15,31A
McKinley, Thomas L.	FL1125	13,10A,12A,34F
McLowry, Sean	NY0700	34D,35G,34E,34F,34H
Wynn, Julie	IN0907	34F,66A,66B

Software Development

Name	Code	Areas
Bennett, Christopher	FL1900	34D,34G,34H
Christensen, Carl J.	CA2150	13,38,37,34G,13A
Crawford, Langdon C.	NY2750	34D,34G
Didkovsky, Nick	NY2750	34G
Falvey, Joseph	VA0150	63B,37,34G,32E,49
Girton, Irene	CA3300	13,34B,34G
Groff, Dale	WA0480	34D,34G,34C,34F,29B
Jaskowiak, Jeffrey	IL3370	34H,34D,34G
Martin, John	KY1550	70,11,34B,34G,41
McCormick, Scott	MA0260	29B,32F,32H,20G,34G
Meng, Chuiyuan	IN0907	34A,66A,34G
Naphtali, Dafna L.	NY2750	34G,34H
Pirkle, William C.	FL1900	34,34D,34G,35C,35G
Wagner, Chad A.	NY2750	34G
Wojcik, Leszek M.	NY2750	34G

New Media

Name	Code	Areas
Anderson, Robert	NY3250	11,34D,34H,35,13A
Bennett, Christopher	FL1900	34D,34G,34H
Bryden, Kristy	IA0850	13,10A,10F,34A,34H
Century, Michael	NY3300	12,13,43,34H,66A
Fried, Joshua	NY2750	34A,34H
Jaskowiak, Jeffrey	IL3370	34H,34D,34G
Lerner, Neil	NC0550	11,12,34H,66H
Lewis, George E.	NY0750	10A,10B,12E,29E,34H
Lewis, Jeremy	IN1800	34D,34H
Lindroth, Scott A.	NC0600	13,34D,34H,10A,10B
Louchouarn, Bruno E.	CA3300	10C,34H
McAllister, Margaret	MA0260	10,13,34H,10A,34
McKinney, Matthew	AL1200	34D,34H,35C,35G
McLowry, Sean	NY0700	34D,35G,34E,34F,34H
Moseley, Roger S.	NY0900	12,13,14D,34H
Naphtali, Dafna L.	NY2750	34G,34H
Nixon, Janis	AG0130	34H
Riley, Raymond G.	MI0150	66A,13,34,34H
Roland, Tomm	NE0610	65,20,34H,50
Schindler, Allan	NY1100	10A,10B,10C,34H
Turner, Patrick	VA1700	11,29,34D,34H,35C
Twombly, Kristian	MN1300	10B,34H,12B,10,11
Watts, Christopher M.	NY3550	10B,34,34D,34H,10
Yen, Chianan	NY2750	32F,34A,34B,34H

Music Business and Industry (All Areas)

Name	Code	Areas
Abrams, Ira	NC0050	35,35A,35E
Aczon, Michael	CA1560	35
Ainger, Marc	OH1850	10,34,35
Alexander, Joseph	CA0800	35
Alper, Garth	LA0760	66A,29,35
Altstatt, Hamilton	SC0400	34,35
Ancona, Ted	CA5300	35
Anderson, Carl	IL0400	35
Anderson, James	MA1450	34D,35
Anderson, Robert	NY3250	11,34D,34H,35,13A
Arndt, Kevin	WI1150	35
Artimisi, Tony	NC2700	35,65
Auman, Kevin	NC1450	34,35
Austin, Michael	MO0850	34,35C,13,35,10
Ballard, Jack	OH1350	35,34A,34D,13L,34E
Bargfrede, Allen	MA0260	35
Barstow, Robert S.	NY3765	12A,36,16,35
Bauman, Marcia	CA4700	10,14C,34,35
Beach, Douglas	IL0850	47,53,71,29,35
Beatty, David	CA0250	47,49,35,63C
Bendich, Jon	CA1560	35
Berry, S. David	SC0650	10,13,34,35,12
Bierman, Benjamin	NY0630	63,4,10,13,34,35
Biersach, Bill	CA5300	35
Black, Cary	WA0350	62D,53,29,35,47
Blackley, Terrance J.	CA1900	66D,46,35
Block-Schwenk, Kevin	MA0260	35
Boardman, Christopher	FL1900	10C,35
Boon, Rolf J.	AA0200	13,34,10,35
Boothe, Randall W.	UT0050	61,54,20G,35
Bowers, Michael	NC0750	34,35
Boyer, Peter	CA1050	10,60,35
Brass, Kenneth	MA0260	35
Breon, Timothy	PA2100	34,35,62D,70
Briles, Travis	IL1050	35
Britt, Carol H.	NY3780	35
Brooks, Debbie	TX3420	35
Broome, Dan	AG0130	35
Brown, J. F. Mark	AL0831	61,35,36,11
Brown, Philip	IL2900	62D,29,35
Bullock, Robert	AL1050	34,35
Burchard, Richard	KY0250	10,13,20,34,35
Burdick, David H.	IL1750	10,13,34,70,35
Cable, Howard	AA0200	10,11,35,47,60
Carlson, Robert A.	CA0200	35
Carrabre, T. Patrick	AC0050	13,10,43,20G,35
Casal, David Plans	NH0100	10B,10F,34,13,35
Casey, Michael	NH0100	10B,10F,34,13,35
Cavera, Chris S.	OH2140	34,35,13,70,10
Chang, Melody Jun Yao	CO0100	35,66A,13
Cho, Peter	LA0080	13,34,35,47,66A
Christensen, Janielle	UT0050	12A,36,39,54,35
Christopher, Casey R.	ID0150	11,29B,34,35,37
Chun, Eric	CA0150	35
Clancy, Gary	ME0340	47,70,53,35
Cole, Daniel	CA3500	10D,35
Cole, Steven	MN1625	35
Collins, Christopher	MI2200	47,64E,29A,35
Coobatis, Christy	CA2960	35,34D
Cottrell, David	VA0600	35
Crockett, C. Edgar	IL0300	13,10,47,35,63A
Cronk, Daniel L.	MI0650	34,35
Crowe, Don R.	SD0550	32,63C,72,35
Cunningham, Steve M.	CA5300	35
Davis, Gregory	LA0300	35
Davis, Mark J.	LA0300	35
Dawson, Robert B.	CA1700	13A,35,13,53
De Ritis, Anthony	MA1450	35,62B,34,45
Dean, Curtis	NC1150	35,54
Deardorf, Chuck	WA0200	62D,53,29,35
Deaville, James	AG0100	12,29,35
Dempsey, Harry J.	MI0650	11,35
Derechailo, Melissa	NE0700	63B,11,35
Deutsch, Herbert A.	NY1600	13,10,45,29A,35
Devonish, Jay	AG0130	35
Di Gioia, Robert	AG0130	35
Dicciani, Marc	PA3330	65,35,50
DiCosimo, William J.	NY4150	35,66A
Dillon, Nathan	CA0200	35,14C
Dixon, Joan DeVee	MD0350	66,31A,35
Dixon, Rich	UT0190	70,47,34,35
Dorritie, Frank	CA2775	20G,35,34
Douthit, Pat	NC1600	35
DuBray, Terry E.	NY3550	35
Duffy, Patrick	AG0130	35
Dunbar, Geoffrey	CA3500	35
Dunlap, Phillip	MO1950	35,66A
Dunn, Christopher	MS0570	11,35,70
Dunne, Matthew R.	TX3530	70,29,47,35
Echard, William	AG0100	12,20,29,34,35
Eigenfeldt, Arne	AB0080	10,45,34,35,12F
Engberg, Michael	CO0100	13,70,41,35,47
Ennis, Sue	WA0860	35,10C
Erickson, Christian	WY0150	10,11,13,34,35
Esleck, David	VA1800	11,66A,29,34,35
Esler, Robert	AZ0350	34,35
Espar, Michael	NY0646	32F,34,35
Estrada, Harvey	CA1400	35
Fabrizio, Louis	MA0260	35
Fallon, Kelly	IN0800	35,67,71,72
Farrell, Frankie	CA2420	34,35
Faulcner, James	OK1350	13,10,34,35
Fenwick, Jerry	CA4000	11,66A,54,29,35
Ferre, Stephen G.	NY4150	13,35
Fialkov, Jay	MA0260	35
Fink, Michael Jon	CA0510	12A,12,35,10
Fish, David Lee	NC0350	35,14,34,20C,29
Flanagan, Edward	PA3250	29,35
Flohil, Richard	AG0130	35
Flores, Carlos	MI0250	13,10,35,34,10F
Flynn Cintron, Jorge A.	PR0115	35
Ford, Andrew	CA1000	35,62D
Frazier, Bruce H.	NC2600	10C,10F,35
Frengel, Mike	MA1450	10B,34,35
Fried, Joe	AG0130	35
Frohrip, Kenton R.	MN1300	29A,35,63A
Fuller, Karen	FL0850	35
Gaber, Brian	AG0130	47,35
Gagnon, Paul	AG0130	35
Gallo, Joseph	CA1520	35,34,66A,29,53
Garcia, Antonio	VA1600	29,47,63C,35,46
Garver, Andrew	CA5300	35
George, Kevin	LA0080	11,13,34,35
Glago, Mikeal	VA0600	35
Glancey, Gregory T.	CA5355	10F,13,34,35
Goldstein, Mark	CA5300	35

Index by Area of Teaching Interest

Name	Code	Areas
Gorham, Linda J.	MA0260	35
Gotfrit, Martin	AB0080	10,45,34,35,12F
Gregg, Gary	CA0200	63C,29,35
Griffin, Buddy	WV0350	62,34,35
Gruner, Greg	AL1300	37,63D,60B,32E,35
Gustafson, Steve	NY1850	35
Guthrie, Karl	NJ1400	35
Gutierrez, Charles	CA5300	35
Haddad, Steve	TX3520	63D,34,35
Haefner, Dale F.	MN1000	66D,35
Hamilton, Peter	AG0130	35
Harrington, E. Michael	MA0260	35,10,20,14
Harris, John	AG0130	35
Harrison, Thomas	FL1000	34D,35,35A,35B,35F
Hartman, Tony	AZ0470	35,34D
Harvey, Kathryn	NY4150	35
Haskell, Jeffrey R.	AZ0500	47,46,29,35
Hatschek, Keith N.	CA5350	35
Hayes, Micah	TX3500	34,35
Hays, Timothy O.	IL0850	13,62D,45,34,35
Head, Russell	KS0750	10B,10D,34,35,45
Hebert, Joseph G.	LA0300	32,37,46,35
Henderson, Kate	AG0130	35
Herbeck, Tina	CA0200	35,61
Herman, Matthew	PA2400	10,11,13,34,35
Hest, Jeff	NY3250	11,29,35,37,47
Hinckley, Edwin	UT0190	34,35
Hodgins, Glenn	AG0400	35
Holland, Deborah	CA0830	35,10D
Holroyd, Megan Calgren	MN0050	11,35
Howard-Spink, Sam J.	NY2750	35
Howell, John	VA1700	36,67,35,55
Hubbard, Gary	AG0130	35
Hussain, Azra	AG0130	35
Huus, Brett	MN1400	35
Jackson, Douglas A.	NC0700	63A,35
Jackson, Ernie	NY3250	34,35,70
Jackson, Kymberly	CA4625	14C,29,35
James, Robert R.	KY0550	35,34
Janik, Liz	AG0130	35
Janikian, Leon C.	MA1450	35,34,64C
Jermance, Frank	CO0550	35
Jester, Jennifer	PA2350	35
Johnson, Alfred	NY0640	34,35
Johnson, Andrea	MA0260	35
Johnson, Keith	CA2975	10,20,34,35,13B
Jones, Hilton Kean	FL2000	10,35,13,45,66G
Jones, Steve	GA1050	35
Judson, Tohm	NC2700	10B,62D,70,34,35
Kamprath, Richard	CA1560	34,35
Kantar, Ned D.	MN0050	13C,35
Kearney, Joe	CA0200	13,70,35
Keepe, Michael L.	AZ0480	35,64E
Kellar, Stephanie	MA0260	35
Kellogg, John	MA0260	35
Kelly, Gary	NY0700	35,34,62D,43
Kelly, Kevin M.	NY2550	34,35
Kelly, Todd	IL0400	32,47,63A,35
Kerensky, Pam	MA0260	35
Kessler, Stan	MO0850	35A,35
King, Brian	CA5300	10,35H,35
Kirby, Wayne J.	NC2400	10,45,34,35,62D
Kleiman, Carey D.	FL0200	34,35A,64,35,32E
Koshinski, Eugene	MN1600	47,65,29,20G,35
Kozak, Brian	OH0750	12B,20G,29,35
Kozel, Paul	NY0550	10,45,35
Krugman, Murray	CT0700	35,34
Kuuskoski, Jonathan	MO1800	35
Lackman, Susan Cohn	FL1550	13,10,12A,35
LaCroix, John	CA0200	34,35
Lampl, Kenneth H.	NY1600	35,10,64E,34,11
Lange, Daniel	OR0010	12A,47,64,35
Large, Mike	AG0070	35
Laymon, Michael	IL1080	11,13,35,63C
Lecuyer, Stephane	AG0130	35
Leeds, Steve	NJ1400	35
Legname, Orlando	NY3765	13A,13,10,35
Lester, David T.	OH2140	70,35,45,42
Levinson, Ross	CA0830	35,34A,10C,10D
Lewis, Colin	AG0130	35
Lewis, Marcia	IN1750	61,35
Lockwood, Gayle	UT0050	39,61,54,20G,35
London, Robert	AZ0470	35,14E
Lopez, Kenneth	CA5300	35H,35
Loubriel, Luis E.	IL0275	11,13A,34,63,35
Lovely, Brian	OH0680	29,10C,10D,70,35
Lyons, Matthew	MD0650	35
Mager, Guillermo E.	CT0700	13,12A,34,35,32
Malito, Jim	AZ0490	35
Marcone, Stephen	NJ1400	35
Marschall, Ron	AZ0490	34,35
Martin, Christopher	NC1600	35
Martin, Jeffrey A.	AE0050	32,35
Martindale, Peggy Lee	CA0200	35,39
Mather, Bill	AG0130	35
Matheson, Bryan	CA0900	34D,35
Mattingly, Douglas	MD0060	13,29,35,70
McCluskey, Kevin	MA0260	35
McCully, Michael	CA0200	35,14C
McGee, Isaiah R.	SC0350	35,36,39,61,32D
McIlvery, Richard	CA5300	35
McLuhan, Eric	AG0130	35
Meitin, A. Richard	MN1000	35
Mercer, John	DC0150	35
Merkel, Steve	AL1195	35
Michael, Doug	CA1560	34,35
Middleton, Jonathan N.	WA0250	13,10,35C,34,35
Miglio, Joseph	MA0260	35
Minasian, Mark	HI0160	11,12A,29,34,35
Montalto, Richard Michael	MS0550	13,12A,35,10,13F
Moore, Britt	VT0300	13L,34D,35,61,34E
Moore, Catherine	NY2750	35
Muehleip, Marc	IA1450	35
Mulvey, Bob	MA0260	10,35
Munson, Chris	KY0550	35
Murciano, Raul	FL1900	35,20H,10C
Murphy, Daniel	CA5150	34,35,29
Murray, Mark S.	IN0100	29,63A,34,35
Neal, Mark	AL1450	65,47,34,35
Nelson, Mary Anne	NY0700	34,35
Nepkie, Janet	NY3765	13A,41,51,62C,35
Newton, Jack	NC0050	47,41,64C,72,35
Noah, Laura	AL1300	35,65
Notter, Tim	AG0130	35
Nottingham, Douglas	AZ0350	65,50,45,10B,35
O'Brien, John	MA0260	35
O'Malley, Sean	CA0630	35
Ouellette, Garry	NY2550	16,14C,72,34,35
Panethiere, Darrell	NY4150	35
Paoli, Kenneth N.	IL0630	13,10,11,35,34
Parliament, Roland	AG0130	35
Patton, Denise	TN0100	35
Paulson, John C.	MN1400	47,64,29,34,35
Peacock, Kenneth J.	NY2750	13,10,12,35,34
Perna, Dana	NY3000	11,35
Perry, Gail	CA5300	35
Pfenninger, Rik C.	NH0250	64E,29,35,32E,10B
Philp, David	NJ1400	35
Piechocinski, Theodore J.	IN0800	35
Pignato, Joseph M.	NY3765	35,34,10,13
Pollock, Heather	AG0130	35
Pontbriand, Roget	FL1450	45,46,35,10D,10C
Post, J. Brian	CA2250	34,35,13,10
Powell, Gary	TX3510	35
Proulx, Ron	AG0130	35
Quilico, David	AG0130	35
Radbill, Catherine Fitterman	NY2750	35
Ramsey, Guthrie P.	PA3350	12,35,20G,29,47
Riley, Edward	OH0755	34,35
Rivas, Anita	CA0800	35
Robinson, Curtis	IN0005	13,16,29,34,35
Robinson, Patrece	FL1750	35
Robinson, Stephanie	CA4000	35
Romersa, Henry J.	IL2900	35
Ronkin, Bruce	MA1450	64E,34,35
Roper, Bob	AG0130	35
Rorick, Michael	NY3725	35
Royal, Guericke	DC0150	29,35
Ruff, Willie H.	CT0850	35,10F,13
Rule, Charles	TN0700	11,47,66A,29,35
Ruoso-Loughlin, Alana	AG0130	35
Sabine, David	AA0032	35,13A,13C,37,65
Sage, Steve	CA1560	35,70
Salazar, Jason	MO0400	34,13,35,43,47
Salzenstein, Alan N.	IL0750	35
Sanchez, Scott	AL1195	35
Sanchez-Samper, Alejandro	FL0650	35
Savage, Steve	CA2775	35,34
Saxberg, Catherine	AG0130	35
Scafide, Anthony	NY3765	35,41,47
Schaefer, G. W. Sandy	NE0050	14C,46,65,29,35
Schaller, Thilo	AA0200	34,35
Schenkel, Steve	MO1950	12A,31,45,29,35
Schmidt, Fred	MA0260	10,35
Schmunk, Richard	CA5300	34,35
Schroepfer, Mark	MN1625	35
Schwartz, Andrew	NJ0825	35
Schweitzer, Kenneth	MD1100	20,29,34,35,11
Sernyk, Glenn	AG0130	35
Shanklin, Richard L.	OH2150	47,64E,29,35
Shannon, William	CA0900	13A,13B,34,63B,35
Shaw, George W.	CA2550	47,29,34,35
Sheehan, Dan	NJ0020	35,35G
Sherman, Steve	AA0080	32E,37,63A,46,35
Shiner, Richard	CA2775	35,34
Smalley, Jack	CA5300	35H,35
Smith, Anne-Marie	AG0130	35
Smith, Robert W.	AL1050	35,34
Snyder, Jeffrey S.	PA1900	35,34D,10B,32F,10D
Snyder, John	LA0300	35
Soderstrom, Erik	IL0750	35
Somerton, Clinton	AG0130	35
Spitz, Bruce	WA0860	66,34,35,13L
Steidel, Mark	CA1560	13,35,34
Stein, George	NY2750	35
Stein, Thomas A.	MA0260	35
Stenius, Karla	AZ0470	35
Stevens, John	WI0815	63D,60B,35,10,13
Sudol, Jacob David	FL0700	34,35,45
Summer, Stephen O.	TX3175	35,12A
Surmani, Andrew	CA0835	35
Suvada, Steven	IL1085	70,34,35
Syler, James	TX3530	20G,29,35,10
Tait, Alicia Cordoba	IL0275	20,12A,15,35,11
Talbott, Matthew	IL1750	35
Tallant, Audrey	IL2910	11,35
Tarrant, James	MO1550	36,60A,35,42,66A
Tate, Galen	CT0300	11,35
Taub, Paul	WA0200	41,64A,35
Taylor, Joseph	VA0600	35
Tetreault, Edward	MD0850	35
Theberge, Paul	AG0100	35,35H
Thompson, Bob	ME0340	47,70,53,35
Thompson, David	WI0400	13,11,14,66A,35
Thoms, Jonas	OH2500	13,13C,63B,35
Tini, Dennis J.	MI2200	60,36,29,35
Titus, Anthony	MN1625	35
Todorov, Jassen	CA4200	62A,35,11
Tolley, David	DE0050	10,34,35
Tomasello, Andrew	NY0250	11,12,14,29A,35
Topel, Spencer	NH0100	10B,10F,34,13,35
Towner, John	IL1085	34,35
Udell, Chester	OR1050	10,10B,11,34,35
Ulibarri, Fernando	FL0200	35,70,47
Unsworth, Arthur E.	NC0050	20G,35
Vandermeer, Aaron D.	NC2435	29,35,47
Wagman, Marcy R.	PA1000	35
Wagner, David O.	MI1260	12A,13B,13C,35,66G
Wakeling, Tom	OR0050	11,12A,47,29,35
Walker, Elizabeth	KS0750	39,61,54,35,34C
Walker, Richard L.	IN0907	65,35,34A,50,37
Wall, Jeremy	NY3765	34,35,36,47,66A
Wang, Ge	CA4900	34,35,13L
Wangler, Kim L.	NC0050	35,64D,35A
Ward, Eric	AL1050	65,35
Washington, Shirley A.	NY2750	35
Washington, Shirley	NJ0950	35
Weddle, Jamison	AZ0470	35,34D
Weise, Christopher	NC1000	13,10,34,35
Wells, Prince	IL2910	13,11,29,35
Wetzel, David B.	PA2150	64C,35,34
Whisler, Bruce Allen	SC0400	29A,41,35,34
White, Chris	OK1050	70,35,37
White, Matthew S.	SC0420	63A,46,35,53
White, Timothy J.	CA1560	34,35
Wicke, Peter	AG0100	12,35,12F
Wight, Steve	CA0830	35,34A,10C,10D,10F
Willey, Robert K.	LA0760	13,34,35,10B,45
Wilson, Edward	AG0650	34,35
Wimberly, Michael	VT0050	10,20,29,35,65
Winer, Arthur H.	CA0630	10D,34D,35G,35,10C
Witt, James	CA4000	13A,11,35
Woelfel, Kevin	ID0250	35A,35,63A,35E,35B
Wolter, Bill	CA1560	34,35
Wray, David	KY0950	35
Wright, Steve	MN0750	47,63A,35,46,10

Name	Code	Areas
Wurzbach, George	NJ0760	34,35
Wynne, Scott	NC0050	35G,35D,35C,35
Young, Chris	CA5300	35H,35
Young, Donald	CA3850	20H,34,35
Young, Paul U.	CA5300	35
Young, Shawn David	GA0500	14C,35A,31A,35,11
Zager, Michael	FL0650	34,35
Zeller, Jared	LA0080	35
Zimbel, Ike	AG0130	35

Music Business

Name	Code	Areas
Abbinanti, David A.	NY2550	13A,35A
Abrams, Ira	NC0050	35,35A,35E
Abrams, Ira	FL0650	35A
Alexander, Michael	GA1150	38,60B,12A,35A
Alhadeff, Peter	MA0260	35A
Allee, Steve	IN0907	66A,47,35A,53
Alsobrook, Joseph	MO0650	10F,32E,37,34F,35A
Anderson, Mark	CA1800	34,35A,35B,45,35C
Apple, Trent	KY0250	35A,35E
Applebaum, Terry L.	PA3330	65,35A,50
Aquila, Carmen	NY4460	35A,13A,35D,12A,10A
Auler, Robert M.	NY3770	66A,66D,13A,40,35A
Balogh, Mike	AG0130	35A
Banks, Christy A.	PA2350	35A,64C,64E
Batiste, Alvin	LA0700	64A,64C,29,47,35A
Beckman, Gary D.	NC1700	12A,67G,11,35A,35B
Bell, Lorriane	VA0500	11,61,35A
Bergeron, Tom	OR1250	13,64,47,35A
Betts, David	AG0130	35A
Bingham, James	CO0830	35A
Blakeman, Jennifer	NY2750	35A
Blankenship, Courtney	IL3500	35A
Blomquist, Edwin	MA0260	35A
Bogdan, Valentin Mihai	LA0100	66A,10,35A
Bohannon, Kenneth	OK1400	39,61,35A
Bohnet, Andra	AL1300	12A,41,64A,62E,35A
Bradshaw, Robert J.	MA1650	10A,10C,10F,35A,35G
Breithaupt, Robert	OH0350	65,35A,35E
Brierton, Thomas D.	CA5350	35A
Brumfield, April	KY0550	35A
Brusky, Paula	WI0830	64D,35A
Burger, Markus	CA2600	35A
Burke, Larry	FL0800	32B,63B,29A,49,35A
Butcher, Paul	FL0800	29B,47,35A,63A
Butler, Esq., LL.M., Tonya D.	TN1680	35A,35B,35F
Cabott, Christopher	PA3710	35A
Cahill, Catherine	NY2150	35A
Cantrell, James	AL0330	35A,35B,35C,35D,46
Capps, Joe	VT0250	70,34,35A
Carlisle, Stephen M.	FL0650	35A
Carlson, Dan	MN1100	11,35A,37,46,63
Castillo, Ramon	MA2030	35A
Celentano, James	NY2750	35A
Champniss, Kim Clarke	AG0130	35A
Channell, Timothy L.	VA1100	35A,35G
Chappell, Rebecca Ann	IN0100	64C,64E,35A,64D
Christensen, Carey L.	CA0835	35A
Cima, Alex	CA1900	35A,35D,45
Clark, Roger R.	MI1200	35A,35F
Clayton, Zedric K.	TN1680	35A
Clemons, Kawachi A.	NC1600	35A,35D,35E
Clendenen, Bob	CA0510	35A,35C
Coates, Norma	AG0500	12A,12D,15,35A
Coltman, Charles	TX0900	10F,41,64,35A
Conley, Irene H.	CT0650	35A,35E
Connors, Lori	LA0080	35A
Cook, Stephen	CA6000	66A,35A,34,36,11
Coolen, Michael T.	OR0700	14,54,20,12A,35A
Cooper, Stacey H.	NY2550	35A
Cornblum, Marcy	AG0130	35A
Crawford, Mark	TN1400	35A,35B,45
Crilly, Neil D.	FL0650	35A
Crittenden, Eric	NY4460	35A
Dana, Michael	CA1850	29,47,35A,34
Daniels, Chris	CO0830	35A,29A
Daniels, Michael T.	MI1200	65,35A
Dassinger, George	NJ1400	35A
Davison, Susan	CT0650	35A
Decker, Michael	MD0850	70,35A,41,47
Denis, Kimberley	AA0050	61,35A,36
Dennehy, Martin J.	MA0260	35A
Dent, Cedric	TN1100	12A,10D,35A,13E
Dismore, Roger	TX0370	47,20G,29,35A,35G
Dorenfeld, Jeffrey	MA0260	35A
Eldridge, Scott	AG0130	35A
Elton, Serona	FL1900	35A,35B,35D,35F,35H
Emmanuel, Donna T.	TX3420	32B,32G,20D,20H,35A
Ewing, Monica Emmons	GA1050	35A
Fair, Ed	TX3510	35A
Falzano, Anthony	NY2500	20G,35A
Feves, Julie	CA0510	42,64D,48,35A
Flanigan, Sean G.	CO0225	63C,63D,41,47,35A
Fleckenstein, Charles F.	NY2750	35A
Fordham, Matthew	WA0860	35A,35B,35C,35D,35G
France, Chris T.	AG0130	35A
Franzen, Donald	CA5030	35A
Frayne, Bryant	AG0130	35A
Freas, Thomas	CT0550	63A,35A
Freidline, Noel	NC2420	40,47,35A
Gallagher, Mitchell	IN0905	35A
Gilman, David	MI0520	35A
Gloor, Storm	CO0830	35A
Glynn, Mark D.	LA0300	35A
Golia, Vinny	CA0510	64,35A,53,47
Gomez, Alice	TX2260	10,14,47,65,35A
Goodell, Mark	CT0650	35A
Goodwin, Linda G.	MD0650	35A,35E
Gorder, Donald C.	MA0260	35A
Gregory, Cristen	NY0400	35A
Grimm, James	MO2000	70,35A
Grodsky, Michael	CA1900	35A
Grubb, Jay	NJ0750	14C,35A
Hagen, Sara L.	ND0600	13B,32B,32C,35A
Hahn, David	TN0580	12A,34,35A,36,60
Halligan, Robert S.	NY4150	35A,35B,35D,35F
Hamann, Wolfgang	AB0040	35A,35D,35E,35F
Hans, Ben J.	WI0450	11,35A,50,65
Harrison, Thomas	FL1000	34D,35,35A,35B,35F
Hatfield, Bradley	MA1450	35A,10B
Haynes, Erica	CT0650	35A,35B,35E,35F
Heath, Guy	FL1430	11,36,35A
Helbing, Stockton T.	TX3420	35A,35B
Hellmer, Jeffrey	TX3510	29,35A,35B,46
Henry, James	CA4850	34,35,35B,35C,35D
Heredia, Joel	WA0480	47,63A,46,29,35A
Herlihy, David	MA1450	35A
Hichborn, Jon	MA1450	35A,35D,35F
Higgins, Ramsey	AZ0490	35A,35C
Hlus, Don	AB0060	35A,70
Hood, Gary	MD0175	35A,35F
Hoppmann, Kenneth	IN0005	10,16,20F,35A,66
Hughes, Charles M.	CA2050	35A,35B,35D
Hunt, Marc	NY4460	35A
Izzo, Jeffrey	MN1120	35A
Jacobson, Harry P.	NY3725	13,62D,35A
Jaquette, Tim	CA1000	35A,35C,35D
Jarriel, Janet	GA1300	35A
Jeffrey, Wayne	AB0060	35A,37,49,48,63B
Jermance, Frank J.	CO0830	35A
Johnson, Lee E.	GA1200	10,35B,35A
Johnson, Roger O.	NJ0950	12,14C,35A
Kameria, Kim	CA1290	11,32D,35A,35B,35C
Kamerin, Kim	CA2400	10B,35A,36,61
Kennedy, Karen	NY2150	29,35A
Kerr, Brady	CA3265	66C,35A,35C,35D,35G
Kessler, Stan	MO0850	35A,35
Klee, David A.	IA0150	10C,29A,34D,35A,47
Kleiman, Carey D.	FL0200	34,35A,64,35,32E
Knisely, Carole	PA3710	35A,35B,35F
Konewko, Mark	WI0425	11,35A,34,69
Koop, Ruth B.	AJ0030	13A,31A,35A,35E,61
Krause, Douglas	CO0830	13A,11,35A,35B,35C
Krawezyk, Shelly	CA2550	34,35A,35B
Krikun, Andrew	NJ0020	35A,10D,47,14,20
LaBarbera, John P.	KY1500	47,35A,35C
Laconti, Paul	NY2550	35A
Lagace, Isolde	AI0220	35A,35E,35F
Laky, Beth	LA0080	35A
Lally, Peter	MA2030	35A
Lange, Margaret	MA0260	35A
Latham, Louis S.	VA1000	13A,34,35A,35C,35D
Lebon, Rachel L.	FL1900	47,61,32,35A,54
Liepins, Laura	CA1075	35A,35F
Lippstrew, Lee	CO0600	46,34D,35G,35A
Longshore, Terry	OR0950	65,20,14,47,35A
Lovely, Valerie	MA0260	35A
MacDonald, Don	AB0070	10,61,62A,64E,35A
MacDonald, Robert M.	FL0800	66A,12A,35A,35E,35F
MacHose, Kathleen	CT0650	35A
Makris, Kristina	AZ0440	10,13,35A,29A,61
Malott, Steve	WA0860	35A,35B,35C,35D
Mamey, Norman	CA1000	66A,10,12A,13,35A
Marinelli, Michael	DE0150	35A
Marsalis, Ellis	LA0300	35A,29
Marshack, Rose	IL1150	34,35A
Martin, Greg	CA2550	34,35A,35B
Matthews, Mark	FL1650	10B,13A,34B,35A,70
McCollim, Danny	WA0950	45,66A,35D,47,35A
McIntire, David D.	MO1790	34,35A
Meadows, Melody	WV0800	13,12A,66G,34,35A
Medina, Lindsay	IN0900	35A
Meints, Kenneth	NE0500	63,20,65,35A,32
Millar, Michael W.	CA0630	63C,35E,29A,35A
Miller, Ben F.	WV0400	11,50,65,35A,37
Minter, Kendall	GA1050	35A
Mizma, Michael E.	TX2295	50,65,35A,35C
Moore, Kevin	NY4150	35A
Moulton, William	VT0300	13A,29C,33,34B,35A
Myers, Allen	MO2000	35A,66A,29
Myers, Dana	CA5350	35A
Nagy, Russ	OH0350	35A
Neidhart, Gregory	MN1700	35A,35E,10C
Nesin, Richard	NY2750	35A
Nevela, Andrew	AL0500	29,35A,35C
Newman, Jill	IL1740	35A
Nienkirchen, Red	OH0350	35A,70
Nix, Kathy	IL2970	35A
Nytch, Jeffrey C.	CO0800	35A
Oesterle, Ulf	NY4150	35A,35B,35D,35F
Olson, Adam	VA1350	35A,35B
O'Neill, Golder	VA1350	29,35A,35B
Owens, Jimmy	NY2660	64E,35A,35B,35D,35E
Palmer, Christopher G.	FL1900	35A,35B,35E,35F,35H
Papolos, Janice	NY2150	35A
Parke, Steve	IL2450	10,47,63A,29A,35A
Payack, Peter	MA0260	35A
Payne, James	NE0590	11,63A,63B,46,35A
Perla, Gene	PA1950	35A,35E,62D
Peters, G. David	IN0907	34,12C,12,35C,35A
Polk, Sylvester	FL0100	34,63A,35A,35D,35G
Potaczek, Amanda Lee	IN0100	10D,35A
Potaczek, Steven A.	IN0100	35A
Quintero, Juan Carlos	CA1265	70,35A
Rachlin, Harvey	NY2200	35A,35D,35E
Rattner, Richard D.	MI2200	35A
Redmond, John	FL1900	35A,35B,35D,35H
Rezak, David M.	NY4150	35A,35B,35D
Richards, Lasim	FL0700	63C,35A
Richardson, W. Mack	NY3770	11,35A
Richeson, David T.	AR0750	63A,11,35A
Richter, Glenn	TX3510	60,37,35A
Roberts, Terry	SC0710	11,63,13C,35A,41
Romain, James P.	IA0550	64E,29A,35A,29,47
Roman, Robert	NY3765	29,66A,20D,35A,46
Rosario, Lita	DC0350	35A
Roscetti, Diane	CA0835	42,62C,35A
Rosen, Benjamin	AZ0490	35A,35C
Rosfeld, Ken	OK1200	34D,34E,35A,35C,35D
Rostock, Paul	PA2450	47,62D,46,35A
Russell, Thomas	OH1800	35A
Samball, Michael L.	ID0050	11,12A,29A,35A
Sanchez, Rey	FL1900	10D,34C,35A,20G,43
Sanders, Charles J.	NY2750	35A
Sarro, John	DE0150	35A
Schwoebel, Sandy	AZ0480	64A,48,67D,35A
Seeger, Anthony	CA5031	20H,14A,20G,35A,35D
Seeger, Brian	LA0800	35A,35B,35C,47,70
Seppanen, Keith C.	CA0800	13A,35A,35C,35D
Sherman, Robert	NY1900	35A,29
Shores, Daniel	VA1350	35A,35B
Silberschlag, Jeffrey	MD0750	29,35A,60,38,63A
Simpson, Ron	UT0050	35A,35D,35E,35F
Singh, Vijay	WA0050	47,60,36,61,35A
Sipes, Danny T.	TX2930	63D,35A,35C,35D,35G
Sklut, Thomas	MI1260	35A,35E
Smialek, William	TX1300	34A,34B,35A,35B
Smith, Byron J.	CA2650	36,35A,35B,61,66
Smith, Geoff	NY1250	47,11,35A,35B,35C
Smith, Tony L.	TN0150	35A,35E,35F,10D
Snodgrass, Laura	CA2250	64A,13,35A
Snyder, Jay R.	CA1960	35A,35B
Sodke, James W.	WI0835	13A,29,35A
Soocher, Stan	CO0830	35A

Index by Area of Teaching Interest

Name	Code	Areas
Stevens, Bill	CA5350	35A
Stewart, D. Andrew	AA0200	34D,10B,45,35A
Strasser, Richard	MA1450	35A,35F
Strauman, Edward	PA0650	10F,29A,13D,13B,35A
Stup, Chris	CO0830	35A,35C,35D,35F
Sweeney, Joyce	CA5500	12A,13,35A,61
Tait, Kristen N.	MI1750	11,35A
Taylor, Jeffrey B.	WI0450	34D,35A,35D,35C
Thayer, Marc	MO1950	35A
Thomas, O. T.	AL0950	37,35A,65
Tim, Raotana	CA2550	34,35A,35B
Tint, Judith H.	NY2750	35A
Tomassetti, Gary	CT0650	35A
Tuit, Rhoda	CA4450	66,35A
Ury Greenberg, Linda	NY2750	35A
Van Houten, John	CA0825	49,63D,35A
Van Wagner, Eric	OH2050	35G,35A,47
Van Winkle, Lisa K.	NM0310	64A,35A
Vander Gheynst, John R.	IN0907	29A,10A,63,34D,35A
Vermeulen, Ron	AB0040	35A,35D,35G
Waller, Jim	TX3410	35G,10C,29B,47,35A
Wangler, Kim L.	NC0050	35,64D,35A
Wanner, Dan	CA2600	13,11,35A,66A
Ward, Keith C.	WA1000	11,35A
Weary, Hal	PA0050	35A,35D,35F
Wegner, Rob	AZ0490	34,35A,35C
Wentz, Brooke	CA5350	35A
White, Greg	OK1330	35A,54
Widenhofer, Stephen B.	IL1750	47,35A
Williams, Alan	MA2030	35C,35A,20
Woelfel, Kevin	ID0250	35A,35,63A,35E,35B
Wohlrab, Stephen	NC2600	70,35A
Wright, Robert	VA1000	34,35A,35C,35D,35G
Wyatt, Alan	TN0850	13,47,64E,35A,35B
Young, Shawn David	GA0500	14C,35A,31A,35,11
Zeisler, Nathaniel W.	CA1075	35A,35F

Commercial Business

Name	Code	Areas
Abbott, Wesley	CA2600	36,61,35B,13
Accurso, Joseph	NJ0030	13A,13,60,10,35B
Allen, Nancy	CA2550	34,35B,35C,35D
Anderson, Mark	CA1800	34,35A,35B,45,35C
Andrews, Nancy	ME0270	35B,35C,35F,45,20G
Bayer, Michelle	NY0250	35B
Beckman, Gary D.	NC1700	12A,67G,11,35A,35B
Benedetti, Fred	CA2100	70,53,35B,29
Beresford, Rick	TN0100	35B
Blake, C. Marc	CA2600	13,11,34,45,35B
Blenzig, Charles	NY3785	10,66A,29,35B
Brashear, Wayne	CA2550	34,35B
Breithaupt, Robert	OH0350	65,35A,35B,35E
Butler, Esq., LL.M., Tonya D.	TN1680	35A,35B,35F
Cantrell, James	AL0330	35A,35B,35C,35D,46
Carbonneau, Pierre-Marc	AI0220	35B,35C,35D
Crawford, Mark	TN1400	35A,35B,45
De Boeck, Garry	AA0050	47,65,29,35B
Dean, Suzanne B.	MA0260	35B
Dudley, Bruce	TN0100	66A,35B,53
Dudley, Sandra	TN0100	36,61,35B
Dustman, Tom	CA2550	36,47,35B
Eaton, Roy	NY2150	29,35B
Elton, Serona	FL1900	35A,35B,35D,35F,35H
Erastostene, Mario	FL1310	70,35B
Ferry, Joe	NY3785	10,29,35B,35D
Fisher, Jocelyn	TN0100	61,35B
Fordham, Matthew	WA0860	35A,35B,35C,35D,35G
Gimble, Richard	TX1600	62D,70,53,35B
Goebel, Ellen Tift	TN0100	61,35B
Guiterrez, Charles	CA2550	39,53,46,35B,34
Guttierez, Ruben	TX3520	10,35B,35C
Halligan, Robert S.	NY4150	35A,35B,35D,35F
Hanson, David	CO0900	66A,29,35B,10A,10C
Harrison, Thomas	FL1000	34D,35,35A,35B,35F
Helbing, Stockton T.	TX3420	35A,35B
Heller, Brian	MN1050	10B,34,12A,35B,35G
Hellmer, Jeffrey	TX3510	29,35A,35B,46
Henry, James	CA4850	34,35A,35B,35C,35D
Howard, Bill	TX1600	10D,10,66A,35B,66D
Hughes, Charles M.	CA2050	35A,35B,35D
John, David	OK0850	35B,34,35C
Johnson, Lee E.	GA1200	10,35B,35A
Kameria, Kim	CA1290	11,32D,35A,35B,35C
Kammerer, David	HI0050	10F,37,35B,63A,13C
Kirk, Jeff	TN0100	47,64E,35B
Klein, Jonathan	MA0260	35B
Knisely, Carole	PA3710	35A,35B,35E,35F
Krause, Douglas	CO0830	13A,11,35A,35B,35C
Krawezyk, Shelly	CA2550	34,35A,35B
Kwan, Andrew	AG0450	35B
Lehrman, Paul D.	MA1900	35C,34,35B,45,45
Liebowitz, Marian L.	CA4100	11,41,48,64C,35B
London, Todd	TN0100	65,35B
Love, Maurice	CA2550	46,34,35B
Luca, Nancy	CA2550	34,35B,35C,35D
Malott, Steve	WA0860	35A,35B,35C,35D
Martin, Greg	CA2550	34,35A,35B
Martin, Kyle	MA2300	13A,13,11,66,35B
Masakowski, Steve	LA0800	70,35B,35C,29B,47
McLain, Michael	TN0100	70,53,35B
Millican, Si	TX3530	32E,37,10F,35B
Mossman, Michael	NY0642	29,35B,63A
Murphy, Shawn	IL0750	35B
Oesterle, Ulf	NY4150	35A,35B,35D,35F
Olson, Adam	VA1350	34,35B
O'Neill, Golder	VA1350	29,35A,35B
Owens, Jimmy	NY2660	64E,35A,35B,35D,35E
Palmer, Christopher G.	FL1900	35A,35B,35E,35F,35H
Pell, John	TN0100	70,35B
Perl, Jonathan	NY0550	45,35B,35C,35D
Poellnitz, Michael	AL0310	12A,47,63,35B
Poston, Ken	CA0825	20G,35B,29A
Redmond, John	FL1900	35A,35B,35D,35H
Reid, John	TX2350	11,10D,35B,62D
Reid, Ronald I.	MA0260	35B
Rezak, David M.	NY4150	35A,35B,35D
Scott, Gary	OH0755	47,63A,20G,29,35B
Seeger, Brian	LA0800	35A,35B,35C,47,70
Shepherd, John	AG0100	12B,35B,12E,12C
Shores, Daniel	VA1350	35A,35B
Simpson, Ron	UT0050	35A,35B,35D,35E,35F
Smialek, William	TX1300	34A,34B,35A,35B
Smith, Byron J.	CA2650	36,35A,35B,61,66
Smith, Geoff	NY1250	47,11,35A,35B,35C
Snoza, Melissa	IL0750	35B
Snyder, Jay R.	CA1960	35A,35B
Thompson, Chester	TN0100	65,35B,47
Tim, Raotana	CA2550	34,35A,35B
Van Regenmorter, Merlyn	CA0150	34,35B
Vance, Scott	CA0845	35B,35C,35D,13L
Vogt, Roy	TN0100	70,53,35B
Woelfel, Kevin	ID0250	35A,35,63A,35E,35B
Wolfe, Thomas	AL1170	47,70,29,35B
Wyatt, Alan	TN0850	13,47,64E,35A,35B
Zipay, Terry L.	PA3700	13,35B,34A,13E,11

Sound Technology

Name	Code	Areas
Abbati, Joseph S.	FL1900	10B,34A,35C,45,34E
Abbott, James S.	NY4150	35C,35D,35G
Abraham, Michael	MA0260	35C
Alexander, Prince Charles	MA0260	34,35C,35G
Allen, Nancy	CA2550	34,35B,35C,35D
Altman, John	CA3850	35C,35D
Alverson, D. J.	CA0950	35C,35D,35G
Alves, William	CA1050	12C,35C,34D
Anderson, Mark	CA1800	34,35A,35B,45,35C
Andrews, Bradford	CA5150	35C,13L
Andrews, Nancy	ME0270	35B,35C,35F,45,20G
Angelli, Paul	MA2030	35C
Argiro, James	MA2100	35C,35H,46,10C
Arnarson, Stefan Orn	NJ1100	34A,34D,35C,62,38
Aulenbacher, Dennis	IL2970	35C
Ausfin, Kevin	AI0070	13,10F,10,34,35C
Austin, Michael	MO0850	34,35C,13,35,10
Aymer, Justin	IL1740	35C,35D
Baddorf, Donald	IL3550	34,35C
Bailey, Richard H.	AR0810	34,35C,35G,63A
Balder, Patrick	MN1625	35C,35G
Balins, Andris	NY3765	35C,35D,35G,47,70
Barry, Thomas	IA1600	64B,64E,35C
Bates, Tom	MA2030	35C
Baumgarnder, Brad	KS0590	34D,32F,35C,35D
Beardslee, Tony	NE0460	35C,35D,35G,34D,34E
Belec, Jonathan	NY1250	35C
Benoff, Mitchell J.	MA0260	35C
Berger, Brad	MA0260	34,35C,35G
Biederwolf, Kurt J.	MA0260	45,35C
Bierylo, Michael	MA0260	45,35C
Bissell, Paul	TX0550	10B,34D,34E,35C,35D
Bizianes, Chris	KY0250	35C,35D
Bjur, David	WA1150	35C,35D,35G
Blinman, Chad	MA0260	35C,35G
Bobrowski, Christine	CA1250	45,34,35C
Bondelevitch, David	CO0830	35C,35D,35G
Boulanger, Richard	MA0260	45,35C
Bowyer, Don	AR0110	63C,63D,29,35C,47
Bregitzer, Lorne	CO0830	35C,35D,35G
Brigida, Michael A.	MA0260	45,35C
Broening, Benjamin	VA1500	10,34,13,35C,35D
Bromann, Michael	AZ0440	35C,35D
Brown, Robert	TX2930	46,35C,34D
Brunner, George	NY0500	34,35C,10B
Buchwald, Peter	CO0150	64E,35C,35D,10
Buchwald, Peter	CO0830	35C,35D,35G
Burtner, Matthew	VA1550	10,34,35C,12F
Cairo, Bo	AG0130	35C
Calloway, Edwin S.	GA2300	13C,35C
Calvert, Phil A.	CA0835	35C
Camelio, Brian	NY2660	10,70,35C
Campbell, Todd A.	NC0700	35G,34D,35D,65,35C
Campos, John	MI2250	35C,35D
Cantrell, James	AL0330	35A,35B,35C,35D,46
Carbone, Anthony P.	MA0260	35C
Carbonneau, Pierre-Marc	AI0220	35B,35C,35D
Carman, William	MA2030	35C
Carney, David	CA4100	34D,35C,35G,72
Caruso, John A.	NY3725	35C
Case, Alexander	MA2030	35C,47,13L
Cerniglia, Richard C.	NY0350	35C
Chapdelaine, Jim	CT0650	35C
Chase, Jon	MA0260	10,35C,35G
Chittum, John	KS0590	34D,32F,35C,35D
Clausen, Rick	AZ0440	35C,35D
Clendenen, Bob	CA0510	35A,35C
Clifton, Jeremy J.	OK1050	35C,10,13,13K,13B
Cline, Jeff	TN1680	34,35C,35D
Coffey, Ted	VA1550	10B,10,34,35C,35G
Collins, Dana L.	IN1560	10,12A,34,35C,13
Comotto, Brian	MD0175	10,35C,35D,35G,66A
Cooper, Rychard	CA0825	35C
Corwin, Mark	AI0070	10F,10,45,34,35C
Crotts, Angela	TX2295	35C,35G
Daniel, Omar	AG0500	13,10,10F,34,35C
D'Antonio, Peter	OH0600	35C
Davis, Greg	PA0500	34A,34D,35C,35D,35G
Dean, Ronnie	IL1750	35C,35D
Debes, Edward	PA3710	35C,35D,35G,35H
Decker, Douglas	MI1150	35C
DeJaynes, Luke	IL1050	65,35C
DeLong, Noah	TN1150	36,35C,60A,61
Devine, George M.	RI0300	35C,35D,35G
DiFranco, Paul	VA1350	35C,35D
Dozoretz, Brian	NY1800	35C,34D
Driessen, Peter	AB0150	10B,35C,35D
Dziuba, Mark	NY3760	70,29A,47,35C
Edelstein, Andrew S.	MA0260	35C
Egre, Bruce	OH0600	35C,35G
Egre, Bruce	OH0400	35C,35D
Elliott, Bill	MA0260	10,35C,35G
Elliott, John	CA4050	34,35C
Elsea, Peter	CA5070	45,35C
Erickson, Mark	TX3175	35C,35D,35G
Erskine, John K.	MI1050	35C,35D,34
Esler, Robert	AZ0490	50,14C,35C,10
Fagnano, Frank	NJ1400	35C
Farwell, Douglas G.	GA2150	63C,49,34,35C,35D
Ferraro, David C.	NY2550	35C,35G
Filadelfo, Gary A.	NY1600	45,35C,35D
Filadelfo, Gary A.	NY2750	10,35C
Fink, Jay	NJ1400	35C
Foley, Charles F.	NV0050	35C,35G
Fordham, Matthew	WA0860	35A,35B,35C,35D,35G
Francis, Jeff	SC1110	35C,35G
Frazer, Jonathan	TN1680	34,35C,35D
Fridmann, Dave	NY3725	35C
Furman, Pablo	CA4400	13,10,34,35C
Furr, Ricky	VA1350	35C,35D
Futrell, Stephen A.	NC0750	36,32D,60,35C,40
Gaff, Isaac	IL1550	34,13G,13,35C,35G
Galindo, Guillermo	CA1250	45,34,35C
Gamberoni, Steve	WA0950	35C,35G
Gaston, Leslie	CO0830	35C,35D,35G
Geist, Doug	NM0450	35G,35C

Index by Area of Teaching Interest

Name	Code	Areas
Gitt, Bill	MA0260	34,35C,35G
Glanz, James M.	NY2750	35C,35G
Goomas, Steve	CA2650	35C,35G,13L
Gottinger, Bernd	NY3725	35C
Greenland, John	PA1150	35C,45
Griffin, Gregory W.	OH2275	54,35C,34
Gutierrez, Alfonso	FL0650	35C
Guttierez, Ruben	TX3520	10,35B,35C
Haertel, Tim	IN1010	35C,35G
Haight, Ronald S.	WA0800	34,35C,35D
Harlan, Paul	FL1740	66A,10,34,35C
Harris, Ben	FL0100	34,35C,35G,32F
Hatcher, Charles E.	OH2200	35C
Hatzis, Christos	AG0450	10,35H,34,35C,13L
Hehmsoth, Henry	TX3175	35C,35D,35G,66A
Henry, James	CA4850	34,35A,35B,35C,35D
Henry, William R.	TX3175	35C,35D,35G
Herald, Terry	MI1750	35G,35C,11
Herman, Gabe	CT0650	35C,35D
Hernandez, Bernardo	MA0260	10,35G,35C
Hickinbotham, Gary	TX3175	35C,35D,35G
Higgins, Ramsey	AZ0490	35A,35C
Hodgson, Jay	AG0500	14,29,35C,35D,12
Hoffman, Christopher	NY2660	35C
Honour, Eric C.	MO1790	10,34,13,13F,35C
Hood, Mark	IN0900	35C,35G
Houchin, Blake	TN1600	35C
Howard, David R.	MA0260	10,35C
Huang, Juan	MD0650	35C
Hughes, Thomas	TX3200	66G,34,35C
Hussa, Robert	WY0060	11,12A,35C,36,61
Jackson, Ryan D.	MN1120	34,35C,35D
Jaczko, Robert	MA0260	35C
Jaquette, Tim	CA1000	35A,35C,35D
Jetter, Jonathan	NY3785	35C
John, David	OK0850	35B,34,35C
Johnson, Richard	KS0590	13G,32F,34D,35C,35D
Johnson, Robert M.	CA0150	35G,35C
Johnson, Shawn F.	MD0650	35C,35G
Johnson, Tom	CA3320	35C,35D,35G
Jones, Keith D.	MA2030	35C
Jones, Thomas A.	MD0650	35C
Julian, Michael	CA2750	35D,35C,35G,13C,13D
Kadis, Jay L.	CA4900	45,35C
Kalinowski, Mark	NJ0175	35C,35G
Kameria, Kim	CA1290	11,32D,35A,35B,35C
Karathanasis, Konstantinos	OK1350	34D,10A,10,35C,35G
Kaupp, Gil	NV0050	35C,35G,63A
Kelleher, Kevin	TX2700	35C
Kerr, Brady	CA3265	66C,35A,35C,35D,35G
Kerzner, David	NJ1400	35C
Khamda, Mazdak	CA3250	66A,66D,32F,35C
Kikta, Thomas J.	PA1050	70,34D,35C
Kilpatrick, Terry	WY0115	35C
Kim-Boyle, David	MD1000	34,35C,35G
Kimball, Eugene	CT0850	35C
Kimlicko, Franklin	TX3370	70,34,35C
Kimura, Mari	NY1900	35C
Kindall, Susan C.	SC0200	66A,66B,35C,34
Kirklewski, Duff	MA2030	35C
Klein, Wendy L.	MA0260	10,35C
Kocandrle, Mirek	MA0260	10,35C
Konzelman, Brian	TX1600	35C,35D,35G
Korn, Mitchell	TN1850	35C
Kostusiak, Thomas J.	NY3717	35C,35D,35G
Kothman, Keith K.	IN0150	10B,10,34,13,35C
Krause, Douglas	CO0830	13A,11,35A,35B,35C
Kreiger, Arthur V.	CT0100	13,35C,10,45,34
Kurtz, Justin	CT0650	35C,13L
LaBarbera, John P.	KY1500	47,35A,35C
Lalli, Marcus	NY0350	35C
Landgrave, Phillip	KY1200	10,35C,31A
Laranja, Ricardo	IN0907	34D,35C
Largent, Jeffrey	MA0260	35C
Latham, Louis S.	VA1000	13A,34,35A,35C,35D
Lee, Abe	MA0260	10A,10D,35C,35G
Lehrman, Paul D.	MA1900	35C,34,35B,45,45
Leider, Colby N.	FL1900	34A,35C,10B,34D,35G
Leonard, Neil	MA0260	35C
Lin, Denny	CA2420	35C
Logan, Jennifer	CA3300	10B,13A,13B,13C,35C
Loughrige, Chad	OH0350	34,35C,10B,10D,45
Lovato, James	NM0400	35C
Luca, Nancy	CA2550	34,35B,35C,35D
MacLean, Stephen	MA0260	34,35C
Macy, John	CO0150	35C,35D
Mahin, Bruce P.	VA1100	10,34,13,35C
Malott, Steve	WA0860	35A,35B,35C,35D
Mariasy, David	OH2300	35C,34D
Marsh, Gerry Jon	WA0800	34,35C,37,10
Masakowski, Steve	LA0800	70,35B,35C,29B,47
Mason, John	MA1100	70,35C,35G
Mazurek, Drew	MD0650	35C,35G
McArthur-Brown, Gail	MA0260	10,35C,35G
McGuire, Samuel A.	CO0830	35C,35D,35G
McKinney, Matthew	AL1200	34D,34H,35C,35G
McKinnie, Douglas	IN0900	35C,35G
McManus, Edward	OR0350	63B,34A,35C,35G,13A
McNally, Kirk	AB0150	10B,34D,34E,35C,35D
McNeish, James	CT0100	70,35C
Mendelson, Richard	MA0260	35C
Mercer, James	CA3400	32C,61,35C
Merkel, Jeffrey	CO0830	35C,35D,35G
Messner, Walter	WI0830	35C,35D
Metcalfe, James L.	TX2295	65,35C,35G,46
Metcalfe, Scott	MD0650	35C,35G
Meyer, Pam	WA0950	35C
Middleton, Jonathan N.	WA0250	13,10,35C,34,35
Middleton, Peter	IL2200	45,64A,34,35C,13L
Millar, Cameron	MD0300	13A,34B,35C,13C,34D
Miller, Lance R.	OR1050	35C,35G
Miller, Tim	NE0460	35C,35D,35G,34D,34E
Miller, Tom D.	IL0750	35C
Miller-Brown, Donna	KS0590	34D,32F,35C,35D
Mizma, Michael E.	TX2295	50,65,35A,35C
Moore, F. Richard	CA5050	10,45,34,35C,13L
Moorhead, Jan Paul	MA0260	35C
Mooy, James D.	CA4410	45,35C,34,46,64
Mortenson, Daniel	SD0150	34,35C
Morton, Nye	CA1850	35C,35D
Moseley, William	ME0340	12A,47,64A,35C,29
Moss, Michael	MA0260	35C
Moylan, William D.	MA2030	35C,13E
Mulder, Geoffrey	CA0850	34,35C,35D,12A,62A
Mulet, Mickael	PR0100	34,35C
Myska, David	AG0500	13,10,45,34,35C
Nagel, Jody	IN0150	13,10,45,35C
Nevela, Andrew	AL0500	29,35A,35C
Nie, James Ian	WI0100	66A,66C,35D,35C
Nittoli, Andrew	NY3790	35C,35D
Nyerges, John	NY2500	35C,47
Orth, Scott	MD0650	35C
Paduck, Ted	MA0260	34,35C,35G
Pannell, Larry J.	LA0100	64,34,35C,37,32
Parish, Steven	AB0070	65,20G,34,35C
Patrick, Dennis M.	AG0450	13,45,13L,34,35C
Payne, Maggi	CA2950	10B,35D,35C,35G
Peck, Chant	AZ0440	35C,35D
Pejrolo, Andrea	MA0260	34,10C,10,35C,35G
Perialas, Alexander	NY1800	35C,13L
Perl, Jonathan	NY0550	45,35B,35C,35D
Perrault, Paul	AI0220	45,34,35C,35E,13L
Peters, G. David	IN0907	34,12C,12,35C,35A
Pirkle, William C.	FL1900	34A,34D,34G,35C,35G
Pixton, Clayton	KS0590	34D,32F,35C,35D
Poniatowski, Mark	MA0260	10,35C,35G
Powers, Ollie	CA5360	35G,35C,11,12A,34
Price, Matt	OH0350	35C
Rathbun, Andrew	NY2050	35C,35D,35G,10B,45
Ray, James	FL1550	66D,34D,60A,35C
Rees, Fred J.	IN0907	34,12C,35C,32,12
Renner, Jack L.	OH0600	35C,35D
Reuter, Eric Lehman	MA0260	34,35C,35D
Reynolds, Steve	LA0800	34D,35C,35D,35G
Richardson, Chuck	TX2850	11,45,35C,35G
Richey, Marc	KY1200	35C
Riddle, Donald	MO2000	34,35C
Riley, Justin	OH0350	34,35C,35D,35G,13G
Rinaldi, Jason P.	MA0260	35C
Rodriguez, Alex	MA0260	34,35C,35G
Rodriguez, Elvin	CA2420	11,66A,35G,35C
Rodriguez, Francisco	PA1050	35C
Rogers, Susan	MA0260	35C,13K,13L
Rolls, Timothy	KS0350	10,13,34,35C,35G
Rose, Brian	OR0050	34,35C,35D,35H
Rosen, Benjamin	AZ0490	35A,35C
Rosfeld, Ken	OK1200	34D,34E,35A,35C,35D
Rothbart, Peter	NY1800	45,35C,35D
Rothkopf, Michael S.	NC1650	45,35C,35G
Rowe, Robert	NY2750	10,43,34,35C
Rubel, Mark	IL2350	45,35C,35D
Rubinstein, Mark	OH1850	35C,35D,34D,35G
Rumbolz, Robert C.	WY0130	13,35C,35D,34,20A
Rust, Ty	CA2420	67,35C,34
Sanders, David	NY2400	35C,35D
Sargent, Daniel	CA0800	35C,35G
Schermerhorn, David	NC1450	34D,34E,35C
Schmutte, Peter J.	IN1650	36,45,35C,35G,34
Scholwin, Richard M.	NE0590	35C,35G,34D
Schulz, Riccardo	PA0550	35C,35G
Schulze, Michael	CO0900	35C,35D,35G
Seagle, Andy	AZ0440	35C,35D
Seagrave, Charles	CA3250	35C,34D
Seeger, Brian	LA0800	35A,35B,35C,47,70
Sentgeorge, Aaron Jacob 'Jake'	MO1790	61,35C
Seppanen, Keith C.	CA0800	13A,35A,35C,35D
Setter, Terry A.	WA0350	10F,10,12B,45,35C
Sever, Ivan	MA0260	35C,35D,10C
Severson, Sandi	CA0100	35C
Seymann, Scott	AZ0440	35C,35D
Shade, Neil Thompson	MD0650	35C
Shadley, Jeffrey	OK1450	34D,35C
Sheppard, Craig	AF0100	45,35C
Shirley, John F.	MA2030	35C
Siegel, Dan	CA2960	35C,35D,34D,35G
Sincaglia, Nicolas W.	IL0750	35C
Sipes, Danny T.	TX2930	63D,35A,35C,35D,35G
Smiley, William C.	NC1550	10B,35C,35G,45
Smith, Geoff	NY1250	47,11,35A,35B,35C
Smith, Stuart	MA2030	13,29B,35C
Sokol, Mike	VA1350	35C,35D
Solomonson, Terry	IL3500	11,63D,35C,35D,35G
Spencer, James W.	AR0750	35C,35G
Stearns, Loudon	MA0260	10,35C,35G
Steinman, Paul	NY2400	35C,35D
Stillman, Fallon	IN0900	35C,35G
Stimmel, Matthew D.	OH2275	34,35C
Stinnett, Jim	MA0260	10,35C
Strauss, Konrad	IN0900	35C,35G
Stuck, Les	CA2950	10B,34A,13G,35C,10C
Stucker, Michael D.	IN0900	35C,35G
Stup, Chris	CO0830	35A,35C,35D,35F
Suchy, John	MD0175	35C,34D
Swenson, Thomas S.	NC2205	13A,66B,35C,34,32
Swist, Christopher	MA1100	65,35C
Sykes, Jerilyn	MA0260	10,35C
Taber, Randy	NJ1400	35C
Tadey, Anthony	IN0900	35C,35G
Taylor, Jeffrey B.	WI0450	34D,35A,35D,35C
Tender, Peter	OH1850	34,35C
Testa, Mike	MA2030	35C
Tetreault, Edward	MD0650	35C,35G
Thibodeau, David	MA2030	35C
Thompson, Dan	MA0260	35C
Tomassetti, Benjamin	VA0500	35G,10B,34D,35C,64E
Traube, Caroline	AI0200	13L,35C,34
Truax, Barry D.	AB0080	10,45,34,35C,13L
Turner, Patrick	VA1700	11,29,34D,34H,35C
Ungar, Leanne	MA0260	34,35C,35G
Valcarcel, David Shawn	CA3265	45,65,35C,13G,66A
Valcarcel, David	CA3950	45,65,35C,13G,66A
Valdez, Paul	TX2295	35C
Valera, Philip	NC0100	34D,35G,35C,35D,13L
Vance, Scott	CA0845	35B,35C,35D,13L
VanWick, Brad	KS0590	34D,32F,35C,35D
Vernon, James R.	OK0650	13,10,35C,11
Vince, Matt	AZ0440	70,35C,35D
Waldrep, Mark	CA0805	34,35C,35D
Walker, Saul A.	NY2750	35C
Waters, Joseph	CA4100	10,45,34,35C
Webber, Stephen	MA0260	35C
Wegner, Rob	AZ0490	34,35A,35C
Wessel, Mark	MA0260	35C
White, Andrew	CO0830	35C
Whittaker, Mark	MA2030	35C
Williams, Alan	MA2030	35C,35A,20
Williams, Jeff	MA0260	34,35C
Williams, John Flawn	DC0075	35C,35G,35H
Wilson, Leslie	KY0250	35C
Wong, Sui-Fan	AA0080	35C,35G
Wood, Dan	NY3770	34,35C,35D,35G
Wright, Robert	VA1000	34,35A,35C,35D,35G
Wyner, Jonathan	MA0260	34,35C,35G
Wynne, Scott	NC0050	35G,35D,35C,35
Yandell, Scott	AZ0440	29,35C,35D
Young, Charles R.	WI0850	13,10F,35C,10A

545

Yuasa, Joji	CA5050	10,20D,35H,34,35C
Zoffer, David	MA0260	10,35C,35G

Recording Industry

Abbott, James S.	NY4150	35C,35D,35G
Allen, Nancy	CA2550	34,35B,35C,35D
Altman, John	CA3850	35C,35D
Alverson, D. J.	CA0950	35C,35D,35G
Aquila, Carmen	NY4460	35A,13A,35D,12A,10A
Aymer, Justin	IL1740	35C,35D
Balins, Andris	NY3765	35C,35D,35G,47,70
Barata, Antonio G.	CA0600	10,34D,35D,35G
Baumgarnder, Brad	KS0590	34D,32F,35C,35D
Beardslee, Tony	NE0460	35C,35D,35G,34D,34E
Bengloff, Richard	NY2750	35D
Bissell, Paul	TX0550	10B,34D,34E,35C,35D
Bizianes, Chris	KY0250	35C,35D
Bjur, David	WA1150	35C,35D,35G
Black, Lendell	OK0750	10C,35D,34
Bocanegra, Cheryl	OK0850	13,66A,35D,47
Bondelevitch, David	CO0830	35C,35D,35G
Bordon, Wellington	NC1600	35D,35G
Bregitzer, Lorne	CO0830	35C,35D,35G
Broening, Benjamin	VA1500	10,34,13,35C,35D
Bromann, Michael	AZ0440	35C,35D
Buchwald, Peter	CO0150	64E,35C,35D,10
Buchwald, Peter	CO0830	35C,35D,35G
Bunce, Mark Robert	OH0300	34,35D,35G
Callahan, Timothy	OH0600	35D
Campbell, Todd A.	NC0700	35G,34D,35D,65,35C
Campos, John	MI2250	35C,35D
Cantrell, James	AL0330	35A,35B,35C,35D,46
Carbonneau, Pierre-Marc	AI0220	35B,35C,35D
Casuccio, Anthony	NY4460	35D,35G
Chapman, Don	AF0050	35G,35D
Cherryholmes, Roy	TX2400	35D
Chittum, John	KS0590	34D,32F,35C,35D
Cima, Alex	CA1900	35A,35D,45
Clausen, Rick	AZ0440	35C,35D
Clemons, Kawachi A.	NC1600	35A,35D,35E
Cline, Jeff	TN1680	34,35C,35D
Comotto, Brian	MD0175	10,35C,35D,35G,66A
Corbett, Ian	KS0590	10,34,35D,35G,13G
Coulas, Ben	AB0040	34,35D,35G,34D
Czink, Andrew	AB0040	35D,35G,34D
Davis, Greg	PA0500	34A,34D,35C,35D,35G
Dean, Ronnie	IL1750	35C,35D
Debes, Edward	PA3710	35C,35D,35G,35H
Devine, George M.	RI0300	35C,35D,35G
DiFranco, Paul	VA1350	35C,35D
Dobbis, Richard B.	NY2750	35D
Driessen, Peter	AB0150	10B,35C,35D
Edighoffer, Gary B.	WA0950	64A,64E,35D
Egre, Bruce	OH0400	35C,35D
Elton, Serona	FL1900	35A,35B,35D,35F,35H
Erickson, Gary	IL1050	34B,10A,13G,31A,35D
Erickson, Mark	TX3175	35C,35D,35G
Erskine, John K.	MI1050	35C,35D,34
Farwell, Douglas G.	GA2150	63C,49,34,35C,35D
Feindell, S.	AB0040	35D,35G,34D
Ferry, Joe	NY3785	10,29,35B,35D
Filadelfo, Gary A.	NY1600	45,35C,35D
Fordham, Matthew	WA0860	35A,35B,35C,35D,35G
Forehan, Jeff	CA5510	10B,13A,34D,35G,35D
Frazer, Jonathan	TN1680	34,35C,35D
Furr, Ricky	VA1350	35C,35D
Garrett, Roger	IL1200	37,64C,60B,41,35D
Gaston, Leslie	CO0830	35C,35D,35G
Gonko, Daniel	NC0700	35D,35G
Haight, Ronald S.	WA0800	34,35C,35D
Haines, Thomas	OH2200	35H,35D
Halligan, Robert S.	NY4150	35A,35B,35D,35F
Hamann, Wolfgang	AB0040	35A,35D,35E,35F
Haynes, Erica	CT0650	35A,35D,35E,35F
Hehmsoth, Henry	TX3175	35C,35D,35G,66A
Heldt, Tim	MI0850	34D,35D,35G
Henry, James	CA4850	34,35A,35B,35C,35D
Henry, William R.	TX3175	35C,35D,35G
Herman, Gabe	CT0650	35C,35D
Hichborn, Jon	MA1450	35A,35D,35F
Hickinbotham, Gary	TX3175	35C,35D,35G
Hodgson, Jay	AG0500	14,29,35C,35D,12
Hughes, Charles M.	CA2050	35A,35B,35D
Jackson, Ryan D.	MN1120	34,35C,35D
Jaquette, Tim	CA1000	35A,35C,35D
Johnson, Richard	KS0590	13G,32F,34D,35C,35D
Johnson, Tom	CA3320	35C,35D,35G
Julian, Michael	CA2750	35D,35C,35G,13C,13D
Kerr, Brady	CA3265	66C,35A,35C,35D,35G
Kohn, Steven Mark	OH0600	10B,35D
Konzelman, Brian	TX1600	35C,35D,35G
Kostusiak, Thomas J.	NY3717	35C,35D,35G
Kroth, Richard	NJ0175	35E,35D
Kunz, Kelly	WA0030	35D,13
Langosch, Paul	VA1700	20H,29,35D,46,47
Last, Julie	VT0050	34D,35D,35G
Latham, Louis S.	VA1000	13A,34,35A,35C,35D
Lehrer, Scott	VT0050	34C,35D,35G
Luca, Nancy	CA2550	34,35B,35C,35D
Lyons, Robert	MA1450	35D,35H
MacDonald, Michael	MD0650	35D
Macy, John	CO0150	35C,35D
Malott, Steve	WA0860	35A,35B,35C,35D
Matsumoto, Shane	AZ0470	35D,35G
McCollim, Danny	WA0950	45,66A,35D,47,35A
McGuire, Samuel A.	CO0830	35C,35D,35G
McNally, Kirk	AB0150	10B,34D,34E,35C,35D
Merkel, Jeffrey	CO0830	35C,35D,35G
Messner, Walter	WI0830	35C,35D
Meyer, Andreas K.	DE0150	35D
Meyer, Eric	WI1150	35D
Miller, Tim	NE0460	35C,35D,35G,34D,34E
Miller-Brown, Donna	KS0590	34D,32F,35C,35D
Mitchell, Geoffrey	AI0150	34,35D
Morton, Nye	CA1850	35C,35D
Mosher, Jimm	NC0350	35D,35G,34D
Mulder, Geoffrey	CA0850	34,35C,35D,12A,62A
Nie, James Ian	WI0100	66A,66C,35D,35C
Nittoli, Andrew	NY3790	35C,35D
Oesterle, Ulf	NY4150	35A,35B,35D,35F
Owens, Jimmy	NY2660	64E,35A,35B,35D,35E
Pastrana, Jorge	CA4850	47,46,45,35D,10B
Patton, David	TN0100	35D
Payne, Maggi	CA2950	10B,35D,35C,35D
Peck, Chant	AZ0440	35C,35D
Perl, Jonathan	NY0550	45,35B,35C,35D
Perlman, Marc	RI0050	14,20D,12E,13J,35D
Pierce, Bradley	MA0150	34D,35D,35G
Pixton, Clayton	KS0590	34D,32F,35C,35D
Polk, Sylvester	FL0100	34,63A,35A,35D,35G
Rachlin, Harvey	NY2200	35A,35D,35E
Rasmussen, Ljerka V.	TN1400	20,14C,20F,35D,14
Rathbun, Andrew	NY2050	35C,35D,35G,10B,45
Redmond, John	FL1900	35A,35B,35D,35H
Renner, Jack L.	OH0600	35C,35D
Reuter, Eric Lehman	MA0260	34,35C,35D
Reynolds, Steve	LA0800	34D,35C,35D,35G
Rezak, David M.	NY4150	35A,35B,35D
Riley, Justin	OH0350	34,35C,35D,35G,13G
Rose, Brian	OR0050	34,35C,35D,35H
Rosfeld, Ken	OK1200	34D,34E,35A,35C,35D
Rothbart, Peter	NY1800	45,35C,35D
Rubel, Mark	IL2350	45,35C,35D
Rubinstein, Mark	OH1850	35C,35D,34D,35G
Rumbolz, Robert C.	WY0130	13,35C,35D,34,20A
Rutland, Neil	NM0100	37,50,65,35D
Sanders, David	NY2400	35C,35D
Schmidt, David	AZ0350	47,53,35D,34D
Schulz, Mark Alan	OH1350	34D,35G,35D,62C,29B
Schulze, Michael	CO0900	35C,35D,35G
Seagle, Andy	AZ0440	35C,35D
Seeger, Anthony	CA5031	20H,14A,20G,35A,35D
Seppanen, Keith C.	CA0800	13A,35A,35C,35D
Sever, Ivan	MA0260	35C,35D,10C
Seymann, Scott	AZ0440	35C,35D
Seymour, David	OH1350	35C,35D,35G
Siegel, Dan	CA2960	35C,35D,34D,35G
Simpson, Ron	UT0050	35A,35B,35D,35E,35F
Singletary, Pat	TX0075	64,35D
Sipes, Danny T.	TX2930	63D,35C,35D,35G
Smolik, Vicky	IL2970	11,63A,10D,35D
Sokol, Mike	VA1350	35C,35D
Solomonson, Terry	IL3500	11,63D,35C,35D,35G
Steinman, Mark	NY2400	35C,35D
Stone, George J.	CA1510	13,47,34,66A,35D
Stup, Chris	CO0830	35A,35C,35D,35G
Taylor, Jeffrey B.	WI0450	34D,35A,35D,35C
Teran, Louie	CA2550	35D,35G
Thomas, Steve	OH0350	34A,34B,34D,35D
Tonnies, Mary Kaye	IL2970	35D
Valera, Philip	NC0100	34D,35G,35C,35D,13L
Vance, Scott	CA0845	35B,35C,35D,13L
VanWick, Brad	KS0590	34D,32F,35C,35D
Vermeulen, Ron	AB0040	35A,35D,35G
Vince, Matt	AZ0440	70,35C,35D
Wade, Brett	AB0040	35D,35G
Waldrep, Mark	CA0805	34,35C,35D
Watkinson, Christopher L.	ME0200	13L,34D,35D,35G
Weary, Hal	PA0050	35A,35D,35F
Western, Daniel	AL0650	64,47,35D,13,29A
Williams, Lester C.	TX2295	35D,35G
Wood, Dan	NY3770	34,35C,35D,35G
Woodyard, Jim	AB0040	35D,35G
Wright, Robert	VA1000	34,35A,35C,35D,35G
Wynne, Scott	NC0050	35G,35D,35C,35
Yandell, Scott	AZ0440	29,35C,35D
Young, Jeff	AB0040	34D,35D,35E,35F,35G

Arts Administration

Abrams, Ira	NC0050	35,35A,35E
Albanese, Janet	IA0550	35E
Apple, Trent	KY0250	35A,35E
Ball, Alexandria	PA2900	66C,66D,35E
Barasch, Shirley R.	PA2900	61,32,54,10,35E
Bowser, Bryan L.	OH0200	35E
Breithaupt, Robert	OH0350	65,35A,35B,35E
Caborn, Peter	VA1350	35E
Chandler, Beth E.	VA0600	64A,42,35E
Cleland, Kent D.	OH0200	13,35E,34A
Clemons, Kawachi A.	NC1600	35A,35D,35E
Collins, Verne E.	VA1350	35E
Conley, Irene H.	CT0650	35A,35E
Crabtree, Kacy E.	NC1050	52,35E
Cunningham, Mark T.	IL0750	35E
Dobroski, Bernard J.	IL2250	32H,63D,32,60,35E
Edelman, David	VA1350	35E
Ferlo, Patrick A.	NY3700	35E
Fitzgibbon, Cecelia	PA1000	35E
Flack, Amy L.	NY3780	35E
Fleming, Becky	CA4100	35E
Fogel, Henry	IL0550	35E
Goodwin, Linda G.	MD0650	35A,35E
Haley, Ardith	AF0050	35E,37
Hamann, Wolfgang	AB0040	35A,35D,35E,35F
Hamilton, Jean	OH2200	35E
Hamilton, Margaret J.	MI2250	63B,32,13,35E
Harder, Lillian U.	SC0400	66A,35E
Harding, C. Tayloe	SC1110	10,35E,43
Haynes, Erica	CT0650	35A,35D,35E,35F
Herriott, Jeffrey	WI0865	10,11,43,35E
Hobbs, Wayne C.	TX3200	13,12,35E,20G
Hodges, Anne R.	FL0850	35E
Hose, Anthony	FL1750	38,60,35E
Hubner, Carla	DC0110	12A,12,66A,35E
Hutton, Kelley	OH2275	35E
Johnson, Eric	SD0150	34,35E
Kenworthy, Jane	CA5350	35E
Klein, Rochelle Z.	PA2900	32,35E,66A,11,13A
Knisely, Carole	PA3710	35A,35D,35E,35F
Koop, Ruth B.	AJ0030	13A,31A,35A,35E,61
Krause, William Craig	VA0550	70,11,12A,20H,35E
Kroth, Richard	NJ0175	35E,35D
Kushick, Marilyn M.	MA2000	35E
Lagace, Isolde	AI0220	35A,35E,35F
Lovely, Valerie	MA0260	35A,35E
MacDonald, Robert M.	FL0800	66A,12A,35A,35E,35F
Marion, Ricki	VA1350	35E
McKelvey, Michael E.	PA2900	35E,61,54,10
Melton, James L.	CA5355	60,36,31A,32D,35E
Millar, Michael W.	CA0630	63C,35E,29A,35A
Neidhart, Gregory	MN1700	35A,35E,10C
Owens, Jimmy	NY2660	64E,35A,35B,35D,35E
Palmer, Christopher G.	FL1900	35A,35B,35E,35F,35H
Penick, Pam	AL1170	35E
Perla, Gene	PA1950	35A,35E,62D
Perrault, Paul	AI0220	45,34,35C,35E,13L
Phillips, Edward D.	IN0910	63A,35E
Potter, Joe	MO2050	66A,66G,35H,54,35E
Rachlin, Harvey	NY2200	35A,35D,35E
Rosenzweig, Joyce	NY1450	14,66C,35E
San Martin, Laurie A.	CA5010	10,13,43,35E
Simpson, Ron	UT0050	35A,35B,35D,35E,35F

Index by Area of Teaching Interest

Sklut, Thomas	MI1260	35A,35E
Smith, Brian R.	CT0650	35E
Smith, Tony L.	TN0150	35A,35E,35F,10D
Speer, Janet Barton	NC1050	35H,54,35E
Spiegelman, Ron	MO0350	60B,35E
Swenson, Daniel	MA1400	35E
Thomas, Wendy E.	OK1450	35E
Vodnoy, Robert L.	SD0400	12A,62,38,51,35E
Whitwell, John	GA2100	35E,37,60B
Woelfel, Kevin	ID0250	35A,35,63A,35E,35B
Yaffe, Alan	OH2200	35E
Young, Jeff	AB0040	34D,35D,35E,35F,35G

Talent Management

Andrews, Nancy	ME0270	35B,35C,35F,45,20G
Butler, Esq., LL.M., Tonya D.	TN1680	35A,35B,35F
Clark, Roger R.	MI1200	35A,35F
Crawford, Elizabeth A.	IN0150	64C,35F
Elton, Serona	FL1900	35A,35B,35D,35F,35H
Halligan, Robert S.	NY4150	35A,35B,35D,35F
Hamann, Wolfgang	AB0040	35A,35D,35E,35F
Harrison, Thomas	FL1000	34D,35,35A,35B,35F
Haynes, Erica	CT0650	35A,35D,35E,35F
Hichborn, Jon	MA1450	35A,35D,35F
Hood, Gary	MD0175	35A,35F
Knisely, Carole	PA3710	35A,35B,35E,35F
Kwan, Andrew	AG0300	35F
Lagace, Isolde	AI0220	35A,35E,35F
Liepins, Laura	CA1075	35A,35F
MacDonald, Robert M.	FL0800	66A,12A,35A,35E,35F
Oesterle, Ulf	NY4150	35A,35B,35D,35F
Palmer, Christopher G.	FL1900	35A,35B,35D,35F,35H
Simpson, Ron	UT0050	35A,35B,35D,35E,35F
Smith, Tony L.	TN0150	35A,35E,35F,10D
Strasser, Richard	MA1450	35A,35F
Stup, Chris	CO0830	35A,35C,35D,35F
Thomas, Colby L.	NY3765	39,60A,35F,61,54
Weary, Hal	PA0050	35A,35D,35F
Young, Jeff	AB0040	34D,35D,35E,35F,35G
Zeisler, Nathaniel W.	CA1075	35A,35F

Recording Technology

Abbott, James S.	NY4150	35C,35D,35G
Adams, James M.	ND0600	35G,37,47,49,53
Alexander, Prince Charles	MA0260	34,35C,35G
Alverson, D. J.	CA0950	35C,35D,35G
Alverson, David J.	CA3800	35G
Bailey, Richard H.	AR0810	34,35C,35G,63A
Baker, Frederick	MT0200	35G
Balder, Patrick	MN1625	35C,35G
Balins, Andris	NY3765	35C,35D,35G,47,70
Barata, Antonio G.	CA0600	10,34D,35D,35G
Beardslee, Tony	NE0460	35C,35D,35G,34D,34E
Bech, Soren	AI0150	34,35G
Beck, Robert T.	MO1810	35G
Begault, Durand	AI0150	34,35G
Benson, Robert	IA0300	34D,35G
Berger, Brad	MA0260	34,35C,35G
Bjur, David	WA1150	35C,35D,35G
Blinman, Chad	MA0260	35C,35G
Bondelevitch, David	CO0830	35C,35D,35G
Bordon, Wellington	NC1600	35D,35G
Bouchillon, Joel	AL1150	35G
Bowen, William	NY2750	34D,35G
Braasch, Jonas	AI0150	34,35G
Bradshaw, Robert J.	MA1650	10A,10C,10F,35A,35G
Bregitzer, Lorne	CO0830	35C,35D,35G
Brenner, Martin	CA0825	35G
Brown, Kathryn D.	TX0370	11,35G
Browne, Steve	TX0370	34,35G
Buchwald, Peter	CO0830	35C,35D,35G
Bunce, Mark Robert	OH0300	34,35D,35G
Burgess, William	SC0050	34D,35G
Campbell, Todd A.	NC0700	35G,34D,35D,65,35C
Campion, Edmund	CA5000	20,13,34,35G
Carney, David	CA4100	34D,35C,35G,72
Carr, Thomas	VA0600	35G
Casuccio, Anthony	NY4460	35D,35G
Channell, Timothy L.	VA1100	35A,35G
Chaplin, Clay	CA0510	10,34,35G
Chapman, Don	AF0050	35G,35D
Chase, Jon	MA0260	10,35C,35G
Chesanow, Marc	SC0420	62D,11,10F,13B,35G
Ciarniello, D. Jack	OH2600	35G
Coffey, Ted	VA1550	10B,10,34,35C,35G
Cohen, Alan	NJ0950	34D,35G
Coleman, Todd	NC0750	10,34,62D,35G,45
Comotto, Brian	MD0175	10,35C,35D,35G,66A
Cook, Peter	AI0150	34,35G
Corbett, Ian	KS0590	10,34,35D,35G,13G
Coulas, Ben	AB0040	34,35D,35G,34D
Crawford, Jeff D.	CA5350	35G,34A,34D
Crotts, Angela	TX2295	35C,35G
Crutti, John A.	LA0300	35G
Czink, Andrew	AB0040	35D,35G,34D
Davis, Greg	PA0500	34A,34D,35C,35D,35G
De Francisco, Martha	AI0150	34,35G
Debes, Edward	PA3710	35C,35D,35G,35H
Deuson, Nicolas	GA0050	13,34A,34D,35G,70
Devine, George M.	RI0300	35C,35D,35G
Dismore, Roger	TX0370	47,20G,29,35A,35G
Doczi, Tom F.	NY2750	34D,35G
Drown, Steve	ME0340	35G,34D
Dvorin, David	CA0800	13,10,35G,45
Egre, Bruce	OH0600	35C,35G
Elliott, Bill	MA0260	10,35C,35G
Ellis, Lief	CT0650	35G
Epstein, Steven	AI0150	35G,34
Erickson, Mark	TX3175	35C,35D,35G
Faganel, Gal	CO0950	62C,42,35G,51
Feindell, S.	AB0040	35D,35G,34D
Ferraro, David C.	NY2550	35C,35G
Foley, Charles F.	NV0050	35C,35G
Fordham, Matthew	WA0860	35A,35B,35C,35D,35G
Forehan, Jeff	CA5510	10B,13A,34D,35G,35D
Francis, Jeff	SC1110	35C,35G
Gaff, Isaac	IL1550	34,13G,13,35C,35G
Galo, Gary A.	NY3780	13L,35G
Gamberoni, Steve	WA0950	35C,35G
Gaston, Leslie	CO0830	35C,35D,35G
Geist, Doug	NM0450	35G,35C
Geluso, Paul	NY2750	34D,35G
Germany, Sam	TX0370	13,66D,35G
Gilliam, C.	MA0800	35G
Gilstrap, Kenneth	MT0175	35G
Gitt, Bill	MA0260	34,35C,35G
Glanz, James M.	NY2750	35C,35G
Gonko, Daniel	NC0700	35D,35G
Gonzales, Mario	CA2960	35G
Goomas, Steve	CA2650	35C,35G,13L
Greenspan, Stuart	IL0720	13,35G
Haertel, Tim	IN1010	35C,35G
Hara, Craig	WI0845	35G,11
Harbison, Kevin	CO0800	35G
Harlas, Lou	TX0370	35G,47
Harris, Ben	FL0100	34,35C,35G,32F
Hartzell, William H.	OH0200	35G
Haydon, Rick	IL2910	70,29,35G,53,47
Hehmsoth, Henry	TX3175	35C,35D,35G,66A
Heitsch, Paul	VA0600	35G
Heldt, Tim	MI0850	34D,35D,35G
Heller, Brian	MN1050	10B,34,12A,35B,35G
Henry, William R.	TX3175	35C,35D,35G
Herald, Terry	MI1750	35G,35C,11
Hernandez, Bernardo	MA0260	10,35G,35C
Hickinbotham, Gary	TX3175	35C,35D,35G
Hill, Barry R.	PA1900	35G
Hodan, Thomas	TX0370	70,35G
Hood, Mark	IN0900	35C,35G
Houlihan, Mickey	CO0560	34D,35G
Hurst, Michael Shane	TX0370	61,40,35G
Irwin, Pamela	TX0370	35G
Isaacs, David	TN1400	70,11,35G,45
Jacobsen, Chad	IA0550	29,35G
Johnson, Fred	CO0830	35G
Johnson, Robert M.	CA0150	35G,35C
Johnson, Shawn F.	MD0650	35C,35G
Johnson, Tom	CA3320	35C,35D,35G
Jones, Arlington	TX0370	13,10F,66A,35G
Julian, Michael	CA2750	35D,35C,35G,13C,13D
Kakouberi, Daredjan 'Baya'	TX0370	66A,35G
Kalinowski, Mark	NJ0175	35C,35G
Karathanasis, Konstantinos	OK1350	34D,10A,10,35C,35G
Karnatz, Roland	VA1150	35G,64C
Kaupp, Gil	NV0050	35C,35G,63A
Kendall, David	CA2420	35G,63C,63D
Kerr, Brady	CA3265	66C,35A,35C,35D,35G
Kilianski, Harold	AI0150	34,35G
Kim-Boyle, David	MD1000	34,35C,35G
King, Richard	AI0150	34,35G
Konsbruck, James	IN1750	70,35G
Konzelman, Brian	TX1600	35C,35D,35G
Kostusiak, Thomas J.	NY3717	35C,35D,35G
Lambson, Nick	CA2250	70,41,35G
Last, Julie	VT0050	34D,35D,35G
Latarski, Donald	OR1050	70,35G,41
Lee, Abe	MA0260	10A,10D,35C,35G
Lee, Jordan	WI1150	35G
Lehrer, Scott	VT0050	34C,35D,35G
Leider, Colby N.	FL1900	34A,35C,10B,34D,35G
Levinson, Drew	CO0830	35G
Liikala, Blair	TX3420	35G
Lippstrew, Lee	CO0600	46,34D,35G,35A
Liu-Rosenbaum, Aaron	AI0190	10,34,35G,13,14C
Lotz, James	TN1450	12A,64D,35G
Marlow, William	GA2100	35G
Martens, William	AI0150	34,35G
Mason, John	MA1100	70,35G,35G
Massenburg, George	AI0150	34,35G
Matsumoto, Shane	AZ0470	35D,35G
May, Jim	AZ0470	35G
Mazurek, Drew	MD0650	35C,35G
McArthur-Brown, Gail	MA0260	10,35C,35G
McGuire, Samuel A.	CO0830	35C,35D,35G
McKinney, Matthew	AL1200	34D,34H,35C,35G
McKinnie, Douglas	IN0900	35C,35G
McLowry, Sean	NY0700	34D,35G,34E,34F,34H
McLure, Richard	TX0370	35G,57,53,70
McManus, Edward	OR0350	63B,34A,35C,35G,13A
Merkel, Jeffrey	CO0830	35C,35D,35G
Metcalfe, James L.	TX2295	65,35C,35G,46
Metcalfe, Scott	MD0650	35C,35G
Miles, Dean	AB0040	35G,35H
Miller, Lance R.	OR1050	35C,35G
Miller, Tim	NE0460	35C,35D,35G,34D,34E
Moore, Mike	OR1250	35G
Moore, Raymond D.	GA2100	35G
Morris, Jeffrey M.	TX2900	70,34,35G
Mosher, Jimm	NC0350	35D,35G,34D
Napoli, Robert	NY2550	35G
Neal, Tira	CO0830	35G
Nichols, David	AZ0350	35G
OGrady, Douglas M.	CT0800	13,34,35G,10
Paduck, Ted	MA0260	34,35C,35G
Parkinson, Wm. Michael	OH1900	29,35G,47
Payne, Maggi	CA2950	10B,35D,35C,35G
Pejrolo, Andrea	MA0260	34,10C,10,35C,35G
Peterson, Russell	MN0600	47,48,64D,64E,35G
Pierce, Bradley	MA0150	34D,35D,35G
Pirkle, William C.	FL1900	34A,34D,34G,35C,35G
Polk, Sylvester	FL0100	34,63A,35A,35D,35G
Poniatowski, Mark	MA0260	10,35C,35G
Powers, Ollie	CA5360	35G,35C,11,12A,34
Prochnow, Peter	NE0150	31A,35G
Ragotskie, Scott	CA1900	35G
Rathbun, Andrew	NY2050	35C,35D,35G,10B,45
Reba, Christopher H.	CT0700	34D,10B,35G,62D,13
Rehl, William	MI0300	35G
Reynolds, Steve	LA0800	34D,35C,35D,35G
Richardson, Cathy	TX0370	62A,35G
Richardson, Chuck	TX2850	11,45,35C,35G
Riley, Justin	OH0350	34,35C,35D,35G,13G
Robertson, Ben	WA0250	10B,45,35G,34D
Roditski, William	PA2200	34A,35G
Rodriguez, Alex	MA0260	34,35C,35G
Rodriguez, Elvin	CA2420	11,66A,35G,35C
Rolls, Timothy	KS0350	10,13,34,35C,35G
Roston, John	AI0150	34,35G
Rothkopf, Michael S.	NC1650	45,35C,35G
Rubinstein, Mark	OH1850	35C,35D,34D,35G
Sadler, Trevor	WI1150	35G
Sargent, Daniel	CA0800	35C,35G
Scarano, Robert	CA3265	34,35G,70
Scherschell, Rebecca	TX0370	35G,62E
Schmutte, Peter J.	IN1650	36,45,35C,35G,34
Scholwin, Richard M.	NE0590	35C,35G,34D
Schulz, Mark Alan	OH1350	34D,35G,35D,62C,29B
Schulz, Riccardo	PA0550	35C,35G
Schulze, Michael	CO0900	35C,35D,35G
Schumacher, Craig	AZ0490	35G
Selter, Scott	CO0830	35G
Sewrey, Jacques	WI1150	35G

Index by Area of Teaching Interest

Name	Code	Areas
Seymour, David	OH1350	35D,35G
Sheehan, Dan	NJ0020	35,35G
Siegel, Dan	CA2960	35C,35D,34D,35G
Sipes, Danny T.	TX2930	63D,35A,35C,35D,35G
Smiley, William C.	NC1550	10B,35C,35G,45
Smith, Charlie	AR0400	35G
Smith, Ed	TX0370	65B,35G
Soifer, Tyler	CO0830	35G
Solomonson, Terry	IL3500	11,63D,35C,35D,35G
Solum, Stephen	MN1050	13,20G,10,35G,34
Spencer, James W.	AR0750	35C,35G
Spencer, Larry	TX0370	35G,63A
Spotts, Cory	AZ0490	35G
Springfield, David	GA2150	29,35G,63C
Stark, Melissa	OR0350	35G
Stearns, Loudon	MA0260	10,35C,35G
Stegmann, Matthias	IN0550	70,35G
Steinman, Daniel B.	IL0750	35G
Stillman, Fallon	IN0900	35C,35G
Storyk, John	CO0830	35G
Strauss, Konrad	IN0900	35C,35G
Stucker, Michael D.	IN0900	35C,35G
Tadey, Anthony	IN0900	35C,35G
Teran, Louie	CA2550	35D,35G
Tetreault, Edward	MD0650	35C,35G
Theisen, Alan	NC1250	13,10,34,35G,64E
Thomas, Wayne	MN1250	35G
Tomassetti, Benjamin	VA0500	35G,10B,34D,35C,64E
Traugh, Steven	CA2960	35G
Ungar, Leanne	MA0260	34,35C,35G
Valera, Philip	NC0100	34D,35G,35C,35D,13L
Van Wagner, Eric	OH2050	35G,35A,47
Vermeulen, Ron	AB0040	35A,35D,35G
Villani, A. David	PA2710	34B,35G,29A
Volpicelli, Thomas	PA1900	35G
Wade, Brett	AB0040	35D,35G
Waller, Jim	TX3410	35G,10C,29B,47,35A
Waltl, Herbert	AI0150	34,35G
Warner, Tony	MD0650	35G
Watkinson, Christopher L.	ME0200	13L,34D,35D,35G
Weinberg, Charles	NC2400	35G
Westfall, Ben	IN1025	35G
Williams, John Flawn	DC0075	35C,35G,35H
Williams, Lester C.	TX2295	35D,35G
Winer, Arthur H.	CA0630	10D,34D,35G,35,10C
Wong, Sui-Fan	AA0080	35C,35G
Wood, Dan	NY3770	34,35C,35D,35G
Woodyard, Jim	AB0040	35D,35G
Woszczyk, Wieslaw	AI0150	34,35G
Wright, Robert	VA1000	34,35A,35C,35D,35G
Wyner, Jonathan	MA0260	34,35C,35G
Wynne, Scott	NC0050	35G,35D,35C,35
Young, Jeff	AB0040	34D,35D,35E,35F,35G
Zoffer, David	MA0260	10,35C,35G
Zolner, Robert R.	NY3780	35G

Radio/Television

Name	Code	Areas
Argiro, James	MA2100	35C,35H,46,10C
Borgers, Ken	CA2550	34,35H
Burke, Kevin F.	OH2200	35H
Burke, Thomas	MA0200	35H
Burlingame, Jon	CA5300	35H,10C
Burton, Ray	CA2550	35H
Conrad, Robert	OH0600	35H
Debes, Edward	PA3710	35C,35D,35G,35H
Elton, Serona	FL1900	35A,35B,35D,35F,35H
Fox, Marjorie	OH2200	35H
Grimm, Mark	NY3680	35H
Haines, Thomas	OH2200	35H,35D
Hallgren, Scott	TN1400	35H,10C
Hannah, Mike	NC1050	35H,66C
Hatzis, Christos	AG0450	10,35H,34,35C,13L
Hersh, Robert	CA2550	35H
Hodge, Cheryl	AB0070	10,36,61,53,35H
King, Brian	CA5300	10,35H,35
Lopez, Kenneth	CA5300	35H,35
Lyons, Robert	MA1450	35D,35H
Matthews, Robin L.	CA2050	11,35H
Mehrmann, Dan	IL2970	34D,35H
Miles, Dean	AB0040	35G,35H
Miller, Rebecca S.	MA1000	14,13A,20F,31B,35H
Owens, John W.	OH2200	35H
Palmer, Christopher G.	FL1900	35A,35B,35E,35F,35H
Parenteau, Gilles	AB0070	10F,45,66,35H
Pearce, Peter	CA2550	35H
Potter, Joe	MO2050	66A,66G,35H,54,35E
Redmond, John	FL1900	35A,35B,35D,35H
Rolle, Nina	CO0560	11,35H
Rose, Brian	OR0050	34,35C,35D,35H
Skogstoe, John	NE0460	35H,34E
Smalley, Jack	CA5300	35H,35
Speer, Janet Barton	NC1050	35H,54,35E
Theberge, Paul	AG0100	35,35H
Uhlenkott, Gary	WA0400	13A,66A,13B,35H,47
Wilkins, Donald	MA0260	35H
Williams, John Flawn	DC0075	35C,35G,35H
Wolfram, Manfred K.	OH2200	35H
Young, Chris	CA5300	35H,35
Yuasa, Joji	CA5050	10,20D,35H,34,35C

Choral

Name	Code	Areas
Aagaard, J. Kjersgaard	WI0842	13,11,36,37,49
Aamot, Kirk C.	MT0200	36,40,32D,60A
Abbey, Gail	MA1560	61,36
Abbott, Carol	FL0930	61,36
Abbott, Wesley	CA2600	36,61,35B,13
Abel, Sandra	TX0390	36,61,13A,13B,13C
Abraham, Daniel E.	DC0010	11,12,14C,36,60
Acevedo, Carmen	PR0150	36,60A
Adam, Jennifer	KY1550	32D,13C,36
Adams, Kenny L.	OK0700	60,36,39,54,40
Adkins, Angela	NC1200	36
Adkins, Kathy	AL0750	11,36,61,66A
Afonasyeva, Yekaterina	MD0850	66D,36,66C
Afonso, Daniel R.	CA0850	36,40,13C,32D,60A
Aldrich, Nicole P.	MO1900	36,40,60
Alexander, Cory T.	TX3527	36,32D,61,32,40
Alexander, Marina	NY0644	36,12A,12C,60A
Alexander, Travis	NC1550	12A,36,40,66
Aliapoulis, S. Mark	FL0700	36,61
Allaire, Jean-Sebastien	AG0100	12,13,36,60A
Allbritten, James	NC1650	36,61,39
Allen, Burt	LA0550	36,60A,60,34,61
Allen, Lisa M.	GA1100	20G,32,36,31A
Allen, Nancy	WI1100	60A,32,36,54
Allison, Linda	DC0110	36,61
Allsup, Neal	KS0550	11,12A,36,60,61
Almond, Frank W.	CA4100	60,12A,36
Almquist, Bradley L.	KY0950	60,32,36,13C
Alstat, Sara	IL2500	11,13A,13C,36,61
Alston, John	PA3200	36
Alt, Jerry A.	NM0310	36,61,60
Altevogt, Brian L.	MI0500	36
Althouse, Paul L.	CT0100	11,60A,12A,36
Alviani, Henry	PA0700	36,40,60A,61
Alwes, Chester	IL3300	36,60A
Amante Y Zapata, Joseph J.	RI0101	36,40,11,13A,13B
Amato, Patricia	MD0850	36,39
Ames, Jeffrey	TN0100	36,60A
Amos, Shaun	GA0500	60,36,13B,13C,12A
Amrein, Emilie	IL1400	36,12A,13C,60,11
Amundson, Bret	MN0450	32,36,60A
Anavitarte, David	TX2550	36,61,66A,12A,32B
Andaya, Mitos	PA3250	36,60A
Anders, Micheal F.	OH2275	12A,61,54,36
Anderson, Alerica	MO1100	36
Anderson, Charlotte	TN1150	61,36
Anderson, Cheryl M.	CA0400	13,36,39
Anderson, David	WA0800	36,20G
Anderson, Edward D.	CO0250	60,36
Anderson, Frank	NY0270	36,61
Anderson, Gary L.	KY1350	60A,12A,36
Anderson, Jared L.	WI0600	36,61,66A,13,12A
Anderson, Jared	MI1450	36,40,11,12A
Anderson, Jeff	KS1000	36,32D,60A
Anderson, Kathy T.	MS0570	36,40,61
Anderson, Ken	CA2100	36,61
Anderson, Lyle J.	OH0450	60A,36,31A
Anderson, Michael J.	IL3310	13A,60,36
Anderson, Scott E.	ID0100	36,40,60A,61
Anderson, Seija	CA4300	36,61
Andraso, Margaret B.	KY1100	11,36,61,63A
Andrews, Jane E.	IA1800	32,36
Andrews-Smith, Belinda	OH0850	61,36,39
Angulo, Skye	CA2550	36,61
Antolini, Anthony	ME0200	36,13A,66D
Apple, A. Alan	PA1750	13A,36,61,13C,40
Aprahamian, Lucik	CA2150	36
Archer, Ed	CA3150	36,40
Archer, Gail	NY0200	36,12A
Archibeque, Charlene	CA4400	36,40,60A,32D
Ardrey, Cathleen	PA2350	32,36,61,66A
Armstrong, Anton	MN1450	60A,36,61
Armstrong, Candace	TN0900	13C,36,60A,66A,11
Armstrong, Colin	PA3150	32D,36,13C
Armstrong, James I.	VA0250	36,12A,60,12C
Arnett, Nathan D.	IL1240	11,13C,32A,36,40
Arnold, Craig S.	NY2150	36
Arroe, Cate	MI0650	20,36,66
Arshagouni, Michael H.	CA2750	13B,13C,12A,66A,36
Ashby, Eda	ID0060	36,61,32D
Ashworth, Teresa	MN1100	61,36,40,20,13C
Aspaas, Christopher	MN1450	36,61,60A,32D
Aspling, Carol	CA0350	36,61
Atienza, Anthony	CA4850	66A,36
Atkinson, Monte	CO0225	60,32C,36,61,66A
Atorino, John J.	NY2750	36
Atteberry, Ron	MO0100	10F,36,61,10A
Aucoin, Amy	KY0950	32,36,60A,13C
Augenblick, John	FL0700	60A,36,11
Aune, Gregory	MN0750	60A,36,32D
Ausmann, Stephen	OH2600	32,36
Austin, Stephanie	CA1450	36,61,66A,40,32
Avery, Handy	AL1160	36,60A
Babb, Mark	IN1485	36
Babcock, Jonathan	TX3175	36,61,32D
Babcock, Mark A.	IA0200	36,40,66G,13
Bach, Larry	MN1250	60,36,61
Bacon, Boyd	NE0450	13,36,61,40
Bailey, Brian K.	OH0650	36,61
Bailey, Donald	TX0300	60,36
Bailey, Jon D.	CA3650	60,12A,36,11
Bain, Clare	IN1100	36,31A
Baker, Alan	PA0250	60A,11,36,61,54
Baker, Guy O.	WV0650	60,36,61
Baker, Katherine Ramos	CA0835	32,36
Baker, Kevin L.	MO0300	36,32D,61,60,32
Baker, Meredith E.	NY2550	13,66G,36
Baker, Nicole	CA0815	12A,36
Baker, R. Bryan	CA1250	60A,61,36
Baker, William	IN0005	12,13,60,36,39
Baldwin, Joseph	MA1750	36,60
Bales, Bruce	CA2050	40,61,67,13A,36
Balian, Muriel	CA1960	11,66A,66D,36,55D
Ball, Sheridan J.	CA1520	36,41,61,13A
Ballou, David L.	MD0850	29,53,63A,29A,36
Ballweg, D. Brent	OK0650	36,60A
Balmos, Donald	TX1600	36
Bandermann, Billie	CA1550	61,36
Baptiste, Renee L.	AL0500	32B,32C,32D,32G,36
Bara, Daniel J.	GA2100	60A,36
Barbham, Vicki	OR0350	36,66D
Barland, Charles J.	IA1450	13,11,31A,66A,36
Barnum, Eric	WI0830	36
Barr, Stephen A.	PA3100	13,36,40,34
Barr, Wayne A.	AL1100	36
Barrientos, Paul	NM0350	11,36,61
Barstow, Robert S.	NY3765	12A,36,16,35
Bartlett, Jacob Kenneth	NE0500	36,61,11
Bartlett, Jamie	VA0250	36
Bartley, Mark	TX3750	36,38,60,60B
Barton, Katie	KY1000	36
Barton, Stephen	MI0850	36,40,11,12A,61
Basney, Nyela	TX3527	61,66,36,38,60
Bass, James K.	FL2000	36
Bassett, Jon	FL0670	36,61,51,38,32D
Batchvarova, Madlen T.	IN0650	60A,36,61,66A,12A
Bates, Michael J.	AR0810	36,13,60,12A,66A
Batey, Angela L.	TN1710	32,36
Battipaglia, Diana M.	NY0635	11,32,36,66A,38
Bauchspies, Cindy	MD0900	31A,36
Bauer, David	NE0590	36,61,60A,32D
Bauer, Jeffrey	KS1350	36,66G,66H,31A
Bauman, Jeffrey Milo	GA2300	36,61,54,10F,60A
Bausano, William	OH1450	60A,32C,36,61
Bayen, Diane	NY2450	13C,61,36,60,32
Becker, Gisele	DC0100	36
Becker, Jeral Blaine	MO1250	61,36,11,60,39
Becker, Karen E.	NY3775	66A,66C,13C,13A,36
Becker, Melinda	CA2801	36,61
Beckford, Richard	LA0700	11,36,66G,13
Beckford, Richard E.	SC1050	13,60,11,36,66G

Index by Area of Teaching Interest

Name	Code	Areas
Beckmann-Collier, Aimee	IA0550	
Beckwith, Sterling	AG0650	12,36,61,12F
Belan, William	CA0830	60,36
Belfield, Roy L.	NC2700	66G,36,60A,10F,12A
Bell, Cindy L.	NY1600	32,11,36
Bell, Jeff	IL2300	36,61,54,60
Bell, Joby	NC0050	66G,66H,36,31A
Bell, Vicki	KY0100	13,10,36
Bell, Victor	CA5060	36
Bellamy, Amy J.	NY0450	11,29A,36,61
Belles, David	CT0150	36,40,60,61
Belnap, Michael	HI0050	36,39,40,54,61
Bennett, Glenn	AZ0440	36,61
Bennett, Vicki	AZ0440	61,36
Benson, Will	TN0300	11,13,34B,36,64
Bent, Jenny	CA4700	36
Bentley, Joe	MI1830	12A,32D,60,36
Benz, Terri	IL1650	61,66A,36
Berentsen, Kurt	OR0150	36,60,61,32A,40
Bergstrom, Melissa	MN0040	36,40,12A,38,61
Bernhardt, Ross C.	TX2930	36,61
Best, Nneka	PA1150	36
Bethany, Adeline M.	PA0450	11,20D,32A,32B,36
BeVille, Jesse	VA1600	36
Bhanji, Baomi Butts	CA1800	36
Bible, Kierstin Michelle	MO0260	36,61,12A,13A,54
Biddlecombe, Mary	TN1850	36
Biddlecombe, Thomas 'Tucker'	TN1850	36,42,32D
Bidelman, Mark	CA0400	36
Bieritz, Gerald	TX1300	12A,11,32A,36,60
Bierschenk, Jerome Michael	TX3250	36,37,32D,61,63A
Bigler, Dwight	VA1700	36,60A
Billingham, Lisa A.	VA0450	32D,36,60A
Billington, Ryan	AF0150	36,40,29,61
Billington, Ryan	AF0120	61,29,36
Binger, Adlai	PA0050	36,61,66G,60A,66C
Biscay, Karen T.	OH1330	13,11,12A,36,61
Bishop, Bruce W.	AZ0300	34,36,61,13,60A
Bishop, Jason	PA2715	36
Bishop, Saundra	MS0575	13A,36,66A,66D,13B
Bjella, Richard L.	TX3200	36,40
Blachly, Alexander	IN1700	60,12,36,55,12A
Black, Karen	IA1800	13C,31A,36,66G
Black, Kathryn A.	NY3475	61,36,40
Blackley, Rowland	OH0100	60A,32D,36,40,55D
Blackshear, Glinda	AL0831	60,11,36,39,61
Blackstone, Jerry O.	MI2100	60,36
Blackwell, Leslie	GA1150	36,40,60A
Blanchard, Gerald J.	MI1160	11,36,13,60A,61
Blankenbaker, Scott E.	MN1290	11,13,61,36
Blea, Anthony	CA1020	38,62A,36
Bleiler, Loueda	NY0950	11,12A,13A,13B,36
Blersch, Jeffrey	NE0150	13,36,66G
Bletstein, Beverly	OH1850	32,36
Blodget, Sherril	VT0100	40,36,60,61,11
Blomquist, Jane K.	CA2600	36,61,13
Bloom, Bradley	AG0550	36
Board, Ryan A.	CA3600	11,32C,36,31A,60A
Boccarossa, Jennifer	AR0750	36
Bode, Robert	MO1810	60A,36,61
Boeder, Bethel J.	MN1030	36,66A
Boerger, Kristina G.	WI0200	36
Boers, Geoffrey	WA1050	60,36,38
Boesiger, Kevin	NE0525	36,54
Boga, Cheryl	PA3500	36,37,47,38,51
Bogdan, Thomas	VT0050	36,61,31,40
Bogey, Brian A.	NY1850	36
Bolkovac, Edward	CT0650	36,60
Bollinger, Bernard	CA1000	36,61,54
Bolster, Stephen C.	KY0300	60,32D,36,40,61
Bolton, Bryan	KY0050	11,13A,32,36,61
Bolton, Thomas W.	KY1200	61,31A,36,12A
Bonner, Gary	CA0450	36,38,60
Bonner, Judd	CA0450	36,60
Boos, Kenneth G.	FL1310	13,60,36,41,61
Boozer, John E.	NC2350	60,20,36,31,61
Bordas, Ricard	SC0275	36,61
Borton, Bruce E.	NY3705	60,36,61
Bostic, Bert	TX1660	36,47,66D
Bot, Mary Jo	MN1300	36
Boudreaux, Margaret A.	MD0520	60,12A,32D,36
Bougie, Marc-Andre	TX2850	11,10,13,36
Boullion, Linda	NE0460	13,11,40,36,61
Bouwman, Aaron	MI0520	36,40
Bowen, K. Scott	CA4300	13,36
Bowen, Meredith Y.	MI1200	36,20,13
Bowen, Richard L.	IN1850	36,12,12A,11,12B
Bowers, Judy	FL0850	32,36
Bowers, Teresa M.	PA1400	64A,64B,12A,36,42
Bowles, Kenneth E.	ND0250	36,61,39,60,32C
Boyd, Kim	OH2050	36,60A,32D,13C
Boyer, D. Royce	AL1160	11,12A,36,61,31A
Boyer, Douglas R.	TX3100	36,60,54,32D,13F
Boyer, Maurice C.	IL0730	13C,36,38,44
Bradfield, Bart	IL0720	36
Bradley, Mark	KY0400	12C,32G,36,39,61
Bradley, Randall	TX0300	36,31A
Bradshaw, Keith M.	UT0200	10A,10F,13,36
Bragle, John	MI1650	36
Branch, Stephen F.	CA3975	12A,61,31A,36,40
Brandau, Ryan James	NJ1350	36,60A
Brandenburg, Julie A.	WI0450	10D,36,61,66D
Brandes, David R.	NH0110	13,10F,60,36,66G
Brandon, Joan Lynette	IN0100	32B,36,32C,32D
Brandon, Mack	NJ0950	10B,31F,36,41
Brannon, Patrick V.	IL3370	14,12A,36,60A,40
Bray, Michael R.	PA3260	60,61,11,36,12A
Breden, Mary C.	CA2800	60A,36,32D
Breland, Barron	NE0160	13,36
Breland, Jason	AL1195	36
Brewer, Bert R.	MT0450	36,61
Bridges, Madeline	TN0100	32,36
Briggs, Philip	TX2050	36,40,61,11
Briggs, Robert	UT0150	36,61,12A,60A
Brimmer, Timothy	IN0250	60,32,36,34
Brinckmeyer, Lynn	TX3175	32D,36
Brinegar, Donald L.	CA3500	13A,36,61,60
Brinson, Barbara Ann	NY3725	32,36
Briones, Marella	MO0650	61,11,36,32B,39
Broad-Ginsberg, Elaine	NH0150	13,31B,10A,36
Brodie, Catherine	MI1500	36
Broeker, Angela	MN1625	60A,36
Broman, John M.	GA1500	36,40,61
Bronaugh, Roderic	TN1400	11,36
Bronfman, Joshua	ND0500	36,40,32D,60A
Brooks, C. Thomas	MA0950	60A,36,40,61
Brooks, Jack	TX1510	36,61,40,13C
Brooks, Marguerite	CT0850	60,36
Broomhead, Paul	UT0050	32,36
Brothers, Grey	CA5550	13,36,61,11,12A
Brotherton, Jonathan P.	NC0900	36,13C,32D
Broughton, Gregory	GA2100	36,61
Brower, Kevin	ID0060	36,61,32D
Brower, Nori	ID0060	13C,36
Brown, Aaron	MN1625	36,31A
Brown, Andiel	OR1050	36,31F
Brown, Bruce C.	NY1700	60,11,36,61,31A
Brown, Charles	NY0270	36,61
Brown, Charles P.	IL0730	36,60,32
Brown, J. F. Mark	AL0831	61,35,36,11
Brown, Jeri	AI0070	36,47,61,29
Brown, Linda	CA3750	36,40,61
Brown, Philip	VT0300	11,13A,36,44,47
Brown, Trent R.	FL0680	36,40,60A
Brown, Wes	MA2020	62D,36
Brown-Clayton, Janet	CT0450	36
Brown-Kibble, Gennevieve	TN1350	11,36,60A,61
Browne, Douglas A.	PA1450	13C,60A,36,61
Browne, Peter J.	NY3705	36,13C
Brubaker, Debra	IN0550	39,61,36,31A,20
Bruce, Neely	CT0750	12A,36,20G
Brugh, Lorraine S.	IN1750	36,31A,66G
Brumley, Dianne	TX3515	36,32D,60A
Bruner, G. Edward	CA5040	11,36
Brunner, David L.	FL1800	60,36,32D,10
Brunson, Richard	WI0922	36
Bryan, Karen	CA3460	36,60A
Bryant, Edward	FL1740	13C,36,61,39,40
Bryant, Stephen	NJ1400	60,36,61
Bryson, Amity H.	MO0050	36,61,60A,15,32D
Buchanan, Heather J.	NJ0800	32D,36,40,60A
Buchanan, Scott	IN0800	36,60
Buchierre, Alisa	MA1500	11,13C,36
Buettner, Jeff	VT0350	13A,36,40,13B,13C
Buffington, Blair	IA1750	61,36,40,32A,60A
Bull, Tina	OR0700	32,36
Bullock, Kathy	KY0300	11,20A,36,13A,13C
Bullock, Valerie K.	SC0275	60,32B,32C,36
Bump, Delbert	CA4650	13A,13,36,53
Bumpers, Wayne	FL1300	36,66A,66D,20G,66B
Bundage, Raphael	TN1100	36,39,60A
Burbach, Brock	FL0200	36,61,40
Burgess, Phillipa	OH1750	36,55C,14C,12A,20
Burke, D'Walla Simmons	NC2700	60A,36,61
Burke, Karen M.	AG0650	61,60A,36,32
Burkot, Louis G.	NH0100	36,61,39
Burleson, Jill	CO0950	60A,36,32D
Burnett, Lawrence E.	MN0300	36,40,31F,61,13A
Burnett, Marty Wheeler	NE0100	12A,13,66A,36,66G
Burns, Brian E.	IA0250	36,12A,32C,32D,60
Burns, Portia	GA0350	36
Burricher, Ronald	FL1850	36,61
Burrs, Lisa Edwards	VA1750	11,13A,36,61
Burton, Sean Michael	IA0100	36,61,41,11,13D
Busch, Gregg	MO0200	11,13A,31A,36,61
Busch, Michael	CA1425	36,60,13B,32D
Busselberg, Paul	TX2295	61,36,13C
Bustamante, Tamara A.	KY1100	36,11,13,66C,66A
Butke, Marla A.	OH0100	32,11,66D,36,60A
Buttolph, David	NY3705	60,36
Byerly, Douglas	MD0060	13,36,39
Byrd, Eric B.	MD0520	36,66A,29
Byun, John	CA3800	61,36,11
Byykkonen, Susan E.	MI1450	66,36
Cabrera, Ricardo	PR0100	11,36,61,60,13A
Cairns, Debra	AA0100	60,36
Caldwell, Hansonia	CA0805	20G,36
Caldwell, William	TN0100	36,60
Caldwell, William	OH0500	36,39,61,60
Calhoun, James M.	CA5100	36,40,60
Callahan, Nancy	FL2050	36
Calvo, Francisco	CA1900	36,32,12
Camera, Bede C.	NH0310	36
Cameron, Virginia	OH1600	60A,36,61,40,11
Camp, Philip	TX1550	36,61,13,32,40
Campbell, Andy	MO1550	36,61,13C
Campbell, Derek	DC0350	36,61
Campbell, Dianna	FL1700	61,36,40,11,32D
Campbell, Don	SC1080	13,60,36,61,12A
Campbell, Helen E.	AL0310	13A,13,36,61,66
Campbell, Jayne E.	CA1960	36,55,61,31A
Campbell, John W.	KY0610	60,11,32,61,36
Campbell, Stanford	OR0600	36,61,31A,60A
Campbell, Timothy	WV0750	36
Cancio-Bello, Susan	NH0050	11,54,61,36,33
Canton, Lisette M.	AG0650	36,55,60
Caporella, Cynthia Anne	OH1050	36,12A,66A,66C
Carew, David	MI1985	36,61,40,32D,13C
Carlisle, Mark R.	IN0800	36,61
Carlson, Damon J.	WI0770	60A,61,40,36
Carlson, Karyl K.	IL1150	36,60A
Carney, Horace R.	AL0010	13,60,10,36
Carney, Timothy F.	HI0060	36,11,13A,54,61
Carpenter, Gregory	WI0425	36,11
Carpenter, Tim	OH0850	36
Carr, Sarah	WV0800	36,60A
Carrington, Simon	CT0850	36
Carroll, William P.	NC2430	60,36
Carson, Caroline	LA0800	11,36,32D,60A
Carswell, William	SC0450	31A,61,32,36,40
Carter, Jeffrey Richard	MO1950	60A,36,61,13A
Carter, John R.	CA1375	11,12A,36,61,13C
Carter, Roland M.	TN1700	13,11,36,66A
Case, Del W.	CA3400	66G,44,13,12A,36
Casey, Maurice T.	OH1850	60,36
Casperson, Joseph	ID0075	36
Cassarino, James P.	VT0200	12,14,20,36,37
Castilla, Kathy	MS0650	11,36,61
Castilla, Willenham	MS0350	36,31,32D,61
Castleberry, David	WV0400	60,12A,36,61
Caston, Ben	GA2050	36,60A,61
Castonguay, David O.	VA1100	36,60,61
Cathey, Rodney	CA0250	60,36
Cavanaugh, Alice I.	NY4050	36,12A,11
Cazier, David	WA0150	36,61,29A,40
Celaire, Jaunelle R.	AK0150	36,39,40,61
Cetto, Edward	CA5350	36,32D,13C
Chae, Hyung Sek	TX3650	36,31A,44,60,32D
Chafin, Gerald	KY0860	60A,11,32,36,44
Chagnon, Richard	CA4050	11,12A,36,61
Chamberlain, Bruce B.	AZ0500	36
Chambers, James Alan	IN1050	61,13A,36
Chambers, Martin	CA4100	36,61
Chambers, Robert B.	TN0650	60,61,31A,36,44
Chandler, Deborah L.	LA0770	36,60,40
Chandler, Kyle	AR0110	32,36,47,32D,32G

549

Index by Area of Teaching Interest

Name	ID	Areas
Chang, Donathan	TX2570	31A,31B,61,60A,36
Chapple, Karliss	AR0550	36
Charloff, Ruth	CA5040	60,11,36,38
Chase, David A.	CA3460	13A,13,12A,36,60
Chase, Shannon M.	NJ1130	36
Chen, Xiaolun	FL1500	11,36,61
Cheng, Marietta	NY0650	13,60,11,36,38
Cheng, Wei	OH0850	36
Chernin, Mallorie	MA0100	36,40
Chiaravalloti, Charissa	CO0350	36,40,60,12A,32D
Childs, Kim J.	OK1450	36,40,61
Chin, David	NY3350	36,60A
Chivington, Amy	OH2050	32,36
Christ, Linden	IL0550	36
Christensen, Janielle	UT0050	12A,36,39,54,35
Christensen, Mary	AZ0440	36
Christensen, Russ	OR0700	36
Christeson, Jane	FL1750	61,12A,39,36
Christeson, Norton M.	FL0400	36,38,39,61
Christianson, Donald G.	AA0150	36
Chu, George	MN0800	13,36,61
Cierpke, Timothy H.	TN1600	10F,60,62,36,38
Cinquegrani, David	CT0350	31A,36,41,12
Cipullo, Tom	NY0280	13A,13,10,36,61
Clark, Andrew G.	MA1050	36,60
Clark, Charles 'Bud'	MO0800	36,61,54
Clark, Mark	KS1250	36,32D,13,40
Clark, Michael	FL1570	13,12A,36,66,54
Clausen, Arla	IA0910	36,61
Clausen, Rene	MN0600	60,36
Clemens, Julie	IL1350	36
Clements, Allen	AL0345	32D,36,60A,40,61
Clency, Cleveland	IL0650	11,66,40,36
Clifft, Al	CA0450	13,36,37
Clifft, Al	CA0250	36,60,13
Cline, Lonnie	OR0050	60,36,61
Cloeter, Tim	OH0300	36
Clousing, Harold	CA0250	61,36
Coates, Atina	ID0060	36,61
Cobb, James	NC0915	11,36,66G
Cobbs, Jerry	AL0330	61,36,11
Cock, Christopher M.	IN1750	60,36,61
Cody, David	MT0400	36,61,54,39,60A
Coffman, Teresa S.	RI0200	36,40,32D
Cogdell, Robyn	MS0320	36,54
Cogdill, Susan	NE0200	36
Cogen, Ellen	MA1100	61,40,36,13A,54
Cohen, Allen L.	NJ0400	13,10,54,39,36
Coker, Stephen R.	CA0960	36
Coker, Timothy C.	MS0385	13,60,32,36,66A
Coleman, Barrington	IL3300	36,61
Coleman, David F.	MA1900	36
Coleman, Edryn J.	PA2000	61,36,60A,13B
Coleman, Fred	SC0200	32,36,31A
Coleman, Lilian	TN0700	36,66A
Colleen, Jeffrey	IL1550	13,10,36,66A,31A
Collett, Jacqueline L.	MO1780	32,36,61,39
Collier, Joanne	AA0040	36,61
Collins, Cherie	ND0250	61,36,32D,64B
Collins, David	MN1250	31A,61,36,46
Collins, Drew S.	OH2500	32D,36
Collins, Myrtice J.	AL0500	32B,66D,36
Collister, Phillip	MD0850	61,36,39
Colwitz, Erin E.	AL1160	32B,61,60A,36,32C
Combs, Barry	SC0950	60,36,61,31A
Compton, Beckie	TX0125	66A,13,11,36,47
Con, Adam Jonathan	OH2450	36,32,11,60A,13C
Concordia, Stephen	PA2950	36,31A
Condaris, Christine	MA1185	12,14,36
Conkling, Susan W.	MA0400	32D,36,32C,32F,32G
Conley, Mark	RI0300	13,60,36,61,32D
Conlon, Joan C.	CO0800	60,36
Conner, Stacey	PA0600	36,39,61
Connolly, Michael E.	OR1100	36,12A,10A,61,13
Connors, Patricia Cahalan	MN1295	36,55D,60
Conte, David	CA4150	10,12A,36
Cook, Grant W.	OH2290	36,40,60,12
Cook, Stephen	CA6000	66A,35A,34,36,11
Cook, Warren	SC0200	13,60,36,31A,40
Cooksey, John M.	UT0250	36,32C,32D
Cooksey, Steven	VA1350	12A,36,66G,31A
Cooper, Britt	OH2370	11,12A,14C,36,61
Cooper, Gloria A.	NY2102	13A,61,32C,36,47
Cooper, Marianne G.	OH1850	32,36
Copeland, Louise	PA1350	36,61
Copeland, Philip L.	AL0800	60,36
Copley, Edith A.	AZ0450	60A,36,60
Corley, Sheila	AZ0400	32C,36,39,61
Corliss, Heidi E.	ME0440	36
Corman, David	TX1850	39,36,40
Cornelius, Jeffrey M.	PA3250	60,11,12A,36
Cornish, John	OK0150	36,39,60A,61,13B
Cornwall, Lonieta	NC2300	13,60,36,66D
Corrie, John H.	ME0150	13C,36,61,66G,66H
Cotte, William	VT0300	11,13H,36,61,66
Cottrell, Duane	DE0150	36,32D
Council, Thomas	GA2000	31A,61,36,60,40
Courtney, Craig	OH0350	36
Cowles, Robert	NY1550	13,36,60
Cox, Dennis K.	ME0440	60A,12A,36
Cox, Donna M.	OH2250	20,36,32
Cox, John	NY4310	36,38,40,41,60
Cox, Michael	VA1580	36,61,32D,60A
Cox, Rachel	KY1350	61,36
Cox, Richard G.	NC2430	36,60A
Crabb, Paul	MO1800	36,60A
Crabtree, Joseph C.	TX1425	11,12,36,39
Crane, Andrew	NC0650	60A,36
Crannell, Wayne T.	TX0250	36,61,11,39,60
Crawford, Glenda	OH2550	36,32A,32C,32B,60
Crayton, Mark	IL0550	61,36
Criddle, Reed	UT0325	36,61
Crocker, John	CA0200	36
Crooks, Jamie	AI0050	36
Crosby, Luanne M.	NY0100	11,36,61,54
Crosby, Matthew	TX3415	36,13A,13B
Crossland, Carolyn M.	NC1075	13A,11,32A,36,32B
Crothers-Marley, Shirley Evans	OH2100	12A,32,36,61
Crow, Andrew	IN0150	36
Crowell, Allen	GA2100	60,36
Crull, Terry	KS0350	11,36,40,60A
Cruse, Carolyn S.	TX3200	36,40,32D,32G
Crutchfield, Jonathan	NC2000	36
Cuk, John	NY2200	36,39,54,40
Culloton, Michael	MN0600	36,12A
Culver, Jerry	MI1700	36,13C,60
Culverhouse, William	IN0400	36,12A,60
Cummings, Grace	NY3350	32B,36,61,32C,32D
Cummins, Nicholaus B.	MS0250	36,60A,32D,40
Cunha, Alcingstone DeOliveira	KY0400	31A,36
Cunningham, Chuck	NM0500	66A,66G,32D,36,40
Cunningham, Walt	NH0100	36
Cushing, Diane	NH0150	36,61,54,11
Custer, Gerald	MI2200	36,60A,13
Cutsforth-Huber, Bonnie	PA2710	61,36
Cutter, William	MA1400	36
Cutter, William C.	MA1200	36
Dade, Fred S.	PA3050	20,11,32B,36,66A
Dagenais, Andree	AC0050	36,40,42,60A
Dahlke, Steven	NY3250	11,13,36,60A,61
Dahlman, Hank	OH2500	32,36,60
Dale, Karen M.	TN0300	11,34B,36,54,61
Daley, Caron	AF0100	13A,13C,36
Dalton, Martha	IL2300	36,61
Damaris, Christa	NY3000	36,61,66D
Dana, Julie R.	CA1850	36,61,11
Dandridge, Damon H.	PA0675	36
Danne, Terry	CA2700	36,61
D'Arca, Denise	OH1800	32,36,11,42
Darr, Steven L.	FL2130	60,32,36,61
Darrough, Galen P.	CO0950	60A,36,32D
Daugherty, James F.	KS1350	32,36
Davenport, Dennis	OH2050	54,10,13,36
Davenport, Susan G.	IL2900	36
Davidovich, Theodore C.	MA2100	60A,11,36
Davids, Julia L.	IL2100	36,40
Davies, Thomas H.	CA0600	13,60,36,61
Davies, Thomas	CA1510	36
Davis, Cara	WI0806	36,61,29A,11
Davis, Gene	AL0450	61,36,13C
Davis, Hugh	TX1300	36,11
Davis, Karen	MS0320	11,36
Davis, Nancy	OH1300	13A,11,36,47
Davis, Ollie Watts	IL3300	61,36
Davis, Richard A.	WV0500	13,60,12A,36,61
Davis, Victor	TN1400	11,36,60
De Jaager, Alfred R.	WV0600	36,32D,60,11
De Jager, Ron	AJ0030	60A,36,52,61,32D
Deakins, Mark	KY0650	13A,60,36,31A,40
Dean, Brandon	MN0750	36,13,20,32D,34B
Dean, Sally	CA3460	36,60
Dearing, James C.	PA1600	36,40,12A
Debes, Pier	IL1800	36
Declue, Gary L.	IL1245	12A,13A,11,61,36
Dehning, Margaret	CA0960	36,61
DeHoogh-Kliewer, David	SD0580	60A,11,32D,36,40
Dekaney, Elisa M.	NY4150	32,36,20H,60A
Delcamp, Robert	TN1800	13,12A,36,66G,31A
Delgado-Pelton, Celeste	CO0600	13,11,34,36,47
Delmore, Jack	CO0225	36,39,61,54
DeLong, Noah	TN1150	36,35C,60A,61
Demaree, Robert K.	WI0840	12A,36
DeMichele, Anna	CA0859	36,61,13A,38,11
Demorest, Steven M.	WA1050	32B,32C,36
Denby, Steven	AC0100	36
Denis, Kimberley	AA0050	61,35A,36
Dennee, Peter D.	WI0250	32C,32D,36,60,40
Dennis, David M.	TN1660	13,66A,36
Dering, James	TX0850	36,47,13,13C,11
DeSanto, William	PA3560	36,66,31A,66C
Desmond, Clinton J.	SD0200	36,11,20,60,12
Dettwiler, Peggy	PA2150	60,36,32C,61
Detweiler, Greg J.	KY0900	60,36,61,40
DeVenney, David P.	PA3600	36,39,60A,61
DeVilbiss, Gloria	IA1390	61,41,36
Di Grazia, Donna M.	CA3650	60,11,12A,36
DiCello, Anthony J.	OH0150	36,61,66,31A,34
Dickau, David C.	MN1000	60,36,45,34
Dickerson, Roger	LA0720	10F,10,12A,36,29
Diddle, Laura D.	SD0550	32B,32D,36
Diehl, David J.	TN1600	12A,32C,36
Dillard, Royzell L.	VA0500	36,61
Dillon, Rhonda	CA1750	36,61
Dimmock, Herb R.	MD0475	36
Dingle, Rosetta	SC1050	32,36,66D,13
DiOrio, Dominick	IN0900	60A,36
Dockendorf, Carl	AZ0460	36
Doebler, Lawrence A.	NY1800	60,36
Doherty, Jean	NY1950	11,36
Dolatowski, David	AZ0510	66A,36,11
Dolloff, Lori-Anne	AG0450	32A,32B,60,36,66C
Donaldson, Kathryn	PA1350	36,61
Donelson, David W.	OH1350	36,32D,60A
Doneski, Sandra	MA0950	32,36,13
Donnelly, Molly	MD0550	36,61,42
Doo, Lina J.	HI0150	11,61,36,54,20
Doss, Robert	KY0200	36
Douglas, Bill	CO0560	13,11,12A,36,66A
Dower, Mary R.	PA1700	11,36
Doyle, Melinda S.	AL1200	36,60A,40
Drafall, Lynn	PA2750	32C,36
Drake, Melvyn	NY4250	70,36
Drayton, Keith	MI1100	13,11,36,32,61
Dudley, Sandra	TN0100	36,61,35B
Duensing, Craig	SC0620	36
Duff, Robert P.	NH0100	36,60,10A,40,13C
Duffy, Kathryn Ann Pohlmann	IA0650	11,12,13,36,60
Duggan, Sean B.	LA0600	11,12A,36,66,31A
Duke, Christopher A.	TN0550	36
Dunbar, Brian	MN0620	10,13,36,34,60A
Duncan, Ellen	MI1300	13A,13,60,36,40
Duncan, Norah	MI2200	36,13C,66G
Dunsmore, Douglas	AD0050	36,60A
Dunston, Douglas E.	NM0350	10B,36,38,47,54
Durham, Franklin	AZ0150	36
Durham, Justin W.	SC0400	36,60A
Durlam, Zachary D.	CA1860	36,60,32A,32B,40
Durow, Peter J.	MO1500	36,32D,60A
Dustman, Tom	CA2550	36,47,35B
Earl, R. Daniel	CA4460	36
Eash, William	KS0200	60,36
Eaton, Denise	TX2250	36,32D
Ebrecht, Ronald	CT0750	36,66G
Eby, Kristen	IA1450	44,61,40,36,13
Eby, Patricia	WI0804	13,11,36,60A,47
Eckert, Stacy	IL2650	36,39,61
Ediger, Thomas L.	NE0500	13,12A,32,36,66
Edison, Noel	AG0300	36,60A
Edmonds, Johnnella	VA1750	60,32B,32C,36,61
Edwards, Lawrence	TN1680	60,32,36
Edwards, Linda	NM0400	60,36,41,61,54
Edwards, Malcolm V.	AA0150	32,36,60A
Edwards, T. Matthew	MD0060	66A,13,66C,12,36
Ehly, Ewald	MO1810	60A,61,36
Eifert, Jonathan	TX0400	36,60A,66G,31A

Index by Area of Teaching Interest

Name	Code	Areas
Eklund, Peter A.	NE0600	60,32D,36
Elder, Christine Welch	OR1300	36
Eleazer, Alan G.	TN0600	36,40,11
Ellefsen, Roy	UT0190	13,11,36
Ellingboe, Bradley	NM0450	36,61
Elliott, Anne	TN1150	66A,66D,66B,66C,36
Ellis, Brenda	OH2500	20A,20G,32,36,66A
Ellis, Peter	AA0032	38,62,51,36
Elpus, Kenneth	MD1010	32D,32G,36
Endris, Robert R.	IN1400	60,32B,36
Engebretson, Stan P.	VA0450	36,60A,60,40
Engelhart, Robert	MI1600	39,61,36,11
Engelson, Robert A.	IA0050	13,60,11,36,54
English, Wendell L.	MD0200	36
Enis, Paul	OK0350	13,36,37,61,63
Enns, Leonard J.	AG0470	13,60,10,36
Entsminger, Deen	TN0100	13,10,32C,36,34
Epley, Arnold	MO2000	60A,32C,36,61,40
Erickson, Kim	AG0170	13,36,20,39
Erickson, Shirley	TX0910	11,13,36,61,66
Erwin, John M.	AR0850	60A,36,40
Escalante, Roosevelt	KY0900	13B,13C,32D,36
Eskew-Sparks, Elise	GA0050	36,40
Esparza, Eric Peche	TX2250	36,61
Espel, Ann	IL1085	36
Etcheto, Sally A.	CA0805	11,36,61,54
Etter, David D.	KY1425	36,61,31A,60
Etter, Paul J.	NC0850	60A,36,44,60,31A
Eubanks, Nathaniel	WI0425	36
Evans, Chris	PA2740	36,40,61
Evans, Cory	UT0300	32D,36,40
Evans, David F.	NY3725	36,61
Everett, Beth	MI0600	36,60,32D
Everitt, Allison	FL1430	13,36,61,55
Ewashko, Laurence J.	AG0400	32,36
Faerber, Matthew L.	WI0860	60A,36,32D,40,13C
Falk, Marc	IA0300	36,11,12A,60A,40
Falker, Matt	CA2960	36,66A,47,66D
Faltstrom, Gloria V.	HI0300	13A,11,66D,61,36
Fankhauser, James L.	AB0100	13,36,55,61
Farah, Mariana	KS1350	36
Farris, Daniel King	OK1250	40,42,12,36,13
Fassett, Charles K.	MA2150	60,11,12A,36
Faszer, Ted	SD0450	32,36,31A,34
Feiszli, James D.	SD0500	12A,36,55D,61
Felpe, Miguel	HI0210	36
Fenton, Kevin	FL0850	60,32,36
Ferguson, David	AA0050	36
Ferguson, J. Scott	IL1200	60A,36,61
Ferguson, John	MN1450	36,66G,31A
Ferrantelli, Sal	CA3050	13,36,61
Ferrell, Matthew	MN1300	36,60A
Ferrington, Darryl	LA0400	13A,36,32,31A
Fett, Basil	OH2450	61,36
Fetzer, Elsie J.	CO0600	36
Fields, Tami	NC0915	11,36
Finney, John R.	MA0330	60,36,38,66G
Finney, John W.	KY0700	13,12A,36,61,66A
Fisher, Ryan A.	AR0850	32D,36
Fisher, Will J.	AZ0510	36,11,66D
Fittipaldi, Thomas	NY2500	36,66D,67,70,11
FitzGibbon, Katherine L.	OR0400	36,60,11
Flagg, Darron	CA1500	36
Flanery, John	MS0750	36
Fleitas, Patricia P.	FL0650	60,36,61
Fleming, Gail H.	IL2970	11,36,66A,40,20
Fleming, Kyle J.	CO0150	36,11,31A,60A
Fleming, Nancy P.	AR0350	12A,36,60A
Flemming, Kyle	CO0900	36
Fletcher, Marylynn L.	TX3600	34C,36,11,66A,12A
Fletcher, Terry W.	MS0300	36,61,12A
Floreen, John E.	NJ1140	12,36,66G
Floriano, Gerard F.	NY3730	60,36
Flory, Jennifer Morgan	GA0850	36,32D,15,60A,61
Floyd, Hugh	SC0750	61,60A,36,32D
Floyd-Savage, Karen	VA1750	11,13A,36,61
Flynn, Timothy	MI1800	10A,12,36,39,13
Folger, William M.	MD0800	60A,36,40,54
Fons, Carolyn	WI1155	61,36
Forbes, Guy	IL1750	32,36
Ford, Joseph Kevin	TN1700	36,40,32D,60
Ford, Kelly	IN1350	36,61,60A,12,64E
Ford, Mary E.	OK0350	11,13,36,66
Foreman, Carolyn	AR0750	36
Foster, Christopher	NY0100	36,63,13A,47,41
Foster, Korre	TN0050	36,60A
Foster, Marc A.	NC0930	36
Foust, Diane	WI1100	36,61,13A,40,13B
Fowler, Colin	NY2900	36,13,12A,66A,66G
Fowler-Calisto, Lauren	VA0150	36,60A
Fox, Ryan H	AR0300	36,60A,32D,40
Fox, T. Jeffrey	NY2550	36,11,20G,14C
Fradley, Kerry	FL0570	36
Frame, Gary	OR0250	36
Francis, Lorie	MO0825	11,12A,13,36,66A
Francom, Jeffery D.	NY3780	36,32D
Franklin, Bonita Louise	OK0450	32,36,60A,61
Franklin, James C.	TX2250	36,32D
Fraser, Teresa L.	WA0600	36,47,13A,40
Frasier, Michael	OR0200	36,32D
Frazier, Meg Hulley	LA0300	36
Fredenburgh, Lisa M.	IL0150	36,11,40,60A
Frederick, John	PA3680	36
Frederickson, Karen	AG0250	32,36,60A
Fredrickson, Ann	MN0200	61,36,39,54,13C
Fredstrom, Tim	IL1150	32D,36,60A,32
Free, Christine	NY0270	36,61
Freed, Donald Callen	TX2710	61,36,10A,13C,12A
Freer, Patrick K.	GA1050	32D,32C,32G,36,60A
French, George E.	MN1590	36,37,66A,66G,54
French, John	PA3550	11,12,13,36
French, Paul T.	OR0950	11,12A,36,39,61
Freyermuth, G. Kim	AZ0200	36,44,61,47
Friesen, Elroy	AC0100	36,60A,32D
Friesen, Milton	CA1860	11,36,70
Frisbie, Jodi	KS0150	61,36,39,13C
Fritschel, James E.	CA0550	10A,36
Fritz, Matthew P.	PA1250	36,60A,34,34E,60
Froese, Elvera	AG0600	39,66C,36
Fryling, David N.	NY1600	36,60A,60,32,13A
Fucci, Melissa	OH1110	11,36,
Fuelberth, Brett J.	IA0800	13,36,47,44
Fuelberth, Rhonda J.	NE0600	32D,36
Fukuda, Joni	CA5355	11,13A,32D,36,61
Fuller, Gregory	MS0750	60,36
Fulton, Kenneth	LA0200	60,36
Futrell, Stephen A.	NC0750	36,32D,60,35C,40
Gabrielse, Kenneth J.	LA0400	60,36,31A,12A
Gackle, Lynne	TX0300	36,60A
Galante, Brian Edward	WA0650	36,10,60A,32D
Galbreath, Loretta J.	MS0350	36,40,47,61
Gallagher, James S.	OH1850	36
Gallagher, Marcia	ME0340	36,61
Galloway, Melodie	NC2400	36
Galvan, Janet	NY1800	60A,32,36
Galvez, Luis	IL2750	61,36
Gamblin-Green, Michelle	MO0600	36,43
Gandy, V. Gay	KY1400	36,61,13A,13C,11
Ganus, Clifton L.	AR0250	12A,31A,36,60A
Garber, Joel	OK0770	12A,61,14,36,60
Garber, Ron	KS0210	11,12A,36,41,61
Garcia, William B.	TN0800	60,11,36,61,31A
Garcia-Novelli, Eduardo	WI0250	36,40,32D,13C,60
Gardiner, Katie	NY3650	36,60A
Gardner, David B.	KS1200	36,60,61,60A,54
Gardner, Patrick	NJ1130	60A,36
Garner, Dirk A.	OH0200	36,40,60A
Garrett, Craig	TX0340	36,47,63A
Garrett, Karen	CA3800	61,36
Garrett, Matthew L.	OH0400	36,32D,60A
Garrett, Monte	TX1100	60,36
Gassi, Gloria	AG0500	36,32
Gates, Elaine	NY2750	36
Gehrenbeck, Robert	WI0865	36,40,39,60A
Gelber, Debbie	TX2350	13A,13B,36,61,13C
Geller, Ian R.	IN0005	61,10A,60,36
Gemme, Terese	CT0450	13A,12A,36,66G
Gemmell, Jeffrey S.	CO0800	36,32D,60A
Gentry, Gregory R.	CO0800	36,60A
Gerber, Alan E.	FL2120	11,55,61,36
Gerber, Casey	OK0650	36,32
Gerber, Gary G.	AR0500	36,61,32D,60A
Gerber, Larry	FL0850	36,61
Gerbi, Elizabeth	NY1050	36,40,61
Germond, Melanie	AZ0250	36,61
Gervais, Michel Marc	CA5060	36,60A,55D,40
Geston, Mary K.	MN1280	40,32D,60A,32C,36
Gibeau, Peter	WI0862	13,36,41,62D,66A
Giebler, David	WI0920	13,11,36,41,66A
Giessow, David	MA2010	36,39,61,32B,32C
Gil, Gustavo	CA0950	36,13,46
Gilleland, Katharine	NC2525	66G,11,13A,29A,36
Gillingham, Bryan	AG0100	12A,12,36
Gilson, Catherine	MI1550	36,60A
Ginsberg, Elaine Broad	MA1000	36
Giorgetti, Marisa	CA0450	61,36
Gladstone, Bruce	WI0815	60A,36
Glann, Kerry	OH1100	20,36,39
Glasman, Ilan David	CA1550	36,40,61,11
Glaze, Debbie	OR0850	32,36
Gleckler, Megan	TN0100	36,61
Glenn, James H.	NC2000	36,61,60A,11,12A
Glocke, Jayne	PA2750	36
Goforth, Stephen C.	KY1300	11,36,60A,61,12A
Gokelman, William	TX3410	60,36,66A,66C,31A
Goldman-Moore, Susan J.	OK1450	32,36,61
Goldsmith, John L.	PA3420	60A,36
Gomer, Wesley	TX1650	13,66,69,12A,36
Gonzalez, Ariel	AA0050	36
Goodman, Andrea	MA1400	36
Goold, William C.	KY0150	60,12A,36,61,31A
Gordon, Barbara N.	NJ0500	11,36,60A,66D,61
Gordon, Daniel	FL1740	13,32,60A,36
Gordon, Heidi Cohenour	AR0810	61,13C,66D,36
Gordon, Regina	PA1550	36,40
Gordon, Samuel	OH2150	60,12A,36,61,40
Gorelick, Brian	NC2500	60A,36,55D
Gort, Cristian	AI0150	36,43
Gosselin, Karen	AL0550	32,60,36,40,44
Gotera, Jose	OH1000	61,39,54,36
Gothard, Paul	OH1250	13A,13,10F,11,36
Gothold, Stephen A.	CA5100	36,40,61,60A
Graber, Todd A.	NY3770	61,54,36,12A
Gracia-Nuthmann, Andre	NM0150	13,60,36,55,61
Graf, Greg	MO0750	36,40,60,11
Graham, Lisa E.	MA2050	36,60
Graham, Sarah J.	IL1150	36,60A
Graham, Seong-Kyung	WI0700	61,32D,36,60A
Grahame, Gerald	NY0350	36,61
Grant, Joe W.	IL3300	60,32,36
Grant, Joyce	NY1210	12,13A,36
Gratto, Sharon Davis	OH2250	36,20,32
Graveline, Michelle	MA0200	15,13,36
Graves, Daniel H.	IN0400	11,12A,36,60,41
Graves, Jim F.	OK1200	36,32D,32B,60A,61
Gray, Gerald Thomas	NY3725	61,36
Gray, John	KS0250	36,13,61
Gray, William Jon	IN0900	60,36
Greco, Eugene A.	FL1300	36,12A,67F,12,67
Green, Elvira O.	VI0050	13C,36,61
Green, Jonathan D.	IL1200	36
Green, Martin	CA1000	11,13H,32D,36,39
Green, Peter	CA1960	13A,66A,36,40
Green, Tim	IL2800	36,63
Green, Verna	NY0640	20A,20H,32D,32E,36
Green, William	TN0850	36,40,60A
Greene, Daniel B.	OH2120	36,61
Greenlee, Robert K.	ME0200	60,36,12A,12,55
Greenwald, Laura	NJ0050	36,13C,61,39
Greer, Albert	AG0650	36,61
Gregg-Boothby, Tracey	OK1050	36,61
Grevlos, Lisa	SD0050	39,61,32B,36,32D
Grew, Melody A.	MD0050	11,32,36,61,66A
Grieger, Evelyn	AA0100	36,60A
Griffeath, Kristin	OK1250	12A,61,39,36
Griffen, Jane	MO0500	60A,32A,32B,36,61
Griffin, Andrew	MN0610	36
Griffin, Stephen W.	AL0332	11,36,37,47,64
Griffin-Keller, Betty	CA3500	36
Griffith, Larry D.	TN0930	60A,32C,36,61,32D
Grigsby, Nathan	GA0050	36
Grives, Steven Matthew	IL0750	36,40
Grogan, David C.	TX3500	61,32D,36,39,40
Groh, Jack C.	AR0700	60,36,61
Grohman, Bryon T.	FL1450	61,36
Grundahl, Nancy J.	MN0050	36
Gubrud, Darcy Lease	MN1285	13,11,36,61,40
Guelker-Cone, Leslie	WA1250	36,39,61
Guerin, Constance Ely	TN1850	36
Guilbert, Fred	LA0150	36
Gunderson, Janice	CA0855	36
Guptill-Crain, Nan	NJ1400	61,36
Gustafson, Steven	KS0900	61,66G,40,13B,36
Guthrie, J. Randall	OK0850	31A,60A,36,11,66G
Guy, Todd	IN1025	36,31A,61,60A,11
Guzman, Darryl	CA3320	36

Name	Code	Areas
Haan, Keith A.	IA1300	60,36,32D,61,40
Haberlen, John B.	GA1050	60,32D,36
Hackel, Erin H.	CO0830	36,13,11,10D
Hackworth, Rhonda S.	NJ1130	32B,32C,32A,36,32
Haecker, Allyss	SC0900	61,20,36,39
Hafso, Marc A.	WA1350	60,36,10A,32D,61
Hagel, Clint	AA0020	31A,36,61,66C
Hagen, Julie	MN0600	32,36
Haggans, Kathryn	MO1830	36,61
Hahn, David	TN0580	12A,34,35A,36,60
Hakoda, Ken	KS0700	36,38,32
Halco, Terry	MA2010	36
Haldeman, Randy	NC2420	36,32D
Hale, Roger	MO0850	60A,61,40,36
Hall, Barbara L.	KY0450	13,12A,12,36,60
Hall, Bruce	IL2250	61,36,40
Hall, Daniel	OH1900	60A,32C,36
Hall, Daniel	TX3750	36,60A
Hall, Jonathan B.	NY2750	12A,13,31A,36,66G
Hall, Robert	AG0150	13,60,36,61,10F
Hall, Roberta	OR1020	36,61
Hall, Rosalind	UT0050	60,36
Hall, Thomas E.	MD0400	36
Hallman, Ludlow B.	ME0440	36,61,39
Halsey, Glynn	GA0490	11,36,40,60A
Ham, Robert	IN0200	32D,36,40
Hamilton, Vivian	SC0750	36,66C
Hamm, Laura	WV0440	32,36,66A,66D,66C
Hammond, June C.	FL1600	12A,36,61,66A,37
Hamre, Anna R.	CA0810	36,60A
Han, Jong-Hoon 'James'	TX1400	36,32D
Hanawalt, Michael	KS1450	36
Hancock, Virginia	OR0900	13,12A,36
Handel-Johnson, Brenda	MN0350	36
Hanna, Cassandria	FL1310	13,66A,66D,36
Hannan, Eric	AB0050	36,61
Hanoian, Scott	MI2200	36,60A
Hansen, Deborah	WA1350	60,36,13B
Hansen, Gloria	WI0825	36
Hansen, Kathleen	UT0190	36,66A
Hansen, Sharon A.	WI0825	60,36
Hanson, Jan	OK1400	60,11,12A,32,36
Harbold, Tim	MA2150	60,36,45
Harbor, Ronald	CA5353	36
Harden, Matthew C.	NE0610	36,60A,32D,40
Harder, Glen	AA0040	36,61,47
Harler, Alan	PA3250	36
Harleston, Sheila C.	MD1020	60,36,66A,66D
Harney, Jon M.	MT0200	36,39,40,61
Harper, Kris	PA3650	36,61
Harper, T.J.	RI0150	36,60,32C,32D,61
Harris, David	PA0150	36,61,31A,40,32D
Harris, Duane	MO0350	32,36,61,12A
Harris, Jason W.	OH1700	60,36,61
Harris, Lee	TN1700	32,13C,36
Harris, Melanie	FL1675	36,61
Harris, Ray	MS0570	11,36,66,54
Harris, Robert A.	IL2250	60,36
Harrison, Judy	FL0900	13,36,60A,66
Hart, Steven R.	MT0350	36,61,32D
Hart, Thomas J.	IA0600	60,36,12A
Harvey, Peter J.	CT0240	13,12A,36,54,20G
Harwood, Elizabeth	AF0050	36,66G
Harwood, Susan	NY0700	39,36,61,40
Hasseler, Lynda	OH0350	60A,36,40,32D
Hassevoort, Darrin	TN0260	36,61,47,60,54
Hasty, Barbara P.	CA1700	13A,61,66A,36
Hatteberg, Kent E.	KY1500	36,60
Hauger, Karin	CO0830	11,13,36
Haupt, Dorothy G.	PA0125	12A,32B,36,66G
Hausmann, Charles S.	TX3400	36,61
Hawkins, Allan	MN1300	36
Hawkins, John A.	WV0500	13A,13,11,36,66
Hawkins, Michelle	CA1550	36,47
Haworth, Janice	MN0150	32A,32C,32B,36,20A
Hayes, Casey J.	IN0500	36,32,11
Hayes, Daun	CA4600	36,61,54
Hayes, William Bryce	VA0600	32D,36
Haygood, Christopher D.	OK0800	36,32D
Haygood, James	LA0760	32,36
Head, Paul D.	DE0150	36
Heald, Jason A.	OR1020	13,10,47,36,38
Hearne, Lisa	IA0400	36,61,40
Heath, Guy	FL1430	11,36,35A
Hebert, Ryan	FL2050	60,36,13C,66G
Hegg, Barbara	SD0150	36,61,63B,60
Heller, Ryan	WA0480	36,39,61
Helms, Elizabeth	CA5360	66C,13A,13C,36,39
Henderson, Mark A.	UT0350	60,10,11,36,32D
Henderson, Silvester	CA2775	36,40,60A,61,66A
Hendricks, Steven	MO1500	32,37,34,36
Hendrickson, David Alan	TN1650	36,61
Hendrickson, Daniel	MI1180	11,12A,36,37,61
Hendrickson, Peter A.	MN0050	60,36,13,66G
Henning, Mary	KY0350	20,44,32,36
Henry, James	MO1830	36,40,60A,32D,10F
Henry, Joseph D.	IL0900	12A,20G,36,40,32C
Hensley, David L.	CA3700	11,36
Hensley, Hunter C.	KY0550	36,61,60A,55,32D
Herman, Cheryl	IL2800	36,54,66A,64
Hesse, Ted	IL1750	13,36,61
Hetrick, Esther A.	MI0910	61,60,31A,36,32B
Hetzel, Lori	KY1450	32,36,32D
Heywood, Andre'	MN0350	36
Hibbard, Kevin	GA2130	36,32D,61,60,32C
Hibbard, Therees Tkach	NE0600	36,60A
Hibbett, Michael	WA1200	11,36
Hickey, Katherine M.	CA5150	32,13A,13C,36,40
Hickman, Joe Eugene	NC2440	60,36,41,61
Hickman, Lowell	MT0200	36,61,63A
Hickok, Robert B.	CA5020	60,36
Hiester, Jason A.	OH2000	36,39,40,60A,61
Highben, Zebulon M.	OH1650	36,40,61,32D
Hightower, Allen	IA0950	36,32D,60
Hildebrand, Ed	AC0100	36
Hildebrand, Millie	AC0100	36
Hill, Camille	KY0600	13A,11,36,61,66D
Hill, Cheryl Frazes	IL0550	32,36,60A
Hines, Billy C.	NC0700	13A,36,61
Hines, Robert S.	HI0210	36
Hinson, Lee	OK0650	31A,11,36
Hinson, Wallace	GA1650	60,36,40
Hirsh, Jonathan M.	MA1750	60,36,38
Hobbins, William	GA0250	32,36,61,11
Hobson, David	LA0050	36,11,31A,12A
Hoch, Matthew	AL0200	61,36,39
Hochstetler, Scott	IN0550	36,61,60
Hodge, Cheryl	AB0070	10,36,61,53,35H
Hodge, Stephen	OH2300	36,32C,61,32D,60A
Hodges, Justin	TX0600	36,40,32D
Hodgman, Thomas	MI0050	32,36,40
Hodgson, Ken	MN1620	36,61,34D,11,60A
Hodson, Steven R.	CA5550	11,36,60,66A
Hoffart, Danica	AA0080	36,61,54,13C
Hoffenberg, Rick	PA2200	36,40,60A,61
Holcomb, Al	NJ1350	32,36,60A
Holcombe, Helen	PA0400	13A,36,61,66D
Holden, LuAnn	TN0850	32,12A,36
Holder, Angela	TN0250	61,36,31,11
Holder, Ryan	AZ0450	32D,36,60A
Holdhusen, David	SD0600	60A,36,61
Holland, Geoffrey	FL1450	60,36
Holleman, James A.	MI1000	60,11,36,38
Holler, David	AG0200	36
Holliday, Guy	CA0450	36,37,47
Hollins, John S.	TX3200	60,36,41
Holloway, Peggy A.	NE0610	61,32B,15,36,40
Holm, Thomas	IA1200	12A,36,11,60,61
Holmes, Brad	IL1750	60,32C,36
Holmes, Elizabeth	IL1750	36,61
Holmes, Isaac	GA1600	60A,11,36,61,39
Holmquist, Solveig	OR1250	11,36,60,66G,69
Holquist, Robert A.	NC2600	32C,36,55D,32D
Holz, Beatrice	KY0100	32B,36,39,61,32D
Hondorp, Paul	KY1550	36,60A,32D,61,40
Honea, Richard	MO0400	36,61,60A
Hong, Xiangtang	IL1850	60A,31A,36,44,11
Hood, Marcia Mitchell	GA0150	66A,60A,32B,36,40
Hooper, Randall	TX2955	36,60A,32D,32B,40
Hopkins, Jesse E.	VA0100	32,36,61,44,60A
Hopkins, John R.	AK0150	36,39,61,60
Hopkins, Stephen M.	NC0050	60,36A,32D
Hopper, Mary	IL3550	60,36
Horan, Leta	TX0300	36,66A,66D
Horjus-Lang, Deanna	WI0800	36,61,11
Horst, Amy S.	HI0200	36,13
Horvath, Janos	AA0150	32B,32D,36,42,13C
Hostetler, Jill	IN0200	36,40,61
Houze, Reginald M.	MA0150	10F,36,37,60,63D
Howard, David L.	TX2700	32C,36,60A
Howard, Robert C.	MO0550	36,40
Howard, Sandra	NH0150	32,36,40
Howell, Allen C.	PA1200	11,32,36
Howell, Andrew P.	RI0300	36,66C,66G
Howell, John	VA1700	36,67,35,55
Howell, Matthew	HI0200	36,38,40
Howlett, Christine R.	NY4450	36,13C,61
Hristova, Gabriela	MI2120	36,60
Hudson, Barbara	VA0050	61,36,12A
Hudson, S.	KY0350	11,13,36
Hudspeth, Charles M.	CA1020	36,13A,66D
Huff, Christina	IN1025	32A,32B,32C,11,36
Huff, Daniel M.	NC2410	32,36
Huff, Walter	IN0900	36,60A
Huffman, Donna M.	WA0100	13,13J,36,47,49
Huffman, Pamela G.	TX2400	60A,36
Hufty, Aaron	TX0300	36,11
Hughes, Albert C.	TN0950	13,11,12A,36,61
Hughes, David	CA0250	60,36,61
Hughes, R. Daniel	NY2550	36,13A,61
Hughes, Ralph	CA0150	36,61,66A
Hugo, John William	VA0650	36,61,12A,60A
Hull, Kenneth	AG0470	11,12A,31A,36
Huls, Marvin J.	PA3000	13,36,44
Humble, Dina M.	CA3800	61,36,11,34,29
Hume, Michael	NY0050	61,36
Hunter, Denise	CA1450	36
Hurst, Twyla	MS0370	13A,36,61,66D
Hurty, Jon	IL0100	36
Hurty, Sonja	IL0100	36,61,13C
Hussa, Robert	WY0060	11,12A,35C,36,61
Huszti, Joseph B.	CA5020	60,36,61
Ihm, Dana	CO0275	36,40,47,60A
Ikach, Yugo Sava	PA0500	61,38,11,13A,36
Imler, James R.	SC1200	36,40
Imthurn, Melinda	TX1725	11,36,61
Intintoli, Helen	CA4650	36,61,66A,31A,54
Irwin, Doreen	CA3850	36,41,66A
Irwin, Frederick	NJ1400	36,60A
Isaacs, Kevin	CT0800	13,60,10,12B,36
Isaacs, Robert	NJ0900	36,61
Isele, David	FL2050	10F,10,36,61,66G
Istad, Robert M.	CA0815	36,40
Ivey, Bobby	GA0350	32,36,13C,40
Izdebski, Christy	MD0100	12A,32,66A,66D,36
Jaber, Thomas I.	TX2150	36,60A,66C
Jablow, Lisa	VT0250	60,12A,36,41,61
Jackson, Albert	IL2775	13A,11,36,61
Jackson, Dan	CA3640	31A,36
Jackson, Gregory	AL0050	65,13,20,10,36
Jackson, L. Max	KY0200	13,11,36,66A
Jacobsen, Lesa L.	WI0845	61,32C,32D,60A,36
Jacobson, Joshua R.	MA1450	11,12A,36,13,31B
Jacobson, Marin	CA1425	36,12A,61,11
James, Buddy	CA0807	36,32D,61,60A
Jameson, Joel	NY2900	36,61,60A
Janisch, Joseph	WV0560	36,60,32,13A,32B
Janower, David M.	NY3700	13,60,12A,36
Janzen, Wesley	AB0090	60,12A,36,31A
Jarjisian, Peter G.	OH1900	36
Jaros, Marc	MN1200	12,36,20,40
Jarrell, Boyd	CA1150	13,36,40
Jarrett, Scott	MA0400	36
Jasperse, Gregory P.	CA3500	61,36
Jefferson, Thomas	IL2750	36,66D
Jeffreys, Shannon	GA0950	36,32D
Jenkins, Donald P.	CO0200	60,36,39,41,54
Jenkins, Isaac B.	CA4410	47,36
Jenkins, Jack	MO0700	33,36,60
Jennings, Joseph	SC1110	36
Jennings, Kenneth	MN1450	60A,61,36
Jennings, Mark D.	MO1780	60,36,61
Jennings, Tom	TX1775	11,36,61
Jenrette, Thomas S.	TN0500	36,61,60
Jenschke, Laura	TX3100	36,61,32E
Jensen, Andrew	AR0050	60A,36,11,61,13C
Jensen, Constance	UT0325	61,36
Jensen, Jocelyn	NV0050	36,13B,13C
Jensen, Joni L.	TX3300	13C,36,61,32D,60A
Jensen, Michelle	CA0250	32,36,55
Jermihov, Peter	IL3200	36,13
Jesse, Lynda	MO0200	32D,36,54,60,61
Jewett, Dennis A.	KY0800	61,31A,32,36
Jimerson, David	OR0850	32B,36,61
Jin, Soohyun	OK0850	61,36
Jirak, James	ID0050	36,32D,60A

Index by Area of Teaching Interest

Name	Code	Areas
Jobin-Bevans, Dean	AG0170	60,36,40,39
Jodry, Frederick	RI0050	13,60,12A,36
John, James A.	NY0642	36,40,60A
Johnson, Brad	MS0200	60,11,36,44,61
Johnson, Brandon P.	NY1700	36,60A,61
Johnson, Carl	TX0200	60,12A,32C,36,61
Johnson, Cornelius	IL0450	13A,66A,11,36,20
Johnson, Deral J.	AG0500	60,36
Johnson, Diane	WA0900	36,61,54,11,20
Johnson, Dirk	WV0700	36
Johnson, Elizabeth	TN0100	36,61
Johnson, Eric	IL2200	60,36
Johnson, G. Larry	UT0325	36,60A,13A,13B,13C
Johnson, Henry	GA1600	36,66A,46,47,48
Johnson, Jefferson	KY1450	60,40,36,42
Johnson, Joaquina Calvo	CA6050	36,39,61,67B
Johnson, John Paul	KS1450	32,36
Johnson, Jon S.	TX2350	13,36,61,54,32D
Johnson, Julianne R.	OR0800	36,40,29
Johnson, Nikki	MS0360	11,61,54,36
Johnson, Randall	GU0500	11,36,47,61,64E
Johnson, Sigrid	MN1450	36,61
Johnson, Timothy	ME0340	36,61
Johnson, Valerie	NC0200	60,36,61
Johnson, Velshera	VA0400	61,36,40,66A
Johnston, Joey	AZ0440	36,61
Johnston, Rebecca R.	SC0600	32,36,60,13C,61
Jones, Ann A.	TN0250	36,61,60A
Jones, Anne Howard	MA0400	60,36
Jones, Barry	IA0700	36
Jones, Eddie	AR0700	32,36
Jones, Erik Reid	WV0550	36,39,40,60A,61
Jones, Jeremy D.	OH1450	36,32D
Jones, Joel C.	AL0050	66,36,13A
Jones, Keith	SC0650	61,36,60
Jones, Paul	PA3250	36
Jones, Robert Owen	OH1650	36,61
Jones, Robert B.	OH2250	60A,32C,36,32D
Jones, William Darryl	LA0350	32C,36
Jones, William	DC0350	11,36,61,66A,66G
Jones, Zebedee	MS0600	13A,32,36,66A
Jordahl, Patricia	AZ0300	36,54,66D,61,11
Jordan, Esther	CA2100	36,39,61,54
Jordan, James	NJ1350	66G,36,13,60
Jordanoff, Christine E.	PA1050	32D,32B,32C,32,36
Joseph, Deanna	GA1050	36,40
Jost, John R.	IL0400	60,36,61,38
Jowers, Florence	NC1100	36,44,66G
Jubenville, Suzanne	CA4460	36
Judge, Joseph	NC1900	36,61,31A,40
Jumpeter, Joseph A.		11,29A,20,36,66G
Junda, Mary Ellen	CT0600	32,36
Junker, Tercio	IN0300	60A,36,31A,32D,10E
Kallembach, James	IL3250	36,60A
Kamerin, Kim	CA2400	10B,35A,36,61
Kamm, Charles W.	CA3620	36,11,12,60
Kamm, Charles W.	CA4500	36,12,40,60
Kamm, Charles W.	CA2175	36,11,12,60
Kamm, Charles W.	CA1060	36,11,12,60
Kammerer, Elizabeth	HI0050	61,36
Kantack, Jerri Lamar	MS0150	60,36,61,12A,32
Kaplan, Abraham	WA1050	60,36,38
Karchin, Louis S.	NY2740	10F,60,10,36
Karlin, Brett	FL0930	36,61
Karna, Duane	IN0150	36
Kauffman, Bradley	KS0500	13,36,37
Kauffman, Larry D.	PA0150	12A,36,66A,31A
Kaufhold, Jessica	AL0530	36,11,13A,13B,13C
Kean, Ronald M.	CA0270	36,20B,20H
Keating, Bevan T.	AR0750	36,60,61
Keating, Karen	VA1350	66A,36
Kechley, Gerald	WA1050	13,10,36
Keck, Kimberly	TN0200	36,39,61,60A,13
Keck, Vail	CA3100	36,60,11,13A,61
Kee, Edna Gayles	NY1200	13A,36
Keeler, Paula	IA0150	32,36,39,41,61
Keenan-Takagi, Kathleen D.	NY0400	32,36,12
Keith, David C.	GA1300	60A,36
Keller, Daniel B.	CA3000	11,36,60
Keller, Dennis L.	CA3320	36,61,20,11,40
Keller, James	CO0800	36
Kellert, Aaron	OK1100	11,36,13A,54,61
Kellim, Kevin	KS1400	60A,36,61
Kelly, Bruce	AG0250	61,36
Kelly, Jennifer W.	PA1850	60,36,61
Kelly, Michael F.	NY1850	36,61,66A,46,34
Kelly, Ryan	PA3600	36,40,61,60A
Kelly, Stephen	IL2100	36,66A
Kelsaw, Geoffrey L.	IN1650	36,61
Kemp, Edward	IL1085	36
Kempster, James	CA3400	11,12A,36,61,31A
Kempster, William G.	NH0350	36,32C
Kempton, Randall	ID0060	61,36
Kenaston-French, Karen	TX3500	36,61,32D,40,60A
Kendrick, Donald	CA0840	60,36
Kennedy, Karen	FL1900	60A,36
Kensmoe, Jeffrey	AL0300	61,39,36
Kern, Gene Marie Callahan	NY3650	61,36,13A,39
Kern, Jeffrey	PA3330	13A,36,44,61,66A
Kern, Philip	IN1100	13,10F,36,54,66A
Kershaw, Linda L.	SC0150	11,12,60,66A,36
Kesling, Will	FL1850	36
Kesselman, Lee R.	IL0630	13,10,36,54,60
Keyne, Lori V.	AZ0250	13B,13C,36,66D
Kientz, Ron	CO0100	36
Kilgore Wood, Janice	MD1050	13C,66A,36,66B,31A
Killian, George W.	IN0700	60A,32,36
Killian, Joni	IN0700	61,36,39
Kim, Irene	CA2600	13A,61,36
Kim, Jaeyoon	NC2435	61,60A,36
Kim, James	CO0250	36,60A
Kim, Jong H.	VA0750	36,13,61,60A,40
Kim, Thomas	NJ1050	36,60A
Kim-Infiesto, Marilyn Liu	HI0160	36,61,12A,32,13A
Kimmel, Jim	TN0100	36,60,32C
Kinchen, James B.	WI0835	60,36,32C
Kinchen, Lucy C.	CA2450	12A,36,61,66A
King, Janette	GA1100	66A,36
King, Jonathan	NY3560	13,10F,60,36,10
King, Sandi	CA3520	36,61,31A
King, Tim	TX2700	60A,32C,36
Kinsey, Katherine S.	SC1200	32D,36,60A,40
Kitson, Jeffrey	NE0040	11,13,36,40,61
Kittredge, Brian	AL1150	36,40
Kiver, Christopher A.	PA2750	36
Klassen, Glenn	AA0200	36,38,40,60
Klassen, Roy L.	CA1860	36
Klaus, Kenneth S.	LA0450	60A,11,36,61,40
Klausmeyer, Sue T.	NC2410	36
Klebanow, Susan	NC2410	60,36
Klein, Jim L.	AZ0510	36
Klein, Nancy K.	VA1000	36,60A,32A,32B,32C
Kleinknecht, Daniel E.	IA1140	60,32,36,61
Klement, David A.	NM0310	10,36
Klemme, Paul	OR1300	36,66G
Kliewer, Jan Michael	WY0130	13,36,61,62D,38
Klockow, Stephanie	WI0840	36,32
Knapp, Brady	TX3450	39,40,36
Knapp, Joel	IL2910	60,36,40
Knight, Gerald R.	NC0750	36,60,61,32
Knight, Gloria J.	NC0700	32,36,61
Knutson, John R.	CA1510	36,13,10
Kohrs, Jonathan A.	IL0730	10,36,11,31A,34
Kolb, G. Roberts	NY1350	60,12A,36,40
Koozer, Robin R.	NE0300	36,61
Kornelis, Benjamin	IA0500	20,32D,36,60A,40
Kornelsen, Michael J.	CO0550	36
Kosche, Kenneth	WI0300	13,60,10,36,31A
Kosciesza, Andrew	PA2400	11,12,20,36
Kotowich, Bruce J. G.	IA0940	61,36,31
Koukios, Ann Marie	MI2200	36,12A,66D
Kovacs, Anna	NY2750	32D,36,60A
Kramer, Kenneth	OH1100	11,36,61
Kramlich, Dan P.	WA0800	36,66A
Kramme, Joel I.	MO0825	11,36,55,67,12A
Krasnovsky, Paul J.	IN1650	60A,36,40
Kratochvil, Jirka	NY1400	36,60A,40,61
Kratzer, Dennis L.	OH1800	36,61,54,60A,40
Kreitner, Mona B.	TN1200	12A,36
Kreitzer, Nathan J.	CA4410	61,36,40,55
Kresek, Emme	NY2400	36
Krueger, Carol J.	KS0300	13C,60,36,32D
Krusemark, William	KS1375	36,39,61,54,11
Kukec, Paul E.	IL1900	13A,13,12A,36,66A
Kuzma, Marika C.	CA5000	36,40,60A,61
Kwami, Paul T.	TN0550	20,36,66G,60A,66D
LaBrie, Jesse	NE0300	61,36
Lamartine, Nicole C.	WY0200	36,60A,32D
Lamb, Robert E.	FL0150	36,13,12,60A
Lambert, Doris	OK0150	36,40,61,13C
Lambert, Evin R.	WA0750	11,36,66A,61,13A
Lamkin, Michael D.	CA1050	36,38
Lancaster, Michael	NC2600	60A,55B,61,36,32D
Landis, Melissa McIntosh	CA3200	61,36
Lane, Kathleen	ID0100	39,61,36
Lane, Laura L.	IL1350	12A,60,36,40,61
Laney, Robert	TX3700	11,13,36
Lang, Brenda J.	OH0550	36,60A,61,13A
Lang, Dennis	CA2300	36
Lang, Donald P.	NY3725	60,36
Lang, Linda	MN1175	66,36
Langager, Arlie	CA2960	36,47,40,61
Langager, Graeme	AB0100	36,60A
Langford, Bruce	CA1000	11,12A,32D,36,39
Langner, Gerald	AJ0150	32,36
Langsford, Christopher M.	KS0750	36,32,11,12,13
Lanham, Barbara	IL1610	13A,36,66A,66D
Lanier, Brian	MO0950	32D,36,60A,61
Lanning, Rebecca	GA1260	11,36,61
Lansing, Nathan	WA0950	36,40,13B,13C,13A
LaPierre, Art	CA0150	36,47,29A,61
Lapin, Lawrence	FL1900	13,10,36,47,29
Laprade, Paul	IL2560	13C,36,61,66D,32
Larsen, Robert L.	IA1350	12A,36,39,66A,66C
Larson, Andrew	FL1750	61,36,60A
Larson, Linda L.	NC0050	13A,11,12A,36,61
Larson, Philip	CA5050	13A,11,12A,36,61
Laster, James	VA1350	60,36,66G,31A
Latimer, Marvin E.	AL1170	32D,36,60A
Latta, Matthew	IN1800	61,32B,36,54
LaVertu, Desiree	CA3300	36
Law, Joshua T.	CA1020	36,61
Lawhon, Sharon L.	AL0800	61,36
Lawrence, Kenya L.	LA0650	36,32B
Lawrence, Robert J.	MO1790	32,36,11,47
Lawrence, Wesley	OH0550	36,61
Lawson, Julie	CA1265	36
Leach, Anthony	PA2750	32C,36
Leaf, Henry	NC1700	36,60A,61
Leck, Henry	IN0250	60,36,32
Lee, April	IL0800	36,11
Lee, Bomi	KY1500	36
Lee, Hae-Jong	OH2600	36,61
Lee, Pamela	TX0150	32,36,66A,60
Lee, Sun Min	PA1950	36,40,60,13C
Lefter, Nancy C.	SC0300	36,66G,31A
Lemson, Lee	TX3850	13A,11,36,61
Lennon, Debby	MO1950	36,61,29,47
Lenti, Elizabeth	OH0600	36,66G
Leonardo, Manuel	CA1400	11,12A,36,61
Levey, John C.	PA3400	10,13,11,34,36
Levi, Michael	NY0700	36,29B,13,60A,32D
Levine, Iris S.	CA0630	12A,32,36,60
Lew, Nathaniel G.	VT0400	12A,13,36,40
Lewis, Alexander	FL1745	61,36,39
Lewis, Andrew	IL3310	36
Liebergen, Patrick	WI0855	11,36,61
Lieberman, Amy	MA1400	36
Lieurance, Neil W.	WA0800	36
Lind, Robin A.	PA3650	32C,36,40,61
Linder, J. Michael	TX1775	13,36,61
Lindquist, Arne	MD0175	36,61
Lindsey, Lauren	WV0050	12A,36,40,61
Lindstrom, G. Mikael	AR0900	13,36
Linduska, Mary	CA2975	61,36
Lippens, Nancy Cobb	IN0800	10,13,36
Lippoldt-Mack, Valerie	KS0210	11,36,61,32I,52
Lipton, Jeffrey S.	NY1275	12A,13B,32C,36,61
Lister, Michael C.	NY0700	32D,32C,55D,36,13
Livesay, Charles	MI2000	60,32D,36,40,61
Livingston, Carolyn H.	RI0300	32,36,66D,12C
Lloyd, Thomas	PA1500	36,61
Lock, William R.	CA0350	60,36,61,31A
Locke, Benjamin R.	OH1200	13A,60,36,38,61
Lockery, Glen	ID0250	36,61
Loeppky, Ian R.	AL1250	60,36,41,40
Loewen, Harris	AG0050	60,36
Lofgren, Ronald R.	NE0700	11,32D,36,60A,61
Logan, Joseph C.	NC0050	12A,32,36,61
Logan, Norman	ID0250	36
Logan, P. Bradley	MN0150	60A,36,32D,40
Logan, Shelly	WA0450	36,61
Logue, James	NE0400	36,40
Long, Daniel	TX2200	36,61,60,11,13D
Long, David	GA0600	36,63A,49,55C,40
Long, Nolan W.	OH2120	36,32D,40,42

Index by Area of Teaching Interest

Name	Code	Areas
Long, Wallace H.	OR1300	60,32C,36
Looker, Wendy	NC0910	60,36,70,12A,13A
Lopez, Christine Sotomayor	CA0859	36,66A,66D,11,66B
Lord, Billy Jean	AZ0150	36
Louis, Kenneth	DC0350	36,61,31A
Lowe, Emily	FL0730	36,61
Lucas, Adonna	NC1950	13,36,64A,66,31A
Lucas, Mark	OK1350	60,32,36,41
Lucky, Harrell C.	TX0700	13,12A,36
Lueck, John	CO0250	36,61
Lueth, Faith	MA0950	36
Luethi, Dean A.	WA1150	36,47,61,32D
Luggie, Brenda	TN1250	36,61,11
Lundergan, Edward	NY3760	13A,13B,36,60,12A
Lupica, Anthony J.	CA1700	36,38,13B,70,61
Luther, David	TN0200	60,36,61,31A,41
Lutter, Lisa	NJ0950	36,61,54,12A
Lyman, Anne E.	WA1000	36,13C
Lynch, Shane	VA1850	36,40,61
Lynerd, Betty Ann	IL1850	31A,44,36
Lynn, Daniel	NE0550	60A,61,36,32C,32D
Lynn, Debra J.	IN1050	60,36,61,40,39
Ma, Yunn-Shan	NY1550	36
Maalouf, Janet	DC0110	36,66
Mabrey, Paul	OK1300	13,36,61
Mabry, Gary L.	TX3530	36,61
Macdonald, James	IL0850	36,41
MacDonald, John A.	OH2150	60,12A,12,36
Machlin, Paul S.	ME0250	12A,36,20G,29A
MacIntyre, Bruce C.	NY0500	12A,12,36
Mack-Bervin, Linda	CO0350	11,32D,36,60A
Maclary, Edward	MD1010	60A,36
MacMullen, Michael J.	FL1470	13A,11,36,61,54
MacPherson, Scott A.	OH1100	36
Magee, Robert G.	AR0950	12A,60,36,61,31A
Maglione, Anthony	MO2000	36,32D,60
Mahraun, Daniel A.	MN1120	61,36,60A,40
Major, James	OH1850	32,36
Major, James E.	IL1150	36,40,32D
Malfatti, Dennis	IN1600	36,40,31A
Mammon, Marielaine	NJ0250	12A,32,36,41,61
Maness, David	PA1150	13,60,11,36,61
Mangini, Mark	NY2050	13A,13,11,36
Mangrum, Leslie	KS0700	61,36,39,12A
Mann, Jay	OH0950	61,36
Mannell, David	IN0907	11,61,36,32B
Mapston, Cindy	AZ0510	36
Marcades, Michael	AL0900	12A,12B,13,32,36
Marchant, Susan J.	KS1050	36,66G,66H,60A
Mariman, Devin	PA2800	36
Marlett, Judy	ID0150	32,36,39,54,60A
Maroney, James	PA1100	11,36,61,13C,40
Marsh, Kerry	CA0840	29,36,47
Marsh, Lawrence B.	OR0450	60,12A,32,36
Marshall, Elizabeth	WV0250	61,36,40
Marshall, Lynda	IL1050	61,36
Martell, Vanessa	MN1270	61,12A,36
Martin, Flora	MD0700	11,36,61
Martin, Gayle H.	AE0050	60A,66G,36,12A,55D
Martin, Joey	TX3175	36,32D,60A
Martin, Linda	IA0950	36,13,32B
Martin, Michael D.	NC1350	32,36
Martin-Andrews, Nicholle	CA5150	36
Martinez, Jeordano S.	IL2050	12A,36,39,54,38
Martinez, Taione	NJ1350	31,36
Marzolf, Dennis	MN0200	60,36,31A,61,54
Mason, Don	KS0215	36
Mason, Joyce D.	OH0700	36
Mason, Rodney	TX0350	13,36,61,66A,66D
Mason, Vito	DC0010	36
Massey, LaDamion	CO0550	36,47
Mathews, Christopher W.	TN1660	36,13H,31A,60A,13C
Mathews, Lee	WA0980	36,60A
Mathews, Lee	WA0300	36,60A
Mathews, Teri	MD0850	36
Mathey, Richard D.	OH0300	36
Mattox, Zeritta	NJ0550	36
Matych-Hager, Susan	MI1950	12A,32,36,61
Maxfield, Dennis	NY1250	36
Maxwell, Monte	MD0900	66G,38,36,31A,51
McAdoo, Susan	NJ1140	13,61,36
McCarthy, Marta	AG0350	60A,36,13C
McCauley, William	SC0200	12A,36,39,61
McClain, Charles	PA2550	13,36,66G
McCoy, Jerry	TX3420	60A,36
McCullough, Richard D.	NY2950	13A,36,39,61,66D
McCutchen, Keith	NC0050	36
McDaniel, Carolyn	OH0250	32A,32B,36
McDermid, Aaron	ND0150	36,60A,61,11,32
McDermott, Pamela D. J.	VA0700	61,60,36,13C
McDonald, Timothy L.	MO1010	11,12A,36,20G
McDonnell, John	NJ1350	36
McDonnell, John	NJ0175	36,32
McGahan, Christopher	MA2030	11,13A,36
McGee, Isaiah R.	SC0350	35,36,39,61,32D
McGhee, Janet F.	NY3650	36,13A,40,60A
Mcgill, Stan	TX0700	36
McGillivray, Angie	AA0050	36
McGilvray, Byron	TX3360	61,36,40
McGilvray, Byron	CA4200	60,32C,36
McGushin, Michael	CA0400	36
McHugh, Barbara	IL1500	32A,36
McInnes, Bruce G.	ME0410	36
McIntire, Dennis K.	GA1700	36,13E
McIntosh, William	CA3200	36,61
McIntyre, John	IN1400	13,34,12A,36,10
McIntyre, John	IN1350	13,10,60,36
McKee-Williams, Robin	CA2150	61,36
McManus, Lanny	AL0550	32D,36,12,13E,40
McMillan, William	TX3520	36,61,60
McMillin, Timothy A.	IA1350	60,36,61,32D,12A
McNeely-Bouie, Barbara	FL0550	36
McNeil, Albert J.	CA5010	60,14,32,36
McRoberts, Gary	CA1900	32,36,66A,20G
McSpadden, George	AL0350	13,36,49,66A,66G
McSpadden, Larry D.	MO0300	36,61
McWhirter, Jamila L.	TN1100	32D,36,60A
McWilliams, Paul	CA5353	36
Meaders, James M.	MS0400	60A,36,61
Means, Allen	IL2450	36,61,63D,63C
Mecham, Mark L.	PA1900	32D,36,40,60A
Mechell, Harry A.	MN1700	60,36,32D,61,54
Meder, Randall A.	WI0808	60,11,36,40,32D
Medley, Susan	PA3580	36,60A,40,11,13A
Megginson, Julie	GA1000	61,36,40,60A
Mehaffey, Matthew W.	MN1623	36,13A
Melson, Christine	CT0500	13A,13C,36,66C
Melton, James L.	CA5355	60,36,31A,32D,35E
Melton, Michael D.	IL2150	36,40,32D,61,60A
Mendez, Max	ID0140	61,36,42,47
Mendoza, Michael D.	NJ0175	60A,32D,36
Menk, Nancy L.	IN1450	60,36,40
Menmuir, Dorla	CA4580	36,61
Meredith, Steven	UT0190	13,36,61,34
Meredith, Victoria	AG0500	60,32,36,41
Merrill, Thomas G.	OH2550	12,60,36,32
Messenger, Richard	CA5355	32C,36
Messoloras, Irene	OK0600	36,12,60A,61,40
Metts, Calland	MN1600	61,36
Metzler, James	MI0900	11,36
Meyer, Dyan	IA1600	36,60A
Miano, Jo Ellen	NY3775	13A,36,61,32I,40
Mianulli, Janice	PA1650	61,40,36
Miceli, Jennifer Scott	NY2105	32,36,60A
Michniewicz, John T.	CT0300	36
Mikolajcik, Walter	CA4650	36,37,47,63,66A
Mikolajewski, Alice	DC0100	36,66A,66C,66D
Miles, James	MS0370	13,66A,66C,36
Miller, Al	AL1195	60,61,36,43
Miller, Andrew	ND0050	36,60A,40,13C
Miller, Becky	IL1612	36,32B,32C
Miller, Christian	OH0680	61,36
Miller, Dale	AR0110	60,36,61
Miller, Dan	IN1800	12A,36,44,61
Miller, DaVaughn	NC1150	36,13E,20B,60
Miller, David	OR0010	36,61,13,60
Miller, Everett F.	KS0225	11,36,34,70,20
Miller, Jo Ann	ND0350	60,36,40,56
Miller, Joe	NJ1350	36,60A
Miller, Josh	WV0200	36,61,32D,11,60A
Miller, June Entwisle	IL3100	36,32B
Miller, Karla	MN1260	13A,11,36,61,66A
Miller, Kelly A.	FL1800	32,36
Miller, Kenny	AZ0470	13C,12A,36,40,61
Miller, Michael	WA0980	32D,36,60A
Miller, Ronald L.	PA2300	12A,36,67B,31A,20G
Miller, Ronald E.	PA2050	13A,36,61
Miller, Thomas E.	CA5400	13B,13C,36,39,54
Miller, Thomas A.	OR1150	60A,11,36,61,31A
Miller, Wendy L.	PA0250	11,12A,36,61,54
Millican, Jason	TX1250	13A,60,11,36,31A
Mills, Susan W.	NC0050	20,32B,32C,61,36
Mindell, Pamela Getnick	MA0700	11,36,40
Minotti, Robert	NY1300	36
Mitchell, Aaron Paul	IN0905	32D,36,40,60A
Mitchell, Linda	CA2440	36,60A,11,12A,13A
Mitchell, Michael A.	MI1750	60A,36,11
Mitchell, Robert	MO0600	13,32,36
Mitchell, William	TX3050	36
Mixon, Laura	AL1050	36,32
Mochnick, John	IL2900	36,41
Modica, Joseph	CA5150	13C,36
Moe, Charlette	ND0350	32B,32D,36
Moffett, Brad	TN0850	36,31A,60A
Moir, Jennifer	AG0500	36,61
Moldenhauer, Kermit G.	MN1030	13A,36,66G,31A,60A
Monek, Daniel G.	OH1400	36,61,12A,60
Moninger, Susan	IL0850	36,40,47,61
Montague, Matthew G.	KS1050	36,32,60A,11
Montalvo, Raquel	PR0100	36,61,13B
Moody, Kevin M.	TX0075	54,61,11,36,40
Moody, Philip	GA2100	36,60A,61
Moon, Hosun	NY1275	11,66,13B,32D,36
Moore, Alison	KS0215	36,61
Moore, David A.	OK1450	10,13,11,36
Moore, Edgar	TX2300	11,36,61,12A
Moore, Edward	NY3720	20G,36,66A,11,29A
Moore, Laura M.	AL1300	36,40,60A,61,66C
Mooy, Mary Annaleen	HI0050	60A,32D,36
Morales, David	CA2910	13A,11,36,61,66
Moran, Kathryn	WI0810	36,61
Morant, Trente	CA2200	36
Morel, Vincent	AI0200	47,36,61
Morgan, Robert Huw	CA4900	66G,60,36
Morris, Gary	AR0200	36,40,60A,61
Morrison, Linda	KY1460	11,32,36,66A,66G
Morrow, David E.	GA1450	60,11,36,61,66A
Morrow, James	TX3510	60,36
Morrow, Phil J.	NC0300	60,36,31A,61
Morton, Wyant	CA0550	60,36
Moses, Oral	GA1150	11,36,61
Moses, Richard	WI0803	36
Moss, Orlando	MS0560	13,60,36,61
Mount, Lorna	HI0120	13A,11,12A,70,36
Mountford, Fritz	NE0300	32C,36,60A,10,20
Moxley, Bryant	VA0050	13,66A,60A,31A,36
Mueller, Paul F.	NY0625	10F,60,11,12A,36
Mueller, Susan	OK0825	36
Muilenburg, Harley	CA2250	36,61,60A,40
Mulhall, Karen	NJ0550	36,66A
Muller, Gerald	TX2170	13,11,12A,32,36
Mullinix, Kelli	NC1250	60A,36
Munn, Albert Christopher	TX3525	13,12A,36,67,55B
Munn, Vivian C.	TX3525	13,32C,36,61
Munson, Mark	OH0300	32,36
Murai, Gregory	CA1450	36
Murphy, Michael	ID0250	36,40,32D,12A,32C
Murray, John	AA0025	61,36,13A,13C
Murray, Kris A.	IL2730	36,70,11,51
Murray, Thomas	CT0850	36,66G
Musgrove, Abby R.	IL1100	36,40,11,32C,32D
Musial, Michael A.	NY3450	13A,11,12A,36,66A
Musselwhite, Harry	GA0300	36,60,39,61
Muzzo, Grace	PA3710	32,36,40,60A
Myers, Gerald C.	MO1120	11,36,40,54,13
Nabholz, Mark A.	SC0700	36,60
Nabors, Louis A.	LA0770	36,61
Nachef, Joanna	CA1750	60,11,36,61
Nafziger, Kenneth J.	VA0300	60,36,31A,38,11
Nagel, Douglas	MT0175	61,36,60A,13C
Nahulu, Nola A.	HI0210	36,20I
Nair, Garyth	NJ0300	36,38,61,60,13C
Najar, Michael	CA3270	13G,36,40
Nakamae, Ayumi	NC0450	61,36,40,67F
Nance, Richard	WA0650	60,36
Nash-Robertson, Nina	MI0400	60,36
Natter, Robert	PA1400	34,36,61,60A
Navari, Jude Joseph	CA4625	10,11,13,36,61
Navarrete, Jennifer Shaw	CA2450	66A,36
Navarro, Joel Magus P.	MI0350	36,60A
Neal, David E.	NY3720	61,54,39,36
Neal, Paul	GA2150	36,60A,61,60
Neal, Randall	VT0050	12,36,45
Neas, Michael	FL1100	36,60A
Neidlinger, Erica	IL0750	36,32E
Neill, Kelly	AR0250	32D,36,40,61

Index by Area of Teaching Interest

Name	Code	Areas
Neiweem, David	VT0450	36,61
Nelson, Curt	CA2900	10D,36,40,54
Nelson, Eric	GA0750	60,36,38,41
Nelson, Karl	OK1330	36,40
Nelson, Lee D.	IA1800	36,60A
Nelson, Roger	WA0200	60,36,66A
Nero, Jonathan	SD0100	36,32D,60
Nesheim, Paul	SD0050	36,32D
Nesheim, Paul J.	MN1120	36,40,60A
Ness, Marjorie S.	MA0930	11,20,32,36,66G
Nestor, Leo Cornelius	DC0050	10A,31A,36,40,60A
Nettles, Darryl	TN1400	13B,32D,36,39,61
Neuen, Donald	CA5030	36,40
Neufeld, Charles W.	SC0800	60A,61,36,32D
Neufeld, Gerald	AG0500	36,55D,60,32
Newby, David L.	CA0200	13C,36,38,39
Newby, Stephen M.	WA0800	10,36
Newlin, Georgia A.	NY0050	11,12A,13C,32,36
Ng, Jonathan	AZ0480	36,61
Niblock, James D.	PA0100	36,61,60A,13A,13B
Nicholeris, Carol A.	MA0510	10A,13D,13A,36,13
Nichols, Eugene C.	ME0430	13,36,37,46,12A
Nichols, Will	MI0150	60,36,61,39
Nieuwenhuis, Mary	MI0450	13A,11,36,61
Nigro, Christie	MA2300	13A,11,12A,36,62A
Niles, Carol Ann	CO0225	36,61
Niu, Elaine	WI0750	61,39,36,60A,13C
Nixon, Patricia	VA0950	36,46,13C,61
Noel, Christine	MA0650	36,60
Noel, Debi	OR0350	13A,36
Norris, Charles	MI0900	32D,32G,36
Norris, Elizabeth	VT0300	11,13A,20,61,36
Norris, James Weldon	DC0150	12A,12,36
Norris, Joshua L.	KS0900	36,60,13,32
Norris, Mike	FL1790	36,12A
Nosworthy, Hedley	CA1750	36,61
Novenske-Smith, Janine L.	MI1200	61,36
Nowack, James	WI1155	60,36,13C
Nunez, Rachel	OH1350	61,36,31A
Nunley, David	WI0825	36
Oakley, Paul E.	NC0350	36,40,61,11
Oakley, Paul E.	KY0800	61,31A,36
Oblinger, Amy	VA1650	36
O'Brien, Kevin	DC0050	36,13B,60A,40
Oby, Jason	TX3150	36,39,61
Octave, Thomas	PA2950	61,36,39,40,11
Odom, Donald R.	MS0850	36,13C,11,32D,60A
Odom, Lisa Sain	SC0400	11,61,36
Ogle, Deborah A.	GA1200	36,13A,60,40,61
Oglesby, Donald T.	FL1900	60,12A,36
Oh, Annette	IL1090	11,61,36,13B,13C
Ohl, Ferris E.	OH0950	60,36,61
Olesen, James D.	MA0500	60,36,55D
Olin, Christopher S.	OR1050	32D,36,60A
Oliver, Ronald D.	MI2250	36,60A,32D
Olsen, Ryan	CO0250	36,32
O'Neal, Melinda P.	NH0100	60,11,36
Oppenheim, Joshua	KS0650	32D,36
Orlofsky, Diane	AL1050	32,12C,36
Orr, Gerald	TX1250	13,11,36,37,66A
Orr, Philip	NJ1000	36,66A
Orr, Sue Butler	SC0710	11,36,61
Orton, Billy H.	AL1160	36,60A,60B,61,63C
O'Shea, Patrick	MN1400	60,12A,36,61,10A
Otal, Monica D.	MD0175	36,61,11
Ottley, Jerold	HI0050	32D,36,60A
Ouimet, Francois	AI0150	36
Owen, Christopher S.	IL2150	36,32D
Owen, Kenneth L.	WA0750	11,61,36,66A,13A
Owen, William E.	WA0550	36,60,12A,40,31A
Owens, Walter	IL0720	36
Owren, Betty Ann	CA1760	36,61,13C,13A,11
Oyen, Valerie	TN1600	36,61
Pace, Mark	NC1750	66G,36,61
Packwood, Gary D.	MS0500	36
Page, Fran M.	NC1300	36,32
Page, Gordon	TX1725	11,13,36
Page, Robert	PA0550	36,39
Pahel, Tim A.	IL1350	36,60
Pahel, Timothy	IL1800	32,36,61,12A
Paiement, Nicole	CA5070	60,36,38
Palmore, James	IL3100	36
Palomaki, Jonathan	TX3800	60,12A,36,61,70
Palomaki, Jonathan	IL0300	12A,32B,36,70,61
Pals, Joel	ID0130	36
Pape, Madlyn	TX1900	36,61
Pardue, Dan	NC1400	36,61
Pardue, Jane	NC1400	36,66A,66D,13A,13B
Park, Jong-Won	WI0845	36,40,61,60A
Parker, Everrett G.	LA0200	36
Parker, Gregory B.	NC0400	36,61,60A,40,32D
Parker, Kara	FL1430	61,36
Parker, Steven	SD0100	36
Parker, Teresa B.	NY0250	36
Parks, Andrew	WA0800	61,31A,12A,36
Parks, Sarah S.	WI0750	36,32D,60A,61
Parnell, Dennis	CA2700	11,36,61
Parnell, Dennis	CA4450	61,36
Parr, Carlotta	CT0050	32A,32B,32C,36,32G
Parr, Clayton G.	MI0100	36,40,60A,32D
Parrish, Eric	MN1175	11,13,36,61
Parsons, Larry R.	WV0800	36,61,31A
Parton-Stanard, Susan	IL1500	61,40,36,11,32D
Patterson, Thomas	WI0960	29A,36,11,63C
Patterson, Trent A.	MO1950	60A,61,32,36,39
Patton, Patrick	WY0050	36,61,40
Paul, Philip	NC0050	13,36,63B
Paul, Sharon J.	OR1050	60A,36,40
Paulk, Jason	NM0100	60A,32C,36
Paulsen, Kent D.	WI0750	36,32D,61,60,13C
Pauly, Elizabeth	MN1050	61,60A,11,36,13A
Paxton, Alexis G.	KY1500	36
Payn, William A.	PA0350	36,44,66G,66H,31A
Payton, Denise	NC0800	20A,36,39,60A,61
Pedersen, David	VA1500	36
Pedersen, Keith	CA3640	36,11,60A
Pedersen, Thomas	DC0050	36,39,54,56,61
Pedroza, Ricardo	PR0125	13,60,36,66A,66D
Pence, Suzanne M.	TX3510	32,36
Pendergrass, Ken E.	WA0800	36
Penniman, G. Victor	MO1010	55,12A,62,11,36
Pennington, Randy	KY1000	60,36,47
Peppo, Bret	CA1560	36,29A,60
Pereira, Hoffmann Urquiza	CA4600	36
Perkins, Daniel R.	NH0200	36,61,12A,32D,60A
Perkins, Leeman L.	NY0750	11,12,31A,36
Perlau, Anita	AA0050	36,32A
Perrin, Raymond	AI0200	36
Perry, Pamela J.	CT0050	32B,32C,36,32D,60A
Peter, Sandra K.	IA0950	60,36
Peter, Timothy	FL1750	36
Peterson, Christopher	CA0815	32D,36
Peterson, Dean	MT0400	60A,32D,36,40
Peterson, Gene D.	TN1710	32,36,40
Peterson, Jon C.	OH0250	36,12A,44,11,54
Peterson, Ken	UT0150	36,39,40,61
Peterson, Mark	NC0100	36,38,66G,66A
Peterson, Robert L.	MN0950	36,61,60A
Peterson, Scott R.	WA0050	36
Peterson, Vince	NY0500	36,60A,32D,13,11
Petrik, Rebecca	ND0250	32,13A,61,70,36
Petzet, John M.	LA0200	11,36
Pfeiffer, Ruth Imperial	HI0160	13A,12A,32,36,66
Pfutzenreuter, Leslie D.	CA2840	11,36,38,39,61
Phelps, Matthew	OH2550	36
Philipsen, Michael D.	IA0750	13,11,36,61,66A
Phillips, Sheena	OH2050	36
Phillips, Sheila A.	MO0950	36,11
Piattoly, Lindsay	LA0650	36
Pierce, Edward A.	OK0850	40,61,36
Pilkington, Steve	NJ1350	36,31A
Pindell, Reginald	PA3330	36,39,61
Piper, Shenita	IN0400	36
Pisciotta, Eva Mae	AZ0200	36,61,29A
Plant, Lourin	NJ1050	60,36,41,61
Plew, Paul T.	CA2810	60,36,61,31A
Ploeger, Kristina	WA0250	32,36,60A
Plummer, Mark W.	IL0150	36,32D,40
Poch, Gail B.	PA3250	60,36
Poland, Jeffrey T.	WV0300	32D,36,61,60
Polochick, Edward	NE0600	36
Polochick, Edward L.	MD0650	60,36
Poniros, Risa	NC1500	32B,40,36,61
Pool, Ellen	MI0900	32D,36,60A
Poole, Eric	SC0850	36,61,60A,32D,40
Poovey, Gena E.	NC2150	13,60,20G,36,41
Popejoy, Melanie	ND0500	36
Popowich, Jamie	AA0050	32A,36
Port, Dennis	MN0250	60A,36
Porter, Beth Cram	OH0450	36,61
Porter, Michael C.	ID0050	36
Porter, Michael	NC0250	36,40,60,61,32D
Porter, Thomas	ND0400	36,13B,10A,32D,31A
Porterfield, Priscilla J.	NC0050	61,36
Potter, Kenney	NC2650	36,13C,60A
Potterton, Matthew	KS0050	60,36,32D
Powell, Aaron	IA0420	70,36
Powell, Curtis Everett	GA0490	36,13,32,32D
Powell, Rosephanye	AL0200	61,36
Powell, Steven S.	PA1000	36,61,34,12A,32D
Powell, William C.	AL0200	60A,36
Preston, Byron L.	NY4050	36
Pretzat, Julie	NY3770	13,60,36
Price, Clayborn	NY3770	13A,36
Prichard, Sheila Grace	MA1600	36,44
Prickett, Todd O.	AR0700	36,32D
Provencio, Robert	CA0650	60,32,36
Prowse, Robert W.	NJ0825	36,40,61,12A
Psurny, Robert D.	MT0075	29A,36,40,54,61
Puchala, Mark	MI1650	12A,36,61,34,41
Puderbaugh, David J.	IA1550	36
Pufall, Molly	WI0050	36
Pullan, Bruce	AB0100	36
Pursino, Peter	GA1990	36,40
Puschendorf, Gunther F.	CA1100	13A,36,38,66A
Pysh, Gregory	TX3527	10,13,61,60A,36
Quantz, Don E.	AA0010	12A,32D,36,40,41
Quash, Jonathan	NY0646	36,54,61
Quesada, Milagros	OH1100	11,32,36
Quinlan, Gloria H.	TX1150	32,36,61,66C,31A
Quinn, Christopher	UT0400	13,36
Quintana, Ariel	CA0845	36,32D
Quist, Amanda R.	NJ1350	32D,36,60
Rada, Raphael	TX0550	61,11,13C,32B,36
Ragland, Janice	MO0850	61,36,32C
Railton, Marlene	MO2050	36,61
Raines, Alan L.	TX0300	36,60A,40
Ramo, Suzanne D.	TX1425	61,11,36
Ramsey, James	CO0900	36
Ramsey, William H.	CA4900	60,36
Ransom, Judy L.	WY0115	13B,13F,36,40,66D
Rao, Doreen	AG0450	32,36,60,61
Rasmussen, Brenda	WA0550	11,31A,36,13A
Rasmussen, Bruce	CA3400	60A,36,61,40,66G
Ratledge, John	AL1170	60A,36
Ratzlaff, Leonard	AA0100	60,36
Rawdon, Kenneth	CA0900	36
Ray, Robert	MO1830	20G,36,66A
Ray, W. Irwin	GA1550	60,11,41,36,40
Rayam, Curtis	FL0100	36,61,40,39
Raybon, Leonard	LA0750	36,61,60A,54
Rayl, David C.	MI1400	36,60A
Reagan, Billy R.	AL0350	36,37,41,47,63
Reager, John	CA2450	36,66A,61,12A
Reames, Rebecca	NY3780	60A,32,36
Redding, Eric	AK0050	11,36,66A,70,53
Redding, Jeffery	WV0750	36,60A
Redfearn, Christopher	ND0600	36,40,60A,61
Rediger, JoAnn K.	IN1560	36,31A,60A,11,40
Reed, Joel F.	NC1250	20G,60A,36,61,31A
Reed, Jonathan I.	MI1400	60A,32C,36
Reese, Jodi	KS0265	36,11,13C,61,60A
Reeves, Bethany	NY0270	11,36,39,60A,61
Reid, Steven D.	IN0005	63A,36,37,38,13
Reigles, B. Jean	NY1700	36,39,60A,61
Reimers-Parker, Nancy	MN0250	36
Renfroe, Dennis C.	NC1025	11,12A,32,36,63
Renner-Hughes, Marty	MO1110	12A,36,54
Replogle, Rebecca	OR1010	36,61,13A,13C,40
Retzko, Barbara	NJ1130	36
Reynolds, Jeff W.	AL1150	60,36,39
Reznicek, Steven	MN0150	36,32B,32C
Ricciardone, Michael	NY2750	36,54,66A
Rice, JoAnn	NY1860	36,60
Rice, Susan	WI0100	40,36,13A
Richard, Monique M.	AE0100	32,36,40,60A
Richards, E. Earl	CA2420	32D,36,60A
Richards, Gwyn	IN0900	36
Richardson, Celia	TX2850	11,36,61,32B,13C
Richardson, David	WI0810	36
Richardson, Dennis	TX0550	36,40,32B,66D,60A
Richardson, James K.	VA0300	61,11,36,54,39
Richardson, Ouida	TX0550	36,64A,32A
Richmond, Brad	MI1050	36,40,60A,61
Richmond, John W.	NE0600	32D,32G,36,32
Richter, Tiffany	AL1450	13,36,40,61

Name	Code	Areas
Rickard, Jeffrey H.	CA5150	10,60,36,31A
Rieck, Alan J.	WI0803	32C,36
Riehl, Jeffrey S.	VA1500	11,36,61,60
Ries, Ardelle	AA0110	13C,36,60A
Rieth, Dale	FL0950	13,36,47,61,66A
Riggs, Ben	CO0650	36
Riley, Blake	FL2100	36,60A
Riley, Denise	MS0200	13,36,61
Ringwall, Lauren	GA1650	32,60,36
Rink, Jeffrey	MA2010	36
Rios, Giselle Elgarresta	FL0050	61,36,60,32,41
Ristow, Gregory C.	IN0350	36,40
Ritchey, Mary Lynn	MA0150	61,36,60A,40,11
Ritter, Paul	MT0370	36
Ritter-Bernardini, Denise	OH2300	61,36
Rivera Ortiz, William	PR0115	13A,13C,36,60A
Rivera, Jose	NC2435	32,36,61,60
Rivers, Cynthia	GA1100	66A,66G,66C,31A,36
Rivers, Earl G.	OH2200	60,36
Rivers, Sylvia	TX0250	61,36
Roberson, Heather D.	CO1050	61,36,11,60A,32D
Roberts, John	OH2290	36
Roberts, Stanley L.	GA1300	60A,36,31A
Robertson, Kaestner	MA0250	66A,13,36,66B,66C
Robertson, Ruth M.	MO0600	36,39,61
Robertson, Troy David	TX2750	60,32C,36,61
Robins, Linda	TX2570	32B,36,66A,66B
Robinson, Charles R.	MO1810	36,32D,32H
Robinson, Russell	FL1850	32,36
Rocco, Emma S.	PA2713	13A,11,20F,36,54
Rockabrand, Sarah	IL2400	36,61,60A
Rodde, James	IA0850	36,60,32D
Rodde, Kathleen	IA0850	36,66A,66C
Rogers, Bruce	CA3200	36,61,60A
Rogers, Eugene C.	MI2100	36
Rogers, Sean	ID0070	36,39,60,66A,66G
Rohlfing, Mimi	MA2030	61,36,47,40
Rolsten, Kathy	MN1120	32A,32B,32D,36,61
Romano, Darlene	CA1270	36,61,11,13A,40
Romano, Patrick	NY3560	60,36,61
Romeo, Tony B.	MA1550	36
Romey, Kathy Saltzman	MN1623	36
Romines, Dee	TX0900	32D,36
Rommereim, John Christian	IA0700	60,10,36,61
Rorex, Michael	LA0550	36,39,61
Rose, Cameron J.	TX3535	36,32D,11,10
Rose, John E.	FL0700	36
Rose, John	CT0500	36,66G,69,31A
Roseberry, Lynn	OH0350	61,39,40,36
Rosenbaum, Harold L.	NY4320	36
Rosenfeld, Andrew	MD0610	11,12,13,20F,36
Rosenmeyer, David G.	NY2750	36
Rosensteel Way, Nancy	PA2500	11,36
Rosewall, Michael	WI0750	36,61,12A,13A,13B
Ross Mehl, Margaret	PA0600	36,39,61,11,12A
Ross, Gregory	PA1000	36
Ross, Jared	KS0060	13,60,31A,36,61
Ross-Hammond, Amelia	VA0950	13,13J,36,66
Rossi, Richard Robert	IL0800	60A,36,38,66G
Rossomando, Fred E.	CT0250	36,11
Rossow, Stacie	FL0650	61,36,13A
Roste, Vaughn	OK0550	60,12A,36,61,20
Rothlisberger, Rodney	MN1120	32D,36,66G
Roueche, Michelle	TX3415	60,36,66C
Rowe, Alissa	LA0650	36,61,60A
Rowehl, John	NY0900	36,40,60A
Rowell, Michael	GA0700	31A,60A,47,36
Rudari, David J.	WV0100	61,36,12A,32B,54
Rudo, Sandy	CA2150	36,61
Rundus, Katharin	CA1900	36,61
Runefors, Bjorn	AE0120	36,37,13,11,64A
Runestad, Kurt	NE0200	36,32D,60A,47
Runyan, Donald	IL1612	36,32D,61
Russell, John	CA0845	36,40,32D,60A
Russell, John K.	CA1520	32D,36,40,60A
Russell, Nathan	TX3370	36,11,61,13C
Russell, Robert J.	ME0500	12A,36,60
Russell, Teresa P.	CA4850	60,36,61,54,32A
Rutledge, Kevin	FL1310	36,61
Ryan, Rebecca	PA2250	36,32C,60A
Ryder, Carol	CA2250	61,36,11
Ryder, Carol	CA1280	36,54,61
Ryner, Jayson	IA1170	32C,36,61,11,13C
Sacalamitao, Melonie	CA4850	32A,32B,32C,66D,36
Saeverud, Trond	ME0430	11,13A,41,36
Sager, Gene	WY0150	36,40,61,11
Sailor, Catherine	CO0900	36,60
Saladino, Jean	WI1100	61,36,13C
Salamunovich, Paul	CA2800	36
Salucka, Ray	IA0930	13,36,60,11,47
Salyer, Douglas W.	CT0200	13,34,12A,36,66
Sametz, Steven P.	PA1950	13,60,10,36
Sanchez, Cynthia	TX2260	36,61,64A,66A
Sandborg, Jeff R.	VA1250	60,11,12A,36,61
Sandefur, Lynn	FL1675	11,13A,36,40,61
Sanders, Paul	OH1850	32,36
Sano, Stephen M.	CA4900	60,36,20C,20I
Santana, Priscilla	TX2800	61,36,40
Satre, Paul J.	IL3150	36,66A,66G,60,13
Savage, Charles M.	OH1910	13,12A,20G,36,61
Sawyer, Charsie Randolph	MI0350	61,36
Sawyer, Timothy K.	MN1280	60,36
Scarbrough, Michael	TX0050	36,61,60A
Schaefer, Elaine	CA1300	13A,36,54,61,40
Schaffer, Donna	MS0050	36,61,60A
Schane-Lydon, Cathy	MA1850	10,36,66
Schantz, Cory Neal	SD0550	61,36,60A
Schantz, Richard	PA2450	36
Schauer, Elizabeth	AZ0500	36,32D,61
Scheib, Curt A.	PA3000	61,36,66C,60,60
Scheibe, Jo-Michael	CA5300	36,60A
Schildkret, David	AZ0100	36,60A
Schlesinger, Scott L.	NC2525	66G,11,13A,29A,36
Schmauk, Doris	PA0650	36,61
Schmidt, Jack W.	PA0900	11,12A,36,37,49
Schmidt, Karl	CA1800	36,61
Schmutte, Peter J.	IN1650	36,45,35C,35G,34
Schnack, Michael B.	PA2550	36,40,61
Schnipke, Richard	OH1850	32D,36
Schoenberg, Kathe	NJ0550	61,36
Schoenecker, Ann Elise	WI1100	61,36
Schoening, Benjamin S.	WI0801	11,13,36,61,63
Schoenlein, Laila	CA4460	36
Scholz, David M.	CA0800	36,61,32C,60
Scholz, Robert	MN1450	36,61,60A
Schreier, Kathleen	IA0790	13,11,36,54
Schreuder, Joel T.	NE0050	60A,36,61,40,32D
Schubert, Peter	AI0150	13,13J,36
Schultz, Ryan	IL2300	37,63C,36
Schulz, Russell E.	TX0750	36,66G,31A
Schulze, Otto	IN0005	62A,67,10,13,36
Schuppener, James	TX1700	36,61,32D
Schutt, Jackie T.	IL2050	32,13C,36
Schwartzhoff, Gary R.	WI0803	60,36
Scinta, Frank	NY0400	61,31A,32C,36
Scott, Chris	IL0100	36,61,13C
Scott, Karla	MD0900	36,31A
Scott, Kraig	WA1100	36,31A,60A,66G,66H,60A
Scott, L. Brett Cornish	OH2200	60A,36
Scott, Sandra C.	GA1600	36,40,60A,32D,66A
Scott, Stuart	MI1250	40,36,61
Scraper, Joel	SC1100	40,60A,32D,36,60
Scully, Joseph D.	IL0450	13A,11,36,20
Scully, Mathew	CA3950	36,61,13
Seaton, Kira J.	OH0755	13A,13,11,36,61
Seaward, Jeffery A.	CA1290	13A,36,41,61,54
Sedonis, Robert D.	OH1850	32,36
Seeley, Gilbert	OR0400	60,12A,36,41
Seeley, Jeffery	NY1150	11,20,36
Seeman, Rebecca	CA5353	13A,11,36,38,61
Seigel, Lester C.	AL0300	60,36,39,66C,13F
Seighman, Gary B.	TX3350	36
Sepulveda, Sonja	NC2205	36,47,13,60
Seuffert, Maria C.	GA0160	36
Severing, Richard	WI0865	36,40,54,61
Shadle-Peters, Jennifer	CO0275	12A,20,32,36,67
Shafer, Robert	VA1350	60,36
Shanahan, Ellen Cooper	MA0280	13,12A,36,54,29A
Shane, Lynn	MA1650	11,61,32B,32D,36
Shangkuan, Pearl	MI0350	60A,36
Shanklin, Bart	IL3500	61,60A,36,32D
Shankman, Ira	NY2750	32,40,36,60
Shankman, Nancy Ellen	NY2750	32,36,60
Shannon, Kathleen	WV0750	36,32,60
Shapiro, Mark L.	NY2105	60A,36,40,13
Shapovalov, Dimitri	WI0250	12A,66D,36,66A
Sharpe, Avery G.	MA2250	62D,41,36
Sharples, Pamela	NJ0750	13C,36,66A,66C
Shasberger, Michael	CA5550	36,31A,38,60,61
Shaw, Lisa	DC0170	61,36
Shaw, Martha	GA1700	36,32D,60A
Shearin, Arthur Lloyd	AR0250	11,36,61
Sheftz, Stephen Walter Robert	NE0160	36
Shelby, Karla	OK1500	10D,13A,60A,66A,36
Sheldon, Janene	NE0450	61,32B,36,40,16
Shelley, Russ	PA1650	11,12B,36
Shelt, Christopher A.	MS0100	60A,36,31A,61,40
Shelton, Tom	NJ1350	31,32,36,60A
Sheppard, Chris	SC0900	36,60A,61,40,34
Sheppard, Kenny	TX2650	60A,36,32D
Sherman, Joy	WA0850	11,36,40,61
Sherwin, Ronald G.	MA0150	11,31A,60A,36,32
Shetler, Timothy	MA0800	60,32C,36,61
Shields, Lisa	MT0100	13,36,37,64E
Shimeo, Barbara	IL1612	61,36
Shirtz, Michael	OH2140	36,60,61,13,29
Shockey, David M.	PA2800	36,61,40
Shover, Blaine F.	PA3050	11,12A,36,61,54
Shrader, James A.	GA2150	60,12A,61,36,39
Shrock, Dennis R.	TX3000	60,36
Shrope, Douglas	CA1000	36,61,60A,40,54
Sichel, John	NJ0975	13,10,11,12A,36
Sieck, Stephen	VA0350	36,61,60A,32D
Sieck, Steven	WI0350	36,60A
Sigmon, Susan McEwen	GA0940	13,36,66A,66G,40
Sikora, Stephanie R.	OH0100	36,39,61
Silantien, John J.	TX3530	60,36
Silverberg, Marc E.	NY1275	36
Simmons, Mark	TN1720	36,32D,60A
Simons, Diane	CA1750	36
Simons, Kevin	MI1850	61,36,32D,60A
Simpson, Alexander T.	KY0250	11,12A,36,44,60A
Simpson, Michael	VA1600	36
Sincell-Corwell, Kathryn	MD0450	36,61
Sinclair, John V.	FL1550	60,32,36,41,38
Sinclair, Robert L.	IL3450	36,32,60A
Sinclair, Terri	SC0420	36,61,32D,60A
Singh, Vijay	WA0050	47,60,36,61,35A
Singleton, H. Craig	CA1650	36,61,31A
Singley, H. E.	IL1850	66A,66G,11,36,31A
Sirett, Mark G.	AG0250	36,60
Sisk, Lawrence T.	IL1520	38,12A,36,31A
Skeris, Robert	DC0050	31A,36
Skinner, Kent	AR0800	60A,36,61,39,54
Skoog, William M.	TN1200	36,61
Slawson, John G.	IL0840	60,12A,36,38,54
Sledge, Larry	FL0800	60,12A,31A,36,13
Slon, Michael	VA1550	36,39,60
Slotterback, Floyd	MI1600	60,36,11
Small, Ann R.	FL1750	32,36
Smalley, Charles	AZ0150	13C,11,36,61,20G
Smith, Aaron	MD0900	31A,36,54,40
Smith, Angie	NC2370	11,36
Smith, Billy	TX0390	36
Smith, Byron J.	CA2650	36,35A,35B,61,66
Smith, Carl H.	KY0750	60,32B,32C,36
Smith, Charles	NE0300	36,39,61,54
Smith, Curtis F.	CO0810	13,34D,36,66A
Smith, David K.	KS0950	36,11,61,13,66A
Smith, David	MD1000	36,39,60,61
Smith, Gayle	AL0335	66D,36,61
Smith, James S.	NC1800	36,41,61
Smith, James E.	CA4450	13,60,36,38
Smith, Jason	IA1400	13,36,61,60A
Smith, Jeffrey	NY2650	36
Smith, Jennifer	MI1550	36,61,66
Smith, John	MO1830	36
Smith, Justin	OR0500	36,11,60
Smith, Kathryn L.	CA1500	61,36,60A
Smith, Kevin	MN0625	36,60,40,10A
Smith, Marilyn	MS0420	36,32A,32B
Smith, Marion	FL0450	13,12A,36
Smith, Paul A.	CA0835	36,60A
Smith, Paul B.	AR0400	60,36,61
Smith, Roy C.	IN0005	61,11,10A,60,36
Smith, Susan A.	MS0360	61,40,13,36,13B
Smith, Vernon L.	FL1300	11,36,61
Smoak, Jeff C.	KY1425	32,36,61,40,43
Smucker, Angela Young	IN1750	36,61
Snow, Sandra	MI1400	32D,36
Snyder, Timothy	FL1000	36,40,12A,32D,60A
Soderberg, Karen	MD0350	61,36,40,32D,60A
Soich, Leslie	CO0830	36,13,11,10D
Sokol, Thomas A.	NY0900	60,36,40
Somer, Gena	IL1090	36
Song, Anna	OR0450	13C,36,55B,55A,40

Index by Area of Teaching Interest

Name	Code	Areas
Song, MyungOk Julie	NY2750	32,36,60,61
Song, Tom	TX2600	36,60A,31A
Songer, Loralee	TN0850	60A,36,61
Sonntag, Dawn Lenore	OH1000	36,61,66C,10A,10
Sorenson, Allin	MO0350	60,11,36,61
Soto, Ricardo	CA3350	36,61,38
Southard, Bruce	ND0100	36,60A,12A,61,60
Sowers, Richard L.	IN0100	60A,36,32D
Sparfeld, Tobin	CA2660	61,36
Sparkman, Carol Joy	MS0400	66C,66D,36,66A
Sparks, Michael	AL1450	12A,36,66A,31A,34
Sparks, Richard	TX3420	60A,36,55D
Spears, Samuel B.	WV0300	32D,36,61,60A
Speck, R. Floyd	TN0450	36,46
Speer, Randall	VA1125	61,36,60A,40
Speer, Shari	MN0610	36,39,61
Spencer, Philip	IL1250	20,61,66A,36,60A
Spencer, Theresa Forrester	MO0250	36,40,61,14C
Sperry, Ethan L.	OR0850	36,60A
Spicer, Donna	OR1020	36,61,66A,66D
Spicer, Nan	GA1750	36
Spillane, Jamie D.	CT0600	36,60A
Sposato, Jeffrey S.	TX3400	12,36
Sprenger, Curtis	CA4460	36
Sprenkle, David	PA3600	36,41,61
Spurgeon, Debra L.	MS0700	32C,36
St. Clair, Nike'	CA0630	36
St. Claire, Jason	NE0250	36
St. Jean, Donald	RI0250	36,61
St. Marie, John	CA0830	36
Stadnicki, Tisha	MA1450	36,61
Stafford, John	KS0590	36,40,47,11,13A
Stafslien, Judy	WI1100	66C,36,61
Staheli, Ronald	UT0050	60,36,41,61,66A
Staininger, Lynn L.	MD0300	36,66A,13B,40,61
Staininger, Lynn	MD0500	36,40
Stallsmith, John	AL0260	12A,36,47,66,31A
Stalter, Timothy J.	IA1550	36
Stam, Carl L.	KY1200	36,31A
Stanley, David	AR0500	61,36
Stark, Eric	IN0250	36
Stauch, Thomas J.	IL1085	36,40,61,32D,11
Steele, Janet	NY0550	13A,55,61,66A,36
Steele, Rebecca W.	FL0100	36,61
Stegall, James C.	IL3500	36,32D,60A
Stegman, Sandra Frey	OH0300	32,36
Steinbuck, Caroline	CA4460	36
Stern, Jeffrey S.	NY0650	36,61
Stern, Kalai	HI0110	11,36,40,13A,13C
Stern, Margaret	NY4300	36,40
Stevens, Alan E.	TN0500	36,61
Stevens, Brian	NY2650	36
Stevens, James M.	TN0580	10A,36,13E,13B
Stevens, Mitchell	LA0900	61,36
Stevenson, George	OK0850	12A,14,36,61
Stewart, Jonathan	OK0825	32D,11,13B,36,61
Stewart, Shawna	CA0350	60,36,32
Stewart, Shirley	LA0720	11,36,61,31A,32
Stich, Adam	AZ0490	36,60A,61,40,13A
Stickler, Larry W.	WV0400	36,32B,32C,61,32D
Stinner, Rita	NE0710	13,36,20G
Stock, Jesse	TN0250	36,61,60A,54
Stokes, Porter	SC1000	36,61,60,32
Stoltzfus, Fred A.	IL3300	60A,36
Stornetta, Catherine	MA0850	60A,32D,36
Stowe, Daniel	IN1700	12,36,38
Strauser, Matthew L.	OR0175	36,60,13C,32D
Stringer, Sandra	AA0200	61,36,11
Stripling, Allen	GA0810	11,36,66,32,40
Stroope, Z. Randall	OK0800	36,60A,40,10A
Stumpf, Robert	IL3370	36,13
Stutzenberger, David R.	TN1710	36
Suderman, Gail	AB0060	36,61,40,39
Suderman, Mark	OH0250	60A,32D,32B,36,61
Sulahian, Nancy	CA0500	36,40
Summer, Robert J.	FL2000	60,36
Sundberg, Gerard	IL3550	36,61
Sundby, Candace	FL0500	61,36
Supeene, Susan	AA0040	32A,61,36
Sussuma, Robert	CO0560	36,55D
Sutton, John	CA0250	60,31A,36
Svenningsen, Russell	SD0050	13,36,61
Svoboda, Matt	OR0350	36,40
Swaim, Doris	NC2640	32A,36,61,66D
Swan, Phillip A.	WI0350	36,60,61,32D,60A
Swaney, Susan	IN0900	36
Swanson, Barry	ID0150	31,36,40
Swift, Robert F.	NH0250	11,32,36
Swisher, Martha	IL2650	36,60A
Taddie, Daniel L.	AR0900	12A,36,61
Taft, Burns	CA5360	13,60,36,66A,38
Tagg, Barbara M.	NY4150	32,36,60A
Takacs, Miklos	AI0210	32,36
Talberg, Jonathan	CA0825	36
Talley, Sue	NY2900	66A,12A,36,31A,31B
Tallman, Donna	IL0850	36,60A,44
Tam, Jing Ling	TX3500	36,61,60A
TangYuk, Richard	NJ0900	36,39,40
Tapanes-Inojosa, Adriana	IL1080	11,20,36,12,66
Tarantino, Cassandra	CA1510	36,60A
Taranto, Vernon	FL1650	10,11,13B,36,13C
Tarrant, James	MO1550	36,60A,35,42,66A
Tasher, Cara S.	FL1950	60A,61,36
Tate, David L.	VA0800	32,36
Tate, Shelia D.	VA1800	11,32,16,36
Tavernier, Jane	VA1475	61,36,39,40
Tavianini, Marie A.	PA0900	36,61
Taylor, Allan	MA2100	13E,66G,36
Taylor, Arlecia Jan	TX2100	11,36,32,66A
Taylor, Betty Sue	NY2400	13A,12,36,61,66
Taylor, Beverly	WI0815	60,36
Taylor, James	NC1050	41,36,61,31A,11
Taylor, Jim	TX1350	36,40,61
Taylor, Mark A.	MS0360	36
Taylor, Robert J.	SC0500	11,36,61,60
Taylor, Una D.	NE0050	36,61,32B,11,40
Teal, Terri	KS0570	11,40,61,36
Tebay, John	CA1900	36,61,66D,66A,12A
Tebay, John	CA0350	36
Tebbets, Gary	KS0040	12A,11,36,54,62
Tedford, Linda	PA2300	60A,36,61
Tegnell, John Carl	CA4200	36,61
Tel, Martin	NJ0850	36,66G,31A
Templon, Paul	NC2400	66A,66C,36
TenBrink, Karen	MI0100	36
Terenzi, Mark J.	NJ0700	36,40,60A,13C
Teske, Deborah Jenkins	CO0200	36,40,60A
Thayer, Fred M.	PA2100	13,60,10,36
Thayer, Lucinda J.	WI0850	60A,36,32D
Theimer, Axel K.	MN0350	60A,36,61,32D
Thevenot, Maxine R.	NM0450	11,36
Thielen-Gaffey, Tina	MN1600	36,61,40,32
Thomas, Andre J.	FL0850	60A,32,36
Thomas, Darrin	MN1450	36
Thomas, Jeffrey	CA5010	60,36,12A
Thomas, Nicholas	IL1890	60A,66D,13A,36,61
Thomas, Steven L.	PA3700	36,61,40
Thompson, Bruce A.	NC1000	36,13,66A,61
Thompson, Edgar	UT0250	36
Thompson, Jonathan	AB0090	11,36,12A,60,38
Thompson, Laura	LA0250	32C,32D,36,60A,61
Thompson, Lynn	IL3500	61,54,39,36
Thompson, Paul	WI0825	60,36
Thompson, Paul	WI0817	36,13B,13C,11
Thoms, Jason A.	NY0850	36,32D,61,55D,12A
Thomson, Jacqueline	IA1400	13,36,61,60A
Thorn, Julia	PA3150	36,60A,61
Thorngate, Russell	WI0925	11,13A,36,40,61
Thornton, Tony	MA2000	36
Thorp, Steven	NM0250	13,11,36,61,40
Thorpe, Austin	UT0400	36
Thorson, Eric	TN0250	32,36,60
Thulin, Jeanette	MN1250	36
Thye, David R.	TX2600	60,32D,32E,36,38
Tidmore, Natasha	AL0850	36,29
Timmerman, David	TX1750	13A,13,36,41,61
Timothy, Sarah O.	AL0890	61,11,36,13,32
Tindall, Danny H.	FL1740	36,37,65,11
Tini, Dennis J.	MI2200	60,36,29,35
Tinsley, David	AL0400	11,36,61
Tipps, Angela	TN1100	66G,36,11
Tipps, James	OH2500	32,36,66A,66D,60
Tobia, Riccardo	PA2900	61,36
Tocheff, Robert	OH1600	60,11,32,36,66D
Todd, Allen F.	TN1680	36
Todd, Colette	WI0250	32D,36,47
Tolbert, Clinton	MI0350	36
Toman, Sharon Ann	PA2775	11,13A,29A,14C,36
Toomer, Charlie	FL0600	60,36,61
Torres, Barry A.	NY3550	55,36,61
Tosh, Melissa Denise	CA5150	61,36,39,54
Town, Stephen	MO0950	13,61,36
Tramm, Jason	NJ1160	36,40,60A
Tresler, Matthew T.	CA2390	36,61,11
Tresler, Matthew	CA1425	36
Tritle, Kent	NY2150	36
Tritle, Kent	NY1900	36
Tropp, Thomas	IL2100	36
Trotta, Michael J.	VA1830	32D,12A,36,40
Trotter, John William	IL3550	36,60A
Trussel, Jacque	NY3785	36,39,61
Tucker, Carlton	KS1350	36
Tucker, Scott	NY0900	60,36,40,13A,20A
Tuning, Mark	CA3920	36,40,61
Turgeon, Melanie E.	AA0035	60,36,42,13C,32D
Turner, Anne Z.	NY3650	36,39,61
Turner, Gregory E.	KS0400	13,38,36,60,61
Turner, James	MI1150	36,61
Turner, Kelly J.	TX3400	36
Turner, Kevin P.	AL1150	36
Tuttle, John	AG0450	36,31A
Tuttle, Marshall	OR0550	13,36,38
Tuzicka, William	KS0700	61,36
Tweed, Randall L.	CA2100	38,36,12A
Tworek-Gryta, Adrienne	NY4460	61,36
Tyler, Edward	CT0050	36
Tyree, Rebecca	VA1600	36,32
Tyson, LaDona	MS0580	11,40,36,61
Udland, Matt	KS0210	11,36,43,61
Ulrich, Jerry	GA0900	10,36,32,32D,60A
Unger, Melvin P.	OH0200	16,12A,36
Upton-Hill, Diana	IA0750	36
Usher, Ann L.	OH2150	32,36,60A
Vail, Leland	CA0825	36,61,60
Vaillancourt, Josee	AI0190	32,36
Valentine, Claudette	NE0160	66A,36,66D
van den Honert, Peter	PA1200	60A,36,11,13A
Van Wyck, Helen J.	IL3100	13,60A,11,36,32D
VanDam, Lois	FL1430	66A,36,60A
Vander Linden, Dan	WI0848	36,61,66
Vanderpool, Linda	IA0550	36
VanDyke, Susanne	MS0575	36,61,13B,13C
VanWeelden, Kimberly	FL0850	60,32,36
Vascan, Ligia	WI0500	40,61,36,54,29
Vaughn, Beverly Joyce	NJ0990	36,11,13A,20G,61
Vazquez-Ramos, Angel M.	CA0960	60A,36,32D,32B
Vickery, Robert	MN1625	36
Voelker, Dale	IL1300	13A,13B,60A,36,66G
Vogel, Bradley D.	KS1300	60,32B,36,61,31A
Vogt, Sean F.	SD0300	60A,36,66G,32D,40
Volk, David Paul	VA1580	13,36,12A,66A,10
Von Ellefson, Randi	OK0750	36,60A,40
Von Kampen, Kurt E.	NE0150	36,60A,32
Vote, Larry	MD0750	60,32,36,61
Vowan, Ruth A.	AR0225	61,12A,36,39
Wade, Michael	IN0910	36
Wagner, Randel	WA0250	36,40,61,54,60A
Wagner, Wayne L.	MN1030	13A,32,36,66G,66D
Wagstrom, Beth Robison	CO0050	36,40,47,60A
Wahl, Shelbie L.	VA0550	13C,36
Wait, Gregory A.	CA4900	36,61
Walker, Alicia W.	SC1110	36,32D,60A
Walker, Cherilee	KS0590	36,13,11,61,29A
Walker, Gayle	OH2050	13C,60,12A,36
Walker, Keith H.	GA0625	36,61,60
Walker, Linda B.	OH1100	32,36
Walker, Steve	OK0300	61,36,60,60A
Wall, Jeremy	NY3765	34,35,36,47,66A
Wallace, James A.	GA1070	36,13C,40,11
Wallace, Thomas	ME0270	36,61
Wallis, David N.	MO0650	36,10A,11,13,32D
Walters, Kent	MI0520	36,60A
Walters, Teresa	NJ0200	13,60,11,12A,36
Walth, Gary Kent	WI0810	60,11,32C,36,54
Ward, Allison	TX3000	36
Ward, Jeffrey	NC0650	32D,36
Ward, Robert J.	OH1850	60,36
Ware, John Earl	LA0900	11,36,39,41,61
Warford, Allison	TN1850	36
Warren, Jane	TN0100	36,60A
Warren, John	IL1900	36,11,12A,13B,13C
Warren, John F.	NY4150	36,32D,60A
Washington, Henry	TX2220	36,11,66A,66D,66G
Waterfield, Elizabeth	CA4550	36,61,40,13A,39
Waters, Richard	KY0550	36,60A,32D,40
Watkins, Wilbert O.	IL0275	36,40,32

Name	Code	Areas
Watson, Tim M.	IA1100	32D,47,36,60A
Wayman, John B.	GA2300	32,36,61
Weaver, Brent	TN0650	36,37,34,13
Weaver, Brent	OR0250	10,61,13,34,36
Webb, Brian P.	VT0125	13A,13,11,12A,36
Webb, Guy B.	MO0775	60,36,61
Webb, Jeffrey L.	PA3410	29A,36,13A,60,13
Webb, Lewis	AL1050	61,36,66A
Webb, Merrilee	UT0150	36,66D,66A
Webb, Robert	VA0975	11,36,13
Weber, Betsy Cook	TX3400	32C,36
Weber, Paul	NC1100	60,36
Weber, Steven T.	TX0100	36,41,61
Weeda, Linn	AK0100	11,36,49,63,63A
Weger, Stacy	OK1150	60A,32D,36
Weglein, Carolyn	MD0100	60,36,66G
Weidenaar, Gary	WA0050	36
Weidner, Raymond	MD0060	12,13,36
Weiller, David B.	NV0050	60A,32D,36
Weinel, John	TX1450	61,60,36,39,40
Weinert, William	NY1100	36,38,60
Welcher, Jeffrey	NY4150	36
Wells, Bradley C.	MA2250	13C,36,40,60A,61
Wendel, Joyce	OH2450	32,36,61,60A
Wesby, Roger	NY4500	11,29A,32D,36,40
Wesche, Nancy	KS0210	36,61,11
Wesley, Charles E.	MS0050	36,61,12A,11
Westfall, Claude R.	MO0100	32B,32D,36,60A,70
Westgate, Phillip Todd	AL0950	13,36,66A,66G,66C
Westlund, John	KY1000	36
Wetzel, James	NY0625	36,60A
Whaley, Mary Susan	OK0500	11,36,61,54,13
Wheeler, W. Keith	TN1550	36,61,13C,11
White, Angela S.	FL0350	36
White, Christopher Dale	TX2955	32D,36,40,60A,61
White, Cindy	MO1710	64,13,36,61,66A
White, Janice	CA5500	11,13A,36,61,66A
White, Perry D.	WI0770	36,40
Whitney, Nadine C.	GA2200	12A,36,61,40,39
Whitworth, Albin C.	KY0150	13A,13,10,36,66
Wiberg, Janice	MT0300	13,12A,32,36,66
Wickman, Ethan F.	TX3530	10A,13,36,10
Wiebe, John	AA0110	36,60A
Wiebe, Laura	IA0300	36,11
Wiens, Paul W.	IL3550	13C,60A,36
Wiest, Lori J.	WA1150	36,55B,61,60A
Wikan, Cory	LA0050	36,60A
Wilcoxson, Nancy	SD0580	13A,61,36,11,12A
Wilds, Timothy	NC1450	61,31A,36,40
Wiles, John L.	IA1600	36,60A,61,32
Wiliams, David B.	TN1850	13C,36
Wilkes, Eve-Anne	CA3250	36,61,54,60
Wilkins, Sharon	MO0400	32,36,66A
Willer, Beth C.	MA0350	36
Williams, Bernard	AL0650	36
Williams, Charles	DC0170	61,36
Williams, Deborah	IL0600	32C,36,61,32D
Williams, Dennis	PA1750	54,36,61,60
Williams, John W.	NY2100	13,11,36,61,54
Williams, Kenneth D.	TX2960	36,61,60A,40,39
Williams, Mark D.	CA2440	13,36,61,38,34
Williams, Robert	NC0800	11,12A,36,61
Williamson, Richard A.	SC0050	13C,36,40,60A
Williamson, Scott	VA1700	36,39,40,60,61
Williamson, Steven C.	NJ0550	60A,61,36
Willingham, Lee	AG0600	32,36
Willoughby, Judith A.	OK0750	36,60A,40,32
Wilner, Stacey	TN1000	12A,36,11,60A
Wilson, Frances	NC2210	13A,36,61,11
Wilson, Gary P.	TN0930	60A,32C,36,61,32D
Wilson, Grover	NC1600	11,36,66A,66C,66D
Wilson, Jeffrey S.	IL1050	60,36,61,40,31A
Wilson, Jill	IA1100	63B,36,32B,60,13C
Wilson, Ken	WA0030	11,36,61
Wilson, Larry K.	CA3975	60,32C,13,66A,36
Wilson, Russell G.	UT0305	11,13,36,61
Wilson, Stephen B.	NY3720	13,60,36,41,61
Wilson, T. Rex	TX2710	60,12A,32C,36,61
Wimberly, Brenda	LA0100	36,61
Windt, Nathan J.	TN1550	60A,61,11,32D,36
Wine, Thomas	KS1450	32,36,60A
Winfield, Jeffrey	MD0850	36
Wing, Henry	NH0350	36,40,61
Wingate, Owen K.	FL0675	13,11,12A,61,36
Wingert, Bradley	NY2800	61,36
Winston, Jeremy	OH2400	36,61,47,13E,60A
Wis, Ramona M.	IL2050	60A,42,32D,36
Witakowski, Thomas E.	NY3717	36,40,61,60A
Witvliet, John	MI0350	36,31A
Wlodarski, Amy	PA0950	36,12
Wojcik, Richard J.	IL3400	11,12A,36,61,31A
Wojkylak, Michael	PA1900	36,61
Wolcott, Sylvia	KS0215	36,66
Wold, Stanley R.	MN1600	60A,36,40,61
Wolff, Lisa	NV0100	36,40,61,13C
Wollan, Barbara	CO0650	61,36
Wong, K. Carson	ID0075	36,61
Wong, Yau-Sun	NM0200	11,60,13B,36,37
Wood, Gary F.	MA1650	36,61,60,13A
Wood, Stanley D.	OH1600	32,36,66D,13C,34
Woodruff, Neal	IL2300	60,36,38,61,12A
Woods, Timothy E.	SD0400	60A,12A,36,61,40
Wordelman, Peter	OR0200	60A,36,61,54
Wright, Chantel R.	NY2750	36
Wright, Clell E.	TX0900	31A,36,60
Wright, Debbie K.	OH1905	36
Wright, J. Clay	KS0440	11,13,36,40,61
Wright, William B.	PA1300	11,13,36,60
Wu, Chieh-Mei Jamie	NY3500	11,13B,61,32D,36
Wu, Yiping	NY3600	61,36
Wurgler, Norman F.	KY1540	11,36,20G,61,54
Wyatt, Gwendolyn	CA3750	36,61
Wyatt, Larry D.	SC1110	60,32,36
Wyers, Giselle Eleanor	WA1050	36,61
Wyman, William A.	NE0450	36,39,61,60,40
Wynkoop, Rodney A.	NC0600	13,60,36
Wynne, Patricia	CA1020	36
Wyrick, Ginger	NC2650	36,32B
Wyss, Jane	PA3600	36,61
Xiques, David	CA4200	13A,13C,36
Yamron, Janet M.	PA3250	60,32,36
Yancey, Patty	CA5400	11,61,36
Yanson, Eliezer G.	SC0200	32D,13,60A,36,40
Yarrington, John	TX1000	60A,36
Yau, Eugenia Oi Yan	NY0270	11,36,61,40,60A
Yeung, Ian	TX3540	36,60A,40,31A,38
Yon, John	PA2710	36
Yoo, Esther	HI0110	36
Yoon, Sujin	MO1350	36,66G,66H,31A,60A
Young, H. G.	WV0760	13,11,12A,36,54
Young, Steven	MA0510	36,11,55,66A,20G
Young, Susan	AB0150	61,36,13C,39
Young, Welborn E.	NC2430	36,60
Youngdahl, Janet Ann	AA0200	36,12A,61
Younger, J. Sophia	IL0450	13A,66A,11,36
Yozviak, Lisa	OH0700	36,32
Ypma, Nancy S.	IL1740	12A,36,66G
Yu-Oppenheim, Julie	KS0650	32D,36,60A
Yun, Gerard J.	AG0600	36
Zabelsky, Bill	NV0150	36,47
Zabriskie, Alan N.	MO1790	11,40,36,60A
Zachow, Barbara	IL2350	36,20G
Zamer, Craig T.	TN1450	36,60A,32D
Zavadsky, Julia	PA3250	36
Zavadsky, Julia	NJ1100	11,13A,36,60A
Zegree, Stephen	IN0900	36,47,40
Zeigler, Mark C.	NY2650	32D,36,40,60A
Zemek, Michael D.	IL0100	32,36,60A
Zerkle, Paula R.	PA2450	36,60,15,11,54
Zhou, Tianxu	MA2020	36,61,12A
Zielinski, Richard	OK1350	60,36,40
Zielke, Gregory D.	NE0250	60,32C,36,61,31A
Zielke, Steven M.	OR0700	36,60,32D
Zimmermann, Carlyn	IL2900	36
Zobel, Elizabeth W.	IL0350	12,13,36,60,61
Zogleman, Deanne	KS0980	12A,13,20G,36,40
Zophi, Steven	WA1000	36,60A,61
Zork, Stephen	MI0250	36,61,60,10,39

Band

Name	Code	Areas
Aagaard, J. Kjersgaard	WI0842	13,11,36,37,49
Aarhus, Craig	MS0500	37,60
Ackley, Dan	WI0862	11,37,64E
Acklin, Amy	KY1500	32E,37,60B
Adams, Bobby L.	FL1750	32,37,60B
Adams, Dave	CA1800	37
Adams, Gary	AF0100	37,48
Adams, James M.	ND0600	35G,37,47,49,53
Adams, Paul	VA0950	63D,12A,37
Adsit, Glen	CT0650	37
Alderson, Erin	IL1800	11,13A,32E,37,64
Aldrich, Mark L.	MA1650	37,32E,32F,37,34D,60B
Allen, David	MS0420	37,63A,65
Allen, Donald F.	FL1800	37
Allen, Fred J.	TX2700	60B,32C,37,41
Allen, Mark	OR1000	37,49,63A,63C,63B
Allen, Sarah	TX2400	32E,37,32,60B,32B
Allen, Virginia	PA3330	37,38
Allmark, John	RI0150	29,37
Alme, Joseph	ND0250	63C,63B,37,60
Alsobrook, Joseph	MO0650	10F,32E,37,34F,35A
Altman, Timothy	NC2435	60,32,37,63A,63B
Alverson, J. Michael	SC0300	13,37,60
Alvis, Jonathan	SD0600	63D,37,63C
Ambrose, Robert J.	GA1050	37,32E,60B
Ammann, Bruce T.	SD0050	60B,37,32E,64E
Ancona, James	DE0150	37,65
Anderson, Christopher	AR0200	60,32C,37
Anderson, Christopher M.	TX3200	37,32E
Anderson, James N.	GA0200	12A,32,37
Anderson, John	CA3050	13,11,37,64A
Angerstein, Fred	TX3450	63D,37
Anglley, Tamey	TX2700	60B,32C,37,41
Anthony, Bob	CA1520	37
Anthony, Johnny	MS0350	32C,37,49,63
Anthony, Robert	CA0815	37
Aquilanti, Giancarlo	CA4900	13,10F,60,37,49
Aranda, Patrick	CA0950	13A,37,47,63C,29A
Araujo, Ramon	PR0125	13,10,37,64C
Archambo, Larry	TX1700	60,32C,37,34,63C
Archer, Robert	TX0250	63D,37
Ardovino, Joseph	AL1200	63A,37,47,49
Arendt, Michael J.	WI0817	37,47
Armstrong, James E.	NC2700	63A,13A,37,46,49
Armstrong, Joshua	MS0250	65,50,37,41
Arnold, Edwin P.	PA1450	32E,37,60B,48,49
Arnold, Ellen	PA1450	32,37
Asbill, M. Miller	NC0250	37,32E
Asch, Arthur	WI0862	13,12A,37,48
Ash, Corey	TX1100	37,49,63A,32E,60B
Atchison, Scott-Lee	KY1450	37,63A
Austin, Kenneth L.	IL3100	13,32C,37,49,46
Austin, Terry	VA1600	32,37,60
Ayres, Carol	IA0800	11,37,47,64,29A
Babcock, Andrew	TX1550	60B,63D,37,13,47
Babcock, Richard	CA2650	37
Bailey, Kalomo	KY0750	37,32E
Bailey, Mark	TN0850	13,32E,32C,37
Bairos, Monte	CA1560	37,41,48,49,50
Baker, Eric	TX1850	11,37,46,63A
Baldauff, Brian	WV0600	65,37
Ball, Greg L.	TX2750	37,48,64,20G,29
Ballenger, William	TX3200	10A,32E,37,63A
Ballereau, Laurence	NY1600	32,37,64
Balog, George	NJ0175	37,32
Banks, Matthew	IL1500	37
Bannon, John	FL1650	37
Baransky, Paul	OH0250	63A,10F,60B,32E,37
Barber, Carolyn	NE0600	60,37
Barnes, Arthur P.	CA4900	13,10F,37
Barnes, Hugh W.	MD0200	37
Barnes, James E.	PA2450	37,38,60,34,41
Barnett, Steven	WV0400	10F,32E,37,60
Barnett, Thomas	WI0845	63A,37,13
Barr, Dustin	CA3200	37,11
Barr, Sammy	MS0360	37,65
Barrera, Ramiro	CA0900	37
Bartels, Bruce	IA0910	37
Bartram, Kevin P.	VA1475	37,60B,38,32E
Bass, Michael	MS0580	11,49,37,63
Batcheller, James C.	MI0400	37
Bates, Charles N.	OH1800	11,32E,37,47,60
Baugh, Kim C.	VA1300	13A,37
Baumgartner, Christopher	MO1800	37,60B
Baxter, David A.	KS0980	63,37
Bayless, Robert R.	AZ0500	32C,32E,37,60B
Bean, Robert G.	AL1450	13,37,47,63,29
Beard, Michael R.	NE0590	37,32C
Beason, Christine F.	TX3250	37,48,63B,32,10F
Beatrice, Anthony B.	MA1500	37
Beatty, Caroline	TX3175	37,32E,60B
Bechen, Gene	IA1300	37,32E,60,32
Beck, Brandon	WA1100	37,63,60B,38,32C
Becker, David M.	OR0400	60,32C,37,29,64

Index by Area of Teaching Interest

Name	Code	Areas
Beckett, Scott	TX0100	11,12,13,37,63
Beckler, Terry	SD0400	65,50,37,46,11
Bednarzyk, Stephen C.	GU0500	60,37,64C,66A
Beeks, Graydon F.	CA3650	60,12A,37,16,54
Beeks, Graydon	CA1050	37
Beery, John	MI1650	32,37,47,63,11
Beghtol, Jason W.	MS0570	37,13A,46,63,49
Behm, Gary	MT0175	37,64C,64E,64A
Behnke, Martin K.	OR1300	60,37,66A,29
Belcher, Jeff	MO0060	37,70
Bell, John	IL2910	32,32C,37,60B
Bell, Ken	CA3460	37,60
Belongia, Daniel A.	IL1150	60,37
Belser, Robert S.	WY0200	37,63D,11
Benkert, Stuart M.	TN1700	37,47,32E,60B
Benson, Gregory V.	UT0305	37
Benya, Susan	IA1140	37,13,11
Berens, Brad	SD0200	37
Berg, Steve	MO1000	37
Bergstrom, Samuel	MN0040	20,32,37,41,47
Berinbaum, Martin C.	AB0100	60B,37,49,63A
Bernard-Stevens, Sarah	KS0700	37,38,13,64D
Bernhardt, Barry W.	FL0700	37,47,63,29A
Berry, James	PA3100	11,37,60,32B,48
Bersaglia, G. Scott	KY0400	13A,60,37
Bertman, David	TX3400	32C,37
Bertrand, Jerry	IA0150	63A,37
Bertucci, Ronald	OR0350	37,13A,47,63C,13C
Berz, William L.	NJ1130	32,37
Betancourt, David	CA0859	37,46,38,32E,60B
Bethea, William	VA0950	65,11,37,50
Bhasin, Paul K.	VA0250	37,63A,38,42,41
Bianchi, Douglas	MI2200	37,13,60B
Bianco, Christopher	WA1250	37,38
Bicigo, James Michael	AK0150	12A,32,37,41,63D
Biddle, Paul D.	NY0400	60B,37
Bierman, Duane	NE0590	37,65,50
Bierschenk, Jerome Michael	TX3250	36,37,32D,61,63A
Bierschenk, Kenny P.	OH0680	37
Biggs, Dana M.	CO0800	37,32E
Bilden, Jeff	CA1290	37,47,29,63,64
Bill, Jennifer	RI0150	32E,37
Bilotta, Lee	PA3560	60,32B,37,63,31A
Bing, Charles S.	FL0600	32C,37,63C,63D
Bing, William	CA3300	37
Bing, William W.	CA0500	37,47,49,63A
Bingham, Thomas	HI0210	32E,37,60
Birch, Robert M.	DC0100	49,63A,37,48
Birden, Larry	OK0450	13A,32E,10F,63,37
Birk, Richard	TX0350	13,11,37,47,63
Birkner, Chip	FL1850	37
Bishop, James	FL0150	12A,37,38,47,64E
Bivens, Pat	TN0250	11,47,63C,48,37
Black, Alan	TX1700	11,37,47,50,65
Blackshear, Alan	AL0831	37,13,11,29
Blackstock, Adam	AL1050	37,65
Blake, Harry D.	TX0340	37
Blankenship, Harold	AL0450	37
Blatti, Richard L.	OH1850	60,37
Bleyle, William B.	OH0950	65,50,37
Blocher, Larry	AL1050	32E,37
Block, Tyrone	TX2570	32E,37,47,60B,63
Bloomquist, Paul	IA0790	11,63,60B,13,37
Blose, Dennis	NJ0175	37,32
Bocook, Jay A.	SC0750	37,10F
Bodiford, Kenneth	AL0500	60,37,63D
Bodolosky, Michael	PA3410	37,47,29A
Boeckman, Jeffrey	HI0210	37,60B
Boehmke, Erik A.	IL1600	63A,66,47,37,49
Boerma, Scott	MI2100	60,37
Boga, Cheryl	PA3500	36,37,47,38,51
Boggs, David G.	IL1740	37,32E,60B
Bohnert, David A.	NE0700	63A,60B,37,11,32E
Bolstad, Stephen P.	VA0600	37,60B
Bolton, Chuck	OR1150	32,37,49,63D
Bone, Lloyd E.	WV0350	12A,49,63,37,11
Booker, Kenneth A.	TX1450	37,46,47,60,13A
Boonshaft, Peter Loel	NY1600	60B,32C,37
Booth, David M.	OH2500	60,37,63D,65
Bott, Darryl J.	NJ1130	32,37
Bough, Thomas	IL2200	37
Boulden, George	KY1450	37,60,32E
Boumpani, Neil M.	GA1070	13,37
Bourque, David	AG0450	48,37,38,64C,60B
Bovenschen, Wayne	OK0800	65,37,50,32E
Bowen, Charles Kevin	NC2500	37,47,49,63A
Boyer, Charles G.	CO0050	32,11,32E,37
Boysen, Andrew A.	NH0350	37,60B,10F
Bracey, Jerry A.	VA0500	37,38,47,62,29
Bradshaw, Eric E.	GA2150	63D,32E,37,60
Brammer, Ron L.	MO0775	37
Brandes, Gary W.	MO1830	37,60,32E
Brashier, Joe H.	GA2150	32,37,60
Bratcher, Nicholas O.	GA1750	37
Breaux, Troy Jude	LA0760	37,65,50
Brechting, Gail	MI1550	60B,63C,37
Breiling, Roy	AZ0510	37,38,46,47,63A
Brekke, Jeremy	ND0350	63,37,49,63A,47
Brennan, Adam	PA2150	60B,37,50,65,10F
Brent, William	LA0550	37,72
Bressler, Mark	IL2730	37,63
Brewer, Paul S.	MI0300	60B,37,32E,29,63C
Bridge, Robert	NY2950	65,37,50,20A
Bridges, Cynthia	TX0550	37,32H,60B,13C,32C
Bright, Jeff R.	KY1550	37,32E,34
Britt, Brian	OK1350	37
Brock, Gordon R.	FL1950	37,48,64E,60B,10A
Brock, Joplin	NC0700	37
Brock, Tomisha	NC0700	37
Bronk, Mary Beth	TX3100	32E,37,60,63A
Brooks, John Patrick	ID0100	60B,37,63C,47,63D
Brooks, Ricky W.	AR0850	60B,37
Brooks, William Robert	ND0500	37
Brough, Ronald P.	UT0050	60,32C,37,65,72
Brown, Andrea E.	GA0900	37,38,11
Brown, Beverly	NC1400	11,29A,47,37,64C
Brown, Charles	NC2300	37,47,65
Brown, George	CA2975	37
Brown, Jeff	MS0360	37,65,50,46
Brown, Jeremy S.	AA0150	37,64E,29,12G,48
Brown, Marcellus	ID0050	37,60B
Brown, Rogers	VA0950	10F,37,47,63D,29
Brozak, George A.	IL2900	37,32H
Brubeck, Dave W.	FL1300	13,37,47,63C,49
Brunner, Matthew	PA3250	37
Bruno, Zachary	CA4625	11,32,37,47,41
Buckner, Bob	NC2600	37
Bueckert, Darrell	AJ0150	50,65,37
Bull, Douglas	WY0050	37,63,11,32E
Bundy, O. Richard	PA2750	32C,37
Burch-Pesses, Michael	OR0750	60,32C,37,47,45
Burden, Douglas	AG0400	63C,37,41
Burdett, John	CA0630	32E,37,60B
Burge, James	FL0930	37
Burks, Ricky	AL1450	48,64,46,29B,37
Burns, Patrick	NJ0825	37
Burrack, Frederick	KS0650	32,12B,11,32,37
Bush, Doug W.	NE0600	32E,37
Bush, Eric W.	NY4050	37,47,63A,13A,11
Bushman, Catharine Sinon	SC1200	37,32E,42
Bustos, Pamela B.	WI0860	32E,37,48,60B,64C
Butler, Rebecca G.	PA0050	11,64A,37,34,13B
Butrico, Michael	NC0400	32E,37,46,60B,63
Buttery, Gary	CT0100	63D,37,47
Byrd, Joshua	GA2130	37,10A,13G,48,10F
Byrne, Gregory	KY1500	65,37,50
Cable, Ron C.	OH2275	37
Cadelago, Harry	CA3250	37,38,60B,49
Cailliet, Claude	WI0800	11,13,63,37,47
Cain, Richard	MA0650	62D,37
Caldwell, Brendan	WI0850	37,32E,60B
Caldwell, Gary	UT0150	13,60,37,63A
Calissi, Jeff L.	CT0150	37,65B,11
Calkin, Joshua	NE0700	63D,37,11,49,63C
Calonico, Robert M.	CA5000	37
Cameron, James Scott	MO0775	37,50,65
Cameron, Robert C.	PA1050	60,32C,37
Cameron, Scott	DC0010	37,63D,63C
Caminiti, Joseph D.	PA2800	60,38,37,63B,32E
Camp, James L.	GA0490	37,49,63B,63C,63D
Campbell, Kathleen M.	PA3000	60,37,38,48
Campbell, Larry	TX0340	37,47,63B,63C,63D
Camphouse, Mark D.	VA0450	10,60B,37
Campo, David	TX2700	32E,32C,37,60B
Caneva, Thomas	IN0150	37,48
Cannon, Cormac	MI1400	37
Cantwell, Richard E.	KS1300	13,60,10A,37,38
Canty, Dean R.	TX3525	60,37,63A,63B,11
Caproni, Christopher	MA2250	37
Caputo, Michael	NJ0200	12A,14,37,64,20G
Caputo, Michael	NJ0250	12A,14,37,48,64
Cardany, Brian M.	RI0300	32E,32G,37,60B
Carlson, Dan	MN1100	11,35A,37,46,63
Carlson, Mark	MD0610	63,11,12,13,37
Carmichael, John C.	FL2000	37
Carnahan, John	CA0825	37
Carnochan, Robert M.	TX3510	37,48,32
Carpenter, Charles M.	CA3500	37,50,65
Carrell, Cynthia T.	AR0250	11,13,32E,37,63A
Carroll, John	TX1900	63A,49,37,41,47
Carroll, Kenneth D.	AR0110	29,64E,37,46
Carson, William S.	IA0300	60B,37,12A,32E,64C
Carter, Drew	NC2000	37
Carter, Robert Scott	NC0650	60B,37,41,32E
Casagrande, John E.	VA0450	37,32C,32E,32G
Caslor, Jason	AD0050	37,38,60B
Cassarino, James P.	VT0200	12,14,20,36,37
Cesario, Robert James	MO0825	37,38,60B,41
Chadwick, John	IL2750	37
Chambers, Timothy	NC0800	37,48,64,60B
Champagne, Kevin	NY3700	37
Chance, Mike	AR0250	32E,37,38,63C,63D
Chapman, Christopher	OR0700	32,37,46,63A,60B
Chase, Jared	NY2650	37
Chen, Jay	OR1300	37,63A,41
Chen, Jay	OR0450	60B,49,37,63A
Chenette, Stephen	AG0450	37,41,63A
Chesebrough, James C.	NH0150	37,60,32,63D,32E
Chesnutt, Rod M.	FL0680	37,38,60,32E,32F
Chevalier, Jason	CA3200	13A,37,20G
Chipman, Shelby R.	FL0600	60,32C,37,63A
Chodoroff, Arthur D.	PA3250	37,47
Christensen, Carl J.	CA2150	13,38,37,34G,13A
Christopher, Casey R.	ID0150	11,29B,34,35,37
Ciabattari, William S.	PA2100	13,63D,32,37,47
Cieplych, Gary	OH0400	60,32,37,48
Cipolla, Frank J.	NY4320	37
Clark, Allen	TX3515	32C,37,63D
Clark, Brenda J.	IN1650	32,11,37
Clark, Norman Alan	GA1400	11,37,49,64
Clark, Tad	OK1450	37
Clark, Wallace	FL0600	12A,32C,37
Clark, William D.	NM0310	32,37
Clayville, Michael	PA0950	37,47
Clements, Phillip L.	TX2955	60B,37,63D,13A,12A
Clements, Tony	CA3320	37
Clemons, Gregory G.	IL1085	37,63A,41,13
Clickard, Stephen D.	PA0250	37,63,47,60B
Clifft, Al	CA0450	13,36,37
Clifton, Artie	FL1000	37,64C
Climer, John	WI0825	60,37,43
Coates, Gary	FL1790	47,37,46,66F
Cochrane, Keith A.	NM0400	60,12A,32B,37,47
Cofer, R. Shayne	IL2150	32,37,49
Cohen, Richard Scott	MI0650	11,37,38
Coleman, Randall	AL1170	37,60B,32E
Collerd, Gene J.	IL3310	13A,60,37,64C
Collins, Kevin	WI0808	37,63D
Collinsworth, Andy	CA4700	13A,32,37,41,60B
Colonna, Jim	UT0325	63A,32,37
Colwell, Brent	TX2800	37,11,12A,63C,63D
Compton, Adam	OK0500	13B,63,37,46,13
Compton, Michael	ND0100	64,37,41,47,60B
Connelly, Marianne	MN0450	37,32,47,64,60B
Connors, Thomas	NJ0700	37,11,32E,60B
Copeland, David	IN0907	37
Copenhaver, James K.	SC1110	32E,37
Corbin, Dwayne V.	CA4600	37,38,65,29
Corcoran, Gary J.	NH0250	37,60B,63A,32E
Cordingley, Allen	WI0840	11,64E,37,47
Corinthian, Randy	FL0200	34D,37
Corkern, David	MO0500	46,63A,37,47,10F
Corley, Alton L.	TX3175	37,32E
Corley, Scott R.	WI0825	37
Corn, Paul	NY0500	37,47
Cornish, Craig S.	TN1100	37
Corporon, Eugene Migliaro	TX3420	60B,37
Correll, Allen	OK0300	37,32E,47,60B,63A
Cosenza, Frank	OH1100	37
Couch, Roy L.	OK0150	37,63D,49,32E
Coull, James	SD0550	37,70,13
Cox, Ishbah	IN1310	37,60B
Craig, Mary Ann	AG0250	37,64C,48,38,41
Craig, Mary Ann	NJ0800	32,37,63D,49
Crawford, Peter	WA1300	34,48,37,66A
Crawford, Stephen J.	TX3415	37,12A,50,65

559

Index by Area of Teaching Interest

Name	Code	Areas
Creasap, Susan D.	KY0900	32E,37
Cressley, Scott	IA1950	37
Crim, Mark	TX0600	37,32E,60B,44
Crochet, Lourinda S.	SC1200	37,32E,42
Cross, Travis J.	VA1700	32E,37,60
Crowder, James	IL0300	37
Culvahouse, John N.	GA1150	37,32C,32E,60B
Cummings, Paul C.	CA2250	32,37,38,64C
Cunningham, Geoffrey A.	MA1100	13A,37
Cunningham, Gregory M.	MI1750	60B,38,37
Curley, Jason	NY1400	60B,63B,37,49,32E
Curry, Jeffrey P.	NE0040	11,13C,32,37,49
D'Addio, Daniel F.	CT0050	13,32,37,49,63A
Dale, Randall N.	MS0700	37
Dally, John	CA3640	37,32
Daniels, Sean	TN1400	37,50,65
Daniels, William B.	KY1100	32B,37,47,49,63
Darling, John A.	ND0050	37,60B,47,13,41
David, Andy	GA1500	37
Davis, Charles	TX1510	11,63,64,37
Davis, Hope	CA2300	13A,12,11,37,13B
Davis, J. Craig	NJ1400	37,63A,41
Davis, John E.	GA0300	60,11,37,64A,64E
Davis, Paul G.	MO1950	60B,37,38,32E
Davis, Peter A.	RI0250	13A,37,47,64
Davis, Randy	AL1195	37,38,60,13,48
Day, Greg	SC1080	13,10F,37,47,63
De Melo, Dorvalino	AI0220	60,32C,37,47,64E
DeAlbuquerque, Joan	CA0825	32,37
DeBenedetto, Patricia	CA1860	32E,37,64E,64C,48
Decuir, Michael	GA0150	11,20,29,37,47
DeGroff, Jason	CT0700	32E,37,46
DeJournett, William	MS0700	37,12B,11
Delaney, Douglas	CA1150	13,11,37,47,64
Delaney, Jack	TX2400	60,37
Deloney, Rick	VA0600	37
Deppe, Scott M.	TX1400	37,60B,32G,32C
DeSpain, Geoff	AZ0300	37,63,46,47,11
Dickerson, Randy C.	WI0803	60,32C,37
Dickey, Marc R.	CA0815	32,37,64
Dickey, Nathaniel H.	MN0600	37,63C,63D,32E,49
DiCuirci, Michael	OH0950	63C,63D,37,32E
DiCuirci, Michael P.	OH0450	32B,32C,37,63D,46
Diden, Benjamin	GA0900	37,13
Diehl, Richard C.	VT0100	13,60,47,10,37
Diem, Timothy W.	MN1623	37,41
Dietrich, Kurt R.	WI0700	13,32,37,47,29
Diggs, David B.	PA1950	13A,13B,37,64B,48
Dillahey, Samuel J.	SC0300	20F,37
DiMeo, Mike J.	NY4400	37,11,47
Ditmer, Nancy	OH0700	32,37,60B
Dodson, Brent	IA1750	63,64,37,60B,48
Doebler, Jeffrey S.	IN1750	11,32,37
Doiel, Mark	CA2900	10D,11,12A,13,37
Dorn, Mark	CO0150	37,63A,46,60B,49
Dorothy, Wayne F.	TX0900	32C,32E,37,60B
Dorsey, Rodney	MI2100	60,37
Douglas, Kenneth	IN0910	32,37,60B
Douglass, Ronald L.	MI1100	13,37,41,63,29
Douglass, Zane S.	NV0050	37
Douthit, LaTika	NC2700	11,37,64A
Dover, Cory	NC2420	37
Downes, Suzanne	IL2310	66D,47,11,37,65
Doyle, Brian K.	NY3780	37,60B
Doyle, Timothy	GA0950	37
Doyle, William	CA1750	11,37,38,63,60
Drake, Thomas	IL1520	37
Drane, Gregory	PA2750	37
Drobnak, Kenneth Paul	SD0500	63D,37,11,47,49
Droste, Paul E.	OH1850	37,63D
Drury, Jay	WV0750	37
Dueitt, David P.	MS0420	37,48,64,65
Duffy, Thomas	CT0850	13,37,47
Dunham, Robert W.	GA0950	32E,37
Dunnigan, Patrick	FL0850	32C,37,60B
Durst, Aaron M.	WI0855	11,37,47,64E
Dvorak, Thomas	WI0825	60,37
Dye, Keith G.	TX3200	60B,37,32C,32E
Dye, Kenneth W.	IN1700	10,37
Dyess, J. Wayne	TX1400	37,47,63C,49
East, David	MS0320	37,47,48,63C
Easter, Wallace E.	VA1700	37,63B,13
Eaton, Daniel	MN1600	37,63D,49
Eckerty, Michael	IA1350	64D,32C,37,60,48
Edgar, Scott N.	IL1400	37,32,11,13A
Edgett, Bryan	PA1150	63A,37
Edwards, Brent	WA1150	37
Edwards, Richard D.	OH2000	37,32,60B,12F,32A
Edwards, Ricky	DE0050	37
Eggleston, Steven	IL1200	60B,37,38,63A
Ehrlich, Barry	WA0860	13,11,37,63C,63D
Eichner, Mark J.	WI0835	60,32C,37,63A,32A
Elkus, Jonathan B.	CA5010	37
Elliott, Richard	OR0250	37,41
Elliott, Richard	OH0680	65,50,37,11,32E
Ellis, Barry L.	WI0840	60,37,64D,64E,32
Ellis, Kim S.	TX1400	37,64C,64E,48
Ellis, Ron	TX3530	37
Ely, Mark	UT0250	32C,37,64E
Emge, Jeffrey D.	TX3535	32,37,60,64B
Endahl, John R.	MI1200	37
Endsley, Gerald	CO0550	37
Engel, Bruce E.	NY3790	37
Engle, Tiffany J.	MI0350	64E,60B,37,32E
Engstrom, Dale	CA1850	13A,37,49
Enis, Paul	OK0350	13,36,37,61,63
Enloe, Loraine D.	ID0250	32E,64,37,64C,32C
Entzi, John A.	NC2400	37,63B,41
Enz, Nicholas J.	MI1450	37,41,64E,47
Erb, Andrew	PA3260	63A,63C,37,47,49
Espinosa, Ricardo	TX0300	37
Ethington, Bradley P.	NY4150	60B,37,32E
Etters, Stephen C.	NC0350	60,32,37,63D,13A
Evans, Garry W.	TX3300	64C,37,12A,41,60B
Evans, Joel	NY3760	37,64B,12A,13B,20
Evans, Thomas	MI1150	37,47,63C,29A,32
Ewing, Lee	GA1650	37,63,64
Fague, Kyla	WA1350	37,60
Fair, Gary	CA3000	11,37
Fairbanks, Will	IL1050	37,63A,46,49,63B
Falcone, Anthony M.	NE0600	37,65,50
Falkner, Dan	OK0200	37
Fallin, Nicky G.	GA0250	37,32E,63A,49,60B
Falskow, John	WA0960	37,63A,38,11,13
Falvey, Joseph	VA0150	63B,37,34G,32E,49
Fambrough, Gene	AL1150	50,37,65
Famulare, Trever R.	PA3050	11,37,47,49,60
Fannin, John E.	KY0950	32,37,10F
Fannin, Karen M.	AR0350	29,11,13A,47,37
Fansler, Michael J.	IL3500	37,60B,32E
Farnham, Curvin G.	ME0440	60B,32E,37
Farris, Daniel J.	IL2250	47,37,60B,60
Feinstein, Allen G.	MA1450	13,10F,60,37,48
Fejeran, Vince	WA0900	47,63C,37,46
Felder, Mark	MI1500	37
Feldman, Evan	NC2410	37,60B
Feller, Robert	CA0350	11,37,49,63,60
Fenderson, Mark W.	MT0175	11,37,63A,63B
Fennell, Mitchell	CA0815	60,32,37
Ferrari, Lois	TX2650	37,38,60B
Filzen Etzel, Laurel Kay	IL1350	63B,60B,37
Fischer, Richard R.	IL0730	37,60B
Fisher, Blair	AB0050	37,47,63A,63,46
Fisher, Dennis W.	TX3420	60B,32C,37
Fisher, Tammy M.	WI0810	60,37,65,32,11
Flanagin, Michael	IN1025	37,63A,63B,41,60B
Fleming, Ricky L.	NY3717	60B,37,47,49,63C
Fletcher, John M.	OK0700	10F,60,37,13
Fleury, August	LA0720	63,37
Flora, Sim	AR0500	32,37,47,63,13
Flowe, Barry	VA1150	37
Floyd, C. Chad	KY0400	37,65,50
Flynn, Michael P.	WY0150	11,37,41,47,63
Fonder, Mark	NY1800	60B,32,37
Fooster, Harold	AR0810	60,11,37,50,65
Forlenza, Ray	IL1890	37
Forrester, Ellard	NC0700	65,37
Forrester, Marshall	SC0275	10,11,37,60
Forsberg, Peggy	KS0560	37
Forsythe, Jada P.	MS0570	11,64C,64E,37,48
Fortney, Patrick	NE0500	60,37,47
Foster, William P.	FL0600	60,37
Fox, Jason	NY3475	37,49,63
Fox, Jeremy	IA1400	13,10F,37,50,34
Francis, Bobby R.	TX3000	37,60,32E
Francis, Joseph Corey	IL0800	37
Frankel, James Thomas	NY4200	34,37,32,32F
Franklin, Cary J.	MN0950	10,37,38,42,60B
Franklin, Kenneth	NC0250	37
Franzblau, Robert	RI0200	32E,37
Fraschilla, Tom	GA1700	37,60B,32E
Frechou, Paul A.	LA0650	64C,37,32C,32E
Freeman, Wendy	AA0200	37,13C
French, George E.	MN1590	36,37,66A,66G,54
French, Otis C.	PA1100	11,37,63,64,65
Frey, Richard	CO0250	37
Friedrichs, Charles	CA4100	11,37,63C,13A,32
Fritz, Benno P.	DC0100	37,49,60,11
Frye, Brian	DC0170	37
Frye, Danny	NC0930	65,50,37,65B,32C
Fuchs, Craig	KS1050	60B,37,32E
Fuchs, Jeffrey W.	NC2410	32E,37
Fuller, John A.	NC1700	37,13C
Furlow, Shaw	MS0200	13,11,10,37,47
Furman, Lisa J.	MI1800	37,60B,11,13,32
Gackstatter, Gary	MO1120	37,11,38
Gage, Stephen	OH2600	37,60
Gaines, Adam W.	WI0808	63,47,37,63A,29
Gallo, Reed P.	SC0800	37,60B,32E,63A,49
Gallops, R. Wayne	VA1100	13A,32C,32E,29,37
Galvan, Alex	CA1000	10,13,37,60
Galyean, Richard D.	VA1580	37,60B,49,63D,32E
Galyen, S. Daniel	IA1600	37,41,32E,60B,32
Garasi, Michael J.	FL1800	37,60B
Garcia, Paul D.	NC1700	37,46,50,65
Gardner, Allen D.	PA0675	37
Gardner, Gary D.	OK1500	11,62,63,37,47
Garmon, Randy	TX1725	37,46,47,63
Garofalo, Robert	DC0050	32E,37,60B
Garrett, Roger	IL1200	37,64C,60B,41,35D
Garrido, Glenn	TX3450	60B,32E,20H,37
Gauger, David	IL1850	37,38,45,63A
Gay, Nathan	KS0300	63C,63D,60B,37
Gazda, Frank S.	DE0050	63D,37,49,63C,42
Gehring, Joseph	PA1550	37,38,60,63
Gemberling, Alan	ID0250	37,63C,47,60,41
Genevro, Bradley	PA2300	37,64C,64E,32E
George, Matthew J.	MN1625	60,41,37
George, Roby	IN0800	37,60
George, Roby G.	IL3300	37,60B
Gephart, Jay S.	IN1310	37,60B
Geraldi, Kevin M.	NC2430	37
Gerhart, David	CA0825	65,20H,37,50
Gershman, Jeffrey D.	IN0900	37
Ghiglione, Brent	AJ0100	37,60B
Gibble, David L.	FL1470	29,47,37,53,49
Gibbs, Brian	TX2250	37,32C
Gibbs, Lawrence	LA0250	11,29A,37,47,64C
Gibson, Clarence	TX3150	11,37,41,42
Gibson, Richard L.	AE0100	13,10F,10,37,63
Gibson, Robert	AI0150	37,32
Gilbert, Jay W.	NE0200	37
Giles, Glenn	VT0100	63C,63D,60,37,46
Giles, Leonard	GA0810	11,32,37,47,63
Gillan, Michael	MI0850	11,37,63C,63D,47
Gillespie, Clint	AL0500	60,37,65
Gilley, John	TX2550	37,64
Gillis, Glen	AJ0150	60,32C,37,48,64E
Gilmore, Jimmy	NC1300	37,64C
Gilroy, Gary P.	CA0810	13C,10F,60B,37
Gindin, Suzanne B.	IN1050	32,37,38,41,63B
Ginocchio, John	MN1500	37,13,47,32E,60B
Girtmon, Paxton	MS0100	37,47,64E,10F,60
Glaze, Richard T.	FL2100	60,32,37,48,64
Glickman, Joel	WI0600	60,32,37,38,47
Glocke, Dennis	PA2750	60,37
Golemo, Michael	IA0850	37,60,64E,32
Gonano, Max A.	PA0500	11,12A,13A,29A,37
Good, Jonathan E.	NV0050	60B,32,37,32E
Good, Richard D.	AL0200	37,63D
Goodwin, Casey S.	NH0350	37,32D,47,60B
Goodwin, Don	WA0250	13,66A,37,46
Goodwin, Mark A.	GA0700	13,32,37,64
Gookin, Larry D.	WA0050	60,37,49,63C
Gordillo, Richard	MI0900	37
Gordon, Daniel J.	NY3775	64E,11,37,48
Gould, Valerie	WV0050	32E,34,37,41,60B
Gowan, Andrew D.	SC1110	60,32,37,64
Gowen, Dennis	ND0400	37,49,63A,63B,60
Graham, Brenda J.	IN1250	13A,32,37,62,31A
Graham, John	AR0810	37,64E,64C,48
Graham, Marques	FL0550	37
Grandy, Larry	CA4550	37,47,64,29,14C
Grant, Denise	AG0600	37,60
Grant, Gary S.	PA1200	37,60,47
Grass, Ken G.	OK1450	37,64E,60B

Index by Area of Teaching Interest

Name	Code	Areas
Graves, Edward	TN1400	37,32
Gray, Donavon D.	CA0250	37,44,49,32,48
Green, Gary D.	FL1900	60,37
Green, Kenneth	LA0550	37,65,41
Green, Ronald	PA2000	37,50,65
Greene, Janet E.	MN0800	32E,13A,37,64C
Greene, Sean	TN0900	63D,13,37,32,42
Greenwald, Fred	IL1610	63A,63B,37
Gregg, Matthew D.	WI0840	37,13
Greggs, Isaac	LA0700	37,63A,46
Gregory, Gary J.	OH0550	44,13,60,37,63C
Gregory, M. David	GA1700	32E,37,32F,60B
Greig, R. Tad	PA3650	32E,37,47,60B,63C
Griffin, Larry	OH2000	60B,37,47,49,63A
Griffin, Peter J.	IL0850	32,37,60B,63C,63D
Griffin, Samuel L.	MS0050	60,37,63D
Griffin, Stephen W.	AL0332	11,36,37,47,64
Griffith, David	TX0075	11,37,46,63
Griffiths, Brian	OR0175	63D,46,37
Griffiths, Curt	ID0070	37
Griggs, Kevin D.	MT0400	37,60B,32E
Grimes, Judith	IL0850	60,14,32,37
Grise', Monte	MN1120	64E,32E,47,37,60B
Groeling, Charles	IL3200	32,37
Gross, Ernest H.	IL1300	37,49,60B,63D,12A
Grugin, Stephen	MI1600	37,63D,12A,32C,32E
Gruner, Greg	AL1300	37,63D,60B,32E,35
Grutzmacher, Patricia Ann	OH1100	32,41,64B,37,20
Guenoit, Eric	LA0450	60B,11,37,65,50
Gustafson, Karen	AK0150	37,63A,41,11,60B
Haberman, Peter J.	MN0600	37,32E
Haddix, Ken	KY0550	37,63C
Haenfler, Eric	AZ0470	37
Hagen, Scott	UT0250	37,32E,60B
Hahn, Christopher D.	SD0100	63,37,60,11
Haithcock, Michael	MI2100	60,37
Haldeman, Michael	SC0275	11,37,65,50
Haley, Ardith	AF0050	35E,37
Hallback, Alan	CA0859	37,63A
Halsell, George K.	ID0075	13,37,63,11,71
Halseth, Robert E.	CA0840	60,37
Hamilton, Brian	CA2550	37,50
Hamilton, Craig V.	AR0500	63A,60B,46,37
Hammer, Eric	CA5350	60B,37,32E
Hammond, June C.	FL1600	12A,36,61,66A,37
Hammond, Tony	MT0350	37,47,32
Hampton, Neal	MA0500	60,37,38,41,48
Hanan, David	OK1330	37,60B,10F,34,63A
Hancock, Craig A.	IA1800	37,60B,63C,63D,72
Hanes, Michael D.	IL2900	37,50,65
Hanman, Theodore	KS0100	65,60B,47,37,32E
Hanna, Frederick	NE0160	13,37,38,10
Hanna, Scott S.	TX3510	60,37
Hannum, Thomas P.	MA2000	37,50
Hansbrough, Robert S.	NY0700	32E,42,37,65
Hansen, Eric	WI0808	64C,37,13,32E
Hansen, Neil E.	WY0130	37,47,63A,32,49
Hansen, Richard K.	MN1300	60B,37,20G,12A
Hansford, James	OK0650	38,32G,37,63D,41
Hanson, Dan L.	OK1400	13,10,32C,47,37
Hanson, Gregg I.	AZ0500	60,37
Harden, Bill	TX3527	64D,37,38
Harper, Larry D.	WI0200	60,37,41,63B
Harper, Rhonda	MO0600	37,46,47
Harris, Brian P.	TX1600	37
Harris, Edward C.	CA4400	37,60B
Harris, Eric	TN1450	37,32E
Harris, Fred	MA1200	37,47
Harris, Howard	TX3150	13A,10,37,47,39
Harris, Timothy	CA0900	37,11,12A,32E
Harrison, Albert D.	IN1560	60B,37,47,63D,32E
Hart, Michael	CA0550	37,13B,13C,63C,63D
Hart, Michael D.	LA0030	37,63A,11,13,47
Hartley, Linda A.	OH2250	32E,37,64E,32G
Haston, Warren	CT0650	32E,37,32G
Hatcher, Oeida M.	VA0750	32,37,41,38,11
Hausey, Collette J.	CA2050	11,37,41,65
Hawkins, Ben	KY1350	60B,32,37,38,63B
Hayes, Glenn C.	WI0865	60,32,37
Hayslett, Dennis J.	FL1450	37,32E
Hayward, Carol M.	OH0300	37
Hearn, Sidney T.	IN1100	32,32E,34,37,63A
Hearne, Martin	IA0400	37,38,50,60
Heasley, Tim	CA0270	37
Hebert, Joseph G.	LA0300	32,37,46,35
Heddens, Jared	MI0520	37
Hedgecoth, David	OR1050	32,32E,37
Heffner, Christopher J.	PA1900	32E,37,60,63
Hegg, Dennis	SD0150	37,47,63,64,65
Heidel, Richard Mark	IA1550	37
Heidenreich, Christopher	MI2120	37,49,11,10F
Heidner, Eric C.	CA4410	37,47,13,29,12A
Heisler, Jeff A.	OH1100	64E,42,37
Held, Jeffrey	CA1425	11,12A,37,32E,10F
Heller, Lauren B.	CT0050	37,32E,60B,64A
Hemberger, Glen J.	LA0650	60B,32C,37,63C,47
Hemenway, Langston	IL2050	11,32E,37,41
Henderson, Douglas S.	OK0800	37,32E
Henderson, Gordon L.	CA5030	37
Hendricks, John	WV0750	32,37
Hendricks, Steven	MO1500	32,37,34,36
Hendrickson, Daniel	MI1180	11,12A,36,37,61
Hendrix, Michael	LA0100	37,63C
Hengst, Michael	CO0550	63A,37
Henley, Matthew	NC2600	37
Hennessey, Patrick D.	HI0110	37,47,29A,12A,63C
Hepler, Lowell E.	PA0100	12A,12C,37,66A,63D
Herbert, Jeffery	TX3050	37
Herlihy, John S.	MN1280	60B,49,37,46
Hermann, Joseph W.	TN1450	37,60B,32E
Heslink, Daniel M.	PA2350	11,14,37,65
Hess, H. Carl	PA1050	37,38,60,63A
Hesse, Robert	AR0500	37,11
Hest, Jeff	NY3250	11,29,35,37,47
Hettle, Mark	TX1725	13,11,37,47,63A
Heuchemer, Dane O.	OH1200	11,12A,12,37,67
Heukeshoven, Janet	MN1400	37,32,60,11,41
Heywood, David John	SC0500	11,37,64A,29,47
Hicken, Leslie W.	SC0750	60,37,32
Higgins, Edward	OR0850	37,32E,60B
Hill, Dennis	FL0500	37,47,64A,64E,29
Hill, Douglas M.	GA1300	60B,32C,37,49,63A
Hill, Gary W.	AZ0100	60,37
Hill, Kyle W.	MS0580	13B,11,37,50,65
Hill, Monty K.	NM0310	37,32
Hinton, Eric L.	PA3150	37,60B,63A
Hinton, Jeffrey	MO0850	60,32C,37,64E
Hochkeppel, William J.	LA0760	37,32C
Hodge, Randy	MO0550	37,64E
Hoefle, Andrew	IL2775	11,37,47,63D,29
Hoehler, Martin R.	OH1050	37,47
Hofer, Calvin	CO0225	32,37,49,63A,60B
Holcomb, Paula K.	NY3725	37,60
Holcomb, Teddy	NC2500	37
Holden, James	VA1750	13,20G,37,64E,46
Holland, Nicholas V.	TN1680	37,32E
Holland, Nicholas V.	SC0275	11,37
Holliday, Guy	CA0450	36,37,47
Hollinger, Trent A.	MO0300	64,37,13C,13A,60B
Holloway, John R.	SC0650	63D,32,37,60B
Holmes, Rasan	VA0500	63C,37,34
Holton, Arthur	CA4300	37,64C,48,49
Hoover, Jerry W.	MO0775	60B,37,46
Hoover, Lloyd W.	DC0350	32,37
Hopkins, Bruce	MA0200	37
Hopkins, Mark E.	AF0050	37,32C,60,60B
Hopwood, Brian	MO1550	32E,37,38,63
Houck, Alan	OH1350	37
House, Richard E.	SC0350	37,63A,32E,60B
House, Richard	SC1000	37,63A,32
Houze, Reginald M.	MA0150	10F,36,37,60,63D
Howarth, Gifford	PA0250	65,37
Hower, Don	WA1150	37,63C
Howey, Robert J.	AA0025	12A,13B,37,46,64
Hubbs, Holly J.	PA3550	11,37,47,29A,20
Hubbs, Randall	WA0150	13,37,47,63A,29A
Huber, Deborah	MA2030	37,60B
Huber, Wayne	CA1860	37,49,63A,67C,13
Hudson, James	AZ0100	37
Hudson, Milton	TX3360	11,37
Huff, Michael H.	AL1050	63A,42,49,67E,37
Huffman, Valarie A.	WV0300	37,32,63D,32E,49
Hufstetler, Ron	TX3520	60,37,38
Hughes, Brian L.	IA0940	60,11,32,37,47
Hughes, Christopher A.	NM0310	37,60B,32E,63A,38
Hulett, Christopher M.	AZ0490	37
Humbert, William	AZ0350	37,64,63,13A,60
Hunter, Andrew	LA0150	37,65,32
Hunter, Robert	AZ0440	32E,63A,37,46,29A
Huntoon, John Richard	IN0100	63C,63D,47,37,49
Hurlburt, Timothy R.	SC0400	37,46,47,11
Hurst, Craig W.	WI0960	11,37,47,41,63A
Hutton, Cynthia	OR0950	60,37,49,63B
Hyden, Derek	VA0600	37
Immel, Dean	CA2750	37
Inkster, Matthew	WV0600	63A,63B,37,47,49
Irizarry, Rafael E.	PR0115	37,12A,63B,42,49
Irving, David	TX0550	47,70,46,29A,37
Irwin, David E.	FL0450	64C,64E,37,41
Isakson, Aaron	MN0610	32E,37,50,60B,65
Izzett, Robert K.	OR0800	37
Izzo, Victor	NY4300	37,38,13A
Jackson, Sharon Sue	IN1800	37,50,65,65B
Jacobs, Ed	IL2970	63D,11,13A,37,46
Jacobs, Jay N.	LA0350	37,41,42,48
Jaeschke, Rick	IL0100	32,37,34
Jagow, Shelley	OH2500	64E,48,37
James, Jeffrey R.	NE0250	13,60,32,37,63
James, Ray	KS0050	37,63D,32E,49
Janners, Erik N.	WI0425	37,47,60,12,13
Janzen, Eldon A.	AR0700	60,32C,37
Jeffrey, Wayne	AB0060	35A,37,49,48,63B
Jenkins, John A.	MA2000	11,37
Jenkins, Neil	FL0200	37
Jenner, Bryan	NJ0760	11,37
Jerosch, Anita	ME0410	37,63C
Jester, Erik	CA0845	37,60B,63C
Jewell, Vickie L.	AL0345	11,37,63B,66A
Jimenez, Fernando	CT0800	60B,37,63C
Johns, Michael	PA3200	48,37,42
Johnson, Clarence J.	GA1900	37
Johnson, David A.	IA0900	60,32,37,47,65
Johnson, Dennis	KY0950	60,37,38
Johnson, H. Wade	PA2000	37,63,11
Johnson, Mark	GA0200	32E,37,60B,63C
Johnson, Nathaniel	NE0710	60,37,64C,64E
Johnson, Randolph J.	DE0050	37,47
Johnson, Ronald	IA1600	60,37
Johnson, Sigurd	ND0350	65,50,37
Johnston, Keith	CT0300	37,63C,63D
Johnston, Stephen K.	VA1350	37,48,64C
Joly, Rene	AI0190	37
Jones, Brandon D.	OH2450	37,38,32E,60
Jones, Cheryl	FL1430	37,66A,66B,47,61
Jones, Eric W.	MI1000	32E,37,50,65
Jones, Gareth	AA0150	37,49
Jones, Herman	SC0150	11,37,47,48,64
Jones, Lloyd	AL1250	64,37,47,32E,34A
Jones, Lloyd E.	AL1250	60B,37,63
Jones, Max	IN1310	37,60B
Jones, Melvin	GA1450	11,37,29,63A
Jones, Scott A.	GA2100	37,60B
Jones, Scott A.	OH1850	37,60B,32E
Jones, Susie	OR0550	13,37,47,29
Jones, Terry	ID0140	37,47,49,63A,29
Jones, Tony	IL1090	37,63,13A,11
Jones, Troy V.	FL0680	32E,37,65
Joosten, Mike	WI0801	37
Jordan, Edward	LA0720	11,20G,37,47,64
Jordan, Jeff	KS0350	37,32E,60B,63B,10
Jorgensen, Robert	OH2150	37,60
Jorgensen, Trevor	NY3770	37,64,48,11
Joss, Laura L.	OH0200	32,37,60
Jossim, J.	FL0800	64B,37,32C
Junkin, Jerry	TX3510	60,37
Justeson, Jeremy	PA1750	64E,37,32E,43,11
Kalman, Zoltan	AG0050	64C,48,64E,37
Kambeitz, Gus	CA5510	46,37,47,29,13A
Kaminsky, Bruce	PA1000	62D,12A,37,50
Kammerer, David	HI0050	10F,37,35B,63A,13C
Karahalis, Dean	NY1275	32E,37
Karrick, Brant	KY1000	37,60B,32E
Karriker, Galen	OH2150	37,60
Kastens, Kevin	IA1550	37
Kauffman, Bradley	KS0500	13,36,37
Kays, Mark	IN1485	12A,13B,37,47,60B
Keck, Thomas B.	FL1900	37,60B
Keech, Christopher	MI1985	64C,64E,37,48,47
Kehler, David T.	GA1150	37,60B,11
Kehrberg, Donald A.	KS0200	64B,37,32
Keiser, Douglas	IN0800	37,32
Kellan, Ross	IL0850	60,32,37,11,13
Kelley, Constance L.	TX0150	37,32E,64A
Kelley, Scott	NY1150	37,63A
Kelley, Timothy S.	TX3650	60,37,49,63,41
Kelly, Mark	OH0300	37

Index by Area of Teaching Interest

Name	Code	Areas
Kelly, Steven N.	FL0850	32,37
Kendall, Michael	IN0200	60,37,32,20,34
Kennedy, Rajah B.	OK0450	11,37,46,49,63
Kenny, William	PA0350	60,11,37,63A,63B
Kephart, Donald B.	PA1350	32C,37,63,46,60
Kerr, Stephen P.	VA0650	63,37,60B,48
Kesner, Fred	WV0500	37,47
Key, Ramon	OH0500	37,60B
Kihle, Jason J.	TX2960	11,37,50,65
Kimball, Marshall C.	OH1400	32,37,47,60B
Kinder, Keith	AG0200	37,41,49,63
King, Gerald	AB0150	32,37,60B
King, Roy M.	LA0200	37
King, Steve E.	VA1700	32E,32G,37
Kirchhoff, Craig	MN1623	60,37,41
Kirk, Jeremy	KS0250	37,13,20A,50,65
Kirkpatrick, Leon	KY0250	37,38,41,51,60B
Kirkpatrick, Linda M.	MD0520	60,37,41,48,64A
Kirsch, Gary	CT0450	37
Kiser, Daniel W.	NC1100	13A,10F,60B,37,63A
Kish, David	CO0550	37,32E,60B,32
Kitelinger, Shannon	CA4100	37,60B
Kizer, Tremon B.	OH2250	37,32E,11
Klemas, John	IA1170	37,47,63,64,65
Kleppinger, Stanley V.	NE0600	13,63A,37,12C
Klickman, Philip	MD0350	63B,37,32E,60B
Kline, W. Peter	TX2260	13A,11,37,49,63D
Kluball, Jeff L.	GA0625	37,63,29,13,10
Knier, Lawrence	MD0800	37,13C,63,13K,11
Knight, Michael D.	WI0750	37,60B,32E,64C,64E
Knight, Steven M.	AR0300	37,32E
Knighten, Christopher	AR0700	32E,37
Knopps, Amy	MI0600	32E,37
Knudtsen, Jere	WA0750	11,37,47,64A,29A
Koch, Andrew	VA1550	37,63
Koch, Christopher	MO0350	37,38,60B
Kofford, Brooke	CA2300	37
Kohlenberg, Kenneth	OH2120	37,60B,12A,11,63A
Kolar, Andrew	CT0300	37,65
Kolman, Barry	VA1850	13,37,38,64C,60
Koops, Alexander	CA0250	37,32
Kopetz, Barry E.	OH0350	60B,37
Koponen, Glenn	NY2900	60,37,41,63A,31A
Korak, John	IL2910	60,37,63A,49,42
Korzun, Jonathan	MI1985	32E,37,47,13
Kraus, Barry N.	TN0100	37,32E,60B
Kravchak, Richard	CA0805	11,64,38,37,32
Kretzer, Scott	OH2275	37
Kretzer, Scott	MI0050	37,41,65
Kroesche, Kenneth	MI1750	63D,63C,49,37
Kugler, Roger T.	KS1000	32E,63,13,37
Kuhn, Michael	AZ0250	37,47
Kuhn, William	OR0150	37,11,63C,60,13A
Kurschner, James	MN1200	37,64E,41,66D
Laarz, Bill	TN0580	37,38,41,63
LaBounty, Anthony	NV0050	37,32E
Labovitz, Sarah J.	KS1400	37
LaCognata, John P.	NC2440	37,49,63
Lacy, Charles	LA0100	37,63D
Laddy, Jason	WI0425	38,37
Laflen, Betty Jo	KS0400	11,13C,32B,37,64
Laing, Daniel R.	NE0300	60B,37,49,63A,63B
Lamb, Brian	OK1330	60B,32,37
Lamb, William	NM0250	13,11,37,47,63
Lambert, Adam E.	NE0050	32E,37,60B,63,49
Lambert, James	OK0150	65,50,37,13,12D
Lambrecht, James M.	IL0100	37,49,63A,60B,13C
Lamkin, John R.	MD1020	10F,37,47,63
Lammers, Ed	KS0040	46,37,65,63,11
Lance, Elva Kaye	MS0500	37,46
Land, Mary	GA2300	37,32
Landsberg, Nils F.	TX3415	37,60B,46
Lane, Mark	WA0050	37,32
Langford, Jeremy	FL1100	37
Langford, R. Gary	FL1850	37,47,29A
Lares, Joseph	CA5353	37
Larragoity, Ingrid	AR0300	37,32E,13B,48
Larsen, Vance	UT0190	60,37,49,32
Larson, Danelle	IL0800	32E,37
Larson, Stacey L.	IL3450	32E,37,60B
LaRue, Peter	KY0610	60,11,32,37,63D
Latten, James E.	PA1650	11,13A,37,50,65
Laverty, John M.	NY4150	60B,37,32,63A
LaVoie, Karen R.	MA2100	13C,60B,37,63A
Law, Charles P.	AR0750	65,50,37
Lawrence, Patrick	WI0850	63C,63D,37,32E
Lawrence, Torrey	ID0250	63D,37
Lawson, Stephen J.	WV0400	13,63B,29,49,37
LeBlanc, Robert L.	OH1850	37,41,63D
Leckrone, Michael E.	WI0815	60,37,20G
LeClair, Paul	VT0400	13,12A,48,37,64E
Ledbetter, Robert	MT0400	37,50,65,20H,14C
Lee, D. Thomas	CA5030	37,48
Lee, Mark	TN0350	37
Lee, Richard F.	TX3150	37,63A
Lee, Ronald T.	RI0300	32,37,12B,12C
Lefevre, Donald	TX3750	37,64E,48
Lefkowitz, Aaron M.	FL1550	63C,37
LeFlore, Maurice	NC0700	64E,37
Legette, Lee David	NC2700	11,32B,37,47,64E
Legutki, Allen R.	IL0275	37,38,32
Lemke, Jeffrey J.	LA0350	32,37,60
Leonard, Angela	OH0100	37
Lesk, Sally	AG0150	37
Leslie, James M.	OH2250	65,47,32B,37
Leslie, Tom	NV0050	37,60B
Lethco, Leigh-Ann M.	WI0830	32E,37,63A,32
Lewis, Cecil	CO0100	47,53,64E,37
Lewis, David P.	WV0350	64,37,41,12A,32E
Lewis, Roger	KS0210	13,10,37,47,53
Leyva, Jesse	IL3300	60B,37,32E
Lill, Joseph	IL2100	47,49,63A,37,42
Lindhal, Gregory	FL0700	37,48,60B
Lindroth, James	OK0550	32,37
Linklater, Fraser	AC0100	63A,32E,37,48,60B
Linn, Don	KS0650	37,32E,10F
Lippard, Michael S.	TX2710	13A,37,46,64,13B
Lipsey, Michael	NY0642	37,50,65
Little, Steve	IA0050	37
Llewellyn, Raymond	CA0815	32B,37,65
Lloyd, Joe	AZ0400	32C,37,63A,11,60
Lo, Adrian	MN0200	12A,37,38,47,62
Lockard, Douglas T.	TX0600	63A,37,47
Locke, Gary	CA3800	37,50
Locke, John R.	NC2430	60,32C,37
Locke, Sheila	CA3800	37
Long, Bill	SC0900	37,47,65,60B,32E
Long, Derle R.	LA0770	60,32E,37
Longfield, Richard O.	AZ0510	13,60,37,38,47
Lopez, John A.	TX3175	37,65
Lorenzo, Benjamin	OK0800	37,32E
Lovejoy, Donald G.	MN1700	37,63A,41,60,32E
Lovely, Aaron	MD0300	63C,63D,37
Lowe, Frederick W.	IL1615	37,46
Lowe, Phillip	TX0910	13,12A,37,47,63
Lowry, Douglas	NY1100	37,38,10A,10B,10C
Lubaroff, Scott C.	MO1790	37,32E,10F,60
Lucas, Michael	CO0625	37,47,64C
Luck, Kyle	CA3500	37,47,11
Luckhardt, Jerry	MN1623	60,37,41
Lum, Richard	HI0210	37
Lutch, Mitchell	IA0700	37
Lutch, Mitchell B.	IA0200	10F,32E,37,60
Lute, Charles	PA1200	37
Luttrell, Matthew	TX3500	37,32
Lutz, Daniel	MA2030	37,46
Lychner, John	MI2250	32,37
Lydeen, Brian	WI0804	37,64
Lydeen, Brian	WI0400	64,47,37,42,64E
Lynch, John P.	GA2100	37,60A
Lynn, Mark J.	KY1500	37
Lynn, Robert	IN0700	13,37,38,62C,63D
Lytle, Stephen	OH1450	37,48
Mack, Kyle	ND0350	60,37,47,63C,29
Mack, William G.	MO0850	60,32C,37,49,63A
MacKay, Gillian	AG0450	37,42,63A,60B,60
Madden, John	MI1400	37,32
Magruder, Michael	NC2700	10F,37,64C
Mahr, Timothy	MN1450	60B,37,10
Maiello, Anthony J.	VA0450	60,37,38,41
Mailman, Matthew	OK0750	60,37
Maki, Daniel H.	IL0840	13,11,37,64A,66D
Maki, Erik	CA3000	37,11,63,64,65
Malambri, William F.	SC1200	37
Malecki, Jeffrey	IL2650	37,60B,63C,63D,38
Maltester, John	CA2775	37,41,60B,63C
Manfredo, Joseph	IL1150	32E,60B,37,32
Mann, Michael	TN1660	37,42,60B,65
Mapes, Randy K.	MS0300	64,37
Marciniak, Alex B.	MI0700	13A,37,66A,13,11
Marinello, Anthony	TX3510	60B,37
Markovich, Victor A.	KS1450	37,60B
Marks, Laurence L.	NC2420	37,64C,32C,41
Marks, Martin	MI0050	37,46,32
Marsh, Gerry Jon	WA0800	34,35C,37,10
Marshall, Jason	CA0835	37
Marshall, Jeffrey	IL2350	37,41
Marsit, Matthew	NH0100	37
Marston, Karen L.	TX2295	37,63C,11,13A,34C
Martin, Barry	MI0900	60,37,32
Martin, Blair	KS1250	13C,37,46,41,32
Martin, Freddie	GA1700	37,32E
Martin, James	MO1950	11,37,47,63D
Martin, John T.	MI0900	37
Martin, Joseph	CO0900	37,63C,63D,41,60
Martin, Kent	PA2710	37
Martin, Mark Gregory	PA3600	37,32
Martin, Peter J.	ME0500	60,32C,37
Martinez, Jesus E.	CA1700	13,29A,37,46
Martinez, Manuel	TX0390	37
Martins, David	MA2030	37,64C,60,42
Martyn, Charles F.	WV0650	37,47,64A,64C,64E
Martynuik, David G.	PA1600	37,13,32
Mason, Craig	IA1450	37
Mast, Andrew	WI0350	37,41,42,60
Matchael, Michael	TX3360	37,48,64
Mathews, Jeffrey	LA0550	37,32C
Mayes, Robert	TX3400	60,32C,37
Mayfield, Gray	GA1450	64E,37
Mayne, Richard	CO0950	32E,37
Mayse, Kevin A.	CA3800	37,63A,38
Mazzaferro, Anthony	CA1900	13,63,37,12A
Mazzio, Carl	NY3725	63C,37
McAllister, James	KS0440	37,10A,63,60B,32C
McBride, M. Scott	KY0900	60B,32,10F,63C,37
McCabe, Brent Poe	MT0450	37,11,32E,70
McCallum, Gregory	VA1800	37,64C,64E
McCallum, Wendy M.	AC0050	64E,32E,37,60B,32
McCann, John	MA1900	13A,11,37
McCarty, Patrick	MO0050	11,32E,37,65,50
McCauley, Thomas E.	NJ0800	37,60B,32
McClary, Michael	GA0940	11,37,47,63
McCloud, Daniel	TX0150	37,65
McClung, Sam W.	FL0365	60B,37,13,47,46
McClure, Matthew	NC2410	37,64E
McCreary, Teresa J.	HI0110	37,13A,13C,38,47
McCullough, David	IN0250	37,32
McCumber, Gary	AG0500	37,41
McCutchen, Matt	FL2000	37
McCutcheon, Russell G.	PA1400	37,32E,60,34,32C
McDonald, Reginald	TN1400	32E,37,41,64E
McGarrell, Matthew	RI0050	37,41,47,46
McGarvey, Timothy	IA1200	37,60,32E,41,29A
McGee, Michael	AL0850	37,47,63,64,65
McGinnis, Donald E.	OH1850	37
McGowan, Mike	TX2000	11,37,49,13,29
McGowan, Thomas	TX3370	37,41,50,65
McGrannahan, A. Graydon	NV0100	37,32C,41,63C,63D
McGrannahan, Grady	IA0550	63C,37,63D
McIlhagga, Samuel D.	MI0100	10F,37,14C,32E
McInnis, Fred	UT0050	37
McIntosh, Lawrence	HI0155	37
McInturf, Matthew	TX2250	32C,37,60B
McKay, James R.	AG0500	37,38,41,64D,12F
McKee, David	VA1700	37
McKeithen, Steven	LA0550	11,32,37
McKenzie, Colin	GA0950	37
McKeown, Kevin	CA4450	37,63,64
McKinney, David	KS0265	13,37,63D,64,29
McKoin, Sarah	TX3200	60B,37
McLamore, L. Alyson	CA3500	37
McMahan, Andrew	CA0600	60,37,63A,54,34
McMahel, Donald	IN1010	37,38,60B
McMullian, Neal	IL2300	13B,32E,64D,60,37
McMullin, Brendan	CA3100	37,46,47
McMurray, Allan R.	CO0800	60,37
McNeill, George	VA1700	37
McNeill, Marvin	CT0600	37,32E
McRoy, James W.	NY2105	60B,37,63,32E
McWilliams, Robert	WI0830	37,32,29A,60B
Means, Arthur	AL0650	37
Meccia, Lauren L.	SC1100	37,41,47
Meeker, Howard G.	OH0650	37,60
Meffert-Nelson, Karrin	MN0750	64C,37,48,32E,12A
Melley, Eric	LA0200	37,60B
Menchaca, Louis A.	WI0300	13A,13,60,37,29

Index by Area of Teaching Interest

Name	Code	Areas
Menghini, Charles T.	IL3450	60,37,32
Mensch, Thomas	TX3370	37,41,63C,49,48
Mensh, Heather	TX3370	37,41,46,48,63D
Mertens, Michael	CA2750	13B,11,63,64,37
Mertz, Justin J.	NY4150	37,60B,32
Meunier, Robert W.	IA0550	60B,37,65,32E
Mickey, Sarah	AR0600	37,48,64C,11
Middleton, Polly K.	VA1700	32E,32G,37,41
Miedema, Bradley	IA0500	32E,37,38,60B
Mietus, Raymond	NC2700	13A,37,50,65
Mikkelson, Russel	OH1850	37,60
Mikolajcik, Walter	CA4650	36,37,47,63,66A
Mikulay, Mark	IL2500	37,66A
Miles, Melvin N.	MD0600	60,37,47,49,63A
Miles, Richard B.	KY0900	60,37
Miliauskas, John	MD0850	37
Miller, Allan	CA6050	11,12,37,47,63
Miller, Ben F.	WV0400	11,50,65,35A,37
Miller, Bryan	IL0850	37
Miller, Donald K.	TX3530	37,60
Miller, James Patrick	MA2000	37,32,60B
Miller, Ward	AL1300	37,63D,41,32E,60B
Millican, Si	TX3530	32E,37,10F,35B
Milligan, Terence G.	OH2200	60,37,32
Millner, William	FL1745	37
Mills, Alan W.	CO0275	37,66A,63A,32E,60B
Mills, David	OR0050	13,10,12A,37,63A
Mills, David	CT0600	32C,37,49
Mills, Ralph L.	TX2250	37
Millsapp, Brian	NC1550	37,49,60B
Missal, Jason	TX0050	37,32E,63B
Missal, Joseph	OK0800	37,60B,49
Mitchell, Adrian	MS0350	11,63A,37,32C,49
Mitchell, Alan	MI0250	60,32,37,49,48
Mitchell, Bryan P.	MS0570	11,37,46,65,50
Mitchell, John	DC0050	37
Mixon, John	MS0575	37,11,63
Mongrain, Richard	CO0625	37,47
Monte, Tobias	MA2020	37,49,60,63A
Montgomery, David L.	MI2250	32,37
Moor, Ric	AG0550	37
Moore, Christopher J.	GA0900	37,65
Moore, J. Steven	MO1790	37,32E,60B
Moore, James H.	WV0800	37,47,29A,11
Moore, Joe D.	MS0250	37,32E,60B
Moore, Michael W.	SC0200	32C,32E,32G,37,13
Moore, Phil	OK1200	37,49
Moore, Rick	AZ0200	13,11,37,46,49
Moore, Selma	NY2950	13,37,41,64A,66D
Moorefield, Bob	CA4425	37,46
Morales, Raimundo	TX3750	63C,37,49
Morehouse, Christopher L.	IL2900	37
Morgan, Charles	IL1250	13A,60B,37,47,63
Morgan, Philip	NC2500	37,47,50,11
Mori, Paul	CA5550	37,64B
Morneau, John P.	ME0200	37,64C,64E
Morong, Eric	IL0850	37
Morris, Gerard	WA1000	37,60B,11
Morris, Willie L.	OH2250	37,47,64E,32
Morrison, David	IL3310	37
Morrison, Nicholas	UT0300	37,64C,48,41
Mose, John	IL0650	37,63C,63D
Mosenbichler-Bryant, Verena	NC0600	37,11
Moses, Kenneth J.	FL1900	60,37
Moss, Bruce B.	OH0300	60,37
Moss, Myron D.	PA1000	10,11,29,37,60
Mruzek, David M.	IN0650	11,37,38,47
Mueller, Marc	OK1250	37,63A,32E,60,34
Murdock, Matthew	TN1600	13C,32E,29,37,47
Murphy, Patrick C.	OR1100	13B,37,32,41
Murray, Renardo	MS0050	37,32,63,13A
Murray, Renardo	MS0350	37,11,32C,49,63D
Murray, Sean	FL0650	37
Naff, George	NC0350	37
Nail, James I. (Ike)	OR1250	38,37,60B,32E
Nakamura, Gwen H.	HI0210	37,64E
Narducci, Kenneth	CA2420	10,37,32E,46,13
Nave, Pamela J.	IN1310	37,65,50
Necessary, Andrew	VA0050	12A,32B,37,46,63C
Neiderhiser, Jonathan	SD0580	37,47,32E,13B,13C
Neiman, Marcus	OH1100	37,60B
Neitzke, Jeff	OH2290	41,65,37
Nelson, David L.	NC2430	13,60,37
Nelson, Jon R.	NY4320	37,47,63A
Nelson, Mark	AZ0480	37,13,63D,34
Nelson, Scott	VA1350	48,46,63A,37
Neuenschwander, Daniel	PA1750	37,32,63C
Neuharth, Randall	NE0460	11,37,47,63
Neumeyer, Albert J.	PA2550	47,37
Neumeyer, Albert J.	PA1950	37
Nevill, Tom	TX3515	65,13A,13C,50,37
Newell, Meri	MS0360	11,32,64,37,48
Newkirk, Brian	CA1280	37
Newlin, Yvonne	IL1612	13,60,37,66,47
Nguyen, Albert	TN1680	37
Nicholas, Christopher J.	CO0250	37,60B
Nicholls, Bud	MT0370	37
Nichols, Eugene C.	ME0430	13,36,37,46,12A
Nicholson, Chad	DE0150	37,32E
Nichter, Christopher	WV0750	32E,37,60B
Nickens, Michael W.	VA0450	37,13C,11
Niemisto, Paul	MN1450	49,63C,63D,37,42
Niethamer, David B.	VA1500	64C,37
Nimmo, Douglas	MN0750	60B,37,32C,32E
Nissen, James	MI1900	13A,13,37,34
Nix, Jamie L.	GA0550	37,60B
Noble, Jason	NY1600	32,37
Norcross, Brian H.	PA1300	60,37,38,60B
Nordgren, Jon	CA0400	13,37,46,47,60
Noreen, Ken	WA0860	37
Norman, Mark	KS1400	37,41,60B,63D
Norris, Paul	DC0170	47,37
Nowak, Gerald C.	PA0400	13,37,47,64
Nyberg, Gary B.	WA0480	13,10,37,63D,54
Nyline, Fred	IA0950	37
Oakley, Tom	TN0150	37,47,32H,10F
Odajima, Isaiah	TX0300	37,60B
Oelrich, John A.	TN1720	37,32E,60B
Okamura, Grant K.	HI0210	60,32C,37,63A
Olfert, Warren	ND0350	60,32C,37,63C
Oliver, James	AL0050	37
Oliver, Sylvester	MS0600	12A,20G,37,46
Oliver, Timothy	AR0110	37,32
Olson, Rolf	SD0600	37,47,49,63A,46
Opfer, Stephen R.	CA2810	32,37,38,60B,47
Orey, Pedro	FL0100	37,50,65
Orovich, Nicholas	NH0350	13C,37,63C,63D
Orr, Gerald	TX1250	13,11,36,37,66A
Orzolek, Douglas	MN1625	11,32,37,60
Osterloh, Elijah	MD1010	37
Ostrander, Phillip A.	WI0803	37,63C
Overmier, Douglas R.	MO0950	60B,60A,37,47,10
Owen, John E.	OH0950	60B,37,47,63A
Ozzello, Kenneth B.	AL1170	60B,32C,37
Packard, John	OH1600	37,49,63A,60B,10F
Paddock, Joan Haaland	OR0450	60,32,49,63A,37
Palma, Donald	MA1400	37,62D
Panacciulli, Louis M.	NY2550	37
Pannell, Larry J.	LA0100	64,34,35C,37,32
Pare', Craig T.	IN0350	32,37,65,60
Parisi, Joseph	MO1810	32E,32F,37
Parker, Grant	CA1500	13,11,12A,49,37
Parker, Wesley	AR0250	65,11,20,37
Parkinson, John S.	CA2840	37,38,47,49,45
Parr, J. D.	KS0050	37,47,48,64,29
Parsons, Kenneth	TN1350	60B,49,37,46,34
Pastin, John R.	NJ1050	37,60,29,46,48
Pattishall, Teresa	FL1700	11,37
Paul, Timothy A.	OR1050	32E,37,60B
Paulson, Brent	CO0625	63A,63,64,37
Payne, Brandt A.	OH2600	37,60B
Pease, William	VA1550	37
Pecorilla, John	OR1020	37,64,65
Pederson, Steven A.	KY0800	37,41,47,64
Pelischek, Jeff	KS0550	11,37,48,64C,64E
Perez, Frank	IA0600	37,47,32,29,63C
Perkins, Boyd	SD0400	63C,63D,37,60B,72
Perry, Dawn A.	NC2650	63C,32E,37,47,60B
Perry, Timothy B.	NY3705	60,37,38,64C
Petersen, William	AL1300	32E,37,63D,60B,49
Peterson, Dan L.	MO1780	37,65
Peterson, Douglas A.	FL0400	11,37,38,64C
Peterson, Elizabeth	NY1800	37,32E
Peterson, Eric	SD0550	63D,37,60B
Peterson, Stephen G.	NY1800	60B,37
Phillips, Chester B.	GA1050	37
Phillips, Mark W.	VA1750	32C,37,49,63C,63D
Phillips, Rebecca L.	SC1110	32E,37,60B
Piazza, Stephen	CA2700	37,64
Pickerell, Kevin	KS0210	63A,37
Pickering, Matthew	MS0360	63,37,11,49,60B
Pier, Fordyce C.	AA0100	37,49,63A
Pierce, Michael	LA0720	37,41,64A,11
Pierson, Scott	CA4400	37
Pilato, Nikk	CA0825	63,37,38,32E,60B
Place, Logan B.	LA0650	63A,37,12A
Plack, David	FL0850	37
Platter, Donald R.	MI2200	37,32
Poitier, James	FL0100	37,49,63,32F,41
Pollard, Shawn	AZ0150	13A,37,11,63D
Pollart, Gene J.	RI0300	60,32,37,29A
Ponto, Robert	OR1050	60B,37,41
Popejoy, James R.	ND0500	37,60B,32E
Popiel, Paul W.	KS1350	37,60B
Posch, Carl	AZ0150	13,11,37,47,63D
Posegate, Stephen C.	IL3150	32,37,49,34
Posey, Benjamin C.	AL0300	32,37,60B,63A
Posey, William	VA0600	37
Powell, Edwin C.	WA0650	37,41,32E,60B
Pratchard, Jeremy	AR0700	37
Pratt, Gary W.	CA0835	60,37,38,47
Pratt, Stephen Wayne	IN0900	37
Predl, Ronald E.	OK1450	37,63A
Premeau, Chad	WI0925	37,63
Prescott, Kyle	FL0650	37
Prescott, Steve C.	IN1400	32E,11,60B,64,37
Presley, Douglas L.	SC0850	37,50,32B,32C,65
Price, Berkeley	CA0200	13,37,48,64
Price, David	TN1650	37
Pridmore, Craig	CA5400	37,49,12
Prins, Rene	NY3765	64B,37,13,41
Procopio, Mary J.	MI0450	11,20,37,64
Proctor, Freda	KS1375	66,64A,13,37,41
Prudchenko, Slava	GA0940	37,13A,13B,13C
Pursell, Anthony	TX2750	37,41,48,60,63C
Purslow, Vicki T.	OR0950	11,37,64E,29
Purves-Smith, Michael	AG0600	60,37,55,10F
Raboy, Asher	CA3400	37,13D,10F,13E,11
Rager, Dan	WI0804	37,13,46
Ragsdale, Aaron	SD0550	37,65,50
Ragsdale, C. David	AL1160	37,60,11,64E
Rainwater, Brian	FL0670	60,37,13C,63C,47
Raisor, Steve C.	NC0500	11,13,37,47,70
Ramirez, Abel	TX0550	37,13A
Rams, Robert	NY4500	37
Ramsdell, Gregory A.	OH0950	37,55D,32B,32D,32C
Rand, Catherine	MS0750	60,32C,37
Raney, Earl	MA0250	37,63A
Rankin, Charles	FL1950	32,37
Ransom, Bryan K.	CA4100	37
Rasmusson, Ralph	NY1850	37,47,63,64,65
Rassier, Daniel	MN0350	63,37
Raymond, Rusty	MO0800	37,63A,60B
Reagan, Billy R.	AL0350	36,37,41,47,63
Redfield, Clayborn	CA0840	11,32E,37
Rees, Jay C.	AZ0500	37
Reeves, Gary L.	SD0600	60B,13G,37,63B
Reeves, M. Bryan	AL0050	37,32E,11,49,60
Reid, Jorim	NC1600	37
Reid, Lynda L.	TX2350	13A,32B,37,48,64C
Reid, Steven	IN0005	63A,36,37,38,13
Reimer, Mark U.	VA0150	13C,60B,37
Renoud, Doug	NY0050	37
Renshaw, Jeffrey	CT0600	60,37,43
Resnick, David	IA0250	10B,10F,13A,37,48
Rettedal, Dean	SD0300	37,60B,47,63,64
Reuss, Dale	MI1180	37,60
Reynolds, H. Robert	CA5300	37
Reynolds, Jeffrey L.	AG0450	49,63A,37,29A
Reynolds, Martin C.	MO1500	37,63C,41,47,32E
Reynolds, Patrick A.	OH2250	60,32E,37,38
Rhea, Tim B.	TX2900	10,37,64E
Rhodes, Andrew L.	OH2300	37,32E,49
Rhodes, Steve	TN0930	60B,32E,37,47,63D
Richards, Eric J.	NE0400	63C,37,10A,13B,47
Richards, Erik W.	IA0850	37,32E
Richardson, Colleen	AG0500	60B,37,32E,41,42
Richardson, Kevin	NC0050	37,32E
Richardson, Robert C.	WA0450	13,11,37,38,47
Richter, Glenn	TX3510	60,37,35A
Ricks, Edward	SC1050	65A,65B,37,50,13A
Ricotta, Charles	MI2100	65,37
Rife, Jerry E.	NJ1000	13,11,12A,12,37
Rikkers, Scott D.	VA0600	37
Rinehart, Jason	LA0770	60B,37,38,41
Ring, Gordon L.	VA0700	13,10,37,34

563

Index by Area of Teaching Interest

Name	Code	Areas
Rinnert, Nathan	PA2150	60,37,32E
Ripley, James	WI0250	37,41,32E,60B,38
Riseling, Robert A.	AG0500	13,37,38,41,64C
Risinger, Ed	IL1200	63D,32E,37
Rivet, Joe	LA0150	37,63
Rizzo, Rick	IL0720	37
Roach, L. Leroy	CA4200	32C,49,63,37
Robblee, Timothy	IL2250	37,47,32E
Robinson, Michael C.	GA2100	37,60,32E,60B
Robinson, Michael L.	NC1250	32E,60B,37
Robken, Jim	LA0250	37,60B
Rochford, Stephen M.	CA2390	37,38,11
Rockwell, Owen P.	MS0350	11,32C,37,65A,65B
Rodman, Ronald	MN0300	13,37,63C,63D,12D
Rodriquez, Raquel H.	KY1000	37,42,63A
Roeder, Matthew J.	CO0800	37,32E,60B
Rogers, Mark	TX2260	37
Rohrer, Thomas	UT0300	37,32
Roisum Foley, Amy K.	MN1000	37
Rombach-Kendall, Eric	NM0450	32C,37
Romeo, James	CA4050	11,37,47,48,29
Romines, Fred David	PA2200	37,60B,64E,32E
Root, Thomas R.	UT0350	13,10,37,41
Rosado-Nazario, Samuel	PR0100	63,37,34
Rosario, Harry	PR0150	13A,13C,37,60B,64B
Rosener, Douglas	AL0200	37,50,65
Ross, John Stanley	NC0050	37,32E
Rothlisberger, Dana	MD0850	32C,37
Rox, David	MA0950	10F,60,32,37,41
Rucker, Lee	OK1330	37,47,63A,46,29
Ruff, Kenneth	NC1550	37
Runefors, Bjorn	AE0120	36,37,13,11,64A
Running, Donald	MA0510	37,38,46,47,11
Rutland, Neil	NM0100	37,50,65,35D
Ryder, Donald D.	TN1710	37
Sabine, David	AA0032	35,13A,13C,37,65
Sackman, Marc L.	WI0806	13B,37,64A,47,11
Sagen, Dwayne P.	TN1850	37
Saker, James	NE0610	32E,37,60B
Sakomoto, Leo	CA0650	37
Salvo, Leonard P.	OH0100	60B,32C,37,41,32E
Salzman, Timothy	WA1050	60,37,49,63D
Sampson, Kenneth C.	TN0800	10F,32B,32C,37,63
Samuels, Sue	AL1150	37,32E,60B
Samuelson, Linda	MN1270	13,20,37,46,64
Sanders, Stephanie	VA0950	37,64
Sanford, O'Neil	VA0950	37,14A,63A
Sang, Richard C.	NY0642	32C,37
Sarjeant, Ronald	SC1050	10F,60,37,64
Sarver, Heidi	DE0150	32C,37
Satterwhite, H. Dwight	GA2100	60B,37
Saville, Kirt	UT0050	37,60B,64C,32E,32C
Sawyer, Tony	NC0750	37,65,34
Scanling, Paul F.	GA1550	64,37,42,48
Scatterday, Mark	NY1100	37,38,60
Schaefer, Phillip	MO2000	37,47,49,63A
Schafer, Erika L.	TN1700	63A,63,67E,37,46
Schaff, Michael P.	NY3780	60B,37
Schallert, Gary	KY1550	37,60B
Schilf, Paul R.	SD0050	37,49,47,32E,29A
Schmidt, Daniel Joseph	AZ0450	60B,37
Schmidt, Jack W.	PA0900	11,12A,36,37,49
Schmidt, John R.	PA2050	60,14,50,65,37
Schneider, Benjamin D.	ND0150	37,38,60B,64,32
Schneider, Mary K.	MI0600	37
Schnettler, John	TN0050	37
Schreier, David	FL1800	49,37
Schroeder, Angela	AA0100	37,48,60B
Schultz, Andrew J.	NE0150	29,37,60B,63A
Schultz, Dale	TX2200	37,60,32C,63
Schultz, Ryan	IL2300	37,63C,36
Schuman, Mohamad	MS0750	37,32E
Schunks, Dan	MO0750	47,37
Schwartz, Terry R.	IL3550	37,63A
Scott, David L.	CA5150	63A,46,37
Scott, Gary	CA2550	37,50
Scott, Kevin	NY3000	37
Seamons, Nathan	UT0190	37
Sedatole, Kevin	MI1400	37,60B
Seggelke, Martin H.	CA4200	37,41,42,60
Seifert, Dustin	NM0100	37,63C,63D,60B,32E
Sekelsky, Michael J.	MO1790	37,50,65
Self, Cale	GA2130	37,63C,63D,32E,49
Sessoms, Sydney	NC1150	13E,32E,37,60B,11
Sexton, James	TN1400	37,46,63C
Sfraga, Debbie	NJ1160	32,37,47,64
Shade, Timothy	KS0200	63D,38,37,13C,32E
Shank, Kevin	KY0600	11,37
Sharer, Marty	PA0500	11,37,12A,13A,13C
Sharnetzka, Charles S.	MD0475	37,12A,63A
Shaw, Gary R.	IL1750	10F,60,37,63C
Sheldon, Robert	IL1090	37
Shelton, Brian M.	TX2960	37,32,60
Shepherd, William	IA1600	11,32C,37
Sherman, Steve	AA0080	32E,37,63A,46,35
Sherrick, Richard	OH1860	37
Shewan, Paul	NY3350	60B,37,63A,32E,38
Shields, Lisa	MT0100	13,36,37,64E
Shier, Robin	AB0050	37,63A,63,46
Shiver, Todd	WA0050	63A,32,37,47,49
Shrewsbury, Matthew Monroe	SC0420	37
Shuholm, Dan	OR0175	37,46,31A
Sidoti, Vincent	OH0755	13,11,37,64C,64E
Sieben, Patrick	KS0225	37,20,13,46,11
Silvester, William	NJ0175	60B,32,37
Simmons, Matthew	SC1050	37,49,63C,63D
Simon, Philip G.	PA3700	11,37,41,51,63D
Simons, Chad P.	NM0450	37
Simpson, Kyle	PA3580	10,11,37,47
Sims, Stuart	CA0850	37,38,41,60B
Singleton, Darryl	TX3150	37,44,11
Singleton, Kenneth	CO0950	60B,37
Skornia, Dale E.	MI0650	11,32B,37,64
Slabaugh, Thomas E.	CA5010	37,60,65,50,42
Smart, James	MT0400	37,63A,32E,60B
Smedley, Eric M.	IN0900	37
Smisek, James J.	AL0800	60B,37,32E
Smith, D.	FL1730	37
Smith, Eddie	CA5150	60,32C,37,64E
Smith, Gavin	TN1850	32E,37
Smith, Joshua D.	TN0150	37,65,13A,50
Smith, Matthew K.	VT0100	37,32,11,63B,60
Smith, Matthew O.	KS1350	37
Smith, Neal	IL0350	37
Smith, Raymond H.	IL1750	32E,37,32C,13
Smith, Ronald	AL1050	47,37,34,64E,29
Smith, Ryan	NC1950	37,32,63,12A
	TX1400	63D,37
Smith, Shawn T.	TX2930	63A,60B,37,32E
Smith, Timothy G.	NJ1130	37
Smithee, Larry G.	TN1000	60,32,37,47,63
Smyth, Steven	AR0850	37,47
Snow, Bradley	MO1800	37,60B
Snowden, Donald	FL1500	37,47,63D,29A
Snyder, Colleen	CA2400	11,29A,37,66D,60
Snyder, Courtney	NE0610	37
Snyder, David W.	IL1150	32,37
Sochinski, James	VA1700	13,37,63C,63D,34
Solie, Gordon A.	OR0850	60,32,37,64D
Sorenson, Scott	MI1650	63,46,37
Sousa, Gary D.	TN1710	37,32
South, James	OK1250	37,63A
Southall, John K.	FL0950	13,63A,60B,37,32E
Southard, Robert G.	MI1050	37,60B,41,11
Souza, Thomas	MA0500	60B,64C,37,32,46
Spaniol, Douglas E.	IN0250	64D,37
Sparks, L. Richmond	MD1010	37,60B
Speck, Frederick A.	KY1500	10,37,43
Spede, Mark J.	SC0400	37,60,12B
Spence, J. Robert	PA1250	37,38,32,60B
Spencer, Malcolm	LA0100	63,37
Sperling, Russ	CA2100	37
Spevacek, Robert	ID0250	60,37,63D
Spila, Tom	AA0110	37
Spinazzola, James M.	IN1650	37,41,60B
Spittal, Robert	WA0400	37,11,42,48,60B
Spitzer, David Martin	NC2435	37,11,64E
Spradling, Robert	MI2250	60,37
Sprayberry, Shane	MS0300	37,11
Springs, Benjy L.	NC0900	37,47
Sproul, Brian	UT0250	37
Spurlin, Adam Corey	AL0200	37
Squires, Stephen E.	IL0550	60B,37
Stacke, Robert J.	MN0050	37,47,29
Stagg, David L.	MO1790	11,37,63C
Stahel, Ann Marie	IL1100	37
Stamp, John E.	PA1600	60,37,65
Standland, James	MS0750	37,32E
Starnes, David	NC2600	37
Staub, William D.	NC0650	37,32E
Steele, Stephen K.	IL1150	60,32,37
Steinsultz, Kenneth	IN1600	63D,37
Stempel, Mark	NY1600	32,37
Stempien, Jeff	NY1950	37
Stern, David	SC0050	37,63D,47,29A,60B
Stevens, Annie J.	VA0150	65,37,50,34
Stevens, Cynthia C.	TX2310	37,40,61
Stevens, Daniel B.	KS1200	38,41,37,62,51
Stevenson, Roxanne	IL0600	13A,20G,32,37,64
Stewart, Michael	TN1710	37,65
Stewart, Scott A.	GA0750	37,38,71
Stewart, Stanley W.	MS0200	11,37,47,49,48
Stich, Gerald	WI0800	37
Stickney, Mark A.	UT0200	37,63D,41,49,63
Stidham, Thomas M.	KS1350	60,37
Stinson, Ron	KS0570	29,37,41,46,47
Stites, Joseph	KY1550	32C,37
Stith, Gary	NY1700	32,37,60B,65
Stith, Marice W.	NY0900	37,63
Stoffel, Lawrence F.	CA0835	32C,37
Stofko, Diane L.	TN0550	32,11,37,13A,60B
Stolarik, Justin R.	WI0815	37,60B,32E,65,10F
Stoll, Gregory	CA0100	37
Stone, Michael John	OK0600	37,46,60B,63,32
Stotter, Douglas	TX3500	37,41,60B
Stovall, Jeremy	AL0500	13A,37,41,54
Stratton, Matthew	TN1720	63D,11,34,37
Strauch, Richard	WA1350	37,63D,60B,41,12A
Street, William H.	AA0100	60,37,64C
Streider, Will E.	TX3200	37,49,63A
Strickland, Jeremy M.	TX3000	37
Strieby, Ken	IL1612	37,46
Strue, Pattie Jo	CA1375	37
Stubbs, James	TX1750	46,32,13A,37,47
Stuckey, John	TX2310	37
Stufft, David	GA2000	37,41,47,32,60B
Stumbo, Jason A.	OH2300	37,32E
Sudduth, Steven	KY1425	13,32E,37,60B,63C
Suk, Richard	OH1900	32,37
Super, Kevin	VA0650	65,50,37
Svanoe, Erika K.	MN0150	64C,60B,37,32E,45
Swallow, Dan	IL1200	37
Sweets, Nancy	MO0500	37,65,64,66A
Swope, Richard	GA1000	37,63,49
Tackitt, Elliott	AZ0450	37,32E
Talbott, Doug	KS0150	10F,32E,37,47,49
Taliaferro-Jones, Gene	NC0450	11,37
Talley, Damon S.	VA1350	37
Taylor, Brian S.	LA0760	37,32C,60
Taylor, Charles L.	LA0800	37,60B,64C,32C,32E
Taylor, Clifton	MS0500	60,37,47
Taylor, Clifton	MS0420	13,47,49,63C,37
Taylor, Jack S.	CA3500	37
Taylor, Jack M.	OH2275	10,37,47,29
Taylor, James W.	SC1110	37,32E,60B
Taylor, Robert C.	AB0100	37,49,60B,63A
Taylor, Susan Lynnette	IN0100	32E,37,48,60B
Teel, Allen J.	TX0050	65,50,20,37
Teeple, Scott	WI0815	37,60B
Tembras, Dan	IN0905	32E,37,60B
Terrell, Maurice	FL1700	11,29,37,47,60B
Tesch, John	MN1120	32E,37,63C,11
Teter, Francis	CA1750	11,37,38,48,64
Tevis, Royce	CA0800	32,37,63A,60
Teweleit, Russell D.	TX3750	32,46,37
Thiel, Robb G.	IN1350	10F,60B,32,37,65
Thimmesch, Richard	IA0650	13B,13C,32E,37,47
Thoma, August	MI1830	32E,37,64C
Thomas, Eric B.	ME0250	37,47,64C,64E,53
Thomas, Matthew J.	IL3500	37,60B
Thomas, O. T.	AL0950	37,35A,65
Thomas, Raymond D.	TN1100	32E,37,60B
Thomas, William	AG0650	32F,37,38
Thompson, Gerald	DE0200	37
Thompson, Kenneth	OH0300	37
Thompson, Mallory	IL2250	60,37
Thompson, Steven	MN0250	37,60B,63A,32E,49
Thompson, Steven D.	CA0150	37,38,63C,11,13A
Thorpe, Allan	AB0090	13,48,64D,13A,37
Threinen, Emily	PA3250	37,60B
Tillotson, J. Robert	IL1085	37,13,41,64C
Timm, Laurance	CA0815	37,48,64B
Timmey, Zachery	VA0950	63A,11,37
Tindall, Danny H.	FL1740	36,37,65,11
Tinnell, Jennifer L.	KY0400	37,63C,32E,47
Tinnin, Randall C.	FL1950	63A,49,37,32E,20

Index by Area of Teaching Interest

Name	Code	Areas
Tirk, Richard	OK1250	47,63A,37
Tjornehoj, Kris	WI0845	38,11,60B,37,32E
Tobias, Scott C.	FL1800	37,32E,60
Toner, D. Thomas	VT0450	65,20,37,50,60
Toney, Hubert	PA0700	37,47,32E,63A
Tornello, Joseph	ID0050	37
Torres, Gregory J.	LA0450	60B,11,37,34B,32B
Toulouse, Sharon	KS1350	37
Towner, Cliff	GA0850	32E,37,47,60B
Townsend, Bradley G.	OR0700	37,60B,32E
Trachsel, Andrew J.	OH1900	37,43
Tracz, Frank	KS0650	60B,37,32E
Traficante, Debra	OK1350	37,10F
Tramiel, Leonard	MS0560	60,11,37,63C,63D
Traster, Jeff	FL2050	37,49,63D,32
Tredway, Curtis B.	TX3520	37,32
Tremulis, Nick	IL0720	37
Treuden, Terry	WI1155	37,47,32,10F
Trevino, Alexander R.	VA1000	37
Trittin, Brian L.	TX0400	12A,13,29,37,64E
Trout, Marion T.	IN1310	37,47,53
Tuinstra, John	WI0865	11,37,63D
Tully, James	SC0420	37,32E,60B
Tuomaala, Glen	MN1300	37
Turnbull, David	WA1150	49,63A,67E,37
Turner, Charles	KY0300	32,37,63,47,41
Turner, Cynthia Johnston	NY0900	60,37,41,42,38
Turner, Daniel	SC0200	32B,32C,37,63D,34
Turner, Timothy R.	LA0900	13G,10F,32E,34,37
Turrill, David	OH1650	37,32E,60,63A
Tutt, Kevin	MI0900	37,32E,32G
Tynan, Paul	AF0150	37,63A,29
Underwood, Margaret	OH2050	32E,37,60
Underwood, Michael P.	AR0750	13,37,63
Ungurait, John B.	MS0575	37,65,62D,46,50
Vallentine, John	IA1600	32,37,64C
Vallo, Victor	GA0850	32,37,60B
Van Deursen, John	AB0100	49,63C,37
Van Hoy, Jeremy	CO0200	63C,37
Van Oyen, Lawrence G.	IL2050	13,64E,37
Van Winkle, Kenneth	NM0310	37,60
Vandehey, Patrick	OR0250	60,32,37,38,63C
Vandelicht, Roy D. 'Skip'	MO0100	32,37,60B,64A,47
VanDessel, Joan	MI0520	12A,13D,37,64C,48
Vandewalker, David W.	GA1050	37
VanValkenburg, Jamie G.	CO0050	63A,63C,63D,37,41
Vargas, Ruben	TX1425	61,46,37,62,63
Varner, Ed	MT0370	32B,37,65
Vega, Rebecca	NJ0050	32,37,11,64A,60B
Venzen, Austin A.	VI0050	10F,11,32B,37,42
Verrier, Thomas	TN1850	37,60B,32C,32D,32
Viertel, Kyle	TX0390	37,63,64,65,46
Vollmar, Ferdinand	TX3410	37,32E
Vondran, Shawn	IN0150	37,60B
Vroman, David	IL0400	60,32,37,63B
Wacker, John M.	CO1050	60,63,37,49,32E
Waggoner, Dori	MO0100	13E,10F,64A,37,13C
Wagoner, W. Sean	OR1050	65,10F,50,37,11
Wakefield, William	OK1350	60,37,41
Waldrop, Joseph	TX3850	13A,32B,37,13B,64
Walker, James A.	NY3730	60,37,38,41
Walker, Mark	AL1050	63D,37,60B
Walker, Richard L.	IN0907	65,35,34A,50,37
Wallace, Jacob E.	OK1150	37,60B
Walter, Cameron	AG0450	32,63C,63D,37,44
Walter, Jennifer Stewart	NC2430	32E,37
Walters, David	AL0500	13,37,63,60
Walters, Mark A.	CO0350	60,11,48,37,64
Wanhoff, Meryl	CA4460	37,46
Wanken, Matthew	IL1800	37
Ward, Steven D.	TX0050	60B,37,38
Warman, Harold	CA4100	60,37,49
Warner, Thomas	GA0490	37
Warren, W. Dale	AR0700	60B,32E,37
Washington, Darian	SC0950	37,49,63B
Wasiak, Ed	AA0200	32,37,63A
Watabe, Junichiro	AK0150	64C,64E,48,37,46
Waters, Tim	OK0850	47,10,37
Watkins, John M. 'Jay'	FL1850	37
Waybright, David	FL1850	60,37
Weatherall, Maurice	MS0600	64C,37
Weaver, Brent	TN0650	36,37,34,13
Weaver, Lane	KS0350	11,63D,37,49
Webb, Glenn	UT0150	37,41,47,50,65
Webb, John C.	AR0800	41,32E,37,60B,63
Weir, Timothy	VA0100	32C,32E,37,47,42
Wells, Donovan V.	FL0100	37,32E
Wells, Glenn	TX1350	37,11
Wery, Brett L.	NY3600	13,37,41,64C,64E
Wesley, Arthur B.	AL0010	11,37,47,65
West, John T.	NC2600	32E,37,60B
Westbrook, Gary W.	TX2750	50,65,37,32E
Westgate, Matthew	OH2550	37
Wheaton, Dana	CA3350	37,63C,34,53
Whitaker, Jennifer A.	NC2420	32E,37
White, Barry R.	NY1300	37,38
White, Chris	OK1050	70,35,37
White, Christopher G.	ME0440	37,60,32E
White, Dale A.	MN0350	60B,37,41,32E,63
White, Dennine	FL0600	32C,37,64A
White, Joseph M.	WV0100	65,50,37,63,64
White, Julian E.	FL0600	60,32C,37,64A,64B
White, Rick	WA0600	11,29A,20,37,46
White, William	MO1710	11,37,47,65,63
Whitfield, James M. (Matt)	NC0850	10A,13,37,10F,10
Whitis, James	TX3415	37,63D
Whitlock, Mark	MN1600	32,37,49,63C,63D
Whitten, Douglas	KS1050	37,63D,32E,11,49
Whitwell, John	GA2100	35E,37,60B
Wickes, Frank	GA2100	37,60
Widder, David R.	VA1700	12A,37,48,64C
Wiedrich, William	FL2000	60,37,43
Wieligman, Thomas	IN0900	37,38,43,46
Wiggins, Tracy Richard	NC2435	65,11,37,50
Wika, Norman	OK0550	60,37,63C,63D
Wilborn, David F.	TX2900	13,63C,63D,41,37
Wilcox, Don G.	WV0750	60,37
Wilfong, Glen	WI0100	37,63A
Wilke, Adam	CA0810	37
Williams, Eddy	AL0450	65,13B,32C,37,60B
Williams, John J.	IN0800	37
Williams, Kraig	NJ1130	37,60B
Williams, Nicholas	TX3420	60B,37
Williams, Robert	AL0950	37,46,60
Williamson, Brad	WY0200	37,63C
Williamson, John E.	MI0400	60,37
Willis, Jesse	SC0420	65,50,20,37
Willis, Jonathan	OH2290	60B,32C,37,47,46
Willson, David	MS0700	37,60B
Wilson, Brian S.	CA4700	10,37,13,43,60
Wilson, Bruce	MD0150	63C,63D,49,37,32C
Wilson, J. P.	AR0600	37,63D,63C,32E,60B
Wilson, J. Eric	TX0300	37,60B
Wilson, Kathy	OH0300	37
Wilson, Steve	TX3520	63D,29A,37
Wiltshire, Eric	OR1050	37,32E,60B
Windham, Mark	AR0800	11,63,32E,32F,37
Winters, Patrick	WA0250	37,32E
Winther, Rodney	OH2200	37
Wise, Wilson	IA1100	64C,13B,32E,37,60B
Wittemann, Wilbur	NJ0550	37,63,47,60B
Woike, David O.	MI0600	37,32E,32C
Wolf, Donald	AL1195	10F,37,46,47,63A
Wolf, Douglas J.	UT0250	37,65
Wolfe, Chris	MD0175	13A,60,37,64C,64E
Wollner, William	MI1850	11,13B,37,63B,60B
Wolynec, Gregory J.	TN0050	37,38,10F
Wong, Yau-Sun	NM0200	11,60,13B,36,37
Woodard, Scott	WV0700	37,47,32C,63,49
Woodford, Paul	AG0500	60,12B,32,37,63
Woodley, David C.	IN0900	37
Woodruff, Christopher J.	CA0600	37,13,63A
Woodruff, Louis	NJ0750	60,11,37
Woods, Jon R.	OH1850	32,37
Woods, William	NC2150	37
Wooten, Ronnie	IL2200	32,37
Workman, Darin D.	KS1110	60,32,37,47,64
Worman, James	TX3350	32,37,47,29,64E
Worzbty, Jason	PA3000	37
Worzbyt, Jason W.	PA1600	64D,13,37,48
Wray, Ron E.	AL1160	64C,37,13,60
Wren, Bobby	TX2310	37
Wright, Arthur	GA1750	37
Wright, Lauren Denney	OK0650	32E,37,64C,60B
Wright, Lawrence	PA2450	37,41,49,63A
Wuest, Harry	FL0675	37,47,64,63
Wurster, Miles B.	MN1030	37,13A,64,65
Wyatt, Alfred	GA1900	37
Yates, Derrick	AL0010	11,37,47,63A
Yeager, Richard F.	MO0850	37,48,64
Yoelin, Shelley	IL3200	13A,13,37,47,64E
Yoes, Milas	AZ0470	12A,29,37,46,63C
Yonchak, Michael	OH2050	34,37,32E,29,46
Yontz, Timothy	IL3550	32E,37,63A,32
York, Kevin	ID0100	37,47,34,32E
Young, Craig S.	MS0400	60B,37,63,64
Youngblood, Brian	TX3000	37,32E
Yozviak, Andrew J.	PA3600	37,60B
Zacharella, Alexandra	AR0730	63C,63D,11,49,37
Zamek, Brian	NY4050	11,37,47
Zamzow, Beth Ann	IA0930	13,41,42,37,12
Zamzow, Laura	WV0200	11,63D,60B,32,37
Zebley, Matthew	CA5040	37,46,47
Zeisler, Dennis J.	VA1000	11,37,64C,48
Zembower, Christian M.	TN0500	63D,37,60B
Zerbe, David	MI0150	65,37,50,32C,32E
Zerull, David	VA1350	32,37
Ziek, Gary D.	KS0300	60,37,63A
Zingara, James	AL1150	63A,37
Zitek, Sam	NE0450	37,64E,60B,32E
Zyskowski, Marty	WA0950	65,50,37

Orchestra

Name	Code	Areas
Abegg, Paul	UT0150	62A,38,51,54,62B
Abel, Alfred	IN1850	62A,62B,38,48
Adelson, Michael	NY3785	60,38
Adkins, Donald	CA0400	38,62D,66
Agopian, Edmond	AA0150	38,41,51,62A,42
Agopian, Edmond	AA0050	62A,41,38
Ahn, Jooyong	TN1700	38,60B
Alburger, Mark	CA1560	10,13,38
Aldridge, Erin	WI0860	38,62A,13C,51,60B
Alexander, Michael	GA1150	38,60B,12A,35A
Alexander, Michael L.	TX0300	32E,38
Allcott, Dan J.	TN1450	38,60B,62C,11,42
Allen, Virginia	PA3330	37,38
Allman, Garrett N.	IL1100	13,66C,38,66A,60B
Altop, Stephen W.	IL2250	60,38
Altieri, Jason	NV0100	38
Alvarez, Franklin	AZ0300	11,51,62,38,13C
Amundson, Steven	MN1450	13,60B,38,10A
Anderson, David	WI0100	66A,38,66C,13E,42
Anderson, Dean	CA1900	38,62A
Anderson, Douglas K.	NY0270	13,10F,60,10,38
Anderson, Elaine M.	OH2290	62C,13,38,41,42
Anderson, James Allen	DE0150	38
Andre, David	CA1290	38
Angeles, L. Dean	LA0300	38,32E,60B
Armenian, Raffi	AG0450	60,38
Arnarson, Stefan Orn	NJ1100	34A,34D,35C,62,38
Arnold, Mitchell A.	WV0750	38,60B
Arnott, J. David	MN0350	38,62A,62B,51
Arrivee, David	CA0600	38,13,41,13A,13C
Arrowsmith, Jamie	AG0070	38,60B,62,13A,13B
Ashton, John H.	WV0300	38,63A,63B
Aubin, Matthew	WA1150	63B,38
Auerbach, Dan J.	GA0850	60,62A,62B,38,51
Averbach, Ricardo Franco	OH1450	11,38,60B
Averett, Janet M.	CA4400	38,64,48
Avramov, Bogidar	CA2800	38,51,11,10F,60B
Aylward, Ansgarius	NY0400	60B,38,41,62A
Bade, Christopher	IN1560	11,38,48,64,12A
Bair, Sheldon E.	MD0475	38
Bakenhus, Douglas	LA0550	13B,38,60B,64D
Baldini, Christian	CA5010	38,10,13,39
Baldini, Donald	NH0150	38,47,62D,29A
Baldwin, Daniel	IA0950	60,41,38
Baldwin, Philip R.	WA1350	62A,41,38,60B
Baldwin, Robert L.	UT0250	38,60B
Ball, James	MI0100	29A,38,47,63D,60B
Balogh, Lajos	OR0500	38,62A
Bangle, Jerry	NC2640	13,11,38,53,29
Bardston, Robert	AA0040	66H,66B,38,41,62C
Barnes, James E.	PA2450	37,38,60,34,41
Bartley, Mark	TX3750	36,38,60,60B
Bartram, Kevin P.	VA1475	37,60B,38,32E
Bartsch, John T.	OR0175	13B,38,66,10F,10A
Basney, Nyela	TX3527	61,66,36,38,60
Bassett, Jon	FL0670	36,61,51,38,32D
Bassin, Daniel	NY4320	38
Bates, James	OH2050	12A,20,32,38,62D
Battipaglia, Diana M.	NY0635	11,32,36,66A,38
Bebe, David M.	NY0700	38,13,42,62C
Beck, Brandon	WA1100	37,63,60B,38,32C

Name	Code	Areas
Beckett, Christine	AI0070	13,12C,32C,38,62A
Beert, Michael	IL2560	11,12A,13,38,20
Bell Hanson, Jeffrey	WA0650	38
Bell, John	MO0850	32,38,63B
Bell, Richard	GA0500	32E,13,38,60B,62D
Bell, Stephani	PA1850	38,62A,62B
Benjamin, Eric J.	OH0700	38
Benjamin, Eric	OH2290	38,11
Bennett, Dwight	AB0100	38,60B
Bennett, Evan	MA1450	38
Bennett, Joyce	DC0170	64A,38
Benyas, Edward M.	IL2900	60,38,64B
Berard, Jesus Manuel	DC0010	38,60,13,11
Bergonzi, Louis	IL3300	32E,38,62,32G,60B
Bergstrom, Melissa	MN0040	36,40,12A,38,61
Bernal, Sergio	UT0300	38,13C
Bernard-Stevens, Sarah	KS0700	37,38,13,64D
Betancourt, David	CA0859	37,46,38,32E,60B
Bettendorf, Carl	NY2200	38,60
Beyers, Foster	MN0600	38,60B
Bhasin, Paul K.	VA0250	37,63A,38,42,41
Bianco, Christopher	WA1250	37,38
Biava, Luis O.	PA3250	38,62A
Binneweg, Anna	MD0060	38,39
Bishop, James	FL0150	12A,37,38,47,64E
Blaine, Robert	MS0350	11,38,32E,63C,60B
Blaney, Michael S.	LA0760	38,62A
Blea, Anthony	CA1020	38,62A,36
Block, Glenn	IL1150	60,38
Blundell, Reuben E.	NY0625	38,11
Boers, Geoffrey	WA1050	60,36,38
Boga, Cheryl	PA3500	36,37,47,38,51
Bogas, Roy	CA2200	60,12A,38,66A,66B
Boggs, William	OH0350	38,60,41,60B
Bongiorno, Joseph A.	NY2750	62D,38,42,51
Bonner, Gary	CA0450	36,38,60
Bontrager, Charles E.	AZ0500	38
Bordo, Guy V.	OH2150	38
Boring, Daniel	PA2550	13,38,70
Bourque, David	AG0450	48,37,38,64C,60B
Bowen, Jose A.	TX2400	47,12A,29,38,12
Boyer, Maurice C.	IL0730	13C,36,38,44
Bozell, Casey	OR0150	62A,62B,38,62C,51
Bracey, Jerry A.	VA0500	37,38,47,62,29
Bradley-Vacco, Lynda	MN0250	38,62A,62B,51
Brandolino, Tony	MO2000	62A,38,42
Brannen, Malcolm	MI0850	62A,62B,38,32A
Braun, Elizabeth	OH1900	38,32
Brawand, John	SD0550	11,12A,38,62
Breiling, Roy	AZ0510	37,38,46,47,63A
Briles, Charity	IL1050	38,62A,62B
Brown, Andrea E.	GA0900	37,38,11
Brown, Emily Freeman	OH0300	60,38
Brown, James	FL1300	11,12A,38,64C
Brown, Kellie Dubel	TN1150	62A,38,12A,60B,62B
Bruck, Douglas	CA3460	38
Buchman, Heather	NY1350	38,49,51,48,60B
Buddo, J. Christopher	NC0650	62D,38,39
Bujak, Ewa	MN1295	38,62B,62A
Burkhardt, Rebecca L.	IA1600	13,38,60
Burroughs, D. Robert	WA0150	13,11,62A,53,38
Buslje, Sergio	DC0250	38,41
Bustamante, Linda	FL1300	11,38,51,62C,62D
Buswell, James	MA0950	62A,42,38
Butler, Lloyd S.	OH1800	38,54
Cadelago, Harry	CA3250	37,38,60B,49
Cai, Jindong	CA4900	60,38,43
Call, Kevin	ID0060	38
Cameron, Wayne C.	MD1000	38,41,63A
Caminiti, Joseph D.	PA2800	60,38,37,63B,32E
Campbell, Kathleen M.	PA3000	60,37,38,48
Campbell, Roy	MA0510	11,10F,38,46,47
Caniato, Michele	MA0930	10,38,29,13,47
Cantwell, Richard E.	KS1300	13,60,10A,37,38
Caoile, Nikolas	WA0050	38
Carbonara, David	LA0720	38,41,51,62
Carey, Thomas C.	OH2275	62A,62B,38,62C
Carlisle, Benjamin	TX3350	38
Carlsen, Philip	ME0410	13,10,29A,38,34
Carlson, Andrew	OH0850	62A,51,20G,38
Carlson, Marlan	OR0700	38,51
Carrettin, Zachary	TX3450	62A,38
Carrettin, Zachary	TX2250	38,60B
Carter, Monty	MO0950	62A,62B,38
Casey, Brian	NY1700	38,63B,60B,13C
Casey, Neil	SC1110	38,42
Caslor, Jason	AD0050	37,38,60B
Cason, Tony	CA3600	41,32E,60B,38,12A
Cedel, Mark	GA2100	60B,38,62B
Cee, Vincent	AK0150	32,29,38,34B,11
Cesario, Robert James	MO0825	37,38,60B,41
Cha, In-Hong	OH2500	60,38,62A
Chambers, Mark K.	AG0650	38,60,62
Chambers, Robert	OK1250	38,63C,63D,13D,10F
Chance, Mike	AR0250	32E,37,38,63C,63D
Chandler, Susan	WI0865	32E,38,62
Charloff, Ruth	CA5040	60,11,36,38
Charry, Michael	NY2250	38
Chauls, Robert	CA2750	11,38,66A,10A,39
Chen, Melvin	NY0150	66A,42,38
Chen-Beyers, Christina	MN1120	38
Cheng, Marietta	NY0650	13,60,11,36,38
Cherniansky, Fyodor	GA0940	38
Chesnutt, Rod M.	FL0680	37,38,60,32E,32F
Cheung, Teresa	MA2000	38
Chew, Sherlyn	CA2450	20D,38
Chi, Jacob	CO0275	13,38,60B
Chilingarian, Samvel	CA1700	12A,38,62
Chmura-Moore, Dylan Thomas	WI0830	63C,38,11
Chobaz, Raymond	FL1850	13,60,38
Christensen, Carl J.	CA2150	13,38,37,34G,13A
Christeson, Norton M.	FL0400	36,38,39,61
Cierpke, Timothy H.	TN1600	10F,60,62,36,38
Clark, Richard A.	IN0250	38,60
Cleland, George	AA0040	38,41,62A,62B
Cline, Benjamin	KS0350	51,62C,62D,38
Cockrell, Thomas R.	AZ0500	38
Cohen, Fredric T.	MA2000	11,38,64B
Cohen, Richard Scott	MI0650	11,37,38
Cohen, Warren	NJ0700	38
Colantti, Stephen	PA2250	38
Cole, David C.	FL0680	38,51,39,62A,32
Colnot, Cliff C.	IL0750	38
Colosimo, Murray B.	NJ1160	64C,38
Conable, William E.	OH1850	38,62C,32
Converse, Ralph D.	NM0500	64,41,38,48,29
Cook, Thomas	MI1250	13,12A,38,63C
Cooke, David	IN0905	38,60B,49,63C
Cooper, Jameson	IN0910	62A,38,60B
Copenhaver, Lee R.	MI0900	13,11,12A,38,62C
Corbin, Dwayne V.	CA4600	37,38,65,29
Corbin, Dwayne	CA4550	38,20
Cortese, Federico	MA1050	38,12A,12B
Cotter, Daniel	WA0950	38,64C,13B,13C
Couturiaux, Clay	TX3420	60B,38,62C
Cowan, Carole	NY3760	38,66D,62A,62B
Cowell, Jennifer	WY0050	38,41,66D,62A
Cox, Gregory	AB0200	63C,38
Cox, John	NY4310	36,38,40,41,60
Cox, Patricia J.	AR0250	11,32,34C,38,62B
Craig, Gordon	AG0250	37,64C,48,38,41
Crocker, Ronald	NE0590	11,38,65
Croegaert, Roxanne	IL0300	38
Csaba, Ajtony	AB0150	38,60B
Cseszko, Ferenc	ID0250	38,62A,62B,41
Cubek, David	CA1060	38,11,13,60
Cubek, David	CA3620	38,11,13,60
Cubek, David	CA2175	38,11,13,60
Cubek, David	CA4500	38,11,60,13
Culver, Daniel	IL0100	13,60B,12,38
Culver, Eric	MA0700	11,60,10F,38,41
Cummings, Daniel	CA2420	60B,38,66D,66A
Cummings, Paul C.	CA2250	32,37,38,64C
Cunningham, Gregory M.	MI1750	60B,38,37
Currie, David	AG0400	60,38,41,62D
Czarkowski, Stephen	MD0550	38,62C,13A
D'Alimonte, Nancia	DC0100	38
Dalmas, Jennifer	TX2700	38,62A,62B,41
Dangerfield, Joseph Allen	IA0300	10,13,66A,38,43
Danis, Ann	RI0300	60,38,11,62A,62B
David, Marc	AD0050	38
Davidson, Harry L.	NC0600	38,11
Davis, Paul G.	MO1950	60B,37,38,32E
Davis, Rachelle Berthelsen	CA3400	62A,12A,38
Davis, Randy	AL1195	37,38,60,13,48
Davis, William	IN0800	38,62A,62B
De La Bretonne, Beverly	TX0100	13,38,41,62A,64A
De Lyser, David M.	OR1100	13,10,38,41
Deadman, Carey	IL0720	38
Dean, Jay L.	MS0750	60,38,39
Deaver, Susan E.	NY3790	38
DeMichele, Anna	CA0859	36,61,13A,38,11
DePreist, James	NY1900	60B,38
Deutsch, Margery	WI0825	60B,38
Di Vittorio, Salvatore	NY0050	10A,38
Diamond, Douglas	MN0050	60B,38,51,12A
Dietrich, Johannes M.	PA1900	60,38,62A,62B
Dissmore, Larry	MO0400	60,38,51,62A,62B
Dixon, Edward E.	WA1300	38,62C,13C,62D
Dixon, Timothy D.	PA2300	38,12A
Djokic, Philippe	AF0100	62B,38,41,51,62A
Dodson, John	MI0050	10,12,38
Dolbashian, Edward	IL1500	38
Dolbashian, Edward	MO1800	60B,38
Domine, James	CA2700	38,70
Dominick, Daniel L.	TX0250	66A,12,60B,38,60
Doroftei, Mugnr	TX2550	13,38,62
Dowdy, Eugene	TX3530	38
Doyle, William	CA1750	11,37,38,63,60
Drago, Alejandro M.	ND0500	38,62
Droste, Douglas	OK0800	38,60B,32E
Dudgeon, Ralph T.	NY3720	12,67,14,38,63
Duitman, Henry E.	MI0900	51,38,32E,41
Dunston, Douglas E.	NM0350	10B,36,38,47,54
Dura, Marian T.	PA1900	38,62,32,32B,62A
Eccles, David F.	IL3450	51,32E,38
Edelberg, Joe	CA4700	32E,38,42,62A,62B
Edelstein, Gerardo	PA2750	60,38
Edgerton, Sara A.	MO1500	11,12A,38,62D,62C
Edwards, Huw	WA1000	38
Effron, David	IN0900	60,38
Eggleston, Steven	IL1200	60B,37,38,63A
Ehle, Todd	TX0550	62A,62B,38
Eichler, Dennis	TX1450	38
Elias, Carlos	CO0225	32C,38,62A,62B,51
Elliott, Lloyd R.	CA1300	38,61,42
Ellis, Peter	AA0032	38,62,51,36
Ellsworth, E. Victor	AR0750	32,62,38
Elworthy, Joseph	AB0200	62C,42,38
Emerson, Deidre	TN1400	62C,38,51
Endo, Akira	CO0800	38,60
Enyart, John	FL0950	38,62A,51
Erdmann, Thomas R.	NC0750	11,38,13E,13F,63A
Ergo, Jack	IA0600	20,31A,38,66A
Errante, Steven	NC2440	13,10F,60,10,38
Espinosa, Leandro	OR0200	62C,62D,38,13A,11
Evans, Charles	SC0420	38
Evans, Clifton J.	TX3500	38,60B,11
Eylar, Leo B.	CA0840	10,12A,38
Fagen, Arthur H.	IN0900	60,38
Fairbanks, Donna	UT0325	51,62,38
Fairlie, Mary	TX2800	62A,62B,51,14C,38
Falskow, John	WA0960	37,63A,38,11,13
Farkas, Pavel	CA5150	38,41,51,62A,62B
Fashun, Christopher H.	IN0550	38,65,32,47,62B
Feather, Carol Ann	TN0450	13,11,38,63B
Felder, Harvey	CT0600	38,60B
Feldman, Ronald	MA2250	60B,38,41,42
Fellenbaum, James	TN1710	38,60B
Ferington, Paul	NY3717	38
Ferrari, Lois	TX2650	37,38,60B
Ficsor, Philip G.	CA5550	62A,38
Finney, John R.	MA0330	60,36,38,66G
Fiske, Richard Allen	CA4550	11,38,66A,63
Flandreau, Tara	CA1150	12A,13,38,41,62
Flint, Jere	GA1700	38
Forsyth, Malcolm	AA0100	13,10F,10,38
Fountain, Robin	TN1850	60,38,43
Foy, Randolph M.	NC1700	11,12A,38
Franklin, Cary J.	MN0950	10,37,38,42,60B
Frazor, Terance	TX3410	38
Freedman, Deborah	NE0590	11,12A,38,63B
Friedman, Jay	IL0550	63C,38
Friesen-Carper, Dennis	IN1750	60,10,41,38
Fritz, J. Thomas	CA2400	38
Fulbright, Marshall T.	CA2550	38,51,48,62,63
Furumoto, Kimo	CA0815	38,39
Fusco, Randall J.	OH1000	13B,38,66A,12A,11
Gabriel, Todd A.	LA0050	10,13,38
Gackstatter, Gary	MO1120	37,11,38
Gaddis, J. Robert	KY0400	60,32,51,63D,38
Gambetta, Charles L.	NC0900	38,60B,13,62D
Garcia, Alvaro	WI0835	38,62B,60,51
Gardiner, Annabelle	FL1740	62A,62B,51,38
Gardiner, Ronald	FL1740	13,62,60B,51,38
Gatto, Angelo	MD0170	38,62

Index by Area of Teaching Interest

Name	Code	Areas
Gaudette, Nicholas	MN0040	38,62D
Gauger, David	IL1850	37,38,45,63A
Geeting, Daniel	CA0550	64E,64C,38,11,60B
Gehring, Joseph	PA1550	37,38,60,63
George, Andrew	TX3200	38,60B,39,32E
Georgieva, Roumena	GA1450	38
Georgieva, Roumena G.	GA0490	62A,62B,38,51
Gerard, Mary	CA4050	38
Getzov, Israel	AR0850	38,10F
Gibson, Mark I.	OH2200	38,39
Gibson, Michael	CA1800	38
Gilad, Yehuda	CA1075	64C,38,42
Gilbert, Albert	NY1900	38,60
Gilbert, David	NY2150	60,38
Gilman, Grant	VA0250	38,60
Gilman, Kurt	TX1400	38,41,62A,62B,20
Gindin, Suzanne B.	IN1050	32,37,38,41,63B
Ginter, Anthony F.	CA5040	12,38
Ginwala, Cyrus	CA4200	38,13B,11,60B
Giray, Selim	KS1450	62A,62B,51,42,38
Glazebrook, James	VA1700	60,38,62A,62B
Glickman, Joel	WI0600	60,32,37,38,47
Gnam, Adrian	GA0950	38,60,64B
Golan, Lawrence	CO0900	60,38
Goldstein, Howard A.	AL0200	10F,62A,11,12A,38
Goldstein, Joanna	IN1010	13,66A,66C,38,11
Gomez-Giraldo, Julian	WA0250	38,60B,13C
Gonzalez, Claudio	MI0250	38,60B,10F,20,12A
Graf, Hans	TX2150	38,60B
Graybeal, Dana	AZ0470	38
Greene, Kenneth H.	TX3350	14,38,62B,51
Gregg, Robert B.	TN0100	60,11,12A,38
Grenfell, Mary-Jo	MA1650	12A,32,38,41,42
Griebling, Karen	AR0350	13,10,38,62B,14
Griffing, Joan	VA0300	62A,38,41,60B,62B
Griffith, Michael Ted	WY0200	60,38,42
Grinnell, Michael	TX3535	62A,62B,38
Grizzell, Janet	CA1290	38,51,62
Groner, Brian	IL2150	62A,38
Groner, Brian	IL1085	38
Gross, Allen R.	CA0500	38
Gross, Allen	CA3300	11,38,60B,42
Gross, Murray	MI0150	38,13,60B,10,20
Grossman, Liza	OH1100	38
Gutierrez, German A.	TX3000	60,38
Guyver, Russell	CO0950	60B,38
Habitzruther, Bruce E.	VA0750	38,62C
Haddock, Marshall	OH1850	60,38,64C
Hadley, Theodore	ID0075	38
Hagy, David	NC2500	11,38,51
Hakoda, Ken	KS0700	36,38,32
Hall, Michael	IN0150	38
Hallstrom, Jonathan F.	ME0250	13,60,10,38,45
Hammer, Levi	OH2150	38,61
Hampton, Neal	MA0500	60,37,38,41,48
Hampton, Neal	MA2050	60,38
Hanna, Frederick	NE0160	13,37,38,10
Hansen, Eric	UT0050	62D,38,51
Hansen, Frank	NY4050	11,38,62B
Hansford, James	OK0650	38,32G,37,63D,41
Hanson, Eric A.	WA0800	60,12A,38,10,64C
Harden, Bill	TX3527	64D,37,38
Hardin, Garry Joe	TX2600	10A,13,29,38,46
Harman, David	NY4350	60,38,41,11
Harrington, William	CA3520	32,38,41,63B,31A
Harrison, Jacob G.	IA0850	38,60
Harth-Bedoya, Miguel	TX3000	38
Hartke-Towell, Christina	KY0900	38,62A,62B
Hartman, Mark L.	PA3050	62,38,13,62A,29
Hastings, Stella	KS1050	38,13B,13C,66D
Hasty, Robert G.	IL2250	41,38
Hatcher, Oeida M.	VA0750	32,37,41,38,11
Hauser, Alexis	AI0150	38,60
Hauze, Andrew	PA3200	38
Hawes, Preston	MD0150	62A,38
Hawkins, Ben	KY1350	60B,32,37,38,63B
Hayes, David	PA0850	60,38
Hayes, David	NY2250	60,38
Heald, Jason A.	OR1020	13,10,47,36,38
Hearne, Martin	IA0400	37,38,50,60
Hekmatpanah, Kevin	WA0400	11,12A,38,51,62C
Henderson, Luther L.	CA2600	20G,38,62,45
Henigbaum, William	NC2600	62,38
Hersh, Stefan	IL0550	62A,42,38
Hess, H. Carl	PA1050	37,38,60,63A
Hewitt, Michael P.	MD1010	60,32,38
Heyde, Stephen	TX0300	38,60B
Hickman, Roger	CA0825	11,12A,38
Hildreth, Thomas P.	SC1200	62D,38
Hill, Kelly	MI1950	64,38
Hirsh, Jonathan M.	MA1750	60,36,38
Hobson, Ian	IL3300	38,41,66A
Hodel, Martin	MN1450	38,63A,42
Hohstadt, Tom	TX3527	38,41,56,60
Holland, Anthony G.	NY3650	10A,60B,34,38,10
Holleman, James A.	MI1000	60,11,36,38
Holman, Colin	IL1615	38,12A
Holmes, Ramona A.	WA0800	14,32,38,62
Holz, Ronald	KY0100	12,38,41,49,10
Hoose, David M.	MA0400	60,38
Hopwood, Brian	MO1550	32E,37,38,63
Hose, Anthony	FL1750	38,60,35E
Hostetter, Paul K.	GA0550	38,39,60B,43
Howard, Robert	MO1830	38
Howell, Matthew	HI0200	36,38,40
Hsu, Howard	GA2150	38,42,60B
Hsu, John	NY0900	42,62C,67A,38,60B
Huang, Steven	OH1900	38,60B,43
Hudiburg, Howard B.	TX3175	32E,38,60B
Hudson, Timothy	NC0930	63,38
Hufstader, Ron	TX3520	60,37,38
Hughes, Christopher A.	NM0310	37,60B,32E,63A,38
Hughey, Richard	IL3500	38,60B
Hunt, William	OR0250	38,62A,62B
Hutchins, Tim	AI0150	38,64A
Hutchinson, Chad	IA1200	11,38,51
Hynes, Maureen	NY2105	38,67,62C,55,42
Iannaccone, Anthony J.	MI0600	10A,38,13,10,12A
Ichmouratov, Airat	AI0190	38,60B
Ikach, Yugo Sava	PA0500	61,38,11,13A,36
Isaacson, Peter R.	TX0900	62A,38,41
Israelievitch, Jacques	AG0650	62A,62B,38
Itkin, David C.	TX3420	38,60B
Ivry, Jessica	CA1150	51,42,62,13C,38
Ivy, Allen	MO1100	60,38,51,64A
Izzo, Victor	NY4300	37,38,13A
Jackson, James	CT0100	38
Jacob, Heidi	PA1500	38,42,62C
Jacobs, David M.	OR1050	38,60B
Jacobsen, Jeffrey	PA2150	38,32E,32C
Jaffe, Claudio	FL1450	62,38,62C
Jarrett, Jack	NC2430	38
Jarvi, Steven	MO1900	38
Jasinski, Mark	WA0750	62A,38,32
Jasinski, Nathan David	KY0550	62C,32E,38,42,13A
Jelinek, Mark R.	PA0250	60B,11,38,62
Jensen, Byron W.	NE0300	13B,38,12A,62,32C
Jensen, Janet L.	WI0815	32,62A,38,51
Jesselson, Robert M.	SC1110	38,41,62C
Jetter, Katherine	CO0350	38,62C,62D,13,51
Jiang, Pu-Qi	TN1680	60B,38
Jimenez, Alexander	FL0850	38,60B,65A,60,65
Joella, Laura	FL0650	38,12A,62D,60B
Johns, Kynan	NJ1130	38,60B
Johnson, Dennis	KY0950	60,37,38
Johnson, Nick	CA1375	38
Johnson, Roger	CA2550	38,51,48
Johnston, James	OH0050	62,38
Joiner, Thomas	SC0750	38,62A
Jones, Brandon D.	OH2450	37,38,32E,60
Jones, Claire	OH1100	38
Jones, Janet	AZ0150	38,62A,62C,62B,62D
Jones, Rufus	DC0075	38,12A
Jones, William LaRue	IA1550	60,38
Jost, John R.	IL0400	60,36,61,38
Jureit-Beamish, Marie	IL2400	38,64A,66A,10F,11
Kaczynski, Marrisa	NY1050	38
Kahn, Alexander G.	PA1400	38,12A,11,60B
Kalam, Tonu	NC2410	60B,38
Kaplan, Abraham	WA1050	60,36,38
Kaplunas, Daniel	IA1800	38,62C,62B,51,60
Katseanes, Kory L.	UT0050	38,60,62A
Kelts, Christopher M.	KS1400	38
Kenney, Wes	CO0250	38,60B
Keogh, Priscilla	ND0100	38
Kidwell, David	MA1100	38
Kiesler, Kenneth	MI2100	60B,38
Kim, Ariana	IN1650	62A,11,38,32E
Kim, Chris Younghoon	NY0900	38,41,42,60
Kim, Lok	GA0600	38,42,60,66A
King, Andy	IL0400	38
Kirkpatrick, Leon	KY0250	37,38,41,51,60B
Kjelland, James	IL2250	60,32C,38,62
Klassen, Glenn	AA0200	36,38,40,60
Klein, Lonnie	NM0310	11,38,41,60
Klein, Mitchell	CA1250	38,60
Kleszynski, Kenneth	OR1100	13,32,38
Klickman, William	IN0905	38,32E
Kliewer, Jan Michael	WY0130	13,36,61,62D,38
Knable, Robert	CA3850	13,38,34
Knetsch, Rene	CO0100	38,62A,42
Knoepfel, Justin	MN0750	62B,62A,38,42,13
Koch, Christopher	MO0350	37,38,60B
Koehler, Andrew	MI1150	60,38,62A,62B,12A
Koehler, Elisa C.	MD0400	38,63A,60,11,13A
Kolman, Barry	VA1850	13,37,38,64C,60
Kono, Yutaka	VT0450	63D,34,38,60
Konye, Paul	NY3680	13G,12A,38,10,12
Konzen, Richard A.	PA1450	38,51,66G,41,13B
Kordzaia, Alexander	VA1500	38,42
Koshgarian, Richard	KS0150	38,51,63C,63D
Kosma, Lou	NJ0825	38
Kozamchak, David M.	MN1280	38,51,62A,62B,41
Krager, Franz Anton	TX3400	60,38
Kravchak, Richard	CA0805	11,64,38,37,32
Krysa, Taras	NV0050	38,60B
Kujawsky, Eric	CA0855	38
Kumi, Gert	IN0100	62A,38
Kuykendall, James Brooks	SC0700	13,12,11,41,38
La Manna, Juan F.	NY3770	38,66A,66D,11,39
Laarz, Bill	TN0580	37,38,41,63
Laddy, Jason	WI0425	38,37
Lai, Ching-Chun	NY3780	38,60B
Lamkin, Michael D.	CA1050	36,38
Lang, Cynthia	CA3400	38,41,51,62
Lantz, Lisa E.	NY0100	11,38,51,62,13A
Lanza, Joseph	AG0500	38,41,51,62A
Larson, Allen C.	MO1950	13,60,12A,38
Latham, Mark	MA2030	38,60B
Lau, Frederick C.	HI0210	14A,38,43,64A,20C
Laux, Charles	GA1150	32E,34C,38,62,32C
Lawson, Robert	CA1265	10,38,41,66A,66D
Lawton, David	NY3790	60,12A,12,38,39
Laycock, Mark Andrew	KS1450	38,60B
Laycock, Rand	OH0755	11,12A,32C,38,62D
Layendecker, Dennis M.	VA0450	60,38,41
Leach, Brenda	MD0850	38,11,66G
Lee, Richard	AC0100	38
Leger, James K.	NM0150	10,60,12,14,38
Legutki, Allen R.	IL0275	37,38,32
Leon, Tania	NY0500	10,38,41,60
Leung, Jackson	OH2500	66A,66D,66B,38
Levi, Zachary	PA3710	38,62
Levin, Andrew R.	SC0400	11,41,38,13,42
Levin, Rami Y.	IL1400	13,11,38,10A
Levitov, Daniel	PA1400	62C,38,42,11
Lewis, Gary J.	CO0800	60B,38
Li, Li	IN0100	62B,38
Lin, Chloe	MO0060	62A,62B,62C,38
Lin, Ruth	MN0750	38,13
Lindberg, Jeffrey	OH0700	47,38,63C,29A
Lindholm, Eric	CA1050	13C,38,60B
Lindholm, Eric C.	CA3650	13A,60,11,38,41
Lipke, William A.	CO0050	66A,38,67F,66B,66D
Littrell, David	KS0650	38,41,62C,62D,13A
Liva, Victor H.	OH0650	38,62A
Lloyd, Kimcherie	KY1500	60,39,38
Lo, Adrian	MN0200	12A,37,38,47,62
Locke, Benjamin R.	OH1200	13A,60,36,38,61
Loeb, Jaemi	KY0450	38,13A,41,42,60B
Loewenheim, Thomas	CA0810	62C,62D,38
Longfield, Richard O.	AZ0510	13,60,37,38,47
Lopes, Gerald	CA0150	38,62D
Lopez, George	ME0200	66A,38,42
Lowry, Douglas	NY1100	37,38,10A,10B,10C
Lubman, Bradley	NY1100	43,38,60B
Lundy, Ann	TX3150	51,62,38
Lupica, Anthony J.	CA1700	36,38,13B,70,61
Luxner, Michael	IL1750	13,38
Lyndon-Gee, Christopher	NY0050	10A,14A,38,39,42
Lynn, Robert	IN0700	13,37,38,62C,63D
Macelaru, Cristian	TX2150	38,60B
MacMorran, Sande	TN1710	11,38,49,63D
MacNair, Alan	MI1750	38
Madole, Craig	TN1850	38
Mahiet, Damien	OH0850	38

567

Name	Code	Areas
Maiello, Anthony J.	VA0450	60,37,38,41
Malecki, Jeffrey	IL2650	37,60B,63C,63D,38
Maltese, John	AL0500	11,38,62A
Manji, K. C.	CA1265	60,38,49,41,29A
Mann, Sylvia Lee	CA0805	32,62,38
Manning, Lucy	VA1000	38,62A,32E,41,51
Marenstein, Harry	NY2550	38,11,13A,13B
Marinescu, Ovidiu	PA3600	38,62C,51
Markou, Kypros L.	MI2200	10F,38,62A
Markward, Edward	RI0200	38,61,60,39
Marosi, Laszlo	FL1800	38,60
Martin, Anne L.	CA3000	11,62,38
Martin, Spencer L.	IA0950	62A,62B,51,38
Martinez, Everaldo	ND0400	62A,62B,62C,51,38
Martinez, Jeordano S.	IL2050	12A,36,39,54,38
Massey, Andrew J.	VT0350	38
Massey, Michael	AA0110	38
Matos, Lucia Regina	IL2200	38,39,60B,66G,66H
Matthews, Brandon Stephen	CO0550	38,42,32E
Maxwell, Monte	MD0900	66G,38,36,31A,51
May, Joanne	IL0850	13,38,42
Mayer, Uri	AG0300	60B,38
Mayse, Kevin A.	CA3800	37,63A,38
Mazzaferro, Jim	CA1500	38
McAfee, Karen	TX3527	38
McCashin, Robert D.	VA0600	60,38
McClure, Sam	MO1780	13,38,62A,62B
McConnell, Robert	IA0900	38
McCreary, Teresa J.	HI0110	37,13A,13C,38,47
McCreery, Carlton	AL1170	38,62C
McCullough, Thomas Eric	OK1330	10,62C,13,38,10C
McDonald, Steven	KS1000	66,38,60B,12A,41
McHaney, David	IL1240	38
McIntosh, Bruce	OR1300	13,38,62C
McIntyre, Eric L.	IA0700	10,38,60,12A,13
McKay, James R.	AG0500	37,38,41,64D,12F
McKinney, Lori	KS0050	38,62A,62B
McMahel, Donald	IN1010	37,38,60B
McMahon, Kevin	WI0700	38
McNeal, Steve W.	CO0250	38,32E
McNeela, Rico	MO0850	38,11,62A,62B,60
Mendola, Ron	GA0900	38,47
Menzies, Mark	CA0510	62A,62B,38,43,60B
Meyer, Elizabeth C.	MI1450	38,62A,62B,10A
Meyer, Jeffery David	NY1800	38,66A,60B,43
Meyers, Dan	MI1550	60B,38
Miedema, Bradley	IA0500	32E,37,38,60B
Mietz, Joshua	NM0400	64C,64E,13,38
Milarsky, Jeffrey F.	NY0750	38,10F,60
Miles, Michael A.	MS0750	38
Miles, Patrick	WI0850	49,63B,38
Millan, Luis	MT0400	38,70,60B,13
Miller, Kevin D.	MI0600	60,32,38
Miller, Mark	MA0400	38
Miller, Michael	FL1100	38,42,62A
Milnes, David	CA5000	38,43,60B
Mims, Lloyd	FL1450	61,31A,38
Mishra, Michael	IL2910	10F,60,38
Mitchell, Jon	MA2010	10F,60,32,38
Miura, Hiroya	ME0150	10,13,38
Miyamura, Henry	HI0210	32C,38,64C
Montelione, Joseph	TN1200	38,49,42
Moon, Gene H.	TX2700	38,39,66,62A,62B
Moore, Frances	CA2800	60B,41,62A,67B,38
Moore, Hilarie Clark	NY3000	38,41,63B
Morgan, Angela L.	GA0250	32,38,51,62A
Mori, Akira	IA0550	38,51,11
Morris, Ralph	OK1330	38,62A,62B,41,42
Moss, Kirk D.	WI0350	11,32E,38,51,62
Mruzek, David M.	IN0650	11,37,38,47
Mueller-Stosch, Johannes	CA0825	38,60B
Mulholland, Jeremy	KY0550	62A,62B,38,60B
Munro, Anne	WV0550	64A,48,38,51
Murai, Hajime Teri	MD0650	60,38
Muresan, Branden	CA2960	38,62
Murphy, Brian	AZ0440	38
Murray, Jane	RI0300	38,41,48,64B
Myers, Ty	IA0200	13,38
Myssyk, Daniel	VA1600	38,60
Nafziger, Kenneth J.	VA0300	60,36,31A,38,11
Nail, James I. (Ike)	OR1250	38,37,60B,32E
Nair, Garyth	NJ0300	36,38,61,60,13C
Nardolillo, John	KY1450	38,60B
Narmour, Eugene	PA3350	13,12,38
Navega, Eduardo	NY4450	38,41,60
Neale, Alasdair	CA4150	38,60
Neely, David L.	KS1350	38
Nelson, David W.	CA0859	13,13A,10F,10,38
Nelson, Eric	GA0750	60,36,38,41
Nelson, Scott	KS0750	38
Neubert, Christopher D.	NY3700	38
Neumann, Ben	AA0050	32B,38,51,62A
Neves, Joel	MI1450	38,39,42,20G
Newby, David L.	CA0200	13C,36,38,39
Ng, Tian Hui	MA1350	38,60,12A
Nguyen, Co Boi	CA5150	38
Nichols, Christopher Robert	NE0150	64C,64E,38
Nies, Bryan	CA4400	38
Nies, Carol R.	TN1850	60,38,13,32E
Nies, Carol	TN1100	38,60B
Nilles, Benjamin	OK0750	38,10F
Noe, Kevin	MI1400	38,43,60B
Norcross, Brian H.	PA1300	60,37,38,60B
Nordling, Robert	MI0350	38
Nowak, Grzegorz	FL0700	38,60
O'Bryant, Daniel K.	MN1300	38,60B,62D
Ogrizovic-Ciric, Mirna	GA0300	38,42,62
Oh, Kyung-Nam	IN0100	62C,38
Olson, Robert H.	MO1810	60B,38
Oltman, Dwight	OH0200	48,38
Opfer, Stephen R.	CA2810	32,37,38,60B,47
Ordaz, Joseph	CA2975	11,66A,66D,38
Osborne, Larry	CA3320	38
Owen, Marlin	CA0350	38,41,51,62,70
Pabon, Roselin	PR0115	60B,38
Page, John	MA1400	38,51
Paiement, Nicole	CA5070	60,36,38
Palmer, Michael	GA1050	38,60B
Palumbo, Michael A.	UT0350	38,62B,32E,60,41
Para, Christopher	PA0350	13,11,38,62A,62B
Park, Chung	NC0050	38,62A,62B,51,60
Parker, Nathaniel F.	PA2200	38,60B,64,41
Parkinson, John S.	CA2840	37,38,47,49,45
Partridge, Gary	CT0650	38
Pasternack, Jonathan R.	WA1050	38,39,12A,60B
Pecherek, Michael J.	IL1175	13,60,11,38,62C
Pellicano, Julian	MA1175	38,60B
Peress, Maurice	NY0600	60,38
Peress, Maurice	NY0642	60,38,39
Perez-Gomez, Jorge	NM0450	60,38,39
Perrault, Jean R.	MN1600	60,62A,62B,62C,38
Perry, Timothy B.	NY3705	60,37,38,64C
Perttu, Melinda H. Crawford	PA3650	38,62A,62B
Peterson, Douglas A.	FL0400	11,37,38,64C
Peterson, Mark	NC0100	36,38,66G,66A
Pfutzenreuter, Leslie D.	CA2840	11,36,38,39,61
Phillips, Paul Schuyler	RI0050	38,60,13,10,10F
Phillips, Paul	TX2400	60,38
Pickett, Kyle	CA0800	38
Pickney, Linda M.	NC2420	63B,32E,38
Piippo, Richard	MI1050	38,41,51,62C,10F
Pilato, Nikk	CA0825	63,37,38,32E,60B
Placeres, Martha	TX3515	62A,38,13A,13C
Placilla, Christina D.	NC2700	12A,20,38,62A,62B
Plate, Stephen W.	TN0850	38,60,32E,13B,13A
Plotnick, Jeff	AA0050	38,41
Polischuk, Derek Kealii	MI1400	66A,66B,66D,38,29
Polley, Jo Ann	MN1450	38,48,64C
Pophal, Lee	CA0270	38
Portnoy, Donald	SC1110	60,38,62A
Pound, Robert	PA0950	13,10,11,38
Pranno, Arthur J.	FL0800	62A,38,51,62B,12A
Pratt, Gary W.	CA0835	60,37,38,47
Pratt, Michael	NJ0900	60,38,43,39
Price-Brenner, Kevin	IA1300	38
Price-Brenner, Kevin	WI0840	11,38
Princiotti, Anthony F.	NH0100	62A,38
Prior, Richard	GA0750	38,41,42,60B
Pulford, Paul	AG0600	41,62C,38
Pulos, Nick	AA0050	38,62B,41
Purdy, Craig Allen	ID0050	41,42,51,62A,38
Puschendorf, Gunther F.	CA1100	13A,36,38,66A
Quebbeman, Robert C.	MO0775	38,64C,60
Quick, Julia M.	SC1050	11,38,41,51,62A
Rachleff, Larry	TX2150	60B,38
Ramadanoff, David	CA1800	38
Ramael, David R.	NY1600	12,38,39,60B,51
Ramsey, Elmer H.	CA0550	63A,38
Ranney, Jack	IL2350	38,51,62
Rapp, Willis M.	PA1750	38,65
Ray, Emily	CA4425	38,41
Ray, Emily	CA1800	66D,38
Read, Jesse	AB0100	38,41,64D,67E
Reams, John	GA1800	13,38,41,64
Redmer Minner, Laurie K.	TN1350	60B,38,51,32C,62B
Regehr, Vernon	AD0050	62C,38,42
Reichwald, Siegwart	SC0650	12,38,60B
Reid, Steven	IN0005	63A,36,37,38,13
Restesan, Francis'c	KY1000	38,51,39,62A
Restesan, Francise T.	PR0125	13,60,12B,38,41
Restesan, Frank	NE0550	38,13C,62A,51,12A
Reynolds, Patrick A.	OH2250	60,32E,37,38
Rhyneer, Barbara	MI1600	60,38,41,62,11
Riazuelo, Carlos	LA0200	38,60B
Ribchinsky, Julie C.	CT0050	13A,13C,62C,11,38
Richards, E. Michael	MD1000	64C,60,41,38
Richards, James	MO1830	10F,60,38
Richardson, Marguerite	FL1000	38,60B,62A,62B
Richardson, Robert C.	WA0450	13,11,37,38,47
Richter, Jorge Luiz	NC0650	60B,38,42,62A,62B
Rieppel, Daniel	MN1500	66A,11,38,66C,12
Rindt, Steven	WI0865	38
Rinehart, Jason	LA0770	60B,37,38,41
Rintoul, Richard	CA5060	38
Ripley, James	WI0250	37,41,32E,60B,38
Riseling, Robert A.	AG0500	13,37,38,41,64C
Rittenhouse, Virginia Gene	MD0150	38,62A,66A,32I
Rivest, Darlene	WI0250	62B,32E,38,62A,41
Rivest, Jean-Francois	AI0200	38,60B
Roberts, Kay George	MA2030	60,38,51
Robertson, Jon	FL1125	60B,38,66A
Robinson, Bill	TN1000	38,62
Robinson, Gary A.	SC0765	63,64,65,38
Robinson, Susan	FL2050	38
Rochford, Stephen M.	CA2390	37,38,11
Rodgers, Joseph W.	MN1000	38,62C,13,62D
Rognstad, Richard	SD0600	38,13A,62D,13C,11
Roscigno, John A.	CA0835	38
Rose, Gil B.	MA1450	60,38,41,13A
Ross, James	MD1010	38,60B
Ross, Nicholas G. M.	AZ0450	38,60B
Rossi, Richard Robert	IL0800	60A,36,38,66G
Rothman, George	NY0500	38,42,60B
Rouslin, Daniel S.	OR1300	11,38,41,62A,62B
Rowe, Matthew	CA4100	38,60B
Roy, Andre	AI0150	38,62B
Royer, Randall D.	SD0100	64,47,38,32E,70
Rozek, Robert	AB0200	62A,62B,38
Rudge, David T.	NY3725	38,62A
Rudolph, Richard	VA0550	62A,38,62B,62C,65B
Rumney, Jon	ND0250	13,38,41,62A,62B
Running, Donald	MA0510	37,38,46,47,11
Russell, Christopher	CA0250	38
Russell, Timothy	AZ0100	60,38
Rutland, John P.	MO1790	38,62A,62B
Rytting, Bryce	UT0325	12,13,38,60
Sachs, Stephen W.	MS0100	66A,66C,38
Saelzer, Pablo	MD0550	11,13A,13C,38,62A
Saeverud, Trond	ME0410	38,62A
Sandersier, Jeffrey	CA1850	38
Sands, Tracy	NE0200	62,38
Scarpa, Salvatore	NJ1050	60,38,41,63C
Scatterday, Mark	NY1100	37,38,60
Schiff, David	OR0900	13,10A,20G,29,38
Schleicher, Donald J.	IL3300	60B,38
Schneider, Benjamin D.	ND0150	37,38,60B,64,32
Schneider, Charles	NY1400	38,60B
Schoyen, Jeffrey G.	MD0800	62C,38,13A,11,62D
Schram, Albert George	FL1125	38
Schroeder, Michael	CA4150	13,38
Schubert, Barbara	IL3250	38,41,60,43
Schulz, Patrick	CA1750	13,38
Schumann, Laura E.	OH1650	38,60,62A,12A,13A
Schwarze, Penny	MN0450	12A,11,38,62A,67A
Scott, Ronald	TX2930	64C,64E,38,10F,60
Scott, William	KY1550	62D,38,41
Searle, David	DC0050	38,39,41
Seebacher, Robert	AL1300	11,38,51
Seeman, Rebecca	CA5353	13A,11,36,38,61
Segal, Uriel	IN0900	38
Selden, Ken	OR0850	38,43,51,60B
Seliger, Bryce M.	OR0750	38,14A,13,12A
Selle, William	NC0050	38
Semanik, Timothy	MN0300	38
Seto, Mark	CT0100	11,12,13A,13C,38
Shabalin, Alexey	RI0150	62A,51,38,32E

Index by Area of Teaching Interest

Name	Code	Areas
Shade, Timothy	KS0200	63D,38,37,13C,32E
Shaffer, Teren	CA0960	38
Shames, Jonathan	OK1350	38,39
Shasberger, Michael	CA5550	36,31A,38,60,61
Shepard, Matthew C.	KS0100	38
Shepherd, Eugene	CA4460	38
Sheppard, Matthew	PA1650	38
Sherman, Joseph	NY2750	38,32,62
Shewan, Paul	NY3350	60B,37,63A,32E,38
Shiao, Simon	FL1950	51,62A,62B,38
Shimada, Toshiyuki	CT0900	38
Shrader, Steven	TN1800	11,12A,12,66A,38
Shufro, Joseph L.	IA1100	10F,13E,34,38,62C
Sidlin, Murry	DC0500	38,60B
Silberschlag, Jeffrey	MD0750	29A,35A,60,38,63A
Simidtchieva, Marta	IL2910	38,42,41,51,62C
Simons, Dennis	ND0250	11,13,20,38
Sims, Stuart	CA0850	37,38,41,60B
Sinclair, John V.	FL1550	60,32,36,41,38
Sisk, Lawrence T.	IL1520	38,12A,36,31A
Skelton, Robert A.	AG0500	60,38,41,51,62
Skelton, William	NY0650	14,20D,38,64D
Slawson, John G.	IL0840	60,12A,36,38,54
Sleeper, Thomas M.	FL1900	10F,60,10,38
Slocum, William	OH2600	63B,38
Smith, Alan M.	OH0300	62C,42,38
Smith, Carol	TX2250	38,51,60B,62,32E
Smith, Elizabeth Reed	WV0400	38,41,51,62A,62B
Smith, G. D.	KY1200	13,60,38,63A
Smith, James E.	CA4450	13,60,36,38
Smith, James	WI0815	38,51,62,60B
Smith, Mark Russell	MN1623	38
Smith, Orcenith George	IN0350	60,38,63D
Smith, Sam	ID0070	62C,51,38
Smith, Timothy M.	CA2775	60B,38
Snider, Colleen	CA1290	38
Sobieski, Dorothy	NJ0700	38
Sohn, Sung-Rai	NY3560	60,38,41,51,62A
Sohn, Sungrai	NY2900	62A,38
Solomon, Qiao Chen	GA0050	62A,62B,51,41,38
Sommerville, Daniel A.	IL3550	38,10,60B
Song, James J.	CA3100	60,11,12,38,13
Soto, Ricardo	CA3350	36,61,38
Spainhour, Alex	SC0050	38
Sparti, Patricia C.	NC0850	13,60,38,63D
Specht, Barbara	OH0950	11,38,64C,64E,48
Specht, Jeffrey	OR0400	13,38,60,63D
Spence, J. Robert	PA1250	37,38,32,60B
Speth, Uli	NY2900	62A,38
Spieth, Donald	PA2450	38
Sprenger, Kurt	TX2600	62A,38,60B
St. John, Brian	IN1600	38,62A,62B,60B
Stahlke, Jonathan E.	IL0730	13,10,38,10F
Stallsmith, Becki	AL0260	32,38,50,61,66C
Stanichar, Christopher	SD0050	38,60,12A
Staron, Timothy	OH1000	62A,62C,38
Starr, Jeremy A.	KS0300	38,62A,62B,11
Steadman, Russell	TX0100	38,62C
Stepniak, Michael	VA1350	12,38,31A,41,32
Sternfeld, Barbara	CA5400	11,38,62
Stevens, Daniel B.	KS1200	38,41,37,62,51
Stewart, Leslie	CO0250	62A,62B,38,11
Stewart, Scott A.	GA0750	37,38,71
Stowe, Daniel	IN1700	12,36,38
Strelau, Nancy	NY2650	38,60B
Stulberg, Neal	CA5030	38,12C
Suda, Carolyn	IL1800	11,12A,62C,38,42
Sulski, Peter	MA0650	62A,62B,60B,38
Summers, Jerome	AG0500	60,38,64C,67B,43
Sun, Xun	UT0200	60,38,62A
Swanson, Mark L.	MA0100	60B,38,66A,41
Tacchia, Michele	CA0845	38
Taft, Burns	CA5360	13,60,36,66A,38
Tamarkin, Kate	VA1550	38,60B,12A,43
Tao, Ye	LA0100	51,38
Tapia, James R.	NY4150	60B,38,32
Tate, Philip	NJ0175	38,60B,32
Tayerle, Loren	CA1550	12A,38,41
Teichler, Robert Christopher	IL3150	47,10,38
Tentser, Alexander	AZ0480	66A,38
Teter, Francis	CA1750	11,37,38,48,64
Thaller, Gregg	IN0550	65,32,13C,38
Thomas, Phillip E.	TN0850	13,12,38,66A
Thomas, Richard B.	SC1000	62C,11,38,12A,62D
Thomas, William	AG0650	32F,37,38
Thompson, David	WI0804	38
Thompson, J. Lynn	VA0150	38
Thompson, Jason	IN1025	38,62A,62B,51,62C
Thompson, John	AA0050	38,62B,41
Thompson, Jonathan	AB0090	11,36,12A,60,38
Thompson, Steven D.	CA0150	37,38,63C,11,13A
Thomson, George	CA2910	38
Thye, David R.	TX2600	60,32D,32E,36,38
Tjornehoj, Kris	WI0845	38,11,60B,37,32E
Tobey, Forrest	IN0400	38,47,13,34
Todd, Kenneth W.	CO1050	11,38,51,62
Tomaro, Annunziata	OH2200	38,60B
Topilow, Carl	OH0600	60,38
Torok, Debra	PA2450	12A,13,38,66A,20G
Trinkle, Steven W.	NV0050	63,41,42,38,13A
Tucker, Stephen Earl	CA5020	60,38
Tueller, Robert F.	ID0060	38,62C,67B
Turner, Cynthia Johnston	NY0900	60,37,41,42,38
Turner, Gregory E.	KS0400	13,38,36,60,61
Tuttle, Marshall	OR0550	13,36,38
Tweed, Randall L.	CA2100	38,36,12A
Twomey, Michael P.	TX1900	10A,13,10F,38,62
Tyler, Philip	CA3640	62A,38
Underwood, Kirsten F.	OK0150	62,38,11,62C,20
Upham, David	NH0350	38
Valcarcel, Andres	PR0100	62A,62B,51,38
Valdivia, Hector	MN0300	10F,60,11,38,41
Valente, Liana	FL1550	61,38,13E,39,12A
Van Der Sloot, Michael	AA0040	62A,62B,38,41
van Deursen, John	AB0060	47,38,63C,63D
Vance, Paul	MN1700	12A,62D,38,51,62C
Vandehey, Patrick	OR0250	60,32,37,38,63C
VanDieman, Jeremy	AA0050	38,62A
Varon, Neil	NY1100	38,60
Vernon, Ronald	MS0700	38
Viliunas, Brian	AL0800	64C,38,13C,32E,60B
Villa, Tara Towson	NC0550	11,38,60B
Vodnoy, Robert L.	SD0400	12A,62,38,51,35E
Volchansky, Vera	PA2350	11,38
Voldman, Yakov	LA0650	60,32C,38,51,62
Wachs, Daniel Alfred	CA0960	38,60B
Waddelow, Jim M.	NC1300	41,62,38,32E
Wadley, Darin J.	SD0600	65,50,13A,13C,38
Waggener, Joshua A.	NC2350	12A,38,13E
Wagner, Jan	VA1350	60B,38
Wagner, Lawrence R.	PA3250	60,38,48,64C
Wagner, Richard A.	OK1450	38
Waldvogel, Nicolas	CA5350	38,60B
Walker, James A.	NY3730	60,37,38,41
Wallin, Nicholas L.	IL1400	38,13,11,20
Wang, Yung-Hsiang	TX3400	62A,12A,38,11
Ward, Steven D.	TX0050	60B,37,38
Warkentien, Vicky	IN0200	13,66,41,51,38
Watanabe, Hisao	OR0350	13C,13D,13F,38,66D
Wedington-Clark, Darlene	AZ0490	38
Weichel, Cynthia	CA4460	38
Weimann, Viljar P.	AL1250	62A,62B,38,10F
Weinert, William	NY1100	36,38,60
Wheeler, Ron	OK0850	38,60B,62B
White, Barry R.	NY1300	37,38
White, Tyler G.	NE0600	10,38
Widner, Paul	AG0450	62,38
Wieck, Anatole	ME0440	38,62A,62B,11
Wieligman, Thomas	IN0900	37,38,43,46
Wilcox, John	OH2600	38,62A,62B,41
Wiley, Frank	OH1100	13,10,38,60B,43
Wiley, Jennifer Sacher	PA3150	38,62A,32E
Williams, Mark D.	CA2440	13,36,61,38,34
Williams, Shane	MO0650	11,13,32E,38,41
Williams, Tom	AI0150	38,51,62A
Wilson, Peter	OH2050	38
Wilson, Peter Stafford	OH0450	38
Winkler, Frank	IL1085	38
Wolynec, Gregory J.	TN0050	37,38,10F
Wooden, Lori L.	OK1330	64D,41,38,42,48
Woodruff, Neal	IL2300	60,36,38,61,12A
Woods, Carlton	MI0400	38,60
Woolweaver, Scott	MA2010	38,41,51,62B,62A
Wright, Richard	NY4050	13,11,13C,66A,38
Wyman, Pat	AF0120	62A,62B,38
Yampolsky, Victor	IL2250	38,60
Yanovskiy, Leonid	FL2100	62A,62B,38,11,41
Yanovskiy, Leonid	FL1500	62A,62B,38
Yarrow, Anne	NY2450	38,62A
Yasuda, Nobuyoshi	WI0803	38,62A,51
Yates, Jonathan	NY3560	38
Yeung, Angela C.	CA5200	13,38,41,42,62C
Yeung, Ian	TX3540	36,60A,40,31A,38
You, Yali	MN0800	38,41,62C,11,12A
Zacharius, Leanne	AC0050	38,62C,51
Zahab, Roger E.	PA3420	38,13,10F,43,62A
Zelle, Tom	IL2100	60B,38
Zeniodi, Zoe	FL0200	38
Zimmerman, Christopher	CT0650	60,38
Zimmermann, Gerhardt	TX3510	38,60B
Zollman, Ronald	PA0550	38,60B

Opera

Name	Code	Areas
Adams, David	MO1790	39,61
Adams, J. Robert	GA0490	61,14,11,39,40
Adams, Kenny L.	OK0700	60,36,39,54,40
Ahearn, Kathryn	VA1475	61,39
Aks, David M.	CA0835	12A,13C,39,60B,62C
Albano, Michael	AG0450	39
Alderson, Daphne	PA3000	61,39
Allbritten, James	NC1650	36,61,39
Allebach, Robin	ND0600	39,61
Allen, Ivalah	KS0350	61,39,12A,20F
Alley, Laura	NY2250	39
Almy, Mark	CA1270	39,61
Altenbach, Andrew	MA0350	39
Amato, Patricia	MD0850	36,39
Amaya, Joseph	NC0050	39,61
Ambrosini, Rebekah	OK1200	39,61
Amonson, Christina	AL1050	60A,32D,39
Anderson, Alfred	OH2150	39,54,61
Anderson, Cheryl M.	CA0400	13,36,39
Anderson, Juliet V.	GA0490	11,39,61
Anderson, Marilyn E.	CA3100	39,61,54
Anderson, Toni P.	GA1200	61,39
Andrews-Smith, Belinda	OH0850	61,36,39
Anglin, David Ives	CA0825	61,39
Arbogast, Jennifer	TN0260	11,13C,54,61,39
Archambeault, Noel	DE0150	61,39
Armistead, Christine	MO1900	39,61
Arnold, Elizabeth Packard	KY1450	61,39
Arreola, Brian	NC2420	61,39
Ashbaker, Susan	NJ1350	61,39
Ashbaker, Susan	PA0850	39
Astafan, Marc A.	PA3250	39,61
Astafan, Marc	MA1400	39
Astrup, Margaret	CT0800	39,61
Aubrey, Julia	MS0700	39,61
Bado, Richard	TX2150	39
Baerg, Theodore	AG0500	39,61
Baggech, Melody A.	OK0300	61,40,39
Bagwell, Thomas	NY2250	66C,39,40
Baker, Mark A.	OH0350	61,39,54
Baker, William	IN0005	12,13,60,36,39
Baldini, Christian	CA5010	38,10,13,39
Balke, Maureen	MI0100	13C,39,61
Ballam, Michael	UT0300	39,54
Ballinger, Robert W.	OH2300	39,66C,11,13A
Balthrop, Carmen A.	MD1010	61,39
Baltz, Ann	CA0835	39
Bamberger, David	OH0600	39
Banister, Linda	GA0250	11,39,61
Banks, Richard	NC1600	39,61,60A
Bankston, David	SC0420	61,39
Barasorda, Antonio	PR0115	61,39
Barrett, Richard	NY0500	39,61,60
Barsamian, Aram	CA2420	61,39
Basinski, Anne	MT0400	61,54,39
Basney, Nyela	IL2100	39
Bastian, William	MN0450	39,61,11
Baum, Joshua	IL0150	61,11,39,12
Bazell, Marciem	MO1810	39
Beasley, Kimberly	FL1000	61,54,39
Beaupre, Odette	AI0220	39,61
Beck, Barbara Geiser	CO0275	61,39,54,66C,42
Becker, Jeral Blaine	MO1250	61,36,11,60,39
Beebe, Harriet	OH2550	39,61
Belich, Kay	WI0150	39,61,32B
Belnap, Michael	HI0050	36,39,40,54,61
Bender, Susan Maria	WI0850	61,39,40
Bengochea, Sandra	CA5510	61,39,54
Benner, Emily	MI0100	61,39
Benson, Ann	SC0420	61,39
Bentz, Anne Hagan	PA3650	61,39

Index by Area of Teaching Interest

Name	Code	Areas
Benz, David	MO0850	61,39,40
Berg, Gregory	WI0250	11,61,39
Berkeley, Edward	NY1900	39
Berkolds, Paul	CA0510	61,39,40,12A,68
Best, Richard W.	IL2900	39,61
Bickel, Jan	IL2650	39,61
Bickham, Teri	MD0850	61,39
Biernacki, Krzysztof K.	FL1950	61,39
Binneweg, Anna	MD0060	38,39
Blackburn, Royce F.	ND0500	61,54,39
Blackshear, Glinda	AL0831	60,11,36,39,61
Blackwood, Jeremy	OK1150	61,39
Blades, Jennifer A.	MD0650	39
Blaisdell, Gayla Bauer	WA0050	61,39
Blier, Steven	NY1900	39
Boaz, Virginia Lile	TX0600	12,61,39,12A
Bohannon, Kenneth	OK1400	39,61,35A
Boianova, Linda	NY2650	66A,13C,61,39,66C
Bomgardner, Stephen D.	MO0350	61,39,12A,11
Boresi, Matthew	WI0250	54,39
Borowitz, Michael J.	LA0200	39
Bostic-Brown, Tiffany	AL1250	39,61,54,13A
Boswell, Michael	IN1400	39,61,12A
Bouterse, Ami K.	WI0835	61,39
Boutte, Tony L.	FL1900	61,39
Bowles, DeVera	ND0250	61,39
Bowles, Kenneth E.	ND0250	36,61,39,60,32C
Bradley, Mark	KY0400	12C,32G,36,39,61
Brady-Riley, Carolyn	IL2650	39,61
Brandes, Christine	CA4200	11,13C,32D,39,61
Brandt, Robert	DE0150	61,39
Braun, Mel	AC0100	39,61
Brautigam, Keith D.	IN1025	61,39
Breault, Robert	UT0250	39,61
Brecher, Benjamin	CA5060	61,39
Brendel, Cheryl M.	TN0850	39,61
Brendel, Ronald S.	TN0850	61,39
Briante, Kate	MD0060	39,61
Bridges, Alban Kit	IL0750	39
Briones, Marella	MO0650	61,11,36,32B,39
Brockington, Frances N.	MI2200	61,39
Brookens, Karen	UT0350	61,39
Brooks, Susan G.	MA0950	13,39,61
Brou, Melinda A.	TX2960	61,39,54,13C
Brown, Eileen Duffy	FL1300	39,61,54
Brown, James L.	WA0650	61,39
Brown, Melba	AL1195	32,61,11,39
Brown, Robert	CA1270	39
Brown, Samuel B.	AL0500	39,61,31A
Brown, Terrance D.	AL1250	39,54,61
Brubaker, Debra	IN0550	39,61,36,31A,20
Bruce, Garnett R.	MD0650	39
Brunyate, Roger	MD0650	39
Bryan, Alan	MN1625	11,39,61,54
Bryant, Edward	FL1740	13C,36,61,39,40
Buchanan, Mary Lenn	MS0250	39,61
Buck, Robin T.	CA5020	39,61
Buddo, J. Christopher	NC0650	62D,38,39
Budlong, Trisha	PA2450	39,61,32
Buhaiciuc, Mihaela	AL1195	39,13,61
Bullock, Betty	DC0170	66A,39
Bullock, Emily A.	PA3600	61,39
Bultema, Darci A.	SD0400	11,61,39
Bundage, Raphael	TN1100	36,39,60A
Burchinal, Frederick	GA2100	39,61
Burgess, Mary	NY3705	39,61
Burkot, Louis G.	NH0100	36,61,39
Burns, Susan M.	CA0630	13A,11,39,61,54
Bussineau-King, D. E.	TX3410	61,15,39
Butler, Kate S.	NE0600	61,39
Butterfield, Benjamin	AB0150	61,39
Byerly, Douglas	MD0060	13,36,39
Bylsma, Kevin	OH0300	39,61
Bynum, Leroy E.	GA0150	12A,39,61
Cain, Bruce A.	TX2650	39,61
Caldwell, Susan	NY2250	39
Caldwell, William	OH0500	36,39,61,60
Cantu, Jacob	TX2200	61,39
Caporello, Corradina	PA0850	39
Caporello-Szykman, Corradina	NY1900	39
Carballo, Kimberly	IN0900	39
Cardenas, Octavio	TX0300	39
Carey, Milissa	CA4150	39
Carter, Clarence	IL2900	39,61
Carter, LisBeth	NC0750	61,39
Carter, Susan	MO0850	61,40,54,39
Carthy, Nicholas	CO0800	39,54
Carver, Kate	AG0450	39
Castel, Nico	NY1900	39
Castro, Margarita	PR0150	11,39,61
Cataneo, Daniel O.	NY1900	39
Cathcart, Kathryn	CA4150	39
Cazan, Ken	CA5300	39
Celaire, Jaunelle R.	AK0150	36,39,40,61
Chafin, Robert	VA1700	13C,39,34,61
Channing, Lynn	AJ0100	39,61
Charney, Miriam	NY4450	66A,39
Chauls, Robert	CA2750	11,38,66A,10A,39
Cheek, Timothy Mark	MI2100	66C,39,61
Chesko, Elizabeth Unis	OH0650	61,39
Chien, Hsueh-Ching	CA3270	39,61
Chilcote, Kathryn S.	PA3600	39,61
Chipman, Michael	UT0400	61,39
Cho, Tony	CA0960	66C,39
Chookasian, Lili P.	CT0850	39,61
Chown, Andrew	PA3250	39,61
Christensen, Janielle	UT0050	12A,36,39,54,35
Christeson, Jane	FL1750	61,12A,39,36
Christeson, Norton M.	FL0400	36,38,39,61
Christiansen, Philip	OH1900	61,39
Christie, Laury	SC1110	39,61
Christman, Sharon Lynn	DC0050	61,39
Christopher, Edward	PA2750	61,39
Christopherson, Anne	ND0500	39,61
Chun, Soyoun Lim	KS0200	61,39
Chung, Suna	NY3560	13A,13,39,61,13C
Church, Celeste	TX1100	61,39
Church, Gregory E.	TX1100	61,39
Clark, Mark Ross	LA0770	39,54,61,11
Clatworthy, David	NY3705	61,39
Clements, Jon	AR0200	61,39,13C
Cline, Judith A.	VA0550	39,61,54,20G,11
Cloutier, David	TX3420	39,66C
Cody, David	MT0400	36,61,54,39,60A
Cohen, Allen L.	NJ0400	13,10,54,39,36
Colaneri, Joseph	NY2250	39
Cole, David C.	FL0680	38,51,39,62A,32
Coleman, William Dwight	GA1050	61,39
Collett, Jacqueline L.	MO1780	32,36,61,39
Collister, Phillip	MD0850	61,36,39
Colon, Frank	VA0450	66C,39
Coloton, Diane S.	IL2900	61,39
Combs, Ronald	IL2150	39,61
Condacse, Anne Marie	OK0800	61,39
Condy, Steven	PA2800	61,39
Conklin-Bishop, Lisa	TN0050	61,39
Conlon, Francis	DC0100	39,66A,66C,54
Conner, Stacey	PA0600	36,39,61
Connolly, Donna	NJ0825	39,40,54,61
Conoly, Shaaron	TX3100	12A,39,61,54
Cook, Samuel	TX0050	61,39
Cooper, Darryl	CA4150	39,66C
Cooper, Jessica	MA2010	39,61
Corcoran, Kathleen	AA0110	12A,61,39
Corley, Sheila	AZ0400	32C,36,39,61
Corman, David	TX1850	39,36,40
Cornett, Eileen	MD0650	66C,39
Cornish, John	OK0150	36,39,60A,61,13B
Cossa, Dominic	MD1010	39,61
Costigan-Kerns, Louise	CA3270	39,61,66C
Cowart, Robert	NY1900	39
Cox, Kenneth	CO0900	39,61,54
Crabtree, Joseph C.	TX1425	11,12,36,39
Craig, James	AG0450	39
Crannell, Wayne T.	TX0250	36,61,11,39,60
Cravero, Ann	IA0550	39,61
Crawford, Leneida	MD0850	61,39
Creese, Anne	CA2910	39
Creswell, Mary	IA0850	61,39
Cross, Richard	CT0850	39,61
Cuk, John	NY2200	36,39,54,40
Culpepper, Jacquelyn	NC0550	39,61
Culver, Carrie	OH0700	61,39
Cumberledge, Melinda	IN1010	61,39
Cuttino, Walter E.	SC1110	61,39
Daigle, Steven	NY1100	61,39
Daniel-Cox, Minnita D.	OH2250	61,39
Dantzler, Drake M.	MI1750	61,39
Darnell, Debra Jean	FL0680	61,11,39
Davidson, Harry	OH0600	39
Davis, Richard	WI0815	39,61
Dawson, Lisa	IN1025	61,39
Day, Mary	IA0100	41,61,67,31A,39
Day, Melanie	VA1600	39,61
Day, Susan	WI0840	61,39
De Chambrier, Jan	TX2150	39
De La Garza, Rene	RI0300	39,41,61
De La Vega, Anne M.	CA3500	61,54,39
De Sousa, Beth Ann	AG0600	13,39,66C
De Souza, Jordan	AI0150	66C,39
Dean, Jay L.	MS0750	60,38,39
De'Ath, Leslie	AG0600	66A,39
Deaton, Tony	TN0850	61,39
DeBoer, Katharine	NV0100	39,61
DeCaumette, Patrick	PA3330	39,10
DeCoro, Helena	CA1520	61,66A,11,12A,39
Delmore, Jack	CO0225	36,39,61,54
Delos, Michael	WA0200	61,39
DeMaris, Brian	NY1800	39,54
DeMent, Melanie	DE0150	39,61
DeRosa, Julia	MI1800	61,39,13C
DeSimone, Robert A.	TX3510	39
DeVenney, David P.	PA3600	36,39,60A,61
Devol, Luana	NV0050	61,39
Dewey, Cynthia	UT0300	61,54,39,13A
Di Costanzo, John	NY3705	39
Diazmunoz, Eduardo	IL3300	39,43,60B
DiChiera, David	MI2200	39
Dickens, Pierce	GA0950	39,66A,66C,66G
Dickinson, Debra	TX2150	39
Dill, Patrick	LA0550	39,61
DiPalma, Maria	IA1350	12A,39,61
Dobbs, Linda M.	WV0400	39,61
Dolacky, Susan	WA0860	11,39,61,66D,54
Dolter, Gerald	TX3200	39,61,54
Domenici, Gianna	IL0420	39,61
Dorgan, Paul	UT0250	39
Draayer, Suzanne Collier	MN1700	39,61,11
Drews, Richard	IL2250	39,61
Dreyfoos, Dale	AZ0100	39
Dronkers, Marcelle	CA3270	39,42
Dubberly, Stephen	TX3420	39
Ducharme, Michel	AI0190	39,61
Dudley, Sherwood	CA5070	13,10F,12A,39
Dufault, Jenny E.	MN1120	32B,39,61
Dundas, Robert B.	FL0700	39,61
Dunn, Cherry W.	MS0550	61,39,15
Dunn, Susan	NC0600	61,39
Duvall, William	WI0825	39,61
Dybdahl, Gene	OH0300	39
Eckard, Kevin L.	OK1330	39,61
Eckenroth, Karen	OH2050	39,61
Eckert, Stacy	IL2650	36,39,61
Effler, Charles E.	LA0650	66C,39,13C
Eggert, Andrew	IL0550	39
Eggleston, Amy	IN1650	39
Eliasen, Mikael	PA0850	39
Ellis, Diana L.	TX1650	61,39,40
Elser, Albert Christian	SC1000	61,12A,34D,39
Emelio, Melanie	CA3600	40,61,39
Engelhart, Robert	MI1600	39,61,36,11
Engler, Kyle C.	MD0520	39,61,54
Enlow, Charles	WA0860	66D,40,54,39
Enman, Cora	MI0400	39,61
Ensley, Mark	TN1680	39
Epp, Richard	AB0100	39,66C
Erickson, Kim	AG0170	13,36,20,39
Eros, Peter	WA1050	60,39
Errante, Valerie	WI0825	61,39
Esquivel, Karen L.	OR1050	61,39
Estes, Richard A.	TX3000	39,61
Estes, Simon	IA0850	39,61
Eylon, Orit	TX3520	39
Farlow, William	WI0815	39,61
Farquharson, Linda J.	IL1200	39,61
Fee, Constance	NY3350	61,39
Feldmann, Linda	WI0750	61,39
Fern, Terry L.	NC0850	11,39,61,54,69
Ferrara, William	OK1350	39
Ferrell, Mark T.	KS1350	39,61,66C
Field, Jonathon	OH1700	39
Fingalson, Vicki	WI0860	61,39
Fink, Tim J.	IL2900	39,61
Finley, Carolyn Sue	MN0350	39,61
Firestone, Adria	NJ0825	39,61
Fischer, Martha	WI0815	66A,66C,39,41

Index by Area of Teaching Interest

Name	Code	Areas
Fisher, Douglas	FL0850	39
Fithian, Bruce S.	ME0500	39,12A,61
Fitzpatrick, Tod M.	NV0050	61,39
Fletcher, Ryan	VA0250	61,39
Flynn, Timothy	MI1800	10A,12,36,39,13
Foradori, Anne	NE0590	39,61,54
Foster, Julia	FL1550	39,61
Fowler, John H.	SC1200	61,39
Fralick, JR	OH0200	61,39
Franks, Russell	FL1750	61,39
Fraser, Malcolm	OH2200	39
Fraser, Stacey	CA0845	61,39
Frazer, Liz	VA0350	61,11,39
Frazier, Larry R.	GA2130	39,61
Fre, Anna	PA3250	39,61
Fredrickson, Ann	MN0200	61,36,39,54,13C
Freeman, Carroll	GA1050	39
French, Paul T.	OR0950	11,12A,36,39,61
Frey, Loryn E.	LA0150	12A,39,61
Fried, Janet Gottschall	MN0050	61,39
Frisbie, Jodi	KS0150	61,36,39,13C
Fritsch, Greg	CA3270	39,54
Froese, Elvera	AG0600	39,66C,36
Frost, James	TN0850	39,40,61
Furumoto, Kimo	CA0815	38,39
Gable, Garry	AJ0150	61,54,39
Gall, Jeffrey C.	NJ0800	55,61,12A,12,39
Galloway, Melanie	CA0250	39,61
Garfein, Herschel	NY2750	39,54
Garnica, Kevin	CA0350	11,66A,39
Gehrenbeck, Robert	WI0865	36,40,39,60A
George, Andrew	TX3200	38,60B,39,32E
Gerritson, Sasha L.	IL2150	11,13C,39,13A
Gesteland, Tracelyn K.	SD0600	61,39
Geyer, Gwynne	PA1300	39,61
Giampa, Janice	MA2030	61,39
Gibson, Mark I.	OH2200	38,39
Gibson, Mila	TX0100	39,61
Giessow, David	MA2010	36,39,61,32B,32C
Giles, Bob	TX3350	39,61
Gilliam, Christopher	NC0550	39,61
Gilmore, Pamela A.	NJ1130	39
Gilmore, Scott	IL0550	39,61
Givens, Hugh	MN1300	39,61
Glann, Kerry	OH1100	20,36,39
Glenn, Larry M.	CO0900	39,61,54
Goeke, Christopher L.	MO1500	39,41,61,54
Goetzinger, Laurel E.	IN0100	61,39,54
Golden, Joseph	GA0550	39,66G,11,12
Golden, Ruth E.	NY2105	39,61,11
Goldhamer, Brahm	AG0300	66C,39
Goldstein, Steven	OH2200	54,39
Golliver, April	OK0800	61,39
Goodheart, Thomas	NY3705	61,39
Goren, Neal	NY2250	39
Gorham, Dee Ann	TX2955	61,39
Gotera, Jose	OH1000	61,39,54,36
Graham, Carleen R.	NY3780	39
Graham, Elizabeth	FL1850	39,61
Graham, Sandra	AG0400	61,39
Gramelspacher, Addie	IL1100	39,61
Grant, Allison	AG0450	39
Grant, Andrea	AG0450	39
Graves, Tifton	OH2400	39,61
Gray, Colleen G.	PA3100	61,39
Gray, Donald N.	SC1110	39,61
Grayson, Robert E.	LA0200	61,39
Green, Elvira	NC1600	39,61
Green, Martin	CA1000	11,13H,32D,36,39
Greenwald, Laura	NJ0050	36,13C,61,39
Greer, John	MA1400	39
Gregory, Arikka	GA0950	39,61
Greif, Carol	WI0150	61,39
Gresham, Kathryn	NC0250	61,39
Grevlos, Lisa	SD0050	39,61,32B,36,32D
Griffeath, Kristin	OK1250	12A,61,39,36
Grimes, Rebecca	TX2250	39,61
Grives, Julie	IL2050	39,61
Grogan, David C.	TX3500	61,32D,36,39,40
Guarino, Robert	NJ0175	61,55,39
Guccione, Rose	IL2750	39
Guechev, Guenko	PA1050	61,39
Guelker-Cone, Leslie	WA1250	36,39,61
Guenther, Greg	AZ0480	61,39
Guiterrez, Charles	CA2550	39,53,46,35B,34
Gulick, Michelle	VA1600	39,61
Gustafson, Nancy J.	NJ1130	39,61
Hacker, Kathleen M.	IN1650	61,39
Haecker, Allyss	SC0900	61,20,36,39
Haffner, James	CA5350	39,61,54
Hahn, Mari	AK0100	61,39,54,32D
Hak, Rakefet	CA5030	39
Hallman, Ludlow B.	ME0440	36,61,39
Hammett, Hank	TX2400	61,66C,39
Hancock, Kyle	GA0950	39,61
Hand, Angela R.	IL3500	61,39
Hansen, Patrick J.	AI0150	61,39
Hanson, Ellen	GA2200	12A,61,39
Hardy, Janis	MN1450	61,39,54
Harley, Anne	CA4500	61,39,12
Harney, Jon M.	MT0200	36,39,40,61
Harper, David R.	RI0150	11,61,54,39,40
Harrell, Richard	CA4150	39
Harrington, Elisabeth	CA2250	39,61,13C
Harris, Hilda	NY3560	39,61
Harris, Howard	TX3150	13A,10,37,47,39
Harrison, Luvada A.	AL0950	61,39
Harte, Monica	NY0500	61,39
Hartmann, Donald	NC2430	39,61
Hartzell, Richard	MD0400	61,39,54
Harwood, Susan	NY0700	39,36,61,40
Hastings, Mary Logan	PA1600	39,61,54
Hayes-Davis, Lucy	AF0100	39,61
Haynes, Kimberly	FL0100	12A,39,61
Hearne, Clarice	IL3370	61,39
Hedges, Don P.	IL3150	13,31A,11,39
Helfgot, Daniel	CA4400	39
Heller, Ryan	WA0480	36,39,61
Heller, Wendy B.	NJ0900	12A,12,39,14A
Helms, Elizabeth	CA5360	66C,13A,13C,36,39
Helton, Jerry L.	SC1200	61,39
Henderson, Allen C.	GA0950	61,39
Henderson, Elaine	PA2300	39,61,54
Hendrickson, Brandon P.	SD0600	61,39
Hendsbee, Blaine	AA0200	61,39
Hensel, Larry L.	WY0200	39,61
Henson, Bill	MI1800	61,39,13C
Henson, Karen A.	NY0750	11,15,39,12A,12B
Herendeen, David	OK0750	39,54
Hermiston, Nancy	AB0100	12A,39,61
Hess, Benton	NY1100	61,39
Hess, John	AG0500	66A,66C,41,39
Hibbitt, Peyton	NY3705	39,61
Hicks, Lori C.	SC0350	61,39,32D
Hicks, Pamela A.	CA0807	61,39
Hiester, Jason A.	OH2000	36,39,40,60A,61
Higgins, William L.	AR0300	39,61,60A,13C
Hill, Serena	SC0450	39,61
Hinshaw, Susan	WA0480	39,61
Hobbs, William	NJ1350	39
Hoch, Matthew	AL0200	61,36,39
Hoffman, Lee	OH0500	39,61,66C,54
Hogan, George	TX3415	61,39,54
Hogan, Hallie Coppedge	NC0750	39,61
Hogan, Penny	TX3415	61,39,54
Holden, Robert	AR0850	61,39
Holeman, Janet	TN0930	39,61
Holland, Rachel J.	VA0150	61,39
Holley, David	NC2430	39,61
Hollingsworth, Christopher	TX0900	61,39
Holliston, Robert	AB0210	66C,12A,11,39,66A
Holman, Leigh	CO0800	39,61
Holman, Sarah	IL3550	39,61
Holmes, Isaac	GA1600	60A,11,36,61,39
Holz, Beatrice	KY0100	32B,36,39,61,32D
Holzschuh, Craig	AB0100	39
Homer, Paula	TX3420	39
Hopkin, J. Arden	UT0050	39,61,54
Hopkin, Teresa	GA0750	39,61
Hopkins, Janet E.	SC1110	61,39
Hopkins, John R.	AK0150	36,39,61,60
Horst, Sandra	AG0450	39
Hostetter, Paul K.	GA0550	38,39,60B,43
Houghtaling, Paul	AL1170	39,61
Howe, Stuart	AA0100	39,61
Howle, Patrick	KS1050	61,39
Hueber, Thomas E.	MO1780	39,61
Huntington, Tammie M.	IN1025	61,39
Hurst-Wajszczuk, Kristine M.	AL1150	61,39
Hutchings, Doreen L.	MN1280	61,39
Hyberger, Brett	TN0260	61,11,39
Hyberger, Sarah Amanda	TN0260	11,13C,54,61,39
Ilban, Serdar	TX1400	61,39
Im, Miah	AG0450	39
Jackson, Dennis C.	ID0250	39,61
Jacobs, Marc	CA3270	39,54
Jacobs, Patrick	AL1195	61,39
James, Clarity	VA1100	39,61
James, Matthew H.	LA0770	61,13D,39,54,60A
Jameson, Shelley	NY2900	39,61
Janas, Mark	NY2150	39
Jarman, Amy	TN1850	61,39,40
Jemison-Keisker, Lynn C.	UT0300	39,54
Jenkins, Donald P.	CO0200	60,36,39,41,54
Jepson, Angela	MA0400	39
Jobin-Bevans, Dean	AG0170	60,36,40,39
Joffe, Lucy	NY2400	39,61
Johnson, Alan O.	FL1900	61,39
Johnson, Byron	MS0050	13A,13B,13C,61,39
Johnson, Catherine	OH2050	39
Johnson, Craig	CA3640	61,39,11
Johnson, Eric D.	NY4150	61,39
Johnson, Joaquina Calvo	CA6050	36,39,61,67B
Johnson, Laura	IA1550	39
Johnson, Mary Jane	TX0100	39,61
Johnson, Molly	TX3535	61,54,39
Johnson, Teri	TX2800	61,11,39
Johnson-Wilmot, Daniel	WI1100	39,61
Jonason, Louisa	PA2250	39,61
Jones, Byron A.	VA1350	61,39
Jones, Dani S.	AL0650	61,39,31A,60
Jones, David	GA2000	61,39,42
Jones, Erik Reid	WV0550	36,39,40,60A,61
Jones, Jeffrey L.	SC0420	61,39
Jones, Joshua	IL1300	61,11,39,54
Jones, Kimberly	CA2810	39,61,54,53
Jones, Leslie I.	MO1500	61,39,11,54
Jones, Robert J.	ND0350	39,61,54,14
Jordan, Esther	CA2100	36,39,61,54
Jordan, Michael D.	TX1660	13A,13,11,39,61
Judisch, David	IA0950	39,61,32D
Kallick, Jenny L.	MA0100	13,12A,39,41,12
Kanakis, Karen	IA0950	61,39
Kano, Mark A.	KY0450	61,39
Kanouse, Monroe	CA2200	39
Kasper, Kathryn	KS0200	39,61,54,13C
Kazaras, Peter	CA5030	39,54
Keates, Peter	OH0500	39,61
Keck, Kimberly	TN0200	36,39,61,60A,13
Keele, Roger S.	TX1400	39,66A,61
Keeler, Paula	IA0150	32,36,39,41,61
Keitges, Christine	CO0050	39,61,54
Keller, Lisa	PA0850	39
Kelley, Frank	MA0400	39
Kelly, Liza	KY1550	61,39
Kelsey, Philip	WA1050	39
Kennedy, Frederick	TN1450	39,61
Kennedy-Dygas, Margaret	LA0760	61,39
Kenning, Kristin	AL0800	61,39
Kensmoe, Jeffrey	AL0300	61,39,36
Kern, Gene Marie Callahan	NY3650	61,36,13A,39
Kiesgen, Mary Stewart	MI0400	39,61
Killian, Joni	IN0700	61,36,39
Kim, Soo Hong	TX3500	61,39
Kim, Youngsuk	PA2150	12A,39,61
King, Ben R.	NY1700	11,12A,61,39
King, Marie A.	KS1450	39,54
King, Thomas R.	TN0050	39,61
Kirchner, Walter	IL2750	39,61
Kirk, Kenneth P.	GA2150	63A,49,13,39
Kisner, Brad	TX2930	66D,39
Klapis, Ralph	IN1750	61,39
Knapp, Brady	TX3450	39,40,36
Koehler, William D.	WV0750	61,39
Koestner, Bonnie	WI0350	39,61
Kompass, Lynn R.	SC1110	39,66C
Koreski, Jacinta T.	WA0800	61,39
Korjus, Ingemar	AG0400	39,61
Kosowski, Richard	GA1300	61,39
Kotze, Michael	IL2100	39
Kowalke, Kim	NY4350	12A,12,39,54,20G
Kramar, John S.	NC0650	61,54,39
Kraus, Philip	IL2250	39
Krause, Philip	IL2100	39,12C
Krebs, John A.	AR0350	66A,66C,39,11,13
Krogh, Dawn Pawlewski	NE0450	61,39

Name	Code	Areas
Kromm, Nancy Wait	CA4425	39,61
Krusemark, William	KS1375	36,39,61,54,11
Kuhnert, Brian	TX3650	61,39,54,40
Kuhnert, Cloyce	TX3750	61,39
Kunkle, Kristen C.	PA2000	61,39,11
Kuo, Kelly	TX3510	39,60A
Kvach, Konstantin	OR0150	61,39
Kyle, Maryann	MS0750	61,39
Kyriakos, Marika V.	AR0110	61,39
La Manna, Juan F.	NY3770	38,66A,66D,11,39
LaBouff, Kathryn	NY1900	39
LaCosse, Steven R.	NC1650	39,12A
Lacy, Christopher	AR0700	39
Laird, Helen L.	PA3250	39,61
Lake, Mary Kay	TX2250	61,39
Lambert, Debra	CA3270	61,39,54
Landry, Rosemarie	AI0200	61,39
Lane, Betty D.	MI2200	61,39
Lane, Kathleen	ID0100	39,61,36
Langford, Bruce	CA1000	11,12A,32D,36,39
Larkin, Christopher J.	NJ0800	39
Larsen, Robert L.	IA1350	12A,36,39,66A,66C
Larson, Jennifer	IA1800	39,61
Larson, Matthew	MA0400	39
Lassetter, Jacob	IA0950	61,39
Lata, Matthew	FL0850	39
Lavonis, William	WI0825	61,39
Lawrence, Cynthia	KY1450	61,39
Lawton, David	NY3790	60,12A,12,38,39
Leaptrott, Ben	GA0350	11,13,39,66A,66B
Leblanc, Jacques	AI0190	39
LeClair, Ben	IL0600	61,39
Lee, Chia-Wei	TX3350	39,61
Lee, Justina	MD1010	39
Lee, Raejin	CA2420	61,39
Lee, Soojeong	TX3300	61,39
Leeper, Brian K.	WI0865	61,39,54
Lefebvre, Marie-France	OH2200	39
Lehman, Carroll	NH0150	40,39,61
Leonard, Gwenellyn	OR0450	12A,61,39
Lerch, Natalie	WA0200	61,39
Lesenger, Jay	IL2250	39
Levine, Rhoda	NY2150	39
Levinson, Gina	NY1900	39
Levitt, Joseph	IN0150	39
Lewis, Alexander	FL1745	61,36,39
Lewis, Grant	SC0950	39,34,61
Lewis, William	TX3510	39,61
Lewis-Hale, Phyllis	MS0350	61,39,32D
Leyrer-Furumoto, Linda	CA2390	61,39
Liberatore, William	CA3270	39,54,60,61
Liles, B. David	OH1600	61,31A,39
Lilite, Louima	OK0650	61,39
Lindsay, Julia	MI0250	11,61,54,39
Linford, Jon	ID0060	39,61,32D
Liotta, Vincent J.	IN0900	39
Little, David	MI2250	39,61,54
Liu, Xiu-ru	PA1050	39,61
Llewellyn, Cherrie	CA3000	11,61,54,39
Lloyd, Charles	LA0700	13,39,11,66D
Lloyd, Kimcherie	KY1500	60,39,38
Lockwood, Gayle	UT0050	39,61,54,20G,35
Loehnig, Grant A.	TX2150	39
Loewen, Laura	AC0100	66A,39,66C
Loftus, Jean	NY2950	39,61,54,13A,13B
Long, Lillian F.	WV0050	61,66C,66G,39,44
Lopez, Ilca	PR0115	61,39
Lowenstein, Marc	CA0510	13,10,60,39,43
Lucius, Sue Anne	AZ0440	39,61,54
Luedloff, Brian Clay	CO0950	39
Luiken, Jennifer	SC0275	61,39,54
Lumpkin, William	MA0400	39
Lusk, Terry	OH2200	66C,39
Lynch, Kelly	PA0600	39,61,11,12A
Lyndon-Gee, Christopher	NY0050	10A,14A,38,39,42
Lynn, Debra J.	IN1050	60,36,61,40,39
Mabbs, Linda	MD1010	39,61
MacDonald, April	AL0200	61,40,39
MacDonald, Pamela	AF0120	61,39
MacIntyre, David K.	AB0080	13,10,39,43
MacNeil, Robert	CA1000	13A,39,61
Major, Elizabeth	MI0050	11,39,61
Major, Leon	MD1010	39
Malis, David H.	OK0800	61,39
Malone, Martha	GA1300	39,61
Mancusi, Roberto	TN1720	39,61,60A,13C
Mangialardi, Robert	IL1200	61,39
Mangin, Andy	IL3550	39
Mangrum, Leslie	KS0700	61,36,39,12A
Mantel, Sarah J.	PA1600	39,61,54
Marano-Murray, June	NY2150	39
Markham, Matthew E.	WI0850	61,39,40
Markou, Stella	MO1830	61,39,40
Markward, Edward	RI0200	38,61,60,39
Marlett, Judy	ID0150	32,36,39,54,60A
Martin, Jessie Wright	NC2650	61,39
Martindale, Peggy Lee	CA0200	35,39
Martinez, Jeordano S.	IL2050	12A,36,39,54,38
Masters, Richard J.	TX3510	66C,39
Mastrian, Stacey	PA1400	61,39
Mastrodomenico, Carol	MA1900	61,39,54
Mathieson, Carol Fisher	MO0300	12A,39,61,31A,11
Matos, Lucia Regina	IL2200	38,39,60B,66G,66H
Matts, Kathleen	WI1150	39,61
Maxedon, Lisa M.	LA0250	61,11,39
Maxwell, Don	TX1700	61,39
McCargar, Barbara Witham	MI0300	11,61,39
McCauley, William	SC0200	12A,36,39,61
McCormack, Jessica D.	IN0910	61,39,12,15,67H
McCorvey, Everett	KY1450	61,39
McCoy, Julie	TX3250	61,39
McCrary, William	TX3530	39,61
McCullough, Richard D.	NY2950	13A,36,39,61,66D
McDaniel, Jan	OK0750	39,54,66C,12A,61
McDaniel-Milliken, Jennifer L.	SC1200	39,16
McDonald, Shawn	MI1300	61,66C,39
McDonough, James D.	LA0200	39
McEvenue, Kelly	AG0450	39
McGee, Isaiah R.	SC0350	35,36,39,61,32D
McGhee, Jeffrey	NY3350	61,39
McKeel, James	MN1450	61,39,54
McKinney, Jane Grant	NC0900	32C,13B,32D,39
McMahon, Michael	AI0150	39,40,66C,61,66A
McMunn, Brent	CA5300	39
McNeil, Linda	TX3350	39,61,54
McQuade, Jennifer H.	OK0650	61,39
McQuade, Mark A.	OK0650	61,39
Meadows, Christine	OR0850	39,61
Mellins-Bumbulis, Valija	TN0550	39,61
Mercier, Richard E.	GA0950	66A,66C,39
Meredith, Sarah A.	WI0808	39,61,54,15
Merrill, Kenneth	NY1900	39
Metcalf, Mark A.	TX3000	39,61
Meyers, Joseph	IN0905	39,61
Michael, Marilyn	FL1650	39,61
Mihai-Zoeter, Mariana	MD0350	61,39
Mikkelsen, Carol M.	GA2150	61,39
Milenski, Isabel	NY1600	39,54
Miller, Karen Coe	OK0750	54,39
Miller, Patricia A.	VA0450	39,61,54
Miller, Scott D.	WA1350	61,39
Miller, Thomas E.	CA5400	13B,13C,36,39,54
Mills, Kate Irvine	CA3270	39,54
Mims, Marilyn	FL1450	61,39
Minsavage, Susan	PA3700	61,39
Minter, Drew	NY4450	61,40,39
Minter, Karen	KS0100	12A,39,61
Mitchell, Christopher	KY0950	61,39
Modesitt, Carol Ann	UT0200	39,61
Mogle, Dean	OH2200	39,54
Moll, Brian	MA0350	39
Mollicone, Henry	CA3270	10A,12A,39,54,60
Momand, Elizabeth B.	AR0730	39,61,32
Moody, David	NY1900	39,61
Moody, David	PA0850	39
Moon, Gene H.	TX2700	38,39,66,62A,62B
Mooney, Chris	VA0150	61,39
Morelock, David	LA0300	39
Moremen, Eileen	GA1150	61,39
Moreno, Madja	PR0100	39,61
Moriarty, John	MA1400	39
Moritz, Alison	NY1100	39
Morris, Eric	CA3270	13C,39
Morris, Steven	MA1900	39,61,66C
Morrow, Lynne	CA4700	39,54,60A,61
Morrow-King, Janet	CO0250	61,39,12A
Mosher, Allan R.	OH2600	39,61
Mosteller, Steven	IL0750	39,61
Mount, John	HI0210	39,61
Mowry, Mark R.	WI0803	39,61
Moyer, John	PA1050	39
Mullen, Wendy Anne	GA0850	61,54,39
Mungo, Samuel	TX3175	61,39
Muni, Nicholas	OH2200	39
Murphy, Hugh	NY3785	39,66C
Murphy, Kevin	IN0900	39
Murphy, Sheila C.	FL2100	61,39,32D
Musmann, Lois S.	CA3270	12,39,60,66H
Musselman, Susan	OH2450	61,39
Musselwhite, Harry	GA0300	60,36,39,61
Muto, Vicki	CA1750	39,61
Myers, Myron	IL2200	39,61
Nagy, Karen	FL1310	39
Neal, David E.	NY3720	61,54,39,36
Nedvin, Brian A.	VA1000	61,39
Nelson, Alice	MO1950	39
Nelson, Daniel	WI0825	39,61
Nelson, Susan	NY2250	39
Ness, Corinne	WI0250	61,54,32B,39
Nettles, Darryl	TN1400	13B,32D,36,39,61
Neves, Joel	MI1450	38,39,42,20G
Newby, David L.	CA0200	13C,36,38,39
Newell, Julie L.	NY3725	39,61
Nichols, Will	MI0150	60,36,61,39
Nicholson, Hillary	RI0150	61,39
Niederloh, Angela	OR0750	61,39
Niu, Elaine	WI0750	61,39,36,60A,13C
Noonkester, Lila D.	SC0800	13,39,61,11
Norman-Sojourner, Elizabeth	IL0600	61,39,12
Novak, Richard A.	VA0450	61,39
Nowicki, Susan	PA0850	39
O'Brien, Susan	IL0550	39
Oby, Jason	TX3150	36,39,61
Ockwell, Frederick	IL2250	60,39,54
Octave, Thomas	PA2950	61,36,39,40,11
Oeste, Wolfgang	AR0850	39,61
Offerle, Anthony	FL1850	39
Ogle, Nancy Ellen	ME0440	39,61
Oh, Sun-Joo	TN0500	61,39
Olcott, Nicholas	MD1010	39
Ollmann, Kurt	WI0825	61,39
Olsen, David	ID0060	32D,39,61
Olson, Margaret	MD0600	61,39
Olson, Robert	ND0350	39,61,54
Opatz-Muni, Mari	OH1450	39,61
Orlando, Danielle	PA0850	39
Ormond, Nelda C.	DC0350	39,61
Ortega, Anne	PA1200	39,61
Osbun-Manley, Kirsten E.	OH1800	39,61,54
Osmond, Melissa	MI1000	61,39
Ostrowski, Gordon	NY2150	39
Ottley, JoAnn	HI0050	39,61
Ottsen, Linda	CA5360	61,39
Overholt, Sherry	NY0642	39,61
Overton, LeAnn	NY2150	39
Owens, Richard R.	FL1550	61,39
Padula, Dawn M.	WA1000	61,39
Page, Robert	PA0550	36,39
Paige-Green, Jacqueline	LA0700	61,39,11
Pajer, Curt	CA4150	39
Pape, John W.	MA0350	39
Parodi, Jorge	NY2150	39
Parodi, Jorge	NY0500	39,40,41,66C
Partridge, Norma	OK0650	39,61
Pasternack, Jonathan R.	WA1050	38,39,12A,60B
Patterson, Jonathan	AI0150	39
Patterson, Paula K.	MO0775	39,61
Patterson, Trent A.	MO1950	60A,61,32,36,39
Paxton, Laurence	HI0210	39,61,54
Payn, Catherine	PA0350	32,39,61
Payton, Denise	NC0800	20A,36,39,60A,61
Pedersen, Thomas	DC0050	36,39,54,56,61
Penhorwood, Edwin L.	IN0900	39
Pennix, Derrick A.	IN0200	61,39
Penny, Michael K.	TN1660	39,61,31A
Peress, Maurice	NY0642	60,38,39
Perez-Gomez, Jorge	NM0450	60,38,39
Perniciaro, Joseph C.	KS0350	39,61
Perrella, Anthony	IL2200	39
Perron, Francis	AI0200	39,66C
Peterson, Jeffrey Todd	TX0300	39
Peterson, Ken	UT0150	36,39,40,61
Petrie, Anne M.	IA0200	39,61
Pfaltzgraff, Brian	IA1800	61,39
Pfautz, John S.	IL0100	39,61,31
Pfutzenreuter, Leslie D.	CA2840	11,36,38,39,61

Name	Code	Areas
Phillips, Burr Cochran	CA5350	61,39
Pierce, Alice O.	MN1600	61,39
Piersall, Rick	TX0050	39,61,12A
Pilkington, Jonathan	GA1650	61,39,11
Pindell, Reginald	PA3330	36,39,61
Pippin, Donald	CA3270	39
Pittman, Reginald L.	KS0650	39,61,54
Playfair, David M.	AC0050	61,39
Pomfret, Bonnie	MA0400	39,61
Pope, Wayne	KY1550	39,61,41
Popham, Deborah	GA1800	61,39
Poppino, Richard	OR0700	61,39
Porter, Janine	OH0755	61,39
Post, Karen Leigh	WI0350	61,39
Potter, Thomas	FL1800	61,39
Pratt, Michael	NJ0900	60,38,43,39
Prewitt, Kenneth	MI2250	39,61
Price, Andrea M.	GA1650	61,39,14
Price, Henry P.	CA3600	61,39,12A
Pridmore, Helen	AE0050	61,39,41
Priebe, Craig	IN0150	61,39
Prindle, Roma	KY0900	39,61
Puller, Shawn I.	GA0150	11,61,12A,32A,39
Queen, Todd	CO0250	39,61
Quigley-Duggan, Susan E.	MO0100	61,39
Radford, Anthony P.	CA0810	61,39,54
Raffo, Laura	MA0400	39
Rahming, Dara	LA0900	61,39
Rain, Jack	FL2000	61,39
Raines, Scott	TX0150	39,61,11
Ralls, Stephen	AG0450	39
Ramael, David R.	NY1600	12,38,39,60B,51
Randall, Martha	MD1010	61,39
Ranney, Todd	PA2150	61,39
Ratner, Carl J.	MI2250	39,61,54
Rausch, Carol E.	LA0300	39
Rayam, Curtis	FL0100	36,61,40,39
Raynes, Christopher	ID0050	61,39,54
Reber, William F.	AZ0100	39,54,52,66C,60
Rednour, Scott	NY2150	39
Reed, Anne	OR0750	61,39
Reeder, Jefferson	NY3780	39
Reeves, Bethany	NY0270	11,36,39,60A,61
Regan, Patrick	MI1300	61,39,54
Regehr, Leanne	AA0100	39
Reigles, B. Jean	NY1700	36,39,60A,61
Reimer, Jamie M.	NE0600	61,39
Renbarger, Cory James	MN0150	39,61
Resick, Georgine	IN1700	39,61
Restesan, Francis'c	KY1000	38,51,39,62A
Retzlaff, Jonathan	TN1850	61,39,40
Reynolds, Jeff W.	AL1150	60,36,39
Reynolds, Marc	TX2930	61,39,13C
Rhyne-Bray, Constance	NC2000	39,61,20
Rice, Dana R.	MS0400	61,39
Rice, Laura Brooks	NJ1350	39,61
Richardson, David	WI1100	39,66C,61
Richardson, Diane	NY1900	39
Richardson, Diane	NY3705	39,61,66C
Richardson, James K.	VA0300	61,11,36,54,39
Rierson, Don G.	VA0600	39,11
Ripley, David	NH0350	61,39
Roberts, Connie	MS0850	39,61
Robertson, Fritz S.	IN0100	39,61
Robertson, Patricia	IN1560	39,61,32D
Robertson, Ruth M.	MO0600	36,39,61
Robinson, Bobb	NC2410	39,61
Robison, Jeanne	CA0350	61,39
Rockwell, Paula	AF0050	61,39
Rodgers, Elizabeth	NY2150	39
Rodgers, Jane Schoonmaker	OH0300	39,61
Rodgers, Susan	RI0200	61,39
Roe, Charles R.	AZ0500	39,61
Rogers, Sean	ID0070	36,39,60,66A,66G
Roll, Donna	MA1175	39
Rollene, Donna	AR0400	61,39
Rorex, Michael	LA0550	36,39,61
Roseberry, Lynn	OH0350	61,39,40,36
Rosinbum, Ralph R.	WA1050	39
Ross Mehl, Margaret	PA0600	36,39,61,11,12A
Ross, Buck	TX3400	39,54
Rowell, Melanie	SC1080	12A,61,54,39
Rowell, Thomas L.	AL1300	61,39,40
Rowland, Martile	CO0200	39,61
Roy, Lisa	AE0100	39,61
Roy, Shawn	LA0760	61,39
Royce, Matthew M.	CA3270	39,54
Ruck, Tanya Kruse	WI0825	61,39
Rushing-Raynes, Laura	ID0050	61,39,54
Ryvkin, Valery	PA3250	39
Sabo, Marlee	WI1150	39,61
Sachs, Carol	TX3515	39,61
Sadeghpour, Mitra M.	WI0803	61,39
Sadlier, David	VA0150	61,40,39
Sahuc, Paul N.	CA5060	61,39
Saito, Miki	OH0755	61,39
Salters, Mark	CA0815	61,39
Salyards, Shannon	IA1100	61,39
Sanders, Wayne	NY3560	39,61
Sannerud, David	CA0835	39,61
Santo, Amanda M.	RI0101	61,39,11
Saulsbury, Kate	IA1100	61,39,66D
Savage, Karen	VA1800	39,61
Savage, Samuel T.	IN0905	61,39
Savarino, Damian	PA2300	61,39
Saya, Virginia	CA2800	12A,39,12C,11
Sayre, Maya	OH2050	39
Schapman, Marc	IL2910	39,61
Scheib, Joy	WI0845	39,61
Schellen, Nando	AZ0450	39
Schiller, Caroline	AD0050	39,61
Schlaefer, Ellen Douglas	SC1110	39
Schleis, Thomas H.	IL3300	39
Schlimmer, Alexa Jackson	NC0930	39,61
Schlosser, Roberta	NY3705	39,61
Schmidt, Timothy A.	MO1500	61,39,54
Schoonmaker, Bruce W.	SC0750	39,61
Schreiner, Frederick	PA3710	11,12A,12,61,39
Schuetz, Jennifer Hilbish	OH0950	61,39
Sciolla, Anne	PA3330	39,47,61
Scott, Mary Anne Spangler	IN0250	61,39
Searle, David	DC0050	38,39,41
Sears, Peggy	CA0650	13A,39,61
Secrest, Jon	AR0500	39,61,54
Seesholtz, John C.	CO0250	61,39
Seigel, Lester C.	AL0300	60,36,39,66C,13F
Seitz, Carole J.	NE0160	39,61,11
Seitz, Christine	MO1800	39,11
Servant, Gregory W.	AF0100	39,61
Severtson, Kirk A.	NY3780	61,66C,39
Shafer, Sharon Guertin	DC0250	13,10F,12A,39,61
Shahani, Michael M.	CA1020	39,54,13A
Shames, Jonathan	OK1350	38,39
Shapiro, Gail S.	IL2250	39
Shay, Gayle D.	TN1850	39,61
Sheats, Jackson	VA1350	39,61
Sherman, Mozelle C.	KY1200	39,61
Shirley, George I.	MI2100	39,61
Shofner-Emrich, Terree	IL2100	66A,39,66B,66C,66D
Shomos, William	NE0600	39,61
Shrader, James A.	GA2150	60,12A,61,36,39
Shrut, Arlene	NY1900	39
Sicilian, Peter J.	NY3705	39,61
Siena, Jerold	IL3300	61,39
Sievers, David	OH2250	61,39
Sikora, Stephanie R.	OH0100	36,39,61
Silverstein, Harry	IL0750	39
Simmons, John	OH0600	39,12A
Simonson, Donald R.	IA0850	39,61,13L,34C,34D
Singler, Juliette	CA3640	61,39
Sirbaugh, Nora	NJ0750	12A,39,61
Sirota, Robert	NY2150	39,10
Skinner, Kent	AR0800	60A,36,61,39,54
Slon, Michael	VA1550	36,39,60
Small, Allanda	AL1195	61,39
Small, David	TX3510	61,39
Smart, Marilyn	FL1950	11,39,61
Smith, Andrew W.	KY0750	39,61
Smith, Benjamin W.	OH0200	39
Smith, Blake	DE0150	61,54,39
Smith, Brent	UT0190	39,62C,13,12A,51
Smith, Charles	NE0300	36,39,61,54
Smith, David	MD1000	36,39,60,61
Smith, Hannah	NE0200	61,39
Smith, Janet	CA0815	61,39
Smucker, Greg	MA1400	39
Snapp, Patricia	MN0750	61,39,40
Snyder, Linda J.	OH2250	39,61,11
Sokol, Michael	CA4100	39,61
Speedie, Penelope A.	KS0300	39,61
Speer, Shari	MN0610	36,39,61
Spencer, Mark	OH0450	39,61
Spies, Claudio	NJ0900	13,60,10,39
Spillman, Robert	CO0800	66A,39
Spivak, Mandy	WV0800	61,39
Springer, Samuel	MD0600	66A,39
St. Pierre, Donald	PA0850	39
Staab, Jane	MA2200	39,54
Stahl, Diane Willis	FL0800	39,61
Stallard, Tina Milhorn	SC1110	39,61
Starkey, David C.	NC1250	61,39,54
Starkey, Linda	KS1450	61,54,39
Staufenbiel, Brian	CA5070	61,39
Steele, Carol	FL1310	61,39
Steele, Timothy	MA1400	39
Steinau, David S.	PA3150	61,39,12A
Steinhaus, Barbara	GA0350	61,11,39
Stephens, John A.	KS1350	39,61
Stephens, Roger L.	TN1710	39
Stephenson, Geoffrey	OH0300	54,39
Stevens, Damon B.	NV0100	39,66A,66C,66D
Stevens, Jeffrey	MA0400	66C,39
Stieber, Marian	NJ1050	39,61
Stone, Terry	IL1750	61,39
Stone, William	PA3250	61,39
Stoner-Hawkins, Sylvia Frances	KS1400	61,39
Storojev, Nikita	TX3510	61,39
Strauss, Robert	NY2650	61,39
Strawn, Lee	CA3270	12A,39
Stringer, Vincent Dion	MD0600	61,39
Strother, Martin	VA1800	39,61
Strummer, Linda	OK1450	39,61
Sublett, Virginia	ND0350	61,39,54
Suderman, Gail	AB0060	36,61,40,39
Sulich, Stephen	MN0600	39
Sullivan, Melinda	MA1400	39
Sullivan-Friedman, Melinda	MA0400	39
Sutliff, Richard	OK0850	39,61
Sutton, Everett L.	MN1623	39
Svatanova, Lucie	SC0700	61,39
Swanson, Christopher	VA0700	13C,61,12A,11,39
Swanson, Donald	MA1400	39
Swanston, Marcia	AF0100	39,61,40
Swayne, Steven R.	NH0100	12A,12,39,54
Swinson, Beth Ann	IL3150	61,39,41
Tadlock, David	OH1400	61,13C,54,39
Talley, Dana W.	NY2900	61,12A,20,39,11
TangYuk, Richard	NJ0900	36,39,40
Tau, Omari	CA0840	61,39
Tavera, Celeste	CA5550	39
Tavernier, Jane	VA1475	61,36,39,40
Taylor, Steven	CO0150	39,61,31A,44,13C
Taylor, Ted	NY2250	39
Templeton, David M.	SC0500	61,39,11
Thieme, Robert	WV0750	39,66A,66C
Thom, Marcia	VA1400	61,39
Thomas, Colby L.	NY3765	39,60A,35F,61,54
Thomas, Laurel A.	IN1450	39,61
Thomasson, John	FL0800	39,61
Thompson, Jack	FL0800	61,39
Thompson, Lee D.	WA1300	12A,39,66A,66C
Thompson, Lynn	IL3500	61,54,39,36
Thompson, Sonja K.	MN0050	61,39,54,41,42
Thorburn, Melissa R.	NY0400	61,39
Thornton, Diane B.	NC0550	39,61
Thrasher, Lucy	MN0600	61,39
Throness, Dale	AB0060	61,39
Thull, Jonathan	IA0400	39,61,54
Tickner, French A.	AB0100	12A,39,61
Todd, Richard	FL1900	61,39
Toronto, Emily Wood	SD0550	39,61,54
Tosh, Melissa Denise	CA5150	61,36,39,54
Towne, Lora Rost	AZ0440	39,61,54,13
Tracy, William	NY2150	39
Trainer, Susan	WA0600	39,61
Transue, Arlene M.	IL2900	39,61
Transue, Paul A.	IL2900	66C,39
Troup, Nathan	MA0400	39
Truitt, Jon	IN1600	61,39
Trussel, Jacque	NY3785	36,39,61
Tucker, Eric Hoy	MI0400	61,39
Tudor, Robert W.	WV0550	61,39,54
Turner, Anne Z.	NY3650	36,39,61
Turner, Leon P.	TX2100	11,39,61
Turnbull, Elizabeth	AA0100	39,61
Twaddle, Katherine	AC0100	39

Name	Code	Areas		Name	Code	Areas
Twitty, Katrina	CO0100	61,39		Austin, Stephanie	CA1450	36,61,66,40,32
Tyler, Marilyn	NM0450	39,61		Babcock, Mark A.	IA0200	36,40,66G,13
Tynon, Mari Jo	ID0070	39,61,54		Bacon, Boyd	NE0450	13,36,61,40
Uhl, Lise	TX1600	39,61		Baggech, Melody A.	OK0300	61,40,39
Umeyama, Shuichi	IN0900	39		Bagwell, Thomas	NY2250	66C,39,40
Umfrid, Thomas C.	OH2200	39,54		Baird, Julianne C.	NJ1100	12A,12C,40,61,67E
Umphrey, Leslie	NM0450	61,39		Bales, Bruce	CA2050	40,61,67,13A,36
Unger, Shannon M.	OK0550	61,11,13C,39		Barber, Julie	IN1560	66A,61,40,12A
Upchurch, Elizabeth	AG0450	39		Barr, Stephen A.	PA3100	13,36,40,34
Valcu, Mihai	PA3650	39		Barton, Stephen	MI0850	36,40,11,12A,61
Valente, Liana	FL1550	61,38,13E,39,12A		Beckmann-Collier, Aimee	IA0550	60,36,40
Van De Graaff, Kathleen	IL1400	61,39		Belles, David	CT0150	36,40,60,61
Vaughn, Dona	NY2150	39		Belnap, Michael	HI0050	36,39,40,54,61
Versage, Susan Woodruff	NY2250	39		Bender, Susan Maria	WI0850	61,39,40
Vest, Jason	NM0100	61,39		Benz, David	MO0850	61,39,40
Vincent, Lawrence P.	UT0050	39,61		Berentsen, Kurt	OR0150	36,60,61,32A,40
Von Villas, Muriel	DC0100	11,39,54		Bergstrom, Melissa	MN0040	36,40,12A,38,61
Voth, Allison	MA0400	39		Berkolds, Paul	CA0510	61,39,40,12A,68
Vought, J. Michelle	IL1150	39,61		Billington, Ryan	AF0150	36,40,29,61
Vowan, Ruth A.	AR0225	61,12A,36,39		Biser, Larry	MI0300	34B,12A,40,66G
Vrenios, Elizabeth	DC0010	39,61,54		Bjella, Richard L.	TX3200	36,40
Wade, Gail G.	TX1600	13,39,66A,66D,66C		Black, Kathryn A.	NY3475	61,36,40
Wadsworth, Stephen	NY1900	39		Blackley, Rowland	OH0100	60A,32D,36,40,55D
Wagner, Jeanine F.	IL2900	39,61		Blackwell, Leslie	GA1150	36,40,60A
Walden, Sandra	IA1600	39,11,61		Blalock, Angela	SC0150	11,13A,13B,40,61
Walentine, Richard L.	ND0150	61,54,13A,39,12A		Blodget, Sherril	VT0100	40,36,60,61,11
Walker, Elizabeth	KS0750	39,61,54,35,34C		Bobbitt, Kayleen	MI0750	11,66,13,40
Walker, Regina	IN0907	39,40		Bogdan, Thomas	VT0050	36,61,31,40
Walsh, David	MN1623	39		Bohlin, Ragnar	CA4150	40
Walter, Elaine R.	DC0050	11,12A,39		Bolster, Stephen C.	KY0300	60,32D,36,40,61
Walters, Kerry E.	IL0400	61,32,39		Boone, Bridgett	IA1450	40
Ward, Frank	OH2150	61,39,54		Boullion, Linda	NE0460	13,11,40,36,61
Ward, Perry	TN1700	61,39		Bourquin, Cindy	CA4450	40,29A
Ware, John Earl	LA0900	11,36,39,41,61		Bouwman, Aaron	MI0520	36,40
Warfield, Tara	MS0500	61,39		Branch, Stephen F.	CA3975	12A,61,31A,36,40
Warren, Stanley	TN1660	61,39		Brannon, Patrick V.	IL3370	14,12A,36,60A,40
Warrick, Kimberly	OH2500	39,61		Briggs, Philip	TX2050	36,40,61,11
Waterbury, Elizabeth	CA4550	36,61,40,13A,39		Broman, John M.	GA1500	36,40,61
Watson, Tommy L.	SC0050	11,61,39,12A,13A		Bronfman, Joshua	ND0500	36,40,32D,60A
Watts, Ardean W.	UT0250	13,39		Brooks, C. Thomas	MA0950	60A,36,40,61
Webb, Adam	MS0500	61,39		Brooks, Jack	TX1510	36,61,40,13C
Weber, Brent	PA2250	61,32D,39,12A		Brown, Linda	CA3750	36,40,61
Wedow, Gary T.	NY1900	39		Brown, Trent R.	FL0680	36,40,60A
Weinel, John	TX1450	61,60,36,39,40		Brown, Zorriante	IL1520	40
Weinmann, Patricia	MA1400	39		Browning, Doug	MS0550	32,40,42,47,60
Welsch, James O.	NY4150	13,49,39		Bryant, Edward	FL1740	13C,36,61,39,40
Wenaus, Grant	NY2750	39,61,66C,66		Buchanan, Heather J.	NJ0800	32D,36,40,60A
Wentzel, Andrew	TN1710	39,61		Buettner, Jeff	VT0350	13A,36,40,13B,13C
Westergaard, Peter	NJ0900	13,60,10,39		Buffington, Blair	IA1750	61,36,40,32A,60A
Wheeler, Robin	AI0200	39		Burbach, Brock	FL0200	36,61,40
Whipple, Shederick Lee	IN1560	61,39		Burgher, R. Catherine	MO1550	40
White, Edward C.	AR0730	61,39,13		Burnett, Lawrence E.	MN0300	36,40,31F,61,13A
White, Frank	LA0700	13,39,66A,11,60		Cafagna, Carl	MI1750	47,40
Whitfield, Andrew D.	IA0950	61,39		Calhoun, James M.	CA5100	36,40,60
Whitney, Nadine C.	GA2200	12A,36,61,40,39		Cameron, Virginia	OH1600	60A,36,61,40,11
Whitten, Kristi	TN0100	39,61,66		Camp, Philip	TX1550	36,61,13,32,40
Wieck, Julie	WA1150	39,61,54		Campbell, Dianna	FL1700	61,36,40,11,32D
Wiggett, Joseph	CA0850	61,54,39		Carew, David	MI1985	36,61,40,32D,13C
Wight, Nathan N.	AL0500	61,39		Carlson, Damon J.	WI0770	60A,61,40,36
Wilcox-Daehn, Ann Marie	MO0775	39,61		Carswell, William	SC0450	31A,61,32,36,40
Wilcox-Jones, Carol	OH1650	61,39,54		Carter, Susan	MO0850	61,40,54,39
Wiley, Darlene	TX3510	61,39		Cazier, David	WA0150	36,61,29A,40
Will, Jacob	SC1110	61,39		Celaire, Jaunelle R.	AK0150	36,39,40,61
Williams, Ellen	NC1300	12A,39,61		Chandler, Deborah L.	LA0770	36,40
Williams, Kenneth D.	TX2960	36,61,60A,40,39		Chernin, Mallorie	MA0100	36,40
Williams, Stephen C.	PA2550	66G,39		Cherry, Mark	NY2200	54,40,66C
Williams, Steven	NC2550	11,54,39,66G		Chiaravalloti, Charissa	CO0350	36,40,60,12A,32D
Williamson, Scott	VA1700	36,39,40,60,61		Childs, Kim J.	OK1450	36,40,61
Wilson, Elisa	TX3520	61,54,47,39		Clark, Courtney	WV0440	40
Wilson, Ellen M.	TX3520	61,54,39,12		Clark, Mark	KS1250	36,32D,13,40
Wilson, Gran	MD1010	61,39		Clark, Serena Jenkins	ID0075	40,61
Wiltsie, Barbara	MI1260	61,39,54		Clements, Allen	AL0345	32D,36,60A,40,61
Witzke, Ron	MO2000	39,61		Clency, Cleveland	IL0650	11,66,40,36
Wolf, Joyce Hall	KY0550	61,39		Coffman, Teresa S.	RI0200	36,40,32D
Wood, Charles E.	AL1200	61,39,12A		Cogen, Ellen	MA1100	61,40,36,13A,54
Wood, Kenneth E.	VA1600	61,39		Coleman-Evans, Felicia	IL2100	61,40
Woodfield, Randal	PA3710	61,39,11		Connolly, Donna	NJ0825	39,40,54,61
Woodruff, Copeland	TN1680	39		Cook, Grant W.	OH2290	36,40,60,12
Woods, Sheryl	PA3250	39,61		Cook, Warren	SC0200	13,60,36,31A,40
Wozencraft-Ornellas, Jean	NM0100	39,61		Corman, David	TX1850	39,36,40
Wright, John Wesley	MD0800	61,39		Council, Thomas	GA2000	31A,61,36,60,40
Wylie, Ted	TN0100	61,31A,54,39		Cox, John	NY4310	36,38,40,41,60
Wyman, William A.	NE0450	36,39,61,60,40		Crull, Terry	KS0350	11,36,40,60A
Wyneken, Daniel	MA1400	39		Cruse, Carolyn S.	TX3200	36,40,32D,32G
Yarick-Cross, Doris	CT0850	39,61		Cuk, John	NY2200	36,39,54,40
Yasuda, Noriko	MA1175	39		Cummins, Nicholaus B.	MS0250	36,60A,32D,40
Yeh, Ying	CA0800	39,61,12A		Cunningham, Chuck	NM0500	66A,66G,32D,36,40
Yeung, Amy	TN1720	61,39,13		Cunningham, Richard	AG0200	40,61
Yotsumoto, Mayumi	CO0100	61,40,39		Dagenais, Andree	AC0050	36,40,42,60A
Young, Eddye Pierce	NY3560	39		Davids, Julia L.	IL2100	36,40
Young, James Russell	GA1150	40,39,66C,54		Deakins, Mark	KY0650	13A,60,36,31A,40
Young, Karen L.	AL1160	61,11,39		Dearing, James C.	PA1600	36,40,12A
Young, M. Susan	PA1450	61,39		DeHoogh-Kliewer, David	SD0580	60A,11,32D,36,40
Young, Susan	AB0150	61,36,13C,39		Delto, Clare	CA4850	61,40
Young, Thomas	NY3560	39,61		Dennee, Peter D.	WI0250	32C,32D,36,60,40
Zeller, Kurt-Alexander	GA0500	61,39,12A		Dennis, Susan	IL1085	61,54,40
Zemliauskas, Christopher	CO0800	39,61,54		Detweiler, Greg J.	KY0900	60,36,61,40
Ziegler, Delores	MD1010	61,39		Doyle, Laurie	TX1550	61,11,40,54
Ziegler, Marci	KS0050	61,66F,39		Doyle, Melinda S.	AL1200	36,60A,40
Zork, Stephen	MI0250	36,61,60,10,39		Drumm, Melissa Percy	WA0950	61,40
				Duff, Robert P.	NH0100	36,60,10A,40,13C
				Duncan, Ellen	MI1300	13A,13,60,36,40
				Durlam, Zachary D.	CA1860	36,60,32A,32B,40

Vocal Chamber Ensemble

Name	Code	Areas		Name	Code	Areas
Aakre, Brett	OR1000	40,61		Eby, Kristen	IA1450	44,61,40,36,13
Aakre, David	OR1000	40		Edwards, Steven C.	LA0080	11,12,36,40,61
Aamot, Kirk C.	MT0200	36,40,32D,60A		Eleazer, Alan G.	TN0600	36,40,11
Adams, J. Robert	GA0490	61,14,11,39,40		Ellis, Diana L.	TX1650	61,39,40
Adams, Kenny L.	OK0700	60,36,39,54,40		Emelio, Melanie	CA3600	40,61,39
Afonso, Daniel R.	CA0850	36,40,13C,32D,60A		Emerich, Kate	CO0900	61,40
Albrecht, Karen	TX1600	61,54,40		Engebretson, Stan P.	VA0450	36,60A,60,40
Alder, Alan	IN0150	40		Engelson, Thea	IA1300	40,61,54
Aldrich, Nicole P.	MO1900	36,40,60		Enlow, Charles	WA0860	66D,40,54,39
Alexander, Cory T.	TX3527	36,32D,61,32,40		Epley, Michael	MO2000	60A,32C,36,61,40
Alexander, Travis	NC1550	12A,36,40,66		Erwin, John M.	AR0850	60A,36,40
Alviani, Henry	PA0700	36,40,60A,61		Eskew-Sparks, Elise	GA0050	36,40
Amante Y Zapata, Joseph J.	RI0101	36,40,11,13A,13		Espinosa, Gabriel	IA0200	47,53,29,40
Anderson, Jared	MI1450	36,40,11,12A		Evans, Chris	PA2740	36,40,61
Anderson, Kathy T.	MS0570	36,40,61		Evans, Cory	UT0300	32D,36,40
Anderson, Scott E.	ID0100	36,40,60A,61		Evans, Timothy	MA0900	40,66A,61
Apple, A. Alan	PA1750	13A,36,61,13C,40		Faerber, Matthew L.	WI0860	60A,36,32D,40,13C
Arasi, Melissa	GA0900	40,61		Falk, Marc	IA0300	36,11,12A,60A,40
Archer, Ed	CA3150	36,40		Farris, Daniel King	OK1250	40,42,12,36,13
Archibeque, Charlene	CA4400	36,40,60A,32D		Ferreira, David C.	MN1120	40
Arnett, Nathan D.	IL1240	11,13C,32A,36,40		Ferrill, Kyle	ID0250	61,40
Ashe, Jennifer	MA0700	11,61,55D,40		Fleming, Gail H.	IL2970	11,36,66A,40,20
Ashworth, Teresa	MN1100	61,36,40,20,13C		Folger, William M.	MD0800	60A,36,40,54
Auler, Robert M.	NY3770	66A,66D,13A,40,35A		Ford, Joseph Kevin	TN1700	36,40,32D,60
				Foust, Diane	WI1100	36,61,13A,40,13B

Index by Area of Teaching Interest

Name	Code	Areas
Fox, Ryan H	AR0300	36,60A,32D,40
Francis, Deirdre	SC0050	61,40
Fraser, Teresa L.	WA0600	36,47,13A,40
Fredenburgh, Lisa M.	IL0150	36,11,40,60A
Freidline, Noel	NC2420	40,47,35A
Froese, Garry W.	AB0150	40
Frost, James	TN0850	39,40,61
Futrell, Stephen A.	NC0750	36,32D,60,35C,40
Galbreath, Loretta J.	MS0350	36,40,47,61
Garcia-Novelli, Eduardo	WI0250	36,40,32D,13C,60
Garner, Dirk A.	OH0200	36,40,60A
Gehrenbeck, Robert	WI0865	36,40,39,60A
Georgieva, Irina P.	NY4350	40
Gerbi, Elizabeth	NY1050	36,40,61
Gervais, Michel Marc	CA5060	36,60A,55A,40
Geston, Mary K.	MN1280	40,32D,60A,32C,36
Glasman, Ilan David	CA1550	36,40,61,11
Goffi-Fynn, Jeanne C.	NY4200	40,61,13H,32B,32D
Gordon, Regina	PA1550	36,40
Gordon, Samuel	OH2150	60,12A,36,61,40
Gosselin, Karen	AL0550	32,60,36,40,44
Gothold, Stephen A.	CA5100	36,40,61,60A
Graf, Greg	MO0750	36,40,60,11
Green, Peter	CA1960	13A,66A,36,40
Green, William	TN0850	36,40,60A
Grives, Steven Matthew	IL0750	36,40
Grogan, David C.	TX3500	61,32D,36,39,40
Gubrud, Darcy Lease	MN1285	13,11,36,61,40
Gustafson, Steven	KS0900	61,66G,40,13B,36
Haan, Keith A.	IA1300	60,36,32D,61,40
Hagerott, Dawn	ND0050	40,61,11
Hale, Roger	MO0850	60A,61,40,36
Hall, Bruce	IL2250	61,36,40
Hall, Lewis R.	WV0050	32,40,54,61
Hall, Van-Anthoney	NC1550	11,12D,40,42,61
Halsey, Glynn	GA0490	11,36,40,60A
Ham, Robert	IN0200	32D,36,40
Hampton, Bradley	CA0845	10D,40
Hansen, Judith	CA5030	40
Harden, Matthew C.	NE0610	36,60A,32D,40
Harney, Jon M.	MT0200	36,39,40,61
Harper, David R.	RI0150	11,61,54,39,40
Harris, David	PA0150	36,61,31A,40,32D
Harwood, Susan	NY0700	39,36,61,40
Hasseler, Lynda	OH0350	60A,36,40,32D
Hearne, Lisa	IA0400	36,61,40
Hedegaard, Kirsten	IL1615	61,40
Hein, David	WI0400	40,61
Helding, Lynn E.	PA0950	61,40,54
Henderson, Silvester	CA2775	36,40,60A,61,66A
Henjum, Katherine	ND0400	61,40,13C
Henry, James	MO1830	36,40,60A,32D,10F
Henry, Joseph D.	IL0900	12A,20G,36,40,32C
Hickey, Katherine M.	CA5150	32,13A,13C,36,40
Hiester, Jason A.	OH2000	36,39,40,60A,61
Highben, Zebulon M.	OH1650	36,40,61,32D
Hinson, Wallace	GA1650	60,36,40
Hixson, Mary	GA2000	13C,20,40,43
Hodges, Justin	TX0600	36,40,32D
Hodgman, Thomas	MI0050	32,36,40
Hoffenberg, Rick	PA2200	36,40,60A,61
Hoifeldt, Steven	IA0425	61,11,40
Holeman, Kathleen	MO0850	61,40,42
Holloway, Peggy A.	NE0610	61,32B,15,36,40
Hondorp, Paul	KY1550	36,60A,32D,61,40
Hood, Marcia Mitchell	GA0150	66A,60A,32B,36,40
Hooper, Randall	TX2955	36,60A,32D,32B,40
Hostetler, Jill	IN0200	36,40,61
Howard, Robert C.	MO0550	36,40
Howard, Sandra	NH0150	32,36,40
Howell, Matthew	HI0200	36,38,40
Hunter, Denise	CA3920	40
Hurst, Michael Shane	TX0370	61,40,35G
Ihm, Dana	CO0275	36,40,47,60A
Imler, James R.	SC1200	36,40
Isensee, Paul R.	PA2800	31A,40
Istad, Robert M.	CA0815	36,40
Ivey, Bobby	GA0350	32,36,13C,40
James, Kimberly Gratland	MT0400	61,40,13
Jamison, Vicki	PA0100	61,40
Jarman, Amy	TN1850	61,39,40
Jaros, Marc	MN1200	12,36,20,40
Jarrell, Boyd	CA1150	13,36,40
Jennings, Graeme	CA2950	40,41,62A,62B,42
Jobin-Bevans, Dean	AG0170	60,36,40,39
John, James A.	NY0642	36,40,60A
Johnson, Jefferson	KY1450	60,40,36,42
Johnson, Julianne R.	OR0800	36,40,29
Johnson, Velshera	VA0400	61,36,40,66A
Jones, Erik Reid	WV0550	36,39,40,60A,61
Joseph, Deanna	GA1050	36,40
Judge, Joseph	NC1900	36,61,31A,40
Kamm, Charles W.	CA4500	36,12,40,60
Kasch, Catherine Loraine	CO0900	61,40
Kashkin, Allan	NY3250	34,40,61
Keller, Dennis L.	CA3320	36,61,20,11,40
Kelly, Frankie J.	LA0800	66C,40,41,42,11
Kelly, Ryan	PA3600	36,40,61,60A
Kenaston-French, Karen	TX3500	36,61,32D,40,60A
Kibler, Keith E.	MA2250	61,40
Kim, Jong H.	VA0750	36,13,61,60A,40
Kinsey, Katherine S.	SC1200	32D,36,60A,40
Kirkwood, Neal	PA1750	40,66A
Kitson, Jeffrey	NE0040	11,13,36,40,61
Kittredge, Brian	AL1150	36,40
Klassen, Glenn	AA0200	36,38,40,60
Klaus, Kenneth S.	LA0450	60A,11,36,61,40
Klemp, Merilee I.	MN0050	12A,12,64B,48,40
Knapp, Brady	TX3450	39,40,36
Knapp, Joel	IL2910	60,36,40
Kolb, G. Roberts	NY1350	60,12A,36,40
Kompelien, Wayne	VA0650	40,61,60A
Kornelis, Benjamin	IA0500	20,32D,36,60A,40
Krasnovsky, Paul J.	IN1650	60A,36,40
Kratochvil, Jirka	NY1400	36,60A,40,61
Kratzer, Dennis L.	OH1800	36,61,54,60A,40
Kreitzer, Nathan J.	CA4410	61,36,40,55
Kuhnert, Brian	TX3650	61,39,54,40
Kuzma, Marika C.	CA5000	36,40,60A,61
Lambert, Doris	OK0150	36,40,61,13C
Lane, Laura L.	IL1350	12A,60,36,40,61
Langager, Arlie	CA2960	36,47,40,61
Lansing, Nathan	WA0950	36,40,13B,13C,13A
Lee, Sun Min	PA1950	36,40,60,13C
Lehman, Carroll	NH0150	40,39,61
Lew, Nathaniel G.	VT0400	12A,13,36,40
Lewis, Bernice	MA2250	10,40
Lewis, Rod	SC0620	13,70,40
Li, Tai-Wai	AK0100	32D,40
Lind, Robin A.	PA3650	32C,36,40,61
Lindsey, Lauren	WV0050	12A,36,40,61
Lippard, Erin	TX2710	61,13A,13B,40,54
Livesay, Charles	MI2000	60,32D,36,40,61
Loeppky, Ian R.	AL1250	60,36,41,40
Logan, P. Bradley	MN0150	60A,36,32D,40
Logue, James	NE0400	36,40
Long, David	GA0600	36,63A,49,55C,40
Long, Nolan W.	OH2120	36,32D,40,42
Longoria, Cynthia	TX0550	40,61
Lubin, Renee	CA4200	40,61
Lyle, Susan	SC0650	61,40
Lynch, Shane	VA1850	36,40,61
Lynn, Debra J.	IN1050	60,36,61,40,39
MacDonald, April	AL0200	61,40,39
MacLaren, Robert	AC0100	61,40
Mahraun, Daniel A.	MN1120	61,36,60A,40
Major, James E.	IL1150	36,40,32D
Malfatti, Dennis	IN1600	36,40,31A
Mallin, Claire	AF0050	13C,40,61,60A
Mann, Alison	GA1150	40,60A,32C,32D
Markham, Matthew E.	WI0850	61,39,40
Markou, Stella	MO1830	61,39,40
Maroney, James	PA1100	11,36,61,13C,40
Marshall, Elizabeth	WV0250	61,36,40
Mautner, Roselida	FL0200	40,61,11
McCoy, Jane O.	NC2550	61,16,40
McGhee, Janet F.	NY3650	36,13A,40,60A
McGilvray, Byron	TX3360	61,36,40
McMahon, Michael	AI0150	39,40,66C,61,66A
McManus, Lanny	AL0550	32D,36,12,13E,40
McPhee, Rosemary	AF0050	33,40
Mecham, Mark L.	PA1900	32D,36,40,60A
Meder, Randall A.	WI0808	60,11,36,40,32D
Medley, Susan	PA3580	36,60A,40,11,13A
Megginson, Julie	GA1000	61,36,40,60A
Melton, Michael D.	IL2150	36,40,32D,61,60A
Menk, Nancy L.	IN1450	60,36,40
Messoloras, Irene	OK0600	36,12,60A,61,40
Meyer, Beverly	NY2200	54,40,66C
Miano, Jo Ellen	NY3775	13A,36,61,32I,40
Mianulli, Janice	PA1650	61,40,36
Miller, Andrew	ND0050	36,60A,40,13C
Miller, Jo Ann	ND0350	60,36,40,56
Miller, Kenny	AZ0470	13C,12A,36,40,61
Miller, Phillip	CA0450	40,66D
Mindell, Pamela Getnick	MA0700	11,36,40
Minter, Drew	NY4450	61,40,39
Mitchell, Aaron Paul	IN0905	32D,36,40,60A
Moninger, Susan	IL0850	36,40,47,61
Monkelien, Sheryl	PA2150	32,40
Moody, Kevin M.	TX0075	54,61,11,36,40
Moore, Laura M.	AL1300	36,40,60A,61,66C
Moore, Tim	FL0670	40,61,54
Morris, Gary	AR0200	36,40,60A,61
Muilenburg, Harley	CA2250	36,61,60A,40
Murphy, Michael	ID0250	36,40,32D,12A,32C
Musgrove, Abby R.	IL1100	36,40,11,32C,32D
Muzzo, Grace	PA3710	32,36,40,60A
Myers, Gerald C.	MO1120	11,36,40,54,13
Nafziger, Erin	MA2250	61,40
Najar, Michael	CA3270	13G,36,40
Nakamae, Ayumi	NC0450	61,36,40,67F
Naydan, William	PA0650	40,60
Nedecky, Jason	AG0300	40
Neill, Kelly	AR0250	32D,36,40,61
Nelson, Curt	CA2900	10D,36,40,54
Nelson, Karl	OK1330	36,40
Nesheim, Paul J.	MN1120	36,40,60A
Nestor, Leo Cornelius	DC0050	10A,31A,36,40,60A
Neuen, Donald	CA5030	36,40
Oakley, Paul E.	NC0350	36,40,61,11
O'Brien, Kevin	DC0050	36,13B,60A,40
Octave, Thomas	PA2950	61,36,39,40,11
Ogle, Deborah A.	GA1200	36,13A,60,40,61
Olson, Craig	WY0130	64E,48,64A,40,46
Overland, Corin T.	FL1900	40,32,60A
Owen, William E.	WA0550	36,60,12A,40,31A
Owens, Tiffany	OH0680	61,13C,40
Pare', Barbara A.	IN0350	61,40
Park, Jong-Won	WI0845	36,40,61,60A
Parker, Gregory B.	NC0400	36,61,60A,40,32D
Parodi, Jorge	NY0500	39,40,41,66C
Parodi, Jorge	NY2750	40,61,66C
Parr, Clayton G.	MI0100	36,40,60A,32D
Parton-Stanard, Susan	IL1500	61,40,36,11,32D
Pastelak, Marianne	MD0475	61,40
Patton, Patrick	WY0050	36,61,40
Paul, Sharon J.	OR1050	60A,36,40
Perez, Olga	OH1650	61,40,32B
Peterson, Dean	MT0400	60A,32D,36,40
Peterson, Gene D.	TN1710	32,36,40
Peterson, Ken	UT0150	36,39,40,61
Petrenko, Jurgen	AG0300	40
Pierce, Edward A.	OK0850	40,61,36
Pierce, Laura	MA2250	61,40
Plash, Duane	AL1195	13,10,66A,40
Plummer, Mark W.	IL0150	36,32D,40
Poniros, Risa	NC1500	32B,40,36,61
Poovey, Gena E.	SC0850	36,61,60A,32D,40
Porter, Michael	NC0250	36,40,60,61,32D
Pricco, Evelyen	CA1560	40
Prowse, Robert W.	NJ0825	36,40,61,12A
Psurny, Robert D.	MT0075	29A,36,40,54,61
Pursino, Peter	GA1990	36,40
Quagliariello, Rachel M.	VA0800	61,40
Quantz, Don E.	AA0010	12A,32D,36,40,41
Raines, Alan L.	TX0300	36,60A,40
Raines, Sarah	MT0370	40,61
Ransom, Judy L.	WY0115	13B,13F,36,40,66D
Rasmussen, Bruce	CA3400	60A,36,61,40,66G
Ray, W. Irwin	GA1550	60,11,41,36,40
Rayam, Curtis	FL0100	36,61,40,39
Redfearn, Christopher	ND0600	36,40,60A,61
Rediger, JoAnn K.	IN1560	36,31A,60A,11,40
Reiss, Deborah	NY0850	44,40,31A,66C
Replogle, Rebecca	OR1010	36,61,13A,13C,40
Retzlaff, Jonathan	TN1850	61,39,40
Rice, Susan	WI0100	40,36,13A
Richard, Monique M.	AE0100	32,36,40,60A
Richardson, Dennis	TX0550	36,40,32B,66D,60A
Richmond, Brad	MI1050	36,40,60A,61
Richter, Tiffany	AL1450	13,36,40,61
Rischar, Richard A.	MI2110	12,29,40,14,20
Ristow, Gregory C.	IN0350	36,40
Ritchey, Mary Lynn	MA0150	61,36,60A,40,11
Rivera, Natalia	MO1810	40

575

Name	Code	Areas
Rohlfing, Mimi	MA2030	61,36,47,40
Romano, Darlene	CA1270	36,61,11,13A,40
Rose, Melissa K.	TN1850	66C,41,40
Roseberry, Lynn	OH0350	61,39,40,36
Ross, Holli	NJ0800	40,61
Roth, John	MN0610	34,40,41,70
Rowehl, John	NY0900	36,40,60A
Rowell, Thomas L.	AL1300	61,39,40
Rubenstein, Eliza N.	CA3350	40
Russell, John	CA0845	36,40,32D,60A
Russell, John K.	CA1520	32D,36,40,60A
Ryczek, Karyl	MA1175	61,40
Ryder, Christopher O.	VA1150	34,61,32,13,40
Ryer-Parke, Kerry	MA2250	61,40
Sabatino, T. M.	PA1750	11,61,40
Sadlier, David	VA0150	61,40,39
Sager, Gene	WY0150	36,40,61,11
Salerno, Christine	WI0808	40,47,66,61
Sandefur, Lynn	FL1675	11,13A,36,40,61
Santana, Priscilla	TX2800	61,36,40
Schaefer, Elaine	CA1300	13A,36,54,61,40
Schnack, Michael B.	PA2550	36,40,61
Schreuder, Joel T.	NE0050	60A,36,61,40,32D
Scott, Cindy	LA0800	61,40
Scott, Sandra C.	GA1600	36,40,60A,32D,66A
Scott, Stuart	MI1250	40,36,61
Scraper, Joel	SC1100	40,60A,32D,36,60
Severing, Richard	WI0865	36,40,54,61
Shankman, Ira	NY2750	32,40,36,60
Shapiro, Mark L.	NY2105	60A,36,40,13
Shaw, Kirby	OR0950	40
Sheldon, Janene	NE0450	61,32B,36,40,16
Shelt, Christopher A.	MS0100	60A,36,31A,61,40
Sheppard, Chris	SC0900	36,60A,61,40,34
Sherman, Joy	WA0850	11,36,40,61
Shockey, David M.	PA2800	36,61,40
Shrope, Douglas	CA1000	36,61,60A,40,54
Sigmon, Susan McEwen	GA0940	13,36,66A,66G,40
Smith, Aaron	MD0900	31A,36,54,40
Smith, Kandie K.	GA0400	61,40
Smith, Kevin	MN0625	36,60,40,10A
Smith, Leroy	MD0500	40
Smith, Susan A.	MS0360	61,40,13,36,13B
Smoak, Jeff C.	KY1425	32,36,61,40,43
Smolder, Benjamin W.	OH1450	61,40
Snapp, Patricia	MN0750	61,39,40
Snider, Karl William	CA2800	13A,11,61,40
Snyder, Timothy	FL1000	36,40,12A,32D,60A
Soderberg, Karen	MD0350	61,36,40,32D,60A
Sokol, Thomas A.	NY0900	60,36,40
Song, Anna	OR0450	13C,36,55B,55A,40
Speer, Randall	VA1125	61,36,60A,40
Spencer, Theresa Forrester	MO0250	36,40,61,14C
St. Clair, Eniko	CA4450	40
Stafford, John	KS0590	36,40,47,11,13A
Staininger, Lynn L.	MD0300	36,66A,13B,40,61
Staininger, Lynn	MD0500	36,40
Stark, Deborah	GA0700	12A,54,11,61,40
Stauch, Thomas J.	IL1085	36,40,61,32D,11
Stern, Kalai	HI0110	11,36,40,13A,13C
Stern, Margaret	NY4300	36,40
Stevens, Cynthia C.	TX2310	37,40,61
Stevens, James	UT0050	40
Stich, Adam	AZ0490	36,60A,61,40,13A
Stripling, Allen	GA0810	11,36,66,32,40
Stroope, Z. Randall	OK0800	36,60A,40,10A
Suderman, Gail	AB0060	36,61,40,39
Sulahian, Nancy	CA0500	36,40
Summers, Alvin	TN1720	40
Sumner, Melissa M.	VA0800	61,11,40
Svoboda, Matt	OR0350	36,40
Swanson, Barry	ID0150	31,36,40
Swanston, Marcia	AF0100	39,61,40
TangYuk, Richard	NJ0900	36,39,40
Tavernier, Jane	VA1475	61,36,39,40
Taylor, Jim	TX1350	36,40,61
Taylor, Una D.	NE0050	36,61,32B,11,40
Teal, Terri	KS0570	11,40,61,36
Terenzi, Mark J.	NJ0700	36,40,60A,13C
Teske, Deborah Jenkins	CO0200	36,40,60A
Thielen-Gaffey, Tina	MN1600	36,61,40,32
Thomas, Steven L.	PA3700	36,61,40
Thomas, William D.	SC0750	40,61,31A
Thorngate, Russell	WI0925	11,13A,36,40,61
Thorp, Steven	NM0250	13,11,36,61,40
Tichenor, Jean-Marie	WY0050	61,40,12A
Toliver, Nicki Bakko	MN0040	11,13,40,61
Tramm, Jason	NJ1160	36,40,60A
Trotta, Michael J.	VA1830	32D,12A,36,40
Tucker, Scott	NY0900	60,36,40,13A,20A
Tucker, William S.	NY2750	40,54
Tuning, Mark	CA3920	36,40,61
Tyson, LaDona	MS0580	11,40,36,61
Van Brunt, Nancy	WI0960	13A,13B,13C,66D,40
Vascan, Ligia	WI0500	40,61,36,54,29
Vogt, Sean F.	SD0300	60A,36,66G,32D,40
Von Ellefson, Randi	OK0750	36,60A,40
Wagner, Randel	WA0250	36,40,61,54,60A
Wagstrom, Beth Robison	CO0050	36,40,47,60A
Walker, Regina	IN0907	39,40
Walker, Steve	OK0300	61,36,40,60A
Wallace, James A.	GA1070	36,13C,40,11
Walt, Marlene	MA2250	61,40
Waterbury, Elizabeth	CA4550	36,61,40,13A,39
Waters, Richard	KY0550	36,60A,32D,40
Watkins, Wilbert O.	IL0275	36,40,32
Weinel, John	TX1450	61,60,36,39,40
Weiser, Kimberly	NE0610	40,61
Wells, Bradley C.	MA2250	13C,36,40,60A,61
Wesby, Roger	NY4500	11,29A,32D,36,40
West, Cheryl	IN0250	40,32
West, Lara L.	KS0100	40,11,66D,66G,20
Whidden, Collen	AA0150	40
White, Christopher Dale	TX2955	32D,36,40,60A,61
White, Kayla	AR0400	31,40,61
White, Perry D.	WI0770	36,40
Whitney, Nadine C.	GA2200	12A,36,61,40,39
Wilds, Timothy	NC1450	61,31A,36,40
Wilhelm, Philip	IL1740	64D,32,40,11
Williams, Kenneth D.	TX2960	36,61,60A,40,39
Williamson, Richard A.	SC0050	13C,36,40,60A
Williamson, Scott	VA1700	36,39,40,60,61
Willoughby, Judith A.	OK0750	36,60A,40,32
Wilson, Jeffrey S.	IL1050	60,36,40,61,31A
Wing, Henry	NH0350	36,40,61
Witakowski, Thomas E.	NY3717	36,40,61,60A
Wold, Stanley R.	MN1600	60A,36,40,61
Wolff, Lisa	NV0100	36,40,61,13C
Woods, Timothy E.	SD0400	60A,12A,36,61,40
Wright, J. Clay	KS0440	11,13,36,40,61
Wright, John	IN0250	40
Wyman, William A.	NE0450	36,39,61,60,40
Yanson, Eliezer G.	SC0200	32D,13,60A,36,40
Yau, Eugenia Oi Yan	NY0270	11,36,61,40,60A
Yeung, Ian	TX3540	36,60A,40,31A,38
Yotsumoto, Mayumi	CO0100	61,40,39
Young, James Russell	GA1150	40,39,66C,54
Zabriskie, Alan N.	MO1790	11,40,36,60A
Zegree, Stephen	IN0900	36,47,40
Zeigler, Mark C.	NY2650	32D,36,40,60A
Zielinski, Richard	OK1350	60,36,40
Zogleman, Deanne	KS0980	12A,13,20G,36,40

Instrumental Chamber Ensemble

Name	Code	Areas
Abayev, Alexander	NY0050	41
Abend, Elena	WI0825	66A,41
Abernathy, Jennifer	IL0150	41
Abram, Blanche	NY1600	41,66A,66D,66C
Abrams, David	NY2950	13C,11,41,64C,12A
Ackmann, Rodney	OK1350	64D,20G,41
Adams, Liselyn	AI0070	13,12A,41,64A,43
Admiral, Roger	AA0100	41,43
Agopian, Edmond	AA0150	38,41,51,62A,42
Agopian, Edmond	AA0050	62A,41,38
Aide, William	AG0450	66A,66B,41,66C
Akerman, Mary S.	GA1150	41,70
Aki, Syoko	CT0850	41,62A
Albulescu, Eugene	PA1950	11,66A,66C,41
Aldrich, Ralph E.	AG0500	41,51,62A,62B
Alexander, Glenn	NY3560	41,47,70,29
Allen, Fred J.	TX2700	60B,32C,37,41
Allen, Peter	AF0100	66A,66C,66B,41,42
Allen, Susan	CA0510	41,62E,43,53
Allphin, Andrew	DC0050	63A,41
Alvarado, John	IN0907	41,70
Alvarez, Heidi Pintner	KY1550	64A,13B,41
Anderson, Anamae	UT0050	41
Anderson, Elaine M.	OH2290	62C,13,38,41,42
Anderson, Eric	MN0040	11,41
Anderson, William	NY3560	41,70
Andrews, Kenneth B.	NY3780	41,64A,43
Andrus, Deborah E.	PA2450	64C,48,41
Anglley, Tamey	TX2700	60B,32C,37,41
Anop, Lenora Marya	IL2910	62A,41,51,42
Anthony, Janet	WI0350	12A,41,62C,51
Appenheimer-Vaida, Christiane	PA2200	62C,41,32E
Applonie, Brent	UT0400	41
Armstrong, Joshua	MS0250	65,50,37,41
Arnold, John	PA2450	41,70
Arrivee, David	CA0600	38,13,41,13A,13C
Asche, Charles	CA5060	66A,41
Ashton, Ted	ID0060	41,62A,32E
Ashworth, Thomas	MN1623	41,63C
Asteriadou, Maria	PA1750	11,66A,66B,41,42
Atherton, Timothy E.	NH0100	63C,41,42
Averitt, Frances Lapp	VA1350	48,64A,41
Ayick, Paul	FL0200	63A,41
Aylward, Ansgarius	NY0400	60B,38,41,62A
Bach, Timothy	CA4150	12A,41,66C
Bachman, James	CA0600	70,41
Bahcall, Klara	WI0830	41,62A,62B
Bailen, Eliot T.	NY0750	62C,41
Bairos, Monte	CA1560	37,41,48,49,50
Baker, James	RI0050	13,13J,41
Baldwin, Daniel	IA0950	60,41,38
Baldwin, David B.	MN1623	41,49,63A
Baldwin, Philip R.	WA1350	62A,41,38,60B
Balestra, Richard J.	NY3770	41,70
Balkin, Laura M.	NY3730	41,62A
Balkin, Richard A.	NY3730	13A,41,62A
Ball, Sheridan J.	CA1520	36,41,61,13A
Bamonte, David	OR0850	41,42,63A,49
Barcellona, John	CA0825	41,64A
Barczyk, Cecylia	MD0850	41,62C,32E,51
Bardston, Robert	AA0040	66H,66B,38,41,62C
Barham, Phillip	TN1450	64E,41,13B
Barker, John C.	AL1300	64C,41
Barnes, James E.	PA2450	37,38,60,34,41
Barnhill, Allen	TX2150	63C,41,42
Barone, Judith	NY4460	66A,66G,13A,41
Barrick, Christopher	WV0600	64,11,41,34,47
Barron, Jose	CA4300	41
Barton, Mark	TX3400	41,63D
Barwell, Nina	MA1900	64A,41
Baytelman, Pola	NY3650	41,66A,66D,66E
Bazala Kim, Alison E.	MD0150	62C,41
Beals, Andrew	CT0800	64E,41,53
Beaver, Martin	CT0850	41
Beavers, Judith	MI0910	66A,41
Beavers, Sean M.	VA0650	12A,13A,13B,13C,41
Becker, Harris	NY2105	67G,70,41
Beegle, Raymond	NY2150	41
Begian, Jamie	CT0800	41,70,53,47,29
Behn, Bradford	OK0750	64C,41
Behrend, Roger L.	VA0450	63D,41
Belknap, Monte	UT0050	62A,41
Bell, David	WI0350	41,64C
Bell, S.	MA0800	41
Bell, Scott	PA1050	64B,41
Bellamy, Terry	NY3475	41,70
Benedict, Jeffrey W.	CA0830	29,47,64E,41
Bennett, Larry	MO0100	32E,63D,63C,41
Bennett, Marie Micol	IL2050	64A,48,41,13A,42
Benson, Katherine	IL2300	64A,41,44
Berger, Gene P.	IN0150	49,41,63B
Bergeron, Andrew	MI0300	70,41
Bergmann, Elizabeth	AA0050	66A,66C,41
Bergmann, Marcel	AA0050	66,66C,41
Bergstrom, Samuel	MN0040	20,32,37,41,47
Berk, Stacey J.	WI0850	13A,13B,64B,41,10F
Berkowitz, Paul M.	CA5060	66A,41
Berry, Mark S.	KY1550	65,50,41
Bhasin, Ruby	VA0250	37,63A,38,42,41
Biber, Sarah J.	MT0200	13B,41,62C
Bicigo, James Michael	AK0150	12A,32,37,41,63D
Bielish, Aaron J.	TX2295	62A,62B,41,11,13
Binford, Joanna	KY1350	62A,62B,41
Bing, Delores M.	CA0500	62,41,42,62C
Binkley, Lindabeth	MI0400	64B,41,48,11
Bishop, Darcie	MS0350	11,41,49,63A
Biss, Paul	MA1400	41
Bjella, David E.	FL1750	41,62C
Bjella, Steven A.	WI0850	41,62A,32E
Bjork, Mark	MN1623	41,62A

Index by Area of Teaching Interest

Name	Code	Areas
Blakeman, Lee	KY1550	63C,13C,11,41
Bloch, Robert S.	CA5010	13,11,41,62A,62B
Blomster, Jennie	CA5350	63B,41,42
Bobenhouse, Elizabeth	NE0450	41,64A
Boggs, William	OH0350	38,60,41,60B
Bohnet, Andra	AL1300	12A,41,64A,62E,35A
Boisvert, Jean-Guy	AE0100	41,64C,64E
Bolter, Norman	MA1400	41,63C
Book, A. Ryan	NC2210	70,12A,13,41
Booker, Adam	MN1600	29,41,46,62D
Boos, Kenneth G.	FL1310	13,60,36,41,61
Borden, Rita	AZ0450	66A,66C,41
Boren, Mark	ND0250	63A,63B,13A,41
Borror, Ronald	CT0650	41,49,63C,67E,55
Bossart, Eugene	MI1900	41,66A,66C
Botts, Nathan	MA2250	63A,41
Boughton, Janet	CT0300	51,62,41
Bouton, Arthur E.	CO0900	48,64E,41
Boyd, Michael	MS0360	70,62D,41,10,11
Bradley-Kramer, Deborah	NY0750	11,12A,41
Bradshaw, Daniel	HI0050	13D,42,41
Brandon, Mack	NJ0950	10B,31F,36,41
Brandt, Lynne	TX2310	13,64A,41,66A
Brantley, Mitch	MS0370	11,41,70
Bravar, Mimi	NH0350	62B,41
Breuninger, Tyrone	NJ1050	41,63D
Bridges, Scott	AL1170	41,64C
Briggs, Amy	IL3250	41,13
Briseno, Antonio	TX3515	11,20H,41
Britz, Joanne M.	KS1050	64C,64E,41
Brooks, Joseph H.	WA0050	41,48,64B,64C,64E
Brown, Brian	NJ0175	63D,41
Brown, Daniel R.	NV0050	63D,41
Brown, Edward	NY0644	70,41
Brown, Elaine K.	MO2000	41,64A
Brown, Hugh M.	MO1810	41,62A,62B
Brown, Jennie	IL0850	64A,41,42
Brown, Susan	CA0400	41,51,62,32
Brown, Tom	WI0810	11,41,49,63A,63B
Browning, Birch P.	OH0650	32,41
Bruno, Zachary	CA4625	11,32,37,47,41
Bucchianeri, Diane	OK1450	11,12A,41,62C
Buckholz, Christopher John	IA1600	63C,29,41,11
Buranskas, Karen	IN1700	41,62C
Burden, Douglas	AG0400	63C,37,41
Burton, Sean Michael	IA0100	36,61,41,11,13D
Bush, Christopher	NY2750	64C,41,42,48
Buslje, Sergio	DC0250	38,41
Buswell, James	MA1400	41,62A
Butts, Leon	TX3525	70,11,41
Cabalo, Eric	CA4700	70,32E,41
Caban, Francisco J.	PR0115	62A,41,42,51
Caldwell, Robert	AB0050	45,65,34,46,41
Callaway, Patricia	GA1200	61,12A,41
Callus, Helen	CA5060	62B,41
Cameron, Michael J.	IL3300	62D,51,41
Cameron, Robin	NY3775	41,64A
Cameron, Wayne C.	MD1000	38,41,63A
Campbell, Douglas	MO1810	41
Candelaria, Philip	AG0070	70,41
Cantu, Ben	CO0275	70,41,42
Carbonara, David	LA0720	38,41,51,62
Cardin, Michel	AE0100	41,67G,70
Carey, Aaron L.	WV0100	41,62,70
Carlson, Sydney R.	OR0850	41,42,64A
Carney, Laurie	NY2150	41,62A
Carr, Colin	NY3790	41,62C
Carr, Tracy A.	NM0100	64B,12A,41,64D,11
Carrasco, Jacqui	NC2500	62A,62B,51,41,14
Carroll, Amy	MA0150	41
Carroll, Ed J.	NH0100	63A,41
Carroll, John	TX1900	63A,49,37,41,47
Cartagena, Cynthia	PR0115	41,42,64A
Carter, David	MN1450	11,41,62C,42
Carter, Robert Scott	NC0650	60B,37,41,32E
Cason, Tony	CA3600	41,32E,60B,38,12A
Cassidy, Marcia	NH0100	62A,62B,41
Castro-Balbi, Jesus	TX3000	62C,41
Cavender, James L.	AL1160	70,41,46,62D
Cella, Lisa M.	MD1000	64A,13C,41
Cerny, William J.	IN1700	12A,41,66A,66C
Cesario, Robert James	MO0825	37,38,60B,41
Champlin, Terry	NY2250	41
Chang, Wei Tsun	TN1450	11,32E,62A,41,62
Chapdelaine, Michael	NM0450	70,41
Chapman, Lucy	MA1400	41
Chapo, Eliot	FL0850	41,51,62A
Charlton, Susan	PA1850	41,64A
Chasanov, Elliot L.	IL3300	63C,49,41
Cheifetz, Hamilton	OR0850	41,51,62C,20G,20F
Chen, Jay	OR1300	37,63A,41
Chenette, Stephen	AG0450	37,41,63A
Chenoweth, Jonathan N.	IA1600	11,41,62C
Chepaitis, Stanley L.	PA1600	41,62A,62B,51
Chesebro, Robert C.	SC0750	12A,64,41
Chiang, Janice ChenJu	AZ0450	66C,66A,41
Chien, Alec F.	PA0100	11,42,66A,41
Cho, Young-Hyun	TX3500	66A,41,66C,66B,12A
Chun, Peter	KS1350	41,62B
Chunn, Michael	OH1100	41,63A
Cinquegrani, David	CT0350	31A,36,41,12
Cipolla, John M.	KY1550	41,64C,64E
Clardy, Mary Karen	TX3420	41,48,64A
Claudin, Margaret	PA2800	64A,41
Cleland, George	AA0040	38,41,62A,62B
Clemons, Gregory G.	IL1085	37,63A,41,13
Clodfelter, Mark	KY1450	63A,41
Cockerham, Scott	FL0150	41,70,34
Coddington, Robert	OH1400	70,41
Code, Belinda B.	AE0050	41,64A,64B,64D
Codreanu, Christian	TN1400	11,41,63B
Coelho, Tadeu	NC1650	64A,41
Cohen, Jeffrey L.	NY2150	41,66A
Collins, Nancy	WI0808	48,64A,41
Collinsworth, Andy	CA4700	13A,32,37,41,60B
Collison, Craig	AR0110	11,41,50,65
Colon Jimenez, Frances	PR0115	64B,41,42
Coltman, Charles	TX0900	10F,41,64,35A
Compton, Michael	ND0100	64,37,41,47,60B
Conner, Timothy M.	FL1900	63C,41,42
Connie, Meredith	WA0750	70,11,41
Connor, Mark	MO0700	13,20,41,47
Consiglio, Catherine	KS1450	62B,51,41
Converse, Ralph D.	NM0500	64,41,38,48,29
Cook, Scott A.	WI0825	62C,51,41
Coop, Jane A.	AB0100	41,66A
Coreil, Kristine	LA0550	63B,13,41
Corey, Horace E.	NV0100	13A,11,41,70
Corps, Wilfredo	PR0115	41,64E,42
Cosand, Walter	AZ0100	41,66A
Costanza, Christopher	CA4900	62C,41,51
Cottin-Rack, Myriam	CA4300	62A,42,41
Coutsouridis, Peter	MA2100	65,41,29A,11,13B
Coviak, James	MI0450	41,65B
Cowell, Jennifer	WY0050	38,41,66D,62A
Cowens, Kathy	MO0400	64A,41
Cox, Allan	TN1850	63A,49,41
Cox, John	NY4310	36,38,40,41,60
Cox, Mark	MI0400	63D,41
Craig, Gordon	AG0250	37,64C,48,38,41
Craioveanu, Mihai	MI1050	11,62A,41
Cramer, Christopher	WI0100	70,41
Crawford, Roberta	NY3705	41,62B,62A
Cromwell, Anna L.	IL0800	62A,62B,41
Crookall, Christine	GA0250	13A,13,62C,12A,41
Crowley, Lisle	UT0150	70,41
Cseszko, Ferenc	ID0250	38,62A,62B,41
Cullen, Christopher	CT0800	64C,41
Culver, Eric	MA0700	11,60,10F,38,41
Cumming, Danielle	MD0800	70,11,41
Cunliffe, William H.	CA0815	29,47,41
Currie, David	AG0400	60,38,41,62D
Curtis, Charles	CA5050	13A,41,62C
Cykert, Linda	NC0750	64A,41
Dahl, Christina A.	NY3790	41,66A,66C
Dahn, Nancy	AD0050	41,62A,62B
Dalmas, Jennifer	TX2700	38,62A,62B,41
Dalmasi, Martin	FL0930	41,64A,64E
Darling, John A.	ND0050	37,60B,47,13,41
Davey, John	NY1400	62D,29B,41
Davidoff, Judith	NY3560	41,55B,67
Davidson, Ian	TX3175	11,64B,41
Davis, J. Craig	NJ1400	37,63A,41
Davy, Karen	CA2250	62A,62B,62C,62D,41
Dawes, Andrew	AB0200	41
Dawes, Andrew	AB0100	41,51,62A,42
Day, Derek	NC2435	70,41
Day, Mary	IA0100	41,61,67,31A,39
De La Bretonne, Beverly	TX0100	13,38,41,62A,64A
De La Garza, Rene	RI0300	39,41,61
De Lyser, David M.	OR1100	13,10,38,41
De Silva, Rohan	NY1900	66C,41
Deane, Alison	NY0550	66,41,42
Deaville, James A.	AG0200	11,12A,12,41,12C
DeBolt, David	OH1100	11,41,64D
Decker, Charles	TN1450	63A,41,63,49
Decker, Michael	MD0850	70,35A,41,47
Decorsey, James H.	WI0350	12A,41,63B
del Grazia, Nicolas M.	AR0200	32E,41,48,64C
Der Hohannesian, Seta	MA2150	41,64A
DerHovsepian, Joan	TX2150	41
Deveau, David	MA1200	11,41,66A
DeVilbiss, Gloria	IA1390	61,41,36
Deyo, Paul	TN1400	41,63A
Dick, Robert	NY2750	64A,42,41
Diem, Timothy W.	MN1623	37,41
DiGiacobbe, David	NJ0175	64A,41
Dikeman, Philip	TN1850	64A,41,48
DiMartino, Vincent	KY1450	63A,41
Dimick, Glen M.	IN1650	63D,41,49
Djokic, Philippe	AF0100	62B,38,41,51,62A
Dobbs, Wendell B.	WV0400	11,13,41,48,64A
Dochnahl, Jesse	WI0350	64E,41
Donnellan, Grant	WA1250	41,42
Dorfman, Amy	TN1850	41,66A,66C
Dornenburg, John D.	CA4900	41,67A
Douglas, Brent	FL0450	41,66A,66C
Douglass, Ronald L.	MI1100	13,37,41,63,29
Dragonetti, John	PA1550	70,41
Drifmeyer, Kelly B.	NY3780	63B,41
Drucker, Eugene S.	NY3790	41,62A
Druhan, Mary Alice	TX2955	64C,41
Dubberly, James	CA0850	63C,63D,29A,41
Duhaime, Ricky	TX0250	13,47,41,64,60B
Duitman, Henry E.	MI0900	51,38,32E,41
Dulin, Mark C.	SC1200	63A,41
Dunker, Amy	IA0250	13,10,63A,41,49
Dunlop, John	NH0100	62C,41
Dusinberre, Edward	CO0800	41
Dutton, Lawrence	NY3790	41,62B
Earley, Robert W.	NJ1130	63A,41
Edberg, C. Eric	IN0350	41,62C,13A
Eddy, Timothy	NY2250	41,62C
Edge, David	OH2050	41,62A
Edwards, Linda	NM0400	60,36,41,61,54
Ehlen, Timothy	IL3300	66A,41
Ehrke, David	NV0100	13C,64C,64E,41
Ehrlich, Janina	IL0100	11,12,41,62C
Eisenstein-Baker, Paula	TX3450	41,62C
Eissenberg, Judith	MA0350	41
Eissenberg, Judith	MA0500	41,62A,11
Eklund, Jason	GA1150	63B,41
Elisha, Steven K.	GA0950	62C,62D,41,42
Ellenwood, Christian K.	WI0865	13,64C,41
Ellert, Michael	FL1125	64D,41,42
Ellinger, John	MN0300	41,34,70
Elliott, Richard	OR0250	37,41
Ellis, John R.	NY3780	63A,41
Elsing, Evelyn	MD1010	41,62C
Emelianoff, Andre	NY1900	62C,41
Emilson, C. Rudolph	NY3725	60,41,63D
Engberg, Michael	CO0100	13,70,41,35,47
Engle, Marilyn	AA0150	41,66A,66B,66C,12B
Entzi, John A.	NC2400	37,63B,41
Entzi, Karen	NC1450	62,11,41
Enz, Nicholas J.	MI1450	37,41,64E,47
Epstein, Daniel	NY2150	41,66A
Epstein, Frank B.	MA1400	41,65
Eselson, Lauren	AA0050	41,64A
Eshbach, Robert	NH0350	11,62A,41
Estrin, Mitchell	FL1850	41,64C
Evans, Garry W.	TX3300	64C,37,12A,41,60B
Everett, Micah P.	MS0700	63C,63D,13C,41,49
Everett, Paul	IN0150	49,63A,41
Everett, Steve	GA0750	60,10,41,45,34
Ezoe, Magdalena	MI1950	66A,13,12B,12A,41
Fadial, John	WY0200	62A,41,55B
Fairbanks, Ann K.	TX3450	13A,12A,41,64A
Falbush, Arthur	NY3765	11,63,29A,46,41
Falk, Leila Birnbaum	OR0900	11,12A,12B,41
Fallis, Todd	UT0300	32C,63C,63D,47,41
Falls, Sheila E.	MA2150	41,62A
Farkas, Pavel	CA5150	38,41,51,62A,62B
Farrington, Robert	CA1550	41,47,63,64,29A
Fejer, Andras	CO0800	62C,41
Feldkamp, Timothy L.	IA0930	13,41,47,64

577

Name	Code	Areas
Feldman, Marion	NY2150	41,62C
Feldman, Ronald	MA2250	60B,38,41,42
Feldman, Stephen B.	AR0850	11,41,62C
Fellows, Robin B.	WI0865	13A,11,41,64A
Ferguson, Danise J.	AE0050	13,41,62C
Ferguson, James W.	TN1100	62D,47,41,61
Fiala, Michele	OH1900	64B,41,13B,13C,64D
Finckel, David	NY3790	41,62C
Fink, Kathleen	NJ0825	64A,41
Fischer Faw, Victoria	NC0750	12,66A,66B,41
Fischer, Martha	WI0815	66A,66C,39,41
Fisher, Yuko	IL1740	62A,62B,62C,41
Fitz-Gerald, Kevin	CA5300	41,66A,66C
Flanagin, Michael	IN1025	37,63A,63B,41,60B
Flandreau, Tara	CA1150	12A,13,38,41,62
Flanigan, Glen	KY0100	11,32C,41,47,63D
Flanigan, Sean G.	CO0225	63C,63D,41,47,35A
Flores, Amy	IL1750	41,62C
Flyer, Nina	CA5350	62C,41,42
Flynn, Michael P.	WY0150	11,37,41,47,63
Flythe, Bernard	GA1150	32E,63D,41,11
Foreman, Charles	AA0150	66A,66B,66C,20G,41
Foster, Christopher	NY0100	36,63,13A,47,41
Foster-Dodson, Dawn	CA3920	41
Foulk, Lin	MI2250	63B,15,41,48,49
Frabizio, William V.	PA0125	13,11,12A,41
Frandsen, Lars	NY0500	41,70
Frank, Pamela	PA0850	41,62A
Frantz, Jeremy	PA2950	70,41,47
Franzetti-Brewster, Allison	NJ0700	66C,41,13A,13B,13C
Fratino, Michael A.	NY3775	70,41
Fred Carrasquillo, Luis	PR0115	63C,49,41,42
Frederick, Matthew D.	VA0350	63A,12A,41,60B,32E
French, Christopher J.	TX2150	41
Fresonke, Michael	OK0750	13A,70,14C,41
Friesen-Carper, Dennis	IN1750	60,10,41,38
Frisch, Michele	MN1280	41,64A
Frisch, Roger	MN1280	62A,41
Frisof, Sarah A.	TX3500	41,64A
Frittelli, Leslie	VA1000	62C,51,41
Fulkerson, Gregory	OH1700	62A,41
Gaboury, Janine	MI1400	41,49,63B
Gaffke, Todd	MI0900	64E,41
Gagnon, Marie-Elaine	SD0600	11,51,62C,41
Galaganov, Misha	TX3000	62C,41
Galyen, S. Daniel	IA1600	37,41,32E,60B,32
Garber, Ron	KS0210	11,12A,36,41,61
Garcia, Federico	PA0600	10,12A,13,41
Garcia, Jeremy	TX2310	70,11,41
Garrett, Roger	IL1200	37,64C,60B,41,35D
Garriss, Phyllis	NC1300	41,62A
Gaston, Susan Deaver	MS0700	41,62C,62D
Gates, Stephen	AR0700	41,62C
Gatwood, Jody	DC0050	62,62A,41
Gaub, Nancy McFarland	IA0700	62A,13C,41
Gavin, Charles	TX2700	41,49,63B
Gee, Constance	SC1110	11,41,62B,42
Gemberling, Alan	ID0250	37,63C,47,60,41
Genova, Joana	MA2250	62A,41
George, Matthew J.	MN1625	60,41,37
George, Samantha	WI0350	62A,41,51
Giacabetti, Tom	NJ1050	41,53,70
Gibbons, John	MA1400	41,66H,67
Gibeau, Peter	WI0862	13,36,41,62D,66A
Gibson, Clarence	TX3150	11,37,41,42
Gibson, Thomas S.	GA1150	63C,34,41
Giebler, David	WI0920	13,11,36,41,66A
Giles, Sonja	IA0850	64A,41,42
Gillespie, James E.	TX3420	41,64C
Gilliland, Erin	OH2050	41,62A
Gilman, Kurt	TX1400	38,41,62A,62B,20
Gindin, Suzanne B.	IN1050	32,37,38,41,63B
Gippo, Jan	MO1810	41
Glencross, Laurie A.	IL1750	13,41,64A
Glicklich, Martin	CA2420	64A,41
Glise, Anthony	MO0850	70,41,42
Goble, Daniel P.	CT0800	47,64E,53,29,41
Goeke, Christopher L.	MO1500	39,41,61,54
Goh, Soo	PA1750	64C,41,11
Gold, Matthew	MA2250	50,65,43,41
Goldberg, Bernard	NY0500	41,64A
Goldberg, Julie	IL2100	70,41
Goldberg, Marc	NY2250	64D,41
Goldenberg, William	IL2200	66A,66C,41
Goldsmith, Harris	NY2250	41
Gonzalez, Rene	FL1900	41,70
Goodberg, Robert	WI0825	41,48,64A
Goode, Dana	MD0100	41
Gordon, Joshua	MA0500	11,41,42,62,62C
Gordon, Peter L.	NY2750	41,49,63B
Gould, David	NY0500	41,64C
Gould, Matt	AG0070	70,41
Gould, Valerie	WV0050	32E,34,37,41,60B
Grabiec, Andrzej	TX3400	41,62A
Grace, Susan L.	CO0200	41,66A
Graff, Steven	NY0625	41,66A
Grafilo, Zakarias	CA4200	62A,41,42
Grant, Darrell	OR0850	41,47,66A,66D,29
Gratovich, Eugene	TX3510	41,62A
Graves, Daniel H.	IN0400	11,12A,36,60,41
Gray, Charles	OR0850	47,41,29
Gray, Harold R. 'Skip'	KY1450	63D,49,41
Green, Kenneth	LA0550	37,65,41
Greensmith, Clive	CT0850	41
Greider, Cynthia S.	IN0905	64C,41
Greitzer, Deborah	MD0750	41,64D,42
Grenfell, Mary-Jo	MA1650	12A,32,38,41,42
Gresham, Jonathan	KY1000	49,63A,41
Grib, Sonia G.	NY1600	41,66H
Griffin, Dennis	UT0300	50,34,65,13G,41
Griffing, Joan	VA0300	62A,38,41,60B,62B
Grim, Jennifer	NV0050	64A,42,41
Grossman, Arthur	WA1050	41,64D
Grossman, Hal	OK1350	62A,41,51
Grubb, William	OH2200	41
Grudechi, Kevin	MA0150	41
Grutzmacher, Patricia Ann	OH1100	32,41,64B,37,20
Grycky, Eileen J.	DE0150	64A,41,48
Gu, Wen-Lei	WI0350	62A,41
Gudmundson, Jon K.	UT0300	29,64E,47,41
Guenther, Christina	TX2700	64A,20,41
Gustafson, Karen	AK0150	37,63A,41,11,60B
Guy, Charles V.	NY3780	63D,41
Haas, Arthur S.	NY3790	41,66H,67,55B
Habedank, Kathryn	WA0650	41,67C
Hagarty, Scott	TX0550	63A,13A,13C,49,41
Hager, Lawson	TX0900	13,49,63B,41
Hagglund, Heidi	IL0150	64A,41
Haight, Russell P.	TX3175	29,41,64E
Haken, Rudolf	IL3300	62B,51,41
Halen, Eric J.	TX2150	41
Halgedahl, Frederick	IA1600	41,62A
Hampton, Neal	MA0500	60,37,38,41,48
Haney, Joel C.	CA0650	11,12A,41
Hankins, Paul	MS0250	63A,41,47,32E
Hanlon, Jeff	AG0250	70,41
Hansford, James	OK0650	38,32G,37,63D,41
Harding, David	AB0100	51,62A,62B,41,42
Hardy, James	UT0150	62C,11,41
Harman, David	NY4350	60,38,41,11
Harmantas, Frank	AG0450	41,49
Harnish, David D.	CA5200	14,20,31,41
Harper, Larry D.	WI0200	60,37,41,63B
Harrill, Stephen	NC1900	61,41,44
Harrington, William	CA3520	32,38,41,63B,31A
Harris, J. David	IL3300	64C,48,41
Harris, Turman	DC0050	64D,41
Harter, Courtenay L.	TN1200	13,64B,41
Hartman, Mark S.	NY3780	63C,41
Hartman, Scott	CT0850	63C,41
Harvey, Brent M.	NC1900	63C,63D,41
Hasty, Robert G.	IL2250	41,38
Hastings, Todd J.	KS1050	63A,29,11,41,42
Hatch, Ken	AR0110	41,64C,64E,16
Hatcher, Oeida M.	VA0750	32,37,41,38,11
Hausey, Collette J.	CA2050	11,37,41,65
Hayes, Gregory M.	NH0100	66,41,42
Haywood, Carl	VA0950	13,60,41,66G
Heard, Cornelia	TN1850	41,51,62A
Hearn, William	GA0500	11,41,70,20
Hebert, Floyd	MA2250	64B,41
Hedrick, Carmella	NC1900	64A,41
Heiles, William H.	IL3300	66A,66H,41
Heilmair, Barbara	OR0850	12A,41,42,64C,48
Heinze, Thomas	PA2200	64B,46,41
Heiss, John C.	MA1400	10,12A,41,43
Helmer, Terence	AG0450	41,62B
Hemenway, Langston	IL2050	11,32E,37,41
Hersh, Alan	KY1450	66A,66B,66C,41
Hess, John	AG0500	66A,66C,41,39
Hess, Susan M.	ID0250	64D,32E,41
Heukeshoven, Janet	MN1400	37,32,60,11,41
Hickman, Joe Eugene	NC2440	60,36,41,61
Hii, Philip	TX0550	41,70
Hindell, Leonard W.	NY2250	41,64D
Hinkle, Jean	OR1020	11,13A,41,66A,66D
Hipp, Gary O.	SC1000	41
Hoag, Bret	MI1750	70,41,11
Hobson, Ian	IL3300	38,41,66A
Hohstadt, Tom	TX3527	38,41,56,60
Holden, Jonathan	MS0750	64C,41
Hollingsworth, Dina L.	CO0275	64A,64E,29,41,11
Hollins, John S.	TX3200	60,36,41
Holz, Ronald	KY0100	12,38,41,49,10
Hominick, Ian G.	MS0700	66A,66D,41
Horner, Jerry	WI0825	41,62B
Houde, Andrea	WV0750	13C,32,41,42,62B
Howard, Jeffrey	MD0850	62A,41,51
Howell, Michael W.	IN1800	41,67D,70
Huang, Hsin-Yun	NY2250	62B,41
Hubbard, Mary Ann	MI0200	41,64A
Hughes, Walden D.	ID0150	12A,41,42,66
Hughes, William M.	SC1200	13,49,63C,41
Hulen, Peter Lucas	IN1850	13,10,34,34A,41
Hulihan, Charles	AZ0350	70,41,32E,32F
Hung, Li-Shan	CA0350	66A,66B,41
Hunter, Mario	NC0550	64C,41,42
Hurst, Craig W.	WI0960	11,37,47,41,63A
Ikeda, Kikuei	CT0850	41
Imperio, Roy	MA0250	66A,66B,41,66C,11
Irom, Benjamin M.	TX2800	29,29A,47,41,13
Irwin, David E.	FL0450	64C,64E,37,41
Irwin, Doreen	CA3850	36,41,66A
Isaacson, Peter R.	TX0900	62A,38,41
Isachsen, Sten Y.	NY3600	67D,41,70,34,29
Ishigaki, Miles M.	CA0810	48,64C,41,11,14C
Isomura, Kazuhide	CT0850	41
Ivanov, Kalin H.	NY0500	41,62C
Iznaola, Ricardo	CO0900	70,41
Izquierdo, Rene	WI0825	70,41
Jablow, Lisa	VT0250	60,12A,36,41,61
Jackson, Bil	TN1850	64C,41,42
Jackson, Stephen	IL0420	48,11,20,41,47
Jacobs, Jay N.	LA0350	37,41,42,48
Jacobson, Mary Ann	MT0200	64C,14C,41
Jaimes, Judit	WI0825	41,66A,66B,66C,42
Jaquez, Candida	CA4500	14,20,12,41
Jeffries, Jean	MA1350	61,41,49
Jenkins, Carl	MA2250	64B,41
Jenkins, Donald P.	CO0200	60,36,39,41,54
Jenkins, Tim G.	MD0520	70,41
Jennings, Graeme	CA2950	40,41,62A,62B,42
Jensen, Kristin	TX3510	41,64D
Jesselson, Robert M.	SC1110	38,41,62C
Joffe, Edward	NJ0825	41,47,48,64
Johanson, Bryan	OR0850	70,13,41,11,10
Johns, John	TN1850	41,70,67G
Johnson, David	ID0070	13A,41,62B,42,51
Johnson, Ellen C.	TX0400	64A,41
Johnson, Gary	MO0250	41,46,63,65
Johnson, Karen	DC0170	41,64A
Johnson, Tripp	VA0250	41
Jolley, David	NY2250	41,63B
Jones, Emily	FL0040	11,12A,13C,41,70
Jones, Kathleen	PR0115	64C,41,42
Jones, Patrick R.	PA1200	11,29,64,41
Jones, Vanita	MD0150	41,64A
Jones, Vanita	MD0550	64A,41
Jonker, Jacob	MN1600	70,41
Jordan-Anders, Lee	VA1830	13,11,41,66A
Jordheim, Steven	WI0350	41,64E
Jorgensen, Elaine	UT0190	11,41,48,64A
Jorgensen, Jerilyn J.	CO0200	62A,41
Josenhans, Thomas	IN1600	64C,13B,13C,64E,41
Juncker, Arthur	CA1950	13,10,12A,41,34
Kadz, John	AA0050	41,62C
Kagarice, Vern L.	TX3420	41,49,63C,63D
Kahn, Sue Ann	NY2250	41,64A
Kahng, Er-Gene	AR0700	62A,62B,41
Kalish, Gilbert	NY3790	41,66A,66C,43
Kallick, Jenny L.	MA0100	13,12A,39,41,12
Kane, Trudy	FL1900	64A,41,48
Kang, Grace	FL1750	41,63B
Kani, Robin	PA2450	41,48,64A
Kannen, Michael	MD0650	41,42
Kaplanek, Jerzy	AG0600	41,62A

Index by Area of Teaching Interest

Name	Code	Areas
Kappy, David	WA1050	13A,41,48,63B
Karp, Benjamin	KY1450	41,62C,42
Karpowicz, Mike	MO1950	29,41
Kartman, Stefan	WI0825	62C,42,51,41
Kasman, Tatiana	AL1150	66C,41
Katz, Martin E.	MI2100	41,66C
Kautsky, Catherine C.	WI0350	66A,66C,66E,41
Kawamura, Manami	CA0350	41,66A,66C
Kawasaki, Masao	NY0500	41,62A,62B
Keaton, Kenneth D.	FL0650	60,12A,41,67D,70
Keeler, Paula	IA0150	32,36,39,41,61
Kellan, Kurt	AB0150	41,63B
Kelley, Timothy S.	TX3650	60,37,49,63,41
Kelly, Frankie J.	LA0800	66C,40,41,42,11
Kelly, Keith	CA0850	29,47,46,41
Kerber, Ronald	PA3330	47,64A,64E,29,41
Kerchner, Jody L.	OH1700	32,41
Kern, Bradley	KY1450	63C,41
Kile, Nora	TN1350	64A,41
Kim, Chin	NY2250	41,62A
Kim, Chris Younghoon	NY0900	38,41,42,60
Kim, David	RI0300	41,62A
Kim, Min	NJ0825	13,12,66A,66B,41
Kim, Wonkak	TN1450	64C,48,41
Kim, Yeesun	MA1400	41,62C
Kim, Yong Tae	NJ0825	41,62A
Kim, Young-Nam	MN1623	41,62A
Kimball, Will	UT0050	41,63C
Kinder, Keith	AG0200	37,41,49,63
King, Richard	OH0600	63B,49,41
King, Sidney	KY1500	62D,41
Kirby, David S.	NC1900	12A,64C,64E,64D,41
Kirby, Steven	MA1650	41
Kirchhoff, Craig	MN1623	60,37,41
Kirk-Doyle, Julianne	NY3780	64C,42,41
Kirkendoll, Mary	KS1050	41,64A
Kirkpatrick, Leon	KY0250	37,38,41,51,60B
Kirkpatrick, Linda M.	MD0520	60,37,41,48,64A
Kitchen, Nicholas	MA1400	41,62A
Klausner, Tiberius	MO1810	41,62A
Klein, Doug	ND0050	70,41
Klein, Lonnie	NM0310	11,38,41,60
Klugherz, Laura	NY0650	13,11,41,62A,62B
Knepp, Richard	GA2300	70,41,12A
Knight, Katharine	CO0900	62C,41
Knopp, Seth D.	MD0650	41,42
Kochanowski, John	TN1850	41,51,62B,42
Kolkay, Peter	TN1850	41,64D,48
Kolodny, Michael	MA2250	64E,41
Konkol, Korey	MN1623	41,62B
Konzen, Richard A.	PA1450	38,51,66G,41,13B
Koponen, Glenn	NY2900	60,37,41,63A,31A
Kostic, Dina	FL0050	62A,41,42,51
Kozak, Kevin J.	AL0800	63B,13C,41
Kozamchak, David M.	MN1280	38,51,62A,62B,41
Kozlova, Yulia	CA4450	11,13,41,66
Krakauer, David	NY2250	41,64C
Krash, Jessica	DC0100	41,66A
Krause, Kristi	MN1700	64B,41
Krauss, David B.	NJ1130	63A,41
Kravitz, Steve	OR0750	64A,64D,64E,41
Krejci, Mathew	CA5350	64A,42,41
Kretzer, Scott	MI0050	37,41,65
Krieger, David	NY2400	62C,41
Krimsier, Renee	MA1400	41
Krolikowski, Lucas	IL1750	41,70
Kroth, Michael	MI1400	64D,41
Kukec, Catherine	IL1900	11,41,47,50,48
Kurkowicz, Joanna	MA2250	41,62A,43
Kurschner, James	MN1200	37,64E,41,66D
Kush, Jason	PA3100	64E,29,41,53,64C
Kustanovich, Serafima	MA0650	66A,66C,41
Kuster, Nicolasa	CA5350	64D,42,41
Kuykendall, James Brooks	SC0700	13,12,11,41,38
Kvetko, Peter J.	MA1650	14,13A,14C,20E,41
Laarz, Bill	TN0580	37,38,41,63
Ladd, Gita	MD1000	41,42,62C
Lafreniere, Andy	CT0800	41,70
Laib, Susan	PA2150	41,64B,64D
Laimon, Sara	AI0150	66A,41
Lamar, Linda Kline	ID0050	13,62B,41
Lambros, Maria	MD0650	41,42
Lambson, Nick	CA2250	70,41,35G
Land, W. Reese	KY0400	11,13A,41
Landgrebe, Junauro	MA1450	11,14C,41
Lang, Cynthia	CA3400	38,41,51,62
Lange, Richard	MI0050	41,70
Lange-Jensen, Catherine	KY1000	62C,41
Lansdale, Katie	CT0650	41,51,62A
Lanza, Joseph	AG0500	38,41,51,62A
Lanza, Lou	PA2450	61,47,29,41
Lapple, Judith A.	VA0450	64A,41
Larmee, Kent	OH1100	11,41,63B
Larocque, Jacques	AI0220	10,41,48,64E,34
Larsen, Eric	NC1650	41,66A
Larson, Richard	IL0150	70,41
Larson, Steven	CT0650	41,62B
Lasareff-Mirinoff, Claudia	IL2100	41,42
Latarski, Donald	OR1050	70,35G,41
Lateiner, Jacob	NY2250	66A,41
Laut, Edward A.	KS1350	41,62C
Lautar, Rebecca	FL0650	11,41,51,62A,62B
Lawrence, Kevin	NC1650	62A,41
Lawson, Charles E.	CO0250	13,64C,41
Lawson, Robert	CA1265	10,38,41,66A,66D
Layendecker, Dennis M.	VA0450	60,38,41
Leathwood, Jonathan	CO0900	70,41,13D,10A,13E
LeBlanc, Robert L.	OH1850	37,41,63D
Leclair, Jacqueline F.	AI0150	64B,41
Lee, Cassandra	TN1850	41,48,64C,42
Lee, Charles	CO0650	62C,41,51,10F,60
Lee, Gregory	OK1350	62A,41,51
Lee, Patricia Taylor	CA4200	41,66A,66B
LeGrand, Thomas	TX2150	41
Leisenring, John R.	MO1810	41,63C,63D
Leisring, Laura	VA0250	48,64A,64D,41,64C
Lemelin, Stephane	AG0400	66,41
Lemmons, Keith M.	NM0450	64C,41
Leon, Tania	NY0500	10,38,41,60
Leone, Carol	TX2400	41,66A
Leong, Sonia	CA5350	66A,41,42
Leslie, Drew	NC0050	63C,49,42,41
Lessly, Chris Ann	IN1025	32,41,48,64C,64E
Lester, Joel	NY2250	13,41
Levin, Andrew R.	SC0400	11,41,38,13,42
Levin, Robert	MA1050	41,66
Levitz, Jodi	CA4150	41,62B
Levtov, Vladimir	AA0150	41,66A,66C,66D,42
Lewanski, Michael A.	IL0750	41,43
Lewis, Darin	PA1850	41
Lewis, David P.	WV0350	64,37,41,12A,32E
Lewis, Melissa	OK1200	60,41,51,62A
Lewis, Nicholas	DC0150	64C,41
Lewis, Philip J.	TX3420	41,62A
Lezcano, Jose	NH0150	41,70,20H
Lichten, Julia	NY3785	62C,41
Liebowitz, Marian L.	CA4100	11,41,48,64C,35B
Lifsitz, Fred	CA4200	41,62A,42
Lin, I-Bei	HI0210	62C,41,42,13A
Linde-Capistran, Jane	MN0600	41,62A,62B
Lindholm, Eric C.	CA3650	13A,60,11,38,41
Lindquist, George	WI1150	41,70
Lindquist, George C.	WI0835	41,70
Lindsey, Douglas	GA1150	63A,41
Lindsey, Logan	WV0050	29,41,49,63D
Linneroth, Sherry	MT0200	63B,41
Lion, Na'ama	MA0250	41,64A,67D
Lipman, Michael	PA0600	62C,41
Little, Donald C.	TX3420	41,49,63D
Littrell, David	KS0650	38,41,62C,62D,13A
Liu, Meng-Chieh	PA0850	41,66A
Liu, Te-Chiang	MN1600	62A,62B,41
Lizotte, Caroline	AI0150	62,41
Loban, John A.	AB0100	41,51,62A
Loeb, Jaemi	KY0450	38,13A,41,42,60B
Loeppky, Ian R.	AL1250	60,36,41,40
Lorenz, Kevin	NC1450	70,41
Louwenaar, Karyl	FL0850	66E,41,66A,66H
Love, Randolph D.	SC0600	13,10,63,41,14C
Lovejoy, Donald G.	MN1700	37,63A,41,60,32E
Luby, Richard E.	NC2410	41,51,62A,67A
Lucarelli, Humbert	CT0650	41,64B
Lucas, Mark	OK1350	60,32,36,41
Luckhardt, Jerry	MN1623	60,37,41
Lupu, Sherban	IL3300	51,62A,41
Lupu, Virgil I.	OH2140	62A,41,12A,11,34B
Luther, David	TN0200	60,36,61,31A,41
Lydy, Laura	IN0905	70,41
Lyon, Howard	PA1200	62A,62B,41
Macdonald, Elizabeth	MO1900	41,62C
Macdonald, James	IL0850	36,41
Machala, Kazimierz W.	IL3300	63B,49,41
Mack, Peter	WA0200	66A,41,13C
Mackey, Steven	NJ0900	13,10F,10,11,41
Magaziner, Elliot	NY2400	60,41,62A
Magnanini, Luciano	FL1900	41,48,64D
Maiello, Anthony J.	VA0450	60,37,38,41
Maier, Ralph	AA0150	70,41,12,14
Mallard, Manley	IL1750	41,70,34
Maltester, Diane	CA2775	12A,64,41,13C
Maltester, John	CA2775	37,41,60B,63C
Malvern, Gary J.	SC0750	63A,41,12A
Mammon, Marielaine	NJ0250	12A,32,36,41,61
Manji, K. C.	CA1265	60,38,49,41,29A
Manning, Lucy	VA1000	38,62A,32E,41,51
Mannix, Natalie K.	MD0850	63C,63D,41
Manwarren, Matthew C.	SC1200	66A,66B,12,41
Marchione, Jill	PA3150	64B,41
Mark, Douglas L.	MS0250	49,63C,63D,41
Markowski, Victoria	CO0275	66A,66D,41,42
Marks, Laurence L.	NC2420	37,64C,32C,41
Markward, Cheri D.	RI0101	13,11,41,62,12A
Marsh, Peter	CA5300	41,62
Marshall, Jeffrey	IL2350	37,41
Marshall, John	WA0250	62C,70,32E,41,32F
Marshall, Kimberly	AZ0100	41,66G
Martin, Blair	KS1250	13C,37,46,41,32
Martin, Danny Ray	TN0150	70,42,29,41
Martin, John	KY1550	70,11,34B,34G,41
Martin, Joseph	CO0900	37,63C,63D,41,60
Martin, Noel	TX3450	41
Martin, Robert	IA1450	41
Martin, Roger	TN1450	64A,41,64
Martinez, Kurt	TX3525	11,70,41
Martula, Susan	MA2250	64C,41
Mason, Daniel	KY1450	62A,62B,41
Masserini, John	AZ0450	64C,41
Mast, Andrew	WI0350	37,41,42,60
Masterson, Daniel J.	KS0150	13,41,66A,66B,42
Matlick, Eldon	OK1350	41,63B
Maxwell, Sarita J.	SC1200	63D,41
Maxwell, Steven	KS0650	63D,11,41
Mayer, Anne B.	MN0300	13A,41,66A,12A
Mayes, Joseph	NJ1050	41,67,70
Mazo, Vadim	IL1200	41,42,62A,62B,51
McAllister, Elizabeth	NC1750	12A,41,48,64C,64E
McBain, Katherine C.	IL0800	63B,41,11
McCabe, Robin	WA1050	41,66A
McCafferty, Dennis S.	IN1650	62C,41
McCandless, Marty	IL1100	64C,64E,32E,47,41
McCleery, Mark	LA0770	11,41,62C,62D
McCloskey, Diane L.	OH1100	64A,41
McColl, William	WA1050	41,64C
McCray, Mack	CA4150	66A,41
McCumber, Gary	AG0500	37,41
McDonald, Reginald	TN1400	32E,37,41,64E
McDonald, Steven	KS1000	66,38,60B,12A,41
McElwaine, James	NY3785	41,47,20G,29,34
McGarrell, Matthew	RI0050	37,41,47,46
McGarvey, Timothy	IA1200	37,60,32E,41,29A
McGhee, Lorna	AB0100	64A,41
McGovern, Timothy S.	IL3300	64D,48,41
McGowan, Thomas	TX3370	37,41,50,65
McGrannahan, A. Graydon	NV0100	37,32C,41,63C,63D
McGuinness, Peter	NJ1400	13,10,29,41
McKay, Emily Hoppe	AZ0450	64A,41
McKay, James R.	AG0500	37,38,41,64D,12F
McKay, Janis	NV0050	13,41,55,64D
McKinney, John S.	WV0350	50,65,34,60B,41
McLaughlin, Michael G.	MA1900	66A,41
McMickle, Doug	OR0750	70,41
McTeer, Mikylah Myers	WV0750	62A,32E,41,42
McWayne, Dorli	AK0150	48,64A,41
Means, Matthew L.	KS0350	11,62A,62B,41,42
Meccia, Lauren L.	SC1100	37,41,47
Mecham, Bryce	ID0060	63C,41,32E
Meehan, Conor	MA2250	65,41
Melancon, Violaine M.	MD0650	41,62A
Melbinger, Timothy	PA2710	12A,41,13B,13C,13E
Melville, Nicola	MN0300	66A,41
Mendenhall, Judith	NY2250	64A,41
Mendoza, Cristina	LA0450	63,46,49,11,41
Mensch, Thomas	TX3370	37,41,63C,49,48
Mensh, Heather	TX3370	37,41,46,48,63D
Meredith, Victoria	AG0500	60,32,36,41
Merritt, Romona	AL0650	62,41

Index by Area of Teaching Interest

Name	Code	Areas
Mery, John Christian	OR0800	13,10,41,70,34
Meyer, Edgar	TN1850	41,62D
Meyer, Kenneth	NY1550	11,70,41
Michaelian, Patricia	WA1050	41,66A,66B
Michel, John	WA0050	11,41,51,62C
Michelic, Matthew C.	WI0350	41,62B
Michell, Edna	NY2250	41
Middleton, Polly K.	VA1700	32E,32G,37,41
Mieses, Nermis	KY1450	64B,13C,41
Milewski, Piotr	OH2200	41,62A
Millard, Christopher	IL2250	41
Millard, Joshua P.	MA2030	13B,13C,41,47
Miller, Ann Elizabeth	CA5350	62A,42,12A,41
Miller, Anton	CT0650	41,51,62A
Miller, Mark	CO0560	29,13A,41,47,64A
Miller, Matthew	WI0250	70,41
Miller, Tess Anissa	MI0150	64A,11,41
Miller, Ward	AL1300	37,63D,41,32E,60B
Minnis, MaryBeth	MI0400	41,48,64D
Miranda, Michael A.	CA2800	11,67G,70,12A,41
Mizrahi, Michael	WI0350	66A,41
Mochnick, John	IL2900	36,41
Monosoff, Sonya	NY0900	41,62A,62B,67B
Montgomery, William L.	MD1010	41,64A
Moody, Gary E.	CO0250	64B,13,41,64D
Moore, Frances	CA2800	60B,41,62A,67B,38
Moore, Hilarie Clark	NY3000	38,41,63B
Moore, Mark E.	IL3300	63D,49,41
Moore, Matthew	ID0060	34,41,63D
Moore, Selma	NY2950	13,37,41,64A,66D
Morehead, Phillip H.	TN0850	13,41,63A,32E
Morelli, Frank	CT0850	64D,41
Morelli, Frank A.	NY3790	64D,41
Morita, Lina	LA0350	13C,41,66A,66C,66D
Morris, Craig	FL1900	41,49,63A,42
Morris, Quinton	WA0850	41
Morris, Ralph	OK1330	38,62A,62B,41,42
Morris, Winston	TN1450	49,63D,41
Morrison, Chris	CT0800	53,70,41
Morrison, Heather	AG0170	41,66A
Morrison, Nicholas	UT0300	37,64C,48,41
Morse, Elizabeth	MA2250	62E,41
Mowitz, Ira	NJ0750	10,13A,13B,41,66A
Moye, Brenda	TN0850	64E,41,34
Moyer, Cynthia M.	CA2250	13,41,62A,62B
Muchnick, Amy Faye	MO0775	11,12A,62B,41
Muegel, Glenn	NC0050	13,41,62A,62B
Murphy, Patrick C.	OR1100	13B,37,32,41
Murray, Jane	RI0300	38,41,48,64B
Murray, Kathrin	MD0520	70,41
, Muryanto	VA0250	41
Musco, Lynn A.	FL1750	41,64C
Mushabac, Regina M.	OH0200	41,51
Myrick, John	AL1195	32,62A,62B,41,51
Nadel, James	CA4900	41,29
Nagel, Rebecca S.	SC1110	11,64B,41
Natenberg, Reena Berger	KS1050	66A,66C,41
Navega, Eduardo	NY4450	38,41,60
Nazarenko, John	MA2250	66A,41
Negyesy, Janos	CA5050	20F,41,62A,43,34
Neitzke, Jeff	OH2290	41,65,37
Nel, Anton	TX3510	66A,41
Nelson, Elise Buffat	ND0350	62C,41,42
Nelson, Eric	GA0750	60,36,38,41
Nepkie, Janet	NY3765	13A,41,51,62C,35
Nestler, Eric M.	TX3420	41,64E
Neu, Ah Ling	MA2250	62A,41
Neubert, Peter	TX0900	62B,62A,41
Neumann, Mark	OK1350	62A,41,51
Newman, David	WI0100	66A,66D,41
Newman, Michael	NY2250	70,41
Newton, Jack	NC0050	47,41,64C,72,35
Niblock, Howard	WI0350	13,10F,12B,41,64B
Nicholson, Jason	UT0300	65,50,41
Nies, Craig	TN1850	66A,41,66C
Nitsch, Paul A.	NC2000	41,66A,66H
Noland, David	CT0800	64E,41
Norman, Mark	KS1400	37,41,60B,63D
Norton, Leslie	TN1850	41,48,63B,49
Novak, Tom	MA1400	41
Novine-Whitaker, Virginia	NC0750	64E,41
Nugent, Thomas	CA5350	64B,41,42
Nutt, Dorrie	AL1160	63B,41
Nuttall, Geoff	CA4900	62A,41,51
Oehler, Donald L.	NC2410	41,42,43,48,64C
Ogle, Alex	NH0100	64A,41,42
Olbrych, Timothy	VA0250	67B,67G,70,41
Oldham, Barbara	NY0500	41,63B
Oliver, Harold	NJ1050	13,10F,10,41,53
Olson, Matthew W.	SC0750	64E,29,47,41,46
O'Neil, Lorne W.	TX3525	11,41,48,64
O'Neill, Jill L.	SC1200	11,64A,48,14C,41
O'Neill, SC, Alice Ann M.	OH0680	32E,62C,41,62D
Oppens, Ursula	NY0500	66,41,42,43
O'Reilly, Sally	MN1623	41,62A
Osland, Lisa	KY1450	64E,41,47
Osmun, Ross	AI0050	13,41,42,66A,66B
Ostrovsky, Paul	NY3785	41,66A
Otaki, Michiko	GA0500	41,66A,66C,66D
Ott, Hal J.	WA0050	12A,41,48,64A,67D
Ou, Carol	MA1400	41
Oundjian, Peter	CT0850	41,62A
Owen, Marlin	CA0350	38,41,51,62,70
Packard, Jennifer	OH1600	64A,41
Padgham Albrecht, Carol	ID0250	11,12A,64B,32E,41
Padilla, Anthony	WI0350	66A,66C,41,42
Paglalonga, Phillip O.	FL0100	64C,41,48,13A,13B
Paliga, Mitch L.	IL2050	64E,29A,41,47,48
Palmer, Bradley E.	GA0550	63C,11,34,32F,41
Palumbo, Michael A.	UT0350	38,62B,32E,60,41
Papillon, Andre	AI0190	11,41,64A
Paradis, Sarah	OH1900	63C,41
Park, Christine	CA2600	66A,13A,13B,13C,41
Park, Sue-Jean	KY0950	62A,62B,41
Park, Tricia	IN1700	62A,42,41
Parke, Nathaniel	MA2250	62C,43,41
Parker, Laura M.	IL2400	13,41,42,62A,66A
Parker, Mara	PA3680	12A,11,41,51,62C
Parker, Nathaniel F.	PA2200	38,60B,64,41
Parks, Ronald Keith	SC1200	10,13,34,41
Parman, David L.	IN1800	41,62C,62D,21,70,20G
Parodi, Jorge	NY0500	39,40,41,66C
Partain, Gregory L.	KY1350	11,41,66A,66B,12A
Patterson, Ronald	WA1050	41,62A
Payne, Catherine	CA4400	41,64A
Pearson, Ian D.	SC1200	12,55,41
Pederson, Steven A.	KY0800	37,41,47,64
Penne, Cynthia S.	VA1850	62A,62B,41
Pepping, Amanda J.	GA1050	63A,41
Peris, Malinee	DC0100	41,66A,51
Perkins, Jerry	TN1100	66A,41
Perron, Johanne	AI0200	62C,41
Peterman, Lewis E.	CA4100	14A,41,55,11
Petrowska-Quilico, Christina	AG0650	13A,41,66A,66B
Pflueger, Bethany	CA1960	13,41
Phelps, Robert	MA2250	70,41
Pherigo, Johnny L.	FL1800	11,41,49,48,63B
Philbrick, Channing	IL2250	41
Phillips, Daniel	NY2250	41,62A
Phillips, Joe Rea	TN1850	41,70,33
Phillips, Todd	NY2250	41,62A
Pierce, Michael	LA0720	37,41,64A,11
Piippo, Richard	MI1050	38,41,51,62C,10F
Pikler, Charles	IL2250	41
Pineda, Kris	IL2910	66A,66C,41
Pitchon, Joel L.	MA1750	62A,41,42
Plant, Lourin	NJ1050	60,36,41,61
Plotnick, Jeff	AA0050	38,41
Plummer, Carolyn	IN1700	62A,42,41
Plummer, Kathryn	TN1850	41,62A,62B,34
Poitier, James	FL0100	37,49,63,32F,41
Polk, Janet E.	NH0100	64D,41,42
Polk, Joanne	NY2150	41,66A
Ponto, Robert	OR1050	60B,37,41
Poole, Eric	NC2150	13,60,20G,36,41
Pope, Wayne	KY1550	39,61,41
Poper, Roy	OH1700	63A,49,41
Popov, Vasily	DC0170	62C,41
Posnak, Paul	FL1900	41,66A,66H,66C
Potter, Valerie	NM0450	64A,41,48
Powell, Brian T.	FL1900	62D,41
Powell, Edwin C.	WA0650	37,41,32E,60B
Powell, Michael E.	NJ1130	63C,41
Powell, Ross	TX2400	41,64C,43
Premezzi, Renato	WI0100	66A,41
Prescott, Barbara	FL0450	41,64A
Price, Cecilia	GA1150	41
Price, William Roger	OK1450	10A,41,66A,10F
Pridmore, Helen	AE0050	61,39,41
Prins, Rene	NY3765	64B,37,13,41
Prior, Richard	GA0750	38,41,42,60B
Prochazka, Tanya	AA0100	62C,41
Proctor, Freda	KS1375	66,64A,13,37,41
Prosser, Peter	NY2250	41
Protsman, Harold S.	VA1000	66A,66C,41
Provost, Richard C.	CT0650	41,70
Puchala, Mark	MI1650	12A,36,61,34,41
Puchhammer, Jutta	AI0200	62B,41,51
Pulford, Paul	AG0600	41,62C,38
Pulos, Nick	AA0050	38,62B,41
Purdy, Craig Allen	ID0050	41,42,51,62A,38
Pursell, Anthony	TX2750	37,41,48,60,63C
Quantz, Don E.	AA0010	12A,32D,36,40,41
Quantz, Michael	TX3515	11,41,62,20H
Quick, Julia M.	SC1050	11,38,41,51,62A
Radlo, Dolores	MA1600	41
Raimi, Max	IL2250	41
Ramirez Rios, Ruben J.	PR0115	63D,41
Ramos, Mary Ann	AZ0450	62C,41
Ranger, Louis	AB0150	49,63A,41
Raps, Gena	NY2250	41,66A
Raschiatore, Lisa	MI1260	64C,41
Rasmussen, Anne K.	VA0250	14,20G,31,41,12C
Rath, Edward	IL3300	66A,41
Ray, Emily	CA4425	38,41
Ray, Mary Ruth	MA0500	41,62B,11
Ray, W. Irwin	GA1550	60,11,41,36,40
Raychev, Evgeni	TX2700	62C,41,11,62D
Read, Jesse	AB0100	38,41,64D,67E
Reagan, Ann B.	CO0750	11,12A,12,41,66A
Reagan, Billy R.	AL0350	36,37,41,47,63
Reams, John	GA1800	13,38,41,64
Reeds, Elizabeth	NY0400	41,64A
Reese, Marc B.	FL1125	63A,49,41,42,48
Reeves, Shane	SC0710	65,41
Rehkopf-Michel, Carrie	WA0050	41,51,62A,62B
Reid, James	ID0250	11,41,70
Reilly, Paul C.	IN0150	41,70,67D
Reimer, David	MI0350	11,32E,42,62A,41
Remenikova, Tanya	MN1623	41,62C
Remy-Schumacher, Tess	OK1330	62C,41,42
Renard-Payen, Florent	NY1350	41
Renzi, Paul	CA4200	41,64A
Requiro, David	WA1000	62C,41,42
Restesan, Francise T.	PR0125	13,60,12B,38,41
Reyes, Ysmael	CO0650	64A,41,48
Reynerson, Rodney T.	NC0050	66A,66C,66D,11,41
Reynolds, Anne B.	IN0350	64A,41
Reynolds, Kathleen	TX3420	41,64D
Reynolds, Martin C.	MO1500	37,63C,41,47,32E
Rheude, Elizabeth A.	ND0500	41,64C,64E
Rhodes, Samuel	NY1900	51,41,62B
Rhyneer, Barbara	MI1600	60,38,41,62,11
Richards, E. Michael	MD1000	64C,60,41,38
Richards, Patrick	MS0360	41,49
Richardson, Colleen	AG0500	60B,37,32E,41,42
Richter, Elizabeth	IN0150	41,66E,66D
Richtmeyer, Debra A.	IL3300	64E,48,41
Rider, Rhonda	MA0350	41,62C
Riggs, Robert D.	MS0700	12A,12B,41,62A,62B
Rinehart, Jason	LA0770	60B,37,38,41
Rios, Giselle Elgarresta	FL0050	61,36,60,32,41
Ripley, James	WI0250	37,41,32E,60B,38
Rischin, Rebecca M.	OH1900	64C,41
Riseling, Robert A.	AG0500	13,37,38,41,64C
Ritzenthaler, Maria	IL1085	62B,41,42
Rivera, Francesca M.	CA5353	14,20H,41
Rivera, Lino	CA3920	11,41
Rivera, Luis C.	AL1300	20,32E,41,65,50
Rivera, Miguel	PR0100	41,63D
Rivest, Darlene	WI0250	62B,32E,38,62A,41
Rivkin, Evgeny	GA2100	41,66A
Rizner, Dan Joseph	IN0350	41,62A
Robbins, Gerald	NY2150	41
Robert, Lucie	NY2150	41,62A
Roberts, Shannon B.	UT0150	13,41,49,63C,10
Roberts, Terry	SC0710	11,63,13C,35A,41
Robertson, Elizabeth A.	IN1600	64B,11,41
Robertson, Karen	NC0050	49,63A,42,41
Robertson, Lesley N.	CA4900	62B,41,51
Robinson, Melissa Ann	OR0850	41,42,49,63B
Rodriguez, Alberto	PR0115	70,41,42
Rodriguez, Galindo	LA0550	63A,41,47
Roelofs, Laura Leigh	MI2200	62A,32E,41,11
Roggen, Ann	NJ1400	62B,41
Rojak, John	NJ1130	63C,41

Index by Area of Teaching Interest

Name	Code	Areas
Rojas, Luis Miguel	PR0115	62C,41,42
Rokeach, Martin	CA3920	13A,13,11,12A,41
Romm, Ronald	IL3300	63A,41
Roop, Cynthia M.	NC1250	64A,32A,32E,13C,41
Root, Thomas R.	UT0350	13,10,37,41
Rosado, Ana Maria	NJ0825	70,41,11,12A
Rose, Gil B.	MA1450	60,38,41,13A
Rose, Melissa K.	TN1850	66C,41,40
Rose, Saxton	NC1650	48,64D,41
Rosenbaum, Victor	MA1400	41,66A
Rosenberg, Thomas	MN0300	62C,41
Rosengren, Hakan	CA0815	64C,41
Rosenwein, Frank	OH0600	64B,41
Ross, Daniel F.	AR0110	11,41,64B,64D,72
Ross, Julian E.	OH0200	41,62A
Roth, John	MN0610	34,40,41,70
Rouslin, Daniel S.	OR1300	11,38,41,62A,62B
Rousseau, Eugene E.	MN1623	41,64E
Rovkah, Pauline	PA0600	66A,41
Rowell, Chester D.	TX2295	64C,64E,41
Rowlett, Michael T.	MS0700	64C,11,41
Rox, David	MA0950	10F,60,32,37,41
Rozman, Jure	FL0200	66A,13,41
Ruas, Laura M.	MD1000	41,42,62D
Rubin, Joel E.	VA1550	14A,14C,64C,41,31B
Rubio, Douglas	NY3780	12A,41,70
Ruby, Meg	MA2030	41,42,47,66A
Ruck, Jonathan C.	OK1350	62C,41
Rudolph, Robert A.	PA0100	62A,62B,41,42,51
Ruffels, Dave	CT0800	62D,53,41
Rulli, Richard J.	AR0700	63A,42,49,41
Rumney, Jon	ND0250	13,38,41,62A,62B
Rundlett, Jennifer	MD0300	64A,11,41
Russell, Tilden	CT0450	11,12A,12,41
Ruthrauff, Jeremy	IL0730	64E,41
Rutkowski, Geoffrey	CA5060	41,62C
Ryan, Pamela	FL0850	41,62B
Sachs, Joel	NY1900	12A,41,43
Saeverud, Trond	ME0430	11,13A,41,36
Sakakeeny, George	OH1700	64D,48,41
Saks, Toby	WA1050	41,62C
Salaff, Peter	OH0600	41
Salanki, Hedi	FL2100	13C,13E,66A,66H,41
Salem, Ernest	CA0815	13A,41,62A,62B
Salerno, Julia	WA0250	62A,62B,41
Salness, David	MD1010	62A,41
Salvo, Leonard P.	OH0100	60B,32C,37,41,32E
Sanders, Raphael P.	NY3780	64C,41
Santiago, Imer	TN1400	63A,41
Saulter, Gerry	NY1275	12A,13C,70,42,41
Saunders, David	MN0300	41,64E
Saunders, Meg	KY0450	62A,62B,41
Saylor, Jonathan	IL3550	12A,64D,41
Scafide, Anthony	NY3765	35,41,47
Scarnati, Rebecca Kemper	AZ0450	64B,13,41
Scarpa, Salvatore	NJ1050	60,38,41,63C
Schachter, Carl	NY2250	13,41
Scharnberg, William	TX3420	41,49,63B
Schepps, David M.	NM0450	62C,41
Schlabach, John	OH1900	63A,41
Schmidt, Carsten	NY3560	13,11,12A,41,66A
Schmitz, Michael	CA3270	66A,12A,13,20,41
Schneider, David E.	MA0100	12,64C,43,13,41
Schneider, John	CA2700	41,45,70,34
Schneider, Lisa A.	AL1160	11,64B,41
Schoen, Theodore A.	MN1600	64C,64E,41,10F
Schoen, Thomas	AA0110	62A,41
Schranz, Karoly	CO0800	62A,41
Schubert, Barbara	IL3250	38,41,60,43
Schulze-Johnson, Virginia	NJ0300	41,47,48,64A,42
Schwartz, Daniel	OK1350	64B,41
Schwartz, Elliott S.	ME0200	10F,10,11,12A,41
Schwartz, Robert	CA2950	66A,41,42
Schwarz, Timothy J.	PA1950	62A,62B,51,41
Scott, David	CT0800	47,63A,41
Scott, John C.	TX3420	41,64C
Scott, Marshall	KY1550	41,47,63A,29
Scott, William	KY1550	62D,38,41
Scruggs, Richard J.	TN0250	11,13B,41,48,64E
Searle, David	DC0050	38,39,41
Seaward, Jeffery A.	CA1290	13A,36,41,61,54
Seeley, Gilbert	OR0400	60,12A,36,41
Seggelke, Martin H.	CA4200	37,41,42,60
Seligman, Susan	NY3760	13A,13C,11,41,62C
Senn, Geoff	MN0040	29A,63A,34,41,11
Setzer, Ann	NY2250	41,62A
Setzer, Philip E.	NY3790	41,62A
Severs, Alan R.	IN0905	63A,41
Shaffer, Marian	TN1850	62E,41,42
Shands, Patricia	CA5350	64C,42,41
Shannon, Nanette	CO0650	66A,41,66D
Sharp, Wendy	CT0850	41
Sharpe, Avery G.	MA2250	62D,41,36
Sharpe, Paul	NC1650	41,62D
Shaw, Clyde Thomas	VA1350	62C,42,12A,41
Shea, David L.	TX3200	34,41,64A,64C,64E
Shelly, Frances	KS1450	64A,41
Sherman, Paul	CA0960	41
Shiffer, Faith E.	PA1250	64C,64E,41
Shifrin, David	CT0850	41,64C
Shipley, Lori R.	VA0500	48,12A,13A,64A,41
Shipp, Daniel	AG0250	41
Shoop, Stephen S.	TX3515	32,41,60B,63D
Shotola, Marilyn	OR0850	13,64A,41,12A
Sidon, Ashley Sandor	IA0550	62C,32E,41
Siegel, Jeff S.	CT0800	53,41,65,29
Siler, Sandra K.	TX1350	41,45,66A,66D
Silverman, Marc	NY2150	41,66A
Silverstein, Joseph	PA0850	41,62A
Simidtchieva, Marta	IL2910	38,42,41,51,62C
Simon, Philip G.	PA3700	11,37,41,51,63D
Simpson, Peter	KY1450	13,64D,41
Sims, Stuart	CA0850	37,38,41,60B
Sinclair, John V.	FL1550	60,32,36,41,38
Sincoff, Alison J. Brown	OH1900	64A,41
Sindell, Carol A.	OR0850	41,62A,42
Singer, David	NJ0800	41,48,64C,11
Singer, Leigh Ann	IA0910	41,64A,64E
Singley, David	MN0300	70,47,41
Sise, Patrick	MD0350	70,41
Skelton, Robert A.	AG0500	60,38,41,51,62
Skidmore, William	WV0750	13,41,62C
Skogen, Meaghan	NC0750	62C,13,41
Slavich, Richard	CO0900	12A,51,62C,41
Sloan, Rita	MD1010	66C,66A,41
Slowik, Peter	OH1700	62B,41
Small, Elisabeth	TN0100	41,62A,51
Smith, Alan	CA5300	41,66A,66C
Smith, C. Scott	OH1900	13,63B,41
Smith, Elizabeth Reed	WV0400	38,41,51,62A,62B
Smith, James S.	NC1800	36,41,61
Smith, Janice M.	MO1900	41,64A
Smith, Jason R.	OH1900	63D,13A,41
Smith, Judith	CT0800	62C,32E,41
Smith, Lee	CA4950	11,41,62
Smith, Rusty	NC1900	63A,41,46,47
Smith, Rylan	GA1050	70,41
Smith, Thomas	NY2250	63A,41
Snavely, Jack	WI0825	41,64C,64E
Snider, Nancy Jo	DC0010	62C,42,51,67B,41
Snoza, Melissa	WI0250	64A,41
Sohn, Sung-Rai	NY3560	60,38,41,51,62A
Solis, Richard	OH0600	63B,41,49
Solomon, Qiao Chen	GA0050	62A,62B,51,41,38
Solomons, John	TX3500	66A,41,66C
Song, JY	NY2250	66A,41
Soroka, Solomia	IN0550	13,62A,41
Southard, Robert G.	MI1050	37,60B,41,11
Sowers, Jodi L.	IN0907	11,64A,41
Sparrow, James	NC1250	63D,32E,41,63C,63
Speth, Uli	NY1400	62A,41,51
Speziale, Marie	TX2150	63A,41,42
Spinazzola, James M.	IN1650	37,41,60B
Sprenkle, David	PA3600	36,41,61
St. John, Scott	CA4900	62A,41,51
Stabile, Ronald	RI0300	32,41,50,65
Staheli, Ronald	UT0050	60,36,41,61,66A
Stanek, Mark	IN0100	70,13B,13C,41
Stanford, Thomas S.	OR0850	64C,12,48,41
Staryk, Steven S.	WA1050	41,62A
Steffen, Christina	AZ0440	64A,41,13
Stencel, Paul L.	NY1210	13A,11,12A,41,47
Stephan, Michael	MA2250	63D,41
Stepner, Daniel	MA0500	41,62A,11
Stepner, Daniel	MA1050	41
Stepniak, Michael	VA1350	12,38,31A,41,32
Stern, James	MD1010	62A,41,42
Stevens, Daniel B.	KS1200	38,41,37,62,51
Stevens, Delores E.	CA3150	41,66A,66H,66C
Stevenson, Doris J.	MA2250	41,66A,66C,42,43
Stewart, David	AG0400	62A,41
Stickney, Mark A.	UT0200	37,63D,41,49,63
Stillwell, Corinne	FL0850	62A,41
Stimson, Ann	OH1200	64A,41
Stinson, Ron	KS0570	29,37,41,46,47
Stodola, Lynn	AF0100	42,66A,66C,41
Stokes, James M.	NC0050	63A,49,41,42
Stolle, Kara M.	IN0350	64D,41
Stone, Elizabeth	AL1160	64A,41
Storch, Laila	WA1050	41,64B
Stotter, Douglas	TX3500	37,41,60B
Stovall, Jeremy	AL0500	13A,37,41,54
Strain, James A.	MI1600	65,13,41,11
Strauch, Richard	WA1350	37,63D,60B,41,12A
Stufft, David	GA2000	37,41,47,32,60B
Stumpf, Suzanne	MA2050	41,67D,64A
Stupin, Mary	CA1270	12A,41
Suarez, Karen	WI0250	63B,41
Sulski, Peter	MA0200	41,62A,62B
Sumerlin, John	RI0200	41,62A,62B
Summerfield, Susan	VT0400	13,11,41,66
Sundberg, Terri	TX3420	41,64A
Sung, Benjamin H.	FL0850	62A,62B,41,42
Sungarian, Victor	MA2250	63B,41
Suovanen, Charles	CA2600	41,70
Sussman, Michael	MA2000	41,64C
Suvada, Steve	IL0850	70,41,20
Suzano, L. Armenio	VA0650	20F,11,13C,41,64
Svanoe, Anders	WI0100	64E,41
Swanson, Mark L.	MA0100	60B,38,66A,41
Swinson, Beth Ann	IL3150	61,39,41
Tak, Young-Ah	FL1740	66A,60,13A,13B,41
Takacs, Peter	OH1700	66A,41
Tanenbaum, David	CA4150	70,41
Tao, Patricia	AA0100	66A,41
Tapping, Roger	MA1400	41,42
Tardif, Guillaume	AA0100	62B,41
Tate, Elda Ann	MI1600	13,10E,41,64A
Taub, Paul	WA0200	41,64A,35
Tayerle, Loren	CA1550	12A,38,41
Taylor, David	NY2250	41,63C
Taylor, James	NC1050	41,36,61,31A,11
Taylor, Lucille	CA2420	62B,41
Taylor, Priscilla	MA2010	13,10,62C,41
Teal, Christian	TN1850	41,51,62A
Teicholz, Marc S.	CA0807	70,41
Teixeira, Robert	NC2000	70,41
Tejero, Nikolasa	TN1700	13,64C,41
Tenenbom, Steven	PA0850	41
Tessmer, David	PA3650	41,64A
Thiem, Barbara	CO0250	41,62C,42
Thomas, Susan H.	RI0300	41,48,64A,34
Thompson, Christopher	LA0770	41,62A,62B,11
Thompson, Curt	TX3000	62A,41
Thompson, Fred	WA0700	41
Thompson, John	AA0050	38,62B,41
Thompson, Kathy A.	OK0700	13,32B,66A,66B,41
Thompson, Marcus	MA1200	41,62
Thompson, Marcus	MA1400	41,62
Thompson, Marilyn	CA4700	66A,41,42
Thompson, Paul	MO1500	11,41,64A,29A,55C
Thompson, Robert	TN0100	70,41
Thompson, Robert	WI0825	11,41,48,64D
Thompson, Sonja K.	MN0050	61,39,54,41,42
Thornton, Bruce	MN0350	60B,41,47,64
Thurman, Demondrae	AL0650	63C,63D,41
Tillotson, J. Robert	IL1085	37,13,41,64C
Timmerman, David	TX1750	13A,13,36,41,61
Timmons, Leslie	UT0300	32A,32B,64A,48,41
Tocco, James V.	OH2200	41,66A
Todd, Richard	TN1400	13E,13F,41,70
Tomasone, Adeline	NJ1050	64A,41
Tomlinson, Peter	CT0800	66A,53,41
Tong, Kristopher	MA1400	41
Tramposh, Shelly	NY3780	41,62B
Trautman, Mark A.	NJ1130	66G,41
Tremblay, Christian	MD1000	41,42,62A
Trent, Robert S.	VA1100	70,67G,41,57
Trigg, William	NJ0175	65,41
Trinkle, Steven W.	NV0050	63A,41,42,38,13A
Truitt, D. Charles	PA2200	70,13,41,13E,13B
Trynchuck, Carla	MI0250	62,41,51
Tryon, Robin R.	OH2290	41,64A
Tuckwiller, George	VA1750	60,11,41,49,63A
Tudek, Thomas S.	IN1650	41,70
Tully, Amy	SC0420	64A,12A,41

Name	Code	Areas
Tumlinson, Charles	CA0815	47,41,29
Tung, Alice Clair	MD0520	62B,41
Tunis, Andrew	AG0400	41,66A
Turetzky, Bertram	CA5050	12A,41,62D,43,29
Turini, Ronald	AG0500	41,66A
Turner, Aaron	CO0275	50,65A,65B,13,41
Turner, Charles	KY0300	32,37,63,47,41
Turner, Cynthia Johnston	NY0900	60,37,41,42,38
Tymas, Byron	NC1600	11,46,70,47,41
Vaillancourt, Jean-Eudes	AI0200	41,66D
Valdes Vivas, Eduardo	PR0115	70,41
Valdivia, Hector	MN0300	10F,60,11,38,41
Valls De Quesada, Margarita	AL0330	41,70
Van Der Sloot, Michael	AA0040	62A,62B,38,41
Van der Sloot, William	AA0050	62A,41
Van Geem, Jack	CA4150	65,41
Vanderborgh, Beth	WY0200	41,62C,55B
Vanosdale, Mary Kathryn	TN1850	41,62A
VanValkenburg, Jamie G.	CO0050	63A,63C,63D,37,41
Vardi, Amitai	OH1100	64C,41
Varosy, Zsuzshanna	FL0450	41,62C
Vartan, Lynn	UT0200	65,41,20
Vassallo, James	TX3400	41,63A
Vaughan, Charles	NC2420	70,41
Veal, Larry	NH0350	11,62C,13A,41
Veazey, Charles	TX3420	41,64B
Vercelli, Michael B.	WV0750	20,14,31F,41,42
Verdery, Benjamin	CT0850	70,41
Via, Kelly	GA1300	64A,41
Videon, Michael	MT0200	70,41
Vieaux, Jason	OH0600	70,41
Villarrubia, Charles	TX3510	63D,41
Vinci, Jan F.	NY3650	41,64A
Vining, David	AZ0450	63C,41
Vokolek, Pamela	WA1050	62E,41
Volpe, Christopher	MN1625	63A,41
Voris, Dan J.	OH0350	70,41
Vrba, Cenek	AA0050	62A,41
Waddelow, Jim M.	NC1300	41,62,38,32E
Waddley, Craig	AR0950	41,47
Wait, Patricia	AG0650	41,64C,13A,12A
Waite, Janice	AA0050	66A,66C,41
Wakefield, William	OK1350	60,37,41
Walker, James A.	NY3730	60,37,38,41
Walsh, Diane	NY2250	41,66A
Walt, Stephen J.	MA2000	64D,41
Walt, Stephen	MA2250	48,64D,43,41
Walters, Timothy	FL0650	13,41,63A,29
Wang, Felix	TN1850	62C,41,51
Wang, I-Fu	MI1400	41,62A
Wang, Linda	CO0900	62A,41,42
Wang, Sylvia	IL2250	66,41
Ware, John Earl	LA0900	11,36,39,41,61
Warkentien, Vicky	IN0200	13,66,41,51,38
Warner, Carolyn Gadiel	OH0600	41
Warren, Dale E.	KY1450	63C,41
Warren, Jeffrey	MN0625	41,70
Wassermann, Ellen	CA0807	41,66A,66D
Watts, Valerie	OK1350	64A,41
Weaver, Phillip E.	AL1160	70,41
Webb, Glenn	UT0150	37,41,47,50,65
Webb, John C.	AR0800	41,32E,37,60B,63
Weber, Steven T.	TX0100	36,41,61
Wechesler, David J.	NY0644	11,13A,29A,41,64A
Weidman-Winter, Becky	CO1050	64A,41,13
Weiner, Robert A.	FL1900	41,64B
Weinstein, Alan	VA1250	41,62C,62D,70
Weller, Ira	NY2250	62B,41
Wells, Wayne W.	VA1350	49,63C,41
Wentworth, Jean	NY3560	12A,41,66A
Wernick, Richard F.	PA3350	13,60,10,41
Wery, Brett L.	NY3600	13,37,41,64C,64E
West, William	IL1200	13,64A,64E,41,67E
Wexler, Mathias K.	NY3780	41,62C
Wharton, William	ID0250	13,41,62C,62D
Wheeler, John	MA2250	63C,41
Whisler, Bruce Allen	SC0400	29A,41,35,34
White, Dale A.	MN0350	60B,37,41,32E,63
White, Joanna Cowan	MI0400	41,64A
White, Kennen D.	MI0400	41,64C
Whitford, Trudy	IN1560	64A,41
Wiebe, Thomas	AG0500	62C,41
Wiggins, William	TN1850	41,50,65
Wilborn, David F.	TX2900	13,63C,63D,41,37
Wilcox, John	OH2600	38,62A,62B,41
Wiley, Peter	PA0850	41,62C
Wilkinson, Wayne	CO0275	70,47,41,42
Williams, Larry	MI0100	41,70
Williams, Mark	MI0900	63C,49,41
Williams, Shane	MO0650	11,13,32E,38,41
Williams, Yolanda	MN1050	12A,20,47,29A,41
Wilson, Eric J.	AB0100	41,62C
Wilson, Kenyon	TN1700	63D,13,41
Wilson, Miranda	ID0250	13C,41,42,62D,62C
Wilson, Ransom	CT0850	41,64A
Wilson, Sandy	CA4200	41,62C,42
Wilson, Stephen B.	NY3720	13,60,36,41,61
Winant, William	CA2950	65,41,42
Winkler, Fred	WA1000	64E,41,32E
Winner, Andrew	KY1000	70,41
Wittchen, Andrea	PA2450	41,62E
Wogick, Jacqueline	NY2950	62C,41
Wojtowicz, Joanne	KY1000	62A,41
Wolford, Dale	CA4400	64E,41
Wood, Peter J.	AL1300	63A,13,49,41
Woodbury, Todd	UT0350	70,41
Wooden, Lori L.	OK1330	64D,41,38,42,48
Woods, Alexander G.	UT0050	62A,41
Woodworth, William	TN1450	64B,13B,13C,41,66G
Woolly, Kimberly A.	MS0750	64D,12A,41,48,72
Woolweaver, Scott	MA2010	38,41,51,62B,62A
Wortmann, David	NC1100	41
Wright, Elizabeth	MA2250	66A,66C,41
Wright, Lawrence	PA2450	37,41,49,63A
Wright, Margaret	DC0170	41,62A,62B
Wright, Scott	KY1450	64C,41,48
Wubbena, Teresa R.	AR0400	13,32,41,16,64
Wulfhorst, Dieter	CA1860	62C,62D,12A,12C,41
Wyner, Yehudi	MA0500	10F,10,41
Yajima, Hiroko	NY2250	41,62A
Yancho, Mari	MI0450	11,70,41
Yannelli, John A.	NY3560	13,41,45,54,34
Yanovskiy, Leonid	FL2100	62A,62B,38,11,41
Yarbrough, Paul R.	CA4200	41,62B,42
Yehuda, Guy	FL1950	64C,60B,41,32E
Yeung, Angela C.	CA5200	13,38,41,42,62C
Yoshioka, Airi	MD1000	32,41,51,62A
You, Yali	MN0800	38,41,62C,11,12A
Young, Eileen M.	NC2500	64C,64E,41,64,12A
Young, Robert	NY3780	64E,41
Youngblood, Pamela J.	TX3300	41,64A,13A,13B,15
Yu, Xiaoqing	TN0850	62A,62B,41
Zamzow, Beth Ann	IA0930	13,41,42,37,12
Zander, Benjamin	MA1400	41,62C
Zawilak, Alexander	AZ0490	70,13A,42,41
Zhu, Hong	OK1330	62A,41,42,51
Zilberkant, Eduard	AK0150	66A,66B,66C,66D,41
Zilincik, Anthony	OH0350	63D,41,43,10F
Zimmerman, Keith	IL1200	64E,41
Zimmerman, Robert	MA2250	62D,41
Zinn, Daniel L.	CA0807	47,64E,41,29A,11
Zito, William	NY2550	70,41
Zlotkin, Fred	NY0500	41,62C
Zumwalt, Wildy	NY3725	64E,41

Chamber Ensemble Coaching

Name	Code	Areas
Abbott, David	MI0100	12A,66A,42
Abeid, Mellad	WA0400	70,42
Admiral, Roger	AA0110	13B,13C,10A,42
Afanassieva, Veronika	CO0275	62A,42,51
Agopian, Edmond	AA0150	38,41,51,62A,42
Albert, Matthew	TX2400	42,62A
Alexander, Lisa M.	NY1600	64D,42
Allard, Catherine	AL1050	61,42
Allcott, Dan J.	TN1450	38,60B,62C,11,42
Allen, Peter	AF0100	66A,66C,66B,41,42
Altino, Leonardo	TN1680	62C,42
Altino, Soh-Hyun Park	TN1680	62A,42
Amalong, Philip	OH0680	66A,66C,13,11,42
Anderson, David	WI0100	66A,38,66C,13E,42
Anderson, Elaine M.	OH2290	62C,13,38,41,42
Anderson, Gwen	MN0300	63B,42
Anderson, Scott	NE0600	63C,42
Anop, Lenora Marya	IL2910	62A,41,51,42
Arnold, John	OK0750	62A,42
Arnone, Francesca M.	TX0300	64A,42,67D
Artmann, Mary	CO0275	62C,42,51
Asche, Kyle	IL1615	42
Asteriadou, Maria	PA1750	11,66A,66B,41,42
Atapine, Dmitri	NV0100	62C,42,11
Atherton, Timothy E.	NH0100	63C,41,42
Atkinson, Keith	AG0300	64B,42
Auner, Edith	MA1900	13A,13,42
Avery, Dawn	MD0550	20,42,62C
Axinn, Audrey	NY1900	42
Azabagic, Denis	IL0550	70,42
Bae, Ik-Hwan	IN0900	42,62A
Baer, Stephanie	NY2750	62,42
Bagg, Jonathan E.	NC0600	62B,42
Baik-Kim, Eun Ae	PA0950	66A,66C,42
Bailey, John R.	NE0600	64A,42,12A
Bain, Andrew	CA1075	63B,42
Bair, Jeffery J.	NC0650	64E,42,29A
Baldacchino, Laura Falzon	NY4200	64A,32E,42,43
Balija, Ayn	VA1550	62B,51,42
Ballard-Ayoub, Anna Claire	PA1400	64D,42
Ballatori, Cristina	TX3515	64A,11,42,13
Bamonte, David	OR0850	41,42,63A,49
Barber, Susan N.	VA0600	64D,42
Barger, Diane C.	NE0600	42,64C
Bargerstock, Nancy E.	NC0050	51,62A,42,62B
Barnard, William	MN1600	70,29,42
Barnewitz, William	IL2250	63B,42
Barnhill, Allen	TX2150	63C,41,42
Barr, Jean M.	NY1100	66C,42
Barth, Molly	OR1050	64A,42,48,43
Barto, Betsy	CO0275	61,42
Bashford, Christina	IL3300	12A,12C,12D,42,51
Baumgarten, Jonathan	DC0010	64A,42,48
Beaudette, Sylvie	NY1100	42,66C
Beaver, Gregory	NE0600	62C,42
Bebe, David M.	NY0700	38,13,42,62C
Beck, Barbara Geiser	CO0275	61,39,54,66C,42
Becker, Karen A.	NE0600	62C,42,13C
Bednarz, Blanka	PA0950	13A,42,51,62A,62B
Beebe, Jon P.	NC0050	13,48,64D,32E,42
Beene, Richard	CA1075	64D,42
Bell, Kenneth G.	PA1400	63B,42
Bennett, Marie Micol	IL2050	64A,48,41,13A,42
Bernhardsson, Sigurbjorn	IN0900	62A,42
Berry, Brandi	IL0750	42
Betts, Timothy	WA0050	62B,42,11
Bhasin, Paul K.	VA0250	37,63A,38,42,41
Biddlecome, Thomas 'Tucker'	TN1850	36,42,32D
Bing, Delores M.	CA0500	62,41,42,62C
Bitz, Alan	MI0050	62A,63A
Bjerken, Xak	NY0900	66A,42,43
Black, Alan	NC0550	62C,42
Blake, Elise A.	VA0800	62A,62B,42
Blakeslee, Lynn	NY1100	62A,42
Blecha-Wells, Meredith	OK0800	62C,11,42
Blocker, Robert	CT0850	66A,42
Blomster, Jennie	CA5350	63B,41,42
Bobak, Jacqueline	CA0510	12,42,61,32G
Boden-Luethi, Ruth	WA1150	62C,62D,13,51,42
Bongiorno, Joseph A.	NY2750	62D,38,42,51
Borrmann, Kenneth	PA2800	66A,66B,66C,42,44
Bostrand, Eva	AA0100	42
Botterbusch, Duane A.	PA1400	62D,42
Bourne, Trina	OH0600	42
Bowers, Teresa M.	PA1400	64A,64B,12A,36,42
Bradley, Annette	AA0080	66A,32B,13C,66D,42
Bradshaw, Daniel	HI0050	13D,42,41
Brandolino, Tony	MO2000	62A,38,42
Bray, Erin	TN0900	64,42,11
Brightbill, Elizabeth	VA0800	64A,42,11
Broffitt, Virginia	OK0800	64A,42,11,32E
Brofsky, Natasha	NY1900	62C,42
Broussard, George L.	NC0650	42,63C,29A
Brown, Jennie S.	IL3550	64A,12A,13C,42
Brown, Jennie	IL0850	64A,41,42
Brown, Joel	NY3650	70,42
Brown, Richard	TX2150	50,65,42
Browning, Doug	MS0550	32,40,42,47,60
Bruk, Karina	NJ1130	66A,42
Buechner, Sara Davis	AB0100	66A,42
Burke, Kevin R.	IN0500	12,13,20,42,63B
Burleson, Geoffrey	NY0625	66A,13,12A,66,42
Burroughs, Mary	NC0650	42,63B,13C
Burton, James	NY1900	42,29
Burton, John R.	TX3500	62C,42
Bush, Christopher	NY2750	64C,41,42,48
Bushman, Catharine Sinon	SC1200	37,32E,42
Buswell, James	MA0950	62A,42,38

Index by Area of Teaching Interest

Name	Code	Areas
Butler, Jocelyn	WI0250	62C,42
Buyse, Leone	TX2150	42,64A
Caban, Francisco J.	PR0115	62A,41,42,51
Cadieux, Marie-Aline	PA1750	13,11,51,62C,42
Cain, Donna	OK0750	62B,42
Calloway, Jason	FL0700	62C,43,42
Cameron, Michael B.	PA0950	62C,42
Cantu, Ben	CO0275	70,41,42
Caplan, Stephen	NV0050	64B,42,11
Carey, Norman	NY0600	13,42
Carlson, Sydney R.	OR0850	41,42,64A
Carrera, Michael	OH1900	62C,42
Cartagena, Cynthia	PR0115	41,42,64A
Carter, David	MN1450	11,41,62C,42
Carter, Monty	MO2000	62B,42
Casey, Neil	SC1110	38,42
Cass, Howard	MI0600	42,10F
Celidore, Daniel	CA4700	42,64B
Chan, Amanda	AB0100	42,66A
Chandler, Beth E.	VA0600	64A,42,35E
Chang, Joanne	NY3250	11,13,32,42,66
Chang, Peter M.	IL2150	11,14,12,42
Chang, Soo-Yeon Park	CA0650	66,42,13A,13C
Chapman, Susannah	NJ0700	62C,42,11
Chase, Roger	IL0550	62B,42
Chen, Fen-Fang	AL0650	66A,66B,66D,42,66C
Chen, Melvin	NY0150	66A,42,38
Chesher, Michael	IA0950	32E,42,64C,64E
Chien, Alec F.	PA0100	11,42,66A,41
Chin, Wayman	MA1175	66A,66C,42
Ching, Daniel	TX3510	62A,42
Cho, Catherine	NY1900	62A,42
Chou, Shun-Lin	CA0825	42,66
Christensen, Brandon J.	MO1500	62A,62B,42,11
Chua, Emily Yap	VA1125	13B,15,42,66A
Chung, Minna Rose	AC0100	62C,42,51
Clapp, Stephen	NY1900	62A,42
Claussen, Kurt	MN1450	64E,42
Clift, Anna	MN1450	62C,42
Cobb, Kevin D.	NY3790	63A,49,42
Coil, Pat	TN1100	66A,29,42
Cole, Carol	FL1125	62A,42,32E
Cole, David	FL1125	62C,42
Coletti, Paul	CA1075	62B,42
Colon Jimenez, Frances	PR0115	64B,41,42
Colwell, David A.	VA1550	62A,51,42
Compton, Lanette	OK0800	63B,11,32E,42
Connelly, Brian	TX2150	66A,66C,66E,42
Conner, Timothy M.	FL1900	63C,41,42
Cook, Jeffrey	TN0900	63B,12A,42,11
Cook, Nathan J.	AD0050	42,62C
Cooper, James	PA2800	62C,42
Cope, Roger Allen	CA0650	70,42
Corps, Wilfredo	PR0115	41,64E,42
Cottin-Rack, Myriam	CA4300	62A,42,41
Crochet, Lourinda S.	SC1200	37,32E,42
Crowe, Jason	CO0275	62D,42
Crowne, Scott	PA1400	66C,66A,42
Culp, Jennifer	CA4150	42,62C
Curran, Nancy A.	CT0500	42,66A,66H
Da Silva, Fabio Gardenal	NY2750	66A,42,66C
Dagenais, Andree	AC0050	36,40,42,60A
Dalbey, Jenna	AZ0490	62C,42
Daniel, John	WI0350	63A,42
Dann, Steven	AG0300	42,62B
D'Arca, Denise	OH1800	32,36,11,42
Dawes, Andrew	AB0100	41,51,62A,42
Day, James M.	NJ0175	70,42
DeAlmeida, Saulo	KY0400	62C,42
Deane, Alison	NY0550	66,41,42
Decker, Jeffrey C.	VA1550	64E,42,47
Dee, John	IL3300	64B,42
DeLeon, Dorien	OR0400	62C,42
DeMartino, Louis	OR1050	42,48,64C
Derthick, Thomas	CA5350	62D,42
Despres, Jacques C.	AA0100	66A,42
Dibari, Keriann K.	NJ0800	42,64C
Dick, Robert	NY2750	64A,42,41
Dillenbeck, Denise	WA0050	62A,42
DiOrio, Andrea R.	IL2050	64C,11,42,43
Dobrotvorskaia, Ekaterina	CO0275	62B,42,51
Dolezal, Darry	MO1800	62C,42
Dona, Daniel	MA0400	62B,42
Donaghue, Margaret A.	FL1900	64C,42
Donnellan, Grant	WA1250	41,42
Donnelly, Molly	MD0550	36,61,42
Dowling, Eugene	AB0150	42,13C,63C,63D
Downing, Elizabeth A.	ME0440	64A,42
Dronkers, Marcelle	CA3270	39,42
Drucker, Naomi	NY1600	48,64C,42
Duke-Kirkpatrick, Erika	CA0510	42,62C,51
Dukes, Leslie D.	CA4460	66,42,66C
Dunham, James	TX2150	62B,42
Dyachkov, Yegor	AI0150	62C,42
Edelberg, Joe	CA4700	32E,38,42,62A,62B
Een, Andrea	MN1450	42,62A,62B
Eickelman, Diane	CO0275	66C,42
Eischeid, Susan	GA2150	64B,11,48,42
Elgart, Matthew P.	CA0500	70,42
Elisha, Larisa	GA0950	62A,62B,42
Elisha, Steven K.	GA0950	62C,62D,41,42
Ellert, Michael	FL1125	64D,41,42
Elliott, Lloyd R.	CA1300	38,61,42
Elliott-Goldschmid, Ann	AB0150	62A,42
Ellison, Paul	TX2150	42,62D
Elworthy, Joseph	AB0200	62C,42,38
Epperson, Bryan	AG0300	62C,42
Ericksen, Elizabeth	MN0300	62A,62B,42
Erickson, Marty	WI0350	63D,42
Espina-Ruiz, Oskar	NC1650	64C,42
Evans, Jay	AL1200	63C,63D,42
Evans, Mathew J.	CO0275	63B,11,13C,42
Evans, Phillip	FL1125	66D,42
Evoskevich, Paul	NY0700	47,64E,53,29,42
Ewoldt, Patrice R.	PA2300	66A,66C,66B,67F,42
Eyler, David	MN0600	32,50,65,42
Faganel, Gal	CO0950	62C,42,35G,51
Farmer, Harry	VA0750	64E,47,42,43
Farris, Daniel King	OK1250	40,42,12,36,13
Farrugia, Pauline	AI0050	64C,42
Feldman, Marion	NY2750	62C,42
Feldman, Ronald	MA2250	60B,38,41,42
Ferril, Michael J.	CA0835	62A,42,43
Feves, Julie	CA0510	42,64D,48,35A
Fieldhouse, Stephen M.	PA1400	64E,29,42
Finckel, David	NY1900	62C,42
Fink, Seymour	OH0350	66A,66B,42
Fischer, Jeanne Kierman	TX2150	66A,66B,66D,42
Fischer, Norman	TX2150	42,62C
Fischer, Rebecca J.	NE0600	62A,42
Flax, Laura	NY0150	64C,42
Fleck, Allyson	GA1150	62B,42,13B
Fleischer, Tania	CA2800	66A,42
Flick, Daniel K.	FL1550	70,13,42
Flint, Gregory	IL0550	63B,42
Flores, Jose G.	TX2930	62A,62B,51,13C,42
Fluchaire, Olivier	NY0644	62A,62B,11,13A,42
Flyer, Nina	CA5350	62C,41,42
Follet, Diane W.	PA2550	13,15,42,13H
Fonteneau, Jean-Michel	CA4150	62C,42
Fort, Kevin	IL0275	66A,42
Fox, Stuart	CA0510	42,70,55B,67G
Francois, Ronald P.	CO0250	62A,42
Frank, Elliot	NC0650	70,42
Frankel, Joanna	NJ0700	62A,62B,42
Franklin, Cary J.	MN0950	10,37,38,42,60B
Frear, Robert	CA0825	63A,42
Fred Carrasquillo, Luis	PR0115	63C,49,41,42
Fredriksen, Brandt	GA1050	66A,66C,42
Freer, Elinor	NY1100	66C,42
Friedman-Adler, Laurie	NY1600	64C,42
Fuzesy, Brianne	ND0050	11,63,42
Galbraith, Connie	IL1740	64C,42
Ganatra, Simin	IN0900	62A,42
Garcia, Marisa	PR0115	66A,42
Garcia, Washington	TX3175	66A,42
Gardner, Ryan B.	OK0800	63A,49,46,42,47
Garibova, Karine	CO0275	62A,42,51
Gazda, Frank S.	DE0050	63D,37,49,63C,42
Gearhart, Fritz	OR1050	62A,42
Gee, Constance	SC1110	11,41,62B,42
Gendron, Mychal	RI0300	70,42
Gibson, Clarence	TX3150	11,37,41,42
Gilad, Yehuda	CA1075	64C,38,42
Giles, Sonja	IA0850	64A,41,42
Gindele, Joshua	TX3510	62C,42
Gingras, Michele	OH1450	64C,42
Ginn, Stan	KY1000	42,50,65
Giray, Selim	KS1450	62A,62B,51,42,38
Gjevre, Naomi	TX2250	62A,42,12C
Glise, Anthony	MO0850	70,41,42
Gluzman, Vadim	IL0550	62A,42
Gnandt, Edwin E.	AA0010	13A,66A,42,13B,66D
Gogichashvili, Eka Dalrymple	TX0300	62A,42
Goldberg, Marc	NY0150	64D,42,48
Goldsmith, Kenneth	TX2150	42,62A
Goldstein, Tamara B.	CO0550	66A,66C,66B,42
Gongos, Chris	AG0300	63B,42
Goranson, Jocelyn	PA2300	64A,13A,13C,13B,42
Goranson, Todd A.	PA2300	64E,64D,13A,47,42
Gordon, Joshua	MA0500	11,41,42,62,62C
Gordon, Judith	MA1750	66A,42
Gordon, Nina	IL1200	62C,42
Gorenman, Yuliya	DC0010	66A,42
Goto, Midori	CA5300	62A,42
Grafilo, Zakarias	CA4200	62A,41,42
Grant, Kenneth	NY1100	64C,42
Gray, Charles	MN1450	42,62A,62B
Greene, Linda	NY1350	64A,42
Greene, Sean	TN0900	63D,13,37,32,42
Gregorian, Ara	NC0650	62A,62B,42
Greitzer, Deborah	MD0750	41,64D,42
Grenfell, Mary-Jo	MA1650	12A,32,38,41,42
Griffith, Michael Ted	WY0200	60,38,42
Grim, Jennifer	NV0050	64A,42,41
Grose, Michael	OR1050	11,63D,49,42
Gross, Allen	CA3300	11,38,60B,42
Gruber, Emanuel	NC0650	62C,42
Guist, Jonathan B.	TX3515	64C,32,42
Gustafson, Christine	NC0650	42,64A
Guthmiller, Anne	VA1500	61,42
Guzzio-Kregler, Mary Ellen	RI0200	13C,64A,42
Haase, Peter	VA0450	62A,42
Hacker, James	FL0700	63A,42,49
Haines-Eitzen, John	NY0900	62C,42
Hall, Lois	NY2800	61,13C,42
Hall, Van-Anthoney	NC1550	11,12D,40,42,61
Hall-Gulati, Doris J.	PA1300	64C,42
Haney, Julia Lawson	CA0650	62A,42
Hanick, Conor	MA1750	66A,42
Hannah, Barry	TN0900	70,42
Hansbrough, Robert S.	NY0700	32E,42,37,65
Hansbrough, Yvonne	NY0700	64A,67D,12A,42
Hansen, Jeremy C.	TN1450	63B,13C,42
Hansen, Lisa	NJ0700	64A,42
Hanson, Paul	VA1500	66A,42
Hardie, William Gary	TX0300	62C,42
Harding, David	AB0100	51,62A,62B,41,42
Harley, Michael	SC1110	13,42
Harlow, Leslie	UT0325	62B,42
Harrington, Allen	AC0100	64D,64E,42,48
Harrington, Barbara	AL1200	64A,42
Harris, Mary	OH1450	32,62B,51,42
Harriss, Elaine Atkins	TN1720	66A,66B,42,66D
Harrow, Anne Lindblom	NY1100	64A,42
Hartig, Caroline A.	OH1850	64C,42
Hastings, David M.	WI0850	64E,42,13A,13B,13C
Hastings, Todd J.	KS1050	63A,29,11,41,42
Hatch, Montgomery	NY1600	65,42,50
Haunton, Thomas C.	NH0100	63B,42
Hauser, Joshua	TN1450	63C,10F,13B,42
Hawkins Raimi, Jane	NC0600	66A,42
Hayes, Gregory M.	NH0100	66,41,42
Hayes, Jane	AB0060	66A,66D,13B,42,66B
Heilman, Barbara	OR0850	12A,41,42,64C,48
Heim, D. Bruce	KY1500	63B,49,42
Heinen, Julia M.	CA0835	64C,42,13C
Heisler, Jeff A.	OH1100	64E,42,37
Helton, Jonathan	FL1850	64E,42,43
Henderson, David	CA5350	64E,42
Henderson, Peter	MO0700	12A,13,42,66A
Heppner-Harjo, Tianna	NV0050	62B,32E,42
Hersh, Julian E.	IL0750	42
Hersh, Paul	CA4150	12A,42,62B,66A
Hersh, Stefan	IL0550	62A,42,38
Hesh, Joseph	PA2800	47,42,66D
Highbaugh Aloni, Pamela	AB0150	62C,42
Hinson, James M.	IL2910	48,64C,64E,42
Hirschl, Richard	IL0550	62C,42
Hodel, Martin	MN1450	38,63A,42
Hodges, Brian D.	ID0050	62C,11,42
Hoebig, Desmond	TX2150	62C,42
Hofeldt, Elizabeth	OH2450	62A,62B,42
Holeman, Kathleen	MO0850	61,40,42
Holland, David	MI0400	62B,42,51
Holland, David	MI1650	62B,42,51

Name	Code	Areas
Holland, Patricia C.	WI0850	64D,12A,42
Hollander, Alan	NY1600	64B,42
Holzer, Linda	AR0750	66A,66B,42,15,11
Hong, Sojung Lee	IL1300	66A,66D,66B,42,66C
Hood, Joanna	AB0150	62B,42
Horozaniecki, Mary B.	MN0300	62A,62B,42
Horvath, Janos	AA0150	32B,32D,36,42,13C
Houde, Andrea	WV0750	13C,32,41,42,62B
Houghton, Amy	MS0100	70,42
Hsu, Howard	GA2150	38,42,60B
Hsu, John	NY0900	42,62C,67A,38,60B
Huang, Rachel Vetter	CA4500	62A,11,13A,42
Huff, Michael H.	AL1050	63A,42,49,67E,37
Hughes, Walden D.	ID0150	12A,41,42,66
Hunter, Mario	NC0550	64C,41,42
Hunter-Holly, Daniel	TX3515	13,61,42
Hwalek, Ginger Y.	ME0440	42,66D
Hwang, Margery	NY1100	42
Hynes, Maureen	NY2105	38,67,62C,55,42
Im, Sung-Mi	IN0900	42
Irizarry, Rafael E.	PR0115	37,12A,63B,42,49
Ivry, Jessica	CA1150	51,42,62,13C,38
Jackson, Bil	TN1850	64C,41,42
Jacob, Heidi	PA1500	38,42,62C
Jacobs, Jay N.	LA0350	37,41,42,48
Jacobsen, Eric	NY2750	42,62C
Jacobson, Katherine	MD0650	42
Jaimes, Judit	WI0825	41,66A,66B,66C,42
James, Gordon	TN1350	63B,42
Janzen, Henry	AG0350	42,62B,62A
Jasinski, Nathan David	KY0550	62C,32E,38,42,13A
Jeanrenaud, Joan	CA2950	62C,42
Jeffrey, Sarah	AG0300	64B,42
Jellison, Anastasia	VA1500	62E,42
Jennings, Graeme	CA2950	40,41,62A,62B,42
Jensen, Susan	MO1800	62A,42
Jiang, Yi-wen	NY0150	62A,42
Jiang, Yi-wen	NJ0800	62A,42
Jin, Yu	OH1100	62B,42
Johnian, Paul	TN0100	42
Johns, Kristen	GA2150	63B,11,42,49
Johns, Michael	PA3200	48,37,42
Johnson, David	ID0070	13A,41,62B,42,51
Johnson, Jay L.	MN0300	65,50,42
Johnson, Jefferson	KY1450	60,40,36,42
Johnson, Marc Thomas	MA0400	62C,42
Johonnott, Edwin	VA0450	62A,62B,42
Joiner, Anna Barbrey	SC0750	62B,42,32E
Jones, David	GA2000	61,39,42
Jones, John R.	KY1500	49,63D,42
Jones, Kathleen	PR0115	64C,41,42
Jones, Sue	IL1550	42,66A,66C,66D,13C
Jordan, Rachel	MS0350	62A,11,13A,13B,42
Joyce, J. Patrick	WV0300	70,12,42
Kaczorowska, Joanna Maria	NY3790	62A,42
Kamins, Benjamin	TX2150	64D,42
Kanda, Sanae	MA1650	10A,42,66A,66C,66D
Kang, Hyo	CT0850	62A,42
Kannen, Michael	MD0650	41,42
Karp, Benjamin	KY1450	41,62C,42
Karpoff, Fred S.	NY4150	42,66A,66C,66B
Kartman, Stefan	WI0825	62C,42,51,41
Katz, Shmuel D.	NY2750	42,62B
Kavafian, Ida	NY1900	62A,42
Kavafian, Ida	NY0150	62A,42
Kayaleh, Laurence	AI0200	62A,42
Kean, Kristen	KY0550	64A,13A,13,42,48
Keberle, David S.	NY0644	10,10B,64C,42,13A
Kehler Siebert, Judith	AC0100	66A,66C,66D,42
Kellogg, Mark	NY1100	63C,42
Kelly, Frankie J.	LA0800	66C,40,41,42,11
Kem, Randy	OR1300	64E,42
Kent, Adam	NJ0825	66A,42
Kent, David	AG0300	65A,65B,42
Ketter, Craig	NJ0825	66A,66C,42
Kiffner, Paula	AB0210	62C,42
Kim, Chris Younghoon	NY0900	38,41,42,60
Kim, Hye-Jin	NC0650	62A,62B,42
Kim, Hyesook	MI0350	66A,66B,11,42
Kim, Lok	GA0600	38,42,60,66A
Kim, Yeon-Su	PA1400	62A,42
Kirk, David E.	TX2150	63D,42
Kirk-Doyle, Julianne	NY3780	64C,42,41
Kirkendoll, Michael	OK0800	66A,66B,66D,42
Kirkland, Anthony B.	MS0500	63A,42,49,67E,11
Kivrak, Osman	DC0010	62B,42,51
Klein, Susanna	VA1600	62A,42,32E
Klibonoff, Jon	NY2150	42
Klorman, Edward	NY1900	13,42
Klotz, Michael	FL0700	62B,42
Knecht, Melissa Gerber	MI1000	11,32,42,62A,62B
Knetsch, Rene	CO0100	38,62A,42
Knoepfel, Justin	MN0750	62B,62A,38,42,13
Knopp, Seth D.	MD0650	41,42
Knupps, Terri L.	MO1550	12A,20,63C,63D,42
Kobayashi, Hibiki	AI0190	42,62A
Kobrin, Alexander	GA0550	66A,42
Kochanowski, John	TN1850	41,51,62B,42
Kodzas, Peter	NY1100	42
Koelble, Bobby	FL1550	70,42
Koontz, Eric E.	NC0050	62B,62A,67A,42,51
Korak, John	IL2910	60,37,63A,49,42
Kordzaia, Alexander	VA1500	38,42
Kosack, Alicia	PA3710	64A,42,67D
Kostic, Dina	FL0050	62A,41,42,51
Krakauer, David	NY0150	64C,42
Kramer, Karl P.	IL3300	42,43
Krehbiel, A. David	CA1075	63B,42
Krejci, Mathew	CA5350	64A,42,41
Krueger, Charae	GA1150	62C,42
Kuan, Flora	NY2200	13C,66A,42
Kucharsky, Boris	NJ0800	62A,42
Kuster, Nicolasa	CA5350	64D,42,41
Kutz, Eric A.	IA0950	62C,32E,42
Kwak, Eun-Joo	WI0150	66A,66B,66C,42,12A
Kwak, Jason	TX3175	66A,42
Ladd, Gita	MD1000	41,42,62C
LaFitte, Barbara	MA2050	64B,42
Lam, Eri Lee	TX2650	62A,32E,42
Lambert, Nathan T.	CO0350	10F,11,14C,42,51
Lambros, Maria	MD1000	62B,42
Lambros, Maria	MD0650	41,42
Lander, Deborah R.	KY1450	62B,42
Largess, John	TX3510	62B,42
Larson, Elizabeth	CA0350	62A,42
Lasareff-Mirinoff, Claudia	IL2100	41,42
Lastrapes, Jeffrey Noel	TX3200	62C,42,51,11,32E
Laurent, Linda	CT0050	13,12,66A,66D,42
LaVorgna, David	MD0400	64A,42
Lawrence, Mark	CA1075	63C,42
Lazar, Teri	DC0010	62A,42,51
Le, Weiwei	NV0050	62A,42
Ledbetter, Lynn F.	TX3175	62A,62B,42,51
Lederer, Doris M.	VA1350	62B,62A,42
Lee, Cassandra	TN1850	41,48,64C,42
Lee, Donna	OH1100	66A,66B,66C,42
Lee, Sang-Eun	IL1085	62A,42
Leech, Alan B.	MT0200	64D,64E,20,64,42
Leech, Karen	MT0200	64A,42
Lehman, Marilyn J.	NY1600	66A,66C,42
Leon-Shames, Stephanie L.	OK1350	66C,42
Leonard, Lisa	FL1125	66B,66D,42
Leonard, Ronald	CA1075	62C,42
Leong, Sonia	CA5350	66A,41,42
Leslie, Drew	NC0050	63C,49,42,41
Lester, David T.	OH2140	70,35,45,42
Lev, Lara	NY1900	42
LeVelle, Teresa	CA6000	13,10,44,42
Levin, Andrew R.	SC0400	11,41,38,13,42
Levitov, Daniel	PA1400	62C,38,42,11
Levtov, Vladimir	AA0150	41,66A,66C,66D,42
Lewis, Brian D.	TX3510	62A,42
Lewis, Gordon R.	KS0650	62D,47,42,46
Li, Honggang	NJ0800	62B,42,62A
Li, Weigang	NY0150	62A,42
Li, Weigang	NJ0800	62A,42
Lifsitz, Fred	CA4200	41,62A,42
Lill, Joseph	IL2100	47,49,63A,37,42
Lin, Cho-Liang	TX2150	62A,42
Lin, I-Bei	HI0210	62C,41,42,13A
Lin, James	CA5510	13A,13B,42,13C,13D
Lin, Joseph	NY1900	62A,42
Lin, Tao	FL1125	66C,42
Lingen, Peter	IA0950	42,67G,70
Lister-Sink, Barbara	NC2205	66A,66B,66C,42
Littley, Marcia De Arias	FL0700	62A,42
Lloyd, Peter	CA1075	62D,42
Lloyd, William	CO0150	42
Loeb, Jaemi	KY0450	38,13A,41,42,60B
Long, Jeremy A.	OH1450	64E,47,42
Long, Nolan W.	OH2120	36,32D,40,42
Longworth, Peter	AG0300	42,66C
Lopez, George	ME0200	66A,38,42
Love, Randall M.	NC0600	66A,66E,42
Lucktenberg, Kathryn	OR1050	62A,42
Lulloff, Joseph	MI1400	42,64E
Lum, Tammy K.	NY2900	13,66A,66D,42
Lurie, Kenneth P.	NC0050	13A,62C,42
Luzanav, Inna	AA0110	66A,42
Lydeen, Brian	WI0400	64,47,37,42,64E
Lyndon-Gee, Christopher	NY0050	10A,14A,38,39,42
Lynn, Catherine D.	GA1150	62B,42
Lysy, Antonio	CA5030	62C,42
Mabee, Patricia	CA1075	42,55B,66H
MacKay, Gillian	AG0450	37,42,63A,60B,60
MacPhail, Heather	OH1450	66C,42
Maddox, Harry	GA1700	63D,42
Maddox, Meredith R.	AR0750	42,62A,62B
Maddox, Nan	GA1700	62C,42
Madrid, Albert	TX3527	42
Maeda, Dana	MN1450	64B,42
Magney, Lucia	MN0350	62C,62D,32E,42
Mahave-Veglia, Pablo	MI0900	42,62C,55B
Makeever, Gerald	MT0200	13A,42,63A
Maker, Bill	RI0200	42,70
Mann, Michael	TN1660	37,42,60B,65
Mann, Nicholas	NY1900	42
Manning, Dwight C.	NY4200	64,42,32E,11,64B
Mao, Ruotao	NJ0175	62A,62B,42
Markowski, Victoria	CO0275	66A,66D,41,42
Marks, Adam	WI0250	66A,42
Martin, Chris	IL2250	42
Martin, Danny Ray	TN0150	70,42,29,41
Martinez, Gabriela	NJ0700	66A,66D,42
Martins, David	MA2030	37,64C,60,42
Mast, Andrew	WI0350	37,41,42,60
Masterson, Daniel J.	KS0150	13,41,66A,66B,42
Matasy, Katherine V.	MA2050	64C,64E,68,42
Matthews, Brandon Stephen	CO0550	38,42,32E
Mattingly, Alan F.	NE0600	63B,13,42
May, Joanne	IL0850	13,38,42
Mazo, Vadim	IL1200	41,42,62A,62B,51
McArthur, Mark	NV0050	64E,42
McCandless, Andrew	AG0300	63A,42
McCaslin, Tom R.	NC0650	63D,42
McClellan, John	MO1950	42,70
McCourry, Christopher C.	MI1000	29,42,63A
McCutcheon, James R.	OH2250	70,42
McNabney, Douglas	AI0150	51,62B,42
McTeer, Mikylah Myers	WV0750	62A,32E,41,42
Means, Matthew L.	KS0350	11,62A,62B,41,42
Mendez, Max	ID0140	61,36,42,47
Miahky, Stephen A.	OH1900	62A,42
Michel, Dennis	IL0550	64D,42
Michel, Peggy	IL0550	64B,42
Miller, Ann Elizabeth	CA5350	62A,42,12A,41
Miller, Anton M.	NY2750	62A,42
Miller, Esther	TN1660	62A,42
Miller, Gregory	FL1125	63B,42
Miller, Michael	FL1100	38,42,62A
Mills, Jesse A.	NJ0800	42,62A
Mindock, Rebecca A.	AL1300	64B,64D,12A,34,42
Miyamoto, Peter M.	MO1800	66,13,42
Moliner, Eugenia	IL0550	42,64A
Molzan, Brett	AI0190	42,62A
Molzan, Ryan	AI0190	42,62C
Monroe, Douglas	NC0650	64C,42
Montelione, Joseph	TN1200	38,49,42
Moore, Frances	CA5040	62,42
Morales-Matos, Jaime	OH1450	63C,63D,13C,42
Morejon, Adrian	MA0350	64D,42
Morgan, Robert	IL2250	42
Morino, Ayako	NJ0825	66A,42
Morris, Craig	FL1900	41,49,63A,42
Morris, Matthew B.	OH1900	13,42,64D
Morris, Ralph	OK1330	38,62A,62B,41,42
Morris, Theodora	OK1330	62A,62B,67C,42
Muller-Szerwas, Jan	MA0700	62C,42
Mussumeli, Bettina	CA4150	62A,42
Myers, Roger	TX3510	62B,42
Nasatir, Cary	CA3520	65,42,46
Neeley, Henrietta	IL1085	62A,11,42,62B
Neidich, Ayako Oshima	NY3785	64C,42
Nelson, Elise Buffat	ND0350	62C,41,42
Neupert, Gina	TN1200	62E,42
Neves, Joel	MI1450	38,39,42,20G

Index by Area of Teaching Interest

Name	Code	Areas
Newman, Leslie	AG0300	64A,42
Niemisto, Paul	MN1450	49,63C,63D,37,42
Nieto-Dorantes, Arturo	AI0190	66A,42
Ninomiya, Ayano	NY1100	62A,42
Noguera, Darwin	IL0275	66A,42
Nolan, Julia	AB0100	64E,32E,42
Nugent, Thomas	CA5350	64B,41,42
O'Connor, Tara Helen	NY3785	64A,42
O'Connor, Tara	NY0150	64A,42
Oehler, Donald L.	NC2410	41,42,43,48,64C
Ogilvie, Tyler	PA0950	63B,42
Ogle, Alex	NH0100	64A,41,42
Ogrizovic-Ciric, Mirna	GA0300	38,42,62
Oh, Kyung-Nam	IN1560	62C,42
Oh, Yoojin	NY0644	11,42,66
Olcott, James L.	OH1450	47,63A,49,42
Olivier, Rufus	CA4700	42,64D
Olsen, Nina	MN0300	64C,42
Olsen, Timothy	NC2205	66G,31A,66H,42,56
Oppens, Ursula	NY0500	66,41,42,43
Orenstein, Janet	NC1650	62A,42
Osmun, Ross	AI0050	13,41,42,66A,66B
Ou, Carol	MA0950	62C,42
Padilla, Anthony	WI0350	66A,66C,41,42
Paer, Lewis J.	NY2750	42,62D
Page, Paula	TX2150	62E,42
Palma, Susan	NJ0800	64A,42
Palter, Morris	AK0150	12A,29A,42,43,14C
Pan, Huiyu-Penny	CA0830	66A,66D,66B,66C,42
Pandolfi, David	AL1200	63B,42
Papich, George	TX3420	42,62B
Parakilas, James P.	ME0150	13,11,42,12
Pare, Richard	AI0190	66G,66H,55,42
Park, Janice	CA2390	66A,42
Park, Tricia	IN1700	62A,42,41
Parker, Jon Kimura	TX2150	66A,42
Parker, Laura M.	IL2400	13A,41,42,62A,66A
Parrell, Richard N.	VA0450	42,64E
Patcheva, Ralitza	DC0170	66A,42
Pearson, Norman	CA1075	63D,42
Pelletier, Marie Volcy	MA1750	62C,42
Perdicaris, Stephen	CA5350	63C,42
Perkins, John D.	MO0100	63A,63B,12A,42,49
Perna, Leslie	MO1800	62B,42
Perry, John	CA1075	66A,42
Perry, Kathy	SC0700	62,51,42
Pesavento, Ann	MN0750	64D,42
Peshlakai, David	MI1000	42,62C
Petillot, Aurelien	IL2900	62B,62A,42,11,12A
Pfaltzgraff, Philip	NE0700	66C,11,42,12A
Phelps, Amy	IA0300	62C,42
Pikler, Charles	IL2100	62A,51,42,62B
Pilafian, Sam	FL1900	63D,42
Pinell, Javier	TX2250	62A,42,51
Pirard, Guillaume	NY2750	62A,42
Pitchon, Joel L.	MA1750	62A,41,42
Plourde, Jean-Luc	AI0190	42,62B
Plum, Sarah A.	IA0550	62A,62B,11,42
Plumer, Shirley	CO0275	42,64D
Plummer, Carolyn	IN1700	62A,42,41
Pochatko, Amanda R.	OH2140	64B,42
Pohran Dawkins, Alexandra	AB0150	42,64B
Pokhanovski, Oleg	AC0100	62A,51,42
Polifrone, Sharon	IL3550	42
Polk, Janet E.	NH0100	64D,41,42
Pollard, Amy	GA2100	64D,42
Pollard, Denson P.	NY1900	63D,42
Pologe, Steven	OR1050	62C,42
Porter, William Anthony	IL1085	62C,42
Posses, Mary	MO1810	64A,42
Powell, Larry	IN1650	63A,42
Powell, William E.	CA0510	48,64C,42,13E
Primes, Theodora	CA1960	42
Prior, Richard	GA0750	38,41,42,60B
Pritchard, Eric N.	NC0600	62A,42
Pritchett, Kate	OK0750	63B,42,13B,13C
Prosser, Douglas	NY1100	63A,42
Purdy, Craig Allen	ID0050	41,42,51,62A,38
Pyle, Laura	SC0400	62C,42
Qian, Jun	MN1450	42,64C,48
Quintanar, David	CO0275	63C,42
Raab-Pontecorvo, Luiza	NY1600	63B,42,66A,66C
Railsback, Stephanie	CA3520	62B,42
Raimi, Frederic B.	NC0600	62C,42
Ralske, Erik	NY1900	63B,42
Ramirez, Catherine	MN1450	13A,64A,48,42,13B
Ramsey, Cynthia B.	VA0750	66A,12A,66C,13E,42
Rarick, Janet	TX2150	42
Rath, Carl	WI0350	64D,42,14C
Raum, Erika	AG0300	62A,42
Ravnan, John	SC0765	62B,42,13
Ray, Vicki	CA0510	66,42
Ray-Carter, Trilla	MO2000	51,62C,42
Read, Evelyn	VT0450	62A,62B,16,42
Reardon, Melissa	NC0650	62B,42
Redman, Inez	NC2400	62A,62B,42
Reese, Marc B.	FL1125	63A,49,41,42,48
Regehr, Rennie	AG0400	62B,42
Regehr, Vernon	AD0050	62C,38,42
Rehberg, Jeanette	ND0050	11,64,42
Reid, Nola	CO0275	61,42
Reimer, David	MI0350	11,32E,42,62A,41
Remy-Schumacher, Tess	OK1330	62C,41,42
Reneau, Mark	TN1350	62A,42
Renyer, Erinn	KS0050	62C,62D,51,42
Requiro, David	WA1000	62C,41,42
Richard, Charles	CA3800	47,64E,29,34,42
Richardson, Colleen	AG0500	60B,37,32E,41,42
Richter, Jorge Luiz	NC0650	60B,38,42,62A,62B
Rike, Gregory	IN1600	61,42
Riley, David M.	OR1050	66C,66A,42
Ritscher, Karen	NY2750	62B,42
Ritz, Lyn	WA1100	62A,62B,42,13,10F
Ritzenthaler, Maria	IL1085	62B,41,42
Robertson, Karen	NC0050	49,63B,42,41
Robinson, Cathy Meng	OH1100	62C,42
Robinson, Keith	OH1100	62C,42
Robinson, Melissa Ann	OR0850	41,42,49,63B
Rodriguez, Alberto	PR0115	70,41,42
Rodriguez, Samantha	NY3730	62B,42
Rodriguez, Raquel H.	KY1000	37,42,63A
Rojak, John	NY0150	63C,42,49
Rojas, Luis Miguel	PR0115	62C,41,42
Romero, Gustavo	TX3420	66A,42
Roscetti, Diane	CA0835	42,62C,35A
Rosen, Marcy	NY0642	62C,42
Rosensky, Michael	VA1550	70,42,47
Ross, John	TN1200	70,67G,42
Rostad, Masumi Per	IN0900	62B,42
Rothman, George	NY0500	38,42,60B
Rowin, Elizabeth	MI1750	62A,62B,42
Rozenblatt, David I.	NY1600	65,42,50
Ruas, Laura M.	MD1000	41,42,62D
Ruby, Meg	MA2030	41,42,47,66A
Rudolph, Kathleen	AG0300	64A,42
Rudolph, Robert A.	PA0100	62A,62B,41,42,51
Rulli, Richard J.	AR0700	63A,42,49,41
Rust, Roberta	FL1125	42,66A
Ruzevic, Nikola	TX3420	42,62C
Ryan, Michael	CA5100	70,42,10D
Sahlin, Kay	MN1450	64A,42
Sakharova, Julia	MO1830	62A,42
Salas, Jorge Davi	TX2700	63D,62D,42
Salzman, Michael J.	NY1600	63D,42
Sampen, Maria	WA1000	62A,13C,42
Santos, Philip	CA3520	62A,42
Sariti, David J.	VA1550	62A,67B,51,42
Satterfield, Sarah	FL0365	12A,64A,11,42,48
Satterwhite, Dan	FL1125	63C,42
Saulter, Gerry	NY1275	12A,13C,70,42,41
Scanling, Paul F.	GA1550	64,37,42,48
Schene, Daniel	MO1950	66A,42
Schranze, Lenny	TN1680	62B,42
Schulze-Johnson, Virginia	NJ0300	41,47,48,64A,42
Schwartz, Robert	CA2950	66A,41,42
Scott Hoyt, Janet	AA0100	66A,66B,42
Scott, Aaron D.	PA1400	64C,42
Scott, Carla A.	CO0275	64B,42
Scott, Jeffrey	NJ0800	63B,42
Seggelke, Martin H.	CA4200	37,41,42,60
Sevilla, Jean-Paul	AG0400	66A,42
Shaffer, Marian	TN1850	62E,41,42
Shands, Patricia	CA5350	64C,42,41
Sharp, Wendy	CT0900	42
Sharpe, Alexander E.	NY1600	62A,42,51
Shaw, Clyde Thomas	VA1350	62C,42,12A,41
Shiffman, Barry	AG0300	42
Shihor, Ory	CA1075	66,66A,42
Shin, Aera	NJ0825	66A,42
Shinn, Michael A.	NY1900	13,42
Shires, Brent A.	AR0850	63B,32E,42,49
Shiu, Timothy	TN1680	62A,42
Shner, Idit	OR1050	64E,42,47,29
Shorthouse, Tom	AB0060	63A,47,49,42
Shultz, Betty Sue	OH2290	64B,42
Shuster, Brett A.	KY1500	42,63C,49,67E
Silver, Noreen	ME0440	42,32E,13C,62C
Silverman, Robert	AB0100	42,66A
Simidtchieva, Marta	IL2910	38,42,41,51,62C
Simmons, Amy	TN1720	42,64C,64E
Sindell, Carol A.	OR0850	41,62A,42
Sipes, Diana	TX2930	64A,12A,13E,42
Sirota, Jonah B.	NE0600	62B,42
Sirotin, Peter	PA2300	62A,42
Sizer, Todd	CO0275	63D,10F,34,42
Slabaugh, Thomas E.	CA5010	37,60,65,50,42
Smith, Alan M.	OH0300	62C,42,38
Smith, Glenn E.	VA0450	13,10,45,34,42
Smith, Michael K.	IA0950	42,63C,63D,49
Smukler, Laurie	NY0150	62A,42
Smylie, Dennis H.	NJ0800	64C,42
Snider, Nancy Jo	DC0010	62C,42,51,67B,41
Snizek, Suzanne	AB0150	64A,42
Sobol, Deborah	IL0550	66A,42
Sobolewski, Susan F.	NY2550	66D,13C,42,66A
Sokasits, Jonathan F.	NE0300	66A,66D,66B,42,12A
Sokol, Mark	CA4150	42
Solose, Kathleen A.	AJ0150	66A,66H,66B,66C,42
Spaar, Peter	VA1550	62D,42,47
Speed, George M.	OK0800	62D,11,42
Spencer, Patricia L.	NY1600	64A,42,43
Speziale, Marie	TX2150	63A,41,42
Spittal, Robert	WA0400	37,11,42,48,60B
Stanis, Sharon	AB0150	42,62A
Stanley, Ed L.	PA1400	64B,42,13A,13C,11
Statser, Sean J.	NY2750	42
Steinhardt, Arnold	CA1075	42
Stern, James	MD1010	62A,41,42
Stevenson, Doris L.	MA2250	41,66A,66C,42,43
Stewart, Victoria	NJ0700	62A,42
Stodola, Lynn	AF0100	42,66A,66C,41
Stoffan, George C.	MI1750	64C,48,42,32E
Stokes, James M.	NC0050	63A,49,41,42
Stowe, Cameron	NY1900	42
Stoyanov, Svetoslav R.	FL1900	65,50,42,43
Strachan, Heather	GA1650	62,42
Straka, Leslie	OR1050	42,62B
Strauss, Michael	OH1700	62B,42
Stuart, David H.	IA0850	63D,42,34A,34C,11
Sturm, Marina	NV0050	64C,42
Suarez, Jeff	WI0847	10,13,29,42,20G
Suda, Carolyn	IL1800	11,12A,62C,38,42
Suda, Carolyn W.	IL1350	11,42,51,62C
Sulski, Peter	MA0700	62B,62A,42
Sung, Benjamin H.	FL0850	62A,62B,41,42
Sutrisno, Joko	MN1623	42
Sweet, Brennan	NJ0700	62A,42
Sweger, Martin	IN0150	48,64D,42
Swensen, Ian	CA4150	62A,42
Swensen, Ian	CA0840	42,62A
Tacke, Mathias	IL2250	42
Talbott, Laura	OK0800	62A,62B,42
Tan, Kia-Hui	OH1850	62A,51,62B,13,42
Tan, Su Lian	VT0350	10,13,64A,42
Tapping, Roger	MA0350	42,62A
Tapping, Roger	MA1400	41,42
Tarbutton, Butch	SC0050	64E,42
Tarrant, James	MO1550	36,60A,35,42,66A
Taylor, Stephen G.	CT0850	64B,42
Tenenbom, Steven	NY0150	62B,42
Terwilliger, William	SC1110	62A,51,42
Theurer, Britton	NC0650	63A,42
Thiaville, Amy L.	LA0300	62A,42
Thiem, Barbara	CO0250	41,62C,42
Thompson, James	NY1100	63A,42
Thompson, Karin E.	WA1100	62C,20,12A,42,13C
Thompson, Marilyn	CA4700	66A,41,42
Thompson, Sonja K.	MN0050	61,39,54,41,42
Thorpe, Clyde	KY0800	70,42
Tidwell, Dallas	KY1500	64C,48,42
Tiedge, Faun Tanenbaum	OR0450	11,13,12A,20,42
Tinkel, Brian C.	NC1250	65,50,42
Tracy, Winston	KY1500	47,64E,42
Treer, Leonid P.	FL0650	14,66A,66B,42
Tremblay, Christian	MD1000	41,42,62A
Trinkle, Steven W.	NV0050	63A,41,42,38,13A

585

Name	Code	Areas
Troxler, Rebecca	NC0600	13A,64A,42,67D
Tsang, Bion	TX3510	62C,42
Tselyakov, Alexander	AC0050	66A,42,66B
Tung, Mimi	VA1550	66A,42
Tunnell, Michael	KY1500	49,63A,42
Turgeon, Melanie E.	AA0035	60,36,42,13C,32D
Turner, Cynthia Johnston	NY0900	60,37,41,42,38
Turner, Kyle	NJ0800	63D,42
Turovsky, JoAnn	CA1075	62E,42
Tzavaras, Nicholas G.	NJ0800	62C,42
Uyeyama, Jason	CA2420	42,51,62A,62B
Uzur, Viktor	UT0350	13,10F,51,62C,42
Vacchi, Steve	OR1050	64D,42,48
Vallecillo, Irma	CT0600	66A,42
Vamos, Brandon	IN0900	62C,42
Van der Werff, Ivo-Jan	TX2150	62B,42
Van Dreel, Lydia	OR1050	63B,49,42
Van Geem, Jack	CA1075	65,42
Vaneman, Christopher	SC0650	64A,12,42
Vaneman, Kelly McElrath	SC0650	12A,64B,42,55,14
Vaupel, Lisa	MD0400	62A,42
Velickovic, Ljubomir	CA3270	62A,42
Veligan, Igor	CA5350	62B,42,62A
Venzen, Austin A.	VI0050	10F,11,32B,37,42
Vercelli, Michael B.	WV0750	20,14,31F,41,42
VerMeulen, William	TX2150	63B,42
Vigneau, Michelle	TN1680	64B,42,13
Vitenson, Misha	FL0700	62A,42
Vogel, Allan	CA1075	64B,42,55B
Waddell, Rachel Lynn	MI1000	11,12,32E,42,64A
Walker, Jim	CA1075	64A,42
Walther, Geraldine E.	CO0800	42,62B
Wan, Andrew	AI0150	42,62
Wang, Hsiu-Hui	MD0400	66A,66C,42
Wang, Linda	CO0900	62A,41,42
Warner, Wendy	GA0550	62C,42
Warren, John	GA1150	64C,32E,42
Washington, Lecolion	TN1680	64D,42,11
Wasserman, Lisa	OH2140	64C,64D,42
Webster, Michael	TX2150	42,64C
Weckstrom, Virginia	AG0300	42,66C
Weir, Timothy	VA0100	32C,32E,37,47,42
Weiss, Lisa G.	MD0400	13A,11,42,66A,66C
Weller, Ira	NY0150	62B,42
Weller, Ira	NY3785	62B,42,51
Wells, Alison	MD0650	62C,42
Wheeler, Dale J.	AA0080	66A,66B,66D,66C,42
Widner, Paul	AG0300	62C,42
Wiens, Harold H.	AA0100	61,42
Wilder, Ralph	IL2100	64C,32E,64E,11,42
Wiley, Peter	NY0150	62C,42
Wilkinson, Wayne	CO0275	70,47,41,42
Williams, Barbara	UT0050	62A,42
Williams, Linda	NY2800	11,42
Wilson, Miranda	ID0250	13C,41,42,62C,62
Wilson, Ruth	CA4700	32E,42,49,63B
Wilson, Sandy	CA4200	41,62C,42
Wilt, James	CA1075	63A,42
Winant, William	CA2950	65,41,42
Winkler, Kathleen	TX2150	62A,42
Wis, Ramona M.	IL2050	60A,42,32D,36
Wise, Sherwood W.	NY0700	64B,48,13,64D,42
Wittstadt, Kurt	MD0175	11,42,63B
Wolfe, Gordon	AG0300	63C,42
Wong, Jerry	OH1100	66A,66B,66C,42
Woodard, Susan J.	PA3580	11,12,66A,42
Wooden, Lori L.	OK1330	64D,41,38,42,48
Wunsch, Aaron M.	NY1900	12,42
Xie, Song	MS0100	62A,62B,51,42
Xu, MingHuan	IL1615	42
Yamamoto, Sandy	TX3510	62A,42
Yampolsky, Miri	NY0900	42,66A
Yang, Rajung	ID0250	66A,66C,66H,42
Yarbrough, Paul R.	CA4200	41,62B,42
Yelverton, William	TN1100	70,42
Yeung, Angela C.	CA5200	13,38,41,42,62C
Ying, David	NY1100	42,62C
Ying, Janet	NY1100	62A,42
Ying, Phillip	NY1100	42,62B
Yon, Kirsten A.	TX3200	62A,42
Yonetani, Ayako	FL1800	62A,62B,42
Yoon, Hyeyung	NE0600	62A,42
York, Paul	KY1500	51,62C,42
Yost, Hilary W.	SC1200	64D,42
Yun, Soohyun	GA1150	66A,66B,66C,42
Zaerr, Laura	OR1050	62E,42
Zajac, Roy	CA4700	42,64C
Zamzow, Beth Ann	IA0930	13,41,42,37,12
Zawilak, Alexander	AZ0490	70,13A,42,41
Zhu, Hong	OK1330	62A,41,42,51
Zieba, Tomasz	OK0750	62C,42
Zimdars, Richard L.	GA2100	66A,42
Zimmerman, Charlene	IL0550	64C,42
Zombor, Iren	TN1200	62C,42
Zori, Carmit	NY3785	62A,42
Zukerman, Eugenia	NY2750	64A,42

New Music Ensemble

Name	Code	Areas
Adams, Liselyn	AI0070	13,12A,41,64A,43
Admiral, Roger	AA0100	41,43
Alexander, Kathryn J.	CT0900	13,10,34,43
Allen, Susan	CA0510	41,62E,43,53
Allsup, Randall Everett	NY4200	43,32,13,12A,12B
Andrews, Kenneth B.	NY3780	41,64A,43
Annis, Robert L.	NJ1350	64C,43
Anzivino, Steve	MI0300	65,50,43
Asia, Daniel I.	AZ0500	13,10,43
Bahn, Curtis	NY3300	43,13,10,12,45
Baime, Peter	WI0150	70,43
Baldacchino, Laura Falzon	NY4200	64A,32E,42,43
Bales, Kenton W.	NE0610	13,10,43,34
Bancks, Jacob	IL0100	10,10F,43,13,12A
Barth, Molly	OR1050	64A,42,48,43
Bauer, Ross	CA5010	13,10,43,29
Beal, Amy C.	CA5070	12A,12,43,20G
Beall, John	WV0750	13,10F,10,43
Berman, Donald L.	MA1900	43
Bjerken, Xak	NY0900	66A,42,43
Bonsignore, Joseph	OH0755	70,43
Bortolussi, Paolo	AB0100	43
Bresnick, Martin I.	CT0850	10,43
Bridges, Duane	MO1950	43
Briggs, Roger	WA1250	43,10F,10,66A
Browning, Zack D.	IL3300	13,10,43
Brubeck, Matthew	AG0650	43,53,62C
Brust, Paul W.	MA1175	10,13,43
Bunk, Louis	NH0110	34,10,11,13,43
Burns, Christopher	WI0825	10,13,34,43,45
Burr, Anthony	CA5050	64C,43,13D,14C,12D
Butterfield, Christopher	AB0150	13,10,43
Cai, Jindong	CA4900	60,38,43
Calloway, Jason	FL0700	62C,43,42
Carastathis, Aris	AG0170	13,10,43
Carrabre, T. Patrick	AC0050	13,10,43,20G,35
Celona, John	AB0150	13,10,43
Century, Michael	NY3300	12,13,43,34H,66A
Chandra, Arun	WA0350	10A,10B,43,34D,11
Chatman, Stephen G.	AB0100	13,10,43
Childs, Adrian P.	GA2100	10,13,43
Climer, John	WI0825	60,37,43
Coghlan, Michael	AG0650	13,10,29,34,43
Cortez, Juan	WA1200	43
Cowart, Steed D.	CA2950	10,13,43
Current, Brian	AG0300	43
D'Alessio, Greg P.	OH0650	13,10,45,43
Dangerfield, Joseph Allen	IA0300	10,13,66A,38,43
de Murga, Manuel	FL1750	10,10F,13E,34,43
Deemer, Robert	NY3725	10A,10C,43,10,60B
Demos, Nickitas J.	GA1050	10,43
Dempster, Stuart R.	WA1050	63C,43
Denham, Robert	CA0350	13,10,34,43
Desjardins, Jacques	CA4150	43,60B,13
Diamond, Jody	NH0100	14,53,43
Diazmunoz, Eduardo	IL3300	39,43,60B
DiBlassio, Brian	MI2120	47,13,43
Dickinson, Paul J.	AR0850	10,13,43,34
Dillon, Lawrence M.	NC1650	13A,13,10,43
DiOrio, Andrea R.	IL2050	64C,11,42,43
Donato, Dominic	NY3785	65,43
Dong, Kui	NH0100	13,10,20D,45,43
Dorman, Avner	PA1400	10A,10F,13,43
Downey, John W.	WI0825	13,10F,10,45,43
Drummond, Dean J.	NJ0800	13,43,10
Drury, Stephen	MA1400	66A,43,12
DuPree, Mary	ID0250	12A,12,43,14C
Duvall, Matthew	VA1500	43,65
Dwyer, Mac	MN1250	43
Dzubay, David	IN0900	10,43
Eagle, David	AA0150	13,10F,10,34,43
Farmer, Harry	VA0750	64E,47,42,43
Feeney, Kendall	WA0250	66A,43,66C
Feldberg, David	NM0450	43,62A,60B
Feltman, Joshua	NY0500	11,13,43
Ferril, Michael J.	CA0835	62A,42,43
Fitzell, Gordon D.	AC0100	10,34,43
Fonville, John	CA5050	13,10,64A,53,43
Fountain, Robin	TN1850	60,38,43
Fox, David E.	NC0900	66A,12A,66D,43,11
Frith, Fred	CA2950	10A,10B,53,43,11
Froelich, Kenneth D.	CA0810	10,34,43
Gamblin-Green, Michelle	MO0600	36,43
Gibson, Robert L.	MD1010	13,10,45,43
Gold, Matthew	MA2250	50,65,43,41
Gomez-Imbert, Luis	FL0700	62D,43,11
Gort, Cristian	AI0150	36,43
Gort, Cristian	AI0200	43
Grosso, Cheryl	WI0808	50,65,43,14,13C
Hackbarth, Glenn A.	AZ0100	13,10F,10,43
Haladyna, Jeremy	CA5060	10,43
Hanlon, Kevin	TX2400	13,10F,10,43
Harding, C. Tayloe	SC1110	10,35E,43
Harkins, Edwin	CA5050	13A,13,63A,54,43
Hege, Daniel C.	NY4150	43,60B
Heifetz, Robin J.	CA0200	11,20,10A,43,12
Heiss, John C.	MA1400	10,12A,41,43
Heldrich, Claire	NY2150	50,65,43
Helton, Jonathan	FL1850	64E,42,43
Herriott, Jeffrey	WI0865	10,11,43,35E
Hicks, Michael D.	UT0050	13,43
Hixson, Mary	GA2000	13C,20,40,43
Ho, Ting	NJ0800	13,10,45,43
Hoffmann, Paul K.	NJ1130	66A,43
Hostetter, Paul K.	GA0550	38,39,60B,43
Huang, Steven	OH1900	38,60B,43
Hultgren, Craig	AL0300	62C,43
Ince, Kamran	TN1680	13,10,43
Jacobs, Edward	NC0650	10A,10B,13,43
Jazwinski, Barbara M.	LA0750	13,10,43
Jenny, Jack	OH2050	13,10,50,65,43
Johnson, William T.	CA4700	13,10,11,43,12A
Justeson, Jeremy	PA1750	64E,37,32E,43,11
Kalish, Gilbert	NY3790	41,66A,66C,43
Kaplan, Lisa	VA1500	43,66A
Karis, Aleck	CA5050	13,12A,66A,66H,43
Kasparov, Aridrey R.	VA1000	13,66A,10,43
Kehn, Conrad	CO0900	13,43
Kelley, Kevin	TX1350	11,10,13,43
Kelly, Gary	NY0700	35,34,62D,43
Kennedy, John M.	CA0830	10,13F,43,10F,13
Kilstofte, Mark F.	SC0750	10,13,43,13E
Kleinsasser, William	MD0850	10,43
Kramer, Karl P.	IL3300	42,43
Kuehn, Mikel	OH0300	13,10F,10,45,43
Kurkowicz, Joanna	MA2250	41,62A,43
Kyr, Robert	OR1050	10A,10F,43,20D
Lam, Michelle	VA1500	62A,62B,43
Lamb, Marvin L.	OK1350	10,43
Lamneck, Esther	NY2750	64C,43
Lau, Frederick C.	HI0210	14A,38,43,64A,20C
Leandro, Eduardo G.	NY3790	65,50,43
Lebens, James C.	AI0190	63C,49,43
Lee, Brent	AG0550	13,10,45,43,53
Leverence, Dan	MN1280	43
Lewanski, Michael A.	IL0750	41,43
Lewis, James E.	FL2000	13,10F,10,43
Lifchitz, Max	NY3700	10,43,13A,13,10F
Lowenstein, Marc	CA0510	13,10,60,39,43
Lubman, Bradley	NY1100	43,38,60B
Lund, Erik R.	IL3300	13,10,43
Mabrey, Charlotte	FL1950	50,65,43,20G
Maccaferri, Michael	VA1500	43,64C
MacDonald, Payton	NJ1400	65,50,43
MacIntyre, David K.	AB0080	13,10,39,43
Martin, Andree	GA0550	64A,11,43,12
Masaki, Megumi	AC0050	13,66A,66C,43,66B
Matthews, Justus F.	CA0825	13,10,43,34
McDonald, John	MA1900	13,10,12A,43,13
McNutt, Elizabeth	TX3420	64A,43
McWhorter, Brian J.	OR1050	63A,49,43
Meister, Scott R.	NC0050	10,65,43,50
Menzies, Mark	CA0510	62A,62B,38,43,60B
Merritt, Justin W.	MN1450	10,13,43,13A,34
Messick, Heather	AL1195	61,43
Meyer, Jeffery David	NY1800	38,66A,60B,43

Name	Code	Numbers
Miles, Stephen T.	FL1360	13,10,43
Miller, Al	AL1195	60,61,36,43
Milnes, David	CA5000	38,43,60B
Mitchell, Darleen C.	NE0590	13,10,15,43,12B
Moshier, Steve	CA3750	13,11,12A,34,43
Muniz, Jorge	IN0910	10A,13,10B,10,43
Munn, Zae	IN1450	13,10F,10,43
Negyesy, Janos	CA5050	20F,41,62A,43,34
Noe, Kevin	MI1400	38,43,60B
Nohai-Seaman, Alexander	NY4050	13,10,43
Oehler, Donald L.	NC2410	41,42,43,48,64C
Oppens, Ursula	NY0500	66,41,42,43
Osborne, Thomas	HI0210	10A,10F,13,43
Paccione, Paul	IL3500	13,10,43,20G
Paiement, Nicole	CA4150	43,60
Palter, Morris	AK0150	12A,29A,42,43,14C
Parke, Nathaniel	MA2250	62C,43,41
Pearson, Scotty	AZ0490	70,43
Pelo, Mika	CA5010	10,11,13,43
Pelusi, Mario J.	IL1200	10A,10F,13,43,29B
Perron, Alain	AJ0100	10A,10B,10C,43,10F
Phillips, Mark W.	OH1900	43,10,45,34
Photinos, Nicholas	VA1500	43,62C
Piedra, Olman	OH2140	65,50,43,29
Pierce, Forrest D.	KS1350	13,10,43
Plantamura, Carol	CA5050	12A,55,61,54,43
Powell, Ross	TX2400	41,64C,43
Pratt, Michael	NJ0900	60,38,43,39
Prouty, Patrick	MI2120	47,13,43,10
Radford, Laurie	AA0150	10,10F,13,43
Reed, Dennis	NC0350	43
Reed, Jerome A.	TN0930	10A,66A,66B,66C,43
Renshaw, Jeffrey	CT0600	60,37,43
Rindfleisch, Andrew P.	OH0650	10,13,43
Rockmaker, Jody D.	AZ0100	13A,13,10,12A,43
Rodgers, Lloyd A.	CA0815	13,10,43
Rohde, Kurt E.	CA5010	13,10,11,43
Rollin, Robert	OH2600	13,10,43
Rosenak, Karen	CA5000	13A,13C,43
Rosenboom, David	CA0510	10,43,66A
Rowe, Robert	NY2750	10,43,34,35C
Ryan, William E.	MI0900	10,43
Sachs, Joel	NY1900	12A,41,43
Salazar, Jason	MO0400	34,13,35,43,47
Salerni, Paul F.	PA1950	13,10,43
San Martin, Laurie A.	CA5010	10,13,43,35E
Sanchez, Pete	AL1195	31,43
Sanchez, Rey	FL1900	10D,34C,35A,20G,43
Sauerwein, Andrew Mark	MS0100	13,10,29B,43,64B
Sawyer, Eric	MA0100	10,13,34,43
Scharfenberger, Paul E.	NH0110	12,67C,43,55,15
Schelle, Michael	IN0250	13,10,43,10F
Schick, Steven	CA5050	11,50,65,43,29
Schneider, David E.	MA0100	12,64C,43,13,41
Schubert, Mark	IL3250	38,41,60,43
Schwendinger, Laura Elise	WI0815	10,43
Scott, Stephen	CO0200	10,11,45,43,29
Segger, Joachim	AA0035	13,13J,66A,66B,43
Selden, Ken	OR0850	38,43,51,60B
Serghi, Sophia	VA0250	13,10F,10,43,10A
Shapiro, Madeleine	NY2250	43
Simpson, Andrew Earle	DC0050	10,10F,13,66A,43
Sinigos, Louis	MI0300	65,50,43
Sintchak, Matthew A.	WI0865	64E,29,43,47,48
Smith, Robert Thomas	TX3400	13A,13,10,43
Smith, William O.	WA1050	13,10,43
Smoak, Jeff C.	KY1425	32,36,61,40,43
Sokol, Casey	AG0650	13A,66A,53,43
Sollberger, Harvey	CA5050	10F,60,10,64A,43
Sorbara, Joe	AG0350	43,65
Speck, Frederick A.	KY1500	10,37,43
Spencer, Patricia L.	NY1600	64A,42,43
Stadelman, Jeffrey	NY4320	10,43
Stemper, Frank L.	IL2900	13,10,43
Stevenson, Doris J.	MA2250	41,66A,66C,42,43
Stock, David	PA1050	60,43
Stolte, Charles	AA0035	64E,13A,13,10,43
Stoyanov, Svetoslav R.	FL1900	65,50,42,43
Stucky, Steven	NY0900	10,13B,13D,13F,43
Summers, Jerome	AG0500	60,38,64C,67B,43
Sunderland, Paul	IL1050	29B,31A,43,70
Tamarkin, Kate	VA1550	38,60B,12A,43
Tower, Joan	NY0150	10,43
Trachsel, Andrew J.	OH1900	37,43
True, Carolyn E.	TX3350	66A,66B,66D,43
Turetzky, Bertram	CA5050	12A,41,62D,43,29
Udland, Matt	KS0210	11,36,43,61
Underhill, Owen	AB0080	13,60,10,12,43
Vaillancourt, Lorraine	AI0200	43
Vaillancourt, Paul	GA0550	65,50,13C,43
Vassilandonakis, Yiorgos	SC0500	10,11,13,43
Vincent, Kate	MA1175	43
Walt, Stephen	MA2250	48,64D,43,41
Welbourne, Todd G.	WI0815	66A,34A,34D,43
Welcher, Dan E.	TX3510	10,43
Welstead, Jon	WI0825	10,13,34,43,45
Wheeler, Scott	MA0850	13,60,10,54,43
White, Barbara A.	NJ0900	13A,10,13,10F,43
Wiedrich, William	FL2000	60,37,43
Wieligman, Thomas	IN0900	37,38,43,46
Wiley, Frank	OH1100	13,10,38,60B,43
Wilson, Brian S.	CA4700	10,37,13,43,60
Wilson, Ken	MN1250	70,43
Winant, William K.	CA5070	50,65,43
Wolf, Lily	AL1195	54,43
Woll, Greg	CA1900	13,49,63,43
Yannay, Yehuda	WI0825	13,10,45,43
Young, Gene	MD0650	43
Youtz, Gregory	WA0650	10,13,14,43
Zahab, Roger E.	PA3420	38,13,10F,43,62A
Zank, MJ Sunny	OH1800	13,20,10,12A,43
Zbyszynski, Michael F.	CA5353	34,43
Zilincik, Anthony	OH0350	63D,41,43,10F

Bell Choir

Name	Code	Numbers
Behnke, John A.	WI0300	10,44,66G,31A
Belflowers, Timothy	NC0350	44
Benson, Katherine	IL2300	64A,41,44
Blachly, Barbara	KS1000	44
Blackwell, Claire	CA2810	44
Booth, John D.	MO0500	12,44,61,31A,70
Borrmann, Kenneth	PA2800	66A,66B,66C,42,44
Boyer, Maurice C.	IL0730	13C,36,38,44
Brown, Philip	VT0300	11,13A,36,44,47
Bruening, Anne	PA3650	44
Burkett, Darlene	IN0700	44,66G
Busch, Stephen E.	CO0250	32,44,66D
Cadwell, Jennifer	MN1625	44
Case, Del W.	CA3400	66G,44,13,12A,36
Caston, Ben	GA0400	44,61,31
Chae, Hyung Sek	TX3650	36,31A,44,60,32D
Chafin, Gerald	KY0860	60A,11,32,36,44
Chambers, Joe	NY2660	44,65,53
Chambers, Robert B.	TN0650	60,61,31A,36,44
Crim, Mark	TX0600	37,32E,60B,44
Dalton, Sharon	WY0060	13,44,61,66
Davis, Ron A.	SC1000	13B,13C,31,66G,44
Droke, Marilyn	MO0200	13A,32B,44
Durbin, Karen	PA2300	31,44
Eby, Kristen	IA1450	44,61,40,36,13
Eithun, Sandra	WI0770	44
Etter, Paul J.	NC0850	60A,36,44,60,31A
Faber, Trudy	OH2450	12A,44,66G,66H,31A
Forster, Marilyn	OH2140	44,66D
Freyermuth, G. Kim	AZ0200	36,44,61,47
Fuelberth, Brett J.	IA0800	13,36,47,44
Gall, George G.	MA1650	44
Gardstrom, Susan	OH2250	33,12F,44
Garner, Jerald	TX3800	44
Geisler, Herbert G.	CA1425	14,32,44,13,31
Gingrich, Shawn	PA2300	66G,44
Gonzales, Elizabeth	CA1860	44
Gosselin, Karen	AL0550	32,60,36,40,44
Gray, Donavon D.	CA0250	37,44,49,32,48
Gregory, Gary J.	OH0550	44,13,60,37,63C
Hall, Elizabeth W.	PA1350	44
Hammar, Christine	MO0400	44
Harrill, Stephen	NC1900	61,41,44
Henning, Mary	KY0350	20,44,32,36
Hewell, Rob	AR0500	31A,44,11
Hirschmann, Craig	WI1155	10A,44,66G
Hong, Xiangtang	IL1850	60A,31A,36,44,11
Hopkins, Jesse E.	VA0100	32,36,61,44,60A
Huls, Marvin J.	PA3000	13,36,44
Jessup, Nancy	CA1425	44,32E
Johnson, Brad	MS0200	60,11,36,44,61
Johnson, Meg	NC2000	33,44
Jowers, Florence	NC1100	36,44,66G
Kern, Jeffrey	PA3330	13A,36,44,61,66A
Kite, Jessica	NE0150	44
Kwan, Eva	IN1560	12A,32,44,20
Lawhon, Daniel E.	AL0800	66G,44
LeVelle, Teresa	CA6000	13,10,44,42
Long, Lillian F.	WV0050	61,66C,66G,39,44
Lynerd, Betty Ann	IL1850	31A,44,36
Mahr, Jill	MN1450	44,64A
Mathis, Carolynne	MN0610	32E,44,65
McClain, Frances	NC2000	33,44
Miller, Dan	IN1800	12A,36,44,61
Moehlman, Carl B.	IA0900	13,12A,44,66G,31A
Moorman-Stahlman, Shelly	PA1900	44,66A,66G,31A,66D
Moss, Grant R.	MA1750	66G,66H,44
Munoz, Nelida	PR0150	11,13A,13C,44
Myrick, Kenny	MS0420	44,64
Nichols, Lois J.	CA4600	66,32,44,67B,11
Nichols, Peter W.	IN1650	44
Nielsen, John	IA0200	44,32
Nigrelli, Christopher	NC1100	12A,47,44,63C,63D
Parker, Linda	NC0200	11,32,44,13,64
Payn, William A.	PA0350	36,44,66G,66H,31A
Persellin, Diane C.	TX3350	32,44
Peterson, Gregory M.	IA0950	44,66G,31A
Peterson, Jon C.	OH0250	36,12A,44,11,54
Prichard, Sheila Grace	MA1600	36,44
Rasmussen, G. Rosalie	CA3400	32,44,66B,66D,13C
Rauschnabel, June	MN0600	44,61
Reed, Allen	TX1100	13,44,66,31A
Reimer, Joyce L.	NE0250	44,66A,66G
Reiss, Deborah	NY0850	44,40,31A,66C
Retif, T. N.	GA0400	13E,12A,61,44
Sanders, George	CT0600	63C,44
Schell, Cheryl	KY0100	44
Schell, Mark	KY0100	44,66G,31A
Schumacher, Judy	OR0150	44
Scott, Jennifer	NY2900	44
Shaw, Kathleen	NJ1350	44
Shull, Kevin	MN0250	44
Simpson, Alexander T.	KY0250	11,12A,36,44,60A
Singleton, Darryl	TX3150	37,44,11
Smith, Larry Dearman	MS0750	44,61
Stansbury, George	TX3415	60,31A,44
Storm, Linda	IL1550	66A,66G,66B,44
Tallman, Donna	IL0850	36,60A,44
Taylor, Steven	CO0150	39,61,31A,44,13C
Thomason, Jo Carol	NC1100	44
Tully, Cynthia	CA1425	44
Turnquist-Steed, Melody	KS0150	11,13C,31,44,66G
Vail, Kathy	MS0850	66A,66G,69,44
Vaughn, Donna	KY1200	44
Veltman, Joshua	TN1660	11,12A,44
Walter, Cameron	AG0450	32,63C,63D,37,44
Westgard, Jessica	MN0600	44
Westra, Mitzi	IN1650	61,13A,11,44
White, Christie	MO2000	44
Williams, Kimberly	WI0300	44
Wiltse, Stephanie	MI0300	44
Wiltse, Stephanie	MI0350	44
Winterfeldt, Chad	MN0750	66G,44,12
Zabel, Albert	WV0400	44,66G,31A,10,66C

Electronic Music Ensemble

Name	Code	Numbers
Abbati, Joseph S.	FL1900	10B,34A,35C,45,34E
Aberdam, Eliane	RI0300	13,10F,10,12A,45
Allik, Kristi A.	AG0250	10,45,34,32F
Alves, William	CA2175	10,14,45,34
Anderson, Mark	CA1800	34,35A,35B,45,35C
Andrews, Nancy	ME0270	35B,35C,35F,45,20G
Babb, Douglas	IN0907	45
Bahn, Curtis	NY3300	43,13,10,12,45
Bain, Reginald	SC1110	13,10,34,45
Ball, Leonard V.	GA2100	13,10,45,34
Ballora, Mark E.	PA2750	45
Barsom, Paul	PA2750	10,45
Barton, Todd	OR0950	10,45
Beck, Stephen David	LA0200	10,45,34
Bennett, Barbara A.	CA5040	13B,13,11,45,34
Berger, Jonathan	CA4900	13,10,45,34
Berry, Robert C.	CA3950	62D,45
Biederwolf, Kurt J.	MA0260	45,35C
Bielawa, Herbert	CA4200	13A,13,10F,10,45
Bierylo, Michael	MA0260	45,35C
Bischoff, John	CA2950	45,10B,12A,13B,20F

587

Name	Code	Areas
Blake, C. Marc	CA2600	13,11,34,45,35B
Bobrowski, Christine	CA1250	45,34,35C
Boulanger, Richard	MA0260	45,35C
Brigida, Michael A.	MA0260	45,35C
Burch-Pesses, Michael	OR0750	60,32C,37,47,45
Burns, Christopher	WI0825	10,13,34,43,45
Bussiere, Michael	AG0100	13A,13,45,34
Caldwell, James M.	IL3500	13,10,45
Caldwell, Robert	AB0050	45,65,34,46,41
Carenbauer, Michael	AR0750	45,51,70,34
Carl, Robert B.	CT0650	13,10,45
Chadabe, Joel	NY2150	45
Chafe, Chris	CA4900	10,45,34,13L
Chamberlin, Robert	MO1950	13,10F,10,45
Chambers, Evan	MI2100	10,45
Chowning, John M.	CA4900	10,45,34,13L
Ciamaga, Gustav	AG0450	13,10,45,34
Cima, Alex	CA1900	35A,35D,45
Clements, Peter J.	AG0500	13,10,45
Coburn, Robert	CA5350	13,10,45
Coleman, Todd	NC0750	10,34,62D,35G,45
Corwin, Mark	AI0070	10F,10,45,34,35C
Crawford, Mark	TN1400	35A,35B,45
Crist, Timothy D.	AR0110	13,45,10,70
Crum, Martin	TN1400	11,45
Csapo, Gyula	AJ0150	13,10,45,10F
Cullison, Jon	CO0830	13,45
D'Alessio, Greg P.	OH0650	13,10,45,43
Davis, Dennis	KY0550	70,45,34
De Ritis, Anthony	MA1450	35,62B,34,45
Deutsch, Herbert A.	NY1600	13,10,45,29A,35
Dickau, David C.	MN1000	60,36,45,34
Dong, Kui	NH0100	13,10,20D,45,43
Dow, David Charles	CA3000	45,66D,34
Downey, John W.	WI0825	13,10F,10,45,43
Dvorin, David	CA0800	13,10,35G,45
Eigenfeldt, Arne	AB0080	10,45,34,35,12F
Elsea, Peter	CA5070	45,35C
Engelmann, Marcus W.	CA0100	13,10,12A,45,20G
Everett, Steve	GA0750	60,10,41,45,34
Fennelly, Brian	NY2740	13,10,12A,45
Ferguson, Sean	AI0150	10,45
Festinger, Richard	CA4200	13,10,45,34
Fikentscher, Kai	NJ0950	14,20,45
Filadelfo, Gary A.	NY1600	45,35C,35D
First, Craig P.	AL1170	13,10,45,34
Flaherty, Thomas E.	CA3650	13,10,12A,45
Fruehwald, Robert D.	MO1500	13,10,45,64A
Gabel, Gerald R.	TX3000	34,10,13,45
Gabriel, Edgar	IL0850	62A,62B,45
Galindo, Guillermo	CA1250	45,34,35C
Garton, Bradford	NY0750	10,11,45,34
Gauger, David	IL1850	37,38,45,63A
George, Arnold E.	NC1600	47,45,64,34,13
Gibson, Robert L.	MD1010	13,10,45,43
Ginader, Gerhard	AC0050	13,10,45,62A
Gluck, Robert J.	NY3700	10B,34D,31B,34,45
Gompertz, Phil	CA2700	45
Gotfrit, Martin	AB0080	10,45,34,35,12F
Gottschalk, Arthur	TX2150	13,10,45
Greenland, John	PA1150	35C,45
Griffin, Nancy W.	AR0750	66D,45
Gunther, John	CO0800	29,45
Hakutani, Naoki	AR0750	66A,66D,45
Hallstrom, Jonathan F.	ME0250	13,60,10,38,45
Harbold, Tim	MA2150	60,36,45
Harjung, Dan	WI1150	45
Hart, James	OH2550	34,45
Hays, Timothy O.	IL0850	13,62D,45,34,35
Head, Russell	KS0750	10B,10D,34,35,45
Headrick, Samuel P.	MA0400	13,10,45
Hellberg, Eric	CA2440	65,45
Helmuth, Mara M.	OH2200	10,45,34
Henderson, Luther L.	CA2600	20G,38,62,45
Hilmy, Steven C.	DC0100	10,45,34
Hiscocks, Mike	CA2650	11,13A,61,45,10B
Ho, Ting	NJ0800	13,10,45,43
Hoffman, Elizabeth D.	NY2740	12D,13,10,45,34
Howard, David	OR0250	13,10,11,45,66G
Howe, Hubert S.	NY0642	13,45,34
Hunkins, Arthur B.	NC2430	13,10,45,34
Irish, Michael J.	MI1450	13,47,45,53,29
Isaacs, David	TN1400	70,11,35G,45
Jacobs, Kenneth A.	TN1710	13,10,45
Jenks, Alden	CA4150	10,45
Johnson, Marvin	AL1170	13,10,45
Jones, Hilton Kean	FL2000	10,35,13,45,66G
Kadis, Jay L.	CA4900	45,35C
Kapur, Ajay	CA0510	34,20E,45
Kidde, Geoffrey C.	NY2200	10,13,34,45,32F
Kirby, Wayne J.	NC2400	10,45,34,35,62D
Klein, Jim	PA1000	34,32F,45,13G,10C
Kozel, Paul	NY0550	10,45,35
Kreiger, Arthur V.	CT0100	13,35C,10,45,34
Krieger, Ulrich	CA0510	10,34D,12A,45,64E
Kuchera-Morin, JoAnn	CA5060	13,10F,10,45,13L
Kuehn, Mikel	OH0300	13,10F,10,45,43
Kuivila, Ronald	CT0750	10,45
Kuss, Mark	CT0450	13,10,45,66A,34
Lansky, Paul	NJ0900	13,10,45,34
Lee, Brent	AG0550	13,10,45,43,53
Lehrman, Paul D.	MA1900	35C,34,35B,45,45
Leonard, Jeff	OR0400	70,10B,45
Lesemann, Frederick	CA5300	13,10F,10,45
Lester, David T.	OH2140	70,35,45,42
Ligon, Bert	SC1110	46,47,66A,29,45
Lippe, Cort	NY4320	10,45,34
Loughrige, Chad	OH0350	34,35C,10B,10D,45
Lowrey, Norman E.	NJ0300	13A,13,10,45,34
Lucier, Alvin	CT0750	10,45,34
Lum, Anne Craig	HI0150	66D,66A,64A,45,66C
Lyren, Delon	MN0150	63A,63B,49,45
MacDonald, Andrew	AI0050	13,10F,10,45,70
Mandrell, Nelson E.	IL2150	13,10,45,34
Marschner, Joseph A.	MD0450	11,45,70,34
Matthusen, Paula A.	CT0750	34,45,10
McCollim, Danny	WA0950	45,66A,35D,47,35A
McManus, James M.	CA3320	13,45,29A,12A,11
Middleton, Peter	IL2200	45,64A,34,35C,13L
Midgley, Herbert	TX2700	11,70,34,45
Miller, Dennis H.	MA1450	13,10,45,34
Moe, Eric H.	PA3420	13,10,45,10B
Molina, Jose	CA1520	34,45
Moore, F. Richard	CA5050	10,45,34,35C,13L
Mooy, James D.	CA4410	45,35C,34,46,64
Morrill, Dexter G.	NY0650	10,45,29A,34
Mountain, Rosemary	AI0070	13,10F,10,45,34
Mumma, Gordon	CA5070	12A,45
Munson, Jordan	IN0907	45,53,13A
Myska, David	AG0500	13,10,45,34,35C
Nagel, Jody	IN0150	13,10,45,35C
Neal, Randall	VT0050	12,36,45
Nelson, Larry A.	PA3600	13,10,45,34
Nichols, Charles Sabin	MT0400	10A,10B,10,45,34
Nottingham, Douglas	AZ0350	65,50,45,10B,35
O'Donnell, Richard L.	MO1900	45
Ortiz, Pablo	CA5010	13,10,45,29,34
Ovens, Douglas P.	PA2550	13,10,45,65
Parenteau, Gilles	AB0070	10F,45,66,35H
Parkinson, John S.	CA2840	37,38,47,49,45
Pastrana, Jorge	CA4850	47,46,45,35D,10B
Patrick, Dennis M.	AG0450	13,45,13L,34,35C
Pennycook, Bruce	TX3510	45
Perl, Jonathan	NY0550	45,35B,35C,35D
Perrault, Paul	AI0220	45,34,35C,35E,13L
Peterson, Keith L.	NY3725	13,10,45
Phelps, James	IL2200	10,45,34
Phillips, Mark W.	OH1900	43,10,45,34
Phillips, Scott L.	AL1150	32F,34,45
Pinkston, Russell F.	TX3510	10,45,34
Pinto, David	CA2700	45
Pisano, Joseph M.	PA1450	47,45,53,46,34
Polansky, Larry	NH0100	13,10,45,34
Pontbriand, Roget	FL1450	45,46,35,10D,10C
Pounds, Michael S.	IN0150	10,34D,13,45,34
Powell, Jarrad	WA0200	13A,10,20D,45,34
Purse, Lynn Emberg	PA1050	10B,34,45
Rathbun, Andrew	NY2050	35C,35D,35G,10B,45
Repar, Patricia Ann	NM0450	10,45
Reynolds, Todd	NY2150	45
Richardson, Chuck	TX2850	11,45,35C,35G
Richens, James W.	TN1680	13,10,45
Riepe, Russell C.	TX3175	13,10,45
Riley, Madeleine C.	PA1000	11,45,64A,64E,29
Robertson, Ben	WA0250	10B,45,35G,34D
Robinson, Marty	FL0600	47,45,63A,29
Rogalsky, Matt	AG0250	10,45,34,32F
Rolnick, Neil B.	NY3300	13,10,45,34
Rothbart, Peter	NY1800	45,35C,35D
Rothkopf, Michael S.	NC1650	45,35C,35G
Rovan, Joseph 'Butch'	RI0050	10,45,34
Rubel, Mark	IL2350	45,35C,35D
Sandroff, Howard	IL3250	10,45,34,13L
Santos, Erik	MI2100	10,34A,45
Sapieyevski, Jerzy	DC0010	13,10,45,11,34
Schenkel, Steve	MO1950	12A,31,45,29,35
Schmutte, Peter J.	IN1650	36,45,35C,35G,34
Schneider, John	CA2700	41,45,70,34
Schoolfield, Robnet	SC0200	32,45,65,72
Scott, Stephen	CO0200	10,11,45,43,29
Semegen, Daria	NY3790	13,10,45
Setter, Terry A.	WA0350	10F,10,12B,45,35C
Shapiro, Gerald	RI0050	13,10,45,34
Sheppard, Craig	AF0100	45,35C
Siler, Sandra K.	TX1350	41,45,66A,66D
Smiley, William C.	NC1550	10B,35C,35G,45
Smith, Glenn E.	VA0450	13,10,45,34,42
Smith, Wadada Leo	CA0510	63A,29,10,45,53
Sommer, Lesley	WA1250	13,10,45
Stallmann, Kurt D.	TX2150	13,10,45,34
Stanton, Geoffrey	MI1300	13,10,45,34
Steen, Kenneth	CT0650	10,13,45
Stewart, D. Andrew	AA0200	34D,10B,45,35A
Stolet, Jeffrey	OR1050	13,45,10,34,10B
Streder, Mark	IL0850	13,66A,53,34,45
Sudol, Jacob David	FL0700	34,35,45
Svanoe, Erika K.	MN0150	64C,60B,37,32E,45
Sweidel, Martin	TX2400	45,13
Taddie, David	WV0750	13,10,45
Theodore, Michael	CO0800	10,45,34,10
Thompson, Robert Scott	GA1050	10A,10B,10C,45,34
Toensing, Richard E.	CO0800	13,10,45
Towner, John	IL0850	45,34
Trayle, Mark	CA0510	10,34,45
Truax, Barry D.	AB0080	10,45,34,35C,13L
Valcarcel, David	CA3950	45,65,35C,13G,66A
Valcarcel, David Shawn	CA3265	45,65,35C,13G,66A
Vercoe, Barry	MA1200	13,10,45,34
Walczyk, Kevin	OR1250	13,45,63B,29,10
Walker, Gregory	MN0350	13,10,45,34
Waters, Joseph	CA4100	10,45,34,35C
Watts, Mike	CA2700	45
Wells, Thomas H.	OH1850	10,45,34
Welstead, Jon	WI0825	10,13,34,43,45
Werren, Philip	AG0650	10F,10,45
Weymouth, Daniel	NY3790	13,10,45,34
Wheeler, George	CA1520	34,45
Whitehead, Glen	CO0810	63A,47,29,45
Willey, Robert K.	LA0760	13,34,35,10B,45
Willson, Kenneth F.	OR0250	13,45,66A,66B,66C
Winkler, Todd	RI0050	10,45,34
Wolek, Nathan	FL1750	34,11,45
Wright, Geoffrey	MD0650	45,34,10B
Wyatt, Scott A.	IL3300	13,10,34,45
Yannay, Yehuda	WI0825	13,10,45,43
Yannelli, John A.	NY3560	13,41,45,54,34
Yarmolinsky, Benjamin	NY0280	13A,13,10,45,70
Zacharias, Andrew	CA1520	34,45,70

Jazz/Stage Band

Name	Code	Areas
Adair, William 'Billy'	TN1850	29,46,47
Adam, Mark	AF0050	11,13C,46,47,65
Adams, Joel	IL2050	46,63C
Adams, Justin	CO0550	66A,46
Adams, Kurtis B.	WV0550	47,46,13
Aliquo, Don	TN1100	29,64E,46,47
Allen, John	OK0750	63C,46,49
Alva, Albert	CA0960	46
Anderson, Leon	FL0850	47,65,29,46
Anderson, Ray R.	NY3790	46,47,53
Aponte, Jose Porentud	TX3420	50,65,46
Appell, Glen	CA1560	11,29,46,47
Argiro, James	MA2100	35C,35H,46,10C
Armstrong, James E.	NC2700	63A,13A,37,46,49
Arriale, Lynne	FL1950	66A,29B,46
Atkins, Victor	LA0800	29,46,47,66A
AuBuchon, Tim	MO1780	29,46,47
Austerlitz, Paul	PA1400	12,14,46
Austin, Kenneth L.	IL3100	13,32C,37,49,46
Bailey, Don	AR0730	13C,29A,29B,46,64E
Baker, Eric	TX1850	11,37,46,63A
Baker, Kent	VT0100	66A,66D,46,13,10F
Baker, Malcolm Lynn	CO0900	47,53,46,29
Balfany, Gregory J.	WI0810	47,64C,46,29

Index by Area of Teaching Interest

Name	Code	Areas
Banks, Steven	OK0770	46,70
Barclay, Timothy R.	IL0650	13A,64E,46,47
Baril, Ray	AA0100	46
Bass, John	TN1200	70,46,47,67G
Baxter, Kara	NE0200	46,47,62
Beckler, Terry	SD0400	65,50,37,46,11
Beghtol, Jason W.	MS0570	37,13A,46,63,49
Behnke, Martin	OR0950	46,47,29A
Berg, Shelton G.	FL1900	66A,66C,29,46,47
Bergeron, Chuck	FL1900	62D,47,29A,46,12A
Beste, Alan	AZ0460	46
Betancourt, David	CA0859	37,46,38,32E,60B
Bindrim, Don	TN0300	34,46
Bitz, Lori	MI1950	46
Blackley, Terrance J.	CA1900	66D,46,35
Blaha, Joseph L.	VA1250	46,10,12A,48,63C
Boedges, Bob	MO1120	46,14C
Bonsanti, Neal	FL0650	64E,47,46
Booker, Adam	MN1600	29,41,46,62D
Booker, Kenneth A.	TX1450	37,46,47,60,13A
Bouchard, George	NY2550	11,46,47,66D,29
Bradfield, Ann	NM0100	29,46,47,64A,64E
Branker, Anthony D.J.	NJ0900	47,29,46
Brath, Wally	MN0250	46
Bratt, Douglass F.	IL1890	50,47,65A,65B,46
Breiling, Roy	AZ0510	37,38,46,47,63A
Brennan, Bill	AD0050	46
Brewer, Johnny	AL0620	13A,13B,11,46,13C
Briggs, Ray A.	CA0825	14,29,46,47
Britt, Michael J.	AR0600	46,50,65
Britto, Richard	MA2020	64E,11,46
Brockman, Luke	WA0250	29,46,66A
Brown, Jeff	MS0360	37,65,50,46
Brown, Miles	MI1750	62D,47,29A,29B,46
Brown, Robert	TX2930	46,35C,34D
Brueske, Jeffrey	MN0250	46
Brunetto, Rick	OH1600	46
Bruya, Chris	WA0050	46,47,29,13
Buonamassa, John	CA0835	34A,34B,46
Burks, Ricky	AL1450	48,64,46,29B,37
Butrico, Michael	NC0400	32E,37,46,60B,63
Butterfield, Craig	SC1110	62D,29,46,47
Butts, William	CA1290	46
Calderazzo, Joey	NC1600	66A,66C,46,47
Caldwell, Robert	AB0050	45,65,34,46,41
Call, R. Steven	UT0050	47,63D,46,29
Callahan, Gary L.	NC1150	48,64,32,46
Campbell, Roy	MA0510	11,10F,38,46,47
Campbell, Will	NC2420	46,47,53,64E
Camwell, David J.	IA1350	32C,46,47,64E,48
Cannon, Jimmie	CA2300	11,13A,46
Cantrell, James	AL0330	35A,35B,35C,35D,46
Carillo, Dan	NY0550	47,13,46,10,29
Carlson, Dan	MN1100	11,35A,37,46,63
Carlson, Lennis Jay	CA1020	70,46,29A
Carroll, James R.	VA0450	47,64E,29,46
Carroll, Kenneth D.	AR0110	29,64E,37,46
Carubia, Michael R.	NY2550	46,47
Cates, Tim	TX1600	46
Cavanagh, Daniel	TX3500	47,29,46
Cavender, James L.	AL1160	70,41,46,62D
Champouillon, David	TN0500	63A,46,29
Chapman, Christopher	OR0700	32,37,46,63A,60B
Cheesman, Robert	MS0300	63,46,34
Claussen, Tina	MO0350	47,64E,46,29
Clements, Gordon	AB0210	46,47,29B,64E,64C
Clothier, Stephen	CA0630	29,46
Coates, Gary	FL1790	47,37,46,66F
Cohen, Stanley	NY1275	14C,32,46,47,64
Cole, Monty	GA1300	29,32E,46,64C,64E
Collaros, Pandel Lee	WV0100	70,62,66A,46
Collins, David	MN1250	31A,61,36,46
Compton, Adam	OK0500	13B,63,37,46,13
Conley, Gene	ID0075	46
Cook, Mark Andrew	WV0550	13,29B,47,46,10
Coolman, Todd	NY3785	47,62D,53,46,29
Cooper, Jack	TN1680	29,64E,46
Corkern, David	MO0500	46,63A,37,47,10F
Crafton, Jason A.	VA1700	63A,46,47
Craig, Monty S.	SC0400	70,46,47,29B
Crane, Kenneth	NY1700	46,47
Dailey, Raleigh K.	KY1450	29,46
Dallas, Joseph	PA1050	46
Darling, Patricia A.	WI0350	46
Davies, Richard	NY3775	10,29,34,46,63D
Davis, Keith	SC0750	66A,46
Davison, Michael A.	VA1500	11,29,46,47,49
DeGroff, Jason	CT0700	32E,37,46
Deibel, Geoffrey	KS1450	64E,46
Denison, Mark	OR1010	12A,29A,63C,46,60B
Dennis, Thomas A.	MI1700	12A,66A,46
DeSpain, Geoff	AZ0300	37,63,46,47,11
DiCuirci, Michael P.	OH0450	32B,32C,37,63D,46
Diehl, Bruce P.	MA0100	29,64E,47,46
DiLauro, Ronald	AI0200	47,63A,46
Dobbins, William	NY1100	29B,29C,10A,10F,46
Doheny, John	LA0750	46,47
Dorn, Mark	CO0150	37,63A,46,60B,49
Dotas, Charles J.	VA0600	46,29
Doyle, James	CO0050	46,47,65
Doyle, Michael	MI0850	46,47
Drayton, Leslie	CA5360	46,47,29B
Drost, Michael	MI0900	46,47,29
Durst, Alan Edward	CA0810	64E,29,32,46,47
Dust, Tom	AA0100	46
Eastin, Brad	CO0275	64E,48,46,47,64C
Eberhardt, Allan	CO0275	47,63A,46,49,29
Eby, Chad	NC2430	46,47,29
Eifertsen, Dyne	CA0150	29,63C,46,47
Ellis, Lloyd	CA2400	11,46,47
Ellison, Charles	AI0070	47,63A,53,46,29
Encke, William	IA1450	70,46,47,29
Enos, Steve	OH0750	13,47,63A,29,46
Esson, Dennis	AB0100	46
Estes, Adam	ND0250	46,47,64E,64C,64D
Estoque, Kevin S.	LA0650	65,50,46,20H
Fague, David	WA0400	29,46,47
Fairbanks, Will	IL1050	37,63A,46,49,63B
Falbush, Arthur	NY3765	11,63,29A,46,41
Fazecash, Robert	AG0550	46,47,63A,29
Fejeran, Vince	WA0900	47,63C,37,46
Festinger, Kurt	CA1750	46
Fiddmont, Keith	CA4450	11,29,13A,46,47
Fischer, Stewart R.	CA1265	46,29A
Fisher, Blair	AB0050	37,47,63A,63,46
Fletcher, Ashton	MD0175	62D,46,47
Foerch, Kenneth	CA5355	46,47,64C,64E
Formanek, Michael	MD0650	29,46
Forney, Fred	AZ0440	63A,46,29A
Frane, Ryan	MN1600	29,47,66A,46
Franks, Rebecca	NY4300	29,29B,46,47,34D
Fremgen, John	TX3510	62D,29,47,46
Fronczek, Tim	MI0900	29,65,29A,47,46
Fusco, Andrew	NJ0700	64E,47,29,46
Galisatus, Michael	CA1250	47,46,63
Garcia, Antonio	VA1600	29,47,63C,35,46
Garcia, Paul D.	NC1700	37,46,50,65
Gardner, Derrick	AC0100	63A,29A,46,47
Gardner, Ryan B.	OK0800	63A,49,46,42,47
Garlock, Scott E.	OH0100	29,47,63C,63D,46
Garmon, Randy	TX1725	37,46,47,63
Garrison, Kirk A.	IL0750	46
Gaughan, Warren J.	NC2550	47,13,66A,46,29
Gifford, Troy S.	FL2120	11,13,46,70,10
Gil, Gustavo	CA0950	36,13,46
Giles, Glenn	VT0100	63C,63D,60,37,46
Goins, Wayne	KS0650	46,47,70,29
Goodman, Donald	VT0200	46,70
Goodwin, Don	WA0250	13,66A,37,46
Goold, Stephen P.	MN0250	46
Gorrell, Brian	OK1330	64E,46,34,47,29B
Gottlieb, Daniel	FL1950	65,46,34C
Gove, John	CA1800	46,47
Graham, Dave	CA5400	47,13A,11,46,29A
Greene, James S.	CT0800	29,64E,46
Greer, Larry	TX0125	13,14C,29,46,70
Greggs, Isaac	LA0700	37,63A,46
Griffin, Joel	MO0400	64E,46,47,13A,13B
Griffith, David	TX0075	11,37,46,63
Griffiths, Brian	OR0175	63D,46,37
Guiterrez, Charles	CA2550	39,53,46,35B,34
Haffley, Robin	PA2400	11,29,46
Hafteck, Pierre	NJ0700	11,46,47
Hainsworth, Jason D.	FL0200	11,29,46,47,64E
Haley, Timothy R.	NC2210	11,13A,46,34C,34A
Hall, Scott	IL0720	29,46,47
Hamilton, Craig V.	AR0500	63A,60B,46,37
Hanes, Michael	IL1240	46
Hardiman, David A.	CA1020	46,29A,29B
Hardin, Garry Joe	TX2600	10A,13,29,38,46
Harper, Rhonda	MO0600	37,46,47
Harris, Jarrard	IL0720	46
Hartman, Jane	IL1610	13,11,66A,46,47
Haskell, Jeffrey R.	AZ0500	47,46,29,35
Hebert, Joseph G.	LA0300	32,37,46,35
Heglund, Andrew	NV0100	65,46,50,47
Heinze, Thomas	PA2200	64B,46,41
Hellmer, Jeffrey	TX3510	29,35A,35B,46
Helsley, Jack	IN0907	46,47,62D
Henderson, Alan E.	AG0650	47,29,46
Heredia, Joel	WA0480	47,63A,46,29,35A
Herlihy, John S.	MN1280	60B,49,37,46
Hermanson, Erik	MN0200	46
Hibbard, Dave	IL0650	11,47,46
Hill, Todd E.	KY0950	63D,46,47
Hines, Tyrone	IL0600	63C,63D,46
Hitt, Christine	IA0910	66A,47,53,46
Holcombe, Ross	WA0250	63C,46,49
Holden, James	VA1750	13,20G,37,64E,46
Holmes, Jeffrey W.	MA2000	10,47,46,29
Holober, Michael	NY0550	66A,29,10,46,47
Hoover, Jerry W.	MO0775	60B,37,46
Horton, Brian	NC1600	64E,46
Howey, Robert J.	AA0025	12A,13B,37,46,64
Hunter, Robert	AZ0440	32E,63A,37,46,29A
Hurlburt, Timothy R.	SC0400	37,46,47,11
Ingalls, Duane	ME0430	65,53,46
Irving, David	TX0550	47,70,46,29A,37
Ishii, Timothy	TX3500	29,46,47,64E
Jacobs, Ed	IL2970	63D,11,13A,37,46
Jacoby, Marc Max	PA3600	32,46,47
Jaffe, Andy W.	MA2250	29,46,47
James, Matthew T.	OH1900	64E,47,53,46,29
Jarden, Timothy	IL1500	47,46
Jeffreys, Harold L.	NC2150	10F,32,64C,65,46
Jessop, Dustin	TX3100	46,64E
Jodoin, Aaron D.	NJ0800	46
Johnson, Gary	MO0250	41,46,63,65
Johnson, Henry	GA1600	36,66A,46,47,48
Johnston, Glen	MT0200	46,64C
Johnston, Paul R.	IL0800	46,29,53
Jones, Stephen W.	TX3200	46,47
Kambeitz, Gus	CA5510	46,37,47,29,13A
Kapralick, Randy	PA3330	63C,20A,46
Karloff, Michael	AG0550	29,46,66A
Karloff, Michael	MI2200	47,46,29,66A
Kelly, Keith	CA0850	29,47,46,41
Kelly, Michael F.	NY1850	36,61,66A,46,34
Kendrick, Brian	CA4300	46,47,65,54
Kendrick, Corey	IL0300	46
Kendrick, Matt	NC2500	46,53
Kennedy, John	TX2350	14C,13A,46,49,32B
Kennedy, Rajah B.	OK0450	11,37,46,49,63
Kephart, Donald B.	PA1350	32C,37,63,46,60
Ketch, James E.	NC2410	47,63A,46,29
Kidwell, Jeff	OK1330	47,63C,46,29
Klevan, Robert B.	CA5070	48,46
Klugh, Vaughn	AG0550	70,29,46,61
Knific, Thomas	MI2250	47,51,62D,46,29
Knoop, Tracy	WA1000	46
Knox, Carl	CT0050	64E,29A,46,47
Kobuck, Martin	TX1775	13,63C,46,11
Kocher, Christopher John	SD0600	47,64E,53,46,29
Kopplin, David F.	CA0630	10,20,29,14C,46
Kubis, Thomas M.	CA2050	10F,13A,29B,46,47
Kuhn, Michael	AZ0480	29,11,46
Kunkel, Jeffrey	NJ0800	32,47,29,53,46
Kupka, Craig	CA1960	10D,46
Kynaston, Trent	MI2250	47,64E,46,29
Lammers, Ed	KS0040	46,37,65,63,11
Lance, Elva Kaye	MS0500	37,46
Landsberg, Nils F.	TX3415	37,60B,46
Langham, Patrick	CA5350	46,47,29,53
Langosch, Paul	VA1700	20H,29,35D,46,47
Laroche, Yves	AG0400	46,47
Lawn, Richard J.	PA3330	46,29
Levine, Theodore	MA2100	64E,46,29A
Lewis, Gordon R.	KS0650	62D,47,42,46
Ligon, Bert	SC1110	46,47,66A,29,45
Linder, Kevin	IA0500	63A,46
Lington, Aaron	CA4400	29,46,63,29B
Lippard, Michael S.	TX2710	13A,37,46,64,13B
Lippstrew, Lee	CO0600	46,34D,35G,35A
Lohman, Al	MO0200	65,46,47
Love, Maurice	CA2550	46,34,35B
Lowe, Frederick W.	IL1615	37,46

Name	Code	Areas
Lowenthal, Richard	NJ0825	63A,53,46,29
Luer, Thomas D.	CA0630	29,46
Lutz, Daniel	MA2030	37,46
Lynch, Brian	FL1900	63A,10,47,46,29B
Maas, Dan	CA3000	46
MacDonald, Earl M.	CT0600	29,47,46
Magee, Chris	TX3350	63A,46,29,47,53
Mair, Jim	KS0590	11,47,53,46
Malpede, William V.	CA0835	11,46
Maltester, John	CA3920	46
Manhart, Grant L.	SD0400	49,63A,63B,11,46
Marks, Martin	MI0050	37,46,32
Marsalis, Branford	NC1600	47,46,64E
Martin, Blair	KS1250	13C,37,46,41,32
Martinez, Jesus E.	CA1700	13,29A,37,46
Masten, Rob	WV0250	29,63,65,47,46
Masters, Ken	OR1000	46
Mayfield, Irvin	LA0800	63A,46
McCain, Martin G.	TX3175	63C,29,46,49
McClung, Sam W.	FL0365	60B,37,13,47,46
McCutchen, Thomas	GA2100	65,46
McFalls, James	MD0850	63C,29A,46
McGarrell, Matthew	RI0050	37,41,47,46
McManus, Keven M.	PA3000	63C,46
McMosley, William F.	KS0700	46,32
McMullen, George	CA2650	47,46,10F
McMullin, Brendan	CA3100	37,46,47
McNeill, Dean	AJ0150	63A,29,46,47
Meggs, Gary L.	AR0800	60B,64,47,46,29
Mendoza, Cristina	LA0450	63,46,49,11,41
Mensh, Heather	TX3370	37,41,46,48,63D
Merrill, Paul	NY0900	46,47,29B,29C,63A
Metcalfe, James L.	TX2295	65,35C,35G,46
Michelin, Nando	MA1900	46,66A
Michewicz, Michael	MI0850	64E,46
Miglia, Jay	OH2050	29,64E,46,47
Miles, Butch	TX3175	65,29,46
Miley, James	OR1300	10,29,47,46,13
Miller, David	MS0050	13,47,46,29
Miller, Heidi Johanna	MA2250	46
Mills, John	TX3510	64E,29,47,46
Mitchell, Bryan P.	MS0570	11,37,46,65,50
Moore, Rick	AZ0200	13,11,37,46,49
Moorefield, Bob	CA4425	37,46
Mooy, James D.	CA4410	45,35C,34,46,64
Morales, Samuel	PR0150	47,46
Moresi, Matthew S.	MI0650	11,46,66
Moring, Bill F.	NJ0800	46,47,62D
Mossblad, Gunnar	OH2300	64E,46,47,29B,29C
Motley, Gary D.	GA0750	29,46,47
Myers, Marcus	PA3330	46,65
Narducci, Kenneth	CA2420	10,37,32E,46,13
Nasatir, Cary	CA3520	65,42,46
Necessary, Andrew	VA0050	12A,32B,37,46,63C
Neitzke, Jeffrey	OH0100	65,46,50
Nelson, Scott	VA1350	48,46,63A,37
Newsome, Charles	MI2200	29,46,47,70
Nicholas, Lauren P.	PA2450	64E,46,48
Nichols, Eugene C.	ME0430	13,36,37,46,12A
Nielsen, Ryan	ID0060	29,46,47,63A
Nieske, Robert	MA0500	10,47,62D,53,46
Nixon, Patricia	VA0950	36,46,13C,61
Nordgren, Jon	CA0400	13,37,46,47,60
Nurullah, Shahida	AG0550	29,46,61
Ogilvie, Kevin	TX1350	46,63B
Oliver, Sylvester	MS0600	12A,20G,37,46
Olson, Craig	WY0130	64E,48,64A,40,46
Olson, Matthew W.	SC0750	64E,29,47,41,46
Olson, Rolf	SD0600	37,47,49,63A,46
O'Neill, Ben	PA3330	46
Ousley, Larry James	FL0700	62D,46,47,53
Owen, Stephen W.	OR1050	46,47,53,29,64E
Pack, Lester	AR0800	65,46,47,29,70
Paiewonsky, Moises	AZ0500	63C,46
Palacio, Jon	CA0900	29,46,47,66A
Palance, Thomas M.	MA1650	29,46,47,63A
Parillo, Joseph M.	RI0300	13,10,47,46,29
Parker, Alex	TX0300	29,47,46
Parkin, Chris	WA1350	64E,46,47
Parks, John	SC0850	70,46,47
Parsons, Kenneth	TN1350	60B,49,37,46,34
Parsons, Sean	WV0400	29,46,47,66A
Pastin, John R.	NJ1050	37,60,29,46,48
Pastrana, Jorge	CA4850	47,46,45,35D,10B
Patitucci, John	NY0550	10,46,47,51,50
Patneaude, Brian	NY3600	64E,29,46
Patterson, James H.	GA0490	29,32,46,63,47
Payne, James	NE0590	11,63A,63B,46,35A
Pendowski, Michael	AL0200	64E,46,47,11
Perkins, Andrew	NC0450	10A,13A,20G,46,11
Perrillo, Ron J.	IL0750	46,66A
Philbrick, Keith E.	VA1000	46,47
Pickett, Lenny B.	NY2750	46,47,64E,29
Pier, David G.	CA4425	14,46
Pierson, Rod	IA1300	46
Pisano, Joseph M.	PA1450	47,45,53,46,34
Pitchford, Timothy	IL1200	63C,29A,46,47,53
Plamondon, Andrew	WA0250	63A,46,47
Platt, Walter	MA2030	47,46
Platz, Eric	AC0050	46,47,29
Polanco-Safadit, Pavel	IN0400	66,53,46,47
Pontbriand, Roget	FL1450	45,46,35,10D,10C
Poole, Tommy A.	OK0550	29,46,64E,10A
Potter, Christopher	NY2750	46,47,64E,29
Prettyman, Ken	WA0550	10A,13A,13B,46,47
Price, Allen	AR0350	46
Price, Jeffrey	AG0550	64E,29,46
Puga, John	TX3527	46,47
Pugh, Paul William	ID0075	46
Quinn, Karyn	WI0810	47,62D,46,29,13A
Rabbai, George	NJ1050	63A,53,46
Rager, Dan	WI0804	37,13,46
Rankin, John M.	TX2200	11,47,63A,46
Rawls, J. Archie	MS0580	13,11,64,46,48
Reddick, Don	IL2300	32E,46,34,13A
Reid, Doug	WA0860	47,64E,53,46,29
Reynolds, Terrance	NY2200	46,49
Ridgeway, Max A.	OK0600	10,70,11,20,46
Riley, Gregory E.	PA3600	64E,46,48
Riposo, Joseph	NY4150	47,46,32
Rivello, David	NY1100	46
Roberts, Tim	CA3320	46,14C,10D,13
Robinson, Thomas S.	NH0250	66A,46,47,29
Romaine, Paul	CO0550	65,46
Roman, Robert	NY3765	29,66A,20D,35A,46
Rostock, Paul	PA2450	47,62D,46,35A
Roth, Lisa	IA1400	53,61,46,13A,13B
Rucker, Lee	OK1330	37,47,63A,46,29
Rummage, Robert F.	IL0750	46,65
Running, Donald	MA0510	37,38,46,47,11
Rupert, Jeffrey M.	FL1800	29,46
Ryga, Campbell	AB0060	29,46,47,64E
Samuelson, Linda	MN1270	13,20,37,46,64
Sanchez, David	PR0115	64E,46
Sarath, Ed	MI2100	46,29
Sarjeant, Lindsey B.	FL0600	47,49,53,46,29
Sato, Akira	TX2400	46,47
Saunders, John Jay	TX3420	47,63A,29,46
Scarbrough, Russell	NY3350	46,29B
Schaefer, G. W. Sandy	NE0050	14C,46,65,29,35
Schafer, Erika L.	TN1700	63A,63,67E,37,46
Schantz, Jack	OH2150	29,46,47,63A
Schmid, William	GA0950	63A,46,29,49,47
Schwab, David	TN0260	46,62D,66C
Schwartz, Richard A.	LA0650	29,47,64E,11,46
Schweitz, Kurt	IL3550	62D,46
Scott, David L.	CA5150	63A,46,37
Sellers, Elizabeth A.	CA0835	10C,46,60B
Severn, Eddie	PA2050	32,29,46,47,63
Sexton, James	TN1400	37,46,63C
Shanley, Steven	IA0300	32,46,47,53
Shemaria, Rich S.	NY2750	46,47,66A,29
Sherman, Steve	AA0080	32E,37,63A,46,35
Shevitz, Matthew	IL1080	11,13,29,47,46
Shier, Robin	AB0050	37,63A,63,46
Shuholm, Dan	OR0175	37,46,31A
Sieben, Patrick	KS0225	37,20,13,46,11
Simmons, James	TN1100	63A,47,46,29A,29B
Sizemore, Mark	KY1400	48,64,46
Smith, C. Raymond	UT0050	47,64,53,46,29
Smith, Larry G.	UT0300	13,29,47,64E,46
Smith, Rusty	NC1900	63A,41,46,47
Snapp, Doug R.	MN1000	46,47,63A,29
Snow, Thomas	ME0150	29,47,46,66A
Snyder, Dirk	OR1020	46
Snyder, Rory	CA1560	29,46,47
Solot, Evan	PA3330	13,10F,10,47,46
Sommer, Peter J.	CO0250	46,47,64E
Sorenson, Scott	MI1650	63,46,37
Souza, Thomas	MA0500	60B,64C,37,32,46
Spaneas, Demetrius	NY1275	10,29,46,64E,10F
Spaniola, Joseph T.	FL2100	47,46,63D,11,10
Speck, R. Floyd	TN0450	36,46
Speight, Andrew	CA4200	29,64E,46,47
Spurr, Ken	IL0850	66A,46,47
Stabley, Jeff	PA3710	46,47,53,65,50
Stapleson, Donald	MD0750	46,47,64E,13C
Steinberg, Steve	CA3460	46,47,60B
Stephens, John C.	IL3300	29,46,47
Stephens, Michael	NE0050	10,29,46,13,64
Steprans, Janis	AI0190	64E,47,46
Sterbank, Mark	SC0275	64E,47,46,29
Stevens, Eric	WA0960	46
Stinson, Ron	KS0570	29,37,41,46,47
Stitt, Ronald	PA0100	63C,47,29,46,34
Stone, Michael John	OK0600	37,46,60B,63,32
Streeter, David	IN0905	46,48
Strieby, Ken	IL1612	37,46
Stubbs, James	TX1750	46,32,13A,37,47
Stuntz, Lori	CA2600	46
Sturm, Fred	WI0350	10,29,46,47
Tanner, Joel	OR0250	46,64E
Tapper, Robert	MT0400	29,63C,46,47
Taylor, Keith A.	AL1160	66A,29B,46
Taylor, Tom	CO0200	70,29B,46,47
Teweleit, Russell T.	TX3750	32,46,37
Tiana, Mayo	IL2150	29,46,47,10F
Titlebaum, Michael	NY1800	29,46,47
Tolliver, Charles	NY2660	10,46,47,63A
Traylor, Steve	WY0060	13,46,47
Trowers, Robert	NC1600	63C,63D,46,29A
Tyler, Steve	CA1550	46
Tymas, Byron	NC1600	11,46,70,47,41
Unguraii, John B.	MS0575	37,65,62D,46,50
Vanderheyden, Joel	MO0550	64E,46,47,29,13
Vandiver, Joseph	TX3650	29,63,46,47,34
Vangjel, Matthew S.	AR0730	63A,46,13C
Vargas, Ruben	TX1425	61,46,37,62,63
Veilleux, Trever L.	HI0200	46
Vernick, Gordon Jay	GA1050	47,46,29
Viertel, Kyle	TX0390	37,63,64,65,46
Vogler, Paul	GA0940	46
Waddington, Alan	CA1000	12F,14,29,46,47
Walker, Gregory T. S.	CO0830	11,62A,20G,62B,46
Walker, Rob	ID0070	46
Walsh, Allan	AG0150	64E,47,46,29A,29B
Wanhoff, Meryl	CA4460	37,46
Washington, Salim	NY0500	47,46,29,29B
Watabe, Junichiro	AK0150	64C,64E,48,37,46
Watson, J. Stephen	SC0750	29A,70,46
Welge, Jurgen	KS0590	65,46,47
Weller, Robert	CA3460	46,47,66
Wetzel, Neil D.	PA2450	47,64,29A,64E,46
White, Matthew S.	SC0420	63A,46,35,53
White, Rick	WA0600	11,29A,20,37,46
Wicker, Charles	MS0400	46
Widner, James	MO1830	46,29B,29C,47
Wieligman, Thomas	IN0900	37,38,43,46
Wiggins, Ira T.	NC1600	47,64A,64E,29,46
Wilken, David M.	NC2400	63C,46,47,10A
Wilkerson, Andrea	CA3500	47,61,29,46,53
Wilkinson, Donald G.	TX3520	64B,64D,64E,46,32H
Williams, Jay	WA0700	46,47
Williams, Robert	AL0950	37,46,60
Williams, Sandy	IN0907	70,47,46
Willis, Jonathan	OH2290	60B,32C,37,47,46
Wimberly, Larry	MS0150	11,13A,31A,34E,46
Winslow, Robert J.	FL0930	66A,46,13,34D,11
Wolf, Donald	AL1195	10F,37,46,47,63A
Woking, Henry C.	UT0250	13,10F,47,46,29
Wright, Steve	MN0750	47,63A,35,46,10
Yannie, Mark	MN0625	46,64C,64E
Yellin, Peter	NY2102	47,64E,46,29
Yoes, Milas	AZ0470	12A,29,37,46,63C
Yonchak, Michael	OH2050	34,37,32E,29,46
Zebley, Matthew	CA5040	37,46,47

Jazz Ensemble

Name	Code	Areas
Aaberg, David E.	MO1790	47,29,10
Abdullah, Ahmed	NY2660	47,63A
Adair, William 'Billy'	TN1850	29,46,47
Adam, Mark	AF0050	11,13C,46,47,65
Adams, Ernie	IL3310	47,65
Adams, James M.	ND0600	35G,37,47,49,53

Index by Area of Teaching Interest

Name	Code	Areas
Adams, Kurtis B.	WV0550	47,46,13
Adams, Mimmie	AG0650	47
Afifi, Bob	CA4700	47
Agidius, Michael	WA1100	47
Aho, Kyle	MO0775	11,66A,47
Akagi, Kei	CA5020	53,29,47
Akins, Keaton Damir	MI0350	47
Albano, John	CA2900	10D,29,47,70
Aldag, Daniel	CA2250	63D,29,14C,63C,47
Alegria, Gabriel A.	NY2750	29,47,63A
Alessi, Ralph P.	NY2750	63A,47,10D
Alexander, Glenn	NY3560	41,47,70,29
Alfonsetti, Louis	NY0350	47
Alford, Steve W.	NC1250	64E,47,53
Alger, Neal	IL0550	47,70
Aliapoulios, S. Mark	FL1450	61,47
Aliquo, Don	TN1100	29,64E,46,47
Allaire, Denis	MN1625	47
Allard, James	MA0650	64E,47
Allee, Steve	IN0907	66A,47,35A,53
Allen, Carl	NY1900	47,29
Allen, Kristopher	CT0500	47,29A
Allison, Bill	CA1280	47
Alvarez, Ruben	IL0720	47
Alvarez, Ruben	IL0550	47,65
Amend, William	OR1250	62D,47
Ammons, Mark	UT0050	47,29
Anderson, Jeff	IN1560	47,29
Anderson, Jon	ID0250	13C,47,66A,66E
Anderson, Jonathan	TX3600	13,47,64E
Anderson, Larry R.	LA0770	47,50,65
Anderson, Leon	FL0850	47,65,29,46
Anderson, Ray R.	NY3790	46,47,53
Anderson, Robert	AR0350	64B,64C,64D,64E,47
Appell, Glen	CA1560	11,29,46,47
Applegate, Erik	CO0950	29,47
Aranda, Patrick	CA0950	13A,37,47,63C,29A
Arcaro, Peter	FL1100	13B,11,29A,47
Archard, Chuck	FL1550	47,62D,53,29
Ardovino, Joseph	AL1200	63A,37,47,49
Arendt, Michael J.	WI0817	37,47
Ascione, Ray A.	MD0060	47,64C,64E
Assad, Mike	TN1200	65,50,47
Atkins, Victor	LA0800	29B,46,47,66A
AuBuchon, Tim	MO1780	29,46,47
Auwarter, Doug	MO1810	47
Ayres, Carol	IA0800	11,37,47,64,29A
Azzolina, Jay	NY2200	70,29,47
Babad, Andrew	CA1900	47,48,64A,64C,64E
Babcock, Andrew	TX1550	60B,63D,37,13,47
Babcock, Donald J.	MI0600	47,63C,63D
Baca, Robert J.	WI0803	47,63A,29
Bachman, Jerome	NY0350	29,47
Bacon, John	NY4460	65,47
Bailey, Craig	AC0100	47,64E
Baker, Andrew	IL0850	63C,47
Baker, Charles	OH1100	47,29
Baker, David N.	IN0900	47,29
Baker, Malcolm Lynn	CO0900	47,53,46,29
Bakos, Daniel F.	GA2130	13,47,29
Baldini, Donald	NH0150	38,47,62D,29A
Balentine, James S.	TX3530	13,10,47,29A
Balfany, Gregory J.	WI0810	47,64C,46,29
Balins, Andris	NY3765	35C,35D,35G,47,70
Ball, James	MI0100	29A,38,47,63D,60B
Balmer, Dan	OR0400	70,47
Banaszak, Greg J.	OH0200	47,64E,29
Barbee, Larry	NJ0975	13A,47,70,29
Barbuto, Robert C.	NY1550	66A,47
Barclay, Timothy R.	IL0650	13A,64E,46,47
Barduhn, David	OR0550	13,10,47,29
Barrett, Darren	MA0260	47
Barrett, Robert H.	CO1050	11,47,64,34,29
Barrick, Christopher	WV0600	64,11,41,34,47
Barry, Kevin	MA0260	47
Barth, Bruce D.	PA3250	47,29
Barton, Karl S.	GA1990	64,47,12A,34
Bass, John	TN1200	70,46,47,67G
Batchelor, Daryl	KS0550	47,63A,29,29A
Bates, Charles N.	OH1800	11,32E,37,47,60
Bates, James I.	OK1450	47,62D,70
Batiste, Alvin	LA0700	64A,64C,29,47,35A
Battenberg, Thomas V.	OH1850	47,63A,29
Baxter, Kara	NE0200	46,47,62
Bayles, David	WI1150	65,47
Beach, Douglas	IL0850	47,53,71,29,35
Bean, Robert G.	AL1450	13,37,47,63,29
Beasley, Walter	MA0260	47
Beatty, David	CA0250	47,49,35,63C
Becker, Christopher A.	MO1900	47
Beery, John	MI1650	32,37,47,63,11
Begel, Rich	IN0400	63C,47
Begian, Jamie	CT0800	41,70,53,47,29
Behnke, Martin	OR0950	46,47,29A
Bell, Isaac	AL0050	47,63C,63D
Bell, Malcolm E.	AA0080	10,13,47,65
Bell, Timothy R.	WI0835	47,64C,64E,29,48
Bendzsa, Paul	AD0050	60,47,64C,64E
Benedict, Jeffrey W.	CA0830	29,47,64E,41
Benkert, Stuart M.	TN1700	37,47,32E,60B
Benson, Steve C.	NJ0800	70,47
Berardinelli, Paula	NY1600	29,13A,13C,11,47
Berg, Christian	OH2050	62B,47
Berg, Shelton G.	FL1900	66A,66C,29,46,47
Bergeron, Chuck	FL1900	62D,47,29A,46,12A
Bergeron, Tom	OR1250	13,64,47,35A
Bergonzi, Jerry	MA1400	29,64E,47
Bergstrom, Samuel	MN0040	20,32,37,41,47
Berney, Mark C.	RI0300	29,47,63A
Bernhardt, Barry W.	FL0700	37,47,63A,29A
Bernstein, Peter A.	NY2750	29,70,47
Berry, Fredrick J.	CA4900	47,29A
Berry, Rodney	NC0050	47,11
Berry, Steve	IL0550	47,63C
Bertucci, Ronald	OR0350	37,13A,47,63C,13C
Beskrone, Steve	PA3330	62D,47
Beyer, George	CA1520	47,13A,11,20G
Biggs, Gunnar	CA3460	60B,47,29A
Bilden, Jeff	CA1290	37,47,29,63,64
Binek, Justin	PA3330	61,47
Bing, William W.	CA0500	37,47,49,63A
Bingham, W. Edwin	WV0400	47,64E,64D,29
Birk, Richard	TX0350	13,11,37,47,63
Bisesi, Gayle	IL0850	47,61
Bishop, James	FL0150	12A,37,38,47,64E
Bivens, Pat	TN0250	11,47,63C,48,37
Biviano, Franklin Lin	MA0260	47
Black, Alan	TX1700	11,37,47,50,65

Name	Code	Areas
Black, Cary	WA0350	62D,53,29,35,47
Blair, Steve	VT0250	10,47,70
Blake, John	PA3330	47,62A,29
Blanchard, Jeff L.	OH2140	63A,47,49,29
Blanchard, Terence	FL1900	63A,10,47
Bland, Ron	CO0830	47,62D
Blink, David	WA1400	47,13,63A,29
Block, Tyrone	TX2570	32E,37,47,60B,63
Bloom, Jane Ira	NY2660	10,53,64,47
Blue, T. K.	NY2105	47,29,29A,29B
Bocanegra, Cheryl	OK0850	13,66A,35D,47
Bodolosky, Michael	PA3410	37,47,29A
Boehmke, Erik A.	IL1600	63A,66,47,37,49
Boga, Cheryl	PA3500	36,37,47,38,51
Bokar Thiam, Pascal	CA5353	47,20
Bonds, Dennis	MS0100	70,47
Bonenfant, Timothy	TX0150	64C,64E,47
Bongiorno, Frank	NC2440	47,64E,29
Bonness, Will	AC0100	29B,47,66A
Bonsanti, Neal	FL0650	64E,47,46
Booker, Kenneth A.	TX1450	37,46,47,60,13A
Booth, Brian	UT0250	10,47
Borgo, David R.	CA5050	64E,14,29,47
Borgstedt, Bryson	SC1000	64E,47,64C
Boss, Robert	CA4050	47,62D
Bostic, Bert	TX1660	36,47,66D
Bouchard, George	NY2550	11,46,47,66D,29
Boukas, Richard A.	NY2660	61,70,20H,47
Bourcier, Tom	IA0950	47,10A
Bovinette, James	IA0850	47,63A,29
Bowen, Charles Kevin	NC2500	37,47,49,63A
Bowen, Jose A.	TX2400	47,12A,29,38,12
Bowen, Ralph	NJ1130	47,64E,29
Bowyer, Don	AR0110	63C,63D,29,35C,47
Boyd, Craig E.	NY4050	60,11,47,70,29A
Boyd, Lance	MT0400	47,63C,63D,53,29
Boyer, Allen	CA3000	13A,47,61,20G
Boyle, Patrick	AB0150	20A,29B,47,53
Bracey, Jerry A.	VA0500	37,38,47,62,29
Brackeen, Joanne	NY2660	10,66A,47,53
Brader, Kenneth E.	PA1850	47,63A
Bradfield, Ann	NM0100	29,46,47,64A,64E
Bradford, Bobby L.	CA3650	47,29A
Bradford, Lovell	NC0550	66A,47
Braig, Christopher	MO1950	47
Brandao, Fernando	MA0260	47
Branker, Anthony D.J.	NJ0900	47,29,46
Bratt, Douglass F.	IL1890	50,47,65A,65B,46
Breazeale, Edward	WY0200	47
Breiling, Roy	AZ0510	37,38,46,47,63A
Brekke, Jeremy	ND0350	63,37,49,63A,47
Brellochs, Christopher	NY1050	47,10,13,12,64E
Bremer, Jeff	PA3650	47,53,62D
Brennan, David	CA2420	64E,47
Brewer, Paul	AZ0490	11,13,29,32E,47
Brian, Aric	FL2050	63A,47
Bridgewater, Ronald S.	IL3300	47,64E,29
Briggs, Ray A.	CA0825	14,29,46,47
Bristol, Doug S.	AL0050	13,29,63C,47
Britto, Richard	MA2150	47,64E
Broadley-Martin, Sharon	MA0260	47
Brock, Andrew	VA0700	47,64E,32H
Brooks, John Patrick	ID0100	60B,37,63C,47,63D
Brookshire, Eddie L.	OH2250	47,70,62D
Brown, Beverly	NC1400	11,29A,47,37,64C
Brown, Charles	NC2300	37,47,65
Brown, Christopher	OK0850	70,51,53,47
Brown, Donald R.	TN1710	47,66A,29A
Brown, Jeffrey C.	IN1750	47,50,65,11
Brown, Jeri	AI0070	36,47,61,29
Brown, John V.	NC0600	62D,47,29A,29B,29C
Brown, Keith	TN1710	47,67E
Brown, Miles	MI1750	62D,47,29A,29B,46
Brown, Patrick	NC0550	64E,47
Brown, Philip	VT0300	11,13A,36,44,47
Brown, Rogers	VA0950	10F,37,47,63D,29
Brown, Shon	SC0700	47,65
Browning, Doug	MS0550	32,40,42,47,60
Brubeck, Dave W.	FL1300	13,37,47,63C,49
Bruno, Zachary	CA4625	11,32,37,47,41
Bruya, Chris	WA0050	46,47,29,13
Bryant, Dave	MA1175	47
Buchman, Matthew	WI0850	47,53,66A
Bukvich, Daniel J.	ID0250	13,10,47,50,65
Burch-Pesses, Michael	OR0750	60,32C,37,47,45
Burchill, Thomas	TX3000	70,47
Burchill, Thomas	TX2600	70,47
Burnette, Sonny	KY0610	13,47,64E,34
Burns, Howard	MD0300	47
Burns, Scott	IL1615	47
Burns, Timothy	IL1890	70,47
Burrell, Kenneth	CA5030	47
Buselli, Mark	IN0150	63A,29,47
Bush, Eric W.	NY4050	37,47,63A,13A,11
Bush, Jeff	OH2600	47
Butcher, Paul	FL0800	29B,47,35A,63A
Butler, Dorsey Mitchell	SC0350	63C,60B,47,29
Butler, Hunt	KY0750	47,48,64,53,29A
Butterfield, Craig	SC1110	62D,29,46,47
Buttery, Gary A.	RI0300	11,47,49,63D,29A
Buttery, Gary	CT0100	63D,37,47
Butturi, Renato	IN1600	70,11,67G,47,29
Byrdwell, Phyllis	WA1050	31A,47
Cable, Howard	AA0200	10,11,35,47,60
Cado, Michael	AG0650	10A,32,47,70
Cafagna, Carl	MI1750	47,40
Cailliet, Claude	WI0800	11,13,63,37,47
Cain, Michael	AC0050	29,47,66A
Calderazzo, Joey	NC1600	66A,66C,46,47
Call, R. Steven	UT0050	47,63D,46,29
Campbell, Gary	FL0700	64E,29,53,47
Campbell, Jeff	NY1100	29A,29B,29C,62D,47
Campbell, Larry	TX0340	37,47,63B,63C,63D
Campbell, Michael J.	GA2300	60B,47,64E,32E,11
Campbell, Roy	MA0510	11,10F,38,46,47
Campbell, Will	NC2420	46,47,53,64E
Campigna, Paul	GA0625	47,29,53,65
Camwell, David J.	IA1350	32C,46,47,64E,48
Candelaria-Barry, Consuelo	MA0260	47
Caniato, Michele	MA0930	10,38,29,13,47
Cannon, Derek	CA2100	29,63A,47
Carbone, Michael	NY3705	47,29A
Cardenas, Steve	NY2660	47
Carillo, Dan	NY0550	47,13,46,10,29
Carlberg, Frank	MA1400	66A,47
Carmichael, Steve R.	WI0250	47,11,29
Carnes, Maurice J.	MO1900	47
Carroll, James R.	VA0450	47,64E,29,46

Name	Code	Areas
Carroll, John	TX1900	63A,49,37,41,47
Carroll, Tom	OH0850	47,29,70
Carter, Allen L.	MN1120	13,10F,65,47
Carter, Cecil	TX2200	47,53
Carter, Joey	TX3000	65,29A,29B,47
Carter, Joseph	CT0300	70,29A,20G,20H,47
Carter, Kenyon	GA0900	47,64E
Carter, Ronald	IL2200	47,29
Carubia, Michael R.	NY2550	46,47
Casas, Jorge	IL1050	62D,47,10D
Case, Alexander	MA2030	35C,47,13L
Casey, Christopher	CT0650	47,64E
Casey, J. Warren	AR0250	10F,11,32,47,64C
Cashman, Glenn	NY0650	47,64E
Cass, Patrick	MS0320	13,11,47,64,70
Cassino, Peter	MA1175	47,29
Castro, Miguel	GA1400	50,65,11,47
Catalano, Frank K.	IL0650	64E,47
Catlin, Barb A.	CA3650	47
Cavanagh, Daniel	TX3500	47,29,46
Cecco, Jerry	MA0260	47,49
Cecere, Dennis	MA0260	47
Celmer, Joey R.	SC1050	63A,63B,63C,63D,47
Chamberlain, Donald J.	IA0400	13,10F,10,11,47
Chandler, Kyle	AR0110	32,36,47,32D,32G
Chappell, Jeffrey	MD0400	47,66A,29,29B,10
Charles, David	MT0200	14,20,47
Charles, Etienne	MI1400	29,63A,47
Chase, Allan S.	MA1400	47,29,53,64E
Cheetham, Andrew	IL0800	63A,47,66A,11
Chesarek, Justin	GA1150	65,47
Chevan, David	CT0450	11,12A,47,53,29
Cho, Peter	LA0080	13,34,35,47,66A
Chodoroff, Arthur D.	PA3250	37,47
Christopher, Evan	LA0800	64C,47
Ciabattari, William S.	PA2100	13,63D,32,37,47
Clancy, Eric	IN0700	47,29,53
Clancy, Gary	ME0340	47,70,53,35
Clancy, Todd A.	MA1650	47,11,70
Clanton, Wendell	AB0150	64E,47
Clark, Dave	KY0250	29B,47,53,64E
Clark, William F.	CO0830	47,63D,13,49,29
Classen, Andrew B.	IA0550	47,49,63A,29
Claussen, Tina	MO0350	47,64E,46,29
Clayton, Greg	AI0150	47,70,29
Clayville, Michael	PA0950	37,47
Cleary, Thomas	VT0450	66A,47,66D
Clements, Gordon	AB0210	46,47,29B,64E,64C
Clickard, Stephen D.	PA0250	37,63,47,60B
Cline, Rebecca	MA0260	47
Coates, Gary	FL1790	47,37,46,66F
Cochrane, Keith A.	NM0400	60,12A,32B,37,47
Coggiola, John C.	NY4150	32,29,34,47,60B
Cohan, Ryan	IL3310	47,66A
Cohen, Stanley	NY1275	14C,32,46,47,64
Coker, Jerry	TN1710	47,29
Collier, Thomas	WA1050	47,65,20G
Collins, Christopher	MI2200	47,64E,29A,35
Compean, Jose D.	TX1425	13,32,47,63,64
Compton, Beckie	TX0125	66A,13,11,36,47
Compton, Michael	OK0150	64,48,47,60B
Compton, Michael	ND0100	64,37,41,47,60B
Compton, Paul R.	OK0800	63C,63D,47,49
Connelly, Marianne	MN0450	37,32,47,64,60B
Connerley, Jim L.	KY1500	47
Connor, Mark	MO0700	13,20,41,47
Coogan, Chris	CT0550	29,66,47
Cook, Alan	ME0430	70,47
Cook, Andrew	AL0345	60B,63,11,47,64
Cook, Ken	CA4700	66A,47
Cook, Mark Andrew	WV0550	13,29B,47,46,10
Coolman, Todd	NY3785	47,62D,53,46,29
Cooper, David	WI0840	47,49,63A,11,29A
Cooper, Gloria A.	NY2102	13A,61,32C,36,47
Cooper, Matthew J.	OR0200	13,47,66A,66D,29
Cordes, Jerome	OH0350	61,47
Cordingley, Allen	WI0840	11,64E,37,47
Corkern, David	MO0500	46,63A,37,47,10F
Corn, Paul	NY0500	37,47
Cornell, Ernest	WV0440	47
Correll, Allen	OK0300	37,32E,47,60B,63A
Cortese, Michael	NY0450	10,11,20,34,47
Cotter, Steve	CA1000	70,47
Coughran, Steven J.	CA1500	47,20,29A,70
Covey, Jason	GA0750	60,47
Cowan, Scott M.	MI2250	11,47,63,29
Cox, James	IL2050	47,62D
Cox, Thomas E.	AR0750	13,47,66A,66D
Coyle, Brian	MI1050	47,29,53
Crafton, Jason A.	VA1700	63A,46,47
Craig, Monty S.	SC0400	70,46,47,29B
Craig, Sean	AI0150	29,47
Crane, Kenneth	NY1700	46,47
Crawford, Andy J.	IL1350	70,47
Cress, David	MO0825	47,54,63
Crockett, C. Edgar	IL0300	13,10,47,35,63A
Crowell, Jeffrey W.	WI0803	47,65
Crowell, Ken R.	CA3320	47
Culligan, Paul	KY0250	47,65
Cunliffe, William H.	CA0815	29,47,41
Da Silva, Jetro	MA0260	47
Dadurka, Jon	FL0200	62D,47
Dalby, Bruce	NM0450	32C,47,12
Dallabetta, Amanda	AZ0150	63A,47
Dalton, Grant B.	AL0800	65,11,32E,47,50
Dana, Christy L.	CA5000	13A,13C,29B,47,29C
Dana, Michael	CA1850	29,47,35A,34
Daniel, Thomas	AL0335	13,11,47
Daniels, William B.	KY1100	32B,37,47,49,63
Danko, Harold	NY1100	29A,29B,29C,66A,47
Darling, John A.	ND0050	37,60B,47,13,41
Darst, John	AZ0460	70,47
Dashiell, Carroll V.	NC0650	47,62D,29
Dasilva, Mario	KY1460	47,70,20H,29
David, Norman	PA3330	64,47,10,29,13
Davies, Josh	AA0200	63A,47,29A,13C
Davis, Dan	NC2410	47,65
Davis, John Douglas	CA0650	13,10,47,29
Davis, John S.	CO0800	47,29,29A,63A
Davis, Joshua	PA3150	47,29,62D,13C,53
Davis, Mark	WI0150	47,29,53
Davis, Matt	PA3330	47,70
Davis, Nancy	OH1300	13A,11,36,47
Davis, Nathan T.	PA3420	20G,47,64E,29
Davis, Orbert	IL3310	47,63A
Davis, Peter A.	RI0250	13A,37,47,64
Davis, Quincy	AC0100	29,65,47
Davis, Scott	IA0420	29A,47,63A
Davis, Troy	LA0800	65,47
Davis, Xavier	NY1900	47,29
Davison, Michael A.	VA1500	11,29,46,47,49
Dawson, Bradley J.	KS0350	47,49,63A,29
Day, Greg	SC1080	13,10F,37,47,63
De Boeck, Garry	AA0050	47,65,29,35B
De Melo, Dorvalino	AI0220	60,32C,37,47,64E
De Toledo, Rubim	AA0050	47,53
Deacon-Joyner, David	WA0650	47,29
D'earth, John E.	VA1550	20G,47,63A,53
Decker, Jeffrey C.	VA1550	64E,42,47
Decker, Michael	MD0850	70,35A,41,47
Decker, Van A.	CA2300	11,13A,34D,47,10A
Decuir, Michael	GA0150	11,20,29,37,47
Dees, David	TX3200	47,64E,29
DeFade, Eric	PA0550	64E,47,29
Del Vecchio, Peter H.	VA1850	63,49,47
Delaney, Douglas	CA1150	13,11,37,47,64
Delgado-Pelton, Celeste	CO0600	13,11,34,36,47
Delony, Willis	LA0200	47,11
Delto, Clare E.	CA1960	10D,54,11,47
Denny, Michael	OR1050	70,47,29,29A
Dering, James	TX0850	36,47,13,13C,11
DeSpain, Geoff	AZ0300	37,63,46,47,11
Detweiler, Bruce	OK0150	11,47,53
DiBlasio, Denis	NJ1050	10F,47,64E,53,29
DiBlassio, Brian	MI2120	47,13,43
Diehl, Bruce P.	MA0100	29,64E,47,46
Diehl, Richard C.	VT0100	13,60,47,10,37
Dierker, John	MD0850	63A,47,53
Dietrich, Kurt R.	WI0700	13,32,37,47,29
DiLauro, Ron	AI0150	63A,29,47
DiLauro, Ronald	AI0200	47,63A,46
DiMeo, Mike J.	NY4400	37,11,47
Dimond, Raymond R.	AR0300	47,65,53,13,32E
Dippre, Keith	NC1350	13,11,10,47,34
DiSanti, Theodore A.	PA3000	63A,47,49,13,10F
Dismore, Roger	TX0370	47,20G,29,35A,35G
Dixon, Rich	UT0190	70,47,34,35
Dobbins, Sean	MI1750	47,65,29
Dobbins, Sean	MI0500	65,47
Dobry, John T.	LA0750	10A,13B,47
Dockter, Larry	IN1050	47,63A,65
Doheny, John	LA0750	46,47
Domenico, Tony	MD0450	32A,47
Dominguez, Peter	OH1700	47,29
Donaldson, Frank	IL0720	66,47,65
Donato, Michel	AI0200	62D,47
Donelian, Armen	NY2660	13A,13C,10,66A,47
Dos Santos, Adriano	NY2750	47
Douglas, John	CA5550	47,66A
Douglas, Thomas W.	PA0550	47,60
Downes, Suzanne	IL2310	66D,47,11,37,65
Doyle, James	CO0050	46,47,65
Doyle, Michael	MI0850	46,47
Doyle, Phillip	WA0250	64E,47,48
Drayton, Leslie	CA5360	46,47,29B
Drewek, Douglas Alexand	KY0450	64E,64C,47
Drewes, William	NY2750	29,47,64E
Driscoll, Nick	PA3700	47,64E
Drobnak, Kenneth Paul	SD0500	63D,37,11,47,49
Drost, Michael	MI0900	46,47,29
Drummond, Billy R.	NY2750	29,47,65
Duerden, Darren	HI0050	32E,65,50,47,11
Duffy, Thomas	CT0850	13,37,47
Dugan, Leonardo	PA1550	64E,47
Dugan, Michael D.	WI0865	11,47,49,63C
Duhaime, Ricky	TX0250	13,47,41,64,60B
Duncan, Warren L.	AL1100	13,11,47,65
Dunne, Matthew R.	TX3530	70,29,47,35
Dunston, Douglas E.	NM0350	10B,36,38,47,54
Duquesnel-Malbon, Peggy	CA1425	66A,47
Durst, Aaron M.	WI0855	11,37,47,64E
Durst, Alan Edward	CA0810	64E,29,32,46,47
Dustman, Tom	CA2550	36,47,35B
Dyess, J. Wayne	TX1400	37,47,63C,49
Dziuba, Mark	NY3760	70,29A,47,35C
Eade, Dominique	MA1400	61,53,47,29
East, David	MS0320	37,47,48,63C
Eastin, Brad	CO0275	64E,48,46,47,64C
Eberhardt, Allan	CO0275	47,63A,46,49,29
Eby, Chad	NC2430	46,47,29
Eby, Patricia	WI0804	13,11,36,60A,47
Eckard, Steven C.	MD0520	47,62D,29
Eckert, Joseph H.	TX3000	64E,29,47
Eckert, Rosana C.	TX3420	47,61
Eckstrom, William	NY1850	47
Edstrom, Brent	WA1350	10,66A,34,47,13
Eifertsen, Dyne	CA0150	29,63C,46,47
Eis, Jeremiah	WI0770	34,48,47,60B,63
Eisenman, Mark	AG0650	47,66A
Eisensmith, Kevin E.	PA1600	47,49,63A
Ellias, Rod	AI0070	13,47,70,53,29
Elliott, Scott	WV0750	70,47
Ellis, Brian	MA0260	47
Ellis, Lloyd	CA2400	11,46,47
Ellison, Charles	AI0070	47,63A,53,46,29
Elmen, Paul	MA0260	47,49
Elmes, Barry	AG0650	47,29
Emmons, Timothy	CA3300	62D,47
Encke, William	IA1450	70,46,47,29
Engberg, Michael	CO0100	13,70,41,35,47
Engelhardt, Kent	OH2600	64E,29,53,47
Enos, Steve	OH0750	13,47,63A,29,46
Ensor, Robert	MO0260	12A,47,66A,66C,54
Enz, Nicholas J.	MI1450	37,41,64E,47
Epstein, Peter	NV0100	47,20,64E
Erb, Andrew	PA3650	63A,47
Erb, Andrew	PA3260	63A,63C,37,47,49
Erickson, Jeff	WI0925	47,13C,29A,13B
Erjavec, Donald L.	CA0859	13A,47,29,20G
Espinosa, Gabriel	IA0700	66A,47,61
Espinosa, Gabriel	IA0200	47,53,29,40
Espinoza, Andres	ME0340	47,65
Ess, Michael	VA1600	70,29,47
Estes, Adam	ND0250	46,47,64E,64C,64D
Eubanks, Robin	NY2750	47,63C,29
Evans, Darryl	AR0810	32E,47,63D,13A,13B
Evans, Thomas	MI1150	37,47,63C,29A,32
Evans, Valerie L.	KY1350	63C,47
Evoskevich, Paul	NY0700	47,64E,53,29,42
Eychaner, Frank	CO0150	10,32,13,47,60
Faddis, Jon	NY3785	47,63A,29
Fagaly, Sam W.	IL0800	64E,47,29,48
Fague, David	WA0400	29,46,47
Fairlie, Thomas A.	TX2800	47
Falco, Frank	AG0650	47,66A
Falker, Matt	CA2960	36,66A,47,66D

Index by Area of Teaching Interest

Name	Code	Areas
Fallis, Todd	UT0300	32C,63C,63D,47,41
Famulare, Trever R.	PA3050	11,37,47,49,60
Fannin, Karen M.	AR0350	29,11,13A,47,37
Farmer, Harry	VA0750	64E,47,42,43
Farr, Chris	PA3330	47,64E,29
Farrell, Timothy P.	SD0600	47
Farrington, Robert	CA1550	41,47,63,64,29A
Farris, Daniel J.	IL2250	47,37,60B,60
Fashun, Christopher H.	IN0550	38,65,32,47,62B
Fazecash, Robert	AG0550	46,47,63A,29
Fejeran, Vince	WA0900	47,63C,37,46
Feldkamp, Timothy L.	IA0930	13,41,47,64
Ferguson, James W.	TN1100	62D,47,41,61
Ferguson, Paul	OH0400	47,29
Ferreira, David	MN0600	66A,47
Festinger, Kurt	CA5500	13A,29,47
Fiddmont, Keith	CA4450	11,29,13A,46,47
Fienberg, Gary	NJ0175	63A,29A,47,49
Finet, Christopher	AZ0450	29,47,62D
Finn, Neal	NC0800	10A,10F,29A,47,63C
Fischer, Lou	OH0350	47,29B,10F
Fisher, Blair	AB0050	37,47,63A,63,46
Fiuczynski, David	MA1400	47
Flaherty, Mark	MI1600	47,63A,29A,34,63B
Flanigan, Glen	KY0100	11,32C,41,47,63D
Flanigan, Sean G.	CO0225	63C,63D,41,47,35A
Fleg, Jerome	WY0050	64C,29,47,64E
Fleming, Ricky L.	NY3717	60B,37,47,49,63C
Fletcher, Ashton	MD0175	62D,46,47
Flora, Sim	AR0500	32,37,47,63,13
Flynn, Michael P.	WY0150	11,37,41,47,63
Foerch, Kenneth	CA5355	46,47,64C,64E
Fontaine, Paul	MA0260	47
Forman, Dick	VT0350	47,29,66C
Fortney, Patrick	NE0500	60,37,47
Foster, Christopher	NY0100	36,63,13A,47,41
Foster, Daniel	IN0350	47
Foster, Robert	GA0250	13,10,11,47,48
Foureman, Jason	NC2410	47,62D
Fraize, Peter W.	DC0100	47,53,64E,29
Frane, Ryan	MN1600	29,47,66A,46
Frank, Mike	PA3250	47,66A,29
Frank, Steven	NY2950	47
Franks, Rebecca	NY4300	29A,29B,46,47,34D
Frantz, Jeremy	PA2950	70,41,47
Fraser, Teresa L.	WA0600	36,47,13A,40
Freidline, Noel	NC2420	40,47,35A
Fremgen, John	TX3510	62D,29,47,46
Freyermuth, G. Kim	AZ0200	36,44,61,47
Friedman, Bennett	CA4460	29,53,47
Friedman, Don E.	NY2750	47,29,66A
Froncek, Tim	MI0900	29,65,29A,47,46
Fryer, Nicholas	CA5350	47,29B
Fudge, Berkeley	WI1150	47,64E,53,64A,29
Fuelberth, Brett J.	IA0800	13,36,47,44
Fulgham, Joel	TX3400	47,65
Fumo, John	CA0510	47,63A
Funderburk, Wes	GA1150	47
Funderburk, Wes	GA1050	47,63C
Furlow, Shaw	MS0200	13,11,10,37,47
Fusco, Andrew	NJ0700	64E,47,29,46
Gaber, Brian	FL0850	47,35
Gabriel, Charles M.	MA2030	62D,13C,47
Gailes, George	VA1600	47,64E,29B
Gailey, Dan J.	KS1350	47,29
Gailloreto, Jim	IL0550	47,64E
Gaines, Adam W.	WI0808	63,47,37,63A,29
Gairo, Anthony	PA2450	64E,29,47
Galbreath, Loretta J.	MS0350	36,40,47,61
Galisatus, Michael	CA1250	47,46,63
Gallagher, Matt	PA3330	47,63A,29
Gallon, Ray	NY2660	66A,47
Galloway, Michael	PA2150	47,63A,53,29
Galper, Hal	NY3785	66A,47
Galper, Hal	NY2660	66A,47
Gantt, William	CA3250	47,29B,60B
Garcia, Antonio	VA1600	29,47,63C,35,46
Garcia, Paulinho	IL0550	47,70
Gardiner, Robert A.	SC0800	11,29,47,32E,64E
Gardner, Al	TX2350	11,47,50,65
Gardner, Derrick	AC0100	63A,29A,46,47
Gardner, Gary D.	OK1500	11,62,63,37,47
Gardner, Mike	AA0050	13,47,64E
Gardner, Ryan B.	OK0800	63A,49,46,42,47
Garling, Tom	IL0850	47,63C
Garlock, Scott	OH0700	47,63C
Garlock, Scott E.	OH0100	29,47,63C,63D,46
Garmon, Randy	TX1725	37,46,47,63
Garrett, Craig	TX0340	36,47,63A
Garrison, Kirk	IL0730	47,53
Gartner, Kurt	KS0650	65,20H,47,50
Garzone, George	NY2660	64E,47
Garzone, George	MA1400	47,29,64E
Gast, Kim	MN1300	47,64E,29
Gately, Doug T.	VA1475	47,48,29,64
Gatien, Gregory	AC0050	64E,29A,47
Gaughan, Warren J.	NC2550	47,13,66A,46,29
Gaumer, Alan	PA2450	47,63A
Gauthier, Michael	AI0050	70,29A,47,10D
Gemberling, Alan	ID0250	37,63C,47,60,41
Gemberling, John	MT0370	47,29,63
George, Arnold E.	NC1600	47,45,64,34,13
Gewirtz, Jonathan	MI1800	47,64E,64C,11,29
Gewirtz, Jonathon D.	MI1200	47,64E,29A
Giacabetti, Thomas	PA3330	47,70,29
Gibble, David L.	FL1470	29,47,37,53,49
Gibbs, Lawrence	LA0250	11,29A,47,64C
Gibson, David	NY3730	63C,63D,47
Gibson, Robert	IA0100	47,49
Giles, Leonard	GA0810	11,32,37,47,63
Giles, Michael S.	IA0850	64E,47
Gillan, Michael	MI0850	11,37,63C,63D,47
Ginocchio, John	MN1500	37,13,47,32E,60B
Gionfriddo, Mark	MA1350	66A,47,34A
Girtmon, Paxton	MS0100	37,47,64E,10F,60
Gittins, John	AG0650	29,13,47
Glanden, Don	PA3330	47,66A,13A,13,29
Glasgo, Don	NH0100	47
Glasser, David	NY2660	64E,47
Glenn, David B.	WA1300	10,47,63D,29
Glickman, Joel	WI0600	60,32,37,38,47
Glover, David	PA3100	29,50,65,34,47
Gnojek, Vincent	KS1350	47,64E
Goacher, Stephen	TX1100	60,48,64,47,29
Goble, Daniel P.	CT0800	47,64E,53,29,41
Goines, Victor L.	IL2250	47,64E
Goins, Wayne	KS0650	46,47,70,29
Goldstein, Gil B.	NY2750	10D,47,66A,29
Goldstein, Thomas	MD1000	47,50,65
Golia, Vinny	CA0510	64,35A,53,47
Gomez, Alice	TX2260	10,14,47,65,35A
Goodhew, Denney B.	WA0200	47
Goodwin, Casey S.	NH0350	37,32D,47,60B
Goranson, Todd A.	PA2300	64E,64D,13A,47,42
Gorman, Kurt	TN1720	13A,34,63A,47
Gorrell, Brian	OK1330	64E,46,34,47,29B
Gove, John	CA1800	46,47
Gove, John	CA2450	13,47,29
Gradone, Richard	NJ0250	13,12A,12,47,63A
Graham, Dave	CA5400	47,13A,11,46,29A
Graham, R. Douglas	SC1110	47,64C,64E
Grandy, Larry	CA4550	37,47,64,29,14C
Grant, Darrell	OR0850	41,47,66A,66D,29
Grant, Gary S.	PA1200	37,60,47
Grantham, Jennifer	OH2550	29A,47
Gray, Charles	OR0850	47,41,29
Greenblatt, Dan	NY2660	64E,32E,47,29B
Greene, Barry	FL1950	47,70,29
Greenough, Forest G.	CO0250	47,62D,10F,34
Greeson, James R.	AR0700	13,10,70,47
Greig, R. Tad	PA3650	32E,37,47,60B,63C
Grier, George	WA0700	11,13,32D,47,65
Griffin, Joel	MO0400	64E,46,47,13A,13B
Griffin, Larry	OH2000	60B,37,47,49,63A
Griffin, Stephen W.	AL0332	11,36,37,47,64
Griffin, T. Joel	MO0400	29,31A,47,64E
Griffith, Joan E.	MN0950	47,70,29,10,62D
Griffiths, Amy	GA0550	64E,32E,11,47
Grimaldi, Peter	MA1100	63A,47
Grimes, William F.	LA0200	47,29
Grinnell, Melonie	CA2100	66A,47,61
Grise', Monte	MN1120	64E,32E,47,37,60B
Gross, John	OR0750	47
Grover, Steve	ME0340	47,65,66A,29,13
Groves, Todd	DE0150	47,64E
Gudmundson, Jon K.	UT0300	29,64E,47,41
Guerin, Roland	LA0800	62D,47
Guerra, Stephen J.	FL1900	10F,29A,29B,47
Guidi, David	TX2650	47,64E
Guter, Christine	CA0825	47,61,32D
Guter, Gerhard	CA1900	47,61
Guzman, Juan-Tony	IA0950	32,47,14,29,20
Haas, Frederick L.	NH0100	64E,66A,29A,29B,47
Haddad, Orlando	PA3330	47,50
Haden, Charlie	CA0510	47,62D,53
Hadfield, John R.	NY2750	29,47,65
Hafteck, Pierre	NJ0700	11,46,47
Hagedorn, David	MN1450	13A,65,50,47,13B
Hagelganz, David	WA1150	47,64E,29,53
Hageman, Paul M.	TX2960	47,29
Hainsworth, Jason D.	FL0200	11,29,46,47,64E
Haist, Dean	NE0450	47,63A,29
Hall, Gary	WY0115	11,12A,13B,13C,47
Hall, Jeff	MI1850	47,64C,64E,66A,29B
Hall, Rick	PA3330	47,20
Hall, Scott	IL0720	29,46,47
Hall, Steven	WV0400	14,47,50,65
Halliday, David	UT0400	64E,47
Hamada, Brian	CA0810	47,65,29A
Hamann, Jeff	WI1150	62D,29,47
Hamel, Gabriel	AI0190	47,29,70
Hamilton, Chico	NY2660	10,65,47
Hamilton, Frederick	TX3420	47,70,53,29
Hamilton, Ryan	OH0350	63C,47,29B,53
Hamm, Randall P.	MO0775	47,64E,29
Hamme, Albert	NY3705	47,64E,53,29A
Hammond, Tony	MT0350	37,47,32
Hamper, Robert	AG0650	47
Hampton, Herman	MA0260	47
Hamrick, Utah	TX3530	47
Hankins, Paul	MS0250	63A,41,47,32E
Hanman, Theodore	KS0100	65,60B,47,37,32E
Hanrahan, Curt	WI0825	47
Hansen, Neil E.	WY0130	37,47,63A,32,49
Hanson, Dan L.	OK1400	13,10,32C,47,37
Harbison, Patrick L.	IN0900	47,29
Harder, Glen	AA0040	36,61,47
Hardy, Jim	NY2660	61,47
Harlas, Lou	TX0370	35G,47
Harms, Jason	MN0250	47
Harms, Lawrence	IL1090	11,47,64C,64E,29A
Harper, Billy	NY2660	64E,47
Harper, Rhonda	MO0600	37,46,47
Harris, David	MA1400	47
Harris, Fred	MA1200	37,47
Harris, Howard	TX3150	13A,10,37,47,39
Harris, Roger	IN0005	10B,13,29,47,66A
Harris, Roger	IL0550	47,66A
Harrison, Albert D.	IN1560	60B,37,47,63D,32E
Harrison, Charley	CA5031	29,47
Harrison, John	MA2020	47,66A
Hart, Kevin M.	IL1350	29B,53,66A,47,65
Hart, Kevin	IL2350	47,65
Hart, Michael D.	LA0030	37,63A,11,13,47
Hartl, David	PA3330	47,66A,66D,34,29
Hartman, Jane	IL1610	13,11,66A,46,47
Haskell, Jeffrey R.	AZ0500	47,46,29,35
Hassevoort, Darrin	TN0260	36,61,47,60,54
Hausback, Jason	MO0775	63C,47
Hawk, Stephen L.	PA3100	63A,47,29
Hawkins, Michelle	CA1550	36,47
Hawthorne, Leroy	LA0100	70,20G,16,47
Haydon, Rick	IL2910	70,29,35G,53,47
Hayes, Andrew	NC0910	29A,47
Heald, Jason A.	OR1020	13,10,47,36,38
Heavner, Tracy	AL1300	32E,64E,47,53
Hegarty, James	IL2400	10A,29A,34D,47,13A
Hegg, Dennis	SD0150	37,47,63,64,65
Heglund, Andrew	NV0100	65,46,50,47
Heidner, Eric C.	CA4410	37,47,13,29,12A
Helbing, Stockton	TX2600	47,65
Helm, Lenora Zenzalai	NC1600	61,47
Helppie, Kevin	OR1250	61,47,54,20G
Helsley, Jack	IN0907	46,47,62D
Helzer, Richard A.	CA4100	29B,29C,66A,47,53
Hemberger, Glen J.	LA0650	60B,32C,37,63C,47
Hemke, Frederic J. B.	SD0400	47,48,64,29A
Henderson, Alan E.	AG0650	47,29,46
Henderson, Chip	TN1680	70,29A,47
Hendricks, James	IL0600	13A,47,66A,66D,29
Hennessey, Patrick D.	HI0110	37,47,29,12A,63C
Henriquez, Carlos G.	IL2250	47
Henson, Mitchell	GA1700	64E,47,13A
Herb, Thomas	UT0200	13C,34,47,32C,32D
Heredia, Joel	WA0480	47,63A,46,29,35A
Herring, Vincent	NJ1400	64E,29,47

Name	Code	Interests	Name	Code	Interests
Hesh, Joseph	PA2800	47,42,66D	Joseph, Alan	CO0900	70,47
Hest, Jeff	NY3250	11,29,35,37,47	Joyce, David	CA0835	47
Hettle, Mark	TX1725	13,11,37,47,63A	Judy, Ned	MD0700	13,29,66,34,47
Heywood, David John	SC0500	11,37,64A,29,47	Juris, Vic	NY2660	70,47
Hibbard, Dave	IL0650	11,47,46	Kambeitz, Gus	CA5510	46,37,47,29,13A
Hickey, Joan B.	IL3300	47,66B,29	Kamstra, Darin	CO0225	65,29,13B,47,50
High, Eric	WI0750	63C,47,13,12,49	Kana, David	OH2600	47
Hildreth, Todd	KY0250	14,34,47,66A	Kandi, Kareem	WA0750	47,64E
Hill, Dennis	FL0500	37,47,64A,64E,29	Karloff, Michael	MI2200	47,46,29,66A
Hill, Todd E.	KY0950	63D,46,47	Karlsson, Stefan	TX3420	29B,29C,47,66A
Hitt, Christine	IA0910	66A,47,53,46	Karn, Michael	NY2660	64E,47
Hodson, Robert	MI1050	13,29B,47	Karsh, Ken	OH2600	47
Hoefle, Andrew	IL2775	11,37,47,63D,29	Kason, Don T.	OH1650	63A,47
Hoehler, Martin R.	OH1050	37,47	Kays, Mark	IN1485	12A,13B,37,47,60B
Hofbauer, Eric	RI0300	29,47,70	Keberle, Daniel	WA1350	47,63A,29,29A
Hoffman, David	IL1350	47,63A,66A	Keberle, Ryan	NY0625	29,47,11,13,63
Holland, Dave	MA1400	62D,47,29	Keech, Christopher	MI1985	64C,64E,37,48,47
Hollender, David A.	MA0260	47	Keeling, Bruce	TX2350	11,12A,47,49,63D
Hollerbach, Peter	NY0270	13A,11,14,47,70	Kehle, Robert G.	KS1050	11,47,29,63C
Holliday, Guy	CA0450	36,37,47	Keipp, Donald K.	UT0350	13A,11,65,29,47
Holm, Molly	CA2950	61,47,53	Keller, Gary W.	FL1900	64E,29,47
Holmes, Jeffrey W.	MA2000	10,47,46,29	Keller, Karlton	CA3400	13,47,48,49,12
Holober, Michael	NY0550	66A,29,10,46,47	Kelly, Daniel	TX2955	63A,47,13A,13B
Holzman, Adam	NY2660	66A,47	Kelly, James J.	NJ0750	12A,13,29A,47,70
Homzy, Andrew	AI0070	10,47,29,29A,34	Kelly, Keith	CA0850	29,47,46,41
Horlas, Lou	TX0700	47,62D,29	Kelly, Todd	IL0400	32,47,63A,35
Horne, John	OH1900	70,29,47	Kelton, Christopher T.	RI0150	47,64C,64E,29A
Hosley, David B.	NY3700	47	Kendrick, Brian	CA4300	46,47,65,54
Hosten, Kevin	NY2100	11,47,63,64,66D	Kendrick, Johnaye	WA0200	61,47,29
Houghton, Stacey	GA0500	47,29,64E,64C	Kennedy, Donny	AI0150	29,64E,47
Houghton, Steve	IN0900	47,65	Kennedy, William	FL0850	47,29,64E
Howard, Chris	MO0750	47,70	Kerber, Ronald	PA3330	47,64A,64E,29,41
Howard, Vernon D.	OK1450	47,49,63C,63D,29	Kesner, Fred	WV0500	37,47
Hubbs, Holly J.	PA3550	11,37,47,29A,20	Ketch, James E.	NC2410	47,63A,46,29
Hubbs, Randall	WA0150	13,37,47,63A,29A	Kidonakis, Tony G.	IL3450	64E,47
Hucke, Adam	IL2970	11,13A,29A,63A,47	Kidwell, Jeff	OK1330	47,63C,46,29
Huffman, Donna M.	WA0100	13,13J,36,47,49	Kim, Steve	WA0860	62D,47,53
Hughes, Brian L.	IA0940	60,11,32,37,47	Kimball, Marshall C.	OH1400	32,37,47,60B
Hughes, Scott	ME0340	70,47	Kinzer, Charles E.	VA0700	12A,47,64E
Hulling, Cliff	CA0350	13,47,50,10A	Kirby, Anna-Lisa	AC0100	47,61
Hunan, Steve	CA1500	47,29B,70	Kirby, Rick B.	WI0200	47
Hunter, Michael	MI1650	47,63C,29,64E	Kirby, Steve	AC0100	29,47,62D
Hunter, Randy	GA0750	47,64E	Kirk, Jeff	TN0100	47,64E,35B
Huntington, Lawrence	MI1250	47,29B	Kirschenmann, Mark	MI2100	47
Huntoon, John Richard	IN0100	63C,63D,47,37,49	Kjos, Kevin	PA1750	11,47,63A,49
Hurlburt, Timothy R.	SC0400	37,46,47,11	Klee, David A.	IA0150	10C,29A,34D,35A,47
Hurst, Craig W.	WI0960	11,37,47,41,63A	Klemas, John	IA1170	37,47,63,64,65
Hutchens, John	IL2350	47,64	Klingensmith, David	TX3400	47,62D
Hynes, Tom	CA1000	13,29,47,53,70	Klopfenstein, Reginald	IN0200	13A,12A,47,50,65
Ibarra, Susie	VT0050	20,29,50,47,53	Knapp, James	WA0200	10,47,63A,53,29
Ihm, Dana	CO0275	36,40,47,60A	Knepp, Marty	MD0060	29,47
Iles, Alex	CA0510	63C,47	Knific, Thomas	MI2250	47,51,62D,46,29
Imara, Mtafiti	CA0847	13,14,64,47,29	Knox, Carl	CT0050	64E,29A,46,47
Ingber, Jonathan	CA3460	47,60B	Knudtsen, Jere	WA0750	11,37,47,64A,29A
Ingle, Ronnie	ND0500	49,63A,47	Kochen, Timothy	TX2310	47
Ingram, Roger	IL0550	47,63A	Kocher, Christopher John	SD0600	47,64E,53,46,29
Inkster, Matthew	WV0600	63A,63B,37,47,49	Kocour, Michael G.	AZ0100	47
Inoue, Satoshi	NY2660	70,47	Koenigsberg, Tobias R.	OR1050	29,47,66A
Irby, Fred	DC0150	47,49,63A	Kohler, Mark	MA0260	47
Irish, Michael J.	MI1450	13,47,45,53,29	Kohlhase, Charlie	MA1175	47
Irom, Benjamin M.	TX2800	29,29A,47,41,13	Kolstad, Michael L.	MO0400	49,63C,63D,47,34
Irving, David	TX0550	47,70,46,29A,37	Koonse, Larry	CA0510	70,47
Isaac, James G.	MO1790	64E,47	Korb, Ryan	WI0925	29A,65,47
Isaackson, Mark	SD0050	64E,47	Korb, Ryan	WI0850	29A,65,47
Ishii, Timothy	TX3500	29,46,47,64E	Korzun, Jonathan	MI1985	32E,37,47,13
Itzler, Neal L.	MA0260	47	Koshinski, Eugene	MN1600	47,65,29,20G,35
Iwanusa, Charles	MI0450	13,10,11,47,29	Kosmyna, David J.	OH1800	63A,63B,49,47,29
Iyer, Vijay S.	NY2750	29,66,47	Kostur, Glenn	NM0450	47,29
Jacklin, Christopher	AJ0100	47,64E	Kotan, Emrah	GA0050	65,29A,47
Jackson, D. D.	NY0625	29,47	Koziol, John	MN0800	47,48
Jackson, Keith	WV0750	47,49,63C,63D	Krajewski, Michael J.	MN1120	70,47,29
Jackson, Stephen	IL1800	47,62D	Kregler, Michael C.	RI0150	66A,66C,47
Jackson, Stephen	IL0420	48,11,20,41,47	Kreitner, William	FL1310	47,50,65,53
Jacobs, Aletha	SC0600	47	Krikun, Andrew	NJ0020	35A,10D,47,14,20
Jacobson, Alan	IA1800	47,65	Krouseup, Jack	CA3520	10,13B,13A,13F,47
Jacobson, Steve	IL1520	47,70	Kruger, Jonathan H.	NY3730	47,63A,53
Jacoby, Marc Max	PA3600	32,46,47	Kubis, Thomas M.	CA2050	10F,13A,29B,46,47
Jaffe, Andy W.	MA2250	29,46,47	Kuhn, Michael	AZ0250	37,47
James, Joshua	MI1260	32E,47	Kukec, Catherine	IL1900	11,41,47,50,48
James, Matthew T.	OH1900	64E,47,53,46,29	Kunkel, Jeffrey	NJ0800	32,47,29,53,46
James, Woodrow	CA2750	47,13B,13C	Kurokawa, Paul	CA2100	13,47,63,64
Janners, Erik N.	WI0425	37,47,60,12,13	Kurzdorfer, James	NY4460	13,47,62D,53
Janson, Peter	MA2010	70,29,11,20,47	Kynaston, Trent	MI2250	47,64E,46,29
Janzen, Chris	CA1860	47	LaBarbera, Joe	CA0510	65,29A,47
Jarden, Timothy	IL1500	47,46	LaBarbera, John P.	KY1500	47,35A,35C
Jarvis, David	WA1150	10,47,50,65,14C	Laboranti, Jerry B.	PA1300	64E,47
Jarvis, Willie	AG0200	62D,47	Lajoie, Stephen H.	RI0101	47,66A,53,29,13A
Jeffrey, Paul H.	NC0600	47,29	LaLama, David S.	NY1600	47,66A,29
Jekabson, Erik	CA2775	47	Lalama, Ralph	NY2750	29,47,64E
Jemielita, James	NY2102	66A,47	Lamar, Jackie B.	AR0850	47,48,64E
Jenkins, Clay	NY1100	29B,29C,63A,47	Lamb, William	NM0250	13,11,37,47,63
Jenkins, Isaac B.	CA4410	47,36	Lambert, Jean-Francois	AI0190	47,13C
Jennings, Joseph W.	GA1900	47,64C,29,64E	Lamkin, John R.	MD1020	10F,37,47,63
Jensen-Hole, Catherine	MA2000	47,61,29	Lamkin, Martin J.	VI0050	11,12A,32A,47,60B
Jewell, Joe	CA1900	47,70,29	Landry, Dana	CO0950	29,66A,47
Joffe, Edward	NJ0825	41,47,48,64	Landry, Jacques	PR0100	47,70
Johns, James	NY0650	47	Landsberg, Paul	AB0070	13A,70,53,47,29
Johns, Steven S.	NJ0800	65,47	Langager, Arlie	CA2960	36,47,40,61
Johnson, Alphonso	CA0510	70,47	Lange, Martin	OR0010	12A,47,64,35
Johnson, Beverly	CA0900	47	Langford, R. Gary	FL1850	37,47,29A
Johnson, Cory	CA1900	10,47,66A	Langham, Patrick	CA5350	46,47,29,53
Johnson, David A.	IA0900	60,32,37,47,65	Langosch, Paul	VA1700	20H,29,35D,46,47
Johnson, Henry	IL0550	47,70	Lanza, Lou	PA2450	61,47,29,41
Johnson, Henry	GA1600	36,66A,46,47,48	LaPierre, Art	CA0150	36,47,29,61
Johnson, Randall	GU0500	11,36,47,61,64E	Lapin, Lawrence	FL1900	13,10,36,47,29
Johnson, Randolph J.	DE0050	37,47	Lark, Robert J.	IL0750	29,63A,47
Johnson, Russell	WI0835	47,29	Laroche, Yves	AG0400	46,47
Johnston, Randy	CT0650	47,70,53	Laronga, Barbara	CA2600	63A,29,47,63
Johnston, Randy B.	NY2750	29,70,47	LaSpina, Steven	NJ1400	29A,47,62D,29
Johnstone, Bruce	NY3725	29,47	Late, Eric	TX2295	47,62D,11,34C
Jones, Alan	OR0850	47	Latta, Jonathan R.	CO0350	10F,47,50,65,20
Jones, Calvin	DC0350	47,62D,63C,63D,29	Lattini, James	MA2030	65,47
Jones, Cheryl	FL1430	37,66A,66B,47,61	Lawing, William D.	NC0550	29,47,63A,34D,49
Jones, Heath	OK0700	64C,64E,47,72,34	Lawrence, Jay	UT0190	65,47
Jones, Herman	SC0150	11,37,47,48,64	Lawrence, Robert J.	MO1790	32,36,11,47
Jones, Lloyd	AL1250	64,37,47,32E,34A	Lawson, Janet	NY2660	61,47
Jones, Micah	PA3330	47,62D,29,13,34	Lazaro, Andrew A.	PR0115	47,65,53
Jones, Michael C.	KS1200	47,63A,63B,63C,13	Leake, Jerry	MA1400	20A,20E,47,65
Jones, R. Larry	AR0850	47,63A	Leali, Brad	TX3420	29,47,64E
Jones, Rodney	NY1900	47,29	Lebon, Rachel L.	FL1900	47,61,32,35A,54
Jones, Sean	PA1050	47,53,63A	Lecuyer, Michael P.	MA1500	13,47,34
Jones, Stephen W.	TX3200	46,47	Ledgewood, Lee Ann	NY2660	10,66A,47
Jones, Susie	OR0550	13,37,47,29	Leduc, Pierre	AI0200	66A,13B,47
Jones, T. Marshall	GA0150	11,29,47,53	Legette, Lee David	NC2700	11,32B,37,47,64E
Jones, Terry	ID0140	37,47,49,63A,29	Leibinger, Douglas J.	CA4700	47,29B,63C,10A
Jordan, Edward	LA0720	11,20G,37,47,64	Lennon, Debby	MO1950	36,61,29,47
Jordan, Rodney	FL0850	47,62D,29	Leslie, James M.	OH2250	65,47,32B,37
Jorgensen, Nathan A.	SD0550	47,64C,64D	Levy, James D.	DC0100	47,66A,29B

Index by Area of Teaching Interest

Name	ID	Areas
Lewis, Cecil	CO0300	47
Lewis, Cecil	CO0100	47,53,64E,37
Lewis, Gordon R.	KS0650	62D,47,42,46
Lewis, Jim	AG0450	29,47
Lewis, Kevin	MD0500	47
Lewis, Robert S. T.	SC0500	11,47,64E
Lewis, Roger	KS0210	13,10,37,47,53
Lewiston, Cal	TX3700	13,47,11
Libonati, Dana	OR0450	47
LiCalzi, Gary	NY1400	47
Lidral, Karel	ME0440	13B,47,64E,29B
Ligon, Bert	SC1110	46,47,66A,29,45
Lill, Joseph	IL2100	47,49,63A,37,42
Limutau, Jacosa	CA0150	47
Lindberg, Jeffrey	OH0700	47,38,63C,29A
Lindsay, Gary M.	FL1900	47,64E,29
Link, Jeffrey	MA0280	13,34,47
Linke, David	WI0825	70,29,47
Livermore, Allen	MA0280	47,64E,29
Lo, Adrian	MN0200	12A,37,38,47,62
Lobenstein, David	NY0050	29,47
Lockard, Douglas T.	TX0600	63A,37,47
Loeb, David	NV0050	29,10,47
Loehrke, John	NJ0975	11,62D,47,29B
Lofsky, Lorne	AG0650	47,70
Lohman, Al	MO0200	65,46,47
London, Amy	NY2660	61,47
Long, Barry	PA0350	29,47,13,63A,53
Long, Bill	SC0900	37,47,65,60B,32E
Long, Bob	MO0850	29,64E,47
Long, Jeremy A.	OH1450	64E,47,42
Longfield, Richard O.	AZ0510	13,60,37,38,47
Longshore, Terry	OR0950	65,20,14,47,35A
Lopez, Richard	OH0850	47,66A
Lorenz, Michael L.	MI1950	13,47,63,29,34
Lovano, Joe S.	NY2750	29,64E,47
Low, Murray	CA4900	47,66A
Lowe, Phillip	TX0910	13,12A,37,47,63
Lozano, Danilo	CA6000	47,64A,20,29A,14
Lucas, Michael	CO0625	37,47,64C
Luciani, Dante T.	FL1900	47,63C,29
Lucini, Alejandro	DC0100	47,65
Luck, Kyle	CA3500	37,47,11
Luckey, Robert	LA0760	47,64E,29
Luethi, Dean A.	WA1150	36,47,61,12D
Lydeen, Brian	WI0400	64,47,37,42,64E
Lyke, Toby Russell	OH0680	10F,47,29A
Lynch, Brian	FL1900	63A,10,47,46,29B
Lyon, Taylene	AA0040	61,47,53
Lyons, Lisanne	FL0700	47
Lyons, Lisanne E.	FL1900	61,29,53,47
MacConnell, Kevin	PA3330	47,62D,29
Maccow, Winston	MA0260	47
MacDonald, Earl M.	CT0600	29,47,46
MacDonald, R. Richard	MN1700	47,50,65,32E
Mack, Kyle	ND0350	60,37,47,63C,29
Mackie, Henry	LA0800	70,29A,29B,47
Macy, Carleton	MN0950	13,10,67,55,47
Madsen, Christopher	IL2250	47
Madsen, Peter C.	NE0610	63C,47,29,49
Magee, Chris	TX3350	63A,46,29,47,53
Magnusson, Robert	CA4050	47,62D
Mahdi, Ronald O. A.	MA0260	47
Mahe, Darren	AB0070	13,47,70,53,12A
Mair, Jim	KS0590	11,47,53,46
Mallet, Alain	MA0260	47
Malley, Kevin J.	IL1350	64E,47
Malley, Nicole	IL1350	12A,20,47,29,31F
Mance, Junior	NY2660	47,66F
Manley, David	PA1150	47,29,53,70
Manos, Larry	AR0400	47
Manson, David	FL1650	47,63C,63D,53,34
Mapp, Douglas	NJ1050	62D,47,53,34
Marcus, Aaron	IN0907	64E,47
Maret, Kevin	MO0950	65,47
Markley, Ben D.	WY0200	66A,47
Marko, Thomas	IL1150	47,29
Marks, Dennis J.	FL1950	62D,66A,47,29A
Marmolejo, Noe	TX3400	47,29
Marrs, Jeff	CA2775	47
Marsalis, Branford	NC1600	47,46,64E
Marsh, Kerry	CA0840	29,36,47
Martin, James	MO1950	11,37,47,63D
Martinelli, Lisa	AG0450	29,61,47
Martucci, Anthony	VA1600	65,47
Martucci, Vincent	NY3760	29A,29B,66A,66D,47
Martyn, Charles F.	WV0650	37,47,64A,64C,64E
Masakowski, Steve	LA0800	70,35B,35C,29B,47
Mason, Colin M.	TX2800	47,11,64E,29,48
Mason, Elliot J.	IL2250	47
Mason, Thom	CA5300	47,29
Massey, LaDamion	CO0550	36,47
Masten, Rob	WV0250	29,63,65,47,46
Mastroianni, John	CT0600	47
Matalon, Leon	CA0200	13A,47,53,48
Mathis, William B.	OH0300	49,63C,47
Matsuura, Gary	CA0960	47,64E
Matthews, Forrest	SC0710	47,11
Matthews, Michael K.	MO0850	13A,13,10F,47,63C
Mattson, Lucas	IA1400	47,66
Mauceri, Frank	ME0200	47,64E
Mayhew, Sandon	ID0070	47,64E
Mayhue, Terence C.	IL1740	47,65
Maynard, Robert	LA0050	64E,47
McAllister, Michael	NC1750	13,10F,60,11,47
McBee, Cecil	MA1400	29,47,62D
McCandless, Marty	IL1100	64C,64E,32E,47,41
McCarley, Ron	CA1510	47,29B
McClary, Michael	GA0940	11,37,47,63
McClune, David	TN1660	47,64C,64E
McClung, Sam W.	FL0365	60B,37,13,47,46
McClure, Ron D.	NY2750	62D,47
McCollim, Danny	WA0950	45,66A,35D,47,35A
McCord, Adam	OH2450	64E,47
McCormick, Chris	TN1450	47,29,32F
McCreary, Teresa J.	HI0110	37,13A,13C,38,47
McCurdy, Robert	SD0550	29A,47
McDannell, Karl	NY2450	32B,32C,47,60
McDonnell, David	OH2250	10B,10F,34,64E,47
McEachern, Peter J.	CT0250	47
McElwaine, James	NY3785	41,47,20G,29,34
McGarrell, Matthew	RI0050	37,41,47,46
McGee, Michael	AL0850	37,47,63,64,65
McGirr, Tom A.	WI0450	47,62D,53
McGuire, Christopher	TX3420	47
McGuire, David	NY1250	13,10,12A,13A,47
McGuire, K. Christian	MN0050	11,47
McKee, Andy	NY2660	47,62D,53
McLaren, Malena	LA0550	12,64C,64E,47
McLaughlin, Greg	CA4580	64A,64E,47
McLean, Allan	AI0150	47,29
McLean, John	IL0550	47,70,29
McMullen, George	CA2650	47,46,10F
McMullin, Brendan	CA3100	37,46,47
McNeil, John	MA1400	29,47,63A
McNeill, Dean	AJ0150	63A,29,46,47
McVinney, Barry D.	AR0350	47
McWilliams, Larry	IN0150	47,29
Meccia, Lauren L.	SC1100	37,41,47
Meckley, William A.	NY3600	47
Medler, Ben	OR0850	63C,47
Meggs, Gary L.	AR0800	60B,64,47,46,29
Meier, Scott Alan	PA2250	47,53,64E,34,32E
Mejias, Paoli	PR0115	47
Melendez, Carlos	MI0150	47,70
Melford, Myra J.	CA5000	29,47,53
Melito, Tom	CT0050	47
Mendez, Max	ID0140	61,36,42,47
Mendola, Ron	GA0900	38,47
Mendoza, Chico	NJ1400	47
Mendoza, Freddie	TX3175	29,47,63C
Menegon, John	NY3760	12A,47,62D
Mercer, Scott A.	IN1800	13A,13,47,61,53
Merrill, Paul	NY0900	46,47,29B,29C,63A
Mertens, Paul	IL0550	47,64E
Merz, Christopher Linn	IA1600	64E,47,29
Metzger, Jon	NC0750	65,29,47,50,53
Meyers, John	WI0100	63A,47
Michael, George	OH2140	47,64E,29
Michaels, Matthew	MI2200	47,66A,29
Middagh, Ryan	TN1100	11,47
Middleton, Robert M.	NJ0050	47,29,64,13,11
Miedema, Harry F.	IN1650	47,64E,29,53
Miele, David	NY3000	47,14C,65
Miele, William	RI0150	47,62D
Miglia, Jay	OH2050	29,64E,46,47
Mikolajcik, Walter	CA4650	36,37,47,63,66A
Miles, Melvin N.	MD0600	60,37,47,49,63A
Miles, Ron	CO0550	47,63A,29
Miley, James	OR1300	10,29,47,46,13
Millard, Joshua P.	MA2030	13B,13C,41,47
Miller, Aaron D.	ID0060	47,62D
Miller, Allan	CA6050	11,12,37,47,63
Miller, Cercie	MA2050	64E,47
Miller, David	MS0050	13,47,46,29
Miller, Fred	IL2775	70,47,14C
Miller, Harold L.	WI0450	10,13A,13G,20,47
Miller, John A.	IL1350	47,70
Miller, M. Frederick	IL2650	70,47
Miller, Marc	GA1150	62D,47
Miller, Mark	CO0560	29,13A,41,47,64A
Millhouse, Steven	AZ0440	62D,47
Mills, John	TX3510	64E,29,47,46
Mills, Peter	OH0850	64E,47,29
Milne, Andy	NY2750	29,47,66A
Milne, Andy	NY2660	66A,47
Milne, David	WI0845	29A,47,48,64E
Milton, Kenneth	MS0560	11,47,49,63A,63B
Moe, Aaron	MN1200	29,47
Moffett, C. Mondre	NC1550	63A,10F,29A,47,31F
Molinari, Raffaele 'Lello'	MA0260	47
Monaghan, Michael	MA0700	47,64A,64E,53,29
Mongrain, Richard	CO0625	37,47
Moninger, Susan	IL0850	36,40,47,61
Montgomery, Dennis	MA0260	47
Moore, Corey	NJ0500	47,60,64E
Moore, Grant W.	PA1250	49,63D,47
Moore, Gregory	WI0860	13C,47,64E,29,10A
Moore, Harlan	OK1200	47
Moore, James H.	WV0800	37,47,29A,11
Moore, Stephen F.	CA0805	13C,29,47,60,66
Morales, Samuel	PR0150	47,46
Morel, Vincent	AI0200	47,36,61
Morell, Drew	CO0830	70,47,62D
Moreno, Tony	NY2750	47,29,65
Morgan, Charles	IL1250	13A,60B,37,47,63
Morgan, David	OH2600	62D,29,47,53
Morgan, Philip	NC2500	37,47,50,11
Moring, Bill F.	NJ0800	46,47,62D
Morreale, Michael	NY0644	11,63A,29A,47,13A
Morris, Joe	MA1400	29,47,70
Morris, Nancy	MA0260	47
Morris, Willie L.	OH2250	37,47,64E,32
Morrow, Jeff	IL0550	47,61
Moseley, William	ME0340	12A,47,64A,35C,29
Moser, Diane	NY2660	47,10
Moses, Robert	MA1400	47,65,29
Moshier, Josh	IL3550	29,10C,47
Mossblad, Gunnar	OH2300	64E,46,47,29B,29C
Motley, Gary D.	GA0750	29,46,47
Moulder, John	IL0550	47,70
Mouse, Eugene	IL2050	53,47,29A,29B
Mruzek, David M.	IN0650	11,37,38,47
Muehlenbeck Pfotenhauer, Thomas R.	MN1600	63A,47,29,11,11
Mullett, Scott	NH0150	53,47,29B
Munro, Douglas	NY3785	47,29
Murdock, Matthew	TN1600	13C,32E,29,37,47
Murphy, John P.	TX3420	29,14,47,64E
Murphy, Timothy	MD0650	29,47
Musselwhite, Eric	VA0150	47,64E
Musso, Paul J.	CO0830	70,47,53,13A
Myer, Tom	CO0800	47,64E
Nagge, Harold	TN1250	70,53,47,29
Nash, Gary Powell	TN0550	10,13,47,64,10F
Nathan, Jonathan	CA5060	47,50,65
Navarro Romero, Emanuel	PR0115	66D,47
Navidad, Paul J.	CA3350	47
Nazarenko, John J.	NY3650	47,66A,29
Neal, Mark	AL1450	65,47,34,35
Neiderhiser, Jonathan	SD0580	37,47,32E,13B,13C
Nelson, Jon R.	NY4320	37,47,63A
Nelson, Larry	KY0550	64E,53,29,47,29A
Nelson, Michael	ME0340	10,34,13,29,47
Netsky, Hankus H.	MA1400	29,13C,47,53,20F
Neuharth, Randall	NE0460	11,37,47,63
Neumeyer, Albert J.	PA2550	47,37
Newlin, Yvonne	IL1612	13,60,37,66,47
Newman, Timothy	NJ1400	47,63A,29
Newsam, David R.	NH0100	47,70
Newsome, Charles	MI2200	29,46,47,70
Newson, Jeffrey	OK1450	66A,47
Newton, Dean A.	OH2150	70,47
Newton, Jack	NC0050	47,41,64C,72,35
Nichol, John	MI0400	47,48,64E,29
Nicholas, Julie	CA1650	29,61,47
Nielsen, Ryan	ID0060	29,46,47,63A

Name	Code	Areas
Nieske, Robert	MA1400	29,47
Nieske, Robert	MA0500	10,47,62D,53,46
Niess, Matt	VA1350	47
Nifong, Bruce	MA0260	47
Nigrelli, Christopher	NC1100	12A,47,44,63C,63D
Nimmons, Phil	AG0450	32,47,29
Noffsinger, Jonathan	AL1170	47,64E,53
Nordgren, Jon	CA0400	13,37,46,47,60
Norris, Alexander	MD0650	29,47
Norris, Paul	DC0170	47,37
Novros, Paul	CA0510	64E,47,29B
Nowak, Gerald C.	PA0400	13,37,47,64
Nyerges, John	NY2500	35C,47
Oakley, Tom	TN0150	37,47,32H,10F
Oberholtzer, Christopher W.	ME0500	29,47,63C
Obrecht, Guy	AA0050	12A,13,47
O'Connor, Douglas	WI0803	64E,47
O'Connor, Thomas	AR0110	13,32,47,10A,10F
O'Farrill, Arturo	NY3785	47,66A
Offard, Felton	IL0600	13A,11,47,70,29A
Olcott, James L.	OH1450	47,63A,49,42
Oles, Darek	CA0510	62D,47
Olsen, Timothy J.	NY4310	13,10,47,63A,29
Olson, Matthew W.	SC0750	64E,29,47,41,46
Olson, Rolf	SD0600	37,47,49,63A,46
Opfer, Stephen R.	CA2810	32,37,38,60B,47
Orta, Michael	FL0700	66A,29A,29B,47
Osborn, James	NY4450	47,63A,48
Osborne, Charles	CA0100	47
Osby, Greg	MA0260	47
Osland, Lisa	KY1450	64E,41,47
Osland, Miles	KY1450	47,64E,29,53,48
Ott, Joseph	IL0100	53,47,29A
Ousley, Larry James	FL0700	62D,46,47,53
Overmier, Douglas R.	MO0950	60B,60A,37,47,10
Owen, Charles (Chuck) R.	FL2000	47,29,10
Owen, John E.	OH0950	60B,37,47,63A
Owen, Stephen W.	OR1050	46,47,53,29,64E
Owens, Charles Marion	CA5020	47
Owens, Charles	CA5031	29,47,64
Owens, Craig	KS1450	47,70,53,29A,20G
Owens, Douglas T.	VA1000	32,47,60B,29
Owens, Priscilla	NY0625	47,29
Pack, Lester	AR0800	65,46,47,29,70
Padilla, Reginald A.	HI0210	47
Page, Richard L.	NH0110	47,64E,29
Palacio, Jon	CA0900	29,46,47,66A
Palance, Thomas M.	MA1650	29,46,47,63A
Paliga, Mitch L.	IL2050	64E,29A,41,47,48
Paliga, Mitchell L.	IL1400	64E,47,29A
Palmer, David	NC1150	63,47
Palmer, Thomas	DE0150	47
Panella, Lawrence	MS0750	29,64E,47
Pannunzio, Sam	CO0275	66A,53,66D,47
Paolantonio, Ed	NC2410	66A,47
Parillo, Joseph M.	RI0300	13,10,47,46,29
Park, William B.	WA0800	47,63C
Parke, Steve	IL2450	10,47,63A,29A,35A
Parker, Alex	TX0300	29,47,46
Parker, Christopher S.	NY3000	47,66A,66D,53,29
Parker, David K.	OR1100	47
Parker, Wesley	NC1700	65,47
Parkin, Chris	WA1350	64E,46,47
Parkinson, John S.	CA2840	37,38,47,49,45
Parkinson, Wm. Michael	OH1900	29,35G,47
Parks, John	SC0850	70,46,47
Parr, J. D.	KS0050	37,47,48,64,29
Parsons, Longineu	FL0600	47,63A,29
Parsons, Sean	WV0400	29,46,47,66A
Parton, Robert T.	OH0350	63A,29,47,29A,53
Pasqua, Alan	CA5300	47,29
Pastrana, Jorge	CA4850	47,46,45,35D,10B
Patitucci, John	NY0550	10,46,47,51,50
Patnode, Matthew A.	ND0350	64E,64A,29,48,47
Paton, Eric	OH0350	65,20A,20C,20H,47
Patterson, Ann E.	CA2650	29A,29D,47
Patterson, James H.	GA0490	29,32,46,63,47
Patterson, Roy	AG0650	47,70
Paulson, John C.	MN1400	47,64,29,34,35
Pazera, Scott	IN1850	47
Pederson, Steven A.	KY0800	37,41,47,64
Peffer, Ed	CA2390	47,29,53
Pellitteri, Marcello	MA0260	47
Pendowski, Michael	AL0200	64E,46,47,11
Pennington, Randy	KY1000	60,36,47
Pensyl, Kim C.	OH2200	47
Pepitone, Anthony F.	OH2250	70,47
Peplin, Steve W.	WI0450	10A,11,13B,47,70
Perconti, William J.	ID0130	13,11,47,64
Perez Rivera, Pedro	PR0115	62D,47
Perez, Frank	IA0600	37,47,32,29,63C
Perez-Feria, Willy	FL1310	47,61
Perrine, John Mark	OH0650	47,29A,64E
Perry, Dawn A.	NC2650	63C,32E,37,47,60B
Perry, Rich	NJ1400	64E,47
Pershounin, Alexander	GA0550	62D,47
Petersen, Lynn	MT0075	10A,11,13A,66A,47
Peterson, David	WA0200	47,70,29
Peterson, Edward	LA0800	47,64C,29B
Peterson, Russell	MN0600	47,48,64D,64E,35G
Pettit, Darren	NE0610	64E,47
Pfau, Tracy	WY0050	47,70,53
Philbrick, Keith E.	VA1000	46,47
Phillips, Damani	IA0700	29,47
Pickett, Lenny B.	NY2750	46,47,64E,29
Pierce, John	MA0260	47
Pietro, David A.	NY2750	64E,29,47
Pilc, Jean-Michel	NY2750	29,66A,47
Pinto, Mike	IL0850	70,53,47
Piontek, Gregory	NY1210	12A,47,29
Pipho, Robert S.	MI2200	47,29,66A
Pisano, James	KS0200	64C,64E,47,53,13
Pisano, Joseph M.	PA1450	47,45,53,46,34
Pitchford, Timothy	IL1200	63C,29A,46,47,53
Plamondon, Andrew	WA0250	63A,46,47
Platt, Walter	MA2030	47,46
Platz, Eric	AC0050	46,47,29
Platz, Eric	RI0300	65,29,47
Plies, Dennis B.	OR1150	47,65B,66B,66D,13C
Plugge, Scott D.	TX2250	64E,20G,29,47
Poelnitz, Michael	AL0310	12A,47,63,35B
Polanco-Safadit, Pavel	IN0400	66,53,46,47
Polett, Thomas C.	MO0300	63,47,32,13,20
Pope, David J.	VA0600	64E,47
Poplin, Stan E.	CA5070	62D,47
Posch, Carl	AZ0150	13,11,37,47,63D
Postle, Matthew W.	NC2000	47,29A
Potter, Christopher	NY2750	46,47,64E,29
Poudrier, Chris	MA2020	65,47
Powe, Holly	AL0330	61,13,11,60,47
Powell, Daniel	FL0350	11,13,47,63,64
Pratt, Gary W.	CA0835	60,37,38,47
Prettyman, Ken	WA0550	10A,13A,13B,46,47
Price, Emmett G.	MA1450	14,29,66A,47
Price, Harvey	DE0150	50,65,47
Price, Larry	MN1700	47
Priester, Julian	WA0200	10,47,63C,63D,29
Prieto, Dafnis	NY2750	29,47,65
Primatic, Stephen P.	GA0200	65,13,29,11,47
Prince, Curtis L.	IN0005	10,12,20G,65,47
Prokop, Rick	NY2400	47
Promane, Terry	AG0450	29,47
Prouten, William	AA0032	13,47,64,53,29A
Prouty, Patrick	MI2120	47,13,43,10
Provencal, Richard	AI0200	47
Pruiett, Kevin P.	OK0650	47,63A,72,29A,49
Puga, John	TX3527	46,47
Purdie, Bernard	NY2660	47,65
Purvis, Ralph E.	AL0400	47
Pusey, Bill	PA3330	47,63A
Quaile, Michael	PA3330	47,70
Quinn, Karyn	WI0810	47,62D,46,29,13A
Rabbai, George	PA3330	63A,47,49
Raberg, Bruno	MA0260	47
Raby, Lee Worley	CA2801	47,64E,13A,13B,64
Ragsdale, Jeremy	MD0850	61,47
Rainwater, Brian	FL0670	60,37,13C,63C,47
Raisor, Steve C.	NC0500	11,13,37,47,70
Ramsey, Guthrie P.	PA3350	12,35,20G,29,47
Randall, Thomas	MA1000	47,57,72,70
Rankin, John M.	TX2200	11,47,63A,46
Rapport, Evan	NY2660	47
Rapson, John	IA1550	47
Rask, Perry J.	IL1750	47,64E,29
Rasmusson, Ralph	NY1850	37,47,63,64,65
Read, Paul	AG0450	47,29
Reagan, Billy R.	AL0350	36,37,41,47,63
Rebbeck, Lyle	AA0040	47,48,64,53
Rector, Malcolm W.	TX3450	13,10,29,47
Reed, Jeff	MD0850	62D,47
Reed, Sean Scot	AR0200	63C,47
Reese, Randall	GA0200	10F,47,64E,10A,13D
Reeves, Scott	NY0550	13,47,53,29
Reid, Doug	WA0860	47,64E,53,46,29
Rettedal, Dean	SD0300	37,60B,47,63,64
Reyman, Randall	IL1750	47,63A,53,29
Reynolds, Dennis	OH1700	29,47
Reynolds, Martin C.	MO1500	37,63C,41,47,32E
Rhodes, Steve	TN0930	60B,32E,37,47,63D
Ricci, John	FL1000	64E,47,29
Richard, Charles	CA3800	47,64E,29,34,42
Richard, Matthew	MA2020	47
Richards, Eric	NE0600	47,10A,10D,13G
Richards, Eric J.	NE0400	63C,37,10A,13B,47
Richardson, Robert C.	WA0450	13,11,37,38,47
Richardson, William	MO0950	47,63A,11
Richmond, Mike	NY2750	29,47,64D
Richwine, Reginald L.	OH2250	63A,47
Ridley, Larry	NY2150	47,29A,62D,20A,20G
Riegle, Dale	FL1500	47,49,63A
Riekenberg, Dave	PA1950	64E,47,29B
Rieth, Dale	FL0950	13,36,47,61,66A
Riley, John	NY3785	47
Rinear, Jeffrey	MN1625	47
Ringquist, Mikael	MA1400	47,65
Rinzler, Paul	CA0600	13,10,47,66A,29
Riposo, Joseph	NY4150	47,46,32
Roach, Stephen W.	CA0840	47,29
Robblee, Timothy	IL2250	37,47,32E
Roberts, Marvin	AL1150	29,63A,47
Robertson, James D.	MT0175	13,60B,63C,63D,47
Robinson, Marty	WI0830	63A,29A,47
Robinson, Marty	FL0600	47,45,63A,29
Robinson, Thomas S.	NH0250	66A,46,47,29
Robitaille, James	MA2020	70,47
Rodgers, Ernest E.	MI2200	64E,29,47
Rodriguez Curet, Marcos J.	PR0115	29B,47
Rodriguez, Bobby H.	CA3500	47
Rodriguez, Galindo	LA0550	63A,41,47
Rogine, Peter	NY1275	13C,29,47,70
Rohlfing, Mimi	MA2030	61,36,47,40
Roiger, Teresa	NY3760	12A,47,61
Roitstein, David	CA0510	13C,47,29,66A
Romain, James P.	IA0550	64E,29A,35A,29,47
Romeo, James	CA4050	11,37,47,48,29
Romero, Frank	NM0310	63A,47,72,34
Rosa Ramos, Luis S.	PR0115	29,10F,47
Rosenberg, Christopher J.	NY2150	47,29
Rosensky, Michael	VA1550	70,42,47
Rossmiller, Adam	MN0610	29,47
Rossum, Kelly	VA0150	63A,29,67E,47
Rostock, Paul	PA2450	47,62D,46,35A
Roubal, Peter	IL2350	13,10,34B,47
Rowe, Ellen H.	MI2100	47,29,66A
Rowell, Michael	GA0700	31A,60A,47,36
Roy, Dany	AI0200	64E,47
Roy, Larry	AC0100	70,47,53
Royer, Randall D.	SD0100	64,47,38,32E,70
Rozie, Edward Rick	CT0650	20G,47,62D,29
Rubinstein, Matan	WI0865	11,29,32B,47
Ruby, Meg	MA2030	41,42,47,66A
Rucker, Lee	OK1330	37,47,63A,46,29
Rucker, Steve P.	FL1900	65,47,29
Rudkin, Ronald	NC1650	47,29,53
Rudolph, Jon	MN1120	70,47
Rule, Charles	TN0700	11,47,66A,29,35
Runestad, Kurt	NE0200	36,32D,60A,47
Runions, Greg	AG0250	47,50,32,65
Runnels, Brent	GA1550	66A,11,29,47,13A
Running, Donald	MA0510	37,38,46,47,11
Russell, Benjamin A.	MD0475	47,64E,14C
Russell, John	CA1550	47
Ryga, Campbell	AB0060	29,46,47,64E
Sabatella, Marc	CO0650	66A,47
Sabina, Leslie M.	NY3475	29,10,34,13,47
Sackman, Marc L.	WI0806	13B,37,64A,47,11
Salazar, Jason	MO0400	34,13,35,43,47
Salerno, Christine	WI0808	40,47,66,61
Salerno, John	WI0808	13,10,47,48,29
Salerno, Steven	NY0050	29,47,70
Salman, Randy Keith	IN0350	47,64C,64E,29
Salucka, Ray	IA0930	13,36,60,11,47
Samson, David	PA0650	47,13B,32C,63,60
Samuels, David A.	MA0260	47,65B
Samuels, Paul	OH1700	47
Sanabria, Bobby	NY2150	47,29

Index by Area of Teaching Interest

Name	Code	Interests
Sanabria, Bobby	NY2660	47,65
Sandahl, Thomas	OR0500	47,70,29B
Sanders, Robert	TX2100	47,11
Santoro, David N.	MA0260	47
Santos, Elias	PR0115	29A,47,29B,53
Santos-Neto, Jovino	WA0200	47,66A,66D
Sarjeant, Lindsey B.	FL0600	47,49,53,46,29
Sato, Akira	TX2400	46,47
Sato, Akira	TX3420	29,63A,47,60A
Saunders, Bruce	TX3510	70,47
Saunders, John Jay	TX3420	47,63A,29,46
Saunders, Marianne	ID0070	47
Saunders, Martin	WV0400	63A,53,49,47,34
Scafide, Anthony	NY3765	35,41,47
Scanlon, Brian	CA3600	64E,47
Scea, Paul	WV0750	64E,29,47
Schaefer, Phillip	MO2000	37,47,49,63A
Schantz, Jack	OH2150	29,46,47,63A
Schattschneider, Adam	OH0250	13,47,64A,64C,64E
Schiavone, David C.	NY0400	47,48,64C,64E
Schiavone, David C.	NY4320	64C,64E,47
Schilf, Paul R.	SD0050	37,49,47,32E,29A
Schilling, Richard	MA2030	70,47
Schirm, Ronald	AG0600	47,29
Schlamb, Peter	MO1950	47
Schlink, Robert	MA0260	47
Schmid, William	GA0950	63A,46,29,49,47
Schmidt, Alan G.	NY1220	13A,12A,47,20G,29A
Schmidt, David A.	FL0400	47,63C,63D
Schmidt, David	AZ0350	47,53,35D,34D
Schmidt, James	NC0450	66A,29A,66D,47,11
Schmidt, Russell	UT0250	66A,29,47
Schmitz, Eric B.	NY3770	47,65,13B,13C,10A
Schneider, Jim	CA1550	47
Schneller, Aric	TX2250	47,29,63C,61
Schnitter, David	NY2660	13,64E,47
Schoeppach, Brad W.	NY2750	29,47
Schroeder, Dave	NY2750	29,47,65,60B
Schubert, John	MI0200	11,47,13G
Schulte, Dan	OR0850	62D,47
Schulze-Johnson, Virginia	NJ0300	41,47,48,64A,42
Schunks, Dan	MO0750	47,37
Schwartz, Richard A.	LA0650	29,47,64E,11,46
Sciolla, Anne	PA3330	39,47,61
Scofield, John L.	NY2750	47,70
Scott, Christopher	OH0755	47
Scott, David	CT0800	47,63A,41
Scott, Debra L.	TX2700	47,63C,63D
Scott, Gary	OH0755	47,63A,20G,29,35B
Scott, J. B.	FL1950	63A,53,47,29A
Scott, Marshall	KY1550	41,47,63A,29
Scott, Michael E.	TN1380	11,47,53
Seeger, Brian	LA0800	35A,35B,35C,47,70
Seiler, David E.	NH0350	47,48,64C
Selvaggio, Robert	OH1100	47,29
Sepulveda, Sonja	NC2205	36,47,13,60
Serfaty, Aaron	CA0510	47,65
Sessions, Timothy	PA1950	63C,47
Settlemires, Joseph	OK1400	47,70
Severn, Eddie	PA2050	32,29,46,47,63
Sfraga, Debbie	NJ1160	32,37,47,64
Shanefield, Andrew	PA3200	47,29A,29B
Shanklin, Richard L.	OH2150	47,64E,29,35
Shanley, Steven	IA0300	32,46,47,53
Sharp, David	IA0750	13,11,47,64
Shaw, Brian	LA0200	63A,47
Shaw, George W.	CA2550	47,29,34,35
Shemaria, Rich S.	NY2750	46,47,66A,29
Sher, Ben	NY4500	34,47,70
Sher, Benjamin	MA1400	47
Sherman, Hal	WA0030	47
Sherman, Jeff	KY0250	47,53,70
Shevitz, Matthew	IL1080	11,13,29,47,46
Shields, Bob	AG0200	47,70
Shifflett, John	CA4400	53,47,62D
Shinn, Alan	TX3200	50,65,47,29
Shiver, Todd	WA0050	63A,32,37,47,49
Shner, Idit	OR1050	64E,42,47,29
Shorthouse, Tom	AB0060	63A,47,49,42
Shu, Peter	MN1250	66A,47
Sidener, Whitney F.	FL1900	47,64E,29
Sielert, Vanessa	ID0250	64E,47
Sielert, Vern	ID0250	47,63A,29
Sierra-Alonso, Saul	CA0807	47
Silbergleit, Paul	WI1150	70,47,29
Simerly, Rick	TN1150	63,29,49,47,32E
Simmons, James	TN1100	63A,47,46,29A,29B
Simon, Fred	IL0550	47,66A
Simon, Harris W.	VA0250	29A,66A,47,29
Simpson, Kyle	PA3580	10,11,37,47
Sims, Jared N.	RI0300	29,47,64E
Singh, Vijay	WA0050	47,60,36,61,35A
Singley, David	MN0300	70,47,41
Sintchak, Matthew A.	WI0865	64E,29,43,47,48
Skeete, Sean	MA0260	47
Skelton, Sam	GA1150	64E,47,29
Skop, Stephen	MA0150	47
Slabaugh, Stephen	MI1180	47,63A
Slack, Robert	CA1000	47,49,63A,53
Slagle, Steven	NY2150	47,64E,29
Smith, Bruce	AG0500	47
Smith, C. Raymond	UT0050	47,64,53,46,29
Smith, Danny	GA1070	47
Smith, Gene	AF0150	13,47,49,63C,29
Smith, Geoff	NY1250	47,11,35A,35B,35C
Smith, Herbert	VA0975	53,29,47
Smith, James E.	OH0500	29,70,47,12A
Smith, Joel L.	MA1450	47,29
Smith, Joel Larue	MA1900	29,47,10,53,13A
Smith, Joey	AB0210	29B,29C,47
Smith, Langston 'Skip'	MA0260	47
Smith, Larry G.	UT0300	13,29,47,64E,46
Smith, Raymond H.	AL1050	47,37,34,64E,29
Smith, Robbie Malcolm	MI0400	47,29A
Smith, Rusty	NC1900	63A,41,46,47
Smithee, Larry G.	TN1000	60,32,37,47,63
Smoker, Paul	NY2650	47
Smyth, Steven	AR0850	37,47
Snapp, Doug R.	MN1000	46,47,63A,29
Snider, Dave	WA1150	62D,47
Snow, Michelle H.	ME0500	47,61
Snow, Thomas	ME0150	29,47,46,66A
Snowden, Donald	FL1500	37,47,63D,29A
Snyder, Randy L.	TX2300	13A,13,11,47,63
Snyder, Rory	CA1560	29,46,47
Snyder, Steven D.	KY0900	13,47,66A,29
Solomon, Joseph	NY2050	47,53,29A
Solot, Evan	PA3330	13,10F,10,47,46
Sommer, Peter J.	CO0250	46,47,64E
Sorenson, Dean P.	MN1623	47
Spaar, Peter	VA1550	62D,42,47
Spaniola, Joseph T.	FL2100	47,46,63D,11,10
Spataro, Susan M.	VA0400	64A,47,11,32A,32B
Speight, Andrew	CA4200	29,64E,46,47
Spicknell, John P.	IN0800	12A,47,64C
Spielman, Mark	AB0070	13A,47,62D,20G
Springs, Benjy L.	NC0900	37,47
Spurr, Ken	IL0850	66A,46,47
Spurr, Kenneth	IL1085	66A,53,29,47
Stabley, Jeff	PA3710	46,47,53,65,50
Stacke, Robert J.	MN0050	37,47,29
Stafford, John	KS0590	36,40,47,11,13A
Stallsmith, John	AL0260	12A,36,47,66,31A
Stallworth, Lenny	MA0260	47
Stapleson, Donald	MD0750	46,47,64E,13C
Starks, George	PA1000	20,14,47,64E,29
Steed, Scott	WA0250	62D,47
Steffen, Richard	TN0050	60B,49,63A,47,11
Stein, Ken J.	IL2560	11,13B,20,47,64E
Steinberg, Steve	CA3460	46,47,60B
Stencel, Paul L.	NY1210	13A,11,12A,41,47
Stephens, Gerald	TN1200	66A,47
Stephens, John C.	IL3300	29,46,47
Stephens, Sonny	KY0250	47,62D
Steprans, Janis	AI0190	64E,47,46
Sterbank, Mark	SC0275	64E,47,46,29
Stern, David	SC0050	37,63D,47,29A,60B
Sterner, Dave	OH0750	13,47,70,29
Stewart, Alexander	VT0450	14,53,20,29,47
Stewart, Stanley W.	MS0200	11,37,47,49,48
Stiegler, Morgen	OH0300	47
Stinson, Ron	KS0570	29,37,41,46,47
Stitt, Ronald	PA0100	63C,47,29,46,34
Stockham, Jeff	NY0650	63A,47
Stone, George J.	CA1510	13,47,34,66A,35D
Stone, Simon	AI0200	64E,47
Stowman, William	PA2300	47,63A
Strait, Tom	MN1120	63A,29,63B,47
Strid-Chadwick, Karen	AK0100	13,47,66A,66D,29
Stride, Frederick	AB0100	47,29
Strohman, Thomas	PA1900	47,64E,29
Stuart, Rory	NY2660	13,70,47
Stubbs, James	TX1750	46,32,13A,37,47
Stufft, David	GA2000	37,41,47,32,60B
Stuntz, Lori A.	CA3200	63,47
Sturm, Fred	WI0350	10,29,46,47
Such, Rich	OR0175	47,64E
Suchanek, Bronislaw	ME0500	47,62D
Sucherman, Paul	WI0848	47
Sulliman, Jason M.	IN1800	63,49,47
Sullivan, Joe	AI0150	63A,29,47
Sullivan, Kevin M.	AI0050	47
Sully, Eldon	VA0150	47
Sunda, Robert	TN1200	62D,47
Sussman, Richard	NY2150	47,29
Swana, John	PA3330	63A,53,47
Swann, William E.	TN1000	47,13,60B,29B,10D
Swindler, Wil J.	CO0250	29,47,64E
Tabor, Jerry N.	MD0800	13,10,29B,47,11
Tadic, Miroslav	CA0510	70,47,20F
Talbott, Doug	KS0150	10F,37,32E,37,47,49
Tallman, Thomas J.	IL0630	13,11,47,63,29
Tanouye, Nathan	NV0050	29,63C,47
Tapper, Robert	MT0400	29,63C,46,47
Tate, Mark	KY0610	47,65
Taylor, Clifton	MS0500	60,37,47
Taylor, Elizabeth	MS0420	13,47,49,63C,37
Taylor, Jack M.	OH2275	10,37,47,29
Taylor, Tom	CO0200	70,29B,46,47
Teasley, Kevin	VA1800	47,29
Teichler, Robert Christopher	IL3150	47,10,38
Terrell, Maurice	FL1700	11,29,37,47,60B
Terry, Clark	NJ1400	47
Thier, Bethany	WI0750	61,66,47
Thimmesch, Richard	IA0650	13B,13C,32E,37,47
Thimmig, Les	WI0815	10,47,64E,29
Thomas, Anita	MD0300	47
Thomas, Craig	PA3330	47,62D,29
Thomas, Daniel A.	MO1810	64E,47,53
Thomas, Eric B.	ME0250	37,47,64C,64E,53
Thomas, Gary	MD0650	47,29
Thomas, John	CA5300	47,29
Thomas, Russell	MS0350	47,64E,29,13
Thompson, Bob	ME0340	47,70,53,35
Thompson, Chester	TN0100	65,35B,47
Thompson, Phil A.	SC1200	47,64
Thompson, Richard O.	CA4100	47,66A,29A
Thompson, Vance	TN1710	63A,47
Thornton, Bruce	MN0350	60B,41,47,64
Threlkeld, David M.	KY1425	11,12A,47,48,64
Tiana, Mayo	IL2150	29,46,47,10F
Tiberio, William	NY4350	47
Tidaback, Darrell	IN0910	62D,10B,47
Tiemann, Jason E.	KY1500	47,65
Tiner, Kris	CA0650	47,32B
Tiner, Kris	CA0270	47,29A,11
Tinnell, Jennifer L.	KY0400	37,63C,32E,47
Tirk, Richard	OK1250	47,63A,37
Titlebaum, Michael	NY1800	29,46,47
Tobey, Forrest	IN0400	38,47,13,34
Todd, Colette	WI0250	32D,36,47
Tolliver, Charles	NY2660	10,46,47,63A
Tolson, Gerald H.	KY1500	32,47,29,14C
Tomaro, Michael	PA1050	64E,47,53,29
Tomlin, Terry	TX3515	47,64E,29,34,32F
Toney, Hubert	PA0700	37,47,32E,63A
Toomey, John F.	VA1000	66A,29,47
Tot, Zvonimir	IL3310	29,13,13C,70,47
Towell, Gordon L.	KY0900	47,64E,53,29
Towner, Cliff	GA0850	32E,37,47,60B
Tracy, Michael	KY1500	47,64E,42
Trask, Alvin	MD0550	63A,53,29A,14C,47
Traylor, Steve	WY0060	13,46,47
Treuden, Terry	WI1155	37,47,32,10F
Trompeter, Jim W.	IL0550	47,66A
Trout, Marion T.	IN1310	37,47,53
Trudel, Eric	MD0850	47,53
Tumlinson, Charles	CA0815	47,41,29
Turcotte, Kevin	AG0650	47,63A
Turner, Charles	KY0300	32,37,63,47,41
Turner, Michael W.	OR1000	70,29,34,47
Turney, Brent	WI0850	47,29A,63A
Turpen, Scott	WY0200	64E,47,29,60B
Tymas, Byron	NC1600	11,46,70,47,41
Uhlenkott, Gary	WA0400	13A,66A,13B,35H,47
Ulibarri, Fernando	FL0200	35,70,47

Name	Code	Areas
Vaccaro, Brian	MO1120	47,14C
Vadala, Christopher	MD1010	47,64E,53,29
Valentin Pagan, Aldemar	PR0115	62D,47,53
van Deursen, John	AB0060	47,38,63C,63D
Van Wagner, Eric	OH2050	35G,35A,47
VanAllen, Michael	NY3350	29,66A,47
Vandelicht, Roy D. 'Skip'	MO0100	32,37,60B,64A,47
Vanderheyden, Joel	MO0550	64E,46,47,29,13
Vandermeer, Aaron D.	NC2435	29,35,47
Vandiver, Joseph	TX3650	29,63,46,47,34
Vandivort, Roger	WA1200	47
VanMatre, Rick	OH2200	47,64E,29
Vanore, John	PA3680	60,10,47,49,63A
Varner, Tom	WA0200	63B,47
Veasley, Gerald	PA3330	62D,47
Vega, Ray	VT0450	29,47,63A
Vento, Steve	OK1300	10,11,12,47,32E
Vernick, Gordon Jay	GA1050	47,46,29
Vernon, James Farrell	IN0905	64E,47
Villanueva, Jari	MD1000	47
Villanueva, Rodrigo	IL2200	29,47
Villines, Roger	FL1500	63A,47,11
Vincent, Randy	CA4700	70,47
Vinci, Mark A.	NY3650	47,64E,29
Vivian, Jim	AG0650	47,62D
Von Kampen, David W.	NE0200	47
Von Ohlen, John	OH2200	47
VonBerg, Craig	CA0810	29,47,14C
Vosbein, Terry	VA1850	10,13,29A,47,29
Wachala, Greg	NY1550	70,47
Waddel, Nathan	OR0350	20G,47
Waddington, Alan	CA1000	12F,14,29,46,47
Waddley, Craig	AR0950	41,47
Wagner, Craig	KY1500	70,47
Wagstrom, Beth Robison	CO0050	36,40,47,60A
Wakeling, Tom	OR0050	11,12A,47,29,35
Wall, Jeremy	NY3765	34,35,36,47,66A
Wallace, Noel	TX3300	63D,47
Wallace, Wayne	CA4400	47
Wallarab, Brent K.	IN0900	29,47
Waller, Jim	TX3410	35G,10C,29B,47,35A
Walsh, Allan	AG0150	64E,47,46,29A,29B
Walsh, Marty	MA0260	47
Walters, Gary	IN0250	66A,47
Wang, Richard A.	IL3310	10F,12A,47,53,29
Ward, Brian	OR0850	66A,47
Ward-Steinman, Patrice Madura	IN0900	32G,32D,32,29,47
Ware, David N.	MS0350	63A,34C,47,11,13B
Warfield, William	PA1950	47,63A,29
Warren, Jeff	AB0090	12B,13F,47,62D
Warren, Ted	AG0350	47
Warrington, Thomas	NV0050	62D,47,29
Warth, James R.	TX2960	47,64E,64B
Washburne, Christopher	NY0750	14,29,47
Washington, Salim	NY0500	47,46,29,29B
Washut, Robert	IA1600	13,47,29
Wasko, Dennis	PA3330	47,63A,49
Waters, Jeffery L.	MO1550	13B,47,64
Waters, Tim	OK0850	47,10,37
Watkins, Mark	ID0060	47,48,64E
Watson, Robert M.	MO1810	29A,29B,29C,47,64E
Watson, Tim M.	IA1100	32D,47,36,60A
Watson, William E.	MD0175	10,47,14C,20
Waugh, Robert	IN0800	63A,47
Webb, Glenn	UT0150	37,41,47,50,65
Webb, John	TX3535	20,47,64E
Weber, Brent M.	MD0350	64E,64D,29,47,20
Weed, Tad	MI1750	66A,29,47
Wehrmann, Rock	OH2150	47,66A
Weigert, David	MA0260	47
Weir, Tim	ME0340	47,63A,29,32E
Weir, Timothy	VA0100	32C,32E,37,47,42
Weiss, Doug	NY2660	13,47
Welge, Jurgen	KS0590	65,46,47
Weller, Robert	CA3460	46,47,66
Wells, David	ME0340	47,64E
Werner, Kenny	NY2750	47,66A
Wernick, Diane	MA0260	47
Wesley, Arthur B.	AL0010	11,37,47,65
West, George	FL1750	47,29A,53
Western, Daniel	AL0650	64,47,35D,13,29A
Westray, Ron	AG0650	47,63C
Wetzel, Neil D.	PA2450	47,64,29A,64E,46
Wheatley, Jon	MA2030	70,47
Wheeler, Ben A.	MO1900	47,62D
Wheeler, Ben	MO1950	47
Wheeler, Mike	TX3400	47,70
Wheeler, Tyrone	KY1500	47,62D
Whipkey, Steve	IN1100	66A,66C,47
Whitaker, Rodney	MI1400	47,29,62D
White, Arthur	MO1800	47,64C,29B
White, Bill	MN0610	47
White, James	CO0950	29,47,65
White, William	MO1710	11,37,47,65,63
Whitehead, Glen	CO0810	63A,47,29,45
Whitted, Pharez	IL0600	63A,29,47,49
Widenhofer, Stephen B.	IL1750	47,35A
Widner, James	MO1830	46,29B,29C,47
Wiest, Steve	TX3420	10,29,47,63C
Wiggins, Ira T.	NC1600	47,64A,64E,29,46
Wiley, N. Keith	PA2350	32C,47,63A,29
Wilken, David M.	NC2400	63C,46,47,10A
Wilkerson, Andrea	CA3500	47,61,29,46,53
Wilkins, Ashby	FL2000	47,29
Wilkins, Carolyn	MA0260	47
Wilkinson, Jay	OK1350	47,53,29
Wilkinson, Michael	FL1800	63C,47,29B
Wilkinson, Todd R.	KS1000	47,64E,29,32E
Wilkinson, Wayne	CO0275	70,47,41,42
Williams, Anthony N.	ND0400	29,47,63C,63D
Williams, Gary R.	WI0450	47,70,53
Williams, Jay	WA0700	46,47
Williams, Sandy	IN0907	70,47,46
Williams, Yolanda	MN1050	12A,20,47,29A,41
Williamson, Bruce	VT0050	64C,64E,66A,67,47
Willis, Jonathan	OH2290	60B,32C,37,47,46
Wilson, Cheryl	IL0550	47
Wilson, Dennis E.	MI2100	63C,29,47
Wilson, Elisa	TX3520	61,54,47,39
Wilson, Stephen K.	NC0250	47,29,63
Wind, Martin	NY2750	29,47,62D
Winking, Keith R.	TX3175	47,63A,29
Winslow, Michael Rocky	CA0800	29,47,63A
Winston, Jeremy	OH2400	36,61,47,13E,60A
Witt, James	CA4050	13A,11,12A,47,62D
Witt, Woody W.	TX3400	47,64E,29
Wittemann, Wilbur	NJ0550	37,63,47,60B
Wlosok, Pavel	NC2600	47,13F,29,66A
Woger, Scott	IL1600	13,11,66A,47
Wohlwend, Karl	OH2050	70,47
Woitach, Christopher	OR1250	70,47
Wolf, Donald	AL1195	10F,37,46,47,63A
Wolfe, Jeffrey L.	WV0400	34,29A,47
Wolfe, Thomas	AL1170	47,70,29,35B
Woking, Henry C.	UT0250	13,10F,47,46,29
Won, Mel	CA4300	47
Woodard, Peter	CT0650	13B,47,66A,29
Woodard, Scott	WV0700	37,47,32C,63,49
Woodford, Peter	CA0550	70,47
Woods, Michael	NY1350	47,29
Workman, Darin D.	KS1110	60,32,37,47,64
Workman, Reggie	NY2660	10,47,62D,53
Worman, James	TX3350	32,37,47,29,64E
Worthy, Michael D.	MS0700	32C,32E,32G,47
Wright, Prakash	TN1800	47,29
Wright, Steve	MN0750	47,63A,35,46,10
Wright, Todd T.	NC0050	29,47
Wright, Trey	GA1150	70,47,29A,29B,14C
Wuest, Harry	FL0675	37,47,64,63
Wurtz, Gary	TX2700	47,63A
Wyatt, Alan	TN0850	13,47,64E,35A,35B
Wyatt, Paula	TN0850	47,66A
Yanez, Raul	AZ0490	66A,47,14C,29A
Yasinitsky, Greg	WA1150	47,64E,29,10F,10A
Yates, Derrick	AL0010	11,37,47,63A
Ybarra, Anthony L.	CA4410	70,53,47
Yeager, Bill	CA4100	47,63C,29
Yellin, Peter	NY2102	47,64E,46,29
Yoder, M. Dan	PA2750	47,64E
Yoelin, Shelley	IL3200	13A,13,37,47,64E
Yon, Franklin	MI0450	63,47,29A,11
York, Kevin	ID0100	37,47,34,32E
Young, Keith R.	PA1600	48,64E,47
Zabelsky, Bill	NV0150	36,47
Zak, Peter	NY2660	47,66A,53
Zambello, Kenneth	MA0260	47
Zamek, Brian	NY4050	11,37,47
Zebley, Matthew	CA5040	37,46,47
Zegree, Stephen	IN0900	36,47,40
Zeitlin, Paula H.	MA2050	62A,47
Zifer, Timothy	IN1600	47,63,29A,49
Zinn, Daniel L.	CA0807	47,64E,41,29A,11
Zinno, David A.	RI0300	47,62D,29
Ziv, Amir	NY2660	47,65
Zlabinger, Tom	NY0646	62D,29,14,20,47
Zonce, George	MA0260	47
Zuniga, Rodolfo	FL0200	65,47
Zvacek, Bret R.	NY3780	47,29

Woodwind Ensemble

Name	Code	Areas
Abel, Alfred	IN1850	62A,62B,38,48
Adams, Gary	AF0100	37,48
Akins, Lori B.	OH0950	48,64A
Akins, Lori	OH2450	48,64A
Aldrich, Simon	AI0150	64C,48
Altstaetter, Lucinda J.	OH1800	64A,48
Amos, Alvin E.	PA2000	29,13A,13C,48,64
Anderle, Jeffrey	CA4150	64C,48
Anderson, Carl H. C.	AL0500	13,48,64A,64C
Anderson, Claudia	IA0700	64A,48
Anderson, Cynthia	WV0750	13,48,64B
Anderson, Emily	SD0050	48
Anderson, Trudi J.	MN0050	64A,48
Andon, Sarah	CA5150	64A,48
Andrus, Deborah E.	PA2450	64C,48,41
Antonetti, Susan	AR0750	64A,48
Ardovino, Lori	AL1200	12A,48,64C,64E,67C
Arnold, Edwin P.	PA1450	32E,37,60B,48,49
Arrowsmith, Brenda	AG0070	48,64,10F,13A,13B
Asch, Arthur	WI0862	13,12A,37,48
Ator, James	IN0905	13,10,48,64E,29
Averett, Janet M.	CA4400	38,64,48
Averett, Frances Lapp	VA1350	48,64A,41
Ayoub, Anna Claire	PA3150	64D,48
Babad, Bruce	CA1900	47,48,64A,64C,64E
Bacon, Marcy D.	NY2650	64C,48
Bade, Christopher	IN1560	11,38,48,64,12A
Bairos, Monte	CA1560	37,41,48,49,50
Ball, Greg L.	TX2750	37,48,64,20G,29
Bambach, Paul	CA5060	64C,48
Banke, Andrea E.	KS1450	48,64B
Barrett, Gregory M.	IL2200	48,64C
Bartels, Cindi	OR1300	64C,48
Barth, Molly	OR1050	64A,42,48,43
Baumgarten, Jonathan	DC0010	64A,42,48
Beaman, M. Teresa	CA0810	13A,13,48,64A,34
Beard, Christine E.	NE0610	64A,48,11,13
Beason, Christine F.	TX3250	37,48,63B,32,10F
Becraft, Steven C.	AR0300	64C,29A,64E,48,32E
Beebe, Jon P.	NC0050	13,48,64D,32E,42
Behrens, Joel	PA2350	12A,48,64A
Bell, Timothy R.	WI0835	47,64C,64E,29,48
Benda, Karen L.	KS1400	64C,48
Bennett, Marie Micol	IL2050	64A,48,41,13A,42
Bergin, Wendy I.	TX2100	64A,48,13
Berkner, Jane	OH2150	48,64A
Berkner, Jane	OH0100	64A,48
Berry, James	PA3100	11,37,60,32B,48
Binkley, Lindabeth	MI0400	64B,41,48,11
Birch, Robert M.	DC0100	49,63A,37,48
Birdwell, Cody	KY1450	48,60B
Bivens, Pat	TN0250	11,47,63C,48,37
Blaha, Joseph L.	VA1250	46,10,12A,48,63C
Blood, Curt	CT0600	48,64C
Bond, Bronwell	PA0100	64A,48
Bonner, Joe	AR0110	48,64A,20
Bortolussi, Paolo	AB0060	64A,48,13
Boulet, Michele	PA2950	64A,48
Bourque, David	AG0450	48,37,38,64C,60B
Bouton, Arthur E.	CO0900	48,64E,41
Brickman, Nina	AG0600	63B,48
Brightbill, Elizabeth	VA0700	64A,48
Britten, Sandra	AF0050	48,64A
Bro, Paul	IN0800	48,64A
Brock, Gordon R.	FL1950	37,48,64E,60B,10A
Brooks, Joseph H.	WA0050	41,48,64B,64C,64E
Brown, Carolyn K.	AR0850	64A,48
Brown, Jeremy S.	AA0150	37,64E,29,12G,48
Brown, Jill Marie	MI0350	48,64A
Bryan, Carolyn J.	GA0950	64E,48
Bryant, Kelly	GA1700	64A,48
Buchman, Heather	NY1350	38,49,51,48,60B
Burks, Ricky	AL1450	48,64,46,29B,37
Bush, Christopher	NY2750	64C,41,42,48

Index by Area of Teaching Interest

Name	Code	Areas
Bustos, Pamela B.	WI0860	32E,37,48,60B,64C
Butler, Hunt	KY0750	47,48,64,53,29A
Butts, Beverly Ann K.	PA1900	64C,48,64
Byrd, Joshua	GA2130	37,10A,13G,48,10F
Callahan, Gary L.	NC1150	48,64,32,46
Campbell, Kathleen M.	PA3000	60,37,38,48
Camus, Elizabeth	OH0600	48,64B
Camwell, David J.	IA1350	32C,46,47,64E,48
Caneva, Thomas	IN0150	37,48
Caputo, Michael	NJ0250	12A,14,37,48,64
Carlson, Patti	VA0250	48,64C
Carlson, Patti F.	VA1000	48,64C
Carnochan, Robert M.	TX3510	37,48,32
Carter, David	AR0730	64C,64E,48,11
Catalfano, Joyce A.	WV0750	48,64A
Caulder, Stephanie B.	PA1600	12A,12D,48,64B,13C
Cazes, Alain	AI0150	60B,63D,48
Chambers, Timothy	NC0800	37,48,64,60B
Charles, Nicole	OH2250	64A,48
Charles, Nicole M.	OH1650	64A,48
Chernoff, Marea	AB0060	64B,48
Chest, Robert	SC0200	48,64B,64C,64D,64E
Ciepluch, Gary	OH0400	60,32,37,48
Cioffari, Cynthia A.	OH2150	64D,48
Cionitti, Linda A.	GA0950	48,64C
Clardy, Mary Karen	TX3420	41,48,64A
Clark, Antoine	OH1200	64C,64E,48
Clark, Antoine T.	OH0850	12A,72,48,64,64C
Clary, Richard	FL0850	48
Clayton, April	UT0050	63A,48
Climie, Stanley	AA0050	12A,48,64C
Clouser, John	OH0600	64D,48
Cohen, Franklin	OH0600	64C,48
Cohen, Paul	NY2150	48,64E
Cohen, Paul	NJ0800	64E,48
Collins, Nancy	WI0808	48,64A,41
Collins, Shelley	MS0250	11,64A,12A,48
Colwell, Denis R.	PA0550	48
Compton, Michael	OK0150	64,48,47,60B
Contino, Loretta	IN0250	48,64A
Converse, Ralph D.	NM0500	64,41,38,48,29
Cook, Lawrence	HI0050	48,64A,64C,64E
Cornils, Margaret A.	WI0840	64,11,48,66D
Councell-Vargas, Martha	MI2250	64A,48
Cowens, Kathleen	MO0350	64A,48
Cox, Michael W.	OH0350	64E,29,48
Craig, Gordon	AG0250	37,64C,48,38,41
Crawford, Peter	WA1300	34,48,37,66A
Cuffari, Gina	CT0800	64D,48,11
Cullen, Leslie	PA3150	64A,48
Daglar, Fatma	MD0850	64B,48
Dahlke, Andrew	CO0950	64E,48
D'Ambrosio, David	GA0050	66A,66C,48
Dannessa, Karen	PA3600	64C,48
Davis, Lapointe M.	DE0050	32,48,64
Davis, Randy	AL1195	37,38,60,13,48
Dean, Martin	GA1650	64,48
Deaver, Susan E.	NY2105	48,64A
DeBenedetto, Patricia	CA1860	32E,37,64E,64C,48
del Grazia, Nicolas M.	AR0200	32E,41,48,64C
Deloach, Doris	TX0300	48,64B
DeMartino, Louis	OR1050	42,48,64C
Demsey, Karen B.	NJ1400	64A,48,12,11,12A
Denza, William M.	OH0500	64A,48,64E,64C
Desgagne, Alain	AI0150	64C,48
DeVoll, James	MN0750	64A,48
Dicker, Michael H.	IL1150	11,48,64D
Dietz, William D.	AZ0500	64D,48
Diggs, David B.	PA1950	13A,13B,37,64B,48
Dikeman, Philip	TN1850	64A,41,48
Dirlam, Richard	MN0350	64E,48
Dobbs, Wendell B.	WV0400	11,13,41,48,64A
Dodson, Brent	IA1750	63,64,37,60B,48
Doggett, Cynthia Krenzel	IA0200	12A,20,48,64C,64E
Dove-Pellito, Glennda M.	NY3730	48,64A
Doyle, Phillip	WA0250	64E,47,48
Draper, Michelle	MO1550	64A,48
Dreisbach, Paul C.	OH1000	64B,64D,64E,64C,48
Drucker, Naomi	NY1600	48,64C,42
Drury, William	MA1400	60,48
Dueitt, David P.	MS0420	37,48,64,65
Dumouchel, Michael	AI0150	64C,48
East, David	MS0320	37,47,48,63C
Eastin, Brad	CO0275	64E,48,46,47,64C
Eckerty, Michael	IA1350	64D,32C,37,60,48
Edwards, George L.	DC0350	11,32C,48,64A,64C
Edwards, Ross	AG0600	64C,48
Eikrem, Jeanne	OR1300	64A,48
Eis, Jeremiah	WI0770	34,48,47,60B,63
Eischeid, Susan	GA2150	64B,11,48,42
Eisenreich, Samuel	FL0050	64,48,64E
Eldridge, Ronda	TX2750	11,20,48,64A
Eller, Joseph M.	SC1110	64C,48
Ellis, Kim S.	TX1400	37,64C,64E,48
Erickson, Scott	KY0950	48,64B,64D,64E
Ericson, Michael	IL3500	13B,13C,64B,48
Erskine, Bruce	TN1680	48,64A
Espinoza, Dannel	NY3350	64E,48
Evans, David H.	AR0300	13,11,12A,32,48
Fagaly, Sam W.	IL0800	64E,47,29,48
Farmer, Katherine	GA0940	48,64A
Farrell, Heidi	SD0600	64B,48
Feinstein, Allen G.	MA1450	13,10F,60,37,48
Felber, Jill	CA5060	64A,48
Feller, David E.	UT0350	11,12A,48,64,31
Fetz, Teun	OR0200	12A,65,48
Feves, Julie	CA0510	42,64D,48,35A
Fields, Alex	SC0200	48,64,72
Fink, Marc	WI0815	48,64B
Fisher, Mickey	GA0300	64B,64C,64E,48
Flemming, Joy	NH0150	64D,48
Flores, Yasmin A.	AL1250	64C,64E,64D,48,13B
Floyd, Angeleita S.	IA1600	48,64A
Flygare, Karla	WA1000	48,64A
Ford, William	MN1250	64E,48
Forget, Normand	AI0150	64B,48
Forsyth, Paul	LA0550	64E,48
Forsythe, Jada P.	MS0570	11,64C,64E,37,48
Foster, Robert	GA0250	13,10,11,47,48
Foulk, Lin	MI2250	63B,15,41,48,49
Franks, Carol	AL1050	13,64A,48
Fulbright, Marshall T.	CA2550	38,51,48,62,63
Fuller, Melanie	GA2130	64A,48
Furman, Carol	ME0150	64C,48
Futterer, Karen	AR0200	12A,48,64A
Futterer, Kenneth	AR0200	10,48,64B,64D,64E
Gaarder, Jon	DE0150	48,64D
Gallagher, Mark	MD0350	64C,48,13,12A
Gamso, Nancy M.	OH2000	11,29A,48,64,32E
Garcia, Nora Lee	FL1800	64A,48
Gargrave, Eric	RI0101	11,13A,29A,48,13B
Garrison, Karen H.	AL0200	11,64A,48
Garritson, Paul W.	MO1800	64C,48
Gartshore, Donelda	AG0250	64A,48,67C
Gately, Doug T.	VA1475	47,48,29,64
Gholson, James	TN1680	48,64C
Gilchrest, Suzanne M.	NY2750	64A,48
Gilliam, Laura	DC0100	48,67C
Gillis, Glen	AJ0150	60,32C,37,48,64E
Gilpin, Shirley	NC2000	64A,48
Giovannetti, Geralyn	UT0050	13,48,64B
Glaze, Richard T.	FL2100	60,32,37,48,64
Goacher, Stephen	TX1100	60,48,64,47,29
Goddard, John	AG0350	48,65
Godsil, Dan	IL1350	66A,48,49
Goldberg, Marc	NY1900	48
Goldberg, Marc	NY0150	64D,42,48
Goodberg, Robert	WI0825	41,48,64A
Goode, Elizabeth	GA2150	64A,48,13
Gordon, Daniel J.	NY3775	64E,11,37,48
Grabb, Henry	PA3600	64B,48
Graham, Jack	IA1800	64C,48
Graham, John	AR0810	37,64E,64C,48
Grass, Mahlon O.	PA2050	12A,48,64B,64C,64E
Gray, Donavon D.	CA0250	37,44,49,32,48
Greitzer, Ian	RI0200	64C,64E,48
Gresham, David	IL1150	48,64C
Grigorov, Liisa Ambegaokar	NY2650	64A,48
Grycky, Eileen J.	DE0150	64A,41,48
Gythfeldt, Marianne	DE0150	64C,48
Hall, Doris S.	AL0010	11,48,64A,64E
Hall, W. Randall	WV0300	64B,64C,64E,48
Hampton, Neal	MA0500	60,37,38,41,48
Hand, Judith	LA0350	48,64A
Hannigan, Mary	PA0950	48,64A
Harrington, Allen	AC0100	64D,64E,42,48
Harris, Debora	MN1120	64A,48
Harris, J. David	IL3300	64C,48,41
Hartline, Nicholas	TN0260	64C,48
Hartung, Colleen	PA3150	64C,48
Hawkins, Sherwood M.	FL1550	64B,48
Heilmair, Barbara	OR0850	12A,41,42,64C,48
Heller, Marsha	NJ0800	48,64B
Helman, Shandra K.	ID0100	64C,13C,48,20,64E
Hemke, Frederic J. B.	SD0400	47,48,64,29A
Henry, Anna W.	TX2350	64A,48
Hewitt, Eric	MA0350	48
Higbee, David	KS0150	48,64E
Hill, Harry H.	SC0850	11,12A,64C,64E,48
Hinckley, Jaren S.	UT0050	64C,11,48
Hindson, Harry	MN1700	64D,64E,48
Hinkley, Brian	MD0500	63,49,48
Hinson, James M.	IL2910	48,64C,64E,42
Hobbs, Julie	KY1450	64A,48
Hodges, Brian	KY0250	48,64A,64C
Hollinger, Lowell	MS0350	11,13A,32C,48,64E
Holsinger, David	TN0850	60B,10,48
Holton, Arthur	CA4300	37,64C,48,49
Honda, Lorence	CA1850	13,48,64,29
Hooten, David M.	TX1600	64C,11,48,64A
Horn, Lawrence C.	MS0560	11,32A,48,64
Horne, Robin	FL1430	64A,48
Hryniewicki, Donna	MN0625	64A,48
Huff, Douglas M.	IL3500	64D,12A,11,48
Huff, Lori	CA0630	13A,11,48,64E,32
Hunt, Douglas	CA4300	49,48,63D
Ibrahim, Michael	WV0750	64E,32E,48
Ingle, Jennet	IN1750	64B,48
Isaac, James	KS0570	48,64
Ishigaki, Miles M.	CA0810	48,64C,41,11,14C
Jackson, Stephen	IL0420	48,11,20,41,47
Jacobs, Jay N.	LA0350	37,41,42,48
Jacobson, Barbara	FL0800	64A,48
Jagow, Shelley	OH2500	64E,48,37
James, Kortney	WI0750	64A,32,48
Jeffrey, Wayne	AB0060	35A,37,49,48,63B
Jelle, Lisa A.	OH0350	64A,48
Jenkins, Cara M.	NC1250	64B,48
Jessup, Carol A.	TX3500	48,64C
Joffe, Edward	NJ0825	41,47,48,64
Johns, Michael	PA3200	48,37,42
Johnson, Deborah S.	NE0300	13A,11,48,64A,13B
Johnson, Henry	GA1600	36,66A,46,47,48
Johnson, Rebecca R.	IL0800	64A,48
Johnson, Roger	CA2550	38,51,48
Johnston, Stephen K.	VA1350	37,48,64C
Jones, Adah T.	TX3175	48,64A
Jones, Harold	NY2200	64A,48
Jones, Herman	SC0150	11,37,47,48,64
Jones, Lorraine	GA0200	48,64A
Jones-Reus, Angela	GA2100	64A,48
Jorgensen, Elaine	UT0190	11,41,48,64A
Jorgensen, Kristen	NY3770	11,48,64A,62A
Jorgensen, Trevor	NY3770	37,64,48,11
Kagy, Tamara K.	OH2140	64A,48
Kairies, Joy E.	TX0550	64A,34C,11,48
Kalman, Zoltan	AG0050	64C,48,64E,37
Kane, Trudy	FL1900	64A,41,48
Kani, Robin	WA1050	13A,41,48,63B
Kappy, David	PA2450	41,48,64A
Karr, Kathy	KY0450	48,64A
Karr, Kristen	KY1500	64A,48
Kean, Kristen	KY0550	64A,13A,13,42,48
Keeble, Jonathan	IL3300	64A,48
Keech, Christopher	MI1985	64C,64E,37,48,47
Keller, Karlton	CA3400	13,47,48,49,12
Kelley, Cheryl K.	MN1280	13,32,48,64D
Kerr, Stephen P.	VA0650	63,37,60B,48
Kerstetter, Tod	KS0650	13A,48,64C,13B
Kestenberg, Abe	AI0150	48,64C,64E,64A
Kibler, Lea F.	SC0400	64A,48
Kiec, Michelle	PA1750	64,13,64C,64E,48
Kim, Bonnie	VA0150	64A,48
Kim, Wonkak	TN1450	64C,48,41
Kirkbride, Jerry E.	AZ0500	48,64C
Kirkpatrick, Christopher	MT0400	64C,48
Kirkpatrick, Linda M.	MD0520	60,37,41,48,64A
Klazek, Merrie	AG0170	63A,48,49
Klemp, Merilee I.	MN0050	12A,12,64B,48,40
Klevan, Robert B.	CA5070	48,46
Knipschild, Ann	AL0200	13,48,64B,64E
Koch, Elizabeth	AA0035	64A,48
Kolbeck, Karl F.	NE0700	12A,72,48,64,11
Kolkay, Peter	TN1850	41,64D,48
Koons, Keith	FL1800	64C,48
Koprowski, Melissa	WI0803	64C,48

Index by Area of Teaching Interest

Name	Code	Areas
Kostek, Patricia	AB0150	48,64C
Koziol, John	MN0800	47,48
Kramer, Atossa	KY0300	13C,48,64C,66A,67C
Krebs, Jesse D.	MO1780	11,64C,13D,48
Kuehn, John W.	PA1600	32,64C,48,72
Kuhl, Mary	TX1750	48,64
Kukec, Catherine	IL1900	11,41,47,50,48
Labadorf, Tom	CT0050	64C,48
Lamar, Jackie B.	AR0850	47,48,64E
Lampidis, Anna	NC2205	64B,48
Lane, Timothy	WI0803	14,48,64A
Large, Karen McLaughlin	KS0650	13,11,64A,13A,48
Larner, James M.	IN1100	12A,48,10E,64A,29A
Larocque, Jacques	AI0220	10,41,48,64E,34
Larragoity, Ingrid	AR0300	37,32E,13B,48
Lascell, Ernest D.	NY3730	48,64C,64E
Laughlin, Jim	TX0100	13A,12A,48,64C,64E
LeClair, Paul	VT0400	13,12A,48,37,64E
Lee, Cassandra	TN1850	41,48,64C,42
Lee, D. Thomas	CA5030	37,48
Lefevre, Donald	TX3750	37,64E,48
Leisring, Laura	VA0250	48,64A,64D,41,64C
Lemmons, Frederick	NC1250	64C,64E,48
Lessly, Chris Ann	IN1025	32,41,48,64C,64E
Levinsky, Gail B.	PA3150	48,64E,32E
Levitin, Susan	IL2750	48,64A
Levy, Kathryn	NC2500	48,64A
Libby, Cynthia Green	MO0775	13,64B,64D,20,48
Liebowitz, Marian L.	CA4100	11,41,48,64C,35B
Lillya, Ann	GA0050	64B,48
Lindberg, John E.	MN1000	12A,12C,48,64D,72
Lindhal, Gregory	FL0700	37,48,60B
Linklater, Fraser	AC0100	63A,32E,37,48,60B
Lipman, William	TX0550	12A,64C,64E,11,48
Little, Deanna	TN1100	64A,48
Lochrie, Daniel	TN0100	64C,48
Loewy, Susanna L.	PA1750	11,48,64A
Lowe, Shannon R.	GA2150	64D,48,13
Luce, Brian A.	AZ0500	64A,48
Lunte, Sandra K.	LA0770	13A,64A,48
Lytle, Stephen	OH1450	37,48
Magnanini, Luciano	FL1900	41,48,64D
Mangrum, Martin	AI0150	64D,48
Marling, Chisato Eda	NY2650	64E,48
Marrs, Leslie	IA0550	64A,48,13A
Marshall, Elizabeth	WI0100	64A,48
Martin, Jennifer	CA1510	32E,11,13,48,63C
Martin, Sharon	MN1700	64A,48
Martins, David J.	MA0400	48
Mason, Colin M.	TX2800	47,11,64E,29,48
Masters, Suzanna	VA1580	64C,11,13A,64E,48
Matalon, Leon	CA0200	13A,47,53,48
Matathias, Robin	NH0150	64A,48
Matchael, Michael	TX3360	37,48,64
Mathews, Robert P.	CA6050	13,64,48,70
Matsukawa, Daniel	PA0850	48,64D
Maugans, Stacy	IN1750	48,64E,13B
Maurer-Davis, Jill	CT0050	64A,48
McAllister, Elizabeth	NC1750	12A,41,48,64C,64E
McArthur, Lisa R.	KY0400	13,48,64A,12A,12F
McCarthy, Charles J.	CA1020	64,48
McClellan, David Ray	GA2100	64C,48
McColley, Stacey	FL0800	64C,48,13
McGee, Blake Anthony	WY0200	12,64C,48
McGill, Anthony	NY2250	64C,48
McGinnis, Barry E.	SC0900	64,12A,29,48,29A
McGovern, Timothy S.	IL3300	64D,48,41
McKeown, Kevin	CA5020	48
McKinney, Roger W.	NJ0175	64C,12A,48
McMurtery, John M.	IL3500	64A,48
McNerney, Kathleen	ME0200	64B,48
McWayne, Dorli	AK0150	48,64A,41
Meffert-Nelson, Karrin	MN0750	64C,37,48,32E,12A
Melia, Hal	OH0500	29A,29B,48
Mensch, Thomas	TX3370	37,41,63C,49,48
Mensh, Heather	TX3370	37,41,46,48,63D
Messersmith, Charles	SC0275	64C,48
Meyer, Frederick	WV0650	13,32,48,64B
Mezzadri, Danilo	MS0750	64A,12E,48
Mickey, Sarah	AR0600	37,48,64C,11
Miller, Michael	MI2250	13,48,64B
Milne, David	WI0845	29A,47,48,64E
Minnis, MaryBeth	MI0400	41,48,64D
Mitchell, Alan	MI0250	60,32,37,49,48
Montanaro, Donald	PA0850	48,64C
Moore, Julianna	MO1780	13,48,64A
Morales, Gary A.	PR0100	60,32,48,64C
Morales, Ricardo	PA0850	48
Moreau, Leslie M.	ID0050	64C,13A,13B,48
Morrison, Nicholas	UT0300	37,64C,48,41
Moss, Emily A.	NY0500	32,48,64D,60B
Mosteller, Sandra M.	TX3650	64,32E,48,20,31B
Munro, Anne	WV0550	64A,48,38,51
Murchison, Pamela	MD0350	64A,48,20,15
Murphy, Joseph M.	PA2150	48,64E,34A
Murray, Jane	RI0300	38,41,48,64B
Myers, Adam	TX3370	48,64C,64E
Nabb, David	NE0590	64,11,12A,48
Neidich, Charles	NY1900	64C,48
Nelson, Jennifer	WA1000	48,64C
Nelson, Pamela	NC1300	64A,48
Nelson, Paula	PA1550	64A,48
Nelson, Scott	VA1350	48,46,63A,37
Nesbit, James B.	VA0250	64E,48,29
Newell, Meri	MS0360	11,32,64,37,48
Nichol, John	MI0400	47,48,64E,29
Nicholas, Lauren P.	PA2450	64E,46,48
Nichols, Sara	MD0850	64A,48
Nolan, Denise G.	NH0110	48,64A,11,13C
Norton, Leslie	TN1850	41,48,63B,49
Nunemaker, Richard	TX3450	64C,48
Oberbrunner, John	NY1550	64A,48
O'Connor, Kelli A.	RI0300	48,64C
Oehler, Donald L.	NC2410	41,42,43,48,64C
Ohlsson, Eric	FL0850	48,64B
O'Keefe, Patrick	WI0845	64C,48
Oldham, Barbara	NY2750	49,63B,48
Olin, Marissa H.	MI2000	48,64A
Olivieri, Mark A.	NY1550	10,13,20G,29,48
Olson, Craig	WY0130	64E,48,64A,40,46
Olson, Jeffrey K.	GA2150	64C,48,64E
Oltman, Dwight	OH0200	48,38
O'Neil, Lorne W.	TX3525	11,41,48,64
O'Neill, Jill L.	SC1200	11,64A,48,14C,41
Osborn, James	NY4450	47,63A,48
Osland, Miles	KY1450	47,64E,29,53,48
Ott, Hal J.	WA0050	12A,41,48,64A,67D
Overmier, Juliana	OK0300	64A,48
Oviedo, Javier	CT0800	64E,48
Owens, Parthena	OK0750	48,64A,32E
Oxford, Todd	TX3175	64E,48
Oyen, David W.	KY0900	13,48,64D
Padilla, Margaret	WI0825	64,48
Paglialonga, Phillip O.	FL0100	64C,41,48,13A,13B
Paliga, Mitch L.	IL2050	64E,29A,41,47,48
Paluzzi, Rebecca Lile	TN0500	48,64A
Parker-Harley, Jennifer	SC1110	64A,48
Parr, J. D.	KS0050	37,47,48,64,29
Pastin, John R.	NJ1050	37,60,29,46,48
Patnode, Matthew A.	ND0350	64E,64A,29,48,47
Patterson, Vincent L.	MD0550	48,64C
Paul, Randall S.	OH2500	64C,29,48,11
Pedrini, Jamie J.	CA3500	64A,48
Peeples, Georgia	OH2150	12A,64D,15,48
Pelischek, Jeff	KS0550	11,37,48,64C,64E
Peltz, Charles	MA1400	48,60B
Peterson, Russell	MN0600	47,48,64D,64E,35G
Pham, Danh	WA1150	32D,60B,48
Pherigo, Johnny L.	FL1800	11,41,49,48,63B
Phillips, Timothy S.	AL1050	64C,12,48
Polk, Janet	NH0350	64D,48
Polley, Jo Ann	MN1450	38,48,64C
Pool, Scott	TX3500	64D,13,48,11,64E
Pope, George	OH2150	48,64A
Potter, Valerie	NM0450	64A,41,48
Powell, William E.	CA0510	48,64C,42,13E
Prather, Belva W.	MO0775	60B,48,64A
Price, Berkeley	CA0200	13,37,48,64
Pursell, Anthony	TX2750	37,41,48,60,63C
Pyne, James	OH1850	48,64C
Qian, Jun	TX0300	64C,48
Qian, Jun	MN1450	42,64C,48
Ramey, Maxine	MT0400	64C,48
Ramirez, Catherine	MN1450	13A,64A,48,42,13B
Raney, Earl L.	MA2150	49,48,63A
Rawls, J. Archie	MS0580	13,11,64,46,48
Rebbeck, Lyle	AA0040	47,48,64,53
Reed, Thomas T.	OH0100	10F,64C,64E,48
Reese, Marc B.	FL1125	63A,49,41,42,48
Register, P. Brent	PA0700	12A,48,64A,64B,64D
Reid, Lynda L.	TX2350	13A,32B,37,48,64C
Reighley, Kimberly	PA3600	64A,48
Reinoso, Crystal Hearne	NY3717	13B,48,64C,15
Resnick, David	IA0250	10B,10F,13A,37,48
Reyes, Ysmael	CO0650	64A,41,48
Reynolds, Anne	IN1650	48,64A
Rhodes, Debra	NE0300	12A,64,48
Rhodes, Ruth	IL3450	48,64C,32
Richards, Jeanne	MN1620	64A,67C,48
Richmond, James	VA0150	64E,48
Richtmeyer, Debra A.	IL3300	64E,48,41
Ridilla, Andrea	OH1450	64B,48
Rife, Jean	MA1200	48,63B
Riley, Gregory E.	PA3600	64E,46,48
Riner, Nicole	WY0200	64A,14C,32G,48
Ring, Eric	MO1950	64D,48,13C
Rippe, Allen	TN1680	48,64E,67C
Rivera-Vega, Salvador	PR0100	11,32,48,64E
Roberts, Elizabeth 'Ibby'	VA1550	64D,48
Romeo, James	CA4050	11,37,47,48,29
Rose, Gwendolyn	MI2250	13,48,64D
Rose, Saxton	NC1650	48,64D,41
Ross, Laura A.	TN1100	48,64B
Running, Timothy	PA1750	60,11,48,64A
Saguiguit, Leo C.	MO1800	64E,48
Sakakeeny, George	OH1700	64D,48,41
Salerno, John	WI0808	13,10,47,48,29
Sandberg, Scott	ND0400	64,13B,13C,11,48
Satterfield, Sarah	FL0365	12A,64A,11,42,48
Scanling, Paul F.	GA1550	64,37,42,48
Schafer, Carl	CA0450	32,48,64
Scherline, Janine	NY3775	64C,48
Schiavone, David C.	NY0400	47,48,64C,64E
Schiavone, David C.	NY3717	64E,48
Schlacks, Mary M.	OH1650	14,48,64C,11
Schloss, David Lee	TX1725	64,48
Schneeloch-Bingham, Nancy	NC0050	64A,48,32E
Schroeder, Angela	AA0100	37,48,60B
Schuberg, Margaret	MT0400	13,48,64A
Schulze-Johnson, Virginia	NJ0300	41,47,48,64A,42
Schwaegler, Susan	IL0100	64C,48
Schwartz, Richard I.	VA1750	13,48,64C,10
Schwoebel, Sandy	AZ0480	64A,48,67D,35A
Scott, Jan	LA0350	32B,48,64B,64D,64C
Scruggs, Richard J.	TN0250	11,13B,41,48,64E
Seiler, Robert	NH0350	47,48,64C
Shanley, Helen A.	TX0300	48,64A
Shanley, Richard A.	TX0300	48,64C
Sheffield, Robert	AB0060	64C,48
Shikaly, Al	IN0400	64E,48,66
Shipley, Lori R.	VA0500	48,12A,13A,64A,41
Sholl, Martha P.	NY3730	64A,64A
Shorter, Lloyd	DE0150	48,64B,12A
Shuter, Cindy	AI0150	64A,48
Singer, David	NJ0800	41,48,64C,11
Sintchak, Matthew A.	WI0865	64E,29,43,47,48
Sizemore, Mark	KY1400	48,64,46
Slater, Sheri	MO0400	11,48,64C
Smith, Diane	NY3350	64A,48
Smith, John David	DE0150	63B,48,49
Smith, Joshua	OH0600	64A,48
Smith, Kristen	OH2250	64D,48
Snyder, Mark S.	CT0800	64B,48,11
Soelberg, Diane	ID0060	48,64B,60
Sooy, Julie	MI1050	64A,48
Sopata, Kimberly	IL3100	48,64A
Sorton, Bailey	OH1200	64B,48
Sparrow, Sharon W.	MI1750	64A,48
Specht, Barbara	OH0950	11,38,64C,64E,48
Speck, Gary A.	OH1450	60,32C,48
Sperrazza, Rose U.	IL2150	64C,48,13H
Spittal, Robert	WA0400	37,11,42,48,60B
Splittberger-Rosen, Andrea	WI0850	48,64C
Stanford, Thomas S.	OR0850	64C,12,48,41
Steele, Stacey G.	PA3100	32A,32B,48,64A
Stees, Barrick R.	OH0600	64D,48
Steltenpohl, Anna C.	NY3730	64B,48
Stephenson, Michael	NC1550	64,48,64E
Sternberg, Jo-Ann	CT0800	64C,48
Stewart, Stanley W.	MS0200	11,37,47,49,48
Stimpert, Elisabeth	PA0950	64C,48
Stodd, Janet	IL0100	48,64A
Stoffan, George C.	MI1750	64C,48,42,32E
Stone, Julie	MI0600	64A,48
Storochuk, Allison M.	MO0775	64C,13,48
Stowe, Samuel P.	NC0850	11,48,64A

Index by Area of Teaching Interest

Name	ID	Codes
Streeter, David	IN0905	46,48
Strefeler, Jamie	FL1800	64B,48
Sugihara, Masahito	IL3100	48,64E
Sweger, Keith	IN0150	48,64D,42
Sydow, Holly	PA2250	13C,48
Sylvern, Craig	NH0150	64E,34,32F,10,48
Talley, Keith M.	OK1250	64E,32,48,34
Tangarov, Vanguel G.	TX3175	64C,48
Tatman, Neil E.	AZ0500	64B,48
Taylor, Caroline	AR0500	48,64,32E
Taylor, Stephen	NY1900	48
Taylor, Susan Lynnette	IN0100	32E,37,48,60B
Teter, Francis	CA1750	11,37,38,48,64
Thibeault, Anna	GA0950	64A,48
Thomas, Susan H.	RI0300	41,48,64A,34
Thomason-Redus, Caen		48,64A
Thompson, Robert	WI0825	11,41,48,64D
Thornton, Delores	WY0050	48,64A
Thorpe, Allan	AB0090	13,48,64D,13A,37
Threlkeld, David M.	KY1425	11,12A,47,48,64
Tidwell, Dallas	KY1500	64C,48,42
Timm, Laurance	CA0815	37,48,64B
Timmons, Leslie	UT0300	32A,32B,64A,48,41
Titus, Jamie	MO0050	64A,12,13,48
Torres, Michael Rene	OH1650	64E,48,10
Tse, Joel	OH2300	64A,48
Turanchik, Thomas	NC0750	64B,64C,64D,48
Turizziani, Robert	WV0800	64C,60B,48
Turner, Dean W.	WV0200	48,64
Turner, Denise	NM0450	64D,48
Turpen, Jennifer	WY0200	13A,13B,48
Turpin, Mike H.	TX1350	11,48,64
Tyson, Liana	AR0350	64A,11,48
Umiker, Robert C.	AR0700	48,64C,64E
Vacchi, Steve	OR1050	64D,42,48
Van Regenmorter, Paula	LA0450	64,12A,11,48,20
VanDessel, Joan	MI0520	12A,13D,37,64C,48
Variego, Jorge	ND0600	10,13B,48,64C,64B
Via, Kelly	GA0050	64A,48
Voorhees, Jerry L.	LA0650	48,64D,72
Vore, Wallis W.	OH2250	64C,48
Wachmann, Eric	IA1800	13,64C,48
Wacker, Therese M.	PA1600	64A,48,13
Waddell, Charles F.	OH1850	48,63B
Wagner, Lawrence R.	PA3250	60,38,48,64C
Waldecker, Todd	TN1100	64C,48
Walker, Christopher G.	GA0150	11,32,64,48
Walker, Kerry E.	CT0800	32,48,64A
Walt, Stephen	MA2250	48,64D,43,41
Walters, Mark A.	CO0350	60,11,48,37,64
Warren, Tasha	VA1550	64C,48
Watabe, Junichiro	AK0150	64C,64E,48,37,46
Watkins, Mark	ID0060	47,48,64E
Weait, Christopher	OH0350	64D,48
Webster, Thomas R.	TX0600	60A,49,48,13B
Weigand, John	WV0750	48,64C
Weiss, Louise	IL1050	13A,32B,48,64A,66C
Weiss, Timothy	OH1700	60,48
Weremchuk, George	FL1800	64E,48
Werth, Kay	KS0350	64B,64D,48,64A
West, Charles W.	VA1600	48,64C,60
White, Lynn	NC0050	48,64,67
Whitelaw, Ian	CA5040	48
Whitmore, Michael	OK0450	32E,48,64
Whitmore, Michael R.	OK0300	48,64C,64E
Widder, David R.	VA1700	12A,37,48,64C
Wilkinson, Fiona	AG0500	48,64A
Willett, Dan L.	MO1800	64B,48
Williams, Jane	IA1800	64E,48
Williamson, Melissa	KS1200	64A,48,13
Wilson, Dwayne	NC0300	48,60,65
Wilson, Jacqueline M.	WI0803	64D,48,13B,13C
Wilson, Jeanne	NJ0825	64A,48
Wilson, Leah	SC0050	48,64A
Wincenc, Carol	NY1900	64A,48
Wirt, Ronald	GA0550	13,48,64D,10
Wise, Sherwood W.	NY0700	64B,48,13,64D,42
Wolbers, Mark	AK0100	60,12A,32C,64C,48
Wolf, Matthew	MI0500	48,13,60,32H
Wolfe, George	IN0150	64E,48
Wong, Bradley	MI2250	48,64C
Wooden, Lori L.	OK1330	64D,41,38,42,48
Woodhams, Richard	PA0850	48,64B
Woolly, Kimberly A.	MS0750	64D,12A,41,48,72
Worzbyt, Jason W.	PA1600	64D,13,37,48
Wright, Scott	KY1450	64C,41,48
Wytko, Anna Marie	KS0650	64E,13A,48
Yasinitsky, Ann	WA1150	48,64A
Yeager, Richard F.	MO0850	37,48,64
Yost, Regina Helcher	SC0275	64A,48
Young, Keith R.	PA1600	48,64E,47
Zaev, Pance	NE0450	64C,64E,48
Zeisler, Dennis J.	VA1000	11,37,64C,48
Zoro, Eugene S.	WA1250	48,64
Zugger, Gail Lehto	OH0350	64C,48

Brass Ensemble

Name	ID	Codes
Aagaard, J. Kjersgaard	WI0842	13,11,36,37,49
Ackley, James	SC1110	49,63A
Acosta, Darren	RI0300	49,63C
Adams, James M.	ND0600	35G,37,47,49,53
Adams, Richard	MI2250	10,49,13L,13,10F
Adler, John	CO0950	63A,49
Alessi, Joseph	NY1900	63D,63C,49
Alexander, Joe L.	LA0250	10,13,63D,10A,49
Alexander, Lois L.	MI2120	63D,49,12,32
Allen, John	OK0750	63C,46,49
Allen, Jonathan	IA1550	49,63C
Allen, Mark	OR1000	37,49,63A,63C,63B
Almeida, John	FL1800	63A,49
Aloisio, Gerard S.	MN1000	11,49,63C
Amend, Jerome	IN1010	63A,49
Anderson, Matthew T.	SC0400	63D,49
Anthony, Johnny	MS0350	32C,37,49,63
Aquilanti, Giancarlo	CA4900	13,10F,60,37,49
Ardovino, Joseph	AL1200	63A,37,47,49
Armstrong, James E.	NC2700	63A,13A,37,46,49
Arndt, Michael J.	TN1100	63A,49
Arnold, Edwin P.	PA1450	32E,37,60B,48,49
Ash, Corey	TX1100	37,49,63A,32E,60B
Ashton, Graham	NY3785	49,63A
Asper, Lynn K.	MI0850	49,63A
Aspnes, Jane	AK0150	63B,49
Austin, Kenneth L.	IL3100	13,32C,37,49,46
Avitsur, Haim	PA3600	63C,49
Bairos, Monte	CA1560	37,41,48,49,50
Baldwin, David B.	MN1623	41,49,63A
Bamonte, David	OR0850	41,42,63A,49
Barlar, Douglas	FL0670	12A,63D,49,32E
Barrow, Gary	AR0200	49,63A,63B
Bartee, Neale	AR0110	60,12A,49,63C
Bass, Michael	MS0580	11,49,37,63
Batchelder, Donald	NJ0800	63A,49
Bauer, Paul D.	IL2200	49,63C
Bean, Scott	WI0810	63D,12A,11,49
Beatty, David	CA0250	47,49,35,63C
Beaulac, Stephane	AI0150	63A,49
Beghtol, Jason W.	MS0570	37,13A,46,63,49
Bekeny, Amanda K.	OH0100	63A,49,11
Berger, Gene P.	IN0150	49,41,63B
Berinbaum, Martin C.	AB0100	60B,37,49,63A
Bernard, Gilles	NJ0825	13,12A,49,63C,63D
Bernatis, William	NV0050	13A,13,49,63B
Betts, L. David	OH0755	63,49
Bing, William W.	CA0500	37,47,49,63A
Birch, Robert M.	DC0100	49,63A,37,48
Birkemeier, Richard	CA0825	11,63A,49
Bishop, Darcie	MS0350	11,41,49,63A
Black, Phillip	KS1450	49,63D
Blackmore, Lisa	MO0650	49,63A,63B
Blanchard, Jeff L.	OH2140	63A,47,49,29
Boccia, James	NH0150	63A,49
Bock, Stan	OR1300	63C,63D,49
Boehmke, Erik A.	IL1600	63A,66,47,37,49
Bogard, Rick G.	TX3500	63A,49
Bolton, Chuck	OR1150	32,37,49,63D
Bone, Lloyd E.	WV0350	12A,49,63,37,11
Bonnett, Kurt	TX3535	49,63A,63B
Borror, Ronald	CT0650	41,49,63C,67E,55
Botts, Nathan	VT0050	11,29,49,63,67E
Bourgois, Louis	KY0750	11,12A,49,63D,34
Bowen, Charles Kevin	NC2500	37,47,49,63A
Boyd, John W.	TX2550	49,11
Brant, Aaron	OH2250	63B,49
Brekke, Jeremy	ND0350	63,37,49,63A,47
Brevig, Per	NY1900	49,63C
Brevig, Per	NY2250	49,63C
Brewer, Robert G.	CO0250	32C,63D,49
Brickens, Nathaniel O.	TX3510	63C,49
Bright, Robert M.	AR0700	49,63A
Brink, Brian S.	FL0800	63C,49,34
Britt, Mark E.	SC0750	63C,49,32E
Brown, David C.	UT0050	63A,49
Brown, Tom	WI0810	11,41,49,63A,63B
Brownell, Jack	AF0050	49,63D,63C
Brownlow, James A.	TX3515	11,12A,49,63A,20
Brubeck, Dave W.	FL1300	13,37,47,63C,49
Bryant, Steven	TX3510	49,63D
Buchman, Heather	NY1350	38,49,51,48,60B
Buckmaster, Matthew	NC0750	63D,29,63C,49,32
Buckner, James R.	AR0300	49,63A,32E
Budde, Paul J.	MN0750	63D,49,32C
Bumcrot, Charles	NJ0700	63A,49,11
Burdick, Daniel	PA1200	63C,63D,49,11
Burke, Larry	FL0800	32B,63D,29A,49,35A
Burnett, Rodger	WA1000	49,63B
Burt, Jack W.	ME0440	13C,49,63A
Butler, Barbara	IL2250	63A,49
Buttery, Gary A.	RI0300	11,47,49,63D,29A
Cadelago, Harry	CA3250	37,38,60B,49
Calkin, Joshua	NE0700	63D,37,11,49,63C
Camp, James L.	GA0490	37,49,63B,63C,63D
Campbell, Bob	NC0850	63B,49
Campbell, John	VA0750	63A,49
Campbell, Robert	NC1900	63B,49
Carlson, Andrea	SD0050	63B,49
Carlton, David	WI0150	49,62C,62D
Carroll, Edward	CA0510	49,63A
Carroll, John	TX1900	63A,49,37,41,47
Casey, Michael R.	MO0775	49,63A,60,54
Cecco, Jerry	MA0260	47,49
Chasanov, Elliot L.	IL3300	63C,49,41
Chasin, Richard	CA5355	63A,49
Chemay, Frank	LA0700	10,63D,10F,11,49
Chen, Jay	OR0450	60B,49,37,63A
Chen, Jay	OR0700	63A,49
Clark, Jim	TX2955	63C,49,63D
Clark, Jonathan	MA0150	11,49,63A
Clark, Norman Alan	GA1400	11,37,49,64
Clark, William F.	CO0830	47,63D,13,49,29
Classen, Andrew B.	IA0550	47,49,63A,29
Cline, Gilbert D.	CA2250	63A,49,29,67E,63B
Cloutier, Daniel	TN1710	49,63C
Coale, Dean	OK0300	32E,49,63C,63D
Cobb, Kevin D.	NY3790	63A,49,42
Cobb, Kevin	NY1900	63A,49
Cofer, R. Shayne	IL2150	32,37,49
Cole, Robert	PA3650	34A,34B,49,63B,72
Collins, Zachary	PA1600	63D,12A,13B,49
Compton, Paul R.	OK0800	63C,63D,47,49
Conklin, Raymond L.	KY0950	49,63C,63D
Cook, Wayne E.	WI0825	49,63A
Cooke, David	IN0905	38,60B,49,63C
Cooper, David	WI0840	47,49,63A,11,29A
Cooper, Joseph	TX3100	63A,49
Cord, John T.	TX2960	63A,49
Couch, Roy L.	OK0150	37,63D,49,32E
Cox, Allan	TN1850	63A,49,41
Cox, Bruce	SC0200	32C,49,63A
Cox, Gregory	AB0060	63C,49
Craig, Mary Ann	NJ0800	32,37,63D,49
Craswell, Brandon	GA2100	63A,49
Curley, Jason	NY1400	60B,63B,37,49,32E
Curnow, Jeffrey	PA0850	49
Curry, Jeffrey P.	NE0040	11,13C,32,37,49
D'Addio, Daniel F.	CT0050	13,32,37,49,63A
Daniels, William B.	KY1100	32B,37,47,49,63
Daussat, David	TX3525	63D,49
Davis, Garnett R.	TN1850	63D,49
Davis, Joyce	FL1850	49,63A
Davis, Ronald	SC1110	11,49,63D
Davison, Michael A.	VA1500	11,29,46,47,49
Dawson, Bradley J.	KS0350	47,49,63A,29
Dean, Allan	CT0850	49,63A
DeBoer, Angela	TN1100	63B,49,13A,13B,13C
DeBoer, Paul	NY1700	63,12A,49
Decker, Charles	TN1450	63A,41,63,49
DeGoti, Mark D.	AL0200	63A,49,11
Del Vecchio, Peter H.	VA1850	63,49,47
Derome, Denys	AI0150	63B,49
Devito, Albert	AI0200	49,63C
DeWitt, Timothy L.	WV0050	49,63A,13E,63B,63C
Diaz, Oscar	TX2960	63C,49
Dickey, Nathaniel H.	MN0600	37,63C,63D,32E,49

Name	Code	Areas
Dickinson, Christian M.	PA1600	13,49,63C,60B
DiMartino, Gabriel V.	NY4150	49,63A
Dimick, Glen M.	IN1650	63D,41,49
DiSanti, Theodore A.	PA3000	63A,47,49,13,10F
Dix, Trevor	AI0150	63C,49
Dobrzelewski, Jan	PA3600	63A,49
Dodson-Webster, Rebecca	PA2150	63B,13,12A,49
Dolske, Christopher C.	FL1550	63A,49,29A
Dorn, Mark	CO0150	37,63A,46,60B,49
Drew, John	FL0850	49,63C
Drobnak, Kenneth Paul	SD0500	63D,37,11,47,49
DuBeau, Peter	VA0250	63D,49
Dugan, Michael D.	WI0865	11,47,49,63C
Dunker, Amy	IA0250	13,10,63A,41,49
Dutton, Brent	CA4100	13,10F,10,49,63D
Dyess, J. Wayne	TX1400	37,47,63C,49
Eastep, Michael	AA0150	63D
Eaton, Daniel	MN1600	37,63D,49
Eberhardt, Allan	CO0275	47,63A,46,49,29
Edwards, Bradley W.	SC1110	63C,49
Eggers, Carter	MI0600	49,63A
Eisensmith, Kevin E.	PA1600	47,49,63A
Elliott, David	KY1450	49,63B
Elmen, Paul	MA0260	47,49
Elsey, Eddie L.	AL1250	49,13B,63C,63D
Engelke, Luis C.	MD0850	63A,49
Engstrom, Dale	CA1850	13A,37,49
Engstrom, Howard	AA0150	63A,49
Entzi, John A.	NC1250	63A,49
Erb, Andrew	PA3260	63A,63C,37,47,49
Everett, Micah P.	MS0700	63C,63D,13C,41,49
Everett, Paul	IN0150	49,63A,41
Fairbanks, Will	IL1050	37,63A,46,49,63B
Fairchild, Kay	GA0750	49,63
Fallin, Nicky G.	GA0250	37,32E,63A,49,60B
Falvey, Joseph	VA0150	63B,37,34G,32E,49
Famulare, Trever R.	PA3050	11,37,47,49,60
Farwell, Douglas G.	GA2150	63C,49,34,35C,35D
Faust, Randall E.	IL3500	63B,10,63,13,49
Feller, Robert	CA0350	11,37,49,63,60
Fensom, Chris	NC2420	63A,49
Few, Guy	AG0600	63A,49
Fienberg, Gary	NJ0175	63A,29A,47,49
Fifield, Glen	UT0300	13A,32A,32B,49,63A
Fleming, Ricky L.	NY3717	60B,37,47,49,63C
Foley, Joseph	RI0200	49,63A
Foulk, Lin	MI2250	63B,15,41,48,49
Fowler, Jonathon	PA3600	63D,49
Fox, Jason	NY3475	37,49,63
Foy, Leonard C.	IN0350	63A,49,29
Freas, Thomas	NY2200	49,63A
Fred Carrasquillo, Luis	PR0115	63C,49,41,42
Frederickson, Matthew	MO0650	63D,32E,49,63C
Freeman, Jeffrey J.	TX2100	11,63C,49,63D,34
Fritz, Benno P.	DC0100	37,49,60,11
Fulgham, Marc S.	MO1500	11,49,63A,63B
Funderburk, Jeffrey	IA1600	49,63D,72
Furman, John	ME0150	63A,49
Furry, Stephanie	GA0950	63B,49,33,11
Gaboury, Janine	MI1400	41,49,63B
Gallo, Reed P.	SC0800	37,60B,32E,63A,49
Galyean, Richard D.	VA1580	37,60B,49,63D,32E
Gardner, Ryan B.	OK0800	63A,49,46,42,47
Gavin, Charles	TX2700	41,49,63B
Gaynor, Rick	WI0845	63C,49,11
Gazda, Frank S.	DE0050	63D,37,49,63C,42
Geiger, Jeanne	CA0807	63C,49
Geyer, Charles	IL2250	63A,49
Gibbens, Tracey	WI0860	63C,63D,49
Gibble, David L.	FL1470	29,47,37,53,49
Gibson, Marilyn	LA0770	11,63A,49
Gibson, Robert	IA0100	47,49
Gier, David	IA1550	49,63C
Gillis, Richard	AC0100	63A,49
Godsil, Dan	IL1350	66A,48,49
Gookin, Larry D.	WA0050	60,37,49,63C
Gordon, Peter L.	NY2750	41,49,63B
Gould, Mark	NY1900	63A,49
Gowen, Dennis	ND0400	37,49,63A,63B,60
Grabois, Daniel	WI0815	32,49,63A
Granthan, Daniel	OH2250	63A,49
Gray, Donavon D.	CA0250	37,44,49,32,48
Gray, Harold R. 'Skip'	KY1450	63D,49,41
Gresham, Jonathon	KY1000	49,63A,41
Griffin, Larry	OH2000	60B,37,47,49,63A
Grodrian, Ericka	IN1750	11,13C,49,63B
Grose, Michael	OR1050	11,63D,49,42
Gross, Ernest H.	IL1300	37,49,60B,63D,12A
Gross, Steven	CA5060	63B,49
Guarneri, Mario	CA4150	49,53,63A
Guzik, Bernie	OK1450	63,49
Hacker, James	FL0700	63A,42,49
Hagarty, Scott	TX0550	63A,13A,13C,49,41
Hager, H. Stephen	TX3175	13A,13,49,63B
Hager, Lawson	TX0900	13,49,63B,41
Hahn, Marjorie	FL1300	63B,49,60
Hall, Jamie	OR1250	49,63A
Hall, Michael	VA1000	63D,49,63C
Hansen, Neil E.	WY0130	37,47,63A,32,49
Hanson, Frank E.	WI0865	11,49,63A
Hanson, Josef M.	NY4350	13A,49
Harbaugh, John	WA0050	29A,53,49,63A
Harcrow, Michael	PA2300	63B,49,13
Harmantas, Frank	AG0450	41,49
Harry, Don	NY1100	63D,49
Hartman, Kevin	WI0825	49,63A
Haskett, William	TX1600	49,63D,11
Hawkins, William	CA3460	13A,32A,49,63,29
Heath, Travis M.	IL2150	49,63A
Hedwig, Douglas F.	NY0500	49,63A,63D
Heidenreich, Christopher	MI2120	37,49,11,10F
Heim, D. Bruce	KY1500	63B,49,42
Helm, Jon E.	AA0040	13A,13,12A,63,49
Henniger, Henry J.	OR1050	49,63C
Henry, Eric L.	PA3150	63D,49
Henry, Kevin	PA3150	63C,49
Herlihy, John S.	MN1280	60B,49,37,46
Hernandez, Rene	MD0850	63A,49
Hesse, Marian	CO0950	63B,49
Hetzler, Mark	WI0815	63C,49
High, Eric	WI0750	63C,47,13,12,49
Hill, Douglas M.	GA1300	60B,32C,37,49,63A
Hinkley, Brian	MD0500	63,49,48
Hoelscher, Mark A.	WI0835	63C,63D,49
Hofer, Calvin	CO0225	32,37,49,63A,60B
Hoffman, Patrick	DE0050	63A,63B,13,11,49
Holcombe, Ross	WA0250	63C,46,49
Holton, Arthur	CA4300	37,64C,48,49
Holz, Ronald	KY0100	12,38,41,49,10
Horgan, Maureen A.	GA0850	63D,11,49,63C,29A
Howard, Vernon D.	OK1450	47,49,63C,63D,29
Hoyt, William	OH2150	49,63B
Huber, Wayne	CA1860	37,49,63A,67C,13
Hudson, Gary	TX2350	11,49,63A,63B
Huff, Michael H.	AL1050	63A,42,49,67E,37
Huffman, Donna M.	WA0100	13,13J,36,47,49
Huffman, Valarie A.	WV0300	37,32,63D,32E,49
Hughes, William M.	SC1200	13,49,63C,41
Hunsaker, Leigh Anne	TX0900	63A,32,49
Hunt, Douglas	CA4300	49,48,63D
Huntoon, John Richard	IN0100	63C,63D,47,37,49
Hurt, Charles R.	TX3175	49,63C
Hutton, Cynthia	OR0950	60,37,49,63B
Ingle, Ronnie	ND0500	49,63A,47
Inkster, Matthew	WV0600	63A,63B,37,47,49
Irby, Fred	DC0150	47,49,63A
Irish, John E.	TX0150	63A,63B,49,29A
Irizarry, Rafael E.	PR0115	37,12A,63B,42,49
Jackson, Keith	WV0750	47,49,63C,63D
Jackson, Milton	AR0810	13,11,49,63,70
James, Ray	KS0050	37,63D,32E,49
Jameson, Philip	GA2100	49,63C
Jantz, Paul	SC0200	12A,49,63C,63D,34
Jeffrey, Wayne	AB0060	35A,37,49,48,63B
Jeffries, Jean	MA1350	61,41,49
Jerosch, Anita	ME0200	63,49
Johansen, David A.	LA0650	63C,11,63D,49
Johns, Kristen	GA2150	63B,11,42,49
Johnson, Larry	OR0700	63B,49
Johnson, Sasha	AI0150	63D,49
Johnston, Dennis	NY0700	32E,12C,49,63A,60B
Johnston, Jason	WY0200	63B,49,12A
Johnston, Scott	OH2150	49,63A
Jolley, David	NC1650	49,63B
Jolly, Tucker	OH2150	49,63D
Jones, Gareth	AA0150	37,49
Jones, Gregory R.	MO1780	11,63A,49
Jones, John R.	KY1500	49,63D,42
Jones, Stephen	MI2250	49,63A,20G
Jones, Terry	ID0140	37,47,49,63A,29
Joy, Nancy	NM0310	63B,49,13A,11
Julian, Tijuana	MO0350	63A,49,20G
Jumper, David	PA2200	29,63A,32E,49
Kagarice, Vern L.	TX3420	41,49,63C,63D
Kaiser, Keith A.	NY1800	32E,32G,49
Keays, James	CA5150	12A,49,63B
Keelan, Nick	WI0350	32,49,63C,63D
Keeling, Bruce	TX2350	11,12A,47,49,63D
Keener, Michael K.	OH2250	63C,49,11,32E
Keller, Karlton	CA3400	13,47,48,49,12
Kelley, Timothy S.	TX3650	60,37,49,63,41
Kemm, Karl	TX0550	63B,49,67E,14E,14F
Kennedy, John	TX2350	14C,13A,46,49,32B
Kennedy, Rajah B.	OK0450	11,37,46,49,63
Kent, George E.	RI0300	11,49,63A,66G,66H
Kerstetter, Kathleen	NC1500	32,49,34,64A
Kincaid, John	CO1050	49
Kinder, Keith	AG0200	37,41,49,63
King, Richard	OH0600	63B,49,41
Kiradjieff, Chris	OH2550	63A,49
Kirk, Kenneth P.	GA2150	63A,49,13,39
Kirkland, Anthony B.	MS0500	63A,42,49,67E,11
Kjos, Kevin	PA1750	11,47,63A,49
Klazek, Merrie	AG0170	63A,48,49
Kline, W. Peter	TX2260	13A,11,37,49,63D
Knorr, Eric	OH0500	63A,49
Kolstad, Michael L.	MO0400	49,63C,63D,47,34
Korak, John	IL2910	60,37,63A,49,42
Kosmyna, David J.	OH1800	63A,63B,49,47,29
Krantz, Wayne M.	NY2750	29,70,49
Krauss, David	NY2750	49,63A
Kroesche, Kenneth	MI1750	63D,63C,49,37
Krummel, Christopher	OH2600	49,63A
LaCognata, John P.	NC2440	37,49,63
Laing, Daniel R.	NE0300	60B,37,49,63A,63B
Lambert, Adam E.	NE0050	32E,37,60B,63,49
Lambrecht, James M.	IL0100	37,49,63A,60B,13C
Lambreeht, Richard	TX3520	12A,49,63B
Lamprey, Audrey	CA0630	13A,49,63B
Lanier, Michael	GA2130	63A,49
LaRosa, Massimo	OH0600	63C,49
Larsen, Jens	SC0900	10F,63A,49
Larsen, Vance	UT0190	60,37,49,32
Laubach, David	AR0300	63A,49
Laumer, Jack C.	TX3175	49,63A
Lawing, William D.	NC0550	29A,47,63A,34D,49
Laws, Francis	OH2500	11,49,63C,63D
Lawson, Stephen J.	WV0400	13,63B,29,49,37
Leasure, Timothy	OH1850	63A,49
Lebens, James C.	AI0190	63C,49,43
Lee, Rodger	NY2105	63A,49
Leslie, Drew	NC0050	63C,49,42,41
Lewis, H. M.	KY0610	10F,11,12A,49,63A
Lewis, Jeremy	TX3750	63D,49
Ligotti, Albert F.	GA2100	49,63A
Lill, Joseph	IL2100	47,49,63A,37,42
Linch-Parker, Sheryl	NC0800	13A,32B,32C,49,63C
Lindahl, Robert	MI0400	49,63C,29
Lindemann, Jens	CA5030	63A,49
Lindsey, Logan	WV0050	29A,41,49,63D
Lipton, Jamie	AR0300	63D,49,13A
Little, Donald C.	TX3420	41,49,63D
Long, Jamie	GA0600	36,63A,49,55C,40
Loucky, David L.	TN1100	63C,63D,49
Lueschen, David	OH0700	63B,63D,49,11
Lumpkin, Royce E.	NC2420	63C,49
Luscombe, Greg	TN1660	63C,49
Lyon, Matthew	IN0150	49,63D
Lyren, Delon	MN0150	63A,63B,49,45
MacDonald, James	AG0650	63B,49
Machala, Kazimierz W.	IL3300	63B,49,41
Mack, William G.	MO0850	60,32C,37,49,63A
MacMorran, Sande	TN1710	11,38,49,63D
Madeja, James T.	NY3780	32,63A,12C,49
Madsen, Peter C.	NE0610	63C,47,29,49
Malatestinic, Patrice A.	NY3650	63B,49
Manhart, Grant L.	SD0400	49,63A,63B,11,46
Manji, K. C.	CA1265	60,38,49,41,29A
Mark, Douglas L.	MS0250	49,63C,63D,41
Martin, David	AI0200	63C,49
Martin, Michael D.	GA0150	11,12A,13C,32,49
Martin, Rex	IL2250	63D,49
Martin-Williams, Jean F.	GA2100	49,63D
Mase, Raymond	NY1900	63A,49
Mason, Richard	GA0950	63D,49
Mathie, David	ID0050	63C,32E,63D,49

Index by Area of Teaching Interest

Name	Code	Areas
Mathis, William B.	OH0300	49,63C,47
Matlock, Herman	NY3775	63A,29A,49
May, Douglas L.	PA1450	63C,49
Mazzocchi, Anthony J.	NJ0800	63C,49
McCain, Martin G.	TX3175	63C,29,46,49
McFarland, Thomas J.	KY1400	60,12A,32E,49,63
McGowan, Mike	TX2000	11,37,49,13,29
McIlwain, William Benjamin	MS0750	63C,49
McKinney, Harold	NC0050	63C,49
McKinstry, Herb	PA1650	63,49
McManus, Kevin	MD0350	63B,63C,63D,49
McQueen, William F.	TX2100	11,20A,49,63A
McSpadden, George	AL0350	13,36,49,66A,66G
McWhorter, Brian J.	OR1050	63A,49,43
Meixner, Brian	PA3100	12A,63C,49,11
Mendoza, Cristina	LA0450	63,46,49,11,41
Mensch, Thomas	TX3370	37,41,63C,49,48
Meredith, Scott	WY0200	63A,67E,12,32E,49
Merriman, John C.	AL0500	11,49,63A,70
Messersmith, Susan	SC0275	63A,49
Metcalf, John C.	PA1750	34,10,11,49,63C
Metcalf, Michael	OH0100	63B,72,49
Miles, Melvin N.	MD0600	60,37,47,49,63A
Miles, Patrick	WI0850	49,63B,38
Miller, Dennis	AI0150	49,63D
Miller, Gregory	MD1010	49,63B
Miller, James	CA0510	63C,49
Miller, Michael	OH0600	63A,49
Miller, Todd	CA0815	49,50,63B,65
Mills, David	CT0600	32C,37,49
Millsap, Kyle	KY0950	63A,49
Millsapp, Brian	NC1550	37,49,60B
Milton, Kenneth	MS0560	11,47,49,63A,63B
Mindeman, John	IL3500	63D,63C,49,29
Misenheimer, Aaron L.	NC0850	32E,34,11,63,49
Missal, Joseph	OK0800	37,60B,49
Mitchell, Adrian	MS0350	11,63A,37,32C,49
Mitchell, Alan	MI0250	60,32,37,49,48
Monte, Tobias	MA2020	37,49,60,63A
Montelione, Joseph	TN1200	38,49,42
Moore, Albert L.	MN1300	49,63B,63A,11
Moore, D. Scott	MN0750	49,14C
Moore, Grant W.	PA1250	49,63D,47
Moore, Mark E.	IL3300	63D,49,41
Moore, Phil	OK1200	37,49
Moore, Rick	AZ0200	13,11,37,46,49
Moots, John E.	OK0150	32,49,63A,20G
Morales, Raimundo	TX3750	63C,37,49
Morris, Craig	FL1900	41,49,63A,42
Morris, James R.	NY3700	13A,63A,13,11,49
Morris, Winston	TN1450	49,63D,41
Mortenson, Gary	KS0650	63A,49
Moyer, Jon	PA3710	49,63C,63D
Mueller, John T.	TN1680	63C,63D,49
Muntefering, Scott	IA1800	32,63A,49
Murray, Renardo	MS0350	37,11,32C,49,63D
Murray, Robert P.	GA0550	63A,49
Neebe, Paul M.	VA1550	63A,49,13C,13A
Niemisto, Paul	MN1450	49,63C,63D,37,42
Northcut, Timothy	OH2200	49,63D
Norton, Leslie	TN1850	41,48,63B,49
Ochoa, Reynaldo	TX3450	63A,49,13
Odello, Mike	MN1620	63D,72,49
Ogilvie, Tyler	PA3150	63B,49
Olah, John J.	FL1900	13,49,63D
Olcott, James L.	OH1450	47,63A,49,42
Oldham, Barbara	NY2750	49,63B,48
Olson, Rolf	SD0600	37,47,49,63A,46
Olt, Timothy J.	OH1450	63D,49,72,67E
Ordman, Ava	MI1400	63C,49
Oster, Floyd	NH0110	63A,49
Packard, John	OH1600	37,49,63A,60B,10F
Paddock, Joan Haaland	OR0450	60,32,49,63A,37
Pagnard, Charles	OH0450	60B,32E,49,63A
Parker, Grant	CA1500	13,11,12A,49,37
Parkinson, John S.	CA2840	37,38,47,49,45
Parmer, Richard	WY0130	63C,63D,60,49
Parsons, Kenneth	TN1350	60B,49,37,46,34
Peacock, Curtis	WA0050	11,49,63D
Perkins, John D.	MO0100	63A,63B,12A,42,49
Perry, Richard H.	MS0750	49,63D
Petersen, William	AL1300	32E,37,63D,60B,49
Petruzzi, Leon T.	NY1600	63A,49
Pherigo, Johnny L.	FL1800	11,41,49,48,63B
Phillips, Brent	TX0300	63C,49
Phillips, Gregory	OH1450	49,63B,13A
Phillips, Mark W.	VA1750	32C,37,49,63C,63D
Pickering, Matthew	MS0360	63,37,11,49,60B
Pier, Fordyce C.	AA0100	37,49,63A
Pinson, Donald L.	TX0550	11,13A,63C,63D,49
Piper, Jeffrey S.	NM0450	49,63A
Plitnik, Brian	WV0750	63C,49
Poitier, James	FL0100	37,49,63,32F,41
Ponzo, Mark	IL2200	49,63A
Poper, Roy	OH1700	63A,49,41
Posegate, Stephen C.	IL3150	32,37,49,34
Powell, Michael	NY1900	63C,49
Pridmore, Craig	CA5400	37,49,12
Pruiett, Kevin P.	OK0650	47,63A,72,29A,49
Pruzin, Robert S.	SC1110	32C,49,63B
Rabbai, George	PA3330	63A,47,49
Ramirez, Roberto	PR0115	63A,49
Raney, Earl L.	MA2150	49,48,63A
Ranger, Louis	AB0150	49,63A,41
Reed, Marc A.	CO0350	63A,63B,49
Reese, Marc B.	FL1125	63A,49,41,42,48
Reeves, M. Bryan	AL0050	37,32E,11,49,60
Reynolds, Jeffrey L.	AG0450	49,63A,37,29A
Reynolds, Terrance	NY2200	46,49
Rhodes, Andrew L.	OH2300	37,32E,49
Richard, Leon	KY0750	49,63A,63B
Richards, Patrick	MS0360	41,49
Richardson, Edward 'Rex'	VA1600	63A,29,49
Riegle, Dale	FL1500	47,49,63A
Rivard, Gene	MN0625	13,10F,49,63,31A
Roach, L. Leroy	CA4200	32C,49,63,37
Roberts, James E.	AL0500	60,12A,49,63C
Roberts, Shannon B.	UT0150	13,41,49,63C,10
Robertson, Donald C.	NY3705	49,63C,63D
Robertson, Karen	NC0050	49,63B,42,41
Robinson, Melissa Ann	OR0850	41,42,49,63B
Robinson, Ryan	OK0750	63D,49,32E
Roby, Lloyd	CA0800	32C,49,63D
Rodgers, Andy	CT0800	49,63D
Rodriguez, Raul I.	TX3175	49,63D
Rojak, John	NY0150	63C,42,49
Rojak, John D.	NY1900	49,63C
Rose, William G.	LA0350	13,49,34,63D,63C
Rulli, Richard J.	AR0700	63A,42,49,41
Russell, Eileen Meyer	TX2650	63D,13,13C,49,63C
Sachs, Michael	OH0600	63A,49
Salzman, Timothy	WA1050	60,37,49,63D
Sanders, Kevin	TN1680	49,63D
Sanders, Robert	CA0815	63C,49
Sandor, Edward	GA2100	49,63A
Sarjeant, Lindsey B.	FL0600	47,49,53,46,29
Saunders, Martin	WV0400	63A,53,49,47,34
Sawchuk, Terry M.	CO0800	49,63A
Scanga, James V.	PA1450	63B,49
Schaefer, Phillip	MO2000	37,47,49,63A
Schaffer, John D.	WI0815	63D,49
Schaffer, William R.	AL0200	13,11,63B,49
Scharnberg, William	TX3420	41,49,63B
Schilf, Paul R.	SD0050	37,49,47,32E,29A
Schmid, William	GA0950	63A,46,29,49,47
Schmidt, David	FL1750	49,63C,63D
Schmidt, Jack W.	PA0900	11,12A,36,37,49
Schooley, John	WV0300	13,49,63D,62D
Schreckengost, John	IN1750	63B,49,11
Schreier, David	FL1800	49,37
Schuchat, Charles	IL2200	63D,49
Schuchat, Charles	IL0550	63D,49
Schuesselin, John C.	MS0700	63A,49
Schultz, Wendy E.	NE0150	49,63D
Schuman, Leah	IL3450	63A,49
Scott, David R.	LA0350	12A,49,63A
Scott, Judson	WA1000	63A,49
Seidel, John	IN0150	49,63C
Self, Cale	GA2130	37,63C,63D,32E,49
Shaffer, Rebecca Boehm	IA0950	63B,49,12A,32E,13C
Shires, Brent A.	AR0850	63B,32E,42,49
Shiver, Todd	WA0050	63A,32,37,47,49
Shoemaker, Vance	SD0050	63C,63D,49
Shorthouse, Tom	AB0060	63A,47,49,42
Shuster, Brett A.	KY1500	42,63C,49,67E
Simerly, Rick	TN1150	63,29,49,47,32E
Simmons, Matthew	FL0100	49,60B,63C,63D
Simmons, Matthew	SC1050	37,49,63C,63D
Slack, Robert	CA1000	47,49,63A,53
Smith, Donald S.	AZ0350	29A,63A,49
Smith, Gene	AF0150	13,47,49,63C,29
Smith, John David	DE0150	63B,48,49
Smith, Michael K.	IA0950	42,63C,63D,49
Smith, Nicholas	KS1450	63B,49,12A
Snead, Charles G.	AL1170	49,63B
Snedeker, Jeffrey	WA0050	12,49,63B
Solis, Richard	OH0600	63B,49,49
South, Janis	OK1250	63B,11,12A,49,20
Spence, Marcia L.	MO1800	63B,49
Staples, Thomas	AA0200	60,11,49,63
Stark, Cynthia	IL0850	63D,49
Stebleton, Michelle	FL0850	49,63B,67E
Stees, Kevin J.	VA0600	49,63D
Steffen, Richard	TN0050	60B,49,63A,47,11
Stern, Jeffrey	AF0100	63A,49
Stevens, Paul W.	KS1350	49,63B
Stewart, Stanley W.	MS0200	11,37,47,49,48
Stibler, Robert	NH0350	11,63A,67C,49,67E
Stickney, Mark A.	UT0200	37,63D,41,49,63
Stoelzel, Richard	MI0900	63A,49
Stokes, James M.	NC0050	63A,49,41,42
Stoupy, Etienne	TX3300	49,63A,63B
Stout, Richard	OH0600	63C,49
Streider, Will E.	TX3200	37,49,63A
Stroeher, Michael	WV0400	63D,49,63C,32,29
Su, Yu-Ting (Tina)	IA1600	63B,49
Sulliman, Jason M.	IN1800	63,49,47
Swisher, Eric	KY0950	63A,49
Swope, Richard	GA1000	37,63,49
Talbott, Doug	KS0150	10F,32E,37,47,49
Taylor, Clifton	MS0420	13,47,49,63C,37
Taylor, Nancy	TX3520	63A,49
Taylor, Robert C.	AB0100	37,49,60B,63A
Thompson, J. Mark	LA0550	49,63C
Thompson, Steven	MN0250	37,60B,63A,32E,49
Thompson, Virginia M.	WV0750	49,63B
Thornburg, Scott	MI2250	13A,13,49,63A
Tinnin, Randall C.	FL1950	63A,49,37,32E,20
Traster, Jeff	FL2050	37,49,63D,32
Trowbridge, James	NY1550	49,63D
Tuck, Patrick M.	KY1425	10,13,49,63A,63B
Tuckwiller, George	VA1750	60,11,41,49,63A
Tunnell, Michael	KY1500	49,63A,42
Turnbull, David	WA1150	49,63A,67E,37
Van Deursen, John	AB0100	49,63C,37
Van Dreel, Lydia	OR1050	63B,49,42
Van Houten, John	CA0825	49,63D,35A
Vanore, John	PA3680	60,10,47,49,63A
Wacker, John M.	CO1050	60,63,37,49,32E
Wagner, Irvin	OK1350	49,63C,54
Waidelich, Peter J.	FL0400	49,63A
Wakefield, David	NY1900	63B,49
Wallace, Jeb	UT0325	49
Walter, Ross A.	VA1600	63C,63D,34,49
Wardlaw, Jeffrey A.	PA0700	63D,49,13,63C
Warman, Harold	CA4100	60,37,49
Washburn, David	CA0960	49,63
Washington, Darian	SC0950	37,49,63B
Wasko, Dennis	PA3330	47,63A,49
Watabe, Eileen	AK0150	63B,49
Watson, Richard	IN1750	63D,49
Watson, Scott C.	KS1350	11,49,63D
Weaver, Lane	KS0350	11,63D,37,49
Webster, Thomas R.	TX0600	60A,49,48,13B
Weeda, Linn	AK0100	11,36,49,63,63A
Weinstein, Michael	MA2200	13A,11,12A,49
Welcomer, Paul	CA4150	63C,49
Wells, Wayne W.	VA1350	49,63C,41
Welsch, James O.	NY4150	13,49,39
White, Tim	AG0050	63A,49
Whitener, Scott	NJ1130	60,49
Whitlock, Mark	MN1600	32,37,49,63C,63D
Whitted, Pharez	IL0600	63A,29,47,49
Whitten, Douglas	KS1050	37,63D,32E,11,49
Wick, Heidi	OH1200	63B,49
Wickham, Nathaniel	CO0950	63C,49,63D
Wiegard, William James	TX3750	63B,49,11
Wilcox, Mark	TX1650	13C,63A,49,29E,29C
Wilhoit, Mel R.	TN0200	10F,12A,32,49,63
Willard, Michael L.	OH1350	63A,49,63
Williams, Mark	MI0900	63C,49,41
Williams, Steven J.	CA3500	63C,49
Wilson, Bruce	MD0150	63C,63D,49,37,32C
Wilson, Chris	AR0110	49,32E,11
Wilson, Ruth	CA4700	32E,42,49,63B
Winkle, William	ID0050	63D,49

Winkler, John WV0750 49,63A
Winslow, Richard D. CA0800 49,63A,63B,29A,20G
Wolfinbarger, Steve MI2250 49,63C,29A
Woll, Greg CA1900 13,49,63,43
Wood, Peter J. AL1300 63A,13,49,41
Woodard, Scott WV0700 37,47,32C,63,49
Woodring, Mark KY0950 63A,49
Woods, Chris P. IL1050 13A,10F,13C,49,63
Wootton, Tim MO0400 63A,49
Wright, Lawrence PA2450 37,41,49,63A
Young, Kevin TX3527 63D,49,11
Zacharella, Alexandra AR0730 63C,63D,11,49,37
Zadrozny, Edward A. OH2150 49,63C
Zerkel, David GA2100 63D,49
Zifer, Timothy IN1600 47,63A,29A,49
Zimmerman, Larry MN0750 63C,63D,49
Zirk, Willard MI0600 13,49,63B
Zugger, Thomas W. OH0350 63C,63D,49

Percussion Ensemble

Adams, Matthew TX1425 65,50,11,12
Ahima, Kwame TN1850 50
Alamo, Juan NC2410 29,65,50
Albagli, Richard NY3700 65,50
Albin, William R. OH1450 14,50,65
Alexander, Conrad NY1800 50,65
Alexander, Joel MN1280 65,50
Alicea, Jose R. PR0115 65,50
Alico, Gregory H. PA3150 50,65
Alorwoyie, Gideon F. TX3420 20,65,31F,50,52
Altmire, Matt CA3200 50,65
Alviso, Ric CA0835 11,50
Amidon, Bradley PA1200 50,65
Anang, Kofi WA0200 50
Anders, Nathan OH0350 65,50
Anderson, Larry R. LA0770 47,50,65
Anderson, Thad FL1800 65,50,34
Anzivino, Steve MI0300 65,50,43
Aponte, Jose Porentud TX3420 50,65,46
Applebaum, Terry L. PA3330 65,35A,50
Armstrong, James D. PA1250 65,50
Armstrong, Joshua MS0250 65,50,37,41
Assad, Mike TN1200 65,50,47
Astaire, John CA0600 65,50
Auwarter, Douglas KS0570 50,65
Baden, Robert WV0800 50,65
Bairos, Monte CA1560 37,41,48,49,50
Baker, Dale NC2350 50,65
Baker, James NY2250 50
Baldwin, John ID0050 13,50,65
Barber, Amy Lynn IN0350 65,50
Barber, Matthew C. MN0050 65,50
Barnhart, Stephen L. WY0200 65,50,32E
Barrier, Gray CO0950 50,65,32E
Bayles, David S. WI0835 65,50
Beck, John R. NC1650 50,65
Beckler, Terry SD0400 65,50,37,46,11
Bedell, Adam TX3100 50,65,32E
Bennett, Michael ME0270 65,50
Bergeron, Norm TX2800 65,50,10D,11,13A
Bernier, Lucas ND0400 65,50,11,34
Berns, Paul S. IN1650 65,50
Berry, Mark S. KY1550 65,50,41
Bessinger, David K. OK1250 13,50,65
Bethea, William VA0950 65,11,37,50
Beyer, Gregory S. IL2200 50,65
Bierman, Duane NE0590 37,65,50
Biggs, Allen CA4200 50,65
Black, Alan TX1700 11,37,47,50,65
Blake, Michael ND0500 13A,50,53,65
Bleyle, William B. OH0950 65,50,37
Bluestone, Joel OR0850 11,50,65,20G
Bonner, Peggy IL0400 50,65
Bouchard, Jean-Luc AI0190 50,65
Bovenschen, Wayne OK0800 65,37,50,32E
Boyar, Simon M. NY2750 65B,50
Branch, Thomas W. AL1160 50,65
Bratt, Douglass F. IL1890 50,47,65A,65B,46
Bratton, Tripp KY0300 65,50
Braun, Roger OH1900 50,65
Breaux, Troy Jude LA0760 37,65,50
Brennan, Adam PA2150 60B,37,50,65,10F
Breton, Jean-Francois AG0170 65,13C,50
Bridge, Robert NY2950 65,37,50,20A
Britain, Mat TN1850 50
Britt, Michael J. AR0600 46,50,65
Broadway, Kenneth FL1850 50,65
Bronstein, Chase TX2250 65,50
Brosh, Robert PA3330 50,65,20G,14
Brown, Al CA0850 32E,65,50
Brown, Allen CA5350 50,65
Brown, Charles V. NC2150 50,65
Brown, Darrell ID0060 32E,65,50
Brown, Jeff MS0360 37,65,50,46
Brown, Jeffrey C. IN1750 47,50,65,11
Brown, Richard TX2150 50,65,42
Brownell, John AG0650 65,50
Bueckert, Darrell AJ0150 50,65,37
Bukvich, Daniel J. ID0250 13,10,47,50,65
Bull, Michael W. NY4150 50,65
Bump, Michael MO1780 65,50
Burda, Pavel WI0825 13A,60,50,65
Burdett, Kimberly H. OH2000 50,65,32E
Burge, Russell OH2200 65,50
Burgett, Gwendolyn MI1400 65,50
Burke, Sarah M. TX0340 50,65
Burkhead, Ricky MS0560 65A,65B,50,65
Burkhead, Ricky MS0700 50,65
Burnham, Jay K. AL1200 65,50
Butters, Steven G. IL0840 65,50
Butters, Steven IL0600 65,50
Buyer, Paul L. SC0400 65,50,14,20
Byrd, Katherine GA2130 65,50
Byrne, Gregory KY1500 65,37,50
Calabrese, Anthony J. NY1550 50
Caldwell, Robert AB0060 50,65
Cameron, James Scott MO0775 37,50,65
Campbell, James B. KY1450 65,50
Campiglia, Paul GA2150 65,29,71,50,11
Carmenates, Omar SC0750 65,50,20
Carney, Michael CA0825 65,29,20,50
Carpenter, Charles M. CA3500 37,50,65
Caschetta, Todd CA4850 20G,11,12,14,50
Cassara, Frank NY0500 65,50
Cassara, Frank NY2105 65,50
Castro, Miguel GA1400 50,65,11,47

Cates, Mike TN0450 65,50
Cebulski, Michael GA0940 50,65
Cebulski, Michael GA0750 50,65
Chandler, Lloyd HI0050 50
Charles, Benjamin FL0650 50,65
Cheung, Pius OR1050 65,50
Cline, Rick NC1100 50,65
Clive, David NY4500 50,65
Coash, David FL0800 65,50
Cogdell, Jerry MS0320 13,11,50,63,54
Coghlan, Connie CT0050 65,50
Coley, Matthew IA0850 65,50
Collier, David L. IL1150 50,65
Collison, Craig AR0110 11,41,50,65
Condon, Clay IL2150 65,50,11
Connors, Sean WI0850 50,65
Conroy, Gregory MA0510 50,65
Corcoran, James R. KY1425 65,34,11,50
Corsi, Stephen F. PA0100 65,50
Coulter, Monte TN1700 13A,11,50,65
Coulter, Ronald E. IL2900 65,10B,50
Counihan, Emma AZ0440 50,65
Coviak, James MI2120 50,65
Cox, Daniel WA0400 65,50
Cox, Daniel R. ID0140 50,65,53,11
Cox, Kyle MO0750 50
Cozart, Keith IN0400 65,50
Crawford, Michael TX2750 65,50
Crawford, Stephen J. TX3415 37,12A,50,65
Craycraft, Jeremy MN0450 20,50,34,65
Crites, Dennis OH0250 65,50
Crook, Larry FL1850 14,50,20H
Crutchfield, Robert TX3360 50,65
Csicsila, Mell OH0755 65,50,13A
Cudd, Patti MN0350 65,32E,50
Culley, James F. OH2200 50,65
Dachtyl, Cary OH1200 65,50
Dahl, Stanley E. IA0200 50,65,34,65A,65B
Dalton, Grant B. AL0800 65,11,32E,47,50
Damberg, John AK0100 14,50,65
Daniels, Sean TN1400 37,50,65
Darling, Matthew H. CA0810 50,65,14C
David, John GA1500 65,50
Davila, Gerardo TN1100 50,65
Davis, Christopher A. SC0950 11,13,29,50,65
DeQuattro, Michael RI0200 50,65
Deschenes, Michel AE0100 65,50
Deviney, Christopher PA0850 65,50
Dicciani, Marc PA3330 65,35,50
Dimond, Theresa CA5020 65,50
Dior, Rick NC2420 50,65
Dorsey, John F. MI0600 65,50
Douds, Nathan PA3100 11,50,65,66A
Douglass, Mark TN1710 50,65
Dreier, James IL0100 65,50
Dudack, Matthew J. OH1650 65,50
Duerden, Darren HI0050 32E,65,50,47,11
Dunn, Neil KS0650 65,50
Eckert, Jamie D. MA2020 65,50
Edgar, Paul DC0100 50,65
Elliott, Richard OH0680 65,50,37,11,32E
Elstner, Erin MO1950 65,50
Erickson, Ross IN1600 65,50
Esau, Matt KS1250 65,50
Esler, Robert AZ0490 50,14C,35C,10
Estoque, Kevin S. LA0650 65,50,46,20H
Eyler, David MN0600 32,50,65,42
Fabricius, Daniel NY3705 50,65
Falcone, Anthony M. NE0600 37,65,50
Fallin, Mathew D. GA0950 50,65
Falvo, Robert J. NC0050 65,50
Fambrough, Gene AL1150 50,37,65
Fang, I-Jen VA1550 50,65
Feeney, Tim AL1170 65,50
Fernandez, Robert CA0830 65,50
Ferrari, John NJ1400 13A,11,50,65
Fife, Travis TX1400 65,50,32E
Finch, Abraham L. MA1650 32A,50,65A,65B
Finley, Benjamin OK0300 65,50
Finnie, Jimmy IN0800 50,65
Fischer, Jeffrey MA2030 50,65
Flamm, Peter TX3350 65,50
Flood, John CA4100 20A,13A,11,65,50
Flores, Ricardo IL3300 65,50
Flowers, Kevin SC0900 65,50
Floyd, C. Chad KY0400 37,65,50
Floyd, John M. VA1700 50,65
Fluman, John R. TX2960 50,65
Fooster, Harold AR0810 60,11,37,50,65
Ford, Mark TX3420 65,50
Fornelli, Devon AG0050 65,50
Forquer, Ty MI1800 65,50,13C
Forrest, Sam FL0400 50
Fosheim, Karen MS0250 66A,13B,50,20A,10F
Foster, Mark CO0550 50,65,32E
Fox, Jeremy IA1400 13,10F,37,50,34
Frank, Arthur PA3250 32C,50
Franklin, Laura L. NC0250 50,65,20,32E
Freeze, Tracy KS0300 65,50,20,34D
Frye, Danny NC0930 65,50,37,65B,32C
Fung, Jan PA0500 50,65
Fuster, Bradley J. NY3717 65,50
Gaetano, Mario A. NC2600 50,65,11
Gaines, Julia MO1800 65,50
Galm, Eric A. CT0500 14,20,20H,50,65
Garcia, Eric TN1200 65,50
Garcia, Paul D. NC1700 37,46,50,65
Gardner, Al TX2350 11,47,50,65
Gartner, Kurt KS0650 65,20H,47,50
Gatch, Perry PA3650 50,65
Gay, Kirk FL1800 50,65,34
Geary, Michael IA0950 65,50,32E
Gerber, Stuart W. GA1050 65,50
Gerhart, David CA0825 65,20H,37,50
Gibbs, Kory AJ0100 50,65
Gibson, Ian AG0070 65,50
Gilbert, Karl IN1560 65,50
Gilmore, Timothy NH0250 50,65
Ginn, Stan KY1000 42,50,65
Ginorio, Jorge TX1725 20H,50,65
Gipson, Richard C. TX3000 65,50,32G
Gloss, Randy CA0510 65,20D,50
Glover, David PA3100 29,50,65,34,47
Gold, Matthew MA2250 50,65,43,41
Golden, Bruce OH0650 50,65
Goldstein, Thomas MD1000 47,50,65
Gonzalez, Genaro TX3175 50,65
Goodenberger, Mark WA0050 65,50

Name	Code	Areas
Gordy, M. B.	CA2650	50
Gould, Michael	MI2100	50
Gray, D'Arcy	AF0100	50,65
Green, Ronald	PA2000	37,50,65
Griffin, Dennis	UT0300	50,34,65,13G,41
Griffin, Robert	KY0750	13A,11,50,65
Grinwis, Brandan	MI0850	65,50,13A
Grosso, Cheryl	WI0808	50,65,43,14,13C
Guenoit, Eric	LA0450	60B,11,37,65,50
Guidry, Travis	AL1160	65,50
Haas, Jonathan L.	NY2750	50,65
Haddad, Orlando	PA3330	47,50
Hagedorn, David	MN1450	13A,65,50,47,13B
Haldeman, Michael	SC0275	11,37,65,50
Hall, Bob	CO0550	50
Hall, Steven	WV0400	14,47,50,65
Hamaker, Robert	CA2775	50,65
Hamilton, Brian	CA2550	37,50
Hanes, Michael D.	IL2900	37,50,65
Hannum, Thomas P.	MA2000	37,50
Hans, Ben J.	WI0450	11,35A,50,65
Harbaugh, Kurt	WA0480	50
Hardman, David J.	OK1330	50,65
Harris, Scott H.	TX2700	50,65
Harrison, Brady	OH2550	65,50,11
Harrison, Edward	IL0550	65,50
Hartenberger, Russell	AG0450	50,65,53
Hasenpflug, Thom	ID0100	65,13,20,10,50
Hatch, Montgomery	NY1600	65,42,50
Hawkins, Phillip	CA2975	11,20H,34,50
Hawkins, Wes	AZ0470	14C,65,50,29A
Head, Stan	TN1380	50,65
Hearne, Martin	IA0400	37,38,50,60
Hedgepeth, Byron	NC0050	65,50
Heglund, Andrew	NV0100	65,46,50,47
Heldrich, Claire	NY2150	50,65,43
Henry, Matthew	MO1830	65,50
Hepler, David	PA0700	50,65,29A
Hernly, Patrick	FL0930	50,65
Higgins, Scott	CA0550	65,50
Hill, John E.	KY0950	50,65
Hill, Julie	TN1720	65,50
Hill, Kyle W.	MS0580	13B,11,37,50,65
Hill, Paul	MN0750	65,50
Hillyer, Tim	IA1200	65,50
Hinkle, Lee	MD1010	65,50
Hogancamp, Randy	IA1600	50,65
Holder, Brian	FL1675	11,20,13A,65,50
Hollenbeck, Eric R.	CO0250	65,50
Holly, Richard	IL2200	50,65,29
Horner, Ronald G.	PA1600	65,50
Horner, Ronald	MD0350	65,20,50
Howden, Moses Mark	NY3475	50,65
Hughes, Robert	AG0500	32,50,65
Hulling, Cliff	CA0350	13,47,50,10A
Humphries, Stephen	GA0600	13A,20,50,65
Hussey, Peter	IL1500	65,20,11,50,12A
Ibarra, Susie	VT0050	20,29,50,47,53
Isakson, Aaron	MN0610	32E,37,50,60B,65
Jacklin, Matt	IL2300	65,50
Jackson, Herman	LA0700	65,29,50
Jackson, Sharon Sue	IN1800	37,50,65,65B
James, Shaylor L.	FL0600	32C,50,65
Jarrett, Gabriel	NY3775	65,50
Jarvis, David	WA1150	10,47,50,65,14C
Jarvis, Peter	NJ1400	65,50
Jarvis, Peter	CT0100	65,50
Jenny, Jack	OH2050	13,10,50,65,43
Johnson, David	CA0510	13A,65,50
Johnson, Jay L.	MN0300	65,50,42
Johnson, Sigurd	ND0350	65,50,37
Johnson, Todd Alan	CA0845	65,12A,14,50,29A
Jones, Brett	WI0860	65,20,50
Jones, Eric W.	MI1000	32E,37,50,65
Jones, Larry	TX2100	13A,11,50,65
Jones, Richard	NE0450	50,65,34,70
Justison, Brian	IL1750	29A,50,65
Kaminsky, Bruce	PA1000	62D,12A,37,50
Kamstra, Darin	CO0225	65,29,13B,47,50
Kastner, Kathleen	IL3550	13A,13,50,65,20
Katterjohn, Michael	GA0250	50,65
Kaufman, Howard	CA2250	65,20,50
Kestner, Luke	MT0175	50,65
Kettner, Scott	NY2660	50
Kieffer, Olivia	GA1700	65,50
Kihle, Jason J.	TX2960	11,37,50,65
Kingan, Michael G.	PA1600	50,65
Kinzie, John	CO0900	50,65
Kirk, Jeremy	KS0250	37,13,20A,50,65
Klier, Kari	TX3175	65,50
Klopfenstein, Reginald	IN0200	13A,12A,47,50,65
Knight, Joshua	AR0730	65,50,11
Knoles, Amy	CA0510	65,50,13A,10B
Knowles, Eddie Ade	NY3300	20,50
Kocmieroski, Matthew	WA0200	50
Koebel, Carolyn	MI1150	65,50
Koontz, Jason	KY0550	50,65,14,34B
Kozakis, Michael J.	IL0750	65,50
Kramer, Janet	IL3100	50,65
Kranzler, Dean	KS0150	65,50
Kranzler, Dean	KS0350	65,50
Kreitner, William	FL1310	47,50,65,53
Kukec, Catherine	IL1900	11,41,47,50,48
Kumor, Frank	PA1750	50,65,13
Kutz, Jonathan	TX1600	65A,65B,14C,50
Ladzekpo, C. K.	CA2950	20A,20B,50
Lambert, James	OK0150	65,50,37,13,12D
Lang, Scott	KY1000	50,65
Langsam, Stuart	OK0800	65,50,11
Langsam, Stuart	OK0450	65,50
Lasley, Michael	NC1550	50,65
Latta, Jonathan R.	CO0350	10F,47,50,65,20
Latten, James E.	PA1650	11,13A,37,50,65
Law, Charles P.	AR0750	65,50,37
Lawless, John	GA1150	65,50
Lawson, Ronald S.	IA0910	63C,65,11,50
Leandro, Eduardo G.	NY3790	65,50,43
Ledbetter, Robert	MT0400	37,50,65,20H,14C
Lee, Jon	TX2400	50
Lemmon, Galen	CA4400	65,50
Lepper, Kevin	IL3450	65,50
Lesbines, Tele	WI1150	50,65
Lewis, Elizabeth A.	MI1200	50,65
Licata, Julie M.	NY3765	65,33,50,20,10B
Lindberg, John	VA0250	65,50
Lipsey, Michael	NY0642	37,50,65
Lipsey, Michael S.	NJ0800	65,50
Lloyd, L. Keith	TX1650	65,12A,14,12,50
Loach, Deborah	AL1160	65,50
Locke, Gary	CA3800	37,50
Logozzo, Derrick	TX0700	50
Lopez, Robert	TX3175	65,50
Lopez-Trujillo, David	TX3515	11,50,65
Lorbeer, James	CA0815	50
Lyons, Greg	LA0250	32E,65,50
Mabrey, Charlotte	FL1950	50,65,43,20G
MacDonald, Payton	NJ1400	65,50,43
MacDonald, R. Richard	MN1700	47,50,65,32E
Made Suparta, I Dewa	AI0200	50,20E
Magnone, Steve	IL3200	50,65
Maley, Marshall	MD0700	50,65
Mallory, Keith	KS1000	65,50
Mankey, Joel R.	CA0835	50
Manns, Olugbala	OH1000	50
Marandola, Fabrice	AI0150	50,65
Marrs, Stuart	ME0440	12A,65,50,34
Marsh, George	CA4700	65,50
Maslanka, Daniel	MI1750	65,50
Mason, Brian S.	KY0900	50,65
Massini, Ryan	AA0040	50,65
Mast, Murray K.	MA1100	50,65
Mathiesen, Steven	PA2200	10A,10F,50,65
Mathiesen, Steven	PA2450	50,65
Maytum, Jeremiah	WY0115	65,50
McCarty, Patrick	MO0050	11,32E,37,65,50
McClung, Matthew	TX2930	65,12A,50
McCormick, John	AA0020	65,50
McCormick, Robert	FL2000	50,65
McCutchen, Thomas	AL0500	65,50
McGowan, Thomas	TX3370	37,41,50,65
McGuire, Dennis	MN1400	70,50,29
McGuire, Kristen Shiner	NY2650	50,65
McKinney, John S.	WV0350	50,65,34,60B,41
Meehan, Todd	TX0300	50,65
Meister, Scott R.	NC0050	10,65,43,50
Mekler, Joseph	NJ0750	65,50
Mensah, Sowah	MN1623	50
Metzger, Jon	NC0750	65,29,47,50,53
Meyers, Nicholaus S.	ND0600	65,50
Meza, Fernando	MN1623	50,65
Michelin, Rob	MA2250	50
Mietus, Raymond	NC2700	13A,37,50,65
Miller, Ben F.	WV0400	11,50,65,35A,37
Miller, Todd	CA0815	49,50,63B,65
Mitchell, Bryan P.	MS0570	11,37,46,65,50
Mitchell, Joseph	CA2600	50,65
Mizicko, Shane J.	MO1500	11,50,65A,65B,65
Mizma, Michael E.	TX2295	50,65,35A,35C
Moersch, William	IL3300	50,65
Moio, Dominick	AZ0440	50,65
Moonert, Judy	MI2250	14,50,65
Moore, Daniel	IA1550	50,65
Moore, James L.	OH1850	50,65
Moore, Jeffrey M.	FL1800	65,50
Morales-Matos, Rolando	NY2660	50
Morgan, Philip	NC2500	37,47,50,11
Morgan, Tom T.	KS1400	50,65,13C
Morris, J. David	GA2150	65,34,13,50
Morrow, Daniel	PA1350	65,50
Moses, Lennard	OH0500	50,65,20A,20G
Mueller, Erwin	IN0150	50,65
Muldar, Dennis	FL0950	65,50
Munzenrider, James	CA1250	50,65
Murray, Warren	OR1300	65,50
Musto, James	NJ0700	65,50
Nappi, Chris	NC0650	65,50
Nathan, Jonathan	CA5060	47,50,65
Nave, Pamela J.	IN1310	37,65,50
Neitzke, Jeffrey	OH0100	65,46,50
Nero, Joseph	PA3330	50,65
Nevill, Tom	TX3515	65,13A,13C,50,37
Ney, Leonard Scott	NM0450	50,65
Nicholson, Jason	UT0300	65,50,41
Nogarede, Steve	NM0400	50
Norton, Christopher S.	TN0100	50,65
Nottingham, Douglas	AZ0350	65,50,45,10B,35
Novotney, Eugene D.	CA2250	14,50,65,20
Oddis, Frank A.	KY0900	50,65
Oliver, Tony	IL0100	65,50
O'Mahoney, Terrence	AF0150	50,65,29,10D,66A
Orey, Pedro	FL0100	37,50,65
Orlick, James	SC0150	13,34,50
Osrowitz, Michael L.	NY2550	50,65
Otte, Allen C.	OH2200	50,65
Overman, Michael M.	VA0600	65,65B,50
Paradis, Kristian	DE0150	50
Parker, Don	NC0800	13,50,65,29
Parker, Philip	AR0200	13,10F,10,65,50
Passmore, Ken	GA1200	66D,66C,65,50
Patitucci, John	NY0550	10,46,47,51,50
Pawlak, Michael	IA0700	65,50
Peeples, Terrance P.	IL1520	65,14C,11,50
Pennington, John C.	SD0050	13A,65,50,10F
Perkins, Douglas	NH0100	65,50
Peske, Robert	ND0050	50,65
Petercsak, James J.	NY3780	50,65
Peters, Mitchel	CA5030	50,65
Piedra, Olman	OH2300	50,65
Piedra, Olman	OH2140	65,50,43,29
Pongrace, Andrew L.	OH1000	50,65
Potts, Brian	FL0050	65,50
Pourmehdi, Houman	CA0510	65,50,20B
Preiss, James	NY2250	50,65
Presley, Douglas L.	SC0850	37,50,32B,32C,65
Price, Harvey	DE0150	50,65,47
Price, Josselyne	VT0400	14,20,50
Pritchard, Jillian	NY3350	65,50
Pritchard, Jillian	NY1250	65,50
Pultorak, Mark	PA0400	50,65
Quillen, Josh R.	NY2750	50
Rabe, Gigi 'Gee'	CA0835	11,50
Ragsdale, Aaron	SD0550	37,65,50
Ragsdale, Chalon L.	AR0700	50,65
Ramirez, Mark Joseph	TX3525	65,50
Redmond, Daryle	NY3775	50,65
Reeves, Richard	SC0350	65,50
Reiner, Art	IN1650	50,65
Remonko, Guy	OH1900	50,65
Rennick, Paul	TX3420	50,65
Rhodes, Edward	NC1900	65,50
Rice, C. William	VA0600	50,65
Richeson, Dane M.	WI0350	50,65
Richmond, Matthew	NC2400	50,65
Ricks, Edward	SC1050	65A,65B,37,50,13A
Riley, Steve	KS0050	65,50,10
Ripley, Randal	MI1985	65,50

Name	Code	Areas
Rivera, Luis C.	AL1300	20,32E,41,65,50
Roach, Seth	KS0750	65,66,29,70,50
Robbins, David P.	WA0650	13,50,65
Robert, James	NC0750	65,11,50
Robinson, Anthony	TX0600	65,50
Robinson, N. Scott	MD0850	12A,14C,50
Roblee, Thomas	OH0700	65,50
Rockwell, Owen	MS0100	65,50
Rogers, Lisa	TX3200	50,65
Rogers, Seth	OH0850	65,50
Roland, Tomm	NE0610	65,20,34H,50
Romeo, Robert	NJ0825	50,65
Rorie, Alfonso	NC0910	50
Rosen, Michael	OH1700	50,65
Rosener, Douglas	AL0200	37,50,65
Ross, Paul	IL1085	65,50
Roulet, Patrick E.	MD0850	50,65,66C
Rounds, Theodore	OH1100	50,65
Rozenblatt, David I.	NY1600	65,42,50
Rudolph, John	AG0450	50
Rummage, Robert	IL0850	50,65,53
Runions, Greg	AG0250	47,50,32,65
Rutkowski, Gary	NY4460	50,65,11
Rutland, Neil	NM0100	37,50,65,35D
Ryan, Jamie V.	IL0800	65,50
Ryan, Josh T.	OH0200	50,65
Sachdev, Salil	MA0510	10,13A,20A,50,13B
Salisbury, Jeff	VT0250	50,65
Sanderbeck, Rande	TN0500	50,65
Saoud, Erick	AR0350	65,50
Scagnoli, Joseph R.	IN0100	65,50
Schaft, Glenn	OH2600	65,50
Schick, Steven	CA5050	11,50,65,43,29
Schlitt, Bill	CA0630	65,50
Schlitt, Bill	CA5150	50,65
Schlitt, William	CA1425	65,50
Schlitt, William	CA5355	65,50
Schmidt, John R.	PA2050	60,14,50,65,37
Schmidt, Steven	CA3800	65,50
Scholl, Gerald	KS1450	65,50,11
Schoonmaker, Matt	WV0300	65,50
Schuetz, Shaun Nicholas	TN1710	50
Schulze, Theodora	IN0005	61,10A,13,50,51
Scott, Gary	CA2550	37,50
Secor, Greg	MI1050	50,65,32E
Sekelsky, Michael J.	MO1790	37,50,65
Seligman, Jonathan D.	MD0520	50,65,32E
Sestrick, Timothy	PA1400	16,65,50
Shabazz, Hafiz F.	NH0100	14,50
Shaffer, Frank	TN1680	65,50
Shaw, Alison	WI0830	65,50
Shaw, John	FL1650	50,65
Shinn, Alan	TX3200	50,65,47,29
Shirley, Hank	NM0400	65,50
Simmons, Bradley E.	NC0600	50
Sinigos, Louis	MI0300	65,50,43
Sisauyhoat, Neil	TX0550	65,50,13A,13C
Slabaugh, Thomas E.	CA5010	37,60,65,50,42
Smith, Brian	VA0750	50,65
Smith, David	CT0800	13,50,65,34
Smith, Demond	KY0250	50,65
Smith, Joshua D.	TN0150	37,65,13A,50
Smith, Mark	IL0600	13A,50,65,29,20G
Smith, Nancy A.	NH0350	50,65
Smith, Nancy	ME0500	65,50
Smith, Ron	IA1100	65,50
Smith, Roy	OK0550	50,65
Smith, Roy	OK0850	50,65
Smith, Ryan	GA0850	65,50
Smith-Wright, Lovie	TX3450	50,65
Snider, Larry D.	OH2150	50,65
Sorrentino, Ralph	PA3600	65,50
Sorrentino, Ralph	PA1550	65,50
Sparks, Victoria	AC0050	65,50
Sparks, Victoria	AC0100	65,50
Spellissey, Gary	MA0950	50,65
Spencer, Andrew	MI0400	50,65
Spinelli, Donald	MD0750	50,65
Squance, Rod Thomas	AA0150	20,50,65
Sriji, Poovalur	TX3420	65,50
Stabile, Ronald	RI0300	32,41,50,65
Stable, Arturo	PA3330	20H,50
Stabley, Jeff	PA3710	46,47,53,65,50
Stallsmith, Becki	AL0260	32,38,50,61,66C
Steele, Glenn A.	PA3250	50,65
Steffens, David	OK0750	50,65,32E
Steinquest, David	TN0050	13,50,65
Steve, Tony	FL1000	65,50
Stevens, Annie J.	VA0150	65,37,50,34
Stockton, J. Larry	PA1850	14,50,20,60
Stone, Mark	MI1750	20,50
Stonefelt, Kay H.	NY3725	50,65
Storch, Arthur	CA0900	65,50
Storch, Arthur L.	CA0807	65,50
Stout, Gordon B.	NY1800	50,65
Stoyanov, Svetoslav R.	FL1900	65,50,42,43
Strauss, Matthew B.	FL1900	65,50
Strouse, Greg	KY1350	65,50
Strunk, Michael J.	CA0400	65,20,20H,50
Sullivan, Dennis	NY0050	50
Summers, Kim G.	NC0900	65,50
Sundeen, Eric	MN0150	50,65
Sunkett, Mark E.	AZ0100	50,65,29A,14
Super, Kevin	VA0650	65,50,37
Suta, Thomas	FL1745	65,50
Swist, Christopher	NH0110	65,50
Swist, Christopher	NH0150	50,65,13,10
Tanner, Christopher	OH1450	14,50
Tariq, Susan Martin	TX3750	65,50
Taylor, David L.	ID0060	50,65
Teague, Chan	LA0050	50,65
Teel, Allen J.	TX0050	65,50,20,37
Terry, Nicholas	CA0960	50,65
Thieben, Jacob S.	SC0800	50,65
Thomas, John	VA0700	50,65
Thompson, Amanda	CO1050	65,50
Tiller, Jim A.	NY3730	50,65
Tinkel, Brian C.	NC1250	65,50,42
Tolbert, Patti	GA0850	32,65,50
Tomaszewski, Staci	CO0250	50
Toner, D. Thomas	VT0450	65,20,37,50,60
Tones, Daniel	AB0060	20,50,65
Turner, Aaron	CO0275	50,65A,65B,13,41
Tyler, George Tracy	AL0500	50,65
Tyson, Blake W.	AR0850	50,65
Ungurait, John B.	MS0575	37,65,62D,46,50
Vaillancourt, Paul	GA0550	65,50,13C,43
Van Dyke, Gary	NJ1400	65,50
Van Sice, Robert	PA0850	50,65B
Varner, Michael	TX3500	50,65,14,20
Veikley, Avis	ND0250	65,50,62E
Veregge, Mark F.	CA4900	50,65
Vermillion, Terry L.	MN1300	65,50
Versaevel, Stephen	MT0200	65,50,14C
Vigo, Silfredo	CA3460	50
Vincent, Ron	NY2200	65,50,32E
Wacker, Jonathan D.	NC0650	65,65,29
Wadley, Darin J.	SD0600	65,50,13A,13C,38
Wagoner, W. Sean	OR1050	65,10F,50,37,11
Waldrop, Michael	WA0250	65,50
Walker, David L.	VA1000	50,65,60B,11,13A
Walker, Erin	KY1450	12,20,50,65
Walker, K. Dean	OK1200	65,50
Walker, Richard L.	IN0907	65,35,34A,50,37
Warne, David	MI1650	50,65,20
Warren, Alec	TX3400	65,50
Warren, Chris	MS0200	65,50
Warren, Michael	MO1810	50
Webb, Glenn	UT0150	37,41,47,50,65
Weber, Bradley	NE0700	65,50
Weber, Glenn	NJ1160	65,50
Weber, Jonathan	MI1400	65,50
Webster, Peter	FL1300	50,65
Weinberg, Norman G.	AZ0500	50,65
Wells, Mary	CA4300	50,65
Wenzel, Scott	WI0150	14,65,55,50,20A
West, Brian	TX3000	65,50
Westbrook, Gary W.	TX2750	50,65,37,32E
Wetzel, Thomas	WI0825	65,50
Weyer, Matthew	TN0250	65,50
White, James L.	TX3520	50,65
White, Joseph M.	WV0100	65,50,37,63,64
White, Marc M.	OK1150	65,50
Whitt, Roger	SC0050	65,50
Wiggins, Tracy Richard	NC2435	65,11,37,50
Wiggins, William	TN1850	41,50,65
Wilkins, Blake	TX3400	65,50
Wilkinson, Tobie L.	WI0865	65,50
Williams, Barry Michael	SC1200	12A,50,65,20A,20B
Williams, Demetrius	TX3520	65,50
Williams, Kenyon C.	MN1120	65,50,20
Williams, Wade	GA0300	50,65
Willie, Eric	TN1450	50,65
Willis, Jesse	SC0420	65,50,20,37
Wilsey, Jennifer	CA4700	65,50,32E
Winant, William K.	CA5070	50,65,43
Witten, Dean	NJ1050	65,50
Wojtera, Allen F.	VA1100	50,65,29
Wooton, John A.	MS0750	50,65
Wubbenhorst, Thomas M.	ME0440	50,65
Wulff, Steve	MI0100	65,50
Yakas, James	TX3500	65,50,20
Yancich, Paul	OH0600	65A,50
Zarro, Domenico E.	NJ0500	50,65
Zator, Brian	TX2955	50,65
Zerbe, David	MI0150	65,37,50,32C,32E
Zlotnick, Peter	NC0350	50,65
Zyskowski, Martin	WA0250	50,65,60B
Zyskowski, Marty	WA0950	65,50,37

String Ensemble

Name	Code	Areas
Abegg, Paul	UT0150	62A,38,51,54,62B
Abo, Takeshi	MI0100	62A,62B,51
Abo, Takeshi	MI0150	62A,51
Aceto, Jonathan D.	GA0950	51,62A,11,62B,13E
Adams, Lowell	FL2050	51,62C
Adams, Valerie	FL0930	51,62A
Afanassieva, Veronika	CO0275	62A,42,51
Agopian, Edmond	AA0150	38,41,51,62A,42
Ahramjian, Sylvia Davis	PA3600	51,62A,62B
Aldrich, Ralph E.	AG0500	41,51,62A,62B
Aldridge, Erin	WI0860	38,62A,13C,51,60B
Alter, Adam M.	SC0800	64C,51
Alvarez, Franklin	AZ0300	11,51,62,38,13C
Ambartsumian, Levon	GA2100	51,62A,62B
Amorim, George J.	TX3525	62D,13,51
Anderson, Erik	ND0250	62D,62C,13,51,29
Andrews, Pamela	FL0850	51,67A
Anop, Lenora Marya	IL2910	62A,41,51,42
Anthony, Janet	WI0350	12A,41,62C,51
Arnott, J. David	MN0350	38,62A,62B,51
Artmann, Mary	CO0275	62C,42,51
Au, Aaron	AA0100	62A,62B,51
Auerbach, Dan J.	GA0850	60,62A,62B,38,51
Avramov, Bogidar	CA2800	38,51,11,10F,60B
Azimkhodjaeva, Shakida	GA2100	51,62A
Baker, Cynthia	AZ0350	51,62A,62B
Baldridge, Margaret Nichols	MT0400	62A,62B,51
Baldwin, Kurt	MO1830	51,62C
Balija, Ayn	VA1550	62B,51,42
Barczyk, Cecylia	MD0850	41,62C,32E,51
Bargerstock, Nancy E.	NC0050	51,62A,42,62B
Barnet, Lori A.	DC0100	62C,51
Bashford, Christina	IL3300	12A,12C,12D,42,51
Bassett, Jon	FL0670	36,61,51,38,32D
Beall, Stephen J.	TX2955	62A,62B,51
Beaver, Johanna L.	VA1475	62A,62B,51
Becker, Wanda	MO1250	51
Bednarz, Blanka	PA0950	13A,42,51,62A,62B
Bell, Valerie	MO1810	51,62
Bernhardsson, Sigurbjorn	IL3300	51,62A
Biava, Luis Gabriel	OH1200	62C,51
Bird, Paula E.	TX3175	62A,51
Bishop, Matthew	TX1425	51,70,12A
Blaydes, Sharon	OH1600	62A,62B,51
Boden-Luethi, Ruth	WA1150	62C,62D,13,51,42
Bodman, Alan	OH2150	51,62A,62B
Boga, Cheryl	PA3500	36,37,47,38,51
Bongiorno, Joseph A.	NY2750	62D,38,42,51
Boughton, Janet	CT0300	51,62,41
Boyd, Fern Glass	MT0400	12A,51,62C,11
Boyer, Duane	OR0200	70,51
Bozell, Casey	OR0150	62A,62B,38,62C,51
Bradley-Vacco, Lynda	MN0250	38,62A,62B,51
Braun, Joel	IN0150	62D,51
Brey, Carter	PA0850	51,62C
Brown, Christopher	OK0850	70,51,53,47
Brown, J. Bruce	MI2000	13,10,11,34,51
Brown, Lindsay	OH0100	62C,62D,51
Brown, Susan	CA0400	41,51,62,32
Brye, Daniel	PA0950	62A,62B,51
Buchman, Heather	NY1350	38,49,51,48,60B
Burns, Lauren	GA2150	62B,32E,51
Bustamante, Linda	FL1300	11,38,51,62C,62D

Index by Area of Teaching Interest

Name	Code	Areas
Butler-Hopkins, Kathleen M.	AK0150	51,62A,62B
Buxton, Donald	MD1100	51
Caballero, Jorge	NJ0700	70,51
Caban, Francisco J.	PR0115	62A,41,42,51
Cadieux, Marie-Aline	PA1750	13,11,51,62C,42
Calderon, Javier	WI0815	70,51
Cameron, Jennifer	OR1150	13,10F,64,60,51
Cameron, Michael J.	IL3300	62D,51,41
Cantwell, Terry	GA1260	13A,13,70,51
Carbonara, David	LA0720	38,41,51,62
Carenbauer, Michael	AR0750	45,51,70,34
Carlson, Andrew	OH0850	62A,51,20G,38
Carlson, Marlan	OR0700	38,51
Carol, Norman	PA0850	51
Carrasco, Jacqui	NC2500	62A,62B,51,41,14
Carter, Adam C.	VA1550	62C,51
Cary, Neal	VA0250	51,62C
Chang, Pansy Y.	OH1450	62C,51
Chapo, Eliot	FL0850	41,51,62A
Charles, Lewis O.	OH1650	70,51
Cheifetz, Hamilton	OR0850	41,51,62C,20G,20F
Chen, Lambert	AI0150	62B,51
Chepaitis, Stanley L.	PA1600	41,62A,62B,51
Cho, Wan-Soo	KY0400	62B,51
Choi, Eugenia	AB0100	62A,51
Christopher, Paul	LA0550	10,13,51,62C,62D
Chung, Minna Rose	AC0100	62C,42,51
Chung, Miri	IN0907	62A,62B,33,51
Cifani, Elizabeth	IL2250	62E,51
Clifford, Patrick	FL1450	62A,62B,51
Cline, Benjamin	KS0350	51,62C,62D,38
Cohen, Joanne	MN0600	32,51,62A,62B
Cole, David	FL0680	51
Cole, David C.	FL0680	38,51,39,62A,32
Colwell, David A.	VA1550	62A,51,42
Consiglio, Catherine	KS1450	62B,51,41
Cook, Scott A.	WI0825	62C,51,41
Cooper, Cora	KS0650	51,62A,62B
Copes, Ronald	NY1900	62A,51
Costanza, Christopher	CA4900	62C,41,51
Cruz, Mark A.	TX3175	70,51
Czarkowski, Stephen	WV0550	62C,11,51
Dahlstrand, John	AR0350	62D,51
Dallinger, Carol	IN1600	62A,13A,62B,51
Davis, Susan A.	NY2750	32,51,62
Dawes, Andrew	AB0100	41,51,62A,42
Dawson, Andrea	TN1100	62A,51,11
De Leon, Tagumpay	CA5040	20D,51
Dempsey, John D.	RI0300	13A,13,51,62A
DePasquale, Charles	PA1550	51,62
Devroye, Anthony	IL2200	62B,51
Diamond, Douglas	MN0050	60B,38,51,12A
DiCecco, Enrico	NY2150	51
Dissmore, Larry	MO0400	60,38,51,62A,62B
Dixon, Scott	OH0600	62D,51
Djokic, Philippe	AF0100	62B,38,41,51,62A
Dobrotvorskaia, Ekaterina	CO0275	62B,42,51
Doctor, Kirsten	OH0600	51,62B
Dolin, Elizabeth	AI0150	62C,51
Dufour, Francine	AI0220	51,62A
Duitman, Henry E.	MI0900	51,38,32E,41
Duke-Kirkpatrick, Erika	CA0510	42,62C,51
DuWors, Kerry	AC0050	62A,62B,51
Dyck, Calvin	AB0060	51,62A
Eccles, David F.	IL3450	51,32E,38
Eckert, Erika	CO0800	51,62B
Elias, Carlos	CO0225	32C,38,62A,62B,51
Ellis, Peter	AA0032	38,62,51,36
Emerson, Deidre	TN1400	62C,38,51
Emery, Michael	NY3650	62A,62B,51
Enyart, John	FL0950	38,62A,51
Faganel, Gal	CO0950	62C,42,35G,51
Fahy, Alison	MN0610	32E,51
Fairbanks, Donna	UT0325	51,62,38
Fairlie, Mary	TX2800	62A,62B,51,14C,38
Farkas, Pavel	CA5150	38,41,51,62A,62B
Fedkenheuer, William	TX3510	62A,51
Fedotov, Igor	MI2250	51,62B
Ferguson, John	MO0500	62,51
Findley, Mary B.	DC0100	62A,51
Flanagan-Lysy, Margaret	CA5030	51
Flavin, Scott Thomas	FL1900	62A,51
Flores, David	CA4425	51,65
Flores, Jose G.	TX2930	62A,62B,51,13C,42
Fowler, Kurt	IN0800	62C,11,12A,51
Fradette, Amelie	NY3717	62C,51
Fredenburgh, Kim	NM0450	62B,51
Friesen, John	WA1250	13,51,62C
Frittelli, Leslie	VA1000	62C,51,41
Fulbright, Marshall T.	CA2550	38,51,48,62,63
Fullard-Rosenthal, Annie	OH0600	51
Gabriel, Edgar	IL1085	62A,53,51
Gaddis, J. Robert	KY0400	60,32,51,63D,38
Gagnon, Marie-Elaine	SD0600	11,51,62C,41
Gallagher, Mara	IL2050	62A,51
Galluzzo, Jacqueline	NY3717	62A,51
Ganatra, Simin	IL3300	51,62A
Garcia, Alvaro	WI0835	38,62B,60,51
Gardiner, Annabelle	FL1740	62A,62B,51,38
Gardiner, Ronald	FL1740	13,62,60B,51,38
Garibova, Karine	CO0275	62A,42,51
George, Samantha	WI0350	62A,41,51
Georgieva, Roumena G.	GA0490	62A,62B,38,51
Giray, Selim	KS1450	62A,62B,51,42,38
Glidden, Amy	NY3717	62A,51
Glyde, Judith	CO0800	11,51,62C
Golden, Lyman	SC0050	10,51,70
Goldspiel, Alan	AL1200	70,13C,13B,51
Gorevic, Elizabeth	NY3775	51,62A,62B
Greene, Kenneth H.	TX3350	14,38,62B,51
Greensmith, Clive S.	NY2750	51,62C
Greenspan, Bertram	NJ1050	62A,51,12A,12
Gries, Rachel	IN0500	62A,51
Grizzell, Janet	CA1290	38,51,62
Grossman, Hal	OK1350	62A,41,51
Grove, Paul	ID0140	51,70
Hagy, David	NC2500	11,38,51
Haken, Rudolf	IL3300	62B,51,41
Hamar, Jon	WA0550	29,62C,62D,32E,51
Hampton, Ian	AB0060	51,62C
Hansen, Eric	UT0050	62D,38,51
Harding, David	AB0100	51,62A,62B,41,42
Harris, Dennis	TX1850	51,70
Harris, Mary	OH1450	32,62B,51,42
Hayden, William P.	FL2000	62A,62B,51
Hays, David R.	MO0775	62A,51
Heard, Cornelia	TN1850	41,51,62A
Hector-Norwood, Diana	TX1350	51,62
Hekmatpanah, Kevin	WA0400	11,12A,38,51,62C
Hillyer, Giselle	WI0845	62A,62B,51
Hogue, Charles	AL1160	62B,51
Holland, David	MI0400	62B,42,51
Holland, David	MI1650	62B,42,51
Holzemer, Kate C.	NY3717	62B,51
Hope, Garrett E.	PA3550	10,62D,13,34,51
Horvath, Kathleen	OH0400	32,51,62
Hosmer, Christian	NY3550	62,51
Howard, Jeffrey	MD0850	62A,41,51
Hristov, Miroslav P.	TN1710	51,62A
Hsu, Linda Y.	AR0850	62A,51
Hubbard, Eve P.	NC0900	51,62A
Hult, David W.	NY2650	62A,62B,11,51
Hungerford, Del	WA1350	64C,51
Hutchinson, Chad	IA1200	11,38,51
Hutton, Christopher	SC0750	62C,12A,51
Hutton, Deirdre	SC0750	62A,51
Imsand, Patrick K.	AL1300	70,11,51
Ito, Kanako	MO1000	51,62A
Ivry, Jessica	CA1150	51,42,62,13C,38
Ivy, Allen	MO1100	60,38,51,64A
Jackobs, Mark	OH0600	62B,51
James, Douglas	NC0050	70,51
Jay, Sarah	CA1425	51
Jennings, Linda G.	PA1600	62C,62D,13,51
Jensen, Janet L.	WI0815	32,62A,38,51
Jetter, Katherine	CO0350	38,62C,62D,13,51
Johnson, Cecilia	MI0050	62,51
Johnson, David	ID0070	13A,41,62B,42,51
Johnson, Karrell	TX3420	32,51,62B
Johnson, Roger	CA2550	38,51,48
Joiner, Lee	IL3550	51,62A,62B
Jones, Stephen F.	CA3500	51,70
Kadetsky, Mark	NJ0550	62D,51,11
Kaminski, Imelda	IL1890	62A,51
Kaplan, Lewis	NY1900	51,62A
Kaplunas, Daniel	IA1800	38,62C,62B,51,60
Karp, Parry	WI0815	51,62C
Kartman, Stefan	WI0825	62C,42,51,41
Kauffman, Irvin C.	PA1600	70,51
Kenny, Megan	NC2435	62A,62B,51
Kew, Margaret Davis	KS0100	51,62,66A
Kim, Eunho	SD0600	62A,62B,51
Kimler, Wayne	MO0650	51,70
King, Terry B.	CT0650	51,62C
King, Troy	MD0850	70,51
Kirkpatrick, Leon	KY0250	37,38,41,51,60B
Kirkwood, James H.	NY3730	51,62C
Kivrak, Osman	DC0010	62B,42,51
Knific, Renata	MI2250	51,62A
Knific, Thomas	MI2250	47,51,62D,46,29
Kochanowski, John	TN1850	41,51,62B,42
Konzen, Richard A.	PA1450	38,51,66G,41,13B
Koontz, Eric E.	NC0050	62B,62A,67A,42,51
Koshgarian, Richard	KS0150	38,51,63C,63D
Kostic, Dina	FL0050	62A,41,42,51
Kozak, Pawel K	SC1000	51,62A,62B
Kozamchak, David M.	MN1280	38,51,62A,62B
Krishnaswami, Donald	MA0510	11,12A,62A,62B,51
Kromin, Vladimir	VA1100	62A,62B,51
Krosnick, Joel	NY1900	51,62C
Kruse, Penny Thompson	OH0300	51,62A
Kubin, Brian	MO1780	62C,13,51,62D
Laderach, Linda C.	MA1350	51,62A,62B,67B
Lagana, Tom	MD0850	70,29A,51
Lamb, Earnest	NC0800	12A,32C,51,62
Lambert, Nathan T.	CO0350	10F,11,14C,42,51
Lang, Cynthia	CA3400	38,41,51,62
Lansdale, Katie	CT0650	41,51,62A
Lantz, Lisa E.	NY0100	11,38,51,62,13A
Lanza, Joseph	AG0500	38,41,51,62A
Lardinios, John	OH2250	62A,51
Lardinois, Kara	OH2250	62A,51
Lastrapes, Jeffrey Noel	TX3200	62C,42,51,11,32E
Laureano, Victor O.	PR0150	70,51
Lautar, Rebecca	FL0650	11,41,51,62A,62B
Lazar, Teri	DC0010	62A,42,51
Lebo, Joanna	SC0050	51,62A,62B
Ledbetter, Lynn F.	TX3175	62A,62B,42,51
Lee, Charles	CO0650	62C,41,51,10F,60
Lee, Cheng-Hou	IL2200	62C,51
Lee, Christine	CA0630	51
Lee, Gregory	OK1350	62A,41,51
Lee, Seunghee	MI0400	62A,51
Lehmann, Matthew	NY1600	62A,51
Lehnert, Oswald	CO0800	51,62A,62B
Leonhardt, Julie	MO1250	62,51
Lewis, Eric	CT0800	12A,62B,51,62A,12B
Lewis, Melissa	OK1200	60,41,51,62A
Lippincott, Tom	FL0700	70,51
Lipscomb, Ronald	PA1000	51,62C
Liu, Kexi	MO0800	11,51,62A,62B
Loban, John A.	AB0100	41,51,62A
Luby, Richard E.	NC2410	41,51,62A,67A
Luchansky, Andrew	CA0840	13A,51,62C
Lundy, Ann	TX3150	51,62,38
Lupanu, Calin	NC0850	62A,51
Lupu, Sherban	IL3300	51,62A,41
Lyons, Glenn	PA3600	51,70
Maahs, Kristin	IA0700	62C,51
Macomber, Curtis	NY1900	51
Magniere, Blaise	IL2200	62A,51
Maldonado, Ana Maria	CA0845	32,62C,51
Maldonado, Greg	CA0825	51,62A,55,62B
Male, Sara	PA1250	62C,51
Manning, Lucy	VA1000	38,62A,32E,41,51
Mantell, Matthew	IL3100	51,62A,62B
Marinescu, Ovidiu	PA3600	38,62C,51
Markow, Roseann	MD0500	62A,62B,51
Martin, Spencer L.	IA0950	62A,62B,51,38
Martinez, Everaldo	ND0400	62A,62B,62C,51,38
Martinez, Everaldo	ND0050	62,51
Martinson, Kenneth	FL1850	62B,51
Masciardo, Milton	GA2100	51,62D
Maxwell, Monte	MD0900	66G,38,36,31A,51
Mazak, Grant	TX3175	70,51
Mazo, Vadim	IL1200	41,42,62A,62B,51
McFadden, Joseph	GA1150	62D,51
McGrosso, John	MO1830	51,62A
McKnight, Linda	NJ0800	62D,51
McLaughlin, Gary	CA4460	51
McNabney, Douglas	AI0150	51,62B,42
Meineke, Robert	TX2350	62A,62B,62C,62D,51
Melik-Stepanov, Karren	SD0050	62C,51
Michel, John	WA0050	11,41,51,62C
Miedema, Lisa	IA1200	62A,51
Mihai, Julieta	IL3500	62A,51

Name	Code	Areas
Miller, Anton	CT0650	41,51,62A
Miller, Charles	ID0140	51,70
Miller, Ken	MN1250	62C,51
Miller, Peter	VT0100	62,32,51
Molina, Moises	IL3500	62C,51
Morgan, Angela L.	GA0250	32,38,51,62A
Morgan, Lauren R.	MO0250	62A,62B,62C,62D,51
Mori, Akira	IA0550	38,51,11
Morrice, John	CA1850	51
Morrow, Elizabeth N.	TX3500	62C,51,11
Moss, Kirk D.	WI0350	11,32E,38,51,62
Munro, Anne	WV0550	64A,48,38,51
Murasugi, Sachiho	MD0800	62A,62B,11,13A,51
Murray, Kris A.	IL2730	36,70,11,51
Murray, Michael A.	MO0775	13,51,62C
Mushabac, Regina M.	OH0200	41,51
Myrick, John	AL1195	32,62A,62B,41,51
Neher, Patrick K.	AZ0500	62D,51
Nepkie, Janet	NY3765	13A,41,51,62C,35
Neubert, Peter	TX1100	51,62
Neumann, Ben	AA0050	32B,38,51,62A
Neumann, Mark	OK1350	62A,41,51
Nuttall, Geoff	CA4900	62A,41,51
Oakes, Elizabeth	IA1550	51
Ogletree, Mary	PA1750	13,11,62A,62B,51
Olivares, Walter G.	AK0100	12A,51,62
Owen, Marlin	CA0350	38,41,51,62,70
Page, John	MA1400	38,51
Pancella, Peter	IL1500	62A,62B,51
Park, Chung	NC0050	38,62A,62B,51,60
Park, Jenny	CA5355	51,66A,66B
Parker, Mara	PA3680	12A,11,41,51,62C
Patitucci, John	NY0550	10,46,47,51,50
Peckham, Merry	OH0600	51,62C
Peng, Bo	AB0060	62C,51
Perez, Miguel	MA0510	11,62A,51
Peris, Malinee	DC0100	41,66A,51
Perry, Kathy	SC0700	62,51,42
Petrescu, Stefan	TN1400	51,62A
Phoenix-Neal, Diane	IA0200	62,11,12,51
Pickett, Susan	WA1300	13A,13,12A,51,62A
Pierce, Carrie	TX2930	62C,62D,51,31A,13C
Piippo, Richard	MI1050	38,41,51,62C,10F
Pikler, Charles	IL2100	62A,51,42,62B
Pile, Randy	CA3460	51,70
Pinell, Javier	TX2250	62A,42,51
Pogrebnoy, Nikita	AB0060	62B,51
Pokhanovski, Oleg	AC0100	62A,51,42
Potter, Shelley	WA0950	51,62A,20,13A,13D
Pranno, Arthur J.	FL0800	62A,38,51,62B,12A
Presler, Anna H.	CA0840	13A,51
Przygocki, James T.	WY0200	62B,51,32E
Puchhammer, Jutta	AI0200	62B,41,51
Purdy, Carl	GA0250	62A,62B,70,51
Purdy, Craig Allen	ID0050	41,42,51,62A,38
Quick, Julia M.	SC1050	11,38,41,51,62A
Rafferty, J. Patrick	KY1500	62A,51
Ramael, David R.	NY1600	12,38,39,60B,51
Rammon, Andrew	PA3150	62C,51
Ranney, Jack	IL2350	38,51,62
Raschen, Gudrun E.	TX3300	62D,62C,67B,51
Raths, O. Nicholas	MN0050	70,51
Ray-Carter, Trilla	MO2000	51,62C,42
Redfield, Stephen C.	MS0750	62A,51
Redmer Minner, Laurie K.	TN1350	60B,38,51,32C,62B
Redmon, Steve	MI0300	32E,51
Rehkopf-Michel, Carrie	WA0050	41,51,62A,62B
Renyer, Erinn	KS0050	62C,62D,51,42
Restesan, Francis'c	KY1000	38,51,39,62A
Restesan, Frank	NE0550	38,13C,62A,51,12A
Rhodes, Samuel	NY1900	51,41,62B
Richardson, Cathy	TX0250	62A,62B,51
Roberts, Kay George	MA2030	60,38,51
Robertson, Lesley N.	CA4900	62B,41,51
Rodgers, Linda	CA1520	62,51
Rojas, Berta	DC0100	70,51
Rollins, Christopher	MI1200	70,51
Roos, Joni N.	FL1550	62A,62B,51
Rostad, Masumi	IL3300	51,62B
Rowan, Mark	NC0910	70,11,51,12E
Rudolph, Robert A.	PA0100	62A,62B,41,42,51
Rush, Mark	AZ0500	51,62A
Russell, Alex	CA0250	67A,51
Ryan, Patrick	GA0050	51
Salsbury, Ben	FL1450	51
Sandomirsky, Gregory	MO1000	51,66A
Santos, Philip	CA0807	62A,62B,51
Sarch, Kenneth	PA2150	51,62
Sariti, David J.	VA1550	62A,67B,51,42
Sato, Mari	OH0600	51
Sayevich, Ben	MO1000	51,62A
Scharron, Eladio	FL1800	70,51
Schnittgrund, Tammy	SD0500	51
Schrader, David D.	IL0550	12,51
Schulze, Theodora	IN0005	61,10A,13,50,51
Schwarz, Timothy J.	PA1950	62A,62B,51,41
Schwede, Walter	WA1250	51,62,62A
Seebacher, Robert	AL1300	11,38,51
Seitz, Diana	KS1400	62A,51
Selden, Ken	OR0850	38,43,51,60B
Sellitti, Anne	NC2205	62C,51
Shabalin, Alexey	RI0150	62A,51,38,32E
Shand, Patricia	AG0450	32C,51,62A,62B
Sharpe, Alexander E.	NY1600	62A,42,51
Shiao, Simon	FL1950	51,62A,62B,38
Shih, Patricia	AB0060	62A,51
Simidtchieva, Marta	IL2910	38,42,41,51,62C
Simon, Philip G.	PA3700	11,37,41,51,63D
Skelton, Robert A.	AG0500	60,38,41,51,62
Skidmore, Dan	NC0750	62A,51
Slavich, Richard	CO0900	12A,51,62C,41
Small, Elisabeth	TN0100	41,62A,51
Smith, Brent	UT0190	39,62C,13,12A,51
Smith, Carol	TX2250	38,51,60B,62,32E
Smith, Carol F.	TN1850	62A,32E,51
Smith, Elizabeth Reed	WV0400	38,41,51,62A,62B
Smith, James	WI0815	38,51,62,60B
Smith, Sam	ID0070	62C,51,38
Snider, Nancy Jo	DC0010	62C,42,51,67B,41
Soares, Luciana	LA0450	66A,66C,13F,51,13C
Sobrino, Laura	CA5040	20H,51
Sohn, Sung-Rai	NY3560	60,38,41,51,62A
Solomon, Qiao Chen	GA0050	62A,62B,51,41,38
Speth, Uli	NY1400	62A,41,51
St. John, Scott	CA4900	62A,41,51
Starkweather, David A.	GA2100	51,62C
Stearns, Roland H.	AK0100	13,70,51
Stein, Dean A.	ME0200	62A,51
Stevens, Daniel B.	KS1200	38,41,37,62,51
Stewart, Tobin E.	FL0680	51,13A,13C
Stomberg, Lawrence J.	DE0150	62C,51
Storey, Martin	MO1000	51,62C
Story, David	WI0850	62D,53,51,13A,13B
Strachan, Heather	GA2000	51,62A,62C
Struman, Susan Jean	TX0550	51,62C,32A,11,62D
Sturm, Hans	NE0600	51,62D
Suda, Carolyn W.	IL1350	11,42,51,62C
Sullivan, Kimberly	AZ0450	51,62A
Sutre, Guillaume	CA5030	62A,51
Swartz, Jennifer	AI0150	62E,51
Szabo, Istvan	IL3500	62B,51
Szekely, Eva D.	MO1800	62A,51
Tan, Kia-Hui	OH1850	62A,51,62B,13,42
Tao, Ye	LA0100	51,38
Teal, Christian	TN1850	41,51,62A
Terrell, Brett	IN0250	51,70
Terwilliger, William	SC1110	62A,51,42
Thomas, Jennifer	MN0625	51,62A,62B
Thomason, Eliza	TX3100	11,32E,62A,62B,51
Thompson, Fiona	PA2300	62C,51
Thompson, Jason	IN1025	38,62A,62B,51,62C
Thurmer, Harvey	OH1450	51,62A
Ting, Damian	CA2775	51,62
Todd, Kenneth W.	CO1050	11,38,51,62
Tormann, Wolf	AG0250	62C,51
Toyonaga, Shiho	IL2100	62B,51
Troxler, Lorinda	PA1350	51
Trtan, Jacqueline	MO0350	51,62C
Trynchuck, Carla	MI0250	62,41,51
Uchimura, Bruce	MI2250	60,51,62C
Uyeyama, Jason	CA2420	42,51,62A,62B
Uzur, Viktor	UT0350	13,10F,51,62C,42
Valcarcel, Andres	PR0100	62A,62B,51,38
Vamos, Brandon	IL3300	51,62C
Vance, Paul	MN1700	12A,62D,38,51,62C
Vodnoy, Robert L.	SD0400	12A,62,38,51,35E
Voldman, Yakov	LA0650	60,32C,38,51,62
Von Dassow, Sasha	FL1745	51,62C
Wada, Rintaro	NY3475	51,62
Wade-Elkamely, Bobbie	OK0450	51,62
Wagner, Lorraine	WY0115	62A,62B,62C,62D,51
Wagner, Shelbi	OH2250	62C,51,32E
Walvoord, Martha J.	TX3500	62A,51
Wang, Felix	TN1850	62C,41,51
Wang, Marie	IL2200	62A,51
Warkentien, Vicky	IN0200	13,66,41,51,38
Weber, Robert	IL1300	62C,51
Weiss, Richard	OH0600	62C,51
Weller, Ira	NY3785	62B,42,51
White, Al	KY0300	70,51
Williams, Tom	AI0150	38,51,62A
Wissick, Brent S.	NC2410	55,51,62C,67A,67E
Wood, Jasper	AB0100	62A,51
Woolweaver, Scott	MA2010	38,41,51,62B,62A
Work, George P.	IA0850	51,62C,62D,13
Wu, Hai-Xin	MI0400	62A,51
Xie, Song	MS0100	62A,62B,51,42
Yasuda, Nobuyoshi	WI0803	38,62A,51
Yates, Peter	CA0630	11,51,70,13A
Yeung, Ann M.	IL3300	62E,51
York, Paul	KY1500	51,62C,42
Yoshioka, Airi	MD1000	32,41,51,62A
Zabelle, Kim A.	WA0800	62A,62B,67A,51
Zacharius, Leanne	AC0050	38,62C,51
Zafer, Paul	IL3550	62A,51
Zank, Jeremy	OH1800	51,62A,62B
Zaplatynsky, Andrew	NY1550	51,62A,62B
Zelmanovich, Mark	TN1710	51,62A
Zezelj-Gualdi, Danijela	GA0940	62A,62B,51
Zhu, Hong	OK1330	62A,41,42,51
Ziebold, Barbara M.	OH2140	62,51
Zimmer, Don	TN1700	11,51,62A

Dance/Ballet Troupe

Name	Code	Areas
Abbott, Gary Bernard	MO1810	52
Alorwoyie, Gideon F.	TX3420	20,65,31F,50,52
An, Chun Chi	IN0900	52
Anderson, Kris	KS0210	52
Angier, D. Chase	NY0100	52
Arnett, Alan	VA1350	52
Atwood, Jodi	AA0040	52
Augustine, Shari	KS0590	52
Bartlett, Carol A.	MD0650	52
Bender, Rhett	OR0950	64E,13,52,64C
Bolden, Christina	OH2550	52
Braun, Kathleen	MS0420	52
Brodie, Nannette	CA2050	52
Brown, Billbob	MA2000	52
Burgess, Stacey	NC1050	52
Burton, Rachel Anne	IL2150	52
Campbell, Diane	OH2550	52
Carberry, Deirdre	OH2200	52
Cash, Shellie B.	OH2200	52
Cesbron, Jacques	IN0900	52
Chandler, David	CT0650	54,52
Chen, Ting Yu	VA1350	52
Clark, Joan	PA2100	52
Cook-Perez, Paige	CA3270	52,54
Crabtree, Kacy E.	NC1050	52,35E
Crocker, Emily	OR0450	52
Damast, Deborah G.	NY2750	52
Dando, Lee C.	FL1570	52
Davalos, Catherine	CA3920	52
De Jager, Ron	AJ0030	60A,36,52,61,32D
DeBord, Kathryn	VA1350	52
Degnan-Boonin, Kristin	PA3700	52
DeJesus, Ron	MI2100	52,54
Dennis, Paul A.	MA2000	52
Dexter Sawyer, Annetta	DC0250	52
Dexter, Mary	IL1090	52
Dunbar, Ulrike	FL1430	52
English, Nicole	MO1810	52
Falk, Jodi	CT0650	52
Farrell, Jamie	IL2150	52
Follett, Karen	VA1350	52
Fox, Julie C.	WI0803	52
Fraga, Maurice	VA1350	52
Frost, Randi	TX3530	52
Gazdyszyn, Danuta U.	TX1425	52,54
Gibson, Elijah	VA1350	52
Giguere, Miriam	PA1000	52
Gorecki, Maria De La Luz	TX1425	52,54
Goshorn, Jereme	VA1350	52
Grammel, Deborah Lynn	IN0350	52

Name	Code	Areas
Greco, Christine R.	TX1425	52,54
Grossman, Pauline	DC0050	52
Guy, Kathyanne	FL1900	52
Hachiya-Weinrer, Jane	IN0100	52
Ham, Christopher M.	VA1350	52
Harris-Warrick, Rebecca	NY0900	11,12,52
Harsa, Sandra Y.	TX1425	52,54
Hart Stoker, Catherine	MN0950	52
Hart, Sasha	OH2550	52
Helm, Erica	VA1350	52
Helms, Nancy	CA5150	52
Henry, Mary Pat	MO1810	52
Hiett, Dee Anna	MO1810	52
Hosler, Cheryl L.	SC0400	52
Hoyt-Brackman, Brenda	OH2275	52,54
Hurst, Christon	OH2550	52
Jiang, Qi M.	OH2200	52
Johnson, Jill	MA1050	52
Johnson, Maurice	DC0050	52
Judiyaba	CA4700	52,62C
Kaminsky, Carol Frances	FL1900	52
Kane, Angela	MI2100	52
Kelly, Kathleen	GA0500	52,54
King, Douglas	IN0100	52
Komaiko, Libby A.	IL2150	52
Kuite, Anne	FL1900	52
Lacoursiere, Marie-Nathalie	AI0200	52,67H
Lancos, Jonette	NY3730	52
Lester-White, Dottie	CA3270	52,54
Levine, Susan	NE0600	52
Lippoldt-Mack, Valerie	KS0210	11,36,61,32I,52
Mackie, Doug	IA1450	52
Madison-Cannon, Sabrina	MO1810	52
Mahoney, Billie	MO1810	52
Mahtani, Lorena	TX1425	52,54
Martin, Mary Lou	AF0050	52
McCausland, Jacqueline J.	NY3730	52
McDonald, Linn	PA2200	52
McIntosh, Eulaine	TX1050	52
McKinnis, Alicia V.	TX1425	52,54
McNamara, Joann	MI0600	52
Miller, Linda	VA1350	52
Mitchell, Erin	WA0860	52
Mitchell, Rebecca	FL1750	52
Moore, Denise Leetch	CT0650	52
Morales, Hilda	CT0650	52
Moss, Suzan	NY2100	52
Murdock, Kelly	FL1430	52
Murphy, Susan	CT0350	52
Nikitina, Alla	CT0650	52
Petry, Julie	PA0250	52
Pier, Stephen	CT0650	52
Pierce, Ken	MA1175	67H,52
Pietri, Michelle M.	TX3530	54,52
Quinn, Ann	CT0650	52
Quinn, Shannon	DC0050	52
Ray, Scott	NY3730	52
Reber, William F.	AZ0100	39,54,52,66C,60
Reisman, Leana	CT0650	52,13C
Reny, Alison	OH2275	52
Richard, Sarah	WA0860	61,52
Rios, Juan	CA5040	20H,52
Rowe, Larry	CT0650	52
Ruiz, Irma	IL2150	52
Rush, Stephen J.	MI2100	52,34A
Sales, Doricha	IN0900	52
Salzer, Rebecca	WI0350	52
Schaaf, Gary D.	NE0590	52
Schroth, Robyn	VA1350	52
Shepard, Kenny	IN0100	52
Short, Shawn	DC0050	52
Silveus, Debra L.	IN0100	52
Simmons, Phil	MI0600	52
Smith, Sue	MI0050	52,54
Solari, Gia	CA3270	52,54
Staton, Celeste A.	HI0200	52
Steele, Cathy	MS0320	52
Steele, Shauna	IN0100	52
Stevinson-Nollet, Katie	CT0650	52
Stifler, Venetia C.	IL2150	52
Strong, Michael	MO1810	52
Tashpulatov, Oyber N.	IN0100	52
Taylor, Joseph	FL1430	52
Ter-Grigor'yan, Irina	IN0900	52
Terrance, Christine	AA0040	52
Tevlin, Michael J.	OH2200	52
Tice, Ronald	MO1810	52
Tzigalanis, Voula	AA0040	52
Unger, Leslie	CT0650	52
Vacanti, Tom L.	MA2000	52
Verdy, Violette	IN0900	52
Vermeer, Cassidy	IA0790	52
Vernon, Michael	IN0900	52
Wang, Guoping	IN0900	52
Weber, Paula B.	MO1810	52
Weisman, Bonita	CT0650	52
Whitworth, Amanda E.	NH0250	52
Wilkinson, Sherry	MI0600	52
Williams, Megan	TX3530	52
Willis, George R.	WV0750	10D,11,32B,52,65

Improvisation Ensemble

Name	Code	Areas
Adams, James M.	ND0600	35G,37,47,49,53
Aguilar, Gustavo	ME0410	53,34D
Akagi, Kei	CA5020	53,29,47
Albertson, John	DC0100	67B,70,53
Alford, Steve W.	NC1250	64E,47,53
Allee, Steve	IN0907	66A,47,35A,53
Allen, Susan	CA0510	41,62E,43,53
Anderson, Ray R.	NY3790	46,47,53
Anderson, Ross	MN1500	53
Archard, Chuck	FL1550	47,62D,53,29
Artwick, Thomas	VA1850	64E,53
Baker, Malcolm Lynn	CO0900	47,53,46,29
Ballou, David L.	MD0850	29,53,63A,29A,36
Bangle, Jerry	NC2640	13,11,38,53,29
Bastin, Ernest	OH1900	53
Beach, Douglas	IL0850	47,53,71,29,35
Beals, Andrew	CT0800	64E,41,53
Beaugrand, Luc	AI0200	53,66A,29
Begian, Jamie	CT0800	41,70,53,47,29
Bejerano, Martin	FL1900	29,10,66A,53
Benedetti, Fred	CA2100	70,53,35B,29
Benton, Leanne	OK0850	53
Birkner, Tom	IL2970	53
Bisio, Michael	VT0050	62D,53,29
Black, Cary	WA0350	62D,53,29,35,47
Blake, Michael	ND0500	13A,50,53,65
Blake, Ran	MA1400	29,66A,53
Bloom, Jane Ira	NY2660	10,53,64,47
Bonelli, Matt	FL1300	62D,53
Borla, Janice	IL2050	53,29,29A,29B
Bouchard, Jean-Marc	AI0200	64E,53
Boyd, Lance	MT0400	47,63C,63D,53,29
Boyle, Patrick	AB0150	20A,29B,47,53
Brackeen, Joanne	NY2660	10,66A,47,53
Brazelton, Kitty	VT0050	13,10F,10,11,53
Bremer, Jeff	PA3650	47,53,62D
Bridgewater, Cecil	NY2660	10,63A,53
Briggs, Nancy L.	CA4580	29,10,66,53,20
Broderick, James	FL1300	13,63A,53,34
Broms, E.	MA0800	70,53
Brown, Christopher	OK0850	70,51,53,47
Brubeck, Matthew	AG0650	43,53,62C
Buchman, Matthew	WI0850	47,53,66A
Buhr, Glenn	AG0600	10,53
Bump, Delbert	CA4650	13A,13,36,53
Burroughs, D. Robert	WA0150	13,11,62A,53,38
Butler, Hunt	KY0750	47,48,64,53,29A
Campbell, Gary	FL0700	64E,29,53,47
Campbell, Will	NC2420	46,47,53,64E
Campiglia, Paul	GA0625	47,29,53,65
Canfield, Wanda	PA1000	66A,66D,53
Carello, Joseph	NY2950	53,64E
Carter, Cecil	TX2200	47,53
Carter, Edward L.	AZ0510	70,53
Chambers, Joe	NY2660	44,65,53
Chase, Allan S.	MA1400	47,29,53,64E
Chevan, David	CT0450	11,12A,47,53,29
Clancy, Eric	IN0700	47,29,53
Clancy, Gary	ME0340	47,70,53,35
Clark, Dave	KY0250	29B,47,53,64E
Clegg, Neill M.	NC0900	10F,12A,64,53,29A
Colby, Mark	IL0850	64E,53
Coleman, Anthony	MA1400	53,29
Coolman, Todd	NY3785	47,62D,53,46,29
Corbet, Kim	TX2400	53,29A
Cox, Daniel R.	ID0140	50,65,53,11
Coyle, Brian	MI1050	47,29,53
Cyrille, Andrew	NY2660	65,53
D'Angelo, David	GA2100	29,53
Davis, Anthony	CA5050	20G,66A,10,53
Davis, Joshua	PA3150	47,29,62D,13C,53
Davis, Mark	WI0150	47,29,53
Dawson, Robert B.	CA1700	13A,35,13,53
De Toledo, Rubim	AA0050	47,53
Deardorf, Chuck	WA0200	62D,53,29,35
D'earth, John E.	VA1550	20G,47,63A,53
Delfante, Ernest	CA1900	53
DeMarinis, Paul	MO1950	64E,53,29
Detweiler, Bruce	OK0150	11,47,53
Diamond, Jody	NH0100	14,53,43
DiBlasio, Denis	NJ1050	10F,47,64E,53,29
Dickert, Lewis H.	SC1200	70,53,29,13A,14
Dickman, Marcus	FL1950	63D,53,29
Dierker, John	MD0850	63A,47,53
Dimond, Raymond R.	AR0300	47,65,53,13,32E
Dudley, Bruce	TN0100	66A,35B,53
Eade, Dominique	MA1400	61,53,47,29
Ellias, Rod	AI0070	13,47,70,53,29
Ellison, Charles	AI0070	47,63A,53,46,29
Engelhardt, Kent	OH2600	64E,29,53,47
Epstein, Joan O.	FL0450	13,11,12A,53,63A
Escalera, Mario	NY2660	64,53
Espinosa, Gabriel	IA0200	47,53,29,40
Evoskevich, Paul	NY0700	47,64E,53,29,42
Feder, Janet	CO0560	10,70,12A,13A,53
Ferrier, Robert	MA1100	70,53,29,13C
Finucane, David A.	NC0600	53,64E
Fonville, John	CA5050	13,10,64A,53,43
Fox, Jon	TX1600	70,53,13B
Fraize, Peter W.	DC0100	47,53,64E,29
Frey, Kevin T.	CA4350	13,11,14,63,53
Friedman, Bennett	CA4460	29,53,47
Frith, Fred	CA2950	10A,10B,53,43,11
Fudge, Berkeley	WI1150	47,64E,53,64A,29
Gabriel, Edgar	IL1085	62A,53,51
Gallo, Joseph	CA1520	35,34,66A,29,53
Galloway, Michael	PA2150	47,63A,53,29
Garrison, Kirk	IL0730	47,53
Garson, Michael	CA1075	53
Giacabetti, Tom	NJ1050	41,53,70
Gibble, David L.	FL1470	29,47,37,53,49
Gilman, Joe	CA0150	13,66A,53,29
Gimble, Richard	TX1600	62D,70,53,35B
Goble, Daniel P.	CT0800	47,64E,53,29,41
Golia, Vinny	CA0510	64,35A,53,47
Gomez, Edgar	PR0115	62D,53
Green, Bunky	FL1950	64E,53,29
Grigoriev, Igor	CA0859	70,53
Groce-Roberts, Virginia	CA4400	53
Guarneri, Mario	CA4150	49,53,63A
Guiterrez, Charles	CA2550	39,53,46,35B,34
Haddad, Jamey	OH1700	53
Haden, Charlie	CA0510	47,62D,53
Hagelgany, David	WA1150	47,64E,29,53
Halberstadt, Randy	WA0200	13,66A,66D,53,29
Hall, Thomas	MA0500	53,64C
Ham, Lawrence	NY1050	53,29
Hamilton, Frederick	TX3420	47,70,53,29
Hamilton, Ryan	OH0350	63C,47,29B,53
Hamme, Albert	NY3705	47,64E,53,29A
Haque, Fareed	IL2200	70,53,29
Harbaugh, John	WA0050	29A,53,49,63A
Hart, Kevin M.	IL1350	29B,53,66A,47,65
Hartenberger, Russell	AG0450	50,65,53
Haydon, Rick	IL2910	70,29,35G,53,47
Heavner, Tracy	AL1300	32E,64E,47,53
Helzer, Richard A.	CA4100	29B,29C,66A,47,53
Hendricks, Jon	OH2300	29,53
Hitt, Christine	IA0910	66A,47,53,46
Hodge, Cheryl	AB0070	10,36,61,53,35H
Holinaty, William	AG0200	53
Holm, Molly	CA2950	61,47,53
Hurel, Pierre	MA0350	53
Hynes, Tom	CA1000	13,29,47,53,70
Ibarra, Susie	VT0050	20,29,50,47,53
Ingalls, Duane	ME0430	65,53,46
Irish, Michael J.	MI1450	13,47,45,53,29
Jackson, Tyrone	GA1150	66A,29B,66D,53
James, Matthew T.	OH1900	64E,47,53,46,29
Johnston, Noel H.	TX3420	70,53,29
Johnston, Paul R.	IL0800	46,29,53
Johnston, Randy	CT0650	47,70,53

Jones, Kimberlyn	CA2810	39,61,54,53
Jones, Sean	PA1050	47,53,63A
Jones, T. Marshall	GA0150	11,29,47,53
Kaplan, Allan Richard	NM0310	11,63C,53
Karush, Larry	CA3300	66A,53
Katz, Brian	AG0650	70,53
Kendrick, Matt	NC2500	46,53
Kim, Steve	WA0860	62D,47,53
Knapp, James	WA0200	10,47,63A,53,29
Kocher, Christopher John	SD0600	47,64E,53,46,29
Koven, Steven	AG0650	53,66A
Kreitner, William	FL1310	47,50,65,53
Kruger, Jonathan H.	NY3730	47,63A,53
Kunkel, Jeffrey	NJ0800	32,47,29,53,46
Kurzdorfer, James	NY4460	13,47,62D,53
Kush, Jason	PA3100	64E,29,41,53,64C
Lajoie, Stephen H.	RI0101	47,66A,53,29,13A
Landsberg, Paul	AB0070	13A,70,53,47,29
Langham, Patrick	CA5350	46,47,29,53
Lawton, Thomas P.	PA0400	66A,53
Lazaro, Andrew A.	PR0115	47,65,53
Lee, Brent	AG0550	13,10,45,43,53
Lee, Colin	AG0600	53,33
Lewandowski, Annie	NY0900	53,66A
Lewis, Cecil	CO0100	47,53,64E,37
Lewis, Roger	KS0210	13,10,37,47,53
Long, Barry	PA0350	29,47,13,63A,53
Lowenthal, Richard	NJ0825	63A,53,46,29
Lyon, Taylene	AA0040	61,47,53
Lyons, Lisanne E.	FL1900	61,29,53,47
Machleder, Anton	NY2500	70,53
Magee, Chris	TX3350	63A,46,29,47,53
Mahe, Darren	AB0070	13,47,70,53,12A
Mair, Jim	KS0590	11,47,53,46
Malicoate, Todd S.	OK0800	53
Manley, David	PA1150	47,29,53,70
Manson, David	FL1650	47,63C,63D,53,34
Mapp, Douglas	NJ1050	62D,47,53,34
Marlier, Mike	CO0900	65B,53,29
Marsh, David	WV0550	62D,53
Mason, Scott	IL0550	13B,13C,53,29
Matalon, Leon	CA0200	13A,47,53,48
Matsuura, Gary	CA2390	53
McGirr, Tom A.	WI0450	47,62D,53
McKee, Andy	NY2660	47,62D,53
McKee, Pat	TX1600	70,53
McLain, Michael	TN0100	70,53,35B
McLean, John T.	IL2050	70,29,53
McLouth, Ryan	MO0100	53,70
McLure, Richard	TX0370	35G,57,53,70
McMullen, Tracy	ME0200	29,15,12,53,14A
Meier, Scott Alan	PA2250	47,53,64E,34,32E
Melford, Myra J.	CA5000	29,47,53
Mercer, Scott A.	IN1800	13A,13,47,61,53
Metzger, Jon	NC0750	65,29,47,50,53
Miceli, Anthony	NJ1050	53,65B
Miedema, Harry F.	IN1650	47,64E,29,53
Mitchell, Roscoe	CA2950	10,29,53
Monaghan, Michael	MA0700	47,64A,64E,53,29
Morales, Fidel	PR0115	29,65,53
Morgan, David	OH2600	62D,29,47,53
Morrison, Chris	CT0800	53,70,41
Mouse, Eugene	IL2050	53,47,29A,29B
Mullen, Stan	PA2050	29B,53,70,20G,20F
Mullett, Scott	NH0150	53,47,29B
Munson, Jordan	IN0907	45,53,13A
Musso, Paul J.	CO0830	70,47,53,13A
Nagge, Harold	TN1250	70,53,47,29
Nauert, Clark	TX1600	70,53,13B,13C
Nelson, Larry	KY0550	64E,53,29,47,29A
Netsky, Hankus H.	MA1400	29,13C,47,53,20F
Newton, Joseph	NC0750	70,53,29
Nieske, Robert	MA0500	10,47,62D,53,46
Noffsinger, Jonathan	AL1170	47,64E,53
Oliver, Harold	NJ1050	13,10F,10,41,53
Osland, Miles	KY1450	47,64E,29,53,48
Ott, Joseph	IL0100	53,47,29A
Ousley, Larry James	FL0700	62D,46,47,53
Owen, Stephen W.	OR1050	46,47,53,29,64E
Owens, Craig	KS1450	47,70,53,29A,20G
Pannunzio, Sam	CO0275	66A,53,66D,47
Parker, Christopher S.	NY3000	47,66A,66D,53,29
Parton, Robert T.	OH0350	63A,29,47,29A,53
Pasiali, Varvara	NC2000	33,53
Peffer, Ed	CA2390	47,29,53
Persip, Charli	NY2660	65,53
Pfau, Tracy	WY0050	47,70,53
Pinto, Mike	IL0850	70,53,47
Piper, Patrick	IN0400	66A,53
Pisano, James	KS0200	64C,64E,47,53,13
Pisano, Joseph M.	PA1450	47,45,53,46,34
Pitchford, Timothy	IL1200	63C,29A,46,47,53
Pogonowski, Lenore	NY4200	53,32,12A,13
Polanco-Safadit, Pavel	IN0400	66,53,46,47
Portolese, Frank	IL0850	70,53
Prouten, William	AA0032	13,47,64,53,29A
Rabbai, George	NJ1050	63A,53,46
Rebbeck, Lyle	AA0040	47,48,64,53
Redding, Eric	AK0050	11,36,66A,70,53
Reed, Kevin	OH0600	53
Reeves, Scott	NY0550	13,47,53,29
Reid, Doug	WA0860	47,64E,53,46,29
Ressler, Amy	IA1450	54,53
Reyman, Randall	IL1750	47,63A,53,29
Riffel, William	NJ0300	70,53
Ritz, John	KY1500	10B,53
Rivera, Diego	MI1400	29,64E,53
Roth, Lisa	IA1400	53,61,46,13A,13B
Roy, Larry	AC0100	70,47,53
Rudkin, Ronald	NC1650	47,29,53
Ruffels, Dave	CT0800	62D,53,41
Rummage, Robert	IL0850	50,65,53
Santos, Elias	PR0115	29A,47,29B,53
Sarjeant, Lindsey B.	FL0600	47,49,53,46,29
Saunders, Martin	WV0400	63A,53,49,47,34
Savage, Timothy L.	NY3550	53
Saxe, Peter	IL0720	29,66,53
Schlicht, Ursel	NJ0950	13,14,15,53
Schmidt, David	AZ0350	47,53,35D,34D
Scivally, Riner	CA3500	70,53
Scott, J. B.	FL1950	63A,53,47,29A
Scott, Michael E.	TN1380	11,47,53
Selvaggio, Robert	OH0600	53
Sepulveda, Charles	PR0115	29,63A,53
Shanley, Steven	IA0300	32,46,47,53
Sheridan, John	PA0400	70,53,13A
Sherman, Jeff	KY0250	47,53,70
Shew, Jamie	CA1900	53,60,13A,13B,66D

Shifflett, John	CA4400	53,47,62D
Siegel, Jeff S.	CT0800	53,41,65,29
Slack, Robert	CA1000	47,49,63A,53
Smart, Gary	FL1950	13,10F,10,66A,53
Smirl, Terry W.	WI0450	53,66A,66D
Smith, C. Raymond	UT0050	47,64,53,46,29
Smith, Herbert	VA0975	53,29,47
Smith, Joel Larue	MA1900	29,47,10,53,13A
Smith, Vern	IA1400	53
Smith, Wadada Leo	CA0510	63A,29,10,45,53
Sokol, Casey	AG0650	13A,66A,53,43
Solomon, Joseph	NY2050	47,53,29A
Spurr, Kenneth	IL1085	66A,53,29,47
Stabley, Jeff	PA3710	46,47,53,65,50
Stats, Clyde	VT0250	53,20A,20G
Steinel, Michael L.	TX3420	53,29
Stewart, Alexander	VT0450	14,53,20,29,47
Stockdale, Michael	MI0520	70,53,13B
Story, David	WI0850	62D,53,51,13A,13B
Streder, Mark	IL0850	13,66A,53,34,45
Sutherland, Dan	AF0150	62D,53
Swana, John	PA3330	63A,53,47
Swana, John	PA3600	53
Tanksley, Francesca	NY2660	13,66A,53
Thomas, Daniel A.	MO1810	64E,47,53
Thomas, Eric B.	ME0250	37,47,64C,64E,53
Thomas, Reginald	MI1400	29,66A,53
Thompson, Bob	ME0340	47,70,53,35
Tomaro, Michael	PA1050	64E,47,53,29
Tomlinson, Peter	CT0800	66A,53,41
Towell, Gordon L.	KY0900	47,64E,53,29
Trask, Alvin	MD0550	63A,53,29A,14C,47
Trout, Marion T.	IN1310	37,47,53
Trudel, Eric	MD0850	47,53
Turner, Matthew	WI0350	53
Vadala, Christopher	MD1010	47,64E,53,29
Valentin Pagan, Aldemar	PR0115	62D,47,53
Valerio, John	SC0900	29B,53,66A,10
Vogt, Roy	TN0100	70,53,35B
Walton, Scott	CA4850	53
Wang, Richard A.	IL3310	10F,12A,47,53,29
Warden, Loyd	MO0100	53,65
Warren, J. Curt	TX3520	70,53,29
Wells, Jesse R.	KY0900	11,53,62A,70
West, George	FL1750	47,29A,53
Westerholm, Matthew	MI0520	53,66A
Wheaton, Dana	CA3350	37,63C,34,53
White, Kevin	MO0750	13,10F,10,63A,53
White, Matthew S.	SC0420	63A,46,35,53
Wilkerson, Andrea	CA3500	47,61,29,46,53
Wilkinson, Jay	OK1350	47,53,29
Williams, Gary R.	WI0450	47,70,53
Winter, Beth	WA0200	61,53,29
Workman, Reggie	NY2660	10,47,62D,53
Ybarra, Anthony L.	CA4410	70,53,47
Zak, Peter	NY2660	47,66A,53

Theatre Music

Abegg, Paul	UT0150	62A,38,51,54,62B
Abrams, Eugene	NY2250	54
Adams, Catherine W.	MI2100	54,60A
Adams, Jennifer	VA1350	54
Adams, Kenny L.	OK0700	60,36,39,54,40
Adkins, Elizabeth	DC0050	54,62A
Adkins, Kathryn	CA0400	61,54
Agnew, Shawn	MO0850	61,54
Albert, Thomas	VA1350	13,10,54
Albrecht, Karen	TX1600	61,54,40
Allen, Nancy	TN0100	61,54
Allen, Nancy	WI1100	60A,32,36,54
Anders, Micheal F.	OH2275	12A,61,54,36
Anderson, Alfred	OH2150	39,54,61
Anderson, Marilyn E.	CA3100	39,61,54
Anderson, Sally	VA1350	54
Andrews, Deborah	NJ0700	61,54
Anselm, Karen	PA0250	54
Aquilino, Dominic	NC1250	61,54
Arbogast, Jennifer	TN0260	11,13C,54,61,39
Arecchi, Kathleen H.	NH0250	61,54
Arrington, Amanda	KS0650	54,66A,66C
Baker, Alan	PA0250	60A,11,36,61,54
Baker, Mark A.	OH0350	61,39,54
Ballam, Michael	UT0300	39,54
Barasch, Shirley R.	PA2900	61,32,54,10,35E
Basinski, Anne	MT0400	61,54,39
Bauman, Jeffrey Milo	GA2300	36,61,54,10F,60A
Bavaar, Kathleen	DC0170	54,61
Bean, Matt	IL3500	61,54
Bearden-Carver, Julie	GA1800	61,54
Beasley, Kimberly	FL1000	61,54,39
Beck, Barbara Geiser	CO0275	61,39,54,66C,42
Beck-Reed, Jonathan	OK0750	54
Beeks, Graydon F.	CA3650	60,12A,37,16,54
Belflower, Alisa	NE0600	61,54
Bell, Jeff	IL2300	36,61,54,60
Belnap, Michael	HI0050	36,39,40,54,61
Benge, Sharon J.	TX3300	54
Bengochea, Sandra	CA5510	61,39,54
Benshoof, Kenneth W.	WA1050	13,10,54
Berg, Aubrey	OH2200	54
Berger, Reverie Mott	GA1700	61,54
Bible, Kierstin Michelle	MO0260	36,61,12A,13A,54
Blackburn, Royce F.	ND0500	61,54,39
Blackledge, Barbara	PA2200	54
Boesiger, Kevin	NE0525	36,54
Bollinger, Bernard	CA1000	36,61,54
Booth, Nancy Davis	AZ0480	61,54
Boothe, Randall W.	UT0050	61,54,20G,35
Boresi, Matthew	WI0250	54,39
Bostic-Brown, Tiffany	AL1250	39,61,54,13A
Boyer, Douglas R.	TX3100	36,60,54,32D,13F
Bozman, William M.	VA1350	54
Brennan, Maureen	MA0850	54
Brock, Jay D.	NY1100	54
Brock, Jay	DC0050	54
Broderick, Daniela	IL1250	11,66A,66D,20G,54
Brooks, Thomas	VA1350	54
Brou, Melinda A.	TX2960	61,39,54,13C
Brown, Cristy Lynn	NC2205	61,15,54
Brown, Eileen Duffy	FL1300	39,61,54
Brown, Terrance D.	AL1250	39,54,61
Bryan, Alan	MN1625	11,39,61,54
Burks, Jo Lynn	TN0100	61,54
Burnham, Michael	OH2200	54
Burns, Susan M.	CA0630	13A,11,39,61,54
Bussert, Meg	NY2750	54

Index by Area of Teaching Interest

Name	Code	Areas
Bussert, Victoria	OH0200	54
Butler, Lloyd S.	OH1800	38,54
Bynane, Patrick	TX3300	54
Calkins, Mark	KY0300	61,54
Cancio-Bello, Susan	NH0050	11,54,61,36,33
Candlish, Bruce	PA0250	54
Carey, Matthew	AR0110	54,61
Carney, Timothy F.	HI0060	36,11,13A,54,61
Carter, Susan	MO0850	61,40,54,39
Carthy, Nicholas	CO0800	39,54
Casey, Michael R.	MO0775	49,63A,60,54
Cawthon, Daniel D.	CA3920	54
Chandler, David	CT0650	54,52
Chapman, Karen Benjamin	CA3500	54
Chapman, Polly	AZ0490	54
Cheatham-Stricklin, Teresa	AL0500	13A,11,61,54
Cherry, Mark	NY2200	54,40,66C
Childress Orchard, Nan	NJ0050	66,13,54
Christensen, Janielle	UT0050	12A,36,39,54,35
Church, Joseph	NY2750	54,10A,10D
Clark, Charles 'Bud'	MO0800	36,61,54
Clark, Mark Ross	LA0770	39,54,61,11
Clark, Michael	FL1570	13,12A,36,66,54
Cline, Judith A.	VA0550	39,61,54,20G,11
Cody, David	MT0400	36,61,54,39,60A
Cogdell, Jerry	MS0320	13,11,50,63,54
Cogdell, Robyn	MS0320	36,54
Cogen, Ellen	MA1100	61,40,36,13A,54
Cohen, Allen L.	NJ0400	13,10,54,39,36
Conlon, Francis	DC0100	39,66A,66C,54
Connolly, Donna	NJ0825	39,40,54,61
Conoly, Shaaron	TX3100	12A,39,61,54
Cook-Perez, Paige	CA3270	52,54
Coolen, Michael T.	OR0700	14,54,20,12A,35A
Corigliano, John	NY0635	10F,10,11,54
Coulson-Grigsby, Carolyn	VA1350	54
Cox, Kenneth	CO0900	39,61,54
Cress, David	MO0825	47,54,63
Crosby, J. Stephen	NY0100	54
Crosby, Luanne M.	NY0100	11,36,61,54
Crowder, Jarrell	MD0550	66A,66D,54
Cuk, John	NY2200	36,39,54,40
Cushing, Diane	NH0150	36,61,54,11
Dal Vera, Rocco	OH2200	54
Dale, Karen M.	TN0300	11,34B,36,54,61
Dalio, Marc G.	NJ0825	54,61
Danby, Jen	NY2200	54
Davenport, David A.	DC0170	54,66D,66A
Davenport, Dennis	OH2050	54,10,13,36
Davis, Hal	NC2435	61,54
Davis, Robert H.	CT0650	54
De La Vega, Anne M.	CA3500	61,54,39
De Puit, Gerald	MI2100	54
Dean, Curtis	NC1150	35,54
DeJesus, Ron	MI2100	52,54
Delmore, Jack	CO0225	36,39,61,54
Delto, Clare E.	CA1960	10D,54,11,47
DeMaio Caprilli, Barbara J.	OK1330	61,54,11
DeMaris, Brian	NY1800	39,54
Dennis, Susan	IL1085	61,54,40
Dennis, Susan	IL0850	54,61
Dewey, Cynthia	UT0300	61,54,39,13A
DiPinto, John	NJ0825	54
Dolacky, Susan	WA0860	11,39,61,66D,54
Dolter, Gerald	TX3200	39,61,54
Doo, Lina J.	HI0150	11,61,36,54,20
D'Ortenzio, Marie Michuda	IL2250	54
Douglass, Mary	NE0525	54
Doyle, Laurie	TX1550	61,11,40,54
Dunston, Douglas E.	NM0350	10B,36,38,47,54
Duran, Amy	NJ0825	54
Eckermann, Joan E.	OH2140	61,54
Edwards, Linda	NM0400	60,36,41,61,54
Egan, Dan	CT0900	54
Eichelberger, K. V.	DC0150	61,54
Elliot, Mike	MO1650	61,54
Ellsworth-Smith, Pamela	MO1650	61,54
Engelson, Robert A.	IA0050	13,60,11,36,54
Engelson, Thea	IA1300	40,61,54
Engle, Martha Ramm	CA2050	12A,11,54
Engle, Rebecca	CA3920	54
Engler, Kyle C.	MD0520	39,61,54
Enlow, Charles	WA0860	66D,40,54,39
Enman, Thomas	MA1175	66C,12A,54,66A,61
Ensor, Robert	MO0260	12A,47,66A,66C,54
Etcheto, Sally A.	CA0805	11,36,61,54
Farrell, Scott	WA0350	61,66,54
Felstein, Robert	CT0650	54
Fenwick, Jerry	CA4000	11,66A,54,29,35
Fern, Terry L.	NC0850	11,39,61,54,69
Feyer, Paul	CT0650	61,54
Fleming, Rachelle	DC0050	61,54
Fletcher, Donna	AC0100	61,54
Flom, Jonathan	VA1350	54
Folger, William M.	MD0800	60A,36,40,54
Fonte, Henry	CT0650	54
Foradori, Anne	NE0590	39,61,54
Franklin, Janice L.	TX1725	11,66,54,34B
Fransen, Wade	VA1350	54
Fredrickson, Ann	MN0200	61,36,39,54,13C
French, George E.	MN1590	36,37,66A,66G,54
Fritsch, Greg	CA3270	39,54
Gable, Garry	AJ0150	61,54,39
Gage, James H.	OH2200	54
Gagnon, Scott R.	MA0900	54
Gardella, Duane	CA4000	54
Gardner, David B.	KS1200	36,60,61,60A,54
Garfein, Herschel	NY2750	39,54
Garner, Rusty	FL0900	60,11,61,54,64D
Garvin, Jerry	CA1900	63B,54
Gazdyszyn, Danuta U.	TX1425	52,54
Gerlach, Bruce	MO0200	13,10,11,54,66G
Getke, Richard	NJ0700	54
Gifford, Amy L.	FL1550	61,11,54
Glenn, Larry M.	CO0900	39,61,54
Goeke, Christopher L.	MO1500	39,41,61,54
Goetz, Sariva	NJ0825	54
Goetzinger, Laurel E.	IN0100	61,39,54
Goldstein, Steven	OH2200	54,39
Gonzalez, Susan	NY0625	11,61,54
Goodrich, Linda	MI2100	54
Gorecki, Maria De La Luz	TX1425	52,54
Gorman, Rhonda	TX3300	54
Gotera, Jose	OH1000	61,39,54,36
Graber, Todd A.	NY3770	61,54,36,12A
Greciano, Sandra	PA2900	61,54
Greco, Christine R.	TX1425	52,54
Gretz, Ronald	MD0175	13A,13,66A,66C,54
Griffin, Gregory W.	OH2275	54,35C,34
Grodsky, Roger	OH2200	54
Haffner, James	CA5350	39,61,54
Hahn, Mari	AK0100	61,39,54,32D
Halbert, Marjorie	TN0100	61,54
Hall, Lewis R.	WV0050	32,40,54,61
Halley, Sharon	NY2250	54
Hamm, Zachary D.	NY0100	54
Hansen, Kurt R.	IL2250	61,54
Hansen, Robert	TX3750	61,54
Hansen, Victoria	CO0200	61,54
Hapner, David E.	OH2450	66C,54
Hardy, Janis	MN1450	61,39,54
Harkins, Edwin	CA5050	13A,13,63A,54,43
Harper, David R.	RI0150	11,61,54,39,40
Harper, Tamara W.	GA1700	61,54
Harris, Ray	MS0570	11,36,66,54
Harsa, Sandra Y.	TX1425	52,54
Hartzell, Richard	MD0400	61,39,54
Harvey, Peter J.	CT0240	13,12A,36,54,20G
Hassevoort, Darrin	TN0260	36,61,47,60,54
Hastings, Mary Logan	PA1600	39,61,54
Hauan, Catherine	AZ0440	61,54
Hayes, Daun	CA4600	36,61,54
Helding, Lynn E.	PA0950	61,40,54
Helppie, Kevin	OR1250	61,47,54,20G
Henderson, Elaine	PA2300	39,61,54
Henry, Ruth	IL2310	61,66A,54
Herendeen, David	OK0750	39,54
Herman, Cheryl	IL2800	36,54,66A,64
Herman, Harold	VA1350	54
Herman, Linde	VA1350	54
Hess, Richard E.	OH2200	54
Hirsch, Michael	NJ0825	10,54
Hoffart, Danica	AA0080	36,61,54,13C
Hoffman, Lee	OH0500	39,61,66C,54
Hoffman, Susan	DC0050	54
Hogan, George	TX3415	61,39,54
Hogan, Penny	TX3415	61,39,54
Hong, Martha	MT0450	61,54
Hopkin, J. Arden	UT0050	39,61,54
Howard, Michael	LA0750	61,54
Howe, Martha Jane	CA2100	61,54
Howell, Jane	PA2900	66A,66C,13A,54,11
Hoyt-Brackman, Brenda	OH2275	52,54
Hudson, Hope A.	NJ0700	61,54
Huebner, Elizabeth	CT0650	54
Hurleigh, Shannon	OK1330	54
Hurt, Phyllis A.	IL2150	12A,61,54
Hyberger, Sarah Amanda	TN0260	11,13C,54,61,39
Ingham, William	VA1350	54
Intintoli, Helen	CA4650	36,61,66A,31A,54
Jackson, Janice	AF0120	61,54
Jacobs, Marc	CA3270	39,54
James, Clay	NJ0800	54
James, Matthew H.	LA0770	61,13D,39,54,60A
Jeffrey, Bobbie	MO0060	54
Jemison-Keisker, Lynn C.	UT0300	39,54
Jenkins, Donald P.	CO0200	60,36,39,41,54
Jesse, Lynda	MO0200	32D,36,54,60,61
Johnson, Diane	WA0900	36,61,54,11,20
Johnson, Jacquelyn Pualani	HI0200	54
Johnson, Janice	OR1300	61,54
Johnson, Jon S.	TX2350	13,36,61,54,32D
Johnson, Molly	TX3535	61,54,39
Johnson, Nikki	MS0360	11,61,54,36
Johnson, Scott R.	SD0050	32,54,11
Johnston, Jack R.	NY3730	13,66A,54,34
Jolles, Annette	CT0900	54
Jones, Joshua	IL1300	61,11,39,54
Jones, K. Jennifer	OH2200	54
Jones, Kimberlyn	CA2810	39,61,54,53
Jones, Leslie I.	MO1500	61,39,11,54
Jones, Robert J.	ND0350	39,61,54,14
Jordahl, Patricia	AZ0300	36,54,66D,61,11
Jordan, Esther	CA2100	36,39,61,54
Karn, Kitty	IL3500	61,54
Kasper, Kathryn	KS0200	39,61,54,13C
Kay, Michele A.	OH2200	54
Kazaras, Peter	CA5030	39,54
Keitges, Christine	CO0050	39,61,54
Kellert, Aaron	OK1100	11,36,13A,54,61
Kelly, Kathleen	GA0500	52,54
Kelly, Terence	WI0810	11,61,54
Kendrick, Brian	CA4300	46,47,65,54
Kern, Philip	IN1100	13,10F,36,54,66A
Kesselman, Lee R.	IL0630	13,10,36,54,60
Killen, Seth R.	IL0800	61,54
King, Marie A.	KS1450	39,54
Klinebriel, Jill	IA0250	16,54
Kloetzli, Pamela	CO0150	54
Koenigberg, Rebecca Anne	CO0650	61,11,54
Kot, Don	NY2650	66A,61,66D,66C,54
Kowalke, Kim	NY4350	12A,12,39,54,20G
Kramar, John S.	NC0650	61,54,39
Kratzer, Dennis L.	OH1800	36,61,54,60A,40
Krueger, Mary Beth	CO0550	54,61,66C,66D
Krupa, Mary Ann	IL3450	13,54,66A
Krupp, Ethan	PA0250	54
Krusemark, William	KS1375	36,39,61,54,11
Kuhnert, Brian	TX3650	61,39,54,40
Kvapil, Diane	OH2200	54
Lala, Diane	OH2200	54
Lambert, Debra	CA3270	61,39,54
Latta, Matthew	IN1800	61,32B,36,54
Lawler, Douglas	MD0175	10,54
Lawrence, Lisa	FL0100	32,54,61
Lebon, Rachel L.	FL1900	47,61,32,35A,54
Leeper, Brian K.	WI0865	61,39,54
Lentz, Jeffrey	PA0050	61,54
Lester-White, Dottie	CA3270	52,54
Levine, Rhoda	NY2250	54
Liberatore, William	CA3270	39,54,60,61
Lindsay, Julia	MI0250	11,61,54,39
Lindsay, Priscilla	MI2100	54
Linhart, Patricia M.	OH2200	61,54
Lippard, Erin	TX2710	61,13A,13B,40,54
Little, David	MI2250	39,61,54
Livingston-Hakes, Beth	AZ0490	61,54,13A
Llewellyn, Cherrie	CA3000	11,61,54,39
LoBalbo, Anthony C.	NY3500	13,29A,10C,12A,54
Lockwood, Gayle	UT0050	39,61,54,20G,35
Loftus, Jean	NY2950	39,61,54,13A,13B
Lonati, Marianne	MA0750	54
Long, Kevin	IL1750	54,13
Long, Ron	AA0020	61,54
Lovett, Rita	LA0750	61,54
Lualdi, Brenda	IL0850	61,54

611

Index by Area of Teaching Interest

Name	Code	Areas
Lucius, Sue Anne	AZ0440	39,61,54
Luellen, Heather M.	MO0775	54
Luiken, Jennifer	SC0275	61,39,54
Lutter, Lisa	NJ0950	36,61,54,12A
M. de Oca, Patricia	TX3520	66D,66C,54
MacMullen, Michael J.	FL1470	13A,11,36,61,54
Madama, Mark	MI2100	54
Maguire, George	CA4650	54
Mahady, Jim	DC0050	54
Mahtani, Lorena	TX1425	52,54
Mantel, Sarah J.	PA1600	39,61,54
Marks, Martin	MA1200	11,12A,54
Marlett, Judy	ID0150	32,36,39,54,60A
Marlow, Carolyn	NY2150	54
Martinez, Jeordano S.	IL2050	12A,36,39,54,38
Marzolf, Dennis	MN0200	60,36,31A,61,54
Masterson, Stephanie C.	FL1570	12A,61,54
Mastrodomenico, Carol	MA1900	61,39,54
Mathews, Heather	CA4150	54
McBerry, Sue	OR0400	61,54
McClurkin, Vicki J.	OH2275	54
McDaniel, Jan	OK0750	39,54,66C,12A,61
McDevitt, Duane	NJ0825	54
McEnerny, Harry	VT0100	54
McKeel, James	MN1450	61,39,54
McKelvey, Michael E.	PA2900	35E,61,54,10
McKenzie, Art	NJ1350	32,54
McKinnis, Alicia V.	TX1425	52,54
McMahan, Andrew	CA0600	60,37,63A,54,34
McNeil, Linda	TX3350	39,61,54
Mechell, Harry A.	MN1700	60,36,32D,61,54
Meinert, Anita	IA1950	64C,66A,66C,54
Meredith, Sarah A.	WI0808	39,61,54,15
Meyer, Beverly	NY2200	54,40,66C
Middleton, Jaynne	TX0900	61,12A,54
Milenski, Isabel	NY1600	39,54
Miller, Karen Coe	OK0750	54,39
Miller, Lisa	IN1800	32,61,54,12A
Miller, Patricia A.	VA0450	39,61,54
Miller, Thomas E.	CA5400	13B,13C,36,39,54
Miller, Wendy L.	PA0250	11,12A,36,61,54
Mills, Kate Irvine	CA3270	39,54
Mogle, Dean	OH2200	39,54
Mohammed, Michael	CA4150	54
Moller-Marino, Diana	CT0650	54
Mollicone, Henry	CA3270	10A,12A,39,54,60
Moody, Kevin M.	TX0075	54,61,11,36,40
Moon, Kimberle	FL0040	61,54
Moore, Tim	FL0670	40,61,54
Morgiewicz, Kerry L.	VA0550	66A,66B,54
Morris, Joan	MI2100	54
Morris, Michael	CT0650	54
Morrison, Harry	MO1650	61,54
Morrison, Johanna	CT0650	54
Morrison, Malcolm	CT0650	54
Morrow, Lynne	CA4700	39,54,60A,61
Moser, Martin	NY3500	13,12A,54,20G
Moshell, Gerald	CT0500	60,12A,54
Mow, Paul	MI1985	61,54
Mueller, Ronald	CO0800	54
Mullen, Wendy Anne	GA0850	61,54,39
Murphy, Steve	IN0907	66A,66B,54
Murray, Frank	CA3920	54
Myers, Gerald C.	MO1120	11,36,40,54,13
Nazworth, Daniel	TX2350	54
Neal, David E.	NY3720	61,54,39,36
Nelson, Curt	CA2900	10D,36,40,54
Ness, Corinne	WI0250	61,54,32B,39
Nevola, Teresa	PA1150	61,54,20G
Newell, Kathy	OH2275	54
Newell, Lawana	OK0600	61,54
Nies, Bryan	CA4150	54
Noone, Katherine	ND0350	61,54
Norberg, Rebecca	MN1250	61,54,12A,11
Nuccio, David A.	IL1250	11,29A,34,54,66A
Nyberg, Gary B.	WA0480	13,10,37,63D,54
Ockwell, Frederick	IL2250	60,39,54
O'Donnell, Terry	CA4100	60,66A,69,54
Olm, James	WY0050	54,61,13A
Olson, Robert	ND0350	39,61,54
Oosting, Stephen	NJ0800	61,54
Osbun-Manley, Kirsten E.	OH1800	39,61,54
Ott, Daniel	NY1300	12A,29A,54,13B,13C
Owens, Theodore	NV0125	10,11,12A,61,54
Page, Carolann	NJ1350	54,61
Paradise, Kathryn L.	TN0100	61,54
Parrish, Robert E.	NJ0175	54,34
Parrish, Steve	NC1050	61,54
Paulus, Carolyn	CT0650	54
Paxton, Laurence	HI0210	39,61,54
Pedersen, Thomas	DC0050	36,39,54,56,61
Perkins, Ralph	CT0650	54
Perlstein, Marla	CT0650	54
Peterson, Jon C.	OH0250	36,12A,44,11,54
Pierson, William	VA1350	54
Pietri, Michelle M.	TX3530	54,52
Pittman, Reginald L.	KS0650	39,61,54
Planner, Mark	CT0650	54
Plantamura, Carol	CA5050	12A,55,61,54,43
Plate, Scott F.	OH0200	54
Pollock, William	PA1000	54
Potter, Joe	MO2050	66A,66G,35H,54,35E
Prophet, Becky B.	NY0100	54
Psurny, Robert D.	MT0075	29A,36,40,54,61
Puricelli, Denise	DC0050	54
Quash, Jonathan	NY0646	36,54,61
Racine, Melody Lynn	MI2100	61,54
Rader, Stephen M.	OH1400	54
Radford, Anthony P.	CA0810	61,39,54
Radomski, Teresa	NC2500	61,54
Ramach, Michael E.	KY1500	54,12A
Rash, Daniel R.	SC0400	11,60A,54
Ratner, Carl J.	MI2250	39,61,54
Raybon, Leonard	LA0750	36,61,60A,54
Raynes, Christopher	ID0050	61,39,54
Reber, William F.	AZ0100	39,54,52,66C,60
Regan, Patrick	MI1300	61,39,54
Reichert, Ed C.	ME0500	54
Renner-Hughes, Marty	MO1110	12A,36,54
Ressler, Amy	IA1450	54,53
Ricciardone, Michael	NY2750	36,54,66A
Richards, June	CA4000	54
Richards, Scott D.	NJ0800	10D,13B,13C,54
Richardson, James K.	VA0300	61,11,36,54,39
Richardson, W. Randall	AL0800	61,54
Rincon, Alicia	CA4000	54
Rittner, Phillip	CT0650	54
Robinson, Yvonne	PA2450	61,54
Rocco, Emma S.	PA2713	13A,11,20F,36,54
Rosenblum, Joshua	CT0900	54
Rosenshein, Ingrid	FL1675	11,13A,61,66D,54
Rosine, Amy	KS0650	61,54
Ross, Buck	TX3400	39,54
Rowell, Melanie	SC1080	12A,61,54,39
Royce, Matthew M.	CA3270	39,54
Rudari, David J.	WV0100	61,36,12A,32B,54
Ruggaber, Brian J.	OH2200	54
Rupert, Susan	TN1800	13A,61,54
Ruscella, J. J.	VA1350	54
Rushing-Raynes, Laura	ID0050	61,39,54
Russell, Teresa P.	CA4850	60,36,61,54,32A
Rust, Alan	CT0650	54
Ryder, Carol	CA1280	36,54,61
Saad, Olga	IL2750	54
Sage, Raymond	PA2750	61,54
Sanders, Steve	CA3270	54
Sauer-Ferrand, Deborah	CA1860	12A,61,31A,54
Saunders, Mary	PA2750	61,54
Savage Day, Susan	WI0840	61,54
Schaefer, Elaine	CA1300	13A,36,54,61,40
Schager, Christopher J.	MS0570	54
Schirmer, Timothy	IL2350	13,10,34B,54
Schloneger, Matthew	KS0500	61,54,11
Schmid, John	IN0250	54
Schmidt, Timothy A.	MO1500	61,39,54
Schreier, Kathleen	IA0790	13,11,36,54
Seaton, Gayle	FL0850	61,54
Seaward, Jeffery A.	CA1290	13A,36,41,61,54
Secrest, Jon	AR0500	39,61,54
Sellers, Lucy Bell	ME0270	54
Severing, Richard	WI0865	36,40,54,61
Shahani, Michael M.	CA1020	39,54,13A
Shamburger, David	TN0100	61,54
Shanahan, Ellen Cooper	MA0280	13,12A,36,54,29A
Sholer, Jeannie	OK0750	54
Shover, Blaine F.	PA3050	11,12A,36,61,54
Shrope, Douglas	CA1000	36,61,60A,40,54
Simone, Ed	NY3475	54
Simpkins, John	NY2750	54
Skinner, Kent	AR0800	60A,54,61,39,54
Skyles, Michael	SD0400	61,54
Slawson, John G.	IL0840	60,12A,36,38,54
Smeltzer, Steven	OK1330	54
Smiley, Henry	TN0100	61,54
Smith, Aaron	MD0900	31A,36,54,40
Smith, Blake	DE0150	61,54,39
Smith, Charles	NE0300	36,39,61,54
Smith, Christina	MN0750	61,54
Smith, Paul	CA1150	12A,66A,66C,66D,54
Smith, Scott	CA1270	54,13G
Smith, Sue	MI0050	52,54
Solari, Gia	CA3270	52,54
Spangler, Julie M.	OH2200	54
Speer, Janet Barton	NC1050	35H,54,35E
Spencer, Reid	AA0050	54,61
St. Clair, Lisa	AF0050	54
Staab, Jane	MA2200	39,54
Stark, Deborah	GA0700	12A,54,11,61,40
Starkey, David C.	NC1250	61,39,54
Starkey, Linda	KS1450	61,54,39
Stempel, Larry	NY1300	13,12,54,29
Stephenson, Carol	CA5100	61,54
Stephenson, Geoffrey	OH0300	54,39
Stern, Theodore	CA1960	11,12A,54,13A
Steward, Lee A.	CA0807	61,54
Stewart, Aliza	NY2250	54
Stock, Jesse	TN0250	36,61,60A,54
Stoffel, David N.	GA2100	61,54
Stone, William S.	MS0570	54
Stovall, Jeremy	AL0500	13A,37,41,54
Strong, James Anthony	NJ0975	13,12A,66,11,54
Sublett, Virginia	ND0350	61,39,54
Swayne, Steven R.	NH0100	12A,12,39,54
Swears, Marilyn	AL0345	11,54,66A
Tadlock, David	OH1400	61,13C,54,39
Tahere, David	GA0600	11,54,61
Tebbets, Gary	KS0040	12A,11,36,54,62
Tedesco, Anne C.	NY3500	13,66A,54,29A,10
Thomas, Colby L.	NY3765	39,60A,35F,61,54
Thomas, Eric S.	TX0600	61,13C,13A,54
Thomas, Nova	NJ1350	61,54
Thompson, Lynn	IL3500	61,54,39,36
Thompson, Sonja K.	MN0050	61,39,54,41,42
Thull, Jonathan	IA0400	39,61,54
Tivnan, Brian	MA0200	54
Tonkin, Humphrey	CT0650	54
Toronto, Emily Wood	SD0550	39,61,54
Torres, Jose R.	PR0150	61,54
Tosh, Melissa Denise	CA5150	61,36,39,54
Towne, Lora Rost	AZ0440	39,61,54,13
Truhart, Regina A.	OH2200	54
Trump, Antonio	VA1350	54
Tucker, William S.	NY2750	40,54
Tudor, Robert W.	WV0550	61,39,54
Turner, J. Frank	CA4450	13A,11,12A,54,13B
Tynon, Mari Jo	ID0070	39,61,54
Uddenberg, Scott	IL0850	61,54
Umfrid, Thomas C.	OH2200	39,54
Van Dewark, Vicky	CA3250	61,54
Van Hoorn, Valerie	NJ0700	61,54
Vascan, Ligia	WI0500	40,61,36,54,29
Von Villas, Muriel	DC0100	11,39,54
Vrenios, Elizabeth	DC0010	39,61,54
Wagner, Brent	MI2100	54
Wagner, Irvin	OK1350	49,63C,54
Wagner, Kathy	MI0520	61,54
Wagner, Randel	WA0250	36,40,61,54,60A
Walentine, Richard L.	ND0150	61,54,13A,39,12A
Walker, Elizabeth	KS0750	39,61,54,35,34C
Walter, Regina	TX1775	61,54,11
Walth, Gary Kent	WI0810	60,11,32C,36,54
Ward, Frank	OH2150	61,39,54
Warner, C. David	MD0450	54
Watson, W. David	CT0650	54
Weber, Marliss	AA0020	54
Weber, Michael J.	ND0350	60,54
Wesbrooks, William	NY2750	54
Westphal, Cynthia	MI2100	54
Whaley, Mary Susan	OK0500	11,36,61,54,13
Wheeler, Scott	MA0850	13,60,10,54,43
Whitaker, Jane	FL0950	54,11
White, Greg	OK1330	35A,54
Wieck, Julie	WA1150	39,61,54
Wiesner, Terry	WI0801	54
Wiggett, Joseph	CA0850	61,54,39
Wilcox-Jones, Carol	OH1650	61,39,54

Name	Code	Areas
Wilkes, Eve-Anne	CA3250	36,61,54,60
Wilkinson, Judi	TX3520	66,54
Williams, Dennis	PA1750	54,36,61,60
Williams, John W.	NY2100	13,11,36,61,54
Williams, Steven	NC2550	11,54,39,66G
Wilson, Elisa	TX3520	61,54,47,39
Wilson, Ellen M.	TX3520	61,54,39,12
Wilson, Kathleen L.	FL0700	61,54
Wiltsie, Barbara	MI1260	61,39,54
Wolf, Lily	AL1195	54,43
Wolfmann, Melissa	CA1850	61,54
Wood, Graham	SC0450	11,12,63B,54,20
Woodruff, William	PR0115	61,54
Wordelman, Peter	OR0200	60A,36,61,54
Wright, Peter	NJ1350	54
Wurgler, Norman F.	KY1540	11,36,20G,61,54
Wylie, Ted	TN0100	61,31A,54,39
Yancey, Cheryl	VA1350	54
Yannelli, John A.	NY3560	13,41,45,54,34
Yatso, Toby	AZ0100	54
Yeston, Maury	NY1275	10D,54
Young, H. G.	WV0760	13,11,12A,36,54
Young, James Russell	GA1150	40,39,66C,54
Young, Steven	TX3300	54
Yurko, Kelly A.	OH2200	54
Zemliauskas, Christopher	CO0800	39,61,54
Zerkle, Paula R.	PA2450	36,60,15,11,54
Zimmerman, Stevie	CT0650	54

Early Music Ensemble (All Areas)

Name	Code	Areas
Aaron, Kathryn	KY0250	55,61
Alden, Jane	CT0750	12,55
Ashworth, John	KY1500	12A,55,66H,67
Austin, Valerie A.	NC2435	32,55
Beazley, Janet M.	CA5040	55,67
Bennett, Peter	OH0400	12A,55
Benoit, John	IA1350	13,11,63C,10F,55
Berg, Christopher B.	SC1110	55,70
Bergeron, Sylvain	AI0150	67,55
Blachly, Alexander	IN1700	60,12,36,55,12A
Bonus, Alexander	NC0600	55,12
Bookout, Melanie	IN0905	11,12A,12,55,67A
Boorman, Stanley H.	NY2740	11,12A,12,55
Borror, Ronald	CT0650	41,49,63C,67E,55
Bowles, Chelcy L.	WI0815	55,67
Brobeck, John T.	AZ0500	12,55
Brookshire, Bradley	NY3785	12A,12,55,66G,66H
Brown, Jennifer Williams	IA0700	12,55,67,66H
Burleson, Richard F.	AC0100	14,55,67G
Bush, Douglas E.	UT0050	12,55,66G,67,31A
Campbell, Jayne E.	CA1960	36,55,61,31A
Canton, Lisette M.	AG0650	36,55,60
Carslake, Louise	CA2950	12,55,64A,67
Carter, Jay	MO2000	55,61
Carter, Stewart	NC2500	13,11,12A,55,67
Coker, Keller	OR1250	55,12A,63C,10D
Cosart, Jann	TX0300	12A,55
Cudek, Mark	MD0650	55
Curry, Jerry L.	SC1110	13,66H,55,66E
Cyrus, Cynthia	TN1850	12,15,55,20F
Davenport, Mark	CO0650	12,55,67C,29A,14C
Dirst, Matthew	TX3400	12A,55,67C
Dolata, David	FL0700	12,67G,55,56,67H
Duffin, Ross	OH0400	12A,12,55
Elliott, Paul	IN0900	61,67H,55
Ellison, Paul	CA4200	12,31,55
Enrico, Eugene	OK1350	12A,12,55,67
Epstein, Paul A.	PA3250	13,10,55
Everitt, Allison	FL1430	13,36,61,55
Fankhauser, James L.	AB0100	13,36,55,61
Farr, Elizabeth	CO0800	55,66G,66H
Fast, Susan	AG0200	13A,11,12A,12,55
Fisher, Alexander	AB0100	12,55,67D
Gall, Jeffrey C.	NJ0800	55,61,12A,12,39
Gerber, Alan E.	FL2120	11,55,61,36
Gibson, Jonathan B.	VA0600	11,12A,55
Gillespie, Wendy	IN0900	67A,55
Glixon, Jonathan	KY1450	12,55
Grace, Michael	CO0200	11,12A,12,55
Gracia-Nuthmann, Andre	NM0150	13,60,36,55,67
Greenlee, Robert K.	ME0200	60,36,12A,12,55
Gries, Peggy	OR1050	12,55,67
Griffioen, Ruth	VA0250	67D,55,12A
Guarino, Robert	NJ0175	61,55,39
Gustafson, Beverly	MN0750	67,55
Harris, Julie	AA0150	55
Hathaway, Janet J.	IL2200	12A,55,67,12C
Hays, Elizabeth	IA0700	12,55,66H
Hensley, Hunter C.	KY0550	36,61,60A,55,32D
Herreid, Grant	CT0900	55
Hershey, Jane	MA1900	67,55
Hettrick, William E.	NY1600	12A,13,55,55B
Hoekstra, Gerald	MN1450	12A,55,29A
Holmes, Karen	AG0400	55,66G,66H
Houle, George L.	CA4900	12A,55,67B
Howell, John	VA1700	36,67,35,55
Hynes, Maureen	NY2105	38,67,62C,55,42
Jensen, Michelle	CA0250	32,36,55
Jeppesen, Laura	MA2050	55,67A,67B
Kelly, Stephen K.	MN0300	12A,55,29A
Kerley, Jolaine	AA0100	61,55
Kielson, Lisette	IL0400	67,55
Kinslow, Valerie	AI0150	61,55,67
Knox, Hank	AI0150	56,66H,67F,55
Kong, Joanne	VA1500	66A,66H,66C,55
Kordes, Gesa	AL1170	55
Kraaz, Sarah Mahler	WI0700	12A,55,66,11,67C
Kramme, Joel I.	MO0825	11,36,55,67,12A
Kreitner, Kenneth	TN1680	12,67E,55
Kreitzer, Nathan J.	CA4410	61,36,40,55
Kreyszig, Walter	AJ0150	12A,12,20G,55
Lalli, Richard	CT0900	55,61
Lanz, Christopher C.	NY3780	55,60B
Lipkis, Larry	PA2450	13,10F,10,55,67
Lockart, Carol	CA5360	64A,55
Lutzke, Myron	NY2250	55
Maas, Martha C.	OH1850	12A,12,55
MacMillan, Betsy	AI0150	67,55
Macy, Carleton	MN0950	13,10,67,55,47
Mahrt, William P.	CA4900	12A,55,67E,31A
Malafronte, Judith	CT0900	55
Maldonado, Greg	CA0825	51,62A,55,62B
Malyshko, Olga	AG0250	12A,12,71,55
Marsh, Carol	NC2430	12A,12,55,67
Martin, Stephanie	AG0650	12A,55,60
Maute, Matthias	AI0150	67C,55

Name	Code	Areas
McCarthy, Kerry R.	NC0600	12A,12C,31A,55
McCollum, Jonathan Ray	MD0060	12,13,20,55,63C
McCraw, Michael	IN0900	67D,55C,55
McGee, Timothy J.	AG0450	12A,12,55
McKay, Janis	NV0050	13,41,55,64D
Mealy, Robert	CT0900	55
Meconi, Honey	NY1100	12A,12,55
Mentzel, Eric P.	OR1050	61,67H,55,55D,55A
Michaud, Natalie	AI0150	67C,55
Moll, Kevin N.	NC0650	12,55,67A,12A,12B
Monahan, Laurie	MA1175	61,55
Montgomery, Vivian	OH2200	11,12A,55,66H,67F
Montiel, Brenda F.	CA3460	12A,55,66A,67B,67C
Moulin, Jane	HI0210	20D,14A,55,67A
Murray, Russell E.	DE0150	12A,15,55,67D,67B
Nisula, Eric	MI1850	11,55,67
North, Nigel	IN0900	67G,55
Nurse, Ray	AB0100	55
Nutter, David A.	CA5010	12A,12,55
O'Brien, John B.	NC0650	66A,66D,66H,55
O'Connor, Michael B.	FL1450	12A,11,20,55
O'Dette, Paul	NY1100	55,56,67G
O'Grady, Terence J.	WI0808	13,12A,12,14,55
Pare, Richard	AI0190	66G,66H,55,42
Parr, Sean M.	PA0950	12A,55,11
Pearlman, Martin	MA0400	55,67F
Pearson, Ian D.	SC1200	12,55,41
Penniman, G. Victor	MO1010	55,12A,62,11,36
Peterman, Lewis E.	CA4100	14A,41,55,11
Petersen, Alice V. Neff	OH2300	55,67,11
Plantamura, Carol	CA5050	12A,55,61,54,43
Purves-Smith, Michael	AG0600	60,37,55,10F
Reed, Kathryn	IA0950	13C,55,66H
Rice, Eric N.	CT0600	55,12A,13A,12
Roesner, Edward	NY2740	11,12A,12,55
Rogers, Vanessa	TN1200	12,55
Sawyer, John E.	AB0100	55,67A,12A
Scharfenberger, Paul E.	NH0110	12,67C,43,55,15
Schaufele, Fritz	OH0650	55
Schlagel, Stephanie P.	OH2200	12C,12,55,67
Semmens, Richard	AG0500	12,13J,55,67B,13L
Shadinger, Richard C.	TN0100	12A,55,66A,31A,69
Sheinberg, Colleen	NM0450	55
Simms, William	MD0500	67G,70,55
Smith, Jacqueline H.	PA2800	55
Steel, David	MS0700	14,66H,55,66G
Steel, Matthew	MI2250	12A,12,14,55
Steele, Janet	NY0550	13A,55,61,66A,36
Stowe, J. Chappell	WI0815	66G,55
Stucky, Rodney D.	OH2200	55
Swack, Jeanne	WI0815	12A,12,67,55,67D
Tarrant, Fredrick A.	GA1800	11,12,14,20,55
Teply, Lee	VA1000	13,55,66G,66H
Thielmann, Christel	NY1100	55,56,67A
Todd, Kristen Stauffer	OK0650	12,14,20,11,55
Torres, Barry A.	NY3550	55,36,61
Towne, Gary	ND0500	12A,55,12C
Treadwell, Nina K.	CA5070	12A,67G,55
Tuomi, Scott	OR0750	12A,12,14,61,55
Van Boer, Bertil H.	WA1250	13E,12,55,12A
Van Orden, Katherine	CA5000	11,12A,12D,55,67
Vaneman, Kelly McElrath	SC0650	12A,64B,42,55,14
Vanscheeuwijck, Marc	OR1050	55,12,67B
Weller, Ellen	CA3460	12A,55,20,29A,60
Wenzel, Scott	WI0150	14,65,55,50,20A
Wexler, Richard	MD1010	12A,12,55,29A
Wilson, Blake	PA0950	12A,55,11
Wissick, Brent S.	NC2410	55,51,62C,67A,67E
Yardley, Anne B.	NJ0300	12,14,31,55
Young, Steven	MA0510	36,11,55,66A,20G
Zajac, Tom	MA2050	67C,67D,55
Zelley, Richard S.	FL0400	55,66A,66H,67B

Medieval Ensemble

Name	Code	Areas
Alonso, Ernesto	PR0150	12A,11,62A,14A,55A
Cohen, Judith	AG0650	20,55C,55A,32E
Dorf, Samuel N.	OH2250	12A,11,55A,55B,55C
Mentzel, Eric P.	OR1050	61,67H,55,55D,55A
Song, Anna	OR0450	13C,36,55B,55A,40

Baroque Ensemble

Name	Code	Areas
Baer, Sarah	PA2450	64B,55B,12A,13E
Borgerding, Todd Michael	ME0250	13,12A,55B
Braun, William	WI1155	13,10,12,55B,34
Burman-Hall, Linda C.	CA5070	55B,20D,20F,66H,67C
Burns, Carolyn	ND0100	32,20,14,55B
Carberg, Daniel J.	IL1750	61,55B
Cunningham, Tekla	WA0200	67B,55B
Davidoff, Judith	NY3560	41,55B,67
Dorf, Samuel N.	OH2250	12A,11,55A,55B,55C
Eisenstein, Robert	MA2000	12A,55B,67
Fadial, John	WY0200	62A,41,55B
Fishman, Guy	RI0150	62C,55B
Fox, Stuart	CA0510	42,70,55B,67G
Gerber, Thomas E.	IN1650	11,66H,55B,12A
Gordon, Adam	TX3420	67E,55B
Gordon-Seifert, Catherine	RI0150	13,12A,12C,55B,66H
Haas, Arthur S.	NY3790	41,66H,67,55B
Hamman, James	LA0800	11,12A,13A,55B,66G
Hettrick, William E.	NY1600	12A,13,55,55B
Higgins, Brenda L.	FL1550	62C,55B
Hoffman, Richard	TN0100	67C,13,55B
Huener, Thomas J.	NC0650	13,63A,55B
Jackson, Barbara G.	AR0700	13,12A,12,55B,67A
Jamason, Corey	CA4150	66F,66E,12A,55B
Josephson, David	RI0050	12A,12,55B,12E
Laird, Paul R.	KS1350	12A,12,55B,55C
Leenhouts, Paul T.	TX3420	55B,67C
Little, Margaret	AI0200	67A,55B,55D
Mabee, Patricia	CA1075	42,55B,66H
Mabee, Patricia	CA0510	66H,55B
Mahave-Veglia, Pablo	MI0900	42,62C,55B
Mead, Sarah	MA0500	55B,55D,67A,67
Moroney, Davitt	CA5000	11,12,55B,56
Moy, Jason	IL0750	55B,66H
Munn, Albert Christopher	TX3525	13,12A,36,67,55B
Pitzer, Lawrence	OH2450	55B,67C,67D,70,67G
Poirier, Rejean	AI0200	66G,66H,55B,55D
Reed, Elisabeth	CA4150	55B
Roberts, Cynthia	TX3420	55B,62A
Schultz, Stephen	PA0550	12,55B
Shurr, Janet	WI0050	55B,62,67
Song, Anna	OR0450	13C,36,55B,55A,40
Stubbs, Stephen	WA0200	67G,55B

Renaissance Ensemble

Vanderborgh, Beth	WY0200	41,62C,55B
Vogel, Allan	CA1075	64B,42,55B
Vogel, Allan	CA0510	12A,55B,64B,13C
Walker, Nicholas	NY1800	62D,67B,55B
Whear, P. Allen	TX3420	67B,67A,55B
Wiest, Lori J.	WA1150	36,55B,61,60A
Wilson, Nancy	NY2250	55B
Zaslaw, Neal	NY0900	12,55B

Renaissance Ensemble

Burgess, Phillipa	OH1750	36,55C,14C,12A,20
Chapman, Alicia	NC0050	55C,64B,32E
Cohen, Judith	AG0650	20,55C,55A,32E
Dorf, Samuel N.	OH2250	12A,11,55A,55B,55C
Fader, Don	AL1170	55C,67C,12
Krause, Robert	TX3750	64B,13,55C
Kresnicka, Judith	MN0200	12A,66G,55C
Laird, Paul R.	KS1350	12A,12,55B,55C
Long, David	GA0600	36,63A,49,55C,40
McCraw, Michael	IN0900	67D,55C,55
Moersch, Charlotte Mattax	IL3300	67F,66H,12A,55C,12
Ritchie, Stanley	IN0900	67B,55C
Rush, John Phillip	OK1450	64A,67D,12A,55C,56
Thompson, Paul	MO1500	11,41,64A,29A,55C
Winzenburger, Janet B.	OH0200	55C

Early Music Vocal Emsemble

Ashe, Jennifer	MA0700	11,61,55D,40
Balian, Muriel	CA1960	11,66A,66D,36,55D
Beitmen, Cynthia	CA2950	55D
Blackley, Rowland	OH0100	60A,32D,36,40,55D
Connors, Patricia Cahalan	MN1295	36,55D,60
Corbin, Patricia	AL0500	60A,32D,61,55D,60
Dobreff, Kevin J.	MI0850	20F,61,67C,55D,13C
Feiszli, James D.	SD0500	12A,36,55D,61
Gervais, Michel Marc	CA5060	36,60A,55D,40
Gorelick, Brian	NC2500	60A,36,55D
Hanks, N. Lincoln	CA3600	55D,13,10,34,12A
Holquist, Robert A.	NC2600	32C,36,55D,32D
Hudson, William	IL1200	55D,61
Johnson, Jeffrey W.	NY2105	61,12A,55D,12B
Kennedy, Stephen	NY1100	55D,66G
Lancaster, Michael	NC2600	60A,55D,61,36,32D
Lister, Michael C.	NY0700	32D,32C,55D,36,13
Little, Margaret	AI0200	67A,55B,55D
Macey, Patrick	NY1100	12A,12C,55D
Martin, Gayle H.	AE0050	60A,66G,36,12A,55D
McLoskey, Lansing D.	FL1900	10A,10F,13,55D
Mead, Sarah	MA0500	55B,55D,67A,67
Mentzel, Eric P.	OR1050	61,67H,55,55D,55A
Neufeld, Gerald	AG0500	36,55D,60,32
Olesen, James D.	MA0500	60,36,55D
Poirier, Rejean	AI0200	66G,66H,55B,55D
Porterfield, Richard R.	NY2750	12,13,31A,55D
Ramsdell, Gregory A.	OH0950	37,55D,32B,32D,32C
Sparks, Richard	TX3420	60A,36,55D
Sussuma, Robert	CO0560	36,55D
Thoms, Jason A.	NY0850	36,32D,61,55D,12A

Baroque Orchestra

Craig, Phebe	CA5010	13C,56,66H
Cypess, Rebecca	NJ1130	12,66E,66H,56
Dolata, David	FL0700	12,67G,55,56,67H
Hohstadt, Tom	TX3527	38,41,56,60
Knox, Hank	AI0150	56,66H,67F,55
Miller, Jo Ann	ND0350	60,36,40,56
Moroney, Davitt	CA5000	11,12,55B,56
O'Dette, Paul	NY1100	55,56,67G
Olsen, Timothy	NC2205	66G,31A,66H,42,56
Pedersen, Thomas	DC0050	36,39,54,56,61
Rush, John Phillip	OK1450	64A,67D,12A,55C,56
Thielmann, Christel	NY1100	55,56,67A
Xenelis, Nick	CA4460	56

Guitar Ensemble

McLure, Richard	TX0370	35G,57,53,70
Millham, Michael	WA0400	70,57
Morales, Joshua	OK0850	70,57
Mowad, Lou	NC0250	70,57
Padron, Rafael	FL0700	70,57
Randall, Thomas	MA1000	47,57,72,70
Stevens, Keith	VA0600	70,57
Trent, Robert S.	VA1100	70,67G,41,57

Bagpipe Corps

Maffett, Jon D.	OH0700	58

DJ Techniques

Reed, William	AZ0350	59

Conducting (All Areas)

Aarhus, Craig	MS0500	37,60
Abraham, Daniel E.	DC0010	11,12,14C,36,60
Accurso, Joseph	NJ0030	13A,13,60,10,35B
Adams, Kenny L.	OK0700	60,36,39,54,40
Adelson, Michael	NY3785	60,38
Aldrich, Nicole P.	MO1900	36,40,60
Allen, Burt	LA0550	36,60A,60,34,61
Allen, Virginia	NY4200	60
Allen, Virginia	PA0850	60
Allen, Virginia	NY1900	60
Allsup, Neal	KS0550	11,12A,36,60,61
Alltop, Stephen W.	IL2250	60,38
Alme, Joseph	ND0250	63C,63D,37,60
Almond, Frank W.	CA4100	60,12A,36
Almquist, Bradley L.	KY0950	60,32,36,13C
Alt, Jerry A.	NM0310	36,61,60
Altman, Timothy	NC2435	60,32,37,63A,63B
Alverson, P. Michael	SC0300	13,37,60
Amos, Shaun	GA0500	60,36,13B,13C,12A
Amrein, Emilie	IL1400	36,12A,13C,60,11
Anderson, Christopher	AR0200	60,32C,37
Anderson, Douglas K.	NY0270	13,10F,60,10,38
Anderson, Edward D.	CO0250	60,36
Anderson, Michael J.	IL3310	13A,60,36
Aquilanti, Giancarlo	CA4900	13,10F,60,37,49
Archambo, Larry	TX1700	60,32C,37,34,63C
Arian, Merri	NY1450	60,32,70
Armenian, Raffi	AG0450	60,38
Armstrong, James I.	VA0250	36,12A,60,12C
Atkinson, Monte	CO0225	60,32C,36,61,66A
Auerbach, Dan J.	GA0850	60,62A,62B,38,51
Austin, Terry	VA1600	32,37,60
Bach, Larry	MN1250	60,36,61
Bailey, Donald	TX0300	60,36
Bailey, Jon D.	CA3650	60,12A,36,11
Bailey, Wayne A.	AZ0100	60
Baker, Guy O.	WV0650	60,36,61
Baker, Kevin L.	MO0300	36,32D,61,60,32
Baker, William	NY1900	60
Baker, William	IN0005	12,13,60,36,39
Baldwin, Joseph	IA0950	60,41,38
Baldwin, Joseph	MA1750	36,60
Bankhead, James M.	UT0300	60
Barber, Carolyn	NE0600	60,37
Barnes, James E.	PA2450	37,38,60,34,41
Barnett, Steven	WV0400	10F,32E,37,60
Barrett, Richard	NY0500	39,61,60
Barrow, Lee G.	GA1500	13,60,34
Bartee, Neale	AR0110	60,12A,49,63C
Bartley, Mark	TX3750	36,38,60,60B
Basney, Nyela	TX3527	61,66,36,38,60
Bates, Charles N.	OH1800	11,32E,37,47,60
Bates, Michael J.	AR0810	36,13,60,12A,66A
Bayen, Diane	NY2450	13C,61,36,60,32
Bechen, Gene	IA1300	37,32E,60,32
Becker, David M,	OR0400	60,32C,37,29,64
Becker, Jeral Blaine	MO1250	61,36,11,60,39
Beckford, Richard E.	SC1050	13,60,11,36,66G
Beckmann-Collier, Aimee	IA0550	60,36,40
Bednarzyk, Stephen C.	GU0500	37,60,64C,66A
Beeks, Graydon F.	CA3650	60,12A,37,16,54
Behnke, Martin K.	OR1300	60,37,66A,29
Belan, William	CA0830	60,36
Bell, Jeff	IL2300	36,61,54,60
Bell, Ken	CA3460	37,60
Belles, David	CT0150	36,40,60,61
Belongia, Daniel A.	IL1150	60,37
Bendzsa, Paul	AD0050	60,47,64C,64E
Bentley, Joe	MI1830	12A,32D,60,36
Benyas, Edward M.	IL2900	60,38,64B
Berard, Jesus Manuel	DC0010	38,60,13,11
Berentsen, Kurt	OR0150	36,60,61,32A,40
Berry, James	PA3100	11,37,60,32B,48
Bersaglia, G. Scott	KY0400	13A,60,37
Bettendorf, Carl	NY2200	38,60
Bieritz, Gerald	TX1300	12A,11,32A,36,60
Bilotta, Lee	PA3560	60,32B,37,63,31A
Bingham, Thomas	HI0210	32E,37,60
Blachly, Alexander	IN1700	60,12,36,55,12A
Black, Donald	VA1350	13,60
Blackshear, Glinda	AL0831	60,11,36,39,61
Blackstone, Jerry O.	MI2100	60,36
Blatti, Richard L.	OH1850	60,37
Bleuel, John	GA2130	13C,60,64E,64B,64D
Block, Glenn	IL1150	60,38
Blodget, Sherril	VT0100	40,36,60,61,11
Bodiford, Kenneth	AL0500	60,37,63D
Boerma, Scott	MI2100	60,37
Boers, Geoffrey	WA1050	60,36,38
Bogas, Roy	CA2200	60,12A,38,66A,66B
Boggs, William	OH0350	38,60,41,60B
Bohn, Donna M.	PA1550	12A,13B,13C,65,60
Bolkovac, Edward	CT0650	36,60
Bolster, Stephen C.	KY0300	60,32D,36,40,61
Bonner, Gary	CA0450	36,38,60
Bonner, Judd	CA0450	36,60
Booker, Kenneth A.	TX1450	37,46,47,60,13A
Boos, Kenneth G.	FL1310	13,60,36,41,61
Booth, David M.	OH2500	60,37,63D,65
Boozer, John E.	NC2350	60,20,36,31,61
Borton, Bruce E.	NY3705	60,36,61
Bostic, Ronald D.	NC2650	60,12A
Boudreaux, Margaret A.	MD0520	60,12A,32D,36
Boulden, George	KY1450	37,60,32E
Bourgeois, John	LA0300	60
Bowles, Kenneth E.	ND0250	36,61,39,60,32C
Boyd, Craig E.	NY4050	60,11,47,70,29A
Boyer, Douglas R.	TX3100	36,60,54,32D,13F
Boyer, Peter	CA1050	10,60,35
Bradshaw, Eric E.	GA2150	63D,32E,37,60
Brakel, Timothy D.	OH2300	32E,32,64E,13,60
Brandes, David E.	NH0110	13,10F,60,36,66G
Brandes, Gary W.	MO1830	37,60,32E
Brantley, Paul E.	NY2150	60
Brashier, Joe H.	GA2150	32,37,60
Bray, Michael R.	PA3260	60,61,11,36,12A
Brimmer, Timothy	IN0250	60,32,36,34
Brinegar, Donald L.	CA3500	13A,36,61,60
Brody, Ben	WA1350	31A,60,11,12A
Bronk, Mary Beth	TX3100	32E,37,60,63A
Brooks, Marguerite	CT0850	60,36
Brough, Ronald P.	UT0050	60,32C,37,65,72
Brown, Bruce C.	NY1700	60,11,36,61,31A
Brown, Charles P.	IL0730	36,60,32
Brown, Emily Freeman	OH0300	60,38
Browning, Doug	MS0550	32,40,42,47,60
Bruck, Douglas	CA4050	13A,13,66A,60
Brunner, David L.	FL1800	60,36,32D,10
Bryant, Stephen	NJ1400	60,36,61
Buchanan, Scott	IN0800	36,60
Bullock, Valerie K.	SC0275	60,32B,32C,36
Burch-Pesses, Michael	OR0750	60,32C,37,47,45
Burda, Pavel	WI0825	13A,60,50,65
Burkhardt, Rebecca L.	IA1600	13,38,60
Burns, Brian E.	IA0250	36,12A,32C,32D,60
Busch, Michael	CA1425	36,60,13B,32D
Buttolph, David	NY3705	60,36
Cable, Howard	AA0200	10,11,35,47,60
Cabrera, Ricardo	PR0100	11,36,61,60,13A
Cai, Jindong	CA4900	60,38,43
Cairns, Debra	AA0100	60,36
Caldwell, Gary	UT0150	13,60,37,63A
Caldwell, William	TN0100	36,60
Caldwell, William	OH0500	36,39,61,60
Calhoun, James M.	CA5100	36,40,60
Cameron, Jennifer	OR1150	13,10F,64,60,51
Cameron, Robert C.	PA1050	60,32C,37
Caminiti, Joseph D.	PA2800	60,38,37,63B,32E
Campbell, Don	SC1080	13,60,36,61,12A
Campbell, John W.	KY0610	60,11,32,61,36
Campbell, Kathleen M.	PA3000	60,37,38,48
Canton, Lisette M.	AG0650	36,55,60
Cantwell, Richard E.	KS1300	13,60,10A,37,38

Index by Area of Teaching Interest

Name	Code	Areas
Canty, Dean R.	TX3525	60,37,63A,63B,11
Carney, Horace R.	AL0010	13,60,10,36
Carroll, William P.	NC2430	60,36
Casey, Maurice T.	OH1850	60,36
Casey, Michael R.	MO0775	49,63A,60,54
Castle, Troy	SC0200	60
Castleberry, David	WV0400	60,12A,36,61
Castonguay, David O.	VA1100	60,36,61
Cathey, Rodney	CA0250	60,36
Cha, In-Hong	OH2500	60,38,62A
Chae, Hyung Sek	TX3650	36,31A,44,60,32D
Chambers, Mark K.	AG0650	38,60,62
Chambers, Robert B.	TN0650	60,61,31A,36,44
Chandler, Deborah L.	LA0770	36,60,40
Charloff, Ruth	CA5040	60,11,36,38
Charter, Ian R.	AA0010	12A,13A,31A,32E,60
Chase, David A.	CA3460	13A,13,12A,36,60
Cheng, Marietta	NY0650	13,60,11,36,38
Chesebrough, James C.	NH0150	37,60,32,63D,32E
Chesnutt, Rod M.	FL0680	37,38,60,32E,32F
Chiaravalloti, Charissa	CO0350	36,40,60,12A,32D
Chipman, Shelby R.	FL0600	60,32C,37,63A
Chobaz, Raymond	FL1850	13,60,38
Ciepluch, Gary	OH0400	60,32,37,48
Cierpke, Timothy H.	TN1600	10F,60,62,36,38
Clark, Andrew G.	MA1050	36,60
Clark, Richard A.	IN0250	38,60
Clarke, W. Harry	KY1450	60,32E
Clausen, Rene	MN0600	60,36
Clayton, Lisa	CT0600	60
Clifft, Al	CA0250	36,60,13
Climer, John	WI0825	60,37,43
Cline, Lonnie	OR0050	60,36,61
Cochrane, Keith A.	NM0400	60,12A,32B,37,47
Cock, Christopher M.	IN1750	60,36,61
Coker, Timothy C.	MS0385	13,60,32,36,66A
Collerd, Gene J.	IL3310	13A,60,37,64C
Colson, David J.	MI2250	10,65,60
Combs, Barry	SC0950	60,36,61,31A
Conley, Mark	RI0300	13,60,36,61,32D
Conlon, Joan C.	CO0800	60,36
Connors, Patricia Cahalan	MN1295	36,55D,60
Cook, Grant W.	OH2290	36,40,60,12
Cook, Warren	SC0200	13,60,36,31A,40
Copeland, Philip L.	AL0800	60,36
Copley, Edith A.	AZ0450	60A,36,60
Corbin, Patricia	AL0500	60A,32D,61,55D,60
Cornelius, Jeffrey M.	PA3250	60,11,12A,36
Cornwall, Lonieta	NC2300	13,60,36,60D
Council, Thomas	GA2000	31A,61,36,60,40
Covey, Jason	GA0750	60,47
Covey, Jason	NY2900	60,32E
Cowles, Robert	NY1550	13,36,60
Cox, John	NY4310	36,38,40,41,60
Crannell, Wayne T.	TX0250	36,61,11,39,60
Crawford, Glenda	OH2550	36,32A,32C,32B,60
Cross, Travis J.	VA1700	32E,37,60
Crowell, Allen	GA2100	60,36
Cubek, David	CA1060	38,11,13,60
Cubek, David	CA3620	38,11,13,60
Cubek, David	CA2175	38,11,13,60
Cubek, David	CA4500	38,11,60,13
Culver, Eric	MA0700	11,60,10F,38,41
Culver, Jerry	MI1700	36,13C,60
Culverhouse, William	IN0400	36,12A,60
Currie, David	AG0400	60,38,41,62D
Cushman, Kevin	MI1260	60,13C
Cutter, William	MA0350	60A,60
Dabrowski, Peter	TX3525	60,10F
Dahlman, Hank	OH2500	32,36,60
Daniel, Robert	OK0550	13A,60,11,61,13C
Danis, Ann	RI0300	60,38,11,62A,62B
Darr, Steven L.	FL2130	60,32,36,61
Davies, Thomas H.	CA0600	13,60,36,61
Davis, Edward	OH0350	20,60,65
Davis, John E.	GA0300	60,11,37,64A,64E
Davis, Randy	AL1195	37,38,60,13,48
Davis, Richard A.	WV0500	13,60,12A,36,61
Davis, Victor	TN1400	11,36,60
De Jaager, Alfred R.	WV0600	36,32D,60,11
De Melo, Dorvalino	AI0220	60,32C,37,47,64E
Deakins, Mark	KY0650	13A,60,36,31A,40
Dean, Jay L.	MS0750	60,38,39
Dean, Sally	CA3460	36,60
Del Tredici, David	NY0550	60,10
Delaney, Jack	TX2400	60,37
Dennee, Peter D.	WI0250	32C,32D,36,60,40
Desmond, Clinton J.	SD0200	36,11,20,60,12
Dettwiler, Peggy	PA2150	60,36,32C,61
Detweiler, Greg J.	KY0900	60,36,61,40
Deutsch, Margery	WI0825	60,38
Di Grazia, Donna M.	CA3650	60,11,12A,36
Dickau, David C.	MN1000	60,36,45,34
Dickerson, Randy C.	WI0803	60,32C,37
Dickey, Thomas Taylor	IA0250	60,64D
Diehl, Richard C.	VT0100	13,60,47,10,37
Dietrich, Johannes M.	PA1900	60,38,62A,62B
Dissmore, Larry	MO0400	60,38,51,62A,62B
Dobroski, Bernard J.	IL2250	32H,63D,32,60,35E
Doebler, Lawrence A.	NY1800	60,36
Dolloff, Lori-Anne	AG0450	32A,32B,60,36,66C
Dominick, Daniel L.	TX0250	66A,12,60B,38,60
Dorsey, Rodney	MI2100	60,37
Douglas, Thomas W.	PA0550	47,60
Downing, Joseph	NY4150	10,66G,13,13C,60
Doyle, William	CA1750	11,37,38,63,60
Dregalla, Herbert E.	OH2500	12,32,60,64C
Drury, William	MA1400	60,48
Duckett, Alfred	OK0150	11,60
Duff, Robert P.	NH0100	36,60,10A,40,13C
Duffy, Kathryn Ann Pohlmann	IA0650	11,12,13,36,60
Duncan, Ellen	MI1300	13A,13,60,36,40
Durlam, Zachary D.	CA1860	36,60,32A,32B,40
Dvorak, Thomas	WI0825	60,37
Eash, William	KS0200	60,36
Eberl, Carl	NY0642	60
Eckerty, Michael	IA1350	64D,32C,37,60,48
Edelstein, Gerardo	PA2750	60,38
Edmonds, Johnnella	VA1750	60,32B,32C,36,61
Edwards, Lawrence	TN1680	60,32,36
Edwards, Linda	NM0400	60,36,41,61,54
Effron, David	IN0900	60,38
Eichner, Mark J.	WI0835	60,32C,37,63A,32A
Eklund, Peter A.	NE0600	60,32D,36
Ellis, Barry L.	WI0840	60,37,64D,64E,32
Emge, Jeffrey D.	TX3535	32,37,60,64B
Emilson, C. Rudolph	NY3725	60,41,63D
Endo, Akira	CO0800	38,60
Endris, Robert R.	IN1400	60,32B,36
Engebretson, Stan P.	VA0450	36,60A,60,40
Engelson, Robert A.	IA0050	13,60,11,36,54
Enns, Leonard J.	AG0470	13,60,10,36
Eros, Peter	WA1050	60,39
Errante, Steven	NC2440	13,10F,60,10,38
Erwin, Joanne	OH1700	32,60
Etter, David D.	KY1425	36,61,31A,60
Etter, Paul J.	NC0850	60A,36,44,60,31A
Etters, Stephen C.	NC0350	60,32,37,63D,13A
Everett, Beth	MI0600	36,60,32D
Everett, Steve	GA0750	60,10,41,45,34
Eychaner, Frank	CO0150	10,32,13,47,60
Fagen, Arthur H.	IN0900	60,38
Fague, Kyla	WA1350	37,60
Famulare, Trever R.	PA3050	11,37,47,49,60
Farris, Daniel J.	IL2250	47,37,60B,60
Fassett, Charles K.	MA2150	60,11,12A,36
Feinstein, Allen G.	MA1450	13,10F,60,37,48
Feller, Robert	CA0350	11,37,49,63,60
Fennell, Mitchell	CA0815	60,32,37
Fenton, Kevin	FL0850	60,32,36
Finney, John R.	MA0330	60,36,38,66G
Fisher, Tammy M.	WI0810	60,37,65,32,11
FitzGibbon, Katherine L.	OR0400	36,60,11
Fleitas, Patricia P.	FL0650	60,36,61
Fletcher, John M.	OK0700	10F,60,37,13
Floriano, Gerard F.	NY3730	60,36
Fooster, Harold	AR0810	60,11,37,50,65
Ford, Joseph Kevin	TN1700	36,40,32D,60
Forrester, Marshall	SC0275	10,11,37,60
Fortney, Patrick	NE0500	60,37,47
Foster, William P.	FL0600	60,37
Fountain, Robin	TN1850	60,38,43
Francis, Bobby R.	TX3000	37,60,32E
Frangipane, Ron	NJ0760	13,10F,60,10,12A
Freeman, James	PA3200	12,60
Friberg, David	CA3520	60
Fried, Eric	TX3200	60,11
Frierson-Campbell, Carol	NJ1400	32,63B,60
Friesen-Carper, Dennis	IN1750	60,10,41,38
Fritz, Benno P.	DC0100	37,49,60,11
Fritz, Matthew P.	PA1250	36,60A,34,34E,60
Fryling, David N.	NY1600	36,60A,60,32,13A
Fuller, Gregory	MS0750	60,36
Fulton, Kenneth	LA0200	60,36
Funk, Eric	MT0200	10A,10F,60,29,13
Futrell, Stephen A.	NC0750	36,32D,60,35C,40
Gabrielse, Kenneth J.	LA0400	60,36,31A,12A
Gaddis, J. Robert	KY0400	60,32,51,63D,38
Gage, Stephen	OH2600	37,60
Galvan, Alex	CA1000	10,13,37,60
Garber, Joel	OK0770	12A,61,14,36,60
Garcia, Alvaro	WI0835	38,62B,60,51
Garcia, William B.	TN0800	60,11,36,61,31A
Garcia-Novelli, Eduardo	WI0250	36,40,32D,13C,60
Gardner, David B.	KS1200	36,60,61,60A,54
Garner, Rusty	FL0900	60,11,61,54,64D
Garrett, Monte	TX1100	60,36
Gehring, Joseph	PA1550	37,38,60,63
Geller, Ian R.	IN0005	61,10A,60,36
Gemberling, Alan	ID0250	37,63C,47,60,41
George, Matthew J.	MN1625	60,41,37
George, Roby	IN0800	37,60
Gilbert, Albert	NY1900	38,60
Gilbert, David	NY2150	60,38
Giles, Glenn	VT0100	63C,63D,60,37,46
Gillespie, Clint	AL0500	60,37,65
Gillis, Glen	AJ0150	60,32C,37,48,64E
Gilman, Grant	VA0250	38,60
Giordano, John R.	TX3000	60
Girtmon, Paxton	MS0100	37,47,64E,10F,60
Glaze, Richard T.	FL2100	60,32,37,48,64
Glazebrook, James	VA1700	60,38,62A,62B
Glickman, Joel	WI0600	60,32,37,38,47
Glocke, Dennis	PA2750	60,37
Gnam, Adrian	GA0950	38,60,64B
Goacher, Stephen	TX1100	60,48,64,47,29
Gokelman, William	TX3410	60,36,66A,66C,31A
Golan, Lawrence	CO0900	60,38
Golemo, Michael	IA0850	37,60,64E,32
Gookin, Larry D.	WA0050	60,37,49,63C
Goold, William C.	KY0150	60,12A,36,61,31A
Gordon, Samuel	OH2150	60,12A,36,61,40
Gosselin, Karen	AL0550	32,60,36,40,44
Gowan, Andrew D.	SC1110	60,32,37,64
Gowen, Dennis	ND0400	37,49,63A,63B,60
Gracia-Nuthmann, Andre	NM0150	13,60,36,55,61
Graf, Greg	MO0750	36,40,60,11
Graham, Lisa E.	MA2050	36,60
Graham, Lowell	TX3520	13,60
Grant, Denise	AG0600	37,60
Grant, Gary S.	PA1200	37,60,47
Grant, Joe W.	IL3300	60,32,36
Graves, Daniel H.	IN0400	11,12A,36,60,41
Gray, William Jon	IN0900	60,36
Grechesky, Robert	IN0250	60,32
Green, Gary D.	FL1900	60,37
Green, J. Paul	AG0500	60,12B,32,12C
Greenlee, Robert K.	ME0200	60,36,12A,12,55
Gregg, Robert B.	TN0100	60,11,12A,38
Gregory, Gary J.	OH0550	44,13,60,37,63C
Griffin, Samuel S.	MS0050	60,37,63D
Griffith, Michael Ted	WY0200	60,38,42
Grimes, Judith	IL0850	60,14,32,37
Groh, Jack C.	AR0700	60,36,61
Grooms, Pamela	MO0650	12A,20,32D,60,66
Grove-DeJarnett, Doug	TN1150	60
Grzych, Frank J.	TN0500	60,32C
Gustafson, Kirk	CO0225	13,10F,60,62C
Gutierrez, German A.	TX3000	60,38
Haan, Keith A.	IA1300	60,36,32D,61,40
Haberlen, John B.	GA1050	60,32D,36
Haddock, Marshall	OH1850	60,38,64C
Hafso, Marc A.	WA1350	60,36,10A,32D,61
Hahm, Shinik	CT0850	60
Hahm, Shinik	CT0900	60
Hahn, Christopher D.	SD0100	63,37,60,11
Hahn, David	TN0580	12A,34,35A,36,60
Hahn, Marjorie	FL1300	63B,49,60
Haithcock, Michael	MI2100	60,37
Hall, Barbara L.	KY0450	13,12A,12,36,60
Hall, Louis O.	ME0440	60,32,64B,64E
Hall, Robert	AG0150	13,60,36,61,10F
Hall, Wade	UT0050	60,36
Hallstrom, Jonathan F.	ME0250	13,60,10,38,45
Halseth, Robert E.	CA0840	60,37
Hampton, Neal	MA2050	60,38

615

Name	Code	Areas
Hampton, Neal	MA0500	60,37,38,41,48
Hanna, Scott S.	TX3510	60,37
Hansen, Deborah	WA1350	60,36,13B
Hansen, Sharon A.	WI0825	60,36
Hanson, Eric A.	WA0800	60,12A,38,10,64C
Hanson, Gregg I.	AZ0500	60,37
Hanson, Jan	OK1400	60,11,12A,32,36
Harbold, Tim	MA2150	60,36,45
Harleston, Sheila C.	MD1020	60,36,66A,66D
Harman, David	NY4350	60,38,41,11
Harper, Larry D.	WI0200	60,37,41,63B
Harper, T.J.	RI0150	36,60,32C,32D,61
Harris, Carl G.	VA0500	60,12A,66,69
Harris, Jason W.	OH1700	60,36,61
Harris, Robert	GA0200	12A,60,61,11,32D
Harris, Robert A.	IL2250	60,36
Harrison, Jacob G.	IA0850	38,60
Hart, Thomas J.	IA0600	60,36,12A
Hassevoort, Darrin	TN0260	36,61,47,60,54
Hatteberg, Kent E.	KY1500	36,60
Hauser, Alexis	AI0150	38,60
Hayes, David	PA0850	60,38
Hayes, David	NY2250	60,38
Hayes, Glenn C.	WI0865	60,32,37
Haywood, Carl	VA0950	13,60,41,66G
Hearne, Martin	IA0400	37,38,50,60
Hebert, Ryan	FL2050	60,36,13C,66G
Heetderks, David	OH1700	10A,13C,13E,60
Heffner, Christopher J.	PA1900	32E,37,60,63
Hegg, Barbara	SD0150	36,61,63B,60
Henderson, Mark A.	UT0350	60,10,11,36,32D
Hendrickson, Peter A.	MN0050	60,36,13,66G
Hensley, David	CA0810	60,61
Herrick, Dennis R.	AL0450	60,63,34,29A,32C
Hess, H. Carl	PA1050	37,38,60,63A
Hetrick, Esther A.	MI0910	61,60,31A,36,32B
Heukeshoven, Janet	MN1400	37,32,60,11,41
Hewitt, Michael P.	MD1010	60,32,38
Hibbard, Kevin	GA2130	36,32D,61,60,32C
Hicken, Leslie W.	SC0750	60,37,32
Hickman, Joe Eugene	NC2440	60,36,41,61
Hickok, Robert B.	CA5020	60,36
Hicks, Martha K.	MO1550	31A,11,60,13C,32B
Hicks, Sarah Hatsuko	PA0850	13,60
Hightower, Allen	IA0950	36,32D,60
Hill, Gary W.	AZ0100	60,37
Hinson, Wallace	GA1650	60,36,40
Hinton, Jeffrey	MO0850	60,32C,37,64E
Hirsh, Jonathan M.	MA1750	60,36,38
Hochstetler, Scott	IN0550	36,61,60
Hodson, Steven R.	CA5550	11,36,60,66A
Hohstadt, Tom	TX3527	38,41,56,60
Holcomb, Paula K.	NY3725	37,60
Holland, Geoffrey	FL1450	60,36
Holleman, James A.	MI1000	60,11,36,38
Hollinger, Diana	CA4400	32,60
Hollins, John S.	TX3200	60,36,41
Holm, Thomas	IA1200	12A,36,11,60,61
Holmes, Brad	IL1750	60,32C,36
Holmquist, Solveig	OR1250	11,36,60,66G,69
Holoman, D. Kern	CA5010	60,11,12A,12
Hoose, David M.	MA0400	60,38
Hopkins, John R.	AK0150	36,39,61,60
Hopkins, Mark E.	AF0050	37,32E,32C,60,60B
Hopper, Mary	IL3550	60,36
Hornsby, Richard	AE0120	64C,12A,29A,34,60
Hose, Anthony	FL1750	38,60,35E
Houze, Reginald M.	MA0150	10F,36,37,60,63D
Hristova, Gabriela	MI2120	36,60
Hu, Ching-chu	OH0850	13,10,60
Huff, Michael D.	UT0300	60,60A,60B
Hufstader, Ron	TX3520	60,37,38
Hughes, Brian L.	IA0940	60,11,32,37,47
Hughes, David	CA0250	60,36,61
Hull, Barbara A.	NY2650	63A,63,60
Humbert, William	AZ0350	37,64,63,13A,60
Husa, Karel	NY0900	10F,60,10A
Huszti, Joseph B.	CA5020	60,36,61
Hutson, Danny J.	AL0010	12A,13E,60,63C
Hutton, Cynthia	OR0950	60,37,49,63B
Isaacs, Kevin	CT0800	13,60,10,12B,36
Ivy, Allen	MO1100	60,38,51,64A
Jablow, Lisa	VT0250	60,12A,36,41,61
Jackson, Christopher	AI0070	60,66G,66H,67C
Jackson, Jay Craig	NC0050	60,32E
James, Jeffrey R.	NE0250	13,60,32,37,63
Janisch, Joseph	WV0560	36,60,32,13A,32B
Janners, Erik N.	WI0425	37,47,60,12,13
Janower, David M.	NY3700	13,60,12A,36
Janzen, Eldon A.	AR0700	60,32C,37
Janzen, Wesley	AB0090	60,12A,36,31A
Jenkins, Donald P.	CO0200	60,36,39,41,54
Jenkins, Jack	MO0700	33,36,60
Jennings, Mark D.	MO1780	60,36,61
Jenrette, Thomas S.	TN0500	36,61,60
Jesse, Lynda	MO0200	32D,36,54,60,61
Jimenez, Alexander	FL0850	38,60B,65A,60,65
Jimenez, Raphael	OH1700	60
Jobin-Bevans, Dean	AG0170	60,36,40,39
Jodry, Frederick	RI0050	13,60,12A,36
Johnson, Brad	MS0200	60,11,36,44,61
Johnson, Carl	TX0200	60,12A,32C,36,61
Johnson, David A.	IA0900	60,32,37,47,65
Johnson, Dennis	KY0950	60,37,38
Johnson, Deral J.	AG0500	60,36
Johnson, Eric	IL2200	60,36
Johnson, Gordon	MT0370	60
Johnson, Jefferson	KY1450	60,40,36,42
Johnson, Kevin P.	GA1900	60,11,32A,32B,34
Johnson, Nathaniel	NE0710	60,37,64C,64E
Johnson, Ronald	IA1600	60,37
Johnson, Stephen P.	TX2600	10,13,10F,60A,60
Johnson, Valerie	NC0200	60,36,61
Johnston, James W.	IN1100	60,62A,66A
Johnston, Rebecca R.	SC0600	32,36,60,13C,61
Jones, Anne Howard	MA0400	60,36
Jones, Brandon D.	OH2450	37,38,32E,60
Jones, Dani S.	AL0650	61,39,31A,60
Jones, Keith	SC0650	61,36,60
Jones, William LaRue	IA1550	60,38
Jordan, James	NJ1350	66G,36,13,60
Jorgensen, Robert	OH2150	37,60
Joseph, Charles	NY3725	60,62A,62B
Joss, Laura L.	OH0200	32,37,60
Jost, John R.	IL0400	60,36,61,38
Junkin, Jerry	TX3510	60,37
Kamenski, Michael	WI0050	60,13,34
Kamm, Charles W.	CA2175	36,11,12,60
Kamm, Charles W.	CA4500	36,12,40,60
Kamm, Charles W.	CA1060	36,11,12,60
Kamm, Charles W.	CA3620	36,11,12,60
Kantack, Jerri Lamar	MS0150	60,36,61,12A,32
Kaplan, Abraham	WA1050	60,36,38
Kaplunas, Daniel	IA1800	38,62C,62B,51,60
Karchin, Louis S.	NY2740	10F,60,10,36
Karriker, Galen	OH2150	37,60
Katseanes, Kory L.	UT0050	38,60,62A
Keating, Bevan T.	AR0750	36,60,61
Keaton, Kenneth D.	FL0650	60,12A,41,67D,70
Keck, Vail	CA3100	36,60,11,13A,61
Kellan, Ross	IL0850	60,32,37,11,13
Keller, Daniel B.	CA3000	11,36,60
Kelley, Timothy S.	TX3650	60,37,49,63,41
Kelly, Jennifer W.	PA1850	60,36,61
Kendall, Michael	IN0200	60,37,32,20,34
Kendrick, Donald	CA0840	60,36
Kennedy, P. Kevin	CO0625	61,60,12A,66
Kenny, William	PA0350	60,11,37,63A,63B
Kephart, Donald B.	PA1350	32C,37,63,46,60
Kershaw, Linda L.	SC0150	11,12,60,66A,36
Kesselman, Lee R.	IL0630	13,10,36,54,60
Kiesler, Kenneth	NY2150	60
Kim, Chris Younghoon	NY0900	38,41,42,60
Kim, Lok	GA0600	38,42,60,66A
Kimmel, Jim	TN0100	36,60,32C
Kinchen, James B.	WI0835	60,36,32C
King, Dennis W.	WI0150	60,11,32,13
King, Jonathan	NY3560	13,10F,60,36,10
King, Valeria G.	LA0720	13,60,12A,12,20G
KinKennon, Heather Marie	CA0200	11,60,66,66D
Kirchhoff, Craig	MN1623	60,37,41
Kirkpatrick, Linda M.	MD0520	60,37,41,48,64A
Kjelland, James	IL2250	60,32C,38,62
Klassen, Glenn	AA0200	36,38,40,60
Klebanow, Susan	NC2410	60,36
Klein, Lonnie	NM0310	11,38,41,60
Klein, Mitchell	CA1250	38,60
Kleinknecht, Daniel E.	IA1140	60,32,36,61
Knapp, Joel	IL2910	60,36,40
Knight, Gerald R.	NC0750	36,60,61,32
Koehler, Andrew	MI1150	60,38,62A,62B,12A
Koehler, Elisa C.	MD0400	38,63A,60,11,13A
Kolb, G. Roberts	NY1350	60,12A,36,40
Kolman, Barry	VA1850	13,37,38,64C,60
Kolt, Robert P.	AR0500	60,12A,60
Kono, Yutaka	VT0450	63D,34,38,60
Koponen, Glenn	NY2900	60,37,41,63A,31A
Korak, John	IL2910	60,37,63A,49,42
Kosche, Kenneth	WI0300	13,60,10,36,31A
Krager, Franz Anton	TX3400	60,38
Krebill, Kerry	DC0350	60,11
Krueger, Carol J.	KS0300	13C,60,36,32D
Kuhn, William	OR0150	37,11,63C,60,13A
Labuta, Joseph	MI2200	60,32
Laird, Scott	NC1800	60,34
Lane, Laura L.	IL1350	12A,60,36,40,61
Lang, Donald P.	NY3725	60,36
LaRosa, Joseph	NY1275	60
Larsen, Vance	UT0190	60,37,49,32
Larson, Allen C.	MO1950	13,60,12A,38
Larson, Richard	NY3725	60,32
LaRue, Peter	KY0610	60,11,32,37,63D
Laster, James	VA1350	60,36,66G,31A
Lavender, Scott	OH0300	60
Lawton, David	NY3790	60,12A,12,38,39
Layendecker, Dennis M.	VA0450	60,38,41
Leck, Henry	IN0250	60,36,32
Leckrone, Michael E.	WI0815	60,37,20G
Lee, Charles	CO0650	62C,41,51,10F,60
Lee, Pamela	TX0150	32,36,66A,60
Lee, Paul S.	TX1300	66G,13B,11,60,66A
Lee, Sun Min	PA1950	36,40,60,13C
Leger, James K.	NM0150	10,60,12,14,38
Lehmann, Jay	CA2450	60,13,64,63
Lehmann, Robert A.	ME0500	60,62
Lemke, Jeffrey J.	LA0350	32,37,60
Lemons, Robert M.	CT0150	11,60,32,63A
Leon, Tania	NY0500	10,38,41,60
Leon, Tania	NY0600	10,60
Levine, Iris S.	CA0630	12A,32,36,60
Levy, Leesa	ND0600	60
Lewis, Melissa	OK1200	60,41,51,62A
Liberatore, William	CA3270	39,54,60,61
Lindholm, Eric C.	CA3650	13A,60,11,38,41
Livesay, Charles	MI2000	60,32D,36,40,61
Livingston, Larry J.	CA5300	60
Lloyd, Joe	AZ0400	32C,37,63A,11,60
Lloyd, Kimcherie	KY1500	60,39,38
Lock, William R.	CA0350	60,36,61,31A
Locke, Benjamin R.	OH1200	13A,60,36,38,61
Locke, John R.	NC2430	60,32C,37
Loeppky, Ian R.	AL1250	60,36,41,40
Loewen, Harris	AG0050	60,36
Logsdon, Anthony	AL0500	60,32,64E
Long, Daniel	TX2200	36,61,60,11,13D
Long, Derle R.	LA0770	60,32E,37
Long, Wallace H.	OR1300	60,32C,36
Longfield, Richard O.	AZ0510	13,60,37,38,47
Looker, Wendy	NC0910	60,36,70,12A,13A
Lopez Yanez, Ruth	CA3460	13A,60,66,66C
Love, Jason L.	MD1000	60
Lovejoy, Donald G.	MN1700	37,63A,41,60,32E
Lowenstein, Marc	CA0510	13,10,60,39,43
Lubaroff, Scott C.	MO1790	37,32E,10F,60
Lucas, Mark	OK1350	60,32,36,41
Luckhardt, Jerry	MN1623	60,37,41
Lundergan, Edward	NY3760	13A,13B,36,60,12A
Lutch, Mitchell B.	IA0200	10F,32E,37,60
Luther, David	TN0200	60,36,61,31A,41J
Lynn, Debra J.	IN1050	60,36,61,40,39
MacDonald, John A.	OH2150	60,12A,12,36
MacGillivray, Rod	AF0120	60,63C,63D
Mack, Kyle	ND0350	60,37,47,63C,29
Mack, William G.	MO0850	60,32C,37,49,63A
MacKay, Gillian	AG0450	37,42,63A,60B,60
Magaziner, Elliot	NY2400	60,41,62A
Magee, Robert G.	AR0950	12A,60,36,61,31A
Maglione, Anthony	MO2000	60,37,38,41
Maiello, Anthony J.	VA0450	36,32D,60
Mailman, Matthew	OK0750	60,37
Manahan, George	NY2150	60
Mandelbaum, Joel	NY0642	13,60
Maness, David	PA1150	13,60,11,36,61
Manji, K. C.	CA1265	60,38,49,41,29A
Markward, Edward	RI0200	38,61,60,39
Marosi, Laszlo	FL1800	38,60

Index by Area of Teaching Interest

Name	Code	Areas
Marsh, Lawrence B.	OR0450	60,12A,32,36
Martin, Barry	MI0900	60,37,32
Martin, Joseph	CO0900	37,63C,63D,41,60
Martin, Peter J.	ME0500	60,32C,37
Martin, Stephanie	AG0650	12A,55,60
Martins, David	MA2030	37,64C,60,42
Marzolf, Dennis	MN0200	60,36,31A,61,54
Mast, Andrew	WI0350	37,41,42,60
Maurtua, Jose Luis	MI0400	13A,13,10F,60,10
Mayes, Robert	TX3400	60,32C,37
Mayo, Walter S.	NY3725	60,32
Mazzaferro, Tony	CA0630	60
McAllister, Michael	NC1750	13,10F,60,11,47
McCashin, Robert D.	VA0600	60,38
McCormick, Robert	MI0500	60
McCutcheon, Russell G.	PA1400	37,32E,60,34,32C
McDannell, Karl	NY2450	32B,32C,47,60
McDermott, Pamela D. J.	VA0700	61,60,36,13C
McEndarfer, Luke	CA3150	60
McFarland, Thomas J.	KY1400	60,12A,32E,49,63
McGarvey, Timothy	IA1200	37,60,32E,41,29A
McGilvray, Byron	CA4200	60,32C,36
McIntyre, Eric L.	IA0700	10,38,60,12A,13
McIntyre, John	IN1350	13,10,60,36
McKee, Max	OR0950	60
McKellar, Donald A.	AG0500	60,32
McMahan, Andrew	CA0600	60,37,63A,54,34
McMillan, William	TX3520	36,61,60
McMillin, Timothy A.	IA1350	60,36,61,32D,12A
McMullian, Neal	IL2300	13B,32E,64D,60,37
McMurray, Allan R.	CO0800	60,37
McNeela, Rico	MO0850	38,11,62A,62B,60
McNeil, Albert J.	CA5010	60,14,32,36
Mechell, Harry A.	MN1700	60,36,32D,61,54
Meder, Randall A.	WI0808	60,11,36,40,32D
Meeker, Howard G.	OH0650	37,60
Megill, Andrew	NJ1350	60
Meier, Gustav	MD0650	60
Melton, James L.	CA5355	60,36,31A,32D,35E
Menchaca, Louis A.	WI0300	13A,13,60,37,29
Menghini, Charles T.	IL3450	60,37,32
Menk, Nancy L.	IN1450	60,36,40
Mennicke, David	MN0610	31A,32,60,61
Meredith, Victoria	AG0500	60,32,36,41
Merrill, Thomas G.	OH2550	12,60,36,32
Mikkelson, Russel	OH1850	37,60
Milarsky, Jeffrey F.	NY0750	38,10F,60
Miles, Melvin N.	MD0600	60,37,47,49,63A
Miles, Richard B.	KY0900	60,37
Miller, Al	AL1195	60,61,36,43
Miller, Dale	AR0110	60,36,61
Miller, DaVaughn	NC1150	36,13E,20B,60
Miller, David	OR0010	36,61,13,60
Miller, Donald K.	TX3530	37,60
Miller, Jo Ann	ND0350	60,36,40,56
Miller, Kevin D.	MI0600	60,32,38
Millican, Jason	TX1250	13A,60,11,36,31A
Milligan, Terence G.	OH2200	60,37,32
Mishra, Michael	IL2910	10F,60,38
Mitchell, Alan	MI0250	60,32,37,49,48
Mitchell, Jon	MA2010	10F,60,32,38
Mollicone, Henry	CA3270	10A,12A,39,54,60
Monachino, Paul	OH1330	13,10A,66,60
Monek, Daniel G.	OH1400	36,61,12A,60
Monseur, George	MA0260	10,60
Monte, Tobias	MA2020	37,49,60,63A
Moore, Corey	NJ0500	47,60,64E
Moore, Stephen F.	CA0805	13C,29,47,60,66
Morales, Gary A.	PR0100	60,32,48,64C
Morgan, Michael	CA4150	60
Morgan, Robert Huw	CA4900	66G,60,36
Morrow, David E.	GA1450	60,11,36,61,66A
Morrow, James	TX3510	60,36
Morrow, Phil J.	NC0300	60,36,31A,61
Morton, Wyant	CA0550	60,36
Moser, Steven R.	MS0750	60,32C
Moses, Kenneth J.	FL1900	60,37
Moshell, Gerald	CT0500	60,12A,54
Moss, Bruce B.	OH0300	60,37
Moss, Myron D.	PA1000	10,11,29,37,60
Moss, Orlando	MS0560	13,60,36,61
Mueller, Marc	OK1250	37,63A,32E,60,34
Mueller, Otto Werner	PA0850	60
Mueller, Paul F.	NY0625	10F,60,11,12A,36
Murai, Hajime Teri	MD0650	60,38
Musmann, Lois S.	CA2270	12,39,60,66H
Musselwhite, Harry	GA0300	60,36,39,61
Myers-Tegeder, Christine	NJ0550	11,60
Myssyk, Daniel	VA1600	38,60
Nabholz, Mark A.	SC0700	36,60
Nachef, Joanna	CA1750	60,11,36,61
Nafziger, Kenneth J.	VA0300	60,36,31A,38,11
Nair, Garyth	NJ0300	36,38,61,60,13C
Nance, Richard	WA0650	60,36
Nash-Robertson, Nina	MI0400	60,36
Navega, Eduardo	NY4450	38,41,60
Naydan, William	PA0650	40,60
Neal, Paul	GA2150	36,60A,61,60
Neale, Alasdair	CA4150	38,60
Neblett, Sonja	CA4150	13,60
Nelson, David L.	NC2430	13,60,37
Nelson, Eric	GA0750	60,36,38,41
Nelson, Roger	WA0200	60,36,66A
Nemhauser, Frank	NY2250	13,60,61
Nero, Jonathan	SD0100	36,32D,60
Neufeld, Gerald	AG0500	36,55D,60,32
Newlin, Yvonne	IL1612	13,60,37,66,47
Ng, Tian Hui	MA1350	38,60,12A
Nichols, Will	MI0150	60,36,61,39
Nies, Carol R.	TN1850	60,38,13,32E
Nitschke, Brad	IN0005	11,12,13,60,63
Noel, Christine	MA0650	36,60
Norcross, Brian H.	PA1300	60,37,38,60B
Nordgren, Jon	CA0400	13,37,46,47,60
Norris, Joshua L.	KS0900	36,60,13,32
Nowack, James	WI1155	60,36,13C
Nowak, Grzegorz	FL0700	38,60
Nurock, Kirk	NY2660	10F,60,10,13J,29A
Oaten, Gregory	PA2450	60,61
Ockwell, Frederick	IL2250	60,39,54
O'Donnell, Terry	CA4100	60,66A,69,54
Ogle, Deborah A.	GA1200	36,13A,60,40,61
Oglesby, Donald T.	FL1900	60,12A,36
Ohl, Ferris E.	OH0950	60,36,61
Okamura, Grant K.	HI0210	60,32C,37,63A
Olesen, James D.	MA0500	60,36,55D
Olfert, Warren	ND0350	60,32C,37,63C
O'Neal, Melinda P.	NH0100	60,11,36
Orzolek, Douglas	MN1625	11,32,37,60
O'Shea, Patrick	MN1400	60,12A,36,61,10A
Osterlund, David	SC0620	60,14,32,66A
Owen, John Edward	AR0110	60,11,63D
Owen, William E.	WA0550	36,60,12A,40,31A
Paddock, Joan Haaland	OR0450	60,32,49,63A,37
Pahel, Tim A.	IL1350	36,60
Paiement, Nicole	CA4150	43,60
Paiement, Nicole	CA5070	60,36,38
Palomaki, Jonathan	TX3800	60,12A,36,61,70
Palumbo, Michael A.	UT0350	38,62B,32E,60,41
Pare', Craig T.	IN0350	32,37,65,60
Park, Chung	NC0050	38,62A,62B,51,60
Park, Sang Eui	IN0005	10,60,12,13,31A
Parker, Harlan D.	MD0650	60,32
Parmer, Richard	WY0130	63C,63D,60,49
Pastin, John R.	NJ1050	37,60,29,46,48
Paulsen, Kent D.	WI0750	36,32D,61,60,13C
Pecherek, Michael J.	IL1175	13,60,11,38,62C
Pedroza, Ricardo	PR0125	13,60,36,66A,66D
Pender, Charles	TN1380	13,11,61,66A,60
Pennington, Randy	KY1000	60,36,47
Peppo, Bret	CA1560	36,29A,60
Peress, Maurice	NY0642	60,38,39
Peress, Maurice	NY0600	60,38
Perez-Gomez, Jorge	NM0450	60,38,39
Perrault, Jean R.	MN1600	60,62A,62B,62C,38
Perry, Timothy B.	NY3705	60,37,38,64C
Peter, Sandra K.	IA0950	60,36
Pethel, Stan	GA0300	13,60,10,63C,10F
Petters, Robert B.	NC1700	60,11
Phillips, Paul Schuyler	RI0050	38,60,13,10,10F
Phillips, Paul	TX2400	60,38
Plant, Lourin	NJ1050	60,36,41,61
Plate, Stephen W.	TN0850	38,60,32E,13B,13A
Platt, Nathan	KY1200	13,60,61,31A
Plew, Paul T.	CA2810	60,36,61,31A
Poch, Gail B.	PA3250	60,36
Poland, Jeffrey T.	WV0300	32D,36,61,60
Pollart, Gene J.	RI0300	60,32,37,29A
Polochick, Edward L.	MD0650	60,36
Poole, Eric	NC2150	13,60,20G,36,61
Porter, Michael	NC0250	36,40,60,61,32D
Portnoy, Donald	SC1110	60,38,62A
Potterton, Matthew	KS0050	60,36,32D
Powe, Holly	AL0330	61,13,11,60,47
Pratt, Gary W.	CA0835	60,37,38,47
Pratt, Michael	NJ0900	60,38,43,39
Pretzat, Julie	NY3770	13,60,36
Provencio, Robert	CA0650	60,32,36
Pursell, Anthony	TX2750	37,41,48,60,63C
Purves-Smith, Michael	AG0600	60,37,55,10F
Quartuccio, Anthony	CA1950	60
Quebbeman, Robert C.	MO0775	38,64C,60
Quist, Amanda R.	NJ1350	32D,36,60
Ragsdale, C. David	AL1160	37,60,11,64E
Rainwater, Brian	FL0670	60,37,13C,63C,47
Ramsey, William H.	CA4900	60,36
Rand, Catherine	MS0750	60,32C,37
Rao, Doreen	AG0450	32,36,60,61
Ratzlaff, Leonard	AA0100	60,36
Ray, W. Irwin	GA1550	60,11,41,36,40
Reber, William F.	AZ0100	39,54,52,66C,60
Recca, David	NY3785	60,13
Reeves, M. Bryan	AL0050	37,32E,11,49,60
Regelski, Thomas A.	NY3725	60,32
Renshaw, Jeffrey	CT0600	60,37,43
Renwick, William J. M.	AG0200	13,60,13J
Restesan, Francise T.	PR0125	13,60,12B,38,41
Reynolds, Jeff W.	AL1150	60,36,39
Reynolds, Patrick A.	OH2250	60,32E,37,38
Rhyneer, Barbara	MI1600	60,38,41,62,11
Rice, JoAnn	NY1860	36,60
Richards, E. Michael	MD1000	64C,60,41,38
Richards, James	MO1830	10F,60,38
Richter, Glenn	TX3510	60,37,35A
Rickard, Jeffrey H.	CA5150	10,60,36,31A
Riehl, Jeffrey S.	VA1500	11,36,61,60
Ringwall, Lauren	GA1650	32,60,36
Rinnert, Nathan	PA2150	60,37,32E
Rios, Giselle Elgarresta	FL0050	61,36,60,32,41
Rivera, Jose	NC2435	32,36,61,60
Rivers, Earl G.	OH2200	60,36
Roberts, James E.	AL0500	60,12A,49,63C
Roberts, Kay George	MA2030	60,38,51
Robertson, Troy David	TX2750	60,32C,36,61
Robinson, Michael C.	GA2100	37,60,32E,60B
Rodde, James	IA0850	36,60,32D
Rogers, Sean	ID0070	36,39,60,66A,66G
Romano, Patrick	NY3560	60,36,61
Rommereim, John Christian	IA0700	60,10,36,61
Rose, Gil B.	MA1450	60,38,41,13A
Ross, James	NY1900	60
Ross, Jared	KS0060	13,60,31A,36,61
Ross, John G.	NC1100	12,60
Roste, Vaughn	OK0550	60,12A,36,61,20
Roueche, Michelle	TX3415	60,36,66C
Rox, Michael	MA0950	10F,60,32,37,41
Running, Timothy	PA1750	60,11,48,64A
Rushton, David	AB0090	13,60,32C,31A
Russell, Robert J.	ME0500	12A,36,60
Russell, Teresa P.	CA4850	60,36,61,54,32A
Russell, Timothy	AZ0100	60,38
Rytting, Bryce	UT0325	12,13,38,60
Sadin, Robert	NY2660	60,10
Sailor, Catherine	CO0900	36,60
Salucka, Ray	IA0930	13,36,60,11,47
Salzman, Timothy	WA1050	60,37,49,63D
Sametz, Steven P.	PA1950	13,60,10,36
Samson, David	PA0650	47,13B,32C,63,60
Sandborg, Jeff R.	VA1250	60,11,12A,36,61
Sano, Stephen M.	CA4900	60,36,20C,20I
Sarjeant, Ronald	SC1050	10F,60,37,64
Satre, Paul J.	IL3150	36,66A,66G,60,13
Sawyer, Timothy K.	MN1280	60,36
Scarpa, Salvatore	NJ1050	60,38,41,63C
Scatterday, Mark	NY1100	37,38,60
Scheib, Curt A.	PA3000	61,36,66C,60,60
Schmidt, John R.	PA2050	60,14,50,65,37
Schneller, Pamela	TN1850	32C,32B,32D,60
Scholz, David M.	CA0800	36,61,32C,60
Schraer-Joiner, Lyn	NJ0700	32,11,13A,60
Schubert, Barbara	IL3250	38,41,60,43
Schultz, Dale	TX2200	37,60,32C,63
Schumann, Laura E.	OH1650	38,60,62A,12A,13A
Schwartzhoff, Gary R.	WI0803	60,36
Scott, David	TX0150	32,60
Scott, Ronald	TX2930	64C,64E,38,10F,60

Name	Code	Areas
Scraper, Joel	SC1100	40,60A,32D,36,60
Seeley, Gilbert	OR0400	60,12A,36,41
Seggelke, Martin H.	CA4200	37,41,42,60
Seigel, Lester C.	AL0300	60,36,39,66C,13F
Sepulveda, Sonja	NC2205	36,47,13,60
Seybert, John M.	FL1740	60,66A,32,64E,12
Shafer, Robert	VA1350	60,36
Shankman, Ira	NY2750	32,40,36,60
Shankman, Nancy Ellen	NY2750	32,36,60
Shannon, Kathleen	WV0750	36,32,60
Shasberger, Michael	CA5550	36,31A,38,60,61
Shaw, Gary R.	IL1750	10F,60,37,63C
Shelton, Brian M.	TX2960	37,32,60
Shemaria, Rich	NY2660	60,10,66A
Sheridan, Daniel	MN1700	64C,60,32C,13A,11
Sherman, Paul	CA1265	64B,60
Shetler, Timothy	MA0800	60,32C,36,61
Shew, Jamie	CA1900	53,60,13A,13B,66D
Shirtz, Michael	OH2140	36,60,61,13,29
Shrader, James A.	GA2150	60,12A,61,36,39
Shrock, Dennis R.	TX3000	60,36
Silantien, John J.	TX3530	60,36
Silberschlag, Jeffrey	MD0750	29A,35A,60,38,63A
Sinclair, John V.	FL1550	60,32,36,41,38
Singh, Vijay	WA0050	47,60,36,61,35A
Sirett, Mark G.	AG0250	36,60
Skelton, Robert A.	AG0500	60,38,41,51,62
Slabaugh, Thomas E.	CA5010	37,60,65,50,42
Slawson, John G.	IL0840	60,12A,36,38,54
Sledge, Larry	FL0800	60,12A,31A,36,13
Sleeper, Thomas M.	FL1900	10F,60,10,38
Slon, Michael	VA1550	36,39,60
Slotterback, Floyd	MI1600	60,36,11
Smith, Carl H.	KY0750	60,32B,32C,36
Smith, David	MD1000	36,39,60,61
Smith, Eddie	CA5150	60,32C,37,64E
Smith, G. D.	KY1200	13,60,38,63A
Smith, James E.	CA4450	13,60,36,38
Smith, Justin	OR0500	36,11,60
Smith, Kevin	MN0625	36,60,40,10A
Smith, Matthew K.	VT0100	37,32,11,63B,60
Smith, Michael V.	DC0050	60,32,32B,32C,32D
Smith, Orcenith George	IN0350	60,38,63D
Smith, Paul B.	AR0400	60,36,61
Smith, Roy C.	IN0005	61,11,10A,60,36
Smithee, Larry G.	TN1000	60,32,37,47,63
Snyder, Colleen	CA2400	11,29A,37,66D,60
Soelberg, Diane	ID0060	48,64B,60
Sohn, Sung-Rai	NY3560	60,38,41,51,62A
Sokol, Thomas A.	NY0900	60,36,40
Solie, Gordon A.	OR0850	60,32,37,64D
Sollberger, Harvey	CA5050	10F,60,10,64A,43
Song, James J.	CA3100	60,11,12,38,13
Song, MyungOk Julie	NY2750	32,36,60,61
Sorenson, Allin	MO0350	60,11,36,61
Southard, Bruce	ND0100	36,60A,12A,61,60
Spano, Robert V.	OH1700	60
Sparti, Patricia C.	NC0850	13,60,38,63D
Spear, David R.	NY2750	10,10F,60,10C
Specht, Jeffrey	OR0400	13,38,60,63D
Speck, Gary A.	OH1450	60,32C,48
Spede, Mark J.	SC0400	37,60,12B
Spencer, William G.	NC0050	60,32,64D,65
Spevacek, Robert	ID0250	60,37,63D
Spies, Claudio	NJ0900	13,60,10,39
Spradling, Robert	MI2250	60,37
Staheli, Ronald	UT0050	60,36,41,61,66A
Stamp, John E.	PA1600	60,37,65
Stanichar, Christopher	SD0050	38,60,12A
Stansbury, George	TX3415	60,31A,44
Staples, Thomas	AA0200	60,11,49,63
Steele, Stephen K.	IL1150	60,32,37
Stephens, John	DC0350	13,60
Stern, Adam	WA0200	10,60
Stewart, Shawna	CA0350	60,36,32
Stidham, Thomas M.	KS1350	60,37
Stock, David	PA1050	60,43
Stockton, J. Larry	PA1850	14,50,20,60
Stokes, Porter	SC1000	36,61,60,32
Stolberg, Tom	MO0060	10F,34,31A,32B,60
Strauser, Matthew L.	OR0175	36,60,13C,32D
Street, William H.	AA0100	60,37,64E
Strouse, Lewis	PA0550	60,32
Summer, Robert J.	FL2000	60,36
Summers, Jerome	AG0500	60,38,64C,67B,43
Sun, Xun	UT0200	60,38,62A
Sutton, John	CA0250	60,31A,36
Swan, Phillip A.	WI0350	36,60,61,32D,60A
Taft, Burns	CA5360	13,60,36,66A,38
Tak, Young-Ah	FL1740	66A,60,13A,13B,41
Taylor, Beverly	WI0815	60,36
Taylor, Brian S.	LA0760	37,32C,60
Taylor, Bryce B.	TX2960	32C,60
Taylor, Clifton	MS0500	60,37,47
Taylor, Robert J.	SC0500	11,36,61,60
Teichmer, Shawn	MI2000	32,60,64,12A,11
Tevis, Royce	CA0800	32,37,63A,60
Thakar, Markand	MD0650	60
Thayer, Fred M.	PA2100	13,60,10,36
Thomas, Edwin	IN0005	65,11,12,32,60
Thomas, Jeffrey	CA5010	60,36,12A
Thompson, Jonathan	AB0090	11,36,12A,60,38
Thompson, Mallory	IL2250	60,37
Thompson, Paul	WI0825	60,36
Thornton, Paula E.	FL1950	60
Thorson, Eric	TN0250	32,36,60
Thye, David R.	TX2600	60,32D,32E,36,38
Tini, Dennis J.	MI2200	60,36,29,35
Tipps, James	OH2500	32,36,66A,66D,60
Tobias, Scott C.	FL1800	37,32E,60
Tocheff, Robert	OH1600	60,11,32,36,66D
Toner, D. Thomas	VT0450	65,20,37,50,60
Toomer, Charlie	FL0600	60,36,61
Topilow, Carl	OH0600	60,38
Tramiel, Leonard	MS0560	60,11,37,63C,63D
Trimborn, Thomas J.	MO1780	60,11,32
Tsolainou, Constantina	GA0550	60
Tucker, Scott	NY0900	60,36,40,13A,20A
Tucker, Stephen Earl	CA5020	60,38
Tuckwiller, George	VA1750	60,11,41,49,63A
Turgeon, Melanie E.	AA0035	60,36,42,13C,32D
Turner, Cynthia Johnston	NY0900	60,37,41,42,38
Turner, Gregory E.	KS0400	13,38,36,60,61
Turrill, David	OH1650	37,32E,60,63A
Uchimura, Bruce	MI2250	60,51,62C
Udagawa, Yoichi	MA0350	60
Underhill, Owen	AB0080	13,60,10,12,43
Underwood, Margaret	OH2050	32E,37,60
Urban, Guy	MA2150	13,60,11,66A
Vail, Leland	CA0825	36,61,60
Valdivia, Hector	MN0300	10F,60,11,38,41
Van Winkle, Kenneth	NM0310	37,60
Vandehey, Patrick	OR0250	60,32,37,38,63C
Vanore, John	PA3680	60,10,47,49,63A
VanWeelden, Kimberly	FL0850	60,32,36
Varineau, John P.	MI0520	60
Varon, Neil	NY1100	38,60
Vinick, Russ	IL0720	60
Vogel, Bradley D.	KS1300	60,32B,36,61,31A
Voldman, Yakov	LA0650	60,32C,38,51,62
Vorwerk, Paul	CA0510	60,13C,12A
Vote, Larry	MD0750	60,32,36,61
Vroman, David	IL0400	60,32,37,63B
Wacker, John M.	CO1050	60,63,37,49,32E
Wade, Jess E.	TX2900	60,32C,61,66A
Wagner, Lawrence R.	PA3250	60,38,48,64C
Wakefield, William	OK1350	60,37,41
Walker, Gayle	OH2050	13C,60,12A,36
Walker, James A.	NY3730	60,37,38,41
Walker, Keith H.	GA0625	36,61,60
Walters, David	AL0500	13,37,63,60
Walters, Mark A.	CO0350	60,11,48,37,64
Walters, Teresa	NJ0200	13,60,11,12A,36
Walth, Gary Kent	WI0810	60,11,32C,36,54
Ward, Robert J.	OH1850	60,36
Warman, Harold	CA4100	60,37,49
Waybright, David	FL1850	60,37
Weathers, Keith	OR0175	60
Webb, Guy B.	MO0775	60,36,61
Webb, Jeffrey L.	PA3410	29A,36,13A,60,13
Weber, Michael J.	ND0350	60,54
Weber, Paul	NC1100	60,36
Weglein, Carolyn	MD0100	60,36,66G
Weinel, John	TX1450	61,60,36,39,40
Weinert, William	NY1100	36,38,60
Weiss, Timothy	OH1700	60,48
Weller, Ellen	CA3460	12A,55,20,29A,60
Wernick, Richard F.	PA3350	13,60,10,41
West, Charles W.	VA1600	48,64C,60
Westergaard, Peter	NJ0900	13,60,10,39
Wheeler, Scott	MA0850	13,60,10,54,43
White, Christopher G.	ME0440	37,60,32E
White, Frank	LA0700	13,39,66A,11,60
White, Julian E.	FL0600	60,32C,37,64A,64B
Whitener, Scott	NJ1130	60,49
Wickes, Frank	GA2100	37,60
Wiedrich, William	FL2000	60,37,43
Wika, Norman	OK0550	60,37,63C,63D
Wilberg, Mack	UT0250	60
Wilcox, Don G.	WV0750	60,37
Wilkes, Eve-Anne	CA3250	36,61,54,60
Williams, Dennis	PA1750	54,36,61,60
Williams, Lindsey R.	MO1810	32E,60,32H,32G,63C
Williams, Robert	AL0950	37,46,60
Williamson, John E.	MI0400	60,37
Williamson, Scott	VA1700	36,39,40,60,61
Wilson, Brian S.	CA4700	10,37,13,43,60
Wilson, Cecil B.	WV0750	10F,60,12A,12
Wilson, Dwayne	NC0300	48,60,65
Wilson, Jeffrey S.	IL1050	60,36,61,40,31A
Wilson, Jill	IA1100	63B,36,32B,60,13C
Wilson, Larry K.	CA3975	60,32C,13,66A,36
Wilson, Stephen B.	NY3720	13,60,36,41,61
Wilson, T. Rex	TX2710	60,12A,32C,36,61
Wolbers, Mark	AK0100	60,12A,32C,64C,48
Wolf, Matthew	MI0500	48,13,60,32H
Wolfe, Chris	MD0175	13A,60,37,64C,64E
Wong, Yau-Sun	NM0200	11,60,13B,36,37
Wood, Gary F.	MA1650	36,61,60,13A
Woodford, Paul	AG0500	60,12B,32,37,63
Woodruff, Louis	NJ0750	60,11,37
Woodruff, Neal	IL2300	60,36,38,61,12A
Woods, Carlton	MI0400	38,60
Woodward, Greg	LA0400	60
Workman, Darin D.	KS1110	60,32,37,47,64
Wray, David	WV0400	32,60,61
Wray, Ron E.	AL1160	64C,37,13,60
Wright, Clell E.	TX0900	31A,36,60
Wright, William B.	PA1300	11,13,36,60
Wyatt, Larry D.	SC1110	60,32,36
Wyman, William A.	NE0450	36,39,61,60,40
Wynkoop, Rodney A.	NC0600	13,60,36
Yampolsky, Victor	IL2250	38,60
Yamron, Janet M.	PA3250	60,32,36
Young, Welborn E.	NC2430	36,60
Yubovich, Benjamin	IN0005	60,16,12,13,14
Zanutto, Daniel R.	CA0825	32,60
Zerkle, Paula R.	PA2450	36,60,15,11,54
Ziek, Gary D.	KS0300	60,37,63A
Zielinski, Richard	OK1350	60,36,40
Zielke, Gregory D.	NE0250	60,32C,36,61,31A
Zielke, Steven M.	OR0700	36,60,32D
Zimmerman, Christopher	CT0650	60,38
Zobel, Elizabeth W.	IL0350	12,13,36,60,61
Zork, Stephen	MI0250	36,61,60,10,39

Choral and Vocal

Name	Code	Areas
Aamot, Kirk C.	MT0200	36,40,32D,60A
Abbott, Patricia	AI0150	32D,60A
Acevedo, Carmen	PR0150	36,60A
Adams, Catherine W.	MI2100	54,60A
Afonso, Daniel R.	CA0850	36,40,13C,32D,60A
Alexander, Marina	NY0644	36,12A,12C,60A
Allaire, Jean-Sebastien	AG0100	12,13,36,60A
Allen, Burt	LA0550	36,60A,60,34,61
Allen, Nancy	WI1100	60A,32,36,54
Allen, Robert T.	VA0800	11,12A,29A,60A
Althouse, Paul L.	CT0100	11,60A,12A,36
Alviani, Henry	PA0700	36,40,60A,61
Alwes, Chester	IL3300	36,60A
Ames, Jeffrey	TN0100	36,60A
Amonson, Christina	AL1050	60A,32D,39
Amundson, Bret	MN0450	32,36,60A
Andaya, Mitos	PA3250	36,60A
Anderson, Gary L.	KY1350	60A,12A,36
Anderson, Jeff	KS1000	36,32D,60A
Anderson, Lyle J.	OH0450	60A,36,31A
Anderson, Ronald E.	TX2700	60A,11,12A,12C
Anderson, Scott E.	ID0100	36,40,60A,61
Archibeque, Charlene	CA4400	36,40,60A,32D
Armstrong, Anton	MN1450	60A,36,61
Armstrong, Candace	TN0900	13C,36,60A,66A,11
Aspaas, Christopher	MN1450	36,61,60A,32D
Aucoin, Amy	KY0950	32,36,60A,13C

Index by Area of Teaching Interest

Name	Code	Areas
Augenblick, John	FL0700	60A,36,11
Aune, Gregory	MN0750	60A,36,32D
Avery, Handy	AL1160	36,60A
Baird, Sara Lynn	AL0200	60A
Baker, Alan	PA0250	60A,11,36,61,54
Baker, R. Bryan	CA1250	60A,61,36
Ballweg, D. Brent	OK0650	36,60A
Banks, Richard	NC1600	39,61,60A
Bara, Daniel J.	GA2100	60A,36
Basilio, Edwin L.	CA5200	60A,32
Batcho, Michael J.	WI0150	60A
Batchvarova, Madlen T.	IN0650	60A,36,61,66A,12A
Bauer, David	NE0590	36,61,60A,32D
Bauman, Jeffrey Milo	GA2300	36,61,54,10F,60A
Bausano, William	OH1450	60A,32C,36,61
Belfield, Roy L.	NC2700	66G,36,60A,10F,12A
Berg, Joy L.	AA0015	60A,66A
Bigler, Dwight	VA1700	36,60A
Billingham, Lisa A.	VA0450	32D,36,60A
Binger, Adlai	PA0050	36,61,66G,60A,66C
Bishop, Bruce W.	AZ0300	34,36,61,13,60A
Black, Daniel	NY1700	60A
Black, Susan	AG0650	66C,61,60A
Blackley, Rowland	OH0100	60A,32D,36,40,55D
Blackwell, Leslie	GA1150	36,40,60A
Blanchard, Gerald J.	MI1160	11,36,13,60A,61
Bloom, Bradley	MI1750	60A
Board, Ryan A.	CA3600	11,32C,36,31A,60A
Bode, Robert	MO1810	60A,36,61
Bogard, Emily	IN0900	60A
Boyd, Kim	OH2050	36,60A,32D,13C
Brandau, Ryan James	NJ1350	36,60A
Brannon, Patrick V.	IL3370	14,12A,36,60A,40
Breden, Mary C.	CA2800	60A,36,32D
Briggs, Robert	UT0150	36,61,12A,60A
Broeker, Angela	MN1625	60A,36
Bronfman, Joshua	ND0500	36,40,32D,60A
Brooks, C. Thomas	MA0950	60A,36,40,61
Brown, Trent R.	FL0680	36,40,60A
Brown-Kibble, Gennevieve	TN1350	11,36,60A,61
Browne, Douglas A.	PA1450	13C,60A,36,61
Brumley, Dianne	TX3515	36,32D,60A
Bryan, Karen	CA3460	36,60A
Bryson, Amity H.	MO0050	36,61,60A,15,32D
Buchanan, Heather J.	NJ0800	32D,36,40,60A
Buffington, Blair	IA1750	61,36,40,32A,60A
Bundage, Raphael	TN1100	36,39,60A
Burke, D'Walla Simmons	NC2700	60A,36,61
Burke, Karen M.	AG0650	61,60A,36,32
Burleson, Jill	CO0950	60A,36,32D
Burnett, J.D.	NJ0800	32D,60A
Burns, Judith E.	OH0200	60A,32D
Butke, Marla A.	OH0100	32,11,66D,36,60A
Cameron, Virginia	OH1600	60A,36,61,40,11
Campbell, Stanford	OR0600	36,61,31A,60A
Cannon, Carey	NC2420	60A
Carlson, Damon J.	WI0770	60A,61,40,36
Carlson, Karyl K.	IL1150	36,60A
Carr, Deborah	VA1830	66G,60A
Carr, Sarah	WV0800	36,60A
Carson, Caroline	LA0800	11,36,32D,60A
Carter, Christina	FL1550	60A,61,11
Carter, Jeffrey Richard	MO1950	60A,36,61,13A
Caston, Ben	GA2050	36,60A,61
Chafin, Gerald	KY0860	60A,11,32,36,44
Chang, Donathan	TX2570	31A,31B,61,60A,36
Chin, David	NY3350	36,60A
Clements, Allen	AL0345	32D,36,60A,40,61
Cock, Maura	IN1750	61,60A
Cody, David	MT0400	36,61,54,39,60A
Cole, Darlyn	NC1950	61,66D,60A,11,13
Coleman, Edryn J.	PA2000	61,36,60A,13B
Colwitz, Erin E.	AL1160	32B,61,60A,36,32C
Con, Adam Jonathan	OH2450	36,32,11,60A,13C
Conley, David A.	SC0400	60A
Copley, Edith A.	AZ0450	60A,36,60
Corbin, Lynn Ann	GA2150	32,61,60A
Corbin, Patricia	AL0500	60A,32D,61,55D,60
Cornish, John	OK0150	36,39,60A,61,13B
Cox, Dennis K.	ME0440	60A,12A,36
Cox, Michael	VA1580	36,61,32D,60A
Cox, Richard G.	NC2430	36,60A
Crabb, Paul	MO1800	36,60A
Crane, Andrew	NC0650	60A,36
Creswell, Bradley	IA1750	61,60A
Crippin, Glee	IA1200	61,60A
Crull, Terry	KS0350	11,36,40,60A
Cummins, Nicholaus B.	MS0250	36,60A,32D,40
Custer, Gerald	MI2200	36,60A,13
Cutter, William	MA0350	60A,60
Dagenais, Andree	AC0050	36,40,42,60A
Dahlke, Steven	NY3250	11,13,36,60A,61
Daniell-Knapp, Courtney	TX3450	60A,32
Darrough, Galen P.	CO0950	60A,36,32D
Davidovich, Theodore C.	MA2100	60A,11,36
De Jager, Ron	AJ0030	60A,36,52,61,32D
DeHoogh-Kliewer, David	SD0580	60A,11,32D,36,40
Dekaney, Elisa M.	NY4150	32,36,20H,60A
DeLong, Noah	TN1150	36,35C,60A,61
Demaris, Mary Kay	MN1500	61,60A
DeVenney, David P.	PA3600	36,39,60A,61
DiOrio, Dominick	IN0900	60A,36
Donelson, David W.	OH1350	36,32D,60A
Doyle, Melinda S.	AL1200	36,60A,40
Dunbar, Brian	MN0620	10,13,36,34,60A
Dunsmore, Douglas	AD0050	36,60A
Durham, Justin W.	SC0400	36,60A
Durow, Peter J.	MO1500	36,32D,60A
Eby, Patricia	WI0804	13,11,36,60A,47
Edison, Noel	AG0300	36,60A
Edwards, Malcolm V.	AA0150	32,36,60A
Ehly, Ewald	MO1810	60A,61,36
Eifert, Jonathan	TX0400	36,60A,66G,31A
Engebretson, Stan P.	VA0450	36,60A,60,40
Epley, Arnold	MO2000	60A,32C,36,61,40
Erwin, John M.	AR0850	60A,36,40
Etter, Paul J.	NC0850	60A,36,44,60,31A
Faerber, Matthew L.	WI0860	60A,36,32D,40,13C
Falk, Marc	IA0300	36,11,12A,60A,40
Ferguson, J. Scott	IL1200	60A,36,61
Ferrell, Matthew	MN1300	36,60A
Ferrell, Rene	CA0650	32B,32C,60A,32D
Finch, Scott	AJ0030	60A,31A,12A,13A,11
Fleming, Kyle J.	CO0150	36,11,31A,60A
Fleming, Nancy P.	AR0350	12A,36,60A
Flory, Jennifer Morgan	GA0850	36,32D,15,60A,61
Floyd, Hugh	SC0750	61,60A,36,32D
Folger, William M.	MD0800	60A,36,40,54
Ford, Kelly	IN1350	36,61,60A,12,64E
Fordice, William	IA0950	32,60A
Foster, Korre	TN0050	36,60A
Fowler-Calisto, Lauren	VA0150	36,60A
Fox, Ryan H	AR0300	36,60A,32D,40
Franklin, Bonita Louise	OK0450	32,36,60A,61
Fredenburgh, Lisa M.	IL0150	36,11,40,60A
Frederickson, Karen	AG0250	32,36,60A
Fredstrom, Tim	IL1150	32D,36,60A,32
Freer, Patrick K.	GA1050	32D,32C,32G,36,60A
Friese, Kenneth	NY1275	60A,61
Friesen, Elroy	AC0100	36,60A,32D
Fritz, Matthew P.	PA1250	36,60A,34,34E,60
Fryling, David N.	NY1600	36,60A,60,32,13A
Fuller, Stephen	MN1300	60A,11,20D,31A
Gackle, Lynne	TX0300	36,60A
Galante, Brian Edward	WA0650	36,10,60A,32D
Galvan, Janet	NY1800	60A,32,36
Ganus, Clifton L.	AR0250	12A,31A,36,60A
Gardiner, Katie	NY3650	36,60A
Gardner, David B.	KS1200	36,60,61,60A,54
Gardner, Patrick	NJ1130	60A,36
Garner, Dirk A.	OH0200	36,40,60A
Garrett, Matthew L.	OH0400	36,32D,60A
Gehrenbeck, Robert	WI0865	36,40,39,60A
Gemmell, Jeffrey S.	CO0800	36,32D,60A
Gentry, Gregory R.	CO0800	36,60A
Gerber, Gary G.	AR0500	36,61,32D,60A
Gervais, Michel Marc	CA5060	36,60A,55D,40
Geston, Mary K.	MN1280	40,32D,60A,32C,36
Gilson, Catherine	MI1550	36,60A
Gilson, David W.	OH0600	32I,60A
Gladstone, Bruce	WI0815	60A,36
Glenn, James H.	NC2000	36,61,60A,11,12A
Goforth, Stephen C.	KY1300	11,36,60A,61,12A
Goldsmith, John L.	PA3420	60A,36
Gordon, Barbara N.	NJ0500	11,36,60A,66D,61
Gordon, Daniel	FL1740	13,32,60A,36
Gordon, Stefan	FL0350	61,60A
Gorelick, Brian	NC2500	60A,36,55D
Gothold, Stephen A.	CA5100	36,40,61,60A
Graham, Sarah J.	IL1150	36,60A
Graham, Seong-Kyung	WI0700	61,32D,36,60A
Grases, Cristian	CA5300	60A
Graves, Jim F.	OK1200	36,32D,32B,60A,61
Green, William	TN0850	36,40,60A
Grieger, Evelyn	AA0035	60A
Grieger, Evelyn	AA0100	36,60A
Griffen, Jane	MO0500	60A,32A,32B,36,61
Griffith, Larry D.	TN0930	60A,32C,36,61,32D
Guthrie, J. Randall	OK0850	31A,60A,36,11,66G
Guy, Todd	IN1025	36,31A,61,60A,11
Hale, Roger	MO0850	60A,61,40,36
Hall, Daniel	OH1900	60A,32C,36
Hall, Daniel	TX3750	36,60A
Halsey, Glynn	GA0490	11,36,40,60A
Hamre, Anna R.	CA0810	36,60A
Hanoian, Scott	MI2200	36,60A
Harden, Matthew C.	NE0610	36,60A,32D,40
Harder, Melissa	AJ0030	61,11,60A
Harrison, Judy	FL0900	13,36,60A,66
Hasseler, Lynda	OH0350	60A,36,40,32D
Hawkins, Michelle	CA5510	60A
Henderson, Silvester	CA2775	36,40,60A,61,66A
Henry, James	MO1830	36,40,60A,32D,10F
Hensley, Hunter C.	KY0550	36,61,60A,55,32D
Hibbard, Therees Tkach	NE0600	36,60A
Hiester, Jason A.	OH2000	36,39,40,60A,61
Higgins, William L.	AR0300	39,61,60A,13C
Hill, Cheryl Frazes	IL0550	32,36,60A
Hodge, Stephen	OH2300	36,32C,61,32D,60A
Hodgson, Ken	MN1620	36,61,34D,11,60A
Hoffenberg, Rick	PA2200	36,40,60A,61
Holcomb, Al	NJ1350	32,36,60A
Holder, Ryan	AZ0450	32D,36,60A
Holdhusen, David	SD0600	60A,36,61
Holland, Sandra Renee	NC2420	60A
Holmes, Isaac	GA1600	60A,11,36,61,39
Hondorp, Paul	KY1550	36,60A,32D,61,40
Honea, Richard	MO0400	36,61,60A
Hong, Xiangtang	IL1850	60A,31A,36,44,11
Hood, Marcia Mitchell	GA0150	66A,60A,32B,36,40
Hooper, John	AA0015	60A,13,10
Hooper, Randall	TX2955	36,60A,32D,32B,40
Hopkins, Jesse E.	VA0100	32,36,61,44,60A
Hopkins, Stephen M.	NC0050	36,60A,32D
Howard, David L.	TX2700	32C,36,60A
Huff, Michael D.	UT0300	60,60A,60B
Huff, Walter	IN0900	36,60A
Huffman, Pamela G.	TX2400	60A,36
Hugo, John William	VA0650	36,61,12A,60A
Ihm, Dana	CO0275	36,40,47,60A
Irwin, Frederick	NJ1400	36,60A
Jaber, Thomas I.	TX2150	36,60A,66C
Jacobsen, Lesa L.	WI0845	61,32C,32D,60A,36
Jaeb, Mary	CA3460	61,60A
James, Buddy	CA0807	36,32D,61,60A
James, Matthew H.	LA0770	61,13D,39,54,60A
Jameson, Joel	NY2900	36,61,60A
Jennings, Kenneth	MN1450	60A,61,36
Jensen, Andrew	AR0050	60A,36,11,61,13C
Jensen, Joni L.	TX3300	13C,36,61,32D,60A
Jirak, James	ID0050	36,32D,60A
John, James A.	NY0642	36,40,60A
Johnson, Brandon P.	NY1700	36,60A,61
Johnson, G. Larry	UT0325	36,60A,13A,13B,13C
Johnson, Stephen P.	TX2600	10,13,10F,60A,60
Jones, Ann A.	TN0250	36,61,60A
Jones, Craig	OR0600	66A,66D,60A
Jones, Erik Reid	WV0550	36,39,40,60A,61
Jones, Meredith	TX2570	12A,31A,60A,61
Jones, Robert B.	OH2250	60A,32C,36,32D
Julien, Ellis	AR0110	60A
Junker, Tercio	IN0300	60A,36,31A,32D,10E
Kallenbach, James	IL3250	36,60A
Keck, Kimberly	TN0200	36,39,61,60A,13
Kehrberg, Kevin	NC2550	12,14C,20,60A,62D
Keith, David C.	GA1300	60A,36
Kellim, Kevin	KS1400	60A,36,61
Kelly, Ryan	PA3600	36,40,61,60A
Kenaston-French, Karen	TX3500	36,61,32D,40,60A
Kennedy, Karen	FL1900	60A,36
Killian, George W.	IN0700	60A,32,36
Kim, Jaeyoon	NC2435	61,60A,36
Kim, James	CO0250	36,60A
Kim, Jong H.	VA0750	36,13,61,60A,40
Kim, Thomas	NJ1050	36,60A
Kimball, Paul	CA5350	60A

Index by Area of Teaching Interest

Name	Code	Areas
King, Tim	TX2700	60A,32C,36
Kinsey, Katherine S.	SC1200	32D,36,60A,40
Klaus, Kenneth S.	LA0450	60A,11,36,61,40
Klein, Nancy K.	VA1000	36,60A,32A,32B,32C
Kompelien, Wayne	VA0650	40,61,60A
Kornelis, Benjamin	IA0500	20,32D,36,60A,40
Kovacs, Anna	NY2750	32D,36,60A
Krasnovsky, Paul J.	IN1650	60A,36,40
Kratochvil, Jirka	NY1400	36,60A,40,61
Kratzer, Dennis L.	OH1800	36,61,54,60A,40
Kuo, Kelly	TX3510	39,60A
Kurth, Robert	PA1050	60A
Kuzma, Marika C.	CA5000	36,40,60A,61
Kwami, Paul T.	TN0550	20,36,66G,60A,66D
Lamartine, Nicole C.	WY0200	36,60A,32D
Lamb, Robert E.	FL0150	36,13,12,60A
Lancaster, Michael	NC2600	60A,55D,61,36,32D
Lang, Brenda J.	OH0550	36,60A,61,13A
Langager, Graeme	AB0100	36,60A
Lanier, Brian	MO0950	32D,36,60A,61
Larson, Andrew	FL1750	61,36,60A
Latimer, Marvin E.	AL1170	32D,36,60A
Leaf, Nathan	NC1700	36,60A,61
Levi, Michael	NY0700	36,29B,13,60A,32D
Lofgren, Ronald R.	NE0700	11,32D,36,60A,61
Logan, P. Bradley	MN0150	60A,36,32D,40
Lynch, John P.	GA2100	37,60A
Lynn, Daniel	NE0550	60A,61,36,32C,32D
Mack-Bervin, Linda	CO0350	11,32D,36,60A
Maclary, Edward	MD1010	60A,36
Mahraun, Daniel A.	MN1120	61,36,60A,40
Major, Marci L.	MO1800	32D,60A
Mallin, Claire	AF0050	13C,40,61,60A
Malone, Thomas	MA2030	20,32D,60A
Mancusi, Roberto	TN1720	39,61,60A,13C
Mann, Alison	GA1150	40,60A,32C,32D
Marchant, Susan J.	KS1050	36,66G,66H,60A
Marlett, Judy	ID0150	32,36,39,54,60A
Marshall, Allen	OK0300	60A,61,13
Martell, Mary	IL2750	60A
Martin, Gayle H.	AE0050	60A,66G,36,12A,55D
Martin, Joey	TX3175	36,32D,60A
Mathews, Christopher W.	TN1660	36,13H,31A,60A,13C
Mathews, Lee	WA0300	36,60A
Mathews, Lee	WA0980	36,60A
Mauldin, Walter	TN0850	60A,31A
McCaffrey, Maureen	TN1400	11,61,32D,60A
McCarthy, Marta	AG0350	60A,36,13C
McClung, Alan C.	TX3420	32C,32D,32G,60A,13C
McCoy, Jerry	TX3420	60A,36
McDermid, Aaron	ND0150	36,60A,61,11,32
McGhee, Janet F.	NY3650	36,13A,40,60A
McWhirter, Jamila L.	TN1100	32D,36,60A
Meaders, James M.	MS0400	60A,36,61
Mecham, Mark L.	PA1900	32D,36,40,60A
Medley, Susan	PA3580	36,60A,40,11,13A
Megginson, Julie	GA1000	61,36,60A,40
Melton, Michael D.	IL2150	36,40,32D,61,60A
Mendoza, Michael D.	NJ0175	60A,32D,36
Messoloras, Irene	OK0600	36,12,60A,61,40
Meyer, Dyan	IA1600	36,60A
Miceli, Jennifer Scott	NY2105	32,36,60A
Miller, Andrew	ND0050	36,60A,40,13C
Miller, Joe	NJ1350	36,60A
Miller, Josh	WV0200	36,61,32D,11,60A
Miller, Michael	WA0980	32D,36,60A
Miller, Thomas A.	OR1150	60A,11,36,61,31A
Mitchell, Aaron Paul	IN0905	32D,36,40,60A
Mitchell, Linda	CA2440	36,60A,11,12A,13A
Mitchell, Michael A.	MI1750	60A,36,11
Moffett, Brad	TN0850	36,31A,60A
Moldenhauer, Kermit G.	MN1030	13A,36,66G,31A,60A
Montague, Matthew G.	KS1050	32,36,60A,11
Moody, Philip	GA2100	36,60A,61
Moore, Laura M.	AL1300	36,40,60A,61,66C
Moore, Rager H.	AR0730	60A,61
Mooy, Mary Annaleen	HI0050	60A,32D,36
Morris, Gary	AR0200	36,40,60A,61
Morrow, Lynne	CA4700	39,54,60A,61
Mountford, Fritz	NE0300	32C,36,60A,10,20
Moxley, Bryant	VA0050	13,66A,60A,31A,36
Muilenburg, Harley	CA2250	36,61,60A,40
Mullinix, Kelli	NC1250	60A,36
Muzzo, Grace	PA3710	32,36,40,60A
Nagel, Douglas	MT0175	61,36,60A,13C
Natter, Robert	PA1400	34,36,61,60A
Navarro, Joel Magus P.	MI0350	36,60A
Neal, Paul	GA2150	36,60A,61,60
Neas, Michael	FL1100	36,60A
Nelson, Lee D.	IA1800	36,60A
Nesheim, Paul J.	MN1120	36,40,60A
Nestor, Leo Cornelius	DC0050	10A,31A,36,40,60A
Neufeld, Charles W.	SC0800	60A,61,36,32D
Newton, Timothy D.	NY3765	60A,60B,66A,66C
Niblock, James D.	PA0100	36,61,60A,13A,13B
Niu, Elaine	WI0750	61,39,36,60A,13C
O'Brien, Kevin	DC0050	36,13B,60A,40
O'Connell, Brian	MA2030	32D,60A
Odom, Donald R.	MS0850	36,13C,11,32D,60A
Olin, Christopher S.	OR1050	32D,36,60A
Oliver, Ronald D.	MI2250	36,60A,32D
Orton, Billy H.	AL1160	36,60A,60B,61,63C
Ottley, Jerold	HI0050	32D,36,60A
Overland, Corin T.	FL1900	40,32,60A
Overmier, Douglas R.	MO0950	60B,60A,37,47,10
Park, Jong-Won	WI0845	36,40,61,60A
Parker, Gregory B.	NC0400	36,61,60A,40,32D
Parks, Sarah S.	WI0750	36,32D,60A,61
Parr, Clayton G.	MI0100	36,40,60A,32D
Patterson, Trent A.	MO1950	60A,61,32,36,39
Paul, Sharon J.	OR1050	60A,36,40
Paulk, Jason	NM0100	60A,32C,36
Pauly, Elizabeth	MN1050	61,60A,11,36,13A
Payton, Denise	NC0800	20A,36,39,60A,61
Pedersen, Keith	CA3640	36,11,60A
Perkins, Daniel R.	NH0250	36,61,12A,32D,60A
Perry, Pamela J.	CT0050	32B,32C,36,32D,60A
Peterson, Dean	MT0400	60A,32D,36,40
Peterson, Robert L.	MN0950	36,61,60A
Peterson, Vince	NY0500	36,60A,32D,13,11
Petit-Homme, Frederika	AI0150	60A
Picard, Betty	MI1160	60A,61
Ploeger, Kristina	WA0250	32,36,60A
Pool, Ellen	MI0900	32D,36,60A
Poovey, Gena E.	SC0850	36,61,60A,32D,40
Port, Dennis	MN0250	60A,36
Potter, Kenney	NC2650	36,13C,60A
Powell, William C.	AL0200	60A,36
Pysh, Gregory	TX3527	10,13,61,60A,36
Raines, Alan L.	TX0300	36,60A,40
Rardin, Paul	PA3250	60A
Rash, Daniel R.	SC0400	11,60A,54
Rasmussen, Bruce	CA3400	60A,36,61,40,66G
Ratledge, John	AL1170	60A,36
Ray, James	FL1550	66D,34D,60A,35C
Ray, John	TN1600	60A,61
Raybon, Leonard	LA0750	36,61,60A,54
Rayl, David C.	MI1400	36,60A
Reames, Rebecca	NY3780	60A,32,36
Redding, Jeffery	WV0750	36,60A
Redfearn, Christopher	ND0600	36,40,60A,61
Rediger, JoAnn K.	IN1560	36,31A,60A,11,40
Reed, Joel F.	NC1250	20G,60A,36,61,31A
Reed, Jonathan I.	MI1400	60A,32C,36
Reese, Jodi	KS0265	36,11,13C,61,60A
Reeves, B. Jean	NY0270	11,36,39,60A,61
Reigles, B. Jean	NY1700	36,39,60A,61
Richard, Monique M.	AE0100	32,36,40,60A
Richards, E. Earl	CA2420	32D,36,60A
Richardson, Dennis	TX0550	36,40,32B,66D,60A
Richmond, Brad	MI1050	36,40,60A,61
Ries, Ardelle	AA0110	13C,36,60A
Riley, Blake	FL2100	36,60A
Ritchey, Mary Lynn	MA0150	61,36,60A,40,11
Rivera Ortiz, William	PR0115	13A,13C,36,60A
Robbins, Catherine	AC0100	32D,32C,60A
Roberson, Heather D.	CO1050	61,36,11,60A,32D
Roberts, Stanley L.	GA1300	60A,36,31A
Rockabrand, Sarah	IL2400	36,61,60A
Rogers, Bruce	CA3200	36,61,60A
Rossi, Richard Robert	IL0800	60A,36,38,66G
Rowe, Alissa	LA0650	36,61,60A
Rowehl, John	NY0900	36,40,60A
Rowell, Michael	GA0700	31A,60A,47,36
Runestad, Kurt	NE0200	36,32D,60A,47
Rupcich, Matthew	NY0625	60A
Russell, John	CA0845	36,40,32D,60A
Russell, John K.	CA1520	32D,36,40,60A
Ryan, Rebecca	PA2250	36,32C,60A
Sato, Akira	TX3420	29,63A,47,60A
Scarbrough, Michael	TX0050	36,61,60A
Schaffer, Donna	MS0050	36,61,60A
Schantz, Cory Neal	SD0550	61,36,60A
Scheibe, Jo-Michael	CA5300	36,60A
Schildkret, David	AZ0100	36,60A
Scholz, Robert	MN1450	36,61,60A
Schreuder, Joel T.	NE0050	60A,36,61,40,32D
Scott, Kraig	WA1100	36,31A,66G,66H,60A
Scott, L. Brett Cornish	OH2200	60A,36
Scott, Sandra C.	GA1600	36,40,60A,32D,66A
Scraper, Joel	SC1100	40,60A,32D,36,60
Shangkuan, Pearl	MI0350	60A,36
Shanklin, Bart	IL3500	61,60A,36,32D
Shapiro, Mark L.	NY2105	60A,36,40,13
Shapiro, Mark L.	NY2250	60A
Shaw, Martha	GA1700	36,32D,60A
Shelby, Karla	OK1500	10D,13A,60A,66A,36
Shelt, Christopher A.	MS0100	60A,36,31A,61,40
Shelton, Tom	NJ1350	31,32,36,60A
Sheppard, Chris	SC0900	36,60A,61,40,34
Sheppard, Kenny	TX2650	60A,36,32D
Sherwin, Ronald G.	MA0150	11,31A,60A,36,32
Shrope, Douglas	CA1000	36,61,60A,40,54
Sieck, Stephen	VA0350	36,61,60A,32D
Sieck, Steven	WI0350	36,60A
Simmons, Mark	TN1720	36,32D,60A
Simons, Carolyn	CA2810	11,20,60A,12
Simons, Kevin	MI1850	61,36,32D,60A
Simpson, Alexander T.	KY0250	11,12A,36,44,60A
Sinclair, Robert L.	IL3450	36,32,60A
Sinclair, Terri	SC0420	36,61,32D,60A
Sinsoulier, Melisande	AG0650	60A
Skinner, Kent	AR0800	60A,36,61,39,54
Sledge, Sylstea	DC0010	31F,60A
Smith, David Kenneth	PA1350	60A,61
Smith, Jason	IA1400	13,36,61,60A
Smith, Kathryn L.	CA1500	61,36,60A
Smith, Paul A.	CA0835	36,60A
Snyder, Timothy	FL1000	36,40,12A,32D,60A
Soderberg, Karen	MD0350	61,36,40,32D,60A
Song, Tom	TX2600	36,60A,31A
Songer, Loralee	TN0850	36,60,36,61
Southard, Bruce	ND0100	36,60A,12A,61,60
Sowers, Richard L.	IN0100	60A,36,32D
Spalding, Ben A.	NJ1050	60A
Sparks, Richard	TX3420	60A,36,55D
Spears, Samuel B.	WV0300	32D,36,61,60A
Speer, Randall	VA1125	61,36,60A,40
Spencer, Philip	IL1250	20,61,66A,36,60A
Sperry, Ethan L.	OR0850	36,60A
Spicer, Nan	IN0005	61,60A,66A,66G,31A
Spillane, Jamie D.	CT0600	36,60A
Stafford, Timothy	IL1850	60A,11
Stegall, James C.	IL3500	36,32D,60A
Stewart, Amy	TX3000	60A
Stich, Joshua	AZ0490	36,60A,61,40,13A
Stock, Jesse	TN0250	36,61,60A,54
Stoltzfus, Fred A.	IL3300	60A,36
Stornetta, Catherine	MA0850	60A,32D,36
Strimple, Nick	CA5300	12A,60A
Stroope, Z. Randall	OK0800	36,60A,40,10A
Suderman, Mark	OH0250	60A,32D,32B,36,61
Swan, Phillip A.	WI0350	36,60,61,32D,60A
Sweet, Bridget Mary	IL3300	32,11,60A
Swisher, Martha	IL2650	36,60A
Tagg, Barbara M.	NY4150	32,36,60A
Tallman, Donna	IL0850	36,60A,44
Tam, Jing Ting	TX3500	36,61,60A
Tarantino, Cassandra	CA1510	36,60A
Tarrant, James	MO1550	36,60A,35,42,66A
Tasher, Cara S.	FL1950	60A,61,36
Tedford, Linda	PA2300	60A,36,61
Teets, Sean	LA0250	60A,61
Terenzi, Mark J.	NJ0700	36,40,60A,13C
Teske, Deborah Jenkins	CO0200	36,40,60A
Thayer, Lucinda J.	WI0850	60A,36,32D
Theimer, Axel K.	MN0350	60A,36,61,32D
Thomas, Andre J.	FL0850	60A,32,36
Thomas, Colby L.	NY3765	39,60A,35F,61,54
Thomas, Nicholas	IL1890	60A,66D,13A,36,61
Thompson, Laura	LA0250	32C,32D,36,60A,61
Thomson, Jacqueline	IA1400	13,36,61,60A
Thorn, Julia	PA3150	36,60A,61
Tramm, Jason	NJ1160	36,40,60A
Trotter, John William	IL3550	36,60A
Tucker, Debra	OH0850	60A

Name	Code	Areas
Ullman, Beth	TX1600	61,60A
Ulrich, Jerry	GA0900	10,36,32,32D,60A
Usher, Ann L.	OH2150	32,36,60A
van den Honert, Peter	PA1200	60A,36,11,13A
Van Wyck, Helen J.	IL3100	13,60A,11,36,32D
VanDam, Lois	FL1430	66A,36,60A
Vazquez-Ramos, Angel M.	CA0960	60A,36,32D,32B
Voelker, Dale	IL1300	13A,13B,60A,36,66G
Vogt, Sean F.	SD0300	60A,36,66G,32D,40
Von Ellefson, Randi	OK0750	36,60A,40
Von Kampen, Kurt E.	NE0150	36,60A,32
Wagner, Randel	WA0250	36,40,61,54,60A
Wagstrom, Beth Robison	CO0050	36,40,47,60A
Walker, Alicia W.	SC1110	36,32D,60A
Walker, Steve	OK0300	61,36,40,60A
Walters, Kent	MI0520	36,60A
Warren, Jane	TN0100	36,60A
Warren, John F.	NY4150	36,32D,60A
Wasserman, Joanne	CA5550	60A
Waters, Richard	KY0550	36,60A,32D,40
Watson, Tim M.	IA1100	32D,47,36,60A
Webber, Kelly Marie	KS0560	11,13A,12A,61,60A
Webster, Thomas R.	TX0600	60A,49,48,13B
Weger, Stacy	OK1150	60A,32D,36
Weiller, David B.	NV0050	60A,32D,36
Weller, Amy G.	IL2250	60A
Wells, Bradley C.	MA2250	13C,36,40,60A,61
Wendel, Joyce	OH2450	32,36,61,60A
Westerhaus, Timothy P.	WA0400	11,60A,61
Westfall, Claude R.	MO0100	32B,32D,36,60A,70
Wetzel, James	NY0625	36,60A
White, Brad	TX3000	60A
White, Christopher Dale	TX2955	32D,36,40,60A,61
White, Robert	NY0642	60A,61
Wiebe, John	AA0110	36,60A
Wiens, Paul W.	IL3550	13C,60A,36
Wiest, Lori J.	WA1150	36,55B,61,60A
Wikan, Cory	LA0050	36,60A
Wiles, John L.	IA1600	36,60A,61,32
Williams, Kenneth D.	TX2960	36,61,60A,40,39
Williamson, Richard A.	SC0050	13C,36,40,60A
Williamson, Steven C.	NJ0550	60A,61,36
Willoughby, Judith A.	OK0750	36,60A,40,32
Wilner, Stacey	TN1000	12A,36,11,60A
Wilson, Gary P.	TN0930	60A,32C,36,61,32D
Wilson, Mark	CA5000	60A
Windt, Nathan J.	TN1550	60A,61,11,32D,36
Wine, Thomas	KS1450	32,36,60A
Winston, Jeremy	OH2400	36,61,47,13E,60A
Winters, Donald Eugene	MS0850	61,31A,12A,60A
Winters, Jill	UT0050	60A
Wis, Ramona M.	IL2050	60A,42,32D,36
Witakowski, Thomas E.	NY3717	36,40,61,60A
Wold, Stanley R.	MN1600	60A,36,40,61
Woods, Timothy E.	SD0400	60A,12A,36,61,40
Wordelman, Peter	OR0200	60A,36,61,54
Wright, Nathan	UT0050	60A
Xiques, David	NY2750	32,60A,61
Yanson, Eliezer G.	SC0200	32D,13,60A,36,40
Yarrington, John	TX1000	60A,36
Yau, Eugenia Oi Yan	NY0270	11,36,61,40,60A
Yeung, Ian	TX3540	36,60A,40,31A,38
Yoon, Sujin	MO1350	36,66G,66H,31A,60A
Young-Wright, Lorna C.	VI0050	13,66,60A
Yu-Oppenheim, Julie	KS0650	32D,36,60A
Zabriskie, Alan N.	MO1790	11,40,36,60A
Zamer, Craig T.	TN1450	36,60A,32D
Zavadsky, Julia	NJ1100	11,13A,36,60A
Zeigler, Mark C.	NY2650	32D,36,40,60A
Zemek, Michael D.	IL0100	32,36,60A
Zophi, Steven	WA1000	36,60A,61

Instrumental

Name	Code	Areas
Abrahams, Daniel	MI1750	60B
Acklin, Amy	KY1500	32E,37,60B
Adams, Bobby L.	FL1750	32,37,60B
Ahn, Jooyong	TN1700	38,60B
Aks, David M.	CA0835	12A,13C,39,60B,62C
Aldrich, Mark L.	MA1650	37,32E,32F,34D,60B
Aldridge, Ben	NY3765	63A,60B,12A
Aldridge, Erin	WI0860	38,62A,13C,51,60B
Alexander, Michael	GA1150	38,60B,12A,35A
Allcott, Dan J.	TN1450	38,60B,62C,11,42
Allen, Fred J.	TX2700	60B,32C,37,41
Allen, Sarah	TX2400	32E,37,32,60B,32B
Allman, Garrett N.	IL1100	13,66C,38,66A,60B
Ambrose, Robert J.	GA1050	37,32E,60B
Ammann, Bruce T.	SD0050	60B,37,32E,64E
Amundson, Steven	MN1450	13,60B,38,10A
An, Won-Hee	MA1450	11,60B,66
Angeles, L. Dean	LA0300	38,32E,60B
Anglley, Tamey	TX2700	60B,32C,37,41
Arnold, Edwin P.	PA1450	32E,37,60B,48,49
Arnold, Mitchell A.	WV0750	38,60B
Arrowsmith, Jamie	AG0070	38,60B,62,13A,13B
Ash, Corey	TX1100	37,49,63A,32E,60B
Atherton, Leonard	IN0150	60B
Averbach, Ricardo Franco	OH1450	11,38,60B
Avramov, Bogidar	CA2800	38,51,11,10F,60B
Aylward, Ansgarius	NY0400	60B,38,41,62A
Babcock, Andrew	TX1550	60B,63D,37,13,47
Bakenhus, Douglas	LA0550	13B,38,60B,64D
Baldwin, Philip R.	WA1350	62A,41,38,60B
Baldwin, Robert L.	UT0250	38,60B
Ball, James	MI0100	29A,38,47,63D,60B
Baransy, Paul	OH0250	63A,10F,60B,32E,37
Bartley, Mark	TX3750	36,38,60,60B
Bartram, Kevin P.	VA1475	37,60B,38,32E
Baumgartner, Christopher	MO1800	37,60B
Bayless, Robert R.	AZ0500	32C,32E,37,60B
Beatty, Caroline	TX3175	37,32E,60B
Beck, Brandon	WA1100	37,63,60B,38,32C
Belcik, Mark G.	OK0750	60B
Bell, John	IL2910	32,32C,37,60B
Bell, Richard	GA0500	32E,13,38,60B,62D
Bellomia, Paolo	AI0200	60B
Benkert, Stuart M.	TN1700	37,47,32E,60B
Bennett, Dwight	AB0100	38,60B
Bergonzi, Louis	IL3300	32E,38,62,32G,60B
Berinbaum, Martin C.	AB0100	60B,37,49,63A
Betancourt, David	CA0859	37,46,38,32E,60B
Beyers, Foster	MN0600	38,60B
Bianchi, Douglas	MI2200	37,13,60B
Biddle, Paul D.	NY0400	60B,37
Biggs, Gunnar	CA3460	60B,47,29A
Birdwell, Cody	KY1450	48,60B
Blaine, Robert	MS0350	11,38,32E,63C,60B
Block, Tyrone	TX2570	32E,37,47,60B,63
Bloomquist, Paul	IA0790	11,63,60B,13,37
Boeckman, Jeffrey	HI0210	37,60B
Boggs, David G.	IL1740	37,32E,60B
Boggs, William	OH0350	38,60,41,60B
Bohnert, David A.	NE0700	63A,60B,37,11,32E
Bolstad, Stephen P.	VA0600	37,60B
Booker, Charles L.	AR0730	10,32E,13,60B
Boonshaft, Peter Loel	NY1600	60B,32C,37
Bourque, David	AG0450	48,37,38,64C,60B
Boysen, Andrew A.	NH0350	37,60B,10F
Brechting, Gail	MI1550	60B,63C,37
Brennan, Adam	PA2150	60B,37,50,65,10F
Brewer, Paul S.	MI0300	60B,37,32E,29,63C
Bridges, Cynthia	TX0550	37,32H,60B,13C,32C
Briskin, David	AG0450	60B
Brock, Gordon R.	FL1950	37,48,64E,60B,10A
Brooks, John Patrick	ID0100	60B,37,63C,47,63D
Brooks, Ricky W.	AR0850	60B,37
Brown, Kellie Dubel	TN1150	62A,38,12A,60B,62B
Brown, Marcellus	ID0050	37,60B
Buchman, Heather	NY1350	38,49,51,48,60B
Burdett, John	CA0630	32E,37,60B
Burns, Stephen	IL2750	60B
Bustos, Pamela B.	WI0860	32E,37,48,60B,64C
Butler, Dorsey Mitchell	SC0350	63C,60B,47,29
Butrico, Michael	NC0400	32E,37,46,60B,63
Cadelago, Harry	CA3250	37,38,60B,49
Caldwell, Brendan	WI0850	37,32E,60B
Campbell, Michael J.	GA2300	60B,47,64E,32E,11
Camphouse, Mark D.	VA0450	10,60B,37
Campo, David	TX2700	32E,32C,37,60B
Cardany, Brian M.	RI0300	32E,32G,37,60B
Carrettin, Zachary	TX2250	38,60B
Carroll, Kevin	GA1600	10,64,60B,11,13
Carson, William S.	IA0300	60B,37,12A,32E,64C
Carter, Robert Scott	NC0650	60B,37,41,32E
Casey, Brian	NY1700	38,63B,60B,13C
Caslor, Jason	AD0050	37,38,60B
Cason, Tony	CA3600	41,32E,60B,38,12A
Cazes, Alain	AI0150	60B,63D,48
Cedel, Mark	GA2100	60B,38,62B
Cesario, Robert James	MO0825	37,38,60B,41
Chambers, Timothy	NC0800	37,48,64,60B
Chapman, Christopher	OR0700	32,37,46,63A,60B
Chen, Donald	IL0550	60B,13
Chen, Jay	OR0450	60B,49,37,63A
Chi, Jacob	CO0275	13,38,60B
Clements, Phillip L.	TX2955	60B,37,63D,13A,12A
Clickard, Stephen D.	PA0250	37,63,47,60B
Coggiola, John C.	NY4150	32,29,34,47,60B
Coleman, Randall	AL1170	37,60B,32E
Collinsworth, Andy	CA4700	13A,32,37,41,60B
Compton, Michael	OK0150	64,48,47,60B
Compton, Michael	ND0100	64,37,41,47,60B
Conger, Robert B.	MO1500	60B,32C,63C,63D
Connelly, Marianne	MN0450	37,32,47,64,60B
Connors, Thomas	NJ0700	37,11,32E,60B
Cook, Andrew	AL0345	60B,63,11,47,64
Cooke, David	IN0905	38,60B,49,63C
Cooper, Jameson	IN0910	62A,38,60B
Corcoran, Gary J.	NH0250	37,60B,63A,32E
Corporon, Eugene Migliaro	TX3420	60B,37
Correll, Allen	OK0300	37,32E,47,60B,63A
Couturiaux, Clay	TX3420	60B,38,62C
Cox, Eleanor Christman	WI0700	62C,62D,60B
Cox, Ishbah	IN1310	37,60B
Crim, Mark	TX0600	37,32E,60B,44
Csaba, Ajtony	AB0150	38,60B
Cullen, John	AG0450	60B
Culvahouse, John N.	GA1150	37,32C,32E,60B
Culver, Daniel	IL0100	13,60B,12,38
Cummings, Daniel	CA2420	60B,38,66D,66A
Cunningham, Gregory M.	MI1750	60B,38,37
Curley, Jason	NY1400	60B,63B,37,49,32E
Darling, John A.	ND0050	37,60B,47,13,41
Davis, Paul G.	MO1950	60B,37,38,32E
Davis, Steven D.	MO1810	60B
Deemer, Robert	NY3725	10A,10C,43,10,60B
Denison, Mark	OR1010	12A,29A,63C,46,60B
Deppe, Scott M.	TX1400	37,60B,32G,32C
DePriest, James	NY1900	60B,38
DeRusha, Stanley	IN0250	32E,11,60B
Desjardins, Jacques	CA4150	43,60B,13
Diamond, Douglas	MN0050	60B,38,51,12A
Diazmunoz, Eduardo	IL3300	39,43,60B
Dickinson, Christian M.	PA1600	13,49,63C,60B
Dimoff, Maximilian	OH0600	62D,60B
Ditmer, Nancy	OH0700	32,37,60B
Dodson, Brent	IA1750	63,64,37,60B,48
Dolbashian, Edward	MO1800	60B,38
Dominick, Daniel L.	TX0250	66A,12,60B,38,60
Dorn, Mark	CO0150	37,63A,46,60B,49
Dorothy, Wayne F.	TX0900	32C,32E,37,60B
Douglas, Kenneth	IN0910	32,37,60B
Doyle, Brian K.	NY3780	37,60B
Droste, Douglas	OK0800	38,60B,32E
Duhaime, Ricky	TX0250	13,47,41,64,60B
Dundjerski, Petar	AA0020	60B,64A
Dundjerski, Petar	AA0100	60B
Dunnigan, Patrick	FL0850	32C,37,60B
Dye, Keith G.	TX3200	60B,32C,32E
Edwards, Richard D.	OH2000	37,32,60B,12F,32A
Eggleston, Steven	IL1200	60B,37,38,63A
Eis, Jeremiah	WI0770	34,48,47,60B,63
Emile, Mark A.	UT0300	10F,60B,62A,62B
Engle, Tiffany J.	MI0350	64E,60B,37,32E
Ethington, Bradley P.	NY4150	60B,37,32E
Evans, Clifton J.	TX3500	38,60B,11
Evans, Garry W.	TX3300	64C,37,12A,41,60B
Fallin, Nicky G.	GA0250	37,32E,63A,49,60B
Fansler, Michael J.	IL3500	37,60B,32E
Farberman, Harold	NY0150	60B
Farnham, Curvin G.	ME0440	60B,32E,37
Farris, Daniel J.	IL2250	47,37,60B,60
Feldberg, David	NM0450	43,62A,60B
Felder, Harvey	CT0600	38,60B
Feldman, Evan	NC2410	37,60B
Feldman, Ronald	MA2250	60B,38,41,42
Fellenbaum, James	TN1710	38,60B
Ferrari, Lois	TX2650	37,38,60B
Fiese, Richard K.	TX1000	60B,32
Filzen Etzel, Laurel Kay	IL1350	63B,60B,37
Fischer, Richard R.	IL0730	37,60B
Fisher, Dennis W.	TX3420	60B,32C,37
Flanagin, Michael	IN1025	37,63A,63B,41,60B
Fleming, Ricky L.	NY3717	60B,37,47,49,63C

Name	Code	Areas
Fonder, Mark	NY1800	60B,32,37
Franklin, Cary J.	MN0950	10,37,38,42,60B
Fraschillo, Tom	GA1700	37,60B,32E
Frederick, Matthew D.	VA0350	63A,12A,41,60B,32E
Fuchs, Craig	KS1050	60B,37,32E
Furman, Lisa J.	MI1800	37,60B,11,13,32
Gallo, Reed P.	SC0800	37,60B,32E,63A,49
Galyean, Richard D.	VA1580	37,60B,49,63D,32E
Galyen, S. Daniel	IA1600	37,41,32E,60B,32
Gambetta, Charles L.	NC0900	38,60B,13,62D
Gantt, William	CA3250	47,29B,60B
Garasi, Michael J.	FL1800	37,60B
Gardiner, Ronald	FL1740	13,62,60B,51,38
Garofalo, Robert	DC0050	32E,37,60B
Garrett, Roger	IL1200	37,64C,60B,41,35D
Garrido, Glenn	TX3450	60B,32E,20H,37
Gay, Nathan	KS0300	63C,63D,60B,37
Geeting, Daniel	CA0550	64E,64C,38,11,60B
George, Andrew	TX3200	38,60B,39,32E
George, Roby G.	IL3300	37,60B
Gephart, Jay S.	IN1310	37,60B
Ghiglione, Brent	AJ0100	37,60B
Gilman, Matt	OR1010	64,60B
Gilroy, Gary P.	CA0810	13C,10F,60B,37
Ginocchio, John	MN1500	37,13,47,32E,60B
Ginwala, Cyrus	CA4200	38,13B,11,60B
Gomez-Giraldo, Julian	WA0250	38,60B,13C
Gonzalez, Claudio	MI0250	38,60B,10F,20,12A
Gonzalez, Helen	PR0115	60B
Good, Jonathan E.	NV0050	60B,32,37,32E
Goodwin, Casey S.	NH0350	37,32D,47,60B
Gould, Valerie	WV0050	32E,34,37,41,60B
Graf, Hans	TX2150	38,60B
Graham, Alexander	TN0100	64E,60B
Grass, Ken G.	OK1450	37,64E,60B
Gregory, M. David	GA1700	32E,37,32F,60B
Greig, R. Tad	PA3650	32E,37,47,60B,63C
Griffin, Larry	OH2000	60B,37,47,49,63A
Griffin, Peter J.	IL0850	32,37,60B,63C,63D
Griffing, Joan	VA0300	62A,38,41,60B,62B
Griggs, Kevin D.	MT0400	37,60B,32E
Grise', Monte	MN1120	64E,32E,47,37,60B
Gross, Allen	CA3300	11,38,60B,42
Gross, Ernest H.	IL1300	37,49,60B,63D,12A
Gross, Murray	MI0150	38,13,60B,10,20
Gruner, Greg	AL1300	37,63D,60B,32E,35
Guenoit, Eric	LA0450	60B,11,37,65,50
Gustafson, Karen	AK0150	37,63A,60B,41,60B
Guyver, Russell	CO0950	60B,38
Guzman, Ariel	PR0150	60B
Hagen, Scott	UT0250	37,32E,60B
Halverson, Pamela	NC1600	60B,37
Hamilton, Craig V.	AR0500	63A,60B,46,37
Hammer, Eric	CA5350	60B,37,32E
Hanan, David	OK1330	37,60B,10F,34,63A
Hancock, Craig A.	IA1800	37,60B,63C,63D,72
Hanman, Theodore	KS0100	65,60B,47,37,32E
Hansen, Richard K.	MN1300	60B,37,20G,12A
Harris, Edward C.	CA4400	37,60B
Harrison, Albert D.	IN1560	60B,37,47,63D,32E
Hawkins, Ben	KY1350	60B,32,37,38,63B
Hedlund, Kristin	IL2750	60B
Hege, Daniel C.	NY4150	43,60B
Heller, Lauren B.	CT0050	37,32E,60B,64A
Hemberger, Glen J.	LA0650	60B,32C,37,63C,47
Herlihy, John S.	MN1280	60B,49,37,46
Hermann, Joseph W.	TN1450	37,60B,32E
Heyde, Stephen	TX0300	38,60B
Higgins, Edward	OR0850	37,32E,60B
Highfill, Philip	OH1700	66C,60B
Hill, Douglas M.	GA1300	60B,32C,37,49,63A
Hinton, Eric L.	PA3150	37,60B,63A
Hofer, Calvin	CO225	32,37,49,63A,60B
Hoffman, Edward C. 'Ted'	AL1200	11,32C,32E,60B
Holland, Anthony G.	NY3650	10A,60B,34,38,10B
Hollinger, Trent A.	MO0300	64,37,13C,13A,60B
Holloway, John R.	SC0650	63D,32,37,60B
Holsinger, David	TN0850	60B,10,48
Hoover, Jerry W.	MO0775	60B,37,46
Hopkins, Mark E.	AF0050	37,32E,32C,60,60B
Hostetter, Paul K.	GA0550	38,39,60B,43
Houghtalen, Brandon	NM0450	60B,64
House, Richard E.	SC0350	37,63A,32E,60B
Hsu, Howard	GA2150	38,42,60B
Hsu, John	NY0900	42,62C,67A,38,60B
Huang, Steven	OH1900	38,60B,43
Huber, Deborah	MA2030	37,60B
Hudiburg, Howard B.	TX3175	32E,38,60B
Hudson, Mark E.	CO0275	11,32,60B
Huff, Michael D.	UT0300	60,60A,60B
Hughes, Christopher A.	NM0310	37,60B,32E,63A,38
Hughey, Richard	IL3500	38,60B
Ichmouratov, Airat	AI0190	38,60B
Ingber, Jonathan	CA3460	47,60B
Isakson, Aaron	MN0610	32E,37,50,60B,65
Itkin, David C.	TX3420	38,60B
Jacobs, David M.	OR1050	38,60B
Jacobs, Gene	MO1000	60B
Jelinek, Mark R.	PA0250	60B,11,38,62
Jester, Erik	CA0845	37,60B,63C
Jiang, Pu-Qi	TN1680	60B,38
Jimenez, Alexander	FL0850	38,60B,65A,60,65
Jimenez, Fernando	CT0800	60B,37,63C
Joella, Laura	FL0650	38,12A,62D,60B
Johns, Kynan	NJ1130	38,60B
Johnson, Mark	GA0200	32E,37,60B,63C
Johnson, Richard	SC0420	32E,60B,13
Johnston, Dennis	NY0700	32E,12C,49,63A,60B
Jones, Lloyd E.	AL1250	60B,37,63
Jones, Max	IN1310	37,60B
Jones, Patrick Michael	NY4150	32G,60B,32,12A,12E
Jones, Scott A.	OH1850	37,60B,32E
Jones, Scott A.	GA2100	37,60B
Jordan, Jeff	KS0350	37,32E,60B,63B,10
Kahn, Alexander G.	PA1400	38,12A,11,60B
Kalam, Tonu	NC2410	60B,38
Karrick, Brant	KY1000	37,60B,32E
Kays, Mark	IN1485	12A,13B,37,47,60B
Keck, Thomas B.	FL1900	37,60B
Keddy, Michael	AB0150	60B
Kehler, David T.	GA1150	37,60B,11
Keller, Jeffrey	OH0350	32E,60B
Kendall, Christopher	MI2100	60B
Kenney, Wes	CO0250	38,60B
Kerr, Stephen P.	VA0650	63,37,60B,48
Key, Ramon	OH0500	37,60B
Kiesler, Kenneth	MI2100	60B,38
Kimball, Marshall C.	OH1400	32,37,47,60B
King, Gerald	AB0150	32,37,60B
Kirkpatrick, Leon	KY0250	37,38,41,51,60B
Kiser, Daniel W.	NC1100	13A,10F,60B,37,63A
Kish, David	CO0550	37,32E,60B,32
Kitelinger, Shannon	CA4100	37,60B
Klickman, Philip	MD0350	63B,37,32E,60B
Knight, Jonathan	CA2775	12A,13A,60B,63
Knight, Michael D.	WI0750	37,60B,32E,64C,64E
Koch, Christopher	MO0350	37,38,60B
Kohlenberg, Kenneth	OH2120	37,60B,12A,11,63A
Kopetz, Barry E.	OH0350	60B,37
Kraus, Barry N.	TN0100	37,32E,60B
Krysa, Taras	NV0050	38,60B
LaFave, Alan	SD0400	64C,60B
Lai, Ching-Chun	NY3780	38,60B
Laing, Daniel R.	NE0300	60B,37,49,63A,63B
Lamb, Brian	OK1330	60B,32,37
Lambert, Adam E.	NE0050	32E,37,60B,63,49
Lambrecht, James M.	IL0100	37,49,63A,60B,13C
Lamkin, Martin J.	VI0050	11,12A,32A,47,60B
Landsberg, Nils F.	TX3415	37,60B,46
Lanz, Christopher C.	NY3780	55,60B
Larson, Stacey L.	IL3450	32E,37,60B
Latham, Mark	MA2030	38,60B
Laverty, John M.	NY4150	60B,37,32,63A
Lavery, Sharon	CA5300	60B
LaVoie, Karen R.	MA2100	13C,60B,37,63A
Laycock, Mark Andrew	KS1450	38,60B
Lee, Christine	SC0200	62C,60B
Lee, Joseph	TN1800	60B
Lees, Christopher	MI2100	60B
Leslie, Tom	NV0050	37,60B
Lewis, Gary J.	CO0800	60B,38
Leyva, Jesse	IL3300	60B,37,32E
Lindhal, Gregory	FL0700	37,48,60B
Lindholm, Eric	CA1050	13C,38,60B
Linklater, Fraser	AC0100	63A,32E,37,48,60B
Loeb, Jaemi	KY0450	38,13A,41,42,60B
Lofstrom, Douglas	IL0720	60B,10
Long, Bill	SC0900	37,47,65,60B,32E
Lubman, Bradley	NY1100	43,38,60B
Macelaru, Cristian	TX2150	38,60B
MacKay, Gillian	AG0450	37,42,63A,60B,60
Maguda, John	NY3725	60B
Mahr, Timothy	MN1450	60B,37,10
Malecki, Jeffrey	IL2650	37,60B,63C,63D,38
Malone, Michael J.	OH2000	60B
Maltester, John	CA2775	37,41,60B,63C
Manfredo, Joseph	IL1150	32E,60B,37,32
Mann, Michael	TN1660	37,42,60B,65
Marinello, Anthony	TX3510	60B,37
Markovich, Victor A.	KS1450	37,60B
Martin, Michelle Denise	GA0150	11,65,66D,60B
Matos, Lucia Regina	IL2200	38,39,60B,66G,66H
Mayer, Uri	AG0300	60B,38
McAllister, James	KS0440	37,10A,63,60B,32C
McBride, M. Scott	KY0900	60B,32,10F,63C,37
McCallum, Wendy M.	AC0050	64E,32E,37,60B,32
McCaskill, Janet L.	MI2200	63D,32E,60B,32C
McCauley, Thomas E.	NJ0800	37,60B,32
McClung, Sam W.	FL0365	60B,37,13,47,46
McDonald, Steven	KS1000	66,38,60B,12A,41
McInturf, Matthew	TX2250	32C,37,60B
McKinney, John S.	WV0350	50,65,34,60B,41
McKoin, Sarah	TX3200	60B,37
McMahel, Donald	IN1010	37,38,60B
McRoy, James W.	NY2105	60B,37,63,32E
McWilliams, Robert	WI0830	37,32,29A,60B
Meggs, Gary L.	AR0800	60B,64,47,46,29
Melley, Eric	LA0200	37,60B
Menzies, Mark	CA0510	62A,62B,38,43,60B
Mertz, Justin J.	NY4150	37,60B,32
Meunier, Robert W.	IA0560	60B,37,65,32E
Meyer, Jeffery David	NY1800	38,66A,60B,43
Meyers, Dan	MI1550	60B,38
Miedema, Bradley	IA0500	32E,37,38,60B
Milarsky, Jeffrey	NY1900	60B
Millan, Luis	MT0400	38,70,60B,13
Miller, James Patrick	MA2000	37,32,60B
Miller, Ward	AL1300	37,63D,41,32E,60B
Mills, Alan W.	CO0275	37,66A,63A,32E,60B
Millsapp, Brian	NC1550	37,49,60B
Milnes, David	CA5000	38,43,60B
Milosavljevic, Svetozar	IN0005	68,60B
Missal, Joseph	OK0800	37,60B,49
Moore, Frances	CA2800	60B,41,62A,67B,38
Moore, J. Steven	MO1790	37,32E,60B
Moore, Joe D.	MS0250	37,32E,60B
Morgan, Charles	IL1250	13A,60B,37,47,63
Morris, Gerard	WA1000	37,60B,11
Moss, Emily A.	NY0500	32,48,64D,60B
Mueller-Stosch, Johannes	CA0825	38,60B
Mulholland, Jeremy	KY0550	62A,62B,38,60B
Muller, David J.	CA6000	10F,11,12A,60B,64D
Nail, James I. (Ike)	OR1250	37,37,60B,32E
Nardolillo, John	KY1450	38,60B
Neiman, Marcus	OH1100	37,60B
Newton, Timothy D.	NY3765	60A,60B,66A,66C
Nicholas, Christopher J.	CO0250	37,60B
Nichter, Christopher	WV0750	32E,37,60B
Nies, Carol	TN1100	38,60B
Nimmo, Douglas	MN0750	60B,37,32C,32E
Nix, Jamie L.	GA0550	37,60B
Noe, Kevin	MI1400	38,43,60B
Norcross, Brian H.	PA1300	60,37,38,60B
Norman, Mark	KS1400	37,41,60B,63D
O'Bryant, Daniel K.	MN1300	38,60B,62D
Odajima, Isaiah	TX0300	37,60B
Oelrich, John A.	TN1720	37,32E,60B
Olson, Robert H.	MO1810	60B,38
Opfer, Stephen R.	CA2810	32,37,38,60B,47
O'Riordan, Kirk	PA1850	10,60B,13,64E
Orton, Billy H.	AL1160	36,60A,60B,61,63C
Overmier, Douglas R.	MO0950	60B,60A,37,47,10
Owen, John E.	OH0950	60B,37,47,63A
Owens, Douglas T.	VA1000	32,47,60B,29
Ozzello, Kenneth B.	AL1170	60B,32C,37
Pabon, Roselin	PR0115	60B,38
Packard, John	OH1600	37,49,63A,60B,10F
Pagnard, Charles	OH0450	60B,32E,49,63A
Palmer, Michael	GA1050	38,60B
Parker, Nathaniel F.	PA2200	38,60B,64,41
Parsons, Kenneth	TN1350	60B,49,37,46,34
Pasternack, Jonathan R.	WA1050	38,39,12A,60B
Paul, Timothy A.	OR1050	32E,37,60B
Payne, Brandt A.	OH2600	37,60B
Pellicano, Julian	MA1175	38,60B
Peltz, Charles	MA1400	48,60B

Index by Area of Teaching Interest

Name	Code	Areas
Perkins, Boyd	SD0400	63C,63D,37,60B,72
Perry, Dawn A.	NC2650	63C,32E,37,47,60B
Petersen, William	AL1300	32E,37,63D,60B,49
Peterson, Eric	SD0550	63D,37,60B
Peterson, Stephen G.	NY1800	60B,37
Pham, Danh	WA1150	32D,60B,48
Phillips, Rebecca L.	SC1110	32E,37,60B
Pickering, Matthew	MS0360	63,37,11,49,60B
Pilato, Nikk	CA0825	63,37,38,32E,60B
Poff, Sarah	OR1010	60B
Polay, Bruce	IL1350	10A,10F,12A,13B,60B
Ponto, Robert	OR1050	60B,37,41
Popejoy, James R.	ND0500	37,60B,32E
Popiel, Paul W.	KS1350	37,60B
Posey, Benjamin C.	AL0300	32,37,60B,63A
Powell, Edwin C.	WA0650	37,41,32E,60B
Powers, Michael	CA5300	60B
Prather, Belva W.	MO0775	60B,48,64A
Prescott, Steve C.	IN1400	32E,11,60B,64,37
Prior, Richard	GA0750	38,41,42,60B
Rachleff, Larry	TX2150	60B,38
Ramael, David R.	NY1600	12,38,39,60B,51
Raymond, Rusty	MO0800	37,63A,60B
Redmer Minner, Laurie K.	TN1350	60B,38,51,32C,62B
Reeves, Gary L.	SD0600	60B,13G,37,63B
Reichwald, Siegwart	SC0650	12,38,60B
Reimer, Mark U.	VA0150	13C,60B,37
Rettedal, Dean	SD0300	37,60B,47,63,64
Rhodes, Steve	TN0930	60B,32E,37,47,63D
Riazuelo, Carlos	LA0200	38,60B
Richardson, Colleen	AG0500	60B,37,32E,41,42
Richardson, Marguerite	FL1000	38,60B,62A,62B
Richter, Jorge Luiz	NC0650	60B,38,42,62A,62B
Rinehart, Jason	LA0770	60B,37,38,41
Ripley, James	WI0250	37,41,32E,60B,38
Rivest, Jean-Francois	AI0200	38,60B
Robertson, James D.	MT0175	13,60B,63C,63D,47
Robertson, Jon	FL1125	60B,38,66A
Robinson, Michael L.	NC1250	32E,60B,37
Robinson, Michael C.	GA2100	37,60,32E,60B
Robken, Jim	LA0250	37,60B
Roeder, Matthew J.	CO0800	37,32E,60B
Romer, Wayne Allen	PA3710	13A,10F,60B,11,32
Romines, Fred David	PA2200	37,60B,64E,32E
Rosario, Harry	PR0150	13A,13C,37,60B,64B
Ross, James	MD1010	38,60B
Ross, Nicholas G. M.	AZ0450	38,60B
Rothman, George	NY0500	38,42,60B
Rowe, Matthew	CA4100	38,60B
Saker, James	NE0610	32E,37,60B
Salvo, Leonard P.	OH0100	60B,32C,37,41,32E
Samuels, Sue	AL1150	37,32E,60B
Satterwhite, H. Dwight	GA2100	60B,37
Saunders, David E.	ID0050	63B,60B,13E,12A
Saville, Kirt	UT0050	37,60B,64C,32E,32C
Schaff, Michael P.	NY3780	60B,37
Schallert, Gary	KY1550	37,60B
Schallock, Michael G.	NC2600	32E,63D,60B
Schleicher, Donald J.	IL3300	60B,38
Schmidt, Daniel Joseph	AZ0450	60B,37
Schneider, Benjamin D.	ND0150	37,38,60B,64,32
Schneider, Charles	NY1400	38,60B
Schroeder, Angela	AA0100	37,48,60B
Schroeder, Dave	NY2750	29,47,65,60B
Schueller, Rodney C.	TX3175	13A,32E,60B
Schultz, Andrew J.	NE0150	29,37,60B,63A
Sedatole, Kevin	MI1400	37,60B
Seifert, Dustin	NM0100	37,63C,63D,60B,32E
Selden, Ken	OR0850	38,43,51,60B
Sellers, Elizabeth A.	CA0835	10C,46,60B
Sessoms, Sydney	NC1150	13E,32E,37,60B,11
Shaw, Arthur E.	WA1250	60B
Shewan, Paul	NY3350	60B,37,63A,32E,38
Shimada, Toshiyuki	CT0850	60B
Shoop, Stephen S.	TX3515	32,41,60B,63D
Sidlin, Murry	DC0050	38,60B
Silvester, William	NJ0175	60B,32,37
Silvey, Brian A.	MO1800	32E,60B
Simmons, Matthew	FL0100	49,60B,63C,63D
Sims, Stuart	CA0850	37,38,41,60B
Singleton, Kenneth	CO0950	60B,37
Smart, James	MT0400	37,63A,32E,60B
Smisek, James J.	AL0800	60B,37,32E
Smith, Carol	TX2250	38,51,60B,62,32E
Smith, James	WI0815	38,51,62,60B
Smith, Shawn T.	TX2930	63A,60B,37,32E
Smith, Timothy M.	CA2775	60B,38
Snow, Bradley	MO1800	37,60B
Sommerville, Daniel A.	IL3550	38,10,60B
Southall, John K.	FL0950	13,63A,60B,37,32E
Southard, Robert G.	MI1050	37,60B,41,11
Souza, Thomas	MA0500	60B,64C,37,32,46
Sparks, L. Richmond	MD1010	37,60B
Spence, J. Robert	PA1250	37,38,32,60B
Spiegelman, Ron	MO0350	60B,35E
Spinazzola, James M.	IN1650	37,41,60B
Spittal, Robert	WA0400	37,11,42,48,60B
Sprenger, Kurt	TX2600	62A,38,60B
Squires, Stephen E.	IL0550	60B,37
St. John, Brian	IN1600	38,62A,62B,60B
Steffen, Richard	TN0050	60B,49,63A,47,11
Steinberg, Steve	CA3460	46,47,60B
Stelluto, George Edward	NY1900	60B
Stern, David	SC0050	37,63D,47,29A,60B
Stevens, John	WI0815	63D,60B,35,10,13
Stith, Gary	NY1700	32,37,60B,65
Stofko, Diane L.	TN0550	32,11,37,13A,60B
Stolarik, Justin R.	WI0815	37,60B,32E,65,10F
Stone, Brian D.	DE0150	60B
Stone, Michael John	OK0600	37,46,60B,63,32
Stotter, Douglas	TX3500	37,41,60B
Strauch, Richard	WA1350	37,63D,60B,41,12A
Strelau, Nancy	NY2650	38,60B
Stufft, David	GA2000	37,41,47,32,60B
Stuppard, Javier	TX1150	12,60B,63
Sudduth, Steven	KY1425	13,32E,37,60B,63C
Sulski, Peter	MA0650	62A,62B,60B,38
Svanoe, Erika K.	MN0150	64C,60B,37,32E,45
Swann, William E.	TN1000	47,13,60B,29B,10D
Swanson, Mark L.	MA0100	60B,38,66A,41
Tamarkin, Kate	VA1550	38,60B,12A,43
Tapia, James R.	NY4150	60B,38,32
Tate, Philip	NJ0175	38,60B,32
Taylor, Charles L.	LA0800	37,60B,64C,32C,32E
Taylor, James W.	SC1110	37,32E,60B
Taylor, Robert C.	AB0100	37,49,60B,63A
Taylor, Susan Lynnette	IN0100	32E,37,48,60B
Tchivzhel, Edvard	SC0750	60B
Teeple, Scott	WI0815	37,60B
Tembras, Dan	IN0905	32E,37,60B
Terrell, Maurice	FL1700	11,29,37,47,60B
Teske, Casey C.	PA0700	60B,13C,63B,11
Thiel, Robb G.	IN1350	10F,60B,32,37,65
Thomas, Matthew J.	IL3500	37,60B
Thomas, Raymond D.	TN1100	32E,37,60B
Thompson, Steven	MN0250	37,60B,63A,32E,49
Thornton, Bruce	MN0350	60B,41,47,64
Threinen, Emily	PA3250	37,60B
Tjornehoj, Kris	WI0845	38,11,60B,37,32E
Tomaro, Annunziata	OH2200	38,60B
Torres, Gregory J.	LA0450	60B,11,37,34B,32B
Towner, Cliff	GA0850	32E,37,47,60B
Townsend, Bradley G.	OR0700	37,60B,32E
Tracz, Frank	KS0650	60B,37,32E
Troy, Matthew	NC1650	60B
Tully, James	SC0420	37,32E,60B
Turizziani, Robert	WV0800	64C,60B,48
Turner, George	ID0150	10,13,60B,63C,63D
Turpen, Scott	WY0200	64E,47,29,60B
Vallo, Victor	GA0850	32,37,60B
Vandelicht, Roy D. 'Skip'	MO0100	32,37,60B,64A,47
Vega, Rebecca	NJ0050	32,37,11,64A,60B
Verrier, Thomas	TN1850	37,60B,32C,32D,32
Viliunas, Brian	AL0800	64C,38,13C,32E,60B
Villa, Tara Towson	NC0550	11,38,60B
Vondran, Shawn	IN0150	37,60B
Votta, Michael	MD1010	60B
Wachs, Daniel Alfred	CA0960	38,60B
Wade, Mark Alan	OH0850	63A,12A,11,32,60B
Wagner, Jan	VA1350	60B,38
Waldvogel, Nicolas	CA5350	38,60B
Walker, David L.	VA1000	50,65,60B,11,13A
Walker, Mark	AL1050	63D,37,60B
Wallace, Jacob E.	OK1150	37,60B
Ward, Steven D.	TX0050	60B,37,38
Warren, W. Dale	AR0700	60B,32E,37
Webb, John C.	AR0800	41,32E,37,60B,63
West, John T.	NC2600	32E,37,60B
Wheeler, Ron	OK0850	38,60B,62B
White, Dale A.	MN0350	60B,37,41,32E,63
Whitwell, John	GA2100	35E,37,60B
Wiley, Frank	OH1100	13,10,38,60B,43
Williams, Eddy	AL0450	65,13B,32C,37,60B
Williams, Kraig	NJ1130	37,60B
Williams, Nicholas	TX3420	60B,37
Willis, Jonathan	OH2290	60B,32C,37,47,46
Willson, David	MS0700	37,60B
Wilson, J. Eric	TX0300	37,60B
Wilson, J. P.	AR0600	37,63D,63C,32E,60B
Wiltshire, Eric	OR1050	37,32E,60B
Wise, William	IA1100	64C,13B,32E,37,60B
Wittemann, Wilbur	NJ0550	37,63,47,60B
Wolfe, Anne Marie	IN0150	63D,64,32E,10F,60B
Wollner, William	MI1850	11,13B,37,63B,60B
Wright, Lauren Denney	OK0650	32E,37,64C,60B
Yehuda, Guy	FL1950	64C,60B,41,32E
Young, Craig S.	MS0400	60B,37,63,64
Yozviak, Andrew J.	PA3600	37,60B
Zamzow, Laura	WV0200	11,63D,60B,32,37
Zelle, Tom	IL2100	60B,38
Zembower, Christian M.	TN0500	63D,37,60B
Zimmermann, Gerhardt	TX3510	38,60B
Zitek, Sam	NE0450	37,64E,60B,32E
Zollman, Ronald	PA0550	38,60B
Zyskowski, Martin	WA0250	50,65,60B

Voice

Name	Code	Areas
Aakre, Brett	OR1000	40,61
Aaland, Jan	MD0500	61
Aaron, Kathryn	KY0250	55,61
Abbey, Gail	MA1560	61,36
Abbott, Amanda-Joyce	OH2290	61,11
Abbott, Carol	FL0930	61,36
Abbott, Thomas	MN1300	14,61
Abbott, Wesley	CA2600	36,61,35B,13
Abel, Sandra	TX0390	36,61,13A,13B,13C
Abele, Catherine	AA0035	61
Abele, Catherine	AA0100	61
Abell, Jan	CA2750	61
Abelson, Norman	MO1810	61
Abernathy, Kristina	CO0600	61
Abraham, Christine	CA2950	61
Abraham, Christine	CA0807	61
Abramowitsch, Miriam	CA2950	61
Acord, Alison	OH1450	61
Adams, Alison	GA1700	61
Adams, David	OH2200	61
Adams, David	MO1790	39,61
Adams, Greta	KS0400	62C,62D,61
Adams, J. Robert	GA0490	61,14,11,39,40
Adams, Julie R.	MN1120	61,32B
Adams, Kris	MA2050	29,61
Adams, Nell	MS0400	61,12A
Adams-McMillan, Aubrey	UT0400	61
Adedapo, Adekola	WI1150	61,29
Adelsberger, Andrew	MD0750	61
Adkins, Kathryn	CA0400	61,54
Adkins, Kathryn	CA0300	61
Adkins, Kathy	AL0750	11,36,61,66A
Adkins, Paul	PA3330	61
Adkins, Scottye	MO0750	61
Adlington, Stephanie	TN0100	61
Agnew, Shawn	MO0850	61,54
Ahearn, Kathryn	VA1475	61,39
Ahern, Rebecca	IA1390	61,66A
Ahlstedt, Douglas F.	PA0550	61
Aiken, Janice	LA0050	61
Aikman, Merla	AA0035	61
Aiosa, Charlotte	VA1350	61
Albert, Donnie Ray	TX3510	61
Albert, Laurence	TN1200	61
Albrecht, Karen	TX1600	61,54,40
Albrink, Emily	KY1500	61
Alch, Marion R.	OH1850	61
Alderson, Daphne	PA3000	61,39
Aldridge, Rachel	WA0400	61
Alexander, Cory T.	TX3527	36,32D,61,32,40
Alexander, Michelle	MA0350	61
Alexander, Michelle	MA0400	61,66C
Alexopoulos, Christina	CA0960	61
Alfano, Karen	MI0500	61
Alfieri, Gabriel	RI0150	61
Algieri, Stefano	AI0150	61
Ali, Susan B.	CA1900	61

Index by Area of Teaching Interest

Name	Code	Areas
Aliapoulios, S. Mark	FL1450	61,47
Aliapoulis, S. Mark	FL0700	36,61
Alig, Kelley	OK0300	32,61,11
Allan, Diana	TX3530	61
Allan, Kathryn	CA2840	61,66A,66D
Allard, Catherine	AL1050	61,42
Allbritten, James	NC1650	36,61,39
Allebach, Robin	ND0600	39,61
Allebach, Robin K.	MN1120	61
Allen, Ben	MN0250	61
Allen, Benjamin	MN0300	61
Allen, Burt	LA0550	36,60A,60,34,61
Allen, Ferris	AR0700	61
Allen, Helen	OH2050	61
Allen, Ivalah	KS0350	61,39,12A,20F
Allen, Jennifer	AZ0470	61
Allen, Nancy	TN0100	61,54
Allen, Sheila M.	TX3000	61
Allison, James	IL1550	12A,61
Allison, Linda	DC0110	36,61
Allison, Linda	DC0010	61
Allred, Carol Ann	UT0250	61
Allred, Jody	UT0190	61,11
Allsup, Neal	KS0550	11,12A,36,60,61
Almy, Mark	CA1270	39,61
Alonzo, Deborah	VA1650	61
Alstat, Sara	IL2500	11,13A,13C,36,61
Alt, David	CA0960	61
Alt, Jerry A.	NM0310	36,61,60
Alvi, Diba N.	MD0650	61
Alvi, Diba N.	MD0550	61
Alviani, Henry	PA0700	36,40,60A,61
Amato, Michelle	FL1950	61
Amaya, Joseph	NC0050	39,61
Ambert, William J.	PA3650	61
Ambrosini, Jeffrey	OK1200	61
Ambrosini, Rebekah	OK1200	39,61
Amos, Gloria	VA0950	13A,11,61
An, Haekyung	MO0060	61
An, Youngjoo	PA3250	61
Anastasia, Stephen	CA0630	61
Anastasia, Stephen	CA3800	61
Anastasia, Stephen	CA3200	61,11
Anavitarte, David	TX2550	36,61,66A,12A,32B
Andereck, Edwin	IA0950	61
Anders, Micheal F.	OH2275	12A,61,54,36
Andersen, LeGrand	UT0200	61,66D,13C,13B
Andersen, Nancy	CT0650	61
Anderson, Alfonse	NV0050	61
Anderson, Alfred	OH2150	39,54,61
Anderson, Catherine Sentman	MD1100	61
Anderson, Charlotte	TN1150	61,36
Anderson, Christine	PA3250	61
Anderson, Danna	MO0650	61
Anderson, Elizabeth Rene	IN0907	61
Anderson, Frank	NY0270	36,61
Anderson, Jared L.	WI0600	36,61,66A,13,12A
Anderson, Jill	CA1510	61
Anderson, Juliana	MA0650	61
Anderson, Juliet V.	GA0490	11,39,61
Anderson, Kathy T.	MS0570	36,40,61
Anderson, Ken	CA2100	36,61
Anderson, Marilyn E.	CA3100	39,61,54
Anderson, Marilyn E.	CA0550	61
Anderson, Richard	OK1350	61
Anderson, Scott E.	ID0100	36,40,60A,61
Anderson, Seija	CA4300	36,61
Anderson, Sylvia	CA4150	61
Anderson, Toni P.	GA1200	61,39
Anderson, Valdine	AC0100	61
Anderson-Collier, Jean	MA0350	61
Andraso, Margaret B.	KY1100	11,36,61,63A
Andreas, Cassandra	CT0300	61
Andrew, Lesley	AG0550	61
Andrews, Deborah	NJ0700	61,54
Andrews, Joyce	WI0830	61
Andrews, Julibeth	RI0250	61
Andrews, Mary	MI2000	61
Andrews, Rachel	MI1850	61
Andrews-Smith, Belinda	OH0850	61,36,39
Angerhofer, Thomas Erik	CO0550	61
Anglin, David Ives	CA0825	61,39
Angulo, Skye	CA2550	36,61
Antolik, Martha E.	AR0850	61
Antonioli, Laurie A.	CA5000	61
Apple, A. Alan	PA1750	13A,36,61,13C,40
Apple, Warren	FL1745	61,66A
Aquilino, Dominic	NC2600	61
Aquilino, Dominic	NC1250	61,54
Aquino, Diane	CT0050	61,13C
Arania, Orna	IL2200	61
Arasi, Melissa	GA0900	40,61
Arbogast, Jennifer	IN1560	61
Arbogast, Jennifer	TN0260	11,13C,54,61,39
Archambeault, Noel	DE0150	61,39
Ardrey, Cathleen	PA2350	32,36,61,66A
Arecchi, Kathleen H.	NH0250	61,54
Areyzaga, Michelle	IL0150	61
Argenta, Nancy	AB0210	61
Argenti, Mary A.	CA1020	61
Argyros, Maria	NY0625	61
Arita, Junko	NY2660	61,13B,13C
Armendarez, Christina	TX1725	61
Armistead, Christine	MO1900	39,61
Armstrong, Anton	MN1450	60A,36,61
Armstrong, Richard	AL0500	12A,12C,61
Arner, Lucia	NY2250	61
Arneson, Christopher P.	NJ1350	61
Arnold, Clara S.	TX3200	61
Arnold, Elizabeth Packard	KY1450	61,39
Arnold, Johana	NY1400	61
Arnold, Tom	MO0100	61
Arnold, Tony	NY4320	61
Arreola, Brian	NC2420	61,39
Artemova, Alina V.	CA2050	61,66D
Artemova, Alina	CA0825	61
Arthur, Katherine	CA0600	61
Arvin, Gary	IN0900	61
Arzillo, Marisa	FL2050	61
Arzillo, Marisa A.	FL1550	61
Asakura, Iwao	TX2750	61
Asel, Nicole	TX3515	61
Ashbaker, Susan	NJ1350	61,39
Ashby, Eda	ID0060	36,61,32D
Ashby, Michael	PA3550	61
Ashcraft, Eric	IA0950	61
Ashe, Jennifer	CT0150	11,61
Ashe, Jennifer	MA0700	11,61,55D,40
Ashley, Marie	FL1450	61
Ashmore, Lance	OH0300	61
Ashmore, Lance	OH2275	61
Ashmore, Lance	OH1800	61
Ashworth, Teresa	MN1100	61,36,40,20,13C
Aspaas, Christopher	MN1450	36,61,60A,32D
Aspling, Carol	CA0350	36,61
Astafan, Marc A.	PA3250	39,61
Astrachan, Christina	ME0500	61
Astrachan, Christina	ME0200	61
Astrup, Margaret	CT0800	39,61
Atchison-Wood, Dawn	KY0450	61
Atchley, Elizabeth	OR0700	61,66C
Atherton, Peter L.	CA0960	61
Atkinson, Monte	CO0225	60,32C,36,61,66A
Atteberry, Ron	MO0100	10F,36,61,10A
Attrot, Ingrid	AB0210	61
Atwood, Julie	TX2800	61
Aubrey, Julia	MS0700	39,61
Auer, Shelley	TX0075	61,11
Auerbach, Elise M.	PA3250	61
Aultman, Carol	TX2600	61
Austin, Debra	IL1150	61
Austin, Linda B.	AR0750	61
Austin, Linda	AR0350	61
Austin, Melissa	TN0100	61
Austin, Stephanie	CA1450	36,61,66,40,32
Austin, Stephen F.	TX3420	61
Avery, Elizabeth	OK1350	61,31
Avery, Lawrence	NY1860	61
Avitabile, Judy	NY3450	61
Avrett, Martha	OK0700	61
Axtell, Les	TX3050	66A,61
Ayau, Joel T.	VA1350	61
Aye, Jeremy K.	NY2750	61
Azzati, Eduardo	PA2450	61,31A
Babcock, Jonathan	TX3175	36,61,32D
Babidge, Darrell	UT0050	61
Baccus, H. E.	IL0720	61
Bach, Larry	MN1250	60,36,61
Backus, Carolyn A.	TX0300	61
Bacon, Boyd	NE0450	13,36,61,40
Bade, Lori E.	LA0200	61
Baer-Peterson, Jamie	NJ0760	61
Baerg, Theodore	AG0500	39,61
Baggech, Melody A.	OK0300	61,40,39
Baglio, Genevieve	WA1300	61
Bailey, Brian K.	OH0650	36,61
Bailey, Marie	IL1850	61
Baird, Dianne	AG0250	61
Baird, Julianne C.	NJ1100	12A,12C,40,61,67E
Baird, Thomas	NY3785	61
Bak, Edward	OH1850	61
Baker, Alan	PA0250	60A,11,36,61,54
Baker, Guy O.	WV0650	60,36,61
Baker, Kevin L.	MO0300	36,32D,61,60,32
Baker, Mark	FL0150	61
Baker, Mark	WI1150	61
Baker, Mark A.	OH0350	61,39,54
Baker, R. Bryan	CA1250	60A,61,36
Baker, Robert P.	DC0100	61
Baker, Ruth	GA0300	11,61
Baker, Sharon	NH0350	61
Baker, Sonya G.	KY0950	61
Baker, Wade	OR1100	61
Baker, Wade	OR1300	61,32D
Balach, Nancy Maria	MS0700	61
Baldwin, Catherine	PA3400	61
Baldwin, Nathan Taylor	WV0200	66C,61
Balensuela, Peggy	IN0800	61
Bales, Bruce	CA2050	40,61,67,13A,36
Balic, Adriana	CA5300	61
Balke, Maureen	MI0100	13C,39,61
Ball, Sheridan J.	CA1520	36,41,61,13A
Ballard, Jeffrey D.	IN0100	61
Ballard, Timothy Marshall	MD0300	61
Ballerino, John	CA5060	61,66C
Balmaceda, Kelly	GA0950	61
Balmer, Patricia	TX3600	61
Balson, Donna C.	NY1600	61
Balthrop, Carmen A.	MD1010	61,39
Bambrick, Heather	AG0450	61,29
Bandermann, Billie	CA1550	61,36
Banion, Brian	OH0350	61
Banister, Linda	GA0250	11,39,61
Banister, Suzanne	AR0350	61
Banks, Richard	NC1600	39,61,60A
Bankston, David	SC0420	61,39
Bara, Edward	PA2550	61
Barasch, Shirley R.	PA2900	61,32,54,10,35E
Barasorda, Antonio	PR0115	61,39
Barba, Kathy	CA1850	61
Barber, Charles	TN1250	61,66A
Barber, Julie	IN1560	66A,61,40,12A
Barber, June	CA0300	13A,13,61
Barber, Kimberly	AG0600	61
Barber-McCurdy, Sarah	CO0400	61
Barcellona, Mary Anne	MD0060	61
Barclay, Martin	IL0100	61
Barclay, Martin	IA0930	61
Barcza, Peter	AB0100	61
Bardill, Sara	CO0900	61
Barefield, Robert C.	CT0650	61
Baresel, Thomas	OH2200	61
Barish, Sheila	FL1300	61
Barksdale, Lisa Browne	SC0750	61
Barlow-Ware, Jackie	OH0350	61
Barnard, Monty	SD0050	61
Barnard, Rachel	OK0750	61
Barnes, Michael	OR0500	61
Barnes, Peter	AG0450	61
Barnes, Sebronette	PA0675	61
Barnett, Janie	MA0260	61
Barney, Kara	UT0325	61
Barnlund, Anna	IL2300	61
Baroni, Melissa	MA0350	61
Barrett, Celeste	OK0825	61
Barrett, Korey J.	IA1600	61,66C
Barrett, Marianne	NY2250	61
Barrett, Marianne	NY1900	61
Barrett, Richard	NY0500	39,61,60
Barrett, Richard	NY2250	61
Barrett, Wayne	TX2250	61,31
Barrientos, Paul	NM0350	11,36,61
Barsamian, Aram V.	CA3500	61
Barsamian, Aram	CA2420	61,39
Bart, Sean	CA3270	61
Bartlett, Jacob Kenneth	NE0500	36,61,11

Index by Area of Teaching Interest

Name	Code	Areas
Barto, Betsy	CO0275	61,42
Barton, Peter A.	SC1110	61
Barton, Stephen	MI0850	36,40,11,12A,61
Bartz, Martha	NC0350	61
Bashar, Inci	MO1810	61
Basinski, Anne	MT0400	61,54,39
Basney, Nyela	TX3527	61,66,36,38,60
Bassett, Dennis	KS0300	61
Bassett, Jenny	FL0670	61,62
Bassett, Jon	FL0670	36,61,51,38,32D
Bastian, William	MN0450	39,61,11
Batchvarova, Madlen T.	IN0650	60A,36,61,66A,12A
Bates, Jennifer	ME0250	61
Bathurst, Pamela	ID0250	61
Battle, Detra	MD0700	61
Baty, Janna	CT0850	61
Batz, Nancy J.	IA0800	61
Bauer, David	NE0590	36,61,60A,32D
Bauer, Karen	IL2100	61
Bauer, Mary K.	NC2600	61
Baughman, Melissa	MO0100	61
Baum, Joshua	IL0150	61,11,39,12
Bauman, Clyde	ND0050	61
Bauman, Jeffrey Milo	GA2300	36,61,54,10F,60A
Baunoch, Joseph	PA1600	61,32D
Bausano, William	OH1450	60A,32C,36,61
Bavaar, Kathleen	DC0170	54,61
Baxter, Deborah	KS1450	61
Bayen, Diane	NY2450	13C,61,36,60,32
Bays, Jay	MI0350	66C,61
Bean, Matt	IL3500	61,54
Bearden-Carver, Julie	GA1800	61,54
Beasley, Kimberly	FL1000	61,54,39
Beasley, Pamela	VA1550	61
Beattie, Michael	MA0400	61
Beatty, Sarah	IL0730	61
Beaupre, Odette	AI0220	39,61
Beauregard, Jenny	MO0050	61
Beck, Barbara Geiser	CO0275	61,39,54,66C,42
Beck, Gina	MA0850	61
Beck, Lucy	CA3520	61
Becker, Jane	TX0350	61
Becker, Jeral Blaine	MO1250	61,36,11,60,39
Becker, Melinda	CA2801	36,61
Becker, Pam	MO1710	61
Becker-Billie, Elisa	IL1890	61
Beckley, Susan	PA0350	61
Beckwith, Sterling	AG0650	12,36,61,12F
Bedard, Elise	AG0200	61
Bedo, Maria	NJ0700	61
Bedsole, Betty	TN1660	61,31A,32
Beebe, Harriet	OH2550	39,61
Beer, Lucille	NY0700	61
Beer, Lucille	NY3600	61
Behrens, Jeffrey	NY2105	61
Belflower, Alisa	NE0600	61,54
Belich, Kay	WI0150	39,61,32B
Bell, Daniel	KY0650	61
Bell, Donald M.	AA0150	61
Bell, Jeff	IL2300	36,61,54,60
Bell, Lorriane	VA0500	11,61,35A
Bellah, Mary	CA0270	66D,61
Bellamy, Amy J.	NY0450	11,29A,36,61
Belles, David	CT0150	36,40,60,61
Bellini, Brigitte	TX3175	61
Belnap, Lila	HI0050	61
Belnap, Michael	HI0050	36,39,40,54,61
Beloncik, Anne	SD0550	61
Belov, Anton	MA1175	61
Bender, Dennis	KY1450	61
Bender, Judy	MN1260	61
Bender, Sharla A.	AL0345	11,61,66A
Bender, Susan Maria	WI0850	61,39,40
Benedict, Deborah	CA1650	61
Benedict, Deborah	CA5000	61
Bengochea, Sandra	CA5510	61,39,54
Benish, Serena Kanig	UT0325	61
Benjamin, Karen	CA4450	61
Benner, Emily	MI0100	61,39
Bennett, Bruce	TN0100	61
Bennett, Glenn	AZ0440	36,61
Bennett, Sharon K.	OH0350	61
Bennett, Vicki	AZ0440	61,36
Benson, Ann	SC0420	61,39
Benson, Lary	AA0020	61
Bentley, JoAnne	AG0450	61
Bentley, Julia	IL0750	61
Benton, Lisa	TN0580	32,61
Bentz, Anne Hagan	PA3650	61,39
Benz, David	MO0850	61,39,40
Benz, Terri	IL1650	61,66A,36
Berentsen, Kurt	OR0150	36,60,61,32A,40
Berg Oram, Stephanie	CO0625	11,12A,61,34B
Berg, Gregory	WI0250	11,61,39
Berg, Lynn	ID0050	61
Berg, Marla	OH0600	61
Berg, Marla	OH1100	61
Berger, Lisa	VA0450	61
Berger, Reverie Mott	GA1700	61,54
Bergstrom, Melissa	MN0040	36,40,12A,38,61
Berkolds, Paul	CA0510	61,39,40,12A,68
Berman, Gayle	MA0800	61
Bermejo-Greenspan, Mili	MA0260	61
Bernard, David	LA0650	61
Bernhardt, Ross C.	TX2930	36,61
Bernhardt, Valerie	NJ0800	61
Berry, Debbie	TX2700	61
Berry, James	WV0440	11,12,13,33,61
Berry, Richard A.	TX2700	61
Bers, Edith	NY0150	61
Bers, Edith	NY2150	61
Bers, Edith	NY1900	61
Besley, Megan C.	NY2750	61
Best, Michael	IL0550	61
Best, Richard W.	IL2900	39,61
Best, Robert L.	TX0300	61
Beudert, Mark	IN1700	61
Beutler, Marian	NE0050	61,66A
Bewley, Ho Eui Holly	NY3717	61
Bible, Kierstin Michelle	MO0260	36,61,12A,13A,54
Bickel, Jan	IL2650	39,61
Bickham, Teri	MD0850	61,39
Bickley, Ashlee Beth	IN0905	61
Bieber, Elizabeth	IA1800	61
Biernacki, Krzysztof K.	FL1950	61,39
Bierschenk, Jerome Michael	TX3250	36,37,32D,61,63A
Bigler, Nathan	AZ0150	61,66A
Billingsley, Monique Phinney	MA0350	61
Billington, Ryan	AF0150	36,40,29,61
Billington, Ryan	AF0120	61,29,36
Billions, Clifford	OH0600	61
Binek, Claire	PA3330	61
Binek, Justin	PA3330	61,47
Binger, Adlai	PA0050	36,61,66G,60A,66C
Bingham, Martina	HI0210	61
Bingig, Mariann	AG0600	61
Bird-Arvidsson, Jennifer	CO0800	61
Birdwell, Florence H.	OK0750	61
Birgfeld, Kelly	NY4500	61
Birnbaum, Mary	NY1900	61
Birnbaum, Melanie	NY1275	61
Birt, Timothy	TX2260	61
Biscay, Karen T.	OH1330	13,11,12A,36,61
Bisesi, Gayle	IL0850	47,61
Bishop, Bruce W.	AZ0300	34,36,61,13,60A
Bishop, Julie	PA3250	29,61
Bishop, Roberta	RI0250	61
Bitzas, Penelope	MA0400	61
Bizinkauskas, Maryte	MA0510	61,11
Bjerke, Sophie	NY3775	61
Black, Cassandra	TX1450	61
Black, Kathryn A.	NY3475	61,36,40
Black, Randall	KY0950	61
Black, Susan	AG0650	66C,61,60A
Blackburn, Royce F.	ND0500	61,54,39
Blackshear, Glinda	AL0831	60,11,36,39,61
Blackwood, Jeremy	OK1150	61,39
Blaisdell, Gayla Bauer	WA0050	61,39
Blaisdell, Tor	WA0050	61
Blake, Joey	MA0260	61
Blake-Oliver, Tiffany Erin	CO0250	61
Blalock, Angela	SC0150	11,13A,13B,40,61
Blanc, Pamela	CA0960	61
Blanchard, Gerald J.	MI1160	11,36,13,60A,61
Bland, Barbara	MI1750	61
Blankenbaker, Scott E.	MN1290	11,13,61,36
Blankenship, Carole	TN1200	11,61
Blanner, Christine Fortner	IA0550	61
Blaser, Lynn	AG0450	61
Bleckman, Theo	NY2150	29,61
Bletstein, Bev R.	OH1860	11,32,61,70
Blizzard, John T.	NC2650	61
Blodget, Sherril	VT0100	40,36,60,61,11
Blois, Scott	CA3300	61
Blomquist, Jane K.	CA2600	36,61,13
Blooding, Randie	NY1800	61
Bloomfield, Tara	UT0050	61
Blosser, C. Andrew	OH1850	61
Blosser, Dan C.	IN1650	61
Boaz, Virginia Lile	TX0600	12,61,39,12A
Bobak, Jacqueline	CA0510	12,42,61,32G
Boddicker, Maureen	WY0200	61
Boddie, Susan	AF0120	61
Bode, Robert	MO1810	60A,36,61
Bodnar, Marian	CA0825	61
Boehm, Patricia A.	OH2290	61,32,11
Boelling, John F.	OR1100	61
Boelling, John	OR1300	61
Bogdan, Thomas	VT0050	36,61,31,40
Bogle, Stephanie	AG0650	61
Bogle, Stephanie	AG0300	61
Bohannon, Kenneth	OK1400	39,61,35A
Boianova, Linda	NY2650	66A,13C,61,39,66C
Boire, Paula L.	KS0350	61,20F
Bokhout, William	MI0850	61
Boky, Colette	AI0210	61
Bolden-Taylor, Diane	CO0950	61
Boldrey, Richard L.	IL2250	61
Bolling-May, Joan	DC0010	61
Bolling-May, Joan	VA1400	61
Bollinger, Bernard	CA1000	36,61,54
Bolster, Stephen C.	KY0300	60,32D,36,40,61
Bolton, Bryan	KY0050	11,13A,32,36,61
Bolton, Thomas W.	KY1200	61,31A,36,12A
Bolton, Tom	AR0500	61
Bolves, Keith	FL1550	61
Bomgardner, Stephen D.	MO0350	61,39,12A,11
Bonacci, Mary Brown	MA2100	61,11,13A
Bonazzi, Elaine	NY3790	61
Bond, Lawrence	TN0100	61
Bond, Mona	LA0300	61
Bonds, Samuel	VA0450	61
Bone, Amber Sudduth	WA1250	61
Bonin, Brian P.	GA0750	61
Boocock, William	CA0250	61
Book, Andee	MO1710	61
Boos, Kenneth G.	FL1310	13,60,36,41,61
Booth, John D.	MO0500	12,44,61,31A,70
Booth, Nancy Davis	AZ0480	61,54
Boothe, Randall W.	UT0050	61,54,20G,35
Boothman, Donald	MA0650	61
Boothroyd, David	AB0100	61
Boozer, John E.	NC2350	60,20,36,31,61
Bordas, Ricard	SC0275	36,61
Borders, Ann	IL1750	61
Borgia-Petro, Diana	PA1550	61
Borton, Bruce E.	NY3705	60,36,61
Boskovich, Elizabeth	OH2050	61
Bosscher, Scott	MI0850	61,13C
Bostic-Brown, Tiffany	AL1250	39,61,54,13A
Boswell, Michael	IN1400	39,61,12A
Bou, Emmy	NE0150	66A,61
Boudette, Jennifer	FL1430	61
Bouffard, Sophie	AJ0100	12A,61,11,13C
Boukas, Richard A.	NY2660	61,70,20H,47
Bouknight, Tara	VA1125	61
Bouknight, Tara	VA0750	61
Boullion, Linda	NE0460	13,11,40,36,61
Bounous, Barry	UT0050	61
Bounous, Debra	UT0050	61
Bouras-Recktenwald, Christina	KY0250	61
Bourne, Thaddeus	CT0600	61
Bouterse, Ami K.	WI0835	61,39
Boutte, Tony L.	FL1900	61,39
Bovbjorg-Neidung, Helen	FL0500	61
Bowie, Audrey	TN1400	61
Bowles, DeVera	ND0250	61,39
Bowles, Douglas	DC0050	61
Bowles, Douglas	DC0010	61
Bowles, Kenneth E.	ND0250	36,61,39,60,32C
Bowles, Suzanne	TX3300	61
Bowles, Virginia B.	KY0150	61
Bowles, Virginia	KY0100	61
Bowling, Jeanne	IN1100	61
Boyer, Allen	CA3000	13A,47,61,20G
Boyer, D. Royce	AL1160	11,12A,36,61,31A

625

Name	Code	Areas
Boyle, Holly	TX3300	61
Bozeman, Joanne H.	WI0350	61
Bozeman, Kenneth W.	WI0350	61
Braamse, Shudong	FL1740	61,13C
Bracey, Robert D.	NC2430	61
Bracken, Patricia	KY0100	61
Bracken, Patricia	KY0150	61
Bradley, Gwendolyn	NY2900	61
Bradley, Mark	KY0400	12C,32G,36,39,61
Brady-Riley, Carolyn	IL2650	39,61
Branch, Stephen F.	CA3975	12A,61,31A,36,40
Brandenburg, Julie A.	WI0450	10D,36,61,66D
Brandes, Christine	CA4150	61
Brandes, Christine	CA5000	61
Brandes, Christine	CA4200	11,13C,32D,39,61
Brandt, Robert	DE0150	61,39
Braun, Mel	AC0100	39,61
Braun, Sharon	AA0080	61
Brautigam, Keith D.	IN1025	61,39
Bravo, Fabiana	DC0050	61,12A
Bray, Michael R.	PA3260	60,61,11,36,12A
Breault, Robert	UT0250	39,61
Brecher, Benjamin	CA5060	61,39
Brendel, Cheryl M.	TN0850	61,39
Brendel, Ronald S.	TN0850	61,39
Brendel, Wolfgang	IN0900	61
Brennan-Hondorp, Jennifer J.	KY1550	61
Brett, Kathleen	AB0210	61
Brewer, Bert R.	MT0450	36,61
Brewer, Mary Kathryn	IN0100	61
Brewer, Mary Kathryn	IN1560	61
Briante, Kate	MD0060	39,61
Brich, Jeffrey	IA1600	61
Briggs, John	AR0500	61
Briggs, Margery S.	CA3650	13,61
Briggs, Philip	TX2050	36,40,61,11
Briggs, Robert	UT0150	36,61,12A,60A
Brightbill, Alvin	CA1425	61
Brightbill, Alvin	CA0815	61
Briley, Crystal	TN1100	61
Brinegar, Don	CA5300	61
Brinegar, Donald L.	CA3500	13A,36,61,60
Brink, Ann	CO0200	61
Briones, Marella	MO0650	61,11,36,32B,39
Brisbon, Perry	PA0450	61
Brister Rachwal, Wanda	FL0850	61,31A
Britton, David	AZ0100	61
Broadbent, Michelle	ID0060	61
Brock, Andrew	OR0950	13A,61
Brock, David	TX3000	61
Brockington, Frances N.	MI2200	61,39
Broman, John M.	GA1500	36,40,61
Bronner, Eric	RI0250	61
Brookens, Karen	UT0350	61,39
Brooks, Bonnie	CA4700	61
Brooks, C. Thomas	MA0950	60A,36,40,61
Brooks, Jack	TX1510	36,61,40,13C
Brooks, Margaret	VA1350	61
Brooks, Susan G.	MA0950	13,39,61
Brothers, Grey	CA5550	13,36,61,11,12A
Brou, Melinda A.	TX2960	61,39,54,13C
Broughton, Gregory	GA2100	36,61
Brouwer, Kristin	FL1450	61
Brovey-Kovach, Lisa	PA2900	61
Brower, Kevin	ID0060	36,61,32D
Brown, Bruce C.	NY1700	60,11,36,61,31A
Brown, Charlene	AA0110	61,32A
Brown, Charles	NY0270	36,61
Brown, Cristy Lynn	NC2205	61,15,54
Brown, Don	NY2500	61
Brown, Donald G.	AB0100	61
Brown, Donna	AG0400	61
Brown, Eileen Duffy	FL1300	39,61,54
Brown, J. F. Mark	AL0831	61,35,36,11
Brown, James L.	WA0650	61,39
Brown, Janet	NY1350	61
Brown, Janet E.	NY4150	61
Brown, Jeri	AI0070	36,47,61,29
Brown, Kathryn	OH0600	61,66A
Brown, Kathy	MO1550	32B,61
Brown, Kimberly	TX3650	61
Brown, Linda	CA3750	36,40,61
Brown, Linda Noble	CA1150	61
Brown, Melba	AL1195	32,61,11,39
Brown, Michael	IL3100	61
Brown, Nina	PA3710	61
Brown, Samuel B.	AL0500	39,61,31A
Brown, Sharon L.	IN1010	61
Brown, Sharon	MA0260	61
Brown, Susan Tara	CA1900	61
Brown, Terrance D.	AL1250	39,54,61
Brown, Uzee	GA1450	13,10,61,11
Brown-Kibble, Gennevieve	TN1350	11,36,60A,61
Browne, Douglas A.	PA1450	13C,60A,36,61
Broxholm, Julia A.	KS1350	61
Brubaker, Debra	IN0550	39,61,36,31A,20
Bruggeman-Kurp, Jeanne	OH0300	61
Brundage, Cynthian	MI2000	61
Brundage, Laura	SC0200	61
Brunner, Peggy G.	TX3175	61
Brunson, Tomas	SC0600	31,61
Brunssen, Karen	IL2250	61
Bruss, Jillian	WI0835	61
Bryan, Alan	MN1625	11,39,61,54
Bryant, Edward	FL1740	13C,36,61,39,40
Bryant, Jennifer	AL0300	61
Bryant, Jordan	TX3530	61
Bryant, Roger	TX2955	61
Bryant, Stephen	NJ1400	60,36,61
Bryden, Jane G.	MA1750	61
Bryn-Julson, Phyllis	MD0650	61
Bryson, Amity H.	MO0050	36,61,60A,15,32D
Buchanan, Marlette	WA0650	61
Buchanan, Mary Lenn	MS0250	39,61
Buck, Barbara	KY0750	32A,32B,32C,32D,61
Buck, Kristina	AR0200	61
Buck, Robin T.	CA5020	39,61
Buckley, Wendell	MN0600	61
Budlong, Trisha	PA2450	39,61,32
Budway, Maureen	PA1050	61
Buffington, Blair	IA1750	61,36,40,32A,60A
Buglio, Patricia L.	IL0650	61
Buglio, Patricia L.	IL0840	61
Buhaiciuc, Mihaela	AL1195	39,13,61
Buhite, Michelle	NY1850	61
Bulat, Therese Marie	CA3460	61
Bulger, Mary	MA0950	61
Bulli, Marilyn	MA0350	61
Bullock, Emily A.	PA3600	61,39
Bultema, Darci A.	SD0400	11,61,39
Bumbach, Matthew	FL0365	66A,61
Bumgardner, James	NC0910	61
Bunnell, Jane E.	IL0750	61
Burbach, Brock	FL0200	36,61,40
Burbank, Judith	NC1100	61
Burcham, Joel	CO0800	61
Burchinal, Frederick	GA2100	39,61
Burdette, Joy	KY1000	61
Burdick, Barbara E.	MI0150	61
Burgess, Mary	NY3705	39,61
Burgoyne, Carolyn	CA5353	61
Burke, D'Walla Simmons	NC2700	60A,36,61
Burke, Karen M.	AG0650	61,60A,36,32
Burke, Leon	MO1250	61
Burkot, Louis G.	NH0100	36,61,39
Burks, Jo Lynn	TN0100	61,54
Burnakus, David	CA4700	61
Burnett, Lawrence E.	MN0300	36,40,31F,61,13A
Burns, Jim	TN0850	11,61,31A
Burns, Judeth Shay	CO0200	61
Burns, Pamela T.	AL0050	11,32,61
Burns, Patricia Donahue	PA1050	61
Burns, Susan M.	CA0630	13A,11,39,61,54
Burrichter, Ronald	FL1850	36,61
Burrowes, Norma	AG0650	61
Burrs, Lisa Edwards	VA1750	11,13A,36,61
Burton, Amy	NY2250	61
Burton, Sean Michael	IA0100	36,61,41,11,13D
Busarow, Jonathan	IN0905	61
Busch, Gregg	MO0200	11,13A,31A,36,61
Busching, Marianna	MD0650	61
Buschmeyer, Corrinne	AA0050	61
Bush, Abra K.	NY1100	61
Bush, Peter	OH0650	61
Busselberg, Paul	TX2295	61,36,13C
Busselberg, Rebecca Pyper	TX2295	61
Bussineau-King, D. E.	TX3410	61,15,39
Butler, Corey	AG0650	61
Butler, Kate S.	NE0600	61,39
Butterfield, Benjamin	AB0150	61,39
Bybee, Ariel	UT0250	61
Bybee, Luretta	MA1400	61
Bylsma, Kevin	OH0300	39,61
Bynum, Leroy E.	GA0150	12A,39,61
Byrne, Elizabeth	IL0750	61
Byun, Jin Hwan	NJ0700	61
Byun, John	CA3800	61,36,11
Bziukiewicz-Kulig, Brygida	WI0865	61
Cable, Jennifer A.	VA1500	11,61
Cabot, Jennifer C.	MD0850	61
Cabrera, Ricardo	PR0100	11,36,61,60,13A
Cain, Bruce A.	TX2650	39,61
Calabrese, Angela Libertella	NY1550	61
Calas, Tiffany	ID0050	61
Caldwell, J. Timothy	MI0400	61,32I
Caldwell, Philip	IL2750	61
Caldwell, William	OH0500	36,39,61,60
Calkins, Mark	KY0300	61,54
Calkins, Mark R.	KY1350	61
Callaway, Patricia	GA1200	61,12A,41
Calloway, Karen E.	GA2300	61,64A
Caluda, Cherie	CT0650	61
Cameron, Virginia	OH1600	60A,36,61,40,11
Camp, Dewey	CA4200	61
Camp, Laura	PA3250	61
Camp, Philip	TX1550	36,61,13,32,40
Campagna, Alison	TX3535	61
Campbell, Andy	MO1550	36,61,13C
Campbell, Betty	AL0550	61,13C
Campbell, Derek	DC0350	36,61
Campbell, Dianna	FL1700	61,36,40,11,32D
Campbell, Don	SC1080	13,60,36,61,12A
Campbell, Helen E.	AL0310	13A,13,36,61,66
Campbell, Jayne E.	CA1960	36,55,61,31A
Campbell, John W.	KY0610	60,11,32,61,36
Campbell, Sharon O'Connell	NE0590	61
Campbell, Stanford	OR0600	36,61,31A,60A
Campos, LeeAnne	WA0650	61
Cancio, Clint	CA3270	61
Cancio-Bello, Susan	NH0050	11,54,61,36,33
Cancryn, Dina	TN1100	61
Canfield, Nanette G.	OH0200	61
Cangelosi, Casey	WV0200	61,65,29,34
Canova, Diana	NY2200	61
Cansler, Joe Ella	TX3750	61
Canter, Jacqueline S.	NC0900	61
Canter, Jacqueline	NC0930	61
Cantu, Jacob	TX2200	61,39
Capaldo, Jennifer R.	VA0700	61,13C,12A
Capener, Debra A.	MN1625	61
Capezza, June	FL0200	61,13A,13B,13C
Caplan, Joan	NY2150	61
Caplan, Joel	NY1860	61
Capozzoli, Andrea	MA0260	61
Cappon, Ronald	NY2200	61
Carbaugh, Deborah	MN0800	61
Carberg, Daniel J.	IL1750	61,55B
Card, Catherine	CA1960	13A,61,11
Cardinal-Dolan, Michelle	KS0700	61
Carew, David	MI1985	36,61,40,32D,13C
Carey, Barbara	NM0300	61,66A
Carey, Larry	PA2300	61
Carey, Mary	NY2900	61
Carey, Matthew	AR0110	54,61
Cariaga, Marvellee	CA0825	61
Carlisle, Mark R.	IN0800	36,61
Carlson, Damon J.	WI0770	60A,61,40,36
Carlson, Maureen A.	MO1800	61
Carlson, Sharon	IL0720	61
Carlton, Kathleen	OK0410	13,11,12A,61,31A
Carney, Sandra L.	NJ1050	61
Carney, Sandy	PA3560	61
Carney, Timothy F.	HI0060	36,11,13A,54,61
Carnine, Albert J.	MO0800	11,61
Carr, Jennifer	TX3000	61
Carr, Julie Anne	MI2120	61,11
Carr, Karen	MA0260	61
Carrier, Lisa	DC0010	61
Carrier, Lisa	MD0550	61
Carswell, William	SC0450	31A,61,32,36,40
Carter, Brian	WA1150	61
Carter, Christina	FL1550	60A,61,11
Carter, Clarence	IL2900	39,61
Carter, Henrietta McKee	CA2050	11,61,13A
Carter, Jay	MO2000	55,61
Carter, Jeanne	SD0050	61

Index by Area of Teaching Interest

Name	Code	Areas
Carter, Jeffrey Richard	MO1950	60A,36,61,13A
Carter, John R.	CA1375	11,12A,36,61,13C
Carter, Joyce	IL2775	61
Carter, LisBeth	NC0750	61,39
Carter, Lisbeth	NC1300	61
Carter, Susan	MO0850	61,40,54,39
Carubia, Agatha	CA4410	61
Cary, Stephen	AL1170	61
Case, Elaine	AA0050	61
Casselle, Carol	FL1310	61
Castaldo, Kay	MI2100	61
Castilla, Kathy	MS0650	11,36,61
Castilla, Willenham	MS0350	36,31,32D,61
Castle, Joyce	KS1350	61
Castleberry, David	WV0400	60,12A,36,61
Caston, Ben	GA2050	36,60A,61
Caston, Ben	GA0400	44,61,31
Castonguay, David O.	VA1100	60,36,61
Castro, Margarita	PR0150	11,39,61
Cataldi, Diana M.	OH2500	61
Catania, Claudia	NJ1350	61
Cato, Ralph Wayne	CA5040	61
Catsalis, Marie-Louise	CA4900	61
Caudill, Nancy	AK0100	61
Cavendish, Thomas	FL0200	61
Caya, Patricia	ME0430	61
Cazier, David	WA0150	36,61,29A,40
Celaire, Jaunelle R.	AK0150	36,39,40,61
Celona-VanGorden, Julie	NC0750	61
Cencel, Elaine	AR0700	61
Cepeda, Iris	CA0830	61
Cereghino, Rosemarie	MO1950	61
Chafin, Robert	VA1700	13C,39,34,61
Chagnon, Richard	CA4050	11,12A,36,61
Chakrovorty, Sumita	CA0050	61
Chama, Eduardo	NJ1130	61
Chambers, James Alan	IN1050	61,13A,36
Chambers, Lynnette	TX0900	61
Chambers, Martin	CA4100	36,61
Chambers, Robert B.	TN0650	60,61,31A,36,44
Champagne, Salvatore C.	OH1700	61
Chandler, Chuck	GA1700	61
Chang, Donathan	TX2570	31A,31B,61,60A,36
Channing, Lynn	AJ0100	39,61
Chapman, Carol L.	MO0775	61
Character, William	GA2175	61,66A,70
Chase, Constance	CT0800	61
Chase, Jennie Kao	NY2400	61
Chase, Leah	LA0800	61
Chasteen, Terry L.	IL3500	61
Cheatham-Stricklin, Teresa	AL0500	13A,11,61,54
Chebra, Tracy Richards	NJ1350	61
Cheek, Timothy Mark	MI2100	66C,39,61
Chellis, Matthew W.	IL0550	61
Chen, Pei-Wen	NY2250	61
Chen, Xiaolun	FL1500	11,36,61
Chen-Maxham, Li-Chan	NJ1140	61
Cheney, Brian	OH2050	61
Chenez, Raymond	AL1170	61
Chernov, Vladimir	CA5030	61
Cherrington, Joseph	ID0060	61
Chesko, Elizabeth Unis	OH0650	61,39
Chiavola, Kathy	TN0100	61
Chickering, Ellen	ME0500	61
Chien, Hsueh-Ching	CA3270	39,61
Chilcote, Kathryn S.	PA3600	39,61
Childs, Kim J.	OK1450	36,40,61
Chiles, Torin W.	AG0500	61
Chipman, Michael	UT0400	61,39
Chipman, Paula	MD0300	61,13A,13C
Chisholm, Amy B.	OR1250	61
Chisholm, Rose Marie	TX3420	61
Cho, Grace	VA1350	61
Cho, Kyoung	FL2000	61
Cho, Philip Y.	PA3250	61
Cho, Soon	TX0300	61
Cho, Won	AL1150	61
Choi, In Dal	DC0050	61
Chookasian, Lili P.	CT0850	39,61
Chown, Andrew	PA3250	39,61
Christensen, Ruth M.	UT0050	61
Christensen, William Nield	OK0750	61
Christenson, Charlie	FL1750	61,12A,39,36
Christeson, Jane	FL0400	36,38,39,61
Christeson, Norton M.	MA0260	61
Christian, Armstead R.	NJ1350	61
Christiansen, Lindsey	OH1900	61,39
Christiansen, Philip	SC1110	39,61
Christie, Laury	CO0550	61
Christin, Judith	DC0050	61
Christman, Rick	DC0050	61,39
Christman, Sharon Lynn	PA2750	61,39
Christopher, Edward	MO1010	61
Christopher, Un Chong	MO1810	61
Christopher, Un Chong	ND0500	39,61
Christopherson, Anne	PA2550	61
Chu, Brian Ming	NJ1050	61
Chu, Brian	MN0800	13,36,61
Chu, George	KS0200	61,39
Chun, Soyoun Lim	NY3560	13A,13,39,61,13C
Chung, Suna	TX1100	61,39
Church, Celeste	TX1100	61,39
Church, Gregory E.	NY1100	61
Ciesinski, Katherine	MA0260	61
Cifelli, Kristin	NY2150	61
Cilliers, Jeanne-Minette	CT0600	61
Cimino, Matthew	CT0450	61
Cimino, Matthew	NY0280	13A,13,10,36,61
Cipullo, Tom	IL0550	61
Clarey, Cynthia	CA3350	61
Clark, Charles C.	MO0800	36,61,54
Clark, Charles 'Bud'	MA0950	61
Clark, Heidi	NC0650	61
Clark, John Charles	LA0770	39,54,61,11
Clark, Mark Ross	ID0075	40,61
Clark, Serena Jenkins	AG0200	61
Classen, Lita	NY3705	61,39
Clatworthy, David	IA0910	36,61
Clausen, Arla	KY1450	61
Clay, Angelique	MA1100	61
Clay, Sarah	IN0800	61
Claybrook, Kara	TX3400	61
Clayton, Cynthia	TX3415	61
Clement, Lisa	GA1050	61
Clement, Richard	AL0345	32D,36,60A,40,61
Clements, Allen	AR0200	61
Clements, Barbara	AR0200	61,39,13C
Clements, Jon		

Name	Code	Areas
Cleveland, Mark	MA2030	61
Cline, Everett Eugene	ID0250	61,66
Cline, Judith A.	VA0550	39,61,54,20G,11
Cline, Lonnie	OR0050	60,36,61
Clinefelter, Molly	MN0750	61
Cloeter, Chelsea	OH0300	61
Close, Shirley J.	FL0850	61
Cloud, Judith	AZ0450	61
Clousing, Harold	CA0250	61,36
Cluthe, Betty	NJ0200	61
Coale, Laura	OK0700	61
Coates, Atina	ID0060	36,61
Cobb, Cheryl	MA1350	61
Cobb, Joyce	TN1680	61
Cobbs, Jerry	AL0330	61,36,11
Coburn, Pamela	IN0350	61
Cochrane, Amy L.	NY2650	61
Cochrane, Jan	TN1350	61
Cock, Christopher M.	IN1750	60,36,61
Cock, Maura	IN1750	61,60A
Cockerham, Barbara	LA0150	61
Cody, Michael	MT0400	36,61,54,39,60A
Coe, Judith A.	CO0830	61,10D,34,14C,12C
Coefield, Carolyn	MT0350	61
Cofer, Angela F.	TX2600	61
Cogen, Ellen	MA1100	61,40,36,13A,54
Cohen, Nicki S.	TX3300	61,33,20
Cohn, Sanford	CT0650	61
Coker, Cheryl W.	MS0385	15,61
Coldiron, Jack	TX0300	61
Cole, Darlyn	NC1950	61,66D,60A,11,13
Cole, Kathryn	MO0400	61,13A,13C
Cole, Victoria	NH0250	61
Cole, Vinson	MO1810	61
Cole, Vinson	OH0600	61
Coleman, Barrington	IL3300	36,61
Coleman, Earl	GA0550	61,13C
Coleman, Edryn J.	PA2000	61,36,60A,13B
Coleman, Jennifer	TN0100	61
Coleman, William Dwight	GA1050	61,39
Coleman-Evans, Felicia	IL2100	61,40
Colenbrander, Caroline	AG0200	61
Coles, Marilyn J.	IL0800	61
Collett, Jacqueline L.	MO1780	32,36,61,39
Collier, Joanne	AA0040	36,61
Collins, Allison	CA0900	61,13C
Collins, Cherie	ND0250	61,36,32D,64B
Collins, David	NM0400	61
Collins, David	MN1250	31A,61,36,46
Collins, Kimberly	MN0620	61
Collister, Phillip	MD0850	61,36,39
Coloton, Diane S.	IL2900	61,39
Colton, Kendra	OH1700	61
Colwitz, Erin E.	AL1160	32B,61,60A,36,32C
Combs, Barry	SC0950	60,36,61,31A
Combs, Ronald	IN0005	61,13
Combs, Ronald	IL2150	39,61
Compson, Christy	TX1000	61
Condacse, Anne Marie	OK0800	61,39
Condran, Dena	PA3250	33,61
Condy, Steven	PA2800	61,39
Cone, Kimberly	GA0550	61
Conklin-Bishop, Lisa	TN0050	61,39
Conley, Mark	RI0300	13,60,36,61,32D
Conner, Stacey	PA0600	36,39,61
Connolly, Donna	NJ0825	39,40,54,61
Connolly, Martha	VA0250	61
Connolly, Michael E.	OR1100	36,12A,10A,61,13
Connors, David	CA0830	32B,32C,61
Conoly, Shaaron	TX3100	12A,39,61,54
Conrad, Robert	CA4625	13,11,12A,61
Converse, Sheila K.	WA1150	61,15
Cook, Carla	PA3250	29,61
Cook, Catherine	CA4150	61
Cook, Edward	WA1250	61
Cook, Jenni	NH0350	61,11
Cook, Samuel	TX0050	61,39
Cooke, Julia	MD0850	61
Cooke, Julia	MD0600	61
Cooper, Barbara	NY4460	61
Cooper, Britt	OH2370	11,12A,14C,36,61
Cooper, Gloria A.	NY2102	13A,61,32C,36,47
Cooper, Jennifer Goode	OH0300	61
Cooper, Jessica	MA2010	39,61
Cooper, Sean	OH0300	61
Copeland, Louise	PA1350	36,61
Copeland, Rachel	NC0650	61
Corbin, Barbara	TX2250	61
Corbin, Lynn Ann	GA2150	32,61,60A
Corbin, Patricia	AL0500	60A,32D,61,55D,60
Corcoran, Kathleen	AA0110	12A,61,39
Cordes, Jamie	OH0350	61,47
Corley, Sheila	AZ0400	32C,36,39,61
Cornelius, Polly Butler	NC0750	61
Cornett, Stanley O.	MD0650	61
Cornish, John	OK0150	36,39,60A,61,13B
Corpus, Edward	IA0550	61
Corrie, John H.	ME0150	13C,36,61,66G,66H
Corrigan, Ann	OH0300	61
Corron, Patricia J.	NY3725	61
Cosgrove, Julia	MI1050	61
Cossa, Dominic	MD1010	39,61
Costigan-Kerns, Louise	CA3270	39,61,66C
Cotroneo, Sue	NY2650	61
Cotte, William	VT0300	11,13H,36,61,66
Cotten, William	MA1400	61
Cotten, William	MA0350	61
Cotton, Maurice	WI1150	61,66A
Cotton, Patricia	AG0170	61
Cotton, Sandra M.	NC0600	61
Cottrill, Heather	WV0050	61,32A,32B
Cottrill, Lara Lynn	PA3580	61
Cottrill-Nelson, Lara Lynn	PA2950	61
Coulter, Beverly	FL0050	61
Council, Thomas	GA2000	31A,61,36,60,40
Cowan, Elizabeth	MI2250	61
Cowan, Kathryn Jean	IL2150	61,11
Cowan, Linda	WV0600	61
Cowan, Richard D.	PA0550	61
Cowdrick, Kathryn	NY1100	61
Cowgill, Jennifer Griffith	PA2200	61
Cox, Amanda K.	NY1700	61
Cox, Donna	OK1350	61
Cox, Kenneth	CO0900	39,61,54
Cox, Michael	VA1580	36,61,32D,60A
Cox, Rachel	KY1350	61,36
Crabb, Amanda	UT0050	61
Craig, Patricia	CA4150	61

627

Index by Area of Teaching Interest

Name	Code	Areas
Craig, Patricia	MA1400	61
Crane, Teresa Ann	IL1500	66C,61,66,66A,11
Crannell, Wayne T.	TX0250	36,61,11,39,60
Cravero, Ann	IA0550	39,61
Crawford, Leneida	MD0850	61,39
Crawford, Stephen L.	AZ0490	61
Crayton, Mark	IL0550	61,36
Creswell, Bradley	IA1750	61,60A
Creswell, Mary	IA0850	61,39
Crews, Ruth	TX3525	61,11
Criddle, Reed	UT0325	36,61
Crimm, William	TN1400	61
Crippin, Glee	IA1200	61,60A
Crockett, Alison	DC0100	61
Crockett-Hardin, Michelle	OH0500	61
Croft, Richard	TX3420	61
Cromer, Lilianne	CA4425	61
Cron, Nancy	KY1550	61
Crosby, Luanne M.	NY0100	11,36,61,54
Croskery, Virginia	IA1350	61,20
Cross, Alan E.	TN0150	11,12A,61,31A
Cross, Julie A.	WI0865	61
Cross, Richard	CT0850	39,61
Cross, Sandra	IL2750	32A,61
Crothers-Marley, Shirley Evans	OH2100	12A,32,36,61
Crouse, Courtney	OK0750	61
Crouse, David L.	AR0600	66A,13C,61,66G,13B
Crowe, Nancy	WA1200	61
Croy, Elizabeth	MT0200	61
Crum, Dorothy E.	KS1450	61
Crumley, Terri L.	IA0200	61
Cuccaro-Penhorwood, Costanza	IN0900	61
Culpepper, Jacquelyn	NC0550	39,61
Cultice, Thomas	NY2250	61
Cultice, Thomas	NY0500	61
Culver, Carrie	OH0700	61,39
Culver, Timothy	OH1100	61
Cumberledge, Melinda	IN1010	61,39
Cummings, Grace	NY3350	32B,36,61,32C,32D
Cunha, Stephanie	CA4425	61
Cunningham, Richard	AG0200	40,61
Curnow, Lauren	PA2550	61
Cusack, Margaret	NJ1350	61
Cushing, Diane	MA0200	61
Cushing, Diane	NH0150	36,61,54,11
Cutsforth-Huber, Bonnie	PA2710	61,36
Cuttino, Walter E.	SC1110	39,61
Czarnota, Benjamin D.	OH0200	61
Daane, Maggie	OR0250	61
Dacus, Edward	MS0400	12A,61
Dacus, Viola	MS0400	61
Dahl, Tracy	AC0100	61
Dahlen, Sienna	AG0450	61
Dahlin, Christina	CA0960	61
Dahlke, Steven	CA1900	61
Dahlke, Steven	NY3250	11,13,36,60A,61
Dahman, Jamie	IL1850	61
Dahman, Jamie	MI2120	61
Daigle, Steven	NY1100	61,39
Dale, Karen M.	TN0300	11,34B,36,54,61
Dalio, Marc G.	NJ0825	54,61
Dalton, Deborah	TX2700	61
Dalton, Martha	IL2300	36,61
Dalton, Sharon	WY0060	13,44,61,66
Damaris, Christa	NY3000	36,61,66D
Dana, Julie R.	CA1850	36,61,11
Dangi, Suparna	CA5000	61
Daniecki, John B.	SC1100	61
Daniel, Margaret H.	LA0760	61
Daniel, Robert	OK0550	13A,60,11,61,13C
Daniel-Cox, Minnita D.	OH2250	61,39
Daniels, Frances	IL1750	61
Daniels, Jerry L.	IL0800	61
Daniels, Matthew	FL0950	61
Daniels, Sharon	MA0400	61
Danne, Terry	CA2700	36,61
Danton, Jean	MA0800	61
Dantzler, Alta	MI1750	61
Dantzler, Drake M.	MI1750	61,39
Daoust, Julie	AI0200	61
Darling, Sandra	NJ0800	61
Darnell, Debra Jean	FL0680	61,11,39
Daroca, Daniel	FL0050	66C,61
Darr, Steven L.	FL2130	60,32,36,61
Daughtrey, Sarah E.	PA1250	61,11
Dauphinais, Kristin E.	AZ0500	61
Daverso, Denise	WA0650	61
Davidsen, Nancy Jo	NY3650	61
Davidson, Heidi	WA0750	61,66A,11,13A
Davies, Thomas H.	CA0600	13,60,36,61
Davis, Cara	WI0806	36,61,29A,11
Davis, Charlotte	TX2700	61
Davis, Clarissa	MS0300	11,61
Davis, Colleen	IN0800	61
Davis, Diane	ID0075	61,66A
Davis, Duane Shields	MI2250	29,61
Davis, Eileen	OH1850	61
Davis, Eillen	OH0350	61
Davis, Erica	CA0835	61
Davis, Gene	AL0450	61,36,13C
Davis, Gladys	NC0220	66D,61
Davis, Hal	NC2435	61,54
Davis, Jason	AF0120	61
Davis, Kimberley M.	MS0750	61
Davis, Lisa A.	GA1000	61
Davis, Morgan	FL1550	61
Davis, Ollie Watts	IL3300	61,36
Davis, Richard	WI0815	39,61
Davis, Richard A.	WV0500	13,60,12A,36,61
Davis, Vincent	OH2500	61
Davis, Wendell R.	TX3525	61,11
Dawe, Brenda M.	NY0350	13C,61
Dawson, Andrea	ID0140	61
Dawson, Lisa	IN1025	61,39
Day, Angela	WV0600	61
Day, Mary	IA0100	41,61,67,31A,39
Day, Melanie	VA1600	39,61
Day, Susan	WI0840	61,39
De Dobay, Thomas	CA0950	11,12A,61,66D
De Jager, Ron	AJ0030	60A,36,52,61,32D
De La Garza, Rene	RI0300	39,41,61
De La Vega, Anne M.	CA3500	61,54,39
De Launay, Anne M.	MO1810	61,12A
De Ratmiroff, Marina	NC2440	61
De Vault, Christine	PA1150	61
Deal, Kerry	MA0350	61
DeAmbrose, Marci Malone	NE0200	61
Dean, Maria	CA0510	61
Dean, Michael	CA5030	61
Dearie, Megan	LA0800	61
Dearing, Kristi Jo	PA1600	61
Deaton, Tony	TN0850	61,39
DeBoer, Katharine	NV0100	39,61
DeBruyn, Michelle Murphy	GA0550	61
DeCandia, Arthur J.	MA0280	61
Dechaine, Nichole P.	CA4410	61
Dechaine, Nichole	CA5550	61
Decima, Terry	MA1400	61,66C
Declue, Gary L.	IL1245	12A,13A,11,61,36
DeCoro, Helena	CA1520	61,66A,11,12A,39
Decuir, Anthony	LA0300	61,33
Deeter, Alissa Walters	NC2420	61
DeForest, Eric P.	IN0500	61
DeHaan, John D.	MN1623	61
DeHaan, Pam	IA0500	61,64E
Dehning, Margaret	CA0960	36,61
DeJong, Brigid	CA0810	61
DeJong, Diane	MN1620	61
Del Santo, Jean	MN1623	61
DeLaurentis, Amber	VT0450	61
Delay, Jeffrey S.	IL0650	61
Dellal, Pamela	MA0350	61
Delmore, Jack	CO0225	36,39,61,54
DeLong, Noah	TN1150	36,35C,60A,61
Delore, Deanna	CA0100	61
Delos, Michael	WA0200	61,39
Delos, Michael	WA1000	61
Delp, Roy	FL0850	61
Delto, Clare	CA4850	61,40
DeMaio Caprilli, Barbara J.	OK1330	61,54,11
DeMarco, Sherrill	AA0020	61
Demaree, Rebekah	WI0840	61
Demaris, Mary Kay	MN1500	61,60A
DeMent, Melanie	DE0150	39,61
DeMichele, Anna	CA0859	36,61,13A,38,11
Demler, James R.	MA0400	61
DenBeste, LeaAnne	OR0050	61
Denbow, Anne	SC0650	61
Denham, Ellen Louise	IN0400	61
Denis, Kimberley	AA0050	61,35A,36
Denison, Maria Fenty	FL1900	61
Dennis, Susan	IL0850	54,61
Dennis, Susan	IL1085	61,54,40
Dennison, Jessica	GA0850	61,32D
Dent, Karl D.	TX3200	61
Derix, Amye	TX0850	61,13
DeRosa, Julia	MI1800	61,39,13C
DesChamps, Elise	OH0350	61
Desmarais, Gail	AI0200	61
Desmarais, Gail	AI0050	61
Desmond, Mary Ellen	PA3330	61
Dettbarn-Slaughter, Vivian Robles	OH2275	61,66A,11
Dettwiler, Peggy	PA2150	60,36,32C,61
Detweiler, Greg J.	KY0900	60,36,61,40
Detwiler, Gwen	OH2200	61
Deutsch, Jeff	IL0850	61
DeVenney, David P.	PA3600	36,39,60A,61
DeVilbiss, Gloria	IA1390	61,41,36
Devol, Luana	NV0050	61,39
DeVries, Anne	NE0250	61
Dewey, Cynthia	UT0300	61,54,39,13A
Di Fiore, Linda	TX3420	61
Di Ghent, Rita	AG0650	61
Diamond, Brad	FL2000	61
Diaz, Justino	PR0115	61
Diaz, Raymond	NY3785	61
Diaz, Rebekah	FL0700	61
Dibble, Benjamin	PA3250	61
DiCamillo, Matthew	NC0750	61
DiCello, Anthony J.	OH0150	36,61,66,31A,34
Dickson, Adrienne C.	NE0150	61
Dickson, Adrienne	NE0720	61
Didi, Rani	CA5000	61
Diebold, Becky	IA0750	61
Diekhoff, Bill	SC0700	61
Dietert, Dale	TX2400	61
Dietz, Diane	IL1600	61
Diggory, Edith	MI1750	61
Dill, Patrick	LA0550	39,61
Dillard, David A.	IL2900	61
Dillard, Pamela	GA1900	61
Dillard, Royzell L.	VA0500	36,61
Dillon, Rhonda	CA0859	61,11
Dillon, Rhonda	CA1750	36,61
Diltz, Judy	TX1700	61
Dilworth, Helen J.	CA1020	61,66D
Dimiziani, Sylvia	NY4320	61
Dimmock, Megan	MD0175	61
Dingler, Diane	OH1200	61
DiPalma, Maria	IA1350	12A,39,61
Dirksen, Dale B. H.	AJ0030	10,13,32,61,66
DiSimone, Lorraine	TN1710	61
Dismukes, Andrea J.	TN0850	61
Doan, Cheryl	AZ0400	61
Doan, Jerry D.	AZ0100	61
Dobbs, Linda M.	WV0400	39,61
Dobreff, Kevin J.	MI0850	20F,61,67C,55D,13C
Dockendorff, Catherine	AZ0470	61
Dodson, Lisa	MD0500	61
Dody, Teresa	WV0800	61
Dody, Teresa D.	WV0350	61,13C,13K,32B,32D
Doing, James	WI0815	61
Dolacky, Susan	WA0860	11,39,61,66D,54
Dolan, Anastasia	MA0260	61
Dolter, Gerald	TX3200	39,61,54
Domenic, Joe	PA3000	61
Domenici, Gianna	IL0420	39,61
Dominski-Sale, Christina	FL0800	61
Donaldson, Cynthia	NY1400	61
Donaldson, Kathryn	PA1350	36,61
Dondlinger, Lisa	CA3600	61
Donnell, Cynthia S.	VA1600	61
Donnell, Julie	IN0905	61
Donnelly, Molly	MD0550	36,61,42
Doo, Lina J.	HI0150	11,61,36,54,20
Dooley, Gail	IA1100	61
Dorchin, Susan	FL0650	61
Dorff, Carolyn	GA1150	61
Dornak, Alan W.	NY4500	61
Doss, Laura	AL0800	61
Doyle, Laurie	TX1550	61,11,40,54
Doyle, Robert	MI0100	61
Draayer, Suzanne Collier	MN1700	39,61,11
Drackley, Phyllis J.	PA1250	61
Drake, Joshua F.	PA1450	11,61
Drayton, Joanne	MI1100	61

Index by Area of Teaching Interest

Name	Code	Areas
Drayton, Keith	MI1100	13,11,36,32,61
Drazek, Jan B.	CO0225	61
Dresen, Steven	ID0060	61
Dresher, Mary Ann	UT0400	61
Dresher, Mary Ann	UT0250	61
Dressen, Dan F.	MN1450	61
Dressler, Jane	OH1100	12A,61
Drews, Richard	IL2250	39,61
Driedger-Klassen, Robyn	AB0200	61
Driskill, Kristina	CA0960	61
Droba, Romalee	MN1250	61,66A
Druck, Susan S.	MN0050	61
Drumm, Melissa Percy	WA0950	61,40
Dry, Marion	MA2050	61
Duchak, Roberta	IL0720	61
Ducharme, Michel	AI0190	39,61
Dudley, Anna C.	CA4200	61
Dudley, Sandra	TN0100	36,61,35B
Dueck, Jocelyn B.	NY2250	66C,66A,61
Dueker, Hollie	TN0050	11,61
Duensing, Dorothy	MI2200	61
Duensing, Jane	SC0620	61
Duesing, Dale L.	WI0350	61
Dufault, Jenny E.	MN1120	32B,39,61
Duffer, Rodger	CA3800	61,11
Dunbar, Pamela	SC0200	61
Dundas, Robert B.	FL0700	39,61
Dunn, Cherry W.	MS0550	61,39,15
Dunn, Kimberly	NC0200	61
Dunn, Mignon	NY2150	61
Dunn, Mignon	NY0500	61
Dunn, Susan L.	TX2150	61
Dunn, Susan	NC0600	61,39
Dunn-Prosser, Barbara	AG0500	61
Duplessis, Ginette	AG0450	61
Dupuy, Virginia	TX2400	61
Duran, Becca	WA0200	61
Durant, Doug	AZ0440	13,61
Duraski, Anne	GA1200	61
Durham, Gary	MA0400	61
Durham, Gary D.	MA0850	61
Durham-Lozaw, Susan	NC2350	13A,13B,13C,61
Durst, Mary	CA3500	61
Dusdieker, Carol E.	OH0950	61
Duvall, William	WI0825	39,61
Duykers, John	WA0200	61
Dvorak, Celeste	OK0700	61
Dwyer, Peggy	AG0550	61
Dyer, Barbara	CA1750	61
Dyer, Barbara J.	CA2800	,61
DyKema, Laurae	ND0100	61
Dykstra, Crisi	MI0750	61
Dykstra, Linda	MI1050	61
Dymit, Thomas E.	IL2050	61
Eade, Dominique	MA1400	61,53,47,29
Eads, Laura	AR0250	61
Eaglen, Jane	OH0200	61
Easterday, Janice	TX0100	61
Eaton, Wendy	NE0160	61
Eaton, Wendy	NE0610	61
Eaves-Smith, Margaret	MN1450	61
Ebbers, Daniel	CA5350	61
Eberhardt, Terry N.	MD0850	61
Eby, Kristen	IA1450	44,61,40,36,13
Eccles, Elizabeth	VA0500	32,61,66A
Eckard, Kevin L.	OK1330	39,61
Eckenroth, Karen	OH2050	39,61
Eckermann, Joan E.	OH2140	61,54
Eckert, Rosana C.	TX3420	47,61
Eckert, Stacy	IL2650	36,39,61
Eddins, Judy	FL1500	11,61
Eder, Kristen	MI0050	61
Edmonds, Johnnella	VA1750	60,32B,32C,36,61
Edmonds, Kristin	MO0700	61
Edwards, Darryl	AG0450	61
Edwards, Linda	NM0400	60,36,41,61,54
Edwards, Matthew C.	VA1350	61
Edwards, Patricia	CA0250	61
Edwards, Patti Yvonne	SC0420	61,32D
Edwards, Steven C.	LA0080	11,12,36,40,61
Egan, Kate	AK0100	61
Eggleston, Mary	VA0550	61
Ehly, Ewald	MO1810	60A,61,36
Eichelberger, K. V.	DC0150	61,54
Eikum, Carol L.	MN1280	61
Eikum, Rex	OH0300	61
Elder, Joshua Ian	CA4425	61
Eldridge, Peter	NY2150	61,29
Eley, Elem	NJ1350	61
Elias, Daniel	CA0150	61
Elizondo, Madeline	TX2260	61
Elkins, Christina	NC1550	61
Elledge, Nancy	TX3000	61
Ellingboe, Bradley	NM0450	36,61
Elliot, Mike	MO1650	61,54
Elliott, Lloyd R.	CA1300	38,61,42
Elliott, Paul	IN0900	61,67H,55
Ellis, Diana L.	TX1650	61,39,40
Ellis, Rochelle	NJ1350	61
Ellis, Thomas J.	SC0700	61
Ellison, Joan	OH0200	61
Ellison, Rachel	TN1150	61
Ellmore, Laurel	FL1700	61
Ellsworth-Smith, Pamela	MO1650	61,54
Elsbernd, Jerome	MN0610	61
Elser, Albert Christian	SC1000	61,12A,34D,39
Embree, Marc A.	IL0750	61,32B
Embretson, Deborah	MN1100	61,66D,11,20,66C
Emelio, Melanie	CA3600	40,61,39
Emerich, Kate	CO0900	61,40
Engelhart, Cecilia	CA5000	61
Engelhart, Robert	MI1600	39,61,36,11
Engelson, Thea	IA0050	61,66A
Engelson, Thea	IA1300	40,61,54
Engen, Helen	MN1450	61
England, Diane	CA4300	61
Engler, Kyle C.	MD0850	61
Engler, Kyle C.	MD0520	39,61,54
English, Horace	LA0050	61
English, Jonathan R.	NY4150	61
Enis, Paul	OK0350	13,36,37,61,63
Enman, Cora	MI0400	39,61
Enman, Thomas	MA1175	66C,12A,54,66A,61
Enslin, Laura A.	NY4150	61
Epley, Arnold	MO2000	60A,32C,36,61,40
Erickson, Lydia K.	MI1200	61
Erickson, Shirley	TX0910	11,13,36,61,66
Ernest, Lorraine K.	NJ0800	61
Errante, Valerie	WI0825	61,39
Eschen, Elizabeth D.	VA1150	61
Esham, Faith	NY2200	61
Esham, Faith L.	MA0250	61
Esham, Faith	NJ1350	61
Eshleman, Elizabeth	CA2950	61,13C
Esparza, Eric Peche	TX2250	36,61
Espinosa, Gabriel	IA0700	66A,47,61
Espinosa, Teresita	CA3150	11,12A,32,61,20G
Esquivel, Karen L.	OR1050	61,39
Estes, Nancy Bliss	CA3800	61
Estes, Richard A.	TX3000	39,61
Estes, Simon	IA0850	39,61
Etcheto, Sally A.	CA0805	11,36,61,54
Etter, David D.	KY1425	36,61,31A,60
Eubanks, Dawne	FL0450	61
Eubanks, Dawne	FL0930	61
Eustis, Lynn	MA0400	61
Evans, Chris	PA2740	36,40,61
Evans, David F.	NY3725	36,61
Evans, Glyn	AG0350	61
Evans, Harold	NJ1350	61
Evans, Joseph	TX3400	61
Evans, Laura	WV0760	61
Evans, Margarita	IL3550	61
Evans, Timothy	MA0900	40,66A,61
Everitt, Allison	FL1430	13,36,61,55
Everitt, Gena	MS0100	61
Evers, Brooke E.	WV0550	61
Evers, Brooke	DC0010	61
Eversole, Bridgid	VA1550	61
Ewing, Rosella	GA0600	12A,61
Fadell, Rebecca	GA1990	61
Fahnestock, Jeffrey	PA3150	61
Fahnestock, Jeffrey L.	PA1400	61
Fair, Carly	TN0580	61
Falcon, Ruth	NY2250	61
Falconbridge, Vaida	CA3250	61,13C
Falcone, Mary Lou	NY1900	61
Faltstrom, Gloria V.	HI0300	13A,11,66D,61,36
Fankhauser, James L.	AB0100	13,36,55,61
Faracco, Thomas	NJ1350	61
Farlow, William	WI0815	39,61
Farnsworth, Anne	CA5300	61,29
Farquharson, Linda J.	IL1200	39,61
Farr, Sarah	NE0200	61
Farr, Sarah	NE0150	61
Farrell, Brian	CA0825	61
Farrell, Jodi	CA5360	61
Farrell, Scott	WA0350	61,66,54
Faulkner, Julia	WI0815	61
Favazza, Kathleen	IL1740	61,20
Favazza, Kathleen	IL2970	61
Fawcett, Derek	IL0720	61
Fee, Constance	NY3350	61,39
Feener, Raymond	MO1810	61
Feiszli, James D.	SD0500	12A,36,55D,61
Feldmann, Linda	WI0750	61,39
Feldt, Alison	MN1450	61
Fenn, Shiloah	TN1600	61
Fennessy, Ann	WA1350	61
Ferguson, J. Scott	IL1200	60A,36,61
Ferguson, James W.	TN1100	62D,47,41,61
Ferland, Louise	AI0210	61
Fern, Terry L.	NC0850	11,39,61,54,69
Ferrante, Martina	MA0510	61
Ferrantelli, Sal	CA3050	13,36,61
Ferraro, Dolores	PA1550	61
Ferrell, Mark T.	KS1350	39,61,66C
Ferrill, Kyle	ID0250	61,40
Fett, Basil	OH2450	61,36
Feyer, Paul	CT0650	61,54
Field, Sandra T.	SC1100	61
Field, Tana	KY0950	61
Fife, Melissa	ID0060	61
Filliman, Timothy	IL1085	61
Fillmore, Molly	MI1400	61
Fincher, James	SC0710	11,61
Findlen, Kathryn	TX2650	61
Fingalson, Vicki	WI0860	61,39
Fink, Katherine Ann	IA1550	61
Fink, Tim J.	IL2900	39,61
Finlay, Gordon J.	MI2200	61
Finley, Carolyn Sue	MN0350	39,61
Finley, William	CT0300	61,31A
Finney, John W.	KY0700	13,12A,36,61,66A
Finnie, Mary	AR0750	61
Firestone, Adria	NJ0825	39,61
Firkus, Krista	GA1070	61
Fischbach, Tim C.	IL2730	61,66A,66G
Fischer, Jeanne	NC2410	61
Fiscus, Gary	IA0910	61
Fisher, Jocelyn	TN0100	61,35B
Fisher, Robin L.	CA0840	61
Fithian, Bruce S.	ME0500	39,12A,61
FitzPatrick, Carole	AZ0100	61
Fitzpatrick, Tim	WA1250	61
Fitzpatrick, Tod M.	NV0050	61,39
Flagg, Lezlee	OR0010	61
Flanagan, Leslie	OK0750	61
Fleitas, Patricia P.	FL0650	60,36,61
Fleming, Rachelle	DC0050	61,54
Fleming, Susan C.	AL1170	61
Fletcher, Donna	AC0100	61,54
Fletcher, Mary Eason	VA0250	61
Fletcher, Ryan	VA0250	61,39
Fletcher, Terry W.	MS0300	36,61,12A
Fleury, Tacy S.	SC1000	61
Floan, Obed	OK0750	61
Flora, James	OH1650	61
Flora, James	PA2900	61
Flores, Andrea	AZ0350	61
Floriano, Joan H.	NY3730	61
Floriano, Joan	NY2650	61
Flory, Jennifer Morgan	GA0850	36,32D,15,60A,61
Floyd, Hugh	SC0750	61,60A,36,32D
Floyd, Ruth Naomi	PA2800	61
Floyd-Savage, Karen	VA1750	11,13A,36,61
Fogderud, Marla	ND0500	61
Fogderud, Marla G.	MN0600	61
Folan, Andrea	NY2650	61
Foley, Ruth	VA0650	32,61
Folsom, Rebecca L.	MA0350	61
Fons, Carolyn	WI1155	61,36
Foradori, Anne	NE0590	39,61,54
Forbay, Bronwen	TX2250	61
Forbis, Clifton	TX2400	61
Ford, Kelly	IN1350	36,61,60A,12,64E

Index by Area of Teaching Interest

Name	Code	Areas
Forderhase, Jerry	NJ0825	61
Forest, Michael	VA1350	61
Forester, Julie	TN0100	61
Forman, Naomi	AC0050	61
Fortney, Julie T.	NC1250	11,61,34C
Fortunato, D'Anna	MA1400	61
Foss, Treva M.	NY0850	61,20
Foster, Julia	FL1550	39,61
Foster, Melissa	IL2250	61
Foster, Melvin F.	GA1450	61
Fournier, Patricia	AI0190	61
Foust, Diane	WI1100	36,61,13A,40,13B
Fowler, Bruce E.	OK1350	61
Fowler, John H.	SC1200	61,39
Fracker, Richard	MI1400	61
Fralick, JR	OH0200	61,39
Francis, Deirdre	SC0050	61,40
Francoeur-Krzyzek, Damien	MA0350	61
Frank, Jane Ring	MA0850	61
Frank, Joseph	CA4400	61
Frank, Robin Shuford	FL0680	61
Frankenberry, Robert	PA2900	61
Franklin, Bonita Louise	OK0450	32,36,60A,61
Franklin, Jeshua	IL1612	61,66D,10D
Franklin, Nicole	TX2250	61
Franks, Kendra	MO0200	61
Franks, Russell	FL1750	61,39
Franks, Sandra	TN1200	61
Franks, Sandra E.	TN1680	61
Fraser, Stacey	CA0845	61,39
Frater, Betsy	CA4050	61,66A
Frazer, Liz	VA0350	61,11,39
Frazier, Larry R.	GA2130	39,61
Frazier, Margaret J.	RI0300	11,61
Fre, Anna	PA3250	39,61
Fredericks, Jim	NY0050	61
Fredrickson, Ann	MN0200	61,36,39,54,13C
Free, Christine	NY0270	36,61
Freed, Donald Callen	TX2710	61,36,10A,13C,12A
Freeman, Janean	KY1100	61,11
Freeman, Kay Paschal	GA1050	61
Freeman-Miller, Leanne	IA0550	61
Freisen, Naomi	AJ0150	61
French, Annabeth	ME0250	61,66G
French, Paul T.	OR0950	11,12A,36,39,61
French, Shannon	NC1350	61
Frey, Loryn E.	LA0150	12A,39,61
Frey-Monell, Robyn	CA1425	61
Frey-Monell, Robyn	CA1900	61
Freyermuth, G. Kim	AZ0200	36,44,61,47
Fried, Janet Gottschall	MN0050	61,39
Frieder, Raphael	NY1860	61
Friedley, Geoffrey A.	ID0100	61,11,12A
Friese, Kenneth	NY1275	60A,61
Frisbie, Jodi	KS0150	61,36,39,13C
Frohnmayer, Ellen Phillips	LA0300	61
Frohnmayer, Philip	LA0300	61
Frook, Sarah	VA1500	61
Frost, James	TN0850	39,40,61
Froysland-Hoerl, Nancy	NJ1350	61
Fruge, Jonathan	TX1550	61
Fry, Pamela	CA4150	61
Fudge, Tamara	IL0300	61
Fuerstman, Marlena	NY1860	31B,61,20F
Fuhrman, Eugenie	TX3600	61
Fuhrmann, Melanie J.	IL0650	61
Fukuda, Joni	CA5355	11,13A,32D,36,61
Fuller, Agnes M.	VA1000	61
Fuller, Gale	MA2050	61
Fuller, Lisa	TN1380	61,11
Fuller, Mark	KS1400	61
Fuller, Parmer	CA5300	61
Fuller, Trudy H.	SC0750	61
Fulmer, Mimmi	WI0815	61
Fusco-Spera, Barbara	NY2105	61
Gable, Garry	AJ0150	61,54,39
Gabrieli, Anna	MA1175	61
Gaetanne, Marisa	AB0100	61
Gage, Yvonne	IL0550	61
Gagne, Jeannie	MA0260	61
Gal, Zehava	NJ1350	61
Galbreath, Loretta J.	MS0350	36,40,47,61
Gale, Holly Ruth	AR0200	61
Galer, Suzanne J.	FL1450	61
Gall, Jeffrey C.	NJ0800	55,61,12A,12,39
Gall, Sandra J.	OK0450	61
Gallagher, Fulton	MN0150	61
Gallagher, Marcia	ME0340	36,61
Gallet, Coralie	NY0200	61,13
Gallet, Coralie	MI1700	61
Galloway, Melanie	CA0250	39,61
Galvez, Luis	IL2750	61,36
Galvin, Eugene	DC0050	61
Gamez, Denise	IL3550	61
Gandy, V. Gay	KY1400	36,61,13A,13C,11
Gang, Eleanor	AI0050	61
Ganz, Dale	KS0650	61
Ganz, Isabelle	TX1400	61
Ganz, Sara	CA2950	61
Garber, Joel	OK0770	12A,61,14,36,60
Garber, Ron	KS0210	11,12A,36,41,61
Garcia, Victor	IL0550	61
Garcia, William B.	TN0800	60,11,36,61,31A
Gardner, David B.	KS1200	36,60,61,60A,54
Gardner, Jessica	UT0150	61
Gardner, Marvel	CA4460	61
Garner, Rusty	FL0900	60,11,61,54,64D
Garrett, Karen	CA3800	61,36
Garrett, Margaret	AR0500	61
Garrett, Victoria	IN0200	61
Garrison, Jon	NJ1050	61
Garritano, Andrea	KS0300	11,61
Gartshore, Sarah	IN1750	61
Gartshore, Sarah	MI1985	61
Gaspar, Carole	MO1950	12A,61
Gast, Daniel	IA1800	61
Gast, Rosemary	IA1800	61
Gaston, Pamela	TN1680	61
Gates, Giacomo	CT0300	61
Gates, John T.	WI0350	61
Gauvin, Marcelle	MA2020	61,13A,11
Gaylard, Catharine P.	VA1850	61
Gee, Mary Sue	CA1510	61
Gee, Patricia	CA0960	61
Gee, Patricia	CA5150	61,11
Geiger, Gregory	CA3650	61
Geihsler, Rebecca	MS0100	61,12A,14C
Geist, Gretchen	FL2050	61
Gelber, Debbie	TX2350	13A,13B,36,61,13C
Gelbwasser, Kimberly A.	NM0100	61
Geller, Ian R.	IN0005	61,10A,60,36
Gengaro, Christine Lee	CA2600	13A,32A,61
Gentry, Ron	MI1650	61
Gentry, Scott	AZ0460	61,66A
Georg, Klaus	WI0250	61
George, Donald	NY3780	61
George, Mary	TN0100	61
George, Roderick L.	AL1200	61
George, Rosemary	NY0270	66A,61,12A,11
Gerber, Alan E.	FL2120	11,55,61,36
Gerber, Gary G.	AR0500	36,61,32D,60A
Gerber, Larry	FL0850	36,61
Gerbi, Elizabeth	NY1050	36,40,61
Germond, Melanie	AZ0250	36,61
Gerstenkorn, Lisa M.	KS1050	61
Gesteland, Tracelyn K.	SD0600	61,39
Gettel, Jennifer	WI1150	61
Gettel, Jennifer	WI0825	61
Geyer, Gwynne	PA1300	39,61
Giampa, Janice	MA2030	61,39
Giampietro, John	NY1900	61
Gibbons, Helen	IL1750	13,61
Gibbs, Brett	IL2500	61,13
Gibson, David	KY1550	11,61
Gibson, Marie	CA4900	61
Gibson, Melissa	TN1900	61
Gibson, Mila	TX0100	39,61
Giessow, David	MA2010	36,39,61,32B,32C
Gifford, Amy L.	FL1550	61,11,54
Gifford, Gene	AL1250	13A,61,13E
Giles, Bob	TX3350	39,61
Gilfry, Rod	CA5300	61
Gilgallon, Mark	IN0250	61
Gilgallon, Mark T.	IN1650	61
Gill, Brian P.	NY2750	61
Gill, Kimberly	NY2750	61
Gillard, Maria	NY1250	61
Gilliam, Christopher	NC0550	39,61
Gillis, Peter R.	NJ0800	61
Gilmer, Melissa	FL0800	61
Gilmore, Scott	IL0550	39,61
Gilroy, Debra	MN0800	61
Gilroy, Debra	MN1050	61
Giorgetti, Marisa	CA0450	61,36
Giovannetti, Claire	CA4900	61
Givens, Hugh	MN1300	39,61
Givens, Melissa	TX1000	61
Glaros, Pam	OR0250	61
Glasman, Ilan David	CA1550	36,40,61,11
Glass, James W.	AL0450	61
Glassman, Allan H.	AZ0100	61
Glaubitz, Robert	OK1330	61
Glaze, Gary	CA5300	61
Gleckler, Megan	TN0100	36,61
Glenn, James H.	NC2000	36,61,60A,11,12A
Glenn, Larry M.	CO0900	39,61,54
Glenn, Melissa Walker	AZ0490	61
Glenn, Suzetta	AR0500	61
Glicklich, Jocelyn Rose	GA0940	61
Glover, Sandra	WA0460	61
Goble, Jodi	IA0850	61
Goebel, Ellen Tift	TN0100	61,35B
Goeke, Christopher L.	MO1500	39,41,61,54
Goeser, Patrick	CA0960	61
Goetzinger, Laurel E.	IN0100	61,39,54
Goff, Kathleen	WA0300	61
Goff, Terrence	NY2450	61
Goffi-Fynn, Jeanne C.	NY4200	40,61,13H,32B,32D
Goforth, Stephen C.	KY1300	11,36,60A,61,12A
Golden, Ruth E.	NY2105	39,61,11
Goldenbaum, Cathy	PA0400	11,61
Goldman-Moore, Susan J.	OK1450	32,36,61
Goldstein, Sara	MA0350	61
Golliver, April	OK0800	61,39
Gondek, Juliana	CA5030	61
Gonen, Raya	PA2550	61
Gonzalez, Susan	NY0625	11,61,54
Goodheart, Thomas	NY3705	61,39
Goodheart, Thomas	NY3785	61
Goodman, Gabrielle A.	MA0260	61
Goodman, Jonathan M.	NY2550	61
Goodman, Jonathan	NY0050	61
Goodrich, Mark J.	CA0815	61
Goold, William C.	KY0150	60,12A,36,61,31A
Gordon, Barbara N.	NJ0500	11,36,60A,66D,61
Gordon, Gail R.	CA4450	61
Gordon, Heidi Cohenour	AR0810	61,13C,66D,36
Gordon, Jerry L.	TX0300	61
Gordon, Samuel	OH2150	60,12A,36,61,40
Gordon, Stefan	FL0350	61,60A
Gordon, Todd	MA0850	61
Gorham, Dee Ann	TX2955	61,39
Gorham, Fr. Daniel	IN0005	31A,33,61
Gorke, Sarah	WI0250	61
Gorman, Tracey	MN1450	61
Goslin, Gerald H.	MI1700	61,66A,20
Gotera, Jose	OH0650	61
Gotera, Jose	OH1000	61,39,54,36
Gothold, Stephen A.	CA5100	36,40,61,60A
Gottlieb, Elizabeth	IL1400	61
Gould, Monette	AE0050	61
Goulet, David	ME0500	61
Gourley, Sonja	WA1100	61
Govich, Marilyn S.	OK1330	61
Graber, Eric	MI0050	61
Graber, Todd A.	NY3770	61,54,36,12A
Grace, Elizabeth	RI0150	61
Gracia-Nuthmann, Andre	NM0150	13,60,36,55,61
Grady, Tracy R.	OH0200	61
Graham, Elizabeth	FL1850	39,61
Graham, Sandra	AG0400	61,39
Graham, Seong-Kyung	WI0700	61,32D,36,60A
Grahame, Gerald	NY0350	36,61
Gramelspacher, Addie	IL1100	39,61
Gramm, Carol J.	OH1800	61
Grammar, Kathleen	ME0500	61
Granger, Linda	VA0650	61,66C
Granite, Bonita	NJ1050	14,20D,61
Gratis, Lorie A.	PA3250	61
Graupmann, Jennifer	MN1600	61
Graves, Denyce	MD0650	61
Graves, Jim F.	OK1200	36,32D,32B,60A,61
Graves, Paul	KS0980	13,61
Graves, Tifton	OH2400	39,61
Gray, Colleen G.	PA3100	61,39
Gray, Donald N.	SC1110	39,61

Index by Area of Teaching Interest

Name	Code	Areas
Gray, George A.	PA3250	61
Gray, Gerald Thomas	NY3725	61,36
Gray, John	KS0250	36,13,61
Gray, Madeleine C.	MD0475	61
Grayson, Robert E.	LA0200	61,39
Greciano, Sandra	PA2900	61,54
Green, Donna	MI0050	61
Green, Elvira	NC1600	39,61
Green, Elvira O.	VI0050	13C,36,61
Green, Kathryn	VA1350	61
Green, Les	OR0750	61
Green, Patricia D.	AG0500	61
Green, Sharon	MI1600	32,61,70
Green, Sheila	WY0115	61,66A
Green, Wendy	CA4850	61
Greenberg, Barry	MD0170	61,66A
Greene, Cheryl	SC0950	61
Greene, Daniel B.	OH2120	36,61
Greene, Joshua	NY2250	61
Greene, Joy	MD0060	61
Greene, Mary Gayle	NC0050	61
Greenwald, Laura	NJ0050	36,13C,61,39
Greer, Albert	AG0650	36,61
Greer, Jean	SC0200	61
Greer, Sarah	MN1050	61
Gregg, Nan F.	NC0850	11,61
Gregg, Thomas	MA0350	61
Gregg-Boothby, Tracey	OK1050	36,61
Gregory, Arikka	GA0950	39,61
Gregory, David	KY1200	61,16,12
Gregory, Lee	TX3400	61
Greif, Carol	WI0150	61,39
Grenier, Robert M.	SC1050	13,61,11
Greschner, Debra	TX1400	61
Gresham, Ann	CA0859	61
Gresham, Ann	CA3750	61
Gresham, David Allen	NC0250	61,11,34,13
Gresham, Kathryn	NC0250	61,39
Gresock, Mary	MD0300	61
Grevlos, Lisa	SD0050	39,61,32B,36,32D
Grew, Melody A.	MD0050	11,32,36,61,66A
Grice, Wendy	PA2200	61
Griffeath, Kristin	OK1250	12A,61,39,36
Griffeath, Robin	OK1250	11,61
Griffen, Jane	MO0500	60A,32A,32B,36,61
Griffin, Ivan	LA0900	61
Griffin, Jennifer J.	IL2200	11,61
Griffin, Ruth Ann	TX1660	61,66D
Griffin, Tammy	NC0050	61
Griffin, William	FL0680	61,13A
Griffith, Larry D.	TN0930	60A,32C,36,61,32D
Grimaldi, Regina	OK0700	61
Grimaldi, Regina	OK0750	61
Grimes, Rebecca	TX2250	39,61
Grimland, Fredna H.	OR0950	13A,32,61
Grimm, Anne	AB0150	61
Grinnell, Melonie	CA2100	66A,47,61
Grissom, Cole	CA5353	61
Grissom, Jan	GA0350	61
Grives, Julie	IL2050	39,61
Grizzell, Paul W.	IL2050	61
Grogan, David C.	TX3500	61,32D,36,39,40
Groh, Jack C.	AR0700	60,36,61
Grohman, Bryon T.	FL1450	61,36
Groom, Peter	AE0050	61
Grout, Gayle	KY1000	61
Grubb, Thomas	NY1900	61
Gruber, Rebecca C.	IA1350	61
Gruber, Sari	PA2900	61
Gruetter, Joy	OH2140	61,32A
Grunert, Judi	TN0450	61
Guarino, Robert	NJ0175	61,55,39
Guarino, Robin	OH2200	61
Gubrud, Darcy Lease	MN1285	13,11,36,61,40
Gubrud, Irene	NY0500	61
Guebert, Carolyn	IN1560	61
Guechev, Guenko	PA1050	61,39
Guelker-Cone, Leslie	WA1250	36,39,61
Guenther, Greg	AZ0480	61,39
Guernsey, Diane	NY2200	66C,61
Guevara, Amy	NE0450	61
Guevara, Amy	NE0200	61
Guhr, Glen	WA0650	61
Guild, Jane E.	LA0750	13A,13,61
Gulick, Michelle	VA1600	39,61
Gullstrand, Donna	VA1350	61
Gundanas, Susan	CA5000	61
Gunderson, Margaret	AZ0450	61
Gunlogson, Kirsten	UT0250	61
Gunn, Natalie	OR0450	61
Gunn, Nathan	IL3300	61
Gunnarson, Eike	NM0310	61
Gunnarson, Eike	TX3520	61
Guptill-Crain, Nan	NJ1400	61,36
Gurney, James F.	MN1120	61
Gursky, Isreal	NY2150	61
Gustafson, David	OR0350	61,13A
Gustafson, Nancy J.	NJ1130	39,61
Gustafson, Steven	KS0900	61,66G,40,13B,36
Guter, Christine	CA0825	47,61,32D
Guter, Gerhard	CA1900	47,61
Guthmiller, Anne	VA1600	61
Guthmiller, Anne	VA1500	61,42
Gutierrez, Dawn	MO0400	61
Gutierrez, Martha	UT0350	61
Guy, Christine	ME0430	61
Guy, Todd	IN1025	36,31A,61,60A,11
Gyllstrom, Mabeth	MN1300	61
Haag, MaryBeth	CA1050	61
Haagenson, Anna	OR0400	61
Haan, Keith A.	IA1300	60,36,32D,61,40
Haas, Angela Dilkey	NY3725	61
Haas, Connie	WI0825	61
Habegger, Christa	SC0200	61
Haber, Carol	MA1400	61
Hacker, John	IL3150	61
Hacker, Kathleen M.	IN1650	61,39
Hackett, Janet	OR0700	61
Haddad, Layna Chianakas	CA4400	61
Haddon, Judith	IL0550	61
Haecker, Allyss	SC0900	61,20,36,39
Haffner, James	CA5350	39,61,54
Hafso, Marc A.	WA1350	60,36,10A,32D,61
Hagel, Clint	AA0020	31A,36,61,66C
Hagen Givens, Marcie	MN0350	61
Hagerott, Dawn	ND0050	40,61,11
Haggans, Kathryn	MO1830	36,61
Hagness, Jane	PA3600	61
Hagon, Darlene	MA0600	61
Hahn, Mari	AK0100	61,39,54,32D
Haight, Catherine M.	WA0800	61
Haines, Amy	WI0250	11,61
Haines, Stephanie	CA4425	61
Halbert, Marjorie	TN0100	61,54
Hale, Roger	MO0850	60A,61,40,36
Hall, Bianca	CA0815	61
Hall, Bruce	IL2250	61,36,40
Hall, David	PA1550	61
Hall, Heidi	WA0550	61
Hall, Janice	CA4460	61
Hall, Lewis R.	WV0050	32,40,54,61
Hall, Lois	NY2800	61,13C,42
Hall, Robert	AG0150	13,60,36,61,10F
Hall, Roberta	OR1020	36,61
Hall, Sarah	AC0050	13J,61
Hall, Sunny Joy Langton	IL2250	61
Hall, Van-Anthoney	NC1550	11,12D,40,42,61
Halley, Gustavo	MO1810	61
Hallman, Ludlow B.	ME0440	36,61,39
Halvecka, Thomas	OH1910	66D,66A,61
Halverson, Carl	OR0400	61
Halverson, Peter	MN0600	61
Halvorson, Carl	OR0850	61
Halvorson, Marjory	WA0400	61
Hamilton, Bonnie	NY2250	61
Hamilton, Bonnie	NY3785	61
Hamilton, Brian	OK0750	61
Hamilton, David	MN0600	61,12A
Hamilton, Karen	MN0600	61
Hamilton, Sue	IL1610	61
Hamilton-Jenkins, Leah	MO0775	61
Hamling, Phyllis	IA0910	61
Hammer, Janet	CA3460	61
Hammer, Levi	OH2150	38,61
Hammet, Jane	CA4700	61
Hammett, Hank	TX2400	61,66C,39
Hammond, June C.	FL1600	12A,36,61,66A,37
Han, Sang-In	IA0250	61,11
Hancock, John	NJ0825	61
Hancock, Kyle	GA0950	39,61
Hancock, Pollyanna	OR0500	61
Hancock, Sarah	GA0950	61
Hand, Angela R.	IL3500	61,39
Hand, Angela R.	IL0100	61,11
Hanegraaf, Margaret	PA2550	61
Haney, Kristee	MO2000	61
Hangen, Bruce	MA0350	61
Hannan, Eric	AB0050	36,61
Hanne, Walt	KS0980	61
Hannigan Tabon, Katie	NY2650	61
Hannon-Roberts, Emilie	CT0550	61
Hanrahan, Kevin G.	NE0600	61
Hansen, Jack	IN0005	66A,13,61
Hansen, Kurt R.	IL2250	61,54
Hansen, Patrick J.	AI0150	61,39
Hansen, Robert	TX3750	61,54
Hansen, Theresa Brancaccio	IL2250	61
Hansen, Victoria	CO0200	61,54
Hansford, Conchita	OK0650	32A,32B,61,66A,31A
Hanson, Andrea J.	OK1200	61
Hanson, Ellen	GA2200	12A,61,39
Hanson, Melissa	MN1620	61
Hapner, Lee Merrill	OH2450	61
Harchanko, Lois	SD0580	61
Hardenbergh, Esther Jane	FL1900	61
Harder, Caroline	AB0090	61
Harder, Glen	AA0040	36,61,47
Harder, Melissa	AJ0030	61,11,60A
Hardesty, Tamara G.	GA2150	61
Hardin, Jane L.	MS0420	61
Hardy, Janis	MN1450	61,39,54
Hardy, Julie	NY2660	61,47
Harland, Kelly	WA0200	61,29
Harler-Smith, Donna D.	NE0600	61
Harley, Anne	CA4500	61,39,12
Harlin, Juston	NM0200	61
Harney, Jon M.	MT0200	36,39,40,61
Harper, David R.	RI0150	11,61,54,39,40
Harper, Joe Dan	NY3725	61
Harper, Kris	PA3650	36,61
Harper, Richard	NY2660	61,29B
Harper, Sharmi	NY2900	61
Harper, T.J.	RI0150	36,60,32C,32D,61
Harper, Tamara W.	GA1700	61,54
Harper, Thomas	WA1050	61
Harr, James	TN1200	61
Harrell, Ann	MO1800	61
Harrell, Greg	MI2250	61
Harrelson, Neal	NY2105	61
Harrelson, Patricia A.	NC0850	61
Harres, Debra	IL1740	61
Harres, Debra	IL2970	61
Harrill, Stephen	NC1900	61,41,44
Harrington, Elisabeth	CA2250	39,61,13C
Harris, Brenda	NY3790	61
Harris, David	PA0150	36,61,31A,40,32D
Harris, Dawn	IL3300	61
Harris, Duane	MO0350	32,36,61,12A
Harris, Evelyn	UT0350	61
Harris, Hilda	NY3560	39,61
Harris, Hilda	NY2150	61
Harris, Jason W.	OH1700	60,36,61
Harris, Katherine	NJ0700	61
Harris, Melanie	FL1675	36,61
Harris, Ray	AB0090	61
Harris, Robert	GA0200	12A,60,61,11,32D
Harrison, Joy	IA0420	11,61
Harrison, Joy	IA0650	32B,61
Harrison, Luvada A.	AL0950	61,39
Harrison, Robert J.	IN0900	61
Hart, Carolyn	IL3550	61
Hart, Cheryl	UT0400	61
Hart, Craig	MA0950	61
Hart, Martha J.	MO1950	61
Hart, Mary Ann	IN0900	61
Hart, Peter	MA0150	61
Hart, Steven R.	MT0350	36,61,32D
Hart, Victoria	CA0859	61
Harte, Monica	NY0500	61,39
Hartgrove, Kathryn	GA1050	61
Hartmann, Donald	NC2430	39,61
Hartzell, Richard	MD0400	61,39,54
Harvey, Lori Kay	OH2050	61
Harwood, Susan	NY0700	39,36,61,40
Hassevoort, Christine	TN0260	61,11
Hassevoort, Darrin	TN0260	36,61,47,60,54

Name	Code	Areas
Hassler, Desiree	IL1850	61
Hastings, Mary Logan	PA1600	39,61,54
Hasty, Barbara P.	CA1700	13A,61,66A,36
Hatley, H. Jerome	OK0850	10,61,34,13D
Hauan, Catherine	AZ0440	61,54
Hauck, Ross	WA0200	61
Haugen, Jennifer E.	MN1030	61
Hausmann, Charles S.	TX3400	36,61
Havranek, Patricia	IN0900	61
Hawk, Heather	TX2750	61,11
Hawkins, Allan	MN0625	61,32C,32D
Hawkins, Michelle Kennedy	AA0110	32A,61,66A
Hay, Beverly R.	SC0650	61
Hayes, Angela	CA5353	61
Hayes, Daun	CA4600	36,61,54
Hayes, Natlynn	OK0200	61
Hayes, Natlynn	AR0730	61
Hayes, Tyrone	AL0050	61,11
Hayes-Davis, Lucy	AF0100	39,61
Haymon-Coleman, Cynthia	IL3300	61
Haynes, Kimberly	FL0100	12A,39,61
Hays, Jonathan C.	PA3150	61
Hays, Jonathan C.	PA0950	61
Hazelip, Richard	TX2300	13B,66G,61,11
Heape, Mary Willis	TX3050	32,61,13,12A
Heard, Richard	NC2500	61,20G
Heard, Richard	NC2700	61
Hearden, Kathryn	VA0450	61
Hearne, Clarice	IL1890	61
Hearne, Clarice	IL3370	61,39
Hearne, Lisa	IA0400	36,61,40
Hecht, Gerard	NY3785	61,66C
Hecht, Joshua	NY1600	61
Hedberg, Jeffrey	IL1085	61,63A
Hedberg, Kristen	NC2600	61
Hedegaard, Kirsten	IL1615	61,40
Hedrick, David	KY0400	61,32
Hegg, Barbara	SD0150	36,61,63B,60
Heimur, Elena	NY0644	61,66A,66D
Hein, David	WI0400	40,61
Heinz-Thompson, Leslie	MO0850	61,11
Heitzman, Jill M.	IA0450	61,64A,66A,11
Helding, Lynn E.	PA0950	61,40,54
Heldman, Dianna J.	NY2750	61
Heley, Ruth	ND0100	61
Heller, Ryan	WA0480	36,39,61
Helm, Lenora Zenzalai	NC1600	61,47
Helppie, Kevin	OR1250	61,47,54,20G
Helton, Caroline	MI2100	61
Helton, Jerry L.	SC1200	61,39
Helton, Melanie	MI1400	61
Helwing, Anna	CA2440	66A,61
Henderson, Allen C.	GA0950	61,39
Henderson, Donald O.	MI0400	61
Henderson, Elaine	PA2300	39,61,54
Henderson, Lisa	IA0700	61
Henderson, Pamela	NC0750	61
Henderson, Silvester	CA2775	36,40,60A,61,66A
Hendricksen, David Alan	TN1650	36,61
Hendrickson, Brandon P.	SD0600	61,39
Hendrickson, Daniel	MI1180	11,12A,36,37,61
Hendrix, Suzanne R.	MO0050	61
Hendsbee, Blaine	AA0200	61,39
Henjum, Katherine	ND0400	61,40,13C
Henkle, Stephanie	OH0850	61
Henrikson, Steven	AG0550	61
Henry, Ruth	IL2310	61,66A,54
Hensel, Larry L.	WY0200	39,61
Hensley, David	CA0810	60,61
Hensley, Hunter C.	KY0550	36,61,60A,55,32D
Henson, Bill	MI1800	61,39,13C
Hensrud, Tammy J.	NY1600	61
Hepburn, Cathleen	AZ0510	61,66A
Hepworth, Elise M.	NE0700	32D,61,32B,32C,11
Herbeck, Tina	CA0200	35,61
Hermalyn, Joy	NJ0700	61
Hermiston, Nancy	AB0100	12A,39,61
Herrera, Luis Ricardo	IL3300	61
Herron, Teri A.	MS0250	61,11
Herseth, Freda	MI2100	61
Hess, Benton	NY1100	61,39
Hess, Jeffery	MN0750	61
Hess, Jeffrey	MN1200	61,34,32,11
Hesse, Ted	IL1750	13,36,61
Hester, Charlotte	MS0570	61
Hetrick, Esther A.	MI0910	61,60,31,36,32B
Hetrick, Mark	OH1330	11,61,66C
Heyl, Jeffrey	MO0650	61
Hibbard, Kevin	GA2130	36,32D,61,60,32C
Hibbitt, Peyton	NY3705	39,61
Hickman, Joe Eugene	NC2440	60,36,41,61
Hickman, Lowell	MT0200	36,61,63A
Hickman, Suzanne L.	NJ0175	61
Hicks, Angela	CA0550	61
Hicks, Lori C.	SC0350	61,39,32D
Hicks, Pamela	CA0807	61,39
Hiebert, Shannon	AA0020	61,66A
Hiester, Jason A.	OH2000	36,39,40,60A,61
Higgins, William L.	AR0300	39,61,60A,13C
High, Ronald	SC0150	11,12,31F,61,66
Highben, Zebulon M.	OH1650	36,40,61,32D
Hightower, J. Taylor	MS0750	61
Hightower, Kristin	IA0950	61
Hijleh, Kelley	NY1700	61
Hildebrandt, Lorna Young	MI0500	61
Hilderbrand, Monica	IL1612	61,62
Hill, Camille	KY0600	13A,11,36,61,66D
Hill, Leah	VA0800	61
Hill, Mary Ann	GA1550	61
Hill, Phillip	TX3175	61
Hill, Serena	SC0450	39,61
Hillhouse, Wendy	CA4900	61
Hinchman, Pamela	IL2250	61
Hinck, David	ID0060	61
Hindemith, Paul B.	MN0600	61
Hinds, Esther	NY2900	61
Hines, Billy C.	NC0700	13A,36,61
Hines, John T.	IA1600	61
Hinshaw, Susan	WA0480	39,61
Hinshaw, Susan	OR0850	61
Hirst, Edmund V. Grayson	AZ0500	61
Hiscocks, Mike	CA2650	11,13A,61,45,10B
Hiscox, Julie	MD0060	61
Hite, William	MA2000	61
Hix, Michael T.	NM0450	61,13A,12A,12
Hobbins, William	GA0250	32,36,61,11
Hobbs, William	NY2250	61
Hobson, Richard	NJ0700	61
Hoch, Beverly	TX3300	61
Hoch, Matthew	AL0200	61,36,39
Hochstetler, Scott	IN0550	36,61,60
Hodgdon, Brett	CT0600	61
Hodgdon, Elizabeth	CA4300	61
Hodge, Cheryl	AB0070	10,36,61,53,35H
Hodge, Stephen	OH2300	36,32C,61,32D,60A
Hodgson, Ken	MN1620	36,61,34D,11,60A
Hoegberg, Elisabeth Honn	IN1650	61,13A,13B
Hoepfner, Gregory	OK0150	10A,32,61,10,11
Hoffart, Danica	AA0080	36,61,54,13C
Hoffenberg, Rick	PA2200	36,40,60A,61
Hoffman, Cathy	CA0830	61
Hoffman, David E.	IL1400	61
Hoffman, Lee	OH0500	39,61,66C,54
Hoffman, Phyllis	MA0400	61
Hoffmann, Cynthia	NY2150	61
Hoffmann, Cynthia	NY1900	61
Hogan, George	TX3415	61,39,54
Hogan, Hallie Coppedge	NC0750	39,61
Hogan, Penny	TX3415	61,39,54
Hoifeldt, Steven	IA0425	61,11,40
Holborn, George	AG0170	61
Holbrook-Bratka, Branita A.	WV0400	61
Holcombe, Helen	PA0400	13A,36,61,66D
Holden, Robert	AR0850	61,39
Holder, Angela	TN0250	61,36,31,11
Holdhusen, David	SD0600	60A,36,61
Holeman, Janet	TN0930	39,61
Holeman, Kathleen	MO0850	61,40,42
Holland, Heather	MA0510	61
Holland, Rachel J.	VA0150	61,39
Holleman, Brenda	OK0750	61
Holley, David	NC2430	39,61
Holliday, James T.	DC0150	13A,13,61
Hollingsworth, Christopher	TX0900	61,39
Hollinshead, Barbara	DC0010	61
Holloman, Charlotte	DC0350	61
Holloman, Charlotte W.	DC0150	61
Holloway, David	IL0550	61
Holloway, Peggy A.	NE0610	61,32B,15,36,40
Holm, Molly	CA2950	61,47,53
Holm, Thomas	IA1200	12A,36,11,60,61
Holman, Leigh	CO0800	39,61
Holman, Sarah	IL3550	39,61
Holmes, Allison	IA0930	61
Holmes, Daniel	MD0060	61
Holmes, Elizabeth	IL1750	36,61
Holmes, Isaac	SC1100	20,61
Holmes, Isaac	GA1600	60A,11,36,61,39
Holmes, Janet	CA3320	66C,61
Holmes, Phil	MI0520	61
Holsberg, Lisa	NY2105	61
Holst, Kelly Margaret	OK0750	61
Holst, Robert I.	IL1520	12A,12,61
Holt, Anthony	MN1450	61
Holz, Beatrice	KY0100	32B,36,39,61,32D
Holzmeier, Jana	NE0450	61
Hondorp, Paul	KY1550	36,60A,32D,61,40
Honea, Richard	MO0400	36,61,60A
Honeysucker, Robert	MA0350	61
Honeysucker, Robert	MA1175	61
Hong, Ah Young	MD0650	61
Hong, Ah Yong	MD0850	61
Hong, Martha	MT0450	61,54
Honn, Barbara	OH2200	61
Hooper, Terry	GA2300	61
Hoover, Maya	HI0210	61
Hoover, Sarah	NY1600	61
Hopkin, J. Arden	UT0050	39,61,54
Hopkin, Teresa	GA0750	39,61
Hopkins, Alice	IN0907	61,66A
Hopkins, Gregory H.	DC0150	61
Hopkins, Janet E.	SC1110	61,39
Hopkins, Jesse E.	VA0100	32,36,61,44,60A
Hopkins, John R.	AK0150	36,39,61,60
Hopkins, Joseph H.	AL0800	61
Hoppe, Jennifer R.	NY2750	61
Hopper, Alice R.	IN0900	61
Horan, Rachel	MN0600	61
Horan, Sara	GA1000	32,11,61
Horjus-Lang, Deanna	WI0800	36,61,11
Horn, Fred	VA1150	61
Horne, Brian	IN0900	61
Horstman, Dorothy Yanes	FL1450	61
Horton, Virginia	TN0850	12A,61
Hostetler, Jill	IN0200	36,40,61
Hough, Jennifer C.	SC1200	61
Hougham, Bradley	NY1800	61
Houghtaling, Paul	AL1170	39,61
Houghton, Rosemarie	DC0050	61
House, Nicole	NC2410	61
Houston, Janeanne	WA0650	61
Howard, Brad	GA0750	61
Howard, Elisabeth	CA3600	61
Howard, Markus	AG0300	61
Howard, Michael	LA0750	61,54
Howe, Eileen	CA2200	61
Howe, Martha Jane	CA2100	61,54
Howe, Stuart	AA0100	39,61
Howell, Christina	GA0500	61
Hower, Eileen	PA0250	32,11,61
Howes, Sarah Marie	PA1400	61,13C
Howle, Patrick	KS1050	61,39
Howlett, Christine R.	NY4450	36,13C,61
Hoyt, Lucy Owen	VA1350	61
Hrivnak, Christine	MS0100	61
Hronek, Melissa	TX2900	61
Hrynkiw, Patricia	AA0150	61
Hsieh, Lily	VA1550	61
Hubbell, Judy	CA1020	61,66D,13A
Hubert, John	CO0650	61
Hudson, Barbara	VA0050	61,36,12A
Hudson, Hope A.	NJ0700	61,54
Hudson, Nita	TX2700	11,61
Hudson, William	IL1200	55D,61
Hueber, Thomas E.	MO1780	39,61
Hughes, Albert C.	TN0950	13,11,12A,36,61
Hughes, Amanda	OK1250	61
Hughes, David	CA0250	60,36,61
Hughes, Evelyn	GA0940	11,12A,61
Hughes, Laura Weaver	IL1090	61
Hughes, R. Daniel	NY2550	36,13A,61
Hughes, Ralph	CA0150	36,61,66A
Hughes-Lopez, Jennifer	MD0550	61
Hugo, John William	VA0650	36,61,12A,60A
Huisman, Monica	AC0100	61
Huizenga, Trudi	MI0350	61

Index by Area of Teaching Interest

Name	Code	Areas
Hull, Allison	WI0250	61
Hull, Allison R.	WI0835	61
Huls, Shirley	PA3000	13A,32A,32B,61
Hulse, Mark	CA0300	13,11,32B,32C,61
Hultgren, Lori	MD0850	61
Humble, Dina M.	CA3800	61,36,11,34,29
Hume, Michael	NY0050	61,36
Hunnicutt, Heather Winter	KY0610	61,32,11
Hunt, Jeremy	FL1800	61
Hunt, Johanna	FL1800	61
Hunter, Laurie	OR0950	61
Hunter-Holly, Daniel	TX3515	13,61,42
Huntington, Tammie M.	IN1025	61,39
Huntoon, Diana	IN0100	61
Hurst, Michael Shane	TX0370	61,40,35G
Hurst, Twyla	MS0370	13A,36,61,66D
Hurst-Wajsczuk, Kristine M.	AL1150	61,39
Hurt, Phyllis A.	IL2150	12A,61,54
Hurty, Sonja	IL0100	36,61,13C
Hussa, Robert	WY0060	11,12A,35C,36,61
Hussung, Lisa	KY1550	61,11
Huszti, Joseph B.	CA5020	60,36,61
Hutcheson, Mary Beth	GA1500	61
Hutchings, Doreen L.	MN1280	61,39
Hutchings, James	IL0420	11,13B,12A,61,13A
Hutchins, Georgette	RI0200	61
Hutchinson, Nicholas	IL0750	61,66C
Hyberger, Brett	TN0260	61,11,39
Hyberger, Sarah Amanda	TN0260	11,13C,54,61,39
Hyde, Edye Evans	MI0300	61
Hyde, Edye	MI1050	61
Hylton, Fleta	DC0170	61
Hylton, Fleta	DC0050	61
Hynes, Elizabeth	CA5300	61
Idenden, John	NJ0100	13A,11,12A,61,66A
Ihasz, Daniel	NY3725	61
Ikach, Yugo Sava	PA0500	61,38,11,13A,36
Ilban, Serdar	TX1400	61,39
Immel, Conrad	CA0859	61
Imthurn, Melinda	TX1725	11,36,61
Indik, Lawrence R.	PA3250	61
Inger, Leah	MD0850	61
Inselman, Elsie	AG0550	61
Inselman, Rachel	MN1600	61
Intintoli, Helen	CA4650	36,61,66A,31A,54
Ion, Charles	CA1960	61
Ireland, Cathy	CA1000	61
Irland, Jeremy	WA1100	61,11
Irmiter, Kay	NC2000	61
Irmiter, Kristopher	SC1200	61
Irvine, Mary	MI1830	61
Irving, Silvia	MA0150	61
Isaacs, Robert	NJ0900	36,61
Isele, David	FL2050	10F,10,36,61,66G
Isley-Farmer, Christine	TN1100	61
Iwama, Kayo	NY0150	61,66C
Izdebski, Krzysztof	CA4150	61
Izdebski, Pawel	NC2440	61
Jablonski, Darlyn	OR0150	61
Jablow, Lisa	VT0250	60,12A,36,41,61
Jackson, Albert	IL2775	13A,11,36,61
Jackson, Cliff	KY1450	61,66C
Jackson, Dennis C.	ID0250	39,61
Jackson, Jackie	UT0200	61
Jackson, Janice	AF0120	61,54
Jackson, Janice R.	MD1000	61
Jackson, Rosemary	MO0350	61
Jackson-Legris, Erin	KS0590	61
Jacobs, Patrick	AL1195	61,39
Jacobsen, Lesa L.	WI0845	61,32C,32D,60A,36
Jacobson, Jaime	OR0200	61
Jacobson, Marin	CA1425	36,12A,61,11
Jaeb, Mary	CA3460	61,60A
Jagielsky, Kathleen	DC0250	61
Jamerson, Celeste Emmons	NY5000	61
Jamerson, Thomas H.	NY5000	61
James, Buddy	CA0807	36,32D,61,60A
James, Clarity	VA1100	39,61
James, Creighton	MT0400	61
James, Dawn-Marie	GA0050	61
James, Judith R.	ME0500	61
James, Kimberly Gratland	MT0400	61,40,13
James, Laurel	UT0190	61
James, Matthew H.	LA0770	61,13D,39,54,60A
James, Nancy B.	NY4150	61
James, Pamela A.	VA0750	32A,61,13C,66D,32B
Jameson, Joel	NY2900	36,61,60A
Jameson, Shelley	NY2900	61,39
Jamison, Vicki	PA0100	61,40
Jang, Jinyoung	CA3100	61
Jang, Jinyoung	CA0200	61
Janis, Christine	WA1100	61
Jannett, Victor	MA0350	61
Jantsch, Nancy	OH1600	61
Janz, Holly A.	MN0600	61
Jarman, Amy	TN1850	61,39,40
Jasperse, Gregory P.	CA3500	61,36
Javore, James	MA0350	61
Jaworski, Warren	FL2000	61
Jeffers, Amy	IA0600	61
Jeffrey, Andrea	AF0120	61
Jeffries, Jean	MA1350	61,41,49
Jenkins Ainsworth, Jodi	MA0260	61
Jenkins, Judith	PA2900	61
Jennings, Carol	AZ0350	61
Jennings, Harlan	MI1400	61
Jennings, Jori Johnson	IL1850	61,32B
Jennings, Kenneth	MN1450	60A,61,36
Jennings, Kerry L.	IN0350	61
Jennings, Mark D.	MO1780	60,36,61
Jennings, Tom	TX1775	11,36,61
Jenrette, Thomas S.	TN0500	36,61,60
Jenschke, Laura	TX3100	36,61,32E
Jensen, Andrew	AR0050	60A,36,11,61,13C
Jensen, Constance	UT0325	61,36
Jensen, DeNice	OR1010	61
Jensen, Janeen	NE0100	61
Jensen, Joni L.	TX3300	13C,36,61,32D,60A
Jensen, Karen	AC0100	61,11
Jensen, Michael	IA1800	61
Jensen, Penelope C.	NC0600	61
Jensen-Hole, Catherine	MA2000	47,61,29
Jesse, Dennis	LA0200	61
Jesse, Lynda	MO0200	32D,36,54,60,61
Jewell, Renee	GA0625	61
Jewett, Dennis A.	KY0800	61,31A,32,36
Jewett, Dennis A.	NC0350	61
Jimenez, Lissette	FL0700	61,12A,13C
Jimerson, David	OR0850	32B,36,61
Jin, Min	MI0900	61
Jin, Soohyun	OK0850	61,36
Joffe, Lucy	NY2400	39,61
Johanson, Erik	OH2300	61
Johansson, Annette	HI0210	61
Johengen, Carl	NY1800	61
Johnson, Alan O.	FL1900	61,39
Johnson, Amy S.	MA2000	61
Johnson, Ann	CA5355	61
Johnson, Barry	WA0650	61
Johnson, Ben S.	NC2350	61,12A,31
Johnson, Bonnie L.	OR0175	61
Johnson, Brad	MS0200	60,11,36,44,61
Johnson, Brandon P.	NY1700	36,60A,61
Johnson, Brenda Seward	OK1450	61
Johnson, Byron	MS0050	13A,13B,13C,61,39
Johnson, Byron	AL1195	61
Johnson, Candace Y.	CA5000	61
Johnson, Carl	TX0200	60,12A,32C,36,61
Johnson, Craig	CA3640	61,39,11
Johnson, David Lee	GA2150	61
Johnson, Dawn	AA0050	61
Johnson, Diane	WA0900	36,61,54,11,20
Johnson, Elizabeth	TN0100	36,61
Johnson, Eric D.	NY4150	61,39
Johnson, Janice	OR1300	61,54
Johnson, Jeanne	TX1350	13C,11,61
Johnson, Jeffrey W.	NY2105	61,12A,55D,12B
Johnson, Jeffry Blake	PA3580	61
Johnson, Joaquina Calvo	CA6050	36,39,61,67B
Johnson, Jon S.	TX2350	13,36,61,54,32D
Johnson, Katherine L.	NJ1350	61
Johnson, Kerilyn	UT0050	61
Johnson, Kerry	CO0300	61,11
Johnson, Lawrence	UT0200	11,13C,61
Johnson, Mary Jane	TX0100	39,61
Johnson, Michael E.	TX2800	61
Johnson, Molly	TX3535	61,54,39
Johnson, Nathaniel	UT0200	12A,61
Johnson, Nikki	MS0360	11,61,54,36
Johnson, Randall	GU0500	11,36,47,61,64E
Johnson, Shauna	UT0325	32B,61
Johnson, Shirley M.	FL0600	13A,61,66A,66D
Johnson, Sidney	OR0600	61
Johnson, Sigrid	MN1450	36,61
Johnson, Teri	TX2800	61,11,39
Johnson, Timothy	ME0340	36,61
Johnson, Timothy	ME0200	61
Johnson, Valerie	NC0200	60,36,61
Johnson, Velshera	VA0400	61,36,40,66A
Johnson-Wilmot, Daniel	WI1100	39,61
Johnston, Amanda J.	MS0700	66C,61
Johnston, Joey	AZ0440	36,61
Johnston, Rebecca R.	SC0600	32,36,60,13C,61
Jolley, Carolyn L.	NY3717	61
Jonason, Louisa	PA2250	39,61
Jonck, Rachelle	NJ1350	61
Jones, Allison	SC0350	61
Jones, Ann A.	TN0250	36,61,60A
Jones, Bernard	OK1050	13,12A,61,11,64
Jones, Byron A.	VA1350	61,39
Jones, Cheryl	FL1430	37,66A,66B,47,61
Jones, Dani S.	AL0650	61,39,31A,60
Jones, Dani R.	AL0500	11,61
Jones, David	GA2000	61,39,42
Jones, Erik Reid	WV0550	36,39,40,60A,61
Jones, Evan T.	TN1680	61
Jones, Grace	WI0804	61
Jones, Jeffrey L.	SC0420	61,39
Jones, Josh	IL0850	61
Jones, Joshua	IL1300	61,11,39,54
Jones, Keith	SC0650	61,36,60
Jones, Kevin	CT0650	61
Jones, Kimberly	IL2750	61
Jones, Kimberlyn	CA2810	39,61,54,53
Jones, Laurie	PA3000	33,61
Jones, Leslie I.	MO1500	61,39,11,54
Jones, Meredith	TX2570	12A,31A,60A,61
Jones, Pamela	MS0580	11,61,13C
Jones, Robert Owen	OH1650	36,61
Jones, Robert J.	ND0350	39,61,54,14
Jones, Susan	IA1550	61
Jones, Timothy A.	TX3400	65,61
Jones, William	DC0350	11,36,61,66A,66G
Jordahl, Patricia	AZ0300	36,54,66D,61,11
Jordan, Christopher	AL0010	11,61
Jordan, DJ	MO0100	61
Jordan, Esther	CA2100	36,39,61,54
Jordan, Michael D.	TX1660	13A,13,11,39,61
Jordan, Paul	IN0005	10A,61,13,20F,31A
Jorgensen, Michael	MN0750	61,11,32D,14C
Jorstad, Dede	MN1625	61
Joselson, Rachel	IA1550	61
Joseph, Richard	MN0040	11,61
Joseph-Weil, Helene	CA0810	61
Josephson, Kim	OK1350	61
Joslin, Art	MI0300	61
Jost, John R.	IL0400	60,36,61,38
Jost, Paul	PA3330	61
Joyce, David	CA3500	61,10D
Jublonski, Anna	OR0150	61
Judge, Joseph	NC1900	36,61,31A,40
Judisch, David	IA0950	39,61,32D
Julian, Kimm D.	MN1000	61
Jung, Hein	FL2050	61
Kaczmarczyk, Mark	NY2200	61
Kai, Kudisan	MA0260	61
Kalinowski, Diane	PA0100	61
Kalm, Stephen	MT0400	61
Kamerin, Kim	CA2400	10B,35A,36,61
Kammerer, Elizabeth	HI0050	61,36
Kanakis, Karen	IA0950	61,39
Kane, Janet	PA3650	31A,61
Kane, Susan W.	CA0830	61
Kano, Mark A.	KY0450	61,39
Kantack, Jerri Lamar	MS0150	60,36,61,12A,32
Karam, Christiane	MA0260	61
Karlin, Brett	FL0930	36,61
Karn, Kitty	IL3500	61,54
Karpatova, Mariana	NJ0400	61
Karpoff, Rebecca J.	NY4150	61
Kasch, Catherine Loraine	CO0900	61,40
Kashkin, Alexander	NY3250	34,40,61
Kasper, Kathryn	KS0200	39,61,54,13C
Kasten, Martha	IL0730	61
Kataja-Urrey, Taina	NJ1130	61
Katz, Joel	AG0300	61,12A

Index by Area of Teaching Interest

Name	Code	Areas
Kaun, Kathleen	TX2150	61
Kaur, Kamaljeet	AA0100	61,20E
Kavasch, Deborah H.	CA0850	10A,13,61,10,10F
Kay, Jennifer	NY1800	61
Kearley, Kandie	FL0400	61
Keates, Peter	OH0500	39,61
Keating, Bevan T.	AR0750	36,60,61
Keck, Kimberly	TN0200	36,39,61,60A,13
Keck, Vail	CA3100	36,60,11,13A,61
Keele, Jeffrey	NE0200	61
Keele, Jeffrey	NE0150	61
Keele, Roger S.	TX1400	39,66A,61
Keeler, Paula	IA0150	32,36,39,41,61
Keeling, Ryan	WV0600	61
Keitges, Christine	CO0050	39,61,54
Keith, Anna	FL1450	61
Keller, Cheryl	CA2200	61
Keller, Dennis L.	CA3320	36,61,20,11,40
Keller, Larry	OK0750	61
Kellert, Aaron	OK1100	11,36,13A,54,61
Kellert, Carolyn	IL1350	32C,32D,61
Kelley, Marvin	IA0700	61
Kellim, Kevin	KS1400	60A,36,61
Kellock, Judith	NY0900	61
Kelly, Bruce	AG0250	61,36
Kelly, Chris	AJ0150	61,66D
Kelly, Elizabeth	MA0600	11,61
Kelly, Jennifer W.	PA1850	60,36,61
Kelly, Jonathan	NY2150	61
Kelly, Justin M.	OH1000	61,32H
Kelly, Liza	KY1550	61,39
Kelly, Michael F.	NY1850	36,61,66A,46,34
Kelly, Ryan	PA3600	36,40,61,60A
Kelly, Sondra	NJ0825	61
Kelly, Terence	WI0810	11,61,54
Kelsaw, Geoffrey L.	IN1650	36,61
Kelton, Mary Katherine	IN0250	61
Kemp, Julia	NJ1350	61
Kemp, Wayne N.	DC0170	61
Kempster, James	CA3400	11,12A,36,61,31A
Kempton, Randall	ID0060	61,36
Kenaston-French, Karen	TX3500	36,61,32D,40,60A
Kendrick, Johnaye	WA0200	61,47,29
Kenley, Nicole	TX1000	61
Kennedy, Charles	AL0630	11,70,66A,61
Kennedy, Frederick	TN1450	39,61
Kennedy, John S.	PA2550	61
Kennedy, Nancy	KS0570	11,61
Kennedy, P. Kevin	CO0625	61,60,12A,66
Kennedy, Richard R.	PA2750	61
Kennedy-Dygas, Margaret	LA0760	61,39
Kenney, Jessika	WA0200	61
Kenney, Sharon E.	AR0730	61,66D
Kenning, Kristin	AL0800	61,39
Kensmoe, Jeffrey	AL0300	61,39,36
Kent, Patricia A.	MN0350	61
Kent, Patricia	MN0300	61
Kerley, Jolaine	AA0100	61,55
Kern, Gene Marie Callahan	NY3650	61,36,13A,39
Kern, Jeffrey	PA3330	13A,36,44,61,66A
Kesling, Diane	AR0750	61
Ketchie, Diane	CA0835	61
Keys, Keven	IL2150	61
Khan, Shujaat Husain	CA5031	20E,62,61
Kho, Julia	IN0005	61
Kibler, Keith E.	MA2250	61,40
Kidd, Christine	NM0400	13A,61,11
Kidd, Murray	MA0800	61
Kierig, Barbara G.	MN1623	61
Kiesgen, Mary Stewart	MI0400	39,61
Kieval, Robert	NY1860	61
Killen, Seth R.	IL0800	61,54
Killian, Joni	IN0700	61,36,39
Killian, Joni	AZ0400	61
Killion, Jamie	CA0450	61,32,31A
Kim, Eun Hee	VA1350	61
Kim, Gloria	CA1265	61,13A,66A
Kim, Irene	CA2600	13A,61,36
Kim, Jaeyoon	NC2435	61,60A,36
Kim, Jin-Hee	CA3400	61
Kim, Jong H.	VA0750	36,13,61,60A,40
Kim, Jungwoo	MI1050	61
Kim, San-ky	TX3000	61
Kim, Soo Hong	TX3500	61,39
Kim, Soo Yeon	NY2650	61
Kim, Sun Ho	MA0350	61
Kim, You-Seong	OH1900	61
Kim, Youngsuk	PA2150	12A,39,61
Kim-Infiesto, Marilyn Liu	HI0160	36,61,12A,32,13A
Kimball, Carol	NV0050	12A,61
Kinchen, Lucy C.	CA2450	12A,36,61,66A
King, Amanda	TN1100	11,61
King, Ben R.	NY1700	11,12A,61,39
King, Cheryl H.	NY3717	61
King, Curtis R.	FL0600	13A,13,32,61,62
King, John	MI0100	61
King, Megan	AL1300	61
King, Nancy	NC2440	61
King, Pamela	TX3420	61
King, Ryan	AL1195	61
King, Sandi	CA3520	36,61,31A
King, Stephen	TX2150	61
King, Thomas R.	TN0050	39,61
King, Thomas D.	MD1000	61
Kinslow, Valerie	AI0150	61,55,67
Kirby, Anna-Lisa	AC0100	47,61
Kirchner, Walter	IL2750	39,61
Kirk, Betty	IL2775	61
Kirkeby, Gary	MD0700	12A,11,61
Kirkland, Glenda	MI0600	61
Kirkpatrick, Adam	GA1150	61
Kirkwood, David	CA0350	61
Kisselstein, Lisa A.	NY3770	61
Kitic, Milena	CA0960	61
Kitka, Claudia B.	CA0840	61
Kitson, Jeffrey	NE0040	11,13,36,40,61
Klapis, Ralph	IN1750	61,39
Klassen, David	AC0100	61
Klaus, Kenneth S.	LA0450	60A,11,36,61,40
Klein, Heidi	TX3420	61
Kleinecke-Boyer, Ursula Maria	CA3650	61
Kleinknecht, Daniel E.	IA1140	60,32,36,61
Kliewer, Jan Michael	WY0130	13,36,61,62D,38
Kling, Irene	NY2250	61
Klinger, Judith	CA0100	61
Klugh, Vaughn	AG0550	70,29,46,61
Knaub, Maribeth J.	PA3100	11,61,66D
Kness, Karen	MI2250	61
Knie, Robert	PA3250	61
Knight, Gerald R.	NC0750	36,60,61,32
Knight, Gloria J.	NC0700	32,36,61
Kniss, Karla	CA1425	61
Knoll, Richard C.	MO1810	61
Knott, Sarah	NE0610	61
Koch, Cheryl	SD0050	61
Koch, Elizabeth	AI0150	61
Koch, John M.	IL1150	61
Koehler, Hope E.	WV0750	61
Koehler, William D.	WV0750	61,39
Koehn, Daniel	KY0100	61
Koehn, Renita	KY0100	61
Koenig, Paul	NE0610	61
Koenigberg, Rebecca Anne	CO0650	61,11,54
Koestner, Bonnie	WI0350	39,61
Kohane, Sara	CT0900	61
Kolb, Lauralyn	NY1350	61
Kolker, Siobhan	NJ0800	61
Kolomyjec, Joanne	AI0150	61
Kompelien, Wayne	VA0650	40,61,60A
Koop, Ruth B.	AJ0030	13A,31A,35A,35E,61
Koozer, Robin R.	NE0300	36,61
Kopetz, Gail	OH0350	61
Kopta, Anne Elgar	AZ0100	61
Korbitz, Angela Presutti	IL2050	61
Koreski, Jacinta T.	WA0800	61,39
Korjus, Ingemar	AG0400	39,61
Kortz, Owen	CO0830	61,10D
Kosloff, Doris	CT0650	61
Koslowske, Charles T.	OK0750	66C,61
Kosowski, Richard	GA1300	61,39
Kot, Don	NY2650	66A,61,66D,66C,54
Kotowich, Bruce J. G.	IA0940	61,36,31
Kovach Brovey, Lisa	PA0500	61
Kowalski, Christina	WA1000	61
Kramer, John S.	NC0650	61,54,39
Kramer, Kenneth	OH1100	11,36,61
Kratochvil, Jirka	NY1400	36,60A,40,61
Kratzer, Dennis L.	OH1800	36,61,54,60A,40
Krause Wiebe, Anita	AG0500	61
Kreitzer, Jacalyn	CA0600	61
Kreitzer, Nathan J.	CA4410	61,36,40,55
Kress, David	CA5355	61
Kreutz, Michael	MA0850	61
Krogh, Dawn Pawlewski	NE0450	61,39
Kromm, Leroy	CA4150	61
Kromm, Nancy Wait	CA4425	39,61
Kronauer, Steven	CA0825	61
Krone, Claudia	ID0250	61
Krout-Lyons, Susan	IL0730	61
Krueger, Bradley	MI1180	61
Krueger, Joan	NY3785	61
Krueger, Mary Beth	CO0550	54,61,66C,66D
Krueger, Nathan E.	WI0830	61
Krusemark, William	KS1375	36,39,61,54,11
Kubey, Phyllis	NY2105	61
Kubiak, Teresa	IN0900	61
Kuhl, Margaret	NY1700	61
Kuhnert, Brian	TX3650	61,39,54,40
Kuhnert, Cloyce	TX3750	61,39
Kulas, Katherine F.	MN1600	61
Kunkle, Kristen C.	PA2000	61,39,11
Kurau, Pamela B.	NY3730	61
Kurth, Robert	PA2900	13C,61
Kutan, Aline	AI0150	61
Kutner, Michael	CT0650	61
Kutulas, Janet	CA2950	61
Kuzma, Marika C.	CA5000	36,40,60A,61
Kvach, Konstantin	OR0750	61
Kvach, Konstantin	OR0150	61,39
Kwanza, Evelyn	VT0450	61
Kwasniewska, Ewelina	AG0250	61
Kwiram, Bernie	WA0550	61
Kwiram, Bernie R.	WA0800	61
Kwoun, Soo Jin	MO0700	33,61,66A
Kyle, Maryann	MS0750	61,39
Kyles, Jerome Kwame	MA0260	61
Kyriakos, Marika V.	AR0110	61,39
LaBarr, Sarah	KS0590	61
LaBrie, Jesse	NE0300	61,36
Lacy, Randolph A.	KS1450	61
LaGraff, Scott	TX2700	61
Lai, Yun-Ju	CA5355	61
Lail, H. Wayne	NC0600	61
Lain, Larry	OH1600	61
Laine, Karin	NY0850	61
Laird, Helen L.	PA3250	39,61
Lake, Mary Kay	TX2250	61,39
Lakers, Janice	MI1150	61
Lalli, Richard	CT0900	55,61
Lamar, Gregory A.	NJ0800	61
Lamb, William	NM0500	61,63,32E
Lambert, Debra	CA3270	61,39,54
Lambert, Doris	OK0150	36,40,61,13C
Lambert, Evin R.	WA0750	11,36,66A,61,13A
Lammers, Paula	MN0610	29,61
LaNasa, Patricia J.	OH2150	61,11
Lancaster, Michael	NC2600	60A,55D,61,36,32D
Lancaster, Stephen J.	IN1700	61
Landis, Melissa McIntosh	CA6000	61
Landis, Melissa McIntosh	CA3200	61,36
Landry, Rosemarie	AI0200	61,39
Lane, Betty D.	MI2200	61,39
Lane, Diane	WI0300	61
Lane, Jennifer R.	TX3420	61
Lane, Kathleen	ID0100	39,61,36
Lane, Laura L.	IL1350	12A,60,36,40,61
Lang, Brenda J.	OH0550	36,60A,61,13A
Langager, Arlie	CA2960	36,47,40,61
Langan, David	NJ0700	61
Lange, Stephen R.	MI1200	66G,61
Langman, Shannon	TX1450	61
Lanier Miller, Pamela	AL0330	61,11,66A
Lanier, Brian	MO0950	32D,36,60A,61
Lanning, Rebecca	GA1260	11,36,61
Lanza, Lou	PA2450	61,47,29,41
Lanzrein, Valentin Christian	IN0350	61,66C
LaPierre, Art	CA0150	36,47,29A,61
Laprade, Paul	IL2560	13C,36,61,66D,32
Larsen, Catherine	MN1280	61
Larson, Andrew	FL1750	61,36,60A
Larson, Jennifer	IA1800	39,61
Larson, Nicholas A.	OR0700	61
Larson, Philip	CA5050	13A,11,12A,36,61
Larzelere, Raymond	NY1350	61
Lashbrook, Laurie E.	OH2150	61
Lassetter, Jacob	IA0950	61,39

Index by Area of Teaching Interest

Name	Code	Areas
Latimer, Carole	PA1150	61
Latour, Michelle R.	NV0050	61
Latta, Matthew	IN1800	61,32B,36,54
Lattimore, Jonita	IL0550	61
Lauer, Eileen	IL1900	61,11,20
Lavanne, Antonia	NY2250	61
Lavonis, William	WI0825	61,39
Law, Joshua T.	CA1020	36,61
Lawhead, David	FL1650	61
Lawhon, Sharon L.	AL0800	61,36
Lawler, Daniel J.	NY2750	61
Lawler, Daniel	NJ1160	61
Lawler-Johnson, Dian	GA0550	61
Lawley, Mark	MO0400	61
Lawrence, Barry	KY0250	61
Lawrence, Betsy	PA0550	61
Lawrence, Cynthia	KY1450	61,39
Lawrence, Lisa	FL0100	32,54,61
Lawrence, Sarah	WI0860	61
Lawrence, Wesley	ND0500	61
Lawrence, Wesley	OH0550	36,61
Lawson, Janet	NY2660	61,47
Lawson, William	NY3705	61,66C
Lawthers, Carol	CA4000	11,32B,61,66A
Lazarova, Maria	CA0825	61
Lazerow, Erica	CA1265	61
Leach, Margaret C.	AL1160	61
Leaf, Nathan	NC1700	36,60A,61
Leary-Warsaw, Jacqueline J.	AL0300	61,12A
Leathers, Gwendolyn	MA0260	61
Leathersich, Stacey	CA0150	11,61
Leatherwood, John G.	FL1430	61,11
Leblanc, Suzie	AI0200	61
Lebon, Rachel L.	FL1900	47,61,32,35A,54
LeClair, Ben	IL0600	61,39
LeClair, Benjamin	IL1615	61
Lee, Chia-Wei	TX3350	39,61
Lee, Christina	IL2775	61
Lee, Hae-Jong	OH2600	36,61
Lee, Helen	AB0100	61
Lee, In Young	PA3600	61
Lee, Janice	CA1000	61
Lee, Raejin	CA2420	61,39
Lee, Ranee	AI0190	29,61
Lee, Ranee	AI0150	61,29
Lee, Robert E.	OH1450	32,61
Lee, Soojeong	TX3300	61,39
Lee, Sujin	OH0300	61
Leeper, Brian K.	WI0865	61,39,54
Leese, Matthew	IL1750	61
LeFebvre, Timothy	OH1700	61
LeFevre, Carla	NC2430	61
Leffingwell, Dolores	OK1350	61
Lehman, Carroll	NH0150	40,39,61
Lehmann, Kathryn	WA1000	61
Lehmann, Mark	IA1800	61
Leibel, Jane	AD0050	61
Lein, Melinda	NC2650	61,12
LeMay, Lisa A.	NJ0825	61
Lemson, Lee	TX3850	13A,11,36,61
Lennon, Debby	MO1950	36,61,29,47
Lenth, Kristen	WY0050	61
Lentz, Jeffrey	PA0050	61,54
Leonard, Gwenellyn	OR0450	12A,61,39
Leonard, Linda	VA1350	61
Leonardo, Manuel	CA1400	11,12A,36,61
Leonhart, Carolyn	MA0260	61
Lerch, Natalie	WA0200	61,39
Lercia, Louise	TX0700	61
Leschisin, Taras	MA0510	61
Lester, Jason	TX1000	61
Lester, Laurie	TX1000	61
Lester, Timothy	FL1310	61
Letson, Roger	CA1450	61
Leupp Hanig, Nicole	OR1100	61
Levasseur, Susan	CO0100	61
Levy, Arthur	NY2150	61
Levy, Arthur	NY2250	61
Levy, Joanna	CT0650	61
Lewin, Ann	NY2250	61
Lewis, Alexander	FL1745	61,36,39
Lewis, Cheryse McLeod	FL1700	61
Lewis, Cheryse M.	NC2700	61
Lewis, Grant	SC0950	39,34,61
Lewis, Gregory	IL1350	61
Lewis, Jill Terhaar	SC0275	61
Lewis, Lori	MN1250	61
Lewis, Marcia	IN1750	61,35
Lewis, Susan	FL1730	61,66A,66G
Lewis, William	TX3510	39,61
Lewis-Hale, Phyllis	MS0350	61,39,32D
Leyerle, William	NY3730	61
Leyrer, Linda	CA0815	61
Leyrer-Furumoto, Linda	CA2390	61,39
Liberatore, William	CA3270	39,54,60,61
Lichti, Daniel	AG0600	61
Liebergen, Patrick	WI0855	11,36,61
Lightfoot, Peter W.	MI1400	61
Liles, B. David	OH1600	61,31A,39
Lilite, Louima	OK0650	61,39
Lilley, Marc Bryan	DC0050	61
Lillie, Erin	SD0300	61
Lin, Hsin Yi	TX2930	61
Lind, Robin A.	PA3650	32C,36,40,61
Linder, J. Michael	TX1775	13,36,61
Lindquist, Arne	MD0175	36,61
Lindsay, Julia	MI0250	11,61,54,39
Lindsay, Tedrin Blair	KY1450	61,66C
Lindsey, Lauren	WV0050	12A,36,40,61
Linduska, Mary	CA2975	61,36
Linduska, Mary	CA5510	61
Lines, Carol F.	LA0350	61
Linford, Jon	ID0060	39,61,32D
Linhart, Patricia M.	OH2200	61,54
Linkins, Jean Ellen	SC0050	61
Linnartz, Elizabeth Byrum	NC0600	61
Linney, Lloyd	FL1750	13,61,12A
Linton, Deborah	AG0050	61,13C
Lippard, Erin	TX2710	61,13A,13B,40,54
Lippoldt-Mack, Valerie	KS0210	11,36,61,32I,52
Lipscomb, Janice	AL0850	61
Lipton, Jeffrey S.	NY1275	12A,13B,32C,36,61
Lischetti, Robert	FL1745	61
Lissemore, Richard	NY2750	61
Lister, Linda J.	NV0050	61
Lister, Rebecca Crow	PA1900	61
Little, David	MI2250	39,61,54
Little, Gwenlynn	AG0500	61
Little, John A.	VA0600	61
Little, Marica	GA2000	61
Little, Ricky R.	KY0900	61
Liu, Xiu-ru	PA1050	39,61
Livesay, Charles	MI2000	60,32D,36,40,61
Livingston, Jaie	WA0700	61
Livingston-Friedley, Diana	ID0100	61
Livingston-Hakes, Beth	AZ0490	61,54,13A
Llewellyn, Cherrie	CA3000	11,61,54,39
Lloyd, Thomas	PA1500	36,61
Llyod, Adam	FL1550	61
Lo Verde, Carol	IL0720	61
Lobitz, Beverly	AR0800	13E,11,12A,61,13C
Lock, William R.	CA0350	60,36,61,31A
Lockard-Zimmerman, Barbara	OH0300	61
Locke, Benjamin R.	OH1200	13A,60,36,38,61
Locke, Randolph	FL0680	61
Lockery, Glen	ID0250	36,61
Lockett, Wendelyn	WI0050	61
Lockwood, Gayle	UT0050	39,61,54,20G,35
Lodine, Emily	IA1200	61
Loerch, Suzanne	AR0850	61
Loewen, Che Anne	AG0450	61,66A
Lofgren, Ronald R.	NE0700	11,32D,36,60A,61
Lofquist, Louise H.	CA3600	61,66C
Loftus, Jean	NY2950	39,61,54,13A,13B
Logan, Beverly	OH0050	61
Logan, Elizabeth	SD0200	61
Logan, Joseph C.	NC0050	12A,32,36,61
Logan, Shelly	WA0450	36,61
Lokken, Fred	WA0860	61
London, Amy	NY2660	61,47
Long, Daniel	TX2200	36,61,60,11,13D
Long, Lillian F.	WV0050	61,66C,66G,39,44
Long, Ron	AA0020	61,54
Long, Timothy G.	NY3790	61,66C
Longer-Schreck, Corlyn	MI0520	61
Longoria, Cynthia	TX0550	40,61
Loo, Janet	AG0500	61,32D
Loomis, Joy	FL2130	61,66
Loomis, Melinda	OR0600	61
Loos, James C.	IA0420	11,61,66A
Lopez, Barbara	CA0400	61,66A,10
Lopez, Ilca	PR0115	61,39
Lopez, Sarah	CA2960	61
Lopez, Zoraida	PR0115	61
LoPresti, Kathleen M.	FL1550	61
Lorimer, Christopher	IL3550	61
Louis, Kenneth	DC0350	36,61,31A
Loup, Francois	MD0650	61
Loushin, Boris M.	NY3780	61
Love, Lisa Reagan	OK0750	61
Love, Shirley	NY5000	61
Lovett, Rita	LA0750	61,54
Lowe, Emily	FL0730	36,61
Lowe, Nina Kay	TX3400	61
Lowezyk, Victoria	IL2775	61
Lowry, Julie	GA2130	61
Lowry, Lisa	IN1850	61
Lowry, Lisa M.	IN1800	61
Loy, David	MD0300	13C,61
Lualdi, Brenda	IL0850	61,54
Lubin, Renee	CA4200	40,61
Lubke, Sarah	IA1170	61
Lucia, Joyce	MA0260	61
Lucius, Sue Anne	AZ0440	39,61,54
Ludolph, Deborah	AG0600	61
Ludowise, Kathleen D.	CA4425	61
Lueck, John	CO0250	36,61
Luethi, Dean A.	WA1150	36,47,61,32D
Luggie, Brenda	TN1250	36,61,11
Lugo, Noemi	KY1450	61
Luiken, Jennifer	SC0275	61,39,54
Luna, Audrey	OH1450	61
Lund, Henriette	DC0050	61
Lund, Kara	RI0200	61
Lundberg, Steve	IA1100	61
Lundholm, Susan L.	IL0650	61
Lundholm, Susan	IL1085	61
Lundy, Joyce	DC0170	61
Lupica, Anthony J.	CA1700	36,38,13B,70,61
Lusmann, Stephen	MI2100	61
Lust, Patricia D.	VA0700	61,32
Luther, David	TN0200	60,36,61,31A,41
Lutter, Lisa	NJ0950	36,61,54,12A
Luttrell, Carol	PA3330	61
Lykes, Karen S.	OH2200	61
Lyle, Susan	SC0650	61,40
Lynam, Charles A.	NC2430	61
Lynch, Kelly	PA0600	39,61,11,12A
Lynch, Kelly Fiona	PA3000	61
Lynch, Kendra	CA0630	61
Lynch, Kendra	CA2650	61
Lynch, Shane	VA1850	36,40,61
Lynn	NE0550	60A,61,36,32C,32D
Lynn, Debra J.	IN1050	60,36,61,40,39
Lyon, Kristine	IL1650	61,66A
Lyon, Taylene	AA0040	61,47,53
Lyons, Lisanne E.	FL1900	61,29,53,47
Lytle, Gwendolyn	CA1050	61
Lytle, Gwendolyn L.	CA3650	61,20G
Mabbs, Linda	MD1010	39,61
Mabrey, Paul	OK1300	13,36,61
Mabry, Gary L.	TX3530	36,61
Mabry, Sharon	TN0050	61
MacDonald, April	AL0200	61,40,39
MacDonald, Don	AB0070	10,61,62A,64E,35A
MacDonald, Kathleen	MA0280	61
MacDonald, Lorna E.	AG0450	61
MacDonald, Pamela	AF0120	61,39
MacDougall, Tim	CA0825	61
Mack, John	CA0960	61
Mack, Jonathan	CA5100	61
Mack, Jonathan	CA6000	61
Mackus, Boyd A.	OH0200	61
MacLaren, Robert	AC0100	61,40
MacLean, Sherry	FL0150	61
MacLeod, Scott	NC0350	61
MacMullen, Jeffrey	OH1200	61
MacMullen, Michael J.	FL1470	13A,11,36,61,54
MacNeil, Robert	CA1000	13A,39,61
MacPhail, Jean	AG0450	61
MacPhail, Jean	AG0300	61
MacPhail, Valerie	SC0650	61
Maddison, Dorothy E.	VA0600	61
Maddox, Craig	FL1750	34,61
Maddox, Shelley	NC0400	61
Madison, Jeffrey W.	WI0860	61

Name	Code	Areas
Madison, Jeffrey	MN0250	61
Magee, Robert G.	AR0950	12A,60,36,61,31A
Maginnis, Patrice	CA5070	61
Mahaney, Cynthia	OH1200	61
Mahaney, Cynthia	OH1750	61
Mahraun, Daniel A.	MN1120	61,36,60A,40
Mahy, Daune	OH1700	61
Maier, Lori	CA3600	61
Major, Elizabeth	MI0050	11,39,61
Makarina, Olga	NY0500	61
Makris, Kristina	AZ0440	10,13,35A,29A,61
Malafronte, Judith	CT0850	61
Malas, Marlena Kleinman	NY1900	61
Malas, Marlena	PA0850	61
Malas, Marlena K.	NY2150	61
Malas, Spiro	NY2150	61
Malcher, Lindsay	SC0275	61
Malde, Melissa	CO0950	61
Malfitano, Catherine	NY2150	61
Malis, David H.	OK0800	61,39
Mallin, Claire	AF0050	13C,40,61,60A
Mallon, Rachel	AG0500	61
Mallory, Jason	IA0300	61,13C
Malone, Martha	GA1300	39,61
Maloney, Melissa	MI1750	61
Maloney, Patrick H.	IN1700	11,61
Mammon, Marielaine	NJ0250	12A,32,36,41,61
Mancusi, Roberto	TN1720	39,61,60A,13C
Maness, David	PA1150	13,60,11,36,61
Mangialardi, Robert	IL1200	61,39
Mangrum, Leslie	KS0700	61,36,39,12A
Mann, Jay	OH0950	61,36
Mannell, David	IN0907	11,61,36,32B
Mannell, David B.	IN0800	61
Mannion, Grace	MI2250	61
Manoli, Anthony	NY2250	61
Manring, Lesley	CO0950	61
Mantel, Sarah J.	PA1600	39,61,54
Manternach, LaDonna	IA0250	61,32B
Mantione, Meryl E.	IN0150	61
Manz, Lorraine	OH1700	61
Marano, Nancy	NJ1400	61,29
Marcellana, Jennifer	OH1200	61
Marek, Dan	NY2250	61
Mariman, Devin	NJ1350	61
Markham, Matthew E.	WI0850	61,39,40
Markou, Stella	MO1830	61,39,40
Markovic, Lorriana	MD0520	61
Markovic, Lorriana	MD0600	61
Markovic-Prakash, Lorriana	MD1000	61
Markuson, Steve H.	NY3765	11,12A,61
Markward, Edward	RI0200	38,61,60,39
Marlatt, Jeffrey	VA1350	32,61
Maroney, James	PA1100	11,36,61,13C,40
Marrazzo, Randi	PA3250	61
Marrs, Margie V.	IA0300	61,13A,13C
Marsch, Debra	IL1050	12A,61
Marsh, Marian	CA1650	61
Marshall, Allen	OK0300	60A,61,13
Marshall, Alyssa	TX1350	61
Marshall, Elizabeth	WV0250	61,36,40
Marshall, Lynda	IL1050	61,36
Marshall, Sharon	AG0650	61
Martel, Helene	AI0200	61,29
Martell, Vanessa	MN1270	61,12A,36
Martens, Victor	AG0600	61
Martin, Flora	MD0700	11,36,61
Martin, James	MS0385	61
Martin, Jessie Wright	NC2650	61,39
Martin, Melissa	NC2410	61
Martin, Melissa	NC1800	61
Martin, Nancy D.	KY1000	61
Martin, William	NC2600	61,11
Martinelli, Lisa	AG0450	29,61,47
Martinez, Mario E.	NY2650	61
Martins, Sandra Lau	AG0450	61
Martorano, Joseph P.	IL3450	61
Martz, Mary	MN1450	61
Martz, Mary	MN0300	61
Marvin, Marajean M.	OH1850	61
Marx, Susan A.	CO0250	61
Marzolf, Dennis	MN0200	60,36,31A,61,54
Mason, Patrick	CO0800	61
Mason, Rodney	TX0350	13,36,61,66A,66D
Masse, Denise	NY1900	61
Massell, Deborah P.	NY3780	61
Massie Legg, Alicia	TN1000	61,12A
Massie, Robin	NJ1350	61
Masterson, Kyle	NH0250	61
Masterson, Stephanie C.	FL1570	12A,61,54
Mastrian, Stacey	DC0010	61
Mastrian, Stacey L.	MD0650	61
Mastrian, Stacey	PA1400	61,39
Mastrodomenico, Carol	MA1900	61,39,54
Mastrodomenico, Carol	MA1175	61
Mastronicola, Michael	CO0400	61,66A,66D
Mather, Jennifer	IL0850	61
Matherne, Karl	LA0800	61
Mathews, Elisa	PA3560	61
Mathieson, Carol Fisher	MO0300	12A,39,61,31A,11
Mathis, Nancy	AR0730	61
Matson, Erin	NC2435	61
Matson, Jan	MN1400	61
Matsumoto, Shigemi	CA0825	61
Matsumoto-Stark, Shigemi	CA5300	61
Matthews, Andrea	MA2050	61
Matthews, Don	OR0950	61
Matthews, Katherine	SC0275	61
Matthews, Tamara	SC0750	61
Matts, Kathleen	WI0050	61
Matts, Kathleen	WI1150	39,61
Matych-Hager, Susan	MI1950	12A,32,36,61
Matzke, Kathleen	MN1400	61
Maughan, Sarah	NC2650	61
Maurer, Kathleen M.	IN0150	61
Maurice, Glenda A.	MN1623	61
Mautner, Roselida	FL0200	40,61,11
Maxedon, Lisa M.	LA0250	61,11,39
Maxfield, Lynn M.	IL1350	61
Maxwell, Don	TX1700	61,39
Maxwell, Francisca	GA0050	61
May, Judith	CA5353	61
May, Judy	AZ0100	61
May, Pam	MN1250	66A,61
May, Susan	GA1500	61
Maye, Shelia J.	VA0500	11,61,32
Mayer, Deborah L.	IN0910	61
Mayo, Christine H. Donahue	AR0850	61
Mayo, William M.	PA3250	61
Mazzacane, Roy	CT0800	61
McAdoo, Susan	NJ1140	13,61,36
McAmis, Carol	NY1800	61
McBerry, Sue	OR0400	61,54
McBride, Michelle	CT0650	61
McBroom, Deanna H.	SC0500	11,61
McCaffrey, Maureen	TN1400	11,61,32D,60A
McCaffrey, Maureen	TN1100	61
McCaffrey, Patricia	NY0500	61
McCain, Alisa	NC2000	61
McCann, Karen	NV0050	61,66C
McCargar, Barbara Witham	MI0300	11,61,39
McCarther, Sean	NJ1350	61
McCarthy, Cheryl	AF0120	66A,61
McCarthy, Kerry	DC0170	61
McCartney, Lynn R.	NH0300	61,11
McCauley, William	SC0200	12A,36,39,61
McClain, Denise	WA0700	61
McClain, Sandra	FL0650	61
McCleary, Harriet C.	MN1450	61
McClellan, Eleanor	AL1250	61
McClellan, Teresa	TN0600	12A,61
McClendon, Forrest	PA3250	61
McClurg, Bruce	CA0960	61
McCluskey, Eric	IL2900	61
McCluskey, P. Eric	GA1800	61
McConico, Marcus	MN1600	61
McConnaughey, Rebecca H.	MN0750	61
McConnell, Michele	NJ0825	61
McCord, Semenya	IL1350	61
McCormack, Jessica D.	IN0910	61,39,12,15,67H
McCorvey, Everett	KY1450	61,39
McCoy, Jane	NC1450	61
McCoy, Jane O.	NC2550	61,16,40
McCoy, Julie	TX3250	61,39
McCoy, Molly	TX3370	61
McCoy, Scott	OH1850	61
McCrary, William	TX3530	39,61
McCullough, Elizabeth L.	NY4500	61
McCullough, Richard D.	NY2950	13A,36,39,61,66D
McDade, Joanne Estelle	AR0350	61,66A
McDaniel, Alfred	CA4050	61
McDaniel, Catherine	OK0750	61
McDaniel, Jan	OK0750	39,54,66C,12A,61
McDermid, Aaron	ND0150	36,60A,61,11,32
McDermott, Pamela D. J.	VA0700	61,60,36,13C
McDermott, Sheila	LA0080	11,13,61,66D
McDonald, Elizabeth	AG0250	61
McDonald, Jean	IA1600	61
McDonald, Lynn	AG0650	61
McDonald, Shawn	MI1300	61,66C,39
McElligott, Brady R.	OK1450	61
McElroy, Donna	MA0260	61
McEvoy, Jeffrey S.	CT0600	61
McFarland, Joan	MD0750	61
McFarland, Joanne	PA1450	61
McGee, Isaiah R.	SC0350	35,36,39,61,32D
McGhee, Jeffrey	NY3350	61,39
McGhee, Mary	AG0170	61
McGilvray, Byron	TX3360	61,36,40
McGladrey, Cynthia	OR0250	61
McGraw, William E.	OH2200	61
McHugh, Kelli M.	IL1615	61
McIntosh, William	CA3200	36,61
McIntyre, Joy	MA0400	61
McIver, Robert	NY1100	61
McKee, Lindsey L.	MO1810	61
McKee, Lindsey L.	OK1450	61
McKee-Williams, Robin	CA2150	61,36
McKeel, James	MN1450	61,39,54
McKelvey, Michael E.	PA2900	35E,61,54,10
McKenzie-Stubbs, Mary E.	NJ0700	61,11
McKim, Christopher Z.	CO0225	61
McKinstry, Julia D.	NY4150	61
McKnight, Lynda Keith	TX3400	61
McLain, James	DC0010	61
McMahan, Jane	NY0200	61
McMahon, Michael	AI0150	39,40,66C,61,66A
McMillan, Kevin	VA0600	61
McMillan, William	TX3520	36,61,60
McMillin, Timothy A.	IA1350	60,36,61,32D,12A
McMurray, Heather A.	VA1475	61
McMurray, Mary	AF0120	61
McMurtry, Lynne	NY3725	61
McNair, Sylvia	IN0900	61
McNeely, April A.	CA4425	61
McNeil, Kathy J.	TX3200	61
McNeil, Linda	TX3350	39,61,54
McQuade, Jennifer H.	OK0650	61,39
McQuade, Mark A.	OK0650	61,39
McRoy, Danielle M.	NY2105	61
McSpadden, Larry D.	MO0300	36,61
McTyre, Robert A.	GA1400	11,13,61
McVeigh, Janice	CA5300	61
Meaders, James M.	MS0400	60A,36,61
Meadows, Christine	OR0850	39,61
Means, Allen	IL2450	36,61,63D,63C
Meashey, Kelly	PA1550	61,33
Mechell, Harry A.	MN1700	60,36,32D,61,54
Medley, Nathan	IN1100	61
Meehan, Linda Pearce	MI1260	61
Meek, David	AB0200	61
Megginson, Charlotte	IL3500	61
Megginson, Julie	GA1000	61,36,40,60A
Meixner, Micah L.	TX3200	61
Mekeel, Alison R.	PA1250	61
Mellinger, Erma	NH0100	61
Mellins-Bumbulis, Valija	TN0550	39,61
Melnick, Marjorie L.	MA2000	61
Melnick, Marjorie	CT0650	61
Melton, Michael D.	IL2150	36,40,32D,61,60A
Mendelson, Jacob	NY1860	61
Mendez, Genaro	KS1350	61
Mendez, Max	ID0140	61,36,42,47
Mendoza, Eleanor	IN0500	61
Mendoza, Juan Carlos	IL1800	61
Menke, Carol	CA4460	61
Menmuir, Dorla	CA4580	36,61
Mennicke, David	MN0610	31A,32,60,61
Mentzel, Eric P.	OR1050	61,67H,55,55D,55A
Mentzel, Michael G.	MD1050	61
Mentzel, Michael	MD0550	61
Mercer, Gregory S.	NY1600	61
Mercer, James	CA3400	32C,61,35C
Mercer, Scott A.	IN1800	13A,13,47,61,53
Mercier, William	VT0100	61
Meredith, Sarah A.	WI0808	39,61,54,15

Index by Area of Teaching Interest

Name	Code	Areas
Meredith, Steven	UT0190	13,36,61,34
Merrill, Suzanne Kantorski	VT0100	61
Merritt, Myra	OH0300	61
Merseth, Megan	MN0200	61
Messick, Heather	AL1195	61,43
Messoloras, Irene	OK0600	36,12,60A,61,40
Metcalf, Mark A.	TX3000	39,61
Metts, Calland	MN1600	61,36
Meuth, Alison	IL1800	61
Meyer, David	VA1350	61
Meyer, Julie	MI1850	61
Meyers, Carolyn	NC0650	61
Meyers, Heather	AA0020	61
Meyers, Joseph	IN0905	39,61
Miano, Jo Ellen	NY3775	13A,36,61,32I,40
Mianulli, Janice	PA2100	61
Mianulli, Janice	PA1650	61,40,36
Michael, Marilyn	FL1650	39,61
Michaels, Cary	TX3175	61
Michel, Christopher	TX2250	61
Micic, Alma	NY5000	61
Midboe, David J.	WI0801	61
Middleton, Jaynne	TX0900	61,12A,54
Mieske, Lynda	AG0600	61
Mihai-Zoeter, Mariana	MD0350	61,39
Mihalik, Denise	NJ0500	61
Mikkelsen, Carol M.	GA2150	61,39
Miklik, Carlie	WI0842	61
Milanese, Jessica	WA0650	61
Milenkovic, Michelle	AA0020	32A,61
Milham, Edwin M.	MA0510	11,61
Miller, Al	AL1195	60,61,36,43
Miller, Christian	OH0680	61,36
Miller, Cory	AA0020	61
Miller, Dale	AR0110	60,36,61
Miller, Dan	IN1800	12A,36,44,61
Miller, David	OR0010	36,61,13,60
Miller, Donna Z.	NY4150	61
Miller, Jean	TN0930	61
Miller, Josh	WV0200	36,61,32D,11,60A
Miller, Karla	MN1260	13A,11,36,61,66A
Miller, Kathleen A.	NY3780	61
Miller, Kenny	AZ0470	13C,12A,36,40,61
Miller, Kristi	MN1620	61
Miller, Lisa	IN1800	32,61,54,12A
Miller, Maureen	PA2950	61
Miller, Patricia A.	VA0450	39,61,54
Miller, Peter	IN1025	61,11
Miller, Peter	TX3360	66C,61,64C,66G
Miller, Rebecca C.	KY0610	61
Miller, Ronald E.	PA2050	13A,36,61
Miller, Russell	NY1100	61
Miller, Scott D.	WA1350	61,39
Miller, Thomas A.	OR1150	60A,11,36,61,31A
Miller, Timothy	GA1450	61
Miller, Wendy L.	PA0250	11,12A,36,61,54
Miller-Campbell, Tamara J.	MO1900	61
Millet, Wayne	FL1500	61
Mills, Susan W.	NC0050	20,32B,32C,61,36
Milner Howell, Denise	OH0100	61
Milton, Jos	MS0700	61
Mims, Lloyd	FL1450	61,31A,38
Mims, Marilyn	FL1450	61,39
Minneman, Ginger	OH2500	61
Minsavage, Susan	PA3700	61,39
Minter, Drew	NY4450	61,40,39
Minter, Karen	KS0100	12A,39,61
Mismas, James	OH2290	61
Misslin, Patricia	NY0150	61
Misslin, Patricia	NY2150	61
Misslin, Patricia	MA1400	61
Mitchell, Christopher	KY0950	61,39
Mixson, Vonnetta	CA1000	61
Mizell, John	MO0200	61
Mobbs, Daniel	CA4150	61
Modesitt, Carol Ann	UT0200	39,61
Moeller, Cindy R.	IA1200	61
Moham, Carren D.	IL1200	20G,61
Moir, Jennifer	AG0500	36,61
Mokole, Elias	MN1600	61
Moliterno, Mark	NJ0175	61
Moliterno, Mark	NJ1350	61
Momand, Elizabeth B.	AR0730	39,61,32
Monaghan, Megan	PA2550	61
Monahan, Laurie	MA1175	61,55
Monek, Daniel G.	OH1400	36,61,12A,60
Mongiardo, Josephine	NY4200	61
Mongiardo-Cooper, Josephine	NY0200	61
Moninger, Susan	IL0850	36,40,47,61
Monroe, Annetta Y.	FL2000	61
Montalbetti, Barbara	AJ0150	61
Montalvo, Raquel	PR0100	36,61,13B
Montane, Carlos	IN0900	61
Montcrieff, Kathy	NY2950	61
Monteiro, Shawnn	RI0150	61
Monteiro-Huelbig, Shawnn	RI0200	61
Montequt, Dreux	LA0300	61
Montgomery, Alice	MO1950	61
Montgomery, Cheri	TN1850	61
Montgomery, Ron	TX2600	61
Montgomery, Susan	CA0960	61
Montgomery-Cove, Deborah	NY1800	61
Moody, David	NY1900	39,61
Moody, Duane	MA0260	61
Moody, Kevin M.	TX0075	54,61,11,36,40
Moody, Philip	GA2100	36,60A,61
Moon, Kimberle	FL0040	61,54
Mooney, Chris	VA0150	61,39
Moore, Alison	KS0215	36,61
Moore, Andrea	NC2410	61
Moore, Barbara	TX2400	61
Moore, Britt	VT0300	13L,34D,35,61,34E
Moore, Celina	VT0250	61
Moore, Deena	NC2700	61
Moore, Edgar	TX2300	11,36,61,12A
Moore, Eileen Marie	OH0650	61
Moore, Keith	TN0100	61
Moore, Laura M.	AL1300	36,40,60A,61,66C
Moore, Marilyn	DE0050	61
Moore, Marilyn	DC0170	61
Moore, Nora	VA1125	61
Moore, Rager H.	AR0730	60A,61
Moore, Tim	FL0670	40,61,54
Moore-Mitchell, Teresa A.	NC2700	11,61
Moore-Mitchell, Teresa	NC1150	61,11
Mooyman, Lisa	OR0150	61
Morales, David	CA2910	13A,11,36,61,66
Moran, Kathryn	WI0810	36,61
Moran, Leslie Mason	PA2200	61
Moran, Sarah E.	IL1350	61
Morehouse, Dale	MO1810	61
Morel, Vincent	AI0200	47,36,61
Moremen, Eileen	GA1150	61,39
Moreno, Madja	PR0100	39,61
Morgan, Leslie	IA1600	61
Morgan, Nicole	IL1750	61
Morningstar, Timothy P.	NY3775	61,11
Morren, Christian	OK1200	61
Morrical, Sharon	IA0790	61
Morris, Gary	AR0200	36,40,60A,61
Morris, Robert B.	AB0100	61
Morris, Steven	MA1900	39,61,66C
Morrison, Amy	SD0580	61
Morrison, Barbara	CA5031	61,29
Morrison, Becky	OK0300	61
Morrison, Harry	MO1650	61,54
Morrison, Mary	AG0450	61
Morrow, Cindy	TX3510	61
Morrow, David E.	GA1450	60,11,36,61,66A
Morrow, Diane	OK1450	61
Morrow, Jeff	IL0550	47,61
Morrow, Lynne	CA4700	39,54,60A,61
Morrow, Phil J.	NC0300	60,36,31A,61
Morrow-King, Janet	CO0250	61,39,12A
Morscheck, Stephen M.	TX3420	61
Mortier, Steve	WA0250	61
Morton, Glenn	NY2250	66C,61
Morton, Stephen C.	MO1830	61
Moses, Oral	GA1150	11,36,61
Mosher, Allan R.	OH2600	39,61
Mosher, Jennifer Jones	OH2600	61
Moss, Gary	IA0950	61,13C
Moss, Orlando	MS0560	13,60,36,61
Moss, Vivian	TX1660	61
Mosteller, Paul W.	AL1150	61,11
Mosteller, Steven	IL0750	39,61
Moteki, Mutsumi	CO0800	61
Mott, Jammieca	TX2250	61
Moulson, Magdalena	GA1050	61
Mount, John	HI0210	39,61
Mount, Megan M.	HI0210	61
Moura, Juliana	KY0400	61
Mouradjian, Joanne	MA2150	61
Mow, Paul	MI1985	61,54
Mow, Paul	MI1180	61
Mowry, Mark R.	WI0803	39,61
Moxness, Diana	MN1000	32B,61
Moyer, Kathryn	NJ0175	61
Mozzani, Pina	KS1450	61
Muilenburg, Harley	CA2250	36,61,60A,40
Mulholland, James Q.	IN0250	11,61
Mullen, Wendy Anne	GA0850	61,54,39
Muller, Marc	NJ0760	61
Mundinger, Gretchen	NY0500	61
Mungo, Nichelle	MA0260	61
Mungo, Samuel	TX3175	61,39
Munn, Vivian C.	TX3525	13,32C,36,61
Munton, Amanda	NH0250	61
Munzer, Cynthia	CA5300	61
Muriello, John R.	IA1550	61
Murnak, Raina	FL1900	61
Murphree, Martin R.	MO0800	61
Murphree, Scott	NY2750	61
Murphy, Heidi Grant	IN0900	61
Murphy, Joy-Anne	AA0110	61
Murphy, Kevin M.	NY2750	61
Murphy, Sheila C.	FL2100	61,39,32D
Murphy, Suzanne	NY1550	61
Murray, Alan	KS0570	61
Murray, Amy	VA1350	61
Murray, Deanna A.	CA0835	61
Murray, Ellie	OR0950	61
Murray, John	AA0025	61,36,13A,13C
Murray, Monica	MN0610	11,13A,61
Murray, Pamela	MA0850	61
Murray, Paul	CA4425	61
Murray, Susannah	CA4500	61
Murray, Susannah	CA2600	61
Musgrave, Helen	AR0425	61
Mussard, Timothy S.	OH0200	61
Musselman, Susan	OH2450	61,39
Musselwhite, Harry	GA0300	60,36,39,61
Muto, Vicki	CA3500	61
Muto, Vicki	CA5300	61
Muto, Vicki	CA1750	39,61
Myers, Carolyn	NC0650	61
Myers, Myron	IL2200	39,61
Myers, Patricia	GA0250	12A,61,11
Myrick, Kathleen	NJ0760	61
Myrick, Korby	CT0650	61
Nabholz, Fran	GA0250	61
Nabors, Louis A.	LA0770	36,61
Nachef, Joanna	CA1750	60,11,36,61
Nadel, Richard	NY1860	61
Naeve, Denise	IA0790	61,66A,13
Nafziger, Erin	MA2250	61,40
Nagel, Douglas	MT0175	61,36,60A,13C
Nagle, Lynn	CA0630	61
Nagy, Jennifer	AZ0440	61
Nagy, Karen	FL1310	61,39
Nair, Garyth	NJ0300	36,38,61,60,13C
Nakamae, Ayumi	NC0450	61,36,40,67F
Nakasian O'Brian, Stephanie	VA0250	61,29
Nakasian, Stephanie	VA1550	61
Nall, Cecily	TN1710	61
Nam, Esther Hyun	KY1000	61
Nam, MeeAe Cecilia	MI0600	61
Nam, Seong	VA0450	61
Namaradze, Medea	MD0150	61
Nanni, Steven	NY1400	61,32D
Nash, Anne Jennifer	MN0600	61
Natter, Robert	PA1400	34,36,61,60A
Navari, Jude Joseph	CA4625	10,11,13,36,61
Neal, David E.	NY3720	61,54,39,36
Neal, Paul	GA2150	36,60A,61,60
Neblett, Carol	CA0960	61
Nedvin, Brian A.	VA1000	61,39
Neely, Dawn Wells	AL0010	61
Neely, William J.	CA4460	61
Neese, Bethany	CA4460	61
Neill, Kelly	AR0250	32D,36,40,61
Neill, William	OK1350	61
Neisinger, Robert	WA0450	61,65
Neiweem, David	VT0450	36,61
Nelson, Daniel	WI0825	39,61
Nemhauser, Frank	NY2250	13,60,61

Index by Area of Teaching Interest

Name	Code	Areas
Ness, Corinne	WI0250	61,54,32B,39
Nesselroad, Sidney	WA0050	61
Nessinger, Mary	NY4450	61
Nettles, Darryl	TN1400	13B,32D,36,39,61
Neubert, Nils	NJ1400	61
Neubert, Nils	NY5000	61
Neufeld, Charles W.	SC0800	60A,61,36,32D
Neufeld, Hannah	KS0150	61
Neville, Shelley	AD0050	61
Nevola, Teresa	PA1150	61,54,20G
Newby, Linda	TN0550	61
Newell, Julie L.	NY3725	39,61
Newell, Lawana	OK0600	61,54
Newland, Martha	NJ1160	61
Newman, David A.	VA0600	61
Newman, Miranda	TX3535	61
Newman, Miranda	TX1510	11,61
Newsom, Mary Ellen	IN0005	12,14,32,61,62
Newton, Robyn	WA1300	61
Ng, Jonathan	AZ0480	36,61
Ng, Stephen	PA3600	61
Niblock, Carol B.	PA0100	61
Niblock, James D.	PA0100	36,61,60A,13A,13B
Nice, Julie	LA0560	61
Nicholas, Alexander	FL1550	61
Nicholas, Julie	CA1650	29,61,47
Nicholas, Scott	MA0850	61,66A
Nichols, Clinton	MS0360	61
Nichols, Laura L.	MN0950	61
Nichols, Lena	IA0930	61
Nichols, Will	MI0150	60,36,61,39
Nicholson, Hillary	RI0150	61,39
Nicolosi, Ida	CA3600	61,32B
Nicolson, Mark	NJ0825	61
Nicosia, Judith	NJ1130	61
Niederloh, Angela	OR0750	61,39
Niederloh, Angela	OR0850	61
Niehoff, Carolyn	IL1085	61
Nielsen, John	IA0650	61,32
Niemann, Judith A.	FL0400	61
Nieuwenhuis, Mary	MI0450	13A,11,36,61
Nikkel, Laurinda	CA4100	61
Niles, Carol Ann	CO0225	36,61
Nims, Marilyn	OH2000	61,13C,32D
Nims, Robert	OH2050	61
Nine-Zielke, Nicola	OR0700	61,66C
Nishibun, Tiffany	AL0345	11,61
Nishibun, Tiffany	AL0450	13A,61
Nispel, Anne	MI1400	61
Niu, Elaine	WI0750	61,39,36,60A,13C
Nix, Catherine	TX3530	61
Nix, John Paul	TX3530	61,13L,32D
Nixon, Justin Taylor	CA3270	61
Nixon, Patricia	VA0950	36,46,13C,61
Noble, Timothy R.	IN0900	61
Noel, Emily	PA1300	61
Noone, Katherine	ND0350	61,54
Noonkester, Lila D.	SC0800	13,39,61,11
Norberg, Rebecca	MN1250	61,54,12A,11
Nordhorn, Johanna	MO1950	61
Norin-Kuehn, Deborah	OH0950	61
Norman-Sojourner, Elizabeth	IL0600	61,39,12
Norris, Elizabeth	VT0300	11,13A,20,61,36
Northcott, Erica	AB0050	61
Nosworthy, Hedley	CA1750	36,61
Nova, Christian	CA2750	61
Novak, Richard A.	VA0450	61,39
Novenske-Smith, Janine L.	MI1200	61,36
Novick, Martha	NY1860	61
Nubar, Lorraine	NY0150	61
Nubar, Lorraine	MA1400	61
Nunez, Rachel	OH1350	61,36,31A
Nurullah, Shahida	AG0550	29,46,61
Nyetam, Rachel	TN1600	61
Nystrom, Alison	AB0060	61
Nystrom, Alison	AB0090	61
Oakley, Paul E.	KY0800	61,31A,36
Oakley, Paul E.	NC0350	36,40,61,11
Oaten, Gregory	PA2450	60,61
Obermeyer, Janet	AG0650	61
O'Brien, Clara	NC2430	61
O'Brien, Kathleen	CA2960	61
O'Brien, Richard	TX2930	61,13A,13B,13C
O'Brien, Tanya	PA2450	61
Oby, Jason	TX3150	36,39,61
Ocampo, Rebecca	DC0100	61
Ocel, Timothy	MO1900	61
O'Connell, Cynthia	OH0200	61
Octave, Thomas	PA2950	61,36,39,40,11
Odom, Aaron	AL1195	61
Odom, Gale J.	LA0050	61
Odom, Lisa Sain	SC0400	11,61,36
Oeck, Cynthia	IL1750	61
Oehlers, K. Rebecca	PA1000	61
Oehme, Jane	NY2900	61
Oeste, Wolfgang	AR0850	39,61
Offerle, Anthony	FL1850	39,61
Ogden Hagen, Linda	IL2050	61
Ogg, Janette	VA1350	61
Ogle, Deborah A.	GA1200	36,13A,60,40,61
Ogle, Nancy Ellen	ME0440	39,61
Oh, Annette	IL1090	11,61,36,13B,13C
Oh, Jung Eun	OH0600	61
Oh, Sun-Joo	TN0500	61,39
O'Hern, Eilene	CA5355	61
Ohl, Ferris E.	OH0950	60,36,61
Ohrenstein, Dora	NY4500	61
Oie, Cheryl	MN0250	61
Okerlund, David	FL0850	61
Oliver, Gale	CA4450	61
Ollmann, Kurt	WI0825	61,39
Olm, James	WY0050	54,61,13A
Olsen, David	ID0060	32D,39,61
Olsen, Gayle	NY0050	61
Olsen, Rebecca	ID0060	61
Olsen, Ryan	ID0050	61
Olsen, Stanford	MI2100	61
Olson, Margaret	MD0600	61,39
Olson, Robert	ND0350	39,61,54
Olson, Susan	TX3530	61
O'Neill, Patricia A.	LA0200	61
Oosting, Stephen	NJ0800	61,54
Oostwoud, Roelof	AB0100	61
Opalach, Jan	NY1100	61
Opatz-Muni, Mari	OH1450	39,61
Oram, Virginia	IN1750	61
Oreskovich, Kristina	NE0250	61
Ormond, Nelda C.	DC0350	39,61
Orr, Sue Butler	SC0710	11,36,61
Orta, Melissa	TX1850	61
Ortega, Anne	PA1200	39,61
Orton, Billy H.	AL1160	36,60A,60B,61,63C
Orton, Korianne	UT0050	61
Osborne, Brian	OK0750	66C,61
Osborne, Robert	NY4450	61
Osborne, Robert M.	NY2550	61
Osbun-Manley, Kirsten E.	OH1800	39,61,54
O'Shea, Lindsy	MN1400	61
O'Shea, Patrick	MN1400	60,12A,36,61,10A
Osifchin, Matthew	PA1400	61
Osmond, Melissa	MI1000	61,39
Oswald, Mark	NY2150	61
Otal, Monica D.	MD0175	36,61,11
Ottley, JoAnn	HI0050	39,61
Ottsen, Linda	CA5360	61,39
Outland, Randall	NC0050	61
Overholt, Sherry	NY3785	61
Overholt, Sherry	NY0642	39,61
Owen, Kenneth L.	WA0750	11,61,36,66A,13A
Owen-Leinert, Susan	TN1680	61
Owens, Chris	VA1550	61
Owens, Diane	NE0160	61
Owens, Richard R.	FL1550	61,39
Owens, Theodore	NV0125	10,11,12A,61,54
Owens, Tiffany	OH0680	61,13C,40
Owren, Betty Ann	CA1760	36,61,13C,13A,11
Oxler, Cora Jean	TX3370	61,11,13C
Oxley, Michael	IA0700	61
Oyen, Valerie	TN1600	36,61
Oyen-Larsen, Valerie	TN0100	61
Pace, Mark	NC1750	66G,36,61
Pack, Shari	ID0060	61,62E
Padula, Dawn M.	WA1000	61,39
Pagano, Stephen	NY1275	13C,61
Page, Carolann	NJ1350	54,61
Paglialunga, Augusto N.	WV0750	61
Pahel, Timothy	IL1800	32,36,61,12A
Paige-Green, Jacqueline	LA0700	61,39,11
Palmer, Leila S.	SC0600	61
Palmer, Richard	NE0610	61
Palmquist, Krista	WI0845	61
Palomaki, Jonathan	IL0300	12A,32B,36,70,61
Palomaki, Jonathan	TX3800	60,12A,36,61,70
Pampinella, Paul	MA0260	61
Pandolfo, Susan	AG0070	61
Pannill Raiford, Judith	OK0850	61
Paoletti, Karl P.	GA2150	61
Pape, Madlyn	TX1900	36,61
Paradise, Kathryn L.	TN0100	61,54
Pardue, Dan	NC1400	36,61
Pare', Barbara A.	IN0350	61,40
Parent, Yolande	AI0200	61
Parins, Linda	WI0808	61
Park, Dong Hoon	KY1200	61
Park, Jong-Won	WI0845	36,40,61,60A
Park, Kyunghee	MD0700	61
Parker Bennett, Dione	OH0100	61
Parker, Clinton R.	NC0050	11,61
Parker, David	SC0200	61,34
Parker, Gregory B.	NC0400	36,61,60A,40,32D
Parker, Kara	FL1430	61,36
Parks, Andrew	WA0800	61,31A,12A,36
Parks, David	NY1800	61
Parks, Karen	SC0765	61
Parks, Sarah S.	WI0750	36,32D,60A,61
Parnell, Dennis	CA2700	11,36,61
Parnell, Dennis	CA4450	61,36
Parodi, Jorge	NY2750	40,61,66C
Parody, Caroline D.	NJ0800	66D,61
Parr, Kimerica	AA0032	61
Parrish, Cheryl A.	TX3175	61
Parrish, Eric	MN1175	11,13,36,61
Parrish, Steve	NC1050	61,54
Parry, A. Scott	OH1850	61
Parsons, Larry R.	WV0800	36,61,31A
Parton-Stanard, Susan	IL1500	61,40,36,11,32D
Partridge, Norma	OK0650	39,61
Pascale, Joanna	PA3250	29,61
Pastelak, Marianne	MD0475	61,40
Pastore, Patrice	NY1800	61
Patenaude-Yarnell, Joan	PA0850	61
Patenaude-Yarnell, Joan	NY2150	61
Paterson, Janice	AJ0150	61
Pato-Lorenzo, Cristina	NJ0825	61
Paton, John Glenn	CA3100	61
Patrelle, Francis	NY2150	61
Patrick-Harris, Terry	LA0200	61
Patterson, Chris	MN0625	61
Patterson, Heather	MO1950	61
Patterson, Paula K.	MO0775	39,61
Patterson, Trent A.	MO1950	60A,61,32,36,39
Patton, Patrick	WY0050	36,61,40
Patton, Richard	IN1025	61
Paukert, Noriko F.	OH0650	61
Paul, David	NY1900	61
Pauley, John-Bede	MN0350	61,13,11
Paulsen, Kent D.	WI0750	36,32D,61,60,13C
Pauly, Elizabeth	MN1050	61,60A,11,36,13A
Pauly, Elizabeth	MN1295	61
Pavelka, Dee	MO1950	61
Paver, Barbara E.	OH2200	61
Pavloski, Rachael	OH2600	61
Pawlowski, Lauressa	AA0020	61
Paxson, Joyce M.	WA0600	61
Paxton, Laurence	HI0210	39,61,54
Paxton-Mierzejewski, Adele	CT0050	61
Payn, Catherine	PA0350	32,39,61
Payne, Bryon	FL1600	61,62,66A
Payne, Richard Todd	MO0775	61
Payton, Chad	MS0250	11,13C,61
Payton, Denise	NC0800	20A,36,39,60A,61
Peabody, Martha	MA1450	61,33,13C
Pearl, Phillip	WI1150	61
Pearon, Jill R.	NY3780	61
Pearson, Mark	MA1400	61
Pease, Patricia	OH1900	61
Peavler, Robert	MI0600	61
Peck, Andrew	ID0060	61
Peck, David	ID0060	12A,12B,12C,61
Peckham, Anne	MA0260	61
Pedersen, Thomas	DC0050	36,39,54,56,61
Pedigo, Julia N.	NC0050	61
Peebles, Stew	NV0150	61
Peeler, Karen	OH1850	61
Pehlivanian, Elisabeth	CA0825	61,32D
Pendarvis, Janice	MA0260	61

Index by Area of Teaching Interest

Name	Code	Areas
Pender, Charles	TN1380	13,11,61,66A,60
Pendleton, Karen A.	ME0440	61
Peng, Yan	MO0950	61
Penn, Stephen T.	KY1450	61,66C
Penna, J.J.	NY1900	61
Penner, Julie	TN1350	11,61
Penning, Rick	MN0050	61
Penning, Rick	MN0300	61
Penning-Koperski, Diane	MI0850	61
Pennix, Derrick A.	IN0200	61,39
Penny, Michael K.	TN1660	39,61,31A
Pereira, Jose Ricardo	AZ0450	61
Pereira, Kenneth	WI0803	61
Perez, Olga	OH1650	61,40,32B
Perez-Feria, Willy	FL1310	47,61
Peri, Janis-Rozena	WV0750	61
Perinchief, Burt H.	FL1700	61
Perkins, Daniel R.	NH0250	36,61,12A,32D,60A
Perna, Nicholas K.	WV0750	61
Perniciaro, Joseph C.	KS0350	39,61
Perry, Talya	MO1110	61,66A
Peters, Braxton	MD0100	61
Peters, Braxton	MD0175	61
Peters, Maitland	NY2150	61
Peterson, Ken	UT0150	36,39,40,61
Peterson, Melissa	MO0700	61
Peterson, Patti	CO0800	61
Peterson, Robert L.	MN0950	36,61,60A
Petillot, Elizabeth A.	WI0803	61
Petrie, Anne M.	IA0200	39,61
Petrik, Rebecca	ND0250	32,13A,61,70,36
Petrongelli, Amy	OH2150	61
Pfaltzgraff, Brian	IA1800	61,39
Pfaltzgraff, Carita	IA1800	61
Pfautz, John S.	IL0100	39,61,31
Pfeiffer, Dale	MA0260	61
Pfutzenreuter, Leslie D.	CA2840	11,36,38,39,61
Phelps, Mark D.	IN0900	61
Philbrick, Tom	IL1610	61
Philip, Annette	MA0260	13,11,36,61,66A
Philipsen, Michael D.	IA0750	13,11,36,61,66A
Phillips, Burr Cochran	CA5350	61,39
Phillips, Gerald	MD0850	11,61
Phillips, Patricia	NJ0825	61
Phillips, Paula	AF0120	61,32A
Piastro-Tedford, Sasha	PA2100	61
Picard, Annie	IL1890	61
Picard, Annie	IL2100	61
Picard, Betty	MI1160	60A,61
Pickering, Amy	IL0850	61
Pickering, Amy J.	IL3310	61
Pickering, Angela	TX1400	61
Pickreign, Christina	NY3600	61
Picon, Jeffrey	OK0750	61
Pier, Christina	NC0350	61
Pierce, Alice O.	MN1600	61,39
Pierce, Dawn	NY1800	61
Pierce, Edward A.	OK0850	40,61,36
Pierce, John	MN1600	61
Pierce, Karen	ME0200	61
Pierce, Laura	MA2250	61,40
Pierce, Marilyn	MI1200	61
Pierce, Stephanie D.	GA2100	61
Pierpoint, Paula	FL0950	61,66A,66D
Piersall, Paul	TX0050	61
Piersall, Rick	TX0050	39,61,12A
Pilar, Nobleza Garcia	FL1900	61
Pilgrim, Neva	NY0650	61
Pilkington, Jonathan	GA1650	61,39,11
Pilon, Sherri	MI1050	61
Pindell, Reginald	PA3330	36,39,61
Pinkerton, Louise	ND0500	61,12A
Pinza, Claudia	PA1050	61
Piper, Scott	MI2100	61
Pisciotta, Eva Mae	AZ0200	36,61,29A
Pitt-Kaye, Melinda	IL1610	61,11
Pittman, Reginald L.	KS0650	39,61,54
Pittman-Jennings, David	NY3780	61
Pitts, Frank	MI1830	61
Pittson, Suzanne	NY0550	29,61
Plack, Rebecca	CA4150	12,61
Plagemann, Melissa	WA0650	61
Planer, John H.	IN1050	20,12,13,14,61
Planet, Janet	WI0350	61
Plant, Lourin	NJ1050	60,36,41,61
Plantamura, Carol	CA5050	12A,55,61,54,43
Platt, Nathan	KY1200	13,60,61,31A
Playfair, David M.	AC0050	61,39
Pleasure, Ruby	CA4150	61
Plemons, Susan	OH0450	61
Plew, Paul T.	CA2810	60,36,61,31A
Pluer, Robin	WI1150	61
Poetschke, Linda	TX3530	61
Poff, Megan	AL1160	61,11
Poland, Jeffrey T.	WV0300	32D,36,61,60
Pomfret, Bonnie	MA0400	39,61
Ponce, Alma Mora	CA3300	61
Poniros, Risa	NC1500	32B,40,36,61
Poore, Mary Elizabeth	NY5000	61
Poore, Mary Elizabeth	NY2400	61
Poovey, Gena E.	SC0850	36,61,60A,32D,40
Pope, Andrea	IL1750	61
Pope, Beth	KY1550	61
Pope, Beth	KY0800	61
Pope, Jerrold	MA0400	61
Pope, Wayne	KY1550	39,61,41
Popescu, Annamaria	AI0150	61
Popham, Deborah	GA1800	61,39
Poppino, Richard	OR0700	61,39
Poretsky, Susana	CA5060	61
Poris, Jill	OR1100	61
Porter, Amy	WA1350	61
Porter, Beth Cram	OH0450	36,61
Porter, Janine	OH0755	61,39
Porter, Lenore	CA5360	61
Porter, Marcia	FL0850	61
Porter, Michael	NC0250	36,40,60,61,32D
Porter, Miriam	IL1050	61
Porter-Borden, Catherine	MD0500	61
Porterfield, Priscilla J.	NC0050	61,36
Post, Bryan	WI0350	61
Post, Karen Leigh	WI0350	61,39
Posvar, Mildred Miller	PA0550	61
Poteet, Sherry	TX1350	61,11
Pott, Jack	CT0050	61
Potter, Thomas	FL1800	61,39
Poulimenos, Andreas	OH0300	61
Poulimenos, Andreas	IN0900	61
Poulson, Ruby Ann	MN0250	61
Powe, Holly	AL0330	61,13,11,60,47
Powell, Rosephanye	AL0200	61,36
Powell, Steven S.	PA1000	36,61,34,12A,32D
Power, David	UT0250	61
Praniuk, Ingrid	CA1000	61
Pranschke, Janet	NY4500	61
Prentice, Tracy	TN1850	61
Preston, Darnelle	WA0400	61
Presutti Korbitz, Angela	IL3450	61
Prewitt, Kenneth	MI2250	39,61
Price, Andrea M.	GA1650	61,39,14
Price, David	OH2050	61
Price, Henry P.	CA3600	61,39,12A
Price, Holly S.	CA3650	61
Price, Jeffrey	NC2420	61,66D
Price, Kathy Kessler	NJ1350	61
Price, Ruth	CA5031	29,61
Pridmore, Helen	AE0050	61,39,41
Priebe, Craig	IN0150	61,39
Prince, Noel	MO1900	61
Prindle, Roma	KY0900	39,61
Proudfoot, Carol	AZ0490	61
Prowse, Robert W.	NJ0825	36,40,61,12A
Pruett, Julie	TX0050	61
Pruitt, Nate	CA1950	61
Prunty, Patricia	CA0815	61
Pryor, Cheryl	AL0010	61
Psurny, Robert D.	MT0075	29A,36,40,54,61
Puchala, Mark	MI1650	12A,36,61,34,41
Pulgram, Anthony	NY2105	61
Puller, Shawn I.	GA0150	11,61,12A,32A,39
Pulte, John	TN1450	61
Purdy, Winston	AI0150	61
Putnam, Ashley	NY2150	61
Pysh, Greg	TX1660	61,12A
Pysh, Gregory	TX3527	10,13,61,60A,36
Quagliariello, Rachel M.	VA0800	61,40
Quant, Scott	OK0850	11,32,61
Quash, Jonathan	NY0646	36,54,61
Queen, Terrell	CO0250	39,61
Quigley-Duggan, Susan E.	MO0100	61,39
Quinlan, Gloria H.	TX1150	32,36,61,66C,31A
Quintero, Michelle A.	TX3175	61
Rabe-Meyer, Janet	FL0400	61
Racine, Melody Lynn	MI2100	61,54
Rada, Raphael	TX0550	61,11,13C,32B,36
Rader, Jana Elam	TX2310	11,12A,34C,61
Radford, Anthony P.	CA0810	61,39,54
Radke, Gina Funes	WA1050	61
Radomski, Teresa	NC2500	61,54
Raferty, Patrick	AG0450	61
Ragains, Diane	IL2200	61
Ragan, Kari	WA1050	61
Ragland, Janice	MO0850	61,36,32C
Ragsdale, Frank	OK0750	61
Ragsdale, Jeremy	MD0850	61,47
Raheb, Paul J.	CA1290	61
Rahming, Dara	LA0900	61,39
Raiken, Larry	CT0650	61
Railton, Marlene	MO2050	36,61
Rain, Jack	FL2000	61,39
Rainbolt, Steven	MD0650	61
Raines, Sarah	MT0370	40,61
Raines, Scott	TX0150	39,61,11
Rainforth, Eva	PA2900	61
Ramey, Kara	MO0400	61
Ramey, Samuel	IL0550	61
Ramirez, Patricia	AL1195	61
Ramo, Suzanne D.	TX1425	61,11,36
Ramsey, DonnaLee	PA2800	61
Ramsey, Jeffery Evans	MA0260	61
Randall, Martha	MD1010	61,39
Randolph, Jane	CA4150	61
Ranney, Todd	PA2150	61,39
Rao, Doreen	AG0450	32,36,60,61
Rasmussen, Bruce	CA3400	60A,36,61,40,66G
Ratliff, Joy	LA0650	61
Ratner, Carl J.	MI2250	39,61,54
Rauch, Benjamin	CT0650	61,31C
Rauschnabel, June	MN0600	44,61
Ray Westlund, Beth	IA0950	61
Ray, Frederic	MD0060	61
Ray, Jeff	IL1890	61
Ray, Jeffrey	IL2100	61
Ray, Jeffrey	IL3370	61
Ray, John	TN1600	60A,61
Rayam, Curtis J.	FL1550	61
Rayam, Curtis	FL0100	36,61,40,39
Rayapati, Sangeetha	IL0100	11,61
Raybon, Leonard	LA0750	36,61,60A,54
Raycroft, Elizabeth	AA0020	61
Raycroft, Elizabeth	AA0035	61
Raymond, Deborah	AZ0450	61
Raynes, Christopher	ID0050	61,39,54
Read, Katie	OH0550	61
Reager, John	CA2450	36,66A,61,12A
Reash, Aimee	PA0100	61
Rebilas, Richard P.	IN1010	61
Reckner, Lillian	MD0360	66,61,65
Redfearn, Christopher	ND0600	36,40,60A,61
Redington, Britania	DE0200	61
Redman, Carolyn	OH1200	61
Redman, Carolyn	OH1600	61
Redman, Yvonne Gonzales	IL3300	61
Redmon, Robynne	FL1900	61
Reed, Anne	OR0750	61,39
Reed, Joel F.	NC1250	20G,60A,36,61,31A
Reed, W. Joseph	MN1625	61
Reeder, Raymond	MA0260	61
Reese, Jodi	KS0265	36,11,13C,61,60A
Reeves, Bethany	NY0270	11,36,39,60A,61
Regan, Joseph	MD0610	61
Regan, Joseph	WV0550	61
Regan, Patrick	MI1300	61,39,54
Regensburger, Tamara	OH1850	61
Reger, Jeremy J.	IN0900	66C,61
Rehberg, Nancy R.	GA1300	61
Rehberg, Nancy	GA0850	61
Reich, Diane T.	UT0050	61
Reid, Nola	CO0275	61,42
Reifel, Carol-Lynn	AG0250	61
Reiff, Amy	DC0100	61
Reigles, B. Jean	NY1700	36,39,60A,61
Reimer, Alvin H.	AG0500	61
Reimer, Christine E.	NY2750	61
Reimer, Jamie M.	NE0600	61,39
Reinebach, John	CA0450	61

Name	Code	Areas
Reinke, Charlotte	GA2100	61
Relyea, Gary	AG0450	61
Renbarger, Cory James	MN0150	39,61
Renn, Rowena S.	GA0940	61
Rentz, Debra	OH1900	61
Replogle, Rebecca	OR1010	36,61,13A,13C,40
Resick, Georgine	IN1700	39,61
Retana, Cynthia	IN1250	61
Retif, T. N.	GA0400	13E,12A,61,44
Retzlaff, Jonathan	TN1850	61,39,40
Reyes, Iris	CO0150	61
Reynolds, Elaine	CA4650	61
Reynolds, Jerald	FL2050	61
Reynolds, Jerald M.	FL2000	61
Reynolds, Marc	TX2930	61,39,13C
Reynolds, Sharon	NJ0975	61
, Rhiannon	MA0260	61
Rhoades, Vanessa	OK0500	61,11
Rhoads, Shari	IA1550	61,66C
Rhodes, Ann G.	KY0300	11,12A,61,32D,29A
Rhodes, Jami	NC0650	61
Rhodes, Terry Ellen	NC2410	61
Rhyne-Bray, Constance	NC2000	39,61,20
Ribando, Jeremy S.	FL1430	61,13
Rice, Dana R.	MS0400	61,39
Rice, John Robin	OH1850	61
Rice, Laura Brooks	NJ1350	39,61
Rice, Patton	MS0400	61
Rich, Melody	TX0900	61
Rich, Mollie	FL1750	61
Richard, Sarah	WA0860	61,52
Richardson, Celia	TX2850	11,36,61,32B,13C
Richardson, David	WI1100	39,66C,61
Richardson, Diane	MA0260	61
Richardson, Diane	NY3705	39,61,66C
Richardson, Donald G.	CA4450	11,12A,61
Richardson, James K.	VA0300	61,11,36,54,39
Richardson, Paul A.	AL0800	61,31A
Richardson, Sylvia	AC0050	61
Richardson, W. Randall	AL0800	61,54
Richman, Pamela L.	OK1330	13C,13A,61
Richmond, Brad	MI1050	36,40,60A,61
Richstone, Lorne S.	OK1350	61,31
Richt, Cheryl	KS0650	61
Richter, Kimberlie J.	IL2050	13A,61,64E,29
Richter, Tiffany	AL1450	13,36,40,61
Rickards, Steven	IN1100	61
Rickards, Steven	IN1650	61
Rickards, Steven	IN0250	61
Riddle-Jackson, Jackie	UT0150	61
Ridgeway, Betty	MD0400	61
Riebe, Jenice	VA1100	61
Rieger, Eric	NJ1350	61
Riehl, Jeffrey S.	VA1500	11,36,61,60
Rieth, Dale	FL0950	13,36,47,61,66A
Rike, Gregory	IN1600	61,42
Riley, Denise	MS0200	13,36,61
Rimington, James	IL0400	32,61
Rinaldi, Beverley	FL1800	61
Rios, Giselle Elgarresta	FL0050	61,36,60,32,41
Ripley, David	NH0350	61,39
Rippere, Mathew	MA2100	61
Ritchey, Doris Ellen	GA2100	33,61
Ritchey, Mary Lynn	MA0150	61,36,60A,40,11
Ritter, Stacey	IL1050	61
Ritter-Bernardini, Denise	OH2300	61,36
Ritterling, Soojin Kim	WI0810	32B,32C,11,61,32A
Rivard, Michele M.	CA0400	61,34
Rivard, Michelle	CA4425	61
Rivera, Jennifer M.	NJ0800	61
Rivera, Jose	NC2435	32,36,61,60
Rivera, Wayne	CT0650	61
Rivers, Sylvia	TX0250	61,36
Robbin, Catherine	AG0650	61
Robbins, Cheryl	IL0420	61,66A
Robbins, Janice B.	TX2295	61
Roberson, Heather D.	CO1050	61,36,11,60A,32D
Roberson, James	CA5031	20G,61
Roberson, Matt	AL0345	12,61
Roberts, Beth	NY2250	61
Roberts, Connie	MS0850	39,61
Roberts, Gene	CO0830	61,10D
Roberts, Gene	CO0550	61
Roberts, Kate	IA0910	61,11
Roberts, Kimberly	IA1350	61
Roberts, Marie J.	GA1300	61
Roberts, Nancy	SD0100	32,61
Roberts, Patricia	TN0100	61
Robertson, Christine	IL1750	61
Robertson, Fritz S.	IN0100	39,61
Robertson, Patricia	IN1560	39,61,32D
Robertson, Phyllis	MO1780	61
Robertson, Ruth M.	MO0600	36,39,61
Robertson, Troy David	TX2750	60,32C,36,61
Robinson Woliver, Loretta	OH1850	61
Robinson, Bobb	NC2410	39,61
Robinson, Bradley C.	MS0700	61
Robinson, David	TX2600	61
Robinson, Faye L.	AZ0500	61
Robinson, Jennifer	MS0700	61
Robinson, Laura E.	GA1900	61
Robinson, Yvonne	PA2450	61,54
Robinson-Martin, Trineice	NY4200	61
Robinson-Martin, Trineice	NJ0750	11,12A,29,61
Robinson-Oturu, Gail M.	TN0050	61
Robison, Jeanne	CA0350	61,39
Rock, Connie	CT0600	61
Rockabrand, Sarah	IL2400	36,61,60A
Rockwell, Paula	AF0050	61,39
Roden, Stella D.	MO1790	61,11
Rodgers, Jane Schoonmaker	OH0300	39,61
Rodgers, Susan	RI0200	61,39
Roe, Charles R.	AZ0500	39,61
Rogers, Bruce	CA3200	36,61,60A
Rogers, Caroline	MI1300	61
Rohlfing, Mimi	MA2030	61,36,47,40
Rohr, Grant	CA0815	66A,61,66C
Rohrer, Katherine	OH1900	61
Roiger, Teresa	NY3760	12A,47,61
Roland-Wieczorek, Sophie	AG0500	61
Roll, Christianne	VA0350	61,32A,13C
Roll, Marcus	MI1985	61
Rollene, Donna	AR0400	61,39
Rolsten, Kathy	MN1120	32A,32B,32D,36,61
Roman, Ed S.	AZ0510	61,66A
Romano, Darlene	CA1270	36,61,11,13A,40
Romano, Patrick	NY3560	60,36,61
Rommereim, John Christian	IA0700	60,10,36,61
Ronis, David A.	NY1600	61
Roozendaal, Jay	WA1250	61
Rorex, Michael	LA0550	36,39,61
Rosales, Rachel	NY4450	61
Rosales, Rachel A.	VT0050	61,66H
Rose, Alissa	PA2150	61
Rose, Angela	OH1350	61,66D
Rose, Victoria	PA1900	61
Roseberry, Lynn	OH0350	61,39,40,36
Rosen, Marlene Ralis	OH1700	61
Rosenblum, Henry	NY1860	31B,61,20F,13C
Rosenshein, Ingrid	FL1675	11,13A,61,66D,54
Rosenshein, Neil	NY2150	61
Rosevear, Burt L.	TN1000	61,11
Rosewall, Michael	WI0750	36,61,12A,13A,13B
Rosine, Amy	KS0650	61,54
Roslak, Roxolana	AG0300	61
Ross Mehl, Margaret	PA0600	36,39,61,11,12A
Ross, Elizabeth	PA3330	61
Ross, Holli	NJ0800	40,61
Ross, Holli W.	NY1600	61,29
Ross, Jared	KS0060	13,60,31A,36,61
Ross, Mary Anne	NY1400	61
Ross, Tyley	NY2750	61
Rossow, Stacie	FL0650	61,36,13A
Roste, Vaughn	OK0550	60,12A,36,61,20
Roth, Lisa	IA1400	53,61,46,13A,13B
Rothfuss, Guy	NJ1350	61
Rowbottom, Terree	MO1250	61
Rowe, Alissa	LA0650	36,61,60A
Rowe, Devonna	MD0600	61
Rowe, Martha	NM0310	61
Rowe, Paul	WI0815	61
Rowell, Melanie	SC1080	12A,61,54,39
Rowell, Thomas L.	AL1300	61,39,40
Rowland, Martile	CO0200	39,61
Roy, Lisa	AE0100	39,61
Roy, Shawn	LA0760	61,39
Ruby, Eileen	MA1350	61
Ruby, Eileen	MA1100	61
Ruck, Tanya Kruse	WI0825	61,39
Rudari, David J.	WV0100	61,36,12A,32B,54
Rudo, Sandy	CA2150	36,61
Ruff, James	NY4450	61
Ruggles, Nathan	MO1900	61
Ruggles, Patricia	NJ0200	61
Ruhadze, Medea Namoradze	VA1350	61
Ruiz, Kristen	NY2750	61
Rundus, Katharin	CA1900	36,61
Rundus, Katharin	CA0825	61
Runyan, Donald	IL1612	36,32D,61
Rupert, Susan	TN1800	13A,61,54
Rushing, Randal J.	TN1680	61
Rushing, Steven J.	LA0650	61
Rushing-Raynes, Laura	ID0050	61,39,54
Rushton, Christianne	AF0050	12A,15,32D,61
Russell, Cynthia	TX0250	61,66A,66G,32B,32C
Russell, Nathan	TX3370	36,11,61,13C
Russell, Teresa P.	CA4850	60,36,61,54,32A
Russell-Dickson, Marion	TX3450	61
Rutherford, Eric D.	KS0560	61
Rutherford, Pearl	CO0150	61
Rutkowski, Ellen	PA2200	61,11
Rutledge, Kevin	FL1310	36,61
Ryan, Anna	KS1000	61
Ryczek, Karyl	MA1175	61,40
Ryder, Carol	CA2250	61,36,11
Ryder, Carol	CA1280	36,54,61
Ryder, Christopher O.	VA1150	34,61,32,13,40
Ryer-Parke, Kerry	MA2250	61,40
Ryker, Andrew	IA0550	61
Rymal, Karen	AG0650	66C,61
Ryner, Jayson	IA1170	32C,36,61,11,13C
Sabatino, T. M.	PA1750	11,61,40
Sabo, Marlee	WI1150	39,61
Sabo, Vyki	FL0950	61,11
Sabol, Julianna M.	NY4150	61
Sacco Belli, Jeanette	CA4625	61
Sachs, Carol	TX3515	39,61
Sadeghpour, Mitra M.	WI0803	61,39
Sadler, Cindy	TX2170	61
Sadlier, David	VA0150	61,40,39
Sage, Raymond	PA2750	61,54
Sager, Gene	WY0150	36,40,61,11
Sager, Stephanie	FL0930	61
Sahai, Rita	CA0050	61
Sahuc, Paul	CA3600	61
Sahuc, Paul N.	CA5060	61,39
Saito, Miki	OH0755	61,39
Sala, Karen	IL1240	13A,13B,13E,13F,61
Saladino, Jean	WI1100	61,36,13C
Salazar, Shirley	IL0400	61
Salerno, Christine	WI0808	40,47,66,61
Salter, Rebecca	GA1700	61
Salter, Rebecca A.	GA1800	61
Salters, Mark	CA0815	61,39
Salyards, Shannon	IA0100	61
Salyards, Shannon	IA1100	61,39
Salyards, Shannon	NE0610	61
Samaras, Stephanie	NJ0800	61
Samarzea, Kelly J.	VA1000	61
Sams, Jennifer	WI0100	61
Samu, Attila	OH2290	61
Samuelsen, Roy	IN1650	61
Sanchez, Cynthia	TX2260	36,61,64C,66A
Sand, Megan	OR0700	61
Sandborg, Jeff R.	VA1250	60,11,12A,36,61
Sandborg, Marianne	VA1250	61
Sandefur, Lynn	FL1675	11,13A,36,40,61
Sanders, Debbie	OR1150	61
Sanders, Terrie	LA0550	61,66D
Sanders, Wayne	NY3560	39,61
Sanford, Elizabeth	CA3200	61
Sannerud, David	CA0835	39,61
Santana, Priscilla	TX2800	61,36,40
Santer, Renee	NY2250	61
Santo, Amanda M.	RI0100	61
Santo, Amanda M.	RI0101	61,39,11
Santogate, Peter	NY4200	61
Santoro, Stephen	MA0260	61
Sargent, Philip	VA1350	61
Sarkisian, Rebecca	CA1850	61
Sato, Kaori	NY3785	61
Sauer, Maureen	IL0780	61
Sauer-Ferrand, Deborah	CA1860	12A,61,31A,54
Saulsbury, Kate	IA1100	61,39,66D
Saunders, Mary	PA2750	61,54
Saunders, Mary	MA0350	61

Index by Area of Teaching Interest

Name	Code	Areas
Saunders, Robert Allen	AZ0450	61
Savage Day, Susan	WI0840	61,54
Savage, Charles M.	OH1910	13,12A,20G,36,61
Savage, Karen	VA1800	39,61
Savage, Samuel T.	IN0905	61,39
Savarino, Damian	PA2300	61,39
Savarino, Tara	PA2300	61
Savoie, Adrienne	AI0200	61
Savoy, Deborah Ann	NY3600	61
Sawchuk, Judy-Lynn	AA0020	61
Sawyer, Charsie Randolph	MI0350	61,36
Sawyer, Lisa Lee	MN0600	13,61,66A
Scanlan, Roger	MI0350	61
Scanlon, Patricia A.	MO1250	61
Scarbrough, Michael	TX0050	36,61,60A
Scarlata, Randall S.	NY3790	61
Scarlata, Randall	PA3600	61
Scarlett, Millicent	DC0100	61
Scarpelli, Bonnie D.	ME0150	61
Scarpelli, Bonnie	ME0200	61
Scattergood, Joanne	CT0050	61
Schachter, Daniela	MA0260	66A,61
Schaefer, Elaine	CA1300	13A,36,54,61,40
Schaffer, Donna	MS0050	36,61,60A
Schag, Shane	NY2150	61
Schantz, Cory Neal	SD0550	61,36,60A
Schapman, Marc	IL2910	39,61
Schauer, Elizabeth	AZ0500	36,32D,61
Scheff, Fredric S.	RI0200	61
Scheffel, Gwendolyn W.	OH2450	61
Scheib, Curt A.	PA3000	61,36,66C,60,60
Scheib, Joy	WI0845	39,61
Schenck-Crowne, Leah Naomi	PA1400	61
Schepker, Kay	LA0650	61
Schernikau, Burt	NE0450	32B,61
Schiel, Melissa	WA0050	61
Schiller, Caroline	AD0050	39,61
Schiller, Mary	OH0600	61
Schindelmann, Marco	CA5150	61
Schindler, Bonnie	CA3600	61
Schleicher, Elizabeth	IN0910	61
Schlimmer, Alexa Jackson	NC0930	39,61
Schloneger, Matthew	KS0500	61,54,11
Schlosser, Roberta	NY3705	39,61
Schmauk, Doris	PA0650	36,61
Schmidt, Karl	CA1800	36,61
Schmidt, Michael P.	MN0950	61,64D,32
Schmidt, Timothy A.	MO1500	61,39,54
Schmitt, James	OR0100	61
Schnack, Michael B.	PA2550	36,40,61
Schnaible, Mark	NY0500	61
Schneller, Aric	TX2250	47,29,63C,61
Schnitzer, Dana	MA1350	61
Schoenberg, Kathe	NJ0550	61,36
Schoenecker, Ann Elise	WI1100	61,36
Schoening, Benjamin S.	WI0801	11,13,36,61,63
Scholl, Christopher	OH0300	61
Scholl, Ellen Strba	OH0300	61
Scholz, David M.	CA0800	36,61,32C,60
Scholz, Robert	MN1450	36,61,60A
Schoonmaker, Bruce W.	SC0750	39,61
Schoonmaker, Gail	SC0750	61
Schopp, James A.	IL2050	61
Schorsch, Kathleen	CA5300	61
Schramm, Barbara	MN0600	61
Schreck, Corlyn	MI1150	61
Schreck, Judith	SD0050	61
Schreiner, Frederick	PA3710	11,12A,12,61,39
Schreuder, Joel T.	NE0050	60A,36,61,40,32D
Schriemer, Dale	MI0900	61
Schrock, Scharmal K.	LA0650	61
Schrock, Scharmal	IN0900	61
Schubert, David T.	OH2450	61,11
Schuetz, Daniel	IL1150	61
Schuetz, Jennifer Hilbish	IL1200	61
Schuetz, Jennifer Hilbish	OH0950	61,39
Schultz, James	NE0250	61
Schultz, Lucinda D.	GA0200	61
Schultze, Andrew W.	IL0720	61
Schulz, Blanche	IL0600	61
Schulze, Theodora	IN0005	61,10A,13,50,51
Schuppener, James	TX1700	36,61,32D
Schutz, Rachel	HI0210	61
Schwaber, Lorian Stein	WI0250	61
Schwing-Braun, Eraine	AG0450	61
Scifres, Sam G.	IL1200	61
Scinta, Frank	NY0400	61,31A,32C,36
Sciolla, Anne	PA3330	39,47,61
Scott, Chris	IL0100	36,61,13C
Scott, Cindy	LA0800	61,40
Scott, Daniel E.	TX0300	61
Scott, David	MA0260	61
Scott, Judith G.	CA0835	61
Scott, Kenneth	NY2660	61
Scott, Levone Tobin	NC2430	61
Scott, Maggie	MA0260	61
Scott, Mary Anne Spangler	IN0250	61,39
Scott, Michele	UT0050	61
Scott, Stuart	MI1250	40,36,61
Scrivner, Matthew	MO0050	61,12,13
Scroggins, Sterling Edward	DC0010	61,16,11
Scully, Mathew	CA3950	36,61,13
Scurto-Davis, Debra	NJ1350	61
Seals, Debra	PR0125	12A,61
Sears, Peggy	CA0650	13A,39,61
Seaton, Gayle	FL0850	61,54
Seaton, Kira J.	OH0755	13A,13,11,36,61
Seaward, Jeffery A.	CA1290	13A,36,41,61,54
Seay, Sandra	AR0110	11,61,32
Sech, Svetlana	AA0020	61
Seckel, Tamara J.	OH1200	61
Secrest, Glenda	AR0500	61
Secrest, Jon	AR0500	39,61,54
Seeds, Laurel M.	OH1100	66D,61
Seegmiller, Lisa	UT0150	61
Seeman, Rebecca	CA5353	13A,11,36,38,61
Seesholtz, John C.	CO0250	61,39
Seglem-Hocking, Sara	DE0150	61
Seidl, Teresa	WI0350	61
Seifert, James	AZ0440	61,13
Seiger, Jennifer	NC1700	61
Seitz, Carole J.	NE0160	39,61,11
Sellers, Crystal Y.	OH0250	61,11,12,31F
Seminatore, Gerald	CA3600	61
Sentgeorge, Aaron Jacob 'Jake'	MO1790	61,35C
Sepulveda, Richardo	IL1750	61
Serbo, Rico	MI2100	61
Sergi, James	NY4500	61
Servant, Gregory W.	AF0100	39,61
Settle, David	KS1250	61,32D
Sevadjian, Therese	AI0150	61
Severing, Richard	WI0865	36,40,54,61
Severtson, Kirk A.	NY3780	61,66C,39
Sevigny, Catherine	AI0200	61
Shafer, Karen	FL0050	61
Shafer, Sharon Guertin	DC0250	13,10F,12A,39,61
Shaffer, Lori	MO1500	61
Shah, Nikita	NC2300	61
Shaheen, Ronald T.	CA5200	11,12A,13A,61
Shaindlin, Tim	CT0850	61
Shakir, Audrey	GA1050	61
Shamburger, David	TN0100	61,54
Shane, Lynn	MA1650	11,61,32B,32D,36
Shane, Rita	NY1100	61
Shanklin, Bart	IL3500	61,60A,36,32D
Shannon, Pamela	MO0950	11,61
Shapiro, Eve	NY1900	61
Shapiro, Jan	MA0260	61
Sharkey-Pryma, Maura	AA0020	61
Sharma, Nachiketa	CA0050	61
Sharp, Stuart	MI1050	61
Sharp, William	MD0650	61
Sharrock, Barry R.	SC0350	61
Shasberger, Michael	CA5550	36,31A,38,60,61
Shaw, Kenneth	OH2200	61
Shaw, Lisa	DC0170	61,36
Shay, Gayle D.	TN1850	39,61
Shea, Merrill	MA0350	61
Shearer, Allen R.	CA0807	61,10A
Shearer, Allen R.	CA5000	61
Shearin, Arthur Lloyd	AR0250	11,36,61
Sheats, Jackson	VA1350	39,61
Sheehan, Aaron	MA2050	61
Sheehan, Aaron	MD0850	61
Sheil, Martha	MI2100	61
Sheil, Richard F.	NY3725	61
Sheldon, Elisabeth	MA0350	61
Sheldon, Janene	NE0450	61,32B,36,40,16
Shelley, Bonnie J.	AZ0510	61
Shelley, Kenneth	CT0650	61
Shelt, Christopher A.	MS0100	60A,36,31A,61,40
Shelton, Lucy	NY2150	61
Shepherd, Eudora	WI0100	61
Sheppard, Chris	SC0900	36,60A,61,40,34
Shepperson, Sam	NM0450	61
Sherburn, Rebecca	MO1810	61
Sherman, Donna	AG0300	61
Sherman, Joy	WA0850	11,36,40,61
Sherman, Mozelle C.	KY1200	39,61
Sherwood, Gertrude	FL1500	61
Sherwood, Thomas W.	OH2550	61
Shetler, Timothy	MA0800	60,32C,36,61
Shimazaki-Kilburn, Yoko	IN0150	61
Shimeo, Barbara	IL1612	61,36
Shirley, George I.	MI2100	39,61
Shirtz, Michael	OH2140	36,60,61,13,29
Shockey, David M.	PA2800	36,61,40
Shomos, William	NE0600	39,61
Short, Jackalyn	AG0500	61
Short, Kevin	FL1900	61
Shover, Blaine F.	PA3050	11,12A,36,61,54
Shrader, James A.	GA2150	60,12A,61,36,39
Shrope, Douglas	CA1000	36,61,60A,40,54
Shumate, Penny	PA1000	61
Shumway, Allyson	AZ0440	61
Shumway, Angelina	MD0700	11,66D,61,13A
Shumway, Angelina	VA1350	61
Siarris, Cathy Froneberger	SC0850	61,11
Sicilian, Peter J.	NY3705	39,61
Siebert, Glenn	NC1650	61
Sieck, Stephen	VA0350	36,61,60A,32D
Sieden, Cyndia	WA0200	61
Sieden, Cyndia	WA0650	61
Siemon, Brittnee	SC0600	61
Siemon, Brittnee	FL1000	61
Siena, Jerold	IL3300	61,39
Sievers, David	OH2250	61,39
Sigars, Julie Kae	WA0800	61
Sikora, Stephanie R.	OH0100	36,39,61
Siler, Christine	WI0100	61
Silva, LaVista	CA3800	61
Silva, Magda Y.	KS1110	61
Sim, Hoejin	PA3250	61
Simmons, Margaret R.	IL2900	61,66C
Simons, Kevin	MI1850	61,36,32D,60A
Simonson, Donald R.	IA0850	39,61,13L,34C,34D
Simpson, Marietta	IN0900	61
Simpson, Marilyn	CA2840	61
Simpson, Nicholas	TX2650	61
Sims, Gary	MO1950	61
Sims, Loraine	LA0200	61
Sims, Robert	IL2200	61
Simson, Julie	CO0800	61
Sincell-Corwell, Kathryn	MD0450	36,61
Sinclair, Terri	SC0420	36,61,32D,60A
Sinder, Philip	MI1200	66G,61
Singh, Vijay	WA0050	47,60,36,61,35A
Singler, Juliette	CA3640	61,39
Singleton, H. Craig	CA1650	36,61,31A
Sirbaugh, Nora	NJ0750	12A,39,61
Sirbaugh, Nora	NJ0175	61
Sisbarro, Jennifer	NY1550	61
Sisbarro, Jennifer L.	NY1250	13A,11,61
Skelton, Sara	MN1630	61,66A
Skemp-Moran, Kathryn	WI1100	61
Skinner, Kate	ID0060	12,13A,13B,13C,61
Skinner, Kent	AR0800	60A,36,61,39,54
Skok, Heidi	MA1400	61
Skoog, Andrew	TN1710	61
Skoog, William M.	TN1200	36,61
Skyles, Michael	SD0400	61,54
Slater, Jeanne	NY1900	61
Slaughter, Nancy	TN1900	61
Slezak, Heide Marie	MI2000	61
Sly, Marcia Gronewold	ME0440	61
Slye, Lorree	MA0260	61
Small, Allanda	AL1195	61,39
Small, David	TX3510	61,39
Smalley, Charles	AZ0150	13C,11,36,61,20G
Smart, Marilyn	FL1950	11,39,61
Smelser, Nadia	CA1900	61
Smelzer, Nadia	CA3350	61
Smiley, Henry	TN0100	61,54
Smith, Allison	TX1550	11,61
Smith, Andrew W.	KY0750	39,61
Smith, Blake	DE0150	61,54,39

Name	Code	Areas
Smith, Brenda	FL1850	61
Smith, Byron J.	CA2650	36,35A,35B,61,66
Smith, Caroline B.	IN0350	61
Smith, Carolyn J.	MO0775	61
Smith, Carolyn	MO0350	61
Smith, Charles	NE0300	36,39,61,54
Smith, Cherie	IN1350	61,66A
Smith, Christina	MN0750	61,54
Smith, David K.	KS0950	36,11,61,13,66A
Smith, David Kenneth	PA1350	60A,61
Smith, David	MD1000	36,39,60,61
Smith, David J.	AL0300	61,11
Smith, Denise A.	MO1900	61
Smith, Derrick	NY2650	61
Smith, Gayle	AL0335	66D,36,61
Smith, Hannah	NE0200	61,39
Smith, James S.	NC1800	36,41,61
Smith, James	VA1600	61
Smith, James	VA1500	61
Smith, Janet	CA0815	61,39
Smith, Jason B.	TX2400	61
Smith, Jason	IA1400	13,36,61,60A
Smith, Jennifer	MI1550	36,61,66
Smith, Jennifer	UT0150	61
Smith, Kandie K.	FL1950	61,13
Smith, Kandie K.	GA0400	61,40
Smith, Kara	WY0115	61,66A
Smith, Kathryn L.	CA1500	61,36,60A
Smith, Kenneth	IL2250	61
Smith, Kent	NY3760	61
Smith, Larry Dearman	MS0750	44,61
Smith, Malcolm S.	ME0500	61
Smith, Matthew Shepard	NY2750	61
Smith, Melanie	TX3800	61
Smith, Paul B.	AR0400	60,36,61
Smith, Perry	NC0650	61
Smith, Robert C.	MN1450	61
Smith, Roy C.	IN0005	61,11,10A,60,36
Smith, Scott Z.	VA0600	61
Smith, Stephen	TN1100	61
Smith, Susan K.	MO0800	61,13C
Smith, Susan A.	MS0360	61,40,13,36,13B
Smith, Susan	MO0400	16,61,12A
Smith, Trevor	VA1650	61,66A
Smith, Vernon L.	FL1300	11,36,61
Smith, Victoria	MO1950	61
Smith-Emerson, Karen	MA1750	61
Smithey, David B.	LA0350	11,61
Smoak, Jeff C.	KY1425	32,36,61,40,43
Smolder, Benjamin W.	OH1450	61,40
Smoot, Lonna Joy	ID0060	61
Smucker, Angela Young	IN1750	36,61
Snapp, Patricia	MN0750	61,39,40
Snider, Jeffrey	TX3420	61
Snider, Karl William	CA2800	13A,11,61,40
Snodgrass, Linda H.	CA0800	61
Snook, Ann Marie	KS1400	61
Snook, Lee	KS1400	61
Snow, Michelle H.	ME0500	47,61
Snow, Steven	PA2550	61
Snyder, Cindy	CA5150	61
Snyder, Linda J.	OH2250	39,61,11
Soder, Aidan L.	MO1810	61
Soderberg, Karen	MD0350	61,36,40,32D,60A
Soebbing, Steven	MD0350	61,20,15
Sokol, Michael	CA4100	39,61
Solis, Kassi	TX2570	61
Soltero, Jill K.	OR1100	61
Soltero, Jill	OR0500	61
Sommers, Paul B.	MO1810	61
Sones, Rodney	KY1200	61
Song, MyungOk Julie	NY2750	32,36,60,61
Songer, Loralee	TN0850	60A,36,61
Sonnenberg, Melanie	TX3400	61
Sonnentag, Kathleen	WI1150	61
Sonntag, Dawn Lenore	OH1000	36,61,66C,10A,10
Sorenson, Allin	MO0350	60,11,36,61
Sorenson, Gary	UT0350	61
Sorrento, Charles J.	MA0260	61
Soto, Christian	FL1300	61
Soto, Ricardo	CA3350	36,61,38
South, Pam	OR0850	61
Southard, Bruce	ND0100	36,60A,12A,61,60
Spann, Joseph S.	NY3717	61
Sparfeld, Tobin	CA2660	61,36
Sparks, Tim	NC2410	61
Sparrow, Carol	FL0680	61
Spaulding, Laura	FL1745	61
Spears, Samuel B.	WV0300	32D,36,61,60A
Spears, Steven	WI0350	61
Speck, Matthew	MI0520	61
Speedie, Penelope A.	KS0300	39,61
Speer, Randall	VA1125	61,36,60A,40
Speer, Shari	MN0610	36,39,61
Speirs, Phyllis	OH0600	61
Speiser, Paul	NY2750	61
Spencer, Charles	OH1350	61
Spencer, Mark	OH0450	39,61
Spencer, Mia	WA0050	13A,13B,13C,61
Spencer, Philip	IL1250	20,61,66A,36,60A
Spencer, Reid	AA0050	54,61
Spencer, Theresa Forrester	MO0250	36,40,61,14C
Sperry, Paul	NY0500	61
Sperry, Tara	NC0900	61
Spicer, Donna	OR1020	36,61,66A,66D
Spicer, Nan	IN0005	61,60A,66A,66G,31A
Spicer-Lane, Anita	MD0170	11,61
Spinetti, Sharon	NJ0825	61
Spivak, Mandy	WV0800	61,39
Spivak, Mandy A.	WV0750	61
Spivey, Norman	PA2750	61
Sposato, Aime	VA1350	61
Spratlan, Melinda K.	MA1350	61
Sprenkle, David	PA3600	36,41,61
St. Goar, Rebecca	TN1700	61
St. Jean, Donald	RI0200	61
St. Jean, Donald	RI0250	36,61
St. Jean, Flo	RI0200	61
St. Julien, Marcus	LA0300	13B,13C,61,66G
St. Laurent, Mark	MA1400	61
St. Pierre, Donald	PA3250	61
St. Pierre, Laurine Grace	MO0775	61
Stabenow, Crystal	OH0450	61
Stachofsky, Mark	IN0905	61
Stadelman-Cohen, Tara	MA0350	61
Stadnicki, Tisha	MA1450	36,61
Staerkel, Todd C.	KS1400	61
Stafslien, Judy	WI1100	66C,36,61
Staheli, Ronald	UT0050	60,36,41,61,66A
Stahl, Diane Willis	FL0800	39,61
Staininger, Lynn L.	MD0300	36,66A,13B,40,61
Stallard, Tina Milhorn	SC1110	39,61
Stallsmith, Becki	AL0260	32,38,50,61,66C
Stanescu-Flagg, Cristina	NY2250	66C,61
Stanley, Christine	VA1150	61
Stanley, David	AR0500	61,36
Stapp, Marcie	CA4150	61
Stark, Deborah	GA0700	12A,54,11,61,40
Stark-Williams, Turia	AL0450	61,13B
Starkey, David C.	NC1250	61,39,54
Starkey, Linda	KS1450	61,54,39
Starr, Lucia	MD0170	61
Starr, Virginia	OH0300	61
Stasney, C. Richard	TX2150	61
Stauch, Thomas J.	IL1085	36,40,61,32D,11
Staufenbiel, Brian	CA5070	61,39
Stecker-Thorsen, Meg	WA0860	61
Stedry, Patricia	MA1600	61
Steele, Carol	FL1310	61,39
Steele, Edward L.	LA0400	12A,13A,13B,13C,61
Steele, Janet	NY0550	13A,55,61,66A,36
Steele, Rebecca W.	FL0100	36,61
Steele, Sherry	AG0500	61
Stegner, John M.	KY1425	32D,61
Stehly, Theresa	SD0580	61
Stein, Daniel C.	NC0350	61
Stein, Daniel C.	SC1200	61
Steinau, David S.	PA3150	61,39,12A
Steinhauer, Kimberly	PA2900	61
Steinhaus, Barbara	GA0350	61,11,39
Steinsnyder, Faith	NY1860	61
Stephens, Charles R.	WA0650	61
Stephens, Emery	MI2200	61
Stephens, John A.	KS1350	39,61
Stephens, Marjorie	TN1710	61
Stephenson, Carol	CA3200	61
Stephenson, Carol	CA5100	61,54
Stephenson, JoAnne	FL1800	61
Sterling, Robin	IL3550	61
Stern, Jeffrey S.	NY0650	36,61
Sternfeld-Dunn, Emily	KS1450	61
Stevans, Joy	MD0550	61
Stevens, Alan E.	TN0500	36,61
Stevens, Carrie L.	VA0600	61
Stevens, Cynthia C.	TX2310	37,40,61
Stevens, Mitchell	LA0900	61,36
Stevens, Morris	TX2170	61
Stevens, Pamela	NH0150	61
Stevenson, George	OK0850	12A,14,36,61
Stevenson, Sandra	UT0150	61
Steward, Lee A.	CA0807	61,54
Stewart, Diane	MA0260	61
Stewart, Jonathan	OK0825	32D,11,13B,36,61
Stewart, Kasey	NY1150	61
Stewart, Peter A.	NJ0800	61
Stewart, Shirley	LA0720	11,36,61,31A,32
Stich, Adam	AZ0490	36,60A,61,40,13A
Stickler, Larry W.	WV0400	36,32B,32C,61,32D
Stieber, Marian	NJ1050	39,61
Stieler, Kathryn	MI0900	61
Stiles, Patricia J.	IN0900	61
Stilwell, Richard	IL0550	61
Stinson, Jonathan	OH2550	61
Stinson, Lori	CA1700	61
Stiver, David Keith	OH0755	61,13C
Stock, Jesse	TN0250	36,61,60A,54
Stoffel, David N.	GA2100	61,54
Stohrer, Baptist	IL0780	12A,12,61
Stohrer, Sharon	OH0350	61
Stokes, Porter	SC1000	36,61,60,32
Stollberg, Amy	IL2450	61
Stoloff, Bob	MA0260	61
Stolz, Patrick	WY0115	61,70
Stone, Sarah	MI0400	61
Stone, Sylvia	IL3300	61
Stone, Terry	IL1750	61,39
Stone, William	PA3250	61,39
Stone-Taborn, Susan	TX0400	61
Stoner, Elizabeth	MI2250	61
Stoner-Cameron, Elizabeth	MI0400	61
Stoner-Hawkins, Sylvia Frances	KS1400	61,39
Stones, Linda M.	CA0835	61
Stooksbury, Laura	GA2300	61
Stork, David	FL0400	61
Storm, Laura	AR0300	61
Stormes, Sheridan	IN0250	61
Storojev, Nikita	TX3510	61,39
Stott, Susan	MI1850	61
Strandt, Terry W.	IL1850	12A,61,29
Strauss, Anja	AI0150	61
Strauss, Michael	MA0350	61,66C
Strauss, Robert	NY2650	61,39
Streator, Carol	IN1050	61,13C
Streeter, Vicki	WY0130	61
Streets, Barbara S.	OK1330	32B,61
Stremlin, Tatyana	NY4250	13,11,61,66A,67C
Strichman, Sherri	NY3600	61
Strickland, Stanley Leon	MA0260	61
Stricklett, Margaret	DC0170	61
Stringer, Sandra	AA0200	61,36,11
Stringer, Vincent Dion	MD0600	61,39
Strnad, Frank L.	CA1900	61
Strock, Kathryn	AK0100	61
Strother, Kevin L.	DC0050	61
Strother, Martin	VA1800	39,61
Strummer, Linda	OK1450	39,61
Struve, Jonathon Paul	IA0950	61
Stryker, Crystal J.	PA3000	32A,32B,61
Stucki, Brian	UT0400	61
Stucky, Mary Henderson	OH2200	61
Sublett, Virginia	ND0350	61,39,54
Suderman, Gail	AB0060	36,61,40,39
Suderman, Mark	OH0250	60A,32D,32B,36,61
Suess, Jennifer	DC0170	61
Sullivan, Daniel	MA0850	61
Sullivan, Lorraine Yaros	NY3780	61
Sullivan, Melanie	TX1350	12,61
Summers, Michelle	KS0040	61
Sumner, Melissa M.	VA0800	61,11,40
Sun, Liyan	AG0550	61
Sundberg, Gerard	IL3550	36,61
Sundby, Candace	FL0500	61,36
Sundquist, David	TX3420	61
Supeene, Susan	AA0040	32A,61,36
Surowiec, Jozef	MD0150	61
Sutliff, Richard	OK0850	39,61

Index by Area of Teaching Interest

Name	Code	Areas
Sutton, Elizabeth	NJ1350	61
Svatanova, Lucie	SC0700	61,39
Svatonova, Lucie Anna	SC1000	61
Svedaite-Waller, Jurate	CT0100	61
Svenningsen, Russell	SD0050	13,36,61
Swaim, Doris	NC2640	32A,36,61,66D
Swaim, Timothy	CA4300	61
Swalin, Paula	NM0450	61
Swan, Phillip A.	WI0350	36,60,61,32D,60A
Swan, Walter R.	NC0700	61
Swank, Helen	OH1850	61
Swann, Kyle	CT0650	61
Swann, Kyle	CT0850	61
Swanson, Christopher	VA0700	13C,61,12A,11,39
Swanson, Stephen	IA1550	61
Swanston, Marcia	AF0100	39,61,40
Swartzendruber, Holly	KS1300	61
Swearingen, Elaine	IL1520	61
Swedberg, Robert M.	MI2100	61
Sweeney, Joyce	CA5500	12A,13,35A,61
Sweet, Sharon	NJ1350	61
Sweigart, Suzanne	MD0610	66A,61
Swensen, Robert	NY1100	61
Swensen-Mitchell, Allison	OR1300	61
Swenson, Ruth Ann	CA4700	61
Swenson, Ruth Ann	TX3510	61
Swinson, Beth Ann	IL3150	61,39,41
Switzer, Linda	FL1650	61
Swope, Anastasia E.	NJ0800	61
Swope, Matthew	FL1550	61
Sykes, Jeffrey	CA5000	61,66C
Sylvan, Sanford	NY1900	61
Sylvan, Sanford	AI0150	61
Sylvester, Joyce	AL1300	61
Sylvester, Joyce	AL1195	61
Sylvester, Lisa M.	CA5300	61,12A
Sylvester, Michael	IL0750	61
Symons, Kathy	PA0100	61
Taddie, Daniel L.	AR0900	12A,36,61
Tadlock, David	OH1400	61,13C,54,39
Tahere, David	GA0600	11,54,61
Talbert, Rebecca	MO2050	61,66A,13,12A,11
Talbott, Christy	WI0848	61
Talley, Dana W.	NY2900	61,12A,20,39,11
Talmadge, Samantha	CT0100	61,32
Tam, Jing Ling	TX3500	36,61,60A
Tannehill, Sarah	MO2000	61
Tanno-Kimmons, Yoriko	AG0400	61
Tarantine, April A.	PA3260	61
Tarbox, Maurie	UT0350	13,61
Tarr, Jeffrey	DC0010	61
Tasher, Cara S.	FL1950	60A,61,36
Tau, Omari	CA0840	61,39
Tavernier, Jane	VA1475	61,36,39,40
Tavianini, Marie A.	PA0900	36,61
Taylor, Amanda	MO0775	61
Taylor, Amanda	MO1950	61
Taylor, Betty Sue	NY2400	13A,12,36,61,66
Taylor, Charles Edwin	CO0250	61
Taylor, Darryl G.	CA5020	61
Taylor, James	VA1600	61
Taylor, James	NC1050	41,36,61,31A,11
Taylor, James R.	CT0850	61
Taylor, James	VA1550	61
Taylor, Jim	TX1350	36,40,61
Taylor, Livingston	MA0260	61
Taylor, Marilyn S.	NC1650	61
Taylor, Mitchell	IL1500	20,61,34B
Taylor, Robert J.	SC0500	11,36,61,60
Taylor, Steven	CO0150	39,61,31A,44,13C
Taylor, Una D.	NE0050	36,61,32B,11,40
Teal, Kelly	TX0100	61
Teal, Terri	KS0570	11,40,61,36
Tebay, John	CA1900	36,61,66D,66A,12A
Tedards, Ann B.	OR1050	61
Tedeschi, John	CT0650	61
Tedford, Linda	PA2300	60A,36,61
Teed, Pamela	AG0150	61
Teed, Pamela	AG0070	13A,61
Teets, Sean	LA0250	60A,61
Tegnell, John Carl	CA4200	36,61
Temple, Robert P.	NE0250	61
Templeton, David M.	SC0500	61,39,11
Ten Brink, Jonathan	MN0625	12A,61
Tenenbaum, Lucy	VT0200	61
Tener, James R.	IA0850	61
Tennenbaum, Lucy	VT0100	61
Terbeek, Kathleen	TX3000	61
Tewari, Laxmi	CA4700	14,13A,61,10E,31D
Thacker, Elizabeth	OH1400	61,32
Thacker, Hope	TN1660	61
Thacker, Hope	KY0950	61
Theimer, Axel K.	MN0350	60A,36,61,32D
Thibodeau, Theresa	AG0350	61
Thielen-Gaffey, Tina	MN1600	36,61,40,32
Thier, Bethany	WI0750	61,66,47
Thom, Marcia	VA1400	61,39
Thom, Patty J.	MA0350	61
Thomas, Colby L.	NY3765	39,60A,35F,61,54
Thomas, Diane	CA3300	61
Thomas, Eric S.	TX0600	61,13C,13A,54
Thomas, Erica	OK1050	61
Thomas, Erica	OK0450	61
Thomas, June M.	PA2550	61,29
Thomas, Laurel A.	IN1450	39,61
Thomas, Nicholas	IL1890	60A,66D,13A,36,61
Thomas, Nova	NJ1350	61,54
Thomas, Sally	NC0300	61
Thomas, Steven L.	PA3700	36,61,40
Thomas, Tracy	NC2435	61
Thomas, William D.	SC0750	40,61,31A
Thomasson, John	FL0800	39,61
Thomen, Willard	IL3370	61,11
Thomen, Willard	IL0730	61
Thompson, Bradley	CO0550	61
Thompson, Bruce A.	NC1000	36,13,66A,61
Thompson, Christopher E.	MO0775	66C,61
Thompson, Dawn	VA1550	61
Thompson, Jack	FL0800	61,39
Thompson, James	IA0400	61
Thompson, Kenneth	NY2400	61
Thompson, Laura	LA0250	32C,32D,36,60A,61
Thompson, Lynn	IL3500	61,54,39,36
Thompson, Michelle	CO0550	61
Thompson, Patricia A.	KS0650	61
Thompson, Shaw	SC0710	11,61
Thompson, Sonja K.	MN0050	61,39,54,41,42
Thompson-Buechner, Patti	NY4150	61
Thoms, Jason A.	NY0850	36,32D,61,55D,12A
Thomson, Jacqueline	IA1350	61
Thomson, Jacqueline	IA1400	13,36,61,60A
Thomson-Price, Heather	AB0100	61
Thorburn, Melissa R.	NY0400	61,39
Thorn, Julia	PA3150	36,60A,61
Thorngate, Russell	WI0925	11,13A,36,40,61
Thornton, Diane B.	NC0550	39,61
Thorp, Steven	NM0250	13,11,36,61,40
Thorson, Lisa	MA0260	61
Thrasher, Lucy	MN0600	61,39
Throness, Dale	AB0060	61,39
Throness, Dale	AB0100	61
Thull, Jonathan	IA0400	39,61,54
Thurlow, Deborah	MD0150	61
Thurmond, Gloria J.	NJ1160	61,31
Tichenor, Jean-Marie	WY0050	61,40,12A
Tichgraeber, Heidi	KS0210	11,61
Tickner, French A.	AB0100	12A,39,61
Tidwell, Edith	KY1500	61
Tiedemann, Patrice	RI0250	61
Tigges, Kristie M.	MN1295	61,11
Timmerman, David	TX1750	13A,13,36,41,61
Timothy, Sarah O.	AL0890	61,11,36,13,32
Tingler, Stephanie	GA2100	61
Tinsley, David	FL0040	61
Tinsley, David	AL0400	11,36,61
Tinsley, Janis	AL0400	61,66A,66B,66D
Titze, Ingo R.	IA1550	61
Tober, Nina M.	PA3150	61
Tobia, Riccardo	PA2900	61,36
Todd, Jo Ella	MO1800	61
Todd, Richard	FL1900	61,39
Toledo, Patricia	IL1085	61
Toliver, Nicki Bakko	MN0040	11,13,40,61
Tomlinson, Mike	MN1250	61
Toomer, Charlie	FL0600	60,36,61
Toppin, Louise	NC2410	61
Toronto, Emily Wood	SD0550	39,61,54
Torres, Barry A.	NY3550	55,36,61
Torres, Jose R.	PR0150	61,54
Toscano, Patricia	SD0300	61,66A,66G,31A
Tosh, Melissa Denise	CA5150	61,36,39,54
Totter, Stephen	PA0550	61
Touree, Marc	PA3000	61
Town, Stephen	MO0950	13,61,36
Towne, Lora Rost	AZ0440	39,61,54,13
Towse, Joanna	NY3680	11,61
Trabold, William E.	CA4450	61,11,13A,12
Tracy, Gina	IL1612	61
Traficante, Marie	NY2400	61
Trainer, Robert F.	WA0600	61,11
Trainer, Susan	WA0600	39,61
Traino, Dominic	DC0050	61
Tramuta, Laurie	NY3725	61
Transue, Arlene M.	IL2900	39,61
Tremblay, Remy	AI0190	61
Trent, Andrea	TX3370	11,61
Tresler, Matthew T.	CA2390	36,61,11
Trombetta, Adelaide Muir	VA0650	61
Trost, Jennifer	PA2750	61
Trott, Donald L.	MS0700	61
Trout, Susan	MA1560	61
Trowbridge, Wendra	NY1550	61
Troyer, Lara	OH1100	61
Truax, Jenean	PA0150	13A,13C,32D,61,66A
Trubow, Valentina	IN1560	61,13C,13B
Truckenbrod, Emily	IL2910	61
Trudel, Eric	CT0800	61
Truitt, Elizabeth	IN1600	61
Truitt, Jon	IN1600	61,39
Trussel, Jacque	NY3785	36,39,61
Tucker, Eric Hoy	MI0400	61,39
Tucker, Jenna	AR0300	61
Tucker, John	TX2750	61
Tucker, Timothy	AR0550	61
Tucker, Timothy R.	AR0350	61
Tudor, Robert W.	WV0550	61,39,54
Tuning, Mark	CA3920	36,40,61
Tuomi, Scott	OR0750	12A,12,14,61,55
Turchi, Elizabeth	WV0550	61
Turner, Anne Z.	NY3650	36,39,61
Turner, Anthony	NY4500	61
Turner, Gregory E.	KS0400	13,38,36,60,61
Turner, James	MI1150	36,61
Turner, Leon P.	TX2100	11,39,61
Turner, Leon	LA0700	11,61
Turner, Noel	TX1400	61
Turner, Rebecca	SC0650	61
Turner, Ronald A.	KY1200	13,61
Turner, Veronica R.	CO0350	61,13A,13B,13C,13D
Turner-Tsonis, Anne	NM0200	61
Turnhull, Elizabeth	AA0100	39,61
Tuzicka, William	KS0700	61,36
Tweed, Pauline	CA4100	61
Tweed, Pauline	CA2100	66A,61
Twitty, Katrina	CO0900	61
Twitty, Katrina	CO0100	61,39
Tworek-Gryta, Adrienne	NY4460	61,36
Twyman, Nita	OK1030	13A,11,61,66A
Tyler, Marilyn	NM0450	39,61
Tynon, Mari Jo	ID0070	39,61,54
Tyson, LaDona	MS0580	11,40,36,61
Uddenberg, Scott	IL0850	61,54
Udland, Matt	KS0210	11,36,43,61
Uhl, Lise	TX1600	39,61
Uhle, Grant	PA3250	61
Ulen, Ronald	TX3175	61
Ullman, Beth	TX1600	61,60A
Ulloa, Cesar	CA4150	61
Ulmer, Enoch	NE0200	61
Umphrey, Leslie	NM0450	61,39
Umstead, Randall	TX0300	61
Unger, Shannon M.	OK0550	61,11,13C,39
Uniatowski, Joanne M.	OH0200	61
Unice, Charles	PA2200	61
Unice, Charles	PA3700	61
Upcraft-Russ, Kimberly	NY2650	61
Upshaw, Dawn	NY0150	61
Urban, Marshall	MN0250	61
Urbano, Patricia	CA3270	61
Urrey, Frederick E.	NJ1130	61
Urton, John	MO1800	61
Vaccariello, Lois	CA2750	61
Vadlamani, Mallika	NC0550	61
Vaida, John	PA2200	61,62B,62B
Vail, Leland	CA0825	36,61,60
Valente, Liana	FL1550	61,38,13E,39,12A

Name	Code	Areas
Valliant, James	PA3710	61,66A,11
Valliant, James	MD0170	61,66A
Vallieres, Claude	AI0190	61
Van Brunt, Jennifer	WI0960	61,66A,66C,66D
Van Cura, John	TX0300	61
Van Dalsom-Boggs, Mariel	WV0560	61
Van De Graaff, Kathleen	IL1400	61,39
Van der Hooft, Rose	AC0100	61
Van der Loo, Marion	IL1750	61
Van Dewark, Vicky	CA3250	61,54
Van Dewark, Vicky	CA2200	61
Van Hoven, Eric	PA1850	61,66A
Van Hoven, Valerie	NJ0700	61,54
Vancura, Ken	TX1750	61
Vancura, Kim	TX1750	61,66A
Vander Linden, Dan	WI0848	36,61,66
VanDyke, Susanne	MS0575	36,61,13B,13C
Vaness, Carol T.	IN0900	61
Vangelisti, Claire	LA0770	61,11
VanHoven, Valerie S.	NJ0800	61
VanNordstrand, Shelby	IA0910	12A,13,61
Vargas, Milagro	OR1050	61
Vargas, Ruben	TX1425	61,46,37,62,63
Varilek, Stephanie R.	NE0150	61
Varimezova, Tzvetanka	CA5031	20F,61
Vascan, Ligia	WI0500	40,61,36,54,29
Vasquez, Hector	TX3400	61
Vass, Heidi	CA0550	61
Vatz, Shaina V.	MD0475	61
Vaughan, Laura	MO0550	61,66D
Vaughn, Beverly Joyce	NJ0990	36,11,13A,20G,61
Vaughn, Jeanne	IL1890	61
Vaughn, Michael	TX1450	61
Velinova, Gergana	AB0210	61
Venettozzi, Vasile	KY0650	61
Vento, Rosa B.	NY2750	61
Ventura, Maria	OH2550	61
VerHoven, Victoria K.	IL0275	61
VerHoven, Victoria	IL2050	61
Verner, Nakia	NY5000	61
Verrilli, Catherine J.	MN1300	61,20B
Very, Laura Knoop	PA0550	61
Vest, Jason	NM0100	61,39
Vibe, Andrea	CA1265	61
Vik, Siri	OR0350	61
Vilcci, Aldona	NY5000	61
Villareal, Leanne	ND0150	61
Villaverde, Christina	AL0800	61
Vincent, Lawrence P.	UT0050	39,61
Viswanathan, Sundar	AG0650	29,64E,10D,61
Vitro-Wickliffe, Roseanne	NJ0825	29,61
Vleck, Marsha	MA0700	61
Vogel, Bradley D.	KS1300	60,32B,36,61,31A
Vogel, Debora	IA0500	61
Vogt, Harriet	LA0650	61
Voin, Camelia	CA5040	61
Volkar, Carie	OH0750	61
Volker, Alyssa	TN0100	61
Von Goerken, Lisa C.	NY0050	61
Von Kamp, Rebecca	IA0300	61
Von Koenigsloew, Heilwig	AB0090	61
Vote, Larry	MD0750	60,32,36,61
Voth, Alison	MA0350	61
Vought, J. Michelle	IL1150	39,61
Voulgaris, Virginia	WA0550	61
Vowan, Ruth A.	AR0225	61,12A,36,39
Voyer, Jessica	VT0400	61
Vrenios, Elizabeth	DC0010	39,61,54
Wade, Jess E.	TX2900	60,32C,61,66A
Wagner, Jeanine F.	IL2900	39,61
Wagner, Kathy	MI0520	61,54
Wagner, Lauren	MI1950	61
Wagner, Linda	MN0150	61
Wagner, Randel	WA0250	36,40,61,54,60A
Wait, Gregory A.	CA4900	36,61
Walden, Sandra	IA1600	39,11,61
Walentine, Richard L.	ND0150	61,54,13A,39,12A
Walford, Maria	IL3550	61
Walhout, Lisa	MI0350	61
Walker, Angela	MD1050	61
Walker, Anne E.	MO0050	61
Walker, Carmen Diaz	TX3520	61
Walker, Charles	NJ1350	61
Walker, Cherilee	KS0590	36,13,11,61,29A
Walker, Elizabeth	KS0750	39,61,54,35,34C
Walker, Keith H.	GA0625	36,61,60
Walker, Nancy L.	NC2430	61
Walker, Steve	OK0300	61,36,40,60A
Walker, Vicki	MI0150	61
Wall, Donna	IA0940	61
Wallace, Thomas	ME0270	36,61
Wallin, Susan	OH0700	61
Walsh, Michael	TX2250	61
Walt, Marlene	MA2250	61,40
Walter, Regina	TX1775	61,54,11
Walters, Dean	FL0730	61
Walters, Kerry E.	IL0400	61,32,39
Walters, Valerie	GA1150	61
Walton, Charles	ID0250	61
Walton, Madalyn	FL2130	61,32C
Ward, Angela	NC1650	61
Ward, Frank	OH2150	61,39,54
Ward, Perry	TN1700	61,39
Warda, Christa	PA2550	61
Ware, Clifton	MN1623	61
Ware, John Earl	LA0900	11,36,39,41,61
Ware, Rachel J.	IA0950	61
Warfield, Tara	MS0500	61,39
Warner, Michele	IN1450	61
Warren, James	CA2700	11,61,66A
Warren, Stanley	TN1660	61,39
Warrick, Kimberly	OH2500	39,61
Washington, Daniel	MI2100	61
Washington, Nadine	MI1750	61
Waterbury, Elizabeth	CA4550	36,61,40,13A,39
Waterman, Marla	NY2105	11,61
Watermeier, Ethan	MD0550	61
Waters, Willie	CT0600	61
Watkins, Howard	NY2250	61
Watkins, Ron	IL2100	61
Watkins, Russell	GA0850	61
Watson Lyons, Lois	AC0100	61
Watson, Lawrence	MA0260	61
Watson, Rita	IL1900	61,66A
Watson, Tommy L.	SC0050	11,61,39,12A,13
Watter, Hillary	NE0300	61
Wayland, Doug	OH0300	61
Wayman, John B.	GA2300	32,36,61
Wayne, Nicholas	MN0200	61,13C
Wayte, Laura Decher	OR1050	61
Wead, Joyce A.	VA0100	61
Weagraff, Marc A.	OH0200	61
Weaver, Brent	OR0250	10,61,13,34,36
Weaver, James	VA1500	61
Webb, Adam	MS0500	61,39
Webb, Guy B.	MO0775	60,36,61
Webb, Lewis	AL1050	61,36,66A
Webb, Phil	CA2810	61
Webber, Allen L.	FL1470	13,11,61,10A,66A
Webber, Carol	NY1100	61
Webber, Kelly Marie	KS0560	11,13A,12A,61,60A
Weber, Brent	PA2250	61,32D,39,12A
Weber, Carolyn R. T.	NY4150	61
Weber, Deanna F.	GA0150	13A,13B,13C,13D,61
Weber, Jessica	OH2290	61
Weber, Kathleen F.	NY2550	61
Weber, Steven T.	TX0100	36,41,61
Webster, Marc	NY1800	61
Wedding, Alison	MA0260	61
Weekly, Edrie Means	VA1350	61
Weeks, Daniel	KY1500	61
Wegenke, Wendy	MN1250	61
Weger, Bill	OK0700	61
Weichert, Constance E.	CA0850	61
Weidlich, Richard	CT0550	61
Weidlich, Richard H.	CT0800	61
Weinel, John	TX1450	61,60,36,39,40
Weiner-Jamison, Sarah	FL0200	61,11
Weir, Michele	CA5031	61,29
Weis, Patricia	WI0300	12A,61
Weiser, Kimberly	NE0610	40,61
Weiss, Daun L.	CA0800	61
Welch, Kay	IL2300	61
Weld, Kathryn	WA0200	61
Wellborn, Georgia G.	TN1660	61
Weller, Lawrence	MN1623	61
Welling, Jennifer	AA0040	61
Welling, Joelle	AA0150	13,61
Wellman, Steve	DC0100	61
Wells Chenoweth, Andrea	OH2250	61,13A,13C
Wells, Bradley C.	MA2250	13C,36,40,60A,61
Wells, Deanne	AG0070	61
Wells, Mark	MI1160	61,66
Wells, Matthew	IN1750	61
Wells, Robert A.	NC2430	61
Wells-Hunt, Deanne	AG0150	61
Wenaus, Grant	NY2750	39,61,66C,66
Wendel, Joyce	OH2450	32,36,61,60A
Wenner, Debby	VA0450	61
Wentzel, Andrew	TN1710	39,61
Wermuth, Bruce M.	TX3420	29,61
Werner, Susan	MO1830	61
Wesche, Nancy	KS0210	36,61,11
Wesley, Charles E.	MS0050	36,61,12A,11
West, Jayne	MA1175	61
West, Stephen	MI2100	61
Wester, R. Glenn	TX2295	61,66,11,13A
Westerhaus, Timothy P.	WA0400	11,60A,61
Westfall, Kathleen	LA0800	61
Westlake, Walton	IL1085	61
Westra, Mitzi	IN1650	61,13A,11,44
Whalen, Laura	AG0500	61
Whaley, Mary Susan	OK0500	11,36,61,54,13
Wheeler, W. Keith	TN1550	36,61,13C,11
Whicher, Monica	AG0300	61
Whipple, Shederick Lee	IN1560	61,39
Whitaker-Auvil, Melissa	MI1985	11,61
White, Andrew R.	NE0590	61
White, Christopher Dale	TX2955	32D,36,40,60A,61
White, Cindy	MO1710	64,13,36,61,66A
White, Edward C.	AR0730	61,39,13
White, Janice	CA5500	11,13A,36,61,66A
White, Jay G.	OH1100	61,67H
White, Jennifer	MO0850	61
White, John-Paul	MI1750	61
White, Judith	PA3150	61
White, Katherine	AR0730	61,11
White, Kayla	AR0400	31,40,61
White, Robert C.	NY2750	61
White, Robert C.	NY1900	61
White, Robert	NY1900	61
White, Robert	NY0642	60A,61
Whitehead, David	FL1700	61
Whitehead, Jennifer	OH2050	61
Whitfield, Andrew D.	IA0950	61,39
Whitfield, Wesla	CA3270	61
Whitlow, Rebecca	PA1150	61
Whitney, Nadine C.	GA2200	12A,36,61,40,39
Whittaker, Billie	DC0170	61,66C
Whittemore, Joan	MO1120	61
Whitten, Kristi	TN0100	39,61,66
Wichael, Scott	KS0590	13A,61
Wickham, Donna	CO0900	29,61
Wicklund, Karen	MI2250	61
Widney, Jason	VA1850	61
Wieck, Julie	WA1150	39,61,54
Wieczorek, Todd	AG0500	61
Wieneke, Erin	IL1890	61
Wiens, Edith	NY1900	61
Wiens, Harold H.	AA0100	61,42
Wiens, Lynelle	CA5350	61
Wierzbicki, Marishka	CT0650	61
Wiest, Lori J.	WA1150	36,55B,61,60A
Wietszychowski, Stanley	CT0650	61
Wiggett, Joseph	CA0850	61,54,39
Wigginton, James R.	TN0100	61
Wight, Nathan N.	AL0500	61,39
Wilcox-Daehn, Ann Marie	MO0775	39,61
Wilcox-Jones, Carol	OH1650	61,39,54
Wilcoxson, Nancy	SD0580	13A,61,36,11,12A
Wilding, Arla	NY3600	66A,61
Wilds, Timothy	NC1450	61,31A,36,40
Wileman, Harv	TN0260	11,61
Wiles, John L.	IA1600	36,60A,61,32
Wiley, Darlene	TX3510	61,39
Wilkerson, Andrea	CA3500	47,61,29,46,53
Wilkerson, Karen	MN1450	61
Wilkes, Eve-Anne	CA3250	36,61,54,60
Wilkinson, David B.	CA5300	61
Will, Jacob	SC1110	61,39
Willard, David	TN0450	61
Williams, Amy B.	NY4500	61
Williams, Charles	DC0170	61,36
Williams, Deborah	IL0600	32C,36,61,32D
Williams, Dennis	PA1750	54,36,61,60
Williams, Ellen	NC1300	12A,39,61

Name	Code	Areas
Williams, Harry	FL2130	61
Williams, James A.	OH2250	61
Williams, John W.	NY2100	13,11,36,61,54
Williams, Katy Schakleton	PA2900	61
Williams, Katy	PA3580	61
Williams, Kenneth D.	TX2960	36,61,60A,40,39
Williams, Lynne	PA3000	61
Williams, Mark D.	CA2440	13,36,61,38,34
Williams, Melanie B.	AL1200	61
Williams, Milton H.	CA4625	11,61,29,34
Williams, Ralph K.	NY4060	13,12A,11,61
Williams, Ralph K.	NY4050	13,11,61
Williams, Richard Lee	MO1810	66C,61
Williams, Robert	NC0800	11,12A,36,61
Williams, Robin	AR0500	61
Williams, Susan E.	AL1170	61
Williams, Susan	IA0950	61
Williams, William Richard	IN1600	61
Williams-Kennedy, Maria	ND0500	61
Williamson, Deborah K.	TX0300	61
Williamson, Sacha	AG0650	61
Williamson, Scott	VA1700	36,39,40,60,61
Williamson, Steven C.	NJ0550	60A,61,36
Williford-Avrett, Martha	OK0800	61
Willis, Sharon J.	GA0490	10A,11,12,61,13A
Willoughby, Malcolm	MD0600	61
Wilson, Angela Turner	TX3000	61
Wilson, Elisa	TX3520	61,54,47,39
Wilson, Ellen M.	TX3520	61,54,39,12
Wilson, Frances	NC2210	13A,36,61,11
Wilson, Gary P.	TN0930	60A,32C,36,61,32D
Wilson, Gran	MD1010	61,39
Wilson, Granberry	MD0850	61
Wilson, Guy	TX3415	61
Wilson, Jacque Scharlach	CA5510	61
Wilson, James	NJ0800	61
Wilson, Jeffrey S.	IL1050	60,36,61,40,31A
Wilson, Jordan	WI0100	61
Wilson, Kathleen L.	FL0700	61,54
Wilson, Ken	WA0030	11,36,61
Wilson, Kevin	MA0350	61
Wilson, Mark	NJ0760	61,13A
Wilson, Russell G.	UT0305	11,13,36,61
Wilson, Stephen B.	NY3720	13,60,36,41,61
Wilson, T. Rex	TX2710	60,12A,32C,36,61
Wilson, William	CO0950	61
Wilsyn, Bobbi	IL0720	61
Wiltsie, Barbara	MI1260	61,39,54
Wimberly, Brenda	LA0100	36,61
Windham, Susan	WA1350	61
Windham, Susan	WA0250	61
Windt, Nathan J.	TN1550	60A,61,11,32D,36
Wines, Kevin N.	OH0850	61
Wing, Henry	NH0350	36,40,61
Wingate, Owen K.	FL0675	13,11,12A,61,36
Wingert, Bradley	NY2800	61,36
Winstead, Elizabeth	NC1350	61,12A
Winstead, Elizabeth	NC0100	61,11
Winston, Jeremy	OH2400	36,61,47,13E,60A
Winter, Beth	WA0200	61,53,29
Winters, Donald Eugene	MS0850	61,31A,12A,60A
Winters, Ellen	IL0720	29,61
Winthrop, Anna	NY2750	61
Winthrop, Faith	CA2950	61
Wise, Jennifer	TX0340	61
Wise, Patricia	IN0900	61
Wiseman, Jeff	AG0150	61
Witakowski, Thomas E.	NY3717	36,40,61,60A
Witmer, Brenda K.	VA0600	61
Witt-Butler, Susan	CA4700	61
Wittman, Frances P.	NY3700	61,20G
Witzke, Ron	MO2000	39,61
Wohlschlager, Cynthia	OH0600	61
Wohlschlager, Cynthia	OH1350	61
Wojcik, Richard J.	IL3400	11,12A,36,61,31A
Wojkylak, Michael	PA1900	36,61
Wold, Stanley R.	MN1600	60A,36,40,61
Wolf, Joyce Hall	KY0550	61,39
Wolf, Sally	NJ1350	61
Wolff, Lisa	NV0100	36,40,61,13C
Wolfgang, Nancy Anderson	OH2600	61
Wolfmann, Melissa	CA1850	61,54
Woliver, C. Patrick	OH1850	61
Wollan, Barbara	CO0650	61,36
Wolz, Larry	TX0900	12A,20G,61,12C
Wong, K. Carson	ID0075	36,61
Wood, Charles E.	AL1200	61,39,12A
Wood, Dawn	KY0100	61
Wood, Gary F.	MA1650	36,61,60,13A
Wood, Juli	TX3175	61
Wood, Kenneth E.	VA1600	61,39
Wood, Rachel	AG0500	61
Woodall, Jeanne	WI1150	61
Wooderson, Joseph	MO1550	11,61
Woodfield, Randal	PA3710	61,39,11
Woodhouse, Reed	NY1900	61
Woodland, Betty	IN1450	61,66
Woodruff, Neal	IL2300	60,36,38,61,12A
Woodruff, William	NY0500	61
Woodruff, William	PR0115	61,54
Woods, Lonel	NY3780	61
Woods, Sheryl	PA3250	39,61
Woods, Timothy E.	SD0400	60A,12A,36,61,40
Woodul, Lars V.	NY4500	61
Wopat, Ann	WA0850	61,32I,32A,32B,32C
Wordelman, Peter	OR0200	60A,36,61,54
Worthen, Mary	AR0500	61,13B,13C
Worthington, Oliver W.	TX3175	61
Wozencraft-Ornellas, Jean	NM0100	39,61
Wray, Robert	WV0400	32,60,61
Wright, Gina	IL0400	61
Wright, Gina	IL0900	61
Wright, J. Clay	KS0440	11,13,36,40,61
Wright, James	NY0400	61
Wright, John Wesley	MD0800	61,39
Wright, Kathryn	GA2100	61
Wright, Kathryn M.	MA0260	61
Wright, Kathryn	MA0350	61
Wright-Costa, Julie	UT0250	61
Wrighte, Michelle	IL1300	61
Wu, Chieh-Mei Jamie	NY3500	11,13B,61,32D,36
Wu, Yiping	NY3600	61,36
Wunderlich, Kristen A.	SC1200	61
Wurgler, Norman F.	KY1540	11,36,20G,61,54
Wurster, Kathryn	MN0200	61
Wurster, Kathryn M.	MN1030	61
Wyatt, Ariana	WV0200	11,61
Wyatt, Ariana	VA1700	61
Wyatt, Gwendolyn	CA3750	36,61
Wyatt, Scott	KY1000	61
Wyers, Giselle Eleanor	WA1050	36,61
Wylie, Ted	TN0100	61,31A,54,39
Wyman, Wayne	IA1550	61,66C
Wyman, William A.	NE0450	36,39,61,60,40
Wyss, Jane	PA3600	36,61
Xiques, David	NY2750	32,60A,61
Yadeau, Lois J.	IL1750	61
Yancey, Patty	CA5400	11,61,36
Yang, Mira	VA0450	61
Yanish, Dorothy	NH0110	61,13C
Yarick-Cross, Doris	CT0850	39,61
Yates, Rebecca	SC0050	61
Yau, Eugenia Oi Yan	NY0270	11,36,61,40,60A
Yauger, Margaret	ME0500	61
Yeh, Ying	CA0800	39,61,12A
Yekel, Amy L.	OH2150	61
Yeung, Amy	TN1720	61,39,13
Yoes, Janice	AR0700	61
Yonely, Jo Belle	NV0050	61,29
Yoon, Hye	MI1830	61
Yotsumoto, Mayumi	CO0100	61,40,39
Young, Eddye Pierce	NY3560	39,61
Young, Jana	GA1150	61
Young, Karen L.	AL1160	61,11,39
Young, M. Susan	PA1450	61,39
Young, Susan	AB0150	61,36,13C,39
Young, Thomas	NY3560	39,61
Youngdahl, Janet Ann	AA0200	36,12A,61
Youngs, Jennifer	MO0260	61
Yu, Helen	AG0450	61
Yun, Misook	OH2600	61
Zabala, Adriana	MN1623	61
Zaidan, Raouf G.	NJ0825	61
Zakkary, Martha	SC1100	61
Zara, Meredith	GA0050	61
Zaro-Mullins, Wendy	MN1623	61
Zaslove, Diana	CA4450	61
Zawisza, Philip David	MN1623	61
Zeller, Kurt-Alexander	GA0500	61,39,12A
Zemliauskas, Christopher	CO0800	39,61,54
Zenobi, Dana	TX2650	61
Zhdanovskikh, Maksim	CT0100	61
Zhong, Mei	IN0150	61
Zhou, Tianxu	MA2020	36,61,12A
Ziebart, Hailey	OR1020	66A,61
Ziegler, Delores	MD1010	61,39
Ziegler, Delores	MA1400	61
Ziegler, Marci	KS0050	61,66F,39
Ziegler, Meredith	CT0600	61
Ziegler, Shanda	UT0150	61
Zielke, Gregory D.	NE0250	60,32C,36,61,31A
Ziemann, Mark	CA4300	61
Zimmerman, Andrew N.	NM0310	61
Zimmerman, Charles R.	WA1350	61
Zimmerman, Kimberly	NE0525	61,66C
Zizzi, Karen	WA1300	61
Zobel, Elizabeth W.	IL0350	12,13,36,60,61
Zoghby, Linda	AL1300	61
Zook, Katrina J.	WY0200	11,61
Zophi, Steven	WA1000	36,60A,61
Zork, Stephen	MI0250	36,61,60,10,39
Zorn, Amy	NJ1350	61
Zukerman, Arianna	DC0050	61
Zuschin, David	VA1100	13,12A,61
Zylstra, Nancy	WA0200	61
Zylstra, Nancy	WA0650	61

Strings (All Areas)

Name	Code	Areas
Alvarez, Franklin	AZ0300	11,51,62,38,13C
Angebrandt, Lynn	CA2750	62
Angeroth, Kathi	NE0700	62
Arnarson, Stefan Orn	NJ1100	34A,34D,35C,62,38
Arrowsmith, Jamie	AG0070	38,60B,62,13A,13B
Baer, Stephanie	NY2750	62,42
Baker, Sidney	IA0790	11,62
Barston, Gilda R.	IL2250	62
Bassett, Jenny	FL0670	61,62
Baumann, Keith	IL1085	62
Baxter, Kara	NE0200	46,47,62
Baxter, Sarah M.	KS0980	62
Becker, Melissa J.	PA2050	10E,12,32,62
Bell, Valerie	MO1810	51,62
Benoit, Linda	IA1350	62
Bergonzi, Louis	IL3300	32E,38,62,32G,60B
Betz, Michael	WI0300	62
Bing, Delores M.	CA0500	62,41,42,62C
Borok, Emanuel	TX3420	62A,62
Bossuat, Judy	CA0840	32E,62
Both, Christoph	AF0050	13F,62,34
Boucher, Leslie H.	GA0700	12,20,13,62,11
Boughton, Janet	CT0300	51,62,41
Boyd, Jesse	LA0080	11,13,29,62,70
Braccio, Joseph	FL1650	62
Bracey, Jerry A.	VA0500	37,38,47,62,29
Brannan, Victoria	IL1500	62
Brawand, John	SD0550	11,12A,38,62
Briselli, Carol	PA3600	62
Britton, Rex	VA0700	62
Broe, Caroline	AZ0440	62
Brown, Susan	CA0400	41,51,62,32
Buck, Casey	AR0200	62
Bullard, Julia K.	IA1600	62
Carbonara, David	LA0720	38,41,51,62
Carey, Aaron L.	WV0100	41,62,70
Ceo, Joseph	RI0250	62
Chambers, Mark K.	AG0650	38,60,62
Chandler, Susan	WI0865	32E,38,62
Chang, Wei Tsun	TN1450	11,32E,62A,41,62
Changhien, Wenting	OH2200	62D,66C,62
Chavez, Arturo	OR1010	62
Chilingarian, Samvel	CA1700	12A,38,62
Christie, Pamela	NY3717	32E,62
Church, Alan	VT0250	62
Churchill, Mary-Lou	MA1400	62
Ciaschini, Peter	GA0900	62
Cierpke, Timothy H.	TN1600	10F,60,62,36,38
Collaros, Pandel Lee	WV0100	70,62,66A,46
Collins, Lisa	NM0450	62
Crookshank, Esther R.	KY1200	12,14,62
Cumming, Hilary W.	NY3700	62
Cutchen, Dovie	AL1050	62,66A
Dabczynski, Andrew	UT0050	32,62
Dackow, Sandra K.	NJ1400	62
Dalbey, Laura	MT0175	62

Name	Code	Numbers
Davis, Mickey	AR0600	62
Davis, Susan A.	NY2750	32,51,62
Dell, Charlene	OK1350	32E,32H,32,62,62A
DePasquale, Charles	PA1550	51,62
Dexter, Jonathan G.	TX2960	62
Docenko, Gregory	NY3717	62
Doroftei, Mugnr	TX2550	13,38,62
Doucette, Hannah	PA3550	62
Drago, Alejandro M.	ND0500	38,62
Dunn, Phyllis M.	CA4410	62
Dupertuis, Jeff	CA3850	62,63,64,65,66
Dura, Marian T.	PA1900	38,62,32,32B,62A
Dwyer, Jack	OR0400	62
Ellis, Peter	AA0032	38,62,51,36
Ellsworth, E. Victor	AR0750	32,62,38
Ellsworth, Rodger	NH0250	62
Entzi, Karen	NC1450	62,11,41
Evans, Judith	FL0680	62
Fairbanks, Donna	UT0325	51,62,38
Fehrenbach, Paula	CA3500	62,62C
Ferguson, John	MO0500	62,51
Flandreau, Tara	CA1150	12A,13,38,41,62
Freyenberger, Denise	IA0900	62
Friesen, Eugene	MA0260	62
Fudge, James	IL0300	11,62
Fulbright, Marshall T.	CA2550	38,51,48,62,63
Gallagher, Mary Gloria	IN1100	62,66A,66G
Gardiner, Ronald	FL1740	13,62,60B,51,38
Gardner, Gary D.	OK1500	11,62,63,37,47
Garris, Margaret E.	NC2350	62
Gatto, Angelo	MD0170	38,62
Gatwood, Jody	DC0050	62,62A,41
Gazouleas, Ed	MA1400	62
Gennarelli, Franco	NJ1400	62
Gerald, Helen	TX0100	62
Gheith, Sarabeth	TN1100	11,62
Giardina, David	CT0350	62,70
Gibson, Mary	VT0250	62
Gillespie, Alison	PA2450	67H,62
Gillette, Michael	NJ0760	11,62,32E
Gilmore, Susanna Perry	TN1680	32E,62
Glaser, Matthew	MA0260	62
Goldberg, Marjorie	PA3330	62,32
Gordon, Joshua	MA0500	11,41,42,62,62C
Graham, Brenda J.	IN1250	13A,32,37,62,31A
Gratton, Chris	SC0700	62
Griffin, Buddy	WV0350	62,34,35
Grizzell, Janet	CA1290	38,51,62
Gronnier, Henry M.	CA5300	62
Guy, Larry L.	NY2750	62,64C
Haefner, Jaymee	TX3420	62E,62
Hamann, Donald L.	AZ0500	32,62,32E,32G
Hamelin, Karla M.	TX0400	62
Hamilton, Anne	WV0800	62
Hart-Reilly, Kathy M.	TN1710	62
Hartman, Mark L.	PA3050	62,38,13,62A,29
Hayes, Pamela	SC0600	62
Hector-Norwood, Diana	TX1350	51,62
Henderson, Luther L.	CA2600	20G,38,62,45
Henigbaum, William	NC2600	62,38
Hess, Rick	NE0250	62
Hilderbrand, Monica	IL1612	61,62
Hillard, Claire Fox	GA0625	11,62A,62B,66D,62
Hilsee, Amalie	CA0800	62
Hinkle, Laura	IL1300	62,32E
Hodder, Christy	AF0120	62
Holley, Timothy	NC1600	14,62,62C,20G
Holmes, Ramona A.	WA0800	14,32,38,62
Horvath, Kathleen	OH0400	32,51,62
Hosmer, Christian	NY3550	62,51
Howard, Greg	VA1550	62
Howard, Sabrina	NC2650	62
Howe, Melissa	MA0260	62
Hutchison, Callie	AZ0250	62
Irwin, Jeffrey	WV0100	62
Ivry, Jessica	CA1150	51,42,62,13C,38
Jaffe, Claudio	FL1450	62,38,62C
Jelinek, Mark R.	PA0250	60B,11,38,62
Jensen, Byron W.	NE0300	13B,38,12A,62,32C
Jenson, Don	WA0450	62
Johnson, Cecilia	MI0050	62,51
Johnson, Nancy	KS1300	62
Johnson, Yvonne P.	GA0200	62
Johnson, Yvonne P.	DE0050	32,66D,62
Johnston, James	OH0050	62,38
Jussila, Clyde	WA1050	32,62,64
Kempter, Susan	NM0450	62,32A,32B,32C
Kent, Peter	NY3725	62
Kew, Margaret Davis	KS0100	51,62,66A
Khan, Ali Akbar	CA0050	13A,10,11,12A,62
Khan, Shujaat Husain	CA5031	20E,62,61
Kim, Dong Suk	CA5031	20C,62,65
Kime, Ramona	MI1800	62,66A,66D,66H
King, Curtis R.	FL0600	13A,13,32,61,62
Kjelland, James	IL2250	60,32C,38,62
Konecky, Larry	MS0050	13,62,70,34
Kosower, Paula	IL0750	62
Kott, Sandra	MA0260	62
Krieger, Angela	OK1400	62
Kroesen, Irene	CA0960	62
Kunins, Alan	NY2450	62
Kwalwasser, Helen	PA3250	62,62A
Lamb, Earnest	NC0800	12A,32C,51,62
Lambson, Jeanne	MO0100	62
Lang, Cynthia	CA3400	38,41,51,62
Lantz, Lisa E.	NY0100	11,38,51,62,13A
Laux, Charles	GA1150	32E,34C,38,62,32C
Lehmann, Robert A.	ME0500	60,62
Leonhardt, Julie	MO1250	62,51
Leska, Gosia	AL1300	62
Levi, Zachary	PA3710	38,62
Li, Chi	CA5031	20C,62,64,65
Li, Nina	AL0010	62
Lieberman, Carol	MA0700	62A,13,12A,67,62
Liedtke, Kris	WI0750	62
Litera, Ina	NY0270	11,62
Lizotte, Caroline	AI0150	62,41
Lo, Adrian	MN0200	12A,37,38,47,62
London, Betsy	CA4700	62
Long, Janet	SC0900	62,32B,11,32A,32C
Loughran, Robert	NJ1350	62,32E
Luchansky, Andrew	CA4150	62
Lundy, Ann	TX3150	51,62,38
Madriguera, Enric	TX0700	62,70,11,12A
Mainland, Timothy L.	WV0200	13,10,70,10F,62
Mann, Sylvia Lee	CA0805	32,62,38
Markward, Cheri D.	RI0101	13,11,41,62,12A
Marsh, Peter	CA5300	41,62
Martin, Anne L.	CA3000	11,62,38
Martinez, Everaldo	ND0050	62,51
Mathur, Sharmila	AA0100	20E,62
Maxfield, Adele	IN1560	62
McCoy, June	OK0700	62
McGann, John	MA0260	62
McLeland, James K.	TX1000	62
Merideth, Sherry Francis	TN0550	62
Merritt, Romona	AL0650	62,41
Mery, John	OR0400	20H,62
Michels, Joyce	IL2310	62
Mickey, Wendy	KS0265	62
Miller, Peter	VT0100	62,32,51
Monte, Charlene	MA2020	62
Montzka Smelser, Ann	IL3550	32C,62
Moore, Christine E.	TX2100	62,16
Moore, Frances	CA5040	62,42
Morris, Theodora	OK1050	62
Morrison, John	WV0300	62,66C
Moss, Kirk D.	WI0350	11,32E,38,51,62
Mouridian, Linda	CA0835	62
Muller, Riana	PA2100	62
Muresan, Branden	CA2960	38,62
Neault, Sylvian	AI0190	29,62
Neubert, Peter	TX1100	51,62
Neuman, Lawrence	IL0550	62
Neuman, Rahul	CA5031	20F,62
Newsom, Mary Ellen	IN0005	12,14,32,61,62
Nobles, Ron	IN0250	62
Ogrizovic-Ciric, Mirna	GA0300	38,42,62
O'Leary, Jed	NE0400	62,64
Olivares, Walter G.	AK0100	12A,51,62
Oliver, Kristen	AF0120	62
Owen, Marlin	CA0350	38,41,51,62,70
Oyenand, Geronimo	VA0050	62
Payne, Bryon	FL1600	61,62,66A
Peloza, Susan	CA5400	62,11,13A,66D
Penniman, G. Victor	MO1010	55,12A,62,11,36
Perkins, Deborah	TX2400	62
Perry, Kathy	SC0700	62,51,42
Petersons, Erik	PA2800	62
Phoenix-Neal, Diane	IA0200	62,11,12,51
Piltz, Hans-Karl	AB0100	11,62
Pinkney, Rachel	OH0250	62C,62
Pogossian, Movses	CA5030	62A,62
Pomeranz, Felice	MA0260	62E,62
Pulgar, Edward	TN0250	62
Pulgar, Mary	TN0250	62
Quantz, Michael	TX3515	11,41,62,20H
Rabson, Miriam	MA0260	62
Ranney, Jack	IL2350	38,51,62
Reeve, Barbara	AR0425	62
Render, Charles	LA0700	62
Rhyneer, Barbara	MI1600	60,38,41,62,11
Richter, Magdalena	MA1400	62
Robinson, Bill	TN1000	38,62
Rodgers, Linda	CA1520	62,51
Rogers, Paul	AG0450	62
Rushing, Densi	OK1200	62
Saeverud, Trond	ME0340	62
Salvo, Joel	MN1620	62
Sampson, Larry	CA0300	62,63,64,70
Sands, Tracy	NE0200	62,38
Sarch, Kenneth	PA2150	51,62
Schwede, Walter	WA1250	51,62,62A
Scott, Laurie	TX3510	32,62
Sherman, Joseph	NY2750	38,32,62
Shrader, Mary Kathryn	WV0550	62
Shurr, Janet	WI0050	55B,62,67
Silverstein, Joseph	MA0350	62
Skelton, Robert A.	AG0500	60,38,41,51,62
Skoldberg, Phyllis	AZ0440	62
Sloothaak, Bea	MI0750	62
Smith, Carol	TX2250	38,51,60B,62,32E
Smith, James	WI0815	38,51,62,60B
Smith, Lee	CA4950	11,41,62
Spicher, Buddy	TN0100	62
Spiro, Michael E.	IN0900	62
Steede, Marcus	WI0770	62
Stees, Rhonda L.	VA0100	64B,62
Sternfeld, Barbara	CA5400	11,38,62
Steva, Elizabeth Ryland	KY1000	62,11,12
Stevens, Daniel B.	KS1200	38,41,37,62,51
Stierneberg, Donald	IL1085	62
Stotelmyer, Deborah L.	MD0450	62
Strachan, Heather	GA1650	62,42
Strizic, Owen	IA0250	62
Suh, Elizabeth	MO0200	62
Sullivan, Eileen	NM0500	62
Swopes, Polly	OK0500	62
Tebbets, Gary	KS0040	12A,11,36,54,62
Thomas, Rob	MA0260	62
Thompson, John	NJ1400	62
Thompson, Marcus	MA1200	41,62
Thompson, Marcus	MA1400	41,62
Ting, Damian	CA2775	51,62
Todd, Kenneth W.	CO1050	11,38,51,62
Torlina, Mark	MO0550	62
Trynchuck, Carla	MI0250	62,41,51
Twomey, Michael P.	TX1900	10A,13,10F,38,62
Underwood, Kirsten F.	OK0150	62,38,11,62C,20
Vargas, Ruben	TX1425	61,46,37,62,63
Verbesly, Franklin	NY1600	62,62C,62D,11
Verhoeven, Martine	CA4450	62
Vodnoy, Robert L.	SD0400	12A,62,38,51,35E
Voldman, Yakov	LA0650	60,32C,38,51,62
Wada, Rintaro	NY3475	51,62
Waddelow, Jim M.	NC1300	41,62,38,32E
Wade-Elkamely, Bobbie	OK0450	51,62
Wan, Andrew	AI0150	42,62
Wang, Liang-yu	IN0900	66C,62
Wessler, Peter	IL0400	62
Widner, Paul	AG0450	62,38
Wilkinson, Chris	AF0050	62
Williams, R.	MO0650	62
Winey, Richard	PA1250	32E,62
Wirtz, Bob	CA6000	62
Witt, Anne C.	AL1170	62,32
Wood, Bruce	TX3200	32E,62
Ziebold, Barbara M.	OH2140	62,51

Violin

Name	Code	Numbers
Abe, Christie-Keiko	IL2750	62A,66E
Abegg, Paul	UT0150	62A,38,51,54,62B
Abel, Alfred	IN1850	62A,62B,38,48
Abo, Takeshi	MI0150	62A,51

Index by Area of Teaching Interest

Name	Code	Areas
Abo, Takeshi	MI0100	62A,62B,51
Aceto, Jonathan D.	GA0950	51,62A,11,62B,13E
Acosta, Gail	CA2750	62A,62B
Adams, Valerie	FL0930	51,62A
Adderley, Cecil L.	MA0260	32E,32F,32G,62A,64C
Adkins, Elizabeth	DC0050	54,62A
Adkins, Elizabeth	MD1010	62A
Adkins, Elizabeth	DC0170	62A
Afanassieva, Veronika	CO0275	62A,42,51
Agopian, Edmond	AA0050	62A,41,38
Agopian, Edmond	AA0150	38,41,51,62A,42
Agostini, Federico	NY1100	62A
Ahn, Angella	MT0200	62A,62B
Ahramjian, Sylvia Davis	PA3600	51,62A,62B
Aki, Syoko	CT0850	41,62A
Akin, Maurine	WY0130	62A,62B
Albanese, Brynn	CA0600	62A
Albela-Vega, Daniel	NM0310	62A
Albert, Matthew	TX2400	42,62A
Aldrich, Ralph E.	AG0500	41,51,62A,62B
Aldridge, Erin	WI0860	38,62A,13C,51,60B
Alexander, James	LA0450	62A,62B
Alfonzo, Jesus	FL1750	62A,62B
Almond, Frank	IL2250	62A
Alonso, Ernesto	PR0150	12A,11,62A,14A,55A
Althoff, Erin	SC0420	62A,62B
Altino, Soh-Hyun Park	TN1680	62A,42
Ambartsumian, Levon	GA2100	51,62A,62B
Amoroso, Richard	PA3250	62A
Anderson, Dean	CA1900	38,62A
Anderson, Stella N.	MN0950	62A,62B
Andrus, Victoria	UT0150	62A,62B
Anger, Darol	MA0260	62A
Anop, Lenora Marya	IL2910	62A,41,51,42
Anop, Lenora	IL2970	62A
Apperson, Jim	AZ0470	62A,62B
Applegate, Geoffrey	MI2200	62A
Aranovskaya, Alla	KS1450	62A
Arden, Cynthia	IL1400	62A
Arenz, David	GA1550	62A
Arksey, Meredith	WA1150	13,62A,62B
Armstrong, Vahn R.	VA1000	62A
Arnold, John	OK0750	62A,42
Arnott, J. David	MN0350	38,62A,62B,51
Ashkenasi, Samuel	PA0850	62A
Ashton, Alice	UT0190	62A,62B
Ashton, Jack	UT0190	62A,62B
Ashton, Ted	ID0060	41,62A,32E
Atanasiu, Lenuta	NJ1050	62A
Athayde, Juliana	NY1100	62A
Atladottir, Hrabba	CA5000	62A
Au, Aaron	AA0100	62A,62B,51
Auer, Frank	DC0170	62A
Auerbach, Dan J.	GA0850	60,62A,62B,38,51
Austin, Alan S.	TX3450	62A
Austin-Stone, Heather	WV0550	62A,62B,11
Aylward, Ansgarius	NY0400	60B,38,41,62A
Azar, Andree	AI0150	62A
Azimkhodjaeva, Shakida	GA2100	51,62A
Babbitt, Frank	IL0850	62A,62B
Badea, Remus	IL0850	62A,62B
Bae, Ik-Hwan	IN0900	42,62A
Bagley, Marjorie H.	NC2430	62A
Bahcall, Klara	WI0830	41,62A,62B
Bahn, Lina	CO0800	62A
Bai, Millie	PA3250	62A
Baker, Christian Matthew	AR0350	62A
Baker, Cynthia	AZ0350	51,62A,62B
Baldridge, Margaret Nichols	MT0400	62A,62B,51
Baldwin, Philip R.	WA1350	62A,41,38,60B
Balkin, Laura M.	NY3730	41,62A
Balkin, Richard A.	NY3730	13A,41,62A
Ball, Terry	AG0050	62A,62B
Balogh, Lajos	OR0500	38,62A
Baltaian, Aroussiak	CA3300	66A,62A
Bankas, Atis	AG0300	62A
Barantschik, Alexander	CA4150	62A
Barbini, William	CA0840	62A,62B
Bargerstock, Nancy E.	NC0050	51,62A,42,62B
Barnes, Darrel	MO0350	62B,62A,63B
Barnes, Mei Chen	PA3250	62A
Barnum, Justin	MO1900	62A
Barta, Michael	IL2900	12A,62A,62B
Bartley, Peter	AG0500	32A,62A
Barton, Mary	NY2400	62A,62B
Basham, Glenn D.	FL1900	62A
Basta, JoAnna	PA2450	62A
Bates, Alexandra	AF0120	62A,62B
Bath, Joanne	NC0650	62A,32A
Batjer, Margaret	CA5300	62A
Baumgartel, Julie	AG0600	62A
Beacham, Graybert	ME0250	62A,62B
Beall, Stephen J.	TX2955	62A,62B,51
Beaudry, Genevieve	AI0050	62A
Beaver, Johanna L.	VA1475	62A,62B,51
Beaver, Martin P.	NY2750	62A
Beckett, Christine	AI0070	13,12C,32C,38,62A
Bedelian, Haroutune	CA5020	62A
Bednar, Stanley	NY2150	62A
Bednarz, Blanka	PA0950	13A,42,51,62A,62B
Beia, Suzanne	WI0815	62A
Beiler, Jonathan	PA3250	62A
Beilina, Nina	NY2250	62A
Belknap, Monte	UT0050	62A,41
Bell, Jeremy	AG0600	62A
Bell, Joshua	IN0900	62A
Bell, Stephani	PA1850	38,62A,62B
Beluska, Vasile	OH0300	62A
Berard, Marie	AG0450	62A
Berard, Marie	AG0300	62A
Berg, Bruce	TX0300	62A
Berick, Yehonatan M.	MI2100	62A
Berlinsky, Dmitri	MI1400	62A
Bernhardsson, Sigurbjorn	IN0900	62A,42
Bernhardsson, Sigurbjorn	IL3300	51,62A
Berofsky, Aaron	MI2100	62A
Beroukhim, Cyrus	NY3725	62A
Bewick, Bonnie	MA0350	62A
Beyer, Douglas A.	KS0700	62A,62B
Biava, Luis O.	PA3250	38,62A
Bielish, Aaron J.	TX2295	62A,62B,41,11,13
Binford, Joanna	KY1350	62A,62B,41
Bird, Paula E.	TX3175	62A,51
Biskupski, Grazyna	MI1260	62A,62B
Bixler, Judith	MI1000	62A
Bjella, Steven A.	WI0850	41,62A,32E
Bjork, Mark	MN1623	41,62A
Blackwell, Jessica	TN1850	62A
Blake, Elise A.	VA0800	62A,62B,42
Blake, John	PA3330	47,62A,29
Blakeslee, Lynn	NY1100	62A,42
Blalock, Karen	UT0325	62A,62B
Blaney, Michael S.	LA0760	38,62A
Blaszak, Emilia	IL2750	62A,62B
Blaydes, Sharon	OH1600	62A,62B,51
Blea, Anthony	CA1020	38,62A,36
Bloch, Robert S.	CA5010	13,11,41,62A,62B
Bloom, Claudia	CA4425	62A
Blount, Alyssa	NY4150	62A
Boardman, Gregory	ME0150	20G,62A
Boder, Alexander	NY2400	62A
Bodman, Alan	OH2150	51,62A,62B
Boehm, Norbert	AA0200	62A
Bogachek, Zinoviy	VA0450	62A
Boggs, Isabelle	MA1100	20,64C,62A,62B
Bohannon, Helen	IN1010	62A
Bohlen, Tara M.	ND0400	62A,62B
Boico, Efim	WI0825	62A
Booth, Davyd M.	PA3250	62A
Borok, Emanuel	TX3420	62A,62
Borok, Emanuel	TX2400	62A
Borup, Hasse	UT0250	62A
Bossert, Laura	MA1175	62A,62B
Bossert-King, Laura	MA2050	62A,62B
Boucher, Gillian	AF0120	62A
Boutin, Lise	AA0200	62A
Bowlin, David Henderson	OH1700	62A
Boyd, Bonnie	TX2200	62A
Boyd, Bruce	KS1250	62A,62B,70,32E,62C
Boyle, Annie Chalex	TX3200	62A
Bozell, Casey	OR0150	62A,62B,38,62C,51
Bozman, Julissa	CA1265	62A
Bradley-Vacco, Lynda	MN0250	38,62A,62B,51
Brandolino, Tony	MO2000	62A,38,42
Brannen, Malcolm	MI0850	62A,62B,38,32A
Branum, Justin	MO1950	62A
Brasky, Jill T.	FL2000	13,13B,13C,62A
Braus, Leonard P.	UT0250	62A
Bregman, Jacqueline	MN1050	62A
Brenner, Brenda L.	IN0900	62A,32E
Brickman, David	NY1100	62A
Briggs, Kurt	NY0270	11,62A
Briles, Charity	IL1050	38,62A,62B
Brink, Robert	MA1400	62A
Brooks, Davis H.	IN0250	62A
Brooks, Lisa E.	IN0250	62A
Brown, Hugh M.	MO1810	41,62A,62B
Brown, Kellie Dubel	TN1150	62A,38,12A,60B,62B
Brown, LuAnn	UT0200	62A
Brown, Susanne	AF0120	62A,62B
Brunelle, Felicia	FL1745	62A
Brye, Daniel	PA0950	62A,62B,51
Bubanj, Marija	IL2750	62A,62B
Buckles, Michael	LA0350	32E,62A
Bujak, Ewa	MN1295	38,62B,62A
Bujak, Ewa	MN0610	62A,62B
Burchard, Brett	IL1100	62A
Burgess, Gina	AF0120	62A
Burggraff, Allison	ND0350	62A
Burrell, Lisa M.	TX1520	62A
Burroughs, D. Robert	WA0150	13,11,62A,53,38
Burton, Heidi R.	OK1300	13A,13,11,66A,62A
Bushkova, Julia	TX3420	62A
Buswell, James	MA0950	62A,42,38
Buswell, James	MA1400	41,62A
Butler-Hopkins, Kathleen M.	AK0150	51,62A,62B
Buxton, Merideth	MD1100	62A,62B
Byers, Andrea	CA0825	62A
Caban, Francisco J.	PR0115	62A,41,42,51
Campetti, Cynthia	PA1150	62A,62B
Cardenes, Andres J.	PA0550	62A
Carey, Pamela Ruth	CA1650	62A
Carey, Thomas C.	OH2275	62A,62B,38,62C
Carlson, Andrew	OH0850	62A,51,20G,38
Carlson, Paul B.	MO0800	62A
Carnes, Donna	NE0450	62A
Carney, Laurie	NY2150	41,62A
Carper, Nick	WA0400	62A,62B
Carrasco, Jacqui	NC2500	62A,62B,51,41,14
Carrettin, Zachary	TX3450	62A,38
Carter, Monty	MO0950	62A,62B,38
Cassidy, Marcia	NH0100	62A,62B,41
Castleman, Charles	NY1100	62A
Cavadas, Angela	AB0050	62A
Cedeno, Eduardo	NC1400	62A,13A
Cha, In-Hong	OH2500	60,38,62A
Cha, Keum Hwa	ID0100	62A
Chai, Liang	NY0500	62A
Chalifour, Martin	CA5300	62A
Chan, David	NY1900	62A
Chang, Elizabeth E.	MA2000	62A
Chang, Lyn	MA0400	62A
Chang, Lynn	MA0350	62A
Chang, Seanad	TN1850	62A,62B
Chang, Wei Tsun	TN1450	11,32E,62A,41,62
Chang, Wei-Tsun	TN1850	62A
Chapo, Eliot	FL0850	41,51,62A
Chase, Stephanie	NY2750	62A
Chen, Ting-Lan	NE0590	11,13B,62A,62B,13C
Chepaitis, Stanley L.	PA1600	41,62A,62B,51
Ching, Daniel	TX3510	62A,42
Chiu, Cornelius	IL3550	62A
Cho, Catherine	NY1900	62A,42
Cho, Yuri	NV0050	62A
Choi, Eugenia	AB0100	62A,51
Choi, Janey	NY3705	62A
Chong, Daniel	MN1625	62A
Christensen, Brandon J.	MO1500	62A,62B,42,11
Christie, Tim	WA1000	62A
Christy, Jay	GA0750	62A
Chuang, Chun-Chien	KS1000	62A
Chudnovsky, Emil	DC0050	62A
Chung, Carol	NC1300	62A
Chung, Kyung-Wha	NY1900	62A
Chung, Miri	IN0907	62A,62B,33,51
Cirlin, Sunny	MI1200	62A
Ciulei, Lenuta	NJ1130	62A
Clapp, Stephen	NY2900	62A
Clapp, Stephen	NY1900	62A,42
Clark, Charlene K.	MO1900	62A
Clark, Martha	NM0300	62A,67B
Clarke, Karen	TN1850	62A,62B,67B
Cleland, George	AG0050	62A
Cleland, George	AA0040	38,41,62A,62B
Clements, Tania Maxwell	GA1050	62B,62A
Cleveland, Michael	NY0650	62A

Name	Code	Areas
Clifford, Patrick	FL1450	62A,62B,51
Co, Wei-Shu Wang	OH0200	62A
Coffman, Elizabeth	IL0730	62A,62B
Cohen, Bonnie	DC0350	62A
Cohen, Joanne	MN0600	32,51,62A,62B
Cole, Carol	FL1125	62A,42,32E
Cole, David C.	FL0680	38,51,39,62A,32
Cole, Scott	OR0950	62A
Colwell, David A.	VA1550	62A,51,42
Combs, Matt	TN1850	62A
Conklin, Scott A.	IA1550	62A
Contreras, Billy	TN0100	62A
Cooke, India	CA2950	62A,29
Cooper, Cora	KS0650	51,62A,62B
Cooper, Jameson	IN0910	62A,38,60B
Copes, Ronald	NY1900	62A,51
Corwin, Lucille H.	NY4500	62A,62B
Cotik, Tomas	TX3750	62A
Cottin-Rack, Myriam	CA4300	62A,42,41
Cowan, Carole	NY3760	38,66D,62A,62B
Cowell, Jennifer	WY0050	38,41,66D,62A
Cox, Kerry	IA0600	62A,62B
Craioveanu, Mihai	MI1050	11,62A,41
Crane, Emily Hanna	TN0050	62A,62B
Crawford, Roberta	NY3705	41,62B,62A
Craycraft, Nicole	MN0450	62A
Creel, David	TN0260	11,62A
Cromwell, Anna L.	IL0800	62A,62B,41
Cseszko, Ferenc	ID0250	38,62A,62B,41
Cueto, Jose	MD0750	62A
Cummins, Danielle Rosaria	CA0845	62A,62B
Currie, Nicholas W.	MD0520	62A
Cyncynates, Ricardo	DC0170	62A
Dahn, Nancy	AD0050	41,62A,62B
Dakin, Deborah	IL0100	11,62B,62A
Dalbec-Szczesniak, Gisele	AG0250	62A,62B
Dallinger, Carol	IN1600	62A,13A,62B,51
Dalmas, Jennifer	TX2700	38,62A,62B,41
Daly, Kathleen	NJ0700	62A,32E,11
Danchenko, Victor	PA0850	62A
Danchenko, Victor	MD0650	62A
D'Andrea, Daria	CA5353	62A,62B
Danis, Ann	RI0300	60,38,11,62A,62B
Darmiento, Madeleine	PA2350	62A,62B
Darvill, Jackie	NY3770	62A,62C
Daucher, Tim	MO0775	62A
Daugherty, Wendy	TX2570	62A,62B,66A,32E
Davidovici, Robert	FL0700	62A,62B,11
Davis, Michael W.	KY0400	62A
Davis, Rachelle Berthelsen	CA3400	62A,12A,38
Davis, William	IN0800	38,62A,62B
Davy, Karen	CA2250	62A,62B,62C,62D,41
Dawes, Andrew	AB0100	41,51,62A,42
Dawson, Andrea	TN1100	62A,51,11
Day, Geoff	FL0500	62A,62B
De La Bretonne, Beverly	TX0100	13,38,41,62A,64A
De Los Santos, Carmelo	NM0450	62A
DeDominick, Jeanne D.	VA1000	62A
Deforest, June D.	IN1750	62A
Del Castillo, Jose Francisco	PR0115	62A
Delevoryas, Sarah	CO0150	62A,62B
Delin, Diane	IL0720	29,62A,10
Dell, Charlene	OK1350	32E,32H,32,62,62A
Dempsey, John D.	RI0300	13A,13,51,62A
Deng, Lu	OK1330	62A
DeNicola, Alan	VT0200	62A,62B,62C
DeWitt, Dortha	IL0100	62A
Dharamraj, Fabrice B.	NC2500	62A
Di Novo, Nancy	AB0100	62A
DiAdamo, Richard	PA3580	62A
Dicterow, Glenn	NY1900	62A
Dicterow, Glenn	NY2150	62A
Dietrich, Johannes M.	PA1900	60,38,62A,62B
DiEugenio, Nicholas	NY1800	62A
Dillenbeck, Denise	WA0050	62A,42
Dillingham, David	FL0930	62A
Dinino, Aileen	FL1310	62A,62B
Dissmore, Larry	MO0400	60,38,51,62A,62B
Djokic, Philippe	AF0100	62B,38,41,51,62A
Dodd, Kit	NY2950	62A
Dodds, Amy	WA1300	62A,62B,13
Doering, Susan J.	CA1860	62A,62B
Doheny, Anthony J.	CA4900	62A
Dolkas, Bridget	CA0960	62A
Dolphin, Amber	WI0100	62A,62B
Douglas, Madonna	AG0170	62A
Drennen, Edward	DC0100	62A
Drennon, Eddie	DC0170	62A,29
Drexler, Darcy	WI0825	62A,62B
Drucker, Eugene	NY0150	62A
Drucker, Eugene S.	NY3790	41,62A
Duchow, Ann L.	IA0940	62A,62B
Dufour, Francine	AI0220	51,62A
Duggan, Ann	IL3150	62A,62B
Duncan, Craig T.	TN1800	62A
Dura, Marian T.	PA1900	38,62,32,32B,62A
Dutton, Kristina	IL2750	62A
DuWors, Kerry	AC0050	62A,62B,51
Dyck, Calvin	AB0060	51,62A
Eckenrode, Bryan	NY4460	62C,62A
Edelberg, Joe	CA4700	32E,38,42,62A,62B
Edge, David	OH2050	41,62A
Een, Andrea	MN1450	42,62A,62B
Ehle, Todd	TX0550	62A,62B,38
Einfeldt, Teri	CT0650	62A
Eissenberg, Judith	MA0500	41,62A,11
Elias, Carlos	CO0225	32C,38,62A,62B,51
Elias, Gerald A.	UT0250	62A
Elisha, Larisa	GA0950	62A,62B,42
Elliott-Goldschmid, Ann	AB0150	62A,42
Emery, Michael	NY3650	62A,62B,51
Emile, Mark A.	UT0300	10F,60B,62A,62B
Englund, John	UT0250	62A,62B
Enyart, John	FL0950	38,62A,51
Ericksen, Elizabeth	MN0300	62A,62B,42
Eshbach, Robert	NH0350	11,62A,41
Espinosa, Sergio	TX3500	32,11,62A
Espy, Blake	NM0310	62A
Estavez, Evelyn	NJ0500	62A
Evans, Ralph	WI0825	62A
Ewer, Gregory	OR0400	62A
Eyzerovich, Inna	PA2450	62A
Fadial, John	WY0200	62A,41,55B
Fagerburg, Karin	CT0050	62A,62B
Faidley-Solars, Elizabeth	CT0650	62A
Fairlie, Mary	TX2800	62A,62B,51,14C,38
Falls, Sheila E.	MA2150	41,62A
Farkas, Pavel	CA5150	38,41,51,62A,62B
Fedkenheuer, William	TX3510	62A,51
Feigin, Tatiana	NY5000	62A
Feldberg, David	NM0450	43,62A,60B
Feldman, Susan M.	CA5300	62A,67B,12A
Fernandez, Gerardo	DC0170	62A
Ferril, Michael J.	CA0835	62A,42,43
Fewer, Mark	AI0150	62A
Ficsor, Philip G.	CA5550	62A,38
Field, Elizabeth	DC0100	62A,67B
Figard, Kristin	SC0200	62A
Filipovich, Natalie	MN1700	62A,62B,32E
Findlay-Partridge, Marta C.	NC1300	62A
Findley, Mary	DC0170	62A
Findley, Mary B.	DC0100	62A,51
Finegan, James	PA1550	62A,62B
Finkelshteyn, Tracy	IA0600	62A
Fiorentino, Mike	CA5353	70,62A
Fischbach, Garrett	NY2250	62A
Fischbach, Gerald	MD1010	62A
Fischer, Rebecca J.	NE0600	62A,42
Fisher, Kimberly	PA3250	62A
Fisher, Yuko	IL1740	62A,62B,62C,41
Fitzpatrick, William	CA0960	62A
Flaniken, Jeffrey Z.	AL0800	62A,13B,32E
Flavin, Scott Thomas	FL1900	62A,51
Fleezanis, Jorja	IN0900	62A
Fleming, Phyllis	DC0170	62A,62B
Flores, Jose G.	TX2930	62A,62B,51,13C,42
Fluchaire, Olivier	NY0644	62A,62B,11,13A,42
Foard, Sarah	DC0170	62A
Foerster, Frank	NJ0825	62A,62B
Follett, Kathleen J.	OR1100	62A
Folus, Brian H.	MD0475	62D,62A,62C
Fong, Debra	CA4900	62A
Ford, Ronnal	NC2700	64,64B,11,64D,62A
Forestier, Marie	AA0020	62A
Forough, Cyrus	PA0550	62A
Fortin, Nicholas	IN1010	62A
Foster, Daniel	MI0600	62A,62B
Foster, Martin	AI0210	62A
Francavilla, Nadia	AE0120	10C,62A
Francois, Ronald P.	CO0250	62A,42
Frank, Pamela	PA0850	41,62A
Franke, Dean	IN1650	62A
Franke, Jerome	WI1155	62A
Frankel, Joanna	NJ0700	62A,62B,42
Frazier, Virginia	CA1750	62A,62B
French, Nell	KS0590	62A,62B
Frens, Jennifer	IA0500	62A,62B
Freund-Striplen, Pamela	CA3920	62A,62B
Fried, Miriam	MA1400	62A
Frisch, Roger	MN1280	62A,41
Fuchs, Richard	CO0950	62A
Fudge, James	IA1300	62A,11
Fuks, Mauricio	IN0900	62A
Fukuda, Ryo	CA4425	62A
Fulkerson, Gregory L.	NY2750	62A
Fulkerson, Gregory	OH1700	62A,41
Fulks, Kathleen	AL1170	62A
Fuller, Susan	DC0170	62A
Fung-Dumm, Molly	OH0650	62A
Gabriel, Edgar	IL1085	62A,53,51
Gabriel, Edgar	IL0850	62A,62B,45
Gajger, Melina	MD0650	62A
Gale, Marie	AA0020	62A
Galileas, Christos	GA1050	62A
Gallagher, Mara	IL2050	62A,51
Galluzzo, Jacqueline	NY3717	62A,51
Galu, Ioana	OH0950	62A
Gamma, Lorenz	CA0825	62A
Gamma, Lorenz	CA0510	62A
Ganatra, Simin	IL3300	51,62A
Ganatra, Simin	IN0900	62A,42
Gant, Christina	PA3260	62A,62B,62C
Gao, Xiang	DE0150	62A
Garcia, Elisa Mon	WI1150	62A
Gardiner, Annabelle	FL1740	62A,62B,51,38
Gardner, James E.	UT0250	62A,12,31,31A
Gardner, Valerie	GA1500	62A
Garibova, Karine	CO0275	62A,42,51
Garriss, Margaret	NC1300	62A
Garriss, Phyllis	NC1300	41,62A
Gatwood, Jody	DC0050	62,62A,41
Gaub, Nancy McFarland	IA0700	62A,13C,41
Gauthier, Tommy	AI0200	62A,29
Gearhart, Fritz	OR1050	62A,42
Geller, Noah	MO1810	62A
Gendler, Anna	AZ0480	62A
Genova, Joana	MA2250	62A,41
Gentry, Sarah	IL1150	13,62A,62B
Genualdi, Joseph	MO1810	62A
George, Samantha	WI0350	62A,41,51
Georgieva, Roumena G.	GA0490	62A,62B,38,51
Gerard, Eva	NY5000	62A,62B
Geyer, Luba	FL1650	62A,62B
Geyer, Oleg	FL1650	62A,62B
Giammario, Matteo	PA0400	13,11,62A,62B
Gilbert, Diane	CA3100	62A,62B
Gilbert, John Haspel	TX3200	12A,62A
Gilbody, Mila	NC2000	62A
Giles, Kari	SC1200	62A
Gillespie, Robert A.	OH1850	32,62A
Gilliland, Erin	OH0350	62A
Gilliland, Erin	OH2050	41,62A
Gilman, Kurt	TX1400	38,41,62A,62B,20
Ginader, Gerhard	AC0050	13,10,45,62A
Giray, Selim	KS1450	62A,62B,51,42,38
Girko, Beth	TX2260	62A
Girko, Elizabeth	TX1900	62A
Givens, Shirley	NY2250	62A
Gjevre, Naomi	TX2250	62A,42,12C
Glazebrook, James	VA1700	60,38,62A,62B
Glidden, Amy	NY3717	62A,51
Gluzman, Vadim	IL0550	62A,42
Gogichashvili, Eka Dalrymple	TX0300	62A,42
Goldsmith, Kenneth	TX2150	42,62A
Goldstein, Howard A.	AL0200	10F,62A,11,12A,38
Gomez, Routa Kroumovitch	FL1750	12A,62A,62B
Gonzalez, Tamara	IL2750	62A
Goodfriend, Benedict N.	VA1250	62A
Gooding, Alison	TN0100	62A
Goree, Mary Ellen	TX3530	62A
Gorevic, Elizabeth	NY3775	51,62A,62B
Gorevic, Ronald	NY2400	62A,62B
Gorgojo, Jamie	IL2150	62A,62B
Goto, Midori	CA5300	62A,42
Grabiec, Andrzej	TX3400	41,62A
Grafilo, Zakarias	CA4200	62A,41,42

Index by Area of Teaching Interest

Name	Code	Areas
Granat, Endre	CA5300	62A
Gratovich, Eugene	TX3510	41,62A
Gray, Charles	MN1450	42,62A,62B
Gray, Terrance	IL2750	62A
Greenberg, Herbert	MD0650	62A
Greenspan, Bertram	NJ1050	62A,51,12A,12
Gregoire, Jenny	AL1170	62A
Gregorian, Ara	NC0650	62A,62B,42
Gregory, Rohan	MA0700	62A,62B
Greive, Tyrone	WI0815	62A
Gries, Rachel	IN0500	62A,51
Griffing, Joan	VA0300	62A,38,41,60B,62B
Grigoriu, Katrina	AA0050	32A,62A,62B
Grigoryan, Gayane	NC1350	62A
Grinnell, Michael	TX3535	62A,62B,38
Groner, Brian	IL2150	62A,38
Grossman, Hal	OK1350	62A,41,51
Grossman, Phillip	WI1150	62A
Grove, Rebecca	SC0200	62A,62B
Gu, Wen-Lei	WI0350	62A,41
Gullickson, Sigrid	WI1150	62A
Gunn, Lorrie	MI1830	62A
Gunnell, Sarah	UT0190	62A
Haase, Peter	VA0450	62A,42
Habitzruther, Ellen M.	VA0750	62A
Haderer, Walter	CA4200	62A
Hagarty, Mia	TX0550	62A,32A,62B
Hahn, Hae Soon	DC0170	62A
Hahnemann, Hanneberit	OH0650	62A
Hakim, William J.	NJ1160	62A,62B
Halen, David	MI2100	62A
Halgedahl, Frederick	IA1600	41,62A
Hall, Erin	TN1850	62A
Hall, Michael L.	IL3450	62A,62B
Hallberg, Karin	AZ0450	62A
Hamm, Steven	OK0850	62A
Hamme, Nora Ruth	PA1650	62A,62B
Haney, Julia Lawson	CA0650	62A,42
Hanford, Robert A.	IL2250	62A
Hansen, Dallin	ID0060	62A,32E
Hanson, Angela	MN0250	62A
Hanson, Melanie	MN0150	62A,13
Harding, David	AB0100	51,62A,62B,41,42
Harea, Ioan	NY3780	62A
Harms, Dawn L.	CA4900	62A
Harris, Kathy	ID0075	62A
Harrison, Carol	MO1550	62A,62B
Harrison, Rosaura	FL0365	62A
Hartke-Towell, Christina	KY0900	38,62A,62B
Hartman, Mark L.	PA3050	62,38,13,62A,29
Haskins, Jodi	AL1150	62A,62B,11
Hawes, Preston	MD0150	62A,38
Hawryluck, Alan	MA0950	62A,62B
Hayden, William P.	FL2000	62A,62B,51
Hayes, Tara	IL1300	62A
Hays, David R.	MO0775	62A,51
He, Lin	LA0200	62A
He, Wei	CA4150	62A
Heald, Michael	GA2100	62A
Heard, Cornelia	TN1850	41,51,62A
Heberlein, Yuko	MN0250	62A
Hendon, Sally	VT0250	62A
Herrera, Jennifer	PA3710	62A,62B
Hersh, Sarah S.	NY3780	62A,32E
Hersh, Stefan	IL0550	62A,42,38
Hill, Lawrie	AB0200	62A
Hill, Margaret	NY2400	62A
Hillard, Clair Fox	GA0150	62A
Hillard, Claire Fox	GA0625	11,62A,62B,66D,62
Hills, Peggy	AG0650	62A,62B
Hillyer, Giselle	WI0845	62A,62B,51
Hines, Edith	WI0700	62A,62B
Hima, Olena	IL0850	62A,62B
Ho, Frank	AA0020	62A
Ho, Leslie	CA6000	62A,62B
Hofeldt, Elizabeth	OH2450	62A,62B,42
Hoffman, Beth	IA0930	62A
Hoffman, Beth	IA0300	62A
Hoopes, Katherine	MA0600	62A,62B
Hornbacker, Georgia	IL1750	62A
Horozaniecki, Mary Budd	MN0950	62A
Horozaniecki, Mary B.	MN0300	62A,62B,42
Horozaniecki, Mary A.	MN0050	62A,62B
Houston, Ronald	TX3000	62A
Howard, Jeffrey	MD0850	62A,41,51
Howard-Phillips, Amanda	WA0400	62A
Hristov, Miroslav P.	TN1710	51,62A
Hsu, Chia-Ying	IL2650	62A,62B
Hsu, Linda Y.	AR0850	62A,51
Hsueh, Yvonne	OR1250	62A,62B,67A,67B
Huang, Frank	TX3400	62A
Huang, Rachel V.	CA1050	62A,62B
Huang, Rachel Vetter	CA4500	62A,11,13A,42
Huang, Wanchi	VA0600	62A
Hubbard, Eve P.	NC0900	51,62A
Huebl, Carolyn	TN1850	62A,13G,32F,34,11
Hult, David W.	NY2650	62A,62B,11,51
Hunt, William	OR0250	38,62A,62B
Hunter, Rebecca	SC1110	62A
Hutton, Deirdre	SC0750	62A,51
Hyun, June	NY5000	62A
Ingber, Elizabeth	CA4625	66A,62A,62B
Isaacson, Peter R.	TX0900	62A,38,41
Israelievitch, Jacques	AG0650	62A,62B,38
Israelievitch, Jacques	AG0450	62A
Iticovici, Silvian	MO1900	62A
Ito, Kanako	MO1000	51,62A
Iwasaki, Jun	TN1850	62A
Iwata, Nanae	IL2750	62A
Iwazumi, Ray	NY1900	62A
Jacklin, Rachel	IL2300	62A,62B
Jackson, Tom	PA3560	62A
Jamanis, Michael T.	PA1300	62A
Jang, Iggy	HI0050	62A
Jang, Ignace	HI0210	62A
Janzen, Henry	AG0350	42,62B,62A
Jarillo Alvarado, Lyanne	AA0020	62A
Jasinski, Mark	WA0750	62A,38,32
Jenner, Joanna	NY5000	62A
Jennings, Andrew W.	MI2100	62A
Jennings, Graeme	CA2950	40,41,62A,62B,42
Jensen, Janet L.	WI0815	32,62A,38,51
Jensen, Rachel	MN1450	62A
Jensen, Susan	MO1800	62A,42
Jevitt, Amy	FL0150	62A,62B
Jiang, Danwen	AZ0100	62A
Jiang, Yi-wen	NJ0800	62A,42
Jiang, Yi-wen	NY0150	62A,42
Jivaev, Anton	NC1700	62A
Johnson, Alan	TX1450	62A
Johnson, Cecilia	OH2300	32E,62A
Johnson, Cecilia	MI1950	62A,62B
Johnson, Christine	IA0600	62A
Johnson, David	TN1600	62A
Johnson, Elizabeth	CA5355	62A
Johnson, Nancy S.	KS0200	62A
Johnson, Sara	TN1850	62A,32A
Johnson, Sarah	SC0650	62A
Johnson, Sarah	NC1650	62A
Johnston, James W.	IN1100	60,62A,66A
Johonnott, Edwin	VA0450	62A,62B,42
Joiner, Lee	IL3550	51,62A,62B
Joiner, Thomas	SC0750	38,62A
Jones, Janet	AZ0150	38,62A,62C,62B,62D
Jones, Sheila L.	OH1650	62A,62B
Jonsson, Johan	MT0200	62A,12A
Jordan, Rachel	LA0720	11,62A
Jordan, Rachel	MS0350	62A,11,13A,13B,42
Jorgensen, Jerilyn J.	CO0200	62A,41
Jorgensen, Kristen	NY3770	11,48,64A,62A
Jorgenson, Jeri	CO0900	62A
Joseph, Charles	NY3725	60,62A,62B
Ju, Alice	DC0170	62A
Judish, Marion	MN1300	62A,62B
Julyan, Robyn	CO0650	62A
Jurchuk, Tobi	AA0050	32A,62A
Justen, Gloria	CA2950	62A
Kaczorowska, Joanna Maria	NY3790	62A,42
Kahng, Er-Gene	AR0700	62A,62B,41
Kaler, Ilya	IL0750	62A
Kaler, Olga D.	IL0750	62A
Kalinovsky, Grigory	NY2150	62A
Kaminski, Imelda	IL1890	62A,51
Kaminsky, Joseph	MO1950	62A
Kang, Hyo	CT0850	62A,42
Kang, Hyo	NY1900	62A
Kang, Hyo	NY0500	62A
Kantor, Paul	OH0600	62A
Kantor, Paul	AG0300	62A
Kaplan, Burton	NY2150	62A
Kaplan, Lewis	NY1900	51,62A
Kaplan, Lewis	NY2250	62A
Kaplan, Mark S.	IN0900	62A
Kaplanek, Jerzy	AG0600	41,62A
Karp, Margaret B.	KY1450	62A,62B
Karriker, Kendra	OH2150	62A,11
Kashap, Philip	AJ0150	11,62A
Katsarelis, Susan	DC0170	62A
Katseanes, Kory L.	UT0050	38,60,62A
Kavafian, Ani	CT0850	62A
Kavafian, Ida	NY0150	62A,42
Kavafian, Ida	PA0850	62A
Kavafian, Ida	NY1900	62A,42
Kawasaki, Masao	NY1900	62A
Kawasaki, Masao	NY0500	41,62A,62B
Kawasaki, Masao	NY0600	62A,62B
Kayaleh, Laurence	AI0200	62A,42
Kecskemethy, Stephen	ME0200	62A
Keelan, Michael	NE0150	62A,62C
Kelly, Velda	MI1260	62A
Kemp, Sean	AF0120	62A
Kenny, Megan	NC1350	62A
Kenny, Megan	NC2435	62A,62B,51
Kerr, Alexander	IN0900	62A
Ketchum, Joseph	WI1150	62A
Keyes, Bayla	MA0400	62A
Khimm, Christina	NY2250	62A
Khimm, Christina	NY5000	62A
Khimm, Christina	NY2400	62A
Khosrowpour, Iman	CA2390	62A,62B,13B
Kilmer, Richard L.	TX3410	62A
Kim, Ariana	IN1650	62A,11,38,32E
Kim, Ariana	NY0900	62A,62B
Kim, Benny	MO1810	62A
Kim, Chee-Yun	TX2400	62A
Kim, Chin	NY2250	41,62A
Kim, David	RI0300	41,62A
Kim, Eunho	SD0600	62A,62B,51
Kim, Helen	GA1150	62A
Kim, Hye-Jin	NC0650	62A,62B,42
Kim, Ji Hyun	MI2000	62A,62B
Kim, Karen	MN1625	62A
Kim, Kyoungwoon Leah	PA3600	62A
Kim, Leah	PA1150	62A,62B
Kim, Lisa	NJ0825	62A
Kim, Lisa	NY2150	62A
Kim, Michelle	NY2250	62A
Kim, Miera	IA0400	62A
Kim, Soovin	NY0150	62A
Kim, Soovin	NY3790	62A
Kim, Yeon-Su	PA1400	62A,42
Kim, Yong Tae	NJ0825	41,62A
Kim, Young-Nam	MN1623	41,62A
Kimura, Etsuko	AG0450	62A
King, Joan	PA0650	62A,62B,62C,62D,31G
King, Matthew	IL2970	62A
Kinney, Daryl W.	OH1850	32G,32E,62A
Kiradjieff, Amy	OH1450	62A
Kirk, John D.	NY3650	62A,67H,20G
Kirkpatrick, Mary Beth	WV0560	62A,62B,62C,62D
Kistler, Linda	PA2450	62A,62B
Kitchen, Nicholas	MA1400	41,62A
Kitzman, Diane D.	TX2400	62A
Klabunde, Timothy A.	WI0150	62A
Klabunde, Timothy	WI1150	62A
Klausner, Tiberius	MO1810	41,62A
Klein, Susanna	VA1600	62A,42,32E
Klugherz, Laura	NY0650	13,11,41,62A,62B
Klukoff, Ruth	FL0450	62A,62B
Knecht, Melissa Gerber	MI1000	11,32,42,62A,62B
Knetsch, Rene	CO0100	38,62A,42
Knific, Renata	MI2250	51,62A
Knoepfel, Justin	MN0750	62B,62A,38,42,13
Kobayashi, Hibiki	AI0190	42,62A
Kobialka, Daniel	CA2950	62A
Kobialka, Daniel	TX3410	62A
Koehler, Andrew	MI1150	60,38,62A,62B,12A
Koh, Jennifer	NY2750	62A
Kojian, Miran	CA5300	62A
Koontz, Eric E.	NC0050	62B,62A,67A,42,51
Kopec, Patinka	NY2150	62A,62B
Kopelman, Mikhail	NJ1130	62A
Kopelman, Mikhail	NY1100	62A
Kostic, Dina	FL0050	62A,41,42,51
Kothman, Mary	IN0150	62A
Kothman, Mary	IN1560	62A

649

Index by Area of Teaching Interest

Name	Code	Areas
Kozak, Pawel K	SC1000	51,62A,62B
Kozamchak, David M.	MN1280	38,51,62A,62B,41
Kramer, Elizabeth A.	GA2130	12A,14,11,13A,62A
Kriehn, Richard	WA1150	11,70,62A,34
Krishnaswami, Donald	MA0510	11,12A,62A,62B,51
Kromin, Vladimir	VA1100	62A,62B,51
Kruse, Penny Thompson	OH0300	51,62A
Krysa, Oleh	NY1100	62A
Ku, Hsiao-Mei	NC0060	62A
Kucharsky, Boris	NJ0800	62A,42
Kuhns, Philip A.	AZ0510	62A,62B
Kumi, Gert	IN0100	62A,38
Kummernuss, Linda	IN1050	62A
Kurkowicz, Joanna	MA2250	41,62A,43
Kurti, Andrej	LA0550	62A
Kwalwasser, Helen	PA3250	62,62A
Kwok, Daniel	IL2775	62A,62B
Kwon, Su Jin	NY5000	62A,62B
Kwuon, Joan	OH0600	62A
Laderach, Linda C.	MA1350	51,62A,62B,67B
Lafranque, Claude-Lise	CA5550	62A
Lahti, Carol	IL2100	62A
Lakirovich, Mark	IL0550	62A
Lakirovich, Mark	MA1175	62A,62B
Lam, Eri Lee	TX2650	62A,32E,42
Lam, Michelle	VA1500	62A,62B,43
Lambert, Jessica I.	OR0700	62A,62B
Lambert, Marjolaine	AI0150	62A
Laminack, Emily	GA1700	62A
Lamkin, Kathleen J.	CA5100	12A,11,12,62A,66A
LaMotte, Adam	OR0750	62A
Landers, Karen	NY2400	62A
Landsman, Vladimir	AI0200	62A
Lane, Diane	AA0050	62A
Lansdale, Katie	CT0650	41,51,62A
Lanza, Joseph	AG0500	38,41,51,62A
LaPointe, Simon	VA1600	62A
Lardinios, John	OH2250	62A,51
Lardinois, John	IN0400	62A,62B
Lardinois, Kara	OH2250	62A,51
Larson, Elizabeth	CA0350	62A,42
Larson, Jon D.	MN1120	62A,62B
Lautar, Rebecca	FL0650	11,41,51,62A,62B
Lawrence, Kevin	NC1650	62A,41
Lazar, Teri	DC0010	62A,42,51
Le, Weiwei	NV0050	62A,42
League, Leanne	WI0865	62A,62B
Leath, Nate R.	VA1850	62A,70
Lebo, Joanna	SC0050	51,62A,62B
Ledbetter, Lynn F.	TX3175	62A,62B,42,51
Lederer, Doris M.	VA1350	62B,62A,42
Lee, Christopher	NJ0825	62A
Lee, Daniel	CT0100	62A,62B
Lee, Gregory	OK1350	62A,41,51
Lee, Hsiaopei	MS0750	62B,62A
Lee, Hui Yu	PA0650	62A
Lee, Jaesung	IN1450	62A
Lee, Jessica	NY4450	62A
Lee, Joo-Mee	MA2010	62A
Lee, Ki Joo	IN0005	62A
Lee, Sang-Eun	IL1085	62A,42
Lee, Seunghee	MI0400	62A,51
Leenhouts, Margaret A.	NY2650	62A
Lefkowitz, Ronan	MA0350	62A
Lehman, Katherine	TN1800	13A,62A
Lehmann, Matthew	NY1600	62A,51
Lehnert, Oswald	CO0800	51,62A,62B
Lehninger, Marcia	NH0150	11,20H,62A,62B
Letourneau, Jaime H.	VA1850	62A
Leventhal, Sharan	MA0350	62A
Levin, Dmitri	PA3250	62A
Lewis, Brian D.	TX3510	62A,42
Lewis, Eloise	KY0610	62A
Lewis, Eric	CT0800	12A,62B,51,62A,12B
Lewis, Melissa	OK1200	60,41,51,62A
Lewis, Philip J.	TX3420	41,62A
Li, Honggang	NJ0800	62B,42,62A
Li, Weigang	NY0150	62A,42
Li, Weigang	NJ0800	62A,42
Liebenow, Marcia Henry	IL0400	62A,62B
Lieberman, Carol	MA0700	62A,13,12A,67,62
Lifsitz, Fred	CA4200	41,62A,42
Light, Susan	AA0050	62A
Lilleslatten, Espen	LA0200	62A
Lim, Tze Yean	OH1450	62A
Lin, Ching Yi	KY1550	62A
Lin, Chloe	MO0060	62A,62B,62C,38
Lin, Cho-Liang	TX2150	62A,42
Lin, Cho-Liang	NY1900	62A
Lin, Jasmine	IL0550	62A
Lin, Joseph	NY1900	62A,42
Lin, Kelvin	IL3370	62A
Lin, Lucia	MA0400	62A
Lin, Swang	TX3000	62A
Linde-Capistran, Jane	MN0600	41,62A,62B
Lindsey, John R.	NY3780	62A
Lipsett, Robert	CA1075	62A
Littley, Marcia De Arias	FL0700	62A,42
Liu, Kexi	MO0800	11,51,62A,62B
Liu, Lei	FL2050	62A,62B
Liu, Te-Chiang	MN1600	62A,62B,41
Liu, Yang	IL0550	62A
Liva, Ferdinand R.	ME0500	62A,62B
Liva, Victor H.	OH0650	38,62A
Loban, John A.	AB0100	41,51,62A
Locke, Douglas	OH2050	62A
Lopez, Fabian E.	NC2430	62A
Lord-Powell, Karen	KY0250	62A
Lorenzo, Donna A.	NY1700	62B,62A
Louie, Bonnie	AA0050	62A
Lowe, Malcolm	MA1175	62A
Lowe, Malcolm	MA1400	62A
Lowe, Malcolm	MA0400	62A
Lower, Janna	FL1850	62A
Lubiarz, Stephen	AA0050	62A
Luby, Richard E.	NC2410	41,51,62A,67A
Luca, Sergiu	TX2150	62A
Lucernoni Haasler, JoAnn	WI1150	62A
Lucero, Kerry	AZ0150	62A,62B
Luckenberg, Kathryn	OR1050	62A,42
Lundin, Paul	WI0300	62A
Luo, Mei Mei	FL0200	62A
Lupanu, Calin	NC0850	62A,51
Lupien, Denise	AI0150	62A
Lupu, Sherban	IL3300	51,62A,41
Lupu, Virgil I.	OH2140	62A,41,12A,11,34B
Luscher, Alexia	HI0050	62A,62B
Lutow, Justyna	SD0050	62A
Lutz, Nina	GA2150	62A,13A
Lyon, Howard	PA1200	62A,62B,41
Lyon, James	PA2750	62A
MacDonald, Don	AB0070	10,61,62A,64E,35A
Macek, Timothy A.	DC0150	62A,62B
Macomber, Curtis	NY2150	62A
MacQueen, Yuki	UT0400	62A
MacWilliams, Brittany K.	KY1500	62A
Maddox, Meredith R.	AR0750	42,62A,62B
Madura, John	TX3527	62A
Magaziner, Elliot	NY5000	62A,62B
Magaziner, Elliot	NY2400	60,41,62A
Magniere, Blaise	IL2200	62A,51
Mahadeen, Roger	NY2750	62A
Makas, George	IL1085	13,62A
Malan, Roy	CA5070	62A,62B
Maldonado, Greg	CA0825	51,62A,55,62B
Malkin, Isaac	NY2150	62A
Mallette, Marcelle	AI0150	62A
Maltese, John	AL0500	11,38,62A
Malvinni, Valerie	CA5550	62A,62B
Malvinni, Valerie L.	CA4410	62A,62B
Mandl, Alexander	WI0835	62A
Mandl, Alexander B.	WI1150	62A
Mann, Nicholas	NY2150	62A
Mann, Robert	NY2150	62A
Manning, Lucy	VA1000	38,62A,32E,41,51
Manning, Mary	WA0650	62A
Mantell, Matthew	IL3100	51,62A,62B
Mao, Ruotao	NJ0175	62A,62B,42
Mardirossian, Kevork M.	IN0900	62A
Margetts, David	UT0325	62A,62B
Marinic, Boro	IA0850	13,62A,62B
Markou, Kypros L.	MI2200	10F,38,62A
Markov, Albert	NY2150	62A
Markow, Elliott	MA2030	62A,62B
Markow, Roseann	MD0500	62A,62B,51
Markowski, Rebecca	AR0950	62A
Markstein, Igor	FL0150	62A,62B
Martin, Melvin	AG0500	62A
Martin, Spencer L.	IA0950	62A,62B,51,38
Martinez, Everaldo	ND0400	62A,62B,62C,51,38
Mason, Daniel	KY1450	62A,62B,41
Matesky, Elisabeth	IN0005	62A
Mathes, Gerard	ID0140	13,11,13J,62A,34
Matson, Ralph	UT0250	62A
Matthews, Margaret	NY1150	62A,62B,62C
Matthews, Todd	IL0600	62A,62B
Maxson, Carrie	UT0350	62A,32E
May-Patterson, Eleanor	IA1100	32E,62A,62B
Maytan, Gregory	MI0900	62A
Mazo, Vadim	IL1200	41,42,62A,62B,51
Mazurkevich, Dana Pomerantz	MA0400	62A
Mazurkevich, Yuri	MA0400	62A
McClure, Sam	MO1780	13,38,62A,62B
McCollum, Kimberly	MD0060	62A
McCullough, Stephanie	PA1250	62A,62B
McDonald, Marilyn	OH1700	62A,67B
McDuffie, Robert	GA1300	62A
McFaul, Rebecca	UT0300	62A
McGee-Daly, Kathleen	NJ0550	62A,62B
McGrath, Casey	IL1520	62A,62B
McGrosso, John	MO1830	51,62A
McKenna, Fr. Edward	IN0005	10,62A,16,31A,11
McKinney, Lori	KS0050	38,62A,62B
McLarry, Royce	OK0700	62A,62B
McLin, Katherine E.	AZ0100	62A
McNair, Linda	MO0550	62A,11
McNeela, Rico	MO0850	38,11,62A,62B,60
McNeely, Carol	DC0170	62A
McTeer, Mikylah Myers	WV0750	62A,32E,41,42
McWilliams, Bernard	NC0450	62A,62B
Means, Matthew L.	KS0350	11,62A,62B,41,42
Meier-Sims, Kimberly R.	OH0600	62A
Meineke, Robert	TX2350	62A,62B,62C,62D,51
Meints, Ruth	NE0610	62A
Melancon, Violaine M.	MD0650	41,62A
Mennemeyer, Bethany	CA1750	62A,62B
Menzies, Mark	CA0510	62A,62B,38,43,60B
Merrit, Doug	TN0580	13C,62A,62B
Meyer, Elizabeth C.	MI1450	38,62A,62B,10A
Meyers, Stephanie	TX3520	62A,62B
Miahky, Stephen A.	OH1900	62A,42
Miedema, Lisa	IA0500	62A
Miedema, Lisa	IA1200	62A,51
Migliaccio, Tatiana	WI1150	62A
Mihai, Julieta	IL3500	62A,51
Mikhlin, Alexandra	DC0170	62A
Milenkovich, Stefan	IL3300	62A
Miles, Debbie	AF0120	62A
Milewski, Piotr	OH2200	41,62A
Miller, Ann Elizabeth	CA5350	62A,42,12A,41
Miller, Anton	CT0650	41,51,62A
Miller, Anton M.	NY2750	62A,42
Miller, Elizabeth	NJ1140	62A
Miller, Esther	TN1660	62A,42
Miller, Lydia	MN1625	62A
Miller, Michael	FL1100	38,42,62A
Miller, Sharon	VA0100	62A
Miller, Sharon	VA0300	32B,62A,32C,32E
Mills, Jesse A.	NJ0800	42,62A
Milton, Blair	IL2250	62A
Minas-Bekov, Ivan	DC0170	62A
Minevich, Eduard	AJ0100	62A
Miranda, Charles	IA0420	11,62A,62B
Miranda, Charles	IA0650	62A,62B,11
Mizuno, Ikuko	MA0400	62A
Molina, Lindy	MD0475	62A,12A,20
Molzan, Brett	AI0190	42,62A
Monosoff, Sonya	NY0900	41,62A,62B,67B
Monroe, Diane	PA3250	62A
Montzka, Ann	IL2200	62A,62B
Moon, Gene H.	TX2700	38,39,66,62A,62B
Moore, Frances	CA2800	60B,41,62A,67B,38
Moore, Janice	OH1350	62A,62B
Morales, Dara	PA3250	62A
Moravec, Andriana	IN0005	62A,62B
Moretti, Amy Schwartz	GA1300	62A
Morgan, Angela L.	GA0250	32,38,51,62A
Morgan, Lauren R.	MO0250	62A,62B,62C,62D,51
Morgan, LeeAnn	UT0050	62A,62B
Morris, Ralph	OK1330	38,62A,62B,41,42
Morris, Theodora	OK1330	62A,62B,67C,42
Moser, Mary	PA1450	62A,62B
Mott, Jonathan	VA0250	62A,62B
Moye, Felicia K.	WI0815	62A
Moyer, Cynthia M.	CA2250	13,41,62A,62B
Muegel, Glenn	NC0050	13,41,62A,62B

Index by Area of Teaching Interest

Name	Code	Areas
Mulder, Geoffrey	CA0850	34,35C,35D,12A,62A
Mulford, Ruth Stomne	DE0175	13,11,12A,62A,20G
Mulholland, Jeremy	KY0550	62A,62B,38,60B
Muller, Irina	MT0370	62A
Murasugi, Sachiho	MD0800	62A,62B,11,13A,51
Muresan, Branden A.	CA2100	11,62A
Muresanu, Irina	MA0350	62A
Murphy, Jacob P.	IN0910	62A
Mussumeli, Bettina	CA4150	62A,42
Mutchnik, Ronald	MD0060	62A
Myintoo, Sylvia C.	IL2150	62A,11
Myrick, John	AL1195	32,62A,62B,41,51
Nardolillo, Jo	KY0100	62A,62B
Neal, Patrick	FL0680	62A
Neeley, Henrietta	IL1085	62A,11,42,62B
Neely, David C.	NE0600	62A,62B
Negyesy, Janos	CA5050	20F,41,62A,43,34
Nelson, Lisa	IL1200	62A
Neu, Ah Ling	MA2250	62A,41
Neubert, Peter	TX0900	62B,62A,41
Neumann, Ben	AA0050	32B,38,51,62A
Neumann, Mark	OK1350	62A,41,51
Newby, Joanna	IL1300	62A,62B
Ngai, Emlyn	CT0650	62A
Nicholeris, Dian	CA4400	62A
Nies, Camille Day	TX0100	62A
Nigro, Christie	MA2300	13A,11,12A,36,62A
Ninomiya, Ayano	NY1100	62A,42
Niwa, David	OH2000	62A
Nordlund, Caroline	AL0800	62A,32E
Norgaard, Martin	GA1050	32E,32F,62A,29E,32
Norwood, Diana	TX3370	62A,62B
Noyes, Rachel	DC0170	62A
Nuttall, Geoff	CA4900	62A,41,51
O'Boyle, Maureen E.	OK1450	62A
O'Brien, Dean	AA0050	62A,62B
Oeseburg, Beth	MI1180	62A,62B
Ogletree, Mary	PA1750	13,11,62A,62B,51
Oliveira, Elmar	FL1125	62A
Oliver, Abby	AL0500	62A
Oliveros, Nancy	MN1450	62A
Olschofka, Felix	TX3420	62A
Oper, Linda L.	IL0840	62A
O'Reilly, Sally	MN1623	41,62A
Orenstein, Janet	NC1650	62A,42
Orozco, Jorge	DC0170	62A
Osterhause, Sharon	MN1250	62A
Ottesen, Bradley	UT0300	62A
Otto, Peter	OH0650	62A
Oundjian, Peter	CT0850	41,62A
Ouyang, Angel	NY3350	62A
Pagan, Joel G.	TX3525	62B,62A
Pagliarini, Shawn	GA0750	62A
Pan, JiaYe	AZ0440	62A
Pan, Shelly	DC0170	62A
Pancella, Peter	IL1500	62A,62B,51
Pandolfi, Anne	AL0300	62A,62B
Papoulis, Mary	MT0370	62A
Para, Christopher	PA0350	13,11,38,62A,62B
Pardo, Danielle	WI1150	62A,62B
Park, Chung	NC0050	38,62A,62B,51,60
Park, David H.	UT0250	62A
Park, Min	AZ0490	62A
Park, Sue-Jean	KY0950	62A,62B,41
Park, Tricia	IN1700	62A,42,41
Parker, Charles H.	PA3250	62A
Parker, Laura M.	IL2400	13A,41,42,62A,66A
Parnell, Janine	NC0700	62A,32
Patipatanakoon, Annalee	AG0450	62A
Patterson, Ronald	WA1050	41,62A
Paulson, Jennifer Clare	WI0865	62A,62B
Pazin, Eugene	IL1085	62A
Pegis, Damien	FL1745	62A
Pegis, Gabe	OH2200	62A
Pelekh, Anna	NY2400	62A
Pelev, Todor	CA1050	62A
Pelev, Todor D.	CA3650	62A
Pendell, Carter	AZ0400	62A
Penne, Cynthia S.	VA1850	62A,62B,41
Pepper, Ronald D.	OH0950	62A,62B,12A
Pereira, Ernest	NC2000	62A
Perez, Miguel	MA0510	11,62A,51
Perkins, Susan	NC2205	62A
Perlman, Itzhak	NY1900	62A
Peroutka, Leah	NC2410	62A
Perrault, Jean R.	MN1600	60,62A,62B,62C,38
Perry, David	WI0815	11,62A
Perttu, Melinda H. Crawford	PA3650	38,62A,62B
Peters, Maria	SD0580	62A,62B
Peterson, Leroy	CA3400	20,62A
Petillot, Aurelien	IL2900	62B,62A,42,11,12A
Petite, Rachel Maria	NY5000	62A
Petrescu, Stefan	TN1400	51,62A
Petursdottir, Ragga	NY5000	62A
Phelps, Melissa	CA0550	62A,62B
Phillips, Daniel	NY2250	41,62A
Phillips, Daniel	NY0642	62A
Phillips, Holland	MA0950	62A
Phillips, Todd	NJ1130	62A
Phillips, Todd	NY2250	41,62A
Pich, Victoria	OR0450	62A,62B
Pickett, Susan	WA1300	13A,13,12A,51,62A
Pidluski, Eric	IL1900	62A,62B
Pikler, Charles	IL2100	62A,51,42,62B
Pilon, Charles	AA0035	62A
Pinell, Javier	TX2250	62A,42,51
Ping, Jin	NY3760	13,10,62A,20A,20B
Pinner, Dianne	SC0200	62A
Pinner, Jay-Martin	SC0800	62A
Pinney, Greg	MD0550	62A,62B
Pirard, Guillaume	NY2750	62A,42
Pitchon, Joel L.	MA1750	62A,41,42
Placci, Markus	MA0350	62A
Placeres, Martha	TX3515	62A,38,13A,13C
Placilla, Christina D.	NC2700	12A,20,38,62A,62B
Plenert, Keith	NE0160	62A,62B
Plesner, Joy	CO0050	62A,62B
Plohman, Crystal	TN1850	62A
Plum, Sarah A.	IA0550	62A,62B,11,42
Plummer, Carolyn	IN1700	62A,42,41
Plummer, Kathryn	TN1850	41,62A,62B,34
Pogossian, Movses	CA5030	62A,62
Pokhanovski, Oleg	AC0100	62A,51,42
Polanka, William Mark	OH2150	13,62A
Polay, Louise	IL0420	62A
Polay, Louise	IL1350	62A
Polett, Jane	MO0300	62A
Polonsky, Leonid	OH1850	62A
Pope, Cathy	NM0400	62A
Portnoy, Donald	SC1110	60,38,62A
Posadas, John	FL2000	62A,62B
Posey, Dawn	PA2950	62A
Posnock, Jason	NC0250	62A,62B,32E
Potter, Shelley	WA0950	51,62A,20,13A,13D
Povey, Peter	AL0050	62A
Power, Brian E.	AG0050	62A,67,12A,12C,13G
Pranno, Arthur J.	FL0800	62A,38,51,62B,12A
Prefontaine, Paule	AG0400	62A
Preucil, William	SC0750	62A
Preucil, William	OH0600	62A
Price, Jane E.	MO1900	62A
Price-Brenner, Paul Alan	WI0840	11,62A,62B,34
Princiotti, Anthony F.	NH0100	62A,38
Pritchard, Eric N.	NC0600	62A,42
Pritsker, Vladimir	NY1350	62A
Pruss, Melissa	NE0100	62A
Purdy, Carl	GA0250	62A,62B,70,51
Purdy, Craig Allen	ID0050	41,42,51,62A,38
Qian, Wen	NY2250	62A
Quan, Linda	NY4450	62A
Quick, Julia M.	SC1050	11,38,41,51,62A
Quindag, Sue	SC0200	32,62A,62B,34
Quint, Philippe	NJ1130	62A
Rabinovitsj, Max	VA0600	62A
Radicheva, Maria	NY2150	62A
Radloff, Susan	MN1290	62A,62B
Rafferty, Alan	KY1000	62A
Rafferty, J. Patrick	KY1500	62A,51
Rapoport, Katharine	AG0450	62A,62B
Raum, Erika	AG0450	62A
Raum, Erika	AG0300	62A,42
Rawston, Amy	MA0150	62A
Read, Evelyn	VT0450	62A,62B,16,42
Redfield, Stephen C.	MS0750	62A,51
Redman, Inez	NC2400	62A,62B,42
Redmon, Nursun	MI0300	62A,62B
Redpath, Keith	TX3750	62A
Reed, Jane	OH0100	11,13A,62A,66D,62B
Reeves, Derek	IN0905	62A,62B
Rehkopf-Michel, Carrie	WA0050	41,51,62A,62B
Reichert, Matthew R.	NY0500	62A
Reimer, David	MI0350	11,32E,42,62A,41
Reiner-Marcus, Ullricke	CA3460	62A
Reisman, Mickey	CT0650	62A
Reiter, Lois	TX2800	62A
Reneau, Mark	TN1350	62A,42
Restesan, Francis'c	KY1000	38,51,39,62A
Restesan, Frank	NE0550	38,13C,62A,51,12A
Reuning, Sanford	NY1800	62A
Rhodes, Harumi	NY4150	62A
Rhody, Matthew	LA0800	62A
Ribeiro, Gerardo	IL2250	62A
Rich, Shelley	AZ0450	62A
Richard, Claude	AI0200	62A
Richards, Cynthia	UT0325	62A
Richards, Julie	TX2310	11,13A,62A,66C
Richardson, Cathy	TX0250	62A,62B,51
Richardson, Cathy	TX0370	62A,35G
Richardson, Cathy	TX1725	11,62A
Richardson, Marguerite	FL1000	38,60B,62A,62B
Richter, Jorge Luiz	NC0650	60B,38,42,62A,62B
Riggs, Robert D.	MS0700	12A,12B,41,62A,62B
Riley, Kristin	OR1020	62A,62B
Ringwald, Ilana	MA2020	62A
Ripley, Vanessa G.	OH1200	62A,62B
Rittenhouse, Virginia Gene	MD0150	38,62A,66A,32I
Ritz, Lyn	WA1100	62A,62B,42,13,10F
Rivest, Darlene	WI0250	62B,32E,38,62A,41
Rizner, Dan Joseph	IN0350	41,62A
Robert, Anne	AI0200	62A
Robert, Lucie	NY2150	41,62A
Robert, Lucie	NY2250	62A
Roberts, Cynthia	TX3420	55B,62A
Roberts, Richard	AI0150	62A
Robillard, David	OK1250	62A,62B
Rodriguez, Joshua A.	NY3650	62A
Roelofs, Laura Leigh	MI2200	62A,32E,41,11
Rogers King, Tammy	TN0100	62A
Roland, Isabelle	AB0200	62A,62B
Rolf, Alison	MO1950	62A
Ronning, Svend John	WA0650	62A
Rooney, Laura G.	WI1150	62A,62B
Roos, Joni N.	FL1550	62A,62B,51
Rosa, Gerard	CT0050	11,62A,12A
Rosand, Aaron	PA0850	62A
Rosand, Aaron	NY2250	62A
Rose, Linda	CA0825	62A
Rose, Stephen	OH0600	62A
Rosenberg, Sylvia	NY2150	62A
Rosenberg, Sylvia	NY1900	62A
Rosenblith, Eric	MA1175	62A
Rosenfeld, Julie	CT0600	62A
Ross, Jana	VA1125	62A
Ross, Jana	VA1400	62A,62B
Ross, Julian E.	OH0200	41,62A
Rotberg, Barton Samuel	PA2250	62A,62B
Rouslin, Daniel S.	OR1300	11,38,41,62A,62B
Rovit, Peter M.	NY4150	62A,67B
Rowe, Booker	PA3250	62A
Rowin, Elizabeth	MI1750	62A,62B,42
Rowley, Jill	ID0050	62A
Rozek, Robert	AB0200	62A,62B,38
Rudge, David T.	NY3725	38,62A
Rudoff, Patricia L.	NY2550	62A,62B
Rudoi, Natalie	PA2800	62A
Rudolph, Richard	VA0550	62A,38,62B,62C,65B
Rudolph, Robert A.	PA0100	62A,62B,41,42,51
Ruhstrat, Desiree	IN0900	62A
Rumney, Jon	ND0250	13,38,41,62A,62B
Rush, Mark	AZ2500	51,62A
Russell, David	NC2420	62A
Rutland, John P.	MO1790	38,62A,62B
Ruzicka, Carol	OH0600	62A,12A
Ryan, Kate	AR0110	62A,62B
Rylatko, Oleg	VA1350	62A
Saelzer, Pablo	DC0170	62A,62B
Saelzer, Pablo	MD0550	11,13A,13C,38,62A
Saeverud, Trond	ME0410	38,62A
Sakharova, Julia	MO1830	62A,42
Salathe, Leslie	NY0400	62A,62B
Salem, Ernest	CA0815	13A,41,62A,62B
Salerno, Julia	WA0250	62A,62B,41
Salness, David	MD1010	62A,41
Salsbury, Karen	KS0400	62A,62B
Sampen, Maria	WA1000	62A,13C,42
Sant'Ambrogio, Stephanie	NV0100	62A,62B

Name	Code	Areas
Santiago, Gabriella	FL1300	62A
Santos, Philip	CA0807	62A,62B,51
Santos, Philip	CA3520	62A,42
Sariti, David J.	VA1550	62A,67B,51,42
Sasse, Christine T.	MO1900	62A
Sassmannshaus, Kurt	OH2200	62A
Saunders, Meg	KY0450	62A,62B,41
Saunders, Meg	KY0550	62A
Sayevich, Ben	MO1000	51,62A
Saylor, Mary Ann	PA2450	62A,62B
Scales-Neubauer, Sheri	OK0850	62A
Scheirich, Lillian	AG0550	62A
Schmidt, Stephen	VA1600	62A,62B
Schmieder, Eduard	PA3250	62A
Schneider-Gould, Beth Ilana	AG0070	62A
Schoen, Thomas	AA0110	62A,41
Schoenfeld, Alice	CA5300	62A
Schotting, MaryBeth Glasgow	PA0550	62A
Schottman, Margret	PA0500	62A,62B,62C
Schranz, Karoly	CO0800	62A,41
Schultz, David	TX0700	62A,62B
Schulze, Otto	IN0005	62A,67,10,13,36
Schumann, Laura E.	OH1650	38,60,62A,12A,13A
Schuppener, Mark	TX3520	62A,62B,11
Schwartz, Ann Marie Barker	NY3600	62A,62B
Schwartz, Anne-Marie	NY3680	12A,62A
Schwartz, Cornelia	NH0110	62A
Schwartz, Sergiu	GA0550	62A
Schwarz, Timothy J.	PA1950	62A,62B,51,41
Schwarze, Penny	MN0450	12A,11,38,62A,67A
Schwede, Walter	WA1250	51,62,62A
Scott, Jennifer	CO0300	62A,34
Scott, Louise H.	AZ0450	62A
Scott, Yumi Ninomiya	PA0850	62A
Scott, Yumi N.	PA3250	62A
Scowcroft, Barbara Ann	UT0250	62A
Scriggins, Elizabeth	AA0050	32A,62A
Segal, Rachel	CO0650	62A
Seiler, Mayumi	AG0300	62A
Seitz, Diana	KS1400	62A,51
Setzer, Ann	NY2750	62A
Setzer, Ann	NY2250	41,62A
Setzer, Philip E.	NY3790	41,62A
Severtson, Paul	CA0600	62A
Shabalin, Alexey	RI0150	62A,51,38,32E
Shallit, Jonathan O.	NY3770	11,13A,62A
Shand, Patricia	AG0450	32C,51,62A,62B
Shapiro, Laurence	IN0250	62A
Sharp, Molly	VA1600	62A
Sharp, Robin	CA4900	62A
Sharpe, Alex E.	NY2750	62A
Sharpe, Alexander E.	NY1600	62A,42,51
Shatzkin, Merton T.	MO1810	13,12A,62A
Shiao, Simon	FL1950	51,62A,62B,38
Shih, Michael	TX3000	62A
Shih, Patricia	AB0060	62A,51
Shipps, Stephen	MI2100	62A
Shiu, Timothy	TN1680	62A,42
Shows, Ray	MN1450	62A,62B
Sievers, Beth	OK1350	62A
Silveira, Mathias	AA0020	62A
Silverman, Tracy	TN0100	62A
Silverstein, Joseph	PA0850	41,62A
Simonson, Jessica	OR1000	62A,62B,62C
Sims, Stephen S.	OH0600	62A
Sinclair, David W.	PA3000	62A,62B
Sindell, Carol A.	OR0850	41,62A,42
Singer, Mark	MD0600	62A
Sinift, Sherry	WY0200	62A
Sinsabaugh, Katherine Anne	NY4200	62A,62B
Siow, Lee-Chin	SC0500	11,62A
Sirotin, Peter	PA2300	62A,42
Sirotin, Peter	DC0170	62A
Sjobring, Steve	IL3550	62A
Skaar, Alice	SC1080	62A
Skazinetsky, Mark	AG0300	62A
Skazinetsky, Mark	AG0450	62A
Skidmore, Dan	NC0750	62A,51
Skidmore, Dan	NC0350	62A,62B
Skinner, Anita	OH0250	62A,62B
Skrocki, Jeanne	CA5150	62A
Sletner, Ariane	OH1200	62A,62B
Small, Elisabeth	TN0100	41,62A,51
Smiley, Mariko	CA5000	62A
Smirnoff, Joel	OH0600	62A
Smith, Carol F.	TN1850	62A,32E,51
Smith, Cory	OH2150	62A,62B
Smith, Elizabeth	IN0700	13C,62A
Smith, Elizabeth Reed	WV0400	38,41,51,62A,62B
Smith, Gillian	AF0120	62A
Smith, Miriam	GA1700	62A
Smolensky, Marcus H.	PA0350	62A,62B
Smukler, Lauri	NY2150	62A
Smukler, Laurie	NY2250	62A
Smukler, Laurie	NY0150	62A,42
Smukler, Laurie	NY3785	62A
Sobieski, Thomas	OH2500	62A
Sohn, Livia	CA4900	62A
Sohn, Sung-Rai	NY3560	60,38,41,51,62A
Sohn, Sungrai	NY2900	62A,38
Solomon, Qiao Chen	GA0050	62A,62B,51,41,38
Sonderling, Lawrence	CA3300	62A
Song, Xie	MS0400	62A,62B
Sonies, Barbara	PA3250	62A
Sor, Karen Shinozaki	CA5000	62A
Sorensen, Ann	LA0250	62A,62B,62C,62D
Sorgi, Craig	TX3350	62A
Soroka, Solomia	IN0550	13,62A,41
Soykan, Betul	GA0500	62A,62B
Spencer, Stacia C.	IL2250	32B,62A,62B
Speth, Uli	NY1400	62A,41,51
Speth, Uli	NY2900	62A,38
Spicknall, Sharry	IN1310	62A
Sprenger, Kurt	TX2600	62A,38,60B
Spring, Kathleen	CO0900	62A
St. John, Brian	IN1600	38,62A,62B,60B
St. John, Scott	CA4900	62A,41,51
Stanfield, Ashley	IA0550	62A,62B
Stanis, Sharon	AB0150	42,62A
Staples, Sheryl	NY1900	62A
Staron, Timothy	OH1000	62A,62C,38
Starr, Jeremy A.	KS0300	38,62A,62B,11
Staryk, Steven S.	WA1050	41,62A
Staskevicius, Algis	AR0300	62A,62B,32E
Stegeman, Charles	PA1050	62A
Stegeman, Rachel	PA1050	62A
Stein, Dean A.	ME0200	62A,51
Stein, Paul A.	CA3500	62A

Name	Code	Areas
Steinberg, Mark	NY2250	62A
Steinhardt, Arnold	NY0150	62A
Steinhardt, Arnold	PA0850	62A
Stephenson, Mary	NY2400	62A
Stephenson, Mary	NY5000	62A
Stepner, Daniel	MA0500	41,62A,11
Stern, James	MD1010	62A,41,42
Stevens, Frankie	MO0825	62A,62B
Stevens, Thomas	VA1500	62A,62B
Stevens, Thomas	VA1150	62A
Stewart, David	AG0400	62A,41
Stewart, Leslie	CO0250	62A,62B,38,11
Stewart, Lynnette	UT0250	62A
Stewart, Victoria	NJ0700	62A,42
Stieda, Nicki	AB0200	62A
Stillwell, Corinne	FL0850	62A,41
Stockton, Rachel	MD0175	62A
Stone, Susan E.	IL0100	13,62A
Stoub, Amy	MO0550	62A
Strachan, Heather	GA2000	51,62A,62C
Strauss, Axel	AI0150	62A
Strauss, Axel	CA4150	62A
Strauss, Virginia F.	IA0950	62A,13C,13D
Stuart, Carolyn	FL2000	62A,62B
Stuckenbruck, Dale	NY2105	62A
Stultz, Rachel	KS0150	62A,62B
Sturges, Tami	TN1600	62A
Subchak, Bohdan	OH2290	62A,66C
Suda, David	IL1800	62A
Sullivan, Kimberly	AZ0450	51,62A
Sulski, Peter	MA0200	41,62A,62B
Sulski, Peter	MA0650	62A,62B,60B,38
Sulski, Peter	MA0700	62B,62A,42
Sumerlin, John	RI0200	41,62A,62B
Sun, Xun	UT0200	60,38,62A
Sung, Benjamin H.	FL0850	62A,62B,41,42
Sung, Janet	IL0750	62A
Sutre, Guillaume	CA5030	62A,51
Swartz, Jonathan	AZ0100	62A
Sweet, Brennan	NJ0700	62A,42
Swensen, Ian	CA0840	42,62A
Swensen, Ian	CA4150	62A,42
Swic, Piotr T.	NC0850	62A
Sykes, Jean	NC0910	62A,62B
Szabo, Zoltan	MD0850	62A
Szekely, Eva D.	MO1800	62A,51
Szojka, Elisabeth	AA0050	62A
Tacke, Mathias	IL2200	62A
Takarabe, Clara	IN1750	62A,62B
Takayama, Akemi	VA1350	62A
Takebe, Yoko	NY1900	62A
Takebe, Yoko	NY2150	62A
Takemoto, Maya	WA1100	62A
Takemoto, Maya	WA1300	62A
Takeya, Kimiyo	CA0825	62A
Talbott, Laura	OK0800	62A,62B,42
Talvi, Ilkka	WA0800	62A
Tan, Kia-Hui	OH1850	62A,51,62B,13,42
Tanaka, Naoko	NY0500	62A,62B
Tanaka, Naoko	NY1900	62A
Tanaka, Naoko	NY2750	62A
Tanau, Marian	MI2200	62A
Tandberg, Irene	AG0500	62A
Tapping, Roger	MA0350	42,62A
Taylor, David	IL0550	62A
Teal, Christian	TN1850	41,51,62A
Terlaak Poot, Nancy	PA2450	62A,62B
Terwilliger, William	SC1110	62A,51,42
Thayer, Katherine	CO0625	62A,62B
Thiaville, Amy L.	LA0300	62A,42
Thierbach, Sue Ellen	MO1950	62A
Thierbach, Susie	MO0650	62A,62B
Tholl, Andrew	CA3100	62A,62B
Thomas, Jennifer	MN0625	51,62A,62B
Thomas, Sally	NY2750	62A
Thomas, Sally	NY1900	62A
Thomas, Sally	NY2250	62A
Thomason, Eliza	TX3100	11,32E,62A,62B,51
Thompson, Christopher	LA0770	41,62A,62B,11
Thompson, Curt	TX3000	62A,41
Thompson, Jason	IN1025	38,62A,62B,51,62C
Thurmer, Harvey	OH1450	51,62A
Till, Sophie	PA2200	62A,62B,13C,32E
Tobey, Moira	NY5000	62A
Todorov, Jassen	CA4200	62A,35,11
Tognozzi, Victoria	CA0150	62A
Tomenko, Keri	MD0150	62A
Tomlin, Laura A.	GA0250	62A,11,13A
Toren-Immerman, Limor	CA0810	62A,62B,13C
Totenberg, Roman	MA1175	62A
Trabichoff, Geoffrey	ID0070	62A
Tracy, Randy	MT0350	62A
Traver, Ivylyn	CA3400	62A
Travers, Tarn	IA0950	62A
Tremblay, Christian	MD0650	62A
Tremblay, Christian	MD1000	41,42,62A
Trentacosti, Marcella	IN0905	62A
Tretick, Stephanie	PA0600	62A,62B
Tsai, Kevin	NJ0750	62A
Tsai, Tammy	CA0859	13A,11,62A
Tseng, Keng-Yuen	MD0650	62A
Tung, James	MD0300	62A
Tuten, Celeste	TN1850	62A
Tyler, Philip	CA3640	62A,38
Ulman, Erik	CA4900	10,13,12B,62A
Updegraff, David	OH0600	62A
Urdaz, Mayra E.	PR0115	62A
Ushioda, Masuko	MA1400	62A
Uyeyama, Jason	CA2420	42,51,62A,62B
Vaida, John M.	PA3700	62A,62B
Vaida, John	PA2200	61,62A,62B
Valcarcel, Andres	PR0100	62A,62B,51,38
Valli, Ubaldo	NY1350	62A
Vamos, Almita	IL2250	62A
Van Der Sloot, Alexsandra	AA0050	62A
Van Der Sloot, Michael	AA0040	62A,62B,38,41
Van Der Sloot, William	AA0050	62A,41
van Dongen, Antoine	MA2050	62A
Van Hoesen, Catherine	CA4150	62A
VanBecker, Leslie	MI0850	62A
VanBurkleo-Carbonara, Natalie	MN0040	62A,62B
Vanderwerf, Paul	IL3550	62A,62B
VanDieman, Jeremy	AA0050	38,62A
Vanosdale, Mary Kathryn	TN1850	41,62A
Vardanian, Vera	MD0550	62A
Vardanyan, Tigran	NY2650	62A
Vaupel, Lisa	MD0400	62A,42
Vayman, Anna	IN0150	62A

Index by Area of Teaching Interest

Name	Code	Areas
Velazquez, Omar	PR0115	62A
Velickovic, Ljubomir	CA3270	62A,42
Veligan, Igor	CA5350	62B,42,62A
Veligan, Igor	CA0150	62A
Verdehr, Walter	MI1400	62A
Via, Susan	VA0250	62A
Viaman, Philip	CA5360	62A
Vilker-Kuchmen, Valeria	MA1400	62A
Visentin, Peter	AA0200	12A,62A,67B,11
Vitek, Milan	OH1700	62A
Vitenson, Misha	FL0700	62A,42
Vizante, Sonia	AG0200	62A
Vogel, Annette-Barbara	AG0500	62A
Votapek, Kathryn	MI2100	62A
Vrba, Cenek	AA0050	62A,41
Wagner, Lorraine	WY0115	62A,62B,62C,62D,51
Walden, Kathy	OR0750	62A,62B
Walker, Gregory T. S.	CO0830	11,62A,20G,62B,46
Walvoord, Jennifer R.	MI0350	62A
Walvoord, Martha J.	TX3500	62A,51
Wang, Han Yuan	UT0190	62A,66A
Wang, I-Fu	MI1400	41,62A
Wang, Linda	CO0900	62A,41,42
Wang, Marie	IL2200	62A,51
Wang, Shi-Hwa	UT0350	62A,13
Wang, Yung-Hsiang	TX3400	62A,12A,38,11
Warburg, Claudia E.	NC0600	62A
Ward, Miriam English	OR0600	62A,62B
Warlick, Leslie Taylor	SC0400	62A,62B
Warren-Green, Rosemary	NC0550	62A
Washecka, Tim	TX2650	62B,62A
Washiyama, Kaori	VT0050	62A,62B
Waterbury, Susan	NY1800	62A
Watson, Bradley	CO0550	62A
Watson, Larry	NY5000	62A,62B
Watson, Virginia	MN0800	62A
Watts-Foss, Mary	IA0200	62A
Waugh, Bob L.	OH0680	62A
Weaver, Ann	AZ0480	62A,62B
Weaver, Michael A.	SC0950	12A,11,32,62A,62B
Webb, A. H.	MA0800	62A
Weilerstein, Donald	MA1400	62A
Weilerstein, Donald	NY1900	62A
Weimann, Viljar P.	AL1250	62A,62B,38,10F
Weisse, Lisa	ID0060	62A
Wells, Jesse R.	KY0900	11,53,62A,70
Wells, Lillie	OR1050	32A,62A,32E
Westney, Stephanie Teply	TX3530	62A
Wetherbee, Charles	CO0800	62A
Wetherbee, Sarah M.	NY5000	62A,62B
Whang, Yumi	CO0900	62A
White, Manami	OH2550	62A,62B
Wieck, Anatole	ME0440	38,62A,62B,11
Wiersma, Calvin	NY3785	62A
Wilburn, Tricia	TN0450	62A
Wilcox, Fred J.	MD0300	62A,62B
Wilcox, John	OH2600	38,62A,62B,41
Wiley, Jennifer Sacher	PA3150	38,62A,32E
Williams, Anne	TN1850	62A,62C
Williams, Barbara	UT0050	62A,42
Williams, Brent	GA2150	62A,20
Williams, Tom	AI0150	38,51,62A
Willwerth, Valissa	PA3250	62A
Windt, Paul	PA2550	62A,62B
Wingett, Joy	MA0600	62A
Winkler, Kathleen	CA5300	62A
Winkler, Kathleen	TX2150	62A,42
Winograd, Peter	NY2150	62A
Wojtowicz, Joanne	KY1000	62A,41
Wolcott, William A.	NE0610	62A
Wolfe, Katherine	IA1550	62A
Wood, Jasper	AB0100	62A,51
Wood, Jennifer	WV0700	62A
Wood, Thomas G.	OH0700	62A,62B,12A,11
Woods, Alexander G.	UT0050	62A,41
Woolley, Stacey	OH0450	62A
Woolley, Susanne	OK0300	62A
Woolweaver, Scott	MA2010	38,41,51,62B,62A
Wright, Margaret	DC0170	41,62A,62B
Wright, Nicholas	AB0200	62A
Wu, Hai-Xin	MI2200	62A
Wu, Hai-Xin	MI0400	62A,51
Wu, Jessica Shuang	GA0750	62A
Wu, Shuang	GA1450	62A,62B
Wu, Tien-Hsin	CA5300	62A
Wunder, Patricia	MI0350	62A
Wyman, Pat	AF0120	62A,62B,38
Xie, Song	MS0385	62A,62B
Xie, Song	MS0100	62A,62B,51,42
Xu, MingHuan	IL0550	62A
Xue, Suli	CA5300	62A
Yajima, Hiroko	NY2250	41,62A
Yamada, Sojiro	LA0900	62A,62B,62C,62D
Yamamoto, Sandy	TX3510	62A,42
Yancich, Lisa	GA0750	62A
Yanovskiy, Leonid	FL1500	62A,62B,38
Yanovskiy, Leonid	FL2100	62A,62B,38,11,41
Yaron, Yuval	CA5060	62A
Yarrow, Anne	NY2450	38,62A
Yasuda, Nobuyoshi	WI0803	38,62A,51
Yi, Young	WI0100	62A,62B
Yim, Susy	VA1500	62A
Yim, Won-Bin	OH2200	62A
Ying, Janet	NY1100	62A,42
Yon, Kirsten A.	TX3200	62A,42
Yonan, David	IL2100	62A,62B
Yonetani, Ayako	FL1800	62A,62B,42
Yoo, Hyun Hanna	MD0700	62A
Yoon, Hyeyung	NE0600	62A,42
Yoshioka, Airi	MD1000	32,41,51,62A
Yu, Enen	AL1195	62A
Yu, Kyung Hak	CT0850	62A
Yu, Wen-Yih	TN1200	62A
Yu, Xiaoqing	TN0850	62A,62B,41
Yu, Yuan-Qing	IN1750	62A
Yu, Yuan-Qing	IL0550	62A
Yuen, Maureene	NY3725	62A
Yun, Chan Ho	CA0825	62A
Zabelle, Kim A.	WA0800	62A,62B,67A,51
Zabenova, Ainur	NY4320	62A,62B
Zafer, Paul	IL3550	62A,51
Zahab, Roger E.	PA3420	38,13,10F,43,62A
Zalkind, Roberta S.	UT0250	62A
Zamora, Christian	SD0050	62A
Zank, Jeremy	OH1800	51,62A,62B
Zaplatynsky, Andrew	NY2950	62A
Zaplatynsky, Andrew	NY1550	51,62A,62B
Zazofsky, Peter	MA0400	62A
Zeitlin, Paula H.	MA2050	62A,47
Zelmanovich, Mark	TN1710	51,62A
Zezelj-Gualdi, Danijela	GA0940	62A,62B,51
Zezelj-Gualdi, Danijela	NC2440	62A,62B,13C
Zhang, Yun	VA0150	62A,62B
Zhou, Xiao-Fu	PA2800	62A,62B
Zhu, Hong	OK1330	62A,41,42,51
Ziebold, Barbara	OH0950	62A
Zimmer, Don	TN1700	11,51,62A
Zinck, Bernard F.	WI0825	62A
Zori, Carmit	NJ1130	62A
Zori, Carmit	NY3785	62A,42
Zorin, Max	PA2750	62A
Zuckerman, Pinchas	NY2150	62A,62B

Viola

Name	Code	Areas
Aagaard, Kathy	FL2000	62B
Abegg, Paul	UT0150	62A,38,51,54,62B
Abel, Alfred	IN1850	62A,62B,38,48
Ablon, Judith	TN1600	62B
Abo, Takeshi	MI0100	62A,62B,51
Aceto, Jonathan D.	GA0950	51,62A,11,62B,13E
Acosta, Gail	CA2750	62A,62B
Adams, Julia	ME0200	62B
Adelson, Edward H.	OH1850	62B
Agent, Betty	WA0650	62B
Ahn, Angella	MT0200	62A,62B
Ahramjian, Sylvia Davis	PA3600	51,62A,62B
Akin, Maurine	WY0130	62A,62B
Aldrich, Ralph E.	AG0500	41,51,62A,62B
Alexander, James	LA0450	62A,62B
Alfonzo, Jesus	FL1750	62A,62B
Allen-Creighton, Esme	DE0150	62B
Althoff, Erin	SC0420	62A,62B
Ambartsumian, Levon	GA2100	51,62A,62B
Amory, Misha	PA0850	62B
Amory, Misha	NY1900	62B
Anderson, Marc	NY3350	62B
Anderson, Stella N.	MN0950	62A,62B
Andrus, Victoria	UT0150	62A,62B
Ansell, Steven	MA0400	62B
Appel, Toby	NY1900	62B
Apperson, Jim	AZ0470	62A,62B
Arad, Atar	IN0900	62B
Arksey, Meredith	WA1150	13,62A,62B
Arnott, J. David	MN0350	38,62A,62B,51
Asbell, Stephanie Ames	TX3175	62B,32E
Ashton, Alice	UT0190	62A,62B
Ashton, Jack	UT0190	62A,62B
Au, Aaron	AA0100	62A,62B,51
Auerbach, Dan J.	GA0850	60,62A,62B,38,51
Auerbach, David	MN1625	62B
Austin-Stone, Heather	WV0550	62A,62B,11
Avshalomov, Daniel	NY2150	62B
Azikiwe, Amadi	VA0600	62B
Babbitt, Frank	IL0850	62B
Badea, Remus	IL0850	62A,62B
Bagg, Jonathan E.	NC0600	62B,42
Bahcall, Klara	WI0830	41,62A,62B
Baker, Cynthia	AZ0350	51,62A,62B
Baldridge, Margaret Nichols	MT0400	62A,62B,51
Balija, Ayn	VA1550	62B,51,42
Ball, Terry	AG0050	62A,62B
Banaszek, Maurycy	NJ0700	62B
Barach, Daniel P.	NY3770	12A,62B,11
Barbini, William	CA0840	62A,62B
Bargerstock, Nancy E.	NC0050	51,62A,42,62B
Barnes, Darrel	MO0350	62B,62A,63B
Barnes, Gail V.	SC1110	32,62B
Barron, Virginia	AG0500	62B
Barta, Michael	IL2900	12A,62A,62B
Barton, Mary	NY2400	62A,62B
Basrak, Cathy	MA0400	62B
Bates, Alexandra	AF0120	62A,62B
Bauer, Leroy	ID0250	62B
Beacham, Graybert	ME0250	62A,62B
Beall, Stephen J.	TX2955	62A,62B,51
Beaudette, Eileen	AG0250	62B
Beaver, Johanna L.	VA1475	62A,62B,51
Becker, Robert	CA0960	62B
Bednarz, Blanka	PA0950	13,42,51,62A,62B
Beeson, Catherine	CO0650	62B
Belgique, Joel	OR0850	62B
Bell, Stephani	PA1850	38,62A,62B
Bennett, Michelle	IA0400	62B
Berg, Christian	OH2050	62B,47
Berg, Robert	CA0835	62B
Berger, Mark	MA2030	62B
Berlet, Pat	OR0950	62B
Besser, Idalynn	TN1450	62B
Betts, Timothy	WA0050	62B,42,11
Beyer, Douglas A.	KS0700	62A,62B
Bielish, Aaron J.	TX2295	62A,62B,41,11,13
Bigelow, Claudine	UT0050	62B
Binford, Joanna	KY1350	62A,62B,41
Bishop, Martha	GA0750	62B,67A
Biskupski, Grazyna	MI1260	62A,62B
Blackman, Daniel	AG0450	62B
Blake, Elise A.	VA0800	62A,62B,42
Blalock, Karen	UT0325	62A,62B
Blaszak, Emilia	IL2750	62A,62B
Blaydes, Sharon	OH1600	62A,62B,51
Blehm, Denise	KS0700	62B
Bloch, Robert S.	CA5010	13,11,41,62A,62B
Blumberg, Kira	CA0630	62B
Blumberg, Kira	CA5150	62B
Bob, Joan	MD0400	62B
Bodman, Alan	OH2150	51,62A,62B
Bodner, Jessica	MN1625	62B
Boggs, Isabelle	MA1100	20,64C,62A,62B
Bohlen, Tara M.	ND0400	62A,62B
Bossert, Laura	MA1175	62A,62B
Bossert-King, Laura	MA2050	62A,62B
Boyd, Bruce	KS1250	62A,62B,70,32E,62C
Boyko, Lisa	OH0600	62B
Bozell, Casey	OR0150	62A,62B,38,62C,51
Bradley-Vacco, Lynda	MN0250	38,62A,62B,51
Brandfonbrener, Amy	IN1310	62B
Brannen, Malcolm	MI0850	62A,62B,38,32A
Bravar, Mimi	NH0350	62B,41
Brenner, Laura	FL0800	62B
Breslaw, Irene	NY2150	62B
Briles, Charity	IL1050	38,62A,62B
Brockmann, Nicole M.	IN0350	62B,32I,13C
Brooks, Wayne	TX3400	62B
Brown, Hugh M.	MO1810	41,62A,62B

653

Name	Code	Areas
Brown, Kellie Dubel	TN1150	62A,38,12A,60B,62B
Brown, Lila R.	MA0350	62B
Brown, Susanne	AF0120	62A,62B
Browne, Sheila A.	NC1650	62B
Brye, Daniel	PA0950	62A,62B,51
Bubanj, Marija	IL2750	62A,62B
Buck, Nancy N.	AZ0100	62B
Bujak, Ewa	MN1295	38,62B,62A
Bujak, Ewa	MN0610	62A,62B
Burns, Lauren	GA2150	62B,32E,51
Buskirk, Kay	KS0200	62B
Butler-Hopkins, Kathleen M.	AK0150	51,62A,62B
Buxton, Merideth	MD1100	62A,62B
Byrens, Robert	MI0900	62B
Cain, Donna	OK0750	62B,42
Callus, Helen	CA5060	62B,41
Campetti, Cynthia	PA1150	62A,62B
Carey, Thomas C.	OH2275	62A,62B,38,62C
Carper, Nick	WA0400	62A,62B
Carrasco, Jacqui	NC2500	62A,62B,51,41,14
Carroll, Catharine L.	OH2200	62B
Carter, Monty	MO0950	62A,62B,38
Carter, Monty	MO2000	62B,42
Casper, Meghan	IN1010	62B
Cassidy, Marcia	NH0100	62A,62B,41
Castleman, Heidi	NY1900	62B
Causa, Ettore	CT0850	62B
Cedel, Mark	GA2100	60B,38,62B
Chan, Susan	IN1650	62B
Chang, Amy	GA0050	62B
Chang, C. J.	NJ1130	62B
Chang, Li Kuo	MD0650	62B
Chang, Seanad	TN1850	62A,62B
Chang, W. Michael	CA0815	62B
Chao, Philippe	VA0450	62B
Chase, Roger	IL0550	62B,42
Chen, C. Brian	CA0815	62B
Chen, Che-Hung	PA3250	62B
Chen, Chi-Yuan	CA4100	62B
Chen, Lambert	AI0150	62B,51
Chen, Ting-Lan	NE0590	11,13B,62A,62B,13C
Chepaitis, Stanley L.	PA1600	41,62A,62B,51
Chestnut, Louise	MD0060	10,62B
Chiang, Victoria	MD0650	62B
Chisholm, Sally	WI0815	62B
Cho, Wan-Soo	KY0400	62B,51
Christensen, Brandon J.	MO1500	62A,62B,42,11
Chun, Peter	KS1350	41,62B
Chung, Miri	IN0907	62A,62B,33,51
Chung, Sharon	IL1750	62B
Clarke, Karen	TN1850	62A,62B,67B
Cleland, George	AA0040	38,41,62A,62B
Clements, Tania Maxwell	GA1050	62B,62A
Clifford, Patrick	FL1450	62A,62B,51
Coade, Caroline	MI2200	62B
Coade, Caroline	MI2100	62B
Coffman, Elizabeth	IL0730	62A,62B
Cohen, Joanne	MN0600	32,51,62A,62B
Coletti, Paul	CA1075	62B,42
Colston, Daniel	IN0150	62B
Cominskey, Millie M.	IL1350	62B
Consiglio, Catherine	KS1450	62B,51,41
Cooper, Cora	KS0650	51,62A,62B
Corbato, Barbara	MI1050	62B
Cords, Nicholas D.	NY3790	62B
Corwin, Lucille H.	NY4500	62A,62B
Cote, Sarah	TN0100	62B
Cowan, Carole	NY3760	38,66D,62A,62B
Cox, Ann	UT0350	62B
Cox, Kerry	IA0600	62A,62B
Cox, Patricia J.	AR0250	11,32,34C,38,62B
Crane, Emily Hanna	TN0050	62A,62B
Crawford, Roberta	NY3705	41,62B,62A
Cromwell, Anna L.	IL0800	62A,62B,41
Cseszko, Ferenc	ID0250	38,62A,62B,41
Culpo, Susan	RI0150	62B
Culver, Robert L.	MI2100	32,62B
Cummins, Danielle Rosaria	CA0845	62A,62B
Currie, Sheridan	OH0450	62B
Curtiss, Sidney	PA3250	62B
Dahn, Nancy	AD0050	41,62A,62B
Dakin, Deborah	IL0100	11,62B,62A
Dalbec-Szczesniak, Gisele	AG0250	62A,62B
Dallinger, Carol	IN1600	62A,13A,62B,51
Dalmas, Jennifer	TX2700	38,62A,62B,41
D'Andrea, Daria	CA5353	62A,62B
Danis, Ann	RI0300	60,38,11,62A,62B
Dann, Steven	AG0300	42,62B
Darmiento, Madeleine	PA2350	62A,62B
Daugherty, Wendy	TX2570	62A,62B,66A,32E
Davidovici, Robert	FL0700	62A,62B,11
Davies, Karl	IL1300	62B
Davis, William	IN0800	38,62A,62B
Davy, Karen	CA2250	62A,62B,62C,62D,41
Dawkins, Allyson	TX3530	62B
Day, Geoff	FL0500	62A,62B
De Pasquale, Joseph	PA0850	62B
De Ritis, Anthony	MA1450	35,62B,34,45
De Villiers, Liesl-Ann	TX3420	62B
Deighton, Timothy	PA2750	62B
Delevoryas, Sarah	CO0150	62A,62B
DeNicola, Alan	VT0200	62A,62B,62C
DePaolo, Gary	WY0050	62B
Dermody, Joseph	NY0850	62B
DeStefano, Dominic	KY1500	62B
Deubner, Brett D.	PA3250	62B
Devroye, Anthony	IL2200	62B,51
Diaz, Roberto	PA0850	62B
Dietrich, Johannes M.	PA1900	60,38,62A,62B
Dinino, Aileen	FL1310	62A,62B
Dirks, Karen	IL0750	62B
Dissmore, Larry	MO0400	60,38,51,62A,62B
Divis, Judy	NE0610	62B
Djokic, Philippe	AF0100	62B,38,41,51,62A
Dobrotvorskaia, Ekaterina	CO0275	62B,42,51
Doctor, Kirsten	OH0600	51,62B
Dodds, Amy	WA1300	62A,62B,13
Doering, Susan J.	CA1860	62A,62B
Dolphin, Amber	WI0100	62A,62B
Dona, Daniel	MA0400	62B,42
Dong, Kun	KY1000	62B
Drexler, Darcy	WI0825	62A,62B
Dreyfus, Karen	NY2150	62B
Dreyfus, Karen	NY2250	62B
Dreyfus, Karen	NY1900	62B
Dubois, Susan L.	TX3420	62B
Duchow, Ann L.	IA0940	62A,62B
Duckles, Andrew	CA0825	62B

Name	Code	Areas
Duggan, Ann	IL3150	62A,62B
Dunham, James	TX2150	62B,42
Dutt, Hank	CA2950	62B
Dutton, Lawrence	GA1300	62B
Dutton, Lawrence	NY2150	62B
Dutton, Lawrence	NY3790	41,62B
DuWors, Kerry	AC0050	62A,62B,51
Eckert, Erika	CO0800	51,62,B
Edelberg, Joe	CA4700	32E,38,42,62A,62B
Edwards, Renard	PA3250	62B
Een, Andrea	MN1450	42,62A,62B
Ehle, Todd	TX0550	62A,62B,38
Ehrlich, Don	CA4150	62B
Elias, Carlos	CO0225	32C,38,62A,62B,51
Elisha, Larisa	GA0950	62A,62B
Emery, Michael	NY3650	62A,62B,51
Emile, Mark A.	UT0300	10F,60B,62A,62B
English-Ward, Miriam	OR0400	62B
Englund, John	UT0250	62A,62B
Ericksen, Elizabeth	MN0300	62A,62B,42
Eskitch, Paulo S.	OK1450	62B
Fagerburg, Karin	CT0050	62A,62B
Fairlie, Mary	TX2800	62A,62B,51,14C,38
Falkner, Renate M.	FL1950	62B,67B
Farina, Danielle	NY4450	62B
Farkas, Pavel	CA5150	38,41,51,62A,62B
Fashun, Christopher H.	IN0550	38,65,32,47,62B
Fedotov, Igor	MI2250	51,62B
Ferdon, Ellen	NC2420	62B
Fernandez, Alma	CA3600	62B
Field, Richard L.	MD0650	62B
Fielding, Ralph W.	FL1125	62B
Filipovich, Natalie	MN1700	62A,62B,32E
Finegan, James	PA1550	62A,62B
Fisher, Yuko	IL1740	62A,62B,62C,41
Flaniken, Angela M.	AL0800	62B
Fleck, Allyson	GA1150	62B,42,13B
Fleming, Phyllis	DC0170	62A,62B
Flores, Jose G.	TX2930	62A,62B,51,13C,42
Fluchaire, Olivier	NY0644	62A,62B,11,13A,42
Foerster, Frank	NJ0825	62A,62B
Fogg, Cynthia R.	CA3650	62B
Foster, Daniel	MD1010	62B
Foster, Daniel	MI0600	62A,62B
Frankel, Joanna	NJ0700	62A,62B,42
Frantz, Nathan	FL1745	62B
Frazier, Virginia	CA1750	62A,62B
Fredenburgh, Kim	NM0450	62B,51
French, Nell	KS0590	62A,62B
Frens, Jennifer	IA0500	62B
Freund-Striplen, Pamela	CA3920	62A,62B
Frisk, Nora	IN1450	62B
Gabriel, Adrienne Moffitt	LA0050	62B
Gabriel, Edgar	IL0850	62A,62B,45
Gallagher, Maureen	NY0500	62B
Gandelsman, Yuri	MI1400	62B
Gant, Christina	PA3260	62A,62B,62C
Garcia, Alvaro	WI0835	38,62B,60,51
Gardiner, Annabelle	FL1740	62A,62B,51,38
Gazouleas, Edward	MA0400	62B
Gazouleas, Edward	IN0900	62B
Gearman, Mara	WA0200	62B
Gee, Constance	SC1110	11,41,62B,42
Gentry, Sarah	IL1150	13,62A,62B
Georgieva, Roumena G.	GA0490	62A,62B,38,51
Gerard, Eva	NY5000	62A,62B
Geyer, Luba	FL1650	62A,62B
Geyer, Oleg	FL1650	62A,62B
Giammario, Matteo	PA0400	13A,11,62A,62B
Gilbert, Diane	CA3100	62A,62B
Gilman, Kurt	TX1400	38,41,62A,62B,20
Gingras-Roy, Marylene	PA1050	62B
Giray, Selim	KS1450	62A,62B,51,42,38
Glazebrook, James	VA1700	60,38,62A,62B
Goldsmith, Pamela	CA5300	62B
Gomez, Routa Kroumovitch	FL1750	12A,62A,62B
Gorevic, Elizabeth	NY3775	51,62A,62B
Gorevic, Ronald	NY2400	62A,62B
Gorgojo, Jamie	IL2150	62A,62B
Gray, Charles	MN1450	42,62A,62B
Greene, Kenneth H.	TX3350	14,38,62B,51
Gregorian, Ara	NC0650	62A,62B,42
Gregory, Monica	OH2140	62B
Gregory, Rohan	MA0700	62A,62B
Griebling, Karen	AR0350	13,10,38,62B,14
Griffin, Stephanie	NY0500	62B
Griffing, Joan	VA0300	62A,38,41,60B,62B
Grigoriu, Katrina	AA0050	32A,62A,62B
Grinnell, Michael	TX3535	62A,62B,38
Gripp, Neal	AI0200	62B
Grmela, Sylvia	NY4460	62B,20,13A,13C
Grove, Rebecca	SC0200	62A,62B
Gustafson, Eric	NY1350	62B
Hagerty, Mia	TX0550	62A,32A,62B
Haken, Rudolf	IL3300	62B,51,41
Hakim, Will J.	NY3650	62B
Hakim, William J.	NJ1160	62A,62B
Hall, Michael L.	IL3450	62A,62B
Hamilton, Kate	MN0600	62B
Hamme, Nora Ruth	PA1650	62A,62B
Hansen, Frank	NY4050	11,38,62B
Harding, David	AB0100	51,62A,62B,41,42
Harker-Roth, Kerry	PA2300	62B
Harlow, Leslie	UT0325	62B,42
Harris, Kim	KY0250	12A,62B,62C
Harris, Mary	OH1450	32,62B,51,42
Harrison, Carol	MO1550	62A,62B
Hartke-Towell, Christina	KY0900	38,62A,62B
Haskins, Jodi	AL1150	62A,62B,11
Hawryluck, Alan	MA0950	62A,62B
Hayden, William P.	FL2000	62A,62B,51
Hayhurst, John	CA5300	62B
Helmer, Terence	AG0450	41,62B
Henry, Rebecca	PA1400	62B
Henry, Rebecca S.	MD0650	62B
Heppner-Harjo, Tianna	NV0050	62B,32E,42
Herndon, Hillary	TN1710	62B
Herrera, Jennifer	PA3710	62A,62B
Hersh, Paul	CA4150	12A,42,62B,66A
Hillard, Claire Fox	GA0625	11,62A,62B,66D,62
Hills, Peggy	AG0650	62A,62B
Hillyer, Giselle	WI0845	62A,62B,51
Hillyer, Raphael	MA1175	62B
Hines, Edith	WI0700	62A,62B
Hirna, Olena	IL0850	62A,62B
Ho, Leslie	CA6000	62A,62B
Hoeschen, Kevin	WI0860	62B
Hofeldt, Elizabeth	OH2450	62B,20
		62A,62B,42

Index by Area of Teaching Interest

Name	Code	Areas
Hoffman, Miles	SC0650	62B
Hogue, Charles	AL1160	62B,51
Holland, David	MI0400	62B,42,51
Holland, David	MI1650	62B,42,51
Holzemer, Kate C.	NY3717	62B,51
Hood, Joanna	AB0150	62B,42
Hoopes, Katherine	MA0600	62A,62B
Horner, Jerry	WI0825	41,62B
Horozaniecki, Mary B.	MN0300	62A,62B,42
Horozaniecki, Mary A.	MN0050	62A,62B
Houde, Andrea	WV0750	13C,32,41,42,62B
Hsu, Chia-Ying	IL2650	62A,62B
Hsueh, Yvonne	OR1250	62A,62B,67A,67B
Huang, Hsin-Yun	NY1900	62B
Huang, Hsin-Yun	NY2250	62B,41
Huang, Rachel V.	CA1050	62A,62B
Hult, David W.	NY2650	62A,62B,11,51
Hunt, William	OR0250	38,62A,62B
Huyge, Dana	NY1400	62B
Ihas, Dijana	OR0750	62B,11,32
Ingber, Elizabeth	CA4625	66A,62A,62B
Irvine, Jeffrey K.	OH0600	62B
Israelievitch, Jacques	AG0650	62A,62B,38
Jacklin, Rachel	IL2300	62A,62B
Jackobs, Mark	OH0600	62B,51
Jakovcic, Zoran	GA0550	62B
Janda, Susan	MN0800	62B
Janzen, Henry	AG0350	42,62B,62A
Jennings, Graeme	CA2950	40,41,62A,62B,42
Jevitt, Amy	FL0150	62A,62B
Jillings, Cathy	AG0170	62B
Jin, Yu	OH1100	62B,42
Johnson, Cecilia	MI1950	62A,62B
Johnson, David	ID0070	13A,41,62B,42,51
Johnson, Karrell	TX3420	32,51,62B
Johnson, Mildred	UT0300	13,12A,12,62B
Johonnott, Edwin	VA0450	62A,62B,42
Joiner, Anna Barbrey	SC0750	62B,42,32E
Joiner, Lee	IL3550	51,62A,62B
Jones, Janet	AZ0150	38,62A,62C,62B,62D
Jones, Sheila L.	OH1650	62A,62B
Joseph, Charles	NY3725	60,62A,62B
Judish, Marion	MN1300	62A,62B
Kadarauch, Katie	CA4150	62B
Kahng, Er-Gene	AR0700	62A,62B,41
Kaplunas, Daniel	IA1800	38,62C,62B,51,60
Karp, Margaret B.	KY1450	62A,62B
Kashkashian, Kim	MA1400	62B
Katz, Martha	MA1400	62B
Katz, Shmuel D.	NY2750	42,62B
Kawasaki, Masao	NY0500	41,62A,62B
Kawasaki, Masao	NY0600	62A,62B
Kawasaki, Masao	OH2200	62B
Kean, Eric	WA1250	62B
Kenny, Megan	NC2435	62A,62B,51
Khosrowpour, Iman	CA2390	62A,62B,13B
Kim, Ariana	NY0900	62A,62B
Kim, Eunho	SD0600	62A,62B,51
Kim, Hye-Jin	NC0650	62A,62B,42
Kim, Ji Hyun	MI2000	62A,62B
Kim, Leah	PA1150	62A,62B
Kimber, Michael	IA0930	62B
Kimber, Michael	IA0300	62B
King, Joan	PA0650	62A,62B,62C,62D,31G
Kirkpatrick, Mary Beth	WV0560	62A,62B,62C,62D
Kistler, Linda	PA2450	62A,62B
Kivrak, Osman	DC0010	62B,42,51
Klein, Korinthia	WI1150	62B
Klima, Arthur	OH0650	62B
Klotz, Michael	FL0700	62B,42
Klugherz, Laura	NY0650	13,11,41,62A,62B
Klukoff, Ruth	FL0450	62A,62B
Knecht, Melissa Gerber	MI1000	11,32,42,62A,62B
Knoepfel, Justin	MN0750	62B,62A,38,42,13
Kochanowski, John	TN1850	41,51,62B,42
Koehler, Andrew	MI1150	60,38,62A,62B,12A
Kong, Yinzi	GA0750	62B
Konkol, Korey	MN1623	41,62B
Konopka, Stanley	OH0600	62B
Koontz, Eric E.	NC0050	62B,62A,67A,42,51
Kopec, Patinka	NY2150	62A,62B
Kotcherguina, Tatiana	AR0850	62B
Kozak, Pawel K	SC1000	51,62A,62B
Kozamchak, David M.	MN1280	38,51,62A,62B,41
Krishnaswami, Donald	MA0510	11,12A,62A,62B,51
Kromin, Vladimir	VA1100	62A,62B,51
Kruger, Anna R.	CA0840	62B
Kruse, Steven	OH0950	62B
Ku, Rachel	PA3250	62B
Kuhns, Philip A.	AZ0510	62A,62B
Kwo, Kenneth P. C.	FL0930	62B
Kwok, Daniel	IL2775	62A,62B
Kwon, Su Jin	NY5000	62A,62B
Lackschewitz, Anna	MO1950	62B
LaCourse, Michelle	MA0400	62B
Laderach, Linda C.	MA1350	51,62A,62B,67B
Lakirovich, Mark	MA1175	62A,62B
Lam, Michelle	VA1500	62A,62B,43
Lamar, Linda Kline	ID0050	13,62B,41
Lambert, Frederic	AI0150	62B
Lambert, Jessica I.	OR0700	62A,62B
Lambros, Maria	MD1000	62B,42
Lander, Deborah R.	KY1450	62B,42
Lara, Elizabeth K.	TN0050	62C,13,62D,62B
Lardinois, John	IN0400	62A,62B
Largess, John	TX3510	62B,42
Larson, Jon D.	MN1120	62A,62B
Larson, Steven	CT0650	41,62B
Lautar, Rebecca	FL0650	11,41,51,62A,62B
Lawson, Sonya R.	MA2100	12A,62B,29A,12,20
League, Leanne	WI0865	62A,62B
Lebo, Joanna	SC0050	51,62A,62B
Ledbetter, Lynn F.	TX3175	62A,62B,42,51
Lederer, Doris L.	VA1350	62B,62A,42
Lee, Daniel	CT0100	62A,62B
Lee, Hsiaopei	MS0750	62B,62A
Lee, Scott	MO1810	62B
Lehnert, Oswald	CO0800	51,62A,62B
Lehninger, Marcia	NH0150	11,20H,62A,62B
Lehr, Barry	NY2550	62B
Letson, Amy	MT0175	62B
Levitz, Jodi	CA4150	41,62B
Lewis, Eric	CT0800	12A,62B,51,62A,12B
Lewis, Katherine J.	IL1150	11,62B
Li, Honggang	NJ0800	62B,42,62A
Li, Li	IN0100	62B,38
Li, Teng	AG0450	62B
Liao, Chien-Ju	OH2200	62B
Liebenow, Marcia Henry	IL0400	62A,62B
Lim, Michael	WA0200	62B
Lin, Chloe	MO0060	62A,62B,62C,38
Linares, Adriana	PA1750	62B
Linde-Capistran, Jane	MN0600	41,62A,62B
Lionti, Victor C.	NY2200	62B
Liu, Hui	CA0830	62B
Liu, Kexi	MO0800	11,51,62A,62B
Liu, Lei	FL2050	62A,62B
Liu, Te-Chiang	MN1600	62A,62B,41
Liva, Ferdinand R.	ME0500	62A,62B
Lockwood, Kathryn	MA2000	62B
Lorenzo, Donna A.	NY1700	62B,62A
Low, Todd K.	NY1600	62B
Lowe, David	KS0700	62B
Lucero, Kerry	AZ0150	62A,62B
Luise, Evelyn J.	PA3250	62B
Luscher, Alexia	HI0050	62A,62B
Lynn, Catherine D.	GA1150	62B,42
Lyon, Howard	PA1200	62A,62B,41
Macek, Timothy A.	DC0150	62A,62B
Maddox, Meredith R.	AR0750	42,62A,62B
Madura, Melissa	TX3527	62B
Magaziner, Elliot	NY5000	62A,62B
Magaziner, Sari	NY2400	62B
Magnuson, Phillip	OH2250	13,10F,10A,62B
Majerfeld, Paula	MA1175	62B
Malan, Roy	CA5070	62A,62B
Maldonado, Greg	CA0825	51,62A,55,62B
Malvinni, Valerie	CA5550	62A,62B
Malvinni, Valerie L.	CA4410	62A,62B
Mantell, Matthew	IL3100	51,62A,62B
Mao, Ruotao	NJ0175	62A,62B,42
Marcotte, Anna-Belle	AI0150	62B
Margetts, David	UT0325	62A,62B
Maril, Travis	CA4100	62B
Marinic, Boro	IA0850	13,62A,62B
Markow, Elliott	MA2030	62A,62B
Markow, Roseann	MD0500	62A,62B,51
Markstein, Igor	FL0150	62A,62B
Martin, Spencer L.	IA0950	62A,62B,51,38
Martinez, Everaldo	ND0400	62A,62B,62C,51,38
Martinez, Jorge	NM0310	62B
Martinson, Kenneth	FL1850	62B,51
Martz, Dee	WI0850	62B
Mason, Daniel	KY1450	62A,62B,41
Matczynski, Leonard	MA0350	62B
Mathes, Adam	MT0370	62B
Matson, Melissa	NY1100	62B
Matsuda, Kenichiro	OH0350	62B
Matthews, Margaret	NY1150	62A,62B,62C
Matthews, Todd	IL0600	62A,62B
Mattson, Lisa	FL0680	62B
May-Patterson, Eleanor	IA1100	32E,62A,62B
Mayo, Thomas	MA0950	62B
Mazo, Vadim	IL1200	41,42,62A,62B,51
McBride Daline, Matthew	OH0300	62B
McBride-Daline, Matthew S.	LA0200	62B
McClure, Sam	MO1780	13,38,62A,62B
McConnell, Pamela A.	FL1900	62B
McCullough, Stephanie	PA1250	62A,62B
McGann, Christina F.	OH1900	62B
McGee-Daly, Kathleen	NJ0550	62A,62B
McGrath, Casey	IL1520	62A,62B
McInnes, Donald	CA5300	62B
McKinney, Lori	KS0050	38,62A,62B
McLarry, Royce	OK0700	62A,62B
McNabney, Douglas	AI0150	51,62B,42
McNeela, Rico	MO0850	38,11,62A,62B,60
McNiven, Lisa	ID0060	12A,62B
McWilliams, Bernard	NC0450	62A,62B
Means, Matthew L.	KS0350	11,62A,62B,41,42
Meidell, Katrin	TX3200	62B
Meineke, Robert	TX2350	62A,62B,62C,62D,51
Mendoza, Joanna	MO1830	62B
Mennemeyer, Bethany	CA1750	62A,62B
Menzies, Mark	CA0510	62A,62B,38,43,60B
Merrit, Doug	TN0580	13C,62A,62B
Meyer, Elizabeth C.	MI1450	38,62A,62B,10A
Meyer, Robert	CT0600	62B
Meyers, Stephanie	TX3520	62A,62B
Michelic, Matthew C.	WI0350	41,62B
Michels, Maureen	NC2205	62B
Migliozzi, Anastasia E.	VA1000	62B
Miller, Margaret	CO0200	62B
Miller, Margaret J.	CO0250	62B
Miranda, Charles	IA0650	62A,62B,11
Miranda, Charles	IA0420	11,62A,62B
Miskell, Jerome P.	OH2290	34,62B,13A,11
Monke, Kirsten	ME0200	62B
Monosoff, Sonya	NY0900	41,62A,62B,67B
Montzka, Ann	IL2200	62A,62B
Moon, Gene H.	TX2700	38,39,66,62A,62B
Moore, Janice	OH1350	62A,62B
Moravec, Andriana	IN0005	62A,62B
Moree, Debra	NY1800	62B
Morgan, Lauren R.	MO0250	62A,62B,62C,62D,51
Morgan, LeeAnn	UT0050	62A,62B
Morris, Ralph	OK1330	38,62A,62B,41,42
Morris, Theodora	OK1330	62A,62B,67C,42
Moser, Mary	PA1450	62B
Motobuchi, Mai	MA1400	62B
Mott, Jonathan	VA0250	62A,62B
Moyer, Cynthia M.	CA2250	13,41,62A,62B
Mu, Ning	PA1300	62B
Muchnick, Amy Faye	MO0775	11,12A,62B,41
Muegel, Glenn	NC0050	13,41,62A,62B
Mulholland, Jeremy	KY0550	62A,62B,38,60B
Mumm, Craig	NJ1130	62B
Murasugi, Sachiho	MD0800	62A,62B,11,13A,51
Murdock, Katherine	MD1010	62B
Murphy, Paul	GA1300	62B
Murphy, Paul	GA0750	62B
Murrath, Dimitri	MA1175	62B
Myers, Roger	TX3510	62B,42
Myrick, John	AL1195	32,62A,62B,41,51
Nardolillo, Jo	KY0100	62A,62B
Neeley, Henrietta	IL1085	62A,11,42,62B
Neely, David C.	NE0600	62A,62B
Neubauer, Paul	NY1900	62B
Neubauer, Paul	NY2250	62B
Neubert, Peter	TX0900	62B,62A,41
Newby, Joanna	IL1300	62A,62B
Noren, Rictor	MA0350	62B
Norman, Jeffery	AZ0490	62B
Norwitz, Sherrie	MD0850	62B
Norwood, Diana	TX3370	62A,62B
O'Brien, Dean	AA0050	62A,62B

655

Name	Code	Areas
Oeseburg, Beth	MI1180	62A,62B
Ogletree, Mary	PA1750	13,11,62A,62B,51
Ogura, Yukiko	IL0550	62B
Okpebhola, Dorthy White	TN0450	62B
Olivieri, Emmanuel	PR0115	62B,13E,13F
O'Neill, Richard	CA5030	62B
Ostrander, Allison	WI0803	62B
Owen, Bruce M.	LA0300	62B
Pagan, Joel G.	TX3525	62B,62A
Palumbo, Michael A.	UT0350	38,62B,32E,60,41
Pancella, Peter	IL1500	62A,62B,51
Pandolfi, Anne	AL0300	62A,62B
Panner, Daniel	NY1900	62B
Panner, Daniel	NY2250	62B
Panner, Daniel Z.	NY3790	62B
Papich, George	TX3420	42,62B
Para, Christopher	PA0350	13,11,38,62A,62B
Pardo, Danielle	WI1150	62A,62B
Park, Chung	NC0050	38,62A,62B,51,60
Park, Sue-Jean	KY0950	62A,62B,41
Patterson, Joanna	OH0650	62B
Paulson, Jennifer Clare	WI0865	62A,62B
Penne, Cynthia S.	VA1850	62A,62B,41
Penny, Nicholas	AG0550	62B
Pepper, Ronald D.	OH0950	62A,62B,12A
Perna, Leslie	MO1800	62B,42
Pernela, Nathan	HI0050	62B
Perrault, Jean R.	MN1600	60,62A,62B,62C,38
Perttu, Melinda H. Crawford	PA3650	38,62A,62B
Peters, Maria	SD0580	62A,62B
Petillot, Aurelien	IL2900	62B,62A,42,11,12A
Petraborg, Kirsti J.	IA0950	62B
Phelps, Melissa	CA0550	62A,62B
Pich, Victoria	OR0450	62A,62B
Pidluski, Eric	IL1900	62A,62B
Pikler, Charles	IL2100	62A,51,42,62B
Pinney, Greg	MD0550	62A,62B
Placilla, Christina D.	NC2700	12A,20,38,62A,62B
Plenert, Keith	NE0160	62A,62B
Plesner, Joy	CO0050	62A,62B
Plexico, Byron K.	IN1650	62B
Plourde, Jean-Luc	AI0190	42,62B
Plum, Sarah A.	IA0550	62A,62B,11,42
Plummer, Kathryn	TN1850	41,62A,62B,34
Pogrebnoy, Nikita	AB0060	62B,51
Ponton, Lisa	IA0700	62B
Porfiris, Rita	CT0650	62B
Porter, David	UT0400	62B
Posadas, John	FL2000	62A,62B
Posnock, Jason	NC0250	62A,62B,32E
Potter, Clark E.	NE0600	62B
Prager, Madeline	CA4150	62B
Pranno, Arthur J.	FL0800	62A,38,51,62B,12A
Price, Debra	OH0850	62B
Price-Brenner, Paul Alan	WI0840	11,62A,62B,34
Przygocki, James T.	WY0200	62B,51,32E
Puchammer, Sedillot	AI0210	62B
Puchammer, Jutta	AI0200	62B,41,51
Pulos, Nick	AA0050	38,62B,41
Puls, David	OH1400	11,62B
Purdy, Carl	GA0250	62A,62B,70,51
Quindag, Sue	SC0200	32,62A,62B,34
Radloff, Susan	MN1290	62A,62B
Railsback, Stephanie	CA3520	62B,42
Ramee, Joyce	WA1000	62B,32E
Ramsey, Lynne	OH0600	62B
Rapoport, Katharine	AG0450	62A,62B
Ratner, Jody	NY0050	62B
Ravnan, John	SC0765	62B,42,13
Rawls, Scott	NC2430	62B
Ray, Mary Ruth	MA0500	41,62B,11
Read, Evelyn	VT0450	62A,62B,16,42
Reardon, Melissa	NC0650	62B,42
Redman, Inez	NC2400	62A,62B,42
Redmer Minner, Laurie K.	TN1350	60B,38,51,32C,62B
Redmon, Nursun	MI0300	62A,62B
Reed, Jane	OH0100	11,13A,62A,66D,62B
Reed-Lunn, Rebecca	KY1550	62B,11
Reeve, Jay A.	IA1200	62B
Reeves, Derek	IN0905	62A,62B
Regehr, Rennie	AG0400	62B,42
Rehkopf-Michel, Carrie	WA0050	41,51,62A,62B
Reinker, Daniel	TN1850	62B
Rende, Jennifer	MD0750	62B
Reynolds, Katherine	AR0850	62B
Rhodes, Samuel	NY1900	51,41,62B
Richardson, Cathy	TX0250	62A,62B,51
Richardson, Marguerite	FL1000	38,60B,62A,62B
Richter, Jorge Luiz	NC0650	60B,38,42,62A,62B
Riggs, Robert D.	MS0700	12A,12B,41,62A,62B
Riley, Kristin	OR1020	62A,62B
Rinehart, Robert	NY2150	62B
Ringwald, Ilana	MA2150	62B
Rintoul, Richard	CA5550	62B
Ripley, Vanessa G.	OH1200	62A,62B
Ritscher, Karen	NY2750	62B,42
Ritscher, Karen	NY2150	62B
Ritscher, Karen	MA0400	62B
Ritz, Lyn	WA1100	62A,62B,42,13,10F
Ritzenthaler, Maria	IL1085	62B,41,42
Rivest, Darlene	WI0250	62B,32E,38,62A,41
Robertson, Lesley N.	CA4900	62B,41,51
Robillard, David	OK1250	62A,62B
Rodland, Carol	NY1100	62B
Rodland, Carol	MA1400	62B
Rodriguez, Samantha	NY3730	62B,42
Roggen, Ann	NJ1400	62B,41
Rokosny, Dana	MD0300	62B
Roland, Isabelle	AB0200	62A,62B
Rooney, Laura G.	WI1150	62B
Roos, Joni N.	FL1550	62A,62B,51
Rose, David	NY3725	62B
Rose, Ellen	TX2400	62B
Rose, Ellen Ruth	CA5000	62B
Rosove, Lewis E.	WI0825	62B
Ross, Jana	VA1400	62A,62B
Rostad, Masumi Per	IN0900	62B,42
Rostad, Masumi	IL3300	51,62B
Rotberg, Barton Samuel	PA2250	62A,62B
Roth, Michael	NY2400	62B
Rouslin, Daniel S.	OR1300	11,38,41,62A,62B
Rousseau, Karine	AI0200	62B
Rovit, Arvilla	NY4150	62B
Rowin, Elizabeth	MI1750	62A,62B,42
Roy, Andre	AI0150	38,62B
Rozek, Robert	AB0200	62A,62B,38
Rudoff, Patricia L.	NY2550	62A,62B
Rudolph, Richard	VA0550	62A,38,62B,62C,65B
Rudolph, Robert A.	PA0100	62A,62B,41,42,51
Rumney, Jon	ND0250	13,38,41,62A,62B
Rutland, John P.	MO1790	38,62A,62B
Rutledge, Christine	IA1550	62B
Ryan, Kate	AR0110	62A,62B
Ryan, Kerri	PA3250	62B
Ryan, Pamela	FL0850	41,62B
Saelzer, Pablo	DC0170	62A,62B
Salas, Veronica	NY2105	62B
Salathe, Leslie	NY0400	62A,62B
Salazar, Rene	TX2250	62B
Salem, Ernest	CA0815	13,41,62A,62B
Salerno, Julia	WA0250	62A,62B,41
Salsbury, Karen	KS0400	62A,62B
Sant'Ambrogio, Stephanie	NV0100	62A,62B
Santana, Lisa	CA1425	62B
Santos, Philip	CA0807	62A,62B,51
Saunders, Meg	KY0450	62A,62B,41
Saylor, Mary Ann	PA2450	62A,62B
Schani, Steve	WI0804	62B
Schmidt, Stephen	VA1600	62A,62B
Scholz, Dan	AC0100	62B
Schotten, Yizhak	MI2100	62B
Schottman, Margret	PA0500	62A,62B,62C
Schranze, Jane	TN1200	62B
Schranze, Lenny	TN1680	62B,42
Schultz, David	TX0700	62A,62B
Schuppener, Mark	TX3520	62A,62B,11
Schwandt, Jacquelyn Joy	AZ0450	62B
Schwartz, Ann Marie Barker	NY3600	62A,62B
Schwarz, Timothy J.	PA1950	62A,62B,51,41
Shand, Patricia	AG0450	32C,51,62A,62B
Shiao, Simon	FL1950	51,62A,62B,38
Shilling, Scott	OH2500	62B
Showell, Jeffrey A.	OH0300	62B
Shows, Ray	MN1450	62A,62B
Sills, David	CA3500	62B
Silva, Ulisses C.	GA1700	62B,11
Simonson, Jessica	OR1000	62A,62B,62C
Sinclair, David W.	PA3000	62A,62B
Sinsabaugh, Katherine Anne	NY4200	62A,62B
Sirota, Jonah B.	NE0600	62B,42
Sirota, Nadia	NY2150	62B
Skerik, Renee	TX3200	62B
Skidmore, Dan	NC0350	62A,62B
Skinner, Anita	OH0250	62A,62B
Sletner, Ariane	OH1200	62A,62B
Slowik, Peter	OH1700	62B,41
Smith, Cory	OH2150	62A,62B
Smith, Elizabeth Reed	WV0400	38,41,51,62A,62B
Smolensky, Marcus	PA3150	62B
Smolensky, Marcus H.	PA0350	62A,62B
Snyder, Jennifer	TX3750	62B
Snyder, Maggie	GA2100	62B
Solomon, Qiao Chen	GA0050	62A,62B,51,41,38
Solomonow, Rami	IL0750	62B
Song, Xie	MS0400	62A,62B
Sorensen, Ann	LA0250	62A,62B,62C,62D
Soykan, Betul	GA0500	62A,62B
Sparks, Dee	MO1900	62B
Sparr, Kimberly	VA0250	62B
Spencer, Stacia C.	IL2250	32B,62A,62B
St. John, Brian	IN1600	38,62A,62B,60B
Stanfield, Ashley	IA0550	62A,62B
Starr, Jeremy A.	KS0300	38,62A,62B,11
Staskevicius, Algis	AR0300	62A,62B,32E
Steely, Kathryn	TX0300	62B
Stevens, Frankie	MO0825	62A,62B
Stevens, Phillip	CO0550	62B
Stevens, Thomas	VA1500	62A,62B
Stewart, Leslie	CO0250	62A,62B,38,11
Straka, Leslie	OR1050	42,62B
Strauss, Michael	IL0550	62B
Strauss, Michael	OH1700	62B,42
Strawn, Logan	IN0800	62B
Stuart, Carolyn	FL2000	62A,62B
Stultz, Rachel	KS0150	62A,62B
Sudweeks, Barbara	TX2400	62B
Sulski, Peter	MA0200	41,62A,62B
Sulski, Peter	MA0700	62B,62A,42
Sulski, Peter	MA0650	62A,62B,60B,38
Sumerlin, John	RI0200	41,62A,62B
Sung, Benjamin H.	FL0850	62A,62B,41,42
Sweaney, Daniel	AL1170	62B
Sykes, Jean	NC0910	62A,62B
Szabo, Istvan	IL3500	62B,51
Tagg, Graham	AA0200	62B
Takarabe, Clara	IN1750	62A,62B
Takizawa, Marcus	AB0200	62B
Talbott, Laura	OK0800	62A,62B,42
Tan, Kia-Hui	OH1850	62A,51,62B,13,42
Tanaka, Naoka	NY0500	62A,62B
Tardif, Guillaume	AA0100	62B,41
Taylor, George	NY1100	62B
Taylor, Lucille	CA2420	62B,41
Tenenbom, Stephen	NY1900	62B
Tenenbom, Steven	NY0150	62B,42
Terlaak Poot, Nancy	PA2450	62A,62B
Thayer, Katherine	CO0625	62A,62B
Thierbach, Susie	MO0650	62A,62B
Tholl, Andrew	CA3100	62A,62B
Thomas, Jennifer	MN0625	51,62A,62B
Thomason, Eliza	TX3100	11,32E,62A,62B,51
Thompson, Christopher	LA0770	41,62A,62B,11
Thompson, Jason	IN1025	38,62A,62B,51,62C
Thompson, John	AA0050	38,62B,41
Till, Sophie	PA2200	62A,62B,13C,32E
Tirado, Hector	PR0100	62B
Tischer, Raymond	CA3300	62B
Topolovec, David	WI1155	62B,62C,62D
Toren-Immerman, Limor	CA0810	62A,62B,13C
Toyonaga, Shiho	IL2100	62B,51
Tramposh, Shelly	NY3780	41,62B
Tree, Michael	NY0150	62B
Tree, Michael	NY2150	62B
Tree, Michael	PA0850	62B
Tree, Michael	NY1900	62B
Tretick, Stephanie	PA0600	62A,62B
Tuhuilka, Olga	WI0150	62B
Tung, Alice Clair	MD0520	62B,41
Tung, Alice	MD0300	62B
Turner, Thomas	MN1623	62B
Ullery, Benjamin	CA1075	62B
Uscher, Nancy	CA0510	62B
Uyeyama, Jason	CA2420	42,51,62A,62B
Vaida, John M.	PA3700	62A,62B
Vaida, John	PA2200	61,62A,62B
Valcarcel, Andres	PR0100	62A,62B,51,38

Index by Area of Teaching Interest

Name	Code	Areas
Vamos, Roland	IL2250	62B
Van Der Sloot, Michael	AA0040	62A,62B,38,41
Van der Werff, Ivo-Jan	TX2150	62B,42
Van Gee, Jill	TX2260	62B
VanBecker, Leslie	MI0350	62B
VanBurkleo-Carbonara, Natalie	MN0040	62A,62B
Vanderwerf, Paul	IL3550	62A,62B
VanValkenburg, James	MI2200	62B
Vargas, Luis Enrique	IN0910	62B
Vargas, Luis	IN0005	62B
Vela, Gloria	AZ0440	62B
Veligan, Igor	CA5350	62B,42,62A
Vendryes, Basil	CO0900	62B
Vernon, Robert	NY1900	62B
Vernon, Robert	OH0600	62B
Vlajk, Christine	AG0600	62B
Wagner, Lorraine	WY0115	62A,62B,62C,62D,51
Walden, Kathy	OR0750	62A,62B
Walker, Gregory T. S.	CO0830	11,62A,20G,62B,46
Wallace, Elizabeth Kuefler	UT0325	62B
Walther, Geraldine E.	CO0800	42,62B
Ward, Miriam English	OR0600	62A,62B
Warlick, Leslie Taylor	SC0400	62A,62B
Washecka, Tim	TX2650	62B,62A
Washiyama, Kaori	VT0050	62A,62B
Wassertzug, Uri	DC0100	62B
Wassertzug, Uri	DC0150	62B
Watras, Melia	WA1050	62B
Watson, Larry	NY5000	62A,62B
Weaver, Andrew H.	DC0050	12A,12,12C,62B
Weaver, Ann	AZ0480	62A,62B
Weaver, Michael A.	SC0950	12A,11,32,62A,62B
Wedell, Steven	OH2050	62B
Wee-Yang, Jeannette	WA1350	62B
Wei, Sharon	CA4900	62B
Weiler, Ella Lou	MA0950	62B
Weimann, Viljar P.	AL1250	62A,62B,38,10F
Weisberg, Diane K.	FL0650	62B
Weller, Ira	NY0150	62B,42
Weller, Ira	NY2250	62B,41
Weller, Ira	NY3785	62B,42,51
Wetherbee, Sarah M.	NY5000	62A,62B
Wetzel, Minor	CA3300	62B
Wheeler, Ron	OK0850	38,60B,62B
White, Manami	OH2550	62A,62B
White-Smith, Juliet	OH1850	62B
Wieck, Anatole	ME0440	38,62A,62B,11
Wilcox, Fred J.	MD0300	62A,62B
Wilcox, John	OH2600	38,62A,62B,41
Windt, Paul	PA2550	62A,62B
Wirth, Julius	MD0100	62B
Wolf, Annalee	MN1450	62B
Womack, Anna	HI0210	62B
Wood, Thomas G.	OH0700	62A,62B,12A,11
Woodman, Sarah	AA0020	62B
Woolweaver, Scott	MA2010	38,41,51,62B,62A
Wright, Margaret	DC0170	41,62A,62B
Wu, Shuang	GA1450	62A,62B
Wyman, Pat	AF0120	62A,62B,38
Wyrczynski, Stephen	IN0900	62B
Xiao, Hong-Mei S.	AZ0500	62B
Xie, Song	MS0385	62A,62B
Xie, Song	MS0100	62A,62B,51,42
Yamada, Sojiro	LA0900	62A,62B,62C,62D
Yanovskiy, Leonid	FL1500	62A,62B,38
Yanovskiy, Leonid	FL2100	62A,62B,38,11,41
Yarbrough, Paul R.	CA4200	41,62B,42
Yi, Young	WI0100	62A,62B
Ying, Phillip	NY1100	42,62B
Yonan, David	IL2100	62A,62B
Yonetani, Ayako	FL1800	62A,62B,42
Young, Alice	MD0400	62B
Yu, Ling	UT0200	62B
Yu, Xiaoqing	TN0850	62A,62B,41
Yuzefovich, Victor	MD0150	12A,12,62B,32I
Zabelle, Kim A.	WA0800	62A,62B,67A,51
Zabenova, Ainur	NY4320	62A,62B
Zank, Jeremy	OH1800	51,62A,62B
Zaplatynsky, Andrew	NY1550	51,62A,62B
Zaretsky, Michael	MA0400	62B
Zeitlin, Louise R.	OH0200	62B
Zelkowicz, Isaias	PA0550	62B
Zezelj-Gualdi, Danijela	GA0940	62A,62B,51
Zezelj-Gualdi, Danijela	NC2440	62A,62B,13C
Zhang, Yun	VA0150	62A,62B
Zhou, Xiao-fu	PA3250	62B
Zhou, Xiao-Fu	PA2800	62A,62B
Zuckerman, Pinchas	NY2150	62A,62B
Zweig, Mimi	IN0900	62B

Cello

Name	Code	Areas
Aaron, Richard L.	NY1900	62C
Abbott, Norman	AG0500	62C
Abondolo, Gianna	CA2950	62C
Adams, Greta	KS0400	62C,62D,61
Adams, Lowell	FL2050	51,62C
Adams, Norman	AF0120	62C
Adkins, Christopher	TX2400	62C
Adkins, Darrett	OH1700	62C
Adkins, Darrett	NY1900	62C
Aerie, Josh	MN0450	62C
Aerie, Josh	WI0860	62C
Akahoshi, Ole	CT0850	62C
Aks, David M.	CA0835	12A,13C,39,60B,62C
Albers, Julie	GA1300	62C
Albert, Heidi A.	OH0700	62C
Allcott, Dan J.	TN1450	38,60B,62C,11,42
Altino, Leonardo	TN1680	62C,42
Altman, Barbara	GA0850	62C
Anderson, Elaine M.	OH2290	62C,13,38,41,42
Anderson, Elizabeth	IL2100	62C
Anderson, Erik	ND0250	62D,62C,13,51,29
Anderson, Tim H.	MD0520	62C
Anderson, Timothy	MD0475	62C
Anthony, Janet	WI0350	12A,41,62C,51
Appenheimer-Vaida, Christiane	PA2200	62C,41,32E
Archbold, Timothy	IL0400	62C
Arcu, Ariana	AL1250	62C
Armstrong, Alan	NC1500	12A,14B,13,62C,66A
Arndt, Wayne	NJ0550	62C
Arnone, Anthony R.	IA1550	62C
Artmann, Mary	CO0275	62C,42,51
Atanasiu, George	NJ1050	62C
Atapine, Dmitri	NV0100	62C,42,11
Attebery, Brian	ID0100	62C
Audi, Carlos	FL0930	62C
Avery, Dawn	MD0550	20,42,62C
Babich, Christina	OH1000	62C
Bacon, Anthony	AG0170	62C
Baek, Na-Young	NJ0700	62C
Bagratuni, Suren	MI1400	62C
Bai, Pauline	HI0050	62C
Bailen, Eliot T.	NY0750	62C,41
Bailey, Zuill	TX3520	62C
Balderston, Stephen	IL0750	62C
Baldwin, Kurt	MO1830	51,62C
Baldwin, Wesley H. B.	TN1710	62C
Balk, Malcolm	NY3775	62C
Bar-David, Ohad	PA3250	62C,62D
Barbu, Simona	ND0500	62C,62D
Barczyk, Cecylia	MD0175	62C
Barczyk, Cecylia	MD0850	41,62C,32E,51
Bardston, Robert	AA0040	66H,66B,38,41,62C
Barnes, Ariel	AB0200	62C
Barnet, Lori A.	DC0100	62C,51
Bartlett, Eric	NY1900	62C
Bass, Walden	NY1550	62C
Bateman, Nancy	MS0100	62C
Bazala Kim, Alison	MD0500	62C
Bazala Kim, Alison E.	MD0150	62C,41
Bazala-Kim, Allison	MD0060	62C
Beaver, Gregory	NE0600	62C,42
Beavers, Clyde E.	KY1350	62C
Bebe, David M.	NY0700	38,13,42,62C
Becker, Karen A.	NE0600	62C,42,13C
Beevers, Suzanne	NY1350	62C
Ben-Pazi, Tamar	SC0420	62C
Benmann, Martine	IL2750	62C
Bennett, John L.	CA3400	62C
Bent, Catherine	MA0260	13C,62C
Bergamo, Janet	CA5360	62C
Berkhout, Bjorn	NY3250	10,62C,12A,13,14C
Bermudez, Ana Ruth	WI1150	62C
Berry, Sarah	KY1550	62C
Bersin, Michael D.	MO1790	11,12A,62C,62D
Biava, Luis Gabriel	OH1200	62C,51
Biber, Sarah J.	MT0200	13B,41,62C
Billmayer, Veneta A.	AL1160	62C
Binford, Patrick	KY0450	62C
Binford, Patrick	KY0610	62C
Bing, Delores M.	CA0500	62,41,42,62C
Biskupski, Tadeusz	MI1260	62C
Bjella, David E.	FL1750	41,62C
Bjorlie, Carol	WI0845	11,62C
Black, Alan R.	NC0850	62C
Black, Alan	NC0550	62C,42
Black, Jacqueline	PA1200	62C
Blair, Suanne Hower	KY0900	12A,62C,62D,62E
Blalock, James	GA1500	62D,62C
Blecha-Wells, Meredith	OK0800	62C,11,42
Boden-Luethi, Ruth	WA1150	62C,62D,13,51,42
Bookhammer, Evelyn	PA1650	62C
Bootland, Christine	AA0040	62C
Borys, Roman	AG0450	62C
Bottelli, Roberta	WA1350	62C
Boyd, Bruce	KS1250	62A,62B,70,32E,62C
Boyd, Fern Glass	MT0400	12A,51,62C,11
Boyko, Megan	AF0120	62C
Bozell, Casey	OR0150	62A,62B,38,62C,51
Brennand, Meg	WA0800	62C
Brewer, Spencer	GA1450	62C,62D
Brey, Carter	PA0850	51,62C
Brofsky, Natasha	NY1900	62C,42
Brofsky, Natasha	MA1400	62C
Brown, Kayson	UT0050	62C
Brown, Lindsay	OH0100	62C,62D,51
Brubeck, Cornelia	FL0650	62C
Brubeck, Matthew	AG0650	43,53,62C
Bryenton, Andrew	TN0250	62C
Bucchianeri, Diane	OK1450	11,12A,41,62C
Buchholz, Theodore	AZ0480	62C
Buranskas, Karen	IN1700	41,62C
Burns, Elizabeth D.	SC1200	62C
Burns, Elizabeth	NC2000	62C,62D
Burton, John R.	TX3500	62C,42
Burton, Warren L.	UT0300	11,32A,32B,62C
Bustamante, Linda	FL1300	11,38,51,62C,62D
Butler, Jocelyn	WI0250	62C,42
Butler, Louise	WA0950	62C
Cadieux, Marie-Aline	PA1900	62C
Cadieux, Marie-Aline	PA1750	13,11,51,62C,42
Call, Monica	UT0325	62C
Call, Monica	UT0050	62C
Calloway, Jason	FL0700	62C,43,42
Cameron, Michael B.	PA0950	62C,42
Campbell, Glenn	CA3640	62C
Camus, Amy E.	NY2550	62C
Cantrell, Elizabeth K.	VA0800	62C,62D
Caravan, Lisa	AL0200	62C,62D,32E
Carey, Tanya N.	IL0550	62C
Carey, Thomas C.	OH2275	62A,62B,38,62C
Carlton, David	WI0150	49,62C,62D
Carr, Colin	NY3790	41,62C
Carrera, Michael	OH1900	62C,42
Carter, Adam C.	VA1550	62C,51
Carter, Brian	NC0910	62C
Carter, David	MN1450	11,41,62C,42
Carter, Selina	NC2500	62C,67A
Cary, Neal	VA0250	51,62C
Cassel-Greer, Kirsten	TN1850	62C
Cassin, Daniel	LA0650	62C
Castro-Balbi, Jesus	TX3000	62C,41
Cetkovic, Igor	MI0100	62C
Champion, Kyle	CA5150	62C
Chang, Amy	OH2300	62C
Chang, Pansy Y.	OH1450	62C,51
Chang, Yoo-Jung	IA0700	62C
Chanteaux, Marcy K.	MI2200	62C
Chao, Fred	AZ0470	62C
Chapman, Susannah	NJ0700	62C,42,11
Cheifetz, Hamilton	OR0850	41,51,62C,20G,20F
Cheney, Elliott	UT0250	62C,11
Chenoweth, Jonathan	IA1800	62C
Chenoweth, Jonathan N.	IA1600	11,41,62C
Christopher, Paul	LA0550	10,13,51,62C,62D
Chung, Minna Rose	AC0100	62C,42,51
Church, Frank V.	CT0100	62C
Chute, Christina	ME0200	62C
Chute, Christina	ME0150	62C
Clark, Derek	WI0810	62C
Cleland, Gordon	AG0050	62C
Clift, Anna	MN1450	62C,42
Cline, Benjamin	KS0350	51,62C,62D,38
Cline, Daniel	AR0350	62C

Index by Area of Teaching Interest

Name	Code	Areas
Cole, David	FL1125	62C,42
Colon, Emilio	PR0115	62C
Colon, Emilio W.	IN0900	62C
Conable, William E.	OH1850	38,62C,32
Contino, Adriana	IN0900	62C
Cook, Andrew	CA3600	62C
Cook, Kim	PA2750	62C
Cook, Luke	MI1180	62C
Cook, Nathan J.	AD0050	42,62C
Cook, Scott A.	WI0825	62C,51,41
Cooper, James	PA2800	62C,42
Copenhaver, Lee R.	MI0900	13,11,12A,38,62C
Costanza, Christopher	CA4900	62C,41,51
Couturiaux, Clay	TX3420	60B,38,62C
Cox, Eleanor Christman	WI0700	62C,62D,60B
Crookall, Christine	GA0250	13A,13,62C,12A,41
Culp, Jennifer	CA4150	42,62C
Curry, Nick	FL1950	62C,12,11
Curtis, Charles	CA5050	13A,41,62C
Custer, Stephen	CA3100	62C
Czarkowski, Stephen	WV0550	62C,11,51
Czarkowski, Stephen	MD0550	38,62C,13A
Dalbey, Jenna	AZ0490	62C,42
Dalton, Phoebe A.	MN1300	62C
Danson, Joan	AF0120	62C
Darvill, Jackie	NY3770	62A,62C
Davies, Daniel E.	CA0850	62C,13A,11,13B
Davy, Karen	CA2250	62A,62B,62C,62D,41
Day-Javkhlan, Alicia	DC0170	62C
DeAlmeida, Saulo	KY0400	62C,42
DeLeon, Dorien	OR0400	62C,42
Deleury, Nadine	MI1750	62C
Delgado, Jan	NM0450	62C
Dempster, Loren	NY5000	62C
DeNicola, Alan	VT0200	62A,62B,62C
Dial, Frances	NY2400	62C
Diaz, Andres	TX2400	62C
Dikener, Solen	WV0400	11,12A,62C,62D
Ding, Jian	NC2435	62C
Dissmore, Randy L.	WI0835	62C
Dixon, Edward E.	WA1300	38,62C,13C,62D
Doane, Steven	NY1100	62C
Dobrinski, Kathy	OK1250	62C
Dolezal, Darry	MO1800	62C,42
Dolin, Elizabeth	AI0150	62C,51
Donakowski, Carl	VA0600	62C
Duckles, Lee	AB0200	62C
Duke-Kirkpatrick, Erika	CA0510	42,62C,51
Dumm, Bryan	OH0650	62C
Dumm, Bryan	OH0600	62C
Dunbar, Christine	WY0050	62C
Dunegan, Martha	WI0100	62C
Dunlop, John	NH0100	62C,41
Dyachkov, Yegor	AI0200	62C
Dyachkov, Yegor	AI0150	62C,42
Dzhuryn, Nazar V.	IL2150	62C
Dzhuryn, Nazar	IL0840	62C
Eckenrode, Bryan	NY0400	62C
Eckenrode, Bryan	NY4460	62C,62A
Eckstein, John B.	UT0250	62C
Edberg, C. Eric	IN0350	41,62C,13A
Eddy, Timothy	NY2250	41,62C
Eddy, Timothy	NY1900	62C
Edgerton, Sara A.	MO1500	11,12A,38,62D,62C
Edmonton-Boehm, Nigel	AA0050	62C
Eeles, Mark	AA0035	62C
Ehrlich, Janina	IL0100	11,12,41,62C
Eisenstein-Baker, Paula	TX3450	41,62C
Eldan, Amir	OH1700	62C
Elisha, Steven K.	GA0950	62C,62D,41,42
Elliot, William	MO0400	62C
Elliott, Anthony D.	MI2100	62C
Elliott, Rosemary	NY1100	62C
Ellis, Erin L.	GA1550	62C
Ellis, James	IA0400	62C
Elsing, Evelyn	MD1010	41,62C
Elworthy, Joseph	AB0200	62C,42,38
Emelianoff, Andre	NY1900	62C,41
Emerson, Deidre	TN1400	62C,38,51
Emerson, Stephen	UT0250	62C
Enyeart, Carter	MO1810	62C
Epperson, Bryan	AG0300	62C,42
Eppinga, Alicia	MI0850	62C
Eskin, Jules	MA0400	62C
Espinosa, Leandro	OR0200	62C,62D,38,13A,11
Eubanks, Amber	SC0200	62C
Evans, Laurel S.	PA3580	62C
Ewell, Philip	NY0625	13,13F,13I,62C
Ewoldt, Virginia	IL0300	62C
Ezerman, Alexander	NC2430	62C
Faganel, Gal	CO0950	62C,42,35G,51
Farny, Natasha	NY3725	62C
Farrell, Peter S.	CA5050	13,12A,62C,67A
Featherston, Mary	OH2000	62C
Fehrenbach, Paula	CA3500	62,62C
Fejer, Andras	CO0800	62C,41
Feldman, Marion	NY2150	41,62C
Feldman, Marion	NY2750	62C,42
Feldman, Marion	NY0500	62C
Feldman, Ronald	MA1400	62C
Feldman, Stephen B.	AR0850	11,41,62C
Fenner, Richard C.	CA1020	62C,66D
Ferguson, Danise J.	AE0050	13,41,62C
Ferrell, Sarah	PA3000	62C
Fesz, Maria	OH2290	62C
Finch, Mary-Katherine	AG0450	62C
Finckel, David	NY1900	62C,42
Finckel, David	NY3790	41,62C
Fischer, Norman	TX2150	42,62C
Fiser, Lee W.	OH2200	62C
Fisher, Yuko	IL1740	62A,62B,62C,41
Fishman, Guy	MA0510	11,62C
Fishman, Guy	RI0150	62C,55B
Fiste, James A.	MI0400	62C
Fitzgerald, Cheryl	TN1150	62C,62D
Flanagan-Zitoun, Braden	WI1150	62C
Flores, Amy	IL1750	41,62C
Flyer, Nina G.	CA0807	62C
Flyer, Nina	CA5350	62C,41,42
Folus, Brian H.	MD0475	62D,62A,62C
Fong, Leighton	CA5000	62C
Fonteneau, Jean-Michel	CA4150	62C,42
Forry, James L.	VA1475	62C
Forry, James	VA1150	62C
Fouse, Jennifer	CO0625	62C
Fowler, Kurt	IN0800	62C,11,12A,51
Fradette, Amelie	NY3717	62C,51
Francis, Anne	UT0300	62C
Francis, Nancy	TX1450	62C
Fraser, Judith	AB0200	62C
Freer, Karen	GA0750	62C
Freudigman, Ken	TX3530	62C
Friedel, Aileen	MO1250	62C
Friedel, Aileen	IL2970	62C
Friedman, Arnold J.	MA0260	10,62C,13
Friesen, John	WA1250	13,51,62C
Frisch, Miranora O.	NC2420	62C,11
Frittelli, Leslie	VA1000	62C,51,41
Fromme, Randolph	CA5070	62C
Fry, Ben	OH1600	62C
Fryer, Simon	AG0600	62C
Gabbert, Andrew	VA1400	62C
Gabbert, Andrew	VA1125	62C
Gagnon, Marie-Elaine	SD0600	11,51,62C,41
Galaganov, Misha	TX3000	62C,41
Gallego, Ignacio	TX2260	62C
Gant, Christina	PA3260	62A,62B,62C
Garrett, David B.	CA0825	62C
Garritson, Ashley	FL0200	62C
Gaston, Susan Deaver	MS0700	41,62C,62D
Gates, Stephen	AR0700	41,62C
Geber, David	NY2150	62C
Geber, Stephen	OH0600	62C
Geeseman, Katherine	TX3515	11,62C,62D
Geeting, Joyce	CA0550	62C
Gelfand, Michael D.	OH2600	62C,11
Gelfand, Peter	CA4425	62C
Gettes, Gretchen	MD0400	62C
Gilliam-Valls, Jessica	TX1150	13A,62C,62D
Gindele, Joshua	TX3510	62C,42
Gish, Benjamin	WA1100	62C,62D
Glyde, Judith	CO0800	11,51,62C
Goeke, Matthew	NY0270	11,62C
Golove, Jonathan	NY4320	10,62C
Gonzalez, Adam	MD0300	62C
Gordon, Joshua	MA0500	11,41,42,62,62C
Gordon, Nina	IL1200	62C,42
Goudimova, Julia	VA1850	62C
Grabe, Ann	OR0700	62C
Gray, Lawrence	IL3300	29,62C,62D
Green, Stephen	CA5355	62C
Greensmith, Clive S.	NY2750	51,62C
Greensmith, Clive	NY2150	62C
Gregory, George R.	TX2260	62C,62E
Greydanus, Peter	VA0150	62C
Grolman, Ellen K.	MD0350	12A,62C
Groschang, Sascha	KS1000	62C
Grubb, William	IN0250	62C
Gruber, Emanuel	NC0650	62C,42
Gustafson, Kirk	CO0225	13,10F,60,62C
Habitzruther, Bruce E.	VA0750	38,62C
Haimovitz, Matt	AI0150	62C
Haines-Eitzen, John	NY0900	62C,42
Halleran, Sandra	NY2650	62C
Hamar, Jon	WA0550	29,62C,62D,32E,51
Hamilton, Gregory	MN0600	62C
Hampton, Ian	AB0060	51,62C
Hampton, Ian	AB0090	62C
Han, Jinhee	KY0950	62C,62D
Hanani, Yuhuda	OH2200	62C
Harbaugh, Ross T.	FL1900	62C
Harchanko, Joseph	OR1250	10,13,62C
Hardie, William Gary	TX0300	62C,42
Hardy, David	MD0650	62C
Hardy, James	UT0150	62C,11,41
Harran, Roy	GA0050	62C
Harrell, David Alan	OH0650	62C
Harris, Alan	NY1100	62C
Harris, Kim	KY0250	12A,62B,62C
Harrison, Stephen J.	CA4900	62C
Hekmatpanah, Kevin	WA0400	11,12A,38,51,62C
Hekmatpanah, Kevin	ID0140	62C
Hernandez, Teresa	KS0700	62C
Herren, Matthew	KS1050	62C,62D
Hetherington, David	AG0300	62C
Higgins, Brenda L.	FL1550	62C,55B
Highbaugh Aloni, Pamela	AB0150	62C,42
Hillyard, Mary	MI0300	62C
Hirschl, Richard	IL0550	62C,42
Hodges, Brian D.	ID0050	62C,11,42
Hoebig, Desmond	TX2150	62C,42
Holbrook, Ashley	KS0150	62D,62C
Holley, Timothy	NC1600	14,62,62C,20G
Horn, Alisa	DC0170	62C
Hotchkiss, Richard	PA3330	62C
Hsu, John	NY0900	42,62C,67A,38,60B
Huang, Alice	MO0060	62C
Hudson, Virginia	NC1300	62C
Hufnagle, Kathryn	SD0050	62C
Hultgren, Craig	AL0300	62C,43
Hultgren, Craig	AL1150	11,62C
Hunn, Jana	CA4300	62C
Hunsinger, Melita	IN0905	62C
Husby, Betsy	MN1600	62C
Hutton, Christopher	SC0750	62C,12A,51
Huzjak, Amy	TX3527	62C
Hwang, Margery 'Mimi'	NY2650	62C
Hynes, Maureen	NY2105	38,67,62C,55,42
Interlandi, Silvio	CT0550	62C
Isaacson, Kristin	TX0900	13C,62C,62D
Isomura, Sachiya	MN1280	62C
Ivanov, Kalin H.	NY0500	41,62C
Jacob, Heidi	PA1500	38,42,62C
Jacobsen, Eric	NY2750	42,62C
Jacobson, Carol	CA2250	62C
Jacobson, James	MN0050	62C
Jaffe, Claudio	FL1450	62,38,62C
Jasinski, Nathan David	KY0550	62C,32E,38,42,13A
Jeanrenaud, Joan	CA2950	62C,42
Jee, Patrick	IL0550	62C
Jennings, Linda G.	PA1600	62C,62D,13,51
Jensen, Hans Jorgen	GA1300	62C
Jensen, Hans Jorgen	IL2250	62C
Jeon, Hyerim	KS1400	62C
Jesselson, Robert M.	SC1110	38,41,62C
Jetter, Katherine	CO0350	38,62C,62D,13,51
Johansen, Dane	NY1900	62C
Johns, Christopher	NC2440	62C,13A
Johns, Norman	OH2550	62C
Johnson, Marc Thomas	MA0400	62C,42
Jojatu, Mihail	MA1175	62C
Jones, Janet	AZ0150	38,62A,62C,62B,62D
Jones, Kate	AR0300	62C,62D
Joul, Susan	MI1830	62C
Judiyaba,	CA4700	52,62C
Kaatz, Jeffry M.	CA2420	62C

Index by Area of Teaching Interest

Name	Code	Areas
Kadz, John	AA0050	41,62C
Kaplunas, Daniel	IA1800	38,62C,62B,51,60
Kapps, Sarah	TX3525	62C
Karp, Benjamin	IN0900	62C
Karp, Benjamin	KY1450	41,62C,42
Karp, Parry	WI0815	51,62C
Kartman, Stefan	WI0825	62C,42,51,41
Kassarova, Petia	NY3600	62C
Katz, Paul	MA1400	62C
Kauffman, Rachel	PA3710	62C
Kazez, Daniel	OH2450	13A,11,20D,62C,62D
Keelan, Michael	NE0150	62A,62C
Kelly, Susan	DC0170	62C
Kemberling, Nan	GA0500	62C
Kemp, Kathleen	NY1100	62C
Kenney, Mary	GA0750	62C
Khoma, Natalia	SC0500	11,62C
Kiffner, Paula	AB0210	62C,42
Kilchyk, Olena	AA0050	32A,62C
Kim, Chungsun	NY2900	13,62C
Kim, Clara	NY4200	62C
Kim, Eric	IN0900	62C
Kim, Kee-Hyun	MN1625	62C
Kim, Yeesun	MA1400	41,62C
King, Joan	PA0650	62A,62B,62C,62D,31G
King, Terry B.	CT0650	51,62C
King, Terry	MA1175	62C
Kirkpatrick, Mary Beth	WV0560	62A,62B,62C,62D
Kirkscey, Jonathan	AR0110	62C,62D
Kirkwood, James H.	NY3730	51,62C
Kirshbaum, Ralph	CA5300	62C
Klein, Edward	FL0365	62C
Kluksdahl, Scott	FL2000	12A,62C
Knapp, Karl D.	AK0150	12A,62C
Knight, Katharine	CO0200	62C
Knight, Katharine	CO0900	62C,41
Ko, Bongshin	CA0815	62C
Koen, John	PA3250	62C
Koessel, Wolfram	NY2150	62C
Koh, Jonathan	CA5000	62C
Kohanski, Elisa C.	PA1450	62C
Kosower, Mark	OH0600	62C
Kosower, Paula	IL2100	62C
Kosower, Paula	IL2250	62C
Kouguell, Alexander	NY0642	62C
Kouzov, Dmitry	IL3300	62C
Kramer, Jonathan C.	NC1700	11,12A,20D,20A,62C
Kraut, Melissa	OH0600	62C
Krieger, David	NY5000	62C
Krieger, David	NY2400	62C,41
Krosnick, Joel	NY1900	51,62C
Krueger, Charae	GA1150	62C,42
Krummel, Karen	MI0350	62C
Kubin, Brian	MO1780	62C,13,51,62D
Kulosa, Kenneth	MO1950	62C
Kutz, Eric A.	IA0950	62C,32E,42
Kuyvenhoven, Cora	OH0850	62C
Kuyvenhoven, Cora	OH2050	62C
Lacarme, Alexandre	MA0400	62C
Ladd, Gita	MD1000	41,42,62C
Lamb Cook, Susan	CA0150	62C
Landschoot, Thomas V.	AZ0100	62C
Lange-Jensen, Catherine	KY1000	62C,41
Langenberg, Claire Coyle	IL2050	62C
Lapham, Barbara	ME0430	62C
Lapin, Geoff	IN0500	62C
Lara, Elizabeth K.	TN0050	62C,13,62D,62B
Lastrapes, Jeffrey Noel	TX3200	62C,42,51,11,32E
Laufer, Wolfgang	WI0825	62C
Laut, Edward A.	KS1350	41,62C
Law, Cameron	CO0225	62C
Le Guin, Elisabeth C.	CA5032	12A,12,62C,67B,15
Lebow, Roger	CA0960	62C
Lebow, Roger B.	CA3650	62C
Lee, Alexandra	AG0070	62C
Lee, Charles	CO0550	62C
Lee, Charles	CO0650	62C,41,51,10F,60
Lee, Cheng-Hou	IL2200	62C,51
Lee, Christine	SC0200	62C,60B
Lee, Elizabeth	TX3100	62C
Lenz, Eric	IL2900	13,62C
Leonard, Ronald	CA1075	62C,42
Lerner, Paige Stockley	WA0200	62C
Leslie, Evan A.	TX3450	62C
Lesser, Laurence	MA1400	62C
Lessie, Erica	IL2750	62C
Leviton, Lawrence	WI0850	11,62C
Levitov, Daniel	PA1400	62C,38,42,11
Li, Darren Si-Yan	IN0910	62C
Lichten, Julia	NY2150	62C
Lichten, Julia	NY3785	62C,41
Lim, Margaret	NE0100	62C
Lin, Chloe	MO0060	62A,62B,62C,38
Lin, I-Bei	HI0050	62C
Lin, I-Bei	HI0210	62C,41,42,13A
Lipman, Michael	PA0600	62C,41
Lipscomb, Ronald	PA1150	62C,62D
Lipscomb, Ronald	PA1000	51,62C
Littrell, David	KS0650	38,41,62C,62D,13A
Liu, Si-Cheng	FL0500	62C
Liu, Si-Cheng	FL0680	62C
Lockwood, Shannon	FL1000	62C
Loewenheim, Thomas	CA0810	62C,62D,38
Longo, Tatiana	NY5000	62C
Lopez, Emmanuel	TX3750	62C
Low, David G.	NE0610	12A,62C
Lowe, Cameron	AJ0100	62C
Luchansky, Andrew	CA0840	13A,51,62C
Lum, Gloria	CA3300	62C
Lurie, Kenneth P.	NC0050	13A,62C,42
Lyman, Rebecca	ID0060	62C
Lynn, Robert	IN0700	13,37,38,62C,63D
Lysy, Antonio	CA5030	62C,42
Maahs, Kristin	IA0700	62C,51
Macdonald, Elizabeth	MO1900	41,62C
Machavariani, David	IN1750	62C
Maddox, Nan	GA1700	62C,42
Magney, Lucia	MN0350	62C,62D,32E,42
Mahave-Veglia, Pablo	MI0900	42,62C,55B
Maldonado, Ana Marie	CA0630	13A,62C,20H
Maldonado, Ana Maria	CA0845	32,62C,51
Male, Sara	PA1250	62C,51
Manker, Brian	AI0150	62C
Mansell, Bradley	TN1850	62C
Mantell, Emily	IL2650	62C
Mantell, Emily Lewis	IL3100	62C
Marinescu, Ovidiu	PA3600	38,62C,51
Mark, Andrew	MA0350	62C
Markstein, Joan	FL0150	62C
Marlatt, Margot	IN1850	62C
Marleyn, Paul	AG0400	62C
Marshall, John	WA0250	62C,70,32E,41,32F
Martin, CarolAnn F.	MO0800	62C,62D
Martin, Chris	TX2800	62C
Martinez, Everaldo	ND0400	62A,62B,62C,51,38
Matthews, Margaret	NY1150	62A,62B,62C
Mautner-Rodgers, Sharon	MN0750	62C
May, Tom	FL0680	62C
Mayo, Susan	KS0300	62C,62D
McCafferty, Dennis S.	IN1650	62C,41
McCleery, Mark	LA0770	11,41,62C,62D
McComb, Dana	VA1600	62C
McComb, Jason B.	VA1500	62C
McConville, Brendan P.	TN1710	13,13F,13I,62C
McCreery, Carlton	AL1170	38,62C
McCullough, Thomas Eric	OK1330	10,62C,13,38,10C
McIntosh, Andrew	AG0550	62C
McIntosh, Bruce	OR1300	13,38,62C
Meade, Michael	NY2200	62C
Meineke, Robert	TX2350	62A,62B,62C,62D,51
Meir, Eran	IL3450	62C
Melik-Stepanov, Karren	IA1200	62C
Melik-Stepanov, Karren	IA0500	62C
Melik-Stepanov, Karren	SD0050	62C,51
Mercer, Ida K.	OH0600	62C
Mermagen, Michael	DC0050	62C
Metzler, Linda	PA3550	62C
Meyers, Joe	NY2750	62C
Michel, John	WA0050	11,41,51,62C
Miller, Ken	MN1250	62C,51
Mirhady, Tom	AA0050	62C
Molina, Moises	IL3500	62C,51
Mollenauer, David	TX2200	62C
Mollenauer, David	TX3350	62C
Molzan, Ryan	AI0190	42,62C
Monson, Anne	IL0730	62C
Moon, Eileen	NY2750	62C
Moore, Edward	IL0850	62C
Moore, Nancy	IL0275	62C
Morgan, Lauren R.	MO0250	62A,62B,62C,62D,51
Morrow, Elizabeth N.	TX3500	62C,51,11
Morton, Rebecca	AG0200	62C
Morton, Susan	LA0760	62C
Moulton, David	PA2550	62C
Moulton, David	PA2450	62C
Mueller, Joseph	OH0350	62C
Muhly, Alexa	IL2750	62C
Muller-Szerwas, Jan	MA0700	62C,42
Murray, Linda	WY0130	62C
Murray, Michael A.	MO0775	13,51,62C
Myers, Benjamin C.	MD0400	62C
Napper, Susie	AI0200	62C,67B
Nauman, Sharon	OH1350	62C
Neikrug, George	MA0400	62C
Nelson, Elise Buffat	ND0350	62C,41,42
Nelson, Elise	MN1120	62C
Nelson, Gregory	MN1300	62C
Nelson, Paul	TN0100	62C
Nepkie, Janet	NY3765	13A,41,51,62C,35
Nicholas, Keith	TN0100	62C
Niezen, Richard S.	CO0150	62C,62D,13C,13G
Nigro, Christine	MA0150	62C
Nisbet, Allen	LA0300	62C
Nordlund, Samuel	AL0800	62C
Oh, Kyung-Nam	IN1560	62C,42
Oh, Kyung-Nam	IN0100	62C,38
O'Neill, SC, Alice Ann M.	OH0680	32E,62C,41,62D
Onwood, Susannah	IN1010	62C
Opie, Peter	IN0150	62C
Orban, Suzanne	MD0750	62C
Osadchy, Eugene	TX3420	62C
Ou, Carol	MA0950	62C,42
Owen, Drew	DC0150	62C
Padrichelli, Andra	OH0450	62C
Panteleyev, Vladimir	NY0500	62C
Parisot, Aldo S.	CT0850	62C
Park, Mary B.	NY1600	62C
Parke, Nathaniel	VT0050	62C
Parke, Nathaniel	MA2250	62C,43,41
Parke, Nathaniel	NY3650	62C
Parker, Dennis N.	LA0200	62C
Parker, Erica	OK0850	62C
Parker, Mara	PA3680	12A,11,41,51,62C
Parkins, Margaret	CA2390	62C
Parkins, Margaret Clara	CA5020	62C
Parman, David L.	IN1800	41,62C,62D,70,20G
Parnas, Leslie	MA0400	62C
Parrette, Anne	FL0800	62C
Pecherek, Michael J.	IL1175	13,60,11,38,62C
Peckham, Merry	OH0600	51,62C
Pegis, John	IL2250	62C
Peled, Amit	MD0650	62C
Pelletier, Marie Volcy	MA1750	62C,42
Peng, Bo	AB0060	62C,51
Pera, Adriana	NY5000	62C
Perrault, Jean R.	MN1600	60,62A,62B,62C,38
Perron, Johanne	AI0200	62C,41
Peshlakai, David	MI1000	42,62C
Phelps, Amy	IA0300	62C,42
Phillips, Susan	IL1100	62C
Photinos, Nicholas	VA1500	43,62C
Picht-Read, Kathryn	PA3250	62C
Pickart, John	WI0100	62C
Pierce, Carrie	TX2930	62C,62D,51,31A,13C
Piippo, Richard	MI1050	38,41,51,62C,10F
Pinkney, Rachel	OH0250	62C,62
Pinkney, Rachel	OH1800	62C,62D
Pinnell-Jackson, Nicole	UT0325	62C
Polk, Suzanne	VT0450	62C
Pologe, Steven	OR1050	62C,42
Popov, Vasily	DC0170	62C,41
Popwell, Brooks	SC0650	62C
Porter, William Anthony	IL1085	62C,42
Premo, David	PA0550	62C
Price, Matt	MO1550	62C,62D
Prochazka, Tanya	AA0100	62C,41
Pulford, Paul	AG0600	41,62C,38
Puls, Cyndi	OH1400	11,62C,62D
Pyle, Laura	SC0400	62C,42
Pyron, Nona	CA5550	62C
Raimi, Frederic B.	NC0600	62C,42
Rammon, Andrew	PA0350	62C
Rammon, Andrew	PA2100	62C
Rammon, Andrew	PA3150	62C,51
Rammon, Philip A.	PA2150	62C
Ramos, Mary Ann	AZ0450	62C,41

659

Name	Code	Areas
Randman, Bennett	MS0400	62C
Ransom, Adriana LaRosa	IL1150	11,62C
Raschen, Gudrun E.	TX3300	62D,62C,67B,51
Ratzlaff, Dieter	OR1100	62C
Ray-Carter, Trilla	MO2000	51,62C,42
Raychev, Evgeni	TX2700	62C,41,11,62D
Reed, Elizabeth	CA2950	62C
Reeder, Deborah	PA3250	62C
Reeve, Douglas	MO0300	62C,62D
Regehr, Vernon	AD0050	62C,38,42
Remenikova, Tanya	MN1623	41,62C
Remy, Elisabeth	GA1050	62C
Remy-Schumacher, Tess	OK1330	62C,41,42
Renard-Payen, Florent	NY0650	62C
Renyer, Erinn	KS0050	62C,62D,51,42
Requiro, David	WA1000	62C,41,42
Rex, Christopher	GA1050	62C
Reynolds, Michael	MA0400	62C
Ribchinsky, Julie C.	CT0050	13A,13C,62C,11,38
Rice, Alexandria	GA0940	62C
Rider, Rhonda	MA0400	62C
Rider, Rhonda	MA0350	41,62C
Riggs, Paige	PA3100	62C
Riley, Susanna	PA0100	62C
Rivas, Aristides	MA2030	62C
Roberts, Sherill	OR0250	62C
Roberts, Sherill	OR0450	62C
Robertshaw, Manon	CA1750	62C
Robertshaw, Manon	CA5040	62C
Robertshaw, Manon	CA2800	62C
Robertshaw, Manon	CA0859	62C
Robinson, Cathy Meng	OH1100	62C,42
Robinson, Keith	OH1100	62C,42
Rodgers, Joseph	MN0200	62C
Rodgers, Joseph W.	MN1000	38,62C,13,62D
Rodgers, Mark	AA0200	62C
Roebke, Catherine	TX3535	62C
Rogoff, Noah T.	NE0590	62C,62D,13A,13B
Rojas, Luis Miguel	PR0115	62C,41,42
Rolston, Shauna	AG0450	62C
Rondon, Tulio J.	WI0803	62C,32E
Rosborough-Bowman, Monika	UT0050	62C
Roscetti, Diane	CA0835	42,62C,35A
Rosen, Marcy	NY0642	62C,42
Rosen, Marcy	NY2250	62C
Rosenberg, Thomas	MN0300	62C,41
Rosenberg, Thomas A.	MN0950	62C
Ross, Paul	ME0250	62C
Ross, Sally	NC1100	62C,62D
Rosser, Christina	OH2150	62C
Rothmuller, Daniel	CA5300	62C
Round, Sue	AB0050	62C
Rounds, William	ME0500	62C
Rowell, Frances	NJ0825	62C
Rozsnyal, Zoltan	AB0200	62C
Rubenstein, Natasha	MO0650	62C
Ruck, Jonathan C.	OK1350	62C,41
Rudoff, Mark	OH1850	62C
Rudolph, Richard	VA0550	62A,38,62B,62C,65B
Rudolph, Shay	MA0650	62C
Russakovsky, Alexander	MS0750	62C
Russell, Carol	IN1450	62C
Russell, David	MA2050	62C
Rutkowski, Geoffrey	CA5060	41,62C
Ruzevic, Nikola	TX3420	42,62C
Saenz, Daniel	TX2250	62C
Saenz, Daniel	TX2295	62C
Saks, Toby	WA1050	41,62C
Salvo, Joel	MN0040	62C,11
Sambo, Adrienne	MA2100	62C
Sandvoss, Beth Root	AA0050	62C
Sandvoss, Beth Root	AA0150	62C
Saradjian, Vagram	TX3400	62C
Sauer, Gregory D.	FL0850	62C
Schepps, David M.	NM0450	62C,41
Schlaikjer, Katie	CT0600	62C
Schlessinger, Laura	AA0050	62C
Schottman, Margret	PA0500	62A,62B,62C
Schoyen, Jeffrey G.	MD0800	62C,38,13A,11,62D
Schroeder, Thomas	TX1400	62C
Schulz, Mark Alan	OH1350	34D,35G,35D,62C,29B
Schween, Astrid	MA1350	62C
Seitz, Noah	OR0750	62C
Seligman, Susan	NY3760	13A,13C,11,41,62C
Sellitti, Anne	NC0350	62C,62D
Sellitti, Anne	NC2205	62C,51
Semmes, Carol	IL2300	62C
Sepe, Deborah	NY0050	62C
Sexton, Norma	CA0650	62C
Shaar, Erik	NC0450	62C,62D
Shao, Sophie S.	NY4450	62C
Shao, Sophie	NY0150	62C
Shapiro, Jarred	VT0100	62C,11,20
Sharp, Irene	NY2250	62C
Sharp, Irene	CA5000	62C
Sharp, John	IL0550	62C
Shaw, Clyde Thomas	VA1350	62C,42,12A,41
Shaw, Laura	IA0930	62C
Shaw, Olive	AF0120	62C
Shelton, Evan	CO0200	62C
Sherry, Fred	NY2150	62C
Sherry, Fred	NY1900	62C
Sherry, Fred	NY2250	62C
Shufro, Joseph L.	IA1100	10F,13E,34,38,62C
Shukaev, Leonid	KS1450	62C
Shumway, Jeanne	CA0600	62C
Sidon, Ashley Sandor	IA0550	62C,32E,41
Silver, Noreen	ME0440	42,32E,13C,62C
Simidtchieva, Marta	IL2910	38,42,41,51,62C
Simkin, Elizabeth	NY1800	62C
Simon, Benjamin	CA5000	62C
Simons, Audrey K.	PA2450	62C
Simonson, Jessica	OR1000	62A,62B,62C
Sirois, Carole	AI0200	62C
Skidmore, William	WV0750	13,41,62C
Skogen, Meaghan	NC0750	62C,13,41
Slavich, Richard	CO0900	12A,51,62C,41
Smelser, Linc	IL3550	62C
Smelser, Linc	IL2200	62C
Smith, Alan M.	OH0300	62C,42,38
Smith, Andrew	NV0050	62C
Smith, Brent	UT0190	39,62C,13,12A,51
Smith, Brinton Averil	TX2150	62C
Smith, Caitlin Maura	AA0020	62C
Smith, Judith	CT0800	62C,32E,41
Smith, Sam	ID0070	62C,51,38
Snider, Nancy Jo	DC0010	62C,42,51,67B,41
Snider, Nancy	DC0350	62C
Snow, Andrew	IL3150	62C
Solow, Jeffrey G.	PA3250	62C
Sophos, Anthony	NY2400	62C
Sorensen, Ann	LA0250	62A,62B,62C,62D
Soyer, David	NY2150	62C
Soyer, David	PA0850	62C
Spencer, Barbara	CA0600	62C
Spencer, Sandy	MA0600	62C
Spitz, Jonathan	NJ1130	62C
Stalker, Stephen	NY0350	62C
Stalker, Stephen T.	NY3705	62C,62D
Stanley, Parker	KS0200	62C
Stanton, Laurel	FL1800	62C
Starker, Janos	IN0900	62C
Starkweather, David A.	GA2100	51,62C
Staron, Timothy	OH1000	62A,62C,38
Steadman, Russell	TX0100	38,62C
Stein-Mallow, Barbara	NY2250	62C
Steiner, Frances	CA0805	62C
Stepansky, Alan	NY2150	62C
Stepansky, Alan	MD0650	62C
Stephan, Charles	WI0830	62C
Stillwell, Jonathan	FL1700	62C
Stinson, Caroline	NY1900	62C
Stinson, Caroline S.	NY4150	62C
Stomberg, Lawrence J.	DE0150	62C,51
Storey, Martin	MO1000	51,62C
Strachan, Heather	GA2000	51,62A,62C
Streetman, Nancy	FL1745	62C
Stroud, James	TN1350	62C
Struman, Susan Jean	TX0550	51,62C,32A,11,62D
Stumpf, Peter	CA5300	62C
Stumpf, Peter	IN0900	62C
Suda, Carolyn	IL1800	11,12A,62C,38,42
Suda, Carolyn W.	IL1350	11,42,51,62C
Sudderth, Janette	MS0385	66A,62C
Suits, Thad	MT0370	62C
Suleiman, Alexander	CA5300	62C
Sunderland, Jose	AL1300	62C
Sutherland, Enid	MI2100	62C
Swora, Matthew	MI1950	62C,62D
Szepessy, David	NJ0175	62C
Tait, Malcolm	AG0500	62C
Tang, Betty	PA1850	62C
Tang, Pin-Fei	CA2420	62C
Tarr, Carol	CO0900	62C
Tatge, Valorie	OK1200	62C
Tatge, Valorie	OK0700	62C
Taylor, Brant	IL0750	62C
Taylor, Priscilla	MA2010	13,10,62C,41
Taylor, Steve M.	GA2150	62C,11
Tchekmazov, Andrey	MN1625	62C
Tehan, Julie	IL3550	62C
Teie, David	VA0450	62C
Teie, David	MD1010	62C
Terauchi, Kristi	AZ0510	62C
Terkeek, Karen	CO0830	62C
Tetel, Mihai	CT0650	62C
Thiem, Barbara	CO0250	41,62C,42
Thomas, Richard	SC0800	62C
Thomas, Richard B.	SC1000	62C,11,38,12A,62D
Thomas, Steven F.	FL1850	62C
Thompson, Fiona	PA2300	62C,51
Thompson, Jason	IN1025	38,62A,62B,51,62C
Thompson, Karin E.	WA1100	62C,20,12A,42,13C
Thornblade, Rebecca E.	MA2050	62C
Thorson, Lee	IA0150	62C,62D
Tisdel, Scott	WI1150	62C
Tobias, Paul	NY2250	62C
Tomkins, Tanya	CA4400	62C
Topolovec, David	WI1155	62B,62C,62D
Tormann, Wolf	AG0250	62C,51
Tortolano, Jonathan	PA2250	62C
Townsend, Brendan	TX1425	10F,11,12A,13,62C
Treat, Richard	WA0650	62C
Trtan, Jacqueline	MO0350	51,62C
Truelove, Lisa	OR0950	62C
Tsang, Bion	TX3510	62C,42
Tueller, Robert F.	ID0060	38,62C,67B
Turovsky, Yuli	AI0200	62C
Tzvaras, Nicholas G.	NJ0800	62C,42
Uchimura, Bruce	MI2250	60,51,62C
Ultan, Jacqueline	MN1050	62C
Underwood, Kirsten F.	OK0150	62,38,11,62C,20
Uzur, Viktor	UT0350	13,10F,51,62C,42
Vamos, Brandon	IN0900	62C,42
Vamos, Brandon	IL3300	51,62C
Vance, Paul	MN1700	12A,62D,38,51,62C
Vander Weg, Judith B.	MI2200	62C
Vanderborgh, Beth	WY0200	41,62C,55B
Vardi, Uri	WI0815	62C
Varosy, Zsuzsanna	FL1650	62C
Varosy, Zsuzshanna	FL0450	41,62C
Vaska-Haas, Kristina	LA0050	62C
Vazquez, Anna	MN1295	62C
Veal, Larry	NH0350	11,62C,13A,41
Velasco, Wendy	CA6000	62C
Verbsky, Franklin	NY1600	62,62C,62D,11
Vial, Stephanie	NC2410	62C
Vierra, Alice	DC0170	62C
Von Dassow, Sasha	FL1745	51,62C
Votapek, Mark A.	AZ0500	62C
Wada, Rintaro	NY1700	62C
Wade, Adrienne Sambo	MA1100	62C
Wagner, Lorraine	WY0115	62A,62B,62C,62D,51
Wagner, Shelbi	OH2250	62C,51,32E
Walt, Shimon	AF0100	62C
Wampner, Barbara	CA1650	62C
Wang, Felix	TN1850	62C,41,51
Wang, Guang	GA0750	62C
Wang, Hong	MN0250	62C
Warner, Wendy	GA0550	62C,42
Watson, Gwendolyn	GA0300	62C
Watts, Ronald	GA1070	62C
Webb, Jennifer	IN0005	62C,62D
Webber, Sophie C.	IL1400	62C,20,12A
Weber, Robert	IL1300	62C,51
Weilerstein, Alisa	OH0600	62C
Weinstein, Alan	VA1700	62C,62D,12B
Weinstein, Alan	VA1250	41,62C,62D,70
Weiss, Richard	OH0600	62C,51
Wells, Alison	MD0650	62C,42
Wexler, Mathias K.	NY3780	41,62C
Whang, Pegsoon	UT0400	62C
Whang, Pegsoon	UT0250	62C
Wharton, William	ID0250	13,41,62C,62D
Wheatley, Jennifer	IN0400	62C
Whitcomb, Benjamin	WI0865	62C,13C,13E,13K,13

Index by Area of Teaching Interest

Name	Code	Areas
Whitehouse, Brooks	NC1650	62C
Whittenburg, Ben	NY1400	62C
Widner, Paul	AG0300	62C,42
Wiebe, Thomas	AG0500	62C,41
Wiley, Peter	NY0150	62C,42
Wiley, Peter	PA0850	41,62C
Williams, Anne Martindale	PA0550	62C
Williams, Anne	TN1850	62A,62C
Williams, Ifan	AF0120	62C
Wilmeth, Margaret	NE0160	62C
Wilson, Eric J.	AB0100	41,62C
Wilson, Miranda	ID0250	13C,41,42,62D,62C
Wilson, Sandy	CA4200	41,62C,42
Winder, Diane L.	MI0600	62C
Wingert, Jennifer	IN1600	62C
Wissick, Brent S.	NC2410	55,51,62C,67A,67E
Wogick, Jacqueline	NY2950	62C,41
Wolff, Benjamin A.	NY1600	62C
Wondercheck, Debora	CA5355	62C
Wong, Y. Alvin	CT0100	62C
Wood, Gregory J.	NY4150	62C
Work, George P.	IA0850	51,62C,62D,13
Wulfhorst, Dieter	CA1860	62C,62D,12A,12C,41
Wyatt, Benjamin H.	VA1100	62C,67B,12,13I,12B
Yamada, Sojiro	LA0900	62A,62B,62C,62D
Yang, Emily	DC0170	62C
Yeung, Angela C.	CA5200	13,38,41,42,62C
Ying, David	NY1100	42,62C
Ying, Keiko	NY3350	62C
York, Paul	KY1500	51,62C,42
You, Yali	MN0800	38,41,62C,11,12A
Yu, Joanne	AA0020	62C
Yu, Ka-Wai	IL0800	62C,11,13B
Yun, Yeon-Ji	CO0225	62C
Zacharius, Leanne	AC0050	38,62C,51
Zander, Benjamin	MA1400	41,62C
Zhang, Xiao-Fan	TN1100	62C
Zhao, Yao	CA4100	62C
Zheng-Olefsky, Hai	TX2650	62C,62D
Zhou, Jessica	MA0400	62C
Zieba, Tomasz	OK0750	62C,42
Zitoun, Adrien	WI1155	62C
Zitoun, Adrien	WI0150	62C
Zlotkin, Fred	NY0500	41,62C
Zlotkin, Frederick	NY2150	62C
Zollars, Dan	TX3530	62C
Zombor, Iren	TN1200	62C,42

Bass

Name	Code	Areas
Abbott, Tyler	OR1050	62D,29,13
Adams, Greta	KS0400	62C,62D,61
Adams, James	ME0440	62D
Adkins, Don	CA0300	13,10F,10,12A,62D
Adkins, Donald	CA0400	38,62D,66
Ailshie, Tyson	CO0650	62D
Ailshie, Tyson	CO0100	11,13,62D,70,29
Alarie, Frederic	AI0200	62D,29
Albright, James	MO2000	62D
Aldridge, Robert	AA0020	62D
Ali, Kelly S.	VA1600	62D
Allen, Christopher	LA0050	62D
Allen, Jeremy	IN0900	62D,29
Allison, Ian	MN1250	62D
Altemeier, David	IA0600	62D
Altemeier, David	IA0550	62D
Amend, William	OR1250	62D,47
Amorim, George J.	TX3525	62D,13,51
Anderson, Andrew	IL3550	62D
Anderson, Andrew	IL0550	62D
Anderson, Clipper	WA0650	62D
Anderson, Dan	IL0720	62D,63D,29
Anderson, Erik	ND0250	62D,62C,13,51,29
Anderson, Jim	OH2550	62D
Anderson, Robert P.	WI0803	62D
Anderson, Robert	NC2410	62D
Anderson-Himmelspach, Neil	MD0475	10A,13,14C,34,62D
Angulo, Denson	UT0250	62D,70
Angulo, Denson	UT0325	62D
Anthony, Tom	MD1100	70,62D
Appleman, Richard	MA0260	62D
Archard, Chuck	FL1550	47,62D,53,29
Arnold, Larry	NC2435	10,29A,13,34A,62D
Asefiev, Boris	KY1000	62D
Athens, William	OR0250	62D
Attanaseo, Jeremy	IL0400	62D
August, Gregg	CT0600	62D
Babbitt, John	WI1150	62D
Bailey, Steve	NC2440	62D
Baker, Brian	WI0300	62D
Baldini, Donald	NH0150	38,47,62D,29A
Baldini, Donald J.	NH0100	62D
Baldwin, Tom	MD1010	62D
Ball, W. Scott	TN1350	11,12A,62D
Barbu, Simona	ND0500	62C,62D
Barker, Edwin	MA0400	62D
Batchelor, Wayne	NY2900	62D
Bates, James	OH2050	12A,20,32,38,62D
Bates, James I.	OK1450	47,62D,70
Bates, Joanne	PA1750	62D
Bayer, Joshua	DC0010	29,20,13,62D,70
Beaudoin, Jacques	AI0200	62D
Beaudry, Paul	NY4200	62D
Beavers, Clyde	KY0100	62D
Becker, Abraham N.	AL1150	62D
Beecher, Jeffrey	AG0450	62D
Beecher, Jeffrey	AG0300	62D
Beers, Heather	OH0350	62D
Bell, Richard	GA0500	32E,13,38,60B,62D
Belove, David	CA2950	62D
Benne, Steve	TN1450	62D
Benne, Steven	TN0250	62D
Benson, William	CA3100	62D
Berg, Chris	OH0500	13,10,62D
Bergeron, Chuck	FL1900	62D,47,29A,46,12A
Bernstein, Alan	RI0250	62D
Berquist, Peter	GA0200	62D
Berry, Robert C.	CA3950	62D,45
Bersin, Michael D.	MO1790	11,12A,62C,62D
Beskrone, Steve	PA3330	62D,47
Biggerstaff, Corey	IL1085	62D
Bilinski, Janusz	MD0150	62D
Bisio, Michael	VT0050	62D,53,29
Bistrow, Douglas	IL3450	62D
Bjornsen, Lawrence	AF0120	62D
Black, Cary	WA0350	62D,53,29,35,47
Black, David	CA6000	62D
Black, David	CA0960	62D
Black, Robert	CT0650	62D
Black, Robert	NY2150	62D
Blair, Suanne Hower	KY0900	12A,62C,62D,62E
Blalock, James	GA1500	62D,62C
Blanchet, Martin	AG0170	62D
Bland, Ron	CO0830	47,62D
Bland, Ron	CO0150	29,62D
Bland, Ronald	CO0550	62D,70
Boden-Luethi, Ruth	WA1150	62C,62D,13,51,42
Bonelli, Matt	FL1300	62D,53
Bongiorno, Joseph A.	NY2750	62D,38,42,51
Booker, Adam	MN1600	29,41,46,62D
Boone, Michael E.	PA3250	29,62D
Borowicz, Zbigniew Jozef	AI0190	62D
Boss, Robert	CA4050	47,62D
Botterbusch, Duane A.	WV0550	62D
Botterbusch, Duane A.	PA1400	62D,42
Bowman, Bob	MO1810	29,62D
Boyd, Jesse	LA0300	62D
Boyd, Michael	MS0360	70,62D,41,10,11
Bracchitta, Ian	SC0750	62D
Bracchitta, Ian	SC0400	62D
Bracchitta, Ian	NC2400	62D
Bradetich, Jeff	TX3420	62D
Bransby, Bruce	IN0900	62D
Bratic, Dean	MO0550	62D
Braun, Joel	IN0150	62D,51
Brauninger, Eva	IA0650	62D
Bremer, Jeff	PA3650	47,53,62D
Brendle, Ron	NC0050	62D
Breon, Timothy	PA2100	34,35,62D,70
Bretschger, Fred	MN0050	62D
Brewer, Spencer	GA1450	62C,62D
Briskovich, Zebadiah	IL2970	62D
Broad, Daniel	MA0280	62D
Brookshire, Eddie L.	OH2250	47,70,62D
Brotman, Justin	AZ0490	62D,10,32E
Brown, Christopher C.	MN1623	62D
Brown, Craig	IN0900	62D
Brown, Craig	NC2430	62D
Brown, Damon	NC1600	62D
Brown, John V.	NC0600	62D,47,29A,29B,29C
Brown, Kevin E.	NJ0800	62D
Brown, Lindsay	OH0100	62C,62D,51
Brown, Miles	MI1750	62D,47,29A,29B,46
Brown, Pebber	CA5100	70,62D
Brown, Philip	IL2900	62D,29,35
Brown, Richard	MS0100	62D,70
Brown, Wes	MA2020	62D,36
Browne, Whitman	MA0260	62D
Bryant, Robert	KY0100	62D
Bryce, Vincent	TX2800	62D
Brydges, Christopher	VA0250	62D
Buckley, Chris	IL2970	62D
Buda, David	MA0260	62D
Buddo, J. Christopher	NC0650	62D,38,39
Budrow, Jack	MI1400	62D
Bunts, Joseph	VA1850	62D
Burney, Herman	DC0100	62D
Burns, Elizabeth	NC2000	62C,62D
Burns, Robert	AL1050	62D
Bustamante, Linda	FL1300	11,38,51,62C,62D
Bustos, Nixon	WI0860	62D
Butterfield, Craig	SC1110	62D,29,46,47
Byrkit, Douglas	IL1740	62D
Cahill, Susan	CO0900	62D
Cain, Richard	MA0650	62D,37
Calin, Rachel	GA1300	62D
Cameron, Michael J.	IL3300	62D,51,41
Campbell, Jeff	NY1100	29A,29B,29C,62D,47
Cantrell, Elizabeth K.	VA0800	62C,62D
Captein, Dave	OR0400	62D
Caravan, Lisa	AL0200	62C,62D,32E
Carleton, Charles	OH0650	62D
Carlton, David	WI0150	49,62C,62D
Carney, Jeff	NY2660	62D
Casale, Bill	CA5040	62D
Casas, Jorge	IL1050	62D,47,10D
Casey, John	IA1200	62D
Casey, John	IA0500	62D
Casey, Marian	SD0580	62D
Cassarino, Richard	AL0800	62D
Casseday, Kevin	FL1850	62D
Castilano, Edward P.	NY4150	62D
Castillo, Carlos	NY2550	62D
Cavender, James L.	AL1160	70,41,46,62D
Changhens, Wenting	OH2200	62D,66C,62
Chapdelaine, Karine	VA0600	62D
Chapman, John	AZ0470	62D
Chapman, Stan	AL1195	62D
Chappell, Eric	AI0150	62D
Chesanow, Marc	SC0420	62D,11,10F,13B,35G
Chiarello, Mario	SD0050	62D
Chiego, John	TN1680	62D
Chiego, Sara	TN1200	62D
Christie, Lyndon	NY2200	62D
Christopher, Paul	LA0550	10,13,51,62C,62D
Cioffari, Richard J.	OH0300	62D
Clark, Chris	NJ0175	62D
Clark, David W.	MA0260	62D
Clay, William	TX3420	62D
Clements, Emory	GA0940	62D
Clements, Emory Lamar	GA1050	62D
Cline, Benjamin	KS0350	51,62C,62D,38
Clubb, Maurice	WA0650	62D
Cobb, Timothy	FL1125	62D
Cobb, Timothy	NY1900	62D
Cobb, Timothy	NY2150	62D
Cobb, Timothy	NJ1130	62D
Cobb, Timothy B.	NY3785	62D
Colby, Donald	ID0100	62D
Cole, Joseph	PA2200	62D
Coleman, Todd	NC0750	10,34,62D,35G,45
Combs, Mikel	OK0550	62D
Conyers, Joseph	PA3250	62D
Coolman, Todd	NY3785	47,62D,53,46,29
Coulter, Chris	CA1265	62D
Cox, Eleanor Christman	WI0700	62C,62D,60B
Cox, James	IL2050	47,62D
Cox, Jim	IL1400	62D
Crawford, Michael	MI0850	62D,20
Cross, Samuel G.	VA0600	62D
Crowe, Jason	CO0275	62D,42
Culbertson, Mark	CA1650	62D
Cullison, Jonathan	CO0625	62D,10D
Currie, David	AG0400	60,38,41,62D
Curtis, Arlyn	OR0750	62D

Name	Code	Areas
Dadurka, Jon	FL0200	62D,47
Dahlstrand, John	AR0350	62D,51
Damschroder, Norman	OH2300	62D,29A
Damschroder, Norman L.	OH2275	62D,13A,13B
Danders, Dennis	KS0200	62D
Danilow, Marji	NY0150	62D
Danilow, Marji	NY2250	62D
Dashiell, Carroll V.	NC0650	47,62D,29
Davey, John	NY1400	62D,29B,41
Davis, John	KS0700	62D
Davis, Joshua	PA3150	47,29,62D,13C,53
Davis, Kenneth	NJ1130	62D,29
Davy, Karen	CA2250	62A,62B,62C,62D,41
Dawson, David J.	TX3175	32D,62D
Dawson, Tim	AG0450	62D
Deardorf, Chuck	WA0200	62D,53,29,35
Deeter, Constance	CA2800	62D
Deitz, Kevin	OR1300	62D
Deitz, Kevin	OR0050	13,62D
Delache-Feldman, Pascale	MA1175	62D
DeLavan, Bill	TX3527	62D
Denis, Marc	AI0200	62D
Denis, Marc	AI0210	62D
Denis, Marc	AI0150	62D
Derthick, Thomas	CA5350	62D,42
Derthick, Thomas	CA0840	62D
Derthick, Tom	CA4300	62D
Derthick, Tom	CA0150	62D
DeSanto, Donn	IL0600	62D
Desgrange, Richard	FL0150	62D
DeVaney, Fred	IL1500	62D
Dewey, Glenn A.	VA0450	62D
Dicarlo, Tom V.	PA1850	70,62D
Dickenson, Stephanie	TN0100	62D
Dikener, Solen	WV0400	11,12A,62C,62D
Dimoff, Maximilian	OH0600	62D,60B
Dixon, Edward E.	WA1300	38,62C,13C,62D
Dixon, Scott	OH1700	62D
Dixon, Scott	OH0600	62D,51
Dixon, Scott	OH0650	62D
Dixon, Virginia	IL0850	62D
Dole, Frederick	VA1600	62D
Dole, Frederick	VA0250	62D
Donato, Michel	AI0200	62D,47
Dorsey, Roland W.	MD0475	62D
Dostal, Jeffrey	MA2100	62D
Douglas, Samuel O.	SC1110	13,10,62D
Dreger, Neil	NY1250	62D
Dresser, Mark	CA5050	62D,29
Driscoll, Kermit	NY3785	62D,29
Dugan, Greg	IN1850	62D
Dugan, Gregory S.	IN0350	62D
Dunham, Deborah	TX2250	62D
Dunn, Robert	IA0700	70,62D
Dvoskin, Victor	MD0850	62D
Dvoskin, Victor	VA1600	62D,29
Ealum, Ernie	FL1000	62D
Easter, Timothy D.	SC0750	62D
Eckard, Steven C.	MD0520	47,62D,29
Edgerton, Sara A.	MO1500	11,12A,38,62D,62C
Egan, Jered	NY1400	62D
Ehrmantraut, Ben R.	ND0400	62D
Eidbo, Ashley	IA0700	62D
Elisha, Steven K.	GA0950	62C,62D,41,42
Elliott, Robert L.	TN1400	13B,32,62D,11
Ellison, Paul	TX2150	42,62D
Emmons, Tim	CA0830	62D,29
Emmons, Timothy	CA3300	62D,47
Emmons, Timothy	CA5150	70,62D
Enghauser, Chris	GA0850	62D
Enghauser, Christopher M.	AL0500	62D,29
Enos, David	CA1000	62D
Erdahl, Rolf	MN0750	62D
Erdahl, Rolf	IA0950	62D,32E
Erhard, Paul	CO0800	11,62D
Erickson, Thomas	MI0300	62D
Eshima, Shinji	CA4200	62D
Espinosa, Leandro	OR0200	62C,62D,38,13A,11
Eulau, Andrew	NJ0825	29,62D
Evans, Bruce	IN1750	62D
Fedewa, Edward W.	MI1200	62D
Fedewa, Edward	MI0400	62D
Feinberg, Joseph	MI2000	62D
Feltham, Scott	AI0150	62D
Ferdon, Jeff	NC0550	62D
Ferdon, Jeffrey	NC2420	62D
Ferguson, James W.	TN1100	62D,47,41,61
Ferrandino, Blaise J.	TX3000	10,62D,13
Ferraris, Robert	IL1520	62D
Ferris, Joe	TN1100	62D
Fiene, Darrel J.	IN1560	62D
Filiano, Ken	PA2150	62D
Finet, Christopher	AZ0450	29,47,62D
Finkelshteyn, Leonid	NC0650	62D
Fiore, Domenick J.	PA2550	62D
Firak, Paul	NV0050	62D
Fisher, Jonathan	TX3420	29,62D
Fitzgerald, Cheryl	TN1150	62C,62D
Fleming, Lynn	MD0300	62D
Fleming, Lynn	MD0520	62D
Fleming, Lynn	MD0500	62D
Fleming, Lynn	MD0550	62D
Fletcher, Ashton	MD0175	62D,46,47
Floeter, John	IL0550	62D
Floeter, John	IL3310	62D
Floeter, John	IL2200	62D
Foley, Laura	IL2650	62D
Foley, Mark	KS1450	62D,29,13
Folus, Brian H.	MD0475	62D,62A,62C
Ford, Andrew	CA1000	35,62D
Ford, Jonathan	MT0200	62D
Foureman, Jason	NC2410	47,62D
Fournier, Gilles	AC0050	62D,29
Fowler, Garold	IL1350	62D
Frajena, Roger	TX0700	62D
Frazier, Jordan	NY2250	62D
Freeze, Marcus	TX2570	62D
Fremgen, John	TX3510	62D,29,47,46
Friedman, Kenneth J.	AB0100	62D
Fryer, Carolyn	MA2030	62D
Fryer-Davis, Carolyn	MA0400	62D
Gabriel, Charles M.	MA2030	62D,13C,47
Gahler, Jason R.	OH2140	62D,29
Gallagher, John P.	HI0210	62D
Gallagher, Todd	IN0800	62D
Gambetta, Charles	NC0910	62D
Gambetta, Charles L.	NC0900	38,60B,13,62D
Gannett, Diana	MI2100	62D
Garber, Neil	CA5060	62D
Garcia, Gregory	TX1000	62D
Garman, Barry	GA0250	62D
Garrett, Charles	AA0150	62D
Garrett, Sheila	AA0050	62D
Garrison, Greg	CO0550	62D
Gaston, Susan Deaver	MS0700	41,62C,62D
Gaudette, Nicholas	MN0040	38,62D
Gaviria, Carlos	TX2700	62D,11,13A,13B
Geeseman, Katherine	TX3515	11,62C,62D
Geggie, John D.	NY3780	62D
Geib, Michael T.	OK1330	62D
Gellert, Karen	NY2105	62D
Gertz, Bruce	MA0260	62D
Giambussso, Scott	MD0550	62D
Gibeau, Peter	WI0862	13,36,41,62D,66A
Gibson, John	WI0804	62D
Gilliam-Valls, Jessica	TX2650	62D
Gilliam-Valls, Jessica	TX1150	13A,62C,62D
Gilson, Tim	OR0450	62D
Gimble, Richard	TX1600	62D,70,53,35B
Gish, Benjamin	WA1100	62C,62D
Glowacki, T. J.	FL0930	62D
Goetz, Michael	CT0550	62D
Goin, Robert	GA0050	62D
Goines, Lincoln	MA0260	62D
Gold, Ira J.	MD0650	62D
Gold, Ira	DC0050	62D
Gold, Michael	NY2400	62D,29
Gold, Scott	FL1310	62D
Goldstein, Lloyd	FL2050	62D
Gomez, Edgar	PR0115	62D,53
Gomez-Imbert, Luis	FL0700	62D,43,11
Gonzalez, Pepe	DC0170	29,62D
Goodwin, Tim	TN1680	29,62D
Gorcik, Christopher	IL2750	62D
Gowers, Todd B.	WA0800	62D
Grabowski, Donald	PA2350	62D
Graham, Eric	WI0845	62D
Gray, Lawrence	IL3300	29,62C,62D
Green, Barry L.	CA5070	62D
Green, Kyp	TX3000	62D
Greenough, Forest G.	CO0250	47,62D,10F,34
Greer, George	AG0600	62D
Gress, Andrew D.	NY2750	62D
Griffith, Joan E.	MN0950	47,70,29,10,62D
Groat, Stephen P.	PA1850	62D
Grossman, David	NY2150	62D
Grubbs, Jeff	PA3100	62D
Guastafeste, Joseph	IL0550	62D
Gudbaur, Michael A.	WI0835	62D
Guerin, Roland	LA0800	62D,47
Haar, Mark	NE0250	62D
Haas, Peter	LA0050	62D
Haden, Charlie	CA0510	47,62D,53
Haebich, Kenneth	IL0850	62D,10A,10F
Hagen, Susan	MA0950	62D
Haines, Steve J.	NC2430	29,62D
Hall, Andy	NE0610	62D
Hall, Donald L.	VA1100	62D
Halt, Hans	NV0100	29B,62D,66A
Hamann, Jeff	WI1150	62D,29,47
Hamar, Jon	WA0050	62D
Hamar, Jon	WA0550	29,62C,62D,32E,51
Hamilton, Margot E.	OH2500	62D
Han, Jinhee	KY0950	62C,62D
Hanke, Craig	WI0808	62D
Hanna, Alexander	IL0750	62D
Hanna, Judith	IL0730	62D
Hansen, Eric	UT0050	62D,38,51
Hansen, Peter	IN1650	62D
Hanson, David B.	OH0950	62D,70
Hanulik, Christopher	CA5030	62D
Harding, Mark	VT0100	62D,70
Hare, Matthew	CA5020	62D
Hare, Matthew	CA1425	62D
Harris, Erik	MO1950	62D
Harris, Zacc	MN0800	62D,70
Hatch, Jim	AR0850	62D
Hay, David	MI0850	62D
Hayden, Marion	MI2100	29,62D
Hays, Timothy O.	IL0850	13,62D,45,34,35
Head, Joseph	CO0200	62D
Heath, Jason	IL0750	62D
Heffernan, Nancy	TX0250	62D
Heine, Bruce	MN1300	62D
Helsley, Jack D.	IN0350	62D
Helsley, Jack	IN0100	62D
Helsley, Jack	IN0907	46,47,62D
Henderson, Benjamin	UT0350	62D
Hennessy, Michael	WI0750	62D
Henry, Mark	MA2050	62D
Henry, Paul S.	VA1475	62D
Herren, Matthew	KS1050	62C,62D
Hester, John	CA3600	62D
Hester, John	CA0550	62D
Hieronymus, Bryan	OH2600	62D
Hildreth, Thomas P.	SC1200	62D,38
Hildreth, Tom	NC2420	62D
Hill, Don-Michael	FL0800	62D
Hill, Don-Michael A.	FL1800	62D
Hill, Don-Michael A.	FL1550	62D
Hill, John	MI0450	11,29A,62D
Hilliker, Tom	PA3710	62D
Hines, Roger	OH0350	62D,11
Hirsh, Jules	NY0500	62D
Hoats, Charlie	MI1050	70,62D
Holbrook, Ashley	KS0150	62D,62C
Holland, Dave	MA1400	62D,47,29
Hollins, Fraser	AI0150	29,62D
Holloway, Harold	TN1710	62D
Holmes, Glenn	OH0650	62D,70
Holt, Joseph	MA0350	62D
Hood, John	PA3250	62D
Hope, Garrett E.	PA3550	10,62D,13,34,51
Horlas, Lou	TX0700	47,62D,29
Hornick, Scott J.	NJ0750	62D
Horvath, Kathleen	OH0600	62D
Hovnanian, Michael	MI0900	62D
Hovnanian, Michael Aram	MI0350	62D
Hovnanian, Michael J.	IL0750	62D
Howard, Micah	PA1050	62D
Howard, Micah	PA0550	62D
Howell, Devin L.	PA1300	62D
Howell, Devin	PA1250	62D
Huergo, Fernando A.	MA0260	62D
Huff, Mark Y.	AL1160	62D
Huff, Mark	AL1250	62D

Index by Area of Teaching Interest

Name	Code	Areas
Hughes, Luther	CA0815	29,62D
Hughes, Matthew	IL3500	62D,20,29
Hugo, Cliff	CA4700	62D
Huhn, Kevin	PA1650	62D
Hungerford, Jay	MO1950	62D,29
Hunter, John	NH0350	62D
Hurley, Brian	AI0150	62D,29
Hustad, Ken	CA0600	62D
Hustad, Ken	CA1510	62D
Hutchinson, Larry	MI2200	62D
Hutter, Patricia	AB0050	62D
Hyde, John	AA0050	10,13,62D
Insko, Robert	PA3000	29,62D
Isaacson, Kristin	TX0900	13C,62C,62D
Jablonsky, Eugene	WA1350	62D
Jackson, Stephen	IL1800	47,62D
Jackson, Steve	IL1350	62D
Jackson, William	KY1000	62D
Jacobson, Harry P.	NY3725	13,62D,35A
Janke, Tom J.	IN0907	34,62D
Janowsky, Maxim	MI1750	62D
Janowsky, Maxim	MI2200	62D
Jarvis, Willie	AG0200	62D,47
Jennings, Linda G.	PA1600	62C,62D,13,51
Jensen, Jeff	IA0550	62D
Jetter, Katherine	CO0350	38,62C,62D,13,51
Joella, Laura	FL0650	38,12A,62D,60B
Johnson, Jeffrey	OR0850	62D
Johnson, Michael	AL1170	62D
Johnson, Paul L.	MD0650	62D
Jones, Calvin	DC0350	47,62D,63C,63D,29
Jones, Janet	AZ0150	38,62A,62C,62B,62D
Jones, Kate	AR0300	62C,62D
Jones, Kate	TX2750	11,62D
Jones, Micah	PA3330	47,62D,29,13,34
Jones, Thomas	AG0150	62D
Jones, Trevor	IL1200	62D
Jordan, Rodney	FL0850	47,62D,29
Judson, Tohm	NC2700	10B,62D,70,34,35
Jursik, Katherine	WI0100	62D
Kadetsky, Mark	NJ0550	62D,51,11
Kahn, David	PA1450	62D
Kail, Jeffrey E.	MO1810	62D
Kalson, James	TX2200	62D
Kalson, Jim	TX2260	62D
Kaminsky, Bruce	PA1000	62D,12A,37,50
Kashiwagi, Kerry	CA0150	62D
Kasper, Don J.	CA0835	62D,66D
Kasper, Max	AF0100	62D
Kassinger, Robert C.	IL0750	62D
Katz, Robert S.	OK1300	13,11,12A,12,62D
Kaufman, Joe	WA0200	62D
Kausch, Mark	MN0350	62D
Kausch, Mark	MN0800	62D
Kausch, Mark L.	MN0250	62D
Kazez, Daniel	OH2450	13A,11,20D,62C,62D
Keaster, Aaron	MI0050	62D
Kehrberg, Kevin	NC2550	12,14C,20,60A,62D
Keith, Randall J.	CA0850	62D
Keller, Paul	MI2200	62D
Kelly, Gary	NY0700	35,34,62D,43
Kesselman, Robert	PA3250	62D
Kew, Craig	MO0850	62D
Killian, Dwight	AZ0440	62D
Kim, Steve	WA0860	62D,47,53
King, Joan	PA0650	62A,62B,62C,62D,31G
King, Sidney	KY1500	62D,41
Kirby, Steve	AC0100	29,47,62D
Kirby, Wayne J.	NC2400	10,45,34,35,62D
Kirkpatrick, Mary Beth	WV0560	62A,62B,62C,62D
Kirkscey, Jonathan	AR0110	62C,62D
Kleis, Lisa	IL2775	62D
Kliewer, Jan Michael	WY0130	13,36,61,62D,38
Klingensmith, David C.	TX3450	62D
Klingensmith, David	TX3400	47,62D
Klobas, Patrick P.	CA0807	62D
Klobas, Patrick	CA3520	62D
Knific, Thomas	MI2250	47,51,62D,46,29
Koczela, Jeff	DC0100	62D
Koczela, Jeffrey L.	DC0150	62D
Koehler, William	IL1150	32B,32C,62D
Kohn, Andrew	WV0750	62D
Korb, Kristin	CA5300	62D,29
Kosmala, Jerzy S.	CA5020	62D
Kozak, Christopher M.	AL1170	29,62D
Krieger, Eric	IA1400	62D
Kubin, Brian	MO1780	62C,13,51,62D
Kurtz-Harris, Jeremy	CA4100	62D
Kurzdorfer, James	NY4460	13,47,62D,53
LaBrosse, Denis	AI0200	62D,29
Lara, Elizabeth K.	TN0050	62C,13,62D,62B
LaSpina, Steven	NJ1400	29A,47,62D,29
Laszlo, Albert	OH2200	62D
Laszlo, Albert	NY1900	62D
Late, Eric	TX2295	47,62D,11,34C
Latenser, Tom	FL1430	62D
Law, Bill R.	ND0350	62D,29
Lawson, Peter K.	IL2100	62D
Laycock, Rand	OH0755	11,12A,32C,38,62D
Leavitt, Tod J.	GA2150	62D
Lebeda, Wiktor	AB0200	62D
Lederer, Thomas	TX2400	62D
Lee, Carver Scott	PA1750	62D
Lee, Eric	AG0250	62D
Lee, Owen	KY1000	62D
Lessard, Daniel	AI0150	62D,29
Lett, Bruce	CA0825	62D
Leverenz, Chris	VA0150	62D
Levinson, Eugene	NY1900	62D
Levy, Benjamin	MA0400	62D
Levy, Benjamin	MA0350	62D
Lewis, Gordon R.	KS0650	62D,47,42,46
Lewis, Gordon R.	KS1400	62D
Libertini, Richard	CA3800	62D
Lieberman, Barry	WA1050	62D
Light, Chris	AB0090	62D
Light, Chris	AB0060	62D
Lin, Victor	NY4200	29,66A,62D
Lindsay, Jason M.	FL1950	62D
Lindsey, Gerald	NY0646	62D
Lipscomb, Ronald	PA1150	62C,62D
Littrell, David	KS0650	38,41,62C,62D,13A
Lloyd, Peter	CA1075	62D,42
Lockwood, John	MA1400	62D,29
Lockwood, John K.	MA0260	62D
Lockwood, John	MA1175	62D
Lockwood, Tom	MI0900	62D
Lockwood, Tom	MI1000	62D,64E
Loehrke, John	NJ0975	11,62D,47,29B
Loewenheim, Thomas	CA0810	62C,62D,38
Lopes, Gerald	CA0150	38,62D
Lopez, Hiram	PR0100	62D
Loughman, Greg	ME0150	62D
Loughman, Greg	ME0200	62D
Lowi, Ralph	CA4410	12A,11,62D
Lu, Yuan Xiong	TX3000	62D
Lucie, Edwin J.	MA0260	62D
Luty, Christoph	CA1750	62D
Macchia, Salvatore	MA2000	10,62D
MacConnell, Kevin	PA3330	47,62D,29
Machado, Marcos	MS0750	62D
Magney, Lucia	MN0350	62C,62D,32E,42
Magnusson, Robert	CA4100	62D
Magnusson, Robert	CA4050	47,62D
Malaga, Ed	MD0750	62D
Malaga, Edgaro	DC0010	62D
Mangone, Jeffrey	PA1050	62D
Manson, Michael	IL0600	62D
Manspeaker, Rick	WV0800	62D
Mapp, Douglas	NJ1050	62D,47,53,34
Marks, Dennis J.	FL1950	62D,66A,47,29A
Marsh, David	WV0550	62D,53
Martin, CarolAnn F.	MO0800	62C,62D
Martin, Constance	MN0300	62D
Martin, Don R.	MO1900	62D
Martin, Mildred	CA2250	62D
Masciadri, Milton	GA2100	51,62D
Masuzzo, Dennis	NJ1160	62D
Matthews, Zachary P.	CA3500	62D,29,34
Mayo, Susan	KS0300	62C,62D
Mazanec, David	AL0300	62D
McBee, Cecil	MA1400	29,47,62D
McCain, Seward	CA4900	62D
McCann, Brian	WA0400	62D
McCleery, Mark	LA0770	11,41,62C,62D
McClure, Ron D.	NY2750	62D,47
McClure, Theron	OH1850	62D,13
McCormick, Corey	CA1000	62D
McCormick, Gaelen	NY2650	62D
McCormick, Gaelen M.	NY3350	62D
McCormick, Mark	CT0100	62D
McCoy, Jeremy	NY2150	62D
McFadden, Joseph	GA1150	62D,51
McGee, Ray	SC0050	62D
McGirr, Tom A.	WI0450	47,62D,53
McKeage, Kathleen M.	WY0200	11,62D,13C,32
McKee, Andy	NY2660	47,62D,53
McKemy, Bill	KS1000	62D
McKnight, Linda	NY2150	62D
McKnight, Linda	NJ0800	62D,51
McMichael, Stacy	IL2300	62D
McNally, Patrick	WA1350	62D
McNally, Patrick	MT0400	62D
Mcneill, Karl	PA1000	62D
Meashey, Steven	PA2300	62D
Medlock, Matthew	FL0680	62D
Meineke, Robert	TX2350	62A,62B,62C,62D,51
Menegon, John	NY3760	12A,47,62D
Meyer, Edgar	TN1850	41,62D
Meyer, Edgar	PA0850	62D
Meyn, Richard	OR0700	62D
Meza, Oscar M.	CA0835	62D
Michelson, Bliss	PA2800	62D
Miele, William	RI0150	47,62D
Milleker, Troy	AG0200	62D
Miller, Aaron D.	ID0060	47,62D
Miller, David	OR0950	62D
Miller, James E.	PA1900	62D,29
Miller, Jeremy	IL2050	62D
Miller, John	FL1745	62D,70
Miller, Marc	GA1150	62D,47
Miller, Stewart	IL3310	62D,29
Millhouse, Steven	AZ0440	62D,47
Miranda, Roberto	CA5031	29,62D
Mixter, Jan	SC0650	62D
Molina, Stephen	MI2100	62D
Molina, Steven R.	MI2200	62D
Montgomery, Michael R.	AR0700	62D
Moore, David	CA5300	62D
Moore, Glen	OR0850	62D,29
Mooter, Gregory G.	MA0260	62D
Morell, Drew	CO0830	70,47,62D
Morgan, David	OH2600	62D,29,47,53
Morgan, Lauren R.	MO0250	62A,62B,62C,62D,51
Moring, Bill F.	NJ0800	46,47,62D
Morris, Anthony	NY0500	62D
Morris, Daniel	MA0260	62D
Morris, William J.	LA0800	62D
Moses, Dee	FL2000	11,62D
Moyer, Bruce	CA4400	62D
Moyer, Bruce	CA4425	62D
Moyer, Bruce D.	CA4900	62D
Munday, Don	OK1200	29B,62D
Muroki, Kurt K.	NY3790	62D
Muroki, Kurt	GA1300	62D
Murray, David	IN0250	62D,11
Nairn, Robert	PA2750	62D
Nash, Robert	LA0650	62D,11
Nash, Robert	LA0760	62D
Neher, Patrick K.	AZ0500	62D,51
Neill, Douglas	MN0600	62D
Neill, Douglas A.	MN1120	70,62D
Nelson, Craig	TN0100	62D
Nelson, Craig E.	TN1850	62D
Neuenschwander, Mark	FL1650	62D
Neuenschwander, Mark	FL0450	62D
Neuenschwander, Mark L.	FL2000	62D
Neumayr, Anton	IN0400	62D
Newton, Barry	CA3100	62D
Newton, Barry	CA5360	62D,11
Nieske, Robert	MA0500	10,47,62D,53,46
Niezen, Richard S.	CO0150	62C,62D,13C,13G
Nitti, Adam	TN0100	62D
Noah, Sean	AL1300	62D
Novosel, Steve J.	DC0350	62D
O'Brien, Dean	AA0150	62D
O'Brien, Orin	NY2150	62D
O'Brien, Orin	NY1900	62D
O'Brien, Orin	NY2250	62D
O'Bryant, Daniel K.	MN1300	38,60B,62D
O'Connor, Matt T.	AK0100	62D
Oles, Darek	CA5020	62D
Oles, Darek	CA0510	62D,47
Oleszkiewicz, Dariusz	CA0835	62D
Olsen, Alex	AB0150	62D
Olsen, Karl	KY1450	62D

Index by Area of Teaching Interest

Name	Code	Areas
Olsen, Karl	KY0400	62D
Olsen, Karl	IN1010	62D
Olszewski, Thomas	IL0420	63,64,62D
O'Neill, SC, Alice Ann M.	OH0680	32E,62C,41,62D
Oppelt, Robert	MD1010	62D
Orhon, Volkan	IA1550	62D
Orleans, James B.	MA0400	62D
Orleans, James	MA1400	62D
Osborn, Vince	MN0450	62D
Osika, Geoffrey	CA0830	62D
Osterhouse, Carl	MN1280	62D
Ostlund, Sandor	TX0300	62D
Ousley, Larry James	FL0700	62D,46,47,53
Ousley, Paul	MN1450	62D
Paer, Lewis J.	NY2750	42,62D
Paeschst, Matthew	OH1200	62D,70
Paetsch, Matt	OH1600	62D,70
Palma, Donald	MA1400	37,62D
Palma, Donald	CT0850	62D
Palmer, Gary	IL0100	62D
Paolo, James	WI1150	62D
Pappas, Louis	NY4450	62D
Parman, David L.	IN1800	41,62C,62D,70,20G
Pascolini, Jon R.	OH2250	62D
Paulsen, Peter	PA3600	62D
Pearse, Lukas	AF0120	62D
Pendley, Daniel	NY4320	62D,29
Pepin, Pierre	AI0150	62D
Perez Rivera, Pedro	PR0115	62D,47
Perla, Gene	PA1950	35A,35E,62D
Perla, Gene	NY2660	62D
Perry, Brian N.	TX3420	62D
Pershounin, Alexander	GA0550	62D,47
Peters, Tom	CA0825	62D
Peterson, Anne L.	PA3250	62D
Peterson, Ian	AI0220	62D
Peyrebrune, Henry L.	OH0200	62D
Pfiefer, Steve	CA2390	62D
Pharr, Randall	VA1500	62D
Pharr, Randall	VA1600	62D
Piekarski, Kevin J.	IN0905	62D
Pierce, Carrie	TX2930	62C,62D,51,31A,13C
Pingel, Scott	CA4150	62D
Pinkney, Rachel	OH1800	62C,62D
Piontek, Gregory	NY4460	62D
Pitta, Tom	MD0060	62D
Pittman, Dwight	MO0650	62D
Pitts, Timothy	TX2150	62D
Plewniak, Kim	WA0400	62D
Pliskow, Dan J.	MI2200	62D,29
Policastro, Joseph	IL1900	62D
Poplin, Stan E.	CA5070	62D,47
Poppe, Donna	WA0650	62D
Porter, Eliot	RI0300	62D
Porter, Eliot	RI0200	62D
Porter, Eliot	RI0150	62D
Pos, Margie	WA0200	29,62D,66A,13
Posey, Dale	FL0950	62D,29B
Powell, Brian T.	FL1900	62D,41
Powell, Ellen	NY3775	62D
Powell, Timothy W.	OH2150	62D
Price, Matt	MO1550	62C,62D
Priester, John Michael	PA1200	62D
Prisco, Peter	NY0644	70,62D
Pugh, Darryl	NY2950	62D
Pugh, Darryl L.	NY4150	62D
Pugh, Darryl	NY0650	62D
Puls, Cyndi	OH1400	11,62C,62D
Punter, Melanie	FL0850	62D
Quebec, Brian	AG0150	62D
Quinn, Karyn	WI0810	47,62D,46,29,13A
Rai, Diana	IL1750	62D
Randles, Edward	MI1180	62D
Raper, Troy	CO0225	62D
Raschen, Gudrun E.	TX3300	62D,62C,67B,51
Rast, Madison B.	PA3250	29,62D
Ray, Chris	IL0650	62D
Ray, John	NY2105	62D
Raychev, Evgeni	TX2700	62C,41,11,62D
Reba, Christopher H.	CT0700	34D,10B,35G,62D,13
Redzic, Zlatan	TX2260	62D
Reed, Jeff	MD0850	62D,47
Reeve, Douglas	MO0300	62C,62D
Reichgott, Joseph	FL1310	62D
Reid, John	TX2350	11,10D,35B,62D
Reist, Joel	TN1850	62D
Renino, Al	NY5000	62D
Renyer, Erinn	KS0050	62C,62D,51,42
Repucci, John	MA0260	62D
Retzlaff, Dustin	WY0130	62D
Rice, Laurence E.	KS1350	62D
Richeson, Doug	OH0850	62D
Richman, Glenn	CA5000	62D
Richman, Glenn	CA0900	62D
Ridley, Larry	NY2150	47,29A,62D,20A,20G
Rimmington, Rob	FL0650	62D,29
Rivera, Maricarmen	PR0115	62D
Rivers, John	VT0450	62D
Robinson, Brian	AI0150	62D
Robinson, Harold	PA0850	62D
Robinson, Paul G.	OH1850	62D
Robison, Riley	MO0400	62D
Rodgers, Joseph W.	MN1000	38,62C,13,62D
Rodriguez, Art	CA2440	62D
Rodriguez-Hernandez, Gabriel	PR0115	29,62D
Rodriquez, Jose	NJ0700	62D
Roederer, Jason	AZ0480	62D
Roessler, Brian	MN1300	62D
Rofe, Peter	CA0510	62D
Rogers, Jefferson	TN0100	62D
Rogers, JoAnne	OK1250	62D
Rognstad, Richard	SD0600	38,13A,62D,13C,11
Rogoff, Noah T.	NE0590	62C,62D,13A,13B
Rohwer, Robert	OH0300	62D
Rose, Richard F.	FL1300	11,32B,32C,62D,29
Rosenberg, Marlene	IL0550	62D
Rosenberg, Marlene	IL2250	62D
Ross, Sally	NC1100	62C,62D
Rostock, Paul	PA2450	47,62D,46,35A
Rotaru, Catalin	AZ0100	62D
Roth, Arthur	AG0650	62D
Rowell, Tracy	OH1700	62D
Rowell, Tracy	OH2150	62D
Rozie, Edward Rick	CT0650	20G,47,62D,29
Ruas, Laura	MD0400	62D
Ruas, Laura M.	MD1000	41,42,62D
Rubin, Jennifer	MN0610	62D
Rubino, George	ME0150	62D
Ruffels, Dave	CT0800	62D,53,41
Ruffels, David	NY3785	62D
Rumbley, Phil	TX3370	62D
Rupp, Emily	NC1300	62D
Rutley, Thom	ID0140	62D
Sachen, Andrew	WI0830	62D
Salas, Jorge Davi	TX2700	63D,62D,42
Santerre, Joseph	MA0260	62D
Santos, Nathan H.	PA1600	62D
Sarchet, Gregory B.	IL2150	62D
Scaffidi, Pete	CA0650	62D
Scales, Nicholas	TX3750	13,62D,11
Scelba, Anthony	NJ0700	12A,13E,11,62D
Schaller, Edward	IL1750	62D
Schermer, Stephen	WA1000	62D,32E
Schettler, William	LA0800	62D
Schilling, Travis	MN0300	62D
Schimek, John	OK0700	62D
Schimek, John	OK0750	32,62D
Schooler, Jason	OR0400	62D
Schooler, Jason G.	OR1100	62D
Schooler, Jason	OR0150	62D
Schooley, John	WV0300	13,49,63D,62D
Schoyen, Jeffrey G.	MD0800	62C,38,13A,11,62D
Schulte, Dan	OR0850	62D,47
Schwab, David	TN0260	46,62D,66C
Schweitz, Kurt	IL3550	62D,46
Scott, William	KY1550	62D,38,41
Scrima, Vin	MA2010	62D
Seaton, Lynn	TX3420	62D,29
Sedloff, Michael	FL0800	13A,62D
Seeber, Todd	MA1400	62D
Seeber, Todd M.	MA0400	62D
Seigfried, Karl E.	WI0250	70,62D,11
Sellitti, Anne	NC0350	62C,62D
Serna, Phillip Woodrow	IN1750	62D,67A,70,67B
Shaar, Erik	NC0450	62C,62D
Shaffer, Timothy	IL3150	62D
Shaffer, Timothy	IL1300	62D
Shaffer, Timothy	IL1085	62D
Shaffer, Timothy William	IL0840	62D
Sharpe, Avery G.	MA2250	62D,41,36
Sharpe, Paul	NC1650	41,62D
Shaw, Rick	CA3500	62D
Sheinberg, Art	NM0450	62D,32C
Sheldon, Gregory	AG0550	62D
Shentov, Lubima	NY5000	62D
Shetler, Donald	SC0275	62D
Shifflett, John	CA4400	53,47,62D
Shurtliffe, Brett	NY0400	62D
Sill, Kelly	IL2200	62D,29
Sill, Kelly	IL0750	62D
Skinner, Josh	ID0060	12,13A,13B,13C,62D
Smith, Barry	MA0260	62D
Smith, John P.	VA1250	62D
Smith, Robin	OK0850	62D
Snider, Dave	WA1150	62D,47
Snyder, Laura	WI0825	62D
Sommer, Douglas	GA1150	62D
Sorensen, Ann	LA0250	62A,62B,62C,62D
Sowards, James	VT0100	62D
Spaar, Peter	VA1550	62D,42,47
Spaits, Gerald K.	MO1810	62D
Spangler, Martha	FL1450	62D
Spears, Tim	CA2200	62D
Speed, George M.	OK0800	62D,11,42
Sperl, Thomas	OH1700	62D
Spielman, Mark	AB0070	13A,47,62D,20G
Spuller, John	NC0050	62D
Spuller, John	NC2500	62D
Stagnaro, Oscar	MA0260	62D
Stahurski, Brian	PA1050	62D
Stalker, Stephen T.	NY3705	62C,62D
Stam, Martin	NC1350	62D
Stannard, Neil	CA1750	66A,66C,66B,62D
Stanziano, Stephen	OH1000	13,13B,13C,10,62D
Staron, Michael	IL3200	13,11,29,62D
Steed, Scott	WA0250	62D,47
Steinmetz, Demetrius	OH0750	62D,29
Stephens, Sonny	KY0250	47,62D
Steward, Jack	OH2290	62D
Steward, Jack L.	OH0700	62D
Stokes, Donovan	VA1350	62D
Stokes, Jeffrey	AG0500	12,62D
Stone, Geoff	HI0050	62D
Stoops, Anthony	OK1350	62D
Story, David	WI0850	62D,53,51,13A,13B
Stovall, John	MA0400	62D
Stover, Jeff	CA3800	62D
Straus, Melissa	MI1050	62D
Struman, Susan Jean	TX0550	51,62C,32A,11,62D
Stubbs, Sue	MO1800	62D
Stubbs, Sue	MO1830	62D
Stubbs, Sue A.	MO0775	62D
Stubbs, Susan A.	MO1250	62D
Sturm, Hans	NE0600	51,62D
Suchanek, Bronislaw	ME0500	47,62D
Sunda, Robert	TN1200	62D,47
Sutherland, Dan	AF0150	62D,53
Swartzbaugh, Bill	FL2050	62D
Swora, Matthew	MI1000	62D
Swora, Matthew	MI1950	62C,62D
Swygard, Craig	IA0900	62D
Synott, Adrian	NJ0760	62D
Syracuse, Rich	NY3650	62D
Taffet, Robert S.	NY0050	62D
Tait, Edward	AG0650	62D
Tait, Edward	AG0450	62D
Tatum, Mark	NM0450	62D,29A
Tetel, Ioan	AA0020	62D
Thomas, Bryan	OH1100	62D
Thomas, Craig	DE0150	62D
Thomas, Craig	PA3330	47,62D,29
Thomas, Richard B.	SC1000	62C,11,38,12A,62D
Thornblade, Sarah	CA3650	62D
Thorson, Lee	IA0150	62C,62D
Tidaback, Darrel	IN1450	62D
Tidaback, Darrell	IN0910	62D,10B,47
Tilley, William T.	VT0450	62D
Tinsley, Frederick	CA0815	62D
Tinsley, Frederick D.	CA3650	62D
Topolovec, David	WI1155	62B,62C,62D
Torres, Martin	CA5355	62D
Torres, Martin	CA0859	62D,70
Townsend, Bradley	WI0865	62D
Tramontozzi, Stephen	CA4150	62D
Tramontozzi, Stephen	CA2950	62D
Trembly, Dennis	CA5300	62D

Name	Code	Areas
Trexler, Henry	NC0850	62D
Trunk, Joseph	FL0500	62D
Tucker, Nick	IL0800	62D
Turetzky, Bertram	CA5050	12A,41,62D,43,29
Turner, Jeffrey	PA1050	62D
Turner, Jeffrey	PA0550	62D
Ullery, Steve	OH1450	62D
Ungurait, John B.	MS0575	37,65,62D,46,50
Unsworth, Erik	TX3520	62D
Urke, Jan	AA0035	62D
Urke, Jan	AA0100	62D
Urness, Mark	WI0350	62D,29A
Valentin Pagan, Aldemar	PR0115	62D,47,53
Valk, Alexis	TX2250	62D
Van Dyck, Thomas	MA1175	62D
Vance, Paul	MN1700	12A,62D,38,51,62C
VanDemark, James	NY1100	62D
Vaughn, James	CO0950	62D
Veasley, Gerald	PA3330	62D,47
Veazey, Lee	IN1600	62D
Vedady, Adrian	AI0190	62D
Velosky, Ronald A.	PA0400	62D,29
Verbsky, Franklin	NY1600	62,62C,62D,11
Vick, Joe D.	AR0750	62D,70
Viertel, Breton	ID0070	62D
Vitti, Anthony	MA0260	62D
Vivian, Jim	AG0650	47,62D
Vivian, Jim	AG0450	62D,29
Von Hombracht, Willem	MO1950	29,62D
Wadopian, Eliot	NC2600	62D
Wagner, Lorraine	WY0115	62A,62B,62C,62D,51
Wagner, Michael F.	NY4320	62D
Wagor, Rich	IA0400	62D
Wagor, Richard	IA0300	62D
Walker, Kenneth	CO0900	62D,29
Walker, Nicholas	NY1800	62D,67B,55B
Walkington, Alec	AI0150	29,29C,62D
Wanner, Glen	TN1850	62D
Warren, Jeff	AB0090	12B,13F,47,62D
Warrington, Thomas	NV0050	62D,47,29
Wasserman, Garry P.	OH1900	62D
Watson, Michael	WI0845	62D
Webb, Charles	IN0005	62C,62D
Weeks, Rudi	MA1100	62D
Wei, Yung-Chiao	LA0200	62D
Weidenmueller, Johannes	NY2660	62D,13
Weinkum, Harald	AZ0470	62D
Weinstein, Alan	VA1700	62C,62D,12B
Weinstein, Alan	VA1250	41,62C,62D,70
Weisner, Jeffrey D.	MD0650	62D
Weiss, Doug	NY3785	62D
Welch, Jeanette	IA0930	62D
Weller, Derek	MI0600	62D
Wharton, William	ID0250	13,41,62C,62D
Wheeler, Ben A.	MO1900	47,62D
Wheeler, Tyrone	KY1500	47,62D
Whitaker, Rodney	MI1400	47,29,62D
White, Christopher B.	VA1000	62D
Whittaker, Dennis	TX3400	62D
Wicks, Michael J.	NY3600	62D
Wieland, John	FL1750	62D
Wijnands, Aberham	KS0590	66A,66F,62D
Williams, Buster	PA3250	29,62D
Williams, Don	NH0250	62D
Williams, Ray	GA0200	62D
Wilson, Miranda	ID0250	13C,41,42,62D,62C
Wind, Martin	NY1600	62D,29
Wind, Martin	NY2750	29,47,62D
Winters, George	TX3350	62D
Wires, Jonathan	TN1400	62D
Wiseman, Roy	CT0050	62D
Witt, James	CA4050	13A,11,12A,47,62D
Wolanski, Rob	AG0050	62D
Wolfe, Ben	NY1900	29,62D
Wolfe, Lawrence	MA0400	62D
Wolfe, Lawrence	MA0350	62D
Wolfe, Lawrence	MA1400	62D
Woodson, Andrew	OH1850	29,62D
Work, George P.	IA0850	51,62C,62D,13
Workman, Reggie	NY2660	10,47,62D,53
Worn, Richard	CA5000	62D
Wulfhorst, Dieter	CA1860	62C,62D,12A,12C,41
Wyrick, Inez	VA1350	62D
Yamada, Sojiro	LA0900	62A,62B,62C,62D
Yavornitzky, David W.	UT0250	62D
Yazdanfar, Ali	AI0150	62D
Young, David	AG0450	62D
Young, Frederick	PA3400	62D,63D
Zadinsky, Derek A.	OH0650	62D
Zapalowski, Paul	NY3717	62D
Zera, Tom	UT0400	62D
Zeserman, Steven B.	TX3530	62D
Zhang, DaXun	TX3510	62D
Zheng-Olefsky, Hai	TX2650	62C,62D
Zibits, Paul	CA0825	62D
Zimmerman, Karen	CA3400	62D
Zimmerman, Robert	MA2250	62D,41
Zinno, David A.	RI0300	47,62D,29
Zisman, Michael	CA4200	62D
Zlabinger, Tom	NY0646	62D,29,14,20,47

Harp

Name	Code	Areas
Allen, Barbara	NY2900	62E
Allen, Nancy	NY1900	62E
Allen, Susan	CA0510	41,62E,43,53
Allvin, Kerstin	MI1750	62E
Anderson, Leeann	OH1000	11,32B,62E,32A,32C
Asmus, Elizabeth Etters	PA0950	62E
Asmus, Elizabeth	PA2300	62E
Aspnes, Lynne A.	AZ0100	62E
Atz, Karen	WI0815	62E
Augustson, Darice E.	MO0775	62E
Ball, Mindy	CA5355	62E
Ball, Mindy	CA0960	62E
Barber, Gail G.	TX3200	13,62E
Baril, Gianetta	AA0150	62E
Baril, Gianetta	AA0050	62E
Bartlett, Jacquelyn	NC2420	62E
Bartlett, Jacquelyn	NC1650	62E
Bartlett, Jacquelyn	NC0050	62E
Barton, Lorelei	OK0850	62E
Barton, Lorelei	OK1450	62E
Beck, Rosalind	FL1800	62E
Benjamin, Ann	IA0950	62E
Bennett, Hye-Yun Chung	VA1000	62E,66A
Bennett, Susan Brady	GA1700	62E
Bennett, Susan Brady	GA0550	62E
Bershad, Kara	IN0005	62E
Bershad, Kara	IL2100	62E
Bircher, Mary	NE0160	62E
Bircher, Mary	NE0250	62E
Bircher, Mary W.	NE0590	62E
Bishop, Dawn	IL0275	62E
Blair, Suanne Hower	KY0900	12A,62C,62D,62E
Bobetsky, Victor V.	NY0625	11,12A,62E
Bohnet, Andra	AL1300	12A,41,64A,62E,35A
Bracy, Katherine B.	OH2290	62E
Brady, Nicole B.	UT0050	62E
Bride, Kathleen	NY1100	62E
Brinksmeier, Ulrike	OH0680	12A,11,62E,14,20
Brumwell, Gretchen	IA0400	62E
Brumwell, Gretchen	IA1800	62E
Brumwell, Gretchen	IA0300	62E
Bruno, Sophie	PA3250	62E
Buchanan, Laurie	TX3530	62E
Bullen, Sarah	IL0550	62E
Bumanis, N.	AA0100	62E
Bumanis, Nora	AA0020	62E
Bunn, Deette	NY4150	62E
Burroughs-Price, Anita	SC0750	62E
Buzzelli, Julie	OH0300	62E
Byrne, Laura S.	NC0600	62E
Byrne, Laura	NC2410	62E
Casale, Maria	CA3600	62E
Ceo, Joan	RI0200	62E
Ceo, Joan H.	RI0300	62E
Chalifoux, Jeanne	VA0450	62E
Chalifoux, Jeanne D.	VA1475	62E
Chalifoux, Jeanne	DC0010	62E
Chan, Celia	CA2420	62E
Chauvel, Marjorie A.	CA4900	62E
Choate, Ellie	CA0815	62E
Choate, Ellie	CA5020	62E
Cifani, Elizabeth	IL2250	62E,51
Clayton, Cathryn	UT0250	62E,20,12A
Coan, Darryl	IL2910	13,32,62E,67
Coelho-Foust, Jenny	WY0115	62E
Colpean, Elizabeth	MI0350	62E
Cook, Elaine	KY0450	62E
Cook, Elaine Humphreys	KY1450	62E
Cooper, Donna	PA1550	62E
Cowin, Jasmin Bey	NY4200	11,62E,12A,31B
Cox, Natalie	CA1650	62E
Craig, Jennifer	OR0400	62E
Cutler, Sara	NY0500	62E
Davids, Suzann	MI1180	62E
Davidson, Sarah	AG0500	62E
Davis, Jackie	OH1450	62E
Davis, Jackie	OH2550	62E
Davis, Jackie	OH0450	62E
Davis, Kaylynn	GA2000	62E
Dederich-Pejovich, Susan	TX2400	62E
Dickstein, Marcia	CA5550	62E
Dickstein, Marcia	CA0825	62E
Dobyns, Whitney	VA0550	62E
Draughn, Maurice	MI2200	62E,66G
Dropkin, Mary	CA0845	62E
Dropkin, Mary C.	CA3650	62E
Dropkin, Mary	CA5150	62E
Duran, Sally	NC2205	62E
Edwards, Dawn	FL1550	62E
Eilander, Maxine	WA0200	62E
Eisfeller, Anne	NM0450	62E
Elder, Laura	TN1350	62E
Ellins, Rachael Starr	CO0250	62E,11
Elossais, Hannah	AA0035	62E
Elossais, Hannah	AA0020	62E
Espinosa, Angela G.	MT0200	62E
Etheredge, Nelda	TX3350	62E
Fackler, Barbara Ann	IL0730	62E
Falcao, Mario	NY3725	62E
Fan, Heaven H.	IN0100	62E
Fedson, Delaine	TX3510	62E
Fedson, Delaine	TX2650	62E
Ferris, Rachel	TX3410	62E
Flannery, Rebecca	CT0650	62E
Fleming Peters, Lori	MD0100	62E
Foss, Judy	IA0850	62E
Fujikawa, Denise	OR0850	62E
Fuller, Sarah	MD1010	62E
Galante, Gloria	PA3600	62E
Gallo, Paulette M.	PA3700	62E
Gallo, Paulette	PA2200	62E
Gemmell, Lori	AG0600	62E
Gertig, Suzanne	CO0900	62E,16,12
Glennie, Kim	NV0050	62E
Glick, Nancy	OH0250	62E
Glick, Nancy	OH2275	62E,66A
Goodrich, Jara S.	ME0500	62E
Gordon, Valerie Muzzolini	WA1050	62E
Gordon, Valerie Muzzolini	WA0200	62E
Gottlieb, Karen	CA2950	62E
Grafius, Ellen	MI0100	62E
Grafius, Ellen	MI1150	62E
Gregory, George R.	TX2260	62C,62E
Guinn, Caryl	OH0650	62E
Guinn, Caryl	OH0600	62E
Guinn, Jody J.	OH0200	62E
Gwynne, Michelle	KY1000	62E
Haefner, Jaymee	TX3420	62E,62
Haefner, Jaymee	TX3300	62E
Haffner, Paula	TN0100	62E
Hainen, Elizabeth	PA0850	62E
Hainen, Elizabeth	PA3250	62E
Halpern Lewis, Emily	MA0950	62E
Hargrave, Monica E.	GA2100	62E
Hargrave, Monica	GA0050	62E
Harriman, Janet K.	CO0800	62E
Harris, Ruth Berman	NY2400	62E
Hicks, Judy S.	AL0800	62E
Hobson-Pilot, Ann	MA0400	62E
Hobson-Pilot, Ann	MA1400	62E
Hoffman, Deborah	NY2150	62E
Holland, Joan	MI2100	62E
Houser, Kimberly A.	LA0200	62E
Huang, Chen-Yu	IL1200	62E
Hugo, Chilali	UT0300	62E
Huhn, Franziska	MA1400	62E
Huhn, Franziska	MA1175	62E
Hunter, Ruth	PA3150	62E
Huntley, Elizabeth M.	NY3650	62E
Hussong, Suzi R.	WA0800	62E
Inglefield, Ruth K.	MD0650	62E
Irkaeva, Zarina S.	MA2150	62E

Name	Code	Areas
Ishimaru, Kayo	FL1950	62E
Ishimaru, Kayo	FL1000	62E
Jackson, Ashley	NY4450	62E
Jellison, Anastasia I.	VA1550	62E
Jellison, Anastasia	VA1500	62E,42
Jellison, Anastasia	VA0250	62E
Jellison, Anastasia	VA1850	62E
Jennings, Shirley	LA0550	62E
Johnson, Elisabeth Remy	GA0750	62E
Jolles, Susan	NY1600	62E
Jolles, Susan	NY2250	62E
Jolles, Susan	NY2150	62E
Karna, Kathy	IN0150	62E
Kelly, Aileen	CA0150	62E,12A,66A
Kibbey, Bridget A.	NY2750	62E
Kienzle, Kathy	MN1623	62E
Kienzle, Kathy	MN0050	62E
Kienzle, Kathy	MN1450	62E
Kondonassis, Yolanda	OH1700	62E
Kondonassis, Yolanda	OH0600	62E
Krutzen, Heidi	AB0100	62E
Kwasnicka, Ursula	NY1350	62E
Langerak, Terri	MO1830	62E
LeBaron, Anne	CA0510	10,12,62E
LeBlanc, Gaye F.	OK1350	62E,11
Lemire, Janell	MN0450	62E
Lemire, Janell	MN1600	62E
Lemire, Janell	WI0860	62E
Lendrim, Nancy	OH2300	62E
Lepke-Sims, Barbara	CO0150	62E
Lepke-Sims, Barbara	CO0650	62E
Levitan, Dan	CA4700	62E
Ley, Amy	AG0550	62E
Lilly, Elizabeth	FL0680	62E
Lindner, Jenny	OR1100	62E
Liss, Ann Marie	CO0200	62E
Liu, Adam	PA1050	62E
Lizotte, Caroline	AI0200	62E
Lobotzke, Ann	WI0825	62E
Logan, Laura	TX3000	62E
Loman, Judy	PA0850	62E
Loman, Judy	AG0450	62E
Loman, Judy	AG0300	62E
Lorcini, Marie	AG0200	62E
Luchs, Nicole	IL2050	62E
Lynch, Charles	IL2300	62E
Lynch, Charles	IN1750	62E
Lynch, Charles	IN1450	62E
Ma, Shuhui Nettie	MO2000	62E
Mackle, Anne Kate	FL1650	62E
Male, Sara	PA1300	62E
Mancini, Meredith	MD0550	62E
Mangrum, Amanda	MS0100	62E
Mashkovtseva, Elena	CA4100	62E
Masri-Fletcher, Patricia	MI1400	62E
Masri-Fletcher, Patricia	MI1260	62E
McClure, Carol	IN1010	62E
McClure, Carol	TN1660	62E
McClure, Carol	KY1500	62E
McDonald, Susann	IN0900	62E
McLaughlin, Carrol M.	AZ0500	62E
Mitchell, Emily	TX2700	62E
Mollenhauer, Jude	OH2050	62E
Moody, Earecka	WA1350	62E
Moody, Erica	WA0400	62E
Moore, Harriet T.	IN0350	62E,70
Moore, Kathy Bundock	CO0950	62E,13B,13C,13E
Morris, Tahlia	WI1150	62E
Morse, Elizabeth	MA2250	62E,41
Morse-Hambrock, Anne	WI0250	62E
Morse-Hambrock, Anne	WI0835	62E
Muston, Wendy	IN0250	62E
Myers-Brown, Ruth	MI0600	62E
Neill, Lou Anne	CA5030	62E
Neupert, Gina	TN1200	62E,42
Newman, Katherine L.	AL1160	62E
Niemisto, Elinor	MN1450	62E
Niemisto, Elinor	MN0300	62E
Norton, Jeanne	OH1850	62E
O'Brien, Nancy	IL1520	62E
O'Hagan, Cheryl Reid	AF0120	62E
Oliver, Sarah	TX2250	62E
O'Neal, Faith	OK0750	62E
Ortega, Janice	CA2950	62E
Ortega, Janice D.	CA0807	62E
Otake, Miya	AB0200	62E
Ownbey, Shru De Li	UT0250	62E
Pack, Shari	ID0060	61,62E
Page, Paula	TX2150	62E,42
Page, Paula	TX3400	62E
Palser, Caroline	NY3350	62E
Parsons, Jeffrey L.	OR1300	62E
Poeschl-Edrich, Barbara	MA0400	62E
Pollauf, Jacqueline M.	MD1000	62E
Pomeranz, Felice	MA0260	62E,62
Porter, Laura	CA1860	62E
Price-Glynn, Cynthia	MA0350	62E
Rasura, Ricky	TX3527	62E
Rector, Arlene	KY0100	62E
Rector, Arlene	KY1350	62E
Reist-Steiner, Tabitha	KS1400	62E
Reit, Alyssa	NY5000	62E
Remy, Elizabeth	GA1150	62E
Rifas, Helen	NC2500	62E
Rinne, Erzsebet Gaal	IN1600	62E
Rioth, Doug	CA4150	62E
Roberts, Dolly	FL0450	62E
Roberts, Elizabeth 'dolly'	FL2050	62E
Roman, Mary C.	FL0850	62E,66D
Rowe, Kimberly	PA3250	62E
Rowe, Kimberly	NJ1050	62E
Rytting, Lysa	UT0325	62E
Sayre, Jennifer	CA0600	62E
Scandrett, Lucy	PA3000	62E
Scandrett, Lucy	PA1600	62E
Schefter, Hillary	WY0200	62E
Scherschell, Rebecca	TX0370	35G,62E
Schweninger, Virginia	VA1400	62E
Scott, Julia	PA1450	62E
Seeman, Faye	IL3550	62E
Seidman, Barbara	DC0100	62E
Seidman, Barbara	DC0170	62E
Sella, Gillian Benet	OH2200	62E
Sesler, Betsey	NC2000	62E
Shaffer, Marian	TN1680	62E
Shaffer, Marian	TN1850	62E,41,42
Shaul, David	WY0115	62E
Sheldon, Vanessa R.	CA3265	12,13C,13A,62E,66A
Shulman, Amy	CA3300	62E
Smith, Paula M.	WI0803	62E
Soons, Heidi	VT0450	62E
Sparks, Phyllis	TN1400	62E
Spence, Chelsea	WA1100	62E
Stearns, Duncan	PA1150	62E,66A
Stern, Andrea	MN1625	62E
Stern, Andrea	MN0050	62E
Stuckey, Bridgett	VA0600	62E
Stuckey, Bridgett	VA1350	62E
Suchy-Pilalis, Jessica R.	NY3780	13,62E,13H,13C,31A
Sullivan, Anne	DE0150	62E
Sullivan, Judith	AL1170	62E
Swartz, Jennifer	AI0150	62E,51
Szmyt, Elzbieta M.	IN0900	62E
Tai, TanFen	IN0900	62E
Tarantiles, Andre	NJ0175	62E
Tarantiles, Andre C.	NJ0800	62E
Taylor, Sue	MO1950	62E
Tennenbaum, Judie	RI0150	62E
Terry-Ross, Patricia	MI2200	62E
Theriault, Kristen Moss	NY4320	62E
Thielen, Karen	CA4425	62E
Thielen, Karen	CA4400	62E
Thomas, Suzanne M.	NY0400	62E
Thomas, Suzanne	AG0050	62E
Thompson, Janet	OH1600	62E
Thompson, Janet	OH1200	62E,66A
Torres Perez, Elisa	PR0115	62E
Tracy, Phala	MN0750	62E
Turovsky, JoAnn	CA1075	62E,42
Turovsky, JoAnn	CA5300	62E
Valerio, Celia Chan	CA5040	62E
Van Hoesen, Gretchen	PA1050	62E
Van Hoesen, Gretchen	PA0550	62E
VanArsdale, Christine	NC0550	62E
Vanvoorhees, Rachael F.	LA0300	62E
Veikley, Avis	ND0250	65,50,62E
Vickerman, Louise	UT0350	62E
Victorsen, Catherine	MN1280	62E
Victorsen, Catherine	MN0250	62E
Victorsen, Catherine	MN0800	62E
Vokolek, Pamela	WA1050	62E,41
Volpe Bligh, Elizabeth	AB0090	62E
Volpe Bligh, Elizabeth	AB0100	62E
Vorhes, Anna	IA1200	62E
Vorhes, Anna	SD0580	62E
Vorhes, Anna	SD0050	62E
Vorhes, Anna	IA0500	62E
Waggoner, Emily	SC0650	62E
Waggoner, Emily	SC0200	62E,12
Waldvogel, Martha	MI1050	62E
Wallace, Connie	WY0050	62E
Wallace, Sharlene	AG0650	62E
Warren, Jessica	UT0050	62E
Wesner-Hoehn, Beverly	CA0840	62E
Westgate, Karen	OH2140	62E
Wheeler, Teresa	OK0500	62E
Whitman, Jill	WA1250	62E
Wiebe, Jill	KS1450	62E
Wilson, Kathleen	SC0275	62E
Wittchen, Andrea	PA2450	41,62E
Wong, Grace	NY1700	62E
Woodson, Louisa Ellis	TX0300	62E
Wooster, Pat	WA1000	62E
Wooster, Pat	WA0650	62E
Wychulis, Kathleen	NE0610	62E
Yan, Ni	OH0850	62E
Yeung, Ann M.	IL3300	62E,51
Young-Davids, Suzann	IN0910	62E
Younger, Brandee	NY0050	62E
Zaerr, Laura	OR1050	62E,42
Zdorovetchi, Ina	MA0350	62E
Zdorovetchi, Ina	MA2050	62E
Zwicker, Keri	AA0020	62E

Brass (All Areas)

Name	Code	Areas
Acosta, Tim	CA4650	11,63,29A
Adduci, Kathryn James	CA4400	63
Ainanda, Lucy	AR0425	63,64,65
Akinskas, Joseph	NJ1100	32,63
Amy, Robynn	MA0260	63
Anthony, Johnny	MS0350	32C,37,49,63
Barker, Kent	OK1400	63
Barraca, Rudy	AL0335	11,63,65
Bass, Michael	MS0580	11,49,37,63
Baxter, David A.	KS0980	63,37
Bean, Robert G.	AL1450	13,37,47,63,29
Beck, Brandon	WA1100	37,63,60B,38,32C
Beckett, Scott	TX0100	11,12,13,37,63
Beery, John	MI1650	32,37,47,63,11
Beghtol, Jason W.	MS0570	37,13A,46,63,49
Bennett, Cindy	IL3370	63,32B
Bennett, Steve	TX2850	63,64
Benson, Mark	PA0400	13,10,12,63,34
Betts, James E.	IL1800	13,20,29A,63,34
Betts, L. David	OH0755	63,49
Bilden, Jeff	CA1290	37,47,29,63,64
Bilotta, Lee	PA3560	60,32B,37,63,31A
Birden, Larry	OK0450	13A,32E,10F,63,37
Birk, Richard	TX0350	13,11,37,47,63
Bitz, Lori L.	OH2275	63
Block, Tyrone	TX2570	32E,37,47,60B,63
Bloomquist, Paul	IA0790	11,63,60B,13,37
Boden, John C.	ME0500	63
Bogert, Nathan	IA0700	64,63
Bone, Lloyd E.	WV0350	12A,49,63,37,11
Botts, Nathan	VT0050	11,29,49,63,67E
Branning, Ron	FL0040	63,64
Braunagel, Jesse	ND0150	63
Brekke, Jeremy	ND0350	63,37,49,63A,47
Brenan, Craig	AA0100	63
Bressler, Mark	IL2730	37,63
Brinegar, Steve	DC0170	63
Bull, Douglas	WY0050	37,63,11,32E
Butrico, Michael	NC0400	32E,37,46,60B,63
Caillier, Claude	WI0800	11,13,63,37,47
Cameron, Wes	MS0850	11,63,64,65,34
Campbell, Carey	UT0350	12,11,63
Carlson, Dan	MN1100	11,35A,37,46,63
Carlson, Mark	MD0610	63,11,12,13,37
Castellano, Mark	FL0680	63
Cavenecia, Terrance E.	NY3770	63
Cervenka, Ken	MA0260	63
Cheesman, Robert	MS0300	63,46,34
Chiarizzio, R. Kevin	VA0650	63,32B,32C,32F

Index by Area of Teaching Interest

Name	Code	Areas
Cicconi, Christopher M.	FL0050	63
Clark, Wayne R.	OK0700	63D,63C,63
Clickard, Stephen D.	PA0250	37,63,47,60B
Cochran, Martin	AL1150	63,11
Cogdell, Jerry	MS0320	13,11,50,63,54
Compean, Jose D.	TX1425	13,32,47,63,64
Compton, Adam	OK0500	13B,63,37,46,13
Cook, Andrew	AL0345	60B,63,11,47,64
Cook, Gary	MS0420	63
Cowan, Scott M.	MI2250	11,47,63,29
Crawley, James	AL0330	63,64
Cress, William L.	MO0825	47,54,63
Cross, Sandy	OK0770	63,64
Daniels, William B.	KY1100	32B,37,47,49,63
Davis, Charles	TX1510	11,63,64,37
Davis, Tim	MN1290	63
Day, Greg	SC1080	13,10F,37,47,63
DeBoer, Paul	NY1700	63,12A,49
Decker, Charles	TN1450	63A,41,63,49
Del Vecchio, Peter H.	VA1850	63,49,47
DeSpain, Geoff	AZ0300	37,63,46,47,11
Dixon, Howard	TN0800	13A,11,32B,63,64
Dodson, Brent	IA1750	63,64,37,60B,48
Douglass, Ronald L.	MI1100	13,37,41,63,29
Downes, Greg	IL1612	63
Doyle, William	CA1750	11,37,38,63,60
Dragovich, James	NY1600	65,63
Drillinger, David	IL1500	63
Dudgeon, Ralph T.	NY3720	12,67,14,38,63
Dupertuis, Jeff	CA3850	62,63,64,65,66
Eis, Jeremiah	WI0770	34,48,47,60B,63
Enis, Paul	OK0350	13,36,37,61,63
Ewing, Lee	GA1650	37,63,64
Faieta, John	MA0260	63
Fairchild, Kay	GA0750	49,63
Falbush, Arthur	NY3765	11,63,29A,46,41
Farnsley, Stephen	NV0150	64,63
Farrington, Robert	CA1550	41,47,63,64,29A
Faust, Randall E.	IL3500	63B,10,63,13,49
Fawson, Christine	MA0260	63
Feller, Robert	CA0350	11,37,49,63,60
Fisher, Blair	AB0050	37,47,63A,63,46
Fiske, Richard Allen	CA4550	11,38,66A,63
Fleury, August	LA0720	63,37
Flora, Sim	AR0500	32,37,47,63,13
Flynn, Michael P.	WY0150	11,37,41,47,63
Foster, Christopher	NY0100	36,63,13A,47,41
Fox, James	KS0400	63
Fox, Jason	NY3475	37,49,63
French, Otis C.	PA1100	11,37,63,64,65
Frey, Kevin T.	CA4350	13,11,14,63,53
Frutkoff, Peter	NY0050	32E,63,64
Fulbright, Marshall T.	CA2550	38,51,48,62,63
Fuzesy, Brianne	ND0050	11,63,42
Gaines, Adam W.	WI0808	63,47,37,63A,29
Galisatus, Michael	CA1250	47,46,63
Gardner, Gary D.	OK1500	11,62,63,37,47
Gareau, Larry	CT0050	63,29A
Garmon, Randy	TX1725	37,46,47,63
Gehring, Joseph	PA1550	37,38,60,63
Gemberling, John	MT0370	47,29,63
Gerdes, John	MO0700	10F,29A,63
Gibson, Richard L.	AE0100	13,10F,10,37,63
Giles, Leonard	GA0810	11,32,37,47,63
Glashauser, Jason	IN1450	63
Gomez, Adrian	OK0600	63
Grab, Charles	MD0450	63
Green, Tim	IL2800	36,63
Griffith, David	TX0075	11,37,46,63
Gronberg, John	OR1020	63
Guzik, Bernie	OK1450	63,49
Hahn, Christopher D.	SD0100	63,37,60,11
Halsell, George K.	ID0075	13,37,63,11,71
Halverson, Pamela	NC1600	63,60B
Harris, Donald	AJ0150	32,63,12
Hawkins, William	CA3460	13A,32A,49,63,29
Heffner, Christopher J.	PA1900	32E,37,60,63
Heflin, Thomas	NY2150	63,11
Hegg, Dennis	SD0150	37,47,63,64,65
Heinen, Julia	CA2750	63,64
Helm, Jon E.	AA0040	13A,13,12A,63,49
Herrick, Dennis R.	AL0450	60,63,34,29A,32C
Hilley, Byron	SC0700	63
Hinkley, Brian	MD0500	63,49,48
Hooker, Tracy	WA0600	63A,63B,63
Hopwood, Brian	MO1550	32E,37,38,63
Hornig, Tom	CA4400	63
Hosten, Kevin	NY2100	11,47,63,64,66D
Hudson, Timothy	NC0930	63,38
Hull, Barbara A.	NY2650	63A,63,60
Humbert, William	AZ0350	37,64,63,13A,60
Ingalls, Glendon	VT0250	63
Jackson, Lynne A.	TX2400	63
Jackson, Milton	AR0810	13,11,49,63,70
James, Jeffrey R.	NE0250	13,60,32,37,63
Jantsch, Carol	PA3250	63
Jerosch, Anita	ME0200	63,49
Johnson, Gary	MO0250	41,46,63,65
Johnson, H. Wade	PA2000	37,63,11
Jolley, David	NY0642	13C,63
Jones, Daniel	IA0420	63
Jones, Lloyd E.	AL1250	60B,37,63
Jones, Tony	IL1090	37,63,13A,11
Kase, Robert	IL3370	63
Keberle, Ryan	NY0625	29,47,11,13,63
Keebaugh, Aaron	FL1675	11,20,13A,63
Kelley, Timothy S.	TX3650	60,37,49,63,41
Kelly, Tom	NE0200	63
Kennedy, Rajah B.	OK0450	11,37,46,49,63
Kennelly, Patrick	VA1100	63
Kephart, Donald B.	PA1350	32C,37,63,46,60
Kerr, Stephen P.	VA0650	63,37,60B,48
Kinder, Keith	AG0200	37,41,49,63
Klemas, John	IA1170	37,47,63,64,65
Kluball, Jeff L.	GA0625	37,63,29,13,10
Knier, Lawrence	MD0800	37,13C,63,13K,11
Knight, Jonathan	CA2775	12A,13A,60B,63
Knox, Daniel	AL0750	11,70,63,64,13A
Koch, Andrew	VA1550	37,63
Kramer, David	PA2800	63
Kresge, Jeff	VA1100	63
Kugler, Roger T.	KS1000	32E,63,13,37
Kurokawa, Paul	CA2100	13,47,63,64
Laarz, Bill	TN0580	37,38,41,63
LaCognata, John P.	NC2440	37,49,63
Lada, Tony	MA0260	63
Lamb, William	NM0250	13,11,37,47,63
Lamb, William	NM0500	61,63,32E
Lambert, Adam E.	NE0050	32E,37,60B,63,49
Lamkin, John R.	MD1020	10F,37,47,63
Lammers, Ed	KS0040	46,37,65,63,11
Lamprey, Audrey	CA0845	63
Laronga, Barbara	CA2600	63A,29,47,63
Lawton, Richard	AI0150	11,12,63
Lehmann, Jay	CA2450	60,13,64,63
Lesser, Jeffrey	NJ0550	32E,63,10,32C,32F
Limb, Christine M.	PA2000	32,11,63
Lington, Aaron	CA4400	29,46,63,29B
Lorenz, Michael L.	MI1950	13,47,63,29,34
Loubriel, Luis E.	IL0275	11,13A,34,63,35
Love, Randolph D.	SC0600	13,10,63,41,14C
Lowe, Phillip	TX0910	13,12A,37,47,63
Madej, Andrew	NY2105	63D,63
Maki, Erik	CA3000	37,11,63,64,65
Mallarino, Larry	CA2440	29,63,13A
Masten, Rob	WV0250	29,63,65,47,46
Mazzaferro, Anthony	CA1900	13,63,37,12A
McAllister, James	KS0440	37,10A,63,60B,32C
McClary, Michael	GA0940	11,37,47,63
McCready, Matthew A.	MO0550	11,12A,63,13A,20
McCullough, Daryl	TX3600	63,70
McFarland, Thomas J.	KY1400	60,12A,32E,49,63
McFaul, Cathi	TX3800	63
McGee, Michael	AL0850	37,47,63,64,65
McKeown, Kevin	CA4450	37,63,64
McKinnon, John A.	OR0200	13,10,63,34,14
McKinstry, Herb	PA1650	63,49
McRoy, James W.	NY2105	60B,37,63,32E
Meints, Kenneth	NE0500	63,20,65,35A,32
Meltzer, Howard S.	NY0270	11,13,12,66A,63
Mendoza, Cristina	LA0450	63,46,49,11,41
Mertens, Michael	CA2750	13B,11,63,64,37
Metcalf, Curtis	AG0450	63
Mikolajcik, Walter	CA4650	36,37,47,63,66A
Miller, Allan	CA6050	11,12,37,47,63
Misenheimer, Aaron L.	NC0850	32E,34,11,63,49
Mitchell, Katherine Beth	CA3500	63
Mixdorf, Cory Daniel	GA1050	63,63C
Mixon, John	MS0575	37,11,63
Molloy, Steve	KS0590	63
Mooy, James	CA5550	63
Morgan, Charles	IL1250	13A,60B,37,47,63
Murray, Renardo	MS0050	37,32,63,13A
Neilan, Martin	TN1600	63
Nelson, Kent	UT0350	63C,63D,63
Neuharth, Randall	NE0460	11,37,47,63
Newman, Timothy	NJ1400	47,63,29A
Nitschke, Brad	IN0005	11,12,13,60,63
Nolte, Brent J.	MN1030	66G,63
Nuessmeier, Tom	MN0200	63
Olszewski, Thomas	IL0420	63,64,62D
Palmer, David	NC1150	63,47
Parsons, Laura E.	AL0950	63A,63,12A,13A,11
Paterno, Matthew	NJ1400	63
Patterson, James H.	GA0490	29,32,46,63,47
Paulson, Brent	CO0625	63A,63,64,37
Pekas, Joe F.	SD0200	63,64
Perry, Robert	NC1300	63,64
Pickering, Matthew	MS0360	63,37,11,49,60B
Pierson, Steve	IL3550	63,11
Pilato, Nikk	CA0825	63,37,38,32E,60B
Poelnitz, Michael	AL0310	12A,47,63,35B
Poitier, James	FL0100	37,49,63,32F,41
Polett, Thomas C.	MO0300	63,47,32,13,20
Powell, Daniel	FL0350	11,13,47,63,64
Pozzi, David	CA2600	63,64
Premeau, Chad	WI0925	37,63
Rasmusson, Ralph	NY1850	37,47,63,64,65
Rassier, Daniel	MN0350	63,37
Reagan, Billy R.	AL0350	36,37,41,47,63
Reimund, John	TX1425	63D,63
Reit, Peter	CT0650	63
Renfroe, Dennis C.	NC1025	11,12A,32,36,63
Rettedal, Dean	SD0300	37,60B,47,63,64
Rivard, Gene	MN0625	13,10F,49,63,31A
Rivers, John	VT0250	63
Rivet, Joe	LA0150	37,63
Rizzo, Stephen	AL0260	11,63
Roach, L. Leroy	CA4200	32C,47,49,63,37
Roberts, Terry	SC0710	11,63,13C,35A,41
Robertson, Jemmie	IL0800	63,11
Robinson, Gary A.	SC0765	63,64,65,38
Rosado-Nazario, Samuel	PR0100	63,37,34
Roylance, Mike	CT0850	63
Sampson, Kenneth C.	TN0800	10F,32B,32C,37,63
Sampson, Larry	CA0300	62,63,64,70
Samson, David	PA0650	47,13B,32C,63,60
Sapochetti, Daniel	FL0365	63
Schafer, Erika L.	TN1700	63A,63,67E,37,46
Schoening, Benjamin S.	WI0801	11,13,36,61,63
Schultz, Dale	TX2200	37,60,32C,63
Severn, Eddie	PA2050	32,29,46,47,63
Shaw, J.D.	NM0450	63B,63
Shier, Robin	AB0050	37,63A,63,46
Simerly, Rick	TN1150	63,29,49,47,32E
Smith, Carey	MS0370	63,64,65,11,13
Smith, Ronald	NC1950	37,32,63,12A
Smithee, Larry G.	TN1000	60,32,37,47,63
Smither, Robert	MO0200	63
Snyder, Randy L.	TX2300	13A,13,11,47,63
Sorenson, Scott	MI1650	63,46,37
Spampinato, Robert	NY2105	63
Sparrow, James	NC1250	63D,32E,41,63C,63
Spencer, Malcolm	LA0100	63,37
Stanton, Ronald	NY2105	63C,63
Staples, Thomas	AA0200	60,11,49,63
Stewart, Raymond	NY2150	63
Stickney, Mark A.	UT0200	37,63D,41,49,63
Stith, Marice W.	NY0900	37,63
Stone, Michael John	OK0600	37,46,60B,63,32
Stornido, Carl	WI0050	63
Stout, Jeffrey	MA0260	63
Street, Deborah	AL0550	63,64
Stuntz, Lori A.	CA3200	63,47
Stuppard, Javier	TX1150	12,60B,63
Suliman, Jason M.	IN1800	63,49,47
Sumares, Frank	CA4400	63,29
Swope, Richard	GA1000	37,63,49
Tafrow, Tony	NJ0760	63
Tallman, Thomas J.	IL0630	13,11,47,63,29
Tellinghuisen, Harvey	CA3975	64,63
Tercero, David R.	TX0850	70,63,13
Titmus, Jon	CA5360	63,11,13A
Traa, Olav	AA0110	63
Turner, Charles	KY0300	32,37,63,47,41
Underwood, Michael P.	AR0750	13,37,63

667

Name	Code	Areas
Vander Gheynst, John R.	IN0907	29A,10A,63,34D,35A
Vandiver, Joseph	TX3650	29,63,46,47,34
Vargas, Ruben	TX1425	61,46,37,62,63
Viertel, Kyle	TX0390	37,63,64,65,46
Wacker, John M.	CO1050	60,63,37,49,32E
Walters, David	AL0500	13,37,63,60
Wampler, Kris A.	OH0680	63,32E
Washburn, David	CA0960	49,63
Webb, John C.	AR0800	41,32E,37,60B,63
Webb, Mark	MI0300	63,32C,32D,32E,11
Weeda, Linn	AK0100	11,36,49,63,63A
Wellington, Craig	WA0450	63
White, Dale A.	MN0350	60B,37,41,32E,63
White, Joseph M.	WV0100	65,50,37,63,64
White, William	MO1710	11,37,47,65,63
Whitfill, Jim	TX0850	64,63,65
Wilhoit, Mel R.	TN0200	10F,12A,32,49,63
Willard, Michael L.	OH1350	63A,49,63
Williams, Jamelle	LA0080	63
Wilson, Phil	MA0260	63
Wilson, Stephen K.	NC0250	47,29,63
Windham, Mark	AR0800	11,63,32E,32F,37
Wittemann, Wilbur	NJ0550	37,63,47,60B
Woll, Greg	CA1900	13,49,63,43
Woodard, Scott	WV0700	37,47,32C,63,49
Woodford, Paul	AG0500	60,12B,32,37,63
Woods, Chris P.	IL1050	13A,10F,13C,49,63
Wuest, Harry	FL0675	37,47,64,63
Yon, Franklin	MI0450	63,47,29A,11
Young, Craig S.	MS0400	60B,37,63,64

Trumpet

Name	Code	Areas
Abdullah, Ahmed	NY2660	47,63A
Ackley, James	SC1110	49,63A
Adams, Dwight	MI2200	63A
Adams, Mark	MI1160	63A
Adams, Randal	TX2250	63A
Adler, John	CO0950	63A,49
Akhmadullin, Iskander	MO1800	63A
Albach, Carl	NY0150	63A
Aldridge, Ben	NY3765	63A,60B,12A
Aldridge, Ben	NY1400	63A
Aldridge, Benjamin L.	NY3705	63A
Alegria, Gabriel A.	NY2750	29,47,63A
Alessi, Ralph P.	NY2750	63A,47,10D
Aley, John	WI0815	63A
Allen, David	MS0420	37,63A,65
Allen, Eddie	NY0500	63A,29
Allen, Mark	OR1000	37,49,63A,63C,63B
Allen, Steve	IN1450	63A
Alley, Greg	MI0350	63A
Alley, Gregory	MI0300	63A,32E
Allison, Robert	IL2900	63A,29
Allphin, Andrew	DC0050	63A,41
Almargo, Brandon	MD0150	63A
Almeida, John	FL1800	63A,49
Altman, Timothy	NC2435	60,32,37,63A,63B
Alvarado Ortiz, Julio E.	PR0115	63A
Amend, Jerome	IN1010	63A,49
Amstutz, A. Keith	SC1110	63A
Anderson, Michael P.	OK0750	63A
Andraso, Margaret B.	KY1100	11,36,61,63A
Apelgren, Scott	FL0150	63A
Appleby-Wineberg, Bryan K.	NJ1050	63A
Aranda, John	CA1900	63A
Archer, Thaddeus	OH2300	63A
Ardovino, Joseph	AL1200	63A,37,47,49
Armstrong, James E.	NC2700	63A,13A,37,46,49
Armstrong, Robert	OR1010	12A,63A,64C,64A
Arndt, Michael J.	TN1100	63A,49
Arthurs, Robert	NY2400	63A,29
Ash, Corey	TX1100	37,49,63A,32E,60B
Ashton, Graham	NY3785	49,63A
Ashton, John H.	WV0300	38,63A,63B
Asper, Lynn K.	MI0850	49,63A
Aston, Spencer	MA0510	63A,11
Atchison, Scott-Lee	KY1450	37,63A
Atwater, Jennifer	WI0300	63A
Audet, Peter	AG0500	63A
Austin, Trent R.	ME0500	63A
Averrett, Michael	KS1400	63A
Ayick, Paul	FL0200	63A,41
Baca, Robert J.	WI0803	47,63A,29
Bach, Edward	AC0050	63A
Bailey, Richard H.	AR0810	34,35C,35G,63A
Baker, Eric	TX1850	11,37,46,63A
Baker, John	FL0930	63A
Baldwin, David B.	MN1623	41,49,63A
Ballenger, William	TX3200	10A,32E,37,63A
Ballou, David L.	MD0850	29,53,63A,29A,36
Bamonte, David	OR0850	41,42,63A,49
Banks, Ansyn P.	KY1500	63A,29
Banyas, Thomas P.	ID0100	63A
Baransy, Paul	OH0250	63A,10F,60B,32E,37
Barley, Leroy	NC2300	63A,63B
Barnett, Thomas	WI0845	63A,37,13
Barnhart, William	FL0850	29,63A
Barraclough, D. J.	UT0200	63A
Barrett, Bill	CA0550	63A
Barrow, Gary	AR0200	49,63A,63B
Bartels, Justin	CO0650	63A
Batchelder, Donald	NJ0800	63A,49
Batchelor, Daryl	KS0550	47,63A,29,29A
Battenberg, Thomas V.	OH1850	47,63A,29
Battistone, Christopher	DC0170	63A,29
Baxter, David	KS0200	63A
Beaulac, Stephane	AI0150	63A,49
Bekeny, Amanda K.	OH0100	63A,49,11
Bellino, Peter A.	NY3600	63A
Benjamin, Keith	MO1810	63A
Benko, Ron	LA0800	63A
Bennett, Cynthia	IL1520	63A
Bennett, Wayne	NC0750	63A
Berardinelli, George	NY2450	63A
Bergman, Jason	MS0750	63A
Berinbaum, Martin C.	AB0100	60B,37,49,63A
Berlin, Eric M.	MA2000	63A
Berney, Mark C.	RI0300	29,47,63A
Bernhardt, Barry W.	FL0700	37,47,63A,29
Berntsen, Neal	PA0550	63A
Berry, William	WA1100	63A
Berry, William	WA1300	63A
Bertrand, Jerry	IA0150	63A,37
Bhasin, Paul K.	VA0250	37,63A,38,42,41
Biancalana, Jeff	CA5000	63A
Bierman, Benjamin	NY0630	63A,10,13,34,35
Bierschenk, Jerome Michael	TX3250	36,37,32D,61,63A
Bilger, David	PA3250	63A
Bilger, David	PA0850	63A
Bilger, David	GA2100	63A
Bing, William W.	CA0500	37,47,49,63A
Birch, Robert M.	DC0100	49,63A,37,48
Bircher, Craig	NE0160	63A
Bircher, K. Craig	NE0600	63A
Birkemeier, Richard	CA0825	11,63A,49
Bishop, Darcie	MS0350	11,41,49,63A
Bitz, Lori	MI0050	42,63A
Black, Larry	NC0250	63A
Blackinton, David	UT0190	63A
Blackmore, Lisa	MO1830	63A
Blackmore, Lisa	MO0650	49,63A,63B
Blake, Ron	NY1900	63A,29
Blanchard, Jeff L.	OH2140	63A,47,49,29
Blanchard, Terence	FL1900	63A,10,47
Blink, David	WA1400	47,13,63A,29
Bliznik, Karen	GA1150	63A
Bobulinski, Greg	NY1275	63A
Boccia, James	NH0250	63A
Boccia, James	NH0150	63A,49
Boehmke, Erik A.	IL1600	63A,66,47,37,49
Bogard, Rick G.	TX3500	63A,49
Bohnert, David A.	NE0700	63A,60B,37,11,32E
Bonnett, Kurt	TX3535	49,63A,63B
Booth, Rodney	TX3420	63A,29
Booth, Thomas	TX2400	63A
Bordner, Gary	MN1623	63A
Boren, Mark	ND0250	63A,63B,13A,41
Botts, Nathan	MA2250	63A,41
Bouchard, Lise	AI0200	63A
Bovinette, James	IA0850	47,63A,29
Bowen, Charles Kevin	NC2500	37,47,49,63A
Bowie, Lenard C.	GA0150	63A
Bowman, Sean	IN0907	63A
Brader, Kenneth E.	PA1850	47,63A
Brath, Jeff	IL2775	63A
Breedlove, Graham	DC0050	63A
Breiling, Roy	AZ0510	37,38,46,47,63A
Breiwick, Jamie	WI1150	63A
Brekke, Jeremy	ND0350	63,37,49,63A,47
Brian, Aric	FL2050	63A,47
Brian, Aric	FL1650	63A
Bridgewater, Cecil	NY2660	10,63A,53
Bright, Robert M.	AR0700	49,63A
Briney, Bruce C.	IL3500	63A
Brndiar, Jack	OH2150	63A
Brndiar, John J.	OH0200	63A
Brndiar, John	OH0700	63A
Brndiar, John	OH0600	63A
Broderick, James	FL1300	13,63A,53,34
Bromley, Tanya M.	KY1350	63A
Bronk, Mary Beth	TX3100	32E,37,60,63A
Brookens, Justin	IA0550	63A
Brooks, Ronald M.	CO0950	63A
Brown, Chris	NC2000	63A
Brown, David C.	UT0050	63A,49
Brown, Kevin W.	CA3500	63A
Brown, Tom	WI0810	11,41,49,63A,63B
Brownlow, James A.	TX3515	11,12A,49,63A,20
Bryant, Jeff	AA0020	63A
Bryant, Jerry	NJ0700	63A
Bryant, John	GA2300	11,13C,63A,20
Buckner, James R.	AR0300	49,63A,32E
Buehrer, Theodore E.	OH1200	13,10,29,63A,34
Bumcrot, Charles F.	NJ0800	63A
Bumcrot, Charles	NJ0700	63A,49,11
Burgess, Jon	TX3000	63A
Burgstaller, Josef	MD0650	63A
Burkart, Richard	OH1850	63A
Burkhart, David	CA4150	63A
Burkhart, Raymond David	CA3650	63A
Burson, John	IL0730	63A
Burt, Jack W.	ME0440	13C,49,63A
Buselli, Mark	IN0150	63A,29,47
Bush, Eric W.	NY4050	37,47,63A,13A,11
Butcher, Paul	FL0800	29B,47,35A,63A
Butler, Barbara	IL2250	63A,49
Byrd, Richard W.	KY0550	13,63A
Caldwell, Gary	UT0150	13,60,37,63A
Caldwell, Michael D.	CA0810	63A
Cameron, Wayne	WV0550	63A
Cameron, Wayne	MD0600	63A
Cameron, Wayne C.	MD1000	38,41,63A
Campbell, Christopher	PA1900	63A
Campbell, John	VA0750	63A,49
Campbell, William	MI2100	63A
Campos, Frank G.	NY1800	63A
Candelaria, Leonard	AL0300	63A
Cannon, Alexander	AB0200	63A
Cannon, Derek	CA4100	63A
Cannon, Derek	CA2100	29,63A,47
Cannon, Robert V.	TX2650	63A
Canty, Dean R.	TX3525	60,37,63A,63B,11
Cappy, Matt	PA3330	63A
Carlson, Stephen R.	VA1000	63A
Carpenter, Lauraine	OH0300	63A
Carrell, Cynthia T.	AR0250	11,13,32E,37,63A
Carrillo, Christine Ennis	VA0600	63A,13B
Carrillo, Christopher J.	VA0600	63A,29
Carrillo, Teofilo	IL3300	63A
Carroll, Ed J.	NH0100	63A,41
Carroll, Edward	CA0510	49,63A
Carroll, John	TX3410	63A
Carroll, John	TX1900	63A,49,37,41,47
Carroll, John	TX2200	63A
Casano, Joe	MA2030	63A
Casey, Michael R.	MO0775	49,63A,60,54
Casteel, Mike	TN0100	63A
Castellana, Joseph	OH0755	66D,66A,63A
Castellanos, Gilbert	CA5300	29,63A
Castro, Ed	WA0650	63A
Castro, Edward	WA0550	63A,32E
Celmer, Joey R.	SC1050	63A,63B,63C,63D,47
Chambers, Carol	TX3100	63A,13C,32E,10F,32A
Champouillon, David	TN0500	63A,46,29
Chapman, Christopher	OR0700	32,37,46,63A,60B
Chapman, Peter	MA0400	63A
Chapman, Peter	MA1400	63A
Charles, Etienne	MI1400	29,63A,47
Chase, George	TX3400	63A
Chasin, Richard	CA1425	63A
Chasin, Richard	CA5355	63A,49
Chatel, Jean-Louis	AI0200	63A
Cheetham, Andrew	IL0800	63A,47,66A,11
Chen, Jay	OR0450	60B,49,37,63A

Index by Area of Teaching Interest

Name	Code	Areas
Chen, Jay	OR0700	63A,49
Chen, Jay	OR1300	37,63A,41
Chenette, Stephen	AG0450	37,41,63A
Cheney, Kathryn	GA0250	63A,13A,11
Chevanelle, Serge	AI0220	63A
Chipman, Shelby R.	FL0600	60,32C,37,63A
Christian, Henry	AB0090	63A
Chunn, Michael	OH1100	41,63A
Cirba, Anita	NC2205	63A
Clark, Jon	MA0650	63A
Clark, Jonathan	MA0150	11,49,63A
Classen, Andrew B.	IA0550	47,49,63A,29
Clayton, April	UT0050	63A,48
Clemons, Gregory G.	IL1085	37,63A,41,13
Cline, Gilbert D.	CA2250	63A,49,29,67E,63B
Clodfelter, Mark	KY1450	63A,41
Cloutier, Glenda L.	TN0250	63A
Clymer, Richard	NY3785	63A
Clymer, Richard	CT0800	63A
Cobb, Kevin D.	NY3790	63A,49,42
Cobb, Kevin	CT0650	63A
Cobb, Kevin	NY1900	63A,49
Coble, Jay	FL2000	63A
Coleman, Douglas	NY2550	63A
Collins, Phillip	OH2200	63A
Colonna, Jim	UT0325	63A,32,37
Conrow, Steve	OR0750	63A
Cook, Christopher	WA0400	63A,11
Cook, Linda Klein	WI0750	63A,12,13,63B,10F
Cook, Wayne	WI1150	63A
Cook, Wayne E.	WI0825	49,63A
Cooper, David	WI0840	47,49,63A,11,29A
Cooper, John	IL3500	29,63A
Cooper, Joseph	TX3100	63A,49
Cooper, Joseph	TX1450	63A
Cooper, William	KS0050	63A
Copenhaver, John E.	PA1900	63A
Coppenbarger, Casey	NC2400	63A
Corcoran, Gary J.	NH0250	37,60B,63A,32E
Cord, Edmund	IN0900	63A
Cord, John T.	TX2960	63A,49
Corkern, David	MO0500	46,63A,37,47,10F
Corlett, Neil	AA0080	63A
Correll, Allen	OK0300	37,32E,47,60B,63A
Couch, Charles A.	OH0650	63A
Couture, Jocelyn	AI0150	63A,29
Cox, Allan	TN1850	63A,49,41
Cox, Bruce	SC0200	32C,49,63A
Crafton, Jason A.	VA1700	63A,46,47
Craswell, Brandon	GA2100	63A,49
Craven, Todd	FL1745	63A
Cresci, Jonathan	MD0550	63A,34D,13C,34C,14C
Cresci, Jonathan	PA3710	63A,32E
Crockett, C. Edgar	IL0300	13,10,47,35,63A
Crouch, Jay	MI1985	63A,29
Curnow, Jeffrey	PA3250	63A
Curtin, Jeff	OK1200	63A
Curtis, Stanley	VA0450	63A
D'Addio, Daniel F.	CT0050	13,32,37,49,63A
Dallabetta, Amanda	AZ0150	63A,47
D'Angelo, Mark	AB0200	63A
Daniel, John	WI0350	63A,42
Daval, Charles	DC0050	63A
Daversa, John	CA0835	10C,29,63A
Daversa, John	CA5300	63A
Davies, Josh	AA0200	63A,47,29A,13C
Davis, Art	IL2050	63A,14,29A,29B
Davis, Art	IL2200	63A,29
Davis, Charlie	CA1000	63A
Davis, J. Craig	NJ1400	37,63A,41
Davis, James	IL3550	63A
Davis, John S.	CO0800	47,29,29A,63A
Davis, Joyce	FL1850	49,63A
Davis, Michael	IL1085	63A
Davis, Michael	CA0805	63A
Davis, Orbert	IL3310	47,63A
Davis, Scott	IA0420	29A,47,63A
Dawson, Bradley J.	KS0350	47,49,63A,29
Day, Michael	NC1550	11,32E,32F,63A,63B
Deadman, Randall	IL0850	63A,10
Dean, Allan	CT0850	49,63A
Dean, Kevin	AI0150	63A,29
Dearden, Jennifer	PA0100	63A,34,13A,13B,13C
D'earth, John E.	VA1550	20G,47,63A,53
Decker, Charles	TN1450	63A,41,63,49
DeGoti, Mark D.	AL0200	63A,49,11
Deichert, Lynn	MN0300	63A
DelBello, Nicolas	NY4460	63A
Devuyst, Russell	AI0150	63A
DeWitt, Timothy L.	WV0050	49,63A,13E,63B,63C
Deyo, Paul	TN1400	41,63A
Diamond, David	IN0400	63A
Dierker, John	MD0850	63A,47,53
Dietz, Curtis	AF0050	63A
Dietz, Curtis	AF0120	63A
DiLauro, Ron	AI0150	63A,29,47
DiLauro, Ronald	AI0200	47,63A,46
Dilworth, Gary	CA0840	13,63A,20G
DiMartino, Gabriel V.	NY4150	49,63A
DiMartino, Vincent	KY1450	63A,41
DiSanti, Theodore A.	PA3000	63A,47,49,13,10F
Divers, Timothy	CA3300	63A
Dobra, William R.	AZ0470	63A,14C
Dobrzelewski, Jan	PA3600	63A,49
Dockter, Larry	IN1050	47,63A,65
Dolske, Christopher C.	FL1550	63A,49,29A
Donnelly, Karen	AG0400	63A
Dorhauer, John	IL0850	20A,13,63A
Dorn, Mark	CO0150	37,63A,46,60B,49
Dotson, Dennis W.	TX3510	63A,29
Dougherty, Patrick	NY0050	63A
Dovel, Jason L.	OK0550	63A,11,63B,10F
Dresser, Bruce	OR0950	63A
Driscoll, Matthew	IA0200	63A,63C,63D
Dudgeon, Ralph	NY0650	63A
Dulin, Mark C.	SC1200	63A,41
Dunker, Amy	IA0250	13,10,63A,41,49
Dunn, Andrew	AI0150	63A
Dunn, Stephen J.	AZ0450	63A
Dunnick, Kim	NY1800	63A
Duro, David A.	OH1000	63A
Eagle, Don J.	NC0600	63A
Earley, Robert W.	NJ1130	63A,41
Earley, Robert	NJ1050	63A
Earley, Robert	PA3250	63A
Eastwood, Deb A.	KY0900	13,13B,13C,63A
Eberhardt, Allan	CO0275	47,63A,46,49,29
Edelbrock, Dennis E.	VA0450	63A
Edgett, Bryan	PA3560	63A
Edgett, Bryan	PA2800	63A
Edgett, Bryan	PA1150	63A,37
Edggett, Bryan	NJ1050	63A
Edwards, Robert	NC2150	63A
Eggers, Carter	MI0600	49,63A
Eggleston, Steven	IL1200	60B,37,38,63A
Eichner, Mark J.	WI0835	60,32C,37,63A,32A
Eisensmith, Kevin E.	PA1600	47,49,63A
Elkins, Phil	SC0750	11,63A
Ellis, John R.	NY3780	63A,41
Ellis, Margaret J.	IL0100	13C,11,63A
Ellison, Charles	AI0070	47,63A,53,46,29
Ellzey, Michael R.	NM0100	63A,13,32E
Emerich, Justin	WA0200	63A
Emery, Steven	MA0350	63A
Emery, Steven	MA1175	63A
Emery, Steven	MA1400	63A,49
Engelke, Luis C.	MD0850	63A,49
Engstrom, Howard	AA0050	63A
Engstrom, Howard	AA0150	63A,49
Engstrom, Larry M.	NV0100	63A
Enos, Steve	OH0750	13,47,63A,29,46
Entzi, John A.	NC1250	63A,49
Epp, Paul	KS1300	63A
Epstein, Joan O.	FL0450	13,11,12A,53,63A
Erb, Andrew	PA3650	63A,47
Erb, Andrew	PA3260	63A,63C,37,47,49
Erdmann, Thomas R.	NC0750	11,38,13E,13F,63A
Erickson, Lynn M.	MN0950	63A
Erickson, Lynn M.	MN0050	63A
Erickson, Steve	NE0400	63A
Etzler, David	VT0100	63A
Evans, David	CA0825	63A
Everett, Paul	IN0150	49,63A,41
Everson, Terry	MA0400	63A
Faddis, Jon	NY3785	47,63A,29
Fairbanks, Will	IL1050	37,63A,46,49,63B
Fallin, Nicky G.	GA0250	37,32E,63A,49,60B
Falskow, Norin	WA0960	37,63A,38,11,13
Fazecash, Robert	AG0550	46,47,63A,29
Fenderson, Mark W.	MT0175	11,37,63A,63B
Fennell, Drew	PA1450	63A
Fensom, Chris	NC2420	63A,49
Ferguson, David A.	PA1600	63A,32
Ferrone, Joe	CO0050	63A
Few, Guy	AG0600	63A,49
Fiala, Keith	TX2800	63A
Fienberg, Gary	NJ0175	63A,29A,47,49
Fifield, Glen	UT0300	13A,32A,32B,49,63A
Finton, Charles	IL3150	63A
Fisher, Blair	AB0050	37,47,63A,63,46
Fitzgerald, Langston	PA2750	63A
Flaherty, Mark	MI1600	47,63A,29A,34,63B
Flanagin, Michael	IN1025	37,63A,63B,41,60B
Flegg, Mark	MI2200	63A,32E
Flegg, Mark	MI1850	63A
Fluchaire, Olivier	NY2200	32E,63A
Foley, Joe	MA0350	63A
Foley, Joseph	RI0200	49,63A
Ford, James	CA0830	63A,29
Ford, Jim S.	VA1475	63A
Fornero, Dan	CA0825	63A
Forney, Fred	AZ0440	63A,46,29A
Foy, Leonard C.	IN0350	63A,49,29
Fraedrich, Craig	VA1350	63A,29
Frear, Robert	CA0825	63A,42
Freas, Thomas	NY2200	49,63A
Freas, Thomas	CT0550	63A,35A
Frederick, Matthew D.	VA0350	63A,12A,41,60B,32E
Freeman, John S.	CA0850	63A
Frink, Laurie A.	NY2750	63A
Frohrip, Kenton R.	MN1300	29A,35,63A
Fulgham, Marc S.	MO1500	11,49,63A,63B
Fumo, John	CA5300	63A
Fumo, John	CA0510	47,63A
Furman, John	ME0150	63A,49
Gaines, Adam W.	WI0808	63,47,37,63A,29
Gallagher, Jack	OH0700	63A,10,10F,13,12A
Gallagher, Matt	PA3330	47,63A,29
Gallo, Reed P.	SC0800	37,60B,32E,63A,49
Galloway, Michael	PA2150	47,63A,53,29
Garcia, Victor	IL1615	63A
Gardner, Derrick	AC0100	63A,29A,46,47
Gardner, Ryan B.	OK0800	63A,49,46,42,47
Garrett, Craig	TX0340	36,47,63A
Gast, Gene	IA1300	63A
Gates, Charles R.	MS0700	63A,11
Gauger, David	IL1850	37,38,45,63A
Gaumer, Alan	PA2450	47,63A
Gebo, Kevin	VA1600	63A
Geiman, Keith	MI1150	63A
Geraci, Paul	IN1350	13,10,29,63A,32B
Geyer, Charles	IL2250	63A,49
Gibson, Marilyn	LA0770	11,63A,49
Gignac, Andrew	TX2260	63A,13,10,11
Gillis, Richard	AC0100	63A,49
Goode, Bradley	CO0800	63A,29A,29B
Gordon, David	WA1050	63A
Gorman, Kurt	TN1720	13A,34,63A,47
Gould, Mark	NY1900	63A,49
Gould, Mark	NY2150	63A
Gowen, Dennis	ND0400	37,49,63A,63B,60
Grabois, Daniel	WI0815	32,49,63A
Grabowski, Randy	IA1600	63A
Gradone, Richard	NJ0250	13,12A,12,47,63A
Graffam, Allen	ME0200	63A
Grant, Tom	TN0150	63A,63B
Granthan, Daniel	OH2250	63A,49
Grasmick, David M.	CA0630	13A,34,63A,29
Gray, Joel	AA0032	63A
Green, Donald	CA5300	63A
Green, Vincent	WA1250	63A,13
Greenwald, Fred	IL1610	63A,63B,37
Greggs, Isaac	LA0700	37,63A,46
Gresham, Jonathan	KY1000	49,63A,41
Griffin, Larry	OH2000	60B,37,47,49,63A
Grimaldi, Peter	MA1100	63A,47
Guarneri, Mario	CA4150	49,53,63A
Gustafson, Karen	AK0150	37,63A,41,11,60B
Hacker, James	FL0700	63A,42,49
Haefner, Steven	OK0850	63A
Hafner, Kenneth A.	HI0210	63A
Hagarty, Scott	TX0550	63A,13A,13C,49,41
Haist, Dean	NE0450	47,63A,29
Hala, James	NJ0175	63A
Hall, Jamie	OR1250	49,63A
Hall, Timothy	CA0960	63A

Name	Code	Areas
Hall, Timothy	CA2390	63A
Hallback, Alan	CA0859	37,63A
Hamilton, Craig V.	AR0500	63A,60B,46,37
Hammiel, Chris	IA0910	63A
Hanan, David	OK1330	37,60B,10F,34,63A
Hankins, Paul	MS0250	63A,41,47,32E
Hann, Gordon	NC2650	63A
Hansen, Neil E.	WY0130	37,47,63A,32,49
Hanson, Frank E.	WI0865	11,49,63A
Hanson, J. Robert	MN1450	63A
Hanzlik, Louis	CT0600	63A
Hara, Craig	MN0800	63A
Harbaugh, John	WA0050	29A,53,49,63A
Hardcastle, Geoffrey C.	NY0400	63A
Harker, Brian	UT0050	63A
Harkins, Edwin	CA5050	13A,13,63A,54,43
Hart, Michael D.	LA0030	37,63A,11,13,47
Hartman, Kevin	WI0825	49,63A
Harvey, Susan	TX1700	63A,63B,66A,32B,32C
Harvey, William	CA3520	63A
Harvey, William	CA4425	63A
Hasbrouck, Calvin	GA2100	63A
Hastings, Todd J.	KS1050	63A,29,11,41,42
Hawk, Stephen L.	PA3100	63A,47,29
Hawkins, Chase	KY0450	63A
Haynes, Juliana	LA0900	63A,11
Head, John	GA0490	63A
Hearn, Sidney T.	IN1100	32,32E,34,37,63A
Heath, Travis M.	IL2150	49,63A
Hedberg, Jeffrey	IL1085	61,63A
Hedrick, Steve	VA1250	63A
Hedwig, Douglas F.	NY0500	49,63A,63D
Heinzen, Craig	LA0700	11,63A,63B
Henderson, Eddie	NY1900	63A,29
Hendrickson, Steven	MD1010	63A
Hengst, Michael	CO0550	63A,37
Hepler, Nathaniel	PA1550	63A
Heredia, Joel	WA0480	47,63A,46,29,35A
Hernandez, Rene	MD0850	63A,49
Hernon, Bonnie	TN0450	63A
Herrick, Carole	AR0350	63A,63B
Herzog, James	NJ1050	63A
Hess, H. Carl	PA1050	37,38,60,63A
Hettle, Mark	TX1725	13,11,37,47,63A
Hickman, David R.	AZ0100	63A
Hickman, Lowell	MT0200	36,61,63A
Hill, Douglas M.	GA1300	60B,32C,37,49,63A
Hillam, Barry	UT0050	63A
Hillard, Leon H.	PA1250	63A
Hindman, Helen	OK0700	63A
Hinton, Eric L.	PA3150	37,60B,63A
Hitt, Barry	IA0910	63A
Hodel, Martin	MN1450	38,63A,42
Hodges, David	SC0850	63A,63C
Hodgson, Aaron	AG0500	63A
Hofer, Calvin	CO0225	32,37,49,63A,60B
Hoffman, David	IL1350	47,63A,66A
Hoffman, Edward W.	MD0650	63A
Hoffman, Patrick	DE0050	63A,63B,13,11,49
Hofmann, Richard Glenn	CA0835	63A
Hoksbergen, Ross	MI0100	63A
Holland, Greg	GA0050	63A
Holsberg, Peter W.	NY4200	63A
Holt, John	TX3420	63A
Hood, Alan	CO0900	63A,29
Hood, Boyde	CA5300	63A
Hooker, Tracy	WA0600	63A,63B,63
Hoover, Brian	IN1100	63A
Hopkins, Bruce	MA0700	63A
Hopkins, Greg J.	MA2050	63A
Hopkins, Gregory	MA1175	63A
Horton, Dennis	MI0400	10F,63A
House, Richard	SC1000	37,63A,32
House, Richard E.	SC0350	37,63A,32E,60B
Hovorka, Jamie	CA1750	63A
Hoyt, Thomas H.	NY2750	63A
Huang, Hai Tao	IL3310	13A,63A
Hubbs, Randall	WA0150	13,37,47,63A,29A
Huber, Wayne	CA1860	37,49,63A,67C,13
Hucke, Adam	IL2970	11,13A,29A,63A,47
Hudson, Gary	TX2350	11,49,63A,63B
Hudson, Timothy	NC0850	63A
Huener, Thomas J.	NC0650	13,63A,55B
Huff, Michael H.	AL1050	63A,42,49,67E,37
Hughes, Christopher A.	NM0310	37,60B,32E,63A,38
Hughes, Donald L.	PA2550	63A
Hull, Barbara A.	NY2650	63A,63,60
Hume, John	IL1100	32E,63A,63B
Hungerford, Grant	CA5060	63A
Hungerford, Grant	CA1750	63A
Hunsaker, Leigh Anne	TX0900	63A,32,49
Hunsicker, David	KS1450	63A
Hunter, Billy	NJ0825	63A
Hunter, Robert	AZ0440	32E,63A,37,46,29A
Huntoon, Ben	OH2050	63A
Hurley, Patricia	NY2400	63A
Hurst, Craig W.	WI0960	11,37,47,41,63A
Husted, Audrey	IA1350	63A
Hutchinson, Raymond	IL1900	66A,63A,63B,11
Hyatt, Jack	NY0635	13,63A
Illman, Richard	MI1400	63A
Ingle, Ronnie	ND0500	49,63A,47
Ingram, Roger	IL0550	47,63A
Inkster, Matthew	WV0600	63A,63B,37,47,49
Inouye, Mark	CA4150	63A
Irby, Fred	DC0150	47,49,63A
Irish, John E.	TX0150	63A,63B,49,29A
Jablonsky, Stephen	NY0550	11,63A,10A,10F,13
Jackson, Douglas A.	NC0700	63A,35
Jackson, Paul	AL0650	63A
Jarvis, Jeffrey S.	CA0825	63A,29
Jaudes, Christian	NY1900	29,63A
Jekabson, Erik	CA0807	63A,29
Jenkins, Clay	NY1100	29B,29C,63A,47
Jennings, David	MI2200	63A
Jewell, Jim	GA0625	66B,63A
Johansen, Larry	CA3800	63A
Johansen, Lawrence	CA0845	63A
Johnson Hamilton, Joyce	CA4900	63A
Johnson, Carly	AL0345	11,63A
Johnson, Carly J.	AL0050	63A
Johnson, J. Keith	TX3420	63A
Johnson, Jason K.	NE0610	63A
Johnston, Darren	CA5000	63A
Johnston, Dennis	NY0700	32E,12C,49,63A,60B
Johnston, Scott	OH2150	49,63A
Jokipii, Alex	NY3725	63A
Jones, David C.	MD0150	63A
Jones, Gregory R.	MO1780	11,63A,49
Jones, Melvin	GA1450	11,37,29,63A
Jones, Michael C.	KS1200	47,63A,63B,63C,13
Jones, R. Larry	AR0850	47,63A
Jones, Sean	PA1050	47,53,63A
Jones, Stephen	MI2250	49,63A,20G
Jones, Terry	ID0140	37,47,49,63A,29
Jorgensen, Richard	AR0750	63A,63B
Joseph, Mervyn	OH0500	32,63A
Julian, Tijuana	MO0350	63A,49,20G
Jumper, David	PA2200	29,63A,32E,49
Kaderabek, Frank	PA0850	63A
Kammerer, David	HI0050	10F,37,35B,63A,13C
Kason, Don T.	OH1650	63A,47
Kassner, Karl J.	NC0900	63A
Kaupp, Gil	NV0050	35C,35G,63A
Keberle, Daniel	WA1350	47,63A,29,29A
Keeley, Michael	AL1050	63A
Kelley, Darin	NJ1050	63A
Kelley, Scott	NY1150	37,63A
Kelly, Brandon	TX1550	63A
Kelly, Daniel	TX2955	63A,47,13A,13B
Kelly, Darin	PA1000	63A
Kelly, Thomas	NE0150	63A
Kelly, Todd	IL0400	32,47,63A,35
Keminski, Joe	NY2102	20,14,12A,63A
Kenny, William	PA0350	60,11,37,63A,63B
Kent, George E.	RI0300	11,49,63A,66G,66H
Kessler, Stan	MO1810	63A
Ketch, James E.	NC2410	47,63A,46,29
Keys, Jeff	MN1050	63A
Keyser, Allyson	NY3600	63A,13,12A
Kiehn, Mark T.	WI0808	32A,66D,70,63A,32B
King, Dan	OH2050	63A
Kiradjieff, Chris	OH2550	63A,49
Kirk, Kenneth P.	GA2150	63A,49,13,39
Kirkland, Anthony B.	MS0500	63A,42,49,67E,11
Kirsop, Daniel	SC0200	63A
Kiser, Daniel W.	NC1100	13A,10F,60B,37,63A
Kisor, Justin	IA1100	63A
Kjos, Kevin	PA1750	11,47,63A,49
Klages, James L.	OK1330	63A
Klaus, Alan S.	AD0050	63A,63B
Klazek, Merrie	AG0170	63A,48,49
Kleppinger, Stanley V.	NE0600	13,63A,37,12C
Knapp, James	WA0200	10,47,63A,53,29
Knepper, Bruce	IN1310	63A
Knopp, Larry	AB0100	63A
Knorr, Eric	OH0500	63A,49
Knudsvig, Peter	MN0600	63A
Koehler, Elisa C.	MD0400	38,63A,60,11,13A
Koenig, Mark	IN0907	34,63A
Koerselman, Herbert L.	KY1500	63A,32B
Kohlenberg, Kenneth	OH2120	37,60B,12A,11,63A
Koponen, Glenn	NY2900	60,37,41,63A,31A
Korak, John	IL2910	60,37,63A,49,42
Koronka, Kyle	TX3350	63A
Kosmyna, David J.	OH1800	63A,63B,49,47,29
Krauss, David B.	NJ1130	63A,41
Krauss, David	NY2750	49,63A
Kresge, Jeff	VA0550	63A
Kris, Michael	NC2410	63A
Kruger, Jonathan H.	NY3730	47,63A,53
Krummel, Christopher	OH2600	49,63A
Laing, Daniel R.	NE0300	60B,37,49,63A,63B
Lambert, Adam	TX0700	63A
Lambrecht, James M.	IL0100	37,49,63A,60B,13C
Lanier, Michael	GA2130	63A,49
Lark, Robert J.	IL0750	29,63A,47
Laronga, Barbara	CA2600	63A,29,47,63
Larsen, Jens	SC0900	10F,63A,49
Larsen, Jens	SC0650	63A
Larsen, Tage	IL0750	63A
Larson, Dave	NJ1400	63A
Latini, Eric J.	NY3650	63A
Laubach, David	AR0300	63A,49
Laudermilch, Kenneth	PA1300	63A
Laumer, Jack C.	TX3175	49,63A
Laverty, John M.	NY4150	60B,37,32,63A
LaVoie, Karen R.	MA2100	13C,60B,37,63A
Lawing, William D.	NC0550	29A,47,63A,34D,49
Lawrence, Josh	PA3330	63A
Lawson, Matthew	KY0250	13A,63A
Leach, Catherine F.	TN1710	13,63A
Leasure, Timothy	OH1850	63A,49
LeCheminant, Reed	UT0350	63A
Leder, Matthew D.	CO0830	63A
Lee, Kari	IL0850	63A
Lee, Matt	IL0750	63A,32E
Lee, R. Matthew	IL0850	63A
Lee, Richard F.	TX3150	37,63A
Lee, Rodger	NY2105	63A,49
Lehn, Steven	CO0100	63A
Leisring, Stephen W.	KS1350	63A
Lemons, Robert M.	CT0150	11,60,32,63A
Leopold, Timothy	NY2150	63A
Lepine, Joachim	AI0050	63A
Lethco, Leigh-Ann M.	WI0830	32E,37,63A,32
Lewis, Charles A.	MA0260	63A
Lewis, H. M.	KY0610	10F,11,12A,49,63A
Lewis, Jeffrey	CA4400	29,63A
Lichtmann, Jay	CT0650	63A
Ligotti, Albert F.	GA2100	49,63A
Lill, Joseph	IL2100	47,49,63A,37,42
Linahon, Jim	CA1900	11,63A
Lindblom, Peter	NY3725	63A
Lindemann, Jens	CA5030	63A,49
Linder, Kevin	IA0500	63A,46
Linder, Kevin	IA1200	63A
Lindsey, Douglas	GA1150	63A,41
Linehan, Wayne	MS0400	63A
Linklater, Fraser	AC0100	63A,32E,37,48,60B
Lirette, Charles	PA1050	63A
Little, Steve	IL0300	63A
Littleford, James	AB0100	63A
Lloyd, Joe	AZ0400	32C,37,63A,11,60
Lockard, Douglas T.	TX0600	63A,37,47
Long, Barry	PA0350	29,47,13,63A,53
Long, David	GA0600	36,63A,49,55C,40
Loos, Brandon	FL1700	63A
Lott, Peter Tell	AL0010	11,63A
Lovejoy, Donald G.	MN1700	37,63A,41,60,32E
Lowenthal, Richard	NJ0825	63A,53,46,29
Lowrey, Alvin	AA0035	63A
Lowrey, Alvin	AA0100	63A
Lowry, Paul	IL2050	63A
Lucas, William G.	MI2100	63A
Luftman, Adam	CA4150	63A

Index by Area of Teaching Interest

Name	Code	Areas
Luftman, Adam	CA5000	63A
Luftman, Adam	CA4200	63A
Lyman, Zachary	WA0650	13,63A
Lynch, Brian	FL1900	63A,10,47,46,29B
Lynn, Mark J.	KY1500	63A
Lyren, Delon	MN0150	63A,63B,49,45
MacDonald, J. Roderick	NY3725	63A
Machon, Allen	MA0600	63A
Mack, Rodney	PA3250	63A
Mack, William G.	MO0850	60,32C,37,49,63A
MacKay, Gillian	AG0450	37,42,63A,60B,60
MacKenzie, David	VT0200	63A
Macklin, Thomas	FL1750	63A
Macomber, Scott	CA0150	63A
Madeja, James T.	NY3780	32,63A,12C,49
Madonia, Michael	IL2775	63A
Madsen, Brent	MD0350	63A
Magee, Chris	TX3350	63A,46,29,47,53
Magnarelli, Joe	NJ0825	29,63A
Magnarelli, Joe A.	NJ1130	63A,29
Maguda, John K.	NY3717	63A
Mahar, Bill	AI0150	63A,29
Major, Amy Gilreath	IL1150	63A
Makeever, Gerald	MT0200	13A,42,63A
Malvern, Gary J.	SC0750	63A,41,12A
Manhart, Grant L.	SD0400	49,63A,63B,11,46
Manikam, Seelan	MA2010	63A
Marchiando, John R.	NM0450	63A
Marchione, Nick	PA3250	29,63A
Margulies, Peter	UT0250	63A
Martin, Klancy	RI0150	63A
Marx, Steve	CO0250	63A
Mase, Raymond	NY1900	63A,49
Mason, Carl	AR0950	63A
Mason, Roger	CA3100	63A
Matheson, Alan	AB0100	63A,29,49
Matlock, Herman	NY3775	63A,29,49
Matthews, Ron	PA1150	13,10,12A,63A,66A
May, Theresa	OH0755	29,63A
Mayfield, Irvin	LA0800	63A,46
Mayfield, Nathaniel	TX2900	63A
Mayse, Kevin A.	CA3800	37,63A,38
Mazziotta, Laura	NY2400	63A
McAlister, Anita	AG0600	63A
McCabe, Amy	DC0170	63A
McCandless, Andrew	AG0300	63A,42
McCarthy, Daniel	MI1180	63A
McChesney, David	NC2410	63A
McCourry, Christopher C.	MI1000	29,42,63A
McElroy, John	AL0800	63A
McFadden, Tim J.	OK1450	63A
McGrath, Michael	IL2775	63A
McKinney, Brian	IL2750	63A
McKinney, Dustin	CA3600	63A
McMahan, Andrew	CA0600	60,37,63A,54,34
McNeely, Heather	SC0200	12A,12C,63A
McNeil, John	MA1400	29,47,63A
McNeill, Dean	AJ0150	63A,29,46,47
McQueen, William F.	TX2100	11,20A,49,63A
McWhorter, Brian J.	OR1050	63A,49,43
Meachum, Jay	NC0350	63A
Meachum, Jay	NC1600	63A
Meredith, Henry M.	AG0500	32,63A,63B,67E
Meredith, Scott	WY0200	63A,67E,12,32E,49
Merkelo, Paul	AI0150	63A
Merrill, Paul	NY0900	46,47,29B,29C,63A
Merriman, John C.	AL0500	11,49,63A,70
Merritt, Frank	NC1100	63A,63B,32
Messersmith, Susan	SC0275	63A,49
Meyers, John	WI0100	63A,47
Mickey, Brian	AR0600	63A,63B
Miles, Melvin N.	MD0600	60,37,47,49,63A
Miles, Ron	CO0550	47,63A,29
Miller, Alan	IN0250	63A
Miller, Ivan	NJ1400	63A
Miller, Melanie	PA2300	63A
Miller, Michael	OH0600	63A,49
Mills, Alan W.	CO0275	37,66A,63A,32E,60B
Mills, David	OR0050	13,10,12A,37,63A
Millsap, Kyle	KY0950	63A,49
Milton, Kenneth	MS0560	11,47,49,63A,63B
Mitchell, Adrian	MS0350	11,63A,37,32C,49
Mitchell, Clarence T.	DC0350	63A
Mitchell, David W.	OR1100	63A
Mitchell, David	OR0150	63A
Moe, Eric	WA1350	63A
Moffett, C. Mondre	NC1550	63A,10F,29A,47,31F
Molloy, Steve	MO0850	63A,11
Monte, Tobias	MA2020	37,49,60,63A
Moon, Brian	MI1260	63A
Moore, Albert L.	MN1300	49,63B,63A,11
Moore, Christopher	FL0850	63A
Moore, Michael D.	OK1450	63A
Moorehead-Libbs, Jean	MI0500	63A
Moots, John E.	OK0150	32,49,63A,20G
Morden, James	GA2000	13,11,12A,63A
Morehead, Phillip H.	TN0850	13,41,63A,32E
Morgan, Carol	TX2300	63A,29,13B,11
Morreale, Michael	NY0644	11,63A,29A,47,13A
Morris, Craig	FL1900	41,49,63A,42
Morris, Hamilton	WV0650	63A
Morris, James R.	NY3700	13A,63A,13,11,49
Morris, Matt	SD0580	63A
Mortenson, Gary	KS0650	63A,49
Morton, Paul D.	LA0760	63A
Moselio, Joe	NJ0825	63A
Mossman, Matthew I.	NY0642	29,35B,63A
Muckey, Matthew I.	NJ1130	63A
Muehlenbeck Pfotenhauer, Thomas R.	MN1600	63A,47,29,11,11
	OK1250	37,63A,32E,60,34
Mueller, Marc	MI0400	63A
Mueller, Neil	MN1200	63A
Munoz, William	IA1800	32,63A,49
Muntefering, Scott	IA0900	63A
Murphy, Derrick	IN0100	29,63A,34,35
Murray, Mark S.	GA0550	63A,49
Murray, Robert P.	VA1000	63A
Muth, Roy	GA0625	63A
Myers, Steven	WI1155	63A
Najoom, Dennis	IA0300	63A
Naylor, Al	VA1550	63A,49,13C,13A
Neebe, Paul M.	NY4320	37,47,63A
Nelson, Jon R.	NY2150	63A
Nelson, Jon	VA1350	48,46,63A,37
Nelson, Scott	CA4850	63A,20H,10
Nevin, Jeff	AJ0100	63A
Newman, Miles	OR0850	63A,29
Newton, Farnell	ID0060	29,46,47,63A
Nielsen, Ryan		
Norris, Phil	MN1250	63A
Norris, Philip E.	MN1280	10F,11,32E,63A,31A
Norton, Nick M.	UT0250	63A
Novak, George	OH0300	63A
O'Banion, James	OR0400	63A
Ochoa, Reynaldo	TX3450	63A,49,13
Oglesby, Michael	TX3370	63A
Okamura, Grant K.	HI0210	60,32C,37,63A
Okoshi, Tiger	MA0260	63A
Olcott, James L.	OH1450	47,63A,49,42
Olive, Jordan	IL1200	63A
Olive, Jordan	IL2650	63A
Olsen, Timothy J.	NY4310	13,10,47,63A,29
Olson, Rolf	SD0600	37,47,49,63A,46
Olson, Scott	SD0050	63A
Optiz, Robert	GA1700	29,63A
Orris, Dale A.	PA2100	63A
Orris, Dale A.	PA0350	63A
Ortiz, Carlos	PA3580	63A
Osborn, James	NY4450	47,63A,48
Osorio, Claudio	FL1310	63A
Oster, Floyd	NH0110	63A,49
Ott, Leonard	CA0900	63A
Ott, Leonard	CA5350	63A
Owen, John E.	OH0950	60B,37,47,63A
Packard, John	OH1600	37,49,63A,60B,10F
Paddock, Joan Haaland	OR0450	60,32,49,63A,37
Pagnard, Charles	OH0450	60B,32E,49,63A
Palance, Thomas M.	MA1650	29,46,47,63A
Palmer, Kirk	OK0700	63A
Palmer, Kye	CA0815	63A
Panelli, Sal	CA0650	63A,32
Parke, Steve	IL2450	10,47,63A,29A,35A
Parker, Craig B.	KS0650	12A,63A,12
Parsons, Laura E.	AL0950	63A,12A,13A,11
Parsons, Longineu	FL0600	47,63A,29
Parton, Robert T.	OH0350	63A,29,47,29A,53
Pascuzzi, Greg	MD0060	10,63A
Paterson, Amy	UT0150	63A
Paulson, Brent	CO0625	63A,63,64,37
Payne, James	NE0590	11,63A,63B,46,35A
Pearce, Stephen	FL1500	63A
Pedde, Dennis	IA0930	63A,63B,63C,63D
Pedde, Dennis R.	IA0200	63A
Penzarella, Vincent	NY2250	63A
Penzarella, Vincent	NY2750	63A
Penzarella, Vincent	NY2150	63A
Pepping, Amanda J.	GA1050	63A,41
Perkins, Barry	CA0815	63A
Perkins, John D.	MO0100	63A,63B,12A,42,49
Peron, Tom	CA0150	63A
Peters, Grant S.	MO0775	63A
Peters, Michael	IA0600	63A,63B
Peterson, Ben	IL1740	63A
Petruzzi, Leon T.	NY1600	63A,49
Phelps, Joe F.	NC0050	63A
Philbrick, Channing P.	IL0550	63A
Phillips, Edward D.	IN0910	63A,35E
Phillips, Timothy	NC1400	63A,63C
Piatt, Kenneth H.	PA1200	63A,63B
Pickerell, Kevin	KS0210	63A,37
Pier, Fordyce C.	AA0100	37,49,63A
Pierce, Ted	WI0770	63A
Pina, Juan	AL0400	63A
Piper, Jeffrey S.	NM0450	49,63A
Place, Logan B.	LA0650	63A,37,12A
Plamondon, Andrew	WA0250	63A,46,47
Podroskey, Frank	PA0500	63A,63B
Polk, Sylvester	FL0100	34,63A,35A,35D,35G
Ponzo, Mark	IL2200	49,63A
Poper, Roy	OH1700	63A,49,41
Porter, David	WV0700	63A,34
Posey, Benjamin C.	AL0300	32,37,60B,63A
Powell, Larry	IN1650	63A,42
Predl, Ronald E.	OK1450	37,63A
Probst, Christopher	GA1070	63A
Probst, Christopher	GA0850	63A
Probst, Christopher	GA0400	63A,63B
Prosser, Douglas	NY1100	63A,42
Pruiett, Kevin P.	OK0650	47,63A,72,29A,49
Puccini, Dorival	IL1400	63A
Pursell, John	PA1400	63A
Pursell, John	MD0610	63A
Pursell, John	MD0300	63A
Purtle, Jeff	SC0050	63A
Pusey, Bill	PA3330	47,63A
Rabbai, George	PA3330	63A,47,49
Rabbai, George	NJ1050	63A,53,46
Radke, Fred	WA1050	29,63A
Ramirez, Roberto	PR0115	63A,49
Ramsey, Elmer H.	CA0550	63A,38
Raney, Earl	MA0250	37,63A
Raney, Earl L.	MA2150	49,48,63A
Ranger, Louis	AB0150	49,63A,41
Rankin, John M.	TX2200	11,47,63A,46
Ransom, Robert	VA0250	29,63A
Ranti, James	NY5000	63A,63C
Raschella, John	NY1350	63A
Raymond, Rusty	MO0800	37,63A,60B
Recktenwald, James	KY0250	63A
Reed, Jim	OH1200	63A
Reed, Marc A.	CO0350	63A,63B,49
Reese, Marc B.	FL1125	63A,49,41,42,48
Reichenbach, Brian	IL2300	63A
Reid, Edward F.	AZ0500	63A
Reid, Steven	IN0005	63A,36,37,38,13
Reider, Nick	MD0520	63A
Reyman, Randall	IL1750	47,63A,53,29
Reynolds, David	SD0550	12C,63A,63B
Reynolds, Jeffrey L.	AG0450	49,63A,37,29A
Riccomini, Ray	NY2250	63A
Richard, Leon	KY0750	49,63A,63B
Richardson, Edward 'Rex'	VA1600	63A,29,49
Richardson, William	MO0950	47,63A,11
Richeson, David T.	AR0750	63A,11,35A
Richwine, Reginald L.	OH2250	63A,47
Ridenour, Mark	IL0550	63A
Riegle, Dale	FL1500	47,49,63A
Rines, Elizabeth B.	ME0500	63A
Riter, Tye	FL1450	63A
Rittenhouse, Kenneth	VA0450	63A
Rizzetto, Jay	CA2950	63A
Roach, Stephen	CA0150	63A
Roberts, Steven	AL1150	29,63A,47
Robinson, Doug	AZ0490	63C,63A
Robinson, Greg	AG0050	63A
Robinson, Marty	WI0830	63A,29A,47
Robinson, Marty	FL0600	47,45,63A,29

Index by Area of Teaching Interest

Name	ID	Areas
Rodriguez, Bobby	CA5020	63A
Rodriguez, Bobby	CA5031	29,63A
Rodriguez, Michael J.	NY2750	63A
Rodriquez, Galindo	LA0550	63A,41,47
Rodriguez, Raquel H.	KY1000	37,42,63A
Rogers, Dave	NJ1400	29,63A
Rolfs, Thomas	MA1400	63A
Rolfs, Thomas C.	MA0400	63A
Roller, Jan D.	TX3530	63A
Romero, Frank	NM0310	63A,47,72,34
Romm, Ronald	IL3300	63A,41
Rommel, John D.	IN0900	63A
Roper, Richard	CA5070	63A
Roselle, Herbert	NJ1050	63A
Ross, Rashawn	FL0700	63A
Rossmiller, Adam	MN1620	63A
Rossum, Kelly	VA0150	63A,29,67E,47
Rotondi, Jim	NY3785	63A,29
Rowe, Carl	VA1350	63A
Rucker, Lee	OK1330	37,47,63A,46,29
Rudd, Wortley F. 'Wiff'	TX0300	63A
Rulli, Richard J.	AR0700	63A,42,49,41
Rupp, Eric	AG0400	63A
Russian, Dana S.	MA2050	63A
Sachs, Michael	OH0600	63A,49
Saenz, Charles	OH0300	63A
Salemink, Earl	WI0860	63A
Samu, Lex	NY0646	63A
Sanborn, Chase	AG0450	63A,29
Sanders, Carolyn I.	AL1160	13A,11,63A
Sandor, Edward	GA2100	49,63A
Sanford, O'Neil	VA0950	37,14A,63A
Sanheim, Trent	AI0190	63A
Santiago, Imer	TN1400	63A,41
Santorelli, Michael	TX1660	63A
Santorelli, Michael	TX3527	63A
Santos, E. Giovanni	CA2420	63A
Sasaki, Ray	TX3510	63A
Sato, Akira	TX3420	29,63A,47,60A
Saul, Ken D.	OR0700	63A
Saunders, John Jay	TX3420	47,63A,29,46
Saunders, Martin	WV0400	63A,53,49,47,34
Sawchuk, Terry M.	CO0800	49,63A
Saxton, Judith	NC1650	63A
Scarlato, Michael	LA0050	63A
Scaruffi-Klispie, Cindy	FL0500	63A
Schaefer, Phillip	MO2000	37,47,49,63A
Schafer, Erika L.	TN1700	63A,63,67E,37,46
Schaffer, Richard	NY2950	63A
Schantz, Jack	OH2150	29,46,47,63A
Schendel, Amy	IA1550	63A
Scherzinger, Peter	AG0150	63A
Schlabach, John	OH1900	63A,41
Schlueter, Charles	MA1400	63A
Schmid, Alice	GA0200	63A
Schmid, Alice	GA0950	11,63A
Schmid, William	GA0950	63A,46,29,49,47
Schneckenburger, Brian	MD0175	63A
Schodowski, Timothy	TX3370	63A
Schuesselin, John C.	MS0700	63A,49
Schultz, Andrew J.	NE0150	29,37,60B,63A
Schuman, Leah	IL3450	63A,49
Schwartz, Terry R.	IL3550	37,63A
Schweingruber, Eric J.	PA3250	63A
Scoles, Philip	TX2295	63A
Scott, Dave	CA4700	63A,29A
Scott, David L.	CA5150	63A,46,37
Scott, David R.	LA0350	12A,49,63A
Scott, David	CT0800	47,63A,41
Scott, Gary	OH0755	47,63A,20G,29,63B
Scott, J. B.	FL1950	63A,53,47,29A
Scott, Judson	WA1000	63A,49
Scott, Marshall	KY1550	41,47,63A,29
Sebring, Richard	MA1400	63A
Seeling, Ellen	CA5000	63A
Seguin, Philip	AG0650	63A
Seipp, Larry	VA1125	63A
Senn, Geoff	MN0040	29,63A,34,41,11
Senn, Takako	MN1300	63A
Senn, Takako Seimiya	MN0610	63A
Sepulveda, Charles	PR0115	29,63A,53
Severs, Alan R.	IN0905	63A,41
Shadday, Craig	RI0250	63A
Sharnetzka, Charles S.	MD0475	37,12A,63A
Sharp, Bradley	OH2300	63A
Shaw, Brian	LA0200	63A,47
Shear, Howard	CA0835	63A
Sherman, Steve	AA0080	32E,37,63A,46,35
Sherry, James Wallace	IA1450	29,63A
Shewan, Paul	NY3350	60B,37,63A,32E,38
Shier, Robin	AB0050	37,63A,63,46
Shipman, Dan	TX1000	63A
Shiver, Todd	WA0050	63A,32,37,47,49
Shook, Brian A.	TX1400	63A,63D,32E
Shorthouse, Tom	AB0060	63A,47,49,42
Siders, Thomas	MA0350	63A
Siders, Tom	MA0400	63A
Siebert, Alan H.	OH2200	63A
Sielert, Vern	ID0250	47,63A,29
Sienkiewicz, Frederick	MA0950	63A
Sievers, Karl H.	OK1350	63A
Silberschlag, Jeffrey	MD0750	29,35A,60,38,63A
Silver, Patricia	TN1350	63A,64C
Simmons, Gordon	MI1750	63A
Simmons, James	TN1100	63A,47,46,29A,29B
Siroky, Brad	NY2105	63A
Skidgel, Wesley	IL0850	63A,32E
Skoniczin, Robert	DE0150	63A
Slabaugh, Stephen	MI1180	47,63A
Slack, Robert	CA1000	47,49,63A,53
Smart, James	MT0400	37,63A,32E,60B
Smith, Carol	OR0250	63A
Smith, Dennis	TN1660	63A
Smith, Donald S.	AZ0350	29,63A,49
Smith, G. D.	KY1200	13,60,38,63A
Smith, Rusty	NC1900	63A,41,46,47
Smith, Shawn T.	TX2930	63A,60B,37,32E
Smith, Thomas	NY2150	63A
Smith, Thomas	NY2250	63A,41
Smith, Wadada Leo	CA0510	63A,29,10,45,53
Smolik, Vicky	IL2970	11,63A,10D,35D
Snapp, Doug R.	MN1000	46,47,63A,29
Sobieralski, Nathan	CA0810	63A
Sokol, Jill	NJ0700	63A
Sonneborn, Matthew	FL0680	63A
Soper, Lee H.	NY2750	63A
Sorah, Donald	VA1580	34,63A,29,14C,20
Sorensen, Randall J.	LA0250	63A,63B,13,13B,13A
Sorg, A.	MA0800	63A
South, James	OK1250	37,63A
Southall, John K.	FL0950	13,63A,60B,37,32E
Spencer, David	TN1680	63A
Spencer, Larry	TX0370	35G,63A
Speziale, Marie	TX2150	63A,41,42
Spicer, Shawn	AG0500	63A
Spragg, James	AG0450	63A
Stamps, Justin	ID0050	63A,11
Stanley, Brian	FL0650	63A
Stannard, Jeffrey	WI0350	63A
Steck, Charles	IN1750	63A
Steeds, Graham	IA0950	63A
Steffen, Richard	TN0050	60B,49,63A,47,11
Stern, Jeffrey	AF0100	63A,49
Stibler, Robert	NH0350	11,63A,67C,49,67E
Still, Christopher	CA0825	63A
Stockham, Jeff	NY0650	63A,47
Stockham, Jeff	NY1350	63A
Stoelzel, Richard	MI0900	63A,49
Stokes, James M.	NC0050	63A,49,41,42
Stoupy, Etienne	TX3300	49,63A,63B
Stout, Ron	CA0825	63A
Stowman, William	PA2300	47,63A
Strait, Tom	MN1120	63A,29,63B,47
Strawley, Brian	VA1600	63A
Strawley, Steven	PA0950	63A
Strecker, Scott	KS1450	63A
Streider, Will E.	TX3200	37,49,63A
Strohmaier, Chris	IA0550	63A
Subera, Angel	MA0350	63A
Suggs, Robert	MD0100	63A
Sullivan, Joe	AI0150	63A,29,47
Sutte, Jack	OH0200	63A
Swana, John	PA3330	63A,53,47
Swana, John	PA3250	29,63A
Swanson, Isaac	WY0115	63A
Swartz, Craig	IA0700	63A
Swisher, Eric	KY0950	63A,49
Swygert, Jonathan	GA1300	63A
Takacs, William	TX3750	63A,11
Tartell, Joey	IN0900	63A
Taylor, Nancy	TX3520	63A,49
Taylor, Robert C.	AB0100	37,49,60B,63A
Tevis, Royce	CA0800	32,37,63A,60
Theurer, Britton	NC0650	63A,42
Thompson, James	NY1100	63A,42
Thompson, Steven	MN0250	37,60B,63A,32E,49
Thompson, Vance	TN1710	63A,47
Thornburg, Scott	MI2250	13A,13,49,63A
Thornton, Mary	TX2930	63A,29A,13B,13C
Thorstenberg, Roger W.	KS0150	63A,63B
Thrower, Daniel N.	TX3530	63A
Tillman, Joshua	NC2700	63A,11
Timmey, Zachery	VA0950	63A,11,37
Tinnin, Randall C.	FL1950	63A,49,37,32E,20
Tipton, Mark	ME0250	63A
Tirk, Richard	OK1250	47,63A,37
Tiscione, Mike	GA0750	63A
Toll, Yvonne	GA0500	63A
Tolliver, Charles	NY2660	10,46,47,63A
Tomlison, R. Scott	PA2250	63A
Toney, Hubert	PA0700	37,47,32E,63A
Towery, Randy	ID0070	63A
Trask, Alvin	MD0550	63A,53,29A,14C,47
Tremblay, Dan	NY3780	63A
Tremblay, Dan	AG0250	63A
Treybig, Joel	TN0100	63A,13B
Trinkle, Steven W.	NV0050	63A,41,42,38,13A
Tuck, Patrick M.	KY1425	10,13,49,63A,63B
Tuckwiller, George	VA0700	63A,63B
Tuckwiller, George	VA1750	60,11,41,49,63A
Tunnell, Michael	KY1500	49,63A,42
Turcotte, Kevin	AG0650	47,63A
Turcotte, Kevin	AG0450	63A
Turnbull, David	WA1150	49,63A,67E,37
Turner, Lloyd	MS0100	63A
Turner, Ross	AG0550	63A
Turney, Brent	WI0850	47,29A,63A
Turrill, David	OH1650	37,32E,60,63A
Tynan, Paul	AF0150	37,63A,29
Ulrich, Brad	NC2600	63A
Valenzuela, Victor	AZ0480	63A,63B
Van Houzen, Aren	MO0300	63A
Van Houzen, Aren	IA0400	63A
VanFleet, Joseph	KY0550	63A
Vangjel, Matthew S.	AR0730	63A,46,13C
Vanore, John	PA3680	60,10,47,49,63A
VanValkenburg, Jamie G.	CO0050	63A,63C,63D,37,41
Vassallo, James	TX3400	41,63A
Vega, Ray	VT0450	29,47,63A
Villines, Roger	FL1500	63A,47,11
Vizutti, Allen	SC1110	29,63A
Volpe, Christopher	MN1625	63A,41
Volz, Nick R.	LA0300	63A
Vonderheide, David E.	VA0250	63A
Vondracek, Tom	MN1500	63A
Vosburgh, George	PA0550	63A
Vosburgh, George	PA1050	63A
Vu, Cuong	WA1050	29,63A
Wade, Mark Alan	OH0850	63A,12A,11,32,60B
Waidelich, Peter J.	FL0400	49,63A
Walburn, Jacob A.	IL3300	63A,29
Walker, Brian	TX2750	63A
Walker, Michael	TX0250	63A
Walter, Matt	IN0700	63A
Walters, Timothy	FL0650	13,41,63A,29
Ware, David N.	MS0350	63A,34C,47,11,13B
Warfield, William	PA1950	47,63A,29
Warkentin, Steve	TX2250	63A
Washburn, David	CA0825	63A
Washburn, David W.	CA5020	63A
Wasiak, Ed	AA0200	32,37,63A
Wasko, Dennis	PA3330	47,63A,49
Waugh, Robert	IN0800	63A,47
Weber, Carlyle	FL0950	63A,63B
Weber, Jonathan	IL2750	63A
Weber, Mary	MO1900	63A
Weber, Mary	MO1250	63A,13,11
Webster, Gerald	OR0850	63A,12A
Weeda, Linn	AK0100	11,36,49,63A
Weir, Tim	ME0340	47,63A,29,32E
Wells, Larry	NC1350	32,63A
Wendholt, Scott	NY3785	63A
Wenger, Alan J.	MO1790	11,63A
West, James R.	LA0200	63A
Westervelt, Todd G.	FL0100	32,12C,63A
Whaley, Daniel M.	TN1100	63A,11

Name	Code	Areas
Wharton, Keith	MD1100	63A
White, Darryl A.	NE0600	63A,29
White, Kevin	MO0750	13,10F,10,63A,53
White, Matthew S.	SC0420	63A,46,35,53
White, Tim	AG0050	63A,49
White, Timothy	AG0200	63A
White, William	MI1750	63A,29
Whitehead, Glen	CO0810	63A,47,29,45
Whitehead, Patrick	DC0170	63A
Whitehead, Russell	AA0100	63A
Whitford, Keith	IN1560	63A
Whitted, Pharez	IL0600	63A,29,47,49
Wilcox, Mark	TX1650	13C,63A,49,29E,29C
Wilds, John	CA4100	63A
Wiley, N. Keith	PA2350	32C,47,63A,29
Wilfong, Glen	WI0100	37,63A
Wilkes, Corey	IL0550	63A
Willard, Michael	OH2290	63A,32E
Willard, Michael L.	OH1350	63A,49,63
Willenborg, Hal	CA4300	63A
Willey, Rich	SC0400	63A
Wilson, John	PA0550	29,63A
Wilson, Thad	DC0100	63A
Wilson, Thomas	CO0200	63A
Wilt, James	CA1075	63A,42
Wing, Gregory	KY0900	63A
Winking, Keith R.	TX3175	47,63A,29
Winkler, Chad	PA0600	63A
Winkler, John	WV0750	49,63A
Winslow, Michael Rocky	CA0800	29,47,63A
Winslow, Richard D.	CA0800	49,63A,63B,29A,20G
Woelfel, Kevin	ID0250	35A,35,63A,35E,35B
Wolf, Donald	AL1195	10F,37,46,47,63A
Wood, Kevin	WI0250	63A
Wood, Kevin	IL1085	63A
Wood, Peter J.	AL1300	63A,13,49,41
Woodring, Mark	KY0950	63A,49
Woodruff, Christopher J.	CA0600	37,13,63A
Woolf, Vance	LA0900	63A
Woomert, Barton R.	AG0450	63A
Wootton, Tim	MO1550	63A
Wootton, Tim	MO0400	63A,49
Workman, Josh	SC1100	63A
Worley, John L.	CA4900	63A
Wright, Ben	MA1400	63A
Wright, Lawrence	PA2450	37,41,49,63A
Wright, Steve	MN0750	47,63A,35,46,10
Wurtz, Gary	TX2700	47,63A
Wygonik, David	PA2950	63A,63B
Yates, Derrick	AL0010	11,37,47,63A
Yates, Eric	AL1170	63A
Yontz, Timothy	IL3550	32E,37,63A,32
Young, James	MI1800	63A
Zehringer, Daniel	OH2500	63A,13A
Ziek, Gary D.	KS0300	60,37,63A
Zifer, Timothy	IN1600	47,63A,29A,49
Zimmerman, Tim	IN1025	63A
Zingara, James	AL1150	63A,37

Horn

Name	Code	Areas
Agrell, Jeffrey	IA1550	63B
Albrecht, Ken	IN1010	63B
Aldrich, Fred	MA2050	63B
Allen, Mark	OR1000	37,49,63A,63C,63B
Allmann, Kimberly	MN0250	63B
Altman, Timothy	NC2435	60,32,37,63A,63B
Ammons, Anthony	NC1250	63B
Anderer, Joseph T.	NY2750	63B
Anderson, Gwen	MN0300	63B,42
Andrus, Brice	GA1050	63B
Ashton, John H.	WV0300	38,63A,63B
Aspnes, Jane	AK0150	63B,49
Atkinson, James	CA0825	63B
Atwell, Bruce W.	WI0830	63B,13,11
Aubin, Matthew	WA1150	63B,38
Austin, Paul	MI0300	63B
Ayoub, Jason	MD0300	63B
Bain, Andrew	CA1075	63B,42
Baker, James	AL0300	63B
Baker, Michelle	NY2150	63B
Baker, Michelle	NY2250	63B
Baker, Sherry H.	KY0450	63B
Bakkegard, Karen	MD0400	63B
Baldwin, Melvin	CA0650	63B
Banfield-Taplin, Carrie	OH0950	11,63B
Barley, Leroy	NC2300	63A,63B
Barnes, Darrel	MO0350	62B,62A,63B
Barnewitz, William	IL2250	63B,42
Barrow, Gary	AR0200	49,63A,63B
Bartz, Tammy	MN1400	63B
Basler, Paul	FL1850	13,63B,34
Bates, Vincent C.	MO0950	63B,32B,32C,11
Beal, Kaylene	NE0150	63B
Bear, Colvin	OH2450	63B
Beason, Christine F.	TX3250	37,48,63B,32,10F
Beck, Lynn	NC0750	13,63B
Becker, Lauren	NY2650	63B
Bell, Charles	OH2550	63B
Bell, John	MO0850	32,38,63B
Bell, Kenneth G.	PA1400	63B,42
Bendixen-Mahoney, Kirsten	FL0680	63B
Bendixon-Mahoney, Kristen	FL0500	63B
Bennett, Dana	NY0400	63B,13B,13C
Bennett, Travis	NC2600	63B
Benway, Joel	IL0850	63B
Berger, Gene P.	IN0150	49,41,63B
Bernatis, William	NV0050	13A,13,49,63B
Betts, Kendall	NH0350	63B
Billman, Nancy S.	NJ0800	63B
Bisson, Mary	MD0100	63B
Black, Amy King	GA0050	63B
Black, Marjorie	MN0800	63B
Blackmore, Lisa	MO0650	49,63A,63B
Blice, Carolyn	FL1550	63B
Blomster, Jennie	CA5350	63B,41,42
Blomster, Jennie	CA1860	63B
Bloom, Myron	IN0900	63B
Boen, Jonathan C.	IL2250	63B
Boldin, James E.	LA0770	63B,12A,11
Bolen, Patricia	SC0700	63B
Bollino, Damien	VA1475	63B
Bomer, Delain	MI1180	11,63B
Bonnell, Bruce M.	MI0400	63B
Bonnett, Kurt	TX3535	49,63A,63B
Bontrager, Lisa Jane	PA2750	63B
Boren, Mark	ND0250	63A,63B,13A,41
Bosler, Annie J.	CA5020	63B
Boudreault, Mary	NC2700	63B,13A,13D,13E,13B
Bowermaster, Tod	MO1830	63B
Brant, Aaron	OH2250	63B,49
Brenes, Laura	CA5150	63B
Brickman, Nina	AG0600	63B,48
Bridge, Julie	NY2950	63B
Brink-Button, Ilze	NY2950	63B
Britsch, Richard	MI0900	63B
Britsch, Richard	MI0350	63B
Britsch, Richard	MI0850	63B
Britten, Ruth	CA4300	63B
Brockett, David	OH0650	63B
Brown, Tom	WI0810	11,41,49,63A,63B
Brummett, Jennifer	WA0400	63B
Brummett, Jennifer	WA1350	63B
Buck, Brenda	AZ0350	63B
Burch, Jennifer	NY1100	63B
Burdick, Richard	AJ0100	63B
Burgess Amstutz, Cheryl	KY0100	63B
Burke, Kevin R.	IN0500	12,13,20,42,63B
Burnett, Rodger	WA1000	49,63B
Burnett, Rodger	WA0800	63B
Burroughs, Mary	NC0650	42,63B,13C
Butler, Charles Mark	MS0250	63B,32B,13E,13B,66G
Bygrave, Max	FL0450	63B
Caballero, William	PA0550	63B
Callaghan, Marjorie S.	CT0800	12A,13,63B
Callaway, Dan T.	LA0650	63B
Caminiti, Joseph D.	PA2800	60,38,37,63B,32E
Camp, James L.	GA0490	37,49,63B,63C,63D
Campbell, Bob	NC0850	63B,49
Campbell, Larry	TX0340	37,47,63B,63C,63D
Campbell, Robert	NC1900	63B,49
Campbell, Robert	NC2500	63B
Canty, Dean R.	TX3525	60,37,63A,63B,11
Carlson, Andrea	IA0500	63B
Carlson, Andrea	SD0050	63B,49
Carrillo, Oto G.	IL0750	63B
Carter, Daniel	WV0550	63B
Casey, Brian	NY1700	38,63B,60B,13C
Casey, Lisa R.	MO0775	13,63B
Celmer, Joey R.	SC1050	63A,63B,63C,63D,47
Channells, Janet	MI1160	63B
Chenoweth, Richard K.	OH2250	63B,32E
Cheshier, Treneere J.	OH0650	63B
Christain, Ron	CA0650	63C,63B
Clevenger, Dale	IN0900	63B
Clevenger, Dale	IL0550	63B
Cline, Gilbert D.	CA2250	63A,49,29,67E,63B
Cockson, Aaron	MD0150	63B
Codreanu, Christian	TN1400	11,41,63B
Cole, Deb	MA0650	63B
Cole, Robert	PA3650	34A,34B,49,63B,72
Colton, Kathy	UT0050	63B
Compton, Lanette	OK0800	63B,11,32E,42
Conrad, Larry	AZ0440	63B
Conrod, Derek	NY1100	63B
Conrod, Derek	AG0500	63B
Conway, Colleen	MI0050	32,63B
Cook, Jeffrey	TN0900	63B,12A,42,11
Cook, Linda Klein	WI0750	63A,12,13,63B,10F
Cooper, Chris	CA5030	63B
Cordell, Angela	NJ0800	63B
Coreil, Kristine	LA0550	63B,13,41
Cottle, Melanie	IL3550	63B
Covington, Alicia	GA2300	63B
Cox, John	OR0150	63B
Cox, John P.	OR1100	63B
Craig, Genevieve	OK0300	63B
Craig, Genevieve	OK1330	63B
Crane, David	OR0250	63B
Craven, Robert	DC0050	63B
Creasy, Catherine S.	VA1400	63B
Creasy, Catherine	VA0750	63B
Creel, Randall Patrick	TX2650	63B
Crenshaw, Sonja L.	SC0800	63B
Croft, Mathew	CA4400	63B
Crook, Joshua	GA0850	63B
Culbertson, Robert M.	TX1400	11,32B,63B
Curley, Jason	NY1400	60B,63B,37,49,32E
Daly, Rachel	MA0510	63B,11
Danforth, Robert B.	IN0350	63B
Dauer, Robin	AR0110	13,11,63B
Davis, Lisa	MS0100	63B
Day, Michael	NC1550	11,32E,32F,63A,63B
Dean-Gates, Elizabeth	RI0300	63B
Deane, Richard	GA2100	63B
Deane, Richard	GA0750	63B
Deatrick, Linda	MI1950	63B,66D
Deats, Carol	KS1050	32B,63B
DeBoer, Angela	TN1100	63B,49,13A,13B,13C
Decorsey, James H.	WI0350	12A,41,63B
Deiderichs, Patty	MN1300	63B
Deland, Neil	AG0300	63B
DeMattia, Alan	OH0600	63B
DeMers, Peggy	TX2250	63B,13
Demilo, Brad	NY0050	63B
DeMilo, Bradford	NY2550	63B
Denis, Andrea	TX1350	63B
Denis, Andrea	TX0600	63B
Derechailo, Melissa	NE0700	63B,11,35
Derome, Denys	AI0150	63B,49
Dewater, Jason	NE0610	63B
DeWitt, Timothy L.	WV0050	49,63A,13E,63B,63C
Dickow, Robert H.	ID0250	13,10,63B,34
Dirmeier, Kristen	MA0950	63B
Dodd, Anna	GA2130	63B
Dodson Galvan, Jennifer	CA0600	63B
Dodson-Webster, Rebecca	PA2150	63B,13,12A,49
Doughty, Heather	CT0100	63B
Dovel, Jason L.	OK0550	63A,11,63B,10F
Dressler, John C.	KY0950	12A,63B,11,12C
Drifmeyer, Kelly B.	NY3780	63B,41
Dugger, Duane A.	OH2200	63B
Dutton, John	MT0350	63B
Easter, Wallace E.	VA1700	37,63B,13
Edwards, Marilyn	OH0250	63B
Eklund, Jason	GA1150	63B,41
Elliott, David	KY1450	49,63B
Ellsworth, Ann	NY3775	63B
Ellsworth, Ann	NY2750	63B
Ellsworth, Ann	NY3790	63B
Eng, Clare Sher Ling	TN0100	13,13B,13D,63B,66A
Entzi, John A.	NC2400	37,63B,41
Epstein, Eli	MA0350	63B
Ericson, John Q.	AZ0100	63B
Etzel, Laurel	IL1090	11,63B

Index by Area of Teaching Interest

Name	Code	Areas
Evans, Mathew J.	CO0275	63B,11,13C,42
Evans, Patty	AC0100	63B
Fackler, Dan	IL1850	63B
Fackler, Dan	IL0730	63B
Fair, Jeffrey	WA1050	63B
Fairbanks, Will	IL1050	37,63A,46,49,63B
Fairchild, G. Daniel	WI0840	10F,11,32,63B
Fairfield, John	IL2200	11,63B
Falvey, Joseph	VA0150	63B,37,34G,32E,49
Farmer, Joni	KY0400	63B
Fassler-Kerstetter, Jacqueline	KS0650	63B,13E,13B
Faust, Randall E.	IL3500	63B,10,63,13,49
Fearing, Scott M.	DC0100	63B
Fearon, Mary	AA0020	63B
Feather, Carol Ann	TN0450	13,11,38,63B
Feltner, Tiffany	TN0260	63B
Fenderson, Mark W.	MT0175	11,37,63A,63B
Fields, D. Loren	ME0250	63B
Filzen Etzel, Laurel Kay	IL1350	63B,60B,37
Filzen, Sherill	IL1350	63B
Finck, Gabrielle	MD0850	63B
Fitter, Todd	OH0450	63B
Fitzpatrick, Stuart L.	NC0900	63B
Flaherty, Mark	MI1600	47,63A,29A,34,63B
Flanagin, Michael	IN1025	37,63A,63B,41,60B
Flint, Gregory	IL0550	63B,42
Flint, Gregory	WI0825	63B
Ford, Marlene	VA1000	63B
Foulk, Lin	MI2250	63B,15,41,48,49
Fox, Suzanne D.	PA1900	63B
Fralick, Janice	AG0050	63B
Frederick, Jeremiah	IL2750	63B
Frederick, Jeremiah	IL1300	63B
Frederick, Mark	SC0200	32,63B
Freedman, Deborah	NE0590	11,12A,38,63B
French, Allen	MI0900	63B
Frierson-Campbell, Carol	NJ1400	32,63B,60
Fritts, Susan L.	VA1550	63B
Fulgham, Marc S.	MO1500	11,49,63A,63B
Funkhouser, James	KS0050	63B,10
Furry, Stephanie	GA0950	63B,49,33,11
Gaboury, Janine	MI1400	41,49,63B
Gagnon, Jean-Louis	AI0210	63B
Gallahan, Carla A.	AL1050	32,63B
Gandara, Javier	NY2150	63B
Gannon, Thomas	MA2100	13A,63B
Garcia, Jessica	GA0200	63B
Gardner, Randy C.	OH2200	63B
Garland, Jon R.	NY4150	63B
Garland, Jon	NY1350	63B
Garner, Ronald L.	UT0150	13,11,12A,63B
Garrett, Christopher	MI1150	63B
Garvin, Jerry	CA1900	63B,54
Garza, Jeff	TX3350	63B
Garza, Jeff	TX2200	63B
Gast, Michael	MN1623	63B
Gaudreault, Jean	AI0150	63B
Gavin, Charles	TX2700	41,49,63B
Gearheart, Kerri	SC1000	63B,32B
George, Alexander	CO0550	63B
George, Emil	DC0010	63B
George, Ron	AG0500	63B
G'froerer, Brian	AB0200	63B
Gibson, Jeff	AG0170	63B
Gilbert, Robert	MS0700	63B
Gilbert, Robert	TN1200	63B
Gillie, Gina	WA0650	13C,63B
Gindin, Suzanne B.	IN1050	32,37,38,41,63B
Glen, Nancy L.	CO0950	63B,32B
Gollmer, James W.	MD0060	63B
Gongos, Chris	AG0450	63B
Gongos, Chris	AG0300	63B,42
Gorbasew, A. 'Sasha'	AG0500	63B
Gordon, Peter L.	NY2750	41,49,63B
Gordon, William	AC0050	10F,12A,63B
Gowen, Dennis	ND0400	37,49,63A,63B,60
Grabois, Daniel	NY2150	63B
Graf, Kendra	UT0150	63B
Graham, Robin	CA0510	63B
Grant, Tom	TN0150	63A,63B
Greenwald, Fred	IL1610	63A,63B,37
Gress, Daniel	AG0400	63B
Griffin, Christopher	NC2650	63B,13C
Griffith, Lynne	MD0520	63B
Griffiths, Laura	CA1000	63B
Grishkoff, Rob	CA2390	63B
Grishkoff, Robert	CA1425	63B
Grishkoff, Robert	CA5355	63B
Grodrian, Ericka	IN1750	11,13C,49,63B
Groome, Frank	IL1740	63B
Gross, Steven	CA5550	63B
Gross, Steven	CA5060	63B,49
Guy, Marc J.	NY3725	13,63B
Hackleman, Allene	AA0100	63B
Hackleman, Martin	MO1810	63B
Hagelstein, Kim Rooney	TX2750	12A,13D,32E,63B
Hager, H. Stephen	TX3175	13A,13,49,63B
Hager, Lawson	TX0900	13,49,63B,41
Hahn, Marjorie	FL1300	63B,49,60
Hamilton, Margaret J.	MI2250	63B,32,13,35E
Hammond, L. Curtis	KY0900	63B,12A
Hanselman, Jay	GA1300	63B
Hansen, Jeremy C.	TN1450	63B,13C,42
Harcrow, Michael	PA2300	63B,49,13
Harper, Larry D.	WI0200	60,37,41,63B
Harrell, Mark	TN0250	63B
Harrell, Wayne	MO0800	63B
Harrington, William	CA3520	32,38,41,63B,31A
Harris, C. Andrew	IA0300	63B
Harris, Charles	IA0930	63B
Harris, Charles	IA1800	63B
Hartman, Scott	CA4425	63B
Harvey, Susan	TX1700	63A,63B,66A,32B,32C
Haskins, David	AB0200	63B
Haunton, Thomas C.	NH0100	63B,42
Hawkins, Ben	KY1350	60B,32,37,38,63B
Hegg, Barbara	SD0150	36,61,63B,60
Heim, D. Bruce	KY1500	63B,49,42
Heinzen, Craig	LA0700	11,63A,63B
Helfter, Susan	CA5300	11,63B
Hellick, Melanie	MI0500	63B
Helman, Michael	ID0100	63B,11
Henke, Corey	MN1700	63B
Hennigar, Harcus	AG0450	63B
Henniss, Bruce G.	OH1850	63B
Hernon, Mike	TN0450	63B
Heroux, Gerard H.	RI0300	16,63B,11
Herrick, Carole	AR0350	63A,63B
Hesse, Marian	CO0950	63B,49
Hettwer, Mike	OR0450	63B
Hiebert, Thomas N.	CA0810	13,63B
Hillyer, Dirk M.	MA1650	63B,11,12A,13E,13F
Hoberg, Gwen	WI0860	63B
Hoffman, Patrick	DE0050	63A,63B,13,11,49
Honea, Ted	OK1330	12A,16,63B
Hooker, Tracy	WA0600	63A,63B,63
Hoops, Haley S.	TX2400	63B
Hoover, David	CA3100	63B
Hoover, David E.	CA0835	63B
Horner, Erin	TN1850	63B
Hosmer, Christopher D.	AL0500	63B,34C
Houtchens, Alan	TX2900	12A,12,63B
Howard, Howard	NY0500	63B
Howarth, Anne	MA2010	63B
Hoyle, Robert	CT0600	63B
Hoyt, William	OH2150	49,63B
Hrivnak, Michael	NC1350	63B
Hudson, Bruce	CA2420	63B
Hudson, Gary	TX2350	11,49,63A,63B
Hughes, Patrick	TX3510	63B
Hull, Douglas	CA2950	63B
Hume, John	IL1100	32E,63A,63B
Hundemer, Thomas	LA0050	63B,16,10A
Hunt, Mary H.	NY3730	63B
Hunter, Barbara	IL2970	63B
Hustis, Gregory	TX2400	63B
Hutchins, Tony	IA1100	11,29A,63B,63C,32E
Hutchinson, Raymond	IL1900	66A,63A,63B,11
Hutton, Cynthia	OR0950	60,37,49,63B
Inglefield, Deb S.	IN0910	63B
Inkster, Matthew	WV0600	63A,63B,37,47,49
Irish, John E.	TX0150	63A,63B,49,29A
Irizarry, Rafael E.	PR0115	37,12A,63B,42,49
Ivanov, Peter	PA2200	63B
Ivanovic, Predrag	FL1450	63B
Ivey, Carol	TX3370	63B
Jackson, Eric	MO1550	63B
Jackson, Eric	MO0400	63B
Jackson, Randy	AI0050	63B
James, Gordon	TN1350	63B,42
Jeffrey, Wayne	AB0060	35A,37,49,48,63B
Jekabson, Erik	CA0900	63B,29
Jenkins, Ellie M.	GA0300	63B
Jewell, Vickie L.	AL0345	11,37,63B,66A
Jirosek, Peter	IL2650	63B
Jirousek, Peter	IL3450	63B
Joham, Michael	WA0250	63B
Johns, Kristen	GA2150	63B,11,42,49
Johnson, Heather	PA3100	63B
Johnson, Larry	OR0700	63B,49
Johnson, Michelle	OK0850	63B
Johnson, Michelle	OK1450	63B
Johnson, Seth	TX0250	63B
Johnston, Jason	WY0200	63B,49,12A
Jolley, David	NY2250	41,63B
Jolley, David	NC1650	49,63B
Jones, Michael C.	KS1200	47,63A,63B,63C,13
Jordan, Jeff	KS0350	37,32E,60B,63B,10
Jorgensen, Richard	AR0750	63A,63B
Jostlein, Thomas	IL3300	63B
Joy, Nancy	NM0310	63B,49,13A,11
Kang, Grace	FL1750	41,63B
Kaplan, Sara	IL2775	63B,13A
Kappy, David	WA1050	13A,41,48,63B
Karr, Andrew	FL2000	63B
Katzen, Daniel	MA1400	63B
Katzen, Daniel	AZ0500	63B
Keays, James	CA5150	12A,49,63B
Kellan, Kurt	AB0150	41,63B
Kemm, Karl	TX2930	63B
Kemm, Karl	TX0550	63B,49,67E,14E,14F
Kennedy, Bryan	MI2100	63B
Kenny, William	PA0350	60,11,37,63A,63B
Kerley, Eric	FL0700	63B
Kilp, Brian T.	IN0800	63B,13
Kilroe-Smith, Catherine	GA2050	63B
Kim, Jennifer L.	CA0960	63B
Kimball, Linda	WI0865	63B
Kimball, Linda	WI0815	63B
Kimel, Neil	IL0750	63B
King, Richard	OH0600	63B,49,41
Kinsman, Benjamin	AB0100	63B
Kirschen, Jeffry	PA3250	63B
Klaus, Alan S.	AD0050	63A,63B
Klein, Jon	ID0060	11,63B
Klickman, Philip	MD0350	63B,37,32E,60B
Klintworth, Paul	CA3800	63B
Klock, Laura C.	MA2000	63B
Kolwinska, Jeremy	MN1280	63C,63D,11,63B
Kosmyna, David J.	OH1800	63A,63B,49,47,29
Kostyniak, Stephen	PA0550	63B
Kozak, Kevin J.	AL0800	63B,13C,41
Kozelka, David	IL1100	63B
Kramer-Johansen, Karl	NJ1050	63B
Krause-Hardie, Rebecca	NH0150	63B
Kravig, Dean	WA1100	63B
Krehbiel, A. David	CA1075	63B,42
Krubsack, Kathryn	WI1155	63B
Krubsack, Kathy	WI0808	63B
Kurau, Peter	NY1100	63B
Lafferty, Laurie	OH2150	32B,32C,63B
Laing, Daniel R.	NE0300	60B,37,49,63A,63B
Lambrecht, Richard	TX3520	12A,49,63B
Lamprey, Audrey	CA0630	13A,49,63B
Lamprey, Audrey	CA5040	13A,63B
Landis, Margery	ME0150	63B
Landsman, Julie	NY0150	63B
Landsman, Julie	NY1900	63B
Lang, Jeffrey	PA3250	63B
Lang, Jeffrey	NY0150	63B
Langenberg, Kelly	IL2100	63B
Langenberg, Kelly	IL1200	63B
Langor, Suzanne	AA0020	63B
Larmee, Kent	OH1100	11,41,63B
Larose, Anne-Marie	AI0190	63B
Larsen, Karli	WI1150	64B,63B
Lauderdale, Rod	LA0350	11,63B
Laursen, Amy	AR0300	63B,32B
Lawson, Stephen J.	WV0400	13,63B,29,49,37
Leclaire, Dennis	MA0260	10,63B
Lee, Mary	AF0050	63B
Lee, Melvin	OK0700	63B
Leech, Thomas	PA0100	63B
Lemen, Caroline M.	MN0950	63B
Lemen, Caroline	MN1623	63B
Lemire, Carole E.	MO1900	63B

Index by Area of Teaching Interest

Name	Code	Areas
Lemon, Ronald	TX3750	63B,11
Leonard, Charlotte	AG0150	12A,63D,63C,15,63B
Lewellen, Michael	IN0905	63B
Lewellen, Michael	IN0700	63B
Lewis, Gail D.	IN0250	63B,13
Lewis, Walter	MI1830	63B
Linder, Susan	UT0200	63B
Linneroth, Sherry	MT0200	63B,41
Lintz, David	PA3580	63B
Lintz, David	PA3000	63B
Lockwood, Timothy	AG0550	63B
Logan, Roger	MT0400	63B
Lopez, Joel H.	TX3410	63B
Lovinsky, Joseph	DC0150	63B
Lowe, Laurence	UT0050	63B
Lucas, Heidi	MS0750	63B
Luchsinger, Brenda	AL0050	11,63B,13A
Lueschen, David	OH0700	63B,63D,49,11
Lundeen, Douglas	NJ1130	12A,63B
Lyren, Delon	MN0150	63A,63B,49,45
MacDonald, Austin	NC1300	63B
MacDonald, James	AG0650	63B,49
MacDonald, Ken	AC0100	63B
MacGillivray, Louise	CA0550	63B
Machala, Kazimierz W.	IL3300	63B,49,41
Mackey, Richard	MA0400	63B
Mackey, Richard	MA1400	63B
Magoto, Travis	OH2140	63B
Mahpar, Steven	CA0815	63B
Malatestinic, Patrice A.	NY3650	63B,49
Manhart, Grant L.	SD0400	49,63A,63B,11,46
Manz, Paul P.	AZ0510	63B,63C
Marcotte, Paul	AI0200	63B
Marsolais, Louis-Philippe	AI0200	63B
Massinon, Francis	TN0050	11,63B
Matiation, Laurie	AA0050	63B
Matiation, Laurie	AA0150	63B
Matlick, Eldon	OK1350	41,63B
Matras, Stanley	OH1000	63B
Mattingly, Alan F.	NE0600	63B,13,42
Mattingly, Jacqueline	NE0600	63B,12B
Mayne, Anna	IL2150	63B
McAfee, Andrew	NC2410	63B
McBain, Katherine C.	IL0800	63B,41,11
McCann, Kimberly	OH0350	63B
McCann, Kimberly	OH1600	63B
McCann, Kimberly	OH2050	63B
McCann, Kimberly	OH2000	63B
McCormick, Jesse D.	OH0200	63B
McCullough, David M.	AL1250	32B,63B,32C,32E
McCullough, Susan	CO0900	63B
McDaniel, Rory	SC0050	63B
McDowell, Robert	SD0580	63B
McEwen, Mark	MA0400	63B
McGuire, John	CO0250	63B,11
McGuire, John P.	CO0250	63B
McIntyre, Guinevere	IA0700	63B
McIntyre, Guinevere	IA0550	63B
McManus, Edward	OR0350	63B,34A,35C,35G,13A
McManus, Kevin	MD0350	63B,63C,63D,49
McMurray, Louise	AA0080	63B
McNeel, Mary	TX2100	63B
Meeroff, Myrna	FL0200	63B
Mehrtens, Kathryn	NJ0175	63B
Menaul, Richard A.	MA0400	63B
Menkis, Jonathan	MA1400	63B
Meredith, Henry M.	AG0500	32,63A,63B,67E
Merritt, Frank	NC1100	63A,63B,32
Metcalf, Michael	OH0100	63B,72,49
Meyer, Joe	CA3600	63B
Michaud Martins, Ellen	MA2030	63B
Mickey, Brian	AR0600	63A,63B
Mickey, Patricia A.	MO1780	63B,11,13D
Miles, Patrick	WI0850	49,63B,38
Miller, Gregory	FL1125	63B,42
Miller, Gregory	MD1010	49,63B
Miller, Todd	CA0815	49,50,63B,65
Milton, Kenneth	MS0560	11,47,49,63A,63B
Mingus, Richard	AB0090	63B
Mingus, Richard	AB0100	63B
Missal, Jason	TX0050	37,32E,63B
Moe, Sharon	NJ0825	63B
Moe, Sharon	NY2105	63B
Moege, Gary R.	MO1790	11,63B,70,71,12A
Mollenkopf, Jennifer	OH2290	63B
Montgomery, Joy	AG0600	63B
Montone, Jennifer	PA3250	63B
Montone, Jennifer	PA0850	63B
Montone, Jennifer	NY1900	63B
Moore, Albert L.	MN1300	49,63B,63A,11
Moore, Eric	VA0450	63B
Moore, Hilarie Clark	NY3000	38,41,63B
Moran, Margaret A.	IN1100	63B
Mordue, Mark	IN1560	63B
Morgan, Sean	FL1000	63B
Morrill, Dori	AZ0150	63B
Morrow, Michael	TX2955	63B,63D,11
Muller, Carl	TX2300	63B,63C,63D
Munds, Philip C.	MD0650	63B
Murdick, Nick	MT0370	63B
Musselman, Diana	CO0225	63B,32B
Myers, Philip	NY2250	63B
Neisler, Joseph	IL1150	11,63B
Nelsen, Jeff	AG0450	63B
Nelsen, Jeffrey	IN0900	63B
Nelson, Kayla	ND0500	63B
Nesmith, David	OH0850	63B
Nichols, Brandon	SC0275	63B
Nickel, James	DC0050	63B
Norton, Leslie	TN1850	41,48,63B,49
Nowlen, Peter	CA0150	63B
Nowlen, Peter	CA0840	63B
Nutt, Dorrie	AL1160	63B,41
Nutt, Dorrie	AL0010	63B
O'Connell, Daniel P.	IL2050	63B
Odell, Dennis	TX1450	63B
Ogilvie, Kevin	TX1350	46,63B
Ogilvie, Tyler	PA3150	63B,49
Ogilvie, Tyler	PA0950	63B,42
Ohlson, Laurel	DC0050	63B
O'Keefe, Stephanie	CA3300	63B
Oldham, Barbara	NY2750	49,63B,48
Oldham, Barbara	NY5000	41,63B
Oliver, Alise M.	KY0250	63B
Onciul, Gerald	AA0035	63B
Ondarza, Danielle	CA3650	63B
Orgel, Seth H.	LA0200	63B
Ormsby, Verle A.	WI0803	63B
Otto, James	MI0100	63B
Owen, Kevin	MA0350	63B
Pack, Abigail	NC2430	63B
Pandolfi, David	AL1150	63B
Pandolfi, David	AL1200	63B,42
Pandolfi, Roland	OH1700	63B
Panepinto, Tom	NC2435	63B
Parcell, Renee	IN0400	63B
Parker, David	AF0100	63B
Parks, Andrew	WI0845	63B
Parmer, Pat	WY0130	63B
Parrish, Jonathan L.	HI0210	63B
Parshley, Alan O.	VT0450	63B,13A,66D
Parson, Laurie	SC1080	63B
Parsons, Laurie N.	SC0400	63B
Pate, Molly	LA0800	63B
Paul, Philip	NC0050	13,36,63B
Payne, James	NE0590	11,63A,63B,46,35A
Pedde, Dennis	IA0930	63A,63B,63C,63D
Peichl, Dan	IA0550	63B
Pelletier, Andrew J.	OH0300	63B
Perkins, John D.	MO0100	63A,63B,12A,42,49
Peters, Michael	IA0600	63A,63B
Peters, Shelley	MO2000	63B
Peterson, Don L.	UT0050	13,12A,13J,63B
Peterson, Erich	MI1050	63B
Petruconis, Michael	MN1450	63B
Pfaffle, Elizabeth	PA3600	63B
Pfaffle, Elizabeth L.	PA1300	63B
Pherigo, Johnny L.	FL1800	11,41,49,48,63B
Phillips, Daniel	TN1680	63B
Phillips, Gregory	OH1450	49,63B,13A
Piatt, Kenneth H.	PA1200	63A,63B
Pickney, Linda M.	NC2420	63B,32E,38
Pierce, Denise Root	MI0600	63B
Pike, Lisa	NJ0500	63B
Pike, Lisa	NJ0700	63B,11
Pike, Lisa F.	NJ1400	63B
Pituch, Karl	MI2200	63B
Podroskey, Frank	PA0500	63A,63B
Polk, Keith	NH0350	11,12A,12C,63B
Porter, Elizabeth	NY3350	63B
Portone, Frank	NC0550	63B
Pospisil, James	MN1600	63B
Powers, Jeffrey S.	TX0300	63B
Presar, Jennifer	IL2900	63B,13B,13C,13
Pritchett, Kate	OK0750	63B,42,13B,13C
Probst, Christopher	GA0400	63A,63B
Propst, Tonya	SC0420	63B,32,32C
Proser, Stephen	UT0250	63B
Pruzin, Robert S.	SC1110	32C,49,63B
Purvis, William	CT0850	63B
Raab-Pontecorvo, Luiza	NY1600	63B,42,66A,66C
Radford, Gabe	AG0450	63B
Ragent, Lawrence S.	CA4900	63B
Ralske, Eric	NY2250	63B
Ralske, Erik	NY1900	63B,42
Ralske, Erik C.	NY2150	63B
Rapier, Christopher	PA2250	63B
Reed, Eric	NJ1130	63B
Reed, Gavin	TX3400	63B
Reed, Marc A.	CO0350	63A,63B,49
Reed, Richard	WA1250	63B
Reeves, Gary L.	SD0600	60B,13G,37,63B
Reid, Kevin	FL1950	63B
Reit, Peter	NY4450	63B
Reit, Peter	NY3785	63B
Reit, Peter	NY5000	63B
Reuter, Jessica M.	MO1500	63B
Reynolds, David	SD0550	12C,63A,63B
Reynolds, Terence	TX3420	63B
Rice, Suzanne	IN0100	63B
Richard, Leon	KY0750	49,63A,63B
Ricker, Richard	NE0450	63B
Riddle, Paula	SC0750	11,63B
Rider, Wendell	CA4200	63B
Rife, Jean	MA1400	63B
Rife, Jean	MA1200	48,63B
Ring, Jonathan	CA4150	63B
Rivard, Kevin C.	CA0807	63B
Robbins, Mark	WA0200	63B
Roberts, Bruce	CA4150	63B
Robertson, James	AC0100	63B
Robertson, Karen	NC0050	49,63B,42,41
Robinson, Melissa Ann	OR0850	41,42,49,63B
Roche-Wallace, Catherine	LA0760	13,63B
Rod, Steve	IA0900	63B
Rodriguez, Jill	TX3100	63B,11
Rounds, Joseph	PA1050	63B
Rubins, Peter	TX3530	63B
Ruske, Eric	MA0400	63B
Russell, Scott	IN1450	63B,13B,13C
Rusu, Radu	TN0100	63B
Rydel, Robert	NC2000	63B
Rydel, Robert E.	SC1200	63B
Sang, Barry R.	NC0350	63B
Saunders, David E.	ID0050	63B,60B,13E,12A
Scandrett, John F.	PA1600	13,63B,34
Scanga, James V.	PA1450	63B,49
Schaffer, Candler	FL0800	63B
Schaffer, William R.	AL0200	13,11,63B,49
Scharf, Deborah	TX2800	63B
Scharnberg, William	TX3420	41,49,63B
Scheffelman, Matthew	CO0200	63B
Scheider, Karen	KY1000	63B
Schepper, Stephen	IL1750	63B
Schmalenberger, Sarah	MN1625	12A,63B,12,67E,14
Schmann, Phillip M.	KY0550	11,63B
Schmid, Lucinda	WY0115	63B
Schmidt, Jody	OR0950	63B
Schreckengost, John	IN1750	63B,49,11
Schultz, Steve	IA0400	63B
Schuster, James	MI2120	63B
Schwagerl, Renee	MN1620	63B
Scott, Jeffrey	NJ0800	63B,42
Shaffer, Rebecca Boehm	IA0950	63B,49,12A,32E,13C
Shannon, Jackie	CA0805	63B
Shannon, William	CA0900	13A,13B,34,63B,35
Sharnetzka, Sandra	MD0475	63B
Shaw, J.D.	NM0450	63B,63
Sheena, Robert	MA0350	64B,63B
Shiplett, Arlene	AJ0150	63B
Shires, Brent A.	AR0850	63B,32E,42,49
Sholtis, Jennifer Ratchford	TX2960	63B
Showers, Shelley	PA3250	63B
Shuhan, Alexander G.	NY1800	63B
Simonini, John	AG0450	63B
Simpson, Steve	CO0150	63B

Name	Code	Areas
Slocum, William	OH2600	63B,38
Smelser, Jim	IL0750	63B
Smith, C. Scott	OH1900	13,63B,41
Smith, Christopher M.	TX3200	63B
Smith, Christy	PA1650	63B
Smith, John David	DE0150	63B,48,49
Smith, Matthew K.	VT0100	37,32,11,63B,60
Smith, Mike	TX2295	63B
Smith, Nicholas	KS1450	63B,49,12A
Smith, Patrick G.	VA1600	12A,63B
Smith, Zachary	PA1050	63B
Snead, Charles G.	AL1170	49,63B
Snedeker, Gretchen	NY0650	63B
Snedeker, Jeffrey	WA0050	12,49,63B
Snider, Jason	MA1175	63B
Snider, Jason	MA0400	63B
Snider, Jason	MA1400	63B
Snidero, Jim	NY2660	63B,64E
Solis, Richard	OH0600	63B,41,49
Sommerville, James	MA1175	63B
Sommerville, James	MA1400	63B
Sommerville, James	MA0400	63B
Sorensen, Randall J.	LA0250	63A,63B,13,13B,13A
Sorley, Darin S.	IN1650	63B
South, Janis	OK1250	63B,11,12A,49,20
Spanjer, R. Allen	NY2150	63B
Sparrow, Richard	FL2050	63B
Spaulding, Neil	AG0250	63B
Spaulding, Susan	CT0050	63B
Spence, Marcia L.	MO1800	63B,49
Spiradopoulos, S.	MA0800	63B
Spiradopoulos, Sheffra	RI0200	63B
Staherski, Cheryl E.	PA1250	63B
Staherski, Cheryl	PA2350	63B
Stalnaker, Bill	OR0400	63B
Stanton, Philip	TX3400	63B
Starcher, Veronica	CO0050	63B
Stebleton, Michelle	FL0850	49,63B,67E
Stephen, J. Drew	TX3530	12A,63B,67E,12
Sternbach, David J.	VA0450	32G,63B
Sternberg, Brian	NY3705	63B
Stetson, Stephanie	CA6000	63B
Steuck, Beth	MN1500	63B,66A
Stevens, Paul W.	KS1350	49,63B
Stoupy, Etienne	TX3300	49,63A,63B
Strait, Tom	MN1120	63A,29,63B,47
Strobel, Larry	ID0140	63B
Su, Yu-Ting (Tina)	IA1600	63B,49
Suarez, Jeff	WI0100	63B
Suarez, Karen	WI0250	63B,41
Sullivan, Nancy	AZ0450	63B
Sungarian, Victor	MA2250	63B,41
Swanson, Lucy Jane	CA0600	63B
Sweeley, Daniel	NY3717	63B
Taplin, Alan	OH2300	63B
Telford, Alicia	CA5000	63B
Teske, Casey C.	PA0700	60B,13C,63B,11
Test, Heather	TX3000	63B
Thatcher, James	CA5300	63B
Thayer, Edwin C.	VA0450	63B
Thayer, Heather	AR0500	63B,13C
Thibodeau, Gilles	AG0150	63B
Thoman, Jessica	TN1720	63B,12A,11
Thomas, John	MO1950	13B,13C,63B
Thompson, Timothy F.	AR0700	12A,63B
Thompson, Virginia M.	WV0750	49,63B
Thoms, Jonas	OH2500	13,13C,63B,35
Thornton, Michael	CO0800	63B
Thorstenberg, Roger W.	KS0150	63A,63B
Tompkins, Leslie	NY2400	63B
Tremarello, Richard	WI1150	63B
Trotz, Amy	GA0750	63B
Tryon, Denise	PA3250	63B
Tuck, Patrick M.	KY1425	10,13,49,63A,63B
Tuckwiller, George	VA0700	63A,63B
Tung, Margaret M.	IL2300	63B
Unger, Susan	AL1195	63B
Unsworth, Adam	MI2100	63B
Valenzuela, Victor	AZ0480	63A,63B
Valerio, Anthony	MD0750	63B
Van Dreel, K.	FL1745	63B
Van Dreel, Lydia	OR1050	63B,49,42
Van Speybroeck, Jennifer	IA1300	63B
Varner, Tom	WA0200	63B,47
Velazquez, Paulette	IL1520	63B
Vellenga, Curtis W.	KS1400	63B
Velleur, Melody	IL3150	63B
Velvikis, Rachel N.	VA1500	63B
VerMeulen, William	TX2150	63B,42
Vigesaa, Erik	ND0350	63B
Vinson, Danny S.	TX3370	63B
Vollmer, Susan C.	CA5070	63B
Von Pechmann, Lisa	IL1085	63B
Vroman, David	IL0400	60,32,37,63B
Waddell, Charles F.	OH1850	48,63B
Wagner, Corbin	MI1400	63B
Wahl, Carolyn	FL1650	63B
Wakefield, David	NY1900	63B,49
Wakefield, Karin	MN0600	63B,66A
Walczyk, Kevin	OR1250	13,45,63B,29,10
Walker, Heather	AB0050	63B
Walker, Patricia	NY2200	63B,32E
Ward, Margaret S.	NH0250	63B
Ward, Robert	CA5000	63B
Ward, Robert	CA4150	63B
Wardle, Alvin	UT0300	32C,63B,63C,63D
Washington, Darian	SC0950	37,49,63B
Watabe, Eileen	AK0150	63B,49
Watson, Joan	AG0450	63B
Weber, Carlyle	FL0950	63A,63B
Welty, Susan	GA2100	63B
Werling, Helen	GA1700	63B
Wetherill, David	PA1550	63B
Whitney, Valerie	IL1400	63B
Whyman, Valerie	PA2100	63B
Wick, David	VA0250	63B
Wick, Heidi	OH1200	63B,49
Wiegard, William James	TX3750	63B,49,11
Wilkerson, John	FL0150	63B
Williams, Daniel	PA3250	63B
Williams, Gail	IL2250	63B
Williams, Larry	MD0600	63B
Williams, Todd	PA2450	63B
Williams, Todd D.	PA1750	63B
Wilson, Elisha K.	CA0850	63B
Wilson, Jill	IA1100	63B,36,32B,60,13C
Wilson, Matt	MN0750	63B
Wilson, Matthew	MN1280	63B
Wilson, Matthew	MN0050	63B
Wilson, Mike	IA1350	63B
Wilson, Ruth	CA4700	32E,42,49,63B
Winslow, Herbert	MN1450	63B
Winslow, Richard D.	CA0800	49,63A,63B,29A,20G
Winter, Allen	NC0300	63B
Winter, Angela	TX3300	63B
Winter, Michael J.	NY4320	63B
Witte, Tom	GA1150	63B
Wittstadt, Kurt	MD0175	11,42,63B
Wollner, William	MI1850	11,13B,37,63B,60B
Wood, Graham	SC0450	11,12,63B,54,20
Wood, Jodi	AL1300	11,63B
Wood, Michael	MI1000	32E,63B
Woodward, Bruce	UT0190	63B
Wygonik, David	PA2950	63A,63B
Young, Scott	GA0625	63B,66D
Zaik, Santha	OR0750	63B,16
Ziek, Terrisa A.	KS0300	32B,63B
Zirbel, John	AI0150	63B
Zirk, Willard	MI0600	13,49,63B
Zook, Ian R.	VA0600	63B
Zuehlke, Anneka	SC0650	63B
Zyla, Luke	OH1400	63B
Zyla, Marc	IN1600	63B

Trombone

Name	Code	Areas
Abdul Al-Khabyyr, Muhammad	AI0150	63C,29
Acosta, Darren	RI0300	49,63C
Adams, Joel	IL2050	46,63C
Albright, Timothy	NY3785	63C
Aldag, Daniel	CA2250	63D,29,14C,63C,47
Aldana, Milton	MD0600	63C,13,12A
Alessi, Joseph	NY1900	63D,63C,49
Allen, John	OK0750	63C,46,49
Allen, Jonathan	IA1550	49,63C
Allen, Mark	OR1000	37,49,63A,63C,63B
Alme, Joseph	ND0250	63C,63D,37,60
Aloisio, Gerard S.	MN1000	11,49,63C
Alvis, Jonathan	SD0600	63D,37,63C
Amend, Holly	WA0950	63C,63D
Anderson, Matt	SC1080	63C,63D
Anderson, Scott	NE0600	63C,42
Anderson, Tim	OH2200	63C
Antonacci, Jarred M.	PA1550	63C
Applewhite, Willie	UT0190	66,20,29,63C
Aranda, Patrick	CA0950	13A,37,47,63C,29A
Arbogast, Paul	PA3330	63C
Archambo, Larry	TX1700	60,32C,37,34,63C
Armandi, Richard	IL3100	63C,63D
Arnow, Chad A.	OH0680	63C
Arnow, Charles	OH2550	63C
Ashworth, Thomas	MN1623	41,63C
Atherton, Timothy E.	NH0100	63C,41,42
Atherton, Timothy	MA2100	63C,63D,29A
Auman, Richard	PA2950	63C
Avitsur, Haim	PA3600	63C,49
Axsom, Ron	PA0950	63C
Babbitt, Mark	IL1150	63C
Babcock, Donald J.	MI0600	47,63C,63D
Baedke, Ron	VA1500	63C
Baker, Andrew	IL0850	63C,47
Baker, Tony E.	TX3420	63C,29
Baldwin, Todd	DC0010	63C
Ball, Thomas J.	CO0900	63C
Bange, Darren R.	MD1000	63C
Bara, Paul	CO0350	63C
Barnhill, Allen	TX2150	63C,41,42
Barnstead, Scott	GA2300	63C
Barrett, Dan	ME0440	13E,63C
Barron, Ronald	MA1400	63C
Bartee, Neale	AR0110	60,12A,49,63C
Bartlett, Anthony	AZ0440	63C,29
Bartlett, John	NC0550	63C
Bauer, Paul D.	IL2200	49,63C
Bearid, Rolyn	SD0580	63D,63C
Beatty, David	CA1000	63C
Beatty, David	CA0250	47,49,35,63C
Beaudry, Pierre	AI0150	63C
Beckel, James A.	IN0350	63C
Begel, Rich	IN0400	63C,47
Begnoche, David J.	TX3000	63C
Bell, Isaac	AL0050	47,63C,63D
Bellino, Paul	NY4450	63C
Bennett, Larry	MO0100	32E,63D,63C,41
Benoit, John	IA1350	13,11,63C,10F,55
Berkman, Jeremy	AB0100	63C
Bernard, Gilles	NJ0825	13,12A,49,63C,63D
Berry, Steve	IL0550	47,63C
Bertucci, Ronald	OR0350	37,13A,47,63C,13C
Bevington, Mike	OR1250	63C
Bing, Charles S.	FL0600	32C,37,63C,63D
Bivens, Pat	TN0250	11,47,63C,48,37
Blaha, Joseph L.	VA1250	46,10,12A,48,63C
Blaine, Robert	MS0350	11,38,32E,63C,60B
Blake, Paul	NY1400	63C,63D
Blakeman, Lee	KY1550	63C,13C,11,41
Blauer, Matt	KS1450	63C
Bledsoe, Joshua	AR0850	63C,34
Blucker, James	IL0300	63C
Bobe, Larry	IA1300	63C,63D
Bock, Stan	OR1300	63C,63D,49
Bohanon, George	CA5031	63C,29
Bohn, Hans	MA2030	63C
Bollinger, Blair J.	PA3250	63C
Bollinger, Blair	PA0850	63C
Bolter, Norman	MA0350	63C
Bolter, Norman	MA1175	63C
Bolter, Norman	MA1400	41,63C
Bonilla, Luis	NY2150	29,63C
Bonvisutto, Bruce	NY0500	63C
Boone, Robert	AZ0480	63C
Booth, William	CA5060	63C
Borror, Ronald	CT0650	41,49,63C,67E,55
Bowell, Jeffrey T.	WY0115	63C
Bowers, Amy	CA5300	63C
Bowyer, Don	AR0110	63C,63D,29,35C,47
Box, James	AI0150	63C
Boyd, Frederick	NC2420	63D,63C
Boyd, Lance	MT0400	47,63C,63D,53,29
Brame, Steven	IL1500	63C,63D
Brantley, K. Thomas	FL2000	63C
Braverman, Frederick	NY0500	63C
Brechting, Gail	MI1550	60B,63C,37
Brevig, Per	NY2250	49,63C
Brevig, Per	NY2150	63C

Index by Area of Teaching Interest

Name	Code	Areas
Brevig, Per	NY1900	49,63C
Brewer, Paul S.	MI0300	60B,37,32E,29,63C
Brickens, Nathaniel O.	TX3510	63C,49
Bridson, Paul	IA0550	63C
Brink, Brian S.	FL0800	63C,49,34
Bristol, Doug S.	AL0050	13,29,63C,47
Britt, Mark E.	SC0750	63C,49,32E
Brodt, Ralph E.	PA2450	63C
Bromme, Derek	MN1600	63C
Brooks, John Patrick	ID0100	60B,37,63C,47,63D
Broussard, George L.	NC0650	42,63C,29A
Brown, Matthew	PA1300	63D,63C
Brown, Thomas	CT0100	63C
Brownell, Jack	AF0050	49,63D,63C
Brubeck, Dave W.	FL1300	13,37,47,63C,49
Brummel, Jonathan	CA0810	63C
Brunette, Chantal	AG0250	63C,63D
Bryan, Paul	PA3250	63C
Bryan, Stephanie	MO2000	63C,63D
Bubert, Dennis	TX3500	63C
Buckholz, Christopher John	IA1600	63C,29,41,11
Buckmaster, Matthew	NC0750	63D,29,63C,49,32
Bulen, Jay C.	MO1780	12C,12A,63C
Bulmer, Karen	AD0050	63C,63D
Burden, Douglas	AG0400	63C,37,41
Burdick, Daniel	PA1200	63C,63D,49,11
Burroughs, John	TN1350	63C,63D
Butler, Dorsey Mitchell	SC0350	63C,60B,47,29
Byerlotzer, Jason L.	HI0210	63C
Bynum, Josh L.	GA2100	63C,63D,13A
Calkin, Joshua	NE0700	63D,37,11,49,63C
Cameron, Scott	DC0010	37,63D,63C
Camp, James L.	GA0490	37,49,63B,63C,63D
Campbell, Larry	TX0340	37,47,63B,63C,63D
Campbell, Lars	OR0750	63C
Campbell, Lars	OR1100	63C
Campora, Randall S.	MD0650	63C
Capetandes, Gary	NJ1400	63C
Capshaw, Reed	IN0910	63C,63D
Capshaw, Reed	IL0550	63C
Capshaw, Reed	IL1085	63C,63D
Caputo, Charles R.	FL0650	63C
Carlson, Ernie	ID0140	63C
Carpentier, Jean-Pierre	AI0210	63C
Castello, Joseph	AG0600	63C
Celmer, Joey R.	SC1050	63A,63B,63C,63D,47
Chamberlain, Rick E.	PA1850	63C,63D
Chambers, Robert	OK1250	38,63C,63D,13D,10F
Chance, Mike	AR0250	32E,37,38,63C,63D
Chandler, Vincent Arvel	MI1750	63C
Chasanov, Elliot L.	IL3300	63C,49,41
Cheetham, Richard	CA5000	63C
Cherian, Rebecca S.	PA0550	63C
Cherry, Daniel E.	NC2600	63C
Chmura-Moore, Dylan Thomas	WI0830	63C,38,11
Christain, Ron	CA0650	63C,63B
Clark, Jim	TX2955	63C,49,63D
Clark, Richard	NJ1400	63C
Clark, Wayne	OK1330	63C
Clark, Wayne R.	OK0700	63D,63C,63
Clayville, Michael	PA2300	63C
Cloutier, Daniel	TN1710	49,63C
Coale, Dean	OK0300	32E,49,63C,63D
Coberly, Ron	IA0900	63C
Coffman, Timothy J.	IL0750	29,63C
Coker, Keller	OR1250	55,12A,63C,10D
Collins, Anthony	CA4200	63C
Collins, Peter	AG0500	63C
Collins, Tony	CA4700	63C,63D
Colwell, Brent	TX2800	37,11,12A,63C,63D
Colwell, Lynn	IN1850	63C,63D
Compton, Paul R.	OK0800	63C,63D,47,49
Conger, Robert B.	MO1500	60B,32C,63C,63D
Conklin, Raymond L.	KY0950	49,63C,63D
Connelly, Chris	SC0420	63C,63D,11,29
Conner, Timothy M.	FL1900	63C,41,42
Converse, Andrew	TX2960	63C
Cook, Justin	TX2750	63D,63C
Cook, Seth	MD0550	63C,63D
Cook, Thomas	MI1250	13,12A,38,63C
Cooke, David	IN0905	38,60B,49,63C
Coomber, Robert	CA1750	63C,63D
Cooper, Lawrence R.	PA0350	63C,63D
Cottrell, Jeffrey	TX0900	10A,63C,63D
Couture, Robert F.	MA2050	63C
Cox, Gregory	AB0100	63C
Cox, Gregory	AB0200	63C,38
Cox, Gregory	AB0060	63C,49
Cox, Gregory A.	WA1250	63C
Crafton, Colleen	NY0650	63C
Cravens, Terry	CA5300	63C
Crawford, Raphael	IL0720	63C
Crewe, Murray	PA1050	63C
Crewe, Murray	PA0550	63C
Crist, Michael	OH2600	32E,63C,34
Crosby, Tracy	MS0300	63C,11,13
Crowe, Don R.	SD0550	32,63C,72,35
Cummings, Dean	OH1400	12A,13,63C
Cunningham, Blaine E.	IA0700	63C,63D
Curran, George	GA1150	63C
Danner, Zachary	MO1250	63C
Daugherty, Helene	IN1450	63C
Davenport, Roger N.	MO1830	63C,63D
David, James M.	CO0250	13,10,10F,63C
Davidson, Dave	AG0350	63C
Davidson, Michael	KS1350	63C
Davies, Rick A.	VT0450	63C
Davis, JoDee	MO1810	63C
Dawson, Brett	FL0200	63C
Day, David	MI0050	63C
Day, Maxon	WI1150	63C
Dearth, Christopher	OH1400	63C
Dease, Michael	MI1400	29,63C
Decker, James	TX3200	63C
Dekker, Steve	MO1810	63C
Dempster, Stuart R.	WA1050	63C,43
Denison, Mark	OR1010	12A,29A,63C,46,60B
DeSano, James	OH1700	63C
Devito, Albert	AI0200	49,63C
Devlin, Michelle P.	VA1100	63C,63D
DeWitt, Timothy L.	WV0050	49,63A,13E,63B,63C
Diaz Torres, Jorge	PR0115	63C
Diaz, Oscar	TX2960	63C,49
Dickey, Nathaniel H.	MN0600	37,63C,63D,32E,49
Dickinson, Christian M.	PA1600	13,49,63C,60B
DiCuirci, Michael	OH0950	63C,63D,37,32E
Diehl, Brian L.	ME0500	63C
Diller, Alisa	OH0250	63C
Dishman, Nathan	VA1550	63C
Dix, Trevor	AI0150	63C,49
Dowling, Eugene	AB0150	42,13C,63C,63D
Drew, John	FL0850	49,63C
Drill, Daniel	AL1170	63C
Driscoll, Matthew	IA0400	63C,63D
Driscoll, Matthew	IA0200	63A,63C,63D
Dubberly, James	CA0850	63C,63D,29A,41
Duchi, Joseph J.	OH1850	63C
Dudley, Christopher	MD1010	63C
Dugan, Michael D.	WI0865	11,47,49,63C
Duncan, Andrew	OH0500	63C,63D
Duncan, Steven	IL3200	11,63C
Duncan, Steven	IL1085	63C
Dunevant, David L.	KY1000	12A,63C
Dyer, Steve	AC0100	63C
Dyess, J. Wayne	TX1400	37,47,63C,49
Eager, Jim	AF0120	63C
East, David	MS0320	37,47,48,63C
Edwards, Bradley W.	SC1110	63C,49
Ehrlich, Barry	WA0860	13,11,37,63C,63D
Eifertsen, Dyne	CA0150	29,63C,46,47
Elias, Joel	CA0840	63C
Ellefson, Peter	IL0550	63C
Ellefson, Peter E.	IN0900	63C
Elliot, Thomas	PA2800	63C
Ellithorpe, Robert	VA1600	63C,32E
Elsey, Eddie L.	AL1250	49,13B,63C,63D
Enabnit, Brian	IA0250	63C,63D
Engelkes, John	CA4150	63C
Erb, Andrew	PA3260	63A,63C,37,47,49
Erb, Richard	LA0300	63C
Erdman, James A.	PA1900	63C,63D
Eubanks, Robin	NY2750	47,63C,29
Eubanks, Robin	MA1400	63C
Evans, Jay	AL1200	63C,63D,42
Evans, Michael	CA5550	63C
Evans, Thomas	MI1150	37,47,63C,29A,32
Evans, Valerie L.	KY1350	63C,47
Everett, Micah P.	MS0700	63C,63D,13C,41,49
Fagerberg, Kaj	IL1900	63C,63D
Faieta, John J.	MA0350	63C
Falfalios, Anatasi	KY0250	63C
Fallis, Todd	UT0300	32C,63C,63D,47,41
Farrugia, Greg	AB0090	63C
Farwell, Douglas G.	GA2150	63C,49,34,35C,35D
Fay, Terrence	CT0550	63C
Fedchcok, John	PA3250	29,63C
Fedchock, John	NY3785	63C
Fejeran, Vince	WA0900	47,63C,37,46
Ferber, Alan D.	NY2750	63C
Ferber, Alan D.	NJ0800	63C
Ferguson, Paul	OH0600	63C
Fetter, David J.	MD0650	63C
Finlayson, David	NY2150	63C
Finn, Neal	NC0800	10A,10F,29A,47,63C
Fisher, Mark	IL0750	63C,63D
Flanigan, Sean G.	CO0225	63C,63D,41,47,35A
Fleming, Ricky L.	NY3717	60B,37,47,49,63C
Fletcher, Douglas	OK0850	63C
Fletcher, Seth	NE0590	63D,63C,13B,13C,11
Foshager, John	WI1150	63C,66A
Fox, Frances	NC2205	63C
Fralick, Steve	AG0050	63C
Fred Carrasquillo, Luis	PR0115	63C,49,41,42
Frederickson, Matthew	MO0650	63D,32E,49,63C
Freeman, Gregory	DC0170	63C
Freeman, Jeffrey J.	TX2100	11,63C,49,63D,34
Freeman, Phillip I.	TX2150	63C
Freeman, Phillip	TX3400	63C
French, Brian	NC2500	63C
French, Chelsea	IL2050	63C,63D
Friedman, Jay	IL0550	63C,38
Friedrichs, Charles	CA4100	11,37,63C,13A,32
Fry, Mark	IL2750	63C
Frye, Joseph W.	TN1720	63C,13A,13C,11,34
Funderburk, Wes	GA1050	47,63C
Gale, Robert	NJ0175	63C
Galindo, Jeffrey	MA1175	63C
Garcia, Antonio	VA1600	29,47,63C,35,46
Garling, Tom	IL0850	47,63C
Garling, Tom	IL0550	29B,63C
Garling, Tom	IL2200	29,63C
Garlock, Scott	OH0700	47,63C
Garlock, Scott E.	OH0100	29,47,63C,63D,46
Gay, Nathan	KS0300	63C,63D,60B,37
Gaynor, Rick	WI0845	63C,49,11
Gaynor, Rick G.	MN0950	63C
Gazda, Frank S.	DE0050	63D,37,49,63C,42
Geiger, Jeanne	CA0807	63C,49
Gemberling, Alan	ID0250	37,63C,47,60,41
Gerlach, Brent	TN1100	63C,11
Gibbens, Tracey	WI0860	63C,63D,49
Gibson, David	NY3730	63C,63D,47
Gibson, Thomas S.	GA1150	63C,34,41
Gibson, Tom	GA1300	63C
Gier, David	IA1550	49,63C
Giles, Glenn	VT0100	63C,63D,60,37,46
Gillan, Michael	MI0850	11,37,63C,63D,47
Glasmire, David	OH0300	63C
Glendening, Andrew	CA5150	63C
Gookin, Larry D.	WA0050	60,37,49,63C
Gordon, Wycliffe	PA3250	29,63C
Gormley, Lon	NY0400	63C,63D
Gregg, Gary	CA0200	63C,29,35
Gregory, Gary J.	OH0550	44,13,60,37,63C
Greig, R. Tad	PA3650	32E,37,47,60B,63C
Griffin, Peter J.	IL0850	32,37,60B,63C,63D
Guilford, Matthew	MD1010	63C
Haack, Donald	WI1155	63C,63D
Haddix, Ken	KY0550	37,63C
Haecker, Arthur	SC0650	63C
Hall, Michael	VA1000	63D,49,63C
Hall, Michael J.	MD1000	63C
Hamilton, Ryan	OH1600	63C
Hamilton, Ryan	OH0350	63C,47,29B,53
Hamlin, Seth	MA2010	63C,63D
Hancock, Craig A.	IA1800	37,60B,63C,63D,72
Haroz, Nitzan	PA0850	63C
Haroz, Nitzan	PA3250	63C
Harper, Gregory	CO0150	63C,63D
Harper, Greg J.	CO0250	63C
Harris, Daniel	OH2300	63C
Harris, David	MA2050	63C
Harris, William	NY2950	63C,63D
Harris, William H.	NY4150	63C,63D
Hart, Michael	CA0550	37,13B,13C,63C,63D
Hartman, Mark S.	NY3780	63C,41

Index by Area of Teaching Interest

Name	Code	Areas
Hartman, Scott	CT0850	63C,41
Harvey, Brent M.	NC1900	63C,63D,41
Hausback, Jason	MO0775	63C,47
Hauser, Joshua	TN1450	63C,10F,13B,42
Hawes, Randell D.	IL2250	63C
Hay, Jeff	WA0200	63C,29
Hayward, Andre	MA1400	63C,29
Hearn, Barry	DC0050	63C
Heidner, Eric	CA5550	63C
Hellick, Gary J.	MI2200	63C
Helmer, John	AC0100	63C
Helmer, John	AC0050	63D,63C
Hemberger, Glen J.	LA0650	60B,32C,37,63C,47
Henderson, Matthew	GA0250	11,63C,63D
Henderson, Matthew C.	SC1100	63C
Hendrix, Michael	LA0100	37,63C
Hennessey, Patrick D.	HI0110	37,47,29A,12A,63C
Henniger, Henry J.	OR0700	63C,63D
Henniger, Henry J.	OR1050	49,63C
Henry, Kevin	PA3150	63C,49
Herrington, Benjamin	NY2150	63C
Hersey, Joanna R.	NC2435	10F,63C,63D,12A
Herwig, Conrad	NJ1130	29,63C
Herwig, Conrad	NY1900	63C,29
Hetrick, Loy	IN0907	63C,63D
Hetzler, Mark	WI0815	63C,49
Heukeshoven, Eric	MN1400	63C,63D,34,10
Hicks, Gregory	LA0900	63C,63D
Higgins, Timothy	CA4150	63C
High, Eric	WI0750	63C,47,13,12,49
Hill, Mark	TX3410	63C
Hills, Ernie M.	CA0840	13,63C
Hilson, Keith	MN0610	63C,63D
Hines, Clarence	FL1950	63C,29
Hines, Tyrone	IL0600	63C,63D,46
Hinterbichler, Karl	NM0450	12A,12,63C,63D
Hodges, David	SC0850	63A,63C
Hoelscher, Mark	WI0825	63C
Hoelscher, Mark A.	WI0835	63C,63D,49
Hoffman, Michael	CA2390	63C
Hoffman, Michael	CA0815	63C
Holcombe, Ross	WA0250	63C,46,49
Holcombe, Ross	WA0400	63C,63D
Holmes, Rasan	VA0500	63C,37,34
Hongisto, Erik	AG0170	63C
Hooten, Bryan	VA1600	13B,13C,63C
Horgan, Maureen A.	GA0850	63D,11,49,63C,29A
Howard, Vernon D.	OK1450	47,49,63C,63D,29
Howe, Donald	CA3520	12A,29A,14C,63C
Howe, Timothy E.	MO1800	63C,63D
Hower, Don	WA1150	37,63C
Howey, Henry E.	TX2250	63D,63C
Huber, William	TN1600	63C
Hudson, Barbara D.	NC0300	63C,63D
Hudson, Jed	OH0850	63C,63D
Hughes, William M.	SC1200	13,49,63C,41
Hulten, Thomas	TX3400	63C
Human, Richard	MS0500	63C,11
Hunt, Paul B.	KS0650	63C,12A,29A
Hunter, Michael	MI1650	47,63C,29,64E
Hunter, Steven	UT0325	63C
Hunter, Todd	PA2200	63C
Huntoon, John Richard	IN0100	63C,63D,47,37,49
Hurt, Charles R.	TX3175	49,63C
Hutchins, Tony	IA1100	11,29A,63B,63C,32E
Hutchins, Tony	OK1200	63C
Hutchinson, Thomas	NY2750	63C
Hutson, Danny J.	AL0010	12A,13E,60,63C
Huttlin, Edward	MN0600	63C
Iles, Alex	CA0510	63C,47
Ingram, Danny	TX1100	63C,63D
Isaacson, Lawrence	MA0350	63C
Isenhour, Justin	AR0500	63C,63D,11,13C
Isenhour, Justin R.	SC0600	63C
Israel, Shachar	OH0650	63C
Jachens, Darryl	SC1080	11,32,63C
Jackson, David Lee	MI2100	63C
Jackson, Keith	WV0750	47,49,63C,63D
Jacobs, Mark	OR0950	63C
Jameson, Philip	GA2100	49,63C
Jantz, Paul	SC0200	12A,49,63C,63D,34
Jarczyk, Jan	AI0150	29,63C,66A
Jasavala, John	AG0450	63C
Jasavala, John	AG0500	63C
Jenkins, Kate	SC0275	63C
Jennings, Arthur	FL1850	11,63C,63D
Jerosch, Anita	ME0410	37,63C
Jerosch, Sebastian	ME0340	63C,11
Jerosch, Sebastian	ME0250	63C
Jerosch, Sebastian	ME0150	63C
Jester, Erik	CA0845	37,60B,63C
Jimenez, Fernando	CT0800	60B,37,63C
Johansen, David A.	LA0650	63C,11,63D,49
Johnson, Adam	IN0905	63C
Johnson, Daniel C.	NC2440	32,63D,34,32B,63C
Johnson, Mark	GA0200	32E,37,60B,63C
Johnson, Victor	CT0100	63C
Johnston, Keith	CT0300	37,63C,63D
Jones, Calvin	DC0350	47,62D,63C,63D,29
Jones, Michael C.	KS1200	47,63A,63B,63C,13
Kadyk, Folkert	PA1550	63C
Kagarice, Jan M.	TX3420	63C
Kagarice, Vern L.	TX3420	41,49,63C,63D
Kane, Kevin	RI0200	63C,63D
Kane, Kevin	RI0150	63C,63D
Kaplan, Allan Richard	NM0310	11,63C,53
Kapralick, Randy	PA3330	63C,20A,46
Karahalis, Dean	NY2550	63C,63D
Karahalis, Dean	NY4050	11,29,63C
Kauk, Brian	TX3400	63C
Keeble, Carson	CO0830	63C,63D
Keehn, Samantha	IL0100	63C,63D,11
Keelan, Nick	WI0350	32,49,63C,63D
Keen, Phil M.	CA3650	63C
Keener, Michael K.	OH2250	63C,49,11,32E
Kehle, Robert G.	KS1050	11,47,29,63C
Kellogg, Mark	NY1100	63C,42
Kemp, Mildred	IN1010	63C,63D
Kendall, David	CA2420	35G,63C,63D
Kenley, McDowell E.	CA4900	63C
Kenneilly, Donald	CA0900	63C
Kern, Bradley	KY1450	63C,41
Kerns, Brad	KY0100	63C
Kidwell, Jeff	OK1330	47,63C,46,29
Kidwell, Jeff	OK0700	63C
Kilpatrick, Barry M.	NY3725	63C
Kimball, Will	UT0050	41,63C
Kischuk, Ronald K.	MI2200	63C,29
Kitzman, John	TX2400	63C
Kline, Peter	TX2200	63C,63D
Knupps, Terri L.	MO1550	12A,20,63C,63D,42
Kobuck, Martin	TX1775	13,63C,46,11
Kocher, Edward W.	PA1050	32,63C,63D
Kofsky, Allen	OH0200	63C,63D
Kohlenberg, Randy	NC2430	32,63C
Kolstad, Michael L.	MO0400	49,63C,63D,47,34
Kolwinska, Jeremy	MN1280	63C,63D,11,63B
Koonce, Jeff	AL1150	63C
Koonce, Jeff	AL0300	63C
Koonce, Jeffrey C.	AL0800	63C
Koshgarian, Richard	KS0150	38,51,63C,63D
Kraft, James	IN1025	63C,63D
Kris, Michael A.	NC0600	63C
Kris, Mike	NC2350	63C
Kroesche, Kenneth	MI1750	63D,63C,49,37
Kuhn, William	OR0150	37,11,63C,60,13A
Kulesha, Gary	AG0450	10,63C,29
LaChance, Marc	NE0300	63C,63D,13,10F,29
Lambert, David D.	AL0500	63C,29
Lambert, Michelle	NE0050	63C
Langfur, Gabriel	MA0400	63C
Lankford, Andrew	VA0600	63C
LaRosa, Massimo	OH0600	63C,49
Larsen, Arved	IL1150	13,12A,63C
Laukhuf, Dale	OH1800	63C,63D,32E
Lavigne, Julie	AI0220	63C
Lawrence, Mark	CA1075	63C,42
Lawrence, Mark	CA4150	63C
Lawrence, Patrick	WI0850	63C,63D,37,32E
Laws, Francis	OH2500	11,49,63C,63D
Lawson, Ronald S.	IA0910	63C,65,11,50
Laymon, Michael	IL1080	11,13,35,63C
Lebens, James C.	AI0190	63C,49,43
Lee, Vivian	AI0150	63C
Lefkowitz, Aaron M.	FL1550	63C,37
Leibinger, Douglas J.	CA4700	47,29B,63C,10A
Leisenring, John R.	MO1810	41,63C,63D
Lenthe, Carl	IN0900	63C
Leonard, Charlotte	AG0150	12A,63D,63C,15,63B
Leslie, Drew	NC0050	63C,49,42,41
Linch-Parker, Sheryl	NC0800	13A,32B,32C,49,63C
Lindahl, Robert	MI0400	49,63C,29
Lindberg, Jeffrey	OH0700	47,38,63C,29A
Linn, Richard	NJ1050	63C
Linsner, Arthur F.	IL2150	63C
Little, Jeannie E.	LA0200	63C
Logan, Christopher	CT0050	63C
Lombardo, Jonathan R.	NY4320	63C
Lopez, Michael	NC0450	11,63C,63D
Loucky, David L.	TN1100	63C,63D,49
Lovely, Aaron	MD0300	63C,63D,37
Lowe, Edward	TX3450	63C
Lowrey, Alden	AA0020	63C
Lucas, Don	MA0400	63C
Luciani, Dante T.	FL1900	47,63C,29
Lukiwski, Terry	AG0450	29,63C
Lumpkin, Royce E.	NC2420	63C,49
Lund, Steve	MN0050	63C,63D
Lund, Steven	MN0800	63C
Luscombe, Greg	TN1660	63C,49
Lusk, Mark Lancaster	PA2750	63C,63D
Lustrea, Robert	IL3150	63C,63D
MacGillivary, Rod	AF0120	60,63C,63D
MacInnes, Scott	AB0150	63C
Mack, Kyle	ND0350	60,37,47,63C,29
Maday, Casey	IA0550	63C
Madsen, Peter C.	NE0610	63C,47,29,49
Magliocco, Hugo	IL1100	63D,63C
Malecki, Jeffrey	IL2650	37,60B,63C,63D,38
Malloy, Andrew	CA3600	63C
Malloy, Andrew Thomas	CA0835	63C
Maltester, John	CA2775	37,41,60B,63C
Manduca, Mark W.	ME0500	63C,11
Mann, William P.	KY0900	63C
Mannix, Natalie K.	MD0850	63C,63D,41
Manson, David	FL1650	47,63C,63D,53,34
Manz, Paul P.	AZ0510	63B,63C
Marcellus, Tom	NY1100	63C
Mark, Douglas L.	MS0250	49,63C,63D,41
Markey, James	NY2250	63C
Markey, James A.	NY1900	63C
Marple, Ellen	AB0200	63C
Marsalis, Delfeayo	LA0800	63C
Marsteller, Loren	CA0825	63C,63D
Marsteller, Loren	CA3300	63C
Marston, Karen L.	TX2295	37,63C,11,13A,34C
Martell, Rodney	VA0250	63C
Martell, Rodney	VA0150	63C,63D
Martin, David	AI0200	63C,49
Martin, David	AI0150	63C
Martin, Jennifer	CA1510	32E,11,13,48,63C
Martin, Joseph	CO0900	37,63C,63D,41,60
Martinez, Pedro	TX3525	63D,63C
Mason, Elliot J.	NY2750	63C
Mast, Ivan	AA0035	63C
Masters, John	OH1850	63C
Matchett, Robert	PA3650	63C
Mathie, David	ID0050	63C,32E,63D,49
Mathis, Eric	AF0100	63C
Mathis, William B.	OH0300	49,63C,47
Matta, Thomas	IL0750	63C,29
Matthews, Michael K.	MO0850	13A,13,10F,47,63C
Mauldin, Mark K.	DC0150	13A,13B,32,63C
May, Douglas L.	PA1450	63C,49
Mazzio, Carl	NY3725	63C,37
Mazziot, Nicholas	MD0175	63C,63D
Mazzocchi, Anthony	NJ0700	63C,63D
Mazzocchi, Anthony J.	NJ0800	63C,49
McBride, M. Scott	KY0900	60B,32,10F,63C,37
McCain, Martin G.	TX3175	63C,29,46,49
McChesney, Bob	CA0825	63C
McChesney, Bob H.	CA0835	63C
McChesney, Bob	CA1000	63C
McClelland, Phillip	PA3250	63C
McCollum, Jonathan	MD1100	63C,63D,11,12,20
McCollum, Jonathan Ray	MD0060	12,13,20,55,63C
McCroskey, John	TX2250	63C
McEuen, Stephen	PA2150	11,63C,63D
McFalls, James	MD0850	63C,29A,46
McGinness, John	MD0150	63C
McGrannahan, A. Graydon	NV0100	37,32C,41,63C,63D
McGrannahan, Grady	IA0550	63C,37,63D
McIlwain, William Benjamin	MS0750	63C,49
McIntosh, Catherine	AA0035	63C
McKee, Paul	FL0850	29,63C
McKinney, Harold	NC0050	63C,49

Index by Area of Teaching Interest

Name	ID	Codes
McKinney, Russell	UT0190	63C,63D
McKinney, Russell	UT0050	63C
McManus, Keven M.	PA3000	63C,46
McManus, Kevin	MD0350	63B,63C,63D,49
McMullen, George Edward	CA5020	63C
McPherson, John	AA0100	63C
Means, Allen	IL2450	36,61,63D,63C
Mecham, Bryce	ID0060	63C,41,32E
Medler, Ben	OR0850	63C,47
Mehrtens, Russell	PA1150	63C
Meidenbauer, Michael	NY3650	63C
Meidenbauer, Michael	NY3600	63C,63D
Meixner, Brian	PA3100	12A,63C,49,11
Mendoza, Freddie	TX3175	29,47,63C
Mensch, Thomas	TX3370	37,41,63C,49,48
Metcalf, John C.	PA1750	34,10,11,49,63C
Milholland, John	CA3400	63C
Millar, Michael W.	CA0630	63C,35E,29A,35A
Millat, Andrew	OH0450	63C
Millat, Andy	OH1900	63C
Miller, Eric	TN0260	63C
Miller, Greg F.	LA0300	63C
Miller, James	CA0510	63C,49
Miller, James	CA5030	63C
Miller, Rodney L.	OH2140	63D,63C
Miller, Ryan	IL0400	63C
Mindeman, John	IL3550	63C
Mindeman, John	IL3500	63D,63C,49,29
Mindemann, John	IL1350	63C
Mitchell, David	OH1100	63C
Mitchell, Randall	IN0800	63C
Mixdorf, Cory Daniel	GA1050	63,63C
Moeller, Jeremy	IL2200	63C
Morales, Raimundo	TX3750	63C,37,49
Morales-Matos, Jaime	OH1450	63C,63D,13C,42
Morrison, Audrey	IL0720	29,63C
Morrison, Audrey	IL2100	63C,63D
Mose, John	IL0650	37,63C,63D
Moyer, Jon	PA3710	49,63C,63D
Mueller, John T.	TN1680	63C,63D,49
Mulcahy, Craig	MD1010	63C
Mulcahy, Craig	DC0050	63C
Mulcahy, Michael	IL2250	63C
Muller, Carl	TX2300	63B,63C,63D
Murchison, Matthew	PA3580	63C,63D
Myers, Timothy R.	MO1900	63C
Necessary, Andrew	VA0050	12A,32B,37,46,63C
Neff, Matthew	VA0450	63C
Nelson, Kent	UT0350	63C,63D,63
Neuenschwander, Daniel	PA1750	37,32,63C
Neuman, Phil	OR0500	12A,63C
Neurohr, John	WA0050	63C
Nicholson, Edmon	GA0750	63C
Niemisto, Paul	MN1450	49,63C,63D,37,42
Nigrelli, Christopher	NC1100	12A,47,44,63C,63D
Norrell, Stephen	NY2150	63C
Norton, Peter K.	OH2200	63C
Nova, James	PA1050	63C
Oberholtzer, Christopher W.	ME0500	29,47,63C
Oft, Mike	OR0150	63D,63C
Oft, Toby	MA0400	63C
Olfert, Warren	ND0350	60,32C,37,63C
Olin, James R.	MD0650	63C
Olson, John	MN0040	63C
Olsson, John	OH2600	63C
Olsson, John A.	OH2290	63C
Ordman, Ava	MI1400	63C,49
Ormsbee, Timothy	AZ0350	63C,63D
Orovich, Nicholas	NH0350	13C,37,63C,63D
Orton, Billy H.	AL1160	36,60A,60B,61,63C
Osborne, Robert B.	TX2250	63C
Ostrander, Phillip A.	WI0803	37,63C
Overly, Paul	SC0200	11,12,32,63C,63D
Oyster, Roger	MO1790	63C
Pagliuca, Domingo	FL1450	63C
Pagliuca, Domincio	FL0700	63C
Paiewonsky, Moises	AZ0500	63C,46
Palmer, Bradley E.	GA0550	63C,11,34,32F,41
Paradis, Sarah	OH1900	63C,41
Park, William B.	WA0800	47,63C
Parker, Steven C.	TX3530	63C
Parmer, Richard	WY0130	63C,63D,60,49
Patterson, Benjamin	MD1010	63C
Patterson, Mark	PA3250	29,63C
Patterson, Mark	NY2900	63C
Patterson, Thomas	WI0960	29A,36,11,63C
Pedde, Dennis	IA0930	63A,63B,63C,63D
Penpraze, Laurie	FL1745	63C,63D,66D,67E
Perdicaris, Stephen	CA5350	63C,42
Perdicaris, Stephen	CA0150	63C
Perez, Frank	IA0600	37,47,32,29,63C
Perkins, Boyd	SD0400	63C,63D,37,60B,72
Perry, Dawn A.	NC2650	63C,32E,37,47,60B
Peterson, David	MN1500	63C,63D
Peterson, David	MN1300	63C
Pethel, Stan	GA0300	13,60,10,63C,10F
Phillips, Brent	TX0300	63C,49
Phillips, Jeffrey T.	TN0100	63C
Phillips, Mark W.	VA1750	32C,37,49,63C,63D
Phillips, Timothy	NC1400	63A,63C
Pinson, Donald L.	TX0550	11,13A,63C,63D,49
Pinson, Donald	TX2930	63C
Pitchford, Timothy	IL1200	63C,29A,46,47,53
Pitchford, Timothy	IL2900	63C
Plitnik, Brian	WV0750	63C,49
Plsek, Thomas	MA0260	63C,63D
Polci, Mike	AG0200	63C
Pollard, Paul	NY3785	63C
Powell, Michael	NY1900	63C,49
Powell, Michael E.	NJ1130	63C,41
Powell, Michael	NY0500	63C
Powell, Michael E.	NY3790	63C
Presson, Lucy	TN0150	63D,63C
Priester, Julian	WA0200	10,47,63C,63D,29
Pugh, James	IL3300	63C
Pugh, Joel	ND0500	63C,63D,11
Pursell, Anthony	TX2750	37,41,48,60,63C
Purviance, Douglas	NJ1160	63C
Pylinski, Thomas	OH1350	63C,63D
Quinby, Jack	OR0250	63C,63D
Quintanar, David	CO0275	63C,42
Rainwater, Brian	FL0670	60,37,13C,63C,47
Ranti, James	NY5000	63A,63C
Reed, Sean Scot	AR0200	63C,47
Reichart, Alan	IL1610	63C
Reichenbach, Bill	CA0825	63C
Renshaw, Don	AG0400	63C
Reycraft, Jonathan W.	MO1900	63C
Reynolds, Harold	NY1800	63C
Reynolds, Martin C.	MO1500	37,63C,41,47,32E
Rich, Kevin	TX1450	63C
Richards, Eric J.	NE0400	63C,37,10A,13B,47
Richards, Lasim	FL0700	63C,35A
Richey, David	NY3350	63C
Ridge, David	CA3920	63C
Ridge, David P.	CA0807	63C
Ritt, David	WA0200	63C
Rivera Trinidad, Miguel	PR0115	63C
Roberts, James E.	AL0500	60,12A,49,63C
Roberts, Shannon B.	UT0150	13,41,49,63C,10
Robertson, Donald C.	NY3705	49,63C,63D
Robertson, James D.	MT0175	13,60B,63C,63D,47
Robinson, D.	MA0800	63C
Robinson, Doug	AZ0490	63C,63A
Robinson, Evan	WV0600	63C
Rodin, Jared	IN0250	63C
Rodman, Ronald	MN0300	13,37,63C,63D,12D
Rodriguez, Joseph	IL0730	63D,63C
Rogers, Richard	GA0940	63C
Rojak, John	NY2750	63C
Rojak, John	NY0500	63C,63D
Rojak, John	NY0150	63C,42,49
Rojak, John D.	NY1900	49,63C
Rojak, John	NJ1130	63C,41
Rose, William G.	LA0350	13,49,34,63D,63C
Ruetz, Andrew	OH1650	63C,63D
Russell, Eileen Meyer	TX2650	63D,13,13C,49,63C
Ryberg, J. Stanley	IL1085	13B,13C,12A,63C,63D
Ryon, James M.	LA0200	63C
Ryon, James P.	MD0520	63C
Ryon, Jim	WV0550	63C
Sanders, George	CT0600	63C,44
Sanders, Robert	CA0815	63C,49
Sandford, Tim	ID0140	63C
Satterwhite, Dan	FL1125	63C,42
Scarpa, Salvatore	NJ1050	60,38,41,63C
Scarr, Susie	GA0050	63D,63C
Schaefer, Donn	UT0250	63C
Schendel, Todd	IA0300	63C
Schlabach, Blake	IN1650	63C
Schmidt, David A.	FL0400	47,63C,63D
Schmidt, David	FL1750	49,63C,63D
Schmidt, Donald	AJ0150	63C,63D
Schmidt, Henry L.	PA2550	13,12A,63C,26,29A
Schneider, Bernard	FL0500	63C,63D
Schneller, Aric	TX2250	47,29,63C,61
Schultz, Paul	DC0150	63C,13
Schultz, Ryan	IL2300	37,63C,36
Sciannella, David	DC0100	63C
Scott, Debra L.	TX2700	47,63C,63D
Scott, James	AA0150	63C
Seidel, John	IN0150	49,63C
Seifert, Dustin	NM0100	37,63C,63D,60B,32E
Seifried, Denver	OH2450	63C
Self, Cale	GA2130	37,63C,63D,32E,49
Sellers, Joel	CA0815	63C
Sessions, Timothy	PA1950	63C,47
Sexton, James	TN1400	37,46,63C
Shaw, Gary R.	IL1750	10F,60,37,63C
Shields, Larry	AG0450	32,63C
Shoemaker, Vance	SD0050	63C,63D,49
Shoemaker, Vance	IA1200	63C
Shoemaker, Vance	IA0500	63C,63D
Shonkwiler, Joel	OH1200	63C,63D
Shuster, Brett A.	KY1500	42,63C,49,67E
Shynett, Jerald	NC2440	29,63C
Simmons, Garth	OH0300	63C
Simmons, Matthew	FL0100	49,60B,63C,63D
Simmons, Matthew	SC1050	37,49,63C,63D
Sipher, John	NY1350	63C,63D
Sleister, Terry	GA1500	63C
Sloan, Gerald H.	AR0700	63C,63D
Smith, Dean W.	IL1740	63C
Smith, Gene	AF0150	13,47,49,63C,29
Smith, Jason D.	OH0650	63C
Smith, Michael K.	IA0950	42,63C,63D,49
Smith, Susan	TN0050	63C
Snyder, Fred	NY2400	63C
Sochinski, James	VA1700	13,37,63C,63D,34
Solomon, Wayne	CA1860	63C,63D
Solomon, Wayne	CA5070	63C,63D
Soto, Robert	CA0630	63C
Soueidi, Mark	WY0200	63C
Spang, Ron	PA0500	63D,63C
Sparkes, Doug	AB0050	63C
Sparkes, Douglas	AB0100	63C
Sparrow, James	NC1250	63D,32E,41,63C,63
Spencer, Daniel	MI1050	63C,63D
Spiridopoulos, Gregory	MA2000	63C
Spoonamore, Dudley	KY0450	63C
Springer, Mark	MN1300	63D,63C
Springfield, David	GA2150	29,35G,63C
Sprott, Weston	NY3785	63C
Sprott, Weston	NJ1130	63C
Sprott, Weston	NY2250	63C
Stagg, David L.	MO1790	11,37,63C
Stanley, Bill J.	CO0800	13A,13,63C
Stanton, Ronald	NY2105	63C,63
Starr, Eric P.	CA4100	63C
Stetson, David B.	CA5020	63C
Stetson, David	CA0960	63C
Stewart, M. Dee	IN0900	63C
Stitt, Ronald	PA0100	63C,47,29,46,34
Stone, Michael	AG0550	63C
Stout, Richard	OH0600	63C,49
Stoyanov, Simeon N.	MI1200	63C
Stroeher, Michael	WV0400	63D,49,63C,32,29
Sudduth, Steven	KY1425	13,32E,37,60B,63C
Sullivan, Nick A.	AA0200	63D,63C,13C
Sullivan, Peter	PA0550	63C
Sullivan, Peter	PA1050	63C
Summers, C. Oland	NC0850	32,63C,64D,65,72
Swallow, John	CA2950	63C
Swallow, John	CT0850	63C
Swanson, Bob	MO0350	63C
Swanson, Philip	MA1650	63C,10A,13B,13C,13F
Sweeney, Christopher R.	AK0100	32,63,63C,32E,32B
Sweeney, Gordon	AG0450	63C
Tanouye, Nathan	NV0050	29,63C,47
Tapper, Robert	MT0400	29,63C,46,47
Taylor, Clifton	MS0420	13,47,49,63C,37
Taylor, David	NY2250	41,63C
Taylor, J. Chris	AA0100	63C
Tesch, John	MN1120	32E,37,63C,11
Thomas, Rachel	AG0600	63C
Thompson, J. Mark	LA0550	49,63C

Name	Code	Areas
Thompson, Steven D.	CA0150	37,38,63C,11,13A
Thurman, Demondrae	AL0650	63C,63D,41
Tinnell, Jennifer L.	KY0400	37,63C,32E,47
Tramiel, Leonard	MS0560	60,11,37,63C,63D
Trapani, Steve	CA0825	63C
Trottier, Jean-Nicolas	AI0150	29,63C
Trottier, Jean-Nicolas	AI0200	63C,29
Trowers, Robert	NC1600	63C,63D,46,29A
Tucker, Craig	MS0400	63C
Tucker, Kent	PA2250	63C
Tulga, Philip	CA0840	29,63C
Turner, George	ID0150	10,13,60B,63C,63D
Tychinski, Bruce D.	DE0150	63C,63D
Utterstrum, Oscar	TN1400	63C,63D
Vail, Mark	TN1200	63C,63D
Van Deursen, John	AB0100	49,63C,37
van Deursen, John	AB0060	47,38,63C,63D
Van Hoy, Jeremy	CO0200	63C,37
Vandehey, Patrick	OR0250	60,32,37,38,63C
VanValkenburg, Jamie G.	CO0050	63A,63C,63D,37,41
Varpness, Lee	MN1620	63C,63D
Vaughan, Matthew	PA3250	63C
Vernon, Charles G.	IL0750	63C
Vining, David	AZ0450	63C,41
Vinson, Danny	TX3535	63C,63D
Vogt, Nancy	NE0450	63C,63D,11
Von Hoff, Paul	WI0250	63C,63D
Voyement, Jacques	CA0830	63C
Wagner, Irvin	OK1350	49,63C,54
Waid, Tom	FL0150	63C,63D
Walker, Jesse	GA0150	13A,63C,63D,13B,13C
Walsh, Benjamin	TX1850	63C
Walter, Cameron	AG0450	32,63C,63D,37,44
Walter, Ross A.	VA1600	63C,63D,34,49
Wardlaw, Jeffrey A.	PA0700	63D,49,13,63C
Wardle, Alvin	UT0300	32C,63B,63C,63D
Warner, Douglas G.	TN0850	11,63D,13B,13C,63C
Warren, Dale E.	KY1450	63C,41
Watters, Harry	VA0450	63C
Weeks, Douglas	MA0650	63C
Weeks, Douglas	MA0700	63C
Weiss, Robert L.	IL2900	63C
Weisz, Deborah	CT0800	29,63C
Welcomer, Paul	CA4150	63C,49
Wells, Wayne W.	VA1350	49,63C,41
Wenger, Fred	MT0370	63C
Westray, Ron	AG0650	47,63C
Weyersberg, Roger	MI1850	63C,63D
Wheat, James R.	MN1700	63C,63D
Wheaton, Dana	CA3350	37,63C,34,53
Wheeler, John	MA2250	63C,41
Whitaker, Jon	AL1170	63C
White, Brad K.	TX3400	63C
Whitlock, Mark	MN1600	32,37,49,63C,63D
Wickham, Nathaniel	CO0950	63C,49,63D
Wicks, Leonard	CA1425	63C
Widener, Russell D.	KS1450	63C
Wiest, Steve	TX3420	10,29,47,63C
Wigness, Robert Clyde	VT0450	63C
Wika, Norman	OK0550	60,37,63C,63D
Wilborn, David F.	TX2900	13,63C,63D,41,37
Wilken, David M.	NC2400	63C,46,47,10A
Wilkinson, Michael	FL1800	63C,47,29B
Williams, Anthony N.	ND0400	29,47,63C,63D
Williams, Lindsey R.	MO1810	32E,60,32H,32G,63C
Williams, Mark	MI0900	63C,49,41
Williams, Mark	WA1000	63C
Williams, Steve	CA3800	63C
Williams, Steven J.	CA3500	63C,49
Williamson, Brad	WY0200	37,63C
Wilson, Bruce	MD0150	63C,63D,49,37,32C
Wilson, Dennis E.	MI2100	63C,29,47
Wilson, J. P.	AR0600	37,63D,63C,32E,60B
Wilson, Jeremy	TN1850	63C
Wilson, Stephen	SC0750	63C
Winkle, Keith	WA0650	63C
Wise, Colin	PA1400	63C
Wise, Herbert	NY2500	63C,66A,66D,11,32E
Wise, Jay	NE0160	63C
Witmer, Larry	NY0050	63C
Wolfe, Gordon	AG0450	63C
Wolfe, Gordon	AG0300	63C,42
Wolfinbarger, Steve	MI2250	49,63C,29A
Woodman, Ian	AA0020	63C
Workman, K. Darren	TX3100	63C,63D
Wright, Bron	CO0830	63C,63D
Wulfeck, David	NC0900	63C
Yamamoto, Ko-Ichiro	WA1050	63C
Yao, John	NY0646	63C
Yeager, Bill	CA4100	47,63C,29
Yeo, Douglas	AZ0100	63C
Yeo, Douglas	MA1400	63C
Yoes, Milas	AZ0470	12A,29,37,46,63C
Young, Michael	IL3450	63C,63D
Zacharella, Alexandra	AR0730	63C,63D,11,49,37
Zadrozny, Edward A.	OH2150	49,63C
Zadrozny, Edward A.	OH0650	63C
Zalkind, Larry	UT0250	63C
Zawacki, Karen A.	KS1400	63C
Zegel, Don	FL2050	63C
Ziegel, Donald	FL0930	63C
Zimmerman, Larry	MN1625	63C,63D
Zimmerman, Larry	MN0750	63C,63D,49
Zimmerman, Larry	MN1450	63C,63D
Zimmerman, Larry	MN0250	63D,63C
Zion, Mike	FL0680	63C
Zugger, Thomas W.	OH0350	63C,63D,49

Low Brass

Name	Code	Areas
Adams, Brent	AG0500	63D
Adams, Brent	AG0050	63D
Adams, Gary	OH0650	63D
Adams, Paul	VA0950	63D,12A,37
Agnew, Joseph	IL3150	63D
Akins, James	OH1850	63D
Aldag, Daniel	CA2250	63D,29,14C,63C,47
Alessi, Joseph	NY1900	63D,63C,49
Alexander, Joe L.	LA0250	10,13,63D,10A,49
Alexander, Lois L.	MI2120	63D,49,12,32
Allen, Michael	CO0550	63D
Allen, Stephen A.	NJ1130	63D
Alme, Joseph	ND0250	63C,63D,37,60
Alvis, Jonathan	SD0600	63D,37,63C
Amend, Holly	WA0950	63C,63D
Amis, Ken	MA0400	63D
Amis, Kenneth	MA1175	63D
Amis, Kenneth	FL1125	63D
Amis, Kenneth	MA0350	63D
Andersen, Michael	SD0050	63D
Anderson, Dan	IL0720	62D,63D,29
Anderson, Jeffrey	CA4150	63D
Anderson, Matt	SC1080	63C,63D
Anderson, Matthew T.	SC0400	63D,49
Andrew, Isaac	OR1250	63D
Angerstein, Fred	TX3450	63D,37
Angerstein, Fred	TX1000	63D
Antonucci, Robert	PA3650	63D
Archer, Robert	TX0250	63D,37
Armandi, Richard	IL3100	63C,63D
Askew, Dennis	NC2430	63D
Atherton, Timothy	MA2100	63C,63D,29A
Babcock, Andrew	TX1550	60B,63D,37,13,47
Babcock, Donald J.	MI0600	47,63C,63D
Baer, Alan J.	NJ1130	63D
Baer, Alan	NY1900	63D
Baer, Alan	NY2250	63D
Baer, Alan	NY0150	63D
Baer, Alan	NY2150	63D
Baker, Jeff	TX2955	63D
Baker, Stacy A.	KY0900	63D
Ball, James	MI0100	29A,38,47,63D,60B
Barlar, Douglas	FL0670	12A,63D,49,32E
Barnette, Mark	NE0610	63D
Barton, Mark	TX3400	41,63D
Bean, Scott	WI0810	63D,12A,11,49
Bearid, Rolyn	SD0580	63D,63C
Beauchesne, Paul	AB0210	63D
Beaudry, Pierre	AI0200	63D
Behrend, Roger L.	VA0450	63D,41
Bell, Isaac	AL0050	47,63C,63D
Belser, Robert S.	WY0200	37,63D,11
Benavidez, Justin	TX2960	63D
Benedict, Les	CA1265	63D
Benjamin, Richard S.	PA0350	63D
Bennett, Larry	MO0100	32E,63D,63C,41
Benton, Robert	AG0550	63D
Benton, Robert	MI0050	63D
Bernard, Gilles	NJ0825	13,12A,49,63C,63D
Bertolet, Jay	FL0700	63D
Bertolet, Jay	FL0200	63D
Bicigo, James Michael	AK0150	12A,32,37,41,63D
Bing, Charles S.	FL0600	32C,37,63C,63D
Bird, Gary	MN1300	63D
Bird, Gary J.	PA1600	63D
Bishop, Ronald	OH0600	63D
Bishop, Ronald	OH1700	63D
Black, Phillip	KS1450	49,63D
Blaha, Christopher	NC0050	63D
Blake, Paul	NY1400	63C,63D
Bobe, Larry	IA1300	63C,63D
Bock, James D.	OH1650	63D
Bock, Stan	OR1300	63C,63D,49
Bodiford, Kenneth	AL0500	60,37,63D
Bohn, William	OK1200	63D
Bohnhorst, Brendan	MI0300	63D
Bolton, Chuck	OR1150	32,37,49,63D
Booth, David M.	OH2500	60,37,63D,65
Bottomley, John	MA2000	63D
Bourgois, Louis	KY0750	11,12A,49,63D,34
Bourne, Brian	MD0750	63D
Bove, Andrew	NJ0700	63D
Bowman, Brian	TX3420	63D
Bowyer, Don	AR0110	63C,63D,29,35C,47
Boyd, Frederick	NC2420	63D,63C
Boyd, Lance	MT0400	47,63C,63D,53,29
Bozeman, Scott	GA0200	63D
Bradshaw, Eric E.	GA2150	63D,32E,37,60
Brady, Angus	AB0050	63D
Brame, Steven	IL1500	63C,63D
Brantigan, Kathleen	CO0900	63D
Breuninger, Tyrone	NJ1050	41,63D
Brewer, Robert G.	CO0250	32C,63D,49
Brickey, James	UT0150	63D,32
Brooks, John Patrick	ID0100	60B,37,63C,47,63D
Brown, Brian	NJ1050	63D
Brown, Brian	PA2800	63D
Brown, Brian	DE0150	63D
Brown, Brian	NJ0175	63D,41
Brown, Daniel R.	NV0050	63D,41
Brown, Joe Davis	MD0850	63D
Brown, Matthew	PA1300	63D,63C
Brown, Richard L.	WV0600	32,63D,72,11
Brown, Rogers	VA0950	10F,37,47,63D,29
Brown, Velvet	PA2750	63D
Brownell, Jack	AF0100	63D
Brownell, Jack	AF0050	49,63C,63D
Brunette, Chantal	AG0250	63C,63D
Bryan, Stephanie	MO2000	63C,63D
Bryant, Bob	KY0450	63D
Bryant, Steven	TX3510	49,63D
Bryce, Daniel	UT0325	63D
Bubacz, Eric	GA1050	63D
Bubacz, Eric	GA1300	63D
Buckmaster, Matthew	NC0750	63D,29,63C,49,32
Budde, Paul J.	MN0750	63D,49,32C
Bulmer, Jared S.	IL2150	63D
Bulmer, Karen	AD0050	63C,63D
Bunn, Michael	DC0150	63D
Bunn, Michael	MD0850	63D
Bunn, Michael	VA1350	63D
Bunn, Michael	MD0750	63D
Burch, Dwight	MI0350	63D
Burdick, Daniel	PA1200	63C,63D,49,11
Burke, Larry	FL0800	32B,63D,29A,49,35A
Burroughs, John	TN1350	63C,63D
Buttery, Gary A.	RI0300	11,47,49,63D,29A
Buttery, Gary	CT0100	63D,37,47
Bynum, Josh L.	GA2100	63C,63D,13A
Byrnes, Jason	CO0950	63D,32
Calkin, Joshua	NE0700	63D,37,11,49,63C
Call, R. Steven	UT0050	47,63D,46,29
Cameron, Scott	DC0010	37,63D,63C
Camp, James L.	GA0490	37,49,63B,63C,63D
Campbell, Larry	TX0340	37,47,63B,63C,63D
Campbell, Neal	OH2300	63D
Campbell, Steven	MN1623	63D
Capshaw, Reed	IN0910	63C,63D
Capshaw, Reed	IL1085	63C,63D
Carichner, Christian Blake	AR0850	63D
Carlson, Paul	MI0900	63D
Carpenter, Ron	NC1250	63D
Carper, Gary E.	VA1475	63D
Cazes, Alain	AI0150	60B,63D,48
Celmer, Joey R.	SC1050	63A,63B,63C,63D,47

Index by Area of Teaching Interest

Name	Code	Areas
Chamberlain, Rick E.	PA1850	63C,63D
Chambers, Robert	OK1250	38,63C,63D,13D,10F
Chance, Mike	AR0250	32E,37,38,63C,63D
Chemay, Frank	LA0700	10,63D,10F,11,49
Chesebrough, James C.	NH0150	37,60,32,63D,32E
Choate, Jim	AL0400	63D
Ciabattari, William S.	PA2100	13,63D,32,37,47
Clark, Allen	TX3515	32C,37,63D
Clark, Evan	MN0040	63D
Clark, Jim	TX2955	63C,49,63D
Clark, Wayne R.	OK0700	63D,63C,63
Clark, William F.	CO0830	47,63D,13,49,29
Clements, Anthony	CA4900	63D
Clements, Phillip L.	TX2955	60B,37,63D,13A,12A
Clements, Tony	CA0807	63D
Clements, Tony	CA4425	63D
Cline, Nancy	WI1150	63D
Coale, Dean	OK0300	32E,49,63C,63D
Collins, Kevin	WI0808	37,63D
Collins, Tony	CA4700	63C,63D
Collins, Zachary	PA1600	63D,12A,13B,49
Colwell, Brent	TX2800	37,11,12A,63C,63D
Colwell, Lynn	IN1310	63D
Colwell, Lynn	IN1850	63C,63D
Combest, Chris	IL2900	63D,13B
Compton, Paul R.	OK0800	63C,63D,47,49
Conger, Robert B.	MO1500	60B,32C,63C,63D
Conklin, Raymond L.	KY0950	49,63C,63D
Connelly, Chris	SC0420	63C,63D,11,29
Cook, Justin	TX2750	63D,63C
Cook, Seth	VA1550	63D
Cook, Seth	MD0550	63C,63D
Cook, Seth	DC0170	63D
Cooley, Floyd O.	IL0750	63D
Coomber, Robert	CA1750	63D
Cooper, Blake	CA0835	63D
Cooper, Lawrence R.	PA0350	63C,63D
Corella, Gil C.	DC0100	63D
Cottrell, Jeffrey	TX0900	10A,63C,63D
Couch, Roy L.	OK0150	37,63D,49,32E
Cox, Mark	MI0400	63D,41
Cox, Thomas B.	GA2000	63D
Craig, Mary Ann	NJ0800	32,37,63D,49
Cranson, Todd	AR0300	63D
Crawford, Jeremy	AL0050	11,63D
Cunningham, Blaine E.	IA0700	63C,63D
Daniel, Robert	TX2250	63D
Daussat, David	TX3525	63D,49
Davenport, Roger N.	MO1830	63C,63D
Davies, Richard	NY3775	10,29,34,46,63D
Davis, Garnett	TN1400	63D
Davis, Garnett R.	TN0550	63D
Davis, Garnett R.	TN1850	63D,49
Davis, Mark	MS0100	63D
Davis, Ronald	SC1110	11,49,63D
Deck, Warren	CO0900	63D
DeMarsh, Joe	MI0500	63D
Demkee, Ronald	PA2450	63D,32
Demkee, Ronald	PA2550	63D
Demmert, Wade C.	WA0600	63D
Devlin, Michelle P.	VA1100	63C,63D
Dibley, Charles	IA1200	63D
DiCesare, John	OH1100	63D
Dickey, Christopher J.	WA1150	13C,11,63D
Dickey, Nathanial H.	MN0600	37,63C,63D,32E,49
Dickman, Marcus	FL1950	63D,53,29
DiCuirci, Michael	OH0950	63C,63D,37,32E
DiCuirci, Michael P.	OH0450	32B,32C,37,63D,46
Dimick, Glen	IN0907	63D
Dimick, Glen	IN0800	63D
Dimick, Glen M.	IN1650	63D,41,49
Dixon, Julian	CA0840	63D
Dobbins, Brian	OK1350	63D
Dobroski, Bernard J.	IL2250	32H,63D,32,60,35E
Dowling, Eugene	AB0150	42,13C,63C,63D
Driscoll, Matthew	IA0200	63A,63C,63D
Driscoll, Matthew	IA0400	63C,63D
Drobnak, Kenneth Paul	SD0500	63D,37,11,47,49
Droste, Paul E.	OH1850	37,63D
Dubberly, James	CA0850	63C,63D,29A,41
DuBeau, Pete	NC0700	63D
Dubeau, Peter C.	VA1000	63D
DuBeau, Peter	VA0250	63D,49
Dumaine, Stephen	MD1010	63D
Duncan, Andrew	OH0500	63C,63D
Dunn, J. Michael	CO0800	63D
Dunsmore, Matthew	NE0610	63D
Dutton, Brent	CA4100	13,10F,10,49,63D
Eastep, Michael	AA0050	63D
Eastep, Michael	AA0150	63D,49
Eaton, Daniel	MN1600	37,63D,49
Ebbers, Paul	FL0850	63D
Ehrlich, Barry	WA0860	13,11,37,63C,63D
Elsey, Eddie L.	AL1250	49,13B,63C,63D
Emilson, C. Rudolph	NY3725	60,41,63D
Enabnit, Brian	IA0250	63C,63D
Erdman, James A.	PA1900	63C,63D
Erickson, Martin	WI0825	63D
Erickson, Marty	WI0350	63D,42
Eshelman, Kent T.	TX0300	63D
Etters, Stephen C.	NC0350	60,32,37,63D,13A
Evans, Brett	IL1520	63D
Evans, Darryl	AR0810	32E,47,63D,13A,13B
Evans, Jay	AL1200	63C,63D,42
Evans, Paul	WA0650	63D
Everett, Micah P.	MS0700	63C,63D,13C,41,49
Fagerberg, Kaj	IL1900	63C,63D
Faller, Richard	IL1400	63D
Fallis, Todd	UT0300	32C,63C,63D,47,41
Fast, Bobbi	AC0100	63D
Fedderly, David T.	MD0650	63D
Ferguson, John	TX2710	63D
Fernisse, Glenn	GA0400	10,63D,34,32E
Fisher, Mark	IL0750	63C,63D
Flanigan, Glen	KY0100	11,32C,41,47,63D
Flanigan, Sean G.	CO0225	63C,63D,41,47,35A
Fletcher, Seth	NE0590	63D,63C,13B,13C,11
Flythe, Bernard	GA0750	63D
Flythe, Bernard	GA1150	32E,63D,41,11
Folger, Bill	VA0750	63D
Forbes, Michael I.	WI0840	63D,13,34
Formeck, Michael C.	PA1450	63D
Fowler, Jonathon	PA3600	63D,49
Fratia, Salvatore	AG0450	63D
Frederickson, Matthew	MO0650	63D,32E,49,63C
Freeman, Jeffrey J.	TX2100	11,63C,49,63D,34
French, Chelsea	IL2050	63C,63D
French, Todd M.	IL0800	63D,32E
Frey, Adam	GA1050	63D
Frey, Adam	GA0750	63D
Fuller, Craig	NE0600	63D
Fullerton, Kevin T.	KS1400	14C,12A,29A,63D,11
Fulmer, Fred	OK1250	63D
Funderburk, Jeffrey	IA1600	49,63D,72
Gaddis, J. Robert	KY0400	60,32,51,63D,38
Gagnon, Sylvain	AG0250	63D
Gallion, Brian	LA0650	63D
Galvan, Santino	CA0600	63D
Galyean, Richard D.	VA1580	37,60,49,63D,32E
Garlock, Scott E.	OH0100	29,47,63C,63D,46
Gassler, Christopher J.	VA0700	63D,20
Gay, Nathan	KS0300	63C,63D,60B,37
Gazda, Frank S.	DE0050	63D,37,49,63C,42
Gibbens, Tracey	WI0860	63C,63D,49
Gibson, David	NY3730	63C,63D,47
Gibson, Walter	CT0050	63D
Gildow, Kurtis	IL0730	63D
Gildow, Kurtis C.	IL2050	63D
Giles, Glenn	VT0100	63C,63D,60,37,46
Gillan, Michael	MI0850	11,37,63C,63D,47
Gillespie, Robert C.	TX0100	63D
Gilliam, Jason	WA0650	63D
Gilmore, Robert	AL1300	11,63D
Glenn, David B.	WA1300	10,47,63D,29
Gnagey, Sam	IN0905	63D
Good, Matt J.	TX2400	63D
Good, Richard D.	AL0200	37,63D
Gormley, Lon	NY0400	63C,63D
Gormley, Lonna L.	NY3717	63D
Gray, Harold R. 'Skip'	KY1450	63D,49,41
Greene, Fred W.	CA5020	63D
Greene, Fred	CA0960	63D
Greene, Sean	TN0250	63D
Greene, Sean	TN0900	63D,13,37,32,42
Gregory, Jon M.	MO1790	63D
Gregory, Thomas	RI0101	29A,63D
Gregory, Tom	RI0200	63D
Griffin, Peter J.	IL0850	32,37,60B,63C,63D
Griffin, Samuel S.	MS0050	60,37,63D
Griffiths, Brian	OR0175	63D,46,37
Grose, Michael	OR1050	11,63D,49,42
Gross, Ernest H.	IL1300	37,49,60B,63D,12A
Grugin, Stephen	MI1600	37,63D,12A,32C,32E
Gruner, Greg	AL1300	37,63D,60B,32E,35
Guy, Charles V.	NY3780	63D,41
Guzik, Bernard	OK0850	63D
Haack, Donald	WI1155	63C,63D
Haddad, Steve	TX3520	63D,34,35
Haecker, Arthur	SC1000	63D
Hall, Jeffrey	AG0450	63D
Hall, Jeffrey	AG0300	63D
Hall, Michael	VA1000	63D,49,63C
Ham, Jason D.	NJ0800	63D
Hamlin, Seth	MA2010	63C,63D
Hamm, Samuel J.	MT0350	12A,13,63D
Hammond, Ivan	OH0300	63D
Hancock, Craig A.	IA1800	37,60B,63C,63D,72
Hansford, James	OK0650	38,32G,37,63D,41
Hardee, Kelly Ann	NC1350	63D
Harper, Gergory	CO0150	63C,63D
Harrelson, Lee	MO0850	13,63D
Harris, William H.	NY4150	63C,63D
Harris, William	NY2950	63C,63D
Harrison, Albert D.	IN1560	60B,37,47,63D,32E
Harrison, Kevin	IL3550	63D
Harry, Don	NY1100	63D,49
Hart, Michael	CA0550	37,13B,13C,63C,63D
Harvey, Brent M.	NC1900	63C,63D,41
Harvey, Brent	NC2700	11,63D
Haskett, William	TX1600	49,63D,11
Hasselfeld, Bart	AC0050	63D
Hedwig, Douglas F.	NY0500	49,63A,63D
Heinlein, Kenneth	OH0600	63D
Hellick, Gary	MI0500	63D
Helmer, John	AC0050	63D,63C
Helseth, Daniel	WA0250	63D
Henderson, Matthew	GA0250	11,63C,63D
Henniger, Henry J.	OR0700	63C,63D
Henry, Eric L.	PA3150	63D,49
Henry, Eric	PA0950	63D
Henry, Eric	PA2300	63D
Henry, John P.	NC1550	13,63D
Henson, Eric	SC0850	63D
Hepler, Lowell E.	PA0100	12A,12C,37,66A,63D
Hepola, Ralph	MN0800	63D
Hersey, Joanna R.	NC2435	10F,63C,63D,12A
Hetrick, Loy	IN0907	63C,63D
Heukeshoven, Eric	MN1400	63C,63D,34,10
Hicks, Gregory	LA0900	63C,63D
Hill, Todd E.	KY0950	63D,46,47
Hilson, Keith	MN0610	63C,63D
Hines, Tyrone	IL0600	63C,63D,46
Hinterbichler, Karl	NM0450	12A,12,63C,63D
Hipp, Lee	TX2200	63D
Hipp, Lee	TX3350	63D
Hittle, Kevin	NY4460	63D
Hitz, Andrew	PA1400	63D
Hoefle, Andrew	IL2775	11,37,47,63D,29
Hoelscher, Mark A.	WI0835	63C,63D,49
Hogue, Johnson	MD0360	70,12A,63D,13,11
Holben, David	CA3800	63D
Holben, David	CA3600	63D
Holcombe, Ross	WA0400	63C,63D
Holloway, John R.	SC0650	63D,32,37,60B
Horgan, Maureen A.	GA0850	63D,11,49,63C,29A
Houze, Reginald M.	MA0150	10F,36,37,60,63D
Howard, Vernon D.	OK1450	47,49,63C,63D,29
Howe, Timothy E.	MO1800	63C,63D
Howey, Henry E.	TX2250	63D,63C
Hudson, Barbara D.	NC0300	63C,63D
Hudson, Jed	OH0850	63C,63D
Huff, Sharon	IL1750	63D,63C
Huffman, Valarie A.	WV0300	37,32,63D,32E,49
Hull, Edward	CA0810	63D
Hunsberger, Johnson	FL2000	63D
Hunt, Douglas	CA4300	49,48,63D
Huntoon, John Richard	IN0100	63C,63D,47,37,49
Ingram, Danny	TX1100	63C,63D
Ioanna, Philip	PA2200	63D
Isenhour, Justin	AR0500	63C,63D,11,13C
Jackson, James	CT0600	63D
Jackson, James	CT0650	63D
Jackson, Joe	CA1000	63D
Jackson, Keith	WV0750	47,49,63C,63D
Jacobs, James	IL2970	63D,11,13A,37,46
James, Ray	KS0050	37,63D,32E,49

681

Name	Code	Areas
Jantsch, Carol	PA0850	63D
Jantz, Paul	SC0200	12A,49,63C,63D,34
Jarvis, Jeffery W.	AR0850	63D,11,12A
Jenkins, James E.	FL1850	63D
Jennings, Arthur	FL1850	11,63C,63D
Jerosch, Anita	ME0150	63D
Johansen, David A.	LA0650	63C,11,63D,49
Johnson, Daniel C.	NC2440	32,63D,34,32B,63C
Johnson, Daryl	IN1010	63D
Johnson, Sasha	AG0300	63D
Johnson, Sasha	AI0150	63D,49
Johnson, Stephen R.	PA0700	10F,32D,13A,63D
Johnston, Keith	CT0300	37,63C,63D
Jolly, Tucker	OH2150	49,63D
Jones, Calvin	DC0350	47,62D,63C,63D,29
Jones, John R.	KY1500	49,63D,42
Jones, Randy	CA0830	63D
Kaenzig, Fritz	MI2100	63D
Kagarice, Vern L.	TX3420	41,49,63C,63D
Kane, Kevin	RI0200	63C,63D
Kane, Kevin	RI0150	63C,63D
Karahalis, Dean	NY2550	63C,63D
Kashnig, Claude	FL1550	63D
Keck, Bill	VT0100	63D
Keeble, Carson	CO0830	63C,63D
Keehn, Samantha	IL0100	63C,63D,11
Keelan, Nick	WI0350	32,49,63C,63D
Keeling, Bruce	TX2350	11,12A,47,49,63D
Keen, Phil	CA5355	63D
Keen, Phillip M.	CA0835	63D
Keen, Phillip	CA0815	63D
Kelley, Charles	MO1500	63D
Kellner, Steve	MD1010	63D
Kellner, Steven	MD0650	63D
Kemp, Mildred	IN1010	63C,63D
Kendall, David	CA2420	35G,63C,63D
Keyser, Timothy	GA1500	63D
Kingsland, William	MA2020	63D
Kirk, David E.	TX2150	63D,42
Kiser, Brian D.	OH2600	63D
Klein, Stephen T.	CA3650	63D
Kline, Peter	TX2200	63C,63D
Kline, W. Peter	TX2260	13A,11,37,49,63D
Knox, Craig	PA0550	63D
Knox, Craig	PA1050	63D
Knupps, Terri L.	MO1550	12A,20,63C,63D,42
Kocher, Edward W.	PA1050	32,63C,63D
Kofsky, Allen	OH0200	63C,63D
Kolstad, Michael L.	MO0400	49,63C,63D,47,34
Kolwinska, Jeremy	MN1280	63C,63D,11,63B
Kono, Yutaka	VT0450	63D,34,38,60
Kortenkamp, Peter	IA0850	63D
Koshgarian, Richard	KS0150	38,51,63C,63D
Kraft, James	IN1025	63C,63D
Krauss, W. John	OH2290	63D,32E
Kroesche, Kenneth	MI1750	63D,63C,49,37
Krush, Jay P.	PA3250	63D
Krzywicki, Paul	PA0850	63D
Kunkee, Patrick	TN1850	63D
Kunzer, Stephen	OK0800	63D,11,29A
Kuroda, Masahito	LA0550	63D
Labrosse, Martin	AG0400	63D
LaChance, Marc	NE0300	63C,63D,13,10F,29
Lacy, Charles	LA0100	37,63D
LaDuke, Lance	PA0550	63D
LaDuke, Lance	PA1050	63D
Lair, Christopher	MO0350	63D
Landry, Scott P.	LA0760	63D
Lapins, Alexander	AZ0450	63D
LaRue, Peter	KY0610	60,11,32,37,63D
Laukhuf, Dale	OH1800	63C,63D,32E
Lawrence, Patrick	WI0850	63C,63D,37,32E
Lawrence, Torrey	ID0250	63D,37
Laws, Francis	OH2500	11,49,63C,63D
LeBlanc, Robert L.	OH1850	37,41,63D
Leday, Eric	AL1195	63D
Lee, Chris	AC0100	63D
Lee, William R.	TN1700	32,63D,11
Leisenring, John R.	MO1810	41,63C,63D
Leonard, Charlotte	AG0070	63D
Leonard, Charlotte	AG0150	12A,63D,63C,15,63B
Lewis, Jeremy	TX3750	63D,49
Lindsey, Logan	WV0050	29A,41,49,63D
Lipton, Jamie	AR0300	63D,49,13A
Little, Donald C.	TX3420	41,49,63D
Loffler, Robert	MO0775	63D
Long, Gilbert	TN1850	63D
Lopez, Michael	NC0450	11,63C,63D
Lordo, Jacqueline L.	MO0100	11,63D
Loucky, David L.	TN1100	63C,63D,49
Louder, Earle	KY1350	63D
Lovely, Aaron	MD0300	63C,63D,37
Lueschen, David	OH0700	63B,63D,49,11
Lukowicz, Thomas	OH2500	11,63D,13,13D,13E
Lukowicz, Thomas	OH1100	63D
Lum, David	AG0650	63D
Lund, Steve	MN0050	63C,63D
Lusk, Mark Lancaster	PA2750	63C,63D
Lustrea, Robert	IL0850	63D
Lustrea, Robert	IL3150	63C,63D
Lynn, Robert	IN0700	13,37,38,62C,63D
Lyon, Matthew	IN0150	49,63D
MacGillivray, Rod	AF0120	60,63C,63D
MacMorran, Sande	TN1710	11,38,49,63D
Macomber, Jeffrey R.	MO0800	10,11,12A,32E,63D
Maddox, Harry	GA1700	63D,42
Madej, Andrew	NY2105	63D,63
Magliocco, Hugo	IL1100	63D,63C
Malecki, Jeffrey	IL2650	37,60B,63C,63D,38
Maness, Jane	AG0350	63D
Maness, Jane	AG0600	63D
Manning, John	IA1550	63D
Mannix, Natalie K.	MD0850	63C,63D,41
Manson, David	FL1650	47,63C,63D,53,34
Manson, David	FL0450	63D
Manzo, Angelo	MO1800	63D
Marble, Troy	IL1740	63D
Marchison, Matthew	OH2600	63D
Mark, Douglas L.	MS0250	49,63C,63D,41
Marsteller, Loren	CA0825	63C,63D
Martell, Rodney	VA0150	63C,63D
Martin, James	MO1950	11,37,47,63D
Martin, Joseph	CO0900	37,63C,63D,41,60
Martin, Rex	IL2250	63D,49
Martin-Williams, Jean F.	GA2100	49,63D
Martinez, Pedro	TX3525	63D,63C
Mason, Richard	GA0950	63D,49
Mathews, Rod	CA4400	63D
Mathie, David	ID0050	63C,32E,63D,49
Maxwell, Sarita J.	SC1200	63D,41
Maxwell, Steven	KS0650	63D,11,41
Maybery, Paul	MN0950	63D
Mazzaferro, Tony	CA2390	63D
Mazziot, Nicholas	MD0175	63C,63D
Mazzocchi, Anthony	NJ0700	63C,63D
McAllister, Bob	AZ0400	63D
McCalla, Aaron	FL0680	63D
McCanless, Clinton T.	KY1500	63D
McCaskill, Janet L.	MI2200	63D,32E,60B,32C
McCaslin, Tom R.	NC0650	63D,42
McCollum, David	WV0750	63D
McCollum, Jonathan	MD1100	63C,63D,11,12,20
McEuen, Stephen	PA2150	11,63C,63D
McGrannahan, A. Graydon	NV0100	37,32C,41,63C,63D
McGrannahan, Grady	IA0550	63C,37,63D
McKinney, David	KS0265	13,37,63D,64,29
McKinney, Russell	UT0190	63C,63D
McManus, Kevin	MD0350	63B,63C,63D,49
McNally, Blair	AG0070	32F,34D,63D
McNamara, Gretchen	OH2500	63D,13B
McWilliams, Heather	WI0830	32,11,63D
Means, Allen	IL2450	36,61,63D,63C
Meidenbauer, Michael	NY3600	63C,63D
Mendoken, Scott	CT0650	63D
Mensh, Heather	TX3370	37,41,46,48,63D
Miles, Benjamin E.	TN1100	63D,34
Miller, Andrew	AL0300	63D
Miller, Andrew	GA0550	63D
Miller, Dennis	AI0150	49,63D
Miller, Rodney L.	OH2140	63D,63C
Miller, Steve	WY0115	63D
Miller, Tom	OH0250	63D
Miller, Ward	AL1300	37,63D,41,32E,60B
Milnarik, Michael S.	ME0500	63D
Mindeman, John	IL3500	63D,63C,49,29
Mintz, Randy	NC0900	63D
Mitchell, Alan	MI1180	63D
Moore, Grant W.	PA1250	49,63D,47
Moore, Mark E.	IL3300	63D,49,41
Moore, Matthew	ID0060	34,41,63D
Moore, Michael	GA1450	63D
Moore, Michael	GA1150	63D
Moore, Michael	GA0750	63D
Morales-Matos, Jaime	OH1450	63C,63D,13C,42
Morrell, Kristy M.	CA5300	63D
Morris, Winston	TN1450	49,63D,41
Morrison, Audrey	IL2100	63C,63D
Morrow, Michael	TX2955	63B,63D,11
Morton, Ron	IL0300	63D
Mose, John	IL0650	37,63C,63D
Moyer, Jon	PA3710	49,63C,63D
Mueller, John T.	TN1680	63C,63D,49
Muller, Carl	TX2300	63B,63C,63D
Murchison, Matthew	PA3580	63C,63D
Murray, Renardo	MS0350	37,11,32C,49,63D
Murrow, Richard	TX3000	63D
Musa, Ben	WA1250	63D
Nagels, Lance	AI0190	63D
Neill, Doug A.	ND0350	63D
Nelson, Kent	UT0350	63C,63D,63
Nelson, Mark	AZ0480	37,13,63D,34
Newman, Sean	OK0500	63D
Niemisto, Paul	MN1450	49,63C,63D,37,42
Nigrelli, Christopher	NC1100	12A,47,44,63C,63D
Noraker, Dan	MN0040	63D
Norman, Mark	KS1400	37,41,60B,63D
Northcut, Timothy	OH2200	49,63D
Nulty, Dennis	MI2200	63D
Nunez, Robert	LA0800	63D
Nyberg, Gary B.	WA0480	13,10,37,63D,54
Oberhein, Stephen	AC0100	63D
Odello, Mike	MN1620	63D,72,49
Ofenloch, Gary	UT0250	63D
Oft, Mike	OR0150	63D,63C
Olah, John J.	FL1900	13,49,63D
Olka, Christopher	WA1050	63D
Olt, Timothy	OH2450	63D
Olt, Timothy	KY1000	63D
Olt, Timothy J.	OH1450	63D,49,72,67E
Ormsbee, Timothy	AZ0350	63C,63D
Orovich, Nicholas	NH0350	13C,37,63C,63D
Overly, Paul	SC0200	11,12,32,63C,63D
Owen, John Edward	AR0110	60,11,63D
Palatucci, John	NJ0800	63D
Palton, George A.	WV0400	63D
Parmer, Richard	WY0130	63C,63D,60,49
Peacock, Curtis	WA0050	11,49,63D
Pearson, Norm	CA5300	63D
Pearson, Norman	CA1075	63D,42
Peck, Daniel	NJ0825	63D
Pedde, Dennis	IA0930	63A,63B,63C,63D
Penpraze, Laurie	FL1745	63C,63D,66D,67E
Perantoni, Daniel T.	IN0900	63D
Perkins, Boyd	SD0400	63C,63D,37,60B,72
Perry, Richard H.	MS0750	49,63D
Petersen, William	AL1300	32E,37,63D,60B,49
Peterson, David	MN1500	63C,63D
Peterson, Eric	SD0550	63D,37,60B
Petrie, Dean	IL1350	63D
Philbrick, Rebekah	IL1610	63D
Phillips, Mark W.	VA1750	32C,37,49,63C,63D
Pierce, Benjamin	AR0700	63D
Pih, Kevin	WA1100	63D
Pilafian, Sam	FL1900	63D,42
Pino, Brad	NC1350	63D
Pinson, Donald L.	TX0550	11,13A,63C,63D,49
Plewniak, Kim	WA0250	63D
Plsek, Thomas	MA0260	63C,63D
Pokorny, Gene	IL0550	63D
Pollard, Denson P.	NY1900	63D,42
Pollard, Shawn	AZ0150	13A,37,11,63D
Posch, Carl	AZ0150	13,11,37,47,63D
Presson, Lucy	TN0150	63D,63C
Priester, Julian	WA0200	10,47,63C,63D,29
Puckett, Michael	GA0500	63D
Pugh, Joel	ND0500	63C,63D,11
Pylinski, Thomas	OH1350	63C,63D
Quade, Christopher	WV0550	63D
Quinby, Jack	OR0250	63C,63D
Radley, Dan	WI0801	63D
Ramirez Rios, Ruben J.	PR0115	63D,41
Ransom, Matt W.	NC1650	63D
Ransom, Matt	NC2500	63D
Reimund, John	TX1425	63D,63
Reynolds, Don	FL1000	63D
Rhodes, Steve	TN0930	60B,32E,37,47,63D

Index by Area of Teaching Interest

Name	Code	Areas
Rice, Suzanne	IN1560	63D
Ricer, Thomas	HI0210	63D
Richardson, Marc	KY0250	63D
Risinger, Ed	IL1200	63D,32E,37
Ritchie, Michael	IN1350	63D
Rivera, Miguel	PR0100	41,63D
Robertson, Donald C.	NY3705	49,63C,63D
Robertson, James D.	MT0175	13,60B,63C,63D,47
Robertson, R. Scott	AL0800	63D
Robertson, R. Scott	AL1150	63D
Robinson, Greg	CA0805	32,63D
Robinson, Keith	TX3100	32B,63D
Robinson, Ryan	OK0750	63D,49,32E
Roby, Lloyd	CA0800	32C,49,63D
Rodgers, Andy	CT0800	49,63D
Rodman, Ronald	MN0300	13,37,63C,63D,12D
Rodriguez, Joseph	IL0730	63D,63C
Rodriguez, Raul I.	TX3175	49,63D
Rojak, John	NY0500	63C,63D
Rojas, Marcus	NY0500	63D
Rojas, Marcus	NY2750	63D
Rojas, Marcus	NY3785	63D
Rose, William G.	LA0350	13,49,34,63D,63C
Rothrock, Donna K.	NC2205	16,32E,63D
Rousch, John	GA1070	63D
Rowland, Daniel	GA2150	63D
Roylance, Mike	MA1400	63D
Roylance, Mike R.	MA0400	63D
Ruetz, Andrew	OH1650	63C,63D
Rummel, Andrew	IL1150	63D
Russell, Eileen Meyer	TX2650	63D,13,13C,49,63C
Rutschman, Carla J.	WA1250	12A,12,32,63D
Ryberg, J. Stanley	IL1085	13B,13C,12A,63C,63D
Salas, Jorge Davi	TX2700	63D,62D,42
Saliers, James R.	TX3530	63D
Saltzman, David	OH0300	63D
Salzman, Michael J.	NY1600	63D,42
Salzman, Timothy	WA1050	60,37,49,63D
Sanders, Kevin	TN1680	49,63D
Scarr, Susie	GA0050	63D,63C
Schaffer, John D.	WI0815	63D,49
Schallock, Michael G.	NC2600	32E,63D,60B
Scheffel, Rich	IA1800	63D,32E
Schmidt, David A.	FL0400	47,63C,63D
Schmidt, David	FL1750	49,63C,63D
Schmidt, Donald	AJ0150	63C,63D
Schneider, Bernard	FL0500	63C,63D
Schooley, John	WV0300	13,49,63D,62D
Schuchat, Charles	IL2200	63D,49
Schuchat, Charles	IL0550	63D,49
Schultz, Ryan	WA1000	63D
Schultz, Wendy E.	NE0150	49,63D
Scott, Debra L.	TX2700	47,63C,63D
Scott, Paul	NJ1400	63D
Seifert, Dustin	NM0100	37,63C,63D,60B,32E
Self, Cale	GA2130	37,63C,63D,32E,49
Self, James	CA5300	63D
Seward, Steve K.	MO1780	63D
Shade, Timothy	KS0200	63D,38,37,13C,32E
Shearer, James E.	NM0310	63D,12A,11
Sheridan, Patrick	CA5030	63D
Shoemaker, Vance	SD0050	63C,63D,49
Shoemaker, Vance	IA0500	63C,63D
Shonkwiler, Joel	OH1200	63C,63D
Shonkwiler, Joel	OH2050	63D
Shook, Brian A.	TX1400	63A,63D,32E
Shoop, Stephen S.	TX3515	32,41,60B,63D
Short, Michael	IA1350	63D
Short, Michael	IA0550	63D
Shudy, Deryk	MO0400	63D
Sienkewicz, Gary	CT0600	63D
Silvagnoli, Michael F.	NY3650	63D
Simmons, Matthew	FL0100	49,60B,63C,63D
Simmons, Matthew	SC1050	37,49,63C,63D
Simon, Philip G.	PA3700	11,37,41,51,63D
Sinder, Philip	MI1400	63D
Sipes, Danny T.	TX2930	63D,35A,35C,35D,35G
Sipher, John	NY1350	63C,63D
Sisk, Robin	FL1800	63D
Sizer, Todd	CO0275	63D,10F,34,42
Skaar, Trygve	MN1625	63D
Skillen, Joseph	LA0200	63D
Sloan, Gerald H.	AR0700	63C,63D
Smith, James W.	AL1050	63D,32E,11
Smith, Jason R.	OH1900	63D,13A,41
Smith, Michael K.	IA0950	42,63C,63D,49
Smith, Orcenith George	IN0350	60,38,63D
Smith, Ryan	TX1400	63D,37
Smith, Stewart	AC0100	63D,34C
Snowden, Donald	FL1500	37,47,63D,29A
Sochinski, James	VA1700	13,37,63C,63D,34
Solomon, Jeffrey	AL0500	63D
Solomon, Wayne	CA1860	63C,63D
Solomon, Wayne	CA5070	63C,63D
Solomonson, Terry	IL0400	63D
Solomonson, Terry	IL3500	11,63D,35C,35D,35G
Spang, Ron	PA0500	63D,63C
Spaniola, Joseph T.	FL2100	47,46,63D,11,10
Sparrow, James	NC1250	63D,32E,41,63C,63
Sparti, Patricia C.	NC0850	13,60,38,63D
Specht, Jeffrey	OR0400	13,38,60,63D
Spellman, Zachariah	CA4200	63D
Spencer, Daniel	MI1050	63C,63D
Spevacek, Robert	ID0250	60,37,63D
Springer, Mark	MN1300	63D,63C
Stark, Cynthia	IL0850	63D,49
Stees, Kevin J.	VA0600	49,63D
Stein, Thomas G.	MO1810	63D
Steinsultz, Kenneth	IN1600	63D,37
Stephan, Michael	MA2250	63D,41
Stern, David W.	SC0800	63D
Stern, David	SC0050	37,63D,47,29A,60B
Stevens, John	WI0815	63D,60B,35,10,13
Stewart, Raymond G.	NY3725	63D
Stickney, Mark A.	UT0200	37,63D,41,49,63
Stimeling, Travis D.	IL1750	12,63D,12D,14
Stokes, Tayler L.	OR1100	63D
Stoner, Jeremy	NY2650	63D
Stover, Jerome	MA2030	63D
Stratton, Matthew	TN1720	63D,11,34,37
Strauch, Richard	WA1350	37,63D,60B,41,12A
Stroeher, Michael	WV0400	63D,49,63C,32,29
Stuart, Daniel H.	IA0850	63D,42,34A,34C,11
Sugiyama, Yasuhito	OH0650	63D
Sugiyama, Yasuhito	OH0200	63D
Sullivan, Nick A.	AA0200	63D,63C,13C
Surface, Edward	TX0150	11,63D
Sutherland, Craig	NY3350	63D
Sutherland, Scott	CA5150	63D
Sweeney, Christopher R.	AK0100	32,63D,63C,32E,32B
Swoboda, Deanna	AZ0100	63D
Taylor, Michael S.	SC0750	63D
Tegge, Scott	WI0250	63D
Tempas, Fred	CA2250	63D,32B
Tetreault, Mark	AG0450	63D
Thomas, Kelly Gene	AZ0500	63D
Thurman, Demondrae	AL1170	63D
Thurman, Demondrae	AL0650	63C,63D,41
Tignor, Scott	WV0600	63D
Tornquist, Doug	CA0815	63D
Tornquist, Doug	CA0510	63D
Tornquist, Douglas V.	CA5300	63D
Tornquist, Douglas	CA3300	63D
Tramiel, Leonard	MS0560	60,11,37,63C,63D
Tranter, John	MN1623	63D
Traster, Jeff	FL2050	37,49,63D,32
Traster, Jeffry	FL0930	63D
Tropman, Matt	CA5350	63D
Trowbridge, James	NY1550	49,63D
Trowers, Robert	NC1600	63C,63D,46,29A
Truckenbrod, Steve	NC1600	63D
Tuinstra, John	WI0865	11,37,63D
Tumino, Joe	IL1890	63D,11
Turner, George	SC0200	32B,32C,37,63D,34
Turner, George	ID0150	10,13,60B,63C,63D
Turner, Kyle	ID0070	63D
Turner, Kyle	NY2250	63D
Tychinski, Bruce D.	NJ0800	63D,42
Undem, Stewart	DE0150	63C,63D
Unland, David	CA0845	63D
Utterstrum, Oscar	NY1800	63D
Vail, Mark	TN1400	63C,63D
van Deursen, John	TN1200	63C,63D
Van Houten, John	AB0060	47,38,63C,63D
Van Ouse, Philip	CA0825	49,63D,35A
VanValkenburg, Jamie G.	PA1050	63D
Varpness, Lee	CO0050	63A,63C,63D,37,41
Viebranz, Gary A.	MN1620	63C,63D
Villarrubia, Charles	PA2250	63D
Vinson, Danny	TX3510	63D,41
Vinson, Danny	TX3535	63C,63D
Vivio, Chris	TX0600	63D
Vivio, Christopher J.	TN0100	63D
Vogt, Nancy	TN0050	63D,11
Von Hoff, Paul	NE0450	63C,63D,11
Wahrhaftig, Peter	WI0250	63C,63D
Wahrhaftig, Peter	CA4150	63D
Wahrhaftig, Peter	CA2950	63D
Wahrhaftig, Peter	CA3520	63D
Wahrhaftig, Peter	CA5000	63D
Waid, Tom	FL1750	63D
Waid, Tom	FL0150	63C,63D
Walden, Daniel	AL1050	63D
Walker, Jesse	GA0150	13A,63C,63D,13B,13C
Walker, Mark	AL1050	63D,37,60B
Wallace, Noel	TX3300	63D,47
Walter, Cameron	AG0450	32,63C,63D,37,44
Walter, Ross A.	VA1600	63C,63D,34,49
Wardlaw, Jeffrey A.	PA0700	63D,49,13,63C
Wardle, Alvin	UT0300	32C,63B,63C,63D
Ware, Douglas G.	NC0900	63D
Warner, Douglas G.	TN0850	11,63D,13B,13C,63C
Warren, Charles	CA1425	63D
Wass, Kevin	TX3200	63D
Watson, Richard	IN1750	63D,49
Watson, Scott C.	KS1350	11,49,63D
Wazanowski, Charles	MN1300	63D
Wazanowski, Charles	WI0845	63D
Wean, Ellis	AB0100	63D
Weaver, Lane	KS0350	11,63D,37,49
Weber, John	IL2775	63D
Weyersberg, Roger	MI1850	63C,63D
Wheat, James R.	MN1700	63C,63D
Whetham, S.	AA0100	63D
Whetham, Scott	AA0035	63D
White, Richard	NM0450	63D
Whitehead, Geoffrey	NC0550	63D
Whitis, James	TX3415	37,63D
Whitlock, Mark	MN1600	32,37,49,63C,63D
Whitten, Douglas	KS1050	37,63D,32E,11,49
Wickham, Nathaniel	CO0950	63C,49,63D
Wiggins, Marcus	AR0200	63D
Wika, Norman	OK0550	60,37,63C,63D
Wilborn, David F.	TX2900	13,63C,63D,41,37
Wildman, Simon	GA2300	63D
Willett, Jim R.	KY0550	13,63D
Williams, Anthony N.	ND0400	29,47,63C,63D
Williams, Melissa	IN1100	63D
Williams, Melissa	IN0250	63D
Wilson, Bruce	MD0150	63C,63D,49,37,32C
Wilson, J. P.	AR0600	37,63D,63C,32E,60B
Wilson, Kenyon	TN1700	63D,13,41
Wilson, Steve	TX3520	63D,29A,37
Winkle, William	ID0050	63D,49
Wirth, Elijah G.	MD0520	63D
Wolfe, Anne Marie	IN0150	63D,64,32E,10F,60B
Wood, Matthew P.	AL0200	63D,13A
Woodruff, Ernest	MO0950	11,32E,63D
Workman, K. Darren	TX3100	63C,63D
Wright, Bron	CO0830	63C,63D
Wulfeck, David	NC2300	63D
Wulfeck, David	NC2150	63D
Ycaza, Stephanie	VA1500	63D
Yeats, Robert E.	IA0300	63D
Young, Frederick	PA3400	62D,63D
Young, Jerry A.	WI0803	11,32C,63D
Young, Kevin	TX1550	63D
Young, Kevin	TX3527	63D,49,11
Young, Michael	IL3450	63C,63D
Zacharella, Alexandra	AR0730	63C,63D,11,49,37
Zamzow, Laura	WV0200	11,63D,60B,32,37
Zaporta, Ouida I.	TX2960	63D
Zembower, Christian M.	TN0500	63D,37,60B
Zerkel, David	GA2100	63D,49
Zetts, Mary Jo F.	PA3000	63D
Zilincik, Anthony	OH0350	63D,41,43,10F
Zimmerman, Larry	MN0750	63C,63D,49
Zimmerman, Larry	MN1450	63C,63D
Zimmerman, Larry	MN0250	63D,63C
Zimmerman, Larry	MN1625	63C,63D
Zugelder, Steven	NY2650	63D
Zugger, Thomas W.	OH0350	63C,63D,49

Woodwinds (All Areas)

Name	Code	Areas
Ainanda, Lucy	AR0425	63,64,65
Alderson, Erin	IL1800	11,13A,32E,37,64
Almario, Justo	CA5031	29,64
Amos, Alvin E.	PA2000	29,13A,13C,48,64
Aron, William	CA4650	64
Arrowsmith, Brenda	AG0070	48,64,10F,13A,13B
Averett, Janet M.	CA4400	38,64,48
Axelson, Shelley	NJ0800	32,64
Ayres, Carol	IA0800	11,37,47,64,29A
Baca, Danny	TX2300	64,11
Bade, Christopher	IN1560	11,38,48,64,12A
Ball, Greg L.	TX2750	37,48,64,20G,29
Ball, Julia	NM0200	64
Ballard, Marcus	LA0900	64,12A
Ballereau, Laurence	NY1600	32,37,64
Barrett, Robert H.	CO1050	11,47,64,34,29
Barrick, Christopher	WV0600	64,11,41,34,47
Barton, Karl S.	GA1990	64,47,12A,34
Beach, Sue Odem	IA0420	64,13,11
Beard, Charles	OK0500	64
Beard, Jackie	MA0260	64
Becker, David M.	OR0400	60,32C,37,29,64
Bennett, Laura	TX2850	64
Bennett, Steve	TX2850	63,64
Benson, Will	TN0300	11,13,34B,36,64
Bergeron, Tom	OR1250	13,64,47,35A
Berta, Joseph M.	NY1550	11,12A,64
Bilden, Jeff	CA1290	37,47,29,63,64
Bingham, Steve	FL1675	11,13A,20,29,64
Bloom, Jane Ira	NY2660	10,53,64,47
Bogert, Nathan	IA0700	64,63
Bowen, Ron	AZ0200	64,70
Brady, Brandon D.	OK0300	64
Branning, Ron	FL0040	63,64
Bray, Erin	TN0900	64,42,11
Budzinski, Thomas	IN1450	64
Burks, Ricky	AL1450	48,64,46,29B,37
Butler, Benjamin	TX3150	32,64
Butler, Hunt	KY0750	47,48,64,53,29A
Butts, Beverly Ann K.	PA1900	64C,48,64
Callahan, Gary L.	NC1150	48,64,32,46
Cameron, Jennifer	OR1150	13,10F,64,60,51
Cameron, Wes	MS0850	11,63,64,65,34
Caputo, Michael	NJ0200	12A,14,37,64,20G
Caputo, Michael	NJ0250	12A,14,37,48,64
Carroll, Kevin	GA1600	10,64,60B,11,13
Cass, Patrick	MS0320	13,11,47,64,70
Chambers, Timothy	NC0800	37,48,64,60B
Chesebro, Robert C.	SC0750	12A,64,41
Christensen, Donald	NY0500	32E,64C,64
Churchill, Rachel	AG0070	64
Clark, Antoine T.	OH0850	12A,72,48,64,64C
Clark, Norman Alan	GA1400	11,37,49,64
Clegg, Neill M.	NC0900	10F,12A,64,53,29A
Cocking, Roger	PA2800	64
Cohen, Stanley	NY1275	14C,32,46,47,64
Cokkinias, Peter L.	MA0260	64
Coletta, Michelle	CA1900	13,64
Coltman, Charles	TX0900	10F,41,64,35A
Compean, Jose D.	TX1425	13,32,47,63,64
Compton, Michael	ND0100	64,37,41,47,60B
Compton, Michael	OK0150	64,48,47,60B
Connelly, Marianne	MN0450	37,32,47,64,60B
Converse, Ralph D.	NM0500	64,41,38,48,29
Cook, Andrew	AL0345	60B,63,11,47,64
Coppenbarger, Brent	SC0950	13,11,64
Crawley, James	AL0330	63,64
Cross, Sandy	OK0770	63,64
Crossen-Richardson, Phyllis	MD1100	64
Dagradi, Anthony	LA0300	64,64E,29
David, Norman	PA3330	64,47,10,29,13
Davis, Charles	TX1510	11,63,64,37
Davis, Lapointe M.	DE0050	32,48,64
Davis, Peter A.	RI0250	13A,37,47,64
Dean, Martin	GA1650	64,48
Decorso, Theodore	FL2050	11,64
Delaney, Douglas	CA1150	13,11,37,47,64
Dickey, Marc R.	CA0815	32,37,64
Dixon, Howard	TN0800	13A,11,32B,63,64
Dodson, Brent	IA1750	63,64,37,60B,48
Dragovich, Mindy	NY1600	64
Dubyk, Jerrold	AA0100	64
Dueitt, David P.	MS0420	37,48,64,65
Duhaime, Ricky	TX0250	13,47,41,64,60B
Dupertuis, Jeff	CA3850	62,63,64,65,66
Duquaine, Kenneth	MI2120	64,13E
Edwards, Jason R.	IA0900	64,13,10,32E
Eisenreich, Samuel	FL0050	64,48,64E
Enloe, Loraine D.	ID0250	32E,64,37,64C,32C
Ernardt, Eric	CO0300	64
Escalera, Mario	NY2660	64,53
Ewing, Lee	GA1650	37,63,64
Falcone, Sheri A.	MS0500	64
Farnsley, Stephen	NV0150	64,63
Farrington, Robert	CA1550	41,47,63,64,29A
Feldkamp, Timothy L.	IA0930	13,41,47,64
Feller, David E.	UT0350	11,12A,48,64,31
Fetz, Katie	OR0200	64,32E
Fields, Alex	SC0200	48,64,72
Finnsson, Karen	AJ0100	12A,64E,64
Fon-Revutzky, Gerik	IL3370	64
Ford, Ronnal	NC2700	64,64B,11,64D,62A
Forsythe, Dawn	IN1450	64
French, Otis F.	PA1100	11,37,63,64,65
Frutkoff, Peter	NY0050	32E,63,64
Gale, Robert	CO0100	64,66A,66F,72
Gamso, Nancy M.	OH2000	11,29A,48,64,32E
Garzone, George	MA0260	64
Gately, Doug T.	VA1475	47,48,29,64
Gawthorp, Kevin	IL2775	64
George, Arnold E.	NC1600	47,45,64,34,13
Gilley, John	TX2550	37,64
Gilman, Matt	OR1010	64,60B
Glaze, Richard T.	FL2100	60,32,37,48,64
Glazer, Stuart	FL0650	13,10,64
Goacher, Stephen	TX1100	60,48,64,47,29
Goldapp, James	MO0200	64
Golia, Vinny	CA0510	64,35A,53,47
Goodwin, Mark A.	GA0700	13,32,37,64
Gowan, Andrew D.	SC1110	60,32,37,64
Grandy, Larry	CA4550	37,47,64,29,14C
Greco, Christopher J.	KS0100	13,10,64,64E,13F
Green, Feleighta	SC0710	64
Griffin, Stephen W.	AL0332	11,36,37,47,64
Gudmundson, Paula	MN0040	64A,64,12A,14
Harrington, Jeff	MA0260	64
Harris, Paul R.	TX2295	64,11
Heckman, Rick	NJ0825	64
Hedrick, Teresa	VA0050	64
Hegg, Dennis	SD0150	37,47,63,64,65
Heinen, Julia	CA2750	63,64
Hemke, Frederic J. B.	SD0400	47,48,64,29A
Herman, Cheryl	IL2800	36,54,66A,64
Higgins, William R.	PA2300	32,64,72,34
Hill, Kelly	MI1950	64,38
Hindson, Harry	WI0810	64
Holland, Katherine N.	GA1300	64D,32,64
Hollinger, Curtis	AL0450	64
Hollinger, Trent A.	MO0300	64,37,13C,13A,60B
Honda, Lorence	CA1850	13,48,64,29
Hopkins, Ted	TX0600	64
Horn, Laurence C.	MS0560	11,32A,48,64
Hosten, Kevin	NY2100	11,47,63,64,66D
Hostetler, Scott	IL2250	64
Houghtalen, Brandon	NM0450	60B,64
Houser, Steven	MO0600	13,12A,12,64
Howey, Robert J.	AA0025	12A,13B,37,46,64
Humbert, William	AZ0350	37,64,63,13A,60
Husband, Julie	AC0100	64
Hutchens, John	IL2350	47,64
Iannone, Vincent	PA1550	64,10A
Imara, Mtafiti	CA0847	13,14,64,47,29
Isaac, James	KS0570	48,64
Jackson, Brett	KS0590	64
Janelli, Ron	NJ0825	64
Jeffreys, Harold	NC2300	64
Jernigan, Richard	FL1500	11,64
Joffe, Edward	NJ0825	41,47,48,64
Johnson, Pamela	WI0801	66D,66A,64
Jones, Bernard	OK1050	13,12A,61,11,64
Jones, Herman	SC0150	11,37,47,48,64
Jones, Lloyd	AL1250	64,37,47,32E,34A
Jones, Patrick R.	PA1200	11,29,64,41
Jordan, Edward	LA0720	11,20G,37,47,64
Jorgensen, Trevor	NY3770	37,64,48,11
Jussila, Clyde	WA1050	32,62,64
Kasica, Paula	MO1950	64
Katz, Judith	NY0625	64
Kerr, William	CA1265	64
Kiec, Michelle	PA1750	64,13,64C,64E,48
Kiec, Michelle	PA1750	64,13,64C,64E,11
Kiel, Dyke	MO0250	13B,13C,64
Kirchner, Bill	NY2660	10,12,64,29
Kleiman, Carey D.	FL0200	34,35A,64,35,32E
Klemas, John	IA1170	37,47,63,64,65
Knopp, Shawn	KS0900	64
Knox, Daniel	AL0750	11,70,63,64,13A
Koffman, Carrie	CT0650	64,64C
Kolbeck, Karl F.	NE0700	12A,72,48,64,11
Kostaras, Jimmy	DC0170	64E,64
Kravchak, Richard	CA0805	11,64,38,37,32
Kuehner, Eric L.	IN0910	64
Kuhl, Mary	TX1750	48,64
Kuist, Bruce	TN1350	64
Kurokawa, Paul	CA2100	13,47,63,64
LaFitte, Barbara	MA0260	64
Laflen, Betty Jo	KS0400	11,13C,32B,37,64
Lange, Daniel	OR0010	12A,47,64,35
Laughrey, Gary	KY0800	64,32F,12A,13
Lawson, David	WV0700	64
LeClaire, Shannon L.	MA0260	64
Lee, Ardyce	TN1710	64
Leech, Alan B.	MT0200	64D,64E,20,64,42
Lehmann, Jay	CA2450	60,13,64,63
Lewis, David P.	WV0350	64,37,41,12A,32E
Li, Chi	CA5031	20C,62,64,65
Liley, Thomas	IL1250	13,12A,64
Lippard, Michael S.	TX2710	13A,37,46,64,13B
Lipsius, Fred	MA0260	64
Lovelady, Hugh	AZ0440	64
Lydeen, Brian	WI0804	37,64
Lydeen, Brian	WI0400	64,47,37,42,64E
Maher, Donna	SC0700	64
Maher, Donna	SC0050	64
Maki, Erik	CA3000	37,11,63,64,65
Maltester, Diane	CA2775	12A,64,41,13C
Mann, Rochelle	CO0350	10,11,32,64
Manning, Dwight C.	NY4200	64,42,32E,11,64B
Mapes, Randy K.	MS0300	64,37
Margaglione, Louis A.	IL2450	64,13A,13C,11
Martensen, Dave	SD0100	64
Martin, Roger	TN1450	64A,41,64
Matchael, Michael	TX3360	37,48,64
Mathews, Robert P.	CA6050	13,64,48,70
Mattox, Amanda M.	MS0570	64,13,11
McCandless, Amanda	IA1600	64C,64
McCarthy, Charles J.	CA1020	64,48
McGee, Michael	AL0850	37,47,63,64,65
McGhee, Andy	MA0260	64
McGinnis, Barry E.	SC0900	64,12A,29,48,29A
McKeown, Kevin	CA4450	37,63,64
McKinney, David	KS0265	13,37,63D,64,29
McLemore, Jeff	TN0150	64
Meggs, Gary L.	AR0800	60B,64,47,46,29
Mertens, Michael	CA2750	13B,11,63,64,37
Middleton, Robert M.	NJ0050	47,29,64,13,11
Mikkola, Gary	NC1950	70,64
Miller, Russell	MI2200	29,64
Moe, Karla	NY2105	64A,64
Monte, Michael	MA2020	64
Mooy, James D.	CA4410	45,35C,34,46,64
Moran, Nick	IL3310	64
Moreland, Wilbur	AL1195	64
Morris, Gretchen	OK1400	64
Mosteller, Sandra M.	TX3650	64,32E,48,20,31B
Myers, Michael	NC1450	64,13G
Myrick, Kenny	MS0420	44,64
Nabb, David	NE0590	64,11,12A,48
Nash, Gary Powell	TN0550	10,13,47,64,10F
Nelson, Mattew	UT0325	13,64
Nesbit, James	NC0400	64
Newell, Meri	MS0360	11,32,64,37,48
Newton, Jeanne	TN0930	32,64
Norden, Gene	KY0650	64
Nowak, Gerald C.	PA0400	13,37,47,64
Nunemaker-Bressler, Emily B.	IL2730	64
Odgren, Jim	MA0260	64
O'Leary, Jed	NE0400	62,64
Olszewski, Thomas	IL0420	63,64,62D
O'Neil, Lorne W.	TX3525	11,41,48,64
Owens, Charles	CA5031	29,47,64
Owens, Margaret B.	VA0450	11,12A,64
Padilla, Margaret	WI0825	64,48
Pannell, Larry J.	LA0100	64,34,35C,37,32

Name	Code	Areas
Park, Angela	IN0900	66C,64
Parker, Linda	NC0200	11,32,44,13,64
Parker, Nathaniel F.	PA2200	38,60B,64,41
Parr, J. D.	KS0050	37,47,48,64,29
Parran, John D.	NY0270	11,13,20,29,64
Paulson, Brent	CO0625	63A,63,64,37
Paulson, John C.	MN1400	47,64,29,34,35
Pecorilla, John	OR1020	37,64,65
Pederson, Steven A.	KY0800	37,41,47,64
Pekas, Joe F.	SD0200	63,64
Perconti, William J.	ID0130	13,11,47,64
Perry, Robert	NC1300	63,64
Phillips, Margaret A.	MA0260	64D,64
Piazza, Stephen	CA2700	37,64
Piccirillo, Lauren	IN0500	64
Pierce, Bill	MA0260	64
Pimentel, Bret R.	MS0250	64,29,64B,11,64C
Powell, Daniel	FL0350	11,13,47,63,64
Pozzi, David	CA2600	63,64
Prescott, Steve C.	IN1400	32E,11,60B,64,37
Price, Berkeley	CA0200	13,37,48,64
Procopio, Mary J.	MI0450	11,20,37,64
Prouten, William	AA0032	13,47,64,53,29A
Raby, Lee Worley	CA2801	47,64E,13A,13B,64
Rasmusson, Ralph	NY1850	37,47,63,64,65
Rath, Richard	OK0850	64,64B,64E
Rawls, J. Archie	MS0580	13,11,64,46,48
Reams, John	GA1800	13,38,41,64
Rebbeck, Lyle	AA0040	47,48,64,53
Rehberg, Jeanette	ND0050	11,64,42
Reilley, Duane	AZ0250	64
Rettedal, Dean	SD0300	37,60B,47,63,64
Rhodes, Debra	NE0300	12A,64,48
Roach, Rebecca	KS0750	64
Robinson, Gary A.	SC0765	63,64,65,38
Rolfe, Wendy	MA0260	64
Roof, Kimberly	NY2450	64
Rose, Brent	LA0080	29B,64
Royer, Randall D.	SD0100	64,47,38,32E,70
Russo, John	PA0125	64
Rybolt, Scott	MO1710	64
Ryder, Virginia	CA2250	64,16
Ryder, William H.	LA0700	11,32,64,13
Sakins, Renate	PA3100	13,64,64B
Salicondro, Anthony	PA3330	64
Salicondro, Anthony	NJ1050	64
Sampson, Larry	CA0300	62,63,64,70
Samuelson, Linda	MN1270	13,20,37,46,64
Sandberg, Scott	ND0400	64,13B,13C,11,48
Sanders, Stephanie	VA0950	37,64
Sarjeant, Ronald	SC1050	10F,60,37,64
Scanling, Paul F.	GA1550	64,37,42,48
Schafer, Carl	CA0450	32,48,64
Schiavone, David	NY4460	64
Schloss, David Lee	TX1725	64,48
Schneider, Benjamin D.	ND0150	37,38,60B,64,32
Sfraga, Debbie	NJ1160	32,37,47,64
Sharp, David	IA0750	13,11,47,64
Shea, Maurice	FL0950	64
Sheedy-Gardner, Anne	NE0500	64
Shoemaker, Elizabeth	IL1750	64
Shoemaker, Michelle N.	MA1175	12A,64,11,64C
Shroyer, Ronald L.	MO0100	64A,64C,64E,64
Shultz, Dane	PA0500	64
Singletary, Pat	TX0075	64,35D
Sizemore, Mark	KY1400	48,64,46
Skoler, Harry	MA0260	64
Skornia, Dale E.	MI0650	11,32B,37,64
Smith, C. Raymond	UT0050	47,64,53,46,29
Smith, Carey	MS0370	63,64,65,11,13
Smith, Tara	IA0790	64
Smukala, Edward	FL0950	64
Spicer, Luke	WI0842	64
Spivey, Gary	FL1430	64
Stensager, Eugene	WA0450	64
Stephens, Michael	NE0050	10,29,46,13,64
Stephenson, Michael	NC1550	64,48,64E
Stevenson, Roxanne	IL0600	13A,20G,32,37,64
Street, Deborah	AL0550	63,64
Suzano, L. Armenio	VA0650	20F,11,13C,41,64
Sweets, Nancy	MO0500	37,65,64,66A
Taylor, Caroline	AR0500	48,64,32E
Teichmer, Shawn	MI2000	32,60,64,12A,11
Tellinghuisen, Harvey	CA3975	64,63
Teter, Francis	CA1750	11,37,38,48,64
Thomas, Jay	WA0200	64
Thompson, Cindy	KS0980	64
Thompson, Phil A.	SC1200	47,64
Thornton, Bruce	MN0350	60B,41,47,64
Threlkeld, David M.	KY1425	11,12A,47,48,64
Tiberi, Frank	MA0260	64
Trautwein, Barbara	NC2500	64
Turner, Dean W.	WV0200	48,64
Turpin, Mike H.	TX1350	11,48,64
Twehues, Mark A.	TX3530	64,32E
Ung, Chinary	CA5050	10,20D,64
Van Regenmorter, Paula	LA0450	64,12A,11,48,20
Varimezov, Ivan S.	CA5031	20F,64
Vickers, Jeffrey E.	AR0600	64,11,64E,64A,12A
Viertel, Kyle	TX0390	37,63,64,65,46
Wagner, Paul	MA0260	64
Waldrop, Joseph	TX3850	13A,32B,37,13B,64
Walker, Christopher G.	GA0150	11,32,64,48
Walters, Mark A.	CO0350	60,11,48,37,64
Waters, Jeffery L.	MO1550	13B,47,64
Welch, Jennifer	MN1400	64
Wen, Andy	AR0750	11,13,64,64E
Western, Daniel	AL0650	64,47,35D,13,29A
Wetzel, Neil D.	PA2450	47,64,29A,64E,46
White, Christopher K.	VA1100	29,64E,32E,64,12B
White, Cindy	MO1710	64,13,36,61,66A
White, Joseph M.	WV0100	65,50,37,63,64
White, Lynn	NC0050	48,64,67
Whitfill, Jim	TX0850	64,63,65
Whitmore, Michael	OK0450	32E,48,64
Williams, Oscar	LA0700	12A,64,11,29A
Wohletz, Jeremy	KS1000	64
Wolfe, Anne Marie	IN0150	63D,64,32E,10F,60B
Workman, Darin D.	KS1110	60,32,37,47,64
Wubbena, Teresa R.	AR0400	13,32,41,16,64
Wucher, Jay	GA0500	64
Wuest, Harry	FL0675	37,47,64,63
Wurster, Miles B.	MN1030	37,13A,64,65
Yeager, Richard F.	MO0850	37,48,64
Young, Craig S.	MS0400	60B,37,63,64
Young, Eileen M.	NC2500	64C,64E,41,64,12A
Zoro, Eugene S.	WA1250	48,64

Flute

Name	Code	Areas
Ackerman, Barbara	AG0650	64A
Adams, Liselyn	AI0070	13,12A,41,64A,43
Adams, Mary Kay	VA0100	64A
Adams, Pam	TX3000	64A
Adams, Patti	LA0300	64A
Adelson, Andrew D.	NJ0800	64A
Ahlers, Ruth	CT0300	64A,64E
Aitken, Dianne	AG0450	64A
Akins, Lori	OH2450	48,64A
Akins, Lori B.	OH0950	48,64A
Akins, Lori	OH0450	64A
Alancraig, Diane	CA0830	64A
Albrecht, Peg	AG0450	64A
Almarza, Alberto	PA0550	64A
Altstaetter, Lucinda J.	OH1800	64A,48
Alvarez, Heidi Pintner	KY1550	64A,13B,41
Amano, Hideko	IL1085	64A
Ambrose, Sarah Kruser	GA1050	64A
Amox, Jennifer	AR0300	64A,20
Amsler, Eva	FL0850	64A
Anderson, Carl H. C.	AL0500	13,48,64A,64C
Anderson, Claudia	IA0700	64A,48
Anderson, John	CA3050	13,11,37,64A
Anderson, Trudi	MN0250	64A
Anderson, Trudi J.	MN0050	64A,48
Andon, Sarah	CA5150	64A,48
Andres, Rebecca	OH1450	64A
Andres, Rebecca	OH2550	64A
Andrew, Nancy	CO0550	64A
Andrews, Kenneth B.	NY3780	41,64A,43
Anno, Mariko	IL1400	20C,64A
Antonetti, Susan	AR0750	64A,48
Arms, Janet	CT0650	64A
Armstrong, Eleanor Duncan	PA2750	64A
Armstrong, Robert	OR1010	12A,63A,64C,64A
Arnone, Francesca M.	TX0300	64A,42,67D
Averitt, Frances Lapp	VA1350	48,64A,41
Ayres, Rebecca Pollack	CA3400	64A
Babad, Bruce	CA1900	47,48,64A,64C,64E
Bailey, John R.	NE0600	64A,42,12A
Baldacchino, Laura Falzon	NY4200	64A,32E,42,43
Ballatori, Cristina	TX3515	64A,11,42,13
Ballif, Kristi	CO0225	64A
Barbanera, Lisa	FL1745	64A
Barcellona, John	CA0825	41,64A
Baron, Deborah	TX2400	64A
Barraclough, Michelle	PA1900	64A
Barrett, Amanda	SC0200	64A
Barron, Elizabeth	PA1450	66D,64A
Barth, Molly	OR1050	64A,42,48,43
Bartholow, Lisa	GA0500	64A
Bartholow, Lisa Hanson	GA2000	64A
Bartholow, Nina	GA0850	64A
Barto, Mary B.	NY4200	64A
Barwell, Nina	MA1900	64A,41
Batiste, Alvin	LA0700	64A,64C,29,47,35A
Baumgarten, Jonathan	DC0010	64A,42,48
Baxter, Dawn	OR1010	64A
Baxtresser, Jeanne	MA1400	64A
Baxtresser, Jeanne	PA0550	64A
Beaman, M. Teresa	CA0810	13A,13,48,64A,34
Beard, Christine E.	NE0610	64A,48,11,13
Behm, Gary	MT0175	37,64C,64E,64A
Behrens, Joel	PA2350	12A,48,64A
Behrmann, Candice	NE0200	64A
Beland, Sarah	MO0300	64A
Beland, Sarah	IA0600	64A
Bell, Lori	CA4100	64A
Bennett, Joyce	DC0170	64A,38
Bennett, Marie Micol	IL2050	64A,48,41,13A,42
Benson, Jeremy L.	AL0500	64A,64B,12
Benson, Katherine	IL2300	64A,41,44
Bentley, Judith C.	OH0300	64A
Berger, Sally	IN1350	64A
Bergin, Wendy I.	TX2100	64A,48,13
Bergman, Catherine	KS0300	64A,13C
Bergman, Elaine	IN0400	64A
Bergstrom, Anne	AF0120	64A
Berkner, Jane	OH2150	48,64A
Berkner, Jane	OH0100	64A,48
Bernier, Jean-Sebastien	AI0190	64A
Berthelet, Marie-Noelle	AJ0100	64A
Bethea, Stephanie	WA0900	13,10,64A
Binder, Shelley	TN1710	64A
Bishop, Jean	IL1300	64A
Bjorkman, Jan	WI0835	64A
Blackburn, Gregory	IL0850	64A
Blanchett, Madalyn	TX2260	11,64A,66A,66D,67
Bleiler-Conrad, Suzanne	PA2450	64A
Bluteau, Denis	AI0150	64A
Bluteau, Denis	AI0200	64A
Bobenhouse, Elizabeth	NE0450	41,64A
Bobo, Ann	MA0350	64A
Bodden, Bruce	WA0250	64A,34C
Bogorad, Julia A.	MN1623	64A
Bohnet, Andra	AL1300	12A,41,64A,62E,35A
Bond, Bronwell	PA0100	64A,48
Bonner, Joe	AR0110	48,64A,20
Boone, Mary E.	NC1700	64A
Bortolussi, Paolo	AB0090	64A
Bortolussi, Paolo	AB0060	64A,48,13
Bortz, Jodi	PA2450	64A
Boschee, Sharon	ND0500	64A
Boulet, Michele	PA2950	64A,48
Bowers, Sally	IL1400	64A
Bowers, Teresa M.	PA1400	64A,64B,12A,36,42
Bowman, Randy	OH1450	64A
Bowman, Randy C.	OH2200	64A
Boyd, Bonita	NY1100	64A
Boyd, Kathleen A.	MA2050	64A
Boyle, Audrey	CA0650	64A,32
Boyle, Benjamin C. S.	NJ1350	10,64A,13
Bradfield, Ann	NM0100	29,46,47,64A,64E
Brady, Sarah	MA0350	64A
Brallier, Kathryn	OR0250	64A
Brandt, Lynne	TX2310	13,64A,41,66A
Breeden, Barbara	CA3270	64A
Brewster, Cornelia L.	NY4150	64A
Brightbill, Elizabeth	VA0700	64A,48
Brightbill, Elizabeth	VA0800	64A,42,11
Britten, Sandra	AF0120	64A
Britten, Sandra	AF0050	48,64A
Broffitt, Virginia	OK0800	64A,42,11,32E
Brooks-Lyle, Alma B.	AL0050	13,64A,12B,12A
Brouwer, Albert	AI0050	64A
Brown, Carolyn K.	AR0850	64A,48

Name	Code	Areas
Brown, Elaine K.	MO2000	41,64A
Brown, Jennie	IL0850	64A,41,42
Brown, Jennie S.	IL3550	64A,12A,13C,42
Brown, Jill Marie	MI0350	48,64A
Bryant, Kelly	GA1700	64A,48
Bryce, Pandora E.	AG0450	64A
Buck, Elizabeth	AZ0100	64A
Buerkle, Suzanne	LA0650	64A
Bugg, Sue	TX3535	64A,32
Bull, Catherine	GA0900	64A
Bullock, Tunisia	NC1350	64A
Bursill-Hall, Damian	PA1050	64A
Butler, Rebecca G.	PA0050	11,64A,37,34,13B
Butterfield, Emily J.	OK1330	64A
Buyse, Leone	TX2150	42,64A
Bylsma, Ruth	MI0850	64A
Byrne, Mary	AB0210	64A
Byrnes, Lisa B.	UT0250	64A
Caimotto, Michelle	CA2950	64A
Caimotto, Michelle	CA0807	64A
Calloway, Karen E.	GA2300	61,64A
Calzolari, Laura	NY2400	64A
Cameron, Robin	NY3775	41,64A
Campbell, Alicia M.	NC0900	64A
Campbell, Laura	NY0650	64A
Cannon, Maureen McDermott	DE0050	64A
Canton, Jacky	CO0300	64A
Carignan, Danielle	AI0220	64A
Carlson, Mimi	CA4425	64A
Carlson, Sydney R.	OR0850	41,42,64A
Carlson, Tammi	IL1890	13F,11,64A
Carroll, Nancy A.	IA0940	64A
Carslake, Louise	CA2950	12,55,64A,67
Cartagena, Cynthia	PR0150	64A
Cartagena, Cynthia	PR0115	41,42,64A
Carter, Elise	NJ0300	64A
Casillas-Rivera, Josue	PR0115	64A
Cassano, Rhonda	FL1950	64A
Catalfano, Joyce A.	WV0750	48,64A
Cawley, Dominique	IA1800	64A
Cech, Jessica	MI2120	64A,11,12A
Cela, Orlando	MA0700	64A
Cella, Lisa M.	MD1000	64A,13C,41
Chaffee, Christopher	OH2500	64A,20,29A,11
Chandler, Beth E.	VA0600	64A,42,35E
Chao, Barbara Davis	AZ0470	64A
Chao, Barbara	AZ0400	64A
Charles, Nicole	OH2250	64A,48
Charles, Nicole M.	OH1650	64A,48
Charlton, Susan	PA1850	41,64A
Chastain, Kathleen	OH1700	64A
Cheeseman, Sybil	MS0400	64A
Cheesman, Sybil	MS0100	64A
Cheramy, Michelle	AD0050	64A,13B
Cherry, Diana	NC2350	64A
Chesis, Linda	NY2150	64A
Cho, Michelle	DC0050	64A
Christie, Carolyn	AI0150	64A
Churchfield, Camille	AG0400	64A
Churchill, Rachel	AG0150	64A
Ciraldo, Rachel Taratoot	LA0650	64A
Clardy, Mary Karen	TX3420	41,48,64A
Clarke, Penelope	AG0170	13A,64A
Claudin, Margaret	PA2800	64A,41
Clegg, Aaron	CA5000	64A
Clemans, Holly	MI0500	64A
Clew, Nancy	FL0150	64A
Cloud, Patricia	CA5020	64A
Cobert, Claude	MA2020	64A,11,12A
Coble, Deborah C.	NY4150	64A
Cochran, Shelley	IL1100	64A
Code, Belinda B.	AE0050	41,64A,64B,64D
Coelho, Tadeu	NC1650	64A,41
Coleman, Malcolm J.	TX3525	64A
Colgin-Abeln, Melissa	TX3520	12A,64A
Collaros, Rebecca L.	DC0170	13,64A
Collins, Nancy	WI0808	48,64A,41
Collins, Shelley	MS0250	11,64A,12A,48
Conner, Jennifer	PA1050	64A
Contino, Loretta	IN0250	48,64A
Cook, Lawrence	HI0050	48,64A,64C,64E
Cooksey, Denise	IL1090	64A
Cooksey, Denise	IL1350	64A
Copeland-Burns, Carla	NC0930	64A
Cornils Luke, Peg	IA0250	64A
Cornils, Margaret A.	WI0840	64A,11,48,66D
Coticone, Geralyn	MA0400	64A
Coticone, Geralyn	MA0350	64A
Councell-Vargas, Martha	MI2250	64A,48
Councill, Ruben	PA2100	64A
Covert, Kelly	NY1800	64A
Cowens, Kathleen	MO0350	64A,48
Cowens, Kathy	MO0400	64A,41
Cramer, David M.	PA3250	64A
Crawford, Barry J.	NY4320	64A
Crawford, Thomas	VA0350	64A,64C,64E
Crawford, Tom	TN1150	64C,64E,64A
Creighton, Patricia	AF0100	64A
Crone, Elizabeth	VA1700	64A,34C
Cronin, Robert	GA1150	64A
Cross, Debra W.	VA1000	64A
Cruz, Karena	CA3520	64A,66C
Cullen, Leslie	PA3150	64A,48
Cullen, Leslie	PA0350	64A
Cykert, Linda	NC0750	64A,41
Dade, Alice K.	MO1800	64A
Dalmasi, Martin	FL0930	41,64A,64E
Damur, Bill	AA0020	64A,70
Daniel, Kathy	TX2250	64A,32A,32B
Daniels, John	FL0600	13,32C,64A,64C
Daoust, Lise	AI0200	64A
Davis, Immanuel	MN1623	64A
Davis, John E.	GA0300	60,11,37,64A,64E
Davis, Susan	VA1600	64A
Day, Timothy	CA4150	64A
De La Bretonne, Beverly	TX0100	13,38,41,62A,64A
De Wetter-Smith, Brooks	NC2410	64A,29A
Deaver, Susan E.	NY2105	48,64A
Degooyer, Suzan	FL1300	64A
DeHaan, Sue	IA1200	64A
DeJongh, Katherine	OH0600	64A
Del Cid, Sandra	FL1550	64A
Demsey, Karen B.	NJ1400	64A,48,12,11,12A
Dennis, Jeannine M.	CA0850	64A
Denza, William M.	OH0500	64A,48,64E,64C
Der Hohannesian, Seta	MA2150	41,64A
DeVoll, James	MN0750	64A,48
DeWitt, Donald	NY1250	64C,64E,64A
Dick, Robert	NY2750	64A,42,41
DiDonato, Alicia	MA0950	64A
DiGiacobbe, David	NJ0175	64A,41
Dikeman, Philip	TN1850	64A,41,48
Dionne, Aubrie	NH0250	64A
Dior, Jennifer	NC2420	64A
Ditiberio, Lisa	MO0650	64A
Dobbs, Wendell B.	WV0400	11,13,41,48,64A
Dockendorf, Lyle	OR0850	64A
Dockendorf-Boland, Janice	IA0300	64A
Doggett, Thomas J.	IA0200	64A
Donner, Ann	IN1050	64A
Dooley, Ellen	DC0170	64A
Dorough, Aralee	TX3400	64A
Douthit, LaTika	NC2700	11,37,64A
Dove-Pellito, Glennda M.	NY3730	48,64A
Downing, Elizabeth A.	ME0440	64A,42
Downing, Sonja Lynn	WI0350	14,15,20D,64A,32
Doyle, Tracy A.	CO0050	64A,32,32B
Draper, Michelle	MO1550	64A,48
Dufour, Mathieu T.	IL0750	64A
Dundjerski, Petar	AA0020	60B,64A
Dungan, Doris	AG0170	64A
Dunn, Lisa	OK0500	64A
Dunnavant, Jessica Guinn	TN1100	64A,67D,11
Dunnell, Rebecca	MO0950	64A,12A,14,11,20
Dwyer, Doriot	MA0400	64A
Dwyer, Laura L.	FL1950	64A
Dwyer, Laura	FL1000	64A
Dydnansky, Patricia	AG0050	64A
Dzapo, Kyle J.	IL0400	12A,12,64A
Easley, Tabatha	VA1600	64A
Edgar, Donna	NM0500	64A
Edighoffer, Gary B.	WA0950	64A,64E,35D
Edwards, Celeste	IN1310	64A
Edwards, George L.	DC0350	11,32C,48,64A,64C
Egekvist, Deborah	NC2430	64A
Eikrem, Jeanne	OR1300	64A,48
Eldridge, Ronda	TX2750	11,20,48,64A
Elliott, Marsha	AB0210	64A
Elliott, Merrilee	KY1350	64A
Elliott, Paula	AG0200	64A
Endsley, Pamela	CO0900	64A
Erickson, Janette	CA1860	64A
Erskine, Bruce	TN1680	48,64A
Eselson, Lauren	AA0150	64A
Eselson, Lauren	AA0050	41,64A
Esposito, Nicole	IA1550	64A
Ethington, Martha Poleman	DC0170	64A
Ewell, Laurel A.	MD0850	64A
Eyles, Amy	MT0370	64A
Fabrique, Martha H.	TX2260	64A
Fagan, Leslie M.	NE0100	64A
Fairbanks, Ann K.	TX3450	13A,12A,41,64A
Farmer, Katherine	GA0940	48,64A
Farrington, Annette	NY2650	64A
Farrington, Annette	NY1700	64A
Faulkner, Elizabeth	AA0035	64A
Fedele, Andrea	MN0350	64B,64A
Fedele, David	KS1350	64A
Fedoruk, Brenda	AB0200	64A
Fedoruk, Brenda	AB0050	64A
Fedoruk, Brenda	AB0100	64A
Feierabend, Christine	AF0100	64A
Felber, Jill	CA5060	64A,48
Feller, Bart	NJ1130	64A
Fellows, Robin B.	WI0865	13A,11,41,64A
Fenley, J. Franklin	MO1790	11,12A,64A
Ferguson, Mary Kay	OH0600	64A
Ferrandis, Jean	CA0815	64A
Fink, Kathleen	NJ0825	64A,41
Fink, Mary Kay	OH0600	64A
Finn, Danielle	IL1610	64A
Finucan, David	NY2400	64A
Florine, Jane Lynn	IL0600	11,12A,12,20A,64A
Floyd, Angeleita S.	IA1600	48,64A
Flygare, Karla	WA1000	48,64A
Flygstad, Jana	KY0610	64A
Fonville, John	CA5050	13,10,64A,53,43
Franks, Carol	AL1050	13,64A,48
Frescoln, Austin	WY0130	64A
Fries, Susan	CA1425	64A
Frisch, Michele	MN1280	41,64A
Frisof, Sarah A.	TX3500	41,64A
Fruehwald, Robert D.	MO1500	13,10,45,64A
Fudala, Cynthia	IN1750	64A
Fudala, Cynthia T.	IL0730	64A
Fudge, Berkeley	WI1150	47,64E,53,64A,29
Fuller, Marcia	IA0400	64A
Fuller, Melanie	GA2130	64A,48
Futterer, Karen	AR0200	12A,48,64A
Gabriel, Sean	OH0650	64A
Gabriel, Sean F.	OH0200	64A
Galvin, Eugene	DC0170	64A
Ganus, Linda	PA2450	64A
Garcia, Nora Lee	FL1800	64A,48
Gardner, Aaron	WI1150	64E,64A
Gariazzo, Mariana Stratta	TX2900	64A,12A,20,11
Garner, Brad A.	NY2750	64A
Garner, Bradley A.	OH2200	64A
Garnett, Rodney A.	WY0200	64A,20,67H
Garrison, Karen H.	AL0200	11,64A,48
Garrison, Leonard	ID0250	64A,13,12,13B,13C
Gartley, Jennifer	IL1740	64A
Gartshore, Donelda	AG0250	64A,48,67C
Garvin, Jane	MN1625	64A
Gasper, Anne	RI0200	64A
Gasper, Anne	RI0150	64A
Gayler, Liane	AA0020	64A
Gedigian, Marianne	TX3510	64A
Gelb, Philip	CA2950	64A
Gerrish, Jo	ID0075	64A
Gerry, Beth	AG0200	64A
Gettel, Court	VT0100	64A,13,20
Gibson, Chris	MI1180	64A,32B
Gibson, Christina	MI1985	64A
Gieck, Sarah	AA0200	64A
Gifford, Robert R.	AL1160	64A
Gilchrest, Suzanne M.	NY2750	64A,48
Giles, Ruth	MN0200	64A
Giles, Sonja	IA0850	64A,41,42
Gilpin, Shirley	NC2000	64A,48
Glaser, Susan J.	NY2750	64A
Glencross, Laurie M.	IL1750	13,41,64A
Glennon, Barbara	PA0650	20G,13B,13C,64A,64C
Glicklich, Martin	CA2420	64A,41
Gnecco, Jeanne E.	TX3410	64A
Gnecco, Jeanne	TX3100	64A

Name	Code	Areas
Goethe-McGinn, Lisa	IL2750	64A
Goldberg, Bernard	NY0500	41,64A
Goldhorn, Jan	GU0500	64A
Goldman, Aaron	MD1010	64A
Goldstein, Joanna	MA0400	64A
Gonzalez, Ana Laura	NY1400	64A,13A,13B
Goodberg, Robert	WI0825	41,48,64A
Goode, Elizabeth	GA2150	64A,48,13
Goodfellow, Susan S.	UT0250	64A
Goodman, Kimberlee	OH2050	64A,14,13A
Goodman, Lindsey	OH1400	64A
Goodnight, Cheryl	TX3415	64A
Goodnight, Sheryl	TX2800	64A
Goranson, Jocelyn	PA2300	64A,13A,13C,13B,42
Gordon, Rachel	ID0140	64A
Gossage, Dave	AI0150	29,64A
Gottlieb, Donald	KY1500	64A
Graef, Richard	IL2250	64A
Granados, Marco	MA1175	64A
Granger, Shelly	CA0600	64A
Grant, Kristin	AR0500	64A,13A,13B,13C
Greenbaum, Adrianne	MA1350	64A,67D
Greenberg-Norman, Susan	CA3600	64A
Greene, Linda	NY1350	64A,42
Grigorov, Liisa Ambegaokar	NY2650	64A,48
Grim, Jennifer	NV0050	64A,42,41
Grimes, Benjamin	OR0700	20G,64A
Gruenhagen, Lisa M.	OH0300	32A,32B,32G,64A,32
Grycky, Eileen J.	DE0150	64A,41,48
Gudmundson, Paula	MN1600	11,13B,64A
Gudmundson, Paula	MN0040	64A,64,12A,14
Guenther, Christina	TX2700	64A,20,41
Gunn, Jennifer	IL0550	64A
Gurgel, Denise	TX0400	64A
Gustafson, Christine	NC0650	42,64A
Guzzio-Kregler, Mary Ellen	RI0200	13C,64A,42
Hagglund, Heidi	IL0150	64A,41
Hagglund, Heidi	IL3150	64A
Hahn, Richard	ID0250	64A,12A
Hale, Alison	MA1350	64A
Hale, Cheryl	TX3370	64C,64A
Hall, Beth	AL1195	64A
Hall, Carl	GA0750	64A
Hall, Doris S.	AL0010	11,48,64A,64E
Hambelton, Patrice	CA3920	64A
Hamilton, Amy	AG0600	64A
Hammerling, Margaret	ND0600	64A
Hammerling, Margaret	MN0600	64A
Hand, Judith	LA0350	48,64A
Hannigan, Mary	PA0950	48,64A
Hansbrough, Yvonne	NY0700	64A,67D,12A,42
Hansen, Lisa	NJ0700	64A,42
Hansen-Jackson, Dionne	IL0550	64A
Hanson, Sarah Beth	TN1660	64A
Harper, Patricia	CT0100	64A
Harrington, Barbara	AL1200	64A,42
Harris, Debora	MN0600	64A
Harris, Debora	MN1120	64A,48
Harrow, Anne Lindblom	NY1100	64A,42
Hart, Cherie	WI0862	66D,64A
Hartger, Susan	PA3580	64A
Hawkins, Diane	OR0175	64A
Hawkinson, Jennifer	SD0580	64A
Hawley, Alexandra W.	CA4900	64A
Hayes, Kristin Delia	TX3530	64A
Hebert, Floyd	MA2250	64A,41
Hedrick, Carmella	NC1900	64A,41
Hedrick, Teresa	VA0550	64C,64E,64A,64B
Heiss, John	MA0400	64A
Heitzman, Jill M.	IA0450	61,64A,66A,11
Heller, Lauren B.	CT0050	37,32E,60B,64A
Helton, Kimberly	IA1350	64A
Henderson, Cindy	UT0350	64A
Hennen, Nancy	AC0050	64A
Henriques, Yurii	AL0800	64A
Henry, Anna	TX1550	64A
Henry, Anna W.	TX2350	64A,48
Hepner, Jae Lyn	IL1200	64A
Herceg, Melissa	OH1400	64A
Herrera, Cathy	PA1650	64A
Hester, Carol	IA0950	64A,32E
Heyboer, Jill L.	MO0775	64A
Heywood, David John	SC0500	11,37,64A,29,47
Hibler, John	WI1155	64A,64E,64C
Hickcox, Julee	VA1250	64A
Hill, Dennis	FL0500	37,47,64A,64E,29
Hill, Heather	MI0520	64A
Hill-Kretzer, Kathleen	OH2275	64A
Hill-Kretzer, Kelly	MI0050	20,64A
Hinata, Kaoru	NJ1130	64A
Hinojosa, Melissa S.	TX1425	11,13,64A
Ho, Hsing-I	IA0930	64A
Hobbs, Julie	KY1450	64A,48
Hodges, Brian	KY0250	48,64A,64C
Hoehne, Bill	CA1000	10F,12C,64A,13,29
Hoeppner, Susan	AG0450	64A
Hollingsworth, Dina L.	CO0275	64A,64E,29,41,11
Holt, Eileen	CA5040	64A
Holt, Eileen	CA5100	64A
Hooten, David M.	TX1600	64C,11,48,64A
Hopkins, Barbara	CT0600	64A
Hopkins, Cynthia	SC0750	64A
Horak, Sally	LA0050	64A
Horne, Robin	FL1430	64A,48
Hovan, Rebecca	IN0910	64A
Howes, Heather	AI0150	64A
Hryniewicki, Donna	MN0625	64A,48
Hryniewicki, Donna	MN1050	64A
Hubbard, Mary Ann	MI0200	41,64A
Hudson, Virginia	AR0730	64A,11
Hugo, Alycia	VA1400	64A
Hugo, Alycia	VA1125	64A
Hugo, Alycia	VA0750	64A
Hulihan, Theresa	AZ0350	64A
Humphreys, Sally	UT0400	64A
Huntington, Ellen	IL2100	64A
Hutchins, Tim	AI0150	38,64A
Inglis, Adrienne	TX2650	64A
Ionesco, Georgette	NY4500	64A
Isadore, Jennifer L.	TX1400	64A
Ivy, Allen	MO1100	60,38,51,64A
Jacobsen, David C.	VA1700	64A,64E
Jacobson, Barbara	FL0800	64A,48
Jacobson, Sheri	WA1350	64A
Jacobson, Sheri	WA0400	64A
James, Deborah	RI0250	64A
James, Kortney	WI0750	64A,32,48
James, Kortney	WI0850	64A
Jamner, Margaret	IN1010	64A
Jamsa, Martha N.	MN0950	64A
Jamsa, Martha	MN0300	64A
Janson, Anne	VT0450	64A
Janzen, Elizabeth A.	TX2960	64A
Jaque, Maria	CA1750	64A
Jelle, Lisa A.	OH0350	64A,48
Jenkins, E. Morgan	MD0450	64A,64E,70,29B
Jenkins, Pamela	ME0340	64A,64C,64E,32,13E
Jennings, Christina	CO0800	64A
Jobson, Krista	MO0800	64A
Johns, Lana Kay	MS0500	13A,11,64A
Johnson, Alyce	IL0750	64A
Johnson, Deborah S.	NE0300	13A,11,48,64A,13B
Johnson, Ellen C.	TX0400	64A,41
Johnson, Karen	MD0750	64A
Johnson, Karen	DC0170	41,64A
Johnson, Rebecca R.	IL0800	64A,48
Jones, Adah T.	TX3175	48,64A
Jones, Harold	NY2400	64A
Jones, Harold	NY0500	64A
Jones, Harold	NY2200	64A,48
Jones, Harold	NY5000	64A
Jones, Katherine Borst	OH1850	64A
Jones, Lorraine	GA0200	48,64A
Jones, Lucie	AA0050	64A
Jones, Lucie	AA0150	64A
Jones, Vanita	DC0050	64A
Jones, Vanita	MD0150	41,64A
Jones, Vanita	MD0550	64A,41
Jones-Reus, Angela	GA2100	64A,48
Jordheim, Suzanne	WI0350	64A
Jorgensen, Elaine	UT0190	11,41,48,64A
Jorgensen, Kristen	NY3770	11,48,64A,62A
Jureit-Beamish, Marie	IL2400	38,64A,66A,10F,11
Jutt, Stephanie	WI0815	64A
Kagy, Tamara K.	OH2140	64A,48
Kahn, Sue Ann	NY2250	41,64A
Kairies, Joy E.	TX0550	64A,34C,11,48
Kamalidiin, Sais	DC0150	64A,29
Kane, Trudy	FL1900	64A,41,48
Kani, Robin	PA2450	41,48,64A
Kanter, Chris	MI0900	64A
Karr, Kathy	KY0450	48,64A
Karr, Kathy	KY1500	64A,48
Kasica, Paula J.	MO1830	64A
Keach, Candace	GA1900	64A
Kean, Kristen	KY0550	64A,13A,13,42,48
Kearney, Linda	OH0755	64A
Keeble, Jonathan	IL3300	64A,48
Keenan, Maureen	NY0270	11,13,64A
Keeney, Jennifer	TX3400	64A
Kelley, Constance L.	TX0150	37,32E,64A
Kelly, Angela	VA1550	64A
Kelly, Maureen	NC1600	64A
Kemler, Katherine A.	LA0200	64A
Kennard, Bryan E.	OH1000	64A
Kennard, Jennifer C.	MN0610	64A
Kenny, Rhian	PA1050	64A
Kenote, Marie Herseth	NY2900	64A,12A,13B,13C,13D
Kent, Heather	MA0950	64A
Kerber, Ronald	PA3330	47,64A,64E,29,41
Kershaw, Yvonne	AE0120	64A,64D,10A,11,13A
Kerstetter, Kathleen	NC1500	32,49,34,64A
Kestenberg, Abe	AI0150	48,64C,64E,64A
Keyser, Catherine	GA1500	64A
Khaner, Jeffrey	FL1125	64A
Khaner, Jeffrey	NY1900	64A
Khaner, Jeffrey	PA0850	64A
Kibler, Lea	SC1080	64A
Kibler, Lea F.	SC0400	64A,48
Kile, Nora	TN1350	64A,41
Kim, Bonnie	VA0150	64A,48
Kim, Bonnie	VA1000	64A
Kimball, Hillary	UT0050	64A
Kimball, Phebe	OR0950	64A
King, Margaret	AA0020	66A,64A
Kipp, Sandra	CA0835	64A
Kirkendoll, Mary	KS1050	41,64A
Kirkpatrick, Linda M.	MD0520	60,37,41,48,64A
Kirsh, Kristy	KY0100	64A
Kirton, Suzanne	FL0680	64A
Kiss, Boglarka	CA3500	11,12A,64A
Klassen, Gwen	AA0150	64A
Klipp, Barbara A.	IL0650	13A,11,64A
Knudtsen, Jere	WA0750	11,37,47,64A,29A
Koch, Elizabeth	AA0035	64A,48
Kocher, Stephanie	IA0500	64A
Kocher, Stephanie	SD0600	64A
Koenig, Laura J.	AK0100	64A
Koidin, Julie	IL1615	64A
Korducki, Linda Nielsen	WI0150	64A
Koregelos, Angela	CA2950	64A
Kosack, Alicia	PA3710	64A,42,67D
Kotter, Laurie	MD0475	64A
Kraus, Tracy	MA0650	64A
Krause, Melissa M.	MN1300	13,64A,10A,10F
Kravitz, Steve	OR0750	64A,64D,64E,41
Kreft, Anne	IL0275	64A,11
Krejci, Mathew	CA5350	64A,42,41
Krimsier, Renee J.	MA0400	64A
Krueger, Christopher	MA2000	64A
Krueger, Christopher	MA1400	64A,64E
Kujala, Walfrid	IL2250	64A
Kumer, Wendy	WV0600	64A
Kyne, Nadia	AB0200	64A
Lakofsky, Elissa	FL0650	64A
Lakofsky, Elissa	FL0700	64A
Lampert, Judi	NC2400	64A
Lane, Timothy	WI0803	14,48,64A
Langevin, Robert	NY2150	64A
Langevin, Robert	NY1900	64A
Lapple, Judith A.	VA0450	64A,41
Large, Karen McLaughlin	KS0650	13,11,64A,13A,48
Larner, James M.	IN1100	12A,48,10E,64A,29A
Larsen, Bill	FL0680	64A
Larsen, William H.	FL0500	64A
Larson, Anne	NC2300	64A
Larson, Jean	TX2400	64A
Larson, Laura A.	MI2200	64A
Lattimore, Lee	TX3420	64A,67E
Lau, Frederick C.	HI0210	14A,38,43,64A,20C
Lau, Jennifer	NM0450	64A,11
Laupp, Belinda	TN1400	64A
LaVorgna, David	MD0400	64A,42
Lawler, Dawn	WI0700	64A
Lawson, Jennifer	VA0250	64A
Lawson, Jennifer	VA1500	64A

Index by Area of Teaching Interest

Name	Code	Areas
Leadbitter, Robyn	SC0600	64A
Leas, Ashleigh	TX3350	64A
Lee, Richard A.	HI0200	13,10,12A,64E,64A
Leech, Karen	MT0200	64A,42
LeGrand, Catherine M.	NC0300	64A
Leibundguth, Barbara	MN0750	64A
Leifer, Lyon	IL2150	64A
Leisring, Laura	VA0250	48,64A,64D,41,64C
Lesser, Erin	WI0350	64A
Levitan, Susan	IN0005	64A
Levitin, Susan	IL2750	48,64A
Levy, Kathryn	NC2500	48,64A
Likes, Susan	IL1500	64A
Lilarose, Robin	PA1900	64A
Linard, Rita A.	TX3530	13,64A
Lind, Loren N.	PA3250	64A
Lindsey, A. Lish	PA3700	64A
Lion, Na'ama	MA0250	41,64A,67D
Little, Deanna	TN1100	64A,48
Lockart, Carol	CA5360	64A,55
Lockart, Carol	CA3100	64A
Lockett, Bonnie	CA1650	64A
Loewy, Andrea Kapell	LA0760	13,64A
Loewy, Susanna L.	PA1750	11,48,64A
Looking Wolf, Jan Michael	OR0700	20G,64A
Lord, Suzanne	IL2900	64A,12A
Lotspeich, Melissa	TX3527	64A
Lozano, Danilo	CA6000	47,64A,20,29A,14
Lozano, Denise	NY2450	13A,11,64A
Lucas, Adonna	NC1950	13,36,64A,66,31A
Luce, Brian A.	AZ0500	64A,48
Lujan, Bethany	FL1500	64A
Lukas, Kathryn	IN0900	64A
Lukas, Linda D.	CA4200	64A
Luke, Nadine	ID0060	13A,13B,13C,64A
Lum, Anne Craig	HI0150	66D,66A,64A,45,66C
Lundgren, Karen E.	CA0630	64A
Lunte, Sandra K.	LA0770	13A,64A,48
Lynn, Kathie	OH1700	67D,67C,64A
Maaser, Leslie G.	OH0850	64A
MacKay-Galbraith, Janet	IN0700	64A
Maestre, Janet M.	CA4900	64A
Magg, Susan A.	OH0680	64A
Maggs, Patty J.	CA1900	64A
Mahr, Jill	MN1450	44,64A
Mains, Ronda	AR0700	64A,32B,32
Maiolo, Georgetta	NY3705	64A
Maiolo, Georgetta	NY0350	64A
Maki, Daniel H.	IL0840	13,11,37,64A,66D
Maki, Patricia	CA1750	64A
Malamut, Myra Lewinter	NJ0550	11,64A,67B,20G,13A
Malone, William	CO0810	64E,64C,64A,29A,20
Maret, Carmen	MI0300	64A
Marfisi, Nancy G.	CA0550	64A
Mark, Amanda	AF0120	64A
Marrs, Leslie	IA0550	64A,48,13A
Marshall, Elizabeth	WI0100	64A,48
Martchev, Pamela	CA4100	64A
Martin, Andree	GA0550	64A,11,43,12
Martin, Elaine J.	PA2550	64A
Martin, Marya	NY2150	64A
Martin, Roger	TN1450	64A,41,64
Martin, Sharon	MN1700	64A,48
Martyn, Charles F.	WV0650	37,47,64A,64C,64E
Masek, Patricia B.	SD0050	64A
Mason-Christianson, Teri	CA5355	64A
Massey, Angela	SC1000	64A
Matathias, Robin	NH0150	64A,48
Maurer-Davis, Jill	CT0050	64A,48
Maxfield, Jessica	IL1900	64A,64C,64E
May, Brittany	TX1450	64A
McAndrews, Deb	OR1000	64A
McArthur, Lisa R.	KY0400	13,48,64A,12A,12F
McBrearty, Angela S.	NY1700	64A
McCage, Leslie	OH2300	64A
McCallum, Laura	OR0750	64A
McCarthy, Elizabeth	AF0100	64A
McCarthy, Lisa	WA1250	64A
McClard Kirk, Jennifer	KS1250	32E,64A,64C
McCloskey, Diane L.	OH1100	64A,41
McCormick, Kim S.	FL2000	64A
McDermott, Dennette Derby	LA0550	13,64A
McElrath, Katheryn	OR0950	64A
McEntire, Jeremy	VA1150	64A
McEntire, Jeremy R.	VA1500	64A
McGhee, Lorna	AB0100	64A,41
McGowan, Orpha Ellen	AZ0510	64A
McKay, Emily Hoppe	AZ0450	64A,41
Mckenzie, Julie C.	CA5000	64A
McKinney, Kelly	GA1070	64A
McLamb, Victoria	NC0450	64A
McLaughlin, Greg	CA4580	64A,64E,47
McMurtery, John M.	IL3500	64A,48
McNutt, Elizabeth	TX3420	64A,43
McQuinn, Susan	FL1750	64A
McWayne, Dorli	AK0150	48,64A,41
Meador, Rebecca	KS1400	13,64A
Meany, Thomas	PA3550	64A
Measel, Jane	WA0550	64A
Mehne, Wendy	NY1800	64A
Mendenhall, Judith	NY2250	64A,41
Meves, Carol	WI1150	64A
Meyer, Kathy	CA2775	64A
Meyer, Thomas	IN1100	64A,64C
Mezzadri, Danilo	MS0750	64A,12E,48
Middleton, Peter	IL2200	45,64A,34,35C,13L
Milanovich, Donna Z.	IL3310	64A
Miles, Sarah	TN1850	64A
Miller, Jane	WY0115	64A
Miller, Leta	CA5070	11,12A,12,64A,67E
Miller, Mark	CO0560	29,13A,41,47,64A
Miller, Tess Anissa	MI0150	64A,11,41
Miska, Renee	FL0200	64A
Mitchell, Nicole	IL3310	29,29A,64A
Mitchell, Teresa L.	FL1310	64A
Moe, Karla	NY2105	64A,64
Moe, Karla	NY2550	64A
Moliner, Eugenia	IL0550	42,64A
Molumby, Nicole L.	ID0050	64A,32E,32I,13C
Monaghan, Michael	MA0700	47,64A,64E,53,29
Montgomery, William L.	MD1010	41,64A
Moon, Emma	CA5000	64A
Moore, Julianna	MO1780	13,48,64A
Moore, Selma	NY2950	13,37,41,64A,66D
Moratz, Karen	IN0250	64A
Morgenstern, Julia	KS0700	64A
Morris, Amy	MN0800	64A
Morris, Amy	MN1295	64A
Morris, Martha M.	IL2650	12A,32,64A
Moseley, William	ME0340	12A,47,64A,35C,29
Moulton, Christine F.	PA2150	64A,66A
Mourton, Laurie	GA2050	64A
Mudge, Ashley	FL1700	13,64A
Muller, Janet	MD0175	64A
Mulvey, Vanessa Breault	MA1175	64A
Muncy, Robert	MD0700	64A,64E
Munro, Anne	WV0550	64A,48,38,51
Murchison, Pamela	MD0350	64A,48,20,15
Murray, Jack	NC2650	64A
Murray, Jack T.	NC0350	64A,64C,64E
Myers-McKenzie, Laurl	CA3200	64A,13A
Myrick, Barbara	OR0350	13,12A,66A,66D,64A
Nabb, Franziska	NE0590	64A
Nagem, Paul	CO0200	64A
Nelson, Conor	OH0300	64A
Nelson, Pamela	NC1300	64A,48
Nelson, Paula	PA1550	64A,48
Nelson, Paula C.	PA1250	64A
Nelson, Randi	AJ0150	64A
Nelson, Susan	MN0150	64A
Nester, Holly	MN1500	64A
Nester, Kathleen M.	NY2750	64A
Newman, Leslie	AG0450	64A
Newman, Leslie	AG0300	64A,42
Nichols, Sara	MD0850	64A,48
Nielsen, Linda	WI0835	64A
Nielsen, Linda	WI0050	64A
Nolan, Denise G.	NH0110	48,64A,11,13C
Nold, Sherry	PA3260	64A,64C,64E
Nozny, Rachel	ND0100	64A,13C
Nugent, Barli	NY1900	29,64A
Oberbrunner, John	NY1550	64A,48
O'Connor, Tara	NY2150	64A
O'Connor, Tara	NY0150	64A,42
O'Connor, Tara Helen	NY3785	64A,42
Oddsen, Kristine	NJ0200	64A
O'Donnell, Kevin	AG0600	64A
Oestreich, Martha	FL0950	64A
Ogle, Alex	NH0100	64A,41,42
Oleskiewicz, Mary	MA2010	11,12A,12,14B,64A
Olin, Elinor	IL2000	11,12A,12,64A
Olin, Marissa H.	MI2000	48,64A
Olson, Craig	WY0130	64E,48,64A,40,46
O'Neill, Amy	AG0500	64A
O'Neill, Jill L.	SC1200	11,64A,48,14C,41
Ordonez, Karla	TX0900	64A
Orr, Emily G.	NC2435	64A
Ortega, Catalina	AR0700	64A
Ostling, Elizabeth	MA0400	64A
O'Toole, Elizabeth A.	MT0350	64A
Ott, Hal J.	WA0050	12A,41,48,64A,67D
Overmier, Juliana	OK0300	64A,48
Owens, Parthena	OK0750	48,64A,32E
Packard, Jennifer	OH1600	64A,41
Palchak, Mary	CA0960	64A
Palchak, Mary	CA2390	64A,13A
Palma, Susan	NJ0800	64A,42
Paluzzi, Rebecca Lile	TN0500	48,64A
Papillon, Andre	AI0190	11,41,64A
Papp, Anne	DC0170	64A
Park, Soo-Kyung	NY2750	64A
Parker-Harley, Jennifer	SC1110	64A,48
Parloff, Michael	NY2150	64A
Parnicky, Lori M.	WA1300	64A
Patnode, Matthew A.	ND0350	64E,64A,29,48,47
Patterson, Lisa D.	IL2775	64A
Patterson, Paula	KS0150	64A
Pauls, Jill	OR0700	64A
Payne, Catherine	CA4400	41,64A
Pedrini, Jamie J.	CA3500	64A,48
Pendergrast, Celine	TN0550	64A
Pepinsky, Juliana May	NY0900	64A
Pereksta, Linda H.	WI0830	64A
Perez-Tetrault, Rachel	CO0150	64A
Perlove, Nina	KY1000	64A,12A
Pettis, Paula	MN1250	64A
Petty, Byron W.	VA1850	64A,13
Phillips, Moses	NY0640	12,13A,13B,13C,64A
Piccinini, Marina	MD0650	64A
Pierce, Michael	LA0720	37,41,64A,11
Poehls, Jenny	ND0350	64A
Polk, Betty	TN1600	64A
Pope, George	OH2150	48,64A
Pope, George S.	OH0200	64A
Port, Donna	IL0730	64A
Porter, Ami	UT0150	64A
Porter, Amy	MI2100	64A
Posses, Mary	MO1810	64A,42
Potter, Valerie	NM0450	64A,41,48
Prather, Belva W.	MO0775	60B,48,64A
Prescott, Barbara	FL0450	41,64A
Prescott, Barbara	FL2050	64A
Prescott, Barbara	FL1650	64A
Pritchard, Jerrold	OR0500	64A
Proctor, Freda	KS1375	66,64A,13,37,41
Queen, Kristen	TX3000	64A
Rabata, Nicole	ME0250	64A
Racamato, Claire	PA0400	64A
Ramirez, Catherine	MN1450	13,64A,48,42,13B
Rea, Stephanie	KY0950	64A,13
Reeds, Elizabeth	NY0400	41,64A
Register, P. Brent	PA0700	12A,48,64A,64B,64D
Reighley, Kimberly	PA3600	64A,48
Renk, Sheryl	CA4100	64A
Renzi, Paul	CA4200	41,64A
Reside, Judy	AA0050	64A
Reuter-Pivetta, Debra	NC2205	64A
Reyes, Ysmael	CO0650	64A,41,48
Reynolds, Anne	IN1650	48,64A
Reynolds, Anne B.	IN0350	64A,41
Reynolds, Kathleen	CA4700	64A
Rhyne, Jennifer	WA0650	64A
Richards, Jeanne	MN1620	64A,67C,48
Richards, Mary	UT0325	64A
Richardson, Ouida	TX0550	36,64A,32A
Ridd, Laurel	AC0100	64A
Rigler, Jane	CO0810	64A,10B,34D,10
Riley, Madeleine C.	PA1000	11,45,64A,64E,29
Riner, Nicole	WY0200	64A,14C,32G,48
Risinger, Kimberly	IL1150	64A
Robertello, Thomas J.	IN0900	64A
Robertello, Thomas	IL0550	64A
Roberts, Layla	AC0100	64A
Robinson, Dawn	SC0800	64A
Robison, Paula	MA1400	64A
Rodenberg, Elise	IA0930	64A

Index by Area of Teaching Interest

Name	Code	Areas
Rodriguez-Salazar, Martha	CA1250	13,64A
Rohwer, Debbie A.	TX3420	32C,32B,64A
Romano, Charlene	VA1350	64A,13
Rondinelli-Eisenreich, Cassandra	FL0050	64A
Ronen, Yael	CA0800	64A
Roop, Cynthia M.	NC1250	64A,32A,32E,13C,41
Rosenblum, Jean K.	ME0500	64A
Rosinski, Jessi	MA2010	64A
Ross, John	WV0700	13,64A,11
Rotavera-Krain, Denise	OH0700	64A
Roth, Marjorie	NY2650	64A,12
Rowe, Elizabeth	MA1400	64A
Royal, Susan L.	NY3725	64A
Rubio, Jill M.	NY3780	64A
Rudich, Rachel	CA1050	64A
Rudich, Rachel	CA0510	64A
Rudich, Rachel E.	CA3650	64A
Rudolph, Kathleen	AG0300	64A,42
Rudolph, Kathleen	AG0500	64A
Rundlett, Jennifer	MD0610	64A
Rundlett, Jennifer	MD0300	64A,11,41
Runefors, Bjorn	AE0120	36,37,13,11,64A
Running, Timothy	PA1750	60,11,48,64A
Rush, John	OK0850	64A
Rush, John Phillip	OK1450	64A,67D,12A,55C,56
Russell, Peggy	TX3400	64A
Ryker, Pamela R.	WA0600	64A
Sackman, Marc L.	WI0806	13B,37,64A,47,11
Sahlin, Kay	MN1450	64A,42
Saiki-Mita, Sabrina	HI0210	64A
Sanchez, Cynthia	TX2260	36,61,64A,66A
Sander, Marie	WI0300	64A
Santa, Lisa Garner	TX3200	64A
Santos, Denis Almeida	KY0400	64A,13
Sappa, Emily	MN1000	64A
Sarver, Julie	OH1350	64A
Satterfield, Sarah	FL0365	12A,64A,11,42,48
Savage, John	OR1250	64A
Schattschneider, Adam	OH0250	13,47,64A,64C,64E
Schettler, Sarah M.	LA0800	64A
Schilling, Korin	IN1450	64A
Schlabach, Robert	TN0450	64A,64B,64C,64E
Schmidt, Tracey	PA0250	13,64A,11
Schneeloch-Bingham, Nancy	NC0050	64A,48,32E
Schocker, Gary M.	NY2750	64A
Schoen, Kathleen	AA0110	64A,67C
Schroder, Lisa	CA2050	64A
Schroeder, Linda	AF0120	64A
Schroeder, Lisa	CA0859	64A
Schuberg, Margaret	MT0400	13,48,64A
Schulkind, Laura	CO0625	64A
Schultz, Diane Boyd	AL1170	64A
Schulze-Johnson, Virginia	NJ0300	41,47,48,64A,42
Schwoebel, Sandy	AZ0480	64A,48,67D,35A
Scolnik, Julia	MA1175	64A
Scott, Caryl Mae	CA4300	64A,66D
Scott, James C.	TX3420	64A
Scott, Janet	IL2970	64A
Scott, Janet	MO1250	64A
Scott, Jenni Olson	CA1000	64A
Scott, Laurie	MN1600	13A,13C,64A
Seale, Sheryl	AZ0150	64A
Sedgley, Tiffany	UT0250	64A
Seeman, Sharon	NJ0750	64A,64B,64C,64D,11
Seidman, Naomi K.	PA2750	64A
Self, Susanna	MO0700	64A
Sever, Melanie M.	WI0860	64A
Shaffer, Kristin	KS0200	64A
Shanley, Helen A.	TX0300	48,64A
Shea, David L.	TX3200	34,41,64A,64C,64E
Shearer, Greig	CT0650	64A
Shelly, Frances	KS1450	64A,41
Shen, Deborah	NY2900	64A
Shepard, Hilary	KS0350	64A,11,20
Shepley, Mary Ellen	NY2400	64A,67B
Sherman, Richard	MI1400	64A
Sherry, Martin	WA0480	13,11,12A,14,64A
Shin, Donna	WA1050	64A
Shipley, Lori R.	VA0500	48,12A,13A,64A,41
Shirley, Ellen	IA1100	64A
Shogrin, Tina	NE0160	64A
Sholl, Martha P.	NY3730	48,64A
Shostac, David J.	CA0835	64A
Shotola, Marilyn	OR0850	13,64A,41,12A
Shroyer, Jo Ellen	MO0100	64A,64C,64E
Shroyer, Ronald L.	MO0100	64A,64C,64E,64
Shulman, Nora	AG0450	64A
Shulman, Suzanne	AG0200	64A
Shuter, Cindy	AI0150	64A,48
Siebert, Renee	FL1125	64A
Sincoff, Alison J. Brown	OH1900	64A,41
Singer, Leigh Ann	IA0910	41,64A,64E
Sipes, Diana	TX2930	64A,12A,13E,42
Skidmore, Dorothy L.	WV0300	64A
Skitch, Todd	TN1200	64A
Smith, Christina	GA1150	64A
Smith, Diane	NY3350	64A,48
Smith, Fenwick	MA1400	64A
Smith, Janice M.	MO1900	41,64A
Smith, Joshua	OH0600	64A,48
Smith, Lonnie	OR0600	64A
Smith, Vincent	NY0350	64A
Snizek, Suzanne	AB0150	64A,42
Snodgrass, Laura	CA2250	64A,13,35A
Snowden, Jonathan	VA1350	64A
Snoza, Melissa	WI0250	64A,41
Sokoloff, Laurie	MD0650	64A
Solfest-Wallis, Cindy	TN0260	11,64A
Solfest-Wallis, Cindy L.	WI0200	64A
Sollberger, Harvey	CA5050	10F,60,10,64A,43
Solum, John	NY4450	64A
Sooy, Julie	MI1050	64A,48
Sopata, Kimberly	IL3100	48,64A
Sowers, Jodi L.	IN1650	64A,11
Sowers, Jodi L.	IN0907	11,64A,41
Sparfeld, Amanda	MI1750	64A
Sparrow, Sharon W.	MI1750	64A,48
Spataro, Susan M.	VA0400	64A,47,11,32A,32B
Spell, Eldred	NC2600	64A,72
Spencer, Patricia L.	NY1600	64A,42,43
Spicer, Mark J.	NY1150	13,11,64A,66A,20G
Spicher, Barbara	MD0500	64A
Spitler, Carolyn	IN1250	64A,66A,13B,13C,66G
Stanek, Emily	IN0100	64A
Stang-McCusker, Stephani	DC0100	64A
Stanley, Michelle	CO0250	64A
Star, Cheryl	GA2300	64A
Starin, Stefani	NY2400	64A,67B
Starin, Stefani	NY5000	64A
Steele, Stacey G.	PA3100	32A,32B,48,64A
Steffen, Christina	AZ0440	64A,41,13
Stephens, Loren	NE0050	11,64A
Sterling, Amy	MD0800	64C,64E,64B,64D,64A
Stevens, Dwana F.	KY0300	64A,64E
Stevens, Laura	NC0930	64A
Steward, Feodora	OK1200	64A
Stewart, Douglas	AG0450	64A
Still, Alexa	OH1700	64A,20I
Stilson, Alicia	WA1100	64A
Stilwell, Jama Liane	IA0400	11,12,20G,13,64A
Stimson, Ann	OH1200	64A,41
Stingley, Mary-Christine	IL3450	64A
Stinson, Laura	AR0425	64A
Stodd, Janet	IA1300	64A
Stodd, Janet	IL0100	48,64A
Stodd, Janet	IL0300	64A
Stokes, Sheridon	CA5030	64A
Stolper, Mary	IL0750	64A
Stone, Elizabeth	AL1160	64A,41
Stone, Julie	MI0600	64A,48
Stoner, Kristen L.	FL1850	64A
Stoune, Michael	TX3200	13,64A
Stout, Sara	FL1450	64A
Stowe, Samuel P.	NC0850	11,48,64A
Straughn, Marcia	TX0900	64A
Stukart, Lynne	IL0300	64A,11
Stumpf, Suzanne	MA2050	41,67D,64A
Suggs, Nora	PA2450	64A
Suhr, Melissa	TX3400	64A
Sullivan, Anne	IL3550	64A
Sullivan, Mary	AA0050	64A
Sundberg, Terri	TX3420	41,64A
Surman, Patricia J.	OK0550	64A
Surman, Patricia	OK1250	64A,11
Swilley, Sue	TN0250	64A
Swinden, Laurel	AG0350	64A
Swisher, Kristen	TN1720	64A
Syring, Natalie	OK0700	64A
Szlosek, Elaine Saloio	MA1100	64A
Szlosek, Elaine Saloio	MA2100	64A
Tamburrino, Maria	CA5000	64A
Tan, Su Lian	VT0350	10,13,64A,42
Tate, Elda Ann	MI1600	13,10E,41,64A
Taub, Paul	WA0200	41,64A,35
Tempas, Laurel	IL1520	64A
Teskey, Nancy	OR0400	64A,32E
Tessmer, David	PA3650	41,64A
Tessmer, David P.	PA1450	64A
Tessmer, David	PA1350	64A
Thaves, Darrin	CA0825	64A
Thesen, Anita	MD0600	64A,12A
Thibeault, Anna	GA0950	64A,48
Thibodeau, Norman	NY3600	64A
Thiemann, Amy	NE0150	64A
Thivierge, Anne	AI0190	64A
Thomas, Susan H.	RI0300	41,48,64A,34
Thomason-Redus, Caen		48,64A
Thompson, Anne	AG0500	64A
Thompson, Paul	MO1500	11,41,64A,29A,55C
Thompson, Shauna	IN1600	64A
Thornton, Delores	WY0050	48,64A
Tiedemann, Sarah	OR0150	64A
Timmons, Leslie	UT0300	32A,32B,64A,48,41
Titus, Jamie	MO0050	64A,12,13,48
Tokito, Kazuo	PA3250	64A
Tomasone, Adeline	PA3250	64A
Tomasone, Adeline	NJ1050	64A,41
Tomlinson, Rebecca	CA0845	64A,32B
Toote, Linda	MA0350	64A
Toote, Linda	MA0400	64A
Trahan, Kathleen	MD1010	64A
Treybig, Carolyn	TN0100	64A
Tripp, Krysia	ME0150	64A
Tripp, Krysia	ME0200	64A
Tristano, Barbara	WI0810	64A
Trolier, Kimberly A.	PA1300	64A
Trolier, Kimberly	PA1150	64A
Troxler, Rebecca	NC0600	13A,64A,42,67D
Tryon, Robin R.	OH2290	41,64A
Tse, Joel	OH2300	64A,48
Tully, Amy	SC0420	64A,12A,41
Tunstall, Julia	PA3400	64A,11
Turska, Joanna	IL0650	64A
Tyson, Liana	AR0350	64A,11,48
Umble, Kathryn Thomas	OH2600	64A
Underwood, Keith	NY2250	64A
Underwood, Keith W.	NY2750	64A
Urso-Trapani, Rena	CA0825	64A
Vagts, Peggy A.	NH0350	64A
Valley, Myriam	AG0150	64A
Van Pelt, Michael	KY1000	64A
Van Winkle, Lisa K.	NM0310	64A,35A
Vanasse, Guy	AI0210	64A
Vandelicht, Roy D. 'Skip'	MO0100	32,37,60B,64A,47
Vaneman, Christopher	SC0650	64A,12,42
Vega, Rebecca	NJ0050	32,37,11,64A,60B
Verbeck, Heather D.	OH2200	64A
Via, Kelly	GA0050	64A,48
Via, Kelly	GA1300	64A,41
Vickers, Jeffrey E.	AR0600	64,11,64E,64A,12A
Vinci, Jan F.	NY3650	41,64A
Viren, Leslie	WY0150	64A
Vliek, Pamela	CA3800	64A,11
Volet, Richard	AB0210	64A
Volk, Jennifer Regan	IN0905	64A
Wacker, Therese M.	PA1600	64A,48,13
Waddell, Rachel Lynn	MI1000	11,12,32E,42,64A
Wade, Melinda	MD0060	64A
Waggoner, Dori	MO0100	13E,10F,64A,37,13C
Wagner, Jaimie	AG0550	64A
Walker, James	CA5300	64A
Walker, Jim	CA1075	64A,42
Walker, Kerry E.	CT0800	32,48,64A
Waln, Ronald	GA2100	64A
Walter, Laura	CA5550	64A
Wang, Diane	MS0700	64A,66D
Ward, Doug	AA0080	64A,64C,64E
Wargo, Edward	PA2200	64A
Watanabe, Mihoko	IN0150	64A,20
Waterman, Ellen F.	AD0050	64A,14
Watters, Patti	VA1000	64A
Watts, Valerie	OK1350	64A,41
Weber, Linda	TX0550	11,64A,66A,32,66D
Wechesler, David J.	NY0644	11,13A,29A,41,64A
Weidman-Winter, Becky	CO1050	64A,41,13
Weinreb, Alice Kogan	DC0050	64A

689

Name	Code	Areas
Weiss, Louise	IL1050	13A,32B,48,64A,66C
Werth, Kay	KS0350	64B,64D,48,64A
West, Jean	FL1750	12A,64A
West, William	IL1200	13,64A,64E,41,67E
Westby, Denise	OR0450	64A
Wetherill, Linda Marie	NY0050	64A,20
White, Carol	ID0070	64A
White, Dennine	FL0600	32C,37,64A
White, Joanna Cowan	MI0400	41,64A
White, Julian E.	FL0600	60,32C,37,64A,64B
White, Rosemary	MD0100	64A
Whitehead, Amy Orsinger	NC0550	64A
Whitford, Trudy	IN1560	64A,41
Whitford, Trudy	IN1025	64A,11
Wiehe, Beth A.	TX2200	64A
Wienhold, Lisa	AL0300	64A
Wienhold, Lisa J.	AL1150	64A
Wiggins, Ira T.	NC1600	47,64A,64E,29,46
Wilkinson, Fiona	AG0500	48,64A
Williams, Alicia	AR0250	64A
Williamson, Melissa	KS1200	64A,48,13
Willoughby, Robert	MA1175	64A
Wilson, Carla E.	OR1100	64A
Wilson, Jeanne	NJ0825	64A,48
Wilson, Joyce	IN0800	11,64A
Wilson, Leah	SC0050	48,64A
Wilson, Leah	SC0700	64A
Wilson, Ransom	CT0850	41,64A
Wilt, Lois J.	NY1700	32,64A
Wincenc, Carol	NY1900	64A,48
Wincenc, Carol	NY3790	64A
Winter-Jones, Kristin	MD0400	64A
Wistrom, LeAnne	PA1200	64A
Witek, Tanya D.	NJ0800	64A
Witnauer, Marlene P.	NY3717	64A
Witnauer, Marlene	NY3725	64A
Witt, Jeanne	IA0650	64A
Wolfersheim, Linda	WV0800	64A
Wolfson, Greer Ellison	CA5070	64A
Wolynec, Lisa	TN0050	11,64A
Wong, Betsy	MI1150	64A
Woodward, Gary	CA5300	64A
Woodward, Gary	CA3300	64A
Worthen, Douglas	IL2900	12A,64A
Yamamoto, Shirley	CA0805	64A
Yasinitsky, Ann	WA1150	48,64A
Yonce, Tammy Evans	SD0550	11,12A,64A,20
Yonce, Tammy	SC1100	64A
Yoo, Peggy	PA0600	64A
York, Molly	ID0100	64A
Yost, Regina Helcher	SC0275	64A,48
Young, Jay	IN1100	64A,64C,64E
Youngblood, Pamela J.	TX3300	41,64A,13A,13B,15
Younge, Shelley	AA0100	64A
Zellers, Jim A.	GA0750	64A
Zinninger, Heather	LA0900	64A
Zook, D.	MA0800	64A
Zook, Donald	MA0510	64A
Zook, Jeffrey	MI1750	64A
Zucker, Laurel	CA0150	64A
Zucker, Laurel	CA0840	64A,20G
Zukerman, Eugenia	NY2750	64A,42
Zuptich, Lory Lacy	MO0850	64A

Oboe

Name	Code	Areas
Ackerman, Mark	TX3350	64B
Acuff, Rachel	TN1000	64B
Adams, Ann M.	FL1750	64B,11,32C
Adduci, Michael D.	CA4400	64B
Aguirre, Sherrie Lake	VA0250	64B
Aguirre, Sherrie Lake	VA1000	64B
Ahlbeck, Laura	MA1400	64B
Aikens, Bill	MT0370	64B
Albert, Michael	ME0150	64B
Albert, Michael P.	ME0250	64B
Alberts, Katherine	KY0250	64B
Aldrich, Rachel	CA0810	64B
Aldrich, Rachel	CA1860	64B
Alvarez, Euridice	MS0750	64B
Alvarez, Euridice	NY1700	64B
Anderson, Amy B.	TX3200	11,64B
Anderson, Cynthia	WV0750	13,48,64B
Anderson, Robert	AR0350	64B,64C,64D,64E,47
Armfield, Terri E.	NC2600	64B,13
Armstrong, Heather M.	IA0950	13B,64B,32E
Atherholt, Robert	TX2150	64B
Atkinson, Keith	AG0300	64B,42
Atkinson, Keith	AG0450	64B
AuBuchon, Elaine	MO1780	64B,64D,11
Bach, Anne	IL3450	64B
Baer, Sarah	PA2450	64B,55B,12A,13E
Bailey, Mary Lindsey	CO0225	64B,11
Baker, Allison	IL3150	64B,64D
Baker, William	OH1850	64B
Banke, Andrea E.	KS1450	48,64B
Barker, Stephanie	WY0115	64B,64D
Barret, Mary Ashley	NC2430	64B
Barrier, Dawn	IN1450	64B
Barry, Thomas	IA1600	64B,64E,35C
Baskin, Ted	AI0150	64B
Beauchamp, Lise	AI0200	64B
Beerstein, Fred	CA0550	64B
Behr, Erik	NY3350	64B
Belfy, Jeanne M.	ID0050	11,12,64B
Bell, Charles V.	CA3400	64B
Bell, Scott F.	PA0550	64B
Bell, Scott	PA1050	64B,41
Belzer, Terrence	NJ1050	64B
Belzer, Terry	PA2800	64B
Bennett, Janice	MA2030	64B
Bennett, William	CA4150	64B
Bensdorf, Naomi	IL2100	64B
Benson, Beth	PA0400	64B
Benson, Jeremy L.	AL0500	64A,64B,12
Bentley, John E.	OH0300	64B
Benyas, Edward M.	IL2900	60,38,64B
Berk, Stacey J.	WI0850	13A,13B,64B,41,10F
Berkshire-Brown, Lorrie	VA0450	64B
Bernard, Jennifer	TX3100	64B
Bibzak, Ray	IL2650	64D,64B
Bibzak, Ray	IL2775	64B,64D
Bierhaus, Sarah	CO0650	64B
Bingham, Ann Marie	WV0400	12A,64B,64C,32E
Binkley, Lindabeth	MI0400	64B,41,48,11
Bishoff, Cheryl	NY4450	64B
Bishop, Barbara A.	MO1810	64B
Bleuel, John	GA2130	13C,60,64E,64B,64D
Bloomberg, Jennifer Wohlenhaus	IA0550	64B
Blumenfeld, Jonathan H.	PA3250	64B
Blumenfeld, Jonathan	NJ1130	64B
Bodner, Vicki Hope	NY2750	64B
Bolte, Barbara	AG0250	64B
Boone, Kathleen	WA0550	64B,64C,70,32E,13C
Booze, Leanna	TN0100	64B
Botti, Robert	NY2150	64B
Bowers, Teresa M.	PA1400	64A,64B,12A,36,42
Boyer, Neil V.	ME0500	64B
Boyer, Neil V.	NH0100	64B
Bramlett, KaDee	OK1330	64B
Breneman, Marianne Leitch	KY1000	11,64C,32E,64B
Bridges, Theresa	LA0050	64B
Brody, James	CO0800	11,64B
Brooks, Joseph H.	WA0050	41,48,64B,64C,64E
Brudnoy, Rachel	MN0800	64B
Brudnoy, Rachel	MN0950	64B
Brudnoy, Rachel	MN1625	64B
Burks, Robert	TN1350	64B
Burns, Noelle	WA0650	64B
Bussell, Lon	OH2550	64B
Button, James	TN1400	64B
Caltvedt, Emily	NC0250	64B
Campbell, John	CA2390	64B
Camus, Elizabeth	OH0600	48,64B
Caplan, Stephen	NV0050	64B,42,11
Carpenter, Nadine	VT0450	64B
Carr, Tracy A.	NM0100	64B,12A,41,64D,11
Casagrande, Angela	AG0400	64B
Castaneda, J. Ricardo	IL2200	64B
Castaneda, Ricardo	IL0275	64B
Castillo, Francisco J.	CA3650	64B
Castillo, Francisco	CA3500	64B
Castillo, Francisco	CA5150	64B
Castriotta, Gabrielle	CA0600	64B
Cathey, Jill	ID0140	64B
Caulder, Stephanie B.	PA1600	12A,12D,48,64B,13C
Cavanaugh, Jennifer Gookin	MT0400	64B,64D,13
Celidore, Daniel	CA4700	42,64B
Chang, Shirley	NY0050	64B
Chapman, Alicia	NC0050	55C,64B,32E
Chen-Beyers, Christina	ND0350	64B
Chernoff, Marea	AB0090	64B
Chernoff, Marea	AB0050	64B
Chernoff, Marea	AB0200	64B
Chernoff, Marea	AB0060	64B,48
Chest, Robert	SC0200	48,64B,64C,64D,64E
Christman, Ruth	FL0500	64B
Christy, Judy	FL0680	64B
Churchill, Steve	MD0550	64C,64E,64B
Cice, Erica	NC0550	64B
Cice, Erica	NC0850	64B
Cichy, Patricia Wurst	RI0150	32B,13C,64B,11,67D
Clardy, Michael	AR0750	64B
Clardy, Shannon	AR0300	64B
Clausen, Brett	CA0650	64B,32
Code, Belinda B.	AE0050	41,64A,64B,64D
Cohen, Fredric T.	MA2000	11,38,64B
Cohen, Lynne	NJ0700	64B,11
Cohick, Mark	MO2000	64E,64D,64B
Colburn, Steve	WI0825	64B
Cole, Roger	AB0200	64B
Cole, Roger	AB0100	64B
Collins, Amy	FL0930	64B
Collins, Amy	FL2000	64B
Collins, Amy	FL0450	64B
Collins, Cherie	ND0250	61,36,32D,64B
Colon Jimenez, Frances	PR0115	64B,41,42
Combs, Julia C.	MO0775	64B,13B,12A,11,13C
Comstock, Allan D.	KS0300	11,64B,64D,12A
Conaty, Donna	CA4100	64B
Condit, Sonja	SC1000	64B,64D
Cooper, Peter	CO0800	64B
Corbett, George	VA0150	64B
Corcoran, Kenda	NH0250	64B
Corina, John H.	GA2100	13,10,64B
Cosby, Tom	NE0610	64B
Costa, Robyn Dixon	PA1650	64B
Crews, Janice	GA2130	64B
Daglar, Fatma	MD0850	64B,48
Daglar, Fatma	MD0750	64B
Dahl Saville, Lara R.	GA1050	11,64B
Dallesio, Richard	NY2250	64B
Dallesio, Richard	NY0150	64B
Dansker, Judith	NY1600	64B
Davidson, Ian	TX3175	11,64B,41
Davis, Jonathan	CA5030	64B
Davis, Jonathan Doane	CA5020	64B
Davol, Sarah	NJ1400	64B
DeAlmeida, Cynthia K.	PA0550	64B
Dee, John	IL3300	64B,42
Deemer, Geoffrey	PA1550	64B
Deemer, Geoffrey A.	PA1300	64B
DeGruchy, Katherine	OH2500	64B
Del Russo, Catherine	CA3600	64B
Del Russo, Catherine	CA3300	64B
Delaplain, Theresa	AR0700	64B
Deloach, Doris	TX0300	48,64B
DeLuna, Russ	CA4150	64B
Diaz, Pedro	NY3790	64B
Dicker, Judith	IL1150	64B
Diggs, David B.	PA1950	13A,13B,37,64B,48
Diggs, David	PA2450	64B
Dimock, Nancy	CT0600	64B
Ding, Monica	CO0200	64B
Dirks, Jelena M.	IL0750	64B
Donner, George	IN1050	64B
Dorsey, Richard	AG0300	64B
Dorsey, Richard	AG0450	64B
Douglas, Susan	TX2650	64B
Douvas, Elaine	NY2250	64B
Douvas, Elaine	NY1900	64B
Dreisbach, Paul C.	OH1000	64B,64D,64E,64C,48
Driscoll, Robert	NC1650	64B
Driscoll, Robin	WV0600	64B
Drummond, Jayne	UT0325	64B
Dubois, Mark	NY3725	13,64B
Dubois, Mark	PA2250	64B
Dupuy, Kathryn D.	CO0550	64B
Duso, Lorraine	AR0350	64B
Duso, Lorraine C.	AR0850	64B,64D,11
Dutton, David	WA1350	64B
Eakin, Kate	IL2750	64B
Eberle, Jan	MI1400	64B
Edwards, Rachel	AZ0350	64B
Eischeid, Susan	GA2150	64B,11,48,42

Index by Area of Teaching Interest

Name	Code	Areas
Ellis, Randall	NY3650	64B
Emge, Jeffrey D.	TX3535	32,37,60,64B
Erb, Helen	LA0300	64B
Erickson, Scott	KY0950	48,64B,64D,64E
Erickson-Lume, Sarah	MN0750	64B
Ericson, Michael	IL3500	13B,13C,64B,48
Ernest, David J.	MN1300	13A,11,64B
Eubank, Beth	SC0200	32,64B
Evans, Joel	NY3760	37,64B,12A,13B,20
Farndale, Nancy	IA1750	64B,64D,66G
Farrell, Heidi	SD0600	64B,48
Faust, Sharon K.	IL1350	64B
Fedele, Andrea	MN0350	64B,64A
Fedele, Andrea	MN1300	64B
Fels, Carl	NM0310	64B
Ferillo, John	MA0400	64B
Ferrillo, John	MA1400	64B
Fiala, Michele	OH1900	64B,41,13B,13C,64D
Findley, Susan	MD0150	64B
Fink, Marc	WI0815	48,64B
Fisher, Mickey	GA0300	64B,64C,64E,48
Fleer, Lesley	IA0300	64B
Flegg, Lynne Mangan	OH0300	64B
Ford, Ronnal	NC2700	64,64B,11,64D,62A
Forget, Normand	AI0150	64B,48
Fossa, Matthew A.	FL1500	11,64B
Fossner, Alvin K.	NY4200	64B,64C,64E
Fox, Dana	KY1425	64B
Franklin, Ian	AG0500	64B
Freedland, Debra R.	IL0840	64B
Freedland, Debra	IL0850	64B
Freedland, Debra	IL1085	64B
Freedland, Debra	IL1300	64B
Frehner, Celeste Johnson	OK0800	64B,20,32E
French, Pam	IN1100	64B
French, Pamela A.	IN0100	64B
French, Pamela Ajango	IN1650	64B
Fronckowiak, Ann	TX2960	64B,13
Futterer, Kenneth	AR0200	10,48,64B,64D,64E
Gal, Peter	AB0100	64B
Gamerl, Darci	NE0100	64B
Gamerl, Darci	NE0160	64B,32E,67H
Gardner, Rebecca	SC0800	64B
Garvey, Christa N.	WI0803	13B,13C,64B
Geoffrey, Suzanne L.	WI0835	64B
Geoffrey, Suzanne	WI0100	64B
Geoffrey, Suzanne	WI0865	64B
Gershman, Laura	PA1450	64B
Ghez, Ariana	CA0960	64B
Gibson, Christopher A.	MO0950	11,64B,64C,64D,64E
Gibson, Colleen	AG0170	64B
Gibson, David	LA0770	13,64B,64D,29A
Gibson, Gerry	AR0250	64B
Giddings, Lorelei	MN0040	64B
Giddings, Lorelei	MN1050	64B
Gilad, Kimaree T.	CA0835	64B
Gillick, Amy	CA3100	64B,64D
Giovannetti, Geralyn	UT0050	13,48,64B
Glaser, Lise E.	OK1450	64B
Gnam, Adrian	GA1300	64B
Gnam, Adrian	GA0850	64B
Gnam, Adrian	GA0950	38,60,64B
Gomez, Kathleen	MI0520	64B
Gomez, Kathleen	MI0350	64B
Goodall, John W.	TX2700	64B
Gordon, Kirsten	PA3710	64B
Gordon, Kirstin	PA2350	64B,64D
Gornik, Holly	UT0250	64B
Gorton, James	PA1050	64B
Gould, Brooke	IA0600	64B,64C,64D,64E
Grabb, Henry	PA3600	64B,48
Grant, Donald R.	MI1600	64B,64C,64D,64E,13
Grant, Margaret	KY1000	13,64B
Grass, Mahlon O.	PA2050	12A,48,64B,64C,64E
Gresso, Selina	WA0800	64B
Griffiths, Laura	CA4200	64B
Gross-Hixon, Andrea	WI0830	64B
Gross-Hixon, Andrea	WI0750	64B
Grove, Lisa	OH2450	64B
Grove, Lisa	OH0450	64B
Grutzmacher, Patricia Ann	OH1100	32,41,64B,37,20
Grycel, Gail	VT0100	64B
Gullickson, Andrea	IN0250	64B,32
Gunn, Katherine	IN0800	64B
Gustafson-Hinds, Melissa	IL1740	64B
Guthrie, Beverly	MI1150	64B
Hages, Brent	WA0050	64B
Haines, Yvonne Bonnie	TX1400	64B,64D
Haley, Jill	PA2550	64B
Halko, Joe	MA0650	64B
Halko, Joseph	MA0700	64B
Hall, Crystal	WI0250	64B
Hall, Louis O.	ME0440	60,32,64B,64E
Hall, W. Randall	WV0300	64B,64C,64E,48
Hamann, Charles	AG0400	64B
Hamilton, Heather	TX2750	64B,66D
Hamilton, Sarah Jean	NY3725	13,64B
Hammond, Rebecca	MI1750	64B
Hanley, Bede	AC0100	64B
Hannigan, Erin	TX2400	64B
Harel, Jack	OH2150	64B
Harper, Denis B.	CA0850	64B
Harter, Courtenay L.	TN1200	13,64B,41
Harvey-Reed, Lisa	OK0750	64B
Harwood, Karen	GA1500	64B,64D
Hauser, Jared E.	TN1850	64B
Hawkins, Sherwood M.	FL1550	64B,48
Hedrick, Teresa	VA0550	64C,64E,64A,64B
Heersche, Kim	KY0450	64B
Heershe, Kim	KY1350	64B
Heinze, Thomas	PA2200	64B,46,41
Heller, Marsha	NJ0825	64B
Heller, Marsha	NJ0800	48,64B
Helvering, Emily		64B
Henderson, Rebecca	TX3510	64B
Hendrickson, Anna	NY3780	64B,11
Henkel, Sussan	NH0150	64B
Henoch, Michael L.	IL2250	64B
Hensley, Maria	MO0400	64B
Hepler, Julie E.	PA0100	64B,64C,12A,64D,64E
Herbert, David	TX3530	13,64B
Herbert, David	TX2200	13A,64B,32,13B,13C
Herbert, David P.	TX2260	64B
Herlehy, Margaret	NH0350	64B
Heuer, Megan	TX2250	64B
Hida, Kyoko	MA0350	64B
Highstein, Gustav	VA1500	64B
Hill, Aaron S.	VA1550	64B
Hill, Mark	MD1010	64B
Hinkeldey, Jeanette	IA0150	13,64B,64D,66
Hobbs, James D.	TX3300	64B
Hochkeppel, Robin M.	LA0760	64B,64D
Hoffer, Heike	TX3525	64B,11,32
Holden, Valerie	AD0050	64B
Hollander, Alan	NY1600	64B,42
Homann, Ann	MO1830	64B
Homann, J. Oliver	CT0050	64B
Horn, Stuart	CA5550	64B
Horn, Stuart	CA5060	64B
Hosmer, Karen E.	NY3600	64B,13
Hough, Robin Z.	TX3400	64B
Hoy, Andria	OH0100	64B
Huckleberry, Heather	IA0250	11,64B
Hughes, Nathan	NY1900	64B
Hughes, Nathan N.	NJ1130	64B
Hughes, Susan K.	ID0100	64B
Hurley, David R.	KS1050	12,20,64B
Hurtz, Timothy	PA2750	64B
Ignatiou, Connie	KY0550	64B
Iimori, Mitch	OR0250	64B,64D
Iimori, Mitch	OR0400	64B
Iimori, Mitch	OR0150	64B,64D
Iimori, Mitch	OR1300	64B
Iimori, Mitch S.	OR1100	64B,64D
Ingle, Jennet	IN1750	64B,48
Ingliss, Robert B.	NY0500	64B
Ingliss, Robert	NY3785	64B
Izotov, Eugene A.	IL0750	64B
Izotov, Eugene	IL0550	64B
Izquierdo, Pablo	WA1100	64B
Jakubiec, Aaron F.	IL0800	11,64B,13B
Jeffrey, Sarah	AG0300	64B,42
Jenkins, Cara M.	NC1250	64B,48
Jenkins, Carl	MA2250	64B,41
Jinright, John W.	AL1050	13,64D,34,64B,66A
Johnson, Kendra	UT0350	64B
Johnson, Ryann P.	NE0200	64B,64D
Johnson, Ryann	NE0150	64B,64D
Johnson, Trevor	IN1010	64B
Johnson, Trevor	KY0400	64B
Jossim, J.	FL0800	64B,37,32C
Juilianna, Anita	FL0150	64B,64D
Juza, Alan	OR0750	64B
Kehrberg, Donald A.	KS0200	64B,37,32
Kennedy, Sarah	FL1450	64B
Khaner, Lidia	AA0110	64B
Kidwell, Curtis	CA0150	64B
Kiene, Kristi	GA0200	64B
Killmer, Richard	CT0850	64B
Killmer, Richard	NY1100	64B
Killmeyer, Heather N.	TN0500	64B,12A,11,64D
King, Nancy Ambrose	MI2100	64B
King, Stanley	WI0845	64B
Kirkdorffer, Michele B.	VA0600	64B
Kistler, Karen	SC0275	64B
Kitagawa, Nobuo	PA1850	64B
Klemp, Merilee I.	MN0050	12A,12,64B,48,40
Klemp, Merilee	MN0300	64B
Knipschild, Ann	AL0200	13,48,64B,64E
Kobernik, Lynnette	CA3800	64B,11
Koch, Elizabeth	GA1150	64B
Korman, Fred	OR0700	64B
Kostilnik, Rise	PA3000	64B
Kozenko, Lisa A.	NY5000	64B
Krause, Kristi	WI0810	64B
Krause, Kristi	MN1700	64B,41
Krause, Robert	TX3750	64B,13,55C
Kravitz, Steve	OR0450	64B,64E,64C,29,11
Kyle, Janice	NY3775	64B
Laclair, Jaqueline	NY2150	64B
LaFitte, Barbara	MA2050	64B,42
Lagarenne, Cecile	TX2955	64B
Laib, Jean	PA2150	41,64B,64D
Lambrecht, Cynthia A.	IL0100	64B,11
Lampidis, Anna	NC2205	64B,48
Lampidis, Anna	NC2500	64B
Landa, Jean	AA0050	64B
Lande, Vladimir	MD1000	64B
Lande, Vladimir	MD0100	64B
Lanini, Phyllis	NY2400	64B
Larsen, Karli	WI1150	64B,63B
Lathwell, John	NY3705	64B
Lawson, Tonya	TN1100	64C,64E,64B,11
Lay, Lara	AL1250	64B
Lazarus, Gordon	CA0200	64B,66D
LeClair, Jacqueline	NY2150	64B
Leclair, Jacqueline F.	AI0150	64B,41
Leek, Anne	TX3400	64B
Lemieux, Suzanne	AF0100	64B
Lenz, Andrea	NV0100	13,64B,66C
Levia, Beth	AA0100	64B
Lewis, Nora A.	KS0650	64B,12A,11
Libby, Cynthia Green	MO0775	13,64B,64D,20,48
Lillya, Ann	GA0050	64B,48
Lindberg, Martha	MN1000	64B
Lipkens, Kirsten	MA1350	64B
Lisicky, Sandra	MD0650	64B
Liu, Rong-Huey	CA2420	64B
Loch, Kim	OH2300	64B
Logan, Susan	MT0175	64B
Logan, Susan	MT0350	64B
Lorance, Elana	MA0510	64B
Lorch, Kimberly	GA0500	11,64B
Lucarelli, Bert	NY0500	64B
Lucarelli, Humbert	NY2750	64B
Lucarelli, Humbert	NY3785	64B
Lucarelli, Humbert	CT0650	41,64B
Lundberg, Susan	CA0800	64B
MacMillan, Robin	AC0100	64B
Madsen, Emily K.	MD0350	64B,64D
Madura, Julie	MN0250	64B
Maeda, Dana	MN1450	64B,42
Majoy, Jocelyn	OH1400	64B,64D
Manning, Dwight C.	NY4200	64,42,32E,11,64B
Mapes, Randy	MS0100	64B,64D
Marchione, Jill	PA2300	64B
Marchione, Jill	PA3150	64B,41
Marchione, Jill	PA1900	64B
Marchione, Jill	PA0950	64B
Marchione, Jill M.	PA1250	64B
Marco, Margaret	KS1350	64B,13
Markowitz, Audrey	MA0950	64B
Marks, Erin	AB0200	64B
Marks, Melissa	MI0050	64B
Martchev, Valentin	CA4100	64B
Marvine, Jane	MD0650	64B

Index by Area of Teaching Interest

Name	Code	Areas
Marzluf, Jonathan	CA2390	64B
Marzluf, Jonathan	CA1425	64B
Mason, James	AG0600	64B
Masoudnia, Elizabeth	PA3250	64B
Mather-Stow, Andrea	IN0910	64B
Matheson, James	CA4900	64B
Mattix, Anna	NY0400	64B
Mattix, Anna L.	NY3717	64B
Mattix, Anna L.	NY4320	64B
Mattson, Sheri	MO1790	11,64B,64D
Mausolf, Susan	NE0450	64B
Mayhew, Rebecca S.	OH0650	64B
McCarthy, Keri E.	WA1150	64B,12A,13,11,12C
McCarty, Evelyn	TX2930	64B
McCarty, Evelyn	TX0550	64B
McCarty, Karena	PA0350	64B
McEwen, Mark	MA1400	64B
McGarity, Kristin A.	MT0200	10B,34,64B
McGuire, David O.	OH0650	64B
McLemore, Katherine	OK1330	64B
McMullen, William W.	NE0600	13,12A,64B
McNabb, Carol	TX3515	13B,13C,64D,67C,64B
McNerney, Kathleen	ME0200	64B,48
Medisky, Laura M.	WI0840	64B
Meggison, Shelly	AL1170	64B,11
Meretta, Kristy	MI0600	64B
Mertz, Tonya	ND0400	64B
Messich, Reid	GA2100	64B
Meyer, Frederick	WV0650	13,32,48,64B
Michel, Peggy	IL0550	64B,42
Michel, Peggy	IL0730	64B
Mieses, Nermis	KY1450	64B,13C,41
Miller, Jessica	NC2440	64B
Miller, Jessica	SC0420	64B
Miller, Michael	MI2250	13,48,64B
Minch, Claudia	FL1950	64B
Mindock, Rebecca A.	AL1300	64B,64D,12A,34,42
Mitchell, Patricia	CA5070	64B
Modin, Lindsay	KS0700	64B
Moody, Gary E.	CO0250	64B,13,41,64D
Moore, James	CA4150	64B
Morehead, Patricia	IL0720	10F,10,64B
Morgan, Paige	NY1800	64B
Mori, Paul	CA5550	37,64B
Morton, Gregory	IA1800	64B,64D
Murray, Jane	RI0250	64B
Murray, Jane	RI0300	38,41,48,64B
Nagel, Rebecca S.	SC1110	11,64B,41
Nauful, Lisa	CA0600	64B,64D
Needleman, Katherine	MD0650	64B
Nelson, Lizzy	UT0190	64B
Nelson, Nancy	AG0200	64B
Newsome, Bo N.	NC0600	64B
Newsome, Bo	NC0650	64B,13C
Niblock, Howard	WI0350	13,10F,12B,41,64B
Nicholson, Tina	IL1750	13,64B
Niles, Melinda Smith	MD0520	64B
Nugent, Thomas	CA2950	64B
Nugent, Thomas	CA5350	64B,41,42
Ochi-Onishi, Susan M.	HI0210	64B
Odell, Kelly	GA0250	64B
Odello, Denise	MN1620	11,12,64B,14,20
Odem, Susan K.	IA0200	64B,64D
Odem, Susan	IA1350	64B,64D
Odem, Susan	IA0650	64D,20,64B,64E
Odom, Leslie S.	FL1850	13,64B
Oft, Eryn	AL0500	64B,64D,12A,12C
Ohlsson, Eric	FL0850	48,64B
O'Leary, Jay	IA1100	64B,64D
Orson, Beth	AB0100	64B
Ortwein, Mark	IN1100	64B
Ostoich, Mark S.	OH2200	64B
Owens, Douglas A.	TN1720	64B,64D,13
Owens, Meg	DC0010	64B
Padgham Albrecht, Carol	ID0250	11,12A,64B,32E,41
Parker, Andrew	IA1550	64B
Parrish, Bill	VA1125	64B,64C
Parrish, Bill	VA0750	64B
Patterson, Ann	CA1750	29,64B,64E
Paul, Jeffrey	SD0050	64B
Pena, Melissa	OR1050	64B,11
Perkins, Tedrow	OH2600	13,64B
Peterson, Jennifer	MN0600	64B
Peterson, Jennifer L.	MN1120	64B
Peterson, Jon	AG0200	64B
Peyton, Heather	IA0850	64B
Pfeiffer, Karen	OH2000	64B,11
Philipp, Hilary	PA0100	64B
Philipsen, Dane	GA1150	64B
Philipsen, Dane	GA0750	64B
Phillips, Christine	IL1400	64B
Phillips, Christine	IL0730	64B
Piecuch, Katherine H.	MS0700	64B
Pimentel, Bret R.	MS0250	64,29,64B,11,64C
Plaza-Martin, Denise	RI0200	64B
Plowman, Gary	WA0400	64B
Pochatko, Amanda R.	OH2140	64B,42
Pohran Dawkins, Alexandra	AB0150	42,64B
Polcyn, Sandra	WI0700	64D,64B,32E
Poling, Mary	MD0400	64B
Polk, Kristin	KY1550	64B,64D,32E,13A,13B
Popham, Phillip F.	MI2000	64B,10B,13C
Potochnic, Jennifer	KY1500	64B
Preacher, Patrick Dale	SC0600	64B
Price, Andrew	MA0400	64B
Prins, Rene	NY3765	64B,37,13,41
Prins, Rene	NY1400	64B
Quaile, Robert	PA3330	32,64B
Ramsay, Ginger	GA2300	64B
Rath, Richard	OK0850	64,64B,64E
Rathbun, Jeffrey	OH0600	64B
Rathbun, Jeffrey J.	OH0200	64B
Rathke, Sarah	CA5000	64B
Ray, Kathryn	IN0400	64B
Reamsnyder, Richard	OH2275	64B,64D
Reed, Richard	DC0150	64B
Reeve, Basil	MN1623	64B
Register, P. Brent	PA0700	12A,48,64A,64B,64D
Reid, Sally	TN0930	10,13,64B,10C,34
Renteria, Gabriel	MI0100	64B
Resnick, Anna	OK1250	64B,64D
Reynolds, Kristen	MI0500	64B
Reynolds, Kristin	MI1000	64B
Reynolds, Lindsey Bird	WY0115	64B
Reynolds, Lindsey	WY0200	64B
Reynolds, Shawn	PA3650	64B
Rhodes, Rhonda L.	UT0150	64B,64E
Ridilla, Andrea	OH1450	64B,48
Riordan, George T.	TN1100	67D,11,64B
Robertson, Elizabeth A.	IN1600	64B,11,41
Robinson, Joseph	FL1125	64B
Robock, Alison	IL0400	64B,11
Rockett, Susetta	TX0900	64B
Roe, Roger A.	IN0900	64B
Rosario, Harry	PR0150	13A,13C,37,60B,64B
Rosenberg, Steven	OH0850	64B
Rosenwein, Frank	OH0600	64B,41
Ross, Daniel F.	AR0110	11,41,64B,64D,72
Ross, Donald	MO0100	64D,64B
Ross, Laura	MO1900	64B
Ross, Laura Guyer	MO1500	64B,64D
Ross, Laura A.	TN1100	48,64B
Rydlinski, Candy	AK0150	64B
Rygg, Beth	SD0580	64B
Sakins, Renate	PA3100	13,64,64B
Sauerwein, Andrew Mark	MS0100	13,10,29B,43,64B
Savage, Susan	NC2420	64B
Sayre, Lora	GA1700	64B
Scarnati, Rebecca Kemper	AZ0450	64B,13,41
Schabloski, Lana	AF0120	64B
Schaefer, Lora	IL0550	64B
Schlabach, Robert	TN0450	64A,64B,64C,64E
Schlaffer, Machiko Ogawa	AL1200	64B
Schleiffer, Marlene J.	IN0700	10,64B
Schmalzbauer, Julie A.	IL2300	64B
Schneider, David	NJ0175	64B
Schneider, Lisa A.	AL1160	11,64B,41
Schoeff, Bethany	WA0250	64B
Scholfield, Faith	AG0550	64B
Scholtz, Clare	AG0450	64B
Schroeder, Waylon	IL1500	64B,64E
Schultz, Michael	NC2410	64B
Schuring, Martin	AZ0100	64B
Schwartz, Daniel	OK1350	64B,41
Scott, Carla A.	CO0275	64B,42
Scott, Geri	WY0130	64B
Scott, Jan	LA0350	32B,48,64B,64D,64C
Secan, Steve	OH0350	64B
Secrist, Phylis	TN1710	64B
Seedorf, Bethany	IA1300	64B
Seeman, Sharon	NJ0750	64A,64B,64C,64D,11
Seerup, Mark	MN0610	64B
Seshadri, Jaleen	CA4425	64B
Shankle, Robert	TN1600	64B,64C,64E
Shapiro, Stephanie	MI2200	64B
Sharp, Pat	NY1350	64B
Sharrock, James	NH0110	64B
Shatalov, Alexandra	NY2650	64B
Sheena, Robert	MA0400	64B
Sheena, Robert	MA0350	64B,63B
Sheena, Robert	MA1400	64B
Sheena, Robert	MA1175	64B
Sherman, Ellen	MI0300	64B
Sherman, Paul	CA1000	64B
Sherman, Paul	CA1265	64B,60
Shidler, Deborah	CA0900	64B
Shidler, Deborah A.	CA0807	64B
Shidler, Deborah	CA0840	64B
Sholl, Martha	NY3350	64B
Shook, Gregory	WV0550	64B
Shorter, Lloyd	DE0150	48,64B,12A
Shultz, Betty Sue	OH2290	64B,42
Sirotkin, Leonid	IN0350	64B
Skovenski, Michael	NY0650	64B
Skuster, Sarah	CA4100	64B
Smith, Malcolm	IN0250	64B
Smith, Peter	PA3250	64B
Snow, John	MN1623	64B
Snyder, Mark	NY2105	64B
Snyder, Mark S.	CT0800	64B,48,11
Soelberg, Diane	ID0060	48,64B,60
Sorton, Bailey	OH1600	64B
Sorton, Bailey	OH1200	64B,48
Sorton, Robert	OH1850	64B
Southard, Sarah	MI1050	64B,11
Spicciati, Shannon	WA1050	64B
Spires, Henry Ray	SC1080	64B,64C,64D,64E
Stabile-Libelo, Carole	DC0100	64B
Stacy, Thomas	NY2150	64B
Stanichav, Kristi	IA0500	64B
Stanley, Ed L.	PA1400	64B,42,13A,13C,11
Stanley, Ed	MD0500	64B
Stearns, Anna Petersen	NY4150	64B
Stees, Rhonda L.	VA0100	64B,62
Stellar, Krista	IL1100	64B
Steltenpohl, Anna C.	NY3730	64B,48
Sterling, Amy	MD0800	64C,64E,64B,64D,64A
Stevens, Melissa	OH2050	64B
Stevenson, Deborah	IL3550	64B
Stilwell, Kenneth	DC0170	64B
Stine, Maria W.	NC0350	64B,64D
Stitt, Virginia K.	UT0200	11,32B,64B,64D,12A
Stokes, Harvey J.	VA0500	13,10,64B,34
Stolz, Lissa J.	LA0650	64B
Stone, Joseph	CA6000	64B,64E
Stone, Joseph	CA0825	64B
Storch, Laila	WA1050	41,64B
Stovall, Nicholas	DC0050	64B
Strand, Karen	OR0850	64B,11
Strand, Karen	OR0450	64B
Strefeler, Jamie	FL1800	64B,48
Strommen, Linda	IN0900	64B
Strommen, Linda	NY1900	64B
Sullivan, James	AL0300	64B
Sullivan, James B.	AL1150	64B
Sullivan, James B.	AL0800	64B
Sullivan, Matt E.	NY2750	64B
Sulzinski, Valerie	NY2550	64B
Sulzinski, Valerie	NY2105	64B
Sundet, Danna	OH1100	64B
Sussman, David	AA0200	64B
Sussman, David	AA0150	64B
Sussman, David	AA0050	64B
Swanson, Karin	IA1200	64B
Sweeney, Aryn D.	IN0150	64B
Swidnicki, Susan	UT0400	64B
Sycks, Linda	OH1800	64B
Sycks, Linda	OH0250	64B
Sylar, Sherry	NY2250	64B
Takahashi, Hiromi	AA0035	64B
Tatman, Neil E.	AZ0500	64B,48
Taylor, Stephen G.	CT0850	64B,42
Taylor, Stephen	NY2150	64B
Thee, Lawrence	NC0930	64B,64C,64D,64E
Thompson, Cindy	KS0200	64B
Timm, Joel	CA5300	64B

Index by Area of Teaching Interest

Name	Code	Areas
Timm, Laurance	CA0815	37,48,64B
Tomoff, Lisa Geering	CA5040	64B
Tosser, Michele	OH0950	64B
Turanchik, Thomas	NC0750	64B,64C,64D,48
Ulaky, Hollis B.	SC1200	64B
Ulaky, Hollis	NC2000	64B
Van Brunt, Laurie	WI0860	64B
Van Brunt, Laurie	MN1600	64B
Van Brunt, Laurie	MN0450	64B
Van Cleve, Libby	CT0100	64B
Vaneman, Kelly McElrath	SC0650	12A,64B,42,55,14
VanValkenburg, Holly	CO0050	64B
Variego, Jorge	ND0600	10,13B,48,64C,64B
Vavrikova, Marlen	MI0900	64B
Veazey, Charles	TX3420	41,64B
Ventura, Brian J.	MI2200	64B
Vigneau, Kevin	NM0450	64B,13A,13
Vigneau, Michelle	TN1680	64B,42,13
Viton, John	KY0900	13,64B
Vogel, Allan	CA1075	64B,42,55B
Vogel, Allan	CA5300	64B
Vogel, Allan	CA0510	12A,55B,64B,13C
Vogel, Michael	AZ0510	64B
Waddell, Mike	NC2440	64B,64C,64D,11,32
Wagoner, Lisa	OK0550	64B
Wakao, Keisuke	MA1175	64B
Wakao, Keisuke	MA1400	64B
Walker, John L.	VA1700	64B,13,14,20H
Wall, Sarah	NY4050	64B,11
Walters, Robert	OH1700	64B
Wang, Liang	NY2750	64B
Wang, Liang-yu	NY2150	64B
Ward, Ann	FL0400	64B
Warlick, Gerald	OK1200	64B
Warlick, Gerald	OK0700	64B
Warneck, Petrea	SC0400	64B
Warneck, Petrea	SC0750	64B,11
Warren, Cynthia	OH0700	64B
Warth, James R.	TX2960	47,64E,64B
Webster, Kim	PA1750	64B
Weiner, Robert A.	FL1900	41,64B
Weiss, David	CA5300	64B
Weiss, David	CA0825	64B
Welk, Shawn	VA1600	64B
Werth, Kay	KS0350	64B,64D,48,64A
West, Jill	IL1200	64B,64D
Whalen, Eileen M.	OH2250	64B
White, Julian E.	FL0600	60,32C,37,64A,64B
Wiesmeyer, Roger	TN1850	64B
Wilkinson, Donald G.	TX3520	64B,64D,64E,46,32H
Willett, Dan L.	MO1800	64B,48
Williams, Dan	WA1000	64B
Williams, Stewart	TX3000	64B
Wilsden, Melanie	NC1300	64B
Wise, Sherwood W.	NY0700	64B,48,13,64D,42
Wlazlo, Tricia L.	IL2050	64B
Woebling-Paul, Cathy	MO0650	64B
Woebling-Paul, Cathleen	MO1950	64B
Wohlenhaus, Jennifer	IA0700	64B,64D
Womack, Jeffrey	TX0150	12A,64B,64D
Woodard, Leigh Ann	AK0100	64B
Woodhams, Richard	PA0850	48,64B
Woodhams, Richard	PA3250	64B
Woodworth, William	TN1450	64B,13B,13C,41,66G
Woolsey, Katherine E.	KS1400	64B
Wright, Lon	MN1500	64D,64E,64B
Wunch, Doreen	WI1155	64B
Wunsch, Doreen	WI1150	64B
Yingst, Benjamin	AZ0350	64B
Young, Katherine	FL2050	64B
Zyko, Jeanette	TN0050	11,64B,64D

Clarinet

Name	Code	Areas
Abrams, Colleen	OH2275	64C,64E
Abrams, David	NY2950	13C,11,41,64C,12A
Acevedo-Hernandez, Victor	IA0400	64C
Acord, Michael D.	KY1350	64C
Adderley, Cecil L.	MA0260	32E,32F,32G,62A,64C
Aguirre, Ruth	TX2260	64C
Alaniz, Steve	CA5100	64E,64C
Aldrich, Simon	AI0150	64C,48
Aleksander, Elizabeth	NE0400	64C,12A
Allen, David R.	VA1100	64C,64E
Allen, Mark	CA0150	64C
Almich, Michael	OR1000	64C,64E
Alter, Adam M.	SC0800	64C,51
Ambler, Don	CO0150	64C
Amsel, Stephen	AA0150	64C
Anderle, Jeffrey	CA4150	64C,48
Anderson, Carl H. C.	AL0500	13,48,64A,64C
Anderson, Marcia H.	MI1200	64C
Anderson, Robert	AR0350	64B,64C,64D,64E,47
Andrews, Christy D.	OK1450	64C
Andrews, Christy	OK0850	64C
Andrus, Deborah E.	PA2450	64C,48,41
Angerstein, Nancy	TX1450	64C
Annis, Robert L.	NJ1350	64C,43
Araujo, Ramon	PR0125	13,10,37,64C
Ardan, Laura	GA0750	64C
Ardovino, Lori	AL1200	12A,48,64C,64E,67C
Armstrong, Laura D.	MD0300	64C
Armstrong, Robert	OR1010	12A,63A,64C,64A
Arvin, Tammy J.	IL1090	13,64C
Ascione, Ray A.	MD0060	47,64C,64E
Askvig, Jamie	WY0115	64C
Aufmann, Ronald	OH2200	64C
Aufmann, Ronald	KY1000	64C
Ayer, Christopher	TX2700	64C
Babad, Bruce	CA1900	47,48,64A,64C,64E
Bacon, Marcy D.	NY2650	64C,48
Baer, Solomon	IL1750	64C
Baez, Luis	CA4150	64C
Balch, Mary W.	AL1160	64E,64C
Balfany, Gregory J.	WI0810	47,64C,46,29
Ballif, Adam	ID0060	32C,32E,64C
Bambach, Paul	CA5060	64C,48
Banks, Christy A.	PA2350	35A,64C,64E
Barbanera, William	FL1745	64C,64E
Barger, Diane C.	NE0600	42,64C
Barker, John C.	AL1300	64C,41
Barlar, Nancy	FL0670	64C,32B,32C,32E,11
Barnetson, Ginger K.	CA4425	64C
Barrett, Gregory M.	IL2200	48,64C
Barron, Christine	FL1550	64C
Barta, Steven E.	MD0650	64C
Bartels, Cindi	OR1300	64C,48
Bartels, Cindi	OR1250	64C
Bartels, Cindi	OR0250	64C
Bartley, Linda L.	WI0815	64C
Baruth, Lori E.	KY0900	13B,13C,64C
Batiste, Alvin	LA0700	64A,64C,29,47,35A
Beacham, Karen	ME0200	64C
Beard, Charles	KS1050	64C,64E
Becraft, Steven C.	AR0300	64C,29A,64E,48,32E
Bednarzyk, Stephen C.	GU0500	60,37,64C,66A
Begelman, Igor	NY0500	64C
Behm, Gary	MT0175	37,64C,64E,64A
Behn, Bradford	OK0750	64C,41
Bell, Carey	CA4150	64C
Bell, David	WI0350	41,64C
Bell, Timothy R.	WI0835	47,64C,64E,29,48
Bellman, David	IN1650	64C
Belter, Babette	OK0800	32E,64C
Belzer, Katie	GA0850	64C
Benda, Karen L.	KS1400	64C,48
Bender, Rhett	OR0950	64E,13,52,64C
Bendzsa, Paul	AD0050	60,47,64C,64E
Berlin, Janet	PA1650	64C
Bibbey, Marianne	WY0130	64C
Bingham, Ann Marie	WV0400	12A,64B,64C,32E
Bish, Deborah	FL0850	64C
Blackie, Ruth	AF0120	64C,13
Bloch, Gus	VT0200	64C,64E
Blood, Curt	CT0600	48,64C
Blood, Curtis	CT0650	64C
Bloom, J. Lawrie	IL2250	64C
Bocaner, Lawrence	DC0050	64C
Boese, Jessica	IL1050	64C
Boggs, Isabelle	MA1100	20,64C,62A,62B
Boggs, Isabelle	MA2100	20,64C
Boisvert, Jean-Guy	AE0100	41,64C,64E
Bombardier, Bradley A.	MN1600	64C,64E,1
Bonds, Nancy	CA3100	64C
Bonenfant, Timothy	TX0150	64C,64E,47
Bonneau, Sharon J.	VA0450	64C
Boone, Kathleen	WA0550	64B,64C,70,32E,13C
Borchert, Laroy	NM0310	13,32,64C
Borgstedt, Bryson	SC1000	64E,47,64C
Bourque, David	AG0450	48,37,38,64C,60B
Bovyer, Gary S.	CA3650	64C
Bradford, Daron	UT0050	64C,64E
Brandenburg, Mark	CA4900	64C
Brandenburg, Mark	CA5070	64C
Brandon, Mark	AL0500	32B,32C,64C
Brannen, Randall	OH1400	64C,64E
Bratton, Susanna	MI0300	64C
Breneman, Marianne Leitch	KY1000	11,64C,32E,64B
Bresnian, Chester	MA0650	64C
Brewer, Suzann	MO0350	64C
Bridges, Scott	AL1170	41,64C
Britz, Joanne M.	KS1050	64C,64E,41
Brooks, Joseph H.	WA0050	41,48,64B,64C,64E
Brown, Beverly	NC1400	11,29A,47,37,64C
Brown, Frances A.	RI0250	64C,32C
Brown, James	FL1300	11,12A,38,64C
Brumbelow, Denise	MI1180	64E,64C
Brumbelow, Rosemary	WI0830	64C
Brumbelow, Rosemary	IA0950	64C
Bruner, Regina	MO1550	64C
Bryant, Mary	MO0650	64C
Burke, Kelly J.	NC2430	64C
Burr, Anthony	CA5050	64C,43,13D,14C,12D
Burrow, Chad E.	MI2100	64C
Bush, Christopher	NY2750	64C,41,42,48
Bustos, Pamela B.	WI0860	32E,37,48,60B,64C
Butts, Beverly Ann K.	PA1900	64C,48,64
Campbell, Arthur J.	MI0900	64C,64E,13
Campbell, Bonnie H.	IL3450	64C
Campbell, James	IN0900	64C
Campbell, Jeff	AA0100	64C
Campione, Carmine	OH2200	64C
Campos, Wagner	IL0750	64C
Caravan, Ronald L.	NY4150	64C,64E
Card, Patricia P.	TX2250	64C
Carl, Jane	MO1810	64C
Carlson, Patti	VA0150	64C
Carlson, Patti	VA0250	48,64C
Carlson, Patti F.	VA1000	48,64C
Carnahan, Deborah	CA0825	64C
Carney, Anna	TX2800	11,13A,14C,64C
Carney, Anna	TX2650	64C,64E
Carpentier, Gilles	AI0210	64C
Carpentier, Martin	AI0200	64C
Carroll, Donald H.	CA4200	64C
Carson, William S.	IA0300	60B,37,12A,32E,64C
Carter, David	AR0730	64C,64E,48,11
Carucci, Brian	NY3600	64C
Casey, J. Warren	AR0250	10F,11,32,47,64C
Chance, Chris	TX3527	64C
Chance, Christopher	TX1850	64C
Chandler, Sarah	NY3705	64C
Chandra, Bharat	FL1745	64C
Chappell, Rebecca Ann	IN0100	64C,64E,35A,64D
Cheeseman, Andrea L.	NC0050	64C,32E
Chen, Ixi	OH2200	64C
Chesher, Michael	IA0950	32E,42,64C,64E
Chest, Robert	SC0200	48,64B,64C,64D,64E
Cholthitchanta, Nophachai	AR0700	64C
Christensen, Donald	NY0500	32E,64C,64
Christie, Max	AG0450	64C
Christofferson, Carol	AZ0480	64C,13
Christopher, Evan	LA0800	64C,47
Churchill, Steve	MD0550	64C,64E,64B
Cifelli, Cheryl L.	MO0800	64C,64D,12A,11,13E
Cigan, Paul	DC0050	64C
Cigan, Paul	MD1010	64C
Cionitti, Linda A.	GA0950	48,64C
Cipolla, John M.	KY1550	41,64C,64E
Clark, Antoine	OH1200	64C,64E,48
Clark, Antoine T.	OH0850	12A,72,48,64,64C
Clements, Gordon	AB0210	46,47,29B,64E,64C
Clifton, Artie	FL1000	37,64C
Climie, Stan	AA0150	64C
Climie, Stanley	AA0050	12A,48,64C
Coad, Daryl L.	TX3420	64C
Coccagnia, Lou	NY1150	64C,64E
Coggiola, Jill A.	NY4150	32E,64C,64E
Cohen, Franklin	OH0600	64C,48
Cohen, Steven	IL2250	64C
Cohill, Gregory	IL1610	64C,64E
Cohler, Jonathan	MA0350	64C
Cohler, Jonathan	MA1175	64C
Colarusso, Joey	TX2170	64C,11
Cole, Monty	GA1300	29,32E,46,64C,64E

Index by Area of Teaching Interest

Name	ID	Codes
Cole, Roger	ID0250	11,64C
Colella, Lou M.	PA1450	64C,64E
Colella, Louis	PA3650	64C,64E
Coleman, Ron	WA1100	64C
Collerd, Gene J.	IL3310	13A,60,37,64C
Colosimo, Murray B.	NJ1160	64C,38
Colquhoun, Jocelyn	AA0050	64C
Combs, Larry R.	IL0750	64C
Cook, Lawrence	HI0050	48,64A,64C,64E
Coope, Ann-Katherine	AB0200	64C
Corley, Paula	TX3100	64C
Costa, Anthony J.	PA2750	64C
Costigan, Christopher	GA2050	64C,64E
Cotter, Daniel	WA0950	38,64C,13B,13C
Cotter, Daniel	WA0250	64C
Cox, Lauren J.	OK0300	64C,64E,13,13C
Craig, Gordon	AG0250	37,64C,48,38,41
Crawford, Elizabeth A.	IN0150	64C,35F
Crawford, Thomas	VA0350	64A,64C,64E
Crawford, Tom	TN1150	64C,64E,64A
Crews, Norval	TX1700	11,64C,64E,72
Crosson, Gail	IL0850	32,64C
Crowley, Robert	AI0150	64C
Cullen, Christopher	CT0800	64C,41
Cullen, Danielle	PA1550	64C
Cummings, Paul C.	CA2250	32,37,38,64C
Cunningham, Randall	MO2000	64C
Curlette, Bruce	OH0450	13,64C,10F
Curran, Kathryn	GA0050	64C
Daniels, John	FL0600	13,32C,64A,64C
Dannessa, Karen	PA3600	64C,48
Deadman, Alison Patricia	TN0500	12A,64C
Dean, Martin	GA2000	64C
DeBenedetto, Patricia	CA1860	32E,37,64E,64C,48
del Grazia, Nicolas M.	AR0200	32E,41,48,64C
DeLuca, Laura	WA0200	64C
DeLuca, Mike	CO0275	13,64C,11,32
DeMartino, Louis	OR1050	42,48,64C
Demers, Paul	PA3250	64C
DeMol, Karen	IA0500	64C,13C
Denza, William M.	OH0500	64A,48,64E,64C
DeRoche, Julie R.	IL0750	64C
Desgagne, Alain	AI0150	64C,48
DeWitt, Donald	NY1250	64C,64E,64A
Diamond, Shirley A.	WA1100	64E,64C,32E
Dibari, Keriann K.	NJ0800	42,64C
Dieker, R. Joseph	MO0300	64C
Dietz, Tom	FL1550	64C
DiLutis, Robert	MD1010	64C
DiLutis, Robert A.	LA0200	64C
DiOrio, Andrea	IL1615	64C
DiOrio, Andrea R.	IL2050	64C,11,42,43
DiPaolo, Stacey	OK1250	11,12A,64C
Doggett, Cynthia Krenzel	IA0200	12A,20,48,64C,64E
Donaghue, Margaret A.	FL1900	64C,42
Donaldson, Judy	AL0300	64C
Dorman, Diana	CA1650	64C
Dornian, Paul	AA0050	64C
Doucet, Denis	AI0220	64C
Dowling, Thomas	AG0450	32,64C
Dransite, Robert S.	NY2550	64E,64C
Dregalla, Herbert E.	OH2500	12,32,60,64C
Dreisbach, Paul C.	OH1000	64B,64D,64E,64C,48
Drelles, Andrew	NY2400	64C
Drewek, Doug	KY0100	64C,64D
Drewek, Douglas Alexand	KY0450	64E,64C,47
Drosinos, David	WV0550	64C
Drucker, Naomi	NY1600	48,64C,42
Druhan, Mary Alice	TX2955	64C,41
Dufford, Gregory	CO0550	64C,32E
Dumas, Charles	NC1350	64C,64E
Dumouchel, Michael	AI0150	64C,48
Duree, David T.	MD0520	64C,64E
Duree, David	MD0500	64C,64E
Earnest, James	IN1350	64C
East, James	NY3725	64C
Eastin, Brad	CO0275	64E,48,46,47,64C
Eban, Eli	IN0900	64C
Ebert, Brian	CO0650	64C
Edwards, George L.	DC0350	11,32C,48,64A,64C
Edwards, Ross	AG0600	64C,48
Ehrke, David	NV0100	13C,64C,64E,41
Eichhorn, Claire	DC0170	64C
Ellenwood, Christian K.	WI0865	13,64C,41
Eller, Joseph M.	SC1110	64C,48
Ellis, Kim S.	TX1400	37,64C,64E,48
Enloe, Loraine D.	ID0250	32E,64,37,64C,32C
Espina-Ruiz, Oskar	NC1650	64C,42
Estes, Adam	ND0250	46,47,64E,64C,64D
Estrin, Mitchell	FL1850	41,64C
Evans, Garry W.	TX3300	64C,37,12A,41,60B
Fabian, Deborah U.	TX3420	64C
Falwell, Calvin	FL2000	64C
Fancher, Susan	NC0910	64C
Faria, Richard Alan	NY1800	64C
Farrugia, Pauline	AI0050	64C,42
Fay, James	VA0975	13,12A,64C
Feller, Rena	TN1200	64C
Ferguson, Lora	DC0100	64C
Ferguson, Lora	DC0170	64C
Ferreira, Wesley	CO0250	64C
Figueiredo, Virginia Costa	CA0815	64C
Fischer, Thomas	LA0800	64C
Fisher, Mickey	GA0300	64B,64C,64E,48
Fisher, Suzanne D.	AZ0510	64C
Fiterstein, Alexander	MN1623	64C
Flax, Laura	NY0150	64C,42
Fleg, Jerome	WY0050	64C,29,47,64E
Flores, Yasmin A.	AL1250	64C,64E,64D,48,13B
Foerch, Kenneth	CA5355	46,47,64C,64E
Ford, Shannon	MI1950	64C,64E
Ford, Shannon	MI0050	64C,64E
Forrest, Sidney	DC0170	64C
Forsythe, Jada P.	MS0570	11,64C,64E,37,48
Forte, Michael	FL1450	64C
Fossner, Alvin K.	NY4200	64B,64C,64E
Franklin, Kip	MI1850	64C
Frazier, John	PA2800	64C
Frechou, Paul A.	LA0650	64C,37,32C,32E
French, Chris	IN0910	64C,64C
Friedman-Adler, Laurie	NY1600	64C,42
Frye, Christa J.	TN1720	64C
Fryml, Nathan	SC1000	64C
Furman, Carol	ME0150	64C,48
Gadgil, Sunil	TX2100	64E,64C,11
Gai, James R.	MO1790	20,64C,64E
Gainey, Denise A.	AL1150	64C,32
Galbraith, Connie	IL1740	64C,42
Gale, Mary	CA3600	64C
Gallagher, Mark	MD0350	64C,48,13,12A
Galvan, Michael	NY1800	64C
Galvin, Mindy	MD0450	64C
Gambino, Kyle A.	LA0760	64C
Gardner, John	IN0700	64C
Gardner, Joshua	AZ0100	64C
Garesche, Jeanine	MO1950	64C
Garner, Paul	TX2400	64C
Garrett, Dawn	MI1150	64C
Garrett, Roger	IL1200	37,64C,60B,41,35D
Garritson, Paul W.	MO1900	64C
Garritson, Paul W.	MO1800	64C,48
Gatti, Pat	VA0750	64C
Gaver, Angie	NE0160	64C
Geeting, Daniel	CA0550	64E,64C,38,11,60B
Genevro, Bradley	PA2300	37,64C,64E,32E
Georges, Julia	AL1050	64C
Gephardt, Donald L.	NJ1050	64C,32E,32G
Gerbino, Thomas J.	NY3600	64C,64E
Gerth, Jennifer	MN1625	64C
Gerth, Jennifer L.	MN0050	64C
Gewirtz, Jonathan	MI1800	47,64E,64C,11,29
Gholson, James	TN1680	48,64C
Gibbs, Lawrence	LA0250	11,29A,37,47,64C
Gibson, Beverly	IA1200	64C
Gibson, Beverly	IA0500	64C
Gibson, Christopher A.	MO0950	11,64B,64C,64D,64E
Gibson, Deborah	NH0250	64C
Gilad, Yehuda	CA1075	64C,38,42
Gilad, Yehuda	CA5300	64C
Gilbert, Daniel	OH0600	64C
Gilbert, Daniel	MI2100	64C
Gillespie, James E.	TX3420	41,64C
Gilmore, Jimmy J.	NC0600	64C
Gilmore, Jimmy	NC1300	37,64C
Gingras, Michele	OH1450	64C,42
Ginsberg, Eric	IL3500	64C
Girko, Stephen	TX2260	64C
Glennon, Barbara	PA0650	20G,13B,13C,64A,64C
Goh, Soo	PA1750	64C,41,11
Goldberg, Benjamin	CA2950	64C
Gomon, Naoum	AC0100	64C
Goodchild, Melissa	AA0020	64C
Goode-Castro, Helen	CA0830	64C
Goode-Castro, Helen	CA0825	64C
Gould, Brooke	IA0600	64B,64C,64D,64E
Gould, David	NY0500	41,64C
Graham, Jack	IA1800	64C,48
Graham, John	AR0810	37,64E,64C,48
Graham, Patrick	FL0150	64C
Graham, R. Douglas	SC1110	47,64C,64E
Grant, Donald R.	MI1600	64B,64C,64D,64E,13
Grant, Kenneth	NY1100	64C,42
Grass, Mahlon O.	PA2050	12A,48,64C,64E
Graves, Kenneth	MS0100	64C
Gray, Gary	CA5030	64C
Green, Paul	FL0650	64C
Green, Tricia	IL1200	64C
Greene, Janet E.	MN0800	32E,13A,37,64C
Grego, Michael	CA0825	64C
Greider, Cynthia S.	IN0905	64C,41
Greitzer, Ian	RI0200	64C,64E,48
Gresham, David	IL1150	48,64C
Griffin, Randall	TX3400	64C
Grimm, Leslie	IL2250	64C
Gross, Cathryn A.	IN1650	64C
Gross, Louis E.	IN1010	64C
Guist, Jonathan B.	TX3515	64C,32,42
Gunlogson, Elizabeth	NH0350	64C,13B
Gustavson, Mark	NY0050	64C
Gustavson, Mark	NY2550	10,64C,66D,10A,10F
Guy, Larry L.	NY2750	62,64C
Guy, Larry	NY4450	64C
Gythfeldt, Marianne	DE0150	64C,48
Hackett, Hara	TN1400	64C
Haddock, Marshall	OH1850	60,38,64C
Hadesbeck, Robert	IA1300	64C
Haiduck, Neal	NY2200	64C,64E
Hale, Cheryl	TX3370	64C,64A
Hall, Jeff	MI1850	47,64C,64E,66A,29B
Hall, Thomas	MA0500	53,64C
Hall, W. Randall	WV0300	64B,64C,64E,48
Hall-Gulati, Doris J.	PA1300	64C,42
Halloran, Jan	NH0100	64C
Hamilton, Tom	PA2200	64C,64E
Hancock, Richard K.	FL0700	64C
Hankins, Barbara	AG0600	64C
Hansen, Eric	WI0808	64C,37,13,32E
Hanson, Eric A.	WA0800	60,12A,38,10,64C
Hanson, Michael	MN0150	64C
Hanson, Shelley J.	MN0950	64C
Hanson, Sylva	MN1400	32B,64C
Harms, Lawrence	IL1090	11,47,64C,64E,29A
Harms, Lois	IA0650	64C,66
Harrigan, Wilfred	MA0600	64C,64E
Harris, Bill	CT0550	64E,64C
Harris, J. David	IL3300	64C,48,41
Hartig, Caroline A.	OH1850	64C,42
Hartline, Nicholas	TN0260	64C,48
Hartung, Colleen M.	PA0350	64C
Hartung, Colleen	PA3150	64C,48
Harwood, Andy	GA1500	64C
Hatch, Ken	AR0110	41,64C,64E,16
Hawkins, Richard	OH1700	64C
Hawley, Richard R.	OH2200	64C
Hayes, Kelly	AZ0440	64C
Hedrick, Teresa	VA0550	64C,64E,64A,64B
Hefley, Earl	OK1330	11,64C,64E
Heilbrunn, Micah	AC0100	64C
Heilmair, Barbara	OR0850	12A,41,42,64C,48
Heinemann, Steven	IL0400	13,10,64C
Heinen, Julia M.	CA0835	64C,42,13C
Helman, Shandra K.	ID0100	64C,13C,48,20,64E
Hepler, Julie E.	PA0100	64B,64C,12A,64D,64E
Hibler, John	WI1155	64A,64E,64C
Hildebrand, Janet N.	NE0200	64C
Hill, Christopher	SD0050	64C
Hill, Harry H.	SC0850	11,12A,64C,64E,48
Hill, Karen	SC0650	64C,64E
Hinckley, Jaren S.	UT0050	64C,11,48
Hinson, James M.	IL2910	48,64C,64E,42
Hirleman, Laura	MI1160	64C,64E
Hodges, Brian	KY0250	48,64A,64C
Hoeprich, Eric	IN0900	64C,67H
Holden, Jonathan	MS0750	64C,41
Holmes-Davis, Tina	GA1070	64C
Holton, Arthur	CA4300	37,64C,48,49

Index by Area of Teaching Interest

Name	Code	Areas
Honnold, Adrianne L.	MO1830	64C
Hooten, David M.	TX1600	64C,11,48,64A
Hopkins, Harlow	IL2300	64C
Hornsby, Richard	AE0120	64C,12A,29A,34,60
Hotle, Dana	MO0700	11,64C
Houghton, Stacey	GA0500	47,29,64E,64C
Hovnanian, Stephanie	MI2250	64C
Howard, David	CA5300	64C
Howard, Sharon	IN1310	64C
Howdle, Joyce	AA0080	64C
Howell, Jack	PA1050	64C
Hsu, E-Chen	AG0170	64C
Hudelson, Charles	AA0100	64C
Hughes, Larry	CA3300	64C,64E
Hughes, Lawrence P.	CA3500	64C,64E
Humes, Scot A.	LA0770	64C,64E,11
Hungerford, Del	WA1350	64C,51
Hungerford, Delores	ID0250	32B,64C
Hunter, Mario	NC0550	64C,41,42
Hurd Hause, Maureen L.	NJ1130	64C
Ignacio, Arnel	CA0825	64C
Inguanti, Cris	AB0200	64C
Inguanti, Cris	AB0100	64C
Irwin, David	FL1650	64C
Irwin, David E.	FL0450	64C,64E,37,41
Ishigaki, Miles M.	CA0810	48,64C,41,11,14C
Jackson, Bil	TN1850	64C,41,42
Jackson, Sandra	MI0600	64C
Jacobson, Mary Ann	MT0200	64C,14C,41
Janikian, Leon C.	MA1450	35,34,64C
Jankauskas, Sarunas	KS1450	64C
Jech, Lori	OK1400	64C
Jeffreys, Harold L.	NC2150	10F,32,64C,65,46
Jenkins, Pamela	ME0340	64A,64C,64E,32,13E
Jennings, Dunja	OR0400	64C
Jennings, Joseph W.	GA1900	47,64C,29,64E
Jessup, Carol A.	TX3500	48,64C
Jirovec, Mary	WI0050	64C
Jirovec, Mary	WI0150	64C
Johnson, Hubert	ID0075	64C,64D
Johnson, Jeanine	TX2750	64C
Johnson, John	AG0450	64C
Johnson, Kelly A.	AR0850	64C
Johnson, Madeline	UT0190	13,11,34,64C
Johnson, Marie	AG0500	64C
Johnson, Nathaniel	NE0710	60,37,64C,64E
Johnston, Glen	MT0200	46,64C
Johnston, Greg	UT0150	64C
Johnston, Greg	UT0200	64C
Johnston, Stephen K.	VA1350	37,48,64C
Jones, Brian	VA0450	64C
Jones, Brian D.	DC0170	64C
Jones, David	DC0100	64C
Jones, David	MD1010	64C
Jones, Heath	OK0700	64C,64E,47,72,34
Jones, Kathleen	PR0115	64C,41,42
Jones, Kristina Belisle	OH2150	64C
Jones, Linda	WI1150	64C
Jones, Robert	OH2050	64C
Jones, Robert	IN1050	64C
Jorgensen, Nathan A.	SD0550	47,64C,64D
Josenhans, Thomas	IN1600	64C,13B,13C,64E,41
Kajiwara, Greg	MN0040	64C
Kalman, Zoltan	AG0050	64C,48,64E,37
Kalman, Zoltan	AG0200	64C
Kalman, Zoltan	AG0500	64C
Kang, Cecilia	ND0350	64C,13
Kantor, Mary L.	WA0800	64C
Karnatz, Roland	VA1150	35G,64C
Kawaller, Meaghan	IL0850	64C
Kay, Alan R.	NY1900	64C
Kay, Alan B.	NY3790	64C
Kay, Alan	NY2150	64C
Keberle, David S.	NY0644	10,10B,64C,42,13A
Keech, Christopher	MI1985	64C,64E,37,48,47
Kelton, Christopher T.	RI0150	47,64C,64E,29A
Kerstetter, Tod	KS0650	13A,48,64C,13B
Kestenberg, Abe	AI0150	48,64C,64E,64A
Key, Stephanie	TX3350	64C
Kiec, Michelle	PA1750	64,13,64C,64E,48
Kiec, Michelle	PA1750	64,13,64C,64E,11
Kim, Wonkak	TN1450	64C,48,41
Kimball, Roger	IL1610	64E,64C
Kind, Sara	WI0830	64C
King, Bill	MI1000	64C
King, Jeffrey	MN1050	64C,64E
Kingfield, Edward	FL0950	64C
Kirby, David S.	NC1900	12A,64C,64E,64D,41
Kirk-Doyle, Julianne	NY3780	64C,42,41
Kirkbride, Jerry E.	AZ0500	48,64C
Kirkland, Denise	IN1750	64C
Kirkley, William	MA0950	64C
Kirkpatrick, Christopher	MT0400	64C,48
Kiser, Candice C.	PA3100	64C
Klaehn, Andrew	AG0350	64C,64E
Klimowski, Stephen	VT0450	64C,64E
Klimowski, Steve	VT0400	64C,64E
Klinghammer, John	SD0600	64C
Klinghammer, John	NE0100	64C
Klug, Howard D.	IN0900	64C
Kmiecik, Thomas	LA0650	64C
Knapp, Donna	GA0940	64C
Knight, Michael D.	WI0750	37,60B,32E,64C,64E
Knoop, Tracy V.	WA0600	64C,64E
Koffman, Carrie	CT0650	64,64C
Kolman, Barry	VA1850	13,37,38,64C,60
Koons, Keith	FL1800	64C,48
Kopperud, Jean K.	NY4320	64C
Koprowski, Melissa	WI0803	64C,48
Kosmala, Diane	WI0835	64C
Kostek, Patricia	AB0150	48,64C
Kowalsky, Frank	FL0850	64C
Koza, Matt	NY0646	13A,64C,64E
Krakauer, David	NY0150	64C,42
Krakauer, David	NY2150	64C
Krakauer, David	NY2250	41,64C
Krakauer, David	NY2750	64C
Kramer, Atossa	KY0300	13C,48,64C,66A,67C
Kraut, Rena	MN0050	64C
Kraut, Rena	MN1300	64C
Kravitz, Steve	OR0450	64B,64E,64C,29,11
Krebs, Jesse D.	MO1780	11,64C,13D,48
Kuehn, John W.	PA1600	32,64C,48,72
Kuhn, Stephanie	NC0450	64C,11
Kurokawa, John K.	OH2500	11,34,64C,32F
Kush, Jason	PA3100	64E,29,41,53,64C
Labadorf, Thomas	CT0100	64C
Labadorf, Tom	CT0050	64C,48
LaFave, Alan	SD0350	64C,60B
Lai, Juliet	MA0510	11,64C
Lai, Juliet	MA0700	64C
Lamneck, Esther	NY2750	64C,43
Lamy, Andy	NJ1400	64C
Lapin, Eric J.	SC0400	64C,11
Larson, Angela	SD0580	64C
Larson, Angela	SD0050	64C
Lascell, Ernest D.	NY3730	48,64C,64E
Lascell, Ernie	NY1700	64C
Latulippe, Mario	AI0050	64C
Laubenthal, Jennifer	NM0100	64C,11,13A
Laughlin, Jim	TX0100	13A,12A,48,64C,64E
Lawing, Sarah	GA2130	64C
Lawson, Charles E.	CO0250	13,64C,41
Lawson, Tonya	TN1100	64C,64E,64B,11
Ledressay, Joanne	AB0090	64C,32B
Lee, Cassandra	TN1850	41,48,64C,42
Leisring, Laura	VA0250	48,64A,64D,41,64C
Lemmons, Frederick	NC1250	64C,64E,48
Lemmons, Keith M.	NM0450	64C,41
Leonard, Rebecca	MA2030	64C
Lessly, Chris Ann	IN1025	32,41,48,64C,64E
Levin, Marguerite	MD0850	64C
Levine, Andrea	KY0400	64C
Levine, Barry	NJ0550	11,64C,64E,29A
Levy, Todd	WI0825	64C
Lewis, Nicholas	DC0150	64C,41
Liebowitz, Marian L.	CA4100	11,41,48,64C,35B
Lindblade, Dawn Marie	OK1330	64C
Linde, Laurel	MT0350	64C
Linton, Larry	MD0300	64C
Lipa, Noella P.	MD0475	64C
Lipman, William	TX0550	12A,64C,64E,11,48
Little, Robert	DC0170	64C
Livengood, Lee	UT0400	64C
Lochrie, Daniel	TN0100	64C,48
Locke, Scott A.	KY0950	64C,11,20
Loden, Larry	TX1900	64C,64E,32E
London, Larry	CA2950	64C
Long, Kenneth A.	GA1050	13A,64C,64E
Loomer, Deborah W.	SC1200	64C
Lopez, Catherine	WI1150	33,64C
Lopez, David F.	CA0859	64C
Lowenstein, Michael	NY2150	64C
Loy, Susan	PA3710	64C
Lucas, Michael	CO0625	37,47,64C
Luperi, Victoria	TX3510	64C
Luperi, Victoria	TX3000	64C
Maccaferri, Michael	VA1500	43,64C
MacDonald, Campbell	IN0905	64C
Mack, James	CA1750	64C,64E
Magruder, Michael	NC2700	10F,37,64C
Mallinger, Patrick	IN0005	64E,64C
Malone, William	CO0810	64C,64C,64A,29A,20
Maltester, Diane	CA0807	64C
Manasse, Jon	NY1100	64C
Manasse, Jon	FL1125	64C
Mandat, Eric P.	IL2900	13,64C,64E
Manzo, Erica	MO1800	13,64C
Marassa, Jill	IL1350	64C
Marco, John	WI0840	11,13,64C
Marcotte, Tracy	IL2300	64C
Marinelli, Vincent J.	DE0150	64C,64E
Marks, Ed	OH0300	64C
Marks, Laurence L.	NC2420	37,64C,32C,41
Marquardt, John	IL0730	64C
Marquis, Eugene	OH2550	64E,64C
Martin, Don	NC0300	64C,64E
Martin, Thomas	MA1400	64C
Martinez-Forteza, Pascual	NY2750	64C
Martins, David	MA2030	37,64C,60,42
Martula, Susan B.	NY3650	64C
Martula, Susan	MA2250	64C,41
Martyn, Charles F.	WV0650	37,47,64A,64C,64E
Masek, Douglas H.	CA5030	64E,64C
Mason, James	CA1425	64C,64E
Masserini, John	AZ0450	64C,41
Massey, Robert	SC1100	64C
Massey, Taylor	GA2100	64C
Masters, Suzanne	VA1580	64C,11,13A,64E,48
Matasy, Katherine V.	MA2050	64C,64E,68,42
Matteson, Vicki	VT0100	64C,32
Maxfield, Jessica	IL1900	64A,64C,64E
McAllister, Elizabeth	NC1750	12A,41,48,64C,64E
McCallum, Gregory	VA1800	37,64C,64E
McCandless, Amanda	IA1600	64C,64
McCandless, Marty	IL1100	64C,64E,32E,47,41
McCarty, Daniel J.	ID0075	64C,64E
McClard Kirk, Jennifer	KS1250	32E,64A,64C
McClellan, David Ray	GA2100	64C,48
McClune, David	TN1660	47,64C,64E
McColl, William	WA1050	41,64C
McColley, Stacey	FL0800	64C,48,13
McConkie, Dawn	KS0300	32,64C,64E
McElroy, Dennis	KY0610	64C
McGee, Blake Anthony	WY0200	12,64C,48
McGill, Anthony	NY2250	64C,48
McGill, Anthony	NY1900	64C
McGill, Anthony B.	MD0650	64C
McGowan, M.	MA0800	64C
McInchak, Kellie	MI2000	64C
McKelway, Daniel	OH0200	64C
McKinney, Roger W.	NJ0175	64C,12A,48
McLaren, Malena	LA0550	12,64C,64E,47
McPherson, Sandra	CA0150	64C
Mead, Maurita Murphy	IA1550	64C
Meffert-Nelson, Karrin	MN0750	64C,37,48,32E,12A
Meinert, Anita	IA1950	64C,66A,66C,54
Mentzer, Larry E.	TX2200	64C
Mentzer, Larry E.	TX3530	64C
Merciers, Meghan	MI0100	64C
Merriman, Lyle C.	PA2750	64C
Merva Robblee, Carolyn	IL1400	64C
Mesare, Roi	PA3000	64C
Messersmith, Charles	SC0275	64C,48
Meyer, Alice	NY3350	64C
Meyer, Thomas	IN1100	64A,64C
Mezei, Margaret	AA0200	13A,64C,64E
Mickey, Sarah	AR0600	37,48,64C,11
Mietz, Joshua	NM0400	64C,64E,13,38
Miller, Douglas	NC0050	64C
Miller, Leigh	GA2300	13A,13B,64C
Miller, Mary Ellen	MA1350	64C
Miller, Peter	TX3360	66C,61,64C,66G
Minevich, Pauline M.	AJ0100	12A,64C,12C,12D
Minor, Janice L.	VA0600	64C
Miyamura, Henry	HI0210	32C,38,64C

Index by Area of Teaching Interest

Name	Code	Areas
Mohen, Girard	NY5000	64C,64E
Moisan, Andre	AI0200	64C
Moisan, Andre	AI0210	64C
Molina, Osiris J.	AL1170	64C
Moline, Garth	WY0150	64C,64E
Mondie, Eugene	DC0050	64C
Monroe, Douglas	NC0650	64C,42
Montanaro, Donald	PA0850	48,64C
Montgomery, Kip	NY3250	11,12,13,64C
Moore, Joel	IL0150	64E,64C
Moorhead, J. Brian	FL2000	64C
Morales, Gary A.	PR0100	60,32,48,64C
Morales, Ricado J.	PA3250	64C
Morales, Ricardo	NY1900	64C
Moreau, Leslie M.	ID0050	64C,13A,13B,48
Moritsugu, Jim	MS0385	64C
Morneau, John P.	ME0200	37,64C,64E
Morrison, Nicholas	UT0300	37,64C,48,41
Moxness, Paul	MN0200	64C,64E
Murphy, Janice	MD0750	64C
Murray, Jack	NC1100	64C,64E
Murray, Jack T.	NC0350	64A,64C,64E
Musco, Lynn A.	FL1750	41,64C
Myers, Adam	TX3370	48,64C,64E
Naragon, Jayne	OH2290	64C
Neidich, Ayako Oshima	NY3785	64C,42
Neidich, Charles	NY1900	64C,48
Neidich, Charles	NY2150	64C
Neidich, Charles	NY2250	64C
Neidich, Charles	NY0642	64C
Neithamer, David	VA0700	29A,64C,32E
Nelson, Jennifer	WA1000	48,64C
Nelson, Jennifer	WA1050	64C
Nelson, William A.	WI0700	64C,64E
Nereim, Linnea	OH0600	64C
Nevin, Kathryn A.	CA5150	64C
Newton, Jack	NC0050	47,41,64C,72,35
Nichols, Christopher Robert	NE0150	64C,64E,38
Nichols, Cynthia	NE0610	64C
Nicholson, David	CA5360	13A,64C
Nielsen, Aage	ID0070	64C
Niethamer, David B.	VA1500	64C,37
Niethamer, David	VA1600	64C
Niiyama, Kelley	IN0800	64C
Nije, Marilyn	KY1500	64C
Nold, Sherry	PA3260	64A,64C,64E
Nordstrom, Craig	MA1400	64C
Normand, Jean-Francois	AI0200	64C
Norsworthy, Michael	MA0350	64C
Norton, Edgar	NY1700	32,64C
Norton, John	IL1890	64C,11
Nuccio, Mark	NY2150	64C
Nunemaker, Richard	TX3450	64C,48
Oakes, Gregory	IA0850	64C
Oberlander, Lisa M.	GA0550	64C,64E
O'Connor, Kelli A.	RI0300	48,64C
O'Connor, Philip	CA3800	64C
Odom, David H.	AL0200	64C,11
Oehler, Donald L.	NC2410	41,42,43,48,64C
Oien, Theodore	MI1400	64C
Oien, Theodore	MI2200	64C
O'Keefe, Patrick	WI0845	64C,48
Okwabi, Tori	MN1300	64C
Olsen, Nina	MN0300	64C,42
Olson, Jeffrey K.	GA2150	64C,48,64E
Orlowski, Joseph	AG0450	64C
Ortiz, Norberto	PR0150	64C
Ortner-Roberts, Susanne	PA3580	64C
Oshima, Ayako	NY1900	64C
Oshima, Ayako	CT0650	64C
Padilla, Clarence S.	IA0550	64C
Paglialonga, Phillip O.	FL0100	64C,41,48,13A,13B
Parchman, Thomas	ME0500	13A,13,64C
Park, Helen	CA5550	64C
Parrish, Bill	VA1125	64B,64C
Patterson, Tracy	TX1550	64C,64E
Patterson, Vincent L.	MD0550	48,64C
Paul, Randall S.	OH2500	64C,29,48,11
Payne, Mary	IL1520	64C
Peersen, Hild	OH0700	64C
Pelischek, Jeff	KS0550	11,37,48,64C,64E
Peltola, Gilbert	ME0200	64C,64E
Perone, James E.	OH2290	11,13,12E,64C
Perry, David L.	SC0050	12A,13A,64C,32,20A
Perry, Tiffany	DC0170	13,64C
Perry, Timothy B.	NY3705	60,37,38,64C
Peterson, Douglas A.	FL0400	11,37,38,64C
Peterson, Edward	LA0800	47,64C,29B
Phillips, Chip	WA0400	64C
Phillips, Jessica J.	NJ1130	64C
Phillips, Katrina	AL0050	11,64C
Phillips, Timothy S.	AL1050	64C,12,48
Phillips, Tom	LA0050	64C
Pierre, Stephen	AG0450	64C
Pierre, Stephen	AG0200	64C
Pimentel, Bret R.	MS0250	64,29,64B,11,64C
Pino, David J.	TX3175	64C
Pinsonneault, Ona	MN1200	64C
Pisano, James	KS0200	64C,64E,47,53,13
Pisano, Kristin	KS0350	11,64C,64E,12A,14C
Pittman, Deborah M.	CA0840	64C,20G
Polley, Jo Ann	MN1450	38,48,64C
Pope, Kathy	UT0250	64C
Potts, Leo W.	WA1300	64C,64E
Powell, Ross	TX2400	41,64C,43
Powell, William E.	CA0510	48,64C,42,13E
Purkhiser, Beth	IN1850	64C,64E
Pyne, James	OH1850	48,64C
Qian, Jun	MN1450	42,64C,48
Qian, Jun	TX0300	64C,48
Quebbeman, Robert C.	MO0775	38,64C,60
Quigley, Roger N.	VA1250	64C
Quijano, Kellie R.	TX2960	64C
Rabin, Barbara	NY0650	64C
Rabin, Barbara	NY1350	64C
Raifsnider, Chrispher J.	MD0060	12,13,64C
Ramey, Maxine	MT0400	64C,48
Ramsbottom, Gene	AB0100	64C
Ramsbottom, Gene	AB0050	64C
Ranti, Richard J.	MA0400	64C
Rapson, John	AF0100	64C
Raschiatore, Lisa	MI1260	64C,41
Raval, Shanti	NY0270	64C,11,20
Reams, John D.	GA0200	64C,11
Reed, Thomas T.	OH0100	10F,64C,64E,48
Reefer, Russell	PA0700	64C,64E
Reeks, John	LA0300	64C
Regan, Lara	IL2650	64E,64C
Reid, Lynda L.	TX2350	13A,32B,37,48,64C
Reinoso, Crystal Hearne	NY3717	13B,48,64C,15
Renander, Cindy	WA0960	64C,11
Reynolds, Jeremy W.	CO0900	64C,33,13C,13H
Rheude, Elizabeth A.	ND0500	41,64C,64E
Rhoades, Connie A.	KY0550	64C,64E,20G
Rhodes, Ruth	IL3450	48,64C,32
Rice, Michael	AL0010	64C,64E
Richards, E. Michael	MD1000	64C,60,41,38
Ricker, Ramon	NY1100	64C,64E
Rider, Daniel	IL1300	64C,64E
Rine, Craig	WA0650	64C
Rischin, Rebecca M.	OH1900	64C,41
Riseling, Robert A.	AG0500	13,37,38,41,64C
Robe, Carol M.	OR0700	64C
Roberdeau, Dan	WI0100	64C
Rodriguez, Jose	ID0050	64C
Roebuck, Nikole D.	LA0100	32,64C
Roesch, Erin R.	IN0400	64C
Romines, Roann	TN1000	64C
Roper, Gretchen	SC0420	64C
Rose, Brent	LA0800	64C,29A,13A,13B,13C
Rose, Thomas	CA2950	64C
Rosengren, Hakan	CA0815	64C,41
Ross, David	TX3520	12A,64C
Ross, Don	AA0035	64C
Ross, Don	AA0020	64C
Rossi, Achille	IN0250	64C
Roter, Bruce	NY0700	10,13,12A,64C
Rothenberg, Florie	WA0050	64C
Rousseau, Marcel	AI0190	64C
Rowell, Chester	TX3400	64C
Rowell, Chester D.	TX2295	64C,64E,41
Rowlett, Michael T.	MS0700	64C,11,41
Rubin, Joel E.	VA1550	14A,14C,64C,41,31B
Rucker, Jennifer	OK0700	64C
Rusinak, Dennis	AA0110	64E,64C
Rusinek, Michael	PA0550	64C
Russo, Charles	NY2150	64C
Sacchini, Louis V.	IA0940	64C,64E
Sadak, John	NC2420	64C,11
Salman, Randy Keith	IN0350	47,64C,64E,29
Samuels, Ronald I.	PA1050	64C
Sanchez, Steve	CA0900	64C
Sanchez, Steve	CA4150	64C
Sanders, Nancy King	TX2960	64C
Sanders, Raphael P.	NY3780	64C,41
Sapadin, David	NY2105	64C
Saville, Kirt	UT0050	37,60B,64C,32E,32C
Schattschneider, Adam	OH0250	13,47,64A,64C,64E
Schekman, Joel	MI1050	64C
Schempf, Kevin	OH0300	64C
Scherline, Janine	NY3775	64C,48
Schiavone, David C.	NY0400	47,48,64C,64E
Schiavone, David C.	NY4320	64C,64E,47
Schimming, Paul	MN0610	32E,64E,64C
Schimming, Paul	MN1500	64C
Schlabach, Robert	TN0450	64A,64B,64C,64E
Schlacks, Mary M.	OH1650	14,48,64C,11
Schneider, David E.	MA0100	12,64C,43,13,41
Schoen, Theodore A.	MN1600	64C,64E,41,10F
Scholl, Janet	MN1280	64C
Schroeder-Garbar, Lacy	IL1085	64C
Schroerlucke, Leslie	CA5040	64C
Schulz, Paul	MN1625	64C
Schwaegler, Susan	IL0100	64C,48
Schwaegler, Susan	IL0300	64C
Schwartz, Richard I.	VA1750	13,48,64C,10
Scott, Aaron D.	PA1400	64C,42
Scott, Jan	LA0350	32B,48,64B,64D,64C
Scott, John C.	TX3420	41,64C
Scott, Ronald	TX2930	64C,64E,38,10F,60
Scott, Shannon	WA1150	64C,12A
Scruggs, Tara A.	TN0250	13A,64C
Seeman, Sharon	NJ0750	64A,64B,64C,64D,11
Seigel, Andrew	NY3725	64C
Seiler, David E.	NH0350	47,48,64C
Seletsky, Robin	NY1400	64C
Sescilla, Mark Christopher	ID0140	64C
Shachal, Harel	NY2660	20B,64C,64E
Shackleton, Peter	AG0500	64C
Shakhman, Igor	OR1100	64C
Shakhman, Igor	OR0500	64C
Shands, Patricia	CA5350	64C,42,41
Shankle, Robert	TN1600	64B,64C,64E
Shanley, Richard A.	TX0300	48,64C
Shaw, Patricia	AF0120	64C
Shea, David L.	TX3200	34,41,64A,64C,64E
Sheffield, Robert	AB0060	64C,48
Sheldon, Paul	NY0600	64C,64E
Sheridan, Daniel	MN1700	64C,60,32C,13A,11
Shiffer, Faith E.	PA1250	64C,64E,41
Shifrin, David	CT0850	41,64C
Shoemaker, Michelle N.	MA1175	12A,64,11,64C
Shroyer, Jo Ellen	MO0100	64A,64C,64E
Shroyer, Ronald L.	MO0100	64A,64C,64E,64
Shultz, Bud	IL1500	64C,64E
Sidoti, Vincent	OH0755	13,11,37,64C,64E
Sigel, Allen R.	NY4320	64C
Silva, Ellen	CA0630	11,64C
Silver, Daniel	CO0800	64C
Silver, Patricia	TN1350	63A,64C
Simmons, Amy	TN1720	42,64C,64E
Simmons, Sunshine	IL3550	64C
Simons, Anthony R.	PA2550	64C,64E
Singer, David	NJ0800	41,48,64C,11
Slater, Sheri	MO0400	11,48,64C
Sloane, Ethan	MA0400	64C
Smith, Gregory	IL0550	64C
Smith, Gregory E.	MA1400	64C
Smith, Jerry Neil	OK1350	64C
Smith, Joseph	PA1150	64C
Smith, Mary M.	IL0800	64C
Smylie, Dennis H.	NY2750	64C
Smylie, Dennis H.	NJ0800	64C,42
Snavely, Jack	WI0825	41,64C,64E
Sommerfield, Janet	MI0500	64C,64E
Sontz, Allison	MT0370	64C
Souza, Thomas	MA0500	60B,64C,37,32,46
Specht, Barbara	OH0950	11,38,64C,64E,48
Sperl, Gary	TN1710	64C,64E
Sperrazza, Rose U.	IL2150	64C,48,13H
Spicknall, John P.	IN0800	12A,47,64C
Spires, Henry Ray	SC1080	64B,64C,64D,64E
Splittberger-Rosen, Andrea	WI0850	48,64C
Spring, Robert S.	AZ0100	64C
Stanford, Ann	IL2750	64C
Stanford, Thomas S.	OR0850	64C,12,48,41

Name	Code	Areas
Stanley, Justin	NJ0400	64C
Stanley, Justin	CT0300	64C
Stanley, Justin	NY5000	64C
Steffens, Lea	CA2390	64C
Steffens, Lea	CA0960	64C
Stefiuk, Karen	WI0750	64C
Stein, William	OH1800	64C,32E
Steinberg, A. Jay	KS0150	64C,12A
Sterling, Amy	MD0800	64C,64E,64B,64D,64A
Sternberg, Jo-Ann	CT0800	64C,48
Stevens, Anthony	MA0600	64C,64E
Stevens, Daryll	CO0200	64C,16
Stimpert, Elisabeth	PA0950	64C,48
Stimpert, Elisabeth	PA0350	64C
Stimpert, Elisabeth	PA2300	64C
Stinson, Carol	TX1000	64C
Stoffan, George C.	MI1750	64C,48,42,32E
Stoll, Peter	AG0450	64C
Stoltzman, Richard	MA1400	64C
Storey, Douglas	TX3750	64C
Storochuk, Allison M.	MO0775	64C,13,48
Strang, Kevin	FL1700	64C
Striplen, Anthony	CA3920	64C
Striplen, Tony	CA4200	64C
Sturm, Marina	NV0050	64C,42
Suhusky, Craig	MI1800	64C
Sullivan, Aimee M.	NC2400	64C,64E
Summers, Jerome	AG0500	60,38,64C,67B,43
Sussman, Michael	MA2000	41,64C
Sutherland, Daniel	AA0020	64C
Suzuki, Rie	NJ1050	64C
Svanoe, Erika K.	MN0150	64C,60B,37,32E,45
Sykes, Kimball	AG0400	64C
Tangarov, Vanguel G.	TX3175	64C,48
Taylor, Anthony	NC2430	64C
Taylor, Charles L.	LA0800	37,60B,64C,32C,32E
Tejero, Nicolasa	TN1350	64C
Tejero, Nikolasa	TN1700	13,64C,41
Temperley, Joe	NY1900	64C,64E,29
Tesch, Catherine	MN1120	64C
Thai, Mei-Chuan Chen	NC1600	64C
Thee, Lawrence	NC0930	64B,64C,64D,64E
Thoma, August	MI1830	32E,37,64C
Thomas, Eric B.	ME0250	37,47,64C,64E,53
Thompson, Randy	OK0825	64C,66G
Thompson, Shannon	NC2600	64C,11
Thompson, Thomas	PA0550	64C,64E
Thomson, Richard	AG0450	64C
Thornhill, Margaret	CA1425	64C
Thrasher, Michael	TX3535	64C,12A,12C
Tidwell, Dallas	KY1500	64C,48,42
Tillotson, J. Robert	IL1085	37,13,41,64C
Timmerman-Yorty, Carol	NY4460	64C
Tirk, Suzanne	OK1350	64C
Tracy, Shawn	WI0250	64C
Trottier, Alain	AI0190	64C
Tryon, Colleen	OH1350	64C
Tryon, Colleen	OH1600	64C
Turanchik, Thomas	NC0750	64B,64C,64D,48
Turizziani, Robert	WV0800	64C,60B,48
Turner, Don	TX2350	64C,64E
Turner, Katherine L.	SC0350	64C,12A,20,14A
Umiker, Robert C.	AR0700	48,64C,64E
Usher, Barry	AG0500	64C
Usher, Jon	CA0845	64C,32
Valdepenas, Joaquin	AG0450	64C
Valdepenas, Joaquin	AG0300	64C
Vallentine, John	IA1600	32,37,64C
VanDessel, Joan	MI0520	12A,13D,37,64C,48
VanKopp, Kristi	CA0650	64C
Vardi, Amitai	OH1100	64C,41
Vardi, Amitai	OH2150	64C
Variego, Jorge	ND0600	10,13B,48,64C,64B
Varineau, John	MI0850	64C
Varineau, John	MI0350	64C
Varineau, John	MI0900	64C
Viliunas, Brian	AL0800	64C,38,13C,32E,60B
Voigts, Kariann	IA1350	64C
Vore, Wallis W.	OH2250	64C,48
Votapek, Paul	FL0680	64C
Vreeland, Harold	OR0750	64C
Wachmann, Eric	IA1800	13,64C,48
Waddell, Mike	NC2440	64B,64C,64D,11,32
Wagner, Lawrence R.	PA3250	60,38,48,64C
Waibel, Keith	CA0600	64C
Wait, Patricia	AG0650	41,64C,13A,12A
Wakefield, Leigh	MN0600	64C
Waldecker, Todd	TN1100	64C,48
Walker, Amanda Jane	CA5020	64C
Walsh, Eileen	AF0120	64C,13
Walsh, Michael	SD0550	64C,12A,12C
Wang, Alice	OH2600	64C
Wang, Hong	MN0610	64C
Wang, Mingzhe	TN0050	64C,11
Wansley, Ivan	FL0800	64C
Ward, Doug	AA0080	64A,64C,64E
Warren, John	GA1150	64C,32E,42
Warren, Tasha	VA1550	64C,48
Wasserman, Lisa	OH2140	64C,64D,42
Watabe, Junichiro	AK0150	64C,64E,48,37,46
Watson, Anne	OK0550	64C,13A,13B,13C,20
Watts, Camille	AG0450	64C
Wayne, Michael	MA1175	64C
Weatherall, Maurice	MS0600	64C,37
Webber, Janice E.	MD0650	64C
Webster, Michael	TX2150	42,64C
Weddle, John W.	CA0850	32C,32B,20G,64C,11
Wegge, Glen T.	IA1750	13C,13B,13G,64C
Weigand, John	WV0750	48,64C
Weinhold, Scott	DC0050	64C
Weir, Claudia	CO0050	64C
Wellwood, William	CA2420	64C
Welte, John	PA3330	64C,64E
Wery, Brett L.	NY3600	13,37,41,64C,64E
West, Charles W.	VA1600	48,64C,60
Wetzel, David B.	PA2150	64C,35,34
Wheeler, Joyce	IA0550	64C
Whitaker, Howard	IL3550	13,10F,10,64C
White, Arthur	MO1800	47,64C,29B
White, Kennen D.	MI0400	41,64C
Whitman, Gary	TX3000	64C
Whitmore, Michael R.	OK0300	48,64C,64E
Whitmore, Michael	OK1200	64C
Widder, David R.	VA1700	12A,37,48,64C
Wiemann, Beth	ME0440	10F,64C,34,10A,13D
Wilder, Ralph	IL2100	64C,32E,64E,11,42
Williams, Don A.	WV0400	64C,64E
Williams, Nathan L.	TX3510	64C
Williamson, Bruce	VT0050	64C,64E,66A,67,47
Williamson, Stephen	NY2250	64C
Wilson, Margaret	AJ0150	64C
Winkle, Carola	ID0050	64C,32
Wise, Wilson	IA1100	64C,13B,32E,37,60B
Wolbers, Mark	AK0100	60,12A,32C,64C,48
Wolfe, Chris	MD0175	13A,60,37,64C,64E
Wong, Bradley	MI2250	48,64C
Wood, Catherine M.	AC0050	64C,13
Wood, T. Bennett	TX2960	64C
Woodrum, Jennifer	IL3150	64C
Woodrum, Jennifer	WI0250	64C
Wray, Ron E.	AL1160	64C,37,13,60
Wright, Christine	AZ0150	64C
Wright, Joseph	MI2120	64C,11
Wright, Lauren Denney	OK0650	32E,37,64C,60B
Wright, Scott	KY1450	64C,41,48
Wyland, Richard	MN0250	64C
Yacoub, Allison	MD0600	64C,32E,20
Yannie, Mark	MN0625	46,64C,64E
Yeh, John Bruce	IL0550	64C
Yehuda, Guy	FL1950	64C,60B,41,32E
Yin, Jei	AA0110	64C,64E
York, Richard	OH2450	64C
York-Garesche, Jeanine	MO1830	64C
Young, Colin	IA0700	64E,64C
Young, Eileen	NC2205	64C
Young, Eileen M.	NC2500	64C,64E,41,64,12A
Young, Gregory D.	MT0200	13,64C
Young, Jay	IN1100	64A,64C,64E
Zaev, Pance	NE0450	64C,64E,48
Zajac, Roy	CA4700	42,64C
Zeisler, Dennis J.	VA1000	11,37,64C,48
Zelnick, Stephanie	KS1350	64C
Zimmerman, Charlene	IL0550	64C,42
Ziporyn, Evan	MA1200	13,10,20D,64C,29
Zoeter, Garrick A.	VA1350	64C
Zugger, Gail Lehto	OH0350	64C,48
Zukovsky, Michele	CA5300	64C
Zumpella, Clement	OH2600	64C
Zuroeveste, Rodney	ID0050	64C

Bassoon

Name	Code	Areas
Abner, Marita	MO1810	64D
Ackmann, Rodney	OK1350	64D,20G,41
Adams, George	ID0060	64D
Adams, George C.	ID0100	64D
Alesandrini, Joyce L.	OH1650	13,64D,66A
Alexander, Lisa M.	NY1600	64D,42
Anderson, Angela	PA3250	64D
Anderson, Collin	IL2100	64D
Anderson, Collin J.	IL2150	64D
Anderson, Collin	IL1085	64D
Anderson, Eric	TN0260	64D
Anderson, Jennifer J.	NC1250	64D
Anderson, Robert	AR0350	64B,64C,64D,64E,47
Andrews, Susan	LA0300	64D
Atria, Karen	OH0850	64D
Atria, Karen	OH2050	64D
AuBuchon, Elaine	MO1780	64B,64D,11
Ayoub, Anna Claire	MD0500	64D
Ayoub, Anna Claire	PA3150	64D,48
Babinec, Lori	WI0300	64D
Baer, Seth	NY2105	64D
Baer, Seth R.	NJ0800	64D
Bakenhus, Douglas	LA0550	13B,38,60B,64D
Baker, Allison	IL3150	64B,64D
Baker, Amy	PA3100	64D
Ballard-Ayoub, Anna Claire	PA1400	64D,42
Ballard-Ayoub, Anne Claire	MD0300	11,64D
Banti, Mary	MN0250	64D
Barber, Gregory	CA2950	64D
Barber, Susan N.	VA0600	64D,42
Barker, Stephanie	WY0115	64B,64D
Barnum, Ellen M.	NY0400	12A,64D,15
Barnum, Ellen M.	NY3717	64D
Barrett, Paul	HI0210	64D
Barris, Robert A.	IL0750	64D
Bawden, Sue	IL0100	64D
Bawden, Susan	IA1300	64D
Beavers, Gabriel	LA0200	64D
Beck, Carolyn	CA3650	64D
Beck, Carolyn L.	CA5150	64D
Beck, Carolyn L.	CA0835	64D
Bedford, Judith	MA2030	64D
Beebe, Jon P.	NC0050	13,48,64D,32E,42
Beene, Richard	CA1075	64D,42
Bernard-Stevens, Sarah	KS0700	37,38,13,64D
Besch, Joyce	NE0450	64D
Bettez, Michel	AI0200	64D
Bibzak, Ray	IL2650	64D,64B
Bibzak, Ray	IL2775	64B,64D
Bingham, W. Edwin	WV0400	47,64E,64D,29
Bleuel, John	GA2130	13C,60,64E,64B,64D
Bombardier, Brad	WI0860	10F,64D
Borah, Bernard	IL0800	13,64D
Borland, Carolyn	PA2250	64D
Boyd, Sara	ND0400	64D
Brewer, James	OK1200	64D
Brown, Douglas	MT0370	64D
Brown, Susan	OK1450	64D
Brown, Susan	OK0850	64D
Brown, Susan	OK0800	64D,32E
Brown, Susie	OK0550	64D
Brubaker, William	FL0200	64D
Brusky, Paula	WI0830	64D,35A
Bryant, David	KY0450	64D
Bryce, Jackson	MN0300	64D
Bubar, Lisa	MI1180	64D
Buchar-Kelley, Kimberly	PA3710	64D
Buchman, William	IL0750	64D
Burns, Michael J.	NC2430	64D
Busby, Stepanie	MA0650	64D
Butte, Jody	PA1650	64D
Byo, Donald W.	OH2600	64D
Byo, Donald W.	PA1450	64D
Byo, William	PA3650	64D
Campbell, Jefferson	MN1600	11,64D,34
Campbell, John	CA0825	64D
Campbell, John	CA0960	64D
Campbell, Richard	PA2100	64D
Capps, Angela	ME0250	64D
Carpenter, Tina	TX3750	64D,13,11,34C
Carr, Tracy A.	NM0100	64B,12A,41,64D,11
Carroll, Richard P.	NJ1050	64D
Carucci, Christine	KY0550	64D,32

Name	Code	Areas
Casey, John	SD0050	64D
Caufield, Stevi	RI0300	64D
Cavanaugh, Jennifer Gookin	MT0400	64B,64D,13
Chappell, Rebecca Ann	IN0100	64C,64E,35A,64D
Chen-Beyers, Christina	ND0500	64D
Chest, Robert	SC0200	48,64B,64C,64D,64E
Chiu, Ying-Ting	DC0170	64D
Chou, Yueh	CA0900	64D
Christoph, Michael E.	CO0550	64D
Cifelli, Cheryl L.	MO0800	64C,64D,12A,11,13E
Cioffari, Cynthia A.	OH2150	64D,48
Clapp, John	MI0900	64D
Clapp, John	MI1050	64D
Clapp, John	MI0520	64D
Clark, Dale	AR0110	64D
Clouser, John	OH0600	64D,48
Code, Belinda B.	AE0050	41,64A,64B,64D
Coelho, Benjamin A.	IA1550	64D,13
Cognata, Chad	CO0900	64D
Cohick, Mark	MO2000	64E,64D,64B
Coleman, Cedric	AG0600	64D
Comstock, Allan D.	KS0300	11,64B,64D,12A
Condit, Sonja	SC1000	64B,64D
Cooley, Brian	KS0150	64D
Coolidge, Tiffany	VT0100	64D
Coppola, A. J.	NH0250	64D
Corrigan, Rose	CA5300	64D
Cripps, Cynthia L.	TX3525	64E,64D
Crockett, Whitney	NY2150	64D
Cuffari, Gina	CT0800	64D,48,11
Cuffari, Gina Lynn	NY2750	64D
DaGrade, Donald	CA4300	64D,64E
Dahlem, Justin	IL1090	64D
Dansereau, Sophie	AB0200	64D
D'Augelli, Barbara	CA0800	64D
Davenport, Francesca	AA0200	64D
Davenport, Francesca	AA0150	64D
Davis, William	GA2100	13,64D
De La Garza, Luis	TX3527	64D
DeBolt, David	OH1100	11,41,64D
DeFade, Eric	WV0800	64E,64D
DeMio, Mark	OH1100	64D
DeMio, Mark	OH0650	64D
DeMio, Mark	OH0600	64D
Denike, Allan	AJ0100	64D
DeYoung, Tim	MI0350	64D
Dicker, Michael H.	IL1150	11,48,64D
Dickerson, Shane	AL0200	11,64E,64D
Dickey, Thomas Taylor	IA0250	60,64D
Diekman, Susan	OK0150	64D
Dietz, William D.	AZ0500	64D,48
Dircksen, Eric	DC0100	64D
Dircksen, Eric	DC0010	64D
Dixon, Nellie	IL1200	64D
Domingues, Cameron	CA0815	64D,64E
Dooly, Louann	AR0730	64D,11
Douglas, Peter	MN1625	64D
Downey, Gwyn	IL1300	64D
Dreisbach, Paul C.	OH1000	64B,64D,64E,64C,48
Drewek, Doug	KY0100	64C,64D
Duda, Cynthia M.	MI0100	64D
Duke, Barbara	VA1100	64D
Durran, Daryl	PA2750	64D
Duso, Lorraine C.	AR0850	64B,64D,11
Dusold, Patricia	TN1350	64D
Ebersold, Timothy	ME0150	64D
Eckerty, Michael	IA1350	64D,32C,37,60,48
Edwards, Constance	WV0300	64D,12,11,12A,10F
Ellert, Michael	FL1125	64D,41,42
Elliott, Rachael	VT0450	64D
Elliott, Rachael	NC0600	64D
Ellis, Barry L.	WI0840	60,37,64D,64E,32
Ellis, Monica	NY0500	64D
Erickson, Scott	KY0950	48,64B,64D,64E
Ervin, Richard	FL1550	64D
Estes, Adam	ND0250	46,47,64E,64C,64D
Estill, Cynthia	TN1850	64D
Eubanks, Mark G.	OR1100	64D
Eubanks, Mark	OR0400	64D
Ewell, Terry B.	MD0850	64D,13,64E
Fain, Jeremy	TX3535	64D
Fain, Jeremy	TX2700	64D,11,13A,13B
Farmer, Judith	CA5300	64D
Farndale, Nancy	IA1750	64B,64D,66G
Fears, Angela	CA3520	13A,13C,64D,16
Fedderly, Carolyn	MD0400	64D
Feller, Lynne	WA1350	64D
Feller-Marshall, Lynne	WA0250	64D
Feves, Julie	CA0510	42,64D,48,35A
Fiala, Michele	OH1900	64B,41,13B,13C,64D
Flemming, Joy	NH0150	64D,48
Flores, Yasmin A.	AL1250	64C,64E,64D,48,13B
Ford, Ronnal	NC2700	64,64B,11,64D,62A
Foster, Erin	WA1100	64D
Foster, Erin	WA0400	64D
Friedman, Jonathan I.	VA1500	64D
Futterer, Kenneth	AR0200	10,48,64B,64D,64E
Gaarder, Jon	PA3600	64D
Gaarder, Jon	DE0150	48,64D
Gale, Karen	CA0150	64D
Gale, Timothy M.	IA0550	64D
Gallup, Trina	PA0350	64D
Gardner, Larry	CA0810	64D
Garfield, Bernard	PA0850	64D
Garner, Rusty	FL0900	60,11,61,54,64D
Gelman, Robin	DC0350	64D
Giacobassi, Beth	WI0825	64D
Gibson, Christopher A.	MO0950	11,64B,64C,64D,64E
Gibson, David	LA0770	13,64B,64D,29A
Gillette, John C.	NY3725	13,64D,72
Gillick, Amy	CA3100	64B,64D
Gillick, Amy	CA1425	64D,11
Glenn, Susan G.	GA1070	64D
Goeres, Nancy E.	PA0550	64D
Goldberg, Marc	NY0150	64D,42,48
Goldberg, Marc	NY2250	64D,41
Goldberg, Marc	CT0650	64D
Gomez, Kathleen	MI0850	64D
Goodhew, Lee	NY1800	64D
Goranson, Todd A.	PA2300	64E,64D,13A,47,42
Gordon, Kirstin	PA2350	64B,64D
Gott, Andrew	MO1900	64D
Gould, Brooke	IA0600	64D,64C,64D,64E
Granger, David W.	CA5000	64D
Grant, Donald R.	MI1600	64D,64C,64D,64E,13
Gray, Julie	KY1350	64D
Gray, Robert	NJ1400	64D
Grego, Michele	CA0825	64D

Name	Code	Areas
Greitzer, Deborah	MD0750	41,64D,42
Grossman, Arthur	WA1050	41,64D
Guist, Anne P.	TX2960	64D
Gunter, Jenny	AB0150	64D
Gunter, Patricia	TN1400	64D
Hague, Zach	KS0200	64D
Haines, Yvonne Bonnie	TX1400	64B,64D
Hale, Daris Word	TX3175	64D,11
Hall, Charles	TX3000	64D
Hammel, Bruce R.	VA1600	13,64D
Hane, Daniel	NY1400	64D
Hanna, Wendell	CA4200	32B,64D,32
Hansen, Charles	CO0950	64D
Harden, Bill	TX3527	64D,37,38
Hare, Ryan	WA1150	13,64D,10A,10B
Haroutunian, Ronald	MA0400	64D
Haroutunian, Ronald	CT0600	64D
Harrington, Allen	AC0100	64D,64E,42,48
Harris, Janet	FL1650	64D
Harris, Janet	FL0450	64D
Harris, Turman	DC0050	64D,41
Hartley, Dawn	TN0100	64D
Harvell, Matthew	IL1400	64D
Harwood, Karen	GA1500	64B,64D
Hauser, Laura	TN1850	64D
Havrilla, Adam A.	PR0115	64D
Heinemen, Sue	MD1010	64D
Heintzen, Ashley	FL1750	64D
Heitzenrater, John	NC1600	64D,20C,20D,20E
Henegar, Gregg	MA1400	64D
Henegar, Gregg	MA0400	64D
Hepler, Julie E.	PA0100	64B,64C,12A,64D,64E
Herr, Andrea	NJ0700	64D
Herr, Andrea	NJ0825	64D
Hess, Susan M.	ID0250	64D,32E,41
Hesseman, Joseph	OH2450	64D
Hicks, Brian	UT0325	64D
Hicks, Roger	UT0190	64D
Hileman, Lynn	WV0750	64D,13C,13B,13A,13D
Hindell, Leonard W.	NY2750	64D
Hindell, Leonard	NY0500	64D
Hindell, Leonard W.	NY2250	41,64D
Hindson, Harry	MN1700	64D,64E,48
Hinkeldey, Jeanette	IA0150	13,64B,64D,66
Hinkle, Russ	KY1000	64D
Hochkeppel, Robin M.	LA0760	64B,64D
Hodges, Woodrow J.	WI0835	64D
Hodges, Woodrow	WI0250	13,13E,32E,64D
Holland, Katherine N.	GA1300	64D,32,64
Holland, Katie	GA0850	64D
Holland, Patricia C.	WI0850	64D,12A,42
Hood, Joshua	NC0550	64D
Hood, Joshua	NC2420	64D
Hooks, Norma R.	MD0520	64D
Hoskisson, Darin T.	TX2960	13,64D
Hoy, Ian	OH0100	64D
Huddleston, Cheryl	TX3400	64D
Huff, Douglas M.	IL3500	64D,12A,11,48
Humphries, Tracy	NC2650	64D
Hunt, John	NY1100	64D
Husser, John S.	VA1700	64D,64E,34
Iimori, Mitch	OR0250	64B,64D
Iimori, Mitch	OR0150	64B,64D
Iimori, Mitch S.	OR1100	64D
Irchai, Arnold	FL1850	64D
Irvin, Wade	MS0700	64D,64E
Irvine, Erin	CA5070	64D
Ishikawa, Yoshiyuki	CO0800	64D
Ivanov, Krassimir	NY3600	64D
Iverson, Cynde	NY3785	64D
Jackson, Fraser	AG0300	64D
Jackson, Fraser	AG0450	64D
Jackson, Nadina Mackie	AG0600	64D
Jackson, Nadina Mackie	AG0300	64D
Jadus, John	PA1550	64D
James, Helen	IA0950	64D
James, Martin E.	OH2200	64D
Jensen, Kristin	TX3510	41,64D
Jinright, John W.	AL1050	13,64D,34,64B,66A
Jobert, William	OH2500	64D
Johnson, Hubert	ID0075	64C,64D
Johnson, Ryann P.	NE0200	64B,64D
Johnson, Ryann	NE0150	64B,64D
Johnson-Tamai, Eric	CA0550	64D
Jones, Russell L.	KS1050	32,64D
Jorgensen, Nathan A.	SD0550	47,64C,64D
Joseph, David	ME0200	64D
Judge, Kevin	IA0850	64D
Juilianna, Anita	FL0150	64B,64D
Kamins, Benjamin	TX2150	64D,42
Kaplan, William	IL3310	13,12A,64D
Karamanov, Vincent	MI0300	64D
Karr, Matthew L.	KY1500	64D
Keef, Ardith A.	ME0500	13A,11,64D
Keesecker, Jeffrey	FL0850	64D
Kehayas, John	FL2000	64D
Kelley, Cheryl K.	MN1280	13,32,48,64D
Kelley, Kimberly D. Buchar	PA1300	64D
Kelley, Kimberly Buchar	PA0950	64D
Kelley, Mark	MN1450	64D
Kelly, Kimberly	PA3560	64D
Kermode, Walker	OR0950	64D
Kern, Stacy J.	MN0040	64D
Kershaw, Yvonne	AE0120	64A,64D,10A,11,13A
Kershner, Brian	CT0050	10,13,64D
Killmeyer, Heather N.	TN0500	64B,12A,11,64D
Kirby, David S.	NC1900	12A,64C,64E,64D,41
Kirk, Lewis	IL2250	64D
Klimko, Ronald	ID0250	13,64D
Knezovich, Bill	CA1860	64D
Koch, Nathan J.	TX2250	64D,13C,12A
Koepke, Laura	NY3725	64D
Kolkay, Peter	TN1850	41,64D,48
Kolker, Phillip A.	MD0650	64D
Koster, Charles	CA5040	64D
Koster, Charles J.	CA2420	64D
Kramer, Jason	MI1150	64D
Kravitz, Steve	OR0750	64A,64D,64E,41
Krimsky, Seth	WA1050	64D
Krimsky, Seth	WA0200	64D
Kroft, Pat	OH1350	64D
Kroft, Patricia	OH2290	64D
Kroth, Michael	MI1400	64D,41
Krutz, Kim	KS1400	64D
Kuehner, Eric	IN1450	64D
Kuhlmann, Evan	OR0700	64D
Kuhlmann, Evan	OR0850	64D
Kuster, Nicolasa	CA5350	64D,42,41

Index by Area of Teaching Interest

Name	Code	Areas
Kuuskmann, Martin	NY2150	64D
Lacy, Edwin	IN1600	64D
Laib, Susan	PA2150	41,64B,64D
Lano, Matthew	IL0730	64D
Lashinsky, Leslie	CA3600	64D
Laskowski, Kim	NY2150	64D
Laskowski, Kim	NY2250	64D
Laskowski, Kim	NY1900	64D
Lawson, Kay	WV0400	32,64D
LeClair, Judith	NY1900	64D
Leech, Alan B.	MT0200	64D,64E,20,64,42
Legere, Katie	AG0250	64D
Leisring, Laura	VA0250	48,64A,64D,41,64C
Levesque, Stephane	AI0150	64D
Libby, Cynthia Green	MO0775	13,64B,64D,20,48
Libera, Rebecca	NC2500	64D
Lindberg, John E.	MN1000	12A,12C,48,64D,72
Lindberg, John	MN0200	64D
Lipori, Daniel	WA0050	11,64D,12A,12C
Lockhart, Carolyn	CA4400	64D
Logan, Brian	KY1425	64D
Lotz, James	TN1450	12A,64D,35G
Lowe, Carol C.	NY3780	64D,11
Lowe, Shannon R.	GA2150	64D,48,13
Ludwig, William	IN0900	64D
Lussier, Matthieu	AI0200	64D
Lyle, Anne K.	IL1350	64D
Lyman, Jeffrey	MI2100	64D
MacDonald, Elizabeth	ME0440	64D
Mackey, Melissa A.	IL2900	64D,12A
Mackie-Jackson, Nadina	AG0450	64D
MacMullin, Dennis	NJ0175	64D,32
Madsen, Emily K.	MD0350	64B,64D
Magnanini, Luciano	FL1900	41,48,64D
Majoy, Jocelyn	OH1400	64B,64D
Malkiewicz, Martha	NY0400	11,64D
Mangrum, Martin	AI0150	64D,48
Mangrum, Martin	AI0200	64D
Mann, Jenny L.	AL1170	64D,12A,13A
Mapes, Randy	MS0100	64B,64D
Marino, Lori	PA2800	64D
Martchev, Valentin	CA0815	64D
Masri, Tariq	AL1150	64D
Masri, Tariq	AL0800	64D
Matsukawa, Daniel	PA3250	64D
Matsukawa, Daniel	PA0850	48,64D
Mattson, Sheri	MO1790	11,64B,64D
Maxwell, Susan	KS0650	13A,13B,64D
McCallum, Kyle	MN0600	64D
McClelland, Keith	TN1710	13,64D
McCray, Jeffrey	NE0600	64D,13
McGill, David	IL0550	64D
McGinnis, Tracy L.	MA2050	64D
McGovern, Timothy S.	IL3300	64D,48,41
McKay, James R.	AG0500	37,38,41,64D,12F
McKay, Janis	NV0050	13,41,55,64D
McLean, Kathleen	IN0900	64D
McLean, Kathleen	AG0450	64D
McLean, Kathleen	AG0300	64D
McLoughlin, Michelle F.	NY3650	64D
McMullian, Neal	IL2300	13B,32E,64D,60,37
McNabb, Carol	TX3515	13B,13C,64D,67C,64B
Meek, Richard	TX3200	13,64D
Merz, Laurie	MN1300	64D
Merz, Laurie	MN0050	64D
Michel, Dennis	IL0550	64D,42
Micklich, Albie	AZ0100	64D
Millard, Christopher	AG0400	64D
Miller, Eric	TX2650	64D
Miller, John	MN1623	64D
Mindock, Rebecca A.	AL1300	64B,64D,12A,34,42
Minnis, MaryBeth	MI0400	41,48,64D
Moody, Gary E.	CO0250	64B,13,41,64D
Moore, Kent R.	AZ0450	64D
Moore, Robert	OH0300	64D
Morejon, Adrian	MA0350	64D,42
Morelli, Frank	NY2150	64D
Morelli, Frank	CT0850	64D,41
Morelli, Frank	NY1900	64D
Morelli, Frank A.	NY3790	64D,41
Morgan, John	IA0650	64D
Morris, Matthew B.	OH1900	13,42,64D
Morton, Gregory	IA1800	64B,64D
Morton, R. Greg	IA0400	64D
Morton, R. Gregory	IA0300	64D,64E
Moss, Emily A.	NY0500	32,48,64D,60B
Mottl, Robert O.	MO1830	64D
Muller, David J.	CA6000	10F,11,12A,60B,64D
Muncil, Donna	NY0050	64D
Muszynski, Michael	GA1050	64D
Myers, Terry	MA0950	64D
Najarian, Laura	GA1150	64D
Nauful, Lisa	CA0600	64B,64D
Nelsen, Suzanne	MA0400	64D
Nelsen, Suzanne	MA1175	64D
Nelson, Susan J.	OH0300	64D
Nelson, Valanda	NC2440	64D
Newton, Steve	MI1000	64D
Nielubowski, Norbert	MN1623	64D
Nitchie, Carl	GA0750	64D
Noreen, Rebecca	CT0100	64D
Nye, Roger	NY2150	64D
Nye, Roger	NJ1130	64D
Oakes, Scott	KS1450	64D
Ober, Gail E.	PA1250	64D
Oberbillig, Janelle	ID0050	64D
Odem, Susan	IA0650	64D,20,64B,64E
Odem, Susan	IA1350	64B,64D
Odem, Susan K.	IA0200	64B,64D
Oft, Eryn	AL0500	64B,64D,12A,12C
O'Leary, Jay	IA1100	64B,64D
Olivier, Rufus	CA4900	64D
Olivier, Rufus	CA2950	64D
Olivier, Rufus	CA4700	42,64D
Oosterwaal, Amber	WI1150	64D
Opp, Benjamin A.	CA0850	64D
Ortwein, Mark T.	IN1650	64D,64E
Owens, Douglas A.	TN1720	64B,64D,13
Oyen, David W.	KY0900	13,48,64D
Palmer, Christopher	AF0120	64D
Pandolfi, Philip	PA1050	64D
Pandolfi, Philip A.	PA0550	64D
Partridge, Hugh	NC2410	64D
Patricio, Raymond	GA0950	64D
Patricio, Raymond	GA0200	64D
Paulson, Stephen	CA4150	64D
Pederson, John	NC2410	64D
Pederson, John	NC1700	64D
Peebles, William	GA2300	64D
Peebles, William L.	NC2600	64D,20D
Peeples, Georgia	OH2150	12A,64D,15,48
Persson, Diane	AA0035	64D
Persson, Diane	AA0100	64D
Pesavento, Ann	MN0750	64D,42
Peterson, Francine G.	WA0800	64D
Peterson, Francine	WA0650	64D
Peterson, Francine G.	WA1250	64D
Peterson, Russell	MN0600	47,48,64D,64E,35G
Petkovich, Brian T.	TX2200	64D
Phillips, Margaret A.	MA0260	64D,64
Phipps, Danny K.	MI0900	64D,12A,12C,13E
Piccirillo, Lauren	OH2550	64D
Pierce, David M.	MI0600	12A,64D
Pierson, Karen	OH1850	64D
Plumer, Shirley	CO0275	42,64D
Polcyn, Sandra	WI0700	64D,64B,32E
Polk, Janet	NH0350	64D,48
Polk, Janet E.	NH0100	64D,41,42
Polk, Kristin	KY1550	64B,64D,32E,13A,13B
Pollard, Amy	GA2100	64D,42
Polonchak, Richard	WV0550	64D
Pool, Scott	TX3500	64D,13,48,11,64E
Priest, Thomas L.	UT0350	32,64D,11
Pytlewski, Barbara	CO0225	64D
Quick, Gregory	NY4150	64D
Quick, Gregory	NY1350	64D
Rachor, David J.	IA1600	11,64D,64E,72
Radford, Andrew	CA5060	64D
Radford, Andy	CA5360	64D
Radford, Andy	CA5550	64D
Rafanelli, Paul	WA1000	64D
Raker, Robert	OH1600	64D
Ramey, Richard C.	AR0700	13A,64D
Ramsey, Laura	GA0250	11,64D
Ramsey, Laura	SC1100	14,64D
Ranti, Richard	MA1400	64D
Rath, Carl	WI0350	64D,42,14C
Read, Jesse	AB0100	38,41,64D,67E
Reamsnyder, Richard	OH2275	64B,64D
Register, P. Brent	PA0700	12A,48,64A,64B,64D
Rehfeldt, Phillip	CA0845	64D
Reinert, C. Robert	FL1745	64D
Resnick, Anna	OK1250	64B,64D
Resnick, Anna	OK0750	64D
Reynolds, Kathleen	TX3420	41,64D
Rhodes, Amy Patricia	IL2200	64D
Richmond, Mike	NY2750	29,47,64D
Ring, Eric	MO1950	64D,48,13C
Roberts, Elizabeth	VA0750	64D
Roberts, Elizabeth 'Ibby'	VA1550	64D,48
Roberts, Wilfred A.	TX2400	64D
Robinson, Gerald	AG0450	64D
Robinson, Jeff	TX3400	64D
Rockwin, Howard	NY2550	64D
Rodriguez, Javier	TX3530	64D
Rogers, Mark	TX2930	64D
Rogers, Mark	TX3100	64D
Rogers, Mark	TX3350	64D
Rogers, Patricia	NY1900	64D
Rogers, Patricia	NY2150	64D
Romano, Elizabeth	NY4450	64D
Romine, Ryan D.	VA1350	64D,13
Rose, Gwendolyn	MI2250	13,48,64D
Rose, Saxton	NC1650	48,64D,41
Roseland, Chad	IN0800	13,64D
Rosen, Michelle	PA3250	64D
Rosing, Carol A.	WI0865	64D
Rosing, Carol A.	WI0100	64D
Ross, Daniel F.	AR0110	11,41,64B,64D,72
Ross, Donald	MO0100	64D,64B
Ross, Laura Guyer	MO1500	64B,64D
Ruggiero, Mathew	MA0400	64D
Ruggiero, Matthew	MA1175	64D
Ryan, P. Dianne	IL0850	64D
Rydlinski, George	AK0150	64D
Sakakeeny, George	OH1700	64D,48,41
Sales, Christopher	FL1000	64D
Sanguinetti, Melanie	AZ0440	64D
Savedoff, Allen M.	CA3300	64D
Savery, Robert	CO0150	64D
Savige, David	VA1000	64D
Savige, David	VA0150	64D
Saylor, Jonathan	IL3550	12A,64D,41
Schaaf-Walker, Leah	IA0500	64D
Schankin, Nora	MI0500	64D
Schillinger, Christin M.	OH1450	64D,13A
Schmidt, Michael P.	MN0950	61,64D,32
Schoenbeck, Sara	CA3800	64D
Schoenbeck, Sara	CA1000	64D
Schoon, Marcus	MI1750	32E,64D
Schoon, Marcus	MI2200	64D
Scott, Jan	LA0350	32B,48,64B,64D,64C
Scrivner, Scott	SC0420	64D
Searing, Harry G.	NJ0800	64D
Seeman, Sharon	NJ0750	64A,64B,64C,64D,11
Seifert, Kimberly	PA2450	64D
Sharp, Jack	AL0300	64D,64E
Shelly, Daniel P.	NY2750	64D
Sherwin, Jonathan	OH0600	64D
Sherwin, Jonathan	OH0650	64D
Sherwin, Jonathan S.	OH0200	64D
Shioji, Lane	DC0010	64D
Shoemaker, Ann H.	TX0300	64D
Simpson, Peter	KY1450	13,64D,41
Skelton, William	NY0650	14,20D,38,64D
Sleeper, Kathryn	FL1300	64D
Smith, Angela	NJ1130	64D
Smith, Carole Mason	MN0800	64D
Smith, Carole Mason	WI0845	64D
Smith, Christian B.	UT0050	64D
Smith, Emily	IN1750	64D
Smith, Emily M.	IL3450	64D
Smith, J. Benjamin	GA2130	64D
Smith, Kristen	OH2250	64D,48
Solie, Gordon A.	OR0850	60,32,37,64D
Soluri, Theodore	IL0550	64D
Soluri, Theodore	WI0825	64D
Sommer, Maralyn	AR0300	64D
Sonneborn, Kristen	FL0680	64D
Sonneborn, Kristen	FL0500	64D
Soren, Roger	IN1010	64D
Southern, Lia M.	MO0775	64D
Southern, Lia	MO0350	64D
Spaniol, Douglas E.	IN0250	64D,37
Spencer, Helena K.	OR0700	64D
Spencer, William G.	NC0050	60,32,64D,65

Name	Code	Areas
Spires, Henry Ray	SC1080	64B,64C,64D,64E
Stees, Barrick R.	OH0600	64D,48
Stefano, Joseph	PA1150	64D
Steinmetz, John	CA1000	64D,12C
Steinmetz, John	CA5030	64D,12C
Sterling, Amy	MD0800	64C,64E,64B,64D,64A
Stewart, Lawrence	NJ1050	13,64D
Stine, Maria W.	NC0350	64B,64D
Stitt, Virginia K.	UT0200	11,32B,64B,64D,12A
Stolle, Kara M.	IN0350	64D,41
Stomberg, Eric W.	KS1350	64D
Stone, Maya K.	MO1800	64D
Stuneck, Julia	OH0700	64D
Summers, C. Oland	NC0850	32,63C,64D,65,72
Svoboda, Richard	MA1400	64D
Sweeney, Michael	AG0300	64D
Sweeney, Michael	AG0450	64D
Sweger, Keith	IN0150	48,64D,42
Tackling, Sebastian	ND0350	64D
Taylor, Jane	NY0500	64D
Thee, Lawrence	NC0930	64B,64C,64D,64E
Thomas, Hunter	AL1160	64D
Thomas, Loretta	SD0600	64D
Thompson, Robert	WI0825	11,41,48,64D
Thorpe, Allan	AB0060	64D
Thorpe, Allan	AB0090	13,48,64D,13A,37
Timmerman, Mark	NY2750	64D
Tomkins, John	SD0050	64D
Tomkins, John	SD0580	64D
Traba, Fernando	FL1745	64D
Traba, Fernando	FL0800	64D
Trentacosti, Michael J.	IN0905	64D
Trollinger, Valerie L.	PA1750	34,32,64D,11,32C
Trussell, Adam	NE0160	64D
Turanchik, Thomas	NC0750	64B,64C,64D,48
Turner, Denise	NM0450	64D,48
Turner, Richard	WY0050	64D,67C,11
Ulffers, Christopher	NC0650	12A,64D,11
Ullery, Charles	MN1623	64D
Ullery, Charles	MN0950	64D
Unger, Ruth Shelly	GA0750	64D,11
Unger, Ruth Shelly	GA0050	64D
Uno-Jack, Kaori	WY0200	64D
Vacchi, Steve	OR1050	64D,42,48
Vallon, Marc	WI0815	64D
VanBuren, Susan	NY2650	64D
Varner, Eric Van der Veer	AG0550	64D
Venterini, Maurizio	FL0930	64D
Venturini, Maurizio	FL2050	64D
Vieira, Alex	CO0200	64D
Voorhees, Jerry L.	LA0650	48,64D,72
Waddell, Mike	NC2440	64B,64C,64D,11,32
Wagner, Julia P.	PA1900	64D
Walker, Abigail	FL1500	11,64D,66D
Walker, Abigail	AL0345	11,64D
Walt, Stephen J.	MA2000	64D,41
Walt, Stephen	MA2250	48,64D,43,41
Wangler, Kim L.	NC0050	35,64D,35A
Washington, Lecolion	TN1680	64D,42,11
Wasserman, Lisa	OH2140	64C,64D,42
Watson, Frank	SC0650	32E,64D
Watson, Robyn	TX0075	64D
Weait, Christopher	OH0350	64D,48
Weait, Christopher R.	OH1850	64D
Weber, Brent M.	MD0350	64E,64D,29,47,20
Weber, Martha	NY3705	64D
Weiler, Joan	OH2300	64D
Weiss, Abraham	NY1700	64D
Wellman, Wayne	KY0250	64D
Wells, Connie	GA2050	64D
Wells, David	CA0840	64D
Wenberg, Jon	MS0385	64D
Werth, Kay	KS0350	64B,64D,48,64A
West, Jill	IL1200	64B,64D
Wevers, Harold	AG0170	64D
White, Mary Joanna	NC2440	64D
Whitney, Susanna	TN1200	64D
Wike, Lori	UT0400	64D
Wike, Lori J.	UT0250	64D
Wilhelm, Philip	IL1740	64D,32,40,11
Wilkinson, Donald G.	TX3520	64B,64D,64E,46,32H
Williams, Robert S.	MI2200	64D
Wilson, Jacqueline M.	WI0803	64D,48,13B,13C
Winstead, William O.	OH2200	64D
Wirt, Ronald	GA0550	13,48,64D,10
Wise, Sherwood W.	NY0700	64B,48,13,64D,42
Wohlenhaus, Jennifer	IA0700	64B,64D
Womack, Jeffrey	TX0150	12A,64B,64D
Wood, Susan	RI0200	64D
Wood, Susan	RI0150	64D
Wooden, Lori L.	OK1330	64D,41,38,42,48
Wooden, Lori	OK0700	64D
Wooldridge, Jessica M.	NY4320	64D
Woolly, Kimberly A.	MS0750	64D,12A,41,48,72
Worzbyt, Jason W.	PA1600	64D,13,37,48
Wright, Lon	MN1500	64D,64E,64B
Yang, Amy	SC0750	64D
Yost, Hilary W.	SC1200	64D,42
Yost, Jennifer	OH0250	64D
Yost, Jennifer	OH1800	64D
Zantow, Thomas	MI1850	64D
Zimmerman, Dean	MI2120	64D
Zyko, Jeanette	TN0050	11,64B,64D

Saxophone

Name	Code	Areas
Abramo, Joseph M.	CT0600	32,64E
Abrams, Colleen	OH2275	64C,64E
Ackley, Dan	WI0862	11,37,64E
Adams, Richard	PA2100	64E
Adams, Stephen	CA2950	64E
Ahlers, Ruth	CT0300	64A,64E
Alaniz, Steve	CA5100	64E,64C
Alexander, Eric	NY3785	64E
Alford, Steve W.	NC1250	64E,47,53
Aliquo, Don	TN1100	29,64E,46,47
Alkire, Jeff	CA0150	64E
Allard, James	MA0650	64E,47
Allen, David R.	VA1100	64C,64E
Allen, Mark	PA3330	64E
Allen, Roy	TX3300	64E
Almich, Michael	OR1000	64C,64E
Ammann, Bruce T.	SD0050	60B,37,32E,64E
Amon, Jonathan T.	MA0510	64E,70
Amsler, Audrey	IN1350	64E
Anderson, Jonathan	TX3600	13,47,64E
Anderson, Robert	AR0350	64B,64C,64D,64E,47
Angerstein, Nancy	TX1000	64E
Archibald, William	IL1050	64E
Ardovino, Lori	AL1200	12A,48,64C,64E,67C
Aron, William	CA3520	64E
Artwick, Thomas	VA1850	64E,53
Ascione, Ray A.	MD0060	47,64C,64E
Ator, James	IN0905	13,10,48,64E,29
Averhoff, Carlos	FL0700	64E,29A
Babad, Bruce	CA1900	47,48,64A,64C,64E
Bailey, Craig	AC0100	47,64E
Bailey, Don	AR0730	13C,29A,29B,46,64E
Bair, Jeffery J.	NC0650	64E,42,29A
Baker, Jan Berry	GA0750	64E
Baker, Jan Berry	GA1050	64E,11,13E
Balcetis, Allison	AA0100	64E
Balch, Mary W.	AL1160	64E,64C
Banaszak, Greg J.	OH0200	47,64E,29
Banaszak, Gregory	OH0600	64E
Banks, Christy A.	PA2350	35A,64C,64E
Barbanera, William	FL1650	64E
Barbanera, William	FL1745	64C,64E
Barclay, Timothy R.	IL0650	13A,64E,46,47
Bardeguez, Lemuel	OK0750	64E
Barham, Phillip	TN1450	64E,41,13B
Barrera, James	CA0825	64E
Barry, Rebecca	AL1195	29,64E
Barry, Thomas	IA1600	64B,64E,35C
Barton, Leroy	DC0350	64E
Bayes, Michael	MD0850	64E
Bazan, Michael	IL3550	64E,29
Beals, Andrew	CT0800	64E,41,53
Beard, Charles	KS1050	64C,64E
Becker, David	CA1510	64E
Becker, David	CA0600	64E
Becraft, Steven C.	AR0300	64C,29A,64E,48,32E
Beeson, Robert	DC0050	32E,64E
Behm, Gary	MT0175	37,64C,64E,64A
Bell, Timothy R.	WI0835	47,64C,64E,29,48
Bender, Rhett	OR0950	64E,13,52,64C
Bendzsa, Paul	AD0050	60,47,64C,64E
Benedict, Jeffrey W.	CA0830	29,47,64E,41
Benson, George	MI2200	29,64E
Bergeron, Jonathan	AZ0450	64E
Bergonzi, Jerry	MA1400	29,64E,47
Bernardo, Mario	FL0680	64E
Bewley, Rabon	TX1660	11,12A,29,64E,13A
Bill, Jennifer	MA0400	64E
Bilotta, Tony	PA3560	64E
Bingham, W. Edwin	WV0400	47,64E,64D,29
Birkeland, Roger	IL0850	64E
Bishop, James	FL0150	12A,37,38,47,64E
Bishop, James	FL1750	64E
Bixler, David	OH0300	64E,29
Bixler, Ronald	PA0350	64E
Bleuel, John	GA2130	13C,60,64E,64B,64D
Bleuel, John	SC0400	64E
Bloch, Gus	VT0200	64C,64E
Boal, Nathan	OR0700	64E
Bogert, Nathan	IA0400	64E
Bohm, Keith	CA0840	13A,64E
Boisvert, Jean-Guy	AE0100	41,64C,64E
Bolduc, Remi	AI0150	64E,29
Bombardier, Bradley A.	MN1600	64C,64E,11
Bonenfant, Timothy	TX0150	64C,64E,47
Bongiorno, Frank	NC2440	47,64E,29
Bonsanti, Neal	FL0650	64E,47,46
Borgo, David R.	CA5050	64E,14,29,47
Borgstedt, Bryson	SC1000	64E,47,64C
Bouchard, Jean-Marc	AI0200	64E,53
Bouton, Arthur E.	CO0900	48,64E,41
Bovenzi, Michael	FL1950	34,32E,64E
Bowen, Ralph	NJ1130	47,64E,29
Bowland, Jimmy	TN1400	64E
Boyd, Ned	IN1310	64E
Bradfield, Ann	NM0100	29,46,47,64A,64E
Bradfield, Geoffrey	IL2200	64E,29
Bradford, Daron	UT0050	64C,64E
Brakel, Timothy D.	OH2300	32E,32,64E,13,60
Brannen, Randall	OH1400	64C,64E
Brellochs, Christopher	NY1050	47,10,13,12,64E
Brenan, Jim	AA0050	64E
Brennan, David	CA2420	64E,47
Brenzel, Darryl L.	MD0850	64E
Bridgewater, Ronald S.	IL3300	47,64E,29
Brightman, Nicholas	IN0250	64E,72
Brignola, Michael	FL0650	64E
Bristol, Caterina	AL0050	11,12A,64E
Bristow, Brent	AR0250	64E
Britto, Richard	MA2150	47,64E
Britto, Richard	MA2020	64E,11,46
Britz, Joanne M.	KS1050	64C,64E,41
Bro, Paul	IN0800	48,64E
Brock, Andrew	VA0700	47,64E,32H
Brock, Gordon R.	FL1950	37,48,64E,60B,10A
Brockman, Michael	WA1050	64E
Brooks, Joseph H.	WA0050	41,48,64B,64C,64E
Brown, Ari	IL3310	64E,29
Brown, Derek	TX0050	29,13B,64E
Brown, Jeremy S.	AA0150	37,64E,29,12G,48
Brown, Leonard	MA1450	11,14,64E,29A,12E
Brown, Patrick	NC0550	64E,47
Brumbelow, Denise	MI1180	64E,64C
Bryan, Carolyn J.	GA0950	64E,48
Buchwald, Peter	CO0150	64E,35C,35D,10
Bunte, James	OH2200	64E
Burgeson, Eric	IN1650	64E
Burnette, Sonny	KY0610	13,47,64E,34
Cain, Joren R.	GA2150	29,64E
Campbell, Arthur J.	MI0900	64C,64E,13
Campbell, Gary	FL0700	64E,29,53,47
Campbell, Griffin M.	LA0200	64E
Campbell, Michael J.	GA2300	60B,47,64E,32E,11
Campbell, Will	NC2420	46,47,53,64E
Camwell, David J.	IA1350	32C,46,47,64E,48
Caravan, Ronald L.	NY4150	64C,64E
Cardillo, Michael	NY2900	64E
Carello, Joseph	NY2950	53,64E
Carli, Rob	AG0450	64E
Carlon, Paul	NY0644	29A,64E
Carlson, Brian	AZ0150	64E
Carmichael, Matthew J.	VA1350	64E
Carney, Anna	TX2650	64C,64E
Carpenter, Andrew	IL2750	64E
Carroll, James R.	VA0450	47,64E,29,46
Carroll, Kenneth D.	AR0110	29,64E,37,46
Carter, David	AR0730	64C,64E,48,11
Carter, Greg	AF0150	64E,29,10
Carter, Kenyon	GA0900	47,64E

Index by Area of Teaching Interest

Name	Code	Areas
Carter, Kenyon W.	AL0500	64E,29
Carter, Kenyon	GA1500	64E,29
Case, Greg	CT0600	64E
Casey, Christopher	CT0650	47,64E
Cashman, Glenn	NY0650	47,64E
Catalano, Frank K.	IL0650	64E,47
Cemprola, Michael	PA3330	64E
Cessor, Tyler	MN0600	64E
Chappell, Rebecca Ann	IN0100	64C,64E,35A,64D
Chase, Allan S.	MA1400	47,29,53,64E
Chesher, Michael	IA0950	32E,42,64C,64E
Chest, Robert	SC0200	48,64B,64C,64D,64E
Christensen, Tom	NY2900	64E
Churchill, Steve	MD0550	64C,64E,64B
Cipolla, John M.	KY1550	41,64C,64E
Clanton, Wendell	AB0150	64E,47
Clark, Antoine	OH1200	64C,64E,48
Clark, Dave	KY0250	29B,47,53,64E
Claussen, Kurt	MN1450	64E,42
Claussen, Tina	MO0350	47,64E,46,29
Clements, Gordon	AB0210	46,47,29B,64E,64C
Coccagnia, Lou	NY1150	64C,64E
Coggiola, Jill A.	NY4150	32E,64C,64E
Cohen, Paul	NY2150	48,64E
Cohen, Paul	NJ0800	64E,48
Cohen, Paul	NY0500	64E
Cohen, Paul	NJ1130	64E
Cohen, Paul	NY2750	64E
Cohick, Mark	MO2000	64E,64D,64B
Cohill, Gregory	IL1610	64C,64E
Colby, Mark	IL0850	64E,53
Colby, Mark S.	IL0750	64E
Cole, Monty	GA1300	29,32E,46,64C,64E
Colella, Lou M.	PA1450	64C,64E
Colella, Louis	PA3650	64C,64E
Collins, Christopher	MI2200	47,64E,29A,35
Contos, Paul D.	CA5070	64E
Cook, Andrew	AL0050	64E
Cook, Lawrence	HI0050	48,64A,64C,64E
Cook, Susan C.	IL0750	64E
Cooper, Jack	TN1680	29,64E,46
Cooper, John H.	ME0270	10,29,13,64E,10F
Cordingley, Allen	WI0840	11,64E,37,47
Corps, Wilfredo	PR0115	41,64E,42
Costigan, Christopher	GA2050	64C,64E
Cox, Carl	NJ1050	64E
Cox, Lauren J.	OK0300	64C,64E,13,13C
Cox, Michael W.	OH0350	64E,29,48
Crawford, Thomas	VA0350	64A,64C,64E
Crawford, Tom	TN1150	64C,64E,64A
Creviston, Christopher	AZ0100	64E
Crews, Norval	TX1700	11,64C,64E,72
Cripps, Cynthia L.	TX3525	64E,64D
Crowe, Gary	MN0250	64E
Cumming, Christine	NY1400	64E,32E
Cunningham, Jeffrey N.	MO0800	64E
Custer, Seth A.	SC0200	13,64E,10A
DaGrade, Donald	CA4300	64D,64E
Dagradi, Anthony	LA0300	64,64E,29
Dahlke, Andrew	CO0950	64E,48
Dalmasi, Martin	FL0930	41,64A,64E
Danielsson, Tamara	FL0800	64E
D'Augelli, Greg	CA0800	64E
Davidson, Tara	AG0650	64E
Davis, Dan	AA0020	64E
Davis, John E.	GA0300	60,11,37,64A,64E
Davis, Nathan T.	PA3420	20G,47,64E,29
De Melo, Dorvalino	AI0220	60,32C,37,47,64E
Dean, Alex	AG0450	64E
DeBenedetto, Patricia	CA1860	32E,37,64E,64C,48
Debus, David	TX3530	64E
Decker, Jeffrey C.	VA1550	64E,42,47
Dees, David	TX3200	47,64E,29
DeFade, Eric	WV0800	64E,64D
DeFade, Eric	PA0550	64E,47,29
DeHaan, Pam	IA1200	64E
DeHaan, Pam	IA0500	61,64E
Deibel, Geoffrey	KS1450	64E,46
DeMarinis, Paul	MO1950	64E,53,29
Demsey, David	NJ1400	64E,29
Denson, Parker	AL0300	64E
Denza, William M.	OH0500	64A,48,64E,64C
Devlin, Scott	FL2050	64E
DeWitt, Donald	NY1250	64C,64E,64A
Diamond, Shirley A.	WA1100	64E,64C,32E
DiBlasio, Denis	NJ1050	10F,47,64E,53,29
Dickerson, Shane	AL0200	11,64E,64D
Diehl, Bruce P.	MA0100	29,64E,47,46
Dirlam, Richard	MN0350	64E,48
Dochnahl, Jesse	WI0350	64E,41
Doggett, Cynthia Krenzel	IA0200	12A,20,48,64C,64E
Domingues, Cameron	CA0815	64D,64E
Doxas, Chet	AI0150	64E,29
Doyle, Phillip	WA0250	64E,47,48
Doyon, Pierre	AI0190	64E
Dransite, Robert S.	NY2550	64E,64C
Dreisbach, Paul C.	OH1000	64B,64D,64E,64C,48
Drewek, Douglas Alexand	KY0450	64E,64C,47
Drewes, William	NY2750	29,47,64E
Driscoll, Nick	PA3700	47,64E
Dugan, Leonardo	PA1550	64E,47
Dumas, Charles	NC1350	64C,64E
Duncan, Preston	MN0040	64E
Duree, David T.	MD0520	64C,64E
Duree, David	MD0500	64C,64E
Durst, Aaron M.	WI0855	11,37,47,64E
Durst, Alan Edward	CA0810	64E,29,32,46,47
Dygert, James	CT0100	64E
Eastin, Brad	CO0275	64E,48,46,47,64C
Eckert, Joseph H.	TX3000	64E,29,47
Edighoffer, Gary B.	WA0950	64A,64E,35D
Ehrke, David	NV0100	13C,64C,64E,41
Eisenreich, Samuel	FL0050	64,48,64E
El-Farrah, Rami	TX3530	64E
Ellis, Barry L.	WI0840	60,37,64D,64E,32
Ellis, Kim S.	TX1400	37,64C,64E,48
Ellwood, Jeff	CA0815	64E,29
Ely, Mark	UT0250	32C,37,64E
Emmons, Deanna	IN1450	64E
Encarnacion, Jose	WI0350	29,64E
Engebretson, John	MN0750	64E
Engelhardt, Kent	OH2600	64E,29,53,47
Engle, Tiffany J.	MI0350	64E,60B,37,32E
Englert, Don	AG0200	64E
Englert, Don	AG0450	64E
Enz, Nicholas J.	MI1450	37,41,64E,47
Epstein, Peter	NV0100	47,20,64E
Erickson, Scott	KY0950	48,64B,64D,64E
Eriksson, Johan	MT0400	64E,29
Espinoza, Dannel	NY3350	64E,48
Estes, Adam	ND0250	46,47,64E,64C,64D
Evans, David	OR0500	64E
Evans, David	OR0400	64E
Evoskevich, Paul	NY0700	47,64E,53,29,42
Ewell, Terry B.	MD0850	64D,13,64E
Fabian, Donald	TX2400	64E
Fackelman, Harry	NY4320	64E
Fagaly, Sam W.	IL0800	64E,47,29,48
Fancher, Susan L.	NC0600	64E
Farmer, Harry	VA0750	64E,47,42,43
Farr, Chris	PA3330	47,64E,29
Fettig, Mary	CA3920	64E
Fieldhouse, Stephen M.	PA1400	64E,29,42
Fine, Joe	OK1200	64E
Finnsson, Karen	AJ0100	12A,64E,64
Finucane, Dave	NC2410	64E
Finucane, David A.	NC0600	53,64E
Fischer, Stephen M.	GA0850	64E
Fisher, Mickey	GA0300	64B,64C,64E,48
Fleg, Jerome	WY0050	64C,29,47,64E
Flores, Yasmin A.	AL1250	64C,64E,64D,48,13B
Flowers, Jim	PA3650	64E
Foerch, Ken R.	CA3650	64E
Foerch, Kenneth	CA5355	46,47,64C,64E
Foley, Brad	OR1050	64E
Foote, Jack E.	CA0840	32,64E
Ford, Kelly	IN1350	36,61,60A,12,64E
Ford, Shannon	MI1950	64C,64E
Ford, Shannon	MI0050	64C,64E
Ford, William	MN1250	64E,48
Forger, James	MI1400	64E
Forsyth, Paul	LA0550	64E,48
Forsythe, Jada P.	MS0570	11,64C,64E,37,48
Fossner, Alvin K.	NY4200	64B,64C,64E
Foster, N. Gary	CA0815	64E
Fraize, Peter W.	DC0100	47,53,64E,29
Frazee, Nickolas	WY0115	64E
Freeman, Peter	AG0250	64E
Freeman, Peter	AI0150	64E,32
French, Chris	IN0910	64E,64C
Frigo, Connie	GA2100	64E
Fudge, Berkeley	WI1150	47,64E,53,64A,29
Furlow, George	PA1350	64E
Fusco, Andrew	NJ0700	64E,47,29,46
Fusik, James	MI2200	64E
Futterer, Kenneth	AR0200	10,48,64B,64D,64E
Gadgil, Sunil	TX2100	64E,64C,11
Gaffke, Todd	MI0900	64E,41
Gai, James R.	MO1790	20,64C,64E
Gailes, George	VA1600	47,64E,29B
Gailloreto, Jim	IL0550	47,64E
Gairo, Anthony	PA2450	64E,29,47
Gairo, Tony P.	PA1850	64E
Gairo, Tony P.	PA2550	64E
Gallo, Tony	AB0090	64E,14
Gardener, Karen Roll	OH0700	64E
Gardiner, Robert A.	SC0800	11,29,47,32E,64E
Gardner, Aaron	WI1150	64E,64A
Gardner, Mike	AA0050	13,47,64E
Garzone, George	NY2660	64E,47
Garzone, George	MA1400	47,29,64E
Gast, Kim	MN1300	47,64E,29
Gatien, Gregory	AC0050	64E,29A,47
Geeting, Daniel	CA0550	64E,64C,38,11,60B
Gelok, Daniel	TX3400	64E
Genevro, Bradley	PA2300	37,64C,64E,32E
Gerbino, Thomas J.	NY3600	64C,64E
Getz, Noah	DC0170	64E
Getz, Noah	DC0010	64E
Gewirtz, Jonathan	MI1800	47,64E,64C,11,29
Gewirtz, Jonathon D.	MI1200	47,64E,29A
Gibson, Christopher A.	MO0950	11,64B,64C,64D,64E
Giles, Michael S.	IA0850	64E,47
Gillespie, Valerie	FL2000	64E
Gillies, Lee	VT0250	64E
Gillis, Glen	AJ0150	60,32C,37,48,64E
Girtmon, Paxton	MS0100	37,47,64E,10F,60
Glasser, David	NY2660	64E,47
Gnojek, Vincent	KS1350	47,64E
Goble, Daniel P.	CT0800	47,64E,53,29,41
Goines, Victor L.	IL2250	47,64E
Goldberg, Merryl	CA0847	64E,32,11
Golemo, Michael	IA0850	37,60,64E,32
Goranson, Todd A.	PA2300	64E,64D,13A,47,42
Gordon, Daniel J.	NY3775	64E,11,37,48
Gordon, Jon	NY3785	64E
Gorman, Kevin J.	AZ0400	64E
Gorrell, Brian	OK1330	64E,46,34,47,29B
Gottlieb, David	NJ0750	10,13A,13B,34D,64E
Gould, Brooke	IA0600	64B,64C,64D,64E
Govoni, Dino	MA0260	64E
Graham, Alexander	TN0100	64E,60B
Graham, John	AR0810	37,64E,64C,48
Graham, R. Douglas	SC1110	47,64C,64E
Grant, Donald R.	MI1600	64B,64C,64D,64E,13
Grantham, Jennifer	OH0680	64E,29
Graser, Daniel	MI1750	64E
Grass, Ken G.	OK1450	37,64E,60B
Grass, Mahlon O.	PA2050	12A,48,64B,64C,64E
Greco, Christopher J.	KS0100	13,10,64,64E,13F
Green, Bunky	FL1950	64E,53,29
Greenblatt, Dan	NY2660	64E,32E,47,29B
Greene, James S.	CT0800	29,64E,46
Greenfield, Hayes	NY4200	64E
Greitzer, Ian	RI0200	64C,64E,48
Grezeszak, Amanda	SC0600	64E
Griffin, Joel	MO0400	64E,46,47,13A,13B
Griffin, T. Joel	MO0400	29,31A,47,64E
Griffiths, Amy	GA0550	64E,32E,11,47
Grise', Monte	MN1120	64E,32E,47,37,60B
Gross, Mark	NJ1130	64E,29,29A
Groves, Todd	DE0150	47,64E
Guay, Jean-Francois	AI0200	64E
Gudmundson, Jon K.	UT0300	29,64E,47,41
Guida, John	NJ1050	64E
Guidi, David	TX2650	47,64E
Gwozdz, Lawrence S.	MS0750	64E
Haar, Paul	NE0600	29,64E
Haas, Frederick L.	NH0100	64E,66A,29A,29B,47
Hagelganz, David	WA1150	47,64E,29,53
Haiduck, Neal	NY2200	64C,64E
Haight, Russell P.	TX3175	29,41,64E
Hainsworth, Jason D.	FL0200	11,29,46,47,64E
Hall, Doris S.	AL0010	11,48,64A,64E
Hall, J. Scott	OR0850	64E,29
Hall, Jeff	MI1850	47,64C,64E,66A,29B

Name	Code	Areas
Hall, Louis O.	ME0440	60,32,64B,64E
Hall, Randall	IL0100	64E,13
Hall, W. Randall	WV0300	64B,64C,64E,48
Halladay, Wallace	AG0450	64E
Halliday, David	UT0250	64E
Halliday, David	UT0400	64E,47
Hamilton, Tom	PA2200	64C,64E
Hamm, Randall P.	MO0775	47,64E,29
Hamme, Albert	NY3705	47,64E,53,29A
Harms, Lawrence	IL1090	11,47,64C,64E,29A
Harper, Billy	NY2660	64E,47
Harrigan, Wilfred	MA0600	64C,64E
Harrington, Allen	AC0100	64D,64E,42,48
Harris, Anton	GA0050	29,64E
Harris, Bill	CT0550	64E,64C
Harris, Jarrard	IL3150	64E
Harris, Mark	CO0550	64E
Harris, Rod D.	CA1375	13A,11,64E,29B,34
Harrison, Kelvin	LA0800	64E
Hart, Antonio	NY0642	29,64E
Hartley, Linda A.	OH2250	32E,37,64E,32G
Hastings, David M.	WI0850	64E,42,13A,13B,13C
Hatch, Ken	AR0110	41,64C,64E,16
Haugen, Ruben	MN1625	64E
Haynes, Justin	IL1350	64E
Heavner, Tracy	AL1300	32E,64E,47,53
Hedrick, Teresa	VA1250	64E
Hedrick, Teresa	VA0550	64C,64E,64A,64B
Hefley, Earl	OK1330	11,64C,64E
Heisler, Jeff A.	OH1100	64E,42,37
Helman, Shandra K.	ID0100	64C,13C,48,20,64E
Helton, Jonathan	FL1850	64E,42,43
Hemke, Frederick	IL2250	64E
Henderson, David	CA5350	64E,42
Henderson, David D.	CA4900	64E
Henson, Mitchell	GA1700	64E,47,13A
Hepler, Julie E.	PA0100	64B,64C,12A,64D,64E
Herbiet, Victor	AG0400	64E
Herring, Vincent	NJ1400	64E,29,47
Hewett, E.	MA0800	64E
Hibbard, Mace	GA1050	64E
Hibler, John	WI0300	64E
Hibler, John	WI1155	64A,64E,64C
Higbee, David	KS0150	48,64E
Hill, Dennis	FL0500	37,47,64A,64E,29
Hill, Harry H.	SC0850	11,12A,64C,64E,48
Hill, James S.	OH1850	64E
Hill, Karen	SC0650	64C,64E
Hindson, Harry	MN1700	64D,64E,48
Hinson, James M.	IL2910	48,64C,64E,42
Hinton, Jeffrey	MO0850	60,32C,37,64E
Hirleman, Laura	MI1160	64C,64E
Hiscock, Fred	NC2000	64E
Hodge, Randy	MO0550	37,64E
Hogg, William	KY1000	29,64E
Holden, James	VA1750	13,20G,37,64E,46
Hollinger, Lowell	MS0350	11,13A,32C,48,64E
Hollingsworth, Dina L.	CO0275	64A,64E,29,41,11
Holmes, J. Michael	IL3300	64E
Homan, Jeff	OR0150	64E
Homan, Jeff C.	OR1100	64E
Honnold, Adrianne	MO0700	12A,64E
Honnold, Adrianne L.	MO1900	64E
Horner, Brian	TN0050	64E
Horton, Brian	NC1600	64E,46
Houghton, Stacey	GA0500	47,29,64E,64C
Houlik, James	PA1050	64E
Huddleston, Jeffrey L.	TN1680	64E
Huff, Lori	CA0630	13A,11,48,64E,32
Hughes, Larry	CA3300	64C,64E
Hughes, Lawrence P.	CA3500	64C,64E
Humes, Scot A.	LA0770	64C,64E,11
Hunter, Michael	MI1650	47,63C,29,64E
Hunter, Randy	GA0750	47,64E
Hurlburt, Sean	IL0550	64E
Husser, John S.	VA1700	64D,64E,34
Hutton, Joan	MN0050	64E
Ibrahim, Michael	WV0750	64E,32E,48
Infusino, Patrick	IL0275	11,64E,13C
Irvin, Wade	MS0700	64D,64E
Irwin, David E.	FL0450	64C,64E,37,41
Isaac, James G.	MO1790	64E,47
Isaackson, Mark	SD0050	64E,47
Ishii, Timothy	TX3500	29,46,47,64E
Jacklin, Christopher	AJ0100	47,64E
Jacobsen, David C.	VA1700	64A,64E
Jacobson, Michael	TX0300	64E,34
Jagow, Shelley	OH2500	64E,48,37
James, Matthew T.	OH1900	64E,47,53,46,29
Janus, Ryan	CO0050	64E
Jefferson, Kelly	AG0650	29,64E
Jenkins, Chester	OH0450	64E
Jenkins, E. Morgan	MD0450	64A,64E,70,29B
Jenkins, Pamela	ME0340	64A,64C,64E,32,13E
Jennings, Joseph W.	GA1900	47,64C,29,64E
Jensen, Christine	AI0150	29,64E
Jessop, Dustin	TX3350	32E,64E
Jessop, Dustin	TX3100	46,64E
Johnson, Curtis	PA3580	64E
Johnson, Curtis	WV0750	64E,29
Johnson, Greg	OR0200	64E
Johnson, Nathaniel	NE0710	60,37,64C,64E
Johnson, Randall	GU0500	11,36,47,61,64E
Jones, Heath	OK0700	64C,64E,47,72,34
Jordheim, Steven	WI0350	41,64E
Josenhans, Thomas	IN1600	64C,13B,13C,64E,41
Justeson, Jeremy	PA1750	64E,37,32E,43,11
Kallestad, Scott	NC0050	32E,64E
Kalman, Zoltan	AG0050	64C,48,64E,37
Kana, Dave	OH1350	64E
Kandi, Kareem	WA0750	47,64E
Karn, Michael	NY2660	64E,47
Keech, Christopher	MI1985	64C,64E,37,48,47
Keel, Gregory	MN0950	64E
Keepe, Michael L.	AZ0500	64E
Keepe, Michael L.	AZ0480	35,64E
Keller, Gary W.	FL1900	64E,29,47
Kelley, Richard P.	IL2900	64E
Kelton, Christopher T.	RI0150	47,64C,64E,29A
Kem, Randy	OR1300	64E,42
Kennedy, Donny	AI0150	29,64E,47
Kennedy, William	FL0850	47,29,64E
Kennell, Richard P.	OH0300	64E
Kenyon, Steven	NY1600	64E,29
Kerber, Ronald	PA3330	47,64A,64E,29,41
Kestenberg, Abe	AI0150	48,64C,64E,64A
Kidder, Tim	UT0190	29,64E
Kidonakis, Tony G.	IL3450	64E,47
Kiec, Michelle	PA1750	64,13,64C,64E,48
Kiec, Michelle	PA1750	64,13,64C,64E,11
Kieme, Mark	MI1750	64E
Kimball, Roger	IL1610	64E,64C
King, Clarence M.	TX2200	64E
King, Jeffrey	MN1050	64C,64E
King, Morgan	TX2260	64E
Kinzer, Charles E.	VA0700	12A,47,64E
Kirby, David S.	NC1900	12A,64C,64E,64D,41
Kirk, Jeff	TN0100	47,64E,35B
Klaehn, Andrew	AG0350	64C,64E
Klimowski, Stephen	VT0450	64C,64E
Klimowski, Steve	VT0400	64C,64E
Klock, Lynn E.	MA2000	64E
Knight, Michael D.	WI0750	37,60B,32E,64C,64E
Knipschild, Ann	AL0200	13,48,64B,64E
Knoop, Tracy V.	WA0600	64C,64E
Knop, Robert	CA0845	32E,29,64E,11
Knox, Carl	CT0050	64E,29A,46,47
Knudsen, Kasey	CA4700	64E
Koch, Jeremy	WV0550	64E
Kocher, Christopher John	SD0600	47,64E,53,46,29
Kolker, Adam	PA1750	64E
Kolodny, Michael	MA2250	64E,41
Kostaras, Jimmy	DC0170	64E,64
Koza, Matt	NY0646	13A,64C,64E
Kravitz, Steve	OR0450	64B,64E,64C,29,11
Kravitz, Steve	OR0750	64A,64D,64E,41
Krieger, Ulrich	CA0510	10,34D,12A,45,64E
Krueger, Christopher	MA1400	64A,64E
Kuhl, J. C.	VA1600	64E
Kurschner, James	MN1200	37,64E,41,66D
Kush, Jason	PA3100	64E,29,41,53,64C
Kynaston, Trent	MI2250	47,64E,46,29
Laboranti, Jerry B.	PA1300	64E,47
Laidlaw, George	AG0500	64E
Lalama, Ralph	NY2750	29,47,64E
Lalama, Ralph	NY3785	64E
Lamar, Jackie B.	AR0850	47,48,64E
Lampl, Kenneth H.	NY1600	35,10,64E,34,11
Larocque, Jacques	AI0220	10,41,48,64E,34
Lascell, Ernest D.	NY3730	48,64C,64E
Lau, Eric	NM0450	64E
Laughlin, Jim	TX0100	13A,12A,48,64C,64E
Lauver, Eric	PA1050	64E
Lawson, Tonya	TN1100	64C,64E,64B,11
Leali, Brad	TX3420	29,47,64E
Leaman, Clifford L.	SC1110	64E
LeClair, Paul	VT0400	13,12A,48,37,64E
Lee, Richard A.	HI0200	13,10,12A,64E,64A
Leech, Alan B.	MT0200	64D,64E,20,64,42
Leechford, Wayne	NC1700	64E
Lefebvre, Matthew T.	MA0150	64E
Lefevre, Donald	TX3750	37,64E,48
LeFlore, Maurice	NC0700	64E,37
Legette, Lee David	NC2700	11,32B,37,47,64E
Lemmons, Frederick	NC1250	64C,64E,48
Lenox, Michael	VT0100	64E
Leroux, Andre	AI0150	29,64E
Lessly, Chris Ann	IN1025	32,41,48,64C,64E
Levine, Barry	NJ0550	11,64C,64E,29A
Levine, Jonathan	FL0400	64E
Levine, Ted	MA1350	64E
Levine, Theodore	MA1100	64E,29A
Levine, Theodore	MA2100	64E,46,29A
Levinsky, Gail B.	PA3150	48,64E,32E
Lewis, Cecil	CO0100	47,53,64E,37
Lewis, Robert S. T.	SC0500	11,47,64E
Lidral, Karel	ME0440	13B,47,64E,29B
Lin, Chien-Kwan	NY1100	64E
Lindsay, Gary M.	FL1900	47,64E,29
Linney, William E.	VA1350	64E
Linsley, Troy	AJ0150	64E
Lipman, William	TX0550	12A,64C,64E,11,48
Lishman, Steve	CA0150	64E
Litroff, Scott	NY0050	64E
Littel, Sue	MI1850	64E
Livermore, Allen	MA0280	47,64E,29
Lockart, Rob R.	CA0835	64E
Lockwood, Tom	MI1050	64E
Lockwood, Tom	MI0300	64E,70
Lockwood, Tom	MI1000	62D,64E
Loden, Larry	TX1900	64C,64E,32E
Loden, Larry D.	TX3410	64E
Loeffert, Jeffrey	OK0800	64E,13
Logsdon, Anthony	AL0500	60,32,64E
Long, Bob	MO0850	29,64E,47
Long, Jeremy A.	OH1450	64E,47,42
Long, Kenneth A.	GA1050	13A,64C,64E
Loudenback, Daniel	TX1850	64E
Louie, Gary	MD0650	64E
Lovano, Joe S.	NY2750	29,64E,47
Lovano, Joe	MA0260	64E
Lozano, Frank	AI0150	29,64E
Lozano, Sal	CA0825	64E
Lucas, April	NY3705	64E
Luckey, Robert	LA0760	47,64E,29
Luedders, Jerry D.	CA0835	32,64E
Luffey, Gregory	TX3520	64E,11
Lulloff, Joseph	MI1400	42,64E
Luthra, Arun	NY2660	13,64E
Luzeniecki, Jerry	IL2300	64E
Lydeen, Brian	WI0400	64,47,37,42,64E
MacDonald, Colin	AB0050	64E
MacDonald, Don	AB0070	10,61,62A,64E,35A
MacDonald, Scott	AF0120	64E
Mack, James	CA1750	64C,64E
Malach, Robert	NJ0825	64E
Malley, Kevin J.	IL1350	64E,47
Mallinger, Patrick	IN0005	64E,64C
Malone, William	CO0810	64E,64C,64A,29A,20
Manceaux, Reese	NC2420	64E
Mandat, Eric P.	IL2900	13,64C,64E
Mandel, Alan	NY1550	64E
Mandel, Nathan	IL1740	64E
Marcus, Aaron	IN0907	64E,47
Marienthal, Eric	CA0825	64E
Marinelli, Vincent J.	DE0150	64C,64E
Marling, Chisato Eda	NY1700	64E
Marling, Chisato Eda	NY2650	64E,48
Marquis, Eugene	OH2550	64C,64E
Marsalis, Branford	NC1600	47,46,64E
Martin, Don	NC0300	64C,64E
Martyn, Charles F.	WV0650	37,47,64A,64C,64E
Masek, Douglas H.	CA5030	64E,64C
Mason, Colin M.	TX2800	47,11,64E,29,48
Mason, James	CA0825	64E
Mason, James	CA1425	64C,64E

Index by Area of Teaching Interest

Name	Code	Areas
Masters, Suzanna	VA1580	64C,11,13A,64E,48
Matasy, Katherine V.	MA2050	64C,64E,68,42
Matsuura, Gary	CA0960	47,64E
Matzke, Rex	CO0200	64E,29B
Mauceri, Frank	ME0200	47,64E
Maugans, Stacy	IN1750	48,64E,13B
Mauk, Steven	NY1800	64E
Maxfield, Jessica	IL1900	64A,64C,64E
Mayfield, Gray	GA1450	64E,37
Mayhew, Sandon	ID0070	47,64E
Maynard, Robert	LA0050	64E,47
Mazzeo, Frank	PA3250	64E
McAllister, Elizabeth	NC1750	12A,41,48,64C,64E
McArthur, Mark	NV0050	64E,42
McCallum, Gregory	VA1800	37,64C,64E
McCallum, Wendy M.	AC0050	64E,32E,37,60B,32
McCandless, Marty	IL1100	64C,64E,32E,47,41
McCarthy, Charles	CA4900	64E
McCarty, Daniel J.	ID0075	64C,64E
McCaslin, Donny	NY2150	64E
McClune, David	TN1660	47,64C,64E
McClure, Matthew	NC2410	37,64E
McComas, Inez S.	FL1450	64E,13
McConkie, Dawn	KS0300	32,64C,64E
McCord, Adam	OH2450	64E,47
McCord, Adam R.	KY1500	64E
McCormick, Thomas	FL1300	64E,20G,29
McDerment, Christopher	OH1900	64E
McDonald, Heather	KY0400	64E
McDonald, Reginald	TN1400	32E,37,41,64E
McDonnell, David	OH2250	10B,10F,34,64E,47
McFeaters, Jason	DC0170	64E
McLaren, Malena	LA0550	12,64C,64E,47
McLaughlin, Greg	CA4580	64A,64E,47
McMullen, Mike	CA0150	64E
Meier, Scott Alan	PA2250	47,53,64E,34,32E
Meighan, Patrick	FL0850	64E
Mertens, Paul	IL0550	47,64E
Merz, Christopher Linn	IA1600	64E,47,29
Mezei, Margaret	AA0200	13A,64C,64E
Michael, George	OH2140	47,64E,29
Michewicz, Michael	MI0850	64E,46
Miedema, Harry F.	IN1650	47,64E,29,53
Mietz, Joshua	NM0400	64C,64E,13,38
Miglia, Jay	OH2050	29,64E,46,47
Miller, Cercie	MA2050	64E,47
Miller, Joel	AI0150	29,64E
Mills, John	TX3510	64E,29,47,46
Mills, Peter	OH0850	64E,47,29
Milne, David	WI0845	29A,47,48,64E
Mitchell, Kathleen	NJ0175	64E
Modirzadeh, Hafez	CA4200	14,20,64E
Mohen, Girard	NY5000	64C,64E
Molinaro, Lisa M.	PA2950	64E
Moline, Garth	WY0150	64C,64E
Monaghan, Michael	MA0700	47,64A,64E,53,29
Moolenbeek, William J.	AG0200	64E
Moore, Christopher	IN1850	64E
Moore, Corey	NJ0500	47,60,64E
Moore, Gregory	WI0860	13C,47,64E,29,10A
Moore, Joel	IL1520	64E,29A
Moore, Joel	IL0150	64E,64C
Moore, John S.	IN1010	64E
Moore, Rich	IL2200	64E,29
Morgan, Kenyon	MI1150	64E
Morneau, John P.	ME0200	37,64C,64E
Morris, Stanley	AR0700	64E
Morris, Willie L.	OH2250	37,47,64E,32
Morton, R. Gregory	IA0300	64D,64E
Mossblad, Gunnar	OH2300	64E,46,47,29B,29C
Motz, Steve	AL1160	64E
Moxness, Paul	MN0200	64C,64E
Moxness, Paul	MN1000	13A,32,64E
Moye, Brenda	TN0850	64E,41,34
Muncy, Robert	MD0700	64A,64E
Mundy, Paul	IL2750	64E
Murdaugh, Johnnie L.	SC0350	64E,32C
Murley, Michael	AG0450	64E,29
Murphy, John P.	TX3420	29,14,47,64E
Murphy, Joseph M.	PA2150	48,64E,34A
Murphy, Otis	IN0900	64E
Murray, Jack	NC1100	64C,64E
Murray, Jack T.	NC0350	64A,64C,64E
Musselwhite, Eric	VA0150	47,64E
Myer, Tom	CO0800	47,64E
Myers, Adam	TX3370	48,64C,64E
Nabb, Nathan	TX2700	64E
Nakamura, Gwen H.	HI0210	37,64E
Nelson, Larry	KY0550	64E,53,29,47,29A
Nelson, William A.	WI0700	64C,64E
Nesbit, James B.	VA1000	64E
Nesbit, James B.	VA0250	64E,48,29
Nestler, Eric M.	TX3420	41,64E
Nevius, Sheila	MD0400	64E
Newsome, Sam	NY2102	29,20,64E
Nichol, John	MI0400	47,48,64E,29
Nichol, Jonathan	MI0900	64E
Nicholas, Lauren P.	PA2450	64E,46,48
Nichols, Christopher Robert	NE0150	64C,64E,38
Nilson, Shawnda	MT0370	64E
Noffsinger, Jonathan	AL1170	47,64E,53
Nolan, Julia	AB0100	64E,32E,42
Noland, David	CT0800	64E,41
Nold, Sherry	PA3260	64A,64C,64E
Nolen, Paul	IL1150	64E,29A
Novine-Whitaker, Virginia	NC0750	64E,41
Novros, Paul	CA0510	64E,47,29B
Noyes, James	NY0625	64E
Noyes, James R.	NJ1400	64E
Nudell, Geoff A.	CA0835	64E
Oatts, Dick	PA3250	29,64E
Oberlander, Lisa M.	GA0550	64C,64E
O'Connor, Douglas	WI0803	64E,47
O'Dell, Timothy J.	ME0500	29,64E
Odem, Susan	IA0650	64D,20,64B,64E
Olson, Craig	WY0130	64E,48,64A,40,46
Olson, Jeffrey K.	GA2150	64C,48,64E
Olson, Matthew W.	SC0750	64E,29,47,41,46
Olsson, Patricia	OH2290	64E,20
Oore, Danny	AF0050	64E
O'Reilly, Daniel	SC0420	14C,64E,29A
Orgill, Edward	MA2100	20,64E
O'Riordan, Kirk	PA1850	10,60B,13,64E
Ortiz Garcia, Norberto	PR0115	64E
Ortwein, Mark T.	IN1650	64D,64E
Osland, Lisa	KY1450	64E,41,47
Osland, Miles	KY1450	47,64E,29,53,48
Oviedo, Javier	CT0800	64E,48
Owen, Stephen W.	OR1050	46,47,53,29,64E
Owens, Jimmy	NY2660	64E,35A,35B,35D,35E
Oxford, Todd	TX3175	64E,48
Oyan, Sheri	VA1600	64E
Pagan, Leslie	PR0100	64E
Page, Richard L.	NH0110	47,64E,29
Paliga, Mitch L.	IL2050	64E,29A,41,47,48
Paliga, Mitch L.	IL1400	64E,47,29A
Panella, Lawrence	MS0750	29,64E,47
Parkin, Chris	WA1350	64E,46,47
Parkin, Christopher	WA0400	64E
Parrell, Richard N.	VA0450	42,64E
Parrish, William	VA1400	64E
Pate, David	FL1650	64E
Patneaude, Brian	NY3600	64E,29,46
Patnode, Matthew A.	ND0350	64E,64A,29,48,47
Patrick, Lee	KY1350	64E
Patterson, Ann	CA1750	29,64B,64E
Patterson, Tracy	TX1550	64C,64E
Paulo, Gary	GA0750	64E
Pelchat, Andre	AI0210	64E
Pelischek, Jeff	KS0550	11,37,48,64C,64E
Peltola, Gilbert	ME0200	64C,64E
Pendowski, Michael	AL0200	64E,46,47,11
Pepe, Dino	AG0170	64E
Perez, Paul	CA0650	64E
Perrett, Mario	MA2010	64E
Perrine, John Mark	OH0650	47,29A,64E
Perry, Rich	NY2750	64E
Perry, Rich	NJ1400	64E,47
Peterson, Jeff	IA1300	64E
Peterson, Russell	MN0600	47,48,64D,64E,35G
Pettit, Darren	NE0610	64E,47
Pfenninger, Rik C.	NH0250	64E,29,35,32E,10B
Phillips, Katrina R.	AL0050	11,12A,64E
Pickett, Lenny B.	NY2750	46,47,64E,29
Pietro, David A.	NY2750	64E,29,47
Pillow, Charles	NY1100	64E
Pinter, Greg	CA5020	64E
Pisano, James	KS0200	64C,64E,47,53,13
Pisano, Kristin	KS0350	11,64C,64E,12A,14C
Pittel, Harvey	TX3510	64E
Pituch, David A.	IL0750	64E,11,12A
Pivec, Matthew	IN0250	29,64E
Plugge, Scott D.	TX2250	64E,20G,29,47
Pool, Scott	TX3500	64D,13,48,11,64E
Poole, Tommy A.	OK0550	29,46,64E,10A
Pope, David J.	VA0600	64E,47
Potter, Christopher	NY2750	46,47,64E,29
Potts, Leo W.	WA1300	64C,64E
Powell, Timothy J.	MD1010	64E
Price, Jeffrey	MI2120	64E,11
Price, Jeffrey	AG0550	64E,29,46
Purkhiser, Beth	IN1850	64C,64E
Purslow, Vicki T.	OR0950	11,37,64E,29
Quesenberry, Karen	VA0100	64E
Quigley, Fred	PA0950	64E
Raby, Lee Worley	CA2801	47,64E,13A,13B,64
Rachor, David J.	IA1600	11,64D,64E,72
Radnofsky, Kenneth	MA1175	64E
Radnofsky, Kenneth	MA0350	64E
Radnofsky, Kenneth	MA1400	64E
Radnosfky, Kenneth	MA0400	64E
Ragsdale, C. David	AL1160	37,60,11,64E
Rask, Perry J.	IL1750	47,64E,29
Raskin, Jon	CA2950	10,64E
Rath, Richard	OK0850	64,64B,64E
Reed, Thomas T.	OH0100	10F,64C,64E,48
Reefer, Russell	PA0700	64C,64E
Reese, Randall	GA0200	10F,47,64E,10A,13D
Regan, Lara	IL0850	64E
Regan, Lara	IL2650	64E,64C
Regni, Albert G.	MD1010	64E
Regni, Albert	VA1600	64E
Reid, Doug	WA0860	47,64E,53,46,29
Reid, Kenneth	MA2030	64E
Rekevics, John	CA4100	64E
Reminick, David M.	IL2150	64E
Rewoldt, Todd	CA4100	13,29,64E
Rhea, Tim B.	TX2900	10,37,64E
Rheude, Elizabeth A.	ND0500	41,64C,64E
Rhoades, Connie A.	KY0550	64C,64E,20G
Rhodes, Rhonda	UT0200	64E
Rhodes, Rhonda L.	UT0150	64B,64E
Ricci, John	FL1000	64E,47,29
Rice, Michael	AL0010	64C,64E
Richard, Charles	CA3800	47,64E,29,34,42
Richardson, Dustyn	AA0050	64E
Richmond, James	VA0150	64E,48
Richter, Kimberlie J.	IL2050	13A,61,64E,29
Richtmyer, Debra A.	IL3300	64E,48,41
Ricker, Ramon	NY1100	64C,64E
Rider, Daniel	IL1300	64C,64E
Ried, William	NY3725	64E
Riekenberg, Dave	PA1950	64E,47,29B
Riley, Gregory E.	PA3600	64E,46,48
Riley, Madeleine C.	PA1000	11,45,64A,64E,29
Rippe, Allen	TN1680	48,64E,67C
Rivera, Diego	MI1400	29,64E,53
Rivera-Vega, Salvador	PR0100	11,32,48,64E
Roberts, Adam	AZ0350	12A,64E,29A
Roberts, Timothy	VA1350	64E
Roberts, Timothy	VA0450	64E
Robinson, Ian	IL1085	64E
Rodgers, Ernest E.	MI2200	64E,29,47
Rodriguez, Cristina	PR0150	64E
Roehrich, Matthew	NC1350	64E
Romain, James P.	IA0550	64E,29A,35A,29,47
Romines, Fred David	PA2200	37,60B,64E,32E
Romines, Jay	TN1710	64E
Romines, Jeff	TN1000	64E
Ronkin, Bruce	MA1450	64E,34,35
Rossi, Jamal J.	NY1100	64E
Rotter, James	CA0815	64E
Rotter, James	CA5300	64E
Rousseau, Eugene E.	MN1623	41,64E
Rowe, Monk	NY1350	64E
Rowell, Chester D.	TX2295	64C,64E,41
Roy, Dany	AI0200	64E,47
Ruedeman, Tim	NJ1400	64E
Ruedeman, Timothy	NY2105	64E
Rusinak, Dennis	AA0110	64E,64C
Russell, Benjamin A.	MD0475	47,64E,14C
Ruth, Byron	AZ0470	14C,29A,64E
Ruthrauff, Jeremy	IL0730	64E,41
Ruthrauff, Jeremy	IL1085	64E
Ryan, Thomas K.	OH0350	64E,13B,13C,13D,13E
Ryga, Campbell	AB0060	29,46,47,64E

703

Name	Code	Areas
Sacchini, Louis V.	IA0940	64C,64E
Saguiguit, Leo C.	MO1800	64E,48
Salman, Randy Keith	IN0350	47,64C,64E,29
Saltzman, James A.	NJ0300	64E,29,13C
Sampen, John	OH0300	64E
Sanchez, David	PR0115	64E,46
Sargent, Glen	ME0440	64E
Saunders, David	MN0300	41,64E
Scanlon, Brian	CA3600	64E,47
Scea, Paul	WV0750	64E,29,47
Schachter, Benjamin	PA0400	64E,29
Schattschneider, Adam	OH0250	13,47,64A,64C,64E
Scherzinger, Nicolas	NY4150	13,10,34,64E
Schiavone, David C.	NY0400	47,48,64C,64E
Schiavone, David C.	NY3717	64E,48
Schiavone, David C.	NY4320	64C,64E,47
Schimming, Paul	MN0610	32E,64E,64C
Schlabach, Robert	TN0450	64A,64B,64C,64E
Schmitt, Clinton	TN1350	64E,32E
Schneider, Doug	OR0850	64E,66C
Schneider, Matt	WA0800	64E
Schnitter, David	NY2660	13,64E,47
Schoen, Theodore A.	MN1600	64C,64E,41,10F
Schroeder, Waylon	IL1500	64B,64E
Schumacker, Meghan	IA0550	64E
Schwartz, Richard A.	LA0650	29,47,64E,11,46
Scott, Jason B.	VA1500	64E
Scott, Ronald	TX2930	64C,64E,38,10F,60
Scruggs, Richard J.	TN0250	11,13B,41,48,64E
Seybert, John M.	FL1740	60,66A,32,64E,12
Shachal, Harel	NY2660	20B,64C,64E
Shankle, Robert	TN1600	64B,64C,64E
Shanklin, Richard L.	OH2150	47,64E,29,35
Sharp, Jack	AL0300	64D,64E
Shaw, Kimberly	IL1890	64E
Shea, David L.	TX3200	34,41,64A,64C,64E
Sheldon, Paul	NY0600	64C,64E
Shelton, Adam	MO0775	11,64E
Sheppard, Robert	CA5300	64E,29
Shernit, George R.	OH0650	64E
Shields, Lisa	MT0100	13,36,37,64E
Shiffer, Faith E.	PA1250	64C,64E,41
Shikaly, Al	IN0400	64E,48,66
Shner, Idit	OR1050	64E,42,47,29
Shotwell, Amanda	SD0580	64E
Shroyer, Jo Ellen	MO0100	64A,64C,64E
Shroyer, Ronald L.	MO0100	64A,64C,64E,64
Shterenberg, Ilya F.	TX3530	64E
Shultz, Bud	IL1500	64C,64E
Sidener, Whitney F.	FL1900	47,64E,29
Sidoti, Vincent	OH0755	13,11,37,64C,64E
Sielert, Vanessa	ID0250	64E,47
Simmons, Amy	TN1720	42,64C,64E
Simons, Anthony R.	PA2550	64C,64E
Sims, Jared N.	RI0300	29,47,64E
Singer, Leigh Ann	IA0910	41,64A,64E
Sinta, Donald J.	MI2100	64E
Sintchak, Matthew A.	WI0865	64E,29,43,47,48
Skelton, Sam	GA1150	64E,47,29
Slagle, Steven	NY2150	47,64E,29
Slezak, Lawrence L.	TX2295	64E
Smith, Eddie	CA5150	60,32C,37,64E
Smith, Larry G.	UT0300	13,29,47,64E,46
Smith, Mike	IL0550	64E,29
Smith, Randall A.	MO1780	13,64E
Smith, Raymond H.	AL1050	47,37,34,64E,29
Snavely, Jack	WI0825	41,64C,64E
Snidero, Jim	NY2660	63B,64E
Solee, Denis	TN1850	64E
Sommer, Peter J.	CO0250	46,47,64E
Sommerfield, Janet	MI0500	64C,64E
Spaneas, Demetrius	NY1275	10,29,46,64E,10F
Specht, Barbara	OH0950	11,38,64C,64E,48
Speight, Andrew	CA4200	29,64E,46,47
Sperl, Gary	TN1710	64C,64E
Spires, Henry Ray	SC1080	64B,64C,64D,64E
Spitzer, David Martin	NC2435	37,11,64E
Stambler, David B.	PA2750	64E,29
Stapleson, Donald	MD0750	46,47,64E,13C
Stapleton, Chip	IN0907	29A,64E,14C,11
Starks, George	PA1000	20,14,47,64E,29
Steele, Terry	PA0550	64E
Steighner, Erik	WA0650	64E
Stein, Ken J.	IL2560	11,13B,20,47,64E
Stephens, Berin	UT0325	64E
Stephenson, Michael	NC1550	64,48,64E
Stephenson, Robert J.	UT0250	64E
Stepp, Scotty	IN0350	64E
Steprans, Janis	AI0190	64E,47,46
Sterbank, Mark	SC0275	64E,47,46,29
Sterling, Amy	MD0800	64C,64E,64B,64D,64A
Stevens, Anthony	MA0600	64C,64E
Stevens, Dwana F.	KY0300	64A,64E
Stewart, Kevin J.	CA0850	64E
Stolte, Charles	AA0020	64E
Stolte, Charles	AA0035	64E,13A,13,10,43
Stoltie, James	FL1745	64E
Stone, Joseph	CA6000	64B,64E
Stone, Simon	AI0200	64E,47
Street, William	ME0500	64E
Street, William H.	AA0100	60,37,64E
Streng, Bobby	MI0100	64E
Strickland, Stan	MA1175	64E
Strohman, Thomas	PA1900	47,64E,29
Strom, Kirsten	CA4425	64E
Stubbs, Fletcher	NC0450	64E
Stusek, Steven C.	NC2430	64E
Such, Rich	OR0175	47,64E
Sugihara, Masahito	IL3100	48,64E
Sugihara, Masahito	IL2250	64E
Sullivan, Aimee M.	NC2400	64C,64E
Sullivan, Taimur	NC1650	64E
Svanoe, Anders	WI0100	64E,41
Swagler, Jason	IL2970	64E
Swan, Steve	MD0520	64E
Swindler, Wil J.	CO0250	29,47,64E
Sylvern, Craig	NH0150	64E,34,32F,10,48
Talley, Keith M.	OK1250	64E,32,48,34
Tanner, Joel	OR0250	46,64E
Tarbutton, Butch	SC0050	64E,42
Tardy, Gregory	TN1710	64E
Taylor, Marshall	PA2800	64E
Taylor, Marshall T.	PA3250	64E
Taylor, Rhonda	NM0310	64E,13
Temperley, Joe	NY1900	64C,64E,29
Teuber, Hans	WA0200	64E
Thee, Lawrence	NC0930	64B,64C,64D,64E
Theisen, Alan	NC1250	13,10,34,35G,64E
Thibault, Joel	AI0190	64E
Thimmig, Les	WI0815	10,47,64E,29
Thomas, Craig	CA5550	64E
Thomas, Daniel A.	MO1810	64E,47,53
Thomas, Eric B.	ME0250	37,47,64C,64E,53
Thomas, Kelland K.	AZ0500	64E
Thomas, Russell	MS0350	47,64E,29,13
Thompson, Bobbi Amanda	AG0500	64E
Thompson, Thomas	PA0550	64C,64E
Thompson, Timothy D.	FL1450	10,13,34,64E
Thomson, Christopher	MN0800	64E
Timmons, Jeff D.	MO1810	64E
Timmons, Timothy	MO1810	64E
Tomaro, Michael	PA1050	64E,47,53,29
Tomassetti, Benjamin	VA0500	35G,10B,34D,35C,64E
Tomlin, Terry	TX3515	47,64E,29,34,32F
Torres, Michael Rene	OH1650	64E,48,10
Towell, Gordon L.	KY0900	47,64E,53,29
Tracy, Michael	KY1500	47,64E,42
Treadwell, Robin	GA1200	64E
Tritt, Terry	IL2775	64E
Trittin, Brian L.	TX0400	12A,13,29,37,64E
Tse, Kenneth	IA1550	64E
Turner, Dave	AI0150	29,64E
Turner, Don	TX2350	64C,64E
Turner, Mark F.	NY2750	64E
Turpen, Scott	WY0200	64E,47,29,60B
Umble, James C.	OH2600	64E,34
Umiker, Robert C.	AR0700	48,64C,64E
Underwood, Dale W.	FL1900	64E
Utley, Brian	TN1850	64E
Vadala, Christopher	MD1010	47,64E,53,29
Van Goes, Paula	TN1400	64E
Van Oyen, Lawrence G.	IL2050	13,64E,37
Vana, John	IL3500	64E,29A
Vanderheyden, Joel	MO0550	64E,46,47,29,13
VanMatre, Rick	OH2200	47,64E,29
Vatalaro, Charles	NY1400	64E
Velasco, Edmund	CA6000	64E
Vernon, James Farrell	IN0905	64E,47
Vickers, Jeffrey E.	AR0600	64,11,64E,64A,12A
Vinci, Mark A.	NY3650	47,64E,29
Vinci, Mark	NY3785	64E
Viswanathan, Sundar	AG0650	29,64E,10D,61
Walker, Chris	GA0625	64E
Walsh, Allan	AG0070	64E,72
Walsh, Allan	AG0150	64E,47,46,29A,29B
Walsh, Thomas P.	IN0900	64E
Ward, Doug	AA0080	64A,64C,64E
Warfield, Tim	PA3250	29,64E
Warth, James R.	TX2960	47,64E,64B
Watabe, Junichiro	AK0150	64C,64E,48,37,46
Watkins, Mark	ID0060	47,48,64E
Watson, Robert M.	MO1810	29A,29B,29C,47,64E
Webb, John	TX3535	20,47,64E
Weber, Brent M.	MD0350	64E,64D,29,47,20
Weiskopf, Walter	PA3250	29,64E
Wells, David	ME0340	47,64E
Wells, David	ME0150	64E
Welte, John	PA3330	64C,64E
Wen, Andy	AR0750	11,13,64E,64E
Weremchuk, George	FL1800	64E,48
Wery, Brett L.	NY3600	13,37,41,64C,64E
West, William	IL1200	13,64A,64E,41,67E
Western, Bruce	IA0930	64E
Wetzel, Neil D.	PA2450	47,64,29A,64E,46
White, Christopher K.	VA1100	29,64E,32E,64,12B
White, Sallie V.	AL0800	64E
Whitmore, Michael R.	OK0300	48,64C,64E
Wiffen, Dave	AG0600	64E
Wiggins, Ira T.	NC1600	47,64A,64E,29,46
Wilder, Ralph	IL2100	64C,32E,64E,11,42
Wilkinson, Donald G.	TX3520	64B,64D,64E,46,32H
Wilkinson, Todd R.	KS1000	47,64E,29,32E
Williams, Don A.	WV0400	64C,64E
Williams, Jane	IA1800	64E,48
Williamson, Bruce	VT0050	64C,64E,66A,67,47
Wilson, Glenn	IL3300	64E
Wilson, Steven	NY2150	29,64E
Wilson, Steven	NY3785	64E
Winkler, Fred	WA1000	64E,41,32E
Witt, Woody W.	TX3400	47,64E,29
Woelfle, Colin	MN1280	64E
Wolfe, Carl	TN1200	64E
Wolfe, Chris	MD0175	13A,60,37,64C,64E
Wolfe, George	IN0150	64E,48
Wolford, Dale	CA5000	64E
Wolford, Dale	CA4400	64E,41
Won, Allen	NY2250	64E
Wood, Tim	ID0140	64E
Worman, James	TX3350	32,37,47,29,64E
Wright, Lon	MN1500	64D,64E,64B
Wyatt, Alan	TN0850	13,47,64E,35A,35B
Wyatt, Angela	MN1623	64E
Wyman, Laurence	NY3725	64E
Wytko, Anna Marie	KS0650	64E,13A,48
Xiques, Ed	NY4450	64E
Yannie, Mark	MN0625	46,64C,64E
Yasinitsky, Greg	WA1150	47,64E,29,10F,10A
Yellin, Peter	NY2102	47,64E,46,29
Yin, Jei	AA0110	64C,64E
Yoder, M. Dan	PA2750	47,64E
Yoelin, Shelley	IL3200	13A,13,37,47,64E
Yokley, Darryl	PA3600	64E
Yorio, Joseph	FL1000	64E
Young, Charlie	DC0150	64E
Young, Colin	IA0700	64E,64C
Young, Eileen M.	NC2500	64C,64E,41,64,12A
Young, Jay	IN1100	64A,64C,64E
Young, Keith R.	PA1600	48,64E,47
Young, Robert	NY3780	64E,41
Yukumoto, Todd	HI0210	64E
Zaev, Pance	NE0450	64C,64E,48
Zanella, Jean-Pierre	AI0210	64E
Zattiero, Joanna R.	UT0300	12A,64E
Zilber, Michael	CA2775	11,64E,12A,20G,29
Zimmerman, Keith	IL0400	64E
Zimmerman, Keith	IL1200	64E,41
Zinn, Daniel L.	CA0807	47,64E,41,29A,11
Zinn, Dann	CA5000	64E
Zinn, Dann	CA0900	64E,29
Zitek, Sam	NE0450	37,64E,60B,32E
Zsoldos, Michael	VT0450	64E
Zsoldos, Michael	VT0100	64E
Zumwalt, Wildy	NY3725	64E,41

Percussion (All Areas)

Name	Code	Areas
Abel, Alan D.	PA3250	65
Abel, Alan	NJ1130	65
Accurso, Robert	NY0400	65
Adam, Mark	AF0050	11,13C,46,47,65
Adams, Dan	WA0800	65
Adams, Daniel C.	TX3150	10A,13D,13E,65,13
Adams, Ernie	IL3310	47,65
Adams, Matthew	TX1425	65,50,11,12
Adams, Timothy K.	GA2100	65
Agatiello, Gustavo	MA0260	65
Ainanda, Lucy	AR0425	63,64,65
Alamo, Juan	NC2410	29,65,50
Albagli, Richard	NY3700	65,50
Albin, William R.	OH1450	14,50,65
Aleo, Keith	MA0350	65
Alexander, Conrad	PA2150	65
Alexander, Conrad	NY1800	50,65
Alexander, Jason	AL1050	65
Alexander, Joel	MN1280	65,50
Alicea, Jose R.	PR0115	65,50
Alico, Gregory H.	PA3150	50,65
Alico, Gregory	PA0350	65
Allee, Fred	CA3975	65
Allen, Christopher	PA0550	65
Allen, Christopher	PA1050	65
Allen, David	MS0420	37,63A,65
Alorwoyie, Gideon F.	TX3420	20,65,31F,50,52
Altmire, Matt	CA3200	50,65
Altmire, Matthew	CA4450	65
Alvarez, Ruben	IL2250	65
Alvarez, Ruben	IL0550	47,65
Ames, Anthony	MD1010	65
Amidon, Brad T.	PA2250	65,32E
Amidon, Bradley	PA1200	50,65
Ancona, James	DE0150	37,65
Anctil, Gilles	AI0050	65
Anders, Nathan	OH0350	65,50
Anderson, Dean	MA0260	65
Anderson, Larry R.	LA0770	47,50,65
Anderson, Leon	FL0850	47,65,29,46
Anderson, Marc	MN0800	65
Anderson, Thad	FL1800	65,50,34
Antony, Trent	CO0300	65
Anzivino, Steve	MI0300	65,50,43
Aponte, Jose Porentud	TX3420	50,65,46
Applebaum, Terry L.	PA3330	65,35A,50
Armstrong, Daniel C.	PA2750	65
Armstrong, James D.	PA1250	65,50
Armstrong, Joshua	MS0250	65,50,37,41
Arrucci, John	NY5000	65
Arsenauit, Greg	RI0200	65
Artimisi, Tony	NC2700	35,65
Assad, Michael	TN1680	65
Assad, Mike	TN1200	65,50,47
Astaire, John	CA0600	65,50
Atkatz, Edward	FL1125	65
Atterbury, Rick	WA0900	65
Atwood, James H.	LA0300	65
Austin, Joshua	NE0250	65
Auwarter, Doug	MO0850	65
Auwarter, Douglas	KS0570	50,65
Babelay, Paul	NC1250	65
Bacon, John	NY3725	65
Bacon, John	NY4460	65,47
Bacon, Scott D.	PA1000	11,14C,65
Baden, Robert	WV0800	50,65
Baker, Dale	NC2350	50,65
Baker, Hill	CO0625	14C,20,65,34B
Baker, Jason	MS0500	65
Baker, Marc	MO1550	65
Baldauff, Brian	WV0600	65,37
Baldwin, John	ID0050	13,50,65
Ball, Jill	AG0500	65
Baranyk, David	IN1850	65,70
Baratto, German	TN1100	65
Barber, Amy Lynn	IN0350	65,50
Barber, Matthew C.	MN0050	65,50
Barnhart, Stephen L.	WY0200	65,50,32E
Barr, Evan	TN1680	65
Barr, Sammy	MS0360	37,65
Barraca, Rudy	AL0335	11,63,65
Barrick, Christopher	OH0550	65
Barrientos, Victor	CA6000	65
Barrier, Gray	CO0950	50,65,32E
Barsness, Erik	MN1300	65
Barudin, Jeffrey E.	MO0650	65
Baskin, Jason	MO0850	11,65,34
Bassett, Matthew	OH0600	65
Batimana, Ching	GU0500	65
Bauman, Carol	AG0600	13,65
Baxter, Brett	IL2650	65
Baxter, Jillian	GA0625	65,65B
Bayles, David	WI1150	65,47
Bayles, David S.	WI0835	65,50
Baynard, Tim D.	SC0400	65
Beam, Joseph	TX1450	65
Beck, John	NC2500	65
Beck, John R.	NC1650	50,65
Beck, John	NY1100	65
Beck, Matt	MI0350	65
Beckler, Terry	SD0400	65,50,37,46,11
Beckstrom, Tom	OR1000	65
Bedell, Adam	TX3100	50,65,32E
Behrens, Jeff	WI0842	65
Bell, Malcolm E.	AA0080	10,13,47,65
Bellotti, Sergio	MA0260	65
Bennett, Michael	ME0270	65,50
Benoist, Debbie	TX2310	11,13A,34C,65,66
Benoit, Lonny	LA0350	65
Benson, Mark F.	AL0210	13,12A,11,65,20
Bergeron, Norm	TX2800	65,50,10D,11,13A
Bernier, Lucas	ND0400	65,50,11,34
Berns, Paul S.	IN1650	65,50
Berry, Mark S.	KY1550	65,50,41
Berry, Michael	PA3580	65
Berthold, Sherwood	MS0300	65
Bessinger, David K.	OK1250	13,50,65
Best, Ed	CA5040	65
Bethea, William	VA0950	65,11,37,50
Beyer, Gregory S.	IL2200	50,65
Bierman, Duane	NE0590	37,65,50
Biesack, Ryan	OR0700	65
Biggs, Allen	CA4200	50,65
Bishara, Aaron	OH1600	65
Bissonette, Gregg S.	CA0835	65
Black, Alan	TX1700	11,37,47,50,65
Black, David	CA2550	65
Blackstock, Adam	AL1050	37,65
Blake, Michael	ND0500	13A,50,53,65
Blanchet, George A.	IL2050	65
Bleyle, William B.	OH0950	65,50,37
Bluestone, Joel	OR0850	11,50,65,20G
Bobo, Kevin A.	IN0900	65
Boccato, Rogerio	NY2150	65
Bohn, Donna M.	PA1550	12A,13B,13C,65,60
Bolen, Jerry	IL2970	65,20
Bonner, Peggy	IL0400	50,65
Booth, David M.	OH2500	60,37,63D,65
Borghesani, Dean	WI0825	65
Boss, Bonnie	CA3100	65
Bostwick, Stacey	IA0420	11,65
Bouchard, Jean-Luc	AI0190	50,65
Bovenschen, Wayne	OK0800	65,37,50,32E
Bowman, Paul A.	TX0550	65
Boyd, Bob	NJ0760	65
Branch, Thomas W.	AL1160	50,65
Brannock, Robert D.	TX3300	65
Branson, Jeremy	PA0550	65
Bratton, Tripp	KY0300	65,50
Braun, Roger	OH1900	50,65
Breaux, Troy Jude	LA0760	37,65,50
Breithaupt, Robert	OH0350	65,35A,35B,35E
Brennan, Adam	PA2150	60B,37,50,65,10F
Breton, Jean-Francois	AG0170	65,13C,50
Bridge, Robert	NY2950	65,37,50,20A
Britt, Michael J.	AR0600	46,50,65
Broadway, Kenneth	FL1850	50,65
Brochu, Paul	AI0200	65,29
Bronstein, Chase	TX2250	65,50
Broome, Curtis	CO0150	65
Broscious, Timothy L.	MN1600	10E,65
Broscoe, Liz	CA2440	65
Brosh, Robert	PA3330	50,65,20G,14
Brough, Ronald P.	UT0050	60,32C,37,65,72
Brown, Al	CA0850	32E,65,50
Brown, Allen	CA5350	50,65
Brown, Charles	NC2300	37,47,65
Brown, Charles V.	NC2150	50,65
Brown, Darrell	ID0060	32E,65,50
Brown, Eric	GA2300	65,32E
Brown, George	UT0250	65
Brown, Gerald	PA3330	65
Brown, Jeff	MS0360	37,65,50,46
Brown, Jeffrey C.	IN1750	47,50,65,11
Brown, Mel	OR1250	65
Brown, Richard	TX2150	50,65,42
Brown, Shon	SC0700	47,65
Brownell, John	AG0450	32,65
Brownell, John	AG0650	65,50
Brownwell, John	AG0200	32C,65
Bruce, Gary	OK0700	70,65,66F
Brudvig, Robert	OR0700	65,13
Brunk, Jeremy	IL1750	13,12,65,10
Bryant, John	TX2400	65
Bryant, Michael	DE0050	65
Buck, Peter	CA1520	65
Buda, Fred	MA2030	65
Buda, Frederick	MA1400	65,29
Bueckert, Darrell	AJ0150	50,65,37
Bugbee, Fred	NM0310	65,13
Bukvich, Daniel J.	ID0250	13,10,47,50,65
Bull, Michael W.	NY4150	50,65
Bump, Michael	MO1780	65,50
Burda, Pavel	WI0825	13A,60,50,65
Burdett, Kimberly H.	OH2000	50,65,32E
Burge, Russell	OH2200	50,65
Burgett, Gwendolyn	MI1400	65,50
Burke, Sarah M.	TX0340	50,65
Burkhead, Ricky	MS0560	65A,65B,50,65
Burkhead, Ricky	MS0700	50,65
Burnham, Jay	AL0300	65
Burnham, Jay K.	AL1200	65,50
Burritt, Michael	NY1100	65
Burritt, Thomas	TX3510	65
Bush, Doug	TX0250	65
Butters, Steven G.	IL0840	65,50
Butters, Steven	IL0600	65,50
Buyer, Paul L.	SC0400	65,50,14,20
Buyer, Paul	SC1080	65
Buzy, Marilyn	ME0250	65
Byrd, Katherine	GA2130	65,50
Byrd, Katie	GA2000	65
Byrne, Gregory	KY1500	65,37,50
Cahn, William	NY1100	65
Caldwell, Bob	AB0090	65
Caldwell, Robert	AB0050	45,65,34,46,41
Caldwell, Robert	AB0060	50,65
Calkin, Lauren	NE0700	65
Camara, Mohamed Kalifa	MA0260	65
Cameron, Clayton	CA5031	29,65
Cameron, James Scott	MO0775	37,50,65
Cameron, Wes	MS0850	11,63,64,65,34
Campbell, James B.	KY1450	65,50
Campbell, Todd	PA0250	34,11,65
Campbell, Todd A.	NC0700	35G,34D,35D,65,35C
Campiglia, Paul	GA0625	47,29,53,65
Campiglia, Paul	GA2150	65,29,71,50,11
Campion, David	AG0600	65
Cangelosi, Casey	WV0200	61,65,29,34
Cannon, Rodney M.	TX2250	65,29
Carmenates, Omar	SC0750	65,50,20
Carney, Michael	CA0825	65,29,20,50
Carpenter, Charles M.	CA3500	37,50,65
Carpenter, Tyler	OH1350	65
Carrington, Terri Lyne	MA0260	65
Carroll, John	TX1850	65
Carroll, Raynor	CA0825	65
Carrott, Bryan	NY1275	65
Carson, Mark	MD0150	65
Carter, Allen L.	MN1120	13,10F,65,47
Carter, Joey	TX3000	65,29A,29B,47
Cassara, Frank	NY0500	65,50
Cassara, Frank	NY2105	65,50
Cassara, Frank	NY4450	65
Castellanos, Juan	PA0650	65
Castrillo, Manuel E.	MA0260	65
Castro, Miguel	GA1400	50,65,11,47
Cates, Mike	TN0450	65,50
Cebulski, Michael	GA0940	50,65
Cebulski, Michael	GA0750	50,65
Centanni, Barry C.	NJ0800	65
Ceron, Homero	AZ0480	65
Cervantes, Ernest	CA0650	65,32
Chaffee, Gary	MA1400	29,65

Name	Code	Areas
Chambers, Joe	NY2660	44,65,53
Chancler, Ndugu	CA5300	29,65
Charbonneau, Louis	AI0200	65
Charles, Benjamin	FL0650	50,65
Charlston, Erik	NY2150	65
Chaudhuri, Swapan	CA0050	13A,10,12A,65
Chesarek, Justin	GA1150	65,47
Chesarek, Justin	GA0750	65
Cheung, Pius	OR1050	65,50
Chiado, Joshua	WV0050	65
Christianson, Tom	ND0150	65
Chuong, Jason	PA3330	32E,65
Churchill, Marc	MI1180	65
Ciano, Jack	FL1300	65
Cirmo, Michael	NY1350	65
Claeys, Keith	MI2200	65
Clanton, James	KS1050	65
Clarke, Axel	CA0825	65
Clarke, Terry	AG0450	65,29
Claude, Henry	MO1900	65
Clemenson, Andrew	MN0600	65
Cline, Rick	NC1100	65,50
Clive, David	NY4500	50,65
Clive, David	NY0644	65
Coash, David	FL0800	65,50
Coash, David C.	FL2050	65
Coghlan, Connie	CT0050	65,50
Cohen, Greg	CA4100	65
Cohen, Joel D.	IL3310	65
Coleman, Matthew	AZ0350	32,65
Coley, Matthew	IA0850	65,50
Collier, David L.	IL1150	50,65
Collier, Thomas	WA1050	47,65,20G
Collison, Craig	AR0110	11,41,50,65
Colson, David J.	MI2250	10,65,60
Condon, Clay	IL2100	65
Condon, Clay	IL2150	65,50,11
Connell, Joseph C.	DC0100	65
Connors, Michael	MA0650	65
Connors, Sean	WI0850	50,65
Conroy, Gregory	MA0510	50,65
Contrino, Joseph L.	MO1500	65,29A,13A,13C
Converse, Mark	CA0630	65
Converse, Mark	CA1265	65
Conzetti, Florian	OR0450	65
Cook, Gary	NV0050	65
Coons, Kevin	OK0770	65
Cooper, Peter	CO0550	65
Cooper, Peter	CO0200	65
Corbin, Dwayne V.	CA4600	37,38,65,29
Corcoran, James R.	KY1425	65,34,11,50
Corey, Scott	TN1600	65
Corniel, Wilson 'Chembo'	NY3785	65
Corsi, Stephen F.	PA0100	65,50
Coulter, Monte	TN1700	13A,11,50,65
Coulter, Ronald E.	IL2900	65,10B,50
Counihan, Emma	AZ0440	50,65
Coutsouridis, Peter	MA2100	65,41,29A,11,13B
Coviak, James	MI2120	50,65
Cox, Daniel R.	ID0140	50,65,53,11
Cox, Daniel	WA0400	65,50
Coye, Gene	CA0835	29,65
Coz, Brandon	AZ0150	65
Cozart, Keith	IN0400	65,50
Crabiel, Jon	IN0250	65,13A
Craig, Mark	MD0850	32E,65
Crawford, Ken	CA1650	65
Crawford, Michael	TX2750	65,50
Crawford, Pete	NC0900	32E,65
Crawford, Stephen J.	TX3415	37,12A,50,65
Crawford, Ted	AJ0030	65,32B,32C
Crawford, Wesley	MD0400	65
Craycraft, Jeremy	MN0450	20,50,34,65
Cree, Christopher	WA1100	65
Crites, Dennis	OH0250	65,50
Crocker, Ronald	NE0590	11,38,65
Crowell, Jeffrey W.	WI0803	47,65
Crowley, Patrick	AL1195	65
Crusoe, Michael	WA1050	65
Crutchfield, Robert	TX3360	50,65
Crutchfield, Robert	TX3535	65
Cryderman-Weber, Molly	MI1200	12,20,13B,13,65
Csicsila, Mell	OH0755	65,50,13A
Cudd, Patti	MN0350	65,32E,50
Cuenca, Sylvia	NY0646	65
Culley, James F.	OH2200	50,65
Culligan, Paul	KY0250	47,65
Cummings, Azande	NY1275	65
Cunneff, Philip B.	MD0475	13A,65,29A,14C
Curry, Steven	NY1550	65
Cyrille, Andrew	NY2660	65,53
Dachytl, Cary	OH1200	65,50
Dachtyl, Linda D.	OH1200	65
Dahl, Stanley	IA0650	65
Dahl, Stanley E.	IA0200	50,65,34,65A,65B
Dahlgren, Marv	MN0050	65
Dalton, Ed	TN1150	65
Dalton, Grant B.	AL0800	65,11,32E,47,50
Damberg, John	AK0100	14,50,65
Damoulakis, Marc H.	IL0750	65
Daniels, Michael T.	MI1200	65,35A
Daniels, Sean	TN1400	37,50,65
Darling, Matthew H.	CA0810	50,65,14C
David, John	GA1500	65,50
Davila, Gerardo	TN1100	50,65
Davila, Julia	TN1100	65
Davis, Christopher A.	SC0950	11,13,29,50,65
Davis, Dan	NC2410	47,65
Davis, Edward	OH0350	20,60,65
Davis, Glenn	PA1850	65
Davis, Quincy	AC0100	29,65,47
Davis, Troy	LA0800	65,47
De Boeck, Garry	AA0050	47,65,29,35B
De Marchi, Ray	MO2000	65
De Siro, David	NY1400	65
Deal, W. Scott	IN0907	34,65
DeHart, Justin	CA0960	65
DeJaynes, Luke	IL1050	65,35C
Dekaney, Joshua A.	NY4150	20H,65,32E
DeLamater, Elizabeth	OH2600	65
DeLamater, Elizabeth L.	AZ0490	20,29A,12A,65
Dembar, Braham	IN1100	65
Dempsey, Kevin	AG0200	65
DeMull, Mark	MI1850	65
Dennard, Kenwood	MA0260	65
DeQuattro, Michael	RI0200	50,65
Deschenes, Michel	AE0100	50,65
Deschenes, Michel	AE0050	65
Desmond, Robert	OH0300	65
Devillier, Danny S.	LA0760	65
Deviney, Christopher	PA3250	65
Deviney, Christopher	PA0850	65,50
Devitt, Matthew	MT0175	65
Di Sanza, Anthony E.	WI0815	65
Diallo, YaYa	KY0250	20A,65
Diaz, Ernesto	MA0260	65
Diaz, Javier	CT0600	65
Diaz, Javier	NY2250	65
Dicciani, Marc	PA3330	65,35,50
DiCenso, David	MA0260	65
Dietz, Brett William	LA0200	65
Dilling, Rick	NC0050	65
Dillon, Jake R.	IL1350	65
Dillon, Robert	IL1615	65
Dimmick, Penny	IN0250	32,65,34
Dimond, Raymond R.	AR0300	47,65,53,13,32E
Dimond, Theresa	CA6000	65
Dimond, Theresa	CA5020	65,50
Dimond, Theresa A.	CA3650	65
Dimond, Theresa	CA0859	65
Ding, Ian	MI2100	65
Dinitz, Mark	MD0550	65
Dior, Rick	NC2420	50,65
Disney, Dale	TN0900	65
Distefano, Donna	MD0610	65
Distefano, Donna	MD0170	65
Dobbins, Sean	MI1750	47,65,29
Dobbins, Sean	MI0500	65,47
Dockter, Larry	IN1050	47,63A,65
Dodge, Steve W.	OH1910	65
Dominguez, Bob	CA3800	65
Dominguez, Robert	CA5040	65
Dominguez, Robert	CA5100	65
Domonkos, Jason	NE0610	65
Domulot, Fred	FL1430	65
Donaldson, Frank	IL0720	66,47,65
Donato, Dominic	NY3785	65,43
Dorff, Dan	KY1000	65
Dorsey, John F.	MI0600	65,50
Douds, Nathan	PA3100	11,50,65,66A
Douglass, Jamie	CA2420	65
Douglass, Mark	TN1710	50,65
Dove, Barry B.	MD1000	65
Downes, Suzanne	IL2310	66D,47,11,37,65
Doxas, Jim	AI0150	29,65
Doyle, James	CO0050	46,47,65
Dragonjian, James	NY2105	65,32
Dragovich, James	NY1600	65,63
Drake, Michael	TX3420	65
Drake, Randy	CA0825	65
Draper, Charles	MN0200	65
Drege, Lance	OK1350	65
Dreier, James	IL0100	65,50
Dreier, James	IA1550	65
Druckman, Daniel	NY1900	65
Drummond, Billy R.	NY2750	29,47,65
Dudack, Mark	OH2150	65
Dudack, Matthew J.	OH1650	65,50
Dueitt, David P.	MS0420	37,48,64,65
Duerden, Darren	HI0050	32E,65,50,47,11
Dugard, Freddy	NY0646	65
Duncan, Warren L.	AL1100	13,11,47,65
Dunn, Neil	KS0650	65,50
Dupertuis, Jeff	CA3850	62,63,64,65,66
Dutz, Brad	CA0825	65
Duvall, Matthew	VA1500	43,65
Eckert, Jamie D.	MA2020	50,65
Edgar, Paul	DC0100	50,65
Edwards, Tony	TX3510	65
Elford, Scott	WI0804	65
Elliott, Richard	OH0680	65,50,37,11,32E
Elliott, William	MD0175	65
Ellison, Glenn	IL2775	11,65
Elstner, Erin	MO1950	65,50
Elstner, Erin	MO0700	65
Elston, Robert	CA5360	65
Epp, Jeremy	AC0100	65
Epstein, Frank B.	MA1400	41,65
Erickson, Ross	IN1600	65,50
Erskine, Peter C.	CA5300	29,65
Esau, Matt	KS1250	65,50
Espinoza, Andres	ME0340	47,65
Estes, Billy	OK0850	65
Estoque, Kevin S.	LA0650	65,50,46,20H
Evans, Paul J.	PA0550	65
Everson, Robert	IL0730	65
Eyler, David	MN0600	32,50,65,42
Fabricius, Daniel	NY3705	50,65
Faini, Philip J.	WV0750	20A,65
Falcone, Anthony M.	NE0600	37,65,50
Fallin, Mathew D.	GA0950	50,65
Falvo, Robert J.	NC0050	65,50
Fambrough, Gene	AL1150	50,37,65
Fang, I-Jen	VA1550	50,65
Farina, Jack	WI0100	65
Farion, Robert	AA0080	65
Fashun, Christopher H.	IN0550	38,65,32,47,62B
Fay, Edmund	NJ1400	65,34
Feeney, Tim	AL1170	65,50
Feeney, Timothy P.	MA0800	65
Fernandez, Robert	CA0830	65,50
Ferrari, John	NY2150	65
Ferrari, John	NJ1400	13A,11,50,65
Ferraris, Steve	VT0450	65
Fetz, Teun	OR0200	12A,65,48
Fidyk, Steve	PA3250	29,65
Fife, Travis	TX1400	65,50,32E
Figueroa, Angel	CA5300	65,29
Files, Frederick	NY4450	65
Finlayson, Jahmes Anthony	WI1150	14,65
Finley, Benjamin	OK0300	65,50
Finn, Lawrence	MA0260	65
Finnie, Jimmy	IN0800	50,65
Fischer, Jeffrey	MA2030	50,65
Fisher, Don	PA2100	65
Fisher, Tammy M.	WI0810	60,37,65,32,11
Fisk, Martin	AB0200	65
Flamm, Peter	TX3350	65,50
Flanagan, Richard	MA0260	65
Fleming, Tod N.	CA1020	65
Flood, John	CA4100	20A,13A,11,65,50
Flores, David	CA4425	51,65
Flores, Ricardo	IL3300	65,50
Florez, Anthony	IL1080	11,34,65,70,13
Flowers, Kevin	SC0900	65,50
Floyd, C. Chad	KY0400	37,65,50

Index by Area of Teaching Interest

Name	Code	Areas
Floyd, John M.	VA1700	50,65
Floyd, Pharroll	GA0490	65
Fluman, John R.	TX2960	50,65
Folker, Michael	IL1300	65
Folker, Michael	IL3550	65
Folsom, Gunnar	WA1000	65,32E
Fooster, Harold	AR0810	60,11,37,50,65
Ford, Douglass	IL1090	65
Ford, Mark	TX3420	65,50
Fornelli, Devon	AG0050	65,50
Forquer, Ty	MI1800	65,50,13C
Forrester, Ellard	NC0700	65,37
Fosnaugh, Christopher	VA1125	65
Foster, Mark H.	NY3650	65
Foster, Mark	CO0550	50,65,32E
Foster, Marlon A.	VA0600	65
Fradette, Gilbert	AI0200	65,29
Francis, Graeme	TX3530	65
Franklin, Laura L.	NC0250	50,65,20,32E
Freeman, Kendrick	CA4700	65
Freer, Thomas	OH0650	65
Freeze, Tracy	KS0300	65,50,20,34D
French, Otis C.	PA1100	11,37,63,64,65
Fricker, Charles	TX0350	65
Friedson, Steven	TX3420	11,14,65
Froman, Ian	MA0260	65
Froncek, Tim	MI0900	29,65,29A,47,46
Fronzaglia, Brian	MO0800	65
Frost, Ryan	PA3580	65
Frye, Danny	NC0930	65,50,37,65B,32C
Fulgham, Joel	TX3400	47,65
Fung, Jan	PA0500	50,65
Fuster, Bradley J.	NY3717	65,50
Gabrielson, David J.	CA0850	65
Gaetano, Mario A.	NC2600	50,65,11
Gaines, Julia	MO1800	65,50
Galeota, Joseph	MA0260	65
Galm, Eric A.	CT0500	14,20,20H,50,65
Galyen, Tom	VA1250	65
Garcia, Eric	TN1200	65,50
Garcia, Manuel	PR0150	65
Garcia, Paul D.	NC1700	37,46,50,65
Gardner, Al	TX2350	11,47,50,65
Gardner, Brian	OR0500	65
Garretson, Paul	TN1100	65
Garry, Kevin	FL1950	65
Gartner, Kurt	KS0650	65,20H,47,50
Gatch, Perry	PA3650	50,65
Gauthreaux, Guy G.	LA0650	65
Gay, Kirk	FL1800	50,65,34
Geary, Michael	IA0950	65,50,32E
Gelispie, Randle	MI1400	29,65
Gerber, Stuart W.	GA1050	65,50
Gerhart, David	CA0825	65,20H,37,50
Gettys, Joel	IA1400	65
Gianino, Kevin	MO1950	65
Gianino, Kevin	MO1900	65
Giannascoli, B. Greg	NJ0825	65
Gibbs, Kory	AJ0100	50,65
Gibson, Ian	AG0150	65
Gibson, Ian	AG0070	65,50
Gilbert, Karl	IN1560	65,50
Gillan, Lucas	IL3550	65
Gillespie, Clint	AL0500	60,37,65
Gilliam, Jauvon	MD1010	65
Gilmore, Timothy	NH0250	50,65
Ginn, Stan	KY1000	42,50,65
Ginorio, Jorge	TX1725	20H,50,65
Gipson, Richard C.	TX3000	65,50,32G
Glenn, Brian	MN0040	65
Gloss, Randy	CA0510	65,20D,50
Glover, David	PA3100	29,50,65,34,47
Goddard, John	AG0350	48,65
Godoy, John E.	TX3410	65
Gold, Matthew	MA2250	50,65,43,41
Golden, Bruce	OH0650	50,65
Goldstein, Thomas	MD1000	47,50,65
Gomez, Alice	TX2260	10,14,47,65,35A
Gonder, Mark H.	OH2150	65,29
Gonzalez, Genaro	TX3175	50,65
Goodenberger, Mark	WA0050	65,50
Goodman, Ian P.	FL2000	65
Gormly, Shane	TX0075	65
Gottlieb, Daniel	FL1950	65,46,34C
Gottlieb, Gordon	NY1900	65
Graham, Damian	AB0210	65
Gramley, Joseph	MI2100	65
Grant, Courtney	PA3580	65
Gratteau, Phil	IL2100	65
Gray, D'Arcy	AF0100	50,65
Green, Kenneth	LA0550	37,65,41
Green, Michael C.	IL0750	65
Green, Ronald	PA2000	37,50,65
Greenwood, Matthew	AL1300	65,11
Gregoire, Julien	AI0200	65
Grier, George	WA0700	11,13,32D,47,65
Griffin, Dennis	UT0300	50,34,65,13G,41
Griffin, Robert	KY0750	13A,11,50,65
Griffiths, Vern	AB0100	65
Grimes, John	MA0350	65
Grinwis, Brandan	MI0850	65,50,13A
Grissom, Kurt	FL0450	65
Gronemeier, Dean	NV0050	65
Grosso, Cheryl	WI0808	50,65,43,14,13C
Grover, Julien	ME0150	65,66
Grover, Steve	ME0200	65,66A
Grover, Steve	ME0340	47,65,66A,29,13
Guenoit, Eric	LA0450	60B,11,37,65,50
Guidry, Travis	AL1160	65,50
Gullotti, Bob	MA1175	65
Gullotti, Robert	MA0260	65
Gunderson, Terry	WY0050	65,34,29,13,12E
Gunji, Maya	NY2250	65
Guthrie, Mark	MI1150	65
Haas, Jonathan L.	NY2750	50,65
Haddad, Jamey	MA1400	29,20,65
Haddad, Jamey	MA0260	65
Hadden, Dudley 'Skip'	MA0260	65
Hadfield, John R.	NY2750	29,47,65
Hagedorn, David	MN1450	13A,65,50,47,13B
Haldeman, Michael	SC0275	11,37,65,50
Hall, Alan M.	CA0807	65,29
Hall, David	TX3000	65
Hall, James	SC1110	65
Hall, Keith	MI2250	29,65
Hall, Steven	WV0400	14,47,50,65
Hamada, Brian	CA0810	47,65,29A
Hamaker, Robert	CA2775	50,65
Hamilton, Chico	NY2660	10,65,47
Hanes, Michael D.	IL2900	37,50,65
Hanks, John B.	NC0600	65
Hanman, Theodore	KS0100	65,60B,47,37,32E
Hann, Dan	MA2150	65
Hanning, Chris	PA3600	65
Hans, Ben J.	WI0450	11,35A,50,65
Hansbrough, Robert S.	NY0700	32E,42,37,65
Hanson, Terry	IL0300	65
Harbison, Kenneth C.	VA0450	65
Harder, Matthew D.	WV0600	65,34B,34D,10A,10B
Harding, Scott R.	MI0400	10A,13C,29A,65,13A
Hardman, David J.	OK1330	50,65
Hardt, Adam C.	WI0700	65
Hare, Andrew	DC0170	65
Harnell, Jason	CA5020	65
Harris, Les	NH0350	65
Harris, Les	ME0500	65
Harris, Matthew W.	IN1100	65
Harris, Scott H.	TX2700	50,65
Harrison, Brady	OH2550	65,50,11
Harrison, Edward	IL0550	65,50
Harrison, James	ID0050	65
Hart, Billy	MA1400	29,65
Hart, Billy W.	NJ0800	65,29C
Hart, Kevin M.	IL1350	29B,53,66A,47,65
Hart, Kevin	IL2350	47,65
Hartenberger, Russell	AG0450	50,65,53
Hasenpflug, Thom	ID0100	65,13,20,10,50
Hatch, Montgomery	NY1600	65,42,50
Hausey, Collette J.	CA2050	11,37,41,65
Hawkins, Wes	AZ0470	14C,65,50,29A
Haynes, Greg	MO0850	65
Hazilla, Jon	MA1400	65
Hazilla, Jon	MA0260	65
Head, Stan	TN1380	50,65
Hedgepeth, Byron	NC0050	65,50
Hegg, Dennis	SD0150	37,47,63,64,65
Heglund, Andrew	NV0100	65,46,50,47
Heid, R. J.	PA1450	65
Heid, Ronald J.	PA3000	65
Heim, Charlie	PA3330	65
Helbing, Stockton	TX2600	47,65
Heldrich, Claire	NY2150	50,65,43
Hellberg, Eric	CA2440	65,45
Hemingway, Gerry	NY2660	65,20,13
Hemphill, Steven R.	AZ0450	65
Hendry, Robin	MO0350	65
Hendry, Robin	MO0400	65
Henry, Matthew	MO1830	65,50
Hepler, David	PA0700	50,65,29A
Hernly, Patrick	FL2050	20,65
Hernly, Patrick	FL0930	50,65
Herring, David Scott	SC1110	65
Herron, Greg	MD0300	65
Heslink, Daniel M.	PA2350	11,14,37,65
Hetrick, Craig	IN0250	65
Hey, Philip	MN1623	65
Hey, Phillip	MN1450	65
Hey, Phillip	MN0950	65
Hicks, Jarrett	IL0720	65
Hicks, Jarrett	IL2750	32B,32C,32E,65
Higgins, Scott	CA0550	65,50
Higgins, Scott	CA3600	65
Hildebrand, Kirsta	PA2300	32E,65
Hill, Colin	KY0450	65
Hill, John E.	KY0950	50,65
Hill, John	MI2120	65
Hill, Julie	TN1720	65,50
Hill, Kyle W.	MS0580	13B,11,37,50,65
Hill, Paul	MN0750	65,50
Hillyer, Tim	IA1200	65,50
Hillyer, Tim	NE0610	65
Hillyer, Timothy	IA0500	65
Hinds, Evan	IL2970	65
Hinkle, Lee	MD1010	65,50
Hobbs, Gary G.	OR1050	29,65
Hodge, Jeffrey S.	TX3000	65
Hodges, Mark	NY3717	65
Hoenig, Ari M.	NY2750	65,29
Hogancamp, Randy	IA1600	50,65
Holder, Brian	FL1675	11,20,13A,65,50
Holguin, Mike	CA4100	65
Hollenbeck, Eric R.	CO0250	65,50
Holloway, Greg	DC0010	65
Holly, Richard	IL2200	50,65,29
Horn, Robin Franklin	AZ0500	65
Hornby, Tyler	AA0050	65
Horner, Ronald	MD0350	65,20,50
Horner, Ronald G.	PA1600	65,50
Horner, Tim	NJ0825	29,65
Houghton, Steve	IN0900	47,65
Howard, Douglas	TX2400	65
Howarth, Gifford	PA0250	65,37
Howden, Moses Mark	NY3475	50,65
Howell, Todd	IL0850	65
Huang, Aiyun	AI0150	65
Hudgins, Will	MA1400	65
Huff, Cleve	AZ0490	65
Hughes, Chris	NY2900	65
Hughes, Robert	AG0500	32,50,65
Humphreys, Michelle	WV0550	65
Humphries, Stephen	GA0600	13A,20,50,65
Hunter, Andrew	LA0150	37,65,32
Hurst, James	WI0801	65
Hussey, Peter	IL1500	65,20,11,50,12A
Ingalls, Duane	ME0430	65,53,46
Inoo, Yuri	CA3300	65
Isakson, Aaron	MN0610	32E,37,50,60B,65
Israel, Yoron	MA0260	65
Ivester, Mark D.	WA0600	65
Ivester, Mark	WA0200	65,29
Iwasaki, Masahiro	IA1450	65
Iwasaki, Masahiro	IA0940	65
Iwasaki, Masahiro	IA0250	65
Jacklin, Matt	IL2300	65,50
Jackson, Gregory	AL0050	65,13,20,10,36
Jackson, Gregory	AL0345	11,65
Jackson, Herman	LA0700	65,29,50
Jackson, Sharon Sue	IN1800	37,50,65,65B
Jacobs, Malcolm	CO0100	65
Jacobson, Alan	IA1800	47,65
Jalbert, Sylvain	AI0220	65
James, Shaylor L.	FL0600	32C,50,65
Janack, Andrew	NY3600	65
Jarrett, Gabriel	NY3775	65,50
Jarrett, Gabriel	VT0400	65
Jarvis, David	WA1150	10,47,50,65,14C

Name	Code	Areas
Jarvis, Peter	NJ1400	65,50
Jarvis, Peter	CT0100	65,50
Jeffreys, Harold L.	NC2150	10F,32,64C,65,46
Jennings, David J.	IL0650	11,65,13
Jenny, Jack	OH2050	13,10,50,65,43
Jensen, Richard	KY1000	65
Jeyasigam, Sam	MI1750	65
Jimenez, Alexander	FL0850	38,60B,65A,60,65
Johns, Jim	NY1350	65
Johns, Steven S.	NJ0800	65,47
Johnson, Daniel	FL1700	12A,13,65
Johnson, Daniel	FL1550	65
Johnson, David	CA0510	13A,65,50
Johnson, David A.	IA0900	60,32,37,47,65
Johnson, Erik	PA3330	29,65
Johnson, Gary	MO0250	41,46,63,65
Johnson, Jay L.	MN0300	65,50,42
Johnson, Matt	CA1900	65
Johnson, Sigurd	ND0350	65,50,37
Johnson, Todd Alan	CA0845	65,12A,14,50,29A
Johnson, Warren	TX2200	65
Johnston, Beverley	AG0450	65
Jones, Brett	WI0860	65,20,50
Jones, Brian	VA1500	65
Jones, Brian	VA1600	65
Jones, Brian	VA0250	65,29
Jones, Brian	AA0100	65
Jones, Eric W.	MI1000	32E,37,50,65
Jones, Jeffrey	CT0550	65
Jones, Larry	TX2100	13A,11,50,65
Jones, Matthew Craig	SC1000	65
Jones, Matthew	SC0600	65
Jones, Richard	NE0450	50,65,34,70
Jones, Stacey	MI2000	65
Jones, Timothy A.	TX3400	65,61
Jones, Timothy	NV0050	65,12A
Jones, Troy V.	FL0680	32E,37,65
Jones, Wendell	OH0300	65
Jones, Willie	IL2250	65
Jordan, Jason	NC1350	65
Jospe, Robert D.	VA1550	65
Joyner, Maria	WA0650	65
Jung, Ji Hye	KS1350	65
Jurkscheit, Robert	CO0625	65
Justison, Brian	IL1750	29A,50,65
Kamstra, Darin	CO0225	65,29,13B,47,50
Kaptain, Laurence D.	LA0200	65
Karpinos, Vadim	IL0550	65
Kasica, John	MO0700	65
Kastner, Kathleen	IL3550	13A,13,50,65,20
Kataoka, Ayano	MA2000	65
Katterjohn, Michael	GA0250	50,65
Kaufman, Howard	CA2250	65,20,50
Kaufman, Robert	MA0260	65
Kaushal, Abhiman	CA5040	20E,65
Kayne, David	NY3725	65
Keeler, Elden L.	IL0650	11,65,13
Keeny, Jonan	VA0050	65
Keeton, Kristopher	NC2430	65
Keipp, Donald K.	UT0350	13A,11,65,29,47
Kemp, Todd	TN0100	65,13B
Kemperman, William	MN0800	65
Kemperman, William	MN1625	65
Kendrick, Brian	CA5350	65
Kendrick, Brian	CA4300	46,47,65,54
Kennedy, Daniel	CA0150	65
Kennedy, Daniel J.	CA0840	11,65
Kerney, Marja	FL1750	65
Kerrigan, William	PA3250	65
Kerrigan, William	PA1150	65
Kerschner, Jeff	GA1900	65
Kestner, Luke	MT0175	50,65
Kestner, Luke	MT0350	65
Khan, Pranesh	CA0050	13A,10,65
Khoja-Eynatyan, Leon	DC0170	65
Kieffer, Olivia	GA1700	65,50
Kihle, Jason J.	TX2960	11,37,50,65
Kilkenny, John	VA0450	65
Kim, Dong Suk	CA5031	20C,62,65
Kimball, Steve T.	MN0950	65
Kingan, Michael G.	PA1600	50,65
Kinkle, Dan	CA0800	65
Kinzie, John	CO0900	50,65
Kirk, Jeremy	KS0250	37,13,20A,50,65
Kirkpatrick, Daniel	WI1150	65
Kizilarmut, John	IA0550	65
Klee, Michael	NE0460	65,11
Klemas, John	IA1170	37,47,63,64,65
Klier, Kari	TX3175	65,50
Klopfenstein, Reginald	IN0200	13A,12A,47,50,65
Knecht, John	IL2750	65
Knight, Joshua	AR0730	65,50,11
Knoles, Amy	CA0510	65,50,13A,10B
Knowles, Debbie	IL1400	65,11
Knutson, James	MN1400	65
Koba, Dean	CA1750	65
Koebel, Carolyn	MI1150	65,50
Kolar, Andrew	CT0300	37,65
Kolor, Thomas P.	NY4320	65
Koontz, Jason	KY0550	50,65,14,34B
Korb, Ryan	WI0850	29A,65,47
Korb, Ryan	WI0925	29A,65,47
Korn, Steven	WA0550	65,32E
Koshinski, Eugene	MN1600	47,65,29,20G,35
Kotan, Emrah	GA0050	65,29A,47
Kozakis, Michael	WI0250	65
Kozakis, Michael J.	IL0750	65,50
Kramer, Janet	IL3100	50,65
Kranzler, Dean	KS0350	65,50
Kranzler, Dean	KS0700	65
Kranzler, Dean	KS1300	65
Kranzler, Dean	KS0200	65
Kranzler, Dean	KS0150	65,50
Kraus, Jeffrey	NY2900	65
Kreibich, Paul	CA0815	29,65
Kreitner, William	FL1310	47,50,65,53
Kretzer, Scott	MI0050	37,41,65
Krikland, Ricky	FL1000	65
Krohn, Ken	MD0550	65
Kruse, Lacey	MN0625	66A,65
Krutz, James	NE0200	65
Krutz, Jim	NE0150	65
Krygier, Joe	OH1850	29,65
Kuhn, Bret	IL3450	65
Kumor, Frank	PA1750	50,65,13
Kurai, Tom	CA5040	20C,65
Kurasz, Rick	IL3500	65,20
LaBarbera, Joe	CA0510	65,29A,47
Ladzekpo, Kobla	CA5031	20A,65
Laing, David	AI0190	65
Laing, David	AI0150	65,29
LaMattina, Michael	OH0450	65
Lamb, Christopher	NY2150	65
Lambert, James	OK0150	65,50,37,13,12D
Lambert, Michel	AI0150	65,29
Lamey, Phil	VT0100	65
Lammers, Ed	KS0040	46,37,65,63,11
Lane, John W.	TX2250	65
Lang, Scott	KY1000	50,65
Langone, Steve M.	MA2050	65
Langsam, Stuart	OK0800	65,50,11
Langsam, Stuart	OK0450	65,50
Lanter, Mark	AL1170	65
Larrance, Steve	MD0550	65
Larson, Leon	FL1675	20H,65
Lasley, Michael	NC1550	50,65
Latta, Jonathan R.	CO0350	10F,47,50,65,20
Latten, James E.	PA1650	11,13A,37,50,65
Lattini, James	MA2030	65,47
Lavender, Robert	FL0650	65
LaVine, Scott	NY3780	65
Law, Charles P.	AR0750	65,50,37
Lawless, John	GA1150	65,50
Lawrence, Alan	IA0300	65
Lawrence, Alan	IA0400	65
Lawrence, Jay	ID0060	65
Lawrence, Jay	UT0050	65
Lawrence, Jay	UT0250	65
Lawrence, Jay	UT0190	65,47
Lawrence, Steve	OR0250	65
Lawson, Ronald S.	IA0910	63C,65,11,50
Lazaro, Andrew A.	PR0115	47,65,53
Leake, Jerry	MA1400	20A,20E,47,65
Leaman, Jim	OH2275	65
Leandro, Eduardo G.	NY3790	65,50,43
Leckrone, Erik	CA1900	65
LeCroy, Hoyt F.	GA1650	65,32
Ledbetter, Robert	MT0400	37,50,65,20H,14C
Leddy, Thomas	IL0850	65
Lee, Mitch	UT0325	65
Legner, Amanda	IL1200	65
Lehman, Stephanie	NY0270	65,11,13
Lehmann, Bertam	MA0260	65
Lemmon, Galen	CA4400	65,50
Leone, Gary	FL0500	65,11
Lepper, Kevin	IL3450	65,50
Leroux, Robert	AI0200	65
Lesbines, Tele	WI1150	50,65
Leslie, James M.	OH2250	65,47,32B,37
Lewis, Elizabeth A.	MI1200	50,65
Lewis, Jason	CA4400	65
Lewis, Ryan C.	AR0500	65,32E,12A,11
Lewis, Victor	NJ1130	65,29
Lewitt, David	NY3785	65
Li, Chi	CA5031	20C,62,64,65
Licata, Julie M.	NY3765	65,33,50,20,10B
Lienert, Keith	WI0840	65
Lill, Michael	IL2100	65
Lim, Malcolm	AA0050	65
Lindberg, John	VA0250	65,50
Linwood, William	AB0150	65
Lipari, Robert	NY1400	65
Lipsey, Michael	NY0642	37,50,65
Lipsey, Michael S.	NJ0800	65,50
Lipton, John	OR0175	65
Liuzzi, Don	PA0850	65
Lizama, Joe	CA1850	65
Llewellyn, Raymond	CA0815	32B,37,65
Lloyd, Keith	TX0900	65
Lloyd, L. Keith	TX1650	65,12A,14,12,50
Loach, Deborah	AL1160	65,50
Locke, John G.	MD0650	65,32E
Lohman, Al	MO0200	65,46,47
Lohman, Gregg	TN1400	65
Lonardo, Tom	TN1380	11,65
London, Todd	TN0100	65,35B
Long, Bill	SC0900	37,47,65,60B,32E
Long, Gary	CA0845	65
Longshore, Terry	OR0950	65,20,14,47,35A
Lopez, John A.	TX3175	37,65
Lopez, Robert	TX3175	65,50
Lopez-Trujillo, David	TX3515	11,50,65
Lotter, Rick	CA0150	65
Lucini, Alejandro	DC0100	47,65
Ludovico, Vincent	NY2950	65
Lyman, Kristin M.	GA0500	32,65
Lyons, Greg	LA0250	32E,65,50
Mabrey, Charlotte	FL1950	50,65,43,20G
MacDonald, Payton	NJ1400	65,50,43
MacDonald, R. Richard	MN1700	47,50,65,32E
Machold, William	IL2450	65
Machold, William	MO0300	65
Macksoud, Mark G.	ME0250	65
Maekane, Nachiko	NY3600	65
Magnone, Steve	IL3200	50,65
Magnussen, John P.	CA0835	65,13C
Maki, Erik	CA3000	37,11,63,64,65
Maley, Marshall E.	VA1475	65
Maley, Marshall	MD0700	50,65
Mallory, Keith	KS1000	65,50
Malloy, Michael	OH2275	65,20G
Maltz, Richard	SC1100	13,10,65,12,14
Mangini, Michael	MA0260	65
Mangini, Nicholas	NY2400	65
Mangini, Nick	NY5000	65
Mann, Michael	TN1660	37,42,60B,65
Marandola, Fabrice	AI0150	50,65
Maret, Kevin	MO0950	65,47
Markgraf, David	NC2650	65
Marrs, Jeffrey	CA5000	65
Marrs, Stuart	ME0440	12A,65,50,34
Marsalis, Jason	LA0800	65
Marsh, George	CA5070	65
Marsh, George	CA4700	65,50
Marshall, Eddie	CA2950	65
Martin, Michelle Denise	GA0150	11,65,66D,60B
Martin, Peter J.	VA1600	65
Martin, Spencer	WY0130	65
Martin, Spencer	WA1300	65
Martin, Stephen	TX1150	65
Martucci, Anthony	VA1600	65,47
Martysz, Erin	TX2650	65
Marucic, Mat	CA0150	65
Maslanka, Daniel	MI1750	65,50
Mason, Adam	AA0200	13A,11,65
Mason, Brian S.	KY0900	50,65

Index by Area of Teaching Interest

Name	Code	Areas
Massini, Ryan	AA0040	50,65
Mast, Murray K.	MA1100	50,65
Masten, Rob	WV0250	29,63,65,47,46
Masuko, Takaaki	MA1175	65
Mathiesen, Steven	PA2200	10A,10F,50,65
Mathiesen, Steven	PA2450	50,65
Mathis, Carolynne	MN0610	32E,44,65
Mativetsky, Shawn	AI0150	32,65
Matney, William	TX3300	65
Matthews, Britton	NY2450	32,12,65
Maurreau, Robert	LA0080	65
Mayhue, Terence C.	IL1740	47,65
Maytum, Jeremiah	WY0115	65,50
McBain, Mike	MO1790	65
McCann, Chris	AI0150	65,29
McCarty, Patrick	MO0050	11,32E,37,65,50
McCloud, Daniel	TX0150	37,65
McClung, Matthew	TX2930	65,12A,50
McCombs, Steven	IA1350	65
McCormick, John	AA0020	65,50
McCormick, John	AA0035	65
McCormick, John	AA0100	65
McCormick, Robert	FL2000	50,65
McCurdy, Roy	CA5300	65,29
McCutchen, Thomas	GA2100	65,46
McCutchen, Thomas	AL0500	65,50
McDaniel, Adena	SC0650	65
McDonald, Aaron	AB0100	65
McGee, Michael	AL0850	37,47,63,64,65
McGowan, Thomas	TX3370	37,41,50,65
McGrath, Kenneth	CA0815	65
McGrath, Thomas	NY3770	65
McGuire, Kristen Shiner	NY2650	50,65
McHugh, Steve	NC0930	65
McKinney, John S.	WV0350	50,65,34,60B,41
McKissick, Charles	GA2050	65
McLafferty, Tim	CT0550	65
McLaren, Robert	AG0450	65,29
McLaurin, Christopher	MO1810	65
McNamara, Ray	CA1900	65
McNutt, Craig	MA2050	65
McPartland, Dennis	IA0750	65
Meckley, Rod	PA3710	65
Meehan, Conor	MA2250	65,41
Meehan, Todd	TX0300	50,65
Meints, Kenneth	NE0500	63,20,65,35A,32
Meister, Scott R.	NC0050	10,65,43,50
Mekler, Joseph	NJ0750	65,50
Menconi, Audra M.	TX2200	65
Mendoza, Victor	MA0260	65
Merusi, Rebecca	OR0950	65
Merz, Albert	DC0010	65
Merz, Albert	DC0050	65
Messerschmidt, William H.	VA1600	65
Metcalfe, James L.	TX2295	65,35C,35G,46
Metzger, Jon	NC0750	65,29,47,50,53
Meunier, Catherine	NY3780	65
Meunier, Robert W.	IA0550	60B,37,65,32E
Meyers, Nicholaus S.	ND0600	65,50
Meza, Fernando	MN1623	50,65
Miceli, Anthony	PA3250	65
Miele, David	NY3000	47,14C,65
Mietus, Raymond	NC2700	13A,37,50,65
Milarsky, Jeffrey	NY2150	65
Miles, Butch	TX3175	65,29,46
Miller, Ben F.	WV0400	11,50,65,35A,37
Miller, Jim D.	NJ1050	65
Miller, Thomas	CO0900	65
Miller, Todd	CA0815	49,50,63B,65
Miller, Zach	MN1250	65
Mills, Jackie	AL0400	65
Millstein, Eric J.	IL0750	65
Miranda, Angelo	NY4200	65
Mitchell, Bryan P.	MS0570	11,37,46,65,50
Mitchell, Joseph	CA1750	65
Mitchell, Joseph	CA0805	32,65
Mitchell, Joseph	CA2600	50,65
Mizicko, Shane J.	MO1500	11,50,65A,65B,65
Mizma, Michael E.	TX2295	50,65,35A,35C
Mobley, Mel	LA0770	65,13
Moersch, William	IL3300	65,50
Mohamed, Jamal	TX2400	65
Moio, Dom	AZ0400	65
Moio, Dominick	AZ0440	50,65
Moll, Benjamin	OR0600	65,13A,13B,13C,10A
Monzon, Ricardo	MA0260	65
Moonert, Judy	MI2250	14,50,65
Moore, Christopher J.	GA0900	37,65
Moore, Daniel	IA1550	50,65
Moore, Dean	AZ0150	65
Moore, James L.	OH1850	50,65
Moore, Jeffrey M.	FL1800	65,50
Moorman, Wilson	NY0270	11,20,65,29
Morales, Fidel	PR0115	29,65,53
Morales, Richie	NY3785	65,29
Morales-Matos, Rolando	NJ0825	65
Morales-Matos, Rolando	NY0500	65
Morales-Matos, Rolando	PA0850	65
Moreno, Tony	NY2750	47,29,65
Morgan, Tom T.	KS1400	50,65,13C
Morgenstein, Rod	MA0260	65
Mori, David	CA2440	65
Morris, J. David	GA2150	65,34,13,50
Morrow, Daniel	PA1350	65,50
Morton, James	CA2100	29,65
Moses, Lennard	OH0500	50,65,20A,20G
Moses, Robert	MA1400	47,65,29
Moyer, Iain	AL1250	65,32E
Mueller, Erwin	IN0150	50,65
Mueller, Todd D.		65,12A
Muldar, Dennis	FL0950	65,50
Mulvaney, Thomas	NJ0800	65
Munzenrider, James	CA1250	50,65
Murphy, Tom	AZ0440	65
Murray, Dana A.	NE0610	65
Murray, Edward	TN1680	65
Murray, Warren	OR1300	65,50
Musto, James	NJ0700	65,50
Myers, Brenda	CA1860	65
Myers, Marcus	PA3330	46,65
Nagata, Gary	AG0450	20D,65
Nappi, Chris	NC0650	65,50
Nappi, Chris	NC0400	65
Nasatir, Cary	CA3520	65,42,46
Nathan, Jonathan	CA5060	47,50,65
Nathan, Jonathan	CA5550	65
Nave, Pamela J.	IN1310	37,65,50
Neal, Mark	AL1450	65,47,34,35
Neciosup, Hector	FL0200	65
Neisinger, Robert	WA0450	61,65
Neitzke, Jeff	OH2290	41,65,37
Neitzke, Jeffrey	OH0100	65,46,50
Nelson, David E.	PA3600	65
Nero, Joseph	PA3330	50,65
Netto, Alberto	MA0260	65
Nevill, Tom	TX3515	65,13A,13C,50,37
Ney, Leonard Scott	NM0450	50,65
Nicely, Tiffany	NY3725	13,65
Nichols, Kevin A.	IL3500	65,20
Nicholson, Jason	UT0300	65,50,41
Nissly, Jacob	NY1100	65
Noah, Laura	AL1300	35,65
Noble, Gerald	OH2500	65
Norton, Christopher S.	TN0100	50,65
Nottingham, Douglas	AZ0350	65,50,45,10B,35
Novak, Brad	MI1650	65
Novotney, Eugene D.	CA2250	14,50,65,20
Nowak, Robert A.	PA1900	11,65,29
Ochiltree, Larry	MI1160	65
O'Connor, Brad M.	MD0450	65
Oddis, Frank A.	KY0900	50,65
Okstel, Henry J.	TX3420	65
Olague, Jimmy	TX3527	65
Oliver, Tony	IL0100	65,50
Ollis, Ken	OR0250	65
Ollis, Ken	OR0850	65,29
O'Mahoney, Terrence	AF0150	50,65,29,10D,66A
Orey, Pedro	FL0100	37,50,65
Orpen, Rick	MN1000	65
Osrowitz, Michael L.	NY2550	50,65
Otte, Allen C.	OH2200	50,65
Ovalle, Jonathan	MI2100	65
Ovens, Douglas P.	PA2550	13,10,45,65
Overman, Michael	VA1850	65
Overman, Michael M.	VA0600	65,65B,50
Pack, Lester	AR0800	65,46,47,29,70
Packer, Michael	CA1000	65
Pagano, Vincent	RI0150	65,65B
Palmer, Jason	OR1250	65
Papador, Nicholas G.	AG0550	13A,13B,13D,65,32E
Pappas, J.	MO0550	65,11,34
Pare', Craig T.	IN0350	32,37,65,60
Parish, Steven	AB0070	65,20G,34,35C
Parker, Don	NC0800	13,50,65,29
Parker, Philip	AR0200	13,10F,10,65,50
Parker, Phillip	NE0300	65
Parker, Wesley	AR0250	65,11,20,37
Parker, Wesley	NC1700	65,47
Parks, Gary	TX1400	65,70
Parks, John	FL0850	65
Paschal, Brett E. E.	OR0400	65,13,11
Passmore, Ken	GA1200	66D,66C,65,50
Pastor, Juan	IL0275	65
Paton, Eric	OH0350	65,20A,20C,20H,47
Patton, Duncan	NY2150	65
Pawlak, Michael	IA0700	65,50
Payson, Al E.	IL0750	65
Pecorilla, John	OR1020	37,64,65
Peeples, Terrance P.	IL1520	65,14C,11,50
Peeples, Terry	IL3370	65
Pegher, Lisa	PA1050	65
Penland, Ralph	CA3500	65
Pennington, John C.	SD0050	13A,65,50,10F
Pereira, Joseph	NY1900	65
Pereira, Joseph	CA5300	65
Perez, Jesus	TX2570	65
Perkins, Douglas	NH0100	65,50
Persip, Charli	NY2660	65,53
Peske, Robert	ND0050	50,65
Petercsak, James J.	NY3780	50,65
Peters, Mitchel	CA5030	50,65
Peterson, Dan L.	MO1780	37,65
Peterson, Ralph	MA0260	65
Petrella, Nick E.	MO1810	65
Phillips, Derrek C.	TN1850	65
Phillips, Derrek	TN1100	65
Pias, Ed	NM0310	65,20
Picard, Paul	AI0200	65,20H
Piedra, Olman	OH2140	65,50,43,29
Piedra, Olman	OH2300	50,65
Pillion, Ed	NJ0550	65
Plainfield, Kim	MA0260	65,29
Plante, Jean-Guy	AI0210	65
Platz, Eric	MA2010	65
Platz, Eric	RI0300	65,29,47
Plog-Benavides, Bony	WI1150	65
Pongracz, Andrew L.	OH1000	50,65
Post, Corey	MI0750	65
Potts, Brian	FL0050	65,50
Poudrier, Chris	MA2020	65,47
Pourmehdi, Houman	CA0510	65,50,20B
Povolny, John	MN0250	65
Powell, Susan K.	OH1850	65
Power, Rob	AD0050	65
Preiss, James	NY2250	50,65
Presley, Douglas L.	SC0850	37,50,32B,32C,65
Price, Harvey	DE0150	50,65,47
Priebe, William	PA2800	65
Prieto, Dafnis	NY2750	29,47,65
Primatic, Stephen P.	GA0200	65,13,29,11,47
Prince, Curtis L.	IN0005	10,12,20G,65,47
Pritchard, Jillian	NY3350	65,50
Pritchard, Jillian	NY1250	65,50
Proctor, Andrew	FL0700	65
Pruitt, David	IL1610	65
Przymus, Chad	MN1500	65
Puga, Richy	TX1660	65
Pultorak, Mark	PA0400	50,65
Purcell, William	VA1250	65
Purdie, Bernard	NY2660	47,65
Queen, Jeffrey	IN0250	65
Rack, John	NC2440	32,65,29A
Rael, Eliseo	PA1050	65
Ragsdale, Aaron	SD0550	37,65,50
Ragsdale, Chalon L.	AR0700	50,65
Ramirez, Anthony	WI1150	65
Ramirez, Mark Joseph	TX3525	65,50
Ramsay, John P.	MA0260	65
Ransom, William	OH0650	65
Rao, Nikhail	AA0100	20E,65
Rapp, Willis M.	PA1750	38,65
Rasmussen, Kurt	NV0050	65
Rasmusson, Ralph	NY1850	37,47,63,64,65
Rath, Eric	TX0100	65
Ray, Willy	UT0400	65
Raymond, Paul	WA1350	65

709

Index by Area of Teaching Interest

Name	Code	Areas
Reamer, Andrew	PA1050	65
Reckner, Lillian	MD0360	66,61,65
Redd, Chuck	MD1010	65
Reddick, Marcus	GA1300	65
Redmond, Daryle J.	NY3780	65
Redmond, Daryle	NY3775	65,50
Reedy, Hillary	IL1612	32,65
Reeves, Richard	SC0350	65,50
Reeves, Shane	SC0710	65,41
Regester, Kristen	IL2750	32A,65
Reid, Todd	CO0830	11,20,29,65
Reifel, Edward	NY3780	65
Reiner, Art	IN1650	50,65
Reiner, Craig	AF0120	65
Remonko, Guy	OH1900	50,65
Rennick, Paul	TX3420	65,50
Rhodes, Edward	NC1900	65,50
Rhoten, Markus	NY1900	65
Rice, C. William	VA0600	50,65
Richards, William W.	DC0150	65
Richeson, Dane M.	WI0350	50,65
Richmond, Matthew	NC2400	50,65
Ricotta, Charles	MI2100	65,37
Riehman, Ken	PA3560	65
Rieppi, Pablo	NY3785	65
Riley, Steve	KS0050	65,50,10
Ringquist, Mikael	MA1400	47,65
Ringquist, Mikael	MA0260	65
Ripley, Randal	MI1985	65,50
Rissmiller, Gary	PA2450	65
Rissmiller, Gary	PA2550	65
Rivera, Luis C.	AL1300	20,32E,41,65,50
Roach, Seth	KS0750	65,66,29,70,50
Robbins, David	IN0100	65
Robbins, David P.	WA0650	13,50,65
Robert, James	NC0750	65,11,50
Roberts, Shawn M.	NC0050	11,65
Robertson, Paul	NJ0825	65,11
Robilliard, David	AG0550	65
Robinson, Anthony	TX0600	65,50
Robinson, Gary A.	SC0765	63,64,65,38
Robinson, N. Scott	MD0400	65
Robinson, Rick	NY0270	11,13,65,32
Robinson, Scott	PA0850	65
Robl, James	WI0750	65
Roblee, Thomas	OH0700	65,50
Rockwell, Owen	MS0100	65,50
Rogers, Dennis G.	MO0850	32,65
Rogers, Leonard	PA1050	65
Rogers, Lisa	TX3200	50,65
Rogers, Seth	OH0850	65,50
Rogiewicz, Thomas	IL2730	65
Roland, Tomm	NE0610	65,20,34H,50
Rollins, Ian	TX2900	65,12
Roma, Joseph	NY0350	65
Romaine, Paul	CO0800	65
Romaine, Paul	CO0550	65,46
Romberg, Barry	AG0650	65
Romeo, Robert	NJ0825	50,65
Rometo, Albert A.	NE0600	65
Rosen, Michael	OH1700	50,65
Rosener, Douglas	AL0200	37,50,65
Ross, James R.	IL2250	65
Ross, Paul	IL1085	65,50
Roth, Robert	VT0100	65
Roulet, Patrick E.	MD0850	50,65,66C
Roulx, Rene	AI0190	65
Rounds, Theodore	OH1100	50,65
Rozenblatt, David I.	NY1600	65,42,50
Rubins, Sherry D.	TX3530	65
Rucker, Steve P.	FL1900	65,47,29
Rummage, Robert F.	IL0750	46,65
Rummage, Robert	IL0850	50,65,53
Runions, Greg	AG0250	47,50,32,65
Russo, Frank	MD0850	65
Rutkowski, Gary	NY4460	50,65,11
Rutland, Neil	NM0100	37,50,65,35D
Ruttenberg, Samuel	PA3330	65
Ryan, James	MI2200	65,29
Ryan, Jamie V.	IL0800	65,50
Ryan, Josh T.	OH0200	50,65
Sabine, David	AA0032	35,13A,13C,37,65
Saindon, Ed	MA0260	65
Salisbury, Jeff	VT0250	50,65
Salisbury, Jeff M.	VT0450	65
Salzmann, Wayne W.	TX3510	65
Sanabria, Bobby	NY2660	47,65
Sanchez, Joseph W.	VA1500	65
Sanchez, Samuel L.	IN1450	65
Sanderbeck, Rande	TN0500	50,65
Santiago, Freddie	PR0100	65
Santos, Jackie	MA0260	65
Santos, John	CA1250	20,65
Saoud, Erick	AR0350	65,50
Saporito, James Frederick	NY2750	65
Sark, Brady	OH0300	65
Savage, Matt	NC2410	65
Savage, Ron	MA0260	65
Sawyer, Tony	NC0750	37,65,34
Scagnoli, Joseph R.	IN0100	65,50
Schaal, Joelle E.	OR0800	13,65,11
Schaefer, G. W. Sandy	NE0050	14C,46,65,29,35
Schaft, Glenn	OH2600	65,50
Scheuerell, Casey	MA0260	65
Scheuerell, Doug	OR1050	20D,65
Schick, Steven	NY2150	65
Schick, Steven	CA5050	11,50,65,43,29
Schietroma, Robert J.	TX3420	65
Schlitt, Bill	CA0630	65,50
Schlitt, Bill	CA5150	50,65
Schlitt, William	CA1425	65,50
Schlitt, William	CA5355	65,50
Schmidt, John R.	PA2050	60,14,50,65,37
Schmidt, Steven	CA3800	65,50
Schmitz, Eric B.	NY3770	47,65,13B,13C,10A
Scholl, Gerald	KS1450	65,50,11
Schoolfield, Robnet	SC0200	32,45,65,72
Schoonmaker, Matt	WV0300	65,50
Schroeder, Dave	NY2750	29,47,65,60B
Schuett, Mike	AA0050	65
Schuetz, Shaun	TN1000	65
Schulz, Robert	MA0950	65
Schupp, Roger B.	OH0300	65
Schweikert, Eric	IN0905	65
Scialla, Peter	NY4200	65
Score, Clyde D.	AZ0510	65,70
Scorza, Darren	IL1085	65
Scott, Arvin	GA2100	65
Scott, David	IA1390	65
Seabra, James	RI0200	65
Sebastian, Mario	CA0150	65
Secor, Greg	MI1050	50,65,32E
Secor, Greg	MI0900	65
Sehman, Melanie	NY3250	65,13A,20,11,13
Sekelsky, Michael J.	MO1790	37,50,65
Sekhon, Baljinder S.	FL2000	10,65,13,34
Seligman, Jonathan D.	MD0520	50,65,32E
Selvaggio, Frederick	IL3150	65
Serfaty, Aaron	CA0510	47,65
Sessa, Thomas P.	OR1100	65
Sessa, Thomas	OR0150	65
Sestrick, Timothy	PA1400	16,65,50
Seward, Owen	FL1450	65,11
Sgouros, Michael	NY2450	65
Shaffer, Frank	TN1680	65,50
Shaw, Alison	WI0830	65,50
Shaw, John	FL1650	50,65
Shaw, Ronnie	WV0550	65
Shelley, Kim S.	IL2970	65
Shepard, Brian K.	CA5300	34,10,13,34C,65
Shepherd, Michael	VA0150	65
Sherman, Joshua	WI1150	65
Shin, Eric	MD1010	65
Shinn, Alan	TX3200	50,65,47,29
Shirley, Hank	NM0400	65,50
Short, Charlie	WI0050	65
Siegel, Jeff S.	CT0800	53,41,65,29
Siegel, Jeff S.	NY2660	65
Siegel, Jeff S.	NY3760	65,12A
Sikes, Ron	MO0550	65
Simpson, Brian	CA3250	65
Simpson, Ken	AG0400	65
Sinigos, Louis	MI0300	65,50,43
Sisauyhoat, Neil	TX0550	65,50,13A,13C
Skidmore, David	MD0650	65
Skinkus, Michael	LA0080	65
Slabaugh, Thomas E.	CA5010	37,60,65,50,42
Slack, Rob	CA2390	65
Slack, Robert	CA0815	65
Slawson, Brian	FL0150	65
Smallcomb, Matt	PA3700	65
Smarelli, Mark E.	OH2450	65
Smirl, Terry	WI0300	65
Smith, Aaron Todd	CA0835	65
Smith, Aaron T.	CA2800	65
Smith, Brian	VA0750	50,65
Smith, Bruce	MD1050	65
Smith, Carey	MS0370	63,64,65,11,13
Smith, David	CT0800	13,50,65,34
Smith, Demond	KY0250	50,65
Smith, Ed	TX3420	65
Smith, Jeffrey B.	AZ0100	65
Smith, Jeremy	IA0790	65
Smith, Joshua D.	TN0150	37,65,13A,50
Smith, Mark	IL0600	13A,50,65,29,20G
Smith, Michael	OH1850	65,29,32E
Smith, Murray	AA0100	65
Smith, Nancy A.	NH0350	50,65
Smith, Nancy	ME0500	65,50
Smith, Neal	MA0260	65
Smith, Patrick	CT0800	65
Smith, Ron	IA1100	65,50
Smith, Roy	OK0550	50,65
Smith, Roy S.	OK1450	65
Smith, Roy	OK0850	50,65
Smith, Ryan	GA0850	50,65
Smith, Tony 'Thunder'	MA0260	65,50
Smith-Wright, Lovie	TX3450	50,65
Smith-Wright, Lovie	TX1000	65
Snell, James W.	MO1810	65
Snider, Larry D.	OH2150	50,65
Snow, Adam	NC0550	65
Snow, Adam M.	SC1200	65
Solomon, Sam	MA0400	65
Solomon, Samuel Z.	MA0350	65
Soph, Ed	TX3420	65,29
Sorbara, Joe	AG0350	43,65
Sorrentino, Ralph	PA3600	65,50
Sorrentino, Ralph	PA1550	65,50
Soto, Leonardo	NC2000	65
Souza, Christine	OK1350	65,20
Spann, Thomas	TN1400	65
Sparks, Victoria	AC0050	65,50
Sparks, Victoria	AC0100	65,50
Spellissey, Gary	MA0950	50,65
Spencer, Andrew	MI0400	50,65
Spencer, William G.	NC0050	60,32,64D,65
Spinelli, Donald	MD0750	50,65
Sprague, John L.	NC1700	65,67E
Squance, Rod Thomas	AA0150	20,50,65
Sriji, Poovalur	TX3420	65,50
Stabile, Ronald	RI0300	32,41,50,65
Stabley, Jeff	PA3710	46,47,53,65,50
Stamp, John E.	PA1600	60,37,65
Steele, Glenn A.	PA3250	50,65
Steffens, David	OK0750	50,65,32E
Steinmann, Ronald	TX2710	65
Steinquest, David	TN0050	13,50,65
Stephan, Edward	PA1050	65,65A
Stephens, Wesley	OK0600	65
Steve, Tony	FL1000	65,50
Stevens, Annie J.	VA0150	65,37,50,34
Steward, Nicholas	OK1330	65
Steward, Nick	OK0700	65
Stewart, Michael	TN1710	37,65
Stith, Gary	NY1700	32,37,60B,65
Stolarik, Justin R.	WI0815	37,60B,32E,65,10F
Stonefelt, Kay H.	NY3725	50,65
Stopa, Alex	NV0050	12A,65
Storch, Arthur	CA0900	65,50
Storch, Arthur L.	CA0807	65
Storniolo, Carl	WI0825	65
Stoup, Nicholas	CA3500	65
Stout, Gordon B.	NY1800	50,65
Stoyanov, Svetoslav R.	FL1900	65,50,42,43
Strain, James A.	MI1600	65,13,41,11
Strauss, Matthew B.	FL1900	65,50
Strawbridge, Nathan	FL2050	20,65
Stroman, Shilo	CO0250	65
Strouse, Greg	KY1350	65,50
Strouse, Greg	KY0100	65
Strunk, Michael J.	CA0400	65,20,20H,50
Struyk, Pieter	MA0700	65
Stubbs, Thomas L.	MO1250	65
Summers, C. Oland	NC0850	32,63C,64D,65,72
Summers, Kim G.	NC0900	65,50

Index by Area of Teaching Interest

Name	Code	Areas
Summey, Harold	VA0450	65
Sundeen, Eric	MN0150	50,65
Sunkett, Mark E.	AZ0100	50,65,29A,14
Super, Kevin	VA0650	65,50,37
Suta, Thomas	FL1745	65,50
Svendsen, Dennis	MN1620	65
Sweets, Nancy	MO0500	37,65,64,66A
Swery, James	WI1155	65
Swist, Christopher	NH0110	65,50
Swist, Christopher	MA1100	65,35C
Swist, Christopher	NH0150	50,65,13,10
Sykes, Wiley	NC0910	65
Tabor, Angela	CA3800	11,65
Tafoya, John J.	IN0900	65
Takekawa, Miho	WA0650	65
Tamagni, Robert	MA0260	65
Tana, Akira	CA4200	65
Tanner, Robert	GA1450	10,12A,11,65,34
Tariq, Susan Martin	TX3750	65,50
Tate, Mark	IN1010	65
Tate, Mark	KY0610	47,65
Taylor, David L.	ID0060	50,65
Taylor, David B.	MI2200	29,65
Taylor, Joel	CA5150	65
Taylor, Thomas	NC1600	65
Taylor, Thomas E.	NC2430	65
Teague, Chan	LA0050	50,65
Teague, William C.	LA0100	65
Teasley, Tom	DC0350	65
Tedesco, Anthony C.	NY1600	65
Teel, Allen J.	TX0050	65,50,20,37
Terry, Nicholas	CA0960	50,65
Thaller, Gregg	IN0550	65,32,13C,38
Thieben, Jacob S.	SC0800	50,65
Thiel, Robb G.	IN1350	10F,60B,32,37,65
Thoma, James	NJ0700	65
Thoma, James E.	PA2550	65
Thomas, Benjamin	WA0460	65
Thomas, Edwin	IN0005	65,11,12,32,60
Thomas, John	VA0700	50,65
Thomas, Laura	AG0050	65
Thomas, O. T.	AL0950	37,35A,65
Thompson, Amanda	CO1050	65,50
Thompson, Chester	TN0100	65,35B,47
Thompson, Douglass	IN0910	65
Thompson, Floyd	MN1050	65
Thompson, Rich	NY1100	65
Tiemann, Jason E.	KY1500	47,65
Tiller, Jim	NY1700	65
Tiller, Jim A.	NY3730	50,65
Tindall, Danny H.	FL1740	36,37,65,11
Tinkel, Brian C.	NC1250	65,50,42
Tirado, Jonathan	TX3530	65
Tolbert, Patti	GA0850	32,65,50
Tomlinson, Dan	AZ0470	65
Tompkins, Joseph	NY2250	65
Tompkins, Joseph H.	NJ1130	65
Toner, D. Thomas	VT0450	65,20,37,50,60
Tones, Daniel	AB0060	20,50,65
Toth, Benjamin J.	CT0650	65
Trigg, William	NJ0175	65,41
Trigg, William	NJ1050	65
Tripathi, Nitin	VA1550	65
Triplett, Isaac	IL0420	65
Troy, TJ	CA1000	65
Tucker, Rob	WA1250	65
Tull, David	CA3500	65
Tyler, George Tracy	AL0500	50,65
Tyson, Blake W.	AR0850	50,65
Udow, Michael W.	MI2100	65
Ungurait, John B.	MS0575	37,65,62D,46,50
Vacanti, Jennifer	NY2950	65
Vaillancourt, Paul	GA0550	65,50,13C,43
Valcarcel, David Shawn	CA3265	45,65,35C,13G,66A
Valcarcel, David	CA3950	45,65,35C,13G,66A
Van Dyke, Gary	NJ1400	65,50
Van Geem, Jack	CA4150	65,41
Van Geem, Jack	CA1075	65,42
Van Schaik, Tom	TX1750	65
Van Schoick, Thomas	CO0830	65
Van Sice, Robert	CT0850	65
VanCleave, Timothy	IN1050	65
VanHassel, Joseph	OH1900	65
VanLente, Mike	MI1050	65
Varner, Ed	MT0370	32B,37,65
Varner, Michael	TX3500	50,65,14,20
Varnes, Justin	GA1050	65,29
Vartan, Lynn	UT0200	65,41,20
Veikley, Avis	ND0250	65,50,62E
Velez, Glen	NY2250	65,65A
Veregge, Mark F.	CA4900	50,65
Vermillion, Terry L.	MN1300	65
Versaevel, Stephen	MT0200	65,50,14C
Vidacovich, John	LA0300	65
Viertel, Kyle	TX0390	37,63,64,65,46
Vincent, Ron	NY2200	65,50,32E
Vogler, Paul	TN0260	34,65
Voss, Darrell	CA1510	65
Wacker, Jonathan D.	NC0650	50,65,29
Wade, Jonathan	AG0400	65
Wadley, Darin J.	SD0600	65,50,13A,13C,38
Wagoner, W. Sean	OR1050	65,10F,50,37,11
Wahlund, Ben	IL2050	65
Waldrop, Michael	WA0250	50,65
Walker, David L.	VA1000	50,65,60B,11,13A
Walker, Erin	KY1450	12,20,50,65
Walker, K. Dean	OK1200	65,50
Walker, Mark	MA0260	65
Walker, Richard L.	IN0907	65,35,34A,50,37
Walker, Skip	NC1350	65
Wall, Nathan	AJ0030	65
Wallis, Kelly	UT0400	65
Wallis, Kelly	UT0250	65
Walrath, Brian	MI2000	11,12A,65,31,34
Walter, Douglas	CO0800	65
Wangen, Peter	MN1290	65
Ward, Eric	AL1050	65,35
Warden, Loyd	MO0100	53,65
Warne, David	MI1650	50,65,20
Warren, Alec	TX3400	65,50
Warren, Alec	TX2300	65
Warren, Alec	TX2295	65
Warren, Chris	MS0200	65,50
Washington, Kenny	NY3785	65
Watson, Derico	TN0100	65
Weaver, James	PA2300	32E,65
Weaver, John	GA0400	65
Webb, Glenn	UT0150	37,41,47,50,65
Weber, Bradley	NE0700	65,50
Weber, Glenn	NJ1160	65,50
Weber, Jonathan	MI1400	65,50
Webster, Peter	FL1300	50,65
Weinberg, Norman G.	AZ0500	50,65
Weiner, Richard	OH0600	65
Welge, Jurgen	KS0590	65,46,47
Weller, Richard A.	CA0835	65
Wells, Mary	CA4300	50,65
Wenger, Laurie	MT0370	65
Wenzel, Scott	WI0150	14,65,55,50,20A
Werner, Michael	NY2250	65
Wertico, Paul	IL0550	65,29
Wesley, Arthur B.	AL0010	11,37,47,65
West, Brian	TX3000	65,50
Westbrook, Gary W.	TX2750	50,65,37,32E
Westmacott, John	KS0265	65
Westrick, Rick	WA0950	65
Westrick, Rick	WA1350	65
Wetzel, Thomas	WI0825	65,50
Weyer, Matthew	TN0250	65,50
White, Andre	AI0150	65,66A,29A,29
White, David	AL1195	65
White, James	CO0950	29,47,65
White, James L.	TX3520	50,65
White, Joseph M.	WV0100	65,50,37,63,64
White, Marc M.	OK1150	65,50
White, William	MO1710	11,37,47,65,63
Whitfill, Jim	TX0850	64,63,65
Whitt, Roger	SC0050	65
Whittall, Geoffrey	AA0025	14,65,20,13,11
Wiggins, Tracy Richard	NC2435	65,11,37,50
Wiggins, William	TN1850	41,50,65
Wilkes, Steve	MA1400	65
Wilkes, Steven M.	MA0260	65
Wilkins, Blake	TX3400	65,50
Wilkinson, Tobie L.	WI0865	65,50
Williams, Barry Michael	SC1200	12A,50,65,20A,20B
Williams, Demetrius	TX3520	65,50
Williams, Earl	NY2105	65
Williams, Eddy	AL0450	65,13B,32C,37,60B
Williams, Jan G.	NY4320	65
Williams, Kenyon C.	MN1120	65,50,20
Williams, Paula	GA0750	65
Williams, Wade	GA0300	50,65
Willie, Eric	TN1450	65
Willis, George R.	WV0750	10D,11,32B,52,65
Willis, Jesse	SC0420	65,50,20,37
Willson, Brian S.	NY0500	65,11
Wilsey, Jennifer	CA4700	65,50,32E
Wilson, Dwayne	NC0300	48,60,65
Wimberly, Michael	VT0050	10,20,29,35,65
Winant, William	CA2950	65,41,42
Winant, William K.	CA5070	50,65,43
Winant, William	CA5000	65
Wirth, Jordan	WY0150	65
Witten, Dean	NJ1050	65,50
Wojtera, Allen F.	VA1100	50,65,29
Wolf, Douglas J.	UT0250	37,65
Wooton, John A.	MS0750	50,65
Wozniak, William	PA3250	65
Wrublesky, Albert	WV0750	65
Wu, She-e	NY2150	65
Wu, She-e	IL2250	65
Wubbenhorst, Thomas M.	ME0440	50,65
Wulff, Steve	MI0100	65,50
Wurster, Miles B.	MN1030	37,13A,64,65
Wyant, Frank	CA4425	65
Yakas, James	TX3500	65,50,20
Yingling, Mark T.	PA1300	65
Yohe, Tony	OK1450	65
Yoshida, Ken	NE0610	65
Yowell, Earl R.	VA1350	65
Yslas, Ray V.	CA3500	65
Zakarian, Sylvie	MA1175	65
Zambito, Pete I.	MO0600	65,31
Zarro, Domenico E.	NJ0500	50,65
Zator, Brian	TX2955	50,65
Zator-Nelson, Angela	PA3250	65
Zeglis, Brian	IL1800	65
Zeglis, Brian	IA1300	65
Zeglis, Brian M.	IL1350	65
Zeltsman, Nancy	MA0350	65
Zerbe, David	MI0150	65,37,50,32C,32E
Zirkle, Thomas	MO1110	65,65B
Ziv, Amir	NY2660	47,65
Zlotnick, Peter	NC0350	50,65
Zollars, Robert P.	OH2150	65
Zoro,	TN0100	65
Zuber, Gregory	NY1900	65
Zuniga, Rodolfo	FL0700	65
Zuniga, Rodolfo	FL0200	65,47
Zygmunt, David	PA0950	65
Zyskowski, Ginger	KS0215	65
Zyskowski, Martin	WA0250	50,65,60B
Zyskowski, Marty	WA0950	65,50,37

Timpani

Name	Code	Areas
Babor, James	CA5300	65A
Berthold, Sherwood	MS0400	65A,65B
Bostrom, Sandra	CA0835	66A,10C,12A,34,65A
Bratt, Douglass F.	IL1890	50,47,65A,65B,46
Broubechliev, Bojil	NY5000	65A,65B
Burkhead, Ricky	MS0560	65A,65B,50,65
Cherry, Kalman	TX2400	65A
Dahl, Stanley E.	IA0200	50,65,34,65A,65B
Deane, Christopher	TX3420	65A,65B
Dinion, Steve	HI0210	65A,65B
Egan, Lora	SD0580	65A,65B
Finch, Abraham L.	MA1650	32A,50,65A,65B
Foster, Marlon	VA0100	65A,65B
Genis, Timothy	MA0400	65A
Guzewicz, Rebecca	SC0850	65A,65B
Herbert, David	CA4150	65A
Holland, Michael	TN1850	65A,65B
Jacobson, James	VA1600	65A
Jimenez, Alexander	FL0850	38,60B,65A,60,65
Kent, David	AG0300	65A,65B,42
Kogan, Peter	MN1623	65A
Kutz, Jonathan	TX1600	65A,65B,14C,50
Lewis, Jon L.	CA0835	65A
Lorenz, Nena	LA0900	65A,65B
Mizicko, Shane J.	MO1500	11,50,65A,65B,65
Moore, Norman	NC0850	65A,65B
Nichols, Edward	MD0800	65A,65B,11,34A,34B
Peyton, Jeff	OR0750	65A,65B

711

Index by Area of Teaching Interest

Name	Code	Areas
Ricks, Edward	SC1050	65A,65B,37,50,13A
Rockwell, Owen P.	MS0350	11,32C,37,65A,65B
Roman, Brent	IL1900	65A,65B
Ross, Charles	NY1100	65A
Sartini, Michael R.	MA0750	65A
Stephan, Edward	PA1050	65,65A
Struyk, Pieter	MA0150	13A,65A,65B
Taylor, Earl	NC0450	65A,65B
Turner, Aaron	CO0275	50,65A,65B,13,41
Velez, Glen	NY2250	65,65A
Wildman, Louis	CA0650	65A,65B
Yancich, Mark	GA0750	65A
Yancich, Paul	OH0600	65A,50
Zerna, Kyle	NJ1130	65A

Mallet

Name	Code	Areas
Baxter, Jillian	GA0625	65,65B
Berthold, Sherwood	MS0400	65A,65B
Boyar, Simon M.	NY2750	65B,50
Bratt, Douglass F.	IL1890	50,47,65A,65B,46
Broubechliev, Bojil	NY5000	65A,65B
Burgett, Gwendolyn	OH0650	65B
Burkhead, Ricky	MS0560	65A,65B,50,65
Calissi, Jeff L.	CT0150	37,65B,11
Cloutier, Randy	RI0150	65B
Cotto, Orlando	DE0150	65B
Coviak, James	MI0450	41,65B
Dahl, Stanley E.	IA0200	50,65,34,65A,65B
Deane, Christopher	TX3420	65A,65B
Deffner, David	CA0840	65B
Dinion, Steve	HI0210	65A,65B
Doiron, Michelle E.	WA0800	65B
Egan, Lora	SD0580	65A,65B
Finch, Abraham L.	MA1650	32A,50,65A,65B
Foster, Marlon	VA0100	65A,65B
Frye, Danny	NC0930	65,50,37,65B,32C
Guzewicz, Rebecca	SC0850	65A,65B
Harris, Stefon	NY2750	29,65B
Holland, Michael	TN1850	65A,65B
Howarth, Gifford W.	PA2750	65B
Jackson, Sharon Sue	IN1800	37,50,65,65B
Kent, David	AG0300	65A,65B,42
Kuo, Ming-Hui	KY0900	65B
Kutz, Jonathan	TX1600	65A,65B,14C,50
Lang, Drew	TX2400	65B
Locke, Joe	NY2150	65B
Lorenz, Nena	LA0900	65A,65B
Mancini, Nick	CA0835	29,65B
Marlier, Mike	CO0900	65B,53,29
Miceli, Anthony	NJ1050	53,65B
Miceli, Tony	PA3330	65B,29
Mizicko, Shane J.	MO1500	11,50,65A,65B,65
Moore, Norman	NC0850	65A,65B
Naranjo, Valerie D.	NY2750	65B
Nichols, Edward	MD0800	65A,65B,11,34A,34B
Overman, Michael M.	VA0600	65,65B,50
Pagano, Vincent	RI0150	65,65B
Peyton, Jeff	OR0750	65A,65B
Plies, Dennis B.	OR1150	47,65B,66B,66D,13C
Rackipov, Errol	FL0700	29A,65B,11
Ricks, Edward	SC1050	65A,65B,37,50,13A
Rockwell, Owen P.	MS0350	11,32C,37,65A,65B
Roman, Brent	IL1900	65A,65B
Rudolph, John	AG0300	65B
Rudolph, Richard	VA0550	62A,38,62B,62C,65B
Samuels, David A.	MA0260	47,65B
Sherman, Mark	NJ0825	65B
Smith, Ed	TX0370	65B,35G
Smith, Edward	TX2400	65B
Steinquest, David E.	TN1850	65B
Stevenson, Francois	AI0150	29,65B
Stirtz, Bradley	IL2050	65B
Struyk, Pieter	MA0150	13A,65A,65B
Taylor, Earl	NC0450	65A,65B
Thomas, Ben	WA0200	65B
Turner, Aaron	CO0275	50,65A,65B,13,41
Van Sice, Robert	PA0850	50,65B
Van Sice, Robert	MD0650	65B
Wildman, Louis	CA0650	65A,65B
Zeltsman, Nancy	MA0260	65B
Zirkle, Thomas	MO1110	65,65B

Keyboard (All Areas)

Name	Code	Areas
Aamodt, Rucci R.	HI0210	32,66
Abeyaratne, Harsha D.	OH1650	66,13,13C
Adams, Mark	NY0646	13,66
Adkins, Donald	CA0400	38,62,D,66
Alexander, Travis	NC1550	12A,36,40,66
Alhaddad, Frederick I.	MI1200	13,10,66
Allata, Rachid	CA1560	66
An, Won-Hee	MA1450	11,60B,66
Andersen, Mary Ann	UT0200	66
Anderson, Dianna M.	ND0250	13,66
Angelo, Carl	MI1850	66
Applewhite, Willie	UT0190	66,20,29,63C
Arroe, Cate	MI0650	20,36,66
Aubuchon, Ann Marie	CA2700	11,66
Augustine, William	CA4450	66
Austin, Stephanie	CA1450	36,61,66,40,32
Backlin, William	IA1170	13,66
Baldwin, Gail	IL0100	66,66A
Barone, Marcantonio	PA3200	66
Barr, John	VA0100	13,10,66,31A
Barta, Steve	CO0200	66
Bartsch, John T.	OR0175	13B,38,66,10F,10A
Basinger, Rhonda	IL1245	13,11,66
Basney, Nyela	TX3527	61,66,36,38,60
Bates, Susan	NC2500	66,66H
Baxter, Diane R.	OR1250	66,20,12A,14
Beard, Robert Scott	WV0550	66,13C,13A,66B,66C
Belshaw, Gary D.	TX3650	10F,10,66,34
Benkman, Noel	CA0900	11,20,66
Bennett, Mary Lynne	WV0300	66B,66A,66D,66,66C
Benoist, Debbie	TX2310	11,13A,34C,65,66
Benson, Michael L.	OH1350	66A,66B,12A,11,66
Bianchi, Jay	NY2660	66
Biel, Carol	OR0400	66,66D
Bjorem, Pauline Kung	TX0050	66,13C
Bobbitt, Kayleen	MI0750	11,66,13,40
Boehmke, Erik A.	IL1600	63A,66,47,37,49
Bogard, Theresa L.	WY0200	13C,66
Bosshardt, Heather	UT0190	29,66
Boyer, Laura	WA0450	66
Bradley, Deborah	AG0450	32,66

Name	Code	Areas
Bratz, Jennifer	MT0350	66
Breitman, David	OH1700	66,66E,66A
Briggs, Nancy L.	CA4580	29,10,66,53,20
Brito, Ramon	NC0750	66
Brown, Ellen	AZ0470	66,13
Brown, Jeffrey A.	IL3500	66,66A,66D
Brown, L. Joel	IA0900	13,12A,14,66,11
Burleson, Geoffrey	NY0625	66A,13,12A,66,42
Burnside, Joanna	MS0420	13,12A,66
Byykkonen, Susan E.	MI1450	66,36
Caliri, Lisa	MA0350	66,66A
Camacho-Zavaleta, Martin	AL0050	66,13
Campbell, Helen E.	AL0310	13A,13,36,61,66
Campi-Walters, Lisa	CO0350	13,12A,66,10A
Carroll, Roy W.	IA0940	66,13,12,11,31A
Cash, Carla Davis	TX3200	66B,66D,29B,66A,66
Chang, Joanne	NY3250	11,13,32,42,66
Chang, Soo-Yeon Park	CA0650	66,42,13A,13C
Cherrington Beggs, Sally	SC0900	13D,66,31A,12A
Chiang, Nora	CA4450	66
Childress Orchard, Nan	NJ0050	66,13,54
Choe, EJ	IN0907	13,11,32A,32B,66
Chou, Godwin	IL2775	10A,13,66A,66,10
Chou, Shun-Lin	CA0825	42,66
Clark, Adam	MI1050	66,66A,66C,66B,66D
Clark, Michael	FL1570	13,12A,36,66,54
Clency, Cleveland	IL0650	11,66,40,36
Cleveland, Lisa A.	NH0310	13,11,29A,66
Clifft, Joel	CA0250	66,13C
Clifft, Joel	CA5300	66
Cline, Everett Eugene	ID0250	61,66
Coogan, Chris	CT0550	29,66,47
Cook, Bruce	CA1560	66,14,11,20
Cook, Sally	FL0150	66
Cornut, Sebastien	NJ0825	66,66A,66C
Cotte, William	VT0300	11,13H,36,61,66
Cotton, Haim	NY2660	66
Coulson, Bette	IL0720	66
Counts, Les	CA0200	66
Crane, Teresa Ann	IL1500	66C,61,66,66A,11
Cratty, William	CA2960	13,66
Crawford, Eric	VA0950	13B,66
Creighton, Randall	CA1560	66
Curtin, David	PA2050	66,13
Da Cunha, Cherise Ann	OR0800	66
Dalton, Sharon	WY0060	13,44,61,66
Dauphinais, Michael D.	AZ0500	66
Dean, Michael	OK0650	66
Deane, Alison	NY0550	66,41,42
Deaver, Stuart T.	OK1450	66A,66D,66B,13I,66
DeSanto, William	PA3560	36,66,31A,66C
DeSiro, Lisa	MA0850	66
Desrosiers, Cecile	AG0200	66
DeVasto, David	IL0850	10,13,32E,66
DeWire, James	MD0350	66
DeWitt, Debora	MI0850	66,12
DiCello, Anthony J.	OH0150	36,61,66,31A,34
Dills, Marcia	NC0930	66
Dirksen, Dale B. H.	AJ0030	10,13,32,61,66
Dixon, Joan DeVee	MD0350	66,31A,35
Donaldson, Frank	IL0720	66,47,65
Dries, Eric	CA0815	13,13E,13D,29A,66
Dubois, Laura	NJ0760	10A,11,32E,66
Duggan, Sean B.	LA0600	11,12A,36,66,31A
DuHamel, Ann M.	MN1620	66
Dujka, John	TX0340	66
Dukes, Leslie D.	CA4460	66,42,66C
Dupertuis, Jeff	CA3850	62,63,64,65,66
Earle, Diane K.	KY0800	11,66
Ediger, Thomas L.	NE0500	13,12A,32,36,66
Egan, John B.	IN1350	13,66,66G,11
Eichhorst, Diane	ND0050	13C,66
Elkins, Eleanor	TX0150	66
Ellingson, Peter	CO0830	66,13C,29
Elton, Nancy H.	GA2100	66
Erickson, Kurt	CA1500	66,11,13C
Erickson, Shirley	TX0910	11,13,36,61,66
Everist, Rachel	IA1170	66
Evers, Carol	AL1195	66
Ezhokina, Oksana	WA0650	66A,66B,66C,66
Farbood, Morwaread Mary	NY2750	34,10,66
Farrell, Scott	WA0350	61,66,54
Fay, Fern	CA5360	66
Ferrara, Lawrence	NY2750	13,12,32,66
Fiske, Jane	MA0930	11,15,32,66
Flack, Michael	IL0650	11,66,13,29,32B
Flynt, Ben	CA1560	66
Foote, Ed V.	TN1850	66
Ford, Mary E.	OK0350	11,13,36,66
Fountain, Richard	TX3650	66
Franco-Summer, Mariana	CA5360	11,13A,66
Frank, Bruce	NY4350	66,13
Franklin, Janice L.	TX1725	11,66,54,34B
Frederick, Amy	TN0100	66
Fredrickson, Don	CA4450	66
Gabay, Darya	DC0170	66
Gach, Peter F.	CA3460	66,11,13
Gershfeld, Tatyana	FL1745	66
Gianforte, Matthew P.	KY0950	66A,66D,66B,66,12A
Goldman, Lawrence	MS0560	66A,66D,66,11,66C
Goldston, Chris	IL0720	66,13
Golightly, John Wesley	KY0650	12A,31A,66,34,13D
Gomer, Wesley	TX1650	13,66,69,12A,36
Gonzalez-Matos, Adonis	AL0050	66,13A
Gorgichuk, Carmen	AA0025	11,13,66
Gray, Arlene	ND0050	66
Gray, Gary	CA4450	66
Green, Dana S.	OR0800	13A,11,66
Gregorich, Shellie Lynn	PA2150	13,66
Griest, Jennifer	CA1450	66
Grooms, Maria	MO0650	12A,20,32D,60,66
Grover, Stephen	ME0150	65,66
Guenette, Maria	TX3535	66
Gunther, Thomas	IL0720	66
Ham, Donna	TX2350	11,13A,66
Hamilton, Anna	SC1100	66
Hampton, Edwin Kevin	GA0200	13,66
Hanks, Kenneth B.	FL0930	66,13,11
Harms, Janet	CA0630	13A,11,66
Harms, Lois	IA0650	64C,66
Harris, B. Joan	MS0200	11,12A,66
Harris, Brenda	IL1612	66,32A
Harris, Carl G.	VA0500	60,12A,66,69
Harris, Ray	MS0570	11,36,66,54
Harrison, Judy	FL0900	13,36,60A,66
Hartzel, Marcie	KS0225	66
Hawkins, John A.	WV0500	13A,13,11,36,66
Hayes, Gregory M.	NH0100	66,41,42

Index by Area of Teaching Interest

Name	Code	Areas
Hayner, Joy	GA1650	11,13,66
Healey, Martha M.	AR0425	66
Heard, Rachel P.	MS0385	66
Henry, Barbara	WI1150	66D,66
Herris, Keith	TN0150	66,13B
Hess, Nathan A.	NY1800	66A,66D,66C,66,66B
High, Ronald	SC0150	11,12,31F,61,66
Hinkeldey, Jeanette	IA0150	13,64B,64D,66
Hirota, Yoko	AG0150	66,13B,12A,66A,12B
Hirshfield, L. Russell	CT0800	16,13,66,66B,66A
Hohlstein, Marjorie Rahima	MA0280	66,13,66A
Hoppmann, Kenneth	IN0005	10,16,20F,35A,66
Hord, John	CA1850	66,66C
Hostetter, Elizabeth	AL0550	66A,66D,66C,13,66
House, LeAnn	MN0450	13,12,66
Huckleberry, Alan R.	IA1550	66A,66B,66C,66
Huebner, Eric H.	NY4320	66
Hughes, Walden D.	ID0150	12A,41,42,66
Hulteen, Rhonda L.	IL2730	66
Hunnicutt, Bradley C.	NC2300	13,66,34,13A,13E
Huydts, Sebastian	IL0720	66
Hwang, Okon	CT0150	14,66,11,12,13
Hyman, Adah	NY1860	66
Iacona, Richard	NY2105	66
Iyer, Vijay S.	NY2750	29,66,47
Janssen, Brett	KS0215	66,13
Janzen, Dorothy	KS0900	66
Jenson, Joyce	MN0040	66
Ji, Hye-Gyung	TX2350	66
Johnson, Joyce F.	GA1900	13,66
Jones, Christine	MO1100	11,66
Jones, Dena Kay	TX3520	66,32,20F,14F,15
Jones, Joel C.	AL0050	66,36,13A
Judy, Ned	MD0700	13,29,66,34,47
Kahan, Sylvia	NY0644	12A,12C,66,13A,13C
Kallay, Aron T.	CA5300	66
Kallian, Sandra	WI0800	66
Kanovich, Leokadia	AG0200	66
Karan, Leon	AG0200	66
Kearney, Kevin	CA2550	66
Kennedy, P. Kevin	CO0625	61,60,12A,66
Ker-Hackleman, Kelly	VA0450	66,13C,11
Kester, Nancie	CA1560	66
Kim, Jung Eun	CA4450	66,13A
Kim, Soyeon	IL1740	66
King, Bryan T.	AL0200	11,66
KinKennon, Heather Marie	CA0200	11,60,66,66D
Kinzer, Lisa B.	VA0700	66
Klassen, Carolyn	KS0440	66,34,13,20F
Kleiankina, Olga	NC1700	66
Klein, Gary	NY2105	66
Klein, Laura	NJ1350	66
Klinder-Badgley, Marcia	CA1290	66
Knauth, Dorcinda	NY1050	11,66
Knecht, Jasminka	CA3800	66
Knier, Veronica T.	MD1020	13B,13E,66
Knudsen, Joel	KS0210	13,11,66
Ko, Priscilla	MD0150	66
Koehler, Raymund	IL3200	29,66
Koehner, Leon	IA1170	66,11
Komisaruk, Kevin M.	AG0450	66
Koopmann, Robert	MN0350	66
Koutsoukos, Sheree	TN1850	66,66D
Kozlova, Yulia	CA4450	11,13,41,66
Kraaz, Sarah Mahler	WI0700	12A,55,66,11,67C
Kwon, Yeeseon	IL0550	66A,66B,66D,66
Lang, Linda	MN1175	66,36
Lau, Sylvia	CA3800	66
Laubmeir, George	WI0842	66
Lavner, Jeffrey	CA1075	66
Lease, Nancy	IA0250	12A,66,11
Leffert, Kristine Lund	SD0200	66,31
Lemelin, Stephane	AG0400	66,41
Lepley, Louise	CA4450	66
Levin, Robert	MA1050	41,66
Lew, Jackie Chooi-Theng	MD0800	32A,32B,20,32C,66
Li-Bleuel, Linda	SC0400	66C,11,32,12A,66
Liao, Amber Yiu-Hsuan	UT0190	66,13
Liaropoulos, Panagiotis	MA2010	66,11
Liefer, David	NJ1350	66
Lim, Chan Kiat	LA0760	66
Lis, Anthony	SD0550	13,10F,10,66,20D
Litke, Sheila	KS1300	66,13,66A,66B,13A
Livingston, Jannine	CA3750	66
Loomis, Joy	FL2130	61,66
Lopez Yanez, Ruth	CA3460	13A,60,66,66C
Lower, Nancy	CA3850	66
Luangkesorn, Sha	PA1350	13,66
Lucas, Adonna	NC1950	13,36,64A,66,31A
Lushtak, Faina	LA0750	66
Luxion, Dennis	IL0720	66
Lyddon, Paul W.	HI0210	66
Maalouf, Janet	DC0110	36
Macchioni, Oscar E.	TX3520	66A,66B,66D,66,14
Madlangsakay, Roselle	CA4450	66
Magrath, Jane	OK1350	66B,66A,66D,66,66C
Majors, Gayle	KY1425	32,66,11
Manley, Douglas H.	TN1550	12,66,31,66G,12C
Margetts, James A.	NE0050	66,12A,13,32A
Markiw, Victor R.	CT0700	66,13,12A,66A,11
Marsh, Gordon E.	VA1250	10,66,13,10A,66A
Martin, Kyle	MA2300	13A,13,11,66,35B
Mattson, Lucas	IA1400	47,66
Maurey, Ronald D.	IN1400	66
May, Nathanael A.	MO0850	66,66B,66C,66D
Mays, Kenneth R.	CA2810	66
Mazullo, Mark	MN0950	12,66
McDonald, Steven	KS1000	66,38,60B,12A,41
McFarland, Kay Dawn	KY1400	66
McGrew, David	PA0150	10,13,66,31A,11
McKellip, Hope	MS0580	11,66
McMullen, Dianne M.	NY4310	13,12,66,31
Meeks, Joseph D.	GA1150	13,12A,66,66B
Menth, Christelle	CO0150	66,12A,20
Mercer, Amy	MN0600	66
Metcalfe, Evelyn	FL2130	13,66
Milbauer, John P.	AZ0500	66
Millar, Robert R.	CA4625	13A,13,11,12A,66
Miller, Bruce	CA1900	13,66
Miller, Heather	IL1740	66,13A
Miller, Sue	ID0075	13,32B,66
Mills, Joan G.	CA4450	13,66
Miyama, Yoko	OR0050	66,13,12A,66C,66D
Miyamoto, Peter M.	MO1800	66,13,42
Mok, Gwendolyn	CA4400	66
Monachino, Paul	OH1330	13,10A,66,60
Moon, Gene H.	TX2700	38,39,66,62A,62B
Moon, Hosun	NY1275	11,66,13B,32D,36
Moore, Stephen F.	CA0805	13C,29,47,60,66
Moore-Hubert, Edith	FL1000	66
Moorman, Joyce E.	NY0270	11,13,20A,34D,66
Morales, David	CA2910	13A,11,36,61,66
Moresi, Matthew S.	MI0650	11,46,66
Morgenstern, Inara E.	CA4200	66
Morrow, Ruth E.	TX1700	66,12A,66A,13D,13E
Mouledous, Pierrette	TX0700	66
Myers, Jeff	MS0320	11,66,13
Nelson, Sharon	OH2500	32B,66
Neve, Vicki	CA4200	66
Newlin, Yvonne	IL1612	13,60,37,66,47
Nichols, Beverly	IA0250	66
Nichols, Lois J.	CA4600	66,32,44,67B,11
O'Conor, John	VA1350	66
Oh, Yoojin	NY0644	11,42,66
Ohls, Ray	WA0600	66A,66
Olson, Kevin R.	UT0300	66,66A,66B
Onalbayeva, Kadisha	FL1500	11,66
Oppens, Ursula	NY0500	66,41,42,43
Otwell, Margaret	WI0825	66
Owens, Jeremy	IA0100	11,12A,66
Oye, Deanna	AA0200	66A,66C,66,13C,66B
Paat, Joel	CA3800	66,29
Pape, Louis W.	SD0150	13,10,11,32,66
Parenteau, Gilles	AB0070	10F,45,66,35H
Park, Hana	TX2600	66
Park, Sung-Hwa	CA5300	66
Parker, Bradley	SC0700	66,13
Parrish, Clifford	NJ0400	66
Perkyns, Jane E.	TX3150	66A,13,12A,66,66C
Pettaway, Charles H.	PA2000	13,11,12A,66,66C
Petteys, Leslie	WV0400	66,66A,66B,66C,12
Pfeiffer, Ruth Imperial	HI0160	13A,12A,32,36,66
Phillips-Farley, Barbara	NY3550	66,13,12
Polanco-Safadit, Pavel	IN0400	66,53,46,47
Polusmiak, Sergei	KY1000	66
Powell, Patricia	PA3600	66,66D
Pretzel, Mark W.	KS0570	66A,66
Proctor, Freda	KS1375	66,64A,13,37,41
Quercia, Olga	CA1850	66,66C
Rauscher, James	TX0100	66
Ray, Vicki	CA0510	66,42
Reckner, Lillian	MD0360	66,61,65
Redfern, Nancy	MI1600	66,11,66D,66B,66G
Reed, Allen	TX1100	13,44,66,31A
Reise, Adriene	OR0010	66
Resnianski, Igor	PA3600	66,66D
Richman, Josh	PA3330	66
Roach, Seth	KS0750	65,66,29,70,50
Roberts, Wesley	KY0400	12,14,31,66
Robinson, Emily	OK1050	13,66
Robinson, Florence	FL0600	12A,66A,66,66D
Rojas, Nuria Mariela	SC0150	11,12,13,34,66
Rojek, Justin J.	AL0345	11,66,13
Roseman, Molly J.	WI0850	66,66A,66B,66D,66C
Ross-Hammond, Amelia	VA0950	13,13J,36,66
Roth, Nicholas	IA0550	66A,66B,66C,66
Rotman, Sam	CA2810	66
Rowlett, Donn	OK1500	13,11,66
Sabak, Linda	WV0800	12A,66,11
Salerno, Christine	WI0808	40,47,66,61
Salyer, Douglas W.	CT0200	13,34,12A,36,66
Sanchez, Theresa	MS0360	11,66
Sands-Pertel, Judith	CA1500	32A,32B,66
Saxe, Peter	IL0720	29,66,53
Scarambone, Bernardo	KY0550	66A,66D,66B,66,66C
Schane-Lydon, Cathy	MA1850	10,36,66
Schneiders, Carson	KY0550	66
Scholl, Tim	TX2550	13A,13E,32A,66,70
Scholz, Steve	CA1560	29,66
Schreiner, Gregory	CA4450	66
Schumann, Michelle	TX3415	66
Schwartz, Robert	CA4625	12,66
Scully, Lawrence L.	GA2150	66,12A
Shihor, Ory	CA1075	66,66A,42
Shikaly, Al	IN0400	64E,48,66
Shipwright, Edward	HI0210	66
Shirar, Ryan	KY0300	66,66C
Shirey, Julie	TX1050	66
Shkoda, Natalya	CA0800	66,13,13A,13B,12A
Shpachenko, Nadia	CA0630	66A,66C,66B,66,34D
Shuster, Richard J.	TX3300	66
Siebert, Sonya	IA0650	66
Sifford, Jason	IA1550	66B,66D,66,29B,66A
Sims, Lori E.	MI2250	66
Slavin, Peter	IN0005	10,13,66,66A,11
Smith, Byron J.	CA2650	36,35A,35B,61,66
Smith, Jan	WV0760	66
Smith, Jennifer	MI1550	36,61,66
Smith, Kimo	CA2420	66,13A
Smith, Robert C.	TX2600	66
Soto-Medina, Victor	TX1725	11,13,66,34B
Spiller, W. Terrence	CA0600	66,11
Spitz, Bruce	WA0860	66,34,35,13L
Stallsmith, John	AL0260	12A,36,47,66,31A
Steinbach, Richard	IA0100	13,10,66,34
Stewart, Barbara	OR0250	66
Stiles, Joan	NY2660	66,13
Stinson, Russell	AR0425	13,11,12A,12,66
Stripling, Allen	GA0810	11,36,66,32,40
Strong, James Anthony	NJ0975	13,12A,66,11,54
Studdard, Shane	TX1775	66,66C,11
Stumpo, Ryan	MI0900	66
Su, Wei-Han	MO0775	66
Subotic, Vedrana	UT0400	66
Summerfield, Susan	VT0400	13,11,41,66
Summers, Shane	CA5100	66
Sweigart, Dennis W.	PA1900	13,66
Takesue, Sumy A.	CA4450	13A,66,12F,13B,13C
Tapanes-Inojosa, Adriana	IL1080	11,20,36,12,66
Taylor, Betty Sue	NY2400	13A,12,36,61,66
Taylor, Kristin Jonina	IA1750	12A,20,66A,66D,66
Taylor, Rachel	KY0550	66
Tchougounov, Evgueni	AG0170	66,66A,13C
Theisen, Kathleen Ann	CT0800	13,66
Thier, Bethany	WI0750	61,66,47
Thomas, Jennifer	NC2210	66
Thomas, Joel Wayne	KS0265	11,13,29,66
Thompson, Catherine	CA2775	66
Thompson, David B.	SC0850	12A,13,66
Thompson, Linda	FL2130	66
Thompson, Stephanie	OR0400	66,66C
Tsai, I-Ching	CA3800	66
Tsang-Hall, Dale Y.	CA2450	66
Tsong, Mayron K.	MD1010	13A,66A,66
Tuit, Rhoda	CA4450	66,35A
Tuttle, Elise	UT0305	66

Name	Code	Areas
Tuttle, Julie	AZ0470	13,66
Twyman, Venita	OK1050	66
Uzeki, Yoichi	NY0646	66
Van Weelden, Pam	AG0200	66
Vander Linden, Dan	WI0848	36,61,66
Violett, Martha Watson	CO1050	11,12,66
Virgoe, Betty	CA1520	66,11,13A,20G
Waddell, Dan	CA1270	66
Walsh, C. Peter	CA5100	66
Wan, Agnes	TN0930	66
Wang, Sylvia	IL2250	66,41
Wang, Yung-Chui	TX2900	66
Ware, John	VA1800	13,10,12,66
Warkentien, Vicky	IN0200	13,66,41,51,38
Warren, Jacquelyn	OH0750	66,29
Waseen, Symeon	SD0100	10A,10B,10F,13,66
Watkins, David	GA1150	66
Watt, Stephanie	NY2105	13,66,66A,66B
Weinbeck, Benedict J.	MN0950	66
Weisbrod, Liza	AL0200	16,66
Weller, Robert	CA3460	46,47,66
Wells, Mark	MI1160	61,66
Wenaus, Grant	NY2750	39,61,66C,66
Weng, Lei	CO0950	66
Wesley, Dee	IL1612	66,32B
Wester, R. Glenn	TX2295	61,66,11,13A
Whang, Hyunsoon	OK0150	11,12A,66
Wheeler, Candace	FL0200	66,11,32,10,66A
White, Anita	WV0350	66
Whitis, Jessye	TX3415	66,13
Whitten, Kristi	TN0100	39,61,66
Whitworth, Albin C.	KY0150	13A,13,10,36,66
Wiberg, Janice	MT0300	13,12A,32,36,66
Wiemer, Gerta	UT0350	66,13
Wilkinson, Judi	TX3520	66,54
Winn, James	NV0100	66,13,10
Wolcott, Sylvia	KS0215	36,66
Wong Doe, Henry	PA1600	66A,66,11,13,66D
Woodland, Betty	IN1450	61,66
Woodward, Roger	CA4200	66
Wright, Patricia	AG0450	66
Yang, Frances K.	LA0550	66
Yoo, Shirley S.	PA2250	66
Young, Margaret	OH1860	11,32,66
Young-Wright, Lorna C.	VI0050	13,66,60A
Zhao, Grace Xia	CA5100	66,14,13,66A,66C
Zheng, Yin	VA1600	66
Ziemba, Chris	NY0646	66

Piano

Name	Code	Areas
Aamodt, Rucci R.	HI0150	32,11,66A,66D
Abbott, David	MI0100	12A,66A,42
Abbott-Kirk, Jane	TX0300	66A
Abend, Elena	WI0825	66A,41
Aber, Stephen	TN0100	66A,66C
Abercrombie, Marilyn	MO0260	66A,66D
Abram, Blanche	NY1600	41,66A,66D,66C
Abramovic, Charles	PA3250	66A
Abramovitch, Ruti	IL3450	66A
Acevedo, Maria Teresa	PR0115	66A,66D
Achucarro, Joaquin	TX2400	66A
Adamek, Magdalena	AA0100	66A,66C
Adams, Andrew	NC2600	66C,11,66A,66D
Adams, Fay	TN1710	66A,66C
Adams, Jan	GA2130	66A,66D
Adams, Justin	CO0550	66A,46
Adams, K. Gary	VA0100	11,12A,12,66A
Adams, Robert L.	MO0700	11,12A,12,66A
Adamson, Philip I.	AG0550	66A,66B,66D,13C,66C
Addamson, Paul	NC1050	66A,66C,66D,13A,13
Adkins, Kathy	AL0750	11,36,61,66A
Ahern, Rebecca	IA1390	61,66A
Ahlquist, Janet S.	PA1550	66A
Ahn, Hyeson Sarah	MN1200	66A,66D
Ahn, Hyojin	FL0050	66A
Ahn, Jungeun	NY2900	66A
Aho, Kyle	MO0775	11,66A,47
Aide, William	AG0450	66A,66B,41,66C
Aiken, Barry	ID0140	66A,66C
Aitken, Deborah	CA1750	66A
Ake, David	NV0100	12,20,29A,14,66A
Albergo, Cathy	IL1085	66A,66B,66D
Albrecht, Ronald	IA1350	13A,13,66A,11
Albulescu, Eugene	PA1950	11,66A,66C,41
Alcalay, Eugene C.	WI0840	66A,66B,66C
Aldredge, Steven	OH2500	66A,66D
Aldridge, Glenda	AR0500	66A
Alekseyeva, Marina	DC0170	66A
Alesandrini, Joyce L.	OH1650	13,64D,66A
Alexander, Charles Reid	IL3300	66B,66D,66A
Alexander, Mark	TX2260	66A
Alexander, Mark W.	TX1900	66A,66C,66D
Alexeyev, Anya	AG0600	66A
Aliyeva, Narmina	OH0350	66A,66C
Allan, Kathryn	CA2840	61,66A,66D
Allee, Steve	IN1650	66A
Allee, Steve	IN0907	66A,47,35A,53
Allen, Christine	LA0550	66A,66D
Allen, Frances	MD0170	13A,66A
Allen, Gregory	TX3510	66A
Allen, James O.	MS0550	11,12A,16,66A,66C
Allen, Peter	AF0100	66A,66C,66B,41,42
Allen, Stephen	ID0060	66A,66C,66B
Allen, Susan	VA0050	13C,11,66A,66D
Allen, Thomas O.	MN1300	66A,66B,66D
Allesee, Eric	NJ0750	66A,13C
Allison, Rees	MN0800	12A,66A,66H
Allman, Garrett N.	IL1100	13,66C,38,66A,60B
Allred, Nancy C.	UT0150	66A,66B,66D,66C
Alm, Gina	CA5355	11,66A,66B,66C,66D
Alper, Garth	LA0760	66A,29,35
Alstadter, Judith	NY1275	66A
Altman, I. H.	GA1300	11,66A
Altstaetter, Dean E.	OH1800	66A
Alvarado, Julieta	MN1500	66A,66H
Alvey, Mary	NJ0200	66A
Amalong, Philip	OH0680	66A,66C,13,11,42
Amano, Gary	UT0300	13,66A,66B,66C
Ambrose, Lorraine	AB0200	66A
Amend, James M.	GA1990	66A,66C
Amendola, Vergie	CO0950	66A,66C
Amin, Kimberly	CA5040	66A
Amirault, Steve	AI0150	66A,29
Amirkhanian, Maria	CA1950	66A
Amoriello, Laura	NJ0175	66A
Amper, Leslie	MA2150	66A,66D

Name	Code	Areas
Amper, Leslie	MA1175	66A
Amrod, Paula J.	PA0700	66A,66D
Amrozowicz, Mary Barbara	NY4460	13A,13,66A,13C,13B
Amstutz, Peter	WV0750	66A,66C
An, Ning	TN0850	66A,66C
Anagnoson, James	AG0300	66A
Anavitarte, David	TX2550	36,61,66A,12A,32B
Anderson, Charles A.	IL2150	66A
Anderson, Connie	OH0450	66A,66B,66D
Anderson, David	WI0100	66A,38,66C,13E,42
Anderson, Diana	CO0200	32B,66A,66G
Anderson, H. Gerald	IL2300	66A,66C,66D,12A
Anderson, Jared L.	WI0600	36,61,66A,13,12A
Anderson, Jerry L.	MO0850	66A,66B,66C,66D
Anderson, Jon	ID0250	13C,47,66A,66E
Anderson, Lois	NJ0700	66A
Anderson, Richard P.	UT0050	66A,66B,66C,66D
Anderson, Shane	TX2930	13A,13B,13C,66A,66B
Andes, Tom	MO1800	66A
Andjaparidze, Eteri	NY2750	66A
Andrews, Anita	UT0325	66A
Andrews, Rick	SD0050	66A,66B,13
Andrievsky, Alexandra	AA0050	66A
Anthony, Carl	AR0850	13,66A
Antonacos, Anastasia	ME0150	66A
Antonacos, Anastasia	PA1600	66A,13,11,66C,66D
Antonova, Natalya	NY1100	66A
Apple, Warren	FL1745	61,66A
Applegate, Ann	WI0925	66D,13A,13B,66A
Appleman, Harry	MD0550	66A
Aquino, Robert	NY2102	13A,13,10,66A,66B
Araujo, Ilka Vasconcelos	TX3250	66A,11,12A,20G
Arcaro, John	MA0260	66A
Archer, Esther	CA5510	66A,13A
Archer, Kelly	MO1650	13A,66A
Archer, Naida	AJ0150	13A,13,66A,66D
Archibald, Laurie	OH1300	66A
Ard, Ken	CA4050	66A,66B,66C,66D
Ard, Kenneth	CA2100	66A,29
Ardrey, Cathleen	PA2350	32,36,61,66A
Arellano, Kristina	MN1250	66A
Argersinger, Charles	WA1150	13,10,66A
Armstrong, Alan	NC1500	12A,14B,13,62C,66A
Armstrong, Candace	TN0900	13C,36,60A,66A,11
Arnay, David	CA5300	66A,29
Arnay, David	CA3500	66A
Arnold, Robert D.	PA2550	29,66A
Aronov, Arkady	NY2150	66A
Aronov, Arkady	NY2250	66A
Arriale, Lynne	FL1950	66A,29B,46
Arrigotti, Stephanie	NV0150	13A,11,66A,66B,66D
Arrington, Amanda	KS0650	54,66A,66C
Arshagouni, Michael H.	CA2750	13B,13C,12A,66A,36
Artinian, Annie	IL0730	66A
Artymiw, Lydia	MN1623	66A
Arul, Kumaran	CA4900	66A
Asada, Chi	CA0825	66A
Aschbrenner, Charles C.	MI1050	66A,32I
Asche, Charles	CA5060	66A,41
Ashley, Douglas D.	SC0500	11,12A,66A
Ashmore, Michel	MO0250	11,66A,13A
Ashmore, Pamela J.	OH1800	66A,66C
Ashton, J. Bruce	TN1350	10A,31A,66A,10F,66C
Asteriadou, Maria	PA1750	11,66A,66B,41,42
Asuncion, Victor S.	TN1680	66A,66C
Athayde, Robert L.	CA0807	66A
Athparia, Colleen	AA0050	66A
Atienza, Anthony	CA4850	66A,36
Atkins, Victor	LA0800	29B,46,47,66A
Atkinson, Monte	CO0225	60,32C,36,61,66A
Attaway, Aiya	OK0450	66A,66C,66D
Atzinger, Christopher	MN1450	66A,66B,66D,66C
Au, Kingchi	TX2300	66A
Auer, Edward	IN0900	66A
August, David	NY2900	66A
Augustine, Joseph R.	OH2150	66A
Auler, Robert M.	NY3770	66A,66D,13A,40,35A
Aultman, Gerald	TX2600	13A,13,66A,66G
Austin, Jennifer N.	SC1200	66A,66D,66C,66B
Austin, Mary Jane	VT0250	66A
Autry, Philip E.	TN0550	66A,66B,66C,66D
Avanesian-Weinstein, Karina	IN1800	66A
Ax, Emanuel	NY1900	66A
Axtell, Les	TX3050	66A,61
Ayers, Steven	WI1150	66A
Ayesh, Kevin	NC0220	13,11,12A,66A,66D
Azevedo, Helena	WA0860	66A,66D
Azzoni-Dow, Christine	CA2390	66A
Babal, Gregory	CT0650	66A,66D
Babayan, Naira	DC0170	66A,66C
Babayan, Sergei	OH0600	66A
Babcock, Michael	VA0650	66A,11
Bachelder, Elizabeth Y.	VA1250	66A,66B
Bachmann, Nancy	CA2775	13A,13B,12A,66A,66B
Baciu, Bianca	AA0020	66A,66B,66C
Badami, Charles A.	MO0950	66C,66A,66D,11
Badgerow, Justin A.	PA1250	66A,66C,66D,13
Badgley, Clifford	CA1850	66A
Badridze, Ketevan	IN0910	66A
Baer, Matthew Kevin	CA4300	66A,66C,66D
Bagg, Joseph	CA1000	29B,66A
Baham, Kerry M.	TX3370	13B,66A,11,66C,12A
Baik-Kim, Eun Ae	PA0950	66A,66C,42
Bailey, Sally	NY0450	66A,66B,66C,66D
Baird, Melinda Lambert	DC0170	66A
Baker, Kent	VT0100	66A,66D,46,13,10F
Baker, Kristi A.	KS1000	66A
Baker, Steve	CA2100	66A,13,29
Baker, Walter W.	OH0300	66A
Balakerskaia, Anna	VA0450	66A,66D
Baldoria, Charisse J.	PA0250	66A,66D,12A,11
Baldus, Kara A.	MO1900	66A
Baldwin, Dalton	NJ1350	66C,66D
Baldwin, Gail	IL0100	66,66A
Bales, Ann	CA2050	66A
Balge, Bethel	MN0200	66A
Balge, Bethel A.	MN1030	66A
Balian, Muriel	CA1960	11,66A,66D,36,55D
Ball, Karen	IL2300	10A,66A,66B,13B,13C
Ballard, Alice	MS0300	66A,66G,66D,11
Ballin, Carolyn	NY1275	66A,66D
Baltaian, Aroussiak	CA3300	66A,62
Bang, In Hyuk	NY3785	66A,66C
Banner, Lucy	MA0600	66A,66G,66H,66B,66C
Bannister, Hazen Duane	SC0400	66A
Banowetz, Joseph M.	TX3420	66A
Barber, Charles	TN1250	61,66A
Barber, Daniel R.	OH0650	66A,13D,12A,66G

Index by Area of Teaching Interest

Name	Code	Areas
Barber, Julie	IN1560	66A,61,40,12A
Barbuto, Robert	NY1250	66A,29
Barbuto, Robert C.	NY1550	66A,47
Bardin, Joan	CA1520	66A
Barfield, Sally	TX2350	66A,66D
Bargas, Nanci	CA3400	66A
Barkley, Elizabeth F.	CA1800	11,12A,66A,66C,66D
Barland, Charles J.	IA1450	13,11,31A,66A,36
Barlar, Rebecca	FL0670	13,66A,66B,66C
Barnes, Paul	NE0600	66A
Barolsky, Ruth	VA1550	66A
Baron, Michael	FL0680	66A,66C,66B,66D
Barone, Judith	NY4460	66A,66G,13A,41
Barrington, Barrie	AB0050	66A,66D
Barron, Kenny	NY1900	66A,29
Barskaya, Galina	CA3300	66A,66C
Barth, George	CA4900	13,66A,67C
Bartles, Martha	TN1850	66A
Bartman, Karen	DC0170	66A
Bartolomeo, Andrea	IL2750	66A
Bartolomeo, Luke	IL2750	66A
Barton, Ena	NJ1350	66A
Bartz, Karen	MN0610	66A,66D
Bascom, Brandon R.	ID0060	32F,66A,66C
Bass, Jonathan	MA0350	66A
Bastian, William M.	MI1200	66A,29
Batchelor-Glader, Brian	OH2550	66A
Batchvarova, Madlen T.	IN0650	60A,36,61,66A,12A
Bates, Elaine	OK1250	32B,66A,13
Bates, Michael J.	AR0810	36,13,60,12A,66A
Bates, Pamela	IL0900	12A,13,66A,66C,66D
Battersby, Edmund	IN0900	66A
Battipaglia, Diana M.	NY0635	11,32,36,66A,38
Bauer, David T.	MN1030	13A,34,66A,66G
Baugh-Bennett, Grace	IN1010	66A
Bax, Alessio	TX2400	66A
Bays, Tatiana	TX0850	66A
Baytelman, Pola	NY3650	41,66A,66D,66E
Beach, Wade	VA0450	66A,29B
Beachley, Laine	MD0500	66A
Beachley, Laine	PA3710	66A,66C
Beale, Nancy	PA2800	66A
Beamish, Gwen	AG0500	66A,66B
Beams, Mahala	MA1560	11,12A,66A,13A
Bean, Robert D.	IN0905	13A,66A,66B,66C,66D
Beane, Diane	IA1800	66A
Beaugrand, Luc	AI0200	53,66A,29
Beavers, Judith	MI0910	66A,41
Becker, Juanita	WI1155	66A,13,66B,66C,66D
Becker, Karen E.	NY3775	66A,66C,13C,13A,36
Becker, Nicole M.	NY4200	66A
Becker, Paul	AR0800	66A,66B,66C,66D,11
Becker, Richard	VA1500	10A,66A
Beckley, Jane E.	OH2140	66A,66C
Beckman, Bradley J.	TX3420	66A,66B
Beckman, Linda L.	AR0400	66A,11,10F,34,66C
Beckman, Seth	FL0850	66A,66C
Bedelian, Lorna Griffitt	CA5020	66A
Bedford, Robert M.	PA3600	66A,66B
Bednarzyk, Stephen C.	GU0500	60,37,64C,66A
Bedner, Edward C.	MA0260	66A
Beecher, Betty	UT0300	66A,66D
Beecher, Randy	CA2100	66A,11
Beecher, Randy	CA4050	66A,66B,66C,66D,12
Beedle, Helen E.	PA1950	66A,66D
Bees, Julie	KS1450	66A
Behnke, Martin K.	OR1300	60,37,66A,29
Bejerano, Martin	FL1900	29,10,66A,53
Bela, Marcin	TN1100	10,66A,66D
Belcher, Deborah	NC2400	66A
Belden, Carol Beck	FL0400	66A,66C
Belfiglio, Anthony	TN0100	66A,13B
Bell, Carol Ann	OK0650	66A,66D
Bell, James	AL1050	66A
Bell, Jane H.	OH1650	66A,66D
Belland, Diana R.	KY1000	66A
Bellassai, Marc C.	AZ0250	11,12A,66A,66F,66G
Bellemare, Yvon	AI0220	66A,66C
Bemberg, Stephanie	MO1110	12A,66A
Bemis, Jennifer	AL1300	66A,66C,66D
Bender, Sharla A.	AL0345	11,61,66A
Benham, Helen	NJ0030	13,66A,66H,66B,66C
Benjamin, John A.	OH2250	66A,66C,66D
Bennett, Cameron	WA0650	66A
Bennett, Elena	TN0100	66A
Bennett, Elizabeth S.	NC0850	66A,66G
Bennett, Erin K.	FL1950	66A,66B,66D
Bennett, Hye-Yun Chung	VA1000	62E,66A
Bennett, Mary Lynne	WV0300	66B,66A,66D,66,66C
Benson, Kelley	MI2100	66A,66B
Benson, Michael L.	OH1350	66A,66B,12A,11,66
Benz, Terri	IL1650	61,66A,36
Berardinelli, Paula	NY2450	29A,13,66A
Berenson, Gail	OH1900	66A,66B
Berg, Joy L.	AA0015	60A,66A
Berg, Reinhard	AA0020	13,10,12A,66A,66G
Berg, Shelton G.	FL1900	66A,66C,29,46,47
Bergey, Matthew	WI1150	66A
Bergmann, Elizabeth	AA0050	66A,66C,41
Bergmann, Marcel	AA0050	66A,66C,41
Berkman, David	NY0642	29,66A
Berkowitz, Paul M.	CA5060	66A,41
Berlinsky, Elena	WY0200	66A
Berman, Boris	CT0850	66A
Berman, Kenneth M.	CA5000	66A
Berns, Kathleen	WI0842	66A
Bernstein, Seymour	NY2750	66A
Berthiaume, Gerald B.	WA1150	66A
Bertsch, Rolf	AA0050	66A
Besalyan, Raffi	WI0850	66A,66D
Bespalko, Polina	OH2550	66A
Best, Raelene	IA1350	66A
Best, Stephen	NY1350	66A,66G
Betancourt, Nilda	PR0100	13,66A,66C,12A
Bethea, Kay	VA1030	13,11,12A,66A,66D
Betts, Donald	MN0950	66A,10
Betts, Steven	OK1200	66A,66B,66D,13,11
Beus, Stephen	OH1450	66A
Beutler, Marian	NE0050	61,66A
Bevelander, Brian E.	OH0950	66A,10A,10B,13E,13G
Beyer, LaVaun	CA1520	66A
Beyer, Loretta	MI0200	13,66A,32B,11
Bezaire, Fionna	IL0730	66A,66D
Bickel, Ronald E.	PA1050	66A
Bidwell, Louise B.	CA5000	66A
Biegel, Jeffrey	NY0500	66A
Bien, Leander	DC0170	66A
Biggs, Charlene	AG0070	11,66A,66B,66C
Biggs, Charlene	AG0150	66A
Bighley, Mark	OK0550	12A,66A,66G,66D
Bigler, Nathan	AZ0150	61,66A
Billias, Anna	VA1400	66C,66A
Billings, Carolyn A.	NC0850	13,12,66A,66B
Billings, Judson	OH0600	66A
Billock, Becky	WV0600	66A
Bills, Mary Ann	NC2500	66A
Bilson, Malcolm	NY0900	66A,66E
Bingener, Bonnie	AZ0470	66A
Bingham, Roxanne Laycock	AA0050	66A,66D
Biran, Dror	KY1500	66A
Bird, Carolyn	AF0120	66A
Birdsong, Nikki S.	TX1150	66A,66D
Birr, Diane	NY1800	66A,66C,66D
Bischoff, Janet	PA2250	20,66A
Bishop, Genevieve	KS0150	66A
Bishop, Marla	GA1700	66A,66D
Bishop, Saundra	MS0575	13A,36,66A,66D,13B
Bittner, Groff S.	MO0650	66A,66D
Bizzell, Gayle	TX1850	12A,66A,66C,66D
Bjerken, Xak	NY0900	66A,42,43
Bjornn, Marsha	ID0060	66A
Blacklow, John	IN1700	66A,66C
Blackwell, Manley	AL1350	11,12A,66A
Blaha, Bernadene	CA5300	66A
Blake, Ran	MA1400	29,66A,53
Blanchett, Madalyn	TX2260	11,64A,66A,66D,67
Blanco, Leo	MA0260	66A
Bland, Sarah	VA0250	66A
Blankenburg, Gayle R.	CA3650	66A,13C
Blankenburg, Gayle	CA4500	66A,66C
Blankenburg, Gayle	CA1050	66A
Blenzig, Charles	NY3785	10,66A,29,35B
Blersch, Carla	NE0150	66A
Blinov, Ilya	PA3150	66A,66C,11
Blocker, Robert	CT0850	66A,42
Bloom, Joe	CA1650	66A
Bluebaugh, Diana	MO0060	66A
Blumfield, Coleman	DC0110	66A
Blyth, Jennifer	PA0950	66A,66B,66C,66D,13
Boatright, Ann	CA4460	66A
Bob, Sarah	MA0700	66A
Bocanegra, Cheryl	OK0850	13,66A,35D,47
Bodaubay, Dina	CO0830	66A,66D
Boddez, Karla	AA0020	66A
Boe, Karen	WI0865	66A,66B,66C,66D
Boeder, Bethel J.	MN1030	36,66A
Boehm, Norman	AR0350	13,10,12A,66A,11
Boemler, Cathy	MO0550	66A,66B,66C,66D
Boepple, Hans C.	CA4425	13,12A,66A,66B,66C
Boerckel, Gary M.	PA2100	11,12A,66A,20G,29
Boespflug, George	CA0350	66A
Boettger, Susan	CA2390	66A,66D
Boey, Hooi Yin	WV0050	66A,66D,20,66B,66C
Bogas, Roy	CA2200	60,12A,38,66A,66B
Bogdan, Valentin Mihai	LA0100	66A,10,35A
Bognar, Joseph A.	IN1750	66A,13,66H,66G
Boguslavsky, Lidia	NJ1050	66A
Bohnenstengel, Christian	UT0200	66A,66C,13A,13B,13C
Boianova, Linda	NY2650	66A,13C,61,39,66C
Bolen, Bradley C.	TX0300	66A,66D
Bomberger, E. Douglas	PA1250	12,66A
Bond, Kori	ID0100	12A,66A,66B,66C
Bonness, Will	AC0100	29B,47,66A
Booker, Sally	MN1600	13C,66A
Boozer, Michael K.	GA0490	13C,66A,66B,66D
Boozer, Pat	NC2350	10,32B,66A,13A,13B
Borbely, Adrienne	NY0050	66A
Borden, Rita	AZ0450	66A,66C,41
Boren, Benjamin J.	CA0850	66A,66B,66C,66D,13B
Bornovalova, Olga	IL0650	66A,66D
Bornovalova, Olga	IL1085	66A,66B,66D
Borrmann, Kenneth	PA2800	66A,66B,66C,42,44
Bos, Ken	MI0850	66C,66A,66D
Bosits, Marcia L.	IL2250	66A,66D
Bossard, Claudia M.	IN1800	66A
Bossart, Eugene	MI1900	41,66A,66C
Bostic, Polly T.	NC2650	66A,66D,66G
Bostick, D. Jane	NC0100	66A,11
Bostock, Anne	MA1100	66A,66C
Boston, Marilyn	MO0400	66A,66D
Boston, Nancy J.	PA2150	66A,66B,66C,66D
Bostonia, Marguerite	WV0800	66A,13F
Bostrom, Sandra	CA0835	66A,10C,12A,34,65A
Botkin, Sean	IA1600	66A
Bou, Emmy	NE0150	66A,61
Boukobza, Laurent	FL1800	66A,66B
Boulanger, Richard	AE0100	12A,12,66A
Boulton, Kenneth	LA0650	66A,66B,66D
Bourgeois, Marilyn	IL2775	66A
Bowden, Derek	MD0800	11,66D,66A
Bowder, Naydene	ME0200	66A,66H
Bowlin, Ellen	IL0300	66A,66G,66C
Bowman, Jennifer	WA0650	66A
Boyce, Emily W.	NY3717	66D,66C,66A,66B
Boyd, Don E.	HI0200	66A
Boyd, Kathleen E.	IN0250	66A
Boyd, Michael	OH2300	66A
Boyd, Sue Marston	VA1350	66A,66H,66C,66D
Braaten-Reuter, Laurie	IA1800	66A,66C,66D
Bracey, John-Paul	AG0500	66A,66B
Brackeen, Joanne	NY2660	10,66A,47,53
Brackeen, JoAnne	MA0260	66A
Brackeen, William	OK0450	66A,66D,10A,13
Bradfield, David	CA0805	13,34,66A
Bradford, Lovell	NC0550	66A,47
Bradford, Mary Pinkney	TX2170	66A,66B,66D
Bradley, Annette	AA0080	66A,32B,13C,66D,42
Bradner, Janice B.	SC1200	66D,66C,66A
Bradshaw, Dean	AF0120	13,66A
Braginsky, Alexander	MN1623	66A
Braid, David	AG0450	29,66A
Branagan, Marcella E.	NY3717	66A
Branagan, Marcella	PA0100	66A
Brancaleone, Francis P.	NY2200	13,66A,66D,66G,66C
Brancart, Evelyne	IN0900	66A
Branch, Kirk	LA0080	66A
Brand, Angela	CA0450	66A,12A
Brandt, Lynne	TX2310	13,64A,41,66A
Brasington, Merewyn	OH1400	66C,66D,13C,66A
Brassard, Henri	AI0210	66A
Braswell, Martha	TX2295	66A,66E,66G,11
Bratuz, Damjana	AG0500	66A,66B
Breckenridge, Carol Lei	IA0200	11,66A,66B,66C,66H
Bree, Wynton	WY0130	66A,66D
Breitman, David	OH1700	66,66E,66A
Brennan, Christopher	CA0960	66A

Index by Area of Teaching Interest

Bresnen, Steven M.	PA0400	13,11,12A,66A,66D	Camp, Cheryl	AR0250	66A
Brett, Douglas	NY4050	66A	Camp, Linda	IL0850	66A
Brewer, Abbie C.	MO0300	66A,66D	Campbell, Cheryl Lynn	PA1900	66A,66D
Brewster, David	WA1350	66D	Campitelli, Stephen	PA1550	66D,66A
Brickman, Martha	AB0200	66A	Campos, David M.	CA4410	66A
Bridgman, Joyce M.	OK0850	66A,66H,66B,66C,66D	Candee, Jan	ND0400	66A,66D,66G,32B,11
Briere, Jimmy	AI0200	66A	Canfield, Wanda	PA1000	66A,66D,53
Briggs, Roger	WA1250	43,10F,10,66A	Canfield, Wanda	PA0450	66A
Brightbill, Janet	WV0560	66C,66A	Canin, Martin	NY2750	66A
Brill, Jodie	VA1150	66A	Canin, Martin	NY1900	66A
Brink, Daniel	CO0200	13A,13,10F,11,66A	Canon, Sherri	CA2660	66A,29A
Briscoe, Anna	IN0250	66A	Canon, Sherri D.	CA2720	20,29A,66A
Briskin, Efrem	NY2400	66A	Capitano, Gay Lyn	FL0365	66A
Briskin, Efrem	NY5000	66A	Capizzi, Christopher	PA0550	66A
Briskin, Natalya	NY5000	66A	Caporale, Matthew	TX1450	66A,66D
Bristol, Cynthia	MI0850	11,66A,20	Caporella, Cynthia Anne	OH1050	36,12A,66A,66C
Britt, Michael	MD0170	66A,66G	Capp, Myrna	WA0800	66A,66B,32I,20A
Britton, Carolyn	WI0845	11,66A,66H	Caramia, Anthony	NY1100	66A,66B,66D
Brockman, Luke	WA0250	29,46,66A	Cardoza, Don	CA3320	66A,66C
Broderick, Daniela	IL1250	11,66A,66D,20G,54	Carey, Barbara	NM0300	61,66A
Broderick, Daniela C.	IL1890	11,66A,66D	Carkeek, Maureen M.	IN0350	66A
Bronola-Dickert, Lannia N.	SC1200	66A	Carlberg, Frank	MA1400	66A,47
Bronson, Janci	IA0850	66A,66B,66D	Carlberg, Frank T.	MA0260	66A
Brook, Sharon D.	CA4400	11,66A,66C,66D	Carleton, Sharon	NC1450	66G,66A
Brooks, Barbara J.	MN0950	66A	Carlin, Kerry	NC0650	66A,66B,66D
Brooks, Ipek	GA0850	66A	Carlin, Maryse	MO1900	66A,66H
Brooks, Melinda K.	AL0850	11,13,66A,66D	Carlin, Seth A.	MO1900	66A,67C
Brossard, Marilyn	WA0900	66A,66D,66B	Carlisle, Kris	GA0300	11,66A,13
Brown, Adrianne	CT0350	66A,66B,66C,66D	Carlson, Stephen J.	MN0150	66A,66B,66C
Brown, Christine A.	IN1010	11,66A,13,66B	Carlton, Elizabeth	NC0350	32,66A,66B,66D
Brown, Dana	OH1100	66D,66A	Carlton, Jan	CA0300	66A,66D
Brown, Donald R.	TN1710	47,66A,29A	Carney, Robert D.	MO1550	66A,66B,66C,11,13C
Brown, Ernest	VA0950	14,66A	Carpenter, Susan	WV0550	66A
Brown, Frank Burch	IN0300	12A,66A,12B,10	Carr, William	PA1550	13B,66D,66A,13D
Brown, Ila	FL1500	66A,66C	Carrell, Scott	AR0250	10A,13,34A,66A,66B
Brown, Jeffrey A.	IL3500	66,66A,66D	Carrell-Coons, Mariah	OK0770	66A,66C,66D,32E
Brown, Kathryn	OH0600	61,66A	Carriere, Marilyn	MN0620	66A,66D
Brown, Lenora N.	UT0250	66A	Carroll-Phelps, Claudia	OK0750	66A
Brown, Stephanie	NY3785	66A	Carrothers, Bill	WI0350	29,66A
Brown, Susan E.	TN0100	66A,66C	Carson, Virginia	VA1800	13,10,66A
Brown-Stanford, Deborah	MD0550	66A	Carter, Beverly H.	PA1450	11,12A,66A,66B
Brown-Stephens, Kelli	OR0750	66A	Carter, Paul S.	NY3765	13A,13B,66A
Brubaker, Bruce	MA1400	66A	Carter, Priscilla	CA3320	66A,66C
Bruck, Douglas	CA4050	13A,13,66A,60	Carter, Roland M.	TN1700	13,11,36,66A
Bruckner, Susan	CA0400	66A,11	Carter, William	PA2200	29A,66A
Bruderer, Conrad D.	CA4100	66A	Cartledge, David O.	IN0900	66A
Bruk, Elfrida	IN0005	66A,13,31B,66C,66H	Caruso, Frank	IL0850	66A
Bruk, Karina	NJ1130	66A,42	Carver, Sylvia	TN0050	11,66A
Brummel, Josephine I.	CA4410	66A,66C	Case, Barbara	TX0250	66A
Brunell, David	TN1710	66A,66C	Casey, Rebecca L.	OH1800	66A,13,66D,66C
Brunelli, Stephanie	KS0150	66A,12A,13,13B	Casgrain, Robert	AA0020	66A
Brunner, Norma	MA0950	66A	Cash, Carla Davis	TX3200	66B,66D,29B,66A,66
Bryant, David	PA1150	66A,66D	Cashwell, Brian	OH0500	66A,29
Bryant, Thomas E.	TN1200	13,11,66A,66C,66H	Casper, Richard	MA0600	66A
Brzozowski, Kazimierz	MI2200	66A	Cassidy, Robert	OH0650	66A
Bucci, Thomas	ME0500	66A	Castellana, Joseph	OH0755	66D,66A,63A
Buchman, Matthew	WI0850	47,53,66A	Castellano, Ann	OH0600	66A
Buckland, Karen W.	SC1000	66A,66C,66D	Caton, Benjamin D.	TN0500	13C,66A,66B
Buckner, Janice	NC0300	66A	Catsalis, Marie-Louise	CA4425	12A,66A
Buckner, Jeremy	TN0250	32B,32C,66A,66D,11	Caviani, Laura	MN1450	66A
Buckner, Nathan	NE0590	66A,66C,66D,13B,13C	Caviani, Laura	MN0300	66A
Buckwalter, Laurel G.	NY0100	66A,66B,66C,69	Cellon, Cheryl	TX3525	66C,66A
Buczynski, Walter	AG0450	13,10F,10,66A	Celotto, Albert Gerard	CT0700	13,12,66A
Budai, William H.	KY0400	66A,66B,66D	Centeno Martell, Ingrid	PR0100	13,66A,66C,32
Budke, Tiffany	KS0300	66A,66C,11	Century, Michael	NY3300	12,13,43,34H,66A
Buechner, Sara Davis	AB0100	66A,42	Cepparulo, Kathie	TN1660	66A
Buelow, William L.	OH1400	13A,13,10,66A,29	Cerny, William J.	IN1700	12A,41,66A,66C
Bugli, David	NV0150	66A	Chabora, Robert J.	MN0600	66A,66B,66D,11,13
Bukvich, Ivana	IL3310	66A	Chamberlain, Julie Rhyne	NC0350	66A,66B,66C,66D,11
Bukvich, Ivana	IL2750	66A	Chambers-Salazar, Polli	CA1750	66A,66G
Bullock, Betty	DC0170	66A,39	Chan, Amanda	AB0200	66A,66C
Bullock, Janie Lee	GA0550	66A	Chan, Amanda	AB0100	42,66A
Bullock, Karen	NC2350	66A,13A,66C	Chan, Jacklyn	IN1650	66A,66D
Bulwinkle, Belle	CA2950	66A,66C,20F	Chan, Joni	IN1800	66A
Bumbach, Matthew	FL0365	66A,61	Chan, Sarah S.	OK0600	66A,66C,66D,13,11
Bumpers, Wayne	FL1300	36,66A,66D,20G,66B	Chan, See Tsai	IL0350	66A,66G,13
Bunchman, Michael	NY5000	66A	Chan, Susan	OR0850	66A,66B,66D,66C
Burch, Alene	TX0550	66A,66C,66D,66B	Chan, Wenyin	DC0170	66A
Burchard, Marcia Earle	CA1650	66A,13	Chan, Yan-Yan	CA3000	66A,66C
Burchard, Marcia	CA4460	66A,13B	Chandler, Gulya	LA0030	66A,66C,66D,11,12A
Burdette, Glenn E.	MI2200	12,66A,66H	Chang, Angelin	OH0650	66A
Burganger-Treer, Judith	FL0650	66A,66B	Chang, Anita L.	CA2650	66A,13A,11
Burger, Markus	CA1900	66A	Chang, Ann	NE0600	66A,66E
Burkett, John	TX2955	13,66A,66G,34,12C	Chang, Helen	IL1085	66A
Burkhart, Annette M.	MO1900	66A,66D	Chang, Jocelyn Hua-Chen	CA0845	66A
Burkhart, Annette	MO1250	66A	Chang, Melody Jun Yao	CO0100	35,66A,13
Burkhart, Charles L.	NY0642	13A,13,66A	Chang, Wan-Chin	CA2960	66A,66D
Burkhead, Phillip	OH2250	66A,29	Chang, Ya-ting	PA2300	66A
Burky, Kenneth	PA1050	66A	Chao, Joanna K.	NJ0175	66A,13C,13B
Burleson, Geoffrey	NY0625	66A,13,12A,66,42	Chapman, Joe C.	GA1500	13,66A,10
Burnaman, Stephen	TX1150	13,66A,66G,66B,66C	Chapman, Norman	MS0600	13A,13,12A,66A
Burnett, Marty Wheeler	NE0100	12A,13,66A,36,66G	Chappell, Jeffrey	DC0170	13,29,66A
Burnham, Stuart	NC1500	12A,13C,66A,20	Chappell, Jeffrey	MD0400	47,66A,29,29B,10
Burns, Chelsea R.	IL2750	66A,66D	Character, William	GA2175	61,66A,70
Burns, Elaina Denney	IA1450	66A,66C	Charney, Miriam	NY4450	66A,39
Burson, Claudia	AR0700	66A	Charoenwongse-Shaw, Chindarat	OK1330	66A,66B,66D,66C
Burt, Patricia A.	IL1200	13A,66A,66D,13B,13C	Chaudoir, Marianne	WI0400	11,66A,66D,13A
Burton, Christopher	MI1300	66A,66C	Chauls, Robert	CA2750	11,38,66A,10A,39
Burton, Heidi R.	OK1300	13A,13,11,66A,62A	Chaverdian, Gregory	AI0070	66A
Busch, Gary D.	NY3780	12A,66A,20G	Checkeye, Jane	PA2450	66A
Bush, Jerry Alan	AL1300	66A,66B	Cheek, John	NC1100	13,11,66A,20G
Bushong, Claire B.	NE0400	12A,13B,13C,66A,66G	Cheetham, Andrew	IL0800	63A,47,66A,11
Bustamante, Tamara A.	KY1100	36,11,13,66C,66A	Chelseth, Gretchen	MN0450	66A
Butler, Beverly	IN1450	66A,66C,66D	Chen, Ann A.	MI1260	66A,66B
Butler, Carol	TN0580	66A,66B,66D	Chen, Claudia S.	MN0950	66A
Butler, Debbie D.	TX3527	66A,66C,66D	Chen, Evelyn	NY4200	66A
Butler, E. Gregory	AG0550	66A,66B	Chen, Fen-Fang	AL0650	66A,66B,66D,42,66C
Butler, Terry	VA0950	13C,32D,66A,66G	Chen, Ginger Jui-Wen	GA0940	66A,66D
Buzzelli-Clarke, Betsy	PA1100	11,13A,12A,66A,66D	Chen, Hsaun-Ya	CA1760	66A,66D
Byington, Jensina	WA0860	13,66A,66D	Chen, Johanna	CA0859	66A,66D
Byrd, Eric B.	MD0520	36,66A,29	Chen, Melvin	NY0150	66A,42,38
Byun, Wha-Kyung	MA1400	66A	Chen, Moh Wei	CA5100	66A,66D,13C
Caceres, Marcelo	MI0250	66A,66B,66C,66D	Chen, Shao Shen	TX0550	66A,66D,66B,66C
Cacioppo, Christine	PA1500	66A	Cheng, Angela	OH1700	66A
Cacioppo, Curt	PA1500	13,10,20G,10F,66A	Cheng, Susan	CT0050	66A,66D
Cademcian, Gerard	IN0005	66A,31A,31B,67F,13	Chernyshev, Alexander	MN1600	66A,66D
Cai, Lei	AR0500	66A	Cherry, Janet	NC1300	66A,66D
Cai, Yi-Min	AL1250	66A,66B,66D,66C	Chertock, Michael S.	OH2200	66G,66A
Cain, Michael	AC0050	29,47,66A	Chesebrough, Constance D.	NH0250	66C,66A
Cain, Michael D.	MA1400	29,66A,34,31,20	Chevalier, Angelis	CA3200	11,66A
Cal, Anna	AB0210	66A	Chew, Jacqueline	CA5000	66A,66D
Calderazzo, Joey	NC1600	66A,66C,46,47	Chiang, Janice ChenJu	AZ0450	66C,66A,41
Caldwell, Ann	GA0850	66A,66D,66G,11	Chien, Alec F.	PA0100	11,42,66A,41
Caldwell, Frances Sherer	NY2400	66A	Chien, Gloria	TN0850	13C,13E,66A,66B
Caldwell, Frances Sherer	NY5000	66A	Chin, Huei Li	IL2910	66A,66B,66D
Caliri, Lisa	MA0350	66A,6	Chin, Wayman	MA1175	66A,66C,42
Caluda, Elizabeth	VA1350	66A,66D	Chioldi, Ronald	OK0550	13B,66A,66D,13D,13E
Camacho, Dionisio	FL0050	66A	Chitwood, Elizabeth	GA0700	66A,66B,66C

Name	Code	Areas		Name	Code	Areas
Cho, Cecilia	DC0170	66A		Cornish, Glenn S.	FL0500	13,11,66A
Cho, Mison	PA3560	66A,66D		Cornut, Sebastien	NJ0825	66A,66A,66C
Cho, Peter	LA0080	13,34,35,47,66A		Correnti, James	PA2800	66A
Cho, Sujung	SC0350	66A,66D,66C		Corrothers, Janette	OH2550	66A
Cho, Young-Hyun	TX3500	66A,41,66C,66B,12A		Cory, Eleanor	NY2050	13,10,11,66A,66D
Chodos, Gabriel	MA1400	66A		Cosand, Walter	AZ0100	41,66A
Choe, Sung	FL1745	66A		Cosgrove, Nancy	MA0600	66A,66G,66H,66B,66C
Choi, Bonnie L.	NY4150	66A,66H,66D		Costa, Jennifer	NC2000	66A,66C
Choi, Bonnie	NY2650	66A,66D,66H		Cotton, Maurice	WI1150	61,66A
Choi, Hyangbin	GA0250	66A		Coulson, Bette	IL2750	66A
Choi, Hye-Jean	TX0900	66A,66G,66H,67C,13		Covell, Jeffrey	MA0260	66A
Choi, Hyunjoo	CA1425	66C,66G,66D,66A		Cowden, Tracy E.	VA1700	66C,66A,66D,13C
Choi, Minju	IN1650	66A,66D		Cowell, Stanley	NJ1130	66A
Choi, Winston	IL0550	66A		Cox, Bradley	MO1000	13J,66A
Choi, Wooyoung	GA0050	66A,66D,66C		Cox, Buford	FL0040	13A,12A,66A,66C
Chou, Godwin	IL2775	10A,13,66A,66,10		Cox, Kellie	TN1600	66A
Chou, Mei-En	LA0150	66A,66B,66C,12A		Cox, Thomas E.	AR0750	13,47,66A,66D
Chow, Alan	IL2250	66A		Cozza, John	CA5350	66A,66C
Chow, Alvin	OH1700	66A		Craig, Vincent	PA3600	66A,66D
Chow-Tyne, June	AZ0480	66A,66D		Craige, Mary Ann	OK1150	66A,66D
Christensen, Linda	NE0700	66A,66D,34,66B,11		Crane, Amy	FL1750	66A
Christian, Kathy P.	IL2050	66A		Crane, Teresa Ann	IL1500	66C,61,66,66A,11
Christiansen, Gregg	NY1250	66A		Cranmer, Carl	PA3600	66A,66C,66D
Christiansen, Gregg S.	NY1550	66A,13A,13B,13C		Crappell, Courtney Joseph	TX3530	66B,66A
Christianson, Paul A.	TN1600	11,66A,66D		Crawford, Donna	SC0200	66A,66G,34
Christopher, Un Chong	MO0060	11,12A,13,66A,66C		Crawford, Jenn	AJ0030	66A,66B,66C,13
Christopherson, Robert	MA0260	66A		Crawford, Lawrence E.	MD0850	13,66A
Chua, Emily Yap	VA1125	13B,15,42,66A		Crawford, Peter	WA1300	34,48,37,66A
Chua, Rosalind Y.	RI0150	66A		Crawley-Mertins, Marilee	IA0425	11,66A,66D,34
Chuang, Ya-Fei	MA0350	66A		Creager, Greg	CO0275	66A
Chung, He-Lyun	CA3100	66A,66D		Cremaschi, Alejandro M.	CO0800	66D,66A,66B
Chung, Hyunjung Rachel	GA1900	66A,13,66C		Crevelli-Sallee, Monica	CA4460	66A
Chung, Jiyun	MO1010	66A		Creviston, Hannah	AZ0100	66A,66B,66C
Chung, Joyce	NY4500	66A,66D		Crisan, Patricia	SC0650	66A,13C
Chung, Mia	MA0950	13,66A,66B		Crissinger, Paula K.	OH0550	66A
Chung, Myung-Hee	WI0865	66A,66B,66C		Crite, Kiera	TN1400	66A
Ciarelli, Katharine	NY2950	66A,66D,11		Crocker, Susan	NY2950	66A,66D
Cifarelli, Joan	CA2775	66A,29,13A		Cromley, Dorothea	MT0175	12A,66A,66B
Cionco, Richard M.	CA0840	66A		Crooks, Mack	CA4650	13,12,66A,34
Cipiti, John	OH2140	13,66A,10,14C		Crosby, Karen	MA0600	66A
Cisler, Valerie C.	NE0590	66A,66B,66D		Crosby, Richard A.	KY0550	66A,66D,12A
Cizewski, Kathleen	IL0650	66A,66D		Crossman, Patricia	MD0175	66A,66C
Clapp, Lawrence	AZ0440	66A		Crouse, David L.	AR0600	66A,13C,61,66G,13B
Clarfield, Ingrid	NJ1350	66A,66B		Crow, Todd	NY4450	66A
Clark, Adam	MI1050	66,66A,66C,66B,66D		Crowder, Jarrell	MD0550	66A,66D,54
Clark, Amber L.	IL1350	66A,66G,66B		Crowne, Scott	PA1400	66C,66A,42
Clark, Jacob	DC0170	66A		Cruciani, Lori L.	WI0803	66A,66D
Clark, Jacob	SC1050	66A,66D,12A		Crummer, Larry D.	CA1760	20,13,11,14,66A
Clark, James W.	SC0050	13,66A,66D,66B		Cruz, Jennifer	OH0500	66A,66B,66D
Clark, Paula	ID0060	66A,66C		Cubbage, John	MT0370	13,12A,66A,10A
Clark, Renee Cherie	MI1000	66A		Cuellar, Martin	KS0300	66A,66B,66C,66D
Clarke, Leland	MA2200	32A,32B,66A,66B		Cumming, Duncan J.	NY3700	66A,13,11
Cleary, Thomas	VT0450	66A,47,66D		Cummings, Daniel	CA2420	60B,38,66D,66A
Cleary, Tom	VT0250	66A		Cunningham, Chuck	NM0500	66A,66G,32D,36,40
Cleland, Sara	MI1160	66A		Curlee, Alisa	NY3350	66A
Clement, Dawn	WA0200	13A,66A,66D,29		Curran, Nancy A.	CT0500	42,66A,66H
Clevenger, Charles	OH0450	66A,66B,66C,66D,12B		Curtis, Laura	WA1300	66A
Clewell, Christine M.	PA1600	66A,66G,66D,13		Curtis, Noma	OK0200	66A
Clinton, Mark K.	NE0600	66A		Curtis-Smith, Curtis O.	MI2250	10,14,66A,20G
Clodes-Jaguaribe, Maria	MA0400	66A		Cushing, Alanna B.	WV0400	66A,66C
Clodfelter, John D.	IN0350	66A,66C,66D		Cushman, Cathy	NY1250	66A,13A,13
Coats, Syble M.	AL0831	66A,66D,11,13A		Cutchen, Dovie	AL1050	62,66A
Cobb, Mary Marden	NY3725	66D,66A		Cutler, Ann	TX0250	66A,66D
Cobb, Susan	IL1750	66A,66B,66D		Cutting, W. Scott	MI1550	13,11,66A,66D,34D
Cochrane, Michael	NJ1140	66A,29		Cymerman, Claude	IN0350	66A
Cockey, Linda E.	MD0800	12A,66A,66B,13E		Da Silva, Fabio Gardenal	NY2750	66A,42,66C
Cockrell, Findlay	NY3700	13A,13,11,66A		Da Silva, Paul	CA0859	13A,66D,66A
Coen, Jean-David	OR1300	12A,66A,66C		D'Abruzzo, Gabriel	PA2950	66A
Cohan, Ryan	IL3310	47,66A		Dade, Fred S.	PA3050	20,11,32B,36,66A
Cohen, Arnaldo	IN0900	66A		Dahl, Christina A.	NY3790	41,66A,66C
Cohen, Jeffrey L.	NY2150	41,66A		Dahl, Christine E.	MN0950	66A
Coil, Pat	TN1100	66A,29,42		Dahl, Laura	CA4900	66A,66C
Coker, Timothy C.	MS0385	13,60,32,36,66A		Dahlman, Barbro	DC0170	66A
Cole, Arlene	RI0050	13A,13,66A		Dahlman, Barbro E.	DC0100	66A,66D
Cole, Pamela	FL0800	66A,66D		Dahn, Luke	IA1200	66A,13B,13C,13D,13E
Cole, Ronald F.	ME0500	12A,12,66A		Daigneault, Sylvain	AI0050	66A
Coleman, Cecilia	CA0825	66A		Dal Porto, Mark	NM0100	10,13,66A,34,13A
Coleman, Lilian	TN0700	36,66A		Dalagar, Martha	NM0450	66A
Coleman, Michael	FL1500	13,10,11,66A,34		Dale, Monica	DC0170	32A,66A
Coleman, Ruth	SC0200	66A,66D		Dalton, Dana	MA1400	66A,12A,12,66C
Collaros, Pandel Lee	WV0100	70,62,66A,46		D'Ambrosio, David	GA0050	66A,66C,48
Colleen, Jeffrey	IL1550	13,10,36,66A,31A		D'Amico, David	RI0250	66A
Collier, Katherine	MI2100	66A		Dang, Thai Son	AI0200	66A
Collins, Cheryl	NM0400	66A,66C,66D		Dangerfield, Joseph Allen	IA0300	10,13,66A,38,43
Collins, Jenny	PA1100	11,13A,66A,66D,66C		Daniel, Wade	OK0825	66A
Collins, Linda	MN1250	66A		Danielsson, Per	FL1800	29,66A
Collins, Peter F.	MO0775	66A,66D,66B		Danko, Harold	NY1100	29A,29B,29C,66A,47
Collins, Rosemary	AG0350	66A		Darling, Ann T.	IL2250	66A
Colter, Nancy	ME0270	66A		Darnell, Robert	NC2430	66A,66D
Coltman, Heather	FL0650	66A		Dashevskaya, Olga	CO0625	11,13A,66A,13B
Comer, Sonya	IL2300	66A		Daub, Eric	TX3100	66A,13A,13B,13C,29A
Comotto, Brian	MD0175	10,35C,35D,35G,66A		Daugherty, Wendy	TX2570	62A,62B,66A,32E
Compton, Beckie	TX0125	66A,13,11,36,47		Davenport, David A.	DC0170	54,66D,66A
Conatser, Brian	AR0200	13A,66A,13B,13C,66C		David, Myrtle	LA0700	11,66A,66B,66C,66D
Conely, James	AL0450	66A,66G		Davidian, Joseph	TN0100	66A
Conlon, Francis	DC0100	39,66A,66C,54		Davidson, Heidi	WA0750	61,66A,11,13A
Connell, Robin	MI0300	66A,13		Davidson, Thalia	IL2750	66A
Connelly, Brian	TX2150	66A,66C,66E,42		Davidson, Thomas	AI0150	13C,66A,13A
Conner, Heather	UT0250	66A,66D		Davidson, Tom	AG0250	13B,66A,66D
Connors, Maureen	MA0150	13A,66A,66C		Davies, James	CA5000	11,12A,12E,20A,66A
Conrad, Kent R.	IL0800	66A,66C,66D		Davies, Paul	CA1800	13,11,13A,66A,10
Conroy, Brenda	IL1090	66A,66D		Davies, Susan Azaret	CA0600	13,66A,66C
Conway, Eric	MD0600	13,66A		D'Avignon, India	CA1510	66A,66C,66D
Conway, Robert	MI2200	66A,66B,66D,12A		D'Avignon, India	CA0600	66A,13
Conway, Vicki J.	TX3535	66A,66B,66D		Davila, William	CA3450	13A,11,12A,66A,67D
Cook, Anne	SC0200	66A		Davis, Anna	GA2050	66A,66D
Cook, Gloria	FL1550	66A,66B,13C,11,66C		Davis, Anthony	CA5050	20G,66A,10,53
Cook, James	NE0590	11,66A,66D		Davis, Diane	ID0075	61,66A
Cook, Jean	SC0200	66A,66B,66D		Davis, Judith Chen	KY0400	66A
Cook, Ken	CA4700	66A,47		Davis, Keith	SC0750	66A,46
Cook, Kent	IL1200	66A,66D		Davis, Mark	WI1150	66A,29
Cook, Stephen	CA6000	66A,35A,34,36,11		Davis, Peter	SC0200	66A,66B,66D,34
Coop, Jane A.	AB0100	41,66A		Davis, Suzanne	MA0260	66A
Cooper, Frank E.	FL1900	12,66A,66H,67		Dawe, Jill A.	MN0050	13,66A,66B,66D
Cooper, Kelli	TX3370	66A		Dawes, Christopher	AG0450	66A
Cooper, Marva W.	DC0350	11,12A,66A,66B,66C		Dawson, Julian S.	IL2250	66A
Cooper, Matthew J.	OR0200	13,47,66A,66D,29		Dawson, Terence	AB0100	66A
Cooper, Peter	TN1350	13,66A		Day, Clinton	CA1450	66A
Cooper, Rex	CA5350	66A,12A		Day-O'Connell, Sarah K.	IL1350	12,14,66A,66E
Cooper, Ted	DC0170	66A,66C		De Burgh, Susan	AB0210	66A
Cooperstock, Andrew	CO0800	66A		De Castro, Paul	CA0830	14,29,20H,66A
Cope, Mary Jane	CA5070	66A		De Freitas, Simon Marc	AA0020	66A
Copeland-Burns, Carla	VA1100	66A		De Mare, Anthony J.	NY2750	66A,66C
Coplan, Lauren Jackson	TN1850	66A		De Margerie, Monique	AI0190	66A
Coppola, Thomas	NC2400	66A,66D,10C,29		De Moura Castro, Luiz	CT0650	66A
Corley, Kirsten M.	PA2350	66A,66C		De Paula, Isidoro	FL1550	66A
Cornelius, John L.	TX2100	66C,66A,66D,13		De Silva, Preethi	CA1050	66A,66H
Cornett-Murtada, Vanessa	MN1625	66A,13,12A,66B		Deahl, Lora	TX3200	66A,66C,66B,12A

Name	Code	Areas
Dean, Lynn	UT0150	11,66A,66B
Deane, Allison	NY0600	66A
De'Ath, Leslie	AG0600	66A,39
Deaver, Stuart T.	OK1450	66A,66D,66B,13I,66
DeCesare, Mona	CA3600	66A
Decesare, Mona Wu	CA3100	66A,66D
DeChellis, Dan	PA2450	66A
Decock, Murray	NY0650	66A
DeCoro, Helena	CA1520	61,66A,11,12A,39
Dedova, Larissa	MD1010	66A
Dees, Pamela Youngdahl	MO1250	66A,66B,66C,11,12A
DeFoor, Cynthia	GA2300	66C,66B,66A
DeFrain, Debbie	NE0500	66A,11,32B
DeGreiff-Beisser, Andrea	WI1150	66A
Deguchi, Tomoko	SC1200	13,66A,13F,13E,13A
DeJong-Pombo, Theresa	CA3350	66A
Dekker, Gretchen	PA3710	66A,66H,13C
Del Aguila, Miguel	CA5360	10,66A,13A,11
Delaplane, Marjorie	IL2750	66A
Delbeau, Marie-Christine	DE0150	66A,66D,66B
Delgado, Derek G.	AK0100	66A
Delgado, Eduardo	CA0815	66A
Delphin, Wilfred	IL2900	66A
Delphin, Wilfred	LA0900	66A,66B,66C,66D
Demme, Elizabeth	ND0250	66A
Dempsey, O. S.	AL0500	66A,66B,13
Demske, Hilary	UT0325	66A,13
Deneff, Peter	CA1520	66A
Denison, William R.	AL1050	66A,66G
Denk, Jeremy	NY0150	66A
Dennihan, James	MN0350	66A
Dennihan, James	MN1300	66A
Dennis, David M.	TN1660	13,66A,36
Dennis, Sandra	MA1350	66A
Dennis, Thomas A.	MI1700	12A,66A,46
Denton, Kristine West	PA1200	66A,66C,66D
Denton, Robert	GA0050	66A
Derfler, Brandon	UT0400	66A,10
Derham, Billie	MO1830	66A,66D
DeRousse, Cathy	LA0050	66A
Derry, Lisa	ID0070	13,10,34,66A,66B
Desai, Nayantara	CO0830	66A,66C,66D
DeSalvo, Nancy J.	PA3650	13A,13B,66A,66B,13C
DeSanto, Jennifer	PA3560	66A,66D
Despres, Jacques C.	AA0100	66A,42
Dettbarn-Slaughter, Vivian Robles	OH2275	61,66A,11
Dettinger, Mary Joyce	OH1330	32A,32B,66A,31A
DeVan, William	AL0300	66A
Deveau, David	MA1200	11,41,66A
Devens, Richard	NY5000	66A
DeYoung, William	IL2775	66A,66G
Di Bella, Karin	AG0050	66A,66B,66C
Di Salvio, Ron	MI1150	66A
Diab, Mary Beth	IL3370	66A,66C,66B,66D
Dibonaventura, Anthony	MA0400	66A
Dickens, Pierce	GA0950	39,66A,66C,66G
Dickens, Pierce	GA0400	13A,13B,13C,13E,66A
Dickinson, Marci	IN1010	66A,13A
Dickinson, Stefanie C.	AR0850	66A,13
DiCosimo, William J.	NY4150	35,66A
Diepeveen, Susan	AF0120	66A,32A
Dietrich, Maria K.	WI0700	66A,66B
Dietzler, Judy	MN0600	66A
Diez, German	NY0500	66A
Dill, Jane	SC1080	13,66A,66G,66C
Dill, John	TX1775	13A,11,66A,66G,12A
Dimaras, Charis	NY1800	66A,66C
DiMedio, Annette	PA3330	12A,12,66A,66D,11
Ding, Xiaoli	KS1400	66A,66B,66D,20
DiPiazza, Joseph	NC2430	66A,66C
DiPinto, Mark	MD0150	66A,66B,66C,13C
Do, Bang Lang	IA1450	66A,66C
Do, Bang Lang	IA0450	66A,66C
Dobek-Shandro, Elaine	AA0040	66A,66C
Dobner, Gabriel	VA0600	66A,66C
Dobrea-Grindahl, Mary	OH0200	66A,66B,66C,32I,66D
Dobrzanski, Slawomir Pawel	KS0650	66A,66C,66B
Docking, Simon	AF0120	66A
Dodd, Susan	FL0200	66A,66C,66D
Doering, James M.	VA1150	13,11,12A,66A,66G
Dokovska, Pavlina	NY2250	66A
Dolatowski, David	AZ0510	66A,36,11
Dolnik, Nata	KS0570	66A
Dominick, Daniel L.	TX0250	66A,12,60B,38,60
Donald, Larry Scott	TX3530	66A
Donald, Scott	NJ0175	66A
Donaldson, Doree	MO0400	66A,13C
Donelian, Armen	NY2660	13A,13C,10,66A,47
Donnelly, Chris	AG0450	66A
Doran, Joy	IL1200	66C,66A,66D
Dorfman, Amy	TN1850	41,66A,66C
Dornian, Kathy	AA0050	66A,66C,32A
Dorris, Dennis	IL1890	66A
Dossin, Alexandre	OR1050	66A
Dotson, Danielle	DC0170	66A
Douds, Nathan	PA3100	11,50,65,66A
Dougherty, Peggy S.	OR0175	66A,66D,13A,66B,13E
Dougherty, Peggy	OR0250	66A,13A
Douglas, Bill	CO0560	13,11,12A,36,66A
Douglas, Brent	FL0450	41,66A,66C
Douglas, John	CA5550	47,66A
Douthit, James Russell	NY2650	66A,66B,66D
Drake, Jennifer	MI1150	66A
Draskovic, Ines	NY1250	66A,13A,13C,13
Drews, Teresa	WI1150	66A
Drifmeyer, Fred	MA0600	66A,66C
Drion, Yoka	CA2975	66A,66D
Driscoll, Katherine	FL1300	66D,66A
Driskell, Daniel	AL1300	66A,66D
Droba, Romalee	MN1250	61,66A
Drontle, Lisa	MN0350	66A
Drury, Stephen	MA1400	66A,43,12
Duane, Carol Rose	WV0550	66A
Duarte, Derison	NC2410	66A
Duarte, Derison	NC0600	66A,66B
Dubbiosi, Stelio	NJ0825	13,10F,66A,66G
Dube', Francis	AI0190	66A,66B
DuBois, May	CA5500	11,13A,66A
Duce, Geoffrey	IN0910	66A,66B
Dudley, Bruce	TN0100	13,66A,66C,66D
Dudley, Bruce J.	TN1850	66A,35B,53
Dueck, Jocelyn B.	NY2250	66A
Duehlmeier, Susan	UT0250	66C,66A,61
Duerden, Jennifer	HI0050	66A,66D
Duggan, Sean	NY3725	11,66A,66C,66D
Dumm, Mary Elizabeth	MD0700	13A,13,11,66A
Dunaway, Lourdes	TN1250	11,66A,70
Dunlap, Larry	CA2950	66A
Dunlap, Phillip	MO1950	35,66A
Duphil, Monique	OH1700	66A
Duquesnel-Malbon, Peggy	CA1425	66A,47
Durand, Marc	AG0300	66A
Durand, Marc	AI0200	66A
Durham, Carol S.	MS0400	66G,66A,66C,66H,12A
Durkovic, Timothy	CA2550	66A,66B
Durnford, Jacqueline	AF0120	66A
Durrenberger, Chris	OH2450	13A,11,66A,66F,12A
Dussault, Michel J.	AI0220	12A,66A,66B
Dutton, Douglas	CA2600	13A,13,11,66A
Dykema, Dan H.	AR0600	13B,11,66A,66D,13C
Dykstra, Brian	OH0700	66A
Dzugan, Eric	PA1450	66A
Earl, Nicole	AF0050	66A
Earnest, JoAnne	PA0050	66A,66D
East, Phyllis	NY3725	66A
Eastman, Patricia	MO1950	13A,13B,13C,66A
Eaton, Alice Butler	AL1160	66A
Eaton, Angela S.	KY1350	66C,66A
Eccles, Elizabeth	VA0500	32,61,66A
Echols, Carol	MO0350	66A,66D,66B
Echols, Charles	MN1300	66H,12A,66A,66G
Eckert, Elizabeth	DC0170	66A
Eckert, Elizabeth	TN1850	66A,66D
Eckes, Sylvia Reynolds	OH1900	66A,66C
Eckhardt, Janet	IL2100	66A,66D
Ecklund, George	IL1610	66A
Eckroth, Rachel	AZ0470	66A,29B,29A
Edel, Theodore	IL3310	11,66A,12A
Edie, Rebecca L.	IN0100	66A,66C
Edlina-Dubinsky, Luba	IN0900	66A
Edson, Tracey D.	OR1100	66A,66D,66C
Edstrom, Brent	WA1350	10,66A,34,47,13
Edward, Ruth	NH0350	66A,66B
Edwards, Alice	IL1610	66A,66G
Edwards, Alison	CA0815	66A,66C
Edwards, Denise	IL1610	13,66A
Edwards, Karen	OH2600	32,66A
Edwards, Karin	IL3550	66A
Edwards, Matthew	MO0850	66A,66B,66C,66D,13
Edwards, T. Matthew	MD0060	66A,13,66C,12,36
Edwards-Henry, Jacqueline	MS5500	13,66A,66B,66C
Eekhoff, CharLee	IA0200	66A
Efremova, Natalia	DC0170	66A
Egan, Anne Marie	IN1350	66A
Eguchi, Akira	NY0500	66A,66C
Ehlen, Timothy	IL3300	66A,41
Ehrman, David	VA0650	66A,66B,66D
Eichelberger, Mary Jane	OH1800	66A,66G
Eide, Christina	AZ0350	11,66A,66D
Eikner, Edward	GA2200	12A,66A,66C,66D,11
Eisenman, Mark	AG0650	47,66A
Elbeck, Lance	AG0200	66A
Elberfeld, Sung Hui	PA2250	66A
Elder, Ellen P.	MS0850	66A,66B,66D,66C
Elder, Ellen	MS0750	66C,66D
Eley, Miriam	NJ1350	66A
Elfine, Robert	IL0100	66A,11,13
Elgersma, Kristin M.	ID0250	66A,66B,66C
Elsi, Enrico	NY1100	66A,66C
Elliott, Anne	TN1150	66A,66D,66B,66C,36
Ellis, Brenda	OH2500	20A,20G,32,36,66A
Ellis, Cynthia	TX2260	66A,66D
Ellis, John S.	MI2100	66A
Elowsky-Fox, Jennifer	MA0260	66A
Elsberry, Kristie B.	TN0100	13,66A,66G
Elshazly, Janet	SC0275	66A,66C,66D
Eng, Clare Sher Ling	TN0100	13,13B,13D,63B,66A
Engbretson, Chris	OR0450	66A,66C
Engebretson, Noel J.	AL1170	66A
Engel, Tiffany	OK1300	13,11,12A,66A
Engelson, Thea	IA0050	61,66A
Engle, Marilyn	AA0150	41,66A,66B,66C,12B
Enlow, David	NY1900	66A
Enman, Thomas	MA1175	66C,12A,54,66A,61
Enns, Alice	AB0100	66A
Ensor, Robert	MO0260	12A,47,66A,66C,54
Epperson, Dean	AK0100	11,12A,66A,66D,66B
Epstein, Daniel	NJ1130	66A
Epstein, Daniel	NY2150	41,66A
Ergo, Jack	IA0600	20,31A,38,66A
Erickson, Stephen	RI0250	66A,66D
Esch, Michael	AG0300	66A,12A
Esleck, David	VA1800	11,66A,29,34,35
Espinosa, Gabriel	IA0700	66A,47,61
Estrin, Morton	NY1600	66A,13A
Etheridge, Kay	CA5200	11,32B,66A,66B,66C
Ethridge, William J.	GA1450	11,66A
Ettinger, Karl Erik	FL1700	66A,11,12A
Eubanks, Erdie	CA1900	13A,66A
Evans, Eugenia H.	VA1350	66A,66B
Evans, Lee	NY1275	66A,66D
Evans, Margaret	NC1300	66A
Evans, Mark	NY3600	66A,66B,66D
Evans, Timothy	MA0900	40,66A,61
Evenson, David N.	LA0650	66A,66D
Everett, Cheryl	IN1850	66A,66G
Ewoldt, Patrice R.	PA2300	66A,66C,66B,67F,42
Ezerova, Maria V.	CA5070	66A,66D
Ezhokina, Oksana	WA0650	66A,66B,66C,66
Ezoe, Magdalena	MI1950	66A,13,12B,12A,41
Fabbro, Renato	OR0500	66A,66D
Fabbro, Renato S.	OR1100	66A
Faflak, Marcela	SD0400	66A,66B,66C
Fahrion, Stacy	CO0300	11,66A,66D
Faith-Slaker, Aubrey	IL2750	66A,66D
Falco, Frank	AG0650	47,66A
Falker, Matt	CA2960	36,66A,47,66D
Fan, Paula	AZ0500	66A,66C
Fandrich, Rita E.	FL0800	13,66A,66B,10
Farouk, Wael	IL0550	66A
Farris, Phillip	OH2250	66A,66C,66D,11
Farrugia, Adrean	AG0650	66A
Fass, YuChing	MA0950	66A
Fast, Barbara	OK1350	66A,66B,66D
Fast, John W.	VA0300	13,66A,66G
Fata, Patrick	IN1560	66A
Faughn, Wendy	AL0500	66A,66B,66C,66D
Faulkner, Lynn	AL1200	66A,66C,66D
Favreau, Janet	CA2800	66A
Favreau, Janet	CA2650	66A,66D,13A,11
Fear, Judith	KS1450	66A,66C
Feder, Donn Alexander	NY2150	66A
Federle, Yong Im Lee	NC2700	66A,66D
Feeney, Kendall	WA0250	66A,43,66C
Feghali, Jose	TX3000	66A
Feket, Robert	AG0200	66A

Index by Area of Teaching Interest

Name	Code	Areas
Feldheim, Michelle	MA1550	66A
Feldman, Damira	FL0200	66A
Fells, Mizue	WA0550	66A,66D,13C,11,20
Feltsman, Vladimir	NY3760	66A,66B,12A
Feltsman, Vladimir	NY2250	66A
Fenster, Laura	IL2750	66A
Fenwick, Jerry	CA4000	11,66A,54,29,35
Ferdinand, Edward	PA0400	66A
Ferguson, Dianne S.	NE0200	13,66A,66C,66D
Feria, Marissa	AA0050	32A,66A
Fernandez, Nohema	CA5020	66A
Ferreira, David	MN0600	66A,47
Ferretti, Joseph A.	AG0600	66A
Fickett, Martha V.	VA1475	11,12A,12E,66A
Fiedler, Anne	IN1600	13B,13C,66A
Fields, Victor	MD0610	66A
Fierro, Nancy	CA3150	66A,66B,66D
Figueroa, Diana	PR0115	66A,66B,66D
Fink, Seymour	OH0350	66A,66B,42
Finkelstein, Marc	NJ0550	32A,32B,66A,70
Finlay, Lois	GA1500	66A
Finney, John W.	KY0700	13,12A,36,61,66A
Fiorillo, Alexander E.	PA3250	66A
Fischbach, Tim C.	IL2730	61,66A,66G
Fischer Faw, Victoria	NC0750	12,66A,66B,41
Fischer, Jeanne Kierman	TX2150	66A,66B,66D,42
Fischer, Kenneth	CT0050	66A
Fischer, Martha	WI0815	66A,66C,39,41
Fischler, Gail	AZ0300	66A,66B,66C
Fishbein, Zenon	NY2150	66A
Fisher, Alexis Z.	PA1850	66A,66D
Fisher, Anna	DC0170	66A,32A
Fisher, Christopher	OH1900	66D,66A,66B
Fisher, Gary	NY2650	66A
Fisher, Jenny	MI0500	66A
Fisher, John	TX3250	13A,13B,10A,15,66A
Fisk, Charles	MA2050	13A,13,12A,66A
Fiske, Richard Allen	CA4550	11,38,66A,63
Fitenko, Nikita	DC0050	66A
Fitz-Gerald, Kevin	CA5300	41,66A,66C
Fleer, Suzanne	IL1085	66A,66D
Fleischer, Tania	CA2800	66A,42
Fleisher, Leon	MD0650	66A
Fleisher, Leon	PA0850	66A
Fleitz, Patrick	FL0800	66A,11
Fleming, Ansley	AR0350	66G,66A
Fleming, Diana M.	WA0550	66A
Fleming, Gail H.	IL2970	11,36,66A,40,20
Fletcher, Marylynn L.	TX3600	34C,36,11,66A,12A
Flick, DaLeesa J.	OK1200	66A,12A
Flippo, David	IL0650	66A
Flood, James	NY4460	66A,66G
Flory, Mary Beth	VA0100	66A
Flournoy-Buford, Debbie	TX3650	32B,32D,34,66C,66A
Flower, Carol	SD0580	66A,66C,66B
Floyd, J. Robert	FL1900	66A
Floyd, Rosalyn	GA0250	13A,13,11,66A,66C
Flugge, Mark	OH1850	29,66A
Flugge, Mark	OH0350	66A,66D,29B
Flurry, Henry	AZ0510	66A
Flyger, Paul	MI1180	66A,66D,11
Fogarty, Rachel	TN0100	66A,66D
Fogg, Matthew	ME0340	66A,13
Fogg, Matthew	ME0200	66A
Fogg, Ryan	TN0250	66A,66D,66B,66C
Follingstad, Karen J.	CA4100	11,66A,66C,66D
Foltz, Kristina	OR0950	66A
Fong, Grace	CA0960	66A,66B,66C
Fong, Ming	NY5000	66A
Forbat, David	OK1330	66A,66B,66C,66D
Ford, Anita	CA3400	66A
Ford, Jeffrey	TX3370	66A,66C
Foreman, Charles	AA0150	66A,66B,66C,20G,41
Forer, Colette	AA0050	66A
Forman, Marilyn T.	VA1000	66A,66D
Forry, Sharon R.	OR0700	66A
Forsha, Heather	NY1400	13C,66A,66C,32E
Fort, Kevin	IL0275	66A,42
Foshager, John	WI1150	63C,66A
Foshee, Anna Harriette	CA4460	66A,66B,66D
Fosheim, Karen	MS0250	66A,13B,50,20A,10F
Foster, Brenda	MO0850	66A,66C
Foster, Linda	NJ0760	66A,66D
Foster, Shimmer	MN0600	66A
Foster, Willene	GA1400	66A
Foster, William	IN1750	66A
Fouse, Kathryn L.	AL0800	66A,66B
Fowler, Colin	NY2900	36,13,12A,66A,66G
Fowler, Lynda	FL1300	66A
Fox, Clinton D.	OH0300	13,66A,66D
Fox, David E.	NC0900	66A,12A,66D,43,11
Fox, Kim	VA1150	66A,66C
Fox, Mary Ann	GA2300	66A
Fox, Rebecca	AL1195	13,11,32,66A
Francis, Edward	CA3100	66A
Francis, Edward	CA0835	66A
Francis, Edward	CA3600	66A
Francis, Lorie	MO0825	11,12A,13,36,66A
Francis, Margreet	CT0650	66A
Francom, Jeffrey D.	NY4050	66A
Frane, Ryan	MN1600	29,47,66A,46
Frank, Claude	PA0850	66A
Frank, Claude	CT0850	66A
Frank, Jolita	WI0150	66A
Frank, Mike	PA3250	47,66A,29
Frankl, Peter	CT0850	66A
Franklin, Rachel F.	MD1000	66A,66D
Frater, Betsy	CA4050	61,66A
Frazier, Ivan	GA2100	66A,66B,66D
Fredriksen, Brandt	GA1050	66A,66C,42
Freeman, Christine L.	IN0905	13A,66C,66A
French, George E.	MN1590	36,37,66A,66G,54
Freyberg, Victoria	NY0500	66A
Fried, Melody	TX1550	66A
Friedman, Don E.	NY2750	47,29,66A
Friedman, Tamara	WA0860	66A
Friedmann, Michael	CT0900	10,13,66A
Frieling, Randall J.	IN0100	66A,66C,66D,66G
Friesen, Darryl	AC0100	66A
Friscioni, Emanuela	OH0600	66A
Fritz, Rachel	WI1150	66A
Froelich, Andrew I.	ND0350	13,12A,66A,66H
Frommeyer, Heinz	TX3530	66A
Fry, Edwin J.	PA1600	11,66A,13
Fugo, Charles Leonard	SC1110	66A,66C
Fukushima, Gary A.	CA0835	66A
Funahashi, Yuri Lily	ME0250	66A
Fung, Eric K.	PA1900	13,66A,66D
Funk, Dana	MN1500	66A
Fuoco, Anthony	OH1300	11,66A
Furr, Barbara	NC2440	12A,66A,66D
Furtado, Danial	FL0050	66A
Fusco, Randall J.	OH1000	13B,38,66A,12A,11
Gable, Kathleen	AJ0150	66D,66A,66C
Gagnon-Matte, Francoise	AI0220	66A,66C
Gaide, Diana	CO0150	66A
Gainsford, Read	FL0850	66A
Gajda, Anne	MI0600	66A,66B,66D
Galasso, Mathew	CA1900	11,12A,66A,13
Gale, Robert	CO0100	64,66A,66F,72
Gallagher, Mary Gloria	IN1100	62,66A,66G
Gallo, Joseph	CA1520	35,34,66A,29,53
Gallo, Pam	CO0150	66A
Gallo, Sergio	GA1050	66A,66B,66C,66D
Gallon, Ray	NY2660	66A,47
Galloway, Robert J.	NY1700	12A,66A
Galper, Hal	NY3785	66A,47
Galper, Hal	NY2660	66A,47
Galusha, Cessaries	OR0750	66A,66D
Galvin, Nancy	ID0050	66A
Galyon, Joseph	KY1000	66A
Ganz, Brian	MD0650	66A
Ganz, Brian	MD0750	66A
Garard-Brewer, Gay	MT0450	66A,32
Garber, Melia	VA0550	66A,66D
Garcia, Jose Manuel	GA2050	66A,66D,11,10A
Garcia, Marisa	PR0115	66A,42
Garcia, Susanna P.	LA0760	66A,66B
Garcia, W. T. Skye	OK0300	66A,66D,13B,13C,66B
Garcia, Washington	TX3175	66A,42
Garcia-Leon, Jose M.	CT0700	11,12A,13,66A,66D
Gardony, Laszlo	MA0260	66A
Garnica, Kevin	CA0350	11,66A,39
Garramone, Suzanne	CA5353	66A
Garrett, Junko Ueno	CA3300	66A
Garrett, Nancy B.	TX3510	66A
Garth, Eliza	MD0750	66A
Gates, Edward	OK1350	66A
Gaub, Eugene	IA0700	13,12A,66A,11
Gaughan, Warren J.	NC2550	47,13,66A,46,29
Gavalchin, John E.	NY4200	66A,12,13
Gavrilova, Julia	AI0150	66A,13A
Gaylard, Timothy R.	VA1850	11,12A,66A,20G
Geary, Sandra	MO1900	66A
Gebhart, Gail Y.	MI2200	66A
Gee, Larry	UT0250	66A
Gehrich, Leonora S.	IL2450	66A,66C,66D
Gekic, Kemal	FL0700	66A
Genge, Anthony	AF0150	13,66A,20G,29
Genova, David	CO0900	66A,66B
Gentry, Scott	AZ0460	61,66A
George, David Alan	KY0250	66A,66C
George, David N.	GA2050	66A
George, Rosemary	NY0270	66A,61,12A,11
Georgieva-Smith, Ralitsa	OH1350	66A
Gerber, Thomas	IN1100	12A,66A
Geringas, Marina	AG0450	66A
Germain, Francois	NY3780	66A,66C
German, Eugenia	CA1510	66A
Gerrish, June	IL1890	66A,11
Gertsenzon, Galina	MA2100	66A,66D,13A
Gessner, Dave	IL0600	66A,29
Gianforte, Matthew P.	KY0950	66A,66D,66B,66,12A
Giasullo, Frank	PA2450	66A,29B
Gibbons, Bruce L.	IL1750	66A,66C
Gibeau, Peter	WI0862	13,36,41,62D,66A
Gibson, Henry	OH0950	66A,66G
Gibson, Robyn	SC0600	66A
Gibson, Tannis L.	AZ0500	66A
Giddens, Scott	FL1000	66A
Giebler, David	WI0920	13,11,36,41,66A
Gifford, Tell	NV0125	11,12A,13,66A
Gilbert, E. Beth	WI0860	66C,66A,66B,13B
Gilbert, Joan	TN1680	66A,66C
Giles, James	IL2250	66A
Giles, Sevgi	IL0550	66A,66D
Gill, Lynette	FL1650	66A
Gille, Tanya	AL1170	66A
Gilliam, Jeffrey	WA1250	66A,66C
Gilman, Joe	CA0150	13,66A,53,29
Gilman, Joseph	CA0840	66A,29
Gingerich, Carol	GA2130	66A,66B,66C
Gingerich, Cheryl F.	PA1250	66B,66A
Gionfriddo, Mark	MA1350	66A,47,34A
Gipson, Ann M.	TX3000	66B,66D,66A
Gitz, Raymond	LA0560	12A,66A,31A
Giunta, Cynthia	IA0550	66D,66C,66A
Glanden, Chris	PA3330	47,66A,13A,13,29
Glasgow, David M.	PA0950	66A,66C,13A
Glass, Anne	TN0050	13,66A,66G,66C
Glazer, Frank	ME0150	66A
Glennon, Maura	NH0150	66A,66C,66D,66H
Gliadkovsky, Anna	UT0200	66A,66B
Gliadkovsky, Kirill	UT0200	66A,12A
Glick, Nancy	OH2275	62E,66A
Glover, Angela	FL0040	66A,66B,66C,66D
Glover, Daniel	CA3270	66A
Glovier, Thomas	PA3000	29,66A
Gnandt, Edwin E.	AA0010	13,66A,42,13B,66D
Godes, Catherine	TN1450	66A,66C,66D
Godsil, Dan	IL1350	66A,48,49
Godsil, Matthew	IL1800	66A,66D
Godwin, Nannette Minor	NC2350	31,66A,66G,32B
Goering, John	KS1450	29,20,66A
Goff, Carolyn	GA1300	13A,66C,66A
Gokelman, William	TX3410	60,36,66A,66C,31A
Golan, Jeanne K.	NY2550	13B,13C,12A,66A,66D
Gold, Maxine	FL1310	66A
Goldenberg, William	IL2200	66A,66C,41
Goldina, Arianna	PA2450	66A,66B
Goldman, Lawrence	MS0560	66A,66D,66,11,66C
Goldray, Martin	NY3560	13A,13,11,12A,66A
Goldsmith, Maryll	CA3850	11,66A
Goldsmith, Michael	MO0750	11,13,66A
Goldstein, Gil B.	NY2750	10D,47,66A,29
Goldstein, Gila	MA0400	66A
Goldstein, Joanna	IN1010	13,66A,66C,38,11
Goldstein, Louis	NC2500	11,66A
Goldstein, Tamara B.	CO0550	66A,66C,66B,42
Goldston, Christopher	IL2750	66A
Goldston, Christopher	IL3310	66A
Goldsworthy, James	NJ1350	66A
Gonder, Jonathan P.	NY3730	66A,66C,11,13A,13B
Goode, Richard	NY2250	66A
Goodheart, Matthew W.	CA2950	66A
Goodloe, Cindy Roden	SC0400	66A

719

Name	Code	Areas
Goodwin, Don	WA0250	13,66A,37,46
Goodwin, Donald	WA0400	66A
Goodwin, Julia	OR0700	66A,66D,11,12A,66C
Gopoian, Juliet	NY5000	66A
Gordon, Judith	MA1750	66A,42
Gordon, Stewart	CA5300	12A,66A
Gordon, Tony A.	MS0050	66A,66D,66B,66C,11
Gordy, Laura	GA0750	66A
Gorecki, Mikolaj P.	TX1425	10,11,13,34,66A
Gorenman, Svetlana	DC0170	66A
Gorenman, Yuliya	DC0010	66A,42
Gorinski, Nancy J.	PA3000	66A
Gorman, John	NJ0250	13,66A
Gorokhovich, Svetlana	NY5000	66A
Gortler, Daniel	NY2750	66A
Goslee, Brenda	TN1250	13A,13,11,66A,66G
Goslin, Gerald H.	MI1700	61,66A,20
Gosswiller, Julie	MT0200	13C,66D,66A
Goter, Arlene	MN1295	66A,66B,13,66D
Gottesman, Mila	NY2400	66A
Gottlieb, Valentina	CA0825	66A
Gould, Brian	CA3350	12A,66A
Gowen, Bradford	MD1010	66A
Gowen, Rhonda	ND0400	66A
Goya, Ruby Cheng	CA0960	66A
Graber, Kenneth	MN1450	66A
Grace, Rose S.	FL0100	66A,66B,66C,66D
Grace, Susan L.	CO0200	41,66A
Graef, Becky	IN1750	66A,66D,13A
Graf, Enrique	PA0550	66A
Graf, Enrique G.	SC0500	66A
Graff, Carleen	NH0250	66A,66D,66B
Graff, Steven	NY0625	41,66A
Graffman, Gary	PA0850	66A
Graham, Edward E.	SC1050	66A,66C,66D,12A
Grandmason, Nicole	OH1350	66A
Graning, Gary Alan	OH2150	66A,66D,66B
Grant, Darrell	OR0850	41,47,66A,66D,29
Grapenthin, Ina	PA1750	11,32B,66A,66G,66D
Graves, Jody C.	WA0250	66A,66B,66C
Gray, Kathryn A.	PA3260	66A,66C,66G
Gray, Sonny	OK1450	66A
Gray, Steven	CA3460	13,66A,66G,66H
Gray, Susan Keith	SD0600	66A,66B,66C,66D
Grayson, W. Norman	NJ0200	66A,66G
Green, Elizabeth	MD0060	66A,66D
Green, Marsha	TX1600	66A,66D
Green, Peter	CA1960	13A,66A,36,40
Green, Sheila	WY0115	61,66A
Greenberg, Barry	MD0170	61,66A
Greenberg, Laura	NY0630	13,10,66A,66D,11
Greenberg, Lionel	CA2700	13,10,66A
Greenberg, Susan R.	NC0600	66A
Greene, Roger W.	MA0150	13,34,66A,13A,10F
Greenlee, Geol	TN1250	13,66A,10F,10,11
Gregory, Rosalie	FL0200	66A
Grenier, Monik	AI0210	66A
Gretz, Ronald	MD0175	13A,13,66A,66C,54
Grew, Melody A.	MD0050	11,32,36,61,66A
Grey, Meg	MO0600	11,12A,32,66A,66G
Gribou, Andre	OH1900	11,10,66A
Griffin-Seal, Mary	FL0500	66A,11,66D,13C
Griffith, Dorothy S.	CA1900	13A,66A,66H
Griggs-Burnham, Patricia	TX0400	66A,11
Grile, Kathy	IN1560	66A,66B,13A
Grimble, Thomas	SC0200	66A,66D
Grimpo, Elizabeth	NE0150	11,13,66A
Grinnell, Melonie	CA2100	66A,47,61
Gritton, Bonnie	UT0250	66A
Grobler, Sophia	OH0950	66A,66C,66D,20
Groesbeck, Rolf A.	AR0750	11,12,14,66A,20
Gronemann, Robert	MN1200	66A,13
Gross, David	SC0750	66A,66C,66B,66D
Gross, Kelly	VA1550	66A
Grossman, Andrea	IN1010	11,66A,13A,66D
Grossman, Morley K.	TX3525	11,66A,66C,66D
Grosz, Gay	LA0050	66A,66C
Grove, Marna	VT0200	66A
Grove, Marna	VT0100	66A
Grover, Elaine	MI1300	13A,13,66A,66G,31A
Grover, Steve	ME0200	65,66A
Grover, Steve	ME0340	47,65,66A,29,13
Groves, Robert W.	ND0350	11,12A,66A,20G,66H
Gualdi, Paolo Andre'	SC0710	66A,11,13,66B,66C
Guenette, Maria Mika	TX3370	66A,66D,66C
Guerrero, Rosi E.	WA0950	66A,66D,13A,13B,13D
Guggenheim, Janet	OR0850	66A
Guiles, Kay	MS0360	11,66A,66D,66G
Gunnson, Eric	CO0900	29,66A
Gurt, Joseph	MI0600	66A,66C
Gurt, Michael	LA0200	66A
Gustofson, Don	IL0300	66A,70
Gutshall, Christi	AZ0400	66A,66B,66D,12A
Guttmann, Hadassah	NY2550	32A,66D,66A
Guynes, Christi	TX2570	66A,66D
Guzasky, G. Frederick	MA0510	66A,66D
Guzman, Christopher	PA2750	66A
Haas, Adam J.	AR0500	66A,66D
Haas, Frederick L.	NH0100	64E,66A,29A,29B,47
Haberkorn, Michael	OH2050	66A,20G,14C,11
Hache, Reginald	FL0570	11,66A
Haddad, George	OH1850	66A
Haddock, Kathleen	NY4150	66A,66C
Haek, Jonathan	OR0500	34D,10A,13,66A
Haerle, Dan	TX3420	66A,34B,29
Hagen, Cathy	MN1270	66A
Hagner, Carolyn Zepf	KY1000	66A,66B,66C
Haguenauer, Jean-Louis	IN0900	66A
Hahn, Carol G.	IN0905	66D,66A
Hahn, Christopher	MT0400	66A,66B,66C,66D
Hahn, Marian	MD0650	66A
Hakken, Lynda S.	IA0400	66G,13,66C,66A,11
Hakutani, Naoki	AR0750	66A,66D,45
Halbeck, Patricia	TN0050	66A,66B,66C,66D
Halberg, Virginia	NY1700	66A,66D
Halberstadt, Randy	WA0200	13,66A,66D,53,29
Halim, Eduardus	NY2750	66A
Hall, Cory	FL1650	66D,66A,12A
Hall, Elena	FL0500	66A,66D,13C
Hall, Jeff	MI1850	47,64C,64E,66A,29B
Hallsted, Nancy	DC0170	66A
Halstead, Amanda R.	VA1000	66A
Halt, Hans	NV0100	29B,62,66A
Halvecka, Thomas	OH1910	66D,66A,61
Ham, Jeongwon	OK1350	66A
Ham, Marilynn	IN0200	66A,66C
Hamilton, Robert	AZ0100	66A
Hamm, Corey D.	AB0100	66A
Hamm, Laura	WV0440	32,36,66A,66D,66C
Hammer, David A.	FL0650	66A
Hammond, Gary	NY0625	11,66A,66D
Hammond, June C.	FL1600	12A,36,61,66A,37
Han, Jiyon	DC0170	13,66A
Hancock, Cindy	MT0370	66A,66G
Haneline, Stacie	IA0910	66A,11
Hanick, Conor	MA1750	66A,42
Hanley, Wells	VA1600	29,66A
Hanley, Wells	VA1550	66A
Hanna, Cassandria	FL1310	13,66A,66D,36
Hannifan, Patricia	CA2600	66G,66A
Hannifan, Patricia	CA2750	66A
Hannigan, Barry T.	PA0350	13,66A
Hanseler, Ryan	NC0650	29,66A
Hansen, Bente	AA0200	66A,13
Hansen, Jack	IN0005	66A,13,61
Hansen, Jessica	AF0050	66A
Hansen, John	AF0050	66A
Hansen, Julia	CA4625	14,66A,20
Hansen, Kathleen	UT0190	36,66A
Hansen, Mark R.	ID0050	66A,13E,11,66G
Hansen, Ted	TX2955	13,10F,10A,66A
Hansen, Thomas	CA3270	66A
Hansford, Conchita	OK0650	32A,32B,61,66A,31A
Hanshaw, Marian C.	MA0700	66A
Hanson, David	CO0900	66A,29,35B,10A,10C
Hanson, F.	NY4060	13,12A,11,66A
Hanson, Paul	VA1500	66A,42
Happel, Rebecca	MI1750	66A,66C
Harada, Tomoko	NJ1160	66A
Harboyan, Patil	AI0150	66A
Hardeman, Anita	IL3500	66G,12A,66A
Harder, Lillian U.	SC0400	66A,35E
Harding, Christopher	MI2100	66A,66C,66D
Harlan, Mary E.	IL1350	66A
Harlan, Mary	IL0420	66A,66G
Harlan, Paul	FL1740	66A,10,34,35C
Harleston, Sheila C.	MD1020	60,36,66A,66D
Harlos, Steven C.	TX3420	66A,66C
Harmon, Linda	TN0100	66A,66D
Harmon, Sally	OR0500	66A,29B
Haroutounian, Joanne	VA0450	66A,66B
Harper, Erin Michelle	NC0350	66A,66C,66D
Harper, Nelson	OH0850	66A
Harrell, Mary	CA1900	66A,66C,66D
Harrell, Paula D.	NC1600	32,66A,66G,66D,31A
Harrington, Karen	OK1450	66A
Harris, Alice Eaton	NY2400	66A,66H
Harris, Amy	NC2000	66A
Harris, Caleb	CO0950	66A,66C
Harris, Roger	IL0550	47,66A
Harris, Roger	IN0005	10B,13,29,47,66A
Harrison, Joanne K.	NC1150	13,66G,31A,66A
Harrison, John F.	PA1250	12A,12,66A
Harrison, John	MA2020	47,66A
Harriss, Elaine Atkins	TN1720	66A,66B,42,66C
Harshenin, Leon A.	IN1560	66A,13B
Harstad, Bonnie	KY0150	66A
Hart, Kevin	IL1150	13,66A
Hart, Kevin M.	IL1350	29B,53,66A,47,65
Hart, Lawrence	NC2430	66A
Harter, Melody	MI2000	66A
Hartl, David	PA3330	47,66A,66D,34,29
Hartman, Jane	IL1610	13,11,66A,46,47
Harty, Jane	WA0650	66A
Harvey, Anne	NH0300	66A
Harvey, Julie	AZ0400	66A,13
Harvey, Susan	TX1700	63A,63B,66A,32B,32C
Hashimoto, Ayumi	NJ1160	66A
Hashimoto, Kyoko	AI0150	66A
Hasty, Barbara P.	CA1700	13A,61,66A,36
Hatem, Jasmine	TX3450	66A,66B,66C
Hatton, Christopher	CO0150	66A
Hatvani, Robert	OR1010	66A,66D
Haubry, Rebekah	FL0800	66A
Haug, Sue E.	PA2750	66A,66B,66C,66D
Haun, Errol	CO0950	66A,66B
Hawkins Raimi, Jane	NC0600	66A,42
Hawkins, Candace	OK0750	66A,66D
Hawkins, Kay	MN0625	66A
Hawkins, Michelle Kennedy	AA0110	32A,61,66A
Hawkinson, Carol	FL1745	66A,66G
Hawkley, Krysta	DC0170	66A,66B
Hay, Dennis	AR0050	13A,13B,11,66A,66C
Hay, James	MA0510	11,12A,66A,66B
Hayase, Takako	IN0400	66A
Hayashida, Mami	KY0610	66A,66G,66D
Haydon, Geoffrey Jennings	GA1050	66A,66F,29B
Hayes, Christina	NC0050	66A,66C,66D
Hayes, Jane	AB0060	66A,66D,13B,42,66B
Hayghe, Jennifer C.	NY1800	66A
Hayner, Phillip A.	GA1650	11,12,66A,66C,66D
Haythorne, Geraldine	AA0020	66A,66B
Hazelip, Richard	TX1450	66A,66G
Hazeltine, David	NY3785	66A
Hearn, Carmelita	AF0120	13A,66A,66D
Hearn, Priscilla	KS0550	66A,11,12,66D,13C
Heaton, Meg Cognetta	NY1550	66A
Hebert, Sandra M.	MA0330	13A,13,66A,66B
Heck, Steve	MA0260	66A
Heersink, Barbara	CO0050	66C,66A
Heffernan, Michele	NJ1100	11,13C,29,33,66A
Hehmsoth, Henry	TX3175	35C,35D,35G,66A
Heid, David	NC0600	66A,66C
Heil, Teri	NE0250	66A,13,11
Heiles, William H.	IL3300	66A,66H,41
Heimur, Elena	NY0644	61,66A,66D
Heitzman, Jill M.	IA0450	61,64A,66A,11
Helder, Annette	MN1620	66A
Hellmann, Mary	NC0700	66A,66D,12A
Hellyar, Kathleen	PA0125	12,66A
Helm, Michael	ND0350	66A
Helmrich, Dennis	IL3300	66A,66C
Helton, James Caton	IN0150	66A,66C
Helvey, Emily	AZ0470	66A,13
Helwing, Anna	CA2440	66A,61
Helzer, Richard A.	CA4100	29B,29C,66A,47,53
Hendelman, Tamir	CA5031	29,66A
Henderson, Jenny	AR0250	66A,32
Henderson, Peter	MO0700	12A,13,42,66A
Henderson, Silvester	CA2775	36,40,60A,61,66A
Hendricks, James	IL0600	13,47,66A,66D,29
Henkel, Kayme	WI1150	66A
Hennel, Daniel	IL0850	13,66A
Henry, Robert	GA1150	66A,66B
Henry, Ruth	IL2310	61,66A,54
Hepburn, Cathleen	AZ0510	61,66A

Index by Area of Teaching Interest

Name	Code	Areas
Hepler, Lowell E.	PA0100	12A,12C,37,66A,63D
Herbener, Catherine	NE0150	66A
Herman, Cheryl	IL2800	36,54,66A,64
Herod, Sheila	TX1750	13,12A,66A,66C,66D
Herrington, Carolyn A.	AG0500	66A
Hersh, Alan	KY1450	66A,66B,66C,41
Hersh, Paul	CA4150	12A,42,62B,66A
Hershberger, Jay	MN0600	66A
Hesla, Steven	MT0400	66A,66B,66C,66D
Hess, John	AG0500	66A,66C,41,39
Hess, Nathan A.	NY1800	66A,66D,66C,66,66B
Hesse, Shannon	TX1000	66A
Hester, Timothy	TX3400	66A,66B,66C
Heydenburg, Audrejean	MI2000	11,12A,66A,66B,66C
Heyman, Steven	NY0650	66A
Heyman, Steven M.	NY4150	66A,66D,66C,66B
Hibbard, James	AG0500	66A
Hibler, Starla	OK0300	12A,66A,66C
Hickman, Melinda	OH0550	11,66A,66B,66D
Hicks, Gail	CA4625	66A,13A
Hicks, Gail	CA1550	66A
Hickson, Carolyn R.	AR0700	13,66A
Hidlay, Rachel	NY2650	66A
Hiebert, Lenore	CA0810	66A,13A
Hiebert, Shannon	AA0020	61,66A
Higdon, Paul	MO1100	13,66A,66B,11,66D
Hijazi, Anne	NY2400	66A
Hildebrandt, Darcy	AJ0030	66A,66B,66C,13
Hildreth, Todd	KY0250	14,34,47,66A
Hill, Barbara F.	NC2430	66A
Hill, Christine F.	OH0650	66A
Hill, Matthew	IN0550	66A,66B,11,12A
Hille, Regina	KS0560	66A,66G
Hilton, Randalin	UT0150	66A
Hinck, Julie	ID0060	66A
Hines, David	NC2000	66A
Hines, Joan	NM0200	66A
Hinkle, Jean	OR1020	11,13A,41,66A,66D
Hinson, G. Maurice	KY1200	12A,66A,31A,66B,66C
Hinton, Hugh D.	MA1175	66A
Hirota, Yoko	AG0150	66,13B,12A,66A,12B
Hirshfield, L. Russell	CT0800	16,13,66,66B,66A
Hirst, Dennis	UT0300	66A,66B,66C,66D
Hirt, James A.	OH0200	13,11,66A,10
Hisey, Andrew	MN1625	66A
Hisey, P. Andrew	MN1450	66A,66B,66D
Hishman, Marcia	IL1200	66C,66A
Hitt, Christine	IA0910	66A,47,53,46
Hlasny, Susan	AA0050	66A,13
Ho, Sarah	AA0020	66A
Ho, Stephanie	NJ0700	66A,66C,11
Hobson, Ian	PR0115	66A
Hobson, Ian	IL3300	38,41,66A
Hochman, Benjamin D.	NC0650	66A
Hodges, Betsi	NC0910	66A
Hodgkinson, Randall	MA1175	66A
Hodgkinson, Randall	MA2050	66A
Hodgkinson, Randall	MA1400	66A
Hodson, Steven R.	CA5550	11,36,60,66A
Hoekman, Timothy	FL0850	66A,66C
Hoffman, David	IL1350	47,63A,66A
Hoffman, Paul K.	NJ1130	66A,43
Hoffmann, Russell	MA0260	66A
Hoffmann, Shulamit	CA1250	66A,11
Hoft, Timothy	NV0050	66A,66C
Hohlstein, Marjorie Rahima	MA0280	66,13,66A
Hoirup, Marlene	NC2500	66A,66C
Hoisington, Linda	MI0350	66A
Hokanson, Randolph	WA1050	66A
Holland, Marianne	SC0950	32,66A
Holland, Samuel S.	TX2400	66A,66B,66D
Hollander, Jeffrey	WI0825	66A,66D
Holliday, K. A.	VA1700	13,66A
Holliday, Stacey A.	SC0350	66A,66C
Hollinger, Deborah	IL3550	66A,11,66D
Hollis, C. Kimm	IN0650	13,66A
Holliston, Robert	AB0210	66C,12A,11,39,66A
Holm, Robert	AL1300	66A,66B,66C,66D,66H
Holmes, Ruth J.	TX1550	12A,66A,66H,66B,13
Holober, Michael	NY0550	66A,29,10,46,47
Holst, Carol	TX0075	66A
Holstrom, Jacqueline	MN1600	66A,66C
Holt, Beverly	IL1890	66A,66G,66C
Holzer, Linda	AR0750	66A,66B,42,15,11
Holzman, Adam	NY2660	66A,47
Hominick, Ian G.	MS0700	66A,66D,41
Hong, Caroline	OH1850	11,66A,66C,66D
Hong, Hye Jung	MO0775	13,66A
Hong, Sojung Lee	IL1300	66A,66D,66B,42,66C
Hong, Sylvia	MS0100	66A,66D
Honigschnabel, Maria	IL0730	66A
Hood, Marcia Mitchell	GA0150	66A,60A,32B,36,40
Hooper, Kay	PA3150	66A
Hoops, Richard	FL1430	66A
Hopkins, Alice	IN0907	61,66A
Hopkins, Karen	IA0790	66A
Hopper, Jeffrey T.	AR0250	66A
Hoppmann, Ken J.	NE0525	66A,66B,20,66C,12A
Hopson, Amanda	IN0350	66A
Horan, Leta	TX0300	36,66A,66D
Horn, Daniel Paul	IL3550	66A,66C
Horning, Rebecca	NY3770	66A
Horsley, Paul J.	MO1000	12A,66A
Horton, Charles T.	AC0100	66A,13D,13E,13F
Horton, Mathew	CA1850	66A
Horvath, Juliane	NM0500	66A,66C
Horvath, Maria	IL1610	66A,66C,13,66D,11
Hostetter, Elizabeth	AL0550	66A,66D,66C,13,66
Houle, Arthur Joseph	CO0225	66A,66C,66B,66D
Houser, Virginia	KS0650	66A,66B,66D
Houston, James	MD0170	66A,66G
Houts, Janice	SD0450	66A
Howard, Beverly A.	CA0450	13,34A,66G,66A,66H
Howard, Bill	TX1600	10D,10,66A,35B,66D
Howard, Billie	IL0730	66A
Howard, Janet	WY0100	66A
Howell, Jane	PA2900	66A,66C,13A,54,11
Hoy, Patricia A.	AB0100	66A
Hrynkiw, Thomas T.	PA2200	66A,66B
Hsiao, Annie C.	IL2250	66A
Hsieh, Annie	MO1900	66A
Hsu, Cindi	NY5000	66A,10
Hsu, Hsing Ay	CO0800	66A
Hsu, Samuel	PA2800	12A,66A,66B,13E
Hsu, Yun-Ling	FL1700	66A
Hsu, Yun-Ling	FL1800	66A,66B,66C,66D
Hu, Chih-Long	TN0500	66A,66B
Hu, Xiao	IA0950	66A,66D
Huang, Du	IA0950	66A,66D
Huang, Grace	OH0600	66A,66D,66B
Huang, Hao	CA1050	66A
Huang, Hao	CA4500	66A,12,20C,20G,29
Huang, Kuang-Hao	IL0730	66A,66C
Huang, Kuang-Hao	IL0550	66A
Huang, Mei-Hsuan	IA0850	66A
Huang, Ming Shiow	FL0550	66A
Huber, John	KS0350	13,66A,66D
Huber, Kenneth	MN0300	66A
Hubner, Carla	DC0170	66A
Hubner, Carla	DC0110	12A,12,66A,35E
Huck, Patricia	AA0050	32A,66A
Huckleberry, Alan R.	IA1550	66A,66B,66C,66
Huddleston, Debra	OR0250	66C,66A,66G
Hudicek, Laurie	DC0170	66A
Hudson, Stephen	NJ0975	66A,66B,66C,11
Hudson, Terry Lynn	TX0300	66A,66D,66B
Hudson, William Andrew	TX1600	66A,11,66C,66D
Huff, Dwayne	MO0200	11,66A,66B,66C,66D
Huffman, Timothy	OH2050	66A,13B,66B,66D,66C
Hughes, Marcia A.	TN0930	12A,32B,66A,66D
Hughes, Ralph	CA0150	36,61,66A
Hukill, Cynthia L.	AR0200	66A,13
Hulbert, Duane	WA1000	66A,13C
Hulbert, Jarl O.	MD0175	66A
Hulin, Charles J.	FL1740	13,66D,66A,66G
Huling, Diane	VT0250	13,66A,66B,66D
Hull, Robert A.	NY3717	66A,66C
Humpherys, Douglas	NY1100	66A
Hund, Jennifer L.	IN1300	12,66A,12A,11
Hundley, Marion S.	FL0100	10A,66A,66C,13
Hung, Emily	CA3350	66A
Hung, Li-Shan	CA0350	66A,66B,41
Hung, Yu-Sui	IL3450	66A,66D,13C
Hunt, Steven	MA0260	66A
Hunter, Colleen	WA0400	66A,66D
Hunter, Judy	AG0200	66A
Hunter, Rosemary Herlong	AL0400	13,66A
Huntley, Yvonne	IL2750	66A,66D
Hurd, James L.	CA1750	11,66A,66G
Hurd, Mary	MI0300	66A,66B,66C,66D,13A
Hurst, Francesca	DC0050	66A
Hurst, Francesca	DC0250	66A
Hussung, Mark	TN0250	66A,66D
Huston, Spencer	KS0590	11,66A
Hutchinson, Raymond	IL1900	66A,63A,63B,11
Hutchison, Amy	OH0450	66A
Hutchison, Lacey	SC0620	66A
Huth, Lori	PA2450	66A
Hutton, Judy F.	NC2650	13,66A,66B,66C,66D
Hutton, Paula R.	OK0700	13,12A,66A,11
Hwang, ChiHee	TN1850	66A
Hynes, Mia M.	MO1790	66A,66B,66D
Hyun, Suk-Yi	MD0300	66A
Idenden, John	NJ0100	13,11,12A,61,66A
Imhoff, Andrea G.	TX2900	13A,11,66C,66A
Immel, Daniel	PA1750	11,66A,66D
Imperio, Roy	MA0250	66A,66B,41,66C,11
Inagawa, Kanako	CA0300	66A
Indergaard, Lyle	GA2150	66A,66C,66D
Ingber, Elizabeth	CA4625	66A,62A,62B
Ingram, David	OR1300	66A,66C
Inkman, Joanne	NC2500	66C,66D,13A
Inouye, Fang-Fang Shi	CA0859	66A,66D
Intintoli, Helen	CA4650	36,61,66A,31A,54
Ioudenitch, Stanislav	MO1000	66A
Ioudenitch, Tatiana	MO1000	66A
Irei, Norito	FL1550	66A,66C
Irvine, Jane	OH1400	66A,32B
Irwin, Doreen	CA3850	36,41,66A
Italiano, Richard	CO0300	13,10,11,66A,66D
Itkin, Ora	MN1625	66A
Ivanov, Svetozar D.	FL2000	66A
Ivanova, Vera	CA0960	10A,10B,10F,10,66A
Izdebski, Christy	MD0100	12A,32,66A,66D,36
Jablonski, Krzysztof	AA0050	66A
Jackson, Jane	CA1250	13,66A
Jackson, L. Max	KY0200	13,11,36,66A
Jackson, Raymond T.	DC0150	66A
Jackson, Russell	PA2450	66A,66G,66C
Jackson, Tyrone	GA1150	66A,29,66D,53
Jacob, Jeffrey	IN0005	66A
Jacob, Jeffrey	IN1450	11,66A,66B
Jacob, Stefanie	WI1150	13A,66A
Jacobi, Bonnie S.	CO0250	32B,66A,13,32I,32
Jacobson, Allan	SD0400	13,10A,66A,66G
Jaimes, Judit	WI0825	41,66,66A,66C,66,42
James, Jo-Sandra	VI0050	66A,66B,66D
James, Karen	VT0100	66A,66D
James, Tim	PA0950	66A,29B
James, William R.	FL1300	66A,66C,66D
Jancewicz, Peter	AA0050	66A
Janleviciute, Egle	CA5550	66A
Janzen, Elaine	TN1350	66A,66D,13A
Jarczyk, Jan	AI0150	29,63C,66A
Jardon, Gloria J.	MO0800	66A
Jarrell, Erinn	CA5355	13,66A,66B,66C,66D
Jasmin, Pierre	AI0210	66A
Jefcoat, Priscilla	GA0350	13A,66A,10F,12A,13D
Jefferson, Thomas	IL2100	66A,66D
Jemielita, James	NY2102	66A,47
Jeng, Rhoda	MD0400	66A
Jenkins, Rosemary	TX2350	66A,66D
Jenkinson, Janet	IN1560	66A
Jennings, Caroline	UT0150	66A,66D
Jennings, Carolyn	MN1450	66A
Jensen, Joan F.	LA0750	66A,66D,13A
Jensen, John	MN1625	66A
Jensen-Abbott, Lia	MI0100	13,66A
Jenson, Matthew	MA0260	66A
Jeon, Hey Rim	MA2030	66A
Jeon, Hey Rim	MA0260	66A,13B
Jewell, Vickie L.	AL0345	11,37,63B,66A
Jin, Jungwon	CA2420	66A
Jinright, John W.	AL1050	13,64D,34,64B,66A
Jo, Marie	FL0365	66A
Jobe, Elena	GA0600	66A,66B,66C
Jochum von Moltke, Veronica	MA1400	66A
Johns, Amy	GA1070	66A,66D,11
Johnson, Barbara C.	CT0650	66A
Johnson, Chrisa	VA0050	66A,13B,13C,11
Johnson, Cornelius	IL0450	13A,66A,11,36,20
Johnson, Cory	CA1900	10,47,66A
Johnson, DeeDee	WY0150	66A
Johnson, Doug	MA2050	66A,29B
Johnson, Douglas	MA0260	66A
Johnson, Gail	CA1375	66A,66D

721

Name	Code	Areas
Johnson, Henry	GA1600	36,66A,46,47,48
Johnson, Herbert	MN0250	11,66A,66B,66C
Johnson, James D.	NE0610	66A,66G,69
Johnson, Jeremiah	NE0200	66A,66C
Johnson, Jessica G.	WI0815	66A,66B
Johnson, Kari M.	MO0050	66A,66B,13
Johnson, Lacey	VA0800	66A,66C
Johnson, Lynn	AE0050	66A
Johnson, Marjorie S.	VA0950	13,66A,66B,66D,34
Johnson, Michelle	TX2600	66A,66B,66C,66D,66E
Johnson, Pamela	WI0801	66D,66A,64
Johnson, Penny	AJ0100	66A,66C
Johnson, Robert	NH0110	66A
Johnson, Ruth	CA5360	13A,66A,66D
Johnson, Sharon L.	NY1700	66C,66A,66D,31A
Johnson, Shirley M.	FL0600	13A,61,66A,66D
Johnson, Tracey	MO2000	66A,66D,13C
Johnson, Velshera	VA0400	61,36,40,66A
Johnson, Victoria	MS0360	11,66A,66D
Johnson, Wayne D.	WA0800	11,12A,66A,66C
Johnston, Jack R.	NY3730	13,66A,54,34
Johnston, James W.	IN1100	60,62A,66A
Johnston, Jeffrey	AI0150	66A,29
Jolly, Donna	NC1300	66A
Jonas, Dorothy	NY2400	66A
Jonas, Dorothy	NY5000	66A
Jones, Arlington	TX0370	13,10F,66A,35G
Jones, Cheryl	FL1430	37,66A,66B,47,61
Jones, Colette	KY0300	32B,11,66A,66D
Jones, Craig	OR0600	66A,66D,60A
Jones, Everett N.	OH2400	12A,66A,66B,66D
Jones, Henry S.	LA0650	66A,66B,66D,13C
Jones, Jeff	KY0450	66G,66H,66A
Jones, Joella	OH0600	66A
Jones, Larry E.	NE0450	66A,66B
Jones, Lawrence	AC0050	66A,12A
Jones, Lis	AR0250	66A,66C,66D
Jones, Martin David	GA0250	11,66A,66H,66B,13
Jones, Maxine	TN1400	66A,66D,11
Jones, Melinda	MO1550	66A,66D,66B,13B,13C
Jones, Robert D.	FL1470	66A,66G,66C,66D,34
Jones, Sue	IL1550	42,66A,66C,66D,13C
Jones, William C.	CA4200	66A
Jones, William	DC0350	11,36,61,66A,66G
Jones, Zebedee	MS0600	13A,32,36,66A
Jong, Pin Pin	NC1300	66A
Jordan, Krassimira	TX0300	66A
Jordan, Robert	NY3725	66A
Jordan-Anders, Lee	VA1830	13,11,41,66A
Jordan-Miller, Rebekah	GA1800	66A,66B
Joseph, Jane	MS0300	11,66A
Josselyn-Cranson, Heather	IA1200	66A,31A,10,20
Jovanovic, Milica Jelaca	WA1250	66A,66B
Joyal, Marc	AI0190	66A
Joyce, Susan	FL1450	66A,66D
Joyner, Rochelle	NC0200	11,66A,66D
Juhn, Hee-Kyung	AR0300	66A,13C,66G,66C,66B
Julian, Suzanne	CA1700	66A,11
Julian, Suzanne	CA3100	11,66A,66D
Jung, Eunsuk	TN0600	13A,66A,66D,66G,13B
Jung, Hyesook	AL0950	66A,66B,66C,13
Junkinsmith, Jeff	WA0860	13,66A,10
Jupinka, Nick	NJ0760	66A
Jureit-Beamish, Marie	IL2400	38,64A,66A,10F,11
Jutras, Peter J.	GA2100	66A,66B,66D,32G
Kahan, Sylvia	NY0600	66A,12A
Kahler, Bette	NY4100	11,12A,33,66A,66G
Kahn, Richard	CA2750	10F,13B,34,66A
Kairoff, Peter	NC2500	11,66A
Kaiser, Audrey K.	RI0101	66A,66D,13
Kaizer, Edward	IL0400	11,12A,66A,66B
Kaizer, Janet	IL0400	66A,66D
Kakouberi, Daredjan 'Baya'	TX0370	66A,35G
Kalhous, David	TX3200	66A,66B
Kalichstein, Joseph	NY1900	66A
Kalish, Gilbert	NY3790	41,66A,66C,43
Kallstrom, Wayne	NE0100	66A,66G,12A
Kalman, Eli	WI0830	66A,66D
Kalson, Dorothy	NY4050	66A,11
Kaltchev, Ivo	DC0050	66A
Kanamaru, Tomoko	NJ0175	66A,66B,66C,66D
Kanda, Sanae	MA1650	10A,42,66A,66C,66D
Kane, Lila	RI0250	66A
Kane, Scott	IN1650	66A
Kaneda, Mariko	OH2000	66C,66A,66D,13B,13C
Kang, Choong Mo	NY1900	66A
Kang, Haysun	IL1615	11,66A,66D
Kang, Heejung	TX3420	66A
Kang, Juyeon	IA1200	66A,66D,66C,13C
Kang, Sang Woo	RI0150	13A,13B,66A
Kang, Sooyoung	NC2150	66A,13
Kania, Robert P.	IL1300	66A,13
Kanno, Sayaka	DC0170	66A
Kantorski, Valrie	MI0050	66A,66D
Kao, Janet	CA1900	66A
Kao, Janet	CA0960	66A
Kaplan, Lisa	VA1500	43,66A
Kaplinsky, Veda	TX3000	66A
Kaplinsky, Yoheved	NY1900	66A
Kargul, Laura J.	ME0500	66A
Karis, Aleck	CA5050	13,12A,66A,66H,43
Karlicek, Martin	AI0150	66A
Karloff, Michael	AG0550	29,46,66A
Karloff, Michael	MI2200	47,46,29,66A
Karlsson, Stefan	TX3420	29B,29C,47,66A
Karp, David	TX2400	13,66A
Karpoff, Fred S.	NY4150	42,66A,66C,66B
Karush, Larry	CA3300	66A,53
Kasling, Kim R.	MN0350	12A,66G,31A,66A
Kasman, Yakov	AL1150	66A
Kasparov, Andrey R.	VA1000	13,66A,10,43
Kates, Christine	PA3710	66A,66G
Kato, Yuko	IL2900	66A
Kats, Irina	DC0170	66A
Kats, Nitza	VA1100	66A,13C
Katz, Steve	TN1380	11,66A
Kauffman, Larry D.	PA0150	12A,36,66A,31A
Kautsky, Catherine C.	WI0350	66A,66C,66E,41
Kawamura, Manami	CA0350	41,66A,66C
Kawashima, Kimi	UT0400	20,66A
Kawin, Phillip	NY2150	66A
Kay, Min Soo	NY5000	66A
Keating, Karen	VA1350	66A,36
Kebuladze, Tatyana	NJ0800	66A,66D,66C
Keck, Ouida	AR0500	66A,66B
Kee, Soyoung	IL0850	66A,11
Keele, Roger S.	TX1400	39,66A,61
Keeling, Kasandra Kennedy	TX3530	66A
Keen, Stephen	UT0400	66A
Keen, Stephen	UT0250	66A
Keenan, Larry W.	KY0900	11,66A,66G,66D,66H
Keene, Theresa	CA0150	13A,66A
Kefferstan, Christine	WV0750	66A,66B,66C,66D
Kehler Siebert, Judith	AC0100	66A,66C,66D,42
Kehner, Kenneth W.	MO1830	66A
Keillor, Elaine	AG0100	12A,12,14,66A,20G
Keiter, Lise	VA0800	13,11,66A,12A,15
Keith, Laura J.	SC0350	12A,66A,66D,32C,32D
Keller Bick, Ingrid P.	OH2250	66A
Keller, Deborah	MI1985	66A,66C,66G
Keller, Elizabeth W.	PA1300	66A
Kelley, Robert T.	SC0800	20,13,66A,66D,10
Kellogg, Hsing-ay	CO0550	66A
Kellogg, Lydia	IL1850	66A
Kelly, Aileen	CA0150	62E,12A,66A
Kelly, Michael F.	NY1850	36,61,66A,46,34
Kelly, Rebecca	AB0200	66A,66D
Kelly, Stephen	IL2100	36,66A
Kennedy, Charles	AL0630	11,70,66A,61
Kennedy, Laura H.	NY0350	66A
Kent, Adam	NJ0825	66A,42
Kent, Adam S.	NY0500	66A
Kenyon, Paul	CA3640	66A,66D
Kern, Jeffrey	PA3330	13A,36,44,61,66A
Kern, Philip	IN1100	13,10F,36,54,66A
Kershaw, Linda L.	SC0150	11,12,60,66A,36
Kersten, Joanne	MN1250	13,66A,32B
Ketter, Craig	NJ0825	66A,66C,42
Kew, Margaret Davis	KS0100	51,62,66A
Khadarin, Linda	KS0570	13,66A
Khamda, Mazdak	CA3250	66A,66D,32F,35C
Kibbe-Hodgkins, Shiela	MA0400	66C,66A
Kiehl, Vicky	AR0200	66A,66H,66B,66D,66C
Kies, Arlene	NH0350	66A,66B,66C
Kies, Christopher	NH0350	13B,10,66A,13F
Kijanowska, Anna	VA0250	66A
Kikuchi, Mayumi	OH2150	66A
Kilburn, Ke-Yin	IN0005	33,66A,66B,13
Kilburn, Ray	IN0150	66A
Kilgore Wood, Janice	MD1050	13C,66A,36,66B,31A
Kim, Adrienne	NY4150	66A
Kim, Aeree	NY2105	66A,66B
Kim, Andrea	NJ0700	66A
Kim, Eileen	AA0020	66A
Kim, Ellen Y.	CA2050	66A,66D
Kim, Eun Hae	MD1100	66A
Kim, Gloria	CA1265	61,13A,66A
Kim, Grace	MD1100	66A
Kim, Heawon	NY2105	66A,66C
Kim, Howard D.	SC0050	66A,66D,13B,66C,11
Kim, Hwa-Jin	NC2400	66A
Kim, Hyesook	MI0350	66A,66B,11,42
Kim, Jean	NY0270	11,13,66A,66C
Kim, JeongSoo	IL2200	66A,66B
Kim, Jisung	NY2550	66A,66D
Kim, Junghyun	IL0350	66A
Kim, Kunyoung	PA0250	66A,13E,11,66B
Kim, Kyung	AC0050	66A
Kim, Kyung-Mi	GA0050	66A,66D
Kim, Linda	HI0050	66A
Kim, Lok	GA0600	38,42,60,66A
Kim, Michael I.	AC0050	66A
Kim, Min	NJ0825	13,12,66A,66B,41
Kim, Mina	NY3785	66A,66C
Kim, Minjung	MI0050	66A,66D
Kim, Nahyun	KS0590	66A,66D
Kim, Namji C.	WI0803	66A,66D
Kim, Paul S.	NY2105	66A,66B,12A
Kim, Seung A.	NY2450	33,66A
Kim, Sungeun	OH0200	66A,66C
Kim, Sungsil	MO0350	66A
Kim, Taeseong	VA0650	66A,66B,13C
Kim, Wonmin	IN0350	66A
Kim, Yona	AA0020	66A
Kim, Yoo-Jung	MI1200	66A,66C,66D
Kim, Youmee	OH1900	66A,66C,66D
Kim, Young	NY0700	13B,13C,66A,66D
Kim, Yuri	NY2250	66A
Kim-Medwin, Sungah	MD0550	66A,66D
Kimball, Sarah	OR1000	66A
Kime, Ramona	MI1800	62,66A,66D,66H
Kimura, Tomoko	WA0250	66A
Kinchen, Lucy C.	CA2450	12A,36,61,66A
Kindall, Susan C.	SC0200	66A,66B,35C,34
Kindt, Allen	NC0050	66A,66B
King, Adam	AL1195	66A,13,66D,66C
King, Anita	OR1300	13,66A,66C
King, Donna Moore	TN0930	11,66A,66D,69
King, Janette	GA1100	66A,36
King, Linda	TN0450	66A
King, Margaret	AA0020	66A,64A
King, Robert	OR1300	66A
King, Vicki B.	TN1400	66A,66D,12A
Kingham, Lesley	AG0050	66G,66C,66A
Kinne, Wafia	WA1100	66A
Kinsley, Diane	MD0060	66A,66D
Kinsley, Eric B.	CA0550	11,66A,66H,66D
Kinton, Leslie	AG0500	66A
Kinton, Leslie	AG0300	66A
Kiorpes, George A.	NC2430	66A,66B,66C
Kirchner, Joann M.	PA3250	66A
Kirchner, Joanne	PA0650	66A
Kirk, Caroline	MN1400	11,66A,66B,66D
Kirkendoll, Michael	OK0800	66A,66B,66D,42
Kirkpatrick, Amanda	MO1900	66A,66D
Kirkpatrick, Gary	NJ1400	66A,66B,66D
Kirkwood, Neal	PA1750	40,66A
Kirson-Jones, Chloe	AF0120	66A
Kisilevitch, Miroslava	MN1250	66A
Kislenko, Natalia	CA5060	66A,66C,66D
Klassen, Masako	CA0815	66A
Klefstad, Kristian I.	TN0100	66A,66B,66D
Klein, Laura	CA5000	66A
Klein, Rochelle Z.	PA2900	32,35E,66A,11,13A
Klemetson, Roxanne	MN1620	66A
Klice, Joseph A.	CA3500	66A,16
Klimaszewska, Alina	TX1450	66A
Klimisch, Mary J.	SD0300	10,13J,66A,66G
Klinder-Badgley, Marcia	CA1850	66A
Klukas, Suzanne	AB0090	66A,66C
Knecht, Karen	CA0960	66A
Knickerbocker, Sharon	IL1900	66A,66B,66C,66D
Knupp, Robert	MS0400	66G,13I,13B,66A
Ko, EunMi	NY1250	11,66A
Kobrin, Alexander	GA0550	66A,42
Kochis, Jane	MN1285	66A,66C,11

Index by Area of Teaching Interest

Name	Code	Areas
Kocyan, Wojciech	CA2800	66A,13C
Koehler, William	IL2200	66A,66C
Koen, Kerry	NY0650	66C,66A
Koenigsberg, Tobias R.	OR1050	29,47,66A
Koester, Eugene	SC0275	66A,66D
Koesterer, Karl	MO1950	66A
Kofman, Irena	FL0650	66A
Koga, Midori	AG0450	66A,66D
Koh-Baker, JoAnn Hwee Been	OH1600	11,12A,66A,13A,13B
Kohl, Jack	NY4050	66A
Kohlbeck-Boeckman, Anne	WI0350	13,66A,66D,13A
Kohls, Shauna	AA0040	66A
Kohn, Margaret S.	CA3650	66A
Kolar, J. Mitzi	CA4100	66A,66B,66D
Kominami, Miko	IA0950	66A,13
Kong, Joanne	VA1500	66A,66H,66C,55
Konstantinov, Tzvetan	DC0100	66A,66C,66D
Koomson, Nathaniel	MD0170	66A
Koppelman, Daniel M.	SC0750	66A,13,34,10
Koranda, Ann	IL1890	66A,66G,66C
Korevaar, David J.	CO0800	66A
Korey, Judith A.	DC0350	13A,13,66A,29,34
Kornicke, Eloise	VA0800	66A,13A
Korsantia, Alexander	MA1400	66A
Korth, Jonathan	HI0210	66A,66B,66C
Kosak, Johanna	NY4050	66A
Kot, Don	NY2650	66A,61,66D,66C,54
Kovacovic, Paul	IA0200	10,12A,66A,66C
Kovalsky, Vladislav D.	NJ0550	66A
Koven, Steven	AG0650	53,66A
Kover, Krisztina	FL0650	66A
Kramer, Atossa	KY0300	13C,48,64C,66A,67C
Kramer, Dean	OR1050	66A
Kramer, Ernest Joachim	MO0950	13,10,11,66A,66H
Kramer, Katya	IN0350	66A
Kramer, Steven	NJ0750	66A
Kramlich, Dan P.	WA0800	36,66A
Kramlich, Daniel	WA0650	66A
Kramlich, Daniel L.	TX1000	13,10F,66A
Krash, Jessica	DC0100	41,66A
Kraus, James	MI1180	66G,13A,66A
Krebs, John A.	AR0350	66A,66C,39,11,13
Kregler, Michael C.	RI0150	66A,66C,47
Kreider, David G.	MD0520	11,66A,66G,66B,66D
Kressler, Jeffrey	MI0400	66A
Krieger, Karen Ann	TN1850	13,66A,66D,66B,68
Krieger, Norman	CA5300	66A
Krislov, Donna	MN1050	66A
Kristof, Rosemary	AF0120	66A
Kroetsch, Terence	AG0600	13,66D,66A
Krontz, Paula	MI1160	66A
Kropidlowski, Monica	IL2650	66A,66D
Krueger, Leslie	WI0825	66A,66D
Krueger, Walter E.	OR0150	13,66A,12A,66G,66D
Kruja, Mira	AL0010	66A,66B,13,11
Krupa, Mary Ann	IL3450	13,54,66A
Kruse, Lacey	MN0625	66A,65
Krusemark, Ruth E.	KS0100	13,10,66A,66G,66D
Krystofiak, Paul	TX3450	66A
Krzywicki, Jan L.	PA3250	13,66A
Kuan, Flora	NY2200	13C,66A,42
Kubik, Paula A.	PA1450	66A
Kudlawiec, Nancy A.	AL1350	11,32,66A,12A,13
Kuehn, Jacquelyn A.	PA1600	66A
Kuhn, Edward M.	PA3000	66A
Kuhn, Lynne	CA3460	66A,66D
Kukec, Paul E.	IL1900	13A,13,12A,36,66A
Kuleshov, Valery	OK1330	66A
Kuliush, Tetyana	FL0950	66A
Kuo, Rita	NY2400	66A
Kushner, Karen	MO1810	66A
Kushnir, Regina	CO0100	13A,66A
Kuss, Mark	CT0450	13,10,45,66A,34
Kustanovich, Serafima	MA0650	66A,66C,41
Kuzmenko, Larysa	AG0450	13,13,66A
Kwak, Eun-Joo	WI0150	66A,66B,66C,42,12A
Kwak, Jason	TX3175	66A,42
Kwok, May Ling	AB0150	66A
Kwok, May Ling	AB0210	66A
Kwon, Min	NJ1130	66A
Kwon, MiYoung	OH0755	66A,66D
Kwon, Yeeseon	IL0550	66A,66B,66D,66
Kwon, Yeeson	IL2750	66A
Kwoun, Soo Jin	MO0700	33,61,66A
La Manna, Juan F.	NY3770	38,66A,66D,11,39
La Rocca, Carla	PA0550	66A,66D
LaBar, Dan	NY1150	66A
Labe, Thomas A.	OK0150	11,12A,66A,66B
Labenske, Victor	CA3640	66A,66D,12A,10
Lacroix, Frederic	AG0400	66A
Laforest, Maurice	AI0190	66A
Laframboise, Damian	AG0150	66A,66D
Laframboise, Damien	AG0070	66A
Laimon, Sara	AI0150	66A,41
Lajoie, Stephen H.	RI0101	47,66A,53,29,13A
Lakey, Richard	PA2100	66A,66G
LaLama, David S.	NY1600	47,66A,29
Lally, Laurie A.	NJ1100	66A
Lam, Sze-Sze	AA0020	66A
Lam, Vincent	TX2650	66A
Lambert, Evin R.	WA0750	11,36,66A,61,13A
Lamkin, Kathleen J.	CA5100	12A,11,12,62A,66A
Lancaster, Carol	CA3100	66A
Land, Michael	ND0400	13C,66A
Landes, Daniel	TN0100	13A,13,66A,66D,31A
Landreth, Janet M.	CO0250	66A,66B
Landrum, Michael	NY3350	66A
Landry, Dana	CO0950	29,66A,47
Lane, Elizabeth	DC0170	66A
Lane, LuAnn	TX1850	11,13,66A,66C,66D
Lane, Mathew	MD0400	13A,13C,66A,66C
Lange, Richard A.	MN1280	66A,66B,66C
Lanham, Barbara	IL1610	13A,36,66A,66D
Lanier Miller, Pamela	AL0330	61,11,66A
Lanners, Heather	OK0800	66A,13C,66C
Lanners, Thomas	OK0800	66A
Lanzer, Kate J.	MN0450	66A
Lapp, Beverly K.	IN0550	66B,66A,11,66C
Larsen, Eric	NC1650	41,66A
Larsen, Laurel	SC0900	66A,66C,66B,13,66D
Larsen, Robert L.	IA1350	12A,36,39,66A,66C
Larson, Lynee	MN1290	66A,66D
Larson, Robert	VA1350	66A
Laskowitz, Lillian	NY5000	66A
Laskowitz, Lillian	NY2400	66A
Latchininsky, Alla	WY0200	66A
Lateiner, Jacob	NY2250	66A,41
Latsabidze, Giorgi	CA1960	66A
Latu, Kalotini	UT0050	66A
Lau, Daniel	MD0150	66A,66C,12A
Lau, Elaine	AG0600	66A
Laubengayer, Karen	MS0350	66A,66B,66C,66D
Lauderdale, Lynne A.	FL2100	12A,66A,66G,66D,66B
Laufer, Milton R.	NC1800	66A,13C
Laughlin, Mark	GA1000	66A,13,12A,66D,13B
Laurendine, Barbara	AL1195	66A,66D
Laurent, Linda	CT0050	13,12,66A,66D,42
Lauterbach, Megan	IL2750	66A
Lavruk, Alexander E.	CA3950	66A
Lawing, Cynthia	NC0550	66A,66D
Lawlor, Catherine	MA2010	66A,66D
Lawrence, Edwin	MA2250	13C,66A,66G,66H,66C
Lawrence-White, Stephanie	NC0200	12A,66A,12C,20F,66B
Lawson, Dianne	IA0910	66A,11
Lawson, Robert	CA1265	10,38,41,66A,66D
Lawthers, Carol	CA4000	11,32B,61,66A
Lawton, Thomas	PA3330	66A
Lawton, Thomas P.	PA0400	66A,53
Lawton, Tom P.	PA3250	66A,29
Lazar, Ludmila	IL0550	66A,66B
Le, Andrew	MI1050	66A
Leaptrott, Ben	GA0350	11,13,39,66A,66B
Leavitt, Edward	NY4300	66A,66D
LeBlond, Gerald	NH0300	66A,66B
Lecuona, Rene	IA1550	66A
Ledgerwood, Lee Ann	NY2660	10,66A,47
Leduc, Pierre	AI0200	66A,13B,47
Lee, Alice	MD0300	66A
Lee, Alice E.	DC0170	66A
Lee, Amanda	TX2570	66A,13C,13B,13E,66B
Lee, Brian	IL1850	66A,11
Lee, Chihchen Sophia	OK1250	33,32F,66A
Lee, Donna	OH1100	66A,66B,66C,42
Lee, Donzell	MS0050	12A,32,66A
Lee, Genevieve Feiwen	CA3650	66A,13
Lee, Gerald K.	WV0600	66A,66B,66C,66D
Lee, Hedy	CA0960	66A
Lee, Hwakyu (Julia)	OR1100	66A
Lee, Hyeweon	DC0170	66A
Lee, Jinah	NY3705	66A
Lee, Julia	OR0850	66A
Lee, Junghwa	IL2900	66A
Lee, Katherine K.		66A,66C
Lee, Kum Sing	AB0200	66A
Lee, Kum-Sing	AA0050	66A
Lee, Lydia	CA1265	66A
Lee, Marian Y.	IA1300	66A,66B,66C,13C,11
Lee, Monica	CA1900	66A,66B
Lee, Pamela	TX0150	32,36,66A,60
Lee, Patricia	IL2650	66A,66H,66B,66C,66D
Lee, Patricia Taylor	CA4200	41,66A,66B
Lee, Patty	TX3100	66A
Lee, Paul S.	TX1300	66G,13B,11,60,66A
Lee, Rebecca	FL1550	66A
Lee, Richard A.	CO0650	66A
Lee, So Yoon	TX3525	66A
Lee, Soh Yeong	PA3550	66A
Lee, Soo Young	IL1400	66A
Lee, Sun Jung	WV0100	66A,66C,66D
Lee, Sung Ae	CA0859	13A,66A,66D
Lee, Won Yong	TX2570	66A
Lee, You Ju	GA2000	66A,66C,66D,66B
LeePreston, Nicole	IN1750	66A,66C
Lehman, David	SC0200	12A,66A,66B
Lehman, Marilyn J.	NY1600	66A,66C,42
Lehman, Shari	IA0790	66A
Lehnert, Doris Pridonoff	CO0800	66A
Lehrer, Phyllis	NJ1350	66A,66B
Leikin, Anatole	CA5070	13,12A,66A
Lein, Susan E.	LA0760	66A
Lemons, Nancy	IL1300	66A,13B
Lemson, Deborah	TX3850	66A,66G,66C,66D
Lenehan, Miriam C.	NY2450	11,12A,32,66A,66D
Lenhart, Andrew Stevens	NY2900	66A
Lenti, Anthony A.	SC0800	11,12A,66A
Lenti, Vincent	NY1100	66A
Leo, Nick	IA0550	66A
Leone, Carol	TX2400	41,66A
Leong, Sonia	CA5350	66A,41,42
Leppert-Largent, Anna	MI1850	11,66A
Lesbines, Melissa	NC0050	11,66A,66C
Leshchinskaya, Ida	MI2120	66A
Lester, Noel K.	MD0500	66A
Lester, William	NY2400	66A,66D,29
Leung, Jackson	OH2500	66A,66D,66B,38
Leventhal, Lois A.	MS0750	66A,66C,66D
Levesque, Gerald	AI0190	66A
Levin, Heather	CA5550	66A
Levin, Oleg	MN0610	66A
Levine, Jerome	NJ1160	11,66D,66A
Levine, Mark	CA2950	66A
Levinson, Max	MA0350	66A
Levtov, Vladimir	AA0150	41,66A,66C,66D,42
Levy, James D.	DC0100	47,66A,29B
Lewandowski, Annie	NY0900	53,66A
Lewin, Michael	MA0400	66A,66D
Lewin, Michael	MA0350	66A
Lewis, Andrew	MD0175	11,66A,66C
Lewis, Andrew J.	MS0350	66A,66C
Lewis, Christopher	VT0050	66A,66B,66C,66D
Lewis, Robert J.	KY0300	13B,11,66A,66B,66D
Lewis, Susan	FL1730	61,66A,66G
Li, Bichuan	HI0210	66A,66D
Li, Chihwei	NY4050	66A
Li, Hanna Wu	PA0550	66A,66B,66D
Li, Juan	MN0250	66A,66D
Li, Lei	IL0650	13A,11,66A,66D
Li, Lin	NY5000	66A
Li, Ping-Hui	PR0150	13A,13C,14A,66A,66C
Li, Simon	NY2900	66A,13A,13B,13C
Libal-Smith, Marie	PA3650	66A
Lieurance, Barbara	MA0510	66A,66D
Lifson, Ludmilla	MA1175	66A
Ligate, Linda	MO0400	12A,66A,31A
Light, Daniel	KY0250	66A
Ligon, Bert	SC1110	46,47,66A,29,45
Liliestedt, Maira	OH2290	12A,66A,66B
Lim, Cheryl	IL1085	66A,66D
Lim, Cheryl	IL3550	66A,66D
Lim, Christine	IL1520	66A
Lim, Jennifer	MO1250	66A,66D
Lim, Mi-Na	TX0345	11,66A,66B
Lim, Philip 'Jay Jay'	CA2100	66A
Lim, Sangmi	MI1400	66A
Lim, Yoon-Mi	TX2600	66G,66A,13A
Limina, David	MA0260	66A

Index by Area of Teaching Interest

Name	Code	Areas
Lin, Anthea	OK1250	66A,66B
Lin, Gloria	TX3000	66A
Lin, Hui-Mei	CT0300	66A
Lin, Melissa	CA4425	66A
Lin, Victor	NY4200	29,66A,62D
Lindeman, Timothy H.	NC0910	13,12A,66A,20
Lindley, Debra	OH2500	66A
Linnenbom, Harriett	MD0700	13A,11,66A,66D
Linstrom, Tracie	CA5400	66D,66A
Lipke, William A.	CO0050	66A,38,67F,66B,66D
Lipke-Perry, Tracy D.	MN1600	66A,66C
Lipkin, Seymour	NY1900	66A
Lipkin, Seymour	PA0850	66A
Lipp, Carolyn	MI0500	14,66A,66H,66B
Lister-Sink, Barbara	NC2205	66A,66B,66C,42
Litke, Sheila	KS1300	66,13,66A,66B,13A
Litzelman, James	DC0050	66A,66B
Liu, Meng-Chieh	PA0850	41,66A
Liu, Meng-Chieh	IL0550	66A
Liu, Pei-Fen	NC0600	66A
Liu, Solungga Fang-Tzu	OH0300	66A
Liu, Susan (Shao-Shan)	TX1425	66A,66D,11,34
Liu, Vivian	CA0960	66A
Lively, Judy	AZ0400	66A,66B
Livesay, Yumi	CA6000	66A
Livingston, Jane	WI0250	66A,66D,66B
Livingston, Lillian	NJ1350	66A,66B
Lloyd, Deborah F.	DC0170	66A
Lo, Wei-Chun Bernadette	TN1800	66A
Lobitz, Kristi	CA2800	66A,66D
Lobitz, Kristi	CA1750	66A,66G
Lobitz, Kristi	CA3500	66A
Lochstampfor, Mark L.	OH0350	13,10A,34A,34B,66A
Loewen, Che Anne	AG0450	61,66A
Loewen, Judy	AA0020	66A,66H
Loewen, Laura	AC0100	66A,39,66C
Lohr, Tom L.	NC1300	66A,10A
Lomazov, Marina	SC1110	66A
Lombard, Becky	GA2050	66A,13B,13C,12A,66C
Lombard, Becky	LA0400	13,12A,66A,66G,12C
Long, Arlene	TX2930	66A,66C,66D
Long, Jason	PA2450	66A
Long, Louanne J.	CA5150	13,66A,66B,66C
Loos, James C.	IA0420	11,61,66A
Lopato, David	NY2660	13,10,66A
Lopez, Barbara	CA0400	61,66A,10
Lopez, Christine Sotomayor	CA0859	36,66A,66D,11,66B
Lopez, Faye	SC0200	13C,66A
Lopez, George	ME0200	66A,38,42
Lopez, Jose R.	FL0700	66A,66C,66H,66B
Lopez, Richard	OH0850	47,66A
Lopez, Richard C.	OH2050	66A,66D
Lopez, Tewanta	IA1300	66A
Lord, Roger	AE0100	13,66A,66D
Loring, George	NH0150	66A,66B,66D,66H
Losey, Mary	SC1100	66A,66D
Lou, Dorothy	AA0020	66A
Louie, David	AG0300	66A
Louise-Turgeon, Anne	FL0650	66A,66C
Louwenaar, Karyl	FL0850	66E,41,66A,66H
Love, Randall M.	NC0600	66A,66E,42
Lovell, Owen C.	WI0803	66A,66D
Lovely, Christopher	AL1195	66A,66C
Low, Linda	AB0210	66A,66B
Low, Murray	CA4900	47,66A
Lowenthal, Jerome	NY1900	66A
Lowrey, Ariane	AA0020	66A
Lu, Alex	CA1960	66A
Lu, Jie	UT0250	66A
Lu, Ning	UT0250	66A
Lubin, Howard	OH1700	66C,66A
Lubin, Steven	NY3785	13,12A,12,66A
Lucia, Margaret E.	PA3050	13,11,12,66A
Luckenberg, George	GA1700	66A,66E,66H
Lum, Anne Craig	HI0150	66D,66A,64A,45,66C
Lum, Tammy K.	NY2900	13,66A,66D,42
Lundberg, Erika	MN1100	66A,66B,66C
Lupinski, Rudy	OK0300	66A,66D,13B,13C,66H
Lupis, Giuseppe	MI0900	66A
Luther, Sigrid	TN0200	13,66A,66B,31A,66C
Lutnes, Patricia	CT0800	66A
Lutsyshyn, Oksana	VA1000	13A,13B,66A,66C
Luzanac, Inna	AA0020	66A
Luzanac, Inna	AA0110	66A,42
Lyerla, Trilla R.	KS0050	13,66A,66B,20
Lyman, Kent M.	NC1300	66A,66B,12A
Lyon, Kristine	IL1650	61,66A
Lyon, William	TX3800	66A
Lyras, Panayis	MI1400	66A
Lysenko, Boris	AG0450	66A
Lytle, Cecil W.	CA5050	66A,29,20G
Lyttle, Eric	VA0250	13A,13C,66A
Macan, Ed	CA1280	66A,13A,13B,13C,12A
Macar, Robert	FL2050	29,66A
MaCaskie, Stuart	NM0450	66A
Macchioni, Oscar E.	TX3520	66A,66B,66D,66,14
MacCrae, Cynthia Perry	AL1200	66A,66B,66C,66D
MacDonald, Laurence E.	MI0450	11,12A,66A,66D
MacDonald, Robert M.	FL0800	66A,12A,35A,35E,35F
MacDougall, Elizabeth	CA2840	66A,66D
MacInnes, James	SD0500	66A
Mack, Ashlee	IL1350	66A
Mack, Ellen	MD0650	66A,66C
Mack, Evan	NY3650	66A
Mack, Peter	WA0200	66A,41,13C
Mackey, Lynne A.	VA0300	66A,66B,66C,66D,13
Mackiewicz-Wolfe, Ewa	NY3705	66A
Mackin, Barbara J.	VA0550	66A,13
MacKown, Rosemary	PA3400	66A
MacNaughton, Roger	MI0300	66A,13G,32F
Madsen, Charles A.	VT0100	66A,12,11,66C
Madsen, Jessica	IN0400	66A
Maes, James	MA1100	66A,66G,66C,66D,11
Magrath, Jane	OK1350	66B,66A,66D,66,66C
Mahamuti, Gulimina	OH2000	66A,66D,66C,66B
Mahany, Michael E.	AZ0510	66A
Maher, Michael	VA1350	66A
Maimine, Anna	NY3717	66A,66B,66C
Maisonpierre, Elizabeth	NC2435	11,13,66A,66B,66D
Maisonpierre, Jonathan	NC2435	11,66A
Malefyt, Norma	MI0350	66A
Malek, Eugenie	MA1350	66A
Mallady, Joan	IL1890	66A,66D
Mallinson, Chai Kyou	NY3705	66A,66C
Mallory, Marie	WV0800	66A
Malone, Joy	KY0800	66A,66C
Mamey, Norman	CA1000	66A,10,12A,13,35A
Mancinelli, Judith	IL1750	66A,66C
Mandel, Alan R.	DC0010	66A
Mandle, William Dee	DC0350	13A,13,32B,66A,66D
Manes, Stephen G.	NY4320	66A,66C
Mankerian, Vatche	CA2750	66A
Mann, George	GA1200	66A
Mann, Janet	UT0250	66A
Mann, Jonathan Edward	NY3725	66A
Mann, Sharon	CA2950	66A
Mann, Sharon	CA4150	66A
Manno, Terrie	MN1120	66A,66B,66C,66D
Manoogian, Peggy Lee	SC0620	66A
Manus, Elizabeth A.	PA2550	66A,66C
Manwarren, Matthew C.	SC1200	66A,66B,12,41
Marcel, Linda A.	NJ0020	12B,66A,66D,32,11
March, James J.	IA1100	66A,66B,66C,12A
March, Kathryn Lucas	IA1100	13C,66A,66D,66C
Marchena, Martha	NJ0700	66A,66C
Marchionni, Raymond	OH2300	66A,11,13
Marchukov, Sergey	PA2900	66A,66D,66C,13A
Marciniak, Alex B.	MI0700	13A,37,66A,13,11
Mares, Michelle	AB0150	66A
Margolis, Sanford	OH1700	66A
Margulis, Jura	AR0700	66A
Marin, Luis	PR0115	29,66A,66D
Markaverich, Michael	FL1745	66A
Markiw, Victor R.	CT0700	66,13,12A,66A,11
Markley, Ben D.	WY0200	66A,47
Markovich, Lucia	OH0600	66A
Markow, Andrew	AG0450	66A
Markowski, Victoria	CO0275	66A,66D,41,42
Marks, Adam	WI0250	66A,42
Marks, Brian	TX0300	66A
Marks, Dennis J.	FL1950	62D,66A,47,29A
Marks, Virginia	OH0300	66A
Markun, Mila M.	WV0400	32A,66A,66C,66D
Marlais, Helen	MI0900	66A,66B
Marler, Robert	TN0100	66A,11,12A
Marlow, Laurine	TX2900	11,12A,66G,66A,66H
Maroon, Gayle E.	ME0250	66A
Marosek, Scott	NC1350	12,66A,66B
Marple, Olive	MA0800	13,12A,66A
Marsh, Gordon E.	VA1250	10,66,13,10A,66A
Marsh, Lisa	OR0850	66A
Marshall, Thomas	VA0250	66A,66G,66H,66D
Marta, Larry W.	TX3370	13A,13,66A,66G
Martens, Judith L.	MN1030	66A
Martin, Bradley	NC2600	11,66A
Martin, Brenda	CA3640	66A,66D
Martin, Deborah	NY1800	66A,66B,66D
Martin, Frank	CA5000	66A
Martin, James	IA0400	13,66A,66B,20G
Martin, Joshua	FL0350	13,11,66A,66D
Martin, Julian	NY1900	66A
Martin, Sherrill	NC2440	12A,66A,66B,20G
Martin, Susan Ryan	MO1950	66A
Martina, Harold	TX3000	66A
Martinez, Gabriela	NJ0700	66A,66D,42
Martorella, Philip	RI0200	66A
Martorella, Stephen T.	RI0200	12A,66A,66G,66H
Martucci, Vincent	NY3760	29A,29B,66A,66D,47
Marzullo, Anne Maria	PA1850	66A
Masaki, Megumi	AC0050	13,66A,66C,43,66B
Mascolo-David, Alexandra	MI0400	66A,66B,66D
Masloski, Deborah	WI0250	66A
Mason, Alan	FL0050	11,12,31B,66A,66C
Mason, Rodney	TX0350	13,36,61,66A,66D
Mason, Sonya G.	NY2150	12A,66A,32
Massey, Mark	CA1750	66A
Masters, Barbara	IL0850	66A,66G,66H
Masterson, Daniel J.	KS0150	13,41,66A,66B,42
Mastrogiacomo, Leonard	FL0850	66A,66C
Mastrogiacomo, Norma	FL0850	66A,66C
Mastrogiacomo, Steven J.	MI2200	66A
Mastroianni, Thomas	DC0050	66A,66B
Mastronicola, Michael	CO0400	61,66A,66D
Matesky, Nancy	WA0860	13,66A,66D
Matheson, Jennifer	AF0120	10,66D,66A
Matsumoto, Kanae	CA5030	66A,66C
Matsuo, Jun	SC0450	66A,66D,66B,66C,13
Matsushita, Hidemi	CO0100	66A,11,12,15,13
Matters, Helene	CA2200	66A,13B,13C
Matthews, Ron	PA1150	13,10,12A,63A,66A
Mattock, David M.	PA1850	66A
Matyukov, Saida	AB0200	66A
Matzke, Laura	MN0200	66A,66G,66C,68,31A
Mauchley, Jay	ID0250	66A,66C
Mauchley, Sandra	ID0250	66A,66H,66B,66D
Mauro, Lucy	WV0750	66A,66C,66B
Maxwell, Margaret	MN0150	66A,66C
May, Pam	MN1250	66A,61
Mayer, Anne B.	MN0300	13A,41,66A,12A
Mayer, Steven	CO0900	66A,66B
Mayerovitch, Robert	OH0200	66A
Mayhood, John	VA1550	66A
McAlister, Andrea	OH1700	66A,66C
McAllister, Lesley Ann	TX0300	66A,66B,66D
McBee, Karen L.	TX0125	12A,11,66A,66C,66D
McCabe, Rachelle	OR0700	66A,66B,12A
McCabe, Robin	WA1050	41,66A
McCachren, Renee	NC0350	13,12A,66A,13E,13J
McCall, Gina	TN1000	66A,66C
McCarrey, Scott	HI0050	66A,66B,13E,12A,11
McCarrey, Stacy	HI0050	66A,66C,66D
McCarthy, Cheryl	AF0120	66A,61
McClung-Guillory, Deborah	LA0770	66A,66B,66D
McClure, Michelle	IA0940	66A
McCollim, Danny	WA0950	45,66A,35D,47,35A
McCollough, Teresa	CA4425	13,12A,66A,66B,66C
McCord, Larry	TX0910	11,13B,14C,34B,66A
McCord, Rebecca	VA1400	13,66A,66C
McCorkle, William	VA1850	66G,66H,66A
McCosh, Ruth	AA0050	13A,66A
McCoy, Darcy	IN0350	66A,66C,12A,66B
McCoy, David	AB0100	66A
McCoy, Steve	FL0400	66A,66C
McCracken, H. Jac	LA0300	66A
McCray, Mack	CA4150	66A,41
McCright, Matthew	MN0300	66A,66C,66B
McCullam, Audrey	MD0600	13,32B,32C,66A,66D
McDade, Joanne Estelle	AR0350	61,66A
McDaniel, Jane	MO1950	66A
McDaniel, Susan E.	OR0450	66A
McDonagh, Brian	AG0450	66A
McDonald, Boyd	AG0600	66A
McDonald, Janelle	TN0260	66A
McDonald, Robert	PA0850	66A
McDonald, Robert	NY1900	66A
McDonough, Lauren	NY2450	33,66A

Index by Area of Teaching Interest

Name	Code	Areas
McFadden, James	CA4460	66A
McFadden, Robert	OK1150	12A,66A
McFarland, Kay Dawn	KY1425	11,66A,66C,66D
McFarland, Timothy	MA2010	13,11,66A
McFarlane, Grace	DC0170	66A
McFatter, Larry E.	CA0845	13,10F,10,66A
McFetridge, George	AB0210	66A
McGee, Lynnette	CA1425	66C,66A
McGee, William James	CA3400	13,10F,10,66A,34
McIntire, Donna	WY0050	66A,66G
McIntosh, W. Legare	AL0500	12A,13,66A,66G
McIntyre, Robert John	MO1810	66A
McKamie, David W.	MO1780	13,12A,66A
McKee, Richard	NC0300	12A,66A
McKeever, James I.	WI0835	12A,66A,66C,66B
McKeever, Susan M.	WI0835	66A
McKirdy, Colleen	ND0100	66A,66B,66C
McLauchlin, Charlotte	OR1000	13A,66D,66A,67C,12A
McLaughlin, Michael G.	MA1900	66A,41
McMahon, Michael	AI0150	39,40,66C,61,66A
McNab, Duncan	MN1623	66A
McNair, Jacqueline	GA1260	66A
McNaughton, Karen	AA0020	66A
McReynolds, Timothy	MD1010	66C,66A
McRoberts, Gary	CA1900	32,36,66A,20G
McRoberts, Terry	TN1660	66A,66C,66D,66B
McSpadden, George	AL0350	13,36,49,66A,66G
McSwain, Jenna	WY0130	66A
McVey, Roger D.	WI0845	12A,66A,66B,66C,66D
McWilliams, Kent M.	MN1450	66A,66C,66D,66E
Mdivani, Marina	AI0150	66A,66D
Meacham, Helen M.	PA2000	66A,66C,11,13A
Meade, Karen	MO0500	32,11,66A,66G
Mears, Perry G.	TN0850	66A,66C
Medford, Sue	WI1150	66A
Medley, William R.	IA1140	66A
Mehta, Phiroze	NY1800	66A
Meinert, Anita	IA1950	64C,66A,66C,54
Mele, Anthony	MA2030	66A
Melendez, Jose	PR0115	66A,66C
Melkonyan, Magdalina	MD0700	66A,11
Mellors, Carol	AA0020	66A
Melton, Laura	OH0300	66A
Meltzer, Howard S.	NY0270	11,13,12,66A,63
Melville, Nicola	MN0300	66A,41
Memmott, Jenny	MO0050	66A,66C,33
Mendez, Jose Ramon	NY2750	66A
Meng, Chuiyuan	IN0907	34A,66A,34G
Mengelkoch, Eva	MD0850	66A,66C,66B,66H,66E
Mercier, Richard E.	GA0950	66A,66C,39
Merfeld, Robert	MA1175	66A,66C
Merfeld, Robert	MA0400	66A
Merrifield, Deborah	CA4450	66A
Merriman, Margarita L.	MA0250	13,10,66A
Messing, Scott	MI0150	11,12A,66A,16,13A
Mesterhazy, George	NJ1050	66A
Metelsky, Lynda	AG0450	66A
Meyer, Jeffery David	NY1800	38,66A,60B,43
Meyer, Sandra G.	OK0650	13B,13C,13E,66A,13
Meyers, Angela	CT0300	66A,11
Michael, Louis	IL1500	29,66A,13,11,34A
Michaelian, Patricia	WA1050	41,66A,66B
Michaels, Matthew	MI2200	47,66A,29
Michelin, Nando	MA0260	66A
Michelin, Nando	MA1900	46,66A
Middleton, R. Hugh	NC0500	11,66A,66C
Middleton, Valerie	TN1850	66A
Mielke, Michelle	WA1150	66A,66B
Mikolajcik, Walter	CA4650	36,37,47,63,66A
Mikolajewski, Alice	DC0100	36,66A,66C,66D
Mikowsky, Solomon	IL0550	66A
Mikowsky, Solomon	NY2150	66A
Mikulay, Mark	IL2500	37,66A
Milenkovic, Vladan	MA0510	29,66A,66D
Miles, Tammy	MS0370	13,66A,66C,36
Milgate, Brooks	MA0650	66A
Millar, Tania	AG0070	66A,66D,13C
Miller, Daniel J.	WV0550	66A
Miller, Elaine	NC2000	13C,66A,66C,66B,13A
Miller, John L.	AL1160	66A
Miller, Karla	MN1260	13A,11,36,61,66A
Miller, Kathryn	PA3650	66A,66C,69
Miller, Marie C.	KS0300	32A,32B,66A
Miller, Michelle	OH2290	66A
Miller, Richard	GA0625	66A
Miller, Robin	CA2250	66A
Miller, Tammy	FL1750	66C,66A,66D
Millican, Brady	MA0800	13,11,12A,66A,66C
Milligan, Thomas	TN0250	13,12A,66A,34
Mills, Alan W.	CO0275	37,66A,63A,32E,60B
Mills, Robert	AZ0440	13,66A,66C
Mills, Robert	AZ0100	66A
Milnar, Veronica Edwards	TN1100	66D,66A
Milne, Andy	NY2750	29,47,66A
Milne, Andy	NY2660	66A,47
Milne, Virginia E.	TX2800	66A,66D
Milovanovic, Biljana	NJ0700	66A,66H,13C
Miltenberger, James E.	WV0750	12A,66A,66B,29
Min, Beverly	CA0960	66A
Minasian, Linda	CA5400	11,66D,66A
Mineva, Daniela	CA2250	66A,66B,66C
Minor, Clark	CA0800	66A
Miotke, David	CA3520	66A,66H,66C,13C
Miropolskaya, Mara	NY2400	66A
Misfeldt, Mark	NE0610	66A
Mitchell, Carol	GA0940	13,66A,66G,66C,66D
Mitchell, Charlene	MO0600	32B,66A,66C,66D
Mitchell, Evelyn	MO1830	66A
Mitchell, Roman	NY0640	29,29B,66A,66B
Mitchell, Yvonne	PA2100	66A
Mizrahi, Michael	WI0350	66A,41
Moak, Elizabeth W.	MS0750	66A,66D,66C
Mobley, Jenny	IN0250	66A,66D
Moegle, Mary Steele A.	LA0250	11,66A,66C,66D
Mogerman, Flora	AZ0490	66A,66C
Mohr, Deanne	MN1700	66A,66C,66B,13B,13C
Molberg, Keith	AJ0030	66A,34D,13,66C,13A
Molinari, Kyounghwa	AR0300	66A,66C,66D
Molinaro, Anthony G.	IL1615	66A,29,13A,13B,13D
Moll, Brian	MA1175	66C,66A
Monear, Clifford E.	MI2200	29,66A
Monroe, Michael	MA0950	66A,66C
Monson, Linda Apple	VA0450	13C,66A
Montalbano, James	NY2450	66A,66G
Montalbano, Richard	NY0650	66A
Montalbano, Rick	NY1350	66A
Montalbano, Rick C.	NY4150	66A
Montano, David R.	CO0900	66A,66B,66D,32
Monteiro, Sergio	OK0750	66A
Montgomery, Glen	AA0050	66A,32A
Montgomery, Glen	AA0200	66A
Montiel, Brenda F.	CA3460	12A,55,66A,67B,67C
Moon, Yong Hi	MD0650	66A
Moore, Barbara	VA1550	66A,66G
Moore, Constance J.	AL0300	66A,66B
Moore, Deanna C.	SC0200	66A,66B,12
Moore, Edward	NY3720	20G,36,66A,11,29A
Moore, John	TX2200	11,66A,66C,12A,66D
Moore, Kevin	NY2950	13,66A,66C,66D,10A
Moore, Ruth	NE0300	66A,66B,66C
Moore, Sharon	TN0650	66A
Moorman, Joyce Solomon	NY2100	13,10,11,66A,66D
Moorman-Stahlman, Shelly	PA1900	44,66A,66G,31A,66D
Moran, Daniel	AI0200	66A
Moreau, Barton	ID0050	13,11,66C,66D,66A
Moreland, Irina	CO0150	66A
Moreland, Irina	CO0830	66A,11,12A
Morelli, Jackie	OR1250	66A,66D
Morelock, Donald	MI1900	13,11,12A,66A,66B
Morenus, Carlyn G.	IL1150	66A,66D
Morgan, Ruby N.	SC0750	66A,66B,66D
Morgiewicz, Kerry L.	VA0550	66A,66B,54
Morgulis, Tali	TX3400	66A
Moriarty, Deborah	MI1400	66A
Morin, Carmen	AA0050	32A,66A
Morino, Ayako	NJ0825	66A,42
Morita, Lina	LA0350	13C,41,66A,66C,66D
Moritz, Benjamin	PA2150	66A,66B,66C,66D
Morken, Randy A.	MN1620	66A,66G
Morlan, Emily Jane	IL0730	66A
Moroz, David	AA0050	66A
Moroz, David	AC0100	66A,66B
Morozova, Irina	NY2250	66A
Morris, Gregory	MO0400	11,66A,66B,13
Morris, Kelley	OK1450	66A,66D
Morris, LoriAnn	ID0060	66A
Morrison, Heather	AG0170	41,66A
Morrison, Linda	KY1460	11,32,36,66A,66G
Morrison, Mable R.	DE0050	11,12A,66A,66D
Morrison, Marian	NC2000	66A
Morrow, David E.	GA1450	60,11,36,61,66A
Morrow, Ruth E.	TX1700	66,12A,66A,13D,13E
Morrow, Ruth	TX3370	66A,66B
Morse, Dana	LA0650	66D,66A
Mort, Bari	NY3560	66A
Mortensen, John J.	OH0450	66A,66C,66D
Mortyakova, Julia V.	MS0550	66A,66D,66B,66C,12B
Moschenross, Ian	IL1800	12A,13E,20,66A,66G
Moser, Bruce	NC0400	12,66A,66B,13,66D
Moser, Janet	IL0850	66A,66D,32A,32
Mosher, Ellen	IL1400	66A
Moslak, Judy	MI1260	32,66A
Moss, Elaine	WI0750	66C,66D,66B,66A,32A
Moss-Sanders, Korby L.	MD0450	66A
Motter, Catherine	CO0150	66A,13C
Moulder, Earline	MO0350	66A,66G
Mouledous, Alfred	TX2400	66A
Moulton, Christine F.	PA2150	64A,66A
Moulton, Joyce	ME0200	66A,66B,66C
Mowitz, Ira	NJ0750	10,13A,13B,41,66A
Mowrey, Peter C.	OH0700	10,66A,13,34
Moxley, Bryant	VA0050	13,66A,60A,31A,36
Moxley, Lisa	VA0050	66A,66D,31A,13A,11
Mrozinski, Lavonne	IL1085	66A,66D
Mrozinski, Mark	IL1085	66A,66D
Mueller, Charlotte G.	TX1450	13,11,66A,66D
Mulhall, Karen	NJ0550	36,66A
Mullenax, Gary	WV0550	66A,11,66D
Mulliken, Erin	IL1200	66A,66D
Mullins, Debra	IN0907	66A,34C
Mulroy, John	MA0260	66A
Muniz, Jennifer	MO0100	66A,66D,13C,13E
Munn, Alexandra	AA0020	66A,66C
Munn, Alexandra M.	AA0100	66A,66B,66C
Murakami, Kazuo	AR0850	66A,66C
Murdoch, Kenneth	AA0050	66A
Murphy, Cynthia	NE0300	16,66A,66D,13
Murphy, Glenda	AA0020	66A
Murphy, John	LA0300	66A,66B
Murphy, Steve	IN0907	66A,66B,54
Murphy, Timothy	MD0850	29,66A,66H
Murray, Bruce J.	OH1450	66A
Murray, David	AZ0440	66A
Murray, David	GA0950	66A,66D
Murray, Janice	NC0250	66A,66C,66D,13
Muscarella, Susan	CA5000	66A
Musial, Michael A.	NY3450	13A,11,12A,36,66A
Mustert, Betty	MI0350	66A
Myers, Allen	MO2000	35A,66A,29
Myrick, Barbara	OR0350	13,12A,66A,66D,64A
Nachman, Myrna	NY2550	66A,13A,12A,13C
Nadgir, Arunesh N.	TN1100	66A,66B,66C
Naegele, Elizabeth M.	IL1850	13A,13,66A,66G,11
Naeve, Denise	IA0790	61,66A,13
Nagai, Yoshikazu	CA4150	66A
Nagatani, Chie	CA1700	66A,13,11
Nagel, Louis B.	MI2100	66A
Nagel, Sue S.	MN1120	66A
Nagell, Ann B.	AZ0440	66A
Nagle, Janice	NY3350	66B,66A
Nagy, Daniel	FL1500	66A,66D
Nagy, Linda Jiorle	MA0400	66A,66B
Nahm, Dorothea A.	DC0350	66A,66D
Nakashima, Rieko	FL1300	66A,66D
Nakashita, Sonomi	HI0050	66A
Nakhmanovich, Raisa	AG0650	66A,66C
Nam, Choong-ha	TX3750	66A,66D
Namer, Dina	AG0250	66A,66C,66H
Namminga, Jaime	ND0600	13C,66C,66A
Naoumoff, Emile	IN0900	66A
Nargizyan, Lucy	CA1700	66A,66C
Naruse, Chiharu	ME0150	66A
Narvey, Lois	DC0170	66A,66H
Natenberg, Reena Berger	KS1050	66A,66C,41
Nathan, Alan	MI1400	66A,66C
Navarrete, Jennifer Shaw	CA2450	66A,36
Naylor, Susan E.	GA1700	13B,66A,13C
Nazarenko, Dmitri	MD0550	66A
Nazarenko, John J.	NY3650	47,66A,29
Nazarenko, John	MA2250	66A,41
Neale, Donald	IL0720	66A
NeCastro, Vicki	ME0430	66A
Neese, Wanda	SC0900	66A,66C
Neil, Mary	IL0100	13,66A,66C,66B
Neiwirth, Mark	ID0100	66A
Nel, Anton	TX3510	66A,41

725

Name	Code	Areas
Nelson, Allison	TN0800	66A
Nelson, Jessica L.	AL1250	66A,66G,66D
Nelson, Roger	WA0200	60,36,66A
Nelson, Timothy	IL2300	13,10F,66A,66G
Nemeth, Rudolph	TN1250	66A,11
Nemko, Deborah G.	MA0510	66A,66C,66D,11
Neriki, Reiko S.	IN0900	66A
Neriki, Shigeo	IN0900	66A
Nersesiyan, Pavel	MA0400	66A
Nestor, Gayleen	NE0720	66A
Newbrough, William J.	NY1700	66A,66B,13C,13E,66C
Newcomb, Suzanne	OH2050	66A,66D,66C
Newman, David	WI0100	66A,66D,41
Newman, Patrice	CT0100	66A
Newson, Jeffrey	OK1450	66A,47
Newton, Timothy D.	NY3765	60A,60B,66A,66C
Nez, Catherine Ketty	MA0400	10,66A,10A
Ng, Elsie	AA0050	66A
Ng, Michelle	OH1330	66A
Ng-Au, Marie	AG0070	66A,66D
Nguyen, Quynh	NY0625	11,66A
Nicholas, Scott	MA0850	61,66A
Nichols, Alan	TN0260	66A,13A,11
Nichols, Kenneth	AC0050	66A,13
Nichols, Margaret	IL2750	66A
Nichols, Sandra	IL1612	11,32E,66A
Nichols, William	MO0200	66A,66D
Nicholson, Bonnie	AJ0150	66A,66D
Nickel, Tony	IA1140	66A
Nie, James Ian	WI0100	66A,66C,35D,35C
Niehaus, Christine J.	VA0250	66A,66D
Nielsen, Lois	PA3710	66A
Nieman, Adam	IL0550	66A
Nies, Craig	TN1850	66A,41,66C
Nieto-Dorantes, Arturo	AI0190	66A,42
Ninoshvili, Lauren	NY0200	14,66A
Nishikiori, Fumi	WI1150	66A
Nishimura, Derek Rikio	OH0600	66A
Niskala, Naomi	PA3150	66A,66C,13
Nitsch, Kevin	NY2650	66A,13A,13C
Nitsch, Paul A.	NC2000	41,66A,66H
Nix, Brad K.	KS1250	66B,66A,66C,10F,66D
Noguera, Darwin	IL0275	66A,42
Nolte, Lanita M.	MN1030	66A,66D
Nonken, Marilyn C.	NY2750	12,13,66A
Noone, Elizabeth	MA0150	66A,66D,11,13A,20B
Norberg, Anna H.	OK1450	66A,66C,66D,15
Norden, James C.	WI0150	66A
Norris, Michael B.	PA3250	66A
Northington, David B.	TN1710	66A
Norton, Diane M.	IN1850	66A,66H
Nosikova, Ksenia	IA1550	66A
Noton, Donna	AA0020	66A
Novak, Christina D.	AZ0490	11,13,66A,10A,66D
Nuccio, David A.	IL1250	11,29A,34,54,66A
Nustad, Corinne	MN0600	66A
Oberacker, Betty	CA5060	66A
O'Brien, Andrew C.	AZ0490	66A,66D
O'Brien, John B.	NC0650	66A,66D,66H,55
O'Brien, Linda	WI1150	66A
O'Connor, Peter J.	NY0100	66A,66C
O'Dell, Debra	ID0140	66A,66C,11,66D,12A
Odnoposoff, Berthe Huberman	TX3420	66A
O'Donnell, Patrick	DC0170	66A,66C
O'Donnell, Terry	CA4100	60,66A,69,54
O'Donohue, Deirdre	NY2750	66A
O'Farrell, Elsa	NC2400	66C,66A
O'Farrill, Arturo	NY3785	47,66A
Ogano, Kumi	CT0100	66A
Oge, Derin	NY3785	66A
Oh, Gregory	AG0450	66A
Oh, Jiyoung	DC0170	66A
Oh, June Choi	CA1650	66A
Ohl, Vicki	OH0950	13,66A,66D
Ohls, Ray	WA0600	66A,66
Ohm, Carlotta L.	MN1030	66A
Oka, Betty A.	CA3500	66D,66A
Olander, Jennifer	TN1000	66A,66B,66C
Oldfather, Christopher	NY2150	66A,66H
Olinyk, George Yuri	CA0150	11,66A,13A
Oliphant, Naomi J.	KY1500	66A
Olmstead, R. Neil	MA0260	66A
Olsen, John F.	NM0100	66A,66B,66D
Olson, Anthony	MO0950	11,66A,66G,66D
Olson, Janna	AA0035	66A,66B
Olson, Kevin R.	UT0300	66A,66A,66B
Oltmanns, Caroline Marianne	OH2600	66A
O'Mahoney, Terrence	AF0150	50,65,29,10D,66A
O'Neal, Andrea	IN0500	66A,66D
O'Neal, Harriet	AR0110	66G,66A
Ono, Momoro	NE0160	66A
Opel, Paul E.	VT0200	66A,70
Oppens, Ursula	NY0600	66A
Ordaz, Joseph	CA2975	11,66A,66D,38
Orgel, Paul	VT0450	66A
Orkis, Lambert T.	PA3250	66A,66C
Orland, Michael	CA5000	13A,66D,66A,13C
Orlando, John	CA0400	12A,66A
Orlov, Irena	DC0170	66A
Orlov, Marietta	AG0300	66A
Orlov, Marietta	AG0450	66A
Orr, Gerald	TX1250	13,11,36,37,66A
Orr, Kevin Robert	FL1850	66A,66B,66D,13A,13
Orr, Philip	NJ1000	36,66A
Orta, Michael	FL0700	66A,29A,29B,47
Oshida, Joanna	UT0325	66A
Oshima-Ryan, Yumiko	MN0750	66A,66B,13C
Osmun, Ross	AI0050	13,41,42,66A,66B
Osorio, Jorge Federico	IL0550	66A
Osowski, Kenneth	PA3710	11,66A,66B
Ostbye, Niels J.	NY0750	66A
Osterlund, David	SC0620	60,14,32,66A
Ostrander, Lonnie	AR0400	66A,66C
Ostrovsky, Paul	NY3785	41,66A
Otaki, Michiko	GA0500	41,66A,66C,66D
Otten, Thomas J.	NC2410	66A,66E,66H
Otto, Noemi	VA0750	66A,66D
Otwell, Margaret V.	WI0500	66A,66C,66D,66B,12A
Ouspenskaya, Anna	DC0170	66A
Outland, Joyanne	IN0905	13,66A,66D,66B
Overmoe, Kirk	TX3360	66A,66D
Owen, Jerri Lee	CA0350	66A,66D
Owen, Kenneth L.	WA0750	11,61,36,66A,13
Owen, Linda	OK1330	66A,66D
Owens, Diane	TX1100	66A,66C,66D,32A,32B
Owens, Kathryn Ananda	MN1450	66A,66C,66D,66E,66B
Owings, John	TX3000	66A
Oye, Deanna	AA0200	66A,66C,66,13C,66B
Ozment, Jon	DC0010	66A
Ozment, Jon	MD1010	66A
Pachak-Brooks, Cheryl	NM0100	66B,66D,66A,66C
Paddleford, Nancy	MN1450	66A,66C,66B,66D
Padilla, Anthony	WI0350	66A,66C,41,42
Pagano, Caio	AZ0100	66A
Page, Cleveland	MD1010	66A,66B
Page, Sandra	AA0050	13A,13,66A
Paik, Wanda	MA1600	66A
Pakman, Mark	NJ0800	66A,66C
Palacio, Jon	CA0900	29,46,47,66A
Palmer, David	AG0550	66A,66G,31A,13C,66H
Palmer, David	NC0550	66A,66C
Palmer, David	NC1900	13A,66A,13B,13C,66G
Palmer, Edit	FL1750	13,66A
Palmer, John M.	IL0275	66A,66G
Palmer, Katherine	NC0250	66A
Palmer, Robert	IN0150	66A,66C
Palmier, Darice	IL2970	66A,66D,11,13A,66C
Pan, Huiyu-Penny	CA0830	66A,66D,66B,66C,42
Panayotova, Miroslava I.	FL2000	66A
Pane, Steven	ME0410	12A,66A,12,12B,11
Paney, Andrew S.	MS0700	32B,13A,66A,32A
Pannunzio, Sam	CO0275	66A,53,66D,47
Paolantonio, Ed	NC2410	66A,47
Paolantonio, Ed	NC1600	66A,67F
Paolantonio, Edmund J.	NC0600	66A
Papatheodoroa, Devvora	IL2750	66A
Papatheodorou, Devovora	IL0780	66A,66B
Parcell, John	OH2120	13,66A,11,29,34C
Pardue, Jane	NC1400	36,66A,66D,13A,13B
Parente, Thomas	NJ1350	66A,66D,32I
Parisot, Elizabeth	CT0850	66A,66C
Park, Angela	AI0200	66A
Park, Christine	CA2600	66A,13A,13B,13C,41
Park, Clara	GA0250	66A,11
Park, Janice	CA2390	66A,42
Park, Janice	CA0960	66A
Park, Jenny	CA5355	51,66A,66B
Park, Jin Young	IA1350	66A,66C
Park, Sohyoung	TX2150	66A,66B,66D
Park-Kim, Phoenix	IN1025	66A,66D,66C
Park-Song, Sophia	CO0830	11,13,66A
Parker, Christopher S.	NY3000	47,66A,66D,53,29
Parker, James	AG0450	66A,66C
Parker, Joan	SC0200	66A,66B,66D
Parker, Jon Kimura	TX2150	66A,42
Parker, Laura M.	IL2400	13A,41,42,62A,66A
Parker, Michael	NC0910	66A,66C
Parker, Patricia	VA0450	66A,66C
Parker, Patricia G.	AL0500	11,66A,66D
Parker, Salli	CA2440	66A,13A,11
Parker, Sylvia	VT0450	13,66A,66D,66B
Parkin, Vera L.	MO1950	66A,66C
Parkinson, Del	ID0050	66A,66B
Parr, Andrew	TX2700	66A,66D
Parr, Patricia	AG0450	66A
Parr, Sharon M.	IN1650	11,66A,66D,12A
Parr-Scanlin, Denise	TX3750	66A,66B,66C
Parrini, Fabio	SC0950	66A,66D,11,66C
Parsche, Paula	FL0800	13,66A,66C,11
Parsons, Derek J.	SC0750	13,66A,66B,66D
Parsons, Sean	WV0400	29,46,47,66A
Partain, Gregory L.	KY1350	11,41,66A,66B,12A
Partlow, Mary Rita	TX1900	66A,66D
Pasbrig, David	PA3250	66A
Paskert, IHM, Joan	PA2200	66A
Paskova, Lyubov	MD0800	66A,66D
Pasternack, Benjamin	MD0650	66A
Pastorello, Cristian	IL0150	66A,66B,66C,11,13
Patcheva, Ralitza	DC0050	66A
Patcheva, Ralitza	DC0170	66A,42
Paterson, Kim	NY1400	66A,66H
Patman, Rebecca	NM0200	11,66A
Patterson, Anthony	MI0150	66A,66C
Patterson, Donald L.	WI0803	66A,66B,66D,66H
Patterson, Michael R.	IA1350	12A,32B,66A,13,10
Patton, Jeb	NY1275	10,13B,29B,29C,66A
Paul, Arryl S.	TX3520	66A
Paul, Pamela Mia	TX3420	66A
Paulk, Kayla Liechty	NM0100	66A,66C,66B,66D
Paulsen, Donna	MN1450	66A
Pauly, Erica	SC0650	66A
Pavlovska, Jana	IL0550	66A
Pavlovskaia, Natalia	AF0120	66A
Pawlicki, Michael	CA2700	11,66A,66D
Payne, Benjamin	FL0670	11,34,13,66A,66D
Payne, Bryon	FL1600	61,62,66A
Pearsall, Tom	GA0950	66A,66B,66D
Pease, Janey L.	NC0850	66A,66G
Pedde, David	MN1250	66A,10B,14C,31A
Pedersen, Gary	MI0600	66A,66B,66C,66D,11
Pedroza, Ricardo	PR0125	13,60,36,66A,66D
Peery Fox, Irene	UT0050	66A
Peh, Alex L.	DC0170	66A
Pelfrey, Patricia	OH1200	66A,66C
Pelfrey, Patricia	OH1600	66A
Pellman, Colleen	NY1350	66A,66C
Pender, Charles	TN1380	13,11,61,66A,60
Penick, Amanda	AL1170	66A
Penneys, Rebecca	NY1100	66A
Pennington, Lynn	AR0950	32,66A,66D
Pepetone, Gregory	GA0850	12A,32,66A,66B,66D
Pepin, Natalie	AI0200	66A
Perez, Samuel	PR0150	11,66A
Peris, Malinee	DC0100	41,66A,51
Perkey, Christine	TN1400	13B,66A,13H
Perkins, Jerry	TN1100	66A,41
Perkyns, Jane E.	TX3150	66A,13,12A,66,66C
Perla, James 'Jack'	CA4425	10A,10B,66A
Permenter, Calvin	MO2000	66A,66B,66C
Perrillo, Ron J.	IL0750	46,66A
Perry, Antoinette	CA5300	66A
Perry, Eileen	AZ0480	66A,13C,66D
Perry, John	CA1075	66A,42
Perry, John	AG0300	66A
Perry, John	CA5300	66A
Perry, Skip	FL0500	66A
Perry, Talya	MO1110	61,66A
Petchersky, Alma	AG0450	66A
Peters, Lorna G.	CA0840	66A,66H,13
Petersen, Lynn	MT0075	10A,11,13A,66A,47
Peterson, Jay	IL1650	13,12A,14,66A,66G
Peterson, Jeffry F.	WI0825	66A,66C,66D
Peterson, Larry	IL0100	66A,66C,11
Peterson, Laura	NY3475	11,12A,66A,20
Peterson, Mark	NC0100	36,38,66A,66A
Peterson, Mark	CA1520	66C,66A

Name	Code	Areas
Peterson, Pamela	FL0400	66A,66D
Peterson, Wayne T.	CA4200	13,10F,10,12A,66A
Petit, Annie	PA2550	66A
Petit, Annie	PA0850	66A
Petitto, Jackie	CA2600	66A
Petitto, Jacqueline	CA3500	66A
Petrella, Diane Helfers	MO1810	66A,66B,66D
Petrowska-Quilico, Christina	AG0650	13A,41,66A,66B
Petteys, Leslie	WV0400	66,66A,66B,66C,12
Petty, Shuko Watanabe	VA1850	66A,66C,13C
Pettyjohn, Emma	GA0700	66A,66B,66C,66G,66D
Phang, May	IN0350	66A,66B
Phemister, William	IL3550	66A
Philcox, Steven	AG0450	66A
Philipsen, Michael D.	IA0750	13,11,36,61,66A
Phillabaum, Katja	WI0825	66A,66C
Phillips, Keith	ID0060	66A
Phillips, Nicholas S.	WI0803	66A,66D
Phipps, Juanita K.	MI1700	66A
Pickens, Willie	IL2200	66A,29
Pickerill, Linda	KY0100	66A,66C
Pickering, David C.	KS0650	66A,66G,66H,13,12A
Pickett, Barbara	WA0050	66C,66D,66A
Pickett, Glen	CA0450	10F,66A,66C
Pickett, John	WA0050	13,11,12A,66A,66B
Pierce, Joshua	NY5000	66A
Pierce, Joshua	NY2400	66A
Pierpoint, Paula	FL0950	61,66A,66D
Piersall, Janie	IL1612	32A,32B,66A
Pifer, Joshua K.	AL0200	66A,66C,66D,13C
Piitz, Lori E.	VA0600	66A
Pilc, Jean-Michel	NY2750	29,66A,47
Pineda, Kris	IL2910	66A,66C,41
Pinkas, Sally	NH0100	66A,67C
Pinkston, Joan	SC0200	13,66A,34
Piper, Patrick	IN0400	66A,53
Pipho, Robert S.	MI2200	47,29,66A
Pirtle, R. Leigh	IA1390	66A,66G,66B,66C
Pirzadeh, Maneli	AI0200	66A
Pitasi, Dennis	FL0200	66A
Pitasi, Dennis	FL1310	66A
Pitts, Ruth	TX1600	13,12A,66A
Pla, Maria	OH0650	66A,66D
Plash, Duane	AL1195	13,10,66A,40
Platt, Rosemary D.	OH1850	66A
Plaunt, Tom	AI0150	66A
Plautz, Gigi	WI0922	66A
Plyler, Wendy	PA0100	66A
Podgurski, Barbara	NY5000	66A,11
Poklewski, Annamarie	CA1550	13,66A
Polcari, Jeanne	NH0300	66A,66B,10A
Poletaev, Ilya	AI0150	66A
Polevoi, Randy M.	CA1900	66A,66D
Polifka, Joyce E.	CO0200	66A
Polischuk, Derek Kealii	MI1400	66A,66B,66D,38,29
Polk, Joanne	NY2150	41,66A
Pollack, Daniel	CA5300	66A
Polonsky, Anna	NY4450	66A
Polyakov, Alina	MA0950	66A
Pompa-Baldi, Antonio	OH0600	66A
Ponce, Walter	CA5030	66A,66B
Ponthus, Marc	NY2250	66A
Pontremoli, Anita	OH0600	66C,66A
Pope, David	OH0300	66A
Pope, Jerry	KS0590	13,66A,11
Popoff-Parks, Linette A.	MI1260	13,66A,66B,66C
Poquette, Linda	IL2300	66A
Portenko, Irena	NY5000	66A
Porter, Randy	OR0250	29,66A
Porter, Randy	OR0850	66A,29
Porter, Randy	OR0400	66A
Porterfield-Pyatt, Chaumonde	CA1290	11,66A,66G,66D
Pos, Margie	WA0200	29,62D,66A,13
Posey, Ann	MO2000	66A,66H
Posnak, Paul	FL1900	41,66A,66H,66C
Potter Faile, Erin	PA1550	66A,33
Potter, Joe	MO2050	66A,66G,35H,54,35E
Potter, Lou Ann	PA0350	66A
Potts, Lana	TX2710	66A
Poulsen, James	IA1350	13,66A,66C,10
Powell, Jason	IN0300	20F,20H,31A,66A,66G
Powell, Philip M.	SC0420	66A,66B,66C,66D
Powell, William	MD0500	66A
Powers, Kathleen	NJ0760	66A
Powrie, Barbara	NY4460	66A
Pracht, Carole	KS0980	66A,66G,66C
Pratt, Scott	CA2450	66A
Prebys, Marylee A.	ND0400	66A,66B,12A
Premezzi, Renato	WI0100	66A,41
Presley, Greg	WA0400	66A
Pressler, Menahem	IN0900	66A
Pressnell, Paula B.	NC0400	66C,66A,66D
Preston, Brian	NY2650	66A,66
Pretzel, Mark W.	KS0570	66A
Price, Emmett G.	MA1450	14,29,66A,47
Price, Jeffrey L.	UT0250	66A
Price, Ruth	MO1950	66A
Price, Scott	SC1110	66A,66B,66D
Price, William Roger	OK1450	10A,41,66A,10F
Pridgen, Elizabeth A.	GA1300	66A,66C
Pridonoff, Elizabeth A.	OH2200	66A
Pridonoff, Eugene A.	OH2200	66A
Prigge, Sarah	MN0600	66A
Prince, Penny	NY0635	32A,66A,66B,66C
Prodan, Angelica	CA5150	66A
Prokop, Rick	NY5000	66A
Prossaird, Didier	MD0550	66A,20
Protsman, Harold S.	VA1000	66A,66C,41
Proulx, John	CA0815	66A
Pryor, Ryan	CA0815	66A
Puckett, Lauren J.	TX0900	66A,66B
Puckett, Mark	TX0900	66A
Puig, Marta	VA1600	66A
Puig, Martha	VA1500	66A,66D
Pulliam, Christine	DC0170	66A
Pullman, Marlene	AJ0030	13A,66A,66B,66D
Purnell, Tom F.	IL0650	11,66A
Puschendorf, Gunther F.	CA1100	13A,36,38,66A
Pyle, Jane	FL1300	13,11,12A,66A,66B
Pyle, Pamela Viktoria	NM0450	66A,66C
Pyle, Sally	FL1300	66A
Qualls, Todd	GA0750	66A
Quist, Pamela	CA4425	13,10,66A,12
Quong, Meijane	AB0060	66A,66D,13C
Raab-Pontecorvo, Luiza	NY1600	63B,42,66A,66C
Rachford, Natalia	IN0350	66A
Rachmanov, Dmitry	CA0835	66A
Radell, Judith M.	PA1600	13,66A,66D,66C
Radosavljevich, Olga	OH0600	66A
Radoslavov, Ilia G.	MO1780	66C,66A,66D,66B
Rae, Wendy	AA0050	13,32A,66A
Raekallio, Matti	NY1900	66A
Rager, Josh	AI0150	29,66A
Ragoini, Ernest	MD0100	13,12A,66A,12C
Raimo, John B.	TX3525	11,12A,66A,66C,66D
Raines, Jean	NC1900	12A,11,66A,32
Raley, Lynn	MS0385	66A,12A,29
Ralston, Jeananne	NY1250	66A
Ralston, Jeananne C.	NY1550	66A
Rambeau, Deborah	WA0700	66A,66B,66C,66D
Ramos, Rene	CA2420	13A,13,12A,12,66A
Ramsay, James Ross	MA0260	66A
Ramsey, Cynthia B.	VA0750	66A,12A,66C,13E,42
Ramsey, David	WI0847	66A
Ramsey, Sarah E.	OH0850	66A
Randall, Jean	MI1830	66A,13D,13E,13B
Randolph, Margaret Ann	TN0300	66A,66C
Ranieri, Anthony	IL1400	66A
Ransom, Keiko	GA0750	66A
Ransom, McCoy	LA0100	13,66A,66G,66C
Ransom, William	GA0750	66A
Rappe, Terri	WA1200	66C,66D,66A
Raps, Gena	NY2250	41,66A
Rath, Edward	IL3300	66A,41
Ratliff, Richard J.	IN1650	13,66A,12D
Ratz, Arlene	AZ0200	66A,66D
Ravitskaya, Irena	KS0350	66A,66B,66C,66D,66G
Ray, Brian	TN1200	66A
Ray, Robert	MO1830	20G,36,66A
Razaq, Janice L.	IL1085	66A,66B,66D
Rea, Edward	SC0200	13,66A,66G,66F
Rea, Judith	SC0200	13,66A
Reagan, Ann B.	CO0750	11,12A,12,41,66A
Reagan, Jama	TN1850	66A,32A
Reager, John	CA2450	36,66A,61,12A
Ream, Duane	SC0200	66A,66D,34
Rearick, Loretta A.	OH1200	66A
Reber, Richard	KS1350	66A
Rebozo, Elizabeth	AA0050	66A
Redding, Eric	AK0050	11,36,66A,70,53
Reddish, Debbie	CA0200	13A,66A
Reed, Jerome A.	TN0930	10A,66A,66B,66C,43
Reed, John Perry	SC0050	66A,66D
Reese, Kirk	PA2300	29,66A
Regehr, Leanne	AA0035	66A,66C
Rehwoldt, Lisa	MD0100	13,12A,66A
Reighard, Mark	OK1200	13A,13,66A,11
Reiman, Erika	AG0050	66A
Reimer, Joyce L.	NE0250	44,66A,66G
Reinhuber, Joachim	TX2960	66A,66D,66C
Reitz, Christina L.	NC2600	12,66A,12A
Reitz, John	OH1200	66A
Reitz, Margaret A.	NY3705	66C,66A
Remek, Robert	FL1310	66A
Renak, Amy	MA0280	66A
Rendleman, Ruth	NJ0800	13,66A,66B
Renfroe, Anita B.	PA2350	66A,66D
Renfrow, Kenon	SC0200	66A,66B,66D,34
Renner, David	TX3510	66A
Renshaw, Kenneth	MO1710	66A,66D
Restivo, Dave	AG0450	66A,29
Reubart, G. Dale	AB0100	66A
Reuter, Ted A.	IA1800	12A,66A
Reuter-Riddle, Pat	IA1800	13A,66A
Reyes, Reynaldo	MD0850	66A,66C,66B
Reynerson, Rodney T.	NC0050	66A,66C,66D,11,41
Reynolds, Robert	KY0860	13A,13,11,66A,20G
Reynolds, Sonya Szabo	OH2550	66A,66D
Rhein, Robert	IN0200	10A,66A,11,12A,13
Rhine, Deborah	TX3350	66A
Rhodebeck, Jacob	NY0270	66A,66C,11,13
Rhoden, Lori E.	IN0150	66A,66B,66D
Rhodes, Beverly	WA1350	66A,66C
Ricci-Rogel, Susan	MD0700	11,66A,66C
Ricciardone, Michael	NY2750	36,54,66A
Rice, Karen	NC2700	66A,66C,66D
Rice, Lorraine	AZ0440	66A
Rice-Young, Lynn	TN1100	66A,66B,66C
Rich, Harvey	UT0050	66A
Rich, Ruth Anne	MO1810	66A
Richards, Doris	MI2200	66A,66D
Richardson, Holly	MI0450	11,66A
Richardson, Lucille K.	NY3725	66A
Richardson, Robert	AC0050	66A
Richey, Craig	CA0825	66A,66C,66B
Richmond, Joshua	PA3250	29,66A
Richmond, Kevin D.	TN1680	66A,66D,66B
Richter, Leonard	WA1100	66A,66B,13A,13B
Rickey, Euni	IN1025	66A,66D,66B,66C
Rickman, Michael	FL1750	66A,12A,66B,66D
Ridges, Lameriel R.	SC1050	13,66A,66C
Ridgway, Meredith K.	TX3410	66A,66D
Ridgway, Zachary M.	TX3410	66A
Riepe, Heidi	IA0900	66A
Rieppel, Daniel	MN1500	66A,11,38,66C,12
Rieth, Dale	FL0950	13,36,47,61,66A
Riffel, Patricia	CA1425	66A,66C
Rigler, Ann Marie	MO2000	66A,66G,31A,12A,12C
Riley, Carole	PA1050	66A,66D
Riley, David M.	OR1050	66C,66A,42
Riley, Mary Lee	IN1750	66A
Riley, Raymond G.	MI0150	66A,13,34,34H
Ringold, Allison	OH0250	66A
Rink, Shelley	CA0150	66A
Rinzler, Paul	CA0600	13,10,47,66A,29
Riske, Barbara	NV0050	66A,66D
Ritt, Morey	NY0642	66A
Ritt, Morey	NY0600	66A
Rittenhouse, Virginia Gene	MD0150	38,62A,66A,32I
Riva-Palacio, Nancy	NC1300	66A
Rivadeneira, Barbara	IA0700	66A
Rivera, Felix	PR0150	11,66A,66D
Rivera-Guzman, Felix	PR0115	66A
Rivers, Cynthia	GA1100	66A,66G,66C,31A,36
Rivers, James	KS1400	11,66A,66C,10
Rivkin, Evgeny	GA2100	41,66A
Rizzer, Gerald	IL2750	66A,13,10
Ro, Betty	AF0120	66A
Roach, Hildred E.	DC0350	20G,66A,66B,66C,66D
Roadfeldt-O'Riordan, Holly K.	PA1850	66A,12A,66C
Robbins, Cheryl	IL0420	61,66A
Roberson, Richard	PA2300	66A,10A,10B
Roberts, Jean	TX2700	66A,13B,13C
Roberts, John Noel	TX2700	66A
Roberts, Lois	CA1750	66A,66G
Roberts, Marcus	FL0850	29,66A

Name	Code	Areas
Roberts, Mary W.	FL0600	66A,66B,66C,66D
Roberts, Melissa	MO1550	66A,66D
Roberts, Ron A.	AL1160	66A,66B
Robertson, Christina N.	AZ0510	66A
Robertson, Jon	FL1125	60B,38,66A
Robertson, Kaestner	MA0250	66A,13,36,66B,66C
Robertson, Masson	IN0905	13,66A,66B,66C
Robertson, Roki	AR0250	66A
Robey, Matthew E.	NY2500	66A,66C,66D,11,32E
Robins, Linda	TX2570	32B,36,66A,66B
Robinson, Florence	FL0600	12A,66A,66,66D
Robinson, Thomas S.	NH0250	66A,46,47,29
Rocchio, Karen	MO0700	66A
Rodde, Kathleen	IA0850	36,66A,66C
Rodewald, Marion	CA2100	66A,32B
Rodgers, Christopher	PA0050	66A,66G,66G
Rodgers, Kenneth	KS0500	66G,66A,66D,66C,11
Rodgers, Reginald G.	IN0100	66A,66B,66D
Rodgers, Stacy D.	MS0700	66A,66B,66C
Roditeleva-Wibe, Maria I.	WA0050	14A,12A,20F,66A,66G
Rodriguez, Ariana	AA0050	66A
Rodriguez, Carlos Cesar	DC0170	66A
Rodriguez, Elvin	CA2420	11,66A,35G,35C
Rodriguez, Linda M.	FL2050	12A,66A
Rodriguez, Santiago	FL1900	66A
Roe, Gail	TX2310	66A,11,66C
Roed, Tom	MO0750	13,11,66A
Roederer, Silvia	MI2250	66A,66B,66C,66D
Rogers, Barbara J.	MN1280	66A,66D,66C
Rogers, Sean	ID0070	36,39,60,66A,66G
Rogizhyna, Maryna	NY5000	66A,11
Rogosin, David	AE0050	66A,12A,66C
Rohr, Grant	CA0815	66A,61,66C
Roitman, Tatiana	AR0750	66A,66D,13
Roitstein, David	CA0510	13C,47,29,66A
Roman, Ed S.	AZ0510	61,66A
Roman, Robert	NY3765	29,66A,20D,35A,46
Romanul, Lisa K.	MA2150	66A
Romero, Gustavo	TX3420	66A,42
Roney, John	AI0150	29,66A
Ronning, Debra D.	PA1250	66A,66B,66D
Rosado, Sara	MD0550	66A,13A
Rose, Jerome	NY2250	66A
Roseman, Molly	KY0900	66A,66D
Roseman, Molly J.	WI0850	66,66A,66B,66D,66C
Rosen, Josh	MA0260	66A
Rosen, Robert	AA0020	66A
Rosenbaum, Victor	MA1400	41,66A
Rosenbaum, Victor	NY2250	66A
Rosenboom, David	CA0510	10,43,66A
Rosenfeld, Steven	NY0650	66A
Rosenkranz, Thomas H.	OH0300	66A
Rosfeld, Marilyn	OK1200	66A
Rosner, Arnold	NY2050	13A,13,11,14,66A
Ross, Nicholas Piers	VA1400	13,66A,66C,12
Rossi, Marc W.	MA0260	66A
Rossman, Pamela	TX2650	66A,66D
Rotella, Gloria	NJ0760	32,66A,66D
Roth, David	PA2450	66A,29
Roth, Nicholas	IA0550	66A,66B,66C,66
Rottmayer, Chris A.	FL2000	66A
Routenberg, Scott	IN0150	29,66A
Roux, Robert	TX2150	66A
Rovkah, Pauline	PA0600	66A,41
Rowe, Arthur	AB0150	66A
Rowe, Ellen H.	MI2100	47,29,66A
Rowe, Paul	OK0300	66A,11,66D,66G
Rowley, Rick E.	TX3510	66A,66C
Rownd, Gary	IL1850	13A,66A,66D,11
Roye, Nedra	OK0500	66A,66D
Royle, Frances	AF0120	13A,66A
Rozman, Jure	FL0200	66A,13,41
Rubin, Justin H.	MN1600	13,34,66G,10,66A
Rubrecht, Karl	LA0100	66A
Ruby, Meg	MA2030	41,42,47,66A
Ruckman, Robert	OH2120	66A,66D
Rudell, Alan M.	SC1000	66A,66C
Ruffin, W. Floyd	GA1450	66A,11
Ruiz, Otmaro	CA5300	66A,10
Ruiz, Sergio	TX2250	66A,66B
Ruiz-Bernal, Gabriel	DC0170	66A
Rule, Charles	TN0700	11,47,66A,29,35
Rule, Tom	GA1260	66A,11
Runge, Stephen M.	AE0050	66A,66B,66C
Runion, Julie	NY3350	66A,66C
Runnels, Brent	GA1550	66A,11,29,47,13A
Runner, David C.	TN1150	13,10F,66A,66G,10A
Runyon, Renee	MI2000	66A,66C
Ruocco, Phyllis	AR0550	13A,13,11,66A,10F
Ruple, Eric K.	VA0600	66A
Rus-Edery, Ilonka Livia	TX2250	66A,66C
Russell, Bruce	CA0859	66A,66D
Russell, Cynthia	TX0250	61,66A,66G,32B,32C
Russell, Joshua D.	IL1150	66A
Russell, Mary Lou	TX2260	11,66A,66C,66D,29
Rust, Roberta	FL1125	42,66A
Rutman, Neil C.	AR0850	66A,66B
Rutman, Paul	CT0650	66A
Rutter, Bronwen	FL1300	66A,66H,66C
Ryabinin, Lev	GA0850	66C,66A
Ryan, Donald	OK0850	66A
Rybak, Alice	CO0900	66A,66C
Ryder, Raymond T.	AZ0480	66A,13A,66D
Ryoo, Soyoung	DC0170	66A
Sabatella, Marc	CO0650	66A,47
Sabre, Alejandro	CA3000	13,66A
Sacco, Kathy	PA0500	66A
Sachs, Daniel	OH0680	66A,66D
Sachs, Stephen W.	MS0100	66A,66C,38
Sadlier, Lelia	VA0150	66D,66A
Sage, Robert	CA0250	66A,12A
Sagripanti, Andrea	DC0170	66A
Sakamoto, Haruyo	DC0170	66A
Salanki, Hedi	FL2100	13C,13E,66A,66H,41
Salas, Jacqueline M.	CA0835	66A,66D
Sale, Craig	IL0730	66A,66B,66D,66C
Salido, Caroline	OH2050	66A,66D
Salmirs, Michael	NY3705	66A
Salmon, John C.	NC2430	66A,66C,29A
Saltzman, Peter	IL2750	66A
Salwen, Barry	NC2440	11,66A,66B,66D
Samaan, Sherilyn	TN1350	32B,11,66A
Sammarco, Donna	LA0450	66A,66B,66C
Samolesky, Jeremy	AL0200	66A,66D,13C
Sanchez, Cynthia	TX2260	36,61,64A,66A
Sanchez, Luis	TX2955	66A,66C,66B
Sanchez, Paul	IL3550	66A
Sanders, Alice	AR0730	66A,66C,66B
Sanders, Donald C.	AL0800	12A,66A
Sandomirsky, Gregory	MO1000	51,66A
Sandor, Alexander	WI0860	66A,66D
Santana, Jose Ramos	DC0050	66A
Santiago, Michelle	AI0200	66A
Santinelli, Silvana	CO0250	66A
Santisi, Ray	MA0260	66A
Santos-Neto, Jovino	WA0200	47,66A,66D
Sarakatsannis, Leonidas N.	FL1745	66A
Sartori, Nicolo A.	PA1600	66A,66F
Satava, Joseph F.	MD0475	66A,66D
Satre, Paul J.	IL3150	36,66A,66G,60,13
Satterlee, Robert S.	OH0300	66A
Sauer, Thomas	NY2250	66A
Saul, Walter B.	CA1860	10A,66A,13,20,10F
Saulnier, Jean	AI0200	66A
Saunders, Ruth	MO1250	66A,66H
Savage, Dylan C.	NC2420	66A,66B,66C
Savage, Jeffrey R.	WA1150	66A,66B,66C,13C
Savage, John	WA0900	66A,70
Savage, Karen Hsiao	WA1150	66A,66C
Savaria, Suzanne	OR0850	66A
Savko, Carolyn	TX3500	66D,66A
Savvidou, Paola	MO1800	66A,66B
Sawyer, Lisa Lee	MN0600	13,61,66A
Sbarboro, Kathlyn	IL1085	66A,66D
Scafidi, Cathy	PA1650	66A
Scagarella, Susan	CA3850	70,66A
Scanlan, Mary	MI0850	66A,66H,66C,66D,20F
Scarambone, Bernardo	KY0550	66A,66D,66B,66,66C
Schachter, Daniela	MA0260	66A,61
Schaffer, Amanda	NC0300	66A
Scharfstein, Tanya	NY2400	66A
Schechter, Dorothy E.	CA0550	12A,66A,66B,66D
Scheck, Carey	IN1750	66A
Schempf, Ruthanne	NY3760	66A,66D,12A,13B
Schene, Daniel	MO1950	66A,42
Schenk, Kathryn E.	MN0610	11,66A,66H
Schenly, Paul	OH0600	66A
Schepkin, Sergey	MA0400	66A
Schepkin, Sergey	PA0550	66A
Scherer, Paul	IL1520	29B,66A
Schilling, Arnie	IA0800	66A,66D
Schilperoort, Anne	WA1400	66A
Schlabach, Eugene	IL3200	11,12A,66A
Schlabaugh, Karen Bauman	KS0200	13,66A,66B,66C,12A
Schlatter, Carolyn	FL1430	66A,13,11
Schlosser, Milton	AA0110	66A,66B
Schmeling, Paul	MA0260	66A
Schmid, Ilo	OR1010	66A,66G
Schmid, Karen	NY0400	66A
Schmidt, Carol	MO1950	66A,29
Schmidt, Carsten	NY3560	13,11,12A,41,66A
Schmidt, Charles	IL0100	11,66A,13
Schmidt, James	NC0450	66A,29A,66D,47,11
Schmidt, Russell	UT0250	66A,29,47
Schmidt, Timothy R.	IA1750	13B,31A,66A,66H
Schmitz, Michael	CA3270	66A,12A,13,20,41
Schneider, Eugene	AA0040	66A,66C
Schneller, Roland	TN1850	66A,66C
Schober, Nathan	NY0642	13,10A,66A,10
Schoenhals, Joel	MI0600	12A,66A
Schoepflin, Judith	WA1350	66A,66D,16,66B
Schoessler, Tim	WY0130	66A,66D,13,12A
Schonthal, Ruth	NY2400	13,10,66A
Schorr, Timothy B.	WI1100	66A,12A,13E,66C
Schott, Kimberly	ND0500	66A,66D
Schrankler, Helene	WI0804	66A
Schreiner, Gregory	CA0859	66A,66D
Schrempel, Martha	PA2450	66A,66C,66B
Schub, Andre-Michel	NY2150	66A
Schubkegel, Joyce C.	MN1030	66G,66A
Schultz, Blaine	KS0100	66A
Schultz, Margaret	NE0460	13C,66A,66C,11,32B
Schultz, Thomas J.	CA4900	66A
Schulze, Sean	OH0600	66A,66B
Schuman, Susan	NY3717	66A,66C
Schuttenberg, Emily Amanda	NC0350	66A,66C,66D
Schwartz, Robert	CA2950	66A,41,42
Scime, Gregory	NJ1160	66A
Scolnik, Nina	CA5020	66A
Scott Goode, Mary	TX2850	66A,11
Scott Hoyt, Janet	AA0100	66A,66B,42
Scott, Frank	AZ0450	66A,66B
Scott, Sandra C.	GA1600	36,40,60A,32D,66A
Scott, Tara	AF0120	66A
Scott, Tatiana	CA0150	66A,13
Seales, Marc	WA1050	66A,29
Sears, E. Ann	MA2150	12A,66A,29A,20G
Sebba, Rosangela Yazbec	MS0500	66A
Segger, Joachim	AA0035	13,13J,66A,66B,43
Segrest, Linda H.	MS0550	13A,13B,66A,66D,13C
Seiler, Richard D.	LA0770	66A,66C,13A,13D
Sekino, Keiko	NC0650	66A,66C
Seldon, Vicki A.	TX2100	11,12A,66A,66C
Selesky, Evelyn C.	NY2450	33,66A
Self, Stephen	MN0250	12A,66A,66G
Selleck, Maria	FL1310	66A
Seo, Seungah	CA5550	66A
Serebryany, Vadim	AL0450	66A,12A,13B
Serkin, Peter	NY0150	66A
Serkin, Robert	MA1175	66A
Serrin, Bret E.	TX3420	66A
Seskir, Sezi	PA0350	12A,13A,66A,66C
Settoon, Donna	LA0080	66A,66D
Severtson, David	WI0808	66A,13,66D,12A,66C
Sevilla, Jean-Paul	AG0400	66A,42
Sexton, Bobby	CA1000	66A
Seybert, John M.	FL1740	60,66A,32,64E,12
Seymore, Sam	KS0215	66A
Shadinger, Richard C.	TN0100	12A,55,66A,31A,69
Shadle, Charles	MA1200	66A
Shafer, Timothy P.	PA2750	66A,66B
Shaffer-Gottschalk, David D.	VA1750	13,66A,66C
Shagdaron, Bair	NC0050	66A,66C,66D
Shandro, Constantine	AA0040	66A,66C
Shank, Nadine E.	MA2000	66A,66C,66D
Shannon, Adrienne	AG0250	66A,66C
Shannon, Nanette	CO0650	66A,41,66D
Shannon, Robert	OH1700	66A
Shapiro, Daniel	OH0600	66A
Shapiro, Lois	MA2050	66A
Shapiro, Marc	CA2950	66A
Shapovalov, Dimitri	WI0250	12A,66D,36,66A
Sharon, Boaz	MA0400	66A
Sharp, Michael D.	LA0400	66A,66B,31A,34,10A
Sharpe, Kevin	FL1850	66A,66C
Sharples, Pamela	NJ0750	13C,36,66A,66C

Index by Area of Teaching Interest

Name	Code	Areas
Shaw, Karen	IN0900	66A
Shaw, Paul	MN1623	66A
Shawn, Allen	VT0050	13,10,66A
Shedd, Kylie	IN1350	66A
Sheeks, Randy	TN0850	66A,31A
Sheie, Sigrid	CA5353	66A
Shelby, Karla	OK1500	10D,13A,60A,66A,36
Sheldon, Vanessa R.	CA3265	12,13C,13A,62E,66A
Shellito, Kelli	PA0100	66A,66D
Shemaria, Rich	NY2660	60,10,66A
Shemaria, Rich S.	NY2750	46,47,66A,29
Shepherd, Dean	CA2390	66A,66C
Sheppard, Craig D.	WA1050	66A
Sher, Daniel	CO0800	66A
Sherman, Russell	MA1400	66A
Shibatani, Naomi	TX1520	66A,66D,11
Shihor, Ory	CA1075	66,66A,42
Shilansky, Mark G.	NH0350	66A
Shim, Jeong-Ja	NY3785	66A,66C
Shimizu, Kumiko	MS0250	66C,66A
Shimpo, Ryoji	OH2150	66A,11
Shimron, Omri D.	NC0750	13,66A,66D
Shin, Aera	NJ0825	66A,42
Shin, Jung-Won	MS0250	66A,66D,66B,66C,13B
Shin, MinKyoo	IL3100	13C,66A,66D,66G
Shinn, Ronald R.	AL0800	66A,66C,13B
Shipley, John	NV0150	66A,34,14C
Shipley, Linda P.	TN0580	13,66A,66G
Shirley, Alicia	TX3400	66A
Shlyam, Eda Mazo	MA1175	66A
Shockey, Mark	PA0650	66A
Shockley, Rebecca P.	MN1623	66A,66B,66D
Shofner-Emrich, Terree	IL2100	66A,39,66B,66C,66D
Shook, Timothy	KS1200	66A,66B,66D,13
Shore, Melanie	UT0250	66A
Shpachenko, Nadia	CA0630	66A,66C,66B,66,34D
Shrader, Steven	TN1800	11,12A,12,66A,38
Shtarkman, Alexander	MD0650	66A
Shteinberg, Dmitri	NC1650	66A
Shu, Peter	MN1250	66A,47
Shumway, Jeffrey	UT0050	66A,66B,66C
Siciliano, Mary	MI1750	66A,66C,66B
Sick, Stella B.	MN0800	66A
Sicsic, Henri-Paul	AG0450	66A
Sicsic, Nancy	AG0450	66A
Siek, Stephen	OH2450	12A,66A,66B,20G
Sifferman, James P.	MO1500	11,66A,66D
Sifford, Jason	IA1550	66B,66D,66,29B,66A
Sifter, Suzanna	MA0260	66A
Sigmon, Susan	GA0900	66A
Sigmon, Susan McEwen	GA0940	13,36,66A,66G,40
Siki, Bela	WA1050	66A
Siler, Sandra K.	TX1350	41,45,66A,66D
Silver, Phillip A.	ME0440	12A,66C,66A,11
Silverman, Ellen	AB0050	66A
Silverman, Laura	OH0700	66A
Silverman, Laura	OH2150	66C,66A
Silverman, Marc	NY2150	41,66A
Silverman, Robert	AB0100	42,66A
Simms, Beverley	IN0800	66A,66D
Simon, Abbey	TX3400	66A
Simon, Dennis	IA0790	66A,13
Simon, Fred	IL0550	47,66A
Simon, Harris W.	VA0250	29,66A,47,29
Simon, Julie	CA4500	66A,66D
Simons, Paul	AF0120	66A
Simons, Penelope	ND0250	66A,66H
Simpson, Andrew Earle	DC0050	10;10F,13,66A,43
Sims, Lamar	MO1000	20B,66A
Singley, H. E.	IL1850	66A,66G,11,36,31A
Sioles, Gregory	LA0200	66A
Sisco, Paul	PA0600	66A
Sitton, Michael R.	NY3780	66A
Skelly, Michael	NY0750	66A
Skelton, Logan	MI2100	66A
Skelton, Sara	MN1630	61,66A
Skoglund, Frances	FL0675	66A,66D,13A,11
Skovorodnikov, Eugene	AB0100	66A
Skyrm, Susanne L.	SD0600	66A,66C,66D,66E
Slater, Vivien H.	NY0650	66A
Slavin, Peter	IN0005	10,13,66A,11
Slawson, Gregory	OH0700	66A
Sloan, Chikako	IN1560	66A
Sloan, Chikako	IN1050	66A
Sloan, Rita	MD1010	66C,66A,41
Slocum, Troy	NY1550	66A
Slovak, Loretta	MA0600	66A
Slowik, Gregory	MA1700	13,11,12A,66A,66C
Sluis, Joyce	IL2775	66A
Slutsky, Boris	MD0650	66A
Smaga, Svitlana	CA1300	13A,66A
Smart, Gary	FL1950	13,10F,10,66A,53
Smedina-Starke, Ruta	VA1600	66A
Smirl, Terry W.	WI0450	53,66A,66D
Smith, Alan	CA5300	41,66A,66C
Smith, Aron	CT0550	66A
Smith, Cameron	IL1615	66A
Smith, Cherie	IN1350	61,66A
Smith, Chuck	ID0050	29,66A
Smith, Curtis F.	CO0810	13,34D,36,66A
Smith, David K.	KS0950	36,11,61,13,66A
Smith, Debbie	TN1200	66A,66G,11
Smith, J. W.	WV0200	11,12A,66A,66B,66D
Smith, Joanne	FL0680	66A,66B
Smith, Kara	WY0115	61,66A
Smith, Karen B.	LA0300	66A
Smith, Kirsten	CA0840	66A,66C,66D
Smith, Marcie	UT0190	66A,66D,13C,11
Smith, Mary L.	CO0600	66A
Smith, Paul	CA1150	12A,66A,66C,66D,54
Smith, Ross	LA0050	11,66A,13A,13B,13C
Smith, Rumi	AK0100	66A
Smith, Sonja	IL2750	66A
Smith, Steven	PA2750	66A
Smith, Timothy C.	AK0100	11,66A,66B,66C
Smith, Timothy	AR0200	13,12A,66A,66C
Smith, Trevor	VA1650	61,66A
Smoker, Beverly A.	NY2650	66A,66B,66D
Smolenski, Scott	FL1675	66A,10,11,13,20
Snitkovsky, Natasha	PA1050	66A,66D
Snow, Julian	OR1300	66A
Snow, Thomas	ME0150	29,47,46,66A
Snyder, Barry	NY1100	66A
Snyder, Maria	MA0600	66A
Snyder, Steven D.	KY0900	13,47,66A,29
Snyder, Vernon G.	CA0630	66A
Soares, Luciana	LA0450	66A,66C,13F,51,13C
Sobkowska-Parsons, Joanna	FL0600	66A
Sobol, Deborah	IL0550	66A,42
Sobolewski, Susan F.	NY2550	66D,13C,42,66A
Soehnlen, Edward J.	MI1850	11,66A,66G
Sohn, Minsoo	MI1400	66A
Sokasits, Jonathan F.	NE0300	66A,66D,66B,42,12A
Sokol, Casey	AG0650	13A,66A,53,43
Sokol-Albert, Andrea C.	PA0950	66A,66C
Sokoloff, Eleanor	PA0850	66A
Solar-Kinderman, Eva	AB0150	66A,66C
Soll, Beverly A.	MA1650	11,66A,66C
Solomon, Mimi	NC0650	66A
Solomon, Nanette Kaplan	PA3100	12A,66A,13C,15
Solomons, John	TX3500	66A,41,66C
Solose, Jane M.	MO1810	66A,66H
Solose, Kathleen A.	AJ0150	66A,66H,66B,66C,42
Solzhenitsyn, Ignat	PA0850	66A
Song, Haewon	OH1700	66A
Song, Hyeyoung	TX3700	66A
Song, J. Z.	WI1150	66A
Song, JY	NY2250	66A,41
Soo Mauldin, Rosalyn	AL1195	66A,66D
Sopher, Rebecca J.	PA1450	66A
Sorel, Suzanne	NY2450	66A,33
Sorley, Rebecca E.	IN1650	66A,66C,66B,66D
Soskin, Mark	NY2150	29,66A
Sothers, Misty K.	CO0225	66A
Soto, Jose	CA1960	66A
Souvorova, Katerina	DC0050	66A,66C
Spang, Lisa	PA2950	66A,66B
Spangler, Douglas	MI1000	66A
Spangler, Pamela	CA2550	11,66A
Sparkman, Carol Joy	MS0400	66C,66D,36,66A
Sparks, David	CA1100	16,10,66A
Sparks, Michael	AL1450	12A,36,66A,31A,34
Spedden, Patricia R.	IN0700	66A,66B,13,66C,66D
Speer, Alesia L.	KY1550	66A,66C
Spencer, Dianthe M.	CA4200	66A,66D,20G,29
Spencer, Philip	IL1250	20,61,66A,36,60A
Spencer, Sarah	TX2295	66A,66C,66D,12A
Spicer, Donna	OR1020	36,61,66A,66D
Spicer, Mark J.	NY1150	13,11,64A,66A,20G
Spicer, Nan	IN0005	61,60A,66A,66G,31A
Spicknall, John	IN0350	66A
Spillman, Robert	CO0800	66A,39
Spires, Rozanne	TX3527	66C,66C,66D
Spitler, Carolyn	IN1250	64A,66A,13B,13C,66G
Spitzer, Laura	NM0310	66A,66B,66C
Spoelstra, Annemieke	VT0400	66A,66C
Spooner, Steven	KS1350	66A
Spotz, Leslie	TX2750	13A,66A,66B,66D
Sprenger, Jill T.	TX2600	66A,66B,66D
Springer, Samuel	MD0600	66A,39
Sprunger, Gina	SC0200	66A
Spurr, Ken	IL0850	66A,46,47
Spurr, Kenneth	IL1085	66A,53,29,47
Squatrito, Fred	CA0400	13,11,66A
Stabinsky, Ron	PA3700	66A,66C
Stackhouse, Eunice Wonderly	NC1450	13,66A,66B,66D,66C
Stacy, Barry	MO0350	66A
Staheli, Ronald	UT0050	60,36,41,61,66A
Stahl, David	CA2600	66A
Staininger, Lynn L.	MD0300	36,66A,13B,40,61
Stallings, Charles	IN1100	66A
Stalnaker, Donna	WV0250	11,12A,32B,66A,66H
Stambuk, Tanya	WA1000	66A,66C,66D
Stampfl, Aaron	IL0275	66A
Stampfli, L. Thomas	IL1050	66A,66B,66D,66C
Stang, Sharon Kay	IA0300	66A,66C,66B
Stangeland, Robert A.	AA0100	66A
Stanley, Amy A.	NY3730	66A,66B
Stannard, Neil	CA1750	66A,66C,66B,62D
Staples, Charles	VA1600	66A
Staples, James G.	PA1600	13,66A
Stauch, Michael	NJ0550	66A,66G
Stearns, Duncan	PA1150	62E,66A
Steele, Janet	NY0550	13A,55,61,66A,36
Steen, Solveig	SD0050	66A
Steeves, Timothy	AD0050	66A
Stefanov, Emi	FL0930	66A
Steffen, Arlene	CA1860	66A,66B,66D
Steffen, Cecil	IL0780	13,66A,66D
Stegall, Gary Miles	SC0420	66A,66D,13A,66C,66G
Steigerwalt, Gary	MA1350	66A,13A
Steinbach, Falko	NM0450	66A,66C,66B
Steinbauer, Robert	TX3415	12A,66A
Steinberg, Paulo	VA0600	66A
Steiner, Sean	UT0350	66A
Stellrecht, Eric	NC0650	66A,66C,13C
Stembler-Smith, Anna	OH0250	66A
Stephens, Gerald	TN1200	66A,47
Stephenson, Angela	NC1300	66A
Sterba, Lydia	IL1900	66A
Sterling, Jolanta	CA4450	66A
Steuck, Beth	MN1500	63B,66A
Stevens, Damon B.	NV0100	39,66A,66C,66D
Stevens, Delores E.	CA3150	41,66A,66H,66C
Stevenson, Doris J.	MA2250	41,66A,66C,42,43
Steward, Gail	AL0500	12A,66A,66D
Stewart, Paul	AI0200	66A
Stewart, Paul B.	NC2430	66A,66C
Stiles, Jennifer	AB0060	13B,66A,66D
Stillman, Judith L.	RI0200	66A
Stillwell, Roy	IL1500	66G,66A,11
Stimson, Kate	TN1200	66A
Stobbe, Melinda	AB0210	66A
Stodola, Lynn	AF0100	42,66A,66C,41
Stokes, Jennifer	IN0907	66A,66B,66D,11,66C
Stoll, Derek	AA0050	66A
Stoloff, Betty	NJ1350	66A,66B,66D
Stolyar, Marina	AA0020	66A
Stone, George J.	CA1510	13,47,34,66A,35D
Storm, Linda	IL1550	66A,66G,66B,44
Stotlar, Curtis	WI1150	66A
Stoudenmire, Myungsook	SC0275	66A,66D,66C
Stoughton, Zachariah	TX3000	66A,12A,67F,11
Stowe, Cameron	AG0450	66A,66C
Stoytcheva, Lilia S.	SC0950	66A,66B,66C,66D
Strabala, Joyce	IA0400	66A
Strahl, Margaret A.	GA2100	11,66A
Strain, Robert L.	VA1350	66A
Strampe, Gregory	WY0200	66A
Strauss, John F.	IA0950	66A
Streder, Mark	IL0850	13,66A,53,34,45
Street, Eric	OH2250	66A,66B,66C,11
Stremlin, Tatyana	NY4250	13,11,61,66A,67C
Strid-Chadwick, Karen	AK0100	13,47,66A,66D,29
Strong, Sar-Shalom	NY1350	66A
Strong, Timothy	WA0650	66A

Name	Code	Areas
Stroud, Cheryl	AI0050	66A
Stryker, Michael S.	IL3500	66A,29
Sturm, Connie Arrau	WV0750	66A,66B,66D
Subotic, Vedrana	UT0250	66A
Sudderth, Janette	MS0385	66A,62C
Sudeith, Mark A.	IL0600	13,66A,66G,66C
Suderman, Betty	AB0090	66A
Sugimura, Kyomi	IL0750	66A
Suh-Rager, Min-Jung	AI0150	66A,29
Suits, Sue	MT0370	66A
Suk, Mykola	NV0050	66A,66B
Sukonik, Inna	NY5000	66A
Sukonik, Inna	NY2400	66A
Sultanov, Namiq	CA4400	66A
Sultanova, Marina	MO1000	66A
Sulton, Randall S.	TX0600	66A,66C,13E,13B,13F
Summer, Averill V.	FL2000	66A,66D
Summers, Billy	NC0750	66A,66C,66D,66G
Sumpter, Teresa L.	NC1250	66A,66B,66D,66C
Surma, Dan	IL2650	66A,66D
Sushel, Michael	CA1000	10D,66A,66B,11,29A
Sutanto, David T.	TX0550	66A,66D,66C,11,66B
Suzuki, Yuko	NJ0500	66A
Svanoe, Kimberly Utke	SD0050	66A,11
Svard, Lois	PA0350	13,66A
Svengalis, Judy	IA0420	32B,66A
Svensen-Smith, Carol	NY1850	66A
Sverjensky, Pamela	DC0170	66A
Svetlanova, Nina	NY2250	66A
Svetlanova, Nina	NY2150	66A
Svistoonoff, Katherine	FL0800	66A,13,12A
Swan, Robert	WA0800	66A
Swanson, Jenny	TX2260	66G,66A
Swanson, Mark L.	MA0100	60B,38,66A,41
Swartzbaugh, Tara	FL2050	66A
Swears, Marilyn	AL0345	11,54,66A
Sweeney, Cecily	CA2600	66A
Sweets, Nancy	MO0500	37,65,64,66A
Sweigart, Suzanne	MD0610	66A,61
Swiatkowski, Chet	CA3150	13B,13C,13E,66A
Swiatkowski, Hak Soon	CA3150	66A,66D
Swigger, Jocelyn A.	PA1400	11,66A,66B,66C,66E
Swingle, Ira	AL0310	12A,66A
Syer, Jamie	AB0210	66A,66B
Sykes, Jeffrey R.	CA0807	66C,66A
Sykes, Robert	DC0170	13,66A,29
Sylvestre, Stephan	AG0500	66A
Synder Jones, Norma	IA0500	66A,66B
Syracuse, Richard D.	OH1900	66A
Szczesniak, Michel	AG0250	66A,66C
Szklarska, Kamilla	FL0700	66A,66C,66D
Szlubowska, Danuta	MS0385	66A
Szutor, Kristina	AD0050	66A,66C,66B
Tadmor, Tali	CA0510	66A,66C,31B
Taft, Burns	CA5360	13,60,36,66A,38
Tak, Young-Ah	FL1740	66A,60,13A,13B,41
Takacs, Peter	OH1700	66A,41
Takasawa, Manabu K.	RI0300	13,66A,66B,66C,66D
Talaga, Steve	MI1050	66A,29A,29B,29C,10
Talbert, Rebecca	MO2050	61,66A,13,12A,11
Tall, Malinda	UT0350	13A,13B,13C,66A,66C
Talley, Sue	NY2900	66A,12A,36,31A,31B
Tam-Wang, Erica	IL2750	66A
Tamagawa, Kiyoshi	TX2650	66A,13,66B
Tambiah, Dharshini	FL2000	66A
Tan, Siok Lian	OH1450	66A,66B,66D
Tanaka, Rieko	MA2020	66C,13C,66A,66D
Tang, Jenny	MA2050	66A,66C,13
Tang, Susan	IL2150	66A
Tanksley, Francesca	MA0260	66A
Tanksley, Francesca	NY2660	13,66A,53
Tao, Patricia	AA0100	66A,41
Tarchalski, Helen Smith	MD0060	66A,66D
Tarrant, James	MO1550	36,60A,35,42,66A
Taubman, Dorothy	PA3250	66A
Tauscheck, Jonathan	IA0930	66A
Taves, Heather	AG0600	66A,66B
Taylor, Annie	AZ0350	66A,66D
Taylor, Arlecia Jan	TX2100	11,36,32,66A
Taylor, Christopher	WI0815	66A
Taylor, Janet	MS0400	13B,13C,66A
Taylor, Karen M.	IN0900	66A,66B
Taylor, Keith A.	AL1160	66A,29B,46
Taylor, Kristin Jonina	IA1750	12A,20,66A,66D,66
Taylor, Larry Clark	VA0100	66A,66G,13B,13D,13E
Taylor, Maria C.	PA3250	66A,66D
Taylor, Paul F.	KY0900	66A,66H,66C,66D
Taylor, Ralph	MS0400	66A
Tchantceva, Irena	RI0150	66A
Tchii, Kent	CA2200	66A,66D
Tchougounov, Evgueni	AG0170	66,66A,13C
Tebay, John	CA1900	36,61,66D,66A,12A
Tedder, Teresa C.	KY1150	10A,10C,10F,66A,11
Tedesco, Anne C.	NY3500	13,66A,54,29A,10
Teel, Susan	TX0050	66A,32B,11,13C
Teicher, Susan C.	IL0800	66A
Teissonniere, Gerardo	OH0600	66A,66B
Telner, Susan	AG0600	66A
Temme, Diane	NE0200	66A
Temple, Elizabeth A.	VA1350	66A
Templeton, Peter	NH0250	66A,66D
Templon, Paul	NC2400	66A,66C,36
Tentser, Alexander	AZ0480	66A,38
Ter-Kazaryan, Marine	CA1960	66A
Termini, Steven	TX0075	11,66A,13A
Tescarollo, Hamilton	IN0905	66A,66B,66C
Teter, Eston	MD0175	66A
Therrian, Dennis	MI1200	66A,34
Thibodeaux, Tatiana	CA4500	66A,12A,13C,66C
Thickstun, Karen	IN0250	66A,66D
Thiedt, Catherine E.	OH0950	13,12A,66A,66G,31A
Thiele, Michael	WI1150	66A
Thiele, Michael	WI0300	66A,66D
Thieme, Robert	WV0750	39,66A,66C
Thiesfeldt, Jeneane M.	MN1030	66A,66A
Thogersen, Chris	IN0550	66A,66B,32B,31A
Thomas, Andy	OR0175	66A
Thomas, Bruce	MA0260	66A
Thomas, Fennoyee	TX3150	66A,66G
Thomas, Martha L.	GA2100	66A,66C
Thomas, Phillip E.	TN0850	13,12,38,66A
Thomas, Reginald	MI1400	29,66A,53
Thomas, Richard Pearson	NY4200	66A,66C,10
Thomas-Lee, Paula	GA1700	66A,66B,32B
Thompson, Barbara Tilden	PA2450	66A,66B,13C,13,13A
Thompson, Bruce A.	NC1000	36,13,66A,61
Thompson, Christopher K.	AR0950	13A,13,10F,10,66A
Thompson, David	WI0400	13,11,14,66A,35
Thompson, Gregory T.	NC1000	66A,66C,12A,31A
Thompson, Janet	OH1200	62E,66A
Thompson, Janice Meyer	AZ0100	66A,66B,66D
Thompson, Kathy A.	OK0700	13,32B,66A,66B,41
Thompson, Lee D.	WA1300	12A,39,66A,66C
Thompson, Marilyn	CA4700	66A,41,42
Thompson, Richard O.	CA4100	47,66A,29A
Thomsen, John David	CA1550	66A,11
Thomsen, Kathy	MN0800	66A,66D,11
Thomson, Philip G.	OH2150	66A
Thomson, Susan N.	GA0950	13B,13E,66A,13
Thorne, Cecilia	UT0050	66A
Thornton, Jim	IL1890	66A,66D
Threadgill, Gwen J.	AL1050	32B,13C,66A,66D
Tian, Tian	MO1790	66A
Tibbs, Elizabeth J.	AZ0150	66A,11,66D
Tice, Loren C.	KY1350	11,66A,66H,66C,66G
Tidwell, Mary	TX1510	66A,66D,13B,13A
Tiernan, Stephany	MA0260	66A
Tierney, Joanne	MN1295	66A
Tili-Trebicka, Thomaidha	NY4150	66A,66D,66C
Timbrell, Charles	DC0150	66A
Timmons, Kathryn Jill	OR0450	12A,66A,66H,66B,66C
Tindall, Josh	PA1900	66A,66D
Tingle, JoDean	AL0300	66A
Tinsley, Janis	AL0400	61,66A,66B,66D
Tipps, James	OH2500	32,36,66A,66D,60
Tipton, Elizabeth	MA0600	66A
Titterington, Connie	OR0850	66A,66D
Tittle, Sandra	OH1000	66A,66G,66H,66D
Titus, Julia	IA0300	11,66A,66D
Tjoelker, Joy	WA0550	66A
Tkachenko, Tanya	AG0450	66A
Tocco, James V.	OH2200	41,66A
Todd, Sarah	IL1050	66A,66C,66D
Tolar, Ron	AL0400	13,11,66A,66G
Tollefson, Arthur R.	NC2430	66A
Tollefson, Mary J.	WI0810	11,66A,66D,66B
Tolmacheka, Tatyana	OH0755	66A
Tomarelli, Ron	AF0050	66A,66B
Tomassetti, Beth	VA0150	66A,66D
Tominaga, Akiko	AA0050	66A,66C
Tomlinson, Peter	NY4450	66A
Tomlinson, Peter	CT0800	66A,53,41
Tompkins, Joshua	MN1250	66A
Tompkins, Ruth	KY0650	66A
Tonnu, Tuyen	IL1150	66A,66B,13B,13C
Toomey, John F.	VA1000	66A,29,47
Toradze, Alexander D.	IN0910	66A
Torkelson, Suzanne	IA1800	11,66A,66B,66C
Tormann, Cynthia	AG0250	66A,13C,66D
Torok, Debra	PA2450	12A,13,38,66A,20G
Torrenti, John	CT0100	66A,66G
Toscano, Patricia	SD0300	61,66A,66G,31A
Toth, Michael S.	PA2550	66A
Toyich, Boyanna	AG0450	66A
Trail, Julian	DC0170	12A,13,66A
Trang, Grace	IL1090	66A,66D
Trechak, Andrew	KS1450	66A
Treer, Leonid P.	FL0650	14,66A,66B,42
Trentham, Donald R.	TN0650	11,12A,66A,31A,13
Trompeter, Jim W.	IL0550	47,66A
Trovato, Vincent	PA2550	66A
Truax, Jenean	PA0150	13A,13C,32D,61,66A
True, Carolbeth	MO1950	66A,29
True, Carolyn E.	TX3350	66A,66B,66D,43
True, Nelita	NY1100	66A
Truelove, Stephen	OR0950	66A,66D
Tryon, Valerie	AG0200	66A
Tsachor, Uriel	IA1550	66A
Tsai, Sin-Hsing	TN1700	66A,66B,66C
Tsao-Lim, May	AR0300	66A,66C,66D,66B,13B
Tsarov, Eugenia M.	NY3780	66A
Tselyakov, Alexander	AC0050	66A,42,66A
Tsinadze, Ana	PA3250	66A
Tsong, Mayron K.	MD1010	13A,66A,66
Tung, Leslie Thomas	MI1150	12A,66A,66C,66E,13
Tung, Mimi	VA1550	66A,42
Tunis, Andrew	AG0400	41,66A
Tunnell, Meme	KY0250	13B,66A,66B,66D
Turcios, Lorri	SC0200	66A,66B,66D
Turgeon, Edward	FL0650	66A,66B
Turini, Ronald	AG0500	41,66A
Turley, Richard L.	MN0350	11,66A,66B,66C
Turnbough, Kimberlee	SC0900	66A,66C
Turner, Sandra	KY1200	66A,66D,66B,66G
Turon, Charles T.	FL1745	11,13,66A,66D
Tusing, Susan	GA0500	66A,66B,13A,13B
Tutt, David	AA0020	66A
Tutunov, Alexander	OR0950	13,66A,66D,66C
Tweed, Pauline	CA2100	66A,61
Twyman, Nita	OK1030	13A,11,61,66A
Uchida, Rika	IA0550	13,66A,66C,66D
Uchimura, Susan	MI2250	66A,66B,66C
Uhlenkott, Gary	WA0400	13A,66A,13B,35H,47
Uitermarkt, Cynthia D.	IL1850	13A,13,66A,31A
Ungar, Garnet	IN1600	66A,66C,66D
Ungar, Tamas	TX3000	66A
Unrath, Wendy	IL0850	66A,66D,12A,11
Unrau, Lucia	OH0250	66A,66B,66D,13C
Uranker, Mark	CA0825	66A,66D
Urban, Guy	MA2150	13,60,11,66A
Urbis, Richard	TX3515	10F,66A,66C
Uricco, Grace E.	RI0300	66C,66A
Utsch, Glenn R.	PA3100	13C,66A,29A,66D
Utterback, David	TX2650	66A,66D
Vagel, Marianne E.	MN1030	66A
Vaicekonis, Dainius	WA0860	66A
Vail, Eleanore	IN0400	11,12A,66A
Vail, Kathy	MS0850	66A,66G,69,44
Valcarcel, David Shawn	CA3265	45,65,35C,13G,66A
Valcarcel, David	CA3950	45,65,35C,13G,66A
Valdes, Cristina	WA0200	66A
Valentine, Claudette	NE0160	66A,36,66D
Valentine, Colette	TX3510	66C,66A
Valerio, John	SC0900	29B,53,66A,10
Valjarevic, Vladimir	NY2250	66A,66B
Valle, Amy	KY1200	66A,66D
Vallecillo, Irma	CT0600	66A,42
Valliant, James	PA3710	61,66A,11
Valliant, James	MD0170	61,66A
Van Brunt, Jennifer	WI0960	61,66A,66C,66D
Van DeLoo, Mary F.	WI0350	66A,66B,66D
Van der Linde, Polly	UT0350	66A,13
Van der Beek, Ralph	VT0050	66A,66B,66C
van der Westhuizen, Petrus	OH0950	66A,66C,66D,13B,13C
Van der Westhuizen, Sophia	OH2600	66A
Van Duyne, Lisa	IL2750	66A,66D

Index by Area of Teaching Interest

Name	Code	Areas
Van Hoose, Matthew	DC0170	66A
Van Hoven, Eric	PA1850	61,66A
Van Kekerix, Todd	NJ0700	66A,66D
Van Nostrand, Carol	MN1295	66A
Van Regenmorter, Heidi	CA0150	66A
Van Slyck, Trudi	MA2010	66A
VanAllen, Michael	NY3350	29,66A,47
Vancura, Kim	TX1750	61,66A
VanDam, Lois	FL1430	66A,36,60A
Vanden Wyngaard, Julianne	MI0900	66A,66B,66C
Vandenberg, Lavonne	MI0350	66A
Vanderbeck, Sue Ann	MI1300	11,12A,66A,66B,66D
Vanderkamp, Herman A.	CA4200	66A
Vanderkooy, Christine	AJ0100	66A,66B,66C,13C
Vanderwall, Barbara S.	IL2050	66A
VanDessel, Peter	MI0520	13C,66A,66D,13E
VanRandwyk, Carol A.	MI0850	13,13C,66A,13D
VanWeelden, Marnie	AG0600	66A
Varlamova, Liudmila	TX3525	66D,66A
Varner, Kenneth	SC0050	66A,66G
Vasquez, Hector	FL1300	13,11,12A,66A
Vasquez, Jerico	GA1800	66A,66D
Vassilev, Mia	FL0050	66A
Vatchnadze, George	IL0750	66A
Vaughan, Jennie	TX2050	13A,13B,13C,66A,11
Vaughn, Michael	IL2000	12A,12,32A,66A
Vauth, Henning	WV0400	66A,66C,66D,13C
Vehar, Persis Parshall	NY0400	10,66A
Vereshagin, Alex	CA1760	66A,66D
Viardo, Vladimir	TX3420	66A
Viemeister, Jane Stave	CA4580	66A,11
Vilker, Sophia	MA1175	66A
Villafranca, Elio	PA3250	29,66A
Vince, Donna	MO1950	66A,66B
Vining-Stauffer, Kristin	WA1100	66A
Vining-Stauffer, Kristin	WA1300	66A
Virelles, Amanda	TN0100	66A
Viscoli, David A.	MN1000	66A,66H,66C
Viviano, Samuel	TN1680	66A,66B
Vlahcevic, Sonia K.	VA1600	13,66A
Vogt, Bruce	AB0150	66A,66C
Vogt, Elaine	IL1200	66A,66C
Vogt-Corley, Christy L.	LA0350	66A,66B,66C,66D
Vokes, Emmett	TX2200	66A
Volchok, Michail	DC0170	66A
Volchok, Mikhail	MD1010	66A
Volk, David Paul	VA1580	13,36,12A,66A,10
Volk, Maureen	AD0050	66A,66B
von Arx, Victoria	NY3700	66A,13,11
Von Spakovsky, Ingrid	AL1160	66A,66D
Von Syberg, Carol	AF0120	66A
Vonsattel, Gilles	MA2000	66A
Voro, Irina	KY1450	66A,66B
Vorobiev, Dmitri	IA1600	66A
Voronietsky, Baycka	ME0440	66A,66B,66C,13A
Vortman, Karma K.	IL1100	66A,66C
Voskoboynikova, Alla	MO1830	66A
Wachsmuth, Karen	IA1140	13,11,12A,66A
Wachter, Claire	OR1050	66A,66B,66D
Wachter, Jeffrey	PA3650	66A,66C
Wade, Gail G.	TX1600	13,39,66A,66D,66C
Wade, James	PA3250	66A
Wade, Jess E.	TX2900	60,32C,61,66A
Wade, Patsy B.	TN1850	66A
Wadsworth, Amanda	LA0080	11,66A,66D
Waggoner, Cathy	TX1350	13A,66A
Wahlstrom, Lynette	AF0100	66A
Wait, Mark	TN1850	66A
Waite, Janice	AA0050	66A,66C,41
Waites, Althea	CA0825	66A,66D,20G
Wakefield, Karin	MN0600	63B,66A
Wakeman, Forrest	MI0300	66A
Waldis, Daniel	UT0250	66A
Waldron, Ann	IL2050	66A,66B
Walgren-Georgas, Carol	IL1085	66A,66D
Walker, Darlene	FL0670	66D,66A
Walker, Deanna	TN1850	66A,10D
Walker, Diana	WA0650	66A
Walker, John M.	SD0550	13,66A
Walker, Michael	CA1510	66A,11
Walker, Tammie Leigh	IL3500	66D,66A,12A
Walker, Vicki	OK0850	13,66A,66D
Wall, Jeremy	NY3765	34,35,36,47,66A
Wallace, Carol	TX2710	66A
Wallace, Elizabeth	TX1100	66A,66B,66C
Wallace, Virginia V.	KS1400	66A
Walley, Steve	IN1560	66A
Walsh, Diane	NY2250	41,66A
Walsh, Megan A.	FL1900	66A
Walsh, Peter	CA1750	66A
Walston, Patricia	MS0400	11,66A,66B
Walters, David	TN0260	29,66A
Walters, Gary	IN0250	66A,47
Waltner, Anne	WV0700	66A
Walton, Michele	NM0200	66A
Walwyn, Karen M.	DC0150	66A
Wang, Esther	MN0750	66A,66C,11
Wang, Han Yuan	UT0190	62A,66A
Wang, Hsiu-Hui	MD0400	66A,66C,42
Wang, Li	AG0300	66A
Wang, Pin-Huey	MD0550	66A,66D
Wang, Rosy	HI0210	66A
Wang, Tianshu	OH0350	66A,66D,66C
Wang, Yung-Chiu	TX1000	66A
Wanner, Dan	CA2600	13,11,35A,66A
Ward, Brian	WA1150	66A,10D,13C,14C,29A
Ward, Brian	WA0250	66A
Ward, Brian	OR0850	66A,47
Ward, Michael	TN0850	66A,13C
Ward, Robert S.	CA0500	66A
Ward, Robert	CA0830	66A
Ward, Robert	CA3300	66A
Ward, Susan	AA0110	66A
Wardson, Greg	MA0260	66A
Warren, James	CA2700	11,61,66A
Warren, Robert	TX2650	66A,66D
Warren, Robert	TX3100	12A,66A,11
Warsaw, Benjamin	GA0940	66A,13
Warshaw, Dalit Hadass	MA0350	10,13,66A,10F,13E
Washington, Henry	TX2220	36,11,66A,66G,66D
Wasley, Martha	CA5000	66A
Wassermann, Ellen	CA0807	41,66A,66D
Watanabe, Vera	UT0250	66A
Waters, Renee	MO1550	13,10,66A,34,11
Watkins, Scott	FL1000	66A,66D
Watson, Cameron	AA0020	66A
Watson, Marva	IL1240	66A,66B,66C,11,12A
Watson, Rita	IL1900	61,66A
Watson, Robert	CA0815	66A,66C
Watson, Teri	CA0815	66A,66D
Watt, Stephanie	NY2105	13,66,66A,66B
Watts, Andre	IN0900	66A
Webb, Lewis	AL1050	61,36,66A
Webb, Merrilee	UT0150	36,66D,66A
Webber, Allen L.	FL1470	13,11,61,10A,66A
Weber, Janice	MA0350	66A
Weber, Linda	TX0550	11,64A,66A,32,66D
Weber, Misato	CA0900	66A
Weber, Misato	CA0807	66A,66D
Weber, Stephen	OK1400	66A,34,66C,66D
Webster, Margee	WA0400	66A
Wedeen, Harvey D.	PA3250	66A,66B
Wee, A. Dewayne	MN1450	66A
Wee, Theo R.	MN1450	66A,66G,66D
Weed, Tad E.	OH0300	66A
Weed, Tad	MI1750	66A,29,47
Weeks, Douglas A.	SC0650	66A
Weems, Nancy	TX3400	66A
Wehr, David	PA1050	66A
Wehrmann, Rock	OH2150	47,66A
Wehrmann, Rock	OH0650	66A
Weidman, James	NJ1400	29,66A
Weilbaecher, Daniel	LA0750	66A,13A
Weilerstein, Vivian Hornik	MA1400	66A
Weilerstein, Vivian Hornik	NY1900	66A
Weinberg, Alan	SC0600	11,66A,12A,66D
Weinstein, Tony	IN1800	66A
Weirich, Robert W.	MO1810	66A
Weiss, Ezra	OR0850	66A,29
Weiss, Lisa G.	MD0400	13A,11,42,66A,66C
Welbourne, Todd G.	WI0815	66A,34A,34D,43
Weldy, Frederick R.	CA4900	66A,66C
Welle, Talman J.	WA0600	66A,66D
Wellman, Samuel	VA0650	66A,66D,10,13A,13B
Wells, Robyn	ID0070	66A,66B,66C
Wells, Ryan	NE0550	13,66A,66B,66C
Wells, Yelena	MI0850	66A,66D,20
Welte, DeEtta	IN1800	66A,66C
Wendland, Kristin	GA0750	13,66A
Weng, Pamela	CO0830	13,11,12A,66A
Wenger, Janice K.	MO1800	66C,66A,66H,66E
Wentworth, Jean	NY3560	12A,41,66A
Werking, Jon	NY2900	66A
Werner, Dianne	AG0300	66A
Werner, Kenny	NY2750	47,66A
Werz, Andreas	CA0810	66A,66B,66C,66D
West, Margaret	CA1760	13A,66A,66D
Westerholm, Matthew	MI0520	53,66A
Westfall, David C.	CT0650	66A,66C
Westgate, Phillip Todd	AL0950	13,36,66A,66G,66C
Westin, Joann	ME0250	66A
Westney, William F.	TX3200	66A
Westphalen, Melinda	IA0700	66A,66D
Wettstein Sadler, Shannon Leigh	MN0050	66A,66C,13F
Whang, Un-Young	IL1850	13,66A,66B
Wharton, Marjorie R.	IA0950	66A,66D
Wheeler, Candace	FL0200	66,11,32,10,66A
Wheeler, Charles Lynn	CA3400	66A,66B,66D,13
Wheeler, Dale J.	AA0080	66A,66B,66D,66C,42
Whipkey, Steve	IN1100	66A,66C,47
Whipple, William P.	IA0930	66A
White, Andre	AI0150	65,66A,29A,29
White, Chris	IL2050	66A,13F,29A,29B,29C
White, Christopher	IL2100	66A
White, Christopher E.	IL1400	66A
White, Cindy	MO1710	64,13,36,61,66A
White, Coralie	LA0770	11,66A,66D
White, Diana	VA1350	66A,66D
White, Frank	LA0700	13,39,66A,11,60
White, Janice	CA5500	11,13A,36,61,66A
White, Laura	VA1600	66A,66D
White, Molly E.	CA2720	66A,13A
White, Pat	NC1950	66A
White, R. Scott	NH0150	66A,66G
Whitehead, Yukiko	TN1200	66A
Whiteley, Dan	IN1310	66A
Whiteman, Richard	AG0650	66A
Whitmore, Judith B.	VA1475	66A
Whitmore, Keith	OK0650	66A,66H,66C,66D
Whittington, Andy	NC2440	66A,29
Whittle, Ralph	MA1100	66A
Wiant, William	RI0250	66A,66G
Wickelgren, John	MD0300	66A,13C,66C,66D
Wickelgren, John	MD0610	66A
Widen, Dennis C.	OK1250	66A,66D,13
Widman, Marcia	MN0300	66A
Wiebe, Allison	AG0500	66A
Wiechman, Elizabeth J.	MN1030	66A,66G
Wieland, William	SD0400	13,66D,66A,34,10
Wielenga, Mary Lou	IA1200	66A,66G,66D
Wielenga, Mary Lou	IA0500	66A,66D,66G
Wiens, Frank	CA5350	66A
Wijnands, Aberham	KS0590	66A,66F,62D
Wijnands, Bram	MO1810	66A
Wilder, Mary Ann	KY0100	66A,66C,66D,13A,13B
Wilder, Roger M.	MO1810	66A
Wilding, Arla	NY3600	66A,61
Wilhite, Carmen	MN1300	66A,66B,66C
Wilkens Wong, Miranda	AB0100	66A
Wilkins, Judy	AZ0250	66A
Wilkins, Sharon	MO0400	32,36,66A
Wilkins, Skip	PA2450	66A
Willcox, Carolyn	AA0110	32A,66A
Willets, Steve	TN0100	66A
Willey, James H.	NY3730	13,10,11,66A
Williams, Brenda	VA1100	66A,66C,66D
Williams, Catherine	MI0300	66A,13C
Williams, Cynthia B.	CA3500	66A,66D
Williams, Dale	FL2050	66A,66C
Williams, Heather	IL2300	66A
Williams, Heidi L.	FL0850	66A
Williams, James	TX0300	66A
Williams, John W.	SC1110	66A
Williams, Kay	TX0050	66A,66C,66D,13A,13B
Williams, Kenneth T.	OH1850	66A,66D,66B
Williams, Leland Page	CA2600	13A,13,66A
Williams, Milton H.	CA1250	11,66A
Williams, Robin	LA0800	66A,66B,66D,66C
Williams, Bruce	VT0050	64C,64E,66A,67,47
Williamson, Gary	AG0450	66A,66H,66C
Willis, Andrew S.	NC2430	12A,66A,66B
Willoughby, Angela	MS0400	12A,66A,66B
Willson, Kenneth F.	OR0250	13,45,66A,66B,66C
Willy, Alan	IN0005	66A,66G,70,13
Wilson, Carol	CO0200	66A,66G
Wilson, Geoffrey	IA1800	12A,13,66A,10F

Name	Code	Areas
Wilson, Grover	NC1600	11,36,66A,66C,66D
Wilson, Jane Ann H.	TX3200	66A,66D,66C
Wilson, Karen	SC0200	12,66A,12C,20G,67
Wilson, Larry K.	CA3975	60,32C,13,66A,36
Wilson, Russell	VA1600	66A,11
Winerock, Jack H.	KS1350	66A
Winfree, James	TN1650	66A,66G
Wing, Barbara	DC0170	66A
Wingreen, Harriet	NY2150	66A
Winslow, Robert J.	FL0930	66A,46,13,34D,11
Winter, Robert	MA0260	66A
Wipf, Elaine	MN1250	66A,66B
Wirtz, Ruth Ann	IN1100	66A
Wise, Herbert	NY2500	63C,66A,66D,11,32E
Wishart, Betty	NC0300	66A
Withers, Lisa Ann	VA0350	66A,66C,13B,13C,13F
Witon, Renee	CA3920	66A,66D
Witte, Diane	IN0907	66A,66B,66D
Witten, David	NJ0800	13B,12A,66A,66B,66C
Wlosok, Pavel	NC2600	47,13F,29,66A
Wodnicki, Adam	TX3420	66A
Woger, Scott	IL1600	13,11,66A,47
Wojnar, William A.	ND0150	12A,66A,66G,31B,31A
Wolf, Debbie Lynn	PA2800	32,66A,66D,66B
Wolf, Eve	NY4200	66A
Wolf, Gary	FL1550	66A
Wolfe, Elizabeth	KY0450	66A,66C
Wolfe-Ralph, Carol	MD0400	13,66A
Wolfe-Ralph, Carol	MD1050	66A,66G,66B,66C,12A
Wolgast, Brett	IA0300	66A,66G,13,12A
Wolgast, Marita	IA0300	66A
Wong Doe, Henry	PA1600	66A,66,11,13,66D
Wong, Jerry	OH1100	66A,66B,66C,42
Wong, Lydia	AG0450	66A
Wong-Abe, Suzanne	CA1900	66A
Woo, Betty	CA5000	66A
Woo, Betty	CA2200	13,12A,66A
Woo, Claudia	AA0050	66A
Woo, Jung-Ja	MA0350	66A
Wood, Jackie Coe	WA1300	66A
Wood, Jeffrey	TN0050	13,10,66A,66D,20G
Wood, Patty	NM0400	66A
Wood, Rose Marie	IL0150	66A
Wood, Winifred	AB0210	66A,66B
Woodard, Peter	CT0650	13B,47,66A,29
Woodard, Susan J.	PA3580	11,12,66A,42
Woodbury, Elizabeth	NY3450	66A
Woodin, Nancy	IA1450	66A,66C
Woods, Rex A.	AZ0500	66A
Woodward-Cooper, Marlene	FL1450	13,66A,66B,66C
Woodworth, Jessica A.	MO0500	11,34,13,66A
Woolley, Clara	IN0010	13,11,32,66A,66G
Worth, David	MN0600	66A
Wotring, Linda	MI1900	11,32A,32B,66A,66B
Wright, Elaine	VA1350	66A,66D
Wright, Elaine	MD0500	66A,66B
Wright, Elizabeth	MA2250	66A,66C,41
Wright, Marylyn	TX3360	13A,66A,66C,66D,66G
Wright, Richard	NY4050	13,11,13C,66A,38
Wright, Sally	VA1000	66A,11
Wristen, Brenda	NE0600	66A,66B,66D
Wu, Chi-Chen	WY0200	66A,66C,66B
Wyatt, Paula	TN0850	47,66A
Wyman, Tamara	NE0450	66A,66D
Wynn, Julie	IN0907	34F,66A,66B
Wyrtzen, Donald	TX2600	10A,31A,66A
Wyse, Debbi	MI1000	66A
Wyse, Paul N.	NY3780	66A
Xian, Tracy	GA1200	66A
YaDeau, William Ronald	IL1750	13,66A,66D
Yamaguchi, Yuko	FL1600	66A,66C
Yamamoto, Travis S.	CO0830	66A,11,13C
Yamazaki, Hiroshi	NY5000	66A
Yampolsky, Miri	NY0900	42,66A
Yanchus, Tina	AG0500	66A
Yandell, Ruth	AZ0440	66A,66G,13
Yanez, Raul	AZ0440	66A
Yanez, Raul	AZ0490	66A,47,14C,29A
Yang, Ben Hoh	LA0150	13,66A,66C
Yang, Clara	NC2410	66A,66B,13
Yang, Hui-Ting	AL1050	66A,66C
Yang, Rajung	ID0250	66A,66C,66H,42
Yang, Tzi-Ming	MD0550	66A,66D
Yang, Yu-Jane	UT0350	66A,66B,66C,66D
Yap, Juliana	PA3580	66A
Yap, Kin	NY2400	66A
Yarnell, Pamela	OH0700	66A,66D
Yazvac, Diane	OH2600	66A,66C,66D
Yee, Thomas	HI0210	13C,66A,66C,66B
Yefimova, Maria	VA0250	66A
Yeh, I-Chen	OH1100	66A,66C
Yeh, I-Chen	OH0300	66A
Yerden, Ruth	OR0600	66A,66G
Yerden, Ruth	OR1150	66A,66G,66D,66C
Yeung, Karay	CO0100	66A,66D
Yi, Ann	CA0855	66A,66D,20H
Yim, Soyoon	DC0170	66A,66C
Ying, Tian	FL1900	66A
Yoder, Roza	CA0250	66A,66B
Yoo, Soyeon Park	IL2250	66A
York, Lela	NM0310	66A
Yoshikawa, Christine	FL0350	66A,13A
Yoshizawa, Haruko	NY4200	66A,29
Yost, Laurel	MT0200	66A,66B,66C,12A
Youn, Gloria	DC0170	66A
Young, Karen	OH1400	66A,66D,66B
Young, Ovid	IL2300	66A,66C,10A
Young, Phillip D.	CA3650	66A,66C
Young, Phillip D.	CA3500	11,66A,66D
Young, Steven	MA0510	36,11,55,66A,20G
Younge, J. Sophia	IL0450	13A,66A,11,36
Yu, Tian-En	CA4425	66A
Yudha, Cicilia I.	OH2600	66A
Yun, Soohyun	GA1150	66A,66B,66C,42
Yurko, Marcia	PA2300	66A
Yurkovskaya, Irina	PA3250	66A
Z, Rachel	NY2660	13B,29B,66A
Zabinski, Marina	RI0150	66A
Zacarelli, Alla	AG0200	66A
Zackery, Harlan H.	MS0350	11,66A,66B,66C,66D
Zak, Peter	NY2660	47,66A,53
Zamparas, Grigorios	FL2050	66A,66H,12A
Zandboer, Sheldon	AA0050	66A
Zanjani, Azadeh	AA0050	32A,66A
Zaretsky, Inessa	NY2250	66A
Zarzeczna, Marion	PA0850	66A
Zavislak, Kay	ID0250	66A
Zavzavadjian, Sylvia	AA0050	32A,66A,66C
Zayarny, Iryna	AA0050	66A
Zeiger, Mikhail	NY5000	66A
Zell, Steven D.	TX0390	13A,13B,13C,11,66A
Zelley, Richard S.	FL0400	55,66A,66H,67B
Zemp, William Robin	SC0500	11,66A,66C,66D
Zent, Donald	KY0100	13E,66B,66A,66C,66D
Zerlang, Timothy	CA4900	66A,69
Zhang, Yi	TX1400	66A
Zhao, Grace Xia	CA5100	66,14,13,66A,66C
Zickafoose, Edward	OH1800	66A,70
Ziebart, Hailey	OR1020	66A,61
Ziedrich, Cheryl	CA4460	66A
Ziedrich, Cheryl	CA1650	66A,66B
Zilberkant, Eduard	AK0150	66A,66B,66C,66D,41
Zimdars, Richard L.	GA2100	66A,42
Zimmer, Susan	MD0800	66A,66C,11,66G
Zimmerman, John	IL3550	13,66A
Zimmerman, Karen Bals	NY3720	13,11,66A,66B,66C
Zimmerman, Lynda	WI0806	13A,66A,66D,11
Zirnitis, Anda	MO0300	13,66A,66C,66D
Zoolalian, Linda A.	CA3650	66A,66C,13C
Zoolalian, Linda A.	CA3500	66A,66C
Zorn, Karen	MA1175	66A
Zuidhof, Jessica	AA0035	66A
Zuk, Ireneus	AG0250	66A,66B
Zuk, Luba	AI0150	66A
Zupko, Mischa	IL3100	10,66A
Zuponcic, Veda	NJ1050	66A,66B
Zwelling, Judith Zwerdling	VA0250	66A

Piano Pedagogy

Name	Code	Areas
Adamson, Philip I.	AG0550	66A,66B,66D,13C,66C
Adderley, Meisha N.	OH0350	13B,13C,66D,66B
Aide, William	AG0450	66A,66B,41,66C
Ajero, Mario	TX2700	66B,66C,66D
Albergo, Cathy	IL1085	66A,66B,66D
Alcalay, Eugene C.	WI0840	66A,66B,66C
Alexander, Charles Reid	IL3300	66B,66D,66A
Allen, Peter	AF0100	66A,66C,66B,41,42
Allen, Stephen	ID0060	66A,66C,66B
Allen, Thomas O.	MN1300	66A,66B,66D
Allred, Nancy C.	UT0150	66A,66B,66D,66C
Alm, Gina	CA5355	11,66A,66B,66C,66D
Amano, Gary	UT0300	13,66A,66B,66C
Anderson, Connie	OH0450	66A,66B,66D
Anderson, Jerry L.	MO0850	66A,66B,66C,66D
Anderson, Richard P.	UT0050	66A,66B,66C,66D
Anderson, Shane	TX2930	13A,13B,13C,66A,66B
Andrade, Juan Pablo	TX3515	13,66B,66C
Andrews, Rick	SD0050	66A,66B,13
Apodaca, Denise R.	CO0250	66B
Aquino, Robert	NY2102	13A,13,10,66A,66B
Ard, Ken	CA4050	66A,66B,66C,66D
Arrigotti, Stephanie	NV0150	13A,11,66A,66B,66D
Asteriadou, Maria	PA1750	11,66A,66B,41,42
Atzinger, Christopher	MN1450	66A,66B,66C,66D
Austin, Jennifer N.	SC1200	66A,66D,66C,66B
Autry, Philip E.	TN0550	66A,66B,66C,66D
Bachelder, Elizabeth Y.	VA1250	66A,66B
Bachmann, Nancy	CA2775	13A,13B,12A,66A,66B
Baciu, Bianca	AA0020	66A,66B,66C
Bailey, Sally	NY0450	66A,66B,66C,66D
Ball, Karen	IL2300	10A,66A,66B,13B,13C
Baltaian, Sarkis	CA1075	66B
Baltazar, Crystl S.	NJ0800	66B,66C
Banner, Lucy	MA0600	66A,66G,66H,66B,66C
Bardston, Robert	AA0040	66H,66B,38,41,62C
Barlar, Rebecca	FL0670	13,66A,66B,66C
Baron, Michael	FL0680	66A,66C,66B,66D
Beamish, Gwen	AG0500	66A,66B
Bean, Robert D.	IN0905	13A,66A,66B,66C,66D
Beard, Robert Scott	WV0550	66,13C,13A,66B,66C
Beattie, Donald P.	IL2900	66B,66D
Becker, Juanita	WI1155	66A,13,66B,66C,66D
Becker, Paul	AR0800	66A,66B,66C,66D,11
Beckman, Bradley J.	TX3420	66A,66B
Bede, Judy	OH0450	66B
Bedford, Robert M.	PA3600	66A,66B
Beecher, Randy	CA4050	66A,66B,66C,66D,12
Bell, Cully	IL2900	66B,66D
Benham, Helen	NJ0030	13A,66A,66H,66B,66C
Bennett, Erin K.	FL1950	66A,66B,66D
Bennett, Mary Lynne	WV0300	66B,66A,66D,66,66C
Benson, Kelley	MI2100	66A,66B
Benson, Michael L.	OH1350	66A,66B,12A,11,66
Berenson, Gail	OH1900	66A,66B
Betts, Steven	OK1200	66A,66B,66D,13,11
Biggs, Charlene	AG0070	11,66A,66B,66C
Billings, Carolyn A.	NC0850	13,12,66A,66B
Blyth, Jennifer	PA0950	66A,66B,66C,66D,13
Boe, Karen	WI0865	66A,66B,66C,66D
Boemler, Cathy	MO0550	66A,66B,66C,66D
Boepple, Hans C.	CA4425	13,12A,66A,66B,66C
Boey, Hooi Yin	WV0050	66A,66D,20,66B,66C
Bogas, Roy	CA2200	60,12A,38,66A,66B
Bond, Kori	ID0100	12A,66A,66B,66C
Boozer, Mark	GA0490	13C,66A,66B,66D
Boren, Benjamin J.	CA0850	66A,66B,66C,66D,13B
Bornovalova, Olga	IL1085	66A,66B,66D
Borrmann, Kenneth	PA2800	66A,66B,66C,42,44
Boston, Nancy J.	PA2150	66A,66B,66C,66D
Boukobza, Laurent	FL1800	66A,66B
Boulton, Kenneth	LA0650	66A,66B,66B
Boyce, Emily W.	NY3717	66D,66C,66A,66B
Bracey, John-Paul	AG0500	66A,66B
Bradford, Mary Pinkney	TX2170	66A,66B,66D
Brady, Patricia L.	VA0600	66B,66D
Bratuz, Damjana	AG0500	66A,66B
Breckenridge, Carol Lei	IA0200	11,66A,66B,66C,66H
Bridgman, Joyce M.	OK0850	66A,66B,66B,66C,66D
Bronson, Janci	IA0850	66A,66B,66D
Brossard, Marilyn	WA0900	66A,66D,66B
Brown, Adrianne	CT0350	66A,66B,66C,66D
Brown, Christine A.	IN1010	11,66A,13,66B
Browne, Lynette	IN0800	66B
Buccheri, Elizabeth	IL2250	66B
Buckwalter, Laurel G.	NY0100	66A,66B,66C,69
Budai, William H.	KY0400	66A,66B,66D
Bumpers, Wayne	FL1300	36,66A,66D,20G,66B
Burch, Alene	TX0550	66A,66B,66D,66B
Burganer-Treer, Judith	FL0650	66A,66B
Burnaman, Stephen	TX1150	13,66A,66G,66B,66C
Bush, Jerry Alan	AL1300	66A,66B
Butler, Carol	TN0580	66A,66B,66B
Butler, E. Gregory	AG0550	66A,66B
Caceres, Marcelo	MI0250	66A,66B,66C,66D

Index by Area of Teaching Interest

Name	Code	Areas
Cai, Yi-Min	AL1250	66A,66B,66D,66C
Camilli, Theresa Chardos	IA1600	66B,32
Capp, Myrna	WA0800	66A,66B,32I,20A
Caramia, Anthony	NY1100	66A,66B,66D
Carlin, Kerry	NC0650	66A,66B,66D
Carlson, Stephen J.	MN0150	66A,66B,66C
Carlton, Elizabeth	NC0350	32,66A,66B,66D
Carney, Robert D.	MO1550	66A,66B,66C,11,13C
Carrell, Scott	AR0250	10A,13,34A,66A,66B
Carter, Beverly H.	PA1450	11,12A,66A,66B
Cash, Carla Davis	TX3200	66B,66D,29A,66A,66
Caton, Benjamin D.	TN0500	13C,66A,66B
Chabora, Robert J.	MN0600	66A,66B,66D,11,13
Chamberlain, Julie Rhyne	NC0350	66A,66B,66C,66D,11
Chan, Susan	OR0850	66A,66B,66D,66C
Charoenwongse-Shaw, Chindarat	OK1330	66A,66B,66D,66C
Chen, Ann A.	MI1260	66A,66B
Chen, Fen-Fang	AL0650	66A,66B,66D,42,66C
Chen, Shao Shen	TX0550	66A,66D,66B,66C
Chien, Gloria	TN0850	13C,13E,66A,66B
Chin, Huei Li	IL2910	66A,66B,66D
Chitwood, Elizabeth	GA0700	66A,66B,66C
Cho, Young-Hyun	TX3500	66A,41,66C,66B,12A
Chou, Mei-En	LA0150	66A,66B,66C,12A
Christensen, Linda	NE0700	66A,66D,34,66B,11
Chung, Mia	MA0950	13,66A,66B
Chung, Myung-Hee	WI0865	66A,66B,66C
Chung, Soon Bin	NY1900	66B
Cisler, Valerie C.	NE0590	66A,66B,66D
Clarfield, Ingrid	NJ1350	66A,66B
Clark, Adam	MI1050	66,66A,66C,66B,66D
Clark, Amber L.	IL1350	66A,66G,66B
Clark, James W.	SC0050	13,66A,66D,66B
Clark, Lauren Schack	AR0110	66C,66D,66B
Clark, Steve H.	GA0550	66B,66D
Clarke, Leland	MA2200	32A,32B,66A,66B
Clevenger, Charles	OH0450	66A,66B,66C,66D,12B
Cleverdon, Suzanne	MA2050	66H,66B
Coats, Sylvia	KS1450	66B,66D
Cobb, Gary W.	CA3600	13,10,12,66G,66B
Cobb, Susan	IL1750	66A,66B,66D
Cockey, Linda E.	MD0800	12A,66A,66B,13E
Collins, Peter F.	MO0775	66A,66D,66B
Conda, J. Michelle	OH2200	66B,66D
Conway, Robert	MI2200	66A,66B,66D,12A
Conway, Vicki J.	TX3535	66A,66B,66D
Cook, Gloria	FL1550	66A,66B,13C,11,66C
Cook, Jean	SC0200	66A,66B,66D
Cooper, Marva W.	DC0350	11,12A,66A,66B,66C
Cornett-Murtada, Vanessa	MN1625	66A,13,12A,66B
Cosgrove, Nancy	MA0600	66A,66,66H,66B,66C
Crappell, Courtney Joseph	TX3530	66B,66A
Crawford, Jenn	AJ0030	66A,66B,66C,13
Cremaschi, Alejandro M.	CO0800	66D,66A,66B
Creviston, Hannah	AZ0100	66A,66B,66C
Cromley, Dorothea	MT0175	12A,66A,66B
Cross, Virginia A.	OR0175	31A,12A,66D,13A,66B
Cruz, Jennifer	OH0500	66A,66B,66D
Cuellar, Martin	KS0300	66A,66B,66C,66D
David, Myrtle	LA0700	11,66A,66B,66C,66D
Davis, Peter	SC0200	66A,66B,66D,34
Dawe, Jill A.	MN0050	13,66A,66B,66D
Deahl, Lora	TX3200	66A,66C,66B,12A
Dean, Lynn	UT0150	11,66A,66B
Deaver, Stuart T.	OK1450	66A,66B,66B,13I,66
Dees, Pamela Youngdahl	MO1250	66A,66B,66C,11,12A
DeFoor, Cynthia	GA2300	66C,66D,66B,66A
Delbeau, Marie-Christine	DE0150	66A,66B,66C,66D
Delphin, Wilfred	LA0900	66A,66B,66C,66D
DeMare, Anthony	NY2150	66B
Dempsey, O. S.	AL0500	66A,66B,13
Derry, Lisa	ID0070	13,10,34,66A,66B
DeSalvo, Nancy J.	PA3650	13A,13B,66A,66B,13C
Di Bella, Karin	AG0050	66A,66,66C
Diab, Mary Beth	IL3370	66A,66C,66B,66D
Dietrich, Maria K.	WI0700	66A,66B
Ding, Xiaoli	KS1400	66A,66B,66D,20
DiPinto, Mark	MD0150	66A,66B,66C,13C
Dobrea-Grindahl, Mary	OH0200	66A,66B,66C,32I,66D
Dobrzanski, Slawomir Pawel	KS0650	66A,66C,66B
Dougherty, Peggy S.	OR0175	66A,66D,13A,66B,13E
Douthit, James Russell	NY2650	66A,66B,66D
Duarte, Derison	NC0600	66A,66B
Dube', Francis	AI0190	66A,66B
Durkovic, Timothy	CA2550	66A,66B
Dussault, Michel J.	AI0220	12A,66A,66B
Echols, Carol	MO0350	66A,66D,66B
Edward, Ruth	NH0350	66A,66B
Edwards, Matthew	MO0850	66A,66B,66C,66D,13
Edwards-Henry, Jacqueline	MS0500	13,66A,66B,66C
Ehrman, David	VA0650	66A,66B,66D
Elder, Ellen P.	MS0850	66A,66B,66C
Elgersma, Kristin M.	ID0250	66A,66B,66C
Elliott, Anne	TN1150	66A,66B,66B,66C,36
Engle, Marilyn	AA0150	41,66A,66B,66C,12B
Epperson, Dean	AK0100	11,12A,66A,66B
Etheridge, Kay	CA5200	11,32B,66A,66B,66C
Evans, Eugenia H.	VA1350	66A,66B
Evans, Mark	NY3600	66A,66B,66D
Ewoldt, Patrice R.	PA2300	66A,66C,66B,67F,42
Ezhokina, Oksana	WA0650	66A,66B,66C,66
Faflak, Marcela	SD0400	66A,66B,66C
Fandrich, Rita E.	FL0800	13,66A,66B,10
Fast, Barbara	OK1350	66A,66B,66D
Faucett, Jim	TX2700	66B
Faughn, Wendy	AL0500	66A,66B,66C,66D
Feltsman, Vladimir	NY3760	66A,66B,12A
Fierro, Nancy	CA3150	66A,66B,66D
Figueroa, Diana	PR0115	66A,66B,66D
Fink, Seymour	OH0350	66A,66B,42
Fischer Faw, Victoria	NC0750	12,66A,66B,41
Fischer, Jeanne Kierman	TX2150	66A,66B,66D,42
Fischler, Gail	AZ0300	66A,66B,66C
Fisher, Christopher	OH1900	66D,66A,66B
Flower, Carol	SD0580	66A,66C,66B
Fogg, Ryan	TN0250	66A,66D,66B,66C
Fong, Grace	CA0960	66A,66B,66C
Forbat, David	OK1330	66A,66B,66C,66D
Foreman, Charles	AA0150	66A,66B,66C,20G,41
Foshee, Anna Harriette	CA4460	66A,66B,66D
Fouse, Kathryn L.	AL0800	66A,66B
Frazier, Ivan	GA2100	66A,66B,66D
Gajda, Anne	MI0600	66A,66B,66C
Gallo, Sergio	GA1050	66A,66B,66C,66D
Garcia, Susanna P.	LA0760	66A,66B
Garcia, W. T. Skye	OK0300	66A,66D,13B,13C,66B
Genova, David	CO0900	66A,66B
Gianforte, Matthew P.	KY0950	66A,66D,66B,66,12A
Gilbert, E. Beth	WI0860	66C,66A,66B,13B
Gilmson, Sophia	TX3510	66B
Gingerich, Carol	GA2130	66A,66B,66C
Gingerich, Cheryl F.	PA1250	66B,66A
Gipson, Ann M.	TX3000	66B,66D,66A
Gladkovsky, Anna	UT0200	66A,66B
Glover, Angela	FL0040	66A,66B,66C,66D
Goldina, Arianna	PA2450	66A,66B
Goldstein, Tamara B.	CO0550	66A,66C,66B,42
Gordon, Tony A.	MS0050	66A,66D,66B,66C,11
Goter, Arlene	MN1295	66A,66B,13,66D
Grace, Rose S.	FL0100	66A,66B,66C,66D
Graff, Carleen	NH0250	66A,66D,66B
Graning, Gary Alan	OH2150	66A,66D,66B
Gravel, Manon	AI0220	32B,32A,66B
Graves, Jody C.	WA0250	66A,66B,66C
Gray, Susan Keith	SD0600	66A,66B,66C,66D
Greene, Arthur	MI2100	66B
Grile, Kathy	IN1560	66A,66B,13A
Gross, David	SC0750	66A,66C,66B,66D
Gualdi, Paolo Andre'	SC0710	66A,11,13,66B,66C
Guest, Ann	SC0750	66B
Gunter, Kevin	TX2400	66B
Gutshall, Christi	AZ0400	66A,66B,66D,12A
Hagner, Carolyn Zepf	KY1000	66A,66B,66C
Hahn, Christopher	MT0400	66A,66B,66C,66D
Halbeck, Patricia	TN0050	66A,66B,66C,66D
Haroutounian, Joanne	VA0450	66A,66B
Harriss, Elaine Atkins	TN1720	66A,66B,42,66D
Hatem, Jasmine	TX3450	66A,66B,66C
Haug, Sue E.	PA2750	66A,66B,66C,66D
Haun, Errol	CO0950	66A,66B
Hawkley, Krysta	DC0170	66A,66B
Hay, James	MA0510	11,12A,66A,66B
Hayes, Jane	AB0060	66A,66D,13B,42,66B
Haythorne, Geraldine	AA0020	66A,66B
Hebert, Sandra M.	MA0330	13A,13,66A,66B
Heighway, Robbi A.	WI0450	11,13C,13D,66B,66D
Henry, Robert	GA1150	66A,66B
Hersh, Alan	KY1450	66A,66B,66C,41
Hesla, Steven	MT0400	66A,66B,66C,66D
Hess, Nathan A.	NY1800	66A,66D,66C,66,66B
Hester, Timothy	TX3400	66A,66B,66C
Heydenburg, Audrejean	MI2000	11,12A,66A,66B,66C
Heyman, Steven M.	NY4150	66A,66D,66C,66B
Hickey, Joan B.	IL3300	47,66B,29
Hickman, Melinda	OH0550	11,66A,66B,66D
Higdon, Paul	MO1100	13,66A,66B,11,66D
Hildebrant, Darcy	AJ0030	66A,66B,66C,13
Hill, Matthew	IN0550	66A,66B,11,12A
Hinson, G. Maurice	KY1200	12A,66A,31A,66,66B
Hirshfield, L. Russell	CT0800	16,13,66,66B,66A
Hirst, Dennis	UT0300	66A,66B,66C,66D
Hisey, P. Andrew	MN1450	66A,66B,66D
Holland, Samuel S.	TX2400	66A,66B,66D
Holm, Robert	AL1300	66A,66B,66C,66D,66H
Holmes, Ruth J.	TX1550	12A,66A,66H,66B,13
Holzer, Linda	AR0750	66A,66B,42,15,11
Hong, Sojung Lee	IL1300	66A,66D,66B,42,66C
Hoppmann, Ken J.	NE0525	66A,66B,20,66C,12A
Houle, Arthur Joseph	CO0225	66A,66C,66B,66D
Houser, Virginia	KS0650	66A,66B,66D
Hrynkiw, Thomas T.	PA2200	66A,66B
Hsu, Samuel	PA2800	12A,66A,66B,13E
Hsu, Yun-Ling	FL1800	66A,66B,66C,66D
Hu, Chih-Long	TN0500	66A,66B
Huang, Grace	OH0600	66A,66D,66B
Huckleberry, Alan R.	IA1550	66A,66B,66C,66
Hudson, Stephen	NJ0975	66A,66B,66C,11
Hudson, Terry Lynn	TX0300	66A,66B,66B
Huff, Dwayne	MO0200	11,66A,66B,66C,66D
Huffman, Timothy	OH2050	66A,13B,66B,66D,66C
Huling, Diane	VT0250	13,66A,66B,66D
Hung, Li-Shan	CA0350	66A,66B,41
Hurd, Mary	MI0300	66A,66B,66C,66D,13A
Hutton, Judy F.	NC2650	13,66A,66B,66C,66D
Hynes, Mia M.	MO1790	66A,66B,66D
Imperio, Roy	MA0250	66A,66B,41,66C,11
Jacob, Jeffrey	IN1450	11,66A,66B
Jaimes, Judit	WI0825	41,66A,66B,66C,42
James, Jo-Sandra	VI0050	66A,66B,66D
Jarrell, Erinn	CA5355	13,66A,66B,66C,66D
Jeffers, Rebecca	OR0700	13A,66B,66C,66D
Jewell, Jim	GA0625	66B,63A
Jobe, Elena	GA0600	66A,66B,66C
Johnson, Amy E.	MI0900	66D,66B
Johnson, Herbert	MN0250	11,66A,66B,66C
Johnson, Herbert	MN1250	12A,13,31A,66B,66C
Johnson, Jessica G.	WI0815	66A,66B
Johnson, Kari M.	MO0050	66A,66B,13
Johnson, Marjorie S.	VA0950	13,66A,66B,66D,34
Johnson, Michelle	TX2600	66A,66B,66C,66D,66E
Johnson, Vicky V.	TX2750	13,32B,14C,32,66B
Jones, Cheryl	FL1430	37,66A,66B,47,61
Jones, Everett N.	OH2400	12A,66A,66B,66D
Jones, Henry S.	LA0650	66A,66B,66D,13C
Jones, Larry E.	NE0450	66A,66B
Jones, Martin David	GA0250	11,66A,66H,66B,13
Jones, Melinda	MO1550	66A,66B,66B,13B,13C
Jordan-Miller, Rebekah	GA1800	66A,66B
Jovanovic, Milica Jelaca	WA1250	66A,66B
Juhn, Hee-Kyung	AR0300	66A,13C,66G,66C,66B
Jung, Hyesook	AL0950	66A,66B,66C,13
Jutras, Peter J.	GA2100	66A,66B,66D,32G
Kaizer, Edward	IL0400	11,12A,66A,66B
Kalhous, David	TX3200	66A,66B
Kanamaru, Tomoko	NJ0175	66A,66B,66C,66D
Karpoff, Fred S.	NY4150	42,66A,66C,66B
Keck, Ouida	AR0500	66A,66B
Kefferstan, Christine	WV0750	66A,66B,66C,66D
Kern, R. Fred	TX3420	13A,66B,66D
Kiehl, Vicky	AR0200	66A,66H,66B,66D,66C
Kies, Arlene	NH0350	66A,66B,66C
Kilburn, Ke-Yin	IN0005	33,66A,66B,13
Kilgore Wood, Janice	MD1050	13C,66A,36,66B,31A
Kim, Aeree	NY2105	66A,66B
Kim, Hyesook	MI0350	66A,66B,11,42
Kim, JeongSoo	IL2200	66A,66B
Kim, Kunyoung	PA0250	66A,13E,11,66B
Kim, Mansoon H.	NJ0800	66B,66C
Kim, Min	NJ0825	13,12,66A,66B,41
Kim, Paul S.	NY2105	66A,66B,12A
Kim, Taeseong	VA0650	66A,66B,13C
Kindall, Susan C.	SC0200	66A,66B,35C,34
Kindt, Allen	NC0050	66A,66B
Kiorpes, George A.	NC2430	66B,66C
Kirk, Caroline	MN1400	11,66A,66B,66D
Kirkendoll, Michael	OK0800	66A,66B,66D,42

Name	Code	Areas	Name	Code	Areas
Kirkpatrick, Gary	NJ1400	66A,66B,66D	Moser, Bruce	NC0400	12,66A,66B,13,66D
Kissack, Christine W.	ME0500	66A,66D	Moss, Elaine	WI0750	66C,66D,66B,66A,32A
Klefstad, Kristian I.	TN0100	66A,66B,66D	Moulton, Joyce	ME0200	66A,66B,66C
Kline, Matthew C.	TX2400	66B,66D	Munn, Alexandra M.	AA0100	66A,66B,66C
Klinefelter, Theresa	PA3600	66B	Murphy, John	LA0300	66A,66B
Klingenstein, Beth Gigante	ND0600	12A,66A,66B,66D	Murphy, Karen Lee	MS0500	66B,66C
Knickerbocker, Sharon	IL1900	66A,66B,66C,66D	Murphy, Steve	IN0907	66A,66B,54
Koch, Patricia Schott	PA2200	66A,66B,66D	Nadgir, Arunesh N.	TN1100	66A,66B,66C
Kolar, J. Mitzi	CA4100	66A,66B,66D	Nagle, Janice	NY3350	66B,66A
Korth, Jonathan	HI0210	66A,66B,66C	Nagy, Linda Jiorle	MA0400	66A,66B
Kreider, David G.	MD0520	11,66A,66G,66B,66D	Neil, Mary	IL0100	13,66A,66C,66B
Krieger, Karen Ann	TN1850	13,66A,66D,66B,68	Newbrough, William J.	NY1700	66A,66B,13C,13E,66C
Kruja, Mira	AL0010	66A,66B,13,11	Nix, Brad K.	KS1250	66B,66A,66C,10F,66D
Kwak, Eun-Joo	WI0150	66A,66B,66C,42,12A	Olander, Jennifer	TN1000	66A,66B,66C
Kwon, Yeeseon	IL0550	66A,66B,66D,66	Olsen, John F.	NM0100	66A,66B,66D
Labe, Thomas A.	OK0150	11,12A,66A,66B	Olson, Janna	AA0035	66A,66B
Lambert, Lerene	LA0300	66B	Olson, Kevin R.	UT0300	66,66A,66B
Landreth, Janet M.	CO0250	66A,66B	Orr, Kevin Robert	FL1850	66A,66B,66D,13A,13
Lange, Richard A.	MN1280	66A,66B,66C	Oshima-Ryan, Yumiko	MN0750	66A,66B,13C
Lapp, Beverly K.	IN0550	66B,66A,11,66C	Osmun, Ross	AI0050	13,41,42,66A,66B
Larsen, Karin	WA0980	66B	Osowski, Kenneth	PA3710	11,66A,66B
Larsen, Laurel	SC0900	66A,66C,66B,13,66D	Otwell, Margaret V.	WI0500	66A,66C,66D,66B,12A
Lau, Daniel	MD0150	66A,66B,66C,12A	Outland, Joyanne	IN0905	13,66A,66D,66B
Laubengayer, Karen	MS0350	66A,66B,66D	Owens, Kathryn Ananda	MN1450	66A,66C,66D,66B,66C
Lauderdale, Lynne A.	FL2100	12A,66A,66G,66D,66B	Oye, Deanna	AA0200	66A,66C,66,13C,66B
Lawrence-White, Stephanie	NC0200	12A,66A,12C,20F,66B	Pachak-Brooks, Cheryl	NM0100	66B,66D,66A,66C
Lazar, Ludmila	IL0550	66A,66B	Paddleford, Nancy	MN1450	66A,66C,66B,66D
Leaptrott, Ben	GA0350	11,13,39,66A,66B	Pagal, Alena M.	SC1110	66B,66D
LeBlond, Gerald	NH0300	66A,66B	Page, Cleveland	MD1010	66A,66B
Lee, Amanda	TX2570	66A,13C,13B,13E,66B	Pan, Huiyu-Penny	CA0830	66A,66D,66B,66C,42
Lee, Donna	OH1100	66A,66B,66C,42	Papatheodorou, Devovora	IL0780	66A,66B
Lee, Gerald K.	WV0600	66A,66B,66C,66D	Park, Jenny	CA5355	51,66A,66B
Lee, Kyung-Ae	TX3175	13,66B	Park, Sohyoung	TX2150	66A,66B,66D
Lee, Marian Y.	IA1300	66A,66B,66C,13C,11	Parker, Joan	SC0200	66A,66B,66D
Lee, Monica	CA1900	66A,66B	Parker, Sylvia	VT0450	13,66A,66D,66B
Lee, Patricia Taylor	CA4200	41,66A,66B	Parkinson, Del	ID0050	66A,66B
Lee, Patricia	IL2650	66A,66H,66A,66B,66C,66D	Parr-Scanlin, Denise	TX3750	66A,66B,66C
Lee, You Ju	GA2000	66A,66C,66D,66B	Parsons, Derek J.	SC0750	13,66A,66B,66D
Lehman, David	SC0200	12A,66A,66B	Partain, Gregory L.	KY1350	11,41,66A,66B,12A
Lehrer, Phyllis	NJ1350	66A,66B	Pastorello, Cristian	IL0150	66A,66B,66C,11,13
Leonard, Lisa	FL1125	66B,66D,42	Patterson, Donald L.	WI0803	66A,66B,66D,66H
Leung, Jackson	OH2500	66A,66D,66B,38	Paulk, Kayla Liechty	NM0100	66A,66C,66B,66D
Lewis, Christopher	VT0050	66A,66B,66C,66D	Pearsall, Tom	GA0950	66A,66B
Lewis, Robert J.	KY0300	13B,11,66A,66B,66D	Pedersen, Gary	MI0600	66A,66B,66C,66D
Li, Hanna Wu	PA0550	66A,66B,66D	Pepetone, Gregory	GA0850	12A,32,66A,66B,66D
Liliestedt, Maira	OH2290	12A,66A,66B	Permenter, Calvin	MO2000	66A,66B,66C
Lim, Mi-Na	TX0345	11,66A,66B	Perry, Margaret	CA5350	66B,66D,66A,66C,13C
Lin, Anthea	OK1250	66A,66B	Petrella, Diane Helfers	MO1810	66A,66B,66C
Lipke, William A.	CO0050	66A,38,67F,66B,66D	Petrowska-Quilico, Christina	AG0650	13A,41,66A,66B
Lipp, Carolyn	MI0500	14,66A,66H,66B	Petteys, Leslie	WV0400	66,66A,66B,66C,12
Lister-Sink, Barbara	NC2205	66A,66B,66C,42	Pettyjohn, Emma	GA0700	66A,66B,66C,66G,66D
Litke, Sheila	KS1300	66,13,66A,66B,13A	Phang, May	IN0350	66A,66B
Litzelman, James	DC0050	66A,66B	Pickett, John	WA0050	13,11,12A,66A,66B
Lively, Judy	AZ0400	66A,66B	Pike, Pamela D.	LA0200	66B,66D
Livingston, Jane	WI0250	66A,66D,66B	Pirtle, R. Leigh	IA1390	66A,66,66B,66C
Livingston, Lillian	NJ1350	66A,66B	Plies, Dennis B.	OR1150	47,65B,66B,66D,13C
Long, Louanne J.	CA5150	13,66A,66B,66C	Polcari, Norma	NH0300	66A,66B,10A
Lopez, Christine Sotomayor	CA0859	36,66A,66D,11,66B	Polischuk, Derek Kealii	MI1400	66A,66B,66D,38,29
Lopez, Jose R.	FL0700	66A,66C,66H,66B	Ponce, Walter	CA5030	66A,66B
Loring, George	NH0150	66A,66B,66D,66H	Popoff-Parks, Linette A.	MI1260	13,66A,66B,66C
Low, Linda	AB0210	66A,66D,66B	Porter, Melana	GA0950	66B
Lundberg, Erika	MN1100	66A,66B,66C	Powell, Philip M.	SC0420	66A,66B,66C,66D
Luther, Sigrid	TN0200	13,66A,66B,31A,66C	Prebys, Marylee A.	ND0400	66A,66B,12A
Lyerla, Trilla R.	KS0050	13,66A,66B,20	Price, Scott	SC1110	66A,66B,66D
Lyman, Kent M.	NC1300	66A,66B,12A	Prince, Penny	NY0635	32,66A,66B,66C
Lysinger, Catherine	TX2400	66B,66D	Puckett, Lauren J.	TX0900	66A,66B
Macchioni, Oscar E.	TX3520	66A,66B,66D,66,14	Pullman, Marlene	AJ0030	13A,66A,66B,66D
MacCrae, Cynthia Perry	AL1200	66A,66B,66C,66D	Pyle, Jane	FL1300	13,11,12A,66A,66B
Mach, Elyse J.	IL2150	11,66D,66B	Radoslavov, Ilia G.	MO1780	66C,66A,66D,66B
Mackey, Lynne A.	VA0300	66A,66B,66C,66D,13	Rambeau, Deborah	WA0700	66A,66B,66C,66D
Magrath, Jane	OK1350	66B,66A,66D,66,66C	Rasmussen, G. Rosalie	CA3400	32,44,66B,66D,13C
Mahamuti, Gulimina	OH2000	66A,66D,66C,66B	Ravitskaya, Irena	KS0350	66A,66B,66C,66D,66G
Maimine, Anna	NY3717	66A,66B,66C	Razaq, Janice L.	IL1085	66A,66B,66D
Maisonpierre, Elizabeth	NC2435	11,13,66A,66B,66D	Redfern, Nancy	MI1600	66,11,66D,66B,66G
Manno, Terrie	MN1120	66A,66B,66C,66D	Reed, Jerome A.	TN0930	10A,66A,66B,66C,43
Manwarren, Matthew C.	SC1200	66A,66B,12,41	Rendleman, Ruth	NJ0800	13,66A,66B
March, James J.	IA1100	66A,66B,66C,12A	Renfrow, Kenon	SC0200	66A,66B,66D,34
Markow, Andrew	AG0300	12A,66B	Reyes, Reynaldo	MD0850	66A,66C,66B
Marlais, Helen	MI0900	66A,66B	Rhoden, Lori E.	IN0150	66A,66B,66D
Marosek, Scott	NC1350	12,66A,66B	Rice-See, Lynn	TN1100	66A,66B,66C
Martin, Deborah	NY1800	66A,66B,66D	Richards, Rebekah	MN0750	66B
Martin, James	IA0400	13,66A,66B,20G	Richey, Craig	CA0825	66A,66C,66B
Martin, Sherrill	NC2440	12A,66A,66B,20G	Richmond, Kevin D.	TN1680	66A,66D,66B
Masaki, Megumi	AC0050	13,66A,66C,43,66B	Richter, Leonard	WA1100	66A,66B,13A,13B
Mascolo-David, Alexandra	MI0400	66A,66B,66D	Rickey, Euni	IN1025	66A,66D,66B,66C
Masterson, Daniel J.	KS0150	13,41,66A,66B,42	Rickman, Michael	FL1750	66A,12A,66B,66D
Mastroianni, Thomas	DC0050	66A,66B	Rivera, Angel Ramon	MA1400	66B
Matsuo, Jun	SC0450	66A,66D,66B,66C,13	Roach, Hildred E.	DC0350	20G,66A,66B,66C,66D
Mauchley, Sandra	ID0250	66A,66H,66B,66D	Roberts, Mary W.	FL0600	66A,66B,66C,66D
Mauro, Lucy	WV0750	66A,66B,66C,66B	Roberts, Ron A.	AL1160	66A,66B
May, Nathanael A.	MO0850	66,66B,66C,66D	Robertson, Kaestner	MA0250	66A,13,36,66B,66C
Mayer, Steven	CO0900	66A,66B	Robertson, Masson	IN0905	13,66A,66B,66C
McAllister, Lesley Ann	TX0300	66A,66B,66D	Robins, Linda	TX2570	32B,36,66A,66B
McArthur, Victoria	FL0850	66B,66D	Rodgers, Reginald G.	IN0100	66A,66B,66D
McCabe, Rachelle	OR0700	66A,66B,12A	Rodgers, Stacy D.	MS0700	66A,66B,66C
McCarrey, Scott	HI0050	66A,66B,13E,12A,11	Roederer, Silvia	MI2250	66A,66B,66C,66D
McClung-Guillory, Deborah	LA0770	66A,66B,66D	Ronning, Debra D.	PA1250	66A,66B,66D
McCollough, Teresa	CA4425	13,12A,66A,66B,66C	Roseman, Molly J.	WI0850	66,66A,66B,66D,66C
McCoy, Darcy	IN0350	66A,66C,12A,66B	Roth, Nicholas	IA0550	66A,66B,66C,66
McCright, Matthew	MN0300	66A,66C,66B	Ruiz, Sergio	TX2250	66A,66B
McKeever, James I.	WI0835	12A,66A,66C,66B	Runge, Stephen M.	AE0050	66A,66B,66C
McKirdy, Colleen	ND0100	66A,66B,66C	Rutman, Neil C.	AR0850	66A,66B
McRoberts, Terry	TN1660	66A,66C,66D,66B	Sachs, Carolyn Reed	MS0100	66B
McVay, Vicki	KY1450	66D,13,66B,13C	Sale, Craig	IL0730	66A,66B,66D,66C
McVey, Roger D.	WI0845	12A,66A,66B,66C,66D	Salwen, Barry	NC2440	11,66A,66B,66D
Meeks, Joseph D.	GA1150	13,12A,66,66B	Sammarco, Donna	LA0450	66A,66B,66D
Meir, Baruch	AZ0100	66B	Sanchez, Luis	TX2955	66A,66C,66B
Mengelkoch, Eva	MD0850	66C,66B,66H,66E	Sanders, Alice	AR0730	66A,66C,66B
Michaelian, Patricia	WA1050	41,66A,66B	Savage, Dylan C.	NC2420	66A,66B,66C
Mielke, Michelle	WA1150	66A,66B	Savage, Jeffrey R.	WA1150	66A,66B,66C,13C
Miller, Elaine	NC2000	13C,66A,66C,66B,13A	Savvidou, Paola	MO1800	66A,66B
Miltenberger, James E.	WV0750	12A,66A,66B,29	Saxon, Kenneth N.	TX3515	66B,66C
Mineva, Daniela	CA2250	66A,66B,66C	Scarambone, Bernardo	KY0550	66A,66D,66B,66,66C
Mitchell, Roman	NY0640	29,29B,66A,66B	Schechter, Dorothy E.	CA0550	12A,66A,66B,66D
Mohr, Deanne	MN1700	66A,66C,66B,13B,13C	Schlabaugh, Karen Bauman	KS0200	13,66A,66B,66C,12A
Molenaar, Mary Beth	IL2250	66B	Schlosser, Milton	AA0110	66A,66B
Montano, David R.	CO0900	66A,66B,66D,32	Schoepflin, Judith	WA1350	66A,66D,16,66B
Moore, Constance J.	AL0300	66A,66B	Schrempel, Martha	PA2450	66A,66C,66B
Moore, Deanna C.	SC0200	66A,66B,12	Schulze, Sean	OH0600	66A,66B
Moore, Ruth	NE0300	66A,66B,66C	Scott Hoyt, Janet	AA0100	66A,66B,42
Morelock, Donald	MI1900	13,11,12A,66A,66B	Scott, Frank	AZ0450	66A,66B
Morgan, Ruby N.	SC0750	66A,66B,66D	Segger, Joachim	AA0035	13,13J,66A,66B,43
Morgiewicz, Kerry L.	VA0550	66A,66B,54	Shafer, Timothy P.	PA2750	66A,66B
Moritz, Benjamin	PA2150	66A,66B,66C,66D	Shank, Dean	TX2150	66B,66F
Moroz, David	AC0100	66A,66B	Sharp, Michael D.	LA0400	66A,66B,31A,34,10A
Morris, Gregory	MO0400	11,66A,66B,13	Shaw, Betty	TX3400	32,66B,66D
Morrow, Ruth	TX3370	66A,66B	Sheftel, Paul	NJ1350	66B
Mortyakova, Julia V.	MS0550	66A,66D,66B,66C,12B	Sheftel, Paul	NY1900	66B

Name	Code	Areas
Sherman, Kathryn D.	NY3780	66D,66B
Shin, Jung-Won	MS0250	66A,66D,66B,66C,13B
Shockley, Rebecca P.	MN1623	66A,66B,66D
Shofner-Emrich, Terree	IL2100	66A,39,66B,66C,66D
Shook, Timothy	KS1200	66A,66B,66D,13
Shpachenko, Nadia	CA0630	66A,66C,66B,66,34D
Shumway, Jeffrey	UT0050	66A,66C,66C
Siciliano, Mary	MI1750	66A,66C,66B
Siek, Stephen	OH2450	12A,66A,66B,20G
Sifford, Jason	IA1550	66B,66D,66,29B,66A
Smith, J. W.	WV0200	11,12A,66A,66B,66D
Smith, Joanne	FL0680	66A,66B
Smith, Scott McBride	KS1350	66B
Smith, Timothy C.	AK0100	11,66A,66B,66C
Smoker, Beverly A.	NY2650	66A,66B,66D
Sokasits, Jonathan F.	NE0300	66A,66B,42,12A
Solose, Kathleen A.	AJ0150	66A,66H,66B,66C,42
Sorley, Rebecca E.	IN1650	66A,66C,66B,66D
Spang, Lisa	PA2950	66A,66B
Spedden, Patricia R.	IN0700	66A,66B,13,66C,66D
Speer, Donald R.	KY1550	66B,66C,66D
Spitzer, Laura	NM0310	66A,66B,66C
Spotz, Leslie	TX2750	13A,66A,66B,66D
Sprenger, Jill T.	TX2600	66A,66B,66D
Stackhouse, Eunice Wonderly	NC1450	13,66A,66B,66D,66C
Stampfli, L. Thomas	IL1050	66A,66B,66D,66C
Stang, Sharon Kay	IA0300	66A,66C,66B
Stanley, Amy A.	NY3730	66A,66B
Stannard, Neil	CA1750	66A,66C,66B,62D
Steffen, Arlene	CA1860	66A,66B,66D
Steinbach, Falko	NM0450	66A,66C,66B
Stokes, Jennifer	IN0907	66A,66B,66D,11,66C
Stoloff, Betty	NJ1350	66A,66B,66D
Storm, Linda	IL1550	66A,66G,66B,44
Stoytcheva, Lilia S.	SC0950	66A,66B,66C,66D
Street, Eric	OH2250	66A,66B,66C,11
Sturgeon, Laura	SC0600	66B
Sturm, Connie Arrau	WV0750	66A,66B,66D
Suk, Mykola	NV0050	66A,66B
Sumpter, Teresa L.	NC1250	66A,66B,66D,66C
Sushel, Michael	CA1000	10D,66A,66B,11,29A
Sutanto, David T.	TX0550	66A,66B,66C,11,66B
Swenson, Thomas S.	NC2205	13A,66B,35C,34,32
Swigger, Jocelyn A.	PA1400	11,66A,66B,66C,66E
Syer, Jamie	AB0210	66A,66B
Synder Jones, Norma	IA0500	66A,66B
Szutor, Kristina	AD0050	66A,66C,66B
Takao, Naoko	FL1900	66B,66C,66D
Takasawa, Manabu K.	RI0300	13A,66A,66B,66C,66D
Tamagawa, Kiyoshi	TX2650	66A,13,66B
Tan, Siok Lian	OH1450	66A,66B,66D
Tanner, Gretchen	UT0250	66B
Taves, Heather	AG0600	66A,66B
Taylor, Karen M.	IN0900	66A,66B
Teissonniere, Gerardo	OH0600	66A,66B
Tescarollo, Hamilton	IN0905	66A,66B,66C
Thomas-Lee, Paula	GA1700	66A,66B,32B
Thompson, Barbara Tilden	PA2450	66A,66B,13C,13,13A
Thompson, Janice Meyer	AZ0100	66A,66B,66D
Thompson, Kathy A.	OK0700	13,32B,66A,66B,41
Thoreson, Deborah	GA0750	66B,66C
Timmons, Kathryn Jill	OR0450	12A,66A,66H,66B,66C
Tinsley, Janis	AL0400	61,66A,66B,66C
Tollefson, Mary J.	WI0810	11,66A,66D,66B
Tomarelli, Ron	AF0050	66A,66B
Tonnu, Tuyen	IL1150	66A,66B,13B,13C
Torkelson, Suzanne	IA1800	11,66A,66B,66C
Treer, Leonid P.	FL0650	14,66A,66B,42
True, Carolyn E.	TX3350	66A,66B,66D,43
Tsai, Sin-Hsing	TN1700	66A,66B,66C
Tsao-Lim, May	AR0300	66A,66C,66B,66B,13
Tselyakov, Alexander	AC0050	66A,42,66B
Tsitsaros, Christos	IL3300	66B,66D
Tunnell, Meme	KY0250	13B,66A,66B,66D
Turcios, Lorri	SC0200	66A,66B,66D
Turgeon, Edward	FL0650	66A,66B
Turley, Edward L.	MN0350	11,66A,66B,66C
Turner, Sandra	KY1200	66A,66D,66B,66G
Tusing, Susan	GA0500	66A,66B,13A,13B
Uchimura, Susan	MI2250	66A,66B,66C
Unrau, Lucia	OH0250	66A,66B,66D,13C
Valjarevic, Vladimir	NY2250	66A,66B
Van DeLoo, Mary F.	WI0350	66A,66B,66D
Van der Linde, Polly	VT0050	66A,66B,66C
Vanden Wyngaard, Julianne	MI0900	66A,66B,66C
Vanderbeck, Sue Ann	MI1300	11,12A,66A,66B,66D
Vanderkooy, Christine	AJ0100	66A,66B,66C,13C
Vince, Donna	MO1950	66A,66B
Viviano, Samuel	TN1680	66A,66B
Vogt-Corley, Christy L.	LA0350	66A,66B,66C,66D
Volk, Maureen	AD0050	66A,66B
Voro, Irina	KY1450	66A,66B
Voronietsky, Baycka	ME0440	66A,66B,66C,13A
Wachter, Claire	OR1050	66A,66B,66D
Waldron, Ann	IL2050	66A,66B
Wallace, Elizabeth	TX1100	66A,66B,66C
Walston, Patricia	MS0400	11,66A,66B
Watson, Marva	IL1240	66A,66B,66C,11,12A
Watt, Stephanie	NY2105	13,66,66A,66B
Wedeen, Harvey D.	PA3250	66A,66B
Wellborn, William E	CA4150	66B
Wells, Robyn	ID0070	66A,66B,66C
Wells, Ryan	NE0550	13,66A,66B,66C
Werz, Andreas	CA0810	66A,66B,66C,66D
Whang, Un-Young	IL1850	13,66A,66B
Wheeler, Charles Lynn	CA3400	66A,66B,66D,13
Wheeler, Dale J.	AA0080	66A,66B,66D,66C,42
Wiley, Adrienne E.	MI0400	66B,66D
Wilhite, Carmen	MN1300	66A,66B,66C
Williams, Kenneth T.	OH1850	66A,66D,66B
Williams, Robin	LA0800	66A,66B,66C
Willoughby, Angela	MS0400	12A,66A,66B
Willson, Kenneth F.	OR0250	13,45,66A,66B,66C
Wipf, Elaine	MN1250	66A,66B
Witte, Diane	IN0907	66A,66B,66B
Witten, David	NJ0800	13B,12A,66A,66B,66C
Wolf, Debbie Lynn	PA2800	32,66A,66B,66D
Wolfe-Ralph, Carol	MD1050	66A,66G,66B,66C,12A
Wong, Jerry	OH1100	66A,66B,66C,42
Wood, Winifred	AB0210	66A,66B
Woodward-Cooper, Marlene	FL1450	13,66A,66B,66C
Wotring, Linda	MI1900	11,32A,32B,66A,66B
Wright, Elaine	MD0500	66A,66B
Wristen, Brenda	NE0600	66A,66B,66D
Wu, Chi-Chen	WY0200	66A,66C,66B
Wynn, Julie	IN0907	34F,66A,66B
Yamashita, Wendy	HI0210	66B
Yang, Clara	NC2410	66A,66B,13
Yang, Yu-Jane	UT0350	66A,66B,66C,66D
Yee, Thomas	HI0210	13C,66A,66C,66B
Yoder, Roza	CA0250	66A,66B
Yost, Laurel	MT0200	66A,66B,66C,12A
Young, Karen	OH1400	66A,66B,66B
Yun, Soohyun	GA1150	66A,66B,66C,42
Zackery, Harlan H.	MS0350	11,66A,66B,66C,66D
Zent, Donald	KY0100	13E,66B,66A,66C,66D
Ziedrich, Cheryl	CA1650	66A,66B
Zilberkant, Eduard	AK0150	66A,66B,66C,66D,41
Zimmerman, Karen Bals	NY3720	13,11,66A,66B,66C
Zuk, Ireneus	AG0250	66A,66B
Zuponcic, Veda	NJ1050	66A,66B

Accompanying and Collaborative Piano

Name	Code	Areas
Aber, Stephen	TN0100	66A,66B
Abram, Blanche	NY1600	41,66A,66D,66C
Adamek, Magdalena	AA0100	66A,66C
Adams, Andrew	NC2600	66C,11,66A,66B
Adams, Fay	TN1710	66A,66C
Adamson, Philip I.	AG0550	66A,66B,66D,13C,66C
Addamson, Paul	NC1050	66A,66C,66D,13A,13
Afonasyeva, Yekaterina	MD0850	66D,36,66C
Ahuvia, Saar	NJ0700	66C,11
Aide, William	AG0450	66A,66B,41,66C
Aiken, Barry	ID0140	66A,66C
Ajero, Mario	TX2700	66B,66C,66D
Akahori, Eliko	MA2050	66C
Albright, Robyn	AA0050	66C
Albulescu, Eugene	PA1950	11,66A,66C,41
Alcalay, Eugene C.	WI0840	66A,66B,66C
Alexander, Mark W.	TX1900	66A,66C,66D
Alexander, Michelle	MA0400	61,66C
Aliyeva, Narmina	OH0350	66A,66C
Allen, James O.	MS0550	11,12A,16,66A,66C
Allen, Peter	AF0100	66A,66C,66B,41,42
Allen, Stephen	ID0060	66A,66C,66B
Allman, Garrett N.	IL1100	13,66C,38,66A,60B
Allred, Nancy C.	UT0150	66A,66B,66D,66C
Alm, Gina	CA5355	11,66A,66B,66C,66D
Amalong, Philip	OH0680	66A,66C,13,11,42
Amano, Gary	UT0300	13,66A,66B,66C
Amato, Donna	PA0550	66C
Amend, James M.	GA1990	66A,66C
Amendola, Vergie	CO0950	66A,66C
Amstutz, Peter	WV0750	66A,66C
An, Ning	TN0850	66A,66C
Anderson, David	WI0100	66A,38,66C,13E,42
Anderson, David C.	OK0150	66C
Anderson, H. Gerald	IL2300	66A,66C,66D,12A
Anderson, Jean	MA1400	66C
Anderson, Jerry L.	MO0850	66A,66B,66C,66D
Anderson, Richard P.	UT0050	66A,66B,66C,66D
Andrade, Juan Pablo	TX3515	13,66B,66C
Andrews, Rachel	MD0520	66C
Antonacos, Anastasia	PA1600	66A,13,11,66C,66D
Arakawa, Jasmin	IL3500	66C
Ard, Ken	CA4050	66A,66B,66C,66D
Armstrong, Anne A.	GA1300	66C
Arrington, Amanda	KS0650	54,66A,66C
Arslanian, Paul P.	MA2000	66C
Artesani, Laura	ME0440	12A,66C,15,32B,32C
Asano, Yuiko	LA0300	66C
Ashmore, Pamela J.	OH1800	66A,66C
Ashton, J. Bruce	TN1350	10A,31A,66A,10F,66C
Asuncion, Victor S.	TN1680	66A,66C
Atchley, Elizabeth	OR0700	61,66C
Attaway, Aiya	OK0450	66A,66C,66D
Atzinger, Christopher	MN1450	66A,66B,66D,66C
Aubin, Isabelle	NY3717	66C
Aubin, Isabelle	NY2650	66C
Austin, Jennifer N.	SC1200	66A,66D,66C,66B
Autry, Philip E.	TN0550	66A,66B,66C,66D
Babayan, Naira	DC0170	66A,66C
Babcock, Beverly	MD0750	66C,66D
Bach, Mia	AG0450	66C
Bach, Timothy	CA4150	12A,41,66C
Baciu, Bianca	AA0020	66A,66B,66C
Badami, Charles A.	MO0950	66A,66A,66D,11
Badgerow, Justin A.	PA1250	66A,66C,66D,13
Baer, Matthew Kevin	CA4300	66A,66C,66D
Bagwell, Thomas	NY2250	66C,39,40
Baham, Kerry M.	TX3370	13B,66A,11,66C,12A
Baik-Kim, Eun Ae	PA0950	66A,66C,42
Bailey, Sally	NY0450	66A,66B,66C,66D
Bailey, Scott	MA2100	66C,66D,11
Balakerskaia, Anna	VA0450	66A,66C
Baldwin, Dalton	NJ1350	66C
Baldwin, Nathan Taylor	WV0200	66C,61
Ball, Alexandria	PA2900	66C,66D,35E
Ball, Gerrie	MI2200	66C,66D
Ballerino, John	CA5060	61,66C
Ballinger, Robert W.	OH2300	39,66C,11,13A
Baltazar, Crystl S.	NJ0800	66B,66C
Bang, In-Sun	NY3785	66A,66C
Banner, Lucy	MA0600	66A,66G,66H,66B,66C
Bardi, Elena	IN0905	66C
Barkley, Elizabeth F.	CA1800	11,12A,66A,66C,66D
Barlar, Rebecca	FL0670	13,66A,66B,66C
Baron, Michael	FL0680	66A,66C,66B,66D
Barr, Jean M.	NY1100	66C,42
Barrett, Korey J.	IA1600	61,66C
Barskaya, Galina	CA3300	66A,66C
Bascom, Brandon R.	ID0060	32F,66A,66C
Bass, Louise	GA1650	66C,66G
Bates, Pamela	IL0900	12A,13,66A,66C,66D
Bays, Jay	MI0350	66C,61
Beachley, Laine	PA3710	66A,66C
Bean, Robert D.	IN0905	13A,66A,66B,66C,66D
Beard, Robert Scott	WV0550	66,13C,13A,66B,66C
Beaton, K. Michelle	RI0300	66C
Beaudette, Sylvie	NY1100	42,66C
Beck, Barbara Geiser	CO0275	61,39,54,66C,42
Becker, Juanita	WI1155	66A,13,66B,66C,66D
Becker, Karen E.	NY3775	66A,66C,13C,13A,36
Becker, Paul	AR0800	66A,66B,66C,66D,11
Beckley, Jane E.	OH2140	66A,66C
Beckman, Linda L.	AR0400	66,11,10F,34,66C
Beckman, Seth	FL0850	66A,66C
Beecher, Randy	CA4050	66A,66B,66C,66D,12
Behan, Ryan J.	OH1850	66C
Belden, Carol Beck	FL0400	66A,66C
Bell, Valda	GA1900	66C
Bellemare, Yvon	AI0220	66A,66C
Belleville, Yolande	AI0220	66C
Bemis, Jennifer	AL1300	66A,66C,66D

Name	Code	Areas
Benham, Helen	NJ0030	13,66A,66H,66B,66C
Benjamin, John A.	OH2250	66A,66C,66D
Bennett, Mary Lynne	WV0300	66B,66A,66D,66,66C
Bennett, Mary Beth	VA1500	66C
Bennie, Ron	AA0050	66C
Benyas, Kara	IL2900	66C
Berg, Shelton G.	FL1900	66A,66C,29,46,47
Bergmann, Elizabeth	AA0050	66A,66C,41
Bergmann, Marcel	AA0050	66A,66C,41
Bernard, Anne-Marie	AI0190	66C
Betancourt, Nilda	PR0100	13,66A,66C,12A
Bible, Judith	TN1710	66C
Biggs, Charlene	AG0070	11,66A,66B,66C
Billias, Anna	VA1400	66C,66A
Binger, Adlai	PA0050	36,61,66G,60A,66C
Birr, Diane	NY1800	66A,66C,66D
Bisbano, Tony	NY2650	66C
Bizzell, Gayle	TX1850	12A,66A,66C,66D
Black, Brian	AA0200	12,66C,13E
Black, Susan	AG0650	66C,61,60A
Blacklow, John	IN1700	66A,66C
Blackwell, Raymond	PA0550	66C
Blaich, Tanya	MA1400	66C
Blankenburg, Gayle	CA4500	66A,66C
Blinov, Ilya	PA3150	66A,66C,11
Blood, Charles F.	NH0250	66C
Blood, Elizabeth P.	NH0350	66C,66D
Blyth, Jennifer	PA0950	66A,66B,66C,66D,13
Boatman, Amy	KS0250	66C
Boe, Karen	WI0865	66A,66B,66C,66D
Boemler, Cathy	MO0550	66A,66B,66C,66D
Boepple, Hans C.	CA4425	13,12A,66A,66B,66C
Boey, Hooi Yin	WV0050	66,66D,20,66B,66C
Bohnenstengel, Christian	UT0200	66A,66C,13A,13B,13C
Boianova, Linda	NY3730	66C
Boianova, Linda	NY2650	66A,13C,61,39,66C
Bolshakova, Natalia	MO1800	66C
Bommelje, Ann	PA2250	66C
Bond, Kori	ID0100	12A,66A,66B,66C
Booker, Anthony	AB0150	66C
Borden, Rita	AZ0450	66A,66C,41
Boren, Benjamin J.	CA0850	66A,66B,66C,66D,13B
Born, Kristie	FL1750	66C
Borrmann, Kenneth	PA2800	66A,66B,66C,42,44
Bos, Ken	MI0850	66C,66A,66D
Bossart, Eugene	MI1900	41,66A,66C
Bostock, Anne	MA1100	66A,66C
Boston, Nancy J.	PA2150	66A,66B,66C,66D
Bowles, Adam Alan	AL1200	66C
Bowlin, Ellen	IL0300	66A,66G,66C
Bowman, Jonathan	NY2650	66C
Boyce, Emily W.	NY3717	66D,66C,66A,66B
Boyd, Sue Marston	VA1350	66A,66H,66C,66D
Braaten-Reuter, Laurie	IA1800	66A,66C,66D
Bradley, Nedra	TX1450	66C
Bradner, Janice B.	SC1200	66D,66C,66A
Bradshaw, Dean	AF0100	66C,66D
Bradshaw, Tracey	UT0200	66C,66D
Brancaleone, Francis P.	NY2200	13,66A,66D,66G,66C
Brasington, Merewyn	OH1400	66C,66D,13C,66A
Breckbill, David	NE0200	12,66C
Breckenridge, Carol Lei	IA0200	11,66A,66B,66C,66H
Breindel, Christina	RI0200	66C
Brennan, Mark	NY2650	66C
Brewer, Robert	TX3530	66C
Bridgman, Joyce M.	OK0850	66A,66H,66B,66C,66D
Brightbill, Janet	WV0560	66C,66A
Bringerud, Catherine	IN0250	66C
Brisson, Eric	MN1700	13A,13B,13C,13E,66C
Brook, Sharon D.	CA4400	11,66A,66C,66D
Brown, Adrianne	CT0350	66A,66B,66C,66D
Brown, Dana L.	IL0550	66C
Brown, Ila	FL1500	66A,66C
Brown, Nancy	MI1160	66C
Brown, Susan E.	TN0100	66A,66C
Bruk, Elfrida	IN0005	66A,13,31B,66C,66H
Brummel, Josephine I.	CA4410	66C
Brunell, David	TN1710	66A,66C
Bryant, Ron	MO1950	66C
Bryant, Thomas E.	TN1200	13,11,66A,66C,66H
Buckland, Karen W.	SC1000	66A,66C,66D
Buckner, Nathan	NE0590	66A,66C,66D,13B,13C
Buckwalter, Laurel G.	NY0100	66A,66B,66C,69
Budke, Tiffany	KS0300	66A,66C,11
Budnick, Eve	MA0400	66C
Buice, David	GA1550	66C,66H,66G,69
Bullock, Karen	NC2350	66A,13A,66C
Bulwinkle, Belle	CA2950	66A,66C,20F
Burch, Alene	TX0550	66A,66C,66D,66B
Burnaman, Stephen	TX1150	13,66A,66G,66B,66C
Burns, Elaina Denney	IA1450	66A,66C
Burton, Christopher	MI1300	66A,66C
Bustamante, Tamara A.	KY1100	36,11,13,66C,66A
Butler, Beverly	IN1450	66A,66C,66D
Butler, Debbie D.	TX3527	66A,66C,66D
Caceres, Marcelo	MI0250	66A,66B,66C,66D
Cai, Yi-Min	AL1250	66A,66B,66D,66C
Calderazzo, Joey	NC1600	66A,66C,46,47
Caldwell, Brad	OH1450	66C
Campbell, Andrew	AZ0100	66C
Cantrell, Wanda	GA1700	66C
Capistran, Raul W.	TX3515	66C,66D
Caporella, Cynthia Anne	OH1050	36,12A,66A,66C
Cardamone, Melissa	WI0250	66C
Cardoza, Don	CA3320	66A,66C
Carlson, Stephen J.	MN0150	66A,66B,66C
Carney, Robert D.	MO1550	66A,66B,66C,11,13C
Carpenter, Jean	RI0300	66C
Carpenter, William	NE0200	66C
Carrell-Coons, Mariah	OK0770	66A,66C,66D,32E
Carter, Priscilla	CA3320	66A,66C
Carver, Mark	PA0550	66C
Case, Alan L.	NY3730	66C
Casey, Rebecca L.	OH1800	66A,13,66D,66C
Castiglione, Anita	FL1450	66C,13
Cellon, Cheryl	TX3525	66C,66A
Centeno Martell, Ingrid	PR0100	13,66A,66C,32
Cerny, William J.	IN1700	12A,41,66A,66C
Chamberlain, Julie Rhyne	NC0350	66A,66B,66C,66D,11
Chambers, Steve	TX2750	13A,32B,66C
Champagne, Sebastien	AI0190	66C
Chan, Amanda	AB0200	66A,66C
Chan, Ken	IN0100	66C
Chan, Sarah S.	OK0600	66A,66C,66D,13,11
Chan, Susan	OR0850	66A,66B,66D,66C
Chan, Yan-Yan	CA3000	66A,66C
Chan-Spannagel, Yiu-Ka	OK0150	66D,66C
Chandler, Gulya	LA0030	66A,66C,66D,11,12A
Changchien, Wenting	OH2200	62D,66C,62
Charoenwongse-Shaw, Chindarat	OK1330	66A,66B,66D,66C
Cheek, Timothy Mark	MI2100	66C,39,61
Chen, Chih-Yi	IN0900	66C
Chen, Fen-Fang	AL0650	66A,66B,66D,42,66C
Chen, Shao Shen	TX0550	66A,66D,66B,66C
Cheng, Clara	CA0960	66C
Chernoff, John	CA2250	66C
Cherry, Mark	NY2200	54,40,66C
Chesebrough, Constance D.	NH0250	66C,66A
Cheung, Alissa	AA0035	66C
Chi, Sungha	IL0150	66C
Chiang, Janice ChenJu	AZ0450	66C,66A,41
Chin, Wayman	MA1175	66A,66C,42
Chitwood, Elizabeth	GA0700	66A,66B,66C
Cho, Sujung	SC0350	66A,66D,66C
Cho, Tony	CA0960	66C,39
Cho, Young-Hyun	TX3500	66A,41,66C,66B,12A
Choi, Hyunjoo	CA1425	66C,66G,66D,66A
Choi, Wooyoung	GA0050	66A,66D,66C
Cholakova, Elena	GA0750	66C
Chou, Mei-En	LA0150	66A,66B,66C,12A
Christopher, Un Chong	MO0060	11,12A,13,66A,66C
Chung, Hyunjung Rachel	GA1900	66A,13,66C
Chung, Myung-Hee	WI0865	66A,66B,66C
Church, Gretchen	IL1200	66C
Ciscon, Katherine	TX3400	66C
Clark, Adam	MI1050	66,66A,66C,66B,66D
Clark, Judith	VA1850	66C
Clark, Lauren Schack	AR0110	66C,66D,66B
Clark, Paula	ID0060	66A,66C
Class, Kevin	TN1710	66C
Clearfield, Andrea	PA3330	66C,66D,10,12F
Clegg, Trey	GA1900	66C
Clevenger, Charles	OH0450	66A,66B,66C,66D,12B
Clodfelter, John D.	IN0350	66A,66C,66D
Cloutier, David	TX3420	39,66C
Coen, Jean-David	OR1300	12A,66A,66C
Coggins, Janet	MO1780	66C
Cole, Judith E.	GA1150	11,13C,13A,66C
Coleman, Janet	OR0750	66C
Collins, Cheryl	NM0400	66A,66C,66D
Collins, Jenny	PA1100	11,13A,66A,66D,66C
Colon, Frank	VA0450	66C,39
Conatser, Brian	AR0200	13A,66A,13B,13C,66C
Conlon, Francis	DC0100	39,66A,66C,54
Connelly, Brian	TX2150	66A,66C,66E,42
Connors, Maureen	MA0150	13A,66A,66C
Conrad, Kent R.	IL0800	66A,66C,66D
Cook, Gloria	FL1550	66A,66B,13C,11,66C
Cooper, Darryl	CA4150	39,66C
Cooper, Marva W.	DC0350	11,12A,66A,66B,66C
Cooper, Ted	DC0170	66A,66C
Corley, Kirsten M.	PA2350	66A,66C
Corliss, Frank	NY0150	66C
Cornelius, John L.	TX2100	66C,66A,66D,13
Cornett, Eileen	MD0650	66C,39
Cornut, Sebastien	NJ0825	66,66A,66C
Cosgrove, Nancy	MA0600	66A,66G,66H,66B,66C
Costa, Jennifer	NC2000	66A,66C
Costigan-Kerns, Louise	CA3270	39,61,66C
Cowden, Tracy E.	VA1700	66C,66A,66D,13C
Cox, Buford	FL0040	13A,12A,66A,66C
Cozza, John	CA0840	66C
Cozza, John	CA5350	66A,66C
Crabill, Michael	VA0450	66C
Crane, Teresa Ann	IL1500	66C,61,66,66A,11
Cranmer, Carl	PA3600	66A,66C,66D
Crawford, Jenn	AJ0030	66A,66B,66C,13
Crawford, Steven	NJ0825	66C
Creighton, Elizabeth	IL1750	66C
Creviston, Hannah	AZ0100	66A,66B,66C
Crossman, Patricia	MD0175	66A,66C
Crowne, Scott	PA1400	66C,66A,42
Cruhm, Robert	TX3515	66C
Cruz, Karena	CA3520	64A,66C
Cuellar, Martin	KS0300	66A,66B,66C,66D
Cukrov, Martina	NJ0800	66C
Cukrov, Terezija	NJ0800	66C
Cultise, Theora	NY2400	66C
Cunev, Irina	LA0650	66C
Curry, Nancy	NE0590	66C
Cushing, Alanna B.	WV0400	66A,66C
Da Costa, Fabio Gardenal	NY2750	66A,42,66C
Dahl, Christina A.	NY3790	41,66A,66C
Dahl, Laura	CA4900	66A,66C
Dale, Sarah	IL1200	66C
Dalton, Dana	MA1400	66A,12A,12,66C
D'Ambrosio, David	GA0050	66A,66C,48
Daroca, Daniel	FL0050	66C,61
David, Myrtle	LA0700	11,66A,66B,66C,66D
Davies, Susan Azaret	CA0600	13,66A,66C
D'Avignon, India	CA1510	66A,66C,66D
Davis, Kimberly	PR0115	66C
Davis, Meredyth P.	KY1350	66C
De Lucas, Marina	PR0115	66C
De Mare, Anthony J.	NY2750	66A,66C
De Silva, Rohan	NY1900	66C,41
De Sousa, Beth Ann	AG0600	13,39,66C
De Souza, Jordan	AI0150	66C,39
Deahl, Lora	TX3200	66A,66C,66B,12A
Debow, Faith	TX3350	66C
DeBow, Faith	TX3175	66C,66D
Debus, Christine	TX3530	66C
Decima, Terry	MA1400	61,66C
Dees, Pamela Youngdahl	MO1250	66A,66B,66C,11,12A
DeFoor, Cynthia	GA2300	66C,66D,66B,66A
Delphin, Wilfred	LA0900	66A,66B,66C,66D
DeMio, Elizabeth	OH0600	66C
Denman, Megan A.	OH2150	66C
Denton, Damon	GA2100	66C
Denton, Kristine West	PA1200	66A,66C,66D
Desai, Nayantara	CO0830	66A,66C,66D
DeSanto, William	PA3560	36,66,31A,66C
Devereaux, Deborah	NY2550	66C
Di Bella, Karin	AG0050	66A,66B,66C
Diab, Mary Beth	IL3370	66A,66C,66B,66D
Diamond, Louise	AI0150	66C
DiBiase, Allan	NH0250	66C
Dickens, Pierce	GA0950	39,66A,66C,66G
Dickson, Douglas	CT0850	66C
Dierks, Deborah	KY1500	66C
Dill, Jane	SC1080	13,66A,66G,66C
Dillard, Chuck	TX3510	66C
Dimaras, Charis	NY1800	66A,66C
Dinkins-Matthews, Patricia A.	GA0750	66C
DiPiazza, Joseph	NC2430	66A,66C
DiPinto, Mark	MD0150	66A,66B,66C,13C

Index by Area of Teaching Interest

Name	Code	Areas
Do, Bang Lang	IA1450	66A,66C
Do, Bang Lang	IA0450	66A,66C
Dobek-Shandro, Elaine	AA0040	66A,66C
Dobner, Gabriel	VA0600	66A,66C
Dobrea-Grindahl, Mary	OH0200	66A,66B,66C,32I,66D
Dobrzanski, Slawomir Pawel	KS0650	66A,66C,66B
Dodd, Susan	FL0200	66A,66C,66D
Dollak, Haidee	NC0750	66C
Dolloff, Lori-Anne	AG0450	32A,32B,60,36,66C
Doran, Joy	IL1200	66C,66A,66D
Dore, Christine	NY2105	66A,66C
Dorfman, Amy	TN1850	41,66A,66C
Dornian, Kathy	AA0050	66A,66C,32A
Douglas, Brent	FL0450	41,66A,66C
Douglass, James B.	NC2430	66C
Drifmeyer, Fred	MA0600	66A,66C
Duce, Geoffrey	IN0910	13,66A,66C,66D
Ducharme, Karen	MA2100	66C
Dueck, Jocelyn B.	NY2250	66C,66A,61
Duerden, Jennifer	HI0050	11,66A,66C,66D
Dukes, Leslie D.	CA4460	66,42,66C
Durham, Carol S.	MS0400	66G,66A,66C,66H,12A
Easley, Delana	TN1720	66C
Eaton, Angela S.	KY1350	66C,66A
Ebright, Matthew	OH1850	66C
Eckes, Sylvia Reynolds	OH1900	66A,66C
Edie, Rebecca L.	IN0100	66A,66C
Edson, Tracey D.	OR1100	66A,66C
Edwards, Alison	CA0815	66A,66C
Edwards, Matthew	MO0850	66A,66B,66C,66D,13
Edwards, T. Matthew	MD0060	66A,13,66C,12,36
Edwards-Henry, Jacqueline	MS0500	13,66A,66B,66C
Effler, Charles E.	LA0650	66C,39,13C
Eguchi, Akira	NY0500	66A,66C
Eickelman, Diane	CO0275	66C,42
Eikner, Edward	GA2200	12A,66A,66C,66D,11
Elder, Ellen P.	MS0850	66A,66B,66D,66C
Elder, Ellen	MS0750	66A,66C,66D
Elgersma, Kristin M.	ID0250	66A,66B,66C
Elisi, Enrico	NY1100	66A,66C
Elliott, Anne	TN1150	66A,66D,66B,66C,36
Elliott, Margarett	GA0950	66C
Elshazly, Janet	SC0275	66A,66C,66D
Embretson, Deborah	MN1100	61,66D,11,20,66C
Emerson, Tara M.	TX2400	66C
Engbretson, Chris	OR0450	66A,66C
Engle, Marilyn	AA0150	41,66A,66B,66C,12B
Enman, Thomas	MA1175	66C,12A,54,66A,61
Ensor, Robert	MO0260	12A,47,66A,66C,54
Epp, Richard	AB0100	39,66C
Epperson, Anne	TX3510	66C
Erickson, Margaret	MO0200	66C
Etheridge, Kay	CA5200	11,32B,66A,66B,66C
Evans, Dane	LA0300	66C
Ewoldt, Patrice R.	PA2300	66A,66C,66B,67F,42
Ezhokina, Oksana	WA0650	66A,66B,66C,66
Faflak, Marcela	SD0400	66A,66B,66C
Fan, Paula	AZ0500	66A,66C
Farris, Phillip	OH2250	66A,66C,66D,11
Faughn, Wendy	AL0500	66A,66B,66C,66D
Faulkner, Lynn	AL1200	66A,66C,66C
Favario, Giulio	IL0550	66C
Fear, Judith	KS1450	66A,66C
Feeney, Kendall	WA0250	66A,43,66C
Feldman, Jonathan	NY1900	66C
Ferguson, Dianne S.	NE0200	13,66A,66C,66D
Ferguson, Eva	IL1200	66C,66D
Ferrell, Mark T.	KS1350	39,61,66C
Ferrente, Joseph	NY2550	66C
Ferrer Brooks, Rafael	PR0115	66C
Fielding, Cheryl Lin	CA0960	66C
Fischer, Martha	WI0815	66A,66C,39,41
Fischler, Gail	AZ0300	66A,66B,66C
Fitz-Gerald, Kevin	CA5300	41,66A,66C
Flournoy-Buford, Debbie	TX3650	32B,32D,34,66C,66A
Flower, Carol	SD0580	66A,66C,66B
Floyd, Rosalyn	GA0250	13A,13,11,66A,66C
Fogg, Ryan	TN0250	66A,66D,66B,66C
Follingstad, Karen J.	CA4100	11,66A,66C,66D
Fong, Grace	CA0960	66A,66B,66C
Forbat, David	OK1330	66A,66B,66C,66D
Forconi, John	NY2150	66C
Ford, Jeffrey	TX3370	66A,66C
Foreman, Charles	AA0150	66A,66B,66C,20G,41
Forman, Dick	VT0350	47,29,66C
Forsha, Heather	NY1400	13C,66A,66C,32E
Fortin, Marie	AI0190	66C
Foster, Brenda	MO0850	66A,66C
Fox, Kim	VA1150	66A,66C
Francoeur-Krzyzek, Damien	MA1400	66C
Franzetti, Allison G.	NJ0800	66C
Franzetti-Brewster, Allison	NJ0700	66C,41,13A,13B,13C
Frazer, Dianne	LA0200	66C
Fredriksen, Brandt	GA1050	66A,66C,42
Freeman, Christine L.	IN0905	13A,66C,66A
Freer, Elinor	NY1100	66C,42
Frieling, Randall J.	IN0100	66A,66C,66D,66G
Friesen, Peter	CO0550	66C,66D
Froese, Elvera	AG0600	39,66C,36
Fry, Daniel	MO1830	66C
Fugo, Charles Leonard	SC1110	66A,66C
Fung, Geneva	TX2700	66C
Gable, Kathleen	AJ0150	66D,66A,66C
Gagnon, Allison	NC1650	66C
Gagnon-Matte, Francoise	AI0220	66A,66C
Gallo, Sergio	GA1050	66A,66B,66C,66D
Ganske, Kathy	OR0450	66C
Garcia, Lynda K.	AL1100	66C
Garner, Catherine H.	NC0650	66C
Garrett, Margo	NY1900	66C
Gartner, Janet Sussman	NY2400	66C
Gartz, Michael	MI0050	66C,66G
Garver, Beryl	NY1100	66C
Gaudette, Fannie	AI0050	13C,66C
Gehrich, Leonora S.	IL2450	66A,66C,66D
George, David Alan	KY0250	66A,66C
Gerhart, Martha	TX2400	66C
Germain, Francois	NY3780	66A,66C
Geston, Janet	ND0350	66C
Gheesling, Laurelie	AL0200	66C
Gibbons, Bruce L.	IL1750	66A,66C
Gilbert, E. Beth	WI0860	66C,66A,66B,13B
Gilbert, Joan	TN1680	66A,66C
Gilliam, Alisa	NC0650	66C
Gilliam, Jeffrey	WA1250	66A,66C
Gilwood, Deborah	MA2100	66C
Gingerich, Carol	GA2130	66A,66B,66C
Giunta, Cynthia	IA0550	66D,66C,66A
Glasgow, David M.	PA0950	66A,66C,13A
Glass, Anne	TN0050	13A,66A,66G,66C
Glennon, Maura	NH0150	66A,66C,66D,66H
Glover, Angela	FL0040	66A,66B,66C,66D
Glover, Judy	PA3330	66D,66C
Glover, Robert	FL1450	66C
Godes, Catherine	TN1450	66A,66C,66D
Godin, Olivier	AI0150	66C
Goff, Carolyn	GA1300	13A,66C,66A
Gokelman, William	TX3410	60,36,66A,66C,31A
Goldenberg, William	IL2200	66A,66C,41
Goldhamer, Brahm	AG0300	66C,39
Goldman, Lawrence	MS0560	66A,66D,66,11,66C
Goldstein, Joanna	IN1010	13,66A,66C,38,11
Goldstein, Tamara B.	CO0550	66A,66C,66B,42
Gonder, Jonathan P.	NY3730	66A,66C,11,13A,13B
Gonthier, Esther	AI0150	66C
Gonzalez-Palmer, Barbara	NJ1130	66C
Goodridge, Andrew	MA2030	66C,66D
Goodwin, Julia	OR0700	66A,66D,11,12A,66C
Gordon, Pamela	AL1170	66D,66C
Gordon, Tony A.	MS0050	66A,66D,66B,66C,11
Gourdin, Lori	SC0400	66C
Gourfinkel, Anna	NY1100	66C
Grace, Rose S.	FL0100	66A,66B,66C,66D
Graham, Edward E.	SC1050	66A,66C,66D,12A
Granger, Linda	VA0650	61,66C
Graves, Jody C.	WA0250	66C,66B,66C
Gray, Kathryn A.	PA3260	66A,66C,66G
Gray, Susan Keith	SD0600	66A,66B,66C,66D
Gresham, Momoko	IL1200	66C
Gretz, Ronald	MD0175	13A,13,66A,66C,54
Griffin, John C.	MI2250	10,13,13C,66C
Griffiths, Kenneth R.	OH2200	66C
Grigg, Eric	OK0700	66C
Grimes, Janice	LA0200	66C
Grimes, Sonja	MN1280	66C
Grimm, Marlys	IA0700	66C
Grobler, Pieter J.	OH0950	11,66C
Grobler, Sophia	OH0950	66A,66C,66D,20
Gross, David	SC0750	66A,66C,66B,66D
Grossman, Morley K.	TX3525	11,66A,66C,66C
Grosz, Gay	LA0050	66A,66C
Gualdi, Paolo Andre'	SC0710	66A,11,13,66B,66C
Guenette, Maria Mika	TX3370	66A,66D,66C
Guernsey, Diane	NY2200	66C,61
Gunn, Julie	IL3300	66C
Gurt, Joseph	MI0600	66A,66C
Guy, Robin	IA1600	66C,66D
Haager, Julia	AA0050	32A,66C
Haddock, Kathleen	NY4150	66A,66C
Hagel, Clint	AA0020	31A,36,61,66C
Hagner, Carolyn Zepf	KY1000	66A,66B,66C
Hahn, Christina	OH1850	66C
Hahn, Christopher	MT0400	66A,66B,66C,66D
Hakken, Lynda S.	IA0400	66G,13,66C,66A,11
Halbeck, Patricia	TN0050	66A,66B,66C,66D
Hale, Charlotte	AB0150	66C
Ham, Marilynn	IN0200	66A,66C
Hamilton, Vivian	SC0750	36,66C
Hamm, Laura	WV0440	32,36,66A,66D,66C
Hammett, Hank	TX2400	61,66C,39
Hammond, Gary	NJ0825	66C
Hancock, Robin	UT0050	66C
Hankins, Tyson	NC0750	66C
Hanna, Joan	AR0850	66C
Hannah, Mike	NC1050	35H,66C
Hapner, David E.	OH2450	66C,54
Happel, Rebecca	MI1750	66A,66C
Harding, Christopher	MI2100	66A,66C,66D
Harley, Andrew	NC2430	66C
Harlos, Steven C.	TX3420	66A,66C
Harper, Carole	VA0700	66C
Harper, Erin Michelle	NC0350	66A,66C,66D
Harrell, Jana	GA0850	66C
Harrell, Mary	CA1900	66A,66C,66D
Harris, Ben	TN1850	66C
Harris, Caleb	CO0950	66A,66C
Harris, Kay	SC1080	66C,66D
Hatem, Jasmine	TX3450	66A,66B,66C
Hatley, Paula	CA5550	66C
Hatsuyama, Hiroyo	CA3600	66C
Haug, Sue E.	PA2750	66A,66B,66C,66D
Haughton, Ethel Norris	VA1750	13,12A,12,20G,66C
Hawkins, Ashley	GA1200	66C
Hawkins, Jemmie Peevy	AL0650	32,66C
Hawkins, Randall	SC0275	66C
Hay, Dennis	AR0050	13A,13B,11,66A,66C
Hay, James	MA2020	66C
Hayes, Christina	NC0050	66A,66C,66D
Hayner, Phillip A.	GA1650	11,12,66A,66C,66D
Haynes, Casey	LA0450	66C
Hecht, Gerard	NY3785	61,66C
Heersink, Barbara	CO0050	66C,66A
Heid, David	NC0600	66C
Helmrich, Dennis	IL3300	66A,66C
Helms, Elizabeth	CA0550	66C
Helms, Elizabeth	CA5360	66C,13A,13C,36,39
Helms, Jessica	CA0550	66C
Helms, Warren	NJ1400	66C
Helton, James Caton	IN0150	66A,66C
Henckel, Kristina	OK0150	66C,11
Henderson, V. Douglas	VA1150	66C,66F
Henry, Colleen	MA1600	66C
Henschell, Lana	AA0050	66C
Herbst-Walker, Nikki	AA0050	66C
Herod, Sheila	TX1750	13,12A,66A,66C,66D
Herrington, Carolyn	AA0200	66C,11
Hersh, Alan	KY1450	66A,66B,66C,41
Hesla, Steven	MT0400	66A,66B,66C,66D
Hess, John	AG0500	66A,66C,41,39
Hess, Nathan A.	NY1800	66A,66D,66C,66B,66B
Hester, Timothy	TX3400	66A,66B,66C
Hetrick, Mark	OH1330	11,61,66C
Hewson, Cheryl	ND0100	66C
Heydenburg, Audrejean	MI2000	11,12A,66A,66B,66C
Heyman, Steven M.	NY4150	66A,66D,66C,66B
Hibberd, Gordon	NY3600	66C
Hibler, Starla	OK0300	12A,66A,66C
Hickman, Kathryn	OK0150	66C,11
Higdon, Patricia	MO1810	66C
Highfill, Philip	OH1700	66C,60B
Hildebrandt, Darcy	AJ0030	66A,66B,66C,13
Hill, Christine	OH0600	66C
Hill-Le, Holly	OK0150	66C,13A
Hines, Betsy Burleson	TX1400	66D,66C
Hinson, G. Maurice	KY1200	12A,66A,31A,66B,66C
Hintz, Gail	MO1900	66C

Index by Area of Teaching Interest

Name	Code	Areas
Hironaka-Bergt, Mieko	MO1830	66C
Hirst, Dennis	UT0300	66A,66B,66C,66D
Hirt, Linda L.	IL0750	66C
Hishman, Marcia	IL1200	66C,66A
Hlashweova, Jamila	AK0150	66C
Ho, Stephanie	NJ0700	66A,66C,11
Hoekman, Timothy	FL0850	66A,66C
Hoffman, Lee	OH0500	39,61,66C,54
Hofmann, Cameron	TX0300	66C
Hoft, Timothy	NV0050	66A,66C
Hoirup, Marlene	NC2500	66A,66C
Holden, Jon	NY2750	66C,66D
Holliday, Stacey A.	SC0350	66A,66C
Holliston, Robert	AB0210	66C,12A,11,39,66A
Holm, Robert	AL1300	66A,66B,66C,66D,66H
Holmes, Janet	CA3320	66C,61
Holstrom, Jacqueline	MN1600	66C
Holt, Beverly	IL1890	66A,66G,66C
Holt, Matthew K.	MO0800	66C
Hong, Caroline	OH1850	11,66A,66C,66D
Hong, Sojung Lee	IL1300	66A,66D,66B,42,66C
Hoppmann, Ken J.	NE0525	66A,66B,20,66C,12A
Hord, John	CA1850	66A,66C
Horn, Daniel Paul	IL3550	66A,66C
Horne, Timothy	NY1400	66C
Horneff, Donald C.	MD0520	66F,66C,66D,66H,32E
Horvath, Juliane	NM0500	66A,66C
Horvath, Maria	IL1610	66A,66C,13,66D,11
Hosoda-Ayer, Kae	TX0300	66C
Hostetter, Elizabeth	AL0550	66A,66D,66C,13,66
Houk, Chad M.	NE0200	66C
Houle, Arthur Joseph	CO0225	66A,66C,66B,66D
Howell, Andrew P.	RI0300	36,66C,66G
Howell, Jane	PA2900	66A,66C,13A,54,11
Howenstine, Nancy	OH2290	66C
Howsmon, James	OH1700	66C
Hsieh, Chialing	KY0900	66C
Hsu, Yun-Ling	FL1800	66A,66B,66C,66D
Huang, Kuang-Hao	IL0730	66A,66C
Huang-Davie, Yuling	LA0760	66C
Huckleberry, Alan R.	IA1550	66A,66B,66C,66
Huddleston, Debra	OR0250	66C,66A,66G
Huddleston, Debra	OR0450	66C
Hudson, Stephen	NJ0975	66A,66B,66C,11
Hudson, William Andrew	TX1600	66A,11,66C,66D
Huff, Dwayne	MO0200	11,66A,66B,66C,66D
Huffman, Timothy	OH2050	66A,13B,66B,66D,66C
Hull, Robert A.	NY3717	66A,66C
Hundley, Marion S.	FL0100	10A,66A,66C,13
Hunt, Robert	TX2250	66C
Hunt, Sylvia	ID0070	66G,66C
Hurd, Mary	MI0300	66A,66B,66C,66D,13A
Hutchinson, Nicholas	IL0750	61,66C
Hutchison, Patrick	GA0940	66C
Hutton, Judy F.	NC2650	13,66A,66B,66C,66D
Hyland, Judy	IA1300	13A,66C,11
Imhoff, Andrea G.	TX2900	13A,11,66C,66A
Imperio, Roy	MA0250	66A,66B,41,66C,11
Indergaard, Lyle	GA2150	66A,66C,66D
Ingram, David	OR1300	66A,66C
Inkman, Joanne	NC2500	66A,66C,66D,13A
Irei, Norito	FL1550	66A,66C
Irwin, Roseanna Lee	PA0550	66C
Ishida, Nobuyuki	NY0625	66C
Iwama, Kayo	NY0150	61,66C
Jaber, Thomas I.	TX2150	36,60A,66C
Jackson, Cliff	KY1450	61,66C
Jackson, Russell	PA2450	66A,66G,66C
Jaimes, Judit	WI0825	41,66A,66B,66C,42
James, Donna Bunn	GA1650	66C
James, William R.	FL1300	66A,66C,66D
Jarianes, Stephen	TX1600	66C
Jarrell, Erinn	CA5355	13,66A,66B,66C,66D
Jeffers, Rebecca	OR0700	13A,66B,66C,66D
Jeoung, Ji-Young	IN1050	66C
Jimenez, Pedro J.	PR0115	66C
Jobe, Elena	GA0600	66A,66B,66C
Johansen, Judy	CA3800	11,66C
Johnson, Deborah	OK1400	66C
Johnson, Herbert	MN0250	11,66A,66B,66C
Johnson, Herbert	MN1250	12A,13,31A,66B,66C
Johnson, Jeremiah	NE0200	66A,66C
Johnson, Lacey	VA0800	66A,66C
Johnson, Michelle	TX2600	66A,66B,66C,66D,66E
Johnson, Penny	AJ0100	66A,66C
Johnson, Sharon L.	NY1700	66C,66A,66D,31A
Johnson, Wayne D.	WA0800	11,12A,66A,66C
Johnston, Amanda J.	MS0700	66C,61
Jones, Linda	OH0600	66C
Jones, Lis	AR0250	66A,66C,66D
Jones, Richard	PA2900	66C,11
Jones, Robert D.	FL1470	66A,66G,66C,66D,34
Jones, Sue	IL1550	42,66A,66C,66D,13C
Jones, Warren	NY2150	66C
Joo, Narae	IL3500	66C
Ju, Ara	MO0850	66C,66D
Juhn, Hee-Kyung	AR0300	66A,13C,66G,66C,66B
Jung, Eunice	MD0850	66C
Jung, Hyesook	AL0950	66A,66B,66C,13
Kaarre, Lois	MI1750	66D,66C
Kachelmeier, Diane	WI0300	66C
Kalish, Gilbert	NY3790	41,66A,66C,43
Kanamaru, Tomoko	NJ0175	66A,66B,66C,66D
Kanda, Sanae	MA1650	10A,42,66A,66C,66D
Kane, Lila	RI0200	66C
Kaneda, Mariko	OH2000	66C,66A,66D,13B,13C
Kang, Chun-Wei	NY2105	66C
Kang, Juyeon	IA1200	66A,66D,66C,13C
Karpoff, Fred S.	NY4150	42,66A,66C,66B
Kasman, Tatiana	AL1150	66C,41
Katz, Martin E.	MI2100	41,66C
Kauffman, Mary Adelyn	FL0700	66C
Kautsky, Catherine C.	WI0350	66A,66C,66E,41
Kawamura, Manami	CA0350	41,66A,66C
Kear, Eleanor G.	OH2150	66C
Kebuladze, Tatyana	NJ0800	66A,66C,66D
Keele, Roger	TX2250	66C
Kefferstan, Christine	WV0750	66A,66B,66C,66D
Kehler Siebert, Judith	AC0100	66A,66C,66D,42
Keller, Deborah	MI1985	66A,66C,66G
Kelly, Frankie J.	LA0800	66C,40,41,42,11
Kennedy, Warren	GA1700	66C
Kerr, Brady	CA3265	66C,35A,35C,35D,35G
Ketter, Craig	NJ0825	66A,66C,42
Kibbe-Hodgkins, Shiela	MA0400	66C,66A
Kiehl, Vicky	AR0200	66A,66H,66B,66D,66C
Kies, Arlene	NH0350	66A,66B,66C
Kim, Heawon	NY2105	66A,66C
Kim, Howard D.	SC0050	66A,66D,13B,66C,11
Kim, Hye-Young	CA0960	66C
Kim, Jean	NY0270	11,13,66A,66C
Kim, Joo-Hae	MS0750	66C
Kim, Kay	IL2150	66C
Kim, Mansoon H.	NJ0800	66B,66C
Kim, Mina	NY3785	66A,66C
Kim, Minjung	MI0050	66A,66C
Kim, Seung-Ah	NC2435	11,66D,66C
Kim, Soyeon	NJ0800	66C
Kim, Sung-Im	PA0550	66C
Kim, Sungeun	OH0200	66A,66C
Kim, Yoo-Jung	MI1200	66A,66C,66D
Kim, Youmee	OH1900	66A,66C,66D
Kimme, Glenn	NY0650	66C,66G
Kincade, Gertrude C.	AR0750	66H,66C,66D
King, Adam	AL1195	66A,13,66D,66C
King, Anita	OR1300	13,66A,66C
King, Jennifer	AF0050	66C
Kingham, Lesley	AG0050	66G,66C,66A
Kiorpes, George A.	NC2430	66A,66B,66C
Kirk, Erin	CA0845	66C,66D
Kislenko, Natalia	CA5060	66A,66C,66D
Kline, Rhonda	WA1050	66C
Klinedinst, Sherry	IN1450	66C
Klotzbach, Susan	IL1200	66C,13A,13B,13C
Klukas, Suzanne	AB0090	66A,66C
Knibbs, Lester A.	NC0800	11,66C
Knickerbocker, Sharon	IL1900	66A,66B,66C,66D
Knight, Gregory	AA0200	66C
Ko, EunMi	NY2650	66C
Kochis, Jane	MN1285	66A,66C,11
Koehler, William	IL2200	66A,66C
Koen, Kerry	NY0650	66C,66A
Koenig, Robert	CA5060	66C
Kompass, Lynn R.	SC1110	39,66C
Kong, Gary	NY2650	66C
Kong, Joanne	VA1500	66A,66H,66C,55
Konstantinov, Tzvetan	DC0100	66A,66C,66D
Koranda, Ann	IL1890	66A,66G,66C
Korneev, Dmitri V.	NJ0800	66C
Korth, Jonathan	HI0210	66A,66B,66C
Korzhev, Mikhail	CA0960	66C
Korzhev, Mikhail	CA0815	66C
Koslowske, Charles T.	OK0750	66C,61
Kossodo, Verena	NY2400	66C
Kot, Don	NY2650	66A,61,66D,66C,54
Kovacovic, Paul	IA0200	10,12A,66A,66C
Krasnican, Martha	IN0800	66C
Kraus, Nanette	KS0050	66C,66D
Krebs, Harald M.	AB0150	13,66C
Krebs, John A.	AR0350	66A,66C,39,11,13
Kregler, Michael C.	RI0150	66A,66C,47
Krueger, Mary Beth	CO0550	54,61,66C,66D
Kubus, Daniel	MO1780	66C
Kuo, Ruth	CA0550	66C
Kuroda, Elena	LA0550	66C,66D
Kustanovich, Serafima	MA0650	66A,66C,41
Kwak, Eun-Joo	WI0150	66A,66B,66C,42,12A
Lamb, Virginia P.	NY2150	66C
Lane, LuAnn	TX1850	11,13,66A,66C,66D
Lane, Mathew	MD0400	13A,13C,66A,66C
Lange, Richard A.	MN1280	66A,66B,66C
Lanners, Heather	OK0800	66A,13C,66C
Lanzrein, Valentin Christian	IN0350	61,66C
Lapp, Beverly K.	IN0550	66B,66A,11,66C
Larocco, Sharon Moss	NC0750	66C,66D
Larsen, Laurel	SC0900	66A,66C,66B,13,66D
Larsen, Robert L.	IA1350	12A,36,39,66A,66C
Larson, Deanna	IA0150	66C
Lau, Daniel	MD0150	66A,66B,66C,12A
Laubengayer, Karen	MS0350	66A,66B,66C,66D
Laurel, Edward	NY2750	66C
Lawrence, Edwin	MA2250	13C,66A,66G,66H,66C
Lawson, William	NY3705	61,66C
Lee, A. Ram	MI0100	66C
Lee, Chiayi	IL1085	66C
Lee, Donna	OH1100	66A,66B,66C,42
Lee, Gerald K.	WV0600	66A,66B,66C,66D
Lee, Hsin-Bei	MA1400	66C
Lee, Joohyun	TX2960	66D,66C
Lee, Kaju	TX2250	66C
Lee, Katherine K.		66A,66C
Lee, Kyung	CA3600	66C,66D
Lee, Kyung-A	AA0035	66C
Lee, Marian Y.	IA1300	66A,66B,66C,13C,11
Lee, Patricia	IL2650	66A,66H,66B,66C,66D
Lee, Pei-Shan	CA0835	66C
Lee, Sun Jung	WV0100	66A,66C,66D
Lee, You Ju	GA2000	66A,66C,66D,66B
LeePreston, Nicole	IN1750	66A,66C
Leerstang, Carmen	LA0300	66C
Lehman, Marilyn J.	NY1600	66A,66C,42
Lemmons, Cheryl T.	TX0050	13C,66C
Lemson, Deborah	TX3850	66A,66G,66C,66D
Lenz, Andrea	NV0100	13,64B,66C
Leon-Shames, Stephanie L.	OK1350	66C,42
Lesbines, Melissa	NC0050	11,66A,66C
Leventhal, Lois A.	MS0750	66A,66C,66D
Levtov, Vladimir	AA0150	41,66A,66C,66D,42
Lewis, Andrew	MD0175	11,66A,66C
Lewis, Andrew J.	MS0350	66A,66C
Lewis, Christopher	VT0050	66A,66B,66C,66D
Lewis, Kelly	OH2275	66C
Li, Ping-Hui	PR0150	13A,13C,14A,66A,66C
Li-Bleuel, Linda	SC0400	66C,11,32,12A,66
Lifshen, Faith	PA2250	66C
Lima, Deloise	FL0850	66C
Lin, Hsaio-Ling	CO0800	66C
Lin, Tao	FL1125	66C,42
Lindsay, Tedrin Blair	KY1450	61,66C
Lingren, Allison	NE0200	66C
Lington, Victoria	CA0900	66C
Lionello, Cathy	CA2100	66C
Lipke-Perry, Tracy D.	MN1600	66A,66C
Lisovskaya-Sayevich, Lolita	MO1000	66C
Lister-Sink, Barbara	NC2205	66A,66B,66C,42
Livingston, Christi J.	CO0350	66C
Lockert, Daniel	CA3270	66C
Loewen, Laura	AC0100	66A,39,66C
Loewy, Donna S.	OH2200	66C
Lofquist, Louise H.	CA3600	61,66C
Lohorn, Michiko	CA4100	66C
Lombard, Becky	GA2050	66A,13B,13C,12A,66C
Long, Arlene	TX2930	66A,66C,66D
Long, Lillian F.	WV0050	61,66C,66G,39,44
Long, Louanne J.	CA5150	13,66A,66B,66C
Long, Timothy G.	NY3790	61,66C

Index by Area of Teaching Interest

Name	Code	Areas
Longhi, Ami	AA0050	66C
Longworth, Peter	AG0300	42,66C
Loparits, Elizabeth	NC2440	66C,11
Lopez Yanez, Ruth	CA3460	13A,60,66,66C
Lopez, Jose R.	FL0700	66A,66C,66H,66B
Louise-Turgeon, Anne	FL0650	66A,66C
Lovelace, Timothy	MN1623	66C
Lovely, Christopher	AL1195	66A,66C
Lowrey, Ariane	AA0035	66C
Lubin, Howard	OH1700	66C,66A
Luk, Siu Yan	NY2500	66C
Lum, Anne Craig	HI0150	66D,66A,64A,45,66C
Lundberg, Erika	MN1100	66A,66B,66C
Lusk, Terry	OH2200	66C,39
Luther, Sigrid	TN0200	13,66A,66B,31A,66C
Lutsyshyn, Oksana	VA1000	13A,13B,66A,66C
Lyons, David P.	IL2900	66C
M. de Oca, Patricia	TX3520	66D,66C,54
MacCrae, Cynthia Perry	AL1200	66A,66B,66C,66D
Mack, Ellen	MD0650	66A,66C
Mackey, Lynne A.	VA0300	66A,66B,66C,66D,13
Macovei, Felix	CA5355	66C
MacPhail, Heather	OH1450	66C,42
Madsen, Charles A.	VT0100	66A,12,11,66C
Maes, James	MA1100	66A,66G,66C,66D,11
Magrath, Jane	OK1350	66B,66A,66D,66,66C
Mahamuti, Gulimina	OH2000	66A,66D,66C,66B
Maher, Betty	AG0350	66C
Maher, Dana F.	OK1450	66C
Maimine, Anna	NY3717	66A,66B,66C
Maiullo, David	NJ0825	66C
Mallimo, Katherine	NJ0800	66C
Mallinson, Chai Kyou	NY3705	66A,66C
Malone, Joy	KY0800	66A,66C
Malyuk, Amy	OH2150	66C
Mancinelli, Judith	IL1750	66A,66C
Manes, Stephen G.	NY4320	66A,66C
Manner, Mollie	NE0450	66C
Manno, Terrie	MN1120	66A,66B,66C,66D
Manriquez, Luz	PA0550	66C
Manus, Elizabeth A.	PA2550	66A,66C
March, James J.	IA1100	66A,66B,66C,12A
March, Kathryn Lucas	IA1100	13C,66A,66D,66C
Marchand, Jean	AI0150	66C
Marchena, Martha	NJ0700	66A,66C
Marchukov, Sergey	PA2900	66A,66D,66C,13A
Marinova, Kristina	AR0750	66C
Markham, I-Fei Chen	NY3725	66C
Markun, Mila M.	WV0400	32A,66A,66C,66D
Marshall, Cindy	GA0950	66C
Marshall, Peter M.	GA1050	66C
Martin, Canarissa	KY0550	66C
Martin, Roland E.	NY4320	66G,66H,66C
Masaki, Megumi	AC0050	13,66A,66C,43,66B
Mason, Alan	FL0050	11,12,31B,66A,66C
Masters, Richard J.	TX3510	66C,39
Mastrogiacomo, Leonard	FL0850	66A,66C
Mastrogiacomo, Norma	FL0850	66A,66C
Matsumoto, Kanae	CA5030	66A,66C
Matsuo, Jun	SC0450	66A,66G,66B,66C,13
Matzke, Laura	MN0200	66A,66G,66C,68,31A
Mauchley, Jay	ID0250	66A,66C
Mauro, Lucy	WV0750	66A,66C,66B
May, Nathanael A.	MO0850	66,66B,66C,66D
Mayfield, David C.	NJ0825	66C
Mayo, Nancy	MO1950	66C
Mazonson, Eric	MA2020	66C
McAlister, Andrea	OH1700	66A,66C
McBee, Karen L.	TX0125	12A,11,66A,66C,66D
McCall, Gina	TN1000	66A,66C
McCann, Karen	NV0050	61,66C
McCarrey, Stacy	HI0050	66A,66C,66D
McCarthy, Justin	NH0250	66C
McCollough, Teresa	CA4425	13,12A,66A,66B,66C
McConnell, Joan	OH0950	66C,66G,13C,66D,13B
McCord, Rebecca	VA1400	13,66A,66C
McCoy, Darcy	IN0350	66A,66C,12A,66B
McCoy, Eleanor K.	OH2275	66C,66G
McCoy, Louise	AL1250	66C,66D
McCoy, Steve	FL0400	66A,66C
McCright, Matthew	MN0300	66A,66C,66B
McDaniel, Jan	OK0750	39,54,66C,12A,61
McDonald, Margaret	CO0800	66C
McDonald, Shawn	MI1300	61,66C,39
McElhaney, Carla	TX3100	66C
McFarland, Kay Dawn	KY1425	11,66A,66C,66D
McGee, Lynnette	CA1425	66C,66A
McGuire, Jennifer	TN1850	66C
McIntosh, John S.	AG0500	13,66G,66C,31A
McKee, Holly	MO0550	66C
McKeever, James I.	WI0835	12A,66A,66C,66B
McKirdy, Colleen	ND0100	66A,66B,66C
McLean, Pierre	AI0150	66C
Mcleod Metz, Caroline	AA0050	66C
McMahon, Michael	AI0150	39,40,66C,61,66A
McReynolds, Timothy	MD1010	66C,66A
McRoberts, Terry	TN1660	66A,66C,66D,66B
McVey, Roger D.	WI0845	12A,66A,66C,66D
McWilliams, Kent M.	MN1450	66A,66C,66D,66E
Meacham, Helen M.	PA2000	66A,66C,11,13A
Mears, Perry G.	TN0850	66A,66C
Meinert, Anita	IA1950	64C,66A,66C,54
Melendez, Jose	PR0115	66A,66C
Melgaard, Connie	GA0940	66C
Mellenbruch, Judy	TX0550	66C
Melson, Christine	CT0500	13A,13C,36,66C
Memmott, Jenny	MO0050	66A,66C,33
Mengelkoch, Eva	MD0850	66A,66C,66B,66H,66E
Mercier, Richard E.	GA0950	66A,66C,39
Merfeld, Robert	MA1175	66A,66C
Merrill, Kenneth W.	NY2150	66C
Merrill, Paul	NH0350	66C,66D
Meyer, Beverly	NY2200	54,40,66C
Middaugh, Laurie	AL1200	66C,66D
Middleton, R. Hugh	NC0500	11,66A,66C
Mikolajewski, Alice	DC0100	36,66A,66C,66D
Miles, Tammy	MS0370	13,66A,66C,36
Miller, Elaine	NC2000	13C,66A,66C,66B,13A
Miller, Julie Welsh	NY3780	66C
Miller, Kathryn	PA3650	66A,66C,69
Miller, Peter	TX3360	66C,61,64C,66G
Miller, Tammy	FL1750	66C,66A,66D
Millican, Brady	MA0800	13,11,12A,66A,66C
Mills, Robert	AZ0440	13,66A,66C
Mineva, Daniela	CA2250	66A,66B,66C
Miotke, David	CA3520	66A,66H,66C,13C
Miranda, Julianne M.	IN0250	66C,66D
Mitchell, Carol	GA0940	13,66A,66G,66C,66D
Mitchell, Charlene	MO0600	32B,66A,66C,66D
Miyama, Yoko	OR0050	66,13,12A,66C,66D
Moak, Elizabeth W.	MS0750	66A,66D,66C
Moegle, Mary Steele A.	LA0250	11,66A,66C,66D
Mogerman, Flora	AZ0490	66A,66C
Mohr, Deanne	MN1700	66A,66C,66B,13B,13C
Molberg, Keith	AJ0030	66A,34D,13,66C,13A
Molina, Andrea	IL0400	66C
Molina, Rocio	TX3515	66C,66D
Molinari, Kyounghwa	AR0300	66A,66C,66D
Moll, Brian	MA1175	66C,66A
Monroe, Michael	MA0950	66A,66C
Mood, Aaron	NC2700	66C
Moore, John	TX2200	11,66A,66C,12A,66D
Moore, Kevin	NY2950	13,66A,66C,66D,10A
Moore, Laura M.	AL1300	36,40,60A,61,66C
Moore, Ruth	NE0300	66A,66B,66C
Morales, Leonel	PR0115	66C
Moreau, Barton	ID0050	13,11,66C,66D,66A
Morita, Lina	LA0350	13C,41,66A,66C,66D
Moritz, Benjamin	PA2150	66A,66B,66C,66D
Morris, Richard	NE0450	66C
Morris, Steven	MA1900	39,61,66C
Morrison, John	WV0300	62,66C
Mortensen, John J.	OH0450	66A,66C,66D
Morton, Glenn	NY2250	66C,61
Mortyakova, Julia V.	MS0550	66A,66D,66B,66C,12B
Mosbey, Jerad M.	IL2250	66C
Moseley, Jessica Barnett	SC0750	13,66C,66D
Moss, Elaine	WI0750	66C,66D,66B,66A,32A
Moulton, Joyce	ME0200	66A,66B,66C
Muckenfuss, Robert W.	MD0650	66C
Munn, Alexandra	AA0020	66A,66C
Munn, Alexandra M.	AA0100	66A,66B,66C
Muraco, Thomas	NY2150	66C
Murakami, Kazuo	AR0850	66A,66C
Murphy, Hugh	NY3785	39,66C
Murphy, Karen Lee	MS0500	66B,66C
Murray, Janice	NC0250	66A,66C,66D,13
Myatt, Traci	OH1600	66D,66C
Nadgir, Arunesh N.	TN1100	66A,66B,66C
Nagel, Susan	ND0350	66C
Nakhmanovich, Raisa	AG0650	66A,66C
Namer, Dina	AG0250	66A,66C,66H
Namminga, Jaime	ND0600	13C,66C,66A
Nargizyan, Lucy	CA1700	66A,66C
Narikawa, Masako	TX0250	66C
Natenberg, Reena Berger	KS1050	66A,66C,41
Nathan, Alan	MI1400	66A,66C
Naumchyk, Alena	AA0050	66C
Neese, Charity	GA1700	66C
Neese, Wanda	SC0900	66A,66C
Neil, Mary	IL0100	13,66A,66C,66B
Nelson, Margaret	NJ0975	13A,66C,66D
Nelson, Seth	TX3350	66C
Nemko, Deborah G.	MA0510	66A,66C,66D,11
Nesterov, Dmitry	AA0050	66C
Neufeld-Smith, Cynthia	KS1400	66C
Newbrough, William J.	NY1700	66A,66B,13C,13E,66C
Newcomb, Suzanne	OH2050	66A,66D,66C
Newton, Timothy D.	NY3765	60A,60B,66A,66C
Nguyen, Alexandra	CO0800	66C
Nie, James Ian	WI0100	66A,66C,35D,35C
Nies, Craig	TN1850	66A,41,66C
Nigrim, Dana	AI0150	66C
Nine-Zielke, Nicola	OR0700	61,66C
Nisbett, Robert	CO0250	13,12A,66C
Nishimura, Julie	DE0150	66C
Niskala, Naomi	PA3150	66A,66C,13
Nix, Brad K.	KS1250	66B,66A,66C,10F,66D
Noland, Brenda	OR0175	66C
Norberg, Anna H.	OK1450	66A,66C,66D,15
O'Connor, Peter J.	NY0100	66A,66C
O'Dell, Debra	ID0140	66A,66C,11,66D,12A
O'Donnell, Patrick	DC0170	66A,66C
O'Farrell, Elsa	NC2400	66C,66A
Ogaard, Sigurd	TX3200	66C
O'Grady, Judy	WI0808	66C
Ohl, Dorothy E.	OH0950	66C
Ojeda, Rodrigo	PA0550	66C
Olander, Jennifer	TN1000	66A,66B,66C
Olinger, Kathy A.	CO0350	66C
Orkis, Lambert T.	PA3250	66A,66C
Osborne, Brian	OK0750	66C,61
Osterbers, Janet	WI0808	66C,66D
Ostrander, Lonnie	AR0400	66A,66C
Otaki, Michiko	GA0500	41,66A,66C,66D
Otwell, Margaret V.	WI0500	66A,66C,66D,66B,12A
Overton, LeAnn L.	NJ0800	66C
Owens, Diane	TX1100	66A,66C,66D,32A,32B
Owens, Kathryn Ananda	MN1450	66A,66C,66D,66E,66B
Oye, Deanna	AA0200	66A,66C,66,13C,66B
Pachak-Brooks, Cheryl	NM0100	66B,66D,66A,66C
Paddleford, Nancy	MN1450	66A,66C,66B,66D
Padelford, Anne Marie	TN0050	66C
Padilla, Anthony	WI0350	66A,66C,41,42
Paick, Yoomi	TN1450	11,13C,66C
Pakman, Mark	NJ0800	66A,66C
Palmer, David	NC0550	66A,66C
Palmer, Robert	IN0150	66A,66C
Palmier, Darice	IL2970	66A,66D,11,13A,66C
Pan, Huiyu-Penny	CA0830	66A,66D,66B,66C,42
Parisot, Elizabeth	CT0850	66A,66C
Park, Adrienne	MS0700	66C
Park, Angela	IN0900	66C,64
Park, Eun-Hee	MS0750	66C
Park, Jin Young	IA1350	66A,66C
Park, Meeyoun	KY0950	66C,66D
Park-Kim, Phoenix	IN1025	66A,66D,66C
Parker, James	AG0450	66A,66C
Parker, Michael	NC0910	66A,66C
Parker, Patricia	VA0450	66A,66C
Parker, Rebekah Bruce	OK0750	66C
Parker, Robin Lee	FL1700	66C
Parkin, Vera L.	MO1950	66A,66C
Parodi, Jorge	NY9500	39,40,41,66C
Parodi, Jorge	NY2750	40,61,66C
Parr-Scanlin, Denise	TX3750	66A,66D,66C
Parrini, Fabio	SC0950	66A,66D,11,66C
Parsche, Paula	FL0800	13,66A,66C,11
Passmore, Ken	GA1200	66D,66C,65,50
Pastorello, Cristian	IL0150	66A,66B,66C,11,13
Patterson, Anthony	MI0150	66A,66C
Paul, Jessica	IA0950	66C
Paulk, Kayla Liechty	NM0100	66A,66C,66B,66D
Paulnack, Karl	MA0350	66C
Payne, Mark	AG0500	66C
Payne, Peggy	OK0750	66C

739

Name	Code	Areas
Pedersen, Gary	MI0600	66A,66B,66C,66D
Pelfrey, Patricia	OH1200	66A,66C
Pelletier, Louise	AI0150	66C
Pellman, Colleen	NY1350	66A,66C
Penn, Stephen T.	KY1450	61,66C
Penna, J. J.	NJ1350	66C
Penner, Ruth	KS0750	66C
Perkyns, Jane E.	TX3150	66A,13,12A,66,66C
Permenter, Calvin	MO2000	66A,66B,66C
Perron, Francis	AI0200	39,66C
Perry, Margaret	CA5350	66B,66D,66C,13C
Peterson, Jeffry F.	WI0825	66A,66C,66D
Peterson, Larry	IL0100	66A,66C,11
Peterson, Mark	CA1520	66C,66A
Petteys, Leslie	WV0400	66,66A,66B,66C,12
Petti, Ronald T.	TX2700	66C
Petty, Shuko Watanabe	VA1850	66A,66C,13C
Pettyjohn, Emma	GA0700	66A,66B,66C,66G,66D
Pfaltzgraff, Philip	NE0700	66C,11,42,12A
Philcox, Stephen	AG0300	66C
Phillabaum, Katja	WI0825	66A,66C
Phillips, Lee	IN0900	66C
Pickerill, Linda	KY0100	66A,66C
Pickett, Barbara	WA0050	66C,66D,66A
Pickett, Glen	CA0450	10F,66A,66C
Pifer, Joshua K.	AL0200	66A,66C,66D,13C
Pineda, Kris	IL2910	66A,66C,41
Pinto, Mary	NJ0800	66C
Pirtle, R. Leigh	IA1390	66A,66G,66B,66C
Pitts, James L.	TX2700	66C
Playford, Louis	GA0250	66C
Plyler, Sylvia J.	OH2200	66C
Ponder, Wemberly	GA0950	66C
Pontremoli, Anita	OH0600	66C,66A
Popoff-Parks, Linette A.	MI1260	13,66A,66B,66C
Posnak, Paul	FL1900	41,66A,66H,66C
Poulsen, James	IA1350	13,66A,66C,10
Pounds, Nancy	IL1200	66C
Powell, Philip M.	SC0420	66A,66B,66C,66D
Pracht, Carole	KS0980	66A,66G,66C
Pratt, Awadagin K. A.	OH2200	66C
Pressnell, Paula B.	NC0400	66C,66A,66D
Pridgen, Elizabeth A.	GA1300	66A,66C
Prince, Penny	NY0635	32,66A,66B,66C
Protsman, Harold S.	VA1000	66A,66C,41
Puccinelli, Elvia	TX3420	66C
Pummill, Janet	TX3000	66C
Pyle, Pamela Viktoria	NM0450	66A,66C
Pyron, Donna N.	MO1830	66C
Quercia, Olga	CA1850	66,66C
Quinlan, Gloria H.	TX1150	32,36,61,66C,31A
Raab-Pontecorvo, Luiza	NY1600	63B,42,66A,66C
Rackers, Joseph P.	SC1110	66C
Radell, Judith M.	PA1600	13,66A,66D,66C
Radoslavov, Ilia G.	MO1780	66C,66A,66D,66B
Raimo, John B.	TX3525	11,12A,66A,66C
Rambeau, Deborah	WA0700	66A,66B,66C,66D
Ramos Asillo, Jorge	PR0115	66C
Ramsey, Cynthia B.	VA0750	66A,12A,66C,13E,42
Randolph, Margaret Ann	TN0300	66A,66C
Ransom, McCoy	LA0100	13,66A,66G,66C
Rappe, Terri	WA1200	66C,66D,66A
Ravitskaya, Irena	KS0350	66A,66B,66C,66D,66G
Raynor, Shari	CA3600	66C
Reber, William F.	AZ0100	39,54,52,66C,60
Reed, Jerome A.	TN0930	10A,66A,66B,66C,43
Regehr, Leanne	AA0035	66A,66C
Reger, Jeremy J.	IN0900	66C,61
Reichenberger, Kathy	OH2290	66C,66D
Reid, Debra	SD0050	66C
Reinhuber, Joachim	TX2960	66A,66D,66C
Reiss, Deborah	NY0850	44,40,31A,66C
Reitz, Margaret A.	NY3705	66C,66A
Reyes, Reynaldo	MD0850	66A,66C,66B
Reynerson, Rodney T.	NC0050	66A,66C,66D,11,41
Rhee, Heasook	NY2150	66C
Rhee, Sarah	NY2650	66C
Rhoads, Shari	IA1550	61,66C
Rhodebeck, Jacob	NY0270	66A,66C,11,13
Rhodes, Beverly	WA1350	66A,66C
Ricci-Rogel, Susan	MD0700	11,66A,66C
Rice, Karen	NC2700	66A,66C,66D
Rice, Nancy	MA2100	66C
Rice-See, Lynn	TN1100	66A,66B,66C
Richards, Julie	TX2310	11,13A,62A,66C
Richards, Rebekah	MN0610	66C
Richardson, David	WI1100	39,66C,61
Richardson, Diane	NY3705	39,61,66C
Richey, Craig	CA0825	66A,66C,66B
Rickey, Euni	IN1025	66A,66D,66B,66C
Ridges, Lameriel R.	SC1050	13,66A,66C
Rieppel, Daniel	MN1500	66A,11,38,66C,12
Riffel, Patricia	CA1425	66A,66C
Riley, David M.	OR1050	66C,66A,42
Rivas, David	OR0750	66C
Rivers, Cynthia	GA1100	66A,66G,66C,31A,36
Rivers, James	KS1400	11,66A,66C,10
Rivers, Sandra	OH2200	66C
Roach, Hildred E.	DC0350	20G,66A,66B,66C,66D
Roadfeldt-O'Riordan, Holly K.	PA1850	66A,12A,66C
Roberts, Mary W.	FL0600	66A,66B,66C,66D
Robertson, Kaestner	MA0250	66A,13,36,66B,66C
Robertson, Masson	IN0905	13,66A,66B,66C
Robey, Matthew E.	NY2500	66A,66C,66D,11,32E
Robichaud, Clement	AI0190	66C
Rocco, Robert P.	NC1650	66C,13
Roche, Mildred A.	SC0650	66C,13C
Rocker, Karla J.	GA0950	66C
Rodde, Kathleen	IA0850	36,66A,66C
Rodgers, Christopher	PA0050	66A,66C,66G
Rodgers, Kenneth	KS0500	66G,66A,66D,66C,11
Rodgers, Stacy D.	MS0700	66A,66B,66C
Roe, Gail	TX2310	66A,11,66C
Roederer, Silvia	MI2250	66A,66B,66C,66D
Roethlisberger, Karen L.	PA0550	66C
Rogers, Barbara J.	MN1280	66A,66D,66C
Rogosin, David	AE0050	66A,12A,66C
Rohr, Grant	CA0815	66A,61,66C
Rose, Melissa K.	TN1850	66C,41,40
Roseman, Molly J.	WI0850	66,66A,66B,66D,66C
Rosenzweig, Joyce	NY1450	14,66,35E
Ross, Nicholas Piers	VA1400	13,66A,66C,12
Rosser, Geraldine	OH1600	10A,66C
Rossow, David	FL0650	66C
Roth, Nicholas	IA0550	66A,66B,66C,66
Rothshteyn, Eleonora	NY0270	66C,11
Roueche, Michelle	TX3415	60,36,66C
Roulet, Patrick E.	MD0850	50,65,66C
Roulet, Rachel	MD0850	66C
Roussel, Marc	AI0190	66C
Rowland, Michael	NC0550	66A,66G
Rowley, Rick E.	TX3510	66A,66C
Ruberg-Gordon, Susanne	AA0050	66C
Rudell, Alan M.	SC1000	66A,66C
Rudolph, Gladys	OH2300	66C
Runge, Stephen M.	AE0050	66A,66B,66C
Runion, Julie	NY3350	66A,66C
Runyon, Renee	MI2000	66A,66C
Rus-Edery, Ilonka Livia	TX2250	66A,66C
Russell, Mary Lou	TX2260	11,66A,66C,66D,29
Russell, Steve	MS0200	66C
Rutter, Bronwen	FL1300	66A,66H,66C
Ryabinin, Lev	GA0850	66A,66A
Ryan, Russell	AZ0100	66C
Ryan, Steven	NJ0800	66C
Rybak, Alice	CO0900	66A,66C
Rymal, Karen	AG0650	66C,61
Sachs, Stephen W.	MS0100	66A,66C,38
Sale, Craig	IL0730	66A,66B,66D,66C
Salmon, John C.	NC2430	66A,66C,29A
Sammarco, Donna	LA0450	66A,66B,66C
Sanborne, Deborah	IA1300	12,66A,66C,11
Sanchez, Luis	TX2955	66A,66C,66B
Sanders, Alice	AR0730	66A,66C,66B
Santorelli, Shari	TX1660	13,66C
Sargsyan, Vahan	PA0550	66C
Sauer, Karen	MA2050	66C
Savage, Dylan C.	NC2420	66A,66B,66C
Savage, Jeffrey R.	WA1150	66A,66B,66C,13C
Savage, Karen Hsiao	WA1150	66A,66C
Savenkova-Krasin, Ludmila V.	MA2000	66C
Savoy, Thomas	NY3600	66C,66G
Saxon, Kenneth N.	TX3515	66B,66C
Scanlan, Mary	MI0850	66A,66H,66C,66D,20F
Scarambone, Bernardo	KY0550	66A,66D,66B,66,66C
Scheib, Curt A.	PA3000	61,36,66C,60,60
Schlabaugh, Karen Bauman	KS0200	13,66A,66B,66C,12A
Schlater, Lynn	NE0450	66C
Schloneger, Brent	OH2290	66C
Schneider, Doug	OR0850	64E,66C
Schneider, Eugene	AA0040	66A,66C
Schneller, Roland	TN1850	66A,66C
Schoeff, Kristin	OH1850	66C
Schorr, Timothy B.	WI1100	66A,12A,13E,66C
Schrempel, Martha	PA2450	66A,66C,66B
Schultz, Margaret	NE0460	13C,66A,66C,11,32B
Schuman, Susan	NY3717	66A,66C
Schuttenberg, Emily Amanda	NC0350	66A,66C,66D
Schwab, David	TN0260	46,62D,66C
Schwartz, Paul	FL1900	66C
Scifres, Maxie	IL1200	66C
Scott, F. Johnson	VA0750	34,13B,13A,66G,66C
Scott, Tara	AF0050	66C
Scovill, Janet R.	MN1280	66C
Seigel, Lester C.	AL0300	60,36,39,66C,13F
Seiler, Richard D.	LA0770	66A,66C,13A,13D
Seitz, Christine L.	IN0550	13,66C,34
Sekino, Keiko	NC0650	66A,66C
Seldon, Vicki A.	TX2100	11,12A,66A,66C
Seo, Minjung	IL3500	66C
Seskir, Sezi	PA0350	12A,13A,66A,66C
Seufert, Dana	CA2050	66C
Sever, Allan	NY1450	66C
Severtson, David	WI0808	66A,13,66D,12A,66C
Severtson, Kirk A.	NY3780	61,66C,39
Shackleton, Jean	OK0750	66C
Shaffer-Gottschalk, David D.	VA1750	13,66A,66C
Shagdaron, Bair	NC0050	66A,66C,66D
Shandro, Constantine	AA0040	66A,66C
Shank, Nadine E.	MA2000	66A,66C,66D
Shannon, Adrienne	AG0250	66A,66C
Shannon, Nanette	CO0550	66C,66D
Shannon, Quynh	GA1750	66C
Sharon, Rena	AB0100	66C
Sharon, Robert	FL1450	66C
Sharpe, Kevin	FL1850	66A,66C
Sharples, Pamela	NJ0750	13C,36,66A,66C
Sheffer, Toni	KY1000	66C
Sheludyakov, Anatoly	GA2100	66C
Shen, Yang	FL1125	66C,66D,13C
Shepherd, Dean	CA2390	66A,66C
Shick, Suzanne	CA4100	66C
Shih, Gloria	NJ0800	66C
Shim, Jeong-Ja	NY3785	66A,66C
Shimizu, Kumiko	MS0250	66A,66A
Shin, Jung-Won	MS0250	66A,66D,66B,66C,13B
Shinn, Ronald R.	AL0800	66A,66C,13B
Shirar, Ryan	KY0300	66,66C
Shofner-Emrich, Terree	IL2100	66A,39,66B,66C,66D
Shpachenko, Nadia	CA0630	66A,66C,66B,66,34D
Shrut, Arlene	NJ0800	66C
Shumway, Jeffrey	UT0050	66A,66B,66C
Siciliano, Mary	MI1750	66A,66C,66B
Silver, Phillip A.	ME0440	12A,66C,66A,11
Silverman, Laura	OH2150	66C,66A
Simmons, Margaret R.	IL2900	61,66C
Sinaisky, Ilya	CO0250	66C
Singer, Douglas Michael	IN1560	66C
Skyrm, Susanne L.	SD0600	66A,66C,66D,66E
Slagle, Diane	OH2450	66C
Slingland, Susan	NC0050	66C
Sloan, Rita	MD1010	66C,66A,41
Sloter, Molly	IL0400	66C
Slowik, Gregory	MA1700	13,11,12A,66A,66C
Smith, Alan	CA5300	41,66A,66C
Smith, Becky	SC0900	66C
Smith, Fabia	GA1700	66C
Smith, James	NJ0800	66C
Smith, Kirsten	CA0840	66A,66C,66D
Smith, Paul	CA1150	12A,66A,66C,66D,54
Smith, Timothy	AR0200	13,12A,66A,66C
Smith, Timothy C.	AK0100	11,66A,66B,66C
Snelling, Ann	OR1300	66C
Snow, Jennifer L.	CA5030	66C
Soares, Luciana	LA0450	66A,66C,13F,51,13C
Sohriakoff, Pam	MN0250	66C
Sokol-Albert, Andrea C.	PA0950	66A,66C
Sokolov-Grubb, Silvana I.	NH0350	66C,66D
Solar-Kinderman, Eva	AB0150	66A,66C
Solero, Elena	MI0100	66C
Soll, Beverly A.	MA1650	11,66A,66C
Solomons, John	TX3500	66A,41,66C
Solose, Kathleen A.	AJ0150	66A,66H,66B,66C,42
Sonntag, Dawn Lenore	OH1000	36,61,66C,10A,10
Sorley, Rebecca E.	IN1650	66A,66C,66B,66D
Southard, Ellen	CA4550	66C,66D

Index by Area of Teaching Interest

Name	Code	Areas
Souvorova, Katerina	DC0050	66A,66C
Spain, Steve	TX1660	66C
Sparkman, Carol Joy	MS0400	66C,66D,36,66A
Spedden, Patricia R.	IN0700	66A,66B,13,66C,66D
Speer, Alesia L.	KY1550	66A,66C
Speer, Donald R.	KY1550	66B,66C,66D
Spencer, Sarah	TX2295	66A,66C,66D,12A
Spires, Rozanne	TX3527	66A,66C,66D
Spitzer, Laura	NM0310	66A,66B,66C
Spoelstra, Annemieke	VT0400	66A,66C
Springfield, Maila Gutierrez	GA2150	66C
Stabinsky, Ron	PA3700	66A,66C
Stablein, Maria	OH1850	66C
Stackhouse, Eunice Wonderly	NC1450	13,66A,66B,66D,66C
Stafslien, Judy	WI1100	66C,36,61
Stallsmith, Becki	AL0260	32,38,50,61,66C
Stambuk, Tanya	WA1000	66A,66C,66D
Stampfli, L. Thomas	IL1050	66A,66B,66C,66C
Stanescu-Flagg, Cristina	NY2250	66C,61
Stang, Sharon Kay	IA0300	66A,66C,66B
Stanley, Lynnette	AR0850	66C,32A
Stannard, Neil	CA1750	66A,66C,66B,62D
Startsev, Mila	CO0550	66C
Stegall, Gary Miles	SC0420	66A,66D,13A,66C,66G
Steinbach, Falko	NM0450	66A,66C,66B
Stellrecht, Eric	NC0650	66A,66C,13C
Stevens, Damon B.	NV0100	39,66A,66C,66D
Stevens, Delores E.	CA3150	41,66A,66H,66C
Stevens, Jeffrey	MA0400	66C,39
Stevenson, Doris J.	MA2250	41,66A,66C,42,43
Stewart, Paul B.	NC2430	66A,66C
Stites, Nathan	KY0550	66C,66D
Stodola, Lynn	AF0100	42,66A,66C,41
Stokes, Jennifer	IN0907	66A,66B,66D,11,66C
Stoudenmire, Myungsook	SC0275	66A,66D,66C
Stowe, Cameron	AG0450	66A,66C
Stowe, Cameron	MA1400	66C
Stoytcheva, Lilia S.	SC0950	66A,66B,66C,66D
Strauss, Michael	MA1400	66C
Strauss, Michael	MA0350	61,66C
Street, Eric	OH2250	66A,66B,66C,11
Strickland, Caitlin	CO0650	66C
Studdard, Shane	TX1775	66,66C,11
Subchak, Bohdan	OH2290	62A,66C
Sudeith, Mark A.	IL0600	13,66A,66G,66C
Sueiras, Rafael	PR0115	66C
Suits, Brian	TX3400	66C
Sulton, Randall S.	TX0600	66A,66C,13E,13B,13F
Summers, Billy	NC0750	66A,66C,66D,66G
Sumpter, Teresa L.	NC1250	66A,66B,66D,66C
Sung, Hugh	PA0850	66C
Sutanto, David T.	TX0550	66A,66D,66C,11,66B
Swann, Jeffrey	NY2750	66C
Swigger, Jocelyn A.	PA1400	11,66A,66B,66C,66E
Swope, Monica	CA5350	66C
Sykes, Jeffrey R.	CA0807	66C,66A
Sykes, Jeffrey	CA5000	61,66C
Szczesniak, Michel	AG0250	66A,66C
Szklarska, Kamilla	FL0700	66A,66C,66D
Szutor, Kristina	AD0050	66A,66C,66B
Tadmor, Tali	CA0510	66A,66C,31B
Takagi, Shinobu	NY3725	66C,66D
Takao, Naoko	FL1900	66B,66C,66D
Takasawa, Manabu K.	RI0300	13A,66A,66B,66C,66D
Tall, Malinda	UT0350	13A,13B,13C,66A,66C
Talroze, Olga W.	MA2050	66C
Tanaka, Rieko	MA2020	66C,13C,66A,66D
Tang, Jenny	MA2050	66A,66C,13
Tang, Zhihua	MI0400	66C
Tash, Sharon	MO1900	66C
Taylor, Janda	FL1450	66C
Taylor, Paul F.	KY0900	66A,66H,66C,66D
Tchekina, Tatiana	NY1100	66C
Templon, Paul	NC2400	66A,66C,36
Tenegal, George	IL2100	66C
Tescarollo, Hamilton	IN0905	66A,66B,66C
Thiagarajan, Beverly	CA3600	66C
Thibodeaux, Tatiana	CA4500	66A,12A,13C,66C
Thieme, Robert	WV0750	39,66A,66C
Thomas, Louise	CA0960	66C
Thomas, Martha L.	GA2100	66A,66C
Thomas, Richard Pearson	NY4200	66A,66C,10
Thompson, Christopher E.	MO0775	66C,61
Thompson, Gregory T.	NC1000	66A,66C,12A,31A
Thompson, Lee D.	MO1810	66C
Thompson, Lee D.	WA1300	12A,39,66A,66C
Thompson, Stephanie	OR0400	66,66C
Thoreson, Deborah	GA0750	66B,66C
Throop, Barbara Chandler	MI1160	66C
Thurmond, Paul	TN1450	66D,66C
Tice, Loren C.	KY1350	11,66A,66H,66C,66G
Tiefenbach, Peter	AG0300	12A,66C
Tili-Trebicka, Thomaidha	NY4150	66A,66D,66C
Timmons, Kathryn Jill	OR0450	12A,66A,66H,66B,66C
Tiodang, Jasmin	PR0115	66C
Tipton, Dewitt	SC0750	66C
Todd, Sarah	IL1050	66A,66C,66D
Todd, Sheila	IN1560	66C
Tominaga, Akiko	AA0050	66A,66C
Torkelson, Suzanne	IA1800	11,66A,66B,66C
Toscano, Amy	CA2390	66C
Transue, Paul A.	IL2900	66C,39
Trenfield, Sally	TX3515	32A,32B,66C,66D
Trowbridge, Cynthia	IL3550	66C
Troyer, Claire	CO0050	66C
True, Janice	IN0500	66C
Trujillo, Valerie M.	FL0850	66C
Tsai, I-Hsuan	IL3450	66C
Tsai, Sin-Hsing	TN1700	66A,66B,66C
Tsao-Lim, May	AR0300	66A,66C,66D,66B,13B
Tung, Jennifer	AG0300	66C
Tung, Leslie Thomas	MI1150	12A,66A,66C,66E,13
Turgeon, Bruno	AI0190	66C
Turley, Edward L.	MN0350	11,66A,66B,66C
Turnbough, Kimberlee	SC0900	66A,66C
Turner, Randin	IL0300	66C
Tutunov, Alexander	OR0950	13,66A,66D,66C
Uchida, Rika	IA0550	13,66A,66C,66D
Uchimura, Susan	MI2250	66A,66B,66C
Underwood, Greg	NC2420	66C
Ungar, Garnet	IN1600	66A,66C,66D
Urban, Emily	MN0250	66C
Urbis, Richard	TX3515	10F,66A,66C
Urbis, Sue Zanne Williamson	TX3515	32,66C
Uricco, Grace E.	RI0300	66C,66A
Vaas, Sharon	OH2275	66C
Valentine, Colette	TX3510	66C,66A
Vallecillo, Irma	MA1400	66C
Van Brunt, Jennifer	WI0960	61,66A,66C,66D
Van der Linde, Polly	VT0050	66A,66B,66C
van der Westhuizen, Petrus	OH0950	66A,66C,66D,13B,13C
Van Hoose, Matthew	DC0010	66C
Vanden Wyngaard, Julianne	MI0900	66A,66B,66C
Vanderkooy, Christine	AJ0100	66A,66C,66C,13C
Varineau, Gwen	MI0350	66C
Vauth, Henning	WV0400	66A,66C,66D,13C
Venable, Catherine Anne	NJ0825	66C
Villaveces, John	MO1790	66C
Virelles, Amanda	TN1850	66C
Viscoli, David A.	MN1000	66A,66H,66C
Vitercik, Greg	VT0350	13,12A,12,66C
Viverette, Connie	TX3527	66C
Vogt, Bruce	AB0150	66A,66C
Vogt, Elaine	IL1200	66A,66C
Vogt-Corley, Christy L.	LA0350	66A,66B,66C,66D
Voldman, Raisa	LA0650	66C
Voronietsky, Baycka	ME0440	66A,66B,66C,13A
Vortman, Karma K.	IL1100	66A,66C
Wachter, Jeffrey	PA3650	66A,66C
Wade, Gail G.	TX1600	13,39,66A,66D,66C
Waite, Janice	AA0050	66A,66C,41
Walker, Ben	KY0550	66C
Walker, Joseph V.	TN1100	66C
Walker, Karen	VA1350	66D,66C
Wallace, Elizabeth	TX1100	66A,66B,66C
Wallace, Susan	GA1700	66C
Waltich, Tsukasa	PA3700	66C
Wang, Esther	MN0750	66A,66C,11
Wang, Hsiu-Hui	MD0400	66A,66C,42
Wang, Liang-yu	IN0900	66C,62
Wang, Tianshu	OH0350	66A,66D,66C
Wang, Yien	GA0550	66C
Ward, Patricia	TN1100	66C
Warfel, Jon R.	IL2050	66C
Warren, Ron	MD0150	10F,10,66C
Watson, Marva	IL1240	66A,66B,66C,11,12A
Watson, Robert	CA0815	66A,66C
Weber, Judy	KS0700	66C
Weber, Stephen	OK1400	66A,34,66C,66D
Weckstrom, Virginia	AG0300	42,66C
Weckstrom, Virginia	OH0600	66C
Weiss, Celia	IN0910	66C
Weiss, Lisa G.	MD0400	13A,11,42,66A,66C
Weiss, Louise	IL1050	13A,32B,48,64A,66C
Welch, Nancy	MS0700	66C
Weldy, Frederick R.	CA4900	66A,66C
Wells, Robyn	ID0070	66A,66B,66C
Wells, Ryan	NE0550	13,66A,66B,66C
Welte, DeEtta	IN1800	66A,66C
Wenaus, Grant	NY2750	39,61,66C,66
Wenger, Janice K.	MO1800	66C,66A,66H,66E
Werz, Andreas	CA0810	66A,66B,66C,66D
West, Rachel	IL1200	66C
Westbrook, Randy	KY0550	66C,12,11
Westfall, Casey	OH1850	66C
Westfall, David C.	CT0650	66A,66C
Westgate, Phillip Todd	AL0950	13,36,66A,66G,66C
Wettstein Sadler, Shannon Leigh	MN0050	66A,66C,13F
Whatley, Jay K.		13B,13C,66D,66C,66G
Wheeler, Dale J.	AA0080	66A,66B,66C,42
Whipkey, Steve	IN1100	66A,66C,47
Whitmore, Keith	OK0650	66A,66H,66C,66D
Whittaker, Billie	DC0170	61,66C
Wickelgren, John	MD0300	66A,13C,66C,66D
Widrig, Judith	WA1250	66C
Wilder, Mary Ann	KY0100	66A,66C,66D,13A,13B
Wilhite, Carmen	MN1300	66A,66B,66C
Wilkinson, David	CA3600	66C
Williams, Brenda	VA1100	66A,66C,66D
Williams, Dale	FL2050	66A,66C
Williams, Kay	TX0050	66A,66C,66D,13A,13B
Williams, Melanie	GA1700	66C
Williams, Richard Lee	MO1810	66C,61
Williams, Robin	LA0800	66A,66B,66D,66C
Willis, Andrew S.	NC2430	66A,66H,66C
Willson, Kenneth F.	OR0250	13,45,66A,66B,66C
Wilson, George	TX3800	66C
Wilson, Grover	NC1600	11,36,66A,66C,66D
Wilson, Jane Ann H.	TX3200	66A,66D,66C
Wirth, Jason	NY2105	66C
Withers, Lisa Ann	VA0350	66A,66C,13B,13C,13F
Witten, David	NJ0800	13B,12A,66A,66B,66C
Wolfe, Elizabeth	KY0450	66A,66C
Wolfe, Jennifer	MI1050	13C,66C,12A,11
Wolfe-Ralph, Carol	MD1050	66A,66G,66B,66C,12A
Wong, Jerry	OH1100	66A,66B,66C,42
Woodford, Dorothy	CA1375	66C
Woodin, Nancy	IA1450	66A,66C
Woodward-Cooper, Marlene	FL1450	13,66A,66B,66C
Wright, Elizabeth	MA2250	66A,66C,41
Wright, Marylyn	TX3360	13A,66A,66C,66D,66G
Wtizig, Lu	IL1200	66C
Wu, Angela	KY0950	66C,66D
Wu, Chi-Chen	WY0200	66A,66C,66B
Wutke, Drew	IN0700	66C
Wyman, Wayne	IA1550	61,66C
Yamaguchi, Yuko	FL1600	66A,66C
Yang, Ben Hoh	LA0150	13,66A,66C
Yang, Hui-Ting	AL1050	66A,66C
Yang, Rajung	ID0250	66A,66C,66H,42
Yang, Yu-Jane	UT0350	66A,66B,66C,66D
Yang, Zhao	WA0950	66C,13A,13B,13C,13D
Yazvac, Diane	OH2600	66A,66C,66D
Yee, Thomas	HI0210	13C,66A,66C,66B
Yeh, I-Chen	OH1100	66A,66C
Yerden, Ruth	OR1150	66A,66G,66D,66C
Yeung, Alwen	GA1000	11,66C,13C,66D
Yim, Soyoon	DC0170	66A,66C
Yom, Jeongeun	NY2200	66C
Yost, Laurel	MT0200	66A,66B,66C,12A
Young, James Russell	GA1150	40,39,66C,54
Young, Michael J.	KY0900	66C
Young, Ovid	IL2300	66A,66C,10A
Young, Phillip D.	CA3650	66A,66C
Yount, Matthew W.	MO1500	11,66C
Yu, Jin	OH2150	66C
Yun, Soohyun	GA1150	66A,66B,66C,42
Zabel, Albert	WV0400	44,66G,31A,10,66C
Zackery, Harlan H.	MS0350	11,66A,66B,66C,66D
Zandmane, Inara	NC2430	66C
Zavzavadjian, Sylvia	AA0050	32A,66A,66C
Zeger, Brian	NY1900	66C
Zemke, Vicki	AZ0350	66C
Zemp, William Robin	SC0500	11,66A,66C,66D
Zent, Donald	KY0100	13E,66B,66A,66C,66D
Zhang, Weihua	MA2020	66C

Name	Code	Areas
Zhao, Grace Xia	CA5100	66,14,13,66A,66C
Zilberkant, Eduard	AK0150	66A,66B,66C,66D,41
Zimmer, Susan	MD0800	66A,66C,11,66G
Zimmerman, Karen Bals	NY3720	13,11,66A,66B,66C
Zimmerman, Kimberly	NE0525	61,66C
Zirnitis, Anda	MO0300	13,66A,66C,66D
Zoolalian, Linda A.	CA3650	66A,66C,13C
Zoolalian, Linda A.	CA3500	66A,66C

Group Piano

Name	Code	Areas
Aamodt, Rucci R.	HI0150	32,11,66A,66D
Abercrombie, Marilyn	MO0260	66A,66D
Abram, Blanche	NY1600	41,66A,66D,66C
Academia, Jon	CA4850	66D
Acevedo, Maria Teresa	PR0115	66A,66D
Adams, Andrew	NC2600	66C,11,66A,66D
Adams, Elma	NJ0700	66D
Adams, Jan	GA2130	66A,66D
Adams, Michelle	ID0100	66D,13C
Adamson, Jared	OH0550	66D
Adamson, Philip I.	AG0550	66A,66B,66D,13C,66C
Addamson, Paul	NC1050	66A,66C,66D,13A,13
Adderley, Meisha N.	OH0350	13B,13C,66D,66B
Afonasyeva, Yekaterina	MD0850	66D,36,66C
Ahn, Hyeson Sarah	MN1200	66A,66D
Ahrend, Janet	WA0400	66G,13C,66D
Ajero, Mario	TX2700	66B,66C,66D
Albergo, Cathy	IL1085	66A,66B,66D
Aldi, Barbara	NY3600	66D
Aldredge, Steven	OH2500	66A,66D
Alexander, Charles Reid	IL3300	66B,66D,66A
Alexander, Mark W.	TX1900	66A,66C,66D
Allan, Kathryn	CA2840	61,66A,66D
Allen, Christine	LA0550	66A,66D
Allen, Susan	VA0050	13C,11,66A,66D
Allen, Thomas O.	MN1300	66A,66B,66D
Allred, Nancy C.	UT0150	66A,66B,66D,66C
Alm, Gina	CA5355	11,66A,66B,66C,66D
Amoriello, Laura	NJ1350	66D
Amper, Leslie	MA2150	66A,66D
Amrod, Paula J.	PA0700	66A,66D
Andersen, LeGrand	UT0200	61,66D,13C,13B
Anderson, Connie	OH0450	66A,66B,66D
Anderson, H. Gerald	IL2300	66A,66C,66D,12A
Anderson, Jerry L.	MO0850	66A,66B,66C,66D
Anderson, Richard P.	UT0050	66A,66B,66C,66D
Anderson, Shirley	TX0900	66D
Anthony, John P.	CT0100	13A,11,12A,66D,66G
Antolini, Anthony	ME0200	36,13A,66D
Antonacos, Anastasia	PA1600	66A,13,11,66C,66D
Applegate, Ann	WI0925	66D,13A,13B,66A
Archer, Naida	AJ0150	13A,13,66A,66D
Ard, Ken	CA4050	66A,66B,66C,66D
Arndt, Sandra K.	TN1100	66D
Arnon, Baruch	NY1900	66D
Arrigotti, Stephanie	NV0150	13A,11,66A,66B,66D
Artemova, Alina V.	CA2050	61,66D
Astolfi, Jeri-Mae G.	WI0830	66D,13C
Attaway, Aiya	OK0450	66A,66C,66D
Atzinger, Christopher	MN1450	66A,66B,66D,66C
Auler, Robert M.	NY3770	66A,66D,13A,40,35A
Austin, Jennifer N.	SC1200	66A,66C,66D,66B
Autry, Philip E.	TN0550	66A,66B,66C,66D
Ayesh, Kevin	NC0220	13,11,12A,66A,66D
Azevedo, Helena	WA0860	66A,66D
Babal, Gregory	CT0650	66A,66D
Babcock, Beverly	MD0750	66C,66D
Badami, Charles A.	MO0950	66C,66A,66D,11
Badgerow, Justin A.	PA1250	66A,66C,66D,13
Baer, Matthew Kevin	CA4300	66A,66C,66D
Baglio, Brennan	WA0030	66D
Bailey, Sally	NY0450	66A,66B,66C,66D
Bailey, Scott	MA2100	66C,66D,11
Baker, Chad	OH0350	66G,66D
Baker, Kent	VT0100	66A,66D,46,13,10F
Baker, Susanne R.	IL0750	66D
Baldoria, Charisse J.	PA0250	66A,66D,12A,11
Balian, Muriel	CA1960	11,66A,66D,36,55D
Ball, Alexandria	PA2900	66C,66D,35E
Ball, Gerrie	MI2200	66C,66D
Ballard, Alice	MS0300	66A,66G,66D,11
Ballin, Scott	NY1275	66A,66D
Barbham, Vicki	OR0350	36,66D
Barfield, Sally	TX2350	66A,66D
Barkley, Elizabeth F.	CA1800	11,12A,66A,66C,66D
Baron, Michael	FL0680	66A,66C,66B,66D
Barrington, Barrie	AB0050	66A,66D
Barron, Elizabeth	PA1450	66D,64A
Bartos, Titus	TN1100	66D
Bartz, Ezra	TX3175	66D
Bartz, Karen	MN0610	66A,66D
Basiletti, Sarah	CA2400	13A,66D
Bateman, Melinda	CA3100	66D
Bates, Pamela	IL0900	12A,13,66A,66C,66D
Battersby, Sharyn L.	DC0050	32B,32C,66D,32D,32H
Baytelman, Pola	NY3650	41,66A,66D,66E
Bean, Robert D.	IN0905	13A,66A,66B,66C,66D
Beattie, Donald P.	IL2900	66B,66D
Becker, Juanita	WI1155	66A,13,66B,66C,66D
Becker, Paul	AR0800	66A,66B,66C,66D,11
Beecher, Betty	UT0300	66A,66D
Beecher, Randy	CA4050	66A,66B,66C,66D,12
Beedle, Helen E.	PA1950	66A,66D
Beith, Nancy S.	MD1000	66D
Bela, Marcin	TN1100	10,66A,66D
Bell, Carol Ann	OK0650	66A,66D
Bell, Cully	IL2900	66B,66D
Bell, Jane H.	OH1650	66A,66D
Bell, Paula	TN1100	66D
Bellah, Mary	CA0270	66D,61
Bemis, Jennifer	AL1300	66A,66C,66D
Benjamin, John A.	OH2250	66A,66C,66D
Bennack, Steven	TX2710	70,29A,66D
Bennett, Erin K.	FL1950	66A,66B,66D
Bennett, Mary Lynne	WV0300	66B,66A,66D,66,66C
Berdnikova, Natalya L.	WI0450	11,66D
Beres, Karen E.	NC1650	13A,66D
Besalyan, Raffi	WI0850	66A,66D
Bethea, Kay	VA1030	13,11,12A,66A,66D
Betts, Steven	OK1200	66A,66B,66D,13,11
Bezaire, Fionna	IL0730	66A,66D
Biel, Carol	OR0400	66,66D
Bighley, Mark	OK0550	12A,66A,66G,66D
Billin, Susan	ID0250	66G,66D
Bingham, Roxanne Laycock	AA0050	66A,66D
Birdsong, Nikki S.	TX1150	66A,66D
Birr, Diane	NY1800	66A,66C,66D
Bishop, Marla	GA1700	66A,66D
Bishop, Saundra	MS0575	13A,36,66A,66D,13B
Bittner, Groff S.	MO0650	66A,66D
Bizzell, Gayle	TX1850	12A,66A,66C,66D
Blackley, Terrance J.	CA1900	66D,46,35
Blanchard, Carol	ID0060	66D
Blanchett, Madalyn	TX2260	11,64A,66A,66D,67
Blood, Elizabeth P.	NH0350	66C,66D
Blyth, Jennifer	PA0950	66A,66B,66C,66D,13
Bodaubay, Dina	CO0830	66A,66D
Boe, Karen	WI0865	66A,66B,66C,66D
Boemler, Cathy	MO0550	66A,66B,66C,66D
Boettger, Susan	CA2390	66A,66B,66C,66D
Boey, Hooi Yin	WV0050	66A,66D,20,66B,66C
Bolen, Bradley C.	TX0300	66A,66D
Bondar, Liudmila E.	MI1200	66D,13C
Boozer, Mark	GA0490	13C,66A,66B,66D
Boren, Benjamin J.	CA0850	66A,66B,66C,66D,13B
Boris, Victor R.	PA3150	66D,14C
Bornovalova, Olga	IL1085	66A,66B,66D
Bornovalova, Olga	IL0650	66A,66D
Bos, Ken	MI0850	66C,66A,66D
Bosits, Marcia L.	IL2250	66A,66D
Bostic, Bert	TX1660	36,47,66D
Bostic, Polly T.	NC2650	66A,66D,66G
Boston, Marilyn	MO0400	66A,66D
Boston, Nancy J.	PA2150	66A,66B,66C,66D
Bouchard, George	NY2550	11,46,47,66D,29
Boulton, Kenneth	LA0650	66A,66B,66D
Bowden, Derek	MD0800	11,66D,66A
Boyce, Emily W.	NY3717	66D,66C,66A,66B
Boyd, Sue Marston	VA1350	66A,66B,66C,66D
Boyle, Mary E.	NY3760	70,33,66D
Braaten-Reuter, Laurie	IA1800	66A,66C,66D
Brackeen, William	OK0450	66A,66D,10A,13
Bradford, Mary Pinkney	TX2170	66A,66B,66D
Bradley, Annette	AA0080	66A,32B,13C,66D,42
Bradner, Janice B.	SC1200	66D,66C,66A
Bradshaw, Dean	AF0100	66C,66D
Bradshaw, Tracey	UT0200	66C,66D
Brady, Patricia L.	VA0600	66B,66D
Brancaleone, Francis P.	NY2200	13,66A,66D,66G,66C
Brandenburg, Julie A.	WI0450	10D,36,61,66D
Brasington, Merewyn	OH1400	66C,66D,13C,66A
Brauer, Vincent	AI0190	13C,66D
Bree, Karen	WY0130	66A,66D
Brenner, Christopher	CA3500	66D
Bresnen, Steven M.	PA0400	13,11,12A,66A,66D
Brewer, Abbie C.	MO0300	66A,66D
Brewster, David	WA1350	66A,66D
Brickman, Scott T.	ME0420	14C,13,32B,10B,66D
Bridgman, Joyce M.	OK0850	66A,66H,66B,66C,66D
Bright, Lorna	AZ0150	66D
Britt, Carol	LA0450	13,11,12A,66D
Broderick, Daniela	IL1250	11,66A,66D,20G,54
Broderick, Daniela C.	IL1890	11,66A,66D
Bronson, Janci	IA0850	66A,66B,66D
Brook, Sharon D.	CA4400	11,66A,66C,66D
Brooks, Melinda K.	AL0850	11,13,66A,66D
Brossard, Marilyn	WA0900	66A,66D,66B
Brown, Adrianne	CT0350	66A,66B,66C,66D
Brown, Dana	OH1100	66D,66A
Brown, Jeffrey A.	IL3500	66,66A,66D
Bruce, Cynthia	AF0050	13C,33,66D,12A
Brucker, Clifford	NY3600	11,66D,29
Bryant, David	PA1150	66A,66D
Buccelli, Sylvia	NY3760	66D
Buchman, Nell J.	WI0350	66D
Buckland, Karen W.	SC1000	66A,66C,66D
Buckner, Jeremy	TN0250	32B,32C,66A,66D,11
Buckner, Nathan	NE0590	66A,66C,66D,13B,13C
Budai, William H.	KY0400	66A,66B,66D
Bugos, Kristen	TX0600	32B,66D
Bumpers, Wayne	FL1300	36,66A,66D,20G,66B
Burch, Alene	TX0550	66A,66C,66D,66B
Burger, Cole	OH0300	66D
Burkhart, Annette M.	MO1900	66A,66D
Burns, Chelsea R.	IL2750	66A,66D
Burt, Patricia A.	IL1200	13A,66A,66D,13B,13C
Busch, Stephen E.	CO0250	32,44,66D
Butke, Marla A.	OH0100	32,11,66D,36,60A
Butler, Beverly	IN1450	66A,66C,66D
Butler, Carol	TN0580	66A,66B,66D
Butler, Debbie D.	TX3527	66A,66C,66D
Buzzelli-Clarke, Betsy	PA1100	11,13A,12A,66A,66D
Byington, Jensina	WA0860	13,66A,66D
Caceres, Marcelo	MI0250	66A,66B,66C,66D
Cai, Yi-Min	AL1250	66A,66B,66D,66C
Caldwell, Ann	GA0850	66A,66D,66G,11
Caluda, Elizabeth	VA1350	66A,66D
Campbell, Cheryl Lynn	PA1900	66A,66D
Campitelli, Stephen	PA1550	66D,66A
Candee, Jan	ND0400	66A,66D,66G,32B,11
Canfield, Jennifer K.	AL0450	11,32A,32D,66D,32B
Canfield, Wanda	PA1000	66A,66D,53
Capistran, Raul W.	TX3515	66C,66D
Caporale, Matthew	TX1450	66A,66D
Caramia, Anthony	NY1100	66A,66B,66D
Carlin, Kerry	NC0650	66A,66B,66D
Carlton, Elizabeth	NC0350	32,66A,66B,66D
Carlton, Jan	CA0300	66A,66D
Caron-Gatto, Lisa J.	MI2110	66D
Carr, William	PA1550	13B,66D,66A,13D
Carrell-Coons, Mariah	OK0770	66A,66C,66D,32E
Carriere, Marilyn	MN0620	66A,66D
Carter, Patricia	TN1710	66D
Casey, Rebecca L.	OH1800	66A,13,66D,66C
Cash, Carla Davis	TX3200	66B,66D,29B,66A,66
Castellana, Joseph	OH0755	66D,66A,63A
Cavallo, Gail R.	NY2550	32A,13A,66D
Chabora, Robert J.	MN0600	66A,66B,66D,11,13
Chai, Susan	AB0100	66D
Chamberlain, Julie Rhyne	NC0350	66A,66B,66C,66D,11
Chan, Jacklyn	IN1650	66A,66D
Chan, Sarah S.	OK0600	66A,66C,66D,13,11
Chan, Susan	OR0850	66A,66B,66D,66C
Chan-Spannagel, Yiu-Ka	OK0150	66D,66C
Chancler, Rose	NY3775	66D
Chandler, Gulya	LA0030	66A,66C,66D,11,12A
Chang, Wan-Chin	CA2960	66A,66D
Chang, Ya-Liang	KY1000	66D
Charoenwongse-Shaw, Chindarat	OK1330	66A,66B,66D,66C
Chaudoir, Marianne	WI0400	11,66A,66D,13A
Chen, Fen-Fang	AL0650	66A,66B,66D,42,66C
Chen, Ginger Jui-Wen	GA0940	66A,66B,66D
Chen, Hsaun-Ya	CA1760	66A,66D
Chen, Johanna	CA0859	66A,66D

Index by Area of Teaching Interest

Name	Code	Areas
Chen, Moh Wei	CA5100	66A,66D,13C
Chen, Shao Shen	TX0550	66A,66D,66B,66C
Cheng, Susan	CT0050	66A,66D
Chernyshev, Alexander	MN1600	66A,66D
Chew, Jacqueline	CA5000	66A,66D
Chiang, Ju-Yu (Carol)	OK1330	66D
Chin, Huei Li	IL2910	66A,66B,66D
Chioldi, Ronald	OK0550	13B,66A,66D,13D,13E
Cho, James	TX2250	66D
Cho, Mison	PA3560	66A,66D
Cho, Sujung	SC0350	66A,66D,66C
Choi, Bonnie L.	NY4150	66A,66H,66D
Choi, Bonnie	NY2650	66A,66D,66H
Choi, Chee Hyeong	IL1750	66D
Choi, Hyunjoo	CA1425	66C,66G,66D,66A
Choi, Minju	IN1650	66A,66D
Choi, Wooyoung	GA0050	66A,66D,66C
Chow-Tyne, June	AZ0480	66A,66D
Christensen, Linda	NE0700	66A,66D,34,66B,11
Christianson, Paul A.	TN1600	11,66A,66D
Chui, Eddie	CA1020	66D,13A
Chung, He-Lyun	CA3100	66A,66D
Chung, Joyce	NY4500	66A,66D
Chung, Young-Eun	OK0850	66D
Ciarelli, Katharine	NY2950	66A,66D,11
Cisler, Valerie C.	NE0590	66A,66B,66D
Cizewski, Kathleen	IL0650	66A,66D
Clark, Adam	MI1050	66,66A,66C,66B,66D
Clark, Jacob	SC1050	66A,66D,12A
Clark, James W.	SC0050	13,66A,66D,66B
Clark, Kenneth	CT0600	66D
Clark, Lauren Schack	AR0110	66C,66D,66B
Clark, Steve H.	GA0550	66B,66D
Clearfield, Andrea	PA3330	66C,66D,10,12F
Cleary, Thomas	VT0450	66A,47,66D
Clement, Dawn	WA0200	13A,66A,66D,29
Clevenger, Charles	OH0450	66A,66B,66C,66D,12B
Clewell, Christine M.	PA1600	66A,66G,66D,13
Clodfelter, John D.	IN0350	66A,66C,66D
Coats, Syble M.	AL0831	66A,66D,11,13A
Coats, Sylvia	KS1450	66B,66D
Cobb, Mary Marden	NY3725	66D,66A
Cobb, Susan	IL1750	66A,66B,66D
Cole, Darlyn	NC1950	61,66D,60A,11,13
Cole, Pamela	FL0800	66A,66D
Coleman, Ruth	SC0200	66A,66D
Collins, Cheryl	NM0400	66A,66C,66D
Collins, Jenny	PA1100	11,13A,66A,66D,66C
Collins, Myrtice J.	AL0500	32B,66D,36
Collins, Peter F.	MO0775	66A,66D,66B
Colson, Steve	NJ0800	20,66D
Colunga, Richard	CA2300	66D,11
Conda, J. Michelle	OH2200	66B,66D
Conley, Cheryl	MO1120	66D
Conner, Heather	UT0250	66A,66D
Conrad, Kent R.	IL0800	66A,66C,66D
Conroy, Brenda	IL1090	66A,66D
Conway, Robert	MI2200	66A,66B,66D,12A
Conway, Vicki J.	TX3535	66A,66B,66D
Cook, James	NE0590	11,66A,66D
Cook, Jean	SC0200	66A,66B,66D
Cook, Kent	IL1200	66A,66D
Cooper, Matthew J.	OR0200	13,47,66A,66D,29
Cooper, Ralph	GA0400	66D
Coppola, Thomas	NC2400	66A,66D,10C,29
Corcoran, Catherine T.	CA0847	66D
Cornelius, John L.	TX2100	66C,66A,66D,13
Cornils, Margaret A.	WI0840	64A,11,48,66D
Cornwall, Lonieta	NC2300	13,60,36,66D
Cory, Eleanor	NY2050	13,10,11,66A,66D
Cowan, Carole	NY3760	38,66D,62A,62B
Cowden, Tracy E.	VA1700	66C,66A,66D,13C
Cowell, Jennifer	WY0050	38,41,66D,62A
Cox, Thomas E.	AR0750	13,47,66A,66D
Craig, Vincent	PA3600	66A,66D
Craige, Mary Ann	OK1150	66A,66D
Cranmer, Carl	PA3600	66A,66C,66D
Crawley-Mertins, Marilee	IA0425	11,66A,66D,34
Cremaschi, Alejandro M.	CO0800	66D,66A,66B
Crocker, Susan	NY2950	66A,66D
Crosby, Richard A.	KY0550	66A,66D,12A
Cross, Virginia A.	OR0175	31A,12A,66D,13A,66B
Crowder, Jarrell	MD0550	66A,66D,54
Cruciani, Lori L.	WI0803	66A,66D
Cruz, Jennifer	OH0500	66A,66B,66D
Cuellar, Martin	KS0300	66A,66B,66C,66D
Cummings, Daniel	CA2420	60B,38,66D,66A
Curtis, Ann	NC1550	66D
Cutler, Ann	TX0250	66A,66D
Cutting, W. Scott	MI1550	13,11,66A,66D,34D
Cvetkov, Vasil	LA0650	66D,13
Da Silva, Paul	CA0859	13A,66D,66A
Dahlman, Barbro E.	DC0100	66A,66D
Damaris, Christa	NY3000	36,61,66D
D'Ambrosio, Christina	KY0950	66D
Darnell, Robert	NC2430	54,66D,66A
Davenport, David A.	DC0170	11,66A,66B,66C,66D
David, Myrtle	LA0700	13B,66A,66D
Davidson, Tom	AG0250	66A,66C,66D
D'Avignon, India	CA1510	66A,66D
Davis, Anna	GA2050	66A,66D
Davis, Gladys	NC0220	66A,61
Davis, Peter	SC0200	66A,66B,66D,34
Dawe, Jill A.	MN0050	13,66A,66B,66D
Daya, Shanti Rajaratnam	WI0200	66D
De Dobay, Thomas	CA0950	11,12A,61,66D
Deatrick, Linda	MI1950	63B,66D
Deaver, Stuart T.	OK1450	66A,66D,66B,13I,66
DeBow, Faith	TX3175	66C,66D
Decesare, Mona Wu	CA3100	66A,66D
DeFoor, Cynthia	GA2300	66C,66D,66B,66A
Delbeau, Marie-Christine	DE0150	66A,66D,66B
Delorenzo, Lisa	NJ0800	32,66D
Delphin, Wilfred	LA0900	66A,66B,66C,66D
DeLuccia, Norma	NY2950	66D
Denton, Kristine West	PA1200	66A,66C,66D
Derham, Billie	MO1830	66A,66D
Desai, Nayantara	CO0830	66A,66C,66D
DeSanto, Jennifer	PA3560	66A,66D
D'Haiti, Maxine	AZ0150	66D,11
Diab, Mary Beth	IL3370	66A,66C,66B,66D
Dietrich-Hallak, Christine	MA1500	66D
Dilworth, Helen J.	CA1020	61,66D
DiMedio, Annette	PA3330	12A,12,66A,66D,11
Ding, Xiaoli	KS1400	66A,66B,66D,20
Dingle, Rosetta	SC1050	32,36,66D,13
Dionne, Louise M.	NY3775	66D
Dobrea-Grindahl, Mary	OH0200	66A,66B,66C,32I,66D
Dodd, Susan	FL0200	66A,66C,66D
Dolacky, Susan	WA0860	11,39,61,66D,54
Donovick, Jeffery	FL1650	66D,13A,13B,13C,34C
Doran, Joy	IL1200	66C,66A,66D
Dotson, Ronald	CA5510	11,34C,66D,14C,12A
Dougherty, Peggy S.	OR0175	66A,66D,13A,66B,13E
Douthit, James Russell	NY2650	66A,66B,66D
Dow, David Charles	CA3000	45,66D,34
Downes, Suzanne	IL2310	66D,47,11,37,65
Downey, Sherri	TX3530	66D
Dransfield, Lee Ann	VA1350	66D
Drion, Yoka	CA5510	66D
Drion, Yoka	CA2975	66A,66D
Driscoll, Katherine	FL1300	66D,66A
Driskell, Daniel	AL1300	66A,66D
Dubal, David	NY2150	66D
Duce, Geoffrey	IN0910	13,66A,66C,66D
Duehlmeier, Susan	UT0250	66A,66D
Duerden, Jennifer	HI0050	11,66A,66C,66D
Durham, Kevin	TN1400	13A,66D,11
Dykema, Dan H.	AR0600	13B,11,66A,66D,13C
Earnest, JoAnne	PA0050	66A,66D
Echols, Carol	MO0350	66A,66D,66B
Eckert, Elizabeth	TN1850	66A,66D
Eckhardt, Janet	IL2100	66A,66D
Edmonds, Carol	NC2000	66D
Edson, Tracey D.	OR1100	66A,66D,66C
Edwards, Matthew	MO0850	66A,66B,66C,66D,13
Ehlers, Lisa	AZ0490	66D
Ehrman, David	VA0650	66A,66B,66D
Eide, Christina	AZ0350	11,66A,66D
Eikner, Edward	GA2200	12A,66A,66C,66D,11
Elder, Ellen	MS0750	66A,66C,66D
Elder, Ellen P.	MS0850	66A,66B,66D,66C
Elliott, Anne	TN1150	66A,66D,66B,66C,36
Ellis, Cynthia	TX2260	66A,66D
Elshazly, Janet	SC0275	66A,66C,66D
Elzinga, Cameo	MI0850	66D
Embretson, Deborah	MN1100	61,66D,11,20,66C
Enciso, Franz J.	CA1020	13C,66D,11
Engberg, Kristina L.	IL2350	66D,11,13,34B
Enlow, Martin	WA0860	66D,40,54,39
Epperson, Dean	AK0100	11,12A,66A,66D,66B
Erickson, Stephen	RI0250	66A,66D
Eshelman, Karen	SC0750	13,66D
Evans, Gerald	OH1300	13,10,12A,14,66D
Evans, Lee	NY1275	66A,66D
Evans, Mark	NY3600	66A,66B,66D
Evans, Phillip	FL1125	66D,42
Evenson, David N.	LA0650	66A,66D
Ezerova, Maria V.	CA5070	66A,66D
Fabbro, Renato	OR0500	66A,66D
Fahrion, Stacy	CO0300	11,66A,66D
Faith-Slaker, Aubrey	IL2750	66A,66D
Faiver, Rosemary T.	MI1200	32B,66D
Falker, Matt	CA2960	36,66A,47,66D
Faltstrom, Gloria V.	HI0300	13A,11,66D,61,36
Farris, Phillip	OH2250	66A,66C,66D,11
Fast, Barbara	OK1350	66A,66B,66D
Faughn, Wendy	AL0500	66A,66B,66C,66D
Faulkner, Lynn	AL1200	66A,66C,66D
Favreau, Janet	CA2650	66A,66D,13A,11
Federle, Yong Im Lee	NC2700	66A,66D
Feigin, Eugene	NY2105	66D
Fells, Mizue	WA0550	66A,66D,13C,11,20
Fenner, Richard C.	CA1020	62C,66D
Ferguson, Dianne S.	NE0200	13,66A,66C,66D
Ferguson, Eva	IL1200	66C,66D
Fierro, Nancy	CA3150	66A,66B,66D
Figueroa, Diana	PR0115	66A,66B,66D
Fischer, Jeanne Kierman	TX2150	66A,66B,66D,42
Fisher, Alexis Z.	PA1850	66A,66D
Fisher, Christopher	OH1900	66D,66A,66B
Fisher, Will J.	AZ0510	36,11,66D
Fittipaldi, Thomas	NY2500	36,66D,67,70,11
Fleer, Suzanne	IL1085	66A,66D
Floden, Andrea	MI0450	11,66D
Floyd, Elizabeth M.	LA0300	66D
Flugge, Mark	OH0350	66A,66D,29B
Flyger, Paul	MI1180	66A,66D,11
Fogarty, Rachel	TN0100	66A,66D
Fogg, Ryan	TN0250	66A,66D,66B,66C
Follingstad, Karen J.	CA4100	11,66A,66C,66D
Forbat, David	OK1330	66A,66B,66C,66D
Foreman, Karen C.	CA0100	66D,13A
Forman, Marilyn T.	VA1000	66A,66D
Forrester, Sheila	FL1675	10A,13,66D,13D,13E
Forster, Marilyn	OH2140	44,66D
Foshee, Anna Harriette	CA4460	66A,66B,66D
Foster, Linda	NJ0760	66A,66D
Fox, Clinton D.	OH0300	13,66A,66D
Fox, David E.	NC0900	66A,12A,66D,43,11
Fox, Marilyn F.	NY2550	70,66D
Frank, Jolita Y.	WI0835	66D,13A
Franklin, Christine C.	AR0850	66D
Franklin, Jeshua	IL1612	61,66D,10D
Franklin, Rachel F.	MD1000	66A,66D
Frazier, Ivan	GA2100	66A,66B,66D
French, Jodi	OR0950	66D
Frieling, Randall J.	IN0100	66A,66C,66D,66G
Friesen, Peter	CO0550	66C,66D
Fung, Eric K.	PA1900	13,66A,66D
Fuoco, Christine M.	OH0200	66D
Furr, Barbara	NC2440	12A,66A,66D
Gable, Kathleen	AJ0150	66D,66A,66C
Gable, Laura Beth	AL0800	66D,34
Gajda, Anne	MI0600	66A,66B,66D
Gallo, Patrick	FL1700	66D
Gallo, Sergio	GA1050	66A,66B,66C,66D
Galusha, Cessaries	OR0750	66A,66D
Garber, Melia	VA0550	66A,66D
Garcia, Jose Manuel	GA2050	66A,66D,11,10A
Garcia, W. T. Skye	OK0300	66A,66D,13B,13C,66B
Garcia-Leon, Jose M.	CT0700	11,12A,13,66A,66D
Gardner, Richard	IL1240	11,66D
Gehrich, Leonora S.	IL2450	66A,66C,66D
George, Elizabeth	AZ0450	13A,13B,66D
Gerhold, John	CA0270	13,10,66D,13A
Germany, Sam	TX0370	13,66D,35G
Gertsenzon, Galina	MA2100	66A,66D,13A
Gianforte, Matthew P.	KY0950	66A,66D,66B,66,12A
Giles, Sevgi	IL0550	66A,66D
Gipson, Ann M.	TX3000	66B,66D,66A
Giunta, Cynthia	IA0550	66D,66C,66A
Glennon, Maura	NH0150	66A,66C,66D,66H
Glover, Angela	FL0040	66A,66B,66C,66D
Glover, Judy	PA3330	66D,66C
Gnandt, Edwin E.	AA0010	13A,66A,42,13B,66D

Name	Code	Areas
Godes, Catherine	TN1450	66A,66C,66D
Godsil, Daniel	IL1800	66A,66D
Golan, Jeanne K.	NY2550	13B,13C,12A,66A,66D
Goldman, Lawrence	MS0560	66A,66D,66,11,66C
Goldston, Christopher	IL0550	66D
Goodridge, Andrew	MA2030	66C,66D
Goodwin, Julia	OR0700	66A,66D,11,12A,66C
Gordon, Barbara N.	NJ0500	11,36,60A,66D,61
Gordon, Heidi Cohenour	AR0810	61,13C,66D,36
Gordon, Pamela	AL1170	66D,66C
Gordon, Tony A.	MS0050	66A,66D,66B,66C,11
Gorina, Alena	TX3175	66D
Gosswiller, Julie	MT0200	13C,66D,66A
Goter, Arlene	MN1295	66A,66B,13,66D
Gottesman, Judith F.	CA2050	66D
Grace, Rose S.	FL0100	66A,66B,66C,66D
Graef, Becky	IN1750	66A,66D,13A
Graff, Carleen	NH0250	66A,66D,66B
Graham, Edward E.	SC1050	66A,66C,66D,12A
Graham, Patricia S.	MD0650	13A,66D
Graning, Gary Alan	OH2150	66A,66D,66B
Grant, Darrell	OR0850	41,47,66A,66D,29
Grapenthin, Ina	PA1750	11,32B,66A,66G,66D
Graves, Kim	TN1660	66D,13C
Gray, Susan Keith	SD0600	66A,66B,66C,66D
Green, Elizabeth	MD0060	66A,66D
Green, Marsha	TX1600	66A,66D
Greenberg, Laura	NY0630	13,10,66A,66D,11
Griffin, Karen K.	KY1500	66D
Griffin, Nancy W.	AR0750	66D,45
Griffin, Ruth Ann	TX1660	61,66D
Griffin-Seal, Mary	FL0500	66A,11,66D,13C
Grimble, Thomas	SC0200	66A,66D
Grimwood, Paul	AG0200	66G,66H,66D
Grissom, Paula	GA1900	66D
Grobler, Sophia	OH0950	66A,66C,66D,20
Gross, David	SC0750	66A,66C,66B,66D
Grossman, Andrea	IN1010	11,66A,13A,66D
Grossman, George	NY2550	20G,66D
Grossman, Morley K.	TX3525	11,66A,66C,66D
Groves, Marilyn	NY2250	66D
Groves, Melinda	KS0300	66D
Grubb, Steve	CA3000	11,66D,66G,66H
Guelce, Sayuri	IN0250	66D
Guenette, Maria Mika	TX3370	66A,66D,66C
Guenther, Timothy E.	OH0100	66G,66H,66D
Guerrero, Rosi E.	WA0950	66A,66D,13A,13B,13D
Guiles, Kay	MS0360	11,66A,66D,66G
Gustavson, Mark	NY2550	10,64C,66D,10A,10F
Gutshall, Christi	AZ0400	66A,66B,66D,12A
Guttmann, Hadassah	NY2550	32A,66D,66A
Guy, Robin	IA1600	66C,66D
Guynes, Christi	TX2570	66A,66D
Guzasky, G. Frederick	MA0510	66A,66D
Haas, Adam J.	AR0500	66A,66D
Hadley, Susan J.	PA3100	70,33,11,66D
Haefner, Dale F.	MN1000	66D,35
Hahn, Carol G.	IN0905	66D,66A
Hahn, Christopher	MT0400	66A,66B,66C,66D
Haines, Janice	CA0950	13A,13C,66D
Haines, Janice	CA3200	66D
Hakutani, Naoki	AR0750	66A,66D,45
Halbeck, Patricia	TN0050	66A,66B,66C,66D
Halberg, Virginia	NY1700	66A,66D
Halberstadt, Randy	WA0200	13,66A,66D,53,29
Hall, Cory	FL1650	66D,66A,12A
Hall, Elena	FL0500	66A,66D,13C
Halvecka, Thomas	OH1910	66D,66A,61
Hamilton, Heather	TX2750	64B,66D
Hamilton, Hilree J.	WI0845	11,20,32A,32B,66D
Hamm, Laura	WV0440	32,36,66A,66D,66C
Hammond, Gary	NY0625	11,66A,66D
Hanna, Cassandria	FL1310	13,66A,66D,36
Hansen, Cheryl	ID0060	66D
Hansen, Lisa	ID0060	66D
Harding, Christopher	MI2100	66A,66C,66D
Harleston, Sheila C.	MD1020	60,36,66A,66D
Harmon, Linda	TN0100	66A,66D
Harms, Janet	CA0250	66D,66G
Harper, Erin Michelle	NC0350	66A,66C,66D
Harrell, Mary	CA1900	66A,66C,66D
Harrell, Paula D.	NC1600	32,66A,66G,66D,31A
Harris, Kay	SC1080	66C,66D
Harris, Larry	OH2600	66D
Harriss, Elaine Atkins	TN1720	66A,66B,42,66D
Hart, Cherie	WI0862	66D,64A
Hartl, David	PA3330	47,66A,66D,34,29
Hartway, James	MI2200	13A,10,10F,66D,13B
Hartwell, Robert	CA1800	66D,20G,12A
Hastings, Stella	KS1050	38,13B,13C,66D
Hatvani, Robert	OR1010	66A,66D
Haug, Sue E.	PA2750	66A,66B,66C,66D
Hawkins, Candace	OK0750	66A,66D
Hawley, Lucrecia	AL0010	11,32,66D
Hayashida, Mami	KY0610	66A,66G,66D
Hayes, Christina	NC0050	66A,66C,66D
Hayes, Jane	AB0060	66A,66D,13B,42,66B
Hayner, Phillip A.	GA1650	11,12,66A,66C,66D
Head, Kelley	MO0100	66D
Healey, John	VA0450	66D
Hearn, Carmelita	AF0120	13A,66A,66D
Hearn, Priscilla	KS0550	66A,11,12,66D,13C
Heath, Malissa	KY1540	11,66D,32B,13,12A
Heighway, Robbi A.	WI0450	11,13C,13D,66B,66D
Heimur, Elena	NY0644	61,66A,66D
Heinick, Carol	NY3780	66D
Hellmann, Mary	NC0700	66A,66D,12A
Hendricks, James	IL0600	13A,47,66A,66D,29
Henry, Barbara	WI1150	66D,66
Hernon, Bonnie	TN1720	66D,11
Herod, Sheila	TX1750	13,12A,66A,66C,66D
Hesh, Joseph	PA2800	47,42,66D
Hesla, Steven	MT0400	66B,66C,66D
Hess, Nathan A.	NY1800	66A,66D,66C,66,66B
Heyman, Amy G.	NY4150	66D
Heyman, Steven M.	NY4150	66A,66D,66C,66B
Hibbard, Jason	FL1950	11,66D
Hichborn, Kathryn D.	VA1475	66D
Hickman, Melinda	OH0550	11,66A,66B,66D
Hicks, Sharalynn	SC0650	66D
Higdon, Paul	MO1100	13,66A,66B,11,66D
Hill, Camille	KY0600	13A,11,36,61,66D
Hillard, Claire Fox	GA0625	11,62A,62B,66D,62
Hilley, Martha F.	TX3510	66D
Hines, Betsy Burleson	TX1400	66D,66C
Hinkle, Jean	OR1020	11,13A,41,66A,66D
Hirst, Dennis	UT0300	66D
Hisey, P. Andrew	MN1450	66A,66B,66D
Hoffman, Brian D.	OK0800	13A,13B,13C,66D
Holcombe, Helen	PA0400	13A,36,61,66D
Holden, Jon	NY2750	66C,66D
Holder, Hope	UT0400	66D
Holland, Samuel H.	TX2400	66A,66B,66D
Hollander, Jeffrey	WI0825	66A,66D
Hollinger, Deborah	IL3550	66A,11,66D
Holm, Robert	AL1300	66A,66B,66C,66D,66H
Holt, Danny	CA0510	66D
Holzman, David	NY2105	12A,66D,13
Hominick, Ian G.	MS0700	66A,66D,41
Hong, Caroline	OH1850	11,66A,66C,66D
Hong, Sojung Lee	IL1300	66A,66D,66B,42,66C
Hong, Sylvia	MS0100	66A,66D
Hopkins, Brenda	PR0115	66D
Horan, Leta	TX0300	36,66A,66D
Horneff, Donald C.	MD0520	66F,66C,66D,66H,32E
Horvath, Maria	IL1610	66A,66C,13,66D,11
Hosten, Kevin	NY2100	11,47,63,64,66D
Hostetter, Elizabeth	AL0550	66A,66D,66C,13,66
Houle, Arthur Joseph	CO0225	66A,66C,66B,66D
Houser, Virginia	KS0650	66A,66B,66D
Howard, Bill	TX1600	10D,10,66A,35B,66D
Hsu, Yun-Ling	FL1800	66A,66B,66C,66D
Hu, Xiao	IA0950	66A,66D
Huang, Du	IA0950	66A,66D
Huang, Grace	OH0600	66A,66D,66B
Hubbard, Constance	SD0100	66D
Hubbell, Judy	CA1020	61,66D,13A
Huber, John	KS0350	13,66A,66D
Hudson, Stephen	NJ1350	29,66D
Hudson, Terry Lynn	TX0300	66A,66D,66B
Hudson, William Andrew	TX1600	66A,11,66C,66D
Hudspeth, Charles M.	CA1020	36,13A,66D
Huff, Dwayne	MO0200	11,66A,66B,66C,66D
Huffman, Timothy	OH2050	66A,13B,66B,66D,66C
Hughes, Marcia A.	TN0930	12A,32B,66A,66D
Hughes, Miriam Kartch	NY2250	66D
Hulin, Charles J.	FL1740	13,66D,66A,66G
Huling, Diane	VT0250	13,66A,66B,66D
Hung, Yu-Sui	IL3450	66A,66D,13C
Hunter, Colleen	WA0400	66A,66D
Huntley, Yvonne	IL2750	66A,66D
Hurd, Mary	MI0300	66A,66B,66C,66D,13A
Hurst, Twyla	MS0370	13A,36,61,66D
Hussung, Mark	TN0250	66A,66D
Hutton, Judy F.	NC2650	13,66A,66B,66C,66D
Hwalek, Ginger Y.	ME0440	42,66D
Hwang, Christine	IL1615	11,66D
Hwang-Hoesley, Jae W.	IL0750	66D
Hynes, Mia M.	MO1790	66A,66B,66D
Immel, Daniel	PA1750	11,66A,66D
Indergaard, Lyle	GA2150	66A,66C,66D
Inkman, Joanne	NC2500	66A,66C,66D,13A
Inouye, Fang-Fang Shi	CA0859	66A,66D
Italiano, Richard	CO0300	13,10,11,66A,66D
Izdebski, Christy	MD0100	12A,32,66A,66D,36
Jackson, Tyrone	GA1150	66A,29B,66D,53
James, Jo-Sandra	VI0050	66A,66B,66D
James, Judy A. G.	LA0700	11,32,32I,66D
James, Karen	VT0100	66A,66D
James, Pamela A.	VA0750	32A,61,13C,66D,32B
James, William R.	FL1300	66A,66C,66D
Jang, Hue Jeong	IL1750	66D
Jantzi, John	OR1050	66D
Janzen, Elaine	TN1350	66A,66D,13A
Jarrell, Erinn	CA5355	13,66A,66B,66C,66D
Jeffers, Rebecca	OR0700	13A,66B,66C,66D
Jefferson, Thomas	IL2100	66A,66D
Jefferson, Thomas	IL2750	36,66D
Jenkins, Jeffry	CA4850	32,66D
Jenkins, Rosemary	TX2350	66A,66D
Jennings, Caroline	UT0150	66A,66D
Jensen, Joan F.	LA0750	66A,66D,13A
Jin, Jungwon	CA1960	66D,13A
Johansen, Ken	MD0650	13A,66D
Johns, Amy	GA1070	66A,66D,11
Johnson, Amy	MI0520	66D
Johnson, Amy E.	MI0900	66D,66B
Johnson, Gail	CA1375	66A,66D
Johnson, Kallin	MA0650	66D
Johnson, Kyle E.	CA0550	66G,66D
Johnson, Lura	MD0650	13A,66D
Johnson, Marjorie S.	VA0950	13,66A,66B,66D,34
Johnson, Michelle	TX2600	66A,66B,66C,66D,66E
Johnson, Pamela	WI0801	66D,66A,64
Johnson, Ruth	CA5360	13A,66A,66D
Johnson, Sharon L.	NY1700	66C,66A,66D,31A
Johnson, Shirley M.	FL0600	13A,61,66A,66D
Johnson, Tracey	MO2000	66A,66D,13C
Johnson, Victoria	MS0360	11,66A,66D
Johnson, Yvonne P.	DE0050	32,66D,62
Jones, Colette	KY0300	32B,11,66A,66D
Jones, Craig	OR0600	66A,66D,60A
Jones, Everett N.	OH2400	12A,66A,66B,66D
Jones, Henry S.	LA0650	66A,66B,66D,13C
Jones, Lis	AR0250	66A,66C,66D
Jones, Maxine	TN1400	66A,66D,11
Jones, Melinda	MO1550	66A,66D,66B,13B,13C
Jones, Pamela Palmer	UT0250	66D,13C
Jones, Robert D.	FL1470	66A,66G,66C,66D,34
Jones, Sue	IL1550	42,66A,66C,66D,13C
Jordahl, Patricia	AZ0300	36,54,66D,61,11
Joyce, Susan	FL1450	66A,66D
Joyner, Rochelle	NC0200	11,66A,66D
Ju, Ara	MO0850	66C,66D
Julian, Suzanne	CA3100	11,66A,66D
Jung, Eunsuk	TN0600	13A,66A,66D,66G,13B
Jutras, Peter J.	GA2100	66A,66B,66D,32G
Kaarre, Lois	MI1750	66D,66C
Kaiser, Audrey K.	RI0101	66A,66D,13
Kaizer, Janet	IL0400	66A,66D
Kalman, Eli	WI0830	66A,66D
Kam, Genna	IN0910	11,66D
Kan-Walsh, Karen	IL2250	66D
Kanamaru, Tomoko	NJ0175	66A,66B,66C,66D
Kanda, Sanae	MA1650	10A,42,66A,66C,66D
Kaneda, Mariko	OH2000	66C,66A,66D,13B,13C
Kang, Haysun	IL1615	11,66A,66D
Kang, Juyeon	IA1200	66A,66D,66C,13C
Kang, Leah	CA0200	66D
Kantorski, Valrie	MI0050	66A,66D
Kasper, Don J.	CA0835	62D,66D
Kaurin-Karaca, Natasa	OK0800	66D,13C,11,34B
Keast, Larry	CA0100	66D
Kebuladze, Tatyana	NJ0800	66A,66D,66C
Keenan, Larry W.	KY0900	11,66A,66G,66D,66H
Kefferstan, Christine	WV0750	66A,66B,66C,66D

Index by Area of Teaching Interest

Name	Code	Areas
Kegerreis, Helen M.	NY2550	32A,13C,66D
Kehle, Lori	KS1050	66D
Kehler Siebert, Judith	AC0100	66A,66C,66D,42
Keith, Laura J.	SC0350	12A,66A,66D,32C,32D
Kelley, Robert T.	SC0800	20,13,66A,66D,10
Kelly, Chris	AJ0150	61,66D
Kelly, Pamela	WI1100	66D
Kelly, Rebecca	AB0200	66A,66D
Kenney, James	CA3375	13A,11,14C,66D
Kenney, Sharon E.	AR0730	61,66D
Kenyon, Paul	CA3640	66A,66D
Kern, R. Fred	TX3420	13A,66B,66D
Kerner, Winifred	OR1050	66D
Keyne, Lori V.	AZ0250	13B,13C,36,66D
Khamda, Mazdak	CA3250	66A,66D,32F,35C
Kiehl, Vicky	AR0200	66A,66H,66B,66D,66C
Kiehn, Mark T.	WI0808	32A,66D,70,63A,32B
Kim, Ellen	CA0815	66D
Kim, Ellen Y.	CA2050	66A,66D
Kim, Howard D.	SC0050	66A,66D,13B,66C,11
Kim, Jisung	NY2550	66A,66D
Kim, Kyung-Mi	GA0050	66A,66D
Kim, Nahyun	KS0590	66A,66D
Kim, Namji C.	WI0803	66A,66D
Kim, Seung-Ah	NC2435	11,66D,66C
Kim, Yoo-Jung	MI1200	66A,66C,66D
Kim, Youmee	OH1900	66A,66C,66D
Kim, Young	NY0700	13B,13C,66A,66D
Kim-Medwin, Sungah	MD0550	66A,66D
Kime, Ramona	MI1800	62,66A,66D,66H
Kincade, Gertrude C.	AR0750	66H,66C,66D
King, Adam	AL1195	66A,13,66D,66C
King, Donna Moore	TN0930	11,66A,66D,69
King, Melodie S.	AL0800	66D
King, Vicki B.	TN1400	66A,66D,12A
KinKennon, Heather Marie	CA0200	11,60,66,66D
Kinney, Kaylyn	NY3000	11,66D
Kinsley, Diane	MD0060	66A,66D
Kinsley, Eric B.	CA0550	11,66A,66H,66D
Kirchoff, Leanna	CO0550	66D,13A
Kirk, Caroline	MN1400	11,66A,66B,66D
Kirk, Erin	CA0845	66C,66D
Kirkendoll, Michael	OK0800	66A,66B,66D,42
Kirkpatrick, Amanda	MO1900	66A,66D
Kirkpatrick, Elka	NJ1400	66D
Kirkpatrick, Gary	NJ1400	66A,66B,66D
Kislenko, Natalia	CA5060	66A,66C,66D
Kisner, Brad	TX2930	66D,39
Kissack, Christine W.	ME0500	66B,66D
Klassen, Masako	CA3200	66D
Klecker, Deb J.	WI0450	11,66D
Klefstad, Kristian I.	TN0100	66A,66B,66D
Kline, Matthew C.	TX2400	66B,66D
Klingenstein, Beth Gigante	ND0600	12A,66B,66D
Kloosterman, Jill	MI0900	66D
Knaub, Maribeth J.	PA3100	11,61,66D
Knickerbocker, Sharon	IL1900	66A,66B,66C,66D
Koch, Patricia Schott	PA2200	66B,66D
Koester, Eugene	SC0275	66A,66D
Koga, Midori	AG0450	66D
Kohlbeck-Boeckman, Anne	WI0350	13,66A,66D,13A
Kolar, J. Mitzi	CA4100	66A,66B,66D
Kolean, Lora Clark	MI1050	66D
Konstantinov, Tzvetan	DC0100	66A,66C,66D
Kot, Don	NY2650	66A,61,66D,66C,54
Koukios, Ann Marie	MI2200	36,12A,66D
Koutsoukos, Sheree	TN1850	66,66D
Kraft, Edith	NY1900	66D
Kraus, Nanette	KS0050	66C,66D
Kreider, David G.	MD0520	11,66A,66G,66D
Kreiling, Jean L.	MA0510	13A,11,12A,12,66D
Kresky, Jeffrey	NJ1400	13,10F,11,66D
Krieger, Karen Ann	TN1850	13,66A,66D,66B,68
Kroetsch, Terence	AG0600	13,66D,66A
Kroik, Anna	NJ0700	66D
Kropidlowski, Monica	IL2650	66A,66D
Krueger, Karen Merola	WA1400	66D
Krueger, Leslie	WI0825	66A,66D
Krueger, Mary Beth	CO0550	54,61,66C,66D
Krueger, Walter E.	OR0150	13A,66A,12A,66G,66D
Krusemark, Ruth E.	KS0100	13,10,66A,66G,66D
Kuhn, Lynne	CA3460	66A,66D
Kuroda, Elena	LA0550	66C,66D
Kurschner, James	MN1200	37,64E,41,66D
Kwami, Paul T.	TN0550	20,36,66G,60A,66D
Kwon, MiYoung	OH0755	66A,66D
Kwon, Yeeseon	IL0550	66A,66B,66D,66
La Manna, Juan F.	NY3770	38,66A,66D,11,39
La Rocca, Carla	PA0550	66A,66D
Labenske, Victor	CA3640	66A,66D,12A,10
Laframboise, Damian	AG0150	66A,66D
Lan, Catherine	FL0200	13B,13C,66D
Landes, Daniel	TN0100	13A,13,66A,66D,31A
Lane, LuAnn	TX1850	11,13,66A,66C,66D
Lanham, Barbara	IL1610	13A,36,66,66D
Laprade, Paul	IL2560	13C,36,61,66D,32
Larocco, Sharon Moss	NC0750	66C,66D
Larsen, Laurel	SC0900	66A,66C,66B,13,66D
Larson, Lynee	MN1290	66A,66D
Lassen, Emily	ID0060	66D
Laubengayer, Karen	MS0350	66A,66B,66C,66D
Lauderdale, Lynne A.	FL2100	12A,66A,66G,66D,66B
Lauffer, Peter	NJ1350	66D
Laughlin, Mark	GA1000	66A,13,12A,66D,13B
Laurendine, Barbara	AL1195	66A,66D
Laurent, Linda	CT0050	13,12,66A,66D,42
Lawing, Cynthia	NC0550	66A,66D
Lawlor, Catherine	MA2010	66A,66D
Lawson, Robert	CA1265	10,38,41,66A,66D
Lawson, Robert	CA5360	13,10,11,66D,12A
Lazarus, Gordon	CA0200	64B,66D
Leavitt, Edward	NY4300	66A,66D
Lee, Gerald K.	WV0600	66A,66B,66C,66D
Lee, Jaeryoung	CA2960	66D
Lee, Joohyun	TX2960	66D,66C
Lee, Kyung	CA3600	66C,66D
Lee, Patricia	IL2650	66A,66H,66B,66C,66D
Lee, Sun Jung	WV0100	66A,66C,66D
Lee, Sung Ae	CA0859	13A,66A,66D
Lee, You Ju	GA2000	66A,66G,66D,66B
Lemson, Deborah	TX3850	66A,66G,66C,66D
Lenehan, Miriam C.	NY2450	11,12A,32,66A,66D
Leonard, Lisa	FL1125	66B,66D,42
Leshowitz, Myron	NJ0700	66D
Lester, William	NY2400	66A,66D,29
Leung, Jackson	OH2500	66A,66D,66B,38
Leventhal, Lois A.	MS0750	66A,66,66D
Levine, Dena	NJ1160	11,66D,66A
Levtov, Vladimir	AA0150	41,66A,66C,66D,42
Lew, Howard	NY2700	13A,12,66D
Lewin, Michael	MA0400	66A,66D
Lewis, Alexandra M.	NY0500	11,12,13C,66D
Lewis, Christopher	VT0050	66A,66B,66C,66D
Lewis, Daniel	MD0175	11,13,66D,70
Lewis, Gary	TX1700	11,66D
Lewis, Kimberly	IL2775	66D
Lewis, Robert J.	KY0300	13B,11,66A,66B,66D
Li, Bichuan	HI0210	66A,66D
Li, Hanna Wu	PA0550	66A,66B,66D
Li, Juan	MN0250	66A,66D
Li, Lei	IL0650	13A,11,66A,66D
Lieurance, Barbara	MA0510	66A,66D
Lim, Benedict M.	CA1020	20C,20D,11,66D
Lim, Cheryl	IL1085	66A,66D
Lim, Cheryl	IL3550	66A,66D
Lim, Jennifer	MO1250	66A,66D
Lin, ChiaHui	CA0830	66D
Lindeman, Carolynn A.	CA4200	13A,32,66D,34
Lington, Victoria	CA4400	11,66D
Linnenbom, Harriett	MD0700	13A,11,66A,66D
Linstrom, Tracie	CA5400	66D,66A
Lipke, William A.	CO0050	66A,38,67F,66B,66D
Liu, Susan (Shao-Shan)	TX1425	66A,66D,11,34
Livingston, Carolyn H.	RI0300	32,36,66D,12C
Livingston, Jane	WI0250	66A,66D,66B
Lloyd, Charles	LA0700	13,39,11,66D
Lobitz, Kristi	CA2800	66A,66D
Long, Arlene	TX2930	66A,66C,66D
Long, Gail	IL2970	66D
Lopez, Christine Sotomayor	CA0859	36,66A,66D,11,66B
Lopez, Richard C.	OH2050	66A,66D
Lord, Roger	AE0100	13,66A,66D
Loring, George	NH0150	66A,66B,66D,66H
Losey, Mary	SC1100	66A,66D
Lovell, Owen C.	WI0803	66A,66D
Low, Linda	AB0210	66A,66D,66B
Lowder, Jerry E.	OH1850	32,66D
Lum, Anne Craig	HI0150	66D,66A,64A,45,66C
Lum, Tammy K.	NY2900	13,66A,66D,42
Lupinski, Rudy	OK0300	66A,66D,13B,13C,66H
Lysinger, Catherine	TX2400	66B,66D
M. de Oca, Patricia	TX3520	66D,66C,54
Macchioni, Oscar E.	TX3520	66A,66B,66D,66,14
MacCrae, Cynthia Perry	AL1200	66A,66B,66C,66D
MacDonald, Laurence E.	MI0450	11,12A,66A,66D
MacDougall, Elizabeth	CA2840	66A,66D
Mach, Elyse J.	IL2150	11,66D,66B
Mackey, Lynne A.	VA0300	66A,66B,66C,66D,13
Macon, Connie	AL0800	66D
Maes, James	MA1100	66A,66G,66C,66D,11
Magrath, Jane	OK1350	66B,66A,66D,66,66C
Mahamuti, Gulimina	OH2000	66A,66D,66B,66B
Maisonpierre, Elizabeth	NC2435	11,13,66A,66B,66D
Maki, Daniel H.	IL0840	13,11,37,64A,66D
Mallady, Joan	IL1890	66A,66D
Mandle, William Dee	DC0350	13A,13,32B,66A,66D
Manno, Terrie	MN1120	66A,66B,66C,66D
Marcel, Linda A.	NJ0020	12B,66A,66D,32,11
March, Kathryn Lucas	IA1100	13C,66A,66D,66C
Marchukov, Sergey	PA2900	66A,66D,66C,13A
Marin, Luis	PR0115	29,66A,66D
Markowski, Victoria	CO0275	66A,66D,41,42
Markun, Mila M.	WV0400	32A,66A,66C,66D
Marsh, John	GA1150	66D,11
Marshall, Thomas	VA0250	66A,66G,66H,66D
Martin, Brenda	CA3640	66A,66D
Martin, Deborah	NY1800	66A,66B,66D
Martin, Joshua	FL0350	13,11,66A,66D
Martin, Michelle Denise	GA0150	11,65,66D,60B
Martinez, Gabriela	NJ0700	66A,66D,42
Martinez, Guillermo	TX3000	66D
Martucci, Vincent	NY3760	29,29B,66A,66D,47
Maryanova, Sofya	NY3760	66D
Mascolo-David, Alexandra	MI0400	66A,66B,66D
Maskell, Kathleen D.	MA1600	66D
Mason, Rodney	TX0350	13,36,61,66A,66D
Massicot, Joshua	NY2650	66D
Mastronicola, Michael	CO0400	61,66A,66D
Matesky, Nancy	WA0860	13,66A,66D
Matheson, Jennifer	AF0120	10,66D,66A
Matsuo, Jun	SC0450	66A,66D,66B,66C,13
Mauchley, Sandra	ID0250	66A,66H,66B,66D
Mauleon-Santana, Rebeca	CA1020	66D,20H,10A
May, Luise	GA0550	66D
May, Maureen	TN1850	66D
May, Nathanael A.	MO0850	66,66B,66C,66D
Mayfield, Farren	OK0550	11,66D
Mayor, Pedro	AL0450	66D
McAllister, Lesley Ann	TX0300	66A,66B,66D
McArthur, Victoria	FL0850	66B,66D
McBee, Karen L.	TX0125	12A,11,66A,66C,66D
McCarrey, Stacy	HI0050	66A,66C,66D
McCloskey, Kathleen	PA0650	11,12A,13A,66D
McClung-Guillory, Deborah	LA0770	66A,66B,66D
McConnell, Joan	OH0950	66C,66G,13C,66D,13B
McCord, G. Dawn Harmon	GA2130	32B,32C,32A,13C,66D
McCoy, Louise	AL1250	66C,66D
McCullam, Audrey	MD0600	13,32B,32C,66A,66D
McCullough, Richard D.	NY2950	13A,36,39,61,66D
McDermott, Sheila	LA0080	11,13,61,66D
McDowell, Laura	NC0250	12C,12A,66D,67C
McFadden, Jim L.	CA1020	66D
McFarland, James	TX3600	11,13,66D,66G
McFarland, Kay Dawn	KY1425	11,66A,66C,66D
McGinnis, Beth	AL0800	66D,11,12A
McKamie, Shirley	MO1780	11,66D,66H
McKay, David	TN0100	66D
McLauchlin, Charlotte	OR1000	13,66D,66A,67C,12A
McRoberts, Terry	TN1660	66A,66C,66D,66B
McVay, Vicki	KY1450	66D,13,66B,13C
McVey, Roger D.	WI0845	12A,66A,66B,66C,66D
McWilliams, Kent M.	MN1450	66A,66C,66D,66E
Mdivani, Marina	AI0150	66A,66D
Meadows, Leslie	OH0200	66D
Mechell, Lauren	MN1700	66D
Meier, Margaret	CA3200	13A,11,66D
Melago, Kathleen A.	PA3100	32B,11,66D
Melendez Dohnert, Victor	PR0115	13A,13B,13C,66D
Meng, Mei-Mei	NY2250	13,66D
Merrill, Paul	NH0350	66C,66D
Metcalf, Mary Louise	OH0100	66D
Middaugh, Laurie	AL1200	66C,66D
Mielbrecht, Marie	CA4300	66D
Mikolajewski, Alice	DC0100	36,66A,66C,66D
Milenkovic, Vladan	MA0510	29,66A,66D
Millar, Tania	AG0070	66A,66D,13C

Name	Code	Areas
Miller, Lori	SD0100	66D
Miller, Phillip	CA0450	40,66D
Miller, Sara	MO1550	66D
Miller, Tammy	FL1750	66C,66A,66D
Miller-Thorn, Jill	NY1275	10A,10F,13,66D,12C
Mills, Charlotte	CO0950	32,66D
Mills, Michele D.	OH2150	13A,12A,66D
Milnar, Veronica Edwards	TN1100	66D,66A
Milne, Virginia E.	TX2800	66A,66D
Minasian, Linda	CA5400	11,66D,66A
Miranda, Julianne M.	IN0250	66C,66D
Mitchell, Carol	GA0940	13,66A,66G,66C,66D
Mitchell, Charlene	MO0600	32B,66A,66C,66D
Miyama, Yoko	OR0050	66,13,12A,66C,66D
Moak, Elizabeth W.	MS0750	66A,66D,66C
Mobley, Jenny	IN0250	66A,66D
Moegle, Mary Steele A.	LA0250	11,66A,66C,66D
Molina, Rocio	TX3515	66C,66D
Molinari, Kyounghwa	AR0300	66A,66C,66D
Montano, David R.	CO0900	66A,66B,66D,32
Moore, John	TX2200	11,66A,66C,12A,66D
Moore, Kevin	NY2950	13,66A,66C,66D,10A
Moore, Selma	NY2950	13,37,41,64A,66D
Moorman, Joyce Solomon	NY2100	13,10,11,66A,66D
Moorman-Stahlman, Shelly	PA1900	44,66A,66G,31A,66D
Moreau, Barton	ID0050	13,11,66C,66D,66A
Morelli, Jackie	OR1250	66A,66D
Morenus, Carlyn G.	IL1150	66A,66D
Morgan, Ruby N.	SC0750	66A,66B,66D
Morita, Lina	LA0350	13C,41,66A,66C,66D
Moritz, Benjamin	PA2150	66A,66B,66C,66D
Morris, Amy B.	SC1200	66D
Morris, Kelley	OK1450	66A,66D
Morrison, Mable R.	DE0050	11,12A,66A,66D
Morrow, Jo L.	LA0650	11,66D
Morse, Dana	LA0650	66A,66D
Mortensen, John J.	OH0450	66A,66C,66D
Mortyakova, Julia V.	MS0550	66A,66D,66B,66C,12B
Moseley, Jessica Barnett	SC0750	13,66C,66D
Moser, Bruce	NC0400	12,66A,66B,13,66D
Moser, Janet	IL0850	66A,66D,32A,32
Moss, Elaine	WI0750	66C,66D,66B,66A,32A
Moxley, Lisa	VA0050	66A,66D,31A,13A,11
Mrozinski, Lavonne	IL1085	66A,66D
Mrozinski, Mark	IL1085	66A,66D
Mueller, Charlotte G.	TX1450	13,11,66A,66D
Mueller, Madeline N.	CA1020	66D
Mullenax, Gary	WV0550	66A,11,66D
Mulliken, Erin	IL1200	66A,66D
Muniz, Jennifer	MO0100	66A,66D,13C,13E
Murphy, Cynthia	NE0300	16,66A,66D,13
Murphy, Kathleen	IN1600	33,32B,66D
Murray, David	GA0950	66A,66D
Murray, Janice	NC0250	66A,66C,66D,13
Murray, Michele C.	IN0100	13A,13B,13C,66D
Myatt, Traci	OH1600	66D,66C
Myrick, Barbara	OR0350	13,12A,66A,66D,64A
Nagy, Daniel	FL1500	66A,66D
Nahm, Dorothea A.	DC0350	66A,66D
Nakashima, Rieko	FL1300	66A,66D
Nam, Choong-ha	TX3750	66A,66D
Nam, Song Hun	KY1000	66D
Nargizyan, Lucy	CA1960	66D
Navarro Romero, Emanuel	PR0115	66D,47
Neal, Nedra	NY2550	13C,66D
Neely-Chandler, Thomasina	GA1450	31,66D
Nelson, Jessica L.	AL1250	66A,66G,66D
Nelson, Margaret	NJ0975	13A,66C,66D
Nelson, Marie	MA2020	32A,32B,32C,66D
Nemko, Deborah G.	MA0510	66A,66C,66D,11
Neville, Ruth	SC0750	66D,13
Newcomb, Suzanne	OH2050	66A,66D,66C
Newman, David	WI0100	66A,66D,41
Ng-Au, Marie	AG0070	66A,66D
Nichols, William	MO0200	66A,66D
Nicholson, Bonnie	AJ0150	66A,66D
Niehaus, Christine J.	VA0250	66A,66D
Nikolova, Iliana	AB0050	66D
Nishikiori, Fumi	WI0835	66D,13A
Nix, Brad K.	KS1250	66B,66A,66C,10F,66D
Nobles, Katherine	GA0300	66D
Nolte, Lanita M.	MN1030	66A,66D
Noone, Elizabeth	MA0150	66A,66D,11,13A,20B
Norberg, Anna H.	OK1450	66A,66C,66D,15
Norman, Janet	AZ0490	66D
Novak, Christina D.	AZ0490	11,13,66A,10A,66D
Nye, Karmelle	ID0075	66D
O'Brien, Andrew C.	AZ0490	66A,66D
O'Brien, John B.	NC0650	66A,66D,66H,55
O'Dell, Debra	ID0140	66A,66C,11,66D,12A
Ohl, Vicki	OH0950	13,66A,66D
Oka, Betty A.	CA3500	66D,66A
Olsen, Eric	NJ0800	13A,13B,13C,66D
Olsen, John F.	NM0100	66A,66B,66D
Olson, Anthony	MO0950	11,66A,66G,66D
O'Neal, Andrea	IN0500	66A,66D
Ordaz, Joseph	CA2975	11,66A,66D,38
Orland, Michael	CA5000	13A,66D,66A,13C
Ormenyi, Dina	CA3300	66D
Orr, Kevin Robert	FL1850	66A,66B,66D,13A,13
Osborn, Susan R.	IL2250	66D
Osterbers, Janet	WI0808	66C,66D
Otaki, Michiko	GA0500	41,66A,66C,66D
Otto, Noemi	VA0750	66A,66D
Otwell, Margaret V.	WI0500	66A,66D
Outland, Joyanne	IN0905	66A,66C,66D,66B,12A
Overmoe, Kirk	TX3360	13,66A,66D,66B
Owen, Jerri Lee	CA0350	66A,66D
Owen, Linda	OK1330	66A,66D
Owens, Diane	TX1100	66A,66C,66D,32A,32B
Owens, Janet	FL1450	66D,13,11
Owens, Kathryn Ananda	MN1450	66A,66C,66D,66E,66B
Owens, Robert	NC0800	11,66D,66G
Pachak-Brooks, Cheryl	NM0100	66B,66D,66A,66C
Paddleford, Nancy	MN1450	66A,66C,66B,66D
Pagal, Alena M.	SC1110	66B,66D
Palmer, Jason	OR1020	66D,13,13C,29A,29B
Palmier, Darice	IL2970	66A,66D,11,13A,66C
Palmieri, Gary	NY3760	66D
Pan, Huiyu-Penny	CA0830	66A,66D,66B,66C,42
Pang, Wilma C.	CA1020	66D,11,13A
Pannunzio, Sam	CO0275	66A,53,60D,47
Pardue, Jane	NC1400	36,66A,66D,13A,13B
Parente, Thomas	NJ1350	66A,66D,32I
Park, Meeyoun	KY0950	66C,66D
Park, Sohyoung	TX2150	66A,66B,66D
Park-Kim, Phoenix	IN1025	66A,66B,66C
Parker, Charla	OK0600	66D,32B
Parker, Christopher S.	NY3000	47,66A,66D,53,29
Parker, Joan	SC0200	66A,66B,66D
Parker, Patricia G.	AL0500	11,66A,66D
Parker, Sylvia	VT0450	13,66A,66D,66B
Parody, Caroline D.	NJ0800	66D,61
Parr, Andrew	TX2700	66A,66D
Parr, Sharon M.	IN1650	11,66A,66D,12A
Parrini, Fabio	SC0950	66A,66D,11,66C
Parshley, Alan O.	VT0450	63B,13A,66D
Parsons, Derek J.	SC0750	13,66A,66B,66D
Partlow, Mary Rita	TX1900	66A,66D
Paskova, Lyubov	MD0800	66A,66D
Passmore, Ken	GA1200	66D,66C,65,50
Patterson, Donald L.	WI0803	66A,66B,66D,66H
Paulk, Kayla Liechty	NM0100	66A,66C,66B,66D
Pavese, Frank	NJ1400	66D
Pawlicki, Michael	CA2700	11,66A,66D
Payne, Benjamin	FL0670	11,34,13,66A,66D
Pearsall, Tom	GA0950	66A,66B,66D
Pedersen, Gary	MI0600	66A,66B,66C,66D
Pedroza, Ludim R.	TX3175	12A,20H,66D
Pedroza, Ricardo	PR0125	13,60,36,66A,66D
Peffley, Lynette	OH0100	32A,11,66D
Peirce, Dwight	TX1400	66D
Peloza, Susan	CA5400	62,11,13A,66D
Pennington, Curt	IN0800	13,66D
Pennington, Lynn	AR0950	32,66A,66D
Penpraze, Laurie	FL1745	63C,63D,66D,67E
Pepetone, Gregory	GA0850	12A,32,66A,66B,66D
Peretz, Marc	MI1850	11,32,66D,34
Perry, Eileen	AZ0480	66A,13C,66D
Perry, Margaret	CA5350	66B,66D,66C,13C
Peterson, Jeffry F.	WI0825	66A,66C,66D
Peterson, Pamela	FL0400	66A,66D
Petrella, Diane Helfers	MO1810	66A,66B,66D
Pettyjohn, Emma	GA0700	66A,66B,66C,66G,66D
Phillips, Linda N.	NY3725	12A,66D,29A
Phillips, Nicholas S.	WI0803	66A,66D
Pickering, Melinda C.	IA0600	66D
Pickett, Barbara	WA0050	66C,66D,66A
Piechocinski, Janet	IN0800	66D
Pierpoint, Paula	FL0950	61,66A,66D
Pifer, Joshua K.	AL0200	66A,66C,66D,13C
Pike, Pamela D.	LA0200	66A,66D
Pitts, Frank	MI2120	66D
Pla, Maria	OH0650	66A,66D
Plies, Dennis B.	OR1150	47,65B,66B,66D,13C
Polevoi, Randy M.	CA1900	66A,66D
Polischuk, Derek Kealii	MI1400	66A,66B,66D,38,29
Poltorak, Agnes	NJ1350	66D
Porter, Charles	NY2700	13A,11,12A,66D,29A
Porterfield-Pyatt, Chaumonde	CA1290	11,66A,66G,66D
Powell, Patricia	PA3600	66,66D
Powell, Philip M.	SC0420	66A,66B,66C,66D
Pressnell, Paula B.	NC0400	66C,66A,66D
Price, Jeffrey	NC2420	61,66D
Price, Scott	SC1110	66A,66B,66D
Prigge, Sarah	ND0350	12A,66D
Pritchard, Lee H.	NY3760	66D
Puig, Martha	VA1500	66A,66D
Pulido, Maria Fernanda Nieto	CO0550	66D
Pullman, Marlene	AJ0030	13,66A,66B,66D
Quong, Meijane	AB0060	66A,66D,13C
Radell, Judith M.	PA1600	13,66A,66D,66C
Radoslavov, Ilia G.	MO1780	66C,66A,66D,66B
Raimo, John B.	TX3525	11,12A,66A,66D,66C
Rambeau, Deborah	WA0700	66A,66B,66C,66D
Ransom, Judy L.	WY0115	13B,13F,36,40,66D
Rappe, Terri	WA1200	66A,66D,66A
Rasmussen, G. Rosalie	CA3400	32,44,66B,66D,13C
Ratcliff, Joy	LA0050	66D
Ratz, Arlene	AZ0200	66A,66D
Ravitskaya, Irena	KS0350	66A,66B,66C,66D,66G
Rawlins, Nancy	NJ1050	66D,66G,13,12
Ray, Emily	CA1800	66D,38
Ray, James	FL1550	66D,34D,60A,35C
Razaq, Janice L.	IL1085	66A,66B,66D
Ream, Duane	SC0200	66A,66D,34
Reason, Dana	OR0700	66D
Redfern, Nancy	MI1600	66,11,66D,66B,66G
Reed, Jane	OH0100	11,13A,62A,66D,62B
Reed, John Perry	SC0050	66A,66D
Reeves, Janet	NJ1400	66D
Reichenberger, Kathy	OH2290	66C,66D
Reichling, Mary	LA0760	32,66D
Reilly, Kevin	OH2300	66D
Reinhuber, Joachim	TX2960	66A,66D,66C
Renfroe, Anita B.	PA2350	66A,66D
Renfrow, Kenon	SC0200	66A,66B,66D,34
Renshaw, Kenneth	MO1710	66A,66D
Resnianski, Igor	PA3600	66,66D
Reynerson, Rodney T.	NC0050	66A,66C,66D,11,41
Reynolds, Sonya Szabo	OH2550	66A,66D
Rhoden, Lori E.	IN0150	66A,66B,66D
Rice, Karen	NC2700	66A,66C,66D
Richards, Doris	MI2200	66A,66D
Richardson, Dennis	TX0550	36,40,32B,66D,60A
Richmond, Kevin D.	TN1680	66A,66D,66B
Richter, Elizabeth	IN0150	41,66E,66D
Richter, Lois	GA0200	66D
Rickey, Euni	IN1025	66A,66D,66B,66C
Rickman, Michael	FL1750	66A,12A,66B,66D
Ridgway, Meredith K.	TX3410	66A,66D
Riley, Carole	PA1050	66A,66D
Riley, Kathleen	MI0150	66D
Rippy, Sylvia	NC0050	32E,66D
Risinger, Andrew	TN0100	66D,66G
Riske, Barbara	NV0050	66A,66D
Rivera, Felix	PR0150	11,66A,66D
Roach, Hildred E.	DC0350	20G,66A,66B,66C,66D
Roberts, Mary W.	FL0600	66A,66B,66D,66D
Roberts, Melissa	MO1550	66A,66D
Roberts, Vera	CT0050	66D
Robey, Matthew E.	NY2500	66A,66C,66D,11,32E
Robinson, Florence	FL0600	12A,66A,66,66D
Robinson, Richard	CA3700	66D
Rodgers, Kenneth	KS0500	66G,66A,66D,66C,11
Rodgers, Reginald G.	IN0100	66A,66B,66D
Rodriguez Aponte, Dalia	PR0115	66D
Roederer, Silvia	MI2250	66A,66B,66C,66D
Roessingh, Karel	AB0210	66D
Rogers, Barbara J.	MN1280	66A,66D,66C
Rogers, Timothy	NH0150	66D,11
Roitman, Tatiana	AR0750	66A,66D,13
Roman, Mary C.	FL0850	62E,66D
Ronning, Debra D.	PA1250	66A,66B,66D
Rose, Angela	OH1350	61,66D
Roseman, Molly	KY0900	66A,66D

Name	Code	Areas
Roseman, Molly J.	WI0850	66,66A,66B,66D,66C
Rosenberg, Aaron H.	MA2030	13,66D
Rosenshein, Ingrid	FL1675	11,13A,61,66D,54
Ross-Happy, Linda Mae	MO1810	66D
Rossman, Pamela	TX2650	66A,66D
Rotella, Gloria	NJ0760	32,66A,66D
Rous, Bruce	WV0400	13,66D
Rowden, Charles H.	NY2550	11,12A,66D
Rowe, Paul	OK0300	66A,11,66D,66G
Rownd, Gary	IL1850	13A,66A,66D,11
Roye, Nedra	OK0500	66A,66D
Ruckman, Robert	OH2120	66A,66D
Russell, Bruce	CA0859	66A,66D
Russell, Mary Lou	TX2260	11,66A,66C,66D,29
Rust, Rosalind	AL1150	66D
Ryan, Sarah E.	MO1800	13,66D
Ryder, Raymond T.	AZ0480	66A,13A,66D
Sacalamitao, Melonie	CA4850	32A,32B,32C,66D,36
Sachs, Daniel	OH0680	66A,66D
Sadlier, Lelia	VA0150	66D,66A
Sahr, Barbara	OH0350	66D
Sajnovsky, Cynthia B.	GU0500	13A,12A,20C,66D,67C
Salas, Jacqueline M.	CA0835	66A,66D
Sale, Craig	IL0730	66A,66B,66D,66C
Salido, Caroline	OH2050	66A,66D
Salwen, Barry	NC2440	11,66A,66B,66D
Samolesky, Jeremy	AL0200	66A,66D,13C
Sanders, Terrie	LA0550	61,66D
Sandim, Carmen	CO0550	29A,66D
Sandor, Alexander	WI0860	66A,66D
Santos-Neto, Jovino	WA0200	47,66A,66D
Satava, Joseph F.	MD0475	66A,66D
Sato, Junichi S.	IL0750	66D
Saulsbury, Kate	IA1100	61,39,66D
Savko, Carolyn	TX3500	66D,66A
Sbarboro, Kathlyn	IL1085	66A,66D
Scanlan, Mary	MI0850	66,66A,66H,66C,66D,20F
Scarambone, Bernardo	KY0550	66A,66D,66B,66,66C
Schechter, Dorothy E.	CA0550	12A,66A,66B,66D
Schempf, Ruthanne	NY3760	66A,66D,12A,13B
Scherr, Bernard	TX0900	13,10,66D
Schilling, Arnie	IA0800	66A,66D
Schmidt, James	NC0450	66A,29A,66D,47,11
Schmidt, Susan	MO1120	66D
Schoeplin, Judith	WA1350	66A,66D,16,66B
Schoessler, Tim	WY0130	66A,66D,13,12A
Schons, Suzanne	MN1625	66D
Schott, Kimberly	ND0500	66A,66D
Schreiner, Gregory	CA0859	66A,66D
Schuttenberg, Emily Amanda	NC0350	66A,66C,66D
Scott, Caryl Mae	CA4300	64A,66D
Scott, Diane	PA3150	66D
Scott, Gina	TN1660	66D
Scott, Sarah	CA5355	16,66D
Scott, Tatiana	CA0840	66D
Seeds, Laurel M.	OH1100	66D,61
Segrest, Linda H.	MS0550	13A,13B,66A,66D,13C
Senedak, Irene	CT0450	66D
Servias, David	OR0700	66D
Settoon, Donna	LA0080	66A,66D
Severtson, David	WI0808	66A,13,66D,12A,66C
Shagdaron, Bair	NC0050	66A,66C,66D
Shank, Nadine E.	MA2000	66A,66C,66D
Shannon, Nanette	CO0550	66C,66D
Shannon, Nanette	CO0650	66A,41,66D
Shapovalov, Dimitri	WI0250	12A,66D,36,66A
Sharp, Leanne	GA1500	66D
Shaw, Betty	TX3400	32,66B,66D
Shaw, Nathan	OH0350	66D
Sheehan, Paul J.	NY2550	13A,66D
Shellito, Kelli	PA0100	66A,66D
Shen, Yang	FL1125	66C,66D,13C
Sherman, Kathryn D.	NY3780	66D,66B
Shew, Jamie	CA1900	53,60,13A,13B,66D
Shibatani, Naomi	TX1520	66A,66D,11
Shimron, Omri D.	NC0750	13,66A,66D
Shin, Jung-Won	MS0250	66A,66D,66B,66C,13B
Shin, MinKyoo	IL3100	13C,66A,66D,66G
Shinn, Barbara A.	AL0800	13C,13B,13A,66D
Shires, Terrie A.	AR0850	66D
Shockley, Rebecca P.	MN1623	66A,66B,66D
Shofner-Emrich, Terree	IL2100	66A,39,66B,66C,66D
Shook, Timothy	KS1200	66A,66B,66D,13
Shumway, Angelina	MD0700	11,66D,61,13A
Sifferman, James P.	MO1500	11,66A,66D
Sifford, Jason	IA1550	66B,66D,66,29B,66A
Siler, Sandra K.	TX1350	41,45,66A,66D
Simms, Beverley	IN0800	66A,66D
Simon, Julie	CA4500	66A,66D
Singleton, Lynn	OH1850	66D
Skoglund, Frances	FL0675	66A,66D,13A,11
Skroch, Diana	ND0600	11,66D
Skyrm, Susanne L.	SD0600	66A,66C,66D,66E
Slade, Elizabeth	OH0100	66D
Smale, Marcelyn	MN1300	32A,13C,66D,32B,32D
Smirl, Terry W.	WI0450	53,66A,66D
Smith, Don	IN0250	66D
Smith, Gayle	AL0335	66D,36,61
Smith, J. W.	WV0200	11,12A,66A,66B,66D
Smith, Kirsten	CA0840	66A,66C,66D
Smith, Linda	OH2300	66D
Smith, Marcie	UT0190	66A,66D,13C,11
Smith, Paul	CA1150	12A,66A,66C,66D,54
Smoker, Beverly A.	NY2650	66A,66B,66D
Snitkovsky, Natasha	PA1050	66A,66D
Snyder, Colleen	CA2400	11,29A,37,66D,60
Sobolewski, Susan F.	NY2550	66D,13C,42,66A
Sokasits, Jonathan F.	NE0300	66A,66D,66B,42,12A
Sokolov-Grubb, Silvana I.	NH0350	66C,66D
Soo Mauldin, Rosalyn	AL1195	66A,66D
Sorley, Rebecca E.	IN1650	66A,66C,66B,66D
Southard, Ellen	CA4550	66C,66D
Sparkman, Carol Joy	MS0400	66C,66D,36,66A
Spedden, Patricia R.	IN0700	66A,66B,13,66C,66D
Speer, Donald R.	KY1550	66B,66C,66D
Spelius, Susan M.	ID0075	11,66D,13B,13C
Spencer, Dianthe M.	CA4200	66A,66D,20G,29
Spencer, Sarah	TX2295	66A,66C,66D,12A
Spicer, Donna	OR1020	36,61,66A,66D
Spires, Rozanne	TX3527	66A,66C,66D
Spotz, Leslie	TX2750	13A,66A,66B,66D
Sprenger, Jill T.	TX2600	66A,66B,66D
Springer, Alisha	NC2420	66D
Stackhouse, Eunice Wonderly	NC1450	13,66A,66B,66D,66C
Stambuk, Tanya	WA1000	66A,66C,66D
Stampfl, Aaron	IL0750	66D
Stampfli, L. Thomas	IL1050	66A,66B,66D,66C
Steffen, Arlene	CA1860	66A,66B,66D
Steffen, Cecil	IL0780	13,66A,66D
Stegall, Gary Miles	SC0420	66A,66D,13A,66C,66G
Stephens, William G.	TN1680	66D
Stevens, Damon B.	NV0100	39,66A,66C,66D
Steward, Gail	AL0500	12A,66A,66D
Stiles, Allen	AB0060	13B,66A,66D
Stites, Nathan	KY0550	66C,66D
Stokes, Jennifer	IN0907	66A,66B,66D,11,66C
Stoloff, Betty	NJ1350	66A,66B,66D
Stott, Jacob	RI0200	66D
Stoudenmire, Myungsook	SC0275	66A,66D,66C
Stoytcheva, Lilia S.	SC0950	66A,66B,66C,66D
Strait, Cindy J.	KS1400	66D
Strid-Chadwick, Karen	AK0100	13,47,66A,66D,29
Strouf, Linda Kay	MI1050	11,66D
Stubbe, Joan H.	CA5510	66D
Stubbe, Joan	CA4400	11,66D
Sturm, Connie Arrau	WV0750	66A,66B,66D
Summer, Averill V.	FL2000	66A,66D
Summers, Billy	NC0750	66A,66C,66D,66G
Sumpter, Teresa L.	NC1250	66A,66B,66D,66C
Suniga, Rosemarie	NY3780	66D
Surma, Dan	IL2650	66A,66D
Sutanto, David T.	TX0550	66A,66D,66C,11,66B
Swaim, Doris	NC2640	32A,36,61,66D
Swiatkowski, Hak Soon	CA3150	66A,66D
Szklarska, Kamilla	FL0700	66A,66C,66D
Takagi, Shinobu	NY3725	66C,66D
Takao, Naoko	FL1900	66B,66C,66D
Takasawa, Manabu K.	RI0300	13A,66A,66B,66C,66D
Tam, TinShi	IA0850	69,66,11,34B,66D
Tan, Siok Lian	OH1450	66A,66B,66D
Tanaka, Rieko	MA2020	66C,13C,66A,66D
Taniguchi, Naoki	CA5510	13,66D
Tarchalski, Helen Smith	MD0060	66A,66D
Taylor, Annie	AZ0350	66A,66D
Taylor, Kristin Jonina	IA1750	12A,20,66A,66D,66
Taylor, Maria C.	PA3250	66A,66D
Taylor, Paul F.	KY0900	66A,66H,66C,66D
Tchii, Kent	CA2200	66A,66D
Teare, Racquel	OH1100	66D
Tebay, John	CA1900	36,61,66D,66A,12A
Templeton, Peter	NH0250	66A,66D
Thallander, Mark	CA1960	66D,66G
Thickstun, Karen	IN0250	66A,66D
Thiele, Michael	WI0300	66A,66D
Thomas, David	PA3330	66D
Thomas, Nicholas	IL1890	60A,66D,13A,36,61
Thompson, Janice Meyer	AZ0100	66A,66B,66D
Thomsen, Kathy	MN0800	66A,66D,11
Thornton, Jim	IL1890	66A,66D
Threadgill, Gwen J.	AL1050	32B,13C,66A,66D
Thurmond, Paul	TN1450	66D,66C
Tibbs, Elizabeth J.	AZ0150	66A,11,66D
Tidwell, Mary	TX1510	66A,66D,13B,13A
Tili-Trebicka, Thomaidha	NY4150	66A,66D,66C
Tincher, Brenda M.	NE0590	66D
Tindall, Josh	PA1900	66A,66D
Tinsley, Janis	AL0400	61,66A,66B,66D
Tipps, James	OH2500	32,36,66A,66D,60
Titterington, Connie	OR0850	66A,66D
Tittle, Sandra	OH1000	66A,66,66H,66D
Titus, Julia	IA0300	11,66A,66D
Tocheff, Robert	OH1600	60,11,32,36,66D
Todd, Sarah	IL1050	66A,66C,66D
Tollefson, Mary J.	WI0810	11,66A,66D,66B
Tomassetti, Beth	VA0150	66A,66D
Tomlinson, Judy	CA1500	66D
Tormann, Cynthia	AG0250	66A,13C,66D
Toro, Cesar	PR0100	66D
Townsend, Norma	CA3800	66D,11
Trang, Grace	IL1090	66A,66D
Trauth, Vincent	IL2350	66D,11
Trenfield, Sally	TX3515	32A,32B,66C,66D
Triest, Amelia	CA5010	13A,13C,66D
True, Carolyn E.	TX3350	66A,66B,66D,43
Truelove, Stephen	OR0950	66A,66D
Trussell, Adam	NE0610	66D
Tsao-Lim, May	AR0300	66A,66C,66D,66B,13B
Tsitsaros, Christos	IL3300	66B,66D
Tunnell, Meme	KY0250	13B,66A,66B,66D
Turcios, Lorri	SC0200	66A,66B,66D
Turner, Sandra	KY1200	66A,66,66B,66D,66G
Turon, Charles T.	FL1745	11,13,66A,66D
Tutunov, Alexander	OR0950	13,66A,66D,66C
Uchida, Rika	IA0550	13,66A,66C,66D
Ungar, Garnet	IN1600	66A,66C,66D
Unrath, Wendy	IL0850	66A,66D,12A,11
Unrau, Lucia	OH0250	66A,66B,66D,13C
Uranker, Mark	CA0825	66A,66D
Urrutia, Lara	CA5150	66D
Utsch, Glenn R.	PA3100	13C,66A,29A,66D
Utterback, David	TX2650	66A,66D
Vaillancourt, Jean-Eudes	AI0200	41,66D
Valentine, Claudette	NE0160	66A,36,66D
Valeria, Anna	FL1310	32B,66D
Valle, Amy	KY1200	66A,66D
Van Brunt, Jennifer	WI0960	61,66A,66C,66D
Van Brunt, Nancy	WI0960	13A,13B,13C,66D,40
Van DeLoo, Mary F.	WI0350	66A,66B,66D
van der Westhuizen, Petrus	OH0950	66A,66C,66D,13B,13C
Van Duyne, Lisa	IL2750	66A,66D
Van Kekerix, Todd	NJ0700	66A,66D
Vanderbeck, Sue Ann	MI1300	11,12A,66A,66B,66D
VanDessel, Peter	MI0520	13C,66A,66D,13E
Varellas, Barbara A.	CA3200	66D
Varlamova, Liudmila	TX3525	66D,66A
Vasquez, Jerico	GA1800	66A,66D
Vaughan, Laura	MO0550	61,66D
Vauth, Henning	WV0400	66A,66C,66D,13C
Vereshagin, Alex	CA1760	66A,66D
Verhaalen, Marion	WI0150	66D
Vest, Johnathan	TN1720	32,66D
Vogel, Dorothy	MI1650	66D,11
Vogt-Corley, Christy L.	LA0350	66A,66B,66C,66D
Von Spakovsky, Ingrid	AL1160	66A,66D
Vuori, Ruston	AA0080	66D,13
Wachter, Claire	OR1050	66A,66B,66D
Wade, Elaine San Juan	TX3515	66D
Wade, Gail G.	TX1600	13,39,66A,66D,66C
Wade, Thomas	NJ1050	13,66D
Wadsworth, Amanda	LA0080	11,66A,66D
Wagner, Wayne L.	MN1030	13A,32,36,66G,66D
Waites, Althea	CA0825	66A,66D,20G
Walby, Catherine	WI0350	66D
Waldon, Stanley H.	MI2200	32,66D
Walgren-Georgas, Carol	IL1085	66A,66D
Walker, Abigail	FL1500	11,64D,66D

Index by Area of Teaching Interest

Name	Code	Areas
Walker, Darlene	FL0670	66D,66A
Walker, Karen	VA1350	66D,66C
Walker, Mary	SD0550	66D
Walker, Tammie Leigh	IL3500	66D,66A,12A
Walker, Vicki	OK0850	13,66A,66D
Wallace-Boaz, Krista B.	KY1500	66D
Wang, Diane	MS0700	64A,66D
Wang, Pin-Huey	MD0550	66A,66D
Wang, Tianshu	OH0350	66A,66D,66C
Ward, Arlene	NM0450	66D,66G
Warren, Robert	TX2650	66A,66D
Washington, Henry	TX2220	36,11,66A,66G,66D
Wassermann, Ellen	CA0807	41,66A,66D
Watanabe, Hisao	OR0350	13C,13D,13F,38,66D
Watkins, Scott	FL1000	66A,66D
Watson, Teri	CA0815	66A,66D
Watts, Joel	CA4850	11,66D
Webb, Merrilee	UT0150	36,66D,66A
Weber, Linda	TX0550	11,64A,66A,32,66D
Weber, Misato	CA0807	66A,66D
Weber, Stephen	OK1400	66A,34,66C,66D
Wee, Theo R.	MN1450	66A,66G,66D
Weinberg, Alan	SC0600	11,66A,12A,66D
Welle, Talman J.	WA0600	66A,66D
Wellman, Samuel	VA0650	66A,66D,10,13A,13B
Wells, Yelena	MI0850	66A,66D,20
Werz, Andreas	CA0810	66A,66B,66C,66D
West, Lara L.	KS0100	40,11,66D,66G,20
West, Margaret	CA1760	13A,66A,66D
Westphalen, Melinda	IA0700	66A,66D
Wharton, Marjorie R.	IA0950	66A,66D
Whatley, Jay K.		13B,13C,66D,66C,66G
Wheeler, Charles Lynn	CA3400	66A,66B,66D,13
Wheeler, Dale J.	AA0080	66A,66B,66D,66C,42
Wheeler, Heather L.	NY3780	66D
White, Coralie	LA0770	11,66A,66D
White, Diana	VA1350	66A,66D
White, Laura	VA1600	66A,66D
White, Susan	GA1150	66D
Whitmore, Keith	OK0650	66A,66H,66C,66D
Wickelgren, John	MD0300	66A,13C,66C,66D
Widen, Dennis C.	OK1250	66A,66D,13
Wieland, William	SD0400	13,66D,66A,34,10
Wielenga, Mary Lou	IA1200	66A,66G,66D
Wielenga, Mary Lou	IA0500	66A,66D,66G
Wilcox, Eileen	ID0060	66D
Wilder, Mary Ann	KY0100	66A,66C,66D,13A,13B
Wildman, Randall D.	MO0800	66D
Wildman, Randall	MO0400	66D
Wiley, Adrienne E.	MI0400	66B,66D
Williams, Brenda	VA1100	66A,66C,66D
Williams, Christa	TN1100	66D
Williams, Cynthia B.	CA3500	66A,66D
Williams, Kay	TX0050	66A,66C,66D,13A,13B
Williams, Kenneth T.	OH1850	66A,66D,66B
Williams, Nancy	CA0950	66D,16,11
Williams, Robin	LA0800	66A,66B,66D,66C
Wilson, Grover	NC1600	11,36,66A,66C,66D
Wilson, Jane Ann H.	TX3200	66A,66D,66C
Wilson, Lorraine P.	PA1600	32,66D,20G
Wise, Herbert	NY2500	63C,66A,66D,11,32E
Witon, Renee	CA3920	66A,66D
Witte, Diane	IN0907	66A,66B,66D
Wolf, Debbie Lynn	PA2800	32,66A,66D,66B
Wolinsky, Robert A.	NY2550	66D,67F
Wong Doe, Henry	PA1600	66A,66,11,13,66D
Wood, Jeffrey	TN0050	13,10,66A,66D,20G
Wood, Rose Ann	CA2050	13A,13B,13C,11,66D
Wood, Stanley D.	OH1600	32,36,66D,13C,34
Woodford, Martha	AL1250	66D
Wright, Elaine	VA1350	66A,66D
Wright, Marylyn	TX3360	13A,66A,66C,66D,66G
Wristen, Brenda	NE0600	66A,66B,66D
Wu, Angela	KY0950	66C,66D
Wutke, Drew	IN0700	66D,66C
Wyman, Tamara	NE0450	66A,66D
Wyse, Philip	CO0225	66H,66D
YaDeau, William Ronald	IL1750	13,66A,66D
Yang, Tzi-Ming	MD0550	66A,66D
Yang, Yu-Jane	UT0350	66A,66B,66C,66D
Yarnell, Pamela	OH0700	66A,66D
Yazvac, Diane	OH2600	66A,66C,66D
Yerden, Ruth	OR1150	66A,66G,66D,66C
Yeung, Alwen	GA1000	11,66C,13C,66D
Yeung, Karay	CO0100	66A,66D
Yi, Ann	CA0855	66A,66D,20H
Young, Karen	OH1400	66A,66D,66B
Young, Margaret	OH1850	32,66D
Young, Phillip D.	CA3500	11,66A,66D
Young, Scott	GA0625	63B,66D
Zackery, Harlan H.	MS0350	11,66A,66B,66C,66D
Zatorski, Thomas	NY2550	66D
Zdechlik, Lisa J.	AZ0500	66D
Zemp, William Robin	SC0500	11,66A,66C,66D
Zent, Donald	KY0100	13E,66B,66A,66C,66D
Zilberkant, Eduard	AK0150	66A,66B,66C,66D,41
Zimmerman, Lynda	WI0806	13A,66A,66D,11
Zirnitis, Anda	MO0300	13,66A,66C,66D
Zuidema, Jeannie	MT0175	13E,66D

Fortepiano

Name	Code	Areas
Abe, Christie-Keiko	IL2750	62,66E
Anderson, Jon	ID0250	13C,47,66A,66E
Baytelman, Pola	NY3650	41,66A,66D,66E
Beghin, Tom	AI0150	66E,12
Bilson, Malcolm	NY0900	66A,66E
Braswell, Martha	TX2295	66A,66E,66G,11
Breitman, David	OH1700	66,66E,66A
Chang, Ann	NE0600	66A,66E
Connelly, Brian	TX2150	66A,66C,66E,42
Curry, Jerry L.	SC1110	13,66H,55,66E
Cypess, Rebecca	NJ1130	12,66E,66H,56
Day-O'Connell, Sarah K.	IL1350	12,14,66A,66E
Hammer, Christoph	TX3420	66E,66G,67F
Heater, Katherine	CA5000	66H,66E
Jamason, Corey	CA4150	66H,66E,12A,55B
Johnson, Michelle	TX2600	66A,66B,66C,66D,66E
Kautsky, Catherine C.	WI0350	66A,66C,66E,41
Kroll, Mark	MA0400	66H,66E,12,67F,13
Louwenaar, Karyl	FL0850	66E,41,66A,66H
Love, Randall M.	NC0600	66A,66E,42
Lucktenberg, George	GA1700	66A,66E,66H
McWilliams, Kent M.	MN1450	66A,66C,66D,66E
Mengelkoch, Eva	MD0850	66A,66G,66B,66H,66E
Otten, Thomas J.	NC2410	66A,66E,66H
Owens, Kathryn Ananda	MN1450	66A,66C,66D,66E,66B

Name	Code	Areas
Richter, Elizabeth	IN0150	41,66E,66D
Skyrm, Susanne L.	SD0600	66A,66C,66D,66E
Swigger, Jocelyn A.	PA1400	11,66A,66B,66C,66E
Tilney, Colin	AB0150	12A,66E
Tung, Leslie Thomas	MI1150	12A,66A,66C,66E,13
Wenger, Janice K.	MO1800	66C,66A,66H,66E

Piano Technician

Name	Code	Areas
Adkins, Richard C.	IA0300	16,71,66F
Aikawa, Atsundo	NY2750	66F
Baird, John	IL1750	66F
Beck, Chuck	IL1750	66F
Bellassai, Marc C.	AZ0250	11,12A,66A,66F,66G
Berryhill, Dennis	WI0860	66F
Bledsoe, Lee	TN1450	66F,71
Breakall, Raymond	VA1500	66F
Briant, Peter	MT0370	66F
Bruce, Gary	OK0700	70,65,66F
Byrd-Anderson, Shelley	IL2100	66F
Byrley, Michael	IL1085	66F
Cady-Willanger, Susan	WA1050	66F
Calhoun, William	RI0300	66F
Cloutier, Robert F.	CO0800	66F
Coates, Gary	FL1790	47,37,46,66F
Crane, Alan	KS1450	66F
Cristy-Couch, Martha	MI1150	66F
Cundiff, Larry	KY0400	66F
D'Alessandro, Joseph	PA3700	66F
Dempsey, Paul E.	WV0400	66F
Doss, Efwood	TN1720	66F,11
Durrenberger, Chris	OH2450	13A,11,66A,66F,12A
Fielding, Crystal	NH0100	66F
Gagliardo, Don	OH2000	66F
Gale, Robert	CO0100	64,66A,66F,72
Garee, Anne	FL0850	66F
Gibbs, Don	KY0900	66F
Gilbert, David	TN0900	66F
Graham, Mark W.	OH0200	66F
Granoff, Gregory J.	CA2250	66F
Griffith, Ben	KY1350	66F
Grijalva, Robert	MI2100	66F
Hargabus, Bruce	FL0850	66F
Haydon, Geoffrey Jennings	GA1050	66A,66F,29B
Heaford, Christian	ND0350	66F
Henderson, V. Douglas	VA1150	66C,66F
Hettinger, Bruce A.	AA0100	66F
Higgins, Scott	TN1680	66F
Hong, Yat-Lam	MI2250	66F
Hook, Terry	VA0600	66F
Horcher, Nick	IL2650	66F
Horneff, Donald C.	MD0520	66F,66C,66D,66H,32E
Houston, James	IL0850	66F
Howes, Graham	NY3725	66F
Hulbert, David	WI0825	66F
Hulbert, David	WI0850	66F
Imobersteg, John	WI0830	72,66F
Johnson, Mick	NE0590	66F
Kabat, Stephen	OH0650	66F
Kaplan, Adam	CA5100	66F
Krippenstapel, George	IL1200	66F
LaBorn, John	IL1085	66F
Lee, Robert W.	NY4150	66F,72
Lehman, Paul R.	MI0600	66F
Lord, Albert P.	NJ0800	66F
Malenich, Thomas	NY3790	66F
Mance, Junior	NY2660	47,66F
Mattison, Nate	MN1120	66F
Mazarak, Eric	NY1400	66F
McCoy, Alan	WA0250	66F
McKechnie, Donald	NY1800	66F
Mihopulos, Michael	WI0150	66F
Miller, Lane E.	NY3780	66F
Mix, Ryan	IA0950	66F
Miyashiro, Ralph	CA4100	66F
Moberg, Jonathan	WI0825	66F
Owen, Wesley	IL0550	66F
Plaster, Amos	IN0650	66F
Ralinovsky, John	OH0500	66F
Rea, Edward	SC0200	13,66A,66G,66F
Rivers, Laurel R.	NY3725	66F
Sartori, Nicolo A.	PA1600	66A,66F
Schroeder, Jerry	MN1120	66F
Schumaker, Alan	NY2550	66F
Senko, Robert	NY3770	66F
Severance, David	WA1150	66F
Sexton, Greg	KY0550	66F
Shank, Dean	TX2150	66B,66F
Shaver, Stephen R.	IN0900	66F
Sieberg, Michael	OH0950	66F,72
Staples, Mitch	OH1850	66F
Steege, David J.	WA1250	66F
Stevenson, Patricia	WI0825	66F
Swafford, Kent	MO1810	66F
Thile, Scott	KY0950	66F,72
Treuhaft, Ben	NY2750	66F
Tucker, Kenneth	MD0700	66F
Vesely, Blaine	OH1100	66F
Whitmire, Sam D.	LA0760	66F
Wiencek, Joe R.	NY2750	66F
Wijnands, Aberham	KS0590	66A,66F,62D
Williams, Russell	AL0300	66F
Wolf, Lee A.	IA1390	66F
Wood, Douglas	WA1050	66F
Wood, Zeno D.	NY0500	66F,13C
Young, Lonnie	MS0750	66F,72
Ziegler, Marci	KS0050	61,66F,39
Ziesemer, Bruce	WI0350	66F

Organ

Name	Code	Areas
Adam, Joseph J.	WA1000	66G,66H
Adkins, Cathy L.	NC1250	12A,66G
Ahrend, Janet	WA0400	66G,13C,66D
Ahrend, Janet	WA0250	66G
Aikin, Diane	NE0300	66G,13A
Akers, Diana L.	FL0650	66G
Albrecht, Timothy	GA0750	11,12A,66G,31A
Anderson, Diana	CO0200	32B,66A,66G
Andrews, Linda	IL3500	66G
Anthony, John P.	CT0100	13A,11,12A,66D,66G
Archbold, Lawrence	MN0300	11,12A,66G,15,12D
Archer, Gail	NY4450	66G,66H
Athas, James	WI0865	66G
Ator, Irene S.	IN0905	66G
Aultman, Gerald	TX2600	13A,13,66A,66G

Index by Area of Teaching Interest

Name	Code	Areas
Babcock, Mark A.	IA0200	36,40,66G,13
Bacon, Joel	CO0250	66G,12A,66H
Bacon, Masako	NE0450	66G
Baird, Barbara M.	OR1050	66G,66H,67F,11
Baker, Chad	OH0350	66G,66D
Baker, Meredith E.	NY2550	13,66G,36
Ballard, Alice	MS0300	66A,66G,66D,11
Banner, Lucy	MA0600	66A,66G,66H,66B,66C
Barber, Daniel R.	OH0650	66A,13D,12A,66G
Barnard, Dene	OH0350	66G
Barone, Judith	NY4460	66A,66G,13A,41
Barte, Paul T.	OH1900	12A,11,66G,66H
Bass, Louise	GA1650	66C,66G
Bates, Robert F.	TX3400	66G
Bates, William H.	SC1110	12A,66G,31A
Bauer, David T.	MN1030	13A,34,66A,66G
Bauer, Michael J.	KS1350	36,66G,66H,31A
Beckford, Richard	LA0700	11,36,66G,13
Beckford, Richard E.	SC1050	13,60,11,36,66G
Behnke, John A.	WI0300	10,44,66G,31A
Belfield, Roy L.	NC2700	66G,36,60A,10F,12A
Bell, Joby	NC0050	66G,66H,36,31A
Bellassai, Marc C.	AZ0250	11,12A,66A,66F,66G
Benedum, Richard P.	OH2250	11,12A,66G
Bennett, Elizabeth S.	NC0850	66A,66G
Berg, Reinhard	AA0020	13,10,12A,66A,66G
Berghout, Elizabeth	KS1350	66G,69
Bernthal, John P.	IN1750	13,66G
Best, Stephen	NY1350	66A,66G
Bickers, Elisa	MO1810	66G
Bickers, Elisa	KS1400	66G
Biggers, Jonathan E.	NY3705	12A,66G,66H
Bighley, Mark	OK0550	12A,66A,66G,66D
Bill, Darlene	SD0450	66G
Billin, Susan	ID0250	66G,66D
Billmeyer, Dean W.	MN1623	66G,66H
Binckes, Fred B.	MT0350	13,10,11,66G
Binger, Adlai	PA0050	36,61,66G,60A,66C
Birch, Kevin	ME0440	66G,66H
Biser, Larry	MI0300	34B,12A,40,66G
Bittmann, Antonius O.	NJ1130	12,66G
Black, Karen	IA1800	13C,31A,36,66G
Blersch, Jeffrey	NE0150	13,36,66G
Bodinger, John	WA1350	66G
Bogey, Brian	NY3725	66G
Bognar, Joseph A.	IN1750	66A,13,66H,66G
Bordignon, Paolo	NJ1350	66G
Borthwick-Aiken, Rebecca A.	PA0100	66G
Bostic, Polly T.	NC2650	66A,66D,66G
Boud, Ronald E.	TN1660	66G
Bowdidge, Mark	MO1550	66G
Bowlin, Ellen	IL0300	66A,66G,66C
Brancaleone, Francis P.	NY2200	13,66A,66D,66G,66C
Brandes, David E.	NH0110	13,10F,60,36,66G
Brandes, Lambert	MA0800	13,66G,13L
Braswell, Martha	TX2295	66A,66E,66G,11
Brewer, Robert S.	TX3450	66H,66G
Brillhart, Jeffrey	CT0850	66G
Brisson, Philip	KY0250	66G
Britt, Michael	MD0170	66A,66G
Brock, John	TN1710	66G,66H,31A
Brock, John	TN0250	66G
Brookshire, Bradley	NY3785	12A,12,55,66G,66H
Brown, Thomas K.	TX3300	66G
Brugh, Lorraine S.	IN1750	36,31A,66G
Brunner, Roy	MA0950	13,10,66G,66H,31A
Bruns, Jeremy	TX2700	66G
Bryant, Linda	IA0700	66G
Buice, David	GA1550	66C,66H,66G,69
Bull, Christoph	CA5030	66G
Bunbury, Richard R.	MA0400	12,66G,32H,31A,32
Bunn, Greg	TN0100	66G
Bunn, Gregg	TN1400	66G
Burell, J. Ashley	TN1000	66G,66H
Burkett, Darlene	IN0700	44,66G
Burkett, John	TX2955	13,66A,66G,34,12C
Burnaman, Stephen	TX1150	13,66A,66G,66B,66C
Burnett, Marty Wheeler	NE0100	12A,13,66A,36,66G
Burton-Brown, David	GA2100	66G
Busarow, Donald A.	OH2450	13A,10A,66G,31A
Bush, Douglas E.	UT0050	12,55,66G,67,31A
Bushong, Claire B.	NE0400	12A,13B,13C,66A,66G
Butler, Charles Mark	MS0250	63B,32B,13E,13B,66G
Butler, H. Joseph	TX3000	66G,12,31
Butler, Terry	VA0950	13C,32D,66A,66G
Cabena, Barrie	AG0600	66G
Caldwell, Ann	GA0850	66A,66D,66G,11
Cameron, David	AG0250	66G
Candee, Jan	ND0400	66A,66D,66G,32B,11
Carleton, Sharon	NC1450	66G,66A
Carr, Deborah	VA1830	66G,60A
Cary, Kathy	MI1160	66G
Case, Del W.	CA3400	66G,44,13,12A,36
Cassarino, James	VT0100	66G,66H
Cauley, Susan	LA0150	66G
Chambers-Salazar, Polli	CA1750	66A,66G
Chan, See Tsai	IL0350	66A,66G,13
Cherry, Janet	NC1300	66G,66A
Chesman, Jeremy A.	MO0775	13,66G,69
Chidester, James	OH2300	66G
Choi, Hye-Jean	TX0900	66A,66G,66H,67C,13
Choi, Hyunjoo	CA1425	66C,66G,66D,66A
Choi, Kyong Mee	IL0550	10,13,66G
Christensen, David	CA5040	66G,69
Christiansen, David	IL0850	66G,31A
Christiansen, Rulon	UT0350	66G
Christie, James David	OH1700	66G
Christie, James	MA2050	66G,66H
Christie, James David	MA0700	66G,66H,31A
Ciucci, Anthony A.	PA1250	66G
Claar, Elizabeth	MI0520	66G
Clark, Amber L.	IL1350	66A,66G,66B
Clewell, Christine M.	PA1600	66A,66G,66D,13
Cobb, Gary W.	CA3600	13,10,12,66G,66B
Cobb, James	NC0915	11,36,66G
Cockburn, Neil	AA0050	66G,67F,12A
Cole, Malcolm S.	CA5032	11,12A,12,66G,31A
Conely, James	AL0450	66A,66G
Congdon, Judy A.	NY1700	13,66G,66H,31A
Constantine, Cyprian G.	PA2950	66G,31A
Conte, Peter Richard	NJ1350	66G
Cook, Don	UT0050	66G,69,31A
Cook, James H.	AL0300	66G
Cooksey, Steven	VA1350	12A,36,66G,31A
Cooper, Nancy Joyce	MT0400	13,66G,66H,69
Cornelius-Bates, Benjamin	PA1050	31A,66G
Cornils, Ray	ME0500	66G
Cornils, Ray	ME0200	66G
Corrie, John H.	ME0150	13C,36,61,66G,66H
Corzine, Michael L.	FL0850	66G
Cosgrove, Nancy	MA0600	66A,66G,66H,66B,66C
Coulthard, Anita	VA0350	66G,32A,32B,31A
Courtney, Ken H.	SC1100	11,66G,20
Cramer, Craig	IN1700	12A,66G
Crawford, Donna	SC0200	66A,66G,34
Criswell, James Anthony	GA1200	66G
Crouse, David L.	AR0600	66A,13C,61,66G,13B
Crowell, Gregory	MI0900	13,12,66G,66H
Cunningham, Chuck	NM0500	66A,66G,32D,36,40
Currie, Randolph	OH1330	13,10,66G
Danek, Leonard P.	MN1280	13,10,66G
Davis, Jolene	GA2100	13,66G,31A
Davis, Kevin	AL1300	11,66G,13C
Davis, Lynne	KS1450	66G
Davis, Ron A.	SC1000	13B,13C,31,66G,44
Davis, Scott	TX3510	31A,66G
Deaver, John	OH2200	66G
Decker, Pamela A.	AZ0500	66G,13
Deffner, David	CA0150	66G,13A
DeFoor, Keith	GA2300	66G
Dehaven, Frederic	MI1750	66G,66H
Delcamp, Robert	TN1800	13,12A,36,66G,31A
DelGiorno, Nichol	IL1100	66G
Demers, Isabelle	TX0300	66G
Denison, William R.	AL1050	66A,66G
Denman, James L.	OR1300	13,12A,66G,13F,13H
DeVaney, Camille	NC2435	66G
Deville, Mary	LA0550	66G,12
DeYoung, William	IL2775	66A,66G
Dickens, Pierce	GA0950	39,66A,66C,66G
Dill, Jane	SC1080	13,66A,66G,66C
Dill, John	TX1775	13A,11,66A,66G,12A
Dinda, Robin	MA0930	10,11,13,29,66G
Ditto, John A.	MO1810	66G,31A
Dix, Ted	MD0520	66G,13C
Dixon, Paul	FL1650	66G
Doering, James M.	VA1150	13,11,12A,66A,66G
Dorroh, William J.	AL0800	66G
Downey, Mark	IL2650	66G
Downing, Joseph	NY4150	10,66G,13,13C,60
Drake, James	ID0100	66G
Draughn, Maurice	MI2200	62E,66G
Dubbiosi, Stelio	NJ0825	13,10F,66A,66G
DuBois, Peter	NY1100	66G
Duckett, Linda B.	MN1000	13,66G,66H
Dunbar, Edward	SC0200	13,12A,66G,34
Duncan, Norah	MI2200	36,13C,66G
Dunphy, Janice	OH2050	66G
Durham, Carol	MS0385	66G
Durham, Carol	MS0100	66G
Durham, Carol S.	MS0400	66G,66A,66C,66H,12A
Dzuris, Linda	SC0400	69,20,66G,34
Eaton, David D.	TX3530	66G,13,66H,67F
Ebrecht, Ronald	CT0750	36,66G
Eby, Pam	AI0050	66G
Echols, Charles	MN1300	66H,12A,66A,66G
Eckert, William H.	DC0110	13,12A,32A,66G
Edman, Laura	WI0845	66G
Edwards, Alice	IL1610	66A,66G
Edwards, Carla Grace	IN0350	66G,13F
Egan, John B.	IN1350	13,66,66G,11
Eggert, John	MN0610	10,13,31A,66G
Egler, Steven	MI0400	12A,66H,66G,31A
Eichelberger, Mary Jane	OH1800	66A,66G
Eifert, Jonathan	TX0400	36,60A,66G,31A
Ellis, Laura	FL1850	66G,69,66H,31
Ellison, Ross W.	PA2350	66G
Elsberry, Kristie B.	TN0100	13,66A,66G
Embloom, George	CA5000	66G
Ennulat, Egbert M.	GA2100	12A,66G,66H
Eppink, Joseph A.	NY0700	32B,66G,66H,32C,32A
Erickson, Neal	MN1290	66G
Ericsson, Hans-Ola	AI0150	66G
Eschbach, Jesse	TX3420	66G
Eskey, Kathryn F.	NC2430	13,66G
Evans, Margaret R.	OR0950	12A,66G
Everett, Cheryl	IN1850	66A,66G
Faber, Nancy	OH2450	12A,44,66G,66H,31A
Farndale, Nancy	IA1750	64B,64D,66G
Farr, Elizabeth	CO0800	55,66G,66H
Fast, John W.	VA0300	13,66A,66G
Ferguson, John	MN1450	36,66G,31A
Files, Kari	ND0250	66G
Filsell, Jeremy	DC0050	66G
Finney, John R.	MA0330	60,36,38,66G
Fischbach, Tim C.	IL2730	61,66A,66G
Fishell, Janette S.	IN0900	66G
Fix, Lou Carol	PA2450	66G,69,31A,67B
Flannery, William	OK0500	66G
Fleming, Ansley	AR0350	66G,66A
Floeter, Valerie	WI1155	66G,31A
Flood, James	NY4460	66A,66G
Floreen, John E.	NJ1140	12,36,66G
Fowler, Colin	NY2900	36,13,12A,66A,66G
Fowler, Jeffrey	PA1150	66G
Frank, Gerald	OK0800	66G
Freese, Faythe R.	AL1170	66G,66H,69
Freese, James	WI0300	66G
French, Annabeth	ME0250	61,66G
French, George E.	MN1590	36,37,66A,66G,54
Frieling, Randall J.	IN0100	66A,66C,66D,66G
Furr, Rhonda	TX1000	12A,16,66G
Galema, Joseph M.	CO0900	66G
Gallagher, Mary Gloria	IN1100	62,66A,66G
Gallant, Mark W.	OH1650	66G,32
Garrett, Lee R.	OR0400	66G
Gartz, Michael	MI0050	66C,66G
Gary, Roberta S.	OH2200	66G
Geerlings, Matthew	IA0500	66G
Gehrke, Rodney	CA4150	66G
Gehrke, Rodney P.	CA5000	66G
Gemme, Terese	CT0450	13A,12A,36,66G
George, John Brian	IN1750	66G
Gerlach, Bruce	MO0200	13,10,11,54,66G
Gibson, Henry	OH0950	66A,66G
Giesbrecht, Marnie	AA0035	66G
Giesbrecht-Segger, Marnie	AA0100	66G
Gilleland, Katharine	NC2525	66G,11,13A,29A,36
Gingrich, Shawn	PA2300	66G,44
Glarner, Robert L.	VA1100	13,10,32I,66G,12
Glass, John	TN0050	13A,66A,66G,66H
Glass, Judith	TN1350	13,66G,66H,31A
Glick, Robert P.	SC0700	66G,31A,11
Godwin, Nannette Minor	NC2350	31,66A,66G,32B
Golden, Joseph	GA0550	39,66G,11,12
Gonzalez, Fr. George	IN0005	11,14,20,66G,32

Name	Code	Areas
Gorman, Sharon L.	AR0900	12A,66G
Goslee, Brenda	TN1250	13A,13,11,66A,66G
Grapenthin, Ina	PA1750	11,32B,66A,66G,66D
Gratz, Robin	IN1050	66G
Gravander, Carl	IA1350	66G
Gray, Kathryn A.	PA3260	66A,66C,66G
Gray, Steven	CA3460	13,66A,66G,66H
Grayson, W. Norman	NJ0200	66A,66G
Greenlee, Anita	PA1550	66G
Greenlee, Anita	PA3600	66G
Grew, John	AI0150	66G,66H,67
Grey, Meg	MO0600	11,12A,32,66A,66G
Griffin, Jackie	SC0950	13,10,12A,66G,34
Griffith, Robert A.	OH2000	66G
Grimwood, Paul	AG0200	66G,66H,66D
Grogan, Robert	DC0050	66G
Groom, Mitzi	KY1550	32,69,66G
Grover, Elaine	MI1300	13A,13,66A,66G,31A
Grubb, Steve	CA3000	11,66D,66G,66H
Guenther, Eileen Morris	DC0100	66G
Guenther, Timothy E.	OH0100	66G,66H,66D
Guiles, Kay	MS0360	11,66A,66D,66G
Gustafson, Steven	KS0900	61,66G,40,13B,36
Guthrie, J. Randall	OK0850	31A,60A,36,11,66G
Guthrie, James M.	NC0400	13,10,34,66G,66H
Ha, Jaehyuk	TX3410	66G
Haakenson, Matthew A.	FL1750	10A,66G,13,13D,13J
Hakken, Lynda S.	IA0400	66G,13,66C,66A,11
Hall, Janean	MN0300	66G,66H
Hall, Jonathan B.	NY2750	12A,13,31A,36,66G
Hall, Thomas	FL0450	66G
Haller, William P.	WV0750	13,12A,66G,31A
Hamilton, Janet	IN1010	11,66G
Hamilton, MaryAnn	NY1550	66G
Hamman, James	LA0800	11,12A,13A,55B,66G
Hammer, Christoph	TX3420	66E,66G,67F
Hancock, Cindy	MT0370	66A,66G
Hancock, Judith E.	TX3510	66G,31A
Hand, Gregory	IA1550	66G,66H
Handford, Kathrine	WI0350	66G,66H
Hannifan, Patricia	CA2600	66G,66A
Hansen, Mark R.	ID0050	66A,13E,11,66G
Hanson, Craig	OR0700	66G
Harbach, Barbara	MO1830	66G,67F,15,66H,34A
Hardeman, Anita	IL3500	66G,12A,66A
Hardin, Dan	FL0700	16,66G
Harlan, Mary	IL0420	66A,66G
Harms, Janet	CA0250	66D,66G
Harrell, Paula D.	NC1600	32,66A,66G,66D,31A
Harris, Ruth	IA0550	66G
Harrison, Joanne K.	NC1150	13,66G,31A,66A
Harwood, Elizabeth	AF0050	36,66G
Haupt, Dorothy G.	PA0125	12A,32B,36,66G
Hawkinson, Carol	FL1745	66A,66G
Hawley, Thomas E.	MD1000	66G
Hayashida, Mami	KY0610	66A,66G,66D
Haywood, Carl	VA0950	13,60,41,66G
Hazelip, Richard	TX1450	66A,66G
Hazelip, Richard	TX2300	13B,66G,61,11
Headlee, Will	NY2950	66G
Hebert, Ryan	FL2050	60,36,13C,66G
Held, Wilbur C.	OH1850	66G,31A
Hell, Felix	PA1400	66G
Heller, David	TX3350	13,66G,66H,31A
Henderson, Andrew Elliot	NY4200	66G
Hendrickson, Peter A.	MN0050	60,36,13,66G
Hesselink, Paul	NV0050	66G
Hester, Danny	NC0300	66G
Hettrick, Jane S.	NY1600	12A,66G
Higdon, James M.	KS1350	66G,66H,31A
Higgs, David	NY1100	66G
Highberger, Edgar B.	PA3000	12A,66G,31A
Hill, Doris	IL1200	66G,66H
Hille, Regina	KS0560	66A,66G
Hilse, Walter	NY2150	66G
Hinton, Heather	IN0250	66G
Hirschmann, Craig	WI1155	10A,44,66G
Hoffman, Steven	WY0200	66G,13D
Hofmann, John T.	NY3725	66G
Hohman, Frederick	IN0005	66G
Holland, Patricia	FL1450	66G
Hollingsworth, Devon	IN0005	10A,12,13,32,66G
Holloway, Clyde	TX2150	66G
Holman, Andrew	MA2010	66G
Holmes, Karen	AG0400	55,66G,66H
Holmquist, Solveig	OR1250	11,36,60,66G,69
Holt, Beverly	IL1890	66A,66G,66C
Hoskins, Richard	WI0250	66G,31A
Houston, James	MD0170	66A,66G
Howard, Beverly A.	CA0450	13,34A,66G,66A,66H
Howard, David	OR0250	13,10,11,45,66G
Howard, Timothy P.	CA0835	13B,13C,66G
Howell, Andrew P.	RI0300	36,66C,66G
Huber, Laurel	CA0810	66G
Huber, Laurell	CA1860	66G,66H
Huddleston, Debra	OR0250	66C,66A,66G
Hueller, Mary	WI0050	66G
Huey, Daniel J.	GA1800	13,66G
Hughes, Thomas	TX3200	66G,34,35C
Hulin, Charles J.	FL1740	13,66D,66A,66G
Hunt, Sylvia	ID0070	66G,66C
Hurd, James L.	CA1750	11,66A,66G
Huss, Adeline	OH0600	13,66G
Isele, David	FL2050	10F,10,36,61,66G
Jackson, Christopher	AI0070	60,66G,66H,67C
Jackson, Russell	PA2450	66A,66G,66C
Jacobs, Paul	NY1900	66G
Jacobson, Allan	SD0400	13,10A,66A,66G
James, Dean G.	MI1000	66G
Jean, Martin D.	CT0850	66G
Jenkins, David	MN1625	66G,31A
Johns, Michele S.	MI2100	66G
Johnson, Calvert	GA0050	66G,15,31,66H,12A
Johnson, Campbell	AR0700	10F,66G
Johnson, James D.	NE0610	66A,66G,69
Johnson, Kyle E.	CA0550	66G,66D
Jones, Betty McLellan	TN0450	66G
Jones, Boyd M.	FL1750	13,66G
Jones, Esther	CA0815	66G
Jones, Esther	CA1425	66G
Jones, Hilton Kean	FL2000	10,35,13,45,66G
Jones, Jeff	KY0450	66G,66H,66A
Jones, Robert D.	FL1470	66A,66G,66C,66D,34
Jones, William	DC0350	11,36,61,66A,66G
Jordan, James	NJ1350	66G,36,13,60
Jordan, Paul	NY3705	66G,67B
Jowers, Florence	NC1100	36,44,66G
Juhn, Hee-Kyung	AR0300	66A,13C,66G,66C,66B
Jumpeter, Joseph A.		11,29A,20,36,66G
Jung, Eunsuk	TN0600	13A,66A,66D,66G,13B
Kaehler, Winston H.	MN0950	66G,66H
Kahler, Bette	NY4100	11,12A,33,66A,66G
Kallstrom, Wayne	NE0100	66A,66G,12A
Kallstrom, Wayne	NE0610	66G
Kaminski, Michael	NY0500	66G
Kasling, Kim R.	MN0350	12A,66G,31A,66A
Kates, Christine	PA3710	66A,66G
Kaufman, Roseann Penner	KS0200	66G,66H
Kaye, G. Donald	MI2120	66G
Kazimir, David	IN0900	66G,69,71
Keenan, Larry W.	KY0900	11,66A,66G,66D,66H
Keller, Deborah	MI1985	66A,66C,66G
Kemper, Margaret M.	IL2250	66G,31A
Kennedy, Stephen	NY1100	55D,66G
Kent, George E.	RI0300	11,49,63A,66G,66H
Kerr, Daniel	ID0060	10A,13,66G,10F
Kibbie, James W.	MI2100	66G
Kimme, Glenn	NY0650	66C,66G
King, Mark	WV0550	66G,66H
King, Shirley S.	PA0950	66G,66H
Kingham, Lesley	AG0050	66G,66C,66A
Klemme, Paul	OR1300	36,66G
Klimisch, Mary J.	SD0300	10,13J,66A,66G
Kloeckner, Phillip	TX2150	66G,13C
Kloppers, Jacobus	AA0035	11,12A,12,66G,31A
Knupp, Robert	MS0400	66G,13I,13B,66A
Konzen, Richard A.	PA1450	38,51,66G,41,13B
Koranda, Ann	IL1890	66A,66G,66C
Koriath, Kirby L.	IN0150	66G,66H,31A,34
Kosnik, James W.	VA1000	12A,66G
Kraus, James	MI1180	66G,13A,66A
Kreider, David G.	MD0520	11,66A,66G,66B,66D
Kresnicka, Judith	MN0200	12A,66G,55C
Krieger, Marcos F.	PA3150	13C,66H,66G,11,12A
Krigbaum, Charles	CT0850	66G
Krueger, Walter R.	OR0150	13A,66A,12A,66G,66D
Krusemark, Ruth E.	KS0100	13,10,66A,66G,66D
Kwami, Paul T.	TN0550	20,36,66G,60A,66D
Labounsky, Ann	PA1050	66G,31A
Lakey, Richard	PA2100	66A,66G
Lange, Stephen R.	MI1200	66G,61
Langlois, Kristina	MN0610	66G
Lash, Andre D.	NC2430	66G
Laster, James	VA1350	60,36,66G,31A
Laubach, Mark	PA2200	31A,66G,66H
Lauderdale, Lynne A.	FL2100	12A,66A,66G,66D,66B
Lawhon, Daniel E.	AL0800	66G,44
Lawrence, Edwin	MA2250	13C,66A,66G,66H,66C
Leach, Brenda	MD0850	38,11,66G
Lee, Paul S.	TX1300	66G,13B,11,60,66A
Lefter, Nancy C.	SC0300	36,66G,31A
Leland, James	KS1200	66G,66H
Lemson, Deborah	TX3850	66A,66G,66C,66D
Lenti, Elizabeth	OH0600	36,66G
Lewis, Huw R.	MI1050	13D,66G,66H,31A
Lewis, Matthew	NJ1350	66G
Lewis, Susan	FL1730	61,66A,66G
Lewis, Tim	NY2400	66G
Lewis, Tim	NY5000	66G
Lim, Yoon-Mi	TX2600	66G,66A,13A
Livesay, Jackie	MI0100	66G
Lobitz, Kristi	CA1750	66A,66G
Locklair, Dan	NC2500	13,10,11,31A,66G
Logan, Kenneth	MI0250	66G,34,10,10F,31A
Lohuis, Ardyth J.	VA1600	66G,12A,12C
Loman, Janet	NM0310	66G,66H
Lombard, Becky	LA0400	13,12A,66A,66G,12C
Long, Lillian F.	WV0050	61,66C,66G,39,44
Lord, Robert S.	PA3420	66G
Lorenz, Jim	FL0500	66G
Louprette, Renee A.	NJ0800	66G
Lowry, David	SC0600	66G
Luckner, Brian	WI1100	66G,31A
Lynch, W. David	NC1300	66G
MacPherson, William A.	MA2150	11,12,66G,66H
Maes, James	MA1100	66A,66G,66C,66D,11
Maher, John	IN1025	13,12A,66G,16,34
Maki, Paul-Martin	NY2150	66G
Malone, Patrick R.	FL0040	13,66G
Malone, Ryan M.	PA0350	66G
Manley, Douglas H.	TN1550	12,66,31,66G,12C
Marchant, Susan J.	KS1050	36,66G,66H,66A
Mardirosian, Haig L.	DC0010	13,10,66G,11
Marek, Tim	OK1200	66G
Margetts, Linda	UT0250	66G
Marks, Christopher	NE0600	66G,66H,13
Marks, Gary	AK0100	66G
Marlow, Laurine	TX2900	11,12A,66G,66A,66H
Marrier, Susan	AG0170	66G
Marshall, Kimberly	AZ0100	41,66G
Marshall, Thomas	VA0250	66A,66G,66H,66D
Marta, Larry W.	TX3370	13A,13,66A,66G
Martin, Gayle H.	AE0050	60A,66G,36,12A,55D
Martin, Les K.	WA0800	66G,66H
Martin, Roland E.	NY0400	66G
Martin, Roland E.	NY4320	66G,66H,66C
Martin, Sarah	GA1050	66G
Martinez, David	RI0150	66G,31A
Martorella, Stephen T.	RI0200	12A,66A,66G,66H
Mason, Marilyn	MI2100	66G
Masters, Barbara	IL0850	66A,66G,66H
Mathias, Brian	KS1400	66G
Matos, Lucia Regina	IL2200	38,39,60B,66G,66H
Matzke, Laura	MN0200	66A,66G,66C,68,31A
Maxwell, Margaret	MN0150	66A,66H,66G
Maxwell, Monte	MD0900	66G,38,36,31A,51
May, Ernest D.	MA2000	12A,12,66G
Maynard-Christensen, Dianne	NY2650	66G
Maynard-Christensen, Dianne	NY3350	66G
McCandless, Terry	OH1200	66G,66H
McClain, Charles	PA2550	13,36,66G
McConnell, Joan	OH0950	66C,66G,13C,66D,13B
McCorkle, William	VA1850	66G,66H,66A
McCoy, Eleanor K.	OH2275	66C,66G
McCoy, William F.	VA1475	66G
McDaniel, Carol	CA1425	32B,13C,31A,66G
McDonough, Raenell	TX0100	66G
McFarland, James	TX3600	11,13,66D,66G
McGhee, Michael	GA2200	13,11,12A,66G,66H
McIntire, Donna	WY0050	66A,66G
McIntosh, John S.	AG0500	13,66G,66C,31A
McIntosh, W. Legare	AL0500	12A,13,66A,66G
McLean, Hugh J.	AG0100	12,14A,66G,31A
McSpadden, George	AL0350	13,36,49,66A,66G
Meade, Karen	MO0500	32,11,66A,66G
Meadows, Melody	WV0800	13,12A,66G,34,35A

Index by Area of Teaching Interest

Name	Code	Areas
Mellichamp, James F.	GA1650	66G
Miller, David L.	AL1160	66G
Miller, Peter	TX3360	66C,61,64C,66G
Mitchell, Carol	GA0940	13,66A,66G,66C,66D
Moehlman, Carl B.	IA0900	13,12A,44,66G,31A
Moeser, Susan	NC2410	66G
Mohr, Bette	IL0420	66G
Mojica, Andres	PR0150	11,66G
Mok, April H.	LA0900	10,66G
Moldenhauer, Kermit G.	MN1030	13A,36,66G,31A,60A
Montalbano, James	NY2450	66A,66G
Moore, Barbara	VA1550	66A,66G
Moorman-Stahlman, Shelly	PA1900	44,66A,66G,31A,66D
Morgan, Robert Huw	CA4900	66G,60,36
Morken, Randy A.	MN1620	66A,66G
Morris, Gayle	TX3100	66G
Morrison, Alan	NJ1350	66G
Morrison, Alan	PA3550	66G
Morrison, Alan	PA0850	66G
Morrison, Linda	KY1460	11,32,36,66A,66G
Moschenross, Ian	IL1800	12A,13E,20,66A,66G
Moss, Grant R.	MA1750	66G,66H,44
Moulder, Earline	MO0350	66A,66G
Moyer, Jonathan W.	OH0200	66G,66H
Mozelle, Mary M.	FL1550	66G,66H
Muehlig, Carol	MI0500	66G
Murray, Michael	AB0100	66G
Murray, Thomas	CT0850	36,66G
Musick, Marilyn J.	NE0590	66G
Myers, Geoffrey	UT0150	66G
Naegele, Elizabeth M.	IL1850	13A,13,66A,66G,11
Nagtegaal, Marlin	AG0600	66G
Near, John R.	IL2400	11,12A,12C,66G
Neil, William W.	VA0450	66G
Nelson, Jessica L.	AL1250	66A,66G,66D
Nelson, Leon	IL2100	66G
Nelson, Timothy	IL2300	13,10F,66A,66G
Nennmann, Jill	IN1350	66G
Ness, Marjorie S.	MA0930	11,20,32,36,66G
Neswick, Bruce	IN0900	66G
Newman, Margaret	AA0050	66G
Nolte, Brent J.	MN1030	66G,63
Nord, James	GA0250	66G
Norman, Edward	AB0090	66G
Nott, Kenneth	CT0650	12A,12,66G
Nowik, John	NJ1160	66G
Olsen, Timothy	NC1650	66G
Olsen, Timothy	NC2205	66G,31A,66H,42,56
Olson, Anthony	MO0950	11,66A,66G,66D
Olson, Michael	ND0350	66G
O'Neal, Harriet	AR0110	66G,66A
Ore, Charles	NE0150	66G
Orlando, Hilary	PA2800	66G
Owens, Robert	NC0800	11,66D,66G
Owolabi, Okuola P.	NY4150	66G,13
Pace, Mark	NC1750	66G,36,61
Palmer, David	NC1900	13A,66A,13B,13C,66G
Palmer, David	AG0550	66A,66G,31A,13C,66H
Palmer, John M.	IL0275	66A,66G
Palmer, Larry	TX2400	66G,66H
Pare, Richard	AI0190	66G,66H,55,42
Parkins, Robert	NC0600	66G,13A,13B,13C
Parkinson, Rebecca	ID0060	66G
Parsons, Charles	MN0800	66G
Partridge, William	MO1950	66G
Patterson, Myron	UT0250	66G
Paul, Lanetta	OR0200	66G
Payn, William A.	PA0350	36,44,66G,66H,31A
Pearson, Ronald	OK1450	66G
Pease, Janey L.	NC0850	66A,66G
Perrin, Raymond	AI0220	66G
Peterson, Gregory M.	IA0950	44,66G,31A
Peterson, Jay	IL1650	13,12A,14,66A,66G
Peterson, John David	TN1680	66G,31A,12A
Peterson, Mark	NC0100	36,38,66G,66A
Peterson, William J.	CA3650	11,12A,66G,66H
Peterson, William	CA1050	66G
Petricic, Marko	IN1650	12A,66G
Pettaway, Charles H.	PA2000	13,11,12A,66,66G
Pettit, Joseph	WA0650	66G
Pettyjohn, Emma	GA0700	66A,66B,66C,66G,66D
Pickering, David C.	KS0650	66A,66G,66H,13,12A
Pirtle, R. Leigh	IA1390	66A,66G,66B,66C
Plamann, Melissa M.	OK0750	66G,31A
Poirier, Rejean	AI0200	66G,66H,55B,55D
Polley, David	TX2650	31,66G
Porter, William	AI0150	66G
Porter, William	NY1100	66G,66H
Porterfield-Pyatt, Chaumonde	CA1290	11,66A,66G,66D
Potratz, Robert C.	MN1030	11,12A,66G,13A
Potter, Joe	MO2050	66A,66G,35H,54,35E
Powell, Jason	IN0300	20F,20H,31A,66A,66G
Powell, Linton	TX3500	12,66G,66H
Pracht, Carole	KS0980	66A,66G,66C
Prowse, Ronald H.	MI2200	66G
Pursell, William	TN0100	10,12A,13,11,66G
Pyle, Daniel S.	GA0500	11,66G
Radice, Jean	NY1800	66G,66H
Raedeke, Barbara A.	MO1900	66G
Rakich, Christa	MA1400	66G
Ransom, McCoy	LA0100	13,66A,66G,66C
Rasmussen, Bruce	CA3400	60A,36,61,40,66G
Rau, George	PA3580	66G
Ravitskaya, Irena	KS0350	66A,66B,66C,66D,66G
Rawlins, Nancy	NJ1050	66D,66G,13,12
Rea, Edward	SC0200	13,66A,66G,66F
Redfern, Nancy	MI1600	66,11,66D,66B,66G
Reed, Douglas	IN1600	66G,66H,13D,31A
Reimer, Joyce L.	NE0250	44,66A,66G
Rhodes, Cherry	CA5300	66G
Rice, Betty	FL1300	66G
Richards, Annette	NY0900	12,13A,13B,66G
Rigler, Ann Marie	MO2000	66A,66G,31A,12A,12C
Risinger, Andrew	TN0100	66D,66G
Rivers, Cynthia	GA1100	66A,66G,66C,31A,36
Roberts, David Scott	TN1720	66G,13,10F
Roberts, Lois	CA1750	66A,66G
Roberts, Stephen	CT0800	66G
Robertson, Carey	CA1050	66G
Robinson, Dana M.	IL3300	66G
Robinson, McNeil	NY2150	66G
Robinson, Schuyler	KY1450	13,66G,66H,31A
Rodgers, Christopher	PA0050	66A,66C,66G
Rodgers, Kenneth	KS0500	66G,66A,66D,66C,11
Roditeleva-Wibe, Maria I.	WA0050	14A,12A,20F,66A,66G
Rodland, Catherine	MN1450	13,66G
Roehrig, Helmut J.	OH2550	66G
Rogers, Sean	ID0070	36,39,60,66A,66G
Rohlig, Harald	AL0450	10,66G,31A
Rose, John	CT0500	36,66G,69,31A
Ross, William	TX2200	66G
Rossi, Richard Robert	IL0800	60A,36,38,66G
Rothlisberger, Rodney	MN1120	32D,36,66G
Rowe, Paul	OK0300	66A,11,66D,66G
Rowland, Michael	NC0550	66C,66G
Rubin, Justin H.	MN1600	13,34,66G,10,66A
Runner, David C.	TN1150	13,10F,66A,66G,10A
Russell, Carlton T.	MA2150	11,12A,66G,31A
Russell, Cynthia	TX0250	61,66A,66G,32B,32C
Salcedo, Angela	CT0600	66G
Sanborne, Deborah	IA1300	12,66G,66C,11
Satre, Paul J.	IL3150	36,66A,66G,60,13
Savoy, Thomas	NY3600	66C,66G
Scanlon, Andrew	NC0650	66G,31
Schaefer, John	MO1000	66G
Schaeffer, Vicki J.	OK1350	66G
Scharf, Margaret	OH0650	66G
Scharf, Margaret R.	OH0200	66G
Scheide, Kathleen	NJ1350	66G,12A,67F,66H
Schell, Mark	KY0100	44,66G,31A
Schempp, Marilyn	SD0050	66G,66H
Scherperel, Loretta	FL0200	13,11,66G
Schipull, Larry D.	MA1350	13,66G,66H
Schlesinger, Scott L.	NC2525	66G,11,13A,29A,36
Schmid, Ilo	OR1010	66A,66G
Schmidt, John C.	TX3175	13,12A,66G
Schneider, Jill L.	WA1150	66G
Schou, Larry B.	SD0600	66G,66H,20
Schrock, Karl	MI2250	66G
Schubkegel, Joyce C.	MN1030	66G,66A
Schulte, Gregory	AJ0150	66G
Schulz, Russell E.	TX0750	36,66G,31A
Schwandt, John	OK1350	66G,66H
Scott, F. Johnson	VA0750	34,13B,13A,66G,66C
Scott, Kraig	WA1300	66G
Scott, Kraig	WA1100	36,31A,66G,66H,60A
Scott, P. Mark	TX3420	66G
Seidel, William	GA1700	66G
Self, Stephen	MN0250	12A,66A,66G
Shelton, Frank	CO0200	11,66G
Shilling, Ronald L.	MN1030	66G
Shin, MinKyoo	IL3100	13C,66A,66D,66G
Shipley, Linda P.	TN0580	13,66A,66G
Sigmon, Susan McEwen	GA0940	13,36,66A,66G,40
Simi, David R.	CA4400	11,66G
Sinder, Philip	MI1200	66G,61
Singleton, Beth	CA1650	66G
Singley, H. E.	IL1850	66A,66G,11,36,31A
Smith, Debbie	TN1200	66A,66G,11
Smith, Robert	NC1100	11,13,66G
Smith, Sally	IL1090	66G
Snyder, Patricia	CT0650	66G
Soderlund, Sandra	CA2950	66G,66H,12A
Soehnlen, Edward J.	MI1850	11,66A,66G
Sparzak, Monica	NC1350	66G
Spayde, Ruth	MO0100	66G
Spicer, Nan	IN0005	61,60A,66A,66G,31A
Spillman, Herndon	LA0200	66G
Spitler, Carolyn	IN1250	64A,66A,13B,13C,66G
Sproat, Joel	OK1350	66G
St. Julien, Marcus	LA0300	13B,13C,61,66G
Stauch, Michael	NJ0550	66A,66G
Stauffer, George B.	NJ1130	12A,66G
Steel, David	MS0700	14,66H,55,66G
Steele, Charlie W.	NC0250	66G
Stegall, Gary Miles	SC0420	66A,66D,13A,66C,66G
Stein, Ken	KY1550	66G
Stevens, Bruce	VA1500	66G
Stevlingson, Norma	WI0860	13B,12A,66G,13E,13D
Still, Tamara	OR0750	66G
Stillwell, Roy	IL1500	66G,66A,11
Stolk, Ronald	DC0050	66G
Storm, Linda	IL1550	66A,66G,66B,44
Stowe, J. Chappell	WI0815	66G,55
Strong, Alan D.	TX0345	11,32,66G
Stuber, Jon	OR1100	66G
Sudeith, Mark A.	IL0600	13,66A,66G,66C
Summers, Billy	NC0750	66A,66C,66D,66G
Sutherland, Donald S.	MD0650	66G
Swanson, Carl B.	CA0550	66G,31A
Swanson, Jenny	TX2260	66G,66A
Sykes, Peter	MA0400	66G,67F
Sykes, Peter	MA1400	66G
Sykes, Peter	MA1175	66G,66H
Szafron, Brennan	SC0650	66G
Tam, TinShi	IA0850	69,66G,11,34B,66D
Tappa, Richard J.	TX0250	11,66G,69
Taylor, Allan	MA2100	13E,66G,36
Taylor, Larry Clark	VA0100	66A,66G,13B,13D,13E
Taylor, William	AL1195	66G
Tegels, Paul	WA0650	66G
Tel, Martin	NJ0850	36,66G,31A
Teply, Lee	VA1000	13,55,66G,66H
Terry, Carole	WA1050	66G,66H,67E
Thallander, Mark	CA1960	66D,66G
Thewes, Mark	OH1350	66G
Thiedt, Catherine E.	OH0950	13,12A,66A,66G,31A
Thiesfeldt, Jeneane M.	MN1030	66G,66A
Thogersen, Chris	IN0550	66A,66G,32B,31A
Thomas, Fennoyee	TX3150	66A,66G
Thomas, Ladd	CA5300	66G
Thompson, Randy	OK0825	64C,66G
Thorson, Valerie	OH2150	66G
Thorson, Valerie	OH0700	66G
Tice, Loren C.	KY1350	11,66A,66H,66C,66G
Tikker, Timothy	MI1150	66G
Tipps, Angela	TN1100	66G,36,11
Tittle, Sandra	OH1000	66A,66G,66H,66D
Tolar, Ron	AL0400	13,11,66A,66G
Tompkins, Charles B.	SC0750	13,66G,66H,31A
Toops, Gary	CA3200	13,11,66G
Torrans, Richard	TN1600	66G
Torrenti, John	CT0100	66A,66G
Toscano, Patricia	SD0300	61,66A,66G,31A
Totter, John	RI0250	66G
Trautman, Mark A.	NJ1130	66G,41
Turner, Sandra	KY1200	66A,66D,66B,66G
Turnquist-Steed, Melody	KS0150	11,13C,31,44,66G
Udy, Kenneth L.	UT0250	66G
Vail, Kathy	MS0850	66A,66G,69,44
Van Buren, Harvey	DC0350	13A,13,10F,10,66G
Vance, Virginia L.	NC1800	13,66G
Vanderford, Brenda M.	WV0700	13A,13,11,66G,31A
Varner, Kenneth	SC0050	66A,66G
Verkuilen, Jeffrey	WI0750	66G
Vincent, Stephen	KS1300	66G

Name	Code	Areas
Voelker, Dale	IL1300	13A,13B,60A,36,66G
Vogt, Sean F.	SD0300	60A,36,66G,32D,40
Wagner, David O.	MI1260	12A,13B,13C,35,66G
Wagner, James	MI0600	66G
Wagner, Wayne L.	MN1030	13A,32,36,66G,66D
Walker, John C.	MD0650	66G
Ward, Arlene	NM0450	66D,66G
Washington, Henry	TX2220	36,11,66A,66G,66D
Watson, Holly	LA0050	66G
Watson, Nancy	NC2000	66G
Webb, Marianne	IL2900	66G
Wee, Theo R.	MN1450	66A,66G,66D
Weglein, Carolyn	MD0100	60,36,66G
Weiss, Linda	TX1725	66G
Welch, James	CA4425	66G
Wells, William	CA0960	66G
Wente, Steven F.	IL0730	13,66G,12A,31A
Werner, J. Ritter	OH2500	11,66G
West, Lara L.	KS0100	40,11,66D,66G,20
Westgate, Phillip Todd	AL0950	13,36,66A,66G,66C
Whatley, Jay K.		13B,13C,66D,66C,66G
White, R. Scott	NH0150	66A,66G
Wiant, William	RI0250	66A,66
Wiechman, Elizabeth J.	MN1030	66A,66G
Wielenga, Mary Lou	IA0500	66A,66D,66G
Wielenga, Mary Lou	IA1200	66A,66G,66D
Wilkins, Donald G.	PA0550	13,12A,66G
Willey, Mark	MD0150	13,66G
Williams, Anthony E.	TN0550	66G
Williams, Craig S.	NY2900	66G
Williams, Stephen C.	PA2550	66G,39
Williams, Steven	NC2550	11,54,39,66G
Willy, Alan	IN0005	66A,66G,70,13
Wilson, Carol	CO0200	66A,66G
Wilson, Todd	OH0600	66G
Winfree, James	TN1650	66A,66G
Winterfeldt, Chad	MN0750	66G,44,12
Wojnar, William A.	ND0150	12A,66A,66G,31B,31A
Wolcott, Vernon	OH0300	66G
Wold, Wayne L.	MD0500	13,66G,66H,10
Wolfe-Ralph, Carol	MD1050	66A,66G,66B,66C,12A
Wolgast, Brett	IA1550	66G
Wolgast, Brett	IA0300	66A,66G,13,12A
Woodworth, William	TN1450	64B,13B,13C,41,66G
Woolley, Clara	IN0010	13,11,32,66A,66G
Wright, Barbara	WV0560	13A,13,12A,12,66G
Wright, Marylyn	TX3360	13,66A,66C,66D,66G
Wright, Robert	TX0600	66G
Wright, William	AG0450	13,66G
Wubbena, Jan Helmut	AR0400	13,66G,12A,11
Yandell, Ruth	AZ0440	66A,66G,13
Yearsley, David	NY0900	12,13,11,66H,66G
Yerden, Ruth	OR0600	66A,66G
Yerden, Ruth	OR1150	66A,66G,66D,66C
Yoon, Sujin	MO1350	36,66G,66H,31A,60A
Yost, Jacqueline	NC2420	13,66G
Young, Christopher	IN0900	66G
Yount, Max	WI0100	66G,66H
Yount, Terry A.	FL1550	66G
Ypma, Nancy S.	IL1740	12A,36,66G
Zabel, Albert	WV0400	44,66G,31A,10,66C
Zec, John	NJ0550	12A,31,66G,13,11
Zimmer, Susan	MD0800	66A,66C,11,66G
Zimmerman, R. Edward	IL3550	11,66G,66H,31A

Harpsichord

Name	Code	Areas
Adam, Joseph J.	WA1000	66G,66H
Agee, Richard J.	CO0200	13,11,12,66H,67D
Allison, Rees	MN0800	12A,66A,66H
Alvarado, Julieta	MN1500	66A,66H
Archer, Gail	NY4450	66G,66H
Ashworth, John	KY1500	12A,55,66H,67
Bacon, Joel	CO0250	66G,12A,66H
Baird, Barbara M.	OR1050	66G,66H,67F,11
Banner, Lucy	MA0600	66A,66G,66H,66B,66C
Bardston, Robert	AA0040	66H,66B,38,41,62C
Barte, Paul T.	OH1900	12A,11,66G,66H
Bates, Susan	NC2500	66,66H
Bauer, Michael J.	KS1350	36,66G,66H,31A
Bedford, Frances M.	WI0835	66H
Bell, Joby	NC0050	66G,66H,36,31A
Benham, Helen	NJ0030	13A,66A,66H,66B,66C
Bennight, Brad	TX0300	66H
Bennight, Bradley J.	TX3420	66H
Bezuidenhout, Kristian	NY1100	66H
Biggers, Jonathan E.	NY3705	12A,66G,66H
Billmeyer, Dean W.	MN1623	66G,66H
Birch, Kevin	ME0440	66G,66H
Birney, Allan	PA2450	66H
Bloomfield, Ruta	CA2810	66H,11
Bognar, Joseph A.	IN1750	66A,13,66H,66G
Bowder, Naydene	ME0200	66A,66H
Boyd, Sue Marston	VA1350	66A,66H,66C,66D
Breckenridge, Carol Lei	IA0200	11,66A,66B,66C,66H
Brendler, Charlene	CA5000	66H
Brewer, Robert S.	TX3450	66H,66G
Bridgman, Joyce M.	OK0850	66A,66H,66B,66C,66D
Britton, Carolyn	WI0845	11,66A,66H
Brock, John	TN1710	66G,66H,31A
Brookshire, Bradley	NY3785	12A,12,55,66G,66H
Brown, Jennifer Williams	IA0700	12,55,67,66H
Bruk, Elfrida	IN0005	66A,13,31B,66C,66H
Brunner, Roy	MA0950	13,10,66G,66H,31A
Bryant, Thomas E.	TN1200	13,11,66A,66C,66H
Buice, David	GA1550	66C,66H,66G,69
Burdette, Glenn E.	MI2200	12,66A,66H
Burell, J. Ashley	TN1000	66G,66H
Burman-Hall, Linda C.	CA5070	55,20D,20F,66H,67C
Carlin, Maryse	MO1900	66A,66H
Carver, Lucinda	CA5300	66H
Cary, Jane G.	NY0400	11,12A,66H
Case-Stott, Angeline	TN1680	66H
Cassarino, James	VT0100	66G,66H
Catello, Darlene	IN1450	66H
Ceaser, Janina Kuzma	OH0600	66H
Chase, Robert	NY2400	13,12A,66H
Choi, Bonnie L.	NY4150	66A,66H,66D
Choi, Bonnie	NY2650	66A,66D,66H
Choi, Hye-Jean	TX0900	66A,66G,66H,67C,13
Christie, James David	MA0700	66G,66H,31A
Christie, James	MA2050	66G,66H
Cleverdon, Suzanne	MA2050	66H,66B
Comparone, Elaine	NY0050	66H
Congdon, Judy A.	NY1700	13,66G,66H,31A
Cooper, Frank E.	FL1900	12,66A,66H,67
Cooper, Kenneth	NY2150	66H
Cooper, Nancy Joyce	MT0400	13,66G,66H,69
Corrie, John H.	ME0150	13C,36,61,66G,66H
Corrigan, Vincent J.	OH0300	12,66H
Cosgrove, Nancy	MA0600	66A,66G,66H,66B,66C
Craig, Phebe	CA5010	13C,56,66H
Crowell, Gregory	MI0900	13,12,66G,66H
Curran, Nancy A.	CT0500	42,66A,66H
Curry, Jerry L.	SC1110	13,66H,55,66E
Cypess, Rebecca	NJ1130	12,66E,66H,56
De Silva, Preethi	CA1050	66A,66H
Dehaven, Frederic	MI1750	66G,66H
Dekker, Gretchen	PA3710	66A,66H,13C
Dorsa, James	CA0835	66H,10A,67F,13C,12A
Duckett, Linda B.	MN1000	13,66G,66H
Dupree, Jillon Stoppels	WA0200	66H
Durham, Carol S.	MS0400	66G,66A,66C,66H,12A
Eaton, David D.	TX3530	66G,13,66H,67F
Echols, Charles	MN1300	66H,12A,66A,66G
Egler, Steven	MI0400	12A,66H,66G,31A
Ellis, William	FL1850	66G,69,66H,31
Ennulat, Egbert M.	GA2100	12A,66G,66H
Eppink, Joseph A.	NY0700	32B,66G,66H,32C,32A
Faber, Trudy	OH2450	12A,44,66G,66H,31A
Farr, Trudy	CO0800	55,66G,66H
Fisher, George	NY2250	13,66H
Freese, Faythe R.	AL1170	66G,66H,69
Froelich, Andrew I.	ND0350	13,12A,66A,66H
Gascho, Joseph	DC0100	66H
Gerber, Thomas E.	IN1650	11,66H,55B,12A
Gerber, Tom	IN0250	13,66H
Gibbons, John	MA1400	41,66H,67
Glass, Judith	TN1350	13,66G,66H,31A
Glennon, Maura	NH0150	66A,66C,66D,66H
Gordon-Seifert, Catherine	RI0150	13,12A,12C,55B,66H
Gray, Steven	CA3460	13,66A,66G,66H
Grew, John	AI0150	66G,66H,67
Grib, Sonia G.	NY1600	41,66H
Griffith, Dorothy S.	CA1900	13A,66A,66H
Grimwood, Paul	AG0200	66G,66H,66D
Groves, Robert W.	ND0350	11,12A,66A,20G,66H
Grubb, Steve	CA3000	11,66G,66G,66H
Guenther, Timothy E.	OH0100	66G,66H,66D
Guthrie, James M.	NC0400	13,10,34,66G,66H
Haas, Arthur S.	NY3790	41,66H,67,55B
Haas, Arthur S.	NY2250	66H
Hall, Janean	MN0300	66G,66H
Hand, Gregory	IA1550	66G,66H
Handford, Kathrine	WI0350	66G,66H
Harbach, Barbara	MO1830	66G,67F,15,66H,34A
Harris, Alice Eaton	NY2400	66A,66H
Haupert, Mary Ellen	WI1100	12A,13,34,66H
Hays, Elizabeth	IA0700	12,55,66H
Heater, Katherine	CA5000	66H,66E
Heiles, William H.	IL3300	66A,66H,41
Heller, David	TX3350	13,66G,66H,31A
Hiebert, Cynthia	AG0600	66H
Higdon, James M.	KS1350	66G,66H,31A
Hill, Doris	IL1200	66G,66H
Holm, Robert	AL1300	66A,66G,66C,66D,66H
Holmes, Karen	AG0400	55,66G,66H
Holmes, Ruth J.	TX1550	12A,66A,66H,66B,13
Horneff, Donald C.	MD0520	66F,66C,66D,66H,32E
Howard, Beverly A.	CA0450	13,34A,66G,66A,66H
Huber, Laurell	CA1860	66G,66H
Hudson, Barton	WV0750	12A,12,66H
Jackson, Christopher	AI0070	60,66G,66H,67C
Jamason, Corey	CA4150	66H,66E,12A,55B
Jenne, Natalie	IL0730	66H
Johnson, Calvert	GA0050	66G,15,31,66H,12A
Jones, Jeff	KY0450	66G,66H,66A
Jones, Martin David	GA0250	11,66A,66H,66B,13
Kaehler, Winston H.	MN0950	66G,66H
Karis, Aleck	CA5050	13,12A,66A,66H,43
Kaufman, Roseann Penner	KS0200	66G,66H
Keenan, Larry W.	KY0900	11,66A,66G,66D,66H
Kent, George E.	RI0300	11,49,63A,66G,66H
Kiehl, Vicky	AR0200	66A,66H,66B,66D,66C
Kime, Ramona	MI1800	62,66A,66H,66G
Kincade, Gertrude G.	AR0750	66H,66C,66D
King, Mark	WV0550	66G,66H
King, Shirley S.	PA0950	66G,66H
Kinsley, Eric B.	CA0550	11,66A,66H,66D
Knox, Hank	AI0150	56,66H,67F,55
Kong, Joanne	VA1500	66A,66H,66C,55
Koriath, Kirby L.	IN0150	66G,66H,31A,34
Kramer, Ernest Joachim	MO0950	13,10,11,66A,66H
Krieger, Marcos F.	PA3150	13C,66H,66G,11,12A
Kroll, Mark	MA1450	11,66H
Kroll, Mark	MA0400	66H,66E,12,67F,13
Larkowski, Charles S.	OH2500	12A,12,66H
Laubach, Mark	PA2200	31A,66G,66H
Laudon, Robert	MN1623	11,12A,12,66H
Lawrence, Edwin	MA2250	13C,66A,66G,66H,66C
Lee, Patricia	IL2650	66A,66H,66B,66C,66D
Leland, James	KS1200	66G,66H
Lerner, Neil	NC0550	11,12,34H,66H
Lewis, Huw R.	MI1050	13D,66G,66H,31A
Lindorff, Joyce Zankel	PA3250	12A,12,66H,67C
Lipp, Carolyn	MI0500	14,66A,66H,66B
Livingston, Don	MN0610	66H
Loewen, Harold	AA0020	66A,66H
Loman, Janet	NM0310	66G,66H
Lopez, Jose R.	FL0700	66A,66C,66H,66B
Loring, George	NH0150	66A,66B,66D,66H
Louwenaar, Karyl	FL0850	66E,41,66A,66H
Lucktenberg, George	GA1700	66A,66E,66H
Lupinski, Rudy	OK0300	66A,66D,13B,13C,66H
Mabee, Patricia	CA1075	42,55B,66H
Mabee, Patricia	CA0510	66H,55B
MacPherson, William A.	MA2150	11,12,66G,66H
Mangsen, Sandra	AG0500	12,66H
Marchant, Susan J.	KS1050	36,66G,66H,60A
Marks, Christopher	NE0600	66G,66H,13
Marlow, Laurine	TX2900	11,12A,66G,66A,66H
Marshall, Thomas	VA0250	66A,66G,66H,66D
Martin, Les K.	WA0800	66G,66H
Martin, Margot	CA1750	12A,12B,20,66H,12E
Martin, Roland E.	NY4320	66G,66H
Martorella, Stephen T.	RI0200	12A,66A,66G,66H
Masters, Barbara	IL0850	66A,66G,66H
Matos, Lucia Regina	IL2200	38,39,60B,66G,66H
Mauchley, Sandra	ID0250	66A,66H,66D
Maxwell, Margaret	MN0150	66A,66H,66G
McCandless, Terry	OH1200	66G,66H
McCorkle, William	VA1850	66G,66H,66A
McGhee, Michael	GA2200	13,11,12A,66G,66H
McKamie, Shirley	MO1780	11,66D,66H
Mengelkoch, Eva	MD0850	66A,66C,66B,66H,66E

Index by Area of Teaching Interest

Milovanovic, Biljana	NJ0700	66A,66H,13C
Miotke, David	CA3520	66A,66H,66C,13C
Moersch, Charlotte Mattax	IL3300	67F,66H,12A,55C,12
Montgomery, Vivian	OH2200	11,12A,55,66H,67F
Moss, Grant R.	MA1750	66G,66H,44
Moy, Jason	IL0750	55B,66H
Moyer, Jonathan W.	OH0200	66G,66H
Mozelle, Mary M.	FL1550	66G,66H
Murphy, Timothy	MD0850	29,66A,66H
Musmann, Lois S.	CA3270	12,39,60,66H
Myers, Patricia Ann	NY1550	11,12,14,66H,20
Namer, Dina	AG0250	66A,66C,66H
Narvey, Lois	DC0170	66A,66H
Nediger, Charlotte	AG0450	66H
Newton, Jean	NY5000	66H
Nitsch, Paul A.	NC2000	41,66A,66H
Norton, Diane M.	IN1850	66A,66H
O'Brien, John B.	NC0650	66A,66D,66H,55
Oke, Doreen	AB0100	66H
Oldfather, Christopher	NY2150	66A,66H
Olsen, Timothy	NC2205	66G,31A,66H,42,56
Otten, Thomas J.	NC2410	66A,66E,66H
Palmer, David	AG0550	66A,66G,31A,13C,66H
Palmer, Larry	TX2400	66G,66H
Panneton, Helene	AI0210	66H
Pare, Richard	AI0190	66G,66H,55,42
Parmentier, Edward L.	MI2100	12A,12,66H
Party, Lionel	PA0850	66H
Paterson, Kim	NY1400	66A,66H
Patterson, Donald L.	WI0803	66A,66B,66G,66H,31A
Payn, William A.	PA0350	36,44,66G,66H,31A
Peters, Lorna G.	CA0840	66A,66H,13
Peterson, William J.	CA3650	11,12A,66G,66H
Pickering, David C.	KS0650	66A,66G,66H,13,12A
Poirier, Rejean	AI0200	66G,66H,55B,55D
Porter, William	NY1100	66G,66H
Posey, Ann	MO2000	66A,66H
Posnak, Paul	FL1900	41,66A,66H,66C
Powell, Linton	TX3500	12,66G,66H
Radice, Jean	NY1800	66G,66H
Reed, Douglas	IN1600	66G,66H,13D,31A
Reed, Kathryn	IA0950	13C,55,66H
Robinson, Schuyler	KY1450	13,66G,66H,31A
Rosales, Rachel A.	VT0050	61,66H
Rutter, Bronwen	FL1300	66A,66H,66C
Salanki, Hedi	FL2100	13C,13E,66A,66H,41
Saunders, Ruth	MO1250	66A,66H
Saunders, Steven E.	ME0250	11,12A,12,66H
Scanlan, Mary	MI0850	66A,66H,66C,66D,20F
Scheide, Kathleen	NJ1350	66G,12A,67F,66H
Schempp, Marilyn	SD0050	66G,66H
Schenk, Kathryn E.	MN0610	11,66A,66H
Schenkman, Byron	WA0200	66H
Schipull, Larry D.	MA1350	13,66G,66H
Schmidt, Timothy R.	IA1750	13B,31A,66A,66H
Schou, Larry B.	SD0600	66G,66H,20
Schwandt, John	OK1350	66G,66H
Scott, Kraig	WA1100	36,31A,66G,66H,60A
Simons, Penelope	ND0250	66A,66H
Skernick, Linda	CT0100	66H
Soderlund, Sandra	CA2950	66G,66H,12A
Solose, Jane M.	MO1810	66A,66H
Solose, Kathleen A.	AJ0150	66A,66H,66B,66C,42
Stalnaker, Donna	WV0250	11,12A,32B,66A,66H
Steel, David	MS0700	14,66H,55,66G
Stevens, Delores E.	CA3150	41,66A,66H,66C
Stewart, Jocelyn	NY2150	66H
Stewart, Jocelyn	NY4200	66H
Sykes, Peter	MA1175	66G,66H
Taylor, Paul F.	KY0900	66A,66H,66C,66D
Teply, Lee	VA1000	13,55,66G,66H
Terry, Carole	WA1050	66G,66H,67E
Thornburgh, Elaine	CA4900	66H
Throgmorton, Debra	CO0950	66H
Tice, Loren F.	KY1350	11,66A,66H,66C,66G
Timmons, Kathryn Jill	OR0450	12A,66A,66H,66B,66C
Tittle, Sandra	OH1000	66A,66G,66H,66D
Tompkins, Charles B.	SC0750	13,66G,66H,31A
Toth, Gwen J.	NJ0800	66H
Veleta, Richard	PA1550	66H
Viscoli, David A.	MN1000	66A,66H,66C
Weiss, Kenneth	NY1900	66H
Wenger, Janice K.	MO1800	66C,66A,66H,66E
Whitmore, Keith	OK0650	66A,66H,66C,66D
Wiggins, Webb	OH1700	66H
Willis, Andrew S.	NC2430	66A,66H,66C
Wold, Wayne L.	MD0500	13,66G,66H,10
Wright, Elisabeth B.	IN0900	66H
Wyse, Philip	CO0225	66H,66D
Yang, Rajung	ID0250	66A,66C,66H,42
Yearsley, David	NY0900	12,13,11,66H,66G
Yoon, Sujin	MO1350	36,66G,66H,31A,60A
Yount, Max	WI0100	66G,66H
Zamparas, Grigorios	FL2050	66A,66H,12A
Zappulla, Robert	CA1050	12A,12C,13,66H
Zelley, Richard S.	FL0400	55,66A,66H,67B
Zimmerman, R. Edward	IL3550	11,66G,66H,31A

Early Instruments (All Areas)

Ashworth, John	KY1500	12A,55,66H,67
Bales, Bruce	CA2050	40,61,67,13A,36
Beazley, Janet M.	CA5040	55,67
Bergeron, Sylvain	AI0150	67,55
Blanchett, Madalyn	TX2260	11,64A,66A,66D,67
Bowles, Chelcy L.	WI0815	55,67
Brown, Jennifer Williams	IA0700	12,55,67,66H
Bush, Douglas E.	UT0050	12,55,66G,67,31A
Carslake, Louise	CA2950	12,55,64A,67
Carter, Stewart	NC2500	13,11,12A,55,67
Coan, Darryl	IL2910	13,32,62E,67
Cooper, Frank E.	FL1900	12,66A,66H,67
Davidoff, Judith	NY3560	41,55B,67
Day, Mary	IA0100	41,61,67,31A,39
Dudgeon, Ralph T.	NY3720	12,67,14,38,63
Eisenstein, Robert	MA1350	67,34A
Eisenstein, Robert	MA2000	12A,55B,67
Enrico, Eugene	OK1350	12A,12,55,67
Fallon, Kelly	IN0800	35,67,71,72
Ferencz, Jane Riegel	WI0865	67,11,12,15
Fittipaldi, Thomas	NY2500	36,66D,67,70,11
Forney, Kristine	CA0825	12A,67,11
Gibbons, John	MA1400	41,66H,67
Gilbert, Kenneth	AI0150	67
Greco, Eugene A.	FL1300	36,12A,67F,12,67
Grew, John	AI0150	66G,66H,67
Gries, Peggy	OR1050	12,55,67

Gustafson, Beverly	MN0750	67,55
Haas, Arthur S.	NY3790	41,66H,67,55B
Haines, Mary Enid	AG0450	67
Hathaway, Janet J.	IL2200	12A,55,67,12C
Hershey, Jane	MA1900	67,55
Heuchemer, Dane O.	OH1200	11,12A,12,37,67
Howell, John	VA1700	36,67,35,55
Hynes, Maureen	NY2105	38,67,62C,55,42
Kielson, Lisette	IL0400	67,55
Kinslow, Valerie	AI0150	61,55,67
Kirk, Douglas	AI0150	67
Kramme, Joel I.	MO0825	11,36,55,67,12A
Kwapis, Kris	IN0900	67
Lieberman, Carol	MA0700	62A,13,12A,67,62
Lipkis, Larry	PA2450	13,10F,10,55,67
MacMillan, Betsy	AI0150	67,55
Macy, Carleton	MN0950	13,10,67,55,47
Marsh, Carol	NC2430	12A,12,55,67
Mayes, Joseph	NJ1050	41,67,70
Mead, Sarah	MA0500	55B,55D,67A,67
Mealy, Robert	NY1900	67
Morton, Joelle	AG0450	67
Munn, Albert Christopher	TX3525	13,12A,36,67,55B
Nisula, Eric	MI1850	11,55,67
Olson, Marjean A.	NY2150	67
Petersen, Alice V. Neff	OH2300	55,67,11
Power, Brian E.	AG0050	62A,67,12A,12C,13G
Robison, John O.	FL2000	13,12A,12,67
Rust, Ty	CA2420	67,35C,34
Schlagel, Stephanie P.	OH2200	12C,12,55,67
Schulze, Otto	IN0005	62A,67,10,13,36
Shadle-Peters, Jennifer	CO0275	12A,20,32,36,67
Shubeck, Scott	CA5300	67
Shurr, Janet	WI0050	55B,62,67
Simons, Mark	AI0150	67
Sosland, Benjamin	NY1900	67
Swack, Jeanne	WI0815	12A,12,67,55,67D
Turner, Charles	CT0650	12A,12,67
Van Orden, Katherine	CA5000	11,12A,12D,55,67
Weman, Lena	AI0150	67,67D
White, Lynn	NC0050	48,64,67
Wiemken, Robert	PA3250	67
Williamson, Bruce	VT0050	64C,64E,66A,67,47
Wilson, Karen	SC0200	12,66A,12C,20G,67
Young, Alphonso	VA1350	67
Yui, Lisa	NY2150	67

Viols

Andrews, Pamela	FL0850	51,67A
Bishop, Martha	GA0750	62B,67A
Bookout, Melanie	IN0905	11,12A,12,55,67A
Carter, Selina	NC2500	62C,67A
Cunningham, Sarah	NY1900	67A
Dornenburg, John D.	CA4900	41,67A
Farrell, Peter S.	CA5050	13,12A,62C,67A
Gillespie, Wendy	IN0900	67A,55
Glosson, Sarah	VA0250	67A
Hershey, Jane	MA1175	67A
Hopkins, Christopher	IA0850	13,10B,34,10,67A
Hsu, John	NY0900	42,62C,67A,38,60B
Hsueh, Yvonne	OR1250	62A,62B,67A,67B
Jackson, Barbara G.	AR0700	13,12A,12,55B,67A
Jamieson, Robert	MN0950	67A
Jeppesen, Laura	MA2050	55,67A,67B
Koontz, Eric A.	NC0050	62B,62A,67A,42,51
Little, Margaret	AI0200	67A,55B,55D
Luby, Richard E.	NC2410	41,51,62A,67A
Mead, Sarah	MA0500	55B,55D,67A,67
Meints, Catharina	OH1700	67A,67B
Moll, Kevin N.	NC0650	12,55,67A,12A,12B
Moran, John	MD0650	67A,12A
Moulin, Jane	HI0210	20D,14A,55,67A
Muratore, John D.	NH0100	67A,70
Plouffe, Helene	AI0150	67A,67B
Reed, Elisabeth	CA5000	67A
Russell, Alex	CA0250	67A,51
Sawyer, John E.	AB0100	55,67A,12A
Schwarze, Penny	MN0450	12A,11,38,62A,67A
Serna, Phillip Woodrow	IN1750	62D,67A,70,67B
Slowik, Kenneth	MD1010	67A
Taurins, Ivars	AG0450	67A
Thielmann, Christel	NY1100	55,56,67A
Tindemans, Margriet	WA0200	67A
Whear, P. Allen	TX3420	67B,67A,55B
Wissick, Brent S.	NC2410	55,51,62C,67A,67E
Zabelle, Kim A.	WA0800	62A,62B,67A,51
Zusman, Shannon	CA5300	67A,67B
Zusman, Shanon P.	CA4450	67A,12,11

Baroque Strings

Abreu, Aldo	MA1400	67B
Albertson, John	DC0100	67B,70,53
Bergeron, Sylvain	AI0200	67B,67G
Blumenstock, Elizabeth	CA4150	67B
Browder, Risa	MD0650	67B
Carrai, Phoebe	MA1175	67B
Clark, Martha	NM0300	62A,67B
Clarke, Karen	TN1850	62A,62B,67B
Cunningham, Tekla	WA0200	67B,55B
Falkner, Renate M.	FL1950	62B,67B
Feldman, Susan M.	CA5300	62A,67B,12A
Field, Elizabeth	DC0100	62A,67B
Fix, Lou Carol	PA2450	66G,69,31A,67B
Freiberg, Sarah	MA0400	67B
Hoover, Tracy	KS1450	67B
Houle, George L.	CA4900	12A,55,67B
Hsueh, Yvonne	OR1250	62A,62B,67A,67B
Huggett, Monica	NY1900	67B
Jeppesen, Laura	MA0400	67B
Jeppesen, Laura	MA2050	55,67A,67B
Johnson, Joaquina Calvo	CA6050	36,39,61,67B
Jordan, Paul	NY3705	66G,67B
Krusemeyer, Mark	MN0300	67B
Laderach, Linda C.	MA1350	51,62A,62B,67B
Lamon, Jeanne	AG0300	67B
Le Guin, Elisabeth C.	CA5032	12A,12,62C,67B,15
Lynn, Michael	OH1700	67B,67E
Maiben, Dana	MA1175	67B
Malamut, Myra Lewinter	NJ0550	11,64A,67B,20G,13A
Matthews, Ingrid	WA0200	67B
McDonald, Marilyn	OH1700	62A,67B
Meints, Catharina	OH1700	67A,67B
Melville, Alison	AG0450	32,67B
Miller, Ronald L.	PA2300	12A,36,67B,31A,20G

753

Name	Code	Areas
Monosoff, Sonya	NY0900	41,62A,62B,67B
Montiel, Brenda F.	CA3460	12A,55,66A,67B,67C
Moore, Carla	CA5000	67B
Moore, Frances	CA2800	60B,41,62A,67B,38
Mueller, Geri	MD0150	67B
Murray, Russell E.	DE0150	12A,15,55,67D,67B
Myers, Herbert W.	CA4900	67B,71
Nairn, Robert	NY1900	67B
Napper, Susie	AI0200	62C,67B
Napper, Susie	AI0150	67B
Nichols, Lois J.	CA4600	66,32,44,67B,11
Olbrych, Timothy	VA0250	67B,67G,70,41
Olivieri, Guido	TX3510	12A,12,67B
Plouffe, Helene	AI0150	67A,67B
Purves-Smith, Shannon	AG0600	67B
Raschen, Gudrun E.	TX3300	62D,62C,67B,51
Remillard, Chantal	AI0150	67B
Ritchie, Stanley	IN0900	67B,55C
Roberts, Cynthia	NY1900	67B
Rovit, Peter M.	NY4150	62A,67B
Russell, Craig H.	CA0600	11,12A,12,67B,70
Sariti, David J.	VA1550	62A,67B,51,42
Semmens, Richard	AG0500	12,13I,55,67B,13L
Serna, Phillip Woodrow	IN1750	62D,67A,70,67B
Shepley, Mary Ellen	NY2400	64A,67B
Skeen, William	CA5300	67B
Snider, Nancy Jo	DC0010	62C,42,51,67B,41
Starin, Stefani	NY2400	64A,67B
Starkman, Jane	MA0400	67B
Starkman, Jane E.	MA2050	67B
Sullivan, Robert	MA0700	67B,70
Summers, Jerome	AG0500	60,38,64C,67B,43
Trout, Anne	MA1175	67B
Tueller, Robert F.	ID0060	38,62C,67B
Tyson, John	MA1400	67B
Vanscheeuwijck, Marc	OR1050	55,12,67B
Visentin, Peter	AA0200	12A,62A,67B,11
Walker, Nicholas	NY1800	62D,67B,55B
Whear, P. Allen	TX3420	67B,67A,55B
Whitaker, Nathan	WA0200	67B
Wyatt, Benjamin H.	VA1100	62C,67B,12,13I,12B
Young, Ann	CA4450	13,67B,11
Zelley, Richard S.	FL0400	55,66A,66H,67B
Zusman, Shannon	CA5300	67A,67B

Recorders

Name	Code	Areas
Abreu, Aldo	MA0400	67C
Ardovino, Lori	AL1200	12A,48,64C,64E,67C
Barth, George	CA4900	13,66A,67C
Boeckman, Vicki	WA0200	67C
Burman-Hall, Linda C.	CA5070	55B,20D,20F,66H,67C
Carlin, Seth A.	MO1900	66A,67C
Choi, Hye-Jean	TX0900	66A,66G,66H,67C,13
Davenport, Mark	CO0650	12,55,67C,29A,14C
Dirst, Matthew	TX3400	12A,55,67C
Dobreff, Kevin J.	MI0850	20F,61,67C,55D,13C
Ekberg, Nancy	CO0200	67C
Fader, Don	AL1170	55C,67C,12
Galhano, Clea	MN0950	67C
Gartshore, Donelda	AG0250	64A,48,67C
Gilliam, Laura	DC0100	48,67C
Habedank, Kathryn	WA0650	41,67C
Hoffman, Richard	TN0100	67C,13,55B
Huber, Wayne	CA1860	37,49,63A,67C,13
Jackson, Christopher	AI0070	60,66G,66H,67C
Jean, Rachel	AA0035	67C
Kraaz, Sarah Mahler	WI0700	12A,55,66,11,67C
Kramer, Atossa	KY0300	13C,48,64C,66A,67C
Lamb, Roberta	AG0250	32,15,67C
Lamothe, Donat	MA0200	12A,67C,20G,20H
Le Comte, Louise	AI0190	67C
Leenhouts, Paul T.	TX3420	55B,67C
Lindblad, Sonja	MA1175	67C
Lindorff, Joyce Zankel	PA3250	12A,12,66H,67C
Lynn, Kathie	OH1700	67D,67C,64A
Maute, Matthias	AI0150	67C,55
McDowell, Laura	NC0250	12C,12A,66D,67C
McLauchlin, Charlotte	OR1000	13A,66D,66A,67C,12A
McNabb, Carol	TX3515	13B,13C,64D,67C,64B
Michaud, Natalie	AI0150	67C,55
Miller, Jody	GA0050	67C
Montiel, Brenda F.	CA3460	12A,55,66A,67B,67C
Montoya, Kathryn	OH1700	67C
Morris, Theodora	OK1330	62A,62B,67C,42
Nie, Emily	WI0100	67C
Pinkas, Sally	NH0100	66A,67C
Pitzer, Lawrence	OH2450	55B,67C,67D,70,67G
Richards, Jeanne	MN1620	64A,67C,48
Rippe, Allen	TN1680	48,64E,67C
Roberts, Gwyn	MD0650	67C
Rogentine, Carole	DC0170	67C
Rosenberg, Steven E.	SC0500	11,67C
Sajnovsky, Cynthia B.	GU0500	13A,12A,20C,66D,67C
Scharfenberger, Paul E.	NH0110	12,67C,43,55,15
Schoen, Kathleen	AA0110	64A,67C
Smiley, Marilynn J.	NY3770	12A,67C
Stern, Nina	NY1900	67C
Stibler, Robert	NH0350	11,63A,67C,49,67E
Stremlin, Tatyana	NY4250	13,11,61,66A,67C
Summers, William J.	NH0100	12A,12,67C
Turner, Richard	WY0050	64D,67C,11
Van Proosdij, Hanneke	CA5000	67C
Zajac, Tom	MA2050	67C,67D,55

Baroque Winds

Name	Code	Areas
Abberger, John	AG0300	67D
Agee, Richard J.	CO0200	13,11,12,66H,67D
Amos, C. Nelson	MI0600	12A,12,67D,70
Arnone, Francesca M.	TX0300	64A,42,67D
Benoit, Marcel	AI0220	67D,70
Burgess, Geoffrey	NY1100	67D
Carslake, Louise	CA5000	67D
Cichy, Patricia Wurst	RI0150	32B,13C,64B,11,67D
Collins, C. Keith	TX3420	67D
Davila, William	CA3450	13A,11,12A,66A,67D
Dunnavant, Jessica Guinn	TN1100	64A,67D,11
Fisher, Alexander	AB0100	12,55,67D
Greenbaum, Adrianne	MA1350	64A,67D
Griffioen, Ruth	VA0250	67D,55,12A
Guimond, Claire	AI0150	67D
Hammer, Stephen	MA1175	67D
Hansbrough, Yvonne	NY0700	64A,67D,12A,42
Hildebrand, Virginia	MD0060	70,67D
Howell, Michael W.	IN1800	41,67D,70
Isachsen, Sten Y.	NY3600	67D,41,70,34,29
Jennejohn, Matthew	AI0150	67D
Jones, M. Douglas	KY1460	20G,67D,70
Kallaur, Barbara	IN0900	67D
Keaton, Kenneth D.	FL0650	60,12A,41,67D,70
Kosack, Alicia	PA3710	64A,42,67D
Lee, Janet	WA0200	67D
Lion, Na'ama	MA1175	67D
Lion, Na'ama	MA0250	41,64A,67D
Lorusso, Mary Ann	NY2400	67D,70
Lussier, Mathieu	AI0150	67D
Lynn, Kathie	OH1700	67D,67C,64A
Manderen, Michael	OH1700	67D
McClain, Washington	IN0900	67D
McCraw, Michael	IN0900	67D,55C,55
McKenna, Terry	AG0600	70,67D
Miller, Dale	CO0200	67D,70
Miller, Sandra	NY1900	67D
Murray, Russell E.	DE0150	12A,15,55,67D,67B
Noonan, Jeffrey J.	MO1900	67D
Noonan, Jeffrey	MO1500	12A,14,67D,70,20G
Ott, Hal J.	WA0050	12A,41,48,64A,67D
Partington, Michael	WA1050	67D
Patterson, R. Thomas	AZ0500	67D,70
Pfau, Marianne Richert	CA5200	12A,67D
Pitzer, Lawrence	OH2450	55B,67C,67D,70,67G
Reilly, Paul C.	IN0150	41,70,67D
Riordan, George T.	TN1100	67D,11,64B
Roth, Kathryn	RI0150	67D
Rubinoff, Kailan	NC2430	67D,14,12
Ruiz, Gonzalo	NY1900	67D
Rush, John Phillip	OK1450	64A,67D,12A,55C,56
Schachman, Marc H.	MA0400	67D
Schneiderman, John H.	CA5020	67D,70
Schwartz, Andrew	MA1175	67D
Schwoebel, Sandy	AZ0480	64A,48,67D,35A
Scott, Joseph	MA0600	67D,70
Stumpf, Suzanne	MA2050	41,67D,64A
Swack, Jeanne	WI0815	12A,12,67,55,67D
Tayler, David	CA5000	67D,67G
Teresi, Dominic	NY1900	67D
Troxler, Rebecca	NC0600	13A,64A,42,67D
Ullman, Richard	VT0100	70,67D,13C
Walker, Dave	KY0250	70,67D,67H
Weman, Lena	AI0150	67D,67D
Willard, Jerry	NY3790	67D,70
Zajac, Tom	MA2050	67C,67D,55

Brass

Name	Code	Areas
Baird, Julianne C.	NJ1100	12A,12C,40,61,67E
Borror, Ronald	CT0650	41,49,63C,67E,55
Botts, Nathan	VT0050	11,29,49,63,67E
Brown, Keith	TN1710	47,67E
Cline, Gilbert D.	CA2250	63A,49,29,67E,63B
Gordon, Adam	TX3420	67E,55B
Huff, Michael H.	AL1050	63A,42,49,67E,37
Ingles, Greg	MA0400	67E
Kelley, R. J.	NY1900	67E
Kemm, Karl	TX0550	63B,49,67E,14E,14F
Kimball, James W.	NY3730	13A,11,14,67E,70
Kirkland, Anthony B.	MS0500	63A,42,49,67E,11
Kreitner, Kenneth	TN1680	12,67E,55
Krogol, D.J.	MI1000	20F,67E
Krueger, Christopher	MA0400	67E
Kwapis, Kris	WA0200	67E
Lattimore, Lee	TX3420	64A,67E
Lortie, Dominique	AI0150	67E
Lynn, Michael	OH1700	67B,67E
Mahrt, William P.	CA4900	12A,55,67E,31A
Martin, Anthony P.	CA4900	67E
Meredith, Henry M.	AG0500	32,63A,63B,67E
Meredith, Scott	WY0200	63A,67E,12,32E,49
Miller, Leta	CA5070	11,12A,12,64A,67E
Olt, Timothy J.	OH1450	63D,49,72,67E
Pearse, Linda	IN0900	67E
Penpraze, Laurie	FL1745	63C,63D,66D,67E
Pyle, Robinson	MA0400	67E
Read, Jesse	AB0100	38,41,64D,67E
Rife, Jean	MA1175	67E
Rossum, Kelly	VA0150	63A,29,67E,47
Schafer, Erika L.	TN1700	63A,63,67E,37,46
Schmalenberger, Sarah	MN1625	12A,63B,12,67E,14
Seraphinoff, Richard M.	IN0900	67E
Shuster, Brett A.	KY1500	42,63C,49,67E
Sprague, John L.	NC1700	65,67E
Stebleton, Michelle	FL0850	49,63B,67E
Stephen, J. Drew	TX3530	12A,63B,67E,12
Stibler, Robert	NH0350	11,63A,67C,49,67E
Terry, Carole	WA1050	66G,66H,67E
Thiessen, John	NY1900	67E
Turnbull, David	WA1150	49,63A,67E,37
Walker, Scot	PA2450	67E
West, William	IL1200	13,64A,64E,41,67E
Wissick, Brent S.	NC2410	55,51,62C,67A,67E

Keyboard

Name	Code	Areas
Baird, Barbara M.	OR1050	66G,66H,67F,11
Cademcian, Gerard	IN0005	66A,31A,31B,67F,13
Cockburn, Neil	AA0050	66G,67F,12A
Crawford, Penelope	MI2100	67F
Dorsa, James	CA0835	66H,10A,67F,13C,12A
Eaton, David D.	TX3530	66G,13,66H,67F
Ewoldt, Patrice R.	PA2300	66A,66C,66B,67F,42
Greco, Eugene A.	FL1300	36,12A,67F,12,67
Haas, Arthur	NY1900	67F
Hammer, Christoph	TX3420	66E,66G,67F
Harbach, Barbara	MO1830	66G,67F,15,66H,34A
Kalis, Dawn	IN0900	67F
Knox, Hank	AI0150	56,66H,67F,55
Kroll, Mark	MA0400	66H,66E,12,67F,13
Lipke, William A.	CO0050	66A,38,67F,66B,66D
Lovallo, Lee T.	CA3258	11,34B,67F,12A
Moersch, Charlotte Mattax	IL3300	67F,66H,12A,55C,12
Montgomery, Vivian	OH2200	11,12A,55,66H,67F
Nakamae, Ayumi	NC0450	61,36,40,67F
Nediger, Charlotte	AG0300	67F
Paolantonio, Ed	NC1600	66A,67F
Pearl, Adam J.	MD0650	67F
Pearlman, Martin	MA0400	55,67F
Rollett, Rebecca	PA1050	67F
Scheide, Kathleen	NJ1350	66G,12A,67F,66H
Stoughton, Zachariah	TX3000	66,12A,67F,11
Sykes, Peter	MA0400	66G,67F
Wolinsky, Robert A.	NY2550	66D,67F

Index by Area of Teaching Interest

Lute

Appello, Patrick	NJ0550	70,67G,13B,13A,12A
Bass, John	TN1200	70,46,47,67G
Becker, Harris	NY2105	67G,70,41
Beckman, Gary D.	NC1700	12A,67G,11,35A,35B
Bergeron, Sylvain	AI0200	67B,67G
Berget, Paul	MN1625	67G
Burleson, Richard F.	AC0100	14,55,67G
Butturi, Renato	IN1600	70,11,67G,47,29
Cardin, Michel	AE0100	41,67G,70
Cinelli, Dennis J.	NJ0800	67G,70
Collver-Jacobson, Glorianne	MA2050	67G,70
Dolata, David	FL0700	12,67G,55,56,67H
Fox, Stuart	CA0510	42,70,55B,67G
Freundlich, Douglas	MA1175	67G
Johns, John	TN1850	41,70,67G
Liddell, Catherine	MA0400	67G
Lingen, Peter	IA0950	42,67G,70
Martin, Edward	MN0450	67G
Miranda, Michael A.	CA2800	11,67G,70,12A,41
North, Nigel	IN0900	67G,55
O'Brien, Patrick	NY1900	67G
O'Dette, Paul	NY1100	55,56,67G
Olbrych, Timothy	VA0250	67B,67G,70,41
Pitzer, Lawrence	OH2450	55B,67C,67D,70,67G
Ross, John	TN1200	70,67G,42
Simms, William	MD0500	67G,70,55
Stone, Richard	MD0650	67G
Stubbs, Stephen	WA0200	67G,55B
Tayler, David	CA5000	67D,67G
Treadwell, Nina K.	CA5070	12A,67G,55
Trent, Robert S.	VA1100	70,67G,41,57
Zito, William F.	NY1600	70,67G
Zito, William	NY0050	67G,70

Other

Bajekal, Nirmal	VA1500	67H
Dazia, Mitzuki	OR0500	67H
De Aeth, Ross	KY1350	67H
Dolata, David	FL0700	12,67G,55,56,67H
Doles, Kurt	OH0300	67H
Elliott, Paul	IN0900	61,67H,55
Espinosa, Vladimir	VA0550	67H
Evans, David	MD0400	67H
Gamerl, Darci	NE0160	64B,32E,67H
Garnett, Rodney A.	WY0200	64A,20,67H
Gillespie, Alison	PA2450	67H,62
Hoeprich, Eric	IN0900	64C,67H
Kirk, John D.	NY3650	62A,67H,20G
Lacoursiere, Marie-Nathalie	AI0200	52,67H
McCormack, Jessica D.	IN0910	61,39,12,15,67H
Mentzel, Eric P.	OR1050	61,67H,55,55D,55A
Monoyios, Ann	AG0300	67H
Nelson, Jocelyn C.	NC0650	70,12A,67H,11
O'Connell, Tim	OR0400	67H
Pierce, Ken	MA1175	67H,52
Reed, Keith	CO0200	67H
Regan, Patrick	PA1200	67H
Sheehan, Aaron	MA0400	67H
Showman, Deke	PA0100	67H
Walker, Dave	KY0250	70,67D,67H
White, Jay G.	OH1100	61,67H
You, Daisy	CA4900	67H,20E

Accordion

Berkolds, Paul	CA0510	61,39,40,12A,68
Bonsiero, Philip	MD0400	68
Cimarusti, Thomas M.	TX3200	12A,13E,20,12C,68
DiPippo, Angelo	NY1275	10C,10D,68
Krieger, Karen Ann	TN1850	13,66A,66D,66B,68
Langley, DeeAnna	MN1050	68
Macerollo, Joseph	AG0450	68
Matasy, Katherine V.	MA2050	64C,64E,68,42
Matzke, Laura	MN0200	66A,66G,66C,68,31A
Milosavljevic, Svetozar	IN0005	68,60B
Sanders, Murl Allen	WA0200	68
Schantz, Allen P.	CO0150	11,12B,13,68
Sommers, Joan C.	MO1810	68

Carillon

Anderson, Lyle	WI0815	69
Ball, Steven	MI2100	69
Berghout, Elizabeth	KS1350	66G,69
Buckwalter, Laurel G.	NY0100	66A,66B,66C,69
Buice, David	GA1550	66C,66H,66G,69
Chesman, Jeremy A.	MO0775	13,66G,69
Christensen, David	CA5040	66G,69
Cook, Don	UT0050	66G,69,31A
Cooper, Nancy Joyce	MT0400	13,66G,66H,69
Davis, Jeff	CA5000	69
Dzuris, Linda	SC0400	69,20G,66G,34
Ellis, Laura	FL1850	66G,69,66H,31
Fern, Terry L.	NC0850	11,39,61,54,69
Fix, Lou Carol	PA2450	66G,69,31A,67B
Freese, Faythe R.	AL1170	66G,66H,69
Gomer, Wesley	TX1650	13,66,69,12A,36
Groom, Mitzi	KY1550	32,69,66G
Harris, Carl G.	VA0500	60,12A,66,69
Holmquist, Solveig	OR1250	11,36,60,66G,69
Husarik, Stephen	AR0730	11,69,12A
Jinkling-Lens, Carol	CO0900	69
Johnson, James D.	NE0610	66A,66G,69
Kazimir, David	IN0900	66G,69,71
King, Donna Moore	TN0930	11,66A,66D,69
Knight, Stephen B.	AL0800	69
Konewko, Mark	WI0425	11,35A,34,69
McLellan, Ray	MI1400	69
Miller, Kathryn	PA3650	66A,66C,69
O'Donnell, Terry	CA4100	60,66A,69,54
Rose, John	CT0500	36,66G,69,31A
Scanlon, Russell J.	TX3175	69
Shadinger, Richard C.	TN0100	12A,55,66A,31A,69
Tam, TinShi	IA0850	69,66G,11,34B,66D
Tappa, Richard J.	TX0250	11,66G,69
Vail, Kathy	MS0850	66A,66G,69,44
Zerlang, Timothy	CA4900	66A,69

Guitar

Abeid, Mellad	WA0400	70,42

Abercrombie, John	NY3785	70
Abrams, Paul E.	TN0100	70
Abrams, Paul E.	TN1100	70
Abril, Mario	TN1700	13,10F,70
Abruzzo, Luke A.	PA1000	70,10A,13,29
Accardo, Frank	CA3750	70
Achen, Mori	CA3920	70
Acosta, Anibal A.	VA1000	70
Acsadi, Daniel	MA0510	70,11
Adams, Daniel B.	OH1300	11,70
Adams, Gerard	NH0300	70
Adams, Richard C.	VA0100	70
Adamy, Paul	NY2400	70,29
Adan, Jose	FL0050	70,13,13C,11,29A
Adan, Jose	FL1300	11,70,13A
Adcock, Elizabeth	MT0175	70
Adele, David	CA3200	70
Afshar, Lily	TN1680	70
Aglinskas, Peter	IL1085	70,14C
Ailshie, Tyson	CO0100	11,13,62D,70,29
Akerman, Mary S.	GA1150	41,70
Alba, James J.	NH0250	70
Albano, John	CA2900	10D,29,47,70
Albaugh, John	IA0550	29,70
Albertson, John	DC0100	67B,70,53
Aldcroft, Ken	AG0350	70
Alexander, Glenn	NY3560	41,47,70,29
Alger, Neal	IL0550	47,70
Allen, Tom	MO1710	70,32B
Alvarado, John	IN0907	41,70
Alves, Julio	WV0400	70,13
Amaral, Jorge A.	OH0200	70
Amirault, Greg	AI0150	70,29
Amon, Jonathan T.	MA0510	64E,70
Amos, C. Nelson	MI0600	12A,12,67D,70
Anderman, Mark	CA4460	13,34,10,70,13A
Anderson, Jeff	IN1310	70
Anderson, Mark	IL1200	70
Anderson, Mark	GA1500	70,13C
Anderson, Matt	GA1700	70,13B
Anderson, Matthew M.	NY3560	41,70
Anderson, William	UT0250	62D,70
Angulo, Denson	MN0900	11,13A,13B,70,14C
Annoni, Maria T.	NM0450	70
Anthony, Michael	CA2700	70
Anthony, Ron	MD1100	70,62D
Anthony, Tom	PA1350	70
Antonich, Mark	PA3650	70
Antonich, Mark E.	AI0150	70
Antonio, Garry	CA0510	70
Aplanalp, Woody	NJ0550	70,67G,13B,13A,12A
Appello, Patrick	MI0910	13,12,70,11
Apple, Ryan	CT0550	70
Arcameon, Dan	CA1900	70
Arcila, Billy	CA1520	70
Arcila, Billy	NY1450	60,32,70
Arian, Merri	CA1270	70
Arizaga, Anthony	MD0610	70
Armato, John	MO1790	70
Armetta, Joseph F.	FL0200	70
Arne, Devin	PA2450	41,70
Arnold, John	NY1250	13A,11,70
Arnold, Mark	AA0050	70
Arnold, Scott	TX1775	70,11
Arnold, Stacy	OH1700	70
Aron, Stephen	OH2150	70
Aron, Stephen	MA0260	70
Aronson, Abigail	VA1500	70
Arthur, Charles	VT0450	70
Asbell, Paul	TX2650	70,11,34,13C
Asbury, David	IL1900	70
Asche, Kyle	VA1600	70,13B,13C
Ashby, Steven	WY0150	70
Ashear, Aaron	OR1100	70
Ashton, Jeff C.	CA0350	31A,70
Askew, Jeff	CA4150	70
Assad, Sergio	AL1150	70
Attar, Yaniv	ND0400	70
Augustadt, David W.	NY1050	70
Avakian, Helen	NE0150	70
Avey, Kevin	AJ0100	70
Ayre, Ron	IL0550	70,42
Azabagic, Denis	NY2200	70,29,47
Azzolina, Jay	MA0260	70
Baboian, John	CA0600	70,41
Bachman, James	OH1100	70,11
Bachmann, George	OH0650	70
Bachmann, George	AL0345	11,70
Back, Douglas	PR0100	70
Baez, Alberto	KS1000	70
Baggett, Brian	IN0400	70
Bailey, Rex	MA0260	70
Bailey, Sheryl	WI0825	70
Baime, Peter	WI0150	70,43
Baime, Peter	WI1150	70
Baime, Peter	MA0260	70
Baione, Larry	NY0650	70
Balestra, Richard	NY3770	41,70
Balestra, Richard J.	NY1350	70
Balestra, Rick	NY3765	35C,35D,35G,47,70
Balins, Andris	OR0400	70,47
Balmer, Dan	PA1300	70
Banks, Rusty	OK0770	46,70
Banks, Steven	IN0907	70
Baranyk, David S.	IN1850	65,70
Baranyk, David	NJ0975	13A,47,70,29
Barbee, Larry	AR0200	34,32B,10D,70,32C
Barber, Deborah L.	NY1220	70
Barber, Jerome	OH2140	70,29
Barber, Keith	MN1600	70,29,42
Barnard, William	NC2400	70
Barnes, Michael	OH2550	70
Barone, Steve	LA0750	70
Barreiro, Elias	LA0900	70
Barrientos, Carlos	PR0115	70
Barrueco, Manuel	MA0260	70
Bartlett, Bruce	NY0270	11,20A,20G,29A,70
Bartow, James	NY0625	20A,20G,70
Bartow, James	WI0350	70
Baruth, Philip A.	TN1200	70,46,47,67G
Bass, John	MD0650	70
Bastepe-Gray, Serap E.	OK1450	47,62D,70
Bates, James I.	PR0150	11,12A,13A,13C,70
Batista, Gustavo	TN1600	70
Bauer, Mike	IL1400	70
Baur, James	DC0010	29,20,13,62D,70
Bayer, Joshua	NY4460	70
Beaudreau, Jason	NY2800	70
Beaudreau, Jason		

Name	Code	Areas
Beaumont, Lance	TX1100	70
Beaumont, Lance	TX2295	70
Beauvais, William	AG0650	70
Becker, Harris	NY2105	67G,70,41
Becker, Thomas R.	KS0050	70,13
Becker, Tia	MO0350	70
Becker, Tia	MO0200	70
Beckner, Woody	VA0250	70,29
Beers, Al	KY0100	70
Beers, Alva E.	KY0150	70
Begian, Jamie	CT0800	41,70,53,47,29
Behroozi, Bahram	CA4350	13A,11,12A,14,70
Belajonas, Michael	NY4050	70
Belcher, Jeff	MO0060	37,70
Belfer, Beverly	WI0825	13A,70
Belford, Rick	VT0400	70
Bell, Tim	ID0130	70
Bellamy, Terry	NY3475	41,70
Belz, Kevin	MA0260	70
Bendickson, Sean	WA0980	10D,70
Benedetti, Fred	CA2100	70,53,35B,29
Benedetti, Fred	CA4100	70
Benham, Jeremiah	IL2750	70
Bennack, Steven	TX2710	70,29A,66D
Bennett, John	KS0400	70
Benoit, Marcel	AI0220	67D,70
Benson, Steve C.	NJ0800	70,47
Berg, Christopher B.	SC1110	55,70
Bergeron, Andrew	MI0850	70,13A,13D
Bergeron, Andrew	MI0300	70,41
Berimeldze, Tariel	IA0930	70
Berman, Ronald M.	CA3500	70,29
Berman, Ronald	CA3300	70
Bernstein, Brandon	CA3500	70
Bernstein, Peter A.	NY2750	29,70,47
Better, Donald	OH0600	70
Bianculli, Pasquale A.	NY2105	70
Bibace, Kenny	AI0150	70
Bier, Ken	IN1350	70
Billmann, Peter	WI0825	70
Binkley, Paul	CA2950	70
Bishop, Matthew	TX1425	51,70,12A
Bishop, Richard	ME0250	70
Bitetti, Ernesto	IN0900	70
Black, David	MO1950	29,70
Blair, Steve	VT0250	10,47,70
Blake, Cory	VA1500	70
Blakey, David	CA1650	70
Bland, Ronald	CO0550	62D,70
Blaszkiewicz, Michael J.	MI1700	70
Bletstein, Bev R.	OH1860	11,32,61,70
Boling, Mark E.	TN1710	70,29
Bolton, Gregory	FL1745	70
Bonds, Dennis	MS0100	70,47
Bonsignore, Joseph	OH0755	70,43
Book, A. Ryan	NC2210	70,12A,13,41
Book, Ryan	VA0050	70
Boone, Kathleen	WA4550	64B,64C,70,32E,13C
Booth, Doug	CA2100	70,29
Booth, John D.	MO0500	12,44,61,31A,70
Boothe, Greg	UT0190	70
Borczon, Ronald M.	CA0835	70,33
Borczon, Ronald	CA3100	70
Boring, Daniel	PA2550	13,38,70
Boris, William	IL0720	70,29
Bos, Daniel	CA5550	70
Boss, Robert	CA4100	70
Boucher, Remi	AI0190	70
Bouffard, Peter P.	NE0600	70
Bouissieres, Ben	MN0625	70
Boukas, Richard A.	NY2660	61,70,20H,47
Bowden, Dan B.	MA0260	70
Bowen, Ron	AZ0200	64,70
Boyce, Cody	OH2050	70
Boyd, Bruce	KS1250	62A,62B,70,32E,62C
Boyd, Craig E.	NY4050	60,11,47,70,29A
Boyd, Jesse	LA0080	11,13,29,62,70
Boyd, Michael	MS0360	70,62D,41,10,11
Boye, David	NE0200	70
Boyer, Duane	OR0200	70,51
Boyette, Larry J.	NY3550	70,12
Boyle, E. C. McGregor	MD0400	70
Boyle, Mary E.	NY3760	70,33,66D
Boyle, Sharon	IN1400	33,70
Boyles, John	VA0150	70
Bozina, Robert P.	CA1020	13A,70
Bozina, Robert	CA4425	20H,70,13A,14F,14C
Branch, Robert	NM0500	34,70
Brantley, Mitch	MS0370	11,41,70
Brazzel, Russel	IL1100	70,12A
Brazzel, Russell	IL1610	70
Bredice, Vincent	FL1310	70
Breon, Timothy	PA2100	34,35,62D,70
Brettschneider, William	MI0350	70
Brewer, Aaron	IL1612	70
Brewer, Curt	IL1740	70
Breznikar, Joseph	IL2900	70
Britton, Jason	IA0950	13,12A,70,13I
Brodie, Trenton	CA2050	70
Brody, David C.	KS1450	70
Broms, E.	MA0800	70,53
Brookshire, Eddie L.	OH2250	47,70,62D
Brophy, Nicholas	NE0250	70
Brouillette, Luke	LA0550	70
Brown, Bruce	IA1350	70
Brown, Christopher	OK0850	70,51,53,47
Brown, David	NY2950	70
Brown, David	MA0280	70
Brown, Edward	NY0644	70,41
Brown, Edward E.	NY4500	70
Brown, Elizabeth	WA0650	70
Brown, Joel	NY3650	70,42
Brown, Leon	LA0050	70
Brown, Pebber	CA5100	70,62D
Brown, Richard	MS0100	62D,70
Brown, Robert	OH0680	70
Brownlee, Jordan	CA1550	70,11
Bruce, Gary	OK0700	70,65,66F
Brunkhorst, Kevin	AF0150	70,34,29
Bryan, David	LA0650	13G,13C,70
Buck, Dave	AZ0350	70
Buckland, James P.	SC1000	70,13
Budds, Cain	LA0250	70,11,13A,13B,13C
Burak, Jeff	IA1800	70
Burchill, Thomas	TX3000	70,47
Burchill, Thomas	TX2600	70,47
Burdick, David H.	IL1750	10,13,34,70,35
Burgess, Richard	GA1550	70
Burleson, Brett	OH0850	70
Burleson, Brett	OH0350	70
Burleson, Brett	OH1850	70
Burleson, Brett J.	OH2000	70,32E
Burns, Logan	MN0200	70
Burns, Timothy	IL1890	70,47
Buschmeyer, Ralf	AA0050	70
Buser, Charles	WA0960	70
Bustos, Isaac	TX2900	20,70
Buthman, Luke	OK1200	70
Butler, Justin	TN1150	70
Butts, Leon	TX3525	70,11,41
Butturi, Renato	IN1600	70,11,67G,47,29
Buzzelli, Christopher	OH0300	70
Byrne, Tom	MO1950	29,70
Caballero, Jorge	NJ0700	70,51
Cabalo, Eric	CA4700	70,32E,41
Cado, Michael	AG0650	10A,32,47,70
Cahueque, David	CA0960	70
Cahueque, David A.	CA0630	11,13A,70
Cahueque, David	CA3200	11,13A,13B,13C,70
Calandrino, Jo	IL1610	70
Calderon, Javier	WI0815	70,51
Calderon, John	TX0075	70
Callahan, Clare	OH2200	70
Caluda, Glenn	VA1350	70
Camelio, Brian	NY2660	10,70,35C
Cameron, Tristan	AA0020	10A,10C,10D,70
Campos, Homero	TX0100	70
Canafax, Bruce	TX1700	70
Candelaria, Philip	AG0400	70
Candelaria, Philip	AG0070	70,41
Cantu, Ben	CO0275	70,41,42
Cantwell, Guy	CA0400	13A,70
Cantwell, Terry	GA1300	70
Cantwell, Terry	GA1260	13A,13,70,51
Capocchi, Roberto	NM0425	70
Capocchi, Roberto	CO0050	70
Capps, Joe	VT0250	70,34,35A
Capps, Joseph	VT0450	70
Caraway, Dan	IA0400	70
Cardillo, Kenneth	TN0260	70,13,11,12B
Cardin, Michel	AE0100	41,67G,70
Carenbauer, Michael	AR0750	45,51,70,34
Carey, Aaron L.	WV0100	41,62,70
Carey, Charles	NE0050	11,13A,70
Carey, Kevin	MN0620	70
Carlin, Eric	NY2650	70
Carlson, Lennis Jay	CA1020	70,46,29A
Carlson, Risa	DC0170	70
Carmona, Marcos	WA0200	70
Carpente, John	NY2450	33,70
Carroll, Tom	OH0850	47,29,70
Carryer, Steven J.	MI2200	70,29
Carter, Edward L.	AZ0510	70,53
Carter, Joseph	CT0300	70,29A,20G,20H,47
Carter, Terry	CA2600	70
Carter, Terry	CA4450	70
Case, David	OR1050	70,11
Cashen, Jeffrey A.	MA2150	70
Cass, Patrick	MS0320	13,11,47,64,70
Castellani, Joanne C.	NY4320	70
Castellote, Javier	NE0100	70
Catford, Julian	WA0800	70
Cathey, Tully J.	UT0250	13,70
Caulkins, Tamara	WA1200	70,13A,13B,13C,13D
Cavallaro, Giorgia	MD1010	70
Cavallini, Francesco	MI2120	70
Cavanagh, Leo	CA4650	70
Cavender, James L.	AL1160	70,41,46,62D
Cavera, Chris S.	OH2140	34,35,13,70,10
Chamis, Michael	NC0910	70
Champlin, Terry	NY4450	70
Chapdelaine, Michael	NM0450	70,41
Chapman, David	CA3000	11,70,20
Chapman, Michael	PA1050	70
Character, William	GA2175	61,66A,70
Charbonneau, Paul	NY1350	70
Charles, Jean	VT0300	11,70
Charles, Lewis O.	OH1650	70,51
Charnofsky, Jordan	CA3100	70
Charupakorn, Joseph	NY0850	70
Cheesman, Jimmy	CA4450	70
Chekan, Elina	WI0825	70
Chellouf, Linda	PR0100	70,13
Cheramy, Rob	AB0210	70
Chester, Ray G.	MD0650	70
Christ, Chip	TX3000	70
Christensen, Eric	RI0200	70
Christiansen, Corey	UT0300	70
Christiansen, Corey M.	IN0900	70,29
Christiansen, Michael	UT0300	70
Christopulos, Paul	CA4460	70
Churm, George W.	PA1450	70
Cinelli, Dennis J.	NJ0800	67G,70
Ciraldo, Nicholas A.	MS0750	70
Clancy, Gary	ME0340	47,70,53,35
Clancy, Todd A.	MA1650	47,11,70
Clark, Matt	IL2800	70
Clayton, Greg	AI0150	47,70,29
Clemens, Peter	IL1500	70
Clemente, Peter	MA0200	11,13A,13,70,20
Cline, James E.	CO0400	70,11
Cline, James	CO0650	70
Clippert, Thomas	WI1150	70
Coates, Michael	ND0350	70
Coates, Michael	MN0600	70
Cobo, Ricardo	NV0050	70,13B
Cochran, Matthew	GA0625	11,70
Cockerham, Scott	FL0150	41,70,34
Coddington, Robert	OH1400	70,41
Coddington, Robert	WV0760	70
Coehlo, Jerry M.	CA0100	70
Coffey, Matthew	OH0550	70
Cogan, Jeff	CA0960	70,34
Cohen, Pablo	NY1800	70
Collaros, Pandel Lee	WV0100	70,62,66A,46
Collins, Darryl	AD0050	70
Collins, Phillip	CA2150	70
Collins, Roger	CA2440	70
Collver-Jacobson, Glorianne	MA2050	67G,70
Comanescu, Anastasios	CA3600	70
Comartin, Keenan	AG0070	70
Combe, Charles	WI0804	70
Concepcion, Elman O.	FL1550	70
Conn, Troy	NC1900	70
Connie, Meredith	WA0750	70,11,41
Connolly, James	CA5550	70

Index by Area of Teaching Interest

Name	Code	Areas
Conway, Mark	MN1290	70
Cook, Alan	ME0430	70,47
Cook, Casey	OH0850	70
Cook, Ed	WY0130	70
Cooper, Jim	MN1600	70
Cooper, Kevin	CA1850	11,70,13A
Cope, Roger Allen	CA0650	70,42
Cord, Adam	OH1350	70
Corey, Horace E.	NV0100	13A,11,41,70
Cormier, Eugene	AF0050	13A,34,70
Corvino, William	NJ0750	11,70
Cosentino, Mike	IL1050	70
Cote, Alejandro	GA0750	70
Cotroneo, P. J.	NJ0950	29,70,13
Cotter, Steve	CA1000	70,47
Cotton, Wilbur P.	CA1400	70
Coughran, Steven J.	CA1500	47,20,29A,70
Coull, James	SD0550	37,70,13
Coulter, William D.	CA5070	70
Cox, Jeff	TN1600	70,13B
Cox, Robert	OH1600	70
Cox, Robert D.	OH1200	70
Cox, Timothy	OR1010	70
Crabbs, David	IA1400	70
Crabbs, David	IA0550	70
Crago, Bartholemy	AI0210	70
Craig, Monty S.	SC0400	70,46,47,29B
Cramer, Christopher	WI0100	70,41
Crawford, Andy J.	IL1350	70,47
Creaghan, Andrew	AA0020	70
Crist, Timothy D.	AR0110	13,45,10,70
Crittenden, David	MN0800	70
Crittenden, David	MN0250	70
Crook, Keith R.	ME0500	13,70
Crowley, Lisle	UT0150	70,41
Crowson, James	MD0550	70
Cruz, Mark A.	TX3175	70,51
Cullen, David	PA0050	70
Cullen, David T.	PA1250	70
Cullen, David	PA1750	70
Cullen, David	PA3600	70
Cumming, Danielle	MD0800	70,11,41
Cummiskey, Tim	OH1850	70
Curtis, Michael	OH0700	70
Curtis, Michael	OH1350	70
Curtis, Peter	CA3800	11,70,14,20,29
Dadian, Clinton M.	CO0300	70
Dahl-Shanks, Deborah	CA1560	70
Damian, Jon	MA0260	70
Damur, Bill	AA0020	64A,70
D'Angelo, Joe	MA0650	70
Daniels, Mathew	MO1250	70
Darst, John	AZ0460	70,47
DaSilva, Mario	TN1600	70
DaSilva, Mario	TN0100	70
DaSilva, Mario	IN1010	70
Dasilva, Mario	KY1460	47,70,20H,29
Davidson, Ryan	AA0020	70
Davila, William	CA0200	70
Davis, Bob	CA1020	70,20G
Davis, Daniel W.	AZ0440	70
Davis, Dennis	KY0550	70,45,34
Davis, Matt	PA3330	47,70
Davis, Michael	OR1150	70
Davis, Mike	OR0050	70
Davis, Stephen	TN0100	70,72
Dawkins, Kyle	GA1650	70
Dawson, Shane	KS0215	70
Day, Derek	NC2435	70,41
Day, Derek	NC2350	70
Day, James M.	NJ0175	70,42
De Fremery, Phillip	MA1350	70
De Fremery, Phillip	MA1100	70
De La Barrera, Carlos	MI0900	70
Deardorf, Glen	CA3520	70
Dearing, Steven	AG0550	70
Dearman, John	CA1750	70
Dearman, John	CA0835	70
Decker, Michael	MD0850	70,35A,41,47
DeFemery, Philip	MA2100	70
Del Monte, Adam	CA5300	70
Dell, Craig	WA0600	70
Delpriora, Mark	NY2150	70
Delto, Byron	CA1960	34,70,13A
Demas, John	FL0930	70
Demas, John	FL2050	70
DeMicco, Mike	NY4450	70
Denman, Matt	OK1200	70
Dennewitz, John K.	RI0101	70
Denny, Michael	OR1050	70,47,29,29A
DeRoche, Brad	MI0550	70
DeRoche, Brad	MI0400	70
DeRoche, Brad	MI1850	70
Deuson, Nicolas	GA0050	13,34A,34D,35G,70
Devine, David	CO0550	70
Devine, Jeff S.	CA0100	70
Di Tomaso, Nick	AI0200	70
Diaz, Reuben	CA1280	70
Dicarlo, Tom V.	PA1850	70,62D
DiChiacchio, Joshua	CA3250	70
Dickenson, Andrew	MD0175	11,70
Dickert, Lewis H.	SC1200	70,53,29,13A,14
Dievendorf, Matthew	DC0170	70
DiFusco, Salvatore	MA0260	70
Digman, Gary	CA4460	70
Dimow, Carl	ME0250	70
Dina, James L.	CT0150	70
Dinger, Gregory	NY4300	13,12A,70
Dixon, Patricia	NC2500	70,20H
Dixon, Rich	UT0190	70,47,34,35
Doan, John	OR1300	70
Doan, John	OR1250	70
Dobby, Tim	AI0150	70
Dodson, Gordon	AL0400	70
Dollar, Kevin	NC0750	70
Domine, James	CA2700	38,70
Donegani, Denis	AG0400	70
Doody, Jeremy	AA0080	70
Dorsey, Sam Brian	VA0950	12A,70
Dragonetti, John	PA1550	70,41
Drake, Melvyn	NY4250	70,36
Draper, Frederick	NY5000	70
Druck, William	PA3710	70
Drummond, Evan	NY3725	70
Drummond, Evan E.	NY3717	12A,13A,70
Ducharme, Jerome	AI0150	70
Duckworth, James	NC0350	70
Duenas, David	CA4425	70
Dunaway, Lourdes	TN1250	11,66A,70
Dunn, Alexander	AB0210	70
Dunn, Alexander	AB0150	70,13A
Dunn, Christopher	MS0570	11,35,70
Dunn, Robert	IA0700	70,62D
Dunn, Ron	CA1550	70,14
Dunne, Matthew R.	TX3530	70,29,47,35
Dunson, Judith	NC1300	70
Durkee, James	WA0050	70
Durkee, Jim	WA1400	70
Dyament, Lee	MI2200	70
Dyotte, Claude	AI0220	70
Dziuba, Mark	NY3760	70,29A,47,35C
Earp, Jonathan	AG0050	70
Ebert, Kevin	OH2550	70,11
Ebner, Craig	PA3250	29,70
Eckhart, Michael	NJ0975	13A,34,70
Eden, Gregg	NE0160	70
Egger, Cynthia	MO1010	70
Ehret, Don	AA0020	70
Eisel, Gunnar	CA1900	70
Elgart, Matthew P.	CA0500	70,42
Elgart, Matthew	CA0830	70,10,13
Ellias, Rod	AI0070	13,47,70,53,29
Ellinger, John	MN0300	41,34,70
Elliott, Scott	WV0600	70
Elliott, Scott	WV0750	70,47
Emerson, Smokey	AR0850	70
Emmons, Timothy	CA5150	70,62D
Encke, William	IA1450	70,46,47,29
Engberg, Michael	CO0100	13,70,41,35,47
Engel, T. G.	TN0950	70
England, George	CA0835	70
Englar, Marcia L.	PA2350	70,29
English, Joseph R.	MO0050	70
Enloe, Luther D.	GA0300	70,11
Erastostene, Mario	FL1310	70,35B
Erbsen, Wayne	NC2550	20G,70
Erickson, James M.	NY4060	13,12A,11,70
Eschete, Ron	CA0815	29,70
Eschete, Ron	CA0825	70
Espinoza, Juan	AZ0150	70
Ess, Michael	VA1600	70,29,47
Estes, Charlie	IN0400	70
Eylands, Kristian	ND0500	70
Fader, Oren	NY2150	70
Fairfield, Patrick K.	MI1850	11,15,20,70
Falcon, Richard	KS0265	70
Falkenstein, Richard	NY0400	11,12A,70
Fanella, Keith	NJ0500	70
Farber, Mitchell	FL1300	70
Fasola, Bryan	CA0835	70
Favis, Angelo L.	IL1150	70
Feasley, William	MD0150	70
Feasly, William	WV0550	70,13C
Feder, Janet	CO0560	10,70,12A,13A,53
Feingold, David W.	WA1250	11,70,13
Fennell, Arden	CO0600	70
Ferguson, Charles Alan	CA1250	10,70
Ferguson, Charles A.	CA4900	70
Ferguson, James	CA1760	13A,11,70
Ferguson, Robert	IN0905	70
Ferguson, Roger L.	WA0600	70
Ferla, James	PA0550	70
Ferlazzo, Gaetano	FL0680	70
Ferrara, Lawrence David	CA4200	70
Ferrara, Lawrence	CA4150	70
Ferrara, Lawrence	CA1020	11,70,34C
Ferrier, Robert A.	MA2000	70
Ferrier, Robert	MA1100	70,53,29,13C
Fewell, A. Garrison	MA0260	70
Fiegl, Ryan	CO0100	70
Figueiroa, Joao Paulo M.	DC0050	70
Filbrun, John	OH0450	70
Finkelstein, Marc	NJ0550	32A,32B,66A,70
Finn, Jon	MA0260	70
Fiorentino, Mike	CA5353	70,62A
Fisk, Eliot	MA1400	70
Fisk, Peter	CA2390	70
Fittipaldi, Thomas	NY2500	36,66D,67,70,11
Fitzer, Harvey	KS0570	70
Fitzhugh, William	TN1400	11,70
Fiuczynski, David	MA0260	70
Flandorffer, Frank M.	PA1850	70
Fleeman, Rod	MO1810	70
Fleeman, Rodney	KS0590	70
Flegel, James	MN0950	70
Flegel, James	MN1620	70
Fleming, Mark	IA1170	70
Flick, Daniel K.	FL1550	70,13,42
Flippin, Thomas	NY5000	70,11
Flores, Richard A.	CA0850	70
Flores, Rick	CA0900	13A,70
Florez, Anthony	IL1080	11,34,65,70,13
Flynn, Patrick	SC0650	70
Fogleman, Matthew	PA3710	70
Fogler, Michael	KY0610	70
Forestier, Michel	AA0035	70
Forestier, Michel	AA0020	70
Forman, Bruce	CA5300	70
Forshee, Zane	NC1650	70
Forshee, Zane F.	MD1000	70
Forte, Chris	IL0720	70
Foster, Adam	GA1990	70
Foster, Eric	CA2960	70
Fowler, Francois	OH2600	70
Fowler, Michael R.	OK1450	70
Fox, Jon	TX1600	70,53,13B
Fox, Marilyn F.	NY2550	70,66D
Fox, Stuart	CA0510	42,70,55B,67G
Francis, Patrick	CA4400	70
Frandsen, Lars	NY2900	12A,13,70
Frandsen, Lars	NY0500	41,70
Frank, Adam	GA2130	70
Frank, Elliot	NC0650	70,42
Franken, Fred	IL2300	70
Frantz, Jeremy	PA2950	70,41,47
Frantz, Jeremy	PA1350	70
Franzen, David	OR0850	70
Frary, Peter Kun	HI0160	13,11,12A,70,34
Fraser, Robert	OH0650	70
Fraser, Robert W.	OH2150	70
Fratino, Michael A.	NY3775	70,41
Frederiksen, Clifford	WI0800	70
French, Bruce	AG0350	70
French, Mark	MA0260	70
Fresonke, Michael	OK0750	13A,70,14C,41
Friesen, Milton	CA1860	11,36,70

757

Index by Area of Teaching Interest

Name	Code	Areas
Frigon, Matthew A.	CA4850	70
Frizzell, Shannon	AA0080	70
Froman, James	PA0100	70,29
Fuchs, Stuart	NY0400	70
Fujita, Tomohisa	MA0260	70
Gaboury, Tony	MA0260	70
Gagnon, Claude	AI0190	70
Galambos, Joe	CA3250	70
Galen, Ron	CA2450	70
Galen, Ronald	CA1450	11,70
Galvan, Gary	PA1830	12,70,29A,34A
Gangi, Jonathan	SC1100	11,70
Garcia, Eduardo	CA0847	20H,11,70
Garcia, Jeremy	TX2310	70,11,41
Garcia, Paulinho	IL0550	47,70
Gardner, TK	CA0815	70
Garry, Kevin M.	CO0400	70,13A,11,12A,14C
Garvin, Marc	TX1400	70
Gaschen, Terry	TX3450	70
Gaspero, Carmen	PA0125	70,29
Gates, Jim	CA3975	70
Gaudino, Brian J.	LA0760	70
Gauthier, Michael A.	AI0200	70
Gauthier, Michael	AI0150	70,29
Gauthier, Michael	AI0050	70,29A,47,10D
Gearey, Jon	AI0150	29,70
Gehle, Keith	GA2000	70
Gekker, Chris	MD1010	70,29
Gendelman, Martin	GA0950	10,13,70,34A
Gendron, Mychal	RI0300	70,42
Gestwicki, Tom	NY3725	70
Giacabetti, Thomas	PA3330	47,70,29
Giacabetti, Tom	NJ1050	41,53,70
Giardina, David	CT0350	62,70
Gibson, Gary	IA0930	70
Gibson, Robbie L.	AL0345	11,70
Gibson, Robert L.	AL1050	70
Gifford, Troy S.	FL2120	11,13,46,70,10
Giglid, Joseph	NY2400	70,29
Gildea, Dan	OR0850	70,29
Gilmore, David	MA0260	70
Gimble, Richard	TX1600	62D,70,53,35B
Ginn, Glenn A.	KY0900	29,70
Girardi, Steve	NJ0400	70
Glanton, Howard	KS0500	70
Glanton, Howard	KS0200	70
Gleason, Jeff	CO0550	70
Glenn, Richard B.	CA3350	70
Glise, Anthony	MO1800	70
Glise, Anthony	MO0850	70,41,42
Godwin, L. Mark	TN0100	70
Goins, Wayne	KS0650	46,47,70,29
Goldberg, Julie	IL1890	70
Goldberg, Julie	IL2100	70,41
Goldberg, Julie	IL3450	70
Goldberg, Michael K.	CA5000	70
Golden, Arthur	CA3460	70
Golden, Lyman	SC1080	70
Golden, Lyman	SC0700	70
Golden, Lyman	SC0050	10,51,70
Goldsmith, Pamela	OR0450	70
Goldsmith, Robert	HI0050	70
Goldspiel, Alan	AL1200	70,13C,13B,51
Goldstein, Rich	CT0050	70
Goldstein, Richard	CT0650	70,29
Goluses, Nicholas	NY1100	70
Gonzales, Carlos	CA3375	70
Gonzales, Carlos	CA5360	70
Gonzalez, Joe	TX3410	70
Gonzalez, Rene	FL1900	41,70
Goodman, Donald	VT0200	46,70
Goodrick, Mick	MA0260	70
Gorklo, Dan	CO0150	70
Gould, Matt	AG0070	70,41
Goynes, Tim	TX2955	70
Grandstaff, Neil	OR0700	70
Gravelle, Darren	CA0630	70
Graves, James	FL0400	70
Gray, Julian F.	MD0650	70
Gray, Serap Bastepe	MD0300	70,13A
Gray, Sterling	KS1450	70
Green, Larry	UT0050	70
Green, Sharon	MI1600	32,61,70
Green, Stuart	CA5150	29,70
Green, Stuart	CA0845	32,70
Greene, Barry	FL1950	47,70,29
Greene, Richard C.	GA0850	70,13C,11,13E,12A
Greenfield, Thomas A.	NY3730	70
Greer, Clare	TX0700	70
Greer, Larry	TX0125	13,14C,29,46,70
Greeson, James R.	AR0700	13,10,70,47
Greif, Matthew	CA0805	70
Greif, Matthew	CA2650	70
Grief, Matt	CA1750	70
Griffith, Joan E.	MN0950	47,70,29,10,62D
Griffith, Joan	MN1625	11,70,29
Grigoriev, Igor	CA0859	70,53
Grigsby, Brett	NY3650	70
Grimm, James	MO2000	70,35A
Grimm, Stephen	WI1150	70
Grisanti, Susan	TX1550	70
Grismore, Steve	IL0100	70
Grismore, Steve	IL0300	70
Grohovac, Janet	TX3100	70,32E
Grove, Paul	WA1350	70
Grove, Paul	WA0400	70,13A,13B,13C
Grove, Paul	ID0140	51,70
Gruber, Nikolas	MN0600	70
Guillen, Jorge	DC0350	70
Guillen, Seth	TN0050	70
Gunderson, Geoff	IA0500	70
Gunderson, Geoff	SD0050	70
Gustofson, Don	IL0300	66A,70
Guthrie, Robert	TX2400	70
Haarhues, Charles D.	CO0100	10,13,29,70,11
Haas, Karl	CA0270	70
Habib, Mark	AL1195	70
Hadley, Susan J.	PA3100	70,33,11,66D
Hadsell, Nancy A.	TX3300	33,70
Hagedorn, Joseph	WI0845	70
Hagerty, Matthew	RI0250	70
Hague, Joylyn	IN1650	70
Hale, Adam	TN0260	70
Hale, Kris	VA0750	70
Hale, Kristopher	VA1100	70
Haley, Geordie	AF0120	70
Hall, John	MI1750	70
Hall, Kenneth	VA1350	70
Hall, Stefan	WI0808	70
Hamel, Gabriel	AI0190	47,29,70
Hamersma, Carol	NJ1160	11,14C,29A,70
Hamilton, Frederick	TX3420	47,70,53,29
Hamlin, John	KS0560	70
Hammett, Larry D.	OK1350	70,29A
Hamrick, Mark	WV0800	70
Hand, Frederic	VT0050	70
Hand, Frederic	NY2250	70
Hand, Frederic	NY3785	70
Handy, Gabriel	NJ1400	70
Hanlon, Jake	AF0150	29,70
Hanlon, Jeff	AG0250	70,41
Hannah, Barry	TN0900	70,42
Hansel, Robert	TN1350	70
Hansen, Charles	MA0260	70
Hanser, Kirk	MO1900	70
Hanson, David B.	OH0950	62D,70
Hanson, Kevin	PA3330	70
Hanson, Ross	OR1020	70
Haque, Fareed	IL2200	70,53,29
Harding, Kevin	VA1500	70
Harding, Mark	VT0100	62D,70
Harmon, Jim	CA4450	70
Harrell, James	MD0170	70
Harrigan, Robert	MA0260	70
Harris, Dennis	TX3527	70
Harris, Dennis	TX1850	51,70
Harris, Jonathan	FL0450	70
Harris, Zacc	MN0800	62D,70
Harrison, Clint	MO0400	70
Hart, Kevin S.	WY0200	70
Hart, Richard	MA0260	70
Hartley, Brian	CT0300	70
Hartman, Andrew	OH1200	70
Harvey, Anthony	MD1100	70
Harvey, James	TX0075	11,70
Harwood, Carey	NC0750	70
Haskell, Peter	NY1150	70
Haskin, Steven	MN1050	70
Hastings, Richard	CA1750	70
Hatfield, Clancy	KY0650	70
Hatfield, Grover 'Clancy'	WV0400	70
Hauser, Michael	MN1625	70
Hauser, Michael S.	MN0950	70
Hawthorne, Leroy	LA0100	70,20G,16,47
Hayden, Ron	KY0250	70
Haydon, Rick	IL2910	70,29,35G,53,47
Head, Brian	CA5300	13,70
Healy, Eddie	TX0700	70,11
Hearn, William	GA0500	11,41,70,20
Hearrell, Steve	KS1400	70
Heavin, Hadley	NE0610	70
Hedger, John	KY0300	70
Hedger, John R.	KY1350	70
Hedquist, Seth	IA1350	70
Heikalo, Daniel	AF0050	70
Helble, Mitch	CO0650	70
Helton, Johann	ID0050	70
Henderson, Chip	TN1680	70,29A,47
Henderson, Paul	TN1400	11,70
Henderson, Paul	TN0100	70
Hennings, Dieter	KY1450	70
Henry, Paul	IL0730	70
Henry, Paul	IN0005	70,13
Herberman, Steve	MD0850	70
Hernandez, Thomas	CA2050	70
Hesse, Scott A.	IL0800	70
Hicks, Charles	AR0250	70
Higgins, Michael	CA0825	70
Higham, Peter	AE0050	70
Hii, Philip	TX0550	41,70
Hii, Philip	TX2930	70
Hildebrand, Virginia	MD0060	70,67D
Hilson, Mike	SD0600	70
Hilson, Mike	NE0460	70
Himmelhoch, Seth	NJ1400	70
Hinesley, Terry	IA1390	70
Hirschheimer, Evan	CA2650	70
Hixson, Wesley	IL0850	70
Hlady, Craig M.	MA0260	70
Hlus, Don	AB0060	35A,70
Hmura, Harry	IL0720	70
Hoag, Bret	MI1830	70,20
Hoag, Bret	MI1750	70,41,11
Hoats, Charlie	MI1050	70,62D
Hochstetler, Tim	IN0910	70
Hodan, Daniel	TX0370	70,35G
Hoeffgen, Thomas E.	KS1200	70
Hoeflicker, Cale	IN0500	70
Hofbauer, Eric	RI0300	29,47,70
Hoffelt, Tim	ND0350	70
Hofmeister, Walter	AJ0150	70
Hofsess, Dustin	NC0550	70
Hogarth, Thaddeus	MA0260	70
Hogue, Harry	MD0360	70,12A,63D,13,11
Hole, Kristopher	VA0350	70
Hollerbach, Peter	NY0270	13A,11,14,47,70
Holmes, Glenn	OH0650	62D,70
Holzman, Adam	TX3510	70
Holzman, Bruce	FL0850	70
Homan, Steve	CA0150	70
Homan, Steven	CA0840	29,70
Hontz, James R.	MD0475	70
Hontz, James	MD0300	70
Hontz, James	PA0950	70,13A
Hontz, James R.	PA1400	70
Hooan, Dan	TX1725	11,70
Hopson, John Casey	CA5550	70
Horel, Charles	GA0950	10A,70,13A,13C
Horne, John	OH1900	70,29,47
Houghton, Amy	MS0100	70,42
Howard, Chris	MO0750	47,70
Howell, Michael W.	IN1800	41,67D,70
Howland, Stephen	WA0650	70
Hudson, Roger	TN1100	70
Huerta, Edgar	IL1085	70
Huff, Adam	IL1300	70
Hughes, Scott	ME0340	70,47
Hulihan, Charles	AZ0350	70,41,32E,32F
Hull, Daniel	SC0710	70
Hull, Daniel	SC0420	70,11
Hull, Michael	IL1090	70
Hull, Michael	IL0400	70
Hummer, Ken	OH1330	11,70
Humphrey, Roger G.	MI1800	70
Hunan, Steve	CA1500	47,29B,70
Hunt, Justin Trevor	MS0850	70

Index by Area of Teaching Interest

Name	Code	Areas
Hunt, Trevor	MS0580	11,70,13C,13G
Hunter, James	NC2650	70
Hyde, Michael	MI0300	70
Hyde, Michael	MI1050	70
Hyman, Victor G.	NH0110	70
Hynes, Tom	CA1000	13,29,47,53,70
Hyslop, Greg	NC0910	70,29
Hyslop, Greg	NC0900	70
Iguina, Jose R.	PR0150	13A,13C,11,70
Ihde, Mike	MA0260	70
Ikner, W. Joseph	AL0200	70,11
Imamovic, Almer	CA3300	70
Imsand, Patrick K.	AL1300	70,11,51
Ingwerson, John	MS0300	70,11
Inoue, Satoshi	NY2660	70,47
Insalaco, Vince	PA3700	70
Irving, David	TX0550	47,70,46,29A,37
Isaacs, David	TN1400	70,11,35G,45
Isaacs, David	CA0859	70
Isachsen, Sten Y.	NY3600	67D,41,70,34,29
Isbin, Sharon	NY1900	70
Iula, Dave	OR0600	70
Iznaola, Ricardo	CO0900	70,41
Izquierdo, Rene	WI0825	70,41
Jackson, Ernie	NY3250	34,35,70
Jackson, Milton	AR0810	13,11,49,63,70
Jacobowski, Richard	NY4200	70
Jacobson, Steve	IL1520	47,70
Jacques, David	AI0190	70
James, Douglas	NC0050	70,51
Jamison, Phil A.	NC2550	72,70,20G
Jankovic, Petar S.	IN0900	70
Janson, Peter	MA2010	70,29,11,20,47
Jemmott, Thomas	FL2050	29,70
Jenkins, E. Morgan	MD0450	64A,64E,70,29B
Jenkins, Tim G.	MD0520	70,41
Jentsch, Christopher	NY4060	13,12A,11,70
Jewell, Joe	CA1900	47,70,29
Jimenez, Carlos	AI0150	70,29
Jirak, Steve	KS0150	70
Johansen, Keven W.	UT0250	70,29,11
Johanson, Bryan	OR0850	70,13,41,11,10
Johns, Brian	IN1100	70
Johns, John	TN1850	41,70,67G
Johnson, Aaron E.	MO1250	10A,34D,13,70
Johnson, Alphonso	CA0510	70,47
Johnson, Christopher R.	SD0500	70
Johnson, Dylan	CA1510	11,70
Johnson, Henry	IL0550	47,70
Johnson, James	TX2250	70
Johnson, Jamie	IN1560	70
Johnson, Ken	IN1025	13E,70
Johnson, Scott	OK1330	70
Johnson, Scott	MA0260	70
Johnson, Thomas M.	TX3420	70
Johnston, Noel H.	TX3420	70,53,29
Johnston, Randy B.	NY2750	29,70,47
Johnston, Randy	NY3785	70
Johnston, Randy	CT0650	47,70,53
Johnston, Steve	KS1300	70
Johnstone, John	ME0200	70
Jones, Emily	FL0040	11,12A,13C,41,70
Jones, Fernando	IL0720	70
Jones, M. Douglas	KY1460	20G,67D,70
Jones, Nathan	TX2570	70
Jones, Richard	NE0450	50,65,34,70
Jones, Stephen F.	CA3500	51,70
Jones, Steve	MD0150	70
Jonker, Jacob	MN1600	70,41
Joseph, Alan	CO0900	70,47
Joyce, J. Patrick	WV0300	70,12,42
Judson, Tohm	NC2700	10B,62D,70,34,35
Julia, Luis Enrique	PR0115	70
Jurek, Shaun	MD0700	70
Juris, Vic	NJ1130	70,29
Juris, Vic	NY2660	70,47
Justus, Keith	TX0550	70,13C,14C,29B
Kachian, Christopher	MN1625	11,70,20
Kaiser, Tyler	WI0860	10A,70
Kaiser, Tyler	MN0450	70,10,13
Kammin, Benjamin	WI1150	70
Kanengiser, William	CA5300	70
Kapner, Harriet H.	NY2550	70,13A,13B,13C
Karas, Ted	KY1000	70
Karsh, Ken	PA0500	70
Karsh, Kenneth M.	PA1050	70,29B
Kasper, Julien	MA0260	70
Kassner, Eli	AG0450	70
Katz, Brian	AG0650	70,53
Kauffman, Irvin C.	PA1600	70,51
Kaufman, Jacob	KS0215	70
Kay, Lalene	OH0700	70,33
Kay, Lalene D.	OH0200	33,70
Kaye, Jordan	IL2350	70
Kearney, Joe	CA0200	13,70,35
Kearney, Joseph B.	CA1265	10A,29,13B,70
Keaton, Kenneth D.	FL0650	60,12A,41,67D,70
Keifer, John	TX1450	70
Kelley, Linda	IL2775	70
Kelley, Pat	CA5300	70
Kellogg, Robbie	IL1850	70
Kelly, James J.	NJ0750	12A,13,29A,47,70
Kelly, James	MA0260	70
Kelly, Linda	IL1890	70
Kelly, Patrick	TX0300	70
Kendrick, Richard	CA3320	70
Kenefic, Richard	ME0440	70
Kennedy, Charles	AL0630	11,70,66A,61
Kennedy, Mike	PA3330	70
Kennedy, Rebecca	KS0900	70
Kennedy, Rebecca	TX1750	70
Kenney, James	PA3550	70
Kerber, Patrick C.	LA0650	70,11
Ketcheson, Dale	AA0200	70
Kiehn, Mark T.	WI0808	32A,66D,70,63A,32B
Kikta, Thomas J.	PA1050	70,34D,35C
Kimball, James W.	NY3730	13A,11,14,67E,70
Kimball, Newel	ID0060	70
Kimbrough, Jerome	TN1850	70
Kimler, Wayne	MO0650	51,70
Kimlicko, Franklin	TX3370	70,34,35C
Kimmel, Pamela J.	IL0550	13A,70
King, Troy	MD0850	70,51
Kinnaman, Hal	HI0155	70
Klasinc, Natasa	MS0420	70
Klasinc-Loncar, Natasa	MS0200	70
Klein, Doug	ND0050	70,41
Klentz, Richard	NE0300	70
Klickstein, Gerald	MD0650	70
Klinghofer, Rhona	CA1750	70
Klugh, Vaughn	AG0550	70,29,46,61
Knepp, Richard	GA2300	70,41,12A
Knight, Adam	GA0900	70
Knight, Alan	SC0600	70,11,20
Knox, Daniel	AL0750	11,70,63,64,13A
Kobza, Tim	CA5300	70,29
Koch, Mark	PA1050	70
Koch, Thomas	FL0680	70
Kodzas, Peter	NY2650	70
Koelble, Bobby	FL1550	70,42
Komodore, Alex	CO0550	70
Konecky, Larry	MS0050	13,62,70,34
Konsbruck, James	IN1750	70,35G
Kooken, Brian	MD0475	70
Koonce, Frank W.	AZ0100	70
Koons, Jessie	TN0450	70
Koonse, Larry	CA0835	70
Koonse, Larry	CA0510	70,47
Kopfstein-Penk, Alicia	DC0010	70,12,13C,11
Koslovsky, Marc S.	NY2550	70,10D
Kostelnik, Steve	TX2650	70
Kozak, Pete E.	OR0700	70
Kozic, Thomas	PA2550	70
Kozic, Tom	PA1850	70
Kozubek, Michael	CA0250	70,13A
Kozubek, Michael	CA2600	70
Krajewski, Michael J.	MN1120	70,47,29
Kramer, Jacob	CA3400	70
Krantz, Allen M.	PA3250	70
Krantz, Wayne M.	NY2750	29,70,49
Kratz, Jay	PA2800	70
Krause, William Craig	VA0550	70,11,12A,20H,35E
Kriehn, Richard	WA1150	11,70,62A,34
Krolikowski, Lucas	IL1750	41,70
Kubica, Robert	AG0500	70
Kuczynski, Christopher	PA0650	70
Kunkel, Gerald	MD1010	70
Kunkel, Gerard F.	DC0150	70
Labrecque, Kenneth J.	ME0150	70
Lacan, Dale	OH1000	70
Lach, Malgorzata	MA1350	70,13A
Lachew, Joseph	NV0150	70
LaCreta, Joseph	MA2100	70
LaCreta, Joseph	MA1100	70,13A
Ladd, Chris	CT0650	70
Ladd, Christopher	CT0050	70
Lafreniere, Andy	CT0800	41,70
Lagana, Thomas V.	MD1000	70
Lagana, Tom	MD0850	70,29A,51
Laguana, Carlos	GU0500	70
Lambert, Gary	IA0800	70
Lambson, Nick	CA2250	70,41,35G
Lammers, James	MO1810	70
Landolfi, Dominic J.	CT0250	70
Landry, Jacques	PR0100	47,70
Landsberg, Paul	AB0070	13A,70,53,47,29
Lange, James	WV0560	70
Lange, Richard	MI0050	41,70
Langley, Mike	IA1100	70
Lano, Joe	NV0050	70
Lapidus, Benjamin	NY0630	14,70,20H
Lappin, Donald P.	MA0260	70
LaQuatra, Jeff	CO0625	70
LaQuatra, Jeff	CO0550	70
Large, Duane	PA3250	70
Larison, Adam	FL0350	70,11
Larrabee, Adam	VA1600	70
Larson, Glen	MN1280	70
Larson, Richard	IL0150	70,41
Lassiter, Stan	TN0100	70
Lassiter, Stan	TN0550	70
Latarski, Donald	OR1050	70,35G,41
Laufersweiler, Jonathan	MO1110	70
Laureano, Orlando	PR0115	70
Laureano, Victor O.	PR0150	70,51
Lawrie, Jim	TX0400	70
Lay, David	TN1200	70
Layne, Darin	TX2170	70
Leach, Troy	TN1660	70
Leasure, Michael	FL0150	29,70
Leath, Nate R.	VA1850	62A,70
Leathwood, Jonathan	CO0900	70,41,13D,10A,13E
LeBlanc, Paul	TX3420	70
Leblanc, Stuart W.	LA0300	70
Leblond, Louis	AI0190	70
Leclerc, Francois	AI0190	70
Lee, Russell	UT0325	70
Lefever, Todd	AA0040	70
LeFevre, Michael	WA1100	70
Leighton, Mark	MA0800	70
Leighton, Mark	ME0250	70
Leisner, David	NY2150	70
Leiter, Joseph W.	MO0800	70
Lenihan, William	MO1900	70,29
Lentini, James P.	OH1450	13,10,70,34
Leonard, George	RI0200	70
Leonard, Jeff	OR0400	70,10B,45
Leonard, Stephen	NY2550	70
Leone, Aaron	NJ0760	70
Lerner, Peter	IL0720	29,70,10
Leslie, Justin	UT0325	70
Lessing, Arnold	CA4450	70
Lester, David T.	OH2140	70,35,45,42
Letkemann, David	AC0050	70
Levenson, Warren	MA0400	70
Lewis, Daniel	MD0175	11,13,66D,70
Lewis, Kate	CA2750	70
Lewis, Rod	SC0620	13,70,40
Lezcano, Jose	NH0150	41,70,20H
Libertino, Dan	CA2960	70
Lile, Drew	NC0600	70
Liles, Reese	TX2800	70
Lindquist, George	WI1150	41,70
Lindquist, George C.	WI0835	41,70
Lindquist, George	WI0865	70
Lingen, Peter	IA0950	42,67G,70
Linke, David	WI0825	70,29,47
Linton, Andrew	TN0850	16,70
Lipman, Agnes	AA0032	70
Lippincott, Tom	FL0700	70,51
Litch, Randy	WA0750	70
Lockwood, Tom	MI0300	64E,70
Lofsky, Lorne	AG0650	47,70
Loo, Ronald	HI0300	70
Looker, Wendy	NC0910	60,36,70,12A,13A
LoPiccolo, Joseph	CA1265	70

Name	Code	Areas
LoPiccolo, Joseph	CA3200	14,70
Loranger, Gene	ID0075	70
Lorenz, Kevin	NC1450	70,41
Lorusso, James	NY2200	70
Lorusso, James	NY2400	70
Lorusso, James	NY5000	70
Lorusso, Mary Ann	NY2400	67D,70
Lothringer, Peter	MN1500	70,10A,13
Lotsberg, Carl	AA0100	70
Loughman, Greg	ME0340	70
Lovely, Brian	OH0680	29,10C,10D,70,35
Lowry, Gary	OR0250	70
Luciano, Stephen	FL1700	70
Lugo, Eddy	FL1650	70
Lugo, Edward	FL0930	70,11
Lugo, Edward	FL0800	70
Lund, Matthew R.	TN1100	70
Lunn, Robert A.	MI1180	13,70
Lunsetter, Gene	MN1270	70
Lupica, Anthony J.	CA1700	36,38,13B,70,61
Lydy, Laura	IN0905	70,41
Lynch, Phil	WA1100	70
Lynch, Phil	WA1300	70
Lyon, Leslie	TX2200	11,70
Lyon, Leslie	TX1900	70
Lyons, Glenn	PA3600	51,70
Lyons, Shawn	AK0100	70
MacDonald, Andrew	AI0050	13,10F,10,45,70
MacDonald, Ben	WI0810	70
MacEachen, Ed	NY2660	70
Machleder, Anton	NY2500	70,53
Machleder, Anton M.	NY1700	70
Mackie, Henry	LA0800	70,29A,29B,47
MacMasters, Dan	MO0200	70
Macmillan, Scott	AF0100	70
Madriguera, Enric	TX0700	62,70,11,12A
Madrya, Paul	AC0050	70
Magurany, John	IL1500	70
Mahe, Darren	AB0070	13,47,70,53,12A
Mahon, Brad	AA0050	70
Maier, Ralph	AA0050	70
Maier, Ralph	AA0150	70,41,12,14
Mainland, Timothy L.	WV0200	13,10,70,10F,62
Maker, Bill	RI0200	42,70
Malfroid, Larry	MI1050	70
Mallard, Manley	IL1750	41,70,34
Maloney, Chris	FL1450	70
Mandel, Jac	SC0620	70
Manderville, Kevin	AL0450	70
Maness, G. Andrew	MA0260	70
Manley, David	PA1150	47,29,53,70
Mann, Erik	PA1200	70
Mann, Erik	OH0600	70
Mann, Ted	NH0150	70,14C,13D
Mannino, Marc P.	FL1745	70
Mantegna, John	VT0450	70
Manuele, James	OR0150	70
Marasco, John	MA0260	70
Marcinizyn, John	PA0600	13,10,70
Marcinizyn, John	PA0550	70
Marcinizyn, John	PA3000	10,70
Marino, Mark	NY2105	70
Mark, Julie	UT0400	70
Markovich, Frank	CA4625	70,34
Marques, Albert	CA1950	70
Marron, James	OH2150	70
Marschner, Joseph A.	MD0450	11,45,70,34
Marshall, John	WA0250	62C,70,32E,41,32F
Marshall, Jonathan	MI0520	70
Marshall, Jonathan	MI0850	13A,70
Marshall, Wolf	CA5031	29,70
Martin, Danny Ray	TN0150	70,42,29,41
Martin, David	MI1050	70
Martin, David J.	MI0350	70
Martin, Jared	TN0580	70,13A,31A
Martin, John	KY1550	70,11,34B,34G,41
Martinez, Kurt	TX3525	11,70,41
Masakowski, Steve	LA0800	70,35B,35C,29B,47
Mason, John	MA2100	70
Mason, John	MA1100	70,35C,35G
Massanari, Jeff	CA5000	70
Masters, Martha	CA2800	70
Masters, Martha	CA0815	70
Matascik, Sheri L.	TN1000	13,10,70,10B,13H
Mateus, Cesar	CA5360	70
Mathews, Robert P.	CA6050	13,64,48,70
Mathieu, Phil	MD0550	70
Matthews, Mark	FL1650	10B,13A,34B,35A,70
Mattina, Fernando	PR0115	29,70
Mattingly, Douglas	MD0060	13,29,35,70
Mattingly, Stephen P.	KY1500	70
Mattingly, Stephen	IN1010	70
Mattison, Travis	IL2970	70,11
Mattison, Travis	IL1500	70,11,13A
Maxson, Mark D.	UT0350	34,70
Maxwell, Mark A.	IL0750	70
May, Ed	ID0060	70
Mayer, Paul	CA4450	70
Mayes, Joseph	NJ1050	41,67,70
Mayeur, Robert G.	CA2750	70
Maynard, Seth	WV0250	70
Mazak, Grant	TX3175	70,51
Mazzoccoli, Jesse	MO0300	70
McCabe, Brent Poe	MT0450	37,11,32E,70
McCann, Jesse	OR0850	70
McCann, Jesse S.	OR0800	70,13A,11
McCarthy, Glen	VA0450	70,32C
McCartney, Ben	AZ0480	70
McChesney, Michael	CA5510	70
McClellan, John	MO0650	70
McClellan, John	MO1950	42,70
McComb, Thomas	WI0850	70
McConnell, Miles	IA0250	11,70
McCullough, Daryl	TX3600	63,70
McCusker, Philip	DC0010	70
McCutcheon, James R.	OH2250	70,42
McCutcheon, James	OH2500	70
McCutcheon, Peter	AI0200	70
McEvoy, Andrew	VA1150	70
McFadden, Jeff	AG0200	70
McFadden, Jeffrey	AG0450	70
McFee, Cathy	PA2710	70
McGann, Daniel	NY2450	13A,13,12A,70
McGillvray, Bruce	AG0350	70
McGlone, Jeff	AZ0400	70,13A
McGuire, Dennis	MN1400	70,50,29
McGuire, James	MN1000	70
McGuire, James	MN0750	70
McIntyre, Chris	AA0025	70,34
McKee, Pat	TX1600	70,53
McKenna, Terry	AG0600	70,67D
McKnight, Danny	TX1450	70
McLain, Michael	TN0100	70,53,35B
McLean, John T.	IL2050	70,29,53
McLean, John	IL0550	47,70,29
McLouth, Ryan	MO0100	53,70
McLure, Richard	TX0370	35G,57,53,70
McLure, Richard	TX3420	70
McMickle, Doug	OR0750	70,41
McNaughton, Barry	CA3800	70
McNeish, James	CT0100	70,35C
McPike, Brent G.	IN0800	70
Meeker, Jared	CA0200	70,34
Melendez, Carlos	MI0150	47,70
Melito, Matthew	AZ0250	70
Mello, Christopher	CA0859	70
Mello, Christopher	CA1750	11,70
Melman, Mort	MO1120	70
Mentschukoff, Andrej	OH1200	70
Mentschukoff, Andrej	OH1600	70
Merriman, John C.	AL0500	11,49,63A,70
Mery, John Christian	OR0800	13,10,41,70,34
Metcalf, Lee	CT0800	29A,70
Metil, Robert	PA0600	14,29A,20G,70
Meyer, Kenneth	NY1550	11,70,41
Meyer, Kenneth R.	NY4150	70
Meyers, Paul	NJ0825	70,29
Meyers, Paul	NJ1400	70,29
Michaels, Ben	TN0300	70
Michaels, Mark	MA2030	70
Michaud, Shaun	MA0260	70
Michell, Ray	OR0350	70
Micic, Rale	NY5000	70
Middle, Bruce H.	VA1475	70
Midgley, Herbert	TX2700	11,70,34,45
Mikkola, Gary	NC1950	70,64
Miley, Jeff	CA1510	70
Miley, Jeff	CA0630	70
Millan, Luis	MT0400	38,70,60B,13
Miller, Charles	ID0140	51,70
Miller, Dale	CO0200	67D,70
Miller, Everett F.	KS0225	11,36,34,70,20
Miller, Fred	IL3100	70
Miller, Fred	IL2775	70,47,14C
Miller, Geoffrey	UT0250	70
Miller, Jane	MA0260	70
Miller, John A.	IL1350	47,70
Miller, John	FL1745	62D,70
Miller, M. Frederick	IL2650	70,47
Miller, Mary	TX1660	70
Miller, Matthew	WI0830	70
Miller, Matthew	WI0250	70,41
Miller, Richard	NJ0825	70
Miller, Tim	MA0260	70
Millham, Michael	WA0250	70
Millham, Michael	WA0400	70,57
Millioto, Thomas	NY0625	70
Mills, Terry	CA4300	70
Minette, A. J.	CA2800	70
Miranda, Michael A.	CA2800	11,67G,70,12A,41
Mitchell, Andrew	DC0170	70
Mitchell, Brian	GA0940	70
Mitchell, Dan	TX0050	70
Mitchell, Dan	TX0900	70
Mitchell, James	WI0500	70
Mitnick, Alex	PA3330	70
Mixon, Joseph D.	PA2450	70
Mixon, Joseph D.	PA1900	70,29
Moege, Gary R.	MO1790	11,63B,70,71,12A
Moeser, Charles	VA1600	70
Molina, Carlos	FL1300	70
Monachino, Jerome	VT0400	70
Monllos, John	RI0300	11,29A,70
Montiel, Alejandro	TX2250	70
Moore, Gary A.	IN0100	70
Moore, Harriet T.	IN0350	62E,70
Moore, James Walter	KY0400	34,13,10,70
Moore, Michael	TX2930	70
Moore, Ryan	GA2050	70
Morales, Joshua	OK0850	70,57
Morell, Drew	CO0830	70,47,62D
Morgan, Christopher	NC0220	70
Morgan, John	OH1850	70
Morgan, Stephen	MN1625	70
Morris, Brian	MI0850	70,13,34D
Morris, Jeffrey M.	TX2900	70,34,35G
Morris, Joe	MA1175	70
Morris, Joe	MA1400	29,47,70
Morris, Scott	CA2650	70,13A
Morris, Scott	CA0805	70
Morris, Scott	CA1900	70
Morrison, Chris	CT0800	53,70,41
Morse, Kevin	ME0270	70
Mortensen, Dan	NY4450	70
Mosby, Todd	MO0700	70
Motto, David	CA3520	70
Mouffe, Jerome	MA0510	70,11
Moulder, John	IL0550	47,70
Moulder, John P.	IL2250	29,70
Moulder, John	IL0275	14C,29,70
Mount, Lorna	HI0120	13A,11,12A,70,36
Mowad, Lou	NC0250	70,57
Mowbray, Candice	MD0300	70
Moynier, Miles	CA3640	70
Mueller, Raymond	WI1150	70,16
Muench, Felicity	CO0150	70
Mullen, Stan	PA2050	29B,53,70,20G,20F
Mullen, Stanley	PA1650	70
Muller, Bryan	PA1550	70,34,33
Mullhall, Kevin	OH0050	70
Mullins, Steve	CO0400	70,11
Mundy, John D.	MN1400	70
Muratore, John D.	NH0100	67A,70
Muratore, John	MA0400	70
Murdy, David H.	CA3350	70
Murphy, Douglas	CA4650	70
Murphy, Michael D.	VA1350	70
Murphy, Paul R.	CA5150	29,70
Murray, Kathrin	MD0520	70,41
Murray, Kris A.	IL2730	36,70,11,51
Muscatello, George	NY3650	29A,70
Musella, Joseph	MA0260	70
Musso, Paul J.	CO0830	70,47,53,13A
Myslewski, David	PA3400	70
Nagatani, Ken	CA1700	70
Nagge, Harold	TN1250	70,53,47,29

Index by Area of Teaching Interest

Name	Code	Areas
Nagge, Harold	TN1000	70
Nago, Stuart H.	HI0150	70
Naito, Shoji	IL1400	70
Nance, Steve	CA1850	70
Nangle, Richard	MA0400	10,70
Napoli, Joseph	PA0450	70
Napoli, Joseph	PA1000	70
Narum, Leighann	NJ1140	70
Nathanson, Robert	NC2440	70,11,13A
Nauert, Clark	TX1600	70,53,13B,13C
Nazario, Angel	PR0100	70
Nebelung, Russell	MI2000	70
Neel, Douglas J.	OH2275	70
Negri, Joseph H.	PA1050	70
Neihof, Marc	CO0200	70
Neill, Douglas A.	MN1120	70,62D
Nelson, Bruce	IL0420	70
Nelson, Jocelyn C.	NC0650	70,12A,67H,11
Nelson, Rob	MI0500	70
Ness, David J.	IL0650	70,11,13
Newell, Michael	SC0800	70
Newman, Michael	NY2250	70,41
Newsam, David	MA0260	70
Newsam, David R.	NH0350	70
Newsam, David R.	NH0100	47,70
Newsome, Charles	MI2200	29,46,47,70
Newton, Dean A.	OH2150	70,47
Newton, Gregory	CA2600	70,11
Newton, Gregory	CA1960	70,13A,11
Newton, Joseph	NC0750	70,53,29
Nguyen, Hanh	AB0200	70
Nichols, Jim	CA4625	70
Nichols, Samuel S.	CA5010	13,10,70,10B
Nickelson, LaRue S.	FL2000	70
Nicolella, Michael	WA0200	70
Nida, Chris	FL1430	70
Niedt, Douglas Ashton	MO1810	70
Nienkirchen, Red	OH0350	35A,70
Nigro, Michael	CA5355	70
Nohe, Eric	CO0225	70
Noonan, Jeffrey	MO1500	12A,14,67D,70,20G
Norberto, Jezimar	KY1200	70
Normandeau, Dale	AC0050	29,70
Novotny, Edward	WY0115	70
Nye, Randall	TX0700	70,11
Ober, Jeremy	IA0790	70
Oberle, Curtis P.	MO1000	11,70
O'Brien, Colin	WI1150	70
O'Brien, Colin	ID0100	70
O'Brien, William J.	IL0650	70
O'Callaghan, Brien	AG0450	70,29
Occhipinti, David	PA2250	70
O'Connor, Martin	MN1200	70
Oden, Wade	IL0600	13A,11,47,70,29A
Offard, Felton	IL2100	70
Offard, Felton	MN1600	70
O'Hara, Thomas	FL0650	70
Okubo, Mack	VA0250	67B,67G,70,41
Olbrych, Timothy	KS0980	70,13
Olivier, Thomas	AB0090	70
Olsen, Tim	CO0950	70
Olson, Jason	PA1850	70
Oltman, Laura G.	AF0120	70
O'Neill, Adrian	NJ0800	70,12C
O'Neill, Darren D.	VT0200	66A,70
Opel, Paul E.	AG0350	70
Orlando, Joe	MN0750	13,70,34,10
Orpen, Rick	HI0210	70
O'Sullivan, Ian	CA1700	70
Osuna, Thomas	WI0300	70
Otto, Clark	MN1050	70
Ouska, Jim	NY0625	70
Overholt, Sara	CA0350	38,41,51,62,70
Owen, Marlin	KS1450	47,70,53,29A,20G
Owens, Craig	CA5070	70
Ozgen, Mesut	AR0800	65,46,47,29,70
Pack, Lester	FL0700	70,57
Padron, Rafael	OH1200	62D,70
Paescht, Matthew	OH1600	62D,70
Paetsch, Matt	NC0050	29A,29B,70
Page, Andy	IL2900	70
Palermo, Joseph M.	IL0550	70
Palfrey, Rossman	MD0060	70
Pallett, Bryan	MI0100	70
Palmer, Dan	TN0100	70
Palmer, Nicholas	IL0750	70
Palmieri, Bob	IL0300	12A,32B,36,70,61
Palomaki, Jonathan	TX3800	60,12A,36,61,70
Palomaki, Jonathan	MI1180	70
Pantaleo, Patrick	NC0300	70
Parashevov, Milen	OR0400	70
Pardew, Mike	CA5000	70
Pardo, Brian	CA2950	70
Pardo, Brian	CA0807	70,29
Pardo-Tristan, Emiliano	NY2750	70,10A
Parkening, Christopher	CA3600	70
Parks, Gary	TX1400	65,70
Parks, John	SC0850	70,46,47
Parks, John	NC2000	70
Parman, David L.	IN1800	41,62C,62D,70,20G
Parnell, Scott	OH0250	11,70,13
Parris, John	FL1600	70
Passarelli, Lauren	MA0260	70
Patilla, Michael K.	AL0260	70
Patterson, David	MA1175	70
Patterson, David	MA0950	70
Patterson, R. Thomas	AZ0500	67D,70
Patterson, Richard	CA3270	70
Patterson, Roy	AG0650	47,70
Pattishall, Jeffrey	FL1550	70
Patykula, John	VA1600	70
Pearson, Don	OK0825	70
Pearson, Ryan	IA0300	70
Pearson, Scotty	AZ0490	70,43
Peck, Gordon	NM0400	70,13G
Peckham, Charles R.	MA0260	70
Pell, John	TN0100	70,35B
Pelton, Carmen	MI2100	70
Pemberton, Rick	WI0100	70
Penkala, Dan	MI1850	70
Pepitone, Anthony F.	OH2250	70,47
Peplin, Steve	WI0350	70
Peplin, Steve W.	WI0450	10A,11,13B,47,70
Perez, Michael	TX0550	70
Perez, Pedro	AZ0470	70
Perron, Bruno	AI0200	70
Perry, Francis	TN0100	70
Peske, Robert T.	ND0400	70
Peterson, David	WA0200	47,70,29
Peterson, James L.	MA0260	70
Peterson, Lynn	TN1900	70
Petric, Paul L.	OH1000	70
Petrides, Ron T.	NY2660	10,29,70,13,12
Petrik, Rebecca	ND0250	32,13A,61,70,36
Pezanelli, Jack	MA0260	70
Pezzimenti, Carlo	TX3300	70
Pfau, Tracy	WY0050	47,70,53
Phagoo, Curtis	AA0080	70
Phelps, Robert	MA2250	70,41
Phillips, Joe Rea	TN1850	41,70,33
Phillips, Tom	CA0150	70
Piche, Rick	AG0500	70
Pickard, Jason A.	NC0850	70
Pierri, Alvaro	AI0210	70
Pierri, Alvaro	AI0190	70
Pile, Randy	CA3350	70
Pile, Randy	CA2390	70
Pile, Randy	CA3460	51,70
Pile, Randy	CA4050	70
Piltz, Peter	RI0250	70
Pinno, John	TX2800	70
Pinto, Mike	IL0850	70,53,47
Piorkowski, James P.	NY3725	70
Pisano, John J.	CA0835	70
Pitzer, Lawrence	OH2450	55B,67C,67D,70,67G
Pitzer, Lawrence	OH0450	70
Platino, Franco	MD0100	70
Platino, Franco	DC0170	70
Plato, Scott	GA1070	70
Pobanz, Randy	IL0300	70
Pobanz, Randy F.	IL1350	70
Pobanz, Randy	IL0100	70
Poltarack, Sanford	FL1300	70
Pomeroy, Loren	VA1850	70
Poole, Jeff	OH1200	70
Porter, Jacob	TX1660	70
Porter, John	NC0400	70
Portolese, Frank	IL0850	70,53
Poshek, Joe	CA3350	13,70
Potenza, Frank	CA5300	70,29
Powell, Aaron	IA0420	70,36
Powell, Aaron	IA0650	70,13A
Powell, Aaron	IA1350	70
Powers, Bob	AZ0470	70
Prenkert, Richard	CA4460	70
Prince, Gary	DC0170	70
Prisco, Peter	NY0644	70,62D
Proulx, Sylvie	AD0050	70
Provost, Richard C.	CT0650	41,70
Pucci, Michael	AI0200	70
Puls, Kenneth	FL0500	70
Purdy, Carl	GA0250	62A,62B,70,51
Purse, William E.	PA1050	70,34
Putterman, Jeff	OR0850	70,29
Quaile, Michael	PA3330	47,70
Quinn, Brian	PA3260	70
Quintero, Juan Carlos	CA1265	70,35A
Rabuse, Brian	MA0280	70
Radovanlija, Maja	MN1623	70
Raisor, Steve C.	NC0500	11,13,37,47,70
Raitt, Donovan	CA1425	70
Ramos-Kittrell, Jesus	TX2400	12,70
Ramsdell, Steve	IL3550	70
Randall, Thomas	MA1000	47,57,72,70
Rankin, John B.	LA0300	70
Rankin, John	LA0800	70
Raths, O. Nicholas	MN0350	70,13C
Raths, O. Nicholas	MN0050	70,51
Ray, Eric J.	CA2720	13A,70
Ray, Eric	CA1900	70
Rayner, William S.	NY2750	32E,70
Reach, Douglas	AF0100	70
Read, Patrick	CA3800	70
Redding, Eric	AK0050	11,36,66A,70,53
Redman, Bill M.	CA4410	70
Reed, Randy	NC0600	70
Reese, Donald T.	PA1830	11,12A,70,13A,14C
Regnier, Marc	SC0500	11,70
Reid, James	ID0250	11,41,70
Reilly, Paul C.	IN0150	41,70,67D
Reyes, William	OK0550	70
Reyes, William	AR0730	70
Reynolds, David B.	MD1050	70
Rezende Lopes, Joao Luiz	NJ0825	70
Rhodes, Aaron	DE0050	70
Rice, Douglas	WA1000	70
Richter, Michael	TX3530	70
Ridgeway, Max A.	OK0600	10,70,11,20,46
Rieken, Justin	MN0625	70
Riffel, William	NJ0300	70,53
Rijos, Ivan	PR0115	70
Riley, David	RI0150	13,70
Riley, Jason	KS0100	70
Riley, Jason	MO0850	70
Riley, William	MA2020	70,11,13C
Rinaldo, Ben	AG0150	70
Rizzuto, Thomas	NY2450	70,12A
Roach, Seth	KS0750	65,66,29,70,50
Roberts, Brian	MI2200	70
Roberts, Brian S.	MI2110	70
Roberts, Russ	OK1050	70
Robinett, Henry	CA0150	70
Robinett, Henry	CA1500	70
Robinson, David	VA1600	70
Robinson, Gary	NH0050	70
Robinson, Stephen	FL1750	70
Robitaille, James	MA2020	70,47
Rodriguez, Alberto	PR0115	70,41,42
Rodriguez, Eleazer	NY2900	70
Rodriguez, Elimiano	CA2550	70
Rodriguez, Francisco	CO0800	70
Rodriquez, Frank	TX2295	70
Rogers, David	OR0950	70
Rogers, Douglas	DC0170	70
Rogers, Joseph	MA0260	70
Rogine, Peter	NY1275	13C,29,47,70
Rojas, Berta	DC0100	70,51
Rojas, Ner	IN1025	70
Roldan, Francisco	NJ0825	70
Roller, Peter	WI0050	20G,70,20H
Rollins, Christopher	MI1200	70,51
Roman, Dan	CT0500	34,70,10A,10F,13
Roman, Orlando	MD0750	70
Romano, Tony	NY1275	70
Romero, Celin	CA4100	70
Romero, Jose	CA5300	70

Name	Code	Areas
Roos, Randy	MA0260	70
Rosado, Ana Maria	NJ0825	70,41,11,12A
Rosenkoetter, Alan C.	MO1830	70
Rosenkoetter, Alan	MO1900	70
Rosenn, Jamie	CA0835	29,70
Rosensky, Michael	VA1550	70,42,47
Ross, John	TN1200	70,67G,42
Roth, John	MN0610	34,40,41,70
Rottenberg, Helene	MI1260	70,11
Roux, Patrick	AG0400	70
Rowan, Kami	NC0910	70,11,51,12E
Rowe, Alex	UT0400	70
Roy, Joseph	AG0170	70,13E
Roy, Larry	AC0100	70,47,53
Roye, Tobin	CA0800	70,13
Royer, Randall D.	SD0100	64,47,38,32E,70
Rubio, Douglas	NY3780	12A,41,70
Rubright, Dan	MO0700	70
Rudolph, Jon	ND0600	11,13A,70
Rudolph, Jon	MN1120	70,47
Ruiz, Norman	IL0720	70
Ruiz, Norman	IL3150	70
Rumpel, Greg	AA0050	70
Ruscoe, Christopher	CA5353	70
Russell, Brian	FL1900	70
Russell, Brian E.	FL0050	70
Russell, Craig H.	CA0600	11,12A,12,67B,70
Russell, Robert A.	NC2440	70,29
Ryan, Michael	CA5100	70,42,10D
Sage, Steve	CA1560	35,70
Salazar, Dennis A.	IL3370	70
Salerno, Steven	NY0050	29,47,70
Sales, Gregory	NE0590	70
Sales, Humberto O.	VA0800	70
Salter, Tim	TX0075	70
Sampson, Larry	CA0300	62,63,64,70
Samsa, Louis	MN0150	70
Sanchez, Scott R.	MA1850	70
Sanchez, Scott	NH0110	70
Sandahl, Thomas	OR0500	47,70,29B
Sanders, Jack D.	CA3650	70
Sanders, Jack	CA1050	70
Sanders, Trevor	AA0110	13A,70,13B,13C
Sanders, Trevor	AA0020	70
Sano, Anthony M.	NY3600	70
Santiago, Nephtali	GA2150	70,29,11
Saraquse, Sandy	CA0150	70
Sarata, Adam	OH0100	70
Sarata, Adam	OH2290	70
Saulter, Gerry	NY1275	12A,13C,70,42,41
Saunders, Bruce	MA0260	70
Saunders, Bruce	TX3510	70,47
Savage, John	WA0900	66A,70
Savino, Richard	CA4150	70
Savino, Richard	CA0840	70
Sawyer, Scott	NC0650	29,70
Scagarella, Susan	CA3850	70,66A
Scannura, Roger	AG0650	70
Scarano, Robert	CA5040	70
Scarano, Robert	CA3265	34D,35G,70
Scarano, Robert	CA0950	70
Scarfullery, Rafael	VA1125	70
Scarfullery, Rafael	VA1400	70
Scharron, Eladio	FL1800	70,51
Scheffler, Jeff	IA0910	70,11
Scheffler, Jeff E.	NE0610	70
Schiller, Andrew	MI1950	70
Schilling, Richard	MA2030	70,47
Schmid, William	WI0825	20G,32C,70
Schmidt, Timothy	NY2950	70,11,13C
Schmunk, Richard	CA1900	70
Schneider, John	CA2700	41,45,70,34
Schneiderman, John H.	CA5020	67D,70
Schneiderman, John	CA2390	70
Scholl, Tim	TX2550	13A,13E,32A,66,70
Schramm, David	CA1850	70
Schroeder, Matthew	WI1150	70
Schulman, Jory	CA4450	70
Schumaker, Adam	MI1150	10A,10B,10C,10D,70
Schurger, Phillip	IN0700	70,10
Schuttenhelm, Thomas	CT0050	11,13,70,34
Schweizer, Kiel Jay	AK0100	70
Schwindt, Dan	CO0830	13C,70
Scivally, Riner	CA3300	70
Scivally, Riner	CA3500	70,53
Scofield, John L.	NY2750	47,70
Scollard, Dan T.	OR0700	70
Score, Clyde D.	AZ0510	65,70
Scott, Joseph	MA0600	67D,70
Scott, Michael	CA1900	70
Seeger, Brian	LA0800	35A,35B,35C,47,70
Seeger, Brian	LA0300	70
Seigfried, Karl E.	WI0250	70,62D,11
Senasi, Karlo	AL0300	70
Senasi, Karlo	AL0800	70
Serna, Phillip Woodrow	IN1750	62D,67A,70,67B
Serpas, Roberto	AA0050	70
Settlemires, Joseph	OK1400	47,70
Shebesta, Bob	WI0770	70
Sheeley, Thomas	AZ0450	70
Sheffer, Jake	MD0550	70
Sher, Ben	NY4500	34,47,70
Sher, Ben	MA0260	70
Sheridan, John	PA0400	70,53,13A
Sherman, Bob	IL2750	70
Sherman, Jeff	KY0250	47,53,70
Sherrod, Ron	TX3535	70,11
Shields, Bob	AG0200	47,70
Shields, John Paul	WA0950	70
Shumate, Curtis	MA0260	70
Silbergleit, Paul	WI1150	70,47,29
Silva, Ben	NM0450	70
Silvers, Travis	CA5350	70
Silvers, Travis	CA3000	70
Simms, William	MD0500	67G,70,55
Simms, William	MD0610	70
Simonds, Judy	MA1550	70
Singleton, Jon	NC0550	70
Singleton, Ron	OK0500	70
Singley, David	MN0300	70,47,41
Siqueiros, John	TX3520	70
Sise, Patrick	MD0350	70,41
Skantar, David	FL1450	70
Skelton, Neal	CT0450	70
Skurtu, Jasmine J.	HI0210	70
Slotkin, Matthew	PA2150	70
Slotkin, Matthew C.	PA0250	70
Smart, Jonathan	CA2440	70
Smith, Brian	GA1200	70
Smith, James	NY4050	70,11
Smith, James E.	OH0500	29,70,47,12A
Smith, James	CA5300	70
Smith, Matthew	SC0900	70
Smith, Michael Cedric	NY2700	70,13A
Smith, Pat	IA0700	70
Smith, Peter D.	FL0365	70
Smith, Richard	CA5300	70
Smith, Rylan	GA1050	70,41
Smith, Stan	OH0350	70,10D
Smith, Tom	FL0200	70
Smith, Tracy Anne	DC0170	70
Smith, William D.	NC1350	70,11
Smyser, Peter	PA2450	70
Sneider, Robert	NY1100	29,70
Snitzler, Larry J.	VA0450	70
Snitzler, Larry	DC0010	70
Snyder, Craig	NY1250	70,29
Snyder, Jerrold	CA1550	70
Snyder, Philip	GA2100	70
Sorroche, Juan	PR0150	13A,11,70,13C
Spann, Joseph	AL0890	11,13,70,34A,34D
Sparks, Glenn	NY2900	70
Sparks, Jeremy	NY4460	70
Spell, Cindy	NC0100	70
Spell, Cindy	NC0450	70,11
Spence, Gary	NC1250	70,20G
Spera, Nicolo	CO0800	70
Spicer, Jeffrey	PA2800	70
Spradley, Bruce	GA0200	70
Sprayberry, Tom	TX2260	70
Spring, Howard	AG0350	14,70,29,12A,13D
St. Hilaire, Jon	WA1300	70
Stahurski, Brian	PA0500	70
Stallings, Joe	FL1500	13,11,70,34
Standard, Richard	GA0200	70
Stanek, Mark	IN1560	70
Stanek, Mark	IN0100	70,13B,13C,41
Stano, Richey	FL1675	70,10
Starling, Gary	FL1000	70,29
Starobin, David	NY2150	70
Starr, Jeff M.	MI1200	70
Steadman, Robert	NC1100	70
Stearns, Roland H.	AK0100	13,70,51
Steele, Louis L.	CO0350	70
Steen, Larry	CA1750	70
Stegmann, Matthias	IN0910	70
Stegmann, Matthias	IN0550	70,35G
Stephenson, Edward	NC1300	70
Sterner, Dave	OH0750	13,47,70,29
Stevens, Keith	VA0600	70,57
Stevenson, David E.	SC0400	70
Stevenson, David	NC2400	70
Stevenson, Janis	CA1800	13A,10,70
Stewart, Billy	NC2410	70
Stewart, Mark	NY2150	70
Stine, Steve	ND0350	70
Stockdale, Michael	MI0520	70,53,13B
Stoddard, David	MN1100	70,13I
Stoican, Michael	WA0600	70
Stolz, Patrick	WY0115	61,70
Stone, Kerry 'Doc'	TN1450	70
Stone, Richard J.	NY1600	70
Stone, Robin	MA0260	70
Stone, Scott	DC0170	70
Stoubis, Nick	CA5300	70
Stowell, John	OR0750	70,29
Strauss, Richard	NY4460	70
Strickler, John A.	MO0775	70
Strickler, John	MO0350	70
Strickler, John	MO1550	70
Strong, Bent	MA0510	70,11
Stropes, John	WI0825	70
Strunsky, Mark	NY3000	11,12A,70,14C
Struthers, Steve	AR0750	70
Strutt, Michael	AB0050	70
Strutt, Michael	AB0100	70
Stuart, Rory	NY2660	13,70,47
Stump, Joseph	MA0260	70
Suchow, Paul	NY2100	70
Sullivan, Keith	AL0850	70,11
Sullivan, Robert	MA0650	70
Sullivan, Robert	MA0700	67B,70
Sullivan, Robert P.	MA1400	70
Sult, Michael	CA1800	13,70,29,13A
Sumi, Akiko	DC0170	70
Summers, George	AZ0440	70,13
Sumner, Richard	CA5400	70
Sunderland, Paul	IL1050	29B,31A,43,70
Suovanen, Charles	CA2600	41,70
Sutherland, John	GA2100	70
Suvada, Steve	IL1615	70
Suvada, Steve	IL0850	70,41,20
Suvada, Steven	IL1085	70,34,35
Svoboda, George	CA4050	70,12A
Sweeny, Paul	NY0350	70
Switzer, Mark	FL0930	11,70
Switzer, Mark	FL0800	70
Sylvester, Eric	LA0350	70
Tabaka, Jim	MN1500	70,20,12A
Tadic, Miroslav	CA0510	70,47,20F
Taft, Kenneth	MA0260	70
Taggart, Christian	DE0150	70
Tamburello, John	WI1155	70,20A,20B
Tamez, Ray	TX3410	70
Tamez, Raymundo	TX3350	70
Tanenbaum, David	CA4150	70,41
Tarulli, Scott	MA0260	70
Taylor, Sam	NC2205	70
Taylor, Tom	CO0200	70,29B,46,47
Tebbs, Mckay	UT0200	70
Teicholz, Marc S.	CA0807	70,41
Teicholz, Marc	CA4150	70
Teixeira, Robert	NC0550	70
Teixeira, Robert	NC2000	70,41
Tennant, Scott	CA5300	70
Tercero, David R.	TX0850	70,63,13
Terrell, Brett	IN0250	51,70
Terrien, Paul	WI1150	70
Terry, Patrick L.	UT0250	70
Teves, Christopher	SC0275	70,11
Thachuk, Steve J.	CA0835	70
Thomas, John	MA0260	70
Thompson, Bob	ME0340	47,70,53,35
Thompson, Robert	TN0100	70,41
Thorpe, Clyde	KY0800	70,42
Thurston, Andrew	MD0170	70

Name	Code	Areas
Thygeson, Jeffrey	MN1295	70
Thygeson, Jeffrey K.	MN1625	70
Tisch, Don	IL0650	70
Todd, Richard	TN1400	13E,13F,41,70
Tokar, David A.	PA0900	12A,12C,70,12,11
Tomlin, Charles	MI1650	70
Tompkins, Daniel	VA0350	70
Torbert, Jeffrey	AF0100	70
Torosian, Brian	IL3550	70,32E
Torosian, Brian L.	IL2150	70,11,13H
Torres, Douglas	CA3320	70
Torres, Martin	CA0859	62D,70
Tot, Zvonimir	IL3310	29,13,13C,70,47
Toussaint, David	VA1600	70
Towey, Dan	IA0930	70
Towill, John	AA0020	70
Townson, Kevin	TX2750	70,11
Trail, Robert	IN1800	70
Tremura, Welson Alves	FL1850	70,20
Trent, Robert S.	VA1100	70,67G,41,57
Trepanier, Louis	AG0400	70
Trinckes, John	FL0365	70
Trindade, Walter	CA0400	70
Tronzo, David	MA0260	70
Trovato, Stephen	CA5300	70
Troxel, Jeffrey C.	MT0350	70
Truitt, D. Charles	PA2200	70,13,41,13E,13B
Tschannen, James	FL1700	70
Tu, Gary	IL1900	70
Tucker, Kerry	IA1300	70
Tudek, Thomas S.	IN1650	41,70
Tunstall, Charles	TN1650	70
Tupik, Justin	NJ0760	70
Turechek, Dennis	NY1400	70,29A
Turechek, Dennis	NY3765	70,29
Turley, Steve	PA1150	70
Turner, George	IL3500	29,70
Turner, James	MS0385	70
Turner, Kevin P.	OH1850	70
Turner, Michael W.	OR1000	70,29,34,47
Turner, Richard	CA0815	70
Tyborowski, Richard	AC0100	70
Tymas, Byron	NC1600	11,46,70,47,41
Tzvetkov, Atanas	IN0900	70
Uch, Mandeda	CA3800	70
Ulibarri, Fernando	FL0200	35,70,47
Ullman, Richard	VT0100	70,67D,13C
Ulreich, Eric	DC0170	70
Umble, Jay	PA0350	70
Umble, Jay	PA2300	70
Umble, Jay	PA3150	70
Valdes Vivas, Eduardo	PR0115	70,41
Valdes, Eduardo	PR0150	70,11
Valentine, Bob	AL1250	70
Valeras, Michael	TN0100	70
Valls De Quesada, Margarita	AL0330	41,70
Van Berkel, Wilma	AG0500	70
Van Duser, Guy	MA0260	70
Vance, Howard	TN0450	70
Vander Hart, Gary	IA1200	70
Vanderlinde, David	SD0580	70
Vandivier, Rick	CA4900	70
Vandivier, Rick	CA4400	70
VanEchaute, Michael	IA1300	70
VanGent, Wendy	SD0400	32,70
Vanselow, Jason	MN0040	20,70
Vargas, Philip	CA2975	70
Varvel, Vince	MO1900	70
Vaughan, Charles	NC2420	70,41
Vaughan, Danny	OK1330	70
Vaughan, John	WV0050	70
Vazquez, Steven	IL1085	70
Velykis, Theodore	NJ1100	20,70
Ventura, Anthony C.	DE0150	70
Vera, Juan-Carlos	FL1310	70
Verdery, Benjamin	CT0850	70,41
Vick, Joe D.	AR0750	62D,70
Videon, Michael	MT0200	70,41
Vieaux, Jason	OH0600	70,41
Vince, Matt	AZ0440	70,35C,35D
Vincent, Larry	TN1250	11,70
Vincent, Larry F.	TN1710	70
Vincent, Randy	CA4700	70,47
Visscher, Murray	AA0050	70
Vogt, Roy	TN0100	70,53,35B
Voris, Dan J.	OH0350	70,41
Wachala, Greg	NY1550	70,47
Wachs, Dean	IN1450	70
Wagner, Craig	KY1500	70,47
Walbridge, William	MI2000	70
Waldon, Reed	MI1300	70
Walker, Dave	KY0250	70,67D,67H
Waller, Anne	IL2250	70
Walter, Steven	SC0750	70,11,12A
Ward, Robert J.	MA1450	70,11,13,20G
Wardenski, Ian	MD0060	70
Warnock, Matthew	IL0350	29,70
Warren, J. Curt	TX3520	70,53,29
Warren, Jeff	MN1250	70
Warren, Jeffrey	MN0625	41,70
Washington, Phil	WV0700	11,29B,70
Watson, J. Stephen	SC0750	29A,70,46
Wayne, Barbara	ID0060	70
Weatherford, Benjamin	AL0500	70,11
Weaver, Daniel	WI0808	70
Weaver, Joseph	PA0500	70
Weaver, Phillip E.	AL1160	70,41
Webb, Chuck	IL0720	70
Webber, Danny R.	MD0450	11,70,13
Webster, Brent	KY0950	70
Weik, Jay C.	OH2300	70
Weinkum, Harald	AZ0350	70
Weinstein, Alan	VA1250	41,62C,62D,70
Welch, Leo	FL0850	70
Wells, Jesse R.	KY0900	11,53,62A,70
Werkema, Jason	MI0350	70
Werkema, Jason R.	MI0750	70,13,29,34
Wessel, Kenneth	NY2400	70,29
Wessel, Kenneth	NY5000	70
Westerholm, Joel M.	IA1200	70
Westfall, Claude R.	MO0100	32B,32D,36,60A,70
Wetzel, Robert	CA4100	70
Wetzel, Robert	CA2100	70
Whalen, Marc	AF0120	70
Wheatley, Jon	MA0260	70
Wheatley, Jon	MA2030	70,47
Wheeler, Brent	TX2350	70
Wheeler, Edwin	OR1010	70
Wheeler, Michael	TX3450	70,29
Wheeler, Mike	TX3400	47,70
White, Al	KY0300	70,51
White, Chris	OK1050	70,35,37
White, Mark	MA0260	70
White, Richard H.	CO0350	70
Whitehead, Corey	CA1860	70
Whitehead, Corey	CA0810	70,11,14C
Whitehead, Richard	VA1350	70,29
Whitehead, Richard	VA0450	70
Wight, Doug	WA0550	70
Wilke, Christopher	NY2650	70
Wilkins, John	MA0260	70
Wilkinson, Wayne	CO0275	70,47,41,42
Willard, Jerry	NY3790	67D,70
William, Jacob	MA0510	70
Williams, Alexander W.	IN0350	70
Williams, Gary R.	WI0450	47,70,53
Williams, Larry	MI2000	70
Williams, Larry	MI1000	70
Williams, Larry	MI0100	41,70
Williams, Michael	CA3920	70
Williams, Michael	CA2775	70,12A
Williams, Mike	MA0260	70
Williams, Sandy	IN0907	70,47,46
Williams, Sean	WA0350	11,12,14,20G,70
Williamson, Andy	AL1050	70
Willis, A. Rexford	FL1745	13,10,70,13A
Willmott, Bret	MA0260	70
Willy, Alan	IN0005	66A,66G,70,13
Wilson, James	NY3600	70
Wilson, Ken	MN1250	70,43
Wilson, Mark	WA0030	70,12A
Winchell, Jill	CA2550	70
Winner, Andrew	KY1300	70
Winner, Andrew	KY1000	70,41
Winter, Brandon	AJ0030	70
Winter, Robert	MD0175	70,11
Wittner, Gary	ME0200	70
Wittner, Gary D.	ME0500	70
Witzel, James	CA4425	70
Witzel, James F.	CA4200	70
Wohlrab, Stephen	NC2600	70,35A
Wohlwend, Karl	OH1850	70
Wohlwend, Karl	OH2050	70,47
Woitach, Christopher	OR1250	70,47
Wolf, Scott	CA6000	70
Wolf, Scott	CA3460	70,11
Wolfe, Thomas	AL1170	47,70,29,35B
Woodard, Eve	TX1000	29,70
Woodbury, Todd K.	UT0250	70
Woodbury, Todd	UT0400	70
Woodbury, Todd	UT0350	70,41
Woodford, Peter	CA0550	70,47
Woodruff, Sidney	GA0250	70,11
Woods, William	CA4550	70
Worley, Dan	KY0450	70,10A,10B,10C,34B
Wright, Trey	GA1150	70,47,29A,29B,14C
Wysock, Nathan	WI0350	70
Wysock, Nathan	WI1150	70
Yancey, James	AZ0470	70
Yancho, Mari	MI2120	70
Yancho, Mari	MI0450	11,70,41
Yankee, Steve	MD0400	70
Yarmolinsky, Benjamin	NY0280	13A,13,10,45,70
Yasui, Byron K.	HI0210	70,10A,10F,13,20B
Yates, Peter F.	CA5030	70
Yates, Peter	CA0630	11,51,70,13A
Yates, Stanley	TN0050	70
Ybarra, Anthony L.	CA4410	70,53,47
Yelverton, William	TN1100	70,42
Yip, Brandon	CA0150	70
Yoshida, Jason	CA3650	70
Young, David	MN1250	70
Young, Geoff	AG0450	70
Young, Mike	MT0370	70
Youngstrom, Kenton	CA1700	70
Youngstrom, Kenton D.	CA3500	70
Youngstrom, Kenton	CA3600	70
Ysereef, Alan	AG0070	70
Yzereef, Allan	AG0150	70
Zacharias, Andrew	CA1520	34,45,70
Zamora, Gloria	TX0550	70
Zanter, Mark J.	WV0400	13,29,10,70,34
Zawilak, Alexander	AZ0490	70,13A,42,41
Zeidel, Scott	CA3200	13A,11,70
Zeidel, Scott	CA1520	70,11
Zickafoose, Edward	OH1800	66A,70
Zimmer, Lee	CA2420	70
Zimmerman, Brian	AC0050	29,70
Zimmerman, Ronald J.	PA1050	70
Zisa, Peter	OR0500	70
Zito, William	NY2550	70,41
Zito, William	NY0050	67G,70
Zito, William F.	NY1600	70,67G
Zocher, Norman	MA0260	70
Zohn, Andrew	GA0550	70,10
Zuluaga, Daniel	CA1960	11,70
Zwally, Randall S.	PA2300	11,70

Music Instrument Curator

Name	Code	Areas
Adkins, Richard C.	IA0300	16,71,66F
Banks, Margaret	SD0600	71
Beach, Douglas	IL0850	47,53,71,29,35
Bledsoe, Lee	TN1450	66F,71
Borders, James M.	MI2100	12,14B,71
Campiglia, Paul	GA2150	65,29,71,50,11
Crenshaw, Timothy	SC1110	71,72
Fallon, Kelly	IN0800	35,67,71,72
Halsell, George K.	ID0075	13,37,63,11,71
Hill, Jackson	PA0350	10,12A,12,14,71
Kazimir, David	IN0900	66G,69,71
Klauss, Sabine	SD0600	71
Koster, John	SD0600	71,72
Larson, Andre	SD0600	71,16
Malyshko, Olga	AG0250	12A,12,71,55
Moege, Gary R.	MO1790	11,63B,70,71,12A
Moore, Dennis	CO0275	71,72
Myers, Herbert W.	CA4900	67B,71
Petersen, Mark	CA2390	71
Skweir, Michael	CA2250	71,72
Stewart, Scott A.	GA0750	37,38,71

Music Instrument Repair

Balmer, Bill	OH2275	72
Blakely, Doug	NY1800	72
Bliton, Nathaniel	MI0900	72,34
Brent, William	LA0550	37,72
Brightman, Nicholas	IN0250	64E,72
Brough, Ronald P.	UT0050	60,32C,37,65,72
Brown, Richard L.	WV0600	32,63D,72,11
Carney, David	CA4100	34D,35C,35G,72
Cheyne, Donald R.	GA1700	32,72
Clark, Antoine T.	OH0850	12A,72,48,64,64C
Cole, Robert	PA3650	34A,34B,49,63B,72
Cooper, Justin L.	TX3420	72
Crenshaw, Timothy	SC1110	71,72
Crews, Norval	TX1700	11,64C,64E,72
Crowe, Don R.	SD0550	32,63C,72,35
Davis, Stephen	TN0100	70,72
Diaz, Manuel	GA0550	72
Dixon, Walter	NY0646	13A,72
Durocher, Michael	AA0032	72
Eversole, Tom	KS1350	72
Fallon, Kelly	IN0800	35,67,71,72
Fields, Alex	SC0200	48,64,72
Funderburk, Jeffrey	IA1600	49,63D,72
Gale, Robert	CO0100	64,66A,66F,72
Gillette, John C.	NY3725	13,64D,72
Grigel, Glen M.	NY3780	72
Hancock, Craig A.	IA1800	37,60B,63C,63D,72
Haunstein, Jim	PA2300	72
Higgins, William R.	PA2300	32,64,72,34
Imobersteg, John	WI0830	72,66F
James, Steve	WI0250	72
Jamison, Phil A.	NC2550	72,70,20G
Jones, Heath	OK0700	64C,64E,47,72,34
Jusino, Christopher	NY2550	13A,72
Kolbeck, Karl F.	NE0700	12A,72,48,64,11
Koster, John	SD0600	71,72
Kuehn, John W.	PA1600	32,64C,48,72
Lee, Robert W.	NY4150	66F,72
Lindberg, John E.	MN1000	12A,12C,48,64D,72
MacMillan, Ann E.	TX3420	72
Metcalf, Michael	OH0100	63B,72,49
Moore, Dennis	CO0275	71,72
Murph, Charles	NC0900	72
Newton, Jack	NC0050	47,41,64C,72,35
Odello, Mike	MN1620	63D,72,49
Olt, Timothy J.	OH1450	63D,49,72,67E
Ouellette, Garry	NY2550	16,14C,72,34,35
Perkins, Boyd	SD0400	63C,63D,37,60B,72
Petchulat, David	TN0100	72
Pruiett, Kevin P.	OK0650	47,63A,72,29A,49
Rachor, David J.	IA1600	11,64D,64E,72
Randall, Thomas	MA1000	47,57,72,70
Risk, Lee	KY0550	72
Ritzenhein, Mark	MI1800	72
Romero, Frank	NM0310	63A,47,72,34
Ross, Daniel F.	AR0110	11,41,64B,64D,72
Scarbrough, Eric	OH1850	72
Schmidt, Daniel	CA2950	72,10E,20D
Schoolfield, Robnet	SC0200	32,45,65,72
Sieberg, Michael	OH0950	66F,72
Skweir, Michael	CA2250	71,72
Sparks, Thomas G.	IN0900	72
Spell, Eldred	NC2600	64A,72
Streibel, Bruce	AA0200	72
Summers, C. Oland	NC0850	32,63C,64D,65,72
Thile, Scott	KY0950	66F,72
Vandermark, Mark S.	LA0200	72
Voorhees, Jerry L.	LA0650	48,64D,72
Walsh, Allan	AG0070	64E,72
Wong, Baldwin	CA0840	72
Woolly, Kimberly A.	MS0750	64D,12A,41,48,72
Young, Lonnie	MS0750	66F,72

Alphabetical Listing of Faculty

Alphabetical Listing of Faculty

Name	Code
Aaberg, David E.	MO1790
Aagaard, J. Kjersgaard	WI0842
Aagaard, Kathy	FL2000
Aakre, Brett	OR1000
Aakre, David	OR1000
Aaland, Jan	MD0500
Aamodt, Rucci R.	HI0150
Aamodt, Rucci R.	HI0210
Aamodt-Nelson, Norma	WA0980
Aamot, Kirk C.	MT0200
Aarhus, Craig	MS0500
Aaron, Elizabeth	NY2250
Aaron, Kathryn	KY0250
Aaron, Richard L.	NY1900
Abad, Andy	CA5300
Abadey, Nasar	MD0650
Abate, Greg	RI0200
Abayev, Alexander	NY0050
Abbate, Carolyn	PA3350
Abbate, Elizabeth	MA0350
Abbati, Joseph S.	FL1900
Abberger, John	AG0300
Abbey, Gail	MA1560
Abbinanti, David A.	NY2550
Abbot, Louis	FL0200
Abbott, Amanda-Joyce	OH2290
Abbott, Carol	FL0930
Abbott, David	MI0100
Abbott, Elaine	PA1050
Abbott, Gary Bernard	MO1810
Abbott, James S.	NY4150
Abbott, Norman	AG0500
Abbott, Patricia	AI0150
Abbott, Thomas	MN1300
Abbott, Tyler	OR1050
Abbott, Wesley	CA2600
Abbott-Kirk, Jane	TX0300
Abdul Al-Khabyyr, Muhammad	AI0150
Abdullah, Ahmed	NY2660
Abe, Christie-Keiko	IL2750
Abe, Marie	MA0400
Abegg, Paul	UT0150
Abeid, Mellad	WA0400
Abel, Alan	NJ1130
Abel, Alan D.	PA3250
Abel, Alfred	IN1850
Abel, Jonathan	CA4900
Abel, Sandra	TX0390
Abel, Sean	CA1300
Abele, Catherine	AA0035
Abele, Catherine	AA0100
Abeles, Harold F.	NY4200
Abell, Jan	CA2750
Abelson, Norman	MO1810
Abelson, Robert	NY1450
Abend, Elena	WI0825
Aber, Stephen	TN0100
Abercrombie, John	NY3785
Abercrombie, Marilyn	MO0260
Aberdam, Eliane	RI0300
Abernathy, Jennifer	IL0150
Abernathy, Kristina	CO0600
Abeyaratne, Harsha D.	OH1650
Abigana, Brett	MA0400
Abigana, Brett K.	MA1400
Ablon, Judith	TN1600
Abner, Marita	MO1810
Abo, Takeshi	MI0100
Abo, Takeshi	MI0150
Abondolo, Gianna	CA2950
Abraham, Christine	CA2950
Abraham, Christine	CA0807
Abraham, Daniel E.	DC0010
Abraham, Deborah	MA0260
Abraham, Michael	MA0260
Abrahams, Daniel	MI1750
Abrahams, Ellen M.	NJ1350
Abrahams, Frank E.	NJ1350
Abram, Blanche	NY1600
Abramo, Joseph M.	CT0600
Abramovic, Charles	PA3250
Abramovitch, Ruti	IL3450
Abramowitsch, Miriam	CA2950
Abrams, Brian	NY0500
Abrams, Brian	NJ0800
Abrams, Colleen	OH2275
Abrams, David	NY2950
Abrams, Eugene	NY2250
Abrams, Ira	NC0050
Abrams, Ira	FL0650
Abrams, Paul E.	TN0100
Abrams, Paul E.	TN1100
Abreu, Aldo	MA0400
Abreu, Aldo	MA1400
Abril, Carlos	FL1900
Abril, Mario	TN1700
Abruzzo, Luke A.	PA1000
Academia, Jon	CA4850
Accardo, Frank	CA3750
Accurso, Joseph	NJ0030
Accurso, Robert	NY0400
Aceto, Jonathan D.	GA0950
Acevedo, Carmen	PR0150
Acevedo, Maria Teresa	PR0115
Acevedo, Michael	TX3530
Acevedo-Hernandez, Victor	IA0400
Achen, Mori	CA3920
Achucarro, Joaquin	TX2400
Acker, Gregory	IN1010
Acker-Mills, Barbara E.	AL0200
Ackerly, Olga	MO1810
Ackerman, Barbara	AG0650
Ackerman, Mark	TX3350
Ackley, Dan	WI0862
Ackley, James	SC1110
Acklin, Amy	KY1500
Ackmann, Rodney	OK1350
Acord, Alison	OH1450
Acord, Michael D.	KY1350
Acosta, Anibal A.	VA1000
Acosta, Darren	RI0300
Acosta, Gail	CA2750
Acosta, Tim	CA4650
Acsadi, Daniel	MA0510
Acuff, Rachel	TN1000
Aczon, Michael	CA1560
Adair, William 'Billy'	TN1850
Adam, Jennifer	KY1550
Adam, Joseph J.	WA1000
Adam, Mark	AF0050
Adam, Nathaniel	CT0050
Adamek, Magdalena	AA0100
Adamek, Mary	IA1550
Adams, Alison	GA1700
Adams, Andrew	NC2600
Adams, Ann M.	FL1750
Adams, Bob	WA0030
Adams, Bobby L.	FL1750
Adams, Brant	OK0800
Adams, Brent	AG0500
Adams, Brent	AG0050
Adams, Byron	CA5040
Adams, Catherine W.	MI2100
Adams, Clifford	OH2200
Adams, Clinton	MD0650
Adams, Dan	WA0800
Adams, Daniel B.	OH1300
Adams, Daniel C.	TX3150
Adams, Dave	CA1800
Adams, David	MO1790
Adams, David	OH2200
Adams, Dwight	MI2200
Adams, Elma	NJ0700
Adams, Ernie	IL3310
Adams, Fay	TN1710
Adams, Gary	AF0100
Adams, Gary	OH0650
Adams, George	ID0060
Adams, George C.	ID0100
Adams, Gerard	NH0300
Adams, Greta	KS0400
Adams, J. Robert	GA0490
Adams, Jacquelyn	AL1050
Adams, James M.	ND0600
Adams, James	ME0440
Adams, Jan	GA2130
Adams, Jennifer	VA1350
Adams, Joel	IL2050
Adams, Julia	ME0200
Adams, Julie R.	MN1120
Adams, Justin	CO0550
Adams, K. Gary	VA0100
Adams, Kenny L.	OK0700
Adams, Kris	MA2050
Adams, Kristine	MA0260
Adams, Kurtis B.	WV0550
Adams, Kyle	IN0900
Adams, Liselyn	AI0070
Adams, Lowell	FL2050
Adams, Margaret Ann	OK1200
Adams, Margarethe A.	NY3790
Adams, Marilyn	TN0350
Adams, Mark	NY0646
Adams, Mark	MI1160
Adams, Mary Kay	VA0300
Adams, Mary Kay	VA0100
Adams, Matthew	TX1425
Adams, Michelle	ID0100
Adams, Mimmie	AG0650
Adams, Nell	MS0400
Adams, Norman	AF0120
Adams, Pam	TX3000
Adams, Patti	LA0300
Adams, Paul	VA0950
Adams, Randal	TX2250
Adams, Richard C.	VA0100
Adams, Richard	MI2250
Adams, Richard	PA2100
Adams, Robert C.	GA0875
Adams, Robert L.	MO0700
Adams, Stephen	CA2950
Adams, Timothy K.	GA2100
Adams, Valerie	FL0930
Adams-McMillan, Aubrey	UT0400
Adamson, Jared	OH0550
Adamson, Philip I.	AG0550
Adamy, Paul	NY2400
Adan, Jose	FL0050
Adan, Jose	FL1300
Adashi, Judah E.	MD0650
Adcock, Elizabeth	MT0175
Addamson, Paul	NC1050
Adderley, Cecil L.	MA0260
Adderley, Meisha N.	OH0350
Addington, Joe	CA3300
Addison, Don F.	OR0800
Addo, Akosua O.	MN1623
Adduci, Kathryn James	CA4400
Adduci, Michael D.	CA4400
Adedapo, Adekola	WI1150
Adele, David	CA3200
Adelsberger, Andrew	MD0750
Adelson, Andrew D.	NJ0800
Adelson, Edward H.	OH1850
Adelson, Michael	NY3785
Adkins, Angela	NC1200
Adkins, Cathy L.	NC1250
Adkins, Christopher	TX2400
Adkins, Darrett	OH1700
Adkins, Darrett	NY1900
Adkins, Don	CA0300
Adkins, Donald	CA0400
Adkins, Elizabeth	DC0050
Adkins, Elizabeth	MD1010
Adkins, Elizabeth	DC0170
Adkins, Kathryn	CA0400
Adkins, Kathryn	CA0300
Adkins, Kathy	AL0750
Adkins, Paul	PA3330
Adkins, Richard C.	IA0300
Adkins, Scottye	MO0750
Adler, Christopher A.	CA5200
Adler, John	CO0950
Adler, Samuel	NY1900
Adlington, Stephanie	TN0100
Admiral, Roger	AA0110
Admiral, Roger	AA0100
Adnyana, I Dewa Ketut Alit	WI0350
Adsit, Glen	CT0650
Aduonum, Ama Oforiwaa Konadu	IL1150
Adzenyah, Abraham	CT0750
Aerie, Josh	WI0860
Aerie, Josh	MN0450
Afanassieva, Veronika	CO0275
Afifi, Bob	CA4700
Afonasyeva, Yekaterina	MD0850
Afonso, Daniel R.	CA0850
Afshar, Lily	TN1680
Agatiello, Gustavo	MA0260
Agawu, V. Kofi	NJ0900
Agee, Richard J.	CO0200
Agen, Kristine	IN0905
Agent, Betty	WA0650
Aghababian, Vartan	MA0400
Agidius, Michael	WA1100
Aglinskas, Peter	IL1085
Agnew, Joseph	IL3150
Agnew, Shawn	MO0850
Agopian, Edmond	AA0150
Agopian, Edmond	AA0050
Agostini, Federico	NY1100
Agrell, Jeffrey	IA1550
Aguilar, Carla E.	CO0550
Aguilar, Gustavo	ME0410
Aguirre, Ruth	TX2260
Aguirre, Sherrie Lake	VA1000
Aguirre, Sherrie Lake	VA0250
Ahearn, Kathryn	VA1475
Ahern, Patty	KS0265
Ahern, Rebecca	IA1390
Ahima, Kwame	TN1850
Ahlbeck, Laura	MA1400
Ahlers, Ruth	CT0300
Ahlquist, Janet S.	PA1550
Ahlquist, Karen	DC0100
Ahlstedt, Douglas F.	PA0550
Ahn, Angella	MT0200
Ahn, Christina H.	CA5350
Ahn, Hyeson Sarah	MN1200
Ahn, Hyojin	FL0050
Ahn, Jean	CA5350
Ahn, Jooyoung	TN1700
Ahn, Jungeun	NY2900
Ahn, Suhnne	MD0650
Ahner, Sally R.	TN1850
Aho, Kyle	MO0775
Ahola, Mark	NY3600
Ahonen-Eerikainen, Heidi	AG0600
Ahramjian, Sylvia Davis	PA3600
Ahrend, Janet	WA0250

Name	Code	Name	Code	Name	Code
Ahrend, Janet	WA0400	Aldrich, Fred	MA2050	Allen, David	IL3300
Ahuvia, Saar	NJ0700	Aldrich, Jon	MA0260	Allen, David	MS0420
Aicher, Carol Ann	NY2150	Aldrich, Mark L.	MA1650	Allen, Donald F.	FL1800
Aide, William	AG0450	Aldrich, Nicole P.	MO1900	Allen, Eddie	NY0500
Aigen, Kenneth	PA3250	Aldrich, Rachel	CA0810	Allen, Ferris	AR0750
Aikawa, Atsundo	NY2750	Aldrich, Rachel	CA1860	Allen, Frances	MD0170
Aiken, Barry	ID0140	Aldrich, Ralph E.	AG0500	Allen, Fred J.	TX2700
Aiken, Janice	LA0050	Aldrich, Simon	AI0150	Allen, Geri	MI2100
Aikens, Bill	MT0370	Aldridge, Ben	NY3765	Allen, Greg	IL1740
Aikin, Diane	NE0300	Aldridge, Ben	NY1400	Allen, Gregory	TX3510
Aikman, Merla	AA0035	Aldridge, Benjamin L.	NY3705	Allen, Helen	OH2050
Ailshie, Tyson	CO0650	Aldridge, Erin	WI0860	Allen, Ivalah	KS0350
Ailshie, Tyson	CO0100	Aldridge, Glenda	AR0500	Allen, James O.	MS0550
Ainanda, Lucy	AR0425	Aldridge, Rachel	WA0400	Allen, Jeffrey L.	CA5300
Ainger, Marc	OH1850	Aldridge, Robert	AA0020	Allen, Jennifer	AZ0470
Aiosa, Charlotte	VA1350	Aldridge, Robert	NJ1130	Allen, Jeremy	IN0900
Aipperspach, Candice Lane	TX2350	Alegant, Brian	OH1700	Allen, JoAnna	PA1750
Aipperspach, Ian B.	TX2350	Alegria, Gabriel A.	NY2750	Allen, Jodi Leigh	MA0260
Aitken, Deborah	CA1750	Aleksander, Elizabeth	NE0400	Allen, John	OK0750
Aitken, Dianne	AG0450	Alekseyeva, Marina	DC0170	Allen, Jonathan	IA1550
Ajero, Mario	TX2700	Aleo, Keith	MA0350	Allen, Kristopher	CT0500
Akagi, Kei	CA5020	Alesandrini, Joyce L.	OH1650	Allen, Lisa M.	GA1100
Akahori, Eliko	MA2050	Alesi-Pazian, Melody	NJ0800	Allen, Mark	OR1000
Akahoshi, Ole	CT0850	Alessi, Joseph	NY1900	Allen, Mark	PA3330
Akaka, Sheryl	WA0460	Alessi, Ralph P.	NY2750	Allen, Mark	CA0150
Akarepi, Ekaterini	OK1350	Alewine, Murry L.	TX2850	Allen, Matthew H.	MA2150
Ake, David	NV0100	Alexander, Charles Reid	IL3300	Allen, Michael	CO0550
Akerman, Mary S.	GA1150	Alexander, Conrad	PA2150	Allen, Nancy	TN0100
Akers, Diana L.	FL0650	Alexander, Conrad	NY1800	Allen, Nancy	NY1900
Akers, Ruth	FL0850	Alexander, Cory T.	TX3527	Allen, Nancy	WI1100
Akhmadullin, Iskander	MO1800	Alexander, Eric	NY3785	Allen, Nancy	CA2550
Aki, Syoko	CT0850	Alexander, Eric	CO0950	Allen, Peter	AF0100
Akin, Maurine	WY0130	Alexander, Glenn	NY3560	Allen, Ray	NY0500
Akin, Willie	MO1950	Alexander, J. Heywood	OH0650	Allen, Ray	NY0600
Akins, James	OH1850	Alexander, James	LA0450	Allen, Robert J.	NY3770
Akins, Keaton Damir	MI0350	Alexander, Jason	AL1050	Allen, Robert T.	VA0800
Akins, Lori B.	OH0950	Alexander, Joe L.	LA0250	Allen, Roy	TX3300
Akins, Lori	OH2450	Alexander, Joel	MN1280	Allen, Sarah	TX2400
Akins, Lori	OH0450	Alexander, Joseph	CA0800	Allen, Sheila M.	TX3000
Akinskas, Joseph	NJ1100	Alexander, Kathryn J.	CT0900	Allen, Stephen A.	NJ1130
Akrong, Isaac	AG0650	Alexander, Lisa M.	NY1600	Allen, Stephen Arthur	NJ1000
Aks, David M.	CA0835	Alexander, Lois L.	MI2120	Allen, Stephen	ID0060
Aksoy, Ozan	NY0625	Alexander, Marina	NY0644	Allen, Steve	IN1450
Al-Zand, Karim	TX2150	Alexander, Mark	TX2260	Allen, Susan	VA0050
Alajaji, Sylvia A.	PA1300	Alexander, Mark W.	TX1900	Allen, Susan	CA0510
Alamo, Juan	NC2410	Alexander, Michael	GA1150	Allen, Thomas O.	MN1300
Alancraig, Diane	CA0830	Alexander, Michael L.	TX0300	Allen, Tom	MO1710
Alaniz, Steve	CA5100	Alexander, Michelle	MA0350	Allen, Travis	UT0050
Alarie, Frederic	AI0200	Alexander, Michelle	MA0400	Allen, Virginia	NY4200
Alba, James J.	NH0250	Alexander, Prince Charles	MA0260	Allen, Virginia	PA3330
Albach, Carl	NY0150	Alexander, Travis	NC1550	Allen, Virginia	PA0850
Albagli, Richard	NY3700	Alexeyev, Anya	AG0600	Allen, Virginia	NY1900
Albanese, Brynn	CA0600	Alexopoulos, Christina	CA0960	Allen, William T.	NY1700
Albanese, Janet	IA0550	Aley, John	WI0815	Allen-Creighton, Esme	DE0150
Albano, John	CA2900	Alfano, Karen	MI0500	Allesee, Eric	NJ0750
Albano, Michael	AG0450	Alfieri, Gabriel	RI0150	Alley, Amy	TN1850
Albaugh, John	IA0550	Alfonsetti, Louis	NY0350	Alley, Greg	MI0350
Albela-Vega, Daniel	NM0310	Alfonzo, Jesus	FL1750	Alley, Gregory	MI0300
Albergo, Cathy	IL1085	Alford, Steve W.	NC1250	Alley, Laura	NY2250
Albers, Julie	GA1300	Alger, Neal	IL0550	Alley, Rob	AR0110
Albert, Donnie Ray	TX3510	Algieri, Stefano	AI0150	Allik, Kristi A.	AG0250
Albert, Heidi A.	OH0700	Alhaddad, Frederick I.	MI1200	Allison, Adrian	MN1295
Albert, Kristen A.	PA3600	Alhadeff, Peter	MA0260	Allison, Bill	CA1280
Albert, Laurence	TN1200	Ali, Kelly S.	VA1600	Allison, Edward	NC0050
Albert, Matthew	TX2400	Ali, Susan B.	CA1900	Allison, Elizabeth Catherine	MA0260
Albert, Michael P.	ME0250	Aliapoulios, S. Mark	FL1450	Allison, Ian	MN1250
Albert, Michael	ME0150	Aliapoulis, S. Mark	FL0700	Allison, James	IL1550
Albert, Thomas	VA1350	Alicea, Jose R.	PR0115	Allison, Joseph	KY0550
Alberts, Katherine	KY0250	Alico, Gregory	PA0350	Allison, Linda	DC0010
Albertson, John	DC0100	Alico, Gregory H.	PA3150	Allison, Linda	DC0110
Albin, William R.	OH1450	Alig, Kelley	OK0300	Allison, Rees	MN0800
Albo, Francisco Javier	GA1050	Aliquo, Don	TN1100	Allison, Robert	IL2900
Albrecht, Karen	TX1600	Aliyeva, Narmina	OH0350	Allman, Garrett N.	IL1100
Albrecht, Ken	IN1010	Alkire, Jeff	CA0150	Allmann, Kimberly	MN0250
Albrecht, Peg	AG0450	Allaire, Denis	MN1625	Allmark, John	RI0150
Albrecht, Ronald	IA1350	Allaire, Jean-Sebastien	AG0100	Allphin, Andrew	DC0050
Albrecht, Tamara	GA0750	Allan, Diana	TX3530	Allred, Carol Ann	UT0250
Albrecht, Theodore	OH1100	Allan, Kathryn	CA2840	Allred, Jody	UT0190
Albrecht, Timothy	GA0750	Allard, Catherine	AL1050	Allred, Nancy C.	UT0150
Albright, Bruce Randall	IN0907	Allard, James	MA0650	Allsbrook, Nancy Boone	TN1100
Albright, James	MO2000	Allata, Rachid	CA1560	Allsen, J. Michael	WI0865
Albright, Robyn	AA0050	Allbritten, James	NC1650	Allsup, Neal	KS0550
Albright, Timothy	NY3785	Allcott, Dan J.	TN1450	Allsup, Randall Everett	NY4200
Albrink, Emily	KY1500	Allebach, Robin	ND0600	Alltop, Stephen W.	IL2250
Albulescu, Eugene	PA1950	Allebach, Robin K.	MN1120	Allvin, Kerstin	MI1750
Alburger, Mark	CA1560	Allee, Fred	CA3975	Alm, Gina	CA5355
Albury, Robert T.	AZ0350	Allee, Steve	IN0907	Almargo, Brandon	MD0150
Alcalay, Eugene C.	WI0840	Allee, Steve	IN1650	Almario, Justo	CA5031
Alch, Marion R.	OH1850	Allemeier, John	NC2420	Almarza, Alberto	PA0550
Alcorn, Allison A.	IL3150	Allen, Aaron S.	NC2430	Alme, Joseph	ND0250
Aldag, Daniel	CA2250	Allen, Barbara	NY2900	Almeida, Artie	FL1800
Aldana, Milton	MD0600	Allen, Ben	MN0250	Almeida, John	FL1800
Aldcroft, Ken	AG0350	Allen, Benjamin	MN0300	Almen, Byron Paul	TX3510
Alden, Jane	CT0750	Allen, Burt	LA0550	Almich, Michael	OR1000
Alder, Alan	IN0150	Allen, Carl	NY1900	Almond, Frank	IL2250
Alderson, Daphne	PA3000	Allen, Christine	LA0550	Almond, Frank W.	CA4100
Alderson, Erin	IL1800	Allen, Christopher	LA0050	Almquist, Bradley L.	KY0950
Aldi, Barbara	NY3600	Allen, Christopher	PA0550	Alms, Anthony	MA0350
Aldins, Peter	MA1175	Allen, Christopher	PA1050	Alms, Anthony	NJ0175
Aldredge, Steven	OH2500	Allen, David R.	VA1100	Almy, Mark	CA1270

Alphabetical Listing of Faculty

Name	Code	Name	Code	Name	Code	Name	Code
Aloisio, Gerard S.	MN1000	Amis, Kenneth	MA0350	Anderson, Elizabeth Rene	IN0907
Alonso, Ernesto	PR0150	Amis, Kenneth	FL1125	Anderson, Emily	SD0050
Alonso-Minutti, Ana R.	TX3420	Amis, Kenneth	MA1175	Anderson, Eric	TN0260
Alonzo, Deborah	VA1650	Amlin, Martin	MA0400	Anderson, Eric	MN0040
Alorwoyie, Gideon F.	TX3420	Ammann, Bruce T.	SD0050	Anderson, Erik	ND0250
Alper, Garth	LA0760	Ammons, Anthony	NC1250	Anderson, Frank	NY0270
Alpern, Wayne	NY2250	Ammons, Mark	UT0050	Anderson, Gary L.	KY1350
Alsobrook, Joseph	MO0650	Amon, Jonathan T.	MA0510	Anderson, Gene	VA1500
Alstadter, Judith	NY1275	Amonson, Christina	AL1050	Anderson, Gwen	MN0300
Alstat, Sara	IL2500	Amoriello, Laura	NJ1350	Anderson, H. Gerald	IL2300
Alston, John	PA3200	Amoriello, Laura	NJ0175	Anderson, James Allen	DE0150
Alt, David	CA0960	Amorim, George J.	TX3525	Anderson, James	MA1450
Alt, Jerry A.	NM0310	Amoroso, Richard	PA3250	Anderson, James N.	GA0200
Altemeier, David	IA0550	Amory, Misha	PA0850	Anderson, Jared	MI1450
Altemeier, David	IA0600	Amory, Misha	NY1900	Anderson, Jared L.	WI0600
Altenbach, Andrew	MA0350	Amos, Alvin E.	PA2000	Anderson, Jay	NY2150
Alter, Adam M.	SC0800	Amos, C. Nelson	MI0600	Anderson, Jean	MA1400
Altevogt, Brian L.	MI0500	Amos, Gloria	VA0950	Anderson, Jeff	KS1000
Althoff, Erin	SC0420	Amos, Shaun	GA0500	Anderson, Jeff	IN1310
Althouse, Paul L.	CT0100	Amox, Jennifer	AR0300	Anderson, Jeff	IN1560
Altieri, Jason	NV0100	Amper, Leslie	MA2150	Anderson, Jeffrey	CA4150
Altino, Leonardo	TN1680	Amper, Leslie	MA1175	Anderson, Jennifer J.	NC1250
Altino, Soh-Hyun Park	TN1680	Amrein, Emilie	IL1400	Anderson, Jerry L.	MO0850
Altman, Barbara	GA0850	Amrod, Paula J.	PA0700	Anderson, Jill	CA1510
Altman, I. H.	GA1300	Amrozowicz, Mary Barbara	NY4460	Anderson, Jim	OH2550
Altman, John	CA3850	Amsel, Stephen	AA0150	Anderson, John	CA3050
Altman, Timothy	NC2435	Amsler, Audrey	IN1350	Anderson, Jon	ID0250
Altmire, Matt	CA3200	Amsler, Eva	FL0850	Anderson, Jonathan	MI2200
Altmire, Matthew	CA4450	Amstutz, A. Keith	SC1110	Anderson, Jonathan	TX3600
Altstaetter, Dean E.	OH1800	Amstutz, Peter	WV0750	Anderson, Juliana	MA0650
Altstaetter, Lucinda J.	OH1800	Amundson, Bret	MN0450	Anderson, Juliet V.	GA0490
Altstatt, Alison	IA1600	Amundson, Steven	MN1450	Anderson, Kathy T.	MS0570
Altstatt, Hamilton	SC0400	Amy, Robynn	MA0260	Anderson, Kay	TX3750
Alva, Albert	CA0960	An, Chun Chi	IN0900	Anderson, Ken	CA2100
Alvarado Ortiz, Julio E.	PR0115	An, Haekyung	MO0060	Anderson, Kris	KS0210
Alvarado, John	IN0907	An, Ning	TN0850	Anderson, Kristian	MN1260
Alvarado, Julieta	MN1500	An, Won-Hee	MA1450	Anderson, Larry R.	LA0770
Alvarez, Euridice	MS0750	An, Youngjoo	PA3250	Anderson, Leeann	OH1000
Alvarez, Euridice	NY1700	Anagnoson, James	AG0300	Anderson, Leon	FL0850
Alvarez, Franklin	AZ0300	Anang, Kofi	WA0200	Anderson, Lois	NJ0700
Alvarez, Heidi Pintner	KY1550	Anastasia, Stephen	CA0630	Anderson, Lyle	WI0815
Alvarez, Ian M.	WA0800	Anastasia, Stephen	CA3800	Anderson, Lyle J.	OH0450
Alvarez, Luis M.	PR0150	Anastasia, Stephen	CA3200	Anderson, Marc	MN0800
Alvarez, Ruben	IL0720	Anavitarte, David	TX2550	Anderson, Marc	NY3350
Alvarez, Ruben	IL2250	Ancona, James	DE0150	Anderson, Marcia H.	MI1200
Alvarez, Ruben	IL0550	Ancona, Ted	CA5300	Anderson, Marilyn E.	CA3100
Alverson, D. J.	CA0950	Anctil, Gilles	AI0050	Anderson, Marilyn E.	CA0550
Alverson, David J.	CA3800	Andaya, Mitos	PA3250	Anderson, Mark	IL1200
Alverson, J. Michael	SC0300	Andereck, Edwin	IA0950	Anderson, Mark	CA1800
Alves, Julio	WV0400	Anderer, Joseph T.	NY2750	Anderson, Matt	SC1080
Alves, William	CA1050	Anderle, Jeffrey	CA4150	Anderson, Matt	GA1500
Alves, William	CA2175	Anderman, Mark	CA4460	Anderson, Matthew	NJ0500
Alvey, Mary	NJ0200	Anders, Micheal F.	OH2275	Anderson, Matthew M.	GA1700
Alvi, Diba N.	MD0550	Anders, Nathan	OH0350	Anderson, Matthew T.	SC0400
Alvi, Diba N.	MD0650	Andersen, LeGrand	UT0200	Anderson, Michael Alan	NY1100
Alviani, Henry	PA0700	Andersen, Mary Ann	UT0200	Anderson, Michael P.	OK0750
Alvis, Jonathan	SD0600	Andersen, Michael	SD0050	Anderson, Michael J.	IL3310
Alviso, Ric	CA0835	Andersen, Nancy	CT0650	Anderson, Miles	CA4150
Alviso, Ric	CA4450	Anderson, Alerica	MO1100	Anderson, Ray R.	NY3790
Alwes, Chester	IL3300	Anderson, Alfonse	NV0050	Anderson, Richard	OK1350
Amador Medina, Ruben J.	PR0115	Anderson, Alfred	OH2150	Anderson, Richard P.	UT0050
Amalong, Philip	OH0680	Anderson, Allen L.	NC2410	Anderson, Robert	NY3250
Amano, Gary	UT0300	Anderson, Amy B.	TX3200	Anderson, Robert	NC2410
Amano, Hideko	IL1085	Anderson, Anamae	UT0050	Anderson, Robert P.	WI0803
Amante Y Zapata, Joseph J.	RI0101	Anderson, Andrew	IL3550	Anderson, Robert J.	CA5300
Amaral, Jorge A.	OH0200	Anderson, Andrew	IL0550	Anderson, Robert	AR0350
Amati-Camperi, Alexandra	CA5353	Anderson, Andrew E.	TX0075	Anderson, Ronald E.	TX2700
Amato, Beatrice	MO0700	Anderson, Angela	PA3250	Anderson, Ross	MN1500
Amato, Donna	PA0550	Anderson, Carl	IL0400	Anderson, Sally	VA1350
Amato, Michelle	FL1950	Anderson, Carl H. C.	AL0500	Anderson, Scott E.	ID0100
Amato, Patricia	MD0850	Anderson, Catherine Sentman	MD1100	Anderson, Scott	NE0600
Amaya, Jennifer	CA0630	Anderson, Charles A.	IL2150	Anderson, Seija	CA4300
Amaya, Joseph	NC0050	Anderson, Charlotte	TN1150	Anderson, Shane	TX2930
Ambartsumian, Levon	GA2100	Anderson, Cheryl M.	CA0400	Anderson, Shirley	TX0900
Ambert, William J.	PA3650	Anderson, Christine	PA3250	Anderson, Stella N.	MN0950
Ambler, Don	CO0150	Anderson, Christopher	AR0200	Anderson, Stephen	NC2410
Ambrose, Lorraine	AB0200	Anderson, Christopher	IL2510	Anderson, Sylvia	CA4150
Ambrose, Robert J.	GA1050	Anderson, Christopher M.	TX3200	Anderson, Thad	FL1800
Ambrose, Sarah Kruser	GA1050	Anderson, Claudia	IA0700	Anderson, Tim	OH2200
Ambrosini, Armand	OK1350	Anderson, Clipper	WA0650	Anderson, Tim H.	MD0520
Ambrosini, Jeffrey	OK1200	Anderson, Collin	IL2100	Anderson, Timothy	MD0475
Ambrosini, Rebekah	OK1200	Anderson, Collin J.	IL2150	Anderson, Toni P.	GA1200
Ambush, June	MA1560	Anderson, Collin	IL1085	Anderson, Trudi	MN0250
Amchin, Robert A.	KY1500	Anderson, Connie	OH0450	Anderson, Trudi J.	MN0050
Amend, Holly	WA0950	Anderson, Cynthia	WV0750	Anderson, Valdine	AC0100
Amend, James M.	GA1990	Anderson, Dan	IL0720	Anderson, William	NY3560
Amend, Jerome	IN1010	Anderson, Danna	MO0650	Anderson-Collier, Jean	MA0350
Amend, William	OR1250	Anderson, David C.	OK0150	Anderson-Himmelspach, Neil	MD0475
Amendola, James	NC2435	Anderson, David	WI0100	Andes, Tom	MO1800
Amendola, Vergie	CO0950	Anderson, David	WA0800	Andjaparidze, Eteri	NY2750
Ames, Anthony	MD1010	Anderson, Dean	CA1900	Andon, Sarah	CA5150
Ames, Jeffrey	TN0100	Anderson, Dean	MA0260	Andrade, Juan Pablo	TX3515
Amico, Stephen	NJ0020	Anderson, Dennis W.	CA3350	Andrade, Ken	CA1760
Amidon, Brad T.	PA2250	Anderson, Dennis	CA3200	Andraso, Margaret B.	KY1100
Amidon, Bradley	PA1200	Anderson, Diana	CO0200	Andre, David	CA1290
Amin, Kimberly	CA5040	Anderson, Dianna M.	ND0250	Andreacchi, Peter	NY2150
Amirault, Greg	AI0150	Anderson, Douglas K.	NY0270	Andreas, Cassandra	CT0300
Amirault, Steve	AI0150	Anderson, Edward D.	CO0250	Andres, Hoyt	CO0550
Amirkhanian, Maria	CA1950	Anderson, Elaine M.	OH2290	Andres, Rebecca	OH1450
Amis, Ken	MA0400	Anderson, Elizabeth	IL2100	Andres, Rebecca	OH2550

Name	Code	Name	Code	Name	Code
Andrew, Isaac	OR1250	Appello, Patrick	NJ0550	Arlen, Walter	CA2800
Andrew, Lesley	AG0550	Appenheimer-Vaida, Christiane	PA2200	Armandi, Richard	IL3100
Andrew, Nancy	CO0550	Apperson, Jim	AZ0470	Armato, John	MD0610
Andrews, Adrianna	IL3500	Apple, A. Alan	PA1750	Armendarez, Christina	TX1725
Andrews, Anita	UT0325	Apple, Marjorie	PA0400	Armenian, Raffi	AG0450
Andrews, Bradford	CA5150	Apple, Nancy K.	TN1680	Armer, Elinor	CA4150
Andrews, Christy D.	OK1450	Apple, Ryan	MI0910	Armetta, Joseph F.	MO1790
Andrews, Christy	OK0850	Apple, Trent	KY0250	Armfield, Terri E.	NC2600
Andrews, Deborah	NJ0700	Apple, Warren	FL1745	Armistead, Christine	MO1900
Andrews, Dwight D.	GA0750	Applebaum, Mark S.	CA4900	Armour, Janet E.	TN1680
Andrews, Jane E.	IA1800	Applebaum, Terry L.	PA3330	Arms, Janet	CT0650
Andrews, Jennifer	MA0260	Appleby-Wineberg, Bryan K.	NJ1050	Armstrong, Alan	NC1500
Andrews, Joyce	WI0830	Applegate, Ann	WI0925	Armstrong, Anne A.	GA1300
Andrews, Julibeth	RI0250	Applegate, Erik	CO0950	Armstrong, Anton	MN1450
Andrews, Kenneth B.	NY3780	Applegate, Geoffrey	MI2200	Armstrong, Candace	TN0900
Andrews, Laura J.	KS0350	Applegate, Janice	IN1300	Armstrong, Colin	PA3150
Andrews, Linda	IL3500	Appleman, Harry	MD0550	Armstrong, Daniel C.	PA2750
Andrews, Mary	MI2000	Appleman, Richard	MA0260	Armstrong, Eleanor Duncan	PA2750
Andrews, Nancy	ME0270	Appleman, Tom	MA0260	Armstrong, Heather M.	IA0950
Andrews, Pamela	FL0850	Applewhite, Willie	UT0190	Armstrong, James E.	NC2700
Andrews, Paul	AL0400	Applin, Richard	MA0260	Armstrong, James I.	VA0250
Andrews, Rachel	MD0520	Applonie, Brent	UT0400	Armstrong, James D.	PA1250
Andrews, Rachel	MI1850	Applonie, Jean	UT0050	Armstrong, Jeff	NY1050
Andrews, Rick	SD0050	Aprahamian, Lucik	CA2150	Armstrong, John	AG0400
Andrews, Susan	LA0300	Aquila, Carmen	NY4460	Armstrong, Joshua	MS0250
Andrews-Smith, Belinda	OH0850	Aquilanti, Giancarlo	CA4900	Armstrong, Kathy	AG0100
Andrievsky, Alexandra	AA0050	Aquilino, Dominic	NC2600	Armstrong, Laura D.	MD0300
Andrus, Brice	GA1050	Aquilino, Dominic	NC1250	Armstrong, Richard	AL0500
Andrus, Deborah E.	PA2450	Aquina, Carmen	NY0400	Armstrong, Robert	OR1010
Andrus, Victoria	UT0150	Aquino, Diane	CT0050	Armstrong, Robin E.	MD0520
Angebrandt, Lynn	CA2750	Aquino, Robert	NY2102	Armstrong, Stephen	AG0130
Angeles, L. Dean	LA0300	Arad, Atar	IN0900	Armstrong, Vahn R.	VA1000
Angelillo, Vic	AI0210	Arakawa, Jasmin	IL3500	Arnarson, Stefan Orn	NJ1100
Angelli, Paul	MA2030	Arana, Miranda	OK1350	Arnason, Carolyn	AG0600
Angelo, Carl	MI1850	Aranda, John	CA1900	Arnay, David	CA5300
Anger, Darol	MA0260	Aranda, Patrick	CA0950	Arnay, David	CA3500
Angerhofer, Thomas Erik	CO0550	Arania, Orna	IL2200	Arndt, Kevin	WI1150
Angeroth, Kathi	NE0700	Aranovskaya, Alla	KS1450	Arndt, Matthew J.	IA1550
Angerstein, Fred	TX3450	Arasi, Melissa	GA0900	Arndt, Michael J.	TN1100
Angerstein, Fred	TX1000	Arauco, Ingrid	PA1500	Arndt, Sandra K.	TN1100
Angerstein, Nancy	TX1450	Araujo, Ilka Vasconcelos	TX3250	Arndt, Wayne	NJ0550
Angerstein, Nancy	TX1000	Araujo, Ramon	PR0125	Arne, Devin	FL0200
Angier, D. Chase	NY0100	Arbogast, Jennifer	TN0260	Arner, Lucia	NY2250
Anglin, David Ives	CA0825	Arbogast, Jennifer	IN1560	Arneson, Christopher P.	NJ1350
Anglley, Tamey	TX2700	Arbogast, Paul	PA3330	Arnett, Alan	VA1350
Angulo, Denson	UT0325	Arcamone, Dan	CT0550	Arnett, Nathan D.	IL1240
Angulo, Denson	UT0250	Arcaro, John	MA0260	Arnold, Alison E.	NC1700
Angulo, Skye	CA2550	Arcaro, Peter	FL1100	Arnold, Ben	KY1450
Anhalt, Istvan	AG0250	Archambault, Ellen	OH0350	Arnold, Clara S.	TX3200
Annicchiarico, Michael	NH0350	Archambault, Ellen J.	OH1850	Arnold, Craig S.	NY2150
Annis, Robert L.	NJ1350	Archambeault, Noel	DE0150	Arnold, David C.	PA3250
Anno, Mariko	IL1400	Archambo, Larry	TX1700	Arnold, Edwin P.	PA1450
Annoni, Maria T.	MN0900	Archard, Chuck	FL1550	Arnold, Elizabeth Packard	KY1450
Anop, Lenora	IL2970	Archbold, Lawrence	MN0300	Arnold, Ellen	PA1450
Anop, Lenora Marya	IL2910	Archbold, Timothy	IL0400	Arnold, Horacee	NJ1400
Ansari, Emily	AG0500	Archer, Ed	CA3150	Arnold, Johana	NY1400
Ansell, Steven	MA0400	Archer, Esther	CA5510	Arnold, John	OK0750
Anselm, Karen	PA0250	Archer, Gail	NY4450	Arnold, John	PA2450
Anson-Cartwright, Mark	NY0600	Archer, Gail	NY0200	Arnold, Larry	NC2435
Anson-Cartwright, Mark	NY0642	Archer, Gail	NY2150	Arnold, Mark	NY1250
Antal, Tom	CA0825	Archer, Kelly	MO1650	Arnold, Mitchell A.	WV0750
Anthon, Gina	LA0650	Archer, Kimberly K.	IL2910	Arnold, Robert D.	PA2550
Anthony, Bob	CA1520	Archer, Naida	AJ0150	Arnold, Roger	CT0700
Anthony, Carl	AR0850	Archer, Robert	TX0250	Arnold, Scott	AA0050
Anthony, James	MD0850	Archer, Thaddeus	OH2300	Arnold, Stacy	TX1775
Anthony, Janet	WI0350	Archetto, Maria	GA0755	Arnold, Tom	MO0100
Anthony, John P.	CT0100	Archibald, Becky H.	IN0100	Arnold, Tony	NY4320
Anthony, Johnny	MS0350	Archibald, Elizabeth	MD0650	Arnon, Baruch	NY1900
Anthony, Michael	NM0450	Archibald, Laurie	OH1300	Arnone, Anthony R.	IA1550
Anthony, Robert	CA0350	Archibald, William	IL1050	Arnone, Francesca M.	TX0300
Anthony, Robert	CA0815	Archibeque, Charlene	CA4400	Arnott, J. David	MN0350
Anthony, Ron	CA2700	Arcila, Billy	CA1900	Arnow, Chad A.	OH0680
Anthony, Tom	MD1100	Arcila, Billy	CA1520	Arnow, Charles	OH2550
Antokoletz, Elliott M.	TX3510	Arcu, Ariana	AL1250	Arnwine, James A.	CA3500
Antolik, Martha E.	AR0850	Ard, Ken	CA4050	Aron, Stephen	OH2150
Antolini, Anthony	ME0200	Ard, Kenneth	CA2100	Aron, Stephen	OH1700
Antonacci, Jarred M.	PA1550	Ard, Sharon	AR0600	Aron, William	CA3520
Antonacos, Anastasia	ME0150	Ardan, Laura	GA0750	Aron, William	CA4650
Antonacos, Anastasia	PA1600	Arden, Cynthia	IL1400	Aronov, Arkady	NY2250
Antonelli, Amy	DC0050	Ardovino, Joseph	AL1200	Aronov, Arkady	NY2150
Antonellis, Evan	OH1900	Ardovino, Lori	AL1200	Aronson, Abigail	MA0260
Antonetti, Susan	AR0750	Ardrey, Cathleen	PA2350	Arell, Christopher A.	MA0700
Antonich, Mark	PA1350	Arecchi, Kathleen H.	NH0250	Arreola, Brian	NC2420
Antonich, Mark E.	PA3650	Arellano, Kristina	MN1250	Arriale, Lynne	FL1950
Antonio, Garry	AI0150	Arendsen, Benjamin D.	NY2550	Arrigotti, Stephanie	NV0150
Antonioli, Laurie A.	CA5000	Arendt, Michael J.	WI0817	Arrington, Amanda	KS0650
Antonova, Natalya	NY1100	Arenson, Michael	DE0150	Arrivee, David	CA0600
Antonucci, Robert	PA3650	Arenz, David	GA1550	Arroe, Cate	MI0650
Antony, Trent	CO0300	Areyzaga, Michelle	IL0150	Arrowsmith, Brenda	AG0070
Anzivino, Steve	MI0300	Argenta, Nancy	AB0210	Arrowsmith, Jamie	AG0070
Apel, Ted R.	ID0050	Argenti, Mary A.	CA1020	Arucci, John	NY5000
Apelgren, Scott	FL0150	Argento, Dominick J.	MN1623	Arsenauit, Greg	RI0200
Apfelstadt, Hilary	AG0450	Argersinger, Charles	WA1150	Arshagouni, Michael H.	CA2750
Aplanalp, Woody	CA0510	Argiro, James	MA2100	Arslanian, Paul P.	MA2000
Apodaca, Denise R.	CO0250	Argyros, Maria	NY0625	Artemova, Alina	CA0825
Aponte, Jose Porentud	TX3420	Arian, Merri	NY1450	Artemova, Alina V.	CA2050
Aponte, Maria P.	PR0150	Arita, Junko	NY2660	Artesani, Laura	ME0440
Aponte, Pedro R.	VA0600	Arizaga, Anthony	CA1270	Arthur, Charles	VA1500
Appel, Toby	NY1900	Arjomand, Ramin Amir	NY2750	Arthur, Katherine	CA0600
Appell, Glen	CA1560	Arksey, Meredith	WA1150	Arthurs, Robert	NY2400

Alphabetical Listing of Faculty

Name	Code	Name	Code	Name	Code
Artimisi, Tony	NC2700	Athayde, Juliana	NY1100	Austin, Melissa	TN0100
Artinian, Annie	IL0730	Athayde, Robert L.	CA0807	Austin, Michael	MO0850
Artmann, Mary	CO0275	Athens, William	OR0250	Austin, Paul	MI0300
Artwick, Thomas	VA1850	Atherholt, Robert	TX2150	Austin, Stephanie	CA1450
Artymiw, Lydia	MN1623	Atherton, Leonard	IN0150	Austin, Stephen F.	TX3420
Arul, Kumaran	CA4900	Atherton, Peter L.	CA0960	Austin, Terry	VA1600
Arvin, Gary	IN0900	Atherton, Susan	IN0150	Austin, Trent R.	ME0500
Arvin, Tammy J.	IL1090	Atherton, Timothy E.	NH0100	Austin, Valerie A.	NC2435
Arzigian, Arleen	MA0260	Atherton, Timothy	MA2100	Austin-Stone, Heather	WV0550
Arzillo, Marisa A.	FL1550	Athparia, Colleen	AA0050	Autry, Philip E.	TN0550
Arzillo, Marisa	FL2050	Atienza, Anthony	CA4850	Auwarter, Doug	MO1810
Asada, Chi	CA0825	Atkatz, Edward	FL1125	Auwarter, Doug	MO0850
Asai, Rika	IN0900	Atkins, Victor	LA0800	Auwarter, Douglas	KS0570
Asai, Susan M.	MA1450	Atkinson, Charles M.	OH1850	Avakian, Helen	NY1050
Asakura, Iwao	TX2750	Atkinson, James	CA0825	Avanesian-Weinstein, Karina	IN1800
Asano, Yuiko	LA0300	Atkinson, Keith	AG0300	Avdeeff, Melissa	AA0110
Asbell, Paul	VT0450	Atkinson, Keith	AG0450	Averbach, Ricardo Franco	OH1450
Asbell, Stephanie Ames	TX3175	Atkinson, Monte	CO0225	Averett, Janet M.	CA4400
Asbill, M. Miller	NC0250	Atkinson, Sean E.	TX3500	Averhoff, Carlos	FL0700
Asbo, Kayleen	CA4150	Atkisson, Lovelle	TN1250	Averill, Gage	AB0100
Asbury, David	TX2650	Atladottir, Hrabba	CA5000	Averitt, Frances Lapp	VA1350
Ascani, Argeo	NY2150	Atlas, Allan W.	NY0600	Averitt, William E.	VA1350
Asch, Arthur	WI0862	Atlas, Allan	NY0500	Averrett, Michael	KS1400
Aschbrenner, Charles C.	MI1050	Atlas, Raphael	MA1750	Avery, Dawn	MD0550
Asche, Charles	CA5060	Ator, Irene S.	IN0905	Avery, Elizabeth	OK1350
Asche, Kyle	IL1615	Ator, James	IN0905	Avery, Handy	AL1160
Asche, Kyle	IL1900	Atorino, John J.	NY2750	Avery, Lawrence	NY1860
Ascione, Ray A.	MD0060	Atria, Karen	OH0850	Avery, Susan J.	NY1800
Asefiev, Boris	KY1000	Atria, Karen	OH2050	Avey, Kevin	NE0150
Asel, Nicole	TX3515	Attanaseo, Jeremy	IL0400	Avidon, Scott	NJ0700
Ash, Corey	TX1100	Attar, Yaniv	AL1150	Aviguetero, Anthony	CA2800
Ashbaker, Susan	NJ1350	Attaway, Aiya	OK0450	Avitabile, Judy	NY3450
Ashbaker, Susan	PA0850	Atteberry, Ron	MO0100	Avitsur, Haim	PA3600
Ashby, Arved M.	OH1850	Attebery, Brian	ID0100	Avramov, Bogidar	CA2800
Ashby, Eda	ID0060	Atterbury, Rick	WA0900	Avrett, Martha	OK0700
Ashby, Jay	OH1700	Attrep, Kara	OH0300	Avshalomov, Daniel	NY2150
Ashby, Michael	PA3550	Attrot, Ingrid	AB0210	Awe, Francis P.	CA3500
Ashby, Steven	VA1600	Atwater, Jennifer	WI0300	Ax, Emanuel	NY1900
Ashcraft, Eric	IA0950	Atwell, Bruce W.	WI0830	Axelrod, Lawrence	IL0720
Ashe, Jennifer	CT0150	Atwood, James H.	LA0300	Axelson, Shelley	NJ0800
Ashe, Jennifer	MA0700	Atwood, Jodi	AA0040	Axinn, Audrey	NY1900
Ashear, Aaron	WY0150	Atwood, Julie	TX2800	Axsom, Ron	PA0950
Ashkenasi, Samuel	PA0850	Atz, Karen	WI0815	Axtell, Katherine L.	VA0600
Ashley, Douglas D.	SC0500	Atzinger, Christopher	MN1450	Axtell, Les	TX3050
Ashley, Marie	FL1450	Au, Aaron	AA0100	Axworthy, Tamra	CO0275
Ashley, Richard	IL2250	Au, Hiu-Wah	NC0050	Ayau, Joel T.	VA1350
Ashmore, Lance	OH0300	Au, Kingchi	TX2300	Aye, Jeremy K.	NY2750
Ashmore, Lance	OH2275	Aubin, Isabelle	NY3717	Ayer, Christopher	TX2700
Ashmore, Lance	OH1800	Aubin, Isabelle	NY2650	Ayers, Jesse M.	OH1350
Ashmore, Michel	MO0250	Aubin, Matthew	WA1150	Ayers, Steven	WI1150
Ashmore, Pamela J.	OH1800	Aubin, Stephane	AI0210	Ayesh, Kevin	NC0220
Ashton, Alice	UT0190	Aubrey, Julia	MS0700	Ayick, Paul	FL0200
Ashton, Graham	NY3785	Aubrey, Robert	MS0700	Ayllon, Robert	MO1950
Ashton, J. Bruce	TN1350	Aubuchon, Ann Marie	CA2700	Aylward, Ansgarius	NY0400
Ashton, Jack	UT0190	AuBuchon, Elaine	MO1780	Aylward, John J.	MA0650
Ashton, Jeff C.	OR1100	AuBuchon, Tim	MO1780	Aymer, Justin	IL1740
Ashton, John H.	WV0300	Aucoin, Amy	KY0950	Ayoub, Anna Claire	PA3150
Ashton, Ted	ID0060	Audet, Peter	AG0500	Ayoub, Anna Claire	MD0500
Ashworth, John	KY1500	Audi, Carlos	FL0930	Ayoub, Jason	MD0300
Ashworth, Teresa	MN1100	Auer, Edward	IN0900	Ayre, Ron	AJ0100
Ashworth, Thomas	MN1623	Auer, Frank	DC0170	Ayres, Carol	IA0800
Asia, Daniel I.	AZ0500	Auer, Shelley	TX0075	Ayres, Rebecca Pollack	CA3400
Askew, Dennis	NC2430	Auerbach, Brent	MA2000	Azabagic, Denis	IL0550
Askew, Jeff	CA0350	Auerbach, Dan J.	GA0850	Azar, Andree	AI0150
Askren, David	CA0830	Auerbach, David	MN1625	Azevedo, Helena	WA0860
Askvig, Jamie	WY0115	Auerbach, Elise M.	PA3250	Azikiwe, Amadi	VA0600
Asly, Monica	AI0150	Aufmann, Ronald	OH2200	Azimkhodjaeva, Shakida	GA2100
Asmus, Edward P.	FL1900	Aufmann, Ronald	KY1000	Azzara, Christopher D.	NY1100
Asmus, Elizabeth Etters	PA0950	Augenblick, John	FL0700	Azzati, Eduardo	PA2450
Asmus, Elizabeth	PA2300	August, David	NY2900	Azzolina, Jay	NY2200
Asnawa, I Ketut Gede	IL3300	August, Gregg	CT0600	Azzoni-Dow, Christine	CA2390
Aspaas, Christopher	MN1450	Augustadt, David W.	ND0400	Babad, Bruce	CA1900
Asper, Lynn K.	MI0850	Augustine, Joseph R.	OH2150	Babal, Gregory	CT0650
Asplin, David	WA1350	Augustine, Shari	KS0590	Babayan, Naira	DC0170
Aspling, Carol	CA0350	Augustine, William	CA4450	Babayan, Sergei	OH0600
Asplund, Christian	UT0050	Augustson, Darice E.	MO0775	Babb, Douglas	IN1100
Aspnes, Jane	AK0150	Aulenbacher, Dennis	IL2970	Babb, Douglas	IN0907
Aspnes, Lynne A.	AZ0100	Auler, Robert M.	NY3770	Babb, Mark	IN1485
Assad, Michael	TN1680	Aultman, Carol	TX2600	Babb, Tim	NC1250
Assad, Mike	TN1200	Aultman, Gerald	TX2600	Babbitt, Frank	IL0850
Assad, Sergio	CA4150	Auman, Kevin	NC1450	Babbitt, John	WI1150
Astafan, Marc A.	PA3250	Auman, Richard	PA2950	Babbitt, Mark	IL1150
Astafan, Marc	MA1400	Aune, Gregory	MN0750	Babbitt, Milton	NJ0900
Astaire, John	CA0600	Auner, Edith	MA1900	Babcock, Andrew	TX1550
Asteriadou, Maria	PA1750	Ausch, Adriana	MA1175	Babcock, Beverly	MD0750
Asti, Martha S.	NC2650	Ausmann, Stephen	OH2600	Babcock, Donald J.	MI0600
Astolfi, Jeri-Mae G.	WI0830	Austerlitz, Paul	PA1400	Babcock, Jonathan	TX3175
Aston, Janis	TN1600	Austern, Linda	IL2250	Babcock, Mark A.	IA0200
Aston, Spencer	MA0510	Austin, Alan S.	TX3450	Babcock, Michael	VA0650
Astrachan, Christina	ME0200	Austin, Debra	IL1150	Babcock, Richard	CA2650
Astrachan, Christina	ME0500	Austin, Diane Snow	NY2750	Babcock, Ronald	OR0850
Astrup, Margaret	CT0800	Austin, Glenda K.	MO0800	Babcock, Windy	TX1550
Asuncion, Victor S.	TN1680	Austin, James R.	CO0800	Babelay, Paul	NC1250
Atanasiu, George	NJ1050	Austin, Jennifer N.	SC1200	Baber, Joseph W.	KY1450
Atanasiu, Lenuta	NJ1050	Austin, Joshua	NE0250	Baber, Katherine	CA5150
Atapine, Dmitri	NV0100	Austin, Kenneth L.	IL3100	Babich, Christina	OH1000
Atchison, Scott-Lee	KY1450	Austin, Kevin	AI0070	Babidge, Darrell	UT0050
Atchison-Wood, Dawn	KY0450	Austin, Linda B.	AR0750	Babinec, Lori	WI0300
Atchley, Elizabeth	OR0700	Austin, Linda	AR0350	Babiracki, Carol M.	NY4100
Athas, James	WI0865	Austin, Mary Jane	VT0250	Baboian, John	MA0260

Name	Code	Name	Code	Name	Code
Babor, James	CA5300	Bailey, Sheryl	MA0260	Balboa, Javier	TX3515
Baca, Danny	TX2300	Bailey, Steve	NC2440	Balcetis, Allison	AA0100
Baca, Robert J.	WI0803	Bailey, Terence	AG0500	Balch, Mary W.	AL1160
Baccus, H. E.	IL0720	Bailey, Walter B.	TX2150	Baldacchino, Laura Falzon	NY4200
Baccus, Jessica	MD0150	Bailey, Wayne A.	AZ0100	Baldauff, Brian	WV0600
Bach, Anne	IL3450	Bailey, Zuill	TX3520	Balder, Patrick	MN1625
Bach, Edward	AC0050	BaileyShea, Matthew	NY1100	Balderston, Stephen	IL0750
Bach, Larry	MN1250	BaileyShea, Matthew L.	NY4350	Baldini, Christian	CA5010
Bach, Mia	AG0450	Baime, Peter	WI1150	Baldini, Donald J.	NH0100
Bach, Timothy	CA4150	Baime, Peter	WI0825	Baldini, Donald	NH0150
Bachelder, Elizabeth Y.	VA1250	Baime, Peter	WI0150	Baldo, Jonathan	NY1100
Bachman, James	CA0600	Bain, Andrew	CA1075	Baldoria, Charisse J.	PA0250
Bachman, Jerome	NY0350	Bain, Clare	IN1100	Baldridge, Margaret Nichols	MT0400
Bachmann, George	OH0650	Bain, Jennifer	AF0100	Baldus, Kara A.	MO1900
Bachmann, George	OH1100	Bain, Reginald	SC1110	Baldwin, Catherine	PA3400
Bachmann, Nancy	CA2775	Baione, Larry	MA0260	Baldwin, Dalton	NJ1350
Baciu, Bianca	AA0020	Bair, Jeffery J.	NC0650	Baldwin, Daniel	IA0950
Back, Douglas	AL0345	Bair, Sheldon E.	MD0475	Baldwin, David B.	MN1623
Backlin, William	IA1170	Baird, Barbara M.	OR1050	Baldwin, Gail	IL0100
Backus, Carolyn A.	TX0300	Baird, Dianne	AG0250	Baldwin, John	ID0050
Bacon, Anthony	AG0170	Baird, John	IL1750	Baldwin, Joseph	MA1750
Bacon, Boyd	NE0450	Baird, Julianne C.	NJ1100	Baldwin, Karen	WA1350
Bacon, Joel	CO0250	Baird, Melinda Lambert	DC0170	Baldwin, Karen	WA0250
Bacon, John	NY4320	Baird, Sara Lynn	AL0200	Baldwin, Kurt	MO1830
Bacon, John	NY4460	Baird, Thomas	NY3785	Baldwin, Melvin	CA0650
Bacon, John	NY3725	Bairos, Monte	CA1560	Baldwin, Nathan Taylor	WV0200
Bacon, Marcy D.	NY2650	Bajekal, Nirmal	VA1500	Baldwin, Philip R.	WA1350
Bacon, Masako	NE0450	Bak, Edward	OH1850	Baldwin, Robert L.	UT0250
Bacon, Scott D.	PA1000	Bakan, Jonathon E.	AG0500	Baldwin, Todd	DC0010
Badami, Charles A.	MO0950	Bakan, Michael	FL0850	Baldwin, Tom	MD1010
Baddorf, Donald	IL3550	Bakenhus, Douglas	LA0550	Baldwin, Wesley H. B.	TN1710
Bade, Christopher	IN1560	Baker, Alan	PA0250	Balensuela, Matthew	IN0350
Bade, Lori E.	LA0200	Baker, Allison	IL3150	Balensuela, Peggy	IN0800
Badea, Remus	IL0850	Baker, Amy	PA3100	Balentine, James S.	TX3530
Baden, Robert	WV0800	Baker, Andrew	IL0850	Bales, Ann	CA2050
Badgerow, Justin A.	PA1250	Baker, Brian	WI0300	Bales, Bruce	CA2050
Badgley, Clifford	CA1850	Baker, Chad	OH0350	Bales, Kenton W.	NE0610
Bado, Richard	TX2150	Baker, Charles	OH1100	Bales, Kevin	GA1050
Badolato, James V.	MD0550	Baker, Christian Matthew	AR0350	Balestra, Richard J.	NY3770
Badridze, Ketevan	IN0910	Baker, Cynthia	AZ0350	Balestra, Richard	NY0650
Bae, Ik-Hwan	IN0900	Baker, Dale	NC2350	Balestra, Rick	NY1350
Baedke, Ron	VA1500	Baker, David N.	IN0900	Baley, Virko	NV0050
Baek, Na-Young	NJ0700	Baker, Eric	TX1850	Balfany, Gregory J.	WI0810
Baer, Alan J.	NJ1130	Baker, Frederick	MT0200	Balge, Bethel	MN0200
Baer, Alan	NY1900	Baker, Guy O.	WV0650	Balge, Bethel A.	MN1030
Baer, Alan	NY0150	Baker, Hill	CO0625	Balian, Muriel G.	CA1700
Baer, Alan	NY2150	Baker, James	AL0300	Balian, Muriel	CA1960
Baer, Alan	NY2250	Baker, James	RI0050	Balic, Adriana	CA5300
Baer, Matthew Kevin	CA4300	Baker, James	NY2250	Balija, Ayn	VA1550
Baer, Sarah	PA2450	Baker, Jan Berry	GA0750	Balins, Andris	NY3765
Baer, Seth	NY2105	Baker, Jan Berry	GA1050	Balk, Malcolm	NY3775
Baer, Seth R.	NJ0800	Baker, Jason	MS0500	Balke, Maureen	MI0100
Baer, Solomon	IL1750	Baker, Jeff	TX2955	Balkin, Laura M.	NY3730
Baer, Stephanie	NY2750	Baker, Jessica	IL2750	Balkin, Richard A.	NY3730
Baer-Peterson, Jamie	NJ0760	Baker, John	FL0930	Ball, Alexandria	PA2900
Baerg, Theodore	AG0500	Baker, Katherine Ramos	CA0835	Ball, David	VA1700
Baez, Alberto	PR0100	Baker, Kent	VT0100	Ball, Gerrie	MI2200
Baez, Luis	CA4150	Baker, Kevin L.	MO0300	Ball, Greg L.	TX2750
Bagg, Jonathan E.	NC0600	Baker, Kristi A.	KS1000	Ball, James	MI0100
Bagg, Joseph	CA1000	Baker, Malcolm Lynn	CO0900	Ball, Jill	AG0500
Baggech, Melody A.	OK0300	Baker, Marc	MO1550	Ball, Julia	NM0200
Baggett, Brian	KS1000	Baker, Mark	FL0150	Ball, Karen	IL2300
Bagley, Marjorie H.	NC2430	Baker, Mark	WI1150	Ball, Leonard V.	GA2100
Baglio, Brennan	WA0030	Baker, Mark A.	OH0350	Ball, Mindy	CA5355
Baglio, Genevieve	WA1300	Baker, Meredith E.	NY2550	Ball, Mindy	CA0960
Bagratuni, Suren	MI1400	Baker, Michael	KY1450	Ball, Sheridan J.	CA1520
Bagwell, Thomas	NY2250	Baker, Michelle	NY2150	Ball, Steven	MI2100
Baham, Kerry M.	TX3370	Baker, Michelle	NY2250	Ball, Terry	AG0050
Bahcall, Klara	WI0830	Baker, Nathan A.	WY0050	Ball, Thomas J.	CO0900
Bahn, Curtis	NY3300	Baker, Nicole	CA0815	Ball, W. Scott	TN1350
Bahn, Lina	CO0800	Baker, R. Bryan	CA1250	Ball, Wesley A.	CT0800
Bahr, Jason	FL0680	Baker, Robert P.	DC0100	Ballam, Michael	UT0300
Bai, Millie	PA3250	Baker, Ron	MI1180	Ballard, Alice	MS0300
Bai, Pauline	HI0050	Baker, Ruth	GA0300	Ballard, Dennis L.	IN0800
Baik-Kim, Eun Ae	PA0950	Baker, Sharon	NH0350	Ballard, Jack	OH1350
Bailen, Eliot T.	NY0750	Baker, Sherry H.	KY0450	Ballard, Jeffrey D.	IN0100
Bailey, Brandon	SC0050	Baker, Sidney	IA0790	Ballard, Marcus	LA0900
Bailey, Brian K.	OH0650	Baker, Sonya G.	KY0950	Ballard, Timothy Marshall	MD0300
Bailey, Candace L.	NC1600	Baker, Stacy A.	KY0900	Ballard-Ayoub, Anna Claire	PA1400
Bailey, Craig	AC0100	Baker, Steve	CA2100	Ballard-Ayoub, Anne Claire	MD0300
Bailey, Darrell	IN0907	Baker, Susanne R.	IL0750	Ballatori, Cristina	TX3515
Bailey, Don	AR0730	Baker, Tony E.	TX3420	Ballengee, Chris	FL1675
Bailey, Donald	TX0300	Baker, Vicki	TX3300	Ballenger, William	TX3200
Bailey, Jane	OK0550	Baker, W. Claude	IN0900	Ballereau, Laurence	NY1600
Bailey, John R.	NE0600	Baker, Wade	OR1100	Ballerino, John	CA5060
Bailey, Jon D.	CA3650	Baker, Wade	OR1300	Ballif, Adam	ID0060
Bailey, Kalomo	KY0750	Baker, Walter W.	OH0300	Ballif, Kristi	CO0225
Bailey, Kathryn	AG0500	Baker, Wilbur	NJ0825	Ballin, Scott	NY1275
Bailey, Marie	IL1850	Baker, William	NY1900	Ballinger, Robert W.	OH2300
Bailey, Mark	TN0850	Baker, William	IN0005	Ballmaier, Robert	IL0720
Bailey, Mary Lindsey	CO0225	Baker, William	OH1850	Ballora, Mark E.	PA2750
Bailey, Nancy	TX2150	Bakkegard, Karen	MD0400	Ballou, David L.	MD0850
Bailey, Rex	IN0400	Bakkum, Nathan	IL0720	Ballweg, D. Brent	OK0650
Bailey, Richard H.	AR0810	Bakos, Daniel F.	GA2130	Balmaceda, Kelly	GA0950
Bailey, Robert E.	OK0550	Bakriges, Christopher	MA1550	Balmer, Bill	OH2275
Bailey, Robert	NY2740	Balach, Nancy Maria	MS0700	Balmer, Dan	OR0400
Bailey, Ronda J.	KS0400	Balada, Leonardo	PA0550	Balmer, Patricia	TX3600
Bailey, Sally	NY0450	Balagurchik, James	NM0450	Balmos, Donald	TX1600
Bailey, Scott	MA2100	Balakerskaia, Anna	VA0450	Balog, George	NJ0175
Bailey, Shad	MT0370	Balasubrahmaniyan, B.	CT0750	Balogh, Lajos	OR0500

Alphabetical Listing of Faculty

Name	Code
Balogh, Mike	AG0130
Balough, Teresa	CT0150
Balson, Donna C.	NY1600
Baltaian, Aroussiak	CA3300
Baltaian, Sarkis	CA1075
Baltazar, Crystl S.	NJ0800
Balter, Marcos	IL0720
Balthazar, Scott Leslie	PA3600
Balthrop, Carmen A.	MD1010
Baltz, Ann	CA0835
Balzano, Gerald	CA5050
Bambach, Paul	CA5060
Bamberger, David	OH0600
Bamberger, Jeanne	MA0260
Bambrick, Heather	AG0450
Bamonte, David	OR0850
Banagale, Ryan	CO0200
Banaszak, Greg J.	OH0200
Banaszak, Gregory	OH0600
Banaszek, Maurycy	NJ0700
Bancks, Jacob	IL0100
Bandem, I Made	MA0700
Bandermann, Billie	CA1550
Banducci, Antonia L.	CO0900
Banfield, William	MA0260
Banfield-Taplin, Carrie	OH0950
Bang, In-Sun	NY3785
Bange, Darren R.	MD1000
Bangle, Jerry	NC2640
Banion, Brian	OH0350
Banister, Linda	GA0250
Banister, Suzanne	AR0350
Banister, Suzanne	AR0850
Bankas, Atis	AG0300
Banke, Andrea E.	KS1450
Bankhead, James M.	UT0300
Banks, Ansyn P.	KY1500
Banks, Christy A.	PA2350
Banks, Eric	WA0200
Banks, Margaret	SD0600
Banks, Matthew	IL1500
Banks, Richard	NC1600
Banks, Rusty	PA1300
Banks, Steven	OK0770
Banks, Timothy	AL0800
Bankston, David	SC0420
Banner, Lucy	MA0600
Bannister, Hazen Duane	SC0400
Bannon, John	FL1650
Banowetz, Joseph M.	TX3420
Bansal, Juhi	CA3500
Banti, Mary	MN0250
Banyas, Thomas P.	ID0100
Banzi, Julia	OR0400
Baptiste, Renee L.	AL0500
Bar-David, Ohad	PA3250
Bara, Daniel J.	GA2100
Bara, Edward	PA2550
Bara, Paul	CO0350
Barach, Daniel P.	NY3770
Baransy, Paul	OH0250
Barantschik, Alexander	CA4150
Baranyk, David S.	IN0907
Baranyk, David	IN1850
Barasch, Shirley R.	PA2900
Barasorda, Antonio	PR0115
Barata, Antonio G.	CA0600
Baratto, German	TN1100
Barba, Kathy	CA1850
Barbanera, Lisa	FL1745
Barbanera, William	FL1745
Barbanera, William	FL1650
Barbee, Larry	NJ0975
Barber, Amy Lynn	IN0350
Barber, Carolyn	NE0600
Barber, Charles	TN1250
Barber, Clarence	OH0200
Barber, Daniel R.	OH0650
Barber, Deborah L.	AR0200
Barber, Gail G.	TX3200
Barber, Gregory	CA2950
Barber, Jerome	NY1220
Barber, Julie	IN1560
Barber, June	CA0300
Barber, Keith	OH2140
Barber, Kimberly	AG0600
Barber, Matthew C.	MN0050
Barber, Susan N.	VA0600
Barber-McCurdy, Sarah	CO0400
Barbham, Vicki	OR0350
Barbini, William	CA0840
Barbone, Anthony	SC0420
Barbour, Cass	NY1800
Barbu, Simona	ND0500
Barbuto, Robert	NY1250
Barbuto, Robert C.	NY1550
Barcellona, John	CA0825
Barcellona, Mary Anne	MD0060
Barclay, Martin	IL0100
Barclay, Martin	IA0930
Barclay, Timothy R.	IL0650
Barcza, Peter	AB0100
Barczak, Bonnie Jean	WI1150
Barczyk, Cecylia	MD0175
Barczyk, Cecylia	MD0850
Bardeguez, Lemuel	OK0750
Bardi, Elena	IN0905
Bardill, Sara	CO0900
Bardin, Joan	CA1520
Bardston, Robert	AA0040
Barduhn, David	OR0550
Barefield, Robert C.	CT0650
Bares, William	MA0260
Baresel, Thomas	OH2200
Barfield, Sally	TX2350
Barfield, Susan	MT0175
Barg, Lisa	AI0150
Bargas, Nanci	CA3400
Barger, Diane C.	NE0600
Barger, Laura	NY0630
Barger, Laura Alison	NY0630
Bargerstock, Nancy E.	NC0050
Bargfrede, Allen	MA0260
Barham, Phillip	TN1450
Barham, Terry	MO1810
Baril, Gianetta	AA0150
Baril, Gianetta	AA0050
Baril, Ray	AA0100
Barilari, Elbio Rodriguez	IL3310
Barish, Sheila	FL1300
Barkan, Paul Michael	NY1275
Barker, David	VA1580
Barker, Edwin	MA0400
Barker, Jennifer M.	DE0150
Barker, John C.	AL1300
Barker, Kent	OK1400
Barker, Stephanie	WY0115
Barkhymer, Lyle	OH2050
Barkley, Elizabeth F.	CA1800
Barksdale, Alicia	MD0850
Barksdale, Lisa Browne	SC0750
Barland, Charles J.	IA1450
Barlar, Douglas	FL0670
Barlar, Nancy	FL0670
Barlar, Rebecca	FL0670
Barley, Leroy	NC2300
Barley, Marsha	VA1350
Barlow, Carla	NM0450
Barlow, Clarence	CA5060
Barlow-Ware, Jackie	OH0350
Barnard, Dene	OH0350
Barnard, Monty	SD0050
Barnard, Rachel	OK0750
Barnard, William	MN1600
Barnes, Ariel	AB0200
Barnes, Arthur P.	CA4900
Barnes, Darrel	MO0350
Barnes, Elendar	NY0640
Barnes, Gail V.	SC1110
Barnes, Hugh W.	MD0200
Barnes, James E.	PA2450
Barnes, James	KS1350
Barnes, Jonathan	NJ1050
Barnes, Larry J.	KY1350
Barnes, Mei Chen	PA3250
Barnes, Michael	OR0500
Barnes, Michael	NC2400
Barnes, Paul	NE0600
Barnes, Peter	AG0450
Barnes, Rich	IL0720
Barnes, Sebronette	PA0675
Barnet, Lori A.	DC0100
Barnetson, Ginger K.	CA4425
Barnett, Carol	MN0050
Barnett, Gregory	TX2150
Barnett, Janie	MA0260
Barnett, Steven	WV0400
Barnett, Thomas	WI0845
Barnette, Mark	NE0610
Barnewitz, William	IL2250
Barney, Kara	UT0325
Barnfather, Samantha	FL1675
Barnhart, Michael R.	OH2100
Barnhart, Stephen L.	WY0200
Barnhart, William	FL0850
Barnhill, Allen	TX2150
Barnhill, Eric	NY5000
Barnlund, Anna	IL2300
Barnstead, Scott	GA2300
Barnum, Ellen M.	NY3717
Barnum, Ellen M.	NY0400
Barnum, Eric	WI0830
Barnum, Justin	MO1900
Barolsky, Daniel G.	WI0100
Barolsky, Ruth	VA1550
Baron, Deborah	TX2400
Baron, John H.	LA0750
Baron, Michael	FL0680
Barone, Ann Carmen	OH1330
Barone, Anthony	NV0050
Barone, Judith	NY4460
Barone, Marcantonio	PA3200
Barone, Steve	OH2550
Baroni, Melissa	MA0350
Barr, Cyrilla	DC0050
Barr, Dustin	CA3200
Barr, Evan	TN1680
Barr, Jean M.	NY1100
Barr, John	VA0100
Barr, Sammy	MS0360
Barr, Stephen A.	PA3100
Barr, Wayne A.	AL1100
Barraca, Rudy	AL0335
Barraclough, D. J.	UT0200
Barraclough, Michelle	PA1900
Barreiro, Elias	LA0750
Barrera, J. J.	TX3510
Barrera, James	CA0825
Barrera, Ramiro	CA0900
Barret, Mary Ashley	NC2430
Barreto, Naitsabes	PR0100
Barrett, Amanda	SC0200
Barrett, Bill	CA0550
Barrett, Celeste	OK0825
Barrett, Dan	ME0440
Barrett, Darren	MA0260
Barrett, Gregory M.	IL2200
Barrett, Janet R.	IL2250
Barrett, Korey J.	IA1600
Barrett, Marianne	NY1900
Barrett, Marianne	NY2250
Barrett, Marianne	NY2150
Barrett, Paul	HI0210
Barrett, Richard	NY2250
Barrett, Richard	NY0500
Barrett, Robert H.	CO1050
Barrett, Roland	OK1350
Barrett, Wayne	TX2250
Barrick, Christopher	OH0550
Barrick, Christopher	WV0600
Barrientos, Carlos	LA0900
Barrientos, Paul	NM0350
Barrientos, Victor	CA6000
Barrier, Dawn	IN1450
Barrier, Gray	CO0950
Barrington, Barrie	AB0050
Barris, Robert A.	IL0750
Barron, Christine	FL1550
Barron, Elizabeth	PA1450
Barron, Fran	MD0060
Barron, Jason	AA0200
Barron, Jose	CA4300
Barron, Kenny	NY1900
Barron, Ronald	MA1400
Barron, Virginia	AG0500
Barrow, Gary	AR0200
Barrow, Lee G.	GA1500
Barrueco, Manuel	PR0115
Barry, Barbara R.	FL1125
Barry, JoAnne	LA0650
Barry, Kevin	MA0260
Barry, Rebecca	AL1195
Barry, Thomas	IA1600
Barsamian, Aram V.	CA3500
Barsamian, Aram	CA2420
Barskaya, Galina	CA3300
Barsness, Erik	MN1300
Barsom, Paul	PA2750
Barston, Gilda R.	IL2250
Barstow, Robert S.	NY3765
Bart, Sean	CA3270
Barta, Daniel	NY3350
Barta, Michael	IL2900
Barta, Steve	CO0200
Barta, Steven E.	MD0650
Barte, Paul T.	OH1900
Bartee, Neale	AR0110
Bartel, Lee R.	AG0450
Bartels, Bruce	IA0910
Bartels, Cindi	OR1250
Bartels, Cindi	OR0250
Bartels, Cindi	OR1300
Bartels, Justin	CO0650
Barth, Bruce	NY2102
Barth, Bruce D.	PA3250
Barth, George	CA4900
Barth, Molly	OR1050
Bartholomew, Douglas	MT0200
Bartholow, Lisa Hanson	GA2000
Bartholow, Lisa	GA0500
Bartholow, Lisa	GA0850
Bartig, Kevin	MI1400
Bartle, Barton	NJ1350
Bartles, Martha	TN1850
Bartlett, Anthony	AZ0440
Bartlett, Bruce	MA0260
Bartlett, Carol A.	MD0650
Bartlett, Eric	NY1900
Bartlett, Jacob Kenneth	NE0500
Bartlett, Jacquelyn	NC2420

Alphabetical Listing of Faculty

Name	Code	Name	Code	Name	Code
Bartlett, Jacquelyn	NC0050	Bates, James I.	OK1450	Bazala-Kim, Allison	MD0060
Bartlett, Jacquelyn	NC1650	Bates, Jennifer	ME0250	Bazan, Dale	OH1100
Bartlett, Jamie	VA0250	Bates, Joanne	PA1750	Bazan, Dale E.	NE0600
Bartlett, John	NC0550	Bates, Mason W.	CA4150	Bazan, Michael	IL3550
Bartlette, Christopher A.	TX0300	Bates, Michael J.	AR0810	Bazayev, Inessa	LA0200
Bartley, Linda L.	WI0815	Bates, Pamela	IL0900	Bazell, Marciem	MO1810
Bartley, Mark	TX3750	Bates, Robert F.	TX3400	Bazinet, Ryan	MA0280
Bartley, Peter	AG0500	Bates, Susan	NC2500	Bazler, Corbett D.	NY4350
Bartman, Karen	DC0170	Bates, Tom	MA2030	Bazler, Corbett	NY1100
Barto, Betsy	CO0275	Bates, Vincent C.	MO0950	Beach, David	AG0300
Barto, Mary B.	NY4200	Bates, William H.	SC1110	Beach, David	AG0450
Bartolome, Sarah J.	LA0200	Batey, Angela L.	TN1710	Beach, Douglas	IL0850
Bartolomeo, Andrea	IL2750	Bath, Joanne	NC0650	Beach, Sue Odem	IA0420
Bartolomeo, Luke	IL2750	Bathurst, Pamela	ID0250	Beach, Wade	VA0450
Barton, David	ID0060	Batimana, Ching	GU0500	Beacham, Graybert	ME0250
Barton, Ena	NJ1350	Batista, Gustavo	PR0150	Beacham, Karen	ME0200
Barton, Karl S.	GA1990	Batiste, Alvin	LA0700	Beachley, Laine	PA3710
Barton, Katie	KY1000	Batjer, Margaret	CA5300	Beachley, Laine	MD0500
Barton, Leroy	DC0350	Battenberg, Thomas V.	OH1850	Beal, Amy C.	CA5070
Barton, Lorelei	OK1450	Battersby, Edmund	IN0900	Beal, Elmer	ME0270
Barton, Lorelei	OK0850	Battersby, Sharyn L.	DC0050	Beal, Kaylene	NE0150
Barton, Mark	TX3400	Battipaglia, Diana M.	NY0635	Beale, Nancy	PA2800
Barton, Mary	NY2400	Battistone, Christopher	DC0170	Beall, John	WV0750
Barton, Peter A.	SC1110	Battle, Detra	MD0700	Beall, Stephen J.	TX2955
Barton, Stephen	MI0850	Baty, Janna	CT0850	Beals, Andrew	CT0800
Barton, Todd	OR0950	Batz, Nancy J.	IA0800	Beam, Joseph	TX1450
Bartos, Titus	TN1100	Batzner, Jay C.	MI0400	Beaman, M. Teresa	CA0810
Bartow, James	NY0625	Bauchspies, Cindy	MD0900	Beamish, Gwen	AG0500
Bartow, James	NY0270	Bauer, Amy M.	CA5020	Beams, Mahala	MA1560
Bartram, Kevin P.	VA1475	Bauer, David	NE0590	Bean, Matt	IL3500
Bartsch, John T.	OR0175	Bauer, David T.	MN1030	Bean, Robert D.	IN0905
Bartus Broberg, Kirsten A.	MN1625	Bauer, Elizabeth	IL3550	Bean, Robert G.	AL1450
Bartz, Ezra	TX3175	Bauer, Glen	MO1950	Bean, Scott	WI0810
Bartz, Gary	OH1700	Bauer, Harold	IL0630	Bean, Shirley Ann	MO1810
Bartz, Karen	MN0610	Bauer, Karen	IL2100	Beane, Diane	IA1800
Bartz, Martha	NC0350	Bauer, Leroy	ID0250	Bear, Colvin	OH2450
Bartz, Tammy	MN1400	Bauer, Mary K.	NC2600	Beard, Charles	OK0500
Barudin, Jeffrey E.	MO0650	Bauer, Michael J.	KS1350	Beard, Charles	KS1050
Baruth, Lori E.	KY0900	Bauer, Mike	TN1600	Beard, Christine	MS0850
Baruth, Philip A.	WI0350	Bauer, Paul D.	IL2200	Beard, Christine E.	NE0610
Barwell, Nina	MA1900	Bauer, Ross	CA5010	Beard, Jackie	MA0260
Barz, Gregory F.	TN1850	Bauer, William R.	NY0600	Beard, Michael R.	NE0590
Barzel, Tamar	MA2050	Bauer, William R.	NY0644	Beard, R. Daniel	MS0750
Barzenick, Walter	LA0650	Bauer, William I.	FL1850	Beard, Robert Scott	WV0550
Bascom, Brandon R.	ID0060	Baugh, Kim C.	VA1300	Bearden, Gregory	GA0250
Basham, Glenn D.	FL1900	Baugh-Bennett, Grace	IN1010	Bearden-Carver, Julie	GA1800
Bashar, Inci	MO1810	Baughman, Melissa	MO0100	Beardslee, Thomas	OH1850
Bashaw, Howard	AA0100	Baum, Jamie	NY2150	Beardslee, Tony	NE0460
Bashford, Christina	IL3300	Baum, Joshua	IL0150	Bearid, Rolyn	SD0580
Bashwiner, David M.	NM0450	Bauman, Carol	AG0600	Beaser, Robert	NY1900
Basiletti, Sarah	CA2400	Bauman, Clyde	ND0050	Beasley, Kimberly	FL1000
Basilio, Edwin L.	CA5200	Bauman, Jeffrey Milo	GA2300	Beasley, Pamela	VA1550
Basinger, Bettie Jo	UT0350	Bauman, Marcia	CA4700	Beasley, Walter	MA0260
Basinger, BettieJo	UT0250	Bauman, Thomas	IL2250	Beason, Christine F.	TX3250
Basinger, Rhonda	IL1245	Baumann, Keith	IL1085	Beaster-Jones, Jayson	TX2900
Basini, Laura	CA0840	Baumer, Matthew R.	PA1600	Beaton, K. Michelle	RI0300
Basinski, Anne	MT0400	Baumgarnder, Brad	KS0590	Beatrice, Anthony B.	MA1500
Baskin, Jason	MO0850	Baumgartel, Julie	AG0600	Beattie, Donald P.	IL2900
Baskin, Stanley	TN1100	Baumgarten, Jonathan	DC0010	Beattie, Michael	MA0400
Baskin, Ted	AI0150	Baumgartner, Christopher	MO1800	Beatty, Caroline	TX3175
Basler, Paul	FL1850	Baumgartner, Michael	OH0650	Beatty, David	CA1000
Basney, Nyela	IL2100	Baunoch, Joseph	PA1600	Beatty, David	CA0250
Basney, Nyela	TX3527	Baur, James	IL1400	Beatty, Sarah	IL0730
Basrak, Cathy	MA0400	Baur, John	TN1680	Beauchamp, Lise	AI0200
Bass, Eddie	NC0910	Baur, Steven	AF0100	Beauchesne, Paul	AB0210
Bass, Eddie C.	NC2430	Bausano, William	OH1450	Beaudet, Luce	AI0200
Bass, James K.	FL2000	Baust, Jeffrey P.	MA0260	Beaudette, Eileen	AG0250
Bass, John	TN1200	Bavaar, Kathleen	DC0170	Beaudette, Sylvie	NY1100
Bass, John	TN1680	Bavicchi, John	MA0260	Beaudoin, Jacques	AI0200
Bass, Jonathan	MA0350	Bawden, Sue	IL0100	Beaudoin, Paul	RI0200
Bass, Louise	GA1650	Bawden, Susan	IA1300	Beaudoin, Richard A.	MA1050
Bass, Michael	MS0580	Bax, Alessio	TX2400	Beaudreau, Jason	NY2800
Bass, Richard	CT0600	Baxter, Brett	IL2650	Beaudreau, Jason	NY4460
Bass, Walden	NY1550	Baxter, David	KS0200	Beaudry, Genevieve	AI0050
Bassett, Dennis	KS0300	Baxter, David A.	KS0980	Beaudry, Nicole	AI0210
Bassett, Jenny	FL0670	Baxter, David	AG0130	Beaudry, Paul	NY4200
Bassett, Jon	FL0670	Baxter, Dawn	OR1010	Beaudry, Pierre	AI0150
Bassett, Matthew	OH0600	Baxter, Deborah	KS1450	Beaudry, Pierre	AI0200
Bassin, Daniel	NY4320	Baxter, Diane R.	OR1250	Beaugrand, Luc	AI0210
Bassler, Samantha Elizabeth	NJ1400	Baxter, Jillian	GA0625	Beaugrand, Luc	AI0200
Basta, JoAnna	PA2450	Baxter, Kara	NE0200	Beaulac, Stephane	AI0150
Bastable, Barbara	TX2400	Baxter, Marsha	NY4200	Beaulieu, Cyrille	AI0210
Bastepe-Gray, Serap E.	MD0650	Baxter, Marsha L.	NY3780	Beaumont, Lance	TX1100
Bastian, William M.	MI1200	Baxter, Sarah M.	KS0980	Beaumont, Lance	TX2295
Bastian, William	MN0450	Baxtresser, Jeanne	MA1400	Beaupre, Odette	AI0220
Bastin, Ernest	OH1900	Baxtresser, Jeanne	PA0550	Beauregard, Jennifer	MA0260
Batchelder, Donald	NJ0800	Bayen, Diane	NY2450	Beauregard, Jenny	MO0050
Batcheller, James C.	MI0400	Bayer, Joshua	DC0010	Beauvais, William	AG0650
Batchelor, Daryl	KS0550	Bayer, Michelle	NY0250	Beaver, Dale	OH1850
Batchelor, Wayne	NY2900	Bayes, Michael	MD0850	Beaver, Gregory	NE0600
Batchelor-Glader, Brian	OH2550	Bayles, David	WI1150	Beaver, Johanna L.	VA1475
Batcho, Michael J.	WI0150	Bayles, David S.	WI0835	Beaver, Martin P.	NY2750
Batchvarova, Madlen T.	IN0650	Bayless, Robert R.	AZ0500	Beaver, Martin	CT0850
Bateman, Melinda	CA3100	Baylock, Alan	VA1350	Beavers, Clyde	KY0100
Bateman, Nancy	MS0100	Baynard, Tim D.	SC0400	Beavers, Clyde E.	KY1350
Bates, Alexandra	AF0120	Bays, Jay	MI0350	Beavers, Doug	CA2775
Bates, Charles N.	OH1800	Bays, Tatiana	TX0850	Beavers, Gabriel	LA0200
Bates, Elaine	OK1250	Baytelman, Pola	NY3650	Beavers, Jennifer	TX3530
Bates, Ian	WI0350	Bazala Kim, Alison	MD0500	Beavers, Judith	MI0910
Bates, James	OH2050	Bazala Kim, Alison E.	MD0150	Beavers, Sean M.	VA0650

Alphabetical Listing of Faculty

Name	Code
Beazley, Janet M.	CA5040
Bebe, David M.	NY0700
Becerra, Janelle	MO0850
Bech, Soren	AI0150
Bechen, Gene	IA1300
Beck, Barbara Geiser	CO0275
Beck, Brandon	WA1100
Beck, Carolyn L.	CA0835
Beck, Carolyn	CA3650
Beck, Carolyn L.	CA5150
Beck, Chuck	IL1750
Beck, Donna Marie	PA1050
Beck, Gina	MA0850
Beck, Gina C.	MD1000
Beck, John	NC2500
Beck, John	NY1100
Beck, John R.	NC1650
Beck, Laurel D.	CA3500
Beck, Lucy	CA3520
Beck, Lynn	NC0750
Beck, Matt	MI0350
Beck, Nathan	OR0400
Beck, Nora	OR0400
Beck, Robert T.	MO1810
Beck, Rosalind	FL1800
Beck, Stephen David	LA0200
Beck-Reed, Jonathan	OK0750
Beckel, James A.	IN0350
Becker, Abraham N.	AL1150
Becker, Christopher A.	MO1900
Becker, Daniel	CA4150
Becker, David	CA0600
Becker, David	CA1510
Becker, David M.	OR0400
Becker, Gisele	DC0100
Becker, Harris	NY2105
Becker, J. Harris	NY2550
Becker, Jane	TX0350
Becker, Jeral Blaine	MO1250
Becker, Juanita	WI1155
Becker, Karen E.	NY3775
Becker, Karen A.	NE0600
Becker, Kristina	NY1100
Becker, Lauren	NY2650
Becker, Melinda	CA2801
Becker, Melissa J.	PA2050
Becker, Michael	IL2650
Becker, Michael	IL3450
Becker, Nicole M.	NY4200
Becker, Pam	MO1710
Becker, Paul	AR0800
Becker, Richard	VA1500
Becker, Robert	CA0960
Becker, Thomas R.	KS0050
Becker, Tia	MO0350
Becker, Tia	MO0200
Becker, Wanda	MO1250
Becker-Billie, Elisa	IL1890
Beckerman, Michael	NY2740
Beckett, Christine	AI0070
Beckett, Hal	AB0100
Beckett, Scott	TX0100
Beckford, John S.	SC0750
Beckford, Richard E.	SC1050
Beckford, Richard	LA0700
Beckler, Terry	SD0400
Beckley, Jane E.	OH2140
Beckley, Susan	PA0350
Beckley-Roberts, Lisa	FL1790
Beckman, Bradley J.	TX3420
Beckman, Gary D.	NC1700
Beckman, Linda L.	AR0400
Beckman, Seth	FL0850
Beckmann-Collier, Aimee	IA0550
Beckner, Woody	VA0250
Beckstrom, Tom	OR1000
Beckwith, Hubert	VA0450
Beckwith, John	AG0450
Beckwith, Sterling	AG0650
Becos, Pelarin	IL3310
Becraft, Steven C.	AR0300
Bedard, Elise	AG0200
Bedard, Martin	AI0200
Bede, Judy	OH0450
Bedelian, Haroutune	CA5020
Bedelian, Lorna Griffitt	CA5020
Bedell, Adam	TX3100
Bedford, Frances M.	WI0835
Bedford, Judith	MA2030
Bedford, Robert M.	PA3600
Bednar, Stanley	NY2150
Bednarz, Blanka	PA0950
Bednarzyk, Stephen C.	GU0500
Bedner, Edward C.	MA0260
Bedo, Maria	NJ0700
Bedrossian, Franck	CA5000
Bedsole, Betty	TN1660
Beebe, Harriet	OH2550
Beebe, Jon P.	NC0050
Beecher, Betty	UT0300
Beecher, Jeffrey	AG0450
Beecher, Jeffrey	AG0300
Beecher, Randy	CA4050
Beecher, Randy	CA2100
Beedle, Helen E.	PA1950
Beegle, Raymond	NY2150
Beeks, Graydon F.	CA3650
Beeks, Graydon	CA1050
Beene, Richard	CA1075
Beer, Lucille	NY0700
Beer, Lucille	NY3600
Beerman, Burton	OH0300
Beers, Al	KY0100
Beers, Alva E.	KY0150
Beers, Heather	OH0350
Beerstein, Fred	CA0550
Beert, Michael	IL2560
Beery, John	MI1650
Bees, Julie	KS1450
Beeson, Catherine	CO0650
Beeson, D. Allen	MO1830
Beeson, Robert	DC0050
Beevers, Suzanne	NY1350
Begault, Durand	AI0150
Begel, Rich	IN0400
Begelman, Igor	NY0500
Beghin, Tom	AI0150
Beghtol, Jason W.	MS0570
Begian, Jamie	CT0800
Begnoche, David J.	TX3000
Behan, Ryan J.	OH1850
Behling, John F.	IL0750
Behm, Gary	MT0175
Behn, Bradford	OK0750
Behnke, John A.	WI0300
Behnke, Martin	OR0950
Behnke, Martin K.	OR1300
Behr, Erik	NY3350
Behrend, Roger L.	VA0450
Behrens, Gene Ann	PA1250
Behrens, Jack	AG0500
Behrens, Jeff	WI0842
Behrens, Jeffrey	NY2105
Behrens, Joel	PA2350
Behrens, Lisa	NY1600
Behrmann, Candice	NE0200
Behroozi, Bahram	CA4350
Beia, Suzanne	WI0815
Beiler, Jonathan	PA3250
Beilina, Nina	NY2250
Beisswenger, Donald A.	MO0775
Beith, Nancy S.	MD1000
Beitmen, Cynthia	CA2950
Bejerano, Martin	FL1900
Beken, Munir N.	CA5031
Bekeny, Amanda K.	OH0100
Bela, Marcin	TN1100
Bela, Marcin	TN0100
Belair, Michel	AI0210
Belajonas, Michael	NY4050
Belan, William	CA0830
Beland, Sarah	MO0300
Beland, Sarah	IA0600
Belanger, Marc	AI0210
Belanger, Olivier	AI0200
Belcher, Debbie	KY1550
Belcher, Deborah	NC2400
Belcher, Jeff	MO0060
Belcik, Mark G.	OK0750
Belck, Scott	OH2200
Belden, Carol Beck	FL0400
Belden, George R.	AK0100
Belec, Jonathan	NY1250
Belet, Brian	CA4400
Belfer, Beverly	WI0825
Belfield, Roy L.	NC2700
Belfiglio, Anthony	TN0100
Belflower, Alisa	NE0600
Belflowers, Timothy	NC0350
Belford, Rick	VT0400
Belfy, Jeanne M.	ID0050
Belgiovane, Alicia	CO1050
Belgique, Joel	OR0850
Belgrave, Melita	MO1810
Beliavsky, Daniel	NY0630
Belich, Kay	WI0150
Belkin, Alan	AI0200
Belknap, Monte	UT0050
Bell Hanson, Jeffrey	WA0650
Bell, Allan	AA0150
Bell, Carey	CA4150
Bell, Carol Ann	OK0650
Bell, Charles	OH2550
Bell, Charles V.	CA3400
Bell, Cindy L.	NY1600
Bell, Cully	IL2900
Bell, Daniel	KY0650
Bell, David	WI0350
Bell, Dennis	NY2400
Bell, Donald M.	AA0150
Bell, Isaac	AL0050
Bell, Jacqueline H.	IL3150
Bell, James	AL1050
Bell, Jane H.	OH1650
Bell, Jeff	IL2300
Bell, Jeremy	AG0600
Bell, Joby	NC0050
Bell, John	MO0850
Bell, John	IL2910
Bell, Joshua	IN0900
Bell, Ken	CA3460
Bell, Kenneth G.	PA1400
Bell, Larry	MA0260
Bell, Lori	CA4100
Bell, Lorriane	VA0500
Bell, Malcolm E.	AA0080
Bell, MaryLynn	KS0150
Bell, Paula	TN1100
Bell, Peter J.	MA2030
Bell, Richard	GA0500
Bell, Richard L.	MO0550
Bell, S.	MA0800
Bell, Scott F.	PA0550
Bell, Scott	PA1050
Bell, Stephani	PA1850
Bell, Tim	ID0130
Bell, Timothy R.	WI0835
Bell, Valda	GA1900
Bell, Valerie	MO1810
Bell, Vicki	KY0100
Bell, Victor	CA5060
Bellah, Mary	CA0270
Bellamy, Amy J.	NY0450
Bellamy, Terry	NY3475
Belland, Diana R.	KY1000
Belland, Douglas	KY1000
Belland, Douglas K.	OH2200
Bellassai, Marc C.	AZ0250
Bellemare, Yvon	AI0220
Beller-McKenna, Daniel	NH0350
Belles, David	CT0150
Belleville, Yolande	AI0220
Bellini, Brigitte	TX3175
Bellink, Allyson	NY3785
Bellino, Paul	NY4450
Bellino, Peter A.	NY3600
Bellisario, Kristen	IN0900
Bellman, David	IN1650
Bellman, Jonathan	CO0950
Bello, Juan P.	NY2750
Bellomia, Paolo	AI0200
Bellor, Jennifer K.	NY2650
Bellotti, Sergio	MA0260
Belnap, Lila	HI0050
Belnap, Michael	HI0050
Beloncik, Anne	SD0550
Belongia, Daniel A.	IL1150
Belov, Anton	MA1175
Belove, David	CA2950
Belser, Robert S.	WY0200
Belshaw, Gary D.	TX3650
Belter, Babette	OK0800
Beluska, Vasile	OH0300
Belz, Kevin	MA0260
Belzer, Katie	GA0850
Belzer, Terrence	NJ1050
Belzer, Terry	PA2800
Bemberg, Stephanie	MO1110
Bemis, Jennifer	AL1300
Bempechat, Paul-Andre	NJ1000
Ben-Amots, Ofer	CO0200
Ben-Pazi, Tamar	SC0420
Benadon, Fernando Raul	DC0010
Benamou, Marc	IN0400
Benavides, Raul	NY0625
Benavidez, Justin	TX2960
Benda, Karen L.	KS1400
Bender, Dennis	KY1450
Bender, Judy	MN1260
Bender, Rhett	OR0950
Bender, Sharla A.	AL0345
Bender, Susan Maria	WI0850
Bendich, Jon	CA1560
Bendickson, Sean	WA0980
Bendixen-Mahoney, Kirsten	FL0680
Bendixon-Mahoney, Kirsten	FL0500
Bendzsa, Paul	AD0050
Benedetti, Fred	CA4100
Benedetti, Fred	CA2100
Benedick, Kristi	MO1120
Benedict, Cathy L.	FL0700
Benedict, Deborah	CA1650
Benedict, Deborah	CA5000
Benedict, Jeffrey W.	CA0830
Benedict, Les	CA1265
Benedum, Richard P.	OH2250
Benford, Alexander E.	GA0500
Benge, Sharon J.	TX3300
Bengloff, Richard	NY2750
Bengochea, Sandra	CA5510

Name	Code	Name	Code	Name	Code
Benham, Helen	NJ0030	Benson, Will	TN0300	Bergstrom, Samuel	MN0040
Benham, Jeremiah	IL2750	Benson, William	CA3100	Berick, Yehonatan M.	MI2100
Benham, John	MN1280	Bent, Catherine	MA0260	Berimeladze, Tariel	IA0200
Benham, Stephen J.	PA1050	Bent, Ian	NY0750	Berimeldze, Tariel	IA0930
Benish, Serena Kanig	UT0325	Bent, Jenny	CA4700	Berinbaum, Martin C.	AB0100
Benitez, Vincent P.	PA2750	Bentley, JoAnne	AG0450	Berk, Stacey J.	WI0850
Benjamin Figueroa, Haydee	PR0115	Bentley, Joe	MI1830	Berke, Melissa	NE0610
Benjamin, Ann	IA0950	Bentley, John E.	OH0300	Berkeley, Edward	NY1900
Benjamin, Eric	OH2290	Bentley, Judith C.	OH0300	Berkhout, Bjorn	NY3250
Benjamin, Eric J.	OH0700	Bentley, Julia	IL2100	Berkman, David	NY0642
Benjamin, John A.	OH2250	Bentley, Julia	IL0750	Berkman, Jeremy	AB0100
Benjamin, Karen	CA4450	Benton, Carol W.	GA0200	Berkner, Jane	OH2150
Benjamin, Keith	MO1810	Benton, Leanne	OK0850	Berkner, Jane	OH0100
Benjamin, Richard S.	PA0350	Benton, Lisa	TN0580	Berkolds, Paul	CA0510
Benjamin, Thomas	MD0650	Benton, Robert	MI0050	Berkowitz, Paul M.	CA5060
Benjamin, William E.	AB0100	Benton, Robert	AG0550	Berkshire-Brown, Lorrie	VA0450
Benkert, Stuart M.	TN1700	Bentz, Anne Hagan	PA3650	Berle, Arnie	NY2400
Benkman, Noel	CA0900	Benway, Joel	IL0850	Berlet, Pat	OR0950
Benkman, Noel	CA1950	Benya, Susan	IA1140	Berlin, Eric M.	MA2000
Benko, Ron	LA0800	Benyas, Edward M.	IL2900	Berlin, Janet	PA1650
Benkovitz, Deborah	PA1050	Benyas, Kara	IL2900	Berliner, Paul F.	NC0600
Benmann, Martine	IL2750	Benz, David	MO0850	Berlinsky, Dmitri	MI1400
Bennack, Steven	TX2710	Benz, Fritz	RI0150	Berlinsky, Elena	WY0200
Benne, Steve	TN1450	Benz, Terri	IL1650	Berman, Boris	CT0850
Benne, Steven	TN0250	Benzer, John	TX3400	Berman, Donald L.	MA1900
Benner, Charles	OH1850	Berard, Jesus Manuel	DC0010	Berman, Gayle	MA0800
Benner, Emily	MI0100	Berard, Marie	AG0450	Berman, Kenneth M.	CA5000
Bennes, Gaye	MA1175	Berard, Marie	AG0300	Berman, Melvin	AG0450
Bennet, Pratt H.T.	MA0260	Berardinelli, George	NY2450	Berman, Ronald	CA3300
Bennett, Barbara A.	CA5040	Berardinelli, Paula	NY1600	Berman, Ronald M.	CA3500
Bennett, Bruce	TN0100	Berardinelli, Paula	NY2450	Bermejo-Greenspan, Mili	MA0260
Bennett, Bruce Christian	CA4200	Berdnikova, Natalya L.	WI0450	Bermudez, Ana Ruth	WI1150
Bennett, Cameron	WA0650	Berens, Brad	SD0200	Bermudez, Luis	PR0115
Bennett, Christopher	FL1900	Berenson, Gail	OH1900	Berna, Linda	IL0550
Bennett, Cindy	IL3370	Berentsen, Kurt	OR0150	Bernal, Sergio	UT0300
Bennett, Cynthia	IL1520	Beres, Karen E.	NC1650	Bernard, Anne-Marie	AI0190
Bennett, Dana	NY0400	Beresford, Rick	TN0100	Bernard, David	LA0650
Bennett, Deborah	MA0260	Berg Oram, Stephanie	CO0625	Bernard, Gilles	NJ0825
Bennett, Dwight	AB0100	Berg, Aubrey	OH2200	Bernard, Jennifer	TX3100
Bennett, Elena	TN0100	Berg, Bruce	TX0300	Bernard, Jonathan	WA1050
Bennett, Elizabeth S.	NC0850	Berg, Chris	OH0500	Bernard, Rhoda J.	MA0350
Bennett, Erin K.	FL1950	Berg, Christian	OH2050	Bernard-Stevens, Sarah	KS0700
Bennett, Evan	MA1450	Berg, Christian R.	OH2200	Bernardo, Mario	FL0680
Bennett, Glenn	AZ0440	Berg, Christopher B.	SC1110	Bernatis, William	NV0050
Bennett, Hye-Yun Chung	VA1000	Berg, Gregory	WI0250	Berners, David P.	CA4900
Bennett, Janice	MA2030	Berg, Jason	TX3200	Berners, John	IN1650
Bennett, John L.	CA3400	Berg, Joy L.	AA0015	Berney, Mark C.	RI0300
Bennett, John	KS0400	Berg, Kenneth	AL0800	Bernhard, H. Christian	NY3725
Bennett, Joyce	DC0170	Berg, Lynn	ID0050	Bernhard, Kathryn M.	IL0840
Bennett, Larry	MO0100	Berg, Margaret Haefner	CO0800	Bernhardsson, Sigurbjorn	IN0900
Bennett, Laura	TX2850	Berg, Marla	OH0600	Bernhardsson, Sigurbjorn	IL3300
Bennett, Lawrence E.	IN1850	Berg, Marla	OH1100	Bernhardt, Barry W.	FL0700
Bennett, Marie Micol	IL2050	Berg, Reinhard	AA0020	Bernhardt, Ross C.	TX2930
Bennett, Mary Lynne	WV0300	Berg, Robert	CA0835	Bernhardt, Valerie	NJ0800
Bennett, Mary Beth	VA1500	Berg, Shelton G.	FL1900	Bernier, Jean-Sebastien	AI0190
Bennett, Michael	ME0270	Berg, Steve	MO1000	Bernier, Lucas	ND0400
Bennett, Michelle	IA0400	Berg, Wesley P.	AA0100	Berns, Kathleen	WI0842
Bennett, Peggy D.	OH1700	Bergamo, Janet	CA5360	Berns, Paul S.	IN1650
Bennett, Peter	OH0400	Bergee, Martin	KS1350	Bernstein, Alan	RI0250
Bennett, Rebecca K.	IL2250	Berger, Brad	MA0260	Bernstein, Brandon	CA3500
Bennett, Sharon K.	OH0350	Berger, Gene P.	IN0150	Bernstein, David	OH2150
Bennett, Steve	TX2850	Berger, Harris M.	TX2900	Bernstein, David	CA2950
Bennett, Susan Brady	GA1700	Berger, Jonathan	CA4900	Bernstein, Harry	CA1020
Bennett, Susan Brady	GA0550	Berger, Karol	CA4900	Bernstein, Jane A.	MA1900
Bennett, Travis	NC2600	Berger, Linda	MN1450	Bernstein, Lawrence F.	PA3350
Bennett, Vicki	AZ0440	Berger, Lisa	VA0450	Bernstein, Peter A.	NY2750
Bennett, Wayne	NC0750	Berger, Mark	MA2030	Bernstein, Seymour	NY2750
Bennett, William	CA4150	Berger, Reverie Mott	GA1700	Bernstorf, Elaine D.	KS1450
Bennie, Ron	AA0050	Berger, Sally	IN1350	Bernthal, John P.	IN1750
Bennighof, James	TX0300	Berger, Talya	CA4900	Berntsen, Neal	PA0550
Bennight, Brad	TX0300	Bergeron, Andrew	MI0900	Berofsky, Aaron	MI2100
Bennight, Bradley J.	TX3420	Bergeron, Andrew	MI0850	Beroukhim, Cyrus	NY3725
Beno, Charles W.	NY4400	Bergeron, Andrew	MI0300	Berquist, Peter	GA0200
Benoff, Mitchell J.	MA0260	Bergeron, Chuck	FL1900	Berrett, Joshua	NY2400
Benoist, Debbie	TX0075	Bergeron, Jonathan	AZ0450	Berrocal, Esperanza	DC0050
Benoist, Debbie	TX2310	Bergeron, Katherine	RI0050	Berry, Brandi	IL0750
Benoit, Aline	MA1175	Bergeron, Norm	TX2800	Berry, David Carson	OH2200
Benoit, John	IA1350	Bergeron, Sylvain	AI0150	Berry, Debbie	TX2700
Benoit, Linda	IA1350	Bergeron, Sylvain	AI0200	Berry, Fredrick J.	CA1250
Benoit, Lonny	LA0350	Bergeron, Tom	OR1250	Berry, Fredrick J.	CA4900
Benoit, Marcel	AI0220	Berget, Paul	MN1625	Berry, James	WV0440
Benoit, Patrick	AI0210	Bergey, Matthew	WI1150	Berry, James	PA3100
Benoit-Otis, Marie-Helene	AI0200	Berghout, Elizabeth	KS1350	Berry, Mark S.	KY1550
Bensdorf, Naomi	IL2100	Bergin, Wendy I.	TX2100	Berry, Michael	PA3580
Benshoof, Kenneth W.	WA1050	Berglund, Robert	MN0250	Berry, Michael	TX3200
Benson, Ann	SC0420	Bergman, Catherine	KS0300	Berry, Paul	CT0850
Benson, Beth	PA0400	Bergman, Elaine	IN0400	Berry, Paul	NY3350
Benson, George	MI2200	Bergman, James	CA4450	Berry, Richard A.	TX2700
Benson, Gregory V.	UT0305	Bergman, Jason	MS0750	Berry, Robert C.	CA3950
Benson, Jack D.	TX1400	Bergman, Luke	WA1050	Berry, Rodney	NC0050
Benson, Jeremy L.	AL0500	Bergman, Mark	VA0450	Berry, S. David	SC0650
Benson, John Halvor	WI0350	Bergman, Rachel	VA0450	Berry, Sarah	KY1550
Benson, Katherine	IL2300	Bergmann, Elizabeth	AA0050	Berry, Steve	IL0550
Benson, Kelley	MI2100	Bergmann, Marcel	AA0050	Berry, Whitney	ND0500
Benson, Lary	AA0020	Bergonzi, Jerry	MA1400	Berry, William	WA1100
Benson, Mark	PA0400	Bergonzi, Louis	IL3300	Berry, William	WA1300
Benson, Mark F.	AL0210	Bergs, Roger	AG0450	Berryhill, Dennis	WI0860
Benson, Michael L.	OH1350	Bergseth, Heather	MI0900	Bers, Edith	NY0150
Benson, Robert	IA0300	Bergstrom, Anne	AF0120	Bers, Edith	NY2150
Benson, Steve C.	NJ0800	Bergstrom, Melissa	MN0040	Bers, Edith	NY1900

Alphabetical Listing of Faculty

Name	Code	Name	Code	Name	Code
Bersaglia, G. Scott	KY0400	Bibace, Kenny	AI0150	Binford, Patrick	KY0610
Bershad, Kara	IN0005	Bibbey, Marianne	WY0130	Bing, Charles S.	FL0600
Bershad, Kara	IL2100	Biber, Sarah J.	MT0200	Bing, Delores M.	CA0500
Bersin, Michael D.	MO1790	Bible, Judith	TN1710	Bing, William	CA3300
Berta, Joseph M.	NY1550	Bible, Kierstin Michelle	MO0260	Bing, William W.	CA0500
Bertagnolli, Paul A.	TX3400	Bibzak, Ray	IL2775	Bingener, Bonnie	AZ0470
Berteig, Laurence	WA0550	Bibzak, Ray	IL2650	Binger, Adlai	PA0050
Berthelet, Marie-Noelle	AJ0100	Bicigo, James Michael	AK0150	Bingham, Ann Marie	WV0400
Berthiaume, Gerald B.	WA1150	Bick, Sally M.	AG0550	Bingham, Emelyne	TN1850
Berthold, Sherwood	MS0300	Bickel, Jan	IL2650	Bingham, James	CO0830
Berthold, Sherwood	MS0400	Bickel, Ronald E.	PA1050	Bingham, Martina	HI0210
Bertman, David	TX3400	Bickers, Elisa	MO1810	Bingham, Roxanne Laycock	AA0050
Bertolet, Jay	FL0700	Bickers, Elisa	KS1400	Bingham, Steve	FL1675
Bertolet, Jay	FL0200	Bickham, Teri	MD0850	Bingham, Thomas	HI0210
Bertoncini, Gene	NJ1400	Bickley, Ashlee Beth	IN0905	Bingham, Tom	NY3725
Bertrand, Jerry	IA0150	Biddle, Paul D.	NY0400	Bingham, W. Edwin	WV0400
Bertrand, Lynn Wood	GA0750	Biddlecombe, Mary	TN1850	Bingig, Mariann	AG0600
Bertsch, Rolf	AA0050	Biddlecombe, Thomas 'Tucker'	TN1850	Binkley, Lindabeth	MI0400
Bertucci, Ronald	OR0350	Bidelman, Mark	CA0400	Binkley, Paul	CA2950
Berz, William L.	NJ1130	Bidwell, Louise B.	CA5000	Binneweg, Anna	MD0060
Besalyan, Raffi	WI0850	Bieber, Elizabeth	IA1800	Biondo, Steven A.	CA5100
Besch, Joyce	NE0450	Biebesheimer, Arlene	AR0850	Biran, Dror	KY1500
Besharse, Kari	LA0650	Biederman, Bradley R.	PA3250	Birch, Kevin	ME0440
Beskrone, Steve	PA3330	Biederwolf, Kurt J.	MA0260	Birch, Robert M.	DC0100
Besley, Megan C.	NY2750	Biegel, Jeffrey	NY0500	Birch, Sebastian A.	OH1100
Bespalko, Polina	OH2550	Biel, Carol	OR0400	Bircher, Craig	NE0160
Bess, David	WV0750	Bielawa, Herbert	CA4200	Bircher, K. Craig	NE0600
Besser, Idalynn	TN1450	Bielish, Aaron J.	TX2295	Bircher, Mary W.	NE0590
Bessinger, David K.	OK1250	Bien, Leander	DC0170	Bircher, Mary	NE0250
Bessinger, Marti	OK1250	Bier, Ken	IN1350	Bircher, Mary	NE0160
Best, Ed	CA5040	Bierhaus, Sarah	CO0650	Bird, Carolyn	AF0120
Best, Michael	IL0550	Bieritz, Gerald	TX1300	Bird, Gary	MN1300
Best, Nneka	PA1150	Bierman, Benjamin	NY0630	Bird, Gary J.	PA1600
Best, Raelene	IA1350	Bierman, Duane	NE0590	Bird, Paula E.	TX3175
Best, Richard W.	IL2900	Biermann, Joanna Cobb	AL1170	Bird-Arvidsson, Jennifer	CO0800
Best, Robert L.	TX0300	Biernacki, Krzysztof K.	FL1950	Birden, Larry	OK0450
Best, Stephen	NY1350	Biersach, Bill	CA5300	Birdsong, Nikki S.	TX1150
Beste, Alan	AZ0460	Bierschenk, Jerome Michael	TX3250	Birdwell, Cody	KY1450
Bester, Matthew	OH1850	Bierschenk, Kenny P.	OH0680	Birdwell, Florence H.	OK0750
Betancourt, David	CA0859	Bierylo, Michael	MA0260	Birenbaum Quintero, Michael	ME0200
Betancourt, Nilda	PR0100	Biesack, Ryan	OR0700	Birgfeld, Kelly	NY4500
Beteta, Xavier	CA4100	Bigelow, Claudine	UT0050	Biringer, Gene D.	WI0350
Bethany, Adeline M.	PA0450	Bigelow, Ira	CO0625	Birk, Richard	TX0350
Bethea, Kay	VA1030	Bigelow, Ira	CO0830	Birkeland, Roger	IL0850
Bethea, Stephanie	WA0900	Biggers, Jonathan E.	NY3705	Birkemeier, Richard	CA0825
Bethea, William	VA0950	Biggerstaff, Corey	IL1085	Birkner, Chip	FL1850
Bethel, Phyllis	NY5000	Biggs, Allen	CA4200	Birkner, Tom	IL2970
Betinis, Abbie	MN0610	Biggs, Charlene	AG0150	Birnbaum, Mary	NY1900
Bettcher, Mark T.	IL0840	Biggs, Charlene	AG0070	Birnbaum, Melanie	NY1275
Bettencourt, Blair	MA2030	Biggs, Dana M.	CO0800	Birney, Allan	PA2450
Bettendorf, Carl	NY2200	Biggs, Gunnar	CA3460	Biro, Daniel Peter	AB0150
Better, Donald	OH0600	Biggs, Millard R.	CA4100	Birr, Diane	NY1800
Bettez, Michel	AI0200	Biggs, William Hayes	NY2150	Birt, Timothy	TX2260
Bettison, Oscar	MD0650	Bighley, Mark	OK0550	Bisbano, Tony	NY2650
Betts, David	AG0130	Bigler, Dwight	VA1700	Biscardi, Chester	NY3560
Betts, Donald	MN0950	Bigler, Nathan	AZ0150	Biscay, Karen T.	OH1330
Betts, James E.	IL1800	Bilden, Jeff	CA1290	Bischoff, Janet	PA2250
Betts, Kendall	NH0350	Bilderback, Barry T.	ID0250	Bischoff, John	CA2950
Betts, L. David	OH0755	Bilger, David	GA2100	Biser, Larry	MI0300
Betts, Steven	OK1200	Bilger, David	PA3250	Bisesi, Gayle	IL0850
Betts, Timothy	WA0050	Bilger, David	PA0850	Bish, Deborah	FL0850
Betz, Brian	NJ1050	Bilinski, Janusz	MD0150	Bishai, Alf	NY2750
Betz, Michael	WI0300	Bill, Darlene	SD0450	Bishara, Aaron	OH1600
Beuche, William A.	CA3950	Bill, Jennifer	MA0400	Bishkoff, Cheryl	NY4450
Beudert, Mark	IN1700	Bill, Jennifer	RI0150	Bishop, Andrew	MI2100
Beus, Stephen	OH1450	Billaud, Louise	VA0900	Bishop, Barbara A.	MO1810
Beutler, Marian	NE0050	Billias, Anna	VA1400	Bishop, Bruce W.	AZ0300
Bevan, Charla	CO0550	Billin, Susan	ID0250	Bishop, Darcie	MS0350
Bevelander, Brian E.	OH0950	Billingham, Lisa A.	VA0450	Bishop, Dawn	IL0275
BeVille, Jesse	VA1600	Billings, Carolyn A.	NC0850	Bishop, Genevieve	KS0150
Bevington, Mike	OR1250	Billings, Judson	OH0600	Bishop, James	FL0150
Bewick, Bonnie	MA0350	Billingslea, Sandra	NY0646	Bishop, James	FL1750
Bewlay, Ho Eui Holly	NY3717	Billingsley, Michael	NJ0060	Bishop, Jason	PA2715
Bewley, Rabon	TX1660	Billingsley, Monique Phinney	MA0350	Bishop, Jean	IL1300
Beyer, Douglas A.	KS0700	Billington, Ryan	AF0120	Bishop, Julie	PA3250
Beyer, George	CA1520	Billington, Ryan	AF0150	Bishop, Marla	GA1700
Beyer, Gregory S.	IL2200	Billions, Clifford	OH2150	Bishop, Martha	GA0750
Beyer, LaVaun	CA1520	Billions, Clifford	OH0600	Bishop, Matthew	TX1425
Beyer, Loretta	MI0200	Billman, Nancy S.	NJ0800	Bishop, Richard	ME0250
Beyer, Tom	NY2750	Billmann, Peter	WI0825	Bishop, Roberta	RI0250
Beyers, Foster	MN0600	Billmayer, Veneta A.	AL1160	Bishop, Ronald	OH1700
Beyt, Christopher	IL2510	Billmeyer, Dean W.	MN1623	Bishop, Ronald	OH0600
Bezaire, Fionna	IL0730	Billock, Becky	WV0600	Bishop, Saundra	MS0575
Bezuidenhout, Kristian	NY1100	Bills, Mary Ann	NC2500	Bisio, Michael	VT0050
Bhagwati, Sandeep	AI0070	Billy, Sandra S.	VA1830	Biskupski, Grazyna	MI1260
Bhanji, Baomi Butts	CA1800	Bilotta, Lee	PA3560	Biskupski, Tadeusz	MI1260
Bhasin, Paul K.	VA0250	Bilotta, Tony	PA3560	Biss, Paul	MA1400
Bhattacharya, Subrata	IL3300	Bilous, Edward	NY1900	Bissell, Paul	TX0550
Bhogal, Gurminder	MA2050	Bilson, Malcolm	NY0900	Bisson, Mary	MD0100
Bialosky, Marshall H.	CA0805	Bimm, Greg L.	IL0750	Bissonette, Gregg S.	CA0835
Biamonte, Nicole	AI0150	Binckes, Fred B.	MT0350	Bistrow, Douglas	IL3450
Biancalana, Jeff	CA5000	Binder, Benjamin A.	PA1050	Bitensky, Laurence S.	KY0450
Biancalana, Jeff	CA4150	Binder, Shelley	TN1710	Bitetti, Ernesto	IN0900
Bianchi, Douglas	MI2200	Bindhammer, Heidi	GA1750	Bithell, David	TX3420
Bianchi, Eric	NY1300	Bindrim, Don	TN0300	Bitticks, Meret	IL0750
Bianchi, Jay	NY2660	Binek, Claire	PA3330	Bittmann, Antonius O.	NJ1130
Bianco, Christopher	WA1250	Binek, Justin	PA3330	Bittner, Groff S.	MO0650
Bianculli, Pasquale A.	NY2105	Binford, Hilde M.	PA2450	Bitz, Lori L.	OH2275
Biava, Luis Gabriel	OH1200	Binford, Joanna	KY1350	Bitz, Lori	MI0050
Biava, Luis O.	PA3250	Binford, Patrick	KY0450	Bitz, Lori	MI1950

Alphabetical Listing of Faculty

Name	Code	Name	Code	Name	Code
Bitzas, Penelope	MA0400	Blake, Joey	MA0260	Blomquist, Jane K.	CA2600
Bivens, Pat	TN0250	Blake, John	PA3330	Blomster, Jennie	CA5350
Biviano, Franklin Lin	MA0260	Blake, John	NY2150	Blomster, Kathleen	CA1860
Bixler, David	OH0300	Blake, Marc C.	CA2710	Blood, Charles F.	NH0250
Bixler, Judith	MI1000	Blake, Michael	ND0500	Blood, Curt	CT0600
Bixler, Ronald	PA0350	Blake, Paul	NY1400	Blood, Curtis	CT0650
Bizianes, Chris	KY0250	Blake, Ran	MA1400	Blood, Elizabeth P.	NH0350
Bizinkauskas, Maryte	MA0510	Blake, Ron	NY1900	Blooding, Karen	TN1100
Bizzell, Gayle	TX1850	Blake-Oliver, Tiffany Erin	CO0250	Blooding, Randie	NY1800
Bjella, David E.	FL1750	Blakely, Doug	NY1800	Bloom, Bradley	AG0550
Bjella, Richard L.	TX3200	Blakeman, Jennifer	NY2750	Bloom, Bradley	MI1750
Bjella, Steven A.	WI0850	Blakeman, Lee	KY1550	Bloom, Claudia	CA4425
Bjerke, Sophie	NY3775	Blakemore, Linda	MI0300	Bloom, J. Lawrie	IL2250
Bjerken, Xak	NY0900	Blakeslee, Lynn	NY1100	Bloom, Jane Ira	NY2660
Bjorck, Andreas	MA0260	Blakey, David	CA1650	Bloom, Joe	CA1650
Bjorem, Pauline Kung	TX0050	Blalock, Angela	SC0150	Bloom, Myron	IN0900
Bjork, Mark	MN1623	Blalock, James	GA1500	Bloom, Peter A.	MA1750
Bjorkman, Jan	WI0835	Blalock, Karen	UT0325	Bloomberg, Jennifer Wohlenhaus	IA0550
Bjorlie, Carol	WI0845	Blanc, Pamela	CA0960	Bloomfield, Ruta	CA2810
Bjornn, Marsha	ID0060	Blanchard, Carol	ID0060	Bloomfield, Tara	UT0050
Bjornsen, Lawrence	AF0120	Blanchard, Gerald J.	MI1160	Bloomquist, Paul	IA0790
Bjur, David	WA1150	Blanchard, Jeff L.	OH2140	Blose, Dennis	NJ0175
Blachly, Alexander	IN1700	Blanchard, Scott	MA2100	Blosser, C. Andrew	OH1850
Blachly, Barbara	KS1000	Blanchard, Terence	FL1900	Blosser, Dan C.	IN1650
Black, Alan	TX1700	Blanchet, George A.	IL2050	Blount, Alyssa	NY4150
Black, Alan R.	NC0850	Blanchet, Martin	AG0170	Bloxam, Jennifer	MA2250
Black, Alan	NC0550	Blanchett, Madalyn	TX2260	Blucker, James	IL0300
Black, Amy King	GA0500	Blanco, Leo	MA0260	Blue, T. K.	NY2105
Black, Amy King	GA0050	Blancq, Charles C.	LA0800	Bluebaugh, Diana	MO0060
Black, Brian	AA0200	Bland, Barbara	MI1750	Bluestone, Joel	OR0850
Black, Cary	WA0350	Bland, Leland	OH2500	Blum, Stephen	NY0600
Black, Cassandra	TX1450	Bland, Ron	CO0150	Blumberg, Kira	CA0630
Black, Christina	PA2710	Bland, Ron	CO0830	Blumberg, Kira	CA5150
Black, Claude	OH2300	Bland, Ronald	CO0550	Blumberg, Stephen	CA0150
Black, Daniel	NY1700	Bland, Sarah	VA0250	Blumberg, Stephen F.	CA0840
Black, David	MO1950	Blaney, Michael S.	LA0760	Blume, Philipp G.	IL3300
Black, David	CA6000	Blankenbaker, Scott E.	MN1290	Blumenfeld, Jonathan	NJ1130
Black, David	CA2550	Blankenburg, Gayle	CA1050	Blumenfeld, Jonathan H.	PA3250
Black, David	CA0960	Blankenburg, Gayle R.	CA3650	Blumenstock, Elizabeth	CA4150
Black, Donald	VA1350	Blankenburg, Gayle	CA4500	Blumfield, Coleman	DC0110
Black, Dorothy M.	PA2800	Blankenship, Carole	TN1200	Blumhofer, Jonathan	MA0650
Black, Elizabeth P.	NC0805	Blankenship, Courtney	IL3500	Blumsack, Michelle	TX3000
Black, Jacqueline	PA1200	Blankenship, Harold	AL0450	Blundell, Reuben E.	NY0625
Black, Karen	IA1800	Blankenship, William	NV0150	Blunsom, Laurie	MN1120
Black, Kathryn A.	NY3475	Blanner, Christine Fortner	IA0550	Bluteau, Denis	AI0150
Black, Larry	NC0250	Blasco, Scott	WA1150	Bluteau, Denis	AI0200
Black, Lendell	OK0750	Blaser, Albert	OH0650	Bly, Carl	VA1350
Black, Les	NY1800	Blaser, Lynn	AG0450	Blyth, Jennifer	PA0950
Black, Marjorie	MN0800	Blaser, Melanie	OH0650	Boal, Nathan	OR0700
Black, Phillip	KS1450	Blasius, Leslie	WI0815	Board, Ryan A.	CA3600
Black, Randall	KY0950	Blaszak, Emilia	IL2750	Boardman, Christopher	FL1900
Black, Robert	NY2150	Blaszkiewicz, Michael J.	MI1700	Boardman, Gregory	ME0150
Black, Robert	CT0650	Blatter, Alfred W.	PA0850	Boateng, Kwabena	MA2020
Black, Susan	AG0650	Blatti, Richard L.	OH1850	Boatman, Amy	KS0250
Blackburn, Bradford	FL2050	Blauer, Matt	KS1450	Boatright, Ann	CA4460
Blackburn, Gregory	IL0850	Blaydes, Sharon	OH1600	Boaz, Virginia Lile	TX0600
Blackburn, Royce F.	ND0500	Blazar, Sally	MA0260	Bob, Joan	MD0400
Blackburn, Ruth	MA1175	Blazekovic, Zdravko	NY0600	Bob, Sarah	MA0700
Blackie, Ruth	AF0120	Blea, Anthony	CA1020	Bobak, Jacqueline	CA0510
Blackinton, David	UT0190	Blecha-Wells, Meredith	OK0800	Bobbitt, Kayleen	MI0750
Blackledge, Barbara	PA2200	Bleckman, Theo	NY2150	Bobe, Larry	IA1300
Blackley, Rowland	OH0100	Bledsoe, Joshua	AR0850	Bobenhouse, Elizabeth	NE0450
Blackley, Terrance J.	CA1900	Bledsoe, Lee	TN1450	Bobetsky, Victor V.	NY0625
Blacklow, John	IN1700	Blehm, Denise	KS0700	Bobo, Ann	MA0350
Blackman, Daniel	AG0450	Bleiler, Loueda	NY0950	Bobo, Kevin A.	IN0900
Blackman, Mary Dave	TN0500	Bleiler-Conrad, Suzanne	PA2450	Boboc, Monica	NC0850
Blackmon, Odie	TN1850	Blench, Karl E.	TX1000	Bobrowski, Christine	CA1250
Blackmore, Lisa	MO1830	Blenzig, Charles	NY3785	Bobulinski, Greg	NY1275
Blackmore, Lisa	MO0650	Blersch, Carla	NE0150	Bocanegra, Cheryl	OK0850
Blackshear, Alan	AL0831	Blersch, Jeffrey	NE0150	Bocaner, Lawrence	DC0050
Blackshear, Glinda	AL0831	Blessinger, Martin	TX3000	Boccarossa, Jennifer	AR0750
Blackstock, Adam	AL1050	Bletstein, Bev R.	OH1860	Boccato, Rogerio	NY2150
Blackstone, Jerry O.	MI2100	Bletstein, Beverly	OH1850	Boccia, James	NH0250
Blackwell, Claire	CA2810	Bleuel, John	SC0400	Boccia, James	NH0150
Blackwell, Jessica	TN1850	Bleuel, John	GA2130	Bock, James D.	OH1650
Blackwell, Leslie	GA1150	Bleyle, Carl O.	IA0850	Bock, Stan	OR1300
Blackwell, Manley	AL1350	Bleyle, William B.	OH0950	Bock, Susan V.	IL1150
Blackwell, Raymond	PA0550	Blice, Carolyn	FL1550	Bocook, Jay A.	SC0750
Blackwood, Easley R.	IL3250	Blier, Steven	NY1900	Boczkowska, Eweline	OH2600
Blackwood, Jeremy	OK1150	Blink, David	WA1400	Boda, Dan	SC0750
Blades, Jennifer A.	MD0650	Blinman, Chad	MA0260	Bodaubay, Dina	CO0830
Blaha, Bernadene	CA5300	Blinov, Ilya	PA3150	Bodden, Bruce	WA0250
Blaha, Christopher	NC0050	Bliton, Nathaniel	MI0900	Boddez, Karla	AA0020
Blaha, Joseph L.	VA1250	Bliznik, Karen	GA1150	Boddicker, Maureen	WY0200
Blaha, Kyle	NY1900	Blizzard, John T.	NC2650	Boddie, Susan	AF0120
Blaich, Tanya	MA1400	Bloch, Gus	VT0200	Bode, Robert	MO1810
Blaine, Robert	MS0350	Bloch, Robert S.	CA5010	Boden, John C.	ME0500
Blair, Dean G.	AA0200	Blocher, Larry	AL1050	Boden-Luethi, Ruth	WA1150
Blair, Deborah V.	MI1750	Block, Geoffrey	WA1000	Boder, Alexander	NY2400
Blair, Starla	MO0400	Block, Glenn	IL1150	Bodiford, Kenneth	AL0500
Blair, Steve	VT0250	Block, Steven	NM0450	Bodine, Gerald B.	IN1300
Blair, Suanne Hower	KY0900	Block, Tyrone	TX2570	Bodinger, John	WA1350
Blais, Jerome	AF0100	Block-Schwenk, Kevin	MA0260	Bodley, Muriel M.	NY4150
Blaisdell, Gayla Bauer	WA0050	Blocker, Robert	CT0850	Bodman, Alan	OH2150
Blaisdell, Tor	WA0050	Blodget, Sherril	VT0100	Bodnar, Marian	CA0825
Blake, C. Marc	CA2600	Bloechl, Olivia A.	CA5032	Bodner, Jessica	MN1625
Blake, Cory	VA1500	Blois, Scott	CA3300	Bodner, Vicki Hope	NY2750
Blake, Daniel	NY0500	Bloland, Per A.	OH1450	Bodolosky, Michael	PA3410
Blake, Elise A.	VA0800	Blombach, Ann K.	OH1850	Boe, Karen	WI0865
Blake, Harry D.	TX0340	Blomquist, Edwin	MA0260	Boeckman, Jeffrey	HI0210

Alphabetical Listing of Faculty

Name	Code	Name	Code	Name	Code
Boeckman, Vicki	WA0200	Bolshakova, Natalia	MO1800	Booth, William	CA5060
Boeder, Bethel J.	MN1030	Bolstad, Stephen P.	VA0600	Boothe, Greg	UT0190
Boedges, Bob	MO1120	Bolster, Stephen C.	KY0300	Boothe, Randall W.	UT0050
Boehm, Norbert	AA0200	Bolte, Barbara	AG0250	Boothman, Donald	MA0650
Boehm, Norman	AR0350	Bolter, Norman	MA0350	Boothroyd, David	AB0100
Boehm, Patricia A.	OH2290	Bolter, Norman	MA1175	Bootland, Christine	AA0040
Boehmke, Erik A.	IL1600	Bolter, Norman	MA1400	Booze, Leanna	TN0100
Boelling, John	OR1300	Bolton, Beth M.	PA3250	Boozer, John E.	NC2350
Boelling, John F.	OR1100	Bolton, Bryan	KY0050	Boozer, Mark	GA0490
Boelter, Karl	NY3725	Bolton, Chuck	OR1150	Boozer, Pat	NC2350
Boemler, Cathy	MO0550	Bolton, Gregory	FL1745	Boquiren, Sidney M.	NY0050
Boen, Jonathan C.	IL2250	Bolton, Thomas W.	KY1200	Bor, Mustafa	AA0100
Boepple, Hans C.	CA4425	Bolton, Tom	AR0500	Borah, Bernard	IL0800
Boerckel, Gary M.	PA2100	Bolves, Keith	FL1550	Borbely, Adrienne	NY0050
Boerger, Kristina G.	WI0200	Bombardier, Brad	WI0860	Borchert, Laroy	NM0310
Boerma, Scott	MI2100	Bombardier, Bradley A.	MN1600	Borczon, Ronald M.	CA0835
Boers, Geoffrey	WA1050	Bomberger, E. Douglas	PA1250	Borczon, Ronald	CA3100
Boese, Jessica	IL1050	Bomer, Delain	MI1180	Bordas, Ricard	SC0275
Boesiger, Kevin	NE0525	Bomgardner, Stephen D.	MO0350	Borden, Rita	AZ0450
Boespflug, George	CA0350	Bommelje, Ann	PA2250	Borders, Ann	IL1750
Boettcher, Bonna	NY0900	Bonacci, Andrew	MA2100	Borders, James M.	MI2100
Boettger, Susan	CA2390	Bonacci, Mary Brown	MA2100	Bordignon, Paolo	NJ1350
Boey, Hooi Yin	WV0050	Bonazzi, Elaine	NY3790	Bordner, Gary	MN1623
Boga, Cheryl	PA3500	Boncella, Paul	AL0332	Bordo, Guy V.	OH2150
Bogachek, Zinoviy	VA0450	Bond, Bronwell	PA0100	Bordon, Wellington	NC1600
Bogard, Emily	IN0900	Bond, Judith	WI0850	Boren, Benjamin J.	CA0850
Bogard, Rick G.	TX3500	Bond, Karlyn	UT0400	Boren, Mark	ND0250
Bogard, Theresa L.	WY0200	Bond, Kori	ID0100	Boresi, Matthew	WI0250
Bogas, Roy	CA2200	Bond, Lawrence	TN0100	Borg, Paul	IL1150
Bogdan, Thomas	VT0050	Bond, Mona	LA0300	Borgerding, Todd Michael	ME0250
Bogdan, Valentin Mihai	LA0100	Bondar, Liudmila E.	MI1200	Borgers, Ken	CA2550
Boge, Claire L.	OH1450	Bondari, Brian	TX3350	Borghesani, Dean	WI0825
Bogert, Nathan	IA0400	Bonde, Allen R.	MA1350	Borgia-Petro, Diana	PA1550
Bogert, Nathan	IA0700	Bondelevitch, David	CO0830	Borgo, David R.	CA5050
Bogey, Brian	NY3725	Bonds, Dennis	MS0100	Borgstedt, Bryson	SC1000
Bogey, Brian A.	NY1850	Bonds, Eric	AL0200	Borgstrom, Steven	MN1260
Boggs, David G.	IL1740	Bonds, Mark Evan	NC2410	Boring, Daniel	PA2550
Boggs, Isabelle	MA1100	Bonds, Nancy	CA3100	Boris, Victor R.	PA3150
Boggs, Isabelle	MA2100	Bonds, Samuel	VA0450	Boris, William	IL0720
Boggs, William	OH0350	Bondurant-Koehler, Shela	IL1200	Borja, Eric	IL0720
Bogle, Stephanie	AG0650	Bone, Amber Sudduth	WA1250	Borja, Jonathan	MO1810
Bogle, Stephanie	AG0300	Bone, Lloyd E.	WV0350	Borla, Janice	IL2050
Bognar, Anna Belle	OH0300	Bonelli, Matt	FL1300	Borland, Carolyn	PA2250
Bognar, Joseph A.	IN1750	Bonenfant, Timothy	TX0150	Borling, James E.	VA1100
Bogojevic, Natasha	IL0750	Boner, Jan	GA1150	Borman, Jeana	NC1100
Bogorad, Julia A.	MN1623	Bongiorno, Frank	NC2440	Born, Kristie	FL1750
Bogue, Bryan	WA1350	Bongiorno, Joseph A.	NY2750	Bornovalova, Olga	IL0650
Boguslavsky, Lidia	NJ1050	Bonilla, Luis	NY2150	Bornovalova, Olga	IL1085
Bohannon, Helen	IN1010	Bonin, Brian P.	GA0750	Borok, Emanuel	TX3420
Bohannon, Kenneth	OK1400	Bonkowski, Anita	AB0150	Borok, Emanuel	TX2400
Bohanon, George	CA5031	Bonneau, Sharon J.	VA0450	Borowicz, Zbigniew Jozef	AI0190
Bohlen, Donald A.	NY3725	Bonnefond, James L.	CT0700	Borowitz, Michael J.	LA0200
Bohlen, Tara M.	ND0400	Bonnell, Bruce M.	MI0400	Borrmann, Kenneth	PA2800
Bohlin, Ragnar	CA4150	Bonner, Gary	CA0450	Borroff, Edith	NY3705
Bohlman, Philip V.	IL3250	Bonner, Joe	AR0110	Borror, Gordon L.	OR1210
Bohm, Keith	CA0840	Bonner, Judd	CA0450	Borror, Ronald	CT0650
Bohn, David M.	WI0835	Bonner, Peggy	IL0400	Borthwick-Aiken, Rebecca A.	PA0100
Bohn, Donna M.	PA1550	Bonness, Will	AC0100	Bortolussi, Paolo	AB0100
Bohn, Hans	MA2030	Bonnett, Kurt	TX3535	Bortolussi, Paolo	AB0090
Bohn, James	MA0510	Bonsanti, Neal	FL0650	Bortolussi, Paolo	AB0060
Bohn, James	RI0200	Bonsiero, Philip	MD0400	Borton, Bruce E.	NY3705
Bohn, William	OK1200	Bonsignore, Joseph	OH0755	Bortz, Jodi	PA2450
Bohnenstengel, Christian	UT0200	Bontrager, Charles E.	AZ0500	Borup, Hasse	UT0250
Bohnert, David A.	NE0700	Bontrager, Lisa Jane	PA2750	Borwick, Susan Harden	NC2500
Bohnet, Andra	AL1300	Bonus, Alexander	NC0600	Borys, Roman	AG0450
Bohnet, Keith	AL1300	Bonvisutto, Bruce	NY0500	Bos, Daniel	CA5550
Bohnhorst, Brendan	MI0300	Boocock, William	CA0250	Bos, Ken	MI0850
Boianova, Linda	NY3730	Book, A. Ryan	NC2210	Boschee, Sharon	ND0500
Boianova, Linda	NY2650	Book, Andee	MO1710	Bosco, Frank	NY2750
Boico, Efim	WI0825	Book, Ryan	VA0050	Bose, Judith	MA1175
Boire, Paula L.	KS0350	Booker, Adam	MN1600	Bosi-Goldberg, Marina	CA4900
Boisvert, Claude	AI0220	Booker, Anthony	AB0150	Bosits, Marcia L.	IL2250
Boisvert, Jean-Guy	AE0100	Booker, Charles L.	AR0730	Boskovich, Elizabeth	OH2050
Boivin, Luc	AI0210	Booker, Kenneth A.	TX1450	Bosler, Annie J.	CA5020
Bokar Thiam, Pascal	CA5353	Booker, Sally	MN1600	Boss, Bonnie	CA3100
Bokhout, William	MI0850	Bookhammer, Evelyn	PA1650	Boss, Jack	OR1050
Boky, Colette	AI0210	Bookout, Melanie	IN0905	Boss, Robert	CA4050
Bolcom, William E.	MI2100	Boon, Rolf J.	AA0200	Boss, Robert	CA4100
Bolden, Christina	OH2550	Boone, Benjamin V.	CA0810	Bossard, Claudia M.	IN1800
Bolden-Taylor, Diane	CO0950	Boone, Bridgett	IA1450	Bossart, Eugene	MI1900
Boldin, James E.	LA0770	Boone, Christine	IN0800	Bosscher, Scott	MI0850
Boldrey, Richard L.	IL2250	Boone, Geraldine T.	VA0950	Bosse, Joanna	MI1400
Boldt-Neurohr, Kirsten	WA0050	Boone, Graeme M.	OH1850	Bossert, Laura	MA1175
Bolduan, Kathleen	MO1900	Boone, Kathleen	WA0550	Bossert-King, Laura	MA2050
Bolduc, Remi	AI0150	Boone, Mary E.	NC1700	Bosshardt, Heather	UT0190
Bolen, Bradley C.	TX0300	Boone, Michael E.	PA3250	Bossuat, Judy	CA0840
Bolen, Jerry	IL2970	Boone, Robert	AZ0480	Bostic, Bert	TX1660
Bolen, Patricia	SC0700	Boonshaft, Peter Loel	NY1600	Bostic, Polly T.	NC2650
Bolger, Jean	CO0200	Boorman, Stanley H.	NY2740	Bostic, Ronald D.	NC2650
Bolin, Daniel	IN0250	Boos, Kenneth G.	FL1310	Bostic-Brown, Tiffany	AL1250
Boling, Mark E.	TN1710	Booth, Adam	WV0550	Bostick, D. Jane	NC0100
Bolkovac, Edward	CT0650	Booth, Brian	UT0250	Bostock, Anne	MA1100
Bollenback, Paul	MD0650	Booth, David M.	OH2500	Bostock, Matthew	MA2100
Bolles, Marita	IL0750	Booth, Davyd M.	PA3250	Bostock, Matthew	MA1100
Bolling-May, Joan	VA1400	Booth, Doug	CA2100	Boston, Marilyn	MO0400
Bolling-May, Joan	DC0010	Booth, John D.	MO0500	Boston, Nancy J.	PA2150
Bollinger, Bernard	CA1000	Booth, Nancy Davis	AZ0480	Bostonia, Marguerite	WV0800
Bollinger, Blair J.	PA3250	Booth, Rodney	TX3420	Bostrand, Eva	AA0100
Bollinger, Blair	PA0850	Booth, Thomas	TX2400	Bostrom, Sandra	CA0835
Bollino, Damien	VA1475	Booth, Todd	AG0130	Bostwick, Stacey	IA0420

Name	Code	Name	Code	Name	Code
Boswell, Michael	IN1400	Bowen, Ron	AZ0200	Boyle, Holly	TX3300
Boswell, Ronald L.	AR0750	Bowen, William	NY2750	Boyle, Mary E.	NY3760
Bot, Mary Jo	MN1300	Bowen, William	AG0450	Boyle, McGregor	MD0650
Botelho, Mauro	NC0550	Bower, Calvin	IN1700	Boyle, Patrick	AB0150
Botelho, Paul J.	LA0300	Bower, John E.	DC0050	Boyle, Sharon	IN1400
Both, Christoph	AF0050	Bowermaster, Tod	MO1830	Boyles, John	VA0150
Botkin, Sean	IA1600	Bowers, Amy	CA5300	Boynton, Susan	NY0750
Botly, George	AG0130	Bowers, Greg J.	VA0250	Boysen, Andrew A.	NH0350
Bott, Darryl J.	NJ1130	Bowers, Judy	FL0850	Bozarth, George	WA1050
Bottelli, Roberta	WA1350	Bowers, Kathryn Smith	MO1950	Bozell, Casey	OR0150
Botterbusch, Duane A.	WV0550	Bowers, Michael	NC0750	Bozeman, Joanne H.	WI0350
Botterbusch, Duane A.	PA1400	Bowers, Sally	IL1400	Bozeman, Kenneth W.	WI0350
Bottge, Karen	KY1450	Bowers, Teresa M.	PA1400	Bozeman, Scott	GA0200
Botti, Robert	NY2150	Bowers, Walt M.	OK1450	Bozina, Robert P.	CA1020
Botti, Susan	NY2150	Bowie, Audrey	TN1400	Bozina, Robert	CA4425
Bottomley, John	MA2000	Bowie, Lenard C.	GA0150	Bozman, Julissa	CA1265
Bottorf, Deane	CA5355	Bowker, Barbara E.	IL1085	Bozman, William M.	VA1350
Botts, Nathan	VT0050	Bowland, Jimmy	TN1400	Braamse, Shudong	FL1740
Botts, Nathan	MA2250	Bowlby, Timothy	IL1520	Braasch, Jonas	AI0150
Bou, Emmy	NE0150	Bowles, Adam Alan	AL1200	Braaten, Brenda	AB0210
Boubel, Karen A.	MN1000	Bowles, Chelcy L.	WI0815	Braaten-Reuter, Laurie	IA1800
Bouchard, Frederick	MA0260	Bowles, DeVera	ND0250	Brabant, John-Paul	NY3780
Bouchard, George	NY2550	Bowles, Douglas	DC0010	Bracchitta, Ian	SC0400
Bouchard, Jean-Luc	AI0190	Bowles, Douglas	DC0050	Bracchitta, Ian	SC0750
Bouchard, Jean-Marc	AI0200	Bowles, Kenneth E.	ND0250	Bracchitta, Ian	NC2400
Bouchard, Lise	AI0200	Bowles, Shannon	KY1500	Braccio, Joseph	FL1650
Boucher, Gillian	AF0120	Bowles, Suzanne	TX3300	Bracey, Jerry A.	VA0500
Boucher, Helene	AI0150	Bowles, Virginia	KY0100	Bracey, John-Paul	AG0500
Boucher, Leslie H.	GA0700	Bowles, Virginia B.	KY0150	Bracey, Judson F.	WV0050
Boucher, Remi	AI0190	Bowlin, David Henderson	OH1700	Bracey, Robert D.	NC2430
Bouchillon, Joel	AL1150	Bowlin, Ellen	IL0300	Brack, Brandon J.	CA1900
Boud, Ronald E.	TN1660	Bowling, Jeanne	IN1100	Brackeen, Joanne	NY2660
Boudette, Jennifer	FL1430	Bowman, Bob	MO1810	Brackeen, JoAnne	MA0260
Boudreau, Walter	AI0210	Bowman, Brian	TX3420	Brackeen, William	OK0450
Boudreault, Mary	NC2700	Bowman, J. D.	KS0900	Bracken, Patricia	KY0100
Boudreaux, Margaret A.	MD0520	Bowman, Jennifer	WA0650	Bracken, Patricia	KY0150
Bouffard, Peter P.	NE0600	Bowman, Jonathan	NY2650	Brackett, David	AI0150
Bouffard, Sophie	AJ0100	Bowman, Judith A.	PA1050	Brackett, John	NC2410
Bouffier, Robert	HI0060	Bowman, Paul A.	TX0550	Bracy, Katherine B.	OH2290
Bough, Thomas	IL2200	Bowman, Randy	OH1450	Bradbury, William	CA0847
Boughton, Janet	CT0300	Bowman, Randy C.	OH2200	Brader, Kenneth E.	PA1850
Bougie, Marc-Andre	TX2850	Bowman, Rob	AG0650	Bradetich, Jeff	TX3420
Bouissieres, Ben	MN0625	Bowman, Sean	IN0907	Bradfield, Ann	NM0100
Boukas, Richard A.	NY2660	Bowman, Wayne	NY2750	Bradfield, Bart	IL0720
Bouknight, Tara	VA0750	Bowser, Bryan L.	OH0200	Bradfield, David	CA0805
Bouknight, Tara	VA1125	Bowser, Teresa	TX0700	Bradfield, Geoffrey	IL2200
Boukobza, Laurent	FL1800	Bowyer, Don	AR0110	Bradford, Bobby L.	CA3650
Boulanger, Richard	AE0100	Box, James	AI0150	Bradford, Daron	UT0050
Boulanger, Richard	MA0260	Boyar, Simon M.	NY2750	Bradford, Lovell	NC0550
Boulden, George	KY1450	Boyce, Cody	OH2050	Bradford, Mary Pinkney	TX2170
Boulet, Michele	PA2950	Boyce, Douglas J.	DC0100	Bradley, Annette	AA0080
Bouliane, Denys	AI0150	Boyce, Emily W.	NY3717	Bradley, Deborah	AG0450
Boullion, Linda	NE0460	Boyd, Bob	NJ0760	Bradley, Gwendolyn	NY2900
Boulton, Kenneth	LA0650	Boyd, Bob	IL2250	Bradley, Mark	KY0400
Boumpani, Neil M.	GA1070	Boyd, Bonita	NY1100	Bradley, Nedra	TX1450
Bounds, Kevin S.	AL1160	Boyd, Bonnie	TX2200	Bradley, Randall	TX0300
Bounous, Barry	UT0050	Boyd, Bruce	KS1250	Bradley-Kramer, Deborah	NY0750
Bounous, Debra	UT0050	Boyd, Craig E.	NY4050	Bradley-Vacco, Lynda	MN0250
Bouras-Recktenwald, Christina	KY0250	Boyd, Don E.	HI0200	Bradner, Janice B.	SC1200
Bourassa, Richard N.	OR0450	Boyd, Fern Glass	MT0400	Bradshaw, Curt	TX0700
Bourcier, Tom	IA0950	Boyd, Frederick	NC2420	Bradshaw, Daniel	HI0050
Bourgeois, John	LA0300	Boyd, Jean A.	TX0300	Bradshaw, Dean	AF0100
Bourgeois, Marilyn	IL2775	Boyd, Jesse	LA0300	Bradshaw, Dean	AF0120
Bourgois, Louis	KY0750	Boyd, Jesse	LA0080	Bradshaw, Eric E.	GA2150
Bourion, Sylveline	AI0200	Boyd, John W.	TX2550	Bradshaw, Keith M.	UT0200
Bourland, Roger	CA5030	Boyd, Kathleen A.	MA2050	Bradshaw, Murray C.	CA5032
Bourne, Brian	MD0750	Boyd, Kathleen E.	IN0250	Bradshaw, Robert J.	MA1650
Bourne, Thaddeus	CT0600	Boyd, Kim	OH2050	Bradshaw, Tracey	UT0200
Bourne, Trina	OH0600	Boyd, Lance	MT0400	Brady, Angus	AB0050
Bourque, David	AG0450	Boyd, Melinda J.	IA1600	Brady, Brandon D.	OK0300
Bourquin, Cindy	CA4450	Boyd, Michael	PA0600	Brady, Judith L.	NY3725
Boury, Robert	AR0750	Boyd, Michael	OH2300	Brady, Nicole B.	UT0050
Bouterse, Ami K.	WI0835	Boyd, Michael	MS0360	Brady, Patricia L.	VA0600
Boutet, Danielle	VT0150	Boyd, Ned	IN1310	Brady, Sarah	MA0350
Boutin, Lise	AA0200	Boyd, Robert	IL3550	Brady-Riley, Carolyn	IL2650
Bouton, Arthur E.	CO0900	Boyd, Sara	ND0400	Braginsky, Alexander	MN1623
Boutte, Tony L.	FL1900	Boyd, Sue Marston	VA1350	Bragle, John	MI1650
Boutwell, Brett N.	LA0200	Boye, David	NE0200	Braid, David	AG0450
Bouvier, Monique	RI0101	Boye, Gary	NC0050	Braig, Christopher	MO1950
Bouwman, Aaron	MI0520	Boyer, Allen	CA3000	Brakel, Timothy D.	OH2300
Bovbjorg-Neidung, Helen	FL0500	Boyer, Charles G.	CO0050	Brallier, Kathryn	OR0250
Bove, Andrew	NJ0700	Boyer, D. Royce	AL1160	Brame, Robert	FL1750
Bovenschen, Wayne	OK0800	Boyer, Douglas R.	TX3100	Brame, Steven	IL1500
Bovenzi, Michael	FL1950	Boyer, Duane	OR0200	Bramlett, KaDee	OK1330
Bovinette, James	IA0850	Boyer, Justin	MD0550	Brammeier, Meredith	CA0600
Bovyer, Gary S.	CA3650	Boyer, Laura	WA0450	Brammer, Ron L.	MO0775
Bowden, Dan B.	MA0260	Boyer, Maurice C.	IL0730	Branagan, Marcella	PA0100
Bowden, Derek	MD0800	Boyer, Neil V.	NH0100	Branagan, Marcella E.	NY3717
Bowder, Naydene	ME0200	Boyer, Neil V.	ME0500	Brancaleone, Francis P.	NY2200
Bowdidge, Mark	MO1550	Boyer, Peter	CA1050	Brancart, Evelyne	IN0900
Bowell, Jeffrey T.	WY0115	Boyer, Rene	OH2200	Branch, Kirk	LA0080
Bowen, Ann D.	IL1400	Boyette, Larry J.	NY3550	Branch, Robert	NM0500
Bowen, Charles Kevin	NC2500	Boykan, Martin	MA0500	Branch, Stephen F.	CA3975
Bowen, Jose A.	TX2400	Boykin-Settles, Jessica	DC0150	Branch, Thomas W.	AL1160
Bowen, K. Scott	CA4300	Boyko, Lisa	OH0600	Branchal, Nick	CO0050
Bowen, Meredith Y.	MI1200	Boyko, Megan	AF0120	Brand, Angela	CA0450
Bowen, Nathan	CA3100	Boyle, Annie Chalex	TX3200	Brand, Benjamin D.	TX3420
Bowen, Ralph	NJ1130	Boyle, Audrey	CA0650	Brandao, Fernando	MA0260
Bowen, Richard L.	IN1850	Boyle, Benjamin C. S.	NJ1350	Brandau, Ryan James	NJ1350
Bowen, Robert E.	CA3200	Boyle, E. C. McGregor	MD0400	Brandeburg, Michael	CA4460

Alphabetical Listing of Faculty

Name	Code	Name	Code	Name	Code
Brandenburg, Julie A.	WI0450	Breese, Gretchen	MA1400	Bridge, Julie	NY2950
Brandenburg, Mark	CA4900	Bregitzer, Lorne	CO0830	Bridge, Robert	NY2950
Brandenburg, Mark	CA5070	Bregman, Jacqueline	MN1050	Bridges, Alban Kit	IL0750
Brandes, Christine	CA5000	Breidenbach, Ruth	NY2450	Bridges, Cynthia	IL0600
Brandes, Christine	CA4150	Breiling, Roy	AZ0510	Bridges, Cynthia	TX0550
Brandes, Christine	CA4200	Breindel, Christina	RI0200	Bridges, David	TN0100
Brandes, David E.	NH0110	Breithaupt, Robert	OH0350	Bridges, Duane	MO1950
Brandes, Gary W.	MO1830	Breitman, David	OH1700	Bridges, Jan	TX2570
Brandes, Jan	WI1150	Breiwick, Jamie	WI1150	Bridges, Madeline	TN0100
Brandes, Lambert	MA0800	Brekke, Jeremy	ND0350	Bridges, Scott	AL1170
Brandfonbrener, Amy	IN1310	Breland, Barron	NE0160	Bridges, Theresa	LA0050
Brandolino, Tony	MO2000	Breland, Jason	AL1195	Bridgewater, Cecil	NY2660
Brandon, Joan Lynette	IN0100	Brellochs, Christopher	NY1050	Bridgewater, Cecil	NY2150
Brandon, Mack	NJ0950	Bremer, Carolyn	CA0825	Bridgewater, Ronald S.	IL3300
Brandon, Mark	AL0500	Bremer, Jeff	PA3650	Bridgman, Joyce M.	OK0850
Brandt, Anthony K.	TX2150	Brenan, Craig	AA0100	Bridson, Paul	IA0550
Brandt, Jeffrey	MT0400	Brenan, Jim	AA0050	Brien, April Malone	SC0275
Brandt, Lynne	TX2310	Brendel, Cheryl M.	TN0850	Briere, Jimmy	AI0200
Brandt, Robert	DE0150	Brendel, Ronald S.	TN0850	Brierton, Thomas D.	CA5350
Branker, Anthony D.J.	NJ0900	Brendel, Wolfgang	IN0900	Briggs, Amy	IL3250
Brannan, Victoria	IL1500	Brendle, Ron	NC0050	Briggs, Cynthia	MO0700
Brannen, Malcolm	MI0850	Brendler, Charlene	CA5000	Briggs, John	AR0500
Brannen, Randall	OH1400	Breneman, Marianne Leitch	KY1000	Briggs, Kendall Durelle	NY1900
Branning, Ron	FL0040	Brenes, Laura	CA5150	Briggs, Kurt	NY0270
Brannock, Robert D.	TX3300	Brennan, Adam	PA2150	Briggs, Margery S.	CA3650
Brannon, Patrick V.	IL3370	Brennan, Bill	AD0050	Briggs, Monique	NY2050
Bransby, Bruce	IN0900	Brennan, Christopher	CA0960	Briggs, Nancy L.	CA4580
Branscome, Eric	TN0050	Brennan, David	CA2420	Briggs, Philip	TX2050
Branson, Jeremy	PA0550	Brennan, Mark	NY2650	Briggs, Ray	CA3500
Brant, Aaron	OH2250	Brennan, Maureen	MA0850	Briggs, Ray A.	CA0825
Brantigan, Kathleen	CO0900	Brennan-Hondorp, Jennifer J.	KY1550	Briggs, Robert	UT0150
Brantley, K. Thomas	FL2000	Brennand, Meg	WA0800	Briggs, Roger	WA1250
Brantley, Mitch	MS0370	Brenner, Brenda L.	IN0900	Bright, Jeff R.	KY1550
Brantley, Paul E.	NY2150	Brenner, Christopher	CA3500	Bright, Lorna	AZ0150
Branum, Justin	MO1950	Brenner, Laura	FL0800	Bright, Robert M.	AR0700
Brasch, Peter	NY3725	Brenner, Liza	WV0350	Brightbill, Alvin	CA1425
Brasco, Richard	GA0250	Brenner, Martin	CA0825	Brightbill, Alvin	CA0815
Brashear, Wayne	CA2550	Brent, William	LA0550	Brightbill, Elizabeth	VA0700
Brashier, Joe H.	GA2150	Brenzel, Darryl L.	MD0850	Brightbill, Elizabeth	VA0800
Brasington, Merewyn	OH1400	Breon, Timothy	PA2100	Brightbill, Janet	WV0560
Brasky, Jill T.	FL2000	Brescia, Tina	NY5000	Brightman, Nicholas	IN0250
Brass, Kenneth	MA0260	Brescia, Tina M.	NY2750	Brigida, Michael A.	MA0260
Brassard, Henri	AI0210	Breslaw, Irene	NY2150	Brignola, Michael	FL0650
Braswell, Martha	TX2295	Bresler, Liora	IL3300	Briles, Charity	IL1050
Bratcher, Nicholas O.	GA1750	Bresler, Ross	MA0260	Briles, Travis	IL1050
Brath, Jeff	IL2775	Bresnen, Steven M.	PA0400	Briley, Crystal	TN1100
Brath, Wally	MN0250	Bresniak, Chester	MA0650	Brill, Jodie	VA1150
Bratic, Dean	MO0550	Bresnick, Martin I.	CT0850	Brill, Mark	TX3530
Bratt, Douglass F.	IL1890	Bressler, Mark	IL2730	Brillhart, Jeffrey	CT0850
Bratt, Wallis	ID0050	Breton, Jean-Francois	AG0170	Brimmer, Timothy	IN0250
Bratton, Susanna	MI0300	Bretschger, Fred	MN0050	Brinckmeyer, Lynn	TX3175
Bratton, Tripp	KY0300	Brett, Douglas	NY4050	Brindell, Sarah	MA0260
Bratuz, Damjana	AG0500	Brett, Kathleen	AB0210	Brinegar, Don	CA5300
Bratz, Jennifer	MT0350	Brettschneider, William	MI0350	Brinegar, Donald L.	CA3500
Brauer, Vincent	AI0190	Bretz, Jeffrey	CA0200	Brinegar, Steve	DC0170
Braun, Elizabeth	OH1900	Bretzius, David	PA1550	Briney, Bruce C.	IL3500
Braun, Joel	IN0150	Breuleux, Yan	AI0200	Bringerud, Catherine	IN0250
Braun, Kathleen	MS0420	Breuninger, Tyrone	NJ1050	Brings, Allen	NY0642
Braun, Mel	AC0100	Brevig, Per	NY1900	Brink, Ann	CO0200
Braun, Roger	OH1900	Brevig, Per	NY2150	Brink, Brian S.	FL0800
Braun, Sharon	AA0080	Brevig, Per	NY2250	Brink, Daniel	CO0200
Braun, William	WI1155	Brewer, Aaron	IL1612	Brink, Rhona	TX3400
Braunagel, Jesse	ND0150	Brewer, Abbie C.	MO0300	Brink, Robert	MA1400
Brauner, Mitchell	WI0825	Brewer, Bert R.	MT0450	Brink-Button, Ilze	NY2950
Brauninger, Eva	IA0650	Brewer, Charles E.	FL0850	Brinkman, David J.	WY0200
Braunlich, Helmut	DC0050	Brewer, Curt	IL1740	Brinksmeier, Ulrike	OH0680
Braunschweig, Karl	MI2200	Brewer, James	OK1200	Brinner, Benjamin	CA5000
Braunstein, Riki	NY0500	Brewer, Jane	IN1650	Brinson, Barbara Ann	NY3725
Braus, Ira	CT0650	Brewer, Johnny	AL0620	Briones, Marella	MO0650
Braus, Leonard P.	UT0250	Brewer, Mary Kathryn	IN0100	Brisbon, Perry	PA0450
Brautigam, Keith D.	IN1025	Brewer, Mary Kathryn	IN1560	Briscoe, Anna	IN0250
Bravar, Mimi	NH0350	Brewer, Paul	AZ0440	Briscoe, James R.	IN0250
Braverman, Frederick	NY0500	Brewer, Paul	AZ0490	Briselli, Carol	PA3600
Bravo, Fabiana	DC0050	Brewer, Paul S.	MI0300	Briseno, Antonio	TX3515
Brawand, John	SD0550	Brewer, Robert	TX3530	Briskin, David	AG0450
Braxton, Anthony	CT0750	Brewer, Robert S.	TX3450	Briskin, Efrem	NY2400
Bray, Erin	TN0900	Brewer, Robert G.	CO0250	Briskin, Efrem	NY5000
Bray, Michael R.	PA3260	Brewer, Spencer	GA1450	Briskin, Natalya	NY5000
Brazelton, Kitty	VT0050	Brewer, Suzann	MO0350	Briskovich, Zebadiah	IL2970
Brazofsky, Matthew	NY2500	Brewer, Wesley D.	IL0550	Brisson, Eric	MN1700
Brazzel, Russel	IL1100	Brewster, Cornelia L.	NY4150	Brisson, Philip	KY0250
Brazzel, Russell	IL1610	Brewster, David	WA1350	Bristah, Pamela	MA2050
Breakall, Raymond	VA1500	Brewton, Greg	KY1200	Brister Rachwal, Wanda	FL0850
Breault, Robert	UT0250	Brey, Carter	PA0850	Bristol, Caterina	AL0050
Breaux, Michael L.	NY2750	Breznikar, Joseph	IL2900	Bristol, Cynthia	MI0850
Breaux, Troy Jude	LA0760	Brian, Aric	FL2050	Bristol, Doug S.	AL0050
Breazeale, Edward	WY0200	Brian, Aric	FL1650	Bristow, Brent	AR0100
Brecher, Benjamin	CA5060	Brian, Aric J.	FL2000	Bristow, Brent	AR0250
Brechting, Gail	MI1550	Briant, Peter	MT0370	Britain, Mat	TN1850
Breckbill, Anita	NE0600	Briante, Kate	MD0060	Brito, Ramon	NC0750
Breckbill, David	NE0200	Briare, Maureen K.	OR1100	Britsch, Richard	MI0900
Breckenridge, Carol Lei	IA0200	Bribitzer-Stull, Matthew	MN1623	Britsch, Richard	MI0850
Breckenridge, Stan	CA2390	Brich, Jeffrey	IA1600	Britsch, Richard	MI0350
Breckling, Molly	TN0050	Brickens, Nathaniel O.	TX3510	Britt, Brian	OK1350
Breden, Mary C.	CA2800	Brickey, James	UT0150	Britt, Carol H.	NY3780
Bredice, Vincent	FL1310	Brickman, David	NY1100	Britt, Carol	LA0450
Bree, Karen	WY0130	Brickman, Martha	AB0200	Britt, Joshua	KS0650
Breeden, Barbara	CA3270	Brickman, Nina	AG0600	Britt, Mark E.	SC0750
Breedlove, Graham	DC0050	Brickman, Scott T.	ME0420	Britt, Michael J.	AR0600
Breedon, Daniel	MN0600	Bride, Kathleen	NY1100	Britt, Michael	MD0170

Alphabetical Listing of Faculty

Name	Code	Name	Code	Name	Code
Brittan, Francesca	OH0400	Brooks, Ricky W.	AR0850	Brown, Frank Burch	IN0300
Britten, Ruth	CA4300	Brooks, Ronald M.	CO0950	Brown, George	UT0250
Britten, Sandra	AF0050	Brooks, Susan G.	MA0950	Brown, George	CA2975
Britten, Sandra	AF0120	Brooks, Thomas	VA1350	Brown, Gerald	PA3330
Brittin, Ruth	CA5350	Brooks, Victoria	FL0100	Brown, Gwynne Kuhner	WA1000
Britto, Richard	MA2150	Brooks, Wayne	TX3400	Brown, Helen F.	IN1300
Britto, Richard	MA2020	Brooks, William Robert	ND0500	Brown, Hugh M.	MO1810
Britton, Carolyn	WI0845	Brooks-Lyle, Alma B.	AL0050	Brown, Ila	FL1500
Britton, David	AZ0100	Brooks-Smith, Emma	MS0350	Brown, Isabelle	AI0190
Britton, Jason	IA0950	Brookshire, Bradley	NY3785	Brown, J. Bruce	MI2000
Britton, Rex	VA0700	Brookshire, Eddie L.	OH2250	Brown, J. F. Mark	AL0831
Britton, Robert	CA4150	Broome, Curtis	CO0150	Brown, James L.	WA0650
Britts, Judy	CA0840	Broome, Dan	AG0130	Brown, James	FL1300
Britz, Joanne M.	KS1050	Broomhead, Paul	UT0050	Brown, Janet	NY1350
Brizzi, Paul D.	IA0550	Brophy, Nicholas	NE0250	Brown, Janet E.	NY4150
Brndiar, Jack	OH2150	Brophy, Timothy S.	FL1850	Brown, Jeff	MS0360
Brndiar, John	OH0700	Broscious, Timothy L.	MN1600	Brown, Jeffrey A.	IL3500
Brndiar, John J.	OH0200	Broscoe, Liz	CA2440	Brown, Jeffrey C.	IN1750
Brndiar, John	OH0600	Brosh, Robert	PA3330	Brown, Jenine	MI1260
Bro, Paul	IN0800	Brosius, Amy T.	NJ1000	Brown, Jennie	IL0850
Broad, Daniel	MA0280	Brossard, Marilyn	WA0900	Brown, Jennie S.	IL3550
Broad-Ginsberg, Elaine	NH0150	Brostoff, Neal	CA2700	Brown, Jennifer Williams	IA0700
Broadbent, Michelle	ID0060	Brothers, Grey	CA5550	Brown, Jeremy S.	AA0150
Broadley-Martin, Sharon	MA0260	Brothers, Lester D.	MO1790	Brown, Jeri	AI0070
Broadway, Kenneth	FL1850	Brothers, Thomas	NC0600	Brown, Jill Marie	MI0350
Brobeck, John T.	AZ0500	Brotherton, Jonathan P.	NC0900	Brown, Joe Davis	MD0850
Brochu, Paul	AI0200	Brotman, Justin	AZ0490	Brown, Joel	NY3650
Brock, Andrew	VA0700	Brou, Melinda A.	TX2960	Brown, John V.	NC0600
Brock, Andrew	OR0950	Broubechliev, Bojil	NY5000	Brown, Joseph	IL3500
Brock, David	TX3000	Brough, Ronald P.	UT0050	Brown, Julie Hedges	AZ0450
Brock, Gordon R.	FL1950	Broughton, Gregory	GA2100	Brown, Kathryn D.	TX0370
Brock, Jay D.	NY1100	Brouillette, Luke	LA0550	Brown, Kathryn	OH0600
Brock, Jay	DC0050	Broussard, George L.	NC0650	Brown, Kathy	MO1550
Brock, John	TN1710	Brouwer, Albert	AI0050	Brown, Kayson	UT0050
Brock, John	TN0250	Brouwer, Kristin	FL1450	Brown, Keith	TN1710
Brock, Joplin	NC0700	Brovey-Kovach, Lisa	PA2900	Brown, Kellie Dubel	TN1150
Brock, Tomisha	NC0700	Browder, Risa	MD0650	Brown, Kevin E.	NJ0800
Brockett, Clyde W.	VA0150	Brower, Kevin	ID0060	Brown, Kevin W.	CA3500
Brockett, David	OH0650	Brower, Nori	ID0060	Brown, Kimberly	TX3650
Brockington, Frances N.	MI2200	Brown, Aaron	MN1625	Brown, Kristi A.	CA1075
Brockman, Luke	WA0250	Brown, Adrianne	CT0350	Brown, L. Joel	IA0900
Brockman, Michael	WA1050	Brown, Al	CA0850	Brown, Laura E.	IL3500
Brockmann, Nicole M.	IN0350	Brown, Alise	CO0950	Brown, Leland W.	RI0250
Brodbeck, David	CA5020	Brown, Alison	TN1850	Brown, Lenora N.	UT0250
Broderick, Daniela	IL1250	Brown, Allen	CA5350	Brown, Leon	LA0050
Broderick, Daniela C.	IL1890	Brown, Andiel	OR1050	Brown, Leonard	MA2200
Broderick, James	FL1300	Brown, Andrea E.	GA0900	Brown, Leonard	MA1450
Brodhead, Richard C.	PA3250	Brown, Angeline	NY5000	Brown, Leslie Ellen	WI0700
Brodie, Catherine	MI1500	Brown, Anne	NY1700	Brown, Lila R.	MA0350
Brodie, Nannette	CA2050	Brown, Ari	IL3310	Brown, Linda	CA3750
Brodie, Trenton	CA2050	Brown, Beverly	NC1400	Brown, Linda Noble	CA1150
Brodsky, Seth	CT0900	Brown, Billbob	MA2000	Brown, Linda	CA5300
Brodt, Ralph E.	PA2450	Brown, Breighan M.	MI1985	Brown, Lindsay	OH0100
Brody, Ben	WA1350	Brown, Brian	DE0150	Brown, LuAnn	UT0200
Brody, David C.	KS1450	Brown, Brian	NJ1050	Brown, Malcolm	AA0150
Brody, James	CO0800	Brown, Brian	PA2800	Brown, Marcellus	ID0050
Brody, Martin	MA2050	Brown, Brian	NJ0175	Brown, Matthew	PA1300
Broe, Caroline	AZ0440	Brown, Bruce	IA1350	Brown, Matthew	NY1100
Broeker, Angela	MN1625	Brown, Bruce C.	NY1700	Brown, Mel	OR1250
Broeker, Jay	MN1625	Brown, Bruce	CA5300	Brown, Melba	AL1195
Broening, Benjamin	VA1500	Brown, Carlene J.	WA0800	Brown, Michael	IL3100
Broffitt, Virginia	OK0800	Brown, Carolyn K.	AR0850	Brown, Michael R.	MS0500
Brofsky, Natasha	NY1900	Brown, Charlene	AA0110	Brown, Miles	MI1750
Brofsky, Natasha	MA1400	Brown, Charles V.	NC2150	Brown, Nancy	MI1160
Broman, John M.	GA1500	Brown, Charles	NC2300	Brown, Nina	PA3710
Broman, Per F.	OH0300	Brown, Charles	NY0270	Brown, Patrick	NC0550
Bromann, Michael	AZ0440	Brown, Charles P.	IL0730	Brown, Pebber	CA5100
Bromley, Tanya M.	KY0900	Brown, Chris	NC2000	Brown, Philip	VT0300
Bromley, Tanya M.	KY1350	Brown, Chris	CA2950	Brown, Philip	IL2900
Bromme, Derek	MN1600	Brown, Christine A.	IN1010	Brown, Rae Linda	CA5020
Broms, E.	MA0800	Brown, Christopher C.	MN1623	Brown, Ray	CA0400
Bronaugh, Roderic	TN1400	Brown, Christopher	OK0850	Brown, Richard	CA0835
Bronfman, Joshua	ND0500	Brown, Craig	IN0900	Brown, Richard	TX2150
Bronk, Mary Beth	TX3100	Brown, Craig	NC2430	Brown, Richard L.	WV0600
Bronner, Eric	RI0250	Brown, Cristy Lynn	NC2205	Brown, Richard	MS0100
Bronola-Dickert, Lannia N.	SC1200	Brown, Damon	NC1600	Brown, Robert W.	TN1100
Bronson, Janci	IA0850	Brown, Dana	OH1100	Brown, Robert	TX2930
Bronstein, Chase	TX2250	Brown, Dana L.	IL0550	Brown, Robert	OH0680
Brook, Sharon D.	CA4400	Brown, Daniel R.	NV0050	Brown, Robert	CA1270
Brooke, Nicholas	VT0050	Brown, Darrell	ID0060	Brown, Rogers	VA0950
Brookens, Justin	IA0550	Brown, David	MA0280	Brown, Royal	NY0600
Brookens, Karen	UT0350	Brown, David	NY2950	Brown, Samuel B.	AL0500
Brooks, Barbara J.	MN0950	Brown, David C.	UT0050	Brown, Sarah	TN1100
Brooks, Beth	IN0907	Brown, Debra	KS0570	Brown, Sharon	MA0260
Brooks, BJ	TX3750	Brown, Derek	TX0050	Brown, Sharon L.	IN1010
Brooks, Bonnie	CA4700	Brown, Don	NY2500	Brown, Shon	SC0700
Brooks, C. Thomas	MA0950	Brown, Donald R.	TN1710	Brown, Stephanie	NY3785
Brooks, Darlene M.	PA3250	Brown, Donald G.	AB0100	Brown, Stephen C.	AZ0450
Brooks, Davis H.	IN0250	Brown, Donna	AG0400	Brown, Stephen	AB0210
Brooks, Debbie	TX3420	Brown, Douglas	MT0370	Brown, Susan	OK1450
Brooks, Erin	CA1075	Brown, Edward	NY0644	Brown, Susan E.	TN0100
Brooks, Ipek	GA0850	Brown, Edward E.	NY4500	Brown, Susan	OK0850
Brooks, Jack	TX1510	Brown, Eileen Duffy	FL1300	Brown, Susan	OK0800
Brooks, John Patrick	ID0100	Brown, Elaine K.	MO2000	Brown, Susan Tara	CA1900
Brooks, Jonathan E.	IN0100	Brown, Elizabeth	WA0650	Brown, Susan	CA0400
Brooks, Joseph H.	WA0050	Brown, Ellen	AZ0470	Brown, Susanne	AF0120
Brooks, Lisa E.	IN0250	Brown, Emily Freeman	OH0300	Brown, Susie	OK0550
Brooks, Margaret	VA1350	Brown, Eric	GA2300	Brown, T. Dennis	MA2000
Brooks, Marguerite	CT0850	Brown, Ernest	VA0950	Brown, Terrance D.	AL1250
Brooks, Melinda K.	AL0850	Brown, Frances A.	RI0250	Brown, Thomas P.	FL0550

Name	Code	Name	Code	Name	Code
Brown, Thomas	CT0100	Bruno, Anthony	IL0750	Buck, Peter	CA1520
Brown, Thomas K.	TX3300	Bruno, Sophie	PA3250	Buck, Robin T.	CA5020
Brown, Tom	WI0810	Bruno, Zachary	CA4625	Buck, Stephen M.	NY3785
Brown, Trent R.	FL0680	Bruns, Jeremy	TX2700	Buckholz, Christopher John	IA1600
Brown, Uzee	GA1450	Bruns, Steven	CO0800	Buckingham, Katisse	CA0835
Brown, Velvet	PA2750	Brunson, Richard	WI0922	Buckingham, Steve	TN1850
Brown, Wes	MA2020	Brunson, Tomas	SC0600	Buckland, James P.	SC1000
Brown, Whitman P.	MA0500	Brunssen, Karen	IL2250	Buckland, Karen W.	SC1000
Brown, Zorriante	IL1520	Brunyate, Roger	MD0650	Buckles, Michael	LA0350
Brown-Clayton, Janet	CT0450	Bruscia, Kenneth E.	PA3250	Buckley, Chris	IL2970
Brown-Kibble, Gennevieve	TN1350	Brusky, Paula	WI0830	Buckley, Rhonda	MI1400
Brown-Stanford, Deborah	MD0550	Bruss, Jillian	WI0835	Buckley, Wendell	MN0600
Brown-Stephens, Kelli	OR0750	Brusse, Allan	WI0848	Buckmaster, Matthew	NC0750
Browne, Douglas A.	PA1450	Brust, Paul W.	MA1175	Buckner, Bob	NC2600
Browne, Kimasi L.	CA0250	Bruya, Chris	WA0050	Buckner, James R.	AR0300
Browne, Lynette	IN0800	Bryan, Alan	MN1625	Buckner, Janice	NC0300
Browne, Peter J.	NY3705	Bryan, Carolyn J.	GA0950	Buckner, Jeremy	TN0250
Browne, Sheila A.	NC1650	Bryan, David	LA0650	Buckner, Nathan	NE0590
Browne, Steve	TX0370	Bryan, Karen	CA3460	Buckwalter, Laurel G.	NY0100
Browne, Whitman	MA0260	Bryan, Karen M.	AR0750	Buczynski, Walter	AG0450
Brownell, Jack	AF0100	Bryan, Paul	PA3250	Buda, David	MA0260
Brownell, Jack	AF0050	Bryan, Stephanie	MO2000	Buda, Fred	MA2030
Brownell, John	AG0650	Bryant, Bob	KY0450	Buda, Frederick	MA1400
Brownell, John	AG0450	Bryant, Curtis	GA1050	Budai, William H.	KY0400
Browner, Tara C.	CA5031	Bryant, Dave	MA1175	Budasz, Rogerio	CA5040
Browning, Birch P.	OH0650	Bryant, David	KY0450	Budde, Paul J.	MN1625
Browning, Doug	MS0550	Bryant, David	PA1150	Budde, Paul	MN1300
Browning, Zack D.	IL3300	Bryant, Deanne	IL1200	Budde, Paul J.	MN0750
Brownlee, Jordan	CA1550	Bryant, Dorothy	OH1900	Buddo, J. Christopher	NC0650
Brownlow, James A.	TX3515	Bryant, Edward	FL1740	Budds, Cain	LA0250
Brownlow, Robert J.	OH2150	Bryant, Jann D.	AR0850	Budds, Michael J.	MO1800
Brownwell, John	AG0200	Bryant, Jeff	AA0020	Budginas, Rudolfas	CA1510
Broxholm, Julia A.	KS1350	Bryant, Jennifer	AL0300	Budke, Tiffany	KS0300
Broyles, Michael	FL0850	Bryant, Jerry	NJ0700	Budlong, Trisha	PA2450
Brozak, George A.	IL2900	Bryant, John	GA2300	Budnick, Eve	MA0400
Brozna, Caitlin	CO0900	Bryant, John	TX2400	Budrow, Jack	MI1400
Brubacher, Scott	AG0500	Bryant, Jordan	TX3530	Budway, Maureen	PA1050
Brubaker, Bruce	MA1400	Bryant, Kelly	GA1700	Budzinski, Thomas	IN1450
Brubaker, Debra	IN0550	Bryant, Lei Ouyang	MN0950	Buechner, Sara Davis	AB0100
Brubaker, William	FL0200	Bryant, Lei Ouyang	NY3650	Bueckert, Darrell	AJ0150
Brubeck, Cornelia	FL0650	Bryant, Linda	IA0700	Buehning, Walter P.	AA0150
Brubeck, Dave W.	FL1300	Bryant, Mary	MO0650	Buehrer, Theodore E.	OH1200
Brubeck, Matthew	AG0650	Bryant, Michael	DE0050	Buelow, William L.	OH1400
Bruce, Cynthia	AF0050	Bryant, Richard	CA3050	Buerkle, Suzanne	LA0650
Bruce, Garnett R.	MD0650	Bryant, Robert	KY0100	Buettner, Jeff	VT0350
Bruce, Gary	OK0700	Bryant, Roger	TX2955	Buffington, Blair	IA1750
Bruce, Neely	CT0750	Bryant, Ron	MO1950	Bugbee, Fred	NM0310
Brucher, Katherine	IL0750	Bryant, Stephen	NJ1400	Bugg, Sue	TX3535
Bruck, Douglas	CA3460	Bryant, Steven	TX3510	Bugli, David	NV0150
Bruck, Douglas	CA4050	Bryant, Thomas E.	TN1200	Buglio, Patricia L.	IL0650
Brucker, Clifford	NY3600	Bryant, Wanda	CA0510	Buglio, Patricia L.	IL0840
Bruckner, Susan	CA0400	Bryce, Daniel	UT0325	Bugos, Jennifer A.	FL2000
Bruderer, Conrad D.	CA4100	Bryce, Jackson	MN0300	Bugos, Kristen	TX0600
Brudnak, Sondra	TX2750	Bryce, Pandora E.	AG0450	Buhaiciuc, Mihaela	AL1195
Brudnoy, Rachel	MN0950	Bryce, Vincent	TX2800	Buhite, Michelle	NY1850
Brudnoy, Rachel	MN0800	Bryden, Jane G.	MA1750	Buhler, James	TX3510
Brudnoy, Rachel	MN1625	Bryden, Kristy	IA0850	Buhr, Glenn	AG0600
Brudvig, Robert	OR0700	Brydges, Christopher	VA0250	Buice, David	GA1550
Bruenger, David	OH1850	Brye, Daniel	PA0950	Buis, Johann S.	IL3550
Bruenger, Susan Dill	TX3530	Bryenton, Andrew	TN0250	Bujak, Ewa	MN0610
Bruening, Anne	PA3650	Bryn-Julson, Phyllis	MD0650	Bujak, Ewa	MN1295
Brueske, Jeffrey	MN0250	Bryson, Amity H.	MO0050	Bukvic, Ivica Ico	VA1700
Bruggeman-Kurp, Jeanne	OH0300	Brzozowski, Kazimierz	MI2200	Bukvich, Daniel J.	ID0250
Brugh, Lorraine S.	IN1750	Bubacz, Eric	GA1050	Bukvich, Ivana	IL3310
Bruhn, Christopher	OH0850	Bubacz, Eric	GA1300	Bukvich, Ivana	IL2750
Bruk, Elfrida	IN0005	Bubanj, Marija	IL2750	Bukvich-Nichols, Svetlana	NY2750
Bruk, Karina	NJ1130	Bubar, Lisa	MI1180	Bulat, Therese Marie	CA3460
Brumbeloe, Joseph	MS0750	Bubert, Dennis	TX3500	Bulen, Jay C.	MO1780
Brumbelow, Denise	MI1180	Buccelli, Sylvia	NY3760	Bulger, Mary	MA0950
Brumbelow, Rosemary	IA0950	Buccheri, Elizabeth	IL2250	Bull, Catherine	GA0900
Brumbelow, Rosemary	WI0830	Bucchianeri, Diane	OK1450	Bull, Christoph	CA5030
Brumfield, April	KY0550	Bucci, Thomas	ME0500	Bull, Douglas	WY0050
Brumfield, Susan Hendrix	TX3200	Buchanan, Donna A.	IL3300	Bull, Michael W.	NY4150
Brumley, Dianne	TX3515	Buchanan, Douglas	MD0850	Bull, Tina	OR0700
Brummel, Jonathan	CA0810	Buchanan, Heather J.	NJ0800	Bullard, Julia K.	IA1600
Brummel, Josephine I.	CA4410	Buchanan, Laurie	TX3530	Bullen, Sarah	IL0550
Brummett, Jennifer	WA0400	Buchanan, Marlette	WA0650	Bulli, Marilyn	MA0350
Brummett, Jennifer	WA1350	Buchanan, Mary Lenn	MS0250	Bullock, Betty	DC0170
Brumwell, Gretchen	IA0400	Buchanan, Scott	IN0800	Bullock, Emily A.	PA3600
Brumwell, Gretchen	IA0300	Buchar-Kelley, Kimberly	PA3710	Bullock, Janie Lee	GA0550
Brumwell, Gretchen	IA1800	Buchholz, Theodore	AZ0480	Bullock, Karen	NC2350
Brundage, Cynthian	MI2000	Buchierre, Alisa	MA1500	Bullock, Kathy	KY0300
Brundage, Laura	SC0200	Buchler, Michael	FL0850	Bullock, Robert	AL1050
Brunell, David	TN1710	Buchman, Heather	NY1350	Bullock, Tunisia	NC1350
Brunelle, Felicia	FL1745	Buchman, Matthew	WI0850	Bullock, Valerie K.	SC0275
Brunelli, Stephanie	KS0150	Buchman, Nell J.	WI0350	Bulmer, Jared S.	IL2150
Bruner, G. Edward	CA5040	Buchman, Rachel	TX2150	Bulmer, Karen	AD0050
Bruner, Regina	MO1550	Buchman, William	IL0750	Bulow, Ellen	IN1300
Brunette, Chantal	AG0250	Buchwald, Peter	CO0830	Bulow, Harry T.	IN1300
Brunette, Jessica	WI0848	Buchwald, Peter	CO0150	Bultema, Darci A.	SD0400
Brunetto, Rick	OH1600	Buck, Barbara	KY0750	Bulwinkle, Belle	CA2950
Brunk, Jeremy	IL1750	Buck, Brenda	AZ0350	Bumanis, N.	AA0100
Brunkhorst, Kevin	AF0150	Buck, Casey	AR0200	Bumanis, Nora	AA0020
Brunner, David L.	FL1800	Buck, Dave	AZ0350	Bumbach, Matthew	FL0365
Brunner, George	NY0500	Buck, Elizabeth	AZ0100	Bumcrot, Charles F.	NJ0800
Brunner, Lance	KY1450	Buck, Fred	IA0700	Bumcrot, Charles	NJ0700
Brunner, Matthew	PA3250	Buck, Kristina	AR0200	Bumgardner, James	NC0910
Brunner, Norma	MA0950	Buck, Lynn	IL1200	Bump, Delbert	CA4650
Brunner, Peggy G.	TX3175	Buck, Michael W.	MN0050	Bump, Michael	MO1780
Brunner, Roy	MA0950	Buck, Nancy N.	AZ0100	Bumpers, Wayne	FL1300

Name	Code	Name	Code	Name	Code
Bunbury, Richard R.	MA0400	Burkett, Phil L.	IN0700	Burstein, Poundie	NY2250
Bunce, Mark Robert	OH0300	Burkhalter, N. Laurence	IA0850	Burswold, Lee	IL2100
Bunch, James D.	IL3300	Burkhardt, Rebecca L.	IA1600	Burt, Jack W.	ME0440
Bunch, Ryan	NJ1100	Burkhart, Annette	MO1250	Burt, Patricia A.	IL1200
Bunchman, Michael	NY5000	Burkhart, Annette M.	MO1900	Burtner, Matthew	VA1550
Bundage, Raphael	TN1100	Burkhart, Charles L.	NY0642	Burton, Amy	NY2250
Bundra, Judy Iwata	IL0750	Burkhart, David	CA4150	Burton, Christopher	MI1300
Bundy, O. Richard	PA2750	Burkhart, Raymond David	CA3650	Burton, Deborah	MA0400
Bunk, Louis	NH0110	Burkhead, Phillip	KY1000	Burton, Heidi R.	OK1300
Bunn, Deette	NY4150	Burkhead, Phillip	OH2250	Burton, J. Bryan	PA3600
Bunn, Greg	TN0100	Burkhead, Ricky	MS0560	Burton, James	NY1900
Bunn, Gregg	TN1400	Burkhead, Ricky	MS0700	Burton, John R.	TX3500
Bunn, Michael	VA1350	Burkholder, J. Peter	IN0900	Burton, Justin D.	NJ1000
Bunn, Michael	DC0150	Burkot, Louis G.	NH0100	Burton, Rachel Anne	IL2150
Bunn, Michael	MD0850	Burks, Jo Lynn	TN0100	Burton, Ray	CA2550
Bunn, Michael	MD0750	Burks, Ricky	AL1450	Burton, Sean Michael	IA0100
Bunnell, Jane E.	IL0750	Burks, Robert	TN1350	Burton, Suzanne L.	DE0150
Bunte, James	OH2200	Burky, Kenneth	PA1050	Burton, Warren L.	UT0300
Bunting, Suzanne Kidd	VA1500	Burleigh, Ian G.	AA0200	Burton-Brown, David	GA2100
Bunts, Joseph	VA1850	Burleson, Brett	OH1850	Burwasser, Daniel	NY0625
Buonamassa, John	CA0835	Burleson, Brett	OH0850	Busarow, Donald A.	OH2450
Buonviri, Nathan	PA3250	Burleson, Brett J.	OH2000	Busarow, Jonathan	IN0905
Burak, Jeff	IA1800	Burleson, Brett	OH0350	Busby, Stepanie	MA0650
Buranskas, Karen	IN1700	Burleson, Geoffrey	NY0625	Busch, Gary D.	NY3780
Burbach, Brock	FL0200	Burleson, Jill	CO0950	Busch, Gregg	MO0200
Burbank, Judith	NC1100	Burleson, Richard F.	AC0100	Busch, Michael	CA1425
Burch, Alene	TX0550	Burlingame, Jon	CA5300	Busch, Stephen E.	CO0250
Burch, Dwight	MI0350	Burlingame-Tsekouras, Jill	IL0550	Busching, Marianna	MD0650
Burch, Jennifer	NY1100	Burman-Hall, Linda C.	CA5070	Buschmeyer, Corrinne	AA0050
Burch, Steve	CA3100	Burmeister, James R.	WI0825	Buschmeyer, Ralf	AA0050
Burch-Pesses, Michael	OR0750	Burnakus, David	CA4700	Buselli, Mark	IN0150
Burcham, Joel	CO0800	Burnaman, Stephen	TX1150	Buser, Charles	WA0960
Burchard, Brett	IL1100	Burnett, Henry	NY0642	Bush, Abra K.	NY1100
Burchard, Marcia Earle	CA1650	Burnett, Henry	NY0600	Bush, Christopher	NY2750
Burchard, Marcia	CA4460	Burnett, J.D.	NJ0800	Bush, Deanna D.	TX3420
Burchard, Richard	KY0250	Burnett, Lawrence E.	MN0300	Bush, Doug	TX0250
Burchill, Kent S.	NY3780	Burnett, Marty Wheeler	NE0100	Bush, Doug W.	NE0600
Burchill, Thomas	TX3000	Burnett, Rodger	WA1000	Bush, Douglas E.	UT0050
Burchill, Thomas	TX2600	Burnett, Rodger	WA0800	Bush, Eric W.	NY4050
Burchinal, Frederick	GA2100	Burnette, Sonny	KY0610	Bush, Jeff	OH2600
Burda, Pavel	WI0825	Burney, Herman	DC0100	Bush, Jeffrey E.	VA0600
Burden, Douglas	AG0400	Burnham, Jay	AL0300	Bush, Jerry Alan	AL1300
Burdett, John	CA0630	Burnham, Jay K.	AL1200	Bush, Nathan	CA2550
Burdett, Kimberly H.	OH2000	Burnham, Michael	OH2200	Bush, Peter	OH0650
Burdette, Glenn E.	MI2200	Burnham, Scott	NJ0900	Bushard, Anthony J.	NE0600
Burdette, Joy	KY1000	Burnham, Stuart	NC1500	Bushkova, Julia	TX3420
Burdick, Barbara E.	MI0150	Burns, Brian E.	IA0250	Bushman, Catharine Sinon	SC1200
Burdick, Daniel	PA1200	Burns, Carolyn	ND0100	Bushong, Claire B.	NE0400
Burdick, David H.	IL1750	Burns, Chelsea R.	IL2750	Bushouse, M. David	KS1350
Burdick, Paul	MA1400	Burns, Christopher	WI0825	Buskey, Sherry	MA2000
Burdick, Richard	AJ0100	Burns, Deb S.	IN0907	Buskirk, Kay	KS0200
Burell, J. Ashley	TN1000	Burns, Elaina Denney	IA1450	Buslje, Sergio	DC0250
Burford, Mark	OR0900	Burns, Elizabeth D.	SC1200	Buss, Gary	CO0830
Burganger-Treer, Judith	FL0650	Burns, Elizabeth	NC2000	Busse Berger, Anna Maria	CA5010
Burge, James	FL0930	Burns, Ellen	NY3680	Busselberg, Paul	TX2295
Burge, John	AG0250	Burns, Ellen J.	NY3700	Busselberg, Rebecca Pyper	TX2295
Burge, Russell	OH2200	Burns, Howard	MD0300	Bussell, Lon	OH2550
Burger, Cole	OH0300	Burns, James	NY3705	Bussert, Meg	NY2750
Burger, Larry	WY0050	Burns, Jim	TN0850	Bussert, Victoria	OH0200
Burger, Markus	CA2600	Burns, Judeth Shay	CO0200	Bussiere, Michael	AG0100
Burger, Markus	CA1900	Burns, Judith E.	OH0200	Bussineau-King, D. E.	TX3410
Burgeson, Eric	IN1650	Burns, Lauren	GA2150	Bustamante, Linda	FL1300
Burgess Amstutz, Cheryl	KY0100	Burns, Logan	MN0200	Bustamante, Tamara A.	KY1100
Burgess, Gareth	AG0650	Burns, Lori	AG0400	Bustos, Isaac	TX2900
Burgess, Geoffrey	NY1100	Burns, Michael J.	NC2430	Bustos, Nixon	WI0860
Burgess, Gina	AF0120	Burns, Noelle	WA0650	Bustos, Pamela B.	WI0860
Burgess, Jon	TX3000	Burns, Pamela T.	AL0050	Buswell, James	MA0950
Burgess, Lindy	AG0650	Burns, Patricia Donahue	PA1050	Buswell, James	MA1400
Burgess, Mary	NY3705	Burns, Patrick	NJ0825	Butcher, Paul	FL0800
Burgess, Phillipa	OH1750	Burns, Patrick J.	NJ0800	Buthman, Luke	OK1200
Burgess, Richard	GA1550	Burns, Portia	GA0350	Butke, Marla A.	OH0100
Burgess, Scott	MI0400	Burns, Robert	AL1050	Butler, Abigail	MI2200
Burgess, Stacey	NC1050	Burns, Scott	IL1615	Butler, Barbara	IL2250
Burgess, William	SC0050	Burns, Stephen	IL2750	Butler, Bartlett	IA0950
Burgett, Gwendolyn	OH0650	Burns, Susan M.	CA0630	Butler, Benjamin	TX3150
Burgett, Gwendolyn	MI1400	Burns, Timothy	IL1890	Butler, Beverly	IN1450
Burgett, Paul	NY4350	Burnsed, C. Vernon	VA1700	Butler, Carol	TN0580
Burggraff, Allison	ND0350	Burnside, Joanna	MS0420	Butler, Charles Mark	MS0250
Burgher, R. Catherine	MO1550	Burr, Anthony	CA5050	Butler, Chuck	PA3330
Burgoyne, Carolyn	CA5353	Burrack, Frederick	KS0650	Butler, Corey	AG0650
Burgstaller, Josef	MD0650	Burrell, Kenneth	CA5030	Butler, David	OH1850
Burkart, Rebecca L.	IN0150	Burrell, Kenneth	CA5031	Butler, Debbie D.	TX3527
Burkart, Richard	OH1850	Burrell, Lisa M.	TX1520	Butler, Dorsey Mitchell	SC0350
Burke, D'Walla Simmons	NC2700	Burrichter, Ronald	FL1850	Butler, E. Gregory	AG0550
Burke, Karen M.	AG0650	Burritt, Michael	NY1100	Butler, Erica E.	ME0150
Burke, Kelly J.	NC2430	Burritt, Thomas	TX3510	Butler, Esq., LL.M., Tonya D.	TN1680
Burke, Kevin D.	IN0500	Burroughs, D. Robert	WA0150	Butler, Gregory G.	AB0100
Burke, Kevin F.	OH2200	Burroughs, John	TN1350	Butler, H. Joseph	TX3000
Burke, Larry	FL0800	Burroughs, Mary	NC0650	Butler, Hunt	KY0750
Burke, Leon	MO1250	Burroughs-Price, Anita	SC0750	Butler, Jocelyn	WI0250
Burke, Martha	DE0150	Burrow, Chad E.	MI2100	Butler, Justin	TN1150
Burke, Patrick	PA1050	Burrowes, Norma	AG0650	Butler, Kate S.	NE0600
Burke, Patrick L.	MO1900	Burrows, David	NY2740	Butler, Lloyd S.	OH1800
Burke, Richard	NY0600	Burrs, Lisa Edwards	VA1750	Butler, Louise	WA0950
Burke, Richard N.	NY0625	Burry, Dean	AG0300	Butler, Margaret R.	FL1850
Burke, Sarah M.	TX0340	Bursill-Hall, Damian	PA1050	Butler, Mark J.	IL2250
Burke, Thomas	MA0200	Burson, Claudia	AR0700	Butler, Melvin L.	IL3250
Burkett, Darlene	IN0700	Burson, John	IL0730	Butler, Milton	OH1900
Burkett, Eugenie I.	NV0050	Burstein, L. Poundie	NY0600	Butler, Rebecca G.	PA0050
Burkett, John	TX2955	Burstein, L. Poundie	NY0625	Butler, Steve	CA5550

Alphabetical Listing of Faculty

Name	Code	Name	Code	Name	Code
Butler, Terry	VA0950	Cadieux, Marie-Aline	PA1900	Calloway, Karen E.	GA2300
Butler-Hopkins, Kathleen M.	AK0150	Cadieux, Marie-Aline	PA1750	Callus, Helen	CA5060
Butrico, Michael	NC0400	Cado, Michael	AG0650	Calonico, Robert M.	CA5000
Butte, Jody	PA1650	Cadwallader, Allen	OH1700	Caltvedt, Emily	NC0250
Butterfield, Benjamin	AB0150	Cadwell, Jennifer	MN1625	Caluda, Cherie	CT0650
Butterfield, Christopher	AB0150	Cady-Willanger, Susan	WA1050	Caluda, Elizabeth	VA1350
Butterfield, Craig	SC1110	Cafagna, Carl	MI1750	Caluda, Glenn	VA1350
Butterfield, Emily J.	OK1330	Caffey, H. David	CO0950	Calvert, Phil A.	CA0835
Butterfield, Matthew W.	PA1300	Cagley, Judith L.	PA0550	Calvo, Francisco	CA1900
Butters, Steven G.	IL0840	Cahill, Catherine	NY2150	Calvo, Francisco	CA0960
Butters, Steven	IL0600	Cahill, Sarah	CA4150	Calzolari, Laura	NY2400
Buttery, Gary A.	RI0300	Cahill, Susan	CO0900	Camacho, Dionisio	FL0050
Buttery, Gary	CT0100	Cahn, Steven J.	OH2200	Camacho, Loida	PA2400
Buttolph, David	NY3705	Cahn, William	NY1100	Camacho-Zavaleta, Martin	AL0050
Button, James	TN1400	Cahow, Matthew	CA3200	Camara, Mohamed Kalifa	MA0260
Butts, Beverly Ann K.	PA1900	Cahueque, David	CA0960	Camardella, Dominic P.	CA4410
Butts, Leon	TX3525	Cahueque, David	CA3200	Camelio, Brian	NY2660
Butts, Robert W.	NJ0800	Cahueque, David A.	CA0630	Camera, Bede C.	NH0310
Butts, William	CA1290	Cai, Camilla	OH1200	Cameron, Clayton	CA5031
Butturi, Renato	IN1600	Cai, Jindong	CA4900	Cameron, David	AG0250
Buxton, Donald	MD1100	Cai, Lei	AR0500	Cameron, James Scott	MO0775
Buxton, Merideth	MD1100	Cai, Yi-Min	AL1250	Cameron, Janet	IL0720
Buyer, Paul	SC1080	Cailliet, Claude	WI0800	Cameron, Jennifer	OR1150
Buyer, Paul L.	SC0400	Caimotto, Michelle	CA2950	Cameron, Michael B.	PA0950
Buys, Douglas	MA1400	Caimotto, Michelle	CA0807	Cameron, Michael J.	IL3300
Buyse, Leone	TX2150	Cain, Bruce A.	TX2650	Cameron, Robert C.	PA1050
Buzy, Marilyn	ME0250	Cain, Donna	OK0750	Cameron, Robin	NY3775
Buzza, Scott	KY1000	Cain, Jerry	AI0150	Cameron, Scott	DC0010
Buzzelli, Christopher	OH0300	Cain, Joren R.	GA2150	Cameron, Tristan	AA0020
Buzzelli, Julie	OH0300	Cain, M. Celia	AG0450	Cameron, Virginia	OH1600
Buzzelli-Clarke, Betsy	PA1100	Cain, Michael	NJ1100	Cameron, Wayne	WV0550
Bybee, Ariel	UT0250	Cain, Michael	AC0050	Cameron, Wayne	MD0600
Bybee, Luretta	MA1400	Cain, Michael D.	MA1400	Cameron, Wayne C.	MD1000
Byerlotzer, Jason L.	HI0210	Cain, Richard	MA0650	Cameron, Wes	MS0850
Byerly, Douglas	MD0060	Cain, Sarah	GA1400	Camilli, Theresa Chardos	IA1600
Byers, Andrea	CA0825	Cairns, Debra	AA0100	Caminiti, Joseph D.	PA2800
Byers, Eric	MA0260	Cairns, Whitney	MO1830	Camino, Suzanne	MI0500
Bygrave, Max	FL0450	Cairns, Zachary	MO1830	Camitsis, Georges	AI0210
Byington, Jensina	WA0860	Cairo, Bo	AG0130	Camp, Cheryl	AR0250
Byl, Julia S.	MN1450	Cajas, Edgar	TX2600	Camp, Dewey	CA4200
Bylsma, Kevin	OH0300	Cal, Anna	AB0210	Camp, James L.	GA0490
Bylsma, Ruth	MI0850	Calabrese, Angela Libertella	NY1550	Camp, Laura	PA3250
Bynane, Patrick	TX3300	Calabrese, Anthony J.	NY1550	Camp, Linda	IL0850
Bynum, Josh L.	GA2100	Calandrino, Jo	IL1610	Camp, Marjorie	CO0550
Bynum, Leroy E.	GA0150	Calas, Tiffany	ID0050	Camp, Philip	TX1550
Byo, Donald W.	PA1450	Calcagno, Mauro	NY3790	Campagna, Alison	TX3535
Byo, Donald W.	OH2600	Calderazzo, Joey	NC1600	Campana, Alessandra	MA1900
Byo, James L.	LA0200	Calderon, Javier	WI0815	Campana, Deborah	OH1700
Byo, William	PA3650	Calderon, John	TX0075	Campbell, Alicia M.	NC0900
Byrd, Donald	TN0100	Calderone, Kathleen	NJ0700	Campbell, Andrew	AZ0100
Byrd, Eric B.	MD0520	Caldwell, Ann	GA0850	Campbell, Andy	MO1550
Byrd, Joseph	CA1280	Caldwell, Bob	AB0090	Campbell, Arthur	MN1450
Byrd, Joshua	GA2130	Caldwell, Brad	OH1450	Campbell, Arthur J.	MI0900
Byrd, Katherine	GA2130	Caldwell, Brendan	WI0850	Campbell, Betty	AL0550
Byrd, Katie	GA2000	Caldwell, Frances Sherer	NY5000	Campbell, Bob	NC0850
Byrd, Richard W.	KY0550	Caldwell, Frances Sherer	NY2400	Campbell, Bonnie H.	IL3450
Byrd-Anderson, Shelley	IL2100	Caldwell, Gary	UT0150	Campbell, Brian G.	MN0350
Byrdwell, Phyllis	WA1050	Caldwell, Glenn G.	MD0520	Campbell, Carey	UT0350
Byrens, Robert	MI0900	Caldwell, Hansonia	CA0805	Campbell, Cheryl Lynn	PA1900
Byrket, Patrick S.	IN0907	Caldwell, J. Timothy	MI0400	Campbell, Christopher	PA1900
Byrkit, Douglas	IL1740	Caldwell, James M.	IL3500	Campbell, Debra L.	NY3780
Byrley, Michael	IL1085	Caldwell, Michael D.	CA0810	Campbell, Derek	DC0350
Byrne, David	AC0100	Caldwell, Philip	IL2750	Campbell, Diane	OH2550
Byrne, Elizabeth	IL0750	Caldwell, Robert	AB0060	Campbell, Dianna	FL1700
Byrne, Gregory	KY1500	Caldwell, Robert	AB0050	Campbell, Don	SC1080
Byrne, Laura	NC2410	Caldwell, Susan	NY2250	Campbell, Douglas	MO1810
Byrne, Laura S.	NC0600	Caldwell, William	TN0100	Campbell, Gary	FL0700
Byrne, Madelyn	CA3460	Caldwell, William	OH0500	Campbell, Glenn	CA3640
Byrne, Mary	AB0210	Calhoun, James M.	CA5100	Campbell, Griffin M.	LA0200
Byrne, Tom	MO1950	Calhoun, Valerie J.	GA1070	Campbell, Helen E.	AL0310
Byrnes, Jason	CO0950	Calhoun, William	RI0300	Campbell, James B.	KY1450
Byrnes, Lisa B.	UT0250	Calico, Joy	TN1850	Campbell, James	IN0900
Byros, Vasili	IL2250	Calin, Rachel	GA1300	Campbell, Jayne E.	CA1960
Byun, Jin Hwan	NJ0700	Caliri, Lisa	MA0350	Campbell, Jeff	AA0100
Byun, John	CA3800	Calissi, Jeff L.	CT0150	Campbell, Jeff	NY1100
Byun, Wha-Kyung	MA1400	Calkin, Joshua	NE0700	Campbell, Jefferson	MN1600
Byykkonen, Susan E.	MI1450	Calkin, Lauren	NE0700	Campbell, Jennifer L.	MI0400
Bziukiewicz-Kulig, Brygida	WI0865	Calkins, Katherine Charlton	CA3200	Campbell, John	CA2390
Caballero, Carlo	CO0800	Calkins, Mark	KY0300	Campbell, John	CA0825
Caballero, Jorge	NJ0700	Calkins, Mark R.	KY1350	Campbell, John	VA0750
Caballero, William	PA0550	Call, Kevin	ID0060	Campbell, John W.	KY0610
Cabalo, Eric	CA4700	Call, Monica	UT0325	Campbell, John	CA0960
Caban, Francisco J.	PR0115	Call, Monica	UT0050	Campbell, Kathleen M.	PA3000
Cabaniss, Thomas	NY1900	Call, R. Steven	UT0050	Campbell, Larry	TX0340
Cabena, Barrie	AG0600	Callaghan, Marjorie S.	CT0800	Campbell, Lars	OR1100
Cable, Howard	AA0200	Callahan, Anne	KS1375	Campbell, Lars	OR0750
Cable, Jennifer A.	VA1500	Callahan, Clare	OH2200	Campbell, Laura	NY0650
Cable, Ron C.	OH2275	Callahan, David	MA0260	Campbell, Mark Robin	NY3780
Caborn, Peter	VA1350	Callahan, Gary L.	NC1150	Campbell, Michael J.	GA2300
Cabot, Jennifer C.	MD0850	Callahan, Michael R.	MI1400	Campbell, Neal	OH2300
Cabott, Christopher	PA3710	Callahan, Nancy	FL2050	Campbell, Patricia Shehan	WA1050
Cabrer, Carlos R.	PR0150	Callahan, Timothy	OH0600	Campbell, Richard	PA2100
Cabrera, Ricardo	PR0100	Callaway, Dan T.	LA0650	Campbell, Robert	NC1900
Cabrini, Michele	NY0625	Callaway, Patricia	GA1200	Campbell, Robert	NC2500
Caceres, Abraham	WI0500	Callender, Clifton D.	FL0850	Campbell, Roy	MA0510
Caceres, Marcelo	MI0250	Callis, Cathy	NY1600	Campbell, Sharon O'Connell	NE0590
Cacioppo, Christine	PA1500	Callon, Gordon J.	AF0050	Campbell, Stanford	OR0600
Cacioppo, Curt	PA1500	Calloway, Edwin S.	GA2300	Campbell, Steven	MN1623
Cadelago, Harry	CA3250	Calloway, Jason	FL0700	Campbell, Susan	UT0350
Cademcian, Gerard	IN0005	Calloway, John	CA4200	Campbell, Tim	AA0050

785

Name	Code	Name	Code	Name	Code
Campbell, Timothy	WV0750	Capps, Angela	ME0250	Carlson, Dan	MN1100
Campbell, Todd	PA0250	Capps, Joe	VT0250	Carlson, Ernie	ID0140
Campbell, Todd A.	NC0700	Capps, Joseph	VT0450	Carlson, James	TN1800
Campbell, Will	NC2420	Cappy, Matt	PA3330	Carlson, Karyl K.	IL1150
Campbell, William	MI2100	Caproni, Christopher	MA2250	Carlson, Lennis Jay	CA1020
Campbell, William G.	IA1300	Capshaw, Reed	IN0910	Carlson, Mark	MD0610
Campetti, Cynthia	PA1150	Capshaw, Reed	IL0550	Carlson, Mark	CA5030
Camphouse, Mark D.	VA0450	Capshaw, Reed	IL1085	Carlson, Mark	CA4450
Campi-Walters, Lisa	CO0350	Captein, Dave	OR0400	Carlson, Marlan	OR0700
Campiglia, Paul	GA0625	Caputo, Charles R.	FL0650	Carlson, Mary C.	NY2650
Campiglia, Paul	GA2150	Caputo, Michael	NJ0200	Carlson, Maureen A.	MO1800
Campion, David	AG0600	Caputo, Michael	NJ0250	Carlson, Mimi	CA4425
Campion, Edmund	CA5000	Capuzzo, Guy	NC2430	Carlson, Patti F.	VA1000
Campione, Carmine	OH2200	Caramia, Anthony	NY1100	Carlson, Patti	VA0250
Campitelli, Stephen	PA1550	Carastathis, Aris	AG0170	Carlson, Patti	VA0150
Campo, David	TX2700	Caravan, Lisa	AL0200	Carlson, Paul	MI0900
Campora, Randall S.	MD0650	Caravan, Ronald L.	NY4150	Carlson, Paul B.	MO0800
Campos, David M.	CA4410	Caraway, Dan	IA0400	Carlson, Risa	DC0170
Campos, Frank G.	NY1800	Carballeira, Andy	MA0260	Carlson, Robert A.	CA0200
Campos, Homero	TX0100	Carballo, Kimberly	IN0900	Carlson, Sharon	IL0720
Campos, John	MI2250	Carbaugh, Deborah	MN0800	Carlson, Stephen R.	VA1000
Campos, LeeAnne	WA0650	Carberg, Daniel J.	IL1750	Carlson, Stephen J.	MN0150
Campos, Wagner	IL0750	Carberry, Deirdre	OH2200	Carlson, Sydney R.	OR0850
Camus, Amy E.	NY2550	Carbon, John J.	PA1300	Carlson, Tammi	IL1890
Camus, Elizabeth	OH0600	Carbonara, David	LA0720	Carlton, David	WI0150
Camwell, David J.	IA1350	Carbone, Anthony P.	MA0260	Carlton, Elizabeth	NC0350
Canafax, Bruce	TX1700	Carbone, Kathy	CA0510	Carlton, Jan	CA0300
Cancio, Clint	CA3270	Carbone, Michael	NY3705	Carlton, Kathleen	OK0410
Cancio-Bello, Susan	NH0050	Carbonneau, Pierre-Marc	AI0220	Carman, William	MA2030
Cancryn, Dina	TN1100	Card, Catherine	CA1960	Carmenates, Omar	SC0750
Candee, Jan	ND0400	Card, Patricia P.	TX2250	Carmichael, John C.	FL2000
Candelaria, Leonard	AL0300	Cardamone, Melissa	WI0250	Carmichael, Matthew J.	VA1350
Candelaria, Lorenzo	TX3510	Cardany, Audrey	MD0650	Carmichael, Steve R.	WI0250
Candelaria, Philip	AG0400	Cardany, Audrey	RI0300	Carmona, Marcos	WA0200
Candelaria, Philip	AG0070	Cardany, Brian M.	RI0300	Carnahan, Deborah	CA0825
Candelaria-Barry, Consuelo	MA0260	Cardenas, Octavio	TX0300	Carnahan, John	CA0825
Candlish, Bruce	PA0250	Cardenas, Steve	NY2660	Carnes, Donna	NE0450
Caneva, Thomas	IN0150	Cardenes, Andres J.	PA0550	Carnes, Glenda	TX3175
Canfield, Jennifer K.	AL0450	Cardillo, Kenneth	TN0260	Carnes, Maurice J.	MO1900
Canfield, Nanette G.	OH0200	Cardillo, Michael	NY2900	Carney, Anna	TX2800
Canfield, Wanda	PA0450	Cardin, Michel	AE0100	Carney, Anna	TX2650
Canfield, Wanda	PA1000	Cardinal-Dolan, Michelle	KS0700	Carney, David	CA4100
Cangelosi, Casey	WV0200	Cardon, Sam	UT0325	Carney, Horace R.	AL0010
Cangro, Richard	IL3500	Cardone, Alissa	MA1175	Carney, Jeff	NY2660
Caniato, Michele	MA0930	Cardoza, Don	CA3320	Carney, Laurie	NY2150
Canin, Martin	NY2750	Carello, Joseph	NY2950	Carney, Michael	CA0825
Canin, Martin	NY1900	Carenbauer, Michael	AR0750	Carney, Peter	IL2650
Cannata, David B.	PA3250	Carere, Anthony	GA1500	Carney, Robert D.	MO1550
Cannava, Ruth	NH0300	Carew, David	MI1985	Carney, Sandra L.	NJ1050
Cannon, Alexander	AB0200	Carey, Aaron L.	WV0100	Carney, Sandy	PA3560
Cannon, Carey	NC2420	Carey, Barbara	NM0300	Carney, Timothy F.	HI0060
Cannon, Cormac	MI1400	Carey, Charles	NE0050	Carnine, Albert J.	MO0800
Cannon, Derek	CA4100	Carey, Christian B.	NJ1350	Carnochan, Robert M.	TX3510
Cannon, Derek	CA2100	Carey, Kevin	MN0620	Carol, Norman	PA0850
Cannon, Jimmie	CA2300	Carey, Larry	PA2300	Caron, Sylvain	AI0200
Cannon, Maureen McDermott	DE0050	Carey, Mary	NY2900	Caron-Gatto, Lisa J.	MI2110
Cannon, Robert V.	TX2650	Carey, Matthew	AR0110	Carpente, John	NY2450
Cannon, Rodney M.	TX2250	Carey, Milissa	CA4150	Carpenter, Alexander	AA0110
Canon, Sherri	CA2660	Carey, Norman	NY0600	Carpenter, Andrew	IL2750
Canon, Sherri D.	CA2720	Carey, Pamela Ruth	CA1650	Carpenter, Charles M.	CA3500
Canova, Diana	NY2200	Carey, Peter	TX2260	Carpenter, Ellon D.	AZ0100
Cansler, Joe Ella	TX3750	Carey, Tanya L.	IL0550	Carpenter, Gregory	WI0425
Canter, Jacqueline	NC0930	Carey, Thomas C.	OH2275	Carpenter, Jean	RI0300
Canter, Jacqueline S.	NC0900	Cariaga, Marvellee	CA0825	Carpenter, Keith A.	WI0200
Canton, Jacky	CO0300	Carichner, Christian Blake	AR0850	Carpenter, Kelley K.	WI0350
Canton, Lisette M.	AG0650	Carignan, Danielle	AI0220	Carpenter, Lauraine	OH0300
Cantrell, Elizabeth K.	VA0800	Carillo, Dan	NY2900	Carpenter, Nadine	VT0450
Cantrell, James	AL0330	Carillo, Dan	NY0550	Carpenter, Ron	NC1250
Cantrell, Wanda	GA1700	Carkeek, Maureen M.	IN0350	Carpenter, Susan	WV0550
Cantu, Ben	CO0275	Carl, Jane	MO1810	Carpenter, Thomas H.	NY3725
Cantu, Jacob	TX2200	Carl, Robert B.	CT0650	Carpenter, Tim	OH0850
Cantwell, Guy	CA0400	Carlberg, Frank	MA1400	Carpenter, Tina	TX3750
Cantwell, Richard E.	KS1300	Carlberg, Frank T.	MA0260	Carpenter, Tyler	OH1350
Cantwell, Terry	GA1260	Carleton, Charles	OH0650	Carpenter, William	NE0200
Cantwell, Terry	GA1300	Carleton, Sharon	NC1450	Carpentier, Gilles	AI0210
Canty, Dean R.	TX3525	Carletti, Marina	AG0300	Carpentier, Jean-Pierre	AI0210
Caoile, Nikolas	WA0050	Carli, Rob	AG0450	Carpentier, Martin	AI0200
Capaldo, Jennifer R.	VA0700	Carlin, Dan	MA0260	Carper, Gary E.	VA1475
Cape, Janet	NJ1350	Carlin, Eric	NY2650	Carper, Ken	FL0680
Capener, Debra A.	MN1625	Carlin, Kerry	NC0650	Carper, Nick	WA0400
Capetandes, Gary	NJ1400	Carlin, Maryse	MO1900	Carr, Colin	NY3790
Capezza, June	FL0200	Carlin, Patrick	VA1600	Carr, Deborah	VA1830
Capistran, Raul W.	TX3515	Carlin, Pete	IL0300	Carr, James H.	NC2430
Capitano, Gay Lyn	FL0365	Carlin, Seth A.	MO1900	Carr, Jennifer	TX3000
Capizzi, Christopher	PA0550	Carlisle, Benjamin	TX3350	Carr, Johnny	GA0250
Caplan, Joan	NY2150	Carlisle, David	MS0700	Carr, Julie Anne	MI2120
Caplan, Joel	NY1860	Carlisle, Katie	GA1050	Carr, Karen	MA0260
Caplan, Linda	AG0650	Carlisle, Kris	GA0300	Carr, Maureen A.	PA2750
Caplan, Stephen	NV0050	Carlisle, Mark R.	IN0800	Carr, Sarah	WV0800
Caplin, William	AI0150	Carlisle, Stephen M.	FL0650	Carr, Thomas	VA0600
Capocchi, Roberto	NM0425	Carlon, Paul	NY0644	Carr, Tracy A.	NM0100
Capocchi, Roberto	CO0050	Carlow, Regina	NM0450	Carr, Walter E.	OR0800
Caporale, Matthew	TX1450	Carlsen, James	WA1050	Carr, William	PA1550
Caporella, Cynthia Anne	OH1050	Carlsen, Philip	ME0410	Carr-Richardson, Amy	NC0650
Caporello, Corradina	PA0850	Carlson, Andrea	SD0050	Carrabre, T. Patrick	AC0050
Caporello-Szykman, Corradina	NY1900	Carlson, Andrea	IA0500	Carrai, Phoebe	MA1175
Capozzoli, Andrea	MA0260	Carlson, Andrew	OH0850	Carrasco, Jacqui	NC2500
Capp, Myrna	WA0800	Carlson, Angela	OR0700	Carreira, Jonathan	IL0720
Cappillo, Frances	NY3500	Carlson, Brian	AZ0150	Carrell, Cynthia T.	AR0250
Cappon, Ronald	NY2200	Carlson, Damon J.	WI0770	Carrell, Scott	AR0250

Name	Code	Name	Code	Name	Code
Carrell-Coons, Mariah	OK0770	Carter, Terry	CA4450	Castellano, Mark	FL0680
Carrera, Michael	OH1900	Carter, Timothy	NC2410	Castellanos, Gilbert	CA5300
Carrettin, Zachary	TX2250	Carter, William	PA2200	Castellanos, Juan	PA0650
Carrettin, Zachary	TX3450	Carthy, Nicholas	CO0800	Castelli, James A.	NJ1050
Carrier, Lisa	DC0010	Cartledge, David O.	IN0900	Castello, Joseph	AG0600
Carrier, Lisa	MD0550	Carubia, Agatha	CA4410	Castellote, Javier	NE0100
Carriere, Marilyn	MN0620	Carubia, Michael R.	NY2550	Castiglione, Anita	FL1450
Carrillo, Carlos R.	PR0115	Carucci, Brian	NY3600	Castilano, Edward P.	NY4150
Carrillo, Christine Ennis	VA0600	Carucci, Christine	KY0550	Castilla, Carlos	TN1400
Carrillo, Christopher J.	VA0600	Carucci, Christine	MN1300	Castilla, Carlos	TN1100
Carrillo, Oto G.	IL0750	Caruso, Frank	IL0850	Castilla, Kathy	MS0650
Carrillo, Teofilo	IL3300	Caruso, John A.	NY3725	Castilla, Willenham	MS0350
Carrington, Simon	CT0850	Carver, Kate	AG0450	Castillo, Carlos	NY2550
Carrington, Terri Lyne	MA0260	Carver, Lucinda	CA5300	Castillo, Francisco J.	CA3650
Carroll, Amy	MA0150	Carver, Mark	PA0550	Castillo, Francisco	CA3500
Carroll, Catharine L.	OH2200	Carver, Sylvia	TN0050	Castillo, Francisco	CA5150
Carroll, Debbie	AI0210	Cary, Jane G.	NY0400	Castillo, Ramon	MA2030
Carroll, Don	CA3200	Cary, Kathy	MI1160	Castillo, Ramon	MA0260
Carroll, Don	CA0859	Cary, Neal	VA0250	Castle, Joyce	KS1350
Carroll, Donald H.	CA4200	Cary, Paul	OH0200	Castle, Troy	SC0200
Carroll, Ed J.	NH0100	Cary, Stephen	AL1170	Castleberry, David	WV0400
Carroll, Edward	CA0510	Casagrande, Angela	AG0400	Castleman, Charles	NY1100
Carroll, Gregory D.	NC2430	Casagrande, John E.	VA0450	Castleman, Heidi	NY1900
Carroll, Gwendolyn J.	NY2105	Casal, David Plans	NH0100	Castles, JoAnn	AL1450
Carroll, James R.	VA0450	Casale, Bill	CA5040	Caston, Ben	GA2050
Carroll, John	TX3410	Casale, Maria	CA3600	Caston, Ben	GA0400
Carroll, John	TX1850	Casano, Joe	MA2030	Castonguay, David O.	VA1100
Carroll, John	TX1900	Casano, Steven	HI0210	Castonguay, Gerald	MA0650
Carroll, John	TX2200	Casas, Jorge	IL1050	Castonguay, Lois	VA1100
Carroll, Kenneth D.	AR0110	Caschetta, Todd	CA4850	Castonguay, Roger	AE0100
Carroll, Kevin	GA1600	Case, Alan L.	NY3730	Castrillo, Manuel E.	MA0260
Carroll, Nancy M.	RI0101	Case, Alexander	MA2030	Castriotta, Gabrielle	CA0600
Carroll, Nancy	RI0102	Case, Barbara	TX0250	Castro, Cesar	CA3300
Carroll, Nancy A.	IA0940	Case, David	OR1050	Castro, Chris	CA1510
Carroll, Raynor	CA0825	Case, Del W.	CA3400	Castro, Christi-Anne Salazar	MI2100
Carroll, Richard P.	NJ1050	Case, Elaine	AA0050	Castro, David R.	MN1450
Carroll, Roy W.	IA0940	Case, Greg	CT0600	Castro, Ed	WA0650
Carroll, Tom	OH0850	Case, Nelly Maude	NY3780	Castro, Edward	WA0550
Carroll, William P.	NC2430	Case-Stott, Angeline	TN1680	Castro, Margarita	PR0150
Carroll-Phelps, Claudia	OK0750	Casey, Brian	NY1700	Castro, Miguel	GA1400
Carrothers, Bill	WI0350	Casey, Christopher	CT0650	Castro, Zeke	TX3510
Carrott, Bryan	NY1275	Casey, Donald E.	IL0750	Castro-Balbi, Jesus	TX3000
Carruthers, Ian	AA0050	Casey, J. Warren	AR0250	Casuccio, Anthony	NY4460
Carryer, Steven J.	MI2200	Casey, John	IA1200	Catalano, Frank K.	IL0650
Carslake, Louise	CA5000	Casey, John	SD0050	Catalano, Roberto F.	CA3950
Carslake, Louise	CA2950	Casey, John	IA0500	Catalano, Roberto	CA5100
Carson, Benjamin Leeds	CA5070	Casey, Lisa R.	MO0775	Catalano, Roberto	CA0630
Carson, Caroline	LA0800	Casey, Marian	SD0580	Cataldi, Diana M.	OH2500
Carson, Charles	TX3510	Casey, Maurice T.	OH1850	Catalfano, Joyce A.	WV0750
Carson, Mark	MD0150	Casey, Michael	NH0100	Catallo, Jennifer Kincer	MI1750
Carson, Virginia	VA1800	Casey, Michael R.	MO0775	Catan, Daniel	CA1265
Carson, William S.	IA0300	Casey, Neil	SC1110	Cataneo, Daniel O.	NY1900
Carswell, William	SC0450	Casey, Rebecca L.	OH1800	Catania, Claudia	NJ1350
Cartagena, Cynthia	PR0115	Casey-Nelson, Colleen Mary	CT0050	Cateforis, Theodore P.	NY4100
Cartagena, Cynthia	PR0150	Casgrain, Robert	AA0020	Catello, Darlene	IN1450
Carter, Adam C.	VA1550	Cash, Carla Davis	TX3200	Cates, Deanna S.	IL0840
Carter, Allen L.	MN1120	Cash, Shellie B.	OH2200	Cates, Mike	TN0450
Carter, Beverly H.	PA1450	Cashen, Jeffrey A.	MA2150	Cates, Tim	TX1600
Carter, Brian	WA1150	Cashman, Glenn	NY0650	Catford, Julian	WA0800
Carter, Brian	NC0910	Cashwell, Brian	OH0500	Cathcart, Kathryn	CA4150
Carter, Cecil	TX2200	Cashwell, Brian	OH2500	Cathey, Jill	ID0140
Carter, Chandler	NY1600	Casillas-Rivera, Josue	PR0115	Cathey, Rodney	CA0250
Carter, Christina	FL1550	Casinghino, Justin	MA0400	Cathey, Sheila Clagg	OK0825
Carter, Clarence	IL2900	Caslor, Jason	AD0050	Cathey, Tully J.	UT0250
Carter, Daniel	WV0550	Cason, Tony	CA3600	Catlin, Amy	CA5031
Carter, David	AR0730	Casper, Meghan	IN1010	Catlin, Barb A.	CA3650
Carter, David	MN1450	Casper, Richard	MA0600	Catlin-Smith, Linda	AG0600
Carter, Drew	NC2000	Casperson, Joseph	ID0075	Cato, Ralph Wayne	CA5040
Carter, Edward L.	AZ0510	Cass, Howard	MI0600	Caton, Benjamin D.	TN0500
Carter, Elise	NJ0300	Cass, Patrick	MS0320	Catravas, Nicolas	DC0050
Carter, Greg	AF0150	Cassano, Rhonda	FL1950	Catsalis, Marie-Louise	CA4900
Carter, Henrietta McKee	CA2050	Cassara, Charles	MA0260	Catsalis, Marie-Louise	CA4425
Carter, Jay	MO2000	Cassara, Frank	NY0500	Cattaneo, Susan K.	MA0260
Carter, Jeanne	SD0050	Cassara, Frank	NY4450	Caudill, Nancy	AK0100
Carter, Jeffrey Richard	MO1950	Cassara, Frank	NY2105	Caufield, Stevi	RI0300
Carter, Joey	TX3000	Cassara, James	NY2105	Caulder, Stephanie B.	PA1600
Carter, John R.	CA1375	Cassarino, James	VT0100	Cauley, Susan	LA0150
Carter, Joseph	CT0300	Cassarino, James P.	VT0200	Caulkins, Tamara	WA1200
Carter, Joyce	IL2775	Cassarino, Richard	AL0800	Causa, Ettore	CT0850
Carter, Kenyon	GA0900	Cassaro, James P.	PA3420	Causey, Wayne	TN0100
Carter, Kenyon W.	AL0500	Casseday, Kevin	FL1850	Cavadas, Angela	AB0050
Carter, Kenyon	GA1500	Cassel, David C.	TN1850	Cavallaro, Giorgia	MD1010
Carter, Linda	AR0225	Cassel-Greer, Kirsten	TN1850	Cavallini, Francesco	MI2120
Carter, Lisbeth	NC1300	Casselle, Carol	FL1310	Cavallo, Gail R.	NY2550
Carter, LisBeth	NC0750	Cassidy, Marcia	NH0100	Cavanagh, Daniel	TX3500
Carter, Marva G.	GA1050	Cassidy, Robert	OH0650	Cavanagh, Leo	CA4650
Carter, Monty	MO0950	Cassin, Daniel	LA0650	Cavanagh, Lynn	AJ0100
Carter, Monty	MO2000	Cassini, Corinne	NC0050	Cavanar, Mary	NH0300
Carter, Patricia	TN1710	Cassino, Peter	MA1175	Cavanaugh, Alice I.	NY4050
Carter, Paul S.	NY3765	Cassio, Francesca	NY1600	Cavanaugh, Jennifer Gookin	MT0400
Carter, Priscilla	CA3320	Cassity, Michael	MO0350	Cavender, James L.	AL1160
Carter, Robert Scott	NC0650	Castaldo, Kay	MI2100	Cavendish, Thomas	FL0200
Carter, Roland M.	TN1700	Castaneda, J. Ricardo	IL2200	Cavera, Chris S.	OH2140
Carter, Ron	NY1900	Castaneda, Ricardo	IL0275	Caviani, Laura	MN0300
Carter, Ronald	IL2200	Casteel, Mike	TN0100	Caviani, Laura	MN1450
Carter, Selina	NC2500	Castel, Nico	NY1900	Caviezel, Samuel R.	PA3250
Carter, Shannon	AG0350	Castellana, Joseph	OH0755	Caviness, Terrance E.	NY3770
Carter, Stewart	NC2500	Castellani, Daniel	NY3785	Cavitt, Mary Ellen	TX3175
Carter, Susan	MO0850	Castellani, Joanne C.	NY4320	Cawley, Dominique	IA1800
Carter, Terry	CA2600	Castellano, Ann	OH0600	Cawthon, Daniel D.	CA3920

Alphabetical Listing of Faculty

Name	Code	Name	Code	Name	Code
Caya, Patricia	ME0430	Champagne, Sebastien	AI0190	Chapman, John	AZ0470
Cazan, Ken	CA5300	Champion, David	CA0805	Chapman, Karen Benjamin	CA3500
Cazes, Alain	AI0150	Champion, Kyle	CA5150	Chapman, Lucy	MA1400
Cazier, David	WA0150	Champlin, Terry	NY2250	Chapman, Michael	PA1050
Ceaser, Janina Kuzma	OH0600	Champlin, Terry	NY4450	Chapman, Norman	MS0600
Ceballos, Sara Gross	WI0350	Champney, Morgen	NC2420	Chapman, Peter	MA0400
Cebulski, Michael	GA0750	Champniss, Kim Clarke	AG0130	Chapman, Peter	MA1400
Cebulski, Michael	GA0940	Champouillon, David	TN0500	Chapman, Polly	AZ0490
Cecco, Jerry	MA0260	Chan, Amanda	AB0200	Chapman, Stan	AL1195
Cecere, Dennis	MA0260	Chan, Amanda	AB0100	Chapman, Susannah	NJ0700
Cech, Jessica	MI2120	Chan, Celia	CA2420	Chapo, Eliot	FL0850
Cedel, Mark	GA2100	Chan, David	NY1900	Chappell, Eric	AI0150
Cedeno, Eduardo	NC1400	Chan, Fu-chen	NY0150	Chappell, Jeffrey	DC0170
Cee, Vincent	AK0150	Chan, Jacklyn	IN1650	Chappell, Jeffrey	MD0400
Ceide, Manuel J.	PR0115	Chan, Joni	IN1800	Chappell, Rebecca Ann	IN0100
Cela, Orlando	MA0700	Chan, Ken	IN0100	Chappell, Robert	IL2200
Celaire, Jaunelle R.	AK0150	Chan, Patty	AG0650	Chapple, Karliss	AR0550
Celentano, James	NY2750	Chan, Sarah S.	OK0600	Character, William	GA2175
Celenza, Anna H.	DC0075	Chan, See Tsai	IL0350	Charbonneau, Louis	AI0200
Celidore, Daniel	CA4700	Chan, Susan	OR0850	Charbonneau, Paul	NY1350
Cella, Lisa M.	MD1000	Chan, Susan	IN1650	Charke, Derek	AF0050
Cellon, Cheryl	TX3525	Chan, Wenyin	DC0170	Charles, Benjamin	FL0650
Celmer, Joey R.	SC1050	Chan, Yan-Yan	CA3000	Charles, David	MT0200
Celona, John	AB0100	Chan-Spannagel, Yiu-Ka	OK0150	Charles, Etienne	MI1400
Celona-VanGorden, Julie	NC0750	Chance, Chris	TX3527	Charles, Jean	VT0300
Celotto, Albert Gerard	CT0700	Chance, Christopher	TX1850	Charles, Lewis O.	OH1650
Cemprola, Michael	PA3330	Chance, Mike	AR0250	Charles, Nicole	OH2250
Cencel, Elaine	AR0700	Chancler, Ndugu	CA5300	Charles, Nicole M.	OH1650
Centanni, Barry C.	NJ0800	Chancler, Rose	NY3775	Charles, Sydney R.	CA5010
Centeno Martell, Ingrid	PR0100	Chandler, B. Glenn	TX3510	Charloff, Ruth	CA5040
Century, Michael	NY3300	Chandler, Beth E.	VA0600	Charlston, Erik	NY2150
Ceo, Joan H.	RI0300	Chandler, Chris	GA0200	Charlton, Susan	PA1850
Ceo, Joan	RI0200	Chandler, Chuck	GA1700	Charney, Miriam	NY4450
Ceo, Joseph	RI0250	Chandler, David	CT0650	Charney, Miriam	NY2150
Cepeda, Iris	CA0830	Chandler, Deborah L.	LA0770	Charnofsky, Eric	OH0600
Cepeda, Manny	CA2100	Chandler, Gulya	LA0030	Charnofsky, Jordan	CA3100
Cepparulo, Kathie	TN1660	Chandler, Jean	MA1400	Charoenwongse-Shaw, Chindarat	OK1330
Cerabona, Linda M.	IL3400	Chandler, Kyle	AR0110	Charry, Eric	CT0750
Cereghino, Rosemarie	MO1950	Chandler, Lloyd	HI0050	Charry, Michael	NY2250
Cerniglia, Richard C.	NY0350	Chandler, Sarah	NY3705	Charsky, Thomas	NJ0050
Cerny, William J.	IN1700	Chandler, Susan	WI0865	Charsky, Thomas	NJ1400
Ceron, Homero	AZ0480	Chandler, Vincent Arvel	MI1750	Charter, Ian R.	AA0010
Cerqua, Joe	IL0720	Chandra, Arun	WA0350	Charupakorn, Joseph	NY0850
Cervantes, Elizabeth	CA0270	Chandra, Bharat	FL1745	Chasalow, Eric	MA0500
Cervantes, Ernest	CA0650	Chandra, Veena V.	NY3650	Chasanov, Elliot L.	IL3300
Cervenka, Ken	MA0260	Chaney, Carol	MI2120	Chase, Allan	MA0260
Cesario, Robert James	MO0825	Chang, Amy	GA0050	Chase, Allan S.	MA1400
Cesbron, Jacques	IN0900	Chang, Amy	OH2300	Chase, Constance	CT0800
Cessor, Tyler	MN0600	Chang, Angelin	OH0650	Chase, Corinne Sloan	MA0260
Cetkovic, Igor	MI0100	Chang, Anita L.	CA2650	Chase, David A.	CA3460
Cetto, Edward	CA5350	Chang, Ann	NE0600	Chase, David M.	CA5350
Cevasco, Andrea	AL1170	Chang, C. J.	NJ1130	Chase, George	TX3400
Cha, In-Hong	OH2500	Chang, Donathan	TX2570	Chase, Jared	NY2650
Cha, Jee-Weon	IA0700	Chang, Dorothy	AB0100	Chase, Jennie Kao	NY2400
Cha, Keum Hwa	ID0100	Chang, Elizabeth E.	MA2000	Chase, Jon	MA0260
Chabora, Robert J.	MN0600	Chang, Gary	IL0720	Chase, Leah	LA0800
Chacholiades, Linda P.	MN0610	Chang, Helen	IL1085	Chase, Linda J.	MA0260
Chadabe, Joel A.	NY2750	Chang, Joanne	NY3250	Chase, Robert	NY2400
Chadabe, Joel	NY2150	Chang, Jocelyn Hua-Chen	CA0845	Chase, Roger	IL0550
Chadwick, Donna	MA0260	Chang, Li Kuo	MD0650	Chase, Shannon M.	NJ1130
Chadwick, John	IL2750	Chang, Lyn	MA0400	Chase, Stephanie	NY2750
Chadwick, Sheelagh	AC0050	Chang, Lynn	MA0350	Chasin, Richard	CA1425
Chae, Hyung Sek	TX3650	Chang, Melody Jun Yao	CO0100	Chasin, Richard	CA5355
Chafe, Chris	CA4900	Chang, Pansy Y.	OH1450	Chastain, Kathleen	OH1700
Chafe, Eric	MA0500	Chang, Peter M.	IL2150	Chasteen, Terry L.	IL3500
Chaffee, Christopher	OH2500	Chang, Phillip	CO0800	Chatel, Jean-Louis	AI0200
Chaffee, Gary	MA1400	Chang, Seanad	TN1850	Chatman, Stephen G.	AB0100
Chafin, Gerald	KY0860	Chang, Shirley	NY0050	Chattah, Juan	FL1900
Chafin, Robert	VA1700	Chang, Soo-Yeon Park	CA0650	Chatterjee, Samir	NY2150
Chagas, Paulo	CA5040	Chang, W. Michael	CA0815	Chatterji, Sumita	CA0050
Chagnon, Richard	CA4050	Chang, Wan-Chin	CA2960	Chaudhuri, Swapan	CA0510
Chai, Liang	NY0500	Chang, Wei Tsun	TN1450	Chaudhuri, Swapan	CA0050
Chai, Susan	AB0100	Chang, Wei-Tsun	TN1850	Chaudoir, Marianne	WI0400
Chakrovorty, Sumita	CA0050	Chang, Ya-Liang	KY1000	Chauls, Robert	CA2750
Chalifour, Martin	CA5300	Chang, Ya-ting	PA2300	Chauvel, Marjorie A.	CA4900
Chalifoux, Jeanne D.	VA1475	Chang, Yoo-Jung	IA0700	Chave, George B.	TX3500
Chalifoux, Jeanne	VA0450	Chang, Yu-Hui	MA0500	Chaverdian, Gregory	AI0070
Chalifoux, Jeanne	DC0010	Changchien, Wenting	OH2200	Chavez, Arturo	OR1010
Chama, Eduardo	NJ1130	Channell, Timothy L.	VA1100	Chavez, David E.	VA1350
Chamberlain, Bruce B.	AZ0500	Channells, Janet	MI1160	Chavez, Robert	CA1700
Chamberlain, Donald J.	IA0400	Channing, Lynn	AJ0100	Cheatham-Stricklin, Teresa	AL0500
Chamberlain, Julie Rhyne	NC0350	Chanteaux, Marcy K.	MI2200	Chebra, Tracy Richards	NJ1350
Chamberlain, Rick E.	PA1850	Chao, Barbara Davis	AZ0470	Check, John D.	MO1790
Chamberlin, Robert	MO1950	Chao, Barbara	AZ0400	Checkeye, Jane	PA2450
Chambers, Carol	TX3100	Chao, Fred	AZ0470	Cheek, John	NC1100
Chambers, Evan	MI2100	Chao, Joanna K.	NJ0175	Cheek, Timothy Mark	MI2100
Chambers, James Alan	IN1050	Chao, Philippe	VA0450	Cheeseman, Andrea L.	NC0050
Chambers, Joe	NY2660	Chapdelaine, Jim	CT0650	Cheeseman, Sybil	MS0400
Chambers, Joseph	NC2440	Chapdelaine, Karine	VA0600	Cheesman, Jimmy	CA4450
Chambers, Lynnette	TX0900	Chapdelaine, Michael	NM0450	Cheesman, Robert	MS0300
Chambers, Mark K.	AG0650	Chaplin, Clay	CA0510	Cheesman, Sybil	MS0100
Chambers, Martin	CA4100	Chapman, Alicia	NC0050	Cheetham, Andrew	IL0800
Chambers, Robert B.	TN0650	Chapman, Carol L.	MO0775	Cheetham, Richard	CA5000
Chambers, Robert	OK1250	Chapman, Christopher	OR0700	Cheever, Olivia	MA1175
Chambers, Steve	TX2750	Chapman, Dale E.	ME0150	Cheifetz, Hamilton	OR0850
Chambers, Timothy	NC0800	Chapman, David	CA3000	Chekan, Elina	WI0825
Chambers-Salazar, Polli	CA1750	Chapman, David F.	NJ1130	Chellis, Matthew W.	IL0550
Chamis, Michael	NC0910	Chapman, Don	AF0050	Chellouf, Linda	PR0100
Champagne, Kevin	NY3700	Chapman, Duane	WV0350	Chelseth, Gretchen	MN0450
Champagne, Salvatore C.	OH1700	Chapman, Joe C.	GA1500	Chemay, Frank	LA0700

Alphabetical Listing of Faculty

Name	Code	Name	Code	Name	Code
Chen, Ann A.	MI1260	Chevalier, Angelis	CA3200	Cholthitchanta, Nophachai	AR0700
Chen, C. Brian	CA0815	Chevalier, Jason	CA3200	Chong, Daniel	MN1625
Chen, Che-Hung	PA3250	Chevan, David	CT0450	Chong, John	AG0300
Chen, Chi-Yuan	CA4100	Chevanelle, Serge	AI0220	Chookasian, Lili P.	CT0850
Chen, Chia-Chi	IN0005	Chew, Jacqueline	CA5000	Chopyak, James D.	CA0840
Chen, Chih-Yi	IN0900	Chew, Sherlyn	CA2450	Chordia, Parag	GA0900
Chen, Claudia S.	MN0950	Cheyne, Donald R.	GA1700	Chou, Godwin	IL2775
Chen, Donald	IL0550	Chi, Jacob	CO0275	Chou, Lin-San	CA4450
Chen, Evelyn	NY4200	Chi, Sungha	IL0150	Chou, Mei-En	LA0150
Chen, Fen-Fang	AL0650	Chiado, Joshua	WV0050	Chou, Sarana	AL0800
Chen, Ginger Jui-Wen	GA0940	Chiang, Janice ChenJu	AZ0450	Chou, Shun-Lin	CA0825
Chen, Hsaun-Ya	CA1760	Chiang, Ju-Yu (Carol)	OK1330	Chou, Yueh	CA0900
Chen, Ixi	OH2200	Chiang, Nora	CA4450	Chow, Alan	IL2250
Chen, Jay	OR0700	Chiang, Victoria	MD0650	Chow, Alvin	OH1700
Chen, Jay	OR0450	Chianis, Sam	NY3705	Chow-Tyne, June	AZ0480
Chen, Jay	OR1300	Chiao, Faye	MD0850	Chown, Andrew	PA3250
Chen, Johanna	CA0859	Chiaravalloti, Charissa	CO0350	Chowning, John M.	CA4900
Chen, Lambert	AI0150	Chiarello, Mario	SD0050	Chrisman, Richard	NJ1130
Chen, Melvin	NY0150	Chiarizzio, R. Kevin	VA0650	Christ, Chip	TX3000
Chen, Moh Wei	CA5100	Chiasson, Rachelle	AI0150	Christ, Linden	IL0550
Chen, Pei-Wen	NY2250	Chiavola, Kathy	TN0100	Christain, Ron	CA0650
Chen, Shao Shen	TX0550	Chickering, Ellen	ME0500	Christensen, Beth	MN1450
Chen, Shih-Hui	TX2150	Chidester, James	OH2300	Christensen, Brandon J.	MO1500
Chen, Ting Yu	VA1350	Chiego, John	TN1680	Christensen, Carey L.	CA0835
Chen, Ting-Lan	NE0590	Chiego, Sara	TN1200	Christensen, Carl J.	CA2150
Chen, Xiaolun	FL1500	Chien, Alec F.	PA0100	Christensen, David	CA5040
Chen, Yao	IL3300	Chien, Gloria	TN0850	Christensen, Dieter	NY0750
Chen, Yi	MO1810	Chien, Hsueh-Ching	CA3270	Christensen, Donald	NY0500
Chen-Beyers, Christina	MN1120	Chihara, Paul	CA5030	Christensen, Eric	RI0200
Chen-Beyers, Christina	ND0500	Chikinda, Michael	UT0250	Christensen, James	CA1425
Chen-Beyers, Christina	ND0350	Chilcote, Kathryn S.	PA3600	Christensen, James	AL0210
Chen-Hafteck, Lily	NJ0700	Child, Peter	MA1200	Christensen, Janielle	UT0050
Chen-Maxham, Li-Chan	NJ1140	Childress Orchard, Nan	NJ0050	Christensen, Jean M.	KY1500
Chenette, Jonathan Lee	NY4450	Childs, Adrian P.	GA2100	Christensen, Linda	NE0700
Chenette, Stephen	AG0450	Childs, David T.	MN0600	Christensen, Mary	AZ0440
Chenette, Timothy	MA2000	Childs, Kim J.	OK1450	Christensen, Russ	OR0700
Chenevert, James	TX3300	Childs-Helton, Sally	IN0250	Christensen, Ruth M.	UT0050
Cheney, Brian	OH2050	Chiles, Torin W.	AG0500	Christensen, Thomas	IL3250
Cheney, Elliott	UT0250	Chilingarian, Samvel	CA1700	Christensen, Tom	NY2900
Cheney, Kathryn	GA0250	Chin, David	NY3350	Christensen, William Nield	OK0750
Cheney, Stuart G.	TX3000	Chin, Huei Li	IL2910	Christenson, Charlie	
Chenez, Raymond	AL1170	Chin, Pablo	IL2650	Christeson, Jane	FL1750
Cheng, Angela	OH1700	Chin, Wayman	MA1175	Christeson, Norton M.	FL0400
Cheng, Clara	CA0960	Ching, Daniel	TX3510	Christian, Armstead R.	MA0260
Cheng, Gloria	CA5030	Chinn, Genevieve	NY2105	Christian, Henry	AB0090
Cheng, James	OK0750	Chioldi, Ronald	OK0550	Christian, Kathy P.	IL2050
Cheng, Marietta	NY0650	Chipman, Michael	UT0400	Christiansen, Corey M.	IN0900
Cheng, Susan	CT0050	Chipman, Paula	MD0300	Christiansen, Corey	UT0300
Cheng, Wei	OH0850	Chipman, Shelby R.	FL0600	Christiansen, David	IL0850
Cheng, Ya-Hui	GA0810	Chisholm, Amy B.	OR1250	Christiansen, Gregg	NY1250
Chenoweth, Gerald	NJ1130	Chisholm, Rose Marie	TX3420	Christiansen, Gregg S.	NY1550
Chenoweth, Jonathan	IA1800	Chisholm, Sally	WI0815	Christiansen, Lindsey	NJ1350
Chenoweth, Jonathan N.	IA1600	Chittum, Donald	PA3330	Christiansen, Michael	UT0300
Chenoweth, Richard K.	OH2250	Chittum, John	KS0590	Christiansen, Paul V.	ME0500
Chepaitis, Stanley L.	PA1600	Chitwood, Elizabeth	GA0700	Christiansen, Philip	OH1900
Cheramy, Michelle	AD0050	Chiu, Cornelius	IL3550	Christiansen, Rulon	UT0350
Cheramy, Rob	AB0210	Chiu, Ying-Ting	DC0170	Christianson, Donald G.	AA0150
Cherian, Rebecca S.	PA0550	Chivington, Amy	OH2050	Christianson, Paul A.	TN1600
Cherkaoui, Tsukasa	FL1125	Chmura-Moore, Dylan Thomas	WI0830	Christianson, Tom	ND0150
Cherlin, Michael	MN1623	Cho, Catherine	NY1900	Christie, Carolyn	AI0150
Cherney, Brian	AI0150	Cho, Cecilia	DC0170	Christie, James David	OH1700
Cherniansky, Fyodor	GA0940	Cho, Gene	TX3420	Christie, James David	MA0700
Chernin, Mallorie	MA0100	Cho, Grace	VA1350	Christie, James	MA2050
Chernoff, John	CA2250	Cho, James	TX2250	Christie, Laury	SC1110
Chernoff, Marea	AB0200	Cho, Kyoung	FL2000	Christie, Lyndon	NY2200
Chernoff, Marea	AB0090	Cho, Michelle	DC0050	Christie, Max	AG0450
Chernoff, Marea	AB0060	Cho, Mison	PA3560	Christie, Pamela	NY3717
Chernoff, Marea	AB0050	Cho, Peter	LA0080	Christie, Tim	WA1000
Chernov, Vladimir	CA5030	Cho, Philip Y.	PA3250	Christin, Judith	CO0550
Chernyshev, Alexander	MN1600	Cho, Soon	TX0300	Christman, Rick	DC0050
Cherrington Beggs, Sally	SC0900	Cho, Sujung	SC0350	Christman, Ruth	FL0500
Cherrington, Joseph	ID0060	Cho, Tony	CA0960	Christman, Sharon Lynn	DC0050
Cherry, Amy K.	NC2600	Cho, Wan-Soo	KY0400	Christmas, Pam	WI1150
Cherry, Daniel E.	NC2600	Cho, Won	AL1150	Christofferson, Carol	AZ0480
Cherry, Diana	NC2350	Cho, Young-Hyun	TX3500	Christoph, Michael E.	CO0550
Cherry, Janet	NC1300	Cho, Yuri	NV0050	Christopher, Casey R.	ID0150
Cherry, Kalman	TX2400	Choate, Ellie	CA0815	Christopher, Edward	PA2750
Cherry, Mark	NY2200	Choate, Ellie	CA5020	Christopher, Evan	LA0800
Cherryholmes, Roy	TX2400	Choate, Jim	AL0400	Christopher, Paul	LA0550
Chertock, Michael S.	OH2200	Chobaz, Raymond	FL1850	Christopher, Un Chong	MO1010
Chesanow, Marc	SC0420	Chodacki-Ford, Roberta	GA0550	Christopher, Un Chong	MO0060
Chesarek, Justin	GA1150	Chodoroff, Arthur D.	PA3250	Christopher, Un Chong	MO1810
Chesarek, Justin	GA0750	Chodos, Gabriel	MA1400	Christopherson, Anne	ND0500
Chesebro, Robert C.	SC0750	Choe, EJ	IN0907	Christopherson, Robert	MA0260
Chesebrough, Constance D.	NH0250	Choe, Sung	FL1745	Christopulos, Paul	CA4460
Chesebrough, James C.	NH0150	Choi, Bonnie L.	NY4150	Christy, Jay	GA0750
Chesher, Michael	IA0950	Choi, Bonnie	NY2650	Christy, Judy	FL0680
Cheshier, Treneere J.	OH0650	Choi, Chee Hyeong	IL1750	Christy, William P.	OH1910
Chesis, Linda	NY2150	Choi, Eugenia	AB0100	Chu, Brian Ming	PA2550
Chesko, Elizabeth Unis	OH0650	Choi, Hyangbin	GA0250	Chu, Brian	NJ1050
Chesky, Kris	TX3420	Choi, Hye-Jean	TX0900	Chu, George	MN0800
Chesman, Jeremy A.	MO0775	Choi, Hyunjoo	CA1425	Chua, Emily Yap	VA1125
Chesnutt, Rod M.	FL0650	Choi, In Dal	DC0050	Chua, Rosalind Y.	RI0150
Chessa, Luciano	CA4150	Choi, Janey	NY3705	Chuah, Cheong	CA2775
Chest, Robert	SC0200	Choi, Kyong Mee	IL0550	Chuang, Chun-Chien	KS1000
Chester, Ray G.	MD0650	Choi, Minju	IN1650	Chuang, Ya-Fei	MA0350
Chestnut, Louise	MD0060	Choi, Winston	IL0550	Chuaqui, Miguel Basim	UT0250
Cheung, Alissa	AA0035	Choi, Wooyoung	GA0050	Chudnovsky, Emil	DC0050
Cheung, Pius	OR1050	Choksy, Lois	AA0150	Chui, Eddie	CA1020
Cheung, Teresa	MA2000	Cholakova, Elena	GA0750	Chun, Eric	CA0150

Chun, Peter	KS1350	Clancy, Todd A.	MA1650	Claude, Henry	MO1900
Chun, Soyoun Lim	KS0200	Clanton, James	KS1050	Claudin, Margaret	PA2800
Chung, Carol	NC1300	Clanton, Wendell	AB0150	Clausen, Arla	IA0910
Chung, He-Lyun	CA3100	Clapp, John	MI0520	Clausen, Brett	CA0650
Chung, Heejin	NY2450	Clapp, John	MI0900	Clausen, Rene	MN0600
Chung, Hsieh	IN0005	Clapp, John	MI1050	Clausen, Rick	AZ0440
Chung, Hyunjung Rachel	GA1900	Clapp, Lawrence	AZ0440	Claussen, Kurt	MN1450
Chung, Jiyun	MO1010	Clapp, Stephen	NY2900	Claussen, Tina	MO0350
Chung, Joyce	NY4500	Clapp, Stephen	NY1900	Clay, Angelique	KY1450
Chung, Kyung-Wha	NY1900	Clardy, Mary Karen	TX3420	Clay, Sarah	MA1100
Chung, Mia	MA0950	Clardy, Michael	AR0750	Clay, Shea	VA0350
Chung, Minna Rose	AC0100	Clardy, Shannon	AR0300	Clay, William	TX3420
Chung, Miri	IN0907	Clarey, Cynthia	IL0550	Claybrook, Doug	TX0300
Chung, Myung-Hee	WI0865	Clarfield, Ingrid	NJ1350	Claybrook, Kara	IN0800
Chung, Sharon	IL1750	Clark, Adam	MI1050	Clayton, April	UT0050
Chung, Soon Bin	NY1900	Clark, Alice V.	LA0300	Clayton, Cathryn	UT0250
Chung, Suna	NY3560	Clark, Allen	TX3515	Clayton, Cynthia	TX3400
Chung, Young-Eun	OK0850	Clark, Amber L.	IL1350	Clayton, Greg	AI0150
Chunn, Michael	OH1100	Clark, Andrew G.	MA1050	Clayton, Jay	MD0650
Chuong, Jason	PA3330	Clark, Antoine	OH1200	Clayton, Lisa	CT0600
Church, Alan	VT0250	Clark, Antoine T.	OH0850	Clayton, Zedric K.	TN1680
Church, Celeste	TX1100	Clark, Brenda J.	IN1650	Clayville, Michael	PA0950
Church, Frank V.	CT0100	Clark, Bryan	TN0100	Clayville, Michael	PA2300
Church, Gregory E.	TX1100	Clark, Caryl L.	AG0450	Clearfield, Andrea	PA3330
Church, Gretchen	IL1200	Clark, Charlene K.	MO1900	Cleary, Thomas	VT0450
Church, Joseph	NY2750	Clark, Charles C.	CA3350	Cleary, Tom	VT0250
Churchfield, Camille	AG0400	Clark, Charles 'Bud'	MO0800	Clegg, Aaron	CA5000
Churchill, Marc	MI1180	Clark, Chris	NJ0175	Clegg, Neill M.	NC0900
Churchill, Mary-Lou	MA1400	Clark, Colleen	MD0800	Clegg, Trey	GA1900
Churchill, Rachel	AG0070	Clark, Courtney	WV0440	Cleland, George	AG0050
Churchill, Rachel	AG0150	Clark, Dale	AR0110	Cleland, George	AA0040
Churchill, Steve	MD0550	Clark, Dan	FL0850	Cleland, Gordon	AG0050
Churm, George W.	PA1450	Clark, Daniel	OH2370	Cleland, Kent D.	OH0200
Chusid, Martin	NY2740	Clark, Dave	KY0250	Cleland, Sara	MI1160
Chute, Christina	ME0200	Clark, David W.	MA0260	Clemans, Holly	MI0500
Chute, Christina	ME0150	Clark, Derek	WI0810	Clemens, Julie	IL1350
Chybowski, Julia J.	WI0830	Clark, Evan	MN0040	Clemens, Peter	IL1500
Chyun, Mi-Hye	NJ1350	Clark, Frank L.	GA0900	Clemenson, Andrew	MN0600
Ciabattari, William S.	PA2100	Clark, Heidi	MA0950	Clement, Dawn	WA0200
Ciacca, Antonio	NY1900	Clark, Jacob	SC1050	Clement, Lisa	TX3415
Ciach, Brian	KY0950	Clark, Jacob	DC0170	Clement, Richard	GA1050
Ciamaga, Gustav	AG0450	Clark, James W.	SC0050	Clemente, Peter	MA0200
Ciano, Jack	FL1300	Clark, Jesse	PA0050	Clements, Allen	AL0345
Ciarelli, Katharine	NY2950	Clark, Jim	TX2955	Clements, Ann C.	PA2750
Ciarniello, D. Jack	OH2600	Clark, Joan	PA2100	Clements, Anthony	CA4900
Ciaschini, Peter	GA0900	Clark, Joe	OH1100	Clements, Barbara	AR0200
Cicconi, Christopher M.	FL0050	Clark, John Charles	NC0650	Clements, Emory	GA0940
Cice, Erica	NC0550	Clark, John	CT0100	Clements, Emory Lamar	GA1050
Cice, Erica	NC0850	Clark, John W.	CA4410	Clements, Gordon	AB0210
Cichy, Patricia Wurst	RI0150	Clark, Jon	MA0650	Clements, Jon	AR0200
Cichy, Roger	RI0150	Clark, Jonathan	CA4900	Clements, Peter J.	AG0500
Cienniwa, Paul D.	MA2020	Clark, Jonathan	MA0150	Clements, Phillip L.	TX2955
Ciepluch, Gary	OH0400	Clark, Joseph	IL0750	Clements, Tania Maxwell	GA1050
Cierpke, Timothy H.	TN1600	Clark, Judith	VA1850	Clements, Tony	CA0807
Cies-Muckala, Jennifer	TN0100	Clark, Kenneth	CT0600	Clements, Tony	CA3320
Ciesinski, Katherine	NY1100	Clark, Lauren Schack	AR0110	Clements, Tony	CA4425
Cifani, Elizabeth	IL2250	Clark, Maribeth	FL1360	Clements-Cortes, Amy	AG0550
Cifarelli, Joan	CA2775	Clark, Mark	KS1250	Clemmons, Bill	CA3640
Cifelli, Cheryl L.	MO0800	Clark, Mark Ross	LA0770	Clemmons, Francois	VT0350
Cifelli, Kristin	MA0260	Clark, Martha	NM0300	Clemons, Gregory G.	IL1085
Cigan, Paul	DC0050	Clark, Matt	IL2800	Clemons, Kawachi A.	NC1600
Cigan, Paul	MD1010	Clark, Michael	TN1450	Clency, Cleveland	IL0550
Cilliers, Jeanne-Minette	NY2150	Clark, Michael	FL1570	Clendenen, Bob	CA0510
Cima, Alex	CA1900	Clark, Norman Alan	GA1400	Clendinning, Jane Piper	FL0850
Cimarusti, Thomas M.	TX3200	Clark, Paula	ID0060	Clenman, David	AB0150
Cimino, Matthew	CT0600	Clark, Renee Cherie	MI1000	Cleveland, Lisa A.	NH0310
Cimino, Matthew	CT0450	Clark, Rich	IL0300	Cleveland, Mark	MA2030
Cinelli, Dennis J.	NJ0800	Clark, Richard A.	IN0250	Cleveland, Michael	NY0650
Cinnamon, Howard	NY1600	Clark, Richard	NJ1400	Cleveland, Susannah L.	OH0300
Cinquegrani, David	CT0350	Clark, Roger R.	MI1200	Clevenger, Charles	OH0450
Cioffari, Cynthia A.	OH2150	Clark, Ronald	MA0260	Clevenger, Dale	IN0900
Cioffari, Richard J.	OH0300	Clark, Serena Jenkins	ID0075	Clevenger, Dale	IL0550
Cionco, Richard M.	CA0840	Clark, Steve H.	GA0550	Cleverdon, Suzanne	MA2050
Cionitti, Linda A.	GA0950	Clark, Suzannah	MA1050	Clew, Nancy	FL0150
Ciorba, Charles R.	OK1350	Clark, Suzanne M.	MA0260	Clewell, Christine M.	PA1600
Cipiti, John	OH2140	Clark, Tad	OK1450	Clickard, Stephen D.	PA0250
Cipolla, Frank J.	NY4320	Clark, Thomas S.	TX3175	Clifford, Patrick	FL1450
Cipolla, John M.	KY1550	Clark, Wallace	FL0600	Clifft, Al	CA0450
Cipullo, Tom	NY0280	Clark, Walter A.	CA5040	Clifft, Al	CA0250
Ciraldo, Nicholas A.	MS0750	Clark, Wayne	OK1330	Clifft, Joel	CA0250
Ciraldo, Rachel Taratoot	LA0650	Clark, Wayne R.	OK0700	Clifft, Joel	CA5300
Cirba, Anita	NC2205	Clark, William D.	NM0310	Clift, Anna	MN1450
Cirlin, Sunny	MI1200	Clark, William F.	CO0830	Clifton, Artie	FL1000
Cirmo, Michael	NY1350	Clarke, Axel	CA0825	Clifton, Felecia	ND0500
Ciscon, Katherine	TX3400	Clarke, Garry E.	MD1100	Clifton, Jeremy J.	OK1050
Cisler, Valerie C.	NE0590	Clarke, Karen	TN1850	Clifton, Keith E.	MI0400
Citron, Marcia J.	TX2150	Clarke, Leland	MA2200	Clifton, Kevin	TX2250
Ciucci, Alessandra	MA1450	Clarke, Penelope	AG0170	Climer, John	WI0825
Ciucci, Alessandra	NY0750	Clarke, Terry	AG0450	Climie, Stan	AA0150
Ciucci, Anthony A.	PA1250	Clarke, W. Harry	KY1450	Climie, Stanley	AA0050
Ciulei, Lenuta	NJ1130	Clarkson, Amy LYN	NJ0800	Climis, Sarah	IN0900
Cizewski, Kathleen	IL0650	Clarkson, Austin	AG0650	Cline, Benjamin	KS0350
Claar, Elizabeth	MI1050	Clary, Carol	CA2550	Cline, Christopher	TX3530
Claar, Elizabeth	MI0520	Clary, Philip	KY1000	Cline, Daniel	AR0350
Claeys, Keith	MI2200	Clary, Richard	FL0850	Cline, Everett Eugene	ID0250
Clague, Mark A.	MI2100	Class, Kevin	TN1710	Cline, Gilbert D.	CA2250
Clair, Alicia A.	KS1350	Classen, Andrew B.	IA0550	Cline, James E.	CO0400
Clampitt, David	OH1850	Classen, Jeffrey	MA0750	Cline, James	CO0650
Clancy, Eric	IN0700	Classen, Lita	AG0200	Cline, Jeff	TN1680
Clancy, Gary	ME0340	Clatworthy, David	NY3705	Cline, Judith A.	VA0550

Alphabetical Listing of Faculty

Name	Code	Name	Code	Name	Code
Cline, Lonnie	OR0050	Coddington, Robert	WV0760	Cole, Carol	FL1125
Cline, Nancy	WI1150	Coddington, Robert	OH1400	Cole, Daniel	CA3500
Cline, Rebecca	MA0260	Code, Belinda B.	AE0050	Cole, Darlyn	NC1950
Cline, Rick	NC1100	Code, David Loberg	MI2250	Cole, David	FL0680
Clinefelter, Molly	MN0750	Codreanu, Christian	TN1400	Cole, David	FL1125
Clinkscales, Joyce	GA0750	Cody, David	MT0400	Cole, David C.	FL0680
Clinton, Mark K.	NE0600	Cody, Thomas	PA2750	Cole, Deb	MA0650
Clippert, Thomas	WI1150	Coe, Judith A.	CO0830	Cole, Dennis E.	OH0100
Clive, David	NY4500	Coefield, Carolyn	MT0350	Cole, Joseph	PA2200
Clive, David	NY0644	Coelho, Jerry M.	CA0100	Cole, Judith E.	GA1150
Clodes-Jaguaribe, Maria	MA0400	Coelho, Victor	MA0400	Cole, Judith W.	TX2960
Clodfelter, John D.	IN0350	Coelho, Benjamin A.	IA1550	Cole, Kathryn	MO0400
Clodfelter, Mark	KY1450	Coelho, Tadeu	NC1650	Cole, Malcolm S.	CA5032
Cloer, John	NC2420	Coelho-Foust, Jenny	WY0115	Cole, Mark R.	NC0850
Cloeter, Chelsea	OH0300	Coen, Anne	OH1350	Cole, Melissa	WI1150
Cloeter, Tim	OH0300	Coen, Jean-David	OR1300	Cole, Monty	GA1300
Close, Shirley J.	FL0850	Cofer, Angela F.	TX2600	Cole, Pamela	FL0800
Clothier, Stephen	CA0630	Cofer, R. Shayne	IL2150	Cole, Richard C.	VA1700
Cloud, Judith	AZ0450	Coffey, Matthew	OH0550	Cole, Robert	PA3650
Cloud, Patricia	CA5020	Coffey, Ted	VA1550	Cole, Roger	ID0250
Clouser, John	OH0600	Coffman, Don D.	FL1900	Cole, Roger	AB0100
Clousing, Harold	CA0250	Coffman, Elizabeth	IL0730	Cole, Roger	AB0200
Cloutier, Daniel	TN1710	Coffman, Teresa S.	RI0200	Cole, Ronald F.	ME0500
Cloutier, David	TX3420	Coffman, Timothy J.	IL0750	Cole, Scott	OR0950
Cloutier, Glenda L.	TN0250	Cogan, Jeff	CA0960	Cole, Steven	MN1625
Cloutier, Jean	AI0190	Cogan, Robert	MA1400	Cole, Thomas	CA0815
Cloutier, Randy	RI0150	Cogdell, Jerry	MS0320	Cole, Victoria	NH0250
Cloutier, Robert F.	CO0800	Cogdell, Robyn	MS0320	Cole, Vinson	OH0600
Clower, Rob	IA0700	Cogdill, Susan	NE0200	Cole, Vinson	MO1810
Clubb, Maurice	WA0650	Cogen, Ellen	MA1100	Colella, Lou M.	PA1450
Cluthe, Betty	NJ0200	Coggins, Janet	MO1780	Colella, Louis	PA3650
Clymer, Richard	NY3785	Coggiola, Jill A.	NY4150	Coleman, Anthony	MA1400
Clymer, Richard	CT0800	Coggiola, John C.	NY4150	Coleman, Barrington	IL3300
Co, Wei-Shu Wang	OH0200	Coghill, Jack	AG0100	Coleman, Cecilia	CA0825
Coach, Leo	OH0650	Coghlan, Connie	CT0050	Coleman, Cedric	AG0600
Coad, Daryl L.	TX3420	Coghlan, Michael	AG0650	Coleman, David F.	MA1900
Coade, Caroline	MI2200	Cognata, Chad	CO0900	Coleman, Douglas	NY2550
Coade, Caroline	MI2100	Cohan, Ryan	IL3310	Coleman, Earl	GA0550
Coale, Dean	OK0300	Cohen, Alan	NJ0950	Coleman, Edryn J.	PA2000
Coale, Laura	OK0700	Cohen, Albert	CA4900	Coleman, Fred	SC0200
Coan, Darryl	IL2910	Cohen, Alla Elana	MA0260	Coleman, Ian D.	MO2000
Coash, David	FL0800	Cohen, Allen L.	NJ0400	Coleman, Janet	OR0750
Coash, David C.	FL2050	Cohen, Arnaldo	IN0900	Coleman, Jennifer	TN0100
Coates, Atina	ID0060	Cohen, Bonnie	WI0300	Coleman, Lilian	TN0700
Coates, Gary	FL1790	Cohen, Bonnie	DC0350	Coleman, Malcolm J.	TX3525
Coates, Michael	ND0350	Cohen, David	AI0150	Coleman, Matthew	AZ0350
Coates, Michael	MN0600	Cohen, David E.	NY0750	Coleman, Michael	FL1500
Coates, Norma	AG0500	Cohen, Douglas H.	NY0500	Coleman, Randall	AL1170
Coats, Syble M.	AL0831	Cohen, Flynn	NH0150	Coleman, Randolph E.	OH1700
Coats, Sylvia	KS1450	Cohen, Franklin	OH0600	Coleman, Ron	WA1100
Cobb, Cheryl	MA1350	Cohen, Fred S.	GA0550	Coleman, Ruth	SC0200
Cobb, Gary W.	CA3600	Cohen, Fredric T.	MA2000	Coleman, Todd	NC0750
Cobb, James	NC0915	Cohen, Gerald	NY1860	Coleman, William Dwight	GA1050
Cobb, Joyce	TN1680	Cohen, Greg	CA4100	Coleman-Evans, Felicia	IL2100
Cobb, Kevin D.	NY3785	Cohen, Howard R.	NY3780	Colenbrander, Caroline	AG0200
Cobb, Kevin	CT0650	Cohen, Jean-Luc D.	NY2750	Colenbrander, Caroline	AG0650
Cobb, Kevin	NY1900	Cohen, Jeffrey L.	NY2150	Coles, Marilyn J.	IL0800
Cobb, Mary Marden	NY3725	Cohen, Joanne	MN0600	Coletta, Michelle	CA1900
Cobb, Susan	IL1750	Cohen, Joel D.	IL3310	Coletti, Paul	CA1075
Cobb, Timothy	FL1125	Cohen, Judith	AG0650	Coley, Matthew	IA0850
Cobb, Timothy	NJ1130	Cohen, Lynne	NJ0700	Colgin-Abeln, Melissa	TX3520
Cobb, Timothy B.	NY3785	Cohen, Mary L.	IA1550	Colin, Marie-Alexis	AI0200
Cobb, Timothy	NY1900	Cohen, Nicki S.	TX3300	Coll, Peter	NJ1400
Cobb, Timothy	NY2150	Cohen, Pablo	NY1800	Colla, Ginger	CA3000
Cobbs, Jerry	AL0330	Cohen, Paul	NY0500	Collaros, Pandel Lee	WV0100
Coberly, Ron	IA0900	Cohen, Paul	NY2750	Collaros, Rebecca L.	DC0170
Cobert, Claude	MA2020	Cohen, Paul	NJ1130	Colleen, Jeffrey	IL1550
Coble, Deborah C.	NY4150	Cohen, Paul	NJ0800	Collerd, Gene J.	IL3310
Coble, Jay	FL2000	Cohen, Paul	NY2150	Collett, Jacqueline L.	MO1780
Cobo, Ricardo	NV0050	Cohen, Richard Scott	MI0650	Colletti, Carla	MO1950
Coburn, Pamela	IN0350	Cohen, Sarah Hess	FL0850	Collier, Bethany	PA0350
Coburn, Robert	CA5350	Cohen, Stanley	NY1275	Collier, David L.	IL1150
Coccagnia, Lou	NY1150	Cohen, Steven	IL2250	Collier, Joanne	AA0040
Cochenour, Deborah	PA1350	Cohen, Warren	NJ0700	Collier, Katherine	MI2100
Cochran, Alfred W.	KS0650	Cohick, Mark	MO2000	Collier, Thomas	WA1050
Cochran, Kathy	SC0750	Cohill, Gregory	IL1610	Collins, Allison	CA0900
Cochran, Martin	AL1150	Cohler, Jonathan	MA0350	Collins, Amy	FL0930
Cochran, Matthew	GA0625	Cohler, Jonathan	MA1175	Collins, Amy	FL2000
Cochran, Nathan	PA2950	Cohn, Richard L.	CT0900	Collins, Amy	FL0450
Cochran, Shelley	IL1100	Cohn, Sanford	CT0650	Collins, Anthony	CA4200
Cochran, Timothy	NJ1350	Coia-Gailey, Susan M.	MA0260	Collins, C. Keith	TX3420
Cochrane, Amy L.	NY2650	Coil, Pat	TN1100	Collins, Caron L.	NY3780
Cochrane, Jan	TN1350	Coker, Cheryl W.	MS0385	Collins, Charlotte A.	VA1350
Cochrane, Keith A.	NM0400	Coker, Jerry	TN1710	Collins, Cherie	ND0250
Cochrane, Michael	NJ1140	Coker, Keller	OR1250	Collins, Cheryl	NM0400
Cock, Christopher M.	IN1750	Coker, Stephen R.	CA0960	Collins, Christopher	MI2200
Cock, Maura	IN1750	Coker, Timothy C.	MS0385	Collins, Dana L.	IN1560
Cockburn, Brian	VA0600	Coker, Warren	NJ1000	Collins, Darryl	AD0050
Cockburn, Neil	AA0050	Cokkinias, Peter L.	MA0260	Collins, David	NM0400
Cockerham, Barbara	LA0150	Colaneri, Joseph	NY2250	Collins, David	MN1250
Cockerham, Scott	FL0150	Colantti, Stephen	PA2250	Collins, Drew S.	OH2500
Cockey, Linda E.	MD0800	Colarusso, Joey	TX2170	Collins, Irma H.	VA1350
Cocking, Roger	PA2800	Colatosti, Camille	MA0260	Collins, Jenny	PA1100
Cockle, Katherine G.	IL3550	Colburn, Steve	WI0825	Collins, Kevin	WI0808
Cockrell, Dale	TN1850	Colby, Constance	NY2150	Collins, Kimberly	MN0620
Cockrell, Findlay	NY3700	Colby, Donald	ID0100	Collins, Leo W.	MA2200
Cockrell, Thomas R.	AZ0500	Colby, Mark	IL0850	Collins, Linda	MN1250
Cockson, Aaron	MD0150	Colby, Mark S.	IL0750	Collins, Lisa	NM0450
Coco, Joseph W.	NJ0800	Coldiron, Jack	TX0300	Collins, Myrtice J.	AL0500
Codding, Peggy	MA0260	Cole, Arlene	RI0050	Collins, Nancy	WI0808

Alphabetical Listing of Faculty

Name	Code	Name	Code	Name	Code
Collins, Peter	AG0500	Conger, Robert B.	MO1500	Cook, Casey	OH0850
Collins, Peter F.	MO0775	Congo, John R.	CT0250	Cook, Catherine	CA4150
Collins, Philip M.	CA0400	Conklin, Michael	NJ0175	Cook, Christopher E.	VA0150
Collins, Phillip	CA2150	Conklin, Raymond L.	KY0950	Cook, Christopher	WA0400
Collins, Phillip	OH2200	Conklin, Scott A.	IA1550	Cook, Don	UT0050
Collins, Roger	CA2440	Conklin-Bishop, Lisa	TN0050	Cook, Ed	WY0130
Collins, Rosemary	AG0350	Conkling, Susan W.	MA0400	Cook, Edward	WA1250
Collins, Shelley	MS0250	Conley, Cheryl	MO1120	Cook, Elaine Humphreys	KY1450
Collins, Susan	SC0700	Conley, David A.	SC0400	Cook, Elaine	KY0450
Collins, Tony	CA4700	Conley, Gene	ID0075	Cook, Gary	MS0420
Collins, Verne E.	VA1350	Conley, Irene H.	CT0650	Cook, Gary	NV0050
Collins, Willa	FL1900	Conley, Mark	RI0300	Cook, Gloria	FL1550
Collins, Zachary	PA1600	Conley, Nancy S.	NY3780	Cook, Grant W.	OH2290
Collinsworth, Andy	CA4700	Conlon, Francis	DC0100	Cook, James	NE0590
Collison, Craig	AR0110	Conlon, Joan C.	CO0800	Cook, James H.	AL0300
Collister, Phillip	MD0850	Conlon, Kelly	RI0200	Cook, Jean	SC0200
Collver-Jacobson, Glorianne	MA2050	Conlon, Paula J.	OK1350	Cook, Jeffrey	TN0900
Colman, Alfredo C.	TX0300	Conn, Troy	NC1900	Cook, Jenni	NH0350
Colnot, Cliff C.	IL0750	Connell, Andrew M.	VA0600	Cook, Justin	TX2750
Colon Carrion, Ismar	PR0115	Connell, Joseph C.	DC0100	Cook, Ken	CA4700
Colon Jimenez, Frances	PR0115	Connell, Robin	MI0300	Cook, Kenneth	NY1275
Colon, Daisy	PR0100	Connell, Robin L.	MI0850	Cook, Kent	IL1200
Colon, Emilio	PR0115	Connelly Bush, Judith	VA1350	Cook, Kim	PA2750
Colon, Emilio W.	IN0900	Connelly, Brian	TX2150	Cook, Lawrence	HI0050
Colon, Frank	VA0450	Connelly, Chris	SC0420	Cook, Linda Klein	WI0750
Colonna, Jim	UT0325	Connelly, Marianne	MN0450	Cook, Lisa M.	CO0550
Colorado, Jose	PR0150	Conner, Heather	UT0250	Cook, Luke	MI1180
Colosimo, Murray B.	NJ1160	Conner, Jennifer	PA1050	Cook, Mark Andrew	WV0550
Coloton, Diane S.	IL2900	Conner, Jennifer A.	OH0200	Cook, Nathan J.	AD0050
Colpean, Elizabeth	MI0350	Conner, Stacey	PA0600	Cook, Peter	AI0150
Colprit, Elaine	OH0300	Conner, Ted A.	PA2550	Cook, Robert C.	IA1550
Colquhoun, Jocelyn	AA0050	Conner, Timothy M.	FL1900	Cook, Sally	FL0150
Colquhoun, Michael	NY0400	Connerley, Jim L.	KY1500	Cook, Samuel	TX0050
Colson, David J.	MI2250	Connie, Meredith	WA0750	Cook, Scott A.	WI0825
Colson, Steve	NJ0800	Connolly, Damien	CT0300	Cook, Seth	VA1550
Colson, William	TX2600	Connolly, Donna	NJ0825	Cook, Seth	DC0170
Colston, Daniel	IN0150	Connolly, James	CA5550	Cook, Seth	MD0550
Colter, Nancy	ME0270	Connolly, Martha	VA0250	Cook, Sophia	DC0170
Coltman, Charles	TX0900	Connolly, Michael E.	OR1100	Cook, Stephen	CA6000
Coltman, Heather	FL0650	Connolly, Thomas H.	PA3350	Cook, Susan C.	IL0750
Colton, Glenn	AG0170	Connor, Jennifer	OH0600	Cook, Thomas	MI1250
Colton, Kathy	UT0050	Connor, Mark	MO0700	Cook, Warren	SC0200
Colton, Kendra	OH1700	Connor, Mark	IL1740	Cook, Wayne E.	WI0825
Colucci, Matthew J.	PA3250	Connors, David	CA0830	Cook, Wayne	WI1150
Colunga, Richard	CA2300	Connors, Lori	LA0080	Cook-Perez, Paige	CA3270
Coluzzi, Seth	MA0500	Connors, Maureen	MA0150	Cooke, David	IN0905
Colvin, Jennifer L.	SC0750	Connors, Michael	MA0650	Cooke, India	CA2950
Colvin, Maura	NC2600	Connors, Patricia Cahalan	MN1295	Cooke, Julia	MD0850
Colwell, Brent	TX2800	Connors, Sean	WI0850	Cooke, Julia	MD0600
Colwell, Cynthia	KS1350	Connors, Thomas	NJ0700	Cooksey, Denise	IL1090
Colwell, David A.	VA1550	Conoly, Shaaron	TX3100	Cooksey, Denise	IL1350
Colwell, Denis R.	PA0550	Conrad, Jon Alan	DE0150	Cooksey, John M.	UT0250
Colwell, Lynn	IN1850	Conrad, Kent R.	IL0800	Cooksey, Steven	VA1350
Colwell, Lynn	IN1310	Conrad, Larry	AZ0440	Coolen, Michael T.	OR0700
Colwitz, Erin E.	AL1160	Conrad, Robert	OH0600	Cooley, Brian	KS0150
Comanescu, Anastasios	CA3600	Conrad, Robert	CA4625	Cooley, Floyd O.	IL0750
Comartin, Keenan	AG0070	Conrod, Derek	NY1100	Cooley, Timothy J.	CA5060
Combe, Charles	WI0804	Conrod, Derek	AG0500	Coolidge, Tiffany	VT0100
Comberiati, Carmelo	NY2200	Conrow, Steve	OR0750	Coolman, Todd	NY3785
Combest, Chris	IL2900	Conroy, Brenda	IL1090	Coomber, Robert	CA1750
Combs, Barry	SC0950	Conroy, Gregory	MA0510	Coons, Kevin	OK0770
Combs, Julia C.	MO0775	Conroy, Thomas	CA4150	Coop, Jane A.	AB0100
Combs, Larry R.	IL0750	Consiglio, Catherine	KS1450	Coope, Ann-Katherine	AB0200
Combs, Matt	TN1850	Consoli, Marc-Antonio	NY2750	Cooper, Barbara	NY4460
Combs, Mikel	OK0550	Constantine, Cyprian G.	PA2950	Cooper, Blake	CA0835
Combs, Ronald	IN0005	Constantinides, Dinos	LA0200	Cooper, Britt	OH2370
Combs, Ronald	IL2150	Conte, David	CA4150	Cooper, Chris	CA5030
Comeau, Gilles	AG0400	Conte, Peter Richard	NJ1350	Cooper, Cora	KS0650
Comeaux, Garrick	MN0050	Conti, Michael	NJ0500	Cooper, Darryl	CA4150
Comer, Sonya	IL2300	Contino, Adriana	IN0900	Cooper, David	WI0840
Cominskey, Millie M.	IL1350	Contino, Loretta	IN0250	Cooper, Donna	PA1550
Comotto, Brian	MD0175	Contos, Paul D.	CA5070	Cooper, Frank E.	FL1900
Comparone, Elaine	NY0050	Contreras, Billy	TN0100	Cooper, Gloria A.	NY2102
Compean, Jose D.	TX1425	Contrino, Joseph L.	MO1500	Cooper, J. Michael	TX2650
Compson, Christy	TX1000	Converse, Andrew	TX2960	Cooper, Jack	TN1680
Compton, Adam	OK0500	Converse, Mark	CA0630	Cooper, James	PA2800
Compton, Beckie	TX0125	Converse, Mark	CA1265	Cooper, Jameson	IN0910
Compton, Lanette	OK0800	Converse, Ralph D.	NM0500	Cooper, Jennifer Goode	OH0300
Compton, Michael	OK0150	Converse, Sheila K.	WA1150	Cooper, Jessica	MA2010
Compton, Michael	ND0100	Conway, Colleen	MI0050	Cooper, Jim	MN1600
Compton, Paul R.	OK0800	Conway, Colleen	MI2100	Cooper, John	IL3500
Comstock, Allan D.	KS0300	Conway, Eric	MD0600	Cooper, John H.	ME0270
Con, Adam Jonathan	OH2450	Conway, Mark	MN1290	Cooper, Joseph	TX1450
Conable, William E.	OH1850	Conway, Nicholas	NY3700	Cooper, Joseph	TX3100
Conatser, Brian	AR0200	Conway, Robert	MI2200	Cooper, Justin L.	TX3420
Conaty, Donna	CA4100	Conway, Vicki J.	TX3535	Cooper, Kelli	TX3370
Concepcion, Elman O.	FL1550	Conyers, Joseph	PA3250	Cooper, Kenneth	NY2150
Concordia, Stephen	PA2950	Conzetti, Florian	OR0450	Cooper, Kevin	CA1850
Conda, J. Michelle	OH2200	Coobatis, Christy	CA2960	Cooper, Lawrence R.	PA0350
Condacse, Anne Marie	OK0800	Coogan, Chris	CT0550	Cooper, Marianne G.	OH1850
Condaris, Christine	MA1185	Coogan, W. Jack	CA1050	Cooper, Marva W.	DC0350
Conde, Moussa	IL3300	Cook Glen, Constance	IN0900	Cooper, Matthew J.	OR0200
Condit, Sonja	SC1000	Cook, Alan	ME0430	Cooper, Nancy Joyce	MT0400
Condon, Clay	IL2100	Cook, Amanda B.	CO1050	Cooper, Peter	CO0550
Condon, Clay	IL2150	Cook, Andrew	AL0050	Cooper, Peter	TN1850
Condran, Dena	PA3250	Cook, Andrew	CA3600	Cooper, Peter	CO0800
Condy, Steven	PA2800	Cook, Andrew	AL0345	Cooper, Peter	TN1350
Cone, Kimberly	GA0550	Cook, Anne	SC0200	Cooper, Peter	CO0200
Conely, James	AL0450	Cook, Bruce	CA1560	Cooper, Ralph	GA0400
Congdon, Judy A.	NY1700	Cook, Carla	PA3250	Cooper, Rex	CA5350

Name	Code	Name	Code	Name	Code
Cooper, Rychard	CA0825	Cornut, Sebastien	NJ0825	Coulter, Monte	TN1700
Cooper, Sean	OH0300	Cornwall, Lonieta	NC2300	Coulter, Ronald E.	IL2900
Cooper, Shelly	AZ0500	Cornwell, Tina	AR0200	Coulter, William D.	CA5070
Cooper, Stacey H.	NY2550	Coroniti, Joseph	MA0260	Coulthard, Anita	VA0350
Cooper, Ted	DC0170	Corporon, Eugene Migliaro	TX3420	Councell-Vargas, Martha	MI2250
Cooper, William	KS0050	Corps, Wilfredo	PR0115	Council, Thomas	GA2000
Coopersmith, Jonathan	PA0850	Corpus, Edward	IA0550	Councill, Ruben	PA2100
Cooperstock, Andrew	CO0800	Correll, Allen	OK0300	Counihan, Emma	AZ0440
Cope, David H.	CA5070	Correll, Larry	VA1350	Counts, Les	CA0200
Cope, Mary Jane	CA5070	Correll, Sue	VA1350	Court, Tom	MI2200
Cope, Roger Allen	CA0650	Correlli, Christopher	MD0850	Courtier, Jessica M.	WI0200
Copeland, David	IN0907	Correnti, James	PA2800	Courtney, Craig	OH0350
Copeland, Louise	PA1350	Corrie, John H.	ME0150	Courtney, Ken H.	SC1100
Copeland, Philip L.	AL0800	Corrigan, Ann	OH0300	Coutsouridis, Peter	MA2100
Copeland, Rachel	NC0650	Corrigan, Rose	CA5300	Coutts, Greg A.	IL2650
Copeland-Burns, Carla	NC0930	Corrigan, Vincent J.	OH0300	Couture, Jocelyn	AI0150
Copeland-Burns, Carla	VA1100	Corron, Patricia J.	NY3725	Couture, Marie	NH0300
Copenhaver, James K.	SC1110	Corrothers, Janette	OH2550	Couture, Robert F.	MA2050
Copenhaver, John E.	PA1900	Corsi, Stephen F.	PA0100	Couturiaux, Clay	TX3420
Copenhaver, Lee R.	MI0900	Corson, Floyd W.	MA2100	Couvillon, Thomas M.	KY0550
Copes, Ronald	NY1900	Cortese, Federico	MA1050	Covach, John	NY1100
Coplan, Lauren Jackson	TN1850	Cortese, Michael	NY0450	Covach, John R.	NY4350
Copley, Edith A.	AZ0450	Cortese, Paul	TX3000	Covell, Jeffrey	MA0260
Coppenbarger, Brent	SC0950	Cortez, Brooke D.	TX3410	Covert, Kelly	NY1800
Coppenbarger, Casey	NC2400	Cortez, Juan	WA1200	Covey, Jason	GA0750
Coppola, A. J.	NH0250	Corvino, William	NJ0750	Covey, Jason	NY2900
Coppola, Catherine	NY0625	Corwin, Lucille H.	NY4500	Coviak, James	MI0450
Coppola, Thomas	NC2400	Corwin, Mark	AI0070	Coviak, James	MI2120
Corbato, Barbara	MI1050	Cory, Craig	CA1290	Covington, Alicia	GA2300
Corbet, Kim	TX2400	Cory, Eleanor	NY2050	Covington, Charles	DC0150
Corbett, George	VA0150	Corzine, Michael L.	FL0850	Cowan, Carole	NY3760
Corbett, Ian	KS0590	Cosand, Walter	AZ0100	Cowan, Elizabeth	MI2250
Corbin, Barbara	TX2250	Cosart, Jann	TX0300	Cowan, Kathryn Jean	IL2150
Corbin, Dwayne	CA4550	Cosby, Tom	NE0610	Cowan, Linda	WV0600
Corbin, Dwayne V.	CA4600	Coscarelli, William F.	GA2100	Cowan, Richard D.	PA0550
Corbin, Lynn Ann	GA2150	Cosentino, Mike	IL1050	Cowan, Scott M.	MI2250
Corbin, Patricia	AL0500	Cosenza, Frank	OH1100	Cowart, Georgia	OH0400
Corbus, Dave	CO0800	Cosenza, Glenda L.	IL2200	Cowart, Robert	NY1900
Corcoran, Catherine T.	CA0847	Cosgrove, Julia	MI1050	Cowart, Steed D.	CA2950
Corcoran, Gary J.	NH0250	Cosgrove, Nancy	MA0600	Cowden, Tracy E.	VA1700
Corcoran, James R.	KY1425	Cosma, Tina	PA1250	Cowdery, James R.	NY0600
Corcoran, Kathleen	AA0110	Cossa, Dominic	MD1010	Cowdrick, Kathryn	NY1100
Corcoran, Kenda	NH0250	Cossette, Isabelle	AI0150	Cowell, Jennifer	WY0050
Cord, Adam	OH1350	Costa, Anthony J.	PA2750	Cowell, Kimberly S.	MO1830
Cord, Edmund	IN0900	Costa, Jennifer	NC2000	Cowell, Stanley	NJ1130
Cord, John T.	TX2960	Costa, John V.	UT0250	Cowens, Kathleen	MO0350
Cordell, Angela	NJ0800	Costa, Robyn Dixon	PA1650	Cowens, Kathy	MO0400
Cordell, Debra	OH1900	Costa-Giomi, Eugenia	TX3510	Cowger, Kelsey	AF0100
Cordell, Tim	NC2000	Costanza, A. Peter	OH1850	Cowgill, Jennifer Griffith	PA2200
Cordes, Jamie	OH0350	Costanza, Christopher	CA4900	Cowin, Jasmin Bey	NY4200
Cordingley, Allen	WI0840	Costanzo, Samuel R.	CT0250	Cowles, Robert	NY1550
Cords, Nicholas D.	NY3790	Costen, Melva Wilson	GA1100	Cox, Allan	TN1850
Coreil, Kristine	LA0550	Costigan, Christopher	GA2050	Cox, Amanda K.	NY1700
Corella, Gil C.	DC0100	Costigan-Kerns, Louise	CA3270	Cox, Ann	UT0350
Corey, Horace E.	NV0100	Cote, Alejandro	GA0750	Cox, Arnie	OH1700
Corey, Jason	MI2100	Cote, Gerald	AI0190	Cox, Bradley	MO1000
Corey, Scott	TN1600	Cote, Sarah	TN0100	Cox, Bruce	SC0200
Corigliano, John	NY0635	Coticone, Geralyn	MA0350	Cox, Buford	FL0040
Corigliano, John	NY0600	Coticone, Geralyn	MA0400	Cox, Carl	NJ1050
Corigliano, John	NY1900	Cotik, Tomas	TX3750	Cox, Cindy	CA5000
Corin, Amy R.	CA3100	Cotner, John S.	TX2700	Cox, Daniel	WA0400
Corina, John H.	GA2100	Cotroneo, P. J.	NJ0950	Cox, Daniel R.	ID0140
Corinthian, Randy	FL0200	Cotroneo, Sue	NY2650	Cox, Dennis K.	ME0440
Corkern, David	MO0500	Cotte, William	VT0300	Cox, Donna	OK1350
Corkey, Jim	ID0070	Cotten, Paul	MS0850	Cox, Donna M.	OH2250
Corlett, Neil	AA0080	Cotten, William	MA1400	Cox, Eleanor Christman	WI0700
Corley, Alton L.	TX3175	Cotten, William	MA0350	Cox, Franklin	OH2500
Corley, Kirsten M.	PA2350	Cotter, Daniel	WA0250	Cox, Gregory	AG0550
Corley, Paula	TX3100	Cotter, Daniel	WA0950	Cox, Gregory A.	WA1250
Corley, Scott R.	WI0825	Cotter, Steve	CA1000	Cox, Gregory	AB0060
Corley, Sheila	AZ0400	Cottin-Rack, Myriam	CA4300	Cox, Gregory	AB0100
Corliss, Frank	NY0150	Cottle, David M.	UT0250	Cox, Gregory	AB0200
Corliss, Heidi E.	ME0440	Cottle, Melanie	IL3550	Cox, Ishbah	IN1310
Corman, David	TX1850	Cottle, W. Andrew	DE0150	Cox, James	IL2050
Cormier, Elizabeth	TN1850	Cotto, Orlando	DE0150	Cox, Jeff	TN1600
Cormier, Eugene	AF0050	Cotton, Haim	NY2660	Cox, Jim	IL1400
Cormier, Pierre	AI0210	Cotton, Maurice	WI1150	Cox, John	OR0150
Corn, Paul	NY0500	Cotton, Patricia	AG0170	Cox, John	NY4310
Cornacchio, Rachel	PA2300	Cotton, Sandra M.	NC0600	Cox, John P.	OR1100
Cornblum, Marcy	AG0130	Cotton, Wilbur P.	CA1400	Cox, Kellie	TN1600
Cornejo, Robert Joseph	CA5510	Cottrell, David	VA0600	Cox, Kenneth	CO0900
Cornelius, Jeffrey M.	PA3250	Cottrell, Duane	DE0150	Cox, Kerry	IA0600
Cornelius, John L.	TX2100	Cottrell, Jeffrey	TX0900	Cox, Kris	IL1100
Cornelius, Polly Butler	NC0750	Cottrill, Heather	WV0050	Cox, Kyle	MO0750
Cornelius-Bates, Benjamin	PA1050	Cottrill, Lara Lynn	PA3580	Cox, Lauren J.	OK0300
Cornell, Ernest	WV0440	Cottrill-Nelson, Lara Lynn	PA2950	Cox, Mark	MI0400
Cornell, Richard	MA0400	Couch, Charles A.	OH0650	Cox, Mary A.	NY1900
Cornett, Eileen	MD0650	Couch, Leon	WI0200	Cox, Melissa	GA0750
Cornett, Stanley O.	MD0650	Couch, Roy L.	OK0150	Cox, Michael	VA1580
Cornett-Murtada, Vanessa	MN1625	Couderc, Valerie	NY1100	Cox, Michael W.	OH0350
Cornfoot, James	TN1200	Coughran, Steven J.	CA1500	Cox, Natalie	CA1650
Cornicello, Anthony	CT0150	Coulas, Ben	AB0040	Cox, Patricia J.	AR0250
Corniel, Wilson 'Chembo'	NY3785	Coull, James	SD0550	Cox, Rachel	KY1350
Cornils Luke, Peg	IA0250	Coulson, Bette	IL0720	Cox, Richard G.	NC2430
Cornils, Margaret A.	WI0840	Coulson, Bette	IL2750	Cox, Robert	OH1600
Cornils, Ray	ME0200	Coulson-Grigsby, Carolyn	VA1350	Cox, Robert D.	OH1200
Cornils, Ray	ME0500	Coulter, Beverly	FL0050	Cox, Robin V.	CA0825
Cornish, Craig S.	TN1100	Coulter, Chris	CA1960	Cox, Terrance	AG0050
Cornish, Glenn S.	FL0500	Coulter, Chris	CA1700	Cox, Thomas B.	GA2000
Cornish, John	OK0150	Coulter, Chris	CA1265	Cox, Thomas E.	AR0750

Cox, Timothy	OR1010	Craycraft, Jeremy	MN0450	Cross, Julie A.	WI0865
Coxe, Stephen	VA1000	Craycraft, Nicole	MN0450	Cross, Richard	CT0850
Coye, Gene	CA0835	Crayton, Mark	IL0550	Cross, Ronald W.	NY4500
Coyle, Brian	MI1050	Creager, Greg	CO0275	Cross, Samuel G.	VA0600
Coz, Brandon	AZ0150	Creaghan, Andrew	AA0020	Cross, Sandra	IL2750
Cozart, Keith	IN0400	Creasap, Susan D.	KY0900	Cross, Sandy	OK0770
Cozza, John	CA0840	Creasy, Catherine S.	VA1400	Cross, Travis J.	VA1700
Cozza, John	CA5350	Creasy, Catherine	VA0750	Cross, Virginia A.	OR0175
Crabb, Amanda	UT0050	Creasy, Kathleen	GA1150	Crossen-Richardson, Phyllis	MD1100
Crabb, Paul	MO1800	Cree, Christopher	WA1100	Crossland, Carolyn M.	NC1075
Crabbs, David	IA0550	Creel, David	TN0260	Crossman, Patricia	MD0175
Crabbs, David	IA1400	Creel, Randall Patrick	TX2650	Crosson, Gail	IL0850
Crabiel, Jon	IN0250	Creese, Anne	CA2910	Crothers-Marley, Shirley Evans	OH2100
Crabill, Michael	VA0450	Creighton, Elizabeth	IL1750	Crotts, Angela	TX2295
Crabtree, Cecile	OK0150	Creighton, Patricia	AF0100	Crotty, John E.	WV0750
Crabtree, John M.	TX2250	Creighton, Randall	CA1560	Crouch, Jay	MI1985
Crabtree, Joseph C.	TX1425	Cremaschi, Alejandro M.	CO0800	Crouse, Courtney	OK0750
Crabtree, Kacy E.	NC1050	Crenshaw, Sonja L.	SC0800	Crouse, David L.	AR0600
Crafton, Colleen	NY0650	Crenshaw, Timothy	SC1110	Crow, Andrew	IN0150
Crafton, Jason A.	VA1700	Cresci, Jonathan	PA3710	Crow, Todd	NY4450
Crago, Bartholemy	AI0210	Cresci, Jonathan	MD0550	Crowder, James	IL0300
Craig, Ed	CA0350	Crespo, Fabra Desamparados	NJ0825	Crowder, Jarrell	MD0550
Craig, Genevieve	OK1330	Cress, David	MO0825	Crowe, Barbara	AZ0100
Craig, Genevieve	OK0300	Cressley, Scott	IA1950	Crowe, Don R.	SD0550
Craig, Gordon	AG0250	Creswell, Bradley	IA1750	Crowe, Gary	MN0250
Craig, James	AG0450	Creswell, Mary	IA0850	Crowe, Jason	CO0275
Craig, Jennifer	OR0400	Crevelli-Sallee, Monica	CA4460	Crowe, Nancy	WA1200
Craig, Mark	MD0850	Creviston, Christopher	AZ0100	Crowell, Allen	GA2100
Craig, Mary Ann	NJ0800	Creviston, Hannah	AZ0100	Crowell, Gregory	MI0900
Craig, Monty S.	SC0400	Crewe, Murray	PA0550	Crowell, Jeffrey W.	WI0803
Craig, Patricia	CA4150	Crewe, Murray	PA1050	Crowell, Ken R.	CA3320
Craig, Patricia	MA1400	Crews, Janice	GA2130	Crowley, James F.	WI0835
Craig, Phebe	CA5010	Crews, Joel	MO1110	Crowley, Lisle	UT0150
Craig, Sean	AI0150	Crews, Norval	TX1700	Crowley, Patrick	AL1195
Craig, Susan	CA0350	Crews, Ruth	TX3525	Crowley, Robert	AI0150
Craig, Vincent	PA3600	Criazzo, Rocco	OH2600	Crowne, Scott	PA1400
Craige, Mary Ann	OK1150	Criddle, Reed	UT0325	Crowson, James	MD0550
Crain, Michael	CA0150	Crider, Joe	VA0650	Croy, Elizabeth	MT0200
Crain, Michael R.	CA0840	Crilly, Neil D.	FL0650	Crozier, Daniel G.	FL1550
Crain, Timothy M.	MA2030	Crim, Mark	TX0600	Cruciani, Lori L.	WI0803
Craioveanu, Mihai	MI1050	Crimm, William	TN1400	Cruhm, Robert	TX3515
Cramer, Alfred W.	CA3650	Crimmins, Andrea	IL1150	Crull, Terry	KS0350
Cramer, Christopher	WI0100	Crippin, Glee	IA1200	Crum, Dorothy E.	KS1450
Cramer, Craig	IN1700	Cripps, Cynthia L.	TX3525	Crum, Martin	TN1400
Cramer, David M.	PA3250	Crisan, Patricia	SC0650	Crumb, David	OR1050
Cramer, Eugene	AA0150	Criss, Mary Ann	MD0850	Crumb, George H.	PA3350
Crandell, Adam	PA1500	Crissinger, Paula K.	OH0550	Crumley, Terri L.	IA0200
Crane, Alan	KS1450	Crist, Michael	OH2600	Crummer, Larry D.	CA1760
Crane, Amy	FL1750	Crist, Stephen A.	GA0750	Crump, Jason	NC2700
Crane, Andrew	NC0650	Crist, Timothy D.	AR0110	Cruse, Carolyn S.	TX3200
Crane, David	OR0250	Cristy-Couch, Martha	MI1150	Crusoe, Michael	WA1050
Crane, Emily Hanna	TN0050	Criswell, James Anthony	GA1200	Crutchfield, Jonathan	NC2000
Crane, Kenneth	NY1700	Criswell, Paul D.	SC0800	Crutchfield, Robert	TX3360
Crane, Rachel L.	KS1450	Crite, Kiera	TN1400	Crutchfield, Robert	TX3535
Crane, Teresa Ann	IL1500	Crites, Dennis	OH0250	Crutti, John A.	LA0300
Craney-Welch, Karen	WI1150	Crittenden, David	MN0800	Cruz, Gabriela G.	MI2100
Cranford, Dennis	MS0100	Crittenden, David	MN0250	Cruz, Jennifer	OH0500
Cranmer, Carl	PA3600	Crittenden, Eric	NY4460	Cruz, Karena	CA3520
Cranna, Kip	CA4150	Crochet, Lourinda S.	SC1200	Cruz, Mark A.	TX3175
Crannell, Wayne T.	TX0250	Crocker, Emily	OR0450	Cruz, Samantha	WI0500
Cranson, Todd	AR0300	Crocker, John	CA0200	Cryderman-Weber, Molly	MI1200
Crappell, Courtney Joseph	TX3530	Crocker, Ronald	NE0590	Csaba, Ajtony	AB0150
Craswell, Brandon	GA2100	Crocker, Susan	NY2950	Csapo, Gyula	AJ0150
Cratty, William	CA4050	Crockett, Alison	DC0100	Cseszko, Ferenc	ID0250
Cratty, William	CA2960	Crockett, C. Edgar	IL0300	Csicsila, Mell	OH0755
Craven, Robert	DC0050	Crockett, Donald	CA5300	Cubbage, John	MT0370
Craven, Todd	FL1745	Crockett, Whitney	NY2150	Cubek, David	CA2175
Cravens, Terry	CA5300	Crockett-Hardin, Michelle	OH0500	Cubek, David	CA1060
Cravero, Ann	IA0550	Croegaert, Roxanne	IL0300	Cubek, David	CA4500
Crawford, Andy J.	IL1350	Croft, Mathew	CA4400	Cubek, David	CA3620
Crawford, Barry J.	NY4320	Croft, Richard	TX3420	Cuccaro-Penhorwood, Costanza	IN0900
Crawford, Donna	SC0200	Crofts, Tim	AF0100	Cuciurean, John D.	AG0500
Crawford, Elizabeth A.	IN0150	Cromer, Lilianne	CA4425	Cuckson, Robert	NY2250
Crawford, Eric	VA0950	Cromley, Dorothea	MT0175	Cuckson, Robert	PA0850
Crawford, Glenda	OH2550	Cromwell, Anna L.	IL0800	Cucunato, Lou	WI0825
Crawford, Jeff D.	CA5350	Cron, Nancy	KY1550	Cudd, Patti	MN0350
Crawford, Jenn	AJ0030	Crone, Elizabeth	VA1700	Cudek, Mark	MD0650
Crawford, Jeremy	AL0050	Cronin, Robert	GA1150	Cudmore, Faye	MA0260
Crawford, Ken	CA1650	Cronk, Daniel L.	MI0650	Cuellar, Martin	KS0300
Crawford, Langdon C.	NY2750	Cronk, M. Sam	CA4500	Cuenca, Sylvia	NY0646
Crawford, Lawrence E.	MD0850	Crook, David	WI0815	Cueto, Jose	MD0750
Crawford, Leneida	MD0850	Crook, Harold	MA0260	Cuffari, Gina	CT0800
Crawford, Mark	TN1400	Crook, Joshua	GA0850	Cuffari, Gina Lynn	NY2750
Crawford, Michael	TX2750	Crook, Keith R.	ME0500	Cuk, John	NY2200
Crawford, Michael	MI0850	Crook, Larry	FL1850	Cukrov, Martina	NJ0800
Crawford, Penelope	MI2100	Crookall, Christine	GA0250	Cukrov, Terezija	NJ0800
Crawford, Pete	NC0900	Crooks, Jamie	AI0050	Culbertson, Mark	CA1650
Crawford, Peter	WA1300	Crooks, Mack	CA4650	Culbertson, Robert M.	TX1400
Crawford, Raphael	IL0720	Crookshank, Esther R.	KY1200	Cullen, Burke	AG0300
Crawford, Richard	FL0200	Crosby, Alison	TX2250	Cullen, Christopher	CT0800
Crawford, Roberta	NY3705	Crosby, J. Stephen	NY0100	Cullen, Danielle	PA1550
Crawford, Stephen L.	AZ0490	Crosby, Karen	MA0600	Cullen, David	PA0050
Crawford, Stephen J.	TX3415	Crosby, Luanne M.	NY0100	Cullen, David	PA1750
Crawford, Steven	NJ0825	Crosby, Matthew	TX3415	Cullen, David	PA3600
Crawford, Ted	AJ0030	Crosby, Richard A.	KY0550	Cullen, David T.	PA1250
Crawford, Thomas	VA0350	Crosby, Tracy	MS0300	Cullen, John	AG0450
Crawford, Tom	TN1150	Croskery, Virginia	IA1350	Cullen, Leslie	PA3150
Crawford, Wesley	MD0400	Croson, James M.	FL1550	Cullen, Leslie	PA0350
Crawley, James	AL0330	Cross, Alan E.	TN0150	Culley, James F.	OH2200
Crawley-Mertins, Marilee	IA0425	Cross, Debra W.	VA1000	Culligan, Paul	KY0250

Alphabetical Listing of Faculty

Name	Code	Name	Code	Name	Code
Cullison, Jon	CO0830	Cusack, Margaret	NJ1350	Dal Porto, Mark	NM0100
Cullison, Jonathan	CO0625	Cushing, Alanna B.	WV0400	Dal Vera, Rocco	OH2200
Culloton, Michael	MN0600	Cushing, Diane	MA0200	Dalagar, Martha	NM0450
Culp, Jennifer	CA4150	Cushing, Diane	NH0150	Dalbec-Szczesniak, Gisele	AG0250
Culpepper, Jacquelyn	NC0550	Cushman, Cathy	NY1250	Dalbey, Jenna	AZ0490
Culpo, Susan	RI0150	Cushman, Kevin	MI1260	Dalbey, Laura	MT0175
Cultice, Thomas	NY2250	Cusick, Suzanne G.	NY2740	Dalby, Bruce	NM0450
Cultice, Thomas	NY0500	Custer, Beth	CA2950	Dalby, Kathy	NE0200
Cultise, Theora	NY2400	Custer, Gerald	MI2200	Dale, Karen M.	TN0300
Culvahouse, John N.	GA1150	Custer, Seth A.	SC0200	Dale, Monica	DC0170
Culver, Carrie	OH0700	Custer, Stephen	CA3100	Dale, Randall N.	MS0700
Culver, Daniel	IL0100	Custodero, Lori A.	NY4200	Dale, Sarah	IL1200
Culver, Eric	MA0700	Cutchen, Dovie	AL1050	Dale, Stephen	MA0260
Culver, Jerry	MI1700	Cutler, Ann	TX0250	Dalen, Brenda	AA0100
Culver, Robert L.	MI2100	Cutler, David	SC1110	D'Alessandro, Joseph	PA3700
Culver, Timothy	OH1100	Cutler, Sara	NY0500	D'Alessio, Greg P.	OH0650
Culverhouse, William	IN0400	Cutler, Timothy S.	OH0600	Daley, Caron	AF0100
Cumberledge, Melinda	IN1010	Cutsforth-Huber, Bonnie	PA2710	D'Alimonte, Nancia	DC0100
Cumming, Christine	NY1400	Cutsforth-Huber, Bonnie	MD0095	Dalio, Marc G.	NJ0825
Cumming, Danielle	MD0800	Cutter, William	MA1400	Dallabetta, Amanda	AZ0150
Cumming, Duncan J.	NY3700	Cutter, William	MA0350	Dallas, Joseph	PA1050
Cumming, Hilary W.	NY3700	Cutter, William C.	MA1200	Dallesio, Richard	NY0150
Cumming, Julie	AI0150	Cutting, Linda	MA1175	Dallesio, Richard	NY2250
Cummings, Anthony M.	PA1850	Cutting, W. Scott	MI1550	Dallinger, Carol	IN1600
Cummings, Azande	NY1275	Cuttino, Walter E.	SC1110	Dally, John	CA3640
Cummings, Craig	NY1800	Cvetkov, Vasil	LA0650	Dalmas, Jennifer	TX2700
Cummings, Daniel	CA2420	Cykert, Linda	NC0750	Dalmasi, Martin	FL0930
Cummings, Dean	OH1400	Cymerman, Claude	IN0350	Dalton, Dana	MA1400
Cummings, Grace	NY3350	Cyncynates, Ricardo	DC0170	Dalton, Deborah	TX2700
Cummings, Paul C.	CA2250	Cypess, Rebecca	NJ1130	Dalton, Ed	TN1150
Cummins, Danielle Rosaria	CA0845	Cyrille, Andrew	NY2660	Dalton, Grant B.	AL0800
Cummins, Linda P.	AL1170	Cyrus, Cynthia	TN1850	Dalton, James	MA0350
Cummins, Nicholas B.	MS0250	Czarkowski, Stephen	WV0550	Dalton, Lester	KS0590
Cummiskey, Tim	OH1850	Czarkowski, Stephen	MD0550	Dalton, Martha	IL2300
Cundiff, Larry	KY0400	Czarnota, Benjamin D.	OH0200	Dalton, Phoebe A.	MN1300
Cunev, Irina	LA0650	Czernowin, Chaya	MA1050	Dalton, Sharon	WY0060
Cunha, Alcingstone DeOliveira	KY0400	Czink, Andrew	AB0040	Daly, Kathleen	NJ0700
Cunha, Stephanie	CA4425	Da Cunha, Cherise Ann	OR0800	Daly, Pat	OR0950
Cunliffe, William H.	CA0815	Da Silva, Fabio Gardenal	NY2750	Daly, Rachel	MA0510
Cunneff, Philip B.	MD0475	Da Silva, Jetro	MA0260	Damaris, Christa	NY3000
Cunningham, Blaine E.	IA0700	Da Silva, Paul	CA0859	Damast, Deborah G.	NY2750
Cunningham, Chuck	NM0500	Da Silva, Pedro Henriques	NY2750	Damberg, John	AK0100
Cunningham, Geoffrey A.	MA1100	Daane, Maggie	OR0250	D'Ambrosio, Christina	KY0950
Cunningham, Gregory M.	MI1750	Dabback, William M.	VA0600	D'Ambrosio, David	GA0050
Cunningham, James E.	FL0650	Dabczynski, Andrew	UT0050	D'Ambrosio, Kara Ireland	CA4400
Cunningham, Jeffrey N.	MO0800	Dabrowski, Peter	TX3525	D'Ambrosio, Michael	KY0950
Cunningham, Jennifer	OK0825	D'Abruzzo, Gabriel	PA2950	Dameron, Beth	CA4400
Cunningham, Mark T.	IL0750	D'Accone, Frank A.	CA5032	Dameron, Stuart	CO0250
Cunningham, Randall	MO2000	Dachtyl, Cary	OH1200	Damian, Jon	MA0260
Cunningham, Richard	AG0200	Dachtyl, Linda D.	OH1200	D'Amico, David	RI0250
Cunningham, Sarah	NY1900	Dackow, Sandra K.	NJ1400	D'Amico, John	PA0450
Cunningham, Steve M.	CA5300	Dacus, Edward	MS0400	Damicone, Tiffany	OH2000
Cunningham, Tekla	WA0200	Dacus, Viola	MS0400	Damm, Robert J.	MS0500
Cunningham, Walt	NH0100	D'Addio, Daniel F.	CT0050	Dammers, Richard J.	NJ1050
Curfman, George D.	PA1900	Daddy, S. Kwaku	CA1020	Damoulakis, Marc H.	IL0750
Curinga, Nick	CA1700	Dade, Alice K.	MO1800	Damschroder, David	MN1623
Curlee, Alisa	NY3350	Dade, Fred S.	PA3050	Damschroder, Norman	OH2300
Curlee, J. Matthew	NY1100	Dadian, Clinton M.	CO0300	Damschroder, Norman L.	OH2275
Curlette, Bruce	OH0450	Dadurka, Jon	FL0200	Damur, Bill	AA0020
Curley, Jason	NY1400	Daegling, Sharon	CA4300	Damuth, Laura	NE0600
Curnow, Jeffrey	PA3250	Dagenais, Andree	AC0050	Dana, Christy L.	CA5000
Curnow, Jeffrey	PA0850	Daglar, Fatma	MD0850	Dana, Julie R.	CA1850
Curnow, Lauren	PA2550	Daglar, Fatma	MD0750	Dana, Michael	CA1850
Curran, George	GA1150	DaGrade, Donald	CA4300	Danby, Jen	NY2200
Curran, Kathryn	GA0050	Dagradi, Anthony	LA0300	Danby, Judd	IN1310
Curran, Nancy A.	CT0500	Dahl Saville, Lara R.	GA1050	Danchenko, Victor	PA0850
Curren, Christina	NY1100	Dahl, Christina A.	NY3790	Danchenko, Victor	MD0650
Current, Brian	AG0300	Dahl, Christine E.	MN0950	Danchenko-Stern, Vera	MD0650
Currie, David	AG0400	Dahl, Laura	CA4900	Danders, Dennis	KS0200
Currie, Gabriela	MN1623	Dahl, Stanley	IA0650	Dando, Lee C.	FL1570
Currie, James Robert	NY4320	Dahl, Stanley E.	IA0200	D'Andrea, Daria	CA5353
Currie, Neil	AJ0150	Dahl, Tracy	AC0100	Dandridge, Damon H.	PA0675
Currie, Nicholas W.	MD0520	Dahl-Shanks, Deborah	CA1560	Danek, Leonard P.	MN1280
Currie, Randolph	OH1330	Dahlem, Justin	IL1090	Danforth, Robert B.	IN0350
Currie, Scott	MN1623	Dahlen, Sienna	AG0450	Dang, Thai Son	AI0200
Currie, Sheridan	OH0450	Dahlenburg, Jane	AR0850	D'Angelo, David	GA2100
Curry, Jeffrey P.	NE0040	Dahlgren, Marv	MN0050	D'Angelo, Gerard	NY2150
Curry, Jerry L.	SC1110	Dahlgren, Winnie	MA0260	D'Angelo, Gerard	NY2660
Curry, Nancy	NE0590	Dahlin, Christina	CA0960	D'Angelo, Joe	MA0650
Curry, Nick	FL1950	Dahlke, Andrew	CO0950	D'Angelo, Mark	AB0200
Curry, Paul	IN1010	Dahlke, Steven	NY3250	Dangerfield, Joseph Allen	IA0300
Curry, Steven	NY1550	Dahlke, Steven	CA1900	Dangi, Suparna	CA5000
Curry, Vicki L.	VA0600	Dahlman, Barbro	DC0170	Daniecki, John B.	SC1100
Curtin, David	PA2050	Dahlman, Barbro E.	DC0100	Daniel, Anne Margaret	NY2250
Curtin, Jeff	OK1200	Dahlman, Hank	OH2500	Daniel, Jane	WV0400
Curtis, Ann	NC1550	Dahlstrand, John	AR0350	Daniel, John	WI0350
Curtis, Arlyn	OR0750	Dahman, Jamie	IL1850	Daniel, Kathy	TX2250
Curtis, Charles	CA5050	Dahman, Jamie	MI2120	Daniel, Margaret H.	LA0760
Curtis, Cynthia R.	TN0100	Dahn, Luke	IA0500	Daniel, Omar	AG0500
Curtis, Laura	WA1300	Dahn, Luke	IA1200	Daniel, Robert	TX2250
Curtis, Michael	OH1350	Dahn, Nancy	AD0050	Daniel, Robert	OK0550
Curtis, Michael	OH0700	Daigle, Paulin	AI0190	Daniel, Thomas	AL0335
Curtis, Noma	OK0200	Daigle, Steven	NY1100	Daniel, Wade	OK0825
Curtis, Peter	CA3800	Daigneault, Sylvain	AI0050	Daniel-Cox, Minnita D.	OH2250
Curtis, Robert C.	IL0840	Dailey, Colleen M.	NY3770	Daniell-Knapp, Courtney	TX3450
Curtis, Stanley	VA0450	Dailey, Jeff	NY1275	Danielpour, Richard	NY2150
Curtis, Stanley	NY3000	Dailey, Raleigh K.	KY1450	Danielpour, Richard	PA0850
Curtis, Steven	OK1350	Dakin, Deborah	IL0100	Daniels, Chris	CO0830
Curtis-Smith, Curtis O.	MI2250	Dakon, Jacob M.	KS1350	Daniels, Frances	IL1750
Curtiss, Sidney	PA3250	Dal Farra, Ricardo	AI0070	Daniels, Jerry L.	IL0800

Daniels, John	FL0600	Davids, Julia L.	IL2100	Davis, John S.	CO0800
Daniels, Mathew	MO1250	Davids, Suzann	MI1180	Davis, Jolene	GA2100
Daniels, Matthew	FL0950	Davidsen, Nancy Jo	NY3650	Davis, Jonathan	CA5030
Daniels, Michael T.	MI1200	Davidson, Charles	NY1860	Davis, Jonathan Doane	CA5020
Daniels, Sean	TN1400	Davidson, Dave	AG0350	Davis, Joshua	PA3150
Daniels, Sharon	MA0400	Davidson, Doris	NY2400	Davis, Joyce	FL1850
Daniels, William B.	KY1100	Davidson, Harry	OH0600	Davis, Judith Chen	KY0400
Danielsson, Per	FL1800	Davidson, Harry L.	NC0600	Davis, Karen	MS0320
Danielsson, Tamara	FL0800	Davidson, Heidi	WA0750	Davis, Kaylynn	GA2000
Danilow, Marji	NY0150	Davidson, Ian	TX3175	Davis, Keith	SC0750
Danilow, Marji	NY2250	Davidson, Lyle	MA1400	Davis, Kenneth	NJ1130
Danis, Ann	RI0300	Davidson, Michael	KS1350	Davis, Kevin	AL1300
Danko, Harold	NY1100	Davidson, Ryan	AA0020	Davis, Kimberley M.	MS0750
Dann, Steven	AG0300	Davidson, Sarah	AG0500	Davis, Kimberly	PR0115
Danne, Terry	CA2700	Davidson, Steve	OR0950	Davis, Lapointe M.	DE0050
Danner, Greg	TN1450	Davidson, Tara	AG0650	Davis, Lisa	MS0100
Danner, Zachary	MO1250	Davidson, Thalia	IL2750	Davis, Lisa A.	GA1000
Dannessa, Karen	PA3600	Davidson, Thomas	AI0150	Davis, Lynne	KS1450
Dansereau, Diana R.	MA0400	Davidson, Tom	AG0250	Davis, Mark	MS0100
Dansereau, Sophie	AB0200	Davies, Daniel E.	CA0850	Davis, Mark J.	LA0300
Dansker, Judith	NY1600	Davies, David H.	NY1700	Davis, Mark	WI1150
Danson, Joan	AF0120	Davies, Drew Edward	IL2250	Davis, Mark	WI0150
Danton, Jean	MA0800	Davies, James	CA5000	Davis, Mary E.	OH0400
D'Antonio, Peter	OH0600	Davies, Josh	AA0200	Davis, Matt	PA3330
Dantzler, Alta	MI1750	Davies, Karl	IL1300	Davis, Meredyth P.	KY1350
Dantzler, Drake M.	MI1750	Davies, Paul	CA1800	Davis, Michael	IL1085
Daoust, Julie	AI0200	Davies, Richard	NY3775	Davis, Michael	CA0805
Daoust, Lise	AI0200	Davies, Rick A.	VT0450	Davis, Michael W.	KY0400
Dapogny, James	MI2100	Davies, Susan Azaret	CA0600	Davis, Michael	OR1150
Darabie, Mohammed	OH0300	Davies, Thomas	CA1510	Davis, Mickey	AR0600
Darby, Joseph E.	NH0150	Davies, Thomas H.	CA0600	Davis, Mike	MI1650
D'Arca, Denise	OH1800	Davies-Wilson, Dennis	NM0450	Davis, Mike	OR0050
Darcy, Warren J.	OH1700	D'Avignon, India	CA1510	Davis, Mindy	ID0060
Darga, Karen	WI1150	D'Avignon, India	CA0600	Davis, Morgan	FL1550
Darling, Alan T.	IL2250	Davila, Gerardo	TN1100	Davis, Nancy	OH1300
Darling, John A.	ND0050	Davila, Julia	TN1100	Davis, Nathan T.	PA3420
Darling, Matthew H.	CA0810	Davila, William	CA3450	Davis, Ollie Watts	IL3300
Darling, Patricia A.	WI0350	Davila, William	CA0200	Davis, Orbert	IL3310
Darling, Sandra	NJ0800	Davis, Alfred L.	VA0500	Davis, Paul G.	MO1950
Darlington, Mahlon S.	IA0850	Davis, Andrew	TX3400	Davis, Peter A.	RI0250
Darmiento, Madeleine	PA2350	Davis, Anna	GA2050	Davis, Peter	SC0200
Darnell, Debra Jean	FL0680	Davis, Anthony	CA5050	Davis, Quincy	AC0100
Darnell, Robert	NC2430	Davis, Art	IL2050	Davis, Rachelle Berthelsen	CA3400
Daroca, Daniel	FL0050	Davis, Art	IL2200	Davis, Randy	AL1195
Darr, Steven L.	FL2130	Davis, Beth A.	AL1160	Davis, Richard	WI0815
Darrough, Galen P.	CO0950	Davis, Bob	CA1020	Davis, Richard A.	WV0500
Darrow, Alice-Ann	FL0850	Davis, Cara	WI0806	Davis, Richard	MA0260
Darst, John	AZ0460	Davis, Caroline	IL2250	Davis, Robert H.	CT0650
Darvill, Jackie	NY3770	Davis, Charles	TX1510	Davis, Ron A.	SC1000
Dascher, Debra M.	PA2675	Davis, Charlie	CA1000	Davis, Ronald	SC1110
Dash, Robin	MA1400	Davis, Charlotte	TX2700	Davis, Scott	TX3510
Dashevskaya, Olga	CO0625	Davis, Chris	PA2300	Davis, Scott	IA0420
Dashiell, Carroll V.	NC0650	Davis, Christopher A.	SC0950	Davis, Stacey	TX3530
DaSilva, Mario	TN0100	Davis, Clarissa	MS0300	Davis, Stephen	TN0100
DaSilva, Mario	TN1600	Davis, Colin	TX2250	Davis, Steve	CT0650
Dasilva, Mario	KY1460	Davis, Colleen	IN0800	Davis, Steven D.	MO1810
DaSilva, Mario	IN1010	Davis, D. Edward	NY0500	Davis, Susan A.	NY2750
Dassinger, George	NJ1400	Davis, Dan	NC2410	Davis, Susan	VA1600
Daub, Eric	TX3100	Davis, Dan	AA0020	Davis, Suzanne	MA0260
Daucher, Tim	MO0775	Davis, Dana Dinsmore	OK0200	Davis, Thomas L.	TN1400
Dauer, Robin	AR0110	Davis, Daniel	NC0600	Davis, Tim	MN1290
D'Augelli, Barbara	CA0800	Davis, Daniel	NM0450	Davis, Troy	LA0800
D'Augelli, Greg	CA0800	Davis, Daniel W.	AZ0440	Davis, Victor	TN1400
Daugherty, Helene	IN1450	Davis, Dennis	KY0550	Davis, Vincent	OH2500
Daugherty, James F.	KS1350	Davis, Diane	ID0075	Davis, Virginia Wayman	TX3525
Daugherty, Michael	MI2100	Davis, Duane Shields	MI2250	Davis, Wendell R.	TX3525
Daugherty, Wendy	TX2570	Davis, Edward	OH0350	Davis, William	NV0150
Daughtrey, Sarah E.	PA1250	Davis, Eileen	OH1850	Davis, William	TX1600
Daughtry, J. Martin	NY2740	Davis, Eillen	OH0350	Davis, William B.	CO0250
Dauphin, Claude	AI0210	Davis, Elizabeth	NY0750	Davis, William	IN0800
Dauphinais, Kristin E.	AZ0500	Davis, Erica	CA0835	Davis, William	GA2100
Dauphinais, Michael D.	AZ0500	Davis, Garnett	TN1400	Davis, Xavier	NY1900
Daussat, David	TX3525	Davis, Garnett R.	TN1850	Davison, Dorothy	CA4460
Daval, Charles	DC0050	Davis, Garnett R.	TN0550	Davison, Michael A.	VA1500
Davalos, Catherine	CA3920	Davis, Gene	AL0450	Davison, Susan	CT0650
Davenport, David A.	DC0170	Davis, Gladys	NC0220	Davol, Sarah	NJ1400
Davenport, Dennis	OH2050	Davis, Glen Roger	OH1450	Davy, Karen	CA2250
Davenport, Francesca	AA0200	Davis, Glenn	PA1850	Dawe, Brenda M.	NY0350
Davenport, Francesca	AA0150	Davis, Greg	PA0500	Dawe, Jill A.	MN0050
Davenport, Mark	CO0650	Davis, Gregory	LA0300	Dawe, Jonathan	NY1900
Davenport, Roger N.	MO1830	Davis, Hal	NC2435	Dawe, Karla	AC0100
Davenport, Susan G.	IL2900	Davis, Hope	CA2300	Dawes, Andrew	AB0200
Daversa, John	CA0835	Davis, Hugh	TX1300	Dawes, Andrew	AB0100
Daversa, John	CA5300	Davis, Immanuel	MN1623	Dawes, Christopher	AG0450
Daverso, Denise	WA0650	Davis, J. Craig	NJ1400	Dawkins, Allyson	TX3530
Davey, John	NY1400	Davis, Jackie	OH2550	Dawkins, Kyle	GA1650
David, Andy	GA1500	Davis, Jackie	OH0450	Dawson, Andrea	ID0140
David, James M.	CO0250	Davis, Jackie	OH1450	Dawson, Andrea	TN1100
David, John	GA1500	Davis, James	IL3550	Dawson, Bradley J.	KS0350
David, Marc	AD0050	Davis, James A.	NY3725	Dawson, Brett	FL0200
David, Myrtle	LA0700	Davis, Jan	MO1830	Dawson, David J.	TX3175
David, Norman	PA3250	Davis, Jason	AF0120	Dawson, Julian S.	IL2250
David, Norman	PA3330	Davis, Jeff	CA5000	Dawson, Lisa	IN1025
David, William M.	IA0850	Davis, JoDee	MO1810	Dawson, Robert B.	CA1700
Davidian, Joseph	TN0100	Davis, Joel Scott	CA2810	Dawson, Shane	KS0215
Davidian, Teresa	TX2750	Davis, Joel	AL0800	Dawson, Terence	AB0100
Davidoff, Judith	NY3560	Davis, John Douglas	CA0650	Dawson, Tim	AG0450
Davidovich, Theodore C.	MA2100	Davis, John	KS0700	Day, Angela	WV0600
Davidovici, Robert	FL0700	Davis, John Henry	NY2100	Day, Clinton	CA1450
Davidovsky, Mario	NY2250	Davis, John E.	GA0300	Day, David	MI0050

Name	Code	Name	Code	Name	Code
Day, Derek	NC2350	Dean, Maria	CA0510	DeFade, Eric	PA0550
Day, Derek	NC2435	Dean, Martin	GA1650	DeFemery, Philip	MA2100
Day, Gary	AJ0150	Dean, Martin	GA2000	Deffner, David	CA0150
Day, Geoff	FL0500	Dean, Michael	CA5030	Deffner, David	CA0840
Day, Greg	SC1080	Dean, Michael	OK0650	DeFoor, Cynthia	GA2300
Day, James G.	NJ0175	Dean, Myron	KY1000	DeFoor, Keith	GA2300
Day, James M.	NJ0175	Dean, Roger A.	PA3250	DeFord, Ruth	NY0600
Day, John	KY0600	Dean, Ronnie	IL1750	DeFord, Ruth	NY0625
Day, Mary	IA0100	Dean, Sally	CA3460	DeForest, Eric P.	IN0500
Day, Maxon	WI1150	Dean, Suzanne B.	MA0260	Deforest, June D.	IN1750
Day, Melanie	VA1600	Dean, Terry Lynn	IN0800	DeFrain, Debbie	NE0500
Day, Michael	NC1550	Dean-Gates, Elizabeth	RI0300	DeGarmeaux, Mark	MN0200
Day, Susan	WI0840	Deane, Alison	NY0550	Degnan-Boonin, Kristin	PA3700
Day, Thomas Charles	RI0250	Deane, Allison	NY0600	Degooyer, Suzan	FL1300
Day, Timothy	CA4150	Deane, Christopher	TX3420	DeGoti, Mark D.	AL0200
Day-Javkhlan, Alicia	DC0170	Deane, Richard	GA2100	DeGraffenreid, George	CA0830
Day-O'Connell, Jeremy	IL1350	Deane, Richard	GA0750	DeGreg, Philip A.	OH2200
Day-O'Connell, Sarah K.	IL1350	DeAngelo, Brian	NY4460	DeGreiff-Beisser, Andrea	WI1150
Daya, Shanti Rajaratnam	WI0200	Dearborn, Keith	OH0300	DeGroff, Jason	CT0700
Dazia, Mitzuki	OR0500	Dearden, Jennifer	PA0100	DeGruchy, Katherine	OH2500
De Aeth, Ross	KY1350	Dearden, Katherine Norman	ND0500	Deguchi, Tomoko	SC1200
De Barros, Paul	WA0800	Deardorf, Chuck	WA0200	DeHaan, John D.	MN1623
De Boeck, Garry	AA0050	Deardorf, Glen	CA3520	DeHaan, Pam	IA1200
De Burgh, Susan	AB0210	Dearie, Megan	LA0800	DeHaan, Pam	IA0500
De Castro, Margaret	AI0150	Dearing, James C.	PA1600	DeHaan, Sue	IA1200
De Castro, Paul	CA0830	Dearing, Kristi Jo	PA1600	DeHart, Justin	CA0960
De Chambrier, Jan	TX2150	Dearing, Steven	AG0550	Dehaven, Frederic	MI1750
De Clercq, Trevor O.	NY1800	Dearman, John	CA1750	Dehning, Margaret	CA0960
De Dobay, Thomas	CA0950	Dearman, John	CA0835	DeHoog, David	FL1100
De Francisco, Martha	AI0150	Dearth, Christopher	OH1400	DeHoogh-Kliewer, David	SD0580
De Freitas, Simon Marc	AA0020	D'earth, John E.	VA1550	Deibel, Geoffrey	KS1450
De Fremery, Phillip	MA1100	Dease, Michael	MI1400	Deichert, Lynn	MN0300
De Fremery, Phillip	MA1350	De'Ath, Leslie	AG0600	Deiderichs, Patty	MN1300
de Ghize, Susan K.	TX3515	Deaton, Tony	TN0850	Deighton, Timothy	PA2750
de Graaf, Melissa J.	FL1900	Deatrick, Linda	MI1950	Deisler, Ann	NY1400
De Jaager, Alfred R.	WV0600	Deats, Carol	KS1050	Deitz, Kevin	OR0050
De Jager, Ron	AJ0030	Deaver, John	OH2200	Deitz, Kevin	OR1300
De La Barrera, Carlos	MI0900	Deaver, Stuart T.	OK1450	DeJaynes, Luke	IL1050
De La Bretonne, Beverly	TX0100	Deaver, Susan E.	NY3790	DeJesus, Ron	MI2100
De La Garza, Luis	TX3527	Deaver, Susan E.	NY2105	DeJong, Brigid	CA0810
De La Garza, Rene	RI0300	Deaville, James	AG0100	DeJong, Diane	MN1620
De La Torre, Javier	PR0150	Deaville, James A.	AG0200	DeJong-Pombo, Theresa	CA3350
De La Vega, Anne M.	CA3500	DeBacco, Maria	TN1680	DeJongh, Katherine	OH0600
De Launay, Erin	MO1810	DeBakcsy, Erin	CA4150	DeJournett, William	MS0700
De Leo, Joseph A.	NY2750	DeBenedetto, Patricia	CA1860	Dekaney, Elisa M.	NY4150
De Leon, Tagumpay	CA5040	Debes, Edward	PA3710	Dekaney, Joshua A.	NY4150
De L'Etoile, Shannon K.	FL1900	Debes, Pier	IL1800	Dekker, Gretchen	PA3710
De Los Santos, Carmelo	NM0450	Debly, Patricia	AG0050	Dekker, Steve	MO1810
De Lucas, Marina	PR0115	DeBoer, Angela	TN1100	Del Aguila, Miguel	CA5360
De Lyser, David M.	OR1100	DeBoer, Jack	MI0900	Del Castillo, Jose Francisco	PR0115
De Marchi, Ray	MO2000	DeBoer, James	MI1050	Del Cid, Sandra	FL1550
De Mare, Anthony J.	NY2750	DeBoer, Katharine	NV0100	del Grazia, Nicolas M.	AR0200
De Margerie, Monique	AI0190	DeBoer, Paul	NY1700	Del Monte, Adam	CA5300
De Medicis, Francois	AI0200	DeBolt, David	OH1100	Del Nero, Paul	MA0260
De Melo, Dorvalino	AI0220	DeBord, Kathryn	VA1350	Del Russo, Catherine	CA3600
De More, Christine	CA5300	DeBow, Faith	TX3175	Del Russo, Catherine	CA3300
De Moura Castro, Luiz	CT0650	Debow, Faith	TX3350	Del Santo, Jean	MN1623
de Murga, Manuel	FL1750	DeBruyn, Michelle Murphy	GA0550	Del Tredici, David	NY0550
De Pasquale, Joseph	PA0850	Debus, Christine	TX3530	Del Tredici, David	NY0600
De Pasquale, Lawrence	NJ1050	Debus, David	TX3530	Del Vecchio, Peter H.	VA1850
De Paula, Isidoro	FL1550	DeCandia, Arthur J.	MA0280	Delache-Feldman, Pascale	MA1175
De Puit, Gerald	MI2100	DeCaumette, Patrick	PA3330	DeLamater, Elizabeth L.	AZ0490
de Quadros, Andre F.	MA0400	DeCesare, Mona	CA3600	DeLamater, Elizabeth	OH2600
De Ratmiroff, Marina	NC2440	Decesare, Mona Wu	CA3100	Deland, Neil	AG0300
De Ritis, Anthony	MA1450	Dechaine, Nichole P.	CA4410	DeLand, Robert	IL3450
De Silva, Preethi	CA1050	Dechaine, Nichole	CA5550	Delaney, Carrie Ann	VA0450
De Silva, Rohan	NY1900	DeChellis, Dan	PA2450	Delaney, Douglas	CA1150
De Siro, David	NY1400	Decima, Terry	MA1400	Delaney, Jack	TX2400
De Sousa, Beth Ann	AG0600	Deck, Warren	CO0900	Delannoy Pizzini, Jose R.	PR0115
De Souza, Jordan	AI0150	Decker, Bradley	IL0800	DeLaO, Armalyn	CA0845
De Souza, Michele	WI1150	Decker, Charles	TN1450	Delaplain, Theresa	AR0700
De Stefano, Reno	AI0200	Decker, Douglas	MI1150	Delaplane, Marjorie	IL2750
De Toledo, Rubim	AA0050	Decker, Greg	OH0300	DeLaRosa, Lou	CA5510
De Val, Dorothy	AG0650	Decker, James	TX3200	DeLaurenti, Christopher	WA0200
De Vault, Christine	PA1150	Decker, Jeffrey C.	VA1550	DeLaurentis, Amber	VT0450
De Villiers, Liesl-Ann	TX3420	Decker, Michael	MD0850	DeLavan, Bill	TX3527
De Wetter-Smith, Brooks	NC2410	Decker, Pamela A.	AZ0500	Delay, Jeffrey S.	IL0650
Deacon-Joyner, David	WA0650	Decker, Todd R.	MO1900	Delbeau, Marie-Christine	DE0150
Deadman, Alison Patricia	TN0500	Decker, Van A.	CA2300	DelBello, Nicolas	NY4460
Deadman, Carey	IL0720	Declue, Gary L.	IL1245	Delcamp, Robert	TN1800
Deadman, Randall	IL0850	Decock, Murray	NY0650	DelDonna, Anthony R.	DC0075
Deagan, Gail	IN1300	DeCoro, Helena	CA1520	DeLeon, Dorien	OR0400
Deahl, Lora	TX3200	Decorsey, James H.	WI0350	Deleury, Nadine	MI1750
Deakin, Paul	TN1850	Decorso, Theodore	FL2050	Delevoryas, Sarah	CO0150
Deakins, Mark	KY0650	Decuir, Anthony	LA0300	Delfante, Ernest	CA1900
Deal, John J.	NC2430	Decuir, Michael	GA0150	Delgado, Derek G.	AK0100
Deal, Kerry	MA0350	Dederich-Pejovich, Susan	TX2400	Delgado, Eduardo	CA0815
Deal, W. Scott	IN0907	DeDominick, Jeanne D.	VA1000	Delgado, Jan	NM0450
DeAlbuquerque, Joan	CA0825	Dedova, Larissa	MD1010	Delgado, Kevin M.	CA4100
DeAlmeida, Cynthia K.	PA0550	Dee, John	IL3300	Delgado-Pelton, Celeste	CO0600
DeAlmeida, Saulo	KY0400	Deemer, Geoffrey	PA1550	DelGiorno, Nichol	IL1100
DeAmbrose, Marci Malone	NE0200	Deemer, Geoffrey A.	PA1300	Delin, Diane	IL0720
Dean, Alex	AG0450	Deemer, Robert	NY3725	DeLio, Thomas	MD1010
Dean, Allan	CT0850	Dees, David	TX3200	DeLise, Louis	PA2700
Dean, Brandon	MN0750	Dees, Jennifer	TX3200	DeLise, Louis Anthony	PA3250
Dean, Curtis	NC1150	Dees, Pamela Youngdahl	MO1250	Dell Aquila, Paul	KY1500
Dean, Jay L.	MS0750	Deeter, Alissa Walters	NC2420	Dell, Charlene	OK1350
Dean, Julie	TX3000	Deeter, Constance	CA2800	Dell, Craig	WA0600
Dean, Kevin	AI0150	Deeter, Gary	CA1850	Dell, Kay	CA0835
Dean, Lynn	UT0150	DeFade, Eric	WV0800	Dellal, Pamela	MA0350

Name	Code	Name	Code	Name	Code
Dell'Antonio, Andrew	TX3510	Denman, Matt	OK1200	Detwiler, Gwen	OH2200
Dello Joio, Justin N.	NY2750	Denman, Megan A.	OH2150	Deubner, Brett D.	PA3250
Delmore, Jack	CO0225	Denmon, Alan	GA2300	Deuson, Nicolas	GA0050
Deloach, Doris	TX0300	Dennard, Kenwood	MA0260	Deutsch, Herbert A.	NY1600
Deloney, Rick	VA0600	Dennee, Peter D.	WI0250	Deutsch, Jeff	IL0850
DeLong, Kenneth	AA0150	Dennehy, Martin J.	MA0260	Deutsch, Margery	WI0825
DeLong, Noah	TN1150	Dennewitz, John	RI0102	DeVan, William	AL0300
Delony, Willis	LA0200	Dennewitz, John K.	RI0101	DeVaney, Camille	NC2435
Delore, Deanna	CA0100	Dennihan, James	MN1300	DeVaney, Fred	IL1500
Delorenzo, Lisa	NJ0800	Dennihan, James	MN0350	Devaney, Johanna C.	OH1850
Delos, Michael	WA0200	Dennis, David M.	TN1660	DeVaron, Alexander	PA3200
Delos, Michael	WA1000	Dennis, Jeannine M.	CA0850	deVaron, Alexander	PA3250
Delp, Roy	FL0850	Dennis, Paul A.	MA2000	DeVasto, David	IL0850
Delphin, Wilfred	LA0900	Dennis, Sandra	MA1350	Deveau, David	MA1200
Delphin, Wilfred	IL2900	Dennis, Susan	IL0850	DeVeaux, Scott K.	VA1550
Delpriora, Mark	NY2150	Dennis, Susan	IL1085	DeVenney, David P.	PA3600
Delto, Byron	CA1960	Dennis, Thomas A.	MI1700	Devens, Richard	NY5000
Delto, Clare E.	CA1960	Dennison, Jessica	GA0850	Devereaux, Deborah	NY2550
Delto, Clare	CA4850	Denny, Michael	OR1050	Devereaux, Kent	WA0200
DeLuca, Laura	WA0200	Denny, Mike	OR0350	DeVilbiss, Gloria	IA1390
DeLuca, Mike	CO0275	Denson, Keith	NC0860	Deville, Mary	LA0550
DeLuccia, Norma	NY2950	Denson, Parker	AL0300	Devillier, Danny S.	LA0760
DeLuna, Russ	CA4150	Dent, Cedric	TN1100	Devine, Dave	CO0830
Delvin, Robert	IL1200	Dent, Geoffrey	CA2800	Devine, David	CO0550
DeMaio Caprilli, Barbara J.	OK1330	Dent, Karl D.	TX3200	Devine, George M.	RI0300
DeMarco, Sherrill	AA0020	Denton, Damon	GA2100	Devine, Jeff S.	CA0100
DeMare, Anthony	NY2150	Denton, David B.	PA1200	Devine, Timothy	CA1250
Demaree, Rebekah	WI0840	Denton, Kristine West	PA1200	Deviney, Christopher	PA3250
Demaree, Robert K.	WI0840	Denton, Robert	GA0050	Deviney, Christopher	PA0850
DeMarinis, Paul	MO1950	Denza, William M.	OH0500	Devito, Albert	AI0200
Demarinis, Paul	MO1900	DeOgburn, Scott	MA0260	Devitt, Matthew	MT0175
DeMaris, Brian	NY1800	Depalle, Philippe	AI0150	Devlin, Michelle P.	VA1100
Demaris, Mary Kay	MN1500	DePaolo, Gary	WY0050	Devlin, Scott	FL2050
Demars, James R.	AZ0100	DePasquale, Charles	PA1550	Devol, Luana	NV0050
DeMarsh, Joe	MI0500	Deppe, Scott M.	TX1400	DeVoll, James	MN0750
DeMartino, Louis	OR1050	DePreist, James	NY1900	Devonish, Jay	AG0130
Demas, John	FL2050	DePue, Wallace E.	OH0300	Devore, Richard O.	OH1100
Demas, John	FL0930	DeQuattro, Anthony	CT0250	DeVries, Anne	NE0250
DeMattia, Alan	OH0600	DeQuattro, Anthony	CT0550	Devroye, Anthony	IL2200
Dembar, Braham	IN1100	DeQuattro, Michael	RI0200	Devuyst, Russell	AI0150
Dembski, Stephen	WI0815	Der Hohannesian, Seta	MA2150	Dewater, Jason	NE0610
DeMent, Melanie	DE0150	D'Ercole, Kendra	AZ0470	Dewey, Cynthia	UT0300
Demers, Isabelle	TX0300	D'Ercole, Patricia	WI0850	Dewey, Glenn A.	VA0450
Demers, Joanna	CA5300	Derechailo, Melissa	NE0700	Dewey, Kevin	MI0950
Demers, Paul	PA3250	Derfler, Brandon	UT0400	DeWire, James	MD0350
DeMers, Peggy	TX2250	Derham, Billie	MO1830	DeWitt, Debora	MI0850
DeMicco, Mike	NY4450	DerHovsepian, Joan	TX2150	DeWitt, Donald	NY1250
DeMichele, Anna	CA0859	Dering, James	TX0850	DeWitt, Dortha	IL0100
Demilo, Brad	NY0050	Derix, Amye	TX0850	DeWitt, Mark F.	LA0760
DeMilo, Bradford	NY2550	Dermody, Joseph	NY0850	DeWitt, Timothy L.	WV0050
DeMio, Elizabeth	OH0600	DeRoche, Brad	MI1850	Dexter Sawyer, Annetta	DC0250
DeMio, Mark	OH1100	DeRoche, Brad	MI0400	Dexter, Jonathan G.	TX2960
DeMio, Mark	OH0650	DeRoche, Brad	MI0550	Dexter, Mary	IL1090
DeMio, Mark	OH0600	DeRoche, Julie R.	IL0750	Dexter-Schabow, Nancy	WI0050
Demitry, E. Hope	NJ0175	Derome, Denys	AI0150	Deyo, Paul	TN1400
Demkee, Ronald	PA2450	DeRosa, Julia	MI1800	DeYoung, Tim	MI0350
Demkee, Ronald	PA2550	DeRosa, Richard J.	TX3420	DeYoung, William	IL2775
Demler, James R.	MA0400	DeRosa, Richard	NY2150	DeZeeuw, Anne Marie	KY1500
Demme, Elizabeth	ND0250	DeRousse, Cathy	LA0050	D'Haiti, Maxine	AZ0150
Demmert, Wade C.	WA0600	Derrickson, Keith W.	MD0850	Dharamraj, Fabrice B.	NC2500
Demmond, Edward C.	CA3100	Derry, Lisa	ID0070	Di Bacco, Giuliano	IN0900
DeMol, Karen	IA0500	Derthick, Thomas	CA5350	Di Bella, Karin	AG0050
Demorest, Steven M.	WA1050	Derthick, Thomas	CA0840	Di Costanzo, John	NY3705
Demos, Nickitas J.	GA0150	Derthick, Tom	CA0150	Di Fiore, Linda	TX3420
DeMotta, David	NY0625	Derthick, Tom	CA4300	Di Ghent, Rita	AG0650
Dempf, Linda	NJ0175	DeRusha, Stanley	IN0250	Di Gioia, Robert	AG0130
Dempsey, Harry J.	MI0650	Desai, Nayantara	CO0830	Di Grazia, Donna M.	CA3650
Dempsey, John D.	RI0300	DeSalvo, Nancy J.	PA3650	Di Novo, Nancy	AB0100
Dempsey, Kevin	AG0200	DeSano, James	OH1700	Di Salvio, Ron	MI1150
Dempsey, O. S.	AL0500	DeSanto, Donn	IL0600	Di Sanza, Anthony E.	WI0815
Dempsey, Paul E.	WV0400	DeSanto, Jennifer	PA3560	Di Tomaso, Nick	AI0200
Dempster, Loren	NY5000	DeSanto, William	PA3560	Di Vittorio, Salvatore	NY0050
Dempster, Stuart R.	WA1050	Desby, Neal	CA5300	Diab, Mary Beth	IL3370
Demsey, David	NJ1400	DesChamps, Elise	OH0350	DiAdamo, Richard	PA3580
Demsey, Karen B.	NJ1400	Deschenes, Michel	AE0050	Dial, Frances	NY2400
Demske, Hilary	UT0325	Deschenes, Michel	AE0100	Dial, Garry	NY2150
DeMull, Mark	MI1850	Desgagne, Alain	AI0150	Diallo, YaYa	KY0250
DeNardo, Gregory F.	IL3300	Desgrange, Richard	FL0150	Diamond, Beverley	AD0050
DenBeste, LeaAnne	OR0050	DeSimone, Robert A.	TX3510	Diamond, Brad	FL2000
Denbow, Anne	SC0650	DeSiro, Lisa	MA0850	Diamond, David	IN0400
Denby, Steven	AC0100	Desjardins, Jacques	CA4150	Diamond, Douglas	MN0050
Deneff, Peter	CA1520	Desmarais, Gail	AI0050	Diamond, Jody	NH0100
Denenberg, Peter	NY3785	Desmarais, Gail	AI0200	Diamond, Louise	AI0150
Deng, Lu	OK1330	Desmond, Clinton J.	SD0200	Diamond, Shirley A.	WA1100
Denham, Ellen Louise	IN0400	Desmond, Mary Ellen	PA3330	Diamond, Tom	AG0300
Denham, Robert	CA0350	Desmond, Robert	OH0300	Diaz Torres, Jorge	PR0115
DeNicola, Alan	VT0200	DeSpain, Geoff	AZ0300	Diaz, Andres	TX2400
Denike, Allan	AJ0100	Despres, Jacques C.	AA0100	Diaz, Ernesto	MA0260
Denis, Andrea	TX0600	Desroches, Monique	AI0200	Diaz, Frank M.	OR1050
Denis, Andrea	TX1350	Desrosiers, Cecile	AG0200	Diaz, Javier	NY2250
Denis, Kimberley	AA0050	Dessen, Michael J.	CA5020	Diaz, Javier	CT0600
Denis, Marc	AI0150	DeStefano, Dominic	KY1500	Diaz, Justino	PR0115
Denis, Marc	AI0200	Dethlefson, James	CA0650	Diaz, Manuel	GA0550
Denis, Marc	AI0210	Dethlefson, John	CA0270	Diaz, Oscar	TX2960
Denisch, Beth	MA0260	Dettbarn-Slaughter, Vivian Robles	OH2275	Diaz, Pedro	NY3790
Denison, Maria Fenty	FL1900	Dettinger, Mary Joyce	OH1330	Diaz, Raymond	NY3785
Denison, Mark	OR1010	Dettwiler, Peggy	PA2150	Diaz, Rebekah	FL0700
Denison, William R.	AL1050	DeTurk, Mark	NH0350	Diaz, Reuben	CA1280
Denk, Jeremy	NY0150	Detweiler, Bruce	OK0150	Diaz, Roberto	PA0850
Denman, James L.	OR1300	Detweiler, Greg J.	KY0900	Diaz-Cassou, Isabel	NY2750

Diazmunoz, Eduardo	IL3300	DiFranco, Paul	VA1350	DiPippo, Angelo	NY1275
Dibari, Keriann K.	NJ0800	DiFusco, Salvatore	MA0260	Dippre, Keith	NC1350
Dibble, Benjamin	PA3250	Diggory, Edith	MI1750	Dircksen, Eric	DC0010
DiBella, Donna J.	WI0350	Diggs, David	PA2450	Dircksen, Eric	DC0100
DiBiase, Allan	NH0250	Diggs, David B.	PA1950	Dirks, Jelena M.	IL0750
DiBlasio, Denis	NJ1050	DiGiacobbe, David	NJ0175	Dirks, Karen	IL0750
DiBlassio, Brian	MI2120	DiGiallonardo, Richard L.	IN0150	Dirksen, Dale B. H.	AJ0030
Dibley, Charles	IA1200	Digman, Gary	CA4460	Dirlam, Richard	MN0350
Dibley, Charles	IA0500	Dikeman, Philip	TN1850	Dirmeier, Kristen	MA0950
Dibner, Steven	CA4150	Dikener, Solen	WV0400	Dirst, Matthew	TX3400
Dibonaventura, Anthony	MA0400	DiLauro, Ron	AI0150	DiSanti, Theodore A.	PA3000
DiBucci, Michelle	NY1900	DiLauro, Ronald	AI0200	Dishman, Nathan	VA1550
DiCamillo, Matthew	NC0750	Dileo, Cheryl L.	PA3250	DiSimone, Lorraine	TN1710
Dicarlo, Tom V.	PA1850	Dill, Charles	WI0815	Dismore, Roger	TX0370
Dicciani, Marc	PA3330	Dill, Jane	SC1080	Dismukes, Andrea J.	TN0850
DiCecco, Enrico	NY2150	Dill, John	TX1775	Disney, Dale	TN0900
DiCello, Anthony J.	OH0150	Dill, Patrick	LA0550	Dissmore, Larry	MO0400
DiCenso, Daniel J.	MA0700	Dillahey, Samuel J.	SC0300	Dissmore, Randy L.	WI0835
DiCenso, David	MA0260	Dillard, Chuck	TX3510	Distefano, Donna	MD0610
DiCesare, John	OH1100	Dillard, David A.	IL2900	Distefano, Donna	MD0170
DiChiacchio, Josh	CA1760	Dillard, Pamela	GA1900	Dithrich, William	CA4460
DiChiacchio, Joshua	CA3250	Dillard, Royzell L.	VA0500	Ditiberio, Lisa	MO0650
DiChiera, David	MI2200	Dillenbeck, Denise	WA0050	Ditmer, Nancy	OH0700
DiCioccio, Justin	NY2150	Dillenger, Robert	CA2775	Ditto, Charles J.	TX3175
Dick, Robert	NY2750	Diller, Alisa	OH0250	Ditto, John A.	MO1810
Dickau, David C.	MN1000	Dilling, Rick	NC0050	Divers, Timothy	CA3300
Dicke, Ian	CA5040	Dillingham, David	FL0930	Divis, Judy	NE0610
Dicke, Ian	CA5040	Dillon, Cheryl	MA1400	Dix, Ted	MD0520
Dickens, Pierce	GA0950	Dillon, Christopher	MD0850	Dix, Trevor	AI0150
Dickens, Pierce	GA0400	Dillon, Emma	PA3350	Dixon, Edward E.	WA1300
Dickensheets, Janice	CO0950	Dillon, Jake R.	IL1350	Dixon, Gail S.	AG0500
Dickenson, Andrew	MD0175	Dillon, James	MN1623	Dixon, Howard	TN0800
Dickenson, Stephanie	TN0100	Dillon, Lawrence M.	NC1650	Dixon, Joan DeVee	MD0350
Dicker, Judith	IL1150	Dillon, Nathan	CA0200	Dixon, Julian	CA0840
Dicker, Michael H.	IL1150	Dillon, Rhonda	CA1750	Dixon, Kara	AC0050
Dickerson, Randy C.	WI0803	Dillon, Rhonda	CA0859	Dixon, Nellie	IL1200
Dickerson, Roger	LA0720	Dillon, Robert	IL1615	Dixon, Patricia	NC2500
Dickerson, Shane	AL0200	Dills, Marcia	NC0930	Dixon, Paul	FL1650
Dickert, Lewis H.	SC1200	Dilthey, Michael R.	MA2250	Dixon, Rich	UT0190
Dickey, Christopher J.	WA1150	Dilthey, Michael R.	MA1185	Dixon, Scott	OH0600
Dickey, Marc R.	CA0815	Diltz, Judy	TX1700	Dixon, Scott	OH0650
Dickey, Nathaniel H.	MN0600	DiLutis, Robert	MD1010	Dixon, Scott	OH1700
Dickey, Thomas Taylor	IA0250	DiLutis, Robert A.	LA0200	Dixon, Timothy D.	PA2300
Dickey, Timothy J.	OH2000	Dilworth, Gary	CA0840	Dixon, Virginia	IL0850
Dickinson, Christian M.	PA1600	Dilworth, Helen J.	CA1020	Dixon, Walter	NY0646
Dickinson, Debra	TX2150	Dilworth, Rollo A.	PA3250	DjeDje, Jacqueline Cogdell	CA5031
Dickinson, Marci	IN1010	Dimaras, Charis	NY1800	Djokic, Philippe	AF0100
Dickinson, Paul J.	AR0850	DiMartino, Gabriel V.	NY4150	Do, Bang Lang	IA1450
Dickinson, Stefanie C.	AR0850	DiMartino, Vincent	KY1450	Do, Bang Lang	IA0450
Dickman, Marcus	FL1950	DiMedio, Annette	PA3330	Doak, Bridget A.	MN0050
Dickow, Robert H.	ID0250	DiMeo, Mike J.	NY4400	Doan, Cheryl	AZ0400
Dickson, Adrienne	NE0720	Dimick, Glen	IN0800	Doan, Gerald R.	OH2200
Dickson, Adrienne C.	NE0150	Dimick, Glen	IN0907	Doan, Jerry D.	AZ0100
Dickson, Douglas R.	CT0250	Dimick, Glen M.	IN1650	Doan, John	OR1250
Dickson, Douglas	CT0850	Dimitrov, Georges	AI0070	Doan, John	OR1300
Dickson, Robert	GA1050	Dimitrov, Georges	AI0200	Doane, Christopher	KY1500
Dickstein, Marcia	CA5550	Dimiziani, Sylvia	NY4320	Doane, Steven	NY1100
Dickstein, Marcia	CA0825	Dimmick, Penny	IN0250	Dobbins, Brian	OK1350
DiCosimo, William J.	NY4150	Dimmock, Herb R.	MD0475	Dobbins, Evan	NY2500
Dicterow, Glenn	NY1900	Dimmock, Megan	MD0175	Dobbins, Francis	AI0200
Dicterow, Glenn	NY2150	Dimock, Nancy	CT0600	Dobbins, Lori E.	NH0350
DiCuirci, Michael	OH0950	Dimoff, Maximilian	OH0600	Dobbins, Sean	MI1750
DiCuirci, Michael P.	OH0450	Dimond, Raymond R.	AR0300	Dobbins, Sean	MI2200
Diddle, Laura D.	SD0550	Dimond, Theresa	CA6000	Dobbins, Sean	MI0500
Diden, Benjamin	GA0900	Dimond, Theresa	CA0859	Dobbins, William	NY1100
Didi, Rani	CA5000	Dimond, Theresa A.	CA3650	Dobbis, Richard B.	NY2750
Didkovsky, Nick	NY2750	Dimond, Theresa	CA5020	Dobbs, Linda M.	WV0400
DiDonato, Alicia	MA0950	Dimow, Carl	ME0250	Dobbs, Teryl L.	WI0815
Diebold, Becky	IA0750	DiMuzio, Richard J.	MA0260	Dobbs, Wendell B.	WV0400
Dieffenbach, Larry S.	IL0840	Dina, James L.	CT0150	Dobby, Tim	AI0150
Diehl, Brian L.	ME0500	Dinda, Robin	MA0930	Dobek-Shandro, Elaine	AA0040
Diehl, Bruce P.	MA0100	Dineen, P. Murray	AG0400	Dobner, Gabriel	VA0600
Diehl, David J.	TN1600	Ding, Ian	MI2100	Dobos, Lora Gingerich	OH1850
Diehl, Richard C.	VT0100	Ding, Jian	NC2435	Dobra, William R.	AZ0470
Dieker, R. Joseph	MO0300	Ding, Monica	CO0200	Dobrea-Grindahl, Mary	OH0200
Diekhoff, Bill	SC0700	Ding, Xiaoli	KS1400	Dobreff, Kevin J.	MI0850
Diekman, Susan	OK0150	Dinger, Gregory	NY4300	Dobrian, Christopher	CA5020
Diem, Timothy W.	MN1623	Dingle, Rosetta	SC1050	Dobrinski, Kathy	OK1250
Diemer, Emma Lou	CA5060	Dingler, Diane	OH1200	Dobroski, Bernard J.	IL2250
Diepeveen, Susan	AF0120	Dingo, Matt	PA1650	Dobrotvorskaia, Ekaterina	CO0275
Dierker, John	MD0850	Dinino, Aileen	FL1310	Dobry, John T.	LA0750
Dierks, Deborah	KY1500	Dinion, Steve	HI0210	Dobrzanski, Slawomir Pawel	KS0650
Dierolf, Wallace	TX3175	Dinitz, Mark	MD0550	Dobrzelewski, Jan	PA3600
Dies, David	WI0830	Dinkins-Matthews, Patricia A.	GA0750	Dobyns, Whitney	VA0550
Dietert, Dale	TX2400	Dinnerstein, Noe	NY0630	Docenko, Gregory	NY3717
Dietrich, Johannes M.	PA1900	Dinsmore, Ann	PA1250	Dochnahl, Jesse	WI0350
Dietrich, Kurt R.	WI0700	Dion, David	CT0600	Dockendorf, Carl	AZ0460
Dietrich, Maria K.	WI0700	Dionne, Aubrie	NH0250	Dockendorf, Lyle	OR0850
Dietrich-Hallak, Christine	MA1500	Dionne, Louise M.	NY3775	Dockendorf-Boland, Janice	IA0300
Dietz, Brett William	LA0200	Dior, Jennifer	NC2420	Dockendorff, Catherine	AZ0470
Dietz, Christopher J.	OH0300	Dior, Rick	NC2420	Dockery, Darryl D.	KY1550
Dietz, Curtis	AF0050	DiOrio, Andrea R.	IL2050	Docking, Simon	AF0120
Dietz, Curtis	AF0120	DiOrio, Andrea	IL1615	Dockter, Larry	IN1050
Dietz, Diane	IL1600	DiOrio, Dominick	IN0900	Doctor, Kirsten	OH0600
Dietz, Tom	FL1550	DiPalma, Maria	IA1350	Doczi, Tom F.	NY2750
Dietz, William D.	AZ0500	DiPaolo, Daniel M.	NY2750	Dodd, Anna	GA2130
Dietzler, Judy	MN0600	DiPaolo, Stacey	OK1250	Dodd, Kit	NY2950
DiEugenio, Nicholas	NY1800	DiPiazza, Joseph	NC2430	Dodd, Susan	FL0200
Dievendorf, Matthew	DC0170	DiPinto, John	NJ0825	Dodds, Amy	WA1300
Diez, German	NY0500	DiPinto, Mark	MD0150	Dodds, Michael R.	NC1650

Name	Code	Name	Code	Name	Code
Dodge, Leanne E.	NY2750	Donnelly, Margaret	CA5355	Douvas, Elaine	NY2250
Dodge, Steve W.	OH1910	Donnelly, Molly	MD0550	Douyon, Marcaisse	FL1310
Dodson Galvan, Jennifer	CA0600	Donner, Ann	IN1050	Dove, Barry B.	MD1000
Dodson, Alan	AB0100	Donner, George	IN1050	Dove-Pellito, Glennda M.	NY3730
Dodson, Brent A.	CA4450	Donofrio, Anthony	OH1100	Dovel, Jason L.	OK0550
Dodson, Brent	IA1750	Donovick, Jeffery	FL1650	Dovel, Suzanne	OK0550
Dodson, Gordon	AL0400	Doo, Lina J.	HI0150	Dovel, Teresa	CA5355
Dodson, John	MI0050	Doody, Jeremy	AA0080	Dover, Cory	NC2420
Dodson, Lisa	MD0500	Dooley, Ellen	DC0170	Dow, David Charles	CA3000
Dodson-Webster, Rebecca	PA2150	Dooley, Gail	IA1100	Dowdy, Eugene	TX3530
Dody, Teresa	WV0800	Doolittle, Emily L.	WA0200	Dowdy, James	OH0350
Dody, Teresa D.	WV0350	Doolittle, Quenten D.	AA0150	Dower, Mary R.	PA1700
Doebler, Jeffrey S.	IN1750	Dooly, Louann	AR0730	Dower-Gold, Catherine A.	MA2100
Doebler, Lawrence A.	NY1800	Dor, George	MS0700	Dowling, Eugene	AB0150
Doepke, Kari J.	WI0200	Doran, David Stephen	KY1460	Dowling, Thomas	AG0450
Doering, James M.	VA1150	Doran, Joy	IL1200	Downes, Greg	IL1612
Doering, Susan J.	CA1860	Dorchin, Susan	FL0650	Downes, Suzanne	IL2310
Doerksen, Paul F.	PA1050	Dore, Christine	NY2105	Downey, Gwyn	IL1300
Doezema, Robert	MA0260	Dorenfeld, Jeffrey	MA0260	Downey, John W.	WI0825
Doggett, Cynthia Krenzel	IA0200	Dorey, Christine S.	OH0200	Downey, Mark	IL2650
Doggett, Thomas J.	IA0200	Dorf, Samuel N.	OH2250	Downey, Sherri	TX3530
Doheny, Anthony J.	CA4900	Dorff, Carolyn	GA1150	Downey, Wayne	CA1560
Doheny, John	LA0750	Dorff, Dan	KY1000	Downing, Andrew	AG0450
Doherty, Jean	NY1950	Dorfman, Amy	TN1850	Downing, Elizabeth A.	ME0440
Doherty, Keith	MA0260	Dorfman, Jay	MA0400	Downing, Joseph	NY4150
Doherty, Mary Lynn	IL2200	Dorgan, Paul	UT0250	Downing, Sonja Lynn	WI0350
Dohoney, Ryan	KS1350	Dorhauer, John	IL0850	Downs, Philip	AG0500
Dohr, Richard William	CA5300	Dorian, Patrick	PA1100	Doxas, Chet	AI0150
Dohrmann, Diana	NJ0550	Dorin, Ryan	NY0644	Doxas, Jim	AI0150
Doiel, Mark	CA2900	Dorman, Avner	PA1400	Doyen, Rob	MO1650
Doing, James	WI0815	Dorman, Diana	CA1650	Doyle, Alicia M.	CA0825
Doiron, Michelle E.	WA0800	Dorn, Mark	CO0150	Doyle, Brian K.	NY3780
Dokovska, Pavlina	NY2250	Dornak, Alan W.	NY4500	Doyle, James	CO0050
Dolacky, Susan	WA0860	Dornberger, Laura	NY3725	Doyle, Jennifer	MD1010
Dolan, Anastasia	MA0260	Dornenburg, John D.	CA4900	Doyle, Joseph	TN1400
Dolan, Drew	GA1150	Dornian, Kathy	AA0050	Doyle, Laurie	TX1550
Dolan, Emily I.	PA3350	Dornian, Paul	AA0050	Doyle, Melinda S.	AL1200
Dolas, Helen G.	CA0835	Doroftei, Mugnr	TX2550	Doyle, Michael	MI0850
Dolata, David	FL0700	Dorothy, Wayne F.	TX0900	Doyle, Phillip	WA0250
Dolatowski, David	AZ0510	Dorough, Aralee	TX3400	Doyle, Robert	MI0100
Dolbashian, Edward	IL1500	Dorough, Prince	IL1090	Doyle, Sean	NY3725
Dolbashian, Edward	MO1800	Dorris, Dennis	IL1890	Doyle, Timothy	GA0950
Dole, Frederick	VA1600	Dorris, Jennifer	CO0625	Doyle, Tracy A.	CO0050
Dole, Frederick	VA0250	Dorritie, Frank	CA2775	Doyle, William	CA1750
Doles, Kurt	OH0300	Dorroh, William J.	AL0800	Doyon, Pierre	AI0190
Dolezal, Darry	MO1800	Dorsa, James	CA0835	Dozier, Lamont	CA5300
Dolin, Elizabeth	AI0150	Dorsey, John F.	MI0600	Dozoretz, Brian	NY1800
Dolkas, Bridget	CA0960	Dorsey, Richard	AG0300	Draayer, Suzanne Collier	MN1700
Doll, Christopher	NJ1130	Dorsey, Richard	AG0450	Drackley, Phyllis J.	PA1250
Dollak, Haidee	NC0750	Dorsey, Rodney	MI2100	Drafall, Lynn	PA2750
Dollar, Kevin	NC0750	Dorsey, Roland W.	MD0475	Drago, Alejandro M.	ND0500
Dolloff, Lori-Anne	AG0450	Dorsey, Sam Brian	VA0950	Dragonetti, John	PA1550
Dolnik, Nata	KS0570	D'Ortenzio, Marie Michuda	IL2250	Dragonvich, James	NY2105
Dolp, Laura A.	NJ0800	Dos Santos, Adriano	NY2750	Dragovich, James	NY1600
Dolphin, Amber	WI0100	dos Santos, Silvio J.	FL1850	Dragovich, Mindy	NY1600
Dolske, Christopher C.	FL1550	Doss, Elwood	TN1720	Drake, Erwin	NY1275
Dolter, Gerald	TX3200	Doss, Laura	AL0800	Drake, James	ID0100
Domek, Richard C.	KY1450	Doss, Robert	KY0200	Drake, Jennifer	MI1150
Domencic, Joe	PA3000	Dossin, Alexandre	OR1050	Drake, Joshua F.	PA1450
Domencic, Mark L.	PA0550	Dostal, Jeffrey	MA2100	Drake, Melvyn	NY4250
Domenici, Gianna	IL0420	Dosunmu, Oyebade A.	MA2250	Drake, Michael	TX3420
Domenico, Tony	MD0450	Dotas, Charles J.	VA0600	Drake, Mike	TX0700
Domine, James	CA2700	Dotson, Danielle	DC0170	Drake, Randy	CA0825
Domingues, Cameron	CA0815	Dotson, Dennis W.	TX3510	Drake, Thomas	IL1520
Domingues, Cameron	CA3200	Dotson, Ronald	CA5510	Drane, Gregory	PA2750
Dominguez, Bob	CA3800	Doucet, Denis	AI0220	Drannon, Andrew	TN1200
Dominguez, Peter	OH1700	Doucette, Hannah	PA3550	Dransfield, Lee Ann	VA1350
Dominguez, Robert	CA5100	Douds, Nathan	PA3100	Dransite, Robert S.	NY2550
Dominguez, Robert	CA5040	Dougall, Sean	CA5300	Draper, Charles	MN0200
Dominick, Daniel L.	TX0250	Dougherty, Patrick	NY0050	Draper, Frederick	NY5000
Dominski-Sale, Christina	FL0800	Dougherty, Peggy S.	OR0175	Draper, Michelle	MO1550
Domonkos, Jason	NE0610	Dougherty, Peggy	OR0250	Draskovic, Ines	NY1250
Doms, David	MA0260	Dougherty, William P.	IA0550	Draughn, Maurice	MI2200
Domulot, Fred	FL1430	Doughty, Heather	CT0100	Draves, Tami	AZ0500
Don, Gary W.	WI0803	Doughty, Ryan	KY1550	Drayson, Susan	AA0050
Dona, Daniel	MA0400	Douglas, Bill	CO0560	Drayton, Joanne	MI1100
Donaghue, Margaret A.	FL1900	Douglas, Brent	FL0450	Drayton, Keith	MI1100
Donakowski, Carl	VA0600	Douglas, Gavin D.	NC2430	Drayton, Leslie	CA5360
Donald, Larry Scott	TX3530	Douglas, John	CA5550	Drayton, Leslie	CA4450
Donald, Scott	NJ0175	Douglas, Kenneth	IN0910	Drazek, Jan B.	CO0225
Donaldson, Cynthia	NY1400	Douglas, Madonna	AG0170	Dregalla, Herbert E.	OH2500
Donaldson, Doree	MO0400	Douglas, Peter	MN1625	Drege, Lance	OK1350
Donaldson, Frank	IL0720	Douglas, Samuel O.	SC1110	Dreger, Neil	NY1250
Donaldson, Judy	AL0300	Douglas, Susan	TX2650	Dreier, James	IL0100
Donaldson, Kathryn	PA1350	Douglas, Thomas W.	PA0550	Dreier, James	IA1550
Donato, Dominic	NY3785	Douglass, James B.	NC2430	Dreisbach, Paul C.	OH1000
Donato, Michel	AI0200	Douglass, Jamie	CA2420	Dreisbach, Tina Spencer	OH1000
Dondlinger, Lisa	CA3600	Douglass, Mark	MI2120	Drelles, Andrew	NY2400
Donegani, Denis	AG0400	Douglass, Mark	TN1710	Drennan, Jennifer	IL2970
Donelian, Armen	NJ1400	Douglass, Mary	NE0525	Drennen, Edward	DC0100
Donelian, Armen	NY2660	Douglass, Ronald L.	MI1100	Drennon, Eddie	DC0170
Donelson, David W.	OH1350	Douglass, Zane S.	NV0050	Dresel, Bernie	NV0050
Doneski, Sandra	MA0950	Doukhan, Lilianne	MI0250	Dresen, Steven	ID0060
Dong, Kui	NH0100	Douma, Jeffrey	CT0850	Dresher, Mary Ann	UT0400
Dong, Kun	KY1000	Dousa, Dominic	TX3520	Dresher, Mary Ann	UT0250
Donnell, Cynthia S.	VA1600	Douthit, James Russell	NY2650	Dressen, Dan F.	MN1450
Donnell, Julie	IN0905	Douthit, LaTika	NC2700	Dresser, Bruce	OR0950
Donnellan, Grant	WA1250	Douthit, Pat	NC1600	Dresser, Mark	CA5050
Donnelly, Chris	AG0450	Doutt, Kathleen C.	PA1550	Dressler, Jane	OH1100
Donnelly, Karen	AG0400	Douvas, Elaine	NY1900	Dressler, John C.	KY0950

Alphabetical Listing of Faculty

Name	Code	Name	Code	Name	Code
Drew, John	FL0850	Dubyk, Jerrold	AA0100	Duncan, Craig T.	TN1800
Drewek, Doug	KY0100	Duce, Geoffrey	IN0910	Duncan, David	OK0150
Drewek, Douglas Alexand	KY0450	Duchak, Roberta	IL0720	Duncan, Ellen	MI1300
Drewes, William	NY2750	Duchan, Joshua S.	MI2200	Duncan, Norah	MI2200
Drews, Michael R.	IN0907	Ducharme, Jay	MA2100	Duncan, Preston	MN0040
Drews, Richard	IL2250	Ducharme, Jerome	AI0150	Duncan, Steven	IL3200
Drews, Teresa	WI1150	Ducharme, Karen	MA2100	Duncan, Steven	IL1085
Drexler, Darcy	WI0825	Ducharme, Michel	AI0190	Duncan, Warren L.	AL1100
Drexler, Richard	FL1800	Duchesneau, Michel	AI0200	Dundas, Robert B.	FL0700
Dreyfoos, Dale	AZ0100	Duchi, Joseph J.	OH1850	Dundjerski, Petar	AA0020
Dreyfus, Karen	NY2250	Duchow, Ann L.	IA0940	Dundjerski, Petar	AA0100
Dreyfus, Karen	NY1900	Duckett, Alfred	OK0150	Dunegan, Martha	WI0100
Dreyfus, Karen	NY2150	Duckett, Linda B.	MN1000	Dunevant, David L.	KY1000
Driankova, Ivanka	NY2650	Duckles, Andrew	CA0825	Dungan, Doris	AG0170
Driedger-Klassen, Robyn	AB0200	Duckles, Lee	AB0200	Dunham, Deborah	TX2250
Dries, Eric	CA0815	Duckworth, James	NC0350	Dunham, James	TX2150
Driessen, Peter	AB0150	Duckworth, William	PA0350	Dunham, Robert W.	GA0950
Drifmeyer, Fred	MA0600	Duda, Cynthia M.	MI0100	Dunker, Amy	IA0250
Drifmeyer, Kelly B.	NY3780	Duda, Theodor	OH0700	Dunlap, Larry	CA2950
Driggers, Dawn	SC0900	Dudack, Mark	OH2150	Dunlap, Phil	MO1830
Driggers, Doris	CA2400	Dudack, Matthew J.	OH1650	Dunlap, Phillip	MO1950
Drill, Daniel	AL1170	Dudas, Libor	MA1175	Dunlop, John	NH0100
Drillinger, David	IL1500	Dudgeon, Ralph	NY0650	Dunn, Alexander	AB0210
Drion, Yoka	CA5510	Dudgeon, Ralph T.	NY3720	Dunn, Alexander	AB0150
Drion, Yoka	CA2975	Dudley, Anna C.	CA4200	Dunn, Andrew	AI0150
Driscoll, Katherine	FL1300	Dudley, Bruce J.	TN1850	Dunn, Cherry W.	MS0550
Driscoll, Kermit	NY3785	Dudley, Bruce	TN0100	Dunn, Christopher	MS0570
Driscoll, Matthew	IA0400	Dudley, Christopher	MD1010	Dunn, J. Michael	CO0800
Driscoll, Matthew	IA0200	Dudley, Sandra	TN0100	Dunn, John	LA0550
Driscoll, Nick	PA3700	Dudley, Shannon	WA1050	Dunn, Kimberly	NC0200
Driscoll, Robert	NC1650	Dudley, Sherwood	CA5070	Dunn, Lisa	OK0500
Driscoll, Robin	WV0600	Dudt, Jay	PA1050	Dunn, Mignon	NY2150
Driskell, Daniel	AL1300	Dueck, Jocelyn B.	NY2250	Dunn, Mignon	NY0500
Driskill, Kristina	CA0960	Duehlmeier, Susan	UT0250	Dunn, Neil	KS0650
Droba, Romalee	MN1250	Dueitt, David P.	MS0420	Dunn, Phyllis M.	CA4410
Drobnak, Kenneth Paul	SD0500	Dueker, Hollie	TN0050	Dunn, Robert	IA0700
Droe, Kevin	IA1600	Duenas, David	CA4425	Dunn, Robert	UT0050
Droke, Marilyn	MO0200	Duensing, Craig	SC0620	Dunn, Ron	CA1550
Dronkers, Marcelle	CA3270	Duensing, Dorothy	MI2200	Dunn, Stephen J.	AZ0450
Drontle, Lisa	MN0350	Duensing, Jane	SC0620	Dunn, Susan L.	TX2150
Dropkin, Mary	CA0845	Duerden, Darren	HI0050	Dunn, Susan	NC0600
Dropkin, Mary C.	CA3650	Duerden, Jennifer	HI0050	Dunn-Prosser, Barbara	AG0500
Dropkin, Mary	CA5150	Duerksen, George L.	KS1350	Dunnavant, Jessica Guinn	TN1100
Drosinos, David	WV0550	Duerksen, Marva G.	OR1300	Dunne, Matthew R.	TX3530
Drost, Michael	MI0900	Duesing, Dale L.	WI0350	Dunnell, Rebecca	MO0950
Droste, Douglas	OK0800	Dufault, Jenny E.	MN1120	Dunnick, Kim	NY1800
Droste, Paul E.	OH1850	Duff, Jim	AD0050	Dunnigan, Patrick	FL0850
Drott, Eric	TX3510	Duff, John A.	FL1850	Dunphy, Janice	OH2050
Drown, Steve	ME0340	Duff, Robert P.	NH0100	Dunsby, Jonathan	NY1100
Druck, Susan S.	MN0050	Duffer, Rodger	CA3800	Dunsmore, Douglas	AD0050
Druck, William	PA3710	Duffin, Greg	UT0350	Dunsmore, Matthew	NE0610
Drucker, Eugene	NY0150	Duffin, Ross	OH0400	Dunson, Judith	NC1300
Drucker, Eugene S.	NY3790	Dufford, Gregory	CO0550	Dunston, Douglas E.	NM0350
Drucker, Naomi	NY1600	Duffy, Kathryn Ann Pohlmann	IA0650	Dunston, Michael	VA1700
Druckman, Daniel	NY1900	Duffy, Patrick	AG0130	Dunyo, Fred	AG0450
Druckman, Joel	CA4450	Duffy, Thomas	CT0850	Dunyo, Kwasi	AG0650
Druhan, Mary Alice	TX2955	Dufour, Francine	AI0220	Dupee, Donald	SC1100
Drumheller, John	CO0800	Dufour, Mathieu T.	IL0750	Dupertuis, Jeff	CA3850
Drumm, Melissa Percy	WA0950	Dufrasne, J. Emmanuel	PR0115	Duphil, Monique	OH1700
Drummond, Barry	MA1900	Dugan, Greg	IN1850	Duplessis, Ginette	AG0450
Drummond, Billy R.	NY2750	Dugan, Gregory S.	IN0350	Dupont, Donald	NY1600
Drummond, Billy	NY1900	Dugan, Leonardo	PA1550	Dupree, Jillon Stoppels	WA0200
Drummond, Dean J.	NJ0800	Dugan, Michael D.	WI0865	DuPree, Mary	ID0250
Drummond, Evan E.	NY3717	Dugard, Freddy	NY0646	Dupuy, Kathryn D.	CO0550
Drummond, Evan	NY3725	Duggan, Ann	IL3150	Dupuy, Virginia	TX2400
Drummond, Jayne	UT0325	Duggan, Sean	NY3725	Duquaine, Kenneth	MI2120
Drummond, Ray	NY1900	Duggan, Sean B.	LA0600	Duquaine, Kenneth	MI0450
Drury, Jay	WV0750	Dugger, Clay	IL1740	Duquesnel-Malbon, Peggy	CA1425
Drury, Stephen	MA1400	Dugger, Duane A.	OH2200	Dura, Marian T.	PA1900
Drury, William	MA1400	Duhaime, Ricky	TX0250	Duran, Amy	NJ0825
Dry, Marion	MA2050	DuHamel, Ann M.	MN1620	Duran, Becca	WA0200
Du, Yun	NY3785	Duitman, Henry E.	MI0900	Duran, Sally	NC2205
Duane, Carol Rose	WV0550	Dujka, John	TX0340	Durand, Joel F.	WA1050
Duarte, Derison	NC0600	Duke, Barbara	VA1100	Durand, Marc	AG0300
Duarte, Derison	NC2410	Duke, Christopher A.	TN0550	Durand, Marc	AI0200
Dubal, David	NY2150	Duke, Richard	UT0050	Durant, David Z.	AL1300
Dubal, David	NY1900	Duke, Robert	CA1075	Durant, Doug	AZ0440
Dubberly, James	CA0850	Duke, Robert A.	TX3510	Durant, Douglas F.	MA1450
Dubberly, Stephen	TX3420	Duke-Kirkpatrick, Erika	CA0510	Duraski, Anne	GA1200
Dubbiosi, Stelio	NJ0825	Duker, Philip	DE0150	Durbin, Karen	PA2300
Dube', Francis	AI0190	Dukes, Leslie D.	CA4460	Durbin, Timothy T.	KY1500
DuBeau, Pete	NC0700	Dulaney, John	OR1250	Duree, David T.	MD0520
Dubeau, Peter C.	VA1000	Dulin, Mark C.	SC1200	Duree, David	MD0500
DuBeau, Peter	VA0250	Dumaine, Stephen	MD1010	Durham, Carol	MS0385
Dubiel, Joseph	NY0750	Dumas, Charles	NC1350	Durham, Carol	MS0100
Dubikovsky, Nadya	IN1300	Dumbauld, Benjamin	NY0625	Durham, Carol S.	MS0400
Dubnjakovic, Ana	SC1110	Dumm, Bryan	OH0600	Durham, Franklin	AZ0150
Dubnov, Shlomo	CA5050	Dumm, Bryan	OH0650	Durham, Gary	MA0400
Dubois, Chantal	AI0190	Dumm, Mary Elizabeth	MD0700	Durham, Gary D.	MA0850
Dubois, Chantal	AI0210	Dumouchel, Michael	AI0150	Durham, Justin W.	SC0400
Dubois, Laura	NJ0760	Dunafin, Cathy A.	IL2050	Durham, Kevin	TN1400
Dubois, Mark	NY3725	Dunaway, Lourdes	TN1250	Durham, Linda Eileen	VA1840
Dubois, Mark	PA2250	Dunbar, Brian	MN0620	Durham, Thomas L.	UT0050
DuBois, May	CA5500	Dunbar, Christine	WY0050	Durham-Lozaw, Susan	NC2350
DuBois, Peter	NY1100	Dunbar, Edward	SC0200	Durkee, James	WA0050
Dubois, Susan L.	TX3420	Dunbar, Geoffrey	CA3500	Durkee, Jim	WA1400
DuBois, Ted	TX3750	Dunbar, Pamela	SC0200	Durkovic, Timothy	CA2550
DuBose, E. L.	AL0210	Dunbar, Ulrike	FL1430	Durlam, Zachary D.	CA1860
Dubowchik, Rosemary	CT0450	Duncan, Andrew	OH0500	Durland, James	CA0400
DuBray, Terry E.	NY3550	Duncan, Christine	AG0450	Durnford, Jacqueline	AF0120

Alphabetical Listing of Faculty

Name	Code	Name	Code	Name	Code
Duro, David A.	OH1000	Easley, Delana	TN1720	Edgett, Bryan	PA3560
Durocher, Michael	AA0032	Easley, Tabatha	VA1600	Edgett, Bryan	PA1150
Durow, Peter J.	MO1500	East, David	MS0320	Edggett, Bryan	NJ1050
Durran, Daryl	PA2750	East, James	NY3725	Edie, Rebecca L.	IN0100
Durrani, Aahminah	TX3400	East, Mary Ann H.	VA0450	Ediger, Thomas L.	NE0500
Durrenberger, Chris	OH2450	East, Phyllis	NY3725	Edighoffer, Gary B.	WA0950
Durst, Aaron M.	WI0855	Eastep, Michael	AA0150	Edington-Hogg, Lynn	CA4100
Durst, Alan Edward	CA0810	Eastep, Michael	AA0050	Edison, Andrew	NY1450
Durst, Dean	IL2560	Easter, Timothy D.	SC0750	Edison, Noel	AG0300
Durst, Mary	CA3500	Easter, Wallace E.	VA1700	Edlina-Dubinsky, Luba	IN0900
Dusdieker, Carol E.	OH0950	Easterday, Janice	TX0100	Edman, Laura	WI0845
Dusinberre, Edward	CO0800	Eastin, Brad	CO0275	Edmonds, Carol	NC2000
Dusman, Linda J.	MD1000	Eastman, George	MA0260	Edmonds, Johnnella	VA1750
Duso, Lorraine	AR0350	Eastman, Patricia	MO1950	Edmonds, Kristin	MO0700
Duso, Lorraine C.	AR0850	Eastwood, Deb A.	KY0900	Edmonton-Boehm, Nigel	AA0050
Dusold, Patricia	TN1350	Eaton, Alice Butler	AL1160	Edmund, Carina	MN1600
Dussault, Michel J.	AI0220	Eaton, Angela S.	KY1350	Edmund, David	MN1600
Dust, Tom	AA0100	Eaton, Daniel	MN1600	Edson, Tracey D.	OR1100
Dustman, Tom	CA2550	Eaton, David D.	TX3530	Edstrom, Brent	WA1350
Dutoit, Tatiana Grecic	NM0150	Eaton, Denise	TX2250	Edward, Ruth	NH0350
Dutt, Hank	CA2950	Eaton, Rebecca M. Doran	TX3175	Edwards, Alice	IL1610
Dutton, Brent	CA4100	Eaton, Roy	NY2150	Edwards, Alison	CA0815
Dutton, David	WA1350	Eaton, Wendy	NE0160	Edwards, Bradley W.	SC1110
Dutton, Douglas	CA2600	Eaton, Wendy	NE0610	Edwards, Brent	WA1150
Dutton, John	MT0350	Eaves-Smith, Margaret	MN1450	Edwards, Carla Grace	IN0350
Dutton, Kristina	IL2750	Eban, Eli	IN0900	Edwards, Celeste	IN1310
Dutton, Lawrence	GA1300	Ebbers, Daniel	CA5350	Edwards, Constance	WV0300
Dutton, Lawrence	NY2150	Ebbers, Paul	FL0850	Edwards, Darryl	AG0450
Dutton, Lawrence	NY3790	Eben, Michael	PA0050	Edwards, Dawn	FL1550
Dutz, Brad	CA0825	Ebener, Ben	MI1400	Edwards, Denise	IL1610
Duvall, Matthew	VA1500	Eberenz, Gina	KY0250	Edwards, Eric F.	KS1450
Duvall, William	WI0825	Eberhardt, Allan	CO0275	Edwards, Geoff	IL0150
DuWors, Kerry	AC0050	Eberhardt, Terry N.	MD0850	Edwards, George H.	NY0750
Duykers, John	WA0200	Eberl, Carl	NY0642	Edwards, George L.	DC0350
Dvorak, Celeste	OK0700	Eberle, Jan	MI1400	Edwards, Huw	WA1000
Dvorak, Thomas	WI0825	Ebersold, Timothy	ME0150	Edwards, Jan	OH1850
Dvorin, David	CA0800	Ebert, Brian	CO0650	Edwards, Jason R.	IA0900
Dvorkin, Janice	TX3410	Ebert, Kevin	OH2550	Edwards, Julie	CA3950
Dvoskin, Victor	VA1600	Ebert, Shari E.	IL1330	Edwards, Julie	IN0800
Dvoskin, Victor	MD0850	Ebner, Craig	PA3250	Edwards, Karen	OH2600
Dworak, Paul E.	TX3420	Ebrecht, Ronald	CT0750	Edwards, Karin	IL3550
Dwyer, Doriot	MA0400	Ebright, Matthew	OH1850	Edwards, Kay L.	OH1450
Dwyer, Jack	OR0400	Eby, Carole	SC0200	Edwards, Lawrence	TN1680
Dwyer, Laura	FL1000	Eby, Chad	NC2430	Edwards, Leo	NY2250
Dwyer, Laura L.	FL1950	Eby, John D.	AI0050	Edwards, Linda	NM0400
Dwyer, Mac	MN1250	Eby, Kristen	IA1450	Edwards, Mahiri	MD1010
Dwyer, Peggy	AG0550	Eby, Pam	AI0050	Edwards, Malcolm V.	AA0150
Dyachkov, Yegor	AI0200	Eby, Patricia	WI0804	Edwards, Marilyn	OH0250
Dyachkov, Yegor	AI0150	Eccles, David F.	IL3450	Edwards, Matthew C.	VA1350
Dyament, Lee	MI2200	Eccles, Elizabeth	VA0500	Edwards, Matthew	MO0850
Dybdahl, Gene	OH0300	Eccleston, Colleen	AB0150	Edwards, Patricia	CA0250
Dyck, Calvin	AB0060	Echard, William	AG0100	Edwards, Patti Yvonne	SC0420
Dydnansky, Patricia	AG0050	Echols, Carol	MO0350	Edwards, Rachel	AZ0350
Dye, Keith G.	TX3200	Echols, Charles	MN1300	Edwards, Renard	PA3250
Dye, Kenneth W.	IN1700	Eckard, Kevin L.	OK1330	Edwards, Richard D.	OH2000
Dyer, Barbara	CA1750	Eckard, Steven C.	MD0520	Edwards, Ricky	DE0050
Dyer, Barbara J.	CA2800	Eckardt, Jason	NY0600	Edwards, Robert	NC2150
Dyer, Steve	AC0100	Eckardt, Jason K.	NY0500	Edwards, Ross	AG0600
Dyess, J. Wayne	TX1400	Eckelmeyer, Judith A.	OH0650	Edwards, Stacey	IN0150
Dygert, James	CT0100	Eckenrode, Bryan	NY0400	Edwards, Steven C.	LA0080
Dykema, Dan H.	AR0600	Eckenrode, Bryan	NY4460	Edwards, T. Matthew	MD0060
DyKema, Laurae	ND0100	Eckenroth, Karen	OH2050	Edwards, Timothy D.	IL0720
Dykstra, Brian	OH0700	Eckermann, Joan E.	OH2140	Edwards, Tony	TX3510
Dykstra, Crisi	MI0750	Eckert, Elizabeth	TN1850	Edwards-Henry, Jacqueline	MS0500
Dykstra, Linda	MI1050	Eckert, Elizabeth	DC0170	Eekhoff, CharLee	IA0200
Dymit, Thomas E.	IL2050	Eckert, Erika	CO0800	Eeles, Mark	AA0035
Dyotte, Claude	AI0220	Eckert, Jamie D.	MA2020	Een, Andrea	MN1450
Dzapo, Kyle J.	IL0400	Eckert, Joseph H.	TX3000	Effler, Charles E.	LA0650
Dzhuryn, Nazar V.	IL2150	Eckert, Michael	IA1550	Effron, David	IN0900
Dzhuryn, Nazar	IL0840	Eckert, Rosana C.	TX3420	Efremova, Natalia	DC0170
Dziuba, Mark	NY3760	Eckert, Stacy	IL2650	Egan, Anne Marie	IN1350
Dzubay, David	IN0900	Eckert, Stefan	IL0800	Egan, Dan	CT0900
Dzugan, Eric	PA1450	Eckert, William H.	DC0110	Egan, Jered	NY1400
Dzuik, Youlee	DC0170	Eckerty, Michael	IA1350	Egan, John B.	IN1350
Dzuris, Linda	SC0400	Eckes, Sylvia Reynolds	OH1900	Egan, Kate	AK0100
Eade, Dominique	MA1400	Eckhardt, Janet	IL2100	Egan, Lora	SD0580
Eads, Laura	AR0250	Eckhart, Michael	NJ0975	Egekvist, Deborah	NC2430
Eager, Jim	AF0120	Ecklund, George	IL1610	Egger, Cynthia	MO1010
Eagle, David	AA0150	Eckroth, Rachel	AZ0470	Eggers, Carter	MI0600
Eagle, Don J.	NC0600	Eckroth-Riley, Joan	ND0050	Eggert, Andrew	IL0550
Eagle, Keith	NC0860	Eckstein, John B.	UT0250	Eggert, John	MN0610
Eaglen, Jane	OH0200	Eckstrom, William	NY1850	Eggert, Scott H.	PA1900
Eagleson, Ian	CT0050	Edberg, C. Eric	IN0350	Eggleston, Amy	IN1650
Eakin, Kate	IL2750	Eddins, Judy	FL1500	Eggleston, Mary	VA0550
Ealum, Ernie	FL1000	Eddy, Timothy	NY1900	Eggleston, Steven	IL1200
Eanes, Edward	GA1150	Eddy, Timothy	NY2250	Egler, Steven	MI0400
Earl, Nicole	AF0050	Edel, Theodore	IL3310	Egre, Bruce	OH0600
Earl, R. Daniel	CA4460	Edelberg, Joe	CA4700	Egre, Bruce	OH0400
Earle, Diane K.	KY0800	Edelbrock, Dennis E.	VA0450	Eguchi, Akira	NY0500
Earles, Randy A.	ID0100	Edelman, David	VA1350	Ehle, Robert	CO0950
Earley, Robert W.	NJ1130	Edelstein, Andrew S.	MA0260	Ehle, Todd	TX0550
Earley, Robert	PA3250	Edelstein, Gerardo	PA2750	Ehlen, Timothy	IL3300
Earley, Robert	NJ1050	Eden, Gregg	NE0160	Ehlers, Lisa	AZ0490
Earnest, James	IN1350	Eder, Kristen	MI0050	Ehly, Ewald	MO1810
Earnest, JoAnne	PA0050	Edgar, Donna	NM0500	Ehret, Don	AA0020
Earnest, John David	WA1300	Edgar, Paul	DC0100	Ehrke, David	NV0100
Earp, Jonathan	AG0050	Edgar, Scott N.	IL1400	Ehrlich, Barry	WA0860
Earp, Lawrence	WI0815	Edge, David	OH2050	Ehrlich, Don	CA4150
Eash, William	KS0200	Edgerton, Sara A.	MO1500	Ehrlich, Janina	IL0100
Easley, David B.	OK0750	Edgett, Bryan	PA2800	Ehrlich, Martin L.	MA1000

Alphabetical Listing of Faculty

Name	Code	Name	Code	Name	Code
Ehrman, David	VA0650	Elliott, Anthony D.	MI2100	Emerich, Kate	CO0900
Ehrmantraut, Ben R.	ND0400	Elliott, Barbara	TX3175	Emerson, Deidre	TN1400
Eichelberger, K. V.	DC0150	Elliott, Bill	MA0260	Emerson, Smokey	AR0850
Eichelberger, Mary Jane	OH1800	Elliott, David J.	NJ1130	Emerson, Stephen	UT0250
Eichenbaum, Daniel	WV0300	Elliott, David J.	NY2750	Emerson, Tara M.	TX2400
Eichhorn, Claire	DC0170	Elliott, David	KY1450	Emerson, Timothy	NY2950
Eichhorst, Diane	ND0050	Elliott, John	CA4050	Emery, Marian L.	IN0910
Eichler, Dennis	TX1450	Elliott, Lloyd R.	CA1300	Emery, Michael	NY3650
Eichner, Mark J.	WI0835	Elliott, Mandy	NY2650	Emery, Steven	MA1400
Eickelman, Diane	CO0275	Elliott, Margarett	GA0950	Emery, Steven	MA1175
Eidbo, Ashley	IA0700	Elliott, Marsha	AB0210	Emery, Steven	MA0350
Eide, Christina	AZ0350	Elliott, Merrilee	KY1350	Emerzian, Jimmy	CA0825
Eidsheim, Nina	CA5032	Elliott, Paul	IN0900	Emge, Jeffrey D.	TX3535
Eidson, Joseph M.	PA1400	Elliott, Paula	AG0200	Emge, Steven	OK1150
Eifert, Jonathan	TX0400	Elliott, Rachael	NC0600	Emigh, Elizabeth	CA1560
Eifertsen, Dyne	CA0150	Elliott, Rachael	VT0450	Emile, Mark A.	UT0300
Eigenfeldt, Arne	AB0080	Elliott, Richard	OH0680	Emilson, C. Rudolph	NY3725
Eikner, Edward	GA2200	Elliott, Richard	OR0250	Emmanuel, Donna T.	TX3420
Eikrem, Jeanne	OR1300	Elliott, Robert L.	TN1400	Emmons, Deanna	IN1450
Eikum, Carol L.	MN1280	Elliott, Robin W.	AG0450	Emmons, Scott	WI0825
Eikum, Rex	OH0300	Elliott, Rosemary	NY1100	Emmons, Stephen D.	TX0150
Eilander, Maxine	WA0200	Elliott, Scott	WV0600	Emmons, Tim	CA0830
Einfeldt, Teri	CT0650	Elliott, Scott	WV0750	Emmons, Timothy	CA5150
Eis, Jeremiah	WI0770	Elliott, William	MD0175	Emmons, Timothy	CA3300
Eischeid, Susan	GA2150	Elliott-Goldschmid, Ann	AB0150	Emoff, Ronald	OH1850
Eisel, Gunnar	CA1000	Ellis, Barry L.	WI0840	Emond, Paul	AG0500
Eisel, Gunnar	CA1900	Ellis, Brenda	OH2500	Enabnit, Brian	IA0250
Eisenbach, David	NY2150	Ellis, Brian	MA0260	Encarnacion, Jose	WI0350
Eisenman, Mark	AG0650	Ellis, Cynthia	TX2260	Enciso, Franz J.	CA1020
Eisenreich, Samuel	FL0050	Ellis, Diana L.	TX1650	Encke, William	IA1450
Eisensmith, Kevin E.	PA1600	Ellis, Erin L.	GA1550	Endahl, John R.	MI1200
Eisenstein, Robert	MA1350	Ellis, James	IA0400	Endo, Akira	CO0800
Eisenstein, Robert	MA2000	Ellis, John S.	MI2100	Endris, Robert R.	IN1400
Eisenstein-Baker, Paula	TX3450	Ellis, John R.	NY3780	Endsley, Gerald	CO0550
Eisfeller, Anne	NM0450	Ellis, Kim S.	TX1400	Endsley, Pamela	CO0900
Eisman, Lawrence W.	NY0642	Ellis, Laura	FL1850	Eng, Clare Sher Ling	TN0100
Eissenberg, Judith	MA0350	Ellis, Lief	CT0650	Engberg, Kristina L.	IL2350
Eissenberg, Judith	MA0500	Ellis, Lloyd	CA2400	Engberg, Michael	CO0100
Eithun, Sandra	WI0770	Ellis, Margaret J.	IL0100	Engbretson, Chris	OR0450
Ekberg, Nancy	CO0200	Ellis, Mark Carlton	OH1850	Engebretsen, Nora A.	OH0300
Eklund, Jason	GA1150	Ellis, Monica	NY0500	Engebretson, John	MN0750
Eklund, Jason	GA0750	Ellis, Peter	AA0032	Engebretson, Mark	NC2430
Eklund, Peter A.	NE0600	Ellis, Randall	NY3650	Engebretson, Noel J.	AL1170
El-Farrah, Rami	TX3530	Ellis, Rochelle	NJ1350	Engebretson, Stan P.	VA0450
Elbeck, Lance	AG0200	Ellis, Ron	TX3530	Engel, Bruce E.	NY3790
Elberfeld, Sung Hui	PA2250	Ellis, Sarah	OK1350	Engel, T. G.	TN0950
Eldan, Amir	OH1700	Ellis, Thomas J.	SC0700	Engel, Tiffany	OK1300
Elder, Christine Welch	OR1300	Ellison, Charles	AI0070	Engelhardt, Jeffers	MA0100
Elder, Ellen	MS0750	Ellison, Glenn	IL2775	Engelhardt, Kent	OH2600
Elder, Ellen P.	MS0850	Ellison, Joan	OH0200	Engelhart, Cecilia	CA5000
Elder, Joshua Ian	CA4425	Ellison, Paul	CA4200	Engelhart, Robert	MI1600
Elder, Laura	TN1350	Ellison, Paul	TX2150	Engelke, Luis C.	MD0850
Eldridge, Peter	NY2150	Ellison, Rachel	TN1150	Engelkes, John	CA4150
Eldridge, Ronda	TX2750	Ellison, Ross W.	PA2350	Engelmann, Marcus W.	CA0100
Eldridge, Ronda	TX1510	Ellison, Sue	CO0550	Engelsdorfer, Amy L.	IA0950
Eldridge, Scott	AG0130	Ellithorpe, Robert	VA1600	Engelson, Robert A.	IA0050
Eleazar, Alan G.	TN0600	Ellmore, Laurel	FL1700	Engelson, Thea	IA1300
Eleazar, Alan	TN1250	Ellsworth, Ann	NY3775	Engelson, Thea	IA0050
Eley, Elem	NJ1350	Ellsworth, Ann	NY3790	Engen, Helen	MN1450
Eley, Miriam	NJ1350	Ellsworth, Ann	NY2750	Engen, Rebecca	NC2000
Elezovic, Ivan	FL1850	Ellsworth, E. Victor	AR0750	Enghauser, Chris	GA0850
Elfline, Robert	IL0100	Ellsworth, Jane	WA0250	Enghauser, Christopher M.	AL0500
Elford, Scott	WI0804	Ellsworth, Rodger	NH0250	England, Diane	CA4300
Elgart, Matthew P.	CA0500	Ellsworth-Smith, Pamela	MO1650	England, George	CA0835
Elgart, Matthew	CA0830	Ellwood, Jeff	CA0815	England, Peter	AJ0150
Elgersma, Kristin M.	ID0250	Ellwood, Jeffrey	CA3200	Englar, Marcia L.	PA2350
Elias, Carlos	CO0225	Ellzey, Michael R.	NM0100	Engle, Marilyn	AA0150
Elias, Cathy A.	IL0750	Elmen, Paul	MA0260	Engle, Martha Ramm	CA2050
Elias, Daniel	CA0150	Elmes, Barry	AG0650	Engle, Rebecca	CA3920
Elias, Gerald A.	UT0250	Elmore, Ashlee	OK0825	Engle, Tiffany J.	MI0350
Elias, Joel	CA0840	Elmore, Doug	KY1500	Engler, Kyle C.	MD0850
Eliasen, Mikael	PA0850	Elossais, Hannah	AA0035	Engler, Kyle C.	MD0520
Eliason, Linda J.	IA1950	Elossias, Hannah	AA0020	Englert, David	TX2250
Elisha, Larisa	GA0950	Elowsky-Fox, Jennifer	MA0260	Englert, Don	AG0450
Elisha, Steven K.	GA0950	Elpus, Kenneth	MD1010	Englert, Don	AG0200
Elisi, Enrico	NY1100	Elsbernd, Jerome	MN0610	English, Aaron	WA0650
Elizabeth, Lori	OR0500	Elsberry, Kristie B.	TN0100	English, Christopher	MD0800
Elizondo, Madeline	TX2260	Elsea, Peter	CA5070	English, Horace	LA0050
Elkins, Christina	NC1550	Elser, Albert Christian	SC1000	English, Jonathan R.	NY4150
Elkins, Eleanor	TX0150	Elsey, Eddie L.	AL1250	English, Joseph R.	MO0050
Elkins, Phil	SC0750	Elshazly, Janet	SC0275	English, Nicole	MO1810
Elkus, Jonathan B.	CA5010	Elsing, Evelyn	MD1010	English, Wendell L.	MD0200
Elledge, Nancy	TX3000	Elstner, Erin	MO1950	English-Ward, Miriam	OR0400
Ellefsen, Roy	UT0190	Elstner, Erin	MO0700	Englund, John	UT0250
Ellefson, Peter	IL0550	Elston, Robert	CA5360	Engstrom, Dale	CA1850
Ellefson, Peter E.	IN0900	Elswick, Beth L.	MO1810	Engstrom, Greg	KY0550
Ellenwood, Christian K.	WI0865	Elton, Nancy H.	GA2100	Engstrom, Howard	AA0050
Eller, Joseph M.	SC1110	Elton, Serona	FL1900	Engstrom, Howard	AA0150
Ellert, Michael	FL1125	Elwood, Paul	CO0950	Engstrom, Larry M.	NV0100
Ellias, Marjorie K.	NJ0800	Elworthy, Joseph	AB0200	Enis, Paul	OK0350
Ellias, Rod	AI0070	Ely, Mark	UT0250	Enloe, Loraine D.	ID0250
Ellingboe, Bradley	NM0450	Elzinga, Cameo	MI0850	Enloe, Luther D.	GA0300
Ellinger, John	MN0300	Elzinga, Harry	TX0300	Enlow, Charles	WA0860
Ellingson, Peter	CO0830	Embloom, George	CA5000	Enlow, David	NY1900
Ellingson, Ter	WA1050	Embree, Marc A.	IL0750	Enman, Cora	MI0400
Ellins, Rachael Starr	CO0250	Embretson, Deborah	MN1100	Enman, Thomas	MA1175
Elliot, Mike	MO1650	Embrey, Danny	MO1810	Ennis, Sue	WA0860
Elliot, Thomas	PA2800	Emelianoff, Andre	NY1900	Enns, Alice	AB0100
Elliot, William	MO0400	Emelio, Melanie	CA3600	Enns, Leonard J.	AG0470
Elliott, Anne	TN1150	Emerich, Justin	WA0200	Enns, Ruth	AB0200

Name	Code	Name	Code	Name	Code
Ennulat, Egbert M.	GA2100	Esau, Matt	KS1250	Eustis, Lynn	MA0400
Enos, David	CA1000	Escalante, Roosevelt	KY0900	Evangelista, Jose	AI0200
Enos, Steve	OH0750	Escalera, Mario	NY2660	Evans, Amanda	OH1100
Enrico, Eugene	OK1350	Esch, Michael	AG0300	Evans, Brett	IL1520
Ensel, Amy	KY1500	Eschbach, Jesse	TX3420	Evans, Bruce	IN1750
Ensley, Mark	TN1680	Eschen, Elizabeth D.	VA1150	Evans, Charles	SC0420
Enslin, Laura A.	NY4150	Eschete, Ron	CA0815	Evans, Chris	PA2740
Ensor, Robert	MO0260	Eschete, Ron	CA0825	Evans, Clifton J.	TX3500
Entsminger, Deen	TN0100	Escot, Pozzi	MA1400	Evans, Cory	UT0300
Entwistle, Erik	MA1175	Eselson, Lauren	AA0150	Evans, Dane	LA0300
Entzi, John A.	NC1250	Eselson, Lauren	AA0050	Evans, Darryl	AR0810
Entzi, John A.	NC2400	Esguerra, Ruben	AG0650	Evans, David	OR0500
Entzi, Karen	NC1450	Esham, Faith	NY2200	Evans, David	MD0400
Enyart, John	FL0950	Esham, Faith L.	MA0250	Evans, David	OR0400
Enyeart, Carter	MO1810	Esham, Faith	NJ1350	Evans, David	TN1680
Enz, Nicholas J.	MI1450	Eshbach, Robert	NH0350	Evans, David H.	AR0300
Epley, Arnold	MO2000	Eshelman, Darla	OK1330	Evans, David F.	NY3725
Epp, Jeremy	AC0100	Eshelman, Karen	SC0750	Evans, David	CA0825
Epp, Paul	KS1300	Eshelman, Kent T.	TX0300	Evans, Eugenia H.	VA1350
Epp, Richard	AB0100	Eshima, Shinji	CA4200	Evans, Garry W.	TX3300
Epperson, Anne	TX3510	Eshleman, Elizabeth	CA2950	Evans, Gary	VA0400
Epperson, Bryan	AG0300	Eskew-Sparks, Elise	GA0050	Evans, Gerald	OH1300
Epperson, Dean	AK0100	Eskey, Kathryn F.	NC2430	Evans, Glyn	AG0350
Eppinga, Alicia	MI0850	Eskin, Jules	MA0400	Evans, Harold	NJ1350
Eppink, Joseph A.	NY0700	Eskitch, Paulo S.	OK1450	Evans, Jay	AL1200
Epstein, Daniel	NJ1130	Esleck, David	VA1800	Evans, Joel	NY3760
Epstein, Daniel	NY2150	Esleck, David	VA1500	Evans, Joseph D.	TN1500
Epstein, Eli	MA0350	Esler, Robert	AZ0490	Evans, Joseph	TX3400
Epstein, Frank B.	MA1400	Esler, Robert	AZ0350	Evans, Judith	FL0680
Epstein, Joan O.	FL0450	Esler, Robert	AZ0470	Evans, Laura	WV0760
Epstein, Marti J.	MA0260	Espar, Michael	NY0646	Evans, Laurel S.	PA3580
Epstein, Nomi R.	IL0750	Esparza, Eric Peche	TX2250	Evans, Lee	NY1275
Epstein, Paul A.	PA3250	Espel, Ann	IL1085	Evans, Lorraine	CO0830
Epstein, Peter	NV0100	Espina-Ruiz, Oskar	NC1650	Evans, Margaret R.	OR0950
Epstein, Steven	AI0150	Espinosa, Angela G.	MT0200	Evans, Margaret	NC1300
Erastostene, Mario	FL1310	Espinosa, Gabriel	IA0700	Evans, Margarita	IL3550
Erb, Andrew	PA3260	Espinosa, Gabriel	IA0200	Evans, Mark	NY3600
Erb, Andrew	PA3650	Espinosa, Leandro	OR0200	Evans, Mathew J.	CO0275
Erb, Helen	LA0300	Espinosa, Ricardo	TX0300	Evans, Michael	CA5550
Erb, Jack	CA4100	Espinosa, Sergio	TX3500	Evans, Patty	AC0100
Erb, James B.	VA1500	Espinosa, Teresita	CA3150	Evans, Paul	WA0650
Erb, Richard	LA0300	Espinosa, Vladimir	VA0550	Evans, Paul J.	PA0550
Erbsen, Wayne	NC2550	Espinoza, Andres	ME0340	Evans, Peter J.	MA1175
Erdahl, Rolf	MN0750	Espinoza, Dannel	NY3350	Evans, Phillip	FL1125
Erdahl, Rolf	IA0950	Espinoza, Juan	AZ0150	Evans, Ralph	WI0825
Erdman, James A.	PA1900	Esposito, Nicole	IA1550	Evans, Richard L.	MA0260
Erdmann, Thomas R.	NC0750	Espy, Blake	NM0310	Evans, Thomas	MI1150
Ergo, Jack	IA0600	Esquillin, June	TN0050	Evans, Timothy	MA0900
Erhard, Paul	CO0800	Esquivel, Karen L.	OR1050	Evans, Valerie L.	KY1350
Ericksen, Elizabeth	MN0300	Ess, Michael	VA1600	Evans, William	MD1010
Erickson, Christian	WY0150	Esse, Melina	NY1100	Evans, William	CA2950
Erickson, Gary	IL1050	Essex, Malinda W.	OH1850	Evelyn, George E.	AA0200
Erickson, James	NY2105	Essl, Georg	MI2100	Evenson, David N.	LA0650
Erickson, James M.	NY2550	Esson, Dennis	AB0100	Everett, Beth	MI0600
Erickson, James M.	NY4060	Estabrook, Peter	CA4460	Everett, Cheryl	IN1850
Erickson, Janette	CA1860	Estavez, Evelyn	NJ0500	Everett, Micah P.	MS0700
Erickson, Jeff	WI0925	Ester, Don P.	IN0150	Everett, Paul	IN0150
Erickson, Kim	AG0170	Estes, Adam	ND0250	Everett, Steve	GA0750
Erickson, Kurt	CA1500	Estes, Billy	OK0850	Everett, Walter T.	MI2100
Erickson, Lydia K.	MI1200	Estes, Charlie	IN0400	Everett, William A.	MO1810
Erickson, Lynn M.	MN0950	Estes, Linda	GA0200	Everett, Yayoi Uno	GA0750
Erickson, Lynn M.	MN0050	Estes, Nancy Bliss	CA3800	Everist, Rachel	IA1170
Erickson, Margaret	MO0200	Estes, Richard A.	TX3000	Everitt, Allison	FL1430
Erickson, Mark	TX3175	Estes, Russell G.	CA4100	Everitt, Gena	MS0100
Erickson, Martin	WI0825	Estes, Simon	IA0850	Evers, Brooke E.	WV0550
Erickson, Marty	WI0350	Estes, William V.	WI0810	Evers, Brooke	DC0010
Erickson, Neal	MN1290	Estill, Cynthia	TN1850	Evers, Carol	AL1195
Erickson, Ross	IN1600	Estoque, Kevin S.	LA0650	Eversole, Bridgid	VA1550
Erickson, Scott	KY0950	Estrada, Harvey	CA1400	Eversole, Tom	KS1350
Erickson, Sheryl	WA0550	Estrin, Mitchell	FL1850	Everson, Robert	IL0730
Erickson, Shirley	TX0910	Estrin, Morton	NY1600	Everson, Terry	MA0400
Erickson, Stephen	RI0250	Etcheto, Sally A.	CA0805	Evoskevich, Paul	NY0700
Erickson, Steve	NE0400	Etheredge, Nelda	TX3350	Ewashko, Laurence J.	AG0400
Erickson, Thomas	MI0300	Etheridge, Kay	CA5200	Ewazen, Eric	NY1900
Erickson-Lume, Sarah	MN0750	Ethington, Bradley P.	NY4150	Ewell, Laurel A.	MD0850
Ericson, John Q.	AZ0100	Ethington, Martha Poleman	DC0170	Ewell, Philip	NY0625
Ericson, Margaret D.	ME0250	Ethridge, William J.	GA1450	Ewell, Terry B.	MD0850
Ericson, Michael	IL3500	Etienne, David	AR0300	Ewer, Gregory	OR0400
Ericsson, Hans-Ola	AI0150	Etienne, Pierre	CA0510	Ewing, Lee	GA1650
Eriksson, Johan	MT0400	Etlinger, David	OR0500	Ewing, Monica Emmons	GA1050
Erjavec, Donald L.	CA0859	Etter, David D.	KY1425	Ewing, Randy	IA1200
Erken, Emily	OH1850	Etter, Paul J.	NC0850	Ewing, Rosella	GA0600
Erken, Emily	OH0350	Etter, Troy L.	NY1600	Ewoldt, Patrice R.	PA2300
Erlandson, Elise	WI1150	Etters, Stephen C.	NC0350	Ewoldt, Virginia	IL0300
Erlmann, Veit	TX3510	Ettinger, Karl Erik	FL1700	Eychaner, Frank	CO0150
Ernardt, Eric	CO0300	Etzel, Laurel	IL1090	Eyerly, Heather E.	NY3780
Ernest, David J.	MN1300	Etzler, David	VT0100	Eyerly, Sarah J.	IN0250
Ernest, Lorraine K.	NJ0800	Euba, Akin	PA3420	Eyerly, Scott	NY1900
Ernst, John	NJ1000	Eubank, Beth	SC0200	Eylands, Kristian	ND0500
Ernste, Kevin	NY0900	Eubanks, Amber	SC0200	Eylar, Leo B.	CA0840
Eros, John	CA0807	Eubanks, Dawne	FL0930	Eyler, David	MN0600
Eros, Peter	WA1050	Eubanks, Dawne	FL0450	Eyles, Amy	MT0370
Errante, Steven	NC2440	Eubanks, Erdie	CA1900	Eylon, Orit	TX3520
Errante, Valerie	WI0825	Eubanks, Mark G.	OR1100	Eyre, Lillian	PA1550
Erskine, Bruce	TN1680	Eubanks, Mark	OR0400	Eyzerovich, Inna	PA2450
Erskine, John K.	MI1050	Eubanks, Nathaniel	WI0425	Ezerman, Alexander	NC2430
Erskine, Peter C.	CA5300	Eubanks, Robin	MA1400	Ezerova, Maria V.	CA5070
Ervin, Richard	FL1550	Eubanks, Robin	NY2750	Ezhokina, Oksana	WA0650
Erwin, Joanne	OH1700	Eubanks, Robin	OH1700	Ezoe, Magdalena	MI1950
Erwin, John M.	AR0850	Eulau, Andrew	NJ0825	Fabbro, Renato	OR0500

Alphabetical Listing of Faculty

Name	Code	Name	Code	Name	Code
Fabbro, Renato S.	OR1100	Fang, I-Jen	VA1550	Fawson, Christine	MA0260
Faber, Trudy	OH2450	Fang, Man	SC1110	Fay, Edmund	NJ1400
Fabian, Deborah U.	TX3420	Fang, Man 'Mandy'	OH0200	Fay, Fern	CA5360
Fabian, Donald	TX2400	Fankhauser, Gabe	NC0050	Fay, James	VA0975
Fabricius, Daniel	NY3705	Fankhauser, James L.	AB0100	Fay, Terrence	CT0550
Fabrique, Martha H.	TX2260	Fannin, John E.	KY0950	Fazecash, Robert	AG0550
Fabrizio, Louis	MA0260	Fannin, Karen M.	AR0350	Feagans, David	TN1100
Fackelman, Harry	NY4320	Fansler, Michael J.	IL3500	Fear, Judith	KS1450
Fackler, Barbara Ann	IL0730	Fantova, Marketa	NY0100	Fearing, Scott M.	DC0100
Fackler, Dan	IL1850	Faracco, Thomas	NJ1350	Fearon, Mary	AA0020
Fackler, Dan	IL0730	Farah, Mariana	KS1350	Fears, Angela	CA3520
Faddis, Jon	NY3785	Faraone, John	TX2930	Feasley, William	MD0150
Fadell, Rebecca	GA1990	Farber, Andy	NY1900	Feasly, William	WV0550
Fader, Don	AL1170	Farber, Mitchell	FL1300	Feather, Carol Ann	TN0450
Fader, Oren	NY2150	Farberman, Harold	NY0150	Featherston, Mary	OH2000
Fadial, John	WY0200	Farbood, Morwaread Mary	NY2750	Feay-Shaw, Sheila J.	WI0825
Faerber, Matthew L.	WI0860	Faria, Richard Alan	NY1800	Fedchcok, John	PA3250
Faflak, Marcela	SD0400	Farina, Danielle	NY4450	Fedchock, John	NY3785
Fagaly, Sam W.	IL0800	Farina, Geoff	IL0750	Fedderly, Carolyn	MD0400
Fagan, Leslie M.	NE0100	Farina, Jack	WI0100	Fedderly, David T.	MD0650
Faganel, Gal	CO0950	Farion, Rob	AA0080	Fedele, Andrea	MN1300
Fagen, Arthur H.	IN0900	Faris, Marc R.	NC0650	Fedele, Andrea	MN0350
Fagerberg, Kaj	IL1900	Farkas, Pavel	CA5150	Fedele, David	KS1350
Fagerburg, Karin	CT0050	Farley, Michael	NY3550	Feder, Donn Alexander	NY2150
Fagnano, Frank	NJ1400	Farlow, Peggy	IN0905	Feder, Janet	CO0560
Fague, David	WA0400	Farlow, William	WI0815	Federle, Yong Im Lee	NC2700
Fague, Kyla	WA1350	Farmer, Dawn	ID0050	Fedewa, Edward	MI0400
Fahnestock, Jeffrey	PA3150	Farmer, Harry	VA0750	Fedewa, Edward W.	MI1200
Fahnestock, Jeffrey L.	PA1400	Farmer, Joni	KY0400	Fedkenheuer, William	TX3510
Fahrion, Stacy	CO0300	Farmer, Judith	CA5300	Fedoruk, Brenda	AB0050
Fahy, Alison	MN0610	Farmer, Katherine	GA0940	Fedoruk, Brenda	AB0100
Faidley-Solars, Elizabeth	CT0650	Farndale, Nancy	IA1750	Fedoruk, Brenda	AB0200
Faieta, John	MA0260	Farnham, Allen	NJ0825	Fedoruk, Claire	CA0250
Faieta, John J.	MA0350	Farnham, Curvin G.	ME0440	Fedotov, Igor	MI2250
Fain, Jeremy	TX2700	Farnsley, Stephen	NV0150	Fedson, Delaine	TX2650
Fain, Jeremy	TX3535	Farnsworth, Anne	CA5300	Fedson, Delaine	TX3510
Faini, Philip J.	WV0750	Farny, Natasha	NY3725	Fee, Constance	NY3350
Fair, Carly	TN0580	Farouk, Wael	IL0550	Fee, Daniel	WI0830
Fair, Ed	TX3510	Farquharson, Linda J.	IL1200	Feener, Raymond	MO1810
Fair, Gary	CA3000	Farquharson, Michael	MA0260	Feeney, Kendall	WA0250
Fair, Jeffrey	WA1050	Farr, Chris	PA3330	Feeney, Tim	AL1170
Fairbanks, Ann K.	TX3450	Farr, Elizabeth	CO0800	Feeney, Timothy P.	MA0800
Fairbanks, Donna	UT0325	Farr, Sarah	NE0150	Feezell, Mark	TX2400
Fairbanks, Will	IL1050	Farr, Sarah	NE0200	Feghali, Jose	TX3000
Fairchild, G. Daniel	WI0840	Farrell, Brian	CA0825	Fehleisen, Fred	NY1900
Fairchild, Kay	GA0750	Farrell, David E.	CO0550	Fehleisen, Fred	NY2250
Fairchild, Nancy	WI0840	Farrell, Diane	NJ0800	Fehrenbach, Paula	CA3500
Fairfield, John	IL2200	Farrell, Frankie	CA2420	Fei, James	CA2950
Fairfield, Patrick K.	MI1850	Farrell, Heidi	SD0600	Feierabend, Christine	AF0100
Fairlie, Mary	TX2800	Farrell, Jamie	IL2150	Feierabend, John	CT0650
Fairlie, Thomas A.	TX2800	Farrell, Jodi	CA5360	Feigin, Eugene	NY2105
Fairtile, Linda B.	VA1500	Farrell, Peter S.	CA5050	Feigin, Joel	CA5060
Faison, Vernice	NC1600	Farrell, Scott	WA0350	Feigin, Tatiana	NY5000
Faith-Slaker, Aubrey	IL2750	Farrell, Timothy P.	SD0600	Feinberg, Henry A.	MI1700
Faiver, Rosemary T.	MI1200	Farrin, Suzanne	NY3785	Feinberg, Joseph	MI2000
Falbush, Arthur	NY3765	Farrington, Annette	NY2650	Feinberg, Joshua	OR0400
Falby, Vern C.	MD0650	Farrington, Annette	NY1700	Feindell, S.	AB0040
Falcao, Mario	NY3725	Farrington, Robert	CA1550	Feiner, Susan	NY2750
Falck, Robert A.	AG0450	Farris, Daniel King	OK1250	Feingold, David W.	WA1250
Falco, Frank	AG0650	Farris, Daniel J.	IL2250	Feinstein, Allen G.	MA1450
Falcon, Richard	KS0265	Farris, Phillip	OH2250	Feisst, Sabine M.	AZ0100
Falcon, Ruth	NY2250	Farrugia, Adrean	AG0650	Feiszli, James D.	SD0500
Falconbridge, Vaida	CA3250	Farrugia, Greg	AB0090	Fejer, Andras	CO0800
Falcone, Anthony M.	NE0600	Farrugia, Pauline	AI0050	Fejeran, Vince	WA0900
Falcone, Mary Lou	NY1900	Farwell, Douglas G.	GA2150	Feket, Robert	AG0200
Falcone, Sheri A.	MS0500	Farzinpour, Peyman	MA2020	Felber, Jill	CA5060
Falfalios, Anatasi	KY0250	Fashun, Christopher H.	IN0550	Feldberg, David	NM0450
Falk Romaine, Diane	NJ1400	Fasola, Bryan	CA0835	Felder, David C.	NY4320
Falk, Jodi	CT0650	Fass, YuChing	MA0950	Felder, Harvey	CT0600
Falk, Leila Birnbaum	OR0900	Fassett, Charles K.	MA2150	Felder, Mark	MI1500
Falk, Marc	IA0300	Fassler-Kerstetter, Jacqueline	KS0650	Feldhausen, Scott	TX1400
Falkenberger, Kristen	AG0600	Fassnacht, Therese	CA3150	Feldheim, Michelle	MA1550
Falkenstein, Richard	NY0400	Fast, Barbara	OK1350	Feldhusen, Roberta	NY2750
Falker, Matt	CA2960	Fast, Bobbi	AC0100	Feldkamp, Timothy L.	IA0930
Falkner, Dan	OK0200	Fast, John W.	VA0300	Feldman, Bernardo	CA1265
Falkner, Dianne	MS0700	Fast, Susan	AG0200	Feldman, Damira	FL0200
Falkner, Renate M.	FL1950	Fastenow, William David	NY2750	Feldman, Evan	NC2410
Faller, Richard	IL1400	Faszer, Ted	SD0450	Feldman, Jonathan	NY1900
Falli, Caterina	NY1100	Fata, Patrick	IN1560	Feldman, Marion	NY2750
Fallin, Mathew D.	GA0950	Fatone, Gina Andrea	ME0150	Feldman, Marion	NY2150
Fallin, Nicky G.	GA0250	Faucett, Jim	TX2700	Feldman, Marion	NY0500
Fallis, David	AG0450	Faugerstrom, Morris	IL3150	Feldman, Martha	IL3250
Fallis, Todd	UT0300	Faughn, Wendy	AL0500	Feldman, Ronald	MA1400
Fallon, Kelly	IN0800	Faulconer, James	OK1350	Feldman, Ronald	MA2250
Fallon, Robert	PA0550	Faulkner, Elizabeth	AA0035	Feldman, Stephen B.	AR0850
Falls, Sheila E.	MA2150	Faulkner, Julia	WI0815	Feldman, Susan M.	CA5300
Falskow, John	WA0960	Faulkner, Lynn	AL1200	Feldmann, Linda	WI0750
Faltstrom, Gloria V.	HI0300	Fauser, Annegret	NC2410	Feldt, Alison	MN1450
Falvey, Joseph	VA0150	Faust, Randall E.	IL3500	Felice, Frank	IN0250
Falvo, Robert J.	NC0050	Faust, Sharon K.	IL1350	Fellenbaum, James	TN1710
Falwell, Calvin	FL0200	Faux, Tom	IL1150	Feller, Bart	NJ1130
Falzano, Anthony	NY2500	Fava, Cristina	NY2650	Feller, David E.	UT0350
Fambrough, Gene	AL1150	Favario, Giulio	IL0550	Feller, Lynne	WA1350
Famulare, Trever R.	PA3050	Favazza, Kathleen	IL1740	Feller, Rena	TN1200
Fan, Heaven H.	IN0100	Favazza, Kathleen	IL2970	Feller, Robert	CA0350
Fan, Paula	AZ0500	Favis, Angelo L.	IL1150	Feller, Ross	OH1200
Fancher, Susan	NC0910	Favreau, Janet	CA2800	Feller-Marshall, Lynne	WA0250
Fancher, Susan L.	NC0600	Favreau, Janet	CA2650	Fellows, Robin B.	WI0865
Fandrich, Rita E.	FL0800	Fawcett, Derek	IL0720	Fells, Mizue	WA0550
Fanella, Keith	NJ0500	Fawcett-Yeske, Maxine	CO0750	Felpe, Miguel	HI0210

Fels, Carl	NM0310	Ferrebee, Sarah	CT0050	Filipovich, Natalie	MN1700
Felstein, Robert	CT0650	Ferreebee, Sarah	CT0650	Fillerup, Jessie	VA1500
Feltham, Scott	AI0150	Ferreira, Copper	CO0250	Filliman, Timothy	IL1085
Feltman, Joshua	NY0500	Ferreira, David	MN0600	Fillingim, Debra K.	MO1810
Feltner, Tiffany	TN0260	Ferreira, David C.	MN1120	Fillion, Michelle	AB0150
Felton, Jukube	IL0600	Ferreira, Wesley	CO0250	Fillmore, Molly	MI1400
Felts, Randolph C.	MA0260	Ferrell, Mark T.	KS1350	Filsell, Jeremy	DC0050
Feltsman, Vladimir	NY3760	Ferrell, Matthew	MN1300	Filzen Etzel, Laurel Kay	IL1350
Feltsman, Vladimir	NY2250	Ferrell, Rene	CA0650	Filzen, Sherill	IL1350
Fenderson, Mark W.	MT0175	Ferrell, Sarah	PA3000	Finch, Abraham L.	MA1650
Fenimore, Ross	NC0550	Ferrente, Joseph	NY2550	Finch, Mary-Katherine	AG0450
Fenley, J. Franklin	MO1790	Ferrer Brooks, Rafael	PR0115	Finch, Scott	AJ0030
Fenn, Shiloah	TN1600	Ferretti, Joseph A.	AG0600	Fincher, James	SC0710
Fennell, Arden	CO0600	Ferri, John P.	NC1650	Finck, Gabrielle	MD0850
Fennell, Drew	PA1450	Ferrier, Robert A.	MA2000	Finckel, David	NY1900
Fennell, Mitchell	CA0815	Ferrier, Robert	MA1100	Finckel, David	NY3790
Fennelly, Brian	NY2740	Ferril, Michael J.	CA0835	Findlay-Partridge, Marta C.	NC1300
Fenner, Richard C.	CA1020	Ferrill, Kyle	ID0250	Findlen, Kathryn	TX2650
Fenner, Roger	WY0050	Ferrillo, John	MA1400	Findley, Mary	DC0170
Fennessy, Ann	WA1350	Ferrington, Darryl	LA0400	Findley, Mary B.	DC0100
Fensom, Chris	NC2420	Ferris, David	TX2150	Findley, Susan	MD0150
Fenster, Laura	IL2750	Ferris, Joe	TN1100	Fine, Joe	OK1200
Fenton, Kevin	FL0850	Ferris, Rachel	TX3410	Fine, Perry	NY1860
Fenwick, Jerry	CA4000	Ferrone, Joe	CO0050	Fine, R. Samuel	MD0850
Ferber, Alan	MD0650	Ferry, Joe	NY3785	Fineberg, Joshua	MA0400
Ferber, Alan D.	NY2750	Fessler, Scott	MA0260	Finegan, James	PA1550
Ferber, Alan D.	NJ0800	Festinger, Kurt	CA1750	Finegold, Michael G.	MA1500
Ferdinand, Edward	PA0400	Festinger, Kurt	CA5500	Finet, Christopher	AZ0450
Ferdon, Ellen	NC2420	Festinger, Richard	CA4200	Fingalson, Vicki	WI0860
Ferdon, Jeff	NC0550	Fesz, Maria	OH2290	Fink, Gary	NJ1400
Ferdon, Jeffrey	NC2420	Fetler, Paul	MN1623	Fink, Katherine	NY0646
Ferenc, Anna	AG0600	Fett, Basil	OH2450	Fink, Katherine Ann	IA1550
Ferencz, George J.	WI0865	Fett, Darlene L.	SD0600	Fink, Kathleen	NJ0825
Ferencz, Jane Riegel	WI0865	Fetter, David J.	MD0650	Fink, Marc	WI0815
Ferer, Mary T.	WV0750	Fetter, John	NY1100	Fink, Mary Kay	OH0600
Fergus, Brian S.	CA1020	Fettig, Mary	CA3920	Fink, Michael Jon	CA0510
Ferguson, Charles Alan	CA1250	Fettig, Mary	CA4150	Fink, Robert W.	CA5032
Ferguson, Charles A.	CA4900	Fetz, Katie	OR0200	Fink, Seymour	OH0350
Ferguson, Daniel	UT0325	Fetz, Teun	OR0200	Fink, Simon B.	MO0850
Ferguson, Danise J.	AE0050	Fetzer, Elsie J.	CO0600	Fink, Tim J.	IL2900
Ferguson, David A.	PA1600	Feurzeig, David K.	VT0450	Finkelshteyn, Leonid	NC0650
Ferguson, David	AA0050	Feurzeig, Lisa	MI0900	Finkelshteyn, Tracy	IA0600
Ferguson, Dianne S.	NE0200	Feves, Julie	CA0510	Finkelstein, Marc	NJ0550
Ferguson, Eva	IL1200	Few, Guy	AG0600	Finlay, Gordon J.	MI2200
Ferguson, J. Scott	IL1200	Fewell, A. Garrison	MA0260	Finlay, Lois	GA1500
Ferguson, James W.	TN1100	Fewer, Mark	AI0150	Finlayson, David	NY2150
Ferguson, James	CA1760	Fey, Alan	TN0100	Finlayson, Jahmes Anthony	WI1150
Ferguson, John	TX2710	Feyer, Paul	CT0650	Finley, Benjamin	OK0300
Ferguson, John	MO0500	Fiala, Joy	AR0110	Finley, Carolyn Sue	MN0350
Ferguson, John	MN1450	Fiala, Keith	TX2800	Finley, William	CT0300
Ferguson, Laura S.	PA1600	Fiala, Michele	OH1900	Finn, Danielle	IL1610
Ferguson, Linda C.	IN1750	Fialkov, Jay	MA0260	Finn, Geraldine	AG0100
Ferguson, Lora	DC0100	Fickett, Martha V.	VA1475	Finn, Jon	MA0260
Ferguson, Lora	DC0170	Ficsor, Philip G.	CA5550	Finn, Lawrence	MA0260
Ferguson, Mary Kay	OH0600	Fiday, Michael	OH2200	Finn, Neal	NC0800
Ferguson, Paul	OH0400	Fiddmont, Keith	CA4450	Finnerty, Rachel	AG0600
Ferguson, Paul	OH0600	Fidelibus, Joseph	NY5000	Finney, John R.	MA0330
Ferguson, Robert	IN0905	Fidyk, Steve	PA3250	Finney, John W.	KY0700
Ferguson, Roger L.	WA0600	Fiedler, Anne	IN1600	Finney, R. Terrell	OH2200
Ferguson, Sean	AI0150	Fiegl, Ryan	CO0100	Finnie, Jimmy	IN0800
Ferguson, Vivian	OH1100	Field, Elizabeth	DC0100	Finnie, Mary	AR0750
Feria, Marissa	AA0050	Field, Jonathon	OH1700	Finnsson, Karen	AJ0100
Ferillo, John	MA0400	Field, Richard L.	MD0650	Finson, Jon W.	NC2410
Ferington, Paul	NY3717	Field, Sandra T.	SC1100	Finton, Charles	IL3150
Ferla, James	PA0550	Field, Tana	KY0950	Finucan, David	NY2400
Ferland, Louise	AI0210	Fielder, Jonathan	OH0300	Finucane, Dave	NC2410
Ferlazzo, Gaetano	FL0680	Fieldhouse, Stephen M.	PA1400	Finucane, David A.	NC0600
Ferlo, Patrick A.	NY3700	Fielding, Cheryl Lin	CA0960	Fiol, Stefan	OH2200
Fern, Terry L.	NC0850	Fielding, Crystal	NH0100	Fiore, Domenick J.	PA2550
Fernandez, Alma	CA3600	Fielding, Ralph W.	FL1125	Fiorentino, Mike	CA5353
Fernandez, David D.	FL0700	Fieldman, Hali	MO1810	Fiorillo, Alexander E.	PA3250
Fernandez, Gerardo	DC0170	Fields, Alex	SC0200	Firak, Paul	NV0050
Fernandez, Nohema	CA5020	Fields, D. Loren	ME0250	Firestone, Adria	NJ0825
Fernandez, Robert	CA0960	Fields, Donna	SC1200	Firkus, Krista	GA1070
Fernandez, Robert	CA0830	Fields, Kenneth	AA0150	First, Craig P.	AL1170
Fernando, Nathalie	AI0200	Fields, Marc E.	OH2200	Fischbach, Garrett	NY2250
Ferneding, Mary Jo	IL0550	Fields, Melinda	CT0600	Fischbach, Gerald	MD1010
Ferneyhough, Brian	CA4900	Fields, Tami	NC0915	Fischbach, Tim C.	IL2730
Fernisse, Glenn	GA0400	Fields, Victor	MD0610	Fischer Faw, Victoria	NC0750
Fernisse, Susan	GA0400	Fields-Moffitt, Rebecca	IA0300	Fischer, Jeanne Kierman	TX2150
Ferrandino, Blaise J.	TX3000	Fienberg, Gary	NJ0175	Fischer, Jeanne	NC2410
Ferrandis, Jean	CA0815	Fiene, Darrel J.	IN1560	Fischer, Jeffrey	MA2030
Ferrante, Martina	MA0510	Fierro, Nancy	CA3150	Fischer, Kenneth	CT0050
Ferrante, Russell K.	CA5300	Fiese, Richard K.	TX1000	Fischer, Lou	OH0350
Ferrantelli, Sal	CA3050	Fife, Melissa	ID0060	Fischer, Martha	WI0815
Ferrara, Dominick J.	MA0260	Fife, Travis	TX1400	Fischer, Norman	TX2150
Ferrara, Lawrence David	CA4200	Fifield, Glen	UT0300	Fischer, Peter H.	TX3200
Ferrara, Lawrence	NY2750	Figard, Kristin	SC0200	Fischer, Rebecca J.	NE0600
Ferrara, Lawrence	CA4150	Figueiredo, Virginia Costa	CA0815	Fischer, Richard R.	IL0730
Ferrara, Lawrence	CA1020	Figueiroa, Joao Paulo M.	DC0050	Fischer, Stephen M.	GA0850
Ferrara, William	OK1350	Figueroa, Angel	CA5300	Fischer, Stewart R.	CA1265
Ferrari, John	NY2150	Figueroa, Diana	PR0115	Fischer, Thomas	LA0800
Ferrari, John	NJ1400	Figueroa, Robert	WI1150	Fischler, Gail	AZ0300
Ferrari, Lois	TX2650	Fikentscher, Kai	NJ0950	Fiscus, Gary	IA0910
Ferraris, Robert	IL1520	Filadelfo, Gary A.	NY2750	Fiser, Lee W.	OH2200
Ferraris, Steve	VT0450	Filadelfo, Gary A.	NY1600	Fish, David Lee	NC0350
Ferraro, David C.	NY2550	Filbrun, John	OH0450	Fish, Mark	CA1250
Ferraro, Dolores	PA1550	Files, Frederick	NY4450	Fishbein, Zenon	NY2150
Ferrazza, Robert	OH1700	Files, Kari	ND0250	Fishell, Janette S.	IN0900
Ferre, Stephen G.	NY4150	Filiano, Ken	PA2150	Fishell, John C.	IN0150

Alphabetical Listing of Faculty

Name	Code	Name	Code	Name	Code
Fisher, Alexander	AB0100	Fleer, Lesley	IA0300	Flowe, Barry	VA1150
Fisher, Alexis Z.	PA1850	Fleer, Suzanne	IL1085	Flower, Carol	SD0580
Fisher, Alfred	AG0250	Fleet, Ken	AG0500	Flowers, Alan	AL1250
Fisher, Anna	DC0170	Fleezanis, Jorja	IN0900	Flowers, Jim	PA3650
Fisher, Blair	AB0050	Fleg, Jerome	WY0050	Flowers, Kevin	SC0900
Fisher, Chad	AL1150	Flegel, James	MN1620	Flowers, Patricia J.	OH1850
Fisher, Christopher	OH1900	Flegel, James	MN0950	Floyd, Angeleita S.	IA1600
Fisher, Daniel	IN0905	Flegg, Lynne Mangan	OH0300	Floyd, C. Chad	KY0400
Fisher, Dennis W.	TX3420	Flegg, Mark	MI1850	Floyd, Elizabeth M.	LA0300
Fisher, Don	PA2100	Flegg, Mark	MI2200	Floyd, Eva	OH2200
Fisher, Douglas	FL0850	Fleischer, Tania	CA2800	Floyd, Hugh	SC0750
Fisher, Gary	NY2650	Fleischman, John F.	NY3717	Floyd, J. Robert	FL1900
Fisher, George	NY2250	Fleischmann, Rob	FL1790	Floyd, John M.	VA1700
Fisher, Jenny	MI0500	Fleisher, Leon	PA0850	Floyd, Pharroll	GA0490
Fisher, Jocelyn	TN0100	Fleisher, Leon	MD0650	Floyd, Rosalyn	GA0250
Fisher, John	TX3250	Fleisher, Robert J.	IL2200	Floyd, Ruth Naomi	PA2800
Fisher, Jonathan	TX3450	Fleitas, Patricia P.	FL0650	Floyd-Savage, Karen	VA1750
Fisher, Kimberly	PA3250	Fleitz, Patrick	FL0800	Fluchaire, Olivier	NY2200
Fisher, Mark	IL0750	Fleming Peters, Lori	MD0100	Fluchaire, Olivier	NY0644
Fisher, Mickey	GA0300	Fleming, Ansley	AR0350	Flugge, Mark	OH1850
Fisher, Robin L.	CA0840	Fleming, Becky	CA4100	Flugge, Mark	OH0350
Fisher, Ryan A.	AR0850	Fleming, Beth	OK0750	Fluman, John R.	TX2960
Fisher, Stan F.	AF0050	Fleming, Diana M.	WA0550	Flurry, Henry	AZ0510
Fisher, Suzanne D.	AZ0510	Fleming, Drew	NY0625	Flyer, Nina G.	CA0807
Fisher, Tammy M.	WI0810	Fleming, Gail	MO1830	Flyer, Nina	CA5350
Fisher, Will J.	AZ0510	Fleming, Gail H.	IL2970	Flygare, Karla	WA1000
Fisher, Yuko	IL1740	Fleming, Kyle J.	CO0150	Flyger, Paul	MI1180
Fishman, Guy	RI0150	Fleming, Lynn	MD0520	Flygstad, Jana	KY0610
Fishman, Guy	MA0510	Fleming, Lynn	MD0300	Flynn Cintron, Jorge A.	PR0115
Fisk, Charles	MA2050	Fleming, Lynn	MD0500	Flynn, Michael P.	WY0150
Fisk, Eliot	MA1400	Fleming, Lynn	MD0550	Flynn, Patrick	SC0650
Fisk, Martin	AB0200	Fleming, Mark	IA1170	Flynn, Timothy	MI1800
Fisk, Peter	CA2390	Fleming, Nancy P.	AR0350	Flynt, Ben	CA1560
Fiske, Harold	AG0500	Fleming, Pat W.	TX3175	Flythe, Bernard	GA1150
Fiske, Jane	MA0930	Fleming, Phyllis	DC0170	Flythe, Bernard	GA0750
Fiske, Richard Allen	CA4550	Fleming, Rachelle	DC0050	Foard, Sarah	DC0170
Fisken, Patricia B.	NH0100	Fleming, Ricky L.	NY3717	Foerch, Ken R.	CA3650
Fiste, James A.	MI0400	Fleming, Susan	VT0150	Foerch, Kenneth	CA5355
Fitch, Frances	MA1175	Fleming, Susan C.	AL1170	Foerster, Frank	NJ0825
Fitch, Keith	OH0600	Fleming, Tod N.	CA1020	Fogarty, Rachel	TN0100
Fitenko, Nikita	DC0050	Flemming, Joy	NH0150	Fogderud, Marla	ND0500
Fiterstein, Alexander	MN1623	Flemming, Kyle	CO0900	Fogderud, Marla G.	MN0600
Fithian, Bruce S.	ME0500	Fletcher, Ashton	MD0175	Fogel, Henry	IL0550
Fitter, Todd	OH0450	Fletcher, Donna	AC0100	Fogelquist, Mark	CA4100
Fittipaldi, Thomas	NY2500	Fletcher, Douglas	OK0850	Fogg, Cynthia R.	CA3650
Fitz-Gerald, Kevin	CA5300	Fletcher, Harold	OK0700	Fogg, Matthew	ME0200
Fitzell, Gordon D.	AC0100	Fletcher, John M.	OK0700	Fogg, Matthew	ME0340
Fitzer, Harvey	KS0570	Fletcher, Mary Eason	VA0250	Fogg, Ryan	TN0250
Fitzgearld, Gayl	NM0310	Fletcher, Marylynn L.	TX3600	Fogle, Megan R.	SC0350
Fitzgerald, Cheryl	TN1150	Fletcher, Ryan	VA0250	Fogleman, Matthew	PA3710
Fitzgerald, Chris	KY1500	Fletcher, Seth	NE0590	Fogler, Michael	KY0610
Fitzgerald, Gregory	MI2250	Fletcher, Terry W.	MS0300	Foglesong, Scott	CA4150
Fitzgerald, Langston	PA2750	Fleury, August	LA0720	Folan, Andrea	NY2650
Fitzgibbon, Cecelia	PA1000	Fleury, Tacy S.	SC1000	Foley, Brad	OR1050
FitzGibbon, Katherine L.	OR0400	Flick, DaLeesa J.	OK1200	Foley, Charles F.	NV0050
Fitzhugh, William	TN1400	Flick, Daniel K.	FL1550	Foley, Christopher	AG0300
FitzPatrick, Carole	AZ0100	Flint, Gregory	IL0550	Foley, Gretchen C.	NE0600
Fitzpatrick, Kate R.	MI2100	Flint, Gregory	WI0825	Foley, Joe	MA0350
Fitzpatrick, Stuart L.	NC0900	Flint, Jere	GA1700	Foley, Joseph	RI0200
Fitzpatrick, Tim	WA1250	Flippin, Jay	KY0900	Foley, Laura	IL2650
Fitzpatrick, Tod M.	NV0050	Flippin, Thomas	NY5000	Foley, Mark	KS1450
Fitzpatrick, William	CA0960	Flippo, David	IL0650	Foley, Megan J.	CA1700
Fitzsimmons, Patricia	AL0530	Floan, Obed	OK0750	Foley, Ruth	VA0650
Fiuczynski, David	MA1400	Floden, Andrea	MI0450	Folger, Bill	VA0750
Fiuczynski, David	MA0260	Floeter, John	IL0550	Folger, William M.	MD0800
Fix, Lou Carol	PA2450	Floeter, John	IL3310	Folio, Cynthia J.	PA3250
Flack, Amy L.	NY3780	Floeter, John	IL2200	Folker, Michael	IL1300
Flack, Michael	IL0650	Floeter, Valerie	WI1155	Folker, Michael	IL3550
Flagg, Darron	CA1500	Flohil, Richard	AG0130	Follet, Diane W.	PA2550
Flagg, Lezlee	OR0010	Flom, James H.	MN1300	Follett, Karen	VA1350
Flaherty, Mark	MI1600	Flom, Jonathan	VA1350	Follett, Kathleen J.	OR1100
Flaherty, Thomas E.	CA1050	Flood, James	NY4460	Follingstad, Karen J.	CA4100
Flaherty, Thomas E.	CA3650	Flood, John	CA4100	Folse, Stuart J.	IL0550
Flamm, Ernest C.	OH2500	Flora, James	PA2900	Folsom, Gunnar	WA1000
Flamm, Peter	TX3350	Flora, James	OH1650	Folsom, Rebecca L.	MA0350
Flanagan, Edward	PA3250	Flora, Sim	AR0500	Foltz, Kristina	OR0950
Flanagan, Leslie	OK0750	Florea, Luminita D.	IL0800	Foltz, Roger	NE0610
Flanagan, Richard	MA0260	Floreen, John E.	NJ1140	Folus, Brian H.	MD0475
Flanagan, Sean	MA1400	Flores, Amy	IL1750	Fon-Revutzky, Gerik	IL3370
Flanagan-Lysy, Margaret	CA5030	Flores, Andrea	AZ0350	Fonder, Mark	NY1800
Flanagan-Zitoun, Braden	WI1150	Flores, Carlos	MI0250	Fong, Debra	CA4900
Flanagin, Michael	IN1025	Flores, Carolina	CT0650	Fong, Grace	CA0960
Flandorffer, Frank M.	PA1850	Flores, David	CA4425	Fong, Leighton	CA5000
Flandreau, Tara	CA1150	Flores, Jose G.	TX2930	Fong, Ming	NY5000
Flanery, John	MS0750	Flores, Lisa	IL2750	Fons, Carolyn	WI1155
Flanigan, Glen	KY0100	Flores, Ricardo	IL3300	Fontaine, Paul	MA0260
Flanigan, Nina	MI1750	Flores, Richard	CA1560	Fonte, Henry	CT0650
Flanigan, Sean G.	CO0225	Flores, Richard A.	CA0850	Fonteneau, Jean-Michel	CA4150
Flaniken, Angela M.	AL0800	Flores, Rick	CA0900	Fontijn, Claire	MA2050
Flaniken, Jeffrey Z.	AL0800	Flores, Yasmin A.	AL1250	Fonville, John	CA5050
Flannery, Katie	CO0550	Florez, Anthony	IL1080	Foor, Morris	GA0550
Flannery, Rebecca	CT0650	Floriano, Gerard F.	NY3730	Fooster, Harold	AR0810
Flannery, William	OK0500	Floriano, Joan H.	NY3730	Foote, Ed V.	TN1850
Flauding, Richard (Ric) G.	TX2600	Floriano, Joan	NY2650	Foote, Jack E.	CA0840
Flavin, Scott Thomas	FL1900	Florine, Jane Lynn	IL0600	Foradori, Anne	NE0590
Flax, Laura	NY0150	Flory, Andrew	MN0300	Forbat, David	OK1330
Fleck, Allyson	GA1150	Flory, Jennifer Morgan	GA0850	Forbay, Bronwen	TX2250
Fleckenstein, Charles F.	NY2750	Flory, Mary Beth	VA0100	Forbes, Douglas	CA1265
Fleeman, Rod	MO1810	Flory, Neil	WA0050	Forbes, Guy	IL1750
Fleeman, Rodney	KS0590	Flournoy-Buford, Debbie	TX3650	Forbes, Michael I.	WI0840

807

Name	Code	Name	Code	Name	Code
Forbis, Clifton	TX2400	Foster, Erin	WA1100	Francese, Ellen	MA0260
Forconi, John	NY2150	Foster, Erin	WA0400	Francini, Kerri	IL1340
Ford, Andrew	CA1000	Foster, Erin	WA0250	Francis, Anne	UT0300
Ford, Anita	CA3400	Foster, Gary	TX2400	Francis, Bobby R.	TX3000
Ford, Barry M.	NE0610	Foster, Gary A.	OK0550	Francis, Deirdre	SC0050
Ford, Douglass	IL1090	Foster, Julia	FL1550	Francis, Edward	CA3600
Ford, James	CA0830	Foster, Korre	TN0050	Francis, Edward	CA0835
Ford, Jeffrey	TX3370	Foster, Linda	NJ0760	Francis, Edward	CA3100
Ford, Jim S.	VA1475	Foster, Marc A.	NC0930	Francis, Graeme	TX3530
Ford, Jonathan	MT0200	Foster, Mark H.	NY3650	Francis, Jeff	SC1110
Ford, Joseph Kevin	TN1700	Foster, Mark	CO0550	Francis, Joseph Corey	IL0800
Ford, Kelly	IN1350	Foster, Marlon	VA0100	Francis, Kelly A.	GA1150
Ford, Mark	TX3420	Foster, Marlon A.	VA0600	Francis, Kimberly	AG0350
Ford, Marlene	VA1000	Foster, Martin	AI0210	Francis, Lorie	MO0825
Ford, Mary E.	OK0350	Foster, Melissa	IL2250	Francis, Margreet	CT0650
Ford, Peter	MI0050	Foster, Melvin F.	GA1450	Francis, Nancy	TX1450
Ford, Philip	IN0900	Foster, N. Gary	CA0815	Francis, Patrick	CA4400
Ford, Ronnal	NC2700	Foster, Robert	GA0250	Franck, Peter	AG0500
Ford, Shannon	MI1950	Foster, Robert E.	KS1350	Franco-Summer, Mariana	CA5360
Ford, Shannon	MI0050	Foster, Rodney W.	NY4100	Francoeur-Krzyzek, Damien	MA0350
Ford, William	MN1250	Foster, Shimmer	MN0600	Francoeur-Krzyzek, Damien	MA1400
Forderhase, Jerry	NJ0825	Foster, Stephen Wolf	MA0260	Francois, Ronald P.	CO0250
Fordham, Matthew	WA0860	Foster, Willene	GA1400	Francom, Jeffery D.	NY3780
Fordice, William	IA0950	Foster, William P.	FL0600	Francom, Jeffery D.	NY4050
Forehan, Jeff	CA5510	Foster, William	IN1750	Frandsen, Lars	NY2900
Foreman, Carolyn	AR0750	Foster-Dodson, Dawn	CA3920	Frandsen, Lars	NY0500
Foreman, Charles	AA0150	Foughty, Sharon	IA1200	Frandsen, Mary E.	IN1700
Foreman, George C.	GA2100	Foulk, Lin	MI2250	Frane, Ryan	MN1600
Foreman, Karen C.	CA0100	Foulkes-Levy, Laurdella	MS0700	Frangipane, Ron	NJ0760
Foreman, Kelly	OH1100	Fountain, Marcia	TX3520	Frank, Adam	GA2130
Foreman, Kelly	MI2200	Fountain, Richard	TX3650	Frank, Andrew D.	CA5010
Forer, Colette	AA0050	Fountain, Robin	TN1850	Frank, Arthur	PA3250
Forest, Michael	VA1350	Foureman, Jason	NC2410	Frank, Bruce	NY4350
Forester, Julie	TN0100	Foureman, Jason	NC1700	Frank, Bruce	NY1100
Forestier, Marie	AA0020	Fournier, Donna	PA3200	Frank, Claude	PA0850
Forestier, Michel	AA0020	Fournier, Gilles	AC0050	Frank, Claude	CT0850
Forestier, Michel	AA0035	Fournier, Karen J.	MI2100	Frank, Elliot	NC0650
Forger, James	MI1400	Fournier, Patricia	AI0190	Frank, Gerald	OK0800
Forget, Georges	AI0200	Fouse, Jennifer	CO0625	Frank, Gloria	TN0050
Forget, Normand	AI0150	Fouse, Kathryn L.	AL0800	Frank, Jane Ring	MA0850
Forlenza, Ray	IL1890	Foust, Diane	WI1100	Frank, Jolita	WI0150
Forlin, Gino	CA1560	Fowler, Andrew J.	SC0420	Frank, Jolita Y.	WI0835
Forman, Bruce	CA5300	Fowler, Bruce.E.	OK1350	Frank, Joseph	CA4400
Forman, Dick	VT0350	Fowler, Colin	NY2900	Frank, Mary Lou	IN1010
Forman, Marilyn T.	VA1000	Fowler, Francois	OH2600	Frank, Mike	PA3250
Forman, Naomi	AC0050	Fowler, Garold	IL1350	Frank, Pamela	PA0850
Forman, Robert B.	CA4100	Fowler, Jeffrey	PA1150	Frank, Robert J.	TX2400
Formanek, Michael	MD0650	Fowler, John H.	SC1200	Frank, Robin Shuford	FL0680
Formeck, Michael C.	PA1450	Fowler, Jonathan	PA3600	Frank, Steven	NY2950
Fornelli, Devon	AG0050	Fowler, Kurt	IN0800	Franke, Dean	IN1650
Fornero, Dan	CA0825	Fowler, Lynda	FL1300	Franke, Jerome	WI1155
Forney, Fred	AZ0440	Fowler, Michael R.	OK1450	Frankel, James Thomas	NY4200
Forney, Kristine	CA0825	Fowler-Calisto, Lauren	VA0150	Frankel, Joanna	NJ0700
Forough, Cyrus	PA0550	Fox, Aaron A.	NY0750	Franken, Fred	IL2300
Forquer, Ty	MI1800	Fox, Clinton D.	OH0300	Frankenberry, Robert	PA2900
Forrest, Sam	FL0400	Fox, Dana	KY1425	Frankl, Peter	CT0850
Forrest, Sidney	DC0170	Fox, David E.	NC0900	Franklin, Bonita Louise	OK0450
Forrester, Ellard	NC0700	Fox, Donna Brink	NY1100	Franklin, Cary J.	MN0950
Forrester, Marshall	SC0275	Fox, Elizabeth	WI1100	Franklin, Christine C.	AR0850
Forrester, Sheila	FL1675	Fox, Frances	NC2205	Franklin, Don O.	PA3420
Forry, James L.	VA1475	Fox, James	KS0400	Franklin, Ian	AG0500
Forry, James	VA1150	Fox, Jason	NY3475	Franklin, James C.	TX2250
Forry, Sharon R.	OR0700	Fox, Jeremy	IA1400	Franklin, Janice L.	TX1725
Forsberg, Charles	MN1450	Fox, Jon	TX1600	Franklin, Jeshua	IL1612
Forsberg, Peggy	KS0560	Fox, Julie C.	WI0803	Franklin, Kenneth	NC0250
Forsha, Heather	NY1400	Fox, Kim	VA1150	Franklin, Kip	MI1850
Forshee, Zane	NC1650	Fox, Marilyn F.	NY2550	Franklin, Laura L.	NC0250
Forshee, Zane F.	MD1000	Fox, Marjorie	OH2200	Franklin, Nicole	TX2250
Forster, Marilyn	OH2140	Fox, Mary Ann	GA2300	Franklin, Rachel F.	MD1000
Forsyth, Malcolm	AA0100	Fox, Rachelle	CA5300	Franklin, Virgil	IN1800
Forsyth, Paul	LA0550	Fox, Rebecca	AL1195	Franks, Carol	AL1050
Forsythe, Dawn	IN1450	Fox, Ronald	IA0950	Franks, Kendra	MO0200
Forsythe, Jada P.	MS0570	Fox, Ryan H	AR0300	Franks, Rebecca	NY4300
Forsythe, Jere L.	OH1850	Fox, Stuart	CA0510	Franks, Russell	FL1750
Fort, Kevin	IL0275	Fox, Suzanne D.	PA1900	Franks, Sandra	TN1200
Forte, Chris	IL0720	Fox, T. Jeffrey	NY2550	Franks, Sandra E.	TN1680
Forte, Michael	FL1450	Fox, William	GA2300	Fransen, Wade	VA1350
Fortin, Marie	AI0190	Foy, Leonard C.	IN0350	Frantz, Charles	NJ1350
Fortin, Nicholas	IN1010	Foy, Patricia S.	SC0650	Frantz, Jeremy	PA1350
Fortney, Julie T.	NC1250	Foy, Randolph M.	NC1700	Frantz, Jeremy	PA2950
Fortney, Patrick	NE0500	Foy, Regina	PA1550	Frantz, Nathan	FL1745
Fortunato, D'Anna	MA1400	Frabizio, William V.	PA0125	Franzblau, Robert	RI0200
Foshager, John	WI1150	Frackenpohl, David J.	GA1050	Franzen, David	OR0850
Foshee, Anna Harriette	CA4460	Fracker, Richard	MI1400	Franzen, Donald	CA5030
Fosheim, Karen	MS0250	Fradette, Amelie	NY3717	Franzetti, Allison G.	NJ0800
Fosler-Lussier, Danielle	OH1850	Fradette, Gilbert	AI0200	Franzetti-Brewster, Allison	NJ0700
Fosnaugh, Christopher	VA1125	Fradley, Kerry	FL0570	Frary, Peter Kun	HI0160
Foss, Mary	IA0850	Fraedrich, Craig	VA1350	Fraschillo, Tom	GA1700
Foss, Treva M.	NY0850	Fraga, Maurice	VA1350	Fraser, Amy	NE0720
Fossa, Matthew A.	FL1500	Fragomeni, Richard	IN1350	Fraser, Jennifer	OH1700
Fossner, Alvin K.	NY4200	Fraize, Peter W.	DC0100	Fraser, Jo-Anne	AI0190
Foster, Adam	GA1990	Frajena, Roger	TX0700	Fraser, Jo-Anne	AI0210
Foster, Adam	AL1050	Frakes, Louise	IA0900	Fraser, Judith	AB0200
Foster, Brenda	MO0850	Fralick, Janice	AG0050	Fraser, Malcolm	OH2200
Foster, Christopher	NY0100	Fralick, JR	OH0200	Fraser, Robert	OH0650
Foster, Daniel	IN0350	Fralick, Steve	AG0050	Fraser, Robert W.	OH2150
Foster, Daniel	MD1010	Fralin, Sandra L.	KY1200	Fraser, Stacey	CA0845
Foster, Daniel	MI0600	Frame, Gary	OR0250	Fraser, Teresa L.	WA0600
Foster, Donald H.	OH2200	Francavilla, Nadia	AE0120	Frasier, Michael	OR0200
Foster, Eric	CA2960	France, Chris T.	AG0130	Frater, Betsy	CA4050

Alphabetical Listing of Faculty

Name	Code
Fratia, Salvatore	AG0450
Fratino, Michael A.	NY3775
Frayne, Bryant	AG0130
Frazee, Nickolas	WY0115
Frazelle, Kenneth	NC1650
Frazer, Dianne	LA0200
Frazer, Jonathan	TN1680
Frazer, Liz	VA0350
Frazier, Bruce H.	NC2600
Frazier, Damon	OK1350
Frazier, Ivan	GA2100
Frazier, John	PA2800
Frazier, Jordan	NY2250
Frazier, Larry R.	GA2130
Frazier, Margaret J.	RI0300
Frazier, Meg Hulley	LA0300
Frazier, Virginia	CA1750
Frazor, Terance	TX3410
Fre, Anna	PA3250
Frear, Robert	CA0825
Freas, Thomas	NY2200
Freas, Thomas	CT0550
Frechou, Paul A.	LA0650
Fred Carrasquillo, Luis	PR0115
Fredenburgh, Kim	NM0450
Fredenburgh, Lisa M.	IL0150
Frederick, Amy	TN0100
Frederick, Jeremiah	IL2750
Frederick, Jeremiah	IL1300
Frederick, John	PA3680
Frederick, Mark	SC0200
Frederick, Matthew D.	VA0350
Fredericks, Jim	NY0050
Frederickson, Karen	AG0250
Frederickson, Matthew	MO0650
Frederiksen, Clifford	WI0800
Fredrick, Samuel	AL1050
Fredrickson, Ann	MN0200
Fredrickson, Don	CA4450
Fredrickson, William E.	FL0850
Fredriksen, Brandt	GA1050
Fredstrom, Tim	IL1150
Free, Christine	NY0270
Free, Scott	MA0260
Freed, Donald Callen	TX2710
Freedland, Debra	IL1085
Freedland, Debra R.	IL0840
Freedland, Debra	IL0850
Freedland, Debra	IL1300
Freedman, Deborah	NE0590
Freedman, Richard	PA1500
Freeman, Alexander	MN0300
Freeman, Carroll	GA1050
Freeman, Christine L.	IN0905
Freeman, Dowyal	TN0350
Freeman, Gary	NC0860
Freeman, Graham	AG0450
Freeman, Gregory	DC0170
Freeman, Jack	MA0260
Freeman, James	PA3200
Freeman, Janean	KY1100
Freeman, Jason A.	GA0900
Freeman, Jeffrey J.	TX2100
Freeman, John S.	CA0850
Freeman, Kay Paschal	GA1050
Freeman, Kendrick	CA4700
Freeman, Peter	AG0250
Freeman, Peter	AI0150
Freeman, Phillip I.	TX2150
Freeman, Phillip	TX3400
Freeman, Robert S.	TX3510
Freeman, Wendy	AA0200
Freeman-Miller, Leanne	IA0550
Freemyer, Janice	CA1960
Freer, Elinor	NY1100
Freer, Karen	GA0750
Freer, Patrick K.	GA1050
Freer, Thomas	OH0650
Freese, Faythe R.	AL1170
Freese, James	WI0300
Freeze, Marcus	TX2570
Freeze, Timothy	IN0900
Freeze, Tracy	KS0300
Frego, R. J. David	TX3530
Frehner, Celeste Johnson	OK0800
Frehner, Paul	AG0500
Freiberg, Sarah	MA0400
Freidline, Noel	NC2420
Freisen, Naomi	AJ0150
Freitas, Roger	NY1100
Frelly, Robert	CA0960
Fremgen, John	TX3510
French, Allen	MI0900
French, Annabeth	ME0250
French, Brian	NC2500
French, Bruce	AG0350
French, Chelsea	IL2050
French, Chris	IN0910
French, Christopher J.	TX2150
French, George E.	MN1590
French, Jodi	OR0950
French, John	PA3550
French, Mark	MA0260
French, Nell	KS0590
French, Otis C.	PA1100
French, Pam	IN1100
French, Pamela A.	IN0100
French, Pamela Ajango	IN1650
French, Paul T.	OR0950
French, Shannon	NC1350
French, Todd M.	IL0800
Frengel, Michael	MA0350
Frengel, Mike	MA1450
Frens, Jennifer	IA0500
Frescoln, Austin	WY0130
Fresne, Jeannette	AL1300
Fresonke, Michael	OK0750
Freudigman, Ken	TX3530
Freund, Don	IN0900
Freund, Stefan	MO1800
Freund-Striplen, Pamela	CA3920
Freundlich, Douglas	MA1175
Frey, Adam	GA1050
Frey, Adam	GA0750
Frey, Kevin T.	CA4350
Frey, Loryn E.	LA0150
Frey, Richard	CO0250
Frey-Monell, Robyn	CA1425
Frey-Monell, Robyn	CA1900
Freyberg, Victoria	NY0500
Freyenberger, Denise	IA0900
Freyermuth, G. Kim	AZ0200
Friberg, David	CA3520
Fricker, Charles	TX0350
Fridmann, Dave	NY3725
Fried, Eric	TX3200
Fried, Janet Gottschall	MN0050
Fried, Joe	AG0130
Fried, Joshua	NY2750
Fried, Melody	TX1550
Fried, Miriam	MA1400
Friedel, Aileen	MO1250
Friedel, Aileen	IL2970
Frieder, Raphael	NY1860
Friedley, Geoffrey A.	ID0100
Friedman, Arnold J.	MA0260
Friedman, Bennett	CA4460
Friedman, Don E.	NY2750
Friedman, Eve A.	NJ1050
Friedman, Jay	IL0550
Friedman, Jeffrey A.	MA0260
Friedman, Joel Phillip	CA4425
Friedman, Jonathan I.	VA1500
Friedman, Kenneth J.	AB0100
Friedman, Stanley Arnold	MS0700
Friedman, Tamara	WA0860
Friedman-Adler, Laurie	NY1600
Friedmann, Michael	CT0900
Friedmann, Michael L.	CT0850
Friedrichs, Charles	CA4100
Friedson, Steven	TX3420
Frieling, Randall J.	IN0100
Frierson-Campbell, Carol	NJ1400
Fries, Susan	CA1425
Friese, Kenneth	NY1275
Friesen, Darryl	AC0100
Friesen, Elroy	AC0100
Friesen, Eugene	MA0260
Friesen, John	WA1250
Friesen, Milton	CA1860
Friesen, Peter	CO0550
Friesen-Carper, Dennis	IN1750
Frigo, Connie	GA2100
Frigon, Matthew A.	CA4850
Frink, Laurie	NY2150
Frink, Laurie A.	NY2750
Frisbie, Jodi	KS0150
Frisch, Andrea	NY2400
Frisch, Michele	MN1280
Frisch, Miranora O.	NC2420
Frisch, Roger	MN1280
Frisch, Walter	NY0750
Friscioni, Emanuela	OH0600
Frishkopf, Michael	AA0100
Frisk, Nora	IN1450
Frisof, Sarah A.	TX3500
Frith, Fred	CA2950
Fritsch, Greg	CA3270
Fritschel, James E.	CA0550
Frittelli, Leslie	MD0850
Fritts, C. Nelson	IA1550
Fritts, Lawrence	VA1550
Fritts, Susan L.	DC0100
Fritz, Benno P.	CA2400
Fritz, J. Thomas	PA1250
Fritz, Matthew P.	WI1150
Fritz, Rachel	MA0260
Fritze, Gregory P.	AA0050
Frizzell, Patricia	AA0080
Frizzell, Shannon	
Froelich, Andrew I.	ND0350
Froelich, Kenneth D.	CA0810
Froese, Elvera	AG0600
Froese, Garry W.	AB0150
Frogley, Alain	CT0600
Frogley, Jane	CT0600
Frohnmayer, Ellen Phillips	LA0300
Frohnmayer, Philip	LA0300
Frohrip, Kenton R.	MN1300
Frolick, Jeanne	OR1150
Froman, Ian	MA0260
Froman, James	PA0100
Fromme, Randolph	CA5070
Frommeyer, Heinz	TX3530
Froncek, Tim	MI0900
Fronckowiak, Ann	TX2960
Fronzaglia, Brian	MO0800
Frook, Sarah	VA1500
Froom, David	MD0750
Frost, James	TN0850
Frost, Randi	TX3530
Frost, Richard P.	PA1150
Frost, Ryan	PA3580
Froysland-Hoerl, Nancy	NJ1350
Fruehauf, Tina	NY0500
Fruehwald, Robert D.	MO1500
Fruge, Jonathan	TX1550
Frutkoff, Peter	NY0050
Fry, Ben	OH1600
Fry, Daniel	MO1830
Fry, Edwin J.	PA1600
Fry, James	MD1010
Fry, Laura	TN0100
Fry, Mark	IL2750
Fry, Pamela	CA4150
Fry, Robert Webb	TN1850
Frye, Brian	DC0170
Frye, Christa J.	TN1720
Frye, Christopher B.	WI0810
Frye, Danny	NC0930
Frye, Joseph W.	TN1720
Fryer, Carolyn	MA2030
Fryer, Nicholas	CA5350
Fryer, Simon	AG0600
Fryer-Davis, Carolyn	MA0400
Fryling, David N.	NY1600
Fryml, Nathan	SC1000
Fryns, Jennifer	FL0365
Fucci, Melissa	OH1110
Fucci, Melissa	OH1100
Fuchs, Craig	KS1050
Fuchs, Jeffrey W.	NC2410
Fuchs, Kenneth	CT0600
Fuchs, Richard	CO0950
Fuchs, Stuart	NY0400
Fudala, Cynthia	IN1750
Fudala, Cynthia T.	IL0730
Fudge, Berkeley	WI1150
Fudge, James	IA1300
Fudge, James	IL0300
Fudge, Tamara	IL0300
Fuelberth, Brett J.	IA0800
Fuelberth, Rhonda J.	NE0600
Fuentes, Alfonso	PR0115
Fuentes, David	MI0350
Fuerstman, Marlena	NY1860
Fuertges, Dan H.	IL0400
Fueting, Reiko	NY2150
Fugo, Charles Leonard	SC1110
Fuhrman, Eugenie	TX3600
Fuhrmann, Christina E.	OH0100
Fuhrmann, Melanie J.	IL0650
Fujikawa, Denise	OR0850
Fujinaga, Ichiro	AI0150
Fujioka, Takako	CA4900
Fujita, Tomohisa	MA0260
Fuks, Mauricio	IN0900
Fukuda, Joni	CA5355
Fukuda, Ryo	CA4425
Fukushima, Gary A.	CA0835
Fulbright, Marshall T.	CA2550
Fulcher, Jane	MI2100
Fulgham, Joel	TX3400
Fulgham, Marc S.	MO1500
Fulkerson, Gregory L.	NY2750
Fulkerson, Gregory	OH1700
Fulks, Jubal	AL1170
Fullard-Rosenthal, Annie	OH0600
Fuller, Agnes M.	VA1000
Fuller, Craig	NE0600
Fuller, Gale	MA2050
Fuller, Gregory	MS0750
Fuller, John A.	NC1700
Fuller, Karen	FL0700
Fuller, Lisa	TN1380
Fuller, Marcia	IA0400
Fuller, Mark	KS1400
Fuller, Matthew	CO0950
Fuller, Melanie	GA2130
Fuller, Parmer	CA5300

Fuller, Sarah	MD1010	Gaetano, Mario A.	NC2600	Gallo, Patrick	FL1700
Fuller, Sarah	NY3790	Gaff, Isaac	IL1550	Gallo, Paulette M.	PA3700
Fuller, Stephen	MN1300	Gaffke, Todd	MI0900	Gallo, Paulette	PA2200
Fuller, Susan	DC0170	Gage, Darren J.	NJ1130	Gallo, Reed P.	SC0800
Fuller, Trudy H.	SC0750	Gage, Darren J.	NJ1400	Gallo, Sergio	GA1050
Fuller, Wesley M.	MA0650	Gage, James H.	OH2200	Gallo, Tony	AB0090
Fullerton, J. Graeme	AB0100	Gage, Stephanie	OH2600	Gallon, Ray	NY2660
Fullerton, Kevin T.	KS1400	Gage, Stephen	OH2600	Gallon, Ray	NY0550
Fulmer, Daniel	FL0570	Gage, Yvonne	IL0550	Gallops, R. Wayne	VA1100
Fulmer, Daniel	FL0550	Gagliardo, Don	OH2000	Galloway, Melanie	CA0250
Fulmer, Fred	OK1250	Gagne, David	NY0642	Galloway, Melodie	NC2400
Fulmer, Mimmi	WI0815	Gagne, Jeannie	MA0260	Galloway, Michael	PA2150
Fulton, Carolyn J.	WA0960	Gagnon, Allison	NC1650	Galloway, Robert J.	NY1700
Fulton, Judy	IL1100	Gagnon, Claude	AI0190	Gallup, Trina	PA0350
Fulton, Kenneth	LA0200	Gagnon, Jean-Louis	AI0210	Galluzzo, Jacqueline	NY3717
Fulton, Ruby	MD0650	Gagnon, Marie-Elaine	SD0600	Galm, Eric A.	CT0500
Fumo, John	CA5300	Gagnon, Paul	AG0130	Galo, Gary A.	NY3780
Fumo, John	CA0510	Gagnon, Scott R.	MA0900	Galper, Hal	NY2660
Funahashi, Yuri Lily	ME0250	Gagnon, Sylvain	AG0250	Galper, Hal	NY3785
Funderburk, Jeffrey	IA1600	Gagnon, Yvaine	AI0190	Galu, Ioana	OH0950
Funderburk, Wes	GA1050	Gagnon-Matte, Francoise	AI0220	Galusha, Cessaries	OR0750
Funderburk, Wes	GA1150	Gahler, Jason R.	OH2140	Galvan, Alex	CA1000
Fung, C. Victor	FL2000	Gai, James R.	MO1790	Galvan, Gary	PA1830
Fung, Eric K.	PA1900	Gaide, Diana	CO0150	Galvan, Janet	NY1800
Fung, Geneva	TX2700	Gailes, George	VA1600	Galvan, Michael	NY1800
Fung, Jan	PA0500	Gailey, Dan J.	KS1350	Galvan, Santino	CA0600
Fung-Dumm, Molly	OH0650	Gailloreto, Jim	IL0550	Galvez, Luis	IL2750
Funk, Curtis H.	IL3550	Gaines, Adam W.	WI0808	Galvin, Eugene	DC0170
Funk, Dana	MN1500	Gaines, Julia	MO1800	Galvin, Eugene	DC0050
Funk, Eric	MT0200	Gainey, Denise A.	AL1150	Galvin, Mindy	MD0450
Funkhouser, James	KS0050	Gainsford, Read	FL0850	Galvin, Nancy	ID0050
Funkhouser, John	MA0260	Gairo, Anthony	PA2450	Galyean, Richard D.	VA1580
Fuoco, Anthony	OH1300	Gairo, Tony P.	PA1850	Galyen, S. Daniel	IA1600
Fuoco, Anthony	OH0200	Gairo, Tony P.	PA2550	Galyen, Tom	VA1250
Fuoco, Christine M.	OH0200	Gaither, Tiffany	OR0175	Galyon, Joseph	KY1000
Furby, Victoria J.	NY3717	Gajda, Anne	MI0600	Gamberoni, Steve	WA0950
Furlong, Allison	OH1850	Gajger, Melina	MD0650	Gambetta, Charles	NC2700
Furlow, George	PA1350	Gal, Peter	AB0100	Gambetta, Charles	NC0910
Furlow, Shaw	MS0200	Gal, Zehava	NJ1350	Gambetta, Charles L.	NC0900
Furman, Carol	ME0150	Galaganov, Misha	TX3000	Gambino, Kyle A.	LA0760
Furman, John	ME0150	Galambos, Joe	CA3250	Gamble, Sue G.	MI0400
Furman, Lisa J.	MI1800	Galand, Joel	FL0700	Gamblin-Green, Michelle	MO0600
Furman, Pablo	CA4400	Galante, Brian Edward	WA0650	Gamer, Carlton	CO0200
Furr, Barbara	NC2440	Galante, Gloria	PA3600	Gamerl, Darci	NE0100
Furr, Rhonda	TX1000	Galasek, Judith	IL0720	Gamerl, Darci	NE0160
Furr, Ricky	VA1350	Galasso, Mathew	CA1900	Gamez, Denise	IL3550
Furry, Stephanie	GA0950	Galbraith, Connie	IL1740	Gamma, Lorenz	CA0825
Furtado, Danial	FL0050	Galbraith, Nancy	PA0550	Gamma, Lorenz	CA0510
Furumoto, Kimo	CA0815	Galbreath, Loretta J.	MS0350	Gammon, Richard	KS0590
Fuschetto, W.	AB0040	Galdston, Philip E.	NY2750	Gamso, Nancy M.	OH2000
Fusco, Andrew	NJ0700	Gale, Holly Ruth	AR0200	Ganatra, Simin	IN0900
Fusco, Randall J.	OH1000	Gale, Jack	NY2150	Ganatra, Simin	IL3300
Fusco-Spera, Barbara	NY2105	Gale, Karen	CA0150	Gandara, Javier	NY2150
Fusik, James	MI2200	Gale, Marie	AA0020	Gandelsman, Yuri	MI1400
Fuson, Tim Abdellah	CA5000	Gale, Mary	CA3600	Gandolfi, Michael	MA1400
Fussell, Charles	NJ1130	Gale, Robert	NJ0175	Gandy, V. Gay	KY1400
Fuster, Bradley J.	NY3717	Gale, Robert	CO0100	Gang, Eleanor	AI0050
Futrell, Stephen A.	NC0750	Gale, Timothy M.	IA0550	Gangi, Jonathan	SC1100
Futterer, Karen	AR0200	Galema, Joseph M.	CO0900	Gannett, Diana	MI2100
Futterer, Kenneth	AR0200	Galen, Ron	CA2450	Gannon, Thomas	MA2100
Fuzesy, Brianne	ND0050	Galen, Ronald	CA1450	Gano, Peter W.	OH1850
Gaarder, Jon	PA3600	Galeota, Joseph	MA0260	Ganske, Kathy	OR0450
Gaarder, Jon	DE0150	Galer, Suzanne J.	FL1450	Gant, Christina	PA3260
Gabay, Darya	DC0170	Galhano, Clea	MN0950	Gant, Edward	VA0600
Gabbart, Ryan	TX3400	Galieva-Szokolay, Julia	AG0300	Gantt, William	CA3250
Gabbert, Andrew	VA1400	Galileas, Christos	GA1050	Ganus, Clifton L.	AR0250
Gabbert, Andrew	VA1125	Galindo, Guillermo	CA1250	Ganus, Linda	PA2450
Gabel, Gerald R.	TX3000	Galindo, Jeffrey	MA1175	Ganz, Brian	MD0650
Gaber, Brian	FL0850	Galindo, Jeffrey A.	MA0260	Ganz, Brian	MD0750
Gable, Christopher	ND0500	Galisatus, Michael	CA1250	Ganz, Dale	KS0650
Gable, David D.	GA0490	Gall, George G.	MA1650	Ganz, Isabelle	TX1400
Gable, Frederick K.	CA5040	Gall, Jeffrey C.	NJ0800	Ganz, Sara	CA2950
Gable, Garry	AJ0150	Gall, Sandra J.	OK0450	Gao, Xiang	DE0150
Gable, Kathleen	AJ0150	Gallagher, Fulton	MN0150	Garard-Brewer, Gay	MT0450
Gable, Laura Beth	AL0800	Gallagher, Jack	OH0700	Garasi, Michael J.	FL1800
Gabour, James	LA0300	Gallagher, James S.	OH1850	Garber, Joel	OK0770
Gaboury, Janine	MI1400	Gallagher, John P.	HI0210	Garber, Melia	VA0550
Gaboury, Tony	MA0260	Gallagher, Kevin	CA1250	Garber, Neil	CA5060
Gabriel, Adrienne Moffitt	LA0050	Gallagher, Lisa	OH0200	Garber, Ron	KS0210
Gabriel, Arnald D.	VA0450	Gallagher, Mara	IL2050	Garbutt, Don	AG0130
Gabriel, Charles M.	MA2030	Gallagher, Marcia	ME0340	Garcia, Alvaro	WI0835
Gabriel, Edgar	IL0850	Gallagher, Mark	MD0350	Garcia, Antonio	VA1600
Gabriel, Edgar	IL1085	Gallagher, Mary Gloria	IN1100	Garcia, David F.	NC2410
Gabriel, Sean F.	OH0200	Gallagher, Matt	PA3330	Garcia, Eduardo	CA0847
Gabriel, Sean	OH0650	Gallagher, Maureen	NY0500	Garcia, Elisa Mon	WI1150
Gabriel, Todd A.	LA0050	Gallagher, Mitchell	IN0905	Garcia, Eric	TN1200
Gabrieli, Anna	MA1175	Gallagher, Patty	IL0780	Garcia, Federico	PA0600
Gabrielse, Kenneth J.	LA0400	Gallagher, Sean	MA0400	Garcia, Gabriel	TX1850
Gabrielsen, Dag	NY0625	Gallagher, Todd	IN0800	Garcia, Glynn	TX0550
Gabrielsen, Stephen M.	MN0050	Gallahan, Carla A.	AL1050	Garcia, Glynn A.	TX2960
Gabrielson, David J.	CA0850	Gallant, Mark W.	OH1650	Garcia, Gregory	TX1000
Gach, Peter F.	CA3460	Gallas, Heidi	AG0600	Garcia, Jeremy	TX2310
Gackle, Lynne	TX0300	Gallego, Ignacio	TX2260	Garcia, Jessica	GA0200
Gackstatter, Gary	MO1120	Gallet, Coralie	NY0200	Garcia, Jose Manuel	GA2050
Gadberry, Anita	PA2200	Gallet, Coralie	MI1700	Garcia, Lynda K.	AL1100
Gadberry, David	PA3150	Gallion, Brian	LA0650	Garcia, Manuel	PR0150
Gaddis, J. Robert	KY0400	Gallo, Donna	IL0750	Garcia, Marisa	PR0115
Gadgil, Sunil	TX2100	Gallo, Franklin J.	IL0750	Garcia, Nora Lee	FL1800
Gaedeke-Riegel, Turid L.	OH2000	Gallo, Joseph	CA1520	Garcia, Orlando Jacinto	FL0700
Gaetanne, Marisa	AB0100	Gallo, Pam	CO0150	Garcia, Paul D.	NC1700

Alphabetical Listing of Faculty

Name	Code
Garcia, Paulinho	IL0550
Garcia, Peter J.	CA0835
Garcia, Susanna P.	LA0760
Garcia, Thomas George Caracas	OH1450
Garcia, Tim	MO0700
Garcia, Tim	MO1950
Garcia, Victor	IL0550
Garcia, Victor	IL1615
Garcia, W. T. Skye	OK0300
Garcia, Washington	TX3175
Garcia, William B.	TN0800
Garcia, William Burres	AL0830
Garcia-Leon, Jose M.	CT0700
Garcia-Novelli, Eduardo	WI0250
Gardella, Duane	CA4000
Gardener, Karen Roll	OH0700
Gardiner, Annabelle	FL1740
Gardiner, Katie	NY3650
Gardiner, Robert A.	SC0800
Gardiner, Ronald	FL1740
Gardner, Aaron	WI1150
Gardner, Al	TX2350
Gardner, Allen D.	PA0675
Gardner, Brian	OR0500
Gardner, Charles	IN1100
Gardner, David B.	KS1200
Gardner, David	AG0100
Gardner, Derrick	AC0100
Gardner, Gary D.	OK1500
Gardner, James E.	UT0250
Gardner, Jessica	UT0150
Gardner, John	IN0700
Gardner, Joshua	AZ0100
Gardner, Kara	CA4150
Gardner, Kara	CA5353
Gardner, Larry	CA0810
Gardner, Marvel	CA4460
Gardner, Mike	AA0050
Gardner, Patrick	NJ1130
Gardner, Peter S.	MA0260
Gardner, Randy C.	OH2200
Gardner, Rebecca	SC0800
Gardner, Richard	IL1240
Gardner, Robert	PA2750
Gardner, Ryan B.	OK0800
Gardner, Stefanie	AZ0350
Gardner, TK	CA0815
Gardner, Valerie	GA1500
Gardony, Laszlo	MA0260
Gardstrom, Susan	OH2250
Gareau, Larry	CT0050
Garee, Anne	FL0850
Garesche, Jeanine	MO1950
Garfein, Herschel	NY2750
Garfield, Bernard	PA0850
Gargrave, Eric	RI0101
Gariazzo, Mariana Stratta	TX2900
Garibova, Karine	CO0275
Garland, Jon	NY1350
Garland, Jon R.	NY4150
Garling, Tom	IL0850
Garling, Tom	IL0550
Garling, Tom	IL2200
Garlington, Aubrey S.	NC2430
Garlock, Scott	OH0700
Garlock, Scott E.	OH0100
Garman, Barry	GA0250
Garman, Michelle	PA3650
Garmon, Randy	TX1725
Garner, Brad A.	NY2750
Garner, Bradley A.	OH2200
Garner, Catherine H.	NC0650
Garner, David	CA4150
Garner, Dirk A.	OH0200
Garner, Jerald	TX3800
Garner, Paul	TX2400
Garner, Ronald L.	UT0150
Garner, Rusty	FL0900
Garnett, Guy E.	IL3300
Garnett, Rodney A.	WY0200
Garnica, Kevin	CA0350
Garofalo, Angelo	PA3500
Garofalo, Robert	DC0050
Garramone, Suzanne	CA5353
Garretson, Paul	TN1100
Garrett, Charles	MI2100
Garrett, Charles	AA0150
Garrett, Christopher	MI1150
Garrett, Craig	TX0340
Garrett, David B.	CA0825
Garrett, Dawn	MI1150
Garrett, Glen R.	CA0835
Garrett, Junko Ueno	CA3300
Garrett, Karen	CA3800
Garrett, Lee R.	OR0400
Garrett, Margaret	AR0500
Garrett, Margo	NY1900
Garrett, Matthew L.	OH0400
Garrett, Monte	TX1100
Garrett, Nancy B.	TX3510
Garrett, Roger	IL1200
Garrett, Sheila	AA0050
Garrett, Victoria	IN0200
Garrido, Glenn	TX3450
Garris, Margaret E.	NC2350
Garrison, Greg	CO0550
Garrison, Jon	NJ1050
Garrison, Karen H.	AL0200
Garrison, Kirk A.	IL0750
Garrison, Kirk	IL0730
Garrison, Leonard	ID0250
Garriss, Margaret	NC1300
Garriss, Phyllis	NC1300
Garritano, Andrea	KS0300
Garritson, Ashley	FL0200
Garritson, Paul W.	MO1900
Garritson, Paul W.	MO1800
Garrop, Stacy	IL0550
Garry, Kevin	FL1950
Garry, Kevin M.	CO0400
Garson, Michael	CA1075
Garth, Eliza	MD0750
Garthee, Jeffrey A.	WI0825
Garthwaite, Lucinda	VT0150
Gartley, Jennifer	IL1740
Gartner, Janet Sussman	NY2400
Gartner, Kurt	KS0650
Garton, Bradford	NY0750
Gartshore, Donelda	AG0250
Gartshore, Sarah	MI1985
Gartshore, Sarah	IN1750
Gartz, Michael	MI0050
Garver, Andrew	CA5300
Garver, Beryl	NY1100
Garvey, Bradford	NY0625
Garvey, Christa N.	WI0803
Garvin, Jane	MN1625
Garvin, Jerry	CA1900
Garvin, Marc	TX1400
Gary, Roberta S.	OH2200
Garza, Jeff	TX3350
Garza, Jeff	TX2200
Garzone, George	NY2660
Garzone, George	MA0260
Garzone, George	MA1400
Gaschen, Terry	TX3450
Gascho, Joseph	DC0100
Gaspar, Carole	MO1950
Gasper, Anne	RI0150
Gasper, Anne	RI0200
Gaspero, Carmen	PA0125
Gass, Glenn	IN0900
Gassi, Gloria	AG0500
Gassler, Christopher J.	VA0700
Gast, Daniel	IA1800
Gast, Gene	IA1300
Gast, Kim	MN1300
Gast, Michael	MN1623
Gast, Rosemary	IA1800
Gastler, Bernard	TX0400
Gaston, Greg	MN0150
Gaston, Leslie	CO0830
Gaston, Pamela	TN1680
Gaston, Susan Deaver	MS0700
Gatch, Perry	PA3650
Gatch, Perry	PA1050
Gately, Doug T.	VA1475
Gates, Charles R.	MS0700
Gates, Edward	OK1350
Gates, Elaine	NY2105
Gates, Elaine	NY2750
Gates, Gerald	MA0260
Gates, Giacomo	CT0300
Gates, Jim	CA3975
Gates, John T.	WI0350
Gates, Stephen	AR0700
Gates, Steven	CA3500
Gatien, Gregory	AC0050
Gatti, Annmarie	NY3785
Gatti, Pat	VA0750
Gatto, Angelo	MD0170
Gatwood, Jody	DC0050
Gaub, Eugene	IA0700
Gaub, Nancy McFarland	IA0700
Gaudette, Fannie	AI0050
Gaudette, Nicholas	MN0040
Gaudino, Brian J.	LA0760
Gaudreault, Jean	AI0150
Gauger, David	IL1850
Gaughan, Warren J.	NC2550
Gault, Brent M.	IN0900
Gaumer, Alan	PA2450
Gauthier, Delores	MI2250
Gauthier, Michael A.	AI0200
Gauthier, Michael	AI0150
Gauthier, Michael	AI0050
Gauthier, Thierry	AI0200
Gauthier, Tommy	AI0200
Gauthreaux, Guy G.	LA0650
Gauvin, Marcelle	MA2020
Gavalchin, John E.	NY4200
Gaver, Angie	NE0160
Gavin, Charles	TX2700
Gavin, Russell	TX0300
Gaviria, Carlos	TX2700
Gavito, Cory M.	OK0750
Gavrilova, Julia	AI0150
Gawboy, Anna	OH1850
Gawlick, Ralf	MA0330
Gawthorp, Kevin	IL2775
Gay, Kirk	FL1800
Gay, Leslie C.	TN1710
Gay, Nathan	KS0300
Gaylard, Catharine P.	VA1850
Gaylard, Timothy R.	VA1850
Gayler, Liane	AA0020
Gaynor, Rick G.	MN0950
Gaynor, Rick	WI0845
Gazda, Frank S.	DE0050
Gazdyszyn, Danuta U.	TX1425
Gazouleas, Ed	MA1400
Gazouleas, Edward	MA0400
Gazouleas, Edward	IN0900
Ge, Tao	GA0550
Geans, Jeannine	OH0550
Gearey, Jon	AI0150
Gearhart, Fritz	OR1050
Gearheart, Kerri	SC1000
Gearman, Mara	WA0200
Geary, Jason D.	MI2100
Geary, Michael	IA0950
Geary, Sandra	MO1900
Geber, David	NY2150
Geber, Stephen	OH0600
Gebhart, Gail Y.	MI2200
Gebo, Kevin	VA1600
Gebuhr, Ann K.	TX1000
Gedigian, Marianne	TX3510
Gee, Constance	SC1110
Gee, Larry	UT0250
Gee, Mary Sue	CA1510
Gee, Patricia	CA0960
Gee, Patricia	CA5150
Geerlings, Matthew	IA0500
Geers, Douglas E.	NY0500
Geeseman, Katherine	TX3515
Geeting, Daniel	CA0550
Geeting, Joyce	CA0550
Geggie, John D.	NY3780
Gehl, Robin	OH2200
Gehle, Keith	GA2000
Gehrenbeck, Robert	WI0865
Gehrich, Leonora S.	IL2450
Gehring, Joseph	PA1550
Gehrke, Rodney	CA4150
Gehrke, Rodney P.	CA5000
Geib, Michael T.	OK1330
Geib, Sally	TN1100
Geiger, Gregory	CA3650
Geiger, Jeanne	CA0807
Geihsler, Rebecca	MS0100
Geiman, Keith	MI1150
Geisler, Herbert G.	CA1425
Geist, Doug	NM0450
Geist, Gretchen	FL2050
Geist, Kamile	OH1900
Gekic, Kemal	FL0700
Gekker, Chris	MD1010
Gelb, Philip	CA2950
Gelbart, Matthew	NY1300
Gelber, Debbie	TX2350
Gelbwasser, Kimberly A.	NM0100
Gelfand, Alexander Lyon	NY3500
Gelfand, Michael D.	OH2600
Gelfand, Peter	CA4425
Gelineau, Phyllis	CT0450
Gelispie, Randle	MI1400
Geller, Ian R.	IN0005
Geller, Noah	MO1810
Gellert, Karen	NY2105
Gellman, Steven	AG0400
Gelman, Robin	DC0350
Gelman, Stephanie	CA0400
Gelok, Daniel	TX3400
Geluso, Paul	NY2750
Gemberling, Alan	ID0250
Gemberling, John	MT0370
Gemme, Terese	CT0450
Gemmell, Jeffrey S.	CO0800
Gemmell, Lori	AG0600
Gemmill, Matthew	IL3550
Gendelman, Martin	GA0950
Gendler, Anna	AZ0480
Gendron, Mychal	RI0300
Genest, Sylvie	AI0210
Genevro, Bradley	PA2300
Gengaro, Christine Lee	CA2600
Genge, Anthony	AF0150
Genis, Timothy	MA0400
Gennarelli, Franco	NJ1400

Name	Code	Name	Code	Name	Code
Gennaro, Joe	FL1800	Gesteland, Tracelyn K.	SD0600	Gibson, Michael	CA1800
Genova, David	CO0900	Geston, Janet	ND0350	Gibson, Mila	TX0100
Genova, Joana	MA2250	Geston, Mary K.	MN1280	Gibson, Richard L.	AE0100
Genovese, John	MA0400	Gestwicki, Tom	NY3725	Gibson, Robbie L.	AL0345
Gentry, Gregory R.	CO0800	Getke, Richard	NJ0700	Gibson, Robert L.	AL1050
Gentry, Philip	DE0150	Gettel, Court	VT0100	Gibson, Robert	IA0100
Gentry, Ron	MI1650	Gettel, Jennifer	WI1150	Gibson, Robert	AI0150
Gentry, Sarah	IL1150	Gettel, Jennifer	WI0825	Gibson, Robert L.	MD1010
Gentry, Scott	AZ0460	Getter, Joseph	CT0050	Gibson, Robyn	SC0600
Genualdi, Joseph	MO1810	Getter, Joseph	CT0450	Gibson, Tannis L.	AZ0500
Genzlinger, Cleve K.	CA4100	Gettes, Gretchen	MD0400	Gibson, Thomas S.	GA1150
Geoffrey, Suzanne L.	WI0835	Gettys, Joel	IA1400	Gibson, Tom	GA1300
Geoffrey, Suzanne	WI0100	Getz, Christine S.	IA1550	Gibson, Walter	CT0050
Geoffrey, Suzanne	WI0865	Getz, Noah	DC0170	Giddens, Scott	FL1000
Georg, Klaus	WI0250	Getz, Noah	DC0010	Giddings, Lorelei	MN0040
George, Alexander	CO0550	Getzov, Israel	AR0850	Giddings, Lorelei	MN1050
George, Andrew	TX3200	Gewirtz, Jonathan	MI1800	Giebler, David	WI0920
George, Arnold E.	NC1600	Gewirtz, Jonathon D.	MI1200	Gieck, Sarah	AA0200
George, David Alan	KY0250	Geyer, Charles	IL2250	Gier, Christina B.	AA0100
George, David N.	GA2050	Geyer, Gwynne	PA1300	Gier, David	IA1550
George, Donald	NY3780	Geyer, Luba	FL1650	Giersch, Sandra	CA0810
George, Elizabeth	AZ0450	Geyer, Oleg	FL1650	Giesbrecht, Marnie	AA0035
George, Emil	DC0010	Gfeller, Kate	IA1550	Giesbrecht-Segger, Marnie	AA0100
George, John Brian	IN1750	G'froerer, Brian	AB0200	Giessow, David	MA2010
George, Kevin	LA0080	Gheesling, Laurelie	AL0200	Gifford, Amy L.	FL1550
George, Mary	TN0100	Gheith, Sarabeth	TN1100	Gifford, Gene	AL1250
George, Matthew J.	MN1625	Ghez, Ariana	CA0960	Gifford, Jewell A.	KS0040
George, Roby	IN0800	Ghiglione, Brent	AJ0100	Gifford, Robert R.	AL1160
George, Roby G.	IL3300	Gholson, James	TN1680	Gifford, Tell	NV0125
George, Roderick L.	AL1200	Ghuman, Nalini G.	CA2950	Gifford, Troy S.	FL2120
George, Ron	AG0500	Giacabetti, Thomas	PA3330	Giger, Andreas	LA0200
George, Rosemary	NY0270	Giacabetti, Tom	PA3250	Giglid, Joseph	NY2400
George, Samantha	WI0350	Giacabetti, Tom	NJ1050	Gignac, Andrew	TX2260
Georges, Julia	AL0800	Giacobassi, Beth	WI0825	Giguere, Miriam	PA1000
Georges, Julia	AL1050	Giacona, Christina	OK1350	Gil, Gustavo	CA0950
Georgieva, Irina P.	NY4350	Giambrone, Marcia	NY1700	Gilad, Kimaree T.	CA0835
Georgieva, Roumena	GA1450	Giambrone, Marcia	NY3725	Gilad, Yehuda	CA1075
Georgieva, Roumena	GA1900	Giambussso, Scott	MD0550	Gilad, Yehuda	CA5300
Georgieva, Roumena G.	GA0490	Giammario, Matteo	PA0400	Gilbert, Adam	CA5300
Georgieva-Smith, Ralitsa	OH1350	Giampa, Janice	MA2030	Gilbert, Albert	NY1900
Gephardt, Donald L.	NJ1050	Giampietro, John	NY1900	Gilbert, Daniel	MI2100
Gephart, Jay S.	IN1310	Giampietro, Matilda	CT0800	Gilbert, Daniel	OH0600
Geraci, Anthony	VT0250	Gianforte, Matthew P.	KY0950	Gilbert, David	TN0900
Geraci, Paul	IN1350	Gianino, Kevin	MO1900	Gilbert, David	NY2150
Gerald, Helen	TX0100	Gianino, Kevin	MO1950	Gilbert, Diane	CA3100
Geraldi, Kevin M.	NC2430	Giannascoli, B. Greg	NJ0825	Gilbert, E. Beth	WI0860
Gerard, Eva	NY5000	Giardina, David	CT0350	Gilbert, Jan M.	MN0950
Gerard, Mary	CA4050	Giarusso, Richard	MD0650	Gilbert, Jay W.	NE0200
Gerber, Alan E.	FL2120	Giasullo, Frank	PA2450	Gilbert, Joan	TN1680
Gerber, Casey	OK0650	Gibbens, Tracey	WI0860	Gilbert, John	NY2750
Gerber, Gary G.	AR0500	Gibble, David L.	FL1470	Gilbert, John Haspel	TX3200
Gerber, Heidi	DC0170	Gibbons, Bruce L.	IL1750	Gilbert, Karl	IN1560
Gerber, Larry	FL0850	Gibbons, Helen	IL1750	Gilbert, Kenneth	AI0150
Gerber, Rebecca L.	NY3780	Gibbons, Henry	TX3420	Gilbert, Peter A.	NM0450
Gerber, Stephen K.	VA0450	Gibbons, John	MA1400	Gilbert, Pia	NY1900
Gerber, Stuart W.	GA1050	Gibbons, William J.	TX3000	Gilbert, Robert	MS0700
Gerber, Thomas E.	IN1650	Gibbs, Beth	MI0900	Gilbert, Robert	TN1200
Gerber, Thomas	IN1100	Gibbs, Brett	IL2500	Gilbert, Rotem	CA5300
Gerber, Timothy A.	OH1850	Gibbs, Brian	TX2250	Gilbody, Mila	NC2000
Gerber, Tom	IN0250	Gibbs, Christopher	NY0150	Gilchrest, Suzanne M.	NY2750
Gerberg, Miriam	MN0800	Gibbs, Don	KY0900	Gildea, Dan	OR0850
Gerbi, Elizabeth	NY1050	Gibbs, Geoffrey D.	RI0300	Gildow, Kurtis C.	IL2050
Gerbino, Giuseppe	NY0750	Gibbs, George E.	KS1350	Gildow, Kurtis	IL0730
Gerbino, Thomas J.	NY3600	Gibbs, Kory	AJ0100	Giles, Bob	TX3350
Gerdes, John	MO0700	Gibbs, Lawrence	LA0250	Giles, Glenn	VT0100
Gerhart, David	CA0825	Gibbson, Jef	AB0090	Giles, James	IL2250
Gerhart, Martha	TX2400	Gibeau, Peter	WI0862	Giles, Jennifer	AG0100
Gerhold, John	CA0270	Gibson, Alan	VT0200	Giles, Kari	SC1200
Geringas, Marina	AG0450	Gibson, Beverly	IA1200	Giles, Leonard	GA0810
Geringer, John M.	FL0850	Gibson, Beverly	IA0500	Giles, Martha M.	VA0450
Gerk, Sarah	OH1700	Gibson, Chris	MI1180	Giles, Michael S.	IA0850
Gerlach, Brent	TN1100	Gibson, Christina Taylor	MD0550	Giles, Ruth	MN0200
Gerlach, Bruce	MO0200	Gibson, Christina	MI1985	Giles, Sevgi	IL0550
Gerlach, Paul D.	PA0550	Gibson, Christopher A.	MO0950	Giles, Sonja	IA0850
Germain, Anthony	MA0260	Gibson, Clarence	TX3150	Gilfry, Rod	CA5300
Germain, Francois	NY3780	Gibson, Colleen	AG0170	Gilgallon, Mark T.	IN1650
German, Eugenia	CA1510	Gibson, David	NY3730	Gilgallon, Mark	IN0250
Germany, Sam	TX0370	Gibson, David	KY1550	Gill, Brian P.	NY2750
Germer, Mark	PA3330	Gibson, David	LA0770	Gill, Kimberly	NY2750
Germond, Melanie	AZ0250	Gibson, Deborah	NH0250	Gill, Lynette	FL1650
Gerrish, Jo	ID0075	Gibson, Don	FL0850	Gill-Gurtan, Denise	MO1900
Gerrish, June	IL1890	Gibson, Elijah	VA1350	Gillan, Lucas	IL3550
Gerritson, Sasha L.	IL2150	Gibson, Gary	IA0930	Gillan, Michael	MI0850
Gerrity, Kevin W.	IN0150	Gibson, Gerry	AR0250	Gillard, Maria	NY1250
Gerry, David	AG0200	Gibson, Henry	OH0950	Gille, Tanya	AL1170
Gershfeld, Tatyana	FL1745	Gibson, Ian	AG0070	Gilleland, Katharine	NC2525
Gershman, Jeffrey D.	IN0900	Gibson, Ian	AG0150	Gillespie, Alison	PA2450
Gershman, Laura	PA1450	Gibson, Jeannette	FL1500	Gillespie, Clint	AL0500
Gerstenkorn, Lisa M.	KS1050	Gibson, Jeff	AG0170	Gillespie, James E.	TX3420
Gerstin, Julian	NH0150	Gibson, John	WI0804	Gillespie, Jeffrey L.	IN0250
Gerth, Jennifer	MN1625	Gibson, John	IN0900	Gillespie, Luke O.	IN0900
Gerth, Jennifer L.	MN0050	Gibson, Joice Waterhouse	CO0550	Gillespie, Robert C.	TX0100
Gertig, Suzanne	CO0900	Gibson, Jonathan B.	VA0600	Gillespie, Robert A.	OH1850
Gertsch, Emily	GA2100	Gibson, Mara	MO1810	Gillespie, Valerie	FL2000
Gertsenzon, Galina	MA2100	Gibson, Marie	CA4900	Gillespie, Wendy	IN0900
Gertz, Bruce	MA0260	Gibson, Marilyn	LA0770	Gillette, John C.	NY3725
Gervais, Jean	AI0190	Gibson, Mark I.	OH2200	Gillette, Michael	NJ0760
Gervais, Michel Marc	CA5060	Gibson, Mary	VT0250	Gilley, John	TX2550
Geslison, Mark	UT0050	Gibson, Maya	MO1800	Gilley, Richard S.	NY2550
Gessner, Dave	IL0600	Gibson, Melissa	TN1900	Gilliam, Alisa	NC0650

Alphabetical Listing of Faculty

Name	Code	Name	Code	Name	Code
Gilliam, Bryan	NC0600	Givens, Hugh	MN1300	Gnandt, Edwin E.	AA0010
Gilliam, C.	MA0800	Givens, Melissa	TX1000	Gnecco, Jeanne	TX3100
Gilliam, Christopher	NC0550	Givens, Shirley	NY2250	Gnecco, Jeanne E.	TX3410
Gilliam, Jason	WA0650	Gjerdingen, Robert	IL2250	Gnojek, Vincent	KS1350
Gilliam, Jauvon	MD1010	Gjevre, Naomi	TX2250	Goacher, Stephen	TX1100
Gilliam, Jeffrey	WA1250	Gladstone, Bruce	WI0815	Goble, Daniel P.	CT0800
Gilliam, Laura	DC0100	Gladysheva, Alla	CA4150	Goble, Jodi	IA0850
Gilliam-Valls, Jessica	TX2650	Glago, Mikael	VA0600	Goddard, John	AG0350
Gilliam-Valls, Jessica	TX1150	Glancey, Gregory T.	CA5355	Godes, Catherine	TN1450
Gillick, Amy	CA3100	Glanden, Don	PA3330	Godfrey, Daniel S.	NY4150
Gillick, Amy	CA1425	Glandorf, Matthew	PA0850	Godin, Jon-Thomas	AG0400
Gillie, Gina	WA0650	Glann, Kerry	OH1100	Godin, Olivier	AI0150
Gillies, Lee	VT0250	Glanton, Howard	KS0500	Godoy, John E.	TX3410
Gillies, Peter	AL1160	Glanton, Howard	KS0200	Godsil, Dan	IL1350
Gilligan, Heather M.	NH0150	Glanz, James M.	NY2750	Godsil, Daniel	IL1800
Gilliland, Erin	OH0350	Glarner, Robert L.	VA1100	Godwin, Joscelyn	NY0650
Gilliland, Erin	OH2050	Glaros, Pam	OR0250	Godwin, L. Mark	TN0100
Gillingham, Bryan	AG0100	Glaser, Lise E.	OK1450	Godwin, Nannette Minor	NC2350
Gillingham, David R.	MI0400	Glaser, Matthew	MA0260	Godwin, Paul M.	TN0100
Gillis, Glen	AJ0150	Glaser, Michael P.	AL1150	Goebel, Ellen Tift	TN0100
Gillis, Peter R.	NJ0800	Glaser, Steven	OH1850	Goehring, Edmund J.	AG0500
Gillis, Richard	AC0100	Glaser, Susan J.	NY2750	Goeke, Christopher L.	MO1500
Gillis, Ron	CA2100	Glasgo, Don	NH0100	Goeke, Matthew	NY0270
Gilman, David	MI0520	Glasgow, David M.	PA0950	Goeller, Dan	SD0580
Gilman, Grant	VA0250	Glasgow, Scott	CA0835	Goeres, Nancy E.	PA0550
Gilman, Joe	CA0150	Glashauser, Jason	IN1450	Goering, John	KS1450
Gilman, Joseph	CA0840	Glasman, Ilan David	CA1550	Goeringer, Lyn	OH1700
Gilman, Kurt	TX1400	Glasmire, David	OH0300	Goertzen, Christopher	MS0750
Gilman, Matt	OR1010	Glass, Anne	TN0050	Goertzen, Valerie Woodring	LA0300
Gilmer, Melissa	FL0800	Glass, James W.	AL0450	Goeser, Patrick	CA0960
Gilmore, Bernard H.	CA5020	Glass, Judith	TN1350	Goethe-McGinn, Lisa	IL2750
Gilmore, David	MA0260	Glass, Susan	NY2750	Goetz, Michael	CT0550
Gilmore, Jimmy J.	NC0600	Glasser, David	NY2660	Goetz, Sariva	NJ0825
Gilmore, Jimmy	NC1300	Glassman, Allan H.	AZ0100	Goetzinger, Laurel E.	IN0100
Gilmore, Pamela A.	NJ1130	Glassman, Bill	CA1900	Goff, Carolyn	GA1300
Gilmore, Robert	AL1300	Glaubitz, Robert	OK1330	Goff, Kathleen	WA0300
Gilmore, Scott	IL0550	Glaze, Debbie	OR0850	Goff, Terrence	NY2450
Gilmore, Susanna Perry	TN1680	Glaze, Gary	CA5300	Goffi-Fynn, Jeanne C.	NY4200
Gilmore, Timothy	NH0250	Glaze, Richard T.	FL2100	Goforth, Stephen C.	KY1300
Gilmour, F. Matthew	MO0850	Glazebrook, James	VA1700	Gogichashvili, Eka Dalrymple	TX0300
Gilmson, Sophia	TX3510	Glazer, Frank	ME0150	Goh, Soo	PA1750
Gilpin, Mary Ann	WA0940	Glazer, Stuart	FL0650	Goin, Robert	GA0050
Gilpin, Shirley	NC2000	Gleason, Bruce	MN1625	Goines, Lincoln	MA0260
Gilroy, Debra	MN0800	Gleason, Jeff	CO0550	Goines, Victor L.	IL2250
Gilroy, Debra	MN1050	Gleason, Stephen	NY1275	Goins, Wayne	KS0650
Gilroy, Gary P.	CA0810	Gleckler, Megan	TN0100	Gokelman, William	TX3410
Gilson, Catherine	MI1550	Glen, Nancy L.	CO0950	Golan, Jeanne K.	NY2550
Gilson, David W.	OH0600	Glencross, Laurie A.	IL1750	Golan, Lawrence	CO0900
Gilson, Tim	OR0450	Glendening, Andrew	CA5150	Gold, Christopher A.	NY2650
Gilstrap, Kenneth	MT0175	Glenn, Brian	MN0040	Gold, Ira	DC0050
Gilwood, Deborah	MA2100	Glenn, David B.	WA1300	Gold, Ira J.	MD0650
Gimble, Richard	TX1600	Glenn, James H.	NC2000	Gold, Lisa R.	CA5000
Gimeno, Montserrat	NY3760	Glenn, Larry M.	CO0900	Gold, Matthew	MA2250
Ginader, Gerhard	AC0050	Glenn, Melissa Walker	AZ0490	Gold, Maxine	FL1310
Gindele, Joshua	TX3510	Glenn, Richard B.	CA3350	Gold, Michael	NY2400
Gindin, Suzanne B.	IN1050	Glenn, Susan G.	GA1070	Gold, Scott	FL1310
Ginenthal, Robin	MA0260	Glenn, Suzetta	AR0500	Goldapp, James	MO0200
Gingerich, Carol	GA2130	Glennie, Kim	NV0050	Goldberg, Benjamin	CA2950
Gingerich, Cheryl F.	PA1250	Glennon, Barbara	PA0650	Goldberg, Bernard	NY0500
Gingerich, John M.	MD0650	Glennon, Maura	NH0150	Goldberg, Halina	IN0900
Gingras, Michele	OH1450	Gliadkovsky, Anna	UT0200	Goldberg, Julie	IL1890
Gingras-Roy, Marylene	PA1050	Gliadkovsky, Kirill	UT0200	Goldberg, Julie	IL2100
Gingrich, Shawn	PA2300	Glick, Nancy	OH0250	Goldberg, Julie	IL3450
Ginn, Glenn A.	KY0900	Glick, Nancy	OH2275	Goldberg, Marc	NY0150
Ginn, Stan	KY1000	Glick, Robert P.	SC0700	Goldberg, Marc	NY1900
Ginocchio, John	MN1500	Glicklich, Jocelyn Rose	GA0940	Goldberg, Marc	NY2250
Ginorio, Jorge	TX1725	Glicklich, Martin	CA2420	Goldberg, Marc	CT0650
Ginsberg, Elaine Broad	MA1000	Glickman, Eugene	NY2550	Goldberg, Marjorie	PA3330
Ginsberg, Eric	IL3500	Glickman, Joel	WI0600	Goldberg, Merryl	CA0847
Ginter, Anthony F.	CA5040	Glidden, Amy	NY3717	Goldberg, Michael K.	CA5000
Ginther, Kathleen C.	IL2900	Glidwell, Delrae	MO1550	Goldberg, Randall	OH2600
Ginwala, Cyrus	CA4200	Glinsky, Albert	PA2250	Goldblatt, David Nathan	FL1675
Gionfriddo, Mark	MA1350	Glise, Anthony	MO1800	Golden, Arthur	CA3460
Giordano, John R.	TX3000	Glise, Anthony	MO0850	Golden, Bruce	OH0650
Giorgetti, Marisa	CA0450	Glixon, Beth	KY1450	Golden, Joseph	GA0550
Giovannetti, Claire	CA4900	Glixon, Jonathan	KY1450	Golden, Lyman	SC1080
Giovannetti, Geralyn	UT0050	Glocke, Dennis	PA2750	Golden, Lyman	SC0050
Gippo, Jan	MO1810	Glocke, Jayne	PA2750	Golden, Lyman	SC0700
Gipson, Ann M.	TX3000	Glofcheskie, John	AB0050	Golden, Rachel	TN1710
Gipson, Crystal	AL0050	Gloor, Storm	CO0830	Golden, Ruth E.	NY2105
Gipson, Richard C.	TX3000	Gloss, Randy	CA0510	Goldenbaum, Cathy	PA0400
Girard, Sharon	CA4200	Glosson, Sarah	VA0250	Goldenberg, William	IL2200
Girardi, Steve	NJ0400	Glover, Angela	FL0040	Goldhamer, Brahm	AG0300
Giray, Selim	KS1450	Glover, Daniel	CA3270	Goldhorn, Jan	GU0500
Girdham, Jane C.	MI1850	Glover, David	PA3100	Goldin, Amy	NY2750
Girko, Beth	TX2260	Glover, Judy	PA3330	Goldina, Arianna	PA2450
Girko, Elizabeth	TX1900	Glover, Robert	FL1450	Goldman, Aaron	MD1010
Girko, Stephen	TX2260	Glover, Sandra	WA0460	Goldman, Edward 'Ted'	NY1100
Giron, Arsenio	AG0500	Glovier, Thomas	PA3000	Goldman, Jason	CA5300
Girtmon, Paxton	MS0100	Glowacki, T. J.	FL0930	Goldman, Jonathan	AB0150
Girton, Irene	CA3300	Gluck, David	NY3785	Goldman, Lawrence	MS0560
Gise, Max E.	OH2200	Gluck, Robert J.	NY3700	Goldman, Robert J.	MA0750
Gish, Benjamin	WA1100	Glunt, Patricia A.	NY2750	Goldman-Moore, Susan J.	OK1450
Giteck, Janice	WA0200	Gluzman, Vadim	IL0550	Goldmark, Daniel	OH0400
Gitler, Ira	NY2150	Glyde, Judith	CO0800	Goldray, Martin	NY3560
Gitt, Bill	MA0260	Glynn, Mark D.	LA0300	Goldsmith, Harris	NY2250
Gittins, John	AG0650	Gnagey, Sam	IN0905	Goldsmith, Jeremy	NY2200
Gitz, Raymond	LA0560	Gnam, Adrian	GA0950	Goldsmith, John L.	PA3420
Giunta, Cynthia	IA0550	Gnam, Adrian	GA0850	Goldsmith, Kenneth	TX2150
Givan, Ben	NY3650	Gnam, Adrian	GA1300	Goldsmith, Maryll	CA3850

Alphabetical Listing of Faculty

Name	Code	Name	Code	Name	Code
Goldsmith, Michael	MO0750	Goodfellow, Susan S.	UT0250	Gorevic, Elizabeth	NY3775
Goldsmith, Pamela	OR0450	Goodfriend, Benedict N.	VA1250	Gorevic, Ronald	NY2400
Goldsmith, Pamela	CA5300	Goodheart, Matthew W.	CA2950	Gorgichuk, Carmen	AA0025
Goldsmith, Robert	HI0050	Goodheart, Thomas	NY3705	Gorgojo, Jamie	IL2150
Goldspiel, Alan	AL1200	Goodheart, Thomas	NY3785	Gorham, Dee Ann	TX2955
Goldstaub, Paul R.	NY3705	Goodhew, Denney B.	WA0200	Gorham, Fr. Daniel	IN0005
Goldstein, Gil B.	NY2750	Goodhew, Lee	NY1800	Gorham, Linda J.	MA0260
Goldstein, Gila	MA0400	Goodin, Glenda	TN1100	Gorina, Alena	TX3175
Goldstein, Howard A.	AL0200	Gooding, Alison	TN0100	Gorinski, Nancy J.	PA3000
Goldstein, Joanna	MA0400	Gooding, Lori	KY1450	Gorke, Sarah	WI0250
Goldstein, Joanna	IN1010	Goodloe, Cindy Roden	SC0400	Gorklo, Dan	CO0150
Goldstein, Lloyd	FL2050	Goodman, Andrea	MA1400	Gorman, John	NJ0250
Goldstein, Louis	NC2500	Goodman, David	CA4450	Gorman, Kevin J.	AZ0400
Goldstein, Mark	CA5300	Goodman, Donald	VT0200	Gorman, Kurt	TN1720
Goldstein, Perry	NY3790	Goodman, Gabrielle A.	MA0260	Gorman, Rhonda	TX3300
Goldstein, Rich	CT0050	Goodman, Glenda	CA1075	Gorman, Sharon L.	AR0900
Goldstein, Richard	CT0650	Goodman, Ian P.	FL2000	Gorman, Tracey	MN1450
Goldstein, Sara	MA0350	Goodman, James A.	ID0050	Gormley, Daniel	NY2750
Goldstein, Steven	OH2200	Goodman, Jonathan	NY0050	Gormley, Lon	NY0400
Goldstein, Tamara B.	CO0550	Goodman, Jonathan M.	NY2550	Gormley, Lonna L.	NY3717
Goldstein, Thomas	MD1000	Goodman, Joseph	NY0642	Gormly, Shane	TX0075
Goldston, Chris	IL0720	Goodman, Karen D.	NJ0800	Gornik, Holly	UT0250
Goldston, Christopher	IL0550	Goodman, Kimberlee	OH2050	Gorokhovich, Svetlana	NY5000
Goldston, Christopher	IL2750	Goodman, Lindsey	OH1400	Gorrell, Brian	OK1330
Goldston, Christopher	IL3310	Goodness, Donald R.	NY3780	Gorrie, Gregg	AB0040
Goldsworthy, James	NJ1350	Goodnight, Cheryl	TX3415	Gort, Cristian	AI0200
Golemo, Michael	IA0850	Goodnight, Sheryl	TX2800	Gort, Cristian	AI0150
Golia, Vinny	CA0510	Goodrich, Andrew M.	MA0400	Gortler, Daniel	NY2750
Golightly, John Wesley	KY0650	Goodrich, Jara S.	ME0500	Gorton, James	PA1050
Golijov, Osvaldo	MA0700	Goodrich, Linda	MI2100	Goshorn, Jereme	VA1350
Goll-Wilson, Kathleen	IL2250	Goodrich, Mark J.	CA0815	Gosine, C. Jane	AD0050
Gollihar, Stephen	TX2260	Goodrick, Mick	MA0260	Goslee, Brenda	TN1250
Gollin, Ed	MA2250	Goodridge, Andrew	MA2030	Goslin, Gerald H.	MI1700
Golliver, April	OK0800	Goodwin, Casey S.	NH0350	Gosman, Alan	MI2100
Gollmer, James W.	MD0060	Goodwin, Don	WA0250	Goss, Kim	MI1500
Gollner, Marie L.	CA5032	Goodwin, Donald	WA0400	Gossage, Dave	AI0150
Golove, Jonathan	NY4320	Goodwin, Julia	OR0700	Gosselin, Karen	AL0550
Goluses, Nicholas	NY1100	Goodwin, Linda G.	MD0650	Gosselin, Nathalie	AI0200
Gomer, Wesley	TX1650	Goodwin, Mark A.	GA0700	Gossett, Philip	IL3250
Gomez, Adalberto	TX2260	Goodwin, Sydney	TX3515	Gosswiller, Julie	MT0200
Gomez, Adrian	OK0600	Goodwin, Tim	TN1680	Goter, Arlene	MN1295
Gomez, Alice	TX2260	Gookin, Larry D.	WA0050	Gotera, Jose	OH0650
Gomez, Edgar	PR0115	Goold, Stephen P.	MN0250	Gotera, Jose	OH1000
Gomez, Kathleen	MI0520	Goold, William C.	KY0150	Gotfrit, Martin	AB0080
Gomez, Kathleen	MI0850	Gooley, Dana	RI0050	Gothard, Paul	OH1250
Gomez, Kathleen	MI0350	Goomas, Steve	CA2650	Gothold, Stephen A.	CA5100
Gomez, Routa Kroumovitch	FL1750	Gopinath, Sumanth	MN1623	Goto, Midori	CA5300
Gomez-Giraldo, Julian	WA0250	Gopoian, Juliet	NY5000	Gott, Andrew	MO1900
Gomez-Imbert, Luis	FL0700	Goranson, Jocelyn	PA2300	Gottesman, Judith F.	CA2050
Gomon, Naoum	AC0100	Goranson, Todd A.	PA2300	Gottesman, Mila	NY2400
Gompertz, Phil	CA2700	Gorbachow, Yuri	AG0130	Gottinger, Bernd	NY3725
Gompper, David	IA1550	Gorbasew, A. 'Sasha'	AG0500	Gottlieb, BettyAnne	OH2200
Gonano, Max A.	PA0500	Gorbos, Stephen	DC0050	Gottlieb, Daniel	FL1950
Gondek, Juliana	CA5030	Gorcik, Christopher	IL2750	Gottlieb, David	NJ0750
Gonder, Jonathan P.	NY3730	Gorder, Donald C.	MA0260	Gottlieb, Donald	KY1500
Gonder, Mark H.	OH2150	Gordillo, Richard	MI0900	Gottlieb, Elizabeth	IL1400
Gonen, Raya	PA2550	Gordon, Adam	TX3420	Gottlieb, Gordon	NY1900
Gongos, Chris	AG0450	Gordon, Barbara N.	NJ0500	Gottlieb, Jane	NY1900
Gongos, Chris	AG0300	Gordon, Daniel	FL1740	Gottlieb, Karen	CA2950
Gonko, Daniel	NC0700	Gordon, Daniel J.	NY3775	Gottlieb, Valentina	CA0825
Gonthier, Esther	AI0150	Gordon, David	WA1050	Gottschalk, Arthur	TX2150
Gonzales, Carlos	CA5360	Gordon, David M.	IL3550	Goudimova, Julia	VA1850
Gonzales, Carlos	CA3375	Gordon, Douglas L.	AL0500	Gougeon, Denis	AI0200
Gonzales, Cynthia I.	TX3175	Gordon, Gail R.	CA4450	Gould, Brian	CA3350
Gonzales, Elizabeth	CA1860	Gordon, Heidi Cohenour	AR0810	Gould, Brooke	IA0420
Gonzales, Mario	CA2960	Gordon, Jerry L.	TX0300	Gould, Brooke	IA0600
Gonzalez, Adam	MD0300	Gordon, Jon	NY3785	Gould, David	NY0500
Gonzalez, Ana Laura	NY1400	Gordon, Joshua	MA0500	Gould, Elizabeth	AG0450
Gonzalez, Ariel	AA0050	Gordon, Judith	MA1750	Gould, Mark	NY2150
Gonzalez, Claudio	MI0250	Gordon, Kirsten	PA3710	Gould, Mark	NY1900
Gonzalez, Fr. George	IN0005	Gordon, Kirstin	PA2350	Gould, Matt	AG0070
Gonzalez, Genaro	TX3175	Gordon, Michael	NY2750	Gould, Michael	MI2100
Gonzalez, Helen	PR0115	Gordon, Nina	IL1200	Gould, Monette	AE0050
Gonzalez, Joe	TX3410	Gordon, Pamela	AL1170	Gould, Valerie	WV0050
Gonzalez, Pepe	DC0700	Gordon, Patricia	MI0900	Goulet, David	ME0500
Gonzalez, Ramon	TX2260	Gordon, Peter L.	NY2750	Goulet, Marie-Maude	AI0190
Gonzalez, Rene	FL1900	Gordon, Rachel	ID0140	Gourdin, Lori	SC0400
Gonzalez, Roberto-Juan	CA3250	Gordon, Regina	PA1550	Gourfinkel, Anna	NY1100
Gonzalez, Susan	NY0625	Gordon, Samuel	OH2150	Gourley, Sonja	WA1100
Gonzalez, Tamara	IL2750	Gordon, Stefan	FL0350	Gove, John	CA1800
Gonzalez-Matos, Adonis	AL0050	Gordon, Stewart	CA5300	Gove, John	CA2450
Gonzalez-Palmer, Barbara	NJ1130	Gordon, Thomas	AD0050	Govich, Marilyn S.	OK1330
Gonzol, David J.	WV0550	Gordon, Todd	MA0850	Govoni, Dino	MA0260
Gooch, Warren P.	MO1780	Gordon, Tony A.	MS0050	Gowan, Andrew D.	SC1110
Good, Jonathan E.	NV0050	Gordon, Valerie Muzzolini	WA0200	Gowen, Bradford	MD1010
Good, Kevin	MI0900	Gordon, Valerie Muzzolini	WA1050	Gowen, Dennis	ND0400
Good, Matt J.	TX2400	Gordon, William	AC0050	Gowen, Rhonda	ND0400
Good, Richard D.	AL0200	Gordon, Wycliff	NY2150	Gowers, Todd B.	WA0800
Goodall, John W.	TX2700	Gordon, Wycliffe	PA3250	Goya, Ruby Cheng	CA0960
Goodberg, Robert	WI0825	Gordon-Seifert, Catherine	RI0150	Goynes, Tim	TX2955
Goodchild, Melissa	AA0020	Gordy, Laura	GA0750	Goza, David	OK1350
Goode, Bradley	CO0800	Gordy, M. B.	CA2650	Grab, Charles	MD0450
Goode, Dana	MD0100	Gore, Art	OH2200	Grabb, Henry	PA3600
Goode, Elizabeth	GA2150	Gorecki, Maria De La Luz	TX1425	Grabe, Ann	OR0700
Goode, Gloria	PA2400	Gorecki, Mikolaj P.	TX1425	Graber, Eric	MI0050
Goode, Richard	NY2250	Goree, Mary Ellen	TX3530	Graber, Kenneth	MN1450
Goode-Castro, Helen	CA0825	Gorelick, Brian	NC2500	Graber, Todd A.	NY3770
Goode-Castro, Helen	CA0830	Goren, Neal	NY2250	Grabiec, Andrzej	TX3400
Goodell, Mark	CT0650	Gorenman, Svetlana	DC0170	Grabois, Daniel	NY2150
Goodenberger, Mark	WA0050	Gorenman, Yuliya	DC0010	Grabois, Daniel	WI0815

Alphabetical Listing of Faculty

Name	Code	Name	Code	Name	Code
Grabowski, Donald	PA2350	Graser, Daniel	MI1750	Green, Les	OR0750
Grabowski, Randy	IA1600	Grases, Cristian	CA5300	Green, Maria	NJ0825
Grabowski, Robert	FL0700	Grashel, John W.	IL3300	Green, Marsha	TX1600
Grace, Elizabeth	RI0150	Grasmick, David M.	CA0630	Green, Martin	CA1000
Grace, Michael	CO0200	Grass, Ken G.	OK1450	Green, Michael C.	IL0750
Grace, Rose S.	FL0100	Grass, Mahlon O.	PA2050	Green, Patricia D.	AG0500
Grace, Susan L.	CO0200	Grasse, Jonathan B.	CA0805	Green, Paul	FL0650
Gracia-Nuthmann, Andre	NM0150	Grasso, Eliot	OR1050	Green, Peter	CA1960
Gradone, Richard	NJ0250	Gratis, Lorie A.	PA3250	Green, Richard D.	OH1450
Grady, Tracy R.	OH0200	Gratovich, Eugene	TX3510	Green, Ronald	PA2000
Graef, Becky	IN1750	Gratteau, Phil	IL2100	Green, Scott	WV0800
Graef, Richard	IL2250	Gratto, Sharon Davis	OH2250	Green, Sharon	MI1600
Graef, Sara Carina	CA0830	Gratton, Chris	SC0700	Green, Sheila	WY0115
Graf, Enrique G.	SC0500	Gratz, Reed	CA5100	Green, Stephen	CA5355
Graf, Enrique	PA0550	Gratz, Robin	IN1050	Green, Stuart	CA5150
Graf, Greg	MO0750	Grau-Schmidt, Anna K.	IL0750	Green, Stuart	CA0845
Graf, Hans	TX2150	Graupmann, Jennifer	MN1600	Green, Tim	IL2800
Graf, Kendra	UT0150	Gravander, Carl	IA1350	Green, Tricia	IL1200
Graff, Carleen	NH0250	Grave, Floyd	NJ1130	Green, Verna	NY0640
Graff, Steven	NY0625	Gravel, Manon	AI0220	Green, Vincent	WA1250
Graffam, Allen	ME0200	Graveline, Michelle	MA0200	Green, Wendy	CA4850
Graffman, Gary	PA0850	Gravelle, Darren	CA0630	Green, William	TN0850
Grafilo, Zakarias	CA4200	Graves, Daniel H.	IN0400	Greenan, April	VA1475
Grafius, Ellen	MI1150	Graves, Denyce	MD0650	Greenbaum, Adrianne	MA1350
Grafius, Ellen	MI0100	Graves, Edward	TN1400	Greenbaum, Matthew J.	PA3250
Graham, Alexander	TN0100	Graves, James	FL0400	Greenberg, Barry	MD0170
Graham, Alta Elizabeth	CO0350	Graves, Jim F.	OK1200	Greenberg, Herbert	MD0650
Graham, Brenda J.	IN1250	Graves, Jody C.	WA0250	Greenberg, Laura	NY0630
Graham, Carleen R.	NY3780	Graves, Kenneth	MS0100	Greenberg, Lionel	CA2700
Graham, Damian	AB0210	Graves, Kim	TN1660	Greenberg, Marvin	HI0210
Graham, Dave	CA5400	Graves, Larry	AG0650	Greenberg, Russell	NY4050
Graham, Edward E.	SC1050	Graves, Paul	KS0980	Greenberg, Susan R.	NC0600
Graham, Elizabeth	FL1850	Graves, Paul	AR0500	Greenberg-Norman, Susan	CA3600
Graham, Eric	WI0845	Graves, Tifton	OH2400	Greenblatt, Dan	NY2660
Graham, Jack	IA1800	Gray, Arlene	ND0050	Greenblatt, Richard	MA0260
Graham, John	AR0810	Gray, Charles	OR0850	Greene, Arthur	MI2100
Graham, Lisa E.	MA2050	Gray, Charles	MN1450	Greene, Barry	FL1950
Graham, Lowell	TX3520	Gray, Colleen G.	PA3100	Greene, Cheryl	SC0950
Graham, Mark W.	OH0200	Gray, D'Arcy	AF0150	Greene, Daniel B.	OH2120
Graham, Marques	FL0550	Gray, D'Arcy	AF0100	Greene, Doug	IA1400
Graham, Patricia S.	MD0650	Gray, Donald N.	SC1110	Greene, Elisabeth Mehl	TX1100
Graham, Patrick	FL0150	Gray, Donavon D.	CA0250	Greene, Fred	CA0960
Graham, R. Douglas	SC1110	Gray, Ellen	NY0750	Greene, Fred W.	CA5020
Graham, Richard M.	GA2100	Gray, Gary	CA4450	Greene, Gary A.	IL0850
Graham, Robin	CA0510	Gray, Gary	CA5030	Greene, Gordon K.	AG0600
Graham, Sandra J.	MA0255	Gray, George A.	PA3250	Greene, James S.	CT0800
Graham, Sandra	AG0400	Gray, Gerald Thomas	NY3725	Greene, Janet E.	MN0800
Graham, Sarah J.	IL1150	Gray, Harold R. 'Skip'	KY1450	Greene, Joshua	NY2250
Graham, Seong-Kyung	WI0700	Gray, Joel	AA0032	Greene, Joy	MD0060
Grahame, Gerald	NY0350	Gray, John	KS0250	Greene, Kenneth H.	TX3350
Gramelspacher, Addie	IL1100	Gray, Julian F.	MD0650	Greene, Kimberly	CA0815
Gramit, David	AA0100	Gray, Julie	KY1350	Greene, Linda	NY1350
Gramley, Joseph	MI2100	Gray, Kathryn A.	PA3260	Greene, Mary Gayle	NC0050
Gramm, Carol J.	OH1800	Gray, Laura J.	AG0470	Greene, Oliver N.	GA1050
Grammar, Kathleen	ME0500	Gray, Lawrence	IL3300	Greene, Richard C.	GA0850
Grammel, Deborah Lynn	IN0350	Gray, Lori F.	MT0400	Greene, Roger W.	MA0150
Gran, Charles	MO1780	Gray, Madeleine C.	MD0475	Greene, Sean	TN0250
Granade, S. Andrew	MO1810	Gray, Patricia	NC2430	Greene, Sean	TN0900
Granados, Marco	MA1175	Gray, Robert	NJ1400	Greene, Ted	AB0060
Granat, Bozena	NY2650	Gray, Serap Bastepe	MD0300	Greene, Terry L.	NY4050
Granat, Endre	CA5300	Gray, Sonny	OK1450	Greene, Thomas E.	RI0100
Granat, Zbigniew	NY2650	Gray, Sterling	KS1450	Greenfield, Hayes	NY4200
Granat, Zbigniew	MA0280	Gray, Steven	CA3460	Greenfield, Thomas A.	NY3730
Granberry, Marsha	KS1200	Gray, Susan Keith	SD0600	Greenhut, Barry	NY2750
Grandmason, Nicole	OH1350	Gray, Terrance	IL2750	Greenidge, Evelyn	AG0600
Grandstaff, Neil	OR0700	Gray, William Jon	IN0900	Greenidge-Copprue, Delano	NY2150
Grandy, Larry	CA4550	Graybeal, Dana	AZ0470	Greenland, John	PA1150
Granet, Peter	CA0550	Graybill, Roger	MA1400	Greenlee, Anita	PA1550
Granger, David W.	CA5000	Grayburn, Margaret	GA1150	Greenlee, Anita	PA3600
Granger, Linda	VA0650	Grayson, David	MN1623	Greenlee, Geol	TN1250
Granger, Shelly	CA0600	Grayson, Robert E.	LA0200	Greenlee, Robert K.	ME0200
Graning, Gary Alan	OH2150	Grayson, W. Norman	NJ0200	Greennagel, David J.	VA1600
Granite, Bonita	NJ1050	Graziano, Amy	CA0960	Greenough, Forest G.	CO0250
Granoff, Gregory J.	CA2250	Greaves, Robert	NY0350	Greensmith, Clive	NY2150
Grant, Allison	AG0450	Grechesky, Robert	IN0250	Greensmith, Clive S.	NY2750
Grant, Andrea	AG0450	Greciano, Sandra	PA2900	Greensmith, Clive	CT0850
Grant, Courtney	PA3580	Greco, Christine R.	TX1425	Greenspan, Bertram	NJ1050
Grant, Darrell	OR0850	Greco, Christopher J.	KS0100	Greenspan, Stuart	IL0720
Grant, David	IL2050	Greco, Eugene A.	FL1300	Greenwald, Fred	IL1610
Grant, David	IL0750	Green, Alan	OH1850	Greenwald, Helen	MA1400
Grant, David	IL0720	Green, Barry L.	CA5070	Greenwald, Laura	NJ0050
Grant, Denise	AG0600	Green, Bunky	FL1950	Greenwood, Andrew	TX2400
Grant, Donald R.	MI1600	Green, Burdette L.	OH1850	Greenwood, James	OR0350
Grant, Gary S.	PA1200	Green, Dana S.	OR0800	Greenwood, Joanna E.	MD0400
Grant, Joe W.	IL3300	Green, Donald	CA5300	Greenwood, Matthew	AL1300
Grant, Joyce	NY1200	Green, Donna	MI0050	Greer, Albert	AG0650
Grant, Joyce	NY1210	Green, Edward	NY2750	Greer, Clare	TX0700
Grant, Kenneth	NY1100	Green, Edward	NY2150	Greer, George	AG0600
Grant, Kerry S.	NY4320	Green, Elizabeth	MD0060	Greer, Jean	SC0200
Grant, Kristin	AR0500	Green, Elvira	NC1600	Greer, John	MA1400
Grant, Margaret	KY1000	Green, Elvira O.	VI0050	Greer, Larry	TX0125
Grant, Roger Mathew	OR1050	Green, Feleighta	SC0710	Greer, Sarah	MN1050
Grant, Roy	GA2100	Green, Gary D.	FL1900	Greer, Taylor A.	PA2750
Grant, Tom	TN0150	Green, Georgia	TX0300	Greeson, James R.	AR0700
Grantham, Donald	TX3510	Green, J. Paul	AG0500	Gregg, Gary	CA0200
Grantham, Jennifer	OH2550	Green, Jonathan D.	IL1200	Gregg, Matthew D.	WI0840
Grantham, Jennifer	OH0680	Green, Kathryn	VA1350	Gregg, Nan F.	NC0850
Granthan, Daniel	OH2250	Green, Kenneth	LA0550	Gregg, Robert B.	TN0100
Grapenthin, Ina	PA1750	Green, Kyp	TX3000	Gregg, Thomas	MA0350
Grapes, Dawn	CO0250	Green, Larry	UT0050	Gregg-Boothby, Tracey	OK1050

Greggs, Isaac	LA0700	Griffin, Stephen W.	AL0332	Grogan, David C.	TX3500
Grego, Michael	CA0825	Griffin, T. Joel	MO0400	Grogan, Robert	DC0050
Grego, Michele	CA0825	Griffin, Tammy	NC0050	Groh, Jack C.	AR0700
Gregoire, Carole	AI0190	Griffin, William	FL0680	Grohman, Bryon T.	FL1450
Gregoire, Jenny	AL1170	Griffin-Keller, Betty	CA3500	Grohovac, Janet	TX3100
Gregoire, Julien	AI0200	Griffin-Seal, Mary	FL0500	Grolman, Ellen K.	MD0350
Gregorian, Ara	NC0650	Griffing, Joan	VA0300	Gromko, Joyce	OH0300
Gregorich, Shellie Lynn	PA2150	Griffioen, Ruth	VA0250	Gronberg, John	OR1020
Gregory, Arikka	GA0950	Griffith, Ben	KY1350	Gronemann, Robert	MN1200
Gregory, Cristen	NY0400	Griffith, David	TX0075	Gronemeier, Dean	NV0050
Gregory, David	KY1200	Griffith, Dorothy S.	CA1900	Groner, Brian	IL2150
Gregory, Dianne	FL0850	Griffith, Glenn	OR0350	Groner, Brian	IL1085
Gregory, Gary J.	OH0550	Griffith, Joan E.	MN0950	Gronnier, Henry M.	CA5300
Gregory, George R.	TX2260	Griffith, Joan	MN1625	Groom, Cody	WA0860
Gregory, Jon M.	MO1790	Griffith, Larry D.	TN0930	Groom, Joan	TX3420
Gregory, Lee	TX3400	Griffith, Lynne	MD0520	Groom, Mitzi	KY1550
Gregory, M. David	GA1700	Griffith, Marshall	OH0600	Groom, Peter	AE0050
Gregory, Monica	OH2140	Griffith, Michael Ted	WY0200	Groome, Frank	IL1740
Gregory, Rohan	MA0700	Griffith, Robert A.	OH2000	Grooms, Pamela	MO0650
Gregory, Rosalie	FL0200	Griffiths, Amy	GA0550	Groos, Arthur	NY0900
Gregory, Thomas	RI0102	Griffiths, Brian	OR0175	Groschang, Sascha	KS1000
Gregory, Thomas	RI0101	Griffiths, Curt	ID0070	Grose, Michael	OR1050
Gregory, Tom	RI0200	Griffiths, Kenneth R.	OH2200	Groskreutz, Shannon	FL1750
Greher, Gena R.	MA2030	Griffiths, Laura	CA4200	Gross, Allen R.	CA0500
Greider, Cynthia S.	IN0905	Griffiths, Laura	CA1000	Gross, Allen	CA3300
Greif, Carol	WI0150	Griffiths, Vern	AB0100	Gross, Anne	DE0150
Greif, Matthew	CA2650	Grigel, Glen M.	NY3780	Gross, Austin	PA3600
Greif, Matthew	CA0805	Grigg, Eric	OK0700	Gross, Cathryn A.	IN1650
Greig, R. Tad	PA3650	Griggs, Kevin D.	MT0400	Gross, David	SC0750
Greitzer, Deborah	MD0750	Griggs-Burnham, Patricia	TX0400	Gross, Ernest H.	IL1300
Greitzer, Ian	RI0200	Grigoriev, Igor	CA0859	Gross, Jeffrey	TN1100
Greitzer, Mary	NY1100	Grigoriu, Katrina	AA0050	Gross, John	OR0750
Greive, Tyrone	WI0815	Grigorov, Liisa Ambegaokar	NY2650	Gross, Kelly	VA1550
Grenfell, Mary-Jo	MA1650	Grigoryan, Gayane	NC1350	Gross, Louis E.	IN1010
Grenier, Monik	AI0210	Grigsby, Brett	NY3650	Gross, Mark	NJ1130
Grenier, Robert M.	SC1050	Grigsby, Nathan	GA0050	Gross, Murray	MI0150
Greschner, Debra	TX1400	Grijalva, Robert	MI2100	Gross, Robert W.	TX2150
Gresham, Ann	CA3750	Grile, Kathy	IN1560	Gross, Steven	CA5550
Gresham, Ann	CA0859	Grill, Joyce	WI0810	Gross, Steven	CA5060
Gresham, David Allen	NC0250	Grim, Jennifer	NV0050	Gross-Hixon, Andrea	WI0830
Gresham, David	IL1150	Grimaldi, Peter	MA1100	Gross-Hixon, Andrea	WI0750
Gresham, Jonathan	KY1000	Grimaldi, Regina	OK0700	Grossman, Andrea	IN1010
Gresham, Kathryn	NC0250	Grimaldi, Regina	OK0750	Grossman, Arthur	WA1050
Gresham, Momoko	IL1200	Grimble, Thomas	SC0200	Grossman, David	NY2150
Gresock, Mary	MD0300	Grimes, Benjamin	OR0700	Grossman, George	NY2550
Gress, Andrew D.	NY2750	Grimes, Calvin B.	GA1450	Grossman, Hal	OK1350
Gress, Daniel	AG0400	Grimes, Janice	LA0200	Grossman, Liza	OH1100
Gresso, Selina	WA0800	Grimes, John	MA0350	Grossman, Morley K.	TX3525
Gretz, Ronald	MD0650	Grimes, Judith	IL0850	Grossman, Pauline	DC0050
Gretz, Ronald	MD0175	Grimes, Rebecca	TX2250	Grossman, Phillip	WI1150
Grevlos, Lisa	SD0050	Grimes, Robert R.	NY1300	Grossmann, Jorge V.	NY1800
Grew, John	AI0150	Grimes, Sonja	MN1280	Grosso, Cheryl	WI0808
Grew, Melody A.	MD0050	Grimes, William F.	LA0200	Grosz, Gay	LA0050
Grey, Benoit	CA0835	Grimland, Fredna H.	OR0950	Grothkopp, William	CA1020
Grey, Meg	MO0600	Grimm, Anne	AB0150	Grott, Dave	AI0150
Grey, Thomas S.	CA4900	Grimm, James	MO2000	Groulx, Timothy J.	IN1600
Greydanus, Peter	VA0150	Grimm, Leslie	IL2250	Grout, Gayle	KY1000
Grezeszak, Amanda	SC0600	Grimm, Mark	NY3680	Grove, Karla	TN1100
Grib, Sonia G.	NY1600	Grimm, Marlys	IA0700	Grove, Lisa	OH2450
Gribbroek, Michael	NJ1400	Grimm, Stephen	WI1150	Grove, Lisa	OH0450
Gribou, Andre	OH1900	Grimpo, Elizabeth	NE0150	Grove, Marna	VT0100
Grice, June	KY0900	Grimshaw, Jeremy	UT0050	Grove, Marna	VT0200
Grice, Wendy	PA2200	Grimwood, Paul	AG0200	Grove, Paul	WA0400
Grieb, Scott	IN0900	Grinnell, Justin	CA2100	Grove, Paul	ID0140
Griebling, Karen	AR0350	Grinnell, Melonie	CA2100	Grove, Paul	WA1350
Grief, Matt	CA1750	Grinnell, Michael	TX3535	Grove, Rebecca	SC0200
Grieger, Evelyn	AA0035	Grinwis, Brandan	MI0850	Grove-DeJarnett, Doug	TN1150
Grieger, Evelyn	AA0100	Gripp, Neal	AI0200	Grover, Elaine	MI1300
Grier, George	WA0700	Grippo, James	CA5360	Grover, Morgan	WY0130
Grier, James	AG0500	Grisanti, Susan	TX1550	Grover, Stephen	ME0150
Grier, Jon Jeffrey	SC0765	Grise', Monte	MN1120	Grover, Steve	ME0200
Gries, Peggy	OR1050	Grishkoff, Rob	CA2390	Grover, Steve	ME0340
Gries, Rachel	IN0500	Grishkoff, Robert	CA1425	Groves, Edgar S.	PA3650
Griesheimer, James	IA0950	Grishkoff, Robert	CA5355	Groves, Marilyn	NY2250
Griest, Jennifer	CA1450	Grismore, Steve	IL0300	Groves, Matthew	OH0350
Griffeath, Kristin	OK1250	Grismore, Steve	IL0100	Groves, Melinda	KS0300
Griffeath, Robin	OK1250	Grismore, Steven D.	IA1550	Groves, Robert W.	ND0350
Griffel, L. Michael	NY1900	Grissom, Cole	CA5353	Groves, Todd	DE0150
Griffen, Jane	MO0500	Grissom, Jan	GA0350	Grubb, Jay	NJ0750
Griffin, Andrew	MN0610	Grissom, Kurt	FL0450	Grubb, Steve	CA3000
Griffin, Buddy	WV0350	Grissom, Paula	GA1900	Grubb, Thomas	NY1900
Griffin, Christopher	NC2650	Griswold, Randall L.	CA0847	Grubb, William	OH2200
Griffin, Dennis	UT0300	Gritton, Bonnie	UT0250	Grubb, William	IN0250
Griffin, Gregory W.	OH2275	Grives, Julie	IL2050	Grubbs, David	NY0500
Griffin, Ivan	LA0900	Grives, Steven Matthew	IL0750	Grubbs, Jeff	PA3100
Griffin, J. Chris	NY2750	Grizzell, Janet	CA1290	Gruber, Emanuel	NC0650
Griffin, Jackie	SC0950	Grizzell, Paul W.	IL2050	Gruber, Nikolas	MN0600
Griffin, Jennifer J.	IL2200	Grmela, Sylvia	NY4460	Gruber, Rebecca C.	IA1350
Griffin, Joel	MO0400	Groat, Stephen P.	PA1850	Gruber, Sari	PA2900
Griffin, John C.	MI2250	Grobler, Pieter J.	OH0950	Grudechi, Kevin	MA0150
Griffin, Karen K.	KY1500	Grobler, Sophia	OH0950	Grudzinski, Richard	MA0260
Griffin, Larry	OH2000	Groce-Roberts, Virginia	CA4400	Gruenhagen, Lisa M.	OH0300
Griffin, Nancy W.	AR0750	Grodrian, Ericka	IN1750	Grueschow, Andrew	CA0510
Griffin, Peter J.	IL0850	Grodsky, Michael	CA1900	Gruetter, Joy	OH2140
Griffin, Randall	TX3400	Grodsky, Roger	OH2200	Grugin, Stephen	MI1600
Griffin, Robert	KY0750	Groeling, Charles	IL3200	Gruhn, Charles	CA1700
Griffin, Rose	IL3550	Groene, Robert W.	MO1810	Grundahl, Nancy J.	MN0050
Griffin, Ruth Ann	TX1660	Groesbeck, Rolf A.	AR0750	Gruner, Greg	AL1300
Griffin, Samuel S.	MS0050	Groff, Dale	WA0480	Grunert, Judi	TN0450
Griffin, Stephanie	NY0500	Grogan, Charles L.	OH2450	Grunow, Richard F.	NY1100

Name	Code	Name	Code	Name	Code
Grutzmacher, Patricia Ann	OH1100	Gunn, Nancy E.	ME0500	Haan, Keith A.	IA1300
Gryc, Stephen Michael	CT0650	Gunn, Natalie	OR0450	Haar, Mark	NE0250
Grycel, Gail	VT0100	Gunn, Nathan	IL3300	Haar, Paul	NE0600
Grycky, Eileen J.	DE0150	Gunnarson, Eike	NM0310	Haarhues, Charles D.	CO0100
Grymes, James A.	NC2420	Gunnarson, Eike	TX3520	Haas, Adam J.	AR0500
Grzych, Frank J.	TN0500	Gunnell, Jonathan	PA1050	Haas, Angela Dilkey	NY3725
Gu, Wen-Lei	WI0350	Gunnell, Sarah	UT0190	Haas, Arthur	NY1900
Gualdi, Paolo Andre'	SC0710	Gunnson, Eric	CO0900	Haas, Arthur S.	NY3790
Guarino, Robert	NJ0175	Gunter, Jenny	AB0150	Haas, Arthur	NY2250
Guarino, Robin	OH2200	Gunter, Kevin	TX2400	Haas, Connie	WI0825
Guarneri, Mario	CA4150	Gunter, Patricia	TN1400	Haas, David	GA2100
Guastafeste, Joseph	IL0550	Gunter, Trey	TX3000	Haas, Frederick L.	NH0100
Guastavino, Catherine	AI0150	Gunther, John	CO0800	Haas, Janet	MA0260
Guay, Jean-Francois	AI0200	Gunther, Thomas	IL0720	Haas, Jonathan L.	NY2750
Gubanov, Yakov	MA0260	Guntren, Alissa	IN0900	Haas, Karl	CA0270
Guberman, Daniel	NC0650	Guptill-Crain, Nan	NJ1400	Haas, Peter	LA0050
Gubrud, Darcy Lease	MN1285	Guralnick, Elissa	CO0800	Haase, Peter	VA0450
Gubrud, Irene	NY0500	Gurevich, Michael	MI2100	Habedank, Kathryn	WA0650
Guccione, Rose	IL0780	Gurgel, Denise	TX0400	Habegger, Christa	SC0200
Guccione, Rose	IL2750	Gurin, Shelley Foster	IL2150	Haber, Carol	MA1400
Guck, Marion A.	MI2100	Gurin, Vladimir	MA0350	Haberkorn, Michael	OH2050
Gudbaur, Michael A.	WI0835	Gurney, James F.	MN1120	Haberlen, John B.	GA1050
Guderian, Lois Veenhoven	WI0860	Gursky, Isreal	NY2150	Haberman, Peter J.	MN0600
Gudmundson, Jon K.	UT0300	Gurt, Joseph	MI0600	Habib, Kenneth S.	CA0600
Gudmundson, Paula	MN0040	Gurt, Michael	LA0200	Habib, Mark	AL1195
Gudmundson, Paula	MN1600	Gustafson, Beverly	MN0750	Habitzruther, Bruce E.	VA0750
Guebert, Carolyn	IN1560	Gustafson, Christine	NC0650	Habitzruther, Ellen M.	VA0750
Guechev, Guenko	PA1050	Gustafson, David	OR0350	Hache, Reginald	FL0570
Guegold, William K.	OH2150	Gustafson, Eric	NY1350	Hachiya-Weinrer, Jane	IN0100
Guelce, Sayuri	IN0250	Gustafson, Karen	AK0150	Hackbarth, Glenn A.	AZ0100
Guelker-Cone, Leslie	WA1250	Gustafson, Kirk	CO0225	Hackel, Erin H.	CO0830
Guenette, Maria	TX3535	Gustafson, Nancy J.	NJ1130	Hacker, James	FL0700
Guenette, Maria Mika	TX3370	Gustafson, Steve	NY1850	Hacker, John	IL3150
Guenoit, Eric	LA0450	Gustafson, Steven	KS0900	Hacker, Kathleen M.	IN1650
Guenther, Christina	TX2700	Gustafson-Hinds, Melissa	IL1740	Hackett, Hara	TN1400
Guenther, Eileen Morris	DC0100	Gustavson, Mark	NY0050	Hackett, Janet	OR0700
Guenther, Greg	AZ0480	Gustavson, Mark	NY2550	Hackett, Patricia	CA4200
Guenther, Roy J.	DC0100	Gustofson, Don	IL0300	Hackleman, Allene	AA0100
Guenther, Timothy E.	OH0100	Guter, Christine	CA0825	Hackleman, Martin	MO1810
Guentner, Francis J.	MO1250	Guter, Gerhard	CA3800	Hackworth, Rhonda S.	NJ1130
Guerin, Constance Ely	TN1850	Guter, Gerhard	CA1900	Haddad, George	OH1850
Guerin, Roland	LA0800	Guthmiller, Anne	VA1600	Haddad, Jamey	OH1700
Guernsey, Diane	NY2200	Guthmiller, Anne	VA1500	Haddad, Jamey	MA1400
Guerra, Stephen J.	FL1900	Guthrie, Beverly	MI1150	Haddad, Jamey	OH0600
Guerrero, Jean	NY1100	Guthrie, J. Randall	OK0850	Haddad, Jamey	MA0260
Guerrero, Rosi E.	WA0950	Guthrie, James M.	NC0400	Haddad, Layna Chianakas	CA4400
Guerriero, Angela	PA3600	Guthrie, Karl	NJ1400	Haddad, Orlando	PA3330
Guerrini, Susan C.	NJ0175	Guthrie, Mark	MI1150	Haddad, Steve	TX3520
Guertin, Ghyslaine	AI0200	Guthrie, Robert	TX2400	Hadden, Dudley 'Skip'	MA0260
Guertin, Marcelle	AI0200	Gutierrez, Alfonso	FL0650	Haddix, Ken	KY0550
Guessford, Jesse	VA0450	Gutierrez, Charles	CA0859	Haddock, Kathleen	NY4150
Guest, Ann	SC0750	Gutierrez, Charles	CA5300	Haddock, Lynette	CA3200
Guevara, Amy	NE0450	Gutierrez, Dawn	MO0400	Haddock, Marshall	OH1850
Guevara, Amy	NE0200	Gutierrez, German A.	TX3000	Haddon, Judith	IL0550
Guggenheim, Janet	OR0850	Gutierrez, Martha	UT0350	Haden, Charlie	CA0510
Guha-Thakurta, Sonya	AA0150	Gutshall, Christi	AZ0400	Haderer, Walter	CA4200
Guhr, Glen	WA0650	Guttierez, Ruben	TX3520	Hadesbeck, Robert	IA1300
Guida, John	NJ1050	Guttmann, Hadassah	NY2550	Hadfield, John R.	NY2750
Guidi, David	TX2650	Guy, Charles V.	NY3780	Hadley, Katie	OR0700
Guidobaldi Chittolina, Alberto	PR0115	Guy, Christine	ME0430	Hadley, Susan J.	PA3100
Guidry, Travis	AL1160	Guy, Kathyanne	FL1900	Hadley, Theodore	ID0075
Guilbault, Denise	RI0200	Guy, Larry L.	NY2750	Hadlock, Heather L.	CA4900
Guilbault, Jocelyne	CA5000	Guy, Larry	NY4450	Hadsell, Nancy A.	TX3300
Guilbert, Fred	LA0150	Guy, Marc J.	NY3725	Haebich, Kenneth	IL0850
Guild, Jane E.	LA0750	Guy, Nancy	CA5050	Haecker, Allyss	SC0900
Guiles, Kay	MS0360	Guy, Robin	IA1600	Haecker, Arthur	SC0650
Guilford, Matthew	MD1010	Guy, Todd	IN1025	Haecker, Arthur	SC1000
Guillen, Jorge	DC0350	Guynes, Christi	TX2570	Haefliger, Kathleen	IL0600
Guillen, Seth	TN0050	Guyver, Russell	CO0950	Haefner, Dale F.	MN1000
Guimond, Claire	AI0150	Guzasky, G. Frederick	MA0510	Haefner, Jaymee	TX3300
Guinn, Caryl	OH0600	Guzewicz, Rebecca	SC0850	Haefner, Jaymee	TX3420
Guinn, Caryl	OH0650	Guzik, Bernard	OK0850	Haefner, Steven	OK0850
Guinn, Jody J.	OH0200	Guzik, Bernie	OK1450	Haek, Jonathan	OR0500
Guinn, John R.	MI2200	Guzman, Ariel	PR0150	Haenfler, Eric	AZ0470
Guist, Anne P.	TX2960	Guzman, Ariel	PR0115	Haerle, Dan	TX3420
Guist, Jonathan B.	TX3515	Guzman, Christopher	PA2750	Haertel, Tim	IN1010
Guiterrez, Charles	CA2550	Guzman, Darryl	CA3320	Hafer, Edward	MS0750
Gulick, Michelle	VA1600	Guzman, Jesus	CA5031	Haffley, Robin L.	PA2700
Gullickson, Andrea	IN0250	Guzman, Joel J.	TX3510	Haffley, Robin	PA2400
Gullickson, Sigrid	WI1150	Guzman, Juan-Tony	IA0950	Haffley, Robin L.	PA1830
Gullings, Kyle	TX3535	Guzman, Ronald P.	NY2550	Haffner, James	CA5350
Gullotti, Bob	MA1175	Guzski, Carolyn	NY3717	Haffner, Paula	TN0100
Gullotti, Robert	MA0260	Guzzi, Ralph	PA0500	Hafner, Kenneth A.	HI0210
Gullstrand, Donna	VA1350	Guzzio-Kregler, Mary Ellen	RI0200	Hafso, Marc A.	WA1350
Gumm, Alan	MI0400	Guzzo, Anne M.	WY0200	Hafteck, Pierre	NJ0700
Gundanas, Susan	CA5000	Gwiazda, Henry	MN1120	Hagarty, Mia	TX0550
Gunderman, Jennifer	TN1850	Gwozdz, Lawrence S.	MS0750	Hagarty, Scott	TX0550
Gunderson, Frank	FL0850	Gwynne, Michelle	KY1000	Hagedorn, David	MN1450
Gunderson, Geoff	IA0500	Gwynne, William G.	OH2200	Hagedorn, Joseph	WI0845
Gunderson, Geoff	SD0050	Gyllstrom, Mabeth	MN1300	Hagedorn, Katherine J.	CA3650
Gunderson, Janice	CA0855	Gythfeldt, Marianne	DE0150	Hagedorn, Katherine	CA1050
Gunderson, Margaret	AZ0450	Ha, Jaehyuk	TX3410	Hagel, Clint	AA0020
Gunderson, Terry	WY0050	Ha, Youngmi	NY2750	Hagelganz, David	WA1150
Gunji, Maya	NY2250	Haack, Donald	WI1155	Hagelstein, Kim Rooney	TX2750
Gunlogson, Elizabeth	NH0350	Haack, Paul	MN1623	Hageman, Paul M.	TX2960
Gunlogson, Kirsten	UT0250	Haag, MaryBeth	CA1050	Hagen Givens, Marcie	MN0350
Gunn, Jennifer	IL0550	Haagenson, Anna	OR0400	Hagen, Cathy	MN1270
Gunn, Julie	IL3300	Haager, Julia	AA0050	Hagen, Julie	MN0600
Gunn, Katherine	IN0800	Haaheim, Bryan Kip	KS1350	Hagen, Sara L.	ND0600
Gunn, Lorrie	MI1830	Haakenson, Matthew A.	FL1750	Hagen, Scott	UT0250

Name	Code	Name	Code	Name	Code
Hagen, Susan	MA0950	Hall, Alan M.	CA0807	Halsey, Glynn	GA0490
Hager, H. Stephen	TX3175	Hall, Amy	MI2120	Halsey, Jeff	OH0300
Hager, Lawson	TX0900	Hall, Andy	NE0610	Halstead, Amanda R.	VA1000
Hager, Nancy M.	NY0500	Hall, Barbara L.	KY0450	Halt, Hans	NV0100
Hagerott, Dawn	ND0050	Hall, Beth	AL1195	Halvecka, Thomas	OH1910
Hagerty, Matthew	RI0250	Hall, Bianca	CA0815	Halversen, Paul J.	WA0950
Hages, Brent	WA0050	Hall, Bob	CO0550	Halverson, Carl	OR0400
Haggans, Kathryn	MO1830	Hall, Bruce	IL2250	Halverson, Janelle C.	MN1120
Haggh-Huglo, Barbara	MD1010	Hall, Carl	GA0750	Halverson, Pamela	NC1600
Hagglund, Heidi	IL3150	Hall, Carolyn F.	NC0930	Halverson, Peter	MN0600
Hagglund, Heidi	IL0150	Hall, Charles	TX3000	Halvorson, Carl	OR0850
Haglund, Richard	IL0350	Hall, Cory	FL1650	Halvorson, Marjory	WA0400
Hagner, Carolyn Zepf	KY1000	Hall, Crystal	WI0250	Ham, Christopher M.	VA1350
Hagness, Jane	PA3600	Hall, Crystal	IL0750	Ham, Donna	TX2350
Hagon, Darlene	MA0600	Hall, Dana	IL0750	Ham, Jason D.	NJ0800
Hagon, John	MA0260	Hall, Daniel	OH1900	Ham, Jeongwon	OK1350
Hague, Joylyn	IN1650	Hall, Daniel	TX3750	Ham, Lawrence	NY1050
Hague, Zach	KS0200	Hall, David	PA1550	Ham, Marilynn	IN0200
Haguenauer, Jean-Louis	IN0900	Hall, David	TX3000	Ham, Robert	IN0200
Hagwood, Angela	VA1100	Hall, Donald L.	VA1100	Hamada, Brian	CA0810
Hagy, David	NC2500	Hall, Doreen	AG0450	Hamaker, Robert	CA2775
Hahm, Shinik	CT0900	Hall, Doris S.	AL0010	Hamann, Charles	AG0400
Hahm, Shinik	CT0850	Hall, Elena	FL0500	Hamann, Donald L.	AZ0500
Hahn, Carol G.	IN0905	Hall, Elizabeth W.	PA1350	Hamann, Jeff	WI1150
Hahn, Christina	OH1850	Hall, Erin	TN1850	Hamann, Keitha Lucas	MN1623
Hahn, Christopher	MT0400	Hall, Frederick A.	AG0200	Hamann, Wolfgang	AB0040
Hahn, Christopher D.	SD0100	Hall, Gail R.	OK1350	Hamant, Alan D.	DE0150
Hahn, David	TN0580	Hall, Gary	WY0115	Hamar, Jon	WA0550
Hahn, Hae Soon	DC0170	Hall, Heidi	WA0550	Hamar, Jon	WA0050
Hahn, Mari	AK0100	Hall, J. Scott	OR0850	Hambelton, Patrice	CA3920
Hahn, Marian	MD0650	Hall, James	SC1110	Hamberlin, Larry D.	VT0350
Hahn, Marjorie	FL1300	Hall, Jamie	OR1250	Hamblin, Michael	UT0350
Hahn, Richard	ID0250	Hall, Janean	MN0300	Hamel, Gabriel	AI0190
Hahn, Tomie	NY3300	Hall, Janice	CA4460	Hamel, Keith A.	AB0100
Hahna, Nicole	PA3100	Hall, Jeff	MI1850	Hamelin, Karla M.	TX0400
Hahnemann, Hanneberit	OH0650	Hall, Jeffrey	AG0450	Hamer, Jan	PA3200
Haiduck, Neal	NY2200	Hall, Jeffrey	AG0300	Hamera, Judith	TX2900
Haight, Catherine M.	WA0800	Hall, John	MI1750	Hamersma, Carol	NJ1160
Haight, Ronald S.	WA0800	Hall, Jonathan B.	NY2750	Hames, Elizabeth	TX3000
Haight, Russell P.	TX3175	Hall, Keith	MI2250	Hamessley, Lydia	NY1350
Hailstork, Aldolphus C.	VA1000	Hall, Kenneth	VA1350	Hamill, Chad	AZ0450
Haimo, Ethan	IN1700	Hall, Lewis R.	WV0050	Hamilton, Alexander W.	MO1810
Haimovitz, Matt	AI0150	Hall, Lois	NY2800	Hamilton, Amy	AG0600
Hainen, Elizabeth	PA0850	Hall, Louis O.	ME0440	Hamilton, Anna	SC1100
Hainen, Elizabeth	PA3250	Hall, Michael	IN0150	Hamilton, Anne	WV0800
Haines, Amy	WI0250	Hall, Michael	VA1000	Hamilton, Bonnie	NY2250
Haines, James L.	PA1250	Hall, Michael L.	IL3450	Hamilton, Bonnie	NY3785
Haines, Janice	CA0950	Hall, Michael J.	MD1000	Hamilton, Brian	OK0750
Haines, Janice	CA3200	Hall, Nadine	CA3500	Hamilton, Brian	CA2550
Haines, John D.	AG0450	Hall, Patricia	MI2100	Hamilton, Bruce	WA1250
Haines, Mary Enid	AG0450	Hall, Randall	IL0100	Hamilton, Chico	NY2660
Haines, Stephanie	CA4425	Hall, Richard D.	TX3175	Hamilton, Craig V.	AR0500
Haines, Steve J.	NC2430	Hall, Rick	PA3330	Hamilton, David	MN0600
Haines, Thomas	OH2200	Hall, Robert	AG0150	Hamilton, Frederick	TX3420
Haines, Yvonne Bonnie	TX1400	Hall, Roberta	OR1020	Hamilton, Gregory	MN0600
Haines-Eitzen, John	NY0900	Hall, Rosalind	UT0050	Hamilton, Heather	TX2750
Hainsworth, Jason D.	FL0200	Hall, Sarah	AC0050	Hamilton, Hilree J.	WI0845
Hair, Harriet	GA2100	Hall, Scott	IL0720	Hamilton, Janet	IN1010
Hairston, Michelle P.	NC0650	Hall, Stefan	WI0808	Hamilton, Jean	OH2200
Haist, Dean	NE0450	Hall, Steven	WV0400	Hamilton, Karen	MN0600
Haithcock, Michael	MI2100	Hall, Sunny Joy Langton	IL2250	Hamilton, Kate	MN0600
Hajda, John M.	CA5060	Hall, Teddy	VA0500	Hamilton, Margaret J.	MI2250
Hak, Rakefet	CA5030	Hall, Thomas	MA0500	Hamilton, Margot E.	OH2500
Haken, Rudolf	IL3300	Hall, Thomas	FL0450	Hamilton, MaryAnn	NY1550
Hakim, Will J.	NY3650	Hall, Thomas E.	MD0400	Hamilton, Peter	AG0130
Hakim, William J.	NJ1160	Hall, Timothy	CA0960	Hamilton, Robert	AZ0100
Hakken, Lynda S.	IA0400	Hall, Timothy	CA2390	Hamilton, Ryan	OH0350
Hakoda, Ken	KS0700	Hall, Van-Anthoney	NC1550	Hamilton, Ryan	OH1600
Hakutani, Naoki	AR0750	Hall, W. Randall	WV0300	Hamilton, Sarah Jean	NY3725
Hala, James	NJ0175	Hall, William D.	CA0960	Hamilton, Sue	IL1610
Haladyna, Jeremy	CA5060	Hall-Gulati, Doris J.	PA1300	Hamilton, Tom	PA2200
Halbeck, Patricia	TN0050	Halladay, Wallace	AG0450	Hamilton, Vivian	SC0750
Halberg, Virginia	NY1700	Hallahan, Robert	VA0600	Hamilton, William R.	SC0420
Halberstadt, Randy	WA0200	Hallback, Alan	CA0859	Hamilton-Jenkins, Leah	MO0775
Halbert, Marjorie	TN0100	Hallberg, Carol	IA0500	Hamlin, John	KS0560
Halco, Terry	MA2010	Hallberg, Karin	AZ0450	Hamlin, Peter S.	VT0350
Haldeman, Michael	SC0275	Halle, John	NY0150	Hamlin, Seth	MA2010
Haldeman, Randy	NC2420	Haller, William P.	WV0750	Hamling, Phyllis	IA0910
Haldey, Olga	MD1010	Halleran, Sandra	NY2650	Hamm, Bruce	CA0050
Hale, Adam	TN0260	Halley, Gustavo	MO1810	Hamm, Corey D.	AB0100
Hale, Alison	MA1350	Halley, Sharon	NY2250	Hamm, Laura	WV0440
Hale, Charlotte	AB0150	Hallgren, Scott	TN1400	Hamm, Randall P.	MO0775
Hale, Cheryl	TX3370	Halliday, Anna Rebecca	AL1200	Hamm, Samuel J.	MT0350
Hale, Connie L.	SC1200	Halliday, David	UT0250	Hamm, Steven	OK0850
Hale, Daris Word	TX3175	Halliday, David	UT0400	Hamm, Zachary D.	NY0100
Hale, Kris	VA0750	Halligan, Robert S.	NY4150	Hamman, James	LA0800
Hale, Kristopher	VA1100	Hallman, Diana R.	KY1450	Hammar, Christine	MO0400
Hale, Nancy	TX1400	Hallman, Ludlow B.	ME0440	Hamme, Albert	NY3705
Hale, Roger	MO0850	Hallmark, Anne Vaughan	MA1400	Hamme, Nora Ruth	PA1650
Halen, David	MI2100	Hallmark, Rufus	NJ1130	Hammel, Alice	VA1600
Halen, Eric J.	TX2150	Halloran, Jan	NH0100	Hammel, Alice M.	VA0150
Haley, Ardith	AF0050	Halloran, Stephen	MA0350	Hammel, Bruce R.	VA1600
Haley, Geordie	AF0120	Hallsted, Nancy	DC0170	Hammer, Christoph	TX3420
Haley, Jill	PA2550	Hallstrom, Jonathan F.	ME0250	Hammer, David A.	FL0650
Haley, Julia W.	OK0800	Halm, Jack L.	WA0800	Hammer, Eric	CA5350
Haley, Timothy R.	NC2210	Halmo, Joan	AJ0150	Hammer, Janet	CA3460
Halgedahl, Frederick	IA1600	Halper, Matthew R.	NJ0700	Hammer, Levi	OH2150
Halim, Eduardus	NY2750	Halpern Lewis, Emily	MA0950	Hammer, Stephen	MA1175
Halko, Joe	MA0650	Halsell, George K.	ID0075	Hammerling, Margaret	MN0600
Halko, Joseph	MA0700	Halseth, Robert E.	CA0840	Hammerling, Margaret	ND0600

Alphabetical Listing of Faculty

Name	Code	Name	Code	Name	Code
Hammers, Eric	WI1150	Hannan, Eric	AB0050	Hanzelin, Fred	IL2775
Hammet, Jane	CA4700	Hanne, Matt	KS0980	Hanzlik, Louis	CT0600
Hammett, Hank	TX2400	Hannesson, Mark	AA0100	Hapner, David E.	OH2450
Hammett, Larry D.	OK1350	Hannifan, Patricia	CA2600	Hapner, Lee Merrill	OH2450
Hammiel, Chris	IA0910	Hannifan, Patricia	CA2750	Happel, Rebecca	MI1750
Hammond, Barbara	GA1150	Hannigan Tabon, Katie	NY2650	Haque, Fareed	IL2200
Hammond, Gary	NJ0825	Hannigan, Barry T.	PA0350	Hara, Craig	MN0800
Hammond, Gary	NY0625	Hannigan, Erin	TX2400	Hara, Craig	WI0845
Hammond, Ivan	OH0300	Hannigan, Mary	PA0950	Hara, Kunio	SC1110
Hammond, June C.	FL1600	Hanninen, Dora A.	MD1010	Harada, Tomoko	NJ1160
Hammond, L. Curtis	KY0900	Hanning, Barbara	NY0600	Haramaki, Gordon	CA4400
Hammond, Rebecca	MI1750	Hanning, Barbara Russano	NY0550	Harbach, Barbara	MO1830
Hammond, Tony	MT0350	Hanning, Chris	PA3600	Harbaugh, John	WA0050
Hamper, Robert	AG0650	Hannon-Roberts, Emilie	CT0550	Harbaugh, Kurt	WA0480
Hampton, Anitra C.	AL0650	Hannum, Thomas P.	MA2000	Harbaugh, Ross T.	FL1900
Hampton, Barbara	NY0600	Hanoian, Scott	MI2200	Harbec, Jacinthe	AI0200
Hampton, Barbara L.	NY0625	Hanrahan, Curt	WI0825	Harbert, Benjamin J.	DC0075
Hampton, Bradley	CA0845	Hanrahan, Kevin G.	NE0600	Harbinson, William G.	NC0050
Hampton, Edwin Kevin	GA0200	Hans, Ben J.	WI0450	Harbison, John H.	MA1200
Hampton, Herman	MA0260	Hansbrough, Robert S.	NY0700	Harbison, Kenneth C.	VA0450
Hampton, Ian	AB0090	Hansbrough, Yvonne	NY0700	Harbison, Kevin	CO0800
Hampton, Ian	AB0060	Hansel, Robert	TN1350	Harbison, Patrick L.	IN0900
Hampton, Neal	MA2050	Hanseler, Ryan	NC0650	Harbold, Mark A.	IL0850
Hampton, Neal	MA0500	Hanselman, Jay	GA1300	Harbold, Tim	MA2150
Hamre, Anna R.	CA0810	Hansen, Alicia S.	LA0300	Harbor, Ronald	CA5353
Hamrick, Mark	WV0800	Hansen, Bente	AA0200	Harboyan, Patil	AI0150
Hamrick, Utah	TX3530	Hansen, Brad	OR0850	Harchanko, Joseph	OR1250
Hamway, Jane	NY3350	Hansen, Charles	MA0260	Harchanko, Lois	SD0580
Han, Jinhee	KY0950	Hansen, Charles	CO0950	Harcrow, Michael	PA2300
Han, Jiyon	DC0170	Hansen, Cheryl	ID0060	Hardaway, Travis	MD0650
Han, Jong-Hoon 'James'	TX1400	Hansen, Dallin	ID0060	Hardcastle, Geoffrey C.	NY0400
Han, June Young	CT0850	Hansen, Deborah	WA1350	Hardee, Kelly Ann	NC1350
Han, Sang-In	IA0250	Hansen, Demaris	CT0650	Hardeman, Anita	IL3500
Hanagan, Joyce	CO0200	Hansen, Eric	WI0808	Harden, Bill	TX3527
Hanan, David	OK1330	Hansen, Eric	UT0050	Harden, Matthew C.	NE0610
Hanani, Yuhuda	OH2200	Hansen, Frank	NY4050	Harden, Patricia A.	NC2050
Hanawalt, Anita	CA5100	Hansen, Gloria	WI0825	Harden, Shirley	MI1900
Hanawalt, Michael	KS1450	Hansen, Jack	IN0005	Hardenbergh, Esther Jane	FL1900
Hancock, Carl B.	AL1170	Hansen, Jeremy C.	TN1450	Harder, Caroline	AB0090
Hancock, Cindy	MT0370	Hansen, Jessica	AF0050	Harder, Glen	AA0040
Hancock, Craig A.	IA1800	Hansen, John	AF0050	Harder, Lane	TX2400
Hancock, John	NJ0825	Hansen, Judith	CA5030	Harder, Lillian U.	SC0400
Hancock, Judith E.	TX3510	Hansen, Julia	CA4625	Harder, Matthew D.	WV0600
Hancock, Kyle	GA0950	Hansen, Kathleen	UT0190	Harder, Melissa	AJ0030
Hancock, Pollyanna	OR0500	Hansen, Kathleen	MT0175	Hardesty, Tamara G.	GA2150
Hancock, Richard K.	FL0700	Hansen, Kristen S.	GA0550	Hardie, William Gary	TX0300
Hancock, Robin	UT0050	Hansen, Kurt R.	IL2250	Hardiman, David A.	CA1020
Hancock, Sarah	GA0950	Hansen, Lisa	NJ0700	Hardin, Dan	FL0700
Hancock, Virginia	OR0900	Hansen, Lisa	ID0060	Hardin, Garry Joe	TX2600
Hand, Angela R.	IL3500	Hansen, Mark R.	ID0050	Hardin, Jane L.	MS0420
Hand, Angela R.	IL0100	Hansen, Neil E.	WY0130	Hardin, Larry E.	AL0500
Hand, Frederic	NY3785	Hansen, Patrick J.	AI0150	Harding, C. Tayloe	SC1110
Hand, Frederic	VT0050	Hansen, Peter	NY1275	Harding, Christopher	MI2100
Hand, Frederic	NY2250	Hansen, Peter	IN1650	Harding, David	AB0100
Hand, Gregory	IA1550	Hansen, Richard K.	MN1300	Harding, Kevin	VA1150
Hand, Judith	LA0350	Hansen, Robert	TX3750	Harding, Kevin	VA1500
Handel, Greg	LA0550	Hansen, Sharon A.	WI0825	Harding, Mark	VT0100
Handel, Thomas	MA1400	Hansen, Steven	TX0550	Harding, Scott R.	MI0400
Handel-Johnson, Brenda	MN0350	Hansen, Ted	TX2955	Hardman, David J.	OK1330
Handford, Kathrine	WI0350	Hansen, Theresa Brancaccio	IL2250	Hardt, Adam C.	WI0700
Handy, Gabriel	NJ1400	Hansen, Thomas	CA3270	Hardy, Bruce	CA5360
Hane, Daniel	NY1400	Hansen, Victoria	CO0200	Hardy, David	MD0650
Hanegraaf, Margaret	PA2550	Hansen-Jackson, Dionne	IL0550	Hardy, James	UT0150
Haneline, Stacie	IA0910	Hanser, Kirk	MO1900	Hardy, Janis	MN1450
Hanes, Jill	WI0848	Hanser, Suzanne	MA0260	Hardy, Julie	NY2660
Hanes, Michael	IL1240	Hanserd, Mary	AL0550	Hare, Andrew	DC0170
Hanes, Michael D.	IL2900	Hansford, Conchita	OK0650	Hare, Matthew	CA1425
Haney, Jason	VA0600	Hansford, James	OK0650	Hare, Matthew	CA5020
Haney, Joel C.	CA0650	Hanshaw, Marian C.	MA0700	Hare, Robert	OH1850
Haney, Julia Lawson	CA0650	Hanson, Alice	MN1450	Hare, Ryan	WA1150
Haney, Kristee	MO2000	Hanson, Andrea J.	OK1200	Harea, Ioan	NY3780
Hanford, Robert A.	IL2250	Hanson, Angela	MN0250	Harel, Jack	OH2150
Hangen, Bruce	MA0350	Hanson, Brian L.	LA0650	Hargabus, Bruce	FL0850
Hanick, Conor	MA1750	Hanson, Craig	OR0700	Hargrave, Monica	GA0050
Hanke, Craig	WI0808	Hanson, Dan L.	OK1400	Hargrave, Monica	GA1100
Hankins, Barbara	AG0600	Hanson, David B.	OH0950	Hargrave, Monica E.	GA2100
Hankins, Paul	MS0250	Hanson, David	CO0900	Hargrove, D'Ann	OK0550
Hankins, Tyson	NC0750	Hanson, Ellen	GA2200	Harguindey, Jose	AI0210
Hanks, John B.	NC0600	Hanson, Eric A.	WA0800	Haringer, Andrew	MA2250
Hanks, Kenneth B.	FL0930	Hanson, F.	NY4060	Haritun, Rosalie	IN0905
Hanks, N. Lincoln	CA3600	Hanson, Frank E.	WI0865	Harjito, I. M.	MA2020
Hanley, Bede	AC0100	Hanson, Gregg I.	AZ0500	Harjito, I.	CT0750
Hanley, Wells	VA1600	Hanson, J. Robert	MN1450	Harjung, Dan	WI1150
Hanley, Wells	VA1550	Hanson, Jan	OK1400	Harker, Brian	UT0050
Hanlon, Jake	AF0150	Hanson, John R.	NY3705	Harker-Roth, Kerry	PA2300
Hanlon, Jeff	AG0250	Hanson, Jordan	AB0150	Harkins, Edwin	CA5050
Hanlon, Kenneth	NV0050	Hanson, Josef M.	NY4350	Harkness, Lisa	TN1100
Hanlon, Kevin	TX2400	Hanson, Kevin	PA3330	Harlan, Evan	MA1400
Hanman, Theodore	KS0100	Hanson, Mark	CA1250	Harlan, Mary E.	IL1350
Hann, Dan	MA2150	Hanson, Melanie	MN0150	Harlan, Mary	IL0420
Hann, Gordon	NC2650	Hanson, Melissa	MN1620	Harlan, Paul	FL1740
Hanna, Alexander	IL0750	Hanson, Michael	MN0150	Harland, Kelly	WA0200
Hanna, Cassandria	FL1310	Hanson, Paul	VA1500	Harlas, Lou	TX0370
Hanna, Frederick	NE0160	Hanson, Ross	OR1020	Harlen, Benjamin	LA0400
Hanna, Joan	AR0850	Hanson, Sarah Beth	TN1660	Harler, Alan	PA3250
Hanna, Judith	IL0730	Hanson, Shelley J.	MN0950	Harler-Smith, Donna D.	NE0600
Hanna, Scott S.	TX3510	Hanson, Sylva	MN1400	Harleston, Sheila C.	MD1020
Hanna, Wendell	CA4200	Hanson, Terry	IL0300	Harley, Andrew	NC2430
Hannah, Barry	TN0900	Hanson-Abromeit, Deanna	MO1810	Harley, Anne	CA4500
Hannah, Mike	NC1050	Hanulik, Christopher	CA5030	Harley, Gretta	WA0200

Harley, James I.	AG0350	Harris, Carl G.	VA0500	Harriss, Elaine Atkins	TN1720
Harley, Michael	SC1110	Harris, Carole J.	NY0400	Harrod, John	KY0450
Harlin, Juston	NM0200	Harris, Charles	IA0930	Harrow, Anne Lindblom	NY1100
Harlos, Steven C.	TX3420	Harris, Charles	IA1800	Harry, Don	NY1100
Harlow, Leslie	UT0325	Harris, Daniel	OH2300	Harsa, Sandra Y.	TX1425
Harman, Chris	AI0150	Harris, David	MA2050	Harshenin, Leon A.	IN1560
Harman, David	NY4350	Harris, David	MA0260	Harstad, Bonnie	KY0150
Harmantas, Frank	AG0450	Harris, David	PA0150	Hart Stoker, Catherine	MN0950
Harmon, Jim	CA4450	Harris, David	MA1400	Hart, Antonio	NY0642
Harmon, Linda	TN0100	Harris, Dawn	IL3300	Hart, Billy	MA1400
Harmon, Richard	FL1700	Harris, Debora	MN0600	Hart, Billy W.	NJ0800
Harmon, Sally	OR0500	Harris, Debora	MN1120	Hart, Billy	OH1700
Harms, Dawn L.	CA4900	Harris, Dennis	TX1850	Hart, Bonny	NY2250
Harms, Janet	CA0250	Harris, Dennis	TX3527	Hart, Brian J.	IL2200
Harms, Janet	CA0630	Harris, Donald	OH1850	Hart, Carolyn	IL3550
Harms, Jason	MN0250	Harris, Donald	AJ0150	Hart, Cherie	WI0862
Harms, Lawrence	IL1090	Harris, Duane	MO0350	Hart, Cheryl	UT0400
Harms, Lois	IA0650	Harris, Edward C.	CA4400	Hart, Craig	MA0950
Harms, Melanie	IA1800	Harris, Ellen T.	MA1200	Hart, Edward B.	SC0500
Harnell, Jason	CA5020	Harris, Eric	TN1450	Hart, James	OH2550
Harness, Kelley	MN1623	Harris, Erik	MO1950	Hart, Kenneth W.	TX2400
Harney, Jon M.	MT0200	Harris, Esther L.	NY2750	Hart, Kevin	IL2350
Harney, Kristin	MT0200	Harris, Evelyn	UT0350	Hart, Kevin S.	WY0200
Harnish, David D.	CA5200	Harris, Fred	MA1200	Hart, Kevin M.	IL1350
Haroutounian, Joanne	VA0450	Harris, Hilda	NY2150	Hart, Kevin	IL1150
Haroutunian, Ronald	CT0600	Harris, Hilda	NY3560	Hart, Lawrence	NC2430
Haroutunian, Ronald	MA0400	Harris, Howard	TX3150	Hart, Martha J.	MO1950
Haroz, Nitzan	PA3250	Harris, J. David	IL3300	Hart, Mary Ann	IN0900
Haroz, Nitzan	PA0850	Harris, Janet	FL1650	Hart, Michael	CA0550
Harp, James	MD0650	Harris, Janet	FL0450	Hart, Michael D.	LA0030
Harper, Billy	NY2660	Harris, Jarrard	IL2750	Hart, Peter	MA0150
Harper, Carole	VA0700	Harris, Jarrard	IL0720	Hart, Richard	MA0260
Harper, Darryl	VA1600	Harris, Jarrard	IL3150	Hart, Sasha	OH2550
Harper, David R.	RI0150	Harris, Jason W.	OH1700	Hart, Steven R.	MT0350
Harper, Denis B.	CA0850	Harris, John	AG0130	Hart, Thomas J.	IA0600
Harper, Erin Michelle	NC0350	Harris, Jonathan	FL0450	Hart, Victoria	CA0859
Harper, Gergory	CO0150	Harris, Julie	AA0150	Hart-Reilly, Kathy M.	TN1710
Harper, Greg J.	CO0250	Harris, Karin	CA5300	Harte, Monica	NY0500
Harper, Joe Dan	NY3725	Harris, Katherine	NJ0700	Hartenberger, Aurelia	MO1950
Harper, Kris	PA3650	Harris, Kathy	ID0075	Hartenberger, Aurelia	MO1830
Harper, Larry D.	WI0200	Harris, Kay	SC1080	Hartenberger, Russell	AG0450
Harper, Nelson	OH0850	Harris, Kim	KY0250	Harter, Courtenay L.	TN1200
Harper, Patricia	CT0100	Harris, Larry	OH2600	Harter, Melody	MI2000
Harper, Rhonda	MO0600	Harris, Lee	TN1700	Hartger, Susan	PA3580
Harper, Richard	NY2660	Harris, Les	NH0350	Hartgrove, Kathryn	GA1050
Harper, Sharmi	NY2900	Harris, Les	ME0500	Harth-Bedoya, Miguel	TX3000
Harper, Steven A.	GA1050	Harris, Mark	CO0550	Hartig, Caroline A.	OH1850
Harper, T.J.	RI0150	Harris, Mary	OH1450	Hartig, Hugo J.	WI0200
Harper, Tamara W.	GA1700	Harris, Matthew W.	IN1100	Hartigan, Royal	MA2020
Harper, Thomas	WA1050	Harris, Melanie	FL1675	Hartke, Stephen	CA5300
Harr, James	TN1200	Harris, Mitzi	IA1300	Hartke-Towell, Christina	KY0900
Harran, Roy	GA0050	Harris, Olga	TN1400	Hartl, David	PA3330
Harrel, Shawn	MO1810	Harris, Paul R.	TX2295	Hartley, Brian	CT0300
Harrell, Ann	MO1800	Harris, Paul K.	WA1000	Hartley, Dawn	TN0100
Harrell, David Alan	OH0650	Harris, Rachel	LA0200	Hartley, Linda A.	OH2250
Harrell, Greg	MI2250	Harris, Ray	AB0090	Hartley, Walter S.	NY3725
Harrell, James	MD0170	Harris, Ray	MS0570	Hartline, Nicholas	TN0260
Harrell, Jana	GA0850	Harris, Rob	AG0600	Hartman, Andrew	OH1200
Harrell, Mark	TN0250	Harris, Robert	GA0200	Hartman, Jane	IL1610
Harrell, Mary	CA1900	Harris, Robert A.	IL2250	Hartman, Kevin	WI0825
Harrell, Paula D.	NC1600	Harris, Rod D.	CA1375	Hartman, Lee	MO1790
Harrell, Richard	CA4150	Harris, Roger	IL0550	Hartman, Mark L.	PA3050
Harrell, Wayne	MO0800	Harris, Roger	IN0005	Hartman, Mark S.	NY3780
Harrelson, Lee	MO0850	Harris, Ruth	IA0550	Hartman, Scott	CA4425
Harrelson, Neal	NY2105	Harris, Ruth Berman	NY2400	Hartman, Scott	CT0850
Harrelson, Patricia A.	NC0850	Harris, Scott H.	TX2700	Hartman, Tony	AZ0470
Harres, Debra	IL1740	Harris, Scott	ME0500	Hartmann, Donald	NC2430
Harres, Debra	IL2970	Harris, Stefon	NY2750	Hartt, Jared C.	OH1700
Harrigan, Robert	MA0260	Harris, Timothy	CA0900	Hartung, Colleen M.	PA0350
Harrigan, Wilfred	MA0600	Harris, Turman	DC0050	Hartung, Colleen	PA3150
Harrill, Stephen	NC1900	Harris, Ward	MD0550	Hartway, James	MI2200
Harriman, Janet K.	CO0800	Harris, William	NY2950	Hartwell, Hugh	AG0200
Harrington, Allen	AC0100	Harris, William H.	NY4150	Hartwell, Robert	CA1800
Harrington, Barbara	AL1200	Harris, Zacc	MN0800	Hartwig, Judy	NE0250
Harrington, Danny	MA0260	Harris-Warrick, Rebecca	NY0900	Hartwig, Judy	NE0610
Harrington, E. Michael	MA0260	Harrison, Albert D.	IN1560	Harty, Jane	WA0650
Harrington, Edward	NM0150	Harrison, Brady	OH2550	Hartzel, Marcie	KS0225
Harrington, Elisabeth	CA2250	Harrison, Carol	MO1550	Hartzell, K. Drew	NY3700
Harrington, Jeff	MA0260	Harrison, Charley	CA5031	Hartzell, Richard	MD0400
Harrington, Karen	OK1450	Harrison, Clint	MO0400	Hartzell, William H.	OH0200
Harrington, Richard	CA0050	Harrison, Daniel	CT0900	Harvell, Matthew	IL1400
Harrington, Roger J.	PA3250	Harrison, David E.	GA1700	Harvey, Anne	NH0300
Harrington, William	CA3520	Harrison, Edward	IL0550	Harvey, Anthony	MD1100
Harriott, Janette	NE0590	Harrison, Jacob G.	IA0850	Harvey, Brent	NC2700
Harris Walsh, Kristen	AD0050	Harrison, James	ID0050	Harvey, Brent M.	NC1900
Harris, Alan	NY1100	Harrison, Jane	OH1850	Harvey, James	TX0075
Harris, Alice Eaton	NY2400	Harrison, Joanne K.	NC1150	Harvey, Julie	AZ0400
Harris, Alonzo	MA0260	Harrison, John F.	PA1250	Harvey, Kathryn	NY4150
Harris, Amy	NC2000	Harrison, John	MA2020	Harvey, Lori Kay	OH2050
Harris, Anton	GA0050	Harrison, Joy	IA0650	Harvey, Mark	MA1200
Harris, B. Joan	MS0200	Harrison, Joy	IA0420	Harvey, Peter J.	CT0240
Harris, Ben	FL0100	Harrison, Judy	FL0900	Harvey, Susan	TX1700
Harris, Ben	TN1850	Harrison, Kelvin	LA0800	Harvey, Susan	CA4150
Harris, Bill	CT0550	Harrison, Kevin	IL3550	Harvey, Trevor	IA1550
Harris, Brenda	NY3790	Harrison, Leslie Anne	WY0115	Harvey, Wallace	CA0050
Harris, Brenda	IL1612	Harrison, Luvada A.	AL0950	Harvey, William	CA3520
Harris, Brian T.	NY2750	Harrison, Robert J.	IN0900	Harvey, William	CA4425
Harris, Brian P.	TX1600	Harrison, Rosaura	FL0365	Harvey-Reed, Lisa	OK0750
Harris, C. Andrew	IA0300	Harrison, Stephen J.	CA4900	Harwood, Andy	GA1500
Harris, Caleb	CO0950	Harrison, Thomas	FL1000	Harwood, Baxter	WA0100

Alphabetical Listing of Faculty

Name	Code	Name	Code	Name	Code
Harwood, Carey	NC0750	Hawkins Raimi, Jane	NC0600	Hazeltine, David	NY3785
Harwood, Craig	CT0900	Hawkins, Allan	MN1300	Hazilla, Jon	MA1400
Harwood, Elizabeth	AF0050	Hawkins, Allan	MN0625	Hazilla, Jon	MA0260
Harwood, Eve E.	IL3300	Hawkins, Anne	FL2000	He, Jianjun	FL1000
Harwood, Gregory	GA0950	Hawkins, Ashley	GA1200	He, Lin	LA0200
Harwood, Karen	GA1500	Hawkins, Ben	KY1350	He, Wei	CA4150
Harwood, Susan	NY0700	Hawkins, Candace	OK0750	Head, Brian	CA5300
Hasbrouck, Calvin	GA2100	Hawkins, Chase	KY0450	Head, John	GA0490
Hasegawa, Robert	AI0150	Hawkins, Diane	OR0175	Head, Joseph	CO0200
Hasenpflug, Thom	ID0100	Hawkins, Jemmie Peevy	AL0650	Head, Kelley	MO0100
Hash, Phillip M.	MI0350	Hawkins, John A.	WV0500	Head, Paul D.	DE0150
Hashimoto, Ayumi	NJ1160	Hawkins, Kay	MN0625	Head, Russell	KS0750
Hashimoto, Kyoko	AI0150	Hawkins, Michelle	CA5510	Head, Stan	TN1380
Haskell, Jeffrey R.	AZ0500	Hawkins, Michelle	CA1550	Headlam, David	NY1100
Haskell, Peter	NY1150	Hawkins, Michelle Kennedy	AA0110	Headlee, Will	NY2950
Haskett, Brandon L.	GA1500	Hawkins, Phillip	CA2975	Headrick, Samuel P.	MA0400
Haskett, William	TX1600	Hawkins, Randall	SC0275	Heaford, Christian	ND0350
Haskin, Steven	MN1050	Hawkins, Richard	OH1700	Heald, Jason A.	OR1020
Haskins, David	AB0200	Hawkins, Sherwood M.	FL1550	Heald, Michael	GA2100
Haskins, Jodi	AL1150	Hawkins, Wes	AZ0470	Healey, John	VA0450
Haskins, Robert	NH0350	Hawkins, William	CA3460	Healey, Martha M.	AR0425
Hass, Jeffrey E.	IN0900	Hawkinson, Carol	FL1745	Healy, Eddie	TX0700
Hasseler, Lynda	OH0350	Hawkinson, Jennifer	SD0580	Heap, Matthew	DC0010
Hasselfield, Bart	AC0050	Hawkley, Krysta	DC0170	Heape, Mary Willis	TX3050
Hassevoort, Christine	TN0260	Hawkshaw, Paul	CT0850	Heard, Alan	AG0500
Hassevoort, Darrin	TN0260	Hawley, Alexandra W.	CA4900	Heard, Cornelia	TN1850
Hassler, Desiree	IL1850	Hawley, Lucrecia	AL0010	Heard, Rachel P.	MS0385
Hastings, David M.	WI0850	Hawley, Richard R.	OH2200	Heard, Richard	NC2700
Hastings, Gena M.	IN0905	Hawley, Thomas E.	MD1000	Heard, Richard	NC2500
Hastings, Mary Logan	PA1600	Hawn, Mary	AC0100	Hearden, Kathryn	VA0450
Hastings, Richard	CA1750	Haworth, Janice	MN0150	Hearn, Barry	DC0050
Hastings, Stella	KS1050	Haworth, Laurie	AL0530	Hearn, Carmelita	AF0120
Hastings, Todd J.	KS1050	Hawryluck, Alan	MA0950	Hearn, Elizabeth	IN1100
Haston, Warren	CT0650	Hawthorne, Leroy	LA0100	Hearn, Priscilla	KS0550
Hasty, Barbara P.	CA1700	Hay, Beverly R.	SC0650	Hearn, Sidney T.	IN1100
Hasty, Christopher	MA1050	Hay, David	MI0850	Hearn, William	GA0500
Hasty, Robert	CA1700	Hay, Dennis	AR0050	Hearne, Clarice	IL1890
Hasty, Robert G.	IL2250	Hay, James	MA2020	Hearne, Clarice	IL3370
Hatch, Jim	AR0850	Hay, James	MA0510	Hearne, Lisa	IA0400
Hatch, Ken	AR0110	Hay, Jeff	WA0200	Hearne, Martin	IA0400
Hatch, Martin	NY0900	Hayase, Takako	IN0400	Hearns, Maureen	UT0300
Hatch, Montgomery	NY1600	Hayashida, Mami	KY0610	Hearnsberger, Keith	AR0750
Hatch, Peter	AG0600	Hayden, Marion	MI2100	Hearrell, Steve	KS1400
Hatcher, Charles E.	OH2200	Hayden, Paulina	IN1450	Hearson, Robert H.	PA1900
Hatcher, George	NC2300	Hayden, Ron	KY0250	Heasley, Tim	CA0270
Hatcher, Oeida M.	VA0750	Hayden, William P.	FL2000	Heater, Katherine	CA5000
Hatchett, Yvonne	NY0630	Haydon, Geoffrey Jennings	GA1050	Heath, Guy	FL1430
Hatem, Jasmine	TX3450	Haydon, Rick	IL2910	Heath, James	NY0642
Hatfield, Bradley	MA1450	Hayes, Andrew	NC0910	Heath, Jason	IL0750
Hatfield, Clancy	KY0650	Hayes, Angela	CA5353	Heath, Malissa	KY1540
Hatfield, D. J.	MA0260	Hayes, Beth Tura	LA0800	Heath, Travis M.	IL2150
Hatfield, Gaye Tolan	MA0260	Hayes, Casey J.	IN0500	Heaton, Meg Cognetta	NY1550
Hatfield, Grover 'Clancy'	WV0400	Hayes, Christina	NC0050	Heavin, Hadley	NE0610
Hathaway, Cheryl	MN0625	Hayes, Christopher	OH1900	Heavner, Tabitha	CT0050
Hathaway, Janet J.	IL2200	Hayes, Daun	CA4600	Heavner, Tracy	AL1300
Hathaway, Matt	MI1650	Hayes, David	PA0850	Heberlein, Yuko	MN0250
Hatley, H. Jerome	OK0850	Hayes, David	NY2250	Hebert, Floyd	MA2250
Hatley, Paula	CA5550	Hayes, Eileen M.	MD0850	Hebert, Joseph G.	LA0300
Hatmaker, J. E.	IL2200	Hayes, Glenn C.	WI0865	Hebert, Pierre	AI0210
Hatschek, Keith N.	CA5350	Hayes, Gregory M.	NH0100	Hebert, Ryan	FL2050
Hatsuyama, Hiroyo	CA3600	Hayes, Jane	AB0060	Hebert, Sandra M.	MA0330
Hatteberg, Kent E.	KY1500	Hayes, Kelly	AZ0440	Hecht, Gerard	NY3785
Hatten, Robert S.	TX3510	Hayes, Kristin Delia	TX3530	Hecht, Joshua	NY1600
Hatton, Christopher	CO0150	Hayes, Micah	TX3500	Heck, Steve	MA0260
Hatvani, Robert	OR1010	Hayes, Natlynn	OK0200	Heckman, Rick	NJ0825
Hatzis, Christos	AG0450	Hayes, Natlynn	AR0730	Hector-Norwood, Diana	TX1350
Hauan, Catherine	AZ0440	Hayes, Pamela	SC0600	Hedberg, Jeffrey	IL1085
Haubry, Rebekah	FL0800	Hayes, Tara	IL1300	Hedberg, Judy L.	OR0800
Hauck, Ross	WA0200	Hayes, Truman	WI0810	Hedberg, Kristen	NC2600
Haug, Sue	IA0850	Hayes, Tyrone	AL0050	Hedden, Debra Gordon	KS1350
Haug, Sue E.	PA2750	Hayes, William Bryce	VA0600	Hedden, Laura	NJ1000
Haugen, Jennifer E.	MN1030	Hayes-Davis, Lucy	AF0100	Heddens, Jared	MI0520
Haugen, Ruben	MN1625	Hayghe, Jennifer C.	NY1800	Hedegaard, Kirsten	IL1615
Hauger, Karin	CO0830	Haygood, Christopher D.	OK0800	Hedgecoth, David	OR1050
Haughton, Ethel Norris	VA1750	Haygood, James	LA0760	Hedgepeth, Byron	NC0050
Haun, Errol	CO0950	Hayhurst, John	CA5300	Hedger, John	KY0300
Haunstein, Jim	PA2300	Haymon-Coleman, Cynthia	IL3300	Hedger, John R.	KY1350
Haunton, Thomas C.	NH0100	Hayner, Joy	GA1650	Hedges, Don P.	IL3150
Haupers, James Mitch	MA0260	Hayner, Phillip A.	GA1650	Hedges, John B.	NY3760
Haupert, Mary Ellen	WI1100	Haynes, Casey	LA0450	Hedlund, Kristin	IL2750
Haupt, Dorothy G.	PA0125	Haynes, Erica	CT0650	Hedquist, Seth	IA1350
Hausback, Jason	MO0775	Haynes, Greg	MO0850	Hedrick, Carmella	NC1900
Hauser, Alexis	AI0150	Haynes, Juliana	LA0900	Hedrick, David	KY0400
Hauser, Jared E.	TN1850	Haynes, Justin	IL1350	Hedrick, Steve	VA1250
Hauser, Joshua	TN1450	Haynes, Kimberly	FL0100	Hedrick, Teresa	VA1250
Hauser, Kristin	TN1450	Haynes, Philip	PA0350	Hedrick, Teresa	VA0550
Hauser, Laura	TN1850	Hays, David R.	MO0775	Hedrick, Teresa	VA0050
Hauser, Michael	MN1625	Hays, Elizabeth	IA0700	Hedwig, Douglas F.	NY0500
Hauser, Michael S.	MN0950	Hays, Jonathan C.	PA3150	Heersche, Kim	KY0450
Hausey, Collette J.	CA2050	Hays, Jonathan C.	PA0950	Heershe, Kim	KY1350
Hausmann, Charles S.	TX3400	Hays, Sorrel	GA2130	Heersink, Barbara	CO0050
Hausmann, John P.	KY1500	Hays, Timothy O.	IL0850	Heetderks, David	OH1700
Hauze, Andrew	PA3200	Hayslett, Dennis J.	FL1450	Heffernan, Michele	NJ1100
Havranek, Patricia	IN0900	Haythorne, Geraldine	AA0020	Heffernan, Nancy	TX0250
Havrilla, Adam A.	PR0115	Hayward, Andre	MA1400	Heffner, Christopher J.	PA1900
Hawes, Preston	MD0150	Hayward, Carol M.	OH0300	Hefley, Earl	OK1330
Hawes, Randell D.	IL2250	Haywood, Carl	VA0950	Heflin, Thomas	NY2150
Hawk, Heather	TX2750	Haywood, Jennifer	NY1800	Hefling, Stephen	OH0400
Hawk, Stephen L.	PA3100	Hazelip, Richard	TX1450	Hegarty, James	IL2400
Hawkey, Walter	TX3540	Hazelip, Richard	TX2300	Hege, Daniel C.	NY4150

Name	Code	Name	Code	Name	Code
Hegg, Barbara	SD0150	Helms, Jessica	CA0550	Hennigar, Harcus	AG0450
Hegg, Dennis	SD0150	Helms, Nancy	CA5150	Henniger, Henry J.	OR1050
Heglund, Andrew	NV0100	Helms, Warren	NJ1400	Henniger, Henry J.	OR0700
Hehmsoth, Henry	TX3175	Helmuth, Mara M.	OH2200	Henning, Mary	KY0350
Hehr, Milton G.	MO1810	Helppie, Kevin	OR1250	Henninger, Jacqueline	TX3510
Heid, David	NC0600	Helsen, Katherine E.	AG0500	Hennings, Dieter	KY1450
Heid, R. J.	PA1450	Helseth, Daniel	WA0250	Henniss, Bruce G.	OH1850
Heid, Ronald J.	PA3000	Helsley, Jack	IN0100	Henoch, Michael L.	IL2250
Heidel, Richard Mark	IA1550	Helsley, Jack	IN0907	Henrikson, Steven	AG0550
Heidenreich, Christopher	MI2120	Helsley, Jack D.	IN0350	Henriques, Donald A.	CA0810
Heidlberger, Frank	TX3420	Helton, Caroline	MI2100	Henriques, J. Tomas	NY3717
Heidner, Eric	CA5550	Helton, James Caton	IN0150	Henriques, Yurii	AL0800
Heidner, Eric C.	CA4410	Helton, Jerry L.	SC1200	Henriquez, Carlos G.	IL2250
Heifetz, Robin J.	CA0200	Helton, Johann	ID0050	Henry, Anna	TX1550
Heighway, Robbi A.	WI0450	Helton, Jonathan	FL1850	Henry, Anna W.	TX2350
Heikalo, Daniel	AF0050	Helton, Kimberly	IA1350	Henry, Barbara	WI1150
Heil, Leila T.	CO0800	Helton, Melanie	MI1400	Henry, Colleen	MA1600
Heil, Teri	NE0250	Helvering, David A.	WI0350	Henry, Eric L.	PA3150
Heilbrunn, Micah	AC0100	Helvering, Emily		Henry, Eric	PA0950
Heiles, William H.	IL3300	Helvering, R. Douglas	NJ1350	Henry, Eric	PA2300
Heilmair, Barbara	OR0850	Helvey, Emily	AZ0470	Henry, James	MO1830
Heilman, Annette	NY3600	Helwing, Anna	CA2440	Henry, James	CA4850
Heim, Charlie	PA3330	Helzer, Richard A.	CA4100	Henry, John P.	NC1550
Heim, D. Bruce	KY1500	Hemberger, Glen J.	LA0650	Henry, Joseph W.	MN0610
Heim, Matthew	OH2050	Hemenway, Langston	IL2050	Henry, Joseph D.	IL0900
Heim, Sean	CA0960	Hemingway, Gerry	NY2660	Henry, Kevin	PA3150
Heiman, Lawrence F.	IN1350	Hemke, Frederic J. B.	SD0400	Henry, Leslie	WI1150
Heimarck, Brita Renee	MA0400	Hemke, Frederick	IL2250	Henry, Mark	MA2050
Heimbecker, Sara	CO0950	Hemmel, Ronald A.	NJ1350	Henry, Mary Pat	MO1810
Heimur, Elena	NY0644	Hemphill, Steven R.	AZ0450	Henry, Matthew	MO1830
Hein, David	WI0400	Henckel, Kristina	OK0150	Henry, Michele L.	TX0300
Heine, Bruce	MN1300	Hendelman, Tamir	CA5031	Henry, Paul	IN0005
Heine, Erik	OK0750	Henderson, Alan E.	AG0650	Henry, Paul	IL0730
Heinemann, Steven	IL0400	Henderson, Allen C.	GA0950	Henry, Paul S.	VA1475
Heinemen, Sue	MD1010	Henderson, Andrew Elliot	NY4200	Henry, Rebecca	PA1400
Heinen, Julia	CA2750	Henderson, Benjamin	UT0350	Henry, Rebecca S.	MD0650
Heinen, Julia M.	CA0835	Henderson, Chip	TN1680	Henry, Robert	GA1150
Heinick, Carol	NY3780	Henderson, Cindy	UT0350	Henry, Robert	TX3200
Heinick, David G.	NY3780	Henderson, David	CA5350	Henry, Ruth	IL2310
Heinlein, Kenneth	OH0600	Henderson, David D.	CA4900	Henry, Warren	TX3420
Heinrichs, William C.	WI0825	Henderson, David R.	NY3550	Henry, William R.	TX3175
Heintzen, Ashley	FL1750	Henderson, Donald O.	MI0400	Henschell, Lana	AA0050
Heinz-Thompson, Leslie	MO0850	Henderson, Douglas S.	OK0800	Hensel, Larry L.	WY0200
Heinze, Thomas	PA2200	Henderson, Eddie	NY1900	Hensley, David	CA0810
Heinzelmann, Sigrun B.	OH1700	Henderson, Elaine	PA2300	Hensley, David L.	CA3700
Heinzen, Craig	LA0700	Henderson, Gordon L.	CA5030	Hensley, Hunter C.	KY0550
Heisler, Jeff A.	OH1100	Henderson, Jean	NE0450	Hensley, Maria	MO0400
Heisler, Wayne H.	NJ0175	Henderson, Jenny	AR0250	Henson, Bill	MI1800
Heiss, John	MA0400	Henderson, Kate	AG0130	Henson, Blake R.	WI0750
Heiss, John C.	MA1400	Henderson, Lisa	IA0700	Henson, Eric	SC0850
Heitsch, Paul	VA0600	Henderson, Luther L.	CA2600	Henson, Karen A.	NY0750
Heitzenrater, John	NC1600	Henderson, Mark A.	UT0350	Henson, Mitchell	GA1700
Heitzman, Jill M.	IA0450	Henderson, Matthew C.	SC1100	Hensrud, Tammy J.	NY1600
Hekmatpanah, Kevin	WA0400	Henderson, Matthew	GA0250	Hentges, Londa	MN1250
Hekmatpanah, Kevin	ID0140	Henderson, Pamela	NC0750	Hepburn, Cathleen	AZ0510
Helbig, Adriana	PA3420	Henderson, Paul	TN0100	Hepler, David	PA0700
Helbing, Stockton T.	TX3420	Henderson, Paul	TN1400	Hepler, Julie E.	PA0100
Helbing, Stockton	TX2600	Henderson, Peter	MO0700	Hepler, Lowell E.	PA0100
Helble, Mitch	CO0650	Henderson, Rebecca	TX3510	Hepler, Nathaniel	PA1550
Held, Jeffrey	CA1425	Henderson, Silvester	CA2775	Hepner, Jae Lyn	IL1200
Held, Wilbur C.	OH1850	Henderson, V. Douglas	VA1150	Hepokoski, James	CT0900
Helder, Annette	MN1620	Hendon, Sally	VT0250	Hepola, Ralph	MN0800
Helding, Lynn E.	PA0950	Hendricks, Allen	SC0275	Heppner-Harjo, Tianna	NV0050
Heldman, Dianna J.	NY2750	Hendricks, Hermina	VA1125	Hepworth, Elise M.	NE0700
Heldrich, Claire	NY2150	Hendricks, James	IL0600	Herald, Terry	MI1750
Heldt, Tim	MI0850	Hendricks, John	WV0750	Herb, Thomas	UT0200
Heley, Ruth	ND0100	Hendricks, Jon	OH2300	Herbeck, Tina	CA0200
Helfgot, Daniel	CA4400	Hendricks, Karin S.	IN0150	Herbener, Catherine	NE0150
Helfter, Susan	CA5300	Hendricks, Karin S.	IL3300	Herberman, Steve	MD0850
Hell, Felix	PA1400	Hendricks, Steven	MO1500	Herbert, David	TX3530
Hellberg, Eric	CA2440	Hendricksen, David Alan	TN1650	Herbert, David	TX2200
Heller, Brian	MN1050	Hendrickson, Anna	NY3780	Herbert, David	CA4150
Heller, David	TX3350	Hendrickson, Brandon P.	SD0600	Herbert, David P.	TX2260
Heller, Jack J.	FL2000	Hendrickson, Daniel	MI1180	Herbert, Jeffery	TX3050
Heller, Lauren B.	CT0050	Hendrickson, Peter A.	MN0050	Herbiet, Victor	AG0400
Heller, Lora	NY2450	Hendrickson, Steven	MD1010	Herbst-Walker, Nikki	AA0050
Heller, Marsha	NJ0825	Hendrix, Michael	LA0100	Herceg, Melissa	OH1400
Heller, Marsha	NJ0800	Hendrix, Suzanne R.	MO0050	Herdan, Eric S.	CA3500
Heller, Ryan	WA0480	Hendry, Robin	MO0350	Heredia, Joel	WA0480
Heller, Wendy B.	NJ0900	Hendry, Robin	MO0400	Herendeen, David	OK0750
Hellick, Gary	MI0500	Hendsbee, Blaine	AA0200	Heritage, Lee	OH2300
Hellick, Gary J.	MI2200	Henegar, Gregg	MA1400	Herl, Joseph	NE0150
Hellick, Melanie	MI0500	Henegar, Gregg	MA0400	Herlehy, Margaret	NH0350
Hellman, Daniel S.	MO0775	Heneghan, Aine	WA1050	Herlihy, David	MA1450
Hellmann, Mary	NC0700	Henes, John M.	IL0750	Herlihy, John S.	MN1280
Hellmer, Jeffrey	TX3510	Henes, John	IL2250	Hermalyn, Joy	NJ0700
Hellyar, Kathleen	PA0125	Hengst, Michael	CO0550	Herman, Cheryl	IL2800
Helm, Erica	VA1350	Henigbaum, William	NC2600	Herman, Gabe	CT0650
Helm, Jon E.	AA0040	Henjum, Katherine	ND0400	Herman, Harold	VA1350
Helm, Lenora Zenzalai	NC1600	Henke, Corey	MN1700	Herman, Linde	VA1350
Helm, Michael	ND0350	Henkel, Karl		Herman, Martin	CA0825
Helm, Patricia	PA2550	Henkel, Kayme	WI1150	Herman, Matthew	PA2400
Helman, Michael	ID0100	Henkel, Sussan	NH0150	Herman, Matthew James	VA1350
Helman, Shandra K.	ID0100	Henkle, Stephanie	OH0850	Hermann, Joseph W.	TN1450
Helmer, John	AC0100	Henley, Matthew	NC2600	Hermann, Richard	NM0450
Helmer, John	AC0050	Hennel, Daniel	IL0850	Hermanson, Erik	MN0200
Helmer, Terence	AG0450	Hennen, Nancy	AC0050	Hermiston, Nancy	AB0100
Helmrich, Dennis	IL3300	Hennessey, Patrick D.	HI0110	Hernandez Candelas, Marta	PR0115
Helms, Elizabeth	CA0550	Hennessy, Jeff	AF0050	Hernandez Guzman, Nestor	PR0115
Helms, Elizabeth	CA5360	Hennessy, Michael	WI0750	Hernandez Mergal, Luis A.	PR0115

Alphabetical Listing of Faculty

Name	Code	Name	Code	Name	Code
Hernandez, Bernardo	MA0260	Heuchemer, Dane O.	OH1200	Higgins, Michael	CA0825
Hernandez, Edgar	CA0830	Heuer, Megan	TX2250	Higgins, Ramsey	AZ0490
Hernandez, Rafael	CA0807	Heuermann, Beryl Lee	MT0400	Higgins, Scott	CA3600
Hernandez, Rene	MD0850	Heukeshoven, Eric	MN1400	Higgins, Scott	CA0550
Hernandez, Richard	CA4450	Heukeshoven, Janet	MN1400	Higgins, Scott	TN1680
Hernandez, Teresa	KS0700	Heuser, David	NY3780	Higgins, Timothy	CA4150
Hernandez, Thomas	CA2050	Heuser, Frank	CA5030	Higgins, William R.	PA2300
Herndon, Hillary	TN1710	Hevia, Lonnie	MD0850	Higgins, William L.	AR0300
Hernly, Patrick	FL2050	Hewell, Rob	AR0500	Higgs, David	NY1100
Hernly, Patrick	FL0930	Hewett, E.	MA0800	High, Eric	WI0750
Hernon, Bonnie	TN1720	Hewitt, Eric	MA0350	High, Linda	NC0650
Hernon, Bonnie	TN0450	Hewitt, Michael P.	MD1010	High, Ronald	SC0150
Hernon, Michael A.	TN1720	Hewlett, Walter	CA4900	Higham, Peter	AE0050
Hernon, Mike	TN0450	Hewson, Cheryl	ND0100	Highbaugh Aloni, Pamela	AB0150
Herod, Sheila	TX1750	Hey, Darryl	NY3000	Highben, Zebulon M.	OH1650
Heroux, Gerard H.	RI0300	Hey, Philip	MN1623	Highberger, Edgar B.	PA3000
Herr, Andrea	NJ0825	Hey, Phillip	MN1450	Highfill, Philip	OH1700
Herr, Andrea	NJ0700	Hey, Phillip	MN0950	Highman, Daniel R.	CA0807
Herreid, Grant	CT0900	Heyboer, Jill L.	MO0775	Highstein, Gustav	VA1500
Herren, Matthew	KS1050	Heyde, Stephen	TX0300	Hightower, Allen	IA0950
Herrera, Cathy	PA1650	Heydenburg, Audrejean	MI2000	Hightower, J. Taylor	MS0750
Herrera, Jennifer	PA3710	Heyer, David	OR1050	Hightower, Kristin	IA0950
Herrera, Luis Ricardo	IL3300	Heyl, Jeffrey	MO0650	Hightshoe, Robert B.	OH1850
Herrick, Carole	AR0350	Heyman, Amy G.	NY4150	Higney, John	AG0100
Herrick, Dennis R.	AL0450	Heyman, Michael B.	MA0260	Hii, Philip	TX2930
Herrick, Matthew	OH1100	Heyman, Steven	NY0650	Hii, Philip	TX0550
Herring, David Scott	SC1110	Heyman, Steven M.	NY4150	Hijazi, Anne	NY2400
Herring, Vincent	NJ1400	Heywood, Andre'	MN0350	Hijleh, Kelley	NY1700
Herrington, Benjamin	NY2150	Heywood, David John	SC0500	Hijleh, Mark D.	NY1700
Herrington, Brian P.	TX2250	Hibbard, Dave	IL0650	Hilbun, Aaron Ichiro	FL1550
Herrington, Carolyn	AA0200	Hibbard, James	AG0500	Hildebrand, David K.	MD0650
Herrington, Carolyn A.	AG0500	Hibbard, Jason	FL1950	Hildebrand, Ed	AC0100
Herriott, Jeffrey	WI0865	Hibbard, Kevin	GA2130	Hildebrand, Janet N.	NE0200
Herris, Keith	TN0150	Hibbard, Mace	GA1050	Hildebrand, Kirsta	PA2300
Herrmann, Tracy	OH0350	Hibbard, Sarah	IL2150	Hildebrand, Millie	AC0100
Herron, Greg	MD0300	Hibbard, Therees Tkach	NE0600	Hildebrand, Virginia	MD0060
Herron, Teri A.	MS0250	Hibberd, Gordon	NY3600	Hildebrandt, Darcy	AJ0030
Hersch, Michael	MD0650	Hibbett, Michael	WA1200	Hildebrandt, Lorna Young	MI0500
Herseth, Freda	MI2100	Hibbitt, Peyton	NY3705	Hilderbrand, Monica	IL1612
Hersey, Joanna R.	NC2435	Hibler, John	WI0300	Hildreth, John W.	IL0100
Hersh, Alan	KY1450	Hibler, John	WI1155	Hildreth, Thomas P.	SC1200
Hersh, Julian E.	IL0750	Hibler, Starla	OK0300	Hildreth, Todd	KY0250
Hersh, Paul	CA4150	Hichborn, Jon	MA1450	Hildreth, Tom	NC2420
Hersh, Robert	CA2550	Hichborn, Kathryn D.	VA1475	Hileman, Lynn	WV0750
Hersh, Sarah S.	NY3780	Hickcox, Julee	VA1250	Hiles, Karen	PA2550
Hersh, Stefan	IL0550	Hicken, Ken	AA0200	Hill, Aaron S.	VA1550
Hershaft, Lisa	WI1150	Hicken, Leslie W.	SC0750	Hill, Barbara F.	NC2430
Hershberger, Jay	MN0600	Hickey, Joan B.	IL3300	Hill, Barry R.	PA1900
Hershey, Jane	MA1175	Hickey, Katherine M.	CA5150	Hill, Bill	CO0900
Hershey, Jane	MA1900	Hickey, Maud	IL2250	Hill, Camille	KY0600
Hertz, Talmon	AA0150	Hickinbotham, Gary	TX3175	Hill, Cheryl Frazes	IL0550
Herwig, Conrad	NY1900	Hickman, David R.	AZ0100	Hill, Christine	OH0600
Herwig, Conrad	NJ1130	Hickman, Joe Eugene	NC2440	Hill, Christine F.	OH0650
Herzog, James	NJ1050	Hickman, Kathryn	OK0150	Hill, Christopher	SD0050
Hesh, Joseph	PA2800	Hickman, Lowell	MT0200	Hill, Colin	KY0450
Hesla, Steven	MT0400	Hickman, Melinda	OH0550	Hill, Dennis	FL0500
Heslink, Daniel M.	PA2350	Hickman, Roger	CA0825	Hill, Don-Michael	FL0800
Hess, Benton	NY1100	Hickman, Suzanne L.	NJ0175	Hill, Don-Michael A.	FL1800
Hess, Carol A.	CA5010	Hickok, Robert B.	CA5020	Hill, Don-Michael A.	FL1550
Hess, Debra L.	FL0680	Hicks, Andrew	NY0900	Hill, Doris	IL1200
Hess, Fred	CO0550	Hicks, Angela	CA0550	Hill, Douglas M.	GA1300
Hess, H. Carl	PA1050	Hicks, Ann M.	IN0150	Hill, Gary W.	AZ0100
Hess, Jeffery	MN0750	Hicks, Brian	UT0325	Hill, George R.	NY0250
Hess, Jeffrey	MN1200	Hicks, Calvin	MA1175	Hill, Harry H.	SC0850
Hess, John	AG0500	Hicks, Charles E.	NC2700	Hill, Heather	MI0520
Hess, Nathan A.	NY1800	Hicks, Charles	AR0250	Hill, Jackson	PA0350
Hess, Richard E.	OH2200	Hicks, G.	CA1950	Hill, James S.	OH1850
Hess, Rick	NE0250	Hicks, Gail	CA4625	Hill, John	MI2120
Hess, Susan M.	ID0250	Hicks, Gail	CA1550	Hill, John	MI0450
Hesse, Marian	CO0950	Hicks, Gregory	LA0900	Hill, John E.	KY0950
Hesse, Robert	AR0500	Hicks, Jarrett	IL0720	Hill, Julie	TN1720
Hesse, Scott A.	IL0800	Hicks, Jarrett	IL2750	Hill, Karen	SC0650
Hesse, Shannon	TX1000	Hicks, Judy S.	AL0800	Hill, Kelly	MI1950
Hesse, Ted	IL1750	Hicks, Lori C.	SC0350	Hill, Kyle W.	MS0580
Hesselink, Nathan	AB0100	Hicks, Martha K.	MO1550	Hill, Lawrie	AB0200
Hesselink, Paul	NV0050	Hicks, Michael D.	UT0050	Hill, Leah	VA0800
Hesseman, Joseph	OH2450	Hicks, Pamela	CA0807	Hill, Margaret	NY2400
Hesser, Barbara	NY2750	Hicks, Roger	UT0190	Hill, Mark	TX3410
Hest, Jeff	NY3250	Hicks, Sarah Hatsuko	PA0850	Hill, Mark	MD1010
Hester, Carol	IA0950	Hicks, Sharalynn	SC0650	Hill, Mary Ann	GA1550
Hester, Charlotte	MS0570	Hicks, V. Douglas	OH2150	Hill, Matthew	IN0550
Hester, Danny	NC0300	Hickson, Carolyn R.	AR0700	Hill, Monty K.	NM0310
Hester, John	CA3600	Hida, Kyoko	MA0350	Hill, Paul	MN0750
Hester, John	CA0550	Hidlay, Rachel	NY2650	Hill, Phillip	TX3175
Hester, Karlton E.	CA5070	Hiebert, Cynthia	AG0600	Hill, Serena	SC0450
Hester, Timothy	TX3400	Hiebert, Lenore	CA0810	Hill, Thomas H.	VA0450
Hetherington, David	AG0300	Hiebert, Shannon	AA0020	Hill, Todd E.	KY0950
Hetrick, Craig	IN0250	Hiebert, Thomas N.	CA0810	Hill, Willie L.	MA2000
Hetrick, Esther A.	MI0910	Hieronymus, Bryan	OH2600	Hill-Kretzer, Kathleen	OH2275
Hetrick, Loy	IN0907	Hiester, Jason A.	OH2000	Hill-Kretzer, Kelly	MI0050
Hetrick, Mark	OH1330	Hiett, Dee Anna	MO1810	Hill-Le, Holly	OK0150
Hettenhausen, Amy	IL1740	Higbee, David	KS0150	Hillam, Barry	UT0050
Hettinger, Bruce A.	AA0100	Higdon, James M.	KS1350	Hillard, Clair Fox	GA0150
Hettle, Mark	TX1725	Higdon, Jennifer	PA0850	Hillard, Claire Fox	GA0625
Hettrick, Jane S.	NY1600	Higdon, Patricia	MO1810	Hillard, Leon H.	PA1250
Hettrick, William E.	NY1600	Higdon, Paul	MO1100	Hille, Regina	KS0560
Hettwer, Mike	OR0450	Higgins, Brenda L.	FL1550	Hiller, Brian	NY1600
Hetu, Jacques	AI0210	Higgins, Edward	OR0850	Hiller, James	OH2250
Hetzel, Lori	KY1450	Higgins, Lee D.	MA0400	Hilley, Byron	SC0700
Hetzler, Mark	WI0815	Higgins, Lynn	OR1150	Hilley, Martha F.	TX3510

Alphabetical Listing of Faculty

Name	Code	Name	Code	Name	Code
Hillhouse, Wendy	CA4900	Hirt, James	OH0600	Hoeflicker, Cale	IN0500
Hilliard, John S.	VA0600	Hirt, James A.	OH0200	Hoefnagels, Anna	AG0100
Hilliard, Quincy C.	LA0760	Hirt, Linda L.	IL0750	Hoegberg, Elisabeth Honn	IN1650
Hilliker, Tom	PA3710	Hisama, Ellie M.	NY0750	Hoehler, Martin R.	OH1050
Hills, Ernie M.	CA0840	Hiscock, Fred	NC2000	Hoehne, Bill	CA1000
Hills, Peggy	AG0650	Hiscock, Fred	NC0860	Hoekman, Timothy	FL0850
Hillyard, Mary	MI0300	Hiscocks, Mike	CA2650	Hoekstra, Gerald	MN1450
Hillyer, Dirk M.	MA1650	Hiscox, Julie	MD0060	Hoelscher, Mark	WI0825
Hillyer, Giselle	WI0845	Hiser, Beth A.	OH0200	Hoelscher, Mark	WI0300
Hillyer, Raphael	MA1175	Hisey, Andrew	MN1625	Hoelscher, Mark A.	WI0835
Hillyer, Tim	NE0610	Hisey, Ernest	OH0650	Hoenig, Ari M.	NY2750
Hillyer, Tim	IA1200	Hisey, P. Andrew	MN1450	Hoepfner, Gregory	OK0150
Hillyer, Timothy	IA0500	Hishman, Marcia	IL1200	Hoeppner, Susan	AG0450
Hilmy, Steven C.	DC0100	Hite, William	MA2000	Hoeprich, Eric	IN0900
Hilowski-Fowler, Ann	PA3600	Hitsky, Seth	IL2750	Hoeschen, Kevin	WI0860
Hilse, Walter	NY2150	Hitt, Barry	IA0910	Hofbauer, Eric	RI0300
Hilsee, Amalie	CA0800	Hitt, Christine	IA0910	Hofbauer, Eric	MA0850
Hilson, Keith	MN0610	Hittle, Kevin	NY4460	Hofeldt, Elizabeth	OH2450
Hilson, Mike	NE0460	Hitz, Andrew	PA1400	Hofer, Calvin	CO0225
Hilson, Mike	SD0600	Hix, Michael T.	NM0450	Hoferer, Kevin	PA2150
Hilton, Ellis	NJ0300	Hixson, Mary	GA2000	Hoffart, Danica	AA0080
Hilton, Randalin	UT0150	Hixson, Wesley	IL0850	Hoffelt, Tim	ND0350
Hilton, Suzanne	MD0550	Hlady, Craig M.	MA0260	Hoffenberg, Rick	PA2200
Hime, Michael	TN1850	Hlashweova, Jamila	AK0150	Hoffer, Charles	FL1850
Himmelhoch, Seth	NJ1400	Hlasny, Susan	AA0050	Hoffer, Heike	TX3525
Himrod, Gail P.	RI0150	Hlus, Don	AB0060	Hoffman, Adrian	AF0100
Hinata, Kaoru	NJ1130	Hmura, Harry	IL0720	Hoffman, Beth	IA0930
Hinchman, Pamela	IL2250	Ho, Allan	IL2910	Hoffman, Beth	IA0300
Hinck, David	ID0060	Ho, Frank	AA0020	Hoffman, Brian D.	OK0800
Hinck, Julie	ID0060	Ho, Hsing-I	IA0930	Hoffman, Cathy	CA0830
Hinckley, Edwin	UT0190	Ho, Hubert	MA1450	Hoffman, Christopher	NY2660
Hinckley, Jaren S.	UT0050	Ho, Leslie	CA6000	Hoffman, David	IL1350
Hindell, Leonard W.	NY2750	Ho, Meilu	MI2100	Hoffman, David E.	IL1400
Hindell, Leonard W.	NY2250	Ho, Sarah	AA0020	Hoffman, Deborah	NY2150
Hindell, Leonard	NY0500	Ho, Stephanie	NJ0700	Hoffman, Edward W.	MD0650
Hindemith, Paul B.	MN0600	Ho, Ting	NJ0800	Hoffman, Edward C. 'Ted'	AL1200
Hinderlie, Sanford E.	LA0300	Hoag, Bret	MI1830	Hoffman, Elizabeth D.	NY2740
Hindman, Dorothy Elliston	FL1900	Hoag, Bret	MI1750	Hoffman, Joel H.	OH2200
Hindman, Helen	OK0700	Hoag, Melissa E.	MI1750	Hoffman, Julia	NM0450
Hinds, Esther	NY2900	Hoats, Charlie	MI1050	Hoffman, Lee	OH0500
Hinds, Evan	IL2970	Hobbins, William	GA0250	Hoffman, Matt	CO0550
Hindson, Harry	WI0810	Hobbs, Gary G.	OR1050	Hoffman, Michael	CA0815
Hindson, Harry	MN1700	Hobbs, James D.	TX3300	Hoffman, Michael	CA2390
Hines, Betsy Burleson	TX1400	Hobbs, Julie	KY1450	Hoffman, Miles	SC0650
Hines, Billy C.	NC0700	Hobbs, Sandy	IN1350	Hoffman, Patrick	DE0050
Hines, Clarence	FL1950	Hobbs, Wayne C.	TX3200	Hoffman, Phyllis	MA0400
Hines, David	NC2000	Hobbs, William	NJ1350	Hoffman, Richard	TN0100
Hines, Edith	WI0700	Hobbs, William	NY2250	Hoffman, Steven	WY0200
Hines, Joan	NM0200	Hoberg, Gwen	WI0860	Hoffman, Susan	DC0050
Hines, John T.	IA1600	Hobson, David	LA0050	Hoffmann, Cynthia	NY1900
Hines, Robert S.	HI0210	Hobson, Ian	PR0115	Hoffmann, Cynthia	NY2150
Hines, Roger	OH0350	Hobson, Ian	IL3300	Hoffmann, Paul K.	NJ1130
Hines, Terry	WA0300	Hobson, Richard	NJ0700	Hoffmann, Russell	MA0260
Hines, Tyrone	IL0600	Hobson-Pilot, Ann	MA0400	Hoffmann, Shulamit	CA1250
Hinesley, Terry	IA1390	Hobson-Pilot, Ann	MA1400	Hofmann, Cameron	TX0300
Hinkeldey, Jeanette	IA0150	Hoch, Beverly	TX3300	Hofmann, John T.	NY3725
Hinkie, William H.	CO0950	Hoch, Christopher	OH1850	Hofmann, Richard Glenn	CA0835
Hinkle, Jean	OR1020	Hoch, Matthew	AL0200	Hofmeister, Walter	AJ0150
Hinkle, Laura	IL1300	Hochkeppel, Robin M.	LA0760	Hofmockel, Jeff	CA2100
Hinkle, Lee	MD1010	Hochkeppel, William J.	LA0760	Hofsess, Dustin	NC0550
Hinkle, Russ	KY1000	Hochman, Benjamin D.	NC0650	Hoft, Timothy	NV0050
Hinkley, Brian	MD0500	Hochstetler, Scott	IN0550	Hogan, George	TX3415
Hinojosa, Melissa S.	TX1425	Hochstetler, Tim	IN0910	Hogan, Hallie Coppedge	NC0750
Hinsey, Jackie	IN0905	Hodan, Daniel	TX0370	Hogan, Lisa	NJ0800
Hinshaw, Susan	OR0850	Hodder, Christy	AF0120	Hogan, Penny	TX3415
Hinshaw, Susan	WA0480	Hodel, Martin	MN1450	Hogancamp, Randy	IA1600
Hinson, Amalie	NC1100	Hodgdon, Brett	CT0600	Hogarth, Thaddeus	MA0260
Hinson, G. Maurice	KY1200	Hodgdon, Elizabeth	CA4300	Hogg, Merle E.	CA4100
Hinson, James M.	IL2910	Hodge, Cheryl	AB0070	Hogg, Wililam	KY1000
Hinson, Lee	OK0650	Hodge, Jeffrey S.	TX3000	Hoggard, Jay	CT0750
Hinson, Wallace	GA1650	Hodge, R. Matthew	KY0400	Hoglund, Richard E.	CA3950
Hinterbichler, Karl	NM0450	Hodge, Randy	MO0550	Hogue, Charles	AL1160
Hinton, Eric L.	PA3150	Hodge, Stephen	OH2300	Hogue, Harry	MD0360
Hinton, Heather	IN0250	Hodges, Anne R.	FL0850	Hohlstein, Marjorie Rahima	MA0280
Hinton, Hugh D.	MA1175	Hodges, Betsi	NC0910	Hohman, Frederick	IN0005
Hinton, Jeffrey	MO0850	Hodges, Betsi	ID0050	Hohmann, Nikolaus	CA4150
Hinton, Jennifer	PA1250	Hodges, Brian D.	ID0050	Hohstadt, Tom	TX3527
Hinton, Stephen W.	CA4900	Hodges, Brian	KY0250	Hoifeldt, Steven	IA0425
Hintz, Gail	MO1900	Hodges, David	SC0850	Hoirup, Marlene	NC2500
Hipp, Gary O.	SC1000	Hodges, Don	NC2430	Hoisington, Linda	MI0350
Hipp, Lee	TX3350	Hodges, Justin	TX0600	Hojnacki, Thomas W.	MA0260
Hipp, Lee	TX2200	Hodges, Mark	NY3717	Hokanson, Randolph	WA1050
Hipskind, Tom	IL0720	Hodges, William Robert	CA3700	Hoke, S. Kay	PA1400
Hiranpradist, Barbara	MI1200	Hodges, Woodrow	WI0250	Hokin, Harlan B.	AZ0480
Hirleman, Laura	MI1160	Hodges, Woodrow J.	WI0835	Hoksbergen, Ross	MI0100
Hirna, Olena	IL0850	Hodgins, Glenn	AG0400	Holben, David	CA3600
Hirokawa, Joy	PA2450	Hodgkinson, Randall	MA2050	Holben, David	CA3800
Hironaka-Bergt, Mieko	MO1830	Hodgkinson, Randall	MA1400	Holborn, George	AG0170
Hirota, Yoko	AG0150	Hodgkinson, Randall	MA1175	Holbrook, Amy K.	AZ0100
Hirsch, Marjorie	MA2250	Hodgman, Thomas	MI0050	Holbrook, Ashley	KS0150
Hirsch, Michael	NJ0825	Hodgson, Aaron	AG0500	Holbrook-Bratka, Branita A.	WV0400
Hirsch, Scott	NY2750	Hodgson, Jay	AG0500	Holcomb, Al	NJ1350
Hirschelman, Evan	CA2650	Hodgson, Ken	MN1620	Holcomb, Paula K.	NY3725
Hirschl, Richard	IL0550	Hodkinson, Sydney P.	FL1750	Holcomb, Teddy	NC2500
Hirschmann, Craig	WI1155	Hodson, Robert	MI1050	Holcombe, Candace	SC0450
Hirsh, Jonathan M.	MA1750	Hodson, Steven R.	CA5550	Holcombe, Helen	PA0400
Hirsh, Jules	NY0500	Hoebig, Desmond	TX2150	Holcombe, Ross	WA0400
Hirshfield, L. Russell	CT0800	Hoeckner, Berthold	IL3250	Holcombe, Ross	WA0250
Hirst, Dennis	UT0300	Hoeffgen, Thomas E.	KS1200	Holden, James	VA1750
Hirst, Edmund V. Grayson	AZ0500	Hoefle, Andrew	IL2775	Holden, Jon	NY2750

Holden, Jonathan	MS0750	Holmes, Isaac	GA1600	Hood, John	PA3250
Holden, LuAnn	TN0850	Holmes, J. Michael	IL3300	Hood, Joshua	NC0550
Holden, Robert	AR0850	Holmes, Janet	CA3320	Hood, Joshua	NC2420
Holden, Valerie	AD0050	Holmes, Jeffrey	CA0960	Hood, Marcia Mitchell	GA0150
Holder, Angela	TN0250	Holmes, Jeffrey W.	MA2000	Hood, Mark	IN0900
Holder, Brian	FL1675	Holmes, Karen	AG0400	Hoogenstyn, Don	MI1550
Holder, Hope	UT0400	Holmes, Michael	MD0850	Hoogerhyde, Jason	TX2650
Holder, Ryan	AZ0450	Holmes, Phil	MI0520	Hook, Julian L.	IN0900
Holdhusen, David	SD0600	Holmes, Ramona A.	WA0800	Hook, Terry	VA0600
Hole, Kristopher	VA0350	Holmes, Rasan	VA0500	Hooker, Tracy	WA0600
Holeman, Janet	TN0930	Holmes, Ruth J.	TX1550	Hooks, Norma R.	MD0520
Holeman, Kathleen	MO0850	Holmes-Davis, Tina	GA1070	Hooper, Jason	MA2000
Holguin, Mike	CA4100	Holmquist, Solveig	OR1250	Hooper, John	AA0015
Holinaty, William	AG0200	Holober, Michael	NY0550	Hooper, Kay	PA3150
Holland, Anthony G.	NY3650	Holoman, D. Kern	CA5010	Hooper, Randall	TX2955
Holland, Dave	MA1400	Holquist, Robert A.	NC2600	Hooper, Terry	GA2300
Holland, David	MI1650	Holroyd, Megan Calgren	MN0050	Hoopes, Katherine	MA0600
Holland, David	MI0400	Holsberg, Lisa	NY2105	Hoops, Haley S.	TX2400
Holland, Deborah	CA0830	Holsberg, Peter W.	NY4200	Hoops, Richard	FL1430
Holland, Geoffrey	FL1450	Holsinger, Bruce	VA1550	Hoose, David M.	MA0400
Holland, Greg	GA0050	Holsinger, David	TN0850	Hooten, Bryan	VA1600
Holland, Heather	MA0510	Holst, Carol	TX0075	Hooten, David M.	TX1600
Holland, Joan	MI2100	Holst, Kelly Margaret	OK0750	Hoover, Brian	IN1100
Holland, Jonathan Bailey	MA0260	Holst, Robert I.	IL1520	Hoover, David	CA3100
Holland, Katherine N.	GA1300	Holstedt, Lucile	MA0260	Hoover, David E.	CA0835
Holland, Katie	GA0850	Holstrom, Jacqueline	MN1600	Hoover, Elizabeth	OH1450
Holland, Linda L.	CA4410	Holt, Anthony	MN1450	Hoover, Jerry W.	MO0775
Holland, Margaret	NJ0175	Holt, Beverly	IL1890	Hoover, Lloyd W.	DC0350
Holland, Marianne	SC0950	Holt, Danny	CA0510	Hoover, Maya	HI0210
Holland, Michael	TN1850	Holt, Dennis	FL1950	Hoover, Sarah	NY1600
Holland, Nicholas V.	SC0275	Holt, Drew	CA4450	Hoover, Tracy	KS1450
Holland, Nicholas V.	TN1680	Holt, Eileen	CA5100	Hope, Colleen	CO0150
Holland, Patricia	FL1450	Holt, Eileen	CA5040	Hope, Garrett E.	PA3550
Holland, Patricia C.	WI0850	Holt, John	TX3420	Hopkin, J. Arden	UT0050
Holland, Rachel J.	VA0150	Holt, Joseph	MA0350	Hopkin, Teresa	GA0750
Holland, Samuel S.	TX2400	Holt, Matthew K.	MO0800	Hopkins, Alice	IN0907
Holland, Sandra Renee	NC2420	Holt, Robert	WI0847	Hopkins, Barbara	CT0600
Hollander, Alan	NY1600	Holton, Arthur	CA4300	Hopkins, Brenda	PR0115
Hollander, Jeffrey	WI0825	Holz, Beatrice	KY0100	Hopkins, Bruce	MA0700
Hollander, Jeffrey M.	IN1750	Holz, Ronald	KY0100	Hopkins, Bruce	MA0200
Holleman, Brenda	OK0750	Holzemer, Kate C.	NY3717	Hopkins, Christopher	NY2105
Holleman, James A.	MI1000	Holzer, Linda	AR0750	Hopkins, Christopher	IA0850
Hollenbeck, Eric R.	CO0250	Holzer, Robert R.	CT0850	Hopkins, Cynthia	SC0750
Hollenbeck, Lisa	NY3770	Holzman, Adam	TX3510	Hopkins, Greg J.	MA2050
Hollender, David A.	MA0260	Holzman, Adam	NY2660	Hopkins, Gregory H.	DC0150
Holler, David	AG0200	Holzman, Bruce	FL0850	Hopkins, Gregory	MA1175
Hollerbach, Peter D.	NY0600	Holzman, David	NY2105	Hopkins, Gregory	MA0260
Hollerbach, Peter	NY0270	Holzmeier, Jana	NE0450	Hopkins, Harlow	IL2300
Holley, David	NC2430	Holzschuh, Craig	AB0100	Hopkins, Janet E.	SC1110
Holley, Timothy	NC1600	Homan, Jeff	OR0150	Hopkins, Jesse E.	VA0100
Holliday, Guy	CA0450	Homan, Jeff C.	OR1100	Hopkins, John R.	AK0150
Holliday, James T.	DC0150	Homan, Jim W.	NE0610	Hopkins, Joseph H.	AL0800
Holliday, K. A.	VA1700	Homan, Steve	CA0150	Hopkins, Karen	IA0790
Holliday, Stacey A.	SC0350	Homan, Steven	CA0840	Hopkins, Mark E.	AF0050
Hollinden, Andrew J.	IN0900	Homann, Ann	MO1830	Hopkins, Michael	MI2100
Hollinger, Curtis	AL0450	Homann, J. Oliver	CT0050	Hopkins, Robert	NY1350
Hollinger, Deborah	IL3550	Homburg, Andrew H.	MO0775	Hopkins, Stephen O.	PA2750
Hollinger, Diana	CA4400	Homer, Paula	TX3420	Hopkins, Stephen M.	NC0050
Hollinger, Lowell	MS0350	Hominick, Ian G.	MS0700	Hopkins, Ted	TX0600
Hollinger, Trent A.	MO0300	Homsey, Ryan	NY3785	Hopkins, William T.	CA4200
Hollingsworth, Christopher	TX0900	Homzy, Andrew	AI0070	Hoppe, Frank	CA3500
Hollingsworth, Devon	IN0005	Honda, Lorence	CA1850	Hoppe, Jennifer R.	NY2750
Hollingsworth, Dina L.	CO0275	Hondorp, Paul	KY1550	Hopper, Alice R.	IN0900
Hollingsworth, Mark	OK0300	Honea, Richard	MO0400	Hopper, Jeffrey T.	AR0250
Hollins, Fraser	AI0150	Honea, Ted	OK1330	Hopper, Kerrin A.	SC1200
Hollins, John S.	TX3200	Honeysucker, Robert	MA1175	Hopper, Mary	IL3550
Hollinshead, Barbara	DC0010	Honeysucker, Robert	MA0350	Hoppmann, Ken J.	NE0525
Hollis, Brenda	KY1540	Hong, Ah Young	MD0650	Hoppmann, Kenneth	IN0005
Hollis, C. Kimm	IN0650	Hong, Ah Yong	MD0850	Hopson, Amanda	IN0350
Holliston, Robert	AB0210	Hong, Caroline	OH1850	Hopson, John Casey	CA5550
Holloman, Charlotte W.	DC0150	Hong, Charles	AG0650	Hopwood, Brian	MO1550
Holloman, Charlotte	DC0350	Hong, Gao	MN0300	Horak, Sally	LA0050
Holloway, Clyde	TX2150	Hong, Hye Jung	MO0775	Horan, Leta	TX0300
Holloway, David	IL0550	Hong, Martha	MT0450	Horan, Rachel	MN0600
Holloway, Greg	DC0010	Hong, Sojung Lee	IL1300	Horan, Sara	GA1000
Holloway, Harold	TN1710	Hong, Sylvia	MS0100	Horcher, Nick	IL2650
Holloway, John R.	SC0650	Hong, Xiangtang	IL1850	Hord, John	CA1850
Holloway, Peggy A.	NE0610	Hong, Yat-Lam	MI2250	Horel, Charles	GA0950
Holly, Janice E.	MD1010	Hongisto, Erik	AG0170	Horgan, Maureen A.	GA0850
Holly, Janice	MD0300	Honigschnabel, Maria	IL0730	Horjus-Lang, Deanna	WI0800
Holly, Richard	IL2200	Honisch, Erika	MO1810	Horlacher, Gretchen G.	IN0900
Holm, Molly	CA2950	Honn, Barbara	OH2200	Horlas, Lou	TX0700
Holm, Robert	AL1300	Honn, Linda	WA0250	Horn, Alisa	DC0170
Holm, Thomas	IA1200	Honnold, Adrianne L.	MO1830	Horn, Daniel Paul	IL3550
Holm-Hudson, Kevin	KY1450	Honnold, Adrianne	MO1120	Horn, Fred	VA1150
Holman, Andrew	MA2010	Honnold, Adrianne L.	MO1900	Horn, Goffery C.	FL0600
Holman, Colin	IL1615	Honnold, Adrianne	MO0700	Horn, Lawrence C.	MS0560
Holman, Colin	IL2100	Honour, Eric C.	MO1790	Horn, Robin Franklin	AZ0500
Holman, Derek	AG0450	Hontos, Margaret Ellen	CA4410	Horn, Stuart	CA5550
Holman, Leigh	CO0800	Hontz, James R.	PA1400	Horn, Stuart	CA5060
Holman, Sarah	IL3550	Hontz, James	PA0950	Hornbach, Christina M.	MI1050
Holmberg, Teri	KS0650	Hontz, James R.	MD0475	Hornbacker, Georgia	IL1750
Holmes, Alena	WI0865	Hontz, James	MD0300	Hornby, Tyler	AA0050
Holmes, Allison	IA0930	Hooan, Dan	TX1725	Horne, Brian	IN0900
Holmes, Brad	IL1750	Hood, Alan	CO0900	Horne, John	OH1900
Holmes, Christopher	IN0100	Hood, Boyde	CA5300	Horne, Robin	FL1430
Holmes, Daniel	MD0060	Hood, Gary	MD0175	Horne, Timothy	NY1400
Holmes, Elizabeth	IL1750	Hood, Heather	MN1280	Horne, William P.	LA0300
Holmes, Glenn	OH0650	Hood, Jo Ann	TN1400	Horneff, Donald C.	MD0520
Holmes, Isaac	SC1100	Hood, Joanna	AB0150	Horner, Brian	TN0050

Alphabetical Listing of Faculty

Name	Code	Name	Code	Name	Code
Horner, Erin	TN1850	Howard, Brad	GA0750	Hsieh, Fang-Lan	TX2600
Horner, Jerry	WI0825	Howard, Chris	MO0750	Hsieh, Lily	VA1550
Horner, Ronald G.	PA1600	Howard, David L.	TX2700	Hsu, Chia-Ying	IL2650
Horner, Ronald	MD0350	Howard, David	OR0250	Hsu, Cindi	NY5000
Horner, Tim	NJ0825	Howard, David	CA5300	Hsu, Dolores M.	CA5060
Hornick, Scott J.	NJ0750	Howard, David R.	MA0260	Hsu, E-Chen	AG0170
Hornig, Tom	CA4400	Howard, Douglas	TX2400	Hsu, Howard	GA2150
Horning, Rebecca	NY3770	Howard, Elisabeth	CA3600	Hsu, Hsing Ay	CO0800
Hornsby, Richard	AE0120	Howard, Greg	VA1550	Hsu, John	NY0900
Horowitz, Robert	NY4200	Howard, Howard	NY0500	Hsu, Linda Y.	AR0850
Horozaniecki, Mary A.	MN0050	Howard, Jacqueline	GA1450	Hsu, Pattie	CA5353
Horozaniecki, Mary B.	MN0300	Howard, Janet	WY0100	Hsu, Samuel	PA2800
Horozaniecki, Mary Budd	MN0950	Howard, Jason	PA3650	Hsu, Yu-Pin	NY2150
Horsley, Paul J.	MO1000	Howard, Jeffrey	MD0850	Hsu, Yun-Ling	FL1700
Horst, Amy S.	HI0200	Howard, Karen	OH1100	Hsu, Yun-Ling	FL1800
Horst, Martha C.	IL1150	Howard, Markus	AG0300	Hsueh, Yvonne	OR1250
Horst, Sandra	AG0450	Howard, Micah	PA0550	Hu, Chih-Long	TN0500
Horstman, Dorothy Yanes	FL1450	Howard, Micah	PA1050	Hu, Ching-chu	OH0850
Horton, Brian	NC1600	Howard, Michael	LA0750	Hu, Xiao	IA0950
Horton, Charles T.	AC0100	Howard, Robert	MO1830	Huang, Aiyun	AI0150
Horton, Christian	GA1260	Howard, Robert C.	MO0550	Huang, Alice	MO0060
Horton, Dennis	MI0400	Howard, Sabrina	NC2650	Huang, Chen-Yu	IL1200
Horton, Mathew	CA1850	Howard, Sandra	NH0150	Huang, Du	IA0950
Horton, Ron	AR0110	Howard, Sharon	IN1310	Huang, Frank	TX3400
Horton, Virginia	TN0850	Howard, Timothy P.	CA0835	Huang, Grace	OH0600
Horvath, Janos	AA0150	Howard, Vernon D.	OK1450	Huang, Hai Tao	IL3310
Horvath, Juliane	NM0500	Howard-Phillips, Amanda	WA0400	Huang, Hao	CA1050
Horvath, Kathleen	OH0600	Howard-Spink, Sam J.	NY2750	Huang, Hao	CA4500
Horvath, Kathleen	OH0400	Howarth, Anne	MA2010	Huang, Hsin-Yun	NY1900
Horvath, Maria	IL1610	Howarth, Gifford	PA0250	Huang, Hsin-Yun	NY2250
Horvitz, Wayne B.	WA0200	Howarth, Gifford W.	PA2750	Huang, Juan	MD0650
Hose, Anthony	FL1750	Howden, Moses Mark	NY3475	Huang, Kuang-Hao	IL0730
Hoskins, Richard	WI0250	Howdle, Joyce	AA0080	Huang, Kuang-Hao	IL0550
Hoskisson, Darin T.	TX2960	Howe, Blake	LA0200	Huang, Mei-Hsuan	IA0850
Hosler, Cheryl L.	SC0400	Howe, Donald	CA3520	Huang, Ming Shiow	FL0550
Hosler, Mark	SC0400	Howe, Eric	CA2200	Huang, Rachel V.	CA1050
Hosley, David B.	NY3700	Howe, Hubert S.	NY0642	Huang, Rachel Vetter	CA4500
Hosley, Robyn L.	NY3780	Howe, Hubert S.	NY0600	Huang, Steven	OH1900
Hosmer, Christian	NY3550	Howe, Martha Jane	CA2100	Huang, Wanchi	VA0600
Hosmer, Christopher D.	AL0500	Howe, Melissa	MA0260	Huang-Davie, Yuling	LA0760
Hosmer, Karen E.	NY3600	Howe, Ryan	IA1400	Hubbard, Constance	SD0100
Hosoda-Ayer, Kae	TX0300	Howe, Stuart	AA0100	Hubbard, Eve P.	NC0900
Hossain, Hamid	MD1000	Howe, Timothy E.	MO1800	Hubbard, Gary	AG0130
Hosten, Kevin	NY2100	Howell, Allen C.	PA1200	Hubbard, Kathy A.	NY3780
Hostetler, Jill	IN0200	Howell, Andrew P.	RI0300	Hubbard, Mary Ann	MI0200
Hostetler, Scott	IL2250	Howell, Christina	GA0500	Hubbell, Judy	CA1020
Hostetter, Elizabeth	AL0550	Howell, Devin	PA1250	Hubbert, Julie	SC1110
Hostetter, Paul K.	GA0550	Howell, Devin L.	PA1300	Hubbs, Holly J.	PA3550
Hotchkiss, Richard	PA3330	Howell, Jack	PA1050	Hubbs, Randall	WA0150
Hotchkiss, Shelia	TN1600	Howell, Jane	PA2900	Huber, Deborah	MA2030
Hotle, Dana	MO1120	Howell, John	VA1700	Huber, John	KS0350
Hotle, Dana	MO0700	Howell, Matthew	HI0200	Huber, Kenneth	MN0300
Houchin, Blake	TN1600	Howell, Michael W.	IN1800	Huber, Laurel	CA0810
Houchins, Andrew	KS0300	Howell, Todd	IL0850	Huber, Laurell	CA1860
Houck, Alan	OH1350	Howenstine, Nancy	OH2290	Huber, Wayne	CA1860
Houde, Andrea	WV0750	Hower, Don	WA1150	Huber, William	TN1600
Houde, Marc	AG0600	Hower, Eileen	PA0250	Hubert, John	CO0650
Hough, Jennifer C.	SC1200	Howery, Lydia	PA2250	Hubner, Carla	DC0170
Hough, Robin Z.	TX3400	Howes, Graham	NY3725	Hubner, Carla	DC0110
Hougham, Bradley	NY1800	Howes, Heather	AI0150	Huck, Patricia	AA0050
Houghtalen, Brandon	NM0450	Howes, Sarah Marie	PA1400	Hucke, Adam	IL2970
Houghtaling, Paul	AL1170	Howey, Henry E.	TX2250	Huckleberry, Alan R.	IA1550
Houghton, Amy	MS0100	Howey, Robert J.	AA0025	Huckleberry, Heather	IA0250
Houghton, Edward F.	CA5070	Howiler, Robert W.	SC1000	Huddleston, Cheryl	TX3400
Houghton, Monica	OH0600	Howland, John L.	NJ1140	Huddleston, Debra	OR0450
Houghton, Rosemarie	DC0050	Howland, Kathleen	MA0260	Huddleston, Debra	OR0250
Houghton, Stacey	GA0500	Howland, Pamela	NC2500	Huddleston, Jeffrey L.	TN1680
Houghton, Steve	IN0900	Howland, Patricia L.	NJ1130	Hudelson, Charles	AA0100
Houk, Chad M.	NE0200	Howland, Stephen	WA0650	Hudgens, Helen	IL2100
Houlahan, Michael	PA2350	Howle, Patrick	KS1050	Hudgins, Will	MA1400
Houle, Arthur Joseph	CO0225	Howlett, Christine R.	NY4450	Hudiburg, Howard B.	TX3175
Houle, George L.	CA4900	Howsmon, James	OH1700	Hudicek, Laurie	DC0170
Houlihan, Mickey	CO0560	Hoy, Andria	OH0100	Hudson, Barbara D.	NC0300
Houlihan, Patrick	AR0500	Hoy, Ian	OH0100	Hudson, Barbara	VA0050
Houlik, James	PA1050	Hoy, Patricia A.	AB0100	Hudson, Barton	WV0750
Hourigan, Amy	IN0150	Hoydich, George	PA1050	Hudson, Bruce	CA2420
Hourigan, Ryan M.	IN0150	Hoyer, John	MI1050	Hudson, Gary	TX2350
House, LeAnn	MN0450	Hoyle, Robert	CT0600	Hudson, Hope A.	NJ0700
House, Nicole	NC2410	Hoyt, Lucy Owen	VA1350	Hudson, James	AZ0100
House, Richard	SC1000	Hoyt, Reed J.	NY3700	Hudson, Jed	OH0850
House, Richard E.	SC0350	Hoyt, Thomas H.	NY2750	Hudson, Mark E.	CO0275
Houser, Kimberly A.	LA0200	Hoyt, William	OH2150	Hudson, Michael	KY1450
Houser, Steven	MO0600	Hoyt-Brackman, Brenda	OH2275	Hudson, Milton	TX3360
Houser, Virginia	KS0650	Hricko-Fay, Maria	PA2200	Hudson, Nita	TX2700
Houston, James	MD0170	Hristov, Maria N.	TN1710	Hudson, Richard	CA5032
Houston, James	IL0850	Hristov, Miroslav P.	TN1710	Hudson, Roger	TN1100
Houston, Janeanne	WA0650	Hristova, Gabriela	MI2120	Hudson, S.	KY0350
Houston, Ronald	TX3000	Hrivnak, Christine	MS0100	Hudson, Stephen	NJ1350
Houtchens, Alan	TX2900	Hrivnak, Michael	NC1350	Hudson, Stephen	NJ0975
Houts, Janice	SD0450	Hronek, Melissa	TX2900	Hudson, Terry Lynn	TX0300
Houze, Reginald M.	MA0150	Hryniewicki, Donna	MN1050	Hudson, Timothy	NC0930
Hovan, Rebecca	IN0910	Hryniewicki, Donna	MN0625	Hudson, Timothy	NC0850
Hovnanian, Michael	MI0900	Hrynkiw, Patricia	AA0150	Hudson, Virginia	AR0730
Hovnanian, Michael Aram	MI0350	Hrynkiw, Thomas T.	PA2200	Hudson, Virginia	NC1300
Hovnanian, Michael J.	IL0750	Hsaio, Fei-Lin	CA5350	Hudson, William	IL1200
Hovnanian, Stephanie	MI2250	Hsiang, Cynthia H.	CA3500	Hudson, William Andrew	TX1600
Hovorka, Jamie	CA1750	Hsiao, Annie C.	IL2250	Hudspeth, Charles M.	CA1020
Howard, Beverly A.	CA0450	Hsieh, Ai-Liu	PA1900	Hueber, Thomas E.	MO1780
Howard, Bill	TX1600	Hsieh, Annie	MO1900	Huebl, Carolyn	TN1850
Howard, Billie	IL0730	Hsieh, Chialing	KY0900	Huebner, Elizabeth	CT0650

Alphabetical Listing of Faculty

Name	Code	Name	Code	Name	Code
Huebner, Eric H.	NY4320	Hull, Edward	CA0810	Hunter-Holly, Daniel	TX3515
Huebner, Steven	AI0150	Hull, Kenneth	AG0470	Huntington, Ellen	IL2100
Hueller, Mary	WI0050	Hull, Michael	IL1090	Huntington, Lawrence	MI1250
Huener, Thomas J.	NC0650	Hull, Michael	IL0400	Huntington, Tammie M.	IN1025
Huergo, Fernando A.	MA0260	Hull, Robert A.	NY3717	Huntley, Elizabeth M.	NY3650
Huerta, Edgar	IL1085	Hulling, Cliff	CA0350	Huntley, Lawrence	NC0250
Huey, Daniel J.	GA1800	Hulme, Lance	NC1600	Huntley, Yvonne	IL2750
Huff, Adam	IL1300	Huls, Marvin J.	PA3000	Huntoon, Ben	OH2050
Huff, Christina	IN1025	Huls, Shirley	PA3000	Huntoon, Diana	IN0100
Huff, Cleve	AZ0490	Hulse, Barney	CA3050	Huntoon, John Richard	IN0100
Huff, Daniel M.	NC2410	Hulse, Brian	VA0250	Huovinen, Erkki	MN1623
Huff, Douglas M.	IL3500	Hulse, Mark	CA0300	Hurd Hause, Maureen L.	NJ1130
Huff, Dwayne	MO0200	Hult, David W.	NY2650	Hurd, James L.	CA1750
Huff, Jay	OH1850	Hulteen, Rhonda L.	IL2730	Hurd, Mary	MI0300
Huff, Kelly A.	KS1400	Hulten, Thomas	TX3400	Hurel, Pierre	MA0350
Huff, Lori	CA0630	Hultgren, Craig	AL1150	Hurlburt, Sean	IL0550
Huff, Mark	AL1250	Hultgren, Craig	AL0300	Hurlburt, Timothy R.	SC0400
Huff, Mark Y.	AL1160	Hultgren, Lori	MD0850	Hurleigh, Shannon	OK1330
Huff, Michael H.	AL1050	Human, Richard	MS0500	Hurley, Brian	AI0150
Huff, Michael D.	UT0300	Humbert, William	AZ0350	Hurley, David R.	KS1050
Huff, Sharon	IL1750	Humble, Dina M.	CA3800	Hurley, Gregory	NC0650
Huff, Walter	IN0900	Hume, John	IL1100	Hurley, Patricia	NY2400
Huffman, Donna M.	WA0100	Hume, Michael	NY0050	Hurley-Glowa, Susan M.	TX3515
Huffman, Pamela G.	TX2400	Humes, Scot A.	LA0770	Huron, David	OH1850
Huffman, Timothy	OH2050	Humiston, Robert G.	MI2250	Hurst, Chloe	AB0200
Huffman, Valarie A.	WV0300	Hummel, Linda W.	PA1900	Hurst, Christon	OH2550
Hufft, Bradley	CA0810	Hummer, Ken	OH1330	Hurst, Craig W.	WI0960
Hufnagle, Kathryn	SD0050	Humperys, Douglas	NY1100	Hurst, Derek	MA0260
Hufstader, Ron	TX3520	Humphrey, AnDrue R.	NE0610	Hurst, Francesca	DC0050
Hufty, Aaron	TX0300	Humphrey, Mark Aaron	TX3415	Hurst, Francesca	DC0250
Huggett, Monica	NY1900	Humphrey, Roger G.	MI1800	Hurst, James	WI0801
Hugghins, Linda	OK0770	Humphreys, Jere T.	AZ0100	Hurst, Michael Shane	TX0370
Huggins, Mark	AZ0350	Humphreys, Michelle	WV0550	Hurst, Robert	MI2100
Hughes, Albert C.	TN0950	Humphreys, Paul W.	CA2800	Hurst, Twyla	MS0370
Hughes, Amanda	OK1250	Humphreys, Sally	UT0400	Hurst-Wajszczuk, Kristine M.	AL1150
Hughes, Andrew	AG0450	Humphries, Stephen	GA0600	Hurt, Charles R.	TX3175
Hughes, Brian L.	IA0940	Humphries, Terri	TX3400	Hurt, Phyllis A.	IL2150
Hughes, Bryn	FL1900	Humphries, Tracy	NC2650	Hurtado, Jose-Luis	NM0450
Hughes, Charles M.	CA2050	Hunan, Steve	CA1500	Hurty, Jon	IL0100
Hughes, Chris	NY2900	Hund, Jennifer L.	IN1300	Hurty, Sonja	IL0100
Hughes, Christopher A.	NM0310	Hundemer, Thomas	LA0050	Hurtz, Timothy	PA2750
Hughes, Constance M.	IL0840	Hundley, Marion S.	FL0100	Husa, Karel	NY0900
Hughes, Curtis K.	MA0350	Hung, Emily	CA3350	Husarik, Stephen	AR0730
Hughes, David	CA0250	Hung, Eric Hing-tao	NJ1350	Husband, Julie	AC0100
Hughes, Donald L.	PA2550	Hung, Li-Shan	CA0350	Husby, Betsy	MN1600
Hughes, Evelyn	GA0940	Hung, Yu-Sui	IL3450	Huseynova, Aida N.	IN0900
Hughes, Julayne	MI1830	Hungerford, Del	WA1150	Huss, Adeline	OH0600
Hughes, Larry	CA3300	Hungerford, Del	WA1350	Hussa, Robert	WY0060
Hughes, Laura Weaver	IL1090	Hungerford, Delores	ID0250	Hussain, Azra	AG0130
Hughes, Lawrence P.	CA3500	Hungerford, Grant	CA1750	Husser, David	MI1650
Hughes, Luther	CA0815	Hungerford, Grant	CA5060	Husser, John S.	VA1700
Hughes, Marcia A.	TN0930	Hungerford, Jay	MO1950	Hussey, Peter	IL1500
Hughes, Matthew	IL3500	Hunkins, Arthur B.	NC2430	Hussey, William G.	IL0550
Hughes, Miriam Kartch	NY2250	Hunn, Jana	CA4300	Hussong, Suzi R.	WA0800
Hughes, Nathan N.	NJ1130	Hunnicutt, Bradley C.	NC2300	Hussung, Lisa	KY1550
Hughes, Nathan	NY1900	Hunnicutt, Heather Winter	KY0610	Hussung, Mark	TN0250
Hughes, Patricia	IN1350	Hunsaker, Leigh Anne	TX0900	Hustad, Ken	CA0600
Hughes, Patrick	TX3510	Hunsberger, Johnson	FL2000	Hustad, Ken	CA1510
Hughes, R. Daniel	NY2550	Hunsicker, David	KS1450	Husted, Audrey	IA1350
Hughes, Ralph	CA0150	Hunsinger, Melita	IN0905	Hustis, Gregory	TX2400
Hughes, Robert L.	MO1250	Hunt, Catherine	KS1400	Huston, Spencer	KS0590
Hughes, Robert	AG0500	Hunt, Douglas	CA4300	Huszti, Joseph B.	CA5020
Hughes, Scott	ME0340	Hunt, Emily	GA2130	Hutchens, John	IL2350
Hughes, Susan K.	ID0100	Hunt, Graham G.	TX3500	Hutcheson, Jere T.	MI1400
Hughes, Thomas	TX3200	Hunt, Jeffrey S.	IL0840	Hutcheson, Mary Beth	GA1500
Hughes, Walden D.	ID0150	Hunt, Jeremy	FL1800	Hutchings, Doreen L.	MN1280
Hughes, William M.	SC1200	Hunt, Johanna	FL1800	Hutchings, James	IL0420
Hughes, Winston	NJ0175	Hunt, John	NY1100	Hutchins, Georgette	RI0200
Hughes-Lopez, Jennifer	MD0550	Hunt, Justin Trevor	MS0850	Hutchins, Tim	AI0150
Hughey, Richard	IL3500	Hunt, Keena Redding	GA0350	Hutchins, Tony	OK1200
Huglo, Michel	MD1010	Hunt, Marc	NY4460	Hutchins, Tony	IA1100
Hugo, Alycia	VA1125	Hunt, Mary H.	NY3730	Hutchinson, Chad	IA1200
Hugo, Alycia	VA1400	Hunt, Paul B.	KS0650	Hutchinson, Jean Leslie	KY1500
Hugo, Alycia	VA0750	Hunt, Robert	TX2250	Hutchinson, Larry	MI2200
Hugo, Chilali	UT0300	Hunt, Steven	MA0260	Hutchinson, Nicholas	IL0750
Hugo, Cliff	CA4700	Hunt, Sylvia	ID0070	Hutchinson, Raymond	IL1900
Hugo, John William	VA0650	Hunt, Trevor	MS0580	Hutchinson, Robert G.	WA1000
Huhn, Franziska	MA1175	Hunt, William	OR0250	Hutchinson, Sydney	NY4100
Huhn, Franziska	MA1400	Hunter, Andrew	LA0150	Hutchinson, Thomas	NY2750
Huhn, Kevin	PA1650	Hunter, Barbara	IL2970	Hutchison, Amy	OH0450
Hui, Melissa	AI0150	Hunter, Billy	NJ0825	Hutchison, Callie	AZ0250
Huisman, Monica	AC0100	Hunter, Bryan C.	NY2650	Hutchison, Lacey	SC0620
Huizenga, Trudi	MI0350	Hunter, Colleen	WA0400	Hutchison, Patrick	GA0940
Hukill, Cynthia L.	AR0200	Hunter, David	TX3510	Huth, Lori	PA2450
Hulbert, David	WI0850	Hunter, Denise	CA3920	Hutsko, Mark	OH0350
Hulbert, David	WI0825	Hunter, Denise	CA1450	Hutson, Danny J.	AL0010
Hulbert, Duane	WA1000	Hunter, James	NC2650	Hutter, Greg J.	IL0750
Hulbert, Jarl O.	MD0175	Hunter, John	NH0350	Hutter, Patricia	AB0050
Hulen, Peter Lucas	IN1850	Hunter, Judy	AG0200	Huttlin, Edward	MN0600
Hulett, Christopher M.	AZ0490	Hunter, Laurie	OR0950	Hutton, Christopher	SC0750
Hulihan, Charles	AZ0350	Hunter, Mario	NC0550	Hutton, Cynthia	OR0950
Hulihan, Theresa	AZ0350	Hunter, Mary K.	ME0200	Hutton, Deirdre	SC0750
Hulin, Charles J.	FL1740	Hunter, Michael	MI1650	Hutton, Joan	MN0050
Huling, Diane	VT0250	Hunter, Randy	GA0750	Hutton, Judy F.	NC2650
Hull, Allison R.	WI0835	Hunter, Rebecca	SC1110	Hutton, Kelley	OH2275
Hull, Allison	WI0250	Hunter, Robert	AZ0440	Hutton, Paula R.	OK0700
Hull, Barbara A.	NY2650	Hunter, Rosemary Herlong	AL0400	Huus, Brett	MN1400
Hull, Daniel	SC0710	Hunter, Ruth	PA3150	Huydts, Sebastian	IL0720
Hull, Daniel	SC0420	Hunter, Steven	UT0325	Huyge, Dana	NY1400
Hull, Douglas	CA2950	Hunter, Todd	PA2200	Huzjak, Amy	TX3527

Hwalek, Ginger Y.	ME0440	Inglis, Adrienne	TX2650	Isomura, Sachiya	MN1280
Hwang, ChiHee	TN1850	Ingliss, Robert B.	NY0500	Israel, Shachar	OH0650
Hwang, Christine	IL1615	Ingliss, Robert	NY3785	Israel, Yoron	MA0260
Hwang, Margery 'Mimi'	NY2650	Ingraham, Mary	AA0100	Israelievitch, Jacques	AG0450
Hwang, Margery	NY1100	Ingram, Charles	CA2710	Israelievitch, Jacques	AG0650
Hwang, Mary	IL1340	Ingram, Danny	TX1100	Istad, Robert M.	CA0815
Hwang, Okon	CT0150	Ingram, David	OR1300	Italiano, Richard	CO0300
Hwang-Hoesley, Jae W.	IL0750	Ingram, Joe	OR1050	Iticovici, Silvian	MO1900
Hyatt, Garey A.	MD0200	Ingram, Roger	IL0550	Itkin, David C.	TX3420
Hyatt, Jack	NY0635	Inguanti, Cris	AB0100	Itkin, Ora	MN1625
Hyberger, Brett	TN0260	Inguanti, Cris	AB0200	Ito, John Paul	PA0550
Hyberger, Sarah Amanda	TN0260	Ingwerson, John	MS0300	Ito, Kanako	MO1000
Hyde, Edye Evans	MI0300	Inkman, Joanne	NC2500	Itoh, Takuma	HI0210
Hyde, Edye	MI1050	Inks, Kimberly	IN0150	Itzler, Neal L.	MA0260
Hyde, John	AA0050	Inkster, Matthew	WV0600	Iula, Dave	OR0600
Hyde, Martha M.	NY4320	Inoo, Yuri	CA3300	Ivanov, Kalin H.	NY0500
Hyde, Michael	MI0300	Inoue, Satoshi	NY2660	Ivanov, Krassimir	NY3600
Hyde, Michael	MI1050	Inouye, Fang-Fang Shi	CA0859	Ivanov, Peter	PA2200
Hyden, Derek	VA0600	Inouye, Mark	CA4150	Ivanov, Svetozar D.	FL2000
Hyer, Brian	WI0815	Insalaco, Vince	PA3700	Ivanova, Vera	CA0960
Hyla, Lee	IL2250	Inselman, Elsie	AG0550	Ivanovic, Predrag	FL1450
Hyland, Greg	AG0130	Inselman, Rachel	MN1600	Ivanovitch, Roman M.	IN0900
Hyland, Judy	IA1300	Inserto, Ayn	MA1400	Iverson, Cynde	NY3785
Hylton, Doris	MO1830	Inserto, Ayn	MA0260	Iverson, Jennifer	IA1550
Hylton, Fleta	DC0050	Inserto, Ayn	MA1175	Ivester, Mark	WA0200
Hylton, Fleta	DC0170	Insko, Robert	PA3000	Ivester, Mark D.	WA0600
Hylton, John B.	MO1830	Interlandi, Silvio	CT0550	Ivey, Bobby	GA0350
Hyman, Adah	NY1860	Intintoli, Helen	CA4650	Ivey, Carol	TX3370
Hyman, Victor G.	NH0110	Ioanna, Philip	PA2200	Ivry, Jessica	CA1150
Hynes, Elizabeth	CA5300	Ion, Charles	CA1960	Ivy, Allen	MO1100
Hynes, Maureen	NY2105	Ionesco, Georgette	NY4500	Ivy, Julie	NV0050
Hynes, Mia M.	MO1790	Ioudenitch, Stanislav	MO1000	Iwaasa, Juel	WA1200
Hynes, Tom	CA1000	Ioudenitch, Tatiana	MO1000	Iwama, Kayo	NY0150
Hynson, Bernard	MD0850	Irby, Fred	DC0150	Iwanusa, Charles	MI0450
Hyslop, Greg	NC0900	Irchai, Arnold	FL1850	Iwasaki, Jun	TN1850
Hyslop, Greg	NC0910	Irei, Norito	FL1550	Iwasaki, Masahiro	IA1450
Hyun, June	NY5000	Ireland, Cathy	CA1000	Iwasaki, Masahiro	IA0940
Hyun, Suk-Yi	MD0300	Irish, John E.	TX0150	Iwasaki, Masahiro	IA0250
Iacona, Richard	NY2150	Irish, Michael J.	MI1450	Iwata, Nanae	IL2750
Iannaccone, Anthony J.	MI0600	Irizarry, Rafael E.	PR0115	Iwazumi, Ray	NY1900
Ianni, Davide	MA0400	Irkaeva, Zarina S.	MA2150	Iyer, Vijay	NY2150
Iannone, Vincent	PA1550	Irland, Jeremy	WA1100	Iyer, Vijay S.	NY2750
Ibarra, Susie	VT0050	Irmiter, Kay	NC2000	Izdebski, Christy	MD0100
Ibershoff, Emily	KY1500	Irmiter, Kristopher	SC1200	Izdebski, Krzysztof	CA4150
Ibrahim, Michael	WV0750	Irom, Benjamin M.	TX2800	Izdebski, Pawel	NC2440
Ichikawa, Andrew	AA0200	Irvin, Virginia	TX2250	Iznaola, Ricardo	CO0900
Ichmouratov, Airat	AI0190	Irvin, Wade	MS0700	Izotov, Eugene A.	IL0750
Idenden, John	NJ0100	Irvine, Erin	CA5070	Izotov, Eugene	IL0550
Ignacio, Arnel	CA0825	Irvine, Jane	OH1400	Izquierdo, Pablo	WA1100
Ignatiou, Connie	KY0550	Irvine, Jeffrey K.	OH0600	Izquierdo, Rene	WI0825
Iguina, Jose R.	PR0150	Irvine, Mary	MI1830	Izzett, Robert K.	OR0800
Ihas, Dijana	OR0750	Irving, David	TX0550	Izzo, Jeffrey	MN1120
Ihasz, Daniel	NY3725	Irving, Howard L.	AL1150	Izzo, Victor	NY4300
Ihde, Mike	MA0260	Irving, Marcy	CA1510	Jaber, Thomas I.	TX2150
Ihm, Dana	CO0275	Irving, Silvia	MA0150	Jablonski, Darlyn	OR0150
Iimori, Mitch	OR0150	Irwin, David	FL1650	Jablonski, Krzysztof	AA0050
Iimori, Mitch	OR0400	Irwin, David E.	FL0450	Jablonsky, Eugene	WA1350
Iimori, Mitch	OR0250	Irwin, Donna	KY0400	Jablonsky, Stephen	NY0550
Iimori, Mitch	OR1300	Irwin, Doreen	CA3850	Jablow, Lisa	VT0250
Iimori, Mitch S.	OR1100	Irwin, Frederick	NJ1400	Jaccard, Jerry L.	UT0050
Ikach, Yugo Sava	PA0500	Irwin, Jeffrey	WV0100	Jachens, Darryl	SC1080
Ikeda, Kikuei	CT0850	Irwin, Pamela	TX0370	Jacklin, Christopher	AJ0100
Ikner, W. Joseph	AL0200	Irwin, Roseanna Lee	PA0550	Jacklin, Matt	IL2300
Ilban, Serdar	TX1400	Isaac, Cecil	TX0250	Jacklin, Rachel	IL2300
Iles, Alex	CA0510	Isaac, James G.	MO1790	Jackman, Sean M.	OH2150
Illari, Bernardo	TX3420	Isaac, James	KS0570	Jackobs, Mark	OH0600
Illman, Richard	MI1400	Isaackson, Mark	SD0050	Jackson, Albert	IL2775
Im, Miah	AG0450	Isaacs, David	TN1400	Jackson, Ashley	NY4450
Im, Sung-Mi	IN0900	Isaacs, David	CA0859	Jackson, Barbara G.	AR0700
Imamovic, Almer	CA3300	Isaacs, Kevin	CT0800	Jackson, Bil	TN1850
Imara, Mtafiti	CA0847	Isaacs, Robert	NJ0900	Jackson, Brett	KS0590
Imhoff, Andrea G.	TX2900	Isaacson, Eric J.	IN0900	Jackson, Christopher	AI0070
Imler, James R.	SC1200	Isaacson, Kristin	TX0900	Jackson, Cliff	KY1450
Immel, Conrad	CA0859	Isaacson, Lawrence	MA0350	Jackson, D. D.	NY0625
Immel, Daniel	PA1750	Isaacson, Peter R.	TX0900	Jackson, Dan	CA3640
Immel, Dean	CA2750	Isachsen, Sten Y.	NY3600	Jackson, David Lee	MI2100
Immel, Dean	CA5300	Isacoff, Stuart M.	NY3785	Jackson, Dennis C.	ID0250
Imobersteg, John	WI0830	Isadore, Jennifer L.	TX1400	Jackson, Douglas A.	NC0700
Imperio, Roy	MA0250	Isakson, Aaron	MN0610	Jackson, Eric	MO1550
Imsand, Patrick K.	AL1300	Isbell, Dan	NY1800	Jackson, Eric	MO0400
Imthurn, Melinda	TX1725	Isbin, Sharon	NY1900	Jackson, Ernie	NY3250
Inagawa, Kanako	CA0300	Isele, David	FL2050	Jackson, Fraser	AG0300
Ince, Kamran	TN1680	Isenberg-Grzeda, Connie	AI0210	Jackson, Fraser	AG0450
Indergaard, Lyle	GA2150	Isenhour, Justin	AR0500	Jackson, Gregory	AL0345
Indik, Lawrence R.	PA3250	Isenhour, Justin R.	SC0600	Jackson, Gregory	AL0050
Infusino, Patrick	IL0275	Isenor, Ted	AA0080	Jackson, Herman	LA0700
Ingalls, Duane	ME0430	Isensee, Paul R.	PA2800	Jackson, Isaiah	MA1175
Ingalls, Glendon	VT0250	Isenstead, Lisa	NY2150	Jackson, Isaiah	MA0260
Ingber, Elizabeth	CA4625	Isgro, Robert M.	NY3730	Jackson, J.P. Christopher	AA0200
Ingber, Jeffrey	VA1400	Ishida, Nobuyuki	NY0625	Jackson, Jackie	UT0200
Ingber, Jonathan	CA3460	Ishigaki, Miles M.	CA0810	Jackson, James	CT0100
Inger, Leah	MD0850	Ishii, Timothy	TX3500	Jackson, James	AL1250
Ingersoll, Orbie D.	CA3100	Ishikawa, Chikae	NY5000	Jackson, James	CT0600
Ingham, William	VA1350	Ishikawa, Yoshiyuki	CO0800	Jackson, James	CT0650
Ingle, Jennet	IN1750	Ishimaru, Kayo	FL1950	Jackson, Jane	CA1250
Ingle, Ronnie	ND0500	Ishimaru, Kayo	FL1000	Jackson, Janice	AF0120
Inglefield, Deb S.	IN0910	Ishizuka, Eiko	MA1175	Jackson, Janice R.	MD1000
Inglefield, Ken P.	OH0300	Iskowitz, David	NJ0300	Jackson, Jay Craig	NC0050
Inglefield, Ruth K.	MD0650	Isley-Farmer, Christine	TN1100	Jackson, Joe	CA1000
Ingles, Greg	MA0400	Isomura, Kazuhide	CT0850	Jackson, Keith	WV0750

Name	Code	Name	Code	Name	Code
Jackson, Kymberly	CA4625	James, Deborah	RI0250	Jarman, Amy	TN1850
Jackson, L. Max	KY0200	James, Donna Bunn	GA1650	Jaros, Marc	MN1200
Jackson, Lynne A.	TX2400	James, Douglas	NC0050	Jaroszewicz, Martin	CA0835
Jackson, Milton	AR0810	James, Gordon	TN1350	Jarred, Jennifer	FL0950
Jackson, Nadina Mackie	AG0600	James, Helen	IA0950	Jarrell, Boyd	CA1150
Jackson, Nadina Mackie	AG0300	James, Jeffrey R.	NE0250	Jarrell, Erinn	CA5355
Jackson, Nancy	IN0905	James, Jo-Sandra	VI0050	Jarrett, Gabriel	VT0400
Jackson, Paul	AL0650	James, Joshua	MI1260	Jarrett, Gabriel	NY3775
Jackson, Randy	AI0050	James, Judith R.	ME0500	Jarrett, Jack	NC2430
Jackson, Raymond T.	DC0150	James, Judy A. G.	LA0700	Jarrett, Scott	MA0400
Jackson, Roland	CA1050	James, Karen	VT0100	Jarriel, Janet	GA1300
Jackson, Roland	CA2710	James, Kimberly Gratland	MT0400	Jarvi, Steven	MO1900
Jackson, Rosemary	MO0350	James, Kortney	WI0850	Jarvis, David	WA1150
Jackson, Russell	PA2450	James, Kortney	WI0750	Jarvis, Jeffery W.	AR0850
Jackson, Ryan D.	MN1120	James, Laurel	UT0190	Jarvis, Jeffrey S.	CA0825
Jackson, Sandra	MI0600	James, Martin E.	OH2200	Jarvis, Peter	CT0100
Jackson, Sharon Sue	IN1800	James, Matthew H.	LA0770	Jarvis, Peter	NJ1400
Jackson, Stephen	IL1800	James, Matthew T.	OH1900	Jarvis, Willie	AG0200
Jackson, Stephen	IL0420	James, Matthew C.	IN1650	Jasavala, John	AG0450
Jackson, Steve	IL1350	James, Nancy B.	NY4150	Jasavala, John	AG0500
Jackson, Timothy L.	TX3420	James, Pamela A.	VA0750	Jasinski, Mark	WA0750
Jackson, Tom	PA3560	James, Ray	KS0050	Jasinski, Nathan David	KY0550
Jackson, Travis A.	IL3250	James, Richard	FL1700	Jaskot, Matthew	MD0550
Jackson, Tyrone	GA1150	James, Robert R.	KY0550	Jaskowiak, Jeffrey	IL3370
Jackson, William	KY1000	James, Sandy L.	PA3250	Jasmin, Pierre	AI0210
Jackson-Legris, Erin	KS0590	James, Shaylor L.	FL0600	Jasperse, Gregory P.	CA3500
Jacob, Heidi	PA1500	James, Steve	WI0250	Jaudes, Christian	NY1900
Jacob, Jeffrey	IN0005	James, Tim	PA0950	Javore, James	MA0350
Jacob, Jeffrey	IN1450	James, William R.	FL1300	Jaworski, Warren	FL2000
Jacob, Stefanie	WI1150	James, Woodrow	CA2750	Jay, Sarah	CA1425
Jacobi, Bonnie S.	CO0250	Jameson, Joel	NY2900	Jazwinski, Barbara M.	LA0750
Jacobowski, Richard	NY4200	Jameson, Philip	GA2100	Jean, Martin D.	CT0850
Jacobs, Aletha	SC0600	Jameson, Shelley	NY2900	Jean, Rachel	AA0035
Jacobs, David M.	OR1050	Jamieson, Jake	CA5031	Jeanrenaud, Joan	CA2950
Jacobs, Ed	IL2970	Jamieson, Robert	MN0950	Jech, Lori	OK1400
Jacobs, Edward	NC0650	Jamison, Phil A.	NC2550	Jee, Patrick	IL0550
Jacobs, Gene	MO1000	Jamison, Vicki	PA0100	Jefcoat, Priscilla	GA0350
Jacobs, Jay N.	LA0350	Jamner, Margaret	IN1010	Jeffers, Amy	IA0600
Jacobs, Kenneth A.	TN1710	Jampel, Peter F.	NY2750	Jeffers, Rebecca	OR0700
Jacobs, Malcolm	CO0100	Jamsa, Martha N.	MN0950	Jefferson, Kelly	AG0650
Jacobs, Marc	CA3270	Jamsa, Martha	MN0300	Jefferson, Thomas	IL2100
Jacobs, Mark	OR0950	Janack, Andrew	NY3600	Jefferson, Thomas	IL2750
Jacobs, Nicole	NE0150	Janas, Mark	NY2150	Jeffery, Peter	NJ0900
Jacobs, Patrick	AL1195	Jancewicz, Peter	AA0050	Jeffrey, Andrea	AF0120
Jacobs, Paul	NY1900	Janco, Steve	IN1350	Jeffrey, Bobbie	MO0060
Jacobsen, Chad	IA0550	Janda, Susan	MN0800	Jeffrey, Paul H.	NC0600
Jacobsen, David C.	VA1700	Jander, Owen	MA2050	Jeffrey, Sarah	AG0300
Jacobsen, Eric	NY2750	Janeczko, Jeffrey M.	CA5031	Jeffrey, Wayne	AB0060
Jacobsen, Jeffrey	PA2150	Janelli, Ron	NJ0825	Jeffreys, Harold	NC2300
Jacobsen, Lesa L.	WI0845	Janello, Mark	MD0650	Jeffreys, Harold L.	NC2150
Jacobson, Alan	IA1800	Jang, Hue Jeong	IL1750	Jeffreys, Shannon	GA0950
Jacobson, Allan	SD0400	Jang, Iggy	HI0050	Jeffries, Curt	NE0700
Jacobson, Barbara	FL0800	Jang, Ignace	HI0210	Jeffries, Jean	MA1350
Jacobson, Carol	CA2250	Jang, Jae Hyeok	IL1850	Jekabson, Erik	CA0807
Jacobson, Daniel C.	MI2250	Jang, Jinyoung	CA3100	Jekabson, Erik	CA0900
Jacobson, Harry P.	NY3725	Jang, Jinyoung	CA0200	Jekabson, Erik	CA2775
Jacobson, Jaime	OR0200	Janik, Liz	AG0130	Jelinek, Mark R.	PA0250
Jacobson, James	VA1600	Janikian, Leon C.	MA1450	Jelle, Lisa A.	OH0350
Jacobson, James	MN0050	Janis, Christine	WA1100	Jellison, Anastasia	VA1850
Jacobson, Joshua R.	MA1450	Janisch, Joseph	WV0560	Jellison, Anastasia	VA0250
Jacobson, Katherine	MD0650	Jankauskas, Sarunas	KS1450	Jellison, Anastasia I.	VA1550
Jacobson, Marin	CA1425	Janke, Tom J.	IN0907	Jellison, Anastasia	VA1500
Jacobson, Mary Ann	MT0200	Jankovic, Petar S.	IN0900	Jellison, Judith A.	TX3510
Jacobson, Michael	TX0300	Jankowsky, Rich	MA1900	Jemian, Rebecca	NY1800
Jacobson, Mikael	CA1270	Janners, Erik N.	WI0425	Jemielita, James	NY2102
Jacobson, Sheri	WA0400	Jannett, Victor	MA0350	Jemison-Keisker, Lynn C.	UT0300
Jacobson, Sheri	WA1350	Janower, David M.	NY3700	Jemmott, Thomas	FL2050
Jacobson, Steve	IL1520	Janowsky, Maxim	MI1750	Jeng, Rhoda	MD0400
Jacobus, Rhea Beth	SC0400	Janowsky, Maxim	MI2200	Jenkins Ainsworth, Jodi	MA0260
Jacoby, Marc		Janson, Anne	VT0450	Jenkins, Cara M.	NC1250
Jacoby, Marc Max	PA3600	Janson, Peter	MA2010	Jenkins, Carl	MA2250
Jacques, David	AI0190	Janson, Thomas	OH1100	Jenkins, Chadwick	NY0600
Jaczko, Robert	MA0260	Janssen, Brett	KS0215	Jenkins, Chester	OH0450
Jadus, John	PA1550	Jantsch, Carol	PA3250	Jenkins, Clay	NY1100
Jaeb, Mary	CA3460	Jantsch, Carol	PA0850	Jenkins, David	MN1625
Jaeschke, Rick	IL0100	Jantsch, Nancy	OH1600	Jenkins, Donald P.	CO0200
Jaffe, Andy W.	MA2250	Jantz, Paul	SC0200	Jenkins, E. Morgan	MD0450
Jaffe, Claudio	FL1450	Jantzi, John	OR1050	Jenkins, Ellie	GA0610
Jaffe, Stephen	NC0600	Januleviciute, Egle	CA5550	Jenkins, Ellie M.	GA0300
Jagielsky, Kathleen	DC0250	Janus, Ryan	CO0050	Jenkins, Isaac B.	CA4410
Jagow, Shelley	OH2500	Janz, Holly A.	MN0600	Jenkins, Jack	MO0700
Jaimes, Judit	WI0825	Janz, Tim	AA0050	Jenkins, James E.	FL1850
Jakelski, Lisa	NY1100	Janzen, Chris	CA1860	Jenkins, Jeff C.	CO0800
Jakovcic, Zoran	GA0550	Janzen, Dorothy	KS0900	Jenkins, Jeffry	CA4850
Jakubiec, Aaron F.	IL0800	Janzen, Elaine	TN1350	Jenkins, Jennifer R.	IL2250
Jalbert, David	AG0400	Janzen, Eldon A.	AR0700	Jenkins, John Daniel	SC1110
Jalbert, Pierre	TX2150	Janzen, Elizabeth A.	TX2960	Jenkins, John A.	MA2000
Jalbert, Sylvain	AI0220	Janzen, Henry	AG0350	Jenkins, Joseph W.	PA1050
Jalilian, Zeinab	AA0050	Janzen, Wesley	AB0090	Jenkins, Judith	PA2900
Jamanis, Michael T.	PA1300	Jaque, Maria	CA1750	Jenkins, Kate	SC0275
Jamason, Corey	CA4150	Jaquette, Tim	CA1000	Jenkins, Lisa Davenport	PA2750
Jamerson, Celeste Emmons	NY5000	Jaquez, Candida	CA4500	Jenkins, Martin D.	OH2500
Jamerson, Thomas H.	NY5000	Jarczyk, Jan	AI0150	Jenkins, Miriam R.	MA2000
James, Buddy	CA0807	Jarden, Timothy	IL1500	Jenkins, Neil	FL0200
James, Candace	KY0550	Jardon, Gloria J.	MO0800	Jenkins, Pamela	ME0340
James, Clarity	VA1100	Jarianes, Stephen	TX1600	Jenkins, Rosemary	TX2350
James, Clay	NJ0800	Jarillo Alvarado, Lyanne	AA0020	Jenkins, Tim G.	MD0520
James, Creighton	MT0400	Jarjisian, Catherine	CT0600	Jenkins-Turner, Christy	MS0650
James, Dawn-Marie	GA0050	Jarjisian, Peter G.	OH1900	Jenkinson, Janet	IN1560
James, Dean G.	MI1000	Jarjour, Tala	IN1700	Jenks, Alden	CA4150

Alphabetical Listing of Faculty

Name	Code	Name	Code	Name	Code
Jenne, Natalie	IL0730	Jeyasigam, Sam	MI1750	Johnson, Birgitta	SC1110
Jennejohn, Matthew	AI0150	Jhaveri, Shweta	CA0050	Johnson, Bonnie L.	OR0175
Jenner, Bryan	NJ0760	Ji, Hye-Gyung	TX2350	Johnson, Brad	MS0200
Jenner, Joanna	NY5000	Ji, Ming Sheng	IN0005	Johnson, Brandon P.	NY1700
Jennings, Andrew W.	MI2100	Jiang, Danwen	AZ0100	Johnson, Brenda Seward	OK1450
Jennings, Arthur	FL1850	Jiang, Pu-Qi	TN1680	Johnson, Bryan	FL2130
Jennings, Carol	AZ0350	Jiang, Qi M.	OH2200	Johnson, Byron	MS0050
Jennings, Caroline	UT0150	Jiang, Yi-wen	NY0150	Johnson, Byron	AL1195
Jennings, Carolyn	MN1450	Jiang, Yi-wen	NJ0800	Johnson, Calvert	GA0050
Jennings, Christina	CO0800	Jillings, Cathy	AG0170	Johnson, Campbell	AR0700
Jennings, David J.	IL0650	Jimenez, Alexander	FL0850	Johnson, Candace Y.	CA5000
Jennings, David	MI2200	Jimenez, Carlos	AI0150	Johnson, Carl	TX0200
Jennings, Dunja	OR0400	Jimenez, Fernando	CT0800	Johnson, Carly	AL0345
Jennings, Graeme	CA2950	Jimenez, Lissette	FL0700	Johnson, Carly J.	AL0050
Jennings, Harlan	MI1400	Jimenez, Pedro J.	PR0115	Johnson, Catherine	OH2050
Jennings, Jori Johnson	IL1850	Jimenez, Raphael	OH1700	Johnson, Cecilia	MI0050
Jennings, Joseph	SC1110	Jimerson, David	OR0850	Johnson, Cecilia	OH2300
Jennings, Joseph W.	GA1900	Jin, Jungwon	CA2420	Johnson, Cecilia	MI1950
Jennings, Kenneth	MN1450	Jin, Jungwon	CA1960	Johnson, Charles	CA5350
Jennings, Kerry L.	IN0350	Jin, Min	MI0900	Johnson, Chrisa	VA0050
Jennings, Linda G.	PA1600	Jin, Soohyun	OK0850	Johnson, Christine	IA0600
Jennings, Mark D.	MO1780	Jin, Yu	OH1100	Johnson, Christopher R.	SD0500
Jennings, Shirley	LA0550	Jinkling-Lens, Carol	CO0900	Johnson, Christopher	KS1350
Jennings, Tom	TX1775	Jinright, John W.	AL1050	Johnson, Clarence J.	GA1900
Jennings, Vance	FL2000	Jirak, James	ID0050	Johnson, Clifford	CT0450
Jenny, Jack	OH2050	Jirak, Steve	KS0150	Johnson, Cornelius	IL0450
Jenrette, Thomas S.	TN0500	Jirosek, Peter	IL2650	Johnson, Cory	CA1900
Jenschke, Laura	TX3100	Jirousek, Peter	IL3450	Johnson, Craig	CA3640
Jensen, Andrew	AR0050	Jirovec, Mary	WI0150	Johnson, Craig R.	IL2100
Jensen, Brent	ID0075	Jirovec, Mary	WI0050	Johnson, Curtis	PA3580
Jensen, Byron W.	NE0300	Jivaev, Anton	NC1700	Johnson, Curtis	WV0750
Jensen, Christine	AI0150	Jo, Marie	FL0365	Johnson, Daniel	IL1200
Jensen, Constance	UT0325	Jobe, Elena	GA0600	Johnson, Daniel	FL1700
Jensen, DeNice	OR1010	Jobert, William	OH2500	Johnson, Daniel	FL1550
Jensen, Espen	IN0900	Jobin-Bevans, Dean	AG0170	Johnson, Daniel C.	NC2440
Jensen, Gary J.	IL0800	Jobson, Krista	MO0800	Johnson, Daryl	IN1010
Jensen, Hans Jorgen	GA1300	Jochum von Moltke, Veronica	MA1400	Johnson, David H.	GA0850
Jensen, Hans Jorgen	IL2250	Jocoy, Stacey	TX3200	Johnson, David	TN1600
Jensen, Janeen	NE0100	Jodoin, Aaron D.	NJ0800	Johnson, David A.	IA0900
Jensen, Janet L.	WI0815	Jodry, Frederick	RI0050	Johnson, David	CA0510
Jensen, Jeff	IA0550	Joe, Jeongwon	OH2200	Johnson, David Lee	GA2150
Jensen, Joan F.	LA0750	Joella, Benjamin R.	FL0650	Johnson, David	ID0070
Jensen, Jocelyn	NV0050	Joella, Laura	FL0650	Johnson, David	MA0260
Jensen, John	MN1625	Joffe, Edward	NJ0825	Johnson, Dawn	AA0050
Jensen, Joni L.	TX3300	Joffe, Lucy	NY2400	Johnson, Deborah	OK1400
Jensen, Karen	AC0100	Joham, Kristin	WA0250	Johnson, Deborah S.	NE0300
Jensen, Kristin	TX3510	Johanningsmeier, Scott	IN1010	Johnson, DeeDee	WY0150
Jensen, Michael	IA1800	Johannsen, Ann	TX3600	Johnson, Dennis	KY0950
Jensen, Michelle	CA0250	Johansen, Dane	NY1900	Johnson, Deral J.	AG0500
Jensen, Penelope C.	NC0600	Johansen, David A.	LA0650	Johnson, Derek Martin	IN0150
Jensen, Rachel	MN1450	Johansen, Judy	CA3800	Johnson, Diane	WA0900
Jensen, Richard	KY1000	Johansen, Ken	MD0650	Johnson, Dirk	WV0700
Jensen, Shane	PA2000	Johansen, Keven W.	UT0250	Johnson, Doug	MA2050
Jensen, Susan	MO1800	Johansen, Larry	CA3800	Johnson, Douglas	MA0260
Jensen-Abbott, Lia	MI0100	Johansen, Lawrence	CA0845	Johnson, Douglas	NJ1130
Jensen-Hole, Catherine	MA2000	Johansen-Werner, Bonnie	IL3370	Johnson, Dylan	CA1510
Jensen-Moulton, Stephanie	NY0500	Johanson, Bryan	OR0850	Johnson, Edmond	CA3300
Jenson, Don	WA0450	Johanson, Erik	OH2300	Johnson, Elisabeth Remy	GA0750
Jenson, Joyce	MN0040	Johanson, Michael	OR0400	Johnson, Elizabeth	CA5355
Jenson, Matthew	MA0260	Johansson, Annette	HI0210	Johnson, Elizabeth	TN0100
Jentsch, Christopher T.	NY4050	Johengen, Carl	NY1800	Johnson, Elizabeth	TN1850
Jentsch, Christopher	NY4060	John, Bina	AG0450	Johnson, Ellen C.	TX0400
Jeon, Hey Rim	MA0260	John, David	OK0850	Johnson, Eric	SD0150
Jeon, Hey Rim	MA2030	John, James A.	NY0642	Johnson, Eric D.	NY4150
Jeon, Hyerim	KS1400	Johnian, Paul	TN0100	Johnson, Eric	IL2200
Jeoung, Ji-Young	IN1050	Johnkoski, Stephen V.	MI1160	Johnson, Erik A.	CO0250
Jeppesen, Laura	MA0400	Johns, Amy	GA1070	Johnson, Erik	PA3330
Jeppesen, Laura	MA2050	Johns, Brian	IN1100	Johnson, Fred	CO0830
Jepson, Angela	MA0400	Johns, Christopher	NC2440	Johnson, G. Larry	UT0325
Jermance, Frank	CO0550	Johns, Donald C.	CA5040	Johnson, Gail	CA1375
Jermance, Frank J.	CO0830	Johns, James	NY0650	Johnson, Gary V.	IL2730
Jermihov, Peter	IL3200	Johns, Jim	NY1350	Johnson, Gary	MO0250
Jernigan, Richard	FL1500	Johns, John	TN1850	Johnson, Gary	IL1340
Jerosch, Anita	ME0410	Johns, Kristen	GA2150	Johnson, Gordon	UT0350
Jerosch, Anita	ME0340	Johns, Kynan	NJ1130	Johnson, Gordon	MT0370
Jerosch, Anita	ME0200	Johns, Lana Kay	MS0500	Johnson, Greg	OR0200
Jerosch, Anita	ME0150	Johns, Michael	PA3200	Johnson, H. Wade	PA2000
Jerosch, Sebastian	ME0340	Johns, Michele S.	MI2100	Johnson, Heather	PA3100
Jerosch, Sebastian	ME0250	Johns, Norman	OH2550	Johnson, Henry	GA1600
Jerosch, Sebastian	ME0150	Johns, Stephen	FL1745	Johnson, Henry	IL0550
Jesse, Dennis	LA0200	Johns, Steven S.	NJ0800	Johnson, Herbert	MN0250
Jesse, Lynda	MO0200	Johnson Hamilton, Joyce	CA4900	Johnson, Herbert	MN1250
Jesselson, Robert M.	SC1110	Johnson, Aaron E.	MO1250	Johnson, Hubert	ID0075
Jessop, Dustin	TX3350	Johnson, Adam	IN0905	Johnson, J. Keith	TX3420
Jessop, Dustin	TX3100	Johnson, Alan	TX1450	Johnson, Jacquelyn Pualani	HI0200
Jessup, Carol A.	TX3500	Johnson, Alan O.	FL1900	Johnson, Jake	OK0750
Jessup, Nancy	CA1425	Johnson, Alfred	NY0640	Johnson, James	TX2250
Jester, Erik	CA0845	Johnson, Alphonso	CA5300	Johnson, James D.	NE0610
Jester, Jennifer	PA2350	Johnson, Alphonso	CA0510	Johnson, James R.	MN1300
Jetter, Jonathan	NY3785	Johnson, Alyce	IL0750	Johnson, Jamie	IN1560
Jetter, Katherine	CO0350	Johnson, Amy	MI0520	Johnson, Janice	OR1300
Jetton, Caroline K.	IN0350	Johnson, Amy S.	MA2000	Johnson, Jason K.	NE0610
Jevitt, Amy	FL0150	Johnson, Amy E.	MI0900	Johnson, Jason	AR0730
Jewell, Jim	GA0625	Johnson, Andrea	MA0260	Johnson, Jay L.	MN0300
Jewell, Joe	CA1900	Johnson, Ann	CA5355	Johnson, Jeanine	TX2750
Jewell, Renee	GA0625	Johnson, Barbara C.	CT0650	Johnson, Jeanne	TX1350
Jewell, Vickie L.	AL0345	Johnson, Barry	WA0650	Johnson, Jefferson	KY1450
Jewett, Dennis A.	KY0800	Johnson, Barry	KY0750	Johnson, Jeffrey	CT0550
Jewett, Dennis A.	NC0350	Johnson, Ben S.	NC2350	Johnson, Jeffrey W.	NY2105
Jex, David	OH2300	Johnson, Beverly	CA0900	Johnson, Jeffrey	OR0850

Alphabetical Listing of Faculty

Name	Code	Name	Code	Name	Code
Johnson, Jeffry Blake	PA3580	Johnson, Scott	MA0260	Jones, Alan	OR0850
Johnson, Jenny O.	MA2050	Johnson, Scott	OK1330	Jones, Allison	SC0350
Johnson, Jeremiah	NE0200	Johnson, Seth	TX0250	Jones, Ann A.	TN0250
Johnson, Jessica G.	WI0815	Johnson, Sharon L.	NY1700	Jones, Anne Howard	MA0400
Johnson, Jill	MA1050	Johnson, Shauna	UT0050	Jones, Arlington	TX0370
Johnson, Joaquina Calvo	CA6050	Johnson, Shauna	UT0325	Jones, Arnold	NJ0950
Johnson, Joel C.	SC1050	Johnson, Shawn F.	MD0650	Jones, Barry	IA0700
Johnson, John Paul	KS1450	Johnson, Sherry A.	AG0650	Jones, Bernard	OK1050
Johnson, John	AG0450	Johnson, Shersten	MN1625	Jones, Betty McLellan	TN0450
Johnson, John F.	PA3250	Johnson, Shirley M.	FL0600	Jones, Boyd M.	FL1750
Johnson, Jon S.	TX2350	Johnson, Sidney	OR0600	Jones, Brandon D.	OH2450
Johnson, Joyce F.	GA1900	Johnson, Sigrid	MN1450	Jones, Brett	WI0860
Johnson, Julianne R.	OR0800	Johnson, Sigurd	ND0350	Jones, Brian	VA0250
Johnson, Kallin	MA0650	Johnson, Stephen P.	TX2600	Jones, Brian	VA1500
Johnson, Karen	MD0750	Johnson, Stephen R.	PA0700	Jones, Brian	VA1600
Johnson, Karen	DC0170	Johnson, Steven P.	UT0050	Jones, Brian	VA0450
Johnson, Kari M.	MO0050	Johnson, Teagan	OR1050	Jones, Brian D.	DC0170
Johnson, Karrell	TX3420	Johnson, Teri	TX2800	Jones, Brian	AA0100
Johnson, Katherine L.	NJ1350	Johnson, Thomas M.	TX3420	Jones, Byron A.	VA1350
Johnson, Keith V.	CA1250	Johnson, Timothy	KY0100	Jones, Calvin	DC0350
Johnson, Keith	CA2975	Johnson, Timothy	ME0340	Jones, Cheryl	FL1430
Johnson, Kelly A.	AR0850	Johnson, Timothy	ME0200	Jones, Christine	MO1100
Johnson, Ken	IN1025	Johnson, Timothy A.	NY1800	Jones, Christopher	IL0750
Johnson, Kendra	UT0350	Johnson, Todd Alan	CA0845	Jones, Christopher	NY3350
Johnson, Kenneth W.	IN0905	Johnson, Tom	CA3320	Jones, Claire	OH1100
Johnson, Kerilyn	UT0050	Johnson, Tracey	MO2000	Jones, Colby	ID0075
Johnson, Kerry	CO0300	Johnson, Trevor	KY0400	Jones, Colette	KY0300
Johnson, Kevin P.	GA1900	Johnson, Trevor	IN1010	Jones, Craig	OR0600
Johnson, Kris	OH1850	Johnson, Tripp	VA0250	Jones, Dani R.	AL0500
Johnson, Kyle E.	CA0550	Johnson, Valerie	NC0200	Jones, Dani S.	AL0650
Johnson, Lacey	VA0800	Johnson, Velshera	VA0400	Jones, Daniel	IA0420
Johnson, Larry	OR0700	Johnson, Vicky V.	TX2750	Jones, David	NJ1400
Johnson, Laura	IA1550	Johnson, Victor	CT0100	Jones, David P.	WA0700
Johnson, Lawrence	UT0200	Johnson, Victoria	MS0360	Jones, David	MD1010
Johnson, Lee E.	GA1200	Johnson, Warren	TX2200	Jones, David C.	MD0150
Johnson, Lindsay	CA4500	Johnson, Wayne D.	WA0800	Jones, David	DC0100
Johnson, Lura	MD0650	Johnson, Will	CA4460	Jones, David	GA2000
Johnson, Lynn	AE0050	Johnson, William T.	CA4700	Jones, David Evan	CA5070
Johnson, Lynne	HI0210	Johnson, Yvonne P.	GA0200	Jones, Deborah	TX3415
Johnson, Madeline	UT0190	Johnson, Yvonne P.	DE0050	Jones, Dena Kay	TX3520
Johnson, Marc Thomas	MA0400	Johnson-Tamai, Eric	CA0550	Jones, Douglas	KY1500
Johnson, Maria V.	IL2900	Johnson-Wilmot, Daniel	WI1100	Jones, Eddie	AR0700
Johnson, Marie	AG0500	Johnston, Amanda J.	MS0700	Jones, Emily	FL0040
Johnson, Marjorie S.	VA0950	Johnston, Ben	NC1750	Jones, Eric W.	MI1000
Johnson, Mark	GA0200	Johnston, Beverley	AG0450	Jones, Erik Reid	WV0550
Johnson, Marvin	AL1170	Johnston, Blair	IN0900	Jones, Esther	CA0815
Johnson, Mary Jane	TX0100	Johnston, Darren	CA5000	Jones, Esther	CA1425
Johnson, Matt	CA1900	Johnston, Dennis	NY0700	Jones, Evan T.	TN1680
Johnson, Maurice	DC0050	Johnston, Gary	KY1000	Jones, Evan	FL0850
Johnson, Meg	NC2000	Johnston, Glen	MT0200	Jones, Everett N.	OH2400
Johnson, Melody	MN1280	Johnston, Grace	CA1250	Jones, Fernando	IL0720
Johnson, Michael	PA3330	Johnston, Greg	UT0150	Jones, Gail	PA1400
Johnson, Michael	MO0600	Johnston, Greg	UT0200	Jones, Gareth	AA0150
Johnson, Michael E.	TX2800	Johnston, Gregory	AG0450	Jones, Gordon	TX3175
Johnson, Michael	RI0250	Johnston, Jack R.	NY3730	Jones, Grace	WI0804
Johnson, Michael	AL1170	Johnston, James W.	IN1100	Jones, Gregory R.	MO1780
Johnson, Michael	MA0260	Johnston, James	OH0050	Jones, Harold	NY0500
Johnson, Michelle	OK0850	Johnston, Jason	WY0200	Jones, Harold	NY5000
Johnson, Michelle	TX2600	Johnston, Jeffrey	AI0150	Jones, Harold	NY2400
Johnson, Michelle	OK1450	Johnston, Jesse A.	MI2110	Jones, Harold	NY2200
Johnson, Mick	NE0590	Johnston, Joey	AZ0440	Jones, Heath	OK0700
Johnson, Mildred	UT0300	Johnston, Keith	CT0300	Jones, Henry S.	LA0650
Johnson, Molly	TX3535	Johnston, Margaret	IL0750	Jones, Herman	SC0150
Johnson, Nancy	KS1300	Johnston, Mindy	OR0400	Jones, Hilton Kean	FL2000
Johnson, Nancy S.	KS0200	Johnston, Noel H.	TX3420	Jones, Hugh	MO1830
Johnson, Nathaniel	UT0200	Johnston, Paul R.	IL0800	Jones, J. Franklin	MA1400
Johnson, Nathaniel	NE0710	Johnston, Randy B.	NY2750	Jones, Janet	AZ0150
Johnson, Nicholas	OH1850	Johnston, Randy	NY3785	Jones, Jeff	KY0450
Johnson, Nick	CA1375	Johnston, Randy	CT0650	Jones, Jeff	CA3200
Johnson, Nikki	MS0360	Johnston, Rebecca R.	SC0600	Jones, Jeffrey	CT0550
Johnson, Pamela A.	WV0400	Johnston, Scott	OH2150	Jones, Jeffrey L.	SC0420
Johnson, Pamela	WI0801	Johnston, Stephen K.	VA1350	Jones, Jennifer D.	IL3500
Johnson, Patricia	KY1550	Johnston, Steve	KS1300	Jones, Jeremy D.	OH1450
Johnson, Paul L.	MD0650	Johnston, Susan	DC0170	Jones, Joel C.	AL0050
Johnson, Paul	IN1700	Johnstone, Bruce	NY3725	Jones, Joella	OH0600
Johnson, Peggy J.	MN0600	Johnstone, John	ME0200	Jones, John W.	PA1400
Johnson, Penny	AJ0100	Johonnott, Edwin	VA0450	Jones, John R.	KY1500
Johnson, Randall	GU0500	Joiner, Anna Barbrey	SC0750	Jones, Josh	IL0850
Johnson, Randolph B.	OK0650	Joiner, Lee	IL3550	Jones, Joshua	IL1300
Johnson, Randolph J.	DE0050	Joiner, Thomas	SC0750	Jones, Judy	NM0450
Johnson, Rebecca R.	IL0800	Jojatu, Mihail	MA1175	Jones, K. Jennifer	OH2200
Johnson, Richard	KS0590	Jokipii, Alex	NY3725	Jones, Kate	TX2750
Johnson, Richard	SC0420	Jokisch, Kelly	SC0710	Jones, Kate	AR0300
Johnson, Robert	TX2750	Jolles, Annette	CT0900	Jones, Katherine Borst	OH1850
Johnson, Robert M.	CA0150	Jolles, Susan	NY1600	Jones, Kathleen	PR0115
Johnson, Robert	NH0110	Jolles, Susan	NY2150	Jones, Keith D.	MA2030
Johnson, Roger O.	NJ0950	Jolles, Susan	NY2250	Jones, Keith	SC0650
Johnson, Roger	CA2550	Jolley, Carolyn L.	NY3717	Jones, Kelly	CA0630
Johnson, Ronald	IA1600	Jolley, David	NY2250	Jones, Kevin	CT0650
Johnson, Russell	WI0835	Jolley, David	NY0642	Jones, Kimberly	IL2750
Johnson, Ruth	CA5360	Jolley, David	NC1650	Jones, Kimberlyn	CA2810
Johnson, Ryann	NE0150	Jolley, Jennifer	OH2000	Jones, Kristina Belisle	OH2150
Johnson, Ryann P.	NE0200	Jolly, Donna	NC1300	Jones, Larry	TX2100
Johnson, Sara	TN1850	Jolly, Tucker	OH2150	Jones, Larry E.	NE0450
Johnson, Sarah	SC0650	Joly, Rene	AI0190	Jones, Laurie	PA3000
Johnson, Sarah	NC1650	Jonas, Dorothy	NY5000	Jones, Lawrence	AC0050
Johnson, Sarah	CO0250	Jonas, Dorothy	NY2400	Jones, Leslie I.	MO1500
Johnson, Sasha	AI0150	Jonason, Louisa	PA2250	Jones, Linda	WI1150
Johnson, Sasha	AG0300	Jonck, Rachelle	NJ1350	Jones, Linda	OH0600
Johnson, Scott R.	SD0050	Jones, Adah T.	TX3175	Jones, Lis	AR0250

831

Jones, Lloyd	AL1250	Jordan, Paul	IN0005	Jung, Hein	FL2050
Jones, Lloyd E.	AL1250	Jordan, Paul	NY3705	Jung, Hyesook	AL0950
Jones, Lorraine	GA0200	Jordan, Rachel	MS0350	Jung, Ji Hye	KS1350
Jones, Lucie	AA0050	Jordan, Rachel	LA0720	Junker, Jay	HI0210
Jones, Lucie	AA0150	Jordan, Rebecca	NY1800	Junker, Tercio	IN0300
Jones, M. Douglas	KY1460	Jordan, Robert	NY3725	Junkin, Jerry	TX3510
Jones, Martin David	GA0250	Jordan, Rodney	FL0850	Junkinsmith, Jeff	WA0860
Jones, Marvin	TN1600	Jordan, William S.	AA0150	Junokas, Michael	IL0850
Jones, Matthew	SC0600	Jordan-Anders, Lee	VA1830	Jupinka, Nick	NJ0760
Jones, Matthew Craig	SC1000	Jordan-Miller, Rebekah	GA1800	Jurcevic, S. Annette	TX2170
Jones, Max	IN1310	Jordanoff, Christine E.	PA1050	Jurchuk, Tobi	AA0050
Jones, Maxine	TN1400	Jordening, Jon	CA1425	Jurcisin, Mark	NJ0750
Jones, Melinda	MO1550	Jordheim, Steven	WI0350	Jureit-Beamish, Marie	IL2400
Jones, Melvin	GA1450	Jordheim, Suzanne	WI0350	Jurek, Shaun	MD0700
Jones, Melvin Rusty	IN0250	Jorgensen, Elaine	UT0190	Juris, Vic	NY2660
Jones, Meredith	TX2570	Jorgensen, Estelle R.	IN0900	Juris, Vic	NJ1130
Jones, Micah	PA3330	Jorgensen, Jerilyn J.	CO0200	Jurkowski, Edward	AA0200
Jones, Michael C.	KS1200	Jorgensen, Kristen	NY3770	Jurkscheit, Robert	CO0625
Jones, Nathan	TX2570	Jorgensen, Michael	MN0750	Jursik, Katherine	WI0100
Jones, Pamela Palmer	UT0250	Jorgensen, Nathan A.	SD0550	Jusino, Christopher	NY2550
Jones, Pamela	MS0580	Jorgensen, Richard	AR0750	Jussila, Clyde	WA1050
Jones, Patrick R.	PA1200	Jorgensen, Robert	OH2150	Justen, Gloria	CA2950
Jones, Patrick Michael	NY4150	Jorgensen, Trevor	NY3770	Justen, Wolfgang H.	MD0650
Jones, Paul	PA3250	Jorgenson, Jeri	CO0900	Justeson, Jeremy	PA1750
Jones, Peter	WA0750	Jorstad, Dede	MN1625	Justice, Roberta	MI0600
Jones, R. Larry	AR0850	Joselson, Rachel	IA1550	Justice, Roberta	OH1330
Jones, Ralph Miles	OH1700	Josenhans, Thomas	IN1600	Justison, Brian	IL1750
Jones, Randy	CA0830	Joseph, Alan	CO0900	Justus, Keith	TX0550
Jones, Rebecca	GA1650	Joseph, Annabelle	PA0550	Justus, Timothy W.	TX1700
Jones, Richard	PA2900	Joseph, Charles	NY3725	Jutras, Peter J.	GA2100
Jones, Richard	NE0450	Joseph, David	ME0200	Jutt, Stephanie	WI0815
Jones, Robert	OH2050	Joseph, Deanna	GA1050	Juza, Alan	OR0750
Jones, Robert Owen	OH1650	Joseph, Jane	MS0300	Kaarre, Lois	MI1750
Jones, Robert J.	ND0350	Joseph, Mervyn	OH0500	Kaatz, Jeffry M.	CA2420
Jones, Robert B.	OH2250	Joseph, Richard	MN0040	Kabat, Stephen	OH0650
Jones, Robert D.	FL1470	Joseph-Weil, Helene	CA0810	Kabir, Chaitanya Mahmud	CO0560
Jones, Robert	IN1050	Josephson, David	RI0050	Kachelmeier, Diane	WI0300
Jones, Rodney	NY1900	Josephson, Kim	OK1350	Kachian, Christopher	MN1625
Jones, Rodney	NY2150	Joslin, Art	MI0300	Kachulis, James A.	MA0260
Jones, Rufus	DC0075	Jospe, Robert D.	VA1550	Kacos, Lisa	MI0850
Jones, Russell L.	KS1050	Joss, Laura L.	OH0200	Kaczmarczyk, Mark	NY2200
Jones, Ryan C.	NY1600	Josselyn-Cranson, Heather	IA1200	Kaczorowska, Joanna Maria	NY3790
Jones, Ryan Patrick	WI0803	Jossim, J.	FL0800	Kaczynski, Marrisa	NY1050
Jones, Scott A.	OH1850	Jost, John R.	IL0400	Kadarauch, Katie	CA4150
Jones, Scott A.	GA2100	Jost, Paul	PA3330	Kaderabek, Frank	PA0850
Jones, Sean	OH1700	Jostlein, Thomas	IL3300	Kadetsky, Mark	NJ0550
Jones, Sean	PA1050	Jothen, Michael	MD0850	Kadis, Jay L.	CA4900
Jones, Sheila L.	OH1650	Joubert, Estelle	AF0100	Kadyk, Folkert	PA1550
Jones, Stacey	MI2000	Joul, Susan	MI1830	Kadz, John	AA0050
Jones, Stephen W.	TX3200	Jovanovic, Milica Jelaca	WA1250	Kaehler, Winston H.	MN0950
Jones, Stephen F.	CA3500	Jowers, Florence	NC1100	Kaenzig, Fritz	MI2100
Jones, Stephen	MI2250	Joy, Nancy	NM0310	Kafumbe, Damascus	VT0350
Jones, Steve	GA1050	Joy, Sharon	LA0550	Kagan, Alan L.	MN1623
Jones, Steve	MD0150	Joyal, Marc	AI0190	Kagarice, Jan M.	TX3420
Jones, Sue	IL1550	Joyce, Brooke	IA0950	Kagarice, Vern L.	TX3420
Jones, Susan	IA1550	Joyce, David	CA0835	Kagin, Roberta S.	MN0050
Jones, Susie	OR0550	Joyce, David	CA3500	Kagy, Tamara K.	OH2140
Jones, T. Marshall	GA0150	Joyce, J. Patrick	WV0300	Kahan, Sylvia	NY0600
Jones, Terry	ID0140	Joyce, John J.	LA0750	Kahan, Sylvia	NY0644
Jones, Thomas A.	MD0650	Joyce, Michael	IL0840	Kahler, Bette	NY4100
Jones, Thomas	AG0150	Joyce, Robert	SD0050	Kahler, Edward P.	TX3750
Jones, Timothy	NV0050	Joyce, Susan	FL1450	Kahn, Alexander G.	PA1400
Jones, Timothy A.	TX3400	Joyner, Maria	WA0650	Kahn, David	PA1450
Jones, Tony	IL1090	Joyner, Rochelle	NC0200	Kahn, Richard	CA2600
Jones, Trevor	IL1200	Ju, Alice	DC0170	Kahn, Richard	CA2750
Jones, Trevor	IL0750	Ju, Ara	MO0850	Kahn, Sue Ann	NY2250
Jones, Troy V.	FL0680	Jubenville, Suzanne	CA4460	Kahng, Er-Gene	AR0700
Jones, Vanita	DC0050	Jublonski, Anna	OR0150	Kai, Kudisan	MA0260
Jones, Vanita	MD0150	Juchniewicz, Jay	NC0650	Kail, Jeffrey E.	MO1810
Jones, Vanita	MD0550	Judge, Joseph	NC1900	Kairies, Joy E.	TX0550
Jones, Warren Puffer	OK0750	Judge, Kevin	IA0850	Kairoff, Peter	NC2500
Jones, Warren	NY2150	Judisch, David	IA0950	Kaiser, Audrey K.	RI0101
Jones, Wendell	OH0300	Judish, Marion	MN1300	Kaiser, Keith A.	NY1800
Jones, William LaRue	IA1550	Judiyaba,	CA4700	Kaiser, Pat	WI1150
Jones, William Darryl	LA0350	Judkins, Jennifer	CA5030	Kaiser, Tyler	WI0860
Jones, William	DC0350	Judson, Tohm	NC2700	Kaiser, Tyler	MN0450
Jones, William C.	CA4200	Judy, Ned	MD0700	Kaizer, Edward	IL0400
Jones, Willie	IL2250	Juengling, Pamela K.	MA2000	Kaizer, Janet	IL0400
Jones, Zebedee	MS0600	Juhl, Aaron	WI0806	Kajikawa, Loren	OR1050
Jones-Bamman, Richard	CT0150	Juhn, Hee-Kyung	AR0300	Kajiwara, Greg	MN0040
Jones-Reus, Angela	GA2100	Juilianna, Anita	FL0150	Kakish, Wael	CA3500
Jong, Pin Pin	NC1300	Julia, Luis Enrique	PR0115	Kakouberi, Daredjan 'Baya'	TX0370
Jonker, Jacob	MN1600	Julian, Ester	KY1540	Kalam, Tonu	NC2410
Jonsson, Johan	MT0200	Julian, Kimm D.	MN1000	Kalanduyan, Danongan	CA4625
Joo, Narae	IL3500	Julian, Michael	CA1700	Kaler, Ilya	IL0750
Joosten, Mike	WI0801	Julian, Michael	CA2750	Kaler, Olga D.	IL0750
Jordahl, Patricia	AZ0300	Julian, Suzanne	CA1700	Kalhous, David	TX3200
Jordan, Christopher	AL0010	Julian, Suzanne	CA3100	Kalib, Sylvan	MI0600
Jordan, DJ	MO0100	Julian, Tijuana	MO0350	Kalichstein, Joseph	NY1900
Jordan, Edward	LA0720	Julien, Ellis	AR0110	Kalinovsky, Grigory	NY2150
Jordan, Esther	CA2100	Julien, Patricia A.	VT0450	Kalinowski, Diane	PA0100
Jordan, Grace	FL1800	Julin, Patti	CA0400	Kalinowski, Mark	NJ0175
Jordan, James	NJ1350	Julyan, Robyn	CO0650	Kalis, Dawn	IN0900
Jordan, Jason	NC1350	Jumper, David	PA2200	Kalish, Gilbert	NY3790
Jordan, Jeff	KS0350	Jumpeter, Joseph A.		Kallaur, Barbara	IN0900
Jordan, John M.	IN1600	Juncker, Arthur	CA1950	Kallay, Aron	CA0960
Jordan, Krassimira	TX0300	Junda, Mary Ellen	CT0600	Kallay, Aron T.	CA5300
Jordan, L. Thomas	KY1000	Jung, Eun-Young	CA5050	Kallberg, Jeffrey	PA3350
Jordan, Michael D.	TX1660	Jung, Eunice	MD0850	Kallembach, James	IL3250
Jordan, Patrick	AG0300	Jung, Eunsuk	TN0600	Kallestad, Scott	NC0050

Alphabetical Listing of Faculty

Name	Code	Name	Code	Name	Code
Kallian, Sandra	WI0800	Kantorski, Valrie	MI0050	Kasper, Don J.	CA0835
Kallick, Jenny L.	MA0100	Kantorski, Vincent J.	OH0300	Kasper, Julien	MA0260
Kallmann, Helmut	AG0100	Kanyan, Joseph M.	VA0450	Kasper, Kathryn	KS0200
Kallstrom, Michael	KY1550	Kao, Janet	CA0960	Kasper, Max	AF0100
Kallstrom, Wayne	NE0100	Kao, Janet	CA1900	Kassarova, Petia	NY3600
Kallstrom, Wayne	NE0610	Kaplan, Abraham	WA1050	Kassel, Philip	ID0070
Kalm, Stephen	MT0400	Kaplan, Adam	CA5100	Kassinger, Robert C.	IL0750
Kalman, Eli	WI0830	Kaplan, Allan Richard	NM0310	Kassner, Eli	AG0450
Kalman, Zoltan	AG0200	Kaplan, Amelia S.	IN0150	Kassner, Karl J.	NC0900
Kalman, Zoltan	AG0050	Kaplan, Burton	NY2150	Kasten, Martha	IL0730
Kalman, Zoltan	AG0500	Kaplan, Chester	NY2750	Kastens, Kevin	IA1550
Kalogeras, Alexandros	MA0260	Kaplan, Lewis	NY1900	Kastner, Kathleen	IL3550
Kaloyanides, Michael G.	CT0700	Kaplan, Lewis	NY2250	Kasun, Scott	AZ0480
Kalson, Dorothy	NY4050	Kaplan, Lisa	VA1500	Kasunic, David M.	CA3300
Kalson, James	TX2200	Kaplan, Mark S.	IN0900	Katahn, Enid	TN1850
Kalson, Jim	TX2260	Kaplan, Sara	IL2775	Kataja-Urrey, Taina	NJ1130
Kaltchev, Ivo	DC0050	Kaplan, William	IL3310	Kataoka, Ayano	MA2000
Kalyn, Andrea	OH1700	Kaplanek, Jerzy	AG0600	Kates, Christine	PA3710
Kam, Dennis	FL1900	Kaplinsky, Veda	TX3000	Kato, Yuko	IL2900
Kam, Genna	IN0910	Kaplinsky, Yoheved	NY1900	Katona, Brian	NJ1130
Kamalidiin, Sais	DC0150	Kaplunas, Daniel	IA1800	Kats, Irina	DC0170
Kamatani, Pamela	CA5353	Kapner, Harriet H.	NY2550	Kats, Nitza	VA1100
Kamatani, Pamela M.	CA1020	Kapps, Sarah	TX3525	Katsarelis, Susan	DC0170
Kambeitz, Gus	CA5510	Kappy, David	WA1050	Katseanes, Kory L.	UT0050
Kambouris, Panagiota A.	MA1400	Kapralick, Randy	PA3330	Kattari, Kim	TX2900
Kamenski, Michael	WI0050	Kaptain, Laurence D.	LA0200	Kattari, Kim	TX3510
Kameria, Kim	CA1290	Kapur, Ajay	CA0510	Katterjohn, Michael	GA0250
Kamerin, Kim	CA2400	Kapuscinski, Jaroslaw	CA4900	Katz, Brian	AG0650
Kamien, Roger	NY0642	Karaca, Igor	OK0800	Katz, Brian	AG0450
Kamins, Benjamin	TX2150	Karahalis, Dean	NY1275	Katz, Bruce	MA0260
Kaminski, Imelda	IL1890	Karahalis, Dean	NY2550	Katz, Darrell	MA0260
Kaminski, Michael	NY0500	Karahalis, Dean	NY4060	Katz, Derek	CA5060
Kaminsky, Bruce	PA1000	Karahalis, Dean	NY4050	Katz, Dick	NY2150
Kaminsky, Carol Frances	FL1900	Karam, Christiane	MA0260	Katz, Joel	AG0300
Kaminsky, Joseph	MO1950	Karamanov, Vincent	MI0300	Katz, Judith	NY0625
Kaminsky, Laura	NY3785	Karan, Leon	AG0200	Katz, Mark	NC2410
Kaminsky, Peter	CT0600	Karas, Ted	KY1000	Katz, Martha	MA1400
Kamm, Charles W.	CA2175	Karass, Alan M.	MA0700	Katz, Martin E.	MI2100
Kamm, Charles W.	CA1060	Karathanasis, Konstantinos	OK1350	Katz, Max	VA0250
Kamm, Charles W.	CA3620	Karchin, Louis S.	NY2740	Katz, Paul	MA1400
Kamm, Charles W.	CA4500	Kargul, Laura J.	ME0500	Katz, Robert S.	OK1300
Kammerer, David	HI0050	Karis, Aleck	CA5050	Katz, Sheila H.	MA0260
Kammerer, Elizabeth	HI0050	Karlicek, Martin	AI0150	Katz, Shmuel D.	NY2750
Kammin, Benjamin	WI1150	Karlin, Brett	FL0930	Katz, Steve	TN1380
Kamprath, Richard	CA1560	Karloff, Michael	AG0550	Katzen, Daniel	MA1400
Kamstra, Darin	CO0225	Karloff, Michael	MI2200	Katzen, Daniel	AZ0500
Kamtman, Leslie E.		Karlsson, Stefan	TX3420	Kauffman, Bradley	KS0500
Kan-Walsh, Karen	IL2250	Karn, Kitty	IL3500	Kauffman, Deborah	CO0950
Kana, Dave	OH1350	Karn, Michael	NY2660	Kauffman, Irvin C.	PA1600
Kana, David	OH2600	Karna, Duane	IN0150	Kauffman, Larry D.	PA0150
Kanakis, Karen	IA0950	Karna, Kathy	IN0150	Kauffman, Mary Adelyn	FL0700
Kanamaru, Tomoko	NJ0175	Karnatz, Roland	VA0700	Kauffman, Rachel	PA3710
Kanda, Sanae	MA1650	Karnatz, Roland	VA1150	Kaufhold, Jessica	AL0530
Kandi, Kareem	WA0750	Karnes, Kevin C.	GA0750	Kaufman, Howard	CA2250
Kane, Angela	MI2100	Karp, Benjamin	IN0900	Kaufman, Jacob	KS0215
Kane, Dreena	HI0160	Karp, Benjamin	KY1450	Kaufman, Joe	WA0200
Kane, Janet	PA3650	Karp, David	TX2400	Kaufman, Robert	MA0260
Kane, Kevin	RI0200	Karp, Margaret B.	KY1450	Kaufman, Roseann Penner	KS0200
Kane, Kevin	RI0250	Karp, Parry	WI0815	Kaufman, Steve	MA0260
Kane, Kevin	RI0150	Karpatova, Mariana	NJ0400	Kauk, Brian	TX3400
Kane, Kevin	RI0200	Karpen, Richard	WA1050	Kaun, Kathleen	TX2150
Kane, Lila	RI0250	Karpf, Nita	OH0400	Kaupp, Gil	NV0050
Kane, Lila	RI0101	Karpinos, Vadim	IL0550	Kaur, Kamaljeet	AA0100
Kane, Marie A.	RI0100	Karpinski, Gary S.	MA2000	Kaurin-Karaca, Natasa	OK0800
Kane, Marie A.	IN1650	Karpoff, Fred S.	NY4150	Kausch, Mark	MN0800
Kane, Scott	CA0830	Karpoff, Rebecca J.	NY4150	Kausch, Mark	MN0350
Kane, Susan W.	FL1900	Karpowicz, Mike	MO1950	Kausch, Mark L.	MN0250
Kane, Trudy	OH2000	Karr, Andrew	FL2000	Kaushal, Abhiman	CA5040
Kaneda, Mariko	CA5300	Karr, John	CA0810	Kaushal, Abhiman	CA5031
Kanengiser, William	HI0210	Karr, Kathy	KY0450	Kautsky, Catherine C.	WI0350
Kaneshiro, Norman	DC0010	Karr, Kathy	KY1500	Kavafian, Ani	CT0850
Kang, Ann Teresa	ND0350	Karr, Matthew L.	KY1500	Kavafian, Ida	NY1900
Kang, Cecilia	NY1900	Karrick, Brant	KY1000	Kavafian, Ida	NY0150
Kang, Choong Mo	NY2105	Karriker, Galen	OH2150	Kavafian, Ida	PA0850
Kang, Chun-Wei	FL1750	Karriker, Kendra	OH2150	Kavasch, Deborah H.	CA0850
Kang, Grace	IL1615	Karsh, Ken	OH2600	Kawaller, Meaghan	IL0750
Kang, Haysun	TX3420	Karsh, Ken	PA0500	Kawaller, Meaghan	IL0850
Kang, Heejung	CT0850	Karsh, Kenneth M.	PA1050	Kawamura, Manami	CA0350
Kang, Hyo	NY1900	Kartman, Stefan	WI0825	Kawarsky, Jay A.	NJ1350
Kang, Hyo	NY0500	Karush, Larry	CA3300	Kawasaki, Masao	NY1900
Kang, Hyo	SC0350	Karyagina, Tanya	CA5355	Kawasaki, Masao	OH2200
Kang, Hyun-Ku	IA1200	Kasch, Catherine Loraine	CO0900	Kawasaki, Masao	NY0500
Kang, Juyeon	CA0200	Kaschub, Alan R.	ME0500	Kawasaki, Masao	NY0600
Kang, Leah	RI0150	Kaschub, Michele E.	ME0500	Kawashima, Kimi	UT0400
Kang, Sang Woo	NC2150	Kase, Robert	IL3370	Kawin, Phillip	NY2150
Kang, Sooyoung	CA4500	Kashap, Philip	AJ0150	Kay, Alan B.	NY3790
Kang, YouYoung	TX3400	Kashino, Motoaki	WI0200	Kay, Alan R.	NY1900
Kangas, Ryan R.	PA2450	Kashiwagi, Kerry	CA0150	Kay, Alan	NY2150
Kani, Robin	IL1300	Kashkashian, Kim	MA1400	Kay, Jennifer	NY1800
Kania, Robert P.	MD0650	Kashkin, Allan	NY3250	Kay, Lalene D.	OH0650
Kannen, Michael	DC0170	Kashnig, Claude	FL1550	Kay, Lalene	OH0700
Kanno, Sayaka	KY0450	Kasica, John	MO0700	Kay, Lalene D.	OH0200
Kano, Mark A.	CA2200	Kasica, Paula	MO1950	Kay, Michele A.	OH2200
Kanouse, Monroe	AG0200	Kasica, Paula J.	MO1830	Kay, Min Soo	NY5000
Kanovich, Leokadia	MS0150	Kasling, Kim R.	MN0350	Kayaleh, Laurence	AI0200
Kantack, Jerri Lamar	MN0050	Kasling, Tess	MN0350	Kaye, G. Donald	MI2120
Kantar, Ned D.	MI0900	Kasman, Tatiana	AL1150	Kaye, Jordan	IL2350
Kanter, Chris	WA0800	Kasman, Yakov	AL1150	Kayne, David	NY3725
Kantor, Mary L.	AG0300	Kason, Don T.	OH1650	Kays, Mark	IN1485
Kantor, Paul	OH0600	Kasparov, Andrey R.	VA1000	Kazaras, Peter	CA5030
Kantor, Paul					

Name	Code	Name	Code	Name	Code
Kazez, Daniel	OH2450	Keith, David C.	GA1300	Kelly, Tom	NE0200
Kazimir, David	IN0900	Keith, Douglas	GA0850	Kelly, Velda	MI1260
Keach, Candace	GA1900	Keith, Kristopher D.	OH1850	Kelly-McHale, Jacqueline	IL0750
Kean, Eric	WA1250	Keith, Laura J.	SC0350	Kelsaw, Geoffrey L.	IN1650
Kean, Kristen	KY0550	Keith, Randall J.	CA0850	Kelsey, Philip	WA1050
Kean, Ronald M.	CA0270	Kellan, Kurt	AB0150	Kelton, Anne	MA0350
Keane, David R.	AG0250	Kellan, Ross	IL0850	Kelton, Christopher T.	RI0150
Kear, Eleanor G.	OH2150	Kellar, Stephanie	MA0260	Kelton, Mary Katherine	IN0250
Kearley, Kandie	FL0400	Kelleher, Kevin	TX2700	Kelts, Christopher M.	KS1400
Kearney Guigne, Anna	AD0050	Keller Bick, Ingrid P.	OH2250	Kem, Randy	OR1300
Kearney, Joe	CA0200	Keller, Cheryl	CA2200	Kemberling, Nan	GA0500
Kearney, Joseph B.	CA1265	Keller, Daniel	CA2650	Keminski, Joe	NY2102
Kearney, Kevin	CA2550	Keller, Daniel B.	CA3000	Kemler, Katherine A.	LA0200
Kearney, Linda	OH0755	Keller, Deborah	MI1985	Kemm, Karl	TX2930
Keast, Dan A.	TX3527	Keller, Dennis L.	CA3320	Kemm, Karl	TX0550
Keast, Larry	CA0100	Keller, Elizabeth W.	PA1300	Kemp, Edward	IL1085
Keast, Michelle	TX3527	Keller, Gary W.	FL1900	Kemp, Julia	NJ1350
Keaster, Aaron	MI0050	Keller, James	CO0800	Kemp, Kathleen	NY1100
Keates, Peter	OH0500	Keller, Jeffrey	OH0350	Kemp, Mildred	IN1010
Keathley, Elizabeth L.	NC2430	Keller, Justin	NY0644	Kemp, Sean	AF0120
Keating, Bevan T.	AR0750	Keller, Karlton	CA3400	Kemp, Todd	TN0100
Keating, Karen	VA1350	Keller, Larry	OK0750	Kemp, Wayne N.	DC0170
Keaton, Kenneth D.	FL0650	Keller, Lisa	PA0850	Kemper, Margaret M.	IL2250
Keays, James	CA5150	Keller, Merry	MO1950	Kemperman, William	MN0800
Keberle, Daniel	WA1350	Keller, Paul	MI2200	Kemperman, William	MN1625
Keberle, David S.	NY0644	Kellert, Aaron	OK1100	Kempster, James	CA3400
Keberle, Ryan	NY0625	Kellert, Carolyn	IL1350	Kempster, William G.	NH0350
Kebuladze, Tatyana	NJ0800	Kelley, Anthony M.	NC0600	Kempter, Susan	NM0450
Kechley, David S.	MA2250	Kelley, Charles	MO1500	Kempton, Randall	ID0060
Kechley, Gerald	WA1050	Kelley, Cheryl K.	MN1280	Kenaston-French, Karen	TX3500
Keck, Bill	VT0100	Kelley, Constance L.	TX0150	Kendall, Christopher	MI2100
Keck, Kimberly	TN0200	Kelley, Darin	NJ1050	Kendall, David	CA2420
Keck, Ouida	AR0500	Kelley, Frank	MA0400	Kendall, Michael	IN0200
Keck, Thomas B.	FL1900	Kelley, Kevin	TX1350	Kendall, Roger A.	CA5031
Keck, Vail	CA3100	Kelley, Kimberly D. Buchar	PA1300	Kendrick, Brian	CA5350
Kecskemethy, Stephen	ME0200	Kelley, Kimberly Buchar	PA0950	Kendrick, Brian	CA4300
Keddy, Michael	AB0150	Kelley, Linda	IL2775	Kendrick, Corey	IL0300
Kee, Edna Gayles	NY1200	Kelley, Mark	MN1450	Kendrick, Donald	CA0840
Kee, Soyoung	IL0850	Kelley, Marvin	IA0700	Kendrick, Johnaye	WA0200
Keebaugh, Aaron	FL1675	Kelley, Pat	CA5300	Kendrick, Matt	NC2500
Keeble, Carson	CO0830	Kelley, R. J.	NY1900	Kendrick, Richard	CA3320
Keeble, Jonathan	IL3300	Kelley, Richard P.	IL2900	Kendrick, Robert L.	IL3250
Keech, Christopher	MI1985	Kelley, Robert T.	SC0800	Kenefic, Richard	ME0440
Keef, Ardith A.	ME0500	Kelley, Scott	NY1150	Kenehan, Garrett	MA0260
Keehn, Samantha	IL0100	Kelley, Timothy S.	TX3650	Kenins, Talivaldis	AG0450
Keel, Gregory	MN0950	Kellim, Kevin	KS1400	Kenley, McDowell E.	CA4900
Keelan, Michael	NE0150	Kellner, Steve	MD1010	Kenley, Nicole	TX1000
Keelan, Nick	WI0350	Kellner, Steven	MD0650	Kennard, Bryan E.	OH1000
Keele, Jeffrey	NE0200	Kellock, Judith	NY0900	Kennard, Jennifer C.	MN0610
Keele, Jeffrey	NE0150	Kellogg, Daniel	CO0800	Kennedy, Bryan	MI2100
Keele, Roger	TX2250	Kellogg, Hsing-ay	CO0550	Kennedy, Charles	AL0630
Keele, Roger S.	TX1400	Kellogg, John	MA0260	Kennedy, Daniel	CA0150
Keeler, Elden L.	IL0650	Kellogg, Lydia	IL1850	Kennedy, Daniel J.	CA0840
Keeler, Paula	IA0150	Kellogg, Mark	NY1100	Kennedy, Donny	AI0150
Keeley, Michael	AL1050	Kellogg, Michael	OH1900	Kennedy, Frederick	TN1450
Keeling, Bruce	TX2350	Kellogg, Robbie	IL1850	Kennedy, John	TX2350
Keeling, Kasandra Kenneda	TX3530	Kelly, Aileen	CA0150	Kennedy, John S.	PA2550
Keeling, Kenneth	PA0550	Kelly, Alex	CA1150	Kennedy, John M.	CA0830
Keeling, Ryan	WV0600	Kelly, Angela	VA1550	Kennedy, Karen	NY2150
Keen, Phil M.	CA3650	Kelly, Brandon	TX1550	Kennedy, Karen	FL1900
Keen, Phil	CA5355	Kelly, Bruce	AG0250	Kennedy, Laura E.	SC0750
Keen, Phillip M.	CA0835	Kelly, Chris	AJ0150	Kennedy, Laura E.	TX3420
Keen, Phillip	CA0815	Kelly, Daniel	TX2955	Kennedy, Laura H.	NY0350
Keen, Stephen	UT0250	Kelly, Darin	PA1000	Kennedy, Martin P.	MO1900
Keen, Stephen	UT0400	Kelly, Elizabeth	MA0600	Kennedy, Matthew	CA4150
Keenan, Larry W.	KY0900	Kelly, Frankie J.	LA0800	Kennedy, Mike	PA3330
Keenan, Maureen	NY0270	Kelly, Gary	NY0700	Kennedy, Nancy	KS0570
Keenan-Takagi, Kathleen D.	NY0400	Kelly, James J.	NJ0750	Kennedy, Nathan	MN0610
Keene, Theresa	CA0150	Kelly, James	MA0260	Kennedy, P. Kevin	CO0625
Keener, Michael K.	OH2250	Kelly, Jennifer W.	PA1850	Kennedy, Patricia E.	IN0905
Keeney, Jennifer	TX3400	Kelly, Jonathan	NY2150	Kennedy, Rajah B.	OK0450
Keeny, Jonan	VA0050	Kelly, Justin M.	OH1000	Kennedy, Rebecca	KS0900
Keepe, Michael L.	AZ0500	Kelly, Kathleen	GA0500	Kennedy, Rebecca	TX1750
Keepe, Michael L.	AZ0480	Kelly, Kathryn	MA0260	Kennedy, Richard R.	PA2750
Keesecker, Jeffrey	FL0850	Kelly, Keith	CA0850	Kennedy, Roy	GA2100
Keeton, Kristopher	NC2430	Kelly, Kevin	GA2100	Kennedy, Sarah	FL1450
Keever, Howard	MS0850	Kelly, Kevin J.	CA2600	Kennedy, Stephen	NY1100
Keever, Tom Dale	NY2150	Kelly, Kevin M.	NY2550	Kennedy, T. Frank	MA0330
Kefferstan, Christine	WV0750	Kelly, Kimberly	PA3560	Kennedy, Warren	GA1700
Kegerreis, Helen M.	NY2550	Kelly, Laura L.	TX3530	Kennedy, William	FL0850
Kehayas, John	FL2000	Kelly, Linda	IL1890	Kennedy-Dygas, Margaret	LA0760
Kehle, Lori	KS1050	Kelly, Liza	KY1550	Kennell, Richard P.	OH0300
Kehle, Robert G.	KS1050	Kelly, Mark	OH0300	Kennelly, Donald	CA0900
Kehler Siebert, Judith	AC0100	Kelly, Maureen	NC1600	Kennelly, Patrick	VA1100
Kehler, David T.	GA1150	Kelly, Michael	OH1450	Kenneson, Claude E.	AA0100
Kehler, Harry	PA3710	Kelly, Michael A.	OH2200	Kenney, James	PA3550
Kehn, Conrad	CO0900	Kelly, Michael F.	NY1850	Kenney, James	CA3375
Kehner, Kenneth W.	MO1830	Kelly, Pamela	WI1100	Kenney, Jessika	WA0200
Kehrberg, Donald A.	KS0200	Kelly, Patrick	TX0300	Kenney, Mary	GA0750
Kehrberg, Kevin	NC2550	Kelly, Rebecca	AB0200	Kenney, Sharon E.	AR0730
Keifer, John	TX1450	Kelly, Ryan	PA3600	Kenney, Susan H.	UT0050
Keiler, Allan R.	MA0500	Kelly, Sondra	NJ0825	Kenney, Wes	CO0250
Keillor, Elaine	AG0100	Kelly, Stephen	IL2100	Kenning, Kristin	AL0800
Keipp, Donald K.	UT0350	Kelly, Stephen K.	MN0300	Kennison, Kendall	MD0400
Keiser, Douglas	IN0800	Kelly, Steven N.	FL0850	Kenny, Megan	NC1350
Keister, Jay	CO0800	Kelly, Susan	DC0170	Kenny, Megan	NC2435
Keister, Mami Itasaka	CO0800	Kelly, Terence	WI0810	Kenny, Rhian	PA1050
Keiter, Lise	VA0800	Kelly, Thomas	NE0150	Kenny, William	PA0350
Keitges, Christine	CO0050	Kelly, Thomas Forrest	MA1050	Kenote, Marie Herseth	NY2900
Keith, Anna	FL1450	Kelly, Todd	IL0400	Kensmoe, Jeffrey	AL0300

Alphabetical Listing of Faculty

Name	Code	Name	Code	Name	Code
Kent, Adam	NJ0825	Khan, Pranesh	CA0050	Kim, David	RI0300
Kent, Adam S.	NY0500	Khan, Shujaat Husain	CA5031	Kim, Dong Suk	CA5031
Kent, David	AG0300	Khaner, Jeffrey	FL1125	Kim, Eileen	AA0020
Kent, George E.	RI0300	Khaner, Jeffrey	NY1900	Kim, Ellen	CA0815
Kent, Heather	MA0950	Khaner, Jeffrey	PA0850	Kim, Ellen Y.	CA2050
Kent, James	MN1590	Khaner, Lidia	AA0110	Kim, Eric	IN0900
Kent, Libbie	AZ0400	Khannanov, Ildar	MD0650	Kim, Eun Hae	MD1100
Kent, Patricia A.	MN0350	Khare, Kimberly	MA0260	Kim, Eun Hee	VA1350
Kent, Patricia	MN0300	Khimm, Christina	NY2250	Kim, Eunho	SD0600
Kent, Peter	NY3725	Khimm, Christina	NY2400	Kim, Gloria	CA1265
Kenworthy, Dan	NJ1000	Khimm, Christina	NY5000	Kim, Grace	MD1100
Kenworthy, Jane	CA5350	Kho, Julia	IN0005	Kim, Heawon	NY2105
Kenyon, Paul	CA3640	Khoja-Eynatyan, Leon	DC0170	Kim, Helen	GA1150
Kenyon, Steven	NY1600	Khoma, Natalia	SC0500	Kim, Hi Kyung	CA5070
Keogh, Priscilla	ND0100	Khosrowpour, Iman	CA2390	Kim, Howard D.	SC0050
Keough, Laurie	NY2650	Kibbe-Hodgkins, Shiela	MA0400	Kim, Hwa-Jin	NC2400
Kephart, Donald B.	PA1350	Kibbey, Bridget A.	NY2750	Kim, Hye-Jin	NC0650
Keppel, Patrick	MA1400	Kibbie, James W.	MI2100	Kim, Hye-Young	CA0960
Ker-Hackleman, Kelly	VA0450	Kibler, Keith E.	MA2250	Kim, Hyesook	MI0350
Kerber, Patrick C.	LA0650	Kibler, Lea	SC1080	Kim, Hyun Kyung	MD0400
Kerber, Ronald	PA3330	Kibler, Lea F.	SC0400	Kim, Irene	CA2600
Kerchner, Jody L.	OH1700	Kickasola, Matthew	PA1350	Kim, Jaeyoon	NC2435
Kerensky, Pam	MA0260	Kidd, Christine	NM0400	Kim, James	CO0250
Kerley, Eric	FL0700	Kidd, Murray	MA0800	Kim, Jean	NY0270
Kerley, Jolaine	AA0100	Kidd, Teri D.	VA0700	Kim, Jennifer L.	CA0960
Kerlin, Jerry	NY2750	Kidd-Szymczak, Deanna	MA0260	Kim, JeongSoo	IL2200
Kerlin, Jerry D.	NY2200	Kidde, Geoffrey C.	NY2200	Kim, Ji Hyun	MI2000
Kermode, Walker	OR0950	Kidder, Tim	UT0190	Kim, Jin-Hee	CA3400
Kern, Bradley	KY1450	Kidger, David M.	MI1750	Kim, Jisung	NY2550
Kern, Gene Marie Callahan	NY3650	Kidonakis, Tony G.	IL3450	Kim, Jong H.	VA0750
Kern, Jeffrey	PA3330	Kidula, Jean	GA2100	Kim, Joo-Hae	MS0750
Kern, Philip	IN1100	Kidwell, Curtis	CA0150	Kim, Jung Eun	CA4450
Kern, R. Fred	TX3420	Kidwell, David	MA1100	Kim, Junghyun	IL0350
Kern, Stacy J.	MN0040	Kidwell, Jeff	OK0700	Kim, Jungwoo	MI1050
Kerner, Winifred	OR1050	Kidwell, Jeff	OK1330	Kim, Karen	MN1625
Kerney, Marja	FL1750	Kiec, Michelle	PA1750	Kim, Kay	IL2150
Kernis, Aaron Jay	CT0850	Kiec, Michelle	PA1750	Kim, Kee-Hyun	MN1625
Kernodle, Tammy L.	OH1450	Kieffer, Olivia	GA1700	Kim, Kunyoung	PA0250
Kerns, Brad	KY0100	Kiehl, Vicky	AR0200	Kim, Kyoungwoon Leah	PA3600
Keroack, Marc	MA2030	Kiehn, Mark T.	WI0808	Kim, Kyung	AC0050
Kerr, Alexander	IN0900	Kiel, Dyke	MO0250	Kim, Kyung-Mi	GA0050
Kerr, Brady	CA3265	Kielian-Gilbert, Marianne	IN0900	Kim, Leah	PA1150
Kerr, Daniel	ID0060	Kielson, Lisette	IL0400	Kim, Linda	HI0050
Kerr, Hugh	FL0050	Kieme, Mark	MI1750	Kim, Lisa	NJ0825
Kerr, Stephen P.	VA0650	Kiene, Kristi	GA0200	Kim, Lisa	NY2150
Kerr, William	CA1265	Kientz, Ron	CO0100	Kim, Lok	GA0600
Kerr, William	CA1000	Kienzle, Kathy	MN0050	Kim, Mansoon H.	NJ0800
Kerrigan, William	PA3250	Kienzle, Kathy	MN1450	Kim, Michael I.	AC0050
Kerrigan, William	PA1150	Kienzle, Kathy	MN1623	Kim, Michelle	NY2250
Kerschner, Jeff	GA1900	Kierig, Barbara G.	MN1623	Kim, Miera	IA0400
Kershaw, Linda L.	SC0150	Kies, Arlene	NH0350	Kim, Mijin	NY2750
Kershaw, Yvonne	AE0120	Kies, Christopher	NH0350	Kim, Min	NJ0825
Kershner, Brian	CT0050	Kiesgen, Mary Stewart	MI0400	Kim, Mina	NY3785
Kersten, Joanne	MN1250	Kiesler, Kenneth	NY2150	Kim, Minjung	MI0050
Kerstetter, Kathleen	NC1500	Kiesler, Kenneth	MI2100	Kim, Misook	IL3550
Kerstetter, Tod	KS0650	Kieval, Robert	NY1860	Kim, Myung Whan	KY1200
Kerzner, David	NJ1400	Kiffner, Paula	AB0210	Kim, Nahyun	KS0590
Kesling, Diane	AR0750	Kihle, Jason J.	TX2960	Kim, Namji C.	WI0803
Kesling, Will	FL1850	Kijanowska, Anna	VA0250	Kim, Paul S.	NY2105
Kesner, Fred	WV0500	Kikta, Thomas J.	PA1050	Kim, Rebecca Y.	MA1450
Kesselman, Lee R.	IL0630	Kikuchi, Mayumi	OH2150	Kim, San-ky	TX3000
Kesselman, Robert	PA3250	Kilburn, Ke-Yin	IN0005	Kim, Seung A.	NY2450
Kessler, Jennifer	NY3780	Kilburn, Ray	IN0150	Kim, Seung-Ah	NC2435
Kessler, Stan	MO1810	Kilby, Shelton	OH2400	Kim, Soo Hong	TX3500
Kessler, Stan	MO0850	Kilchyk, Olena	AA0050	Kim, Soo Yeon	NY2650
Kessner, Dolly Eugenio	CA3100	Kile, Nora	TN1350	Kim, Soovin	NY3790
Kestenberg, Abe	AI0150	Kilgore Wood, Janice	MD1050	Kim, Soovin	MD0650
Kester, Nancie	CA1560	Kilianski, Harold	AI0150	Kim, Soovin	NY0150
Kestner, Luke	MT0175	Kilkenny, John	VA0450	Kim, Soyeon	NJ0800
Kestner, Luke	MT0350	Killen, Seth R.	IL0800	Kim, Soyeon	IL1740
Ketch, James E.	NC2410	Killian, Dwight	AZ0440	Kim, Steve	WA0860
Ketcheson, Dale	AA0200	Killian, George W.	IN0700	Kim, Sun Ho	MA0350
Ketchie, Diane	CA0835	Killian, Janice N.	TX3200	Kim, Sung-Im	PA0550
Ketchum, Joseph	WI1150	Killian, Joni	IN0700	Kim, Sungeun	OH0200
Ketter, Craig	NJ0825	Killian, Joni	AZ0400	Kim, Sungsil	MO0350
Kettinger, Gregory S.	PA3250	Killion, Jamie	CA0450	Kim, Taeseong	VA0650
Kettner, Scott	NY2660	Killmer, Richard	NY1100	Kim, Thomas	NJ1050
Kew, Craig	MO0850	Killmer, Richard	CT0850	Kim, Wonkak	TN1450
Kew, Margaret Davis	KS0100	Killmeyer, Heather N.	TN0500	Kim, Wonmin	IN0350
Key, Ramon	OH0500	Kilmer, Richard L.	TX3410	Kim, Yeesun	MA1400
Key, Stephanie	TX3350	Kilp, Brian T.	IN0800	Kim, Yeon-Su	PA1400
Keyes, Bayla	MA0400	Kilpatrick, Barry M.	NY3725	Kim, Yona	AA0020
Keyes, Cheryl L.	CA5031	Kilpatrick, Terry	WY0115	Kim, Yong Tae	NJ0825
Keyl, Stephen M.	AZ0500	Kilroe-Smith, Catherine	GA2050	Kim, Yoo-Jung	MI1200
Keyne, Lori V.	AZ0250	Kilstofte, Anne C.	AZ0350	Kim, You-Seong	OH1900
Keys, Jeff	MN1050	Kilstofte, Mark F.	SC0750	Kim, Youmee	OH1900
Keys, Keven	IL2150	Kim, Adrienne	NY4150	Kim, Young	NY0700
Keys, Kevin M.	IL2250	Kim, Aeree	NY2105	Kim, Young-Nam	MN1623
Keys, Scarlet	MA0260	Kim, Andrea	NJ0700	Kim, Youngsuk	PA2150
Keyser, Allyson	NY3600	Kim, Ariana	NY0900	Kim, Yuri	NY2250
Keyser, Catherine	GA1500	Kim, Ariana	IN1650	Kim-Boyle, David	MD1000
Keyser, Dorothy	ND0500	Kim, Benny	MO1810	Kim-Infiesto, Marilyn Liu	HI0160
Keyser, Timothy	GA1500	Kim, Bonnie	VA1000	Kim-Medwin, Sungah	MD0550
Khadavi, Linda	KS0570	Kim, Bonnie	VA0150	Kim-Quathamer, Chan Ji	FL0150
Khalsa, Gurjeet	DC0170	Kim, Chee-Yun	TX2400	Kimball, Carol	NV0050
Khamda, Mazdak	CA3250	Kim, Chi Gook	MA0260	Kimball, Eugene	CT0850
Khan, Aashish	CA0510	Kim, Chin	NY2250	Kimball, Hillary	UT0050
Khan, Alam	CA0050	Kim, Chris Younghoon	NY0900	Kimball, James W.	NY3730
Khan, Ali Akbar	CA0050	Kim, Chungsun	NY2900	Kimball, Linda	WI0865
Khan, Lori Conlon	ID0050	Kim, Clara	NY4200	Kimball, Linda	WI0815

Alphabetical Listing of Faculty

Name	Code	Name	Code	Name	Code
Kimball, Marshall C.	OH1400	Kinne, Wafia	WA1100	Kislenko, Natalia	CA5060
Kimball, Newel	ID0060	Kinnett, Randy	TX3420	Kisliuk, Michelle	VA1550
Kimball, Paul	CA5350	Kinney, Daryl W.	OH1850	Kisner, Brad	TX2930
Kimball, Phebe	OR0950	Kinney, Kaylyn	NY3000	Kisner, Janna	WV0750
Kimball, Roger	IL1610	Kinney, Michael	NY0350	Kisor, Justin	IA1100
Kimball, Sarah	OR1000	Kinsey, Katherine S.	SC1200	Kiss, Boglarka	CA3500
Kimball, Steve T.	MN0950	Kinsley, Diane	MD0060	Kissack, Christine W.	ME0500
Kimball, Will	UT0050	Kinsley, Eric B.	CA0550	Kisselstein, Lisa A.	NY3770
Kimbell, Sara	OH2600	Kinslow, Valerie	AI0150	Kistler, Karen	SC0275
Kimber, Michael	IA0930	Kinsman, Benjamin	AB0100	Kistler, Linda	PA2450
Kimber, Michael	IA0300	Kinton, Leslie	AG0500	Kitagawa, Nobuo	PA1850
Kimbrough, Frank	NY1900	Kinton, Leslie	AG0300	Kitchen, Jennifer	MI0400
Kimbrough, Jerome	TN1850	Kinzer, Charles E.	VA0700	Kitchen, Nicholas	MA1400
Kime, Ramona	MI1800	Kinzer, Lisa B.	VA0700	Kitchen, Otis D.	PA1250
Kimel, Neil	IL0750	Kinzie, John	CO0900	Kite, Jessica	NE0150
Kimler, Wayne	MO0650	Kiorpes, George A.	NC2430	Kitelinger, Shannon	CA4100
Kimlicko, Franklin	TX3370	Kipp, Sandra	CA0835	Kitic, Milena	CA0960
Kimme, Glenn	NY0650	Kippen, James R.	AG0450	Kitka, Claudia B.	CA0840
Kimmel, Jim	TN0100	Kiradjieff, Amy	OH1450	Kitson, Jeffrey	NE0040
Kimmel, Pamela J.	IL0550	Kiradjieff, Chris	OH2550	Kittredge, Brian	AL1150
Kimura, Etsuko	AG0450	Kirby, Anna-Lisa	AC0100	Kitzman, Diane D.	TX2400
Kimura, Mari	NY1900	Kirby, Brett	VA0600	Kitzman, John	TX2400
Kimura, Tomoko	WA0250	Kirby, Catharine C.	VA1500	Kiver, Christopher A.	PA2750
Kincade, Gertrude C.	AR0750	Kirby, David S.	NC1900	Kivrak, Osman	DC0010
Kincaid, John	CO1050	Kirby, Rick B.	WI0200	Kiyama, Wynn	OR0850
Kincaid, Sam	OR0700	Kirby, Steve	AC0100	Kizer, Kay	IN0910
Kinchen, James B.	WI0835	Kirby, Steven	MA0260	Kizer, Tremon B.	OH2250
Kinchen, Lucy C.	CA2450	Kirby, Steven	MA1650	Kizilarmut, John	IA0550
Kind, Sara	WI0830	Kirby, Wayne J.	NC2400	Kjelland, James	IL2250
Kind, Sara	WI0350	Kircher, Bill	NY2150	Kjorness, Christopher	VA0700
Kindall, Susan C.	SC0200	Kirchhoff, Craig	MN1623	Kjos, Kevin	PA1750
Kinder, Keith	AG0200	Kirchner, Bill	NY2660	Klabunde, Timothy A.	WI0150
Kinderman, William A.	IL3300	Kirchner, Jane	TN1850	Klabunde, Timothy	WI1150
Kindred, Janis B.	FL1750	Kirchner, Joann M.	PA3250	Klaehn, Andrew	AG0350
Kindred, Kyle	TX2250	Kirchner, Joanne	PA0650	Klages, James L.	OK1330
Kindt, Allen	NC0050	Kirchner, Walter	IL2750	Klakowich, Robert	AA0020
King, Adam	AL1195	Kirchner, William	NJ0825	Klapis, Ralph	IN1750
King, Amanda	TN1100	Kirchoff, Leanna	CO0900	Klasinc, Natasa	MS0420
King, Andy	IL0400	Kirchoff, Leanna	CO0550	Klasinc-Loncar, Natasa	MS0200
King, Anita	OR1300	Kireilis, Ramon J.	CO0900	Klassen, Carolyn	KS0440
King, Ben R.	NY1700	Kirilov, Kalin	MD0850	Klassen, David	AC0100
King, Betsey	NY2650	Kirk, Betty	IL2775	Klassen, Glenn	AA0200
King, Bill	MI1000	Kirk, Caroline	MN1400	Klassen, Gwen	AA0150
King, Brian	CA5300	Kirk, David E.	TX2150	Klassen, Masako	CA0815
King, Bryan T.	AL0200	Kirk, Douglas	AI0150	Klassen, Masako	CA3200
King, Cheryl H.	NY3717	Kirk, Elizabeth	NC0860	Klassen, Roy L.	CA1860
King, Clarence M.	TX2200	Kirk, Erin	CA5400	Klaus, Alan S.	AD0050
King, Curtis R.	FL0600	Kirk, Erin	CA0845	Klaus, Kenneth S.	LA0450
King, Dan	OH2050	Kirk, Jeff	TN0100	Klausmeyer, Sue T.	NC2410
King, Dennis W.	WI0150	Kirk, Jeremy	KS0250	Klausner, Tiberius	MO1810
King, Donna Moore	TN0930	Kirk, John D.	NY3650	Klauss, Sabine	SD0600
King, Douglas	IN0100	Kirk, John	VT0050	Klazek, Merrie	AG0170
King, Fredericka	MA0850	Kirk, Jonathon J.	IL2050	Klebanow, Susan	NC2410
King, Gerald	AB0150	Kirk, Kenneth P.	GA2150	Klecker, Deb J.	WI0450
King, Janette	GA1100	Kirk, Lewis	IL2250	Klee, David A.	IA0150
King, Jeffrey	MN1050	Kirk-Doyle, Julianne	NY3780	Klee, Michael	NE0460
King, Jennifer	AF0050	Kirkbride, Jerry E.	AZ0500	Klefstad, Kristian I.	TN0100
King, Joan	PA0650	Kirkdorffer, Michele B.	VA0600	Klefstad, Terry	TN0100
King, John	MI0100	Kirkeby, Gary	MD0700	Kleiankina, Olga	NC1700
King, Jonathan	NY3560	Kirkell, Lorie	CA2100	Kleiman, Carey D.	FL0200
King, Linda	TN0450	Kirkendoll, Mary	KS1050	Klein, Benjamin	CT0050
King, Margaret	AA0020	Kirkendoll, Michael	OK0800	Klein, Doug	ND0050
King, Marie A.	KS1450	Kirkland, Anthony B.	MS0500	Klein, Edward	FL0365
King, Mark	WV0550	Kirkland, Denise	IN1750	Klein, Gary	NY2105
King, Mary J.	CA0450	Kirkland, Glenda	MI0600	Klein, Heidi	TX3420
King, Matthew	IL2970	Kirklewski, Duff	MA2030	Klein, James A.	MA1400
King, Megan	AL1300	Kirkley, William	MA0950	Klein, Jim	PA1000
King, Melodie S.	AL0800	Kirkpatrick, Adam	GA1150	Klein, Jim L.	AZ0510
King, Morgan	TX2260	Kirkpatrick, Amanda	MO1900	Klein, Jon	ID0060
King, Morgan	TX3530	Kirkpatrick, Christopher	MT0400	Klein, Jonathan	MA0260
King, Nancy Ambrose	MI2100	Kirkpatrick, Daniel	WI1150	Klein, Joseph	TX3420
King, Nancy	NC2440	Kirkpatrick, Elka	NJ1400	Klein, Korinthia	WI1150
King, Pamela	TX3420	Kirkpatrick, Gary	NJ1400	Klein, Laura	CA5000
King, Richard	AI0150	Kirkpatrick, Leon	KY0250	Klein, Laura	NJ1350
King, Richard G.	MD1010	Kirkpatrick, Linda M.	MD0520	Klein, Lonnie	NM0310
King, Richard	OH0600	Kirkpatrick, Mary Beth	WV0560	Klein, Michael L.	PA3250
King, Robert	OR1300	Kirkscey, Jonathan	AR0110	Klein, Mitchell	CA1250
King, Roy M.	LA0200	Kirkwood, David	CA0350	Klein, Nancy K.	VA1000
King, Ryan	AL1195	Kirkwood, James H.	NY3730	Klein, Rochelle Z.	PA2900
King, Sandi	CA3520	Kirkwood, Neal	PA1750	Klein, Stephen T.	CA3650
King, Shirley S.	PA0950	Kiros, Teodros	MA0260	Klein, Susanna	VA1600
King, Sidney	KY1500	Kirov, Milen	CA0960	Klein, Wendy L.	MA0260
King, Stanley	WI0845	Kirov, Milen	CA0835	Kleinecke-Boyer, Ursula Maria	CA3650
King, Stephen	TX2150	Kirsch, Gary	CT0450	Kleinknecht, Daniel E.	IA1140
King, Steve E.	VA1700	Kirschen, Jeffry	PA3250	Kleinsasser, Jerome S.	CA0650
King, Terry B.	CT0650	Kirschenmann, Mark	MI2100	Kleinsasser, William	MD0850
King, Terry	MA1175	Kirschstein, Natalie	CO0650	Kleis, Lisa	IL2775
King, Thomas D.	MD1000	Kirsh, Kristy	KY0100	Klemas, John	IA1170
King, Thomas R.	TN0050	Kirshbaum, Ralph	CA5300	Klement, David A.	NM0310
King, Tim	TX2700	Kirshner, Andrew	MI2100	Klemetson, Roxanne	MN1620
King, Troy	MD0850	Kirson-Jones, Chloe	AF0120	Klemme, Paul	OR1300
King, Valeria G.	LA0720	Kirsop, Daniel	SC0200	Klemp, Merilee I.	MN0050
King, Vicki B.	TN1400	Kirst, Patrick	CA5300	Klemp, Merilee	MN0300
Kingan, Michael G.	PA1600	Kirton, Suzanne	FL0680	Klentz, Richard	NE0300
Kingfield, Edward	FL0950	Kischuk, Ronald K.	MI2200	Kleppinger, Stanley V.	NE0600
Kingham, Lesley	AG0050	Kiser, Brian D.	OH2600	Kleszynski, Kenneth	OR1100
Kingsland, William	MA2020	Kiser, Candice C.	PA3100	Klevan, Robert B.	CA5070
KinKennon, Heather Marie	CA0200	Kiser, Daniel W.	NC1100	Klibonoff, Jon	NY2150
Kinkle, Dan	CA0800	Kish, David	CO0550	Klice, Joseph A.	CA3500
Kinnaman, Hal	HI0155	Kisilevitch, Miroslava	MN1250	Klich, Chris	CA2100

Alphabetical Listing of Faculty

Name	Code
Klickman, Philip	MD0350
Klickman, William	IN0905
Klickstein, Gerald	MD0650
Klier, Kari	TX3175
Kliewer, Jan Michael	WY0130
Kligman, Mark L.	NY1450
Klima, Arthur	OH0650
Klimaszewska, Alina	TX1450
Klimisch, Mary J.	SD0300
Klimko, Ronald	ID0250
Klimowski, Stephen	VT0450
Klimowski, Steve	VT0400
Klinder-Badgley, Marcia	CA1850
Klinder-Badgley, Marcia	CA1290
Kline, Matthew C.	TX2400
Kline, Peter	TX2200
Kline, Rhonda	WA1050
Kline, W. Peter	TX2260
Klinebriel, Jill	IA0250
Klinedinst, Sherry	IN1450
Klinefelter, Theresa	PA3600
Kling, Irene	NY2250
Klingbeil, Michael	CT0900
Klingensmith, David C.	TX3450
Klingensmith, David	TX3400
Klingenstein, Beth Gigante	ND0600
Klinger, Judith	CA0100
Klinghammer, John	SD0600
Klinghammer, John	NE0100
Klinghofer, Rhona	CA1750
Klintworth, Paul	CA3800
Klipp, Barbara A.	IL0650
Klobas, Patrick P.	CA0807
Klobas, Patrick	CA3520
Klock, Laura C.	MA2000
Klock, Lynn E.	MA2000
Klockow, Stephanie	WI0840
Kloeckner, Phillip	TX2150
Kloetzli, Pamela	CO0150
Klonoski, Edward	IL2200
Kloosterman, Jill	MI0900
Klopfenstein, Reginald	IN0200
Kloppers, Jacobus	AA0035
Klorman, Edward	NY1900
Klotz, Michael	FL0700
Klotzbach, Susan	IL1200
Kluball, Jeff L.	GA0625
Klug, Howard D.	IN0900
Klugh, Vaughn	AG0550
Klugherz, Laura	NY0650
Klukas, Suzanne	AB0090
Klukoff, Ruth	FL0450
Kluksdahl, Scott	FL2000
Klumpenhouwer, Henry	AA0100
Kmiecik, Thomas	LA0650
Knable, Robert	CA3850
Knapp, Brady	TX3450
Knapp, Donna	GA0940
Knapp, James	WA0200
Knapp, Joel	IL2910
Knapp, Karl D.	AK0150
Knapp, Peter J.	CA2550
Knapp, Raymond L.	CA5032
Knaub, Maribeth	PA1050
Knaub, Maribeth J.	PA3100
Knauth, Dorcinda	NY1050
Knecht, Jasminka	CA3800
Knecht, John	IL2750
Knecht, Karen	CA0960
Knecht, Melissa Gerber	MI1000
Knechtges, Eric T.	KY1000
Knehans, Douglas	OH2200
Knelman, Jennifer	AG0350
Knepp, Marty	MD0060
Knepp, Richard	GA2300
Knepper, Bruce	IN1310
Kness, Karen	MI2250
Knetsch, Rene	CO0100
Knezovich, Bill	CA1860
Knibbs, Lester A.	NC0800
Knickerbocker, Sharon	IL1900
Knie, Robert	PA3250
Knier, Lawrence	MD0800
Knier, Veronica T.	MD1020
Knific, Renata	MI2250
Knific, Thomas	MI2250
Knight, Adam	GA0900
Knight, Alan	SC0600
Knight, Andrew	ND0500
Knight, Diane	WI0050
Knight, Edward	OK0750
Knight, Gerald R.	NC0750
Knight, Gloria J.	NC0700
Knight, Gregory	AA0200
Knight, Jonathan	CA2775
Knight, Joshua	AR0730
Knight, Katharine	CO0900
Knight, Katharine	CO0200
Knight, Michael D.	WI0750
Knight, Stephen B.	AL0800
Knight, Steven M.	AR0300
Knighten, Christopher	AR0700
Knighten, Janet W.	AR0700
Knipschild, Ann	AL0200
Knisely, Carole	PA3710
Kniss, Karla	CA1425
Knoeloch, Glenn	IL2970
Knoepfel, Justin	MN0750
Knoles, Amy	CA0510
Knoll, Richard C.	MO1810
Knoop, Tracy	WA1000
Knoop, Tracy V.	WA0600
Knop, Robert	CA0845
Knopp, Larry	AB0100
Knopp, Seth D.	MD0650
Knopp, Shawn	KS0900
Knopps, Amy	MI0600
Knorr, Eric	OH0500
Knott, Sarah	NE0610
Knotts, Clara	FL1750
Knowles, Debbie	IL1400
Knowles, Eddie Ade	NY3300
Knowles, Gregory	NY1900
Knowles, William A.	TN1500
Knox, Carl	CT0050
Knox, Charles C.	GA1050
Knox, Craig	PA1050
Knox, Craig	PA0550
Knox, Daniel	AL0750
Knox, Hank	AI0150
Knudsen, Joel	KS0210
Knudsen, Kasey	CA4700
Knudson, Donna	WA0650
Knudsvig, Peter	MN0600
Knudtsen, Jere	WA0750
Knupp, Robert	MS0400
Knupps, Terri L.	MO1550
Knutson, James	MN1400
Knutson, John R.	CA1510
Knyt, Erinn	MA2000
Ko, Bongshin	CA0815
Ko, EunMi	NY2650
Ko, EunMi	NY1250
Ko, Priscilla	MD0150
Koba, Dean	CA1750
Kobayashi, Hibiki	AI0190
Kobayashi, Ron	CA0350
Kobernik, Lynnette	CA3800
Kobialka, Daniel	TX3410
Kobialka, Daniel	CA2950
Kobler, Linda	PA2250
Koblyakov, Lev	IL2350
Kobrin, Alexander	GA0550
Kobuck, Martin	TX1775
Kobza, Tim	CA5300
Kocandrle, Mirek	MA0260
Koch, Andrew	VA1550
Koch, Cheryl	SD0050
Koch, Christopher	MO0350
Koch, Danielle	MO0350
Koch, Elizabeth	AI0150
Koch, Elizabeth	GA1150
Koch, Elizabeth	AA0035
Koch, Jeremy	WV0550
Koch, John M.	IL1150
Koch, Mark	PA1050
Koch, Nathan J.	TX2250
Koch, Patricia Schott	PA2200
Koch, Thomas	FL0680
Koch, Thomas	NC1700
Kochanowski, John	TN1850
Kochavi, Jonathan	PA3200
Kochen, Timothy	TX2310
Kocher, Christopher John	SD0600
Kocher, Edward W.	PA1050
Kocher, Stephanie	IA0500
Kocher, Stephanie	SD0600
Kochis, Jane	MN1285
Kocmieroski, Matthew	WA0200
Kocour, Michael G.	AZ0100
Kocyan, Wojciech	CA2800
Koczela, Jeff	DC0100
Koczela, Jeffrey L.	DC0150
Kodzas, Peter	NY1100
Kodzas, Peter	NY2650
Koebel, Carolyn	MI1150
Koeble, Robert	FL1800
Koegel, John	CA0815
Koehler, Andrew	MI1150
Koehler, Elisa C.	MD0400
Koehler, Hope E.	WV0750
Koehler, Raymond	IL3200
Koehler, Reimund G.	IL0840
Koehler, William D.	WV0750
Koehler, William	IL1150
Koehler, William	IL2200
Koehn, Daniel	KY0100
Koehn, Renita	KY0100
Koehner, Leon	IA1170
Koelble, Bobby	FL1550
Koeller, David	IL2100
Koen, Benjamin D.	FL0850
Koen, John	PA3250
Koen, Kerry	NY0650
Koenig, Chris	NH0300
Koenig, Laura J.	AK0100
Koenig, Mark	IN0907
Koenig, Paul	NE0610
Koenig, Robert	CA5060
Koenigberg, Rebecca Anne	CO0650
Koenigsberg, Tobias R.	OR1050
Koepke, Laura	NY3725
Koeppel, James	NY3785
Koepsel, Keith	CO1050
Koerselman, Herbert L.	KY1500
Koessel, Wolfram	NY2150
Koester, Eugene	SC0275
Koesterer, Karl	MO1950
Koestner, Bonnie	WI0350
Koffman, Carrie	CT0650
Kofford, Brooke	CA2300
Kofman, Irena	FL0650
Kofsky, Allen	OH0200
Koga, Midori	AG0450
Kogan, Peter	MN1623
Koh, Jennifer	NY2750
Koh, Jonathan	CA5000
Koh-Baker, JoAnn Hwee Been	OH1600
Kohane, Sara	CT0900
Kohanski, Elisa C.	PA1450
Kohl, Jack	NY4050
Kohl, Jack	NY4060
Kohlbeck-Boeckman, Anne	WI0350
Kohlenberg, Kenneth	OH2120
Kohlenberg, Randy	NC2430
Kohler, Mark	MA0260
Kohler-Ghiorzi, Elizabeth	PA1250
Kohlhase, Charlie	MA1175
Kohls, Shauna	AA0040
Kohn, Andrew	WV0750
Kohn, Douglas C.	MA0260
Kohn, Karl G.	CA3650
Kohn, Margaret S.	CA3650
Kohn, Steven Mark	OH0600
Kohrs, Jonathan A.	IL0730
Koidin, Julie	IL1615
Kojian, Miran	CA5300
Kok, Roe-Min	AI0150
Kolar, Andrew	CT0300
Kolar, J. Mitzi	CA4100
Kolb, Barbara	RI0200
Kolb, G. Roberts	NY1350
Kolb, Lauralyn	NY1350
Kolbeck, Brandi	NE0700
Kolbeck, Karl F.	NE0700
Kolean, Lora Clark	MI1050
Kolek, Adam J.	MA1100
Kolkay, Peter	TN1850
Kolker, Adam	PA1750
Kolker, Phillip A.	MD0650
Kolker, Siobhan	NJ0800
Kolman, Barry	VA1850
Kolodny, Michael	MA2250
Kolomyjec, Joanne	AI0150
Kolor, Thomas P.	NY4320
Kolstad, Michael L.	MO0400
Kolt, Robert P.	AR0500
Kolthammer, Stacy	OH1100
Kolwinska, Jeremy	MN1280
Komaiko, Libby A.	IL2150
Komara, Edward M.	NY3780
Kominami, Miko	IA0950
Komisaruk, Kevin M.	AG0450
Komodore, Alex	CO0550
Kompanek, Rudolph W.	NY2750
Kompanek, Rudolph (Sonny)	NY2660
Kompass, Lynn R.	SC1110
Kompelien, Wayne	VA0650
Kondonassis, Yolanda	OH1700
Kondonassis, Yolanda	OH0600
Konecky, Larry	MS0050
Konewko, Mark	WI0425
Kong, Gary	NY2650
Kong, Joanne	VA1500
Kong, Yinzi	GA0750
Konkol, Korey	MN1623
Kono, Yutaka	VT0450
Konopka, Stanley	OH0600
Konoval, Brandon	AB0100
Konsbruck, James	IN1750
Konstantinov, Tzvetan	DC0100
Konye, Paul	NY3680
Konzelman, Brian	TX1600
Konzen, Richard A.	PA1450
Kooken, Brian	MD0475
Koolsbergen, William J.	NY2100
Koomson, Nathaniel	MD0170
Koonce, Frank W.	AZ0100
Koonce, Jeff	AL0300
Koonce, Jeff	AL1150

Alphabetical Listing of Faculty

Name	Code
Koonce, Jeffrey C.	AL0800
Koonce, Paul C.	FL1850
Koons, Jessie	TN0450
Koons, Keith	FL1800
Koonse, Larry	CA0835
Koonse, Larry	CA0510
Koonts, Cortlandt	SC0700
Koontz, Eric E.	NC0050
Koontz, Jason	KY0550
Koop, Ruth B.	AJ0030
Koopmann, Robert	MN0350
Koops, Alexander	CA0250
Koops, Lisa	OH0400
Koozer, Robin R.	NE0300
Koozin, Timothy	TX3400
Kopec, Patinka	NY2150
Kopelman, Mikhail	NJ1130
Kopelman, Mikhail	NY1100
Kopelson, Robert	NY2150
Kopetz, Barry E.	OH0350
Kopetz, Gail	OH0350
Kopfstein-Penk, Alicia	DC0010
Koplow, Philip	KY1000
Koponen, Glenn	NY2900
Kopp, David	MA0400
Koppel, Mary Montgomery	MA0400
Koppelman, Daniel M.	SC0750
Kopperud, Jean K.	NY4320
Kopplin, David F.	CA0630
Koprowski, Melissa	WI0803
Koprowski, Peter P.	AG0500
Kopta, Anne Elgar	AZ0100
Korak, John	IL2910
Koranda, Ann	IL1890
Korb, Kristin	CA5300
Korb, Ryan	WI0925
Korb, Ryan	WI0850
Korbitz, Angela Presutti	IL2050
Korbitz, Ronald S.	IL3450
Korde, Shirish	MA0700
Kordes, Gesa	AL1170
Korducki, Linda Nielsen	WI0150
Kordzaia, Alexander	VA1500
Koregelos, Angela	CA2950
Koreski, Jacinta T.	WA0800
Korevaar, David J.	CO0800
Korey, Judith A.	DC0350
Koriath, Kirby L.	IN0150
Korjus, Ingemar	AG0400
Korman, Clifford	NY2150
Korman, Fred	OR0700
Korn, Mitchell	TN1850
Korn, Steve	WA1050
Korn, Steven	WA0550
Korneev, Dmitri V.	NJ0800
Korneitchouk, Igor	CA4050
Kornelis, Benjamin	IA0500
Kornelsen, Michael J.	CO0550
Kornfield, Jono	CA4200
Kornick, Rebecca	IL1615
Kornicke, Eloise	VA0800
Koronka, Kyle	TX3350
Korsantia, Alexander	MA1400
Korstvedt, Benjamin M.	MA0650
Korsyn, Kevin E.	MI2100
Kortenkamp, Peter	IA0850
Korth, Jonathan	HI0210
Kortz, Owen	CO0830
Korzhev, Mikhail	CA0960
Korzhev, Mikhail	CA0815
Korzun, Jonathan	MI1985
Kos, Ronald P.	MA0400
Kosack, Alicia	PA3710
Kosak, Johanna	NY4050
Kosar, Anthony	NJ1350
Kosche, Kenneth	WI0300
Kosciesza, Andrew	PA2400
Koshgarian, Richard	KS0150
Koshinski, Eugene	MN1600
Koskoff, Ellen	NY1100
Kosloff, Doris	CT0650
Koslovsky, Marc S.	NY2550
Koslowske, Charles T.	OK0750
Kosma, Lou	NJ0825
Kosmala, Diane	WI0835
Kosmala, Jerzy S.	CA5020
Kosmyna, David J.	OH1800
Kosnik, James W.	VA1000
Kosower, Mark	OH0600
Kosower, Paula	IL0750
Kosower, Paula	IL2250
Kosower, Paula	IL2100
Kosowski, Richard	GA1300
Kossodo, Verena	NY2400
Kostaras, Jimmy	DC0170
Kostek, Patricia	AB0150
Kostelnik, Steve	TX2650
Koster, Charles	CA5040
Koster, Charles J.	CA2420
Koster, John	SD0600
Koster, Keith	NY2650
Kostic, Dina	FL0050
Kostilnik, Rise	PA3000
Kostlan, Robert	CA0847
Kostner, Douglas	NY2400
Kostur, Glenn	NM0450
Kostusiak, Thomas J.	NY3717
Kostyniak, Stephen	PA0550
Kot, Don	NY2650
Kotan, Emrah	GA0050
Kotcherguina, Tatiana	AR0850
Kothman, Keith K.	IN0150
Kothman, Mary	IN1560
Kothman, Mary	IN0150
Kotowich, Bruce J. G.	IA0940
Kott, Sandra	MA0260
Kotter, Laurie	MD0475
Kotze, Michael	IL2100
Kouguell, Alexander	NY0642
Koukios, Ann Marie	MI2200
Kouratachvili, Tinatin	WA0850
Koury, Daniel J.	MA2100
Koutsoukos, Sheree	TN1850
Kouzov, Dmitry	IL3300
Kovach Brovey, Lisa	PA0500
Kovacovic, Paul	IA0200
Kovacs, Anna	NY2750
Kovacs, Jolan	AI0150
Kovalcheck, Steve	CO0950
Kovalsky, Vladislav D.	NJ0550
Koven, Steven	AG0650
Kover, Krisztina	FL0650
Kowalke, Kim	NY4350
Kowalke, Kim H.	NY1100
Kowalkowski, Jeffrey F.	IL2150
Kowalkowski, Jeffrey F.	IL0750
Kowalkowski, Paula	IL0720
Kowalski, Christina	WA1000
Kowalsky, Frank	FL0850
Koza, John	CA2150
Koza, Julia Eklund	WI0815
Koza, Matt	NY0646
Kozak, Brian	OH0750
Kozak, Christopher M.	AL1170
Kozak, Kevin J.	AL0800
Kozak, Pawel K	SC1000
Kozak, Pete E.	OR0700
Kozakis, Michael J.	IL0750
Kozakis, Michael	WI0250
Kozamchak, David M.	MN1280
Kozel, Paul	NY0550
Kozelka, David	IL1100
Kozenko, Lisa A.	NY5000
Kozic, Thomas	PA2550
Kozic, Tom	PA1850
Kozinn, Allan	NY2750
Koziol, John	MN0800
Kozlova, Yulia	CA4450
Kozlovsky, Danielle Godbout	AI0220
Kozubek, Michael	CA0250
Kozubek, Michael	CA2600
Kpogo, Robert	AA0100
Kraakevik, Kari	CO0550
Kraaz, Sarah Mahler	WI0700
Kraft, Edith	NY1900
Kraft, James	IN1025
Kraft, Leo	NY0642
Krager, Franz Anton	TX3400
Krajewski, Michael J.	MN1120
Krakauer, David	NY0150
Krakauer, David	NY2750
Krakauer, David	NY2150
Krakauer, David	NY2250
Kramar, John S.	NC0650
Kramer, Atossa	KY0300
Kramer, David	PA2800
Kramer, Dean	OR1050
Kramer, Elizabeth A.	GA2130
Kramer, Ernest Joachim	MO0950
Kramer, Jacob	CA3400
Kramer, Janet	IL3100
Kramer, Jason	MI1150
Kramer, Jonathan C.	NC1700
Kramer, Karl P.	IL3300
Kramer, Katya	IN0350
Kramer, Keith A.	CT0050
Kramer, Kelly B.	TN1380
Kramer, Kenneth	OH1100
Kramer, Lawrence	NY1300
Kramer, Paul	WI0825
Kramer, Richard	NY0600
Kramer, Steven	NJ0750
Kramer, Timothy	IL1100
Kramer-Johansen, Karl	NJ1050
Kramlich, Dan P.	WA0800
Kramlich, Daniel	WA0650
Kramlich, Daniel L.	TX1000
Kramme, Joel I.	MO0825
Krantz, Allen M.	PA3250
Krantz, Wayne M.	NY2750
Kranzler, Dean	KS0200
Kranzler, Dean	KS1300
Kranzler, Dean	KS0700
Kranzler, Dean	KS0150
Kranzler, Dean	KS0350
Krash, Jessica	DC0100
Krasner, Orly	NY0550
Krasnican, Martha	IN0800
Krasnovsky, Paul J.	IN1650
Kratochvil, Jirka	NY1400
Kratus, John	MI1400
Kratz, Girard	PA3250
Kratz, Jay	PA2800
Kratzer, Dennis L.	OH1800
Kraus, Barry N.	TN0100
Kraus, James	MI1180
Kraus, Jeffrey	NY2900
Kraus, Joseph C.	FL0850
Kraus, Nanette	KS0050
Kraus, Philip	IL2250
Kraus, Tracy	MA0650
Krausas, Veronika	CA5300
Krause Wiebe, Anita	AG0500
Krause, Douglas	CO0830
Krause, Drew S.	NY2750
Krause, Kristi	WI0810
Krause, Kristi	MN1700
Krause, Melissa M.	MN1300
Krause, Philip	IL2100
Krause, Robert	TX3750
Krause, Stephen	TX3530
Krause, William Craig	VA0550
Krause-Hardie, Rebecca	NH0150
Krauss, David B.	NJ1130
Krauss, David	NY2750
Krauss, W. John	OH2290
Kraut, Melissa	OH0600
Kraut, Rena	MN1300
Kraut, Rena	MN0050
Kravchak, Richard	CA0805
Kravig, Dean	WA1100
Kravitz, Steve	OR0450
Kravitz, Steve	OR0750
Krawezyk, Shelly	CA2550
Krebill, Kerry	DC0350
Krebs, Harald M.	AB0150
Krebs, Jesse D.	MO1780
Krebs, John A.	AR0350
Kreft, Anne	IL0275
Kregler, Michael C.	RI0150
Kregor, Jonathan	OH2200
Krehbiel, A. David	CA1075
Kreibich, Paul	CA0815
Kreider, David G.	MD0520
Kreider, J. Evan	AB0100
Kreiger, Arthur V.	CT0100
Kreiger, Donna	WY0100
Kreiling, Jean L.	MA0510
Kreinberg, Steven	PA3250
Kreitner, Kenneth	TN1680
Kreitner, Mona B.	TN1680
Kreitner, Mona B.	TN1200
Kreitner, William	FL1310
Kreitzer, Jacalyn	CA0600
Kreitzer, Mark	MN0300
Kreitzer, Nathan J.	CA4410
Krejci, Mathew	CA5350
Kremer, Kelly	MO0550
Krenek, Catherine	MI1300
Kresek, Emme	NY2400
Kresge, Jeff	VA1100
Kresge, Jeff	VA0550
Kresky, Jeffrey	NJ1400
Kresnicka, Judith	MN0200
Kress, David	CA5355
Kress, Richard	MA0260
Kressler, Jeffrey	MI0400
Kretchner, Darlene	CA0830
Kretzer, Scott	MI0050
Kretzer, Scott	OH2275
Kreutz, Michael	MA0850
Kreuze, Brandon R.	GA0600
Kreuzer, Gundula	CT0900
Krewitsky, Michael	CA2100
Kreyszig, Walter	AJ0150
Krieger, Angela	OK1400
Krieger, David	NY2400
Krieger, David	NY5000
Krieger, Eric	IA1400
Krieger, Karen Ann	TN1850
Krieger, Marcos F.	PA3150
Krieger, Norman	CA5300
Krieger, Ulrich	CA0510
Kriehn, Richard	WA1150
Krigbaum, Charles	CT0850
Krikland, Ricky	FL1000
Krikun, Andrew	NJ0020
Krimsier, Renee J.	MA0400
Krimsier, Renee	MA1400
Krimsky, Seth	WA0200

Name	Code	Name	Code	Name	Code
Krimsky, Seth	WA1050	Kuchar, Evan	IL0600	Kurzdorfer, James	NY4460
Krippenstapel, George	IL1200	Kucharsky, Boris	NJ0800	Kush, Jason	PA3100
Kris, Michael	NC2410	Kuchera-Morin, JoAnn	CA5060	Kushick, Marilyn M.	MA2000
Kris, Michael A.	NC0600	Kuczynski, Christopher	PA0650	Kushner, David Z.	FL1850
Kris, Mike	NC2350	Kudlawiec, Nancy A.	AL1350	Kushner, Karen	MO1810
Krishnaswami, Donald	MA0510	Kudo, Takeo	HI0210	Kushnir, Regina	CO0100
Krislov, Donna	MN1050	Kuehn, Jacquelyn A.	PA1600	Kuss, Mark	CT0450
Kristiansen, Morten	OH2550	Kuehn, John W.	PA1600	Kustanovich, Serafima	MA0650
Kristjanson, William	AC0100	Kuehn, Mikel	OH0300	Kuster, Kristin P.	MI2100
Kristof, Rosemary	AF0120	Kuehne, Jane M.	AL0200	Kuster, Nicolasa	CA5350
Kritzmire, Judith A.	MN1600	Kuehner, Denise	IN1450	Kutan, Aline	AI0150
Kroesche, Kenneth	MI1750	Kuehner, Eric	IN1450	Kutner, Michael	CT0650
Kroesen, Irene	CA0960	Kuehner, Eric L.	IN0910	Kutulas, Janet	CA2950
Kroetsch, Terence	AG0600	Kuentz, Charles	TX3530	Kutz, Eric A.	IA0950
Kroft, Pat	OH1350	Kugler, Roger T.	KS1000	Kutz, Jonathan	TX1600
Kroft, Patricia	OH2290	Kuhl, J. C.	VA1600	Kuuskmann, Martin	NY2150
Krogh, Dawn Pawlewski	NE0450	Kuhl, Margaret	NY1700	Kuuskoski, Jonathan	MO1800
Krogol, D.J.	MI1000	Kuhl, Mary	TX1750	Kuykendall, James Brooks	SC0700
Krohn, Ken	MD0550	Kuhlman, Kristyn	NY3350	Kuyvenhoven, Cora	OH2050
Kroik, Anna	NJ0700	Kuhlman, William	IA0950	Kuyvenhoven, Cora	OH0850
Krolikowski, Lucas	IL1750	Kuhlmann, Evan	OR0700	Kuzma, Marika C.	CA5000
Kroll, Mark	MA1450	Kuhlmann, Evan	OR0850	Kuzmenko, Larysa	AG0450
Kroll, Mark	MA0400	Kuhn, Bret	IL3450	Kvach, Konstantin	OR0150
Kromin, Vladimir	VA1100	Kuhn, Edward M.	PA3000	Kvach, Konstantin	OR0750
Kromm, Leroy	CA4150	Kuhn, Judith	WI0825	Kvam, Nancy E.	CA0400
Kromm, Nancy Wait	CA4425	Kuhn, Lois	WV0550	Kvapil, Diane	OH2200
Kronauer, Steven	CA0825	Kuhn, Lynne	CA3460	Kvet, Edward J.	LA0300
Krone, Claudia	ID0250	Kuhn, Michael	AZ0250	Kvetko, Peter J.	MA1650
Kronengold, Charles	CA4900	Kuhn, Michael	AZ0480	Kwak, Eun-Joo	WI0150
Kronour, Dianne	OH2200	Kuhn, Stephanie	NC0450	Kwak, Jason	TX3175
Kronour, Dianne	OH2250	Kuhn, William	OR0150	Kwalwasser, Helen	PA3250
Krontz, Paula	MI1160	Kuhnert, Brian	TX3650	Kwami, Paul T.	TN0550
Kropidlowski, Monica	IL2650	Kuhnert, Cloyce	TX3750	Kwan, Andrew	AG0450
Krosnick, Joel	NY1900	Kuhns, Philip A.	AZ0510	Kwan, Andrew	AG0300
Kroth, Michael	MI1400	Kuist, Bruce	TN1350	Kwan, Eva	IN1560
Kroth, Richard	NJ0175	Kuite, Anne	FL1900	Kwanza, Evelyn	VT0450
Krouse, Ian	CA5030	Kuivila, Ronald	CT0750	Kwapis, Kris	WA0200
Krouseup, Jack	CA3520	Kujala, Walfrid	IL2250	Kwapis, Kris	IN0900
Krout, Robert E.	TX2400	Kujawsky, Eric	CA0855	Kwasnicka, Ursula	NY1350
Krout-Lyons, Susan	IL0730	Kukec, Catherine	IL1900	Kwasniewska, Ewelina	AG0250
Krubsack, Kathryn	WI1155	Kukec, Paul E.	IL1900	Kwiram, Bernie R.	WA0800
Krubsack, Kathy	WI0808	Kukrechtova, Daniela	MA0260	Kwiram, Bernie	WA0550
Kruckenberg, Lori	OR1050	Kula, Jeff	AC0100	Kwo, Kenneth P. C.	FL0930
Krueger, Bradley	MI1180	Kulas, Katherine F.	MN1600	Kwok, Daniel	IL2775
Krueger, Carol J.	KS0300	Kulenovic, Vuk	MA0260	Kwok, May Ling	AB0210
Krueger, Charae	GA1150	Kulesha, Gary	AG0450	Kwok, May Ling	AB0150
Krueger, Christopher	MA2000	Kuleshov, Valery	OK1330	Kwok, Sarita	CT0900
Krueger, Christopher	MA0400	Kuliush, Tetyana	FL0950	Kwon, Donna L.	KY1450
Krueger, Christopher	MA1400	Kull, James A.	IL0840	Kwon, Hea-Kyung	NY2750
Krueger, Joan	NY3785	Kuller, Ronnie	IL2750	Kwon, Min	NJ1130
Krueger, Karen Merola	WA1400	Kulma, David T.	SC1200	Kwon, MiYoung	OH0755
Krueger, Leslie	WI0825	Kulosa, Kenneth	MO1950	Kwon, Su Jin	NY5000
Krueger, Mary Beth	CO0550	Kulp, Jonathan	LA0760	Kwon, Yeeseon	IL0550
Krueger, Nathan E.	WI0830	Kulpa, John	NJ0750	Kwon, Yeeson	IL2750
Krueger, Pat	WA1000	Kumer, Wendy	WV0600	Kwoun, Soo Jin	MO0700
Krueger, Timothy	CO0550	Kumi, Gert	IN0100	Kwuon, Joan	OH0600
Krueger, Walter E.	OR0150	Kumme, Karl	CT0050	Kyker, Jennifer	NY1100
Kruger, Anna R.	CA0840	Kummernuss, Linda	IN1050	Kyle, Janice	NY3775
Kruger, Jonathan H.	NY3730	Kumor, Frank	PA1750	Kyle, Maryann	MS0750
Krugman, Murray	CT0700	Kunda, Keith	IN0250	Kyle, Scott	CA4100
Kruja, Mira	AL0010	Kunda, Keith	IN1560	Kyles, Jerome Kwame	MA0260
Krumbholz, Gerald A.	WA0950	Kunderna, Jerry	CA1560	Kynaston, Trent	MI2250
Krummel, Christopher	OH2600	Kung, Hsiong-Ning	OH1850	Kyne, Nadia	AB0200
Krummel, Karen	MI0350	Kunin, Ben	CA0050	Kyr, Robert	OR1050
Krumrei, Randall	CA0200	Kunins, Alan	NY2450	Kyriakos, Marika V.	AR0110
Krupa, Mary Ann	IL3450	Kunkee, Patrick	TN1850	Kyser, Ramon	SC0750
Krupp, Ethan	PA0250	Kunkel, Gerald	MD1010	La Barbara, Joan	NY2750
Kruse, Lacey	MN0625	Kunkel, Gerard F.	DC0150	La Manna, Juan F.	NY3770
Kruse, Nathan B.	TX3420	Kunkel, Jeffrey	NJ0800	La Rocca, Carla	PA0550
Kruse, Penny Thompson	OH0300	Kunkle, Kristen C.	PA2000	La Rocca, Frank J.	CA0807
Kruse, Steven	OH0950	Kuntz, Tammy	OH1100	Laarz, Bill	TN0580
Krusemark, Ruth E.	KS0100	Kunz, Jean-Willy	AI0200	Labadorf, Thomas	CT0100
Krusemark, William	KS1375	Kunz, Kelly	WA0030	Labadorf, Tom	CT0050
Krusemeyer, Mark	MN0300	Kunzer, Stephen	OK0800	LaBar, Arthur T.	TN1450
Krush, Jay P.	PA3250	Kuo, Kelly	TX3510	LaBar, Dan	NY1150
Kruspe, John	AG0450	Kuo, Ming-Hui	KY0900	LaBarbera, Joe	CA0510
Krutz, James	NE0200	Kuo, Rita	NY2400	LaBarbera, John P.	KY1500
Krutz, Jim	NE0150	Kuo, Ruth	CA0550	Labaree, Robert	MA1400
Krutz, Kim	KS1400	Kupfer, Peter A.	TX2400	LaBarr, Sarah	KS0590
Krutzen, Heidi	AB0100	Kupka, Craig	CA1960	Labe, Paul E.	MD0475
Krygier, Joe	OH1850	Kurai, Tom	CA5040	Labe, Thomas A.	OK0150
Krysa, Oleh	NY1100	Kurasz, Rick	IL3500	Labenske, Victor	CA3640
Krysa, Taras	NV0050	Kurau, Pamela	NY1100	Labonte, Celeste	RI0200
Krystofiak, Paul	TX3450	Kurau, Pamela B.	NY3730	Labonville, Marie E.	IL1150
Krzywicki, Jan L.	PA3250	Kurau, Peter	NY1100	Labor, Tim A.	CA5040
Krzywicki, Paul	PA0850	Kurek, Michael	TN1850	Laboranti, Jerry B.	PA1300
Ku, Hsiao-Mei	NC0600	Kurkowicz, Joanna	MA2250	LaBorn, John	IL1085
Ku, Rachel	PA3250	Kuroda, Elena	LA0550	LaBouff, Kathryn	NY1900
Kuan, Flora	NY2200	Kuroda, Masahito	LA0550	Labouff, Kathryn	NY2150
Kubesheski, Cindy	IA0250	Kurokawa, John K.	OH2500	Labounsky, Ann	PA1050
Kubey, Phyllis	NY2105	Kurokawa, Paul	CA2100	LaBounty, Anthony	NV0050
Kubiak, Paul	CA0859	Kurschner, James	MN1200	Labovitz, Sarah J.	KS1400
Kubiak, Teresa	IN0900	Kurth, Richard	AB0100	Labrecque, Kenneth J.	ME0150
Kubica, Robert	AG0500	Kurth, Robert	PA2900	LaBrie, Jesse	NE0300
Kubik, Ladislav	FL0850	Kurth, Robert	PA1050	LaBron, Wendy	MA1400
Kubik, Paula A.	PA1450	Kurti, Andrej	LA0550	LaBrosse, Denis	AI0200
Kubin, Brian	MO1780	Kurtz, James	NY1900	Labrosse, Martin	AG0400
Kubis, Jon-Michael	CA2050	Kurtz, Justin	CT0650	Labuta, Joseph	MI2200
Kubis, Thomas M.	CA2050	Kurtz-Harris, Jeremy	CA4100	Lacaille, Nathalie	AI0210
Kubus, Daniel	MO1780	Kurtzman, Jeffrey	MO1900	Lacan, Dale	OH1000

Lacarme, Alexandre	MA0400	Lalli, Marcus	NY0350	Landau, Gregory P.	CA1020
Lacasse, Serge	AI0190	Lalli, Marcus	NY3705	Landay, Lori	MA0260
Lacelle, Diane	AI0210	Lalli, Richard	CT0900	Lande, Vladimir	MD1000
Lach, Malgorzata	MA1350	Lally, Laurie A.	NJ1100	Lande, Vladimir	MD0100
LaChance, Marc	NE0300	Lally, Peter	MA2030	Lander, Deborah R.	KY1450
Lachew, Joseph	NV0150	Lalonde, Alain	AI0200	Landers, Joseph	AL1200
Lackey, Mark A.	MD0850	Lam, Eri Lee	TX2650	Landers, Karen	NY2400
Lackey, William J.	MO1800	Lam, Joseph S. C.	MI2100	Landes, Daniel	TN0100
Lackman, Susan Cohn	FL1550	Lam, Michelle	VA1500	Landey, Peter	AG0050
Lackschewitz, Anna	MO1950	Lam, Sze-Sze	AA0020	Landgrave, Phillip	KY1200
Laclair, Jaqueline	NY2150	Lam, Vincent	TX2650	Landgrebe, Junauro	MA1450
LaCognata, John P.	NC2440	Lamar, Gregory A.	NJ0800	Landis, Margery	ME0150
Laconti, Paul	NY2550	Lamar, Jackie B.	AR0850	Landis, Melissa McIntosh	CA3200
LaCosse, Steven R.	NC1650	Lamar, Linda Kline	ID0050	Landis, Melissa McIntosh	CA6000
Lacoste, Debra	AG0600	LaMarca, Perry	CA0825	Landis, Stella Baty	LA0750
LaCourse, Michelle	MA0400	Lamarche, Andre	AI0210	Landolfi, Dominic J.	CT0250
Lacoursiere, Marie-Nathalie	AI0200	Lamartine, Nicole C.	WY0200	Landreth, Janet M.	CO0250
LaCreta, Joseph	MA2100	LaMattina, Michael	OH0450	Landrum, Michael	NY3350
LaCreta, Joseph	MA1100	Lamb Cook, Susan	CA0150	Landry, Dana	CO0950
Lacroix, Frederic	AG0400	Lamb, Brian	OK1330	Landry, Jacques	PR0100
LaCroix, John	CA0200	Lamb, Christopher	NY2150	Landry, Rosemarie	AI0200
Lacy, Charles	LA0100	Lamb, Earnest	NC0800	Landry, Scott P.	LA0760
Lacy, Christopher	AR0700	Lamb, Marvin L.	OK1350	Landsberg, Nils F.	TX3415
Lacy, Edwin	IN1600	Lamb, Robert E.	FL0150	Landsberg, Paul	AB0070
Lacy, Randolph A.	KS1450	Lamb, Roberta	AG0250	Landschoot, Thomas V.	AZ0100
Lada, Tony	MA0260	Lamb, Sally	NY1800	Landsman, Julie	NY0150
Ladd, Chris	CT0650	Lamb, Virginia P.	NY2150	Landsman, Julie	NY1900
Ladd, Christopher	CT0050	Lamb, William	NM0500	Landsman, Vladimir	AI0200
Ladd, Gita	MD1000	Lamb, William	NM0250	Lane, Betty D.	MI2200
Ladd, Karen	TN1710	Lambert, Adam E.	NE0050	Lane, Brandie	NY2750
Laddy, Jason	WI0425	Lambert, Adam	TX0700	Lane, Diane	WI0300
Laderach, Linda C.	MA1350	Lambert, David D.	AL0500	Lane, Diane	AA0050
Laderman, Ezra	CT0850	Lambert, Debra	CA3270	Lane, Elizabeth	DC0170
Laderman, Michael	NY3100	Lambert, Doris	OK0150	Lane, Jennifer R.	TX3420
Ladewig, James L.	RI0300	Lambert, Evin R.	WA0750	Lane, Jeremy S.	SC1110
LaDuke, Lance	PA0550	Lambert, Frederic	AI0150	Lane, John W.	TX2250
LaDuke, Lance	PA1050	Lambert, Gary	IA0800	Lane, Kathleen	ID0100
Ladzekpo, Alfred K.	CA0510	Lambert, James	OK0150	Lane, Laura L.	IL1350
Ladzekpo, C. K.	CA5000	Lambert, Jean-Francois	AI0190	Lane, LuAnn	TX1850
Ladzekpo, C. K.	CA2950	Lambert, Jessica I.	OR0700	Lane, Mark	WA0050
Ladzekpo, Kobla	CA5031	Lambert, Kevin	TX0150	Lane, Mathew	MD0400
LaFave, Alan	SD0400	Lambert, Lerene	LA0300	Lane, Roger	NC0900
Lafferty, Laurie	OH2150	Lambert, Marjolaine	AI0150	Lane, Stephen S.	IA0200
LaFitte, Barbara	MA2050	Lambert, Michel	AI0150	Lane, Timothy	WI0803
LaFitte, Barbara	MA0260	Lambert, Michelle	NE0050	Laney, Robert	TX3700
Laflen, Betty Jo	KS0400	Lambert, Nathan T.	CO0350	Lang, Brenda J.	OH0550
Laforest, Maurice	AI0190	Lambert, Philip	NY0600	Lang, Cynthia	CA3400
Laframboise, Damian	AG0150	Lambert, Philip	NY0250	Lang, David	CT0850
Laframboise, Damien	AG0070	Lambert, Sterling	MD0750	Lang, Dennis	CA2300
Lafranque, Claude-Lise	CA5550	Lamberton, Elizabeth	AB0060	Lang, Donald P.	NY3725
Lafreniere, Andy	CT0800	Lambrecht, Cynthia A.	IL0100	Lang, Drew	TX2400
Lagace, Isolde	AI0220	Lambrecht, James M.	IL0100	Lang, Jeffrey	PA3250
Lagana, Thomas V.	MD1000	Lambrecht, Richard	TX3520	Lang, Jeffrey	NY0150
Lagana, Tom	MD0850	Lambright, Spencer N.	TN1100	Lang, Linda	MN1175
Laganella, David	DE0200	Lambros, Maria	MD1000	Lang, Scott	KY1000
Lagarenne, Cecile	TX2955	Lambros, Maria	MD0650	Lang, Zoe	FL2000
Lagasse, Blythe	CO0250	Lambson, Jeanne	MO0100	Langager, Arlie	CA2960
Laginya, Daniel	OH2600	Lambson, Nick	CA2250	Langager, Graeme	AB0100
LaGraff, Scott	TX2700	Lamendola, Gene	NY4060	Langan, David	NJ0700
LaGruth, Anthony	NJ0550	Lamendola, Gene	NY4050	Langdon, Gillian S.	NY2750
Laguana, Carlos	GU0500	Lamey, Phil	VT0100	Lange, Daniel	OR0010
LaGuardia, Frank	CA0550	Laminack, Emily	GA1700	Lange, Diane	TX3500
Lahti, Carol	IL2100	Lamkin, John R.	MD1020	Lange, James	WV0560
Lai, Ching-Chun	NY3780	Lamkin, Kathleen J.	CA5100	Lange, Jesse	OH2150
Lai, Eric C.	TX0300	Lamkin, Lynn B.	TX3400	Lange, Magaret	MA0260
Lai, Juliet	MA0510	Lamkin, Martin J.	VI0050	Lange, Peter V.	WI0200
Lai, Juliet	MA0700	Lamkin, Michael D.	CA1050	Lange, Richard	MI0050
Lai, Yun-Ju	CA5355	Lammers, Ed	KS0040	Lange, Richard A.	MN1280
Laib, Susan	PA2150	Lammers, James	MO1810	Lange, Rose	TX3400
Laidlaw, George	AG0500	Lammers, Mark E.	MN0750	Lange, Stephen R.	MI1200
Lail, H. Wayne	NC0600	Lammers, Paula	MN0610	Lange-Jensen, Catherine	KY1000
Laimon, Sara	AI0150	Lamneck, Esther	NY2750	Langenberg, Claire Coyle	IL2050
Lain, Larry	OH1600	Lamon, Jeanne	AG0300	Langenberg, Kelly	IL1200
Laine, Karin	NY0850	Lamothe, Donat	MA0200	Langenberg, Kelly	IL0750
Laing, Daniel R.	NE0300	Lamothe, Peter	TN0100	Langenberg, Kelly	IL2100
Laing, David	AI0190	Lamothe, Virginia Christy	TN0100	Langer, Kenneth P.	MA1500
Laing, David	AI0150	Lamott, Bruce	CA4150	Langerak, Terri	MO1830
Laing, Laurence 'Corky'	AG0500	LaMotte, Adam	OR0750	Langevin, Robert	NY2150
Lair, Christopher	MO0350	Lampert, Judi	NC2400	Langevin, Robert	NY1900
Laird, Helen L.	PA3250	Lampert, Steven	NY0050	Langford, Bruce	CA1000
Laird, Paul R.	KS1350	Lampidis, Anna	NC2205	Langford, Jeffrey	NY2150
Laird, Scott	NC1800	Lampidis, Anna	NC2500	Langford, Jeremy	FL1100
Laird, Tracey	GA0050	Lampl, Kenneth H.	NY1600	Langford, R. Gary	FL1850
Laitz, Steven	NY1100	Lamprey, Audrey	CA0845	Langfur, Gabriel	MA0400
Lajoie, Stephen H.	RI0101	Lamprey, Audrey	CA5040	Langham, Patrick	CA5350
Lake, Mary Kay	TX2250	Lamprey, Audrey	CA0630	Langley, DeeAnna	MN1050
Lake, William E.	OH0300	Lamy, Andy	NJ1400	Langley, Jeff	CA4700
Lakers, Janice	MI1150	Lan, Catherine	FL0200	Langley, Mike	IA1100
Lakey, Richard	PA2100	LaNasa, Patricia J.	OH2150	Langlois, Kristina	MN0610
Lakirovich, Mark	IL0550	Lancaster, Carol	CA3100	Langman, Shannon	TX1450
Lakirovich, Mark	MA1175	Lancaster, Linda K.	KY1200	Langner, Gerald	AJ0150
Lakofsky, Elissa	FL0700	Lancaster, Michael	CO0830	Langol, Stefani	MA0260
Lakofsky, Elissa	FL0650	Lancaster, Michael	NC2600	Langol, Stefani	
Laky, Beth	LA0080	Lancaster, Stephen J.	IN1700	Langone, Steve M.	MA2050
Lala, Diane	OH2200	Lance, Elva Kaye	MS0500	Langor, Suzanne	AA0020
Lalama, David	NY2150	Lancos, Jonette	NY3730	Langosch, Paul	VA1700
LaLama, David S.	NY1600	Land, Mary	GA2300	Langsam, Stuart	OK0800
Lalama, Ralph	NY2750	Land, Michael	ND0400	Langsam, Stuart	OK0450
Lalama, Ralph	NY3785	Land, W. Reese	KY0400	Langsford, Christopher M.	KS0750
Lallerstedt, Ford	PA0850	Landa, Jean	AA0050	Lanham, Barbara	IL1610

Name	Code	Name	Code	Name	Code	Name	Code
Lanier Miller, Pamela	AL0330	Larson, Leon	FL1675	Laurance, Emily R.	CA4150
Lanier, Brian	MO0950	Larson, Linda L.	NC0050	Laureano, Orlando	PR0115
Lanier, Michael	GA2130	Larson, Lynee	MN1290	Laureano, Victor O.	PR0150
Lanini, Phyllis	NY2400	Larson, Matthew	MA0400	Laurel, Edward	NY2750
Lankford, Andrew	VA0600	Larson, Nancy	MD0850	Laurendine, Barbara	AL1195
Lanners, Heather	OK0800	Larson, Nicholas A.	OR0700	Laurent, Linda	CT0050
Lanners, Thomas	OK0800	Larson, Paul	PA2450	Lauridsen, Morten	CA5300
Lanning, Rebecca	GA1260	Larson, Philip	CA5050	Laursen, Amy	AR0300
Lano, Joe	NV0050	Larson, Richard	IL0150	Laut, Edward A.	KS1350
Lano, Matthew	IL0730	Larson, Richard	NY3725	Lautar, Rebecca	FL0650
Lansdale, Katie	CT0650	Larson, Robert	VA1350	Lauterbach, Megan	IL2750
Lansing, Nathan	WA0950	Larson, Stacey L.	IL3450	Lautzenheiser, Tim	IN0905
Lansky, Paul	NJ0900	Larson, Steven	CT0650	Lautzenheiser, Tim N.	IN0150
Lanter, Mark W.	AL1150	Larson, Tom	NE0600	Lauver, Eric	PA1050
Lanter, Mark	AL1170	LaRue, Peter	KY0610	Laux, Charles	GA1150
Lantz, Lisa E.	NY0100	Larzelere, Raymond	NY1350	Lauzon, Paul	AF0050
Lanz, Christopher C.	NY3780	Lasareff-Mirinoff, Claudia	IL2100	Lavanne, Antonia	NY2250
Lanza, Alcides	AI0150	Lascell, Ernest D.	NY3730	Lavenda, Richard A.	TX2150
Lanza, Joseph	AG0500	Lascell, Ernie	NY1700	Lavender, Robert	FL0650
Lanza, Lou	PA2450	Lash, Andre D.	NC2430	Lavender, Scott	OH0300
Lanzer, Kate J.	MN0450	Lashbrook, Laurie E.	OH2150	Laverne, Andrew	CT0650
Lanzrein, Valentin Christian	IN0350	Lashinsky, Leslie	CA3600	LaVertu, Desiree	CA3300
LaPerna, Eric	ME0150	Laskey, Anne	CA2200	Laverty, John M.	NY4150
Lapham, Barbara	ME0430	Laskowitz, Lillian	NY5000	Laverty, Mary	NY4150
Lapidis, Rachael	CA0960	Laskowitz, Lillian	NY2400	Lavery, Sharon	CA5300
Lapidus, Benjamin	NY0630	Laskowski, Kim	NY1900	Lavigne, Julie	AI0220
LaPierre, Art	CA0150	Laskowski, Kim	NY2250	LaVine, Scott	NY3780
Lapin, Eric J.	SC0400	Laskowski, Kim	NY2150	Lavner, Jeffrey	CA1075
Lapin, Geoff	IN0500	Lasley, Michael	NC1550	LaVoie, Karen R.	MA2100
Lapin, Lawrence	FL1900	Lasmawan, I. Made	CO0800	Lavoie, Mathieu	AI0200
Lapins, Alexander	AZ0450	Lasmawan, I. Made	CO0200	Lavonis, William	WI0825
Lapka, Christine	IL3500	LaSpina, Steven	NJ1400	LaVorgna, David	MD0400
LaPointe, Simon	VA1600	Lassen, Emily	ID0060	Lavruk, Alexander E.	CA3950
Lapp, Beverly K.	IN0550	Lasser, Philip	NY1900	Law, Bill R.	ND0350
Lappin, Donald P.	MA0260	Lassetter, Jacob	IA0950	Law, Cameron	CO0225
Lapple, Judith A.	VA0450	Lassiter, Stan	TN0100	Law, Charles P.	AR0750
Laprade, Paul	IL2560	Lassiter, Stan	TN0550	Law, Joshua T.	CA1020
LaQuatra, Jeff	CO0550	Last, Julie	VT0050	Law, Zada	TN1850
LaQuatra, Jeff	CO0625	Laster, James	VA1350	Lawhead, David	FL1650
Lara, Elizabeth K.	TN0050	Lastrapes, Jeffrey Noel	TX3200	Lawhon, Daniel E.	AL0800
Laranja, Ricardo	IN0907	Laszlo, Albert	NY1900	Lawhon, Sharon L.	AL0800
Lardinios, John	OH2250	Laszlo, Albert	OH2200	Lawing, Cynthia	NC0550
Lardinois, John	IN0400	Lata, Matthew	FL0850	Lawing, Hollie	GA1150
Lardinois, Kara	OH2250	Latarski, Donald	OR1050	Lawing, Sarah	GA2130
Lares, Joseph	CA5353	Latartara, John	MS0700	Lawing, William D.	NC0550
Large, Duane	PA3250	Latchininsky, Alla	WY0200	Lawler, Daniel	NJ1160
Large, Karen McLaughlin	KS0650	Late, Eric	TX2295	Lawler, Daniel J.	NY2750
Large, Mike	AG0070	Lateiner, Jacob	NY2250	Lawler, Dawn	WI0700
Largent, Jeffrey	MA0260	Latenser, Tom	FL1430	Lawler, Douglas	MD0175
Largess, John	TX3510	Latham, Edward D.	PA3250	Lawler-Johnson, Dian	GA0550
Largey, Michael	MI1400	Latham, Louis S.	VA1000	Lawless, John	GA1150
Larish, Charles	IA0910	Latham, Mark	MA2030	Lawley, Mark	MO0400
Larison, Adam	FL0350	Lathom-Radocy, Wanda	MO1810	Lawlor, Catherine	MA2010
Lark, Robert J.	IL0750	Lathrum, Linda	FL0700	Lawluvi, Beatrice	CA0510
Larkin, Christopher J.	NJ0800	Lathwell, John	NY3705	Lawn, Richard J.	PA3330
Larkowski, Charles S.	OH2500	Latimer, Carole	PA1150	Lawrence, Alan	IA0400
Larmee, Kent	OH1100	Latimer, Marvin E.	AL1170	Lawrence, Alan	IA0300
Larner, James M.	IN1100	Latini, Eric J.	NY3650	Lawrence, Barry	KY0250
Larocco, Sharon Moss	NC0750	Latour, Michelle R.	NV0050	Lawrence, Betsy	PA0550
Laroche, Yves	AG0400	Latsabidze, Giorgi	CA1960	Lawrence, Cynthia	KY1450
Larocque, Jacques	AI0220	Latta, Jonathan R.	CO0350	Lawrence, Deborah	MD0750
Laronga, Barbara	CA2600	Latta, Matthew	IN1800	Lawrence, Edwin	MA2250
LaRosa, Joseph	NY1275	Latten, James E.	PA1650	Lawrence, Jay	ID0060
LaRosa, Massimo	OH0600	Lattimore, Jonita	IL0550	Lawrence, Jay	UT0190
Larose, Anne-Marie	AI0190	Lattimore, Lee	TX3420	Lawrence, Jay	UT0250
Larose, Christine	AI0190	Lattini, James	MA2030	Lawrence, Jay	UT0050
Larose, Thomas	VA1750	Latts, Ginny	MA1175	Lawrence, Josh	PA3330
Larrabee, Adam	VA1550	Latu, Kalotini	UT0050	Lawrence, Kenya L.	LA0650
Larrabee, Adam	VA1600	Latulippe, Mario	AI0050	Lawrence, Kevin	NC1650
Larragoity, Ingrid	AR0300	Lau, Daniel	MD0150	Lawrence, Lisa	FL0100
Larrance, Steve	MD0550	Lau, Elaine	AG0600	Lawrence, Mark	CA1075
Larsen, Arved	IL1150	Lau, Eric	NM0450	Lawrence, Mark	CA4150
Larsen, Bill	FL0680	Lau, Frederick C.	HI0210	Lawrence, Patrick	WI0850
Larsen, Catherine	MN1280	Lau, Jennifer	NM0450	Lawrence, Robert C.	OH2000
Larsen, Eric	NC1650	Lau, Sylvia	CA3800	Lawrence, Robert J.	MO1790
Larsen, Jens	SC0900	Laubach, David	AR0300	Lawrence, Sarah	WI0860
Larsen, Jens	SC0650	Laubach, Mark	PA2200	Lawrence, Sidra	OH0300
Larsen, Karin	WA0980	Laubengayer, Karen	MS0350	Lawrence, Steve	OR0250
Larsen, Karli	WI1150	Laubenthal, Jennifer	NM0100	Lawrence, Torrey	ID0250
Larsen, Laurel	SC0900	Lauber, Anne	AI0210	Lawrence, Wesley	ND0500
Larsen, Robert L.	IA1350	Laubmeir, George	WI0842	Lawrence, Wesley	OH0550
Larsen, Tage	IL0750	Lauderdale, Lynne A.	FL2100	Lawrence-White, Stephanie	NC0200
Larsen, Vance	UT0190	Lauderdale, Rod	LA0350	Lawrie, Jim	TX0400
Larsen, William H.	FL0500	Laudermilch, Kenneth	PA1300	Laws, Francis	OH2500
Larson, Allen C.	MO1950	Laudon, Robert	MN1623	Lawson, Charles E.	CO0250
Larson, Andre	SD0600	Lauer, Eileen	IL1900	Lawson, David	WV0700
Larson, Andrew	FL1750	Laufer, Milton R.	NC1800	Lawson, Dianne	IA0910
Larson, Angela	SD0580	Laufer, Wolfgang	WI0825	Lawson, Janet	NY2660
Larson, Angela	SD0050	Laufersweiler, Jonathon	MO1110	Lawson, Jennifer	VA0250
Larson, Anne	NC2300	Lauffer, Peter	NJ1000	Lawson, Jennifer	VA1500
Larson, Danelle	IL0800	Lauffer, Peter	NJ1350	Lawson, Julie	CA1265
Larson, Dave	NJ1400	Laughlin, Jim	TX0100	Lawson, Kay	WV0400
Larson, Deanna	IA0150	Laughlin, Mark	GA1000	Lawson, Matthew	KY0250
Larson, Elizabeth	CA0350	Laughlin, Tina	IL0750	Lawson, Peter K.	IL2100
Larson, Glen	MN1280	Laughrey, Gary	KY0800	Lawson, Robert	CA1265
Larson, Jean	TX2400	Lauinger, Robert	OR0250	Lawson, Robert	CA5360
Larson, Jennifer	IA1800	Laukhuf, Dale	OH1800	Lawson, Ronald S.	IA0910
Larson, John	IL0400	Laumer, Jack C.	TX3175	Lawson, Sonya R.	MA2100
Larson, Jon D.	MN1120	Launius, Michael	GA0550	Lawson, Stephen J.	WV0400
Larson, Laura A.	MI2200	Laupp, Belinda	TN1400	Lawson, Tonya	TN1100

Name	Code	Name	Code	Name	Code
Lawson, William	NY3705	Ledbetter, Steven	MA1400	Lee, Owen J.	CA1560
Lawthers, Carol	CA4000	Leddy, Thomas	IL0850	Lee, Pamela Perec	DC0170
Lawton, David	NY3790	Ledeen, Lydia Hailparn	NJ0300	Lee, Pamela	TX0150
Lawton, Richard	AI0150	Leder, Matthew D.	CO0830	Lee, Patricia Taylor	CA4200
Lawton, Thomas	PA3330	Lederer, Doris M.	VA1350	Lee, Patricia	IL2650
Lawton, Thomas P.	PA0400	Lederer, Thomas	TX2400	Lee, Patty	TX3100
Lawton, Tom P.	PA3250	Ledgerwood, Lee Ann	NY2660	Lee, Paul	NY2750
Lay, David	TN1200	Ledressay, Joanne	AB0090	Lee, Paul S.	TX1300
Lay, Jean	OR0450	Leduc, Pierre	AI0200	Lee, Pei-Shan	CA0835
Lay, Lara	AL1250	Leduc, Yolande	AI0210	Lee, R. Matthew	IL0850
Laycock, Mark Andrew	KS1450	Lee, A. Ram	MI0100	Lee, Raejin	CA2420
Laycock, Rand	OH0755	Lee, Abe	MA0260	Lee, Ranee	AI0190
Layendecker, Dennis M.	VA0450	Lee, Alexandra	AG0070	Lee, Ranee	AI0150
Layman, Deborah	OH0650	Lee, Alice	MD0300	Lee, Rebecca	FL1550
Laymon, Michael	IL1080	Lee, Alice E.	DC0170	Lee, Richard A.	CO0650
Layne, Darin	TX2170	Lee, Amanda	TX2570	Lee, Richard	AC0100
Layne, R. Dennis	MN1300	Lee, April	IL0800	Lee, Richard F.	TX3150
Layton, Myrna	UT0325	Lee, Ardyce	TN1710	Lee, Richard A.	HI0200
Layton, Richard Douglas	MD1010	Lee, Bomi	KY1500	Lee, Robert E.	OH1450
Lazar, Ludmila	IL0550	Lee, Brent	AG0550	Lee, Robert W.	NY4150
Lazar, Richard	AG0650	Lee, Brian	IL1850	Lee, Rodger P.	NY2550
Lazar, Teri	DC0010	Lee, Byong Won	HI0210	Lee, Rodger	NY2105
Lazaro, Andrew A.	PR0115	Lee, Carver Scott	PA1750	Lee, Ronald T.	RI0300
Lazarova, Maria	CA0825	Lee, Cassandra	TN1850	Lee, Rosey	MA0260
Lazarus, Gordon	CA0200	Lee, Charles	CO0550	Lee, Russell	UT0325
Lazerow, Erica	CA1265	Lee, Charles	CO0650	Lee, Sang-Eun	IL1085
Le Comte, Louise	AI0190	Lee, Cheng-Hou	IL2200	Lee, Sang-Hie	FL2000
Le Guin, Elisabeth C.	CA5032	Lee, Chia-Wei	TX3350	Lee, Scott	MO1810
Le, Andrew	MI1050	Lee, Chiayi	IL1085	Lee, Seunghee	MI0400
Le, Weiwei	NV0050	Lee, Chihchen Sophia	OK1250	Lee, So Yoon	TX3525
Leach, Anthony	PA2750	Lee, Chris	AC0100	Lee, Soh Yeong	PA3550
Leach, Brenda	MD0850	Lee, Christina	IL2775	Lee, Soo Young	IL1400
Leach, Catherine F.	TN1710	Lee, Christine	CA0630	Lee, Soojeong	TX3300
Leach, Margaret C.	AL1160	Lee, Christine	SC0200	Lee, Sujin	OH0300
Leach, Troy	TN1660	Lee, Christopher	NJ0825	Lee, Sun Jung	WV0100
Leadbitter, Robyn	SC0600	Lee, Christopher	MA2030	Lee, Sun Min	PA1950
Leaf, Nathan	NC1700	Lee, Colin	AG0600	Lee, Sung Ae	CA0859
Leafstedt, Carl S.	TX3350	Lee, D. Thomas	CA5030	Lee, Thomas Oboe	MA0330
League, Leanne	WI0865	Lee, Damon Thomas	NE0600	Lee, Tong Soon	GA0750
Leahy, Eugene J.	IN1700	Lee, Daniel	CT0100	Lee, Vivian	AI0150
Leake, Jerry	MA1400	Lee, Donna	OH1100	Lee, William R.	TN1700
Leali, Brad	TX3420	Lee, Donzell	MS0050	Lee, Won Yong	TX2570
Leaman, Clifford L.	SC1110	Lee, Douglas	TN1850	Lee, You Ju	GA2000
Leaman, Jim	OH2275	Lee, Elizabeth	TX3100	Lee-Keller, Derek	CA1500
Leandro, Eduardo G.	NY3790	Lee, Eric	AG0250	Leech, Alan B.	MT0200
Leaptrott, Ben	GA0350	Lee, Genevieve Feiwen	CA3650	Leech, Karen	MT0200
Leary-Warsaw, Jacqueline J.	AL0300	Lee, Gerald K.	WV0600	Leech, Thomas	PA0100
Leas, Ashleigh	TX3350	Lee, Gordon	OR1250	Leechford, Wayne	NC1700
Lease, Gus	CA4400	Lee, Gregory	OK1350	Leeds, Steve	NJ1400
Lease, Nancy	IA0250	Lee, Hae-Jong	OH2600	Leek, Anne	TX3400
Leasure, Michael	FL0150	Lee, Hayoung Heidi	CA4150	Leenhouts, Margaret A.	NY2650
Leasure, Timothy	OH1850	Lee, Hedy	CA0960	Leenhouts, Paul T.	TX3420
Leath, Nate R.	VA1850	Lee, Helen	AB0100	Leeper, Brian K.	WI0865
Leathers, Gwendolyn	MA0260	Lee, Hsiaopei	MS0750	LeePreston, Nicole	IN1750
Leathersich, Stacey	CA0150	Lee, Hsin-Bei	MA1400	Leerstang, Carmen	LA0300
Leatherwood, John G.	FL1430	Lee, Hui Yu	PA0650	Lees, Christopher	MI2100
Leathwood, Heidi Brende	CO0900	Lee, Hwakyu (Julia)	OR1100	Lees, Priscilla	MI2100
Leathwood, Jonathan	CO0900	Lee, HyeKyung	OH0850	Leese, Matthew	IL1750
Leavitt, Edward	NY4300	Lee, Hyeweon	DC0170	Lefebvre, Claire	AI0210
Leavitt, Tod J.	GA2150	Lee, In Young	PA3600	Lefebvre, Marie-France	OH2200
LeBaron, Anne	CA0510	Lee, Jaeryoung	CA4050	Lefebvre, Marie-Therese	AI0200
Lebeda, Wiktor	AB0200	Lee, Jaeryoung	CA2960	Lefebvre, Matthew T.	MA0150
Lebens, James C.	AI0190	Lee, Jaesung	IN1450	LeFebvre, Timothy	OH1700
LeBlanc, Eric	AB0210	Lee, James	AZ0200	Lefever, Todd	AA0040
LeBlanc, Gaye F.	OK1350	Lee, Janet	WA0200	LeFevre, Carla	NC2430
Leblanc, Jacques	AI0190	Lee, Janice	CA1000	Lefevre, Donald	TX3750
Leblanc, Mario	AI0200	Lee, Jessica	NY4450	LeFevre, Michael	WA1100
LeBlanc, Paul	TX3420	Lee, Jinah	NY3705	Leffert, Kristine Lund	SD0200
LeBlanc, Robert L.	OH1850	Lee, Jon	TX2400	Lefferts, Peter M.	NE0600
Leblanc, Stuart W.	LA0300	Lee, Joo-Mee	MA2010	Leffingwell, Dolores	OK1350
Leblanc, Suzie	AI0200	Lee, Joohyun	TX2960	Lefkowitz, Aaron M.	FL1550
LeBlond, Gerald	NH0300	Lee, Jordan	WI1150	Lefkowitz, David	NY1450
Leblond, Louis	AI0190	Lee, Joseph	TN1800	Lefkowitz, David S.	CA5030
Lebo, Joanna	SC0050	Lee, Julia	OR0850	Lefkowitz, Ronan	MA0350
Lebon, Rachel L.	FL1900	Lee, Junghwa	IL2900	LeFlore, Maurice	NC0700
Lebow, Roger	CA0960	Lee, Justina	MD1010	Lefrance, Manon	AI0210
Lebow, Roger B.	CA3650	Lee, Kaju	TX2250	Lefter, Nancy C.	SC0300
Lebron, Nelie	PR0115	Lee, Kari	IL0850	Leger, James K.	NM0150
LeCheminant, Reed	UT0350	Lee, Katherine In-Young	CA5010	Legere, Katie	AG0250
Leck, Henry	IN0250	Lee, Katherine K.		Legette, Lee David	NC2700
Leckrone, Erik	CA1900	Lee, Ki Joo	IN0005	Legette, Roy M.	GA2100
Leckrone, Michael E.	WI0815	Lee, Kum Sing	AB0200	Leggatt, Jacqueline	AB0200
LeClair, Ben	IL0600	Lee, Kum-Sing	AA0050	Leglar, Mary A.	GA2100
LeClair, Benjamin	IL1615	Lee, Kyung	CA3600	Legname, Orlando	NY3765
Leclair, Francois-Hugues	AI0200	Lee, Kyung-A	AA0035	Legner, Amanda	IL1200
LeClair, Jacqueline	NY2150	Lee, Kyung-Ae	TX3175	LeGrand, Catherine M.	NC0300
Leclair, Jacqueline F.	AI0150	Lee, LaToya	GA0490	LeGrand, Thomas	TX2150
LeClair, Judith	NY1900	Lee, Lydia	CA1265	Legutki, Allen R.	IL0275
LeClair, Paul	VT0400	Lee, Marian Y.	IA1300	Lehane, Gregory J.	PA0550
Leclaire, Dennis	MA0260	Lee, Mark	TN0350	Lehman, Carroll	NH0150
LeClaire, Shannon L.	MA0260	Lee, Mary	AF0050	Lehman, David	SC0200
Leclerc, Francois	AI0190	Lee, Matt	IL0750	Lehman, Frank M.	RI0050
LeCroy, Hoyt F.	GA1650	Lee, Melvin	OK0700	Lehman, Katherine	TN1800
Lecuona, Rene	IA1550	Lee, Michael	CA0250	Lehman, Lowell	OK0550
Lecuyer, Michael P.	MA1500	Lee, Michael E.	OH1100	Lehman, Marilyn J.	NY1600
Lecuyer, Stephane	AG0130	Lee, Michael	OK1350	Lehman, Paul R.	MI0600
L'Ecuyer, Sylvia	AI0200	Lee, Mitch	UT0325	Lehman, Shari	IA0790
Leday, Eric	AL1195	Lee, Monica	CA1900	Lehman, Stephanie	NY0270
Ledbetter, Lynn F.	TX3175	Lee, Nancy	MN1450	Lehmann, Bertam	MA0260
Ledbetter, Robert	MT0400	Lee, Owen	KY1000	Lehmann, Jay	CA2450

Alphabetical Listing of Faculty

Name	Code	Name	Code	Name	Code
Lehmann, Kathryn	WA1000	Leone, Carol	TX2400	Levine, Dena	NJ1160
Lehmann, Mark	IA1800	Leone, Gary	FL0500	Levine, Iris S.	CA0630
Lehmann, Matthew	NY1600	Leone, Gustavo	IL1615	Levine, Jonathan	FL0400
Lehmann, Robert A.	ME0500	Leong, Daphne	CO0800	Levine, Josh	OH1700
Lehmberg, Lisa J.	MA2000	Leong, Sonia	CA5350	Levine, Mark	CA2950
Lehn, Steven	CO0100	Leonhardt, Angela J.	TX3530	Levine, Rhoda	NY2250
Lehnert, Doris Pridonoff	CO0800	Leonhardt, Julie	MO1250	Levine, Rhoda	NY2150
Lehnert, Oswald	CO0800	Leonhart, Carolyn	MA0260	Levine, Susan	NE0600
Lehninger, Marcia	NH0150	Leopold, Timothy	NY2150	Levine, Ted	MA1350
Lehr, Barry	NY2550	Leotar, Frederic	AI0200	Levine, Theodore	MA1100
Lehr, Joan	OH1850	Lepine, Joachim	AI0050	Levine, Theodore	MA2100
Lehrer, Phyllis	NJ1350	Lepke-Sims, Barbara	CO0150	Levine, Victoria Lindsay	CO0200
Lehrer, Scott	VT0050	Lepke-Sims, Barbara	CO0650	LeVines, T. Allen	MA0260
Lehrman, Paul D.	MA1900	Lepley, Louise	CA4450	Levinowitz, Lili	NJ1050
Leibel, Jane	AD0050	Lepper, Kevin	IL3450	Levinsky, Gail B.	PA3150
Leibensperger, Peter	NY0625	Leppert-Largent, Anna	MI1850	Levinson, Drew	CO0830
Leibinger, Douglas J.	CA4700	Lepson, Ruth	MA1400	Levinson, Eugene	NY1900
Leibundguth, Barbara	MN0750	Lerch, Natalie	WA0200	Levinson, Gerald C.	PA3200
Leider, Colby N.	FL1900	Lercia, Louise	TX0700	Levinson, Gina	NY1900
Leifer, Lyon	IL2150	Lerdahl, Fred	NY0750	Levinson, Ilya	IL0720
Leighton, Mark	MA0800	Lerner, Edward	NY0642	Levinson, Max	MA0350
Leighton, Mark	ME0250	Lerner, Neil	NC0550	Levinson, Ross	CA0830
Leikin, Anatole	CA5070	Lerner, Paige Stockley	WA0200	Levitan, Dan	CA4700
Lein, Melinda	NC2650	Lerner, Peter	IL0720	Levitan, Susan	IN0005
Lein, Susan E.	LA0760	Leroux, Andre	AI0150	Levitin, Daniel	AI0150
Leinberger, Charles	TX3520	Leroux, Philippe	AI0150	Levitin, Susan	IL2750
Leisawitz, Jeffrey	WA0650	Leroux, Robert	AI0200	Leviton, Lawrence	WI0850
Leisenring, John R.	MO1810	Lesage, Jean	AI0150	Levitov, Daniel	PA1400
Leisner, David	NY2150	Lesbines, Melissa	NC0050	Levitt, Joseph	IN0150
Leisring, Laura	VA0250	Lesbines, Tele	WI1150	Levitz, Jodi	CA4150
Leisring, Stephen W.	KS1350	Leschisin, Taras	MA0510	Levitz, Tamara	CA5032
Leist, Christine	NC0050	Lesemann, Frederick	CA5300	Levtov, Vladimir	AA0150
Leistra-Jones, Karen	PA1300	Lesenger, Jay	IL2250	Levy, Arthur	NY2150
Leiter, Cherise D.	CO0550	Leshchinskaya, Ida	MI2120	Levy, Arthur	NY2250
Leiter, Joseph W.	MO0800	Leshnoff, Jonathan	MD0850	Levy, Ben	AZ0100
Leive, Cynthia	AI0150	Leshowitz, Myron	NJ0700	Levy, Benjamin	MA0400
Leland, James	KS1200	Lesiuk, Teresa L.	FL1900	Levy, Benjamin	MA0350
LeMay, Lisa A.	NJ0825	Lesk, Sally	AG0150	Levy, Beth E.	CA5010
Lemay, Robert	AG0150	Leska, Gosia	AL1300	Levy, Byron	MD0650
Lemelin, Stephane	AG0400	Leslie, Drew	NC0050	Levy, David B.	NC2500
Lemen, Caroline	MN1623	Leslie, Evan A.	TX3450	Levy, Fabien	NY0750
Lemen, Caroline M.	MN0950	Leslie, James M.	OH2250	Levy, James D.	DC0100
LeMessurier, Susan	AG0600	Leslie, Justin	UT0325	Levy, Joanna	CT0650
Lemieux, Christiane	AI0190	Leslie, Tom	NV0050	Levy, Katherine M.	NY3725
Lemieux, Suzanne	AF0100	Leslie, Tracy	KY1540	Levy, Kathryn	NC2500
Lemire, Carole E.	MO1900	Lessard, Brigitte-Louise	AI0190	Levy, Kenneth	NJ0900
Lemire, Janell	WI0860	Lessard, Daniel	AI0150	Levy, Leesa	ND0600
Lemire, Janell	MN0450	Lesser, Erin	WI0350	Levy, Mark	OR1050
Lemire, Janell	MN1600	Lesser, Jeffrey	NJ0550	Levy, Sharon	NY1900
Lemire-Ross, Dominique	PA2200	Lesser, Laurence	MA1400	Levy, Sharon G.	MD0650
Lemke, Jeffrey J.	LA0350	Lessie, Erica	IL2750	Levy, Todd	WI0825
Lemmon, Galen	CA4400	Lessing, Arnold	CA4450	Lew, Howard	NY2700
Lemmons, Cheryl T.	TX0050	Lessly, Chris Ann	IN1025	Lew, Jackie Chooi-Theng	MD0800
Lemmons, Frederick	NC1250	Lester, David T.	OH2140	Lew, Nathaniel G.	VT0400
Lemmons, Keith M.	NM0450	Lester, Jason	TX3850	Lewandowski, Annie	NY0900
Lemon, Ronald	TX3750	Lester, Jason	TX1000	Lewanski, Michael A.	IL0750
Lemons, Chris H.	IL0750	Lester, Joel	NY2250	Lewellen, Michael	IN0905
Lemons, Mary L.	PA1900	Lester, Laurie	TX1000	Lewellen, Michael	IN0700
Lemons, Nancy	IL1300	Lester, Noel K.	MD0500	Lewin, Ann	NY2250
Lemons, Robert M.	CT0150	Lester, Timothy	FL1310	Lewin, Ann	NY2150
Lemson, Deborah	TX3850	Lester, William	NY2400	Lewin, Michael	MA0400
Lemson, Lee	TX3850	Lester-White, Dottie	CA3270	Lewin, Michael	MA0350
Lendrim, Nancy	OH2300	Lethco, Leigh-Ann M.	WI0830	Lewis, Alexander	FL1745
Lenehan, Miriam C.	NY2450	Letkemann, David	AC0050	Lewis, Alexandra M.	NY0500
Lenhart, Andrew Stevens	NY2900	Letourneau, Jaime H.	VA1850	Lewis, Andrew	MD0175
Lenihan, William	MO1900	Letson, Amy	MT0175	Lewis, Andrew J.	MS0350
Lenney, James	NJ0700	Letson, Roger	CA1450	Lewis, Andrew	IL3310
Lennon, Debby	MO1950	Lett, Bruce	CA0825	Lewis, Barbara E.	ND0500
Lennon, John A.	GA0750	Leung, Jackson	OH2500	Lewis, Bernice	MA2250
Lenox, Michael	VT0100	Leupold, John K.	MD1100	Lewis, Brian D.	TX3510
Lenth, Kristen	WY0050	Leupp Hanig, Nicole	OR1100	Lewis, Brian	MA0260
Lenthe, Carl	IN0900	Lev, Lara	NY1900	Lewis, Cecil	CO0100
Lenti, Anthony A.	SC0800	Levasseur, Susan	CO0100	Lewis, Cecil	CO0300
Lenti, Elizabeth	OH0600	Leve, James	AZ0450	Lewis, Charles A.	MA0260
Lenti, Vincent	NY1100	LeVelle, Teresa	CA6000	Lewis, Cheryse M.	NC2700
Lentini, James P.	OH1450	Levenson, Warren	MA0400	Lewis, Cheryse McLeod	FL1700
Lentsner, Dina	OH0350	Leventhal, Lois A.	MS0750	Lewis, Christopher	VT0050
Lentz, Jeffrey	PA0050	Leventhal, Sharan	MA0350	Lewis, Colin	AG0130
Lenz, Andrea	NV0100	Leverence, Dan	MN1280	Lewis, D. Andrew	IL0840
Lenz, Eric	IL2900	Leverenz, Chris	VA0150	Lewis, Daniel	MD0175
Leo, Nick	IA0550	Levesque, Craig	NJ1130	Lewis, Daniel	CA1560
Leon, Javier F.	IN0900	Levesque, Gerald	AI0190	Lewis, Darin	PA1850
Leon, Tania	NY0500	Levesque, Stephane	AI0150	Lewis, David P.	WV0350
Leon, Tania	NY0600	Levey, John C.	PA3400	Lewis, Don R.	WI0450
Leon-Shames, Stephanie L.	OK1350	Levey, Joseph A.	OH1850	Lewis, Elizabeth A.	MI1200
Leonard, Angela	OH0100	Levi, Michael	NY0700	Lewis, Eloise	KY0610
Leonard, Charlotte	AG0070	Levi, Zachary	PA3710	Lewis, Eric	CT0800
Leonard, Charlotte	AG0150	Levia, Beth	AA0100	Lewis, Gail D.	IN0250
Leonard, George	RI0200	Levin, Andrew R.	SC0400	Lewis, Gary	TX1700
Leonard, Jeff	OR0450	Levin, Dmitri	PA3250	Lewis, Gary J.	CO0800
Leonard, Gwenellyn	OR0400	Levin, Heather	CA5550	Lewis, George E.	NY0750
Leonard, Katy E.	AL0300	Levin, Marguerite	MD0850	Lewis, Gordon R.	KS1400
Leonard, Linda	VA1350	Levin, Neil	NY1860	Lewis, Gordon R.	KS0650
Leonard, Lisa	FL1125	Levin, Oleg	MN0610	Lewis, Grant	SC0950
Leonard, Neil	MA0260	Levin, Rami Y.	IL1400	Lewis, Gregory	IL1350
Leonard, Rebecca	MA2030	Levin, Robert	MA1050	Lewis, H. M.	KY0610
Leonard, Ronald	CA1075	Levin, Theodore C.	NH0100	Lewis, Huw R.	MI1050
Leonard, Stephen	NY2550	Levine, Andrea	KY0400	Lewis, Ian	CA2750
Leonardo, Manuel	CA1400	Levine, Art D.	AG0650	Lewis, James E.	FL2000
Leone, Aaron	NJ0760	Levine, Barry	NJ0550	Lewis, Jason	CA4400

Lewis, Jeffrey	CA4400	Lien, Joelle L.	UT0250	Lindahl, Susan	MI0400
Lewis, Jeremy	IN1800	Lienert, Keith	WI0840	Lindau, Elizabeth Ann	PA1400
Lewis, Jeremy	TX3750	Lienert, Keith	AZ0440	Lindberg, Jeffrey	OH0700
Lewis, Jill Terhaar	SC0275	Lienert, Keith A.	IL0840	Lindberg, John	MN0200
Lewis, Jim	AG0450	Liepins, Laura	CA1075	Lindberg, John	VA0250
Lewis, Jon L.	CA0835	Liesch, Barry	CA0350	Lindberg, John E.	MN1000
Lewis, Kate	CA2750	Lieurance, Barbara	MA0510	Lindberg, Martha	MN1000
Lewis, Katherine J.	IL1150	Lieurance, Neil W.	WA0800	Lindblad, Sonja	MA1175
Lewis, Kelly	OH2275	Lieuwen, Peter	TX2900	Lindblade, Dawn Marie	OK1330
Lewis, Kevin	MD0500	Lifchitz, Max	NY3700	Lindblom, Peter	NY3725
Lewis, Kimberly	IL2775	Lifshen, Faith	PA2250	Linde, Laurel	MT0350
Lewis, Leonard Mark	SC1200	Lifsitz, Fred	CA4200	Linde-Capistran, Jane	MN0600
Lewis, Lori	MN1250	Lifson, Ludmilla	MA1175	Lindekugel, Denise	MD0550
Lewis, Marcia	IN1750	Ligate, Linda	MO0400	Lindeman, Carolynn A.	CA4200
Lewis, Mary S.	PA3420	Light, Chris	AB0090	Lindeman, Stephan	UT0050
Lewis, Matthew	NJ1350	Light, Chris	AB0060	Lindeman, Timothy H.	NC0910
Lewis, Melissa	OK1200	Light, Daniel	KY0250	Lindemann, Jens	CA5030
Lewis, Nicholas	DC0150	Light, Susan	AA0050	Lindenfelser, Kathryn	MN0040
Lewis, Nora A.	KS0650	Lightfoot, Peter W.	MI1400	Linder, J. Michael	TX1775
Lewis, Philip J.	TX3420	Ligon, Bert	SC1110	Linder, Kevin	IA0500
Lewis, Robert S. T.	SC0500	Ligotti, Albert F.	GA2100	Linder, Kevin	IA1200
Lewis, Robert J.	KY0300	Lih, Lars	AI0150	Linder, Susan	UT0200
Lewis, Rod	SC0620	Liikala, Blair	TX3420	Lindgren, Lowell	MA1200
Lewis, Roger	KS0210	Likes, Susan	IL1500	Lindhal, Gregory	FL0700
Lewis, Ryan C.	AR0500	Lilarose, Robin	PA1900	Lindholm, Eric	CA1050
Lewis, Susan	FL1730	Lile, Drew	NC0600	Lindholm, Eric C.	CA3650
Lewis, Tim	NY2400	Liles, B. David	OH1600	Lindley, Debra	OH2500
Lewis, Tim	NY5000	Liles, Reese	TX2800	Lindner, Jenny	OR1100
Lewis, Victor	NJ1130	Liley, Thomas	IL1250	Lindorff, Joyce Zankel	PA3250
Lewis, Walter	MI1830	Liliestedt, Maira	OH2290	Lindquist, Arne	MD0175
Lewis, William	TX3510	Lilite, Louima	OK0650	Lindquist, George	WI1150
Lewis-Hale, Phyllis	MS0350	Lill, Joseph	IL2100	Lindquist, George C.	WI0835
Lewis-Hammond, Susan	AB0150	Lill, Michael	IL2100	Lindquist, George	WI0865
Lewiston, Cal	TX3700	Lilleslatten, Espen	LA0200	Lindroth, James	OK0550
Lewitt, David	NY3785	Lilley, Marc Bryan	DC0050	Lindroth, Scott A.	NC0600
Ley, Amy	AG0550	Lillie, Erin	SD0300	Lindsay, Gary M.	FL1900
Leydon, Rebecca	OH1700	Lillios, Elainie	OH0300	Lindsay, Jason M.	FL1950
Leyerle, William	NY3730	Lilly, Elizabeth	FL0680	Lindsay, Julia	MI0250
Leyrer, Linda	CA0815	Lillya, Ann	GA0050	Lindsay, Priscilla	MI2100
Leyrer-Furumoto, Linda	CA2390	Lim, Benedict	CA1250	Lindsay, Tedrin Blair	KY1450
Leyva, Jesse	IL3300	Lim, Benedict M.	CA1020	Lindsey, A. Lish	PA3700
Lezcano, Jose	NH0150	Lim, Chan Kiat	LA0760	Lindsey, Douglas	GA1150
L'Hommedieu, Randi L.	MI0400	Lim, Cheryl	IL1085	Lindsey, Gerald	NY0646
Li, Bichuan	HI0210	Lim, Cheryl	IL3550	Lindsey, John R.	NY3780
Li, Chi	CA5031	Lim, Christine	IL1520	Lindsey, Lauren	WV0050
Li, Chihwei	NY4050	Lim, Hayoung Audrey	TX2250	Lindsey, Logan	WV0050
Li, Darren Si-Yan	IN0910	Lim, Jennifer	MO1250	Lindsey, Roberta	IN0907
Li, Hanna Wu	PA0550	Lim, Malcolm	AA0050	Lindstrom, G. Mikael	AR0900
Li, Honggang	NJ0800	Lim, Margaret	NE0100	Linduska, Mary	CA5510
Li, Juan	MN0250	Lim, Mi-Na	TX0345	Linduska, Mary	CA2975
Li, Lei	IL0650	Lim, Michael	WA0200	Lineberger, Rhonda	WA1100
Li, Li	IN0100	Lim, Philip 'Jay Jay'	CA2100	Linehan, Wayne	MS0400
Li, Lin	NY5000	Lim, Rachel	AL0800	Lines, Carol F.	LA0350
Li, Nina	AL0010	Lim, Sangmi	MI1400	Linford, Jon	ID0060
Li, Ping-Hui	PR0150	Lim, Tze Yean	OH1450	Lingen, Peter	IA0950
Li, Simon	NY2900	Lim, Yoon-Mi	TX2600	Lingren, Allison	NE0200
Li, Tai-Wai	AK0100	Lima, Deloise	FL0850	Lington, Aaron	CA4400
Li, Teng	AG0450	Limb, Christine M.	PA2000	Lington, Victoria	CA0900
Li, Weigang	NY0150	Limbert, Thom	IN0910	Lington, Victoria	CA4400
Li, Weigang	NJ0800	Limina, David	MA0260	Linhart, Patricia M.	OH2200
Li-Bleuel, Linda	SC0400	Limutau, Jacosa	CA0150	Linial, Christine A.	TX3530
Liang, Lei	CA5050	Lin, Anthea	OK1250	Link, Dorothea	GA2100
Liao, Amber Yiu-Hsuan	UT0190	Lin, C.	CA1950	Link, Jeffrey	MA0280
Liao, Chien-Ju	OH2200	Lin, Chen-Chi	IN0005	Link, John	NJ1400
Liaropoulos, Panagiotis	MA0260	Lin, ChiaHui	CA0830	Link, Nathan	KY0450
Liaropoulos, Panagiotis	MA2010	Lin, Chien-Kwan	NY1100	Link, Stan	TN1850
Lias, Stephen J.	TX2700	Lin, Ching Yi	KY1550	Linke, David	WI0825
Libal-Smith, Marie	PA3650	Lin, Chloe	MO0060	Linkins, Jean Ellen	SC0050
Libby, Amos	ME0150	Lin, Cho-Liang	TX2150	Linklater, Fraser	AC0100
Libby, Cynthia Green	MO0775	Lin, Cho-Liang	NY1900	Linklater, Joan	AC0100
Libera, Rebecca	NC2500	Lin, Denny	CA2420	Linn, Don	KS0650
Liberatore, John	NY4150	Lin, Gloria	TX3000	Linn, Richard	NJ1050
Liberatore, William	CA3270	Lin, Hsaio-Ling	CO0800	Linnartz, Elizabeth Byrum	NC0600
Libertini, Richard	CA3800	Lin, Hsin Yi	TX2930	Linnenbom, Harriett	MD0700
Libertino, Dan	CA2960	Lin, Hui-Mei	CT0300	Linnerooth, Sherry	MT0200
Libin, Kathryn L.	NY4450	Lin, I-Bei	HI0050	Linney, Lloyd	FL1750
Libonati, Dana	OR0450	Lin, I-Bei	HI0210	Linney, William E.	VA1350
LiCalzi, Gary	NY1400	Lin, James	CA5510	Linsley, Troy	AJ0150
Licata, Julie M.	NY3765	Lin, Jasmine	IL0550	Linsner, Arthur F.	IL2150
Licata, Thomas V.	NC0050	Lin, Jolie	MD0650	Linstrom, Tracie	CA5400
Lichten, Julia	NY3785	Lin, Joseph	NY1900	Linton, Andrew	TN0850
Lichten, Julia	NY2150	Lin, Kelvin	IL3370	Linton, Deborah	AG0050
Lichti, Daniel	AG0600	Lin, Lucia	MA0400	Linton, Larry	MD0300
Lichtmann, Jay	CT0650	Lin, Mei-Fang	TX3200	Linton, Michael	TN1100
Liddell, Catherine	MA0400	Lin, Melissa	CA4425	Lintz, David	PA3000
Lidge, Kenneth	MO1810	Lin, Ruth	MN0750	Lintz, David	PA3580
Lidov, David	AG0650	Lin, Swang	TX3000	Linwood, William	AB0150
Lidral, Karel	ME0440	Lin, Tao	FL1125	Lion, Na'ama	MA1175
Liebenow, Marcia Henry	IL0400	Lin, Victor	NY4200	Lion, Na'ama	MA0250
Liebergen, Patrick	WI0855	Linahon, Jim	CA1900	Lionello, Cathy	CA2100
Lieberman, Amy	MA1400	Linard, Rita A.	TX3530	Lionti, Victor C.	NY2200
Lieberman, Barry	WA1050	Linares, Adriana	PA1750	Liotta, Vincent J.	IN0900
Lieberman, Bernard	NY2750	Linch-Parker, Sheryl	NC0800	Liotti, Ernest J.	MD0650
Lieberman, Carol	MA0700	Lincoln, Harry B.	NY3705	Lipa, Noella P.	MD0475
Lieberman, Fredric	CA5070	Lincoln-DeCusatis, Nathan J.	WV0550	Lipari, Robert	NY1400
Liebhaber, Barbara	PA2550	Lind, Loren N.	PA3250	Lipartito, Robert	NJ1050
Liebman, David	NY2150	Lind, Robin A.	PA3650	Lipe, Anne	VA1350
Liebowitz, Marian L.	CA4100	Lind, Stephanie	AG0250	Liperote, Kathy	NY1100
Liedtke, Kris	WI0750	Lind, Vicki R.	AR0750	Lipke, William A.	CO0050
Liefer, David	NJ1350	Lindahl, Robert	MI0400	Lipke-Perry, Tracy D.	MN1600

Alphabetical Listing of Faculty

Name	Code	Name	Code	Name	Code
Lipkens, Kirsten	MA1350	Livermore, Allen	MA0280	Loewen, Judy	AA0020
Lipkin, Seymour	NY1900	Livesay, Charles	MI2000	Loewen, Laura	AC0100
Lipkin, Seymour	PA0850	Livesay, Jackie	MI0100	Loewen, Peter V.	TX2150
Lipkis, Larry	PA2450	Livesay, Yumi	CA6000	Loewenheim, Thomas	CA0810
Lipman, Agnes	AA0032	Livingston, Carolyn H.	RI0300	Loewy, Andrea Kapell	LA0760
Lipman, Michael	PA0600	Livingston, Christi J.	CO0350	Loewy, Donna S.	OH2200
Lipman, William	TX0550	Livingston, Don	MN0610	Loewy, Susanna L.	PA1750
Lipori, Daniel	WA0050	Livingston, Edwin U.	CA5300	Loffler, Robert	MO0775
Lipp, Carolyn	MI0500	Livingston, Jaie	WA0700	Lofgren, Ronald R.	NE0700
Lippard, Erin	TX2710	Livingston, Jane	WI0250	Lofquist, Louise H.	CA3600
Lippard, Michael S.	TX2710	Livingston, Jannine	CA3750	Lofsky, Lorne	AG0650
Lippe, Cort	NY4320	Livingston, Larry J.	CA5300	Lofstrom, Douglas	IL0720
Lippens, Nancy Cobb	IN0800	Livingston, Lavinia	CA0400	Lofthouse, Charity	NY1550
Lippincott, Tom	FL0700	Livingston, Lillian	NJ1350	Loftus, Jean	NY2950
Lippoldt-Mack, Valerie	KS0210	Livingston-Friedley, Diana	ID0100	Logan, Beverly	OH0050
Lippstrew, Lee	CO0600	Livingston-Hakes, Beth	AZ0490	Logan, Brian	KY1425
Lipscomb, Janice	AL0850	Lizama, Joe	CA1850	Logan, Cameron	CT0600
Lipscomb, Ronald	PA1000	Lizotte, Caroline	AI0200	Logan, Christopher	CT0050
Lipscomb, Ronald	PA1150	Lizotte, Caroline	AI0150	Logan, Elizabeth	SD0200
Lipscomb, Scott D.	MN1623	Llewellyn, Cherrie	CA3000	Logan, Hal	OR1100
Lipsett, Robert	CA1075	Llewellyn, Raymond	CA0815	Logan, Jennifer	CA3300
Lipsey, Michael S.	NJ0800	Lloyd, Charles	LA0700	Logan, Joseph C.	NC0050
Lipsey, Michael	NY0642	Lloyd, Deborah F.	DC0170	Logan, Kenneth	MI0250
Lipsius, Fred	MA0260	Lloyd, Gerald J.	MA2030	Logan, Laura	TX3000
Liptak, David	NY1100	Lloyd, Joe	AZ0400	Logan, Norman	ID0250
Lipton, Jamie	AR0300	Lloyd, Keith	TX0900	Logan, P. Bradley	MN0150
Lipton, Jeffrey S.	NY1275	Lloyd, Kimcherie	KY1500	Logan, Roger	MT0400
Lipton, John	OR0175	Lloyd, L. Keith	TX1650	Logan, Shelly	WA0450
Lipton, Kay	TX3175	Lloyd, Leslie	KY1550	Logan, Susan	MT0175
Lirette, Charles	PA1050	Lloyd, Peter	CA1075	Logan, Susan	MT0350
Lis, Anthony	SD0550	Lloyd, Thomas	PA1500	Logozzo, Derrick	TX0700
Lischetti, Robert	FL1745	Lloyd, William	CO0150	Logsdon, Anthony	AL0500
Lisek, Carol A.	CA3500	Llyod, Adam	FL1550	Logue, James	NE0400
Lishman, Steve	CA0150	Lo Verde, Carol	IL0720	Lohman, Al	MO0200
Lisicky, Sandra	MD0650	Lo, Adrian	MN0200	Lohman, Gregg	TN1400
Lisius, Peter	OH1100	Lo, Wei-Chun Bernadette	TN1800	Lohman, Laura Ann	CA0815
Liske, Kenneth L.	WI0830	Loach, Deborah	AL1160	Lohninger, Elisabeth	NY2660
Lisovskaya-Sayevich, Lolita	MO1000	LoBalbo, Anthony C.	NY3500	Lohorn, Michiko	CA4100
Liss, Ann Marie	CO0200	Loban, John A.	AB0100	Lohr, Tom L.	NC1300
Lissance, Alizon J.	MA0260	Lobenstein, David	NY0050	Lohr, Tom L.	NC1750
Lissemore, Richard	NY2750	Lobitz, Beverly	AR0800	Lohuis, Ardyth J.	VA1600
List, Andrew	MA0260	Lobitz, Kristi	CA1750	Lokken, Fred	WA0860
Lister, Linda J.	NV0050	Lobitz, Kristi	CA3500	Loman, Janet	NM0310
Lister, Michael C.	NY0700	Lobitz, Kristi	CA2800	Loman, Judy	PA0850
Lister, Rebecca Crow	PA1900	Lobotzke, Ann	WI0825	Loman, Judy	AG0450
Lister, Rodney	MA0400	Loch, Kim	OH2300	Loman, Judy	AG0300
Lister-Sink, Barbara	NC2205	Lochhead, Judith	NY3790	Lomazov, Marina	SC1110
Liston, Robin	KS0050	Lochrie, Daniel	TN0100	Lombard, Becky	GA2050
Litch, Randy	WA0750	Lochstampfor, Mark L.	OH0350	Lombard, Becky	LA0400
Litera, Ina	NY0270	Lock, William R.	CA0350	Lombardi, Paul	SD0600
Litke, David	AG0550	Lockard, Douglas T.	TX0600	Lombardi, Paul	NM0450
Litke, Sheila	KS1300	Lockard-Zimmerman, Barbara	OH0300	Lombardo, Jonathan R.	NY4320
Litroff, Scott	NY0050	Lockart, Carol	CA3100	Lonardo, Tom	TN1380
Littel, Sue	MI1850	Lockart, Carol	CA5360	Lonati, Marianne	MA0750
Litteral, Ron	UT0190	Lockart, Rob R.	CA0835	London, Amy	NY2660
Litterick, Louise	MA1350	Locke, Benjamin R.	OH1200	London, Betsy	CA4700
Little, David	VA1350	Locke, Brian	IL3500	London, Edwin	OH0650
Little, David	MI2250	Locke, David	MA1900	London, Frank	NY3785
Little, Deanna	TN1100	Locke, Douglas	OH2050	London, Justin	MN0300
Little, Donald C.	TX3420	Locke, Gary	CA3800	London, Larry	CA2950
Little, Gwenlynn	AG0500	Locke, Joe	NY2150	London, Lawrence	CA3320
Little, Jeannie E.	LA0200	Locke, John R.	NC2430	London, Robert	AZ0470
Little, John A.	VA0600	Locke, John G.	MD0650	London, Todd	TN0100
Little, Julie Evans	MI2250	Locke, Ralph P.	NY1100	Long, Arlene	TX2930
Little, Lynn	WI0300	Locke, Randolph	FL0680	Long, Barry	PA0350
Little, Margaret	AI0200	Locke, Scott A.	KY0950	Long, Bill	SC0900
Little, Marica	GA2000	Locke, Sheila	CA3800	Long, Bill	AR0100
Little, Ricky R.	KY0900	Locker, Fred	OH2150	Long, Bob	MO0850
Little, Robert	DC0170	Lockert, Daniel	CA3270	Long, Daniel	TX2200
Little, Steve	IL0300	Lockery, Glen	ID0250	Long, David	GA0600
Little, Steve	IA0050	Lockett, Bonnie	CA1650	Long, David J.	VA1475
Littleford, James	AB0100	Lockett, Wendelyn	WI0050	Long, Derle R.	LA0770
Littler, William	AG0300	Lockhart, Carolyn	CA4400	Long, Gail	IL2970
Littley, Marcia De Arias	FL0700	Locklair, Dan	NC2500	Long, Gary	CA0845
Littrell, David	KS0650	Lockwood, Gayle	UT0050	Long, Gilbert	TN1850
Litvin, Michail	WI1150	Lockwood, John	MA1175	Long, Janet	SC0900
Litzelman, James	DC0050	Lockwood, John K.	MA0260	Long, Jason	PA2450
Liu, Adam	PA1050	Lockwood, John	MA1400	Long, Jeremy A.	OH1450
Liu, Hsien-Ping	IN0005	Lockwood, Kathryn	MA2000	Long, John M.	AL1050
Liu, Hui	CA0830	Lockwood, Shannon	FL1000	Long, Kenneth A.	GA1050
Liu, Kexi	MO0800	Lockwood, Timothy	AG0550	Long, Kevin	IL1750
Liu, Lei	FL2050	Lockwood, Tom	MI0300	Long, Lillian F.	WV0050
Liu, Meng-Chieh	IL0550	Lockwood, Tom	MI1050	Long, Louanne J.	CA5150
Liu, Meng-Chieh	PA0850	Lockwood, Tom	MI0900	Long, Michael	IN0900
Liu, Pei-Fen	NC0600	Lockwood, Tom	MI1000	Long, Michael P.	NY4320
Liu, Rong-Huey	CA2420	Loden, Larry D.	TX3410	Long, Nolan W.	OH2120
Liu, Si-Cheng	FL0680	Loden, Larry	TX1900	Long, Patrick A.	PA3150
Liu, Si-Cheng	FL0500	Lodine, Emily	IA1200	Long, Rebecca	NC1250
Liu, Solungga Fang-Tzu	OH0300	Loeb, David	NV0050	Long, Ron	AA0020
Liu, Susan (Shao-Shan)	TX1425	Loeb, David	NY2250	Long, Timothy G.	NY3790
Liu, Te-Chiang	MN1600	Loeb, Jaemi	KY0450	Long, Wallace H.	OR1300
Liu, Vivian	CA0960	Loeffert, Jeffrey	OK0800	Longer-Schreck, Corlyn	MI0520
Liu, Xiu-ru	PA1050	Loeffler, Rodney J.	MN1280	Longfield, Richard O.	AZ0510
Liu, Yang	IL0550	Loehnig, Grant A.	TX2150	Longhi, Ami	AA0050
Liu-Rosenbaum, Aaron	AI0190	Loehrke, John	NJ0975	Longhin, Daniel	MI0750
Liuzzi, Don	PA0850	Loeppky, Ian R.	AL1250	Longo, Tatiana	NY5000
Liva, Ferdinand R.	ME0500	Loera, Francisco	TX3525	Longoria, Cynthia	TX0550
Liva, Victor H.	OH0650	Loerch, Suzanne	AR0850	Longshore, Terry	OR0950
Lively, Judy	AZ0400	Loewen, Che Anne	AG0450	Longtin, Michel	AI0200
Livengood, Lee	UT0400	Loewen, Harris	AG0050	Longworth, Peter	AG0300

Lonich, Nancy L.	PA0500	Louder, Earle	KY1350	Lubben, Joseph	OH1700
Loo, Janet	AG0500	Loughman, Greg	ME0200	Lubet, Alex	MN1623
Loo, Ronald	HI0300	Loughman, Greg	ME0150	Lubiarz, Stephen	AA0050
Looker, Wendy	NC0910	Loughman, Greg	ME0340	Lubin, Howard	OH1700
Looking Wolf, Jan Michael	OR0700	Loughran, Robert	NJ1350	Lubin, Renee	CA4200
Loomer, Deborah W.	SC1200	Loughrige, Chad	OH0350	Lubin, Steven	NY3785
Loomis, Joy	FL2130	Louie, Bonnie	AA0050	Lubke, Sarah	IA1170
Loomis, Melinda	OR0600	Louie, David	AG0300	Lubman, Bradley	NY1100
Loong, ChetYeng	HI0210	Louie, Gary	MD0650	Luby, Richard E.	NC2410
Loos, Brandon	FL1700	Louis, Kenneth	DC0350	Luca, Nancy	CA2550
Loos, James C.	IA0420	Louise-Turgeon, Anne	FL0650	Luca, Sergiu	TX2150
Loparits, Elizabeth	NC2440	Loup, Francois	MD0650	Lucarelli, Bert	NY0500
Lopato, David	NJ0800	Louprette, Renee A.	NJ0800	Lucarelli, Humbert	NY2750
Lopato, David	NY2660	Loushin, Boris M.	NY3780	Lucarelli, Humbert	NY3785
Lopes, Gerald	CA0150	Louth, Joseph Paul	OH2600	Lucarelli, Humbert	CT0650
Lopez Yanez, Ruth	CA3460	Louwenaar, Karyl	FL0850	Lucas, Adonna	NC1950
Lopez, Barbara	CA0400	Lovallo, Lee T.	CA3258	Lucas, Ann E.	MA0500
Lopez, Catherine	WI1150	Lovano, Joe S.	NY2750	Lucas, Ann D.	CA0100
Lopez, Christine Sotomayor	CA0859	Lovano, Joe	MA0260	Lucas, April	NY3705
Lopez, David F.	CA0859	Lovato, James	NM0400	Lucas, Don	MA0400
Lopez, Eduardo	OK1350	Love, Diana	WV0750	Lucas, Elena	MA0260
Lopez, Emmanuel	TX3750	Love, Jason L.	MD1000	Lucas, Heidi	MS0750
Lopez, Fabian E.	NC2430	Love, Lisa Reagan	OK0750	Lucas, James A.	IL2150
Lopez, Faye	SC0200	Love, Maurice	CA2550	Lucas, M. Jayne	PA3500
Lopez, George	ME0200	Love, Randall M.	NC0600	Lucas, Mark	OK1350
Lopez, Hiram	PR0100	Love, Randolph D.	SC0600	Lucas, Michael	CO0625
Lopez, Ilca	PR0115	Love, Shirley	NY5000	Lucas, William G.	MI2100
Lopez, Joel H.	TX3410	Lovejoy, Donald G.	MN1700	Luce, Brian A.	AZ0500
Lopez, John A.	TX3175	Lovelace, Jason R.	DC0050	Lucente, Jill	NY2450
Lopez, Jose R.	FL0700	Lovelace, Timothy	MN1623	Lucernoni Haasler, JoAnn	WI1150
Lopez, Kenneth	CA5300	Lovelady, Hugh	AZ0440	Lucero, Kerry	AZ0150
Lopez, Michael	NC0450	Lovell, Owen C.	WI0803	Luchansky, Andrew	CA4150
Lopez, Richard	OH0850	Lovell, Stephanie	CA5150	Luchansky, Andrew	CA0840
Lopez, Richard C.	OH2050	Lovely, Aaron	MD0300	Luchese, Diane	MD0850
Lopez, Robert	TX3175	Lovely, Brian	OH0680	Luchs, Nicole	IL2050
Lopez, Sarah	CA2960	Lovely, Christopher	AL1195	Luchsinger, Brenda	AL0050
Lopez, Tewanta	IA1300	Lovely, Valerie	MA0260	Lucia, Joyce	MA0260
Lopez, Thomas Handman	OH1700	Lovensheimer, James A.	TN1850	Lucia, Margaret E.	PA3050
Lopez, Zoraida	PR0115	Lovett, Rita	LA0750	Luciani, Dante T.	FL1900
Lopez-Gonzalez, Monica	MD0650	Lovinsky, Joseph	DC0150	Luciano, Stephen	FL1700
Lopez-Trujillo, David	TX3515	Low, David G.	NE0610	Lucie, Edwin J.	MA0260
LoPiccolo, John	ID0100	Low, Linda	AB0210	Lucier, Alvin	CT0750
LoPiccolo, Joseph	CA1265	Low, Murray	CA4900	Lucini, Alejandro	DC0100
LoPiccolo, Joseph	CA3200	Low, Todd K.	NY1600	Lucius, Sue Anne	AZ0440
Lopinski, Janet	AG0300	Lowder, Jerry E.	OH1850	Luck, Kyle	CA3500
LoPresti, Kathleen M.	FL1550	Lowe, Cameron	AJ0100	Luckey, Robert	LA0760
Lorance, Elana	MA0510	Lowe, Carol C.	NY3780	Luckhardt, Jerry	MN1623
Loranger, Dennis	OH2500	Lowe, David	KS0700	Luckner, Brian	WI1100
Loranger, Gene	ID0075	Lowe, Donald R.	GA2100	Lucktenberg, George	GA1700
Lorbeer, James	CA0815	Lowe, Edward	TX3450	Lucktenberg, Kathryn	OR1050
Lorch, Kimberly	GA0500	Lowe, Emily	FL0730	Lucky, Harrell C.	TX0700
Lorcini, Marie	AG0200	Lowe, Frederick W.	IL1615	Ludemann, Hans	PA3200
Lord, Albert P.	NJ0800	Lowe, Laurence	UT0050	Ludolph, Deborah	AG0600
Lord, Billy Jean	AZ0150	Lowe, Malcolm	MA1175	Ludovico, Vincent	NY2950
Lord, Robert S.	PA3420	Lowe, Malcolm	MA0400	Ludowise, Kathleen D.	CA4425
Lord, Roger	AE0100	Lowe, Malcolm	MA1400	Ludwig, David	PA0850
Lord, Suzanne	IL2900	Lowe, Melanie D.	TN1850	Ludwig, Mary	NC0450
Lord-Powell, Karen	KY0250	Lowe, Nina Kay	TX3400	Ludwig, William	IN0900
Lordo, Jacqueline L.	MO0100	Lowe, Phillip	TX0910	Luebke, Linda M.	IN0800
Lorek, Mary Jo	MO1810	Lowe, Shannon R.	GA2150	Lueck, John	CO0250
Lorenz, James	FL0680	Lowell, Richard L.	MA0260	Luedders, Jerry D.	CA0835
Lorenz, Jim	FL0500	Lowenstein, Marc	CA0510	Luedloff, Brian Clay	CO0950
Lorenz, Kevin	NC1450	Lowenstein, Michael	NY2150	Luellen, Heather M.	MO0775
Lorenz, Michael L.	MI1950	Lowenthal, Jerome	NY1900	Luer, Thomas D.	CA0630
Lorenz, Nena	LA0900	Lowenthal, Richard	NJ0825	Lueschen, David	OH0700
Lorenz, Ralph	OH1100	Lower, Janna	FL1850	Lueth, Faith	MA0950
Lorenz, Ricardo	MI1400	Lower, Nancy	CA3850	Lueth, Faith	MA0260
Lorenz, Shanna	CA3300	Lowery, Christopher	IL1520	Luethi, Dean A.	WA1150
Lorenzetti, Kristen	NJ0700	Lowery, Daryl	MA0260	Luffey, Gregory	TX3520
Lorenzino, Lisa	AI0150	Lowezyk, Victoria	IL2775	Luftman, Adam	CA5000
Lorenzo, Benjamin	OK0800	Lowi, Ralph	CA4410	Luftman, Adam	CA4200
Lorenzo, Donna A.	NY1700	Lowrey, Alden	AA0020	Luftman, Adam	CA4150
Lorenzo, Elizabeth	CT0300	Lowrey, Alvin	AA0035	Luggie, Brenda	TN1250
Lorenzo, Elizabeth	CT0050	Lowrey, Alvin	AA0100	Lugo, Eddy	FL1650
Lorimer, Christopher	IL3550	Lowrey, Ariane	AA0020	Lugo, Edward	FL0930
Loring, George	NH0150	Lowrey, Ariane	AA0035	Lugo, Edward	FL0800
Lornell, Christopher 'Kip'	DC0100	Lowrey, Norman E.	NJ0300	Lugo, Noemi	KY1450
Lorrey, Haidee	MA0260	Lowry, Carol S.	TN1680	Luiken, Jennifer	SC0275
Lortie, Dominique	AI0150	Lowry, David	SC0600	Luise, Evelyn J.	PA3250
Lortz, Mark E.	MD0520	Lowry, Douglas	NY1100	Lujan, Bethany	FL1500
Lorusso, James	NY2450	Lowry, Gary	OR0250	Luk, Siu Yan	NY2500
Lorusso, James	NY2200	Lowry, Julie	GA2130	Lukas, Kathryn	IN0900
Lorusso, James	NY5000	Lowry, Lisa M.	IN1800	Lukas, Linda D.	CA4200
Lorusso, Mary Ann	NY2400	Lowry, Lisa	IN1850	Luke, Nadine	ID0060
Losada, Cristina Catherine	OH2200	Lowry, Paul	IL2050	Luker, Morgan James	OR0900
Losey, Mary	SC1100	Loy, David	MD0300	Lukiwski, Terry	AG0450
Lothringer, Peter	MN1500	Loy, Susan	PA3710	Luko, Alexis	AG0100
Lotsberg, Carl	AA0100	Loza, Steven	CA5031	Lukowicz, Thomas	OH2500
Lotspeich, Melissa	TX3527	Lozano, Danilo	CA0830	Lukowicz, Thomas	OH1100
Lott, Marian J.	OH2150	Lozano, Danilo	CA6000	Lulloff, Joseph	MI1400
Lott, Peter Tell	AL0010	Lozano, Denise	NY2450	Lum, Anne Craig	HI0150
Lott, R. Allen	TX2600	Lozano, Frank	AI0150	Lum, David	AG0650
Lotter, Rich	CA0840	Lozano, Sal	CA0825	Lum, Gloria	CA3300
Lotter, Rick	CA0150	Lu, Alex	CA1960	Lum, Richard	HI0210
Lotz, James	TN1450	Lu, Jie	UT0250	Lum, Tammy K.	NY2900
Lou, Dorothy	AA0020	Lu, Ning	UT0250	Lumpkin, Royce E.	NC2420
Loubriel, Luis E.	IL0275	Lu, Yuan Xiong	TX3000	Lumpkin, William	MA0400
Louchouarn, Bruno E.	CA3300	Lualdi, Brenda	IL0850	Lumsden, Rachel	OK1350
Loucky, David L.	TN1100	Luangkesorn, Sha	PA1350	Luna, Audrey	OH1450
Loudenback, Daniel	TX1850	Lubaroff, Scott C.	MO1790	Lund, Erik R.	IL3300

Name	Code	Name	Code	Name	Code
Lund, Henriette	DC0050	Lynch, Kelly Fiona	PA3000	MacDonald, Ken	AC0100
Lund, Kara	RI0200	Lynch, Kelly	PA0600	MacDonald, Kirk	AG0450
Lund, Matthew R.	TN1100	Lynch, Kendra	CA0630	MacDonald, Laurence E.	MI0450
Lund, Steve	MN0050	Lynch, Kendra	CA2650	MacDonald, Lorna E.	AG0450
Lund, Steven	MN0800	Lynch, Phil	WA1100	MacDonald, Mary Carla	MA0150
Lundak, Gayle	IA0420	Lynch, Phil	WA1300	MacDonald, Michael	MD0650
Lundberg, Erika	MN1100	Lynch, Shane	VA1850	MacDonald, Michael	AA0100
Lundberg, Kim	AG0500	Lynch, Timothy	CA1290	MacDonald, Pamela	AF0120
Lundberg, Steve	IA1100	Lynch, W. David	NC1300	MacDonald, Payton	NJ1400
Lundberg, Susan	CA0800	Lyndon-Gee, Christopher	NY0050	MacDonald, R. Richard	MN1700
Lundblad, Genevieve	MD0450	Lynerd, Betty Ann	IL1850	MacDonald, Robert M.	FL0800
Lundeen, Douglas	NJ1130	Lynn, Catherine D.	GA1150	MacDonald, Scott	AF0120
Lundergan, Edward	NY3760	Lynn, Daniel	NE0550	MacDonald, Scott	PA1550
Lundgren, Karen E.	CA0630	Lynn, Debra J.	IN1050	MacDougall, Elizabeth	CA2840
Lundholm, Susan L.	IL0650	Lynn, Kathie	OH1700	MacDougall, Tim	CA0825
Lundholm, Susan	IL1085	Lynn, Mark J.	KY1500	MacEachen, Ed	NY2660
Lundin, Claudia	GA0850	Lynn, Mark J.	KY1500	Macek, Timothy A.	DC0150
Lundin, Paul	WI0300	Lynn, Michael	OH1700	Macelaru, Cristian	TX2150
Lundquist, Barbara Reeder	WA1050	Lynn, Robert	IN0700	Macerollo, Joseph	AG0450
Lundy, Alexis	GA1070	Lynn, Sarah B.	TX3410	Macey, Patrick	NY1100
Lundy, Ann	TX3150	Lyon, Howard	PA1200	MacFarlane, Thomas	NY2750
Lundy, Joyce	DC0170	Lyon, James	PA2750	MacGilliviray, Rod	AF0120
Lunn, Robert A.	MI1180	Lyon, Kristine	IL1650	MacGillivray, Louise	CA0550
Lunsetter, Gene	MN1270	Lyon, Leslie	TX2200	MacGregor, Barbara J.	OH2150
Lunte, Sandra K.	LA0770	Lyon, Leslie	TX1900	Mach, Elyse J.	IL2150
Luo, Mei Mei	FL0200	Lyon, Matthew	IN0150	Machado, Marcos	MS0750
Lupanu, Calin	NC0850	Lyon, Taylene	AA0040	Machala, Kazimierz W.	IL3300
Luperi, Victoria	TX3510	Lyon, William	TX3800	Machavariani, David	IN1750
Luperi, Victoria	TX3000	Lyons, David P.	IL2900	Machleder, Anton	NY2500
Lupica, Anthony J.	CA1700	Lyons, Glenn	PA3600	Machleder, Anton M.	NY1700
Lupien, Denise	AI0150	Lyons, Greg	LA0250	Machlin, Paul S.	ME0250
Lupinski, Rudy	OK0300	Lyons, James H.	MD0350	Machold, William	IL2450
Lupis, Giuseppe	MI0900	Lyons, Lisanne	FL0700	Machold, William	MO0300
Lupo, Michael	NY0630	Lyons, Lisanne E.	FL1900	Machon, Allen	MA0600
Lupu, Sherban	IL3300	Lyons, Lyndel	AL0530	MacHose, Kathleen	CT0650
Lupu, Virgil I.	OH2140	Lyons, Matthew	MD0650	MacInnes, James	SD0500
Lurie, Kenneth P.	NC0050	Lyons, Robert	MA1450	MacInnes, Scott	AB0150
Luscher, Alexia	HI0050	Lyons, Shawn	AK0100	MacInnis, John	IA0500
Luscombe, Greg	TN1660	Lyras, Panayis	MI1400	MacIntyre, Bruce C.	NY0500
Lushtak, Faina	LA0750	Lyren, Delon	MN0150	MacIntyre, Bruce C.	NY0600
Lusk, Mark Lancaster	PA2750	Lysenko, Boris	AG0450	MacIntyre, David K.	AB0080
Lusk, Terry	OH2200	Lysinger, Catherine	TX2400	Mack, Ashlee	IL1350
Lusmann, Stephen	MI2100	Lysloff, Rene T.A.	CA5040	Mack, Dianne	TX3150
Lussier, Mathieu	AI0150	Lysy, Antonio	CA5030	Mack, Ellen	MD0650
Lussier, Matthieu	AI0200	Lytle, Cecil W.	CA5050	Mack, Evan	NY3650
Lust, Patricia D.	VA0700	Lytle, Gwendolyn L.	CA3650	Mack, George	RI0200
Lustig, Andrea	NJ1050	Lytle, Gwendolyn	CA1050	Mack, James	CA1750
Lustig, Raymond J.	NY1900	Lytle, Stephen	OH1450	Mack, John	CA0960
Lustrea, Robert	IL0850	Lyttle, Eric	VA0250	Mack, Jonathan	CA5100
Lustrea, Robert	IL3150	M. de Oca, Patricia	TX3520	Mack, Jonathan	CA6000
Lutch, Mitchell	IA0700	Ma, Shuhui Nettie	MO2000	Mack, Kyle	ND0350
Lutch, Mitchell B.	IA0200	Ma, Yunn-Shan	NY1550	Mack, Peter	WA0200
Lute, Charles	PA1200	Maahs, Kristin	IA0700	Mack, Rodney	PA3250
Luther, David	TN0200	Maalouf, Janet	DC0110	Mack, William G.	MO0850
Luther, Sigrid	TN0200	Maas, Dan	CA3000	Mack-Bervin, Linda	CO0350
Luthra, Arun	NY2660	Maas, Martha C.	OH1850	MacKay, Gillian	AG0450
Lutnes, Patricia	CT0800	Maaser, Leslie G.	OH0850	MacKay, James S.	LA0300
Lutow, Justyna	SD0500	Mabary, Judith A.	MO1800	MacKay-Galbraith, Janet	IN0700
Lutsyshyn, Oksana	VA1000	Mabbs, Linda	MD1010	Mackenzie, Barbara Dobbs	NY0600
Lutter, Lisa	NJ0950	Mabee, Patricia	CA1075	MacKenzie, David	VT0200
Luttinger, Elizabeth	CA0960	Mabee, Patricia	CA0510	Mackey, Lynne A.	VA0300
Luttmann, Stephen	CO0950	Mabern, Harold	NJ1400	Mackey, Melissa A.	IL2900
Luttrell, Carol	PA3330	Mabrey, Charlotte	FL1950	Mackey, Richard	MA0400
Luttrell, Matthew	TX3500	Mabrey, Paul	OK1300	Mackey, Richard	MA1400
Luty, Christoph	CA1750	Mabry, Gary L.	TX3530	Mackey, Ryan	KS0215
Lutz, Daniel	MA2030	Mabry, Sharon	TN0050	Mackey, Steven	NJ0900
Lutz, Nina	GA2150	Macan, Ed	CA1280	Mackie, Doug	IA1450
Lutzke, Myron	NY2250	Macar, Robert	FL2050	Mackie, Henry	LA0800
Luu, Bing	CA4050	MaCaskie, Stuart	NM0450	Mackie-Jackson, Nadina	AG0450
Luxion, Dennis	IL0720	MacAulay, Suzanne	CO0810	Mackiewicz-Wolfe, Ewa	NY3705
Luxner, Michael	IL1750	MacAyeal, Gregory	IL2100	Mackin, Barbara J.	VA0550
Luzanac, Inna	AA0020	Macbride, David	CT0650	Mackin, Glenn	NY1100
Luzanac, Inna	AA0110	Maccaferri, Michael	VA1500	Mackle, Anne Kate	FL1650
Luzeniecki, Jerry	IL2300	MacCallum, Jeanette	TN0100	Macklin, Christopher B.	GA1300
Luzko, Daniel	CA2390	MacCallum, John	CA5000	Macklin, Thomas	FL1750
Lyashenko, Natalia E.	IL2250	MacCallum, John	MA1450	MacKown, Rosemary	PA3400
Lybarger, Lowell H.	AR0200	Macchia, Salvatore	MA2000	Macksoud, Mark G.	ME0250
Lychner, John	MI2250	Macchioni, Oscar E.	TX3520	Mackus, Boyd A.	OH0200
Lyddon, Paul W.	HI0210	MacConnell, Kevin	PA3330	MacLachlan, Heather M.	OH2250
Lydeen, Brian	WI0804	Maccow, Winston	MA0260	MacLaren, Robert	AC0100
Lydeen, Brian	WI0400	MacCrae, Cynthia Perry	AL1200	Maclary, Edward	MD1010
Lydy, Laura	IN0905	MacDonald, Andrew	AI0050	MacLaughlin, Heather	MN1260
Lyerla, Trilla R.	KS0050	MacDonald, April	AL0200	MacLean, Alasdair	AE0050
Lyke, Toby Russell	OH0680	MacDonald, Austin	NC1300	MacLean, Sherry	FL0150
Lykes, Karen S.	OH2200	MacDonald, Ben	WI0810	MacLean, Stephen	MA0260
Lyle, Anne K.	IL1350	MacDonald, Campbell	IN0905	MacLeod, Rebecca	NC2430
Lyle, Susan	SC0650	Macdonald, Claudia	OH1700	MacLeod, Scott	NC0350
Lyman, Anne E.	WA1000	MacDonald, Colin	AB0050	MacMasters, Dan	MO0200
Lyman, Jeffrey	MI2100	Macdonald, David	AG0150	MacMillan, Ann E.	TX3420
Lyman, Kent M.	NC1300	Macdonald, David	NY2150	MacMillan, Betsy	AI0150
Lyman, Kristin M.	GA0500	MacDonald, Don	AB0070	MacMillan, Robin	AC0100
Lyman, Rebecca	ID0060	MacDonald, Earl M.	CT0600	Macmillan, Scott	AF0100
Lyman, Zachary	WA0650	MacDonald, Elizabeth	ME0440	MacMorran, Sande	TN1710
Lynam, Charles A.	NC2430	Macdonald, Elizabeth	MO1900	MacMullen, Jeffrey	OH1200
Lynch, Brian	FL1900	MacDonald, J. Roderick	NY3725	MacMullen, Michael J.	FL1470
Lynch, Charles	IL2300	Macdonald, James	IL0850	MacMullin, Dennis	NJ0175
Lynch, Charles	IN1450	MacDonald, James M.	IL0720	MacNair, Alan	MI1750
Lynch, Charles	IN1750	MacDonald, James	AG0650	MacNaughton, Roger	MI0300
Lynch, Christopher	IN0350	MacDonald, John A.	OH2150	MacNeil, Anne E.	NC2410
Lynch, John P.	GA2100	MacDonald, Kathleen	MA0280	MacNeil, Robert	CA1000

Name	Code	Name	Code	Name	Code
Macomber, Curtis	NY2150	Mahadeen, Roger	NY2750	Malenich, Thomas	NY3790
Macomber, Curtis	NY1900	Mahady, Jim	DC0050	Maley, Marshall E.	VA1475
Macomber, Jeffrey R.	MO0800	Mahamuti, Gulimina	OH2000	Maley, Marshall	MD0700
Macomber, Scott	CA0150	Mahaney, Cynthia	OH1200	Malfatti, Dennis	IN1600
Macon, Connie	AL0800	Mahaney, Cynthia	OH1750	Malfitano, Catherine	NY2150
Macovei, Felix	CA5355	Mahany, Michael E.	AZ0510	Malfroid, Larry	MI1050
MacPhail, Heather	OH1450	Mahar, Bill	AI0150	Malicoate, Todd S.	OK0800
MacPhail, Jean	AG0450	Mahave-Veglia, Pablo	MI0900	Malin, Yonatan	CO0800
MacPhail, Jean	AG0300	Mahdi, Ronald O. A.	MA0260	Malinverni, Peter	NY3785
MacPhail, Valerie	SC0650	Mahe, Darren	AB0070	Malis, David H.	OK0800
MacPherson, Scott A.	OH1100	Maher, Betty	AG0350	Malito, Jim	AZ0490
MacPherson, William A.	MA2150	Maher, Dana F.	OK1450	Malkiewicz, Martha	NY0400
MacQueen, Yuki	UT0400	Maher, Donna	SC0700	Malkin, Isaac	NY2150
Macrae, Craig	MA0260	Maher, Donna	SC0050	Mallady, Joan	IL1890
MacWilliams, Brittany K.	KY1500	Maher, James	NJ1350	Mallak, Augustine	IL0275
Macy, Carleton	MN0950	Maher, John	IN1025	Mallard, Manley	IL1750
Macy, Elizabeth	CA5031	Maher, Michael	VA1350	Mallarino, Larry	CA2440
Macy, Elizabeth	CA0960	Mahiet, Damien	OH0850	Mallet, Alain	MA0260
Macy, John	CO0150	Mahin, Bruce P.	VA1100	Mallett, Lawrence R.	OK1350
Madama, Mark	MI2100	Mahinka, Janice	NY0625	Mallette, Marcelle	AI0150
Maday, Casey	IA0550	Mahon, Brad	AA0150	Malley, Kevin J.	IL1350
Madden, Andrew	NY2750	Mahon, Brad	AA0050	Malley, Nicole	IL1350
Madden, John	MI1400	Mahon, Maureen	NY2740	Mallia, John	MA1400
Maddison, Dorothy E.	VA0600	Mahoney, Billie	MO1810	Mallimo, Katherine	NJ0800
Maddox, Craig	FL1750	Mahoney, John A.	LA0300	Mallin, Claire	AF0050
Maddox, Eric	GA0550	Mahoney, Shafer	NY1900	Mallinger, Patrick	IN0005
Maddox, Harry	GA1700	Mahoney, Shafer	NY0625	Mallinson, Chai Kyou	NY3705
Maddox, Meredith R.	AR0750	Mahonske, Adam	MD0600	Mallon, Rachel	AG0500
Maddox, Nan	GA1700	Mahpar, Steven	CA0815	Mallory, Jason	IA0300
Maddox, Shelley	NC0400	Mahr, Jill	MN1450	Mallory, Joan	NY2900
Maddox, Timothy	NC1075	Mahr, Timothy	MN1450	Mallory, Keith	KS1000
Maddren, Chauncey	CA2750	Mahraun, Daniel A.	MN1120	Mallory, Marie	WV0800
Made Suparta, I Dewa	AI0200	Mahrenholz, Simone	AC0100	Malloy, Andrew	CA3600
Madeira, David	TN0100	Mahrt, William P.	CA4900	Malloy, Andrew Thomas	CA0835
Madej, Andrew	NY2105	Mahtani, Lorena	TX1425	Malloy, Chris	CO0900
Madeja, James T.	NY3780	Mahy, Daune	OH1700	Malloy, Michael	OH2275
Madison, Jeffrey	MN0250	Maiben, Dana	MA1175	Maloff, Nikolai	AB0100
Madison, Jeffrey W.	WI0860	Maiello, Anthony J.	VA0450	Malone, Joy	KY0800
Madison, Vicki	KY0950	Maiello, James V.	TN1850	Malone, Mark H.	MS0850
Madison-Cannon, Sabrina	MO1810	Maier, Lori	CA3600	Malone, Martha	GA1300
Madlangsakay, Roselle	CA4450	Maier, Ralph	AA0150	Malone, Michael J.	OH2000
Madole, Craig	TN1850	Maier, Ralph	AA0050	Malone, Patrick R.	FL0040
Madonia, Michael	IL2775	Mailman, Matthew	OK0750	Malone, Ryan M.	PA0350
Madrid, Albert	TX3527	Maimine, Anna	NY3717	Malone, Thomas	MA2030
Madriguera, Enric	TX0700	Maimonis, Nina	IL0850	Malone, William	CO0810
Madrya, Paul	AC0050	Main, Alexander	OH1850	Maloney, Chris	FL1450
Madsen, Brent	MD0350	Mainland, Timothy L.	WV0200	Maloney, Melissa	MI1750
Madsen, Charles A.	VT0100	Mains, Ronda	AR0700	Maloney, Patrick H.	IN1700
Madsen, Christopher	IL2250	Maiolo, Georgetta	NY3705	Maloney, Timothy	MN1623
Madsen, Clifford K.	FL0850	Maiolo, Georgetta	NY0350	Maloney-Titland, Patricia	NY3400
Madsen, Emily K.	MD0350	Mair, Jim	KS0590	Malott, Steve	WA0860
Madsen, Farrell D.	UT0300	Maisonpierre, Elizabeth	NC2435	Maloy, Kris	OK0750
Madsen, Jessica	IN0400	Maisonpierre, Jonathan	NC2435	Maloy, Rebecca	CO0800
Madsen, Pamela	CA0815	Maiullo, David	NJ0825	Malpede, William V.	CA0835
Madsen, Peter C.	NE0610	Majerfeld, Paula	MA1175	Malsky, Matthew	MA0650
Madura, John	TX3527	Major, Amy Gilreath	IL1150	Maltais, Helene	AI0200
Madura, Julie	MN0250	Major, Elizabeth	MI0050	Maltas, Carla Jo	MO1790
Madura, Melissa	TX3527	Major, James	OH1850	Maltese, John	AL0500
Maeda, Dana	MN1450	Major, James E.	IL1150	Maltester, Diane	CA0807
Maekane, Nachiko	NY3600	Major, Leon	MD1010	Maltester, Diane	CA2775
Maes, James	MA1100	Major, Marci L.	MO1800	Maltester, John	CA3920
Maestre, Janet M.	CA4900	Majors, Gayle	KY1425	Maltester, John	CA2775
Maffett, Jon D.	OH0700	Majoy, Jocelyn	OH1400	Maltz, Richard	SC1100
Magaldi, Cristina	MD0850	Makan, Keeril	MA1200	Malvern, Gary J.	SC0750
Magaziner, Elliot	NY2400	Makarina, Olga	NY0500	Malvinni, David J.	CA4410
Magaziner, Elliot	NY5000	Makas, George	IL1085	Malvinni, Valerie L.	CA4410
Magaziner, Sari	NY2400	Makeever, Gerald	MT0200	Malvinni, Valerie	CA5550
Magee, Chris	TX3350	Makela, Steven L.	MN0600	Malyshko, Olga	AG0250
Magee, Gayle Sherwood	IL3300	Maker, Bill	RI0200	Malyuk, Amy	OH2150
Magee, Jeffrey	IL3300	Maki, Daniel H.	IL0840	Mamey, Norman	CA1000
Magee, Robert G.	AR0950	Maki, David J.	IL2200	Mammon, Marielaine	NJ0250
Mager, Guillermo E.	CT0700	Maki, Erik	CA3000	Mamula, Stephen	RI0150
Magg, Susan A.	OH0680	Maki, Patricia	CA1750	Mamula, Stephen	RI0200
Maggio, Robert	PA3600	Maki, Paul-Martin	NY2150	Manabe, Noriko	NJ0900
Maggs, Patty J.	CA1900	Makris, Kristina	AZ0440	Manabe, Noriko	NY0500
Maginnis, Patrice	CA5070	Makubuya, James	IN1850	Manahan, George	NY2150
Magliocco, Hugo	IL1100	Malach, Robert	NJ0825	Manasia, Jeremy	NY2150
Maglione, Anthony	MO2000	Malafronte, Judith	CT0900	Manasse, Jon	FL1125
Magnani, Victor A.	NY0644	Malafronte, Judith	CT0850	Manasse, Jon	NY1100
Magnanini, Luciano	FL1900	Malaga, Ed	MD0750	Mance, Junior	NY2660
Magnarelli, Joe A.	NJ1130	Malaga, Edgaro	DC0010	Manceaux, Reese	NC2420
Magnarelli, Joe	NY1900	Malambri, William F.	SC1200	Manchester, John	MS0300
Magnarelli, Joe	NJ0825	Malamut, Myra Lewinter	NJ0550	Mancinelli, Judith	IL1750
Magney, Lucia	MN0350	Malan, Roy	CA5070	Mancini, David	TX2400
Magniere, Blaise	IL2200	Malas, Marlena Kleinman	NY1900	Mancini, Meredith	MD0550
Magnone, Steve	IL3200	Malas, Marlena K.	NY2150	Mancini, Nick	CA0835
Magnuson, John	TN0930	Malas, Marlena	PA0850	Mancino, Kim	NY3725
Magnuson, Phillip	OH2250	Malas, Spiro	NY2150	Mancusi, Roberto	TN1720
Magnussen, John P.	CA0835	Malatestinic, Patrice A.	NY3650	Mancuso, Charles	NY3717
Magnusson, Robert	CA4100	Malcher, Lindsay	SC0275	Mandat, Eric P.	IL2900
Magnusson, Robert	CA4050	Malde, Melissa	CO0950	Mandel, Alan	NY1550
Magoto, Travis	OH2140	Maldonado, Ana Marie	CA0630	Mandel, Alan R.	DC0010
Magrath, Jane	OK1350	Maldonado, Ana Maria	CA0845	Mandel, Jac	SC0620
Magrill, Samuel	OK1330	Maldonado, Anna Maria	CA0950	Mandel, Nathan	IL1740
Magruder, Michael	NC2700	Maldonado, Greg	CA0825	Mandelbaum, Joel	NY0642
Maguda, John	NY3725	Male, Sara	PA1250	Manderen, Michael	OH1700
Maguda, John K.	NY3717	Male, Sara	PA1300	Manderville, Kevin	AL0450
Maguire, George	CA4650	Malecki, Jeffrey	IL2650	Mandl, Alexander	WI0835
Magurany, John	IL1500	Malefyt, Norma	MI0350	Mandl, Alexander B.	WI1150
Magyar, Paul R.	TN0930	Malek, Eugenie	MA1350	Mandle, William Dee	DC0350

Alphabetical Listing of Faculty

Name	Code
Mandrell, Nelson E.	IL2150
Manduca, Mark W.	ME0500
Manes, Stephen G.	NY4320
Maness, David	PA1150
Maness, G. Andrew	MA0260
Maness, Jane	AG0350
Maness, Jane	AG0600
Manfredo, Joseph	IL1150
Mangels, Jeffrey W.	MD0550
Mangeni, Andrew	RI0200
Mangi, Mary	WI1150
Mangialardi, Robert	IL1200
Mangin, Andy	IL3550
Mangini, Mark	NY2050
Mangini, Michael	MA0260
Mangini, Nicholas	NY2400
Mangini, Nick	NY5000
Mangone, Jeffrey	PA1050
Mangrum, Amanda	MS0100
Mangrum, Leslie	KS0700
Mangrum, Martin	AI0150
Mangrum, Martin	AI0200
Mangsen, Sandra	AG0500
Manhart, Grant L.	SD0400
Manhollan, John W.	OH2600
Maniates, Maria R.	AG0450
Manik, Rich	MN1300
Manikam, Seelan	MA2010
Manji, K. C.	CA1265
Manker, Brian	AI0150
Mankerian, Vatche	CA2750
Mankey, Joel R.	CA0835
Manley, David	PA1150
Manley, Douglas H.	TN1550
Mann, Alison	GA1150
Mann, Brian R.	NY4450
Mann, Erik	OH0600
Mann, Erik	PA1200
Mann, George	AR0730
Mann, George	GA1200
Mann, Hummie	IL0720
Mann, Janet	UT0250
Mann, Jay	OH0950
Mann, Jenny L.	AL1170
Mann, Jonathan Edward	NY3725
Mann, Michael	TN1660
Mann, Nicholas	NY1900
Mann, Nicholas	NY2150
Mann, Robert	NY2150
Mann, Rochelle	CO0350
Mann, Sharon	CA2950
Mann, Sharon	CA4150
Mann, Sylvia Lee	CA0805
Mann, Ted	NH0150
Mann, Victoria	PA3650
Mann, William P.	KY0900
Mannell, David	IN0907
Mannell, David B.	IN0800
Manner, Mollie	NE0450
Manning, Dwight C.	NY4200
Manning, John	IA1550
Manning, Lucy	VA1000
Manning, Mary	WA0650
Manning, Sheri	NV0050
Mannino, Marc P.	FL1745
Mannion, Grace	MI2250
Mannix, Natalie K.	MD0850
Manno, John	WI1150
Manno, Terrie	MN1120
Manns, Olugbala	OH1000
Manoli, Anthony	NY2250
Manoogian, Peggy Lee	SC0620
Manos, Larry	AR0400
Manoury, Philippe	CA5050
Manring, Lesley	CO0950
Manriquez, Luz	PA0550
Mansell, Bradley	TN1850
Mansfield, Cynthia	CT0800
Manson, David	FL0450
Manson, David	FL1650
Manson, Michael	IL0600
Manspeaker, Rick	WV0800
Mansure, Victor N.	NC0050
Mantegna, John	VT0450
Mantel, Sarah J.	PA1600
Mantell, Emily Lewis	IL3100
Mantell, Emily	IL2650
Mantell, Matthew	IL3100
Manternach, LaDonna	IA0250
Mantie, Roger	MA0400
Mantini, David	MN1260
Mantione, Meryl E.	IN0150
Manuel, Peter G.	NY0600
Manuel, Peter	NY0630
Manuele, James	OR0150
Manus, Elizabeth A.	PA2550
Manwarren, Matthew C.	SC1200
Manz, Lorraine	OH1700
Manz, Paul P.	AZ0510
Manzo, Angelo	MO1800
Manzo, Erica	MO1800
Manzo, V.J.	NJ0800
Mao, Ruotao	NJ0175
Mapes, Randy	MS0100
Mapes, Randy K.	MS0300
Mapp, Douglas	NJ1050
Mapston, Cindy	AZ0510
Marandola, Fabrice	AI0150
Marano, Nancy	NY2150
Marano, Nancy	NJ1400
Marano-Murray, June	NY2150
Marasco, John	MA0260
Marassa, Jill	IL1350
Marble, Jamie	IL2970
Marble, Troy	IL1740
Marcades, Michael	AL0900
Marcel, Linda A.	NJ0020
Marcellana, Jennifer	OH1200
Marcellus, John	NY1100
March, Hunter	TX3510
March, James J.	IA1100
March, Kathryn Lucas	IA1100
Marchand, Jean	AI0150
Marchand, Rebecca	MA0350
Marchand, Rebecca G.	MA1175
Marchant, Susan J.	KS1050
Marchena, Martha	NJ0700
Marchiando, John R.	NM0450
Marchione, Jill	PA1900
Marchione, Jill	PA0950
Marchione, Jill	PA2300
Marchione, Jill	PA3150
Marchione, Jill M.	PA1250
Marchione, Nick	PA3250
Marchionni, Raymond	OH2300
Marchison, Matthew	OH2600
Marchukov, Sergey	PA2900
Marciniak, Alex B.	MI0700
Marcinizyn, John	PA0600
Marcinizyn, John	PA0550
Marcinizyn, John	PA3000
Marco, John	WI0840
Marco, Margaret	KS1350
Marcone, Stephen	NJ1400
Marcotte, Anna-Belle	AI0150
Marcotte, Paul	AI0200
Marcotte, Tracy	IL2300
Marcozzi, Rudy T.	IL0550
Marcus, Aaron	IN0907
Marcus, David	GA0490
Marcus, Edward	MN0800
Marcus, Scott	CA5060
Marcuzzi, Michael	AG0650
Mardirosian, Haig L.	DC0010
Mardirossian, Kevork M.	IN0900
Marek, Dan	NY2250
Marek, Tim	OK1200
Marenstein, Harry	NY2550
Mares, Michelle	AB0150
Maret, Carmen	MI0300
Maret, Kevin	MO0950
Marfisi, Nancy G.	CA0550
Margaglione, Louis A.	IL2450
Margetts, David	UT0325
Margetts, James A.	NE0050
Margetts, Linda	UT0250
Margolis, Sanford	OH1700
Margulies, Peter	UT0250
Margulies, Elizabeth	AR0700
Margulis, Jura	AR0700
Mariani, Angela	TX3200
Mariano, Dennis	NY2500
Mariasy, David	OH2300
Marienthal, Eric	CA0825
Maril, Travis	CA4100
Mariman, Devin	PA2800
Mariman, Devin	NJ1350
Marin, Luis	PR0115
Marinelli, Michael	DE0150
Marinelli, Vincent J.	DE0150
Marinello, Anthony	TX3510
Mariner, Justin	AI0150
Marinescu, Liviu	CA0835
Marinescu, Ovidiu	PA3600
Maring, Eric	DC0170
Maring, Marvel A.	NE0610
Marinic, Boro	IA0850
Marino, Lori	PA2800
Marino, Mark	NY2105
Marinova, Kristina	AR0750
Marion, Pierre	AI0210
Marion, Ricki	VA1350
Marissen, Michael	PA3200
Mark, Amanda	AF0120
Mark, Andrew	MA0350
Mark, Douglas L.	MS0250
Mark, Julie	UT0400
Markaverich, Michael	FL1745
Markey, James A.	NY1900
Markey, James	NY2250
Markgraf, David	NC2650
Markham, I-Fei Chen	NY3725
Markham, Matthew E.	WI0850
Markham, Michael	NY3725
Markiewicz, Larry	NJ0800
Markiw, Victor R.	CT0700
Markley, Ben D.	WY0200
Marko, Thomas	IL1150
Markoff, Irene	AG0650
Markou, Kypros L.	MI2200
Markou, Stella	MO1830
Markov, Albert	NY2150
Markovic, Lorriana	MD0520
Markovic, Lorriana	MD0600
Markovic-Prakash, Lorriana	MD1000
Markovich, Frank	CA4625
Markovich, Kimberly	CA3250
Markovich, Lucia	OH0600
Markovich, Victor A.	KS1450
Markow, Andrew	AG0300
Markow, Andrew	AG0450
Markow, Elliott	MA2030
Markow, Roseann	MD0500
Markowitz, Audrey	MA0950
Markowitz, Phil	NY2150
Markowski, Rebecca	AR0950
Markowski, Victoria	CO0275
Marks, Adam	WI0250
Marks, Brian	TX0300
Marks, Christopher	NE0600
Marks, Dennis J.	FL1950
Marks, Ed	OH0300
Marks, Erin	AB0200
Marks, Gary	AK0100
Marks, Laurence L.	NC2420
Marks, Martin	MI0050
Marks, Martin	MA1200
Marks, Melissa	MI0050
Marks, Randall J.	PA1900
Marks, Virginia	OH0300
Markstein, Igor	FL0150
Markstein, Joan	FL0150
Markstrom, Kurt	AC0100
Markun, Mila M.	WV0400
Markuson, Stephen	NY1400
Markuson, Steve H.	NY3765
Markward, Cheri D.	RI0101
Markward, Edward	RI0200
Markworth, Wayne	OH2500
Marlais, Helen	MI0900
Marlatt, Jeffrey	VA1350
Marlatt, Margot	IN1850
Marler, Robert	TN0100
Marlett, Judy	ID0150
Marleyn, Paul	AG0400
Marlier, Mike	CO0900
Marling, Chisato Eda	NY2650
Marling, Chisato Eda	NY1700
Marlow, Carolyn	NY2150
Marlow, Laurine	TX2900
Marlow, William	GA2100
Marlowe, Sarah	NY2750
Marmolejo, Noe	TX3400
Maroney, James	PA1100
Maroney, Marcus K.	TX3400
Maroon, Gayle E.	ME0250
Marosek, Scott	NC1350
Marosi, Laszlo	FL1800
Marple, Ellen	AB0200
Marple, Olive	MA0800
Marquardt, John	IL0730
Marques, Albert	CA1950
Marques, Alfredo	NY2250
Marquez-Barrios, Victor	MI0900
Marquez-Reyes, John D.	PR0115
Marquis, Eugene	OH2550
Marr, John	CA2390
Marr, John	CA0859
Marrazzo, Randi	PA3250
Marrier, Susan	AG0170
Marron, James	OH2150
Marrs, Jeff	CA2775
Marrs, Jeffrey	CA5000
Marrs, Leslie	IA0550
Marrs, Margie V.	IA0300
Marrs, Stuart	ME0440
Marsalis, Branford	NC1600
Marsalis, Delfeayo	LA0800
Marsalis, Ellis	LA0300
Marsalis, Jason	LA0800
Marsch, Debra	IL1050
Marschall, Ron	AZ0490
Marschner, Joseph A.	MD0450
Marsden, Frances	CA3300
Marsh, Carol	NC2430
Marsh, David	WV0550
Marsh, George	CA4700
Marsh, George	CA5070
Marsh, Gerry Jon	WA0800
Marsh, Gordon E.	VA1250

Name	Code	Name	Code	Name	Code
Marsh, John	GA1150	Martin, Les K.	WA0800	Mascolo-David, Alexandra	MI0400
Marsh, Kerry	CA0840	Martin, Linda	IA0950	Mase, Raymond	NY1900
Marsh, Lawrence B.	OR0450	Martin, Margo	CA3200	Masek, Douglas H.	CA5030
Marsh, Lisa	OR0850	Martin, Margot	CA1750	Masek, Patricia B.	SD0050
Marsh, Marian	CA1650	Martin, Mark Gregory	PA3600	Mash, David S.	MA0260
Marsh, Peter	CA5300	Martin, Mary Lou	AF0050	Mashkovtseva, Elena	CA4100
Marsh, Peter K.	CA0807	Martin, Marya	NY2150	Maske, Dan	WI0150
Marshack, Rose	IL1150	Martin, Melissa	NC2410	Maskell, Kathleen D.	MA1600
Marshall, Allen	OK0300	Martin, Melissa	NC1800	Masko, Meganne	ND0500
Marshall, Alyssa	TX1350	Martin, Melvin	AG0500	Maslanka, Daniel	MI1750
Marshall, Christopher J.	FL1800	Martin, Michael D.	NC1350	Masloski, Deborah	WI0250
Marshall, Cindy	GA0950	Martin, Michael D.	GA0150	Mason, Adam	AA0200
Marshall, Eddie	CA2950	Martin, Michelle Denise	GA0150	Mason, Alan	FL0050
Marshall, Elizabeth	WI0100	Martin, Mildred	CA2250	Mason, Brian S.	KY0900
Marshall, Elizabeth	WV0250	Martin, Monique	AI0210	Mason, Carl	AR0950
Marshall, Herbert D.	OH0200	Martin, Morris	TX3420	Mason, Charles Norman	FL1900
Marshall, Ingram	CT0850	Martin, Nancy D.	KY1000	Mason, Colin M.	TX2800
Marshall, Jason	CA0835	Martin, Noel	TX3450	Mason, Craig	IA1450
Marshall, Jean V.	KS1400	Martin, Peter J.	VA1600	Mason, Daniel	KY1450
Marshall, Jeffrey	IL2350	Martin, Peter H.	IL2250	Mason, Don	KS0215
Marshall, John	WA0250	Martin, Peter J.	ME0500	Mason, Elliot J.	IL2250
Marshall, Jonathan	MI0520	Martin, Rex	IL2250	Mason, Elliot J.	NY2750
Marshall, Jonathan	MI0850	Martin, Robert	IA1450	Mason, Emily J.	NY1800
Marshall, Kimberly	AZ0100	Martin, Roger	TN1450	Mason, James	CA1425
Marshall, Lynda	IL1050	Martin, Roland E.	NY0400	Mason, James	CA0825
Marshall, Peter M.	GA1050	Martin, Roland E.	NY4320	Mason, James	AG0600
Marshall, Robert L.	MA0500	Martin, Sarah	GA1050	Mason, John	MA2100
Marshall, Ruth	IL0750	Martin, Sharon	MN1700	Mason, John	MA1100
Marshall, Sharon	AG0650	Martin, Sherrill	NC2440	Mason, Joyce D.	OH0700
Marshall, Thomas	VA0250	Martin, Spencer	WY0130	Mason, Justin	OH2150
Marshall, Wolf	CA5031	Martin, Spencer	WA1300	Mason, Kaley R.	IL3250
Marshall-McClure, Clara	IN0907	Martin, Spencer L.	IA0950	Mason, Keith	TN0100
Marsit, Matthew	NH0100	Martin, Stephanie	AG0650	Mason, Marilyn	MI2100
Marsolais, Louis-Philippe	AI0200	Martin, Stephen	TX1150	Mason, Mike	MA0260
Marsteller, Loren	CA3300	Martin, Stephen	OR0850	Mason, Patrick	CO0800
Marsteller, Loren	CA0825	Martin, Susan Ryan	MO1950	Mason, Richard	GA0950
Marston, Karen L.	TX2295	Martin, Thomas	MA1400	Mason, Rodney	TX0350
Marta, Larry W.	TX3370	Martin, William	NC2600	Mason, Roger	CA3100
Martchev, Pamela	CA4100	Martin, William R.	OH0650	Mason, Scott	IL0550
Martchev, Valentin	CA0815	Martin-Andrews, Nicholle	CA5150	Mason, Sonya G.	NY2150
Martchev, Valentin	CA4100	Martin-Atwood, Michelle R.	NY3780	Mason, Thom	CA5300
Martel, Helene	AI0200	Martin-Williams, Jean F.	GA2100	Mason, Vicki	TX0200
Martell, Mary	IL2750	Martina, Harold	TX3000	Mason, Vito	DC0010
Martell, Rodney	VA0250	Martindale, Peggy Lee	CA0200	Mason-Christianson, Teri	CA5355
Martell, Rodney	VA0150	Martinelli, Lisa	AG0450	Masonson, Norman	CA1150
Martell, Vanessa	MN1270	Martinez Ortiz, Laura	PR0115	Masoudnia, Elizabeth	PA3250
Martens, Judith L.	MN1030	Martinez, Adriana	AZ0470	Masri, Tariq	AL0800
Martens, Peter A.	TX3200	Martinez, David	RI0150	Masri, Tariq	AL1150
Martens, Victor	AG0600	Martinez, Everaldo	ND0050	Masri-Fletcher, Patricia	MI1400
Martens, William	AI0150	Martinez, Everaldo	ND0400	Masri-Fletcher, Patricia	MI1260
Martensen, Dave	SD0100	Martinez, Gabriela	NJ0700	Massanari, Jeff	CA5000
Martin, Andree	GA0550	Martinez, Guillermo	TX3000	Masse, Denise	NY1900
Martin, Anne L.	CA3000	Martinez, Jeordano S.	IL2050	Massell, Deborah P.	NY3780
Martin, Anthony P.	CA4900	Martinez, Jesus E.	CA1700	Massenburg, George	AI0150
Martin, Barry	MI0900	Martinez, Jorge	NM0310	Masserini, John	AZ0450
Martin, Blair	KS1250	Martinez, Kurt	TX3525	Massey, Andrew J.	VT0350
Martin, Bradley	NC2600	Martinez, Manuel	TX0390	Massey, Angela	SC1000
Martin, Brenda	CA3640	Martinez, Mario E.	NY2650	Massey, LaDamion	CO0550
Martin, Canarissa	KY0550	Martinez, Pedro	TX3525	Massey, Mark	CA1750
Martin, CarolAnn F.	MO0800	Martinez, Robby	CA0270	Massey, Michael	AA0110
Martin, Cathy	AI0150	Martinez, Taione	NJ1350	Massey, Robert	SC1100
Martin, Chris	TX2800	Martinez-Forteza, Pascual	NY2750	Massey, Taylor	GA2100
Martin, Chris	IL2250	Martinovic, Nada	OH1100	Massicot, Joshua	NY2650
Martin, Christopher	NC1600	Martins, David J.	MA0400	Massie Legg, Alicia	TN1000
Martin, Constance	MN0300	Martins, David	MA2030	Massie, Robin	NJ1350
Martin, Danny Ray	TN0150	Martins, Jose Oliveira	NY1100	Massini, Ryan	AA0040
Martin, David J.	MI0350	Martins, Sandra Lau	AG0450	Massinon, Francis	TN0050
Martin, David	AI0200	Martinson, Kenneth	FL1850	Mast, Andrew	WI0350
Martin, David	MI1050	Martorano, Joseph P.	IL3450	Mast, Ivan	AA0035
Martin, David	AI0150	Martorella, Philip	RI0200	Mast, Murray	CT0050
Martin, Deborah	NY1800	Martorella, Stephen T.	RI0200	Mast, Murray K.	MA1100
Martin, Don R.	MO1900	Martucci, Anthony	VA1600	Masten, Rob	WV0250
Martin, Don	NC0300	Martucci, Vincent	NY3760	Masters, Barbara	IL0850
Martin, Edward P.	WI0830	Martula, Susan B.	NY3650	Masters, Jim	OH1850
Martin, Edward	MN0450	Martula, Susan	MA2250	Masters, Ken	OR1000
Martin, Elaine J.	PA2550	Martyn, Charles F.	WV0650	Masters, Martha	CA0815
Martin, Flora	MD0700	Martynuik, David G.	PA1600	Masters, Martha	CA2800
Martin, Frank	CA5000	Martysz, Erin	TX2650	Masters, Richard J.	TX3510
Martin, Freddie	GA1700	Martz, Dee	WI0850	Masters, Suzanna	VA1580
Martin, Gayle H.	AE0050	Martz, Mary	MN1450	Masterson, Daniel J.	KS0150
Martin, Greg	CA2550	Martz, Mary	MN0300	Masterson, Kyle	NH0250
Martin, Gregg	DC0050	Marucci, Mat	CA0150	Masterson, Rik	OR0400
Martin, Henry	NJ1140	Marvin, Clara	AG0250	Masterson, Stephanie C.	FL1570
Martin, James	MS0385	Marvin, Elizabeth W.	NY1100	Mastrian, Stacey	DC0010
Martin, James	MO1950	Marvin, John W.	CA0850	Mastrian, Stacey	PA1400
Martin, James	CA4450	Marvin, Marajean M.	OH1850	Mastrian, Stacey L.	MD0650
Martin, James	IA0400	Marvin, William	NY1100	Mastrodomenico, Carol	MA1175
Martin, Jared	TN0580	Marvine, Jane	MD0650	Mastrodomenico, Carol	MA1900
Martin, Jeffrey A.	AE0050	Marvit, Betsy	CA4150	Mastrogiacomo, Leonard	FL0850
Martin, Jennifer	CA1510	Marx, Steve	CO0250	Mastrogiacomo, Norma	FL0850
Martin, Jessie Wright	NC2650	Marx, Susan A.	CO0250	Mastrogiacomo, Steven J.	MI2200
Martin, Joey	TX3175	Maryanova, Sofya	NY3760	Mastroianni, John	CT0600
Martin, John T.	MI0900	Marzluf, Jonathan	CA2390	Mastroianni, Thomas	DC0050
Martin, John	KY1550	Marzluf, Jonathan	CA1425	Mastronicola, Michael	CO0400
Martin, Joseph	CO0900	Marzolf, Dennis	MN0200	Masuko, Takaaki	MA1175
Martin, Joshua	FL0350	Marzullo, Anne Maria	PA1850	Masuzzo, Dennis	NJ1160
Martin, Julian	NY1900	Masaki, Megumi	AC0050	Matalon, Leon	CA0200
Martin, Kent	PA2710	Masakowski, Steve	LA0800	Matascik, Sheri L.	TN1000
Martin, Klancy	RI0150	Masci, Michael J.	NY3730	Matasy, Katherine V.	MA2050
Martin, Kyle	MA2300	Masciadri, Milton	GA2100	Matathias, Robin	NH0150

Matchael, Michael	TX3360	Matthys, Joel W.	WI0200	Mayer, Steven	CO0900
Matchett, Robert	PA3650	Mattin, Gary	IL1340	Mayer, Uri	AG0300
Matchim, David	MD0650	Mattina, Fernando	PR0115	Mayerovitch, Robert	OH0200
Matczynski, Leonard	MA0350	Mattingly, Alan F.	NE0600	Mayes, Catherine	UT0250
Mateiescu, Carmen	NJ1000	Mattingly, Douglas	MD0060	Mayes, Frank	LA0300
Mateiescu, Carmen	NJ1350	Mattingly, Jacqueline	NE0600	Mayes, Joseph	NJ1050
Matejka, Merle	AJ0030	Mattingly, Stephen P.	KY1500	Mayes, Kathleen	NJ1050
Matesky, Elisabeth	IN0005	Mattingly, Stephen	IN1010	Mayes, Robert	TX3400
Matesky, Nancy	WA0860	Mattison, Nate	MN1120	Mayeur, Robert G.	CA2750
Mateus, Cesar	CA5360	Mattison, Travis	IL2970	Mayfield, David C.	NJ0825
Mather, Bill	AG0130	Mattison, Travis	IL1500	Mayfield, Farren	OK0550
Mather, Jennifer	IL0850	Mattix, Anna	NY0400	Mayfield, Gray	GA1450
Mather, Pierrette	AI0150	Mattix, Anna L.	NY3717	Mayfield, Irvin	LA0800
Mather-Stow, Andrea	IN0910	Mattix, Anna L.	NY4320	Mayfield, Nathaniel	TX2900
Matherne, Karl	LA0800	Mattix, Daniel J.	IL1850	Mayhew, Rebecca S.	OH0650
Mathes, Adam	MT0370	Mattock, David M.	PA1850	Mayhew, Sandon	ID0070
Mathes, Gerard	ID0140	Mattox, Amanda M.	MS0570	Mayhood, Erin L.	VA1550
Mathes, James	FL0850	Mattox, Zeritta	NJ0550	Mayhood, John	VA1550
Matheson, Alan	AB0100	Matts, Kathleen	WI1150	Mayhue, Terence C.	IL1740
Matheson, Bryan	CA0900	Matts, Kathleen	WI0050	Maynard, Keith	NY2400
Matheson, James	CA4900	Mattson, Lisa	FL0680	Maynard, Lisa M.	VA0600
Matheson, Jennifer	AF0120	Mattson, Lucas	IA1400	Maynard, Robert	LA0050
Mathew, Nicholas	CA5000	Mattson, Sheri	MO1790	Maynard, Seth	WV0250
Mathews, Christopher W.	TN1660	Mattson-Hill, Jodi	MT0075	Maynard-Christensen, Dianne	NY2650
Mathews, Elisa	PA3560	Maturani, Marilyn Muns	KY0550	Maynard-Christensen, Dianne	NY3350
Mathews, Heather	CA4150	Matych-Hager, Susan	MI1950	Mayne, Anna	IL2150
Mathews, Jeffrey	LA0550	Matyukov, Saida	AB0200	Mayne, Richard	CO0950
Mathews, Lee	WA0980	Matzke, Kathleen	MN1400	Mayo, Christine H. Donahue	AR0850
Mathews, Lee	WA0300	Matzke, Laura	MN0200	Mayo, John	AG0450
Mathews, Paul	MD0650	Matzke, Rex	CO0200	Mayo, Nancy	MO1950
Mathews, Peter	FL1950	Mauceri, Frank	ME0200	Mayo, Susan	KS0300
Mathews, Robert P.	CA6050	Mauceri, Frank	ME0340	Mayo, Thomas	MA0950
Mathews, Rod	CA4400	Mauchley, Jay	ID0250	Mayo, Walter S.	NY3725
Mathews, Teri	MD0850	Mauchley, Sandra	ID0250	Mayo, William M.	PA3250
Mathey, Richard D.	OH0300	Maugans, Stacy	IN1750	Mayor, Jeff	CA3350
Mathias, Brian	KS1400	Maughan, Sarah	NC2650	Mayor, Pedro	AL0450
Mathie, David	ID0050	Mauk, Steven	NY1800	Mayrose, John S.	IN0910
Mathiesen, Steven	PA2450	Mauldin, Mark K.	DC0150	Mays, Kenneth R.	CA2810
Mathiesen, Steven	PA2200	Mauldin, Steve	TN0100	Mays, Michael E.	TN1500
Mathieson, Carol Fisher	MO0300	Mauldin, Walter	TN0850	Mays, Walter A.	KS1450
Mathieu, Louise	AI0190	Mauleon-Santana, Rebeca	CA1020	Mayse, Kevin A.	CA3800
Mathieu, Phil	MD0550	Maureau, Wayne	LA0300	Mayse, Susie	CA3800
Mathis, Carolynne	MN0610	Maurer, Kathleen M.	IN0150	Maytan, Gregory	MI0900
Mathis, Eric L.	AL0800	Maurer-Davis, Jill	CT0050	Maytan, Sandra	MI0900
Mathis, Eric	AF0100	Maurey, Ronald D.	IN1400	Maytum, Jeremiah	WY0115
Mathis, Nancy	AR0730	Maurice, Glenda A.	MN1623	Maz, Andrew	CA1900
Mathis, William B.	OH0300	Mauro, Lucy	WV0750	Mazak, Grant	TX3175
Mathur, Sharmila	AA0100	Maurreau, Robert	LA0080	Mazanec, David	AL0300
Matiation, Laurie	AA0050	Maurtua, Jose Luis	MI0400	Mazarak, Eric	NY1400
Matiation, Laurie	AA0150	Maus, Fred Everett	VA1550	Mazer, Susan	CT0300
Mativetsky, Shawn	AI0150	Mausolf, Susan	NE0450	Mazo, Margarita L.	OH1850
Matlick, Eldon	OK1350	Maute, Matthias	AI0150	Mazo, Vadim	IL1200
Matlock, Herman	NY3775	Mauthe, Holger	AA0050	Mazonson, Eric	MA2020
Matney, William	TX3300	Mauthe, Timothy	VA0250	Mazullo, Mark	MN0950
Matos, Lucia Regina	IL2200	Mautner, Roselida	FL0200	Mazurek, Drew	MD0650
Matras, Stanley	OH1000	Mautner-Rodgers, Sharon	MN0750	Mazurkevich, Dana Pomerantz	MA0400
Matrone, Tom	MO0400	Mavromatis, Panayotis	NY2750	Mazurkevich, Yuri	MA0400
Matson, Erin	NC2435	Maxedon, Lisa M.	LA0250	Mazzacane, Roy	CT0800
Matson, Jan	MN1400	Maxfield, Adele	IN1560	Mazzaferro, Anthony	CA1900
Matson, Melissa	NY1100	Maxfield, Dennis	NY1250	Mazzaferro, Jim	CA1500
Matson, Ralph	UT0250	Maxfield, Jessica	IL1900	Mazzaferro, Tony	CA2390
Matsos, Christopher	OH2275	Maxfield, Lynn M.	IL1350	Mazzaferro, Tony	CA0630
Matsuda, Kenichiro	OH0350	Maxile, Horace J.	TX0300	Mazzatenta, Mark	NC0915
Matsue, Jennifer	NY4310	Maxon, James	NY5000	Mazzeo, Frank	PA3250
Matsukawa, Daniel	PA3250	Maxson, Carrie	UT0350	Mazzio, Carl	NY3725
Matsukawa, Daniel	PA0850	Maxson, Mark D.	UT0350	Mazziot, Nicholas	MD0175
Matsumoto, Kanae	CA5030	Maxwell, Don	TX1700	Mazziotta, Laura	NY2400
Matsumoto, Shane	AZ0470	Maxwell, Francisca	GA0050	Mazzocchi, Anthony	NJ0700
Matsumoto, Shigemi	CA0825	Maxwell, Margaret	MN0150	Mazzocchi, Anthony J.	NJ0800
Matsumoto-Stark, Shigemi	CA5300	Maxwell, Mark A.	IL0750	Mazzoccoli, Jesse	MO0300
Matsuo, Jun	SC0450	Maxwell, Monte	MD0900	Mazzola, Guerino	MN1623
Matsuoka, Yumiko	MA0260	Maxwell, Sarita J.	SC1200	McAdams, Stephen	AI0150
Matsushita, Hidemi	CO0100	Maxwell, Steven	KS0650	McAdoo, Susan	NJ1140
Matsuura, Gary	CA2390	Maxwell, Susan	KS0650	McAdow, Seth	TX2250
Matsuura, Gary	CA0960	May, Andrew D.	TX3420	McAfee, Andrew	NC2410
Matta, Thomas	IL0750	May, Brittany	TX1450	McAfee, Karen	TX3527
Matters, Helene	CA2200	May, Douglas L.	PA1450	McAlister, Andrea	OH1700
Matteson, Vicki	VT0100	May, Ed	ID0060	McAlister, Anita	AG0600
Matthay, Christopher D.	NY2750	May, Eldonna	MI2200	McAllister, Bob	AZ0400
Matthews, Andrea	NH0150	May, Ernest D.	MA2000	McAllister, DeeAnn	AZ0400
Matthews, Andrea	MA2050	May, Jim	AZ0470	McAllister, Elizabeth	NC1750
Matthews, Bill	ME0150	May, Joanne	IL0850	McAllister, James	KS0440
Matthews, Brandon Stephen	CO0550	May, Judith	CA5353	McAllister, Lesley Ann	TX0300
Matthews, Britton	NY2450	May, Judy	AZ0100	McAllister, Margaret	MA0260
Matthews, Don	OR0950	May, Juliana	CT0450	McAllister, Michael	NC1750
Matthews, Forrest	SC0710	May, Lissa F.	IN0900	McAllister, Peter A.	AZ0500
Matthews, Ingrid	WA0200	May, Luise	GA0550	McAllister, Scott	TX0300
Matthews, Justus F.	CA0825	May, Maureen	TN1850	McAmis, Carol	NY1800
Matthews, Katherine	SC0275	May, Nathanael A.	MO0850	McAndrews, Deb	OR1000
Matthews, Margaret	NY1150	May, Pam	MN1250	McAneny, Marc	MA0350
Matthews, Mark	FL1650	May, Susan	GA1500	McAneny, Marc A.	NY3717
Matthews, Michael	AC0100	May, Theresa	OH0755	McAneny, Marc	MA0500
Matthews, Michael K.	MO0850	May, Tom	FL0680	McArthur, Lisa R.	KY0400
Matthews, Robin L.	CA2050	May, William V.	TX0300	McArthur, Mark	NV0050
Matthews, Ron	PA1150	May-Patterson, Eleanor	IA1100	McArthur, Victoria	FL0850
Matthews, Tamara	SC0750	Maybery, Paul	MN0950	McArthur-Brown, Gail	MA0260
Matthews, Todd	IL0600	Maye, Shelia J.	VA0500	McAulliffe, Harold F.	NY4350
Matthews, Wendy K.	MI2200	Mayer, Anne B.	MN0300	McBain, Jeremy	IL0800
Matthews, Zachary P.	CA3500	Mayer, Deborah L.	IN0910	McBain, Katherine C.	IL0800
Matthusen, Paula A.	CT0750	Mayer, Paul	CA4450	McBain, Mike	MO1790

Name	Code	Name	Code	Name	Code
McBay, Brian	AG0600	McClary, Michael	GA0940	McCoy, Jerry	TX3420
McBee, Cecil	MA1400	McCleary, Harriet C.	MN1450	McCoy, Julie	TX3250
McBee, Karen L.	TX0125	McCleery, Mark	LA0770	McCoy, June	OK0700
McBerry, Sue	OR0400	McClellan, David Ray	GA2100	McCoy, Louise	AL1250
McBeth, Christopher	UT0250	McClellan, Eleanor	AL1250	McCoy, Marilyn L.	MA1400
McBrearty, Angela S.	NY1700	McClellan, John	MO0650	McCoy, Matthew T.	KS0650
McBride Daline, Matthew	OH0300	McClellan, John	MO1950	McCoy, Molly	TX3370
McBride, M. Scott	KY0900	McClellan, Robinson	NY4500	McCoy, Pamela	TN1400
McBride, Michael S.	IL2100	McClellan, Teresa	TN0600	McCoy, Peter M.	NY3780
McBride, Michelle	CT0650	McClelland, Keith	TN1710	McCoy, Scott	OH1850
McBride, Nick	NJ1350	McClelland, Phillip	PA3250	McCoy, Steve	FL0400
McBride-Daline, Matthew S.	LA0200	McClelland, Ryan	AG0450	McCoy, William F.	VA1475
McBroom, Deanna H.	SC0500	McClement, Doug	AG0130	McCracken, H. Jac	LA0300
McCabe, Amy	DC0170	McClendon, Forrest	PA3250	McCrane, Barbara	NY2150
McCabe, Brent Poe	MT0450	McCloskey, Diane L.	OH1100	McCrary, William	TX3530
McCabe, Matthew	GA0550	McCloskey, Kathleen	PA0650	McCraw, Michael	IN0900
McCabe, Melissa	MD0850	McCloud, Daniel	TX0150	McCray, James	CO0250
McCabe, Rachelle	OR0700	McClune, David	TN1660	McCray, Jeffrey	NE0600
McCabe, Robin	WA1050	McClung, Alan C.	TX3420	McCray, Mack	CA4150
McCachren, Renee	NC0350	mcclung, bruce d.	OH2200	McCready, Matthew A.	MO0550
McCafferty, Dennis S.	IN1650	McClung, Matthew	TX2930	McCreary, Teresa J.	HI0110
McCaffrey, Maureen	TN1400	McClung, Sam W.	FL0365	McCreery, Carlton	AL1170
McCaffrey, Maureen	TN1100	McClung-Guillory, Deborah	LA0770	McCreless, Patrick	CT0900
McCaffrey, Patricia	NY0500	McClure, Carol	IN1010	McCrickard, Eleanor	NC2430
McCage, Leslie	OH2300	McClure, Carol	TN1660	McCright, Matthew	MN0300
McCain, Alisa	NC2000	McClure, Carol	KY1500	McCroskey, John	TX2250
McCain, Martin G.	TX3175	McClure, Matthew	NC2410	McCullam, Audrey	MD0600
McCain, Seward	CA4900	McClure, Michelle	IA0940	McCulloch, Doug	HI0210
McCall, Gina	TN1000	McClure, Ron D.	NY2750	McCulloch, Peter	NY4450
McCalla, Aaron	FL0680	McClure, Ryan	NE0250	McCullough, Allen	GA1300
McCallum, Gregory	VA1800	McClure, Sam	MO1780	McCullough, Brian	MN1623
McCallum, Kyle	MN0600	McClure, Theron	OH1850	McCullough, Daryl	TX3600
McCallum, Laura	OR0750	McClurg, Bruce	CA0960	McCullough, David M.	AL1250
McCallum, Wendy M.	AC0050	McClurkin, Vicki J.	OH2275	McCullough, David	IN0250
McCandless, Amanda	IA1600	McCluskey, Eric	IL2900	McCullough, Elizabeth L.	NY4500
McCandless, Andrew	AG0300	McCluskey, Kevin	MA0260	McCullough, Michael	CA0200
McCandless, Marty	IL1100	McCluskey, P. Eric	GA1800	McCullough, Richard D.	NY2950
McCandless, Terry	OH1200	McClymonds, Marita P.	VA1550	McCullough, Stephanie	PA1250
McCanless, Clinton T.	KY1500	McColl, William	WA1050	McCullough, Susan	CO0900
McCann, Brian	WA0400	McColley, Stacey	FL0800	McCullough, Thomas Eric	OK1330
McCann, Chris	AI0150	McCollim, Danny	WA0950	McCully, Michael	CA0200
McCann, Jesse	OR0850	McCollough, Sean	TN1710	McCumber, Gary	AG0500
McCann, Jesse S.	OR0800	McCollough, Teresa	CA4425	McCurdy, Robert	SD0550
McCann, John	MA1900	McCollum, David	WV0750	McCurdy, Ronald	CA5300
McCann, Karen	NV0050	McCollum, Jonathan	MD1100	McCurdy, Roy	CA5300
McCann, Kimberly	OH0350	McCollum, Jonathan Ray	MD0060	McCusker, IHM, Joan	PA2200
McCann, Kimberly	OH2000	McCollum, Kimberly	MD0060	McCusker, Philip	DC0010
McCann, Kimberly	OH1600	McComas, Inez S.	FL1450	McCutchen, Keith	NC0050
McCann, Kimberly	OH2050	McComb, Dana	VA1600	McCutchen, Matt	FL2000
McCann, William J.	NY3760	McComb, Jason B.	VA1500	McCutchen, Thomas	GA2100
McCardell, Stephen	WI0350	McComb, Thomas	WI0850	McCutchen, Thomas	AL0500
McCardell, Susan L.	WI0350	McCombs, Steven	IA1350	McCutcheon, James	OH2500
McCardle, Dennis	KY0150	McConico, Marcus	MN1600	McCutcheon, James R.	OH2250
McCargar, Barbara Witham	MI0300	McConkey, Michelle	CA0800	McCutcheon, Peter	AI0200
McCarley, Ron	CA1510	McConkie, Dawn	KS0300	McCutcheon, Russell G.	PA1400
McCarrey, Scott	HI0050	McConnaughey, Rebecca H.	MN0750	McDade, Joanne Estelle	AR0350
McCarrey, Stacy	HI0050	McConnell, Douglas W.	OH0950	McDaniel, Adena	SC0650
McCarrick-Dix, Patricia	PA3250	McConnell, Joan	OH0950	McDaniel, Alfred	CA4050
McCarther, Sean	NJ1350	McConnell, Michele	NJ0825	McDaniel, Carol	CA1425
McCarthy, Charles	CA4900	McConnell, Miles	IA0250	McDaniel, Carolyn	OH0250
McCarthy, Charles J.	CA1020	McConnell, Pamela A.	FL1900	McDaniel, Catherine	OK0750
McCarthy, Cheryl	AF0120	McConnell, Robert	IA0900	McDaniel, Jan	OK0750
McCarthy, Daniel	MI1180	McConnell, Roger	IN0150	McDaniel, Jane	MO1950
McCarthy, Daniel	OH2150	McConville, Brendan P.	TN1710	McDaniel, Rory	SC0050
McCarthy, David	NY2650	McCool, Jason	MD0550	McDaniel, Susan E.	OR0450
McCarthy, Elizabeth	AF0100	McCord, Adam R.	KY1500	McDaniel, William T.	OH1850
McCarthy, Glen	VA0450	McCord, Adam	OH2450	McDaniel-Milliken, Jennifer L.	SC1200
McCarthy, Justin	NH0250	McCord, G. Dawn Harmon	GA2130	McDannell, Karl	NY2450
McCarthy, Keri E.	WA1150	McCord, Kimberly A.	IL1150	McDerment, Christopher	OH1900
McCarthy, Kerry R.	NC0600	McCord, Larry	TX0910	McDermid, Aaron	ND0150
McCarthy, Kerry	DC0170	McCord, Rebecca	VA1400	McDermott, Dennette Derby	LA0550
McCarthy, Lisa	WA1250	McCord, Semenya	IL1350	McDermott, Pamela D. J.	VA0700
McCarthy, Marie F.	MI2100	McCord, Vicki	IL0420	McDermott, Sheila	LA0080
McCarthy, Marta	AG0350	McCorkle, William	VA1850	McDermott, Tom	CA2800
McCartney, Ben	AZ0480	McCormack, Jessica D.	IN0910	McDevitt, Duane	NJ0825
McCartney, Lynn R.	NH0300	McCormick, Chris	TN1450	McDonagh, Brian	AG0450
McCarty, Daniel J.	ID0075	McCormick, Corey	CA1000	McDonald, Aaron	AB0100
McCarty, Diane	KS0300	McCormick, David	LA0650	McDonald, Boyd	AG0600
McCarty, Evelyn	TX2930	McCormick, Gaelen	NY2650	McDonald, Elizabeth	AG0250
McCarty, Evelyn	TX0550	McCormick, Gaelen M.	NY3350	McDonald, Heather	KY0400
McCarty, Karena	PA0350	McCormick, Jesse D.	OH0200	McDonald, Janelle	TN0260
McCarty, Patrick	MO0050	McCormick, John	AA0035	McDonald, Jean	IA1600
McCashin, Robert D.	VA0600	McCormick, John	AA0100	McDonald, John	MA1900
McCaskill, Janet L.	MI2200	McCormick, John	AA0020	McDonald, Linn	PA2200
McCaslin, Donny	NY2150	McCormick, Kim S.	FL2000	McDonald, Lynn	AG0650
McCaslin, Tom R.	NC0650	McCormick, Mark	CT0100	McDonald, Margaret	CO0800
McCauley, Thomas E.	NJ0800	McCormick, Robert	MI0500	McDonald, Marilyn	OH1700
McCauley, William	SC0200	McCormick, Robert	FL2000	McDonald, Matthew	MA1450
McCausland, Jacqueline J.	NY3730	McCormick, Scott	MA0260	McDonald, Nan	CA4100
McChesney, Bob	CA0825	McCormick, Thomas	FL1300	McDonald, Reginald	TN1400
McChesney, Bob	CA1000	McCorvey, Everett	KY1450	McDonald, Richard F.	TX2930
McChesney, Bob H.	CA0835	McCosh, Ruth	AA0050	McDonald, Robert	PA0850
McChesney, David	NC2410	McCourry, Christopher C.	MI1000	McDonald, Robert	NY1900
McChesney, Michael	CA5510	McCoy, Alan	WA0250	McDonald, Shawn	MI1300
McClain, Charles	PA2550	McCoy, Darcy	IN0350	McDonald, Steven	KS1000
McClain, Denise	WA0700	McCoy, David	AB0100	McDonald, Susan M.	PA1830
McClain, Frances	NC2000	McCoy, Eleanor K.	OH2275	McDonald, Susann	IN0900
McClain, Sandra	FL0650	McCoy, Jane	NC1450	McDonald, Timothy L.	MO1010
McClain, Washington	IN0900	McCoy, Jane O.	NC2550	McDonnell, David	OH2250
McClard Kirk, Jennifer	KS1250	McCoy, Jeremy	NY2150	McDonnell, Donald	MA0260

Alphabetical Listing of Faculty

Name	Code	Name	Code	Name	Code
McDonnell, John	NJ1350	McGowan, Mike	TX2000	McKeithen, Steve	SC1110
McDonnell, John	NJ0175	McGowan, Orpha Ellen	AZ0510	McKeithen, Steven	LA0550
McDonough, James D.	LA0200	McGowan, Sean C.	CO0830	McKellar, Donald A.	AG0500
McDonough, Lauren	NY2450	McGowan, Thomas	TX3370	McKellip, Hope	MS0580
McDonough, Raenell	TX0100	McGrann, Jeremiah	MA0330	McKelvey, Berke	MA0260
McDowell, Laura	NC0250	McGrannahan, A. Graydon	NV0100	McKelvey, Michael E.	PA2900
McDowell, Robert	SD0580	McGrannahan, Grady	IA0550	McKelway, Daniel	OH0200
McDuffie, Robert	GA1300	McGrath, Casey	IL1520	McKemy, Bill	KS1000
McEachern, Peter J.	CT0250	McGrath, Edward J.	MA0260	McKenna, Fr. Edward	IN0005
McElhaney, Carla	TX3100	McGrath, Kenneth	CA0815	McKenna, Terry	AG0600
McElligott, Brady R.	OK1450	McGrath, Michael	IL2775	McKenney, W. Thomas	MO1800
McElrath, Katheryn	OR0950	McGrath, Thomas	NY3770	McKenzie, Art	NJ1350
McElroy, Dennis	KY0610	McGraw, Andrew	VA1500	McKenzie, Colin	GA0950
McElroy, Donna	MA0260	McGraw, William E.	OH2200	Mckenzie, Julie C.	CA5000
McElroy, John	AL0800	McGregor, Cynthia	CA4850	McKenzie-Stubbs, Mary E.	NJ0700
McElwaine, James	NY3785	McGrew, David	PA0150	McKeown, Kevin	CA5020
McEnaney, Rick	NV0050	McGrosso, John	MO1830	McKeown, Kevin	CA4450
McEndarfer, Luke	CA3150	McGuinness, Peter	NJ1400	McKim, Christopher Z.	CO0225
McEnerny, Harry	VT0100	McGuire, Charles E.	OH1700	McKinley, Kathy	AG0100
McEntire, Jeremy	VA1150	McGuire, Christopher	TX3420	McKinley, Thomas L.	FL1125
McEntire, Jeremy R.	VA1500	McGuire, David O.	OH0650	McKinney, Brian	IL2750
McEuen, Stephen	PA2150	McGuire, David	NY1250	McKinney, Cathy	NC0050
McEvenue, Kelly	AG0450	McGuire, Dennis	MN1400	McKinney, David	KS0265
McEvoy, Andrew	VA1150	McGuire, James	MN0750	McKinney, Dustin	CA3600
McEvoy, Jeffrey S.	CT0600	McGuire, James	MN1000	McKinney, Harold	NC0050
McEwen, Mark	MA0400	McGuire, Jennifer	TN1850	McKinney, Jane Grant	NC0900
McEwen, Mark	MA1400	McGuire, John	CO0250	McKinney, John S.	WV0350
McFadden, James	CA4460	McGuire, John P.	CO0250	McKinney, Kelly	GA1070
McFadden, Jeff	AG0200	McGuire, Joshua	TN1850	McKinney, Kevin	GA1900
McFadden, Jeffrey	AG0450	McGuire, K. Christian	MN0050	McKinney, Lori	KS0050
McFadden, Jim L.	CA1020	McGuire, Kenneth	AL1170	McKinney, Matthew	AL1200
McFadden, Joseph	GA1150	McGuire, Kristen Shiner	NY2650	McKinney, Roger W.	NJ0175
McFadden, Robert	OK1150	McGuire, Samuel A.	CO0830	McKinney, Russell	UT0190
McFadden, Tim J.	OK1450	McGushin, Michael	CA0400	McKinney, Russell	UT0050
McFalls, James	MD0850	McHaney, David	IL1240	McKinney, Timothy R.	TX0300
McFarland, Alison	LA0200	McHugh, Barbara	IL1500	McKinnie, Douglas	IN0900
McFarland, Ann L.	PA3600	McHugh, David	IL0720	McKinnis, Alicia V.	TX1425
McFarland, James	TX3600	McHugh, Ernestine	NY1100	McKinnon, John A.	OR0200
McFarland, Joan	MD0750	McHugh, Kelli M.	IL1615	McKinnon, Taryn	AG0600
McFarland, Joanne	PA1450	McHugh, Larisa	OH2250	McKinstry, Herb	PA1650
McFarland, Kay Dawn	KY1425	McHugh, Steve	NC0930	McKinstry, Julia D.	NY4150
McFarland, Kay Dawn	KY1400	McIlhagga, Samuel D.	MI0100	McKirdy, Colleen	ND0100
McFarland, Mark J.	GA1050	McIlvery, Richard	CA5300	McKissick, Charles	GA2050
McFarland, Thomas J.	KY1400	McIlwain, William Benjamin	MS0750	McKissick, Marvin L.	CA0250
McFarland, Timothy	MA2010	McInchak, Kellie	MI2000	McKittrick, Cam	AG0350
McFarlane, Grace	DC0170	McInnes, Bruce G.	ME0410	McKittrick, Cam	AG0600
McFatter, Larry E.	CA0845	McInnes, Donald	CA5300	McKnight, Charles M.	NC2400
McFaul, Cathi	TX3800	McInnis, Fred	UT0050	McKnight, Danny	TX1450
McFaul, Rebecca	UT0300	McIntire, David D.	MO1790	McKnight, Linda	NJ0800
McFeaters, Jason	DC0170	McIntire, Dennis K.	GA1700	McKnight, Linda	NY2150
McFee, Cathy	PA2710	McIntire, Donna	WY0050	McKnight, Lynda Keith	TX3400
McFerron, Mike	IL1520	McIntire, Jean	PA1150	McKnight, Mark	TX3420
McFetridge, George	AB0210	McIntosh, Andrew	AG0550	McKoin, Sarah	TX3200
McGah, Thomas J.	MA0260	McIntosh, Bruce	OR1300	McKoy, Constance L.	NC2430
McGahan, Christopher	MA2030	McIntosh, Catherine	AA0035	McLafferty, Tim	CT0550
McGann, Christina F.	OH1900	McIntosh, Eulaine	TX1050	McLain, Barbara	HI0210
McGann, Daniel	NY2450	McIntosh, Jim	NV0050	McLain, James	DC0010
McGann, John	MA0260	McIntosh, John S.	AG0500	McLain, Michael	TN0100
McGarity, Kristin A.	MT0200	McIntosh, Lawrence	HI0155	McLamb, Victoria	NC0450
McGarrell, Matthew	RI0050	McIntosh, W. Legare	AL0500	McLamore, Alyson	CA0600
McGarvey, Timothy	IA1200	McIntosh, William	CA3200	McLamore, L. Alyson	CA3500
McGaughey, Martha	NY2250	McInturf, Matthew	TX2250	McLane, Alec	CT0750
McGee, Blake Anthony	WY0200	McIntyre, Chris	AA0025	McLane, Brian	AZ0460
McGee, Deron	KS1350	McIntyre, Daniel P.	IL0840	McLaren, Malena	LA0550
McGee, Isaiah R.	SC0350	McIntyre, Eric L.	IA0700	McLaren, Robert	AG0450
McGee, Lynnette	CA1425	McIntyre, Guinevere	IA0700	McLarry, Royce	OK0700
McGee, Michael	AL0850	McIntyre, Guinevere	IA0550	McLauchlin, Charlotte	OR1000
McGee, Ray	SC0050	McIntyre, John	IN1400	McLaughlin, Carrol M.	AZ0500
McGee, Timothy J.	AG0450	McIntyre, John	IN1350	McLaughlin, Gary	CA4460
McGee, William James	CA3400	McIntyre, Joy	MA0400	McLaughlin, Greg	CA4580
McGee-Daly, Kathleen	NJ0550	McIntyre, Robert John	MO1810	McLaughlin, Kevin	CA4150
McGhee, Andy	MA0260	McIntyre, Sarah Elizabeth	IL2750	McLaughlin, Michael	IL0780
McGhee, Janet F.	NY3650	McIver, Robert	NY1100	McLaughlin, Michael G.	MA1900
McGhee, Jeffrey	NY3350	McKamie, David W.	MO1780	McLaurin, Christopher	MO1810
McGhee, Lorna	AB0100	McKamie, Shirley	MO1780	McLaurine, Marcus	NJ1400
McGhee, Mary	AG0170	McKay, Anthony L.	PA0550	McLay, Mark	AG0130
McGhee, Michael	GA2200	McKay, David	TN0100	McLean, Allan	AI0150
McGill, Anthony	NY1900	McKay, Emily Hoppe	AZ0450	McLean, Greg	GA0940
McGill, Anthony	NY2250	McKay, Frances	DC0170	McLean, Hugh J.	AG0500
McGill, Anthony B.	MD0650	McKay, James R.	AG0500	McLean, John T.	IL2050
McGill, David	IL0550	McKay, Janis	NV0050	McLean, John	IL0550
Mcgill, Stan	TX0700	McKay, Neil	HI0210	McLean, Kathleen	IN0900
McGillivray, Angie	AA0050	McKeage, Kathleen M.	WY0200	McLean, Kathleen	AG0300
McGillvray, Bruce	AG0350	McKechnie, Donald	NY1800	McLean, Kathleen	AG0450
McGilvray, Byron	TX3360	McKee, Andy	NY2660	McLean, Kim	TN1600
McGilvray, Byron	CA4200	McKee, Angela	GA1150	McLean, Pierre	AI0150
McGinness, John	MD0150	McKee, David	VA1700	McLean, Rene	CT0650
McGinness, John R.	NY3780	McKee, Eric John	PA2750	McLeland, James K.	TX1000
McGinney, William L.	TX3420	McKee, Holly	MO0550	McLellan, Ray	MI1400
McGinnis, Barry E.	SC0900	McKee, Lindsey L.	MO1810	McLemore, Jeff	TN0150
McGinnis, Beth	AL0800	McKee, Lindsey L.	OK1450	McLemore, Katherine	OK1330
McGinnis, Donald E.	OH1850	McKee, Max	OR0950	Mcleod Metz, Caroline	AA0050
McGinnis, Tracy L.	MA2050	McKee, Pat	TX1600	McLeod, Lindy	AL1000
McGirr, Tom A.	WI0450	McKee, Paul	FL0850	McLin, Katherine E.	AZ0100
McGladrey, Cynthia	OR0250	McKee, Richard	GA1150	McLoskey, Lansing D.	FL1900
McGlinn, Margaret	NY2400	McKee, Richard	NC0300	McLoughlin, Michelle F.	NY3650
McGlone, Jeff	AZ0400	McKee-Williams, Robin	CA2150	McLouth, Ryan	MO0100
McGovern, Timothy S.	IL3300	McKeel, James	MN1450	McLowry, Sean	NY0700
McGowan, James	AG0200	McKeever, James I.	WI0835	McLucas, Anne Dhu	OR1050
McGowan, M.	MA0800	McKeever, Susan M.	WI0835	McLuhan, Eric	AG0130

853

Name	Code	Name	Code	Name	Code
McLure, Richard	TX3420	McQuinn, Julie	WI0350	Megill, Andrew	NJ1350
McLure, Richard	TX0370	McQuinn, Susan	FL1750	Megill, David W.	CA2960
McMahan, Andrew	CA0600	McQuiston, Kate	HI0210	Megill, Donald D.	CA2960
McMahan, Cassandra	NE0150	McReynolds, Clifton	IL0720	Mehaffey, Matthew W.	MN1623
McMahan, Jane	NY0200	McReynolds, Timothy	MD1010	Mehling, Gordon	CA0650
McMahan, Robert Y.	NJ0175	McRoberts, Gary	CA1900	Mehne, Wendy	NY1800
McMahel, Donald	IN1010	McRoberts, Terry	TN1660	Mehringer, Richard	AG0300
McMahon, Kevin	WI0700	McRoy, Danielle M.	NY2105	Mehrmann, Dan	IL2970
McMahon, Michael	AI0150	McRoy, James W.	NY2105	Mehrtens, Kathryn	NJ0175
McManus, Edward	OR0350	McSpadden, George	AL0350	Mehrtens, Russell	PA1150
McManus, Emily	TX2900	McSpadden, Larry D.	MO0300	Mehta, Phiroze	NY1800
McManus, James M.	CA3320	McSwain, Jenna	WY0130	Meidell, Katrin	TX3200
McManus, Keven M.	PA3000	McTee, Cindy K.	TX3420	Meidenbauer, Michael	NY3650
McManus, Kevin	MD0350	McTeer, Mikylah Myers	WV0750	Meidenbauer, Michael	NY3600
McManus, Lanny	AL0550	McTyre, Robert A.	GA1400	Meier, Gustav	MD0650
McManus, Laurie	VA1350	McVay, Vicki	KY1450	Meier, Margaret	CA3200
McMichael, Stacy	IL2300	McVeigh, Janice	CA5300	Meier, Scott Alan	PA2250
McMickle, Doug	OR0750	McVey, Elyse Nicole	TN1100	Meier, Steven	GA1500
McMillan, Bart	TX1775	McVey, Roger D.	WI0845	Meier-Sims, Kimberly R.	OH0600
McMillan, Brian	AI0150	McVinney, Barry D.	AR0350	Meighan, Patrick	FL0850
McMillan, Glenn	NY0640	McWain, Andrew J.	MA2020	Meineke, Robert	TX2350
McMillan, Kevin	VA0600	McWayne, Dorli	AK0150	Meinert, Anita	IA1950
McMillan, William	TX3520	McWhirter, Jamila L.	TN1100	Meinhart, Michelle	OH2550
McMillin, Timothy A.	IA1350	McWhorter, Brian J.	OR1050	Meintjes, Louise	NC0600
McMorrow, Kathleen	AG0450	McWilliams, Bernard	NC0450	Meints, Catharina	OH1700
McMosley, William F.	KS0700	McWilliams, Heather	WI0830	Meints, Kenneth	NE0500
McMullen, Dianne M.	NY4310	McWilliams, Kent M.	MN1450	Meints, Ruth	NE0610
McMullen, George	CA2650	McWilliams, Larry	IN0150	Meir, Baruch	AZ0100
McMullen, George Edward	CA5020	McWilliams, Paul	CA5353	Meir, Eran	IL3450
McMullen, Michael	CA0840	McWilliams, Robert	WI0830	Meissner, Marla	NJ0800
McMullen, Mike	CA0150	Mdivani, Marina	AI0150	Meister, Blake	MD0650
McMullen, Tracy	ME0200	Meacham, Helen M.	PA2000	Meister, Scott R.	NC0050
McMullen, William W.	NE0600	Meachum, Jay	NC0350	Meitin, A. Richard	MN1000
McMullian, Neal	IL2300	Meachum, Jay	NC1600	Meitrott, Gary	VT0200
McMullin, Brendan	CA3100	Mead, Andrew W.	MI2100	Meixner, Brian	PA3100
McMunn, Ben	IL0750	Mead, Maurita Murphy	IA1550	Meixner, Micah L.	TX3200
McMunn, Brent	CA5300	Mead, Sarah	MA0500	Meizel, Katherine L.	OH0300
McMurray, Allan R.	CO0800	Meade, David B.	NY2750	Mejias, Paoli	PR0115
McMurray, Heather A.	VA1475	Meade, Karen	MO0500	Mekeel, Alison R.	PA1250
McMurray, Louise	AA0080	Meade, Michael	NY2200	Mekler, Joseph	NJ0750
McMurray, Mary	AF0120	Meader, Darmon	NY2150	Melago, Kathleen A.	PA3100
McMurray, William	MO0850	Meaders, James M.	MS0400	Melamed, Daniel R.	IN0900
McMurtery, John M.	IL3500	Meador, Rebecca	KS1400	Melancon, Violaine M.	MD0650
McMurtry, Lynne	NY3725	Meadows, Anthony	PA1550	Melbinger, Timothy	PA2710
McNab, Duncan	MN1623	Meadows, Christine	OR0850	Mele, Anthony	MA2030
McNabb, Carol	TX3515	Meadows, Erin	TN0930	Melendez Dohnert, Victor	PR0115
McNabney, Douglas	AI0150	Meadows, Leslie	OH0200	Melendez, Carlos	MI0150
McNair, Jacqueline	GA1260	Meadows, Melody	WV0800	Melendez, Jose	PR0115
McNair, Jonathan B.	TN1700	Mealy, Robert	NY1900	Melendres, Henry	NV0150
McNair, Linda	MO0550	Mealy, Robert	CT0900	Melford, Myra J.	CA5000
McNair, Sylvia	IN0900	Means, Allen	IL2450	Melgaard, Connie	GA0940
McNally, Blair	AG0070	Means, Arthur	AL0650	Melia, Hal	OH0500
McNally, Kirk	AB0150	Means, Matthew L.	KS0350	Melik-Stepanov, Karren	IA1200
McNally, Patrick	MT0400	Meany, Thomas	PA3550	Melik-Stepanov, Karren	IA0500
McNally, Patrick	WA1350	Mears, Perry G.	TN0850	Melik-Stepanov, Karren	SD0050
McNamara, Gretchen	OH2500	Measel, Jane	WA0550	Melito, Matthew	AZ0250
McNamara, Joann	MI0600	Measels, Clark	TN0250	Melito, Tom	CT0050
McNamara, Ray	CA1900	Meashey, Kelly	PA1550	Melkonyan, Magdalina	MD0700
McNamara, Robert	CA3050	Meashey, Steven	PA2300	Mellenbruch, Judy	TX0550
McNaughton, Barry	CA3800	Meccia, Lauren L.	SC1100	Melley, Eric	LA0200
McNaughton, Karen	AA0020	Mecham, Bryce	ID0060	Mellichamp, James F.	GA1650
McNeal, Steve W.	CO0250	Mecham, Jessica	ID0060	Mellinger, Erma	NH0100
McNeel, Mary	TX2100	Mecham, Mark L.	PA1900	Mellins-Bumbulis, Valija	TN0550
McNeela, Rico	MO0850	Mechell, Harry A.	MN1700	Mello, Christopher	CA1750
McNeely, April A.	CA4425	Mechell, Lauren	MN1700	Mello, Christopher	CA0859
McNeely, Carol	DC0170	Meckler, David C.	CA0855	Mello, S.	CA1950
McNeely, Heather	SC0200	Meckley, Rod	PA3710	Melloni, Romeo	NH0250
McNeely, James	NY2150	Meckley, William A.	NY3600	Mellors, Carol	AA0020
McNeely, James	NJ1400	Meconi, Honey	NY1100	Melman, Mort	MO1120
McNeely, Joel	CA5300	Meconi, Honey	NY4350	Melnick, Marjorie	CT0650
McNeely-Bouie, Barbara	FL0550	Medeiros, Peter	HI0210	Melnick, Marjorie L.	MA2000
McNeil, Albert J.	CA5010	Meder, Randall A.	WI0808	Melnikoff, Anna	AG0650
McNeil, Carol	MI0520	Medford, Sue	WI1150	Melson, Christine	CT0500
McNeil, John	MA1400	Medina, Lindsay	IN0900	Melton, James L.	CA5355
McNeil, Kathy J.	TX3200	Medisky, Laura M.	WI0840	Melton, Laura	OH0300
McNeil, Linda	TX3350	Medler, Ben	OR0850	Melton, Michael D.	IL2150
McNeill, Charles	IL3300	Medley, Nathan	IN1100	Meltzer, Harold	NY4450
McNeill, Dean	AJ0150	Medley, Susan	PA3580	Meltzer, Howard S.	NY0270
McNeill, George	VA1700	Medley, William R.	IA1140	Melville, Alison	AG0450
Mcneill, Karl	PA1000	Medlock, Matthew	FL0680	Melville, Nicola	MN0300
McNeill, Marvin	CT0600	Medwin, Marc	DC0010	Memmott, Jenny	MO0050
McNeish, James	CT0100	Meehan, Conor	MA2250	Memory, Barbara	NC0650
McNellie, Myra	TX2700	Meehan, Jill	PA3680	Menard, Aileen	AG0500
McNerney, Kathleen	ME0200	Meehan, Jill	PA3250	Menard, Elizabeth	OH0300
McNiven, Lisa	ID0060	Meehan, Linda Pearce	MI1260	Menaul, Richard A.	MA0400
McNutt, Craig	MA2050	Meehan, Todd	TX0300	Menchaca, Louis A.	WI0300
McNutt, Elizabeth	TX3420	Meek, Darla	TX2955	Menconi, Audra M.	TX2200
McPartland, Dennis	IA0750	Meek, David	AB0200	Mendel, Traci R.	AL1050
McPhail, Ann Marie	GA1900	Meek, Richard	TX3200	Mendelson, Jacob	NY1450
McPhee, Rosemary	AF0050	Meeker, Christopher	NY2500	Mendelson, Jacob	NY1860
McPherson, Eve	OH1100	Meeker, Howard G.	OH0650	Mendelson, Richard	MA0260
McPherson, John	AA0100	Meeker, Jared	CA0200	Mendelson, Ruth J.	MA0260
McPherson, Sandra	CA0150	Meeks, Joseph D.	GA1150	Mendenhall, Eddie	CA3050
McPike, Brent G.	IN0800	Meeroff, Myrna	FL0200	Mendenhall, Judith	NY2250
McQuade, Jennifer H.	OK0650	Meffert-Nelson, Karrin	MN0750	Mendez, Genaro	KS1350
McQuade, Mark A.	OK0650	Megas, Alexander	CA3800	Mendez, Jose Ramon	NY2750
McQuarrie, Sarah	MA0510	Megginson, Charolette	IL3500	Mendez, Max	ID0140
McQueen, William F.	TX2100	Megginson, Julie	GA1000	Mendoken, Scott	CT0650
McQuere, Gordon	KS1400	Meggison, Shelly	AL1170	Mendola, Ron	GA0900
McQuilkin, Terry P.	OR1050	Meggs, Gary L.	AR0800	Mendonca, Maria Alice	OH1200

Alphabetical Listing of Faculty

Name	Code	Name	Code	Name	Code
Mendoza, Chico	NJ1400	Mery, John	OR0400	Mianulli, Janice	PA1650
Mendoza, Cristina	LA0450	Mery, John Christian	OR0800	Miceli, Anthony	PA3250
Mendoza, Eleanor	IN0500	Merz, Albert	DC0050	Miceli, Anthony	NJ1050
Mendoza, Freddie	TX3175	Merz, Albert	DC0010	Miceli, Jennifer Scott	NY2105
Mendoza, Joanna	MO1830	Merz, Christopher Linn	IA1600	Miceli, Tony	PA3330
Mendoza, Juan Carlos	IL1800	Merz, Laurie	MN0050	Michael, Doug	CA1560
Mendoza, Michael D.	NJ0175	Merz, Laurie	MN1300	Michael, George	OH2140
Mendoza, Victor	MA0260	Mesare, Roi	PA3000	Michael, Louis	IL1500
Mendoza, Vince	CA5300	Meschi, John	NY2105	Michael, Marilyn	FL1650
Menegon, John	NY3760	Messenger, Joseph	IA0850	Michaelian, Patricia	WA1050
Menendez Abovici, Natalia E.	PR0115	Messenger, Richard	CA5355	Michaels, Ben	TN0300
Meng, Chuiyuan	IN0907	Messer, Benjamin	AZ0470	Michaels, Cary	TX3175
Meng, Mei-Mei	PA0850	Messerschmidt, William H.	VA1600	Michaels, Mark	MA2030
Meng, Mei-Mei	NY2250	Messersmith, Charles	SC0275	Michaels, Matthew	MI2200
Mengelkoch, Eva	MD0850	Messersmith, Susan	SC0275	Michaelsen, Garrett	MA2030
Menghini, Charles T.	IL3450	Messich, Reid	GA2100	Michalek, Thomas	NE0300
Mengozzi, Stefano	MI2100	Messick, Heather	AL1195	Michaud Martins, Ellen	MA2030
Menhart, Donna	CT0650	Messing, Scott	MI0150	Michaud, Natalie	AI0150
Menk, Nancy L.	IN1450	Messner, Walter	WI0830	Michaud, Pierre	AI0200
Menke, Carol	CA4460	Messoloras, Irene	OK0600	Michaud, Shaun	MA0260
Menkis, Jonathan	MA1400	Mesterhazy, George	NJ1050	Michel, Christopher	TX2250
Menmuir, Dorla	CA4580	Metcalf, Curtis	AG0450	Michel, Dennis	IL0550
Mennemeyer, Bethany	CA1750	Metcalf, Joanne	WI0350	Michel, John	WA0050
Mennicke, David	MN0610	Metcalf, John C.	PA1750	Michel, Peggy	IL0550
Menoche, Charles Paul	CT0050	Metcalf, Lee	CT0800	Michel, Peggy	IL0730
Menon, Rekha	MA0260	Metcalf, Mark A.	TX3000	Micheletti, Joan	MT0350
Mensah, Sowah	MN1623	Metcalf, Mary Louise	OH0100	Michelic, Leslie O.	WI0350
Mensah, Sowah	MN1625	Metcalf, Michael	OH0100	Michelic, Matthew C.	WI0350
Mensah, Sowah	MN0950	Metcalf, Steve P.	CT0650	Michelin, Nando	MA0260
Mensch, Thomas	TX3370	Metcalfe, Evelyn	FL2130	Michelin, Nando	MA1900
Mensh, Heather	TX3370	Metcalfe, James L.	TX2295	Michelin, Rob	MA2250
Menth, Christelle	CO0150	Metcalfe, Scott	MA0400	Michell, Edna	NY2250
Menton, Allen W.	CA0845	Metcalfe, Scott	MD0650	Michell, Ray	OR0350
Mentschukoff, Andrej	OH1600	Metelsky, Lynda	AG0450	Michels, Joyce	IL2310
Mentschukoff, Andrej	OH1200	Methe, Daniel	CA0815	Michels, Maureen	NC2205
Mentzel, Eric P.	OR1050	Metil, Robert	PA0600	Michelson, Bliss	PA2800
Mentzel, Michael G.	MD1050	Metlicka, Scott D.	IL0840	Michewicz, Michael	MI0850
Mentzel, Michael	MD0550	Metts, Calland	MN1600	Michki, Kevin	NY3725
Mentzer, Larry E.	TX2200	Metz, Andreas	OH0200	Michniewicz, John T.	CT0300
Mentzer, Larry E.	TX3530	Metz, Donald E.	OH2200	Micic, Alma	NY5000
Menzies, Mark	CA0510	Metz, Ken	TX3410	Micic, Rale	NY5000
Mercado, Chesley	GA0850	Metz, Paul W.	CO0250	Mickey, Brian	AR0600
Mercer, Amy	MN0600	Metz, Sue	CA0840	Mickey, Patricia A.	MO1780
Mercer, Bjorn M.	AZ0440	Metzer, David	AB0100	Mickey, Sarah	AR0600
Mercer, Christopher A.	IL2250	Metzger, Jon	NC0750	Mickey, Wendy	KS0265
Mercer, Gregory S.	NY1600	Metzler, James	MI0900	Micklich, Albie	AZ0100
Mercer, Ida K.	OH0600	Metzler, Linda	PA3550	Micznik, Vera G.	AB0100
Mercer, James	CA3400	Meunier, Catherine	NY3780	Midboe, David J.	WI0801
Mercer, John	DC0150	Meunier, Robert W.	IA0550	Middagh, Ryan	TN1100
Mercer, Scott A.	IN1800	Meuth, Alison	IL1800	Middaugh, Laurie	AL1200
Mercer-Taylor, Peter	MN1623	Meves, Carol	WI1150	Middle, Bruce H.	VA1475
Merchant, Tanya H.	CA5070	Mewaldt, David	WI0810	Middleton, Jaynne	TX0900
Merchlewitz, Brenda	MN1700	Meyer, Alice	NY3350	Middleton, Jonathan N.	WA0250
Mercier, Richard E.	GA0950	Meyer, Andreas K.	DE0150	Middleton, Peter	IL2200
Mercier, William	VT0100	Meyer, Beverly	NY2200	Middleton, Polly K.	VA1700
Merciers, Meghan	MI0100	Meyer, David	VA1350	Middleton, R. Hugh	NC0500
Meredith, Henry M.	AG0500	Meyer, Donald C.	IL1400	Middleton, Robert M.	NJ0050
Meredith, Sarah A.	WI0808	Meyer, Dyan	IA1600	Middleton, Valerie	TN1850
Meredith, Scott	WY0200	Meyer, Edgar	PA0850	Midgley, Herbert	TX2700
Meredith, Steven	UT0190	Meyer, Edgar	TN1850	Midha, Chris	MO0825
Meredith, Victoria	AG0500	Meyer, Elizabeth C.	MI1450	, Midiyanto	CA5000
Meredith, William	CA4400	Meyer, Eric	WI1150	Miedema, Bradley	IA0500
Meretta, Kristy	MI0600	Meyer, Eve R.	PA3250	Miedema, Harry F.	IN1650
Merfeld, Robert	MA1175	Meyer, Frederick	WV0650	Miedema, Lisa	IA1200
Merfeld, Robert	MA0400	Meyer, Jeffery David	NY1800	Miedema, Lisa	IA0500
Merideth, Sherry Francis	TN0550	Meyer, Jeffrey	MN0600	Mielbrecht, Marie	CA4300
Merkel, Jeffrey	CO0830	Meyer, Joe	CA3600	Mielcarz, Kelly	IL2050
Merkel, Steve	AL1195	Meyer, Julie	MI1850	Miele, David	NY3000
Merkelo, Paul	AI0150	Meyer, Kathy	CA2775	Miele, William	RI0150
Merkley, Paul	AG0400	Meyer, Kenneth	NY1550	Mielke, Michelle	WA1150
Merkowitz, Jennifer Bernard	OH2050	Meyer, Kenneth R.	NY4150	Mieses, Nermis	KY1450
Mermagen, Michael	DC0050	Meyer, Kenton	PA0850	Mieske, Lynda	AG0600
Merrifield, Deborah	CA4450	Meyer, Lisa M.	MI2200	Mietus, Raymond	NC2700
Merrill, Allison	OH0300	Meyer, Pam	WA0950	Mietz, Joshua	NM0400
Merrill, Amy	MA0260	Meyer, Peter	MN0050	Miglia, Jay	OH2050
Merrill, Brian G.	TX2400	Meyer, Robert	CT0600	Migliaccio, Tatiana	WI1150
Merrill, Kenneth	NY1900	Meyer, Sandra G.	OK0650	Miglio, Joseph	MA0260
Merrill, Kenneth W.	NY2150	Meyer, Stephen C.	NY4100	Migliozzi, Anastasia E.	VA1000
Merrill, Paul	NH0350	Meyer, Thomas	IN1100	Mihai, Julieta	IL3500
Merrill, Paul	NY0900	Meyers Sawa, Suzanne	AG0450	Mihai-Zoeter, Mariana	MD0350
Merrill, Suzanne Kantorski	VT0100	Meyers, Angela	CT0300	Mihalik, Denise	NJ0500
Merrill, Theresa R.	MI0600	Meyers, Carolyn	NC0650	Mihopulos, Michael	WI0150
Merrill, Thomas G.	OH2550	Meyers, Dan	MI1550	Mikalunas, Robin	TX3540
Merriman, John C.	AL0500	Meyers, Heather	AA0020	Mikhalevsky, Nina	DC0110
Merriman, Lyle C.	PA2750	Meyers, Joe	NY2750	Mikhaylova, Ekaterina	AI0200
Merriman, Margarita L.	MA0250	Meyers, John	WI0100	Mikhlin, Alexandra	DC0170
Merrit, Doug	TN0580	Meyers, Joseph	IN0905	Mikkelsen, Carol M.	GA2150
Merritt, Frank	NC1100	Meyers, Nicholaus S.	ND0600	Mikkelson, Russel	OH1850
Merritt, Justin W.	MN1450	Meyers, Paul	NJ0825	Mikkola, Gary	NC1950
Merritt, Myra	OH0300	Meyers, Paul	NJ1400	Miklik, Carlie	WI0842
Merritt, Romona	AL0650	Meyers, Stephanie	TX3520	Mikolajcik, Walter	CA4650
Merryman, Marjorie	NY2150	Meyn, Richard	OR0700	Mikolajewski, Alice	DC0100
Merseth, Megan	MN0200	Meyn, Till MacIvor	TX3000	Mikowsky, Solomon	IL0550
Mertens, Michael	CA2750	Meza, Fernando	MN1623	Mikowsky, Solomon	NY2150
Mertens, Paul	IL0550	Meza, Oscar M.	CA0835	Miksch, Bonnie	OR0850
Mertz, Amy	NY4150	Mezei, Margaret	AA0200	Miksza, Peter J.	IN0900
Mertz, Justin J.	NY4150	Mezzadri, Danilo	MS0750	Mikulay, Mark	IL2500
Mertz, Tonya	ND0400	Miahky, Stephen A.	OH1900	Milam, Brent	GA1050
Merusi, Rebecca	OR0950	Miano, Jo Ellen	NY3775	Milam, Michael R.	VA0550
Merva Robblee, Carolyn	IL1400	Mianulli, Janice	PA2100	Milam, Timothy A.	FL0100

Name	Code	Name	Code	Name	Code
Milanese, Jessica	WA0650	Miller, Gabriel	LA0150	Miller, Sandra	NY1900
Milanovich, Donna Z.	IL3310	Miller, Gary	MA0260	Miller, Sara	MO1550
Milarsky, Jeffrey	NY1900	Miller, Geoffrey	UT0250	Miller, Scott D.	WA1350
Milarsky, Jeffrey	NY2150	Miller, Greg F.	LA0300	Miller, Scott L.	MN1300
Milarsky, Jeffrey F.	NY0750	Miller, Gregory	FL1125	Miller, Sharon	VA0100
Milbauer, John P.	AZ0500	Miller, Gregory	MD1010	Miller, Sharon	VA0300
Milenkovic, Michelle	AA0020	Miller, Harold L.	WI0450	Miller, Stephen R.	TN1800
Milenkovic, Vladan	MA0510	Miller, Heather	IL1740	Miller, Steve	WY0115
Milenkovic, Vladan	MN0050	Miller, Heidi Johanna	MA2250	Miller, Stewart	IL3310
Milenkovich, Stefan	IL3300	Miller, Ivan	NJ1400	Miller, Sue	ID0075
Milenski, Isabel	NY1600	Miller, James	CA0510	Miller, Tammy	FL1750
Miles, Benjamin E.	TN1100	Miller, James	CA5030	Miller, Tess Anissa	MI0150
Miles, Butch	TX3175	Miller, James Patrick	MA2000	Miller, Thomas	CO0900
Miles, Charles F.	MS0700	Miller, James E.	PA1900	Miller, Thomas A.	OR1150
Miles, Dean	AB0040	Miller, Jane	WY0115	Miller, Thomas E.	CA5400
Miles, Debbie	AF0120	Miller, Jane	MA0260	Miller, Tim	MA0260
Miles, Melvin N.	MD0600	Miller, Jean	TN0930	Miller, Tim	NE0460
Miles, Michael A.	MS0750	Miller, Jeffrey L.	CA0807	Miller, Timothy	GA1450
Miles, Patrick	WI0850	Miller, Jeremy	IL2050	Miller, Todd	CA0815
Miles, Richard B.	KY0900	Miller, Jessica	SC0420	Miller, Tom	OH0250
Miles, Ron	CO0550	Miller, Jessica	NC2440	Miller, Tom D.	IL0750
Miles, Sarah	TN1850	Miller, Jim D.	NJ1050	Miller, Ward	AL1300
Miles, Stacey	MS0750	Miller, Jo Ann	ND0350	Miller, Wendy L.	PA0250
Miles, Stephen T.	FL1360	Miller, Joan	MN1300	Miller, Zach	MN1250
Miles, Tammy	MS0370	Miller, Jody	GA0050	Miller-Brown, Donna	KS0590
Milewski, Barbara Ann	PA3200	Miller, Joe	NJ1350	Miller-Campbell, Tamara J.	MO1900
Milewski, Piotr	OH2200	Miller, Joel	AI0150	Miller-Thorn, Jill	NY1275
Miley, James	OR1300	Miller, John A.	IL1350	Millet, Wayne	FL1500
Miley, Jeff	CA0630	Miller, John L.	AL1160	Millett, Michael J.	TX3535
Miley, Jeff	CA1510	Miller, John	FL1745	Millham, Michael	WA0250
Milford, Gene F.	OH2150	Miller, John	ND0350	Millham, Michael	WA0400
Milgate, Brooks	MA0650	Miller, John	MN1623	Millhouse, Steven	AZ0440
Milgram-Luterman, Joni F.	NY3725	Miller, Joseph P.	SC1200	Millican, Brady	MA0800
Milham, Edwin M.	MA0510	Miller, Josh	WV0200	Millican, Jason	TX1250
Milholland, John	CA3400	Miller, Julie Welsh	NY3780	Millican, Si	TX3530
Miliauskas, John	MD0850	Miller, June Entwisle	IL3100	Milligan, Terence G.	OH2200
Milicevic, Zeljko	MI1750	Miller, Karen Epps	TX2250	Milligan, Thomas	TN0250
Miljkovic, Katarina	MA1400	Miller, Karen Coe	OK0750	Millioto, Thomas	NY0625
Millan, Luis	MT0400	Miller, Karla	MN1260	Millner, William	FL1745
Millar, Cameron	MD0300	Miller, Kathleen A.	NY3780	Mills, Alan W.	CO0275
Millar, Jana	TX0300	Miller, Kathryn	PA3650	Mills, Charlotte	CO0950
Millar, Michael W.	CA0630	Miller, Kelly A.	FL1800	Mills, David	OR0050
Millar, Robert R.	CA4625	Miller, Ken	MN1250	Mills, David	CT0600
Millar, Tania	AG0070	Miller, Kenneth E.	MO1830	Mills, Jackie	AL0400
Millard, Christopher	IL2250	Miller, Kenny	AZ0470	Mills, Jesse A.	NJ0800
Millard, Christopher	AG0400	Miller, Kevin D.	MI0600	Mills, Joan G.	CA4450
Millard, Joshua P.	MA2030	Miller, Kiri	RI0050	Mills, John	TX3510
Millat, Andrew	OH0450	Miller, Kristi	MN1620	Mills, Kate Irvine	CA3270
Millat, Andy	OH1900	Miller, Lance R.	OR1050	Mills, Michele D.	OH2150
Milleker, Troy	AG0200	Miller, Lane E.	NY3780	Mills, Peter	OH0850
Miller, Aaron D.	ID0060	Miller, Leigh	GA2300	Mills, Ralph L.	TX2250
Miller, Al	AL1195	Miller, Leta	CA5070	Mills, Robert	AZ0100
Miller, Alan	IN0250	Miller, Linda	VA1350	Mills, Robert	AZ0440
Miller, Allan	CA6050	Miller, Lisa	IN1800	Mills, Robert P.	VA0650
Miller, Andrew	ND0050	Miller, Lori	SD0100	Mills, Susan W.	NC0050
Miller, Andrew	AL0300	Miller, Lydia	MN1625	Mills, Terry	CA4300
Miller, Andrew	GA0550	Miller, M. Frederick	IL2650	Millsap, Kyle	KY0950
Miller, Ann Elizabeth	CA5350	Miller, Marc	GA1150	Millsapp, Brian	NC1550
Miller, Anna Maria	TN0100	Miller, Margaret	CO0200	Millstein, Eric J.	IL0750
Miller, Anton	CT0650	Miller, Margaret J.	CO0250	Milnar, Veronica Edwards	TN1100
Miller, Anton M.	NY2750	Miller, Marie C.	KS0300	Milnarik, Michael S.	ME0500
Miller, Becky	IL1612	Miller, Mark	MA0400	Milne, Andy	NY2750
Miller, Ben F.	WV0400	Miller, Mark	CO0560	Milne, Andy	NY2660
Miller, Brett	WV0800	Miller, Mary	TX1660	Milne, David	WI0845
Miller, Brigetta F.	WI0350	Miller, Mary Ellen	MA1350	Milne, Virginia E.	TX2800
Miller, Bruce E.	CA1075	Miller, Matthew	WI0250	Milner Howell, Denise	OH0100
Miller, Bruce	CA1900	Miller, Matthew	WI0830	Milnes, David	CA5000
Miller, Bryan	IL0850	Miller, Maureen	PA2950	Milosavljevic, Svetozar	IN0005
Miller, Cercie	MA2050	Miller, Melanie	PA2300	Milovanovic, Biljana	NJ0700
Miller, Charles	ID0140	Miller, Michael	WA0980	Milstein, Amir	MA0510
Miller, Christian	OH0680	Miller, Michael	FL1100	Miltenberger, James E.	WV0750
Miller, Christopher J.	NY0900	Miller, Michael	OH0600	Milton, Blair	IL2250
Miller, Connaitre	DC0150	Miller, Michael	MI2250	Milton, Jos	MS0700
Miller, Cory	AA0020	Miller, Michelle	OH2290	Milton, Kenneth	MS0560
Miller, Cynthia F.	AL1170	Miller, Mulgrew	NJ1400	Mims, Herbert	CA1100
Miller, Dale	AR0110	Miller, Patricia A.	VA0450	Mims, Lloyd	FL1450
Miller, Dale	CO0200	Miller, Patricia M.	NY3650	Mims, Marilyn	FL1450
Miller, Dan	IN1800	Miller, Patrick	CT0650	Mims, Mary	MO1500
Miller, Daniel J.	WV0550	Miller, Paul W.	PA2740	Min, Beverly	CA0960
Miller, DaVaughn	NC1150	Miller, Paul V.	CO0800	Mina, Niloofar	NJ0825
Miller, David L.	AL1160	Miller, Peter	TX3360	Minard, Juliet	IL0300
Miller, David	MS0050	Miller, Peter	IN1025	Minas-Bekov, Ivan	DC0170
Miller, David	OR0010	Miller, Peter	VT0100	Minasian, Linda	CA5400
Miller, David	OR0950	Miller, Phillip	CA0450	Minasian, Mark	HI0160
Miller, Dennis	AI0150	Miller, R J	CO0550	Minch, Claudia	FL1950
Miller, Dennis H.	MA1450	Miller, Randy	MI0520	Mindell, Pamela Getnick	MA0700
Miller, Donald K.	TX3530	Miller, Rebecca C.	KY0610	Mindeman, John	IL3550
Miller, Donna Z.	NY4150	Miller, Rebecca S.	MA1000	Mindeman, John	IL3500
Miller, Douglas	NC0050	Miller, Richard	NJ0825	Mindemann, John	IL1350
Miller, Elaine	NC2000	Miller, Richard	GA0625	Mindock, Rebecca A.	AL1300
Miller, Elizabeth	NJ1140	Miller, Rob	AG0450	Minear, Carolyn	MO1950
Miller, Eric	TN0260	Miller, Robert F.	CT0600	Minette, A. J.	CA2800
Miller, Eric	TX2800	Miller, Robin	CA2250	Mineva, Daniela	CA2250
Miller, Eric	TX2650	Miller, Rodney L.	OH2140	Minevich, Eduard	AJ0100
Miller, Esther	TN1660	Miller, Roger L.	UT0250	Minevich, Pauline M.	AJ0100
Miller, Ethan	OH1100	Miller, Ronald L.	PA2300	Mingus, Richard	AB0090
Miller, Everett F.	KS0225	Miller, Ronald E.	PA2050	Mingus, Richard	AB0100
Miller, Franklin	WI0825	Miller, Russell	MI2200	Minichiello, Molly J.	NJ0800
Miller, Fred	IL3100	Miller, Russell	NY1100	Minneman, Ginger	OH2500
Miller, Fred	IL2775	Miller, Ryan	IL0400	Minnis, MaryBeth	MI0400

Alphabetical Listing of Faculty

Name	Code	Name	Code	Name	Code
Minor, Clark	CA0800	Miyakawa, Felicia M.	TN1100	Moll, Kevin N.	NC0650
Minor, Janice L.	VA0600	Miyake, Jan	OH1700	Mollenauer, David	TX2200
Minor, Ryan	NY3790	Miyama, Yoko	OR0050	Mollenauer, David	TX3350
Minorgan, Bruce	AI0150	Miyamoto, Peter M.	MO1800	Mollenhauer, Jude	OH2050
Minotti, Robert	NY1300	Miyamura, Henry	HI0210	Mollenhauer, Shawn	CO0550
Minsavage, Susan	PA3700	Miyashiro, Darin	HI0210	Mollenkopf, Jennifer	OH2290
Minter, Drew	NY4450	Miyashiro, Kurt	IL2800	Moller-Marino, Diana	CT0650
Minter, Karen	KS0100	Miyashiro, Ralph	CA4100	Mollicone, Henry	CA1950
Minter, Kendall	GA1050	Mizell, John	MO0200	Mollicone, Henry	CA3270
Minturn, Neil	MO1800	Mizener, Charlotte P.	TX1400	Molloy, Steve	KS0590
Mintz, Randy	NC0900	Mizener, Gary	TX1400	Molloy, Steve	MO0850
Mintzer, Bob	CA5300	Mizicko, Shane J.	MO1500	Mols, Robert W.	NY4320
Miotke, David	CA3520	Mizma, Michael E.	TX2295	Moltoni, Giovanni	MA0260
Miranda, Angelo	NY4200	Mizrahi, Michael	WI0350	Molumby, Nicole L.	ID0050
Miranda, Charles	IA0650	Mizuno, Ikuko	MA0400	Molzan, Brett	AI0190
Miranda, Charles	IA0420	Mo, Sung Hoon	IL0840	Molzan, Ryan	AI0190
Miranda, Julianne M.	IN0250	Moak, Elizabeth W.	MS0750	Momand, Elizabeth B.	AR0730
Miranda, Martina	CO0800	Mobberley, James C.	MO1810	Monachino, Jerome	VT0400
Miranda, Michael A.	CA2800	Mobbs, Daniel	CA4150	Monachino, Paul	OH1330
Miranda, Roberto	CA5031	Moberg, Jonathan	WI0825	Monaghan, Daniel	PA3250
Mirchandani, Sharon	NJ1350	Mobley, Jenny	IN0250	Monaghan, Megan	PA2550
Mirhady, Tom	AA0050	Mobley, Mel	LA0770	Monaghan, Michael	MA0700
Miropolskaya, Mara	NY2400	Mochnick, John	IL2900	Monahan, Katie	WI1150
Mirowitz, Sheldon P.	MA0260	Mocny, Timothy S.	MI0400	Monahan, Laurie	MA1175
Misenheimer, Aaron L.	NC0850	Moder, Jennifer	KS0590	Monahan, Seth	NY1100
Misenhelter, Dale D.	AR0700	Moder, Jennifer	IL1090	Monchick, Alexandra	CA0835
Misfeldt, Mark	NE0610	Modesitt, Carol Ann	UT0200	Mondie, Eugene	DC0050
Mishra, Jennifer	MO1830	Modica, Joseph	CA5150	Monear, Clifford E.	MI2200
Mishra, Michael	IL2910	Modin, Lindsay	KS0700	Monek, Daniel G.	OH1400
Miska, Renee	FL0200	Modirzadeh, Hafez	CA4200	Mongiardo, Josephine	NY4200
Miskell, Jerome P.	OH2290	Moe, Aaron	MN1200	Mongiardo-Cooper, Josephine	NY0200
Mismas, James	OH2290	Moe, Charlette	ND0350	Mongrain, Richard	CO0625
Missal, Jason	TX0050	Moe, Eric H.	PA3420	Monhardt, Jonathan	WI0825
Missal, Joseph	OK0800	Moe, Eric	WA1350	Monhardt, Maurice	IA0950
Misslin, Patricia	NY0150	Moe, Jean	CA4100	Monical, Dwight	IN1300
Misslin, Patricia	MA1400	Moe, Judy	IL0550	Monier, Shelly	MO1100
Misslin, Patricia	NY2150	Moe, Karla	NY2550	Moninger, Susan	IL0850
Mitchell, Aaron Paul	IN0905	Moe, Karla	NY2105	Moniz, Michael	MA0260
Mitchell, Adrian	MS0350	Moe, Sharon	NY2105	Monke, Kirsten	ME0200
Mitchell, Alan	MI1180	Moe, Sharon	NJ0825	Monkelien, Sheryl	PA2150
Mitchell, Alan	MI0250	Moebus-Bergeron, Susanne	MA0260	Monllos, John	RI0300
Mitchell, Alice L.	NY3705	Moege, Gary R.	MO1790	Monosoff, Sonya	NY0900
Mitchell, Andrew	AG0200	Moegle, Mary Steele A.	LA0250	Monoyios, Ann	AG0300
Mitchell, Andrew	DC0170	Moehle, Matthew	OH1100	Monroe, Annetta Y.	FL2000
Mitchell, Brenda	OH1450	Moehlman, Carl B.	IA0900	Monroe, Diane	PA3250
Mitchell, Brian	GA0940	Moeller, Cindy R.	IA1200	Monroe, Douglas	NC0650
Mitchell, Bryan P.	MS0570	Moeller, Jeremy	IL2200	Monroe, Marc	KY0600
Mitchell, Carol	GA0940	Moersch, Charlotte Mattax	IL3300	Monroe, Martha Frances	MS0570
Mitchell, Charlene	MO0600	Moersch, William	IL3300	Monroe, Michael	MA0950
Mitchell, Christopher	KY0950	Moes, Brook	CA5350	Monseur, George	MA0260
Mitchell, Clarence T.	DC0350	Moeser, Charles	VA1600	Monson, Anne	IL0730
Mitchell, Dan	TX0900	Moeser, James	NC2410	Monson, Craig	MO1900
Mitchell, Dan	TX0050	Moeser, Susan	NC2410	Monson, Dale E.	GA2100
Mitchell, Dan	CA1550	Moffett, Brad	TN0850	Monson, Ingrid	MA1050
Mitchell, Danlee G.	CA4100	Moffett, C. Mondre	NC1550	Monson, Linda Apple	VA0450
Mitchell, Darleen C.	NE0590	Mogerman, Flora	AZ0490	Montagnier, Jean-Paul	AI0150
Mitchell, David	OR0150	Mogle, Dean	OH2200	Montague, Eugene	DC0100
Mitchell, David W.	OR1100	Moham, Carren D.	IL1200	Montague, Matthew G.	KS1050
Mitchell, David	OH1100	Mohamed, Jamal	TX2400	Montalbano, James	NY2450
Mitchell, Deborah H.	CA0825	Mohammed, Michael	CA4150	Montalbano, Richard	NY0650
Mitchell, Elizabeth	AG0600	Mohar, Barbara	NY2105	Montalbano, Rick C.	NY4150
Mitchell, Emily	TX2700	Mohen, Gerald	NY2400	Montalbano, Rick	NY1350
Mitchell, Erin	WA0860	Mohen, Girard	NY5000	Montalbetti, Barbara	AJ0150
Mitchell, Evelyn	MO1830	Mohr, Bette	IL0420	Montalto, Richard Michael	MS0550
Mitchell, Geoffrey	AI0150	Mohr, Deanne	MN1700	Montalvo, Raquel	PR0100
Mitchell, Ian	AZ0150	Moidel, Jeffrey	WA0300	Montanaro, Donald	PA0850
Mitchell, James	WI0500	Moio, Dom	AZ0100	Montane, Carlos	IN0900
Mitchell, Jennifer	GA1150	Moio, Dom	AZ0400	Montano, David R.	CO0900
Mitchell, John	DC0050	Moio, Dominick	AZ0440	Montcrieff, Kathy	NY2950
Mitchell, Jon	MA2010	Moir, Jennifer	AG0500	Monte, Charlene	MA2020
Mitchell, Joseph	CA0805	Moisan, Andre	AI0210	Monte, Michael	MA2020
Mitchell, Joseph	CA1750	Moisan, Andre	AI0200	Monte, Tobias	MA2020
Mitchell, Joseph	CA2600	Mojica, Andres	PR0150	Monteiro, Sergio	OK0750
Mitchell, Katherine Beth	CA3500	Mojica, Porfirio Antonio	CA3200	Monteiro, Shawn	CT0650
Mitchell, Kathleen	NJ0175	Mok, April H.	LA0900	Monteiro, Shawnn	RI0150
Mitchell, Linda	CA2400	Mok, Gwendolyn	CA4400	Monteiro-Huelbig, Shawnn	RI0200
Mitchell, Michael A.	MI1750	Mokole, Elias	MN1600	Montelione, Joseph	TN1200
Mitchell, Nicole	IL3310	Molberg, Keith	AJ0030	Montello, Louise	NY2400
Mitchell, Patricia	CA5070	Moldenhauer, Kermit G.	MN1030	Montemayor, Mark	CO0950
Mitchell, Rachel E.	TX3420	Molenaar, Mary Beth	IL2250	Montequt, Dreux	LA0300
Mitchell, Randall	IN0800	Molina, Andrea	IL0400	Montford, Kimberlyn	TX3350
Mitchell, Rebecca	FL1750	Molina, Carlos	FL1300	Montgomery, Alice	MO1950
Mitchell, Robert	MO0600	Molina, Jose	CA1520	Montgomery, Andrea	MS0650
Mitchell, Roman	NY0640	Molina, Linda	MD0475	Montgomery, Annette	MI2250
Mitchell, Roscoe	CA2950	Molina, Moises	IL3500	Montgomery, Cheri	TN1850
Mitchell, Teresa L.	FL1310	Molina, Osiris J.	AL1170	Montgomery, David L.	MI2250
Mitchell, William	TX3050	Molina, Rocio	TX3515	Montgomery, Dennis	MA0260
Mitchell, Yvonne	PA2100	Molina, Stephen	MI2100	Montgomery, Glen	AA0050
Mitnick, Alex	PA3330	Molina, Steven R.	MI2200	Montgomery, Glen	AA0200
Mitschell, P. Bryan	OK1330	Molinari, Kyounghwa	AR0300	Montgomery, Janet	MD1010
Mitts, Thomas	VA1350	Molinari, Raffaele 'Lello'	MA0260	Montgomery, Joy	AG0600
Miura, Hiroya	ME0150	Molinaro, Anthony G.	IL1615	Montgomery, Kip	NY3250
Mix, Ryan	IA0950	Molinaro, Lisa M.	PA2950	Montgomery, Michael R.	AR0700
Mixdorf, Cory Daniel	GA1050	Moline, Garth	WY0150	Montgomery, Ron	TX2600
Mixon, John	MS0575	Moliner, Eugenia	IL0550	Montgomery, Susan	CA0960
Mixon, Joseph D.	PA2450	Moliterno, Mark	NJ0175	Montgomery, Vivian	OH2200
Mixon, Joseph D.	PA1900	Moliterno, Mark	NJ1350	Montgomery, William L.	MD1010
Mixon, Laura	AL1050	Moll, Benjamin	OR0600	Montgomery-Cove, Deborah	NY1800
Mixson, Vonnetta	CA1000	Moll, Brian	MA1175	Montiel, Alejandro	TX2250
Mixter, Jan	SC0650	Moll, Brian	MA0350	Montiel, Brenda F.	CA3460

Montone, Jennifer	PA3250	Moore, Marilyn	DE0050	Morell, Drew	CO0830
Montone, Jennifer	NY1900	Moore, Marilyn	DC0170	Morell, Martin	FL1800
Montone, Jennifer	PA0850	Moore, Mark E.	IL3300	Morelli, Frank A.	NY3790
Montoya, Kathryn	OH1700	Moore, Marvelene C.	TN1710	Morelli, Frank	NY1900
Montoya, Tomas	CA1950	Moore, Matthew	MO0400	Morelli, Frank	NY2150
Monts, Lester P.	MI2100	Moore, Matthew	ID0060	Morelli, Frank	CT0850
Montzka Smelser, Ann	IL3550	Moore, Michael	GA1450	Morelli, Jackie	OR1250
Montzka, Ann	IL2200	Moore, Michael	TX2930	Morelli, Sarah	CO0900
Monzon, Ricardo	MA0260	Moore, Michael W.	SC0200	Morelock, David	LA0300
Mood, Aaron	NC2700	Moore, Michael D.	OK1450	Morelock, Donald	MI1900
Moody, David	NY1900	Moore, Michael	GA1150	Moremen, Eileen	GA1150
Moody, David	PA0850	Moore, Michael	GA0750	Moreno, Jairo	PA3350
Moody, Duane	MA0260	Moore, Mike	OR1250	Moreno, Madja	PR0100
Moody, Earecka	WA1350	Moore, Nancy	IL0275	Moreno, Maria Teresa	AI0190
Moody, Erica	WA0400	Moore, Nancy	OH0350	Moreno, Tony	NY2750
Moody, Gary E.	CO0250	Moore, Nora	VA1125	Morenus, Carlyn G.	IL1150
Moody, Kevin M.	TX0075	Moore, Norman	NC0850	Moresi, Matthew S.	MI0650
Moody, Philip	GA2100	Moore, Phil	OK1200	Moretti, Amy Schwartz	GA1300
Mook, Richard W.	AZ0100	Moore, Rager H.	AR0730	Moretti, Daniel D.	MA0260
Moolenbeek, William J.	AG0200	Moore, Raymond D.	GA2100	Morey, Carl	AG0450
Moon, Brian A.	AZ0500	Moore, Rich	IL2200	Morgan, Angela L.	GA0250
Moon, Brian C.	AL1150	Moore, Rick	AZ0200	Morgan, Carol	TX2300
Moon, Brian	MI1260	Moore, Robert	OH0300	Morgan, Charles	IL1250
Moon, Eileen	NY2750	Moore, Robert S.	CA5300	Morgan, Christopher	NC0220
Moon, Emma	CA5000	Moore, Robin D.	TX3510	Morgan, David	OH2600
Moon, Gene H.	TX2700	Moore, Ruth	NE0300	Morgan, John	IA0650
Moon, Hosun	NY1275	Moore, Ryan	GA2050	Morgan, John	OH1850
Moon, Kathleen	CA3150	Moore, Selma	NY2950	Morgan, Kenyon	MI1150
Moon, Kimberle	FL0040	Moore, Sharon	TN0650	Morgan, Kerri	TX2260
Moon, Yong Hi	MD0650	Moore, Stephen F.	CA0805	Morgan, Lauren R.	MO0250
Moonert, Judy	MI2250	Moore, Tim	FL0670	Morgan, LeeAnn	UT0050
Mooney, Chris	VA0150	Moore, Vicki	CA0270	Morgan, Leslie	IA1600
Mooney, Kevin E.	TX3175	Moore-Hubert, Edith	FL1000	Morgan, Michael	CA4150
Mooney, Kevin	AG0500	Moore-Mitchell, Teresa	NC1150	Morgan, Nicole	IL1750
Moor, Ric	AG0550	Moore-Mitchell, Teresa A.	NC2700	Morgan, Paige	NY1800
Moore, Albert L.	MN1300	Moorefield, Bob	CA4425	Morgan, Philip	NC2500
Moore, Alison	KS0215	Moorehead-Libbs, Jean	MI0500	Morgan, Philip G.	PA1900
Moore, Andrea	NC2410	Moorhead, J. Brian	FL2000	Morgan, Robert	IL2250
Moore, Anthony	NC1450	Moorhead, Jan Paul	MA0260	Morgan, Robert Huw	CA4900
Moore, Barbara	VA1550	Moorman, Joyce E.	NY0270	Morgan, Ruby N.	SC0750
Moore, Barbara	TX2400	Moorman, Joyce Solomon	NY2100	Morgan, Sean	FL1000
Moore, Brian	NE0600	Moorman, Wilson	NY0270	Morgan, Stephen	MN1625
Moore, Britt	VT0300	Moorman-Stahlman, Shelly	PA1900	Morgan, Tom T.	KS1400
Moore, Carla	CA5000	Mooter, Gregory G.	MA0260	Morgenstern, Rod	MA0260
Moore, Carol A.	WI0200	Moots, John E.	OK0150	Morgenstern, Inara E.	CA4200
Moore, Catherine	NY2750	Mooy, James	CA5550	Morgenstern, Julia	KS0700
Moore, Celina	VT0250	Mooy, James D.	CA4410	Morgiewicz, Kerry L.	VA0550
Moore, Christine	AL0050	Mooy, Mary Annaleen	HI0050	Morgulis, Tali	TX3400
Moore, Christine E.	TX2100	Mooyman, Lisa	OR0150	Mori, Akane	CT0650
Moore, Christopher	IN1850	Mora, Richard	CA4450	Mori, Akira	IA0550
Moore, Christopher	AG0400	Moral, Carmen	MA0260	Mori, David	CA2440
Moore, Christopher	FL0850	Morales, Dara	PA3250	Mori, Paul	CA5550
Moore, Christopher J.	GA0900	Morales, David	CA2910	Moriarty, Deborah	MI1400
Moore, Constance J.	AL0300	Morales, Fidel	PR0115	Moriarty, John	MA1400
Moore, Corey	NJ0500	Morales, Gary A.	PR0100	Morin, Carmen	AA0050
Moore, D. Scott	MN0750	Morales, Hilda	CT0650	Morin, Eric	AI0190
Moore, Daniel	IA1550	Morales, Joshua	OK0850	Morin, Joseph C.	MD1000
Moore, David A.	OK1450	Morales, Leonel	PR0115	Moring, Bill F.	NJ0800
Moore, David	CA5300	Morales, Raimundo	TX3750	Morino, Ayako	NJ0825
Moore, Dean	AZ0150	Morales, Ricado J.	PA3250	Morita, Lina	LA0350
Moore, Deanna C.	SC0200	Morales, Ricardo	PA0850	Moritsugu, Jim	MS0385
Moore, Deena	NC2700	Morales, Ricardo	NY1900	Moritz, Alison	NY1100
Moore, Denise Leetch	CT0650	Morales, Richie	NY3785	Moritz, Benjamin	PA2150
Moore, Dennis	CO0275	Morales, Samuel	PR0150	Moritz, Kristina	PA2150
Moore, Edgar	TX2300	Morales-Matos, Jaime	OH1450	Morken, Randy A.	MN1620
Moore, Edward	NY3720	Morales-Matos, Rolando	NJ0825	Morlan, Emily Jane	IL0730
Moore, Edward	IL0850	Morales-Matos, Rolando	NY0500	Morneau, John P.	ME0200
Moore, Eileen Marie	OH0650	Morales-Matos, Rolando	NY2660	Morningstar, Timothy P.	NY3775
Moore, Eric	VA0450	Morales-Matos, Rolando	PA0850	Moroney, Davitt	CA5000
Moore, F. Richard	CA5050	Moran, Daniel	AI0200	Morong, Eric	IL0850
Moore, Frances	CA5040	Moran, John	MD0650	Moroz, David	AA0050
Moore, Frances	CA2800	Moran, Kathryn	WI0810	Moroz, David	AC0100
Moore, Gary A.	IN0100	Moran, Kenny	AG0130	Morozova, Irina	NY2250
Moore, Glen	OR0850	Moran, Leslie Mason	PA2200	Morreale, Michael	NY0644
Moore, Grant W.	PA1250	Moran, Margaret A.	IN1100	Morrell, Kristy M.	CA5300
Moore, Gregory	WI0860	Moran, Nick	IL3310	Morren, Christian	OK1200
Moore, Harlan	OK1200	Moran, Sarah E.	IL1350	Morrical, Sharon	IA0790
Moore, Harriet T.	IN0350	Moran, Tom	WA0860	Morrice, John	CA1850
Moore, Hilarie Clark	NY3000	Morant, Trente	CA2200	Morrill, Dexter G.	NY0650
Moore, J. Steven	MO1790	Moratz, Karen	IN0250	Morrill, Dori	AZ0150
Moore, James	CA4150	Moravec, Andriana	IN0005	Morris, Amy B.	SC1200
Moore, James H.	WV0800	Moravec, Paul	NY2250	Morris, Amy	MN0800
Moore, James L.	OH1850	Moravec, Paul	NY0050	Morris, Amy	MN1295
Moore, James Walter	KY0400	Morawetz, Oskar	AG0450	Morris, Anthony	NY0500
Moore, Janet L. S.	FL2000	Morden, James	GA2000	Morris, Brian	MI0850
Moore, Janice	OH1350	Mordue, Mark	IN1560	Morris, Christopher	AA0200
Moore, Jeffrey M.	FL1800	Moreau, Barton	ID0050	Morris, Craig	FL1900
Moore, Joe D.	MS0250	Moreau, Leslie M.	ID0050	Morris, Daniel	MA0260
Moore, Joel	IL0150	Moree, Debra	NY1800	Morris, Eric	CA3270
Moore, Joel	IL1520	Morehead, Patricia	IL0720	Morris, Gary	HI0060
Moore, John	TX2200	Morehead, Phillip H.	TN0850	Morris, Gary	AR0200
Moore, John S.	IN1010	Morehouse, Christopher L.	IL2900	Morris, Gayle	TX3100
Moore, Julianna	MO1780	Morehouse, Dale	MO1810	Morris, Gerard	WA1000
Moore, Kathy Bundock	CO0950	Morehouse, Katherine	GA1150	Morris, Gregory	MO0400
Moore, Keith	TN0100	Morejon, Adrian	MA0350	Morris, Gretchen	OK1400
Moore, Kent R.	AZ0450	Morel, Vincent	AI0200	Morris, Hamilton	WV0650
Moore, Kevin	AL0890	Moreland, Irina	CO0150	Morris, J. David	GA2150
Moore, Kevin	NY4150	Moreland, Irina	CO0830	Morris, James R.	NY3700
Moore, Kevin	NY2950	Moreland, Michael	KS0570	Morris, Jeffrey M.	TX2900
Moore, Laura M.	AL1300	Moreland, Wilbur	AL1195	Morris, Joan	MI2100

Alphabetical Listing of Faculty

Name	Code	Name	Code	Name	Code
Morris, Joe	MA1175	Morton, Stephen C.	MO1830	Mow, Paul	MI1985
Morris, Joe	MA1400	Morton, Susan	LA0760	Mow, Paul	MI1180
Morris, Kelley	OK1450	Morton, Wyant	CA0550	Mowad, Lou	NC0250
Morris, LoriAnn	ID0060	Mortyakova, Julia V.	MS0550	Mowbray, Candice	MD0300
Morris, Marjorie	NJ1050	Mosbey, Jerad M.	IL2250	Mowitz, Ira	NJ0750
Morris, Martha M.	IL2650	Mosby, Todd	MO0700	Mowrer, Tony	CA0810
Morris, Matt	SD0580	Mosca, John	NY2150	Mowrey, Peter C.	OH0700
Morris, Matthew B.	OH1900	Mosca, John	NJ1400	Mowry, Mark R.	WI0803
Morris, Michael	CT0650	Moschenross, Ian	IL1800	Moxley, Bryant	VA0050
Morris, Mitchell B.	CA5032	Mose, John	IL0650	Moxley, Lisa	VA0050
Morris, Nancy	MA0260	Moseley, Brian	SC0750	Moxness, Diana	MN1000
Morris, Quinton	WA0850	Moseley, Jessica Barnett	SC0750	Moxness, Paul	MN0200
Morris, Ralph	OK1330	Moseley, Roger S.	NY0900	Moxness, Paul	MN1000
Morris, Richard	NE0450	Moseley, William	ME0340	Moy, Jason	IL0750
Morris, Robert D.	NY1100	Mosello, Joe	NJ0825	Moye, Brenda	TN0850
Morris, Robert B.	AB0100	Mosenbichler-Bryant, Verena	NC0600	Moye, Felicia K.	WI0815
Morris, Scott	CA2650	Moser, Bruce	NC0400	Moyer, Bruce	CA4425
Morris, Scott	CA0805	Moser, Diane	NY2660	Moyer, Bruce D.	CA4900
Morris, Scott	CA1900	Moser, Janet	IL0850	Moyer, Bruce	CA4400
Morris, Stanley	AR0700	Moser, Martin	NY3500	Moyer, Cynthia M.	CA2250
Morris, Stephen	GA0050	Moser, Mary	PA1450	Moyer, Iain	AL1250
Morris, Steven	MA1900	Moser, Steven R.	MS0750	Moyer, J. Harold	KS0200
Morris, Tahlia	WI1150	Moses, Dee	FL2000	Moyer, John	PA1050
Morris, Theodora	OK1050	Moses, Kenneth J.	FL1900	Moyer, Jon	PA3710
Morris, Theodora	OK1330	Moses, Lennard	OH0500	Moyer, Jonathan W.	OH0200
Morris, William J.	LA0800	Moses, Leonard	MD0060	Moyer, Kathryn	NJ0175
Morris, Willie L.	OH2250	Moses, Mark	AL1195	Moylan, William D.	MA2030
Morris, Winston	TN1450	Moses, Oral	GA1150	Moynier, Miles	CA3640
Morrison, Alan	NJ1350	Moses, Richard	WI0803	Mozelle, Mary M.	FL1550
Morrison, Alan	PA3550	Moses, Robert	MA1400	Mozetich, Marjan	AG0250
Morrison, Alan	PA0850	Moshaver, Maryam A.	AA0100	Mozzani, Pina	KS1450
Morrison, Amy	SD0580	Moshell, Gerald	CT0500	Mroziak, Jordan	PA1050
Morrison, Audrey	IL2100	Mosher, Allan R.	OH2600	Mrozinski, Lavonne	IL1085
Morrison, Audrey	IL0720	Mosher, Ellen	IL1400	Mrozinski, Mark	IL1085
Morrison, Barbara	CA5031	Mosher, Jennifer Jones	OH2600	Mruzek, David M.	IN0650
Morrison, Becky	OK0300	Mosher, Jimm	NC0350	Mu, Ning	PA1300
Morrison, Charles D.	AG0600	Moshier, Josh	IL3550	Muchmore, Pat	NY3560
Morrison, Chris	CT0800	Moshier, Steve	CA3750	Muchnick, Amy Faye	MO0775
Morrison, Chuck	AZ0400	Mosko, Beth	CO0250	Muckenfuss, Robert W.	MD0650
Morrison, David	IL3310	Moskowitz, David V.	SD0600	Muckey, Matthew I.	NJ1130
Morrison, Harry	MO1650	Moslak, Judy	MI1260	Mudge, Ashley	FL1700
Morrison, Heather	AG0170	Moss, Bruce B.	OH0300	Mudry, Karen	PA0650
Morrison, Johanna	CT0650	Moss, Elaine	WI0750	Muegel, Glenn	NC0050
Morrison, John	WV0300	Moss, Emily A.	NY0500	Muehleip, Marc	IA1450
Morrison, John H.	MA1350	Moss, Frances	AL0330	Muehlenbeck Pfotenhauer, Thomas R.	MN1600
Morrison, Kenneth	AB0100	Moss, Gary	IA0950	Muehlenbeck, Bettina	MN1600
Morrison, Leah A.	CA5300	Moss, Grant R.	MA1750	Muehlig, Carol	MI0500
Morrison, Linda	KY1460	Moss, Kirk D.	WI0350	Mueller, Alicia K.	MD0850
Morrison, Mable R.	DE0050	Moss, Lawrence	MD1010	Mueller, Charlotte G.	TX1450
Morrison, Malcolm	CT0650	Moss, Michael	MA0260	Mueller, Erwin	IN0150
Morrison, Mandy	TX1600	Moss, Myron D.	PA1000	Mueller, Frank	WI0835
Morrison, Marian	NC2000	Moss, Orlando	MS0560	Mueller, Gerald A.	CA1020
Morrison, Mary	AG0450	Moss, Patricia J.	AL0650	Mueller, Geri	MD0150
Morrison, Nicholas	UT0300	Moss, Suzan	NY2100	Mueller, John T.	TN1680
Morrison, Simon	NJ0900	Moss, Vivian	TX1660	Mueller, Joseph	OH0350
Morrison, Steven J.	WA1050	Moss-Sanders, Korby L.	MD0450	Mueller, Madeline N.	CA1020
Morrongiello, Christopher	NY1600	Mossblad, Gunnar	OH2300	Mueller, Marc	OK1250
Morrow, Cindy	TX3510	Mossman, Michael	NY0642	Mueller, Neil	MI0400
Morrow, Daniel	PA1350	Mosteller, Paul W.	AL1150	Mueller, Otto Werner	PA0850
Morrow, David E.	GA1450	Mosteller, Sandra M.	TX3650	Mueller, Paul F.	NY0625
Morrow, Diane	OK1450	Mosteller, Steven	IL0750	Mueller, Raymond	WI1150
Morrow, Elizabeth N.	TX3500	Moteki, Mutsumi	CO0800	Mueller, Rena Charnin	NY2740
Morrow, James	TX3510	Motley, Gary D.	GA0750	Mueller, Robert K.	AR0700
Morrow, Jeff	IL0550	Motobuchi, Mai	MA1400	Mueller, Ronald	CO0800
Morrow, Jo L.	LA0650	Mott, David	AG0650	Mueller, Ruth	NY2400
Morrow, Lance	TN0050	Mott, Jammieca	TX2250	Mueller, Susan	NV0050
Morrow, Lynne	CA4700	Mott, Jonathan	VA0250	Mueller, Susan	OK0825
Morrow, Mary Sue	OH2200	Motter, Catherine	CO0150	Mueller, Todd D.	
Morrow, Matthew	NY1100	Mottl, Robert O.	MO1830	Mueller-Stosch, Johannes	CA0825
Morrow, Michael	TX2955	Motto, David	CA3520	Muench, Felicity	CO0150
Morrow, Phil J.	NC0300	Motz, Steve	AL1160	Muhl, Erica	CA5300
Morrow, Ruth E.	TX1700	Mouffe, Jerome	MA0510	Muhly, Alexa	IL2750
Morrow, Ruth	TX3370	Moulder, Earline	MO0350	Muilenburg, Harley	CA2250
Morrow, Sharon	NJ1350	Moulder, John P.	IL2250	Mukuna, Kazadi Wa	OH1100
Morrow-King, Janet	CO0250	Moulder, John	IL0550	Mulcahy, Craig	DC0050
Morscheck, Stephen M.	TX3420	Moulder, John	IL0275	Mulcahy, Craig	MD1010
Morse, Dana	LA0650	Mouledous, Alfred	TX2400	Mulcahy, Michael	IL2250
Morse, Elizabeth	MA2250	Mouledous, Pierrette	TX0700	Muldar, Dennis	FL0950
Morse, Kevin	ME0270	Moulin, Jane	HI0210	Mulder, Axel	AI0150
Morse-Hambrock, Anne	WI0835	Moulson, Magdalena	GA1050	Mulder, Erin	GA1070
Morse-Hambrock, Anne	WI0250	Moulton, Christine F.	PA2150	Mulder, Geoffrey	CA0850
Mort, Bari	NY3560	Moulton, David	PA2550	Mulet, Mickael	PR0100
Mortensen, Dan	NY4450	Moulton, David	PA2450	Muley, Nandkishor	FL1750
Mortensen, John J.	OH0450	Moulton, Elizabeth	NJ0700	Mulford, Ruth Stomne	DE0175
Mortenson, Daniel	SD0150	Moulton, Joyce	ME0200	Mulhall, Karen	NJ0550
Mortenson, Gary	KS0650	Moulton, Paul F.	ID0070	Mulhall, Sean	KY1500
Mortenson, Kristin	KS0650	Moulton, William	VT0300	Mulholland, James Q.	IN0250
Mortier, Steve	WA0250	Mount, Andre	NY3780	Mulholland, Jeremy	KY0550
Morton, Glenn	NY2150	Mount, John	HI0210	Mulholland, Joseph	MA0260
Morton, Glenn	NY2250	Mount, Lorna	HI0120	Mullen, Stan	PA2050
Morton, Gregory	IA1800	Mount, Megan M.	HI0210	Mullen, Stanley	PA1650
Morton, James	CA2100	Mountain, Rosemary	AI0070	Mullen, Wendy Anne	GA0850
Morton, Joelle	AG0450	Mountain, Toby	MA0700	Mullenax, Gary	WV0550
Morton, Leonard	TN1400	Mountford, Fritz	NE0300	Muller, Bryan	PA1550
Morton, Nye	CA1850	Moura, Juliana	KY0400	Muller, Carl	TX2300
Morton, Paul D.	LA0760	Mouradjian, Joanne	MA2150	Muller, Carol A.	PA3350
Morton, R. Greg	IA0400	Mouridian, Linda	CA0835	Muller, David J.	CA6000
Morton, R. Gregory	IA0300	Mourton, Laurie	GA2050	Muller, Gerald	TX2170
Morton, Rebecca	AG0200	Mouse, Eugene	IL2050	Muller, Irina	MT0370
Morton, Ron	IL0300	Moushey, Suzanne Z.	OH2290	Muller, Janet	MD0175

Muller, John J. H.	NY1900	Murphy, Hugh	NY3785	Mustert, Betty	MI0350
Muller, Marc	NJ0760	Murphy, Jacob P.	IN0910	Musto, James	NJ0700
Muller, Riana	PA2100	Murphy, James L.	ID0250	Muston, Wendy	IN0250
Muller-Szeraws, Jan	MA0700	Murphy, Janice	MD0750	Muszynski, Michael	GA1050
Mullett, Scott	NH0150	Murphy, Joanna	FL0200	Mutchnik, Ronald	MD0060
Mullhall, Kevin	OH0050	Murphy, John	LA0300	Muth, Roy	VA1000
Mulliken, Erin	IL1200	Murphy, John P.	TX3420	Muto, Vicki	CA1750
Mullinix, Kelli	NC1250	Murphy, Joseph M.	PA2150	Muto, Vicki	CA3500
Mullins, Debra	IN0907	Murphy, Joy-Anne	AA0110	Muto, Vicki	CA5300
Mullins, Devoyne	NE0400	Murphy, Karen Lee	MS0500	Muxfeldt, Kristina	IN0900
Mullins, Steve	CO0400	Murphy, Kathleen	IN1600	Muzzo, Grace	PA3710
Mulroy, John	MA0260	Murphy, Kathy	PA3250	Myatt, Traci	OH1600
Mulvaney, Thomas	NJ0800	Murphy, Kevin M.	NY2750	Myer, Tom	CO0800
Mulvey, Bob	MA0260	Murphy, Kevin	IN0900	Myers, Adam	TX3370
Mulvey, Vanessa Breault	MA1175	Murphy, Michael	ID0250	Myers, Allen	MO2000
Mumford, Larry	CA0350	Murphy, Michael D.	VA1350	Myers, Andre K.	CA3300
Mumford, Lawrence R.	CA5355	Murphy, Otis	IN0900	Myers, Benjamin C.	MD0400
Mumm, Craig	NJ1130	Murphy, Patrick C.	OR1100	Myers, Brenda	CA1860
Mumm, Daniel C.	NJ0800	Murphy, Paul	GA1300	Myers, Carolyn	NC0650
Mumma, Gordon	CA5070	Murphy, Paul T.	NY3725	Myers, Dana	CA5350
Muncil, Donna	NY0050	Murphy, Paul	GA0750	Myers, David E.	MN1623
Muncy, Robert	MD0700	Murphy, Paul R.	CA5150	Myers, Geoffrey	UT0150
Munday, Don	OK1200	Murphy, Scott	KS1350	Myers, Gerald C.	MO1120
Mundinger, Gretchen	NY0500	Murphy, Shawn	IL0750	Myers, Herbert W.	CA4900
Munds, Philip C.	MD0650	Murphy, Sheila C.	FL2100	Myers, Jeff	MS0320
Mundy, John	MN1700	Murphy, Steve	IN0907	Myers, Marcus	PA3330
Mundy, John	MN1400	Murphy, Susan	CT0350	Myers, Michael	NC1450
Mundy, Paul	IL2750	Murphy, Suzanne	NY1550	Myers, Myron	IL2200
Mundy, Rachel	PA3420	Murphy, Timothy	MD0650	Myers, Patricia Ann	NY1550
Munger, Philip	AK0100	Murphy, Timothy	MD0850	Myers, Patricia	GA0250
Mungo, Nichelle	MA0260	Murphy, Tom	AZ0440	Myers, Philip	NY2250
Mungo, Samuel	TX3175	Murphy, Vanissa B.	WI0803	Myers, Roger	TX3510
Muni, Nicholas	OH2200	Murphy-Manley, Sheryl K.	TX2250	Myers, Steven	GA0625
Muniz, Jennifer	MO0100	Murrath, Dimitri	MA1175	Myers, Terry	MA0950
Muniz, Jorge	MO0100	Murray, Alan	KS0570	Myers, Timothy R.	MO1900
Muniz, Jorge	IN0910	Murray, Amy	VA1350	Myers, Ty	IA0200
Munn, Albert Christopher	TX3525	Murray, Bruce J.	OH1450	Myers-Brown, Ruth	MI0600
Munn, Alexandra	AA0020	Murray, Dana A.	NE0610	Myers-McKenzie, Laurl	CA3200
Munn, Alexandra M.	AA0100	Murray, David	GA0950	Myers-Tegeder, Christine	NJ0550
Munn, Vivian C.	TX3525	Murray, David	AZ0440	Mygatt, Louise	NY1800
Munn, Zae	IN1450	Murray, David	IN0250	Myintoo, Sylvia C.	IL2150
Munoz, Nelida	PR0150	Murray, Deanna A.	CA0835	Myrick, Barbara	OR0350
Munoz, William	MN1200	Murray, Edward	TN1680	Myrick, John	AL1195
Munro, Anne	WV0550	Murray, Ellie	OR0950	Myrick, Kathleen	NJ0760
Munro, Douglas	NY3785	Murray, Eric	OH1110	Myrick, Kenny	MS0420
Munson, Chris	KY0550	Murray, Frank	CA3920	Myrick, Korby	CT0650
Munson, Jordan	IN0907	Murray, Jack	NC1100	Myska, David	AG0500
Munson, Mark	OH0300	Murray, Jack T.	NC0350	Myslewski, David	PA3400
Munson, Paul A.	PA1450	Murray, Jack	NC2650	Myssyk, Daniel	VA1600
Muntefering, Scott	IA1800	Murray, Jane	RI0300	Nabb, David	NE0590
Munton, Amanda	NH0250	Murray, Jane	RI0250	Nabb, Franziska	NE0590
Munzenrider, James	CA1250	Murray, Janice	NC0250	Nabb, Nathan	TX2700
Munzer, Cynthia	CA5300	Murray, John	AA0025	Nabholz, Fran	GA0250
Muparutsa, Tendai	MA2250	Murray, Kathrin	MD0520	Nabholz, Mark A.	SC0700
Muraco, Thomas	NY2150	Murray, Kathy	MO0775	Nabors, Louis A.	LA0770
Murai, Gregory	CA1450	Murray, Kris A.	IL2730	Nachef, Joanna	CA1750
Murai, Hajime Teri	MD0650	Murray, Linda	WY0130	Nachman, Myrna	NY2550
Murail, Tristan C.	NY0750	Murray, Mark S.	IN0100	Nadas, John L.	NC2410
Murakami, Kazuo	AR0850	Murray, Melissa M.	TX2400	Nadel, James	CA4900
Murasugi, Sachiho	MD0800	Murray, Michael F.	MO0775	Nadel, Richard	NY1860
Murata, Margaret K.	CA5020	Murray, Michael	OH1850	Nadgir, Arunesh N.	TN1100
Muratore, John	MA0400	Murray, Michael A.	MO0775	Naegele, Elizabeth M.	IL1850
Muratore, John D.	NH0100	Murray, Michael	AB0100	Naeve, Denise	IA0790
Murawski, Marianne	NJ0990	Murray, Michele C.	IN0100	Naff, George	NC0350
Murchison, Gayle	VA0250	Murray, Monica	MN0610	Nafziger, Erin	MA2250
Murchison, Matthew	PA3580	Murray, Pamela	MA0850	Nafziger, Kenneth J.	VA0300
Murchison, Pamela	MD0350	Murray, Paul	CA4425	Nagai, Yoshikazu	CA4150
Murciano, Raul	FL1900	Murray, Renardo	MS0050	Nagata, Gary	AG0450
Murdaugh, Johnnie L.	SC0350	Murray, Renardo	MS0350	Nagatani, Chie	CA1700
Murdick, Nick	MT0370	Murray, Robert P.	GA0550	Nagatani, Ken	CA1700
Murdie, Lorelei T.	NY3780	Murray, Russell E.	DE0150	Nagel, Douglas	MT0175
Murdoch, Kenneth	AA0050	Murray, Sean	FL0650	Nagel, Jody	IN0150
Murdock, Katherine	MD1010	Murray, Stephen	MA0280	Nagel, Louis B.	MI2100
Murdock, Kelly	FL1430	Murray, Susannah	CA4500	Nagel, Rebecca S.	SC1110
Murdock, Matthew	TN1600	Murray, Susannah	CA2600	Nagel, Sue S.	MN1120
Murdy, David H.	CA3350	Murray, Thomas	CT0850	Nagel, Susan	ND0350
Muresan, Branden	CA2960	Murray, Warren	OR1300	Nagell, Ann B.	AZ0440
Muresan, Branden A.	CA2100	Murrow, Richard	TX3000	Nagels, Lance	AI0190
Muresanu, Irina	MA0350	, Muryanto	VA0250	Nagem, Paul	CO0200
Muriello, John R.	IA1550	Musa, Ben	WA1250	Nagge, Harold	TN1250
Murillo, Julie	AZ0100	Muscarella, Susan	CA5000	Nagge, Harold	TN1000
Murley, Michael	AG0450	Muscatello, George	NY3650	Nagle, Donna	MA2030
Murnak, Raina	FL1900	Musco, Lynn A.	FL1750	Nagle, Janice	NY3350
Muroki, Kurt K.	NY3790	Musella, Joseph	MA0260	Nagle, Lynn	CA0630
Muroki, Kurt	GA1300	Musgrave, Helen	AR0425	Nagler, Joseph	NY3250
Murph, Charles	NC0900	Musgrave, Thea	NY0642	Nago, Stuart H.	HI0150
Murphey, Maura	WI0250	Musgrove, Abby R.	IL1100	Nagtegaal, Marlin	AG0600
Murphree, John	MA0350	Mushabac, Regina M.	OH0200	Nagy, Daniel	FL1500
Murphree, Martin R.	MO0800	Musial, Michael A.	NY3450	Nagy, Jennifer	AZ0440
Murphree, Scott	NY2750	Music, David W.	TX0300	Nagy, Karen	FL1310
Murphy, Barbara A.	TN1710	Musick, Marilyn J.	NE0590	Nagy, Linda Jiorle	MA0400
Murphy, Bill S.	MD0475	Musmann, Lois S.	CA3270	Nagy, Russ	OH0350
Murphy, Brian	AZ0440	Mussard, Timothy S.	OH0200	Nagy, Zvonimir	PA1050
Murphy, Cynthia	NE0300	Musselman, Diana	CO0225	Nahm, Dorothea A.	DC0350
Murphy, Daniel	CA5150	Musselman, Susan	OH2450	Nahulu, Nola A.	HI0210
Murphy, Derrick	IA0900	Musselwhite, Eric	VA0150	Naidoo, Shaun	CA0960
Murphy, Douglas	CA4650	Musselwhite, Harry	GA0300	Nail, James I. (Ike)	OR1250
Murphy, Edward W.	AZ0500	Musser, Amanda	TX3000	Naimpally, Ravi	AG0650
Murphy, Glenda	AA0020	Musso, Paul J.	CO0830	Nair, Garyth	NJ0300
Murphy, Heidi Grant	IN0900	Mussumeli, Bettina	CA4150	Nairn, Robert	NY1900

Alphabetical Listing of Faculty

Name	Code	Name	Code	Name	Code
Nairn, Robert	PA2750	Neal, David E.	NY3720	Nelson, Daniel	WI0825
Naito, Shoji	IL1400	Neal, Jocelyn	NC2410	Nelson, David E.	PA3600
Najar, Michael	CA3270	Neal, Mark	AL1450	Nelson, David	CT0750
Najarian, Laura	GA1150	Neal, Mary Elizabeth	AL0300	Nelson, David P.	NC2350
Najoom, Dennis	WI1155	Neal, Nedra	NY2550	Nelson, David W.	CA0859
Nakamae, Ayumi	NC0450	Neal, Patrick	FL0680	Nelson, David L.	NC2430
Nakamura, Gwen H.	HI0210	Neal, Paul	GA2150	Nelson, Elise Buffat	ND0350
Nakashima, Rieko	FL1300	Neal, Randall	VT0050	Nelson, Elise	MN1120
Nakashita, Sonomi	HI0050	Neal, Tira	CO0830	Nelson, Eric	GA0750
Nakasian O'Brian, Stephanie	VA0250	Neale, Alasdair	CA4150	Nelson, Gary R.	OR0050
Nakasian, Stephanie	VA1550	Neale, Donald	IL0720	Nelson, Gregory	MN1300
Nakhmanovich, Raisa	AG0650	Near, John R.	IL2400	Nelson, Jennifer	WA1050
Nakra, Teresa Marrin	NJ0175	Neas, Michael	FL1100	Nelson, Jennifer	WA1000
Nalesnik, David A.	MO1950	Neault, Sylvain	AI0190	Nelson, Jessica L.	AL1250
Nall, Cecily	TN1710	Nebelung, Russell	MI2000	Nelson, Jocelyn C.	NC0650
Nam, Choong-ha	TX3750	Neblett, Carol	CA0960	Nelson, Jon	NY2150
Nam, Esther Hyun	KY1000	Neblett, Sonja	CA4150	Nelson, Jon C.	TX3420
Nam, Jason	CA0845	NeCastro, Vicki	ME0430	Nelson, Jon R.	NY4320
Nam, MeeAe Cecilia	MI0600	Necessary, Andrew	VA0050	Nelson, Jon	CA4460
Nam, Seong	VA0450	Neciosup, Hector	FL0200	Nelson, Josh	CA0835
Nam, Song Hun	KY1000	Nedbal, Martin	AR0700	Nelson, Joy	OK1350
Namer, Dina	AG0250	Nedecky, Jason	AG0300	Nelson, Joy	AJ0150
Namminga, Jaime	ND0600	Nediger, Charlotte	AG0450	Nelson, Karl	OK1330
Namoradze, Medea	MD0150	Nediger, Charlotte	AG0300	Nelson, Kayla	ND0500
Nance, Richard	WA0650	Nedvin, Brian A.	VA1000	Nelson, Kent	UT0350
Nance, Steve	CA1850	Neebe, Paul M.	VA1550	Nelson, Kristen	TX2700
Nance, Virginia	TX2150	Needelman, William	NY2250	Nelson, Larry A.	PA3600
Nangle, Richard	MA0400	Needleman, Gail	CA2200	Nelson, Larry	KY0550
Nangle, Richard P.	MA2030	Needleman, Katherine	MD0650	Nelson, Lee D.	IA1800
Nanni, Steven	NY1400	Neel, Douglas J.	OH2275	Nelson, Leon	IL2100
Nanongkham, Priwan Keo	OH1100	Neeley, Henrietta	IL1085	Nelson, Lisa	IL1200
Naoumoff, Emile	IN0900	Neelly, Linda Page	CT0600	Nelson, Lizzy	UT0190
Naphtali, Dafna L.	NY2750	Neely, David C.	NE0600	Nelson, Margaret	NJ0975
Napoles, Jessica	UT0250	Neely, David L.	KS1350	Nelson, Margaret	WI0855
Napoli, Joseph	PA0450	Neely, Dawn Wells	AL0010	Nelson, Marie	MA2020
Napoli, Joseph	PA1000	Neely, Stephen	PA0550	Nelson, Mark	AZ0480
Napoli, Robert	NY2550	Neely, William J.	CA4460	Nelson, Mary Anne	NY0700
Napper, Susie	AI0200	Neely-Chandler, Thomasina	GA1450	Nelson, Mattew	UT0325
Napper, Susie	AI0150	Neese, Bethany	CA4460	Nelson, Nancy	AG0200
Nappi, Chris	NC0650	Neese, Charity	GA1700	Nelson, Pamela	NC1300
Nappi, Chris	NC0400	Neese, Wanda	SC0900	Nelson, Paul	TN0100
Naragon, Jayne	OH2290	Neff, Lyle	DE0150	Nelson, Paula C.	PA1250
Naranjo, Valerie D.	NY2750	Neff, Matthew	VA0450	Nelson, Paula	PA1550
Nardini, Luisa	TX3510	Neff, Severine	NC2410	Nelson, Randi	AJ0150
Nardo, Rachel L.	UT0250	Neff, Teresa M.	MA1200	Nelson, Richard B.	OH0600
Nardolillo, Jo	KY0100	Negrete, Merida	NC2410	Nelson, Richard	ME0340
Nardolillo, John	KY1450	Negri, Joseph H.	PA1050	Nelson, Rob	MI0500
Narducci, Kenneth	CA2420	Negyesy, Janos	CA5050	Nelson, Robert S.	TX3400
Nargizyan, Lucy	CA1960	Neher, Patrick K.	AZ0500	Nelson, Roger	WA0200
Nargizyan, Lucy	CA1700	Nehre, Heather	MO1950	Nelson, Ron	AG0650
Narikawa, Masako	TX0250	Neiderhiser, Jonathan	SD0580	Nelson, Scott	VA1350
Narmour, Eugene	PA3350	Neidhart, Gregory	MN1700	Nelson, Scott	KS0750
Naroditskaya, Inna	IL2250	Neidhoefer, Christoph	AI0150	Nelson, Seth	TX3350
Narum, Jessica	MN0600	Neidich, Ayako Oshima	NY3785	Nelson, Sharon	OH2500
Narum, Leighann	NJ1140	Neidich, Charles	NY2150	Nelson, Sheri	CA0630
Naruse, Chiharu	ME0150	Neidich, Charles	NY1900	Nelson, Susan J.	OH0300
Narvey, Lois	DC0170	Neidich, Charles	NY2250	Nelson, Susan	NY2250
Nasatir, Cary	CA3520	Neidich, Charles	NY0642	Nelson, Susan	MN0150
Nash, Anne Jennifer	MN0600	Neidlinger, Erica	IL0750	Nelson, Timothy	IL2300
Nash, Gary Powell	TN0550	Neidlinger, Robert D.	OH2150	Nelson, Troy	MI1300
Nash, Robert	LA0760	Neihof, Marc	CO0200	Nelson, Valanda	NC2440
Nash, Robert	LA0650	Neikrug, George	MA0400	Nelson, William A.	WI0700
Nash-Robertson, Nina	MI0400	Neil, Mary	IL0100	Nelson-Raney, Steven	WI0825
Natale, Michael A.	PA3250	Neil, William W.	VA0450	Nemeth, Rudolph	TN1250
Natenberg, Reena Berger	KS1050	Neilan, Martin	TN1600	Nemhauser, Frank	NY2250
Nathan, Alan	MI1400	Neill, Dave	AG0450	Nemko, Deborah G.	MA0510
Nathan, Jonathan	CA5550	Neill, Doug A.	ND0350	Nennmann, Jill	IN1350
Nathan, Jonathan	CA5060	Neill, Douglas A.	MN1120	Nepkie, Janet	NY3765
Nathanson, Robert	NC2440	Neill, Douglas	MN0600	Nereim, Linnea	OH0600
Natter, Robert	PA1400	Neill, Kelly	AR0250	Neriki, Reiko S.	IN0900
Nattiez, Jean-Jacques	AI0200	Neill, Lou Anne	CA5030	Neriki, Shigeo	IN0900
Natvig, Mary	OH0300	Neill, Roger	CA0630	Nero, Jonathan	SD0100
Nauert, Clark	TX1600	Neill, Sheri L.	TX3000	Nero, Joseph	PA3330
Nauert, Paul	CA5070	Neill, William	OK1350	Nersesiyan, Pavel	MA0400
Nauful, Lisa	CA0600	Neilson, Brian	CA4150	Nesbit, James B.	VA0250
Nauman, Sharon	OH2150	Neilson, Duncan	OR0150	Nesbit, James B.	VA1000
Nauman, Sharon	OH1350	Neiman, Marcus	OH1100	Nesbit, James	NC0400
Naumchyk, Alena	AA0050	Neimoyer, Susan	UT0250	Nesheim, Paul	SD0050
Naus, Jesse	PA1050	Neisinger, Robert	WA0450	Nesheim, Paul J.	MN1120
Navari, Jude Joseph	CA4625	Neisler, Joseph	IL1150	Nesin, Richard	NY2750
Navarrete, Jennifer Shaw	CA2450	Neithamer, David	VA0700	Neske, Joe	MO1950
Navarro Romero, Emanuel	PR0115	Neitzke, Jeff	OH2290	Nesmith, David	OH0850
Navarro, Gloria	PR0115	Neitzke, Jeffrey	OH0100	Ness, Corinne	WI0250
Navarro, Joel Magus P.	MI0350	Neiweem, David	VT0450	Ness, David J.	IL0650
Nave, Pamela J.	IN1310	Neiwirth, Mark	ID0100	Ness, Marjorie S.	MA0930
Navega, Eduardo	NY4450	Nel, Anton	TX3510	Nesselroad, Sidney	WA0050
Navidad, Paul J.	CA3350	Nelms, Morris H.	TX3175	Nessinger, Mary	NY4450
Naydan, William	PA0650	Nelsen, Jack	ID0075	Nester, Holly	MN1500
Naylor, Al	IA0300	Nelsen, Jeff	AG0450	Nester, Kathleen M.	NY2750
Naylor, Earl	MO1950	Nelsen, Jeffrey	IN0900	Nesterov, Dmitry	AA0050
Naylor, Michael L.	MI2200	Nelsen, Suzanne	MA0400	Nestler, Eric M.	TX3420
Naylor, Stephen	AF0050	Nelsen, Suzanne	MA1175	Nestor, Gayleen	NE0720
Naylor, Susan E.	GA1700	Nelson, Alice	MO1950	Nestor, Leo Cornelius	DC0050
Nazarenko, Dmitri	MD0550	Nelson, Allison	TN0800	Neswick, Bruce	IN0900
Nazarenko, John	MA2250	Nelson, Beth P.	OH0600	Netsky, Hankus H.	MA1400
Nazarenko, John J.	NY3650	Nelson, Bruce	IL0420	Nettl, Bruno	IL3300
Nazario, Angel	PR0100	Nelson, Conor	OH0300	Nettles, Darryl	TN1400
Nazworth, Daniel	TX2350	Nelson, Craig	TN0100	Netto, Alberto	MA0260
Ndaliko, Cherie Rivers	NC2410	Nelson, Craig E.	TN1850	Netz, Anthony R.	NY1900
Neal, Anna	TN1680	Nelson, Curt	CA2900	Neu, Ah Ling	MA2250

Alphabetical Listing of Faculty

Name	Code
Neubauer, Paul	NY1900
Neubauer, Paul	NY2250
Neubert, Christopher D.	NY3700
Neubert, Nils	NY5000
Neubert, Nils	NJ1400
Neubert, Peter	TX1100
Neubert, Peter	TX0900
Neuen, Donald	CA5030
Neuenschwander, Daniel	PA1750
Neuenschwander, Mark	FL0450
Neuenschwander, Mark L.	FL2000
Neuenschwander, Mark	FL1650
Neufeld, Charles W.	SC0800
Neufeld, Gerald	AG0500
Neufeld, Hannah	KS0150
Neufeld, Julia R.	CA4410
Neufeld-Smith, Cynthia	KS1400
Neuharth, Randall	NE0460
Neuman, Daniel M.	CA5031
Neuman, Dard A.	CA5070
Neuman, Gayle	OR0500
Neuman, Lawrence	IL0550
Neuman, Phil	OR0500
Neuman, Rahul	CA5031
Neumann, Ben	AA0050
Neumann, Kyle	KY0250
Neumann, Mark	OK1350
Neumayr, Anton	IN0400
Neumeyer, Albert J.	PA1950
Neumeyer, Albert J.	PA2550
Neumeyer, David	TX3510
Neupert, Gina	TN1200
Neurohr, John	WA0050
Neve, Vicki	CA4200
Nevela, Andrew	AL0500
Neves, Joel	MI1450
Nevill, Tom	TX3515
Neville, Donald	AG0500
Neville, Ruth	SC0750
Neville, Shelley	AD0050
Nevin, Jeff	CA4850
Nevin, Kathryn A.	CA5150
Nevius, Sheila	MD0400
Nevola, Teresa	PA1150
New, Laura L.	MO1810
New, Laura	KS0570
Newborn, Ira	NY2750
Newbrough, William J.	NY1700
Newby, David L.	CA0200
Newby, Joanna	IL1300
Newby, Linda	TN0550
Newby, Stephen M.	WA0800
Newcomb, Anthony A.	CA5000
Newcomb, Suzanne	OH2050
Newell, Julie L.	NY3725
Newell, Kathy	OH2275
Newell, Lawana	OK0600
Newell, Meri	MS0360
Newell, Michael	SC0800
Newkirk, Brian	CA1280
Newland, Martha	NJ1160
Newlin, Georgia A.	NY0050
Newlin, Yvonne	IL1612
Newman, David A.	VA0600
Newman, David	WI0100
Newman, Diane M.	NY0500
Newman, Jill	IL1740
Newman, Katherine L.	AL1160
Newman, Leslie	AG0450
Newman, Leslie	AG0300
Newman, Margaret	AA0050
Newman, Michael	NY2250
Newman, Miles	AJ0100
Newman, Miranda	TX1510
Newman, Miranda	TX3535
Newman, Nancy	NY3700
Newman, Patrice	CT0100
Newman, Ronald	MI1400
Newman, Sean	OK0500
Newman, Timothy	NJ1400
Newsam, David R.	NH0100
Newsam, David R.	NH0350
Newsam, David	MA0260
Newsom, Daniel	MA0260
Newsom, Mary Ellen	IN0005
Newsome, Bo N.	NC0600
Newsome, Bo	NC0650
Newsome, Charles	MI2200
Newsome, Leigh	NY2750
Newsome, Sam	NY2102
Newson, Jeffrey	OK1450
Newton, Barry	CA3100
Newton, Barry	CA5360
Newton, Dean A.	OH2150
Newton, Farnell	OR0850
Newton, Gregory	CA2600
Newton, Gregory	CA1960
Newton, Jack	NC0050
Newton, James	CA5031
Newton, Jean	NY5000
Newton, Jeanne	TN0930
Newton, Jon	OR0850
Newton, Jon	OR0450
Newton, Joseph	NC0750
Newton, Robyn	WA1300
Newton, Steve	MI1000
Newton, Timothy D.	NY3765
Ney, Leonard Scott	NM0450
Nez, Catherine Ketty	MA0400
Ng, Elsie	AA0050
Ng, Jonathan	AZ0480
Ng, Michelle	OH1330
Ng, Samuel	OH2200
Ng, Stephen	PA3600
Ng, Tian Hui	MA1350
Ng-Au, Marie	AG0070
Ngai, Emlyn	CT0650
Nguyen, Albert	TN1680
Nguyen, Alexandra	CO0800
Nguyen, Co Boi	CA5150
Nguyen, Hanh	AB0200
Nguyen, Quynh	NY0625
Niblock, Carol B.	PA0100
Niblock, Howard	WI0350
Niblock, James D.	PA0100
Nice, Julie	LA0560
Nicely, Tiffany M.	NY3717
Nicely, Tiffany	NY3725
Nichol, John	MI0400
Nichol, Jonathan	MI0900
Nicholas, Alexander	FL1550
Nicholas, Christopher J.	CO0250
Nicholas, Julie	CA1650
Nicholas, Keith	TN0100
Nicholas, Lauren P.	PA2450
Nicholas, Scott	MA0850
Nicholeris, Carol A.	MA0510
Nicholeris, Dian	CA4400
Nicholl, Matthew J.	MA0260
Nicholls, Bud	MT0370
Nichols, Alan	TN0260
Nichols, Beverly	IA0250
Nichols, Brandon	SC0275
Nichols, Charles Sabin	MT0400
Nichols, Christopher Robert	NE0150
Nichols, Clinton	MS0360
Nichols, Cynthia	NE0610
Nichols, David	AZ0350
Nichols, Edward	MD0800
Nichols, Eugene C.	ME0430
Nichols, James	CA1250
Nichols, Jeff	NY0600
Nichols, Jeff W.	NY0642
Nichols, Jim	CA4625
Nichols, Kenneth	AC0050
Nichols, Kevin A.	IL3500
Nichols, Laura L.	MN0950
Nichols, Lena	IA0930
Nichols, Lois J.	CA4600
Nichols, Margaret	IL2750
Nichols, Peter W.	IN1650
Nichols, Samuel S.	CA5010
Nichols, Sandra	IL1612
Nichols, Sara	MD0850
Nichols, Will	MI0150
Nichols, William	MO0200
Nichols, William	LA0770
Nicholson, Bonnie	AJ0150
Nicholson, Chad	DE0150
Nicholson, Daniel	IL0750
Nicholson, David	CA5360
Nicholson, Edmon	GA0750
Nicholson, Hillary	RI0150
Nicholson, Jason	UT0300
Nicholson, Tina	IL1750
Nichter, Christopher	WV0750
Nickel, James	DC0050
Nickel, Tony	IA1140
Nickelson, LaRue S.	FL2000
Nickens, Michael W.	VA0450
Nicolella, Michael	WA0200
Nicolosi, Ida	CA3600
Nicolson, Mark	NJ0825
Nicolucci, Sandra	MA0400
Nicosia, Judith	NJ1130
Nida, Chris	FL1430
Nie, Emily	WI0100
Nie, James Ian	WI0100
Niebur, Louis	NV0100
Niederberger, Maria	TN0500
Niederloh, Angela	OR0850
Niederloh, Angela	OR0750
Niedermaier, Edward G.	IL0550
Niedt, Douglas Ashton	MO1810
Niehaus, Christine J.	VA0250
Niehoff, Carolyn	IL1085
Nielsen, Aage	ID0070
Nielsen, John	IA0650
Nielsen, John	IA0200
Nielsen, Kenneth L.	AA0150
Nielsen, Linda	WI0835
Nielsen, Linda	WI0050
Nielsen, Lois	PA3710
Nielsen, Robert	CA1850
Nielsen, Ryan	ID0060
Nielson, Lewis	OH1700
Nielubowski, Norbert	MN1623
Niemann, Adam	IL0550
Niemann, Judith A.	FL0400
Niemisto, Elinor	MN0300
Niemisto, Elinor	MN1450
Niemisto, Paul	MN1450
Nienkirchen, Red	OH0350
Nierman, Glenn E.	NE0600
Nies, Bryan	CA4400
Nies, Bryan	CA4150
Nies, Camille Day	TX0100
Nies, Carol	TN1100
Nies, Carol R.	TN1850
Nies, Craig	TN1850
Nieske, Robert	MA1400
Nieske, Robert	MA0500
Niess, Matt	VA1350
Niethamer, David B.	VA1500
Niethamer, David	VA1600
Nieto-Dorantes, Arturo	AI0190
Nieuwenhuis, Bruce	MI0450
Nieuwenhuis, Mary	MI0450
Niezen, Richard S.	CO0150
Nifong, Bruce	MA0260
Nigrelli, Christopher	NC1100
Nigrim, Dana	AI0150
Nigro, Christie	MA2300
Nigro, Christine	MA0150
Nigro, Michael	CA5355
Niiyama, Kelley	IN0800
Nije, Marilyn	KY1500
Nikitina, Alla	CT0650
Nikkel, Laurinda	CA4100
Nikolova, Iliana	AB0050
Niles, Carol Ann	CO0225
Niles, Melinda Smith	MD0520
Nilles, Benjamin	OK0750
Nilson, Shawnda	MT0370
Nilsson, Donna	GA0525
Nimmer, Rebecca	WI0750
Nimmo, Douglas	MN0750
Nimmons, Phil	AG0450
Nims, Marilyn	OH2000
Nims, Robert	OH2050
Nims, Robert D.	OH2000
Nin, Chan Ka	AG0450
Nine-Zielke, Nicola	OR0700
Ninomiya, Ayano	NY1100
Ninoshvili, Lauren	NY0200
Ninov, Dimitar	TX3175
Niren, Ann Glazer	IN1010
Nisbet, Allen	LA0300
Nisbett, Robert	CO0250
Nishibun, Tiffany	AL0345
Nishibun, Tiffany	AL0450
Nishikiori, Fumi	WI0835
Nishikiori, Fumi	WI1150
Nishimura, Derek Rikio	OH0600
Nishimura, Julie	DE0150
Niskala, Naomi	PA3150
Nisnevich, Anna V.	PA3420
Nispel, Anne	MI1400
Nissen, James	MI1900
Nissen, James C.	MI2110
Nissly, Jacob	NY1100
Nisula, Eric	MI1850
Nitchie, Carl	GA0750
Nitsch, Kevin	NY2650
Nitsch, Paul A.	NC2000
Nitschke, Brad	IN0005
Nitti, Adam	TN0100
Nittoli, Andrew	NY3790
Nitzberg, Roy J.	NY0642
Niu, Elaine	WI0750
Nivans, David	CA2050
Nivans, David	CA0805
Niwa, David	OH2000
Nix, Brad K.	KS1250
Nix, Catherine	TX3530
Nix, Jamie L.	GA0550
Nix, John Paul	TX3530
Nix, Kathy	IL2970
Nixon, Janis	AG0130
Nixon, Justin Taylor	CA3270
Nixon, Patricia	VA0950
Nixon, Roger A.	CA4200
Nketia, Joseph K.	PA3420
Noah, Laura	AL1300
Noah, Sean	AL1300
Noble, Gerald	OH2500
Noble, James	MI1800
Noble, Jason	NY1600
Noble, Jason L.	NJ0700
Noble, Jeremy	NY4320

Name	Code	Name	Code	Name	Code
Noble, Karen	WA0250	Norton, Kevin	NJ1400	O'Banion, James	OR0400
Noble, Steve L.	KY1500	Norton, Leslie	TN1850	O'Banion, Philip R.	PA3250
Noble, Timothy R.	IN0900	Norton, Michael	VA0600	Ober, Gail E.	PA1250
Noble, Weston H.	IA0950	Norton, Nick M.	UT0250	Ober, Jeremy	IA0790
Nobles, Katherine	GA0300	Norton, Peter K.	OH2200	Oberacker, Betty	CA5060
Nobles, Ron	IN0250	Norwine, Doug	SC0050	Oberbillig, Janelle	ID0050
Nocella, Peter S.	PA2700	Norwitz, Sherrie	MD0850	Oberbrunner, John	NY1550
Noe, Kevin	MI1400	Norwood, Diana	TX3370	Oberheu, Stephen	AC0100
Noel, Christine	MA0650	Noseworthy, Susan	NH0350	Oberholtzer, Christopher W.	ME0500
Noel, Debi	OR0350	Nosikova, Ksenia	IA1550	Oberlander, Lisa M.	GA0550
Noel, Emily	PA1300	Nosworthy, Hedley	CA1750	Oberle, Curtis P.	MO1000
Noel, John	NC1800	Notareschi, Loretta K.	CO0650	Obermeyer, Janet	AG0650
Noffsinger, Jonathan	AL1170	Notley, Margaret	TX3420	Obermueller, Karola	NM0450
Nogarede, Steve	NM0400	Noton, Donna	AA0020	Oblak, Jerica	NY2750
Noguera, Darwin	IL0275	Nott, Kenneth	CT0650	Oblinger, Amy	VA1650
Noh, Gerrey	OH1100	Notter, Tim	AG0130	O'Boyle, Maureen E.	OK1450
Nohai-Seaman, Alexander	NY4050	Nottingham, Douglas	AZ0350	Obrecht, Guy	AA0050
Nohe, Eric	CO0225	Nova, Christian	CA2750	O'Brien, Andrew C.	AZ0490
Nolan, Catherine	AG0500	Nova, James	PA1050	O'Brien, Clara	NC2430
Nolan, Denise G.	NH0110	Novak, Brad	MI1650	O'Brien, Colin	WI1150
Nolan, Julia	AB0100	Novak, Christina D.	AZ0490	O'Brien, Dean	AA0150
Noland, Brenda	OR0175	Novak, David	CA5060	O'Brien, Dean	AA0050
Noland, David	CT0800	Novak, George	OH0300	O'Brien, Eugene	IN0900
Nold, Sherry	PA3260	Novak, John K.	IL2200	O'Brien, John	MA0260
Nole, Nancy	WA0650	Novak, Richard A.	VA0450	O'Brien, John B.	NC0650
Nolen, Paul	IL1150	Novak, Tom	MA1400	O'Brien, Kathleen	CA2960
Nolker, D. Brett	NC2430	Novenske-Smith, Janine L.	MI1200	O'Brien, Kevin	DC0050
Nolte, Brent J.	MN1030	Novick, Martha	NY1860	O'Brien, Linda	WI1150
Nolte, John P.	MN1030	Novick, Martha	NY1450	O'Brien, Michael S.	IA0950
Nolte, Lanita M.	MN1030	Novine-Whitaker, Virginia	NC0750	O'Brien, Nancy	IL1520
Nonken, Marilyn C.	NY2750	Novosel, Steve J.	DC0350	O'Brien, Orin	NY1900
Noon, David	NY2150	Novotney, Eugene D.	CA2250	O'Brien, Orin	NY2150
Noonan, Jeffrey	MO1500	Novotny, Edward	WY0115	O'Brien, Orin	NY2250
Noonan, Jeffrey J.	MO1900	Novros, Paul	CA0510	O'Brien, Patrick	NY1900
Noonan, Timothy	WI0825	Nowack, James	WI1155	O'Brien, Richard	TX2930
Noone, Elizabeth	MA0150	Nowacki, Edward C.	OH2200	O'Brien, Susan	IL0550
Noone, Katherine	ND0350	Nowak, Gerald C.	PA0400	O'Brien, Tanya	PA2450
Noone, Michael J.	MA0330	Nowak, Grzegorz	FL0700	O'Brien, William J.	ID0100
Noonkester, Lila D.	SC0800	Nowak, Robert A.	PA1900	O'Bryant, Daniel K.	MN1300
Noraker, Dan	MN0040	Nowicki, Susan	PA0850	Oby, Jason	TX3150
Norberg, Anna H.	OK1450	Nowik, John	NJ1160	O'Callaghan, Brien	IL0650
Norberg, Rebecca	MN1250	Nowlen, Peter	CA0150	Ocampo, Rebecca	DC0100
Norberto, Jezimar	KY1200	Nowlen, Peter	CA0840	Occhipinti, David	AG0450
Norcross, Brian H.	PA1300	Noya, Francisco	MA0260	Ocel, Timothy	MO1900
Nord, James	GA0250	Noyes, Christopher R.	MA0260	Ochi-Onishi, Susan M.	HI0210
Nord, Merilee	NY1800	Noyes, James	NY0625	Ochiltree, Larry	MI1160
Nord, Michael	OR1300	Noyes, James R.	NJ1400	Ochoa, Reynaldo	TX3450
Nord, Timothy	NY1800	Noyes, Rachel	DC0170	Ochs, Hunter	CA0960
Norden, Gene	KY0650	Nozny, Brian	ND0100	Ockwell, Frederick	IL2250
Norden, James C.	WI0150	Nozny, Rachel	ND0100	O'Connell, Brian	MA2030
Nordgren, Jon	CA0400	Nubar, Lorraine	NY0150	O'Connell, Cynthia	OH0200
Nordhorn, Johanna	MO1950	Nubar, Lorraine	MA1400	O'Connell, Daniel P.	IL2050
Nordling, Robert	MI0350	Nuccio, David	IL2650	O'Connell, Debora S.	NC2700
Nordlund, Caroline	AL0800	Nuccio, David A.	IL1250	O'Connell, Jason	CA4150
Nordlund, Moya L.	AL0800	Nuccio, Mark	NY2150	O'Connell, Tim	OR0400
Nordlund, Samuel	AL0800	Nudell, Geoff A.	CA0835	O'Connell, William	NJ1130
Nordman, Robert W.	MO1830	Nuessmeier, Tom	MN0200	O'Connor, Brad M.	MD0450
Nordstrom, Craig	MA1400	Nugent, Barli	NY1900	O'Connor, Douglas	WI0803
Nordstrom, Erland	NJ1400	Nugent, Thomas	CA2950	O'Connor, Kelli A.	RI0300
Noreen, Ken	WA0860	Nugent, Thomas	CA5350	O'Connor, Margaret	NJ1400
Noreen, Rebecca	CT0100	Nulty, Dennis	MI2200	O'Connor, Martin	PA2250
Noren, Rictor	MA0350	Nunemaker, Richard	TX3450	O'Connor, Matt T.	AK0100
Norfleet, Dawn	CA0630	Nunemaker-Bressler, Emily B.	IL2730	O'Connor, Michael B.	FL1450
Norgaard, Martin	GA1050	Nunez, John	CA1700	O'Connor, Peter J.	NY0100
Noriega, Scott	NY0625	Nunez, Rachel	OH1350	O'Connor, Philip	CA3800
Norin-Kuehn, Deborah	OH0950	Nunez, Robert	LA0800	O'Connor, Susan	NJ0175
Norman, Edward	AB0090	Nunley, David	WI0825	O'Connor, Tara	NY2150
Norman, Janet	AZ0490	Nurock, Kirk	NY2660	O'Connor, Tara	NY0150
Norman, Jeffery	AZ0490	Nurse, Ray	AB0100	O'Connor, Tara Helen	NY3785
Norman, John L.	CA1270	Nurullah, Shahida	AG0550	O'Connor, Thomas	AR0110
Norman, Mark	KS1400	Nuss, Patricia	GA1400	O'Conor, John	VA1350
Norman-Sojourner, Elizabeth	IL0600	Nuss, Steven R.	ME0250	Octave, Thomas	PA2950
Normand, Jean-Francois	AI0200	Nustad, Corinne	MN0600	Odajima, Isaiah	TX0300
Normandeau, Dale	AC0050	Nutt, Dorrie	AL0010	Oddis, Frank A.	KY0900
Normandeau, Robert	AI0200	Nutt, Dorrie	AL1160	Oddsen, Kristine	NJ0200
Norrell, Stephen	NY2150	Nuttall, Geoff	CA4900	Ode, James	TX2400
Norris, Alexander	MD0650	Nutter, David A.	CA5010	Odell, Andrew	NY1400
Norris, Charles	MI0900	Nuzzo, Nancy B.	NY4320	O'Dell, Debra	ID0140
Norris, Elizabeth	VT0300	Nyberg, Gary B.	WA0480	Odell, Dennis	TX1450
Norris, James Weldon	DC0150	Nye, Karmelle	ID0075	Odell, Kelly	GA0250
Norris, Joshua L.	KS0900	Nye, Randall	TX0700	O'Dell, Timothy J.	ME0500
Norris, Michael B.	PA3250	Nye, Roger	NY2150	Odello, Denise	MN1620
Norris, Mike	FL1790	Nye, Roger	NJ1130	Odello, Mike	MN1620
Norris, Paul	DC0170	Nyerges, John	NY2500	Odem, Susan	IA0650
Norris, Phil	MN1250	Nyetam, Rachel	TN1600	Odem, Susan	IA1350
Norris, Philip E.	MN1280	Nyline, Fred	IA0950	Odem, Susan K.	IA0200
Norris, Renee Lapp	PA1900	Nystrom, Alison	AB0060	Oden, Wade	MN1200
Norsworthy, Michael	MA0350	Nystrom, Alison	AB0090	O'Dette, Paul	NY1100
North, Geoffrey	IN0905	Nytch, Jeffrey C.	CO0800	Odgren, Jim	MA0260
North, Nigel	IN0900	Oakes, Elizabeth	IA1550	Odnoposoff, Berthe Huberman	TX3420
Northcott, Erica	AB0050	Oakes, Gregory	IA0850	Odom, Aaron	AL1195
Northcut, Timothy	OH2200	Oakes, Scott	KS1450	Odom, David H.	AL0200
Northington, David B.	TN1710	Oakley, Paul E.	KY0800	Odom, Donald R.	MS0850
Northrop, Jonathan	CT0050	Oakley, Paul E.	NC0350	Odom, Gale J.	LA0050
Norton, Christopher S.	TN0100	Oakley, Tom	TN0150	Odom, Leslie S.	FL1850
Norton, Diane M.	IN1850	Oare, Steven	KS1450	Odom, Lisa Sain	SC0400
Norton, Edgar	NY1700	Oaten, Gregory	PA2450	O'Donnell, Jennifer M.	CT0246
Norton, Jeanne	OH1850	Oates, Jennifer Lynn	NY0600	O'Donnell, Kevin	AG0600
Norton, John	IL1890	Oatts, Dick	PA3250	O'Donnell, Patrick	DC0170
Norton, Kay	AZ0100	Oba, Junko	MA1000	O'Donnell, Richard L.	MO1900

Alphabetical Listing of Faculty

Name	Code	Name	Code	Name	Code
O'Donnell, Shaugn	NY0600	Olcott, James L.	OH1450	Olson, Rolf	SD0600
O'Donnell, Shaugn	NY0550	Olcott, Nicholas	MD1010	Olson, Scott	SD0050
O'Donnell, Terry	CA4100	Oldani, Robert	AZ0100	Olson, Susan	TX3530
O'Donohue, Deirdre	NY2150	Oldfather, Christopher	NY2150	Olson, Willis R.	OH2000
O'Donohue, Deirdre	NY2750	Oldham, Barbara	NY2750	Olsson, John	OH2600
Oeck, Cynthia	IL1750	Oldham, Barbara	NY0500	Olsson, John A.	OH2290
Oehler, Donald L.	NC2410	Oldham, Ryan P.	MO1810	Olsson, Patricia	OH2290
Oehlers, K. Rebecca	PA1000	O'Leary, James	OH1700	Olszewski, Thomas	IL0420
Oehme, Jane	NY2900	O'Leary, Jay	IA1100	Olt, Timothy	KY1000
Oelrich, John A.	TN1720	O'Leary, Jed	NE0700	Olt, Timothy J.	OH1450
Oelschlaeger-Fischer, Curtis	IL0300	O'Leary, Jed	NE0400	Olt, Timothy	OH2450
Oeseburg, Beth	MI1180	Oles, Darek	CA5020	Olthafer, Rebecca	IL2100
Oeste, Wolfgang	AR0850	Oles, Darek	CA0510	Oltman, Dwight	OH0200
Oesterle, Ulf	NY4150	Olesen, Bradley C.	LA0200	Oltman, Laura G.	PA1850
Oestreich, Martha	FL0950	Olesen, James D.	MA0500	Oltmanns, Caroline Marianne	OH2600
O'Farrell, Elsa	NC2400	Oleskiewicz, Mary	MA2010	Olvera, Victor	KS0570
O'Farrill, Arturo	NY3785	Oleson, Bradley	PA3600	O'Mahoney, Terrence	AF0150
Ofenloch, Gary	UT0250	Oleszkiewicz, Dariusz	CA0835	O'Malley, Sean	CA0630
Offard, Felton	IL2100	Oleszkiewicz, Dariusz	CA5300	O'Meally, Christine	WI0200
Offard, Felton	IL0600	Olfert, Warren	ND0350	O'Meara, Caroline	TX3510
Offerle, Anthony	FL1850	Olin, Christopher S.	OR1050	O'Modhrain, Sile	MI2100
Oft, Eryn	AL0500	Olin, Elinor	IL2000	Omojola, Olabode	MA1350
Oft, Mike	OR0150	Olin, James R.	MD0650	Omoumi, Hossein	CA5020
Oft, Toby	MA0400	Olin, Marissa H.	MI2000	Onalbayeva, Kadisha	FL1500
Ogaard, Sigurd	TX3200	Olinger, Kathy A.	CO0350	Onciul, Gerald	AA0035
Ogano, Kumi	CT0100	Olinyk, George Yuri	CA0150	Ondarza, Danielle	CA3650
Ogden Hagen, Linda	IL2050	Oliphant, Naomi J.	KY1500	Onderdonk, Julian	PA3600
Ogdon, Will L.	CA5050	Olivares, Walter G.	AK0100	O'Neal, Andrea	IN0500
Oge, Derin	NY3785	Olive, Jordan	IL2650	O'Neal, Faith	OK0750
Ogg, Janette	VA1350	Olive, Jordan	IL1200	O'Neal, Harriet	AR0110
Ogilvie, Jessica	TX3535	Oliveira, Elmar	FL1125	O'Neal, Kevin	CA4450
Ogilvie, Kevin	TX1350	Oliver, Abby	AL0500	O'Neal, Melinda P.	NH0100
Ogilvie, Tyler	PA3150	Oliver, Alise M.	KY0250	O'Neal, Thomas	MO1800
Ogilvie, Tyler	PA0950	Oliver, Brenda	NH0300	O'Neal, Whitney	AL1250
Ogle, Alex	NH0100	Oliver, Gale	CA4450	O'Neel, Roger	OH0450
Ogle, Deborah A.	GA1200	Oliver, Harold	NJ1050	O'Neil, Lorne W.	TX3525
Ogle, Nancy Ellen	ME0440	Oliver, Holly E.	NH0250	O'Neill, Adrian	AF0120
Oglesby, Donald T.	FL1900	Oliver, James	AL0050	O'Neill, Amy	AG0500
Oglesby, Michael	TX3370	Oliver, Jon	KY1400	O'Neill, Ben	PA3330
Ogletree, Mary	PA1750	Oliver, Kristen	AF0120	O'Neill, Darren D.	NJ0800
OGrady, Douglas M.	CT0800	Oliver, Murray	CO0250	O'Neill, Golder	VA1350
O'Grady, Judy	WI0808	Oliver, Ronald D.	MI2250	O'Neill, Jill L.	SC1200
O'Grady, Terence J.	WI0808	Oliver, Sarah	TX2250	O'Neill, Patricia A.	LA0200
Ogrizovic-Ciric, Mirna	GA0300	Oliver, Sylvester	MS0600	O'Neill, Richard	CA5030
Ogura, Yukiko	IL0550	Oliver, Timothy	AR0110	O'Neill, SC, Alice Ann M.	OH0680
Oh, Annette	IL1090	Oliver, Tony	IL0100	O'Neill, Susan	AG0500
Oh, Gregory	AG0450	Oliverio, James C.	FL1850	Ong, Seow-Chin	KY1500
Oh, Jiyoung	DC0170	Oliveros, Nancy	MN1450	Ongaro, Giulio M.	CA5350
Oh, June Choi	CA1650	Oliveros, Pauline	NY3300	Ono, Momoro	NE0160
Oh, Jung Eun	OH0600	Oliveros, Pauline	CA2950	Onofrio, Marshall	NJ1350
Oh, Kyung-Nam	IN0100	Olivier, Rufus	CA2950	Onofrio, Susan	NJ1350
Oh, Kyung-Nam	IN1560	Olivier, Rufus	CA4700	Onwood, Susannah	IN1010
Oh, Seung-Ah	IL0750	Olivier, Rufus	CA4900	Oore, Danny	AF0050
Oh, Sun-Joo	TN0500	Olivier, Thomas	KS0980	Oorts, Paul	MD0650
Oh, Yoojin	NY0644	Olivieri, Emmanuel	PR0115	Oosterwaal, Amber	WI1150
O'Hagan, Cheryl Reid	AF0120	Olivieri, Guido	TX3510	Oosting, Stephen	NJ0800
O'Hara, Thomas	MN1600	Olivieri, Mark A.	NY1550	Oostwoud, Roelof	AB0100
O'Hern, Eilene	CA5355	Olka, Christopher	WA1050	Opalach, Jan	NY1100
Ohia, Chinyerem	DC0150	Ollen, Joy	AB0050	Opatz-Muni, Mari	OH1450
Ohl, Dorothy E.	OH0950	Ollis, Ken	OR0850	Opel, Paul E.	VT0200
Ohl, Ferris E.	OH0950	Ollis, Ken	OR0250	Oper, Linda L.	IL0840
Ohl, Vicki	OH0950	Ollmann, Kurt	WI0825	Opfer, Stephen R.	CA2810
Ohlman, Kathleen	NE0200	Olm, James	WY0050	Opie, Benjamin	PA0550
Ohls, Ray	WA0600	Olmstead, R. Neil	MA0260	Opie, Peter	IN0150
Ohlson, Laurel	DC0050	Olschofka, Felix	TX3420	Opp, Benjamin A.	CA0850
Ohlsson, Eric	FL0850	Olsen, Alex	AB0150	Oppelt, Maren	ID0075
Ohm, Carlotta L.	MN1030	Olsen, David	ID0060	Oppelt, Robert	MD1010
Ohrenstein, Dora	NY4500	Olsen, Eric	NJ0800	Oppenheim, Joshua	KS0650
Ohriner, Mitchell S.	VA1350	Olsen, Gayle	NY0050	Oppens, Ursula	NY0600
Oie, Cheryl	MN0250	Olsen, John F.	NM0100	Oppens, Ursula	NY0500
Oien, Theodore	MI1400	Olsen, Karl	KY1450	Optiz, Robert	GA1700
Oien, Theodore	MI2200	Olsen, Karl	IN1010	Oquin, Wayne	NY1900
Oja, Carol J.	MA1050	Olsen, Karl	KY0400	Oram, Virginia	IN1750
Ojeda, Rodrigo	PA0550	Olsen, Lance	NJ0990	Oravitz, Michael	IN0150
Oka, Betty A.	CA3500	Olsen, Nina	MN0300	Orban, Suzanne	MD0750
Oka, Hirono	PA3250	Olsen, Rebecca	ID0060	Orchard, Joseph T.	NJ0050
Okamoto, Kyoko M.	VA0450	Olsen, Ryan	CO0250	Ordaz, Joseph	CA2975
Okamoto, Kyoko	MD1010	Olsen, Ryan	ID0050	Ordman, Ava	MI1400
Okamura, Grant K.	HI0210	Olsen, Stanford	MI2100	Ordonez, Karla	TX0900
Oke, Doreen	AB0100	Olsen, Tim	AB0090	Ore, Charles	NE0150
O'Keefe, Patrick	WI0845	Olsen, Timothy	NC2205	O'Rear, Susan A.	TX3420
O'Keefe, Stephanie	CA3300	Olsen, Timothy	NC1650	O'Reilly, Daniel	SC0420
Okerlund, David	FL0850	Olsen, Timothy J.	NY4310	O'Reilly, Sally	MN1623
Okigbo, Austin	CO0800	Olson, Adam	VA1350	Orenstein, Arbie	NY0642
Okins, Ann	SD0580	Olson, Adrienne	TN1350	Orenstein, Arbie	NY0600
Okoshi, Tiger	MA0260	Olson, Anthony	MO0950	Orenstein, Janet	NC1650
Okpebhola, Dorthy White	TN0450	Olson, Craig	WY0130	Oreskovich, Kristina	NE0250
Okpebholo, Shawn E.	IL3550	Olson, Janna	AA0035	Orey, Pedro	FL0100
Okstel, Henry J.	TX3420	Olson, Jason	CO0950	Orfe, John	IL0400
Okubo, Mack	FL0650	Olson, Jeffrey K.	GA2150	Organ, Wayne	CA1450
Okumura, Lydie	MA0260	Olson, Jennifer	CA3500	Orgel, Paul	VT0450
Okun, Matthew J.	WA0800	Olson, John	MN0040	Orgel, Seth H.	LA0200
Okwabi, Tori	MN1300	Olson, Kevin R.	UT0300	Orgill, Edward	MA2100
Olague, Jimmy	TX3527	Olson, Margaret	MD0600	Orhon, Volkan	IA1550
Olah, John J.	FL1900	Olson, Marjean A.	NY2150	O'Riordan, Kirk	PA1850
Olan, David M.	NY0250	Olson, Matthew W.	SC0750	Orkis, Lambert T.	PA3250
Olan, David	NY0600	Olson, Mia	MA0260	Orland, Michael	CA5000
Olander, Jennifer	TN1000	Olson, Michael	ND0350	Orlando, Courtney Sian	MD0650
Olander, Virginia	LA0300	Olson, Robert	ND0350	Orlando, Danielle	PA0850
Olbrych, Timothy	VA0250	Olson, Robert H.	MO1810	Orlando, Hilary	PA2800

Alphabetical Listing of Faculty

Name	Code	Name	Code	Name	Code
Orlando, Joe	AG0350	Ostrander, Jeanette Davis	OH0600	Owens, Robert	NC0800
Orlando, John	CA0400	Ostrander, Lonnie	AR0400	Owens, Rose Mary	MO0775
Orleans, James	MA1400	Ostrander, Phillip A.	WI0803	Owens, Theodore	NV0125
Orleans, James B.	MA0400	Ostrovsky, Paul	NY3785	Owens, Thomas C.	VA0450
Orlick, James	SC0150	Ostrowski, Gordon	NY2150	Owens, Tiffany	OH0680
Orlofsky, Diane	AL1050	O'Sullivan, Ian	HI0210	Owens, Walter	IL0720
Orlov, Irena	DC0170	O'Sullivan, Laila K.	TN1680	Owings, John	TX3000
Orlov, Marietta	AG0450	Osuna, Thomas	CA1700	Ownbey, Shru De Li	UT0250
Orlov, Marietta	AG0300	Oswald, Mark	NY2150	Owolabi, Olukola P.	NY4150
Orlowski, Joseph	AG0450	Oswalt, Lewis	MS0400	Owren, Betty Ann	CA1760
Orman, Evelyn	LA0200	Otake, Miya	AB0200	Oxford, Todd	TX3175
Ormandy, Paul	AG0650	Otaki, Michiko	GA0500	Oxler, Cora Jean	TX3370
Ormenyi, Dina	CA3300	Otal, Monica D.	MD0175	Oxley, Michael	IA0700
Ormond, Nelda C.	DC0350	Otero, Erica	NM0450	Oyan, Sheri	VA1600
Ormsbee, Timothy	AZ0350	O'Toole, Elizabeth A.	MT0350	Oye, Deanna	AA0200
Ormsby, Verle A.	WI0803	Ott, Daniel P.	NY1900	Oyen, David W.	KY0900
Orovich, Nicholas	NH0350	Ott, Daniel	NY1300	Oyen, Valerie	TN1600
Orozco, Eduardo	ND0350	Ott, Hal J.	WA0050	Oyen-Larsen, Valerie	TN0100
Orozco, Jorge	DC0170	Ott, Joseph	IL0100	Oyenard, Geronimo	VA0050
Orpen, Rick	MN1000	Ott, Leonard	CA0900	Oyer, Mary K.	IN0550
Orpen, Rick	MN0750	Ott, Leonard	CA5350	Oyster, Roger	MO1790
Orr, Emily G.	NC2435	Otte, Allen C.	OH2200	Ozah, Marie Agatha	PA1050
Orr, Gerald	TX1250	Otten, Thomas J.	NC2410	Ozaki, Yukio	HI0060
Orr, Kevin Robert	FL1850	Ottervik, Jennifer	MD0650	Ozeas, Natalie	PA0550
Orr, Philip	NJ1000	Ottesen, Bradley	UT0300	Ozgen, Mesut	CA5070
Orr, Sue Butler	SC0710	Ottley, Jerold	HI0050	Ozment, Jon	DC0010
Orris, Dale A.	PA2100	Ottley, JoAnn	HI0050	Ozment, Jon	MD1010
Orris, Dale A.	PA0350	Otto, Clark	WI0300	Ozzello, Kenneth B.	AL1170
Orson, Beth	AB0100	Otto, James	MI0100	Paar, Sara	NY2050
Orta, Melissa	TX1850	Otto, Noemi	VA0750	Paat, Joel	CA3800
Orta, Michael	FL0700	Otto, Peter	OH0650	Pabon, Roselin	PR0115
Ortega, Anne	PA1200	Otto, Steven	AG0650	Paccione, Paul	IL3500
Ortega, Catalina	AR0700	Ottsen, Linda	CA5360	Pace, Mark	NC1750
Ortega, Janice	CA2950	Otwell, Margaret V.	WI0500	Pace, Matthew	MO1950
Ortega, Janice D.	CA0807	Otwell, Margaret	WI0825	Pace, Roberto J.	NJ1050
Orth, Scott	MD0650	Ou, Carol	MA0950	Pachak-Brooks, Cheryl	NM0100
Ortiguera, Joseph	AL1200	Ou, Carol	MA1400	Pack, Abigail	NC2430
Ortiz Garcia, Norberto	PR0115	Ouellette, Antoine	AI0210	Pack, Lester	AR0800
Ortiz, Carlos	PA3580	Ouellette, Garry	NY2550	Pack, Shari	ID0060
Ortiz, Gabriela	NY2450	Ouimet, Francois	AI0150	Pack, Tim S.	OR1050
Ortiz, Norberto	PR0150	Oundjian, Peter	CT0850	Packales, Joseph	ME0500
Ortiz, Pablo	CA5010	Ouska, Jim	MN1050	Packard, Jennifer	OH1600
Ortiz, Sheila	PR0115	Ousley, Larry James	FL0700	Packard, John	OH1600
Ortiz, William	PR0115	Ousley, Paul	MN1450	Packer, Michael	CA1000
Ortner-Roberts, Susanne	PA3580	Ouspenskaya, Anna	DC0170	Packman, Jeffrey L.	AG0450
Orton, Billy H.	AL1160	Outland, Joyanne	IN0905	Packwood, Gary D.	MS0500
Orton, Korianne	UT0050	Outland, Randall	NC0050	Pacun, David E.	NY1800
Ortwein, Mark	IN1100	Ouyang, Angel	NY3350	Paddleford, Nancy	MN1450
Ortwein, Mark T.	IN1650	Ovalle, Jonathan	MI2100	Paddock, Joan Haaland	OR0450
Orzolek, Douglas	MN1625	Ovens, Douglas P.	PA2550	Padelford, Anne Marie	TN0050
Osadchy, Eugene	TX3420	Overfield-Zook, Kathleen	VA0600	Padgham Albrecht, Carol	ID0250
Osborn, Bradley T.	OH1900	Overholt, Sara	NY0625	Padilla, Anthony	WI0350
Osborn, James	NY4450	Overholt, Sherry	NY0642	Padilla, Clarence S.	IA0550
Osborn, Susan R.	IL2250	Overholt, Sherry	NY3785	Padilla, Margaret	WI0825
Osborn, Vince	MN0450	Overland, Corin T.	FL1900	Padilla, Reginald A.	HI0210
Osborne, Brian	OK0750	Overly, Paul	SC0200	Padrichelli, Andra	OH0450
Osborne, Charles	CA0100	Overman, Michael	VA1850	Padron, Rafael	FL0700
Osborne, Larry	CA3320	Overman, Michael M.	VA0600	Paduck, Ted	MA0260
Osborne, Michelle M.	NY2950	Overmier, Douglas R.	MO0950	Padula, Dawn M.	WA1000
Osborne, Robert B.	TX2250	Overmier, Juliana	OK0300	Paer, Lewis J.	NY2750
Osborne, Robert M.	NY2550	Overmoe, Kirk	TX3360	Paescht, Matthew	OH1200
Osborne, Robert	NY4450	Overton, LeAnn L.	NJ0800	Paetsch, Matt	OH1600
Osborne, Tam	WA0300	Overton, LeAnn	NY2150	Pagal, Alena M.	SC1110
Osborne, Thomas	HI0210	Overy, Charles	AI0200	Pagan, Joel G.	TX3525
Osbun-Manley, Kirsten E.	OH1800	Oviedo, Javier	CT0800	Pagan, Leslie	PR0100
Osburn, Carmen E.	MS0550	Owen, Bruce M.	LA0300	Pagano, Caio	AZ0100
Osby, Greg	MA0260	Owen, Charles (Chuck) R.	FL2000	Pagano, John J.	NY2150
O'Shea, Lindsy	MN1400	Owen, Christopher S.	IL2150	Pagano, Stephen	NY1275
O'Shea, Patrick	MN1400	Owen, Drew	DC0150	Pagano, Vincent	RI0150
Oshida, Joanna	UT0325	Owen, Edward 'Ted'	OR0500	Page, Andy	NC0050
Oshima, Ayako	CT0650	Owen, Jerri Lee	CA0350	Page, Carolann	NJ1350
Oshima, Ayako	NY1900	Owen, John E.	OH0950	Page, Cleveland	MD1010
Oshima-Ryan, Yumiko	MN0750	Owen, John Edward	AR0110	Page, Fran M.	NC1300
Osifchin, Matthew	PA1400	Owen, Kenneth L.	WA0750	Page, Gordon	TX1725
Osika, Geoffrey	CA0830	Owen, Kevin	MA0350	Page, Janet K.	TN1680
Osland, Lisa	KY1450	Owen, Linda	OK1330	Page, John	MA1400
Osland, Miles	KY1450	Owen, Marlin	CA0350	Page, Paula	TX2150
Osmond, Melissa	MI1000	Owen, Stephen W.	OR1050	Page, Paula	TX3400
Osmun, Ross	AI0050	Owen, Wesley	IL0550	Page, Richard L.	NH0110
Osorio, Claudio	FL1310	Owen, William E.	WA0550	Page, Robert	PA0550
Osorio, Jorge Federico	IL0550	Owen-Leinert, Susan	TN1680	Page, Sandra	AA0050
Osowski, Kenneth	PA3710	Owens, Charles	CA5031	Page, Tim	CA5300
Osrowitz, Michael L.	NY2550	Owens, Charles Marion	CA5020	Paglialonga, Phillip O.	FL0100
Ossi, Massimo M.	IN0900	Owens, Chris	VA1550	Paglialunga, Augusto N.	WV0750
Ostbye, Niels J.	NY0750	Owens, Craig	KS1450	Pagliarini, Shawn	GA0750
Osteen, Kim	AZ0200	Owens, Diane	TX1100	Pagliuca, Domingo	FL1450
Osten, Mark	CA3250	Owens, Diane	NE0160	Pagluica, Domincio	FL0700
Osten, Mark	CA4460	Owens, Douglas A.	TN1720	Pagnard, Charles	OH0450
Oster, Andrew	PA2550	Owens, Douglas T.	VA1000	Pahel, Tim A.	IL1350
Oster, Floyd	NH0110	Owens, Janet	FL1450	Pahel, Timothy	IL1800
Osterbers, Janet	WI0808	Owens, Jeremy	IA0100	Paick, Yoomi	TN1450
Osterfield, Paul	TN1100	Owens, Jessie Ann	CA5010	Paiement, Nicole	CA4150
Osterhause, Sharon	MN1250	Owens, Jimmy	NY2660	Paiement, Nicole	CA5070
Osterhouse, Carl	MN1280	Owens, John W.	OH2200	Paiewonsky, Moises	AZ0500
Osterloh, Elijah	MD1010	Owens, Kathryn Ananda	MN1450	Paige, Diane M.	NY1400
Osterlund, David	SC0620	Owens, Margaret B.	VA0450	Paige-Green, Jacqueline	LA0700
Ostling, Elizabeth	MA0400	Owens, Meg	DC0010	Paik, Wanda	MA1600
Ostlund, Sandor	TX0300	Owens, Parthena	OK0750	Painter, Karen	MN1623
Ostoich, Mark S.	OH2200	Owens, Priscilla	NY0625	Painter, Noel	FL1750
Ostrander, Allison	WI0803	Owens, Richard R.	FL1550	Paise, Michele	TN1100

Alphabetical Listing of Faculty

Name	Code	Name	Code	Name	Code
Pajer, Curt	CA4150	Panteleyev, Vladimir	NY0500	Parkening, Christopher	CA3600
Pakman, Mark	NJ0800	Pantoja, Rique	CA0350	Parker Bennett, Dione	OH0100
Palac, Judith A.	MI1400	Paolantonio, Ed	NC2410	Parker, Alex	TX0300
Palacio, Jon	CA0900	Paolantonio, Ed	NC1600	Parker, Andrew	IA1550
Palance, Thomas M.	MA1650	Paolantonio, Edmund J.	NC0600	Parker, Bradley	SC0700
Palatucci, John	NJ0800	Paoletti, Karl P.	GA2150	Parker, Charla	OK0600
Palchak, Mary	CA0960	Paoli, Kenneth N.	IL0630	Parker, Charles H.	PA3250
Palchak, Mary	CA2390	Paolo, James	WI1150	Parker, Christopher S.	NY3000
Palecek, Brian	ND0400	Paolucci, Roland	OH2150	Parker, Clinton R.	NC0050
Palej, Norbert	AG0450	Papador, Nicholas G.	AG0550	Parker, Craig B.	KS0650
Palermo, Joseph M.	IL2900	Papanikolaou, Eftychia	OH0300	Parker, David	SC0200
Palese, Richard	IL3450	Paparo, Stephen A.	MA2000	Parker, David	AF0100
Palestrant, Christopher	NC0700	Paparone, Stacy A.	PA1450	Parker, David K.	OR1100
Palfrey, Rossman	IL0550	Papatheodoroa, Devvora	IL2750	Parker, Dennis N.	LA0200
Paliga, Mitch L.	IL2050	Papatheodorou, Devovora	IL0780	Parker, Don	NC0800
Paliga, Mitchell L.	IL1400	Pape, John W.	MA0350	Parker, Elizabeth	GA0550
Palkovic, Mark	OH2200	Pape, Louis W.	SD0150	Parker, Erica	OK0850
Pallett, Bryan	MD0060	Pape, Madlyn	TX1900	Parker, Everett G.	LA0200
Palma, Donald	CT0850	Papich, George	TX3420	Parker, Gene	MI2200
Palma, Donald	MA1400	Papillon, Andre	AI0190	Parker, Grant	CA1500
Palma, Susan	NJ0800	Papolos, Janice	NY2150	Parker, Gregory B.	NC0400
Palmer, Anthony J.	MA0400	Papoulis, Mary	MT0370	Parker, Harlan D.	MD0650
Palmer, Bradley E.	GA0550	Papp, Anne	DC0170	Parker, James	AG0450
Palmer, Caroline	AI0150	Pappano, Annalisa	OH2200	Parker, Joan	SC0200
Palmer, Christopher G.	FL1900	Pappas, J.	MO0550	Parker, Jon Kimura	TX2150
Palmer, Christopher	AF0120	Pappas, Joan H.	WV0400	Parker, Kara	FL1430
Palmer, Dan	MI0100	Pappas, Louis	NY4450	Parker, Laura M.	IL2400
Palmer, David	NC1150	Pappas, Mark	MI0600	Parker, Laura J.	MD0650
Palmer, David	NC0550	Paquette-Abt, Mary	MI2200	Parker, Linda	NC0200
Palmer, David	NC1900	Para, Christopher	PA0350	Parker, Lisa	MA1175
Palmer, David	AG0550	Paradis, Kristian	DE0150	Parker, Mara	PA3680
Palmer, Edit	FL1750	Paradis, Sarah	OH1900	Parker, Mark	SC0200
Palmer, Gary	IL0100	Paradise, Kathryn L.	TN0100	Parker, Mary Ann	AG0450
Palmer, Jason	OR1020	Parakilas, James P.	ME0150	Parker, Michael	NC0910
Palmer, Jason	OR1250	Paranosic, Milica	NY1900	Parker, Nancy	MN0610
Palmer, John	CA4700	Parashevov, Milen	NC0300	Parker, Nancy	MN1300
Palmer, John M.	IL0275	Paraskevas, Apostolos	MA0260	Parker, Nathaniel F.	PA2200
Palmer, Katherine	NC0250	Parcell, John	OH2120	Parker, Olin G.	GA2100
Palmer, Kirk	OK0700	Parcell, Renee	IN0400	Parker, Patricia	VA0450
Palmer, Kye	CA0815	Parchman, Thomas	ME0500	Parker, Patricia G.	AL0500
Palmer, Larry	TX2400	Pardew, Mike	OR0400	Parker, Philip	AR0200
Palmer, Leila S.	SC0600	Pardini, Eithne	CA4150	Parker, Phillip	NE0300
Palmer, Michael	GA1050	Pardo, Brian	CA5000	Parker, Rebekah Bruce	OK0750
Palmer, Nicholas	TN0100	Pardo, Brian	CA0807	Parker, Robin Lee	FL1700
Palmer, Patricia	MD0650	Pardo, Brian	CA2950	Parker, Salli	CA2440
Palmer, Richard	NE0610	Pardo, Danielle	WI1150	Parker, Steven C.	TX3530
Palmer, Robert	NC0250	Pardo-Tristan, Emiliano	NY2750	Parker, Steven	SD0100
Palmer, Robert	IN0150	Pardue, Dan	NC1400	Parker, Sylvia	VT0450
Palmer, Thomas	DE0150	Pardue, Jane	NC1400	Parker, Teresa B.	NY0250
Palmier, Darice	IL2970	Pare', Barbara A.	IN0350	Parker, Val	GA0490
Palmieri, Bob	IL0750	Pare', Craig T.	IN0350	Parker, Webster	MS0750
Palmieri, Gary	NY3760	Pare, Richard	AI0190	Parker, Wesley	NC1700
Palmore, James	IL3100	Parent, Marie-Danielle	AI0210	Parker, Wesley	AR0250
Palmquist, Jane E.	NY0500	Parent, Yolande	AI0200	Parker-Brass, Myran	MA1175
Palmquist, Krista	WI0845	Parente, Thomas	NJ1350	Parker-Harley, Jennifer	SC1110
Palomaki, Jonathan	IL0300	Parenteau, Gilles	AB0070	Parkes, Kelly Anne	VA1700
Palomaki, Jonathan	TX3800	Parillo, Joseph M.	RI0300	Parkhurst, Melissa	OR0750
Pals, Joel	ID0130	Parins, Linda	WI0808	Parkhurst, Raymond	IL2350
Palser, Caroline	NY3350	Paris, John	IL0720	Parkin, Chris	WA1350
Palter, Morris	AK0150	Parish, Steven	AB0070	Parkin, Christopher	WA0400
Palton, George A.	WV0400	Parisi, Joseph	MO1810	Parkin, Vera L.	MO1950
Palumbo, Michael A.	UT0350	Parisot, Aldo S.	CT0850	Parkins, Margaret	CA2390
Paluzzi, Rebecca Lile	TN0500	Parisot, Elizabeth	CT0850	Parkins, Margaret Clara	CA5020
Pampin, Juan	WA1050	Park, Adrienne	MS0700	Parkins, Robert	NC0600
Pampinella, Paul	MA0260	Park, Angela	CA0350	Parkinson, Del	ID0050
Pan, Huiyu-Penny	CA0830	Park, Angela	IN0900	Parkinson, John S.	CA2840
Pan, JiaYe	AZ0440	Park, Angela	AI0200	Parkinson, Rebecca	ID0060
Pan, Shelly	DC0170	Park, Christine	CA2600	Parkinson, Wm. Michael	OH1900
Panacciulli, Louis M.	NY2550	Park, Christopher	NY2250	Parks, Andrew	WA0800
, Panaiotis	FL1750	Park, Chung	NC0050	Parks, Andrew	WI0845
Panayotova, Miroslava I.	FL2000	Park, Clara	GA0250	Parks, David	NY1800
Pancella, Peter	IL1500	Park, David H.	UT0250	Parks, Gary	TX1400
Pandolfi, Anne	AL0300	Park, Dong Hoon	KY1200	Parks, John	NC2000
Pandolfi, David	AL1200	Park, Eun-Hee	MS0750	Parks, John	FL0850
Pandolfi, David	AL1150	Park, Hana	TX2600	Parks, John	SC0850
Pandolfi, Philip A.	PA0550	Park, Helen	CA5550	Parks, Karen	SC0765
Pandolfi, Philip	PA1050	Park, In-Sook	AL1160	Parks, Richard S.	AG0500
Pandolfi, Roland	OH1700	Park, Janice	CA0960	Parks, Ronald Keith	SC1200
Pandolfo, Susan	AG0070	Park, Janice	CA2390	Parks, Sarah S.	WI0750
Pane, Steven	ME0410	Park, Jenny	CA5355	Parliament, Roland	AG0130
Panella, Lawrence	MS0750	Park, Jin Young	IA1350	Parloff, Michael	NY2150
Panelli, Sal	CA0650	Park, Jong-Won	WI0845	Parman, David L.	IN1800
Panepinto, Tom	NC2435	Park, Kyunghee	MD0700	Parmentier, Edward L.	MI2100
Panethiere, Darrell	NY4150	Park, Mary B.	NY1600	Parmer, Dillon	AG0400
Panetti, Joan	CT0850	Park, Meeyoun	KY0950	Parmer, Pat	WY0130
Paney, Andrew S.	MS0700	Park, Min	AZ0490	Parmer, Richard	WY0130
Pang, Wilma C.	CA1020	Park, Sang Eui	IN0005	Parnas, Leslie	MA0400
Pangburn, Chuck	TX0700	Park, Sohyoung	TX2150	Parnell, Dennis	CA2700
Panion, Henry	AL1150	Park, Soo-Kyung	NY2750	Parnell, Dennis	CA4450
Pankratz, Timothy	AZ0480	Park, Sue-Jean	KY0950	Parnell, Janine	NC0700
Pann, Carter N.	CO0800	Park, Sung-Hwa	CA5300	Parnell, Scott	OH0250
Pannell, Larry J.	LA0100	Park, Tae Hong	NY2750	Parnicky, Lori M.	WA1300
Panner, Daniel Z.	NY3790	Park, Tricia	IN1700	Parodi, Jorge	NY2150
Panner, Daniel	NY1900	Park, William B.	WA0800	Parodi, Jorge	NY2750
Panner, Daniel	NY2250	Park-Kim, Phoenix	IN1025	Parodi, Jorge	NY0500
Panneton, Helene	AI0210	Park-Song, Sophia	CO0830	Parody, Caroline D.	NJ0800
Panneton, Isabelle	AI0200	Parke, Nathaniel	NY3650	Parr, Andrew	TX2700
Pannill Raiford, Judith	OK0850	Parke, Nathaniel	VT0050	Parr, Carlotta	CT0050
Pannunzio, Sam	CO0275	Parke, Nathaniel	MA2250	Parr, Clayton G.	MI0100
Pantaleo, Patrick	MI1180	Parke, Steve	IL2450	Parr, J. D.	KS0050

Alphabetical Listing of Faculty

Name	Code	Name	Code	Name	Code
Parr, Kimerica	AA0032	Patrick-Harris, Terry	LA0200	Payette, Jessica	MI1750
Parr, Patricia	AG0450	Patterson, Ann	CA1750	Payn, Catherine	PA0350
Parr, Sean M.	NH0310	Patterson, Ann E.	CA2650	Payn, William A.	PA0350
Parr, Sean M.	PA0950	Patterson, Anne L.	WV0300	Payne, Benjamin	FL0670
Parr, Sharon M.	IN1650	Patterson, Anthony	MI0150	Payne, Brandt A.	OH2600
Parr-Scanlin, Denise	TX3750	Patterson, Benjamin	MD1010	Payne, Bryon	FL1600
Parran, John D.	NY0270	Patterson, Chris	MN0625	Payne, Catherine	CA4400
Parrell, Richard N.	VA0450	Patterson, David	MA1175	Payne, Doris	CA1860
Parrette, Anne	FL0800	Patterson, David	MA0950	Payne, James	NE0590
Parrini, Fabio	SC0950	Patterson, David N.	MA2010	Payne, Maggi	CA2950
Parris, John	FL1600	Patterson, Donald L.	WI0803	Payne, Mark	AG0500
Parrish, Bill	VA1125	Patterson, Heather	MO1950	Payne, Mary	IL1520
Parrish, Bill	VA0750	Patterson, James H.	GA0490	Payne, Peggy	OK0750
Parrish, Cheryl A.	TX3175	Patterson, Joanna	OH0650	Payne, Phillip	KS0650
Parrish, Clifford	NJ0400	Patterson, Jonathan	AI0150	Payne, Richard Todd	MO0775
Parrish, Eric	MN1175	Patterson, Lisa D.	IL2775	Payne, Thomas B.	VA0250
Parrish, Jonathan L.	HI0210	Patterson, Mark	PA3250	Payne, Tony L.	IL3550
Parrish, Regina T.	AL1170	Patterson, Mark	NY2900	Payne, William	WA1150
Parrish, Robert E.	NJ0175	Patterson, Michael	NY2150	Payson, Al E.	IL0750
Parrish, Steve	NC1050	Patterson, Michael R.	IA1350	Payton, Chad	MS0250
Parrish, Susan K.	CA0400	Patterson, Myron	UT0250	Payton, Denise	NC0800
Parrish, William	VA1400	Patterson, Paula K.	MO0775	Pazera, Scott	IN1850
Parry, A. Scott	OH1850	Patterson, Paula	KS0150	Pazin, Eugene	IL1085
Parsche, Paula	FL0800	Patterson, R. Thomas	AZ0500	Peabody, Martha	MA1450
Parshley, Alan O.	VT0450	Patterson, Richard	CA3270	Peacock, Curtis	WA0050
Parson, Laurie	SC1080	Patterson, Ronald	WA1050	Peacock, Kenneth J.	NY2750
Parsons, Charles	MN0800	Patterson, Roy	AG0650	Peak, Linda	WV0200
Parsons, Derek J.	SC0750	Patterson, Roy	AG0450	Pearce, Peter	CA2550
Parsons, Donna S.	IA1550	Patterson, Thomas	WI0960	Pearce, Stephen	FL1500
Parsons, James B.	MO0775	Patterson, Tracy	TX1550	Pearcy, Robert W.	TN1850
Parsons, Jeffrey L.	OR1300	Patterson, Trent A.	MO1950	Pearl, Adam J.	MD0650
Parsons, Jeffrey L.	OR0700	Patterson, Vincent L.	MD0550	Pearl, Phillip	WI1150
Parsons, Kenneth	TN1350	Patterson, William M.	NY2750	Pearlman, Martin	MA0400
Parsons, Larry R.	WV0800	Pattila, Michael	MS0500	Pearon, Jill R.	NY3780
Parsons, Laura E.	AL0950	Pattishall, Jeffrey	FL1550	Pearsall, Edward	TX3510
Parsons, Laurie N.	SC0400	Pattishall, Teresa	FL1700	Pearsall, Tom	GA0950
Parsons, Longineu	FL0600	Pattison, C. Pat	MA0260	Pearse, Linda	IN0900
Parsons, Sean	WV0400	Patton, David	TN0100	Pearse, Lukas	AF0120
Partain, Gregory L.	KY1350	Patton, Denise	TN0100	Pearson, Don	OK0825
Partington, Michael	WA1050	Patton, Duncan	NY2150	Pearson, Glen	CA1100
Partlow, Mary Rita	TX1900	Patton, Jeb	NY1275	Pearson, Holly	NJ0700
Parton, Robert T.	OH0350	Patton, Patrick	WY0050	Pearson, Ian D.	SC1200
Parton-Stanard, Susan	IL1500	Patton, Richard	IN1025	Pearson, Mark	MA1400
Partridge, Gary	CT0650	Patton, Robert	MA0260	Pearson, Norm	CA5300
Partridge, Hugh	NC2410	Patty, Austin T.	TN0850	Pearson, Norman	CA1075
Partridge, Norma	OK0650	Patykula, John	VA1600	Pearson, Ronald	OK1450
Partridge, William	MO1950	Pau, Andrew Yat-Ming	OH1700	Pearson, Ryan	IA0300
Party, Daniel	IN1450	Paugh, Rob	KY1550	Pearson, Scotty	AZ0490
Party, Lionel	PA0850	Paukert, Noriko F.	OH0650	Pease, Janey L.	NC0850
Pasbrig, David	PA3250	Paul, Arryl S.	TX3520	Pease, Patricia	OH1900
Pascale, Joanna	PA3250	Paul, David	NY1900	Pease, William	VA1550
Paschal, Brett E. E.	OR0400	Paul, David	CA5060	Peattie, Matthew	OH2200
Pascolini, Jon R.	OH2250	Paul, Helene	AI0210	Peattie, Thomas A.	MA0400
Pascuzzi, Greg	MD0060	Paul, Jeffrey	SD0050	Peavler, Robert	MI0600
Pashkin, Elissa Brill	MA1100	Paul, Jessica	IA0950	Pecherek, Michael J.	IL1175
Pasiali, Varvara	NC2000	Paul, John F.	OR0500	Peck, Andrew	ID0060
Paskert, IHM, Joan	PA2200	Paul, Lanetta	OR0200	Peck, Chant	AZ0440
Paskova, Lyubov	MD0800	Paul, Pamela Mia	TX3420	Peck, Daniel	NJ0825
Paslawski, Gordon	AB0100	Paul, Philip	NC0050	Peck, David	ID0060
Pasler, Jann C.	CA5050	Paul, Phyllis M.	OR1050	Peck, Gordon	NM0400
Pasqua, Alan	CA5300	Paul, Randall S.	OH2500	Peck, Jamie	WV0600
Pasqua, Ferdinand A.	CT0250	Paul, Sharon J.	OR1050	Peck, Robert W.	LA0200
Passarelli, Lauren	MA0260	Paul, Timothy A.	OR1050	Peck, Thomas	MI0520
Passaretti, Sumalee	MA0260	Pauley, John-Bede	MN0350	Peckham, Anne	MA0260
Passmore, Ken	GA1200	Paulk, Jason	NM0100	Peckham, Charles R.	MA0260
Pastelak, Marianne	MD0475	Paulk, Kayla Liechty	NM0100	Peckham, Merry	OH0600
Pasternack, Benjamin	MD0650	Paull, Eric	TN0050	Pecorilla, John	OR1020
Pasternack, Jonathan R.	WA1050	Paulnack, Karl	MA0350	Pedatella, R. Anthony	NY2150
Pastin, John R.	NJ1050	Paulo, Gary	GA0750	Pedatella, Stefan	NY2150
Pastor, Elizabeth M.	OH0100	Pauls, Jill	OR0700	Pedde, David	MN1250
Pastor, Juan	IL0275	Paulsen, Donna	MN1450	Pedde, Dennis	IA0930
Pastore, Patrice	NY1800	Paulsen, Kent D.	WI0750	Pedde, Dennis R.	IA0200
Pastorello, Cristian	IL0150	Paulsen, Peter	PA3600	Pedersen, David	VA1500
Pastrana, Jorge	CA4850	Paulson, Brent	CO0625	Pedersen, Gary	MI0600
Patch, Justin	NY4450	Paulson, Jennifer Clare	WI0865	Pedersen, Jean	NY1100
Patcheva, Ralitza	DC0050	Paulson, John C.	MN1400	Pedersen, Kathy	WI0848
Patcheva, Ralitza	DC0170	Paulson, Stephen	CA4150	Pedersen, Keith	CA3640
Pate, David	FL1650	Paulus, Carolyn	CT0650	Pedersen, Thomas	DC0050
Pate, Molly	LA0800	Pauly, Elizabeth	MN1050	Pederson, Donald	TN1710
Patenaude-Yarnell, Joan	PA0850	Pauly, Elizabeth	MN1295	Pederson, John	NC1700
Patenaude-Yarnell, Joan	NY2150	Pauly, Erica	SC0650	Pederson, John	NC2410
Paterno, Matthew	NJ1400	Pauly, Reinhard G.	OR0400	Pederson, Robin	OR0450
Paterson, Amy	UT0150	Pavasaris, Walter	MA0350	Pederson, Sanna	OK1350
Paterson, Janice	AJ0150	Pavelek, Robert	MI1650	Pederson, Steven A.	KY0800
Paterson, Kim	NY1400	Pavelka, Dee	MO1950	Pedigo, Julia A.	NC0050
Patilla, Michael K.	AL0260	Paver, Barbara E.	OH2200	Pedneault-Deslauriers, Julie	AG0400
Patipatanakoon, Annalee	AG0450	Pavese, Frank	NJ1400	Pedrini, Jamie J.	CA3500
Patitucci, John	NY0550	Pavlik, Charleen	PA1050	Pedroza, Ludim R.	TX3175
Patman, Rebecca	NM0200	Pavloski, Rachael	OH2600	Pedroza, Ricardo	PR0125
Patneaude, Brian	NY3600	Pavlovska, Jana	IL0550	Peebles, Crystal	AZ0450
Patnode, Matthew A.	ND0350	Pavlovskaia, Natalia	AF0120	Peebles, Stew	NV0150
Pato-Lorenzo, Cristina	NJ0825	Pawlak, Keith V.	AZ0500	Peebles, William	GA2300
Paton, Eric	OH0350	Pawlak, Michael	IA0700	Peebles, William L.	NC2600
Paton, John Glenn	CA3100	Pawlicki, Michael	CA2700	Peel, John	OR1300
Patrelle, Francis	NY2150	Pawlowski, Lauressa	AA0020	Peeler, Karen	OH1850
Patricio, Raymond	GA0950	Paxson, Joyce M.	WA0600	Peeples, Georgia	OH2150
Patricio, Raymond	GA0200	Paxton, Alexis G.	KY1500	Peeples, Terrance P.	IL1520
Patrick, Dennis M.	AG0450	Paxton, Laurence	HI0210	Peeples, Terry	IL3370
Patrick, Lee	KY1350	Paxton-Mierzejewski, Adele	CT0050	Peersen, Hild	OH0700
Patrick, Louise R.	FL0680	Payack, Peter	MA0260	Peery Fox, Irene	UT0050

Name	Code	Name	Code	Name	Code
Peffer, Ed	CA2390	Peppo, Bret	CA1560	Perry, Gail	CA5300
Peffley, Lynette	OH0100	Pera, Adriana	NY5000	Perry, Jeffery S.	MA0260
Pegher, Lisa	PA1050	Peraino, Judith A.	NY0900	Perry, Jeffrey	LA0200
Pegis, Damien	FL1745	Perantoni, Daniel T.	IN0900	Perry, John	CA1075
Pegis, Gabe	OH2200	Perconti, William J.	ID0130	Perry, John	AG0300
Pegis, John	IL2250	Perdicaris, Stephen	CA0150	Perry, John	CA5300
Pegley, Kip	AG0250	Perdicaris, Stephen	CA5350	Perry, Kathy	SC0700
Peh, Alex L.	DC0170	Pereira, David	CA5000	Perry, Margaret	CA5350
Pehlivanian, Elisabeth	CA0825	Pereira, Ernest	NC2000	Perry, Mark E.	GA1500
Peichl, Dan	IA0550	Pereira, Hoffmann Urquiza	CA4600	Perry, Pamela J.	CT0050
Peirce, Dwight	TX1400	Pereira, Jose Ricardo	AZ0450	Perry, Rich	NY2750
Pejril, Veronica	IN0350	Pereira, Joseph	NY1900	Perry, Rich	NJ1400
Pejrolo, Andrea	MA0260	Pereira, Joseph	CA5300	Perry, Richard H.	MS0750
Pekas, Joe F.	SD0200	Pereira, Kenneth	WI0803	Perry, Robert	NC1300
Peknik, Patricia	MA0260	Pereksta, Linda H.	WI0830	Perry, Skip	FL0500
Pelchat, Andre	AI0210	Perera, Selina	CA3500	Perry, Talya	MO1110
Peled, Amit	MD0650	Peress, Maurice	NY0600	Perry, Tiffany	DC0170
Pelekh, Anna	NY2400	Peress, Maurice	NY0642	Perry, Timothy B.	NY3705
Peles, Stephen	AL1170	Peretz, Marc	MI1850	Persellin, Diane C.	TX3350
Pelev, Todor	CA1050	Perez Rivera, Pedro	PR0115	Pershing, Drora	NY0642
Pelev, Todor D.	CA3650	Perez, Danilo	MA0260	Pershounin, Alexander	GA0550
Pelfrey, Patricia	OH1600	Perez, Danilo	MA1400	Persip, Charli	NY2660
Pelfrey, Patricia	OH1200	Perez, Erin	TN1850	Person, Philip	MA0260
Pelischek, Jeff	KS0550	Perez, Frank	IA0600	Persson, Diane	AA0100
Pell, John	TN0100	Perez, Jesus	TX2570	Persson, Diane	AA0035
Pellay-Walker, Michelle T.	TN1380	Perez, Michael	TX0550	Pertl, Brian G.	WI0350
Pellegrin, Richard S.	MO1800	Perez, Miguel	MA0510	Perttu, Daniel E.	PA3650
Pellegrino, Francesco	AG0450	Perez, Olga	OH1650	Perttu, Melinda H. Crawford	PA3650
Pellegrino, Kristen	TX3530	Perez, Paul	CA0650	Pesavento, Ann	MN0750
Pellegrino, Larry	NV0050	Perez, Pedro	AZ0470	Pesce, Dolores	MO1900
Pelletier, Andrew J.	OH0300	Perez, Samuel	PR0150	Peshlakai, David	MI1000
Pelletier, Christina	OH1850	Perez-Feria, Willy	FL1310	Peske, Robert	ND0050
Pelletier, Louise	AI0150	Perez-Gomez, Jorge	NM0450	Peske, Robert T.	ND0400
Pelletier, Marie Volcy	MA1750	Perez-Tetrault, Rachel	CO0150	Petchersky, Alma	AG0450
Pellicano, Julian	MA1175	Pergola, Joseph	NY2105	Petchulat, David	TN0100
Pellitteri, Marcello	MA0260	Peri, Janis-Rozena	WV0750	Peter, Sandra K.	IA0950
Pellman, Colleen	NY1350	Perialas, Alexander	NY1800	Peter, Timothy	FL1750
Pellman, Samuel	NY1350	Perinchief, Burt H.	FL1700	Petercsak, James J.	NY3780
Pelo, Mika	CA5010	Peris, Malinee	DC0100	Petering, Mark D.	WI0250
Peloza, Susan	CA5400	Perkey, Christine	TN1400	Peterman, Lewis E.	CA4100
Pelto, William L.	NC0050	Perkins, Andrew	NC0450	Peters, Braxton	MD0100
Peltola, Gilbert	ME0200	Perkins, Barry	CA0815	Peters, Braxton	MD0175
Pelton, Carmen	MI2100	Perkins, Boyd	SD0400	Peters, G. David	IN0907
Peltz, Charles	MA1400	Perkins, Daniel R.	NH0250	Peters, Grant S.	MO0775
Pelusi, Mario J.	IL1200	Perkins, Deborah	TX2400	Peters, Gretchen	WI0803
Pemberton, Rick	WI0100	Perkins, Douglas	NH0100	Peters, Lorna G.	CA0840
Pen, Ronald	KY1450	Perkins, Jerry	TN1100	Peters, Maitland	NY2150
Pena, Melissa	OR1050	Perkins, John D.	MO0100	Peters, Maria	SD0580
Pence, Suzanne M.	TX3510	Perkins, Leeman L.	NY0750	Peters, Mark	IL3100
Pendarvis, Janice	MA0260	Perkins, Ralph	CT0650	Peters, Michael	IA0600
Pendell, Carter	AZ0400	Perkins, Richard	MN0040	Peters, Mitchel	CA5030
Pender, Charles	TN1380	Perkins, Scott	IN0350	Peters, Shelley	MO2000
Pendergrass, Ken E.	WA0800	Perkins, Susan	NC2205	Peters, Tom	CA0825
Pendergrast, Celine	TN0550	Perkins, Tedrow	OH2600	Peters, Valerie	AI0190
Pendleton, Karen A.	ME0440	Perkyns, Jane E.	TX3150	Petersen, Alice V. Neff	OH2300
Pendley, Daniel	NY4320	Perl, Jonathan	NY0550	Petersen, Lynn	MT0075
Pendowski, Michael	AL0200	Perla, Gene	NY2660	Petersen, Marian F.	MO1810
Peng, Bo	AB0060	Perla, Gene	PA1950	Petersen, Mark	CA2390
Peng, Yan	MO0950	Perla, James 'Jack'	CA4425	Petersen, William	AL1300
Penhorwood, Edwin L.	IN0900	Perlau, Anita	AA0050	Peterson, Amber Dahlen	OH1100
Penick, Amanda	AL1170	Perlis, Vivian M.	CT0850	Peterson, Anne L.	PA3250
Penick, Pam	AL1170	Perlman, Itzhak	NY1900	Peterson, Ben	IL1740
Penkala, Dan	MI1850	Perlman, Marc	RI0050	Peterson, Christopher	CA0815
Penland, Ralph	CA3500	Perlongo, Daniel J.	PA1600	Peterson, Dan L.	MO1780
Penn, Stephen T.	KY1450	Perlove, Nina	KY1000	Peterson, David	MN1300
Penna, J. J.	NJ1350	Perlstein, Marla	CT0650	Peterson, David	WA0200
Penna, J.J.	NY1900	Perman, Anthony	IA0700	Peterson, David	MN1500
Penne, Cynthia S.	VA1850	Permenter, Calvin	MO2000	Peterson, Dean	MT0400
Penner, Julie	TN1350	Perna, Dana	NY3000	Peterson, Don L.	UT0050
Penner, Ruth	KS0750	Perna, Leslie	MO1800	Peterson, Douglas	NV0050
Penneys, Rebecca	NY1100	Perna, Nicholas K.	WV0750	Peterson, Douglas A.	FL0400
Penniman, G. Victor	MO1010	Pernela, Nathan	HI0050	Peterson, Edward	LA0800
Penning, Rick	MN0300	Perniciaro, Joseph C.	KS0350	Peterson, Elizabeth	NY1800
Penning, Rick	MN0050	Peron, Tom	CA0150	Peterson, Eric	SD0550
Penning-Koperski, Diane	MI0850	Perone, James E.	OH2290	Peterson, Erich	MI1050
Pennington, Curt	IN0800	Peroutka, Leah	NC2410	Peterson, Floyd	ID0250
Pennington, John C.	SD0050	Perrault, Jean R.	MN1600	Peterson, Francine	WA0650
Pennington, Lynn	AR0950	Perrault, Paul	AI0220	Peterson, Francine G.	WA0800
Pennington, Randy	KY1000	Perrella, Anthony	IL2200	Peterson, Francine G.	WA1250
Pennington, Stephen	MA1900	Perrett, Mario	MA2010	Peterson, Gene D.	TN1710
Pennix, Derrick A.	IN0200	Perricone, Jack	MA0260	Peterson, Gregory M.	IA0950
Penny, Michael K.	TN1660	Perricone, Rebecca	MA0260	Peterson, Ian	AI0220
Penny, Nicholas	AG0550	Perrillo, Ron J.	IL0750	Peterson, James L.	MA0260
Pennycook, Bruce	TX3510	Perriment, Andrew	AB0200	Peterson, Jason P.	VA1000
Penpraze, Laurie	FL1745	Perrin, Raymond	AI0200	Peterson, Jay	IL1650
Pensyl, Kim C.	OH2200	Perrin, Raymond	AI0220	Peterson, Jeff	IA1300
Penzarella, Vincent	NY2750	Perrine, John Mark	OH0650	Peterson, Jeffrey Todd	TX0300
Penzarella, Vincent	NY2150	Perris, Arnold	MO1830	Peterson, Jeffry F.	WI0825
Penzarella, Vincent	NY2250	Perron, Alain	AJ0100	Peterson, Jennifer L.	MN1120
Peot, Deborah L.	IL0750	Perron, Bruno	AI0200	Peterson, Jennifer	MN0600
Pepe, Dino	AG0170	Perron, Francis	AI0200	Peterson, John David	TN1680
Pepetone, Gregory	GA0850	Perron, Johanne	AI0200	Peterson, Jon C.	OH0250
Pepin, Natalie	AI0200	Perrotte, Jean-Paul	NV0100	Peterson, Jon	AG0200
Pepin, Pierre	AI0150	Perry, Antoinette	CA5300	Peterson, Keith L.	NY3725
Pepinsky, Juliana May	NY0900	Perry, Brian N.	TX3420	Peterson, Ken	UT0150
Pepitone, Anthony F.	OH2250	Perry, David L.	SC0050	Peterson, Kirsten	CT0450
Peplin, Steve	WI0350	Perry, David	WI0815	Peterson, Larry	IL0100
Peplin, Steve W.	WI0450	Perry, Dawn A.	NC2650	Peterson, Laura	NY3475
Pepper, Ronald D.	OH0950	Perry, Eileen	AZ0480	Peterson, Leroy	CA3400
Pepping, Amanda J.	GA1050	Perry, Francis	TN0100	Peterson, Lynn	TN1900

Alphabetical Listing of Faculty

Name	Code	Name	Code	Name	Code
Peterson, Mark	NC0100	Philbrick, Channing	IL2250	Pickering, Matthew	MS0360
Peterson, Mark	CA1520	Philbrick, Channing P.	IL0550	Pickering, Melinda C.	IA0600
Peterson, Melissa	MO0700	Philbrick, Keith E.	VA1000	Pickett, Barbara	WA0050
Peterson, Pamela	FL0400	Philbrick, Rebekah	IL1610	Pickett, Glen	CA0450
Peterson, Patti	CO0800	Philbrick, Tom	IL1610	Pickett, John	WA0050
Peterson, Rai	WA0860	Philcox, Stephen	AG0300	Pickett, Kyle	CA0800
Peterson, Ralph	MA0260	Philcox, Steven	AG0450	Pickett, Lenny B.	NY2750
Peterson, Robert L.	MN0950	Philip, Annette	MA0260	Pickett, Susan	WA1300
Peterson, Russell	MN0600	Philipp, Hilary	PA0100	Pickney, Linda M.	NC2420
Peterson, Scott R.	WA0050	Philipsen, Dane	GA1150	Pickreign, Christina	NY3600
Peterson, Stephen G.	NY1800	Philipsen, Dane	GA0750	Picon, Jeffrey	OK0750
Peterson, Vince	NY0500	Philipsen, Michael D.	IA0750	Pidluski, Eric	IL1900
Peterson, Wayne T.	CA4200	Phillabaum, Katja	WI0825	Piechocinski, Janet	IN0800
Peterson, William	CA1050	Phillips, Brent	TX0300	Piechocinski, Theodore J.	IN0800
Peterson, William J.	CA3650	Phillips, Burr Cochran	CA5350	Piecuch, Katherine H.	MS0700
Peterson, William F.	FL0850	Phillips, Chester B.	GA1050	Piedra, Olman	OH2300
Petersons, Erik	PA2800	Phillips, Chip	WA0400	Piedra, Olman	OH2140
Pethel, Stan	GA0300	Phillips, Christine	IL1400	Piekarski, Kevin J.	IN0905
Petilot, Aurelien	IL2900	Phillips, Christine	IL0730	Piekut, Benjamin	NY0900
Petillot, Elizabeth A.	WI0803	Phillips, Damani	IA0700	Pier, Christina	NC0350
Petit, Annie	PA2550	Phillips, Daniel	NY0642	Pier, David G.	CA4425
Petit, Annie	PA0850	Phillips, Daniel	NY2250	Pier, Fordyce C.	AA0100
Petit-Homme, Frederika	AI0150	Phillips, Daniel	TN1680	Pier, Stephen	CT0650
Petite, Rachel Maria	NY5000	Phillips, Derrek	TN1100	Pierard, George	IL3370
Petitto, Jackie	CA2600	Phillips, Derrek C.	TN1850	Pierce, Alice O.	MN1600
Petitto, Jacqueline	CA1075	Phillips, Dorie	OH2250	Pierce, Benjamin	AR0700
Petitto, Jacqueline	CA3500	Phillips, Edward D.	IN0910	Pierce, Bill	MA0260
Petkovich, Brian T.	TX2200	Phillips, Gary J.	MD0350	Pierce, Bradley	MA0150
Petraborg, Kirsti J.	IA0950	Phillips, Gerald	MD0850	Pierce, Carrie	TX2930
Petrella, Diane Helfers	MO1810	Phillips, Gregory	OH1450	Pierce, David M.	MI0600
Petrella, Nick E.	MO1810	Phillips, Holland	MA0950	Pierce, Dawn	NY1800
Petrenko, Jurgen	AG0300	Phillips, Jeffrey T.	TN0100	Pierce, Denise Root	MI0600
Petrescu, Stefan	TN1400	Phillips, Jessica J.	NJ1130	Pierce, Edward A.	OK0850
Petric, Paul L.	OH1000	Phillips, Joe Rea	TN1850	Pierce, Forrest D.	KS1350
Petricic, Marko	IN1650	Phillips, Joel	NJ1350	Pierce, James	MS0850
Petrides, Ron T.	NY2660	Phillips, Katrina	AL0050	Pierce, John	MN1600
Petrie, Anne M.	IA0200	Phillips, Katrina R.	AL0050	Pierce, John	MA0260
Petrie, Dean	IL1350	Phillips, Keith	ID0060	Pierce, Joshua	NY2400
Petrik, Rebecca	ND0250	Phillips, Kenneth	FL1450	Pierce, Joshua	NY5000
Petrongelli, Amy	OH2150	Phillips, Kenneth H.	MA0950	Pierce, Karen	ME0200
Petrovic, Ankica	CA5031	Phillips, Lee	IN0900	Pierce, Ken	MA1175
Petrowska-Quilico, Christina	AG0650	Phillips, Linda N.	NY3725	Pierce, Laura	MA2250
Petruconis, Michael	MN1450	Phillips, Margaret A.	MA0260	Pierce, Marilyn	MI1200
Petruzzi, Leon T.	NY1600	Phillips, Mark W.	OH1900	Pierce, Michael	LA0720
Petry, Julie	PA0250	Phillips, Mark W.	VA1750	Pierce, Stephanie D.	GA2100
Pettaway, Charles H.	PA2000	Phillips, Matt K.	PA1250	Pierce, Ted	WI0770
Petters, Robert B.	NC1700	Phillips, Moses	NY0640	Pierpoint, Paula	FL0950
Petteys, Leslie	WV0400	Phillips, Nicholas S.	WI0803	Pierre, Stephen	AG0450
Petti, Ronald T.	TX2700	Phillips, Patricia	NJ0825	Pierre, Stephen	AG0200
Pettis, Paula	MN1250	Phillips, Paul Schuyler	RI0050	Pierri, Alvaro	AI0190
Pettit, Darren	NE0610	Phillips, Paul	TX2400	Pierri, Alvaro	AI0210
Pettit, Joseph	WA0650	Phillips, Paula	AF0120	Piersall, Janie	IL1612
Petty, Byron W.	VA1850	Phillips, Rebecca L.	SC1110	Piersall, Paul	TX0050
Petty, Judith V.	MI2100	Phillips, Scott L.	AL1150	Piersall, Rick	TX0050
Petty, Shuko Watanabe	VA1850	Phillips, Sheena	OH2050	Pierson, Karen	OH1850
Petty, Wayne C.	MI2100	Phillips, Sheila A.	MO0950	Pierson, Rod	IA1300
Pettyjohn, Emma	GA0700	Phillips, Susan	IL1100	Pierson, Scott	CA4400
Petursdottir, Ragga	NY5000	Phillips, Timothy S.	AL1050	Pierson, Steve	IL3550
Petzet, John M.	LA0200	Phillips, Timothy	NC1400	Pierson, William	VA1350
Pevac, Karen	MD0650	Phillips, Todd	NJ1130	Pieslak, Jonathan	NY0600
Peyrebrune, Henry L.	OH0200	Phillips, Todd	NY2250	Pieslak, Jonathan	NY0550
Peyton, Claudia	IL1085	Phillips, Tom	CA0150	Pietri, Michelle M.	TX3530
Peyton, Heather	IA0850	Phillips, Tom	LA0050	Pietro, David A.	NY2750
Peyton, Jeff	OR0750	Phillips-Farley, Barbara	NY3550	Pifer, Joshua K.	AL0200
Peyton, Malcolm C.	MA1400	Phillipus, Donna	AL0500	Pigg, Dewayne	TN1100
Pezanelli, Jack	MA0260	Philp, David	NJ1400	Pignato, Joseph M.	NY3765
Pezzimenti, Carlo	TX3300	Phipps, Danny K.	MI0900	Pih, Kevin	WA1100
Pezzullo, Louis	RI0200	Phipps, Dennis	IN1450	Piippo, Richard	MI1050
Pfaff, William P.	NY3775	Phipps, Graham H.	TX3420	Piitz, Lori E.	VA0600
Pfaffle, Elizabeth	PA3600	Phipps, Juanita K.	MI1700	Pike, Lisa	NJ0500
Pfaffle, Elizabeth L.	PA1300	Phipps, Nathaniel J.	NY3600	Pike, Lisa F.	NJ1400
Pfaltzgraff, Brian	IA1800	Phoenix-Neal, Diane	IA0200	Pike, Lisa	NJ0700
Pfaltzgraff, Carita	IA1800	Photinos, Nicholas	VA1500	Pike, Pamela D.	LA0200
Pfaltzgraff, Philip	NE0700	Piagentini, Susan M.	IL2250	Pikler, Charles	IL2250
Pfau, Marianne Richert	CA5200	Pias, Ed	NM0310	Pikler, Charles	IL2100
Pfau, Tracy	WY0050	Piastro-Tedford, Sasha	PA2100	Pilafian, Sam	FL1900
Pfautz, John S.	IL0100	Piatt, Kenneth H.	PA1200	Pilar, Nobleza Garcia	FL1900
Pfeiffer, Dale	MA0260	Piattoly, Lindsay	LA0650	Pilato, Nikk	CA0825
Pfeiffer, Karen	OH2000	Piazza, Stephen	CA2700	Pilc, Jean-Michel	NY2750
Pfeiffer, Ruth Imperial	HI0160	Picard, Annie	IL1890	Pilchner, Martin	AG0130
Pfenninger, Rik C.	NH0250	Picard, Annie	IL2100	Pile, Randy	CA3350
Pfiefer, Steve	CA2390	Picard, Betty	MI1160	Pile, Randy	CA2390
Pflueger, Bethany	CA1960	Picard, Paul	AI0200	Pile, Randy	CA3460
Pfutzenreuter, Leslie D.	CA2840	Piccinini, Marina	MD0650	Pile, Randy	CA4050
Phagoo, Curtis	AA0080	Piccirillo, Lauren	IN0500	Pilgrim, Neva	NY0650
Pham, Danh	WA1150	Piccirillo, Lauren	OH2550	Pilkington, Jonathan	GA1650
Phan, P. Q.	IN0900	Piccone, James	NJ1050	Pilkington, Robert	MA0260
Phang, May	IN0350	Pich, Victoria	OR0450	Pilkington, Steve	NJ1350
Pharr, Randall	VA1500	Piche, Jean	AI0200	Piller, Paul R.	OH2200
Pharr, Randall	VA1600	Piche, Rick	AG0500	Pillich, G. Simeon	CA3300
Phelps, Amy	IA0300	Picht-Read, Kathryn	PA3250	Pillion, Ed	NJ0550
Phelps, James	IL2200	Pickard, Jason A.	NC0850	Pillow, Charles	NY1100
Phelps, Joe F.	NC0050	Pickart, John	WI0100	Pilon, Charles	AA0035
Phelps, Mark D.	IN0900	Pickens, Willie	IL2200	Pilon, Sherri	MI1050
Phelps, Matthew	OH2550	Pickerell, Kevin	KS0210	Piltz, Hans-Karl	AB0100
Phelps, Melissa	CA0550	Pickerill, Linda	KY0100	Piltz, Peter	RI0250
Phelps, Robert	MA2250	Pickering, Amy J.	IL3310	Piltzecker, Ted	NY3785
Phemister, William	IL3550	Pickering, Amy	IL0850	Pilzer, Joshua	AG0450
Pherigo, Johnny L.	FL1800	Pickering, Angela	TX1400	Pilzer, Joshua	NY0750
Phifer, Larry	IL2500	Pickering, David C.	KS0650	Pimentel, Bret R.	MS0250

Name	Code	Name	Code	Name	Code
Pina, Juan	AL0400	Planet, Janet	WI0350	Polcari, Jeanne	NH0300
Pinckney, Warren R.	CA0800	Plank, Steven E.	OH1700	Polci, Mike	AG0200
Pincock, Christian P.	NM0450	Planner, Mark	CT0650	Polcyn, Sandra	WI0700
Pindell, Reginald	PA3330	Plant, Lourin	NJ1050	Poletaev, Ilya	AI0150
Pineda, Gerry	CA0840	Plantamura, Carol	CA5050	Polett, Jane	MO0300
Pineda, Gerry	CA5350	Plante, Alison	MA0260	Polett, Thomas C.	MO0300
Pineda, Kris	IL2910	Plante, Gilles	AI0210	Polevoi, Randy M.	CA1900
Pinell, Javier	TX2250	Plante, Jean-Guy	AI0210	Policastro, Joseph	IL1900
Ping, Jin	NY3760	Plash, Duane	AL1195	Polifka, Joyce E.	CO0200
Pingel, Scott	CA4150	Plaskett, Anna	AF0050	Polifrone, Sharon	IL3550
Pinkas, Sally	NH0100	Plaster, Amos	IN0650	Poling, Mary	MD0400
Pinkerton, Louise	ND0500	Plate, Scott F.	OH0200	Polischuk, Derek Kealii	MI1400
Pinkney, Rachel	OH0250	Plate, Stephen W.	TN0850	Polk, Ben	KY1550
Pinkney, Rachel	OH1800	Platino, Franco	MD0100	Polk, Betty	TN1600
Pinkston, Dan	CA4600	Platino, Franco	DC0170	Polk, Janet	NH0350
Pinkston, Joan	SC0200	Plato, Scott	GA1070	Polk, Janet E.	NH0100
Pinkston, Russell F.	TX3510	Platoff, John	CT0500	Polk, Joanne	NY2150
Pinnell-Jackson, Nicole	UT0325	Platow, Beth	MA0260	Polk, Keith	NH0350
Pinner, Dianne	SC0200	Platt, Heather	IN0150	Polk, Kristin	KY1550
Pinner, Jay-Martin	SC0800	Platt, Melvin C.	MO1800	Polk, Suzanne	VT0450
Pinney, Greg	MD0550	Platt, Nathan	KY1200	Polk, Sylvester	FL0100
Pinno, John	TX2800	Platt, Rosemary D.	OH1850	Pollack, Daniel	CA5300
Pinnock, Rob	AE0120	Platt, Walter	MA2030	Pollack, Howard	TX3400
Pino, Brad	NC1350	Platter, Donald R.	MI2200	Pollard, Amy	GA2100
Pino, Carlos E.	AL1150	Platz, Eric	RI0300	Pollard, Catherine	NV0100
Pino, David J.	TX3175	Platz, Eric	AC0050	Pollard, Denson P.	NY1900
Pinson, Donald	TX2930	Platz, Eric	MA2010	Pollard, Paul	NY3785
Pinson, Donald L.	TX0550	Plaunt, Tom	AI0150	Pollard, Shawn	AZ0150
Pinson, Joseph Warren	TX3300	Plautz, Gigi	WI0922	Pollart, Gene J.	RI0300
Pinsonneault, Ona	MN1200	Playfair, David M.	AC0050	Pollauf, Jacqueline M.	MD1000
Pinter, Jerry	CA5020	Playford, Louis	GA0250	Polley, David	TX2650
Pinto, David	CA2700	Plaza-Martin, Denise	RI0200	Polley, Jo Ann	MN1450
Pinto, Mary	NJ0800	Plazak, Joseph S.	IL1200	Pollock, Heather	AG0130
Pinto, Mike	IL0850	Pleasure, Ruby	CA4150	Pollock, William	PA1000
Pinza, Claudia	PA1050	Plemons, Susan	OH0450	Polman, Bert	MI0350
Piontek, Gregory	NY4460	Plenert, Keith	NE0160	Polochick, Edward	NE0600
Piontek, Gregory	NY1210	Plesner, Joy	CO0050	Polochick, Edward L.	MD0650
Piorkowski, James P.	NY3725	Plew, Paul T.	CA2810	Pologe, Steven	OR1050
Piper, Deirdre	AG0100	Plewniak, Kim	WA0250	Polonchak, Richard	WV0550
Piper, Jeffrey S.	NM0450	Plewniak, Kim	WA0400	Polonsky, Anna	NY4450
Piper, Patrick	IN0400	Plexico, Byron K.	IN1650	Polonsky, Leonid	OH1850
Piper, Scott	MI2100	Plies, Dennis B.	OR1150	Polot, Barton L.	MI1900
Piper, Shenita	IN0400	Pliskow, Dan J.	MI2200	Poloz, Zimfira	AG0450
Pipho, Robert S.	MI2200	Plitnik, Brian	WV0750	Poltarack, Sanford	FL1300
Pippin, Donald	CA3270	Ploeger, Kristina	WA0250	Poltorak, Agnes	NJ1350
Pirard, Guillaume	NY2750	Plog-Benavides, Bony	WI1150	Polusmiak, Sergei	KY1000
Pirkle, William C.	FL1900	Ploger, Marianne	TN1850	Polyakov, Alina	MA0950
Pirtle, R. Leigh	IA1390	Plohman, Crystal	TN1850	Pomerantz, James	CA0050
Pirzadeh, Maneli	AI0200	Plotkin, Richard	NY4320	Pomerantz, Mark	TX3410
Pisani, Michael	NY4450	Plotnick, Jeff	AA0050	Pomeranz, Felice	MA0260
Pisano, James	KS0200	Plouffe, Helene	AI0150	Pomeroy, David Boyd	AZ0500
Pisano, John J.	CA0835	Plourde, Jean-Luc	AI0190	Pomeroy, Loren	VA1850
Pisano, Joseph M.	PA1450	Plowman, Gary	WA0400	Pomfret, Bonnie	MA0400
Pisano, Kristin	KS0350	Plsek, Thomas	MA0260	Pompa-Baldi, Antonio	OH0600
Pisaro, Kathryn G.	CA0510	Plude, Patricia	CA4425	Ponce, Adriana	IL1200
Pisaro, Michael J.	CA0510	Pluer, Robin	WI1150	Ponce, Alma Mora	CA3300
Pisciotta, Eva Mae	AZ0200	Plugge, Scott D.	TX2250	Ponce, Julie	IL0650
Pitasi, Dennis	FL0200	Plum, Sarah A.	IA0550	Ponce, Walter	CA5030
Pitasi, Dennis	FL1310	Plumer, Shirley	CO0275	Pond, Steven	NY0900
Pitchford, Timothy	IL1200	Plummer, Carolyn	IN1700	Ponder, Wemberly	GA0950
Pitchford, Timothy	IL2900	Plummer, Kathryn	TN1850	Pongracz, Andrew L.	OH1000
Pitchon, Joel L.	MA1750	Plummer, Mark W.	IL0150	Poniatowski, Mark	MA0260
Pittman, Grover A.	PA3650	Plummer, William	KY0250	Poniros, Risa	NC1500
Pitt-Kaye, Melinda	IL1610	Plyler, Sylvia J.	OH2200	Pontbriand, David	ME0150
Pitta, Tom	MD0060	Plyler, Wendy	PA0100	Pontbriand, Roget	FL1450
Pittel, Harvey	TX3510	Pobanz, Randy	IL0300	Ponte, Nora	PR0150
Pittman, Daniel	GA0950	Pobanz, Randy	IL0100	Ponthus, Marc	NY2250
Pittman, Deborah M.	CA0840	Pobanz, Randy F.	IL1350	Ponto, Robert	OR1050
Pittman, Dwight	MO0650	Poch, Gail B.	PA3250	Ponton, Lisa	IA0700
Pittman, Dwight	MO1120	Pochatko, Amanda R.	OH2140	Pontremoli, Anita	OH0600
Pittman, Reginald L.	KS0650	Podgurski, Barbara	NY5000	Ponzner, Joseph	OH1850
Pittman-Jennings, David	NY3780	Podolka, Deborah	MI1650	Ponzo, Mark	IL2200
Pitts, Frank	MI2120	Podroskey, Frank	PA0500	Pool, Ellen	MI0900
Pitts, Frank	MI1830	Poehls, Jenny	ND0350	Pool, Scott	TX3500
Pitts, James L.	TX2700	Poellnitz, Michael	AL0310	Poole, Elissa	AB0150
Pitts, Larry	CA2250	Poeschl-Edrich, Barbara	MA0400	Poole, Eric	NC2150
Pitts, Ruth	TX1600	Poetschke, Linda	TX3530	Poole, Jeff	OH1200
Pitts, Timothy	TX2150	Poff, Megan	AL1160	Poole, Mary Ada	SC0650
Pittson, Suzanne	NY0550	Poff, Sarah	OR1010	Poole, Tommy A.	OK0550
Pituch, David A.	IL0750	Pogonowski, Lenore	NY4200	Poor, Andrew F.	GA0550
Pituch, Karl	MI2200	Pogossian, Movses	CA5030	Poore, Mary Elizabeth	NY2400
Pitzer, Lawrence	OH2450	Pogrebnoy, Nikita	AB0060	Poore, Mary Elizabeth	NY5000
Pitzer, Lawrence	OH0450	Pohly, Linda L.	IN0150	Poovey, Gena E.	SC0850
Pitzer, Robert M.	WA1250	Pohran Dawkins, Alexandra	AB0150	Pope, Andrea	IL1750
Pivec, Matthew	IN0250	Poirier, Rejean	AI0200	Pope, Beth	KY0800
Pixton, Clayton	KS0590	Poissant, Michael	MD0850	Pope, Beth	KY1550
Piza, Antoni	NY0600	Poitier, James	FL0100	Pope, Cathy	NM0400
Pla, Maria	OH0650	Pokhanovski, Oleg	AC0100	Pope, David	OH0300
Placci, Markus	MA0350	Poklewski, Annamarie	CA1550	Pope, David J.	VA0600
Place, Logan B.	LA0200	Pokorny, Gene	IL0550	Pope, George S.	OH0200
Placek, Robert W.	GA2100	Polack, Eric	NJ1100	Pope, George	OH2150
Placeres, Martha	TX3515	Polancich, Ronald	IL0550	Pope, Jerrold	MA0400
Placilla, Christina D.	NC2700	Polanco-Safadit, Pavel	IN0400	Pope, Jerry	KS0590
Plack, David	FL0850	Poland, Jeffrey T.	WV0300	Pope, Kathy	UT0250
Plack, Rebecca	CA4150	Polanka, William Mark	OH1100	Pope, Wayne	KY1550
Plagemann, Melissa	WA0650	Polanka, William Mark	OH2150	Popejoy, James R.	ND0500
Plainfield, Kim	MA0260	Polansky, Larry	NH0100	Popejoy, Melanie	ND0500
Plamann, Melissa M.	OK0750	Polay, Bruce	IL1350	Popeney, Mark	CA5300
Plamondon, Andrew	WA0250	Polay, Louise	IL0420	Poper, Roy	OH1700
Planer, John H.	IN1050	Polay, Louise	IL1350	Popescu, Annamaria	AI0150

Alphabetical Listing of Faculty

Name	Code	Name	Code	Name	Code
Pophal, Lee	CA0270	Pott, Jack	CT0050	Pray, Keith	NY3600
Popham, Deborah	GA1800	Potter Faile, Erin	PA1550	Preacher, Patrick Dale	SC0600
Popham, Phillip F.	MI2000	Potter, Christopher	NY2750	Prebys, Marylee A.	ND0400
Popiel, Paul W.	KS1350	Potter, Clark E.	NE0600	Prechtl, Sylvanna	OK0550
Poplin, Stan E.	CA5070	Potter, Jane	MA0260	Predl, Ronald E.	OK1450
Popoff-Parks, Linette A.	MI1260	Potter, Joe	MO2050	Prefontaine, Paule	AG0400
Popoli, Gary	MD0650	Potter, Kenney	NC2650	Preiss, James	NY2250
Popov, Vasily	DC0170	Potter, Lou Ann	PA0350	Premeau, Chad	WI0925
Popowich, Jamie	AA0050	Potter, Pamela	WI0815	Premezzi, Renato	WI0100
Popp, Harold	KS1450	Potter, Sharon	PA1550	Premo, David	PA0550
Poppe, Donna	WA0650	Potter, Shelley	WA0950	Prenkert, Richard	CA4460
Poppino, Richard	OR0700	Potter, Thomas	FL1800	Prentice, Tracy	TN1850
Popwell, Brooks	SC0650	Potter, Valerie	NM0450	Presar, Jennifer	IL2900
Poquette, Linda	IL2300	Potterton, Matthew	KS0050	Prescott, Anne	IL3300
Poretsky, Susana	CA5060	Potthoff, Joseph	MO1110	Prescott, Barbara	FL2050
Porfiris, Rita	CT0650	Potts, Brian	FL0050	Prescott, Barbara	FL0450
Poris, Jill	OR1100	Potts, Lana	TX2710	Prescott, Barbara	FL1650
Poris, Valerie Jill	OR0500	Potts, Leo W.	WA1300	Prescott, John S.	MO0775
Poriss, Hilary	MA1450	Poudrier, Chris	MA2020	Prescott, Kyle	FL0650
Port, Dennis	MN0250	Poudrier, Eve	CT0900	Prescott, Steve C.	IN1400
Port, Donna	IL0730	Poulimenos, Andreas	OH0300	Presler, Anna H.	CA0840
Portenko, Irena	NY5000	Poulimenos, Andreas	IN0900	Presley, Douglas L.	SC0850
Porter, Ami	UT0150	Poulsen, James	IA1350	Presley, Greg	WA0400
Porter, Amy	WA1350	Poulson, Ruby Ann	MN0250	Press, Daisy	NY2150
Porter, Amy	MI2100	Poulter, Patricia S.	IL0800	Press, Stephen D.	IL1200
Porter, Ann M.	OH2200	Pound, Robert	PA0950	Pressler, Menahem	IN0900
Porter, Beth Cram	OH0450	Pounds, Michael S.	IN0150	Pressnell, Paula B.	NC0400
Porter, Charles	NY2400	Pounds, Nancy	IL1200	Presson, Lucy	TN0150
Porter, Charles	NY2700	Pourmehdi, Houman	CA0510	Preston, Brian	NY2650
Porter, David	WV0700	Povey, Peter	AL0050	Preston, Byron L.	NY4050
Porter, David	UT0400	Povolny, John	MN0250	Preston, Darnelle	WA0400
Porter, Eliot	RI0150	Powe, Holly	AL0330	Preston, Katherine K.	VA0250
Porter, Eliot	RI0200	Powell, Aaron	IA0420	Presutti Korbitz, Angela	IL3450
Porter, Eliot	RI0300	Powell, Aaron	IA0650	Prettyman, Ken	WA0550
Porter, Elizabeth	NY3350	Powell, Aaron	IA1350	Pretzat, Julie	NY3770
Porter, Jacob	TX1660	Powell, Brian T.	FL1900	Pretzel, Mark W.	KS0570
Porter, Janine	OH0755	Powell, Clay	KY1550	Preucil, William	SC0750
Porter, John	NC0400	Powell, Curtis Everett	GA0490	Preucil, William	OH0600
Porter, Judith	NC0860	Powell, Daniel	FL0350	Prevost, Roxane	AG0400
Porter, Laura	CA1860	Powell, Edwin C.	WA0650	Prewitt, Kenneth	MI2250
Porter, Lenore	CA5360	Powell, Ellen	NY3775	Pricco, Evelyen	CA1560
Porter, Lewis R.	NJ1140	Powell, Gary	TX3510	Price, Allen	AR0350
Porter, Marcia	FL0850	Powell, Glendora	NC1200	Price, Andrea M.	GA1650
Porter, Mark	MO0400	Powell, Jarrad	WA0200	Price, Andrew	MA0400
Porter, Melana	GA0950	Powell, Jason	IN0300	Price, Berkeley	CA0200
Porter, Michael C.	ID0050	Powell, John S.	OK1450	Price, Cecilia	GA1150
Porter, Michael	NC0250	Powell, Larry	IN1650	Price, Clayborn	NY3770
Porter, Michael S.	TN1850	Powell, Linton	TX3500	Price, David	TN1650
Porter, Miriam	IL1050	Powell, Michael	NY0500	Price, David	OH2050
Porter, Randy	OR0850	Powell, Michael E.	NJ1130	Price, Debra	OH0850
Porter, Randy	OR0250	Powell, Michael	NY1900	Price, Emmett G.	MA1450
Porter, Randy	OR0400	Powell, Michael E.	NY3790	Price, Hannah E.	NC0050
Porter, Thomas	ND0400	Powell, Patricia	PA3600	Price, Harry E.	GA1150
Porter, William	AI0150	Powell, Philip M.	SC0420	Price, Harvey	DE0150
Porter, William	NY1100	Powell, Rosephanye	AL0200	Price, Henry P.	CA3600
Porter, William Anthony	IL1085	Powell, Ross	TX2400	Price, Holly S.	CA3650
Porter-Borden, Catherine	MD0500	Powell, Sean	GA0550	Price, Jane E.	MO1900
Porterfield, Priscilla J.	NC0050	Powell, Steven S.	PA1000	Price, Jeffrey	AG0550
Porterfield, Richard R.	NY2750	Powell, Susan K.	OH1850	Price, Jeffrey	MI2120
Porterfield, Richard	NY2250	Powell, Timothy J.	MD1010	Price, Jeffrey	NC2420
Porterfield-Pyatt, Chaumonde	CA1290	Powell, Timothy W.	OH2150	Price, Jeffrey L.	UT0250
Portis, Vicki	AL0800	Powell, William	MD0500	Price, Josselyne	VT0400
Portnoy, Donald	SC1110	Powell, William C.	AL0200	Price, Kathy Kessler	NJ1350
Portnoy, Kim	MO1950	Powell, William E.	CA0510	Price, Larry	MN1700
Portolese, Frank	IL0850	Power, Brian E.	AG0050	Price, Larry	WA1400
Portone, Frank	NC0550	Power, David	UT0250	Price, Matt	OH0350
Pos, Margie	WA0200	Power, Rob	AD0050	Price, Matt	MO1550
Posadas, John	FL2000	Powers, Bob	AZ0470	Price, Ruth	MO1950
Posch, Carl	AZ0150	Powers, Daniel	IN0800	Price, Ruth	CA5031
Posegate, Stephen C.	IL3150	Powers, David	OH1850	Price, Scott	SC1110
Posey, Ann	MO2000	Powers, Jeffrey S.	TX0300	Price, Thomas A.	TN1100
Posey, Benjamin C.	AL0300	Powers, Kathleen	NJ0760	Price, William Roger	OK1450
Posey, Dale	FL0950	Powers, Michael	CA5300	Price, William M.	AL1150
Posey, Dawn	PA2950	Powers, Ollie	CA5360	Price-Brenner, Kevin	IA1300
Posey, William	VA0600	Powrie, Barbara	NY4460	Price-Brenner, Kevin	WI0840
Poshek, Joe	CA3350	Poynter, Lynn	OH0680	Price-Brenner, Paul Alan	WI0840
Posnak, Paul	FL1900	Poythress, Christine	TN1100	Price-Glynn, Cynthia	MA0350
Posnock, Jason	NC0250	Pozdnyakov, Aleksandr	AI0200	Prichard, Laura D.	MA2030
Pospisil, James	MN1600	Pozzi, Dave A.	CA0835	Prichard, Sheila Grace	MA1600
Poss, Nicholas	OH0100	Pozzi, David	CA2600	Prickett, Carol A.	AL1170
Poss, Nicholas	OH1850	Pracht, Carole	KS0980	Prickett, Todd O.	AR0700
Posses, Mary	MO1810	Prado, Danny	TX3420	Pridgen, Elizabeth A.	GA1300
Post, Bryan	WI0350	Prager, Madeline	CA4150	Pridmore, Craig	CA5400
Post, Corey	MI0750	Pragides, Carol	CA4150	Pridmore, Helen	AE0050
Post, J. Brian	CA2250	Praniuk, Ingrid	CA1000	Pridonoff, Elizabeth A.	OH2200
Post, Julie Goodman	NY2400	Pranno, Arthur J.	FL0800	Pridonoff, Eugene A.	OH2200
Post, Karen Leigh	WI0350	Pranschke, Janet	NY4500	Priebe, Craig	IN0150
Post, Olaf	MA1050	Pras, Amandine	NY2750	Priebe, William	PA2800
Post, William	OH1100	Pratchard, Jeremy	AR0700	Priest, Charles	KY1200
Post, William Dean	AK0150	Prater, Jeffrey L.	IA0850	Priest, Thomas L.	UT0350
Postle, Matthew W.	NC2000	Prather, Belva W.	MO0775	Priester, John Michael	PA1200
Poston, Ken	CA0825	Pratt, Alice	NY2650	Priester, Julian	WA0200
Posvar, Mildred Miller	PA0550	Pratt, Awadagin K. A.	OH2200	Prieto, Dafnis	NY2750
Potaczek, Amanda Lee	IN0100	Pratt, Dennis H.	RI0101	Priez, Robert G.	LA0650
Potaczek, Steven A.	IN0100	Pratt, Dennis H.	RI0100	Prigge, Sarah	ND0350
Poteet, Sherry	TX1350	Pratt, Gary W.	CA0835	Prigge, Sarah	MN0600
Potenza, Frank	CA5300	Pratt, Holly	KY1000	Primatic, Stephen P.	GA0200
Potes, Cesar I.	MI1200	Pratt, Michael	NJ0900	Primeau, Dominique	AI0210
Potochnic, Jennifer	KY1500	Pratt, Scott	CA2450	Primer, Jessie	MS0650
Potratz, Robert C.	MN1030	Pratt, Stephen Wayne	IN0900	Primes, Theodora	CA1960

Name	Code	Name	Code	Name	Code
Primosch, James	PA3350	Pugh, Joel	ND0500	Quick, Gregory	NY4150
Prince, Curtis L.	IN0005	Pugh, Paul William	ID0075	Quick, Julia M.	SC1050
Prince, Gary	DC0170	Puig, Marta	VA1600	Quick, Steve	MI1650
Prince, J. Whitney	MI0600	Puig, Martha	VA1500	Quigley, Fred	PA0950
Prince, Noel	MO1900	Pulford, Paul	AG0600	Quigley, Roger N.	VA1250
Prince, Penny	NY0635	Pulgar, Edward	TN0250	Quigley-Duggan, Susan E.	MO0100
Princiotti, Anthony F.	NH0100	Pulgar, Mary	TN0250	Quijano, Kellie R.	TX2960
Prindle, Daniel	MA2250	Pulgram, Anthony	NY2105	Quilico, David	AG0130
Prindle, Roma	KY0900	Pulido, Maria Fernanda Nieto	CO0550	Quillen, Josh R.	NY2750
Prins, Rene	NY1400	Pullan, Bruce	AB0100	Quinby, Jack	OR0250
Prins, Rene	NY3765	Puller, Shawn I.	GA0150	Quindag, Sue	SC0200
Prior, Richard	GA0750	Pulliam, Christine	DC0170	Quinlan, Gloria H.	TX1150
Priore, Irna	NC2430	Pullig, Kenneth	MA0260	Quinn, Ann	CT0650
Prisco, Peter	NY0644	Pullman, Marlene	AJ0030	Quinn, Brian	PA3260
Pritchard, Bob	AB0100	Pulos, Nick	AA0050	Quinn, Christopher	UT0400
Pritchard, Eric N.	NC0600	Puls, Cyndi	OH1400	Quinn, Ian	CT0900
Pritchard, Gary	CA0859	Puls, David	OH1400	Quinn, Karyn	WI0810
Pritchard, Jerrold	OR0500	Puls, Kenneth	FL0500	Quinn, Kelly	MO1120
Pritchard, Jillian	NY3350	Pulte, Diane	TN1450	Quinn, Kelly	MO1110
Pritchard, Jillian	NY1250	Pultorak, Mark	PA0400	Quinn, Shannon	DC0050
Pritchard, Lee H.	NY3760	Pummill, Janet	TX3000	Quint, Philippe	NJ1130
Pritchett, Kate	OK0750	Punter, Melanie	FL0850	Quintana, Ariel	CA0845
Pritsker, Vladimir	NY1350	Purcell, Julia	KY1500	Quintana, Sylvia	CA1050
Prizer, William	CA5060	Purcell, William	VA1250	Quintanar, David	CO0275
Probst, Christopher	GA1070	Purciello, Maria Anne	PA3600	Quintero, Juan Carlos	CA1265
Probst, Christopher	GA0850	Purciello, Maria Anne	DE0150	Quintero, Michelle A.	TX3175
Probst, Christopher	GA0400	Purdie, Bernard	NY2660	Quist, Amanda R.	NJ1350
Prochazka, Tanya	AA0100	Purdy, Carl	GA0250	Quist, Pamela	CA4425
Prochnow, Peter	NE0150	Purdy, Craig Allen	ID0050	Quong, Meijane	AB0060
Procopio, Mary J.	MI0450	Purdy, Winston	AI0150	Qureshi, Regula	AA0100
Proctor, Andrew	FL0700	Puri, Michael James	VA1550	Raab-Pontecorvo, Luiza	NY1600
Proctor, Freda	KS1375	Puricelli, Denise	DC0050	Rabago, Kathy	TX2170
Proctor, Gregory	OH1850	Purin, Peter	OK0650	Rabata, Nicole	ME0250
Prodan, Angelica	CA5150	Purkhiser, Beth	IN1850	Rabbai, George	PA3330
Profitt, Tommee	MI0750	Purnell, Tom F.	IL0650	Rabbai, George	NJ1050
Prokop, Rick	NY2400	Purse, Lynn Emberg	PA1050	Rabe, Gigi 'Gee'	CA0835
Prokop, Rick	NY5000	Purse, William E.	PA1050	Rabe-Meyer, Janet	FL0400
Proksch, Bryan	LA0350	Pursell, Anthony	TX2750	Raberg, Bruno	MA0260
Promane, Terry	AG0450	Pursell, John	MD0610	Rabin, Barbara	NY0650
Prophet, Becky B.	NY0100	Pursell, John	PA1400	Rabin, Barbara	NY1350
Propst, Tonya	SC0420	Pursell, John	MD0300	Rabinovitsj, Max	VA0600
Proser, Stephen	UT0250	Pursell, William	TN0100	Raboy, Asher	CA3400
Prossaird, Didier	MD0550	Pursino, Peter	GA1990	Rabson, Miriam	MA0260
Prosser, Douglas	NY1100	Purslow, Vicki T.	OR0950	Rabuse, Brian	MA0280
Prosser, Peter	NY2250	Purtle, Jeff	SC0050	Raby, Lee Worley	CA2801
Prosser, Steve	MA0260	Purves-Smith, Michael	AG0600	Racamato, Claire	PA0400
Protopapas, John	PA3710	Purves-Smith, Shannon	AG0600	Rachford, Natalia	IN0350
Protsman, Harold S.	VA1000	Purviance, Douglas	NJ1160	Rachleff, Larry	TX2150
Proudfoot, Carol	AZ0490	Purvis, Ralph E.	AL0400	Rachlin, Harvey	NY2200
Proulx, John	CA0815	Purvis, William	CT0850	Rachmanov, Dmitry	CA0835
Proulx, Ron	AG0130	Puschendorf, Gunther F.	CA1100	Rachor, David J.	IA1600
Proulx, Sylvie	AD0050	Pusey, Bill	PA3330	Racine, Melody Lynn	MI2100
Prouten, William	AA0032	Pusztai, Tibor J.	MA0260	Rack, John	NC2440
Prouty, Kenneth E.	MI1400	Puterbaugh, Parke	NC0910	Rackers, Joseph P.	SC1110
Prouty, Patrick	MI2120	Putnam, Ashley	NY2150	Rackipov, Errol	FL0700
Provencal, Richard	AI0200	Putnam, Fay	OR0500	Rackley, David	CA0100
Provencio, Linda	CA0650	Puts, Kevin M.	MD0650	Rackley, David	CA1510
Provencio, Robert	CA0650	Putterman, Jeff	OR0850	Racy, A. J.	CA5031
Provine, Robert C.	MD1010	Pyle, Daniel S.	GA0500	Rada, Raphael	TX0550
Provost, Richard C.	CT0650	Pyle, Jane	FL1300	Radano, Ronald	WI0815
Provost, Sarah	MA0650	Pyle, Laura	SC0400	Radbill, Catherine Fitterman	NY2750
Prowse, Robert W.	NJ0825	Pyle, Pamela Viktoria	NM0450	Radell, Judith M.	PA1600
Prowse, Ronald H.	MI2200	Pyle, Robinson	MA0400	Rader, Jana Elam	TX2310
Proznick, Jodi	AB0060	Pyle, Sally	FL1300	Rader, Stephen M.	OH1400
Prudchenko, Slava	GA0940	Pylinski, Thomas	OH1350	Radford, Andrew	CA5060
Pruett, Julie	TX0050	Pyne, James	OH1850	Radford, Andy	CA5360
Pruiett, Kevin P.	OK0650	Pyron, Donna N.	MO1830	Radford, Andy	CA5550
Pruiksma, Rose	NH0350	Pyron, Nona	CA5550	Radford, Anthony P.	CA0810
Pruiksma, Rose A.	MA1400	Pysh, Greg	TX1660	Radford, Gabe	AG0450
Pruitt, David	IL1610	Pysh, Gregory	TX3527	Radford, Laurie	AA0150
Pruitt, Nate	CA1950	Pytlewski, Barbara	CO0225	Radice, Jean	NY1800
Prunty, Patricia	CA0815	Qian, Jun	TX0300	Radice, Mark A.	NY1800
Pruss, Melissa	NE0100	Qian, Jun	MN1450	Radicheva, Maria	NY2150
Pruzin, Robert S.	SC1110	Qian, Wen	NY2250	Radke, Fred	WA1050
Pryor, Cheryl	AL0010	Quade, Christopher	WV0550	Radke, Gina Funes	WA1050
Pryor, Ryan	CA0815	Quaglia, Bruce	UT0250	Radley, Dan	WI0801
Przybylowski, Michelle	PA0650	Quagliariello, Rachel M.	VA0800	Radley, Roberta	MA0260
Przygocki, James T.	WY0200	Quaile, Michael	PA3330	Radlo, Dolores	MA1600
Przymus, Chad	MN1500	Quaile, Robert	PA3330	Radloff, Susan	MN1290
Psurny, Robert D.	MT0075	Qualliotine, Armand Guy	MA0260	Radnofsky, Kenneth	MA1175
Ptaszynska, Marta	IL3250	Qualls, Todd	GA0750	Radnofsky, Kenneth	MA0350
Pucci, Michael	AI0200	Quan, Linda	NY4450	Radnofsky, Kenneth	MA1400
Puccinelli, Elvia	TX3420	Quant, Scott	OK0850	Radnosfky, Kenneth	MA0400
Puccini, Dorival	IL1400	Quantz, Don E.	AA0010	Radomski, James V.	CA0845
Puchala, Mark	MI1650	Quantz, Michael	TX3515	Radomski, Teresa	NC2500
Puchammer, Sedillot	AI0210	Quartuccio, Anthony	CA1950	Radosavljevich, Olga	OH0600
Puchhammer, Jutta	AI0200	Quash, Jonathan	NY0646	Radoslavov, Ilia G.	MO1780
Puckett, Joel W.	MD0650	Quathamer, Mark	FL0150	Radovanlija, Maja	MN1623
Puckett, Lauren J.	TX0900	Quebbeman, Robert C.	MO0775	Radspinner, Matthew	PA3150
Puckett, Mark	TX0900	Quebec, Brian	AG0150	Radzynski, Jan	OH1850
Puckett, Michael	GA0500	Queen, Jeffrey	IN0250	Rae, Wendy	AA0050
Puckette, Miller	CA5050	Queen, Kristen	TX3000	Raedeke, Barbara A.	MO1900
Puderbaugh, David J.	IA1550	Queen, Todd	CO0250	Raekallio, Matti	NY1900
Pufall, Molly	WI0050	Quercia, Olga	CA1850	Rael, Eliseo	PA1050
Puga, John	TX3527	Quereau, Quentin	OH0600	Raessler, Daniel	VA1125
Puga, Richy	TX1660	Quereau, Quentin W.	OH0400	Raevens, Jean M.	PA1050
Pugh, Darryl	NY2950	Quesada Agostini, Milagros	OH1120	Rafal, Jeremy	NJ0050
Pugh, Darryl L.	NY4150	Quesada, Milagros	OH1100	Rafanelli, Paul	WA1000
Pugh, Darryl	NY0650	Quesenberry, Karen	VA0100	Raferty, Patrick	AG0450
Pugh, James	IL3300	Quick, Gregory	NY1350	Rafferty, Alan	KY1000

Alphabetical Listing of Faculty

Name	Code
Rafferty, J. Patrick	KY1500
Raffo, Laura	MA0400
Ragains, Diane	IL2200
Ragan, Kari	WA1050
Ragazzi, Claudio	MA0260
Ragent, Lawrence S.	CA4900
Rager, Dan	WI0804
Rager, Josh	AI0150
Ragland, Janice	MO0850
Ragogini, Ernest	MD0100
Ragotskie, Scott	CA1900
Ragsdale, Aaron	SD0550
Ragsdale, C. David	AL1160
Ragsdale, Chalon L.	AR0700
Ragsdale, Frank	OK0750
Ragsdale, Jeremy	MD0850
Rahaim, Matthew	MN1623
Raheb, Paul J.	CA1290
Rahkonen, Carl J.	PA1600
Rahming, Dara	LA0900
Rahn, Jay	AG0650
Rahn, John	WA1050
Rai, Diana	IL1750
Raiber, Michael	OK1350
Raickovich, Milos	NY0644
Raifsnider, Christoper J.	MD0060
Raiken, Larry	CT0650
Railsback, Stephanie	CA3520
Railton, Marlene	MO2050
Raimi, Frederic B.	NC0600
Raimi, Max	IL2250
Raimo, John B.	TX3525
Rain, Jack	FL2000
Rainbolt, Steven	MD0650
Raines, Alan L.	TX0300
Raines, Jean	NC1900
Raines, Sarah	MT0370
Raines, Scott	TX0150
Rainforth, Eva	PA2900
Rainsong, Lisa	OH0600
Rainwater, Brian	FL0670
Raisor, Steve C.	NC0500
Raitt, Donovan	CA1425
Raker, Robert	OH1600
Rakich, Christa	MA1400
Rakowski, David	MA1400
Rakowski, David	MA0500
Raley, Lynn	MS0385
Ralinovsky, John	OH0500
Ralls, Stephen	AG0450
Ralske, Eric	NY2250
Ralske, Erik	NY1900
Ralske, Erik C.	NY2150
Ralston, Jeananne C.	NY1550
Ralston, Jeananne	NY1250
Ramach, Michael E.	KY1500
Ramadanoff, David	CA1800
Ramael, David R.	NY1600
Rambeau, Deborah	WA0700
Rambo, Kathryn	WI1150
Ramee, Joyce	WA1000
Ramey, Kara	MO0400
Ramey, Lauren	TN1850
Ramey, Maxine	MT0400
Ramey, Richard C.	AR0700
Ramey, Samuel	IL0550
Ramirez Rios, Ruben J.	PR0115
Ramirez, Abel	TX0550
Ramirez, Anthony	WI1150
Ramirez, Armando L.	PR0115
Ramirez, Catherine	MN1450
Ramirez, George	CA1850
Ramirez, Mark Joseph	TX3525
Ramirez, Miguel	TN0930
Ramirez, Pamela	TX3515
Ramirez, Patricia	AL1195
Ramirez, Roberto	PR0115
Rammon, Andrew	PA0350
Rammon, Andrew	PA2100
Rammon, Andrew	PA3150
Rammon, Philip A.	PA2150
Ramo, Suzanne D.	TX1425
Ramos Asillo, Jorge	PR0115
Ramos, Mary Ann	AZ0450
Ramos, Rene	CA2420
Ramos-Kittrell, Jesus	TX2400
Rampal, Michelle	NY2450
Rampp, Rose K.	DC0170
Rams, Robert	NY4500
Ramsay, Ginger	GA2300
Ramsay, James Ross	MA0260
Ramsay, John P.	MA0260
Ramsay, Susan	TN1850
Ramsay, Susan	TN0100
Ramsbottom, Gene	AB0100
Ramsbottom, Gene	AB0050
Ramsdell, Gregory A.	OH0950
Ramsdell, Steve	IL3550
Ramsey, Cynthia B.	VA0750
Ramsey, Darhyl S.	TX3420
Ramsey, David	WI0847
Ramsey, DonnaLee	PA2800
Ramsey, Elmer H.	CA0550
Ramsey, Guthrie P.	PA3350
Ramsey, James	CO0900
Ramsey, Jeffery Evans	MA0260
Ramsey, Laura	SC1100
Ramsey, Laura	GA0250
Ramsey, Lynne	OH0600
Ramsey, Sarah E.	OH0850
Ramsey, William H.	CA4900
Ramstrum, Momilani	CA4050
Ramthum, Kerry	WI1150
Ran, Shulamit	IL3250
Rancier, Megan M.	OH0300
Rand, Catherine	MS0750
Randall, Annie Janeiro	PA0350
Randall, James	MT0400
Randall, James K.	NJ0900
Randall, Jean	MI1830
Randall, Martha	MD1010
Randall, Richard R.	PA0550
Randall, Thomas	MA1000
Randel, Julia	MI1050
Randles, Clinton A.	FL2000
Randles, Edward	MI1180
Randlette, Peter	WA0350
Randman, Bennett	MS0400
Randolph, Anthony W.	DC0150
Randolph, Jane	CA4150
Randolph, Margaret Ann	TN0300
Randruut, Avo	IL0750
Raney, Earl	MA0250
Raney, Earl L.	MA2150
Ranganathan, Lakshmi	AG0250
Ranger, Louis	AB0150
Ranieri, Anthony	IL1400
Ranjbaran, Behzad	NY1900
Rankin, Charles	FL1950
Rankin, John M.	TX2200
Rankin, John B.	LA0300
Rankin, John	LA0800
Ranney, Jack	IL2350
Ranney, Todd	PA2150
Ransom, Adriana LaRosa	IL1150
Ransom, Bryan K.	CA4100
Ransom, Judy L.	WY0115
Ransom, Keiko	GA0750
Ransom, Matt W.	NC1650
Ransom, Matt	NC2500
Ransom, McCoy	LA0100
Ransom, Robert	VA0250
Ransom, William	OH0650
Ransom, William	GA0750
Ranti, James	NY5000
Ranti, Richard	MA1400
Ranti, Richard J.	MA0400
Rao, Doreen	AG0450
Rao, Nancy	NJ1130
Rao, Nikhail	AA0100
Raper, Troy	CO0225
Raphael, Honora	NY0500
Rapier, Christopher	PA2250
Rapoport, Alexander	AG0450
Rapoport, Katharine	AG0450
Rapoport, Paul	AG0200
Rapp, Willis M.	PA1750
Rappe, Terri	WA1200
Rappoport, Katharine	AG0300
Rapport, Evan	NY2660
Rapport, Evan	NY0644
Raps, Gena	NY2250
Rapson, John	AF0100
Rapson, John	IA1550
Rardin, Paul	PA3250
Rarick, Janet	TX2150
Rasar, Lee Anna	WI0803
Raschella, John	NY1350
Raschen, Gudrun E.	TX3300
Raschiatore, Lisa	MI1260
Raschiatore, Lisa C.	MI0050
Rash, Daniel R.	SC0400
Rask, Perry J.	IL1750
Raskin, Jon	CA2950
Rasmussen, Anne K.	VA0250
Rasmussen, Brenda	WA0550
Rasmussen, Bruce	CA3400
Rasmussen, G. Rosalie	CA3400
Rasmussen, Josh	UT0190
Rasmussen, Kurt	NV0050
Rasmussen, Ljerka V.	TN1400
Rasmussen, Warren	CA4200
Rasmusson, Ralph	NY1850
Rassier, Daniel	MN0350
Rast, Madison B.	PA3250
Rasura, Ricky	LA0050
Ratcliff, Joy	CA4050
Ratelle, Dan	WI0350
Rath, Carl	IL3300
Rath, Edward	
Rath, Eric	TX0100
Rath, Richard	OK0850
Rathbun, Andrew	NY2050
Rathbun, Jeffrey	OH0600
Rathbun, Jeffrey J.	OH0200
Rathey, Markus	CT0850
Rathke, Sarah	CA5000
Rathnaw, Dennis M.	OH0300
Raths, O. Nicholas	MN0050
Raths, O. Nicholas	MN0350
Ratledge, John	AL1170
Ratliff, Joy	LA0650
Ratliff, Phillip	AL0650
Ratliff, Phillip W.	AL1150
Ratliff, Richard J.	IN1650
Ratner, Carl J.	MI2250
Ratner, Jody	NY0050
Ratte, Michel	AI0210
Ratti, Linda	KY1500
Rattner, Richard D.	MI2200
Ratz, Arlene	AZ0200
Ratzlaff, Dieter	OR1100
Ratzlaff, Leonard	AA0100
Rau, George	PA3580
Rauch, Benjamin	CT0650
Raum, Erika	AG0450
Raum, Erika	AG0300
Rausch, Carol E.	LA0300
Rauscher, James	TX0100
Rauschnabel, June	MN0600
Raval, Shanti	NY0270
Ravenscroft, Brenda	AG0250
Ravitskaya, Irena	KS0350
Ravnan, John	SC0765
Rawdon, Kenneth	CA0900
Rawley, Joseph	TX2310
Rawlins, Deborah	TX2250
Rawlins, Nancy	NJ1050
Rawlins, Robert	NJ1050
Rawls, J. Archie	MS0580
Rawls, Scott	NC2430
Rawston, Amy	MA0150
Ray Westlund, Beth	IA0950
Ray, Brian	TN1200
Ray, Chris	IL0650
Ray, Emily	CA4425
Ray, Emily	CA1800
Ray, Eric J.	CA2720
Ray, Eric	CA1900
Ray, Frederic	MD0060
Ray, James	FL1550
Ray, Jeff	IL1890
Ray, Jeffrey	IL3370
Ray, Jeffrey	IL2100
Ray, John	TN1600
Ray, John	NY2105
Ray, Julia J.	CA0835
Ray, Kathryn	IN0400
Ray, Marcie	MI1400
Ray, Mary Ruth	MA0500
Ray, Robert	MO1830
Ray, Scott	NY3730
Ray, Vicki	CA0510
Ray, W. Irwin	GA1550
Ray, Willy	UT0400
Ray-Carter, Trilla	MO2000
Rayam, Curtis J.	FL1550
Rayam, Curtis	FL0100
Rayapati, Sangeetha	IL0100
Raybon, Leonard	LA0750
Raychev, Evgeni	TX2700
Raycroft, Elizabeth	AA0020
Raycroft, Elizabeth	AA0035
Rayl, David C.	MI1400
Raymond, Deborah	AZ0450
Raymond, Diane	MI1260
Raymond, Paul	WA1350
Raymond, Rusty	MO0800
Rayner, William S.	NY2750
Raynes, Christopher	ID0050
Raynor, Shari	CA3600
Raynovich, William Jason	IL0600
Razaq, Janice L.	IL1085
Rea, Edward	SC0200
Rea, John	AI0150
Rea, Judith	SC0200
Rea, Stephanie	KY0950
Reach, Douglas	AF0100
Read, Evelyn	VT0450
Read, Jesse	AB0100
Read, Katie	OH0550
Read, Kenneth E.	OH0550
Read, Patrick	CA3800
Read, Paul	AG0450
Read, Thomas L.	VT0450
Reagan, Ann B.	CO0750
Reagan, Billy R.	AL0350
Reagan, Jama	TN1850
Reager, John	CA2450
Real-D'Arbelles, Giselle	FL0200

Name	Code	Name	Code	Name	Code
Reale, Steven	OH2600	Reedy, Hillary	IL1612	Reilly, Kevin	OH2300
Ream, Duane	SC0200	Reefer, Russell	PA0700	Reilly, Paul C.	IN0150
Reamer, Andrew	PA1050	Reeks, John	LA0300	Reiman, Erika	AG0050
Reames, Rebecca	NY3780	Rees, Fred J.	IN0907	Reimer, Alvin H.	AG0500
Reams, John	GA1800	Rees, Helen	CA5031	Reimer, Christine E.	NY2750
Reams, John D.	GA0200	Rees, Jay C.	AZ0500	Reimer, David	MI0350
Reams, Lisa	GA0200	Reese, Donald T.	PA1830	Reimer, Jamie M.	NE0600
Reamsnyder, Richard	OH2275	Reese, Jodi	KS0265	Reimer, Joyce L.	NE0250
Reardon, Colleen A.	CA5020	Reese, Kirk	PA2300	Reimer, Mark U.	VA0150
Reardon, Melissa	NC0650	Reese, Marc B.	FL1125	Reimer, Robert	NJ0175
Rearick, Loretta A.	OH1200	Reese, Randall	GA0200	Reimers-Parker, Nancy	MN0250
Reash, Aimee	PA0100	Reeve, Barbara	AR0425	Reimund, John	TX1425
Reason, Dana	OR0700	Reeve, Basil	MN1623	Reinebach, John	CA0450
Reasoner, Eric	MA0260	Reeve, Douglas	MO0300	Reiner, Art	IN1650
Reba, Christopher H.	CT0700	Reeve, Jay A.	IA1200	Reiner, Craig	AF0120
Rebbeck, Lyle	AA0040	Reeves, Bethany	NY0270	Reiner-Marcus, Ullricke	CA3460
Reber, Richard	KS1350	Reeves, Derek	IN0905	Reinert, C. Robert	FL1745
Reber, William F.	AZ0100	Reeves, Gary L.	SD0600	Reinhart, Robert	IL0720
Rebilas, Richard P.	IN1010	Reeves, Janet	NJ1400	Reinhart, Robert A.	IL2250
Rebozo, Elizabeth	AA0050	Reeves, M. Bryan	AL0050	Reinhuber, Joachim	TX2960
Recca, David	NY3785	Reeves, Matthew	MA0400	Reinke, Charlotte	GA2100
Reckner, Lillian	MD0360	Reeves, Nat	CT0650	Reinker, Daniel	TN1850
Recktenwald, James	KY0250	Reeves, Nicholas	NJ1000	Reinoso, Crystal Hearne	NY3717
Recktenwald, Karl	NJ0175	Reeves, Patricia	TN1400	Reiprich, Bruce J.	AZ0450
Rector, Arlene	KY0100	Reeves, Richard	SC0350	Reis, Marzo	CT0300
Rector, Arlene	KY1350	Reeves, Scott	NY0550	Reisch, Carla	CA2390
Rector, Malcolm W.	TX3450	Reeves, Shane	SC0710	Reise, Adriene	OR0010
Redd, Ann	SC1100	Regan, Joseph	WV0550	Reise, Jay	PA3350
Redd, Chuck	MD1010	Regan, Joseph	MD0610	Reish, Gregory N.	IL0550
Reddick, Carissa	CO0950	Regan, Lara	IL0850	Reisman, Leana	CT0650
Reddick, Don	IL2300	Regan, Lara	IL2650	Reisman, Mickey	CT0650
Reddick, Marcus	GA1300	Regan, Martin	TX2900	Reiss, Deborah	NY0850
Redding, Eric	AK0050	Regan, Patrick	PA1200	Reist, Joel	TN1850
Redding, Jeffery	WV0750	Regan, Patrick	MI1300	Reist-Steiner, Tabitha	KS1400
Reddish, Debbie	CA0200	Regehr, Leanne	AA0035	Reit, Alyssa	NY5000
Redfearn, Christopher	ND0600	Regehr, Leanne	AA0100	Reit, Peter	NY5000
Redfern, Nancy	MI1600	Regehr, Rennie	AG0400	Reit, Peter	NY4450
Redfield, Clayborn	CA0840	Regehr, Vernon	AD0050	Reit, Peter	CT0650
Redfield, Stephen C.	MS0750	Regelski, Thomas A.	NY3725	Reit, Peter	NY3785
Rediger, JoAnn K.	IN1560	Regensburger, Tamara	OH1850	Reiter, Burkhardt	PA3420
Redington, Britania	DE0200	Reger, Jeremy J.	IN0900	Reiter, Lois	TX2800
Redman, Bill M.	CA4410	Regester, Kristen	IL2750	Reitz, Christina L.	NC2600
Redman, Carolyn	OH1200	Register, Dena M.	KS1350	Reitz, John	OH1200
Redman, Carolyn	OH1600	Register, P. Brent	PA0700	Reitz, Margaret A.	NY3705
Redman, Inez	NC2400	Regni, Albert G.	MD1010	Rekevics, John	CA4100
Redman, Suzanne	TN1150	Regni, Albert	VA1600	Reller, Paul	FL2000
Redman, Will	MD0850	Regnier, Marc	SC0500	Relyea, Gary	AG0450
Redman, Yvonne Gonzales	IL3300	Rehberg, Jeanette	ND0050	Remek, Robert	FL1310
Redmer Minner, Laurie K.	TN1350	Rehberg, Nancy R.	GA1300	Remele, Rebecca	AL0300
Redmon, Nursun	MI0300	Rehberg, Nancy	GA0850	Remenikova, Tanya	MN1623
Redmon, Robynne	FL1900	Rehding, Alexander	MA1050	Remillard, Chantal	AI0150
Redmon, Steve	MI0300	Rehfeldt, Phillip	CA0845	Reminick, David M.	IL2150
Redmond, Daryle J.	NY3780	Rehkopf-Michel, Carrie	WA0050	Remmel, Rachel	NY1100
Redmond, Daryle	NY3775	Rehl, Mark	MI0300	Remonko, Guy	OH1900
Redmond, James Ryan	AZ0200	Rehwoldt, Lisa	MD0100	Remy, Elisabeth	GA1050
Redmond, John	FL1900	Reich, Amy J.	NJ0800	Remy, Elizabeth	GA1150
Redmond, Michael	IN0907	Reich, Diane T.	UT0050	Remy-Schumacher, Tess	OK1330
Rednour, Scott	NY2150	Reich, Stephanie	MA0260	Renak, Amy	MA0280
Redpath, Keith	TX3750	Reichart, Alan	IL1610	Renander, Cindy	WA0960
Redwood, Andre	IN1700	Reichenbach, Bill	CA0825	Renard-Payen, Florent	NY1350
Redzic, Zlatan	TX2260	Reichenbach, Brian	IL2300	Renard-Payen, Florent	NY0650
Reece, A.	NY3770	Reichenberger, Kathy	OH2290	Renbarger, Cory James	MN0150
Reece, Richard	OH0300	Reichert, Ed C.	ME0500	Rende, Jennifer	MD0750
Reed, Allen	TX1100	Reichert, Matthew R.	NY0500	Render, Charles	LA0700
Reed, Anne	OR0750	Reichgott, Joseph	FL1310	Rendleman, Ruth	NJ0800
Reed, Dennis	NC0350	Reichling, Mary	LA0760	Rendler-McQueeney, Elaine J.	VA0450
Reed, Douglas	IN1600	Reichwald, Siegwart	SC0650	Rene, Benjamin	AI0190
Reed, Elisabeth	CA4150	Reid, Clement	WA0650	Reneau, Mark	TN1350
Reed, Elisabeth	CA5000	Reid, Darlene Chepil	AG0170	Renfroe, Anita B.	PA2350
Reed, Elizabeth	CA2950	Reid, Debra	SD0050	Renfroe, Dennis C.	NC1025
Reed, Eric	NJ1130	Reid, Doug	WA0860	Renfrow, Kenon	SC0200
Reed, Gavin	TX3400	Reid, Edward F.	AZ0500	Renino, Al	NY5000
Reed, James	FL0570	Reid, James	ID0250	Renk, Sheryl	CA4100
Reed, Jane	OH0100	Reid, John	TX2350	Renn, Rowena S.	GA0940
Reed, Jeff	MD0850	Reid, John	AA0150	Renner, David	TX3510
Reed, Jerome A.	TN0930	Reid, Jorim	NC1600	Renner, Jack L.	OH0600
Reed, Jim	OH1200	Reid, Kenneth	MA2030	Renner-Hughes, Marty	MO1110
Reed, Joel F.	NC1250	Reid, Kevin	FL1950	Rennick, Paul	TX3420
Reed, John Perry	SC0050	Reid, Lynda L.	TX2350	Renninger, Laura Ann	WV0550
Reed, John	GA0400	Reid, Nola	CO0275	Renoud, Doug	NY0050
Reed, Jonathan I.	MI1400	Reid, Ronald I.	MA0260	Renshaw, Don	AG0400
Reed, Kathryn	IA0950	Reid, Sally	TN0930	Renshaw, Jeffrey	CT0600
Reed, Keith	CO0200	Reid, Steven	IN0005	Renshaw, Kenneth	MO1710
Reed, Kevin	OH0600	Reid, Susanne M.	CA5355	Renter, David	MI0900
Reed, Marc A.	CO0350	Reid, Ted	CA0825	Renteria, Gabriel	MI0100
Reed, Melissa	NY2650	Reid, Todd	CO0830	Rentz, David Joseph	CA4500
Reed, Randy	NC0600	Reid, Wendy	CA2950	Rentz, Debra	OH1900
Reed, Richard	WA1250	Reider, Nick	MD0520	Renwick, William J. M.	AG0200
Reed, Richard	DC0150	Reifel, Carol-Lynn	AG0250	Reny, Alison	OH2275
Reed, S. Alexander	FL1850	Reifel, Edward	NY3780	Renyer, Erinn	KS0050
Reed, Sean Scot	AR0200	Reiff, Amy	DC0100	Renzi, Paul	CA4200
Reed, Teresa Shelton	OK1450	Reiff, Eric	VA0500	Repar, Patricia Ann	NM0450
Reed, Thomas T.	OH0100	Reifinger, James L.	TX3400	Repass, Deidre	TN0050
Reed, W. Joseph	MN1625	Reifsnyder, Robert	IL1890	Replogle, Rebecca	OR1010
Reed, William	AZ0350	Reighard, Mark	OK1200	Repucci, John	MA0260
Reed-Lunn, Rebecca	KY1550	Reighley, Kimberly	PA3600	Requiro, David	WA1000
Reeder, Deborah	PA3250	Reigler, Susan	IN1010	Resanovic, Nikola	OH2150
Reeder, Jefferson	NY3780	Reigles, B. Jean	NY1700	Resch, Barbara	IN0905
Reeder, Raymond	MA0260	Reilley, Duane	AZ0250	Resick, Georgine	IN1700
Reeds, Elizabeth	NY0400	Reilly, Allyn D.	OH1900	Reside, Judy	AA0050

Alphabetical Listing of Faculty

Name	Code	Name	Code	Name	Code
Resnianski, Igor	PA3600	Rhodes, Amy Patricia	IL2200	Richardson, Colleen	AG0500
Resnick, Anna	OK1250	Rhodes, Andrew L.	OH2300	Richardson, Danene	AZ0440
Resnick, Anna	OK0750	Rhodes, Ann G.	KY0300	Richardson, David	WI0810
Resnick, David	IA0250	Rhodes, Beverly	WA1350	Richardson, David	WI1100
Ressler, Amy	IA1450	Rhodes, Carol	WI1100	Richardson, Dennis	TX0550
Resta, Craig	OH1100	Rhodes, Cherry	CA5300	Richardson, Diane	MA0260
Restesan, Francis'c	KY1000	Rhodes, Debra	NE0300	Richardson, Diane	NY1900
Restesan, Francise T.	PR0125	Rhodes, Edward	NC1900	Richardson, Diane	NY3705
Restesan, Frank	NE0550	Rhodes, Harumi	NY4150	Richardson, Donald G.	CA4450
Restivo, Dave	AG0450	Rhodes, Jami	NC0650	Richardson, Dustyn	AA0050
Retana, Cynthia	IN1250	Rhodes, Phillip	MN0300	Richardson, Edward 'Rex'	VA1600
Retif, T. N.	GA0400	Rhodes, Rhonda	UT0200	Richardson, Holly	MI0450
Rettedal, Dean	SD0300	Rhodes, Rhonda L.	UT0150	Richardson, Jack	AG0130
Retzko, Barbara	NJ1130	Rhodes, Ruth	IL3450	Richardson, James K.	VA0300
Retzlaff, Dustin	WY0130	Rhodes, Samuel	NY1900	Richardson, Kevin	NC0050
Retzlaff, Jonathan	TN1850	Rhodes, Steve	TN0930	Richardson, Lisa	CA4450
Reubart, G. Dale	AB0100	Rhodes, Terry Ellen	NC2410	Richardson, Lucille K.	NY3725
Reul, Barbara M.	AJ0100	Rhody, Matthew	LA0800	Richardson, Marc	KY0250
Reuning, Sanford	NY1800	Rhoten, Markus	NY1900	Richardson, Marguerite	FL1000
Reuss, Dale	MI1180	Rhyne, Jennifer	WA0650	Richardson, Mark Douglas	NC0650
Reuter, Eric Lehman	MA0260	Rhyne, Kathryn	SC0750	Richardson, Neal	MO1950
Reuter, Jessica M.	MO1500	Rhyne-Bray, Constance	NC2000	Richardson, Ouida	TX0550
Reuter, Rocky J.	OH0350	Rhyneer, Barbara	MI1600	Richardson, Paul A.	AL0800
Reuter, Ted A.	IA1800	Riazuelo, Carlos	LA0200	Richardson, Robert C.	WA0450
Reuter-Pivetta, Debra	NC2205	Ribando, Jeremy S.	FL1430	Richardson, Robert	AC0050
Reuter-Riddle, Pat	IA1800	Ribchinsky, Julie C.	CT0050	Richardson, Sylvia	AC0050
Revuluri, Sindhumathi	MA1050	Ribeiro, Gerardo	IL2250	Richardson, Tracy	IL1612
Rewoldt, Todd	CA4100	Ricci, Adam	NC2430	Richardson, Tracy	IN1400
Rex, Christopher	GA1050	Ricci, John	FL1000	Richardson, Vernal	GA2300
Rey, Mario	NC0650	Ricci, Robert	MI2250	Richardson, W. Randall	AL0800
Reycraft, Jonathan W.	MO1900	Ricci-Rogel, Susan	MD0700	Richardson, W. Mack	NY3770
Reyes, Iris	CO0150	Ricciardone, Michael	NY2750	Richardson, William	MO0950
Reyes, James E.	MA0260	Riccomini, Ray	NY2250	Richens, James W.	TN1680
Reyes, Reynaldo	MD0850	Rice, Alexandria	GA0940	Richeson, Dane M.	WI0350
Reyes, William	OK0550	Rice, Betty	FL1300	Richeson, David T.	AR0750
Reyes, William	AR0730	Rice, C. William	VA0600	Richeson, Doug	OH0850
Reyes, Ysmael	CO0650	Rice, Dana R.	MS0400	Richey, Craig	CA0825
Reyman, Randall	IL1750	Rice, Douglas	WA1000	Richey, David	NY3350
Reynerson, Rodney T.	NC0050	Rice, Eric N.	CT0600	Richey, Marc	KY1200
Reynolds, Alison M.	PA3250	Rice, JoAnn	NY1860	Richman, Glenn	CA0900
Reynolds, Anne	IN1650	Rice, John Robin	OH1850	Richman, Glenn	CA5000
Reynolds, Anne B.	IN0350	Rice, Karen	NC2700	Richman, Josh	PA3330
Reynolds, Anne-Marie	NY3730	Rice, Laura Brooks	NJ1350	Richman, Pamela L.	OK1330
Reynolds, Christopher A.	CA5010	Rice, Laurence E.	KS1350	Richman, Yoriko	CA4150
Reynolds, David B.	MD1050	Rice, Lorraine	AZ0440	Richmond, Brad	MI1050
Reynolds, David	SD0550	Rice, Marc	MO1780	Richmond, C. Floyd	PA3560
Reynolds, Dennis	OH1700	Rice, Michael	AL0010	Richmond, James	VA0150
Reynolds, Don	FL1000	Rice, Nancy	MA2100	Richmond, Jeffrey W.	OR0950
Reynolds, Elaine	CA4650	Rice, Patton	MS0400	Richmond, John W.	NE0600
Reynolds, Geoffrey	CT0650	Rice, Paul	AD0050	Richmond, Joshua	PA3250
Reynolds, H. Robert	CA5300	Rice, Susan	WI0100	Richmond, Kevin D.	TN1680
Reynolds, Harold	NY1800	Rice, Suzanne	IN1560	Richmond, Matthew	NC2400
Reynolds, Heidi M.	OH2250	Rice, Suzanne	IN0100	Richmond, Mike	NY2750
Reynolds, Jeff W.	AL1150	Rice, Timothy	CA5031	Richmond, Thomas	MN0600
Reynolds, Jeffrey L.	AG0450	Rice-See, Lynn	TN1100	Richstone, Lorne S.	OK1350
Reynolds, Jerald	FL2050	Ricer, Thomas	HI0210	Richt, Cheryl	KS0650
Reynolds, Jerald M.	FL2000	Rich, Harvey	UT0050	Richter, Elizabeth	IN0150
Reynolds, Jeremy W.	CO0900	Rich, Kevin	TX1450	Richter, Glenn	TX3510
Reynolds, Katherine	AR0850	Rich, Melody	TX0900	Richter, Jorge Luiz	NC0650
Reynolds, Kathleen	TX3420	Rich, Mollie	FL1750	Richter, Julia M.	IL0840
Reynolds, Kathleen	CA4700	Rich, Ruth Anne	MO1810	Richter, Kimberlie J.	IL2050
Reynolds, Kristen	MI0500	Rich, Shelley	AZ0450	Richter, Leonard	WA1100
Reynolds, Kristin	MI1000	Richard, Charles	CA3800	Richter, Lois	GA0200
Reynolds, Lindsey Bird	WY0115	Richard, Claude	AI0200	Richter, Magdalena	MA1400
Reynolds, Lindsey	WY0200	Richard, Leon	KY0750	Richter, Michael	TX3530
Reynolds, Marc	TX2930	Richard, Matthew	MA2020	Richter, Tiffany	AL1450
Reynolds, Martin C.	MO1500	Richard, Monique M.	AE0100	Richtmeyer, Debra A.	IL3300
Reynolds, Michael	MA0400	Richard, Sarah	WA0860	Richwine, Reginald L.	OH2250
Reynolds, Patrick A.	OH2250	Richards, Annette	NY0900	Rickard, Jeffrey H.	CA5150
Reynolds, Robert	KY0860	Richards, Cynthia	UT0325	Rickards, Steven	IN1100
Reynolds, Roger L.	CA5050	Richards, Doris	MI2200	Rickards, Steven	IN1650
Reynolds, Sharon	NJ0975	Richards, Douglas	VA1600	Rickards, Steven	IN0250
Reynolds, Shawn	PA3650	Richards, E. Earl	CA2420	Rickels, David A.	CO0800
Reynolds, Sonya Szabo	OH2550	Richards, E. Michael	MD1000	Ricker, Ramon	NY1100
Reynolds, Steve	LA0800	Richards, Eric J.	NE0400	Ricker, Richard	NE0450
Reynolds, Terence	TX3420	Richards, Eric	NE0600	Rickey, Euni	IN1025
Reynolds, Terrance	NY2200	Richards, Erik W.	IA0850	Rickey, Shirley	AL0400
Reynolds, Todd	NY2150	Richards, Gwyn	IN0900	Rickman, Michael	FL1750
Reynolds, Winton	TX3510	Richards, James	MO1830	Ricks, Edward	SC1050
Rezak, David M.	NY4150	Richards, Jeanne	MN1620	Ricks, Steven L.	UT0050
Rezende Lopes, Joao Luiz	NJ0825	Richards, Julie	TX2310	Ricotta, Charles	MI2100
Reznicek, Steven	MN0150	Richards, June	CA4000	Ridd, Laurel	AC0100
Reznicow, Joshua	IA0300	Richards, Lasim	FL0700	Riddick, Frank C.	OK1350
Rhea, Thomas L.	MA0260	Richards, Mark C.	AA0200	Riddle, Donald	MO2000
Rhea, Tim B.	TX2900	Richards, Mary	UT0325	Riddle, Paula	SC0750
Rheault, Pierre-Daniel	AI0200	Richards, Patrick	MS0360	Riddle-Jackson, Jackie	UT0150
Rhee, Heasook	NY2150	Richards, Paul	FL1850	Ridenour, Mark	IL0550
Rhee, Sarah	NY2650	Richards, Rebekah	MN0610	Rideout, Roger R.	OK1350
Rhein, Robert	IN0200	Richards, Rebekah	MN0750	Rider, Daniel	IL1300
Rheude, Elizabeth A.	ND0500	Richards, Richard	MN1620	Rider, Rhonda	MA0400
, Rhiannon	MA0260	Richards, Scott D.	NJ0800	Rider, Rhonda	MA0350
Rhine, Deborah	TX3350	Richards, Wade	NY1100	Rider, Wendell	CA4200
Rhinehart, James	IN0150	Richards, Walter	FL1790	Ridge, David	CA3920
Rhoades, Connie A.	KY0550	Richards, William W.	DC0150	Ridge, David P.	CA0807
Rhoades, Vanessa	OK0500	Richardson, Abby	AG0450	Ridges, Lameriel R.	SC1050
Rhoads, Mark	MN0250	Richardson, Cathy	TX1725	Ridgeway, Betty	MD0400
Rhoads, Shari	IA1550	Richardson, Cathy	TX0370	Ridgeway, Max A.	OK0600
Rhodebeck, Jacob	NY0270	Richardson, Cathy	TX0250	Ridgway, Meredith K.	TX3410
Rhoden, Lori E.	IN0150	Richardson, Celia	TX2850	Ridgway, Zachary M.	TX3410
Rhodes, Aaron	DE0050	Richardson, Chuck	TX2850	Ridilla, Andrea	OH1450

Name	Code	Name	Code	Name	Code
Ridley, Larry	NY2150	Rios, Juan	CA5040	Rizzo, Rick	IL0720
Riebe, Jenice	VA1100	Rioth, Doug	CA4150	Rizzo, Stephen	AL0260
Rieck, Alan J.	WI0803	Ripley, David	NH0350	Rizzuto, Thomas	NY2450
Ried, Michael	NY3725	Ripley, James	WI0250	Ro, Betty	AF0120
Riedel, Kimberly	NJ1130	Ripley, Randal	MI1985	Roach, Donna Kay	VA1475
Rieger, Eric	NJ1350	Ripley, Vanessa G.	OH1200	Roach, Hildred E.	DC0350
Riegle, Dale	FL1500	Riposo, Joseph	NY4150	Roach, L. Leroy	CA4200
Riehl, Jeffrey S.	VA1500	Rippe, Allen	TN1680	Roach, Rebecca	KS0750
Riehman, Ken	PA3560	Rippere, Mathew	MA2100	Roach, Seth	KS0750
Rieken, Justin	MN0625	Rippy, Sylvia	NC0050	Roach, Stephen	CA0150
Riekenberg, Dave	PA1950	Rischar, Richard A.	MI2110	Roach, Stephen W.	CA0840
Riepe, Heidi	IA0900	Rischin, Rebecca M.	OH1900	Roadfeldt-O'Riordan, Holly K.	PA1850
Riepe, Russell C.	TX3175	Riseling, Robert A.	AG0500	Roads, Curtis	CA5060
Rieppel, Daniel	MN1500	Risinger, Andrew	TN0100	Roane, Steve	NY2400
Rieppi, Pablo	NY3785	Risinger, Ed	IL1200	Robb, P.	CA1950
Rierson, Don G.	VA0600	Risinger, Kimberly	IL1150	Robbin, Catherine	AG0650
Ries, Ardelle	AA0110	Risk, Lee	KY0550	Robbins, Allison	TN1710
Ries, Tim	AG0450	Riske, Barbara	NV0050	Robbins, Catherine	AC0100
Rieth, Dale	FL0950	Risser, Martha	MO2000	Robbins, Cheryl	IL0420
Rifas, Helen	NC2500	Rissman, Maurice Nick	TX1400	Robbins, Daniel C.	CA2050
Rife, Jean	MA1400	Rissmiller, Gary	PA2450	Robbins, David P.	WA0650
Rife, Jean	MA1175	Rissmiller, Gary	PA2550	Robbins, David	IN0100
Rife, Jean	MA1200	Ristow, Gregory C.	IN0350	Robbins, Gerald	NY2150
Rife, Jerry E.	NJ1000	Ritcher, Gary	VA0600	Robbins, Hollis	MD0650
Riffel, Patricia	CA1425	Ritchey, Doris Ellen	GA2100	Robbins, Janet	WV0750
Riffel, William	NJ0300	Ritchey, Mary Lynn	MA0150	Robbins, Janice B.	TX2295
Rifkin, Deborah	NY1800	Ritchie, Michael	IN1350	Robbins, Malcolm Scott	SC0650
Rifkin, Joshua	MA0400	Ritchie, Stanley	IN0900	Robbins, Mark	WA0200
Riggs, Ben	CO0650	Riter, Tye	FL1450	Robblee, Timothy	IL2250
Riggs, Paige	PA3100	Ritscher, Karen	NY2150	Robe, Carol M.	OR0700
Riggs, Robert D.	MS0700	Ritscher, Karen	MA0400	Rober, R. Todd	PA1750
Rigler, Ann Marie	MO2000	Ritscher, Karen	NY2750	Roberdeau, Dan	WI0100
Rigler, Jane	CO0810	Ritt, David	WA0200	Roberdeaux, Dan	WI0300
Riis, Thomas L.	CO0800	Ritt, Morey	NY0600	Roberge, Marc-Andre	AI0190
Rijos, Ivan	PR0115	Ritt, Morey	NY0642	Roberson, Heather D.	CO1050
Rike, Gregory	IN1600	Rittenhouse, Kenneth	VA0450	Roberson, James	CA5031
Rikkers, Scott D.	VA0600	Rittenhouse, Kerry	GA2300	Roberson, Matt	TX0050
Riley, Blake	FL2100	Rittenhouse, Virginia Gene	MD0150	Roberson, Matt	AL0345
Riley, Carole	PA1050	Ritter, Jonathan	CA5040	Roberson, Richard	PA2300
Riley, David	RI0150	Ritter, Michael F.	TN0050	Robert, Anne	AI0200
Riley, David M.	OR1050	Ritter, Paul	MT0370	Robert, James	NC0750
Riley, Denise	MS0200	Ritter, Stacey	IL1050	Robert, Lucie	NY2150
Riley, Edward	OH0755	Ritter-Bernardini, Denise	OH2300	Robert, Lucie	NY2250
Riley, Gregory E.	PA3600	Ritterling, Soojin Kim	WI0810	Robertello, Thomas	IL0550
Riley, Jason	KS0100	Rittner, Phillip	CT0650	Robertello, Thomas J.	IN0900
Riley, Jason	MO0850	Ritz, Dennis W.	PA3050	Roberts, Adam	AZ0350
Riley, John	NY2150	Ritz, John	KY1500	Roberts, Andrew	PA1900
Riley, John	NY3785	Ritz, Lyn	WA1100	Roberts, Beth	NY2250
Riley, Justin	OH0350	Ritzenhein, Mark	MI1800	Roberts, Brian S.	MI2110
Riley, Kathleen	MI0150	Ritzenthaler, Maria	IL1085	Roberts, Brian	MI2200
Riley, Kristin	OR1020	Riva-Palacio, Nancy	NC1300	Roberts, Bruce	CA4150
Riley, Madeleine C.	PA1000	Rivadeneira, Barbara	IA0700	Roberts, Connie	MS0850
Riley, Martha C.	IN1300	Rivard, Gene	MN0625	Roberts, Cynthia	NY1900
Riley, Mary Lee	IN1750	Rivard, Kevin C.	CA0807	Roberts, Cynthia	TX3420
Riley, Patricia E.	VT0450	Rivard, Michele M.	CA0400	Roberts, David Scott	TN1720
Riley, Raymond G.	MI0150	Rivard, Michelle	CA4425	Roberts, Dolly	FL0450
Riley, Steve	KS0050	Rivas, Anita	CA0800	Roberts, Elizabeth 'dolly'	FL2050
Riley, Susanna	PA0100	Rivas, Aristides	MA2030	Roberts, Elizabeth	VA0750
Riley, William	NY0050	Rivas, David	OR0750	Roberts, Elizabeth 'Ibby'	VA1550
Riley, William	MA2020	Riveire, Janine	CA0630	Roberts, Gene	CO0830
Rimington, James	IL0400	Rivello, David	NY1100	Roberts, Gene	CO0550
Rimmington, Rob	FL0650	Rivera Diaz, Almicar	PR0115	Roberts, Gwyn	MD0650
Rimple, Mark T.	PA3600	Rivera Lassen, Carmen L.	PR0115	Roberts, J. Christopher	OH1100
Rinaldi, Beverley	FL1800	Rivera Ortiz, William	PR0115	Roberts, James E.	AL0500
Rinaldi, Jason P.	MA0260	Rivera Ruiz, Alvaro M.	PR0115	Roberts, Jean	TX2700
Rinaldo, Ben	AG0150	Rivera Trinidad, Miguel	PR0115	Roberts, John	OH2290
Rincon, Alicia	CA4000	Rivera, Angel Ramon	MA1400	Roberts, John P.L.	AA0150
Rindfleisch, Andrew P.	OH0650	Rivera, Diego	MI1400	Roberts, John Noel	TX2700
Rindt, Steven	WI0865	Rivera, Felix	PR0150	Roberts, John H.	CA5000
Rine, Craig	WA0650	Rivera, Francesca M.	CA5353	Roberts, Kate	IA0910
Rinear, Jeffrey	MN1625	Rivera, Jennifer M.	NJ0800	Roberts, Kay George	MA2030
Rinehart, Jason	LA0770	Rivera, Jose	NC2435	Roberts, Kimberly	IA1350
Rinehart, John	OH0050	Rivera, Lino	CA3920	Roberts, Layla	AC0100
Rinehart, Robert	NY2150	Rivera, Luis C.	AL1300	Roberts, Lois	CA1750
Riner, Nicole	WY0200	Rivera, Maricarmen	PR0115	Roberts, Marcus	FL0850
Rines, Elizabeth B.	ME0500	Rivera, Miguel	PR0100	Roberts, Marie J.	GA1300
Ring, Eric	MO1950	Rivera, Natalia	MO1810	Roberts, Mary W.	FL0600
Ring, Gordon L.	VA0700	Rivera, Nicole	IL0750	Roberts, Melissa	MO1550
Ring, Jonathan	CA4150	Rivera, Wayne	CT0650	Roberts, Nancy	SD0100
Ring, Richard	AI0210	Rivera-Guzman, Felix	PR0115	Roberts, Patricia	TN0100
Ringold, Allison	OH0250	Rivera-Vega, Salvador	PR0100	Roberts, Richard	AI0150
Ringquist, Mikael	MA1400	Rivers, Cynthia	GA1100	Roberts, Ron A.	AL1160
Ringquist, Mikael	MA0260	Rivers, Earl G.	OH2200	Roberts, Russ	OK1050
Rings, Steven M.	IL3250	Rivers, James	KS1400	Roberts, Sara	CA0510
Ringwald, Ilana	MA2020	Rivers, John	VT0450	Roberts, Shannon B.	UT0150
Ringwald, Ilana	MA2150	Rivers, John	VT0250	Roberts, Shawn M.	NC0050
Ringwall, Lauren	GA1650	Rivers, Joseph L.	OK1450	Roberts, Sherill	OR0250
Rink, Jeffrey	MA2010	Rivers, Laurel R.	NY3725	Roberts, Sherill	OR0450
Rink, Shelley	CA0150	Rivers, Sandra	OH2200	Roberts, Stanley L.	GA1300
Rinne, Erzsebet Gaal	IN1600	Rivers, Sylvia	TX0250	Roberts, Stephen	CT0800
Rinnert, Nathan	PA2150	Rives, Charles L.	TX2750	Roberts, Steven	AL1150
Rintoul, Richard	CA5550	Rivest, Darlene	WI0250	Roberts, Tamara	CA5000
Rintoul, Richard	CA5060	Rivest, Jean-Francois	AI0200	Roberts, Terry	SC0710
Rinzler, Paul	CA0600	Rivet, Joe	LA0150	Roberts, Tim	CA3320
Rio, Robin	AZ0100	Rivkin, Evgeny	GA2100	Roberts, Timothy	VA1350
Riordan, George T.	TN1100	Rizner, Dan Joseph	IN0350	Roberts, Timothy	VA0450
Rios Escribano, Enrique B.	PR0115	Rizzer, Gerald	IL2750	Roberts, Vera	CT0050
Rios, Fernando	MD1010	Rizzer, Gerald M.	IL0750	Roberts, Wesley	KY0400
Rios, Fernando	IL3300	Rizzetto, Jay	CA2950	Roberts, Wilfred A.	TX2400
Rios, Giselle Elgarresta	FL0050	Rizzo, Jacques	NJ1400	Robertshaw, Manon	CA5040

Name	Code	Name	Code	Name	Code
Robertshaw, Manon	CA1750	Robinson, Yvonne	PA2450	Rodriquez, Frank	TX2295
Robertshaw, Manon	CA0859	Robinson-Martin, Trineice	NY4200	Rodriquez, Galindo	LA0550
Robertshaw, Manon	CA2800	Robinson-Martin, Trineice	NJ0750	Rodriquez, Jose	NJ0700
Robertson, Anne Walters	IL3250	Robinson-Oturu, Gail M.	TN0050	Rodriquez, Raquel H.	KY1000
Robertson, Ben	WA0250	Robison, Jeanne	CA0350	Roe, Charles R.	AZ0500
Robertson, Carey	CA1050	Robison, John O.	FL2000	Roe, Gail	TX2310
Robertson, Christina N.	AZ0510	Robison, Paula	MA1400	Roe, Roger A.	IN0900
Robertson, Christine	IL1750	Robison, Riley	MO0400	Roebke, Catherine	TX3535
Robertson, Donald C.	NY3705	Robitaille, James	MA2020	Roebuck, Nikole D.	LA0100
Robertson, Elizabeth A.	IN1600	Robken, Jim	LA0250	Roed, Tom	MO0750
Robertson, Eric	AG0450	Robl, James	WI0750	Roeder, John B.	AB0100
Robertson, Fritz S.	IN0100	Roblee, Thomas	OH0700	Roeder, Matthew J.	CO0800
Robertson, James	AC0100	Robock, Alison	IL0400	Roederer, Jason	AZ0480
Robertson, James D.	MT0175	Roby, Lloyd	CA0800	Roederer, Silvia	MI2250
Robertson, Jemmie	IL0800	Rocchio, Karen	MO0700	Roehrich, Matthew	NC1350
Robertson, Jon	FL1125	Rocco, Emma S.	PA2713	Roehrig, Helmut J.	OH2550
Robertson, Kaestner	MA0250	Rocco, Robert	NJ0700	Roelofs, Laura Leigh	MI2200
Robertson, Karen	NC0050	Rocco, Robert P.	NC1650	Roens, Steven	UT0250
Robertson, Lesley N.	CA4900	Roche, Deryck	AG0130	Roesch, Erin R.	IN0400
Robertson, Marta E.	PA1400	Roche, Mildred A.	SC0650	Roesner, Edward	NY2740
Robertson, Masson	IN0905	Roche-Wallace, Catherine	LA0760	Roessingh, Karel	AB0210
Robertson, Patricia	IN1560	Rochford, Stephen M.	CA2390	Roessler, Brian	MN1300
Robertson, Paul	NJ0825	Rochinski, Stephen	MA0260	Roethlisberger, Karen L.	PA0550
Robertson, Phyllis	MO1780	Rochon, Gaston	AI0210	Rofe, Peter	CA0510
Robertson, R. Scott	AL1150	Rock, Connie	CT0600	Rogalsky, Matt	AG0250
Robertson, R. Scott	AL0800	Rockabrand, Sarah	IL2400	Rogan, Michael J.	MA1900
Robertson, Roki	AR0250	Rockefeller, John D.	MD0650	Rogentine, Carole	DC0170
Robertson, Ruth M.	MO0600	Rocker, Karla J.	GA0950	Rogers King, Tammy	TN0100
Robertson, Troy David	TX2750	Rockett, Susetta	TX0900	Rogers, Barbara J.	MN1280
Robey, Matthew E.	NY2500	Rockmaker, Jody D.	AZ0100	Rogers, Bruce	CA3200
Robichaud, Clement	AI0190	Rockwell, Joti	CA3650	Rogers, Caroline	MI1300
Robillard, David	OK1250	Rockwell, Owen	MS0100	Rogers, Dave	NJ1400
Robilliard, David	AG0550	Rockwell, Owen P.	MS0350	Rogers, David	OR0950
Robinett, Henry	CA1500	Rockwell, Paula	AF0050	Rogers, Dennis G.	MO0850
Robinett, Henry	CA0150	Rockwin, Howard	NY2550	Rogers, Donald M.	SC1200
Robins, Linda	TX2570	Rod, Steve	IA0900	Rogers, Douglas	DC0170
Robinson Woliver, Loretta	OH1850	Rodde, James	IA0850	Rogers, Eugene C.	MI2100
Robinson, Anthony	TX0600	Rodde, Kathleen	IA0850	Rogers, George L.	MA2100
Robinson, Bill	TN1000	Roden, Stella D.	MO1790	Rogers, Jefferson	TN0100
Robinson, Bobb	NC2410	Roden, Timothy J.	OH2000	Rogers, JoAnne	OK1250
Robinson, Bradley C.	MS0700	Rodenberg, Elise	IA0930	Rogers, John E.	NH0350
Robinson, Brian	MA1450	Rodewald, Marion	CA2100	Rogers, John Fitz	SC1110
Robinson, Brian	AI0150	Rodger, Gillian	WI0825	Rogers, Joseph	MA0260
Robinson, Cathy Meng	OH1100	Rodgers, Andy	CT0800	Rogers, Leonard	PA1050
Robinson, Charles R.	MO1810	Rodgers, Christopher	PA0050	Rogers, Lisa	TX3200
Robinson, Curtis	IN0005	Rodgers, Elizabeth	NY2150	Rogers, Lynne	NJ1400
Robinson, D.	MA0800	Rodgers, Ernest E.	MI2200	Rogers, Mark	TX2930
Robinson, Dana M.	IL3300	Rodgers, Jane Schoonmaker	OH0300	Rogers, Mark	TX2260
Robinson, David	VA1600	Rodgers, Joseph	MN0200	Rogers, Mark	TX3350
Robinson, David	TX2600	Rodgers, Joseph W.	MN1000	Rogers, Mark	TX3100
Robinson, Dawn	SC0800	Rodgers, Kenneth	KS0500	Rogers, Martha	MA0350
Robinson, Doug	AZ0490	Rodgers, Linda	CA1520	Rogers, Maurice L.	IA0270
Robinson, Elizabeth	KS0650	Rodgers, Lloyd A.	CA0815	Rogers, Michael	OR1050
Robinson, Emily	OK1050	Rodgers, Mark	AA0200	Rogers, Nancy Marie	FL0850
Robinson, Evan	WV0600	Rodgers, Reginald G.	IN0100	Rogers, Patricia	NY1900
Robinson, Faye L.	AZ0500	Rodgers, Stacy D.	MS0700	Rogers, Patricia	NY2150
Robinson, Florence	FL0600	Rodgers, Stephen	OR1050	Rogers, Paul	AG0450
Robinson, Gary A.	SC0765	Rodgers, Susan	RI0200	Rogers, Richard	GA0940
Robinson, Gary	NH0050	Rodin, Jared	IN0250	Rogers, Rodney	AZ0100
Robinson, Gerald	AG0450	Rodin, Jesse	CA4900	Rogers, Sean	ID0070
Robinson, Greg	CA0805	Roditeleva-Wibe, Maria I.	WA0050	Rogers, Seth	OH0850
Robinson, Greg	AG0050	Roditski, William	PA2200	Rogers, Sharon	AC0050
Robinson, Gregory J.	VA0450	Rodland, Carol	NY1100	Rogers, Susan	MA0260
Robinson, Harold	PA0850	Rodland, Carol	MA1400	Rogers, Timothy	NH0150
Robinson, Ian	IL1085	Rodland, Catherine	MN1450	Rogers, Tom	AG0130
Robinson, Jason	MA0100	Rodman, Ronald	MN0300	Rogers, Vanessa	TN1200
Robinson, Jeff	TX3400	Rodrigue, Jean-Louis	CA5030	Roggen, Ann	NJ1400
Robinson, Jennifer	MS0700	Rodriguez Alvira, Jose	PR0115	Roggenbuck, Therese	WI0810
Robinson, Joseph	FL1125	Rodriguez Aponte, Dalia	PR0115	Rogiewicz, Thomas	IL2730
Robinson, Kathleen E.	MN1280	Rodriguez Curet, Marcos J.	PR0115	Rogine, Peter	NY1275
Robinson, Keith	TX3100	Rodriguez, Alberto	PR0115	Roginska, Agnieska	NY2750
Robinson, Keith	OH1100	Rodriguez, Alex	MA0260	Roginske, Lynn	WI1150
Robinson, Laura E.	GA1900	Rodriguez, Ariana	AA0050	Rogizhyna, Maryna	NY5000
Robinson, Marty	WI0830	Rodriguez, Art	CA2440	Rognstad, Richard	SD0600
Robinson, Marty	FL0600	Rodriguez, Bobby	CA5020	Rogoff, Noah T.	NE0590
Robinson, McNeil	NY2150	Rodriguez, Bobby	CA5031	Rogosin, David	AE0050
Robinson, Melissa Ann	OR0850	Rodriguez, Bobby H.	CA3500	Rohde, Kurt E.	CA5010
Robinson, Michael L.	NC1250	Rodriguez, Carlos Xavier	MI2100	Rohlfing, Mimi	MA2030
Robinson, Michael C.	GA2100	Rodriguez, Carlos Cesar	DC0170	Rohlig, Harald	AL0450
Robinson, Mitchell	MI1400	Rodriguez, Cristina	PR0150	Rohr, Clint	OK1330
Robinson, N. Scott	MD0400	Rodriguez, Eleazer	NY2900	Rohr, Deborah	NY3650
Robinson, N. Scott	MD0850	Rodriguez, Elimiano	CA2550	Rohr, Grant	CA0815
Robinson, Nathalie G.	NY1600	Rodriguez, Elvin	CA2420	Rohrer, Katherine	OH1900
Robinson, Nicole R.	TN1680	Rodriguez, Francisco	CO0800	Rohrer, Thomas	UT0300
Robinson, Patrece	FL1750	Rodriguez, Francisco	PA1050	Rohwer, Debbie A.	TX3420
Robinson, Paul G.	OH1850	Rodriguez, Hugo Marcos	FL0050	Rohwer, Robert	OH0300
Robinson, Richard	CA3700	Rodriguez, Javier	TX3530	Roig-Francoli, Jennifer	OH2550
Robinson, Rick	NY0270	Rodriguez, Jill	TX3100	Roig-Francoli, Miguel A.	OH2200
Robinson, Russell	FL1850	Rodriguez, Jose	ID0050	Roiger, Teresa	NY3760
Robinson, Ryan	OK0750	Rodriguez, Joseph	IL0730	Roisum Foley, Amy K.	MN1000
Robinson, Schuyler	KY1450	Rodriguez, Joshua A.	NY3650	Roitman, Tatiana	AR0750
Robinson, Scott	PA0850	Rodriguez, Linda M.	FL2050	Roitstein, David	CA0510
Robinson, Scott	PA1150	Rodriguez, Michael J.	NY2750	Rojahn, Karolina	MA0350
Robinson, Stephanie	CA4000	Rodriguez, Ramon	PR0100	Rojahn, Rudolf	MA0350
Robinson, Stephanie	MA1750	Rodriguez, Raul I.	TX3175	Rojak, John	NY2750
Robinson, Stephen	FL1750	Rodriguez, Samantha	NY3730	Rojak, John	NY0150
Robinson, Susan	FL2050	Rodriguez, Sandra	PR0115	Rojak, John	NY0500
Robinson, Thomas S.	NH0250	Rodriguez, Santiago	FL1900	Rojak, John D.	NY1900
Robinson, Thomas	AL1170	Rodriguez-Hernandez, Gabriel	PR0115	Rojak, John	NJ1130
Robinson, Vicky	GA0850	Rodriguez-Salazar, Martha	CA1250	Rojas, Berta	DC0100

Name	Code	Name	Code	Name	Code
Rojas, Luis Miguel	PR0115	Root, Jena	OH2600	Rosenfeld, Steven	NY0650
Rojas, Marcus	NY2750	Root, Thomas R.	UT0350	Rosengren, Hakan	CA0815
Rojas, Marcus	NY3785	Roozendaal, Jay	WA1250	Rosenhaus, Steven L.	NY2750
Rojas, Marcus	NY0500	Roper, Bob	AG0130	Rosenholtz-Witt, Jason	CO0250
Rojas, Ner	IN1025	Roper, Gretchen	SC0420	Rosenkoetter, Alan	MO1900
Rojas, Nuria Mariela	SC0150	Roper, Richard	CA4150	Rosenkoetter, Alan C.	MO1830
Rojek, Justin J.	AL0345	Roper, Richard	CA5070	Rosenkranz, Thomas H.	OH0300
Rokeach, Martin	CA3920	Roper, Scott	AZ0490	Rosenmeyer, David G.	NY2750
Rokosny, Dana	MD0300	Ropp, Cindy	IL1150	Rosenn, Jamie	CA0835
Roland, Isabelle	AB0200	Rorex, Michael	LA0550	Rosenshein, Ingrid	FL1675
Roland, Tomm	NE0610	Rorick, Michael	NY3725	Rosenshein, Neil	NY2150
Roland-Silverstein, Kathleen	NY4150	Rorick, William	NY0642	Rosensky, Michael	VA1550
Roland-Wieczorek, Sophie	AG0500	Rorie, Alfonso	NC0910	Rosensteel Way, Nancy	PA2500
Rold, Julie	MA0260	Rorke, Margaret A.	UT0250	Rosenthal, Roseanne K.	IL3450
Roldan, Francisco	NJ0825	Rosa Ramos, Luis S.	PR0115	Rosenthal, Ted	NY2150
Rolf, Alison	MO1950	Rosa, Gerard	CT0050	Rosenwein, Frank	OH0600
Rolf, Marie	NY1100	Rosado, Ana Maria	NJ0825	Rosenzweig, Joyce	NY1450
Rolfe, James	AG0450	Rosado, Sara	MD0550	Rosenzweig, Morris	UT0250
Rolfe, Wendy	MA0260	Rosado-Nazario, Samuel	PR0100	Rosevear, Burt L.	TN1000
Rolfs, Thomas	MA1400	Rosales, Rachel	NY4450	Rosewall, Michael	WI0750
Rolfs, Thomas C.	MA0400	Rosales, Rachel A.	VT0050	Rosfeld, Ken	OK1200
Roll, Christianne	VA0350	Rosand, Aaron	NY2250	Rosfeld, Marilyn	OK1200
Roll, Donna	MA1175	Rosand, Aaron	PA0850	Roshong, Janelle	OH1350
Roll, Marcus	MI1985	Rosand, Ellen	CT0900	Rosinbum, Ralph R.	WA1050
Rolle, Nina	CO0560	Rosario, Harry	PR0150	Rosine, Amy	KS0650
Rollene, Donna	AR0400	Rosario, Lita	DC0350	Rosing, Carol A.	WI0865
Roller, Jan D.	TX3530	Rosborough-Bowman, Monika	UT0050	Rosing, Carol A.	WI0100
Roller, Jonathan	KY0100	Roscetti, Diane	CA0835	Rosinski, Jessi	MA2010
Roller, Peter	WI0050	Roscigno, John A.	CA0835	Roslak, Roxolana	AG0300
Rollett, Rebecca	PA1050	Rose, Alissa	PA2150	Rosner, Arnold	NY2050
Rollin, Gwen	OH2600	Rose, Angela	OH1350	Rosove, Lewis E.	WI0825
Rollin, Robert	OH2600	Rose, Bernard	NY1275	Rosow, Lois	OH1850
Rollins, Christopher	MI1200	Rose, Brent	LA0080	Ross Mehl, Margaret	PA0600
Rollins, Ian	TX2900	Rose, Brent	LA0800	Ross, Buck	TX3400
Rolls, Timothy	KS0350	Rose, Brian	OR0050	Ross, Charles	NY1100
Rolnick, Neil B.	NY3300	Rose, Cameron J.	TX3535	Ross, Clark	AD0050
Rolsten, Kathy	MN1120	Rose, David	NY3725	Ross, Daniel F.	AR0110
Rolston, Shauna	AG0450	Rose, Ellen Ruth	CA5000	Ross, David	TX3520
Roma, Joseph	NY0350	Rose, Ellen	TX2400	Ross, Don	AA0020
Romain, James P.	IA0550	Rose, Francois	CA5350	Ross, Don	AA0035
Romaine, Paul	CO0550	Rose, Gil B.	MA1450	Ross, Donald	MO0100
Romaine, Paul	CO0800	Rose, Gwendolyn	MI2250	Ross, Elaine M.	CA1075
Roman, Brent	IL1900	Rose, Jerome	NY2250	Ross, Elizabeth	PA3330
Roman, Dan	CT0500	Rose, John E.	FL0700	Ross, Emily	OR0500
Roman, Ed S.	AZ0510	Rose, John	CT0500	Ross, Gregory	PA1000
Roman, Joe	IL0400	Rose, Leslie Paige	AR0850	Ross, Holli	NJ0800
Roman, Mary C.	FL0850	Rose, Linda	CA0825	Ross, Holli W.	NY1600
Roman, Orlando	MD0750	Rose, Lloyd	MA0280	Ross, James	MD1010
Roman, Robert	NY3765	Rose, Melissa K.	TN1850	Ross, James R.	IL2250
Roman, Zoltan	AA0150	Rose, Michael	TN1850	Ross, James	NY1900
Romanek, Mary L.	PA2720	Rose, Richard F.	FL1300	Ross, Jana	VA1400
Romano, Charlene	VA1350	Rose, Sarah Elizabeth	NC0050	Ross, Jana	VA1125
Romano, Darlene	CA1270	Rose, Saxton	NC1650	Ross, Jared	KS0060
Romano, Elizabeth	NY4450	Rose, Stephen	OH0600	Ross, John	WV0700
Romano, Patrick	NY3560	Rose, Thomas	CA2950	Ross, John G.	NC1100
Romano, Tony	NY1275	Rose, Victoria	PA1900	Ross, John C.	KS1050
Romanul, Lisa K.	MA2150	Rose, William G.	LA0350	Ross, John	TN1200
Rombach-Kendall, Eric	NM0450	Roseberry, Lynn	OH0350	Ross, John Stanley	NC0050
Romberg, Barry	AG0650	Roseland, Chad	IN0800	Ross, Julian E.	OH0200
Romeo, Arthur	NY1275	Roselle, Herbert	NJ1050	Ross, Laura	MO1120
Romeo, James	CA4050	Roselli, Kathryn	NJ0700	Ross, Laura	MO1900
Romeo, Robert	NJ0825	Roseman, Jacob	KY0900	Ross, Laura Guyer	MO1500
Romeo, Tony B.	MA1550	Roseman, Molly	KY0900	Ross, Laura A.	TN1100
Romer, Wayne Allen	PA3710	Roseman, Molly J.	WI0850	Ross, Mary Anne	NY1400
Romero, Brenda M.	CO0800	Rosen, Benjamin	AZ0490	Ross, Nicholas G. M.	AZ0450
Romero, Celin	CA4100	Rosen, David	NY0900	Ross, Nicholas Piers	VA1400
Romero, Frank	NM0310	Rosen, Josh	MA0260	Ross, Paul	IL1085
Romero, Gustavo	TX3420	Rosen, Marcy	NY0642	Ross, Paul	ME0250
Romero, Jose	CA5300	Rosen, Marcy	NY2250	Ross, Rashawn	FL0700
Romersa, Henry J.	IL2900	Rosen, Marlene Ralis	OH1700	Ross, Ronald	LA0200
Rometo, Albert A.	NE0600	Rosen, Michael	OH1700	Ross, Ryan M.	MS0500
Romeu, Emma	MA0260	Rosen, Michelle	PA3250	Ross, Sally	NC1100
Romey, Kathy Saltzman	MN1623	Rosen, Robert	AA0020	Ross, Tyley	NY2750
Romig, James	IL3500	Rosenak, Karen	CA5000	Ross, William	TX2200
Romine, Ryan D.	VA1350	Rosenbaum, Harold L.	NY4320	Ross-Hammond, Amelia	VA0950
Romines, Dee	TX0900	Rosenbaum, Victor	NY2250	Ross-Happy, Linda Mae	MO1810
Romines, Fred David	PA2200	Rosenbaum, Victor	MA1400	Rosser, Christina	OH2150
Romines, Jay	TN1710	Rosenberg, Aaron H.	MA2030	Rosser, Geraldine	OH1600
Romines, Jeff	TN1000	Rosenberg, Christopher J.	NY2150	Rossi, Achille	IN0250
Romines, Roann	TN1000	Rosenberg, Jesse	IL2250	Rossi, Jamal J.	NY1100
Romm, Ronald	IL3300	Rosenberg, Marlene	IL0550	Rossi, Marc W.	MA0260
Rommel, John D.	IN0900	Rosenberg, Marlene	IL2250	Rossi, Richard Robert	IL0800
Rommen, Timothy	PA3350	Rosenberg, Ruth Emily	IL3310	Rossman, Pamela	TX2650
Rommereim, John Christian	IA0700	Rosenberg, Steven E.	SC0500	Rossmiller, Adam	MN0610
Rondinelli-Eisenreich, Cassandra	FL0050	Rosenberg, Steven	OH0850	Rossmiller, Adam	MN1620
Rondon, Tulio J.	WI0803	Rosenberg, Sylvia	NY1900	Rossomando, Fred E.	CT0250
Ronen, Yael	CA0800	Rosenberg, Sylvia	NY2150	Rossow, David	FL0650
Roney, John	AI0150	Rosenberg, Thomas	MN0300	Rossow, Stacie	FL0650
Ronis, David A.	NY1600	Rosenberg, Thomas A.	MN0950	Rossum, Kelly	VA0150
Ronkin, Bruce	MA1450	Rosenblatt, Jay M.	AZ0500	Rostad, Masumi Per	IN0900
Ronning, Debra D.	PA1250	Rosenblith, Eric	MA1175	Rostad, Masumi	IL3300
Ronning, Svend John	WA0650	Rosenblum, Henry	NY1860	Roste, Vaughn	OK0550
Roof, Kimberly	NY2450	Rosenblum, Jean K.	ME0500	Rostock, Paul	PA2450
Rooney, Laura G.	WI1150	Rosenblum, Joshua	CT0900	Roston, John	AI0150
Rooney, Matthew	CO0550	Rosenblum, Martin J.	WI0825	Rotaru, Catalin	AZ0100
Roop, Cynthia M.	NC1250	Rosenblum, Mathew	PA3420	Rotavera-Krain, Denise	OH0700
Roos, Joni N.	FL1550	Rosenboom, David	CA0510	Rotberg, Barton Samuel	PA2250
Roos, Randy	MA0260	Rosener, Douglas	AL0200	Rotella, Gloria	NJ0760
Root, Deane L.	PA3420	Rosenfeld, Andrew	MD0610	Roter, Bruce	NY0700
Root, Gordon	NY3725	Rosenfeld, Julie	CT0600	Roth, Arthur	AG0650

Alphabetical Listing of Faculty

Name	Code	Name	Code	Name	Code
Roth, David	PA2450	Rowland, Martile	CO0200	Rudolph, Kathleen	AG0300
Roth, Edward	MI2250	Rowland, Michael	NC0550	Rudolph, Richard	VA0550
Roth, John	MN0610	Rowland, Robert	PA0850	Rudolph, Robert A.	PA0100
Roth, Jonathan D.	IN0910	Rowlett, Donn	OK1500	Rudolph, Roy	MA1175
Roth, Kathryn	RI0150	Rowlett, Michael T.	MS0700	Rudolph, Shay	MA0650
Roth, Lisa	IA1400	Rowley, Jill	ID0050	Rudolph, Thomas	PA3330
Roth, Marjorie	NY2650	Rowley, Rick E.	TX3510	Rudy, Paul	MO1810
Roth, Michael	NY2400	Rowley, Terra	IN0700	Rudzik, Sarina Rommedahl	AA0050
Roth, Nicholas	IA0550	Rownd, Gary	IL1850	Ruedeman, Tim	NJ1400
Roth, Robert	VT0100	Rowsey, Les	MI0520	Ruedeman, Timothy	NY2105
Rothbart, Peter	NY1800	Rox, David	MA0950	Ruehr, Elena	MA1200
Rothbaum, Christiane	MD0650	Roy, Andre	AI0150	Ruetz, Andrew	OH1650
Rothenberg, David J.	OH0400	Roy, Bruno	AI0210	Ruff, James	NY4450
Rothenberg, Florie	WA0050	Roy, Dany	AI0200	Ruff, Kenneth	NC1550
Rothfarb, Lee	CA5060	Roy, J. Michael	WI0845	Ruff, Willie H.	CT0850
Rothfuss, Guy	NJ1350	Roy, Joseph	AG0170	Ruffels, Dave	CT0800
Rothgeb, John	NY3705	Roy, Larry	AC0100	Ruffels, David	NY3785
Rothkopf, Michael S.	NC1650	Roy, Lisa	AE0100	Ruffin, Milton	OH1850
Rothlisberger, Dana	MD0850	Roy, Shawn	LA0760	Ruffin, W. Floyd	GA1450
Rothlisberger, Rodney	MN1120	Royal, Guericke	DC0150	Ruggaber, Brian J.	OH2200
Rothman, George	NY0500	Royal, Jacquelyn A.	TN0300	Ruggiero, Charles	MI1400
Rothmuller, Daniel	CA5300	Royal, Matthew	AG0050	Ruggiero, Mathew	MA0400
Rothrock, Donna K.	NC2205	Royal, Susan L.	NY3725	Ruggiero, Matthew	MA1175
Rothshteyn, Eleonora	NY0270	Royce, Matthew M.	CA3270	Ruggles, Nathan	MO1900
Rothstein, William	NY0600	Roye, Nedra	OK0500	Ruggles, Patricia	NJ0200
Rothstein, William	NY0642	Roye, Tobin	CA0800	Ruhadze, Medea Namoradze	VA1350
Rotman, Sam	CA2810	Royem, Dominique	TX1000	Ruhstrat, Desiree	IN0900
Rotola, Albert	MO1250	Royer, Randall D.	SD0100	Ruiz, Gonzalo	NY1900
Rotondi, Jim	NY3785	Roylance, Mike	MA1400	Ruiz, Irma	IL2150
Rottenberg, Helene	MI1260	Roylance, Mike R.	MA0400	Ruiz, Kristen	NY2750
Rotter, James	CA0815	Roylance, Mike	CT0850	Ruiz, Norman	IL0720
Rotter, James	CA5300	Royle, Frances	AF0120	Ruiz, Norman	IL3150
Rottmayer, Chris A.	FL2000	Royo, Johanna	GA2100	Ruiz, Otmaro	CA5300
Roubal, Peter	IL2350	Royse, David M.	TN1710	Ruiz, Sergio	TX2250
Roueche, Michelle	TX3415	Royse, Dennis	CA0250	Ruiz-Bernal, Gabriel	DC0170
Roulet, Patrick E.	MD0850	Roze, Chris	CA5300	Rule, Charles	TN0700
Roulet, Rachel	MD0850	Rozek, Robert	AB0200	Rule, Tom	GA1260
Roulx, Rene	AI0190	Rozenblatt, David I.	NY1600	Rulli, Richard J.	AR0700
Round, Sue	AB0050	Rozie, Edward Rick	CT0650	Rumbley, Phil	TX3370
Rounds, Joseph	PA1050	Rozin, Alexander	PA3600	Rumbolz, Robert C.	WY0130
Rounds, Theodore	OH1100	Rozman, Jure	FL0200	Rummage, Robert F.	IL0750
Rounds, Tyler	OH1100	Rozsnyal, Zoltan	AB0200	Rummage, Robert	IL0850
Rounds, William	ME0500	Rozukalns, Thelma	NC1100	Rummel, Andrew	IL1150
Rous, Bruce	WV0400	Ruas, Laura M.	MD1000	Rumney, Jon	ND0250
Rousch, John	GA1070	Ruas, Laura	MD0400	Rumpel, Greg	AA0050
Rouse, Christopher	NY1900	Rubel, Mark B.	IL0800	Rumpf, Randy	WV0550
Rouse, Steve	KY1500	Rubel, Mark	IL2350	Rumph, Stephen	WA1050
Roush, Clark	NE0720	Rubens, Beth	DC0170	Rundlett, Jennifer	MD0610
Roush, Dean	KS1450	Rubenstein, Eliza N.	CA3350	Rundlett, Jennifer	MD0300
Rouslin, Daniel S.	OR1300	Rubenstein, Natasha	MO0650	Rundus, Katharin	CA0825
Rousseau, Beth	OR0500	Ruberg-Gordon, Susanne	AA0050	Rundus, Katharin	CA1900
Rousseau, Eugene E.	MN1623	Rubin, Anna I.	MD1000	Runefors, Bjorn	AE0120
Rousseau, Karine	AI0200	Rubin, Jennifer	MN0610	Runestad, Kurt	NE0200
Rousseau, Marcel	AI0190	Rubin, Joel E.	VA1550	Runge, Stephen M.	AE0050
Roussel, Marc	AI0190	Rubin, Justin H.	MN1600	Runion, Julie	NY3350
Roust, Colin	IL0550	Rubin, Lauren	OR0950	Runions, Greg	AG0250
Routen, I. J.	AR0750	Rubin-Bosco, Judi F.	NY2750	Runnels, Brent	GA1550
Routenberg, Scott	IN0150	Rubino, George	ME0150	Runnels, Jason	TX2600
Routhier, Christine	MA1650	Rubinoff, Kailan	NC2430	Runner, David C.	TN1150
Roux, Patrick	AG0400	Rubins, Peter	TX3530	Runner, Lisa	NC0050
Roux, Robert	TX2150	Rubins, Sherry D.	TX3530	Running, Donald	MA0510
Rovan, Joseph 'Butch'	RI0050	Rubinstein, Mark	OH1850	Running, Timothy	PA1750
Rovit, Arvilla	NY4150	Rubinstein, Matan	WI0865	Runyan, Donald	IL1612
Rovit, Peter M.	NY4150	Rubio, Douglas	NY3780	Runyan, William E.	CO0250
Rovkah, Pauline	PA0600	Rubio, Jill M.	NY3780	Runyon, Renee	MI2000
Row, Peter	MA1400	Rubrecht, Karl	LA0100	Ruo, Huang	NY3785
Rowan, Kami	NC0910	Rubright, Dan	MO0700	Ruocco, Phyllis	AR0550
Rowbottom, Terree	MO1250	Ruby, Eileen	MA1350	Ruoso-Loughlin, Alana	AG0130
Rowden, Charles H.	NY2550	Ruby, Eileen	MA1100	Rupcich, Matthew	NY0625
Rowe, Alex	UT0400	Ruby, Meg	MA2030	Rupert, Jeffrey M.	FL1800
Rowe, Alissa	LA0650	Ruby, Meg	NY2500	Rupert, Susan	TN1800
Rowe, Arthur	AB0150	Ruck, Jonathan C.	OK1350	Ruple, Eric K.	VA0600
Rowe, Booker	PA3250	Ruck, Tanya Kruse	WI0825	Rupp, Emily	NC1300
Rowe, Carl	VA1350	Rucker, Jennifer	OK0700	Rupp, Eric	AG0400
Rowe, Devonna	MD0600	Rucker, Lee	OK1330	Rupp, Jim	OH1850
Rowe, Elizabeth	MA1400	Rucker, Steve P.	FL1900	Rupp, Susan	AG0400
Rowe, Ellen H.	MI2100	Ruckert, George	MA1200	Rupprecht, Philip	NC0600
Rowe, Kimberly	PA3250	Ruckman, Robert	OH2120	Rus-Edery, Ilonka Livia	TX2250
Rowe, Kimberly	NJ1050	Rudari, David J.	WV0100	Ruscella, J. J.	VA1350
Rowe, Larry	CT0650	Rudd, Stephen W.	CA0950	Rusch, Rene	AI0150
Rowe, Lee	TN1850	Rudd, Wortley F. 'Wiff'	TX0300	Rusche, Marjorie M.	IN0910
Rowe, Martha	NM0310	Rudell, Alan M.	SC1000	Ruscoe, Christopher	CA5353
Rowe, Matthew	CA4100	Rudge, David T.	NY3725	Rush, John	OK0850
Rowe, Monk	NY1350	Rudich, Rachel	CA1050	Rush, John Phillip	OK1450
Rowe, Paul	OK0300	Rudich, Rachel E.	CA3650	Rush, Mark	AZ0500
Rowe, Paul	WI0815	Rudich, Rachel	CA0510	Rush, Stephen J.	MI2100
Rowe, Robert	NY2750	Rudkin, Ronald	NC1650	Rush, Tobias	CO0950
Rowe, Simon B.	CA5350	Rudman, Jessica	NY0600	Rush, Toby	OH2250
Rowe, Victoria	PA1250	Rudnytsky, Susan	OH2600	Rushen, Patrice Louise	CA5300
Rowehl, John	NY0900	Rudo, Sandy	CA2150	Rushing, Densi	OK1200
Rowell, Chester	TX3400	Rudoff, Mark	OH1850	Rushing, Randal J.	TN1680
Rowell, Chester D.	TX2295	Rudoff, Patricia L.	NY2550	Rushing, Steven J.	LA0650
Rowell, Frances	NJ0825	Rudoi, Natalie	PA2800	Rushing-Raynes, Laura	ID0050
Rowell, Melanie	SC1080	Rudolf, Homer	VA1500	Rushton, Christianne	AF0050
Rowell, Michael	GA0700	Rudolph, Gladys	OH2300	Rushton, David	AB0090
Rowell, Thomas L.	AL1300	Rudolph, John	AG0300	Rusinak, Dennis	AA0110
Rowell, Tracy	OH2150	Rudolph, John	AG0450	Rusinek, Michael	PA0550
Rowell, Tracy	OH1700	Rudolph, Jon	MN1120	Ruske, Eric	MA0400
Rowin, Elizabeth	MI1750	Rudolph, Jon	ND0600	Russakovsky, Alexander	MS0750
Rowland, Daniel	GA2150	Rudolph, Kathleen	AG0500	Russell, Alex	CA0250

Name	Code	Name	Code	Name	Code
Russell, Armand	HI0210	Ryczek, Karyl	MA1175	Sakata, Lorraine	CA5031
Russell, Benjamin A.	MD0475	Rydel, Robert	NC2000	Saker, James	NE0610
Russell, Brian	FL1900	Rydel, Robert E.	SC1200	Saker, Marilyn	MI0600
Russell, Brian E.	FL0050	Rydell, Claire	CA2750	Sakharova, Julia	MO1830
Russell, Bruce	CA0859	Ryder, Carol	CA2250	Sakins, Renate	PA3100
Russell, Carlton T.	MA2150	Ryder, Carol	CA1280	Sakomoto, Leo	CA0650
Russell, Carol	IN1450	Ryder, Christopher O.	VA1150	Saks, Toby	WA1050
Russell, Christopher	CA0250	Ryder, Donald D.	TN1710	Sala, Aaron J.	HI0210
Russell, Craig H.	CA0600	Ryder, Raymond T.	AZ0480	Sala, Karen	IL1240
Russell, Cynthia	TX0250	Ryder, Virginia	CA2250	Saladino, Jean	WI1100
Russell, David	MA2050	Ryder, William H.	LA0700	Salaff, Peter	OH0600
Russell, David	NC2420	Rydlinski, Candy	AK0150	Salamunovich, Paul	CA2800
Russell, Eileen Meyer	TX2650	Rydlinski, George	AK0150	Salanki, Hedi	FL2100
Russell, George	MA0260	Ryer-Parke, Kerry	MA2250	Salas, Jacqueline M.	CA0835
Russell, Jennifer	AZ0450	Ryga, Campbell	AB0060	Salas, Jorge Davi	TX2700
Russell, Joan	AI0100	Rygg, Beth	SD0580	Salas, Veronica	NY2105
Russell, John	CA0845	Ryker, Andrew	IA0550	Salathe, Leslie	NY0400
Russell, John K.	CA1520	Ryker, Pamela R.	WA0600	Salazar, Dennis A.	IL3370
Russell, John	CA1550	Rylatko, Oleg	VA1350	Salazar, Jason	MO0400
Russell, Joshua D.	IL1150	Rymal, Karen	AG0650	Salazar, Lauryn C.	CA5031
Russell, Mary Lou	TX2260	Ryner, Jayson	IA1170	Salazar, Rene	TX2250
Russell, Melinda	MN0300	Ryon, James P.	MD0520	Salazar, Shirley	IL0400
Russell, Nathan	TX3370	Ryon, James M.	LA0200	Salcedo, Angela	CT0600
Russell, Peggy	TX3400	Ryon, Jim	WV0550	Sale, Craig	IL0730
Russell, Ralph Anthony	NJ0175	Ryoo, Soyoung	DC0170	Salem, Ernest	CA0815
Russell, Robert A.	NC2440	Rytting, Bryce	UT0325	Salemink, Earl	WI0860
Russell, Robert J.	ME0500	Rytting, Lysa	UT0325	Salerni, Paul F.	PA1950
Russell, Scott	IN1450	Ryvkin, Valery	PA3250	Salerno, Christine	WI0808
Russell, Steve	MS0200	Rzasa, Karl	IL0750	Salerno, John	WI0808
Russell, Teresa P.	CA4850	S., Harvie	NY2150	Salerno, Julia	WA0250
Russell, Thomas	OH1800	Saad, Olga	IL2750	Salerno, Steven	NY0050
Russell, Tilden	CT0450	Saake, Garrett	NC0910	Sales, Christopher	FL1000
Russell, Timothy	AZ0100	Saavedra, Leonora	CA5040	Sales, Doricha	IN0900
Russell, Tracy	TX3400	Sabak, Linda	WV0800	Sales, Gregory	NE0590
Russell-Dickson, Marion	TX3450	Sabatella, Marc	CO0900	Sales, Humberto O.	VA0800
Russian, Dana S.	MA2050	Sabatella, Marc	CO0650	Salfen, Kevin	TX3410
Russo, Charles	NY2150	Sabatino, T. M.	PA1750	Saliba, Raphael	FL0570
Russo, Frank	MD0850	Sabin, Paula	CA0825	Salicandro, Anthony	PA3330
Russo, John	PA0125	Sabina, Leslie M.	NY3475	Salicondro, Anthony	NJ1050
Russo, Tadd	MD0600	Sabine, David	AA0032	Salido, Caroline	OH2050
Rust, Alan	CT0650	Sabino, Robert	CA5010	Saliers, James R.	TX3530
Rust, Douglas	MS0750	Sabo, Marlee	WI1150	Salisbury, Jeff	VT0250
Rust, Roberta	FL1125	Sabo, Vyki	FL0950	Salisbury, Jeff M.	VT0450
Rust, Rosalind	AL1150	Sabol, Julianna M.	NY4150	Salley, Keith P.	VA1350
Rust, Ty	CA2420	Sabourin, Carmen	AI0150	Sallis, Friedemann	AA0150
Rusu, Radu	TN0100	Sabre, Alejandro	CA3000	Sallmen, Mark	NY2650
Ruth, Byron	AZ0470	Sacalamitao, Melonie	CA4850	Salman, Randy Keith	IN0350
Ruth, Christopher	VA1350	Sacchini, Louis V.	IA0940	Salmirs, Michael	NY3705
Rutherford, Eric D.	KS0560	Sacco Belli, Jeanette	CA4625	Salmon, John C.	NC2430
Rutherford, Pearl	CO0150	Sacco, Kathy	PA0500	Salness, David	MD1010
Ruthmann, Alex	MA2030	Sachdev, Salil	MA0510	Saloman, Ora Frishberg	NY0250
Ruthrauff, Jeremy	IL0730	Sachen, Andrew	WI0830	Saloman, Ora Frishberg	NY0600
Ruthrauff, Jeremy	IL1085	Sachs, Carol	TX3515	Salsbury, Ben	FL1450
Rutkowski, Chris	IN0905	Sachs, Carolyn Reed	MS0100	Salsbury, Karen	KS0400
Rutkowski, Ellen	PA2200	Sachs, Daniel	OH0680	Salter, Michael A.	IL0840
Rutkowski, Gary	NY4460	Sachs, Joel	NY1900	Salter, Rebecca A.	GA1800
Rutkowski, Geoffrey	CA5060	Sachs, Michael	OH0600	Salter, Rebecca	GA1700
Rutkowski, Joanne	PA2750	Sachs, Stephen W.	MS0100	Salter, Tim	TX0075
Rutland, John P.	MO1790	Sackman, Marc L.	WI0806	Salters, Mark	CA0815
Rutland, Neil	NM0100	Sadak, John	NC2420	Saltzman, David	OH0300
Rutledge, Christine	IA1550	Sadeghpour, Mitra M.	WI0803	Saltzman, James A.	NJ0300
Rutledge, Kevin	FL1310	Sadin, Robert	NY2660	Saltzman, Peter	IL2750
Rutley, Thom	ID0140	Sadler, Cindy	TX2170	Saltzstein, Jennifer A.	OK1350
Rutman, Neil C.	AR0850	Sadler, Trevor	WI1150	Salucka, Ray	IA0930
Rutman, Paul	CT0650	Sadlier, David	VA0150	Salvador, Karen	MI2120
Rutschman, Carla J.	WA1250	Sadlier, Lelia	VA0150	Salvo, Joel	MN0040
Rutschman, Edward R.	WA1250	Sadoff, Ronald H.	NY2750	Salvo, Joel	MN1620
Ruttenberg, Samuel	PA3330	Sadovnik, Nir	NY2750	Salvo, Leonard P.	OH0100
Rutter, Bronwen	FL1300	Saelzer, Pablo	DC0170	Salwen, Barry	NC2440
Rutty, Alejandro	NC2430	Saelzer, Pablo	MD0550	Salyards, Shannon	IA0100
Rutz, Harold A.	TX0400	Saenz, Charles	OH0300	Salyards, Shannon	NE0610
Ruymann, Karen	MA0350	Saenz, Daniel	TX2250	Salyards, Shannon	IA1100
Ruzevic, Nikola	TX3420	Saenz, Daniel	TX2295	Salyer, Douglas W.	CT0200
Ruzicka, Carol	OH0600	Saeverud, Trond	ME0410	Salzenstein, Alan N.	IL0750
Ryabinin, Lev	GA0850	Saeverud, Trond	ME0430	Salzer, Rebecca	WI0350
Ryan, Anna	KS1000	Saeverud, Trond	ME0340	Salzman, Michael J.	NY1600
Ryan, Charlene	MA0260	Sage, Raymond	PA2750	Salzman, Timothy	WA1050
Ryan, Christine	PA1750	Sage, Robert	CA0250	Salzmann, Wayne W.	TX3510
Ryan, Donald	OK0850	Sage, Steve	CA1560	Samaan, Sherilyn	TN1350
Ryan, Ed	DE0200	Sagen, Dwayne P.	TN1850	Samaras, Stephanie	NJ0800
Ryan, Francis J.	OK1450	Sager, Gene	WY0150	Samarotto, Frank	IN0900
Ryan, James	MI2200	Sager, Stephanie	FL0930	Samarzea, Kelly J.	VA1000
Ryan, Jamie V.	IL0800	Saginario, Donald	FL1100	Samball, Michael L.	ID0050
Ryan, Josh T.	OH0200	Sagripanti, Andrea	DC0170	Sambo, Adrienne	MA2100
Ryan, Kate	AR0110	Sagues, Marie	CA1650	Sametz, Steven P.	PA1950
Ryan, Kathreen A.	IL0800	Saguiguit, Leo C.	MO1800	Sammarco, Donna	LA0450
Ryan, Kerri	PA3250	Sahagian, Robert	MA2300	Samolesky, Jeremy	AL0200
Ryan, Michael	CA5100	Sahai, Rita	CA0050	Sampen, John	OH0300
Ryan, P. Dianne	IL0850	Sahlin, Kay	MN1450	Sampen, Maria	WA1000
Ryan, Pamela	FL0850	Sahr, Barbara	OH0350	Sampsel, Laurie	CO0800
Ryan, Patrick	GA0050	Sahuc, Paul	CA3600	Sampson, Kenneth C.	TN0800
Ryan, Rebecca	PA2250	Sahuc, Paul N.	CA5060	Sampson, Larry	CA0300
Ryan, Russell	AZ0100	Saiki-Mita, Sabrina	HI0210	Sams, Jennifer	WI0100
Ryan, Sarah E.	MO1800	Sailor, Catherine	CO0900	Samsa, Louis	MN0150
Ryan, Steven	NJ0800	Sain, James Paul	FL1850	Samson, David	PA0650
Ryan, Thomas K.	OH0350	Saindon, Ed	MA0260	Samson, Louise	AI0210
Ryan, William E.	MI0900	Saito, Miki	OH0755	Samu, Attila	OH2290
Rybak, Alice	CO0900	Sajnovsky, Cynthia B.	GU0500	Samu, Lex	NY0646
Ryberg, J. Stanley	IL1085	Sakakeeny, George	OH1700	Samuel, Jamuna	NY3790
Rybolt, Scott	MO1710	Sakamoto, Haruyo	DC0170	Samuels, David	NY2740

Alphabetical Listing of Faculty

Name	Code	Name	Code	Name	Code
Samuels, David A.	MA0260	Sano, Stephen M.	CA4900	Sauerwein, Andrew Mark	MS0100
Samuels, David	MA1400	Santa, Lisa Garner	TX3200	Saul, Ken D.	OR0700
Samuels, Paul	OH1700	Santa, Matthew	TX3200	Saul, Walter B.	CA1860
Samuels, Ronald I.	PA1050	Sant'Ambrogio, Stephanie	NV0100	Saulnier, Jean	AI0200
Samuels, Sue	AL1150	Santana, Jose Ramos	DC0050	Saulsbury, Kate	IA1100
Samuelsen, Roy	IN1650	Santana, Lisa	CA1425	Saulter, Gerry	NY1275
Samuelson, Linda	MN1270	Santana, Priscilla	TX2800	Saunders, Bruce	TX3510
San Martin, Laurie A.	CA5010	Santer, Renee	NY2250	Saunders, Bruce	MA0260
Sanabria, Bobby	NY2660	Santerre, Joseph	MA0260	Saunders, David E.	ID0050
Sanabria, Bobby	NY2150	Santiago, Freddie	PR0100	Saunders, David	MN0300
Sanborn, Chase	AG0450	Santiago, Gabriella	FL1300	Saunders, Harris S.	IL3310
Sanborn, Pamela	NH0050	Santiago, Imer	TN1400	Saunders, John Jay	TX3420
Sanborn, Timothy	IN0250	Santiago, Michelle	AI0200	Saunders, Marianne	ID0070
Sanborne, Deborah	IA1300	Santiago, Nephtali	GA2150	Saunders, Martin	WV0400
Sanchez de Fuentes, Luisa	FL1125	Santinelli, Silvana	CO0250	Saunders, Mary	PA2750
Sanchez, Cynthia	TX2260	Santisi, Ray	MA0260	Saunders, Mary	MA0350
Sanchez, David	PR0115	Santo, Amanda M.	RI0100	Saunders, Meg	KY0550
Sanchez, Joseph W.	VA1500	Santo, Amanda M.	RI0101	Saunders, Meg	KY0450
Sanchez, Luis	TX2955	Santo, Joseph A.	DC0050	Saunders, Robert Allen	AZ0450
Sanchez, Paul	IL3550	Santogade, Peter	NY4200	Saunders, Ruth	MO1250
Sanchez, Pete	AL1195	Santore, Jonathan C.	NH0250	Saunders, Steven E.	ME0250
Sanchez, Rey	FL1900	Santorelli, Michael	TX1660	Sausser, Darrell	CA3800
Sanchez, Samuel L.	IN1450	Santorelli, Michael	TX3527	Savage Day, Susan	WI0840
Sanchez, Scott	AL1195	Santorelli, Shari	TX1660	Savage, Charles M.	OH1910
Sanchez, Scott	NH0110	Santoro, David N.	MA0260	Savage, Dylan C.	NC2420
Sanchez, Scott R.	MA1850	Santoro, Stephen	MA0260	Savage, Jeffrey R.	WA1150
Sanchez, Steve	CA0900	Santos, Denis Almeida	KY0400	Savage, John	OR1250
Sanchez, Steve	CA4150	Santos, E. Giovanni	CA2420	Savage, John	WA0900
Sanchez, Theresa	MS0360	Santos, Elias	PR0115	Savage, Karen Hsiao	WA1150
Sanchez-Behar, Alexander	OH0100	Santos, Erik	MI2100	Savage, Karen	VA1800
Sanchez-Gutierrez, Carlos	NY1100	Santos, Jackie	MA0260	Savage, Matt	NC2410
Sanchez-Samper, Alejandro	FL0650	Santos, John	CA1250	Savage, Roger W. H.	CA5031
Sand, Megan	OR0700	Santos, Nathan H.	PA1600	Savage, Ron	MA0260
Sandacata, Lisa	NY2400	Santos, Philip	CA0807	Savage, Samuel T.	IN0905
Sandagata, Lisa	NY5000	Santos, Philip	CA3520	Savage, Steve	CA2775
Sandahl, Thomas	OR0500	Santos-Neto, Jovino	WA0200	Savage, Susan	NC2420
Sandberg, Scott	ND0400	Santosuosso, Alma	AG0600	Savage, Timothy L.	NY3550
Sandborg, Jeff R.	VA1250	Santovetti, Francesca	MA1400	Savaria, Suzanne	OR0850
Sandborg, Marianne	VA1250	Saoud, Erick	AR0350	Savarino, Damian	PA2300
Sandefur, Lynn	FL1675	Sapadin, David	NY2105	Savarino, Tara	PA2300
Sanden, Paul	AA0200	Sapegin, Judith	CO0950	Savedoff, Allen M.	CA3300
Sander, Kurt L.	KY1000	Sapegin, Judy	CO0550	Savenkova-Krasin, Ludmila V.	MA2000
Sander, Marie	WI0300	Saperston, Bruce M.	UT0300	Savery, Robert	CO0150
Sanderbeck, Rande	TN0500	Sapieyevski, Jerzy	DC0010	Savige, David	VA0150
Sanders, Alice	AR0730	Sapochetti, Daniel	FL0365	Savige, David	VA1000
Sanders, Carolyn I.	AL1160	Saporito, James Frederick	NY2750	Saville, Kirt	UT0050
Sanders, Charles J.	NY2750	Sappa, Emily	MN1000	Savino, Richard	CA4150
Sanders, David	NY2400	Saradjian, Vagram	TX3400	Savino, Richard	CA0840
Sanders, Debbie	OR1150	Sarakatsannis, Leonidas N.	FL1745	Savko, Carolyn	TX3500
Sanders, Donald C.	AL0800	Saraquse, Sandy	CA0150	Savoie, Adrienne	AI0200
Sanders, George	CT0600	Sarata, Adam	OH2290	Savoy, Deborah Ann	NY3600
Sanders, Gregory L.	TX2960	Sarata, Adam	OH0100	Savoy, Thomas	NY3600
Sanders, Jack D.	CA3650	Sarath, Ed	MI2100	Savvidou, Paola	MO1800
Sanders, Jack	CA1050	Sarch, Kenneth	PA2150	Sawchuk, Judy-Lynn	AA0020
Sanders, Kevin	TN1680	Sarchet, Gregory B.	IL2150	Sawchuk, Terry M.	CO0800
Sanders, Linda	PA1050	Sargent, Daniel	CA0800	Sawyer, Charsie Randolph	MI0350
Sanders, Murl Allen	WA0200	Sargent, Glen	ME0440	Sawyer, Eric	MA0100
Sanders, Nancy King	TX2960	Sargent, Joseph	AL1200	Sawyer, John 'Del'	TN1850
Sanders, Paul	OH1850	Sargent, Philip	VA1350	Sawyer, John E.	AB0100
Sanders, Raphael P.	NY3780	Sargon, Simon	TX2400	Sawyer, Lisa Lee	MN0600
Sanders, Reginald L.	OH1200	Sargsyan, Vahan	PA0550	Sawyer, Scott	NC0650
Sanders, Robert	CA0815	Sariti, David J.	VA1550	Sawyer, Timothy K.	MN1280
Sanders, Robert	TX2100	Sarjeant, Lindsey B.	FL0600	Sawyer, Tony	NC0750
Sanders, Stephanie	VA0950	Sarjeant, Ronald	SC1050	Saxberg, Catherine	AG0130
Sanders, Steve	CA3270	Sark, Brady	OH0300	Saxe, Peter	IL0720
Sanders, Terrie	LA0550	Sarkisian, Rebecca	CA1850	Saxon, Kenneth N.	TX3515
Sanders, Trevor	AA0020	Sarkissian, Margaret	MA1750	Saxton, Judith	NC1650
Sanders, Trevor	AA0110	Sarma, Barbara	AG0500	Saya, Mark	CA2800
Sanders, Wayne	NY3560	Sarro, John	DE0150	Saya, Virginia	CA2800
Sandersier, Jeffrey	CA1850	Sarte, Ysabel	TX2955	Sayevich, Ben	MO1000
Sandford, Tim	ID0140	Sartini, Michael R.	MA0750	Saylor, Bruce S.	NY0642
Sandim, Carmen	CO0550	Sartor, David	TN1600	Saylor, Bruce	NY0600
Sandler, Felicia A.	MA1400	Sartori, Nicolo A.	PA1600	Saylor, Eric A.	IA0550
Sandness, Dorothy	MN0850	Sarver, Heidi	DE0150	Saylor, Jonathan	IL3550
Sandness, Marilyn I.	OH2250	Sarver, Julie	OH1350	Saylor, Mary Ann	PA2450
Sandomirsky, Gregory	MO1000	Sarver, Sarah	OK0750	Sayre, Charles L.	GA1700
Sandor, Alexander	WI0860	Sasaki, Ray	TX3510	Sayre, Elizabeth	PA3200
Sandor, Edward	GA2100	Saslaw, Janna K.	LA0300	Sayre, Jennifer	CA0600
Sandow, Greg	NY1900	Sasse, Christine T.	MO1900	Sayre, Lisa	GA1700
Sandred, Orjan	AC0100	Sassmannshaus, Kurt	OH2200	Sayre, Maya	OH2050
Sandroff, Howard	IL3250	Satava, Joseph F.	MD0475	Sayre, Paul	IL0780
Sands, Rosita M.	IL0720	Satloff, Laila	CA4460	Sayrs, Elizabeth P.	OH1900
Sands, Tracy	NE0200	Sato, Akira	TX2400	Sbarboro, Kathlyn	IL1085
Sands-Pertel, Judith	CA1500	Sato, Akira	TX3420	Scaffidi, Pete	CA0650
Sandstrom, Boden	MD1010	Sato, Junichi S.	IL0750	Scaffidi, Susan	CA0270
Sandvoss, Beth Root	AA0050	Sato, Kaori	NY3785	Scafide, Anthony	NY3765
Sandvoss, Beth Root	AA0150	Sato, Mari	OH0600	Scafidi, Cathy	PA1650
Sandy, Brent	IA1550	Satre, Paul J.	IL3150	Scagarella, Susan	CA3850
Sanford, David	MA1350	Satterfield, Sarah	FL0365	Scagnoli, Joseph R.	IN0100
Sanford, Elizabeth	CA3200	Satterlee, Robert S.	OH0300	Scales, Nicholas	TX3750
Sanford, O'Neil	VA0950	Satterwhite, Dan	FL1125	Scales-Neubauer, Sheri	OK0850
Sang, Barry R.	NC0350	Satterwhite, H. Dwight	GA2100	Scandrett, John F.	PA1600
Sang, Richard C.	NY0642	Satterwhite, Marc	KY1500	Scandrett, Lucy	PA3000
Sanger, Annette	AG0450	Satyendra, Ramon	MI2100	Scandrett, Lucy	PA1600
Sanguinetti, Melanie	AZ0440	Saucier, Catherine	AZ0100	Scanga, James V.	PA1450
Sanheim, Trent	AI0190	Sauer, Gregory D.	FL0850	Scanlan, Mary	MI0850
Sankaran, Trichy	AG0650	Sauer, Karen	MA2050	Scanlan, Roger	MI0350
Sanlikol, Mehmet	RI0200	Sauer, Maureen	IL0780	Scanling, Paul F.	GA1550
Sannerud, David	CA0835	Sauer, Thomas	NY2250	Scanlon, Andrew	NC0650
Sano, Anthony M.	NY3600	Sauer-Ferrand, Deborah	CA1860	Scanlon, Brian	CA3600

Name	Code	Name	Code	Name	Code
Scanlon, Patricia A.	MO1250	Scheck, Carey	IN1750	Schirmer, Timothy	IL2350
Scanlon, Russell J.	TX3175	Schedel, Margaret	NY3790	Schisler, Charles	GA0750
Scannura, Roger	AG0650	Scheer, Christopher	UT0300	Schlabach, Blake	IN1650
Scarambone, Bernardo	KY0550	Scheff, Fredric S.	RI0200	Schlabach, Eugene	IL3200
Scarano, Robert	CA0950	Scheffel, Gwendolyn W.	OH2450	Schlabach, John	OH1900
Scarano, Robert	CA3265	Scheffel, Rich	IA1800	Schlabach, Robert	TN0450
Scarano, Robert	CA5040	Scheffelman, Matthew	CO0200	Schlabach, Karen Bauman	KS0200
Scarbrough, Eric	OH1850	Scheffield, Eric	WI0865	Schlacks, Mary M.	OH1650
Scarbrough, Michael	TX0050	Scheffler, Jeff	IA0910	Schlaefer, Ellen Douglas	SC1110
Scarbrough, Russell	NY3350	Scheffler, Jeff E.	NE0610	Schlaffer, Machiko Ogawa	AL1200
Scarfullery, Rafael	VA1125	Schefter, Hillary	WY0200	Schlagel, Stephanie P.	OH2200
Scarfullery, Rafael	VA1400	Scheib, Curt A.	PA3000	Schlaikjer, Katie	CT0600
Scarlata, Randall S.	NY3790	Scheib, John W.	IN0150	Schlamb, Peter	MO1950
Scarlata, Randall	PA3600	Scheib, Joy	WI0845	Schlater, Lynn	NE0450
Scarlato, Michael	LA0050	Scheibe, Jo-Michael	CA5300	Schlatter, Carolyn	FL1430
Scarlett, Millicent	DC0100	Scheiby, Benedikte B.	NY2750	Schleeter, Bob	CA1150
Scarnati, Blase S.	AZ0450	Scheide, Kathleen	NJ1350	Schlegel, Amanda L.	MS0750
Scarnati, Rebecca Kemper	AZ0450	Scheider, Karen	KY1000	Schlei, Kevin	WI0825
Scarpa, Salvatore	NJ1050	Scheidker, Barbara	CA4850	Schleicher, Donald J.	IL3300
Scarpa, Tony	NY2400	Scheie, Timothy	NY1100	Schleicher, Elizabeth	IN0910
Scarpelli, Bonnie	ME0200	Scheirich, Lillian	AG0550	Schleifer, Martha Furman	PA3250
Scarpelli, Bonnie D.	ME0150	Schekman, Joel	MI1050	Schleiffer, Marlene J.	IN0700
Scarr, Susie	GA0050	Schelfer, James	NY2700	Schleis, Thomas H.	IL3300
Scartelli, Joseph P.	VA1100	Schell, Cheryl	KY0100	Schlesinger, Scott L.	NC2525
Scaruffi-Klispie, Cindy	FL0500	Schell, Mark	KY0100	Schlessinger, Laura	AA0050
Scatterday, Mark	NY1100	Schelle, Michael	IN0250	Schleuse, Paul	NY3705
Scattergood, Joanne	CT0050	Schellen, Nando	AZ0450	Schlicht, Ursel	NJ0950
Scavone, Gary	AI0150	Schempf, Kevin	OH0300	Schliff, Mary A.	CA0835
Scea, Paul	WV0750	Schempf, Ruthanne	NY3760	Schlimmer, Alexa Jackson	NC0930
Scearce, J. Mark	NC1700	Schempp, Marilyn	SD0050	Schlink, Robert	MA0260
Scelba, Anthony	NJ0700	Schenbeck, Lawrence A.	GA1900	Schlitt, Bill	CA0630
Schaaf, Gary D.	NE0590	Schenck-Crowne, Leah Naomi	PA1400	Schlitt, Bill	CA5150
Schaaf-Walker, Leah	IA0500	Schendel, Amy	IA1550	Schlitt, William	CA5355
Schaal, Joelle E.	OR0800	Schendel, Todd	IA0300	Schlitt, William	CA1425
Schaap, Phil	NY1900	Schene, Daniel	MO1950	Schloneger, Brent	OH2290
Schabas, Ezra	AG0450	Schenk, Kathryn E.	MN0610	Schloneger, Matthew	KS0500
Schabloski, Lana	AF0120	Schenkel, Steve	MO1950	Schloss, Andrew	AB0150
Schachman, Marc H.	MA0400	Schenkman, Byron	WA0200	Schloss, David Lee	TX1725
Schachnick, Gilson	MA0260	Schenly, Paul	OH0600	Schlosser, Milton	AA0110
Schachter, Benjamin	PA0400	Schepker, Kay	LA0650	Schlosser, Roberta	NY3705
Schachter, Carl	NY0642	Schepkin, Sergey	MA0400	Schlueter, Charles	MA1400
Schachter, Carl	NY1900	Schepkin, Sergey	PA0550	Schmalenberger, Sarah	MN1625
Schachter, Carl	NY2250	Schepper, Stephen	IL1750	Schmalfeldt, Janet	MA1900
Schachter, Daniela	MA0260	Schepps, David M.	NM0450	Schmalzbauer, Julie A.	IL2300
Schaefer, Carl	CA0815	Scherer, Paul	IL1520	Schmann, Phillip M.	KY0550
Schaefer, Donn	UT0250	Scherline, Janine	NY3775	Schmauk, Doris	PA0650
Schaefer, Elaine	CA1300	Scherling, John	KS0210	Schmeling, Paul	MA0260
Schaefer, G. W. Sandy	NE0050	Schermer, Stephen	WA1000	Schmelz, Peter	MO1900
Schaefer, John	MO1000	Schermerhorn, David	NC1450	Schmid, Alice	GA0200
Schaefer, Lora	IL0550	Schernikau, Burt	NE0450	Schmid, Alice	GA0950
Schaefer, Phillip	MO2000	Scherperel, Loretta	FL0200	Schmid, Ilo	OR1010
Schaeffer, Greg	AZ0400	Scherr, Bernard	TX0900	Schmid, John	IN0250
Schaeffer, Vicki J.	OK1350	Scherschell, Rebecca	TX0370	Schmid, Karen	NY0400
Schaerrer, Bart	UT0050	Scherzinger, Nicolas	NY4150	Schmid, Lucinda	WY0115
Schafer, Carl	CA0450	Scherzinger, Peter	AG0150	Schmid, William	WI0825
Schafer, Erika L.	TN1700	Schettler, Sarah M.	LA0800	Schmid, William	GA0950
Schaff, Michael P.	NY3780	Schettler, William	LA0800	Schmidt, Alan G.	NY1220
Schaffer, Amanda	NC0300	Scheuerell, Casey	MA0260	Schmidt, Carl B.	MD0850
Schaffer, Candler	FL0800	Scheuerell, Doug	OR1050	Schmidt, Carol	MO1950
Schaffer, Donna	MS0050	Scheusner, Marsha	TN0350	Schmidt, Carsten	NY3560
Schaffer, John D.	WI0815	Scheusner, Ronald	TN0350	Schmidt, Catherine M.	MN1700
Schaffer, Richard	NY2950	Schiano, Michael	CT0650	Schmidt, Charles	IL0100
Schaffer, William R.	AL0200	Schiavo, Joseph C.	NJ1100	Schmidt, Daniel	CA2950
Schaft, Glenn	OH2600	Schiavone, David C.	NY3717	Schmidt, Daniel Joseph	AZ0450
Schag, Shane	NY2150	Schiavone, David C.	NY0400	Schmidt, David	FL1750
Schager, Christopher J.	MS0570	Schiavone, David C.	NY4320	Schmidt, David	AZ0350
Schall, Noah	NY1450	Schiavone, David	NY4460	Schmidt, David A.	FL0400
Schaller, Edward	IL1750	Schick, Steven	NY2150	Schmidt, Donald	AJ0150
Schaller, Thilo	AA0200	Schick, Steven	CA5050	Schmidt, Doris D.	NY1220
Schallert, Gary	KY1550	Schiel, Melissa	WA0050	Schmidt, Eric	CA5300
Schallock, Michael G.	NC2600	Schietroma, Robert J.	TX3420	Schmidt, Fred	MA0260
Schamber, Don	CA3050	Schiff, David	OR0900	Schmidt, Henry L.	PA2550
Schane-Lydon, Cathy	MA1850	Schiff, Lauren	NY1900	Schmidt, Jack W.	PA0900
Schani, Steve	WI0804	Schildkret, David	AZ0100	Schmidt, James	NC0450
Schankin, Nora	MI0500	Schildt, Matthew	OH1100	Schmidt, Jody	OR0950
Schantz, Allen P.	CO0150	Schildt, Matthew C.	CO0050	Schmidt, John C.	TX3175
Schantz, Cory Neal	SD0550	Schilf, Paul R.	SD0050	Schmidt, John R.	PA2050
Schantz, Jack	OH2150	Schiller, Andrew	MI1950	Schmidt, Juliana	WI0855
Schantz, Monica	PA2450	Schiller, Benjie-Ellen	NY1450	Schmidt, Karl	CA1800
Schantz, Richard	PA2450	Schiller, Caroline	AD0050	Schmidt, Margaret	AZ0100
Schaphorst, Kenneth	MA1400	Schiller, Mary	OH0600	Schmidt, Michael P.	MN0950
Schapman, Marc	IL2910	Schiller, Mary	OH2150	Schmidt, Nolan	NE0200
Scharf, Deborah	TX2800	Schilling, Arnie	IA0800	Schmidt, Patrick	FL0700
Scharf, Margaret	OH0650	Schilling, Korin	IN1450	Schmidt, Russell	UT0250
Scharf, Margaret R.	OH0200	Schilling, Richard	MA2030	Schmidt, Stephen	VA1600
Scharf, Scott L.	IL2100	Schilling, Travis	MN0300	Schmidt, Steven	CA3800
Scharfenberger, Paul E.	NH0110	Schillinger, Christin M.	OH1450	Schmidt, Susan	MO1120
Scharfstein, Tanya	NY2400	Schilperoort, Anne	WA1400	Schmidt, Timothy	NY2950
Scharnberg, William	TX3420	Schimek, John	OK0700	Schmidt, Timothy A.	MO1500
Scharper, Alice	CA4410	Schimek, John	OK0750	Schmidt, Timothy R.	IA1750
Scharron, Eladio	FL1800	Schimmel, Carl W.	IL1150	Schmidt, Tracey	PA0250
Schatt, Matthew D.	OH1100	Schimming, Paul	MN0610	Schmieder, Eduard	PA3250
Schattschneider, Adam	OH0250	Schimming, Paul	MN1500	Schmitt, Clinton	TN1350
Schauer, Elizabeth	AZ0500	Schimpf, Peter	CO0550	Schmitt, James	OR0500
Schauer, Jerry	PA0450	Schindelmann, Marco	CA5150	Schmitz, Alan W.	IA1600
Schauert, Paul W.	MI1750	Schindler, Allan	NY1100	Schmitz, Eric B.	NY3770
Schaufele, Fritz	OH0650	Schindler, Bonnie	CA3600	Schmitz, Michael	CA3270
Schecher, Mary	WI0050	Schindler, Karl W.	AZ0470	Schmunk, Richard	CA5300
Schechter, Dorothy E.	CA0550	Schipull, Larry D.	MA1350	Schmunk, Richard	CA1900
Schechter, John M.	CA5070	Schirm, Ronald	AG0600	Schmutte, Peter J.	IN1650

Name	Code	Name	Code	Name	Code
Schnack, Michael B.	PA2550	Schranze, Jane	TN1200	Schulze, Hendrik	IL3300
Schnaible, Mark	NY0500	Schranze, Lenny	TN1680	Schulze, Michael	CO0900
Schnauber, Thomas	MA0900	Schreck, Corlyn	MI1150	Schulze, Otto	IN0005
Schneckenburger, Brian	MD0175	Schreck, Judith	SD0050	Schulze, Sean	OH0600
Schneeloch-Bingham, Nancy	NC0050	Schreckengost, John	IN1750	Schulze, Theodora	IN0005
Schneider, Benjamin D.	ND0150	Schreffler, Gibb	CA3650	Schulze-Johnson, Virginia	NJ0300
Schneider, Bernard	FL0500	Schreiber, David R.	WI0200	Schumacher, Craig	AZ0490
Schneider, Brandt	CT0550	Schreiber, Paul	MS0560	Schumacher, Judy	OR0150
Schneider, Charles	NY1400	Schreibman, Janice	IN0907	Schumacker, Meghan	IA0550
Schneider, David	KY1000	Schreier, David	FL1800	Schumaker, Adam	MI1150
Schneider, David	NJ0175	Schreier, Kathleen	IA0790	Schumaker, Adam T.	MI2250
Schneider, David E.	MA0100	Schreiner, Frederick	PA3710	Schumaker, Alan	NY2550
Schneider, Doug	OR0850	Schreiner, Gregory	CA4450	Schuman, Leah	IL3450
Schneider, Eugene	AA0040	Schreiner, Gregory	CA0859	Schuman, Mohamad	MS0750
Schneider, Jill L.	WA1150	Schrempel, Martha	PA2450	Schuman, Susan	NY3717
Schneider, Jim	CA1550	Schreuder, Joel T.	NE0050	Schumann, Laura E.	OH1650
Schneider, John	CA2700	Schriemer, Dale	MI0900	Schumann, Michelle	TX3415
Schneider, Lisa A.	AL1160	Schrock, Karl	MI2250	Schunks, Dan	MO0750
Schneider, M. Christine	IA0550	Schrock, Scharmal K.	LA0650	Schupp, Roger B.	OH0300
Schneider, Mary K.	MI0600	Schrock, Scharmal	IN0900	Schuppener, James	TX1700
Schneider, Matt	WA0800	Schroder, Lisa	CA2050	Schuppener, Mark	TX3520
Schneider, Wayne J.	VT0450	Schroeder, Angela	AA0100	Schurger, Phillip	IN0700
Schneider-Gould, Beth Ilana	AG0070	Schroeder, Dave	NY2750	Schuricht, Paul	CA1000
Schneiderman, John	CA2390	Schroeder, David	AF0100	Schuring, Martin	AZ0100
Schneiderman, John H.	CA5020	Schroeder, Jerry	MN1120	Schuster, James	MI2120
Schneiders, Carson	KY0550	Schroeder, Joy A.	MI1500	Schuster-Craig, John	MI0900
Schneller, Aric	TX2250	Schroeder, Karen	OH1350	Schutt, Jackie T.	IL2050
Schneller, Pamela	TN1850	Schroeder, Kelly M.	NY2650	Schuttenberg, Emily Amanda	NC0350
Schneller, Roland	TN1850	Schroeder, Linda	AF0120	Schuttenheim, Tom	CT0650
Schnettler, John	TN0050	Schroeder, Lisa	CA0859	Schuttenhelm, Thomas	CT0050
Schnipke, Richard	OH1850	Schroeder, Matthew	WI1150	Schutz, Rachel	HI0210
Schnitter, David	NY2660	Schroeder, Michael	CA4150	Schuyler, Philip	WA1050
Schnittgrund, Tammy	SD0500	Schroeder, Phillip J.	AR0300	Schwab, David	TN0260
Schnitzer, Dana	MA1350	Schroeder, Thomas	TX1400	Schwabe, Jonathan C.	IA1600
Schober, David	NY0642	Schroeder, Waylon	IL1500	Schwaber, Lorian Stein	WI0250
Schocker, Gary M.	NY2750	Schroeder-Garbar, Lacy	IL1085	Schwaberow, Denise	IN0905
Schodowski, Timothy	TX3370	Schroepfer, Mark	MN1625	Schwaegler, Susan	IL0300
SchoederDorn, Jill	CO0300	Schroerlucke, Leslie	CA5040	Schwaegler, Susan	IL0100
Schoeff, Bethany	WA0250	Schroth, Robyn	VA1350	Schwagerl, Renee	MN1620
Schoeff, Kristin	OH1850	Schub, Andre-Michel	NY2150	Schwanda, Grace	MI0850
Schoen, Kathleen	AA0110	Schuberg, Margaret	MT0400	Schwandt, Jacquelyn Joy	AZ0450
Schoen, Theodore A.	MN1600	Schubert, Barbara	IL3250	Schwandt, John	OK1350
Schoen, Thomas	AA0110	Schubert, David T.	OH2450	Schwantes, Melody	NC0050
Schoenbach, Peter Julian	NY3725	Schubert, John	MI0200	Schwarm-Glesner, Elizabeth	CO0550
Schoenbeck, Sara	CA3800	Schubert, Linda	WI0922	Schwartz, Agnes Szekely	CA1265
Schoenbeck, Sara	CA1000	Schubert, Peter	AI0150	Schwartz, Andrew	NJ0825
Schoenberg, Kathe	NJ0550	Schubkegel, Joyce C.	MN1030	Schwartz, Andrew	MA1175
Schoendorff, Matthew	MI2200	Schuchat, Charles	IL2200	Schwartz, Ann Marie Barker	NY3600
Schoenecker, Ann Elise	WI1100	Schuchat, Charles	IL0550	Schwartz, Anne-Marie	NY3680
Schoenfeld, Alice	CA5300	Schueller, Rodney C.	TX3175	Schwartz, Cornelia	NH0110
Schoenfield, Paul	MI2100	Schuesselin, John C.	MS0700	Schwartz, Daniel	OK1350
Schoenhals, Joel	MI0600	Schuessler, Philip T.	LA0650	Schwartz, Elizabeth	NY2450
Schoening, Benjamin S.	WI0801	Schuett, Mike	AA0050	Schwartz, Elliott S.	ME0200
Schoenlein, Laila	CA4460	Schuette, Rebecca C.	IL0800	Schwartz, Paul	FL1900
Schoepflin, Judith	WA1350	Schuetz, Daniel	IL1150	Schwartz, Richard I.	VA1750
Schoeppach, Brad W.	NY2750	Schuetz, Jennifer Hilbish	IL1200	Schwartz, Richard A.	LA0650
Schoessler, Tim	WY0130	Schuetz, Jennifer Hilbish	OH0950	Schwartz, Robert	CA2950
Scholfield, Faith	AG0550	Schuetz, Shaun	TN1000	Schwartz, Robert	CA4625
Scholl, Christopher	OH0300	Schuetz, Shaun Nicholas	TN1710	Schwartz, Roberta Freund	KS1350
Scholl, Ellen Strba	OH0300	Schulenberg, David	NY1900	Schwartz, Sandra M.	WV0750
Scholl, Gerald	KS1450	Schulenberg, David L.	NY4500	Schwartz, Sergiu	GA0550
Scholl, Janet	MN1280	Schuler, Nico S.	TX3175	Schwartz, Terry R.	IL3550
Scholl, Tim	TX2550	Schulkind, Laura	CO0625	Schwartz-Kates, Deborah	FL1900
Scholtz, Clare	AG0450	Schulman, Jory	CA4450	Schwartzberg, Edward	MN1623
Scholwin, Richard M.	NE0590	Schulte, Dan	OR0850	Schwartzhoff, Gary R.	WI0803
Scholz, Dan	AC0100	Schulte, Gregory	AJ0150	Schwartzman, Kenneth	NY2105
Scholz, David M.	CA0800	Schultz, Andrew J.	NE0150	Schwarz, David	TX3420
Scholz, Robert	MN1450	Schultz, Anna	CA4900	Schwarz, Timothy J.	PA1950
Scholz, Steve	CA1560	Schultz, Arlan N.	AA0200	Schwarze, Penny	MN0450
Scholz-Carlson, Miriam	MN1450	Schultz, Blaine	KS0100	Schwede, Walter	WA1250
Schons, Suzanne	MN1625	Schultz, Dale	TX2200	Schween, Astrid	MA1350
Schonthal, Ruth	NY2400	Schultz, David	TX0700	Schweikert, Eric	IN0905
Schooler, Jason	OR0150	Schultz, Diane Boyd	AL1170	Schweingruber, Eric J.	PA3250
Schooler, Jason	OR0400	Schultz, Eric	CA0900	Schweitz, Kurt	IL3550
Schooler, Jason G.	OR1100	Schultz, James	NE0250	Schweitzer, Kenneth	DE0150
Schooley, John	WV0300	Schultz, Kirsten M.	AG0500	Schweitzer, Kenneth	MD1100
Schoolfield, Robnet	SC0200	Schultz, Lucinda D.	GA0200	Schweizer, Kiel Jay	AK0100
Schoon, Marcus	MI1750	Schultz, Marc	NY2800	Schwendener, Ben	MA1175
Schoon, Marcus	MI2200	Schultz, Margaret	NE0460	Schwendener, Benjamin	MA1400
Schoonmaker, Bruce W.	SC0750	Schultz, Michael	NC2410	Schwendinger, Laura Elise	WI0815
Schoonmaker, Gail	SC0750	Schultz, Paul	DC0150	Schweninger, Virginia	VA1400
Schoonmaker, Matt	WV0300	Schultz, Robert D.	MA2000	Schwindt, Dan	CO0830
Schopp, James A.	IL2050	Schultz, Ryan	IL2300	Schwing-Braun, Eraine	AG0450
Schorr, Timothy B.	WI1100	Schultz, Ryan	WA1000	Schwoebel, David	VA1150
Schorsch, Kathleen	CA5300	Schultz, Stephen	PA0550	Schwoebel, Sandy	AZ0480
Schott, Kimberly	ND0500	Schultz, Steve	IA0400	Schyman, Garry	CA5300
Schotten, Yizhak	MI2100	Schultz, Thomas J.	CA4900	Scialla, Carmen J.	NJ0760
Schotting, MaryBeth Glasgow	PA0550	Schultz, Wendy E.	NE0150	Scialla, Peter	NY4200
Schottman, Margret	PA0500	Schultz, Willard	AA0150	Sciannella, David	DC0100
Schou, Larry B.	SD0600	Schultz, Willis Jackson	MA0260	Sciarrotta, Jo-Ann	NJ0175
Schowalter, Elise Anne	KY1000	Schultze, Andrew W.	IL0720	Scifres, Maxie	IL1200
Schoyen, Jeffrey G.	MD0800	Schulz, Blanche	IL0600	Scifres, Sam G.	IL1200
Schrader, Barry	CA0510	Schulz, Maria	TN0350	Scime, Gregory	NJ1160
Schrader, David D.	IL0550	Schulz, Mark Alan	OH1350	Scinta, Frank	NY0400
Schraer-Joiner, Lyn	NJ0700	Schulz, Patrick	CA1750	Sciolla, Anne	PA3330
Schram, Albert George	FL1125	Schulz, Paul	MN1625	Scism, William	MA0260
Schramm, Barbara	MN0600	Schulz, Riccardo	PA0550	Scivally, Riner	CA3300
Schramm, David	CA1850	Schulz, Robert	MA0950	Scivally, Riner	CA3500
Schrankler, Helene	WI0804	Schulz, Russell E.	TX0750	Sclater, James	MS0400
Schranz, Karoly	CO0800	Schulze, Hendrik	TX3420	Scofield, John L.	NY2750

Name	Code	Name	Code	Name	Code
Scoggin, David	OR0950	Scruggs, Richard J.	TN0250	Seipp, Larry	VA1125
Scoles, Philip	TX2295	Scruggs, Tara A.	TN0250	Seis, Catherine	GA2300
Scoles, Shannon	MI2250	Scudder, Howard	TN0050	Seitz, Carole J.	NE0160
Scollard, Dan T.	OR0700	Scull, Erik	IN0907	Seitz, Christine	IN0910
Scolnik, Julia	MA1175	Scully, Francis	LA0560	Seitz, Christine	MO1800
Scolnik, Nina	CA5020	Scully, Joseph D.	IL0450	Seitz, Christine L.	IN0550
Score, Clyde D.	AZ0510	Scully, Lawrence L.	GA2150	Seitz, Diana	KS1400
Scorza, Darren	IL1085	Scully, Mathew	CA3950	Seitz, Elizabeth	MA0350
Scott Goode, Mary	TX2850	Scurich, Kelly	OH2600	Seitz, Jeanette	WI1150
Scott Hoyt, Janet	AA0100	Scurto-Davis, Debra	NJ1350	Seitz, Noah	OR0750
Scott, Aaron D.	PA1400	Seabra, James	RI0200	Seitz, Paul T.	MO1800
Scott, Allen	OK0800	Seabrook, Deborah	AG0600	Sekelsky, Michael J.	MO1790
Scott, Arvin	GA2100	Seachrist, Denise A.	OH1100	Sekhon, Baljinder S.	FL2000
Scott, Carla A.	CO0275	Seagle, Andy	AZ0440	Sekino, Keiko	NC0650
Scott, Caryl Mae	CA4300	Seagrave, Charles	CA3250	Selden, Ken	OR0850
Scott, Chris	IL0100	Seal, Mary Griffin	FL0680	Seldess, Zachary	NY0500
Scott, Christopher	OH0755	Seale, Sheryl	AZ0150	Seldon, Vicki A.	TX2100
Scott, Cindy	LA0800	Seales, Marc	WA1050	Selesky, Evelyn C.	NY2450
Scott, Daniel E.	TX0300	Seals, Debra	PR0125	Seletsky, Robin	NY1400
Scott, Dave	CA4700	Seamons, Nathan	UT0190	Self, Cale	GA2130
Scott, David	CT0800	Searchfield, John W.	AA0150	Self, James	CA5300
Scott, David	IA1390	Searing, Harry G.	NJ0800	Self, Stephen	MN0250
Scott, David L.	CA5150	Searle, David	DC0050	Self, Susanna	MO0700
Scott, David	TX0150	Searles, Julie	MA2150	Selfridge-Field, Eleanor	CA4900
Scott, David	MA0260	Sears, E. Ann	MA2150	Seliger, Bryce M.	OR0750
Scott, David R.	LA0350	Sears, Peggy	CA0650	Seligman, Jonathan D.	MD0520
Scott, Debra L.	TX2700	Seaton, Douglass	FL0850	Seligman, Susan	NY3760
Scott, Diane	PA3150	Seaton, Gayle	FL0850	Sella, Gillian Benet	OH2200
Scott, F. Johnson	VA0750	Seaton, Kira J.	OH0755	Selle, William	NC0050
Scott, Frank	AZ0450	Seaton, Lynn	TX3420	Selleck, Maria	FL1310
Scott, Gary	OH0755	Seaward, Jeffery A.	CA1290	Sellers, Crystal Y.	OH0250
Scott, Gary	CA2550	Seay, Sandra	AR0110	Sellers, Elizabeth A.	CA0835
Scott, Geri	WY0130	Sebastian, Mario	CA0150	Sellers, Joel	CA0815
Scott, Gina	TN1660	Sebba, Rosangela Yazbec	MS0500	Sellers, Lucy Bell	ME0270
Scott, J. B.	FL1950	Sebring, Richard	MA1400	Sellitti, Anne	NC0350
Scott, James	AA0150	Secan, Steve	OH0350	Sellitti, Anne	NC2205
Scott, James C.	TX3420	Secco, Leonardo	AI0200	Selter, Scott	CO0830
Scott, Jan	LA0350	Sech, Svetlana	AA0020	Selvaggio, Frederick	IL3150
Scott, Janet	IL2970	Seckel, Tamara J.	OH1200	Selvaggio, Robert	OH1100
Scott, Janet	MO1250	Secor, Greg	MI1050	Selvaggio, Robert	OH0600
Scott, Jason B.	VA1500	Secor, Greg	MI0900	Semanic, Paul A.	IL0840
Scott, Jeffrey	NJ0800	Secor, Robert	CA4300	Semanik, Timothy	MN0300
Scott, Jenni Olson	CA1000	Secrest, Glenda	AR0500	Semegen, Daria	NY3790
Scott, Jennifer	CO0300	Secrest, Jon	AR0500	Seminatore, Gerald	CA3600
Scott, Jennifer	NY2900	Secrist, Phylis	TN1710	Semmens, Richard	AG0500
Scott, Jerry	KY0450	Sedatole, Kevin	MI1400	Semmes, Carol	IL2300
Scott, John C.	TX3420	Sedgley, Tiffany	UT0250	Semmes, Laurie R.	NC0050
Scott, Joseph	MA0600	Sedloff, Michael	FL0800	Senasi, Karlo	AL0300
Scott, Judith G.	CA0835	Sedonis, Robert D.	OH1850	Senasi, Karlo	AL0800
Scott, Judson	WA1000	Seebacher, Robert	AL1300	Senders, Warren	MA1400
Scott, Julia	PA1450	Seeber, Todd M.	MA0400	Sendler, Greg	FL1300
Scott, Julia K.	TX2400	Seeber, Todd	MA1400	Senedak, Irene	CT0450
Scott, Karla	MD0900	Seedorf, Bethany	IA1300	Senko, Robert	NY3770
Scott, Kenneth	NY2660	Seeds, Laurel M.	OH1100	Senn, Geoff	MN0040
Scott, Kevin	NY3000	Seeger, Anthony	CA5031	Senn, Takako Seimiya	MN0610
Scott, Kraig	WA1100	Seeger, Brian	LA0300	Senn, Takako	MN1300
Scott, Kraig	WA1300	Seeger, Brian	LA0800	Sentgeorge, Aaron Jacob 'Jake'	MO1790
Scott, L. Brett Cornish	OH2200	Seegmiller, Lisa	UT0150	Seo, Ju Ri	IL3300
Scott, Laurie	MN1600	Seel, Nancy	NY3725	Seo, Minjung	IL3500
Scott, Laurie	TX3510	Seeley, Gilbert	OR0400	Seo, Seungah	CA5550
Scott, Levone Tobin	NC2430	Seeley, Jeffery	NY1150	Sepe, Deborah	NY0050
Scott, Louise H.	AZ0450	Seeling, Ellen	CA5000	Seppanen, Keith C.	CA0800
Scott, Maggie	MA0260	Seeman, Faye	IL3550	Sepulveda, Charles	PR0115
Scott, Marshall	KY1550	Seeman, Rebecca	CA5353	Sepulveda, Richardo	IL1750
Scott, Mary Anne Spangler	IN0250	Seeman, Sharon	NJ0750	Sepulveda, Sonja	NC2205
Scott, Michael E.	TN1380	Seeman, Sonia T.	TX3510	Seraphinoff, Richard M.	IN0900
Scott, Michael	CA1900	Seerup, Mark	MN0610	Serbo, Rico	MI2100
Scott, Michael	MA0260	Seesholtz, John C.	CO0250	Serebryany, Vadim	AL0450
Scott, Michele	UT0050	Segal, Rachel	CO0650	Serfaty, Aaron	CA5300
Scott, P. Mark	TX3420	Segal, Uriel	IN0900	Serfaty, Aaron	CA0510
Scott, Paul	NJ1400	Segall, Christopher	AL1170	Serghi, Sophia	VA0250
Scott, Rebecca	NY1900	Seggelke, Martin H.	CA4200	Sergi, James	NY3500
Scott, Ronald	TX2930	Segger, Joachim	AA0035	Sergi, James	NY4500
Scott, Rosemary	GA0250	Seglem-Hocking, Sara	DE0150	Serkin, Peter	NY0150
Scott, Sandra C.	GA1600	Segrest, Linda H.	MS0550	Serkin, Peter	MA1175
Scott, Sarah	CA5355	Seguin, Philip	AG0650	Serna, Phillip Woodrow	IN1750
Scott, Shannon	WA1150	Sehman, Melanie	NY3250	Sernyk, Glenn	AG0130
Scott, Sheila	AC0050	Sehmann, Karin M.	KY0550	Serpas, Roberto	AA0050
Scott, Stanley	CT0450	Seidel, John	IN0150	Serrin, Bret E.	TX3420
Scott, Stephen	CO0200	Seidel, William	GA1700	Servant, Gregory W.	AF0100
Scott, Stuart	MI1250	Seidl, Teresa	WI0350	Servias, David	OR0700
Scott, Tara	AF0050	Seidman, Barbara	DC0100	Sescilla, Mark Christopher	ID0140
Scott, Tara	AF0120	Seidman, Barbara	DC0170	Seshadri, Jaleen	CA4425
Scott, Tatiana	CA0150	Seidman, Mitch	MA0260	Seskler, Sezi	PA0350
Scott, Tatiana	CA0840	Seidman, Naomi K.	PA2750	Sesler, Betsey	NC2000
Scott, Vicky	MO0775	Seidman, William	NY2750	Sessa, Thomas	OR0150
Scott, William	KY1550	Seifert, Dustin	NM0100	Sessa, Thomas P.	OR1100
Scott, Yumi Ninomiya	PA0850	Seifert, James	AZ0440	Sessions, Timothy	PA1950
Scott, Yumi N.	PA3250	Seifert, Kim	PA2550	Sessler, Eric S.	PA0850
Scott-Moncrieff, Suzannah	NY2750	Seifert, Kimberly	PA2450	Sessoms, Sydney	NC1150
Scotto, Ciro G.	FL2000	Seifried, Denver	OH2450	Sestrick, Timothy	PA1400
Scovill, Janet R.	MN1280	Seigel, Andrew	NY3725	Seter, Ronit	MD0650
Scowcroft, Barbara Ann	UT0250	Seigel, Lester C.	AL0300	Seto, Mark	CT0100
Scraper, Joel	SC1100	Seiger, Jennifer	NC1700	Settel, Zack	AI0200
Scriggins, Elizabeth	AA0050	Seigfried, Karl E.	WI0250	Setter, Terry A.	WA0350
Scrima, Vin	MA2010	Seighman, Gary B.	TX3350	Settle, David	KS1250
Scripp, Lawrence	MA1400	Seiler, David E.	NH0350	Settlemires, Joseph	OK1400
Scrivner, Matthew	MO0050	Seiler, Mayumi	AG0300	Settoon, Donna	LA0080
Scrivner, Scott	SC0420	Seiler, Richard D.	LA0770	Setzer, Ann	NY2750
Scroggins, Sterling Edward	DC0010	Sein Siaca, Maria P.	PR0115	Setzer, Ann	NY2250

Alphabetical Listing of Faculty

Name	Code	Name	Code	Name	Code
Setzer, Philip E.	NY3790	Shanklin, Bart	IL3500	Shaw, Olive	AF0120
Setziol, Paul	CA1550	Shanklin, Richard L.	OH2150	Shaw, Patricia	AF0120
Seufert, Dana	CA2050	Shankman, Ira	NY2750	Shaw, Paul	MN1623
Seuffert, Maria C.	GA0160	Shankman, Nancy Ellen	NY2750	Shaw, Rick	CA3500
Sevadjian, Therese	AI0150	Shankovich, Robert L.	PA1050	Shaw, Roger	CA3200
Sever, Allan	NY1450	Shanley, Helen A.	TX0300	Shaw, Ronnie	WV0550
Sever, Ivan	MA0260	Shanley, Richard A.	TX0300	Shaw, Timothy B.	PA2800
Sever, Melanie M.	WI0860	Shanley, Steven	IA0300	Shawn, Allen	VT0050
Severance, David	WA1150	Shannon, Adrienne	AG0250	Shay, Gayle D.	TN1850
Severing, Richard	WI0865	Shannon, Jackie	CA0805	Shay, Robert	MO1800
Severn, Eddie	PA2050	Shannon, Kathleen	WV0750	Shchegolev, Aleksey	AI0200
Severs, Alan R.	IN0905	Shannon, Nanette	CO0650	Shea, David L.	TX3200
Severson, Sandi	CA0100	Shannon, Nanette	CO0550	Shea, Joy	NC2600
Severtson, David	WI0808	Shannon, Pamela	MO0950	Shea, Maurice	FL0950
Severtson, Kirk A.	NY3780	Shannon, Quynh	GA1750	Shea, Merrill	MA0350
Severtson, Paul	CA0600	Shannon, Robert	OH1700	Shear, Howard	CA0835
Sevigny, Catherine	AI0200	Shannon, William	CA0900	Shearer, Allen R.	CA0807
Sevilla, Jean-Paul	AG0400	Shao, Sophie	NY0150	Shearer, Allen R.	CA5000
Sevilla, Tiffany	IL0720	Shao, Sophie S.	NY4450	Shearer, Greig	CT0650
Seward, Owen	FL1450	Shapero, Harold S.	MA0500	Shearer, James E.	NM0310
Seward, Philip	IL0720	Shapiro, Daniel	OH0600	Shearin, Arthur Lloyd	AR0250
Seward, Steve K.	MO1780	Shapiro, Eve	NY1900	Shearon, Stephen	TN1100
Sewrey, Jacques	WI1150	Shapiro, Gail S.	IL2250	Sheats, Jackson	VA1350
Sexton, A. Jeanette	OH1850	Shapiro, Gerald	RI0050	Shebesta, Bob	WI0770
Sexton, Bobby	CA1000	Shapiro, Jan	MA0260	Shedd, Kylie	IN1350
Sexton, Greg	KY0550	Shapiro, Jarred	VT0100	Sheedy-Gardner, Anne	NE0500
Sexton, James	TN1400	Shapiro, Laurence	IN0250	Sheehan, Aaron	MA0400
Sexton, Lucinda	DC0170	Shapiro, Lois	MA2050	Sheehan, Aaron	MA2050
Sexton, Norma	CA0650	Shapiro, Madeleine	NY2250	Sheehan, Aaron	MD0850
Seybert, John M.	FL1740	Shapiro, Marc	CA2950	Sheehan, Dan	NJ0020
Seybold, Donald	IN1300	Shapiro, Mark L.	NY2105	Sheehan, Joseph C.	PA1050
Seyfried, Sheridan	NY2250	Shapiro, Mark L.	NY2250	Sheehan, Paul J.	NY2550
Seymann, Scott	AZ0440	Shapiro, Noah	NY2750	Sheeks, Randy	TN0850
Seymore, Sam	KS0215	Shapiro, Stephanie	MI2200	Sheeley, Thomas	AZ0450
Seymour, David	OH1350	Shapovalov, Dimitri	WI0250	Sheena, Robert	MA0400
Sfraga, Debbie	NJ1160	Sharer, Marty	PA0500	Sheena, Robert	MA1400
Sgouros, Michael	NY2450	Sharkey-Pryma, Maura	AA0020	Sheena, Robert	MA1175
Shaar, Erik	NC0450	Sharlat, Yevgeniy	TX3510	Sheena, Robert	MA0350
Shabalin, Alexey	RI0150	Sharma, Nachiketa	CA0050	Sheffer, Jake	MD0550
Shabani, Afrim	IL2510	Sharnetzka, Charles S.	MD0475	Sheffer, Toni	KY1000
Shabazz, Hafiz F.	NH0100	Sharnetzka, Sandra	MD0475	Sheffield, Robert	AB0060
Shachal, Harel	NY2660	Sharon, Boaz	MA0400	Sheftel, Paul	NJ1350
Shackleton, Jean	OK0750	Sharon, Rena	AB0100	Sheftel, Paul	NY1900
Shackleton, Peter	AG0500	Sharon, Robert	FL1450	Sheftz, Stephen Walter Robert	NE0160
Shackleton, Phil	CA0250	Sharp, Bradley	OH2300	Sheie, Sigrid	CA5353
Shadday, Craig	RI0250	Sharp, Charles	CA0815	Sheil, Martha	MI2100
Shade, Neil Thompson	MD0650	Sharp, David	IA0750	Sheil, Richard F.	NY3725
Shade, Timothy	KS0200	Sharp, Irene	CA5000	Sheinbaum, John J.	CO0900
Shadinger, Marilyn	TN0100	Sharp, Irene	NY2250	Sheinberg, Art	NM0450
Shadinger, Richard C.	TN0100	Sharp, Jack	AL0300	Sheinberg, Colleen	NM0450
Shadle, Charles	MA1200	Sharp, John	IL0550	Shelby, Karla	OK1500
Shadle, Douglas W.	KY1500	Sharp, Leanne	GA1500	Sheldon, Deborah	PA3250
Shadle-Peters, Jennifer	CO0275	Sharp, Michael D.	LA0400	Sheldon, Elisabeth	MA0350
Shadley, Jeffrey	OK1450	Sharp, Molly	VA1600	Sheldon, Gregory	AG0550
Shafer, Karen	FL0050	Sharp, Pat	NY1350	Sheldon, Janene	NE0450
Shafer, Robert	VA1350	Sharp, Robin	CA4900	Sheldon, John M.	CA4100
Shafer, Sharon Guertin	DC0250	Sharp, Stuart	MI1050	Sheldon, Paul	NY0600
Shafer, Timothy P.	PA2750	Sharp, Thom	CA0960	Sheldon, Robert	IL1090
Shaffer, Frank	TN1680	Sharp, Thomas	CA0815	Sheldon, Vanessa R.	CA3265
Shaffer, Kris P.	SC0275	Sharp, Wendy	CT0900	Shelemay, Kay K.	MA1050
Shaffer, Kristin	KS0200	Sharp, Wendy	CT0850	Shellans, Michael	AZ0100
Shaffer, Lori	MO1500	Sharp, William	MD0650	Shelley, Bonnie J.	AZ0510
Shaffer, Marian	TN1680	Sharpe, Alex E.	NY2750	Shelley, Kenneth	CT0650
Shaffer, Marian	TN1850	Sharpe, Alexander E.	NY1600	Shelley, Kim S.	IL2970
Shaffer, Rebecca Boehm	IA0950	Sharpe, Avery G.	MA2250	Shelley, Russ	PA1650
Shaffer, Teren	CA0960	Sharpe, Carlyle	MO0350	Shellhammer, Jeff	OH1850
Shaffer, Timothy	IL3150	Sharpe, Kevin	FL1850	Shellito, Kelli	PA0100
Shaffer, Timothy	IL1085	Sharpe, Paul	NC1650	Shelly, Daniel P.	NY2750
Shaffer, Timothy William	IL0840	Sharpe, Rod L.	IL3500	Shelly, Frances	KS1450
Shaffer, Timothy	IL1300	Sharples, Pamela	NJ0750	Shelt, Christopher A.	MS0100
Shaffer-Gottschalk, David D.	VA1750	Sharrock, Barry R.	SC0350	Shelton, Adam	MO0775
Shaftel, Matthew R.	FL0850	Sharrock, James	NH0110	Shelton, Brian M.	TX2960
Shagdaron, Bair	NC0050	Shasberger, Michael	CA5550	Shelton, Evan	CO0200
Shah, Nikita	NC2300	Shatalov, Alexandra	NY2650	Shelton, Frank	CO0200
Shahani, Michael M.	CA1020	Shatin, Judith	VA1550	Shelton, Lucy	NY2150
Shaheen, Ronald T.	CA5200	Shatzkin, Merton T.	MO1810	Shelton, Tom	NJ1350
Shahouk, Bassam	AG0650	Shaul, David	WY0115	Sheludyakov, Anatoly	GA2100
Shahriari, Andrew	OH1100	Shaver, Cynthia L.	IN0100	Shemaria, Rich S.	NY2750
Shaindlin, Tim	CT0850	Shaver, Stephen R.	IN0900	Shemaria, Rich	NY2660
Shakhman, Igor	OR1100	Shaw, A. Herndon	GA1600	Shen, Deborah	NY2900
Shakhman, Igor	OR0500	Shaw, Alison	WI0830	Shen, Yang	FL1125
Shakir, Audrey	GA1050	Shaw, Arthur E.	WA1250	Shende, Vineet	ME0200
Shallit, Jonathan O.	NY3770	Shaw, Betty	TX3400	Sheng, Bright	MI2100
Shaman, Sila	OR0700	Shaw, Brian	LA0200	Shentov, Lubima	NY5000
Shamburger, David	TN0100	Shaw, Clyde Thomas	VA1350	Shepard, Brian K.	CA5300
Shames, Jonathan	OK1350	Shaw, David	NY2500	Shepard, Hilary	KS0350
Shamoto, Masatoshi	HI0210	Shaw, Gary R.	IL1750	Shepard, James A.	CA2960
Shanahan, Ellen Cooper	MA0280	Shaw, George W.	CA2550	Shepard, Kenny	IN0100
Shand, Patricia	AG0450	Shaw, Giocille	NY2750	Shepard, Matthew C.	KS0100
Shandro, Constantine	AA0040	Shaw, J.D.	NM0450	Shepherd, Dean	CA2390
Shands, Patricia	CA5350	Shaw, John	FL1650	Shepherd, Eudora	WI0100
Shane, Lynn	MA1650	Shaw, Karen	IN0900	Shepherd, Eugene	CA4460
Shane, Rita	NY1100	Shaw, Kathleen	NJ1350	Shepherd, Gregory	HI0155
Shanefield, Andrew	PA3200	Shaw, Kenneth	OH2200	Shepherd, John	AG0100
Shangkuan, Pearl	MI0350	Shaw, Kimberly	IL1890	Shepherd, Michael	VA0150
Shank, Dean	TX2150	Shaw, Kirby	OR0950	Shepherd, William	IA1600
Shank, Jennifer S.	OH1100	Shaw, Laura	IA0930	Shepley, Mary Ellen	NY2400
Shank, Kevin	KY0600	Shaw, Lisa	DC0170	Sheppard, Chris	SC0900
Shank, Nadine E.	MA2000	Shaw, Martha	GA1700	Sheppard, Craig D.	WA1050
Shankle, Robert	TN1600	Shaw, Nathan	OH0350	Sheppard, Craig	AF0100

885

Name	Code	Name	Code	Name	Code
Sheppard, Gregory	NY0630	Shinn, Barbara A.	AL0800	Shu, Peter	MN1250
Sheppard, Kenny	TX2650	Shinn, Michael A.	NY1900	Shubeck, Scott	CA5300
Sheppard, Matthew	PA1650	Shinn, Ronald R.	AL0800	Shuck, Carla	KY0700
Sheppard, Robert	CA5300	Shioji, Lane	DC0010	Shudy, Deryk	MO0400
Sheppard, W. Anthony	MA2250	Shiplett, Arlene	AJ0150	Shufro, Joseph L.	IA1100
Shepperson, Sam	NM0450	Shipley, John	NV0150	Shuhan, Alexander G.	NY1800
Sher, Ben	NY4500	Shipley, Linda P.	TN0580	Shuholm, Dan	OR0175
Sher, Ben	MA0260	Shipley, Lori R.	VA0500	Shukaev, Leonid	KS1450
Sher, Benjamin	MA1400	Shipman, Dan	TX1000	Shull, Kevin	MN0250
Sher, Daniel	CO0800	Shipp, Daniel	AG0250	Shulman, Amy	CA3300
Sherbon, James W.	NC2430	Shipps, Stephen	MI2100	Shulman, Nora	AG0450
Sherburn, Rebecca	MO1810	Shipwright, Edward	HI0210	Shulman, Suzanne	AG0200
Sherer, Kathryn	IN0550	Shirar, Ryan	KY0300	Shulstad, Reeves	NC0050
Sherer, Lon	IN0550	Shires, Brent A.	AR0850	Shultis, Carol	SC0650
Sheridan, Daniel	MN1700	Shires, Terrie A.	AR0850	Shultis, Carol L.	PA3000
Sheridan, John	PA0400	Shirey, Julie	TX1050	Shultis, Christopher	NM0450
Sheridan, Patrick	CA5030	Shirey, Kim F.	AR0600	Shultz, Betty Sue	OH2290
Sheridan, Wilma F.	OR0850	Shirey, Richard	OH2150	Shultz, Bud	IL1500
Sherinian, Zoe	OK1350	Shirley, Alicia	TX3400	Shultz, Dane	PA0500
Sherman, Bob	IL2750	Shirley, Ellen	IA1100	Shumate, Curtis	MA0260
Sherman, Donna	AG0300	Shirley, George I.	MI2100	Shumate, Penny	PA1000
Sherman, Ellen	MI0300	Shirley, Hank	NM0400	Shumway, Allyson	AZ0440
Sherman, Hal	WA0030	Shirley, John F.	MA2030	Shumway, Angelina	VA1350
Sherman, Jeff	KY0250	Shirtz, Michael	OH2140	Shumway, Angelina	MD0700
Sherman, Joseph	NY2750	Shiu, Timothy	TN1680	Shumway, Jeanne	CA0600
Sherman, Joshua	WI1150	Shively, Joseph L.	MI1750	Shumway, Jeffrey	UT0050
Sherman, Joy	WA0850	Shively, Victoria	MI1750	Shurr, Janet	WI0050
Sherman, Kathryn D.	NY3780	Shiver, Todd	WA0050	Shurtliffe, Brett	NY0400
Sherman, Mark	NJ0825	Shkoda, Natalya	CA0800	Shurtz, H. Paul	TN1700
Sherman, Mozelle C.	KY1200	Shlyam, Eda Mazo	MA1175	Shuster, Brett A.	KY1500
Sherman, Paul	CA1265	Shner, Idit	OR1050	Shuster, Richard J.	TX3300
Sherman, Paul	CA5300	Shockey, David M.	PA2800	Shuter, Cindy	AI0150
Sherman, Paul	CA1000	Shockey, Mark	PA0650	Shynett, Jerald	NC2440
Sherman, Paul	CA0960	Shockley, Alan	CA0825	Siarris, Cathy Froneberger	SC0850
Sherman, Richard	MI1400	Shockley, Rebecca P.	MN1623	Sichel, John	NJ0975
Sherman, Robert	NY1900	Shoemaker, Ann H.	TX0300	Sicilia, Sheila	NY2950
Sherman, Russell	MA1400	Shoemaker, Elizabeth	IL1750	Sicilian, Peter J.	NY3705
Sherman, Steve	AA0080	Shoemaker, Michelle N.	MA1175	Siciliano, Mary	MI1750
Shernit, George R.	OH0650	Shoemaker, Vance	SD0050	Sick, Stella B.	MN0800
Sherr, Laurence E.	GA1150	Shoemaker, Vance	IA1200	Sickbert, Murl	TX0900
Sherr, Richard J.	MA1750	Shoemaker, Vance	IA0500	Sicsic, Henri-Paul	AG0450
Sherrick, Richard	OH1860	Shofner-Emrich, Terree	IL2100	Sicsic, Nancy	AG0450
Sherrill, William	TX3530	Shogrin, Tina	NE0160	Sidener, Whitney F.	FL1900
Sherrod, Ron	TX3535	Sholer, Jeannie	OK0750	Siders, Thomas	MA0350
Sherry, Fred	NY2150	Sholes, Jacquelyn	MA0400	Siders, Tom	MA0400
Sherry, Fred	NY2250	Sholl, Martha	NY3350	Sidhu, Inderjeet	IL1085
Sherry, Fred	NY1900	Sholl, Martha P.	NY3730	Sidlin, Murry	DC0050
Sherry, James Wallace	IA1450	Sholtis, Jennifer Ratchford	TX2960	Sidon, Ashley Sandor	IA0550
Sherry, Martin	WA0480	Shomos, William	NE0600	Sidoti, Vincent	ND0600
Sherwin, Jonathan S.	OH0200	Shonekan, Stephanie	MO1800	Sidoti, Vincent	OH0755
Sherwin, Jonathan	OH0600	Shonkwiler, Joel	OH2050	Sieben, Patrick	KS0225
Sherwin, Jonathan	OH0650	Shonkwiler, Joel	OH1200	Siebenaler, Dennis	CA0815
Sherwin, Ronald G.	MA0150	Shook, Brian A.	TX1400	Sieberg, Michael	OH0950
Sherwood, Gertrude	FL1500	Shook, Gregory	WV0550	Siebert, Alan H.	OH2200
Sherwood, Thomas W.	OH2550	Shook, Lee	WA1350	Siebert, Glenn	NC1650
Shetler, Donald	SC0275	Shook, Thomas M.	WA1350	Siebert, Renee	FL1125
Shetler, Timothy	MA0800	Shook, Timothy	KS1200	Siebert, Sonya	IA0650
Sheveloff, Joel L.	MA0400	Shoop, Stephen S.	TX3515	Sieck, Stephen	VA0350
Shevitz, Matthew	IL1080	Shoopman, Chad	FL1550	Sieck, Steven	WI0350
Shew, Jamie	CA1900	Shope, Bradley	TX2930	Sieden, Cyndia	WA0200
Shewan, Paul	NY3350	Shore, Melanie	UT0250	Sieden, Cyndia	WA0650
Shiao, Simon	FL1950	Shores, Daniel	VA1350	Sieg, Jerry	LA0800
Shibatani, Naomi	TX1520	Shorley, Ken	AF0050	Siegel, Dan	CA2960
Shick, Suzanne	CA4100	Shorner-Johnson, Kevin T.	PA1250	Siegel, Hedi	NY2250
Shidler, Deborah	CA0900	Short, Charlie	WI0050	Siegel, Jeff S.	CT0800
Shidler, Deborah A.	CA0807	Short, Jackalyn	AG0500	Siegel, Jeff S.	NY3760
Shidler, Deborah	CA0840	Short, Kevin	FL1900	Siegel, Jeff S.	NY2660
Shields, Bob	AG0200	Short, Michael	IA1350	Siegel, Matthew	CA4150
Shields, John Paul	WA0950	Short, Michael	IA0550	Sieger, Crystal	OH0400
Shields, Larry	AG0450	Short, Shawn	DC0050	Siek, Stephen	OH2450
Shields, Lisa	MT0100	Shorter, Lloyd	DE0150	Sielert, Vanessa	ID0250
Shier, Robin	AB0050	Shorthouse, Tom	AB0060	Sielert, Vern	ID0250
Shiffer, Faith E.	PA1250	Shortt, Paul R.	OH2200	Siemon, Brittnee	FL1000
Shifflett, John	CA4400	Shostac, David J.	CA0835	Siemon, Brittnee	SC0600
Shiffman, Barry	AG0300	Shostak, Anthony	ME0150	Siena, Jerold	IL3300
Shifrin, David	CT0850	Shotola, Marilyn	OR0850	Sienkewicz, Gary	CT0600
Shih, Gloria	NJ0800	Shotwell, Amanda	SD0580	Sienkiewicz, Frederick	MA0950
Shih, Michael	TX3000	Shotwell, Clayton	GA0250	Sierra, Roberto	NY0900
Shih, Patricia	AB0060	Shover, Blaine F.	PA3050	Sierra-Alonso, Saul	CA0807
Shihor, Ory	CA1075	Showell, Jeffrey A.	OH0300	Sievers, Beth	OK1350
Shikaly, Al	IN0400	Showers, Shelley	PA3250	Sievers, David	OH2250
Shilansky, Mark G.	NH0350	Showman, Deke	PA0100	Sievers, Karl H.	OK1350
Shilansky, Mark	MA0260	Shows, Ray	MN1450	Sifferman, James P.	MO1500
Shilling, Ronald L.	MN1030	Shpachenko, Nadia	CA0630	Sifford, Jason	IA1550
Shilling, Scott	OH2500	Shrader, James A.	GA2150	Sifter, Suzanna	MA0260
Shim, Jeong-Ja	NY3785	Shrader, Mary Kathryn	WV0550	Sigars, Julie Kae	WA0800
Shimada, Toshiyuki	CT0850	Shrader, Steven	TN1800	Sigel, Allen R.	NY4320
Shimada, Toshiyuki	CT0900	Shreffler, Anne C.	MA1050	Sigmon, Susan	GA0900
Shimazaki-Kilburn, Yoko	IN0150	Shrewsbury, Matthew Monroe	SC0420	Sigmon, Susan McEwen	GA0940
Shimeo, Barbara	IL1612	Shrock, Dennis R.	TX3000	Siivola, Carolyn	MI1200
Shimizu, Kumiko	MS0250	Shrope, Douglas	CA1000	Sikes, Ron	MO0550
Shimpo, Ryoji	OH2150	Shroyer, Jo Ellen	MO0100	Siki, Bela	WA1050
Shimron, Omri D.	NC0750	Shroyer, Ronald L.	MO0100	Sikora, Stephanie R.	OH0100
Shin, Aera	NJ0825	Shrude, Marilyn	OH0300	Silantien, John J.	TX3530
Shin, Donna	WA1050	Shrut, Arlene	NJ0800	Silbergleit, Paul	WI1150
Shin, Eric	MD1010	Shrut, Arlene	NY1900	Silberman, Peter	NY1800
Shin, Jung-Won	MS0250	Shrut, Arlene	NY2150	Silberschlag, Jeffrey	MD0750
Shin, MinKyoo	IL3100	Shtarkman, Alexander	MD0650	Silbiger, Alexander	NC0600
Shiner, Richard	CA2775	Shteinberg, Dmitri	NC1650	Siler, Christine	WI0100
Shinn, Alan	TX3200	Shterenberg, Ilya F.	TX3530	Siler, Sandra K.	TX1350

Name	Code	Name	Code	Name	Code
Sill, Kelly	IL2200	Simpson, Brian	CA3250	Skaar, Trygve	MN1625
Sill, Kelly	IL0750	Simpson, Ken	AG0400	Skadsem, Julie A.	MI2100
Sills, David	CA3500	Simpson, Kyle	PA3580	Skantar, David	FL1450
Silva, Ben	NM0450	Simpson, Marietta	IN0900	Skazinetsky, Mark	AG0300
Silva, LaVista	CA3800	Simpson, Marilyn	CA2840	Skazinetsky, Mark	AG0450
Silva, Linda	CA0630	Simpson, Michael	VA1600	Skeen, William	CA5300
Silva, Magda Y.	KS1110	Simpson, Nicholas	TX2650	Skeete, Sean	MA0260
Silva, Ulisses C.	GA1700	Simpson, Peter	KY1450	Skeirik, Kaleel	OH2550
Silva-Marin, Guillermo	AG0300	Simpson, R. Eric	TX3000	Skelly, Michael	NY0750
Silvagnoli, Michael F.	NY3650	Simpson, Reynold	MO1810	Skelton, Logan	MI2100
Silveira, Mathias	AA0020	Simpson, Ron	UT0050	Skelton, Neal	CT0450
Silver, Daniel	CO0800	Simpson, Scott	NJ1400	Skelton, Robert A.	AG0500
Silver, Noreen	ME0440	Simpson, Steve	CO0150	Skelton, Sam	GA1150
Silver, Patricia	TN1350	Simpson-Litke, Rebecca	GA2100	Skelton, Sara	MN1630
Silver, Phillip A.	ME0440	Sims, Gary	MO1950	Skelton, William	NY0650
Silver, Sheila	NY3790	Sims, Jared N.	RI0300	Skemp-Moran, Kathryn	WI1100
Silverberg, Ann L.	TN0050	Sims, Lamar	MO1000	Skerik, Renee	TX3200
Silverberg, Laura Gail	NY0750	Sims, Loraine	LA0200	Skeris, Robert	DC0050
Silverberg, Marc E.	NY1275	Sims, Lori E.	MI2250	Skernick, Linda	CT0100
Silverman, Adam B.	PA3600	Sims, Robert	IL2200	Skidgel, Sharon	CO0810
Silverman, Alan	NY2750	Sims, Stephen S.	OH0600	Skidgel, Wesley	IL0850
Silverman, Ellen	AB0050	Sims, Stuart	CA0850	Skidmore, Dan	NC0750
Silverman, Faye-Ellen	NY2250	Sims, Wendy L.	MO1800	Skidmore, Dan	NC0350
Silverman, Laura	OH0700	Simson, Julie	CO0800	Skidmore, David	MD0650
Silverman, Laura	OH2150	Sinaisky, Ilya	CO0250	Skidmore, Dorothy L.	WV0300
Silverman, Marc	NY2150	Sincaglia, Nicolas W.	IL0750	Skidmore, Jon	UT0050
Silverman, Marissa	NY0500	Sincell-Corwell, Kathryn	MD0450	Skidmore, William	WV0750
Silverman, Michael	MN1623	Sinclair, David W.	PA3000	Skillen, Joseph	LA0200
Silverman, Robert	AB0100	Sinclair, John V.	FL1550	Skinkus, Michael	LA0080
Silverman, Tracy	TN0100	Sinclair, Robert L.	IL3450	Skinner, Anita	OH0250
Silvers, Travis	CA5350	Sinclair, Terri	SC0420	Skinner, Josh	ID0060
Silvers, Travis	CA3000	Sinclair, Terrol	AG0650	Skinner, Kate	ID0060
Silverstein, Harry	IL0750	Sincoff, Alison J. Brown	OH1900	Skinner, Kent	AR0800
Silverstein, Joseph	MA0350	Sindberg, Laura K.	MN1623	Skinner, Ryan	OH1850
Silverstein, Joseph	PA0850	Sindell, Carol A.	OR0850	Skitch, Todd	TN1200
Silvester, William	NJ0175	Sinder, Philip	MI1200	Sklut, Thomas	MI1260
Silveus, Debra L.	IN0100	Sinder, Philip	MI1400	Skogen, Meaghan	NC0750
Silvey, Brian A.	MO1800	Sine, Nadine J.	PA1950	Skoglund, Frances	FL0675
Silvey, Philip E.	NY1100	Singer, David	NJ0800	Skogstoe, John	NE0460
Silvio, Will	MA0260	Singer, Douglas Michael	IN1560	Skok, Heidi	MA1400
Sim, Hoejin	PA3250	Singer, Leigh Ann	IA0910	Skoldberg, Phyllis	AZ0440
Simerly, Rick	TN1150	Singer, Mark	MD0600	Skoler, Harry	MA0260
Simi, David R.	CA4400	Singh, Vijay	WA0050	Skoniczin, Robert	DE0150
Simidtchieva, Marta	IL2910	Singler, Juliette	CA3640	Skoog, Andrew	TN1710
Simkin, Elizabeth	NY1800	Singletary, Pat	TX0075	Skoog, William M.	TN1200
Simmonds, Jim	NY2500	Singleton, Beth	CA1650	Skop, Stephen	MA0150
Simmons, Amy	TN1720	Singleton, Darryl	TX3150	Skornia, Dale E.	MI0650
Simmons, Amy L.	TX3175	Singleton, H. Craig	CA1650	Skoumal, Zdenek	AB0060
Simmons, Bradley E.	NC0600	Singleton, Jon	NC0550	Skovenski, Michael	NY0650
Simmons, Garth	OH0300	Singleton, Kenneth	CO0950	Skovorodnikov, Eugene	AB0100
Simmons, Gordon	MI1750	Singleton, Lynn	OH1850	Skroch, Diana	ND0600
Simmons, James	CA2550	Singleton, Ron	OK0500	Skrocki, Jeanne	CA5150
Simmons, James	TN1100	Singley, David	MN0300	Skurtu, Jasmine J.	HI0210
Simmons, Jim	CA0859	Singley, H. E.	IL1850	Skuster, Sarah	CA4100
Simmons, John	OH0600	Sinift, Sherry	WY0200	Skweir, Michael	CA2250
Simmons, Margaret R.	IL2900	Sinigos, Louis	MI0300	Skyles, Michael	SD0400
Simmons, Mark	TN1720	Sink, Damon W.	NC2600	Skyrm, Susanne L.	SD0600
Simmons, Matthew	FL0100	Sink, Patricia E.	NC2430	Slabaugh, Stephen	MI1180
Simmons, Matthew	SC1050	Sinsabaugh, Katherine Anne	NY4200	Slabaugh, Thomas E.	CA5010
Simmons, Phil	MI0600	Sinsoulier, Melisande	AG0650	Slack, Rob	CA2390
Simmons, Sunshine	IL3550	Sinta, Donald J.	MI2100	Slack, Robert	CA0815
Simms, Beverley	IN0800	Sintchak, Matthew A.	WI0865	Slack, Robert	CA1000
Simms, Bryan R.	CA5300	Sioles, Gregory	LA0200	Slade, Elizabeth	OH0100
Simms, Rob	AG0650	Siow, Lee-Chin	SC0500	Slagle, Diane	OH2450
Simms, William	MD0610	Sipes, Danny T.	TX2930	Slagle, Steven	NY2150
Simms, William	MD0500	Sipes, Diana	TX2930	Slagowski, Joshua	OH1450
Simon, Abbey	TX3400	Sipher, John	NY1350	Slaney, Malcolm	CA4900
Simon, Benjamin	CA5000	Sipley, Kenneth L.	MS0575	Slater, Jeanne	NY1900
Simon, Dennis	IA0790	Siqueiros, John	TX3520	Slater, Sheri	MO0400
Simon, Fred	IL0550	Sir, Neil	NH0350	Slater, Vivien H.	NY0650
Simon, Harris W.	VA0250	Sirbaugh, Nora	NJ0175	Slaughter, Nancy	TN1900
Simon, Julie	CA4500	Sirbaugh, Nora	NJ0750	Slavich, Richard	CO0900
Simon, Philip G.	PA3700	Sirett, Mark G.	AG0250	Slavin, Dennis	NY0250
Simoncic, Max	CA4300	Sirguey, Gait	NY2150	Slavin, Dennis	NY0600
Simonds, Judy	MA1250	Sirois, Carole	AI0200	Slavin, Peter	IN0005
Simone, Ed	NY3475	Siroky, Brad	NY2105	Slawek, Stephen M.	TX3510
Simoneau, Brigitte	AI0220	Sirota, Jonah B.	NE0600	Slawson, A. Wayne	CA5010
Simonelli, John	AG0450	Sirota, Nadia	NY2150	Slawson, Brian	FL0150
Simonett, Helena	TN1850	Sirota, Robert	NY2150	Slawson, Gregory	OH0700
Simonot, Colette	AC0050	Sirotin, Peter	DC0170	Slawson, John G.	IL0840
Simonovic Schiff, Jelena	OR0850	Sirotin, Peter	PA2300	Slawson, Wayne	OR0950
Simons, Anthony R.	PA2550	Sirotkin, Leonid	IN0350	Slayton, Michael K.	TN1850
Simons, Audrey K.	PA2450	Sirotta, Michael	NY0644	Sledge, Larry	FL0800
Simons, Carolyn	CA2810	Sisauyhoat, Neil	TX0550	Sledge, Sylstea	DC0010
Simons, Chad P.	NM0450	Sisbarro, Jennifer	NY1550	Sleeper, Kathryn	FL1300
Simons, Dennis	ND0250	Sisbarro, Jennifer L.	NY1250	Sleeper, Thomas M.	FL1900
Simons, Diane	CA1750	Sisco, Paul	PA0600	Sleister, Terry	GA1500
Simons, John	TX2600	Sise, Patrick	MD0350	Sletner, Ariane	OH1200
Simons, Kevin	MI1850	Sisk, Lawrence T.	IL1520	Sletta, Lauren	CO0250
Simons, Mark	AI0150	Sisk, Robin	FL1800	Sletto, Thomas A.	IA0550
Simons, Mark	CA1560	Siskind, Paul A.	NY3780	Slezak, Heide Marie	MI2000
Simons, Paul	AF0120	Sisman, Elaine	NY0750	Slezak, Lawrence L.	TX2295
Simons, Penelope	ND0250	Sitterly, James	CA2650	Slim, H. Colin	CA5020
Simonson, Donald R.	IA0850	Sitton, Michael R.	NY3780	Slingland, Susan	NC0050
Simonson, Jessica	OR1000	Sivan, Noam	NY2250	Sloan, Chikako	IN1560
Simos, Mark	MA0260	Sizemore, Mark	KY1400	Sloan, Chikako	IN1050
Simpkins, John	NY2750	Sizer, Todd	CO0275	Sloan, Donald S.	SC0420
Simpson, Alexander T.	KY0250	Sjobring, Steve	IL3550	Sloan, Gerald H.	AR0700
Simpson, Andrew Earle	DC0050	Sjoquist, Doug P.	MI1200	Sloan, Rita	MD1010
Simpson, Brennetta	NC1600	Skaar, Alice	SC1080	Sloane, Ethan	MA0400

Alphabetical Listing of Faculty

Name	Code	Name	Code	Name	Code
Sloane, Marcia	CA2840	Smith, Carey	MS0370	Smith, Jason	IA1400
Slobin, Mark	CT0750	Smith, Carl	TN1850	Smith, Jeff	CT0800
Slocum, Troy	NY1550	Smith, Carl H.	KY0750	Smith, Jeffrey	NY2650
Slocum, William	OH2600	Smith, Carol	TX2250	Smith, Jeffrey B.	AZ0100
Slominski, Johnandrew	NY1100	Smith, Carol	OR0250	Smith, Jennifer	MI1550
Slominski, Tes	WI0100	Smith, Carol F.	TN1850	Smith, Jennifer	UT0150
Slon, Michael	VA1550	Smith, Carole Mason	WI0845	Smith, Jeremy	IA0790
Sloothaak, Bea	MI0750	Smith, Carole Mason	MN0800	Smith, Jeremy L.	CO0800
Sloter, Molly	IL0400	Smith, Caroline B.	IN0350	Smith, Jerry Neil	OK1350
Slotkin, Matthew	PA2150	Smith, Carolyn J.	MO0775	Smith, Jewel Ann	OH2550
Slotkin, Matthew C.	PA0250	Smith, Carolyn	MO0350	Smith, Joanne	FL0680
Slotterback, Floyd	MI1600	Smith, Charles	NE0300	Smith, Joel L.	MA1450
Slottow, Stephen	TX3420	Smith, Charles J.	NY4320	Smith, Joel Larue	MA1900
Slovak, Loretta	MA0600	Smith, Charlie	AR0400	Smith, Joey	AB0210
Slowik, Gregory	MA1700	Smith, Charlotte R.	SC0750	Smith, John	MO1830
Slowik, Kenneth	MD1010	Smith, Cherie	IN1350	Smith, John P.	VA1250
Slowik, Peter	OH1700	Smith, Christian B.	UT0050	Smith, John David	DE0150
Sluis, Joyce	IL2775	Smith, Christina	AD0050	Smith, John Robert	MI0600
Slusser, Anthony	OH0600	Smith, Christina	MN0750	Smith, Joseph R.	NJ0800
Slutsky, Boris	MD0650	Smith, Christina	GA1150	Smith, Joseph	PA1150
Sly, Gordon C.	MI1400	Smith, Christopher J.	TX3200	Smith, Joseph	MA0260
Sly, Marcia Gronewold	ME0440	Smith, Christopher M.	TX3200	Smith, Joshua D.	TN0150
Slye, Lorree	MA0260	Smith, Christy	PA1650	Smith, Joshua	OH0600
Smaga, Svitlana	CA1300	Smith, Chuck	ID0050	Smith, Judith	CT0800
Smaldone, Edward	NY0642	Smith, Cory	OH2150	Smith, Julius O.	CA4900
Smale, Marcelyn	MN1300	Smith, Craig Steven	KS0040	Smith, Justin	OR0500
Small, Allanda	AL1195	Smith, Curtis F.	CO0810	Smith, Kandie K.	FL1950
Small, Ann R.	FL1750	Smith, D.	FL1730	Smith, Kandie K.	GA0400
Small, David	TX3510	Smith, Daniel Ian	MA0260	Smith, Kara	WY0115
Small, Elisabeth	TN0100	Smith, Danny	GA1070	Smith, Karen B.	LA0300
Smallcomb, Matt	PA3700	Smith, David	MD1000	Smith, Kathleen	NC1400
Smalley, Charles	AZ0150	Smith, David Kenneth	PA1350	Smith, Kathryn L.	CA1500
Smalley, Jack	CA5300	Smith, David K.	KS0950	Smith, Kenneth H.	MI2250
Smallwood, Scott	AA0100	Smith, David J.	AL0300	Smith, Kenneth	IL2250
Smar, Benedict J.	MA2000	Smith, David	CT0800	Smith, Kent	NY3760
Smarelli, Mark E.	OH2450	Smith, David S.	MI2250	Smith, Kent M.	PA3560
Smart, Carlos	CA2910	Smith, Dean W.	IL1740	Smith, Kevin	MN0625
Smart, David	KS0590	Smith, Debbie	TN1200	Smith, Kile	PA2800
Smart, Gary	FL1950	Smith, Deborah	CA1075	Smith, Kimo	CA2420
Smart, James	MT0400	Smith, Deborah	IL2910	Smith, Kirsten	CA0840
Smart, Jonathan	CA2440	Smith, Demond	KY0250	Smith, Kristen	OH2250
Smart, Marilyn	FL1950	Smith, Denise A.	MO1900	Smith, Langston 'Skip'	MA0260
Smart, Mary Ann	CA5000	Smith, Dennis	TN1660	Smith, Larry G.	UT0300
Smathers, Robin H.	NC1250	Smith, Derek T.	MO0600	Smith, Larry Dearman	MS0750
Smedina-Starke, Ruta	VA1600	Smith, Derrick	NY2650	Smith, Larry Alan	CT0650
Smedley, Eric M.	IN0900	Smith, Diane	NY3350	Smith, Lauren	PA1250
Smelser, Jim	IL0750	Smith, Don	IN0250	Smith, Lee	CA4950
Smelser, Linc	IL3550	Smith, Donald S.	AZ0350	Smith, Leland C.	CA4900
Smelser, Linc	IL2200	Smith, Douglas	AB0050	Smith, Leroy	MD0500
Smelser, Nadia	CA1900	Smith, Douglas	AB0200	Smith, Linda	OH2300
Smeltzer, Steven	OK1330	Smith, Ed	TX0370	Smith, Linda S.	KS1400
Smeltzer, Nadia	CA3350	Smith, Ed	TX3420	Smith, Lisa Kingston	CA5300
Smialek, William	TX1300	Smith, Eddie	CA5150	Smith, Lonnie	OR0600
Smigel, Eric	CA4100	Smith, Edward	TX2400	Smith, Malcolm S.	ME0500
Smiley, Henry	TN0100	Smith, Elizabeth Lena	IL1150	Smith, Malcolm	IN0250
Smiley, Jayne	AG0300	Smith, Elizabeth Reed	WV0400	Smith, Marcie	UT0190
Smiley, Mariko	CA5000	Smith, Elizabeth	IN0700	Smith, Marian E.	OR1050
Smiley, Marilynn J.	NY3770	Smith, Emily	IN1750	Smith, Marilyn	MS0420
Smiley, William C.	NC1550	Smith, Emily M.	IL3450	Smith, Marion	FL0450
Smirl, Terry	WI0300	Smith, Fabia	GA1700	Smith, Mark Russell	MN1623
Smirl, Terry W.	WI0450	Smith, Fenwick	MA1400	Smith, Mark	IL0600
Smirnoff, Joel	OH0600	Smith, Fran	CA2200	Smith, Mary L.	CO0600
Smisek, James J.	AL0800	Smith, G. D.	KY1200	Smith, Mary M.	IL0800
Smith, Aaron	MD0900	Smith, Gavin	TN1850	Smith, Matthew Shepard	NY2750
Smith, Aaron Todd	CA0835	Smith, Gayle	AL0335	Smith, Matthew K.	VT0100
Smith, Aaron T.	CA2800	Smith, Gene	AF0150	Smith, Matthew	SC0900
Smith, Ada	NC1100	Smith, Geoff	NY1250	Smith, Matthew	IL1150
Smith, Alan M.	OH0300	Smith, Gillian	AF0120	Smith, Matthew O.	KS1350
Smith, Alan	CA5300	Smith, Glenda G.	CA1700	Smith, Melanie	TX3800
Smith, Allison	TX1550	Smith, Glenn E.	VA0450	Smith, Michael	OH1850
Smith, Andrew	MA0400	Smith, Gordon E.	AG0250	Smith, Michael	CO0950
Smith, Andrew	NV0050	Smith, Gregory E.	MA1400	Smith, Michael K.	IA0950
Smith, Andrew W.	KY0750	Smith, Gregory	IL0550	Smith, Michael Cedric	NY2700
Smith, Angela	NJ1130	Smith, Hannah	NE0200	Smith, Michael V.	DC0050
Smith, Angie	NC2370	Smith, Herbert	VA0975	Smith, Mike	TX2295
Smith, Anne-Marie	AG0130	Smith, Hope Munro	CA0800	Smith, Mike	IL0550
Smith, Arnold	NJ0825	Smith, Howie	OH0650	Smith, Miriam	GA1700
Smith, Aron	CT0550	Smith, J. W.	WV0200	Smith, Murray	AA0100
Smith, Ayana	IN0900	Smith, J. Benjamin	GA2130	Smith, Nancy A.	NH0350
Smith, Barbara B.	HI0210	Smith, Jacqueline H.	PA2800	Smith, Nancy	ME0500
Smith, Barry	MA0260	Smith, James	NY4050	Smith, Neal	MA0260
Smith, Becky	SC0900	Smith, James	WI0815	Smith, Neal	IL0350
Smith, Benjamin W.	OH0200	Smith, James	VA1600	Smith, Neal	IL1750
Smith, Billy	TX0390	Smith, James	NJ0800	Smith, Nicholas	KS1450
Smith, Blake	DE0150	Smith, James E.	OH0500	Smith, Norman E.	PA3350
Smith, Bradley	PA1050	Smith, James S.	NC1800	Smith, Orcenith George	IN0350
Smith, Brenda	FL1850	Smith, James	VA1500	Smith, Pat	IA0700
Smith, Brent	UT0190	Smith, James E.	OH2200	Smith, Patrick	CT0800
Smith, Bret	WA0050	Smith, James	CA5300	Smith, Patrick G.	VA1600
Smith, Brian	GA1200	Smith, James E.	CA4450	Smith, Paul A.	PA3150
Smith, Brian	VA0750	Smith, James W.	AL1050	Smith, Paul A.	CA0835
Smith, Brian R.	CT0650	Smith, James Russell	MA0260	Smith, Paul	CA1150
Smith, Brinton Averil	TX2150	Smith, James A.	KS1350	Smith, Paul B.	AR0400
Smith, Bruce	MD1050	Smith, Jan	WV0760	Smith, Paula M.	WI0803
Smith, Bruce	AG0500	Smith, Janet	CA0815	Smith, Perry	NC0650
Smith, Byron J.	CA2650	Smith, Janice P.	NY0642	Smith, Peter	PA3250
Smith, C. Raymond	UT0050	Smith, Janice M.	MO1900	Smith, Peter D.	FL0365
Smith, C. Scott	OH1900	Smith, Jason B.	TX2400	Smith, Peter H.	IN1700
Smith, Caitlin Maura	AA0020	Smith, Jason D.	OH0650	Smith, Randall A.	MO1780
Smith, Cameron	IL1615	Smith, Jason R.	OH1900	Smith, Raymond H.	AL1050

Alphabetical Listing of Faculty

Name	Code	Name	Code	Name	Code
Smith, Richard	CA5300	Snedeker, Jeffrey	WA0050	Sodke, James W.	WI0835
Smith, Robbie Malcolm	MI0400	Sneider, Robert	NY1100	Soebbing, Steven	MD0350
Smith, Robert W.	AL1050	Snell, Alden	DE0150	Soehnlen, Edward J.	MI1850
Smith, Robert C.	TX2600	Snell, James W.	MO1810	Soelberg, Diane	ID0060
Smith, Robert Thomas	TX3400	Snelling, Ann	OR1300	Sogin, David	KY1450
Smith, Robert	NC1100	Snider, Colleen	CA1290	Sohn, Livia	CA4900
Smith, Robert C.	MN1450	Snider, Dave	WA1150	Sohn, Minsoo	MI1400
Smith, Robin	OK0850	Snider, Denise G.	WA1150	Sohn, Sung-Rai	NY3560
Smith, Ron	IA1100	Snider, Jason	MA1175	Sohn, Sungrai	NY2900
Smith, Ronald	NC1950	Snider, Jason	MA0400	Sohriakoff, Pam	MN0250
Smith, Ronald B.	MA1450	Snider, Jason	MA1400	Soich, Leslie	CO0830
Smith, Ross	LA0050	Snider, Jeffrey	TX3420	Soifer, Tyler	CO0830
Smith, Roy C.	IN0005	Snider, Karl William	CA2800	Sokasits, Jonathan F.	NE0300
Smith, Roy	OK0850	Snider, Larry D.	OH2150	Sokol, Casey	AG0650
Smith, Roy S.	OK1450	Snider, Nancy Jo	DC0010	Sokol, Jill	NJ0700
Smith, Roy	OK0550	Snider, Nancy	DC0350	Sokol, Mark	CA4150
Smith, Rumi	AK0100	Snidero, Jim	NY2660	Sokol, Michael	CA4100
Smith, Rusty	NC1900	Snitkovsky, Natasha	PA1050	Sokol, Mike	VA1350
Smith, Ruth	CA2300	Snitzler, Larry J.	VA0450	Sokol, Thomas A.	NY0900
Smith, Ryan	TX1400	Snitzler, Larry	DC0010	Sokol-Albert, Andrea C.	PA0950
Smith, Ryan	GA0850	Snizek, Suzanne	AB0150	Sokoloff, Eleanor	PA0850
Smith, Rylan	GA1050	Snodgrass, Ann A.	MA0260	Sokoloff, Laurie	MD0650
Smith, Sally	IL1090	Snodgrass, Debra D.	MO0800	Sokolov-Grubb, Silvana I.	NH0350
Smith, Sam	ID0070	Snodgrass, Jennifer Sterling	NC0050	Sokolovic, Ana	AI0200
Smith, Scott McBride	KS1350	Snodgrass, Laura	CA2250	Sokolowski, Elizabeth	PA3330
Smith, Scott Z.	VA0600	Snodgrass, Linda H.	CA0800	Solar-Kinderman, Eva	AB0150
Smith, Scott	CA1270	Snodgrass, William G.	MO0800	Solari, Gia	CA3270
Smith, Shawn T.	TX2930	Snook, Ann Marie	KS1400	Sole, Meryl	NY0050
Smith, Sonja	IL2750	Snook, Lee	KS1400	Solee, Denis	TN1850
Smith, Stan	OH0350	Snow, Adam	NC0550	Solero, Elena	MI0100
Smith, Stephen	TN1100	Snow, Adam M.	SC1200	Solfest-Wallis, Cindy	TN0260
Smith, Steven	PA2750	Snow, Andrew	IL3150	Solfest-Wallis, Cindy L.	WI0200
Smith, Stewart	AC0100	Snow, Bradley	MO1800	Solie, Gordon A.	OR0850
Smith, Stuart	MA2030	Snow, Greg	NY3725	Solis, Gabriel	IL3300
Smith, Stuart Saunders	MD1000	Snow, Jennifer L.	CA5030	Solis, Kassi	TX2570
Smith, Sue	MI0050	Snow, John	MN1623	Solis, Richard	OH0600
Smith, Susan	TN0050	Snow, Julian	OR1300	Solis, Ted	AZ0100
Smith, Susan K.	MO0800	Snow, Lydia F.	IL2150	Soll, Beverly A.	MA1650
Smith, Susan A.	MS0360	Snow, Michelle H.	ME0500	Sollberger, Harvey	CA5050
Smith, Susan	MO0400	Snow, Sandra	MI1400	Solomon, Alan L.	NY3780
Smith, Tara	IA0790	Snow, Steven	PA2550	Solomon, Evan	MD0550
Smith, Tawnya D.	IN0150	Snow, Thomas	ME0150	Solomon, Jason Wyatt	GA0050
Smith, Thomas	NY2250	Snowden, Donald	FL1500	Solomon, Jeffrey	AL0500
Smith, Thomas	NY2150	Snowden, Jonathan	VA1350	Solomon, Joseph	NY2050
Smith, Timothy	AR0200	Snoza, Melissa	IL0750	Solomon, Larry J.	AZ0480
Smith, Timothy G.	NJ1130	Snoza, Melissa	WI0250	Solomon, Marisa	ME0440
Smith, Timothy M.	CA2775	Snukst, Penny	IN0005	Solomon, Mimi	NC0650
Smith, Timothy C.	AK0100	Snyder, Barry	NY1100	Solomon, Nanette Kaplan	PA3100
Smith, Timothy A.	AZ0450	Snyder, Cindy	CA5150	Solomon, Qiao Chen	GA0050
Smith, Tom	FL0200	Snyder, Colleen	CA2400	Solomon, Sam	MA0400
Smith, Tony 'Thunder'	MA0260	Snyder, Courtney	NE0610	Solomon, Samuel Z.	MA0350
Smith, Tony L.	TN0150	Snyder, Craig	NY1250	Solomon, Wayne	CA1860
Smith, Tracy Anne	DC0170	Snyder, David	CT0450	Solomon, Wayne	CA5070
Smith, Trevor	VA1650	Snyder, David W.	IL1150	Solomon, William	CT0050
Smith, Vern	IA1400	Snyder, Dirk	OR1020	Solomonow, Rami	IL0750
Smith, Vernon L.	FL1300	Snyder, Fred	NY2400	Solomons, John	TX3500
Smith, Victoria	MO1950	Snyder, Jacob	PA2710	Solomonson, Terry	IL0400
Smith, Vincent	NY0350	Snyder, Jay R.	CA1960	Solomonson, Terry	IL3500
Smith, W. Lindsay	SC0750	Snyder, Jean E.	PA1200	Solose, Jane M.	MO1810
Smith, Wadada Leo	CA0510	Snyder, Jeffrey S.	PA1900	Solose, Kathleen A.	AJ0150
Smith, William O.	WA1050	Snyder, Jennifer	TX3750	Solot, Evan	PA3330
Smith, William D.	NC1350	Snyder, Jerrold	CA1550	Solow, Jeffrey G.	PA3250
Smith, Zachary	PA1050	Snyder, John	LA0300	Soltero, Jill K.	OR1100
Smith-Emerson, Karen	MA1750	Snyder, John L.	TX3400	Soltero, Jill	OR0500
Smith-Wright, Lovie	TX3450	Snyder, Laura	WI0825	Solum, John	NY4450
Smith-Wright, Lovie	TX1000	Snyder, Laura	AA0100	Solum, Stephen	MN1050
Smithee, Larry G.	TN1000	Snyder, Linda J.	OH2250	Soluri, Theodore	IL0550
Smither, Robert	MO0200	Snyder, Maggie	GA2100	Soluri, Theodore	WI0825
Smithey, David B.	LA0350	Snyder, Maria	MA0600	Solzhenitsyn, Ignat	PA0850
Smoak, Jeff C.	KY1425	Snyder, Mark	NY2105	Somer, Gena	IL1090
Smoje, Dujka	AI0200	Snyder, Mark L.	VA1475	Somerton, Clinton	AG0130
Smoker, Beverly A.	NY2650	Snyder, Mark S.	CT0800	Somma, Sal	NY1275
Smoker, Paul	NY2650	Snyder, Patricia	CT0650	Sommer, Douglas	GA1150
Smolder, Benjamin W.	OH1450	Snyder, Philip	GA2100	Sommer, Lesley	WA1250
Smolenski, Scott	FL1675	Snyder, Randall	NE0500	Sommer, Maralyn	AR0300
Smolensky, Marcus	PA3150	Snyder, Randy L.	TX2300	Sommer, Peter J.	CO0250
Smolensky, Marcus H.	PA0350	Snyder, Rory	CA1560	Sommerfeldt, Jerod	OH1450
Smolik, Vicky	IL2970	Snyder, Sarah A.	MD0650	Sommerfeldt, Jerod	OH2250
Smooke, David	MD0650	Snyder, Steven D.	KY0900	Sommerfield, Janet	MI0500
Smoot, Lonna Joy	ID0060	Snyder, Timothy	FL1000	Sommers, Joan C.	MO1810
Smucker, Angela Young	IN1750	Snyder, Vernon G.	CA0630	Sommers, Paul B.	MO1810
Smucker, Greg	MA1400	Soares, Luciana	LA0450	Sommerville, Daniel A.	IL3550
Smucker, Peter	IN1750	Sobaje, Martha H.	RI0101	Sommerville, David	PA1600
Smukala, Edward	FL0950	Sobaje, Martha H.	RI0100	Sommerville, James	MA0400
Smukler, Lauri	NY2150	Sobaskie, James William	MS0500	Sommerville, James	MA1400
Smukler, Laurie	NY0150	Sobel, Elise	NY2105	Sommerville, James	MA1175
Smukler, Laurie	NY2250	Sobieralski, Nathan	CA0810	Sonami, Laetitia	CA2950
Smukler, Laurie	NY3785	Sobieski, Dorothy	NJ0700	Sonderling, Lawrence	CA3300
Smyla, Adam	CA4150	Sobieski, Thomas	OH2500	Sonenberg, Daniel M.	ME0500
Smylie, Dennis H.	NY2750	Sobke, Catherine	CA4850	Sones, Rodney	KY1200
Smylie, Dennis H.	NJ0800	Sobkowska-Parsons, Joanna	FL0600	Song, Anna	OR0450
Smyser, Peter	PA2450	Sobol, Deborah	IL0550	Song, Haewon	OH1700
Smyth, David H.	LA0200	Sobol, Elise	NY2750	Song, Hyeyoung	TX3700
Smyth, Steven	AR0850	Sobolewski, Susan F.	NY2550	Song, J. Z.	WI1150
Snapp, Doug R.	MN1000	Sobrino, Laura	CA5040	Song, James J.	CA3100
Snapp, Patricia	MN0750	Sochinski, James	VA1700	Song, JY	NY2250
Snarrenberg, Robert	MO1900	Soder, Aidan L.	MO1810	Song, MyungOk Julie	NY2750
Snavely, Jack	WI0825	Soderberg, Karen	MD0350	Song, Tom	TX2600
Snead, Charles G.	AL1170	Soderlund, Sandra	CA2950	Song, Xie	MS0400
Snedeker, Gretchen	NY0650	Soderstrom, Erik	IL0750	Songer, Loralee	TN0850

Name	Code	Name	Code	Name	Code
Sonies, Barbara	PA3250	Sparfeld, Amanda	MI1750	Spicciati, Shannon	WA1050
Sonneborn, Kristen	FL0680	Sparfeld, Tobin	CA2660	Spice, Graham	VA1850
Sonneborn, Matthew	FL0680	Sparkes, Doug	AB0050	Spicer, Donna	OR1020
Sonnenberg, Melanie	TX3400	Sparkes, Douglas	AB0100	Spicer, Jeffrey	PA2800
Sonnenborn, Kristen	FL0500	Sparkman, Carol Joy	MS0400	Spicer, Luke	WI0842
Sonnentag, Kathleen	WI1150	Sparks, David	CA1100	Spicer, Mark	NY0600
Sonntag, Dawn Lenore	OH1000	Sparks, Dee	MO1900	Spicer, Mark J.	NY1150
Sontz, Allison	MT0370	Sparks, Glenn	NY2900	Spicer, Mark	NY0625
Soo Mauldin, Rosalyn	AL1195	Sparks, Jeremy	NY4460	Spicer, Nan	GA1750
Soocher, Stan	CO0830	Sparks, L. Richmond	MD1010	Spicer, Nan	IN0005
Soons, Heidi	VT0450	Sparks, Michael	AL1450	Spicer, Shawn	AG0500
Sooy, Julie	MI1050	Sparks, Phyllis	TN1400	Spicer-Lane, Anita	MD0170
Sopata, Kimberly	IL3100	Sparks, Richard	TX3420	Spicher, Barbara	MD0500
Soper, Kate	MA1750	Sparks, Thomas G.	IN0900	Spicher, Buddy	TN0100
Soper, Lee H.	NY2750	Sparks, Tim	NC2410	Spicknall, John	IN0350
Soph, Ed	TX3420	Sparks, Victoria	AC0050	Spicknall, John P.	IN0800
Sopher, Rebecca J.	PA1450	Sparks, Victoria	AC0100	Spicknall, Sharry	IN1310
Sophos, Anthony	NY2400	Sparr, Kimberly	VA0250	Spiegelberg, Scott C.	IN0350
Sor, Karen Shinozaki	CA5000	Sparrow, Carol	FL0680	Spiegelman, Ron	MO0350
Sorah, Donald	VA1580	Sparrow, James	NC1250	Spielman, Mark	AB0070
Sorbara, Joe	AG0350	Sparrow, Richard	FL2050	Spies, Claudio	NJ0900
Sorce, Richard P.	NJ0950	Sparrow, Sharon W.	MI1750	Spieth, Donald	PA2450
Sorel, Suzanne	NY2450	Sparti, Patricia C.	NC0850	Spila, Tom	AA0110
Soren, Roger	IN1010	Sparzak, Monica	NC1350	Spilker, John D.	NE0450
Sorensen, Ann	LA0250	Spataro, Susan M.	VA0400	Spillane, Jamie D.	CT0600
Sorensen, Julie	ID0100	Spaulding, Laura	FL1745	Spiller, Henry	CA5010
Sorensen, Randall J.	LA0250	Spaulding, Neil	AG0250	Spiller, W. Terrence	CA0600
Sorenson, Allin	MO0350	Spaulding, Sue	CT0650	Spillman, Herndon	LA0200
Sorenson, Dean P.	MN1623	Spaulding, Susan	CT0050	Spillman, Robert	CO0800
Sorenson, Gary	UT0350	Spayde, Ruth	MO0100	Spinazzola, James M.	IN1650
Sorenson, Scott	MI1650	Speake, Constance J.	IL2150	Spinelli, Donald	MD0750
Sorg, A.	MA0800	Spear, David R.	NY2750	Spinetti, Frederico	AA0100
Sorgi, Craig	TX3350	Speare, Mary Jean	VA0600	Spinetti, Sharon	NJ0825
Sorley, Darin S.	IN1650	Spears, Samuel B.	WV0300	Spiradopoulos, S.	MA0800
Sorley, Rebecca E.	IN1650	Spears, Steven	WI0350	Spires, Henry Ray	SC1080
Soroka, Michele R.	MI1750	Spears, Tim	CA2200	Spires, Rozanne	TX3527
Soroka, Solomia	IN0550	Specht, Barbara	OH0950	Spiridopoulos, Gregory	MA2000
Sorrell, Martha	VT0250	Specht, Jeffrey	OR0400	Spiridopoulos, Sheffra	RI0200
Sorrentino, Ralph	PA1550	Speck, Frederick A.	KY1500	Spiro, Michael E.	IN0900
Sorrentino, Ralph	PA3600	Speck, Gary A.	OH1450	Spitler, Carolyn	IN1250
Sorrento, Charles J.	MA0260	Speck, Matthew	MI0520	Spitler, Justin	IN0700
Sorroche, Juan	PR0150	Speck, R. Floyd	TN0450	Spittal, Robert	WA0400
Sorton, Bailey	OH1600	Spedden, Patricia R.	IN0700	Spitz, Bruce	WA0860
Sorton, Bailey	OH1200	Spede, Mark J.	SC0400	Spitz, Jonathan	NJ1130
Sorton, Robert	OH1850	Speed, George M.	OK0800	Spitzer, David Martin	NC2435
Soskin, Mark	NY2150	Speedie, Penelope A.	KS0300	Spitzer, John	CA4150
Sosland, Benjamin	NY1900	Speer, Alesia L.	KY1550	Spitzer, Laura	NM0310
Sothers, Misty K.	CO0225	Speer, Donald R.	KY1550	Spivak, Mandy	WV0800
Soto, Amanda C.	ID0250	Speer, Janet Barton	NC1050	Spivak, Mandy A.	WV0750
Soto, Christian	FL1300	Speer, Randall	VA1125	Spivey, Gary	FL1430
Soto, Jose	CA1960	Speer, Shari	MN0610	Spivey, Norman	PA2750
Soto, Leonardo	NC2000	Speight, Andrew	CA4200	Splittberger-Rosen, Andrea	WI0850
Soto, Ricardo	CA3350	Speirs, Phyllis	OH0600	Spoelstra, Annemieke	VT0400
Soto, Robert	CA0630	Speiser, Paul	NY2750	Spohr, Arne	OH0300
Soto-Medina, Victor	TX1725	Spelius, Susan M.	ID0075	Spoonamore, Dudley	KY0450
Soueidi, Mark	WY0200	Spell, Cindy	NC0100	Spooner, Steven	KS1350
Sousa, Gary D.	TN1710	Spell, Cindy	NC0450	Spoor, Aaron	CA3200
South, James	OK1250	Spell, Eldred	NC2600	Sposato, Aime	VA1350
South, Janis	OK1250	Spellissey, Gary	MA0950	Sposato, Jeffrey S.	TX3400
South, Pam	OR0850	Spellman, Zachariah	CA4200	Spotts, Cory	AZ0490
Southall, John K.	FL0950	Spence, Chelsea	WA1100	Spotz, Leslie	TX2750
Southard, Bruce	ND0100	Spence, Gary	NC1250	Spradley, Bruce	GA0200
Southard, Ellen	CA4550	Spence, J. Robert	PA1250	Spradling, Robert	MI2250
Southard, Robert G.	MI1050	Spence, Marcia L.	MO1800	Spragg, James	AG0450
Southard, Sarah	MI1050	Spence, Stephen	NC0220	Spraggins, Mark	CA0550
Southern, Lia	MO0350	Spencer, Andrew	MI0400	Sprague, John L.	NC1700
Southern, Lia M.	MO0775	Spencer, Barbara	CA0600	Spratlan, Melinda K.	MA1350
Souvorova, Katerina	DC0050	Spencer, Charles	OH1350	Sprayberry, Shane	MS0300
Souza, Christine	OK1350	Spencer, Daniel	MI1050	Sprayberry, Tom	TX2260
Souza, Ricardo A.	OK1350	Spencer, David	TN1680	Sprenger, Curtis	CA4460
Souza, Thomas	MA0500	Spencer, Dianthe M.	CA4200	Sprenger, Jill T.	TX2600
Sovik, Thomas	TX3420	Spencer, Helena K.	OR0700	Sprenger, Kurt	TX2600
Sowards, James	VT0100	Spencer, James W.	AR0750	Sprenkle, David	PA3600
Sowers, Jodi L.	IN1650	Spencer, Larry	TX0370	Sprenkle, Elam Ray	MD0650
Sowers, Jodi L.	IN0907	Spencer, Malcolm	LA0100	Spring, Erin	OH1900
Sowers, Richard L.	IN0100	Spencer, Mark	OH0450	Spring, Howard	AG0350
Soyer, David	PA0850	Spencer, Mia	WA0050	Spring, Kathleen	CO0900
Soyer, David	NY2150	Spencer, Patricia L.	NY1600	Spring, Robert S.	AZ0100
Soykan, Betul	GA0500	Spencer, Philip	IL1250	Springer, Alisha	NC2420
Spaar, Peter	VA1550	Spencer, Reid	AA0050	Springer, Mark	MN1300
Spain, Steve	TX1660	Spencer, Roger A.	TN1850	Springer, Samuel	MD0600
Spainhour, Alex	SC0050	Spencer, Sandy	MA0600	Springfield, David	GA2150
Spaits, Gerald K.	MO1810	Spencer, Sarah	TX2295	Springfield, Maila Gutierrez	GA2150
Spalding, Ben A.	NJ1050	Spencer, Stacia C.	IL2250	Springs, Benjy L.	NC0900
Spampinato, Robert	NY2105	Spencer, Theresa Forrester	MO0250	Sproat, Joel	OK1350
Spaneas, Demetrius	NY1275	Spencer, William G.	NC0050	Sprott, Weston	NY2250
Spang, Lisa	PA2950	Spera, Nicolo	CO0800	Sprott, Weston	NJ1130
Spang, Ron	PA0500	Sperl, Gary	TN1710	Sprott, Weston	NY3785
Spangler, Douglas	MI1000	Sperl, Thomas	OH1700	Sproul Pulatie, Leah	MO0050
Spangler, Julie M.	OH2200	Sperling, Russ	CA2100	Sproul, Brian	UT0250
Spangler, Martha	FL1450	Sperrazza, Rose U.	IL2150	Sprout, Leslie A.	NJ0300
Spangler, Pamela	CA2550	Sperry, Ethan L.	OR0850	Sprow, Margaret	MS0100
Spaniol, Douglas E.	IN0250	Sperry, Paul	NY0500	Sprowles, Michael David	KY1500
Spaniola, Joseph T.	FL2100	Sperry, Paul	NY2150	Sprunger, Gina	SC0200
Spanjer, R. Allen	NY2150	Sperry, Tara	NC0900	Spuller, John	NC0050
Spann, Joseph	AL0890	Speth, Uli	NY1400	Spuller, John	NC2500
Spann, Joseph S.	NY3717	Speth, Uli	NY2900	Spurgeon, Alan L.	MS0700
Spann, Thomas	TN1400	Spethmann, Molly	WI1150	Spurgeon, Debra L.	MS0700
Spano, Fred P.	NC2420	Spevacek, Robert	ID0250	Spurlin, Adam Corey	AL0200
Spano, Robert V.	OH1700	Speziale, Marie	TX2150	Spurr, Ken	IL0850

Name	Code	Name	Code	Name	Code
Spurr, Kenneth	IL1085	Standard, Richard	GA0200	Stauffer, George B.	NJ1130
Squance, Rod Thomas	AA0150	Standerfer, Stephanie	VA1350	Stauffer, Sandra L.	AZ0100
Squatrito, Fred	CA0400	Standland, James	MS0750	Stauffer, Thomas D.	CA4100
Squibbs, Ronald J.	CT0600	Standley, Jayne	FL0850	Steadman, Robert	NC1100
Squire, Anne	MA0260	Stanek, Emily	IN0100	Steadman, Russell	TX0100
Squire, Anne	MA1400	Stanek, Mark	IN1560	Stearns, Anna Petersen	NY4150
Squires, David	AB0090	Stanek, Mark	IN0100	Stearns, Duncan	PA1150
Squires, Stephen E.	IL0550	Stanescu, Christina	NY2150	Stearns, Loudon	MA0260
Sriji, Poovalur	TX3420	Stanescu-Flagg, Cristina	NY2250	Stearns, Roland H.	AK0100
Srinivasan, Asha	WI0350	Stanfield, Ashley	IA0550	Stebleton, Michelle	FL0850
St. Clair, Collette	CO0550	Stanford, Ann	IL2750	Steck, Charles	IN1750
St. Clair, Eniko	CA4450	Stanford, Thomas S.	OR0850	Stecker-Thorsen, Meg	WA0860
St. Clair, Eniko	CA0250	Stang, Sharon Kay	IA0300	Stedry, Patricia	MA1600
St. Clair, Lisa	AF0050	Stang-McCusker, Stephani	DC0100	Steed, Brad B.	CA3500
St. Clair, Nike'	CA0630	Stangeland, Robert A.	AA0100	Steed, Scott	WA0250
St. Claire, Jason	NE0250	Stanichar, Christopher	SD0050	Steede, Marcus	WI0770
St. Goar, Rebecca	TN1700	Stanichav, Kristi	IA0500	Steeds, Graham	IA0950
St. Hilaire, Jon	WA1300	Staniland, Andrew	AD0050	Steege, Benjamin A.	NY3790
St. Jean, Donald	RI0200	Stanis, Sharon	AB0150	Steege, David J.	WA1250
St. Jean, Donald	RI0250	Stanley, Amy A.	NY3730	Steel, David	MS0700
St. Jean, Flo	RI0200	Stanley, Ann Marie	NY1100	Steel, Matthew	MI2250
St. John, Brian	IN1600	Stanley, Bill J.	CO0800	Steele, Anita Louise	OH1900
St. John, Patricia A.	NY4200	Stanley, Brian	FL0650	Steele, Carol	FL1310
St. John, Scott	CA4900	Stanley, Christine	VA1150	Steele, Cathy	MS0320
St. Juliana, Linda	MO0500	Stanley, David	AR0500	Steele, Charlie W.	NC0250
St. Julien, Marcus	LA0300	Stanley, Ed	MD0500	Steele, Daniel L.	MI0400
St. Laurent, Mark	MA1400	Stanley, Ed L.	PA1400	Steele, Edward L.	LA0400
St. Marie, John	CA0830	Stanley, Glenn	CT0600	Steele, Glenn A.	PA3250
St. Onge, Sarah	NY2750	Stanley, John	CA4700	Steele, Janet	NY0550
St. Pierre, Donald	PA3250	Stanley, Justin	NJ0400	Steele, Louis L.	CO0350
St. Pierre, Donald	PA0850	Stanley, Justin	CT0300	Steele, Nalora L.	MA0260
St. Pierre, Laurine Grace	MO0775	Stanley, Justin	NY5000	Steele, Natalie	IA0850
Staab, Jane	MA2200	Stanley, Lynnette	AR0850	Steele, Rebecca W.	FL0100
Stabenow, Crystal	OH0450	Stanley, Michelle	CO0250	Steele, Shauna	IN0100
Stabile, Ronald	RI0300	Stanley, Parker	KS0200	Steele, Sherry	AG0500
Stabile-Libelo, Carole	DC0100	Stannard, Jeffrey	WI0350	Steele, Stacey G.	PA3100
Stabinsky, Ron	PA3700	Stannard, Neil	CA1750	Steele, Stephen K.	IL1150
Stable, Arturo	PA3330	Stano, Richey	FL1675	Steele, Terry	PA0550
Stablein, Maria	OH1850	Stanojevic, Vera	OH0350	Steele, Timothy	MI0350
Stabley, Jeff	PA3710	Stansbury, George	TX3415	Steele, Timothy	MA1400
Stace, Stephen	PA2700	Stanton, Geoffrey	MI1300	Steely, Kathryn	TX0300
Stachofsky, Mark	IN0905	Stanton, Laurel	FL1800	Steen, Kenneth	CT0650
Stacke, Robert J.	MN0050	Stanton, Philip	TX3400	Steen, Larry	CA1750
Stackhouse, Eunice Wonderly	NC1450	Stanton, Ronald	NY2105	Steen, Solveig	SD0050
Stacy, Barry	MO0350	Stanton, Zachary K.	TN0100	Stees, Barrick R.	OH0600
Stacy, Thomas	NY2150	Stanyek, Jason	NY2740	Stees, Kevin J.	VA0600
Stadelman, Jeffrey	NY4320	Stanziano, Stephen	OH1000	Stees, Rhonda L.	VA0100
Stadelman-Cohen, Tara	MA0350	Staples, Charles	VA1600	Steeves, Timothy	AD0050
Stadnicki, Tisha	MA1450	Staples, James G.	PA1600	Stefaniak, Alexander	MO1900
Staerkel, Todd C.	KS1400	Staples, Mitch	OH1850	Stefano, Joseph	PA1150
Stafford, John	KS0590	Staples, Sheryl	NY1900	Stefanov, Emi	FL0930
Stafford, Terell L.	PA3250	Staples, Thomas	AA0200	Steffen, Arlene	CA1860
Stafford, Timothy	IL1850	Stapleson, Donald	MD0750	Steffen, Cecil	IL0780
Stafslien, Judy	WI1100	Stapleton, Chip	IN0907	Steffen, Christina	AZ0440
Stagg, David L.	MO1790	Stapp, Marcie	CA4150	Steffen, Richard	TN0050
Stagnaro, Oscar	MA1400	Star, Allison	AC0050	Steffens, David	OK0750
Stagnaro, Oscar	MA0260	Star, Cheryl	GA2300	Steffens, Lea	CA2390
Stahel, Ann Marie	IL1100	Starcher, Veronica	CO0050	Steffens, Lea	CA0960
Staheli, Ronald	UT0050	Starin, Stefani	NY5000	Stefiuk, Karen	WI0750
Staherski, Cheryl E.	PA1250	Starin, Stefani	NY2400	Stegall, Gary Miles	SC0420
Staherski, Cheryl	PA2350	Stark, Cynthia	IL0850	Stegall, James C.	IL3500
Stahl, David	CA2600	Stark, Deborah	GA0700	Stegall, Pat	AL1250
Stahl, Diane Willis	FL0800	Stark, Eric	IN0250	Stegall, Sydney Wallace	WA0460
Stahlke, Jonathan E.	IL0730	Stark, Melissa	OR0350	Stegeman, Charles	PA1050
Stahura, Raymond	WI0700	Stark-Williams, Turia	AL0450	Stegeman, Rachel	PA1050
Stahurski, Brian	PA0500	Starker, Janos	IN0900	Stegman, Sandra Frey	OH0300
Stahurski, Brian	PA1050	Starkey, David C.	NC1250	Stegmann, Matthias	IN0910
Staininger, Lynn	MD0500	Starkey, Linda	KS1450	Stegmann, Matthias	IN0550
Staininger, Lynn L.	MD0300	Starkman, Jane	MA0400	Stegner, John M.	KY1425
Stalker, Stephen	NY0350	Starkman, Jane E.	MA2050	Stehly, Theresa	SD0580
Stalker, Stephen T.	NY3705	Starks, George	PA1000	Steib, Murray	IN0150
Stallard, Tina Milhorn	SC1110	Starkweather, David A.	GA2100	Steidel, Mark	CA1560
Stallings, Charles	IN1100	Starling, Gary	FL1000	Steiger, Rand	CA5050
Stallings, Jim	GA0940	Starner, Robert	CA0200	Steigerwalt, Gary	MA1350
Stallings, Joe	FL1500	Starnes, David	NC2600	Steighner, Erik	WA0650
Stallings, Kendall	MO1950	Starnes, Timothy J.	NY2750	Stein, Beverly	CA0830
Stallmann, Kurt D.	TX2150	Starobin, David	NY2150	Stein, Daniel C.	NC0350
Stallsmith, Becki	AL0260	Staron, Michael	IL3200	Stein, Daniel C.	SC1200
Stallsmith, John	AL0260	Staron, Michael	IL0750	Stein, Dean A.	ME0200
Stallworth, Lenny	MA0260	Staron, Timothy	OH1000	Stein, Deborah	MA1400
Stalnaker, Bill	OR0400	Starr, Eric P.	CA4100	Stein, George	NY2750
Stalnaker, Donna	WV0250	Starr, Jeff M.	MI1200	Stein, John	MA0260
Stalnaker, William P.	OR0850	Starr, Jeremy A.	KS0300	Stein, Ken	KY1550
Stalter, Timothy J.	IA1550	Starr, Lawrence	WA1050	Stein, Ken J.	IL2560
Stam, Carl L.	KY1200	Starr, Lucia	MD0170	Stein, Louise K.	MI2100
Stam, Martin	NC1350	Starr, Pamela	NE0600	Stein, Paul A.	CA3500
Stambaugh, J. Mark	NY2150	Starr, Virginia	OH0300	Stein, Robin	TX3175
Stambaugh, Laura	GA0950	Startsev, Mila	CO0550	Stein, Thomas G.	MO1810
Stambler, David B.	PA2750	Staryk, Steven S.	WA1050	Stein, Thomas A.	MA0260
Stambuk, Tanya	WA1000	Stasack, Jennifer	NC0550	Stein, William	OH1800
Stamer, Linda	AZ0450	Staskevicius, Algis	AR0300	Stein-Mallow, Barbara	NY2250
Stamer, Rick A.	AZ0450	Stasney, C. Richard	TX2150	Steinau, David S.	PA3150
Stamp, John E.	PA1600	Staton, Celeste A.	HI0200	Steinbach, Falko	NM0450
Stampfl, Aaron	IL0275	Stats, Clyde	VT0250	Steinbach, Richard	IA0100
Stampfl, Aaron	IL0750	Stats, Clyde	VT0450	Steinbauer, Robert	TX3415
Stampfli, L. Thomas	IL1050	Statser, Sean J.	NY2750	Steinbeck, Paul	MO1900
Stamps, Jack W.	NJ1160	Staub, William D.	NC0650	Steinberg, A. Jay	KS0150
Stamps, Justin	ID0050	Stauch, Michael	NJ0550	Steinberg, Mark	NY2250
Stanbridge, Alan	AG0450	Stauch, Thomas J.	IL1085	Steinberg, Michael	RI0050
Stancu, Letitia G.	NJ0800	Staufenbiel, Brian	CA5070	Steinberg, Paulo	VA0600

Steinberg, Steve	CA3460	Sterner, Dave	OH0750	Stewart, Raymond G.	NY3725
Steinbuck, Caroline	CA4460	Sternfeld, Barbara	CA5400	Stewart, Scott A.	GA0750
Steinel, Michael L.	TX3420	Sternfeld, Jessica	CA0960	Stewart, Shawna	CA0350
Steiner, Frances	CA0805	Sternfeld-Dunn, Aleksander	KS1450	Stewart, Shirley	LA0720
Steiner, Ruth	DC0050	Sternfeld-Dunn, Emily	KS1450	Stewart, Stanley W.	MS0200
Steiner, Sean	UT0350	Stetson, David B.	CA5020	Stewart, Tobin E.	FL0680
Steingrover, Reinhild	NY1100	Stetson, David	CA0960	Stewart, Victoria	NJ0700
Steinhardt, Arnold	CA1075	Stetson, Stephanie	CA6000	Stibler, Robert	NH0350
Steinhardt, Arnold	NY0150	Steuck, Beth	MN1500	Stich, Adam	AZ0490
Steinhardt, Arnold	PA0850	Steuer, Jeff	IL1300	Stich, Gerald	WI0800
Steinhauer, Kimberly	PA2900	Steva, Elizabeth Ryland	KY1000	Stickler, Larry W.	WV0400
Steinhaus, Barbara	GA0350	Stevance, Sophie	AI0200	Stickney, Mark A.	UT0200
Steinke, David	FL0950	Stevans, Joy	MD0550	Stidham, Thomas M.	KS1350
Steinman, Daniel B.	IL0750	Steve, Tony	FL1000	Stieber, Marian	NJ1050
Steinman, Paul	NY2400	Stevens, Alan E.	TN0500	Stieda, Nicki	AB0200
Steinmann, Ronald	TX2710	Stevens, Annie J.	VA0150	Stiefel, Van	PA3600
Steinmetz, Demetrius	OH0750	Stevens, Anthony	MA0600	Stiegler, Morgen	OH0300
Steinmetz, John	CA5030	Stevens, Bill	CA5350	Stieler, Kathryn	MI0900
Steinmetz, John	CA1000	Stevens, Blake	SC0500	Stier, Greg	CA3200
Steinquest, David E.	TN1850	Stevens, Brian	NY2650	Stiernberg, Donald	IL1085
Steinquest, David	TN0050	Stevens, Bruce	VA1500	Stifler, Venetia C.	IL2150
Steinsnyder, Faith	NY1860	Stevens, Carrie L.	VA0600	Stiles, Allen	AB0060
Steinsultz, Kenneth	IN1600	Stevens, Cynthia C.	TX2310	Stiles, Joan	NY2660
Stella, Martin	MI1250	Stevens, Damon B.	NV0100	Stiles, Joan	NY2150
Stellar, Krista	IL1100	Stevens, Daniel B.	KS1200	Stiles, Patricia J.	IN0900
Stellrecht, Eric	NC0650	Stevens, Daniel B.	DE0150	Still, Alexa	OH1700
Stelluto, George Edward	NY1900	Stevens, Daryll	CO0200	Still, Christopher	CA0825
Steltenpohl, Anna C.	NY3730	Stevens, Deborah	IA1450	Still, Tamara	OR0750
Stembler-Smith, Anna	OH0250	Stevens, Delores E.	CA3150	Still, Tamara G.	OR0500
Stemen, James A.	CA3100	Stevens, Dwana F.	KY0300	Stiller, Paul	MA0260
Stempel, Larry	NY1300	Stevens, Eric	WA0960	Stillman, Fallon	IN0900
Stempel, Mark	NY1600	Stevens, Frankie	MO0825	Stillman, Judith L.	RI0200
Stemper, Frank L.	IL2900	Stevens, James	UT0050	Stillwell, Corinne	FL0850
Stempien, Jeff	NY1950	Stevens, James M.	TN0580	Stillwell, Jonathan	FL1700
Stencel, Paul L.	NY1210	Stevens, Jane	CA5050	Stillwell, Roy	IL1500
Stenius, Karla	AZ0470	Stevens, Jeffrey	MA0400	Stilson, Alicia	WA1100
Stensager, Eugene	WA0450	Stevens, John	WI0815	Stilwell, Jama Liane	IA0400
Stepansky, Alan	NY2150	Stevens, John L.	MA0260	Stilwell, Kenneth	DC0170
Stepansky, Alan	MD0650	Stevens, Keith	VA0600	Stilwell, Richard	IL0550
Stephan, Charles	WI0830	Stevens, Laura	NC0930	Stilwell, Robyn	DC0075
Stephan, Edward	PA1050	Stevens, Lynn	CA0840	Stimeling, Travis D.	IL1750
Stephan, Michael	MA2250	Stevens, Melissa	OH2050	Stimmel, Matthew D.	OH2275
Stephan-Robinson, Anna K.	WV0600	Stevens, Mitchell	LA0900	Stimpert, Elisabeth	PA2300
Stephansky, Joyce	VA0450	Stevens, Morris	TX2170	Stimpert, Elisabeth	PA0350
Stephen, Anne	NV0050	Stevens, Pamela	NH0150	Stimpert, Elisabeth	PA0950
Stephen, J. Drew	TX3530	Stevens, Paul W.	KS1350	Stimson, Ann	OH1200
Stephens, Berin	UT0325	Stevens, Phillip	CO0550	Stimson, Ann	OH1850
Stephens, Charles R.	WA0650	Stevens, Thomas	VA1500	Stimson, Kate	TN1200
Stephens, Emery	MI2200	Stevens, Thomas	VA1150	Stine, Maria W.	NC0350
Stephens, Gerald	TN1200	Stevenson, David E.	SC0400	Stine, Steve	ND0350
Stephens, John C.	IL3300	Stevenson, David	NC2400	Stingley, Mary-Christine	IL3450
Stephens, John	DC0350	Stevenson, Deborah	IL3550	Stinner, Rita	NE0710
Stephens, John A.	KS1350	Stevenson, Doris J.	MA2250	Stinnett, Jim	MA0260
Stephens, Loren	NE0050	Stevenson, Francois	AI0150	Stinson, Carol	TX1000
Stephens, Marjorie	TN1710	Stevenson, George	OK0850	Stinson, Caroline	NY1900
Stephens, Mary Ann	WI0300	Stevenson, Janis	CA1800	Stinson, Caroline S.	NY4150
Stephens, Michael	NE0050	Stevenson, Patricia	WI0825	Stinson, Jonathan	OH2550
Stephens, Robert W.	CT0600	Stevenson, Robert M.	CA5032	Stinson, Laura	AR0425
Stephens, Roger L.	TN1710	Stevenson, Roxanne	IL0600	Stinson, Lori	CA1700
Stephens, Sonny	KY0250	Stevenson, Sandra	UT0150	Stinson, Ron	KS0570
Stephens, Timothy	OR0750	Stevinson-Nollet, Katie	CT0650	Stinson, Russell	AR0425
Stephens, Wesley	OK0600	Stevlingson, Norma	WI0860	Stinson, Scott	FL1900
Stephens, William G.	TN1680	Steward, Feodora	OK1200	Stirling, Michael	OR0400
Stephenson, Angela	NC1300	Steward, Gail	AL0500	Stirtz, Bradley	IL2050
Stephenson, Carol	CA5100	Steward, Jack	OH2290	Stites, Joseph	KY1550
Stephenson, Carol	CA3200	Steward, Jack L.	OH0700	Stites, Nathan	KY0550
Stephenson, Edward	NC1300	Steward, Lee A.	CA0807	Stith, Gary	NY1700
Stephenson, Geoffrey	OH0300	Steward, Nicholas	OK1330	Stith, Marice W.	NY0900
Stephenson, JoAnne	FL1800	Steward, Nick	OK0700	Stitt, Ronald	PA0100
Stephenson, Kenneth	OK1350	Stewart, Alexander	VT0450	Stitt, Virginia K.	UT0200
Stephenson, Mary	NY5000	Stewart, Aliza	NY2250	Stiver, David Keith	OH0755
Stephenson, Mary	NY2400	Stewart, Amy	TX3000	Stobbe, Linda	AB0210
Stephenson, Michael	NC1550	Stewart, Barbara	OR0250	Stock, David	PA1050
Stephenson, Robert J.	UT0250	Stewart, Billy	NC2410	Stock, Jesse	TN0250
Stepner, Daniel	MA0500	Stewart, Chris	WA0200	Stockdale, Michael	MI0520
Stepner, Daniel	MA1050	Stewart, D. Andrew	AA0200	Stockham, Jeff	NY0650
Stepniak, Michael	VA1350	Stewart, David	AG0400	Stockham, Jeff	NY1350
Stepp, Scotty	IN0350	Stewart, Diane	MA0260	Stockton, J. Larry	PA1850
Steprans, Janis	AI0190	Stewart, Douglas	AG0450	Stockton, Larry	PA2450
Sterba, Lydia	IL1900	Stewart, James	CA0400	Stockton, Rachel	MD0175
Sterbank, Mark	SC0275	Stewart, Jeremy	VT0050	Stodd, Janet	IL0300
Sterling, Amy	MD0800	Stewart, Jesse	AG0100	Stodd, Janet	IA1300
Sterling, Eugene	CA2975	Stewart, Jocelyn	NY2150	Stodd, Janet	IL0100
Sterling, Jolanta	CA4450	Stewart, Jocelyn	NY4200	Stoddard, David	MN1100
Sterling, Robin	IL3550	Stewart, Jon	CO0560	Stodola, Lynn	AF0100
Stern, Adam	WA0200	Stewart, Jonathan	OK0825	Stoecker, Philip S.	NY1600
Stern, Andrea	MN1625	Stewart, Kasey	NY1150	Stoelzel, Richard	MI0900
Stern, Andrea	MN0050	Stewart, Kevin	CA1650	Stoessinger, Carolyn	NY0630
Stern, David W.	SC0800	Stewart, Kevin J.	CA0850	Stoffan, George C.	MI1750
Stern, David	SC0050	Stewart, Lawrence	NJ1050	Stoffel, David N.	GA2100
Stern, James	MD1010	Stewart, Leslie	CO0250	Stoffel, Lawrence F.	CA0835
Stern, Jeffrey S.	NY0650	Stewart, Louis	MA0260	Stofko, Diane L.	TN0550
Stern, Jeffrey	AF0100	Stewart, Lynnette	UT0250	Stohrer, Baptist	IL0780
Stern, Kalai	HI0110	Stewart, M. Dee	IN0900	Stohrer, Sharon	OH0350
Stern, Margaret	NY4300	Stewart, Mark	NY2150	Stoia, Nikki R.	MA2000
Stern, Nina	NY1900	Stewart, Michael	TN1710	Stoican, Michael	WA0600
Stern, Theodore	CA1960	Stewart, Paul	AI0200	Stokes, Donovan	VA1350
Sternbach, David J.	VA0450	Stewart, Paul B.	NC2430	Stokes, Harvey J.	VA0500
Sternberg, Brian	NY3705	Stewart, Peter A.	NJ0800	Stokes, James M.	NC0050
Sternberg, Jo-Ann	CT0800	Stewart, Raymond	NY2150	Stokes, Jeffrey	AG0500

Name	Code	Name	Code	Name	Code
Stokes, Jennifer	IN0907	Stouffer, Janice W.	PA1250	Strichman, Sherri	NY3600
Stokes, Jordan	NY0625	Stoughton, Zachariah	TX3000	Strickland, Caitlin	CO0650
Stokes, Katarina Markovic	MA1400	Stoune, Michael	TX3200	Strickland, Jeremy M.	TX3000
Stokes, Porter	SC1000	Stoup, Nicholas	CA3500	Strickland, Stan	MA1175
Stokes, Sheridon	CA5030	Stoupy, Etienne	TX3300	Strickland, Stanley Leon	MA0260
Stokes, Tayler L.	OR1100	Stout, David L.	TX3420	Strickler, John A.	MO0775
Stokking, William	PA0850	Stout, Gordon B.	NY1800	Strickler, John	MO1550
Stolarik, Justin R.	WI0815	Stout, Jeffrey	MA0260	Strickler, John	MO0350
Stolberg, Tom	MO0060	Stout, Richard	OH0600	Stricklett, Margaret	DC0170
Stolet, Jeffrey	OR1050	Stout, Ron	CA0825	Strid-Chadwick, Karen	AK0100
Stolk, Ronald	DC0050	Stout, Sara	FL1450	Stride, Frederick	AB0100
Stoll, Derek	AA0050	Stovall, Jeremy	AL0500	Strieby, Ken	IL1612
Stoll, Gregory	CA0100	Stovall, John	MA0400	Strimple, Nick	CA5300
Stoll, Joni L.	OH1100	Stovall, Leah	NM0400	Stringer, Sandra	AA0200
Stoll, Peter	AG0450	Stovall, Nicholas	DC0050	Stringer, Vincent Dion	MD0600
Stollberg, Amy	IL2450	Stovall, Sia Liss	MA1400	Stringham, David A.	VA0600
Stolle, Kara M.	IN0350	Stover, Jeff	CA3800	Striplen, Anthony	CA3920
Stoloff, Betty	NJ1350	Stover, Jerome	MA2030	Striplen, Tony	CA4200
Stoloff, Bob	MA0260	Stover, Pamela	OH2300	Stripling, Allen	GA0810
Stolpe, Andrea Kay	CA5300	Stover, Pamela J.	IL2900	Strizic, Owen	IA0250
Stolper, Mary	IL0750	Stowe, Cameron	NY1900	Strnad, Frank L.	CA1900
Stolte, Charles	AA0020	Stowe, Cameron	MA1400	Strobel, Larry	ID0140
Stolte, Charles	AA0035	Stowe, Cameron	AG0450	Strock, Kathryn	AK0100
Stoltie, James	FL1745	Stowe, Daniel	IN1700	Stroeher, Michael	WV0400
Stoltzfus, Fred A.	IL3300	Stowe, J. Chappell	WI0815	Stroeher, Vicki P.	WV0400
Stoltzman, Richard	MA1400	Stowe, Samuel P.	NC0850	Strohmaier, Chris	IA0550
Stolyar, Marina	AA0020	Stowell, John	OR0750	Strohman, Thomas	PA1900
Stolz, Lissa J.	LA0650	Stowman, William	PA2300	Strom, Jeffrey	MN1700
Stolz, Patrick	WY0115	Stoyanov, Simeon N.	MI1200	Strom, Kirsten	CA4425
Stomberg, Eric W.	KS1350	Stoyanov, Svetoslav R.	FL1900	Stroman, Shilo	CO0250
Stomberg, Lawrence J.	DE0150	Stoytcheva, Lilia S.	SC0950	Strommen, Carl	NY2105
Stone, Anne	NY0642	Strabala, Joyce	IA0400	Strommen, Linda	NY1900
Stone, Anne	NY0600	Strachan, Heather	GA1650	Strommen, Linda	IN0900
Stone, Brian D.	DE0150	Strachan, Heather	GA2000	Strong, Alan D.	TX0345
Stone, Christopher	NY2250	Strahl, Margaret A.	GA2100	Strong, Bent	MA0510
Stone, Elizabeth	AL1160	Strain, James A.	MI1600	Strong, J. Anthony	NJ0975
Stone, Geoff	HI0050	Strain, Robert L.	VA1350	Strong, James Anthony	NJ0975
Stone, George J.	CA1510	Strainchamps, Edmond N.	NY4320	Strong, Michael	MO1810
Stone, Jeff	TX2960	Strait, Cindy J.	KS1400	Strong, Sar-Shalom	NY1350
Stone, Joseph	CA0825	Strait, Tom	MN1120	Strong, Timothy	WA0650
Stone, Joseph	CA6000	Straka, Leslie	OR1050	Strong, Willie	SC1100
Stone, Julie	MI0600	Strampe, Gregory	WY0200	Stroope, Z. Randall	OK0800
Stone, Kerry 'Doc'	TN1450	Strand, Julie	MA1450	Stropes, John	WI0825
Stone, Mark	MI1750	Strand, Karen	OR0450	Strother, Kevin L.	DC0050
Stone, Maya K.	MO1800	Strand, Karen	OR0850	Strother, Martin	VA1800
Stone, Michael D.	CA0650	Strand, Katherine D.	IN0900	Stroud, Cheryl	AI0050
Stone, Michael	KY0550	Strandberg, Kristen	IN1850	Stroud, James	TN1350
Stone, Michael	AG0550	Strandt, Terry W.	IL1850	Stroud, Stephen	CA3000
Stone, Michael John	OK0600	Strang, Kevin	FL1700	Strouf, Linda Kay	MI1050
Stone, Richard	MD0650	Strasser, Michael C.	OH0200	Strouse, Greg	KY0100
Stone, Richard J.	NY1600	Strasser, Richard	MA1450	Strouse, Greg	KY1350
Stone, Robin	MA0260	Strathman, Marc	MO1100	Strouse, Lewis	PA0550
Stone, Sarah	MI0400	Strattan, Ken	FL0200	Strue, Pattie Jo	CA1375
Stone, Scott	DC0170	Stratton, Matthew	TN1720	Struman, Susan Jean	TX0550
Stone, Simon	AI0200	Strauch, Richard	WA1350	Strummer, Linda	OK1450
Stone, Stephen C.	MD0650	Straughn, Greg	TX0050	Strunk, Michael	WA0300
Stone, Susan E.	IL0100	Straughn, Marcia	TX0900	Strunk, Michael J.	CA0400
Stone, Sylvia	IL3300	Strauman, Edward	PA0650	Strunsky, Mark	NY3000
Stone, Terry	IL1750	Straus, Joseph N.	NY0600	Struss, Jane	MA1175
Stone, William	PA3250	Straus, Melissa	MI1050	Struthers, Steve	AR0750
Stone, William S.	MS0570	Strauser, Matthew L.	OR0175	Strutt, Michael	AB0100
Stone-Taborn, Susan	TX0400	Strauss, Anja	AI0150	Strutt, Michael	AB0050
Stonefelt, Kay H.	NY3725	Strauss, Axel	AI0150	Struve, Jonathon Paul	IA0950
Stoner, Elizabeth	MI2250	Strauss, Axel	CA4150	Struyk, Pieter	MA0700
Stoner, Jeremy	NY2650	Strauss, Gail	NY1600	Struyk, Pieter	MA0150
Stoner, Kristen L.	FL1850	Strauss, John F.	IA0950	Stryck, Mary	WI0050
Stoner-Cameron, Elizabeth	MI0400	Strauss, Konrad	IN0900	Stryker, Crystal J.	PA3000
Stoner-Hawkins, Sylvia Frances	KS1400	Strauss, Matthew B.	FL1900	Stryker, Michael S.	IL3500
Stones, Linda M.	CA0835	Strauss, Michael	OH1700	Stuart, Carolyn	FL2000
Stooksbury, Laura	GA2300	Strauss, Michael	IL0550	Stuart, David H.	IA0850
Stoops, Anthony	OK1350	Strauss, Michael	MA1400	Stuart, Gregory	SC1110
Stopa, Alex	NV0050	Strauss, Michael	MA0350	Stuart, Rory	NY2660
Storch, Arthur	CA0900	Strauss, Richard	NY4460	Stubbe, Joan	CA4400
Storch, Arthur L.	CA0807	Strauss, Robert	NY2650	Stubbe, Joan H.	CA5510
Storch, Laila	WA1050	Strauss, Virginia F.	IA0950	Stubbs, Fletcher	NC0450
Storey, Douglas	TX3750	Stravato, James	RI0101	Stubbs, Frederick	MA2010
Storey, Martin	MO1000	Strawbridge, Nathan	FL2050	Stubbs, James	TX1750
Stork, David	FL0400	Strawley, Brian	VA1600	Stubbs, Stephen	WA0200
Storm, Laura	AR0300	Strawley, Steven	PA0950	Stubbs, Sue	MO1830
Storm, Linda	IL1550	Strawn, Lee	CA3270	Stubbs, Sue A.	MO0775
Stormes, Sheridan	IN0250	Strawn, Logan	IN0800	Stubbs, Sue	MO1800
Stornetta, Catherine	MA0850	Streator, Carol	IN1050	Stubbs, Susan A.	MO1250
Stornido, Carl	WI0050	Strecker, Scott	KS1450	Stubbs, Thomas L.	MO1250
Storniolo, Carl	WI0825	Streder, Mark	IL0850	Stuber, Jon	OR1100
Storochuk, Allison M.	MO0775	Street, D. Alan	KS1350	Stubley, Eleanor	AI0150
Storojev, Nikita	TX3510	Street, Deborah	AL0550	Stuck, Les	CA2950
Story, David	WI0850	Street, Eric	OH2250	Stuckenbruck, Dale	NY2105
Story, James W.	TN1900	Street, William H.	AA0100	Stucker, Michael D.	IN0900
Story, Kirstin 'Maya'	OR0500	Street, William	ME0500	Stuckey, Bridgett	VA0600
Storyk, John	CO0830	Streeter, David	IN0905	Stuckey, Bridgett	VA1350
Stotelmyer, Deborah L.	MD0450	Streeter, Vicki	WY0130	Stuckey, John	TX2310
Stotlar, Curtis	WI1150	Streetman, Nancy	FL1745	Stucki, Brian	UT0400
Stott, Jacob	RI0101	Streets, Barbara S.	OK1330	Stucky, Mary Henderson	OH2200
Stott, Jacob T.	RI0100	Strefeler, Jamie	FL1800	Stucky, Rodney D.	OH2200
Stott, Jacob	RI0200	Streibel, Bruce	AA0200	Stucky, Steven	NY0900
Stott, Susan	MI1850	Streider, Will E.	TX3200	Studdard, Shane	TX1775
Stotter, Douglas	TX3500	Strelau, Nancy	NY2650	Studebaker, Donald	OK0550
Stoub, Amy	MO0550	Stremlin, Tatyana	NY4250	Studinger, Bob	CO0625
Stoubis, Nick	CA5300	Streng, Bobby	MI0100	Studt-Shoemaker, Lauren	MN0750
Stoudenmire, Myungsook	SC0275	Streng, Richard	MI0300	Stufft, David	GA2000

Stukart, Lynne	IL0300	Sullivan, Jill	AZ0100	Sushel, Michael	CA1000
Stulberg, Neal	CA5030	Sullivan, Joe	AI0150	Susman, Robert E.	NY2750
Stultz, Rachel	KS0150	Sullivan, Judith	TN1450	Sussman, David	AA0200
Stumbo, Jason A.	OH2300	Sullivan, Judith	AL1170	Sussman, David	AA0150
Stump, Joseph	MA0260	Sullivan, Keith	AL0850	Sussman, David	AA0050
Stumpf, Peter	IN0900	Sullivan, Kevin M.	AI0050	Sussman, Michael	MA2000
Stumpf, Peter	CA5300	Sullivan, Kimberly	AZ0450	Sussman, Richard	NY3785
Stumpf, Robert	IL3370	Sullivan, Lorraine Yaros	NY3780	Sussman, Richard	NY2150
Stumpf, Suzanne	MA2050	Sullivan, Mark	MI1400	Sussuma, Robert	CO0560
Stumpo, Ryan	MI0900	Sullivan, Mary	AA0050	Suta, Thomas	FL1745
Stuneck, Julia	OH0700	Sullivan, Matt E.	NY2750	Sutanto, David T.	TX0550
Stuntz, Lori	CA2600	Sullivan, Melanie	TX1350	Suter, Anthony	CA5150
Stuntz, Lori A.	CA3200	Sullivan, Melinda	MA1400	Sutherland, Craig	NY3350
Stup, Chris	CO0830	Sullivan, Michael	TX2200	Sutherland, Dan	AF0150
Stupin, Mary	CA1270	Sullivan, Nancy	AZ0450	Sutherland, Daniel	AA0020
Stuppard, Javier	TX1150	Sullivan, Nick A.	AA0200	Sutherland, Donald S.	MD0650
Sturgeon, Laura	SC0600	Sullivan, Peter	PA0550	Sutherland, Enid	MI2100
Sturges, Tami	TN1600	Sullivan, Peter	PA1050	Sutherland, John	GA2100
Sturm, Connie Arrau	WV0750	Sullivan, Robert	MA0650	Sutherland, Scott	CA5150
Sturm, Fred	WI0350	Sullivan, Robert P.	MA1400	Sutliff, Richard	OK0850
Sturm, Hans	NE0600	Sullivan, Robert	MA0700	Sutre, Guillaume	CA5030
Sturm, Jonathan	IA0850	Sullivan, Shawn	CA2050	Sutrisno, Joko	MN1623
Sturm, Julie	IA0850	Sullivan, Taimur	NC1650	Sutte, Jack	OH0200
Sturm, Marina	NV0050	Sullivan, Timothy R.	NY3780	Sutton, Brigette	PA1050
Sturman, Janet L.	AZ0500	Sullivan, Todd E.	AZ0450	Sutton, Elizabeth	NJ1350
Stusek, Steven C.	NC2430	Sullivan-Friedman, Melinda	MA0400	Sutton, Everett L.	MN1623
Stutes, Ann B.	TX3650	Sully, Eldon	VA0150	Sutton, John	CA0250
Stutzenberger, David R.	TN1710	Sulski, Peter	MA0650	Sutton, Leslie	IN1300
Stutzman, Walter J.	CT0450	Sulski, Peter	MA0200	Sutton, R. Anderson	WI0815
Su, Wei-Han	MO0775	Sulski, Peter	MA0700	Suvada, Steve	IL1615
Su, Yu-Ting (Tina)	IA1600	Sult, Michael	CA1800	Suvada, Steve	IL0850
Suabedissen, Gary	NJ0175	Sultanov, Namiq	CA4400	Suvada, Steven	IL1085
Suadin, I. Ketut	MD1010	Sultanova, Marina	MO1000	Suzano, L. Armenio	VA0650
Suadin, I. Ketut	NY1100	Sulton, Randall S.	TX0600	Suzuki, Dean P.	CA4200
Suadin, Nyoman	PA3200	Sulzinski, Valerie	NY2105	Suzuki, Rie	NJ1050
Suarez, Jeff	WI0100	Sulzinski, Valerie	NY2550	Suzuki, Yuko	NJ0500
Suarez, Jeff	WI0847	Sumares, Frank	CA4400	Svanoe, Anders	WI0100
Suarez, Karen	WI0250	Sumarna, Undang	CA5070	Svanoe, Erika K.	MN0150
Suarez, Luciano	NC1700	Sumarsam,	CT0750	Svanoe, Kimberly Utke	SD0050
Subchak, Bohdan	OH2290	Sumerlin, John	RI0200	Svard, Lois	PA0350
Suber, Stephen C.	LA0650	Sumi, Akiko	DC0170	Svatanova, Lucie	SC0700
Subera, Angel	MA0350	Summer, Averill V.	FL2000	Svatonova, Lucie Anna	SC1000
Sublett, Virginia	ND0350	Summer, Lisa	MA0150	Svedaite-Waller, Jurate	CT0100
Subotic, Vedrana	UT0400	Summer, Robert J.	FL2000	Svendsen, Dennis	MN1620
Subotic, Vedrana	UT0250	Summer, Stephen O.	TX3175	Svengalis, Judy	IA0420
Subotnick, Morton	NY2750	Summerfield, Susan	VT0400	Svenningsen, Russell	SD0050
Such, Rich	OR0175	Summers, Alvin	TN1720	Svensen-Smith, Carol	NY1850
Suchanek, Bronislaw	ME0500	Summers, Billy	NC0750	Sverjensky, Pamela	DC0170
Sucherman, Paul	WI0848	Summers, C. Oland	NC0850	Svetlanova, Nina	NY2150
Suchow, Paul	NY2100	Summers, Debora	MO0700	Svetlanova, Nina	NY2250
Suchy, John	MD0175	Summers, George	AZ0440	Svistoonoff, Katherine	FL0800
Suchy-Pilalis, Jessica R.	NY3780	Summers, Jerome	AG0500	Svoboda, George	CA4050
Suda, Carolyn W.	IL1350	Summers, Kim G.	NC0900	Svoboda, Matt	OR0350
Suda, Carolyn	IL1800	Summers, Michelle	KS0040	Svoboda, Richard	MA1400
Suda, David	IL1800	Summers, Shane	CA5100	Svoboda, Tomas	OR0850
Sudano, Gary R.	IN1300	Summers, Stanley Bryan	KS0040	Svorinich, Victor	NJ0700
Suddaby, Juliet	AG0130	Summers, William J.	NH0100	Swack, Jeanne	WI0815
Sudderth, Janette	MS0385	Summey, Harold	VA0450	Swafford, Jan	MA0350
Sudduth, Steven	KY1425	Summit, Jeffrey	MA1900	Swafford, Kent	MO1810
Sudeith, Mark A.	IL0600	Sumner Lott, Marie	GA1050	Swagler, Jason	IL2970
Suderman, Betty	AB0090	Sumner, Daniel	LA0770	Swaim, Doris	NC2640
Suderman, Gail	AB0060	Sumner, Melissa M.	VA0800	Swaim, Timothy	CA4300
Suderman, Mark	OH0250	Sumner, Richard	CA5400	Swain, Joseph P.	NY0650
Sudol, Jacob David	FL0700	Sumpter, Teresa L.	NC1250	Swalin, Paula	NM0450
Sudweeks, Barbara	TX2400	Sun, Cecilia	CA5020	Swallow, Dan	IL1200
Sue, Phig Choy	AG0650	Sun, Liyan	AG0550	Swallow, John	CT0850
Sueiras, Rafael	PR0115	Sun, Xun	UT0200	Swallow, John	CA2950
Suess, Jennifer	DC0170	Sunardi, Christina	WA1050	Swan, Phillip A.	WI0350
Sugarman, Jane	NY0600	Sunda, Robert	TN1200	Swan, Robert	WA0800
Suggs, Nora	PA2450	Sunday, Shannon	PA1750	Swan, Steve	MD0520
Suggs, Robert	MD0100	Sundberg, Gerard	IL3550	Swan, Walter R.	NC0700
Sugihara, Masahito	IL3100	Sundberg, Terri	TX3420	Swana, John	PA3250
Sugihara, Masahito	IL2250	Sundby, Candace	FL0500	Swana, John	PA3330
Sugimura, Kyomi	IL0750	Sundeen, Eric	MN0150	Swana, John	PA3600
Sugiyama, Yasuhito	OH0650	Sunderland, Jose	AL1300	Swaney, Susan	IN0900
Sugiyama, Yasuhito	OH0200	Sunderland, Paul	IL1050	Swank, Helen	OH1850
Suh, Elizabeth	MO0200	Sundet, Danna	OH1100	Swann, Jeffrey	NY2750
Suh-Rager, Min-Jung	AI0150	Sundquist, David	TX3420	Swann, Kyle	CT0650
Suhr, Melissa	TX3400	Sung, Benjamin H.	FL0850	Swann, Kyle	CT0850
Suhusky, Craig	MI1800	Sung, Hugh	PA0850	Swann, William E.	TN1000
Suits, Brian	TX3400	Sung, Janet	IL0750	Swanson, Barry	ID0150
Suits, Sue	MT0370	Sung, Marion	VA1350	Swanson, Bob	MO0350
Suits, Thad	MT0370	Sungarian, Victor	MA2250	Swanson, Brent	FL0700
Suk, Mykola	NV0050	Suniga, Rosemarie	NY3780	Swanson, Carl B.	CA0550
Suk, Richard	OH1900	Sunkett, Mark E.	AZ0100	Swanson, Christopher	VA0700
Sukonik, Inna	NY5000	Suovanen, Charles	CA2600	Swanson, Donald	MA1400
Sukonik, Inna	NY2400	Suozzo, Mark John	NY2750	Swanson, Isaac	WY0115
Sulahian, Nancy	CA0500	Suparta, I Dewa Made	AI0200	Swanson, Jenny	TX2260
Suleiman, Alexander	CA5300	Supeene, Susan	AA0040	Swanson, Karin	IA1200
Sulich, Stephen	MN0600	Super, Kevin	VA0650	Swanson, Lucy Jane	CA0600
Sulliman, Jason M.	IN1800	Supko, John	NC0600	Swanson, Mark L.	MA0100
Sullivan, Aimee M.	NC2400	Surface, Edward	TX0150	Swanson, Michelle	IA1600
Sullivan, Anne	IL3550	Surma, Dan	IL2650	Swanson, Philip	MA1650
Sullivan, Anne	DE0150	Surman, Patricia	OK1250	Swanson, Robyn	KY1550
Sullivan, Daniel	MA0850	Surman, Patricia J.	OK0550	Swanson, Stephen	IA1550
Sullivan, Dennis	NY0050	Surmani, Andrew	CA0835	Swanson-Ellis, Kathryn	CT0650
Sullivan, Eileen	NM0500	Surowiec, Jozef	MD0150	Swanston, Marcia	AF0100
Sullivan, James B.	AL0800	Survilla, Maria Paula	IA1800	Swantek, Paul	MI0900
Sullivan, James	AL0300	Susa, Conrad	CA4150	Swanzy, David	LA0300
Sullivan, James B.	AL1150	Susens, Sharon K.	CA2440	Swartz, Anne	NY0600

Alphabetical Listing of Faculty

Name	Code	Name	Code	Name	Code
Swartz, Anne	NY0250	Sylvern, Craig	NH0150	Talbott, Doug	KS0150
Swartz, Craig	IA0700	Sylvester, Eric	LA0350	Talbott, Laura	OK0800
Swartz, Jennifer	AI0150	Sylvester, Joyce	AL1300	Talbott, Matthew	IL1750
Swartz, Jonathan	AZ0100	Sylvester, Joyce	AL1195	Taliaferro-Jones, Gene	NC0450
Swartzbaugh, Bill	FL2050	Sylvester, Lisa M.	CA5300	Tall, Malinda	UT0350
Swartzbaugh, Tara	FL2050	Sylvester, Michael	IL0750	Tallant, Audrey	IL2910
Swartzendruber, Holly	KS1300	Sylvestre, Stephan	AG0500	Tallarico, Pat	OH0300
Swayne, Steven R.	NH0100	Symons, Kathy	PA0100	Talle, Andrew	MD0650
Sweaney, Daniel	AL1170	Synder Jones, Norma	IA0500	Talley, Damon S.	VA1350
Swearingen, Elaine	IL1520	Synott, Adrian	NJ0760	Talley, Dana W.	NY2900
Swearingen, James	OH0350	Syracuse, Rich	NY3650	Talley, Keith M.	OK1250
Swears, Marilyn	AL0345	Syracuse, Richard D.	OH1900	Talley, Sue	NY2900
Swedberg, Robert M.	MI2100	Syring, Natalie	OK1330	Talley, Terri	GA1150
Sweeley, Daniel	NY3717	Syring, Natalie	OK0700	Tallman, Donna	IL0850
Sweeney, Aryn D.	IN0150	Syswerda, Todd	IN1025	Tallman, Thomas J.	IL0630
Sweeney, Cecily	CA2600	Szabo, Istvan	IL3500	Talmadge, Samantha	CT0100
Sweeney, Christopher R.	AK0100	Szabo, Natalie	IL0840	Talpash, Andriy	AA0100
Sweeney, Gordon	AG0450	Szabo, Peter	OH2000	Talroze, Olga W.	MA2050
Sweeney, Joyce	CA5500	Szabo, Zoltan	MD0850	Talusan Lacanlale, Mary	CA2800
Sweeney, Michael	AG0300	Szafron, Brennan	SC0650	Talvi, Ilkka	WA0800
Sweeney, Michael	AG0450	Szanto, Judit	AA0050	Tam, Jing Ling	TX3500
Sweeny, Paul	NY0350	Szczesniak, Michel	AG0250	Tam, TinShi	IA0850
Sweet, Brennan	NJ0700	Sze, Eva	NY2750	Tam-Wang, Erica	IL2750
Sweet, Bridget Mary	IL3300	Szego, Kati	AD0050	Tamagawa, Kiyoshi	TX2650
Sweet, Michael	MA0260	Szekely, Eva D.	MO1800	Tamagni, Robert	MA0260
Sweet, Sharon	NJ1350	Szepessy, David	NJ0175	Tamarkin, Kate	VA1550
Sweets, Nancy	MO0500	Szklarska, Kamilla	FL0700	Tambiah, Dharshini	FL2000
Sweger, Keith	IN0150	Szlosek, Elaine Saloio	MA1100	Tamburello, John	WI1155
Sweidel, Martin	TX2400	Szlosek, Elaine Saloio	MA2100	Tamburrino, Maria	CA5000
Sweigart, Brian	OH0600	Szlubowska, Danuta	MS0385	Tamez, Ray	TX3410
Sweigart, Dennis W.	PA1900	Szmyt, Elzbieta M.	IN0900	Tamez, Raymundo	TX3350
Sweigart, Suzanne	MD0610	Szojka, Elisabeth	AA0050	Tan, Kia-Hui	OH1850
Swendsen, Peter V.	OH1700	Szurek, Jaroslaw P.	AL0800	Tan, Siok Lian	OH1450
Swensen, Ian	CA0840	Szutor, Kristina	AD0050	Tan, Siu-Lan	MI1150
Swensen, Ian	CA4150	Taavola, Kristin	CO0900	Tan, Su Lian	VT0350
Swensen, Robert	NY1100	Tabaka, Jim	MN1500	Tana, Akira	CA4200
Swensen-Mitchell, Allison	OR1300	Taber, Randy	NJ1400	Tanaka, Naoka	NY0500
Swenson, Daniel	MA1400	Tabor, Angela	CA3800	Tanaka, Naoko	NY2750
Swenson, Edward E.	NY1800	Tabor, Jerry N.	MD0800	Tanaka, Naoko	NY1900
Swenson, Ruth Ann	TX3510	Tacchia, Michele	CA0845	Tanaka, Rieko	MA2020
Swenson, Ruth Ann	CA4700	Tacconi, Marisa S.	PA2750	Tanau, Marian	MI2200
Swenson, Sonya	CA4950	Tacka, Philip V.	PA2350	Tancredi, Dominick	NY0644
Swenson, Thomas S.	NC2205	Tacke, Mathias	IL2250	Tandberg, Irene	AG0500
Swery, James	WI1155	Tacke, Mathias	IL2200	Tanenbaum, David	CA4150
Swiatek, Thomas	TN0350	Tacke, Tom	AZ0150	Tang, Betty	PA1850
Swiatkowski, Chet	CA3150	Tackett, Jeff	OH1100	Tang, Jenny	MA2050
Swiatkowski, Hak Soon	CA3150	Tackitt, Elliott	AZ0450	Tang, Patricia	MA1200
Swic, Piotr T.	NC0850	Tackling, Sebastian	ND0350	Tang, Pin-Fei	CA2420
Swidnicki, Susan	UT0400	Taddie, Daniel L.	AR0900	Tang, Susan	IL2150
Swift, Arthur	IA0850	Taddie, David	WV0750	Tang, Zhihua	MI0400
Swift, Mark D.	PA3580	Tadey, Anthony	IN0900	Tangarov, Vanguel G.	TX3175
Swift, Robert F.	NH0250	Tadic, Miroslav	CA0510	TangYuk, Richard	NJ0900
Swigger, Jocelyn A.	PA1400	Tadlock, David	OH1400	Taniguchi, Naoki	CA5510
Swilley, Daniel	IL1200	Tadmor, Tali	CA0510	Tanksley, Francesca	MA0260
Swilley, Sue	TN0250	Taffet, Robert S.	NY0050	Tanksley, Francesca	NY2660
Swinden, Kevin J.	AG0600	Tafoya, John J.	IN0900	Tann, Hilary	NY4310
Swinden, Laurel	AG0350	Tafrow, Tony	NJ0760	Tannehill, Sarah	MO2000
Swindler, Wil J.	CO0250	Taft, Burns	CA5360	Tanner, Christopher	OH1450
Swingle, Ira	AL0310	Taft, Kenneth	MA0260	Tanner, Greg	TX3540
Swinson, Beth Ann	IL3150	Tagg, Barbara M.	NY4150	Tanner, Gretchen	UT0250
Swinyar, Carol	MA0250	Tagg, Graham	AA0200	Tanner, Joel	OR0250
Swisher, Eric	KY0950	Taggart, Bruce F.	MI1400	Tanner, Robert	GA1450
Swisher, Kristen	TN1720	Taggart, Charlotte A.	KS1400	Tanno-Kimmons, Yoriko	AG0400
Swisher, Martha	IL2650	Taggart, Christian	DE0150	Tanosaki, Kazuko	MD1000
Swist, Christopher	NH0110	Taggart, Cynthia Crump	MI1400	Tanouye, Nathan	NV0050
Swist, Christopher	NH0150	Taggart, Mark Alan	NC0650	Tao, Patricia	AA0100
Swist, Christopher	MA1100	Tague, Daniel	VA1350	Tao, Ye	LA0100
Switzer, Linda	FL1650	Tahere, David	GA0600	Tapanes-Inojosa, Adriana	IL1080
Switzer, Mark	FL0930	Tai, FanFen	IN0900	Tapia, Doug	CO0625
Switzer, Mark	FL0800	Tait, Alicia Cordoba	IL0275	Tapia, James R.	NY4150
Swoboda, Deanna	AZ0100	Tait, Edward	AG0650	Tapia-Carreto, Veronica	AA0050
Swope, Anastasia E.	NJ0800	Tait, Edward	AG0450	Taplin, Alan	OH2300
Swope, Matthew	FL1550	Tait, Kristen N.	MI1750	Tappa, Richard J.	TX0250
Swope, Monica	CA5350	Tait, Malcolm	AG0500	Tapper, Robert	MT0400
Swope, Richard	GA1000	Tak, Young-Ah	FL1740	Tapping, Roger	MA0350
Swopes, Polly	OK0500	Takacs, Miklos	AI0210	Tapping, Roger	MA1400
Swora, Matthew	MI1950	Takacs, Peter	OH1700	Tarantiles, Andre C.	NJ0800
Swora, Matthew	MI1000	Takacs, William	TX3750	Tarantiles, Andre	NJ0175
Swygard, Craig	IA0900	Takagi, Shinobu	NY3725	Tarantine, April A.	PA3260
Swygert, Jonathan	GA1300	Takahashi, Hiromi	AA0035	Tarantino, Cassandra	CA1510
Sycks, Linda	OH1800	Takamine, Victoria	HI0210	Taranto, Cheryl	NV0050
Sycks, Linda	OH0250	Takao, Naoko	FL1900	Taranto, Vernon	FL1650
Sydow, Holly	PA2250	Takarabe, Clara	IN1750	Tarbox, Maurie	UT0350
Syer, Jamie	AB0210	Takasawa, Manabu K.	RI0300	Tarbutton, Butch	SC0050
Syer, Katherine R.	IL3300	Takayama, Akemi	VA1350	Tarchalski, Helen Smith	MD0060
Sykes, Jean	NC0910	Takebe, Yoko	NY1900	Tarczon, Philip	MI1650
Sykes, Jeffrey	CA5000	Takebe, Yoko	NY2150	Tardif, Guillaume	AA0100
Sykes, Jeffrey R.	CA0807	Takeda, Walter N.	HI0060	Tardy, Gregory	TN1710
Sykes, Jerilyn	MA0260	Takekawa, Miho	WA0650	Taricani, JoAnn	WA1050
Sykes, Kimball	AG0400	Takemoto, Maya	WA1100	Tariq, Susan Martin	TX3750
Sykes, Peter	MA0400	Takemoto, Maya	WA1300	Tarr, Carol	CO0900
Sykes, Peter	MA1400	Takesue, Sumy A.	CA4450	Tarr, Jeffrey	DC0010
Sykes, Peter	MA1175	Takeya, Kimiyo	CA0825	Tarrant, Fredrick A.	GA1800
Sykes, Robert	DC0170	Takizawa, Marcus	AB0200	Tarrant, James	MO1550
Sykes, Wiley	NC0910	Talaga, Steve	MI1050	Tarsi, Boaz	NY1860
Sylar, Sherry	NY2250	Talberg, Jonathan	CA0825	Tartell, Joey	IN0900
Syler, James	TX3410	Talbert, Rebecca	MO2050	Tarulli, Scott	MA0260
Syler, James	TX3530	Talbot, Brent C.	PA1400	Taruskin, Richard	CA5000
Sylvan, Sanford	AI0150	Talbot, Brent	IL3300	Tarver, Jennifer	AG0300
Sylvan, Sanford	NY1900	Talbott, Christy	WI0848	Tash, Sharon	MO1900

Name	Code	Name	Code	Name	Code
Tasher, Cara S.	FL1950	Taylor, Robert C.	AB0100	Templon, Paul	NC2400
Tashjian, B. Charmian	IL0750	Taylor, Robert J.	SC0500	Ten Brink, Jonathan	MN0625
Tashjian, Charmian	IL1085	Taylor, Rowan S.	CA2700	TenBrink, Karen	MI0100
Tashpulatov, Oyber N.	IN0100	Taylor, Sam	NC2205	Tendall, Rosita	IL0100
Tate, Brian	MO1800	Taylor, Sean	OH0500	Tender, Peter	OH1850
Tate, David L.	VA0800	Taylor, Stephen G.	CT0850	Tenegal, George	IL2100
Tate, Elda Ann	MI1600	Taylor, Stephen	NY1900	Tenenbaum, Lucy	VT0200
Tate, Galen	CT0300	Taylor, Stephen	NY2150	Tenenbom, Stephen	NY1900
Tate, Henry Augustine	MA0260	Taylor, Stephen A.	IL3300	Tenenbom, Steven	NY0150
Tate, Mark	KY0610	Taylor, Steve M.	GA2150	Tenenbom, Steven	PA0850
Tate, Mark	IN1010	Taylor, Steven	CO0150	Tener, James R.	IA0850
Tate, Philip	NJ0175	Taylor, Sue	MO1950	Tenison-Willis, MaryJo	AR0750
Tate, Shelia D.	VA1800	Taylor, Sue	MO1900	Tennant, Scott	CA5300
Tatge, Valorie	OK0700	Taylor, Susan Lynnette	IN0100	Tennenbaum, Judie	RI0150
Tatge, Valorie	OK1200	Taylor, Ted	NY2250	Tennenbaum, Lucy	VT0100
Tatman, Neil E.	AZ0500	Taylor, Terry D.	AL0800	Tentser, Alexander	AZ0480
Tatum, Mark	NM0450	Taylor, Thomas E.	NC2430	Tenzer, Michael	AB0100
Tau, Omari	CA0840	Taylor, Thomas	NC1600	Teply, Lee	VA1000
Taub, Paul	WA0200	Taylor, Timothy D.	CA5031	Ter-Grigor'yan, Irina	IN0900
Taube, Heinrich K.	IL3300	Taylor, Timothy D.	CA5032	Ter-Kazaryan, Marine	CA1960
Taubman, Dorothy	PA3250	Taylor, Tom	CO0200	Teran, Louie	CA2550
Taurins, Ivars	AG0450	Taylor, Una D.	NE0050	Terauchi, Kristi	AZ0510
Tauscheck, Jonathan	IA0930	Taylor, Valerie	MA0260	Terbeek, Kathleen	TX3000
Tavaglione, Eunice	TX0700	Taylor, Wayne	VA0450	Tercero, David R.	TX0850
Tavera, Celeste	CA5550	Taylor, William	AL1195	Terefenko, Dariusz	NY1100
Tavernier, Jane	VA1475	Taylor-Bilenki, Jan	AA0050	Terenzi, Mark J.	NJ0700
Taves, Heather	AG0600	Taylor-Gibson, Cristina	DC0050	Teresi, Cindy	CA0150
Tavianini, Marie A.	PA0900	Tchantceva, Irena	RI0150	Teresi, Dominic	NY1900
Tayerle, Loren	CA1550	Tcharos, Stefanie	CA5060	Terey-Smith, Mary	WA1250
Tayler, David	CA5000	Tchekina, Tatiana	NY1100	Terkeek, Karen	CO0830
Taylor, Allan	MA2100	Tchekmazov, Andrey	MN1625	Terlaak Poot, Nancy	PA2450
Taylor, Amanda	MO1950	Tchii, Kent	CA2200	Termini, Steven	TX0075
Taylor, Amanda	MO0775	Tchivzhel, Edvard	SC0750	Terrance, Christine	AA0040
Taylor, Annie	AZ0350	Tchoubar, Katerina	AG0300	Terrell, Brett	IN0250
Taylor, Anthony	NC2430	Tchougounov, Evgueni	AG0170	Terrell, Maurice	FL1700
Taylor, Arlecia Jan	TX2100	Tcimpidis, David	NY2250	Terrien, Paul	WI1150
Taylor, Betty Sue	NY2400	Teachout, David J.	NC2430	Terrigno, Loretta	NY2250
Taylor, Beverly	WI0815	Teager, Michael	MI2000	Terrigno, Loretta	NY1600
Taylor, Bobby G.	TN1850	Teague, Chan	LA0050	Terrigno, Loretta	NY0625
Taylor, Brant	IL0750	Teague, Liam	IL2200	Terry, Carole	WA1050
Taylor, Brian S.	LA0760	Teague, William C.	LA0100	Terry, Clark	NJ1400
Taylor, Bryce B.	TX2960	Teal, Christian	TN1850	Terry, Lesa	CA4450
Taylor, Caroline	AR0500	Teal, Kelly	TX0100	Terry, Nicholas	CA0960
Taylor, Charles Edwin	CO0250	Teal, Kimberly Hannon	NY1100	Terry, Patrick L.	UT0250
Taylor, Charles L.	LA0800	Teal, Terri	KS0570	Terry, Peter R.	OH0250
Taylor, Christopher	WI0815	Teare, Racquel	OH1100	Terry-Ross, Patricia	MI2200
Taylor, Clifton	MS0500	Teasley, Kevin	VA1800	Teruel, Hugo	IL2150
Taylor, Clifton	MS0420	Teasley, Tom	DC0350	Terwilliger, William	SC1110
Taylor, Clint 'Skip'	GA2100	Tebay, John	CA0350	Tescarollo, Hamilton	IN0905
Taylor, Darryl G.	CA5020	Tebay, Johh	CA1900	Tesch, Catherine	MN1120
Taylor, David	IL0550	Tebbets, Gary	KS0040	Tesch, John	MN1120
Taylor, David	NY2250	Tebbs, Mckay	UT0200	Teske, Casey C.	PA0700
Taylor, David	NY2150	Tedards, Ann B.	OR1050	Teske, Deborah Jenkins	CO0200
Taylor, David B.	MI2200	Tedder, Teresa C.	KY1150	Teskey, Nancy	OR0400
Taylor, David L.	ID0060	Tedeschi, John	CT0650	Tessmer, David	PA3650
Taylor, Donald M.	TX3420	Tedesco, Anne C.	NY3500	Tessmer, David P.	PA1450
Taylor, Dowell	MS0350	Tedesco, Anthony C.	NY1600	Tessmer, David	PA1350
Taylor, Earl	NC0450	Tedford, Linda	PA2300	Test, Heather	TX3000
Taylor, Edward J. F.	TX0300	Teed, Pamela	AG0070	Testa, Michael	MA1650
Taylor, George	NY1100	Teed, Pamela	AG0150	Testa, Mike	MA2030
Taylor, Greg	AR0750	Teel, Allen J.	TX0050	Tetel, Ioan	AA0020
Taylor, J. Chris	AA0100	Teel, Susan	TX0050	Tetel, Mihai	CT0650
Taylor, Jack S.	CA3500	Teeple, Scott	WI0815	Teter, Eston	MD0175
Taylor, Jack M.	OH2275	Teeters, Donald	MA1400	Teter, Francis	CA1750
Taylor, James W.	SC1110	Teets, Sean	LA0250	Tetreault, Edward	MD0850
Taylor, James R.	CT0850	Tegels, Paul	WA0650	Tetreault, Edward	MD0650
Taylor, James	VA1550	Tegge, Scott	WI0250	Tetreault, Mark	AG0450
Taylor, James	VA1600	Tegnell, John Carl	CA4200	Teuber, Hans	WA0200
Taylor, James	NC1050	Tehan, Julie	IL3550	TeVelde, Rebecca	OK0800
Taylor, Janda	FL1450	Teicher, Susan C.	IL0800	Teves, Christopher	SC0275
Taylor, Jane	NY0500	Teichler, Robert Christopher	IL3150	Tevis, Royce	CA0800
Taylor, Janet	MS0400	Teichmer, Shawn	MI2000	Tevlin, Michael J.	OH2200
Taylor, Jeffrey B.	WI0450	Teicholz, Marc S.	CA0807	Tewari, Laxmi	CA4700
Taylor, Jeffrey	NY0600	Teicholz, Marc	CA4150	Teweleit, Russell D.	TX3750
Taylor, Jeffrey J.	NY0500	Teie, David	VA0450	Thachuk, Steve J.	CA0835
Taylor, Jim	TX1350	Teie, David	MD1010	Thacker, Elizabeth	OH1400
Taylor, Joel	CA5150	Teissonniere, Gerardo	OH0600	Thacker, Hope	TN1660
Taylor, Joseph	VA0600	Teixeira, Robert	NC0550	Thacker, Hope	KY0950
Taylor, Joseph	FL1430	Teixeira, Robert	NC2000	Thai, Mei-Chuan Chen	NC1600
Taylor, Karen M.	IN0900	Tejada, Rob	IL2250	Thakar, Markand	MD0650
Taylor, Keith A.	AL1160	Tejero, Nicolasa	TN1350	Thallander, Mark	CA1960
Taylor, Kristin Jonina	IA1750	Tejero, Nikolasa	TN1700	Thaller, Gregg	IN0550
Taylor, Larry Clark	VA0100	Tel, Martin	NJ0850	Tharp, Reynold	IL3300
Taylor, Livingston	MA0260	Telesco, Paula	MA2030	Thatcher, James	CA5300
Taylor, Lucille	CA2420	Telford, Alicia	CA5000	Thaut, Michael H.	CO0250
Taylor, Maria C.	PA3250	TellerRatner, Sabina	AI0200	Thaves, Darrin	CA0825
Taylor, Marilyn S.	NC1650	Tellinghuisen, Harvey	CA3975	Thayer, Edwin C.	VA0450
Taylor, Mark	CO0550	Telner, Susan	AG0600	Thayer, Fred M.	PA2100
Taylor, Mark A.	MS0360	Tembras, Dan	IN0905	Thayer, Fred	MD0360
Taylor, Marshall	PA2800	Temme, Diane	NE0200	Thayer, Heather	AR0500
Taylor, Marshall T.	PA3250	Tempas, Fred	CA2250	Thayer, Katherine	CO0625
Taylor, Michael S.	SC0750	Tempas, Laurel	IL1520	Thayer, Lucinda J.	WI0850
Taylor, Mitchell	IL1500	Temperley, David	NY1100	Thayer, Marc	MO1950
Taylor, Nancy	TX3520	Temperley, Joe	NY1900	Thayer, Robert W.	OH0300
Taylor, Paul	DC0050	Temperley, Joe	NY2150	Theberge, Paul	AG0100
Taylor, Paul F.	KY0550	Temple, Elizabeth A.	VA1350	Thee, Lawrence	NC0930
Taylor, Priscilla	MA2010	Temple, Robert P.	NE0250	Theimer, Axel K.	MN0350
Taylor, Rachel	KY0550	Templeman, Robert W.	OH2550	Theisen, Alan	NC1250
Taylor, Ralph	MS0400	Templeton, David M.	SC0500	Theisen, Kathleen Ann	CT0800
Taylor, Rhonda	NM0310	Templeton, Peter	NH0250	Theodore, Michael	CO0800

Alphabetical Listing of Faculty

Name	Code	Name	Code	Name	Code
Theofanidis, Christopher	CT0850	Thomas, Martha L.	GA2100	Thompson, Kenneth	NY2400
Theriault, Kristen Moss	NY4320	Thomas, Matthew J.	IL3500	Thompson, Laura	LA0250
Therrian, Dennis	MI1200	Thomas, Matthew	CA0815	Thompson, Lee D.	MO1810
Therrien, Gabrielle	AI0200	Thomas, Matthew	CA3500	Thompson, Lee D.	WA1300
Thesen, Anita	MD0600	Thomas, Michael	AL0530	Thompson, Linda	FL2130
Theurer, Britton	NC0650	Thomas, Naymond	TX3175	Thompson, Linda K.	TN0850
Thevenot, Maxine R.	NM0450	Thomas, Nicholas	IL1890	Thompson, Lynn	IL3500
Thewes, Mark	OH1350	Thomas, Nova	NJ1350	Thompson, Mallory	IL2250
Thiagarajan, Beverly	CA3600	Thomas, O. T.	AL0950	Thompson, Marcus	MA1200
Thiaville, Amy L.	LA0300	Thomas, Omar	MA0260	Thompson, Marcus	MA1400
Thibault, Joel	AI0190	Thomas, Phillip E.	TN0850	Thompson, Marilyn	CA4700
Thibault, Lorraine	AI0210	Thomas, Rachel	AG0600	Thompson, Michelle	CO0550
Thibeault, Anna	GA0950	Thomas, Raymond D.	TN1100	Thompson, Patricia A.	KS0650
Thibeault, Matthew	IL3300	Thomas, Reginald	MI1400	Thompson, Paul	WI0817
Thibodeau, David	MA2030	Thomas, Richard	SC0800	Thompson, Paul	WI0825
Thibodeau, Gilles	AG0150	Thomas, Richard Pearson	NY4200	Thompson, Paul	MO1500
Thibodeau, Norman	NY3600	Thomas, Richard B.	SC1000	Thompson, Phil A.	SC1200
Thibodeau, Theresa	AG0350	Thomas, Rob	MA0260	Thompson, Randy	OK0825
Thibodeaux, David	AZ0350	Thomas, Robert	NJ1400	Thompson, Rich	NY1100
Thibodeaux, Tatiana	CA4500	Thomas, Robert E.	NY0700	Thompson, Richard O.	CA4100
Thickstun, Karen	IN0250	Thomas, Ronald B.	PA2800	Thompson, Robert	TN0100
Thieben, Jacob S.	SC0800	Thomas, Russell	MS0350	Thompson, Robert	WI0825
Thiedt, Catherine E.	OH0950	Thomas, Sally	NY2750	Thompson, Robert Scott	GA1050
Thiel, Robb G.	IN1350	Thomas, Sally	NC0300	Thompson, Ruth	TX3000
Thiele, Margaret	MI0600	Thomas, Sally	NY1900	Thompson, Sandra D.	OK1330
Thiele, Michael	WI0300	Thomas, Sally	NY2250	Thompson, Shannon	NC2600
Thiele, Michael	WI1150	Thomas, Samuel	NY0630	Thompson, Shauna	IN1600
Thielen, Karen	CA4425	Thomas, Steve	OH0350	Thompson, Shaw	SC0710
Thielen, Karen	CA4400	Thomas, Steven	MO1110	Thompson, Sonja K.	MN0050
Thielen-Gaffey, Tina	MN1600	Thomas, Steven F.	FL1850	Thompson, Stephanie	OR0400
Thielmann, Christel	NY1100	Thomas, Steven L.	PA3700	Thompson, Steven	MN0250
Thiem, Barbara	CO0250	Thomas, Susan R.	GA2100	Thompson, Steven D.	CA0150
Thiemann, Amy	NE0150	Thomas, Susan H.	RI0300	Thompson, Thomas	PA0550
Thieme, Robert	WV0750	Thomas, Suzanne M.	NY0400	Thompson, Timothy D.	FL1450
Thier, Bethany	WI0750	Thomas, Suzanne	AG0050	Thompson, Timothy F.	AR0700
Thierbach, Sue Ellen	MO1950	Thomas, Taryn	NY5000	Thompson, Vance	TN1710
Thierbach, Susie	MO0650	Thomas, Tracy	NC2435	Thompson, Virginia M.	WV0750
Thiesfeldt, Jeneane M.	MN1030	Thomas, Vicky	WA0980	Thompson, William C.	MA0260
Thiessen, John	NY1900	Thomas, Wayne	MN1250	Thompson-Buechner, Patti	NY4150
Thile, Scott	KY0950	Thomas, Wendy E.	OK1450	Thoms, Jason A.	NY0850
Thimmesch, Richard	IA0650	Thomas, William	AG0650	Thoms, Jonas	OH2500
Thimmig, Les	WI0815	Thomas, William D.	SC0750	Thomsen, John David	CA1550
Thivierge, Anne	AI0190	Thomas-Lee, Paula	GA1700	Thomsen, Kathy	MN0800
Thivierge, Jacques	AI0210	Thomason, Eliza	TX3100	Thomson, Christopher	MN0800
Thogersen, Chris	IN0550	Thomason, Jo Carol	NC1100	Thomson, George	CA2910
Tholl, Andrew	CA3100	Thomason-Redus, Caen		Thomson, Jacqueline	IA1400
Thom, Marcia	VA1400	Thomasson, John	FL0800	Thomson, Jacqueline	IA1350
Thom, Patty J.	MA0350	Thome, Diane	WA1050	Thomson, John	IL0550
Thoma, August	MI1830	Thome, Joel H.	NY3785	Thomson, Philip G.	OH2150
Thoma, James	NJ0700	Thomen, Willard	IL3370	Thomson, Richard	AG0450
Thoma, James E.	PA2550	Thomen, Willard	IL0730	Thomson, Susan N.	GA0950
Thomalla, Hans Christian	IL2250	Thompson, Amanda	CO1050	Thomson-Price, Heather	AB0100
Thoman, Jessica	TN1720	Thompson, Anne	MI0900	Thorburn, Melissa R.	NY0400
Thomas, Andre J.	FL0850	Thompson, Anne	AG0500	Thoreson, Deborah	GA0750
Thomas, Andy	OR0175	Thompson, Barbara Tilden	PA2450	Thorman, Marc	NY0500
Thomas, Anita	MD0300	Thompson, Bob	ME0340	Thorn, Becky	MO1950
Thomas, Ben	WA0200	Thompson, Bobbi Amanda	AG0500	Thorn, Julia	PA3150
Thomas, Ben	MA0260	Thompson, Bradley	CO0550	Thornblade, Rebecca E.	MA2050
Thomas, Benjamin	WA0460	Thompson, Bruce A.	NC1000	Thornblade, Sarah	CA3650
Thomas, Bruce	MA0260	Thompson, Catherine	CA2775	Thornburg, Benjamin	OH0550
Thomas, Bryan	OH1100	Thompson, Chester	TN0100	Thornburg, Scott	MI2250
Thomas, Caryl Beth	MA1450	Thompson, Christopher K.	AR0950	Thornburgh, Elaine	CA4900
Thomas, Colby L.	NY3765	Thompson, Christopher E.	MO0775	Thorndike, Oliver	MD0650
Thomas, Craig	DE0150	Thompson, Christopher	LA0770	Thorne, Cecilia	UT0050
Thomas, Craig	PA3330	Thompson, Cindy	KS0200	Thorngate, Russell	WI0925
Thomas, Craig	CA5550	Thompson, Cindy	KS0980	Thornhill, Margaret	CA1425
Thomas, Daniel A.	MO1810	Thompson, Curt	TX3000	Thornton, Bruce	MN0350
Thomas, Darrin	MN1450	Thompson, Dan	MA0260	Thornton, Delores	WY0050
Thomas, David	PA3330	Thompson, David	WI0804	Thornton, Diane B.	NC0550
Thomas, Diane	CA3300	Thompson, David B.	SC0850	Thornton, Jim	IL1890
Thomas, Edwin	IN0005	Thompson, David	WI0400	Thornton, Linda	PA2750
Thomas, Eric S.	TX0600	Thompson, Dawn	VA1550	Thornton, Mary	TX2930
Thomas, Eric B.	ME0250	Thompson, Douglas S.	NJ0500	Thornton, Michael	CO0800
Thomas, Erica	OK1050	Thompson, Douglass	IN0910	Thornton, Paula E.	FL1950
Thomas, Erica	OK0450	Thompson, Edgar	UT0250	Thornton, Robert	FL1800
Thomas, Fennoyee	TX3150	Thompson, Fiona	PA2300	Thornton, Tony	MA2000
Thomas, Gary	MD0650	Thompson, Floyd	MN1050	Thornton, William C.	NY2750
Thomas, Gates	MA0260	Thompson, Fred	WA0700	Thorp, Steven	NM0250
Thomas, Hunter	AL1160	Thompson, Gerald	DE0200	Thorpe, Allan	AB0060
Thomas, Jay	WA0200	Thompson, Gordon R.	NY3650	Thorpe, Allan	AB0090
Thomas, Jeffrey	CA5010	Thompson, Gregory T.	NC1000	Thorpe, Austin	UT0400
Thomas, Jennifer	NC2210	Thompson, Howard	TX1600	Thorpe, Clyde	KY0800
Thomas, Jennifer	MN0625	Thompson, J. Mark	LA0550	Thorson, Eric	TN0250
Thomas, Jennifer	FL1850	Thompson, J. Lynn	VA0150	Thorson, Lee	IA0150
Thomas, Joel Wayne	KS0265	Thompson, Jack	FL0800	Thorson, Lisa	MA0260
Thomas, John	VA0700	Thompson, James	IA0400	Thorson, Valerie	OH2150
Thomas, John	MO1950	Thompson, James	NY1100	Thorson, Valerie	OH0700
Thomas, John	CA5300	Thompson, Janet	OH1600	Thorstenberg, Roger W.	KS0150
Thomas, John	MA0260	Thompson, Janet	OH1200	Thrasher, Alan R.	AB0100
Thomas, June M.	PA2550	Thompson, Janice Meyer	AZ0100	Thrasher, Lucy	MN0600
Thomas, Kelland K.	AZ0500	Thompson, Jason	IN1025	Thrasher, Michael	TX3535
Thomas, Kelly Gene	AZ0500	Thompson, Jewel	NY0625	Threadgill, Gwen J.	AL1050
Thomas, Kenneth B.	AL0340	Thompson, Joan M.	CA3100	Threinen, Emily	PA3250
Thomas, Ladd	CA5300	Thompson, John	NJ1400	Threlkeld, David M.	KY1425
Thomas, Laura	AG0050	Thompson, John	GA0950	Throgmorton, Debra	CO0950
Thomas, Laurel A.	IN1450	Thompson, John	AA0050	Throness, Dale	AB0060
Thomas, Loretta	SD0600	Thompson, Jonathan	AB0090	Throness, Dale	AB0100
Thomas, Louise	CA0960	Thompson, Karin E.	WA1100	Throop, Barbara Chandler	MI1160
Thomas, Margaret E.	CT0100	Thompson, Kathy A.	OK0700	Thrower, Daniel	UT0305
Thomas, Marilyn Taft	PA0550	Thompson, Kenneth	OH0300	Thrower, Daniel N.	TX3530

Thulin, Jeanette	MN1250	Tipps, Angela	TN1100	Tomlinson, Peter	NY4450
Thull, Jonathan	IA0400	Tipps, James	OH2500	Tomlinson, Peter	CT0800
Thurber, Donald W.	CA2420	Tipton, Dewitt	SC0750	Tomlinson, Rebecca	CA0845
Thurgood, George	AG0300	Tipton, Elizabeth	MA0600	Tomlison, R. Scott	PA2250
Thurlow, Deborah	MD0150	Tipton, Mark	ME0250	Tomoff, Lisa Geering	CA5040
Thurmaier, David P.	FL0680	Tirado, Hector	PR0100	Tompkins, Charles B.	SC0750
Thurman, Demondrae	AL0650	Tirado, Jonathan	TX3530	Tompkins, Daniel	VA0350
Thurman, Demondrae	AL1170	Tirk, Richard	OK1250	Tompkins, Joseph H.	NJ1130
Thurmer, Harvey	OH1450	Tirk, Suzanne	OK1350	Tompkins, Joseph	NY2250
Thurmond, Gloria J.	NJ1160	Tisch, Don	IL0650	Tompkins, Joshua	MN1250
Thurmond, Paul	TN1450	Tischer, Raymond	CA3300	Tompkins, Leslie	NY2400
Thursby, Stephen	MD0650	Tischler, Judith	NY1860	Tompkins, Ruth	KY0650
Thurston, Andrew	MD0170	Tiscione, Mike	GA0750	Tonelli, Chris	AD0050
Thwaites, Mary Evelyn Clark	AL1300	Tisdel, Scott	WI1150	Toner, D. Thomas	VT0450
Thye, David R.	TX2600	Titlebaum, Michael	NY1800	Tones, Daniel	AB0060
Thygeson, Jeffrey K.	MN1625	Titmus, Jon	CA4450	Toney, Hubert	PA0700
Thygeson, Jeffrey	MN1295	Titmus, Jon	CA5360	Tong, Kristopher	MA1400
Thym, Jurgen	NY1100	Titon, Jeff	RI0050	Tonkin, Humphrey	CT0650
Tian, Tian	MO1790	Titterington, Beth	MO1810	Tonnies, Mary Kaye	IL2970
Tiana, Mayo	IL2150	Titterington, Connie	OR0850	Tonnu, Tuyen	IL1150
Tibbs, Elizabeth J.	AZ0150	Tittle, Sandra	OH1000	Toomer, Charlie	FL0600
Tiberi, Frank	MA0260	Titus, Anthony	MN1625	Toomey, John F.	VA1000
Tiberio, Albert	PA2950	Titus, Jamie	MO0050	Toops, Gary	CA3200
Tiberio, William	NY4350	Titus, Jason	NY4350	Toote, Linda	MA0350
Tice, Joshua	WI1150	Titus, Joan M.	NC2430	Toote, Linda	MA0400
Tice, Loren C.	KY1350	Titus, Julia	IA0300	Topel, Spencer	NH0100
Tice, Ronald	MO1810	Titze, Ingo R.	IA1550	Topilow, Carl	OH0600
Ticheli, Frank	CA5300	Tivnan, Brian	MA0200	Topolovec, David	WI1155
Tichenor, Jean-Marie	WY0050	Tjoelker, Joy	WA0550	Toppin, Louise	NC2410
Tichgraeber, Heidi	KS0210	Tjornehoj, Kris	WI0845	Toradze, Alexander D.	IN0910
Tick, Judith	MA1450	Tkachenko, Tanya	AG0450	Torbert, Jeffrey	AF0100
Tickner, French A.	AB0100	Tober, Nina M.	PA3150	Toren-Immerman, Limor	CA0810
Tidaback, Darrel	IN1450	Tobey, Forrest	IN0400	Torkelson, Suzanne	IA1800
Tidaback, Darrell	IN0910	Tobey, Moira	NY5000	Torlina, Mark	MO0550
Tidmore, Natasha	AL0850	Tobia, Riccardo	PA2900	Tormann, Cynthia	AG0250
Tidwell, Dallas	KY1500	Tobias, Evan	AZ0100	Tormann, Wolf	AG0250
Tidwell, Edith	KY1500	Tobias, Paul	NY2250	Tornello, Joseph	ID0050
Tidwell, Mary	TX3360	Tobias, Scott C.	FL1800	Tornquist, Doug	CA0510
Tidwell, Mary	TX1510	Tocco, James V.	OH2200	Tornquist, Doug	CA0815
Tiedemann, Patrice	RI0250	Tocheff, Robert	OH1600	Tornquist, Douglas V.	CA5300
Tiedemann, Sarah	OR0150	Todd, Allen F.	TN1680	Tornquist, Douglas	CA3300
Tiedge, Faun Tanenbaum	OR0450	Todd, Charles E.	GA2150	Toro, Cesar	PR0100
Tiefenbach, Peter	AG0300	Todd, Colette	WI0250	Torok, Debra	PA2450
Tiemann, Jason E.	KY1500	Todd, Jo Ella	MO1800	Toronto, Emily Wood	SD0550
Tiernan, Stephany	MA0260	Todd, Kenneth W.	CO1050	Torosian, Brian	IL3550
Tierney, Joanne	MN1295	Todd, Kristen Stauffer	OK0650	Torosian, Brian L.	IL2150
Tietjen, Linda	CO0830	Todd, R. Larry	NC0600	Torpaga, Olivier	OH1850
Tiffe, Janine	OH1100	Todd, Richard	FL1900	Torrans, Richard	TN1600
Tiffin, Corey	IL0750	Todd, Richard	TN1400	Torre, Robert Anthony	GA0050
Tigges, Kristie M.	MN1295	Todd, Sarah	IL1050	Torrenti, John	CT0100
Tignor, Scott	WV0600	Todd, Sheila	IN1560	Torres Navarro, Pedro J.	PR0115
Tikker, Timothy	MI1150	Todorov, Jassen	CA4200	Torres Perez, Elisa	PR0115
Tili-Trebicka, Thomaidha	NY4150	Todorovski, Catherine	AI0200	Torres Rivera, Alfredo	PR0115
Till, Sophie	PA2200	Toensing, Richard E.	CO0800	Torres, Adam A.	CO0250
Tiller, Jim	NY1700	Toft, Robert	AG0500	Torres, Barry A.	NY3550
Tiller, Jim A.	NY3730	Tognozzi, Victoria	CA0150	Torres, David	TX2260
Tilley, Janette M.	NY0635	Tokar, David A.	PA0900	Torres, Douglas	CA3320
Tilley, Marilyn	MI1650	Tokito, Kazuo	PA3250	Torres, George	PA1850
Tilley, William T.	VT0450	Tolar, Ron	AL0400	Torres, Gregory J.	LA0450
Tillman, Joshua	NC2700	Tolbert, Clinton	MI0350	Torres, Jose	TX0550
Tillman-Kemp, Gloria	WI0250	Tolbert, Elizabeth D.	MD0650	Torres, Jose R.	PR0150
Tillotson, J. Robert	IL1085	Tolbert, Patti	GA0850	Torres, Martin	CA5355
Tilman, Ernest	PA2300	Toledo, Patricia	IL1085	Torres, Martin	CA0859
Tilney, Colin	AB0150	Toliver, Brooks	OH2150	Torres, Michael Rene	OH1650
Tim, Raotana	CA2550	Toliver, Nicki Bakko	MN0040	Torres, Stephanie	RI0200
Timbrell, Charles	DC0150	Toll, Yvonne	GA0500	Tortolano, Jonathan	PA2250
Timm, Cynthia L.	OH0700	Tollefson, Arthur R.	NC2430	Toscano, Amy	CA2390
Timm, Joel	CA5300	Tollefson, Mary J.	WI0810	Toscano, Patricia	SD0300
Timm, Laurance	CA0815	Tollefson, Tim	MN0200	Tosh, Melissa Denise	CA5150
Timmerman, David	TX1750	Tolley, David	DE0050	Tosser, Michele	OH0950
Timmerman, Mark	NY2750	Tolliver, Charles	NY2660	Tot, Zvonimir	IL3310
Timmerman-Yorty, Carol	NY4460	Tolmacheka, Tatyana	OH0755	Totenberg, Roman	MA1175
Timmey, Zachery	VA0950	Tolson, Gerald H.	KY1500	Toth, Benjamin J.	CT0650
Timmons, Jeff D.	MO1810	Toman, Sharon Ann	PA2775	Toth, Gwen J.	NJ0800
Timmons, Kathryn Jill	OR0450	Tomarelli, Ron	AF0050	Toth, Michael S.	PA2550
Timmons, Leslie	UT0300	Tomaro, Annunziata	OH2200	Totter, John	RI0250
Timmons, Timothy	MO1810	Tomaro, Michael	PA1050	Totter, Stephen	PA0550
Timothy, Sarah O.	AL0890	Tomaro, Robert	WI0100	Touliatos-Miles, Diane	MO1830
Tincher, Brenda M.	NE0590	Tomasello, Andrew	NY0250	Toulouse, Sharon	KS1350
Tindall, Danny H.	FL1740	Tomasello, Andrew	NY0600	Touree, Marc	PA3000
Tindall, Josh	PA1900	Tomasello, Randal S.	FL1300	Toussaint, David	VA1600
Tindemans, Margriet	WA0200	Tomasone, Adeline	PA3250	Toutant, William P.	CA0835
Tiner, Kris	CA0650	Tomasone, Adeline	NJ1050	Tovey, David G.	OH1850
Tiner, Kris	CA0270	Tomassetti, Benjamin	VA0500	Towell, Gordon L.	KY0900
Ting, Damian	CA2775	Tomassetti, Beth	VA0150	Tower, Joan	NY0150
Tingen, Jolie	NC2500	Tomassetti, Gary	CT0650	Tower, Mollie	TX3175
Tingle, JoDean	AL0300	Tomassi, Edward	MA0260	Towery, Randy	ID0070
Tingler, Stephanie	GA2100	Tomaszewski, Staci	CO0250	Towey, Dan	IA0930
Tini, Dennis J.	MI2200	Tomenko, Keri	MD0150	Towill, John	AA0020
Tinkel, Brian C.	NC1250	Tominaga, Akiko	AA0050	Town, Stephen	MO0950
Tinnell, Jennifer L.	KY0400	Tomkins, John	SD0580	Towne, Gary	ND0500
Tinnin, Randall C.	FL1950	Tomkins, John	SD0050	Towne, Lora Rost	AZ0440
Tinsley, David	AL0400	Tomkins, Tanya	CA4150	Towner, Cliff	GA0850
Tinsley, David	FL0040	Tomkins, Tanya	CA4400	Towner, John	IL1085
Tinsley, Frederick	CA0815	Tomlin, Charles	MI1650	Towner, John	IL0850
Tinsley, Frederick D.	CA3650	Tomlin, Laura A.	GA0250	Townsend, Bradley	WI0840
Tinsley, Janis	AL0400	Tomlin, Terry	TX3515	Townsend, Bradley	WI0865
Tint, Judith H.	NY2750	Tomlinson, Dan	AZ0470	Townsend, Bradley G.	OR0700
Tiodang, Jasmin	PR0115	Tomlinson, Judy	CA1500	Townsend, Brendan	TX1425
Tipei, Sever	IL3300	Tomlinson, Mike	MN1250	Townsend, Norma	CA3800

Alphabetical Listing of Faculty

Name	Code	Name	Code	Name	Code
Townsend, Sid	OH0350	Trigg, William	NJ0175	Tsai, Sin-Hsing	TN1700
Townson, Kevin	TX2750	Trigg, William	NJ1050	Tsai, Tammy	CA0859
Towse, Joanna	NY3680	Trimborn, Thomas J.	MO1780	Tsang, Bion	TX3510
Toyich, Boyanna	AG0450	Trimillos, Ricardo D.	HI0210	Tsang-Hall, Dale Y.	CA2450
Toyonaga, Shiho	IL2100	Trinckes, John	FL0365	Tsangari, Victoria	KY0750
Traa, Olav	AA0110	Trindade, Walter	CA0400	Tsao-Lim, May	AR0300
Traba, Fernando	FL1745	Trinka, Jill L.	SC0420	Tsarov, Eugenia M.	NY3780
Traba, Fernando	FL0800	Trinkle, Karen M.	MO1950	Tschannen, James	FL1700
Trabichoff, Geoffrey	ID0070	Trinkle, Steven W.	NV0050	Tse, Joel	OH2300
Trabold, William E.	CA4450	Tripathi, Nitin	VA1550	Tse, Kenneth	IA1550
Trachsel, Andrew J.	OH1900	Triplett, Isaac	IL0420	Tselyakov, Alexander	AC0050
Tracy, Gina	IL1612	Tripold, David	NJ0760	Tseng, Keng-Yuen	MD0650
Tracy, Janet M.	TX2260	Tripp, Krysia	ME0150	Tsinadze, Ana	PA3250
Tracy, Michael	KY1500	Tripp, Krysia	ME0200	Tsitsaros, Christos	IL3300
Tracy, Phala	MN0750	Tripp, Scott	FL0700	Tsolainou, Constantina	GA0550
Tracy, Randy	MT0350	Tristano, Barbara	WI0810	Tsong, Mayron K.	MD1010
Tracy, Shawn	WI0250	Tritle, Kent	NY2150	Tsontakis, George	NY0150
Tracy, William	NY2150	Tritle, Kent	NY1900	Tsou, Judy	WA1050
Tracz, Frank	KS0650	Tritt, Terry	IL2775	Tu, Gary	IL1900
Traficante, Debra	OK1350	Trittin, Brian L.	TX0400	Tu, Ming	IL1750
Traficante, Frank	CA1050	Trolier, Kimberly A.	PA1300	Tuck, Patrick M.	KY1425
Traficante, Marie	NY2400	Trolier, Kimberly	PA1150	Tucker, Allan	NY2750
Trahan, Kathleen	MD1010	Trollinger, Valerie L.	PA1750	Tucker, Carlton	KS1350
Trail, Julian	DC0170	Trombetta, Adelaide Muir	VA0650	Tucker, Craig	MS0400
Trail, Robert	IN1800	Trompeter, Jim W.	IL0550	Tucker, Debra	OH0850
Trainer, Robert F.	WA0600	Tronzo, David	MA0260	Tucker, Eric Hoy	MI0400
Trainer, Susan	WA0600	Tropman, Matt	CA5350	Tucker, Gary	AE0050
Traino, Dominic	DC0050	Tropp, Thomas	IL2100	Tucker, Jenna	AR0300
Tramiel, Leonard	MS0560	Trost, Jennifer	PA2750	Tucker, John	TX2750
Tramm, Jason	NJ1160	Trosvig, Michael	MN1100	Tucker, Joshua	RI0050
Tramontozzi, Stephen	CA4150	Trott, Donald L.	MS0700	Tucker, Kenneth	MD0700
Tramontozzi, Stephen	CA2950	Trotta, Michael J.	VA1830	Tucker, Kent	PA2250
Tramposh, Shelly	NY3780	Trotter, John William	IL3550	Tucker, Kerry	IA1300
Tramuta, Laurie	NY3725	Trottier, Alain	AI0190	Tucker, Laura	TN0350
Trang, Grace	IL1090	Trottier, Danick	AI0200	Tucker, Melissa	MA1175
Tranquilino, Armando	FL0700	Trottier, Jean-Nicolas	AI0150	Tucker, Nick	IL0800
Transue, Arlene M.	IL2900	Trottier, Jean-Nicolas	AI0200	Tucker, Rob	WA1250
Transue, Paul A.	IL2900	Trotz, Amy	GA0750	Tucker, Scott	NY0900
Tranter, John	MN1623	Troup, Nathan	MA0350	Tucker, Stephen Earl	CA5020
Trantham, Gene S.	OH0300	Troup, Nathan	MA0400	Tucker, Timothy	AR0550
Trapani, Steve	CA0825	Trout, Anne	MA1175	Tucker, Timothy R.	AR0350
Trapp, Ken	CT0550	Trout, Marion T.	IN1310	Tucker, William S.	NY2750
Trask, Alvin	MD0550	Trout, Susan	MA1560	Tuckwiller, George	VA0700
Traster, Jeff	FL2050	Trovato, Stephen	CA5300	Tuckwiller, George	VA1750
Traster, Jeffry	FL0930	Trovato, Vincent	PA2550	Tudek, Thomas S.	IN1650
Traub, Thomas	NJ1050	Trowbridge, Cynthia	IL3550	Tudor, Robert W.	WV0550
Traube, Caroline	AI0200	Trowbridge, James	NY1550	Tueller, Robert F.	ID0060
Traugh, Steven	CA2960	Trowbridge, Wendra	NY1550	Tuhuilka, Olga	WI0150
Traupman-Carr, Carol A.	PA2450	Trowers, Robert	NC1600	Tuinstra, John	WI0865
Traut, Donald G.	AZ0500	Troxel, Jeffrey C.	MT0350	Tuit, Rhoda	CA4450
Trauth, Vincent	IL2350	Troxler, Lorinda	PA1350	Tulga, Philip	CA0840
Trautman, Mark A.	NJ1130	Troxler, Rebecca	NC0600	Tull, David	CA3500
Trautwein, Barbara	NC2500	Troxtel, Diane C.	MI1700	Tully, Amy	SC0420
Trautwein, Mark	MO0550	Troy, Matthew	NC1650	Tully, Cynthia	CA1425
Traver, Ivylyn	CA3400	Troy, TJ	CA1000	Tully, James	SC0420
Travers, Aaron	IN0900	Troyer, Claire	CO0050	Tumino, Joe	IL1890
Travers, Martha	MI2100	Troyer, Lara	OH1100	Tumlinson, Charles	CA0815
Travers, Tarn	IA0950	Trtan, Jacqueline	MO0350	Tung, Alice	MD0300
Trawick, Eleanor	IN0150	Truax, Barry D.	AB0080	Tung, Alice Clair	MD0520
Trayle, Mark	CA0510	Truax, Jenean	PA0150	Tung, James	MD0300
Traylor, Steve	WY0060	Trubow, Valentina	IN1560	Tung, Jennifer	AG0300
Treadwell, Nina	CA5300	Truckenbrod, Emily	IL2910	Tung, Leslie Thomas	MI1150
Treadwell, Nina K.	CA5070	Truckenbrod, Steve	NC1600	Tung, Margaret M.	IL2300
Treadwell, Robin	GA1200	Trucks, Linda	AL0530	Tung, Mimi	VA1550
Treat, Richard	WA0650	Trudel, Eric	MD0850	Tuning, Mark	CA3920
Trechak, Andrew	KS1450	Trudel, Eric	CT0800	Tunis, Andrew	AG0400
Tredway, Curtis B.	TX3520	Trudel, Louise	AI0210	Tunks, Thomas W.	TX2400
Tree, Michael	NY0150	True, Carolbeth	MO1950	Tunnell, Meme	KY0250
Tree, Michael	NY1900	True, Carolyn E.	TX3350	Tunnell, Michael	KY1500
Tree, Michael	NY2150	True, Janice	IN0500	Tunstall, Charles	TN1650
Tree, Michael	PA0850	True, Nelita	NY1100	Tunstall, Julia	PA3400
Treer, Leonid P.	FL0650	Truelove, Lisa	OR0950	Tuohey, Terese M.	MI2200
Trejo, Kyndell	IL2750	Truelove, Stephen	OR0950	Tuomaala, Glen	MN1300
Tremarello, Richard	WI1150	Trueman, Daniel	NJ0900	Tuomi, Scott	OR0750
Tremblay, Christian	MD0650	Truhart, Regina A.	OH2200	Tupik, Justin	NJ0760
Tremblay, Christian	MD1000	Truitt, D. Charles	PA2200	Turanchik, Thomas	NC0750
Tremblay, Dan	NY3780	Truitt, Elizabeth	IN1600	Turchi, Elizabeth	WV0550
Tremblay, Dan	AG0250	Truitt, Jon	IN1600	Turci-Escobar, John	TX3510
Tremblay, Remy	AI0190	Trujillo, Valerie M.	FL0850	Turcios, Lorri	SC0200
Trembly, Dennis	CA5300	Trumbore, Lisa	KY0200	Turcotte, Kevin	AG0650
Tremulis, Nick	IL0720	Trump, Kirsten	VA1350	Turcotte, Kevin	AG0450
Tremura, Welson Alves	FL1850	Truniger, Matthias	MA1400	Turechek, Dennis	NY1400
Trenfield, Sally	TX3515	Trunk, Joseph	FL0500	Turechek, Dennis	NY3765
Trent, Andrea	TX3370	Trussel, Jacque	NY3785	Turek, Ralph	OH2150
Trent, Robert S.	VA1100	Trussell, Adam	NE0160	Turetzky, Bertram	CA5050
Trentacosti, Marcella	IN0905	Trussell, Adam	NE0610	Turgeon, Bruno	AI0190
Trentacosti, Michael J.	IN0905	Trynchuck, Carla	MI0250	Turgeon, Edward	FL0650
Trentham, Donald R.	TN0650	Tryon, Colleen	OH1600	Turgeon, Melanie E.	AA0035
Trepanier, Louis	AG0400	Tryon, Colleen	OH1350	Turini, Ronald	AG0500
Tresler, Matthew T.	CA2390	Tryon, Denise	PA3250	Turino, Thomas R.	IL3300
Tresler, Matthew	CA1425	Tryon, Robin R.	OH2290	Turizziani, Robert	WV0800
Trester, Francine G.	MA0260	Tryon, Valerie	AG0200	Turley, Edward L.	MN0350
Tretick, Stephanie	PA0600	Tsabar, David	AB0100	Turley, Steve	PA1150
Treuden, Terry	WI1155	Tsabary, Eldad	AI0070	Turnbough, Kimberlee	SC0900
Treuhaft, Ben	NY2750	Tsachor, Rachelle P.	IA1550	Turnbull, David	WA1150
Trevino, Alexander R.	VA1000	Tsachor, Uriel	IA1550	Turnbull, Kai	MA0260
Trexler, Henry	NC0850	Tsai, I-Ching	CA3800	Turner, Aaron	CO0275
Treybig, Carolyn	TN0100	Tsai, I-Hsuan	IL3450	Turner, Anne Z.	NY3650
Treybig, Joel	TN0100	Tsai, Kevin	NJ0750	Turner, Anthony	NY4500
Triest, Amelia	CA5010	Tsai, Shang-Ying	CA5400	Turner, Charles	KY0300

Turner, Charles	CT0650	Tymas, Byron	NC1600	Upton, Elizabeth R.	CA5032
Turner, Connie	AC0100	Tymoczko, Dmitri	NJ0900	Upton, Gregory	OH0200
Turner, Corinne	DC0170	Tynan, Paul	AF0150	Upton-Hill, Diana	IA0750
Turner, Cynthia Johnston	NY0900	Tynon, Mari Jo	ID0070	Uranker, Mark	CA0825
Turner, Daniel	SC0200	Tyre, Jess B.	NY3780	Urban, Emily	MN0250
Turner, Dave	AI0150	Tyree, Rebecca	VA1600	Urban, Guy	MA2150
Turner, Dean W.	WV0200	Tyrrell, Sarah	MO1810	Urban, Marshall	MN0250
Turner, Denise	NM0450	Tyson, Blake W.	AR0850	Urban, Tim	NJ1130
Turner, Don	TX2350	Tyson, John	MA1400	Urban, Timothy	NJ1350
Turner, George	IL3500	Tyson, LaDona	MS0580	Urbano, Patricia	CA3270
Turner, George	ID0070	Tyson, Liana	AR0350	Urbis, Richard	TX3515
Turner, George	ID0150	Tzavaras, Nicholas G.	NJ0800	Urbis, Sue Zanne Williamson	TX3515
Turner, Gregory E.	KS0400	Tzigalanis, Voula	AA0040	Urdaz, Mayra E.	PR0115
Turner, J. Frank	CA4450	Tzvetkov, Atanas	IN0900	Uribe, Patrick Wood	MA0400
Turner, James	MS0385	Uch, Mandeda	CA3800	Uricco, Grace E.	RI0300
Turner, James	MI1150	Uchida, Rika	IA0550	Urista, Diane J.	OH0600
Turner, Jeffrey	PA0550	Uchimura, Bruce	MI2250	Urke, Jan	AA0035
Turner, Jeffrey	PA1050	Uchimura, Susan	MI2250	Urke, Jan	AA0100
Turner, Katherine L.	SC0350	Udagawa, Yoichi	MA0350	Urness, Mark	WI0350
Turner, Kelly J.	TX3400	Uddenberg, Scott	IL0850	Urquhart, Peter W.	NH0350
Turner, Kevin P.	OH1850	Udell, Chester	OR1050	Urrey, Frederick E.	NJ1130
Turner, Kevin P.	AL1150	Udland, Matt	KS0210	Urrutia, Lara	CA5150
Turner, Kristen	NC1800	Udow, Michael W.	MI2100	Urso-Trapani, Rena	CA0825
Turner, Kristin Meyers	NC1700	Udy, Kenneth L.	UT0250	Urton, Dan	MO1800
Turner, Kyle	NY2250	Ueno, Ken	CA5000	Ury Greenberg, Linda	NY2750
Turner, Kyle	NJ0800	Uhl, Lise	TX1600	Uscher, Nancy	CA0510
Turner, Leon P.	TX2100	Uhle, Grant	PA3250	Usher, Ann L.	OH2150
Turner, Leon	LA0700	Uhlenkott, Gary	WA0400	Usher, Barry	AG0500
Turner, Lloyd	MS0100	Uitermarkt, Cynthia D.	IL1850	Usher, Jon	CA0845
Turner, Mark F.	NY2750	Ulaky, Hollis B.	SC1200	Ushioda, Masuko	MA1400
Turner, Mark E.	TX2700	Ulaky, Hollis	NC2000	Utley, Brian	TN1850
Turner, Matthew	WI0350	Ulen, Ronald	TX3175	Utsch, Glenn R.	PA3100
Turner, Michael W.	OR1000	Ulffers, Christopher	NC0650	Utter, Hans	OH1850
Turner, Mitchell	GA1200	Ulibarri, Fernando	FL0200	Utterback, David	TX2650
Turner, Noel	TX1400	Ullery, Benjamin	CA1075	Utterback, Joe	CT0300
Turner, Patrick	VA1700	Ullery, Charles	MN0950	Utterstrum, Oscar	TN1400
Turner, Randin	IL0300	Ullery, Charles	MN1623	Uyeyama, Jason	CA2420
Turner, Randy	LA0150	Ullery, Steve	OH1450	Uzeki, Yoichi	NY0646
Turner, Rebecca	SC0650	Ullman, Beth	TX1600	Uzur, Viktor	UT0350
Turner, Richard	WY0050	Ullman, Michael	MA1900	Vaas, Sharon	OH2275
Turner, Richard	CA0815	Ullman, Richard	VT0100	Vacanti, Jennifer	NY2950
Turner, Ronald A.	KY1200	Ulloa, Cesar	CA4150	Vacanti, Tom L.	MA2000
Turner, Ross	AG0550	Ullom, Jack R.	CA4410	Vacca, Anthony	AZ0490
Turner, Sandra	KY1200	Ulman, Erik	CA4900	Vaccariello, Lois	CA2750
Turner, Tammy	KY1540	Ulmer, Allison C.	TX2960	Vaccaro, Brandon C.	OH1100
Turner, Tammy	KY0950	Ulmer, Enoch	NE0200	Vaccaro, Brian	MO1120
Turner, Thomas	MN1623	Ulreich, Douglas	IL2775	Vacchi, Steve	OR1050
Turner, Timothy R.	LA0900	Ulreich, Eric	DC0170	Vaclavik, Jude	UT0300
Turner, Veronica R.	CO0350	Ulrich, Brad	NC2600	Vadala, Christopher	MD1010
Turner-Tsonis, Anne	NM0200	Ulrich, Jerry	GA0900	Vadlamani, Mallika	NC0550
Turney, Brent	WI0850	Ultan, Jacqueline	MN1050	Vagel, Marianne E.	MN1030
Turnhull, Elizabeth	AA0100	Umble, James C.	OH2600	Vaglio, Anthony J.	NC1300
Turnquist-Steed, Melody	KS0150	Umble, Jay	PA2300	Vagts, Peggy A.	NH0350
Turon, Charles T.	FL1745	Umble, Jay	PA0350	Vaicekonis, Dainius	WA0860
Turovsky, JoAnn	CA1075	Umble, Jay	PA3150	Vaida, John M.	PA3700
Turovsky, JoAnn	CA5300	Umble, Kathryn Thomas	OH2600	Vaida, John	PA2200
Turovsky, Yuli	AI0200	Umeyama, Shuichi	IN0900	Vail, Eleanore	IN0400
Turp, Richard	AI0210	Umezaki, Kojiro	CA5020	Vail, Kathy	MS0850
Turpen, Jennifer	WY0200	Umfrid, Thomas C.	OH2200	Vail, Leland	CA0825
Turpen, Scott	WY0200	Umiker, Robert C.	AR0700	Vail, Mark	TN1200
Turpin, Douglas	MO1830	Umphrey, Leslie	NM0450	Vaillancourt, Jean-Eudes	AI0200
Turpin, Mike H.	TX1350	Umstead, Randall	TX0300	Vaillancourt, Josee	AI0190
Turre, Steve	NY1900	Unal, Fureya	CA0815	Vaillancourt, Lorraine	AI0200
Turrill, David	OH1650	Undem, Stewart	CA0845	Vaillancourt, Paul	GA0550
Turrin, Joseph	NJ0700	Underhill, Owen	AB0080	Vaillancourt, Scott J.	ME0500
Turrin, Joseph E.	NJ0800	Underwood, Dale W.	FL1900	Valcarcel, Andres	PR0100
Turry, Alan	NY2750	Underwood, Greg	NC2420	Valcarcel, David Shawn	CA3265
Turska, Joanna	IL0650	Underwood, Keith W.	NY2750	Valcarcel, David	CA3950
Tusa, Michael C.	TX3510	Underwood, Keith	NY2250	Valcu, Mihai	PA3650
Tusing, Susan	GA0500	Underwood, Kent	NY2750	Valdepenas, Joaquin	AG0300
Tuten, Celeste	TN1850	Underwood, Kirsten F.	OK0150	Valdepenas, Joaquin	AG0450
Tutschku, Hans	MA1050	Underwood, Margaret	OH2050	Valdes Vivas, Eduardo	PR0115
Tutt, David	AA0020	Underwood, Michael P.	AR0750	Valdes, Cristina	WA0200
Tutt, Kevin	MI0900	Ung, Chinary	CA5050	Valdes, Eduardo	PR0150
Tuttle, Elise	UT0305	Ungar, Garnet	IN1600	Valdez, Paul	TX2295
Tuttle, John	AG0450	Ungar, Leanne	MA0260	Valdez, Stephen	GA2100
Tuttle, Julie	AZ0470	Ungar, Tamas	TX3000	Valdivia, Hector	MN0300
Tuttle, Marshall	OR0550	Unger, Leslie	CT0650	Valente, Liana	FL1550
Tutunov, Alexander	OR0950	Unger, Melvin P.	OH0200	Valentin Pagan, Aldemar	PR0115
Tuzicka, William	KS0700	Unger, Ruth Shelly	GA0750	Valentine, Bob	AL1250
Twaddle, Katherine	AC0100	Unger, Ruth Shelly	GA0050	Valentine, Claudette	NE0160
Tweed, Pauline	CA4100	Unger, Shannon M.	OK0550	Valentine, Colette	TX3510
Tweed, Pauline	CA2100	Unger, Susan	AL1195	Valenzuela, Victor	AZ0480
Tweed, Randall L.	CA2100	Ungurait, John B.	MS0575	Valera, Philip	NC0100
Twehues, Mark A.	TX3530	Uniatowski, Joanne M.	OH0200	Valeras, Michael	TN0100
Twitty, Katrina	CO0900	Unice, Charles	PA2200	Valeria, Anna	FL1310
Twitty, Katrina	CO0100	Unice, Charles	PA3700	Valerio, Anthony	MD0750
Twombly, Kristian	MN1300	Unland, David	NY1800	Valerio, Celia Chan	CA5040
Twomey, Michael P.	TX1900	Uno-Jack, Kaori	WY0200	Valerio, John	SC0900
Tworek-Gryta, Adrienne	NY4460	Unrath, Wendy	IL0850	Valerio, John B.	SC1110
Twyman, Nita	OK1030	Unrau, Lucia	OH0250	Valerio, Wendy	SC1110
Twyman, Venita	OK1050	Unruh, Elise A.	CA4410	Vali, M. Reza	PA0550
Tyborowski, Richard	AC0100	Unsworth, Adam	MI2100	Valiente, Jessica L.	NJ0800
Tychinski, Bruce D.	DE0150	Unsworth, Arthur E.	NC0050	Valjarevic, Vladimir	NY2250
Tyler, Edward	CT0050	Unsworth, Erik	TX3520	Valk, Alexis	TX2250
Tyler, George Tracy	AL0500	Upchurch, Elizabeth	AG0450	Valle, Amy	KY1200
Tyler, Marilyn	NM0450	Upcraft-Russ, Kimberly	NY2650	Vallecillo, Irma	CT0600
Tyler, Paul	IL2000	Updegraff, David	OH0600	Vallecillo, Irma	MA1400
Tyler, Philip	CA3640	Upham, David	NH0350	Vallee, Mickey	AA0100
Tyler, Steve	CA1550	Upshaw, Dawn	NY0150	Vallentine, John	IA1600

Alphabetical Listing of Faculty

Name	Code
Valley, Myriam	AG0150
Valli, Ubaldo	NY1350
Valliant, James	PA3710
Valliant, James	MD0170
Vallieres, Claude	AI0190
Vallieres, Claude	AI0220
Vallo, Victor	GA0850
Vallon, Marc	WI0815
Valls De Quesada, Margarita	AL0330
Vamos, Almita	IL2250
Vamos, Brandon	IN0900
Vamos, Brandon	IL3300
Vamos, Roland	IL2250
Van Appledorn, Mary Jeanne	TX3200
Van Berkel, Wilma	AG0500
Van Boer, Bertil H.	WA1250
Van Brunt, Jennifer	WI0960
Van Brunt, Laurie	MN0450
Van Brunt, Laurie	MN1600
Van Brunt, Laurie	WI0860
Van Brunt, Nancy	WI0960
Van Buren, Harvey	DC0350
Van Buskirk, Jeremy	MA1175
Van Cleave, Brad	CA0050
Van Cleve, Libby	CT0100
Van Cura, John	TX0300
Van Dalsom-Boggs, Mariel	WV0560
Van De Graaff, Kathleen	IL1400
Van DeLoo, Mary F.	WI0350
van den Honert, Peter	PA1200
Van Den Toorn, Pieter	CA5060
Van der Beek, Ralph	UT0350
Van der Bliek, Rob	AG0650
Van der Hooft, Rose	AC0100
Van der Linde, Polly	VT0050
Van der Loo, Marion	IL1750
Van der Sloot, Alexsandra	AA0050
Van Der Sloot, Michael	AA0040
Van der Sloot, William	AA0050
Van der Vat-Chromy, Jo-Anne	VA0600
Van der Werff, Ivo-Jan	TX2150
van der Westhuizen, Petrus	OH0950
Van der Westhuizen, Sophia	OH2600
Van Deursen, John	AB0100
van Deursen, John	AB0060
Van Deusen, Nancy	CA1050
Van Dewark, Vicky	CA3250
Van Dewark, Vicky	CA2200
Van Dijk, G. Hage	CA4400
van Dongen, Antoine	MA2050
Van Dreel, K.	FL1745
Van Dreel, Lydia	OR1050
Van Duser, Guy	MA0260
Van Duyne, Lisa	IL2750
Van Dyck, Thomas	MA1175
Van Dyke, Gary	NJ1400
Van Evera, Angeline Smith	MD0850
Van Gee, Jill	TX2260
Van Geem, Jack	CA1075
Van Geem, Jack	CA4150
Van Goes, Paula	TN1400
Van Herck, Bert	IA1550
Van Hoesen, Catherine	CA4150
Van Hoesen, Gretchen	PA0550
Van Hoesen, Gretchen	PA1050
Van Hoose, Matthew	DC0010
Van Hoose, Matthew	DC0170
Van Houten, John	CA0825
Van Houzen, Aren	MO0300
Van Houzen, Aren	LA0400
Van Hoven, Eric	PA1850
Van Hoven, Valerie	NJ0700
Van Hoy, Jeremy	CO0200
Van Kekerix, Todd	NJ0700
Van Kooten, Jan	MI0350
Van Nostrand, Carol	MN1295
Van Orden, Katherine	CA5000
Van Ouse, Philip	PA1050
Van Oyen, Lawrence G.	IL2050
Van Pelt, Michael	KY1000
Van Proosdij, Hanneke	CA5000
Van Regenmorter, Heidi	CA0150
Van Regenmorter, Merlyn	CA0150
Van Regenmorter, Paula	LA0450
Van Schaik, Tom	TX1750
Van Schoick, Thomas	CO0830
Van Sice, Robert	PA0850
Van Sice, Robert	MD0650
Van Sice, Robert	CT0850
Van Slyck, Trudi	MA2010
Van Speybroeck, Jennifer	IA1300
Van Wagner, Eric	OH2050
Van Weelden, Pam	AG0200
Van Winkle, Brian	WA0250
Van Winkle, Kenneth	NM0310
Van Winkle, Lisa K.	NM0310
Van Wyck, Helen J.	IL3100
Vana, John	IL3500
VanAllen, Michael	NY3350
VanArsdale, Christine	NC0550
Vanasse, Guy	AI0210
VanBecker, Leslie	MI0850
VanBecker, Leslie	MI0350
VanBuren, Susan	NY2650
VanBurkleo-Carbonara, Natalie	MN0040
Vance, Howard	TN0450
Vance, Jeanne	KS1450
Vance, Paul	MN1700
Vance, Scott	CA0845
Vance, Virginia L.	NC1800
VanCleave, Timothy	IN1050
Vancura, Ken	TX1750
Vancura, Kim	TX1750
VanDam, Lois	FL1430
Vandegriff, Matthew	NY2105
Vandegriff, Matthew M.	NY4050
Vandehey, Patrick	OR0250
Vandelicht, Roy D. 'Skip'	MO0100
VanDemark, James	NY1100
Vanden Wyngaard, Julianne	MI0900
Vandenberg, Lavonne	MI0350
Vander Gheynst, John R.	IN0907
Vander Hart, Gary	IA1200
Vander Linden, Dan	WI0848
Vander Weg, John D.	MI2200
Vander Weg, Judith B.	MI2200
Vander Wel, Stephanie L.	NY4320
Vanderbeck, Sue Ann	MI1300
Vanderborgh, Beth	WY0200
Vanderford, Brenda M.	WV0700
Vanderheyden, Joel	MO0550
Vanderkamp, Herman A.	CA4200
Vanderkooy, Christine	AJ0100
Vanderlinde, David	SD0580
Vandermark, Mark S.	LA0200
Vandermeer, Aaron D.	NC2435
Vandermeer, Philip R.	NC2410
Vanderpool, Linda	IA0550
Vanderwall, Barbara S.	IL2050
Vanderwerf, Paul	IL3550
Vanderwoude, Matt	AG0130
VanderWoude, Matthew	AG0650
VanDessel, Joan	MI0520
VanDessel, Peter	MI0520
Vandewalker, David W.	GA1050
Vandewalker, Eddie R.	TX1050
VanDieman, Jeremy	AA0050
Vandiver, Joseph	TX3650
Vandivier, Rick	CA4900
Vandivier, Rick	CA4400
Vandivort, Roger	WA1200
VanDyke, Susanne	MS0575
VanEchaute, Michael	IA1300
Vaneman, Christopher	SC0650
Vaneman, Kelly McElrath	SC0650
Vaness, Carol T.	IN0900
VanFleet, Joseph	KY0550
Vangelisti, Claire	LA0770
VanGent, Wendy	SD0400
Vangjel, Matthew S.	AR0730
VanHandel, Leigh A.	MI1400
VanHassel, Joseph	OH1900
VanHoven, Valerie S.	NJ0800
VanKopp, Kristi	CA0650
VanLente, Mike	MI1050
VanMatre, Rick	OH2200
Vannatta-Hall, Jennifer E.	TN1100
Vannice, Michael	OR0950
VanNordstrand, Shelby	IA0910
Vanore, John	PA3680
Vanosdale, Mary Kathryn	TN1850
VanRandwyk, Carol A.	MI0850
Vanscheeuwijck, Marc	OR1050
Vanselow, Jason	MN0040
VanValkenburg, Holly	CO0050
VanValkenburg, James	MI2200
VanValkenburg, Jamie G.	CO0050
Vanvoorhees, Rachael F.	LA0300
VanWeelden, Kimberly	FL0850
VanWeelden, Marnie	AG0600
VanWick, Brad	KS0590
Vardanian, Vera	MD0550
Vardanyan, Tigran	NY2650
Vardi, Amitai	OH1100
Vardi, Amitai	OH2150
Vardi, Uri	WI0815
Varellas, Barbara A.	CA3200
Vargas, Luis	IN0005
Vargas, Luis Enrique	IN0910
Vargas, Milagro	OR1050
Vargas, Philip	CA2975
Vargas, Ruben	TX1425
Variego, Jorge	ND0600
Varilek, Stephanie R.	NE0150
Varimezov, Ivan S.	CA5031
Varimezova, Tzvetanka	CA5031
Varineau, Gwen	MI0350
Varineau, John	MI0900
Varineau, John P.	MI0520
Varineau, John	MI0850
Varineau, John	MI0350
Varlamova, Liudmila	TX3525
Varner, Ed	MT0370
Varner, Eric Van der Veer	AG0550
Varner, Kenneth	SC0050
Varner, Michael	TX3500
Varner, Tom	WA0200
Varnes, Justin	GA1050
Varney, John	NY2250
Varon, Neil	NY1100
Varosy, Zsuzsanna	FL1650
Varosy, Zsuzshanna	FL0450
Varpness, Lee	MN1620
Vartan, Lynn	UT0200
Vartanian, Tina M.	CA5300
Varvel, Vince	MO1900
Vasallo, Nicholas R.	CA0807
Vascan, Ligia	WI0500
Vasconcellos, Renato	KY1500
Vascotto, Norma	AG0600
Vasey, Monika	DC0170
Vasimi, James	OH2600
Vaska-Haas, Kristina	LA0050
Vasquez, Hector	TX3400
Vasquez, Hector	FL1300
Vasquez, Jerico	GA1800
Vass, Heidi	CA0550
Vassallo, James	TX3400
Vassilandonakis, Yiorgos	SC0500
Vassilev, Mia	FL0050
Vassiliades, Christopher	NY2150
Vatalaro, Charles	NY1400
Vatchnadze, George	IL0750
Vatz, Shaina V.	MD0475
Vaughan, Charles	NC2420
Vaughan, Danny	OK1330
Vaughan, Jennie	TX2050
Vaughan, John	WV0050
Vaughan, Laura	MO0550
Vaughan, Matthew	PA3250
Vaughn, Beverly Joyce	NJ0990
Vaughn, Dona	NY2150
Vaughn, Donna	KY1200
Vaughn, James	CO0950
Vaughn, Jeanne	IL1890
Vaughn, Michael	TX1450
Vaughn, Michael	IL2000
Vaupel, Lisa	MD0400
Vauth, Henning	WV0400
Vavrikova, Marlen	MI0900
Vayman, Anna	IN0150
Vayo, David J.	IL1200
Vazquez, Anna	MN1295
Vazquez, Carlos	PR0150
Vazquez, Steven	IL1085
Vazquez-Ramos, Angel M.	CA0960
Veal, Larry	NH0350
Veal, Michael E.	CT0900
Veasley, Gerald	PA3330
Veazey, Charles	TX3420
Veazey, Lee	IN1600
Veblen, Kari	AG0500
Vedady, Adrian	AI0190
Veenker, Jonathan	MN0250
Veenstra, Kim	MI1050
Veenstra, Kimberly	MI0900
Veeraraghauen, Lee	AG0600
Vees, Jack	CT0850
Vega, Ray	VT0450
Vega, Rebecca	NJ0050
Vega, Victoria P.	LA0300
Vehar, Persis Parshall	NY0400
Veigel, Loren	OH2150
Veikley, Avis	ND0250
Veilleux, Trever L.	HI0200
Vela, Gloria	AZ0440
Velasco, Edmund	CA6000
Velasco, Wendy	CA6000
Velazquez, Ileana Perez	MA2250
Velazquez, Omar	PR0115
Velazquez, Paulette	IL1520
Veleta, Richard	PA1550
Velez, Gilbert Y.	AZ0500
Velez, Glen	NY2250
Velickovic, Ljubomir	CA3270
Veligan, Igor	CA0150
Veligan, Igor	CA5350
Velinova, Gergana	AB0210
Vellenga, Curtis W.	KS1400
Velleur, Melody	IL3150
Velosky, Ronald A.	PA0400
Veltman, Joshua	TN1660
Velvikis, Rachel N.	VA1500
Velykis, Theodore	NJ1100
Venable, Catherine Anne	NJ0825
Vendryes, Basil	CO0900
Venesile, Christopher J.	OH1100
Venettozzi, Vasile	KY0650
Venterini, Maurizio	FL0930
Vento, Rosa B.	NY2750

Alphabetical Listing of Faculty

Name	Code	Name	Code	Name	Code
Vento, Steve	OK1300	Villanueva, Rodrigo	IL2200	Volk, Jennifer Regan	IN0905
Ventre, Madelaine	NY2450	Villareal, Leanne	ND0150	Volk, Maureen	AD0050
Ventura, Anthony C.	DE0150	Villarrubia, Charles	TX3510	Volkar, Carie	OH0750
Ventura, Brian J.	MI2200	Villaveces, John	MO1790	Volker, Alyssa	TN0100
Ventura, Maria	OH2550	Villaverde, Christina	AL0800	Volker, Mark D.	TN0100
Venturini, Maurizio	FL2050	Villec, John	CA4300	Vollinger, William F.	NY2900
Venzen, Austin A.	VI0050	Villeneuve, Andre	AI0210	Vollmar, Ferdinand	TX3410
Vera, Juan-Carlos	FL1310	Villines, Roger	FL1500	Vollmer, Jeffrey	IN0900
Verbeck, Heather D.	OH2200	Vinao, Ezequiel P.	NY2750	Vollmer, Susan C.	CA5070
Verbsky, Franklin	NY1600	Vince, Donna	MO1950	Vollrath, Carl P.	AL1050
Vercelli, Michael B.	WV0750	Vince, Matt	AZ0440	Volpe Bligh, Elizabeth	AB0100
Vercoe, Barry	MA1200	Vincent, Dennis	FL1000	Volpe Bligh, Elizabeth	AB0090
Vercoe, Elizabeth	MA1600	Vincent, Jennifer J.	IN0800	Volpe, Christopher	MN1625
Verdehr, Walter	MI1400	Vincent, Kate	MA1175	Volpicelli, Thomas	PA1900
Verdery, Benjamin	CT0850	Vincent, Larry F.	TN1710	Volz, Nick R.	LA0300
Verdicchio, Linda	NJ1400	Vincent, Larry	TN1250	von Arx, Victoria	NY3700
Verdie' de Vas-Romero, Adriana	CA0825	Vincent, Lawrence P.	UT0050	Von Dassow, Sasha	FL1745
Verdrager, Martin	NY1900	Vincent, Randy	CA4700	Von Ellefson, Randi	OK0750
Verdy, Violette	IN0900	Vincent, Ron	NY2200	Von Foerster, Richard	CO0900
Veregge, Mark F.	CA4900	Vincent, Stephen	KS1300	Von Glahn, Denise	FL0850
Veres, Fran A.	AZ0500	Vinci, Jan F.	NY3650	Von Goerken, Lisa C.	NY0050
Vereshagin, Alex	CA1760	Vinci, Mark	NY1900	Von Gruenigan, Robert	OH1850
Verfaille, Vincent	AI0200	Vinci, Mark	NY3785	Von Hoff, Paul	WI0250
Verge, Marc-Pierre	AI0150	Vinci, Mark A.	NY3650	Von Hombracht, Willem	MO1950
Verhaalen, Marion	WI0150	Vines, Lisa	AL0530	Von Kamp, Rebecca	IA0300
Verhoeven, Martine	CA4450	Vinick, Russ	IL0720	Von Kampen, David	NE0150
VerHoven, Victoria K.	IL0275	Vining, David	AZ0450	Von Kampen, David W.	NE0200
VerHoven, Victoria	IL2050	Vining-Stauffer, Kristin	WA1100	Von Kampen, Kurt E.	NE0150
Verkuilen, Jeffrey	WI0750	Vining-Stauffer, Kristin	WA1300	Von Koenigsloew, Heilwig	AB0090
Vermeer, Cassidy	IA0790	Vinson, Danny	TX0600	Von Oertzen, Alexandra 'Sasha'	NY2750
Vermeulen, Ron	AB0040	Vinson, Danny	TX3535	Von Ohlen, John	OH2200
VerMeulen, William	TX2150	Vinson, Danny S.	TX3370	Von Pechmann, Lisa	IL1085
Vermillion, Terry L.	MN1300	Vinson, Nancy	AL0200	Von Schweinitz, Wolfgang	CA0510
Verner, Nakia	NY5000	Violett, Martha Watson	CO1050	Von Spakovsky, Ingrid	AL1160
Vernick, Gordon Jay	GA1050	Viragh, Gabor	CT0650	Von Syberg, Carol	AF0120
Vernon, Charles G.	IL0750	Viragh, Katalin	CT0650	Von Villas, Muriel	DC0100
Vernon, James R.	OK0650	Virelles, Amanda	TN1850	VonBerg, Craig	CA1850
Vernon, James Farrell	IN0905	Virelles, Amanda	TN0100	VonBerg, Craig	CA0810
Vernon, Michael	IN0900	Viren, Leslie	WY0150	Vonderheide, David E.	VA0250
Vernon, Robert	NY1900	Virgoe, Betty	CA1520	Vondra, Nancy	NE0610
Vernon, Robert	OH0600	Viscoli, David A.	MN1000	Vondracek, Tom	MN1500
Vernon, Ronald	MS0700	Visentin, Peter	AA0200	Vondran, Shawn	IN0150
Verplank, William	CA4900	Viskontas, Indre	CA4150	Vonsattel, Gilles	MA2000
Verrier, Thomas	TN1850	Visscher, Murray	AA0050	Voorhees, Jerry L.	LA0650
Verrilli, Catherine J.	MN1300	Viswanathan, Sundar	AG0650	Vore, Wallis W.	OH2250
Versaevel, Stephen	MT0200	Vitek, Milan	OH1700	Vores, Andy	MA0350
Versage, Susan Woodruff	NY2250	Vitenson, Misha	FL0700	Vorhes, Anna	SD0580
Very, Laura Knoop	PA0550	Vitercik, Greg	VT0350	Vorhes, Anna	SD0050
Verzatt, Marc	CT0850	Viton, John	KY0900	Vorhes, Anna	IA0500
Verzosa, Noel	MD0500	Vitro-Wickliffe, Roseanne	NJ0825	Vorhes, Anna	IA1200
Vesely, Blaine	OH1100	Vitti, Anthony	MA0260	Voris, Dan J.	OH0350
Vest, Jason	NM0100	Viverette, Connie	TX3527	Voro, Irina	KY1450
Vest, Johnathan	TN1720	Vivian, Jim	AG0650	Vorobiev, Dmitri	IA1600
Vetter, Roger R.	IA0700	Vivian, Jim	AG0450	Voronietsky, Baycka	ME0440
Vetter, Valerie	IA0700	Viviano, Samuel	TN1680	Vortman, Karma K.	IL1100
Vezinho, Ed	NJ1050	Vivio, Chris	TN0100	Vorwerk, Paul	CA0510
Via, Kelly	GA1300	Vivio, Christopher J.	TN0050	Vosbein, Terry	VA1850
Via, Kelly	GA0050	Vizante, Sonia	AG0200	Vosburgh, George	PA0550
Via, Susan	VA0250	Vizutti, Allen	SC1110	Vosburgh, George	PA1050
Vial, Stephanie	NC2410	Vlahcevic, Sonia K.	VA1600	Vose, David	MA0260
Viaman, Philip	CA5360	Vlajk, Christine	AG0600	Vosen, Elyse Carter	MN0450
Viardo, Vladimir	TX3420	Vleck, Marsha	MA0700	Voskoboynikova, Alla	MO1830
Vibe, Andrea	CA1265	Vliek, Pamela	CA3800	Voss, Darrell	CA1510
Vick, Bingham L.	SC0750	Vobejda, Lori	CA4150	Votapek, Kathryn	MI2100
Vick, Joe D.	AR0750	Vodnoy, Robert L.	SD0400	Votapek, Mark A.	AZ0500
Vickerman, Louise	UT0350	Voelker, Dale	IL1300	Votapek, Paul	FL0680
Vickers, Gilbert	MA1850	Vogan, Nancy F.	AE0050	Vote, Larry	MD0750
Vickers, Jeffrey E.	AR0600	Vogel, Allan	CA1075	Voth, Alison	MA0350
Vickery, Robert	MN1625	Vogel, Allan	CA5300	Voth, Allison	MA0400
Victorsen, Catherine	MN0800	Vogel, Allan	CA0510	Votta, Michael	MD1010
Victorsen, Catherine	MN0250	Vogel, Annette-Barbara	AG0500	Vought, J. Michelle	IL1150
Victorsen, Catherine	MN1280	Vogel, Bradley D.	KS1300	Voulgaris, Virginia	WA0550
Vidacovich, John	LA0300	Vogel, Debora	IA0500	Vowan, Ruth A.	AR0225
Videon, Michael	MT0200	Vogel, Dorothy	MI1650	Voyement, Jacques	CA5300
Vidiksis, Adam	PA3250	Vogel, Michael	AZ0510	Voyement, Jacques	CA0830
Vieaux, Jason	OH0600	Vogel, Roger C.	GA2100	Voyer, Jessica	VT0400
Viebranz, Gary A.	PA2250	Vogler, Paul	GA0940	Vranna, Jeff	ND0100
Viebranz, Gary A.	PA2715	Vogler, Paul	TN0260	Vrba, Cenek	AA0050
Viega, Michael	NY2450	Vogt, Bruce	AB0150	Vredenburg, Brenda	NY3780
Vieira, Alex	CO0200	Vogt, Elaine	IL1200	Vredenburg, Jeffrey	NY3780
Viemeister, Jane Stave	CA4580	Vogt, Harriet	LA0650	Vreeland, Harold	OR0750
Vierra, Alice	DC0170	Vogt, Nancy	NE0450	Vrenios, Elizabeth	DC0010
Viertel, Breton	ID0070	Vogt, Roy	TN0100	Vroman, David	IL0400
Viertel, Kyle	TX0390	Vogt, Sean F.	SD0300	Vu, Cuong	WA1050
Vigeland, Nils	NY2150	Vogt, Sebastian	MD0650	Vuori, Ruston	AA0080
Vigesaa, Erik	ND0350	Vogt-Corley, Christy L.	LA0350	Wachala, Greg	NY1550
Vigil, Ryan H.	NH0350	Voigt, Steve	VA0600	Wachmann, Eric	IA1800
Vigneau, Kevin	NM0450	Voigts, Kariann	IA1350	Wachs, Daniel Alfred	CA0960
Vigneau, Michelle	TN1680	Voin, Camelia	CA5040	Wachs, Dean	IN1450
Vigo, Silfredo	CA3460	Vojcic, Aleksandra	MI2100	Wachsmuth, Karen	IA1140
Vij, Andrea	MA1400	Vokes, Emmett	TX2200	Wachter, Claire	OR1050
Vik, Siri	OR0350	Vokolek, Pamela	WA1050	Wachter, Jeffrey	PA3650
Vilcci, Aldona	NY5000	Volchansky, Vera	PA2350	Wacker, John M.	CO1050
Viliunas, Brian	AL0800	Volchok, Michail	DC0170	Wacker, Jonathan D.	NC0650
Vilker, Sophia	MA1175	Volchok, Mikhail	MD1010	Wacker, Lori	NC0650
Vilker-Kuchmen, Valeria	MA1400	Volckhausen, David	NY2150	Wacker, Therese M.	PA1600
Villa, Tara Towson	NC0550	Voldman, Raisa	LA0650	Wacks, Karen S.	MA0260
Villafranca, Elio	PA3250	Voldman, Yakov	LA0650	Wada, Rintaro	NY1700
Villani, A. David	PA2710	Volet, Richard	AB0210	Wada, Rintaro	NY3475
Villanueva, Jari	MD1000	Volk, David Paul	VA1580	Waddel, Nathan	OR0350

Alphabetical Listing of Faculty

Name	Code	Name	Code	Name	Code
Waddell, Charles F.	OH1850	Walczyk, Kevin	OR1250	Wall, Sarah	NY4050
Waddell, Dan	CA1270	Wald, Jean P.	FL1750	Wallace, Carol	TX2710
Waddell, Mike	NC2440	Waldecker, Todd	TN1100	Wallace, Connie	WY0050
Waddell, Rachel Lynn	MI1000	Walden, Daniel	AL1050	Wallace, David	WA1250
Waddelow, Jim M.	NC1300	Walden, Kathy	OR0750	Wallace, David	NY1900
Waddington, Alan	CA1000	Walden, Sandra	IA1600	Wallace, Elizabeth Kuefler	UT0325
Waddley, Craig	AR0950	Walden, Valerie	CA1290	Wallace, Elizabeth	TX1100
Wade, Adrienne Sambo	MA1100	Waldis, Daniel	UT0250	Wallace, Jacob E.	OK1150
Wade, Bonnie C.	CA5000	Waldoff, Jessica	MA0700	Wallace, James A.	GA1070
Wade, Brett	AB0040	Waldon, Eric	CA5350	Wallace, Jeb	UT0325
Wade, Elaine San Juan	TX3515	Waldon, Reed	MI1300	Wallace, John H.	MA0400
Wade, Gail G.	TX1600	Waldon, Stanley H.	MI2200	Wallace, Noel	TX3300
Wade, James	PA3250	Waldrep, Mark	CA0805	Wallace, Robin	TX0300
Wade, Jess E.	TX2900	Waldron, Ann	IL2050	Wallace, Roy	MI0850
Wade, Jonathan	AG0400	Waldron, Janice Lynn	AG0550	Wallace, Sharlene	AG0650
Wade, Mark Alan	OH0850	Waldron, Richard	WA0300	Wallace, Shawn	OH1850
Wade, Melinda	MD0060	Waldrop, Joseph	TX3850	Wallace, Susan	GA1700
Wade, Michael	IN0910	Waldrop, Michael	WA0250	Wallace, Thomas	ME0270
Wade, Patsy B.	TN1850	Waldvogel, Martha	MI1050	Wallace, Virginia V.	KS1400
Wade, Patsy	TN0100	Waldvogel, Nicolas	CA5350	Wallace, Wayne	CA4400
Wade, Thomas	NJ1050	Walentine, Richard L.	ND0150	Wallace, William	AG0200
Wade-Elkamely, Bobbie	OK0450	Walford, Maria	IL3550	Wallace-Boaz, Krista B.	KY1500
Wadley, Darin J.	SD0600	Walgren-Georgas, Carol	IL1085	Wallach, Joelle	TX3420
Wadopian, Eliot	NC2600	Walhout, Lisa	MI0350	Wallarab, Brent K.	IN0900
Wadsworth, Amanda	LA0080	Walicki, Kenneth J.	CA0815	Wallen, Norm	WA0050
Wadsworth, Benjamin K.	GA1150	Walker, Abigail	FL1500	Wallenbrock, Nicole Beth	NY2150
Wadsworth, Stephen	NY1900	Walker, Abigail	AL0345	Waller, Anne	IL2250
Waeber, Jacqueline	NC0600	Walker, Alan	AG0200	Waller, Jim	TX3410
Waggener, Joshua A.	NC2350	Walker, Alicia W.	SC1110	Walley, Steve	IN1560
Waggoner, Andrew B.	NY4150	Walker, Amanda Jane	CA5020	Walley, Steve	IN0905
Waggoner, Cathy	TX1350	Walker, Angela	MD1050	Wallin, Nicholas L.	IL1400
Waggoner, David	AZ0500	Walker, Anne E.	MO0050	Wallin, Susan	OH0700
Waggoner, Dori	MO0100	Walker, Becky	TX2260	Wallis, David N.	MO0650
Waggoner, Emily	SC0650	Walker, Ben	KY0550	Wallis, Kelly	UT0400
Waggoner, Emily	SC0200	Walker, Brian	TX2750	Wallis, Kelly	UT0250
Waggoner, Robert	MO1950	Walker, Carmen Diaz	TX3520	Wallis, Victor E.	MA0260
Wagler, Trevor	AG0600	Walker, Charles	NJ1350	Walls, Kimberly C.	AL0200
Wagman, Marcy R.	PA1000	Walker, Cherilee	KS0590	Waln, Ronald	GA2100
Wagner, Brent	MI2100	Walker, Chris	GA0625	Walrath, Brian	MI2000
Wagner, Chad A.	NY2750	Walker, Christopher G.	GA0150	Walsh, Allan	AG0070
Wagner, Corbin	MI1400	Walker, Christopher	CA3150	Walsh, Allan	AG0150
Wagner, Craig	KY1500	Walker, Darlene	FL0670	Walsh, Benjamin	TX1850
Wagner, David O.	MI1260	Walker, Dave	KY0250	Walsh, C. Peter	CA5100
Wagner, Irvin	OK1350	Walker, David L.	VA1000	Walsh, Craig T.	AZ0500
Wagner, Jaimie	AG0550	Walker, Deanna	TN1850	Walsh, David	MN1623
Wagner, James	MI0600	Walker, Diana	WA0650	Walsh, Diane	NY2250
Wagner, Jan	VA1350	Walker, Elaine	AZ0490	Walsh, Eileen	AF0120
Wagner, Jeanine F.	IL2900	Walker, Elizabeth	KS0750	Walsh, James	LA0300
Wagner, Julia P.	PA1900	Walker, Elizabeth	PA0850	Walsh, Marty	MA0260
Wagner, Kathy	MI0520	Walker, Erin	KY1450	Walsh, Megan A.	FL1900
Wagner, Lauren	MI1950	Walker, Garry	ID0250	Walsh, Michael	TX2250
Wagner, Lawrence R.	PA3250	Walker, Gayle	OH2050	Walsh, Michael	SD0550
Wagner, Linda	MN0150	Walker, Gerald	MS0650	Walsh, Peter	CA1750
Wagner, Linda	WV0800	Walker, Gregory T. S.	CO0830	Walsh, Thomas P.	IN0900
Wagner, Lorraine	WY0115	Walker, Gregory	MN0350	Walston, Patricia	MS0400
Wagner, Marella	WI0770	Walker, Heather	AB0050	Walt, Marlene	MA2250
Wagner, Michael F.	NY4320	Walker, James E.	IL1090	Walt, Shimon	AF0100
Wagner, Paul	MA0260	Walker, James A.	NY3730	Walt, Stephen J.	MA2000
Wagner, Randel	WA0250	Walker, James	CA5300	Walt, Stephen	MA2250
Wagner, Richard A.	OK1450	Walker, Jeri	OK1150	Walter, Cameron	AG0450
Wagner, Shelbi	OH2250	Walker, Jesse	GA0150	Walter, Douglas	CO0800
Wagner, Wayne L.	MN1030	Walker, Jim	CA1075	Walter, Elaine R.	DC0050
Wagoner, Cynthia L.	NC0650	Walker, Joey	IA1550	Walter, Jennifer Stewart	NC2430
Wagoner, Lisa	OK0550	Walker, John C.	MD0650	Walter, Laura	CA5550
Wagoner, W. Sean	OR1050	Walker, John L.	VA1700	Walter, Matt	IN0700
Wagor, Rich	IA0400	Walker, John M.	SD0550	Walter, Regina	TX1775
Wagor, Richard	IA0300	Walker, Joseph V.	TN1100	Walter, Ross A.	VA1600
Wagstaff, Grayson	DC0050	Walker, K. Dean	OK1200	Walter, Steven	SC0750
Wagstrom, Beth Robison	CO0050	Walker, Karen	VA1350	Walters, Andrew B.	PA2150
Wahl, Carolyn	FL1650	Walker, Keith H.	GA0625	Walters, Corinne	LA0080
Wahl, Shelbie L.	VA0550	Walker, Kenneth	CO0900	Walters, Darrel L.	PA3250
Wahlstrom, Lynette	AF0100	Walker, Kerry E.	CT0800	Walters, David	TN0260
Wahlund, Ben	IL2050	Walker, Linda B.	OH1100	Walters, David	AL0500
Wahrhaftig, Peter	CA3520	Walker, Margaret Edith	AG0250	Walters, Dean	FL0730
Wahrhaftig, Peter	CA2950	Walker, Mark	AL1050	Walters, Gary	IN0250
Wahrhaftig, Peter	CA4150	Walker, Mark	MA0260	Walters, Kent	MI0520
Wahrhaftig, Peter	CA5000	Walker, Mary	SD0550	Walters, Kerry E.	IL0400
Waibel, Keith	CA0600	Walker, Michael	CA1510	Walters, Mark A.	CO0350
Waid, Tom	FL1750	Walker, Michael	TX3525	Walters, Robert	OH1700
Waid, Tom	FL0150	Walker, Michael	TX0250	Walters, Teresa	NJ0200
Waidelich, Peter J.	FL0400	Walker, Nancy L.	NC2430	Walters, Timothy	FL0650
Wait, Gregory A.	CA4900	Walker, Nicholas	NY1800	Walters, Valerie	GA1150
Wait, Mark	TN1850	Walker, Patricia	NY2200	Walth, Gary Kent	WI0810
Wait, Patricia	AG0650	Walker, Regina	IN0907	Waltham-Smith, Naomi	PA3350
Waite, Janice	AA0050	Walker, Richard L.	IN0907	Walther, Geraldine E.	CO0800
Waites, Althea	CA0825	Walker, Rob	ID0070	Waltich, Tsukasa	PA3700
Wakao, Keisuke	MA1175	Walker, Saul A.	NY2750	Waltl, Herbert	AI0150
Wakao, Keisuke	MA1400	Walker, Scot	PA2450	Waltner, Anne	WV0700
Wakefield, David	NY1900	Walker, Skip	NC1350	Walton, Charles	ID0250
Wakefield, Karin	MN0600	Walker, Steve	OK0300	Walton, Madalyn	FL2130
Wakefield, Leigh	MN0600	Walker, Tammie Leigh	IL3500	Walton, Michele	NM0200
Wakefield, William	OK1350	Walker, Tim	CA1450	Walton, Scott	CA3460
Wakeley, David A.	WA1350	Walker, Timm	CA2775	Walton, Scott	CA4850
Wakeling, Tom	OR0050	Walker, Vicki	OK0850	Waltz, Sarah Clemmens	CA5350
Wakeman, Forrest	MI0300	Walker, Vicki	MI0150	Walujo, Djoko	CA4100
Waksman, Steve M.	MA1750	Walkington, Alec	AI0150	Walujo, Djoko	CA0510
Walborn, Melanie	PA1250	Wall, Daniel	OH1700	Walvoord, Jennifer R.	MI0350
Walbridge, William	MI2000	Wall, Donna	IA0940	Walvoord, Martha J.	TX3500
Walburn, Jacob A.	IL3300	Wall, Jeremy	NY3765	Walworth, Darcy DeLoach	FL0850
Walby, Catherine	WI0350	Wall, Nathan	AJ0030	Walworth, Darcy	FL0950

Name	Code	Name	Code	Name	Code
Walwyn, Karen M.	DC0150	Ware, John	VA1800	Wasserman, Garry P.	OH1900
Walzer, Barbara	NY3560	Ware, John Earl	LA0900	Wasserman, Joanne	CA5550
Wampler, Kris A.	OH0680	Ware, Rachel J.	IA0950	Wasserman, Lisa	OH2140
Wampner, Barbara	CA1650	Ware, Steve	NC0900	Wassermann, Ellen	CA0807
Wan, Agnes	TN0930	Warfel, Jon R.	IL2050	Wassertzug, Uri	DC0100
Wan, Andrew	AI0150	Warfield, Patrick R.	MD1010	Wassertzug, Uri	DC0150
Wanamaker, Gregory R.	NY3780	Warfield, Scott A.	FL1800	Watabe, Eileen	AK0150
Wanamaker, Tracy S.	NY3780	Warfield, Tara	MS0500	Watabe, Junichiro	AK0150
Wanderley, Marcelo	AI0150	Warfield, Tim	PA3250	Watanabe, Hisao	OR0350
Wang, Alice	OH2600	Warfield, Timothy	PA2300	Watanabe, Mihoko	IN0150
Wang, Cecilia	KY1450	Warfield, William	PA1950	Watanabe, Vera	UT0250
Wang, Diane	MS0700	Warford, Allison	TN1850	Watchorn, Peter G.	MA0350
Wang, Esther	MN0750	Wargo, Edward	PA2200	Waterbury, Elizabeth	CA4550
Wang, Felix	TN1850	Wark, Stephen	MA0260	Waterbury, Susan	NY1800
Wang, Ge	CA4900	Warkentien, Vicky	IN0200	Waterfall, Linda	WA0200
Wang, Guang	GA0750	Warkentin, Steve	TX2250	Waterman, Ellen F.	AD0050
Wang, Guoping	IN0900	Warlick, Gerald	OK1200	Waterman, Marla	NY2105
Wang, Han Yuan	UT0190	Warlick, Gerald	OK0700	Watermeier, Ethan	MD0550
Wang, Hong	MN0610	Warlick, Leslie Taylor	SC0400	Waters, Becky	AL1160
Wang, Hong	MN0250	Warman, Harold	CA4100	Waters, J. Kevin	WA0400
Wang, Hsiu-Hui	MD0400	Warne, David	MI1650	Waters, Jeffery L.	MO1550
Wang, I-Fu	MI1400	Warneck, Petrea	SC0400	Waters, Joseph	CA4100
Wang, Jing	MA2020	Warneck, Petrea	SC0750	Waters, Keith	CO0800
Wang, Jui-Ching	IL2200	Warner, C. David	MD0450	Waters, Renee	MO1550
Wang, Li	AG0300	Warner, Carolyn Gadiel	OH0600	Waters, Richard	KY0550
Wang, Liang	NY2750	Warner, Daniel C.	MA1000	Waters, Robert F.	NJ1160
Wang, Liang-yu	IN0900	Warner, Douglas G.	TN0850	Waters, Sarah S.	OH1800
Wang, Liang-yu	NY2150	Warner, Michele	IN1450	Waters, Tim	OK0850
Wang, Lin-Ti	NC1700	Warner, Thomas	GA0490	Waters, Willie	CT0600
Wang, Linda	CO0900	Warner, Tony	MD0650	Watkins, Cornelia	TX2150
Wang, Marie	IL2200	Warner, Wendy	GA0550	Watkins, David	GA1150
Wang, Mingzhe	TN0050	Warnock, Matthew	IL0350	Watkins, Holly	NY1100
Wang, Pin-Huey	MD0550	Warren, Alec	TX2300	Watkins, Howard	NY2250
Wang, Richard A.	IL3310	Warren, Alec	TX3400	Watkins, John M. 'Jay'	FL1850
Wang, Rosy	HI0210	Warren, Alec	TX2295	Watkins, Lenora	WI1150
Wang, Shi-Hwa	UT0350	Warren, Alicyn	IN0900	Watkins, Mark	ID0060
Wang, Sylvia	IL2250	Warren, Charles	CA1425	Watkins, Ron	IL2100
Wang, Tianshu	OH0350	Warren, Chris	MS0200	Watkins, Russell	GA0850
Wang, Xi	TX2400	Warren, Cynthia	OH0700	Watkins, Scott	FL1000
Wang, Yien	GA0550	Warren, Dale E.	KY1450	Watkins, Timothy D.	TX3000
Wang, Yung-Chiu	TX1000	Warren, J. Curt	TX3520	Watkins, Wilbert O.	IL0275
Wang, Yung-Chui	TX2900	Warren, Jacquelyn	OH0750	Watkinson, Christopher L.	ME0200
Wang, Yung-Hsiang	TX3400	Warren, James	CA2700	Watras, Melia	WA1050
Wangen, Peter	MN1290	Warren, Jane	TN0100	Watrous, Bill	CA5300
Wangler, Kim L.	NC0050	Warren, Jeff	MN1280	Watson Lyons, Lois	AC0100
Wanhoff, Meryl	CA4460	Warren, Jeff	AB0090	Watson, Anne	OK0550
Wanken, Matthew	IL1800	Warren, Jeff	MN1250	Watson, Bradley	CO0550
Wanken, Matthew	IL0400	Warren, Jeffrey	MN0625	Watson, Cameron	AA0020
Wanken, Matthew	IL0420	Warren, Jessica	UT0050	Watson, Derico	TN0100
Wannamaker, Robert	CA0510	Warren, John	IL1900	Watson, Frank	SC0650
Wanner, Dan	CA3150	Warren, John	GA1150	Watson, Gwendolyn	GA0300
Wanner, Dan	CA2600	Warren, John F.	NY4150	Watson, Holly	LA0050
Wanner, Glen	TN1850	Warren, Maredia D. L.	NJ0825	Watson, J. Stephen	SC0750
Wansley, Ivan	FL0800	Warren, Michael	MO1810	Watson, Jed	MI0900
Wapnick, Joel	AI0150	Warren, Robert	TX2650	Watson, Joan	AG0450
Warburg, Claudia E.	NC0600	Warren, Robert	TX3100	Watson, Larry	NY5000
Ward, Allison	TX3000	Warren, Ron	MD0550	Watson, Lawrence	MA0260
Ward, Angela	NC1650	Warren, Ron	MD0150	Watson, Marva	IL1240
Ward, Ann	FL0400	Warren, Stanley	TN1660	Watson, Michael	WI0845
Ward, Arlene	NM0450	Warren, Tasha	VA1550	Watson, Nancy	NC2000
Ward, Brian	OR0850	Warren, Ted	AG0350	Watson, Nessim	MA1850
Ward, Brian	WA1150	Warren, W. Dale	AR0700	Watson, Richard	ND0250
Ward, Brian	WA0250	Warren-Green, Rosemary	NC0550	Watson, Richard	IN1750
Ward, Doug	AA0080	Warrick, Kimberly	OH2500	Watson, Rita	IL1900
Ward, Eric	AL1050	Warrington, Thomas	NV0050	Watson, Robert M.	MO1810
Ward, Frank	OH2150	Warsaw, Benjamin	GA0940	Watson, Robert	CA0815
Ward, Jeffrey	NC0650	Warshaw, Dalit Hadass	MA0350	Watson, Robyn	TX0075
Ward, Keith C.	WA1000	Wartchow, Brett	MN1300	Watson, Scott	PA2800
Ward, Larry F.	IL0630	Warth, James R.	TX2960	Watson, Scott C.	KS1350
Ward, Margaret S.	NH0250	Wartofsky, Michael	MA0260	Watson, Teri	CA0815
Ward, Michael	TN0850	Warwick, Jacqueline	AF0100	Watson, Terry Gutterman	NY2750
Ward, Miriam English	OR0600	Waschka, Rodney A.	NC1700	Watson, Tim M.	IA1100
Ward, Patricia	TN1100	Waseen, Symeon	SD0100	Watson, Tommy L.	SC0050
Ward, Perry	TN1700	Washburn, David	CA0825	Watson, Virginia	MN0800
Ward, Robert S.	CA0500	Washburn, David W.	CA5020	Watson, W. David	CT0650
Ward, Robert J.	OH1850	Washburn, David	CA0960	Watson, William E.	MD0175
Ward, Robert	CA4150	Washburn, Rodney	IL1740	Watt, Stephanie	NY2105
Ward, Robert	CA5000	Washburne, Christopher	NY0750	Watter, Hillary	NE0300
Ward, Robert	CA0830	Washecka, Tim	TX2650	Watters, August	MA0260
Ward, Robert	CA3300	Washington, Daniel	MI2100	Watters, Harry	VA0450
Ward, Robert J.	MA1450	Washington, Darian	SC0950	Watters, Ken G.	AL1160
Ward, Steven D.	TX0050	Washington, Donna	DC0150	Watters, Patti	VA1000
Ward, Susan	AA0110	Washington, Henry	TX2220	Watts, Andre	IN0900
Ward, Tom R.	IL3300	Washington, Kenny	NY1900	Watts, Ardean W.	UT0250
Ward, Wayne	MA0260	Washington, Kenny	NY3785	Watts, Camille	AG0450
Ward-Griffin, Danielle	VA0150	Washington, Kera M.	MA2050	Watts, Christopher M.	NY3550
Ward-Steinman, David	IN0900	Washington, Lecolion	TN1680	Watts, Donald	OH0600
Ward-Steinman, Patrice Madura	IN0900	Washington, Nadine	MI1750	Watts, Joel	CA4850
Ward-Steinman, Susan L.	CA4100	Washington, Phil	WV0700	Watts, Mike	CA0350
Warda, Christa	PA2550	Washington, Salim	NY0500	Watts, Mike	CA2700
Warden, Loyd	MO0100	Washington, Shirley A.	NY2750	Watts, Ronald	GA1070
Wardenski, Ian	MD0060	Washington, Shirley	NJ0950	Watts, Sarah	PA0350
Wardlaw, Jeffrey A.	PA0700	Washington-Harris, Kara E.	AL0050	Watts, Sarah	OH0650
Wardlaw-Bailey, Freya	AK0100	Washiyama, Kaori	VT0050	Watts, Valerie	OK1350
Wardle, Alvin	UT0300	Washut, Robert	IA1600	Watts-Foss, Mary	IA0200
Wardson, Greg	RI0200	Wasiak, Ed	AA0200	Waugh, Bob L.	OH0680
Wardson, Greg	MA0260	Wasko, Dennis	PA3330	Waugh, Robert	IN0800
Wardzinski, Anthony J.	CA3100	Wasley, Martha	CA5000	Way, Marshall R.	CA4410
Ware, Clifton	MN1623	Wason, Robert W.	NY1100	Waybright, David	FL1850
Ware, David N.	MS0350	Wass, Kevin	TX3200	Wayland, Doug	OH0300

Alphabetical Listing of Faculty

Name	Code
Wayman, John B.	GA2300
Waymire, Mark D.	MS0750
Wayne, Barbara	ID0060
Wayne, Michael	MA1175
Wayne, Nicholas	MN0200
Waynick, Mark	AR0730
Wayte, Laura Decher	OR1050
Wayte, Lawrence A.	OR1050
Wazanowski, Charles	MN1300
Wazanowski, Charles	WI0845
Wead, Joyce A.	VA0100
Weagraff, Marc A.	OH0200
Weait, Christopher	OH0350
Weait, Christopher R.	OH1850
Weale, Gerald	MA0400
Wean, Ellis	AB0100
Weary, Hal	PA0050
Weast, Wade P.	NC1650
Weatherall, Maurice	MS0600
Weatherford, Benjamin	AL0500
Weathers, Keith	OR0175
Weaver, Andrew H.	DC0050
Weaver, Ann	AZ0480
Weaver, Brent	TN0650
Weaver, Brent	OR0250
Weaver, Carol Ann	AG0470
Weaver, Daniel	WI0808
Weaver, James	PA2300
Weaver, James	VA1500
Weaver, Jamie G.	TX2700
Weaver, John	GA0400
Weaver, Joseph	PA0500
Weaver, Lane	KS0350
Weaver, Michael A.	SC0950
Weaver, Molly A.	WV0750
Weaver, Phillip E.	AL1160
Weaver, Zac	GA0750
Webb, A. H.	MA0800
Webb, Adam	MS0500
Webb, Brian P.	VT0125
Webb, Charles	IN0005
Webb, Chuck	IL0720
Webb, Glenn	UT0150
Webb, Guy B.	MO0775
Webb, Jeffrey L.	PA3410
Webb, John	TX3535
Webb, John C.	AR0800
Webb, Lewis	AL1050
Webb, Marianne	IL2900
Webb, Mark	MI0300
Webb, Merrilee	UT0150
Webb, Phil	CA2810
Webb, Richard	MA2000
Webb, Robert	VA0975
Webb, William	MN0050
Webber, Allen L.	FL1470
Webber, Carol	NY1100
Webber, Danny R.	MD0450
Webber, David	KY1000
Webber, Janice E.	MD0650
Webber, Kelly Marie	KS0560
Webber, Sophie C.	IL1400
Webber, Stephen	MA0260
Weber, Angela	IL2150
Weber, Betsy Cook	TX3400
Weber, Bradley	NE0700
Weber, Brent M.	MD0350
Weber, Brent	PA2250
Weber, Carlyle	FL0950
Weber, Carolyn R. T.	NY4150
Weber, Deanna F.	GA0150
Weber, Glenn	NJ1160
Weber, Janice	MA0350
Weber, Jessica	OH2290
Weber, John	IL2775
Weber, Jonathan	IL2750
Weber, Jonathan	MI1400
Weber, Judy	KS0700
Weber, Kathleen F.	NY2550
Weber, Linda	TX0550
Weber, Marliss	AA0020
Weber, Martha	NY3705
Weber, Mary	MO1900
Weber, Mary	MO1250
Weber, Michael J.	ND0350
Weber, Misato	CA0900
Weber, Misato	CA0807
Weber, Paul	NC1100
Weber, Paula B.	MO1810
Weber, Robert	IL1300
Weber, Stephen	OK1400
Weber, Steven T.	TX0100
Weber, Susan	MO0700
Webster, Brent	KY0950
Webster, Gerald	OR0850
Webster, James	NY0900
Webster, Kim	PA1750
Webster, Marc	NY1800
Webster, Margee	WA0400
Webster, Michael	TX2150
Webster, Peter	FL1300
Webster, Peter R.	IL2250
Webster, Thomas R.	TX0600
Wechesler, David J.	NY0644
Weckstrom, Virginia	OH0600
Weckstrom, Virginia	AG0300
Wedding, Alison	MA0260
Weddle, Jamison	AZ0470
Weddle, John W.	CA0850
Wedeen, Harvey D.	PA3250
Wedell, Steven	OH2050
Wedington-Clark, Darlene	AZ0490
Wedow, Gary T.	NY1900
Wee, A. Dewayne	MN1450
Wee, Theo R.	MN1450
Wee-Yang, Jeannette	WA1350
Weed, Tad	MI1750
Weed, Tad	OH2300
Weed, Tad E.	OH0300
Weeda, Linn	AK0100
Weekley, Dallas	WI0810
Weekly, Edrie Means	VA1350
Weeks, Daniel	KY1500
Weeks, Douglas	MA0700
Weeks, Douglas A.	SC0650
Weeks, Douglas	MA0650
Weeks, Rudi	MA1100
Weems, Nancy	TX3400
Weesner, Anna	PA3350
Wegenke, Wendy	MN1250
Weger, Bill	OK0700
Weger, Stacy	OK1150
Wegge, Glen T.	IA1750
Weglein, Carolyn	MD0100
Wegman, Rob	NJ0900
Wegner, Rob	AZ0490
Wehr, David	PA1050
Wehr, Erin	IA1550
Wehrmann, Rock	OH2150
Wehrmann, Rock	OH0650
Wei, Sharon	CA4900
Wei, Yung-Chiao	LA0200
Weichel, Cynthia	CA4460
Weichert, Constance E.	CA0850
Weidenaar, Gary	WA0050
Weidenmueller, Johannes	NY2660
Weidlich, Richard	CT0550
Weidlich, Richard H.	CT0800
Weidman, James	NJ1400
Weidman-Winter, Becky	CO1050
Weidner, Raymond	MD0060
Weigand, John	WV0750
Weigert, David	MA0260
Weightman, Lindsay	PA3250
Weightman, Lindsay	PA2700
Weigt, Steven	MA0400
Weik, Jay C.	OH2300
Weil, Susan	CA1520
Weilbaecher, Daniel	LA0750
Weiler, Ella Lou	MA0950
Weiler, Joan	OH2300
Weilerstein, Alisa	OH0600
Weilerstein, Donald	MA1400
Weilerstein, Donald	NY1900
Weilerstein, Vivian Hornik	NY1900
Weilerstein, Vivian Hornik	MA1400
Weiller, David B.	NV0050
Weimann, Viljar P.	AL1250
Weinbeck, Benedict J.	MN0950
Weinberg, Alan	SC0600
Weinberg, Charles	NC2400
Weinberg, Gil	GA0900
Weinberg, Henry	NY0642
Weinberg, Norman G.	AZ0500
Weinel, John	TX1450
Weiner, Richard	OH0600
Weiner, Robert A.	FL1900
Weiner-Jamison, Sarah	FL0200
Weinert, William	NY1100
Weingarten, Frederic	NY2650
Weinhold, Scott	DC0050
Weinkum, Harald	AZ0470
Weinkum, Harald	AZ0350
Weinmann, Patricia	MA1400
Weinreb, Alice Kogan	DC0050
Weinstein, Alan	VA1700
Weinstein, Alan	VA1250
Weinstein, Michael	MA0260
Weinstein, Michael	MA2200
Weinstein, Tony	IN1800
Weinstock, Frank M.	OH2200
Weintraub, Andrew	PA3420
Weinzweig, John	AG0450
Weir, Claudia	CO0050
Weir, Michele	CA5031
Weir, Tim	ME0340
Weir, Timothy	VA0100
Weirich, Robert W.	MO1810
Weis, Patricia	WI0300
Weisberg, David	NJ1400
Weisberg, Diane K.	FL0650
Weisbrod, Liza	AL0200
Weise, Christopher	NC1000
Weisenberg, Marvi	NY2400
Weiser, Kimberly	NE0610
Weiser, Mark L.	CA5300
Weisert, Lee	NC2410
Weiskopf, Walter	PA3250
Weisman, Bonita	CT0650
Weismann, Raymond	NY2250
Weisner, Jeffrey D.	MD0650
Weiss, Abraham	NY1700
Weiss, Celia	IN0910
Weiss, Daniel	IN1300
Weiss, Daun L.	CA0800
Weiss, David	CA0825
Weiss, David	CA5300
Weiss, Doug	NY3785
Weiss, Doug	NY2660
Weiss, Ezra	OR0850
Weiss, Kenneth	NY1900
Weiss, Linda	TX1725
Weiss, Lisa G.	MD0400
Weiss, Louise	IL1050
Weiss, Richard	OH0600
Weiss, Robert L.	IL2900
Weiss, Sarah	CT0900
Weiss, Susan F.	MD0650
Weiss, Timothy	OH1700
Weisse, Lisa	ID0060
Weisz, Deborah	CT0800
Welborn, Daniel C.	GA1050
Welbourne, Todd G.	WI0815
Welch, Chapman	TX3400
Welch, James	CA4425
Welch, Jeanette	IA0930
Welch, Jennifer	MN1400
Welch, Kay	IL2300
Welch, Leo	FL0850
Welch, Nancy	MS0700
Welcher, Dan E.	TX3510
Welcher, Jeffrey	NY4150
Welcomer, Paul	CA4150
Weld, Kathryn	WA0200
Weldon-Stephens, Amber	GA1150
Weldy, Frederick R.	CA4900
Welge, Jurgen	KS0590
Welk, Shawn	VA1600
Wellborn, Georgia G.	TN1660
Wellborn, William E	CA4150
Welle, Talman J.	WA0600
Weller, Amy G.	IL2250
Weller, Derek	MI0600
Weller, Ellen	CA3460
Weller, Ira	NY0150
Weller, Ira	NY2250
Weller, Ira	NY3785
Weller, Lawrence	MN1623
Weller, Richard A.	CA0835
Weller, Robert	CA3460
Welling, Jennifer	AA0040
Welling, Joelle	AA0150
Wellington, Craig	WA0450
Wellman, Samuel	VA0650
Wellman, Steve	DC0100
Wellman, Wayne	KY0250
Wells Chenoweth, Andrea	OH2250
Wells, Alison	MD0650
Wells, Bradley C.	MA2250
Wells, Connie	GA2050
Wells, David	CA0840
Wells, David	ME0340
Wells, David	ME0150
Wells, Deanne	AG0070
Wells, Donovan V.	FL0100
Wells, Elizabeth A.	AE0050
Wells, Glenn	TX1350
Wells, Greg	MI0300
Wells, Jesse R.	KY0900
Wells, Larry	NC1350
Wells, Lillie	OR1050
Wells, Mark	MI1160
Wells, Mary	CA4300
Wells, Matthew	IN1750
Wells, Paul F.	TN1100
Wells, Prince	IL2910
Wells, Rebecca Schaffer	KY1300
Wells, Robert A.	NC2430
Wells, Robyn	ID0070
Wells, Ryan	NE0550
Wells, Thomas H.	OH1850
Wells, Wayne W.	VA1350
Wells, William	CA0960
Wells, Yelena	MI0850
Wells-Hunt, Deanne	AG0150
Wellwood, William	CA2420
Welsch, James O.	NY4150
Welstead, Jon	WI0825
Welte, DeEtta	IN1800
Welte, John	PA3330

Alphabetical Listing of Faculty

Name	Code	Name	Code	Name	Code
Welty, Susan	GA2100	Westfall, Casey	OH1850	Whetstone, David	MN0300
Welwood, Arthur	MA0260	Westfall, Claude R.	MO0100	Whetstone, Joni	PA2710
Weman, Lena	AI0150	Westfall, David C.	CT0650	Whicher, Monica	AG0300
Wen, Andy	AR0750	Westfall, Kathleen	LA0800	Whicker, Monica	AG0450
Wen, Eric	PA0850	Westgard, Jessica	MN0600	Whidden, Collen	AA0150
Wen, Eric	NY2250	Westgate, Karen	OH2140	Whipkey, Steve	IN1100
Wenaus, Grant	NY2750	Westgate, Matthew	OH2550	Whipple, Jennifer	SC0275
Wenberg, Jon	MS0385	Westgate, Phillip Todd	AL0950	Whipple, R. James	PA0550
Wendel, Joyce	OH2450	Westin, Joann	ME0250	Whipple, Shederick Lee	IN1560
Wenderoth, Valeria	HI0210	Westlake, Walton	IL1085	Whipple, William P.	IA0930
Wendholt, Scott	NY2150	Westlund, John	KY1000	Whisler, Bruce Allen	SC0400
Wendholt, Scott	NY3785	Westmacott, John	KS0265	Whitaker, Howard	IL3550
Wendland, Kristin	GA0750	Westney, Stephanie Teply	TX3530	Whitaker, Jane	FL0950
Weng, Lei	CO0950	Westney, William F.	TX3200	Whitaker, Jennifer A.	NC2420
Weng, Pamela	CO0830	Weston, Beth	MI1650	Whitaker, Jon	AL1170
Wenger, Alan J.	MO1790	Weston, Craig A.	KS0650	Whitaker, Nancy L.	WI0835
Wenger, Fred	MT0370	Weston, Trevor L.	NJ0300	Whitaker, Nathan	WA0200
Wenger, Janice K.	MO1800	Westphal, Cynthia	MI2100	Whitaker, Rodney	MI1400
Wenger, Laurie	MT0370	Westphalen, Melinda	IA0700	Whitaker-Auvil, Melissa	MI1985
Wenner, Debby	VA0450	Westra, Mitzi	IN1650	Whitcomb, Benjamin	WI0865
Wennerstrom, Mary H.	IN0900	Westray, Ron	AG0650	Whitcomb, Rachel	PA1050
Wenninger, Karl	NY2660	Westrick, Rick	WA1350	White, Al	KY0300
Wente, Steven F.	IL0730	Westrick, Rick	WA0950	White, Andre	AI0150
Wenten, I. Nyoman	CA5031	Wetherbee, Charles	CO0800	White, Andrew	CO0830
Wenten, I. Nyoman	CA0510	Wetherbee, Sarah M.	NY5000	White, Andrew R.	NE0590
Wenten, Nanik	CA0510	Wetherill, David	PA1550	White, Angela S.	FL0350
Wenten, Nyoman	CA3650	Wetherill, Linda Marie	NY0050	White, Anita	WV0350
Wentworth, Jean	NY3560	Wetherington, John M.	WA0650	White, Arthur	MO1800
Wentz, Brooke	CA5350	Wettstein Sadler, Shannon Leigh	MN0050	White, Barbara A.	NJ0900
Wentzel, Andrew	TN1710	Wetzel, David B.	PA2150	White, Barry R.	NY1300
Wenzel, Scott	WI0150	Wetzel, Don Louis	CA5300	White, Bill	MN0610
Weremchuk, George	FL1800	Wetzel, James	NY0625	White, Brad	TX3000
Werkema, Jason	MI0350	Wetzel, Minor	CA3300	White, Brad K.	TX3400
Werkema, Jason R.	MI0750	Wetzel, Neil D.	PA2450	White, Carol	ID0070
Werking, Jon	NY2900	Wetzel, Richard	OH1900	White, Chris	IL2050
Werling, Helen	GA1700	Wetzel, Robert	CA4100	White, Chris	OK1050
Wermuth, Bruce M.	TX3420	Wetzel, Robert	CA2100	White, Christie	MO2000
Werner, Dianne	AG0300	Wetzel, Thomas	WI0825	White, Christopher	IL2100
Werner, J. Ritter	OH2500	Wevers, Harold	AG0170	White, Christopher T.	KY1500
Werner, Kenny	NY2750	Wexler, Mathias K.	NY3780	White, Christopher B.	VA1000
Werner, Michael	NY2250	Wexler, Richard	MD1010	White, Christopher G.	ME0440
Werner, Susan	MO1830	Weyer, Matthew	TN0250	White, Christopher E.	IL1400
Werner, Wendel V.	TN1710	Weyersberg, Roger	MI1850	White, Christopher K.	VA1100
Wernick, Diane	MA0260	Weymouth, Daniel	NY3790	White, Christopher Dale	TX2955
Wernick, Richard F.	PA3350	Whale, Mark	AG0450	White, Cindy	MO1710
Werntz, Julia	MA1400	Whalen, Eileen M.	OH2250	White, Coralie	LA0770
Werren, Philip	AG0650	Whalen, Laura	AG0500	White, Dale A.	MN0350
Werth, Kay	KS0350	Whalen, Marc	AF0120	White, Darryl A.	NE0600
Wertico, Paul	IL0550	Whalen, Margaret F.	NC2000	White, David	AL1195
Wery, Brett L.	NY3600	Whaley, Daniel M.	TN1100	White, David A.	TX3400
Werz, Andreas	CA0810	Whaley, Mary Susan	OK0500	White, Dennine	FL0600
Wesbrooks, William	NY2750	Whang, Hyunsoon	OK0150	White, Diana	VA1350
Wesby, Barbara K.	NY4500	Whang, Pegsoon	UT0250	White, Edward C.	AR0730
Wesby, Roger	NY4500	Whang, Pegsoon	UT0400	White, Frank	LA0700
Wesche, Nancy	KS0210	Whang, Un-Young	IL1850	White, Greg	OK1330
Wesley, Arthur B.	AL0010	Whang, Yumi	CO0900	White, James	PA2710
Wesley, Charles E.	MS0050	Wharton, Keith	MD1100	White, James	CO0950
Wesley, Dee	IL1612	Wharton, Marjorie R.	IA0950	White, James L.	TX3520
Wesner-Hoehn, Beverly	CA0840	Wharton, William	ID0250	White, Janice	CA5500
Wesolowski, Brian	GA2100	Whatley, Jay K.		White, Jay G.	OH1100
Wessel, David	CA5000	Whear, P. Allen	TX3420	White, Jennifer	MO0850
Wessel, Kenneth	NY2400	Wheat, James R.	MN1700	White, Joanna Cowan	MI0400
Wessel, Kenneth	NY5000	Wheatley, Greg	IL3550	White, John W.	NY1800
Wessel, Mark	MA0260	Wheatley, Jennifer	IN0400	White, John-Paul	MI1750
Wessler, Peter	IL0400	Wheatley, Jon	MA0260	White, Joseph M.	WV0100
Wessler, Robert	WI0810	Wheatley, Jon	MA2030	White, Judith	PA3150
West, Brian	TX3000	Wheatley, Susan E.	PA1600	White, Julian E.	FL0600
West, Charles W.	VA1600	Wheaton, Dana	CA3350	White, Karin	MI1260
West, Cheryl E.	IN1650	Wheaton, J. Randall	VA0600	White, Katherine	AR0730
West, Cheryl	IN0250	Wheaton, Michael	MI2250	White, Kayla	AR0400
West, George	FL1750	Wheeldon, Marianne	TX3510	White, Kennen D.	MI0400
West, Glenn A.	NY1100	Wheeler, Ben	MO1950	White, Kevin	MO0750
West, James R.	LA0200	Wheeler, Ben A.	MO1900	White, Kim	MN0610
West, Jayne	MA1175	Wheeler, Brent	TX2350	White, L. Keith	OK1330
West, Jean	FL1750	Wheeler, Candace	FL0200	White, Laura	VA1600
West, Jill	IL1200	Wheeler, Charles Lynn	CA3400	White, Lynn	NC0050
West, John T.	NC2600	Wheeler, Dale J.	AA0080	White, Manami	OH2550
West, Julie A.	CA0835	Wheeler, Edwin	OR1010	White, Marc M.	OK1150
West, Lara L.	KS0100	Wheeler, George	CA0825	White, Mark	MA0260
West, Margaret	CA1760	Wheeler, George	CA1520	White, Mary Joanna	NC2440
West, Rachel	IL1200	Wheeler, Heather L.	NY3780	White, Matthew S.	SC0420
West, Stephen	MI2100	Wheeler, John	MA2250	White, Michael	NY1900
West, Therese	OR0500	Wheeler, John	GA0940	White, Michael	AG0300
West, William	IL1200	Wheeler, Joyce	IA0550	White, Molly E.	CA2720
Westbrook, Gary W.	TX2750	Wheeler, Kathy	MI0400	White, Pat	NC1950
Westbrook, Randy	KY0550	Wheeler, Lawrence	TX3400	White, Perry D.	WI0770
Westby, Denise	OR0450	Wheeler, Mark	NC0915	White, Phyllis	MI1750
Westcott, William W.	AG0650	Wheeler, Michael	TX3450	White, R. Scott	NH0150
Wester, R. Glenn	TX2295	Wheeler, Mike	TX3400	White, Richard	NM0450
Westerberg, Kurt H.	IL0750	Wheeler, Robin	AI0200	White, Richard H.	CO0350
Westergaard, Peter	NJ0900	Wheeler, Ron	OK0850	White, Rick	WA0600
Westerhaus, Timothy P.	WA0400	Wheeler, Scott	MA0850	White, Robert C.	NY1900
Westerholm, Joel M.	IA1200	Wheeler, Teresa	OK0500	White, Robert	NY0642
Westerholm, Matthew	MI0520	Wheeler, Tyrone	KY1500	White, Robert C.	NY2750
Westermeyer, Paul	MN1450	Wheeler, W. Keith	TN1550	White, Robert	NY1900
Western, Bruce	IA0930	Wheelock, Donald	MA1750	White, Rosemary	MD0100
Western, Daniel	AL0650	Wheelock, Gretchen A.	NY1100	White, Sallie V.	AL0800
Westervelt, Dirck	CT0800	Whetham, S.	AA0100	White, Susan	GA1150
Westervelt, Todd G.	FL0100	Whetham, Scott	AA0035	White, Tim	AG0050
Westfall, Ben	IN1025	Whetstone, David S.	MN0950	White, Timothy J.	CA1560

Name	Code	Name	Code	Name	Code
White, Timothy	AG0200	Wiebe, Jill	KS1450	Wiley, N. Keith	PA2350
White, Tyler G.	NE0600	Wiebe, John	AA0110	Wiley, Peter	NY0150
White, William	MI1750	Wiebe, Laura	IA0300	Wiley, Peter	PA0850
White, William	MO1710	Wiebe, Thomas	AG0500	Wiley, Roland J.	MI2100
White-Smith, Juliet	OH1850	Wiechman, Elizabeth J.	MN1030	Wilfong, Glen	WI0100
Whitehead, Amy Orsinger	NC0550	Wieck, Anatole	ME0440	Wilhelm, Philip	IL1740
Whitehead, Baruch	NY1800	Wieck, Julie	WA1150	Wilhite, Carmen	MN1300
Whitehead, Corey	CA1860	Wieczorek, Todd	AG0500	Wilhoit, Mel	TN0260
Whitehead, Corey	CA0810	Wiedrich, William	FL2000	Wilhoit, Mel R.	TN0200
Whitehead, David	FL1700	Wiegard, William James	TX3750	Wiliams, David B.	TN1850
Whitehead, Geoffrey	NC0550	Wiehe, Beth A.	TX2200	Wilke, Adam	CA0810
Whitehead, Glen	CO0810	Wieland, John	FL1750	Wilke, Christopher	NY2650
Whitehead, Jennifer	OH2050	Wieland, William	SD0400	Wilken, David M.	NC2400
Whitehead, Patrick	DC0170	Wielenga, Mary Lou	IA1200	Wilkerson, Andrea	CA3500
Whitehead, Richard	VA0450	Wielenga, Mary Lou	IA0500	Wilkerson, John	FL0150
Whitehead, Richard	VA1350	Wieligman, Thomas	IN0900	Wilkerson, Karen	MN1450
Whitehead, Russell	AA0100	Wiemann, Beth	ME0440	Wilkerson, Steve	CA3200
Whitehead, Yukiko	TN1200	Wiemer, Gerta	UT0350	Wilkes, Corey	IL0550
Whitehouse, Brooks	NC1650	Wiemken, Robert	PA3250	Wilkes, Eve-Anne	CA3250
Whitehouse, Jackie	CA3320	Wiencek, Joe R.	NY2750	Wilkes, Jamey	GA2000
Whitelaw, Ian	CA5040	Wieneke, Erin	IL1890	Wilkes, Steve	MA1400
Whiteley, Dan	IN1310	Wienhold, Lisa J.	AL1150	Wilkes, Steven M.	MA0260
Whiteman, Richard	AG0650	Wienhold, Lisa	AL0300	Wilkins Wong, Miranda	AB0100
Whitener, Edward	NC0050	Wiens, Edith	NY1900	Wilkins, Ashby	FL2000
Whitener, John L.	CA5300	Wiens, Frank	CA5350	Wilkins, Blake	TX3400
Whitener, Scott	NJ1130	Wiens, Harold H.	AA0100	Wilkins, Carolyn	MA0260
Whitesell, Lloyd	AI0150	Wiens, Lynelle	CA5350	Wilkins, Colette	PA0550
Whitfield, Andrew D.	IA0950	Wiens, Paul W.	IL3550	Wilkins, Donald G.	PA0550
Whitfield, James M. (Matt)	NC0850	Wiersma, Calvin	NY3785	Wilkins, Donald	MA0260
Whitfield, Wesla	CA3270	Wierzbicki, Marishka	CT0650	Wilkins, Jack	NY2150
Whitfill, Jim	TX0850	Wiesmeyer, Roger	TN1850	Wilkins, John	MA0260
Whitford, Keith	IN1560	Wiesner, Terry	WI0801	Wilkins, Judy	AZ0250
Whitford, Trudy	IN1560	Wiest, Lori J.	WA1150	Wilkins, Mariah	NY2150
Whitford, Trudy	IN1025	Wiest, Steve	TX3420	Wilkins, Sharon	MO0400
Whiting, Jennifer	IL1340	Wietzychowski, Stanley	CT0650	Wilkins, Skip	PA2450
Whiting, Steven M.	MI2100	Wiffen, Dave	AG0600	Wilkins, Skip	PA1850
Whitis, James	TX3415	Wiggett, Joseph	CA0850	Wilkinson, Carlton J.	NJ0175
Whitis, Jessye	TX3415	Wiggin, Christine	WI1150	Wilkinson, Chris	AF0050
Whitley, H. Moran	NC0300	Wiggins, David	KS0150	Wilkinson, Christopher	WV0750
Whitley, William	OR1250	Wiggins, Donna	NC2700	Wilkinson, David	CA3600
Whitlock, Christina	IN1560	Wiggins, Ira T.	NC1600	Wilkinson, David B.	CA5300
Whitlock, Mark	MN1600	Wiggins, Jacqueline H.	MI1750	Wilkinson, Donald G.	TX3520
Whitlow, Rebecca	PA1150	Wiggins, Marcus	AR0200	Wilkinson, Fiona	AG0500
Whitman, Gary	TX3000	Wiggins, Tracy Richard	NC2435	Wilkinson, Jay	OK1350
Whitman, Jill	WA1250	Wiggins, Webb	OH1700	Wilkinson, Judi	TX3520
Whitman, Thomas I.	PA3200	Wiggins, William	TN1850	Wilkinson, Leslie	MI0900
Whitmire, Sam D.	LA0760	Wigginton, James R.	TN0100	Wilkinson, Michael	FL1800
Whitmore, Judith B.	VA1475	Wight, Doug	WA0550	Wilkinson, Sherry	MI0600
Whitmore, Keith	OK0650	Wight, Ed	OR0950	Wilkinson, Tobie L.	WI0865
Whitmore, Michael	OK0450	Wight, Nathan N.	AL0500	Wilkinson, Todd R.	KS1000
Whitmore, Michael R.	OK0300	Wight, Steve	CA0830	Wilkinson, Wayne	CO0275
Whitmore, Michael	OK1200	Wigness, Robert Clyde	VT0450	Will, Jacob	SC1110
Whitmore, Peter	OR0500	Wijnands, Aberham	KS0590	Will, Richard	VA1550
Whitney, Nadine C.	GA2200	Wijnands, Bram	MO1810	Will, Udo	OH1850
Whitney, Susanna	TN1200	Wika, Norman	OK0550	Willard, David	TN0450
Whitney, Valerie	IL1400	Wikan, Cory	LA0050	Willard, Jerry	NY3790
Whitt, Roger	SC0050	Wike, Lori	UT0400	Willard, Michael	OH2290
Whittaker, Billie	DC0170	Wike, Lori J.	UT0250	Willard, Michael L.	OH1350
Whittaker, Dennis	TX3400	Wiksyk, Crystal	AB0210	Willcox, Carolyn	AA0110
Whittaker, Mark	MA2030	Wilberg, Mack	UT0250	Willeford, Constance E.	NY3725
Whittall, Geoffrey	AA0025	Wilborn, David F.	TX2900	Willenborg, Hal	CA4300
Whitted, Pharez	IL0600	Wilbourne, Emily	NY0642	Willer, Beth C.	MA0350
Whittemore, Joan	MO1120	Wilbourne, Emily	NY0750	Willet, Gene K.	OH0200
Whitten, Douglas	KS1050	Wilburn, Tricia	TN0450	Willets, Steve	TN0100
Whitten, Kristi	TN0100	Wilcken, Geoff	KS0570	Willett, Dan L.	MO1800
Whittenburg, Ben	NY1400	Wilcox, Don G.	WV0750	Willett, Jim R.	KY0550
Whittington, Andy	NC2440	Wilcox, Eileen	ID0060	Willette, Andrew C.	OR0850
Whittle, Ralph	MA1100	Wilcox, Fred J.	MD0300	Willette, Andrew	OR0750
Whitwell, John	GA2100	Wilcox, James H.	LA0650	Willey, James H.	NY3730
Whitworth, Albin C.	KY0150	Wilcox, John	OH2600	Willey, Jason	NY2650
Whitworth, Amanda E.	NH0250	Wilcox, Mark	TX1650	Willey, Mark	MD0150
Whitworth, J. Ralph	OK0550	Wilcox-Daehn, Ann Marie	MO0775	Willey, Rich	SC0400
Whyman, Valerie	PA2100	Wilcox-Jones, Carol	OH1650	Willey, Robert K.	LA0760
Wiant, William	RI0250	Wilcoxson, Nancy	SD0580	William, Jacob	MA2020
Wiberg, Janice	MT0300	Wild, Jonathan	AI0150	William, Jacob	MA0510
Michael, Scott	KS0590	Wild, Wayne	MA0260	Williams, Alan	MA2030
Wick, David	VA0250	Wilder, Joe	NY1900	Williams, Alexander W.	IN0350
Wick, Heidi	OH1200	Wilder, Mary Ann	KY0100	Williams, Alicia	AR0250
Wicke, Peter	AG0100	Wilder, Matt	TN1850	Williams, Amy B.	NY4500
Wickelgren, John	MD0300	Wilder, Ralph	IL2100	Williams, Amy C.	PA3420
Wickelgren, John	MD0610	Wilder, Roger M.	MO1810	Williams, Anne	TN1850
Wicker, Charles	MS0400	Wilding, Arla	NY3600	Williams, Anne Martindale	PA0550
Wickes, Frank	GA2100	Wilding, James	OH1100	Williams, Anthony N.	ND0400
Wickham, Donna	CO0900	Wilding, Jamie	OH2150	Williams, Anthony E.	TN0550
Wickham, Nathaniel	CO0950	Wildman, Louis	CA0650	Williams, Barbara	UT0050
Wicklund, Karen	MI2250	Wildman, Randall	MO0400	Williams, Barbara	CA5350
Wickman, Ethan F.	TX3530	Wildman, Randall D.	MO0800	Williams, Barry Michael	SC1200
Wicks, Leonard	CA1425	Wildman, Simon	GA2300	Williams, Bernard	AL0650
Wicks, Michael J.	NY3600	Wilds, John	CA4100	Williams, Bonnie Blu	MS0400
Widder, David R.	VA1700	Wilds, Timothy	NC1450	Williams, Brad	IL3550
Widen, Dennis C.	OK1250	Wile, Kip D.	MD0650	Williams, Bradley	IL0750
Widener, Russell D.	KS1450	Wileman, Harv	TN0260	Williams, Brenda	VA1100
Widenhofer, Stephen B.	IL1750	Wilensky, Pamela B.	TN1680	Williams, Brent	GA2150
Widman, Marcia	MN0300	Wiles, John L.	IA1600	Williams, Buster	PA3250
Widner, James	MO1830	Wiley, Adrienne E.	MI0400	Williams, Catherine	MI0300
Widner, Paul	AG0300	Wiley, Darlene	TX3510	Williams, Charles	DC0170
Widner, Paul	AG0450	Wiley, Frank	OH1100	Williams, Christa	TN1100
Widney, Jason	VA1850	Wiley, Jennifer Sacher	PA3150	Williams, Christine	MI1650
Widrig, Judith	WA1250	Wiley, Kevin	CA3200	Williams, Christopher A.	OH2300
Wiebe, Allison	AG0500	Wiley, Mathew S.	AL1150	Williams, Craig S.	NY2900

Name	Code	Name	Code	Name	Code
Williams, Cynthia B.	CA3500	Williams, Todd D.	PA1750	Wilson, Jill	IA1100
Williams, Dale	FL2050	Williams, Todd	PA2450	Wilson, John	PA1050
Williams, Dan	WA1000	Williams, Tom	AI0150	Wilson, John	PA0550
Williams, Daniel	PA3250	Williams, Wade	GA0300	Wilson, Jordan	WI0100
Williams, David A.	FL2000	Williams, William Richard	IN1600	Wilson, Joyce	IN0800
Williams, Deborah	IL0600	Williams, Yolanda	MN0050	Wilson, Karen	SC0200
Williams, Demetrius	TX3520	Williams, Yolanda	MN1050	Wilson, Kathleen	SC0275
Williams, Dennis	PA1750	Williams-Kennedy, Maria	ND0500	Wilson, Kathleen L.	FL0700
Williams, Don A.	WV0400	Williamson, Amber	IL2500	Wilson, Kathy	OH0300
Williams, Don	NH0250	Williamson, Andy	AL1050	Wilson, Ken	MN1250
Williams, Earl	NY2105	Williamson, Brad	WY0200	Wilson, Ken	WA0030
Williams, Eddy	AL0450	Williamson, Bruce	VT0050	Wilson, Kenyon	TN1700
Williams, Ellen	NC1300	Williamson, Deborah K.	TX0300	Wilson, Kevin	MA0350
Williams, Gail	IL2250	Williamson, Emily	NY0625	Wilson, Larry K.	CA3975
Williams, Gary R.	WI0450	Williamson, Gary	AG0450	Wilson, Leah	SC0700
Williams, Harry	FL2130	Williamson, John E.	MI0400	Wilson, Leah	SC0050
Williams, Heather	IL2300	Williamson, Melissa	KS1200	Wilson, Leslie	KY0250
Williams, Heidi L.	FL0850	Williamson, Richard A.	SC0050	Wilson, Lorraine P.	PA1600
Williams, Ifan	AF0120	Williamson, Sacha	AG0650	Wilson, Margaret	AJ0150
Williams, J. Kent	NC2430	Williamson, Scott	VA1700	Wilson, Mark	CA5000
Williams, Jamelle	LA0080	Williamson, Stephen	NY2250	Wilson, Mark	WA0030
Williams, James A.	OH2250	Williamson, Steven C.	NJ0550	Wilson, Mark	NJ0760
Williams, James	TX0300	Willie, Eric	TN1450	Wilson, Mark	MD1010
Williams, Jan G.	NY4320	Willier, Stephen A.	PA3250	Wilson, Matt	MN0750
Williams, Jane	IA1800	Williford-Avrett, Martha	OK0800	Wilson, Matt	NY3725
Williams, Jay	WA0700	Willingham, Lee	AG0600	Wilson, Matthew	MN0050
Williams, Jeff	MA0260	Willis, A. Rexford	FL1745	Wilson, Matthew	MN1280
Williams, John Flawn	DC0075	Willis, Andrew S.	NC2430	Wilson, Mike	IA1350
Williams, John J.	IN0800	Willis, Debbie	CA4100	Wilson, Miranda	ID0250
Williams, John W.	SC1110	Willis, George R.	WV0750	Wilson, Nancy	NY2250
Williams, John W.	NY2100	Willis, Jesse	SC0420	Wilson, Olly W.	CA5000
Williams, Johnny	FL0600	Willis, Jonathan	OH2290	Wilson, Peter Stafford	OH0450
Williams, Julius P.	MA0260	Willis, Sharon J.	GA0490	Wilson, Peter	OH2050
Williams, Katy	PA3580	Willman, Fred	MO1830	Wilson, Phil	MA0260
Williams, Katy Schakleton	PA2900	Willmott, Bret	MA0260	Wilson, Ransom	CT0850
Williams, Kay	TX0050	Willoughby, Angela	MS0400	Wilson, Richard E.	NY4450
Williams, Kenneth T.	OH1850	Willoughby, Judith A.	OK0750	Wilson, Russell G.	UT0305
Williams, Kenneth D.	TX2960	Willoughby, Malcolm	MD0600	Wilson, Russell	VA1600
Williams, Kenyon C.	MN1120	Willoughby, Robert	MA1175	Wilson, Ruth	CA4700
Williams, Kimberly	WI0300	Willoughby, Vicki	VA1000	Wilson, Sandy	CA4200
Williams, Kraig	NJ1130	Wills, Christopher	CA0350	Wilson, Scott	FL1850
Williams, Larry	MI2000	Willson, Brian S.	NY0500	Wilson, Stephen	SC0750
Williams, Larry	MD0600	Willson, David	MS0700	Wilson, Stephen K.	NC0250
Williams, Larry	MI1000	Willson, Kenneth F.	OR0250	Wilson, Stephen B.	NY3720
Williams, Larry	MI0100	Willumstad, Jytte	NY2250	Wilson, Steve	NY1900
Williams, Laura	NC0600	Willumstad, Jytte	NY2150	Wilson, Steve	TX3520
Williams, Leland Page	CA2600	Willwerth, Valissa	PA3250	Wilson, Steve	CA0400
Williams, Lester C.	TX2295	Willy, Alan	IN0005	Wilson, Steven	NY2150
Williams, Linda	NY2800	Wilmeth, Margaret	NE0160	Wilson, Steven	NY3785
Williams, Lindsey R.	MO1810	Wilner, Stacey	TN1000	Wilson, T. Rex	TX2710
Williams, Loni	CA1100	Wilsden, Melanie	NC1300	Wilson, Thad	DC0100
Williams, Lynne	PA3000	Wilsey, Darren	CA2390	Wilson, Thomas	CO0200
Williams, Maria	NM0450	Wilsey, Jennifer	CA4700	Wilson, Todd	OH0600
Williams, Mark D.	CA2440	Wilshusen, Nicole	CO0250	Wilson, Tracy	MA0280
Williams, Mark	MI0900	Wilson Kimber, Marian	IA1550	Wilson, William	CO0950
Williams, Mark	WA1000	Wilson, Angela Turner	TX3000	Wilsyn, Bobbi	IL0720
Williams, Marvin	NY2050	Wilson, Blake	PA0950	Wilt, James	CA1075
Williams, Megan	TX3530	Wilson, Brian S.	CA4700	Wilt, Kevin	MI1260
Williams, Melanie	GA1700	Wilson, Brian	MI2250	Wilt, Lois J.	NY1700
Williams, Melanie B.	AL1200	Wilson, Bruce	MD0150	Wiltse, Stephanie	MI0350
Williams, Melissa	IN1100	Wilson, Carla E.	OR1100	Wiltse, Stephanie	MI0300
Williams, Melissa	IN0250	Wilson, Carol	CO0200	Wiltshire, Eric	OR1050
Williams, Michael M.	MA0260	Wilson, Cecil B.	WV0750	Wiltsie, Barbara	MI1260
Williams, Michael	CA3920	Wilson, Cheryl	IL0550	Wimberly, Brenda	LA0100
Williams, Michael	CA2775	Wilson, Chris	AR0110	Wimberly, Larry	MS0150
Williams, Mike	MA0260	Wilson, Dana	NY1800	Wimberly, Michael	VT0050
Williams, Milton H.	CA1250	Wilson, Darcel	MA0260	Winant, William	CA5000
Williams, Milton H.	CA4625	Wilson, Dean	PA3650	Winant, William K.	CA5070
Williams, Nancy	CA0950	Wilson, Dennis E.	MI2100	Winant, William	CA2950
Williams, Natalie	GA2100	Wilson, Donald	OH0300	Winard, Kevin R.	CA4410
Williams, Nathan L.	TX3510	Wilson, Dora	OH1900	Wincenc, Carol	NY1900
Williams, Nicholas	TX3420	Wilson, Dwayne	NC0300	Wincenc, Carol	NY3790
Williams, Oscar	LA0700	Wilson, Edward	AG0650	Winchell, Jill	CA2550
Williams, Patrick C.	MT0400	Wilson, Elisa	TX3520	Wind, Martin	NY1600
Williams, Paula	GA0750	Wilson, Elisha K.	CA0850	Wind, Martin	NY2750
Williams, Peter F.	NC0600	Wilson, Ellen M.	TX3520	Winder, Diane L.	MI0600
Williams, R.	MO0650	Wilson, Eric	TN1600	Windeyer, Richard	AG0600
Williams, Ralph K.	NY4050	Wilson, Eric J.	AB0100	Windham, Mark	AR0800
Williams, Ralph K.	NY4060	Wilson, Eugene N.	AB0100	Windham, Susan	WA1350
Williams, Ray	AG0650	Wilson, Frances	NC2210	Windham, Susan	WA0250
Williams, Ray	GA0200	Wilson, Gary P.	TN0930	Windt, Nathan J.	TN1550
Williams, Richard	GA0550	Wilson, Geoffrey	IA1800	Windt, Paul	PA2550
Williams, Richard Lee	MO1810	Wilson, George	TX3800	Wine, Thomas	KS1450
Williams, Robert	AL0950	Wilson, Glenn	IL3300	Winer, Arthur H.	CA0630
Williams, Robert S.	MI2200	Wilson, Gran	MD1010	Winerock, Jack H.	KS1350
Williams, Robert	NC0800	Wilson, Granberry	MD0850	Wines, Kevin N.	OH0850
Williams, Robin	AR0500	Wilson, Grover	NC1600	Winett, Kenneth	CA4460
Williams, Robin	LA0800	Wilson, Guy	TX3415	Winey, Richard	PA1250
Williams, Russell	AL0300	Wilson, J. Eric	TX0300	Winfield, Jeffrey	MD0850
Williams, Sandy	IN0907	Wilson, J. P.	AR0600	Winfree, James	TN1650
Williams, Sarah F.	SC1110	Wilson, Jack Forbes	WI1150	Wing, Barbara	DC0170
Williams, Sean	WA0350	Wilson, Jacque Scharlach	CA5510	Wing, Gregory	KY0900
Williams, Shane	MO0650	Wilson, Jacqueline M.	WI0803	Wing, Henry	NH0350
Williams, Stephen C.	PA2550	Wilson, James Dale	CT0100	Wing, Lizabeth A.	OH2200
Williams, Steve	CA3800	Wilson, James	NY3600	Wingard, Alan B.	GA1800
Williams, Steven	NC2550	Wilson, James	NJ0800	Wingate, Mark	FL0850
Williams, Steven J.	CA3500	Wilson, Jane Ann H.	TX3200	Wingate, Owen K.	FL0675
Williams, Stewart	TX3000	Wilson, Jeanne	NJ0825	Wingert, Bradley	NY2800
Williams, Susan E.	AL1170	Wilson, Jeffrey S.	IL1050	Wingert, Jennifer	IN1600
Williams, Susan	IA0950	Wilson, Jeremy	TN1850	Wingett, Joy	MA0600

Alphabetical Listing of Faculty

Name	Code	Name	Code	Name	Code
Wingreen, Harriet	NY2150	Witte, Tom	GA1150	Wolfson, Greer Ellison	CA5070
Winkelman, David	NC1650	Wittemann, Wilbur	NJ0550	Wolgast, Brett	IA1550
Winking, Keith R.	TX3175	Witten, David	NJ0800	Wolgast, Brett	IA0300
Winkle, Carola	ID0050	Witten, Dean	NJ1050	Wolgast, Marita	IA0300
Winkle, Keith	WA0650	Witter, Tim	CA0050	Wolinski, Mary E.	KY1550
Winkle, William	ID0050	Wittgraf, Michael A.	ND0500	Wolinsky, Robert A.	NY2550
Winkler, Amanda Eubanks	NY4100	Wittman, Frances P.	NY3700	Woliver, C. Patrick	OH1850
Winkler, Chad	PA0600	Wittman, Jesse C.	IN1650	Wolking, Henry C.	UT0250
Winkler, Frank	IL1085	Wittner, Gary	ME0200	Woll, Greg	CA1900
Winkler, Fred	WA1000	Wittner, Gary D.	ME0500	Wollan, Barbara	CO0650
Winkler, John	WV0750	Wittstadt, Kurt	MD0175	Wollman, Elizabeth L.	NY0250
Winkler, Kathleen	CA5300	Witvliet, John	MI0350	Wollner, William	MI1850
Winkler, Kathleen	TX2150	Witzel, James	CA4425	Wolter, Bill	CA1560
Winkler, Peter	NY3790	Witzel, James F.	CA4200	Wolters-Fredlund, Benita	MI0350
Winkler, Todd	RI0050	Witzke, Ron	MO2000	Wolverton, Peggy	KY1000
Winn, Jack	MI0520	Witzleben, J. Lawrence	MD1010	Wolverton, Vance D.	KY1000
Winn, James	NV0100	Wiznerowicz, James	VA1600	Wolynec, Gregory J.	TN0050
Winner, Andrew	KY1000	Wlazlo, Tricia L.	IL2050	Wolynec, Lisa	TN0050
Winner, Andrew	KY1300	Wlodarski, Amy	PA0950	Wolz, Larry	TX0900
Winograd, Barry	IL0720	Wlosok, Pavel	NC2600	Wolzinger, Renah	CA2050
Winograd, Peter	NY2150	Wodnicki, Adam	TX3420	Womack, Anna	HI0210
Winslow, Herbert	MN1450	Woebling-Paul, Cathy	MO0650	Womack, Donald Reid	HI0210
Winslow, Michael Rocky	CA0800	Woelbling-Paul, Cathleen	MO1950	Womack, Jeffrey	TX0150
Winslow, Richard D.	CA0800	Woelfel, Kevin	ID0250	Womack, Sara	AL1150
Winslow, Richard	CT0750	Woelfle, Colin	MN1280	Won, Allen	NY2250
Winslow, Robert J.	FL0930	Woger, Scott	IL1600	Won, Mel	CA4300
Winstead, Elizabeth	NC1350	Wogick, Jacqueline	NY2950	Wondercheck, Debora	CA5355
Winstead, Elizabeth	NC0100	Wohl, Daniel	NY3560	Wong Doe, Henry	PA1600
Winstead, William O.	OH2200	Wohlenhaus, Jennifer	IA0700	Wong, Baldwin	CA0840
Winston, Jeremy	OH2400	Wohletz, Jeremy	KS1000	Wong, Betsy	MI1150
Wint, Suzanne	IL2250	Wohlgemuth, J. Leigh	MN0625	Wong, Bradley	MI2250
Winter, Allen	NC0300	Wohlrab, Stephen	NC2600	Wong, Deborah	CA5040
Winter, Angela	TX3300	Wohlschlager, Cynthia	OH0600	Wong, Grace	NY1700
Winter, Beth	WA0200	Wohlschlager, Cynthia	OH1350	Wong, Jerry	OH1100
Winter, Brandon	AJ0030	Wohlwend, Karl	OH1850	Wong, K. Carson	ID0075
Winter, Michael J.	NY4320	Wohlwend, Karl	OH2050	Wong, Ketty	KS1350
Winter, Robert	CA5030	Woideck, Carl	OR1050	Wong, Lydia	AG0450
Winter, Robert	MD0175	Woike, David O.	MI0600	Wong, Sui-Fan	AA0080
Winter, Robert	MA0260	Woitach, Christopher	OR1250	Wong, Wing Ho	IN0005
Winter-Jones, Kristin	MD0400	Wojcik, Leszek M.	NY2750	Wong, Y. Alvin	CT0100
Winteregg, Steven L.	OH0450	Wojcik, Richard J.	IL3400	Wong, Yau-Sun	NM0200
Winterfeldt, Chad	MN0750	Wojkylak, Michael	PA1900	Wong-Abe, Suzanne	CA1900
Winters, Donald Eugene	MS0850	Wojnar, William A.	ND0150	Wonneberger, Alan A.	MD1000
Winters, Ellen	IL0720	Wojtera, Allen F.	VA1100	Woo, Betty	CA5000
Winters, George	TX3350	Wojtowicz, Joanne	KY1000	Woo, Betty	CA2200
Winters, Gregg	CT0800	Wolanski, Rob	AG0050	Woo, Claudia	AA0050
Winters, Jill	UT0050	Wolbers, Mark	AK0100	Woo, Jung-Ja	MA0350
Winters, Patrick	WA0250	Wolcott, Sylvia	KS0215	Wood, Bruce	TX3200
Winters, Thomas D.	PA3600	Wolcott, Vernon	OH0300	Wood, Catherine M.	AC0050
Winther, Rodney	OH2200	Wolcott, William A.	NE0610	Wood, Charles E.	AL1200
Winthrop, Anna	NY2750	Wold, Stanley R.	MN1600	Wood, Charles H.	CA4410
Winthrop, Faith	CA2950	Wold, Wayne L.	MD0500	Wood, Dan	NY3770
Winzenburger, Janet B.	OH0200	Woldu, Gail Hilson	CT0500	Wood, Darrell	OH2000
Wipf, Elaine	MN1250	Wolek, Krzysztof	KY1500	Wood, Dawn	KY0100
Wires, Jonathan	TN1400	Wolek, Nathan	FL1750	Wood, Douglas	WA1050
Wirt, Ronald	GA0550	Wolf, Aaron	CA1510	Wood, Eric	CA5350
Wirth, Elijah G.	MD0520	Wolf, Annalee	MN1450	Wood, Gary F.	MA1650
Wirth, Jason	NY2105	Wolf, Debbie	PA3250	Wood, Graham	SC0450
Wirth, Jordan	WY0150	Wolf, Debbie Lynn	PA2800	Wood, Gregory J.	NY4150
Wirth, Julius	MD0100	Wolf, Donald	AL1195	Wood, Jackie Coe	WA1300
Wirth, Mary Jo	WI1150	Wolf, Douglas J.	UT0250	Wood, Jasper	AB0100
Wirtz, Bob	CA6000	Wolf, Eve	NY4200	Wood, Jeffrey	TN0050
Wirtz, Ruth Ann	IN1100	Wolf, Gary	FL1550	Wood, Jennifer	WV0700
Wis, Ramona M.	IL2050	Wolf, Joyce Hall	KY0550	Wood, Jodi	AL1300
Wischusen, Mary A.	MI2200	Wolf, Lee A.	IA1390	Wood, Juli	TX3175
Wise, Colin	PA1400	Wolf, Lily	AL1195	Wood, Kenneth E.	VA1600
Wise, Herbert	NY2500	Wolf, Matthew	MI0500	Wood, Kevin	IL1085
Wise, Jay	NE0160	Wolf, Richard	MA1050	Wood, Kevin	WI0250
Wise, Jennifer	TX0340	Wolf, Sally	NJ1350	Wood, Matthew P.	AL0200
Wise, Patricia	IN0900	Wolf, Scott	CA6000	Wood, Michael	MI1000
Wise, Phillip C.	MO0800	Wolf, Scott	CA3460	Wood, Pamela	MA1200
Wise, Sherwood W.	NY0700	Wolfe, Anne Marie	IN0150	Wood, Patty	NM0400
Wise, Wilson	IA1100	Wolfe, Ben	NY1900	Wood, Peter J.	AL1300
Wiseman, Jeff	AG0150	Wolfe, Carl	TN1200	Wood, Rachel	AG0500
Wiseman, Roy	CT0050	Wolfe, Chris	MD0175	Wood, Robert	AG0500
Wishart, Betty	NC0300	Wolfe, Elizabeth	KY0450	Wood, Rose Ann	CA2050
Wiskus, Jessica	PA1050	Wolfe, George	IN0150	Wood, Rose Marie	IL0150
Wisler, Jay	KY0700	Wolfe, Gordon	AG0300	Wood, Stanley D.	OH1600
Wissick, Brent S.	NC2410	Wolfe, Gordon	AG0450	Wood, Susan	RI0200
Wistrom, LeAnne	PA1200	Wolfe, Jeffrey L.	WV0400	Wood, Susan	RI0150
Witakowski, Thomas E.	NY3717	Wolfe, Jennifer	MI1050	Wood, T. Bennett	TX2960
Witcher, William	NC0050	Wolfe, Julia	NY2750	Wood, Thomas G.	OH0700
Witek, Tanya D.	NJ0800	Wolfe, Katherine	IA1550	Wood, Tim	ID0140
Withers, Lisa Ann	VA0350	Wolfe, Lawrence	MA0350	Wood, Winifred	AB0210
Witmer, Brenda K.	VA0600	Wolfe, Lawrence	MA0400	Wood, Zeno D.	NY0500
Witmer, Larry	NY0050	Wolfe, Lawrence	MA1400	Woodall, Jeanne	WI1150
Witmer, Robert	AG0650	Wolfe, Thomas	AL1170	Woodard, Eve	TX1000
Witmer, Ruth	FL1550	Wolfe-Ralph, Carol	MD0400	Woodard, Leigh Ann	AK0100
Witmyer, Clyde	MA0260	Wolfe-Ralph, Carol	MD1050	Woodard, Peter	CT0650
Witnauer, Marlene P.	NY3717	Wolfersheim, Linda	WV0800	Woodard, Scott	WV0700
Witnauer, Marlene	NY3725	Wolff, Benjamin A.	NY1600	Woodard, Susan J.	PA3580
Witon, Renee	CA3920	Wolff, Christoph	MA1050	Woodbury, Elizabeth	NY3450
Witt, Anne C.	AL1170	Wolff, David	DC0170	Woodbury, Todd K.	UT0250
Witt, James	CA4000	Wolff, Lisa	NV0100	Woodbury, Todd	UT0400
Witt, James	CA4050	Wolfgang, Nancy Anderson	OH2600	Woodbury, Todd	UT0350
Witt, Jeanne	IA0650	Wolfinbarger, Steve	MI2250	Woodcock, Ruth	WA0100
Witt, Woody W.	TX3400	Wolfmann, Melissa	CA1850	Wooden, Lori	OK0700
Witt-Butler, Susan	CA4700	Wolford, Dale	CA5000	Wooden, Lori L.	OK1330
Wittchen, Andrea	PA2450	Wolford, Dale	CA4400	Wooderson, Joseph	MO1550
Witte, Diane	IN0907	Wolfram, Manfred K.	OH2200	Woodfield, Randal	PA3710

Name	Code	Name	Code	Name	Code
Woodford, Dorothy	CA1375	Worzbyt, Jason W.	PA1600	Wulfhorst, Dieter	CA1860
Woodford, Martha	AL1250	Woszczyk, Wieslaw	AI0150	Wunch, Doreen	WI1155
Woodford, Paul	AG0500	Wotring, Linda	MI1900	Wunder, Patricia	MI0350
Woodford, Peter	CA0550	Wozencraft-Ornellas, Jean	NM0100	Wunderlich, Kristen A.	SC1200
Woodhams, Richard	PA3250	Wozniak, William	PA3250	Wunsch, Aaron M.	NY1900
Woodhams, Richard	PA0850	Wraggett, Wes	AB0210	Wunsch, Doreen	WI1150
Woodhouse, Reed	NY1900	Wramage, Gregg	NJ0050	Wurgler, Norman F.	KY1540
Woodin, Nancy	IA1450	Wray, David	KY0950	Wurgler, Pamela S.	KY0950
Woodland, Betty	IN1450	Wray, Robert	WV0400	Wurster, Kathryn	MN0200
Woodley, David C.	IN0900	Wray, Ron E.	AL1160	Wurster, Kathryn M.	MN1030
Woodman, Ian	AA0020	Wrazen, Louise	AG0650	Wurster, Miles B.	MN1030
Woodman, Sarah	AA0500	Wren, Bobby	TX2310	Wurtz, Gary	TX2700
Woodring, Mark	KY0950	Wright, Arthur	GA1750	Wurzbach, George	NJ0760
Woodruff, Christopher J.	CA0600	Wright, Barbara	WV0560	Wutke, Drew	IN0700
Woodruff, Copeland	TN1680	Wright, Ben	MA1400	Wyant, Frank	CA4425
Woodruff, Ernest	MO0950	Wright, Bron	CO0830	Wyatt, Alan	TN0850
Woodruff, Jennifer A.	ME0150	Wright, Chantel R.	NY2750	Wyatt, Alfred	GA1900
Woodruff, Louis	NJ0750	Wright, Christine	AZ0150	Wyatt, Angela	MN1623
Woodruff, Neal	IL2300	Wright, Clell E.	TX0900	Wyatt, Ariana	WV0200
Woodruff, Sidney	GA0250	Wright, Craig M.	CT0900	Wyatt, Ariana	VA1700
Woodruff, William	PR0115	Wright, Debbie K.	OH1905	Wyatt, Benjamin H.	VA1100
Woodruff, William	NY0500	Wright, Elaine	MD0500	Wyatt, Gwendolyn	CA3750
Woodrum, Jennifer	WI0250	Wright, Elaine	VA1350	Wyatt, Larry D.	SC1110
Woodrum, Jennifer	IL3150	Wright, Elisabeth B.	IN0900	Wyatt, Paula	TN0850
Woods, Alexander G.	UT0050	Wright, Elizabeth	MA2250	Wyatt, Renee	WV0750
Woods, Alyssa	AG0400	Wright, Geoffrey	MD0400	Wyatt, Scott	KY1000
Woods, Benjamin	SC0710	Wright, Geoffrey	MD0650	Wyatt, Scott A.	IL3300
Woods, Bret	AL1050	Wright, Gina	IL0400	Wychulis, Kathleen	NE0610
Woods, Carlton	MI0400	Wright, Gina	IL0900	Wyers, Giselle Eleanor	WA1050
Woods, Chris P.	IL1050	Wright, Helen	NY0642	Wygonik, David	PA2950
Woods, Craig W.	CA4410	Wright, J. Clay	KS0440	Wyland, Richard	MN0250
Woods, Jon R.	OH1850	Wright, James	NY0400	Wylie, Mary Ellen	IN1600
Woods, Lonel	NY3780	Wright, James	AG0100	Wylie, Ted	TN0100
Woods, Michael	NY1350	Wright, Jeffrey	IN0910	Wyman, Laurence	NY3725
Woods, Rex A.	AZ0500	Wright, Jeffrey E.	IN0100	Wyman, Pat	AF0120
Woods, Sheryl	PA3250	Wright, John Wesley	MD0800	Wyman, Tamara	NE0450
Woods, Timothy E.	SD0400	Wright, John	IN0250	Wyman, Wayne	IA1550
Woods, William	NC2150	Wright, Joseph	MI2120	Wyman, William A.	NE0450
Woods, William	CA4550	Wright, Joseph	NY2400	Wyneken, Daniel	MA1400
Woodson, Andrew	OH1850	Wright, Josephine	OH0700	Wyner, Jonathan	MA0260
Woodson, Louisa Ellis	TX0300	Wright, Julie	TN0250	Wyner, Yehudi	MA0500
Woodul, Lars V.	NY4500	Wright, Kathryn	GA2100	Wynkoop, Rodney A.	NC0600
Woodward, Bruce	UT0190	Wright, Kathryn	MA0350	Wynn, Julie	IN0907
Woodward, Gary	CA3300	Wright, Kathryn M.	MA0260	Wynne, Patricia	CA1020
Woodward, Gary	CA5300	Wright, Lauren Denney	OK0650	Wynne, Scott	NC0050
Woodward, Greg	LA0400	Wright, Lawrence	PA2450	Wyrczynski, Stephen	IN0900
Woodward, Gregory S.	NY1800	Wright, Lesley A.	HI0210	Wyrick, Ginger	NC2650
Woodward, James E.	AL0500	Wright, Lon	MN1500	Wyrick, Inez	VA1350
Woodward, Roger	CA4200	Wright, Margaret	DC0170	Wyrtzen, Donald	TX2600
Woodward, Sheila C.	WA0250	Wright, Marylyn	TX3360	Wyse, Debbi	MI1000
Woodward, Todd	KY1550	Wright, Maurice W.	PA3250	Wyse, Paul N.	NY3780
Woodward-Cooper, Marlene	FL1450	Wright, Nathan	UT0050	Wyse, Philip	CO0225
Woodworth, Jessica A.	MO0500	Wright, Nicholas	AB0200	Wysock, Nathan	WI0350
Woodworth, William	TN1450	Wright, Patricia	AG0450	Wysock, Nathan	WI1150
Woody, Gilbert P.	CA3850	Wright, Peter	NJ1350	Wyss, Jane	PA3600
Woody, John	AZ0150	Wright, Prakash	TN1800	Wytko, Anna Marie	KS0650
Woody, Robert H.	NE0600	Wright, Randy	AZ0150	Xenelis, Nick	CA4460
Woodyard, Jim	AB0040	Wright, Richard	NY4050	Xia, Vivian	AG0650
Wooldridge, Jessica M.	NY4320	Wright, Robert	VA1000	Xian, Tracy	GA1200
Wooldridge, Marc	IN1025	Wright, Robert	TX0600	Xiao, Hong-Mei S.	AZ0500
Woolf, Vance	LA0900	Wright, Ruth	AG0500	Xie, Song	MS0385
Woolley, Clara	IN0010	Wright, Sally	VA1000	Xie, Song	MS0100
Woolley, Stacey	OH0450	Wright, Scott	KY1450	Xiques, David	NY2750
Woolley, Susanne	OK0300	Wright, Steve	MN0750	Xiques, David	CA4200
Woolly, Kimberly A.	MS0750	Wright, Todd T.	NC0050	Xiques, Ed	NY4450
Woolsey, Katherine E.	KS1400	Wright, Trey	GA1150	Xu, MingHuan	IL1615
Woolweaver, Scott	MA2010	Wright, Trudi Ann	CO0830	Xu, MingHuan	IL0550
Woomert, Barton R.	AG0450	Wright, Trudi Ann	CO0550	Xue, Suli	CA5300
Wooster, E.	MA0800	Wright, Vincent	NY2105	Xydas, Spiros	MI1750
Wooster, Pat	WA1000	Wright, William B.	PA1300	Yacoub, Allison	MD0600
Wooster, Pat	WA0650	Wright, William	AG0450	Yadeau, Lois J.	IL1750
Wooten, Ronnie	IL2200	Wright-Bower, Linda	IN0905	YaDeau, William Ronald	IL1750
Wooton, John A.	MS0750	Wright-Costa, Julie	UT0250	Yaffe, Alan	OH2200
Wootton, Tim	MO1550	Wright-FitzGerald, Jesse	CA3500	Yaffe, Carl	DC0170
Wootton, Tim	MO0400	Wright-FitzGerald, Jesse	CA0960	Yajima, Hiroko	NY2250
Wopat, Ann	WA0850	Wrighte, Michelle	IL1300	Yakas, James	TX3500
Wordelman, Peter	OR0200	Wristen, Brenda	NE0600	Yamada, Sojiro	LA0900
Work, George P.	IA0850	Wrublesky, Albert	WV0750	Yamaguchi, Yuko	FL1600
Workman, Darin D.	KS1110	Wtzig, Lu	IL1200	Yamamoto, Ko-Ichiro	WA1050
Workman, Josh	SC1100	Wu, Angela	KY0950	Yamamoto, Sandy	TX3510
Workman, K. Darren	TX3100	Wu, Chi-Chen	WY0200	Yamamoto, Shirley	CA0805
Workman, Reggie	NY2660	Wu, Chieh-Mei Jamie	NY3500	Yamamoto, Travis S.	CO0830
Worley, Dan	KY0450	Wu, Hai-Xin	MI0400	Yamashita, Wendy	HI0210
Worley, Daniel T.	KY1500	Wu, Hai-Xin	MI2200	Yamazaki, Hiroshi	NY5000
Worley, John L.	CA4900	Wu, Jessica Shuang	GA0750	Yampolsky, Miri	NY0900
Worlton, James T.	TX3420	Wu, She-e	IL2250	Yampolsky, Philip	IL3300
Worman, James	TX3350	Wu, She-e	NY2150	Yampolsky, Victor	IL2250
Wormhoudt, Pearl	IA1950	Wu, Shuang	GA1450	Yamron, Janet M.	PA3250
Worn, Richard	CA5000	Wu, Tien-Hsin	CA5300	Yan, Ni	OH0850
Woronecki, Stuart	CT0600	Wu, Yiping	NY3600	Yancey, Cheryl	VA1350
Worsley, Margaret	CA3200	Wubbels, Eric	OH1700	Yancey, James	AZ0470
Worster, Larry	CO0550	Wubbena, Jan Helmut	AR0400	Yancey, Patty	CA5400
Worth, David	MN0600	Wubbena, Teresa R.	AR0400	Yancho, Mari	MI2120
Worth, Mike	PA3330	Wubbenhorst, Thomas M.	ME0440	Yancho, Mari	MI0450
Worthen, Douglas	IL2900	Wucher, Jay	GA0500	Yanchus, Tina	AG0500
Worthen, Mary	AR0500	Wuest, Harry	FL0675	Yancich, Lisa	GA0750
Worthington, Oliver W.	TX3175	Wulfeck, David	NC2150	Yancich, Mark	GA0750
Worthy, Michael D.	MS0700	Wulfeck, David	NC0900	Yancich, Paul	OH0600
Wortmann, David	NC1100	Wulfeck, David	NC2300	Yandell, Ruth	AZ0440
Worzbty, Jason	PA3000	Wulff, Steve	MI0100	Yandell, Scott	AZ0440

Name	Code	Name	Code	Name	Code
Yanez, Raul	AZ0490	Yin, Jei	AA0110	Young, Jerry A.	WI0803
Yanez, Raul	AZ0440	Ying, David	NY1100	Young, Judy	OK0550
Yang, Amy	SC0750	Ying, Janet	NY1100	Young, Karen	OH1400
Yang, Ben Hoh	LA0150	Ying, Keiko	NY3350	Young, Karen L.	AL1160
Yang, Clara	NC2410	Ying, Phillip	NY1100	Young, Katherine	FL2050
Yang, Emily	DC0170	Ying, Tian	FL1900	Young, Keith R.	PA1600
Yang, Fengshi	IL0720	Yinger, Olivia	KY1450	Young, Kevin	TX1550
Yang, Frances K.	LA0550	Yingling, Mark T.	PA1300	Young, Kevin	TX3527
Yang, Hao	IN0005	Yingst, Benjamin	AZ0350	Young, Lonnie	MS0750
Yang, Hui-Ting	AL1050	Yip, Brandon	CA0150	Young, Louis G.	AR0850
Yang, Mina	CA5300	Yoder, Dan	PA1650	Young, M. Susan	PA1450
Yang, Mira	VA0450	Yoder, M. Dan	PA2750	Young, Margaret	OH1860
Yang, Rajung	ID0250	Yoder, Roza	CA0250	Young, Margaret	OH1850
Yang, Sandra S.	OH0450	Yoder, Tim	IN1025	Young, Michael J.	KY0900
Yang, Tzi-Ming	MD0550	Yoder-Frantz, Emily	PA1250	Young, Michael	IL3450
Yang, Yu-Jane	UT0350	Yoelin, Shelley	IL3200	Young, Mike	MT0370
Yang, Zhao	WA0950	Yoes, Janice	AR0700	Young, Ovid	IL2300
Yanish, Dorothy	NH0110	Yoes, Milas	AZ0470	Young, Paul U.	CA5300
Yankee, Steve	MD0400	Yohe, Tony	OK1450	Young, Paul G.	OH1905
Yankeelov, Margie L.	TN0100	Yokley, Darryl	PA3600	Young, Phillip D.	CA3650
Yannay, Yehuda	WI0825	Yom, Jeongeun	NY2200	Young, Phillip D.	CA3500
Yannelli, John A.	NY3560	Yon, Franklin	MI0450	Young, Robert	NY3780
Yannie, Mark	MN0625	Yon, John	PA2710	Young, Sam	CO0550
Yanovskiy, Leonid	FL1500	Yon, Kirsten A.	TX3200	Young, Scott	GA0625
Yanovskiy, Leonid	FL2100	Yonan, David	IL2100	Young, Shawn David	GA0500
Yanson, Eliezer G.	SC0200	Yonce, Tammy	SC1100	Young, Stefan	NJ1350
Yao, John	NY0646	Yonce, Tammy Evans	SD0550	Young, Steven	TX3300
Yap, Juliana	PA3580	Yonchak, Michael	OH2050	Young, Steven	MA0510
Yap, Kin	NY2400	Yonely, Jo Belle	NV0050	Young, Susan	IL2250
Yaraman, Sevin H.	NY1300	Yonetani, Ayako	FL1800	Young, Susan	AB0150
Yarbrough, Paul R.	CA4200	Yontz, Timothy	IL3550	Young, Sylvester	OH1900
Yarbrough, Stephen	SD0600	Yoo, Esther	HI0110	Young, Thomas	NY3560
Yardley, Anne B.	NJ0300	Yoo, Hyun Hanna	MD0700	Young, Welborn E.	NC2430
Yarick-Cross, Doris	CT0850	Yoo, In-Sil	NY3550	Young-Davids, Suzann	IN0910
Yarmolinsky, Benjamin	NY0280	Yoo, Peggy	PA0600	Young-Wright, Lorna C.	VI0050
Yarnell, Pamela	OH0700	Yoo, Shirley S.	PA2250	Youngblood, Brian	TX3000
Yarnelle, E.	CA3950	Yoo, Soyeon Park	IL2250	Youngblood, Pamela J.	TX3300
Yaron, Yuval	CA5060	Yoon, Choon Sil	CA3950	Youngdahl, Janet Ann	AA0200
Yarrington, John	TX1000	Yoon, Hye	MI1830	Younge, J. Sophia	IL0450
Yarrow, Anne	NY2450	Yoon, Hyeyung	NE0600	Younge, Pascal Yao	OH1900
Yasinitsky, Ann	WA1150	Yoon, Paul	VA1500	Younge, Shelley	AA0100
Yasinitsky, Greg	WA1150	Yoon, Sujin	MO1350	Younger, Brandee	NY0050
Yasuda, Nobuyoshi	WI0803	Yoon, Sunmin	OH1100	Youngs, Jennifer	MO0260
Yasuda, Noriko	MA1175	Yorgasen, Brent	OH1400	Youngstrom, Kenton	CA3600
Yasui, Byron K.	HI0210	Yorio, Joseph	FL1000	Youngstrom, Kenton	CA1700
Yates, Charles	CA4100	York, Elizabeth F.	SC0650	Youngstrom, Kenton D.	CA3500
Yates, Derrick	AL0010	York, Kevin	ID0100	Younker, Betty Anne	AG0500
Yates, Eric	AL1170	York, Lela	NM0310	Younse, Stuart	CT0650
Yates, Jonathan	NY3560	York, Molly	ID0100	Yount, Matthew W.	MO1500
Yates, Peter F.	CA5030	York, Paul	KY1500	Yount, Max	WI0100
Yates, Peter	CA0630	York, Richard	OH2450	Yount, Terry A.	FL1550
Yates, Rebecca	SC0050	York-Garesche, Jeanine	MO1830	Yourke, Peter	NY0644
Yates, Stanley	TN0050	Yoselevich, Gerald	NJ0700	Youtz, Gregory	WA0650
Yatso, Toby	AZ0100	Yoshida, Jason	CA3650	Yowell, Earl R.	VA1350
Yau, Eugenia Oi Yan	NY0270	Yoshida, Ken	NE0610	Yozviak, Andrew J.	PA3600
Yauger, Margaret	ME0500	Yoshikawa, Christine	FL0350	Yozviak, Lisa	OH0700
Yavornitzky, David W.	UT0250	Yoshioka, Airi	MD1000	Ypma, Nancy S.	IL1740
Yazdanfar, Ali	AI0150	Yoshioka, Masataka	TX3420	Yri, Kirsten	AG0600
Yazvac, Diane	OH2600	Yoshizawa, Haruko	NY4200	Ysereef, Alan	AG0070
Ybarra, Anthony L.	CA4410	Yost, Hilary W.	SC1200	Yslas, Ray V.	CA3500
Ycaza, Stephanie	VA1500	Yost, Jacqueline	NC2420	Yu, Enen	AL1195
Ycaza, Stephanie	VA1600	Yost, Jennifer	OH0250	Yu, Helen	AG0450
Yeager, Bill	CA4100	Yost, Jennifer	OH1800	Yu, Hongmei	AA0150
Yeager, Katherine	CO0250	Yost, Laurel	MT0200	Yu, Jin	OH2150
Yeager, Richard F.	MO0850	Yost, Regina Helcher	SC0275	Yu, Joanne	AA0020
Yearsley, David	NY0900	Yotsumoto, Mayumi	CO0100	Yu, Ka-Wai	IL0800
Yeary, Mark	IN0900	You, Daisy	CA4900	Yu, Kyung Hak	CT0850
Yeats, Robert E.	IA0300	You, JaeSong	NY0625	Yu, Ling	UT0200
Yee, Thomas	HI0210	You, Yali	MN0800	Yu, Tian-En	CA4425
Yefimova, Maria	VA0250	Youens, Susan	IN1700	Yu, Wen-Yih	TN1200
Yeh, I-Chen	OH1100	Youens-Wexler, Laura	DC0100	Yu, Xiaoqing	TN0850
Yeh, I-Chen	OH0300	Youmans, Charles D.	PA2750	Yu, Yuan-Qing	IL0550
Yeh, John Bruce	IL0550	Youn, Gloria	DC0170	Yu, Yuan-Qing	IN1750
Yeh, Ying	CA0800	Young, Alice	MD0400	Yu-Oppenheim, Julie	KS0650
Yehuda, Guy	FL1950	Young, Alphonso	VA1350	Yuasa, Joji	CA5050
Yekel, Amy L.	OH2150	Young, Ann	CA4450	Yubovich, Benjamin	IN0005
Yellin, Peter	NY2102	Young, Barbara G.	WI0803	Yudha, Cicilia I.	OH2600
Yelverton, William	TN1100	Young, Charles R.	WI0850	Yudkin, Jeremy	MA0400
Yen, Chianan	NY2750	Young, Charlie	DC0150	Yuen, Maureen	NY3725
Yeo, Douglas	AZ0100	Young, Chris	CA5300	Yui, Lisa	NY2150
Yeo, Douglas	MA1400	Young, Christopher	IN0900	Yukumoto, Todd	HI0210
Yeomans, David J.	TX3000	Young, Colin	IA0700	Yun, Chan Ho	CA0825
Yerden, Ruth	OR0600	Young, Craig S.	MS0400	Yun, Francis Y.	NJ0800
Yerden, Ruth	OR1150	Young, David	NE0450	Yun, Gerard	AG0650
Yerkins, Gary	IL0720	Young, David	MN1250	Yun, Gerard J.	AG0600
Yeston, Maury	NY1275	Young, David	AG0450	Yun, Misook	OH2600
Yeung, Alwen	GA1000	Young, Donald	CA3850	Yun, Soohyun	GA1150
Yeung, Amy	TN1720	Young, Eddye Pierce	NY3560	Yun, Yeon-Ji	CO0225
Yeung, Angela C.	CA5200	Young, Eileen	NC2205	Yung, Bell	PA3420
Yeung, Ann M.	IL3300	Young, Eileen M.	NC2500	Yurko, Bruce	PA2300
Yeung, Ian	TX3540	Young, Frederick	PA3400	Yurko, Bruce	NJ1050
Yeung, Karay	CO0100	Young, Gene	MD0650	Yurko, Kelly A.	OH2200
Yi, Ann	CA0855	Young, Geoff	AG0450	Yurko, Marcia	PA2300
Yi, Young	WI0100	Young, Gregory D.	MT0200	Yurkovskaya, Irina	PA3250
Yih, Annie	CA3600	Young, H. G.	WV0760	Yust, Jason	MA0400
Yih, Annie	CA5060	Young, James	MI1800	Yuzefovich, Victor	MD0150
Yim, Jay Alan	IL2250	Young, James Russell	GA1150	Yzereef, Allan	AG0150
Yim, Soyoon	DC0170	Young, Jana	GA1150	Z, Rachel	NY2660
Yim, Susy	VA1500	Young, Jay	IN1100	Zabala, Adriana	MN1623
Yim, Won-Bin	OH2200	Young, Jeff	AB0040	Zabel, Albert	WV0400

Name	Code	Name	Code	Name	Code
Zabelle, Kim A.	WA0800	Zegel, Don	FL2050	Zilli, Carol	CA3320
Zabelsky, Bill	NV0150	Zeger, Brian	NY1900	Zimbel, Ike	AG0130
Zabenova, Ainur	NY4320	Zeglis, Brian	IL1800	Zimberg, Todd	WA0460
Zabin, Amy	NY2750	Zeglis, Brian	IA1300	Zimdars, Richard L.	GA2100
Zabinski, Marina	RI0150	Zeglis, Brian M.	IL1350	Zimmer, Don	TN1700
Zabriskie, Alan N.	MO1790	Zegree, Stephen	IN0900	Zimmer, Lee	CA2420
Zabriskie, David	UT0400	Zehringer, Daniel	OH2500	Zimmer, Susan	MD0800
Zacarelli, Alla	AG0200	Zeidel, Scott	CA3200	Zimmerman, Andrew N.	NM0310
Zacharella, Alexandra	AR0730	Zeidel, Scott	CA1520	Zimmerman, Brian	AC0050
Zacharias, Andrew	CA1520	Zeiger, Mikhail	NY5000	Zimmerman, Charlene	IL0550
Zacharius, Leanne	AC0050	Zeigler, Lynn J.	IA0850	Zimmerman, Charles R.	WA1350
Zachow, Barbara	IL2350	Zeigler, Mark C.	NY2650	Zimmerman, Christopher	CT0650
Zackery, Harlan H.	MS0350	Zeinemann, Glenn	WI0848	Zimmerman, Daniel	MD1010
Zadinsky, Derek A.	OH0650	Zeisler, Dennis J.	VA1000	Zimmerman, Dean	MI2120
Zadrozny, Edward A.	OH0650	Zeisler, Nathaniel W.	CA1075	Zimmerman, Franklin B.	PA3350
Zadrozny, Edward A.	OH2150	Zeiss, Laurel E.	TX0300	Zimmerman, John	IL3550
Zaerr, Laura	OR1050	Zeitlin, Louise R.	OH0200	Zimmerman, Karen	CA3400
Zaev, Pance	NE0450	Zeitlin, Paula H.	MA2050	Zimmerman, Karen Bals	NY3720
Zafer, Paul	IL3550	Zelkowicz, Isaias	PA0550	Zimmerman, Keith	IL0400
Zager, Daniel	NY1100	Zell, Steven D.	TX0390	Zimmerman, Keith	IL1200
Zager, Michael	FL0650	Zelle, Tom	IL2100	Zimmerman, Kimberly	NE0525
Zagorski, Marcus	OH0300	Zeller, Jared	LA0080	Zimmerman, Larry	MN0750
Zahab, Roger E.	PA3420	Zeller, Kurt-Alexander	GA0500	Zimmerman, Larry	MN1450
Zahler, Clara	PA0550	Zeller, Richard	OR0250	Zimmerman, Larry	MN1625
Zahler, Noel	NY2105	Zellers, Jim A.	GA0750	Zimmerman, Larry	MN0250
Zahn, George	MN0350	Zelley, Richard S.	FL0400	Zimmerman, Lynda	WI0806
Zaidan, Raouf G.	NJ0825	Zelmanovich, Mark	TN1710	Zimmerman, R. Edward	IL3550
Zaik, Santha	OR0750	Zelnick, Stephanie	KS1350	Zimmerman, Robert	MA2250
Zaimont, Judith Lang	MN1623	Zeltsman, Nancy	MA0260	Zimmerman, Robert R.	NC0600
Zajac, Roy	CA4700	Zeltsman, Nancy	MA0350	Zimmerman, Ronald J.	PA1050
Zajac, Tom	MA2050	Zembower, Christian M.	TN0500	Zimmerman, Stevie	CT0650
Zak, Albin J.	NY3700	Zemek, Michael D.	IL0100	Zimmerman, Tim	IN1025
Zak, Peter	NY2660	Zemke, Lorna	WI0770	Zimmermann, Carlyn	IL2900
Zakarian, Sylvie	MA1175	Zemke, Vicki	AZ0350	Zimmermann, Gerhardt	TX3510
Zaki, Mark	NJ1100	Zemliauskas, Christopher	CO0800	Zinck, Bernard F.	WI0825
Zakkary, Martha	SC1100	Zemp, William Robin	SC0500	Zingara, James	AL1150
Zalantis, Helen	NY0625	Zeniodi, Zoe	FL0200	Zinn, Daniel L.	CA0807
Zalkind, Larry	UT0250	Zenobi, Dana	TX2650	Zinn, Dann	CA0900
Zalkind, Roberta S.	UT0250	Zent, Donald	KY0100	Zinn, Dann	CA5000
Zambello, Kenneth	MA0260	Zera, Tom	UT0400	Zinninger, Heather	LA0900
Zambito, Pete I.	MO0600	Zerbe, David	MI0150	Zinno, David A.	RI0300
Zamek, Brian	NY4050	Zerkel, David	GA2100	Ziolek, Eric E.	OH0650
Zamer, Craig T.	TN1450	Zerkle, Paula R.	PA2450	Zion, Mike	FL0680
Zamora, Christian	SD0050	Zerlang, Timothy	CA4900	Zipay, Terry L.	PA3700
Zamora, Gloria	TX0550	Zerna, Kyle	NJ1130	Ziporyn, Evan	MA1200
Zamparas, Grigorios	FL2050	Zerull, David	VA1350	Zirbel, John	AI0150
Zamzow, Beth Ann	IA0930	Zeserman, Steven B.	TX3530	Zirk, Willard	MI0600
Zamzow, Laura	WV0200	Zetts, Mary Jo F.	PA3000	Zirkle, Thomas	MO1110
Zandboer, Sheldon	AA0050	Zezelj-Gualdi, Danijela	NC2440	Zirnitis, Anda	MO0300
Zander, Benjamin	MA1400	Zezelj-Gualdi, Danijela	GA0940	Zisa, Peter	OR0500
Zanders, Michael	PA3250	Zhang, DaXun	TX3510	Zisman, Michael	CA4200
Zandmane, Inara	NC2430	Zhang, Weihua	MA2020	Zitek, Sam	NE0450
Zanella, Jean-Pierre	AI0210	Zhang, Xiao Feng	CA5000	Zito, Vincent	FL0730
Zaninelli, Luigi	MS0750	Zhang, Xiao-Fan	TN1100	Zito, William	NY0050
Zanjani, Azadeh	AA0050	Zhang, Yi	TX1400	Zito, William	NY2550
Zank, Jeremy	OH1800	Zhang, Yun	VA0150	Zito, William F.	NY1600
Zank, MJ Sunny	OH1800	Zhao, Chen	CA4150	Zitoun, Adrien	WI0150
Zank, Stephen	NY3705	Zhao, Grace Xia	CA5100	Zitoun, Adrien	WI1155
Zanovello, Giovanni	IN0900	Zhao, Wen	AG0650	Ziv, Amir	NY2660
Zanter, Mark J.	WV0400	Zhao, Yao	CA4100	Zizzi, Karen	WA1300
Zantow, Thomas	MI1850	Zhdanovskikh, Maksim	CT0100	Zlabinger, Tom	NY0646
Zanutto, Daniel R.	CA0825	Zheng, Su	CT0750	Zlotkin, Fred	NY0500
Zapalowski, Paul	NY3717	Zheng, Yin	VA1600	Zlotkin, Frederick	NY2150
Zaplatynsky, Andrew	NY2950	Zheng-Olefsky, Hai	TX2650	Zlotnick, Peter	NC0350
Zaplatynsky, Andrew	NY1550	Zhong, Mei	IN0150	Zobel, Elizabeth W.	IL0350
Zaporta, Ouida I.	TX2960	Zhou, Jessica	MA0400	Zocchi, Michael	MN1625
Zappa, John	KY1000	Zhou, Long	MO1810	Zocher, Norman M. E.	MA1400
Zappulla, Robert	CA1050	Zhou, Tianxu	MA2020	Zocher, Norman	MA0260
Zara, Meredith	GA0050	Zhou, Xiao-fu	PA3250	Zoeter, Garrick A.	VA1350
Zaretsky, Inessa	NY2250	Zhou, Xiao-Fu	PA2800	Zoffer, David	MA0260
Zaretsky, Michael	MA0400	Zhu, Hong	OK1330	Zoghby, Linda	AL1300
Zaritzky, Gerald	MA1400	Zibits, Paul	CA0825	Zogleman, Deanne	KS0980
Zaro-Mullins, Wendy	MN1623	Zickafoose, Edward	OH1800	Zohn, Andrew	GA0550
Zarro, Domenico E.	NJ0500	Zieba, Tomasz	OK0750	Zohn, Steven D.	PA3250
Zarzeczna, Marion	PA0850	Ziebart, Hailey	OR1020	Zohn-Muldoon, Ricardo	NY1100
Zaslaw, Neal	NY0900	Ziebold, Barbara M.	OH2140	Zollars, Dan	TX3530
Zaslove, Diana	CA4450	Ziebold, Barbara	OH0950	Zollars, Robert P.	OH2150
Zator, Brian	TX2955	Ziedrich, Cheryl	CA4460	Zollman, Ronald	PA0550
Zator-Nelson, Angela	PA3250	Ziedrich, Cheryl	CA1650	Zolner, Robert R.	NY3780
Zatorski, Thomas	NY2550	Ziegel, Donald	FL0930	Zolper, Stephen T.	MD0850
Zattiero, Joanna R.	UT0300	Ziegler, Delores	MA1400	Zombor, Iren	TN1200
Zavac, Nancy C.	FL1900	Ziegler, Delores	MD1010	Zonce, George	MA0260
Zavadsky, Julia	NJ1100	Ziegler, Marci	KS0050	Zook, D.	MA0800
Zavadsky, Julia	PA3250	Ziegler, Meredith	CT0600	Zook, Donald	MA0510
Zavislak, Kay	ID0250	Ziegler, Shanda	UT0150	Zook, Ian R.	VA0600
Zavzavadjian, Sylvia	AA0050	Ziek, Gary D.	KS0300	Zook, Jeffrey	MI1750
Zawacki, Karen A.	KS1400	Ziek, Terrisa A.	KS0300	Zook, Katrina J.	WY0200
Zawilak, Alexander	AZ0490	Zielinski, Mark D.	NH0350	Zoolalian, Linda A.	CA3650
Zawisza, Philip David	MN1623	Zielinski, Richard	OK1350	Zoolalian, Linda A.	CA3500
Zayarny, Iryna	AA0050	Zielke, Gregory D.	NE0250	Zophi, Steven	WA1000
Zazofsky, Peter	MA0400	Zielke, Steven M.	OR0700	Zori, Carmit	NJ1130
Zazulia, Emily	PA3420	Ziemann, Mark	CA4300	Zori, Carmit	NY3785
Zbikowski, Lawrence	IL3250	Ziemba, Chris	NY0646	Zorin, Max	PA2750
Zbyszynski, Michael F.	CA5353	Ziesemer, Bruce	WI0350	Zork, Stephen	MI0250
Zdechlik, Lisa J.	AZ0500	Zifer, Timothy	IN1600	Zorn, Amy	NJ1350
Zdorovetchi, Ina	MA2050	Zigler, Amy E.	NC2205	Zorn, Karen	MA1175
Zdorovetchi, Ina	MA0350	Zigo, Julie Buras	MA0260	Zoro,	TN0100
Zdzinski, Stephen	FL1900	Zilber, Michael	CA2775	Zoro, Eugene S.	WA1250
Zebley, Matthew	CA5040	Zilberkant, Eduard	AK0150	Zsoldos, Michael	VT0450
Zec, John	NJ0550	Zilincik, Anthony	OH0350	Zsoldos, Michael	VT0100

Zuber, Gregory	NY1900
Zubow, Zachariah	IA0700
Zucker, Laurel	CA0150
Zucker, Laurel	CA0840
Zuckerman, Pinchas	NY2150
Zuehlke, Anneka	SC0650
Zugelder, Steven	NY2650
Zugger, Gail Lehto	OH0350
Zugger, Thomas W.	OH0350
Zuidema, Jeannie	MT0175
Zuidhof, Jessica	AA0035
Zuk, Ireneus	AG0250
Zuk, Luba	AI0150
Zukerman, Arianna	DC0050
Zukerman, Eugenia	NY2750
Zukovsky, Michele	CA5300
Zuluaga, Daniel	CA1960
Zumpella, Clement	OH2600
Zumwalt, Wildy	NY3725
Zuniga, Rodolfo	FL0700
Zuniga, Rodolfo	FL0200
Zupko, Mischa	IL0750
Zupko, Mischa	IL3100
Zuponcic, Veda	NJ1050
Zuptich, Lory Lacy	MO0850
Zurcher, Allen	PA2250
Zuroeveste, Rodney	ID0050
Zuschin, David	VA1100
Zusman, Shannon	CA5300
Zusman, Shanon P.	CA4450
Zuttermeister, Noenoelani	HI0210
Zvacek, Bret R.	NY3780
Zwally, Randall S.	PA2300
Zwartjes, Martijn	CA0510
Zweig, Mimi	IN0900
Zwelling, Judith Zwerdling	VA0250
Zwerneman, Jane	CA2100
Zwicker, Keri	AA0020
Zwilich, Ellen T.	FL0850
Zygmunt, David	PA0950
Zyko, Jeanette	TN0050
Zyla, Luke	OH1400
Zyla, Marc	IN1600
Zylstra, Nancy	WA0200
Zylstra, Nancy	WA0650
Zyman, Samuel	NY1900
Zyskowski, Ginger	KS0215
Zyskowski, Martin	WA0250
Zyskowski, Marty	WA0950

Index by Area of Administration

Contents of the Areas of Administration Index

Chair/Dean/Director/President............. 917

Undergraduate Studies..................... 927

Graduate Studies. 928

Admissions............................. 929

Community/Preparatory Division.......... 930

Festival/Artist Series/Cultural Programs..... 932

Summer Programs....................... 932

Associate/Assistant Chair/Dean............ 933

Chair/Dean/Director/President

Name	Code	Area
Aagaard, J. Kjersgaard	WI0842	80A
Aberasturi, Paul	NV0125	80A
Abrahamson, Kristeen	CA4460	80A
Abrams, David	NY2950	80A
Accurso, Joseph	NJ0030	80A
Adams, Brant	OK0800	80A
Adams, Robert C.	GA0875	80A
Adams-Ramsey, Suzanne	VA1580	80A
Adamson, Philip I.	AG0550	80A
Adlish, John	NV0125	80A
Alaimo, Kathleen	IL2650	80A
Albergo, Cathy	FL0680	80A
Alden, Jane	CT0750	80A
Aldridge, Robert	NJ1130	80A
Alesandrini, Joyce L.	OH1650	80A
Alexander, Bryant Keith	CA2800	80A
Alexander, Jerry	KS0215	80A
Alexander, Lois L.	MI2120	80A
Alig, Kelley	OK0300	80A
Allen, Matthew H.	MA2150	80A
Allison, Rees	MN0800	80A
Allsen, J. Michael	WI0865	80A
Almli, Thomas	WA0030	80A
Alper, Garth	LA0760	80A
Alsobrook, Joseph	MO0650	80A
Alstat, Sara	IL2500	80A
Altevogt, Brian L.	MI0500	80A
Altman, Timothy	NC2435	80A
Alverson, J. Michael	SC0300	80A
Alves, William	CA2175	80A
Amalong, Philip	OH0680	80A
Amati-Camperi, Alexandra	CA5353	80A
Amos, Alvin E.	PA2000	80A
Amrhein, Tim	NY0646	80A
Amrozowicz, Mary Barbara	NY4460	80A
Anagnoson, James	AG0300	80A
Anders, Micheal F.	OH2275	80A
Anderson, Beverly	DC0350	80A
Anderson, Gene	VA1500	80A
Anderson, Jonathan	TX3600	80A
Anderson, Lawrence P.	SC0710	80A
Anderson, Michael J.	IL3310	80A
Anderson, Toni P.	GA1200	80A
Andre, James	MS0150	80A
Andrews, Gregg L.	OH1120	80A
Angle, Terrie Karn	MD0450	80A
Annis, Robert L.	NJ1350	80A
Aquino, Robert	NY2102	80A
Arasimowicz, George Z.	NJ0700	80A
Arata, Michael	CA5500	80A
Arcaro, Peter	FL1100	80A
Archbold, Lawrence	MN0300	80A
Archer, Gail	NY0200	80A
Archetto, Maria	GA0755	80A
Armstrong, Alan	NC1500	80A
Arnade, Peter	HI0210	80A
Arnett, Nathan D.	IL1240	80A
Arnold, Donna	CA4850	80A
Arnold, Edwin P.	PA1450	80A
Arnwine, James A.	CA3500	80A
Arrigotti, Stephanie	NV0150	80A
Arroe, Cate	MI0650	80A
Arshagouni, Michael H.	CA2750	80A
Arthurs, Robert	NY2400	80A
Ashmore, Michel	MO0250	80A
Ashworth, Teresa	MN1100	80A
Atkinson, Michael	IN1250	80A
Auman, Kevin	NC1450	80A
Auner, Joseph	MA1900	80A
Autry, Philip E.	TN0550	80A
Avelar, Linda	CA1250	80A
Averill, Gage	AB0100	80A
Ayres, Carol	IA0800	80A
Babcock, Mark A.	IA0200	80A
Bach, Larry	MN1250	80A
Backlin, William	IA1170	80A
Bahr, Christine	IL1740	80A
Bailey, John R.	NE0600	80A
Bain, Jennifer	AF0100	80A
Baird, Sara Lynn	AL0200	80A
Baker, Eric	TX1850	80A
Baker, Gail	NE0610	80A
Baker, James	RI0050	80A
Baker, Janet Ann	CA3258	80A
Baldwin, Deborah J.	AR0750	80A
Ball, W. Scott	TN1350	80A
Ballenger, William	TX3200	80A
Bankhead, James M.	UT0300	80A
Banocy-Payne, Marge	FL1790	80A
Barland, Charles J.	IA1450	80A
Barlar, Douglas	FL0670	80A
Barnes, Elendar	NY0640	80A
Barrios, Francisco X.	MO1500	80A
Barry, Marilyn R.	AK0050	80A
Bartlett, Melanie	MI1250	80A
Barton, Karl S.	GA1990	80A,80F
Bass, Ruth	NY0280	80A
Bauer, Paul D.	IL2200	80A
Baugh, Kim C.	VA1300	80A
Baxter, Diane R.	OR1250	80A,80F,80G
Beams, Mahala	MA1560	80A
Bean, Robert D.	IN0905	80A
Beckerman, Michael	NY2740	80A
Beckett, Christine	AI0070	80A
Beckford, John S.	SC0750	80A
Beckford, Richard E.	SC1050	80A
Beckstrom, Robert	OH1300	80A
Bednarz, Blanka	PA0950	80A
Beene, Richard	CA1075	80A
Beert, Michael	IL2560	80A,80F
Beeson, Robert	FL0500	80A
Behroozi, Bahram	CA4350	80A
Bell, Susan	CA2840	80A
Bellassai, Marc C.	AZ0250	80A,80F
Ben-Amots, Ofer	CO0200	80A
Benedetti, Fred	CA2100	80A
Benjamin, Jack	SC1100	80A
Bennett, Cameron	WA0650	80A
Bennie, Roanna	CA0100	80A
Benson, Gregory V.	UT0305	80A
Benson, Mark	PA0400	80A
Benson, Mark F.	AL0210	80A,80F
Benson, Will	TN0300	80A,80F
Bentley, Joe	MI1830	80A
Berentsen, Kurt	OR0150	80A
Berg Oram, Stephanie	CO0625	80A
Berg, Jim	CA1270	80A
Berg, Shelton G.	FL1900	80A
Berger, Harris M.	TX2900	80A
Bergstrom, Melissa	MN0040	80A
Berke, Melissa	NE0610	80A
Berkowitz, Paul M.	CA5060	80A
Berna, Linda	IL0550	80A,80H
Berrett, Joshua	NY2400	80A
Bestock, Donna J.	CA4625	80A
Betancourt, David	CA0859	80A
Bethany, Adeline M.	PA0450	80A,80F
Betts, James E.	IL1800	80A
Betts, Steven	OK1200	80A
Beyer, George	CA1520	80A
Beyer, Loretta	MI0200	80A
Bible, Kierstin Michelle	MO0260	80A
Bieritz, Gerald	TX1300	80A
Bighley, Mark	OK0550	80A
Binford, Hilde M.	PA2450	80A
Binger, Adlai	PA0050	80A
Birk, Richard	TX0350	80A
Birkedahl, Walter	CA3320	80A
Birx, Donald L.	PA2715	80A
Biscardi, Chester	NY3560	80A
Biscay, Karen T.	OH1330	80A
Bishop, Darcie	MS0350	80A
Black, John Paul	NC1075	80A
Blackley, Terrance J.	CA1900	80A
Blackshear, Glinda	AL0831	80A
Blackwood, Jothany	CA1850	80A
Blair, Steve	VT0250	80A
Blair, Timothy V.	PA3600	80A
Blanchard, Gerald J.	MI1160	80A
Blankenbaker, Scott E.	MN1290	80A
Blankenship, Daniel	WI0804	80A
Blassingame, Susan	TX1550	80A
Blasting, Ralph	NY3680	80A
Blatti, Richard L.	OH1850	80A
Bleiler, Loueda	NY0950	80A,80F
Bletstein, Bev R.	OH1860	80A
Blewett, Cathy	AG0300	80A
Blocher, Larry	AL1050	80A,80C
Block, Steven	NM0450	80A
Blocker, Robert	CT0850	80A
Blount, Joanna	IN0010	80A
Bobrowski, Christine	CA1250	80A
Boehm, Norman	AR0350	80A
Boehm, Patricia A.	OH2290	80A
Boelter, Karl	NY3725	80A
Boerckel, Gary M.	PA2100	80A
Boespflug, George	CA0350	80A
Boga, Cheryl	PA3500	80A,80F
Bogard, Theresa L.	WY0200	80A
Bognar, Joseph A.	IN1750	80A
Bohn, Donna M.	PA1550	80A,80B
Bolin, Daniel	IN0250	80A
Bolton, Bryan	KY0050	80A
Bolton, Thomas W.	KY1200	80A
Bomberger, E. Douglas	PA1250	80A
Bond, Karlyn	UT0400	80A
Bone, Lloyd E.	WV0350	80A,80B
Bonner, Gary	CA0450	80A
Booth, John D.	MO0500	80A
Boozer, John E.	NC2350	80A,80C
Bordeau, Catherine A.	AR0425	80A
Borror, Gordon L.	OR1210	80A
Bostic, Ronald D.	NC2650	80A
Botelho, Mauro	NC0550	80A
Boubel, Karen A.	MN1000	80A
Boucher, Leslie H.	GA0700	80A
Boudreaux, Margaret A.	MD0520	80A
Boulanger, Richard	AE0100	80A
Boullion, Linda	NE0460	80A
Boulton, Kenneth	LA0650	80A

Name	Code	Area
Bourgois, Louis	KY0750	80A
Boutet, Danielle	VT0150	80A
Bowen, Jose A.	TX2400	80A
Bowles, Kenneth E.	ND0250	80A
Bowyer, Don	AR0110	80A
Boyce, Douglas J.	DC0100	80A
Boyd, Craig E.	NY4050	80A
Boyd, John W.	TX2550	80A
Boyd, Michael	PA0600	80A
Boyer, Douglas R.	TX3100	80A
Bracks, Lean'tin	TN0550	80A
Bradbury, William	CA0847	80A
Bradley, Jennifer	IA0930	80A
Bradshaw, Keith M.	UT0200	80A
Bragg, Christopher	ID0075	80A
Brakel, Timothy D.	OH2300	80A
Brancaleone, Francis P.	NY2200	80A
Branch, Stephen F.	CA3975	80A
Brand, Todd	MS0370	80A
Brandes, David E.	NH0110	80A
Brandes, Lambert	MA0800	80A
Brandon, Maureen	CO0350	80A
Brandon, Rodester	FL1300	80A
Brandt, Lynne	TX2310	80A
Brannon, Patrick V.	IL3370	80A,80F
Braun, Mark	MN0750	80A
Bray, Michael R.	PA3260	80A
Breden, Mary C.	CA2800	80A
Breland, John Roger	AL1195	80A
Brellochs, Christopher	NY1050	80A
Bremer, Carolyn	CA0825	80A
Brenan, Jim	AA0050	80A
Brent, William	LA0550	80A
Brewer, Johnny	AL0620	80A
Brewer, William T.	KS0550	80A
Brickman, Scott T.	ME0420	80A
Bridges, Cynthia	TX0550	80A
Briere, Daniel H.	IN1650	80A
Briggs, Cynthia	MO0700	80A
Brink, Brian S.	FL0800	80A
Brinner, Benjamin	CA5000	80A
Britt, Carol	LA0450	80A
Britt, Mark E.	SC0750	80A
Broaddus, Vivian	MD0360	80A
Brodbeck, David	CA5020	80A
Brooks, C. Thomas	MA0950	80A
Brooks, Charles	SC0150	80A
Brooks, Melinda K.	AL0850	80A
Brown, Chris	CA2950	80A,80F
Brown, J. Bruce	MI2000	80A
Brown, Jennifer Williams	IA0700	80A
Brown, Joel	NY3650	80A
Brown, Kellie Dubel	TN1150	80A
Brown, Leslie Ellen	WI0700	80A
Brown, Michael R.	MS0500	80A
Brown, Richard L.	WV0600	80A
Brown, Roger H.	MA0260	80A
Brown, Terrance D.	AL1250	80A
Brown, Terry	WI0845	80A
Brown, Uzee	GA1450	80A
Browne, Patrick	AJ0150	80A,80F
Browning, Birch P.	OH0650	80A
Brubaker, Debra	IN0550	80A
Brunson, Ty	TX3800	80A
Bryan, Karen M.	AR0750	80A,80B,80D,80F
Bryson, Amity H.	MO0050	80A
Brzezinski, Jamey	CA2900	80A
Buchholz, Cindy	TX3600	80A
Buck, Barbara	KY0750	80A
Buckles, Michael	LA0350	80A
Buckmaster, Matthew	NC0750	80A
Buckner, James R.	AR0300	80A
Buckner, Jeremy	TN0250	80A,80G
Buddo, J. Christopher	NC0650	80A
Bugaj, Albert	WI0920	80A
Bulen, Jay C.	MO1780	80A
Bull, Douglas	WY0050	80A
Bullock, Kathy	KY0300	80A
Bullock, Valerie K.	SC0275	80A
Bulow, Harry T.	IN1300	80A
Bunk, Louis	NH0110	80A
Burbach, Brock	FL0200	80A
Burchard, Richard	KY0250	80A
Burford, Mark	OR0900	80A
Burgess, Phillipa	OH1750	80A
Burke, Kevin R.	IN0500	80A
Burks, Ricky	AL1450	80A
Burnett, Marty Wheeler	NE0100	80A
Burnette, Sonny	KY0610	80A
Burns, Lori	AG0400	80A
Burrell, Dan	WI0450	80A
Burton, Heidi R.	OK1300	80A
Burton, John R.	TX3500	80A
Burwinkel, James J.	MO1250	80A
Bush, Jeffrey E.	VA0600	80A
Busse Tucker, Ann	IL1340	80A
Butler, Charles Mark	MS0250	80A
Butler, Rebecca G.	PA0050	80A
Butler, Steve	CA5550	80A
Butterfield, Matthew W.	PA1300	80A
Buzzelli-Clarke, Betsy	PA1100	80A
Byerly, Douglas	MD0060	80A
Byrne, Mary	AB0210	80A
Caffey, H. David	CO0950	80A
Cailliet, Claude	WI0800	80A
Caldwell, Michael D.	CA0810	80A
Caldwell, William	OH0500	80A
Calkins, Katherine Charlton	CA3200	80A
Call, Kevin	ID0060	80A
Callahan, Gary L.	NC1150	80A
Calloway, Edwin S.	GA2300	80A
Calzolari, Laura	NY2400	80A
Camacho-Zavaleta, Martin	AL0050	80A
Campbell, Helen E.	AL0310	80A
Campbell, Jefferson	MN1600	80A
Campbell, Larry	TX0340	80A
Campbell, Stanford	OR0600	80A
Campbell, William G.	IA1300	80A
Camphouse, Mark D.	VA0450	80A
Canales, M. Cristina	MA1550	80A
Canier, Caren	NY3300	80A
Cannon, Derek	CA2100	80A
Canter, Nancy	CA1550	80A
Cantwell, Richard E.	KS1300	80A,80B
Cardillo, Kenneth	TN0260	80A
Carey, Barbara	NM0300	80A
Carlson, Andrew	OH0850	80A
Carlson, Marlan	OR0700	80A
Carlton, Kathleen	OK0410	80A
Carnahan, John	CA0825	80A
Carney, Horace R.	AL0010	80A
Carney, Timothy F.	HI0060	80A
Carpentier-Alting, Neil	CA1300	80A
Cart, Jon Robert	NJ1050	80A
Carter, Gary M.	CA0900	80A
Carter, Henrietta McKee	CA2050	80A
Carter, Jeffrey Richard	MO1950	80A
Carter, Joseph	CT0300	80A
Carter, Laurie A.	NY1900	80A,80C
Carter, Stewart	NC2500	80A
Cary, Jane G.	NY0400	80A,80C,80F
Casey, Donald E.	IL0750	80A
Casey, Michael	NH0100	80A
Cash, G. Gerald	FL0730	80A
Cassarino, James P.	VT0200	80A
Castleberry, David	WV0400	80A
Caston, Ben	GA2050	80A
Cato, Tom L.	GA0200	80A
Cavalier, Philip	IL0900	80A
Chabora, Robert J.	MN0600	80A
Chaffin, Lon W.	NM0310	80A
Chagas, Paulo	CA5040	80A
Chapman, Norman	MS0600	80A
Charron, Michael	MN1400	80A
Cheesman, Robert	MS0300	80A
Chenevert, James	TX3300	80A
Cherrington Beggs, Sally	SC0900	80A,80B,80F
Chester, Nia	MA1560	80A
Chien, Alec F.	PA0100	80A
Childress Orchard, Nan	NJ0050	80A
Chin, Wayman	MA1175	80A
Chinwah, Lovette	OH0500	80A
Christensen, Linda	NE0700	80A
Christophersen, Rick	CA0960	80A
Christy, William P.	OH1910	80A
Chua, Emily Yap	VA1125	80A,80F
Cid, Carmen	CT0150	80A
Cisler, Valerie C.	NE0590	80A
Clancy, Brian	NH0050	80A
Clark, Frank L.	GA0900	80A
Clark, John W.	CA4410	80A
Clark, Kelly	OK1300	80A
Clark, Thomas S.	TX3175	80A
Clemons, Gregory G.	IL1085	80A
Clervi, Paul	MO2050	80A
Cleveland, Lisa A.	NH0310	80A
Clickard, Stephen D.	PA0250	80A
Cline, Benjamin	KS0350	80A
Cline, Catherine	AR0225	80A
Cline, Judith A.	VA0550	80A,80F
Clinton, John	OK1330	80A
Cloke, Hugh	DC0075	80A
Clow, William	IL3500	80A
Coakley, Thomas	PA2500	80A
Cobb, Gary W.	CA3600	80A
Cochran, Barney	OH1600	80A
Cochran, Nancy	CO0900	80A
Cochran, Nathan	PA2950	80A,80F
Cochrane, Keith A.	NM0400	80A
Cockey, Linda E.	MD0800	80A
Codding, Amparo	NJ0020	80A
Coe, Judith A.	CO0830	80A
Cofer, R. Shayne	IL2150	80A
Cohen, Allen L.	NJ0400	80A
Cohen, David	NY2102	80A
Cohen, Fred S.	GA0550	80A
Cohen, Stanley	NY1275	80A,80B,80E
Coleman, Barbara J.	CO0650	80A
Coleman, Ian D.	MO2000	80A,80F
Coleman, Stephen	NY1150	80A
Coleman, William Dwight	GA1050	80A
Colleen, Jeffrey	IL1550	80A,80G

Index by Area of Administration

Name	Code	Area
Collins, David	MN1250	80A
Collins, Leo W.	MA2200	80A
Colson, David J.	MI2250	80A
Colton, Glenn	AG0170	80A,80F
Combs, Julia C.	MO0775	80A
Comstock, Allan D.	KS0300	80A
Conaty, Donna	CA4100	80A,80E
Condaris, Christine	MA1185	80A
Condon, Jennifer	IA0790	80A
Connelly, Bob J.	TX3410	80A
Connolly, Michael E.	OR1100	80A
Connors, Patricia Cahalan	MN1295	80A
Converse, Ralph D.	NM0500	80A
Conway, Eric	MD0600	80A
Cook, Stephen	CA6000	80A
Cooper, John H.	ME0270	80A
Cooper, Michael	TX2850	80A
Corley, Sheila	AZ0400	80A
Cornelius, John L.	TX2100	80A
Cortese, Michael	NY0450	80A
Cosentino, Joe V.	NY1050	80A
Costanzo, Samuel R.	CT0250	80A
Cotton, Jerry	TX0370	80A
Coutts, Greg A.	IL2650	80A
Covach, John R.	NY4350	80A
Cowan, Carole	NY3760	80A
Cowles, Robert	NY1550	80A
Cox, Jeff R.	MA2000	80A,80C
Crabtree, Joseph C.	TX1425	80A
Cram, Matthew	OH2100	80A
Cramer, Alfred W.	CA3650	80A
Crane, Susan	KS0980	80A
Crannell, Wayne T.	TX0250	80A
Crawford, Leneida	MD0850	80A
Creaser, Cynthia	AF0120	80A
Crist, Michael	OH2600	80A
Croes, Stephen	MA0260	80A
Cromley, Dorothea	MT0175	80A
Crone, Jay	VA1700	80A
Crosby, J. Stephen	NY0100	80A
Crossman, Patricia	MD0175	80A
Crowder, Jarrell	MD0550	80A
Cubbage, John	MT0370	80A
Cucchi, Paolo	NJ0300	80A
Cudjoe, Gwendolyn	TX1300	80A
Culbertson, Robert M.	TX1400	80A
Culver, Daniel	IL0100	80A
Culverhouse, William	IN0400	80A
Curry, Jeffrey P.	NE0040	80A
Curtis, Cynthia R.	TN0100	80A
Curtis, Marvin V.	IN0910	80A
Cusack, Mary	MI0450	80A
Cutietta, Robert A.	CA5300	80A
Cutsforth-Huber, Bonnie	MD0095	80A
Cutting, W. Scott	MI1550	80A
Dahn, Luke	IA1200	80A
Daly, Adrian	OH0600	80A,80B,80C
Dammers, Richard J.	NJ1050	80A
Daniel, Thomas	AL0335	80A
Daniels, Jerry L.	IL0800	80A
Daniels, William B.	KY1100	80A
Danis, Francine	TX1900	80A
Daras, April L.	WV0250	80A
Dark, James	CA4000	80A
Darr, Steven L.	FL2130	80A
Daugherty, Buelane	IA1140	80A
Dauphin, Claude	AI0210	80A
Davalos, Catherine	CA3920	80A
Davenport, Mark	CO0650	80A
David, Andy	GA1500	80A,80F,80C
Davidian, Teresa	TX2750	80A
Davila, William	CA3450	80A
Davis, Clifford	NH0300	80A
Davis, Dana Dinsmore	OK0200	80A
Davis, Gene	AL0450	80A
Davis, Mary E.	OH0400	80A
Davis, Peter A.	RI0250	80A
Dawe, Edmund N.	AC0100	80A
Dawson, Joseph C.	PA3700	80A
Dawson, Robert B.	CA1700	80A
Day, Mary	IA0100	80A
De Mesa, Cindy	CA0500	80A
De Ritis, Anthony	MA1450	80A
Deakins, Mark	KY0650	80A
Deal, John J.	NC2430	80A
Dean, Michael	CA5030	80A
Decker, Van A.	CA2300	80A
Declue, Gary L.	IL1245	80A
Decuir, Anthony	LA0300	80A
DeFord, Ruth	NY0625	80A
DeGraffenreid, George	CA0830	80A
DeLaRosa, Lou	CA5510	80A
DelDonna, Anthony R.	DC0075	80A
DeLongchamp, Jim	CA2975	80A
DeMol, Karen	IA0500	80A,80F
Dennee, Peter D.	WI0250	80A
Dering, James	TX0850	80A
Derrick, Patty	PA3410	80A
DeSanto, William	PA3560	80A
Deschere, Karen	WI1150	80A
DesJardins, Joseph	MN0350	80A
Desmond, Clinton J.	SD0200	80A
Devaney, Margaret	VA1100	80A
Devereaux, Kent	WA0200	80A
Dewey, Cynthia	UT0300	80A
Diaz, Roberto	PA0850	80A
Dicciani, Marc	PA3330	80A
DiCello, Anthony J.	OH0150	80A
Dickerson, Roger	LA0720	80A
Dickey, Bobby	GA0810	80A
Dickey, Marc R.	CA0815	80A
Dickson, John H.	GA1300	80A
Diehl, David J.	TN1600	80A
Dill, Jane	SC1080	80A
Dinielli, Michael	CA0950	80A
DiPalma, Maria	IA1350	80A
Dippre, Keith	NC1350	80A
Dismore, Roger	TX0370	80A
Dizinno, Janet	TX2200	80A
Doane, Christopher	KY1500	80A
Dobreff, Kevin J.	MI0850	80A
Dodds, Dinah	OR0400	80A
Dodson, Robert K.	MA0400	80A
Doherty, Jean	NY1950	80A
Dombrosky, Marc	MI1985	80A
Donelson, David W.	OH1350	80A,80B
Dooley, Gail	IA1100	80A
Dopson, Brian	FL0675	80A
Dornian, Paul	AA0050	80A
Dorsey, Sam Brian	VA0950	80A
Douglass, Ronald L.	MI1100	80A
Douthit, James Russell	NY2650	80A
Dower, Mary R.	PA1700	80A
Downes, Suzanne	IL2310	80A
Downey, Joanna	CA3750	80A
Doyen, Rob	MO1650	80A
Doyle, Laurie	TX1550	80A
Doyle, Tracy A.	CO0050	80A
Draskovic, Ines	NY1250	80A
Draves, Patricia	OH2290	80A
Driskell, Kelly	TX3360	80A
Drury, Jay	CA6050	80A
Dry, Marion	MA2050	80A,80D
Dubman, Shirley	MO0550	80A
Duff, John A.	FL1850	80A
Duffy, Kathryn Ann Pohlmann	IA0650	80A
Duggan, Sean B.	LA0600	80A
Dunbar, Brian	MN0620	80A
Dunbar, Edward	SC0200	80A
Duncan, Warren L.	AL1100	80A
Dunscomb, J. Richard	IL0720	80A
Dunston, Douglas E.	NM0350	80A
Durham, Linda Eileen	VA1840	80A
Dykema, Dan H.	AR0600	80A,80F
Earle, Diane K.	KY0800	80A
Easby, Rebecca	DC0250	80A
Eby, John D.	AI0050	80A
Eby, Patricia	WI0804	80A
Edidin, Aron	FL1360	80A
Ediger, Thomas L.	NE0500	80A
Edwards, Elizabeth	OK1050	80A
Edwards, Linda	NM0400	80A
Edwards, Steven C.	LA0080	80A
Ehlert, Alysia	GA0625	80A
Elderkin, Nicholas P.	TX1660	80A
Ellington, Deborah	TX1520	80A
Elliott, Robert L.	TN1400	80A
Ellis, Diana L.	TX1650	80A
Ellis, Peter	AA0032	80A
Elwell, Jeffery	TN1700	80A
Elworthy, Joseph	AB0200	80A
Endicott, David	WA0960	80A
Engelmann, Marcus W.	CA0100	80A
Engelson, Robert A.	IA0050	80A,80F,80H
Engstrom, Larry M.	NV0100	80A
Enis, Paul	OK0350	80A
Enos, Steve	OH0750	80A
Entz, James	CA3700	80A
Epperson, Douglas	CA0600	80A
Epstein, Joan O.	FL0450	80A
Ergo, Jack	IA0600	80A
Erickson, Christian	WY0150	80A
Erickson, Susan N.	MI2110	80A
Espinosa, Teresita	CA3150	80A
Fabozzi, Paul F.	NY3500	80A
Fagan, Jeffrey	NY3500	80A
Fahey, Paul F.	PA3500	80A
Fahy, Greg	ME0340	80A
Fairchild, G. Daniel	WI0840	80A
Fairlie, Thomas A.	TX2800	80A
Falk, Marc	IA0300	80A
Falker, Matt	CA2960	80A,80F
Falskow, John	WA0960	80A,80H
Famulare, Trever R.	PA3050	80A
Farrell, Timothy P.	SD0600	80A
Farrington, Lisa	NY0630	80A
Farwell, Douglas G.	GA2150	80A
Faszer, Ted	SD0450	80A
Feather, Carol Ann	TN0450	80A
Feeler, William	TX1660	80A
Feiszli, James D.	SD0500	80A
Feldman, Barbara	NJ0825	80A

Name	Code	Area
Feldman, Bernardo	CA1265	80A
Feldman, Martha	IL3250	80A
Feldt, Alison	MN1450	80A
Ferguson, Sean	AI0150	80A
Fernisse, Glenn	GA0400	80A
Fetz, Teun	OR0200	80A
Fields, Phyllis	SC0450	80A,80F
Fienberg, Gary	NJ0175	80A
Fienberg, Nona	NH0150	80A
Fink, Robert W.	CA5032	80A
Fink, Ted	OR1010	80A
Finney, John W.	KY0700	80A
Firmani, Domenico	MD0100	80A
Fisher, Brock L.	AL0950	80A
Fisher, John	TX3250	80A
Fishwick, Greg	OR1020	80A
Fitzgibbon, Cecelia	PA1000	80A,80C
Fitzsimons, Constance	CA1750	80A
Flack, Michael	IL0650	80A
Flagg, Aaron A.	CT0650	80A
Flandreau, Tara	CA1150	80A
Flax, Gale	NC0500	80A
Floreen, John E.	NJ1140	80A
Flores, Carlos	MI0250	80A
Flores, Mary	ID0130	80A
Fluhrer, Roy	SC0765	80A
Flynn, Timothy	MI1800	80A
Fogel, Henry	IL0550	80A
Fohrman, Jonathan	CA4050	80A
Foley, Brad	OR1050	80A,80F
Fonseca, James W.	OH1910	80A
Forbes, Bruce	NE0550	80A
Ford, Charles W.	NC2700	80A
Forger, James	MI1400	80A
Foss, Brian	AG0100	80A
Foster, Elaine	MI1985	80A
Foster, Marc A.	NC0930	80A
Foust, Diane	WI1100	80A
Fowler, Vivia	GA2200	80A
Fox, Aaron A.	NY0750	80A
Fox, Jeremy	IA1400	80A,80F,80G
Fox, T. Jeffrey	NY2550	80A
Foy, Patricia S.	SC0650	80A
Frabizio, William V.	PA0125	80A
Fragnoli, Kristen	NY2500	80A
Franklin, Bonita Louise	OK0450	80A,80F
Franklin, Laura L.	NC0250	80A
Fraser, Teresa L.	WA0600	80A,80F
Fredenburgh, Lisa M.	IL0150	80A
Freedman, Richard	PA1500	80A
Freeman, Gary	NC0860	80A
Frego, R. J. David	TX3530	80A
French, George E.	MN1590	80A
French, John	PA3550	80A
Freyermuth, G. Kim	AZ0200	80A
Friedman, Bennett	CA4460	80A
Frierson-Campbell, Carol	NJ1400	80A
Froom, David	MD0750	80A
Frye, Christopher B.	WI0810	80A
Fryns, Jennifer	FL0365	80A
Fulton, Richard D.	HI0300	80A
Furlons, Scott	WI0808	80A
Furlow, John W.	OH1905	80A
Fusco, Randall J.	OH1000	80A
Fuster, Bradley J.	NY3717	80A
Gach, Peter F.	CA3460	80A
Gaddis, J. Robert	KY0400	80A,80C
Gagnon, Jean-Louis	AI0210	80A
Gallagher, Mark	MD0350	80A
Galm, Eric A.	CT0500	80A,80F
Gammon, Steve	OR0200	80A
Garcia, Alvaro	WI0835	80A
Garcia, Orlando Jacinto	FL0700	80A
Garcia, William B.	TN0800	80A
Gardner, James E.	UT0250	80A
Garner, Rusty	FL0900	80A
Garrido, Glenn	TX3450	80A
Garry, Kevin M.	CO0400	80A
Gates, Charles R.	MS0700	80A
Gaughan, Warren J.	NC2550	80A
Gaylard, Timothy R.	VA1850	80A
Geisler, Herbert G.	CA1425	80A
Gentry, April	GA1750	80A
George, Matthew J.	MN1625	80A
Gephart, Jay S.	IN1310	80A
Gerber, Gary G.	AR0500	80A
Gerber, Richard A.	CT0450	80A
Gerhold, John	CA0270	80A
Gerster, Patrick	CA4350	80A
Gibbs, Phyllis M.	FL0570	80A
Gibeau, Peter	WI0862	80A
Gibson, Don	FL0850	80A
Gibson, Robert L.	MD1010	80A
Gier, David	IA1550	80A
Gifford, Troy S.	FL2120	80A
Gil, Maria Del Carmen	PR0115	80A
Gilbert, E. Beth	WI0860	80A
Gilbert, Jay W.	NE0200	80A,80F
Giles, Glenn	VT0100	80A
Giles, Leonard	GA0810	80A
Gilmour, F. Matthew	MO0850	80A
Gilpin, Mary Ann	WA0940	80A
Ginocchio, John	MN1500	80A
Gipson, Richard C.	TX3000	80A
Girdham, Jane C.	MI1850	80A
Girton, Irene	CA3300	80A
Gitz, Raymond	LA0560	80A
Glendening, Andrew	CA5150	80A
Glennon, Maura	NH0150	80A
Glickman, Joel	WI0600	80A
Glover, David	PA3100	80A
Goble, Daniel P.	CT0800	80A
Goeke, Christopher L.	MO1500	80A
Goetz-Sota, Germaine	IL0780	80A
Goforth, Stephen C.	KY1300	80A
Gokelman, William	TX3410	80A
Goldberg, Joel	VT0450	80A
Goldspiel, Alan	AL1200	80A
Goldstein, Joanna	IN1010	80A,80E
Goldstein, Norma	WA0860	80A
Golemo, Michael	IA0850	80A
Gonano, Max A.	PA0500	80A
Gonder, Jonathan P.	NY3730	80A
Gonzales, Gregory	TX2220	80A
Good, Jonathan E.	NV0050	80A
Goold, William C.	KY0150	80A
Gordon, Barbara N.	NJ0500	80A
Gordon, Daniel J.	NY3775	80A
Gordon-Seifert, Catherine	RI0150	80A
Gorham, Fr. Daniel	IN0005	80A
Gorman, Sharon L.	AR0900	80A
Gotfrit, Martin	AB0080	80A
Gothard, Paul	OH1250	80A
Govang, Don	MO0600	80A
Graber, Todd A.	NY3770	80A
Gracia-Nuthmann, Andre	NM0150	80A,80H
Graf, Greg	MO0750	80A
Graham, Lowell	TX3520	80A
Gramit, David	AA0100	80A
Grandy, Larry	CA4550	80A
Grant, Donald R.	MI1600	80A
Grant, Gary S.	PA1200	80A
Grass, Mahlon O.	PA2050	80A
Gratto, Sharon Davis	OH2250	80A
Gratz, Reed	CA5100	80A,80D
Graulty, John P.	CA0400	80A
Graveline, Michelle	MA0200	80A
Gray, Harold R. 'Skip'	KY1450	80A
Gray, Laura J.	AG0470	80A
Graziano, Amy	CA0960	80A
Green, Gayle	NC1200	80A
Green, Peter	CA1960	80A
Greene, Gayle	NC2525	80A
Greene, Sean	TN0900	80A
Greenlee, Geol	TN1250	80A
Greenlee, Robert K.	ME0200	80A
Gregg, Robert S.	NJ0990	80A
Gregorich, Shellie Lynn	PA2150	80A
Greig, R. Tad	PA3650	80A
Grenfell, Mary-Jo	MA1650	80A
Griffin, Jackie	SC0950	80A,80B
Griffin, Peter J.	IL0850	80A
Griffing, Joan	VA0300	80A
Grigel, Glen M.	NY3780	80A
Gronemann, Robert	MN1200	80A
Groom, Mitzi	KY1550	80A
Grooms, Pamela	MO0650	80A
Gross, Ernest H.	IL1300	80A
Grosso, Cheryl	WI0808	80A
Gruner, Greg	AL1300	80A
Grzych, Frank J.	TN0500	80A
Gubrud, Darcy Lease	MN1285	80A
Guilbert, Fred	LA0150	80A
Guinn, Melani	CA2300	80A
Guretzki, David	AJ0030	80A
Gustafson, Anita K.	SC1000	80A
Guterman, Jeffrey	PA3400	80A
Guthrie, J. Randall	OK0850	80A
Guy, Todd	IN1025	80A
Guzelimian, Ara	NY1900	80A
Haas, Thomas	IA1950	80A
Hachey, Michael C.	MA2300	80A,80B,80F
Hacker, Kathleen M.	IN1650	80A
Hafeli, Mary	NY3760	80A
Hageman, Paul M.	TX2960	80A,80C
Hagen, Patrick	WI0842	80A
Hager, Lawson	TX0900	80A,80G
Hakoda, Ken	KS0700	80A
Haley, Timothy R.	NC2210	80A
Hall, Barbara L.	KY0450	80A
Hall, Gary	WY0115	80A
Hall, Lois	NY2800	80A
Hall, Mark	TN1000	80A
Hall, William	NY0100	80A
Hallstrom, Jonathan F.	ME0250	80A
Ham, Robert	IN0200	80A
Hamlin, Peter S.	VT0350	80A
Hammond, June C.	FL1600	80A
Hammond, L. Curtis	KY0900	80A
Hancock, Blair M.	NC2640	80A
Hankins, Paul	MS0250	80A
Hanks, Kenneth B.	FL0930	80A

Name	Code	Area
Hanley, Darla	MA0260	80A
Hanna, Frederick	NE0160	80A
Hanni, Margaret	MA1700	80A
Hansbrough, Robert S.	NY0700	80A,80G
Hansen, Deborah	WA1350	80A
Hansen, Mark R.	ID0050	80A
Hansen, Neil E.	WY0130	80A
Harden, Patricia A.	NC2050	80A
Harder, Matthew D.	WV0600	80A
Harding, C. Taylee	SC1110	80A
Hardy, Steven	WV0440	80A
Harkey, Gary Don	TX3540	80A
Harnish, David D.	CA5200	80A
Harper, Darryl	VA1600	80A
Harper, Larry D.	WI0200	80A
Harrigan, Peter	VT0400	80A
Harrington, Katherine	CO0750	80A
Harrington, William	CA3520	80A
Harris, Edward C.	CA4400	80A
Harris, John	AG0130	80A
Harris, Lee	TN1700	80A,80F
Harris, Mary Carol C.	IA0940	80A
Harris, Ray	MS0570	80A
Harris, Rod D.	CA1375	80F,80A
Harris, Scott	ME0500	80A
Harris, Scott H.	TX2700	80A
Harrison, Albert D.	IN1560	80A
Harrison, Daniel	CT0900	80A
Harriss, Elaine Atkins	TN1720	80A
Hart, Michael D.	LA0030	80A
Hart, Steven R.	MT0350	80A
Hartenberger, Russell	AG0450	80A
Hartmann, David	SC0400	80A
Hartvig-Nielson, Niels	AB0040	80A
Hartwell, Robert	CA1800	80A
Harvey, Peter J.	CT0240	80A
Hasenpflug, Thom	ID0100	80A
Hatch, Ken	AR0110	80A
Hatcher, George	NC2300	80A
Hatcher, Oeida M.	VA0750	80A,80B
Haug, Sue E.	PA2750	80A
Haury, Clifford	VA1030	80A
Hawkins Raimi, Jane	NC0600	80A
Hawkins, Jemmie Peevy	AL0650	80A
Hawkins, John A.	WV0500	80A
Haworth, Janice	MN0150	80A
Hayes, Christopher	OH1900	80A
Hayes, John W.	OR0750	80A
Hayes, Raymond	WI0855	80A
Haynes, Alexis	NY1950	80A
Haynes, Alora D.	FL1675	80A
Haynes, Christopher A.	MA1850	80A
Haynes, Kimberly	FL0100	80A
Haynes, W. Lance	MO0825	80A
Head, Paul D.	DE0150	80A
Heald, Jason A.	OR1020	80A
Hedges, Don P.	IL3150	80A
Heighway, Robbi A.	WI0450	80A
Heitzman, Jill M.	IA0450	80A
Held, Roger L.	MI1450	80A
Helfers, James	AZ0400	80A
Heller, David	TX3350	80A
Heller, Jennifer	NC1100	80A
Henderson, David R.	NY3550	80A
Henderson, Peter	MO0700	80A
Henderson, Silvester	CA2775	80A
Hendricks, Bob	OK0200	80A
Hendrickson, Daniel	MI1180	80A
Hennessy, Jeff	AF0050	80A
Henning, Mary	KY0350	80A
Henry, Joseph D.	IL0900	80A
Hentschel, Alain R.	FL1570	80A
Herron, Clifford	FL1430	80A,80F
Hetrick, Esther A.	MI0910	80A
Hibbard, Kevin	GA2130	80A
Hick, Steven V.	PA2715	80A
Hicks, Charles E.	NC2700	80A
Hicks, Martha K.	MO1550	80A
Higdon, Paul	MO1100	80A
Hill, Camille	KY0600	80A
Hill, Matthew	IN0550	80A
Hill, William	FL1000	80A
Hilles, Sharon	CA0630	80A
Hills, Ernie M.	CA0840	80A,80C
Himes, A. C. 'Buddy'	TX2700	80A,80F
Hingst, Debra	IL2775	80A
Hinson, Wallace	GA1650	80A
Hinton, Don	UT0150	80A
Hirota, Yoko	AG0150	80A
Hiscocks, Mike	CA2650	80A
Hlus, Don	AB0060	80A
Hodgman, Thomas	MI0050	80A
Hodson, Robert	MI1050	80A
Hoepfner, Gregory	OK0150	80A
Hofer, Calvin	CO0225	80A
Hoffman, Joseph M.	MD0350	80A
Hogan, Larry	NC0805	80A
Hoifeldt, Steven	IA0425	80A
Hoke, S. Kay	PA1400	80A
Holden, LuAnn	TN0850	80A,80B
Holland, Patricia C.	WI0850	80A
Holland, Samuel S.	TX2400	80A,80C,80H
Holleman, James A.	MI1000	80A
Hollingsworth, Mark	OK0300	80A
Hollis, Burney J.	MD0600	80A
Hollis, C. Kimm	IN0650	80A
Holloway, Watson	GA0525	80A
Holly, Janice	MD0300	80A
Holmes, Ramona A.	WA0800	80A
Holt, Earl	TX1520	80A
Holzmeier, Jana	NE0450	80A,80B
Honda, Lorence	CA1850	80A
Hood, Marcia Mitchell	GA0150	80A
Hood, Michael J.	PA1600	80A
Hoogerhyde, Jason	TX2650	80A
Hooper, John	AA0015	80A
Hoover, Jeffrey	IL1090	80A
Hopkins, Jesse E.	VA0100	80A,80F
Hopkins, Joseph H.	AL0800	80A
Horn, Lawrence C.	MS0560	80A
Hornsby, Richard	AE0120	80A,80F,80G,80B
Houlahan, Michael	PA2350	80A,80B,80D,80E,80F
House, LeAnn	MN0450	80A
Hoyt, Reed J.	NY3700	80A
Huber, Wayne	CA1860	80A
Huckabee, KT	PA2710	80A
Hudson, David	CA2050	80A
Hudson-Mairet, Stephen	WI0425	80A
Hudspeth, Gregory	TX2220	80A
Huffman, Donna M.	WA0100	80A
Hughes, Albert C.	TN0950	80A
Hughes, Ralph	CA0150	80A
Hughes, Scott	TX2960	80A
Hugo, John William	VA0650	80A
Hukill, Cynthia L.	AR0200	80A
Hulen, Peter Lucas	IN1850	80A
Hulse, Mark	CA0300	80A
Hume, Michael	NY0050	80A
Humphrey, Mark Aaron	TX3415	80A
Hunt, Jeffrey	TX2260	80A
Hunt, Tom A.	OH1800	80A
Hurst, Carol	VA0900	80A
Hurst, Craig W.	WI0960	80A
Hurty, Jon	IL0100	80A
Hussain, Zac	PA2050	80A
Hutchings, James	IL0420	80A
Hutchinson, Mary Anne	NY4400	80A
Hyatt, Garey A.	MD0200	80A
Ice, Richard	MN0350	80A
Ioudenitch, Stanislav	MO1000	80A
Irving, Howard L.	AL1150	80A
Isaak, JoAnna	NY1300	80A
Isensee, Paul R.	PA2800	80A
Italiano, Richard	CO0300	80A
Ivey, Adriane	GA0755	80A
Jablonsky, Stephen	NY0550	80A
Jablow, Peter	DC0170	80A
Jachens, Darryl	SC1080	80A
Jackson, Albert	IL2775	80A
Jackson, Keith	WV0750	80A
Jackson, Roland	CA2710	80A
Jaeger, Lois	MN0200	80A
James, Robert R.	KY0550	80A,80G
Janisch, Joseph	WV0560	80A
Janners, Erik N.	WI0425	80A
Jarjisian, Catherine	CT0600	80A
Jarvis, Jeffery W.	AR0850	80A
Jarvis, Michelle	IN0250	80A
Jazwinski, Barbara M.	LA0750	80A
Jenkins, Ellie	GA0610	80A
Jennings, Charles R.	CA4300	80A
Jessop, Brad	OK0300	80A
Jessop, Craig D.	UT0300	80A
Johanson, Bryan	OR0850	80A
Johnson, Brad	MS0200	80A
Johnson, Craig R.	IL2100	80A
Johnson, David A.	IA0900	80A
Johnson, Diane	WA0900	80A
Johnson, Jacquelyn Pualani	HI0200	80A
Johnson, Jean	AL0340	80A
Johnson, Jeanne	TX1350	80A
Johnson, Jeffrey	CT0550	80A
Johnson, Kevin P.	GA1900	80A
Johnson, Michelle	IL0300	80A
Johnson, Roger O.	NJ0950	80A
Johnson, Scott R.	SD0050	80A
Johnson, Stephen R.	PA0700	80A
Johnson, Stephen P.	TX2600	80A
Johnson, Todd Alan	CA0845	80A
Johnson, William	CA0800	80A
Johnston, Joe	TX3540	80A
Johnston, Rebecca R.	SC0600	80A
Jonason, Louisa	PA2250	80A
Jones, Nick	KS0225	80A
Jones, Patrick Michael	NY4150	80A
Jones, Russell L.	KS1050	80A,80C
Jones, Suzanne	VT0050	80A
Jordahl, Patricia	AZ0300	80A
Jordan, William S.	AA0150	80A
Jordan-Anders, Lee	VA1830	80A
Josenhans, Thomas	IN1600	80A
Juarez, Benjamin Echenique	MA0400	80A

Name	Code	Area
Judd, Cristle Collins	ME0200	80A
Judy, Ned	MD0700	80A
Juncker, Arthur	CA1950	80A
Junkinsmith, Jeff	WA0860	80A
Jurgensmeier, Charles L.	IL1615	80A
Justus, Timothy W.	TX1700	80A
Juusela, Kari H.	MA0260	80A
Kahan, Sylvia	NY0644	80A
Kale, David	MA0800	80A
Kalm, Stephen	MT0400	80A
Kamm, Charles W.	CA3620	80A
Kamm, Charles W.	CA1060	80A
Kamm, Charles W.	CA4500	80A
Kammerer, David	HI0050	80A
Kampert, James	IL0630	80A
Kanis, David	IL0600	80A
Kantack, Jerri Lamar	MS0150	80A
Kanu, Andrew J.	VA1750	80A
Kaplan, William	IL3310	80A
Kaptain, Laurence D.	LA0200	80A
Kardan, Sel	CA1075	80A
Karnes, Kevin C.	GA0750	80A
Karpen, Richard	WA1050	80A
Katseanes, Kory L.	UT0050	80A
Katz, Mark	NC2410	80A
Kauffman, Bradley	KS0500	80A
Kauffman, Larry D.	PA0150	80A
Kaufhold, Jessica	AL0530	80A
Kaufman, Jacob	KS0215	80A
Kavasch, Deborah H.	CA0850	80A
Kays, Mark	IN1485	80A
Keast, Dan A.	TX3527	80A
Keeler, Steve	NY0450	80A
Keeling, Bruce	TX2350	80A
Keener, Allen	NY4060	80A
Kehrberg, Robert	NC2600	80A
Keiter, Lise	VA0800	80A
Keller, Dorothy	CT0350	80A
Kellert, Aaron	OK1100	80A
Kelley, Danny R.	TX2100	80A
Kelly, James J.	NJ0750	80A
Kelly, Michael F.	NY1850	80A
Kendall, Christopher	MI2100	80A
Kenney, James	CA3375	80A
Kennison, Kendall	MD0400	80A
Kenny, William	PA0350	80A
Kenyon, Paul	CA3640	80A
Kephart, Donald B.	PA1350	80A
Khaleel, Tasneem	MT0175	80A
Kilgore Wood, Janice	MD1050	80A
Killian, George W.	IN0700	80A
Kilpinen, Jonathan	IN1750	80A
Kim, Michael I.	AC0050	80A
Kim, Min	NJ0825	80A
Kimball, Kay	ME0430	80A
King, Anita	OR1300	80A,80F
King, Ben R.	NY1700	80A
King, Dennis W.	WI0150	80A
Kinney, Michael	NY0350	80A
Kinzer, Charles E.	VA0700	80A,80F
Kirby, David S.	NC1900	80A
Kirby, Wayne J.	NC2400	80A
Kirk, Ned	MN1400	80A
Kissick, John	AG0350	80A
Kjellman, Judith	WA1400	80A
Klein, Rochelle Z.	PA2900	80A
Kleinknecht, Daniel E.	IA1140	80A
Kluball, Jeff L.	GA0625	80A
Knapp, Peter J.	CA2550	80A
Knippenberg, Gary	MI1200	80A
Knott, Josef W.	FL2000	80A
Knowles, William A.	TN1500	80A
Knox, Daniel	AL0750	80A
Knudtsen, Jere	WA0750	80A
Kocher, Edward W.	PA1050	80A
Koep, Jeffrey	NV0050	80A
Koffman, David	GA0940	80A
Kolb, G. Roberts	NY1350	80A
Kolstad, Michael L.	MO0400	80A,80G
Kolwinska, Jeremy	MN1280	80A
Konecky, Larry	MS0050	80A
Konschak, Norma	MN1270	80A
Kontos, Julie	PA0250	80A
Koozer, Robin R.	NE0300	80A
Koponen, Glenn	NY2900	80A
Korde, Shirish	MA0700	80A
Korey, Judith A.	DC0350	80A
Kornelis, Benjamin	IA0500	80A
Kornelsen, Michael J.	CO0550	80A
Korstvedt, Benjamin M.	MA0650	80A
Kosciesza, Andrew	PA2400	80A
Kramer, Karl P.	IL3300	80A
Kramer, Timothy	IL1100	80A
Krause, Robert	TX3750	80A
Kravchak, Richard	CA0805	80A
Kreider, Paul K.	WV0750	80A
Kreuze, Brandon R.	GA0600	80A,80B
Krittenbrink, Juanita	OK1030	80A
Kromm, Nancy Wait	CA4425	80A
Krueger, Conrad	TX2260	80A
Krumbholz, Gerald A.	WA0950	80A
Krupansky, Sharla	KY1540	80A
Krusemark, Ruth E.	KS0100	80A
Krusemark, William	KS1375	80A,80B
Kugler, Roger T.	KS1000	80A
Kuhlman, Kristyn	NY3350	80A,80B,80E
Kuhns, Diana L.	PA2675	80A
Kunin, Ben	CA0050	80A
Kurth, Richard	AB0100	80A
Kuykendall, James Brooks	SC0700	80A
Kvam, Robert A.	IN0150	80A
LaBar, Arthur T.	TN1450	80A,80F
Labe, Paul E.	MD0475	80A
Lach, Peter	WV0300	80A
Laderach, Linda C.	MA1350	80A
Laderman, Michael	NY3100	80A
LaFave, Alan	SD0400	80A
Laird, Tracey	GA0050	80A
Lamb, Bill	KS0570	80A
Lamb, Earnest	NC0800	80A
Lamb, Robert E.	FL0150	80A
Lambert, Debra	CA3270	80A,80F,80G
Lambert, James	OK0150	80A
Landes, Heather	AZ0100	80A
Landgren, Peter	OH2200	80A
Langer, Kenneth P.	MA1500	80A
Langsford, Christopher M.	KS0750	80A
Lanning, Rebecca	GA1260	80A
Larcheid, Mary	IA0800	80A
Larner, James M.	IN1100	80A
Larocque, Jacques	AI0220	80A
Larson, David	SC0050	80A
Late, Eric	TX2295	80A
Latham, Michael	NY1300	80A
Laubersheimer, David	IL1610	80A
Laughton, John C.	NJ0175	80A
Lautar, Rebecca	FL0650	80A,80G
Lawrence, David	CA3950	80A
Lawrence-White, Stephanie	NC0200	80A
Lawson, Darren P.	SC0200	80A,80F
Lawson, Robert	CA5360	80A,80F
Lawson, Sonya R.	MA2100	80A
Leader, Jeanne	WA0300	80A
Lee, David	KY1550	80A
Lee, Richard F.	TX3150	80A
Lee, Ronald T.	RI0300	80A
Lees, Priscilla	MI2100	80A
Legname, Orlando	NY3765	80A
Lehmann, Jay	CA2450	80A
Lehtinen, Jennifer	NY3000	80A
Lemelin, Stephane	AG0400	80A
Lentini, James P.	OH1450	80A
Lenz, Andrea	NV0100	80A
Lepage, Peter	NY0900	80A
Lester, Joel	NY2250	80A
Levine, Dena	NJ1160	80A
Levine, Iris S.	CA0630	80A
Lewis, Diane	CA2440	80A
Lewis, Joseph S.	CA5020	80A
Lewis, Kathryn	MS0420	80A
Lewis, Steven D.	MO1710	80A
Lewis-Hammond, Susan	AB0150	80A
Lewiston, Cal	TX3700	80A
L'Hommedieu, Randi L.	MI0400	80A
Libin, Kathryn L.	NY4450	80A
Lieberman, Fredric	CA5070	80A
Lindblom, Michelle	ND0050	80A
Lindeman, Timothy H.	NC0910	80A
Linder, J. Michael	TX1775	80A
Lindsey, Lauren	WV0050	80A
Link, Anne-Marie	AA0110	80A
Lippens, Nancy Cobb	IN0800	80A
Lipton, Jeffrey S.	NY1275	80A,80B
Lister-Sink, Barbara	NC2205	80A
Lites, Wesley	KY1460	80A
Lochhead, Judith	NY3790	80A
Lochstampfor, Mark L.	OH0350	80A
Locke, Mamie	VA0500	80A
Lockwood, Susan	AL0335	80A
Loft, Jan	MN1500	80A
Long, Bill	AR0100	80A
Long, Derle R.	LA0770	80A
Long, Patrick A.	PA3150	80A
Longshore, Terry	OR0950	80A
Loos, James C.	IA0420	80A
Loubriel, Luis E.	IL0275	80A
Loucks, John	KS1110	80A
Lowe, Phillip	TX0910	80A,80F
Lowry, Douglas	NY1100	80A
Lublin, Robert	MA2010	80A
Lucius, Sue Anne	AZ0440	80A
Lucke, Paul	TX1450	80A
Lucky, Harrell C.	TX0700	80A
Ludwig, Mark	OH0755	80A
Lueger, Robert	NE0160	80A
Lum, Anne Craig	HI0150	80A
Lumpkin, Royce E.	NC2420	80A
Lumpp, David	MN0610	80A
Ly, Vi	CA1700	80A
Lyerla, Trilla R.	KS0050	80A
Mabry, Danajean	NC2370	80A
Macan, Ed	CA1280	80A

Name	Code	Area
MacAulay, Suzanne	CO0810	80A
MacDonald, Don	AB0070	80A
Machado, John	CA0950	80A
Machell, Iain	NY4300	80A
MacIntyre, Bruce C.	NY0500	80A
MacKenzie, Louis	IN1700	80A
Mackey, Steven	NJ0900	80A
Mackidon, Michon	NV0150	80A
Macomber, Jeffrey R.	MO0800	80A
Magee, Robert G.	AR0950	80A
Mager, Guillermo E.	CT0700	80A
Maginnis, Hayden	AG0200	80A
Mains, Ronda	AR0700	80A
Maline, Sarah R.	ME0410	80A
Mallett, Lawrence R.	OK1350	80A
Mallinson, Jeff	WA0980	80A
Maloney, Donna J.	OH1200	80A
Maloney-Titland, Patricia	NY3400	80A
Mamey, Norman	CA1000	80A,80F,80G,80H
Mamiya, Christin J.	NE0600	80A
Mammon, Marielaine	NJ0250	80A
Mandle, William Dee	DC0350	80A
Manley, Douglas H.	TN1550	80A
Mann, Bruce	VA0975	80A
Mann, Linda	CA2100	80A
Manning, Dwight C.	NY4200	80A
Manternach, LaDonna	IA0250	80A
Mao, Ruixuan	IL0840	80A
Marcades, Michael	AL0900	80A
Marcel, Linda A.	NJ0020	80A
Marder, Barbara	MD0060	80A
Mardirosian, Haig L.	FL2050	80A
Marissen, Michael	PA3200	80A
Markward, Cheri	RI0102	80A
Markward, Cheri D.	RI0101	80A
Marrs, Rick R.	CA3600	80A
Marschner, Joseph A.	MD0450	80A
Marta, Larry W.	TX3370	80A
Martin, Curtis E.	GA1600	80A
Martin, James	IA0400	80A
Martin, Jennifer	CA1510	80A
Martin, Robert	NY0150	80A
Martin, Valerie G.	PA3150	80A
Martinez, Javier	TX3515	80A
Martinez, Pedro	TX3525	80A
Marvuglio, Matt	MA0260	80A
Marzolf, Dennis	MN0200	80A
Mason, Colin M.	TX2800	80A
Mason, Freddy	TX2000	80A
Mastandrea, Eva	MT0450	80A
Masterson, Daniel J.	KS0150	80A
Matachek, John	MN0800	80A
Mathews, Christopher W.	TN1660	80A
Matsushita, Hidemi	CO0100	80A
Matthews, Ron	PA1150	80A
Mattingly, Bruce	NY3720	80A
Mattys, Joe	VA1150	80A
Matych-Hager, Susan	MI1950	80A
May, William V.	TX0300	80A
Maye, Shelia J.	VA0500	80A
Mayfield, Connie E.	CA0859	80A
McAllister, Michael	NC1750	80A
McAllister, Peter A.	AZ0500	80A
McAlpine, Tim	KY0860	80A
McBee, Karen L.	TX0125	80A
McCachren, Renee	NC0350	80A
McCallister, Ron	TN1650	80A
McCargar, Barbara Witham	MI0300	80A
McClellan, Teresa	TN0600	80A
McCloskey, Kathleen	PA0650	80A
McConnell, Douglas W.	OH0950	80A
McConnell, Patrick	NC0100	80A
McCormick, Robert	MI0500	80A
McCoy, D. Mark	IN0350	80A
McCreary, Teresa J.	HI0110	80A
McCullough, David M.	AL1250	80A
McCurley, Steven	OK0500	80A
McCusker, IHM, Joan	PA2200	80A
Mcelwain, Hugh	IL0780	80A
McFarland, Thomas J.	KY1400	80A
McGee, Gerald	MD0360	80A
McGee, Isaiah R.	SC0350	80A
McGilvray, Byron	TX3360	80A
McGinn, Jeanne	PA0850	80A
McGregor, Jane Butler	AB0210	80A
McGuigan-Sadoff, Kathleen	NY1200	80A
McIlhagga, Samuel D.	MI0100	80A
McIntire, Dennis K.	GA1700	80A
McIntosh, W. Legare	AL0500	80A
McIntyre, John	IN1400	80A
McKay, William	WA0150	80A
McKinney, Jane Grant	NC0900	80A
McLaughlin, Dan	IL1600	80A
McLeod, Lindy	AL1000	80A
McManus, Edward	OR0350	80A
McMullen, Dianne M.	NY4310	80A
McPhail, Mark L.	WI0865	80A
McTyre, Robert A.	GA1400	80A,80F
McWilliams, Robert	WI0830	80A
Meaders, James M.	MS0400	80A
Meadows, Melody	WV0800	80A
Mecham, Mark L.	PA1900	80A
Meckler, David C.	CA0855	80A
Meckley, William A.	NY3600	80A
Meeks, Joseph D.	GA1150	80A
Megginson, Julie	GA1000	80A,80F
Melton, James L.	CA5355	80A,80B
Meltzer, Howard S.	NY0270	80A
Menchaca, Louis A.	WI0300	80A
Mendez, Celestino 'Tino'	NM0150	80A
Menghini, Charles T.	IL3450	80A
Mennicke, David	MN0610	80A
Menoche, Charles Paul	CT0050	80A
Mercier, Richard E.	GA0950	80A
Meredith, Steven	UT0190	80A
Merrill, Dale A.	CA0960	80A
Merrill, Thomas G.	OH2550	80A
Mery, John Christian	OR0800	80A
Messere, Fritz J.	NY3770	80A
Messolaras, Irene	OK0600	80A
Meyer, Donald C.	IL1400	80A
Meyer, Frederick	WV0650	80A
Miceli, Jennifer Scott	NY2105	80A
Middleton, Jonathan N.	WA0250	80A
Mihalyo, Michael	NC0250	80A
Miles, Michael A.	MS0750	80A
Miller, Dan	IN1800	80A
Miller, Gabriel	LA0150	80A
Miller, John	ND0350	80A
Miller, Mark	CO0560	80A
Miller, Michael	WA0980	80A
Miller, Paul W.	PA2740	80A
Miller, Roland G.	IL0650	80A
Miller, Stephen R.	TN1800	80A
Miller, Thomas E.	CA5400	80A
Milne, David	WI0845	80A
Mims, Lloyd	FL1450	80A,80F
Minix, Dean	TX2750	80A
Modesitt, Carol Ann	UT0200	80A
Moffat, Bennet T.	HI0300	80A
Mohr, Deanne	MN1700	80A
Momand, Elizabeth B.	AR0730	80A
Monek, Daniel G.	OH1400	80A
Monson, Dale E.	GA2100	80A
Montgomery, Kip	NY3250	80A
Montgomery, Toni-Marie	IL2250	80A
Moody, Kevin M.	TX0075	80A
Moore, D. Scott	MN0750	80A
Moore, Daryl	CA0850	80A
Moore, J. Steven	MO1790	80A
Moore, Jeffrey M.	FL1800	80A
Moore, John	TX2200	80A
Morgan, Angela L.	GA0250	80A
Morgan, Charles	IL1250	80A,80F
Morin, Jeff	WI0850	80A,80F
Morris, Mellasenah Y.	MD0650	80A,80H
Morris, Valerie Bonita	SC0500	80A
Morrison, Charles D.	AG0600	80A
Morrison-Shetlar, Alison	NC0750	80A
Mortenson, Gary	KS0650	80A
Morton, Wyant	CA0550	80A
Mortyakova, Julia V.	MS0550	80A
Mount, Lorna	HI0120	80A
Mueller, Madeline N.	CA1020	80A
Mueller, Martin	NY2660	80A
Muir, Harry	WI0960	80A
Mulford, Ruth Stomne	DE0175	80A
Muller, Gerald	TX2170	80A
Mullis, Julie	NC2640	80A
Mulvihill, Mary	NY3500	80A
Munro, Chris	AG0130	80A
Murdoch, Colin	CA4150	80A
Murphy, Geraldine	NY0550	80A
Murphy, Vanissa B.	WI0803	80A
Murray, Bruce J.	OH1450	80A
Musial, Michael A.	NY3450	80A
Myers, David E.	MN1623	80A
Nabors, Larry J.	MS0570	80A,80F
Nakamae, Ayumi	NC0450	80A
Navari, Jude Joseph	CA4625	80A
Neal, David E.	NY3720	80A
Nealon, Michael A.	MI1200	80A
Neill, Kelly	AR0250	80A
Nelson, Drew	TX0075	80A
Nelson, Mark	AZ0480	80A
Neufeld, Donald E.	CA0250	80A
Newlin, Yvonne	IL1612	80A,80E
Newton, Jean	NY5000	80A
Nicholls, Barbara	KY0200	80A
Nichols, Eliza	IL0720	80A
Nicosia, Gloria	NY2050	80A
Nix, Brad K.	KS1250	80A,80E
Nolte, Jeffrey L.	OH1110	80A
Nolte, John P.	MN1030	80A
Noone, Michael J.	MA0330	80A
Noonkester, Lila D.	SC0800	80A
Nordeen, Mark	WY0060	80A
Nordman, Robert W.	MO1830	80A
Norris, Elizabeth	VT0300	80A
Norris, Joshua L.	KS0900	80A
Novak, Christina D.	AZ0490	80A
Nowack, James	WI1155	80A

Name	Code	Area	Name	Code	Area
Nunes, Dennis	MN1300	80A,80G	Plugge, Scott D.	TX2250	80A
Nyberg, Gary B.	WA0480	80A	Polay, Bruce	IL1350	80A
O'Bourke, Rosemarie	FL0900	80A	Polisi, Joseph W.	NY1900	80A
O'Connor, Charles 'Chuck'	NE0600	80A	Polman, Bert	MI0350	80A
Odom, Donald R.	MS0850	80A	Pond, Steven	NY0900	80A
Odom, Gale J.	LA0050	80A	Poole, Eric	NC2150	80A
O'Donnell, Jennifer M.	CT0246	80A	Poole, Mary Ellen	CA4150	80A
Olan, David	NY0600	80A	Poovey, Gena E.	SC0850	80A
Olin, Elinor	IL2000	80A	Popoff-Parks, Linette A.	MI1260	80A
Oliver, Sylvester	MS0600	80A	Porter, Beth Cram	OH0450	80A
Ollen, Joy	AB0050	80A	Porter, Charles	NY2700	80A
Ongaro, Giulio M.	CA5350	80A	Porter, Thomas	ND0400	80A
Ordaz, Joseph	CA2975	80A	Post, J. Brian	CA2250	80A
Organ, Wayne	CA1450	80A	Potes, Cesar I.	MI1200	80A
Orihuela, Ruthanne	CO0300	80A	Potts, Christina	TX2310	80A
Orovich, Nicholas	NH0350	80A	Powe, Holly	AL0330	80A
Orr, Clifton	AR0810	80A	Powell, Philip M.	SC0420	80A
Orr, Gerald	TX1250	80A	Power, Brian E.	AG0050	80A
Ortner, Richard	MA0350	80A	Price, Harry E.	GA1150	80A
Osborn, Clifton	AL0350	80A	Price, Marjorie	CA3375	80A
Otwell, Margaret V.	WI0500	80A	Prichard, Sheila Grace	MA1600	80A,80B
Ovens, Douglas P.	PA2550	80A	Priest, Thomas L.	UT0350	80A
Owen, William E.	WA0550	80A	Provencio, Robert	CA0650	80A
Owens, Douglas T.	VA1000	80A	Psurny, Robert D.	MT0075	80A
Oye, Deanna	AA0200	80A	Puchala, Mark	MI1650	80A
Padilla, Clarence S.	IA0550	80A	Puckette, Miller	CA5050	80A
Page, Fran M.	NC1300	80A	Purslow, Vicki T.	OR0950	80A
Page, Robert S.	TX1600	80A	Purvis, Ralph E.	AL0400	80A
Paige, Diane M.	NY1400	80A,80B,80F	Quantz, Don E.	AA0010	80A
Palmer, Douglas B.	OH2370	80A	Queen, Todd	CO0250	80A
Palmier, Darice	IL2970	80A	Quinlan, Gloria H.	TX1150	80A
Panken, Aaron D.	NY1450	80A	Rabinau, Kevin	MI1160	80A
Pannell, Larry J.	LA0100	80A	Raby, Lee Worley	CA2801	80A
Panneton, Isabelle	AI0200	80A	Ralston, Pamela	CA1510	80A
Pape, Louis W.	SD0150	80A	Ramey, Maxine	MT0400	80A
Papillon, Andre	AI0190	80A	Ramos Escobar, Jose Luis	PR0150	80A
Papini, Dennis	SD0550	80A	Rampersad, David	AL0345	80A
Parakilas, James P.	ME0150	80A	Ransom, Judy L.	WY0115	80A
Parasher, Prajna Paramita	PA0600	80A	Rapp, Willis M.	PA1750	80A
Pardue, Jane	NC1400	80A	Rauscher, James	TX0100	80A
Parker, Grant	CA1500	80A	Rawls, J. Archie	MS0580	80A
Parker, Gregory B.	NC0400	80A	Ray, Mary Ruth	MA0500	80A
Parker, Mara	PA3680	80A,80H	Ray, W. Irwin	GA1550	80A
Parker, Mark Edward	OK0750	80A	Read, Kenneth E.	OH0550	80A
Parker, Robin Lee	FL1700	80A	Rebbeck, Lyle	AA0040	80A
Parks, Sarah S.	WI0750	80A	Reddick, Don	IL2300	80A
Parrish, Eric	MN1175	80A	Reed, Dennis J.	CA2750	80A
Parsons, Laura E.	AL0950	80A	Reed, Joel F.	NC1250	80A,80F
Parsons, Stephen	IL1150	80A	Reed, Marc A.	CO0350	80A
Partain, Gregory L.	KY1350	80A	Reed, Teresa Shelton	OK1450	80A
Partin, Bruce	VA1250	80A	Reed, Thomas T.	OH0100	80A
Parton-Stanard, Susan	IL1500	80A,80B,80F	Rees, Fred J.	IN0907	80A
Pashkin, Elissa Brill	MA1100	80A	Rees, Helen	CA5031	80A
Patnoe, Lyneen	WA0030	80A	Reeves, Daniel	AR0110	80A
Patton, Larry	KS0210	80A	Regan, Patrick	MI1300	80A
Paul, John F.	OR0500	80A	Rehding, Alexander	MA1050	80A
Paul, Randall S.	OH2500	80A	Reid, Sally	TN0930	80A
Paulnack, Karl	MA0350	80A	Reimer, Mark U.	VA0150	80A
Paver, Jonathan	IL3200	80A	Reise, Jay	PA3350	80A
Pavlovsky, Taras	NJ0175	80A	Renfroe, Dennis C.	NC1025	80A
Pawlyshyn, Nancy	CA1760	80A	Restesan, Francise T.	PR0125	80A
Paxton, Laurence	HI0210	80A	Reynolds, David	SD0550	80A
Paxton, Steven E.	NM0425	80A	Reynolds, William D.	MI1050	80A
Payne, Thomas B.	VA0250	80A	Rice, Susan	WI0100	80A
Pearce, Jared	IA1950	80A	Richard, Charles	CA3800	80A
Pearson, Glen	CA1100	80A	Richards, E. Michael	MD1000	80A
Pecherek, Michael J.	IL1175	80A	Richards, Eric J.	NE0400	80A
Peebles, William L.	NC2600	80A	Richards, Gwyn	IN0900	80A
Peffer, Tony	VT0100	80A	Richards, James	MO1830	80A
Pelkey, Stanley C.	NY3350	80A	Richardson, Robert C.	WA0450	80A
Pellegrini, David	CT0150	80A	Richmond, John W.	NE0600	80A
Pelto, William L.	NC0050	80A	Richter, Glenn	TX3510	80A
Pelusi, Mario J.	IL1200	80A	Richter, Sara Jane	OK0770	80A
Peppo, Bret	CA1560	80A	Rieth, Dale	FL0950	80A,80E
Perconti, William J.	ID0130	80A	Rife, Jerry E.	NJ1000	80A
Perkins, Boyd	SD0400	80A	Riley, Raymond G.	MI0150	80A
Perrin, Ralph W.	CA4550	80A,80B	Rincon, Alicia	CA4000	80A
Perry, James	WI0806	80A	Rinehart, John	OH0050	80A
Perry, Steven	NJ0950	80A	Riordan, George T.	TN1100	80A
Perry, Timothy B.	NY3705	80A	Rischar, Richard A.	MI2110	80A
Pertl, Brian G.	WI0350	80A	Rivard, Gene	MN0625	80A
Pesavento, Gayle	IL1240	80A	Rivera, Francesca M.	CA5353	80A
Pesce, Dolores	MO1900	80A	Robbins, David P.	WA0650	80A
Peters, Mark	IL3100	80A	Roberson, Matt	AL0345	80A
Peterson, Douglas A.	FL0400	80A	Robertson, Jon	FL1125	80A
Peterson, Jay	IL1650	80A	Robertson, Kaestner	MA0250	80A
Pethel, Stan	GA0300	80A	Robins, Linda	TX2570	80A
Philipsen, Michael D.	IA0750	80A	Robinson, Nathalie G.	NY1600	80A,80C
Phillips, Kenneth	FL1450	80A	Robinson-Oturu, Gail M.	TN0050	80A
Phillips, Mark W.	VA1750	80A	Rocco, Emma S.	PA2713	80A
Philp, Brenda	AA0020	80A	Rochfort, Desmond	AA0200	80A
Phipps, Danny K.	MI0900	80A	Roden, Timothy J.	OH2000	80A
Pilsner, Joseph	TX3450	80A	Rogers, Donald M.	SC1200	80A,80C
Pinard, Mary	MA0255	80A	Roggenstein, Gary	CA0200	80A
Pinder, Kimberly	NM0450	80A	Roller, Peter	WI0050	80A
Pinkston, Dan	CA4600	80A	Rollin, Robert	OH2600	80A
Pirtle, R. Leigh	IA1390	80A	Romanek, Mary L.	PA2720	80A
Planer, John H.	IN1050	80A	Romeo, James	CA4050	80A
Plate, Stephen W.	TN0850	80A	Root, Timothy	FL0550	80A
Plew, Paul T.	CA2810	80A	Rosado-Nazario, Samuel	PR0100	80A
Plies, Dennis B.	OR1150	80A	Rose, Douglas	TN0050	80A

Index by Area of Administration

Name	Code	Area
Rose, Kathleen	CA2150	80A
Roseborough, Barbara	TN1380	80A
Rosenberg, Steven E.	SC0500	80A
Rosenblum, Henry	NY1860	80A
Rosenboom, David	CA0510	80A
Rosenfeld, Andrew	MD0610	80A
Ross, Jared	KS0060	80A
Ross, Nicholas Piers	VA1400	80A
Roush, Clark	NE0720	80A
Rowe, Robert	NY2750	80A
Royal, Guericke	DC0150	80A
Royer, Randall D.	SD0100	80A
Ruben, Bruce	NY1450	80A
Ruckman, Robert	OH2120	80A
Rudari, David J.	WV0100	80A,80F
Rumsey, Esther	TX2710	80A
Runge, Alan	TX0400	80A
Ruocco, Phyllis	AR0550	80A
Rupp, Martin	WI0817	80A
Rushing, Randal J.	TN1680	80A
Russell, Joan	AI0100	80A
Russell, Melinda	MN0300	80A
Russell, Teresa P.	CA4850	80A
Ruth, David E.	PA2700	80A
Rutherford, Eric D.	KS0560	80A
Rytting, Bryce	UT0325	80A
Sabina, Leslie M.	NY3475	80A
Sachdev, Salil	MA0510	80A
Sachs, Stephen W.	MS0100	80A,80F
Sajnovsky, Cynthia B.	GU0500	80A
Salerno, John	WI0808	80A
Salyer, Douglas W.	CT0200	80A
Samiian, Vida	CA0810	80A
Samuelson, Linda	MN1270	80A
Sanchez, George	NY0644	80A
Sander, Kurt L.	KY1000	80A
Sanders, Reginald L.	OH1200	80A
Sandler, Karen W.	PA2700	80A
Sandvick, Jerry	MN1260	80A
Sano, Stephen M.	CA4900	80A
Santana-Santana, Melanie	PR0115	80A
Santore, Jonathan C.	NH0250	80A
Satchell, Ernest R.	MD1020	80A
Sattler, Nancy J.	OH2140	80A
Sawyer, Eric	MA0100	80A
Scearce, J. Mark	NC1700	80A
Scelba, Anthony	NJ0700	80A,80F
Schaberg, David	CA5032	80A
Scharfenberger, Paul E.	NH0110	80A
Scharper, Alice	CA4410	80A
Scheib, Curt A.	PA3000	80A
Scheib, John W.	IN0150	80A
Schell, Mark	KY0100	80A
Schiavo, Joseph C.	NJ1100	80A,80F
Schindler, Karl W.	AZ0470	80A
Schirmer, Timothy	IL2350	80A
Schissel, Wendy	OR0550	80A
Schlabaugh, Karen Bauman	KS0200	80A
Schleppenbach, Barbara	IL2450	80A
Schlesinger, Scott L.	NC2525	80A
Schmidt, Alan G.	NY1220	80A
Schmidt, Jack W.	PA0900	80A,80F
Schmidt, Myron	MA0750	80A,80G
Schnauber, Thomas	MA0900	80A,80H
Schnepf, Chester	CT0200	80A
Schoenberg, Lisa	PA0675	80A
Schoening, Benjamin S.	WI0801	80A
Schorr, Timothy B.	WI1100	80A
Schreiner, Frederick	PA3710	80A,80F
Schreuder, Joel T.	NE0050	80A
Schubert, David T.	OH2450	80A
Schulenberg, David L.	NY4500	80A
Schultz, Jim	MT0100	80A
Schultz, Roger	VA0650	80A
Schultz, Russ A.	TX1400	80A
Schulz, Russell E.	TX0750	80A
Schwarze, Penny	MN0450	80A
Schweitzer, Kenneth	MD1100	80A
Sconyers, David	FL1730	80A
Scott, David	TX0150	80A
Scott, James C.	TX3420	80A
Scott, Sandra C.	GA1600	80A,80F
Scully, Mathew	CA3950	80A
Seachrist, Denise A.	OH1100	80A
Seaward, Jeffery A.	CA1290	80A
Seelbinder, Emily	NC2000	80A
Segger, Joachim	AA0035	80A
Seifert, Dustin	NM0100	80A
Seigel, Lester C.	AL0300	80A
Selby, Sara E.	GA2175	80A
Selesky, Evelyn C.	NY2450	80A
Seliger, Bryce M.	OR0750	80A,80B,80E
Selsor, Mindy	MO0550	80A
Seuffert, Maria C.	GA0160	80A
Shadle-Peters, Jennifer	CO0275	80A
Shanahan, Ellen Cooper	MA0280	80A
Shanklin, Bart	IL3500	80A
Shannon, John	IN1485	80A
Sharkey, Jeffrey N.	MD0650	80A
Shaw, Rolland H.		80A
Shay, Robert	MO1800	80A
Shearer, Erik	CA3250	80A
Sheffler, Jack	WV0200	80A
Shelby, Karla	OK1500	80A
Shelley, Russ	PA1650	80A
Shelton, Beth	TX2050	80A
Shepherd, Gregory	HI0155	80A
Sheppard, W. Anthony	MA2250	80A
Sher, Daniel	CO0800	80A
Sherr, Richard J.	MA1750	80A
Sherwin, Ronald G.	MA0150	80A,80C,80F,80H
Shevitz, Matthew	IL1080	80A
Shirley, John F.	MA2030	80A
Shirtz, Michael	OH2140	80A
Shiver, Todd	WA0050	80A
Shockett, Bernard	NY0635	80A
Shockley, Darlas	IA0750	80A
Shook, Timothy	KS1200	80A
Showell, Jeffrey A.	OH0300	80A
Shroyer, Walter	VA0050	80A
Shuholm, Dan	OR0175	80A
Sievers, Tim	IA0270	80F,80A
Simmons, James	SD0300	80A
Simon, Peter C.	AG0300	80A
Sinclair, John V.	FL1550	80A
Sine, Nadine J.	PA1950	80A
Singleton, H. Craig	CA1650	80A
Sipes, Diana	TX2930	80A
Sipley, Kenneth L.	MS0575	80A
Sirota, Robert	NY2150	80A
Sisk, Lawrence T.	IL1520	80A
Sitton, Michael R.	NY3780	80A
Siu, Lily	IL2510	80A
Skiba, Karin	CA3265	80A
Skoog, William M.	TN1200	80A
Skroch, Diana	ND0600	80A,80B
Smaldone, Edward	NY0642	80A,80G
Smiley, William C.	NC1550	80A
Smirnoff, Joel	OH0600	80A
Smith, Aaron	MD0900	80A
Smith, Ann	AF0120	80A
Smith, Billy	TX0390	80A
Smith, Carey	MS0370	80A
Smith, Charles J.	NY4320	80A
Smith, Dana	CA2960	80A
Smith, David K.	KS0950	80A
Smith, Donald S.	AZ0350	80A
Smith, Elise	MS0385	80A
Smith, Gene	AF0150	80A
Smith, James E.	CA4450	80A
Smith, Kimo	CA2420	80A
Smith, Mark	IL0600	80A
Smith, Nancy	FL1650	80A
Smith, Paul B.	AR0400	80A
Smith, Ronald	NC1950	80A
Smith, Susan A.	MS0360	80A
Smith, Timothy C.	AK0100	80A
Smoak, Jeff C.	KY1425	80A
Snead, Charles G.	AL1170	80A
Snider, Nancy Jo	DC0010	80A
Snook, Ann Marie	KS1400	80A
Snowden, Donald	FL1500	80A
Snyder, Colleen	CA2400	80A
Snyder, Randy L.	TX2300	80A
Solum, Stephen	MN1050	80A
Sommer, Lesley	WA1250	80A
Sonenberg, Janet	MA1200	80A
Song, James J.	CA3100	80A
Sorensen, Randall J.	LA0250	80A
Sorenson, Allin	MO0350	80A
Sorroche, Juan	PR0150	80A,80G
Soto, Ricardo	CA3350	80A
Soto-Medina, Victor	TX1725	80A
Spain, Bruce	CA1750	80A
Spaniola, Joseph T.	FL2100	80A
Sparfeld, Tobin	CA2660	80A
Sparti, Patricia C.	NC0850	80A
Spataro, Susan M.	VA0400	80A
Speer, Janet Barton	NC1050	80A
Spencer, Dianthe M.	CA4200	80A
Spencer, Mark	AR0800	80A
Spencer, Mary	GU0500	80A
Spiller, Henry	CA5010	80A
Spiller, W. Terrence	CA0600	80A
Spitler, Carolyn	IN1250	80A,80B
Spitz, Bruce	WA0860	80A
Spoto, Mary T.	FL1600	80A
Stacke, Robert J.	MN0050	80A
Stadsklev, Joan B.	FL0350	80A,80F
Stamp, John E.	PA1600	80A
Stauffacher, Paul	WI0855	80A
Stauffer, George B.	NJ1130	80A
Steinhaus, Barbara	GA0350	80A
Stencel, Paul L.	NY1210	80A
Stephens, Roger L.	TN1710	80A
Stepniak, Michael	VA1350	80A
Stevens, James M.	TN0580	80A
Stevens, John	WI0815	80A
Stewart, Jonathan	OK0825	80A,80H
Stick, James W.	IA0420	80A
Stockton, J. Larry	PA1850	80A
Stokes, Porter	SC1000	80A,80B,80E,80F

Name	ID	Code	Name	ID	Code
Stolberg, Tom	MO0060	80A	Vallentine, John	IA1600	80A
Stowman, William	PA2300	80A	Vallo, Victor	GA0850	80A
Strain, David	AR0900	80A	Vance, Virginia L.	NC1800	80A
Strait, Tom	MN1120	80A	Vander Weg, John D.	MI1200	80A
Stroker, Robert	PA3250	80A	Vanderford, Brenda M.	WV0700	80A
Strong, Ernie	CA2450	80A	Vandervaart, Len	AA0040	80A
Stufft, David	GA2000	80A	Vanore, John	PA3680	80A
Stull, David H.	OH1700	80A	Vaughan, Jennie	TX2050	80A
Stull, Gregg	VA1475	80A	Veenker, Jonathan	MN0250	80A
Stutes, Ann B.	TX3650	80A,80E	Venker, Josef	WA0850	80A
Suarez, Jeff	WI0847	80A	Vermillion, Terry L.	MN1300	80A
Suchon, Donnetta	TX1450	80A	Villanueva, Donna Mae	CA2700	80A
Suddaby, Juliet	AG0130	80A	Vogt, Sean F.	SD0300	80A
Sudeikis, Barbara	MI1160	80A	Volk, David Paul	VA1580	80A
Sullivan, Todd E.	AZ0450	80A	Von Kampen, Kurt E.	NE0150	80A
Sundquist, Michael	CA3000	80A	Vroman, David	IL0400	80A
Svedlow, Andrew	CO0950	80A	Wachmann, Eric	IA1800	80A
Swain, Joseph P.	NY0650	80A	Wachter, Renee	WI0860	80A
Swann, William E.	TN1000	80A	Wacker, John M.	CO1050	80A
Swanson, Barry	ID0150	80A	Wade, Bonnie C.	CA5000	80A
Swartz, Anne	NY0250	80A	Waggener, Joshua A.	NC2350	80A,80B
Swenson, Sonya	CA4950	80A	Waggoner, Dori	MO0100	80A
Swets, Paul	TX0150	80A	Wagner, Jeanine F.	IL2900	80A
Swift, Mark D.	PA3580	80A	Wagner, Marella	WI0770	80A,80B,80F
Tallant, Audrey	IL2910	80A	Wagstaff, Grayson	DC0050	80A
Talley, Keith M.	OK1250	80A,80G	Wait, Mark	TN1850	80A,80B,80E
Tate, Shelia D.	VA1800	80A	Wakeling, Tom	OR0050	80A
Taylor, Danille	TX3150	80A	Waldrop, Joseph	TX3850	80A
Taylor, Jamie	RI0200	80A	Walentine, Richard L.	ND0150	80A
Taylor, Steven	CO0150	80A	Walker, Cherilee	KS0590	80A
Tebay, John	CA1900	80A	Walker, Larry	KS0440	80A
Tebbets, Gary	KS0040	80A	Walker, Margaret Edith	AG0250	80A
Tedder, Teresa C.	KY1150	80A	Wallace, James A.	GA0170	80A
Tel, Martin	NJ0850	80A	Waller, Jan	MN1290	80A
Thachuk, Steve J.	CA0835	80A	Walters, Teresa	NJ0200	80A
Thiel, Robb G.	IN1350	80A	Walzel, Robert L.	KS1350	80A
Thomas, Benjamin	WA0460	80A	Wanner, Dan	CA2600	80A
Thomas, Cheryl	MI1000	80A	Ward, Keith C.	WA1000	80A
Thomas, Laurel A.	IN1450	80A	Ward, Steve A.	OR0800	80A
Thomas, Margaret E.	CT0100	80A	Ware, John	VA1800	80A
Thomas, Nicholas	IL1890	80A	Warner, Daniel C.	MA1000	80A
Thomas, Phillip E.	TN0850	80A,80B	Warren, John	IL1900	80A
Thompson, David	WI0400	80A	Warwick, Jacqueline	AF0100	80A
Thompson, Gregory T.	NC1000	80A	Waterman, Ellen F.	AD0050	80A
Thompson, Karin E.	WA1100	80A	Waters, Dana	KS0265	80A
Thompson, Kathy A.	OK0700	80A	Waters, Jeffery L.	MO1550	80A
Thompson, Lee D.	WA1300	80A	Watson, Ian D.	NJ1140	80A
Thompson, Paul	WI0817	80A	Watson, Kathy	AZ0150	80A
Thompson, Robert	NY3785	80A	Watson, Shawn	TX3527	80A
Thompson, Scott	CO0600	80A	Watson, William E.	MD0175	80A
Thoms, Jason A.	NY0850	80A	Way, R. Bruce	MI1500	80A
Thorngate, Russell	WI0925	80A	Weast, Wade P.	NC1650	80A
Thorp, Steven	NM0250	80A	Weaver, Brent	OR0250	80A
Thorpe, Allan	AB0090	80A	Webb, Brian P.	VT0125	80A
Thrasher, Michael	TX3535	80A	Webb, Glenn	UT0150	80A
Tidwell, Mary	TX1510	80A	Weber, Stephen	OK1400	80A
Tiedge, Faun Tanenbaum	OR0450	80A	Webster, Thomas R.	TX0600	80A
Timothy, Sarah O.	AL0890	80A	Weger, Stacy	OK1150	80A
Tindall, Danny H.	FL1740	80A,80G	Wegge, Glen T.	IA1750	80A
Tinnin, Randall C.	FL1950	80A	Weinstock, Frank M.	OH2200	80A
Tio, Adrian R.	MA2020	80A	Weintraub, Andrew	PA3420	80A
Tocheff, Robert	OH1600	80A	Weir, Tim	ME0340	80A
Todd, Kristen Stauffer	OK0650	80A	Weissman, Neil	PA0950	80A
Toman, Sharon Ann	PA2775	80A	Wells, Elizabeth A.	AE0050	80A,80G
Toner, D. Thomas	VT0450	80A	Welstead, Jon	WI0825	80A
Toomey, John F.	VA1000	80A	Wener, Richard E.	NY3100	80A
Townsend, Ralph	MN1700	80A	Wente, Steven F.	IL0730	80A
Traster, Jeff	FL2050	80A	Wenzel, Gary	IL0730	80A
Trela, DJ	MI2120	80A	Werkema, Jason R.	MI0750	80A
Trentham, Donald R.	TN0650	80A	Werner, Donna	MO1120	80A
Tresler, Matthew T.	CA2390	80A	West, James	HI0160	80A
Tripold, David	NJ0760	80A	West, Jean	FL1750	80A
Trittin, Brian L.	TX0400	80A	Weston, Trevor L.	NJ0300	80A
Tsubota, Ann	NJ0975	80A	Wheeler, Charles Lynn	CA3400	80A,80F
Tsuquiashi-Daddesio, Eva	PA3100	80A	Wheeler, Dale J.	AA0080	80A
Tubbs, Carol A.	CA0805	80A	Wheeler, Mark	NC0915	80A
Tucker, Robert	TX1100	80A	Wheeler, Scott	MA0850	80A
Tudor, Robert W.	WV0550	80A	Whisenhunt, Ted	GA2300	80A
Tung, Leslie Thomas	MI1150	80A	White, Christopher Dale	TX2955	80A
Turley, Edward L.	MN0350	80A	White, David A.	TX3400	80A
Turner, Gregory E.	KS0400	80A	White, Frank	LA0700	80A
Turner, John	OR0010	80A	White, Julian E.	FL0600	80A
Turner, Michael W.	OR1000	80A	White, L. Keith	OK1330	80A
Turner, Timothy R.	LA0900	80A	White, Molly E.	CA2720	80A
Turon, Charles T.	FL1745	80A	Whitehead, Glen	CO0810	80A
Tusing, Susan	GA0500	80A	Whitelock, Edward	GA1070	80A
Tymas, Byron	NC1600	80A	Whitlatch, Michael	IA0150	80A
Tynon, Mari Jo	ID0070	80A	Whitley, H. Moran	NC0300	80A
Uhlenkott, Gary	WA0400	80A	Whitney, Nadine C.	GA2200	80A
Uitermarkt, Cynthia D.	IL1850	80A	Whittall, Geoffrey	AA0025	80A
Ulibarri, Debbie	CO0700	80A	Wiberg, Janice	MT0300	80A
Underwood, Mark	TX1750	80A	Widener, Russell D.	KS1450	80A
Underwood, Von E.	OK0150	80A	Widenhofer, Stephen B.	IL1750	80A,80E
Unrau, Lucia	OH0250	80A	Wiemann, Beth	ME0440	80A
Unruh, Eric W.	WY0050	80A	Wiggins, Jacqueline H.	MI1750	80A
Urban, Kathleen	WY0115	80A	Wilcoxson, Nancy	SD0580	80A
Urbis, Sue Zanne Williamson	TX3515	80A	Wilder, Michael	IL3550	80A
Urfer, Kristi	IL2310	80A	Wilhoit, Mel R.	TN0200	80A,80F
Usher, Ann L.	OH2150	80A	Wilkinson, Cathryn	IL0630	80A
Valenti, Julie R.	PA1830	80A	Will, Richard	VA1550	80A
Valenti, Nick J.	MI1700	80A	Williams, John W.	NY2100	80A

Name	Code	Area
Williams, Mark D.	CA2440	80A
Williams, Paul	CA5400	80A
Williams, Robin	LA0800	80A
Williamson, Richard A.	SC0050	80A
Willis, Sharon J.	GA0490	80A
Willis, Steve	NC0200	80A
Wilson, Barbara	IL2350	80A
Wilson, Brian S.	CA4700	80A
Wilson, Jeffrey S.	IL1050	80A
Wilson, Josie	OR0950	80A
Wilson, Thomas	IA0790	80A
Winder, Diane L.	MI0600	80A
Wingard, Alan B.	GA1800	80A
Winkler, Amanda Eubanks	NY4100	80A
Winston, Jeremy	OH2400	80A
Winteregg, Steven L.	OH0450	80A
Wis, Ramona M.	IL2050	80A
Withers, Lisa Ann	VA0350	80A
Witte, Peter	MO1810	80A
Wittgraf, Michael A.	ND0500	80A
Woelfel, Kevin	ID0250	80A
Wojtera, Allen F.	VA1100	80A
Wold, Wayne L.	MD0500	80A
Wolf, Matthew	MI0500	80A
Wolff, David	SD0100	80A
Wong, Sandra	CO0200	80A
Wong, Yau-Sun	NM0200	80A
Wood, Robert	AG0500	80A
Wood, Thomas G.	OH0700	80A
Woodruff, Ernest	MO0950	80A
Woods, David G.	CT0600	80A
Woodward, Greg	LA0400	80A
Woodward, Gregory S.	NY1800	80A
Workman, Darin D.	KS1110	80A
Wortley, Gary S.	GA0550	80A
Wrazen, Louise	AG0650	80A
Wright, Emily Powers	NC1350	80A
Wright, J. Clay	KS0440	80A
Wright, Jeffrey	IN0910	80A
Wright, Jeffrey E.	IN0100	80A,80C
Wulfert, Edelgard	NY3700	80A
Wurgler, Pamela S.	KY0950	80A,80C
Yager, David	CA5070	80A
Yarrington, John	TX1000	80A
Yasinitsky, Greg	WA1150	80A
Yates, Christopher	WA0350	80A
Yekovich, Robert	TX2150	80A
Yoon, Sujin	MO1350	80A
Young, Gregory D.	MT0200	80A
Young, H. G.	WV0760	80A,80F
Young, Mark	MO0200	80A
Young, Mary Ellen	TX2850	80A
Young-Wright, Lorna C.	VI0050	80A
Younge, J. Sophia	IL0450	80A
Younker, Betty Anne	AG0500	80A
Ypma, Nancy S.	IL1740	80A
Zagorsky, Joe	CA1300	80A
Zahler, Noel	NY2105	80A
Zamagias, Jim	MD0050	80A
Zappulla, Robert	CA1050	80A
Zarubick, Fran	WA0480	80A
Zec, John	NJ0550	80A
Zielke, Gregory D.	NE0250	80A
Zilberkant, Eduard	AK0150	80A
Zimbelman, Joel	CA0800	80A
Zimmerman, Lynda	WI0806	80A
Ziolek, Eric E.	OH0650	80A
Zirkle, Thomas	MO1110	80A
Zirnitis, Anda	MO0300	80A,80F
Zlabinger, Tom	NY0646	80A
Zobel, Elizabeth W.	IL0350	80A
Zogleman, Deanne	KS0980	80A
Zorn, Karen	MA1175	80A
Zwelling, Judith Zwerdling	VA0250	80A

Undergraduate Studies

Name	Code	Area
Alexander, Kathryn J.	CT0900	80B
Antonelli, Amy	DC0050	80D,80B
Arnold, Elizabeth Packard	KY1450	80B
Austin, James R.	CO0800	80B
Baccus, H. E.	IL0720	80B
Balestracci, Gina L.	NJ0800	80B,80C,80D,80G
Beken, Munir N.	CA5031	80B
Benedict, Jeffrey W.	CA0830	80B,80C
Bernard, David	LA0650	80B
Bohn, Donna M.	PA1550	80A,80B
Bone, Lloyd E.	WV0350	80A,80B
Bowker, Mandy	WA0200	80B
Brechin, Lesley	AF0100	80B,80D,80F
Britt, Brian	OK1350	80B,80H
Brown, Dana	OH1100	80B,80D
Bryan, Karen M.	AR0750	80A,80B,80D,80F
Bryant, Steven	TX3510	80B
Burke, Patrick L.	MO1900	80B
Burky, Kenneth	PA1050	80B
Burnett, Henry	NY0642	80B,80H
Cantwell, Richard E.	KS1300	80A,80B
Cathey, Rodney	CA0250	80B
Chadwick, Sheelagh	AC0050	80B
Champagne, Mario	CA4900	80B,80C
Cherrington Beggs, Sally	SC0900	80A,80B,80F
Chiego, John	TN1680	80B
Citim-Kepic, Mutlu	FL1850	80B,80D
Coelho, Benjamin A.	IA1550	80B,80H
Cohen, Douglas H.	NY0500	80B
Cohen, Stanley	NY1275	80A,80B,80E
Conley, Irene H.	CT0650	80B
Crawford, Mark	TN1400	80B
Cummings, Craig	NY1800	80B
Cunha, Alcingstone DeOliveira	KY0400	80H,80B
Cyrus, Cynthia	TN1850	80H,80B,80E
Daly, Adrian	OH0600	80A,80B,80C
Daughtry, J. Martin	NY2740	80B
Davenport, Susan G.	IL2900	80B,80H
Delony, Willis	LA0200	80H,80B,80C
DeZeeuw, Anne Marie	KY1500	80B
Donelson, David W.	OH1350	80A,80B
Draughn, Maurice	MI2200	80B
Droste, Douglas	OK0800	80B
Duncan, Norah	MI2200	80B,80H
Dunn, Susan	NC0600	80B
Dunnick, Kim	NY1800	80B
Elliott, Robin W.	AG0450	80B,80H
Eppink, Joseph A.	NY0700	80B
Favorito, Barbara	CA2420	80B
Fox, Donna Brink	NY1100	80H,80B
Fujimoto, Elise	CA4900	80B
Gallahan, Carla A.	AL1050	80B
Garton, Bradford	NY0750	80B
Garton, Linda	IL2250	80D,80B,80C
Gatien, Gregory	AC0050	80B
Gay, Kirk	FL1800	80B
Giovannetti, Geralyn	UT0050	80B
Goldsmith, John L.	PA3420	80B
Griffin, Jackie	SC0950	80A,80B
Grymes, James A.	NC2420	80B
Hachey, Michael C.	MA2300	80A,80B,80F
Haefner, Jaymee	TX3420	80B
Haley, Julia W.	OK0800	80B,80E
Hamman, James	LA0800	80H,80B
Handel, Thomas	MA1400	80B
Hatcher, Oeida M.	VA0750	80A,80B
Hayden, William P.	FL2000	80B,80D,80C
Henderson, Douglas S.	OK0800	80B
Henry, Warren	TX3420	80H,80B
Hightower, J. Taylor	MS0750	80B
Hill, Douglas M.	GA1300	80B
Holden, LuAnn	TN0850	80A,80B
Holzmeier, Jana	NE0450	80A,80B
Hope-Cunningham, Catherine	OH1850	80B,80D
Hornsby, Richard	AE0120	80A,80F,80G,80B
Houlahan, Michael	PA2350	80A,80B,80D,80E,80F
Hull, Kenneth	AG0470	80B
Hunt, Paul B.	KS0650	80B
Jensen, Janet L.	WI0815	80B,80H
Kaiser, Keith A.	NY1800	80B,80H
Kalyn, Andrea	OH1700	80B,80E,80H
Kaminsky, Peter	CT0600	80B
Kim, Chris Younghoon	NY0900	80B
Koop, Ruth B.	AJ0030	80B
Kothman, Keith K.	IN0150	80B
Krause, William Craig	VA0550	80B,80F
Kreuze, Brandon R.	GA0600	80A,80B
Kriehn, Richard	WA1150	80B
Kroth, Michael	MI1400	80B
Krusemark, William	KS1375	80A,80B
Kuhlman, Kristyn	NY3350	80A,80B,80E
Langham, Patrick	CA5350	80B
Larsen, Carol W.	LA0200	80B,80D,80H
Larson, Stacey L.	IL3450	80B
Le Guin, Elisabeth C.	CA5032	80B
Leasure, Timothy	OH1850	80H,80B
Leibowitz, Ellen	NJ1130	80B
Lemmons, Keith M.	NM0450	80B
Lipscomb, Scott D.	MN1623	80B,80H
Lipton, Jeffrey S.	NY1275	80A,80B
Livingston-Friedley, Diana	ID0100	80B
Madison-Cannon, Sabrina	MO1810	80B,80H
Martin, Deborah	NY1800	80B
Marvin, Clara	AG0250	80B
Massey, Heather	OH0350	80B,80D
May, Lissa F.	IN0900	80B
McDonald, Reginald	TN1400	80B
Mead, Sarah	MA0500	80B
Meggison, Shelly	AL1170	80B,80H
Melton, James L.	CA5355	80A,80B
Meredith, Victoria	AG0500	80B
Metz, Paul W.	CO0250	80B
Meyer, Stephen C.	NY4100	80B
Miller, Al	AL1195	80B,80H
Miller, Ann Elizabeth	CA5350	80B
Mincocchi, Joseph	OH2150	80B,80C,80D
Molina, Moises	IL3500	80H,80B
Moore, Daniel	IA1550	80B,80H
Moses, Kenneth J.	FL1900	80B,80H
Moulin, Jane	HI0210	80B
Murphy, Barbara A.	TN1710	80B
Negrete, Merida	NC2410	80B
Nettles, Darryl	TN1400	80B
Paige, Diane M.	NY1400	80A,80B,80F

Name	Code	Areas
Parton-Stanard, Susan	IL1500	80A,80B,80F
Paul, Phyllis M.	OR1050	80B,80H
Perrin, Ralph W.	CA4550	80A,80B
Power, David	UT0250	80B
Prichard, Sheila Grace	MA1600	80A,80B
Pruzin, Robert S.	SC1110	80B,80H
Puri, Michael James	VA1550	80B
Racine, Melody Lynn	MI2100	80B,80H
Rath, Edward	IL3300	80B,80H
Reeves, Patricia	TN1400	80B
Rings, Steven M.	IL3250	80B
Ritt, Morey	NY0642	80B
Rose, Melissa K.	TN1850	80H,80B,80E
Sagen, Dwayne P.	TN1850	80B,80D,80H
Saulter, Gerry	NY1275	80B,80F
Schilling, Kevin	IA0850	80B
Schleuse, Paul	NY3705	80B
Schmitz, Alan W.	IA1600	80B
Schneller, Pamela	TN1850	80H,80B,80E
Schwartz, Sandra M.	WV0750	80B
Scott Hoyt, Janet	AA0100	80B
Scott, Sheila	AC0050	80B
Sehmann, Karin M.	KY0550	80H,80B,80C
Seliger, Bryce M.	OR0750	80A,80B,80E
Shinn, Alan	TX3200	80H,80B
Silver, Sheila	NY3790	80B
Skroch, Diana	ND0600	80A,80B
Smith, James W.	AL1050	80B
Smith, Peter H.	IN1700	80B
Song, Tom	TX2600	80B
Spicer, Mark	NY0625	80B
Spitler, Carolyn	IN1250	80A,80B
Sposato, Aime	VA1350	80B,80H
Stamer, Rick A.	AZ0450	80B
Stefanco, Carolyn	GA0050	80B
Stodola, Lynn	AF0100	80B
Stoia, Nikki R.	MA2000	80B
Stokes, Porter	SC1000	80A,80B,80E,80F
Strand, Jonathan	AA0015	80B
Stroh, Elaine M.	NY4350	80B
Sweger, Keith	IN0150	80B,80D
Taylor, Allen	PA3600	80B
Thomas, Phillip E.	TN0850	80A,80B
Thoreson, Deborah	GA0750	80B
Turpen, Jennifer	WY0200	80B
Waggener, Joshua A.	NC2350	80A,80B
Wagner, Marella	WI0770	80A,80B,80F
Wait, Mark	TN1850	80A,80B,80E
Welling, Joelle	AA0150	80B
Winkelman, David	NC1650	80B,80H
Wurtz, Gary	TX2700	80B

Graduate Studies

Name	Code	Areas
Aberdam, Eliane	RI0300	80C
Allen, Virginia	NY1900	80C
Almen, Byron Paul	TX3510	80C
Anderson, Cynthia	WV0750	80C
Anthony, Johnny	MS0350	80C
Atkins, Victor	LA0800	80C
Ausmann, Stephen	OH2600	80C
Austin, Valerie A.	NC2435	80C
Bade, Lori E.	LA0200	80C,80D
Baldwin, Robert L.	UT0250	80C
Balestracci, Gina L.	NJ0800	80B,80C,80D,80G
Barney, Debbie	CA4900	80C,80D
Batey, Angela L.	TN1710	80C
Bauer, Glen	MO1950	80C,80H
Bauer, Mary K.	NC2600	80C
Beaman, M. Teresa	CA0810	80C
Beckman, Seth	FL0850	80C,80H
Belfy, Jeanne M.	ID0050	80C
Bell, Cindy L.	NY1600	80C
Beller-McKenna, Daniel	NH0350	80C
Benedict, Jeffrey W.	CA0830	80B,80C
Benham, Stephen J.	PA1050	80C
Billingham, Lisa A.	VA0450	80C
Blocher, Larry	AL1050	80A,80C
Bloechl, Olivia A.	CA5032	80C
Bluestone, Joel	OR0850	80C,80H
Bonds, Mark Evan	NC2410	80C,80D
Boozer, John E.	NC2350	80A,80C
Borton, Bruce E.	NY3705	80C
Brendel, Ronald S.	TN0850	80C
Brinkman, David J.	WY0200	80C
Brittin, Ruth	CA5350	80C
Broeker, Angela	MN1625	80C
Bruk, Karina	NJ1130	80C
Brunner, Lance	KY1450	80C
Bruns, Steven	CO0800	80C,80G
Bruya, Chris	WA0050	80C,80H
Budasz, Rogerio	CA5040	80C
Bullard, Julia K.	IA1600	80C
Burrack, Frederick	KS0650	80C
Burstein, L. Poundie	NY0625	80C
Burton, J. Bryan	PA3600	80C
Butler, H. Joseph	TX3000	80C
Butler, Melvin L.	IL3250	80C
Cahn, Steven J.	OH2200	80C
Cameron, Michael J.	IL3300	80C
Canton, Lisette M.	AG0650	80C
Carrabre, T. Patrick	AC0050	80C
Carroll, William P.	NC2430	80C,80H
Carter, Laurie A.	NY1900	80A,80C
Cary, Jane G.	NY0400	80A,80C,80F
Caulder, Stephanie B.	PA1600	80C
Cavitt, Mary Ellen	TX3175	80C
Chafe, Eric	MA0500	80C
Chaffee, Christopher	OH2500	80C
Chambers, Lynnette	TX0900	80C
Champagne, Mario	CA4900	80B,80C
Chang, Yu-Hui	MA0500	80C
Childs, Adrian P.	GA2100	80C
Chou, Sarana	AL0800	80C
Chunn, Michael	OH1100	80C
Cohn, Richard L.	CT0900	80C
Cole, Judith W.	TX2960	80C
Coles, Marilyn J.	IL0800	80C
Cox, Jeff R.	MA2000	80A,80C
Cummins, Linda P.	AL1170	80C
Dahlenburg, Jane	AR0850	80C
Daly, Adrian	OH0600	80A,80B,80C
David, Andy	GA1500	80A,80F,80C
Davis, Andrew	TX3400	80C
Davis, William B.	CO0250	80C
De L'Etoile, Shannon K.	FL1900	80C,80H
Delgado, Kevin M.	CA4100	80C
Delony, Willis	LA0200	80H,80B,80C
DeSimone, Robert A.	TX3510	80H,80F,80G,80C
Despres, Jacques C.	AA0100	80C
Dowling, Eugene	AB0150	80C
Doyle, Alicia M.	CA0825	80C
Durham, Thomas L.	UT0050	80C
Eagle, David	AA0150	80C
Eddlman, William	MO1500	80C
Edwards, Kay L.	OH1450	80C
Ehle, Robert	CO0950	80C
Ellsworth, Jane	WA0250	80C
Elsberry, Kristie B.	TN0100	80C
Engelke, Luis C.	MD0850	80C
Evans, Clifton J.	TX3500	80C
Everett, William A.	MO1810	80H,80C
Favis, Angelo L.	IL1150	80C
Fischbach, Gerald	MD1010	80C
Fitzgibbon, Cecelia	PA1000	80A,80C
Foley, Mark	KS1450	80C
Frisch, Walter	NY0750	80C
Fritz, Lawrence	PA0250	80C
Gaddis, J. Robert	KY0400	80A,80C
Galand, Joel	FL0700	80C,80H
Garcia, David F.	NC2410	80C
Garton, Linda	IL2250	80D,80B,80C
Gates, Stephen	AR0700	80C
Gervais, Michel Marc	CA5060	80C
Getz, Christine S.	IA1550	80C,80D,80H
Glanden, Don	PA3330	80C
Goldman, Jonathan	AB0150	80C
Goldstein, Perry	NY3790	80C
Gowan, Andrew D.	SC1110	80C,80H
Guilbault, Denise	RI0200	80C
Hageman, Paul M.	TX2960	80A,80C
Hahn, Tomie	NY3300	80C
Haramaki, Gordon	CA4400	80C
Harper, Steven A.	GA1050	80C
Hartley, Linda A.	OH2250	80C
Harwood, Gregory	GA0950	80C
Haskett, Brandon L.	GA1500	80C
Hathaway, Janet J.	IL2200	80C,80H
Hayden, William P.	FL2000	80B,80D,80C
Heller, Wendy B.	NJ0900	80C,80D
Hemberger, Glen J.	LA0650	80C
Heuser, David	NY3780	80H,80D,80C
Hill, Stephen	IL2250	80C
Hills, Ernie M.	CA0840	80A,80C
Hisama, Ellie M.	NY0750	80H,80C
Hoffman, Elizabeth D.	NY2740	80C
Holland, Samuel S.	TX2400	80A,80C,80H
Holliday, Shawn	OK0600	80C
Honea, Richard	MO0400	80C
Honea, Ted	OK1330	80C
Huffman, Debora L.	CA5300	80H,80C
Hurt, Phyllis A.	IL2150	80C,80H
Indergaard, Lyle	GA2150	80C
Isaacs, Kevin	CT0800	80H,80C
Isaacson, Eric J.	IN0900	80C
Jensen, Karen	AC0100	80C
Jensen-Moulton, Stephanie	NY0500	80C
Johnson, Timothy A.	NY1800	80C,80G
Jones, Russell L.	KS1050	80A,80C
Joubert, Estelle	AF0100	80C
Kageyama, Noa	NY1900	80C
Keiser, Douglas	IN0800	80C
Keith, David C.	GA1300	80C
Kim, Jong H.	VA0750	80C
Kim, Paul S.	NY2105	80C
Klefstad, Terry	TN0100	80C
Klein, Nancy K.	VA1000	80C
Koons, Keith	FL1800	80C,80H
Kreitner, Kenneth	TN1680	80C
Lewis, George E.	NY0750	80C
Lias, Stephen J.	TX2700	80C

Name	Code	Areas
Liva, Victor H.	OH0650	80C
Locke, Brian	IL3500	80C
Loewy, Andrea Kapell	LA0760	80C
Lott, R. Allen	TX2600	80H,80C
Lust, Patricia D.	VA0700	80C
MacIntyre, David K.	AB0080	80C
MacKay, Gillian	AG0450	80C,80H
Marsh, Peter K.	CA0807	80C
Masserini, John	AZ0450	80C
Maus, Fred Everett	VA1550	80C
Mayo, Susanna	OH0350	80C,80D
Mayrose, John S.	IN0910	80C
McClain, Sandra	FL0650	80C
McCracken, H. Jac	LA0300	80C
Meadows, Anthony	PA1550	80C
Mercer-Taylor, Peter	MN1623	80C
Miller, Jo Ann	ND0350	80C
Miller-Thorn, Jill	NY1275	80C
Mincocchi, Joseph	OH2150	80B,80C,80D
Mitchell, Brenda	OH1450	80C
Mizener, Charlotte P.	TX1400	80C
Moe, Eric H.	PA3420	80C
Moffett, Brad	TN0850	80C
Moskowitz, David V.	SD0600	80C
Muehlenbeck Pfotenhauer, Thomas R.	MN1600	80C
Musgrave, Michael	NY1900	80C
Nelson, Eric	GA0750	80C
Neuman, Daniel M.	CA5031	80C
Newman, Timothy	NJ1400	80C
Oquin, Wayne	NY1900	80C
Ott, Daniel P.	NY1900	80C
Owen, John Edward	AR0110	80C
Oyen, David W.	KY0900	80C
Parks, Richard S.	AG0500	80C
Parr, Carlotta	CT0050	80C,80G
Peters, G. David	IN0907	80C
Phipps, Graham H.	TX3420	80C
Pohly, Linda L.	IN0150	80C
Porter, Lewis R.	NJ1140	80C
Quebbeman, Robert C.	MO0775	80C
Rayl, David C.	MI1400	80C,80H
Rhodes, Ruth	IL3450	80C
Rice, Eric N.	CT0600	80C
Robinson, Nathalie G.	NY1600	80A,80C
Rogers, Donald M.	SC1200	80A,80C
Rolf, Marie	NY1100	80C,80H
Rolnick, Neil B.	NY3300	80C
Ross, David	TX3520	80C
Roter, Bruce	NY0700	80C
Rothkopf, Michael S.	NC1650	80C,80H
Rothlisberger, Dana	MD0850	80C
Rothstein, William	NY0642	80C,80D
Royse, Dennis	CA0250	80C
Rupprecht, Philip	NC0600	80C
Rust, Douglas	MS0750	80C
Sallis, Friedemann	AA0150	80C
Santo, Joseph A.	DC0050	80D,80C
Saunders, T. Clark	CT0650	80C,80H
Saxon, Kenneth N.	TX3515	80C
Scott, Allen	OK0800	80C
Sehmann, Karin M.	KY0550	80H,80B,80C
Shearon, Stephen	TN1100	80C
Sheinberg, Colleen	NM0450	80C
Sherwin, Ronald G.	MA0150	80A,80C,80F,80H
Smith, Andrew	NV0050	80C
Smith, Robert W.	AL1050	80C
Snarrenberg, Robert	MO1900	80C
Snodgrass, Jennifer Sterling	NC0050	80C
Sosland, Benjamin	NY1900	80C
Speare, Mary Jean	VA0600	80C
Spurgeon, Alan L.	MS0700	80C
Stark, Eric	IN0250	80C,80H
Steele, Daniel L.	MI0400	80C
Steffens, David	OK0750	80C
Stemper, Frank L.	IL2900	80C
Stoune, Michael	TX3200	80C
Strasser, Richard	MA1450	80C
Stroeher, Michael	WV0400	80C
Stubley, Eleanor	AI0150	80C
Sumarsam	CT0750	80C
Takasawa, Manabu K.	RI0300	80C
Taricani, JoAnn	WA1050	80C
Tedards, Ann B.	OR1050	80C,80H
Thompson, Linda K.	TN0850	80C
Toliver, Brooks	OH2150	80C
Towne, Gary	ND0500	80C
Vigneau, Michelle	TN1680	80C
Wagner, Irvin	OK1350	80C,80H
Walczyk, Kevin	OR1250	80C
Walker, Karen	VA1350	80C,80H
Wallace-Boaz, Krista B.	KY1500	80C
Wallis, David N.	MO0650	80C
Welbourne, Todd G.	WI0815	80C
Wetzel, Richard	OH1900	80C
White, Barbara A.	NJ0900	80C,80D
Whiting, Steven M.	MI2100	80C,80H
Widen, Dennis C.	OK1250	80C
Wieck, Julie	WA1150	80C
Williams, Amy C.	PA3420	80C
Willman, Fred	MO1830	80C
Wischusen, Mary A.	MI2200	80C
Wolff, Christoph	NY1900	80C
Woliver, C. Patrick	OH1850	80C,80H
Woods, Rex A.	AZ0500	80C,80D,80H
Wright, Jeffrey E.	IN0100	80A,80C
Wright, Lesley A.	HI0210	80C
Wurgler, Pamela S.	KY0950	80A,80C
Zaslaw, Neal	NY0900	80C
Zeiss, Laurel E.	TX0300	80C
Zemke, Lorna	WI0770	80C,80E,80G
Zohn, Andrew	GA0550	80C

Admissions

Name	Code	Areas
Adams, Sara	PA3150	80D,80G
Allen, Mark E.	CA0840	80D
Ammons, Mark	UT0050	80D,80H
Anselment, Ken	WI0350	80D
Antonelli, Amy	DC0050	80D,80B
Ardizzone, Matthew	NY1100	80D
Bade, Lori E.	LA0200	80C,80D
Balestracci, Gina L.	NJ0800	80B,80C,80D,80G
Barney, Debbie	CA4900	80C,80D
Beacraft, Ross	IL0750	80D
Benson, Robert	IA0300	80D
Berry, Joe	TX3650	80D
Best, Raelene	IA1350	80D
Bethune, Lawrence E.	MA0260	80D,80H
Bill, Kate	OH0650	80D
Bonds, Mark Evan	NC2410	80C,80D
Bowen, Mara	MO0100	80D
Branch, Robert C.	WA1200	80D
Brechin, Lesley	AF0100	80B,80D,80F
Brown, Dana	OH1100	80B,80D
Brown, Kristi A.	CA1075	80D
Bryan, Karen M.	AR0750	80A,80B,80D,80F
Canfield, Nanette G.	OH0200	80H,80D
Carey, Mary Beth	NJ0300	80D
Caruso, Andrea	IL2650	80D
Centofanto, Troy	PA1050	80D
Cioppa, Lee	NY1900	80D
Citim-Kepic, Mutlu	FL1850	80B,80D
Clark, Jackie	NC2435	80D
Cocco-Mitten, Melissa	CA4150	80D
Criss, Mary Ann	MD0850	80D
Davidson, Elsa Jean	NY2150	80D
Deedrick, Gary	SC0200	80D
Dolan, Laura	IL1200	80D
Dry, Marion	MA2050	80A,80D
Ebener, Ben	MI1400	80D
Ellis, Margaret J.	IL0100	80D,80H
Enns, Ruth	AB0200	80D,80H
Evans, Anita S.	OH0200	80H,80D
Fay, William	OH0600	80D
Feves, Julie	CA0510	80H,80D
Fritz, Matthew P.	PA1250	80D
Ganus, Linda C.	PA1950	80D
Garton, Linda	IL2250	80D,80B,80C
Getz, Christine S.	IA1550	80C,80D,80H
Gonzalez, Helen	PR0115	80D
Gorcik, Christopher	IL2750	80D
Gratz, Reed	CA5100	80A,80D
Griggs, Joyce L.	IL3300	80D,80E,80G
Gruhn, Charles	CA1700	80D
Halligan, Meg	IA1300	80D
Halperin, Allison R.	LA0300	80D
Hayden, William P.	FL2000	80B,80D,80C
Held, Jeffrey	CA1425	80F,80D
Heller, Wendy B.	NJ0900	80C,80D
Heuser, David	NY3780	80H,80D,80C
Hillner, Paul R.	OH2200	80D,80H
Hodson, Luke	KY0300	80D
Hope-Cunningham, Catherine	OH1850	80B,80D
Houlahan, Michael	PA2350	80A,80B,80D,80E,80F
Hull, Janet	AF0120	80D
Jablonski, Jennifer	SC1110	80D
Jackson, Travis A.	IL3250	80D
Johnson, Lynn M.	CT0650	80D
Keller, Christopher	PA0250	80D
Kilpatrick, Barry M.	NY3725	80D,80H
Kirkdorffer, Michele B.	VA0600	80D
Kline, Thomas	NY1800	80D
LaCosse, Steven R.	NC1650	80D,80H
Lamb, Krista	PA2250	80D
Lanier, Marta	SC0750	80D
Larsen, Carol W.	LA0200	80B,80D,80H
Lastoria, Dean	AB0080	80D
Leeson, Susan	AC0100	80D
Leousis, Kim	AL1195	80D
Lockert, Robin	AG0300	80D
Lowe, Curt	IA0050	80D,80G
Lucas, Teri	NY2660	80D
Madsen, Nathan	NY0150	80D
Martin, Laura	GA0050	80D
Massey, Heather	OH0350	80B,80D
Mayo, Susanna	OH0350	80C,80D
McCowen, Heather	IL0550	80D,80H
McGregor, Michele	PA0550	80D
McMahon, Dorothy	AG0550	80D
McQuade, Amy	OK0750	80D
Mertz, Amy	NY4150	80D,80E

Name	Code	Area
Metts, Amanda H.	NC0100	80D
Meyer, Eric	WI1150	80D
Mincocchi, Joseph	OH2150	80B,80C,80D
Mitro, Patricia	MA0400	80H,80D
Monroe, Murphy	IL0720	80D
Moore, Brett	NY1150	80D
Narvey, Lois	DC0170	80D
Newsom, Mary Ellen	IN0005	80D
Oakley, Paul E.	KY0800	80D
O'Connor, Susan	NJ0175	80D
O'Leary, Shelley	AC0100	80D
Olthafer, Rebecca	IL2100	80D
O'Mealey, Ryan	IL2250	80D
O'Neill, Patrick	AI0150	80D
Parsons, Jennifer R.	WV0400	80D
Peach, Christi	IN1600	80D
Pence, Suzanne M.	TX3510	80D
Peterbark, Frederick	CO0800	80D,80H
Philpott, Craig	CA3400	80D
Placenti, Phillip	CA5300	80H,80D
Ponto, Robert	OR1050	80D,80H
Powell, Alex	MA1175	80D
Price, Jerrod J.	CO0900	80D
Priester, Thomas	NY2500	80D,80H
Reister, John	IN0650	80D
Rosen, Marcy	NY0642	80D
Rothstein, William	NY0642	80C,80D
Sagen, Dwayne P.	TN1850	80B,80D,80H
Santo, Joseph A.	DC0050	80D,80C
Schmitt, Georgia	NY2250	80D
Scott, Geoffrey	TX2150	80D
Sherman, Steve	AA0080	80D
Shier, Fuchsia	AB0210	80D
Shistle, Tammy C.	FL1750	80D
Slish, John	MO1800	80D
Sweger, Keith	IN0150	80B,80D
Tesar, Kathleen	CA1075	80H,80D
Thomas, Edwin	IN0005	80D
Thornley, Christopher T.	MA2000	80D
Vega, Rebecca	NJ0050	80D
White, Barbara A.	NJ0900	80C,80D
Wood, Graham	SC0450	80D
Woods, Rex A.	AZ0500	80C,80D,80H
Yager, Kay B.	TN1680	80D
Zaricki, Alexis	NH0350	80D

Community/Preparatory Division

Name	Code	Area
Allison, Edward	NC0050	80E
Baker, Susanne R.	IL0750	80E
Barnes, Gail V.	SC1110	80E
Barrett, Daniel	PA0550	80E
Bedsole, Betty	TN1660	80E
Bielek, Danika	KS0200	80E
Bond, Kori	ID0100	80E
Bowser, Bryan L.	OH0200	80E,80G
Brannen, Malcolm	MI0850	80E
Braun, Elizabeth	OH1900	80E
Bronaugh, Roderic	TN1400	80E
Brooks, Robert Rankin	NY1900	80E
Brown, Charlene	AA0110	80E
Bruno, Karen	WI0350	80E
Bryant, Jann D.	AR0850	80E
Buchman, Rachel	TX2150	80E
Buckley, Rhonda	MI1400	80E,80H
Burns, Lauren	GA2150	80E
Capra, Toni	TX3400	80E
Cespedes Diaz, German A.	PR0115	80E
Chamberlain, Julie Rhyne	NC0350	80E
Chan, Fu-chen	NY0150	80E
Choe, EJ	IN0907	80E
Christ, Lori	TX3000	80E
Clifford, Patrick	FL1450	80E
Cohen, Stanley	NY1275	80A,80B,80E
Conaty, Donna	CA4100	80A,80E
Crane, Teresa Ann	IL1500	80E
Cruz, Jennifer	OH0500	80E
Curtis, Elizabeth A.	VA0450	80E
Cyrus, Cynthia	TN1850	80H,80B,80E
De Pasquale, Lawrence	NJ1050	80E
Delancy, Demetrius	DE0150	80E
Dennison, Amy F.	OH2200	80E
Eckelhoefer, Miriam	MA1175	80E
Elder, Ellen P.	MS0850	80E
Fisher, Gary	NY2650	80E
Floyd, Elizabeth M.	LA0300	80E
Friscioni, Emanuela	OH0755	80E
Fulgham, Rebecca L.	MO1500	80E
Gary, Jonathan	TX3415	80E
Gatewood, Claudia	FL1750	80E
Gee, Constance	SC1110	80E
Gentilesco, Lauren	PA3700	80E
George, Mark	CT0650	80E
Gibson, Mara	MO1810	80E
Goldstein, Joanna	IN1010	80A,80E
Gordon, Joan	CA4150	80E
Griggs, Joyce L.	IL3300	80D,80E,80G
Groves, Melinda	KS0300	80E
Haley, Julia W.	OK0800	80B,80E
Hawn, Mary	AC0100	80E
Hays, Timothy O.	IL0850	80E
Hershkowitz, Michael F.	NY3790	80E
Hoerl, Scott	NJ1350	80E
Hoffman, Julia	NM0450	80E
Houlahan, Michael	PA2350	80A,80B,80D,80E,80F
Hunt, Sylvia	ID0070	80E,80F
Jakovcic, Zoran	GA0550	80E
Jalbert, Julia	TX2150	80E
Jeleva, Jivka	LA0650	80E
Johnson, Julie J.	MN1280	80E
Jones, Lis	AR0250	80E
Jones, Micah	PA3330	80E,80G
Jordan, Paul	IN0005	80E
Joyce, J. Patrick	WV0300	80E
Jutras, Kristin	GA2100	80E
Kalyn, Andrea	OH1700	80B,80E,80H
Kania, Robert P.	IL1300	80E,80H,80G
Klassen, Carolyn	KS0440	80E,80F
Krystofiak, Paul	TX3450	80E
Kuhlman, Kristyn	NY3350	80A,80B,80E
Kuuskoski, Jonathan	MO1800	80E
Larson, Shari	ND0600	80E
Lippert-Coleman, Mary J.	PA3150	80E
Litke, Sheila	KS1300	80E
Lohr, Tom L.	NC1300	80E
Loken, Kent	MN0600	80E
Macon, Connie	AL0800	80E
Manzo, Erica	MO1800	80E
Martin, Blair	KS1250	80E
Mason, Daniel	KY1450	80E
Mattingly, Stephen P.	KY1500	80E
McAllister, Robert C.	CA1075	80H,80E
Meissner, Marla	NJ0800	80E
Mertz, Amy	NY4150	80D,80E
Meyer, Elizabeth C.	MI1450	80E
Mezei, Margaret	AA0200	80E
Miller, Michelle	OH2290	80E
Miller, Sharon	VA0300	80E
Moad, JoBeth	OK0750	80H,80E
Moe, Gordon	MN0600	80E
Molina, Rocio	TX3515	80E
Moore, Grant W.	PA1250	80E,80G
Moore, Gregg	CA2250	80E
Morgan, Lauren	AL1200	80E
Morgan, Paula	SC0650	80E
Murray, Jane	RI0300	80E
Murray, Nicole	MO2000	80E
Neeley, Henrietta	IL1085	80E
Nelson, Lisa	IL1200	80E,80G
Newlin, Yvonne	IL1612	80A,80E
Newman, Diane M.	NY0500	80E
Nix, Brad K.	KS1250	80A,80E
Oswald, Lisa	WV0550	80E
Pagal, Alena M.	SC1110	80E
Parker, Bradley	SC0700	80E
Payne, Carol W.	GA0500	80E
Potter, Howard	NY1100	80E
Purinton, Teresa	MO0060	80E
Ragsdale, Chalon L.	AR0700	80E
Rasmussen, G. Rosalie	CA3400	80E
Reiter, Lois	TX2800	80E
Richards, Rebekah	MN0750	80E
Rieth, Dale	FL0950	80A,80E
Rose, Melissa K.	TN1850	80H,80B,80E
Roselli, Kathryn	NJ0700	80E
Russell, Richard	NY2250	80E
Sale, Craig	IL0730	80E
Sanchez de Fuentes, Luisa	FL1125	80E
Schneider, M. Christine	IA0550	80E
Schneller, Pamela	TN1850	80H,80B,80E
Scott-Williams, Alison	NY1900	80E
Seliger, Bryce M.	OR0750	80A,80B,80E
Shames, Kay W.	OH0650	80E
Shapiro, Sandra	OH0600	80E
Sheeran, Kate	NY2250	80E
Sheffer, Toni	KY1000	80E
Shurtz, H. Paul	TN1700	80E
Sidhom, Samuel	TN1680	80E
Simons, John	TX2600	80E,80H
Smith, Bret	WA0050	80E
Smith, Mary M.	IL0800	80E
Sorley, Rebecca E.	IN1650	80E,80G
Stancu, Letitia G.	NJ0800	80E
Steele, Angela	NC2000	80E
Stokes, Porter	SC1000	80A,80B,80E,80F
Straka, Leslie	OR1050	80E
Stutes, Ann B.	TX3650	80A,80E
Swenson, Thomas S.	NC2205	80E
Swinyar, Carol	MA0250	80E
Tanner, Gretchen	UT0250	80E
Tomm, Karma	AG0250	80E
Tunnell, Meme	KY0250	80E
Tyler, Philip	CA3640	80E
Valerio, Wendy	SC1110	80E
Van der Sloot, William	AA0050	80E
Victory, Lucy	AL0300	80E
Voytko, Christy	NY1800	80E,80F
Wait, Mark	TN1850	80A,80B,80E
Waldron, Ann	IL2050	80E
Walters, Michelle L.	PA3000	80E
Wells, Lillie	OR1050	80E

Name	Code	Area
Widenhofer, Stephen B.	IL1750	80A,80E
Wilson, Tracy	MA0280	80E
Wistrom, LeAnne	PA1200	80E
Wright, Sally	VA1000	80E
Yaeger, Neddi	CA2420	80E
Zemke, Lorna	WI0770	80C,80E,80G

Festival/Artist Series/Cultural Programs

Name	Code	Area
Adams, Mary Kay	VA0300	80F
Adams, Susan	NH0350	80F
Aldridge, Erin	WI0860	80F
Allman, Garrett N.	IL1100	80F
Altermatt, Sarah A.	WI0865	80F
Arseneault, Sylvie	AI0190	80F
Arthur, George N.	VA1250	80F
Atwell, Bruce W.	WI0830	80F
Austin, Alan	TX3400	80F,80G
Austin, Stephanie	CA1450	80F
Ayesh, Kevin	NC0220	80F
Baird, Julianne C.	NJ1100	80F
Baldwin, Daniel	IA0950	80F
Barnett, Steven	WV0400	80F
Barnett, Susan	FL0200	80F
Barton, Karl S.	GA1990	80A,80F
Bass, John	TN1200	80F
Baxter, Diane R.	OR1250	80A,80F,80G
Baxter, Richard	IN1450	80F,80G
Beach, Douglas	IL0850	80F
Beck, Stephen David	LA0200	80F
Beeks, Graydon F.	CA3650	80F
Beert, Michael	IL2560	80A,80F
Behrends, Al	MN0750	80F
Bell, Daniel	KY0650	80F
Bellassai, Marc C.	AZ0250	80A,80F
Bennett, Kate	MD1100	80F
Benson, Mark F.	AL0210	80A,80F
Benson, Will	TN0300	80A,80F
Bethany, Adeline M.	PA0450	80A,80F
Bingham, W. Edwin	WV0400	80F
Biondo, Steven A.	CA5100	80F
Black, Alan	NC0550	80F
Blackford, Nancy	OH2370	80F
Blatt, Allison Quensen	PA1850	80F
Bleiler, Loueda	NY0950	80A,80F
Bliton, Nathaniel	MI0900	80F
Blumberg, Stephen F.	CA0840	80F
Boga, Cheryl	PA3500	80A,80F
Bohannon, Kenneth	OK1400	80F
Bohnet, Keith	AL1300	80F
Boone, Bruce	IL2800	80F
Bowles, Chelcy L.	WI0815	80F,80G
Brannon, Patrick V.	IL3370	80A,80F
Braun, Joan McLean	CO0800	80F
Brechin, Lesley	AF0100	80B,80D,80F
Brockpahler, Jennifer Lynn	WI0803	80F
Brown, Chris	CA2950	80A,80F
Browne, Patrick	AJ0150	80A,80F
Bruenger, Susan Dill	TX3530	80F
Bryan, Karen M.	AR0750	80A,80B,80D,80F
Bryant, Edward	FL1740	80F
Burge, John	AG0250	80F
Buslje, Sergio	DC0250	80F
Carroll, Allison Coyne	VT0350	80F
Carson, Rebecca	CA3600	80F
Carter, Shree	CA5355	80F,80G
Cary, Jane G.	NY0400	80A,80C,80F
Cherrington Beggs, Sally	SC0900	80A,80B,80F
Chua, Emily Yap	VA1125	80A,80F
Chung-Feltsman, Haewon	NY3760	80F
Cipiti, John	OH2140	80F
Clark, Jeff	NC0750	80F
Clements, Tony	CA2250	80F
Clendenen, Bob	CA0510	80F
Cline, Judith A.	VA0550	80A,80F
Cochran, Nathan	PA2950	80A,80F
Coker, Keller	OR1250	80F
Coleman, Ian D.	MO2000	80A,80F
Collins, Christine	CO0550	80F
Colon, Wilma	PR0115	80F
Colson, William	TX2600	80H,80F
Colton, Glenn	AG0170	80A,80F
Cool, Michael P.	NJ0990	80F
Cooper, Timothy	PA0100	80G,80F
Corbin, Frank W.		80F
Coulthard, Anita	VA0350	80F
Creasey, Linda	VA1650	80F
Crossland, Carolyn M.	NC1075	80F
Curry, Nick	FL1950	80F
David, Andy	GA1500	80A,80F,80C
Dean, Jay L.	MS0750	80F
Deane, Alison	NY0550	80F
DeMol, Karen	IA0500	80A,80F
D'Ercole, Patricia	WI0850	80F
DeSimone, Robert A.	TX3510	80H,80F,80G,80C
Dickelman, Karen	IL2100	80F
Dickens, Pierce	GA0400	80F
Dietrich, Kurt R.	WI0700	80F
Dikener, Solen	WV0400	80F
Dixon, Sam	GA0500	80F
Doyle, Phillip	WA0250	80F
Dunn, David	NY3350	80F
DuPree, Mary	ID0250	80F
Dykema, Dan H.	AR0600	80A,80F
East, David	MS0320	80F
Edel, Theodore	IL3310	80F
Engelson, Robert A.	IA0050	80A,80F,80H
Evans, John	OR1050	80F
Falker, Matt	CA2960	80A,80F
Fatone, Gina Andrea	ME0150	80F
Fetchen, Joan	FL0675	80F
Field, Eric G.	WI0865	80G,80F
Fields, Phyllis	SC0450	80A,80F
Finger, Ellis	PA1850	80F
Fischer, Lou	OH0350	80F
Fitzgerald, Betsy	GA1300	80F
Flack, Amy L.	NY3780	80F
Foley, Brad	OR1050	80A,80F
Fortney, Julie T.	NC1250	80F
Fox, Jeremy	IA1400	80A,80F,80G
Fralin, Sandra L.	KY1200	80F
Franklin, Bonita Louise	OK0450	80A,80F
Fraser, Teresa L.	WA0600	80A,80F
Fraser, Wendy	AA0015	80F
Fuller, Gregory	MS0750	80F
Galloway, Robert J.	NY1700	80F
Galm, Eric A.	CT0500	80A,80F
Ganus, Clifton L.	AR0250	80F
Geier, Alan	CA2250	80F
Gelfand, Michael D.	OH2600	80F
Gilbert, Jay W.	NE0200	80A,80F
Gillette, Michael	NJ0760	80F
Gimble, Richard	TX1600	80F
Goff, Nadine	TN0850	80F
Gordon, Mike	IL1200	80F,80G
Grace, Susan L.	CO0200	80F,80H
Greenwald, Laura	NJ0050	80F
Hachey, Michael C.	MA2300	80A,80B,80F
Haefner, Dale F.	MN1000	80F
Haley, Ardith	AF0050	80F
Hall-Gulati, Doris J.	PA1300	80F
Halper, Matthew R.	NJ0700	80F
Hammett, Peter E.	LA0600	80F
Hanes, Wendy L.	KS1450	80F
Hansbrough, Yvonne	NY0700	80F
Hanson, Josef M.	NY4350	80F
Hard, Randi	IL2350	80F
Harder, Lillian U.	SC0400	80F,80G
Harris, Lee	TN1700	80A,80F
Harris, Rod D.	CA1375	80F,80A
Hartig, Hugo J.	WI0200	80F
Hartzell, Lance	MN1030	80F
Hawkins, Phillip	CA2975	80F
Hazewinkel, Jeff	IN1750	80F
He, Wei	CA4150	80F
Healey, Roberta	NY0650	80F
Hearne, Clarice	IL3370	80F
Hearne, Martin	IA0400	80F
Held, Jeffrey	CA1425	80F,80D
Henley, Larry	NV0050	80F
Heroux, Gerard H.	RI0300	80G,80F
Herron, Clifford	FL1430	80A,80F
Hicks, Joe	TX0250	80F
Hightower, Allen	IA0950	80F
Himes, A. C. 'Buddy'	TX2700	80A,80F
Hines, Clarence	FL1950	80F
Hoffman, Steve	KY0450	80F
Hollister, James	PA0250	80F
Hopkins, Jesse E.	VA0100	80A,80F
Hornsby, Richard	AE0120	80A,80F,80G,80B
Houlahan, Michael	PA2350	80A,80B,80D,80E,80F
Howdle, Joyce	AA0080	80F
Hudson, Barbara D.	NC0300	80F
Hughes, Jennifer L.	MA2050	80F
Hunt, Sylvia	ID0070	80E,80F
Imboden, Jeff H.	MO1790	80F
Isaacson, Peter R.	TX0900	80F
Isele, David	FL2050	80F
Jacobson, John	MI0400	80F
James, Jeffrey H.	NH0100	80F
James, Lori	NV0050	80F
Jeffrey, Diane	NH0250	80F
Johns, Shellie	NE0050	80F
Johnson, David	ID0070	80F
Johnson, Valerie	NC0200	80F
Jose, Brian	MN0350	80F
Jureit-Beamish, Marie	IL2400	80F,80G
Kapralick, Randy	PA3330	80F,80G
Kartman, Stefan	WI0825	80F
Kibelsbeck, Erik	NY1800	80F
Kies, Diana	MI1000	80F
King, Anita	OR1300	80A,80F
Kinzer, Charles E.	VA0700	80A,80F
Kirkpatrick, Gary	NJ1400	80F
Kirkwood, Judy	IN1560	80F
Klassen, Carolyn	KS0440	80E,80F
Krause, William Craig	VA0550	80B,80F
Krawchuk, Hali	AG0400	80F
LaBar, Arthur T.	TN1450	80A,80F
Lambert, Debra	CA3270	80A,80F,80G
Langley, Angie D.	MS0570	80F

Name	Code	Area
Lawrence, Margaret A.	NH0100	80F
Lawson, Darren P.	SC0200	80A,80F
Lawson, Robert	CA5360	80A,80F
Learner, Martha L.	NJ0800	80F
Ledeen, Lydia Hailparn	NJ0300	80F
Lee, Hsiaopei	MS0750	80F
Lehman, Deborah	MN0350	80F
Lemieux, Vivian	ME0250	80F
Leonard, Sara R.	MA0100	80F
Liberatore, Patti	OH1450	80F
Ligate, Linda	MO0400	80F
Livingston, Jane	WI0250	80F
Long, Bill	SC0900	80F
Lowe, Phillip	TX0910	80A,80F
Lucia, Margaret E.	PA3050	80F
Luther, David	TN0200	80F
Mabrey, Charlotte	FL1950	80F
Maguet, Kathryn L.	PA0350	80F
Mainland, Timothy L.	WV0200	80F
Malley, Nicole	IL1350	80F
Mamey, Norman	CA1000	80A,80F,80G,80H
Marchant, Susan J.	KS1050	80F
Masciadri, Milton	GA2100	80F,80G
Matson, Krik	CT0600	80F
McGhee, Michael	GA2200	80F
McRoberts, Terry	TN1660	80F
McTyre, Robert A.	GA1400	80A,80F
Megginson, Julie	GA1000	80A,80F
Messmer, Cathy	NJ0300	80F
Millican, Brady	MA0800	80F
Mims, Lloyd	FL1450	80A,80F
Mirabal, Lianell	PR0150	80F
Miskell, Jerome P.	OH2290	80F
Morgan, Charles	IL1250	80A,80F
Morin, Jeff	WI0850	80A,80F
Nabors, Larry J.	MS0570	80A,80F
Napolitano, Daniel	NY0100	80F
Nice, Julie	LA0560	80F
Nyline, Fred	IA0950	80F
Orlando, John	CA0400	80F
Ostman, Jessica	MN1300	80F
Otal, Monica D.	MD0175	80F
Paige, Diane M.	NY1400	80A,80B,80F
Parker, Don	NC0800	80F
Parton-Stanard, Susan	IL1500	80A,80B,80F
Pastor, Elizabeth M.	OH0100	80F
Patton, Patrick	WY0050	80F
Payne, Tony L.	IL3550	80F
Perdue, Greg	NE0610	80F
Perry, Kris	OH2140	80F
Pfau, Tracy	WY0050	80F
Poklewski, Annamarie	CA1550	80F
Prouten, William	AA0032	80F
Race, Kathy	AA0150	80F
Raley, Lynn	MS0385	80F
Ravel, David	WI0050	80F
Reed, Jerome A.	TN0930	80F
Reed, Joel F.	NC1250	80A,80F
Reiser-Memmer, Michelle	NY1350	80F
Reynolds, Tom	VA0450	80F
Ricci-Rogel, Susan	MD0700	80F
Richter, Robert	CT0100	80F
Ries, Kristi D.	PA0550	80F
Rindfleisch, Andrew P.	OH0650	80F
Rinn, Susan	TX3100	80F
Robbins, Kelly	WA1400	80F
Roberts, Randall	KY0300	80F
Rodgers, Heather H.	MI0350	80F
Rodman, Ronald	MN0300	80F
Rose, Francois	CA5350	80F
Rovkah, Pauline	PA0600	80F
Rudari, David J.	WV0100	80A,80F
Russakovsky, Alexander	MS0750	80F
Sachs, Stephen W.	MS0100	80A,80F
Sadlek, Lance	IA1300	80F
Sass, Christopher	GA2300	80F
Saulter, Gerry	NY1275	80B,80F
Scelba, Anthony	NJ0700	80A,80F
Schattschneider, Adam	OH0250	80F
Schiavo, Joseph C.	NJ1100	80A,80F
Schloneger, Matthew	KS0500	80F
Schmidt, Jack W.	PA0900	80A,80F
Schreiner, Frederick	PA3710	80A,80F
Schulze-Johnson, Virginia	NJ0300	80F
Scott, J. B.	FL1950	80F
Scott, Sandra C.	GA1600	80A,80F
Scott, Sue Stone	AC0100	80F
Scruggs, Richard J.	TN0250	80F
Sepulveda, Richardo	OH1100	80F,80G
Shaheen, Ronald T.	CA5200	80F
Shands, Patricia	CA5350	80F
Shearer, James E.	NM0310	80F
Sherwin, Ronald G.	MA0150	80A,80C,80F,80H
Shover, Blaine F.	PA3050	80F
Sievers, Tim	IA0270	80F,80A
Sigmon, Susan McEwen	GA0940	80F
Silberschlag, Jeffrey	MD0750	80F
Smith, Jason	IA1400	80F
Smith, Sam	ID0070	80F
Smith, Tamara L.	DE0150	80F
Snell, Mary E.	ME0500	80F
Sommers, Deborah	VA1500	80F
Sparhawk, Don	ID0060	80F
Stadsklev, Joan B.	FL0350	80A,80F
Stauch, Thomas J.	IL1085	80F
Steinitz, Michael	AF0150	80F
Stevenson, Laura	FL0570	80F
Stillman, Judith L.	RI0200	80F
Stob, Jeff	MI0350	80F
Stokes, Porter	SC1000	80A,80B,80E,80F
Stolte, Charles	AA0035	80F
Strauss, John F.	IA0950	80F
Sutanto, David T.	TX0550	80F
Sutton, John	CA0250	80F
Tate, Rob	FL0800	80F
Taylor, Clint 'Skip'	GA2100	80F
Taylor, Jeffrey J.	NY0500	80F
Taylor, Kristin Jonina	IA1750	80F
Thatcher, Paula	OR0750	80F
Thompson, David B.	SC0850	80F
Townsend, Laurie	AB0100	80F
Trabichoff, Geoffrey	ID0070	80F
Traino, Dominic	DC0050	80F
Unger, Melvin P.	OH0200	80F
Urbis, Richard	TX3515	80F
Vanderhoof, Winston	MO1780	80F
Vasquez, Jerico	GA1800	80F
Vayo, David J.	IL1200	80F
Vos, Ruth	PA1350	80F
Voytko, Christy	NY1800	80E,80F
Wagner, Marella	WI0770	80A,80B,80F
Wales, Lorraine	OH0850	80F
Walker, John M.	SD0550	80F
Walter, Clyde Andrew	IL0100	80F
Walters, C. J.	NV0100	80F
Westgate, Phillip Todd	AL0950	80F
Wheeler, Charles Lynn	CA3400	80A,80F
Whitler, Kellye	IL2800	80F,80G
Wiebe, Brian	IN0550	80F
Wiggins, Tracy Richard	NC2435	80F
Wilhoit, Mel R.	TN0200	80A,80F
Williams, Demetrice	GA0050	80F,80G
Williams, Sean	WA0350	80F
Witucki, Darrin	WI0855	80F
Wohlers, Bill	TN1350	80F
Wolcott, Sylvia	KS0215	80F
Wollenzein, Timothy	MN0600	80F
Woolley, Clara	IN0010	80F
Wu, Chieh-Mei Jamie	NY3500	80F,80G
Yannelli, John A.	NY3560	80F
Yehuda, Guy	FL1950	80F
Young, H. G.	WV0760	80A,80F
Zent, Donald	KY0100	80F
Zilincik, Anthony	OH0350	80F
Zirnitis, Anda	MO0300	80A,80F

Summer Programs

Name	Code	Area
Abeles, Harold F.	NY4200	80G
Adams, Sara	PA3150	80D,80G
Allen, Ivalah	KS0350	80G
Alvis, Jonathan	SD0600	80G
Anderson, Christopher	AR0200	80G
Austin, Alan	TX3400	80F,80G
Baker, Eliott G.	PA3100	80G
Balestracci, Gina L.	NJ0800	80B,80C,80D,80G
Baxter, Diane R.	OR1250	80A,80F,80G
Baxter, Richard	IN1450	80F,80G
Bennett, Erin K.	FL1950	80G
Berinbaum, Martin C.	AB0100	80G
Bernstorf, Elaine D.	KS1450	80G
Boss, Jack	OR1050	80G
Bowles, Chelcy L.	WI0815	80F,80G
Bowser, Bryan L.	OH0200	80E,80G
Brandon, Joan Lynette	IN0100	80G
Brewer, Paul S.	MI0300	80G
Brown, Patti	OH0850	80G
Bruns, Steven	CO0800	80C,80G
Buckner, Jeremy	TN0250	80A,80G
Carter, Shree	CA5355	80F,80G
Chapman, Susannah	NJ0700	80G
Coleman, Randall	AL1170	80G
Colleen, Jeffrey	IL1550	80A,80G
Cooper, Timothy	PA0100	80G,80F
Crothers-Marley, Shirley Evans	OH2100	80G
Curley, Jason	NY1400	80G
Davies, Daniel E.	CA0850	80G
Deaver, Susan E.	NY2105	80G
DeSimone, Robert A.	TX3510	80H,80F,80G,80C
Dickman, Marcus	FL1950	80G
Doyle, LeeAnn	WI0804	80G
Egeness, Michelle	MN1450	80G
Ehle, Todd	TX0550	80G
Entzi, John A.	NC1250	80G
Epperson, Skip A.	CA0400	80G
Fansler, Michael J.	IL3500	80G
Field, Eric G.	WI0865	80G,80F
Filner, David	CA2250	80G
Finch, Abraham L.	MA1650	80G
Fletcher, Tom	PA0250	80G
Foote, Jack E.	CA0840	80G

Name	Code 1	Code 2
Fox, Jeremy	IA1400	80A,80F,80G
Frese, Marcella	SC0750	80G
Gaddis, Roger G.	NC0850	80G
Gash, William H.	NC2435	80G
Goffi-Fynn, Jeanne C.	NY4200	80G
Gordon, Nina	IL1200	80F,80G
Griggs, Joyce L.	IL3300	80D,80E,80G
Hager, Lawson	TX0900	80A,80G
Hansbrough, Robert S.	NY0700	80A,80G
Hansen, Demaris	CT0650	80G
Hardenbergh, Esther Jane	FL1900	80G
Harder, Lillian U.	SC0400	80F,80G
Hauser, Joshua	TN1450	80G
Hawk, Heather	TX2750	80G
Heroux, Gerard H.	RI0300	80G,80F
Hessler, Arthur	VA0100	80G
Hoffman, Edward C. 'Ted'	AL1200	80G
Holsinger, Winona	TN0850	80G
Hornsby, Richard	AE0120	80A,80F,80G,80B
Hynes, Maureen	NY2105	80G
James, Robert R.	KY0550	80A,80G
Janco, Steve	IN1350	80G
Jantz, Paul	SC0200	80G
Jenkins, John A.	MA2000	80G,80H
Johnson, Marjorie S.	VA0950	80G
Johnson, Timothy A.	NY1800	80C,80G
Jones, Micah	PA3330	80E,80G
Jones, Stuart	IN1050	80G
Jones, Sue	IL1550	80G
Judisch, David	IA0950	80G
Jureit-Beamish, Marie	IL2400	80F,80G
Kania, Robert P.	IL1300	80E,80H,80G
Kapralick, Randy	PA3330	80F,80G
Kelly-McHale, Jacqueline	IL0750	80G
Kirk-Doyle, Julianne	NY3780	80G
Klugherz, Laura	NY0650	80G
Knight, Steven M.	AR0300	80G
Kolstad, Michael L.	MO0400	80A,80G
Lambert, Debra	CA3270	80A,80F,80G
Larocque, Monique M.	ME0500	80G
Larsen, Vance	UT0190	80G
Laurendine, Barbara	AL1195	80G
Lautar, Rebecca	FL0650	80A,80G
Laux, Charles	GA1150	80G
Lecourt, Nancy	CA3400	80G
Lee, Jay	ID0140	80G
Lewis, Lynda	KS0050	80G
Lill, Joseph	IL2100	80G
Locke, John R.	NC2430	80G
Lowe, Curt	IA0050	80D,80G
Lubaroff, Scott C.	MO1790	80G
Mamey, Norman	CA1000	80A,80F,80G,80H
Masciadri, Milton	GA2100	80F,80G
Mathews, Jeffrey	LA0550	80G
McCabe, Melissa	MD0850	80G
McWayne, Dorli	AK0150	80G
Meyer, John E.	MN1030	80G
Moore, Grant W.	PA1250	80E,80G
Moore, Jacques R.	ME0250	80G
Nagelbach, Emily	AB0210	80G
Nelson, Lisa	IL1200	80E,80G
Nicholson, Marie	NC1250	80G
Nicolas, Ashton	MD0400	80G
Noon, Rosemary	MA1600	80G
Nunes, Dennis	MN1300	80A,80G
Parker, Alex	TX0300	80G
Parr, Carlotta	CT0050	80C,80G
Perdicaris, Stephen	CA5350	80G
Raisor, Steve C.	NC0500	80G
Ramirez, Abel	TX0550	80G
Rand, Catherine	MS0750	80G
Richardson, Dennis	TX0550	80G
Robinson, Michael L.	NC1250	80G
Rodriguez, Elvin	CA2420	80G
Roseberry, Lynn	OH0350	80G
Schmidt, Myron	MA0750	80A,80G
Scott, Julia K.	TX2400	80G
Seaton, Kira J.	OH0755	80G
Sepulveda, Richardo	OH1100	80F,80G
Smaldone, Edward	NY0642	80A,80G
Smith, Claudia	WI0855	80G
Sorley, Rebecca E.	IN1650	80E,80G
Sorroche, Juan	PR0150	80A,80G
Sparrow, James	NC1250	80G
Stuckenbruck, Dale	NY2105	80G
Talley, Keith M.	OK1250	80A,80G
Thomas, Kanet	CA3600	80G
Tindall, Danny H.	FL1740	80A,80G
Waheed, Mohammed	WY0060	80G
Walker, Ben	KY0550	80G
Webb, John C.	AR0800	80G,80H
Wells, Elizabeth A.	AE0050	80A,80G
White, Angela S.	FL0350	80G
Whitler, Kellye	IL2800	80F,80G
Williams, Demetrice	GA0050	80F,80G
Wilson, J. P.	AR0600	80G
Wooton, John A.	MS0750	80G
Wu, Chieh-Mei Jamie	NY3500	80F,80G
Yeung, Angela C.	CA5200	80G
Zemke, Lorna	WI0770	80C,80E,80G

Associate/Assistant Chair/Dean

Name	Code 1	Code 2
Alfaro, Ricardo	MI2120	80H
Allen, Burt	LA0550	80H
Allen, Susan	CA0510	80H
Amano, Gary	UT0300	80H
Ambrose, Robert J.	GA1050	80H
Amendola, Vergie	CO0950	80H
Ammons, Mark	UT0050	80D,80H
Andraso, Margaret B.	KY1100	80H
Arecchi, Kathleen H.	NH0250	80H
Atlas, Allan W.	NY0600	80H
Aubrey, Julia	MS0700	80H
Averett, Janet M.	CA4400	80H
Axinn, Audrey	NY2250	80H
Baker, Robert P.	DC0100	80H
Banks, Christy A.	PA2350	80H
Barnes, Anne	MN1623	80H
Barnes, Roy	MI2120	80H
Barrett, Roland	OK1350	80H
Bauer, Glen	MO1950	80C,80H
Bayersdorfer, Fred S.	VA1000	80H
Beckman, Seth	FL0850	80C,80H
Belcik, Mark G.	OK0750	80H
Bergee, Martin	KS1350	80H
Berna, Linda	IL0550	80A,80H
Bernatis, William	NV0050	80H
Bethune, Lawrence E.	MA0260	80D,80H
Bluestone, Joel	OR0850	80C,80H
Blum, Stephen	NY0600	80H
Bobak, Jacqueline	CA0510	80H
Bogard, Rick G.	TX3500	80H
Bollinger, Bernard	CA1000	80H
Bolton, Beth M.	PA3250	80H
Bonner, Judd	CA0450	80H
Bott, Darryl J.	NJ1130	80H
Bottge, Karen	KY1450	80H
Boyd, Michael	OH2300	80H
Bridges, Madeline	TN0100	80H
Britt, Brian	OK1350	80B,80H
Broman, Per F.	OH0300	80H
Brooks, Lisa E.	IN0250	80H
Brotherton, Jonathan P.	NC0900	80H
Brown, Billbob	MA2000	80H
Brown, Cristy Lynn	NC2205	80H
Brown, David P.	PA3250	80H
Brown, Janet E.	NY4150	80H
Browne, Colin	AB0080	80H
Bruya, Chris	WA0050	80C,80H
Buckley, Rhonda	MI1400	80E,80H
Bundra, Judy Iwata	IL0750	80H
Burnett, Henry	NY0642	80B,80H
Canfield, Nanette G.	OH0200	80H,80D
Carey, Norman	NY0600	80H
Carillo, Dan	NY0550	80H
Carroll, William P.	NC2430	80C,80H
Carter, Robert Scott	NC0650	80H
Chase, David M.	CA5350	80H
Chen, Melvin	NY0150	80H
Cherry, Amy K.	NC2600	80H
Chipman, Paula	MD0300	80H
Cipullo, Tom	NY0280	80H
Ciraldo, Nicholas A.	MS0750	80H
Clatterbuck, Nanette	MI0300	80H
Clifton, Kevin	TX2250	80H
Coelho, Benjamin A.	IA1550	80B,80H
Colson, William	TX2600	80H,80F
Corron, Patricia J.	NY3725	80H
Cortese, Paul	TX3000	80H
Council, Thomas	GA2000	80H
Cowell, Jennifer	WY0050	80H
Crocker, Ronald	NE0590	80H
Crookshank, Esther R.	KY1200	80H
Cumming, Julie	AI0150	80H
Cunha, Alcingstone DeOliveira	KY0400	80H,80B
Cyrus, Cynthia	TN1850	80H,80B,80E
Davenport, Susan G.	IL2900	80B,80H
Davis, David	NC0220	80H
Davis, John S.	CO0800	80H
Davis, Stacey	TX3530	80H
De Caen, Jeffrey	CA5300	80H
De La Camara, Maria	OH1250	80H
De L'Etoile, Shannon K.	FL1900	80C,80H
De Melo, Dorvalino	AI0220	80H
DeBoy, Lori	MD1010	80H
Delony, Willis	LA0200	80H,80B,80C
Dempsey, John D.	RI0300	80H
DeSimone, Robert A.	TX3510	80H,80F,80G,80C
Di Bella, Karin	AG0050	80H
DiCioccio, Justin	NY2150	80H
Dixon, Timothy D.	PA2300	80H
Domber, Edward	NJ0300	80H
Dressen, Dan F.	MN1450	80H
Duncan, Norah	MI2200	80B,80H
Dunevant, David L.	KY1000	80H
Durand, Joel F.	WA1050	80H
Durran, Daryl	PA2750	80H
Edwards, Constance	WV0300	80H
Eisenmann, Linda	MA2150	80H
Eisensmith, Kevin E.	PA1600	80H
Elliott, Robin W.	AG0450	80B,80H

Name	Code	Areas	Name	Code	Areas
Ellis, John S.	MI2100	80H	Ko, Bongshin	CA0815	80H
Ellis, Margaret J.	IL0100	80D,80H	Koons, Keith	FL1800	80C,80H
Engelson, Robert A.	IA0050	80A,80F,80H	Kreinberg, Steven	PA3250	80H
Enns, Ruth	AB0200	80D,80H	Krueger, Rob W.	IL0750	80H
Eschbach, Jesse	TX3420	80H	LaCosse, Steven R.	NC1650	80D,80H
Evans, Anita S.	OH0200	80H,80D	Laflamme, Christiane	AI0200	80H
Evans, Dina Pannabecker	KS1350	80H	Laimon, Sara	AI0150	80H
Everett, William A.	MO1810	80H,80C	Lamar, Linda Kline	ID0050	80H
Falskow, John	WA0960	80A,80H	Lamkin, Lynn B.	TX3400	80H
Fauser, Annegret	NC2410	80H	Langley, Jeff	CA4700	80H
Fedrizzi-Williams, Linda	NY3000	80H	Lanting, Mark	IL1330	80H
Fernando, Nathalie	AI0200	80H	Larsen, Carol W.	LA0200	80B,80D,80H
Feves, Julie	CA0510	80H,80D	Lau, Eric	NM0450	80H
Finney, R. Terrell	OH2200	80H	Law, Bill R.	ND0350	80H
Fisher, George	NY2250	80H	Leasure, Timothy	OH1850	80H,80B
Flanagan, Edward	PA3250	80H	Leglar, Mary A.	GA2100	80H
Fouse, Kathryn L.	AL0800	80H	Linklater, Joan	AC0100	80H
Fox, Donna Brink	NY1100	80H,80B	Lippoldt-Mack, Valerie	KS0210	80H
Foy, Randolph M.	NC1700	80H	Lipscomb, Scott D.	MN1623	80B,80H
Franzblau, Robert	RI0200	80H	Little, Donald C.	TX3420	80H
Fredrickson, William E.	FL0850	80H	Lopez, Susan Miltner	CA5300	80H
Fredstrom, Tim	IL1150	80H	Lott, R. Allen	TX2600	80H,80C
Fuller, John A.	NC1700	80H	Luby, Paul	FL1700	80H
Furumoto, Kimo	CA0815	80H	Luby, Richard E.	NC2410	80H
Gackstatter, Gary	MO1120	80H	Lynn, Michael	OH1700	80H
Galand, Joel	FL0700	80C,80H	Machado, Rene E.	IL2250	80H
Garcia-Leon, Jose M.	CT0700	80H	MacKay, Gillian	AG0450	80C,80H
Garin, Ross	PA0550	80H	MacMullen, Michael J.	FL1470	80H
Garrett, Michael D.	KS0570	80H	Madison-Cannon, Sabrina	MO1810	80B,80H
Gartner, Kurt	KS0650	80H	Mamey, Norman	CA1000	80A,80F,80G,80H
Geber, David	NY2150	80H	Martin, Joey	TX3175	80H
Getz, Christine S.	IA1550	80C,80D,80H	Mathews, Paul	MD0650	80H
Gibble, David L.	FL1470	80H	Mathieson, Maria	DC0170	80H
Gibson, Michele	NY1100	80H	McAllister, Robert C.	CA1075	80H,80E
Gilson, David W.	OH0600	80H	McCowen, Heather	IL0550	80D,80H
Glancey, Gregory T.	CA5355	80H	McCutchen, Thomas	AL0500	80H
Gowan, Andrew D.	SC1110	80C,80H	McGrann, Jeremiah	MA0330	80H
Grace, Susan L.	CO0200	80F,80H	McMillan, William	TX3520	80H
Gracia-Nuthmann, Andre	NM0150	80A,80H	Meggison, Shelly	AL1170	80B,80H
Gray, Mary Kay	OH1700	80H	Merryman, Marjorie	NY2150	80H
Green, Georgia	TX0300	80H	Middleton, Jaynne	TX0900	80H
Green, Verna	NY0640	80H	Miller, Al	AL1195	80B,80H
Greenblatt, Dan	NY2660	80H	Miller, W Scott	FL0200	80H
Gresham, Georgia	LA0300	80H	Millican, Jason	TX1250	80H
Hamilton, Margaret J.	MI2250	80H	Minnis, MaryBeth	MI0400	80H
Hamman, James	LA0800	80H,80B	Misenhelter, Dale D.	AR0700	80H
Hansen, Charles	CO0950	80H	Mitchell, Michael A.	MI1750	80H
Hanson, Brent	UT0150	80H	Mitro, Patricia	MA0400	80H,80D
Harbach, Barbara	MO1830	80H	Miyakawa, Felicia M.	TN1100	80H
Harris, Timothy	CA0900	80H	Moad, JoBeth	OK0750	80H,80E
Hatch, Mary	IL0840	80H	Molina, Moises	IL3500	80H,80B
Hathaway, Janet J.	IL2200	80C,80H	Monson, Linda Apple	VA0450	80H
Hawkshaw, Paul	CT0850	80H	Moore, Daniel	IA1550	80B,80H
Hayden, Diane	CA1750	80H	Morin, Joseph C.	MD1000	80H
Hellmer, Jeffrey	TX3510	80H	Morris, Mellasenah Y.	MD0650	80A,80H
Henderson, Gordon L.	CA5030	80H	Morrison, Nicholas	UT0300	80H
Henry, Mary Pat	MO1810	80H	Moses, Kenneth J.	FL1900	80B,80H
Henry, Warren	TX3420	80H,80B	Moss, Emily A.	NY0500	80H
Hentschel, Alain	IL0630	80H	Mosteller, Paul W.	AL1150	80H
Hess, Susan M.	ID0250	80H	Moylan, James	MA1175	80H
Heuser, David	NY3780	80H,80D,80C	Murphy, Joseph M.	PA2150	80H
Hewitt, Michael P.	MD1010	80H	Murray, Monica	MN0610	80H
Hillner, Paul R.	OH2200	80D,80H	Murray, Russell E.	DE0150	80H
Hirst, Dennis	UT0300	80H	Myers, Gerald C.	MO1120	80H
Hisama, Ellie M.	NY0750	80H,80C	Nagel, Rebecca S.	SC1110	80H
Hisey, P. Andrew	MN1450	80H	Natvig, Mary	OH0300	80H
Hoefnagels, Anna	AG0100	80H	Nelson, Jon C.	TX3420	80H
Hoffman, Laura	MI2100	80H	Nestler, Eric M.	TX3420	80H
Holcomb, Richard	FL1470	80H	Nierman, Glenn E.	NE0600	80H
Holland, Samuel S.	TX2400	80A,80C,80H	Novak, Tom	MA1400	80H
Hourigan, Ryan M.	IN0150	80H	Oberlander, Lisa M.	GA0550	80H
Howe, Hubert S.	NY0642	80H	O'Brien, Eugene	IN0900	80H
Huffman, Debora L.	CA5300	80H,80C	O'Dell, James	MA0350	80H
Hughes, Marcia A.	TN0930	80H	O'Hara, Michael	IN0150	80H
Hulihan, Charles	AZ0350	80H	Oliphant, Naomi J.	KY1500	80H
Hurt, Phyllis A.	IL2150	80C,80H	Onofrio, Marshall	NJ1350	80H
Isaacs, Kevin	CT0800	80H,80C	Orzolek, Douglas	MN1625	80H
Isaacson, Lawrence	MA0350	80H	Ouzomgi, Samir	PA2700	80H
Jackson, Jay Craig	NC0050	80H	Ozeas, Natalie	PA0550	80H
Jacobson, Michael	TX0300	80H	Painter, Noel	FL1750	80H
James, Matthew T.	OH1900	80H	Parker, Mara	PA3680	80A,80H
James, Matthew H.	LA0770	80H	Patykula, John	VA1600	80H
Janson, Thomas	OH1100	80H	Paul, Phyllis M.	OR1050	80B,80H
Jenkins, John A.	MA2000	80G,80H	Pawek, Peggy	CA2910	80H
Jensen, Janet L.	WI0815	80B,80H	Perkins, Tedrow	OH2600	80H
Jermance, Frank J.	CO0830	80H	Peterbark, Frederick	CO0800	80D,80H
Johns, Lana Kay	MS0500	80H	Petersen, Carol	IL0420	80H
Jones, Tony	IL1090	80H	Peterson, Don L.	UT0050	80H
Jorgensen, Robert	OH2150	80H	Phillips, Moses	NY0640	80H
Kaiser, Audrey K.	RI0101	80H	Pickeral, Charles W.	FL1850	80H
Kaiser, Keith A.	NY1800	80B,80H	Placenti, Phillip	CA5300	80H,80D
Kalyn, Andrea	OH1700	80B,80E,80H	Ponto, Robert	OR1050	80D,80H
Kania, Robert P.	IL1300	80E,80H,80G	Priester, Thomas	NY2500	80D,80H
Kelbley, John R.	OH1910	80H	Pruzin, Robert S.	SC1110	80B,80H
Kiec, Michelle	PA1750	80H	Puschendorf, Gunther F.	CA1100	80H
Kiec, Michelle	PA1750	80H	Queen, Kristen	TX3000	80H
Kilpatrick, Barry M.	NY3725	80D,80H	Racine, Melody Lynn	MI2100	80H
Kim, Gloria	OH1700	80H	Rath, Edward	IL3300	80B,80H
Kirk, Jeff	TN0100	80H	Ray Westlund, Beth	IA0950	80H
Klein, Joseph	TX3420	80H	Rayl, David C.	MI1400	80C,80H
Kleinsasser, William	MD0850	80H	Reale, Steven	OH2600	80H

Name	Code	Areas
Reckzin, Lance	AG0130	80H
Redman, Paul	IL3300	80H
Reese, Marc B.	FL1125	80H
Reid, Susanne M.	CA5355	80H
Reynolds, Winton	TX3510	80H
Ringle, Stephanie Kohl	IL1200	80H
Roberts, Stanley L.	GA1300	80H
Rockmaker, Jody D.	AZ0100	80H
Rohwer, Debbie A.	TX3420	80H
Rolf, Marie	NY1100	80C,80H
Rose, Melissa K.	TN1850	80H,80B,80E
Rose, William G.	LA0350	80H
Rossi, Jamal J.	NY1100	80H
Rothkopf, Michael S.	NC1650	80C,80H
Rowlands, Judith	NJ0060	80H
Rumbolz, Robert C.	WY0130	80H
Ryczek, Karyl	MA1175	80H
Sagen, Dwayne P.	TN1850	80B,80D,80H
Sampson, Christopher	CA5300	80H
Sanchez, Matilde	CA3375	80H
Sands, Rosita M.	IL0720	80H
Satterlee, Robert S.	OH0300	80H
Saunders, T. Clark	CT0650	80C,80H
Scandrett, John F.	PA1600	80H
Schaub, Owen	IN0250	80H
Schimpf, Peter	CO0550	80H
Schmelz, Peter	MO1900	80H
Schnauber, Thomas	MA0900	80A,80H
Schneller, Pamela	TN1850	80H,80B,80E
Schraer-Joiner, Lyn	NJ0700	80H
Scott, Jan	LA0350	80H
Scott, John C.	TX3420	80H
Sehmann, Karin M.	KY0550	80H,80B,80C
Shaw, Rochelle	CA1650	80H
Sheinbaum, John J.	CO0900	80H
Sherwin, Ronald G.	MA0150	80A,80C,80F,80H
Shiffman, Barry	AG0300	80H
Shinn, Alan	TX3200	80H,80B
Simons, Carolyn	CA2810	80H
Simons, John	TX2600	80E,80H
Simpson, Lawrence J.	MA0260	80H
Smith, Eddie	CA5150	80H
Smith, G. D.	KY1200	80H
Smith, Gary A.	TX2150	80H
Smith-Emerson, Karen	MA1750	80H
Snell, James W.	MO1810	80H
Snider, Jeffrey	TX3420	80H
Spangenberg, Saul	NY3785	80H
Sposato, Aime	VA1350	80B,80H
Stadelman, Jeffrey	NY4320	80H
Stark, Eric	IN0250	80C,80H
Starkweather, David A.	GA2100	80H
Stevens, Paul W.	KS1350	80H
Stewart, Jonathan	OK0825	80A,80H
Stoecker, Philip S.	NY1600	80H
Straus, Joseph N.	NY0600	80H
Strong, James Anthony	NJ0975	80H
Strong, Nathan	CA2450	80H
Sundberg, Terri	TX3420	80H
Sweeney, Joyce	CA5500	80H
Sweidel, Martin	TX2400	80H
Tacconi, Marisa S.	PA2750	80H
Tanner, Christopher	OH1450	80H
Taylor, Susan Lynnette	IN0100	80H
Tedards, Ann B.	OR1050	80C,80H
Tesar, Kathleen	CA1075	80H,80D
Thelander, Kristin	IA1550	80H
Thomas, William	AG0650	80H
Thomas-Maddox, Candice	OH1905	80H
Thompson, Kenneth	OH0300	80H
Tidwell, Mary	TX3360	80H
Timmons, Leslie	UT0300	80H
Tomasello, Andrew	NY0250	80H
Trachsel, Andrew J.	OH1900	80H
Traube, Caroline	AI0200	80H
Tutt, Kevin	MI0900	80H
Ulffers, Christopher	NC0650	80H
Vandervoort, Patricia	TX3600	80H
VanLeuven, Denise	OR0900	80H
Villella, John	PA3600	80H
Volk, Maureen	AD0050	80H
Wagner, Alan	TX2400	80H
Wagner, Irvin	OK1350	80C,80H
Wagner, Karen	NY1900	80H
Walker, Karen	VA1350	80C,80H
Washington, Daniel	MI2100	80H
Waters, Tim	OK0850	80H
Webb, John C.	AR0800	80G,80H
Weirich, Robert W.	MO1810	80H
Welch, Leo	FL0850	80H
Weller-Stilson, Rhonda	MO1500	80H
Wenger, Janice K.	MO1800	80H
Wennerstrom, Mary H.	IN0900	80H
West, John T.	NC2600	80H
West, Kevin	MI2250	80H
Wetherbee, Sarah M.	NY5000	80H
Whiting, Steven M.	MI2100	80C,80H
Willett, Dan L.	MO1800	80H
Williams, David A.	FL2000	80H
Wilson, Kathleen L.	FL0700	80H
Winkelman, David	NC1650	80B,80H
Wiznerowicz, James	VA1600	80H
Woliver, C. Patrick	OH1850	80C,80H
Woods, Rex A.	AZ0500	80C,80D,80H
Wurgler, Norman F.	KY1540	80H
Yaffe, Michael C.	CT0850	80H
Yardley, Anne B.	NJ0300	80H
Yee, Thomas	HI0210	80H
Youngblood, Michael	IL2560	80H
Zuk, Ireneus	AG0250	80H

Alphabetical Listing of Administrators

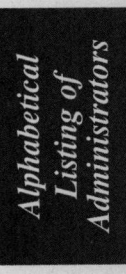

Alphabetical Listing of Administrators

Name	Code	Name	Code	Name	Code
Aagaard, J. Kjersgaard	WI0842	Ashmore, Michel	MO0250	Beert, Michael	IL2560
Abeles, Harold F.	NY4200	Ashworth, Teresa	MN1100	Beert, Michael	IL2560
Aberasturi, Paul	NV0125	Atkins, Victor	LA0800	Beeson, Robert	FL0500
Aberdam, Eliane	RI0300	Atkinson, Michael	IN1250	Behrends, Al	MN0750
Abrahamson, Kristeen	CA4460	Atlas, Allan W.	NY0600	Behroozi, Bahram	CA4350
Abrams, David	NY2950	Atwell, Bruce W.	WI0830	Beken, Munir N.	CA5031
Accurso, Joseph	NJ0030	Aubrey, Julia	MS0700	Belcik, Mark G.	OK0750
Adams, Brant	OK0800	Auman, Kevin	NC1450	Belfy, Jeanne M.	ID0050
Adams, Mary Kay	VA0300	Auner, Joseph	MA1900	Bell, Cindy L.	NY1600
Adams, Robert C.	GA0875	Ausmann, Stephen	OH2600	Bell, Daniel	KY0650
Adams, Sara	PA3150	Austin, Alan	TX3400	Bell, Susan	CA2840
Adams, Sara	PA3150	Austin, Alan	TX3400	Bellassai, Marc C.	AZ0250
Adams, Susan	NH0350	Austin, James R.	CO0800	Bellassai, Marc C.	AZ0250
Adams-Ramsey, Suzanne	VA1580	Austin, Stephanie	CA1450	Beller-McKenna, Daniel	NH0350
Adamson, Philip I.	AG0550	Austin, Valerie A.	NC2435	Ben-Amots, Ofer	CO0200
Adlish, John	NV0125	Autry, Philip E.	TN0550	Benedetti, Fred	CA2100
Alaimo, Kathleen	IL2650	Avelar, Linda	CA1250	Benedict, Jeffrey W.	CA0830
Albergo, Cathy	FL0680	Averett, Janet M.	CA4400	Benedict, Jeffrey W.	CA0830
Alden, Jane	CT0750	Averill, Gage	AB0100	Benham, Stephen J.	PA1050
Aldridge, Erin	WI0860	Axinn, Audrey	NY2250	Benjamin, Jack	SC1100
Aldridge, Robert	NJ1130	Ayesh, Kevin	NC0220	Bennett, Cameron	WA0650
Alesandrini, Joyce L.	OH1650	Ayres, Carol	IA0800	Bennett, Erin K.	FL1950
Alexander, Bryant Keith	CA2800	Babcock, Mark A.	IA0200	Bennett, Kate	MD1100
Alexander, Jerry	KS0215	Baccus, H. E.	IL0720	Bennie, Roanna	CA0100
Alexander, Kathryn J.	CT0900	Bach, Larry	MN1250	Benson, Gregory V.	UT0305
Alexander, Lois L.	MI2120	Backlin, William	IA1170	Benson, Mark	PA0400
Alfaro, Ricardo	MI2120	Bade, Lori E.	LA0200	Benson, Mark F.	AL0210
Alig, Kelley	OK0300	Bade, Lori E.	LA0200	Benson, Mark F.	AL0210
Allen, Burt	LA0550	Bahr, Christine	IL1740	Benson, Robert	IA0300
Allen, Ivalah	KS0350	Bailey, John R.	NE0600	Benson, Will	TN0300
Allen, Mark E.	CA0840	Bain, Jennifer	AF0100	Benson, Will	TN0300
Allen, Matthew H.	MA2150	Baird, Julianne C.	NJ1100	Bentley, Joe	MI1830
Allen, Susan	CA0510	Baird, Sara Lynn	AL0200	Berentsen, Kurt	OR0150
Allen, Virginia	NY1900	Baker, Eliott G.	PA3100	Berg Oram, Stephanie	CO0625
Allison, Edward	NC0050	Baker, Eric	TX1850	Berg, Jim	CA1270
Allison, Rees	MN0800	Baker, Gail	NE0610	Berg, Shelton G.	FL1900
Allman, Garrett N.	IL1100	Baker, James	RI0050	Bergee, Martin	KS1350
Allsen, J. Michael	WI0865	Baker, Janet Ann	CA3258	Berger, Harris M.	TX2900
Almen, Byron Paul	TX3510	Baker, Robert P.	DC0100	Bergstrom, Melissa	MN0040
Almli, Thomas	WA0030	Baker, Susanne R.	IL0750	Berinbaum, Martin C.	AB0100
Alper, Garth	LA0760	Baldwin, Daniel	IA0950	Berke, Melissa	NE0610
Alsobrook, Joseph	MO0650	Baldwin, Deborah J.	AR0750	Berkowitz, Paul M.	CA5060
Alstat, Sara	IL2500	Baldwin, Robert L.	UT0250	Berna, Linda	IL0550
Altermatt, Sarah A.	WI0865	Balestracci, Gina L.	NJ0800	Berna, Linda	IL0550
Altevogt, Brian L.	MI0500	Balestracci, Gina L.	NJ0800	Bernard, David	LA0650
Altman, Timothy	NC2435	Balestracci, Gina L.	NJ0800	Bernatis, William	NV0050
Alverson, J. Michael	SC0300	Balestracci, Gina L.	NJ0800	Bernstorf, Elaine D.	KS1450
Alves, William	CA2175	Ball, W. Scott	TN1350	Berrett, Joshua	NY2400
Alvis, Jonathan	SD0600	Ballenger, William	TX3200	Berry, Joe	TX3650
Amalong, Philip	OH0680	Bankhead, James M.	UT0300	Best, Raelene	IA1350
Amano, Gary	UT0300	Banks, Christy A.	PA2350	Bestock, Donna J.	CA4625
Amati-Camperi, Alexandra	CA5353	Banocy-Payne, Marge	FL1790	Betancourt, David	CA0859
Ambrose, Robert J.	GA1050	Barland, Charles J.	IA1450	Bethany, Adeline M.	PA0450
Amendola, Vergie	CO0950	Barlar, Douglas	FL0670	Bethany, Adeline M.	PA0450
Ammons, Mark	UT0050	Barnes, Anne	MN1623	Bethune, Lawrence E.	MA0260
Ammons, Mark	UT0050	Barnes, Elendar	NY0640	Bethune, Lawrence E.	MA0260
Amos, Alvin E.	PA2000	Barnes, Gail V.	SC1110	Betts, James E.	IL1800
Amrhein, Tim	NY0646	Barnes, Roy	MI2120	Betts, Steven	OK1200
Amrozowicz, Mary Barbara	NY4460	Barnett, Steven	WV0400	Beyer, George	CA1520
Anagnoson, James	AG0300	Barnett, Susan	FL0200	Beyer, Loretta	MI0200
Anders, Micheal F.	OH2275	Barney, Debbie	CA4900	Bible, Kierstin Michelle	MO0260
Anderson, Beverly	DC0350	Barney, Debbie	CA4900	Bielek, Danika	KS0200
Anderson, Christopher	AR0200	Barrett, Daniel	PA0550	Bieritz, Gerald	TX1300
Anderson, Cynthia	WV0750	Barrett, Roland	OK1350	Bighley, Mark	OK0550
Anderson, Gene	VA1500	Barrios, Francisco X.	MO1500	Bill, Kate	OH0650
Anderson, Jonathan	TX3600	Barry, Marilyn R.	AK0050	Billingham, Lisa A.	VA0450
Anderson, Lawrence P.	SC0710	Bartlett, Melanie	MI1250	Binford, Hilde M.	PA2450
Anderson, Michael J.	IL3310	Barton, Karl S.	GA1990	Binger, Adlai	PA0050
Anderson, Toni P.	GA1200	Barton, Karl S.	GA1990	Bingham, W. Edwin	WV0400
Andraso, Margaret B.	KY1100	Bass, John	TN1200	Biondo, Steven A.	CA5100
Andre, James	MS0150	Bass, Ruth	NY0280	Birk, Richard	TX0350
Andrews, Gregg L.	OH1120	Batey, Angela L.	TN1710	Birkedahl, Walter	CA3320
Angle, Terrie Karn	MD0450	Bauer, Glen	MO1950	Birx, Donald L.	PA2715
Annis, Robert L.	NJ1350	Bauer, Glen	MO1950	Biscardi, Chester	NY3560
Anselment, Ken	WI0350	Bauer, Mary K.	NC2600	Biscay, Karen T.	OH1330
Anthony, Johnny	MS0350	Bauer, Paul D.	IL2200	Bishop, Darcie	MS0350
Antonelli, Amy	DC0050	Baugh, Kim C.	VA1300	Black, Alan	NC0550
Antonelli, Amy	DC0050	Baxter, Diane R.	OR1250	Black, John Paul	NC1075
Aquino, Robert	NY2102	Baxter, Diane R.	OR1250	Blackford, Nancy	OH2370
Arasimowicz, George Z.	NJ0700	Baxter, Diane R.	OR1250	Blackley, Terrance J.	CA1900
Arata, Michael	CA5500	Baxter, Richard	IN1450	Blackshear, Glinda	AL0831
Arcaro, Peter	FL1100	Baxter, Richard	IN1450	Blackwood, Jothany	CA1850
Archbold, Lawrence	MN0300	Bayersdorfer, Fred S.	VA1000	Blair, Steve	VT0250
Archer, Gail	NY0200	Beach, Douglas	IL0850	Blair, Timothy V.	PA3600
Archetto, Maria	GA0755	Beacraft, Ross	IL0750	Blanchard, Gerald J.	MI1160
Ardizzone, Matthew	NY1100	Beaman, M. Teresa	CA0810	Blankenbaker, Scott E.	MN1290
Arecchi, Kathleen H.	NH0250	Beams, Mahala	MA1560	Blankenship, Daniel	WI0804
Armstrong, Alan	NC1500	Bean, Robert D.	IN0905	Blassingame, Susan	TX1550
Arnade, Peter	HI0210	Beck, Stephen David	LA0200	Blasting, Ralph	NY3680
Arnett, Nathan D.	IL1240	Beckerman, Michael	NY2740	Blatt, Allison Quensen	PA1850
Arnold, Donna	CA4850	Beckett, Christine	AI0070	Blatti, Richard L.	OH1850
Arnold, Edwin P.	PA1450	Beckford, John S.	SC0750	Bleiler, Loueda	NY0950
Arnold, Elizabeth Packard	KY1450	Beckford, Richard E.	SC1050	Bleiler, Loueda	NY0950
Arnwine, James A.	CA3500	Beckman, Seth	FL0850	Bletstein, Bev R.	OH1860
Arrigotti, Stephanie	NV0150	Beckman, Seth	FL0850	Blewett, Cathy	AG0300
Arroe, Cate	MI0650	Beckstrom, Robert	OH1300	Bliton, Nathaniel	MI0900
Arseneault, Sylvie	AI0190	Bednarz, Blanka	PA0950	Blocher, Larry	AL1050
Arshagouni, Michael H.	CA2750	Bedsole, Betty	TN1660	Blocher, Larry	AL1050
Arthur, George N.	VA1250	Beeks, Graydon F.	CA3650	Block, Steven	NM0450
Arthurs, Robert	NY2400	Beene, Richard	CA1075	Blocker, Robert	CT0850

Name	Code	Name	Code	Name	Code
Bloechl, Olivia A.	CA5032	Bremer, Carolyn	CA0825	Burford, Mark	OR0900
Blount, Joanna	IN0010	Brenan, Jim	AA0050	Burge, John	AG0250
Bluestone, Joel	OR0850	Brendel, Ronald S.	TN0850	Burgess, Phillipa	OH1750
Bluestone, Joel	OR0850	Brent, William	LA0550	Burke, Kevin R.	IN0500
Blum, Stephen	NY0600	Brewer, Johnny	AL0620	Burke, Patrick L.	MO1900
Blumberg, Stephen F.	CA0840	Brewer, Paul S.	MI0300	Burks, Ricky	AL1450
Bobak, Jacqueline	CA0510	Brewer, William T.	KS0550	Burky, Kenneth	PA1050
Bobrowski, Christine	CA1250	Brickman, Scott T.	ME0420	Burnett, Henry	NY0642
Boehm, Norman	AR0350	Bridges, Cynthia	TX0550	Burnett, Henry	NY0642
Boehm, Patricia A.	OH2290	Bridges, Madeline	TN0100	Burnett, Marty Wheeler	NE0100
Boelter, Karl	NY3725	Briere, Daniel H.	IN1650	Burnette, Sonny	KY0610
Boerckel, Gary M.	PA2100	Briggs, Cynthia	MO0700	Burns, Lauren	GA2150
Boespflug, George	CA0350	Brink, Brian S.	FL0800	Burns, Lori	AG0400
Boga, Cheryl	PA3500	Brinkman, David J.	WY0200	Burrack, Frederick	KS0650
Boga, Cheryl	PA3500	Brinner, Benjamin	CA5000	Burrell, Dan	WI0450
Bogard, Rick G.	TX3500	Britt, Brian	OK1350	Burstein, L. Poundie	NY0625
Bogard, Theresa L.	WY0200	Britt, Brian	OK1350	Burton, Heidi R.	OK1300
Bognar, Joseph A.	IN1750	Britt, Carol	LA0450	Burton, J. Bryan	PA3600
Bohannon, Kenneth	OK1400	Britt, Mark E.	SC0750	Burton, John R.	TX3500
Bohn, Donna M.	PA1550	Brittin, Ruth	CA5350	Burwinkel, James J.	MO1250
Bohn, Donna M.	PA1550	Broaddus, Vivian	MD0360	Bush, Jeffrey E.	VA0600
Bohnet, Keith	AL1300	Brockpahler, Jennifer Lynn	WI0803	Buslje, Sergio	DC0250
Bolin, Daniel	IN0250	Brodbeck, David	CA5020	Busse Tucker, Ann	IL1340
Bollinger, Bernard	CA1000	Broeker, Angela	MN1625	Butler, Charles Mark	MS0250
Bolton, Beth M.	PA3250	Broman, Per F.	OH0300	Butler, H. Joseph	TX3000
Bolton, Bryan	KY0050	Bronaugh, Roderic	TN1400	Butler, Melvin L.	IL3250
Bolton, Thomas W.	KY1200	Brooks, C. Thomas	MA0950	Butler, Rebecca G.	PA0050
Bomberger, E. Douglas	PA1250	Brooks, Charles	SC0150	Butler, Steve	CA5550
Bond, Karlyn	UT0400	Brooks, Lisa E.	IN0250	Butterfield, Matthew W.	PA1300
Bond, Kori	ID0100	Brooks, Melinda K.	AL0850	Buzzelli-Clarke, Betsy	PA1100
Bonds, Mark Evan	NC2410	Brooks, Robert Rankin	NY1900	Byerly, Douglas	MD0060
Bonds, Mark Evan	NC2410	Brotherton, Jonathan P.	NC0900	Byrne, Mary	AB0210
Bone, Lloyd E.	WV0350	Brown, Billbob	MA2000	Caffey, H. David	CO0950
Bone, Lloyd E.	WV0350	Brown, Charlene	AA0110	Cahn, Steven J.	OH2200
Bonner, Gary	CA0450	Brown, Chris	CA2950	Cailliet, Claude	WI0800
Bonner, Judd	CA0450	Brown, Chris	CA2950	Caldwell, Michael D.	CA0810
Boone, Bruce	IL2800	Brown, Cristy Lynn	NC2205	Caldwell, William	OH0500
Booth, John D.	MO0500	Brown, Dana	OH1100	Calkins, Katherine Charlton	CA3200
Boozer, John E.	NC2350	Brown, Dana	OH1100	Call, Kevin	ID0060
Boozer, John E.	NC2350	Brown, David P.	PA3250	Callahan, Gary L.	NC1150
Bordeau, Catherine A.	AR0425	Brown, J. Bruce	MI2000	Calloway, Edwin S.	GA2300
Borror, Gordon L.	OR1210	Brown, Janet E.	NY4150	Calzolari, Laura	NY2400
Borton, Bruce E.	NY3705	Brown, Jennifer Williams	IA0700	Camacho-Zavaleta, Martin	AL0050
Boss, Jack	OR1050	Brown, Joel	NY3650	Cameron, Michael J.	IL3300
Bostic, Ronald D.	NC2650	Brown, Kellie Dubel	TN1150	Campbell, Helen E.	AL0310
Botelho, Mauro	NC0550	Brown, Kristi A.	CA1075	Campbell, Jefferson	MN1600
Bott, Darryl J.	NJ1130	Brown, Leslie Ellen	WI0700	Campbell, Larry	TX0340
Bottge, Karen	KY1450	Brown, Michael R.	MS0500	Campbell, Stanford	OR0600
Boubel, Karen A.	MN1000	Brown, Patti	OH0850	Campbell, William G.	IA1300
Boucher, Leslie H.	GA0700	Brown, Richard L.	WV0600	Camphouse, Mark D.	VA0450
Boudreaux, Margaret A.	MD0520	Brown, Roger H.	MA0260	Canales, M. Cristina	MA1550
Boulanger, Richard	AE0100	Brown, Terrance D.	AL1250	Canfield, Nanette G.	OH0200
Boullion, Linda	NE0460	Brown, Terry	WI0845	Canfield, Nanette G.	OH0200
Boulton, Kenneth	LA0650	Brown, Uzee	GA1450	Canier, Caren	NY3300
Bourgois, Louis	KY0750	Browne, Colin	AB0080	Cannon, Derek	CA2100
Boutet, Danielle	VT0150	Browne, Patrick	AJ0150	Canter, Nancy	CA1550
Bowen, Jose A.	TX2400	Browne, Patrick	AJ0150	Canton, Lisette M.	AG0650
Bowen, Mara	MO0100	Browning, Birch P.	OH0650	Cantwell, Richard E.	KS1300
Bowker, Mandy	WA0200	Brubaker, Debra	IN0550	Cantwell, Richard E.	KS1300
Bowles, Chelcy L.	WI0815	Bruenger, Susan Dill	TX3530	Capra, Toni	TX3400
Bowles, Chelcy L.	WI0815	Bruk, Karina	NJ1130	Cardillo, Kenneth	TN0260
Bowles, Kenneth E.	ND0250	Brunner, Lance	KY1450	Carey, Barbara	NM0300
Bowser, Bryan L.	OH0200	Bruno, Karen	WI0350	Carey, Mary Beth	NJ0300
Bowser, Bryan L.	OH0200	Bruns, Steven	CO0800	Carey, Norman	NY0600
Bowyer, Don	AR0110	Bruns, Steven	CO0800	Carillo, Dan	NY0550
Boyce, Douglas J.	DC0100	Brunson, Ty	TX3800	Carlson, Andrew	OH0850
Boyd, Craig E.	NY4050	Bruya, Chris	WA0050	Carlson, Marlan	OR0700
Boyd, John W.	TX2550	Bruya, Chris	WA0050	Carlton, Kathleen	OK0410
Boyd, Michael	PA0600	Bryan, Karen M.	AR0750	Carnahan, John	CA0825
Boyd, Michael	OH2300	Bryan, Karen M.	AR0750	Carney, Horace R.	AL0010
Boyer, Douglas R.	TX3100	Bryan, Karen M.	AR0750	Carney, Timothy F.	HI0060
Bracks, Lean'tin	TN0550	Bryan, Karen M.	AR0750	Carpenter-Alting, Neil	CA1300
Bradbury, William	CA0847	Bryant, Edward	FL1740	Carrabre, T. Patrick	AC0050
Bradley, Jennifer	IA0930	Bryant, Jann D.	AR0850	Carroll, Allison Coyne	VT0350
Bradshaw, Keith M.	UT0200	Bryant, Steven	TX3510	Carroll, William P.	NC2430
Bragg, Christopher	ID0075	Bryson, Amity H.	MO0050	Carroll, William P.	NC2430
Brakel, Timothy D.	OH2300	Brzezinski, Jamey	CA2900	Carson, Rebecca	CA3600
Brancaleone, Francis P.	NY2200	Buchholz, Cindy	TX3600	Cart, Jon Robert	NJ1050
Branch, Robert C.	WA1200	Buchman, Rachel	TX2150	Carter, Gary M.	CA0900
Branch, Stephen F.	CA3975	Buck, Barbara	KY0750	Carter, Henrietta McKee	CA2050
Brand, Todd	MS0370	Buckles, Michael	LA0350	Carter, Jeffrey Richard	MO1950
Brandes, David E.	NH0110	Buckley, Rhonda	MI1400	Carter, Joseph	CT0300
Brandes, Lambert	MA0800	Buckley, Rhonda	MI1400	Carter, Laurie A.	NY1900
Brandon, Joan Lynette	IN0100	Buckmaster, Matthew	NC0750	Carter, Laurie A.	NY1900
Brandon, Maureen	CO0350	Buckner, James R.	AR0300	Carter, Robert Scott	NC0650
Brandon, Rodester	FL1300	Buckner, Jeremy	TN0250	Carter, Shree	CA5355
Brandt, Lynne	TX2310	Buckner, Jeremy	TN0250	Carter, Shree	CA5355
Brannen, Malcolm	MI0850	Budasz, Rogerio	CA5040	Carter, Stewart	NC2500
Brannon, Patrick V.	IL3370	Buddo, J. Christopher	NC0650	Caruso, Andrea	IL2650
Brannon, Patrick V.	IL3370	Bugaj, Albert	WI0920	Cary, Jane G.	NY0400
Braun, Elizabeth	OH1900	Bulen, Jay C.	MO1780	Cary, Jane G.	NY0400
Braun, Joan McLean	CO0800	Bull, Douglas	WY0050	Cary, Jane G.	NY0400
Braun, Mark	MN0750	Bullard, Julia K.	IA1600	Casey, Donald E.	IL0750
Bray, Michael R.	PA3260	Bullock, Kathy	KY0300	Casey, Michael	NH0100
Brechin, Lesley	AF0100	Bullock, Valerie K.	SC0275	Cash, G. Gerald	FL0730
Brechin, Lesley	AF0100	Bulow, Harry T.	IN1300	Cassarino, James P.	VT0200
Brechin, Lesley	AF0100	Bundra, Judy Iwata	IL0750	Castleberry, David	WV0400
Breden, Mary C.	CA2800	Bunk, Louis	NH0110	Caston, Ben	GA2050
Breland, John Roger	AL1195	Burbach, Brock	FL0200	Cathey, Rodney	CA0250
Brellochs, Christopher	NY1050	Burchard, Richard	KY0250	Cato, Tom L.	GA0200

Name	Code	Name	Code	Name	Code
Caulder, Stephanie B.	PA1600	Cole, Judith W.	TX2960	Cyrus, Cynthia	TN1850
Cavalier, Philip	IL0900	Coleman, Barbara J.	CO0650	D'Ercole, Patricia	WI0850
Cavitt, Mary Ellen	TX3175	Coleman, Ian D.	MO2000	Dahlenburg, Jane	AR0850
Centofanto, Troy	PA1050	Coleman, Ian D.	MO2000	Dahn, Luke	IA1200
Cespedes Diaz, German A.	PR0115	Coleman, Randall	AL1170	Daly, Adrian	OH0600
Chabora, Robert J.	MN0600	Coleman, Stephen	NY1150	Daly, Adrian	OH0600
Chadwick, Sheelagh	AC0050	Coleman, William Dwight	GA1050	Daly, Adrian	OH0600
Chafe, Eric	MA0500	Coles, Marilyn J.	IL0800	Dammers, Richard J.	NJ1050
Chaffee, Christopher	OH2500	Colleen, Jeffrey	IL1550	Daniel, Thomas	AL0335
Chaffin, Lon W.	NM0310	Colleen, Jeffrey	IL1550	Daniels, Jerry L.	IL0800
Chagas, Paulo	CA5040	Collins, Christine	CO0550	Daniels, William B.	KY1100
Chamberlain, Julie Rhyne	NC0350	Collins, David	MN1250	Danis, Francine	TX1900
Chambers, Lynnette	TX0900	Collins, Leo W.	MA2200	Daras, April L.	WV0250
Champagne, Mario	CA4900	Colon, Wilma	PR0115	Dark, James	CA4000
Champagne, Mario	CA4900	Colson, David J.	MI2250	Darr, Steven L.	FL2130
Chan, Fu-chen	NY0150	Colson, William	TX2600	Daugherty, Buelane	IA1140
Chang, Yu-Hui	MA0500	Colson, William	TX2600	Daughtry, J. Martin	NY2740
Chapman, Norman	MS0600	Colton, Glenn	AG0170	Dauphin, Claude	AI0210
Chapman, Susannah	NJ0700	Colton, Glenn	AG0170	Davalos, Catherine	CA3920
Charron, Michael	MN1400	Combs, Julia C.	MO0775	Davenport, Mark	CO0650
Chase, David M.	CA5350	Comstock, Allan D.	KS0300	Davenport, Susan G.	IL2900
Cheesman, Robert	MS0300	Conaty, Donna	CA4100	Davenport, Susan G.	IL2900
Chen, Melvin	NY0150	Conaty, Donna	CA4100	David, Andy	GA1500
Chenevert, James	TX3300	Condaris, Christine	MA1185	David, Andy	GA1500
Cherrington Beggs, Sally	SC0900	Condon, Jennifer	IA0790	David, Andy	GA1500
Cherrington Beggs, Sally	SC0900	Conley, Irene H.	CT0650	Davidian, Teresa	TX2750
Cherrington Beggs, Sally	SC0900	Connelly, Bob J.	TX3410	Davidson, Elsa Jean	NY2150
Cherry, Amy K.	NC2600	Connolly, Michael E.	OR1100	Davies, Daniel E.	CA0850
Chester, Nia	MA1560	Connors, Patricia Cahalan	MN1295	Davila, William	CA3450
Chiego, John	TN1680	Converse, Ralph D.	NM0500	Davis, Andrew	TX3400
Chien, Alec F.	PA0100	Conway, Eric	MD0600	Davis, Clifford	NH0300
Childress Orchard, Nan	NJ0050	Cook, Stephen	CA6000	Davis, Dana Dinsmore	OK0200
Childs, Adrian P.	GA2100	Cool, Michael P.	NJ0990	Davis, David	NC0220
Chin, Wayman	MA1175	Cooper, John H.	ME0270	Davis, Gene	AL0450
Chinwah, Lovette	OH0500	Cooper, Michael	TX2850	Davis, John S.	CO0800
Chipman, Paula	MD0300	Cooper, Timothy	PA0100	Davis, Mary E.	OH0400
Choe, EJ	IN0907	Cooper, Timothy	PA0100	Davis, Peter A.	RI0250
Chou, Sarana	AL0800	Corley, Sheila	AZ0400	Davis, Stacey	TX3530
Christ, Lori	TX3000	Cornelius, John L.	TX2100	Davis, William B.	CO0250
Christensen, Linda	NE0700	Corron, Patricia J.	NY3725	Dawe, Edmund N.	AC0100
Christophersen, Rick	CA0960	Cortese, Michael	NY0450	Dawson, Joseph C.	PA3700
Christy, William P.	OH1910	Cortese, Paul	TX3000	Dawson, Robert B.	CA1700
Chua, Emily Yap	VA1125	Cosentino, Joe V.	NY1050	Day, Mary	IA0100
Chua, Emily Yap	VA1125	Costanzo, Samuel R.	CT0250	De Caen, Jeffrey	CA5300
Chung-Feltsman, Haewon	NY3760	Cotton, Jerry	TX0370	De L'Etoile, Shannon K.	FL1900
Chunn, Michael	OH1100	Coulthard, Anita	VA0350	De L'Etoile, Shannon K.	FL1900
Cid, Carmen	CT0150	Council, Thomas	GA2000	De La Camara, Maria	OH1250
Cioppa, Lee	NY1900	Coutts, Greg A.	IL2650	De Melo, Dorvalino	AI0220
Cipiti, John	OH2140	Covach, John R.	NY4350	De Mesa, Cindy	CA0500
Cipullo, Tom	NY0280	Cowan, Carole	NY3760	De Pasquale, Lawrence	NJ1050
Ciraldo, Nicholas A.	MS0750	Cowell, Jennifer	WY0050	De Ritis, Anthony	MA1450
Cisler, Valerie C.	NE0590	Cowles, Robert	NY1550	Deakins, Mark	KY0650
Citim-Kepic, Mutlu	FL1850	Cox, Jeff R.	MA2000	Deal, John J.	NC2430
Citim-Kepic, Mutlu	FL1850	Cox, Jeff R.	MA2000	Dean, Jay L.	MS0750
Clancy, Brian	NH0050	Crabtree, Joseph C.	TX1425	Dean, Michael	CA5030
Clark, Frank L.	GA0900	Cram, Matthew	OH2100	Deane, Alison	NY0550
Clark, Jackie	NC2435	Cramer, Alfred W.	CA3650	Deaver, Susan E.	NY2105
Clark, Jeff	NC0750	Crane, Susan	KS0980	DeBoy, Lori	MD1010
Clark, John W.	CA4410	Crane, Teresa Ann	IL1500	Decker, Van A.	CA2300
Clark, Kelly	OK1300	Crannell, Wayne T.	TX0250	Declue, Gary L.	IL1245
Clark, Thomas S.	TX3175	Crawford, Leneida	MD0850	Decuir, Anthony	LA0300
Clatterbuck, Nanette	MI0300	Crawford, Mark	TN1400	Deedrick, Gary	SC0200
Clements, Tony	CA2250	Creaser, Cynthia	AF0120	DeFord, Ruth	NY0625
Clemons, Gregory G.	IL1085	Creasey, Linda	VA1650	DeGraffenreid, George	CA0830
Clendenen, Bob	CA0510	Criss, Mary Ann	MD0850	Delancy, Demetrius	DE0150
Clervi, Paul	MO2050	Crist, Michael	OH2600	DeLaRosa, Lou	CA5510
Cleveland, Lisa A.	NH0310	Crocker, Ronald	NE0590	DelDonna, Anthony R.	DC0075
Clickard, Stephen D.	PA0250	Croes, Stephen	MA0260	Delgado, Kevin M.	CA4100
Clifford, Patrick	FL1450	Cromley, Dorothea	MT0175	DeLongchamp, Jim	CA2975
Clifton, Kevin	TX2250	Crone, Jay	VA1700	Delony, Willis	LA0200
Cline, Benjamin	KS0350	Crookshank, Esther R.	KY1200	Delony, Willis	LA0200
Cline, Catherine	AR0225	Crosby, J. Stephen	NY0100	Delony, Willis	LA0200
Cline, Judith A.	VA0550	Crossland, Carolyn M.	NC1075	DeMol, Karen	IA0500
Cline, Judith A.	VA0550	Crossman, Patricia	MD0175	DeMol, Karen	IA0500
Clinton, John	OK1330	Crothers-Marley, Shirley Evans	OH2100	Dempsey, John D.	RI0300
Cloke, Hugh	DC0075	Crowder, Jarrell	MD0550	Dennee, Peter D.	WI0250
Clow, William	IL3500	Cruz, Jennifer	OH0500	Dennison, Amy F.	OH2200
Coakley, Thomas	PA2500	Cubbage, John	MT0370	Dering, James	TX0850
Cobb, Gary W.	CA3600	Cucchi, Paolo	NJ0300	Derrick, Patty	PA3410
Cocco-Mitten, Melissa	CA4150	Cudjoe, Gwendolyn	TX1300	DeSanto, William	PA3560
Cochran, Barney	OH1600	Culbertson, Robert M.	TX1400	Deschere, Karen	WI1150
Cochran, Nancy	CO0900	Culver, Daniel	IL0100	DeSimone, Robert A.	TX3510
Cochran, Nathan	PA2950	Culverhouse, William	IN0400	DeSimone, Robert A.	TX3510
Cochran, Nathan	PA2950	Cumming, Julie	AI0150	DeSimone, Robert A.	TX3510
Cochrane, Keith A.	NM0400	Cummings, Craig	NY1800	DeSimone, Robert A.	TX3510
Cockey, Linda E.	MD0800	Cummins, Linda P.	AL1170	DesJardins, Joseph	MN0350
Codding, Amparo	NJ0020	Cunha, Alcingstone DeOliveira	KY0400	Desmond, Clinton J.	SD0200
Coe, Judith A.	CO0830	Cunha, Alcingstone DeOliveira	KY0400	Despres, Jacques C.	AA0100
Coelho, Benjamin A.	IA1550	Curley, Jason	NY1400	Devaney, Margaret	VA1100
Coelho, Benjamin A.	IA1550	Curry, Jeffrey P.	NE0040	Devereaux, Kent	WA0200
Cofer, R. Shayne	IL2150	Curry, Nick	FL1950	Dewey, Cynthia	UT0300
Cohen, Allen L.	NJ0400	Curtis, Cynthia R.	TN0100	DeZeeuw, Anne Marie	KY1500
Cohen, David	NY2102	Curtis, Elizabeth A.	VA0450	Di Bella, Karin	AG0050
Cohen, Douglas H.	NY0500	Curtis, Marvin V.	IN0910	Diaz, Roberto	PA0850
Cohen, Fred S.	GA0550	Cusack, Mary	MI0450	Dicciani, Marc	PA3330
Cohen, Stanley	NY1275	Cutietta, Robert A.	CA5300	DiCello, Anthony J.	OH0150
Cohen, Stanley	NY1275	Cutsforth-Huber, Bonnie	MD0095	DiCioccio, Justin	NY2150
Cohen, Stanley	NY1275	Cutting, W. Scott	MI1550	Dickelman, Karen	IL2100
Cohn, Richard L.	CT0900	Cyrus, Cynthia	TN1850	Dickens, Pierce	GA0400
Coker, Keller	OR1250	Cyrus, Cynthia	TN1850	Dickerson, Roger	LA0720

Name	Code	Name	Code	Name	Code
Dickey, Bobby	GA0810	Elliott, Robin W.	AG0450	Fitzsimons, Constance	CA1750
Dickey, Marc R.	CA0815	Ellis, Diana L.	TX1650	Flack, Amy L.	NY3780
Dickman, Marcus	FL1950	Ellis, John S.	MI2100	Flack, Michael	IL0650
Dickson, John H.	GA1300	Ellis, Margaret J.	IL0100	Flagg, Aaron A.	CT0650
Diehl, David J.	TN1600	Ellis, Margaret J.	IL0100	Flanagan, Edward	PA3250
Dietrich, Kurt R.	WI0700	Ellis, Peter	AA0032	Flandreau, Tara	CA1150
Dikener, Solen	WV0400	Ellsworth, Jane	WA0250	Flax, Gale	NC0500
Dill, Jane	SC1080	Elsberry, Kristie B.	TN0100	Fletcher, Tom	PA0250
Dinielli, Michael	CA0950	Elwell, Jeffery	TN1700	Floreen, John E.	NJ1140
DiPalma, Maria	IA1350	Elworthy, Joseph	AB0200	Flores, Carlos	MI0250
Dippre, Keith	NC1350	Endicott, David	WA0960	Flores, Mary	ID0130
Dismore, Roger	TX0370	Engelke, Luis C.	MD0850	Floyd, Elizabeth M.	LA0300
Dixon, Sam	GA0500	Engelmann, Marcus W.	CA0100	Fluhrer, Roy	SC0765
Dixon, Timothy D.	PA2300	Engelson, Robert A.	IA0050	Flynn, Timothy	MI1800
Dizinno, Janet	TX2200	Engelson, Robert A.	IA0050	Fogel, Henry	IL0550
Doane, Christopher	KY1500	Engelson, Robert A.	IA0050	Fohrman, Jonathan	CA4050
Dobreff, Kevin J.	MI0850	Engstrom, Larry M.	NV0100	Foley, Brad	OR1050
Dodds, Dinah	OR0400	Enis, Paul	OK0350	Foley, Brad	OR1050
Dodson, Robert K.	MA0400	Enns, Ruth	AB0200	Foley, Mark	KS1450
Doherty, Jean	NY1950	Enns, Ruth	AB0200	Fonseca, James W.	OH1910
Dolan, Laura	IL1200	Enos, Steve	OH0750	Foote, Jack E.	CA0840
Domber, Edward	NJ0300	Entz, James	CA3700	Forbes, Bruce	NE0550
Dombrosky, Marc	MI1985	Entzi, John A.	NC1250	Ford, Charles W.	NC2700
Donelson, David W.	OH1350	Epperson, Douglas	CA0600	Forger, James	MI1400
Donelson, David W.	OH1350	Epperson, Skip A.	CA0400	Fortney, Julie T.	NC1250
Dooley, Gail	IA1100	Eppink, Joseph A.	NY0700	Foss, Brian	AG0100
Dopson, Brian	FL0675	Epstein, Joan O.	FL0450	Foster, Elaine	MI1985
Dornian, Paul	AA0050	Ergo, Jack	IA0600	Foster, Marc A.	NC0930
Dorsey, Sam Brian	VA0950	Erickson, Christian	WY0150	Fouse, Kathryn L.	AL0800
Douglass, Ronald L.	MI1100	Erickson, Susan N.	MI2110	Foust, Diane	WI1100
Douthit, James Russell	NY2650	Eschbach, Jesse	TX3420	Fowler, Vivia	GA2200
Dower, Mary R.	PA1700	Espinosa, Teresita	CA3150	Fox, Aaron A.	NY0750
Dowling, Eugene	AB0150	Evans, Anita S.	OH0200	Fox, Donna Brink	NY1100
Downes, Suzanne	IL2310	Evans, Anita S.	OH0200	Fox, Donna Brink	NY1100
Downey, Joanna	CA3750	Evans, Clifton J.	TX3500	Fox, Jeremy	IA1400
Doyen, Rob	MO1650	Evans, Dina Pannabecker	KS1350	Fox, Jeremy	IA1400
Doyle, Alicia M.	CA0825	Evans, John	OR1050	Fox, Jeremy	IA1400
Doyle, Laurie	TX1550	Everett, William A.	MO1810	Fox, T. Jeffrey	NY2550
Doyle, LeeAnn	WI0804	Everett, William A.	MO1810	Foy, Patricia S.	SC0650
Doyle, Phillip	WA0250	Fabozzi, Paul F.	NY3500	Foy, Randolph M.	NC1700
Doyle, Tracy A.	CO0050	Fagan, Jeffrey	NY3500	Frabizio, William V.	PA0125
Draskovic, Ines	NY1250	Fahey, Paul F.	PA3500	Fragnoli, Kristen	NY2500
Draughn, Maurice	MI2200	Fahy, Greg	ME0340	Fralin, Sandra L.	KY1200
Draves, Patricia	OH2290	Fairchild, G. Daniel	WI0840	Franklin, Bonita Louise	OK0450
Dressen, Dan F.	MN1450	Fairlie, Thomas A.	TX2800	Franklin, Bonita Louise	OK0450
Driskell, Kelly	TX3360	Falk, Marc	IA0300	Franklin, Laura L.	NC0250
Droste, Douglas	OK0800	Falker, Matt	CA2960	Franzblau, Robert	RI0200
Drury, Jay	CA6050	Falker, Matt	CA2960	Fraser, Teresa L.	WA0600
Dry, Marion	MA2050	Falskow, John	WA0960	Fraser, Teresa L.	WA0600
Dry, Marion	MA2050	Falskow, John	WA0960	Fraser, Wendy	AA0015
Dubman, Shirley	MO0550	Famulare, Trever R.	PA3050	Fredenburgh, Lisa M.	IL0150
Duff, John A.	FL1850	Fansler, Michael J.	IL3500	Fredrickson, William E.	FL0850
Duffy, Kathryn Ann Pohlmann	IA0650	Farrell, Timothy P.	SD0600	Fredstrom, Tim	IL1150
Duggan, Sean B.	LA0600	Farrington, Lisa	NY0630	Freedman, Richard	PA1500
Dunbar, Brian	MN0620	Farwell, Douglas G.	GA2150	Freeman, Gary	NC0860
Dunbar, Edward	SC0200	Faszer, Ted	SD0450	Frego, R. J. David	TX3530
Duncan, Norah	MI2200	Fatone, Gina Andrea	ME0150	French, George E.	MN1590
Duncan, Norah	MI2200	Fauser, Annegret	NC2410	French, John	PA3550
Duncan, Warren L.	AL1100	Favis, Angelo L.	IL1150	Frese, Marcella	SC0750
Dunevant, David L.	KY1000	Favorito, Barbara	CA2420	Freyermuth, G. Kim	AZ0200
Dunn, David	NY3350	Fay, William	OH0600	Friedman, Bennett	CA4460
Dunn, Susan	NC0600	Feather, Carol Ann	TN0450	Frierson-Campbell, Carol	NJ1400
Dunnick, Kim	NY1800	Fedrizzi-Williams, Linda	NY3000	Frisch, Walter	NY0750
Dunscomb, J. Richard	IL0720	Feeler, William	TX1660	Friscioni, Emanuela	OH0755
Dunston, Douglas E.	NM0350	Feiszli, James D.	SD0500	Fritz, Lawrence	PA0250
DuPree, Mary	ID0250	Feldman, Barbara	NJ0825	Fritz, Matthew P.	PA1250
Durand, Joel F.	WA1550	Feldman, Bernardo	CA1265	Froom, David	MD0750
Durham, Linda Eileen	VA1840	Feldman, Martha	IL3250	Frye, Christopher B.	WI0810
Durham, Thomas L.	UT0050	Feldt, Alison	MN1450	Fryns, Jennifer	FL0365
Durran, Daryl	PA2750	Ferguson, Sean	AI0150	Fujimoto, Elise	CA4900
Dykema, Dan H.	AR0600	Fernando, Nathalie	AI0200	Fulgham, Rebecca L.	MO1500
Dykema, Dan H.	AR0600	Fernisse, Glenn	GA0400	Fuller, Gregory	MS0750
Eagle, David	AA0150	Fetchen, Joan	FL0675	Fuller, John A.	NC1700
Earle, Diane K.	KY0800	Fetz, Teun	OR0200	Fulton, Richard D.	HI0300
Easby, Rebecca	DC0250	Feves, Julie	CA0510	Furlons, Scott	WI0808
East, David	MS0320	Feves, Julie	CA0510	Furlow, John W.	OH1905
Ebener, Ben	MI1400	Field, Eric G.	WI0865	Furumoto, Kimo	CA0815
Eby, John D.	AI0050	Field, Eric G.	WI0865	Fusco, Randall J.	OH1000
Eby, Patricia	WI0804	Fields, Phyllis	SC0450	Fuster, Bradley J.	NY3717
Eckelhoefer, Miriam	MA1175	Fields, Phyllis	SC0450	Gach, Peter F.	CA3460
Eddlman, William	MO1500	Fienberg, Gary	NJ0175	Gackstatter, Gary	MO1120
Edel, Theodore	IL3310	Fienberg, Nona	NH0150	Gaddis, J. Robert	KY0400
Edidin, Aron	FL1360	Filner, David	CA2250	Gaddis, J. Robert	KY0400
Ediger, Thomas L.	NE0500	Finch, Abraham L.	MA1650	Gaddis, Roger G.	NC0850
Edwards, Constance	WV0300	Finger, Ellis	PA1850	Gagnon, Jean-Louis	AI0210
Edwards, Elizabeth	OK1050	Fink, Robert W.	CA5032	Galand, Joel	FL0700
Edwards, Kay L.	OH1450	Fink, Ted	OR1010	Galand, Joel	FL0700
Edwards, Linda	NM0400	Finney, John W.	KY0700	Gallagher, Mark	MD0350
Edwards, Steven C.	LA0080	Finney, R. Terrell	OH2200	Gallahan, Carla A.	AL1050
Egeness, Michelle	MN1450	Firmani, Domenico	MD0100	Galloway, Robert J.	NY1700
Ehle, Robert	CO0950	Fischbach, Gerald	MD1010	Galm, Eric A.	CT0500
Ehle, Todd	TX0550	Fischer, Lou	OH0350	Galm, Eric A.	CT0500
Ehlert, Alysia	GA0625	Fisher, Brock L.	AL0950	Gammon, Steve	OR0200
Eisenmann, Linda	MA2150	Fisher, Gary	NY2650	Ganus, Clifton L.	AR0250
Eisensmith, Kevin E.	PA1600	Fisher, George	NY2250	Ganus, Linda C.	PA1950
Elder, Ellen P.	MS0850	Fisher, John	TX3250	Garcia, Alvaro	WI0835
Elderkin, Nicholas P.	TX1660	Fishwick, Greg	OR1020	Garcia, David F.	NC2410
Ellington, Deborah	TX1520	Fitzgerald, Betsy	GA1300	Garcia, Orlando Jacinto	FL0700
Elliott, Robert L.	TN1400	Fitzgibbon, Cecelia	PA1000	Garcia, William B.	TN0800
Elliott, Robin W.	AG0450	Fitzgibbon, Cecelia	PA1000	Garcia-Leon, Jose M.	CT0700

Alphabetical Listing of Administrators

Gardner, James E.	UT0250	Gorman, Sharon L.	AR0900	Hamilton, Margaret J.	MI2250
Garin, Ross	PA0550	Gotfrit, Martin	AB0080	Hamlin, Peter S.	VT0350
Garner, Rusty	FL0900	Gothard, Paul	OH1250	Hamman, James	LA0800
Garrett, Michael D.	KS0570	Govang, Don	MO0600	Hamman, James	LA0800
Garrido, Glenn	TX3450	Gowan, Andrew D.	SC1110	Hammett, Peter E.	LA0600
Garry, Kevin M.	CO0400	Gowan, Andrew D.	SC1110	Hammond, June C.	FL1600
Gartner, Kurt	KS0650	Graber, Todd A.	NY3770	Hammond, L. Curtis	KY0900
Garton, Bradford	NY0750	Grace, Susan L.	CO0200	Hancock, Blair M.	NC2640
Garton, Linda	IL2250	Grace, Susan L.	CO0200	Handel, Thomas	MA1400
Garton, Linda	IL2250	Gracia-Nuthmann, Andre	NM0150	Hanes, Wendy L.	KS1450
Garton, Linda	IL2250	Gracia-Nuthmann, Andre	NM0150	Hankins, Paul	MS0250
Gary, Jonathan	TX3415	Graf, Greg	MO0750	Hanks, Kenneth B.	FL0930
Gash, William H.	NC2435	Graham, Lowell	TX3520	Hanley, Darla	MA0260
Gates, Charles R.	MS0700	Gramit, David	AA0100	Hanna, Frederick	NE0160
Gates, Stephen	AR0700	Grandy, Larry	CA4550	Hanni, Margaret	MA1700
Gatewood, Claudia	FL1750	Grant, Donald R.	MI1600	Hansbrough, Robert S.	NY0700
Gatien, Gregory	AC0050	Grant, Gary S.	PA1200	Hansbrough, Robert S.	NY0700
Gaughan, Warren J.	NC2550	Grass, Mahlon O.	PA2050	Hansbrough, Yvonne	NY0700
Gay, Kirk	FL1800	Gratto, Sharon Davis	OH2250	Hansen, Charles	CO0950
Gaylard, Timothy R.	VA1850	Gratz, Reed	CA5100	Hansen, Deborah	WA1350
Geber, David	NY2150	Gratz, Reed	CA5100	Hansen, Demaris	CT0650
Gee, Constance	SC1110	Graulty, John P.	CA0400	Hansen, Mark R.	ID0050
Geier, Alan	CA2250	Graveline, Michelle	MA0200	Hansen, Neil E.	WY0130
Geisler, Herbert G.	CA1425	Gray, Harold R. 'Skip'	KY1450	Hanson, Brent	UT0150
Gelfand, Michael D.	OH2600	Gray, Laura J.	AG0470	Hanson, Josef M.	NY4350
Gentilesco, Lauren	PA3700	Gray, Mary Kay	OH1700	Haramaki, Gordon	CA4400
Gentry, April	GA1750	Graziano, Amy	CA0960	Harbach, Barbara	MO1830
George, Mark	CT0650	Green, Gayle	NC1200	Hard, Randi	IL2350
George, Matthew J.	MN1625	Green, Georgia	TX0300	Harden, Patricia A.	NC2050
Gephart, Jay S.	IN1310	Green, Peter	CA1960	Hardenbergh, Esther Jane	FL1900
Gerber, Gary G.	AR0500	Green, Verna	NY0640	Harder, Lillian U.	SC0400
Gerber, Richard A.	CT0450	Greenblatt, Dan	NY2660	Harder, Lillian U.	SC0400
Gerhold, John	CA0270	Greene, Gayle	NC2525	Harder, Matthew D.	WV0600
Gerster, Patrick	CA4350	Greene, Sean	TN0900	Harding, C. Tayloe	SC1110
Gervais, Michel Marc	CA5060	Greenlee, Geol	TN1250	Hardy, Steven	WV0440
Getz, Christine S.	IA1550	Greenlee, Robert K.	ME0200	Harkey, Gary Don	TX3540
Getz, Christine S.	IA1550	Greenwald, Laura	NJ0050	Harnish, David D.	CA5200
Getz, Christine S.	IA1550	Gregg, Robert S.	NJ0990	Harper, Darryl	VA1600
Gibble, David L.	FL1470	Gregorich, Shellie Lynn	PA2150	Harper, Larry D.	WI0200
Gibbs, Phyllis M.	FL0570	Greig, R. Tad	PA3650	Harper, Steven A.	GA1050
Gibeau, Peter	WI0862	Grenfell, Mary-Jo	MA1650	Harrigan, Peter	VT0400
Gibson, Don	FL0850	Gresham, Georgia	LA0300	Harrington, Katherine	CO0750
Gibson, Mara	MO1810	Griffin, Jackie	SC0950	Harrington, William	CA3520
Gibson, Michele	NY1100	Griffin, Jackie	SC0950	Harris, Edward C.	CA4400
Gibson, Robert L.	MD1010	Griffin, Peter J.	IL0850	Harris, John	AG0130
Gier, David	IA1550	Griffing, Joan	VA0300	Harris, Lee	TN1700
Gifford, Troy S.	FL2120	Grigel, Glen M.	NY3780	Harris, Lee	TN1700
Gil, Maria Del Carmen	PR0115	Griggs, Joyce L.	IL3300	Harris, Mary Carol C.	IA0940
Gilbert, E. Beth	WI0860	Griggs, Joyce L.	IL3300	Harris, Ray	MS0570
Gilbert, Jay W.	NE0200	Griggs, Joyce L.	IL3300	Harris, Rod D.	CA1375
Gilbert, Jay W.	NE0200	Gronemann, Robert	MN1200	Harris, Rod D.	CA1375
Giles, Glenn	VT0100	Groom, Mitzi	KY1550	Harris, Scott	ME0500
Giles, Leonard	GA0810	Grooms, Pamela	MO0650	Harris, Scott H.	TX2700
Gillette, Michael	NJ0760	Gross, Ernest H.	IL1300	Harris, Timothy	CA0900
Gilmour, F. Matthew	MO0850	Grosso, Cheryl	WI0808	Harrison, Albert D.	IN1560
Gilpin, Mary Ann	WA0940	Groves, Melinda	KS0300	Harrison, Daniel	CT0900
Gilson, David W.	OH0600	Gruhn, Charles	CA1700	Harriss, Elaine Atkins	TN1720
Gimble, Richard	TX1600	Gruner, Greg	AL1300	Hart, Michael D.	LA0030
Ginocchio, John	MN1500	Grymes, James A.	NC2420	Hart, Steven R.	MT0350
Giovannetti, Geralyn	UT0050	Grzych, Frank J.	TN0500	Hartenberger, Russell	AG0450
Gipson, Richard C.	TX3000	Gubrud, Darcy Lease	MN1285	Hartig, Hugo J.	WI0200
Girdham, Jane C.	MI1850	Guilbault, Denise	RI0200	Hartley, Linda A.	OH2250
Girton, Irene	CA3300	Guilbert, Fred	LA0150	Hartmann, David	SC0400
Gitz, Raymond	LA0560	Guinn, Melani	CA2300	Hartvig-Nielson, Niels	AB0040
Glancey, Gregory T.	CA5355	Guretzki, David	AJ0030	Hartwell, Robert	CA1800
Glanden, Don	PA3330	Gustafson, Anita K.	SC1000	Hartzell, Lance	MN1030
Glendening, Andrew	CA5150	Guterman, Jeffrey	PA3400	Harvey, Peter J.	CT0240
Glennon, Maura	NH0150	Guthrie, J. Randall	OK0850	Harwood, Gregory	GA0950
Glickman, Joel	WI0600	Guy, Todd	IN1025	Hasenpflug, Thom	ID0100
Glover, David	PA3100	Guzelimian, Ara	NY1900	Haskett, Brandon L.	GA1500
Goble, Daniel P.	CT0800	Haas, Thomas	IA1950	Hatch, Ken	AR0110
Goeke, Christopher L.	MO1500	Hachey, Michael C.	MA2300	Hatch, Mary	IL0840
Goetz-Sota, Germaine	IL0780	Hachey, Michael C.	MA2300	Hatcher, George	NC2300
Goff, Nadine	TN0850	Hachey, Michael C.	MA2300	Hatcher, Oeida M.	VA0750
Goffi-Fynn, Jeanne C.	NY4200	Hacker, Kathleen M.	IN1650	Hatcher, Oeida M.	VA0750
Goforth, Stephen C.	KY1300	Haefner, Dale F.	MN1000	Hathaway, Janet J.	IL2200
Gokelman, William	TX3410	Haefner, Jaymee	TX3420	Hathaway, Janet J.	IL2200
Goldberg, Joel	VT0450	Hafeli, Mary	NY3760	Haug, Sue E.	PA2750
Goldman, Jonathan	AB0150	Hageman, Paul M.	TX2960	Haury, Clifford	VA1030
Goldsmith, John L.	PA3420	Hageman, Paul M.	TX2960	Hauser, Joshua	TN1450
Goldspiel, Alan	AL1200	Hagen, Patrick	WI0842	Hawk, Heather	TX2750
Goldstein, Joanna	IN1010	Hager, Lawson	TX0900	Hawkins Raimi, Jane	NC0600
Goldstein, Joanna	IN1010	Hager, Lawson	TX0900	Hawkins, Jemmie Peevy	AL0650
Goldstein, Norma	WA0860	Hahn, Tomie	NY3300	Hawkins, John A.	WV0500
Goldstein, Perry	NY3790	Hakoda, Ken	KS0700	Hawkins, Phillip	CA2975
Golemo, Michael	IA0850	Haley, Ardith	AF0050	Hawkshaw, Paul	CT0850
Gonano, Max A.	PA0500	Haley, Julia W.	OK0800	Hawn, Mary	AC0100
Gonder, Jonathan P.	NY3730	Haley, Julia W.	OK0800	Haworth, Janice	MN0150
Gonzales, Gregory	TX2220	Haley, Timothy R.	NC2210	Hayden, Diane	CA1750
Gonzalez, Helen	PR0115	Hall, Barbara L.	KY0450	Hayden, William P.	FL2000
Good, Jonathan E.	NV0050	Hall, Gary	WY0115	Hayden, William P.	FL2000
Goold, William C.	KY0150	Hall, Lois	NY2800	Hayden, William P.	FL2000
Gorcik, Christopher	IL2750	Hall, Mark	TN1000	Hayes, Christopher	OH1900
Gordon, Barbara N.	NJ0500	Hall, William	NY0100	Hayes, John W.	OR0750
Gordon, Daniel J.	NY3775	Hall-Gulati, Doris J.	PA1300	Hayes, Raymond	WI0855
Gordon, Joan	CA4150	Halligan, Meg	IA1300	Haynes, Alexis	NY1950
Gordon, Nina	IL1200	Hallstrom, Jonathan F.	ME0250	Haynes, Alora D.	FL1675
Gordon, Nina	IL1200	Halper, Matthew R.	NJ0700	Haynes, Christopher A.	MA1850
Gordon-Seifert, Catherine	RI0150	Halperin, Allison R.	LA0300	Haynes, Kimberly	FL0100
Gorham, Fr. Daniel	IN0005	Ham, Robert	IN0200	Haynes, W. Lance	MO0825

Name	Code	Name	Code	Name	Code
Hays, Timothy O.	IL0850	Holland, Samuel S.	TX2400	Jachens, Darryl	SC1080
Hazewinkel, Jeff	IN1750	Holland, Samuel S.	TX2400	Jackson, Albert	IL2775
He, Wei	CA4150	Holland, Samuel S.	TX2400	Jackson, Jay Craig	NC0050
Head, Paul D.	DE0150	Holleman, James A.	MI1000	Jackson, Keith	WV0750
Heald, Jason A.	OR1020	Holliday, Shawn	OK0600	Jackson, Roland	CA2710
Healey, Roberta	NY0650	Hollingsworth, Mark	OK0300	Jackson, Travis A.	IL3250
Hearne, Clarice	IL3370	Hollis, Burney J.	MD0600	Jacobson, John	MI0400
Hearne, Martin	IA0400	Hollis, C. Kimm	IN0650	Jacobson, Michael	TX0300
Hedges, Don P.	IL3150	Hollister, James	PA0250	Jaeger, Lois	MN0200
Heighway, Robbi A.	WI0450	Holloway, Watson	GA0525	Jakovcic, Zoran	GA0550
Heitzman, Jill M.	IA0450	Holly, Janice	MD0300	Jalbert, Julia	TX2150
Held, Jeffrey	CA1425	Holmes, Ramona A.	WA0800	James, Jeffrey H.	NH0100
Held, Jeffrey	CA1425	Holsinger, Winona	TN0850	James, Lori	NV0050
Held, Roger L.	MI1450	Holt, Earl	TX1520	James, Matthew H.	LA0770
Helfers, James	AZ0400	Holzmeier, Jana	NE0450	James, Matthew T.	OH1900
Heller, David	TX3350	Holzmeier, Jana	NE0450	James, Robert R.	KY0550
Heller, Jennifer	NC1100	Honda, Lorence	CA1850	James, Robert R.	KY0550
Heller, Wendy B.	NJ0900	Honea, Richard	MO0400	Janco, Steve	IN1350
Heller, Wendy B.	NJ0900	Honea, Ted	OK1330	Janisch, Joseph	WV0560
Hellmer, Jeffrey	TX3510	Hood, Marcia Mitchell	GA0150	Janners, Erik N.	WI0425
Hemberger, Glen J.	LA0650	Hood, Michael J.	PA1600	Janson, Thomas	OH1100
Henderson, David R.	NY3550	Hoogerhyde, Jason	TX2650	Jantz, Paul	SC0200
Henderson, Douglas S.	OK0800	Hooper, John	AA0015	Jarjisian, Catherine	CT0600
Henderson, Gordon L.	CA5030	Hoover, Jeffrey	IL1090	Jarvis, Jeffery W.	AR0850
Henderson, Peter	MO0700	Hope-Cunningham, Catherine	OH1850	Jarvis, Michelle	IN0250
Henderson, Silvester	CA2775	Hope-Cunningham, Catherine	OH1850	Jazwinski, Barbara M.	LA0750
Hendricks, Bob	OK0200	Hopkins, Jesse E.	VA0100	Jeffrey, Diane	NH0250
Hendrickson, Daniel	MI1180	Hopkins, Jesse E.	VA0100	Jeleva, Jivka	LA0650
Henley, Larry	NV0050	Hopkins, Joseph H.	AL0800	Jenkins, Ellie	GA0610
Hennessy, Jeff	AF0050	Horn, Lawrence C.	MS0560	Jenkins, John A.	MA2000
Henning, Mary	KY0350	Hornsby, Richard	AE0120	Jenkins, John A.	MA2000
Henry, Joseph D.	IL0900	Hornsby, Richard	AE0120	Jennings, Charles R.	CA4300
Henry, Mary Pat	MO1810	Hornsby, Richard	AE0120	Jensen, Janet L.	WI0815
Henry, Warren	TX3420	Hornsby, Richard	AE0120	Jensen, Janet L.	WI0815
Henry, Warren	TX3420	Houlahan, Michael	PA2350	Jensen, Karen	AC0100
Hentschel, Alain	IL0630	Houlahan, Michael	PA2350	Jensen-Moulton, Stephanie	NY0500
Hentschel, Alain R.	FL1570	Houlahan, Michael	PA2350	Jermance, Frank J.	CO0830
Heroux, Gerard H.	RI0300	Houlahan, Michael	PA2350	Jessop, Brad	OK0300
Heroux, Gerard H.	RI0300	Houlahan, Michael	PA2350	Jessop, Craig D.	UT0300
Herron, Clifford	FL1430	Hourigan, Ryan M.	IN0150	Johanson, Bryan	OR0850
Herron, Clifford	FL1430	House, LeAnn	MN0450	Johns, Lana Kay	MS0500
Hershkowitz, Michael F.	NY3790	Howdle, Joyce	AA0080	Johns, Shellie	NE0050
Hess, Susan M.	ID0250	Howe, Hubert S.	NY0642	Johnson, Brad	MS0200
Hessler, Arthur	VA0100	Hoyt, Reed J.	NY3700	Johnson, Craig R.	IL2100
Hetrick, Esther A.	MI0910	Huber, Wayne	CA1860	Johnson, David	ID0070
Heuser, David	NY3780	Huckabee, KT	PA2710	Johnson, David A.	IA0900
Heuser, David	NY3780	Hudson, Barbara D.	NC0300	Johnson, Diane	WA0900
Heuser, David	NY3780	Hudson, David	CA2050	Johnson, Jacquelyn Pualani	HI0200
Hewitt, Michael P.	MD1010	Hudson-Mairet, Stephen	WI0425	Johnson, Jean	AL0340
Hibbard, Kevin	GA2130	Hudspeth, Gregory	TX2220	Johnson, Jeanne	TX1350
Hick, Steven V.	PA2715	Huffman, Debora L.	CA5300	Johnson, Jeffrey	CT0550
Hicks, Charles E.	NC2700	Huffman, Debora L.	CA5300	Johnson, Julie J.	MN1280
Hicks, Joe	TX0250	Huffman, Donna M.	WA0100	Johnson, Kevin P.	GA1900
Hicks, Martha K.	MO1550	Hughes, Albert C.	TN0950	Johnson, Lynn M.	CT0650
Higdon, Paul	MO1100	Hughes, Jennifer L.	MA2050	Johnson, Marjorie S.	VA0950
Hightower, Allen	IA0950	Hughes, Marcia A.	TN0930	Johnson, Michelle	IL0300
Hightower, J. Taylor	MS0750	Hughes, Ralph	CA0150	Johnson, Roger O.	NJ0950
Hill, Camille	KY0600	Hughes, Scott	TX2960	Johnson, Scott R.	SD0050
Hill, Douglas M.	GA1300	Hugo, John William	VA0650	Johnson, Stephen P.	TX2600
Hill, Matthew	IN0550	Hukill, Cynthia L.	AR0200	Johnson, Stephen R.	PA0700
Hill, Stephen	IL2250	Hulen, Peter Lucas	IN1850	Johnson, Timothy A.	NY1800
Hill, William	FL1000	Hulihan, Charles	AZ0350	Johnson, Timothy A.	NY1800
Hilles, Sharon	CA0630	Hull, Janet	AF0120	Johnson, Todd Alan	CA0845
Hillner, Paul R.	OH2200	Hull, Kenneth	AG0470	Johnson, Valerie	NC0200
Hillner, Paul R.	OH2200	Hulse, Mark	CA0300	Johnson, William	CA0800
Hills, Ernie M.	CA0840	Hume, Michael	NY0050	Johnston, Joe	TX3540
Hills, Ernie M.	CA0840	Humphrey, Mark Aaron	TX3415	Johnston, Rebecca R.	SC0600
Himes, A. C. 'Buddy'	TX2700	Hunt, Jeffrey	TX2260	Jonason, Louisa	PA2250
Himes, A. C. 'Buddy'	TX2700	Hunt, Paul B.	KS0650	Jones, Lis	AR0250
Hines, Clarence	FL1950	Hunt, Sylvia	ID0070	Jones, Micah	PA3330
Hingst, Debra	IL2775	Hunt, Sylvia	ID0070	Jones, Micah	PA3330
Hinson, Wallace	GA1650	Hunt, Tom A.	OH1800	Jones, Nick	KS0225
Hinton, Don	UT0150	Hurst, Carol	VA0900	Jones, Patrick Michael	NY4150
Hirota, Yoko	AG0150	Hurst, Craig W.	WI0960	Jones, Russell L.	KS1050
Hirst, Dennis	UT0300	Hurt, Phyllis A.	IL2150	Jones, Russell L.	KS1050
Hisama, Ellie M.	NY0750	Hurt, Phyllis A.	IL2150	Jones, Stuart	IN1050
Hisama, Ellie M.	NY0750	Hurty, Jon	IL0100	Jones, Sue	IL1550
Hiscocks, Mike	CA2650	Hussain, Zac	PA2050	Jones, Suzanne	VT0050
Hisey, P. Andrew	MN1450	Hutchings, James	IL0420	Jones, Tony	IL1090
Hlus, Don	AB0060	Hutchinson, Mary Anne	NY4400	Jordahl, Patricia	AZ0300
Hodgman, Thomas	MI0050	Hyatt, Garey A.	MD0200	Jordan, Paul	IN0005
Hodson, Luke	KY0300	Hynes, Maureen	NY2105	Jordan, William S.	AA0150
Hodson, Robert	MI1050	Ice, Richard	MN0350	Jordan-Anders, Lee	VA1830
Hoefnagels, Anna	AG0100	Imboden, Jeff H.	MO1790	Jorgensen, Robert	OH2150
Hoepfner, Gregory	OK0150	Indergaard, Lyle	GA2150	Jose, Brian	MN0350
Hoerl, Scott	NJ1350	Ioudenitch, Stanislav	MO1000	Josenhans, Thomas	IN1600
Hofer, Calvin	CO0225	Irving, Howard L.	AL1150	Joubert, Estelle	AF0100
Hoffman, Edward C. 'Ted'	AL1200	Isaacs, Kevin	CT0800	Joyce, J. Patrick	WV0300
Hoffman, Elizabeth D.	NY2740	Isaacs, Kevin	CT0800	Juarez, Benjamin Echenique	MA0400
Hoffman, Joseph M.	MD0350	Isaacson, Eric J.	IN0900	Judd, Cristle Collins	ME0200
Hoffman, Julia	NM0450	Isaacson, Lawrence	MA0350	Judisch, David	IA0950
Hoffman, Laura	MI2100	Isaacson, Peter R.	TX0900	Judy, Ned	MD0700
Hoffman, Steve	KY0450	Isaak, JoAnna	NY1300	Juncker, Arthur	CA1950
Hogan, Larry	NC0805	Isele, David	FL2050	Junkinsmith, Jeff	WA0860
Hoifeldt, Steven	IA0425	Isensee, Paul R.	PA2800	Jureit-Beamish, Marie	IL2400
Hoke, S. Kay	PA1400	Italiano, Richard	CO0300	Jureit-Beamish, Marie	IL2400
Holcomb, Richard	FL1470	Ivey, Adriane	GA0755	Jurgensmeier, Charles L.	IL1615
Holden, LuAnn	TN0850	Jablonski, Jennifer	SC1110	Justus, Timothy W.	TX1700
Holden, LuAnn	TN0850	Jablonsky, Stephen	NY0550	Jutras, Kristin	GA2100
Holland, Patricia C.	WI0850	Jablow, Peter	DC0170	Juusela, Kari H.	MA0260

Alphabetical Listing of Administrators

Name	Code	Name	Code	Name	Code
Kageyama, Noa	NY1900	Kleinknecht, Daniel E.	IA1140	Lanning, Rebecca	GA1260
Kahan, Sylvia	NY0644	Kleinsasser, William	MD0850	Lanting, Mark	IL1330
Kaiser, Audrey K.	RI0101	Kline, Thomas	NY1800	Larcheid, Mary	IA0800
Kaiser, Keith A.	NY1800	Kluball, Jeff L.	GA0625	Larner, James M.	IN1100
Kaiser, Keith A.	NY1800	Klugherz, Laura	NY0650	Larocque, Jacques	AI0220
Kale, David	MA0800	Knapp, Peter J.	CA2550	Larocque, Monique M.	ME0500
Kalm, Stephen	MT0400	Knight, Steven M.	AR0300	Larsen, Carol W.	LA0200
Kalyn, Andrea	OH1700	Knippenberg, Gary	MI1200	Larsen, Carol W.	LA0200
Kalyn, Andrea	OH1700	Knott, Josef W.	FL2000	Larsen, Carol W.	LA0200
Kalyn, Andrea	OH1700	Knowles, William A.	TN1500	Larsen, Vance	UT0190
Kaminsky, Peter	CT0600	Knox, Daniel	AL0750	Larson, David	SC0050
Kamm, Charles W.	CA3620	Knudtsen, Jere	WA0750	Larson, Shari	ND0600
Kamm, Charles W.	CA1060	Ko, Bongshin	CA0815	Larson, Stacey L.	IL3450
Kamm, Charles W.	CA4500	Kocher, Edward W.	PA1050	Lastoria, Dean	AB0080
Kammerer, David	HI0050	Koep, Jeffrey	NV0050	Late, Eric	TX2295
Kampert, James	IL0630	Koffman, David	GA0940	Latham, Michael	NY1300
Kania, Robert P.	IL1300	Kolb, G. Roberts	NY1350	Lau, Eric	NM0450
Kania, Robert P.	IL1300	Kolstad, Michael L.	MO0400	Laubersheimer, David	IL1610
Kania, Robert P.	IL1300	Kolstad, Michael L.	MO0400	Laughton, John C.	NJ0175
Kanis, David	IL0600	Kolwinska, Jeremy	MN1280	Laurendine, Barbara	AL1195
Kantack, Jerri Lamar	MS0150	Konecky, Larry	MS0050	Lautar, Rebecca	FL0650
Kanu, Andrew J.	VA1750	Konschak, Norma	MN1270	Lautar, Rebecca	FL0650
Kaplan, William	IL3310	Kontos, Julie	PA0250	Laux, Charles	GA1150
Kapralick, Randy	PA3330	Koons, Keith	FL1800	Law, Bill R.	ND0350
Kapralick, Randy	PA3330	Koons, Keith	FL1800	Lawrence, David	CA3950
Kaptain, Laurence D.	LA0200	Koop, Ruth B.	AJ0030	Lawrence, Margaret A.	NH0100
Kardan, Sel	CA1075	Koozer, Robin R.	NE0300	Lawrence-White, Stephanie	NC0200
Karnes, Kevin C.	GA0750	Koponen, Glenn	NY2900	Lawson, Darren P.	SC0200
Karpen, Richard	WA1050	Korde, Shirish	MA0700	Lawson, Darren P.	SC0200
Kartman, Stefan	WI0825	Korey, Judith A.	DC0350	Lawson, Robert	CA5360
Katseanes, Kory L.	UT0050	Kornelis, Benjamin	IA0500	Lawson, Robert	CA5360
Katz, Mark	NC2410	Kornelsen, Michael J.	CO0550	Lawson, Sonya R.	MA2100
Kauffman, Bradley	KS0500	Korstvedt, Benjamin M.	MA0650	Le Guin, Elisabeth C.	CA5032
Kauffman, Larry D.	PA0150	Kosciesza, Andrew	PA2400	Leader, Jeanne	WA0300
Kaufhold, Jessica	AL0530	Kothman, Keith K.	IN0150	Learner, Martha L.	NJ0800
Kaufman, Jacob	KS0215	Kramer, Karl P.	IL3300	Leasure, Timothy	OH1850
Kavasch, Deborah H.	CA0850	Kramer, Timothy	IL1100	Leasure, Timothy	OH1850
Kays, Mark	IN1485	Krause, Robert	TX3750	Lecourt, Nancy	CA3400
Keast, Dan A.	TX3527	Krause, William Craig	VA0550	Ledeen, Lydia Hailparn	NJ0300
Keeler, Steve	NY0450	Krause, William Craig	VA0550	Lee, David	KY1550
Keeling, Bruce	TX2350	Kravchak, Richard	CA0805	Lee, Hsiaopei	MS0750
Keener, Allen	NY4060	Krawchuk, Hali	AG0400	Lee, Jay	ID0140
Kehrberg, Robert	NC2600	Kreider, Paul K.	WV0750	Lee, Richard F.	TX3150
Keiser, Douglas	IN0800	Kreinberg, Steven	PA3250	Lee, Ronald T.	RI0300
Keiter, Lise	VA0800	Kreitner, Kenneth	TN1680	Lees, Priscilla	MI2100
Keith, David C.	GA1300	Kreuze, Brandon R.	GA0600	Leeson, Susan	AC0100
Kelbley, John R.	OH1910	Kreuze, Brandon R.	GA0600	Leglar, Mary A.	GA2100
Keller, Christopher	PA0250	Kriehn, Richard	WA1150	Legname, Orlando	NY3765
Keller, Dorothy	CT0350	Krittenbrink, Juanita	OK1030	Lehman, Deborah	MN0350
Kellert, Aaron	OK1100	Kromm, Nancy Wait	CA4425	Lehmann, Jay	CA2450
Kelley, Danny R.	TX2100	Kroth, Michael	MI1400	Lehtinen, Jennifer	NY3000
Kelly, James J.	NJ0750	Krueger, Conrad	TX2260	Leibowitz, Ellen	NJ1130
Kelly, Michael F.	NY1850	Krueger, Rob W.	IL0750	Lemelin, Stephane	AG0400
Kelly-McHale, Jacqueline	IL0750	Krumbholz, Gerald A.	WA0950	Lemieux, Vivian	ME0250
Kendall, Christopher	MI2100	Krupansky, Sharla	KY1540	Lemmons, Keith M.	NM0450
Kenney, James	CA3375	Krusemark, Ruth E.	KS0100	Lentini, James P.	OH1450
Kennison, Kendall	MD0400	Krusemark, William	KS1375	Lenz, Andrea	NV0100
Kenny, William	PA0350	Krusemark, William	KS1375	Leonard, Sara R.	MA0100
Kenyon, Paul	CA3640	Krystofiak, Paul	TX3450	Leousis, Kim	AL1195
Kephart, Donald B.	PA1350	Kugler, Roger T.	KS1000	Lepage, Peter	NY0900
Khaleel, Tasneem	MT0175	Kuhlman, Kristyn	NY3350	Lester, Joel	NY2250
Kibelsbeck, Erik	NY1800	Kuhlman, Kristyn	NY3350	Levine, Dena	NJ1160
Kiec, Michelle	PA1750	Kuhlman, Kristyn	NY3350	Levine, Iris S.	CA0630
Kiec, Michelle	PA1750	Kuhns, Diana L.	PA2675	Lewis, Diane	CA2440
Kies, Diana	MI1000	Kunin, Ben	CA0050	Lewis, George E.	NY0750
Kilgore Wood, Janice	MD1050	Kurth, Richard	AB0100	Lewis, Joseph S.	CA5020
Killian, George W.	IN0700	Kuuskoski, Jonathan	MO1800	Lewis, Kathryn	MS0420
Kilpatrick, Barry M.	NY3725	Kuykendall, James Brooks	SC0700	Lewis, Lynda	KS0050
Kilpatrick, Barry M.	NY3725	Kvam, Robert A.	IN0150	Lewis, Steven D.	MO1710
Kilpinen, Jonathan	IN1750	L'Hommedieu, Randi L.	MI0400	Lewis-Hammond, Susan	AB0150
Kim, Chris Younghoon	NY0900	LaBar, Arthur T.	TN1450	Lewiston, Cal	TX3700
Kim, Gloria	OH1700	LaBar, Arthur T.	TN1450	Lias, Stephen J.	TX2700
Kim, Jong H.	VA0750	Labe, Paul E.	MD0475	Liberatore, Patti	OH1450
Kim, Michael I.	AC0050	Lach, Peter	WV0300	Libin, Kathryn L.	NY4450
Kim, Min	NJ0825	LaCosse, Steven R.	NC1650	Lieberman, Fredric	CA5070
Kim, Paul S.	NY2105	LaCosse, Steven R.	NC1650	Ligate, Linda	MO0400
Kimball, Kay	ME0430	Laderach, Linda C.	MA1350	Lill, Joseph	IL2100
King, Anita	OR1300	Laderman, Michael	NY3100	Lindblom, Michelle	ND0050
King, Anita	OR1300	LaFave, Alan	SD0400	Lindeman, Timothy H.	NC0910
King, Ben R.	NY1700	Laflamme, Christiane	AI0200	Linder, J. Michael	TX1775
King, Dennis W.	WI0150	Laimon, Sara	AI0150	Lindsey, Lauren	WV0050
Kinney, Michael	NY0350	Laird, Tracey	GA0050	Link, Anne-Marie	AA0110
Kinzer, Charles E.	VA0700	Lamar, Linda Kline	ID0050	Linklater, Joan	AC0100
Kinzer, Charles E.	VA0700	Lamb, Bill	KS0570	Lippens, Nancy Cobb	IN0800
Kirby, David S.	NC1900	Lamb, Earnest	NC0800	Lippert-Coleman, Mary J.	PA3150
Kirby, Wayne J.	NC2400	Lamb, Krista	PA2250	Lippoldt-Mack, Valerie	KS0210
Kirk, Jeff	TN0100	Lamb, Robert E.	FL0150	Lipscomb, Scott D.	MN1623
Kirk, Ned	MN1400	Lambert, Debra	CA3270	Lipscomb, Scott D.	MN1623
Kirk-Doyle, Julianne	NY3780	Lambert, Debra	CA3270	Lipton, Jeffrey S.	NY1275
Kirkdorffer, Michele B.	VA0600	Lambert, Debra	CA3270	Lipton, Jeffrey S.	NY1275
Kirkpatrick, Gary	NJ1400	Lambert, James	OK0150	Lister-Sink, Barbara	NC2205
Kirkwood, Judy	IN1560	Lamkin, Lynn B.	TX3400	Lites, Wesley	KY1460
Kissick, John	AG0350	Landes, Heather	AZ0100	Litke, Sheila	KS1300
Kjellman, Judith	WA1400	Landgren, Peter	OH2200	Little, Donald C.	TX3420
Klassen, Carolyn	KS0440	Langer, Kenneth P.	MA1500	Liva, Victor H.	OH0650
Klassen, Carolyn	KS0440	Langham, Patrick	CA5350	Livingston, Jane	WI0250
Klefstad, Terry	TN0100	Langley, Angie D.	MS0570	Livingston-Friedley, Diana	ID0100
Klein, Joseph	TX3420	Langley, Jeff	CA4700	Lochhead, Judith	NY3790
Klein, Nancy K.	VA1000	Langsford, Christopher M.	KS0750	Lochstampfor, Mark L.	OH0350
Klein, Rochelle Z.	PA2900	Lanier, Marta	SC0750	Locke, Brian	IL3500

945

Name	Code	Name	Code	Name	Code
Locke, John R.	NC2430	Marsh, Peter K.	CA0807	McWayne, Dorli	AK0150
Locke, Mamie	VA0500	Marta, Larry W.	TX3370	McWilliams, Robert	WI0830
Lockert, Robin	AG0300	Martin, Blair	KS1250	Mead, Sarah	MA0500
Lockwood, Susan	AL0335	Martin, Curtis E.	GA1600	Meaders, James M.	MS0400
Loewy, Andrea Kapell	LA0760	Martin, Deborah	NY1800	Meadows, Anthony	PA1550
Loft, Jan	MN1500	Martin, James	IA0400	Meadows, Melody	WV0800
Lohr, Tom L.	NC1300	Martin, Jennifer	CA1510	Mecham, Mark L.	PA1900
Loken, Kent	MN0600	Martin, Joey	TX3175	Meckler, David C.	CA0855
Long, Bill	SC0900	Martin, Laura	GA0050	Meckley, William A.	NY3600
Long, Bill	AR0100	Martin, Robert	NY0150	Meeks, Joseph D.	GA1150
Long, Derle R.	LA0770	Martin, Valerie G.	PA3150	Megginson, Julie	GA1000
Long, Patrick A.	PA3150	Martinez, Javier	TX3515	Megginson, Julie	GA1000
Longshore, Terry	OR0950	Martinez, Pedro	TX3525	Meggison, Shelly	AL1170
Loos, James C.	IA0420	Marvin, Clara	AG0250	Meggison, Shelly	AL1170
Lopez, Susan Miltner	CA5300	Marvuglio, Matt	MA0260	Meissner, Marla	NJ0800
Lott, R. Allen	TX2600	Marzolf, Dennis	MN0200	Melton, James L.	CA5355
Lott, R. Allen	TX2600	Masciadri, Milton	GA2100	Melton, James L.	CA5355
Loubriel, Luis E.	IL0275	Masciadri, Milton	GA2100	Meltzer, Howard S.	NY0270
Loucks, John	KS1110	Mason, Colin M.	TX2800	Menchaca, Louis A.	WI0300
Lowe, Curt	IA0050	Mason, Daniel	KY1450	Mendez, Celestino 'Tino'	NM0150
Lowe, Curt	IA0050	Mason, Freddy	TX2000	Menghini, Charles T.	IL3450
Lowe, Phillip	TX0910	Masserini, John	AZ0450	Mennicke, David	MN0610
Lowe, Phillip	TX0910	Massey, Heather	OH0350	Menoche, Charles Paul	CT0050
Lowry, Douglas	NY1100	Massey, Heather	OH0350	Mercer-Taylor, Peter	MN1623
Lubaroff, Scott C.	MO1790	Mastandrea, Eva	MT0450	Mercier, Richard E.	GA0950
Lublin, Robert	MA2010	Masterson, Daniel J.	KS0150	Meredith, Steven	UT0190
Luby, Paul	FL1700	Matachek, John	MN0800	Meredith, Victoria	AG0500
Luby, Richard E.	NC2410	Mathews, Christopher W.	TN1660	Merrill, Dale A.	CA0960
Lucas, Teri	NY2660	Mathews, Jeffrey	LA0550	Merrill, Thomas G.	OH2550
Lucia, Margaret E.	PA3050	Mathews, Paul	MD0650	Merryman, Marjorie	NY2150
Lucius, Sue Anne	AZ0440	Mathieson, Maria	DC0170	Mertz, Amy	NY4150
Lucke, Paul	TX1450	Matson, Krik	CT0600	Mertz, Amy	NY4150
Lucky, Harrell C.	TX0700	Matsushita, Hidemi	CO0100	Mery, John Christian	OR0800
Ludwig, Mark	OH0755	Matthews, Ron	PA1150	Messere, Fritz J.	NY3770
Lueger, Robert	NE0160	Mattingly, Bruce	NY3720	Messmer, Cathy	NJ0300
Lum, Anne Craig	HI0150	Mattingly, Stephen P.	KY1500	Messoloras, Irene	OK0600
Lumpkin, Royce E.	NC2420	Mattys, Joe	VA1150	Metts, Amanda H.	NC0100
Lumpp, David	MN0610	Matych-Hager, Susan	MI1950	Metz, Paul W.	CO0250
Lust, Patricia D.	VA0700	Maus, Fred Everett	VA1550	Meyer, Donald C.	IL1400
Luther, David	TN0200	May, Lissa F.	IN0900	Meyer, Elizabeth C.	MI1450
Ly, Vi	CA1700	May, William V.	TX0300	Meyer, Eric	WI1150
Lyerla, Trilla R.	KS0050	Maye, Shelia J.	VA0500	Meyer, Frederick	WV0650
Lynn, Michael	OH1700	Mayfield, Connie E.	CA0859	Meyer, John E.	MN1030
Mabrey, Charlotte	FL1950	Mayo, Susanna	OH0350	Meyer, Stephen C.	NY4100
Mabry, Danajean	NC2370	Mayo, Susanna	OH0350	Mezei, Margaret	AA0200
Macan, Ed	CA1280	Mayrose, John S.	IN0910	Miceli, Jennifer Scott	NY2105
MacAulay, Suzanne	CO0810	McAllister, Michael	NC1750	Middleton, Jaynne	TX0900
MacDonald, Don	AB0070	McAllister, Peter A.	AZ0500	Middleton, Jonathan N.	WA0250
Machado, John	CA0950	McAllister, Robert C.	CA1075	Mihalyo, Michael	NC0250
Machado, Rene E.	IL2250	McAllister, Robert C.	CA1075	Miles, Michael A.	MS0750
Machell, Iain	NY4300	McAlpine, Tim	KY0860	Miller, Al	AL1195
MacIntyre, Bruce C.	NY0500	McBee, Karen L.	TX0125	Miller, Al	AL1195
MacIntyre, David K.	AB0080	McCabe, Melissa	MD0850	Miller, Ann Elizabeth	CA5350
MacKay, Gillian	AG0450	McCachren, Renee	NC0350	Miller, Dan	IN1800
MacKay, Gillian	AG0450	McCallister, Ron	TN1650	Miller, Gabriel	LA0150
MacKenzie, Louis	IN1700	McCargar, Barbara Witham	MI0300	Miller, Jo Ann	ND0350
Mackey, Steven	NJ0900	McClain, Sandra	FL0650	Miller, John	ND0350
Mackidon, Michon	NV0150	McClellan, Teresa	TN0600	Miller, Mark	CO0560
MacMullen, Michael J.	FL1470	McCloskey, Kathleen	PA0650	Miller, Michael	WA0980
Macomber, Jeffrey R.	MO0800	McConnell, Douglas W.	OH0950	Miller, Michelle	OH2290
Macon, Connie	AL0800	McConnell, Patrick	NC0100	Miller, Paul W.	PA2740
Madison-Cannon, Sabrina	MO1810	McCormick, Robert	MI0500	Miller, Roland G.	IL0650
Madison-Cannon, Sabrina	MO1810	McCowen, Heather	IL0550	Miller, Sharon	VA0300
Madsen, Nathan	NY0150	McCowen, Heather	IL0550	Miller, Stephen R.	TN1800
Magee, Robert G.	AR0950	McCoy, D. Mark	IN0350	Miller, Thomas E.	CA5400
Mager, Guillermo E.	CT0700	McCracken, H. Jac	LA0300	Miller, W Scott	FL0200
Maginnis, Hayden	AG0200	McCreary, Teresa J.	HI0110	Miller-Thorn, Jill	NY1275
Maguet, Kathryn L.	PA0350	McCullough, David M.	AL1250	Millican, Brady	MA0800
Mainland, Timothy L.	WV0200	McCurley, Steven	OK0500	Millican, Jason	TX1250
Mains, Ronda	AR0700	McCusker, IHM, Joan	PA2200	Milne, David	WI0845
Maline, Sarah R.	ME0410	McCutchen, Thomas	AL0500	Mims, Lloyd	FL1450
Mallett, Lawrence R.	OK1350	McDonald, Reginald	TN1400	Mims, Lloyd	FL1450
Malley, Nicole	IL1350	Mcelwain, Hugh	IL0780	Mincocchi, Joseph	OH2150
Mallinson, Jeff	WA0980	McFarland, Thomas J.	KY1400	Mincocchi, Joseph	OH2150
Maloney, Donna J.	OH1200	McGee, Gerald	MD0360	Mincocchi, Joseph	OH2150
Maloney-Titland, Patricia	NY3400	McGee, Isaiah R.	SC0350	Minix, Dean	TX2750
Mamey, Norman	CA1000	McGhee, Michael	GA2200	Minnis, MaryBeth	MI0400
Mamey, Norman	CA1000	McGilvray, Byron	TX3360	Mirabal, Lianell	PR0150
Mamey, Norman	CA1000	McGinn, Jeanne	PA0850	Misenhelter, Dale D.	AR0700
Mamey, Norman	CA1000	McGrann, Jeremiah	MA0330	Miskell, Jerome P.	OH2290
Mamiya, Christin J.	NE0600	McGregor, Jane Butler	AB0210	Mitchell, Brenda	OH1450
Mammon, Marielaine	NJ0250	McGregor, Michele	PA0550	Mitchell, Michael A.	MI1750
Mandle, William Dee	DC0350	McGuigan-Sadoff, Kathleen	NY1200	Mitro, Patricia	MA0400
Manley, Douglas H.	TN1550	McIlhagga, Samuel D.	MI0100	Mitro, Patricia	MA0400
Mann, Bruce	VA0975	McIntire, Dennis K.	GA1700	Miyakawa, Felicia M.	TN1100
Mann, Linda	CA2100	McIntosh, W. Legare	AL0500	Mizener, Charlotte P.	TX1400
Manning, Dwight C.	NY4200	McIntyre, John	IN1400	Moad, JoBeth	OK0750
Manternach, LaDonna	IA0250	McKay, William	WA0150	Moad, JoBeth	OK0750
Manzo, Erica	MO1800	McKinney, Jane Grant	NC0900	Modesitt, Carol Ann	UT0200
Mao, Ruixuan	IL0840	McLaughlin, Dan	IL1600	Moe, Eric H.	PA3420
Marcades, Michael	AL0900	McLeod, Lindy	AL1000	Moe, Gordon	MN0600
Marcel, Linda A.	NJ0020	McMahon, Dorothy	AG0550	Moffat, Bennet T.	HI0300
Marchant, Susan J.	KS1050	McManus, Edward	OR0350	Moffett, Brad	TN0850
Marder, Barbara	MD0060	McMillan, William	TX3520	Mohr, Deanne	MN1700
Mardirosian, Haig L.	FL2050	McMullen, Dianne M.	NY4310	Molina, Moises	IL3500
Marissen, Michael	PA3200	McPhail, Mark L.	WI0865	Molina, Moises	IL3500
Markward, Cheri	RI0102	McQuade, Amy	OK0750	Molina, Rocio	TX3515
Markward, Cheri D.	RI0101	McRoberts, Terry	TN1660	Momand, Elizabeth B.	AR0730
Marrs, Rick R.	CA3600	McTyre, Robert A.	GA1400	Monek, Daniel G.	OH1400
Marschner, Joseph A.	MD0450	McTyre, Robert A.	GA1400	Monroe, Murphy	IL0720

Name	Code	Name	Code	Name	Code
Monson, Dale E.	GA2100	Nicosia, Gloria	NY2050	Parsons, Laura E.	AL0950
Monson, Linda Apple	VA0450	Nierman, Glenn E.	NE0600	Parsons, Stephen	IL1150
Montgomery, Kip	NY3250	Nix, Brad K.	KS1250	Partain, Gregory L.	KY1350
Montgomery, Toni-Marie	IL2250	Nix, Brad K.	KS1250	Partin, Bruce	VA1250
Moody, Kevin M.	TX0075	Nolte, Jeffrey L.	OH1110	Parton-Stanard, Susan	IL1500
Moore, Brett	NY1150	Nolte, John P.	MN1030	Parton-Stanard, Susan	IL1500
Moore, D. Scott	MN0750	Noon, Rosemary	MA1600	Parton-Stanard, Susan	IL1500
Moore, Daniel	IA1550	Noone, Michael J.	MA0330	Pashkin, Elissa Brill	MA1100
Moore, Daniel	IA1550	Noonkester, Lila D.	SC0800	Pastor, Elizabeth M.	OH0100
Moore, Daryl	CA0850	Nordeen, Mark	WY0060	Patnoe, Lyneen	WA0030
Moore, Grant W.	PA1250	Nordman, Robert W.	MO1830	Patton, Larry	KS0210
Moore, Grant W.	PA1250	Norris, Elizabeth	VT0300	Patton, Patrick	WY0050
Moore, Gregg	CA2250	Norris, Joshua L.	KS0900	Patykula, John	VA1600
Moore, J. Steven	MO1790	Novak, Christina D.	AZ0490	Paul, John F.	OR0500
Moore, Jacques R.	ME0250	Novak, Tom	MA1400	Paul, Phyllis M.	OR1050
Moore, Jeffrey M.	FL1800	Nowack, James	WI1155	Paul, Phyllis M.	OR1050
Moore, John	TX2200	Nunes, Dennis	MN1300	Paul, Randall S.	OH2500
Morgan, Angela L.	GA0250	Nunes, Dennis	MN1300	Paulnack, Karl	MA0350
Morgan, Charles	IL1250	Nyberg, Gary B.	WA0480	Paver, Jonathan	IL3200
Morgan, Charles	IL1250	Nyline, Fred	IA0950	Pavlovsky, Taras	NJ0175
Morgan, Lauren	AL1200	O'Bourke, Rosemarie	FL0900	Pawek, Peggy	CA2910
Morgan, Paula	SC0650	O'Brien, Eugene	IN0900	Pawlyshyn, Nancy	CA1760
Morin, Jeff	WI0850	O'Connor, Charles 'Chuck'	NE0600	Paxton, Laurence	HI0210
Morin, Jeff	WI0850	O'Connor, Susan	NJ0175	Paxton, Steven E.	NM0425
Morin, Joseph C.	MD1000	O'Dell, James	MA0350	Payne, Carol W.	GA0500
Morris, Mellasenah Y.	MD0650	O'Donnell, Jennifer M.	CT0246	Payne, Thomas B.	VA0250
Morris, Mellasenah Y.	MD0650	O'Hara, Michael	IN0150	Payne, Tony L.	IL3550
Morris, Valerie Bonita	SC0500	O'Leary, Shelley	AC0100	Peach, Christi	IN1600
Morrison, Charles D.	AG0600	O'Mealey, Ryan	IL2250	Pearce, Jared	IA1950
Morrison, Nicholas	UT0300	O'Neill, Patrick	AI0150	Pearson, Glen	CA1100
Morrison-Shetlar, Alison	NC0750	Oakley, Paul E.	KY0800	Pecherek, Michael J.	IL1175
Mortenson, Gary	KS0650	Oberlander, Lisa M.	GA0550	Peebles, William L.	NC2600
Morton, Wyatt	CA0550	Odom, Donald R.	MS0850	Peffer, Tony	VT0100
Mortyakova, Julia V.	MS0550	Odom, Gale J.	LA0050	Pelkey, Stanley C.	NY3350
Moses, Kenneth J.	FL1900	Olan, David	NY0600	Pellegrini, David	CT0150
Moses, Kenneth J.	FL1900	Olin, Elinor	IL2000	Pelto, William L.	NC0050
Moskowitz, David V.	SD0600	Oliphant, Naomi J.	KY1500	Pelusi, Mario J.	IL1200
Moss, Emily A.	NY0500	Oliver, Sylvester	MS0600	Pence, Suzanne M.	TX3510
Mosteller, Paul W.	AL1150	Ollen, Joy	AB0050	Peppo, Bret	CA1560
Moulin, Jane	HI0210	Olthafer, Rebecca	IL2100	Perconti, William J.	ID0130
Mount, Lorna	HI0120	Ongaro, Giulio M.	CA5350	Perdicaris, Stephen	CA5350
Moylan, James	MA1175	Onofrio, Marshall	NJ1350	Perdue, Greg	NE0610
Muehlenbeck Pfotenhauer, Thomas R.	MN1600	Oquin, Wayne	NY1900	Perkins, Boyd	SD0400
Mueller, Madeline N.	CA1020	Ordaz, Joseph	CA2975	Perkins, Tedrow	OH2600
Mueller, Martin	NY2660	Organ, Wayne	CA1450	Perrin, Ralph W.	CA4550
Muir, Harry	WI0960	Orihuela, Ruthanne	CO0300	Perrin, Ralph W.	CA4550
Mulford, Ruth Stomne	DE0175	Orlando, John	CA0400	Perry, James	WI0806
Muller, Gerald	TX2170	Orovich, Nicholas	NH0350	Perry, Kris	OH2140
Mullis, Julie	NC2640	Orr, Clifton	AR0810	Perry, Steven	NJ0950
Mulvihill, Mary	NY3500	Orr, Gerald	TX1250	Perry, Timothy B.	NY3705
Munro, Chris	AG0130	Ortner, Richard	MA0350	Pertl, Brian G.	WI0350
Murdoch, Colin	CA4150	Orzolek, Douglas	MN1625	Pesavento, Gayle	IL1240
Murphy, Barbara A.	TN1710	Osborn, Clifton	AL0350	Pesce, Dolores	MO1900
Murphy, Geraldine	NY0550	Ostman, Jessica	MN1300	Peterbark, Frederick	CO0800
Murphy, Joseph M.	PA2150	Oswald, Lisa	WV0550	Peterbark, Frederick	CO0800
Murphy, Vanissa B.	WI0803	Otal, Monica D.	MD0175	Peters, G. David	IN0907
Murray, Bruce J.	OH1450	Ott, Daniel P.	NY1900	Peters, Mark	IL3100
Murray, Jane	RI0300	Otwell, Margaret V.	WI0500	Petersen, Carol	IL0420
Murray, Monica	MN0610	Ouzomgi, Samir	PA2700	Peterson, Don L.	UT0050
Murray, Nicole	MO2000	Ovens, Douglas P.	PA2550	Peterson, Douglas A.	FL0400
Murray, Russell E.	DE0150	Owen, John Edward	AR0110	Peterson, Jay	IL1650
Musgrave, Michael	NY1900	Owen, William E.	WA0550	Pethel, Stan	GA0300
Musial, Michael A.	NY3450	Owens, Douglas T.	VA1000	Pfau, Tracy	WY0050
Myers, David E.	MN1623	Oye, Deanna	AA0200	Philipsen, Michael D.	IA0750
Myers, Gerald C.	MO1120	Oyen, David W.	KY0900	Phillips, Kenneth	FL1450
Nabors, Larry J.	MS0570	Ozeas, Natalie	PA0550	Phillips, Mark W.	VA1750
Nabors, Larry J.	MS0570	Padilla, Clarence S.	IA0550	Phillips, Moses	NY0640
Nagel, Rebecca S.	SC1110	Pagal, Alena M.	SC1110	Philp, Brenda	AA0020
Nagelbach, Emily	AB0210	Page, Fran M.	NC1300	Philpott, Craig	CA3400
Nakamae, Ayumi	NC0450	Page, Robert S.	TX1600	Phipps, Danny K.	MI0900
Napolitano, Daniel	NY0100	Paige, Diane M.	NY1400	Phipps, Graham H.	TX3420
Narvey, Lois	DC0170	Paige, Diane M.	NY1400	Pickeral, Charles W.	FL1850
Natvig, Mary	OH0300	Paige, Diane M.	NY1400	Pilsner, Joseph	TX3450
Navari, Jude Joseph	CA4625	Painter, Noel	FL1750	Pinard, Mary	MA0255
Neal, David E.	NY3720	Palmer, Douglas B.	OH2370	Pinder, Kymberly	NM0450
Nealon, Michael A.	MI1200	Palmier, Darice	IL2970	Pinkston, Dan	CA4600
Neeley, Henrietta	IL1085	Panken, Aaron D.	NY1450	Pirtle, R. Leigh	IA1390
Negrete, Merida	NC2410	Pannell, Larry J.	LA0100	Placenti, Phillip	CA5300
Neill, Kelly	AR0250	Panneton, Isabelle	AI0200	Placenti, Phillip	CA5300
Nelson, Drew	TX0075	Pape, Louis W.	SD0150	Planer, John H.	IN1050
Nelson, Eric	GA0750	Papillon, Andre	AI0190	Plate, Stephen W.	TN0850
Nelson, Jon C.	TX3420	Papini, Dennis	SD0550	Plew, Paul T.	CA2810
Nelson, Lisa	IL1200	Parakilas, James P.	ME0150	Plies, Dennis B.	OR1150
Nelson, Lisa	IL1200	Parasher, Prajna Paramita	PA0600	Plugge, Scott D.	TX2250
Nelson, Mark	AZ0480	Pardue, Jane	NC1400	Pohly, Linda L.	IN0150
Nestler, Eric M.	TX3420	Parker, Alex	TX0300	Poklewski, Annamarie	CA1550
Nettles, Darryl	TN1400	Parker, Bradley	SC0700	Polay, Bruce	IL1350
Neufeld, Donald E.	CA0250	Parker, Don	NC0800	Polisi, Joseph W.	NY1900
Neuman, Daniel M.	CA5031	Parker, Grant	CA1500	Polman, Bert	MI0350
Newlin, Yvonne	IL1612	Parker, Gregory B.	NC0400	Pond, Steven	NY0900
Newlin, Yvonne	IL1612	Parker, Mara	PA3680	Ponto, Robert	OR1050
Newman, Diane M.	NY0500	Parker, Mara	PA3680	Ponto, Robert	OR1050
Newman, Timothy	NJ1400	Parker, Mark Edward	OK0750	Poole, Eric	NC2150
Newsom, Mary Ellen	IN0005	Parker, Robin Lee	FL1700	Poole, Mary Ellen	CA4150
Newton, Jean	NY5000	Parks, Richard S.	AG0500	Poovey, Gena E.	SC0850
Nice, Julie	LA0560	Parks, Sarah S.	WI0750	Popoff-Parks, Linette A.	MI1260
Nicholls, Barbara	KY0200	Parr, Carlotta	CT0050	Porter, Beth Cram	OH0450
Nichols, Eliza	IL0720	Parr, Carlotta	CT0050	Porter, Charles	NY2700
Nicholson, Marie	NC1250	Parrish, Eric	MN1175	Porter, Lewis R.	NJ1140
Nicolas, Ashton	MD0400	Parsons, Jennifer R.	WV0400	Porter, Thomas	ND0400

Alphabetical Listing of Administrators

Name	Code	Name	Code	Name	Code
Post, J. Brian	CA2250	Richards, Eric J.	NE0400	Rushing, Randal J.	TN1680
Potes, Cesar I.	MI1200	Richards, Gwyn	IN0900	Russakovsky, Alexander	MS0750
Potter, Howard	NY1100	Richards, James	MO1830	Russell, Joan	AI0100
Potts, Christina	TX2310	Richards, Rebekah	MN0750	Russell, Melinda	MN0300
Powe, Holly	AL0330	Richardson, Dennis	TX0550	Russell, Richard	NY2250
Powell, Alex	MA1175	Richardson, Robert C.	WA0450	Russell, Teresa P.	CA4850
Powell, Philip M.	SC0420	Richmond, John W.	NE0600	Rust, Douglas	MS0750
Power, Brian E.	AG0050	Richter, Glenn	TX3510	Ruth, David E.	PA2700
Power, David	UT0250	Richter, Robert	CT0100	Rutherford, Eric D.	KS0560
Price, Harry E.	GA1150	Richter, Sara Jane	OK0770	Ryczek, Karyl	MA1175
Price, Jerrod J.	CO0900	Ries, Kristi D.	PA0550	Rytting, Bryce	UT0325
Price, Marjorie	CA3375	Rieth, Dale	FL0950	Sabina, Leslie M.	NY3475
Prichard, Sheila Grace	MA1600	Rieth, Dale	FL0950	Sachdev, Salil	MA0510
Prichard, Sheila Grace	MA1600	Rife, Jerry E.	NJ1000	Sachs, Stephen W.	MS0100
Priest, Thomas L.	UT0350	Riley, Raymond G.	MI0150	Sachs, Stephen W.	MS0100
Priester, Thomas	NY2500	Rincon, Alicia	CA4000	Sadlek, Lance	IA1300
Priester, Thomas	NY2500	Rindfleisch, Andrew P.	OH0650	Sagen, Dwayne P.	TN1850
Prouten, William	AA0032	Rinehart, John	OH0050	Sagen, Dwayne P.	TN1850
Provencio, Robert	CA0650	Ringle, Stephanie Kohl	IL1200	Sagen, Dwayne P.	TN1850
Pruzin, Robert S.	SC1110	Rings, Steven M.	IL3250	Sajnovsky, Cynthia B.	GU0500
Pruzin, Robert S.	SC1110	Rinn, Susan	TX3100	Sale, Craig	IL0730
Psurny, Robert D.	MT0075	Riordan, George T.	TN1100	Salerno, John	WI0808
Puchala, Mark	MI1650	Rischar, Richard A.	MI2110	Sallis, Friedemann	AA0150
Puckette, Miller	CA5050	Ritt, Morey	NY0642	Salyer, Douglas W.	CT0200
Puri, Michael James	VA1550	Rivard, Gene	MN0625	Samiian, Vida	CA0810
Purinton, Teresa	MO0060	Rivera, Francesca M.	CA5353	Sampson, Christopher	CA5300
Purslow, Vicki T.	OR0950	Robbins, David P.	WA0650	Samuelson, Linda	MN1270
Purvis, Ralph E.	AL0400	Robbins, Kelly	WA1400	Sanchez de Fuentes, Luisa	FL1125
Puschendorf, Gunther F.	CA1100	Roberson, Matt	AL0345	Sanchez, George	NY0644
Quantz, Don E.	AA0010	Roberts, Randall	KY0300	Sanchez, Matilde	CA3375
Quebbeman, Robert C.	MO0775	Roberts, Stanley L.	GA1300	Sander, Kurt L.	KY1000
Queen, Kristen	TX3000	Robertson, Jon	FL1125	Sanders, Reginald L.	OH1200
Queen, Todd	CO0250	Robertson, Kaestner	MA0250	Sandler, Karen W.	PA2700
Quinlan, Gloria H.	TX1150	Robins, Linda	TX2570	Sands, Rosita M.	IL0720
Rabinau, Kevin	MI1160	Robinson, Michael L.	NC1250	Sandvick, Jerry	MN1260
Raby, Lee Worley	CA2801	Robinson, Nathalie G.	NY1600	Sano, Stephen M.	CA4900
Race, Kathy	AA0150	Robinson, Nathalie G.	NY1600	Santana-Santana, Melanie	PR0115
Racine, Melody Lynn	MI2100	Robinson-Oturu, Gail M.	TN0050	Santo, Joseph A.	DC0050
Racine, Melody Lynn	MI2100	Rocco, Emma S.	PA2713	Santo, Joseph A.	DC0050
Ragsdale, Chalon L.	AR0700	Rochfort, Desmond	AA0200	Santore, Jonathan C.	NH0250
Raisor, Steve C.	NC0500	Rockmaker, Jody D.	AZ0100	Sass, Christopher	GA2300
Raley, Lynn	MS0385	Roden, Timothy J.	OH2000	Satchell, Ernest R.	MD1020
Ralston, Pamela	CA1510	Rodgers, Heather H.	MI0350	Satterlee, Robert S.	OH0300
Ramey, Maxine	MT0400	Rodman, Ronald	MN0300	Sattler, Nancy J.	OH2140
Ramirez, Abel	TX0550	Rodriguez, Elvin	CA2420	Saulter, Gerry	NY1275
Ramos Escobar, Jose Luis	PR0150	Rogers, Donald M.	SC1200	Saulter, Gerry	NY1275
Rampersad, David	AL0345	Rogers, Donald M.	SC1200	Saunders, T. Clark	CT0650
Rand, Catherine	MS0750	Roggenstein, Gary	CA0200	Saunders, T. Clark	CT0650
Ransom, Judy L.	WY0115	Rohwer, Debbie A.	TX3420	Sawyer, Eric	MA0100
Rapp, Willis M.	PA1750	Rolf, Marie	NY1100	Saxon, Kenneth N.	TX3515
Rasmussen, G. Rosalie	CA3400	Rolf, Marie	NY1100	Scandrett, John F.	PA1600
Rath, Edward	IL3300	Roller, Peter	WI0050	Scearce, J. Mark	NC1700
Rath, Edward	IL3300	Rollin, Robert	OH2600	Scelba, Anthony	NJ0700
Rauscher, James	TX0100	Rolnick, Neil B.	NY3300	Scelba, Anthony	NJ0700
Ravel, David	WI0050	Romanek, Mary L.	PA2720	Schaberg, David	CA5032
Rawls, J. Archie	MS0580	Romeo, James	CA4050	Scharfenberger, Paul E.	NH0110
Ray Westlund, Beth	IA0950	Root, Timothy	FL0550	Scharper, Alice	CA4410
Ray, Mary Ruth	MA0500	Rosado-Nazario, Samuel	PR0100	Schattschneider, Adam	OH0250
Ray, W. Irwin	GA1550	Rose, Douglas	TN0050	Schaub, Owen	IN0250
Rayl, David C.	MI1400	Rose, Francois	CA5350	Scheib, Curt A.	PA3000
Rayl, David C.	MI1400	Rose, Kathleen	CA2150	Scheib, John W.	IN0150
Read, Kenneth E.	OH0550	Rose, Melissa K.	TN1850	Schell, Mark	KY0100
Reale, Steven	OH2600	Rose, Melissa K.	TN1850	Schiavo, Joseph C.	NJ1100
Rebbeck, Lyle	AA0040	Rose, Melissa K.	TN1850	Schiavo, Joseph C.	NJ1100
Reckzin, Lance	AG0130	Rose, William G.	LA0350	Schilling, Kevin	IA0850
Reddick, Don	IL2300	Roseberry, Lynn	OH0350	Schimpf, Peter	CO0550
Redman, Paul	IL3300	Roseborough, Barbara	TN1380	Schindler, Karl W.	AZ0470
Reed, Dennis J.	CA2750	Roselli, Kathryn	NJ0700	Schirmer, Timothy	IL2350
Reed, Jerome A.	TN0930	Rosen, Marcy	NY0642	Schissel, Wendy	OR0550
Reed, Joel F.	NC1250	Rosenberg, Steven E.	SC0500	Schlabaugh, Karen Bauman	KS0200
Reed, Joel F.	NC1250	Rosenblum, Henry	NY1860	Schleppenbach, Barbara	IL2450
Reed, Marc A.	CO0350	Rosenboom, David	CA0510	Schlesinger, Scott L.	NC2525
Reed, Teresa Shelton	OK1450	Rosenfeld, Andrew	MD0610	Schleuse, Paul	NY3705
Reed, Thomas T.	OH0100	Ross, David	TX3520	Schloneger, Matthew	KS0500
Rees, Fred J.	IN0907	Ross, Jared	KS0060	Schmelz, Peter	MO1900
Rees, Helen	CA5031	Ross, Nicholas Piers	VA1400	Schmidt, Alan G.	NY1220
Reese, Marc B.	FL1125	Rossi, Jamal J.	NY1100	Schmidt, Jack W.	PA0900
Reeves, Daniel	AR0110	Roter, Bruce	NY0700	Schmidt, Jack W.	PA0900
Reeves, Patricia	TN1400	Rothkopf, Michael S.	NC1650	Schmidt, Myron	MA0750
Regan, Patrick	MI1300	Rothkopf, Michael S.	NC1650	Schmidt, Myron	MA0750
Rehding, Alexander	MA1050	Rothlisberger, Dana	MD0850	Schmitt, Georgia	NY2250
Reid, Sally	TN0930	Rothstein, William	NY0642	Schmitz, Alan W.	IA1600
Reid, Susanne M.	CA5355	Rothstein, William	NY0642	Schnauber, Thomas	MA0900
Reimer, Mark U.	VA0150	Roush, Clark	NE0720	Schnauber, Thomas	MA0900
Reise, Jay	PA3350	Rovkah, Pauline	PA0600	Schneider, M. Christine	IA0550
Reiser-Memmer, Michelle	NY1350	Rowe, Robert	NY2750	Schneller, Pamela	TN1850
Reister, John	IN0650	Rowlands, Judith	NJ0060	Schneller, Pamela	TN1850
Reiter, Lois	TX2800	Royal, Guericke	DC0150	Schneller, Pamela	TN1850
Renfroe, Dennis C.	NC1025	Royer, Randall D.	SD0100	Schnepf, Chester	CT0200
Restesan, Francise T.	PR0125	Royse, Dennis	CA0250	Schoenberg, Lisa	PA0675
Reynolds, David	SD0550	Ruben, Bruce	NY1450	Schoening, Benjamin S.	WI0801
Reynolds, Tom	VA0450	Ruckman, Robert	OH2120	Schorr, Timothy B.	WI1100
Reynolds, William D.	MI1050	Rudari, David J.	WV0100	Schraer-Joiner, Lyn	NJ0700
Reynolds, Winton	TX3510	Rudari, David J.	WV0100	Schreiner, Frederick	PA3710
Rhodes, Ruth	IL3450	Rumbolz, Robert C.	WY0130	Schreiner, Frederick	PA3710
Ricci-Rogel, Susan	MD0700	Rumsey, Esther	TX2710	Schreuder, Joel T.	NE0050
Rice, Eric N.	CT0600	Runge, Alan	TX0400	Schubert, David T.	OH2450
Rice, Susan	WI0100	Ruocco, Phyllis	AR0550	Schulenberg, David L.	NY4500
Richard, Charles	CA3800	Rupp, Martin	WI0817	Schultz, Jim	MT0100
Richards, E. Michael	MD1000	Rupprecht, Philip	NC0600	Schultz, Roger	VA0650

Name	Code	Name	Code	Name	Code
Schultz, Russ A.	TX1400	Simons, John	TX2600	Spoto, Mary T.	FL1600
Schulz, Russell E.	TX0750	Simpson, Lawrence J.	MA0260	Spurgeon, Alan L.	MS0700
Schulze-Johnson, Virginia	NJ0300	Sinclair, John V.	FL1550	Stacke, Robert J.	MN0050
Schwartz, Sandra M.	WV0750	Sine, Nadine J.	PA1950	Stadelman, Jeffrey	NY4320
Schwarze, Penny	MN0450	Singleton, H. Craig	CA1650	Stadsklev, Joan B.	FL0350
Schweitzer, Kenneth	MD1100	Sipes, Diana	TX2930	Stadsklev, Joan B.	FL0350
Sconyers, David	FL1730	Sipley, Kenneth L.	MS0575	Stamer, Rick A.	AZ0450
Scott Hoyt, Janet	AA0100	Sirota, Robert	NY2150	Stamp, John E.	PA1600
Scott, Allen	OK0800	Sisk, Lawrence T.	IL1520	Stancu, Letitia G.	NJ0800
Scott, David	TX0150	Sitton, Michael R.	NY3780	Stark, Eric	IN0250
Scott, Geoffrey	TX2150	Siu, Lily	IL2510	Stark, Eric	IN0250
Scott, J. B.	FL1950	Skiba, Karin	CA3265	Starkweather, David A.	GA2100
Scott, James C.	TX3420	Skoog, William M.	TN1200	Stauch, Thomas J.	IL1085
Scott, Jan	LA0350	Skroch, Diana	ND0600	Stauffacher, Paul	WI0855
Scott, John C.	TX3420	Skroch, Diana	ND0600	Stauffer, George B.	NJ1130
Scott, Julia K.	TX2400	Slish, John	MO1800	Steele, Angela	NC2000
Scott, Sandra C.	GA1600	Smaldone, Edward	NY0642	Steele, Daniel L.	MI0400
Scott, Sandra C.	GA1600	Smaldone, Edward	NY0642	Stefanco, Carolyn	GA0050
Scott, Sheila	AC0050	Smiley, William C.	NC1550	Steffens, David	OK0750
Scott, Sue Stone	AC0050	Smirnoff, Joel	OH0600	Steinhaus, Barbara	GA0350
Scott-Williams, Alison	NY1900	Smith, Aaron	MD0900	Steinitz, Michael	AF0150
Scruggs, Richard J.	TN0250	Smith, Andrew	NV0050	Stemper, Frank L.	IL2900
Scully, Mathew	CA3950	Smith, Ann	AF0120	Stencel, Paul L.	NY1210
Seachrist, Denise A.	OH1100	Smith, Billy	TX0390	Stephens, Roger L.	TN1710
Seaton, Kira J.	OH0755	Smith, Bret	WA0050	Stepniak, Michael	VA1350
Seaward, Jeffery A.	CA1290	Smith, Carey	MS0370	Stevens, James M.	TN0580
Seelbinder, Emily	NC2000	Smith, Charles J.	NY4320	Stevens, John	WI0815
Segger, Joachim	AA0035	Smith, Claudia	WI0855	Stevens, Paul W.	KS1350
Sehmann, Karin M.	KY0550	Smith, Dana	CA2960	Stevenson, Laura	FL0570
Sehmann, Karin M.	KY0550	Smith, David K.	KS0950	Stewart, Jonathan	OK0825
Sehmann, Karin M.	KY0550	Smith, Donald S.	AZ0350	Stewart, Jonathan	OK0825
Seifert, Dustin	NM0100	Smith, Eddie	CA5150	Stick, James W.	IA0420
Seigel, Lester C.	AL0300	Smith, Elise	MS0385	Stillman, Judith L.	RI0200
Selby, Sara E.	GA2175	Smith, G. D.	KY1200	Stob, Jeff	MI0350
Selesky, Evelyn C.	NY2450	Smith, Gary A.	TX2150	Stockton, J. Larry	PA1850
Seliger, Bryce M.	OR0750	Smith, Gene	AF0150	Stodola, Lynn	AF0100
Seliger, Bryce M.	OR0750	Smith, James E.	CA4450	Stoecker, Philip S.	NY1600
Seliger, Bryce M.	OR0750	Smith, James W.	AL1050	Stoia, Nikki R.	MA2000
Selsor, Mindy	MO0550	Smith, Jason	IA1400	Stokes, Porter	SC1000
Sepulveda, Richardo	OH1100	Smith, Kimo	CA2420	Stokes, Porter	SC1000
Sepulveda, Richardo	OH1100	Smith, Mark	IL0600	Stokes, Porter	SC1000
Seuffert, Maria C.	GA0160	Smith, Mary M.	IL0800	Stokes, Porter	SC1000
Shadle-Peters, Jennifer	CO0275	Smith, Nancy	FL1650	Stolberg, Tom	MO0060
Shaheen, Ronald T.	CA5200	Smith, Paul B.	AR0400	Stolte, Charles	AA0035
Shames, Kay W.	OH0650	Smith, Peter H.	IN1700	Stoune, Michael	TX3200
Shanahan, Ellen Cooper	MA0280	Smith, Robert W.	AL1050	Stowman, William	PA2300
Shands, Patricia	CA5350	Smith, Ronald	NC1950	Strain, David	AR0900
Shanklin, Bart	IL3500	Smith, Sam	ID0070	Strait, Tom	MN1120
Shannon, John	IN1485	Smith, Susan A.	MS0360	Straka, Leslie	OR1050
Shapiro, Sandra	OH0600	Smith, Tamara L.	DE0150	Strand, Jonathan	AA0015
Sharkey, Jeffrey N.	MD0650	Smith, Timothy C.	AK0100	Strasser, Richard	MA1450
Shaw, Rochelle	CA1650	Smith-Emerson, Karen	MA1750	Straus, Joseph N.	NY0600
Shay, Robert	MO1800	Smoak, Jeff C.	KY1425	Strauss, John F.	IA0950
Shearer, Erik	CA3250	Snarrenberg, Robert	MO1900	Stroeher, Michael	WV0400
Shearer, James E.	NM0310	Snead, Charles G.	AL1170	Stroh, Elaine M.	NY4350
Shearon, Stephen	TN1100	Snell, James W.	MO1810	Stroker, Robert	PA3250
Sheeran, Kate	NY2250	Snell, Mary E.	ME0500	Strong, Ernie	CA2450
Sheffer, Toni	KY1000	Snider, Jeffrey	TX3420	Strong, James Anthony	NJ0975
Sheffler, Jack	WV0200	Snider, Nancy Jo	DC0010	Strong, Nathan	CA2450
Sheinbaum, John J.	CO0900	Snodgrass, Jennifer Sterling	NC0050	Stubley, Eleanor	AI0150
Sheinberg, Colleen	NM0450	Snook, Ann Marie	KS1400	Stuckenbruck, Dale	NY2105
Shelby, Karla	OK1500	Snowden, Donald	FL1500	Stufft, David	GA2000
Shelley, Russ	PA1650	Snyder, Colleen	CA2400	Stull, David H.	OH1700
Shelton, Beth	TX2050	Snyder, Randy L.	TX2300	Stull, Gregg	VA1475
Shepherd, Gregory	HI0155	Solum, Stephen	MN1050	Stutes, Ann B.	TX3650
Sheppard, W. Anthony	MA2250	Sommer, Lesley	WA1250	Stutes, Ann B.	TX3650
Sher, Daniel	CO0800	Sommers, Deborah	VA1500	Suarez, Jeff	WI0847
Sherman, Steve	AA0080	Sonenberg, Janet	MA1200	Suchon, Donnetta	TX1450
Sherr, Richard J.	MA1750	Song, James J.	CA3100	Suddaby, Juliet	AG0130
Sherwin, Ronald G.	MA0150	Song, Tom	TX2600	Sudeikis, Barbara	MI1160
Sherwin, Ronald G.	MA0150	Sorensen, Randall J.	LA0250	Sullivan, Todd E.	AZ0450
Sherwin, Ronald G.	MA0150	Sorenson, Allin	MO0350	Sumarsam,	CT0750
Sherwin, Ronald G.	MA0150	Sorley, Rebecca E.	IN1650	Sundberg, Terri	TX3420
Shevitz, Matthew	IL1080	Sorley, Rebecca E.	IN1650	Sundquist, Michael	CA3000
Shier, Fuchsia	AB0210	Sorroche, Juan	PR0150	Sutanto, David T.	TX0550
Shiffman, Barry	AG0300	Sorroche, Juan	PR0150	Sutton, John	CA0250
Shinn, Alan	TX3200	Sosland, Benjamin	NY1900	Svedlow, Andrew	CO0950
Shinn, Alan	TX3200	Soto, Ricardo	CA3350	Swain, Joseph P.	NY0650
Shirley, John F.	MA2030	Soto-Medina, Victor	TX1725	Swann, William E.	TN1000
Shirtz, Michael	OH2140	Spain, Bruce	CA1750	Swanson, Barry	ID0150
Shistle, Tammy C.	FL1750	Spangenberg, Saul	NY3785	Swartz, Anne	NY0250
Shiver, Todd	WA0050	Spaniola, Joseph T.	FL2100	Sweeney, Joyce	CA5500
Shockett, Bernard	NY0635	Sparfeld, Tobin	CA2660	Sweger, Keith	IN0150
Shockley, Darlas	IA0750	Sparhawk, Don	ID0060	Sweger, Keith	IN0150
Shook, Timothy	KS1200	Sparrow, James	NC1250	Sweidel, Martin	TX2400
Shover, Blaine F.	PA3050	Sparti, Patricia C.	NC0850	Swenson, Sonya	CA4950
Showell, Jeffrey A.	OH0300	Spataro, Susan M.	VA0400	Swenson, Thomas S.	NC2205
Shroyer, Walter	VA0050	Speare, Mary Jean	VA0600	Swets, Paul	TX0150
Shuholm, Dan	OR0175	Speer, Janet Barton	NC1050	Swift, Mark D.	PA3580
Shurtz, H. Paul	TN1700	Spencer, Dianthe M.	CA4200	Swinyar, Carol	MA0250
Sidhom, Samuel	TN1680	Spencer, Mark	AR0800	Tacconi, Marisa S.	PA2750
Sievers, Tim	IA0270	Spencer, Mary	GU0500	Takasawa, Manabu K.	RI0300
Sievers, Tim	IA0270	Spicer, Mark	NY0625	Tallant, Audrey	IL2910
Sigmon, Susan McEwen	GA0940	Spiller, Henry	CA5010	Talley, Keith M.	OK1250
Silberschlag, Jeffrey	MD0750	Spiller, W. Terrence	CA0600	Talley, Keith M.	OK1250
Silver, Sheila	NY3790	Spitler, Carolyn	IN1250	Tanner, Christopher	OH1450
Simmons, James	SD0300	Spitler, Carolyn	IN1250	Tanner, Gretchen	UT0250
Simon, Peter C.	AG0300	Spitz, Bruce	WA0860	Taricani, JoAnn	WA1050
Simons, Carolyn	CA2810	Sposato, Aime	VA1350	Tate, Rob	FL0800
Simons, John	TX2600	Sposato, Aime	VA1350	Tate, Shelia D.	VA1800

Name	Code	Name	Code	Name	Code
Taylor, Allen	PA3600	Ulffers, Christopher	NC0650	Watson, Kathy	AZ0150
Taylor, Clint 'Skip'	GA2100	Ulibarri, Debbie	CO0700	Watson, Shawn	TX3527
Taylor, Danille	TX3150	Underwood, Mark	TX1750	Watson, William E.	MD0175
Taylor, Jamie	RI0200	Underwood, Von E.	OK0150	Way, R. Bruce	MI1500
Taylor, Jeffrey J.	NY0500	Unger, Melvin P.	OH0200	Weast, Wade P.	NC1650
Taylor, Kristin Jonina	IA1750	Unrau, Lucia	OH0250	Weaver, Brent	OR0250
Taylor, Steven	CO0150	Unruh, Eric W.	WY0050	Webb, Brian P.	VT0125
Taylor, Susan Lynnette	IN0100	Urban, Kathleen	WY0115	Webb, Glenn	UT0150
Tebay, John	CA1900	Urbis, Richard	TX3515	Webb, John C.	AR0800
Tebbets, Gary	KS0040	Urbis, Sue Zanne Williamson	TX3515	Webb, John C.	AR0800
Tedards, Ann B.	OR1050	Urfer, Kristi	IL2310	Weber, Stephen	OK1400
Tedards, Ann B.	OR1050	Usher, Ann L.	OH2150	Webster, Thomas R.	TX0600
Tedder, Teresa C.	KY1150	Valenti, Julie R.	PA1830	Weger, Stacy	OK1150
Tel, Martin	NJ0850	Valenti, Nick J.	MI1700	Wegge, Glen T.	IA1750
Tesar, Kathleen	CA1075	Valerio, Wendy	SC1110	Weinstock, Frank M.	OH2200
Tesar, Kathleen	CA1075	Vallentine, John	IA1600	Weintraub, Andrew	PA3420
Thachuk, Steve J.	CA0835	Vallo, Victor	GA0850	Weir, Tim	ME0340
Thatcher, Paula	OR0750	Van der Sloot, William	AA0050	Weirich, Robert W.	MO1810
Thelander, Kristin	IA1550	Vance, Virginia L.	NC1800	Weissman, Neil	PA0950
Thiel, Robb G.	IN1350	Vander Weg, John D.	MI2200	Welbourne, Todd G.	WI0815
Thomas, Benjamin	WA0460	Vanderford, Brenda M.	WV0700	Welch, Leo	FL0850
Thomas, Cheryl	MI1000	Vanderhoof, Winston	MO1780	Weller-Stilson, Rhonda	MO1500
Thomas, Edwin	IN0005	Vandervaart, Len	AA0040	Welling, Joelle	AA0150
Thomas, Kanet	CA3600	Vandervoort, Patricia	TX3600	Wells, Elizabeth A.	AE0050
Thomas, Laurel A.	IN1450	VanLeuven, Denise	OR0900	Wells, Elizabeth A.	AE0050
Thomas, Margaret E.	CT0100	Vanore, John	PA3680	Wells, Lillie	OR1050
Thomas, Nicholas	IL1890	Vasquez, Jerico	GA1800	Welstead, Jon	WI0825
Thomas, Phillip E.	TN0850	Vaughan, Jennie	TX2050	Wener, Richard E.	NY3100
Thomas, Phillip E.	TN0850	Vayo, David J.	IL1200	Wenger, Janice K.	MO1800
Thomas, William	AG0650	Veenker, Jonathan	MN0250	Wennerstrom, Mary H.	IN0900
Thomas-Maddox, Candice	OH1905	Vega, Rebecca	NJ0050	Wente, Steven F.	IL0730
Thompson, David	WI0400	Venker, Josef	WA0850	Wenzel, Gary	IL0730
Thompson, David B.	SC0850	Vermillion, Terry L.	MN1300	Werkema, Jason R.	MI0750
Thompson, Gregory T.	NC1000	Victory, Lucy	AL0300	Werner, Donna	MO1120
Thompson, Karin E.	WA1100	Vigneau, Michelle	TN1680	West, James	HI0160
Thompson, Kathy A.	OK0700	Villanueva, Donna Mae	CA2700	West, Jean	FL1750
Thompson, Kenneth	OH0300	Villella, John	PA3600	West, John T.	NC2600
Thompson, Lee D.	WA1300	Vogt, Sean F.	SD0300	West, Kevin	MI2250
Thompson, Linda K.	TN0850	Volk, David Paul	VA1580	Westgate, Phillip Todd	AL0950
Thompson, Paul	WI0817	Volk, Maureen	AD0050	Weston, Trevor L.	NJ0300
Thompson, Robert	NY3785	Von Kampen, Kurt E.	NE0150	Wetherbee, Sarah M.	NY5000
Thompson, Scott	CO0600	Vos, Ruth	PA1350	Wetzel, Richard	OH1900
Thoms, Jason A.	NY0850	Voytko, Christy	NY1800	Wheeler, Charles Lynn	CA3400
Thoreson, Deborah	GA0750	Voytko, Christy	NY1800	Wheeler, Charles Lynn	CA3400
Thorngate, Russell	WI0925	Vroman, David	IL0400	Wheeler, Dale J.	AA0080
Thornley, Christopher T.	MA2000	Wachmann, Eric	IA1800	Wheeler, Mark	NC0915
Thorp, Steven	NM0250	Wachter, Renee	WI0860	Wheeler, Scott	MA0850
Thorpe, Allan	AB0090	Wacker, John M.	CO1050	Whisenhunt, Ted	GA2300
Thrasher, Michael	TX3535	Wade, Bonnie C.	CA5000	White, Angela S.	FL0350
Tidwell, Mary	TX3360	Waggener, Joshua A.	NC2350	White, Barbara A.	NJ0900
Tidwell, Mary	TX1510	Waggener, Joshua A.	NC2350	White, Barbara A.	NJ0900
Tiedge, Faun Tanenbaum	OR0450	Waggoner, Dori	MO0100	White, Christopher Dale	TX2955
Timmons, Leslie	UT0300	Wagner, Alan	TX2400	White, David A.	TX3400
Timothy, Sarah O.	AL0890	Wagner, Irvin	OK1350	White, Frank	LA0700
Tindall, Danny H.	FL1740	Wagner, Irvin	OK1350	White, Julian E.	FL0600
Tindall, Danny H.	FL1740	Wagner, Jeanine F.	IL2900	White, L. Keith	OK1330
Tinnin, Randall C.	FL1950	Wagner, Karen	NY1900	White, Molly E.	CA2720
Tio, Adrian R.	MA2020	Wagner, Marella	WI0770	Whitehead, Glen	CO0810
Tocheff, Robert	OH1600	Wagner, Marella	WI0770	Whitelock, Edward	GA1070
Todd, Kristen Stauffer	OK0650	Wagner, Marella	WI0770	Whiting, Steven M.	MI2100
Toliver, Brooks	OH2150	Wagstaff, Grayson	DC0050	Whiting, Steven M.	MI2100
Toman, Sharon Ann	PA2775	Waheed, Mohammed	WY0060	Whitlatch, Michael	IA0150
Tomasello, Andrew	NY0250	Wait, Mark	TN1850	Whitler, Kellye	IL2800
Tomm, Karma	AG0250	Wait, Mark	TN1850	Whitler, Kellye	IL2800
Toner, D. Thomas	VT0450	Wait, Mark	TN1850	Whitley, H. Moran	NC0300
Toomey, John F.	VA1000	Wakeling, Tom	OR0050	Whitney, Nadine C.	GA2200
Towne, Gary	ND0500	Walczyk, Kevin	OR1250	Whittall, Geoffrey	AA0025
Townsend, Laurie	AB0100	Waldron, Ann	IL2050	Wiberg, Janice	MT0300
Townsend, Ralph	MN1700	Waldrop, Joseph	TX3850	Widen, Dennis C.	OK1250
Trabichoff, Geoffrey	ID0070	Walentine, Richard L.	ND0150	Widener, Russell D.	KS1450
Trachsel, Andrew J.	OH1900	Wales, Lorraine	OH0850	Widenhofer, Stephen B.	IL1750
Traino, Dominic	DC0050	Walker, Ben	KY0550	Widenhofer, Stephen B.	IL1750
Traster, Jeff	FL2050	Walker, Cherilee	KS0590	Wiebe, Brian	IN0550
Traube, Caroline	AI0200	Walker, John M.	SD0550	Wieck, Julie	WA1150
Trela, DJ	MI2120	Walker, Karen	VA1350	Wiemann, Beth	ME0440
Trentham, Donald R.	TN0650	Walker, Karen	VA1350	Wiggins, Jacqueline H.	MI1750
Tresler, Matthew T.	CA2390	Walker, Larry	KS0440	Wiggins, Tracy Richard	NC2435
Tripold, David	NJ0760	Walker, Margaret Edith	AG0250	Wilcoxson, Nancy	SD0580
Trittin, Brian L.	TX0400	Wallace, James A.	GA1070	Wilder, Michael	IL3550
Tsubota, Ann	NJ0975	Wallace-Boaz, Krista B.	KY1500	Wilhoit, Mel R.	TN0200
Tsuquiashi-Daddesio, Eva	PA3100	Waller, Jan	MN1290	Wilhoit, Mel R.	TN0200
Tubbs, Carol A.	CA0805	Wallis, David N.	MO0650	Wilkinson, Cathryn	IL0630
Tucker, Robert	TX1100	Walter, Clyde Andrew	IL0100	Will, Richard	VA1550
Tudor, Robert W.	WV0550	Walters, C. J.	NV0100	Willett, Dan L.	MO1800
Tung, Leslie Thomas	MI1150	Walters, Michelle L.	PA3000	Williams, Amy C.	PA3420
Tunnell, Meme	KY0250	Walters, Teresa	NJ0200	Williams, David A.	FL2000
Turley, Edward L.	MN0350	Walzel, Robert L.	KS1350	Williams, Demetrice	GA0050
Turner, Gregory E.	KS0400	Wanner, Dan	CA2600	Williams, Demetrice	GA0050
Turner, John	OR0010	Ward, Keith C.	WA1000	Williams, John W.	NY2100
Turner, Michael W.	OR1000	Ward, Steve A.	OR0800	Williams, Mark D.	CA2440
Turner, Timothy R.	LA0900	Ware, John	VA1800	Williams, Paul	CA5400
Turon, Charles T.	FL1745	Warner, Daniel C.	MA1000	Williams, Robin	LA0800
Turpen, Jennifer	WY0200	Warren, John	IL1900	Williams, Sean	WA0350
Tusing, Susan	GA0500	Warwick, Jacqueline	AF0100	Williamson, Richard A.	SC0050
Tutt, Kevin	MI0900	Washington, Daniel	MI2100	Willis, Sharon J.	GA0490
Tyler, Philip	CA3640	Waterman, Ellen F.	AD0050	Willis, Steve	NC0200
Tymas, Byron	NC1600	Waters, Dana	KS0265	Willman, Fred	MO1830
Tynon, Mari Jo	ID0070	Waters, Jeffery L.	MO1550	Wilson, Barbara	IL2350
Uhlenkott, Gary	WA0400	Waters, Tim	OK0850	Wilson, Brian S.	CA4700
Uitermarkt, Cynthia D.	IL1850	Watson, Ian D.	NJ1140	Wilson, J. P.	AR0600

Wilson, Jeffrey S.	IL1050
Wilson, Josie	OR0950
Wilson, Kathleen L.	FL0700
Wilson, Thomas	IA0790
Wilson, Tracy	MA0280
Winder, Diane L.	MI0600
Wingard, Alan B.	GA1800
Winkelman, David	NC1650
Winkelman, David	NC1650
Winkler, Amanda Eubanks	NY4100
Winston, Jeremy	OH2400
Winteregg, Steven L.	OH0450
Wis, Ramona M.	IL2050
Wischusen, Mary A.	MI2200
Wistrom, LeAnne	PA1200
Withers, Lisa Ann	VA0350
Witte, Peter	MO1810
Wittgraf, Michael A.	ND0500
Witucki, Darrin	WI0855
Wiznerowicz, James	VA1600
Woelfel, Kevin	ID0250
Wohlers, Bill	TN1350
Wojtera, Allen F.	VA1100
Wolcott, Sylvia	KS0215
Wold, Wayne L.	MD0500
Wolf, Matthew	MI0500
Wolff, Christoph	NY1900
Wolff, David	SD0100
Woliver, C. Patrick	OH1850
Woliver, C. Patrick	OH1850
Wollenzein, Timothy	MN0600
Wong, Sandra	CO0200
Wong, Yau-Sun	NM0200
Wood, Graham	SC0450
Wood, Robert	AG0500
Wood, Thomas G.	OH0700
Woodruff, Ernest	MO0950
Woods, David G.	CT0600
Woods, Rex A.	AZ0500
Woods, Rex A.	AZ0500
Woods, Rex A.	AZ0500
Woodward, Greg	LA0400
Woodward, Gregory S.	NY1800
Woolley, Clara	IN0010
Wooton, John A.	MS0750
Workman, Darin D.	KS1110
Wortley, Gary S.	GA0550
Wrazen, Louise	AG0650
Wright, Emily Powers	NC1350
Wright, J. Clay	KS0440
Wright, Jeffrey	IN0910
Wright, Jeffrey E.	IN0100
Wright, Jeffrey E.	IN0100
Wright, Lesley A.	HI0210
Wright, Sally	VA1000
Wu, Chieh-Mei Jamie	NY3500
Wu, Chieh-Mei Jamie	NY3500
Wulfert, Edelgard	NY3700
Wurgler, Norman F.	KY1540
Wurgler, Pamela S.	KY0950
Wurgler, Pamela S.	KY0950
Wurtz, Gary	TX2700
Yaeger, Neddi	CA2420
Yaffe, Michael C.	CT0850
Yager, David	CA5070
Yager, Kay B.	TN1680
Yannelli, John A.	NY3560
Yardley, Anne B.	NJ0300
Yarrington, John	TX1000
Yasinitsky, Greg	WA1150
Yates, Christopher	WA0350
Yee, Thomas	HI0210
Yehuda, Guy	FL1950
Yekovich, Robert	TX2150
Yeung, Angela C.	CA5200
Yoon, Sujin	MO1350
Young, Gregory D.	MT0200
Young, H. G.	WV0760
Young, H. G.	WV0760
Young, Mark	MO0200
Young, Mary Ellen	TX2850
Young-Wright, Lorna C.	VI0050
Youngblood, Michael	IL2560
Younge, J. Sophia	IL0450
Younker, Betty Anne	AG0500
Ypma, Nancy S.	IL1740
Zagorsky, Joe	CA1300
Zahler, Noel	NY2105
Zamagias, Jim	MD0050
Zappulla, Robert	CA1050
Zaricki, Alexis	NH0350
Zarubick, Fran	WA0480
Zaslaw, Neal	NY0900
Zec, John	NJ0550
Zeiss, Laurel E.	TX0300
Zemke, Lorna	WI0770
Zemke, Lorna	WI0770
Zemke, Lorna	WI0770
Zent, Donald	KY0100
Zielke, Gregory D.	NE0250
Zilberkant, Eduard	AK0150
Zilincik, Anthony	OH0350
Zimbelman, Joel	CA0800
Zimmerman, Lynda	WI0806
Ziolek, Eric E.	OH0650
Zirkle, Thomas	MO1110
Zirnitis, Anda	MO0300
Zirnitis, Anda	MO0300
Zlabinger, Tom	NY0646
Zobel, Elizabeth W.	IL0350
Zogleman, Deanne	KS0980
Zohn, Andrew	GA0550
Zorn, Karen	MA1175
Zuk, Ireneus	AG0250
Zwelling, Judith Zwerdling	VA0250

Index of Graduate Degrees

Index of Graduate Degrees

Advanced Certificate in Music Education
NY0500   City Univ of New York-Brooklyn

Artist Diploma
AG0300   The Glenn Gould School
AG0500   Univ of Western Ontario
CA1075   Colburn School, The
CT0850   Yale University
DC0050   Catholic Univ of America, The
GA0550   Columbus State University
GA1300   Mercer University
IL3300   Univ of Illinois
IN0150   Ball State University
IN0900   Indiana Univ-Bloomington
IN0910   Indiana Univ-South Bend
MA0350   The Boston Conservatory
MA1175   Longy School of Music
NJ0800   Montclair State University
NY3785   State Univ of New York-Purchase
OH0600   Cleveland Institute of Music
OH2200   Univ of Cincinnati
PA0550   Carnegie Mellon University
PA1050   Duquesne University
TX3000   Texas Christian University
TX3510   Univ of Texas-Austin
VA1350   Shenandoah Conservatory

Artist Diploma in Historical Performance
NY1900   The Juilliard School

Artist Diploma in Instrumental Conducting
FL1900   Univ of Miami

Artist Diploma in Instrumental Performance
FL1900   Univ of Miami

Artist Diploma in Jazz Studies
NY1900   The Juilliard School

Artist Diploma in Keyboard Performance
FL1900   Univ of Miami

Artist Diploma in Music Performance
NY1900   The Juilliard School

Artist Diploma in Opera Studies
NY1900   The Juilliard School

Artist Diploma in String Quartet Studies
NY1900   The Juilliard School

Artist Diploma in Vocal Performance
FL1900   Univ of Miami

Artist's Certificate
CA4150   San Francisco Conserv of Music
MO1810   Univ of Missouri-Kansas City
TN1710   Univ of Tennessee-Knoxville
WI0815   Univ of Wisconsin-Madison

Certificate
CA3270   Notre Dame de Namur University
CT0800   Western Connecticut State Univ
CT0850   Yale University
IL2910   Southern Illinois Univ-Edwardsvle
MA0350   The Boston Conservatory
MA0400   Boston University
NC1650   Univ of North Carolina School of the Arts
OH1900   Ohio University
TX3000   Texas Christian University
VA1350   Shenandoah Conservatory

Diploma
CT0650   Univ of Hartford
MA1400   New England Conservatory
NC1650   Univ of North Carolina School of the Arts
PA0850   Curtis Institute of Music
WI1150   Wisconsin Conservatory of Music

Diploma in Operatic Performance
AG0450   Univ of Toronto

DMA Contemporary Music Performance
CA5050   Univ of California-San Diego

DMA in Brass Performance
WA1050   Univ of Washington

DMA in Chamber Music (Piano)
DC0050   Catholic Univ of America, The

DMA in Choral Conducting
FL1900   Univ of Miami
KS1350   Univ of Kansas
OK1350   Univ of Oklahoma
WA1050   Univ of Washington
WI0815   Univ of Wisconsin-Madison

DMA in Choral Literature & Conducting
CO0800   Univ of Colorado-Boulder

DMA in Choral Music
CA5300   Univ of Southern California
IL3300   Univ of Illinois

DMA in Church Music
KS1350   Univ of Kansas
KY1200   Southern Baptist Theo Seminary
LA0400   New Orleans Baptist Theo Seminary
TX2600   Southwestern Baptist Theo Sem

DMA in Collaborative Keyboard
FL1900   Univ of Miami

DMA in Collaborative Piano
CO0800   Univ of Colorado-Boulder

DMA in Collaborative Piano Performance
NJ1130   Rutgers the State Univ-New Brnswk

DMA in Collaborative Piano/Coaching
MN1623   Univ of Minnesota-Twin Cities

DMA in Composition
AB0100   Univ of British Columbia
AL1170   Univ of Alabama
AZ0100   Arizona State University
AZ0500   Univ of Arizona
CA4900   Stanford University
CA5070   Univ of California-Santa Cruz
CA5300   Univ of Southern California
CO0800   Univ of Colorado-Boulder
CT0650   Univ of Hartford
CT0850   Yale University
DC0050   Catholic Univ of America, The
FL1900   Univ of Miami
GA2100   Univ of Georgia
IL3300   Univ of Illinois
KS1350   Univ of Kansas
KY1450   Univ of Kentucky-Lexington
MA0400   Boston University
MA1400   New England Conservatory
MD0650   Peabody Conservatory of Music
MD1010   Univ of Maryland
MI1400   Michigan State University
MI2100   Univ of Michigan-Ann Arbor
MO1810   Univ of Missouri-Kansas City
MS0750   Univ of Southern Mississippi, The
NE0600   Univ of Nebraska-Lincoln
NY0600   City Univ of New York-Grad Center
NY0750   Columbia University
NY0900   Cornell University
NY1100   Eastman School of Music
NY1900   The Juilliard School
NY2150   Manhattan School of Music
OH0600   Cleveland Institute of Music
OH1850   Ohio State University-Columbus
OH2200   Univ of Cincinnati
OK1350   Univ of Oklahoma
OR1050   Univ of Oregon
PA3250   Temple University
SC1110   Univ of South Carolina-Columbia
TN1680   Univ of Memphis
TX3000   Texas Christian University
TX3200   Texas Tech University
TX3400   Univ of Houston
TX3420   Univ of North Texas
TX3510   Univ of Texas-Austin
WA1050   Univ of Washington
WI0815   Univ of Wisconsin-Madison
WV0750   West Virginia University

DMA in Composition/Arranging
NY1275   Five Towns College

DMA in Conducting
AL1170   Univ of Alabama
AZ0100   Arizona State University
AZ0500   Univ of Arizona
CA5030   Univ of California-Los Angeles
CT0600   Univ of Connecticut
CT0650   Univ of Hartford
GA2100   Univ of Georgia
IA1550   Univ of Iowa
KS1350   Univ of Kansas
KY1450   Univ of Kentucky-Lexington
LA0200   Louisiana State University
MA0400   Boston University
MD0650   Peabody Conservatory of Music
MD1010   Univ of Maryland
MI1400   Michigan State University
MI2100   Univ of Michigan-Ann Arbor
MN1623   Univ of Minnesota-Twin Cities
MO1810   Univ of Missouri-Kansas City
MS0750   Univ of Southern Mississippi, The
NC2430   Univ of North Carolina-Greensboro
ND0350   North Dakota State University
NE0600   Univ of Nebraska-Lincoln
NJ1130   Rutgers the State Univ-New Brnswk
NY1100   Eastman School of Music
OH1850   Ohio State University-Columbus
OH2200   Univ of Cincinnati
SC1110   Univ of South Carolina-Columbia
TN1680   Univ of Memphis
TX3000   Texas Christian University
TX3200   Texas Tech University
TX3400   Univ of Houston
TX3420   Univ of North Texas
UT0250   Univ of Utah
VA0600   James Madison University

DMA in Contemporary Music
OH0300   Bowling Green State University

DMA in Early Music
CA5300   Univ of Southern California
NY1100   Eastman School of Music
OH0400   Case Western Reserve University

DMA in Harp Performance
WA1050   Univ of Washington

DMA in Harpsichord Performance
WA1050   Univ of Washington

DMA in Historical Performance

MA0400   Boston University

DMA in Instrumental Conducting
FL1900   Univ of Miami

DMA in Instrumental Conducting
O0800   Univ of Colorado-Boulder
OK1350   Univ of Oklahoma
WA1050   Univ of Washington

DMA in Instrumental Performance
FL1900   Univ of Miami

DMA in Instrumental Performance - Multi Woodwinds
FL1900   Univ of Miami

DMA in Jazz Composition
FL1900   Univ of Miami

DMA in Jazz Studies
CA5300   Univ of Southern California
CO0800   Univ of Colorado-Boulder
NE0600   Univ of Nebraska-Lincoln

DMA in Keyboard Performance
FL1900   Univ of Miami

DMA in Music
IN0005   American Conservatory of Music
PA2750   Penn State Univ-University Park
TX2150   Rice University

DMA in Music & Human Learning
TX3510   Univ of Texas-Austin

DMA in Music Education
CA5300   Univ of Southern California
CT0650   Univ of Hartford
GA2100   Univ of Georgia
MA0400   Boston University
NJ1130   Rutgers the State Univ-New Brnswk
NY1100   Eastman School of Music
NY1275   Five Towns College
TX3400   Univ of Houston
VA1350   Shenandoah Conservatory

DMA in Music Education (Distance Education)
MA0400   Boston University

DMA in Music History & Literature
NY1275   Five Towns College

DMA in Music Theory
MA1400   New England Conservatory

DMA in Orchestral Conducting
DC0050   Catholic Univ of America, The

DMA in Orchestral Instruments
DC0050   Catholic Univ of America, The

DMA in Organ Performance
WA1050   Univ of Washington

DMA in Percussion Performance
WA1050   Univ of Washington

DMA in Performance
AB0100   Univ of British Columbia
AL1170   Univ of Alabama
AZ0100   Arizona State University
AZ0500   Univ of Arizona
CA5030   Univ of California-Los Angeles
CA5060   Univ of California-Santa Barbara
CA5300   Univ of Southern California
CO0800   Univ of Colorado-Boulder
CT0600   Univ of Connecticut
CT0650   Univ of Hartford
CT0850   Yale University
GA2100   Univ of Georgia
KS1350   Univ of Kansas
KY1450   Univ of Kentucky-Lexington
LA0200   Louisiana State University
MA0400   Boston University
MA1400   New England Conservatory
MD0650   Peabody Conservatory of Music
MD1010   Univ of Maryland
MI1400   Michigan State University
MI2100   Univ of Michigan-Ann Arbor
MN1623   Univ of Minnesota-Twin Cities
MO1810   Univ of Missouri-Kansas City
NC2430   Univ of North Carolina-Greensboro
ND0350   North Dakota State University
NE0600   Univ of Nebraska-Lincoln
NJ1130   Rutgers the State Univ-New Brnswk
NV0050   Univ of Nevada-Las Vegas
NY0600   City Univ of New York-Grad Center
NY1275   Five Towns College
NY1900   The Juilliard School
NY2150   Manhattan School of Music
NY3790   State Univ of New York-Stony Brook
OH0600   Cleveland Institute of Music
OH1850   Ohio State University-Columbus
OH2200   Univ of Cincinnati
OK1350   Univ of Oklahoma
OR1050   Univ of Oregon
PA3250   Temple University
SC1110   Univ of South Carolina-Columbia
TN1680   Univ of Memphis
TX3000   Texas Christian University
TX3200   Texas Tech University
TX3400   Univ of Houston
TX3420   Univ of North Texas
TX3510   Univ of Texas-Austin
UT0250   Univ of Utah
VA0600   James Madison University
VA1350   Shenandoah Conservatory
WI0815   Univ of Wisconsin-Madison
WV0750   West Virginia University

DMA in Performance & Literature
IL3300   Univ of Illinois
NY1100   Eastman School of Music

DMA in Performance & Pedagogy
CO0800   Univ of Colorado-Boulder
IA1550   Univ of Iowa
MS0750   Univ of Southern Mississippi, The

DMA in Performance Practice
NY0900   Cornell University

DMA in Piano Accompanying & Chamber Music
NY1100   Eastman School of Music

DMA in Piano Pedagogy
DC0050   Catholic Univ of America, The
SC1110   Univ of South Carolina-Columbia
TX3000   Texas Christian University
TX3200   Texas Tech University

DMA in Piano Performance
DC0050   Catholic Univ of America, The
WA1050   Univ of Washington

DMA in Sacred Music
DC0050   Catholic Univ of America, The

DMA in String Performance
WA1050   Univ of Washington

DMA in Studio Music & Jazz Instrumental Performance
FL1900   Univ of Miami

DMA in Studio Music & Jazz Vocal Performance
FL1900   Univ of Miami

DMA in Vocal Accompanying
DC0050   Catholic Univ of America, The

DMA in Vocal Accompanying & Coaching
IL3300   Univ of Illinois

DMA in Vocal Pedagogy
DC0050   Catholic Univ of America, The
VA1350   Shenandoah Conservatory

DMA in Vocal Pedagogy & Performance
FL1900   Univ of Miami

DMA in Vocal Performance
DC0050   Catholic Univ of America, The
FL1900   Univ of Miami
WA1050   Univ of Washington

DMA in Woodwind Performance
WA1050   Univ of Washington

DMA Interdisciplinary Digital Media Arts
AZ0100   Arizona State University

DMA Jazz Studies & Contemporary Media
NY1100   Eastman School of Music

DMA Performer-Composer Program
CA0510   Calif Institute of the Arts

DMA Piano Pedagogy & Performance
MI2100   Univ of Michigan-Ann Arbor

Doctor in Music Instrumental/Voice Performance
AI0200   Universite de Montreal

Doctor in Music Performance Conducting
AI0200   Universite de Montreal

Doctor of Art in Performance
IN0150   Ball State University

Doctor of Arts in Conducting
IN0150   Ball State University

Doctor of Arts in Piano Chamber Music/Accompanying
IN0150   Ball State University

Index of Graduate Degrees

Doctor of Education in Music Education
AL1170 Univ of Alabama
GA2100 Univ of Georgia
IL3300 Univ of Illinois
NY4200 Teachers College/Columbia Univ

Doctor of Music Education
IN0900 Indiana Univ-Bloomington

Doctor of Music in Choral Conducting
AA0100 Univ of Alberta
IN0900 Indiana Univ-Bloomington

Doctor of Music in Composition
AA0100 Univ of Alberta
AG0450 Univ of Toronto
AI0150 McGill University
AI0200 Universite de Montreal
FL0850 Florida State University
IL2250 Northwestern University
IN0900 Indiana Univ-Bloomington

Doctor of Music in Conducting
IL2250 Northwestern University

Doctor of Music in Conducting
IL2250 Northwestern University

Doctor of Music in Early Music
IN0900 Indiana Univ-Bloomington

Doctor of Music in Music Literature & Performance
IN0900 Indiana Univ-Bloomington

Doctor of Music in Orchestral Conducting
IN0900 Indiana Univ-Bloomington

Doctor of Music in Organ & Sacred Music
IN0900 Indiana Univ-Bloomington

Doctor of Music in Performance
AA0100 Univ of Alberta
AI0150 McGill University
FL0850 Florida State University
IL2250 Northwestern University

Doctor of Music in Piano Performance & Collaborative Arts
IL2250 Northwestern University

Doctor of Music in Piano Performance & Pedagogy
IL2250 Northwestern University

Doctor of Music in Wind Conducting
IN0900 Indiana Univ-Bloomington

Doctor of Music Ministry
KY1200 Southern Baptist Theo Seminary

Doctorate of Arts in Music
CO0950 Univ of Northern Colorado
IN0150 Ball State University

Doctorate of Arts in Music Education
CO0950 Univ of Northern Colorado
IN0150 Ball State University

Doctorate of Church Music
CA1050 Claremont Graduate University

Doctorate of Musical Arts
CA1050 Claremont Graduate University
UT0250 Univ of Utah

EDDCT in Music Education
NY4200 Teachers College/Columbia Univ

Graduate Cantorial Investiture
NY1450 Hebrew Union College

Graduate Certificate in Music
AR0850 Univ of Central Arkansas

Graduate Certificate in Music Entrepreneurship
NE0600 Univ of Nebraska-Lincoln

Graduate Certificate in Orchestral Studies
MI2200 Wayne State University

Graduate Certificate in Performance
AG0450 Univ of Toronto
IL2200 Northern Illinois University
IL2250 Northwestern University
TX3500 Univ of Texas-Arlington

Graduate Diploma
NY1900 The Juilliard School

Graduate Diploma in Jazz Studies
PA3330 Univ of the Arts

Graduate Diploma in Performance
IL0550 Chicago College of Perf Arts
MA1175 Longy School of Music
MI1400 Michigan State University

Graduate Diploma in Professional Performance
AI0200 Universite de Montreal

Graduate Diploma in Professional Performance
AI0150 McGill University

Graduate Diploma: Pro Performance Orchestral Repertory
AI0200 Universite de Montreal

IPHD in Music Education
MO1810 Univ of Missouri-Kansas City

Master Humanities of Music
OH2500 Wright State University

Master Musical Arts in Composition
CT0850 Yale University

Master Musical Arts in Performance
CT0850 Yale University

Master of Arts
AG0100 Carleton University
CA1050 Claremont Graduate University
CT0900 Yale University
SD0450 Sioux Falls Seminary
WI0300 Concordia University Wisconsin

Master of Arts Collaborative Piano/Instrumental or Vocal
TN1100 Middle Tennessee State University

Master of Arts Education in Music Education
MO1780 Truman State University

Master of Arts in Arts Administration
FL0850 Florida State University
MN1400 St Marys University of Minnesota

Master of Arts in Arts Presenting
FL1900 Univ of Miami

Master of Arts in Audio Sciences
MD0650 Peabody Conservatory of Music

Master of Arts in Church Music
GA1100 Interdenominational Theo Center
IN1350 St Josephs College
KY0150 Asbury Theological Seminary
TX2600 Southwestern Baptist Theo Sem

Master of Arts in Church Music/Christian Education
GA1100 Interdenominational Theo Center

Master of Arts in Composition
AG0650 York University
CA2950 Mills College
CA4200 San Francisco State University
CA4400 San Jose State University
CA5000 Univ of California-Berkeley
CA5010 Univ of California-Davis
CA5030 Univ of California-Los Angeles
CA5050 Univ of California-San Diego
CA5060 Univ of California-Santa Barbara
CA5070 Univ of California-Santa Cruz
IA1550 Univ of Iowa
IL3250 Univ of Chicago
LA0750 Tulane University
MI2100 Univ of Michigan-Ann Arbor
MN1623 Univ of Minnesota-Twin Cities
MO1900 Washington University
NC0600 Duke University
NY0550 City Univ of New York-City Coll
NY0642 City Univ of New York-Queens Coll
NY1100 Eastman School of Music
NY3790 State Univ of New York-Stony Brook
NY4320 Univ at Buffalo (SUNY)
OH1100 Kent State University-Kent
PA3350 Univ of Pennsylvania
TN1100 Middle Tennessee State University

Master of Arts in Composition for Contemporary Media
TN1100 Middle Tennessee State University

Master of Arts in Composition for Visual Media
CA5030 Univ of California-Los Angeles

Master of Arts in Computer Music
CA5050 Univ of California-San Diego

Master of Arts in Conducting

CA4400	San Jose State University
CA5010	Univ of California-Davis
IA1550	Univ of Iowa
MO1790	Univ of Central Missouri
TN1100	Middle Tennessee State University
VA0750	Lynchburg College

Master of Arts in Digital Musics
| H0100 | Dartmouth College |

Master of Arts in Early Music
| CA5300 | Univ of Southern California |
| OH0400 | Case Western Reserve University |

Master of Arts in Education
AL1150	Univ of Alabama-Birmingham
CA1425	Concordia University
MN0800	Hamline University
MO0650	Lindenwood University
NC2600	Western Carolina University
NY1600	Hofstra University
OH1650	Muskingum University
VT0150	Goddard College

Master of Arts in Education: Music Education
| NE0590 | Univ of Nebraska-Kearney |

Master of Arts in Electronic Music & Multimedia
| RI0050 | Brown University |

Master of Arts in Ethnomusicology
AB0100	Univ of British Columbia
AD0050	Memorial Univ of Newfoundland
AG0650	York University
AZ0100	Arizona State University
CA4100	San Diego State University
CA5000	Univ of California-Berkeley
CA5010	Univ of California-Davis
CA5031	Univ of California-Los Angeles
CA5040	Univ of California-Riverside
CA5060	Univ of California-Santa Barbara
CA5070	Univ of California-Santa Cruz
HI0210	Univ of Hawaii-Manoa
IL3250	Univ of Chicago
MD1010	Univ of Maryland
NY1100	Eastman School of Music
OH1100	Kent State University-Kent
PA3420	Univ of Pittsburgh
RI0050	Brown University
WA1050	Univ of Washington
WI0815	Univ of Wisconsin-Madison

Master of Arts in Historical Musicology
AB0150	Univ of Victoria
CA5000	Univ of California-Berkeley
CT0600	Univ of Connecticut
NY0550	City Univ of New York-City Coll
NY0642	City Univ of New York-Queens Coll

Master of Arts in History & Literature
AZ0100	Arizona State University
CA0815	Calif State Univ-Fullerton
CO0900	Univ of Denver
MD1010	Univ of Maryland
MO1790	Univ of Central Missouri
NY2105	Long Island Univ-LIU Post Campus
PA1600	Indiana Univ of Pennsylvania
WV0400	Marshall University

Master of Arts in History & Theory
| L3250 | Univ of Chicago |
| NJ1130 | Rutgers the State Univ-New Brnswk |

Master of Arts in History & Theory of Music
| NY3790 | State Univ of New York-Stony Brook |

Master of Arts in Integrative Studies
| CA5050 | Univ of California-San Diego |

Master of Arts in Interdisciplinary Studies
| OR0700 | Oregon State University |
| TX3535 | Univ of Texas at Tyler |

Master of Arts in Jazz
| AG0650 | York University |

Master of Arts in Jazz Performance & Composition
| NY0642 | City Univ of New York-Queens Coll |

Master of Arts in Jazz Studies
CA4400	San Jose State University
NJ1140	Rutgers the State Univ-Newark
NY0550	City Univ of New York-City Coll
TN1100	Middle Tennessee State University

Master of Arts in Jazz Studies: Music Culture of New Orleans
| LA0750 | Tulane University |

Master of Arts in Kodaly
| MO1790 | Univ of Central Missouri |

Master of Arts in Liberal Studies
| MN0800 | Hamline University |

Master of Arts in Media Arts
| MI2100 | Univ of Michigan-Ann Arbor |

Master of Arts in Music
AA0100	Univ of Alberta
AK0150	Univ of Alaska-Fairbanks
AL0500	Jacksonville State University
CA0807	Calif State Univ-East Bay
CA0810	Calif State Univ-Fresno
CA0830	Calif State Univ-Los Angeles
CA0835	Calif State Univ-Northridge
CT0750	Wesleyan University
FL0650	Florida Atlantic University
FL0850	Florida State University
FL1800	Univ of Central Florida
IA1600	Univ of Northern Iowa
IL0730	Concordia University
IL0800	Eastern Illinois University
IL2150	Northeastern Illinois University
IN0150	Ball State University
KY0400	Campbellsville University
MA0400	Boston University
MA1900	Tufts University
MI0250	Andrews University
MI2200	Wayne State University
MO1780	Truman State University
MO1810	Univ of Missouri-Kansas City
MO1950	Webster University
NH0350	Univ of New Hampshire
NV0100	Univ of Nevada-Reno
NY0625	City Univ of New York-Hunter Coll
NY1700	Houghton College
OR0850	Portland State University
PA2150	Mansfield University
TX2700	Stephen F Austin State University
TX3150	Texas Southern University
TX3420	Univ of North Texas
TX3750	West Texas A&M University
VA1100	Radford University
WA0250	Eastern Washington University
WA1150	Washington State University

Master of Arts in Music Business

| NY2750 | New York University |

Master of Arts in Music Criticism
| AG0200 | McMaster University |

Master of Arts in Music Education
AI0150	McGill University
AL0500	Jacksonville State University
AL1170	Univ of Alabama
CA0815	Calif State Univ-Fullerton
CA0825	Calif State Univ-Long Beach
CA4200	San Francisco State University
CA4400	San Jose State University
CO0900	Univ of Denver
FL2000	Univ of South Florida
GA1650	Piedmont College
HI0210	Univ of Hawaii-Manoa
IA1550	Univ of Iowa
IL2150	Northeastern Illinois University
KY1550	Western Kentucky University
MD1010	Univ of Maryland
MN1623	Univ of Minnesota-Twin Cities
MN1625	Univ of St. Thomas
MO1790	Univ of Central Missouri
MO1800	Univ of Missouri
NC2435	Univ of North Carolina-Pembroke
NJ0800	Montclair State University
NJ0825	New Jersey City University
NJ1050	Rowan University
NY1100	Eastman School of Music
NY2750	New York University
NY4200	Teachers College/Columbia Univ
OH0400	Case Western Reserve University
OH1850	Ohio State University-Columbus
PA1600	Indiana Univ of Pennsylvania
PA2200	Marywood University
PR0100	Interamerican Univ of Puerto Rico
TN1100	Middle Tennessee State University
TX2700	Stephen F Austin State University
TX3300	Texas Woman's University
UT0050	Brigham Young University
WA1050	Univ of Washington
WV0400	Marshall University

Master of Arts in Music Education (Distance Learning)
| TX2700 | Stephen F Austin State University |

Master of Arts in Music History
CA4200	San Francisco State University
CA4400	San Jose State University
CA5300	Univ of Southern California
GA2100	Univ of Georgia
ID0250	Univ of Idaho
MO1800	Univ of Missouri
NY4320	Univ at Buffalo (SUNY)
OH0400	Case Western Reserve University
WA1050	Univ of Washington

Master of Arts in Music History & Musicology
| IA1550 | Univ of Iowa |

Master of Arts in Music Industry Administration
| CA0835 | Calif State Univ-Northridge |

Master of Arts in Music Science & Technology
| LA0750 | Tulane University |

Master of Arts in Music Teaching
| NY0500 | City Univ of New York-Brooklyn |
| NY0635 | City Univ of New York-Lehman Coll |

Master of Arts in Music Technology
| AI0150 | McGill University |
| NY2750 | New York University |

Master of Arts in Music Theory
AB0100	Univ of British Columbia
AG0400	Univ of Ottawa
AG0500	Univ of Western Ontario
AI0150	McGill University
AJ0100	Univ of Regina
CA0825	Calif State Univ-Long Beach
CA4100	San Diego State University
CA4400	San Jose State University
CA5060	Univ of California-Santa Barbara
CO0900	Univ of Denver
CT0600	Univ of Connecticut
IA1550	Univ of Iowa
KY1450	Univ of Kentucky-Lexington
MD1010	Univ of Maryland
MI2100	Univ of Michigan-Ann Arbor
MN1623	Univ of Minnesota-Twin Cities
MO1900	Washington University
NY0550	City Univ of New York-City Coll
NY0642	City Univ of New York-Queens Coll
NY1100	Eastman School of Music
NY4320	Univ at Buffalo (SUNY)
OH1100	Kent State University-Kent
OH1850	Ohio State University-Columbus
OR1050	Univ of Oregon
PA2750	Penn State Univ-University Park
WA1050	Univ of Washington
WA1250	Western Washington University
WI0815	Univ of Wisconsin-Madison

Master of Arts in Music Theory & History
PA2750	Penn State Univ-University Park

Master of Arts in Music Theory Pedagogy
NY1100	Eastman School of Music

Master of Arts in Music Theory-Composition
CA5040	Univ of California-Riverside
MA0500	Brandeis University
MO1790	Univ of Central Missouri
NJ0800	Montclair State University
NJ1130	Rutgers the State Univ-New Brnswk
NY2105	Long Island Univ-LIU Post Campus
PA1600	Indiana Univ of Pennsylvania
PA3420	Univ of Pittsburgh
WV0400	Marshall University

Master of Arts in Music Theory/Gender and Women's Studies
AI0150	McGill University

Master of Arts in Music Therapy
CA5350	Univ of the Pacific
IN1400	St Mary of the Woods College
MO1810	Univ of Missouri-Kansas City
NJ0800	Montclair State University
NY2750	New York University
PA1550	Immaculata University
TX3300	Texas Woman's University

Master of Arts in Music, Science & Technology
CA4900	Stanford University

Master of Arts in Musicology
AA0150	Univ of Calgary
AB0100	Univ of British Columbia
AB0150	Univ of Victoria
AF0100	Dalhousie University
AG0400	Univ of Ottawa
AG0450	Univ of Toronto
AG0500	Univ of Western Ontario
AG0650	York University
AI0150	McGill University
AJ0100	Univ of Regina
CA0825	Calif State Univ-Long Beach
CA4100	San Diego State University
CA5010	Univ of California-Davis
CA5032	Univ of California-Los Angeles
CA5040	Univ of California-Riverside
CA5060	Univ of California-Santa Barbara
HI0210	Univ of Hawaii-Manoa
IN0900	Indiana Univ-Bloomington
KY1450	Univ of Kentucky-Lexington
MA0500	Brandeis University
MI1400	Michigan State University
MI2100	Univ of Michigan-Ann Arbor
MN1623	Univ of Minnesota-Twin Cities
MO1900	Washington University
NC0600	Duke University
NC2410	Univ of North Carolina-Chapel Hill
NJ1130	Rutgers the State Univ-New Brnswk
NY0500	City Univ of New York-Brooklyn
NY1100	Eastman School of Music
OH1850	Ohio State University-Columbus
OR1050	Univ of Oregon
PA2750	Penn State Univ-University Park
PA3420	Univ of Pittsburgh
TN1100	Middle Tennessee State University
UT0050	Brigham Young University
UT0250	Univ of Utah
WI0815	Univ of Wisconsin-Madison

Master of Arts in Musicology with Performance
AB0150	Univ of Victoria

Master of Arts in Musicology, Specialization in New Orleans Music
LA0750	Tulane University

Master of Arts in Musicology/Gender and Women's Studies
AI0150	McGill University

Master of Arts in Musicology/Master of Library Science
IN0900	Indiana Univ-Bloomington

Master of Arts in Musicology/MS in Library Science
DC0050	Catholic Univ of America, The

Master of Arts in Pedagogy
IL2150	Northeastern Illinois University
TX3300	Texas Woman's University

Master of Arts in Performance
CA4400	San Jose State University
CA5050	Univ of California-San Diego
IA1550	Univ of Iowa
MO1790	Univ of Central Missouri
NJ0800	Montclair State University
NY0550	City Univ of New York-City Coll
NY0642	City Univ of New York-Queens Coll
PA1600	Indiana Univ of Pennsylvania
TN1100	Middle Tennessee State University
TX3300	Texas Woman's University
WV0400	Marshall University

Master of Arts in Performance Practice
CA5070	Univ of California-Santa Cruz
MA1050	Harvard University
NC0600	Duke University
NY0500	City Univ of New York-Brooklyn

Master of Arts in Piano Pedagogy
CA0815	Calif State Univ-Fullerton
CA4100	San Diego State University
MO1790	Univ of Central Missouri

Master of Arts in Popular Music
AG0650	York University

Master of Arts in Popular Music & Culture
AG0500	Univ of Western Ontario

Master of Arts in Sacred Music
Y1860	Jewish Theological Seminary

Master of Arts in Teaching
MI0300	Aquinas College
NC2600	Western Carolina University
NY2200	Manhattanville College
OR0700	Oregon State University
OR1300	Willamette University
SC1200	Winthrop University

Master of Arts in Teaching in Music Education
GA1650	Piedmont College
NY0625	City Univ of New York-Hunter Coll
PA3330	Univ of the Arts
WV0400	Marshall University

Master of Arts in Teaching Specialization Music
MA0510	Bridgewater State University
NC2435	Univ of North Carolina-Pembroke
SC0420	Coastal Carolina University

Master of Arts in Worship
KY1200	Southern Baptist Theo Seminary
TX2600	Southwestern Baptist Theo Sem

Master of Arts Musicology/Ethnomusicology
AI0200	Universite de Montreal

Master of Arts Teaching emphasis Choral Music
SC0500	College of Charleston

Master of Arts Teaching Music Education
OR0150	Concordia University

Master of Church Music
IL0730	Concordia University
KY1200	Southern Baptist Theo Seminary
NC2350	Southeast Baptist Theo Seminary
TN0850	Lee University

Master of Divinity emphasis in Church Music
AL0800	Samford University

Master of Divinity in Church Music
KY1200	Southern Baptist Theo Seminary

Master of Divinity in Worship
AJ0030	Briercrest College and Seminary
KY1200	Southern Baptist Theo Seminary

Master of Divinity in Worship Leadership
GA1100	Interdenominational Theo Center
NC2350	Southeast Baptist Theo Seminary
OH0150	Athenaeum of Ohio
SD0450	Sioux Falls Seminary

Master of Education
AJ0150 Univ of Saskatchewan
OK0600 Northwestern Oklahoma State Univ

Master of Education in Music Education
AL0010 Alabama A & M University
AL0200 Auburn University-Auburn
GA2100 Univ of Georgia
MA2100 Westfield State University
MN1400 St Marys University of Minnesota
MO1800 Univ of Missouri
NY4200 Teachers College/Columbia Univ
PA2750 Penn State Univ-University Park

Master of Education with Concentration in Music Education
OH2250 Univ of Dayton

Master of Music
AG0400 Univ of Ottawa
AJ0150 Univ of Saskatchewan
FL1125 Lynn University
IN0005 American Conservatory of Music
KY1200 Southern Baptist Theo Seminary
LA0550 Northwestern State Univ of Louisiana
NY0150 Bard College
NY1900 The Juilliard School
TX2150 Rice University
TX3175 Texas State University-San Marcos

Master of Music Education
AR0110 Arkansas State University-State U
CO0800 Univ of Colorado-Boulder
CT0650 Univ of Hartford
DC0150 Howard University
FL0850 Florida State University
GA0150 Albany State University
GA0850 Georgia College & State University
GA2100 Univ of Georgia
IL3300 Univ of Illinois
IL3450 VanderCook College of Music
IN0900 Indiana Univ-Bloomington
KY0950 Murray State University
KY1500 Univ of Louisville
LA0350 McNeese State University
MO1810 Univ of Missouri-Kansas City
MO1830 Univ of Missouri-St. Louis
MS0350 Jackson State University
MS0750 Univ of Southern Mississippi, The
ND0250 Minot State University
ND0350 North Dakota State University
NJ1350 Westminster Choir College
OK1350 Univ of Oklahoma
SC0200 Bob Jones University
SC1200 Winthrop University
TX2955 Texas A&M University-Commerce
TX3000 Texas Christian University
VA1000 Old Dominion University
VA1350 Shenandoah Conservatory
WV0550 Shepherd University

Master of Music Education in Music Therapy
GA2100 Univ of Georgia
KS1350 Univ of Kansas

Master of Music in Accompanying
CT0650 Univ of Hartford
FL0850 Florida State University
ID0250 Univ of Idaho
MA1400 New England Conservatory
NC0650 East Carolina University
NC2430 Univ of North Carolina-Greensboro
NM0450 Univ of New Mexico
OH2150 Univ of Akron
TN1710 Univ of Tennessee-Knoxville
WI0825 Univ of Wisconsin-Milwaukee

Master of Music in Accompanying & Chamber Music
AG0650 York University
TX3400 Univ of Houston

Master of Music in Afro Latin Music
CA0830 Calif State Univ-Los Angeles

Master of Music in Applied Music
AR0700 Univ of Arkansas-Fayetteville
IL0750 DePaul University
OH2600 Youngstown State University
TX3400 Univ of Houston

Master of Music in Arts Administration
MI2100 Univ of Michigan-Ann Arbor

Master of Music in Brass Performance
WA1050 Univ of Washington

Master of Music in CD Production
OK1330 Univ of Central Oklahoma

Master of Music in Chamber Music
CA4150 San Francisco Conserv of Music
CA4200 San Francisco State University
FL2000 Univ of South Florida
MA1400 New England Conservatory
MI2100 Univ of Michigan-Ann Arbor
WI0825 Univ of Wisconsin-Milwaukee

Master of Music in Chamber Music (Piano)
DC0050 Catholic Univ of America, The

Master of Music in Choral Conducting
AA0100 Univ of Alberta
AL1170 Univ of Alabama
AR0110 Arkansas State University-State U
AZ0450 Northern Arizona University
CA0825 Calif State Univ-Long Beach
FL1900 Univ of Miami
GA0750 Emory University
GA1300 Mercer University
IN0900 Indiana Univ-Bloomington
KS1050 Pittsburg State University
MA1400 New England Conservatory
MN1000 Minnesota State Univ-Mankato
MN1623 Univ of Minnesota-Twin Cities
MS0700 Univ of Mississippi
NE0600 Univ of Nebraska-Lincoln
NJ1350 Westminster Choir College
NM0450 Univ of New Mexico
NY2250 Mannes College
WA1050 Univ of Washington

Master of Music in Choral Music
CA5300 Univ of Southern California
IL3300 Univ of Illinois

Master of Music in Church Music
AL0800 Samford University
GA1300 Mercer University
KS1350 Univ of Kansas
KY0400 Campbellsville University
LA0400 New Orleans Baptist Theo Seminary
MI2100 Univ of Michigan-Ann Arbor
MO1950 Webster University
NC0650 East Carolina University
SC0200 Bob Jones University
TN0100 Belmont University
TX0300 Baylor University
TX0900 Hardin-Simmons University
TX2600 Southwestern Baptist Theo Sem
VA1350 Shenandoah Conservatory

Master of Music in Collaborative Keyboard
CA4150 San Francisco Conserv of Music
FL1900 Univ of Miami

Master of Music in Collaborative Performance
NY1700 Houghton College

Master of Music in Collaborative Piano
AC0050 Brandon University
AZ0100 Arizona State University
CO0800 Univ of Colorado-Boulder
CO0950 Univ of Northern Colorado
IL1150 Illinois State University
IL2100 North Park University
IL2900 Southern Illinois Univ-Carbondale
LA0200 Louisiana State University
MA1175 Longy School of Music
MA2000 Univ of Massachusetts Amherst
MI1400 Michigan State University
MI2100 Univ of Michigan-Ann Arbor
MO1800 Univ of Missouri
OH0600 Cleveland Institute of Music
OH1900 Ohio University
OH2200 Univ of Cincinnati
TX0300 Baylor University
VA1350 Shenandoah Conservatory
WI0815 Univ of Wisconsin-Madison
WI0825 Univ of Wisconsin-Milwaukee
WV0750 West Virginia University

Master of Music in Collaborative Piano Performance
NJ1130 Rutgers the State Univ-New Brnswk

Master of Music in Collaborative Piano/Chamber Music
TX2250 Sam Houston State University

Master of Music in Collaborative Piano/Coaching
MN1623 Univ of Minnesota-Twin Cities

Master of Music in Commercial Music
CA0830 Calif State Univ-Los Angeles
TN0100 Belmont University

Master of Music in Composition
AA0100 Univ of Alberta
AA0150 Univ of Calgary
AB0100 Univ of British Columbia
AB0150 Univ of Victoria
AC0050 Brandon University
AC0100 Univ of Manitoba
AG0450 Univ of Toronto
AG0500 Univ of Western Ontario
AI0150 McGill University
AI0190 Universite Laval
AI0200 Universite de Montreal
AJ0100 Univ of Regina
AL1170 Univ of Alabama
AR0110 Arkansas State University-State U
AR0700 Univ of Arkansas-Fayetteville
AZ0100 Arizona State University
AZ0500 Univ of Arizona
CA0815 Calif State Univ-Fullerton
CA0825 Calif State Univ-Long Beach
CA0830 Calif State Univ-Los Angeles
CA0835 Calif State Univ-Northridge
CA0840 Calif State Univ-Sacramento
CA4100 San Diego State University
CA5150 Univ of Redlands
CA5300 Univ of Southern California
CO0800 Univ of Colorado-Boulder
CO0900 Univ of Denver
CO0950 Univ of Northern Colorado
CT0650 Univ of Hartford
CT0850 Yale University
DC0050 Catholic Univ of America, The
DE0150 Univ of Delaware
FL0700 Florida International Univ
FL0850 Florida State University
FL1850 Univ of Florida
FL1900 Univ of Miami
FL2000 Univ of South Florida
GA0950 Georgia Southern University
GA1050 Georgia State University
GA2100 Univ of Georgia
HI0210 Univ of Hawaii-Manoa

Index of Graduate Degrees

IA1600	Univ of Northern Iowa
ID0250	Univ of Idaho
IL0550	Chicago College of Perf Arts
IL0750	DePaul University
IL1150	Illinois State University
IL3300	Univ of Illinois
IL3500	Western Illinois University
IN0150	Ball State University
IN0250	Butler University
IN0900	Indiana Univ-Bloomington
IN0910	Indiana Univ-South Bend
KS1350	Univ of Kansas
KY1450	Univ of Kentucky-Lexington
KY1500	Univ of Louisville
LA0200	Louisiana State University
LA0800	Univ of New Orleans
MA0350	The Boston Conservatory
MA0400	Boston University
MA1175	Longy School of Music
MA1400	New England Conservatory
MA2000	Univ of Massachusetts Amherst
MD0650	Peabody Conservatory of Music
MD0850	Towson University
MD1010	Univ of Maryland
ME0500	Univ of Southern Maine
MI0400	Central Michigan University
MI0600	Eastern Michigan University
MI1400	Michigan State University
MI2100	Univ of Michigan-Ann Arbor
MI2250	Western Michigan University
MO1800	Univ of Missouri
MO1810	Univ of Missouri-Kansas City
MO1950	Webster University
NC0650	East Carolina University
NC2430	Univ of North Carolina-Greensboro
ND0500	Univ of North Dakota-Grand Forks
NE0600	Univ of Nebraska-Lincoln
NJ1050	Rowan University
NJ1350	Westminster Choir College
NY0500	City Univ of New York-Brooklyn
NY1100	Eastman School of Music
NY1700	Houghton College
NY1800	Ithaca College
NY2150	Manhattan School of Music
NY2250	Mannes College
NY2750	New York University
NY3705	State Univ of New York-Binghamton
NY3780	State Univ of New York-Potsdam
NY3785	State Univ of New York-Purchase
NY4150	Syracuse University
OH0300	Bowling Green State University
OH0600	Cleveland Institute of Music
OH0650	Cleveland State University
OH1850	Ohio State University-Columbus
OH1900	Ohio University
OH2150	Univ of Akron
OH2200	Univ of Cincinnati
OK0750	Oklahoma City University
OK1350	Univ of Oklahoma
OR1050	Univ of Oregon
PA0550	Carnegie Mellon University
PA3250	Temple University
SC1110	Univ of South Carolina-Columbia
TN0100	Belmont University
TN1680	Univ of Memphis
TN1710	Univ of Tennessee-Knoxville
TX0300	Baylor University
TX2250	Sam Houston State University
TX2400	Southern Methodist University
TX3400	Univ of Houston
TX3420	Univ of North Texas
TX3510	Univ of Texas-Austin
UT0050	Brigham Young University
UT0250	Univ of Utah
VA0450	George Mason University
VA1350	Shenandoah Conservatory
WA0050	Central Washington University
WA1050	Univ of Washington
WA1250	Western Washington University
WI0815	Univ of Wisconsin-Madison
WV0750	West Virginia University

Master of Music in Composition/Arranging
NY1275	Five Towns College

Master of Music in Composition/Music Technology
MT0400	Univ of Montana
NC0650	East Carolina University

Master of Music in Computer Music
MD0650	Peabody Conservatory of Music

Master of Music in Computer Music Composition
IN0900	Indiana Univ-Bloomington

Master of Music in Conducting
A0150	Univ of Calgary
AC0050	Brandon University
AC0100	Univ of Manitoba
AD0050	Memorial Univ of Newfoundland
AI0200	Universite de Montreal
AJ0100	Univ of Regina
AR0700	Univ of Arkansas-Fayetteville
AR0850	Univ of Central Arkansas
AZ0500	Univ of Arizona
CA0830	Calif State Univ-Los Angeles
CA0835	Calif State Univ-Northridge
CA0840	Calif State Univ-Sacramento
CA4100	San Diego State University
CA4150	San Francisco Conserv of Music
CA4200	San Francisco State University
CA5150	Univ of Redlands
CA5300	Univ of Southern California
CO0250	Colorado State University
CO0800	Univ of Colorado-Boulder
CO0900	Univ of Denver
CO0950	Univ of Northern Colorado
CT0650	Univ of Hartford
FL0700	Florida International Univ
FL0850	Florida State University
FL1850	Univ of Florida
FL2000	Univ of South Florida
GA0550	Columbus State University
GA0950	Georgia Southern University
GA1050	Georgia State University
GA1700	Reinhardt University
GA2100	Univ of Georgia
IA1600	Univ of Northern Iowa
IL2250	Northwestern University
IL3300	Univ of Illinois
IL3500	Western Illinois University
IN0150	Ball State University
IN0250	Butler University
IN0800	Indiana State University
KS1350	Univ of Kansas
KS1450	Wichita State University
KY0400	Campbellsville University
KY0550	Eastern Kentucky University
KY1450	Univ of Kentucky-Lexington
LA0200	Louisiana State University
LA0760	Univ of Louisiana-Lafayette
LA0770	Univ of Louisiana-Monroe
LA0800	Univ of New Orleans
MA0350	The Boston Conservatory
MA0400	Boston University
MA1400	New England Conservatory
MA2000	Univ of Massachusetts Amherst
MD0650	Peabody Conservatory of Music
ME0500	Univ of Southern Maine
MI0250	Andrews University
MI0400	Central Michigan University
MI1400	Michigan State University
MI1750	Oakland University
MI2100	Univ of Michigan-Ann Arbor
MI2200	Wayne State University
MI2250	Western Michigan University
MO0775	Missouri State University
MO1800	Univ of Missouri
MO1810	Univ of Missouri-Kansas City
MS0400	Mississippi College
MS0750	Univ of Southern Mississippi, The
NC2430	Univ of North Carolina-Greensboro
ND0350	North Dakota State University
ND0500	Univ of North Dakota-Grand Forks
NE0610	Univ of Nebraska-Omaha
NJ1050	Rowan University
NJ1130	Rutgers the State Univ-New Brnswk
NM0310	New Mexico State University
NM0450	Univ of New Mexico
NV0050	Univ of Nevada-Las Vegas
NY1100	Eastman School of Music
NY1700	Houghton College
NY1800	Ithaca College
NY3705	State Univ of New York-Binghamton
NY4150	Syracuse University
OH1100	Kent State University-Kent
OH1700	Oberlin College
OH1850	Ohio State University-Columbus
OH1900	Ohio University
OH2150	Univ of Akron
OH2200	Univ of Cincinnati
OK0750	Oklahoma City University
OR0850	Portland State University
OR0950	Southern Oregon University
OR1050	Univ of Oregon
PA0550	Carnegie Mellon University
PA2300	Messiah College
PA2750	Penn State Univ-University Park
PA3250	Temple University
SC1110	Univ of South Carolina-Columbia
SC1200	Winthrop University
TN0050	Austin Peay State University
TN1680	Univ of Memphis
TN1710	Univ of Tennessee-Knoxville
TX0300	Baylor University
TX2250	Sam Houston State University
TX2400	Southern Methodist University
TX2700	Stephen F Austin State University
TX3000	Texas Christian University
TX3530	Univ of Texas-San Antonio
UT0050	Brigham Young University
UT0250	Univ of Utah
VA0450	George Mason University
VA0600	James Madison University
VA1350	Shenandoah Conservatory
WA0050	Central Washington University
WA1250	Western Washington University
WI0825	Univ of Wisconsin-Milwaukee

Master of Music in Contemporary Improvisation
MA1400	New England Conservatory

Master of Music in Contemporary Music
OR1250	Western Oregon University

Master of Music in Dalcroze Eurhythmics
MA1175	Longy School of Music

Master of Music in Dance Accompanying
VA1350	Shenandoah Conservatory

Master of Music in Digital Arts & Sound Design
FL1900	Univ of Miami

Master of Music in Early Keyboard Instruments
MI2100	Univ of Michigan-Ann Arbor

Master of Music in Early Music
IN0900	Indiana Univ-Bloomington
NY1100	Eastman School of Music

Master of Music in Early Music Performance
MA1175	Longy School of Music

Master of Music in Education
CA5300	Univ of Southern California
PA1050	Duquesne University
RI0200	Rhode Island College

Master of Music in Electro-Acoustic Music
FL2000	Univ of South Florida

Master of Music in Ethnomusicology
OH0300	Bowling Green State University

Master of Music in Harp Performance
WA1050　Univ of Washington

Master of Music in Harpischord Performance
WA1050　Univ of Washington

Master of Music in Historical Performance
MA0400　Boston University
MA1400　New England Conservatory
OH1700　Oberlin College

Master of Music in History & Literature
CO0950　Univ of Northern Colorado
IL2900　Southern Illinois Univ-Carbondale
KS0650　Kansas State University
KS1450　Wichita State University
MA0400　Boston University
MS0750　Univ of Southern Mississippi, The
NY3705　State Univ of New York-Binghamton
OH1900　Ohio University
OH2150　Univ of Akron
TX0300　Baylor University
TX2400　Southern Methodist University
TX3200　Texas Tech University
WA1250　Western Washington University
WI0825　Univ of Wisconsin-Milwaukee
WV0750　West Virginia University

Master of Music in History of Musical Instruments
SD0600　Univ of South Dakota

Master of Music in History-Musicology
IN0150　Ball State University

Master of Music in Improvisation
MI2100　Univ of Michigan-Ann Arbor

Master of Music in Instrumental Conducting
AZ0450　Northern Arizona University
CA0825　Calif State Univ-Long Beach
FL1900　Univ of Miami
NE0600　Univ of Nebraska-Lincoln
TX2400　Southern Methodist University
WA1050　Univ of Washington

Master of Music in Instrumental Pedagogy
AI0190　Universite Laval

Master of Music in Instrumental Performance
L1900　Univ of Miami

Master of Music in Instrumental/Voice Performance
AI0200　Universite de Montreal

Master of Music in Jazz
FL0700　Florida International Univ

Master of Music in Jazz & Studio Music
TN1680　Univ of Memphis

Master of Music in Jazz Composing/Arranging
MA2000　Univ of Massachusetts Amherst

Master of Music in Jazz Pedagogy
IA1600　Univ of Northern Iowa
IL2250　Northwestern University

Master of Music in Jazz Performance
MI2200　Wayne State University
OK1330　Univ of Central Oklahoma

Master of Music in Jazz Performance & Pedagogy
MO1800　Univ of Missouri

Master of Music in Jazz Studies
CA0825　Calif State Univ-Long Beach
CA4100　San Diego State University
CA5300　Univ of Southern California
CO0950　Univ of Northern Colorado
DC0150　Howard University
FL0850　Florida State University
FL2000　Univ of South Florida
GA1050　Georgia State University
IL0750　DePaul University
IL3500　Western Illinois University
IN0900　Indiana Univ-Bloomington
LA0200　Louisiana State University
LA0800　Univ of New Orleans
MA1400　New England Conservatory
ME0500　Univ of Southern Maine
MI1400　Michigan State University
MO1950　Webster University
NC0650　East Carolina University
NE0600　Univ of Nebraska-Lincoln
NJ1050　Rowan University
NJ1130　Rutgers the State Univ-New Brnswk
NJ1400　William Paterson University
NY2150　Manhattan School of Music
OH2150　Univ of Akron
OH2600　Youngstown State University
OR0850　Portland State University
OR1050　Univ of Oregon
PA3330　Univ of the Arts
SC1110　Univ of South Carolina-Columbia
TN1710　Univ of Tennessee-Knoxville
TX3420　Univ of North Texas
UT0250　Univ of Utah

Master of Music in Jazz Studies & Contemporary Media
NY1100　Eastman School of Music

Master of Music in Jazz Studies & Improv Music
WA1050　Univ of Washington

Master of Music in Jazz/Commercial Music Performance
NY1275　Five Towns College

Master of Music in Keyboard Instruments
MI2100　Univ of Michigan-Ann Arbor

Master of Music in Keyboard Performance
FL1900　Univ of Miami

Master of Music in Keyboard Performance & Pedagogy
FL1900　Univ of Miami

Master of Music in Keyboard Studies
MO1900　Washington University

Master of Music in Literature & Pedagogy
TX3510　Univ of Texas-Austin

Master of Music in Media Writing-Production
FL1900　Univ of Miami

Master of Music in Multiple Woodwinds
FL1900　Univ of Miami
IN0150　Ball State University

Master of Music in Music & Human Learning
TX3510　Univ of Texas-Austin

Master of Music in Music Ed with Certification
FL1900　Univ of Miami

Master of Music in Music Ed with String Pedagogy Emphasis
FL1900　Univ of Miami

Master of Music in Music Ed. & Piano Pedagogy
IL2250　Northwestern University

Master of Music in Music Ed. & String Pedagogy
IL2250　Northwestern University

Master of Music in Music Education
AA0150　Univ of Calgary
AC0050　Brandon University
AG0450　Univ of Toronto
AG0500　Univ of Western Ontario
AI0190　Universite Laval
AL0050　Alabama State University
AL0800　Samford University
AR0700　Univ of Arkansas-Fayetteville
AR0850　Univ of Central Arkansas
AZ0100　Arizona State University
AZ0500　Univ of Arizona
CA0250　Azusa Pacific University
CA0830　Calif State Univ-Los Angeles
CA5150　Univ of Redlands
CA5300　Univ of Southern California
CA5350　Univ of the Pacific
CO0250　Colorado State University
CO0950　Univ of Northern Colorado
DE0150　Univ of Delaware
FL1850　Univ of Florida
FL1900　Univ of Miami
GA0550　Columbus State University
GA0950　Georgia Southern University
GA1050　Georgia State University
GA1700　Reinhardt University
GA2130　Univ of West Georgia
GA2150　Valdosta State University
IA1600　Univ of Northern Iowa
ID0050　Boise State University
ID0100　Idaho State University
ID0250　Univ of Idaho
IL0750　DePaul University
IL1150　Illinois State University
IL2200　Northern Illinois University
IL2250　Northwestern University
IL2900　Southern Illinois Univ-Carbondale
IL2910　Southern Illinois Univ-Edwardsvle
IL3500　Western Illinois University
IN0100　Anderson University
IN0150　Ball State University
IN0250　Butler University
IN0800　Indiana State University

KS0300	Emporia State University	VA0600	James Madison University	\	\	\

Index of Graduate Degrees

KS0300	Emporia State University
KS0650	Kansas State University
KS1050	Pittsburg State University
KS1350	Univ of Kansas
KS1450	Wichita State University
KY0400	Campbellsville University
KY0550	Eastern Kentucky University
KY0900	Morehead State University
KY1450	Univ of Kentucky-Lexington
LA0200	Louisiana State University
LA0760	Univ of Louisiana-Lafayette
LA0770	Univ of Louisiana-Monroe
MA0350	The Boston Conservatory
MA0400	Boston University
MA2000	Univ of Massachusetts Amherst
MA2030	Univ of Massachusetts Lowell
MD0650	Peabody Conservatory of Music
MD1010	Univ of Maryland
ME0440	Univ of Maine-Orono
ME0500	Univ of Southern Maine
MI0250	Andrews University
MI0400	Central Michigan University
MI0600	Eastern Michigan University
MI1400	Michigan State University
MI1750	Oakland University
MI2100	Univ of Michigan-Ann Arbor
MI2200	Wayne State University
MI2250	Western Michigan University
MN1000	Minnesota State Univ-Mankato
MN1600	Univ of Minnesota Duluth
MO0775	Missouri State University
MO1950	Webster University
MS0400	Mississippi College
MS0700	Univ of Mississippi
MS0850	William Carey University
MT0400	Univ of Montana
NC0050	Appalachian State University
NC0650	East Carolina University
NC2430	Univ of North Carolina-Greensboro
ND0500	Univ of North Dakota-Grand Forks
NE0600	Univ of Nebraska-Lincoln
NE0610	Univ of Nebraska-Omaha
NJ1130	Rutgers the State Univ-New Brnswk
NJ1350	Westminster Choir College
NJ1400	William Paterson University
NM0310	New Mexico State University
NM0450	Univ of New Mexico
NV0050	Univ of Nevada-Las Vegas
NV0100	Univ of Nevada-Reno
NY1100	Eastman School of Music
NY1275	Five Towns College
NY1800	Ithaca College
NY3350	Roberts Wesleyan College
NY3725	State Univ of New York-Fredonia
NY3780	State Univ of New York-Potsdam
NY4150	Syracuse University
OH0300	Bowling Green State University
OH0650	Cleveland State University
OH1100	Kent State University-Kent
OH1450	Miami University
OH1900	Ohio University
OH2150	Univ of Akron
OH2200	Univ of Cincinnati
OH2300	Univ of Toledo
OH2500	Wright State University
OH2600	Youngstown State University
OK1250	Southwestern Oklahoma State Univ
OK1330	Univ of Central Oklahoma
OR1050	Univ of Oregon
PA0550	Carnegie Mellon University
PA1900	Lebanon Valley College
PA3250	Temple University
PA3600	West Chester University
RI0300	Univ of Rhode Island
SC0650	Converse College
SC1110	Univ of South Carolina-Columbia
SD0600	Univ of South Dakota
TN0050	Austin Peay State University
TN0100	Belmont University
TN0850	Lee University
TN1680	Univ of Memphis
TN1700	Univ of Tennessee-Chattanooga
TN1710	Univ of Tennessee-Knoxville
TX0300	Baylor University
TX0900	Hardin-Simmons University
TX1400	Lamar University
TX2250	Sam Houston State University
TX2400	Southern Methodist University
TX2960	Texas A&M University-Kingsville
TX3175	Texas State University-San Marcos
TX3200	Texas Tech University
TX3400	Univ of Houston
TX3420	Univ of North Texas
TX3500	Univ of Texas-Arlington
TX3515	Univ of Texas-Brownsville
TX3520	Univ of Texas-El Paso
TX3530	Univ of Texas-San Antonio
UT0050	Brigham Young University
UT0250	Univ of Utah
VA0450	George Mason University
VA0600	James Madison University
VA0950	Norfolk State University
VA1600	Virginia Commonwealth Univ
WA0050	Central Washington University
WA1250	Western Washington University
WI0815	Univ of Wisconsin-Madison
WI0825	Univ of Wisconsin-Milwaukee
WI0850	Univ of Wisconsin-Stevens Point
WV0750	West Virginia University
WY0200	Univ of Wyoming

Master of Music in Music Education (Distance Education)

MA0400	Boston University

Master of Music in Music Education (Distance Learning)

TX2750	Tarleton State University

Master of Music in Music Education Instrumental Emphasis

H0350	Capital University

Master of Music in Music Education Jazz Pedagogy Emphasis

OH0350	Capital University

Master of Music in Music Education with Kodaly Emphasis

CA2200	Holy Names University
OH0350	Capital University
WI0770	Silver Lake College of

Master of Music in Music History

AR0700	Univ of Arkansas-Fayetteville
CT0650	Univ of Hartford
IA1600	Univ of Northern Iowa
IN0250	Butler University
MA0350	The Boston Conservatory
MA2000	Univ of Massachusetts Amherst
NE0600	Univ of Nebraska-Lincoln
NY1275	Five Towns College
OH0300	Bowling Green State University
OH2200	Univ of Cincinnati
PA3600	West Chester University
SC1110	Univ of South Carolina-Columbia
SD0600	Univ of South Dakota
UT0250	Univ of Utah

Master of Music in Music History & Literature

FL1850	Univ of Florida
KY1500	Univ of Louisville
NM0450	Univ of New Mexico
OH2600	Youngstown State University
PA3250	Temple University

Master of Music in Music Librarianship

WI0825	Univ of Wisconsin-Milwaukee

Master of Music in Music Literature

CO0800	Univ of Colorado-Boulder
GA2100	Univ of Georgia
TX3400	Univ of Houston

Master of Music in Music Management

NJ1400	William Paterson University

Master of Music in Music Technology

FL0700	Florida International Univ
GA0950	Georgia Southern University
NY1275	Five Towns College
OH2150	Univ of Akron
PA1050	Duquesne University

Master of Music in Music Theatre Direction

AZ0100	Arizona State University

Master of Music in Music Theory

AL1170	Univ of Alabama
AR0700	Univ of Arkansas-Fayetteville
AR0850	Univ of Central Arkansas
AZ0500	Univ of Arizona
CO0800	Univ of Colorado-Boulder
CT0650	Univ of Hartford
FL0850	Florida State University
FL1850	Univ of Florida
FL2000	Univ of South Florida
IL2250	Northwestern University
IL3300	Univ of Illinois
IN0150	Ball State University
IN0250	Butler University
IN0900	Indiana Univ-Bloomington
KS1350	Univ of Kansas
KY1500	Univ of Louisville
LA0200	Louisiana State University
LA0650	Southeastern Louisiana University
MA0400	Boston University
MA1400	New England Conservatory
MA2000	Univ of Massachusetts Amherst
MI1400	Michigan State University
MO1800	Univ of Missouri
MO1810	Univ of Missouri-Kansas City
NC0650	East Carolina University
NC2430	Univ of North Carolina-Greensboro
NE0600	Univ of Nebraska-Lincoln
NY2250	Mannes College
OH0300	Bowling Green State University
OH1900	Ohio University
OH2150	Univ of Akron
OH2200	Univ of Cincinnati
OK1350	Univ of Oklahoma
PA3250	Temple University
TN1710	Univ of Tennessee-Knoxville
TX0300	Baylor University
TX2400	Southern Methodist University
TX3200	Texas Tech University
TX3400	Univ of Houston
TX3420	Univ of North Texas
TX3510	Univ of Texas-Austin
UT0250	Univ of Utah
WV0750	West Virginia University

Master of Music in Music Theory & Composition

MS0750	Univ of Southern Mississippi, The

Master of Music in Music Theory Pedagogy

MD0650	Peabody Conservatory of Music

Master of Music in Music Theory-Composition

AZ0450	Northern Arizona University
IL2900	Southern Illinois Univ-Carbondale
KS0650	Kansas State University
KS1450	Wichita State University
KY0550	Eastern Kentucky University
LA0760	Univ of Louisiana-Lafayette
LA0770	Univ of Louisiana-Monroe
MI2200	Wayne State University
MO0775	Missouri State University
MS0400	Mississippi College
NM0450	Univ of New Mexico
NV0050	Univ of Nevada-Las Vegas
NY3725	State Univ of New York-Fredonia
OH2600	Youngstown State University
PA1050	Duquesne University
PA2750	Penn State Univ-University Park
PA3600	West Chester University
TX0900	Hardin-Simmons University
TX3000	Texas Christian University
TX3520	Univ of Texas-El Paso
VA0600	James Madison University
VA0950	Norfolk State University
WI0825	Univ of Wisconsin-Milwaukee

Master of Music in Music Theory/Master of Library Science

IN0900	Indiana Univ-Bloomington

Master of Music in Music Therapy
AG0600	Wilfrid Laurier University
AZ0100	Arizona State University
CO0250	Colorado State University
FL0850	Florida State University
FL1900	Univ of Miami
IL1150	Illinois State University
MI2250	Western Michigan University
OH1900	Ohio University
PA3250	Temple University
TX2250	Sam Houston State University
TX2400	Southern Methodist University
VA1350	Shenandoah Conservatory

Master of Music in Musical Theatre
AZ0100	Arizona State University
MA0350	The Boston Conservatory
MT0400	Univ of Montana
OK0750	Oklahoma City University

Master of Music in Musicology
AI0190	Universite Laval
AL1170	Univ of Alabama
AZ0450	Northern Arizona University
AZ0500	Univ of Arizona
FL0850	Florida State University
FL1900	Univ of Miami
IL2250	Northwestern University
IL3300	Univ of Illinois
IL3500	Western Illinois University
KS1350	Univ of Kansas
KY0400	Campbellsville University
LA0200	Louisiana State University
MA1400	New England Conservatory
MD0650	Peabody Conservatory of Music
MO1810	Univ of Missouri-Kansas City
NM0450	Univ of New Mexico
TN1680	Univ of Memphis
TN1710	Univ of Tennessee-Knoxville
TX2250	Sam Houston State University
TX3000	Texas Christian University
TX3420	Univ of North Texas
TX3510	Univ of Texas-Austin

Master of Music in Musicology/Ethnomusicology
AL1170	Univ of Alabama

Master of Music in Opera
AB0100	Univ of British Columbia
CA0825	Calif State Univ-Long Beach
KS1350	Univ of Kansas
KS1450	Wichita State University
MA0350	The Boston Conservatory
MA1175	Longy School of Music
MA1400	New England Conservatory
NY1100	Eastman School of Music
NY3705	State Univ of New York-Binghamton
OH1700	Oberlin College
OK0750	Oklahoma City University
PA0850	Curtis Institute of Music

Master of Music in Opera Production
FL0850	Florida State University

Master of Music in Opera-Music Theatre
IL2900	Southern Illinois Univ-Carbondale
SC1110	Univ of South Carolina-Columbia

Master of Music in Orchestral Conducting
DC0050	Catholic Univ of America, The
IN0900	Indiana Univ-Bloomington
MA1400	New England Conservatory
MN1623	Univ of Minnesota-Twin Cities
NE0600	Univ of Nebraska-Lincoln
NY2250	Mannes College
OH0600	Cleveland Institute of Music

Master of Music in Orchestral Instruments
DC0050	Catholic Univ of America, The
NY2250	Mannes College

Master of Music in Orchestral Performance
MO1950	Webster University

Master of Music in Orff Schulwerk
TN1680	Univ of Memphis

Master of Music in Organ & Liturgical Music
CT0650	Univ of Hartford

Master of Music in Organ & Sacred Music
IN0900	Indiana Univ-Bloomington

Master of Music in Organ Performance
GA0750	Emory University
NJ1350	Westminster Choir College
WA1050	Univ of Washington

Master of Music in Pedagogy
FL2000	Univ of South Florida
IN0250	Butler University
KS1050	Pittsburg State University
KS1450	Wichita State University
MI1750	Oakland University
MO0775	Missouri State University
ND0500	Univ of North Dakota-Grand Forks
NY1800	Ithaca College
TN0100	Belmont University
TN1680	Univ of Memphis
TN1710	Univ of Tennessee-Knoxville
TX3000	Texas Christian University
VA0450	George Mason University
VA1350	Shenandoah Conservatory

Master of Music in Pedagogy & Performance
A0760	Univ of Louisiana-Lafayette
MD0650	Peabody Conservatory of Music
OK0800	Oklahoma State University
TX0300	Baylor University

Master of Music in Percussion Performance
WA1050	Univ of Washington

Master of Music in Performance
AA0100	Univ of Alberta
AA0150	Univ of Calgary
AB0100	Univ of British Columbia
AB0150	Univ of Victoria
AC0050	Brandon University
AC0100	Univ of Manitoba
AD0050	Memorial Univ of Newfoundland
AG0450	Univ of Toronto
AI0150	McGill University
AI0190	Universite Laval
AJ0100	Univ of Regina
AL1170	Univ of Alabama
AR0110	Arkansas State University-State U
AR0700	Univ of Arkansas-Fayetteville
AR0850	Univ of Central Arkansas
AZ0100	Arizona State University
AZ0450	Northern Arizona University
AZ0500	Univ of Arizona
CA0250	Azusa Pacific University
CA0815	Calif State Univ-Fullerton
CA0825	Calif State Univ-Long Beach
CA0830	Calif State Univ-Los Angeles
CA0835	Calif State Univ-Northridge
CA0840	Calif State Univ-Sacramento
CA1075	Colburn School, The
CA4100	San Diego State University
CA4150	San Francisco Conserv of Music
CA4200	San Francisco State University
CA5030	Univ of California-Los Angeles
CA5060	Univ of California-Santa Barbara
CA5150	Univ of Redlands
CA5300	Univ of Southern California
CO0250	Colorado State University
CO0800	Univ of Colorado-Boulder
CO0900	Univ of Denver
CO0950	Univ of Northern Colorado
CT0600	Univ of Connecticut
CT0650	Univ of Hartford
CT0850	Yale University
DC0150	Howard University
DE0150	Univ of Delaware
FL0700	Florida International Univ
FL0850	Florida State University
FL1850	Univ of Florida
FL2000	Univ of South Florida
GA0550	Columbus State University
GA0950	Georgia Southern University
GA1050	Georgia State University
GA1300	Mercer University
GA2100	Univ of Georgia
GA2130	Univ of West Georgia
GA2150	Valdosta State University
HI0210	Univ of Hawaii-Manoa
IA1600	Univ of Northern Iowa
ID0050	Boise State University
ID0250	Univ of Idaho
IL0550	Chicago College of Perf Arts
IL0750	DePaul University
IL1150	Illinois State University
IL2100	North Park University
IL2200	Northern Illinois University
IL2250	Northwestern University
IL2900	Southern Illinois Univ-Carbondale
IL2910	Southern Illinois Univ-Edwardsvle
IL3500	Western Illinois University
IN0150	Ball State University
IN0250	Butler University
IN0800	Indiana State University
IN0900	Indiana Univ-Bloomington
IN0910	Indiana Univ-South Bend
KS0300	Emporia State University
KS0650	Kansas State University
KS1050	Pittsburg State University
KS1350	Univ of Kansas
KS1450	Wichita State University
KY0400	Campbellsville University
KY0550	Eastern Kentucky University
KY0900	Morehead State University
KY1450	Univ of Kentucky-Lexington
KY1500	Univ of Louisville
LA0200	Louisiana State University
LA0300	Loyola University
LA0650	Southeastern Louisiana University
LA0760	Univ of Louisiana-Lafayette
LA0770	Univ of Louisiana-Monroe
LA0800	Univ of New Orleans
MA0350	The Boston Conservatory
MA0400	Boston University
MA1175	Longy School of Music
MA1400	New England Conservatory
MA2000	Univ of Massachusetts Amherst
MD0650	Peabody Conservatory of Music
MD0850	Towson University
MD1010	Univ of Maryland
ME0440	Univ of Maine-Orono
ME0500	Univ of Southern Maine
MI0250	Andrews University
MI0400	Central Michigan University
MI0600	Eastern Michigan University
MI1400	Michigan State University
MI1750	Oakland University
MI2100	Univ of Michigan-Ann Arbor
MI2200	Wayne State University
MI2250	Western Michigan University
MN1000	Minnesota State Univ-Mankato
MN1600	Univ of Minnesota Duluth
MN1623	Univ of Minnesota-Twin Cities
MO0775	Missouri State University
MO1800	Univ of Missouri
MO1810	Univ of Missouri-Kansas City
MO1950	Webster University
MS0400	Mississippi College
MS0700	Univ of Mississippi
MS0750	Univ of Southern Mississippi, The
MT0400	Univ of Montana
NC0050	Appalachian State University
NC0650	East Carolina University
NC1650	Univ of North Carolina School of the Arts
NC2430	Univ of North Carolina-Greensboro
NC2600	Western Carolina University

ND0350	North Dakota State University
ND0500	Univ of North Dakota-Grand Forks
NE0600	Univ of Nebraska-Lincoln
NE0610	Univ of Nebraska-Omaha
NJ0825	New Jersey City University
NJ1050	Rowan University
NJ1130	Rutgers the State Univ-New Brnswk
NM0310	New Mexico State University
NM0450	Univ of New Mexico
NV0050	Univ of Nevada-Las Vegas
NV0100	Univ of Nevada-Reno
NY0500	City Univ of New York-Brooklyn
NY1700	Houghton College
NY1800	Ithaca College
NY2150	Manhattan School of Music
NY2250	Mannes College
NY2750	New York University
NY3705	State Univ of New York-Binghamton
NY3725	State Univ of New York-Fredonia
NY3780	State Univ of New York-Potsdam
NY3785	State Univ of New York-Purchase
NY3790	State Univ of New York-Stony Brook
NY4150	Syracuse University
NY4320	Univ at Buffalo (SUNY)
OH0300	Bowling Green State University
OH0600	Cleveland Institute of Music
OH0650	Cleveland State University
OH1100	Kent State University-Kent
OH1450	Miami University
OH1850	Ohio State University-Columbus
OH1900	Ohio University
OH2150	Univ of Akron
OH2200	Univ of Cincinnati
OH2300	Univ of Toledo
OH2500	Wright State University
OK0750	Oklahoma City University
OK1250	Southwestern Oklahoma State Univ
OK1330	Univ of Central Oklahoma
OK1350	Univ of Oklahoma
OR0850	Portland State University
OR1050	Univ of Oregon
PA0550	Carnegie Mellon University
PA1050	Duquesne University
PA2750	Penn State Univ-University Park
PA3250	Temple University
PA3600	West Chester University
RI0300	Univ of Rhode Island
SC0200	Bob Jones University
SC0650	Converse College
SC1110	Univ of South Carolina-Columbia
SC1200	Winthrop University
SD0600	Univ of South Dakota
TN0050	Austin Peay State University
TN0100	Belmont University
TN0850	Lee University
TN1680	Univ of Memphis
TN1700	Univ of Tennessee-Chattanooga
TN1710	Univ of Tennessee-Knoxville
TX0300	Baylor University
TX0900	Hardin-Simmons University
TX1400	Lamar University
TX2250	Sam Houston State University
TX2400	Southern Methodist University
TX2700	Stephen F Austin State University
TX2955	Texas A&M University-Commerce
TX3000	Texas Christian University
TX3200	Texas Tech University
TX3420	Univ of North Texas
TX3500	Univ of Texas-Arlington
TX3510	Univ of Texas-Austin
TX3520	Univ of Texas-El Paso
TX3530	Univ of Texas-San Antonio
TX3750	West Texas A&M University
UT0050	Brigham Young University
UT0250	Univ of Utah
VA0450	George Mason University
VA0600	James Madison University
VA0950	Norfolk State University
VA1350	Shenandoah Conservatory
WA0050	Central Washington University
WA1250	Western Washington University
WI0815	Univ of Wisconsin-Madison
WI0825	Univ of Wisconsin-Milwaukee
WV0750	West Virginia University
WY0200	Univ of Wyoming

Master of Music in Performance & Literature
AC0050	Brandon University
AG0500	Univ of Western Ontario
IL3300	Univ of Illinois
NY1100	Eastman School of Music

Master of Music in Performance & Pedagogy
CO0800	Univ of Colorado-Boulder
TX3400	Univ of Houston
WA0050	Central Washington University

Master of Music in Performance Pedagogy
AZ0100	Arizona State University
OH1900	Ohio University

Master of Music in Piano Accompanying
CT0650	Univ of Hartford
KS1350	Univ of Kansas
MS0750	Univ of Southern Mississippi, The
PA3250	Temple University

Master of Music in Piano Accompanying & Chamber Music
AZ0450	Northern Arizona University
IN0150	Ball State University
NY1100	Eastman School of Music

Master of Music in Piano Accompanying & Coaching
NJ1350	Westminster Choir College

Master of Music in Piano Ensemble Arts
MD0650	Peabody Conservatory of Music

Master of Music in Piano Pedagogy
CA2200	Holy Names University
CO0900	Univ of Denver
CT0650	Univ of Hartford
DC0050	Catholic Univ of America, The
FL0850	Florida State University
GA1050	Georgia State University
GA1700	Reinhardt University
IL2900	Southern Illinois Univ-Carbondale
IL3300	Univ of Illinois
IL3500	Western Illinois University
KY0400	Campbellsville University
LA0200	Louisiana State University
MI0400	Central Michigan University
MI0600	Eastern Michigan University
MI1400	Michigan State University
MO1800	Univ of Missouri
NC0650	East Carolina University
NE0600	Univ of Nebraska-Lincoln
NH0250	Plymouth State University
OR1050	Univ of Oregon
PA3250	Temple University
PA3600	West Chester University
SC0200	Bob Jones University
SC1110	Univ of South Carolina-Columbia

Master of Music in Piano Pedagogy & Performance
IA1600	Univ of Northern Iowa
ID0250	Univ of Idaho
IL2250	Northwestern University
MI2100	Univ of Michigan-Ann Arbor
NJ1350	Westminster Choir College
PA2750	Penn State Univ-University Park
TX3530	Univ of Texas-San Antonio

Master of Music in Piano Performance
DC0050	Catholic Univ of America, The
NJ1350	Westminster Choir College
UT0300	Utah State University
WA1050	Univ of Washington

Master of Music in Piano Performance & Collaborative Arts
IL2250	Northwestern University

Master of Music in Piano Performance & Pedagogy
AL0800	Samford University
IN0150	Ball State University
TX2400	Southern Methodist University

Master of Music in Sacred Music
DC0050	Catholic Univ of America, The
KY1450	Univ of Kentucky-Lexington
MA0400	Boston University
NJ1350	Westminster Choir College
PA1050	Duquesne University

Master of Music in Scoring for Film and Multimedia
NY2750	New York University

Master of Music in Sound Recording
AI0150	McGill University

Master of Music in Sound Recording Arts
FL1900	Univ of Miami

Master of Music in Sound Recording Technology
MA2030	Univ of Massachusetts Lowell

Master of Music in String Development
WI0815	Univ of Wisconsin-Madison

Master of Music in String Pedagogy
NC0650	East Carolina University
PA3250	Temple University

Master of Music in String Performance
WA1050	Univ of Washington

Master of Music in String Performance & Pedagogy
IL2250	Northwestern University

Master of Music in Studio Jazz Writing
FL1900	Univ of Miami

Master of Music in Studio Music & Jazz Instrumental Performance
FL1900	Univ of Miami

Master of Music in Studio Music & Jazz Vocal Performance
FL1900	Univ of Miami

Master of Music in Suzuki Ped & Violin Performance
MN1623	Univ of Minnesota-Twin Cities

Master of Music in Suzuki Pedagogy
CO0900	Univ of Denver
CT0650	Univ of Hartford

Master of Music in Suzuki Piano Pedagogy
CA2200   Holy Names University

Master of Music in Suzuki Violin/Viola
AZ0450   Northern Arizona University

Master of Music in Teaching
AZ0450   Northern Arizona University
MA2030   Univ of Massachusetts Lowell
OH1700   Oberlin College

Master of Music in Vocal Accompanying
DC0050   Catholic Univ of America, The
NY2250   Mannes College

Master of Music in Vocal Accompanying & Coaching
IL3300   Univ of Illinois

Master of Music in Vocal Coaching
OK0750   Oklahoma City University

Master of Music in Vocal Pedagogy
CA2200   Holy Names University
DC0050   Catholic Univ of America, The
MA1400   New England Conservatory
MS0400   Mississippi College
NC2430   Univ of North Carolina-Greensboro
NJ1350   Westminster Choir College

Master of Music in Vocal Performance
AZ0450   Northern Arizona University
DC0050   Catholic Univ of America, The
FL1900   Univ of Miami
MO1900   Washington University
WA1050   Univ of Washington

Master of Music in Voice Pedagogy & Performance
NJ1350   Westminster Choir College
PA2750   Penn State Univ-University Park

Master of Music in Wind Conducting
AL1170   Univ of Alabama
AR0110   Arkansas State University-State U
IN0900   Indiana Univ-Bloomington
KS1050   Pittsburg State University
MA1400   New England Conservatory
MN1000   Minnesota State Univ-Mankato
MN1623   Univ of Minnesota-Twin Cities

Master of Music in Wind Instruments
MI2100   Univ of Michigan-Ann Arbor

Master of Music in Woodwind and Pedagogy
MS0750   Univ of Southern Mississippi, The

Master of Music in Woodwind Performance
WA1050   Univ of Washington

Master of Music in Woodwind Specialties
NE0600   Univ of Nebraska-Lincoln

Master of Music in Woodwinds
IN0150   Ball State University

Master of Music Individual Studies
IL2200   Northern Illinois University

Master of Music Interdisciplinary Digital Media Arts
AZ0100   Arizona State University

Master of Music Intermedia Music Technology
OR1050   Univ of Oregon

Master of Music Suzuki Violin Pedagogy
OH0600   Cleveland Institute of Music

Master of Music Therapy
MO0700   Maryville University
NC0050   Appalachian State University
PA2200   Marywood University
VA1350   Shenandoah Conservatory

Master of Music/Master of Divinity (Joint Degree)
AL0800   Samford University

Master of Sacred Music
GA0750   Emory University
NY1450   Hebrew Union College
TX2400   Southern Methodist University

Master of Science Focus in Music Industry
AL1050   Troy University

Master of Science in Arts Administration
PA1000   Drexel University
VA1350   Shenandoah Conservatory

Master of Science in Creative Arts Therapy Specialization in Music Therapy
NY2650   Nazareth College

Master of Science in Curriculum & Instruction/Music
VA0700   Longwood University

Master of Science in Ed Teaching: Music
MO0950   Northwest Missouri State Univ

Master of Science in Education
NY1600   Hofstra University

Master of Science in Music
OR0850   Portland State University

Master of Science in Music & Technology
PA0550   Carnegie Mellon University

Master of Science in Music Education
AL1050   Troy University
CT0050   Central Connecticut State Univ
CT0550   Univ of Bridgeport
CT0800   Western Connecticut State Univ
FL0700   Florida International Univ
IN0900   Indiana Univ-Bloomington
MD0500   Morgan State University
MD0850   Towson University
MO0775   Missouri State University
NE0700   Wayne State College
NY0642   City Univ of New York-Queens Coll
NY0700   College of St Rose, The
NY1800   Ithaca College
NY2105   Long Island Univ-LIU Post Campus
NY2650   Nazareth College
NY4150   Syracuse University
TN1400   Tennessee State University

Master of Science in Music Engineering Technology
FL1900   Univ of Miami

Master of Science in Music Industry Leadership
MA1450   Northeastern University

Master of Science in Music Technology
GA0900   Georgia Institute of Technology
IN0907   Indiana Univ-Purdue Univ

Master of Science in Music Therapy
IN0907   Indiana Univ-Purdue Univ
NY2450   Molloy College
NY3760   State Univ of New York-New Paltz
VA1100   Radford University

Master of Science in Music w/Teacher Licensure
VA1350   Shenandoah Conservatory

Masters in Education
MI0300   Aquinas College

Masters in Music Therapy
GA0850   Georgia College & State University
LA0300   Loyola University

Masters of Applied Integrated Media
MO0850   Missouri Western State University

MFA
AB0080   Simon Fraser University
IN0150   Ball State University
PA2900   Point Park University
VA1350   Shenandoah Conservatory
VT0050   Bennington College

MFA - Music Composition for the Screen
IL0720   Columbia College Chicago

MFA in Choral Conducting
CA5020   Univ of California-Irvine

MFA in Collaborative Piano
CA5020   Univ of California-Irvine

MFA in Composition
CA0510   Calif Institute of the Arts
NJ0900   Princeton University

Index of Graduate Degrees

MFA in Electronic Art
NY3300   Rensselaer Polytechnic Institute

MFA in Electronic Music
CA2950   Mills College

MFA in Historical Musicology
NJ0900   Princeton University

MFA in Intergrated Composition, Improv and Tech
CA5020   Univ of California-Irvine

MFA in Jazz Studies
CA0510   Calif Institute of the Arts

MFA in Music Tech: Interaction, Intelligence and Design
CA0510   Calif Institute of the Arts

MFA in Music Theory
NJ0900   Princeton University
PA2713   Penn State Univ-Beaver

MFA in Music Theory-Composition
MA0500   Brandeis University

MFA in Musical Theatre
LA0750   Tulane University

MFA in Musicology
MA0500   Brandeis University

MFA in Performance
CA0510   Calif Institute of the Arts
CA3270   Notre Dame de Namur University
CA5020   Univ of California-Irvine
LA0750   Tulane University

MFA in Performance-Literature
CA2950   Mills College

MFA in Specialization in Experimental Sound Practices
CA0510   Calif Institute of the Arts

MFA Performer-Composer Program
CA0510   Calif Institute of the Arts

MFA Performer-Composer Program specialization in African-American Improv Music
CA0510   Calif Institute of the Arts

Non-Degree Music Teacher Certification
DC0050   Catholic Univ of America, The

One Year Performer's Certificate
NJ0800   Montclair State University

Performance Diploma
AG0300   The Glenn Gould School

Performer Diploma
OH0600   Cleveland Institute of Music
TX2400   Southern Methodist University

Performer Diploma Orchestral Studies
IN0900   Indiana Univ-Bloomington

Performer Diploma Solo Performance
IN0900   Indiana Univ-Bloomington

Performer's Certificate
MO1810   Univ of Missouri-Kansas City
NY3785   State Univ of New York-Purchase

PhD Critical & Comparative Studies Music
VA1550   Univ of Virginia

PhD in Church Music
TX2600   Southwestern Baptist Theo Sem

PhD in Composition
AA0150   Univ of Calgary
AI0150   McGill University
CA5000   Univ of California-Berkeley
CA5010   Univ of California-Davis
CA5030   Univ of California-Los Angeles
CA5050   Univ of California-San Diego
CA5060   Univ of California-Santa Barbara
IA1550   Univ of Iowa
IL3250   Univ of Chicago
LA0200   Louisiana State University
MA1050   Harvard University
MN1623   Univ of Minnesota-Twin Cities
NC0600   Duke University
NJ0900   Princeton University
NY0600   City Univ of New York-Grad Center
NY1100   Eastman School of Music
NY2750   New York University
NY3790   State Univ of New York-Stony Brook
NY4320   Univ at Buffalo (SUNY)
OR1050   Univ of Oregon
PA3350   Univ of Pennsylvania
UT0250   Univ of Utah
VA1550   Univ of Virginia

PhD in Computer Based Music Theory and Acoustics
CA4900   Stanford University

PhD in Computer Music
CA5050   Univ of California-San Diego

PhD in Cross Cultural Studies
CA5070   Univ of California-Santa Cruz

PhD in Curriculum & Instruction (Music Education)
MO1800   Univ of Missouri
NY4150   Syracuse University
WI0815   Univ of Wisconsin-Madison

PhD in Electronic Art
NY3300   Rensselaer Polytechnic Institute

PhD in Electronic Music & Multimedia
RI0050   Brown University

PhD in Ethnomusicology
AB0100   Univ of British Columbia
AD0050   Memorial Univ of Newfoundland
AG0650   York University
CA5000   Univ of California-Berkeley
CA5010   Univ of California-Davis
CA5031   Univ of California-Los Angeles
CA5060   Univ of California-Santa Barbara
CT0750   Wesleyan University
IL3250   Univ of Chicago
MA1050   Harvard University
MD1010   Univ of Maryland
NY0600   City Univ of New York-Grad Center
NY0750   Columbia University
PA2713   Penn State Univ-Beaver
PA3350   Univ of Pennsylvania
PA3420   Univ of Pittsburgh
RI0050   Brown University
TX3510   Univ of Texas-Austin
WA1050   Univ of Washington
WI0815   Univ of Wisconsin-Madison

PhD in Ethnomusicology/Speciality in Systemantic Musicology
CA5031   Univ of California-Los Angeles

PhD in Fine Arts
TX3200   Texas Tech University

PhD in Historical Musicology
AB0150   Univ of Victoria
CA5000   Univ of California-Berkeley
MA1050   Harvard University
NJ0900   Princeton University
NY0600   City Univ of New York-Grad Center
NY0750   Columbia University
NY4320   Univ at Buffalo (SUNY)

PhD in History & Music Theory
CT0600   Univ of Connecticut
IL3250   Univ of Chicago
PA3350   Univ of Pennsylvania

PhD in History & Theory of Music
NY3790   State Univ of New York-Stony Brook

PhD in Integrative Studies
A5050   Univ of California-San Diego

PhD in Jazz
AG0650   York University

PhD in Jazz Studies
PA3420   Univ of Pittsburgh

PhD in Music
AA0100   Univ of Alberta
AG0500   Univ of Western Ontario
CA1050   Claremont Graduate University
CA5040   Univ of California-Riverside
FL1850   Univ of Florida
GA2100   Univ of Georgia
HI0210   Univ of Hawaii-Manoa
MN1623   Univ of Minnesota-Twin Cities
NE0600   Univ of Nebraska-Lincoln
NY2740   New York University

PhD in Music & Human Learning
TX3510   Univ of Texas-Austin

PhD in Music Ed with Music Therapy Emphasis
FL1900   Univ of Miami

PhD in Music Education
AA0150   Univ of Calgary
AG0450   Univ of Toronto
AI0150   McGill University
AI0190   Universite Laval
AL0200   Auburn University-Auburn
AZ0100   Arizona State University
AZ0500   Univ of Arizona
CO0800   Univ of Colorado-Boulder
CT0650   Univ of Hartford

FL0850	Florida State University
FL1850	Univ of Florida
FL1900	Univ of Miami
FL2000	Univ of South Florida
GA1050	Georgia State University
IA1550	Univ of Iowa
IL2250	Northwestern University
IL3300	Univ of Illinois
IN0900	Indiana Univ-Bloomington
KS1350	Univ of Kansas
KY1450	Univ of Kentucky-Lexington
LA0200	Louisiana State University
MA2000	Univ of Massachusetts Amherst
MD1010	Univ of Maryland
MI1400	Michigan State University
MI1750	Oakland University
MI2100	Univ of Michigan-Ann Arbor
MS0700	Univ of Mississippi
MS0750	Univ of Southern Mississippi, The
NC2430	Univ of North Carolina-Greensboro
ND0500	Univ of North Dakota-Grand Forks
NY1100	Eastman School of Music
NY2750	New York University
OH0400	Case Western Reserve University
OH1100	Kent State University-Kent
OH1850	Ohio State University-Columbus
OK1350	Univ of Oklahoma
OR1050	Univ of Oregon
PA2750	Penn State Univ-University Park
PA3250	Temple University
SC1110	Univ of South Carolina-Columbia
TN1680	Univ of Memphis
TX3420	Univ of North Texas
UT0250	Univ of Utah
WA1050	Univ of Washington
WV0750	West Virginia University

PhD in Music History
CT0900	Yale University
WA1050	Univ of Washington
WI0815	Univ of Wisconsin-Madison

PhD in Music History & Musicology
IA1550	Univ of Iowa

PhD in Music Literature
IA1550	Univ of Iowa

PhD in Music Technology
AI0150	McGill University
GA0900	Georgia Institute of Technology
NY2750	New York University

PhD in Music Theory
AB0100	Univ of British Columbia
AI0150	McGill University
AZ0500	Univ of Arizona
CA5060	Univ of California-Santa Barbara
CT0900	Yale University
FL0850	Florida State University
IA1550	Univ of Iowa
IN0900	Indiana Univ-Bloomington
KS1350	Univ of Kansas
KY1450	Univ of Kentucky-Lexington
LA0200	Louisiana State University
MA1050	Harvard University
MA2000	Univ of Massachusetts Amherst
MD1010	Univ of Maryland
MI2100	Univ of Michigan-Ann Arbor
MN1623	Univ of Minnesota-Twin Cities
MO1900	Washington University
NJ0900	Princeton University
NY0600	City Univ of New York-Grad Center
NY0750	Columbia University
NY1100	Eastman School of Music
NY4320	Univ at Buffalo (SUNY)
OH1850	Ohio State University-Columbus
OH2200	Univ of Cincinnati
OR1050	Univ of Oregon
TX3420	Univ of North Texas
TX3510	Univ of Texas-Austin
WA1050	Univ of Washington
WI0815	Univ of Wisconsin-Madison

PhD in Music Theory & Cognition
IL2250	Northwestern University

PhD in Music Theory-Composition

MA0500	Brandeis University
MI2100	Univ of Michigan-Ann Arbor
NJ1130	Rutgers the State Univ-New Brnswk
OH1100	Kent State University-Kent
PA3420	Univ of Pittsburgh

PhD in Music Therapy
PA3250	Temple University

PhD in Musicology
AA0150	Univ of Calgary
AB0100	Univ of British Columbia
AG0450	Univ of Toronto
AG0650	York University
AI0150	McGill University
AI0190	Universite Laval
CA4900	Stanford University
CA5010	Univ of California-Davis
CA5032	Univ of California-Los Angeles
CA5060	Univ of California-Santa Barbara
CA5300	Univ of Southern California
CO0800	Univ of Colorado-Boulder
DC0050	Catholic Univ of America, The
FL0850	Florida State University
IL2250	Northwestern University
IL3300	Univ of Illinois
IN0900	Indiana Univ-Bloomington
KS1350	Univ of Kansas
KY1450	Univ of Kentucky-Lexington
LA0200	Louisiana State University
MA0400	Boston University
MA0500	Brandeis University
MD1010	Univ of Maryland
MI2100	Univ of Michigan-Ann Arbor
MN1623	Univ of Minnesota-Twin Cities
MO1900	Washington University
NC0600	Duke University
NC2410	Univ of North Carolina-Chapel Hill
NJ1130	Rutgers the State Univ-New Brnswk
NY0900	Cornell University
NY1100	Eastman School of Music
OH0400	Case Western Reserve University
OH1850	Ohio State University-Columbus
OH2200	Univ of Cincinnati
OR1050	Univ of Oregon
PA3420	Univ of Pittsburgh
TN1680	Univ of Memphis
TX3420	Univ of North Texas
TX3510	Univ of Texas-Austin
WI0815	Univ of Wisconsin-Madison

PhD in Performance Practice
NY2750	New York University

PhD in Popular Music
AG0650	York University

PhD in Sound Recording
AI0150	McGill University

PhD in Sound Recording & Theory
AI0150	McGill University

PhD Musicology/Ethnomusicology
AI0200	Universite de Montreal

PhD/EDD in Education Emphasis Music Education
ID0250	Univ of Idaho

Postgraduate Diploma in Performance
CA4150	San Francisco Conserv of Music

Professional Studies Certificate
CA1075	Colburn School, The

Professional Studies Diploma
NY2250	Mannes College

Specialist in Education
GA1050	Georgia State University

Specialist in Education in Music Education
AL0200	Auburn University-Auburn
GA2100	Univ of Georgia

Specialist in Music: Ethnomusicology (Graduate)
MI2100	Univ of Michigan-Ann Arbor

Specialist in Music: Music Education
IN0900	Indiana Univ-Bloomington

Alphabetical Listing of Institutions

Alphabetical Listing of Institutions

Abilene Christian University	TX0050
Acadia University	AF0050
Adams State University	CO0050
Adelphi University	NY0050
Adrian College	MI0050
Agnes Scott College	GA0050
Alabama A & M University	AL0010
Alabama State University	AL0050
Alaska Pacific University	AK0050
Albany State University	GA0150
Albion College	MI0100
Albright College	PA0050
Alcorn State University	MS0050
Alderson-Broaddus College	WV0050
Alfred University	NY0100
Ali Akbar College of Music	CA0050
Alice Lloyd College	KY0050
Allan Hancock College	CA0100
Allegany College	MD0050
Allegheny College	PA0100
Allen County Community College	KS0040
Alma College	MI0150
Alpena Community College	MI0200
Alverno College	WI0050
Alvin Community College	TX0075
Amarillo College	TX0100
Ambrose University College	AA0010
American Conservatory of Music	IN0005
American River Community College	CA0150
American University	DC0010
Amherst College	MA0100
Ancilla College	IN0010
Anderson University	SC0050
Anderson University	IN0100
Andrew College	GA0160
Andrews University	MI0250
Angelina College	TX0125
Angelo State University	TX0150
Anna Maria College	MA0150
Anne Arundel Community College	MD0060
Anoka Ramsey Community College	MN0040
Antelope Valley College	CA0200
Antioch College	OH0050
Appalachian State University	NC0050
Aquinas College	MI0300
Arapahoe Community College	CO0100
Arcadia University	PA0125
Arizona State University	AZ0100
Arizona Western University	AZ0150
Arkansas Northeastern College	AR0050
Arkansas State University-Beebe	AR0100
Arkansas State University-State U	AR0110
Arkansas Tech University	AR0200
Arlington Baptist College	TX0200
Armstrong Atlantic State Univ	GA0200
Art Institute of Vancouver-Burnaby	AB0040
Asbury Theological Seminary	KY0150
Asbury University	KY0100
Ashford University	IA0050
Ashland Community College	KY0200
Ashland University	OH0100
Assumption College	MA0200
Athenaeum of Ohio	OH0150
Atlantic Union College	MA0250
Auburn University-Auburn	AL0200
Auburn University-Montgomery	AL0210
Augsburg College	MN0050
Augusta State University	GA0250
Augustana College	SD0050
Augustana College	IL0100
Aurora University	IL0150
Austin College	TX0250
Austin Peay State University	TN0050
Avila University	MO0050
Azusa Pacific University	CA0250
Babson College	MA0255
Baker University	KS0050
Bakersfield College	CA0270
Baldwin-Wallace College	OH0200
Ball State University	IN0150
Baptist Bible College of Penn	PA0150
Baptist College of Florida	FL0040
Barclay College	KS0060
Bard College	NY0150
Barnard College	NY0200
Barry University	FL0050
Barton College	NC0100
Baruch College	NY0250
Bates College	ME0150
Baylor University	TX0300
Belhaven University	MS0100
Bellarmine University	KY0250
Bellevue Community College	WA0030
Belmont University	TN0100
Beloit College	WI0100
Bemidji State University	MN0150
Benedict College	SC0150
Benedictine College	KS0100
Benedictine University	IL0275
Bennett College	NC0200
Bennington College	VT0050
Berea College	KY0300
Bergen Community College	NJ0020
Berklee College of Music	MA0260
Berkshire Community College	MA0280
Berry College	GA0300
Bethany College	WV0100
Bethany College	KS0150
Bethany Lutheran College	MN0200
Bethany University	CA0300
Bethel College	KS0200
Bethel College	IN0200
Bethel University	MN0250
Bethel University	TN0150
Bethune-Cookman University	FL0100
Bevill State Community College	AL0260
Biola University	CA0350
Birmingham-Southern College	AL0300
Bishop State Comm College	AL0310
Bishop's University	AI0050
Bismarck State College	ND0050
Black Hawk College	IL0300
Black Hills State University	SD0100
Blackburn College	IL0350
Blinn College	TX0345
Blinn College	TX0340
Bloomsburg University	PA0250
Blue Mountain College	MS0150
Blue Mountain Community College	OR0010
Blue Ridge Community College	NC0220
Bluefield College	VA0050
Bluffton University	OH0250
Bob Jones University	SC0200
Boise State University	ID0050
Borough of Manhattan Comm College	NY0270
Bossier Parish Community College	LA0030
Boston College	MA0330
The Boston Conservatory	MA0350
Boston University	MA0400
Bowdoin College	ME0200
Bowling Green State University	OH0300
Bradley University	IL0400
Brandeis University	MA0500
Brandon University	AC0050
Brazosport College	TX0350
Brenau University	GA0350
Brescia University	KY0350
Brevard College	NC0250
Brevard Community College	FL0150
Brewton-Parker College	GA0400
Briar Cliff University	IA0100
Bridgewater College	VA0100
Bridgewater State University	MA0510
Briercrest College and Seminary	AJ0030
Brigham Young Univ-Hawaii	HI0050
Brigham Young Univ-Idaho	ID0060
Brigham Young University	UT0050
Brock University	AG0050
Bronx Community College	NY0280
Brookdale Community College	NJ0030
Broome Community College	NY0350
Broward College	FL0200
Brown University	RI0050
Bryan College	TN0200
Bucknell University	PA0350
Bucks County Community College	PA0400
Buena Vista University	IA0150
Butler Community College	KS0210
Butler University	IN0250
C.S. Mott Community College	MI0450
Cabrillo College	CA0400
Cabrini College	PA0450
Caldwell College	NJ0050
Calhoun Community College	AL0330
Calif Baptist University	CA0450
Calif Institute of Technology	CA0500
Calif Institute of the Arts	CA0510
Calif Lutheran University	CA0550
Calif Polytechnic State Univ	CA0600
Calif St Polytechnic Univ-Pomona	CA0630
Calif State Univ-Bakersfield	CA0650
Calif State Univ-Chico	CA0800
Calif State Univ-Dominguez Hills	CA0805
Calif State Univ-East Bay	CA0807
Calif State Univ-Fresno	CA0810
Calif State Univ-Fullerton	CA0815
Calif State Univ-Long Beach	CA0825
Calif State Univ-Los Angeles	CA0830
Calif State Univ-Northridge	CA0835
Calif State Univ-Sacramento	CA0840
Calif State Univ-San Bernardino	CA0845
Calif State Univ-San Marcos	CA0847
Calif State Univ-Stanislaus	CA0850
Calif University of Pennsylvania	PA0500
Calvary Bible College	MO0060
Calvin College	MI0350
Cambrian College of Applied Arts	AG0070
Camden County College	NJ0060
Cameron University	OK0150
Campbell University	NC0300
Campbellsville University	KY0400
Canada College	CA0855
Canisius College	NY0400
Cape Cod Community College	MA0600
Capital University	OH0350
Cardinal Stritch University	WI0150
Carl Albert State College	OK0200
Carl Sandburg College	IL0420
Carleton College	MN0300
Carleton University	AG0100
Carnegie Mellon University	PA0550
Carroll College	WI0200
Carroll College	MT0075
Carson-Newman College	TN0250
Carthage College	WI0250
Case Western Reserve University	OH0400
Casper College	WY0050
Castleton State College	VT0100
Catawba College	NC0350
Catholic Univ of America, The	DC0050
Cayuga County Community College	NY0450
Cedar Valley Coll-Dallas Comm Col	TX0370
Cedarville University	OH0450
Centenary College	NJ0100
Centenary College of Louisiana	LA0050
Central Alabama Comm College	AL0332
Central Arizona College	AZ0200
Central Christian College	KS0215
Central College	IA0200
Central Comm College-Columbus	NE0040
Central Connecticut State Univ	CT0050
Central Methodist University	MO0100
Central Michigan University	MI0400
Central State University	OH0500
Central Washington University	WA0050
Central Wyoming College	WY0060
Centralia College	WA0100
Centre College	KY0450
Cerritos College	CA0859
Chabot College	CA0900
Chadron State College	NE0050
Chaffey College	CA0950
Chaminade University of Honolulu	HI0060
Chapman University	CA0960
Charleston Southern University	SC0275
Chatham University	PA0600
Chattahoochee Valley Comm Coll	AL0335
Chattanooga State Comm Coll	TN0260
Chesapeake College	MD0095
Chestnut Hill College	PA0650
Cheyney Univ of Pennsylvania	PA0675
Chicago City College	IL0450
Chicago College of Perf Arts	IL0550
Chicago State University	IL0600
Chipola College	FL0350
Chowan University	NC0400
Christian Theological Seminary	IN0300
Christopher Newport University	VA0150
Cincinnati Christian University	OH0550
Cisco Junior College	TX0390
The Citadel	SC0300
Citrus College	CA1000
City College of San Francisco	CA1020
City Univ of New York-Brooklyn	NY0500
City Univ of New York-City Coll	NY0550
City Univ of New York-Grad Center	NY0600
City Univ of New York-Hunter Coll	NY0625
City Univ of New York-J Jay Coll	NY0630
City Univ of New York-Lehman Coll	NY0635
City Univ of New York-Medgar Ever	NY0640
City Univ of New York-Queens Coll	NY0642
City Univ of New York-Staten Isl	NY0644
City Univ of New York-York College	NY0646
Clackamas Community College	OR0050
Claflin University	SC0350
Claremont Graduate University	CA1050
Claremont McKenna College	CA1060
Clarion Univ of Pennsylvania	PA0700
Clark Atlanta University	GA0490
Clark University	MA0650
Clarke College	IA0250
Clayton State University	GA0500
Clemson University	SC0400
Cleveland Institute of Music	OH0600
Cleveland State Community College	TN0300
Cleveland State University	OH0650
Clinton Community College	IA0270
Cloud County Community College	KS0225
Coastal Carolina Comm College	NC0450
Coastal Carolina University	SC0420
Cochise College	AZ0250
Coe College	IA0300
Coffeyville Community College	KS0250
Coker College	SC0450
Colburn School, The	CA1075
Colby College	ME0250
Colby-Sawyer College	NH0050
Colgate University	NY0650
Coll of St Benedict/St Johns Univ	MN0350
College of Alameda	CA1100

971

College of Central Florida	FL0365
College of Charleston	SC0500
College of Coastal Georgia	GA0525
College of Du Page	IL0630
College of Idaho, The	ID0070
College of Lake County	IL0650
College of Marin	CA1150
College of Mount St Joseph	OH0680
The College of New Jersey	NJ0175
College of Notre Dame of Maryland	MD0100
College of San Mateo	CA1250
College of Siskiyous	CA1300
College of Southern Idaho	ID0075
College of St Elizabeth	NJ0200
College of St Mary	NE0100
College of St Rose, The	NY0700
College of St Scholastica	MN0450
College of the Albemarle	NC0500
College of the Atlantic	ME0270
College of the Canyons	CA1265
College of the Desert	CA1270
College of the Holy Cross	MA0700
College of the Ozarks	MO0200
College of the Redwoods	CA1280
College of the Sequoias	CA1290
College of William and Mary	VA0250
College of Wooster, The	OH0700
Colorado Christian University	CO0150
Colorado College	CO0200
Colorado Mesa University	CO0225
Colorado State University	CO0250
Colorado State University-Pueblo	CO0275
Columbia Basin College	WA0150
Columbia College	CA1375
Columbia College	SC0600
Columbia College Chicago	IL0720
Columbia International University	SC0620
Columbia State Community College	TN0350
Columbia Union College	MD0150
Columbia University	NY0750
Columbus State University	GA0550
Community Coll of Baltimore Cnty	MD0170
Community Coll of Baltimore Cnty	MD0175
Community College of Aurora	CO0300
Community College of Rhode Island	RI0101
Community College of Rhode Island	RI0100
Community College of Rhode Island	RI0102
Community College of Vermont	VT0125
Compton Community College	CA1400
Concord College	WV0200
Concordia College	MN0600
Concordia College	NY0850
Concordia Univ College of Alberta	AA0015
Concordia University	IL0730
Concordia University	NE0150
Concordia University	CA1425
Concordia University	MI0500
Concordia University	AI0070
Concordia University - St. Paul	MN0610
Concordia University Wisconsin	WI0300
Concordia University-Austin	TX0400
Concordia University	OR0150
Connecticut College	CT0100
Contra Costa College	CA1450
Converse College	SC0650
Copiah-Lincoln Comm College	MS0200
Coppin State College	MD0200
Corban University	OR0175
Cornell College	IA0400
Cornell University	NY0900
Cornerstone University	MI0520
Corning Community College	NY0950
Cornish College of the Arts	WA0200
Cosumnes River College	CA1500
Cottey College	MO0250
County College of Morris	NJ0250
Covenant College	GA0600
Creighton University	NE0160
Crossroads College	MN0620
Crowder College	MO0260
Crown College	MN0625
Cuesta College	CA1510
Culver-Stockton College	MO0300
Curtis Institute of Music	PA0850
Cuyahoga Comm College-Metropolitn	OH0750
Cuyahoga Comm College-West	OH0755
Cypress College	CA1520
Dakota State University	SD0150
Dakota Wesleyan University	SD0200
Dalhousie University	AF0100
Dalton State College	GA0610
Dartmouth College	NH0100
Darton College	GA0625
Davidson College	NC0550
Davis & Elkins College	WV0250
Dawson Community College	MT0100
Daytona Beach Community College	FL0400
De Anza College	CA1550
Dean College	MA0750
Del Mar College	TX0550
Delaware State University	DE0050
Delaware Valley College	PA0900
Delgado Community College	LA0080
Delta College	MI0550
Delta State University	MS0250
Denison University	OH0850
DePaul University	IL0750
DePauw University	IN0350
Des Moines Area Community College	IA0425
Des Moines Area Community College	IA0420
Diablo Valley College	CA1560
Dickinson College	PA0950
Dickinson State University	ND0100
Divine Word College	IA0450
Dixie State College of Utah	UT0150
Doane College	NE0200
Dodge City Community College	KS0265
Dominican Univ of California	CA1650
Dominican University	IL0780
Dordt College	IA0500
Douglas College	AB0050
Drake University	IA0550
Drew University	NJ0300
Drexel University	PA1000
Drury University	MO0350
Duke University	NC0600
Duquesne University	PA1050
Dutchess Community College	NY1050
Dyersburg State Community College	TN0450
Earlham College	IN0400
East Arkansas Community College	AR0225
East Carolina University	NC0650
East Central University	OK0300
East Los Angeles College	CA1700
East Stroudsburg University	PA1100
East Tennessee State University	TN0500
East Texas Baptist University	TX0600
Eastern Arizona College	AZ0300
Eastern Connecticut State Univ	CT0150
Eastern Illinois University	IL0800
Eastern Kentucky University	KY0550
Eastern Mennonite University	VA0300
Eastern Michigan University	MI0600
Eastern Nazarene College	MA0800
Eastern New Mexico University	NM0100
Eastern Oklahoma State College	OK0350
Eastern Oregon University	OR0200
Eastern University	PA1150
Eastern Washington University	WA0250
Eastern Wyoming College	WY0100
Eastfield College	TX0700
Eastman School of Music	NY1100
Eckerd College	FL0450
Edinboro Univ of Pennsylvania	PA1200
Edison College-Lee County	FL0500
Edward Waters College	FL0550
El Camino College	CA1750
Elgin Community College	IL0840
Elizabeth City State University-UNC	NC0700
Elizabethtown College	PA1250
Elizabethtown Community College	KY0600
Elmhurst College	IL0850
Elmira College	NY1150
Elon University	NC0750
Emerson College	MA0850
Emmanuel College	GA0700
Emmanuel College	MA0900
Emory & Henry College	VA0350
Emory University	GA0750
Emory University-Oxford College	GA0755
Emporia State University	KS0300
Enterprise State Comm College	AL0340
Episcopal Theological Seminary	TX0750
Erie Comm College-North	NY1210
Erie Comm College-South	NY1220
Erie Community College-City	NY1200
Erskine College	SC0700
Eureka College	IL0900
Evangel University	MO0400
Everett Community College	WA0300
Evergreen State College	WA0350
Evergreen Valley College	CA1760
Fairleigh Dickinson Univ-Madison	NJ0400
Fairmont State University	WV0300
Faulkner University	AL0345
Fayetteville State University	NC0800
Fayetteville Tech Comm College	NC0805
Felician College	NJ0500
Ferris State University	MI0650
Ferrum College	VA0400
Finger Lakes Community College	NY1250
Fisk University	TN0550
Fitchburg State University	MA0930
Five Towns College	NY1275
Flagler College	FL0570
Florida A & M University	FL0600
Florida Atlantic University	FL0650
Florida College	FL0670
Florida Gateway College	FL0675
Florida Gulf Coast University	FL0680
Florida International Univ	FL0700
Florida Keys Community College	FL0730
Florida Southern College	FL0800
Florida State University	FL0850
Foothill College	CA1800
Fordham University	NY1300
Fort Hays State University	KS0350
Fort Lewis College	CO0350
Fort Scott Community College	KS0400
Fort Valley State University	GA0810
Francis Marion University	SC0710
Franklin and Marshall College	PA1300
Franklin College	IN0500
Franklin Pierce University	NH0110
Frederick Community College	MD0300
Free Will Baptist Bible College	TN0580
Fresno City College	CA1850
Fresno Pacific University	CA1860
Front Range Community College	CO0400
Frostburg State University	MD0350
Fullerton College	CA1900
Furman University	SC0750
G C Wallace State Community Coll	AL0400
Gadsden State Junior College	AL0350
Garden City Community College	KS0440
Gardner Webb University	NC0850
Garrett College	MD0360
Gaston College	NC0860
Gateway Community Technical Coll	CT0200
Gavilan College	CA1950
Geneva College	PA1350
George Fox University	OR0250
George Mason University	VA0450
George Washington Univ-Mt Vernon	DC0110
George Washington University	DC0100
Georgetown College	KY0610
Georgetown University	DC0075
Georgia College & State University	GA0850
Georgia Highlands College	GA0875
Georgia Institute of Technology	GA0900
Georgia Perimeter College	GA0940
Georgia Southern University	GA0950
Georgia Southwestern State Univ	GA1000
Georgia State University	GA1050
Georgian Court University	NJ0550
Gettysburg College	PA1400
Glendale College	CA1960
Glendale Community College	AZ0350
The Glenn Gould School	AG0300
Glenville State College	WV0350
Goddard College	VT0150
Gogebic Community College	MI0700
Golden West College	CA2050
Gonzaga University	WA0400
Gordon College	MA0950
Gordon College	GA1070
Goshen College	IN0550
Goucher College	MD0400
Grace Bible College	MI0750
Grace University	NE0250
Graceland University	IA0600
Grambling State University	LA0100
Grand Canyon University	AZ0400
Grand Rapids Comm College	MI0850
Grand Valley State University	MI0900
Grand View University	IA0650
Grande Prairie Regional College	AA0025
Grays Harbor College	WA0450
Grayson County College	TX0850
Great Lakes Christian College	MI0910
Green Mountain College	VT0200
Greensboro College	NC0900
Greenville College	IL1050
Grinnell College	IA0700
Grossmont College	CA2100
Grove City College	PA1450
Guilford College	NC0910
Guilford Tech Community College	NC0915
Gulf Coast Community College	FL0900
Gustavus Adolphus College	MN0750
Hagerstown Community College	MD0450
Hamilton College	NY1350
Hamline University	MN0800
Hampshire College	MA1000
Hampton University	VA0500
Hannibal La Grange College	MO0500
Hanover College	IN0650
Hardin-Simmons University	TX0900
Harding University	AR0250
Harford Community College	MD0475
Harold Washington College	IL1080
Harper College	IL1085
Harris Institute	AG0130
Hartford College for Women-UH	CT0240
Hartnell College	CA2150
Hartwick College	NY1400
Harvard University	MA1050
Harvey Mudd College	CA2175
Hastings College	NE0300
Haverford College	PA1500

Alphabetical Listing of Institutions

Hawaii Pacific University	HI0110
Hebrew Union College	NY1450
Heidelberg College	OH0950
Henderson State University	AR0300
Hendrix College	AR0350
Henry Ford Community College	MI0950
Hesston College	KS0500
Hibbing Community College	MN0850
High Point University	NC0930
Highline Community College	WA0460
Hill College	TX0910
Hillsborough Community College	FL0930
Hillsdale College	MI1000
Hillsdale Free Will Baptist Coll	OK0410
Hinds Community College	MS0300
Hiram College	OH1000
Hiwassee College	TN0600
Hobart & William Smith Colleges	NY1550
Hofstra University	NY1600
Hollins University	VA0550
Holy Names University	CA2200
Holyoke Community College	MA1100
Honolulu Community College	HI0120
Hood College	MD0500
Hope College	MI1050
Houghton College	NY1700
Houston Baptist University	TX1000
Howard College at Big Spring	TX1050
Howard Payne University	TX1100
Howard University	DC0100
Humboldt State University	CA2250
Huntingdon College	AL0450
Huntington University	IN0700
Huston-Tillotson University	TX1150
Hutchinson Comm Junior College	KS0550
Idaho State University	ID0100
Illinois Central College	IL1090
Illinois College	IL1100
Illinois State University	IL1150
Illinois Valley Community College	IL1175
Illinois Wesleyan University	IL1200
Immaculata University	PA1550
Imperial Valley College	CA2300
Independence Community College	KS0560
Indian Hills Community College	IA0750
Indian River State College	FL0950
Indiana State University	IN0800
Indiana Univ of Pennsylvania	PA1600
Indiana Univ-Bloomington	IN0900
Indiana Univ-Purdue Univ	IN0905
Indiana Univ-Purdue Univ	IN0907
Indiana Univ-South Bend	IN0910
Indiana University-Southeast	IN1010
Indiana Wesleyan University	IN1025
Interamerican Univ of Puerto Rico	PR0100
Interdenominational Theo Center	GA1100
Iowa Central Community College	IA0790
Iowa Lakes Community College	IA0800
Iowa State University	IA0850
Iowa Wesleyan College	IA0900
Iowa Western Community College	IA0910
Irvine Valley College	CA2390
Itasca Community College	MN0900
Itawamba Community College	MS0320
Ithaca College	NY1800
Jackson Community College	MI1100
Jackson State University	MS0350
Jacksonville College	TX1250
Jacksonville State University	AL0500
Jacksonville University	FL1000
James Madison University	VA0600
Jamestown College	ND0150
Jamestown Community College	NY1850
Jarvis Christian College	TX1300
Jefferson College	MO0550
Jefferson State Community College	AL0530
Jewish Theological Seminary	NY1860
John A Logan College	IL1240
John Brown University	AR0400
John Carroll University	OH1050
John Wood Community College	IL1245
Johnson C Smith University	NC1000
Johnson County Community College	KS0570
Johnson State College	VT0250
Johnson University	TN0650
Joliet Junior College	IL1250
Jones County Junior College	MS0360
Judson College	AL0550
Judson University	IL1300
The Juilliard School	NY1900
Juniata College	PA1650
Kalamazoo College	MI1150
Kankakee Community College	IL1330
Kansas City Kansas Community Coll	KS0590
Kansas State University	KS0650
Kansas Wesleyan University	KS0700
Kapi'olani Community College	HI0150
Kauai Community College	HI0155
Kean University	NJ0700
Keene State College	NH0150
Kellogg Community College	MI1160
Kennesaw State University	GA1150
Kent State University-Kent	OH1100
Kent State University-Salem	OH1110
Kent State University-Tuscarawas	OH1120
Kentucky Christian University	KY0650
Kentucky Mountain Bible College	KY0700
Kentucky State University	KY0750
Kentucky Wesleyan College	KY0800
Kenyon College	OH1200
Keuka College	NY1950
Keyano College	AA0032
Keystone Junior College	PA1700
Kilgore College	TX1350
The King's University College	AA0035
Kingsborough Community College	NY2050
Kirkwood Community College	IA0930
Kishwaukee College	IL1340
Knox College	IL1350
Knoxville College	TN0700
Kutztown University	PA1750
Kwantlen Polytech University	AB0060
La Grange College	GA1200
La Salle University	PA1830
La Sierra University	CA2420
Labette Community College	KS0750
Lafayette College	PA1850
Laguardia Community College	NY2100
Lake Erie College	OH1250
Lake Forest College	IL1400
Lake Michigan College	MI1180
Lake Sumter Community College	FL1100
Lake Tahoe Community College	CA2440
Lakehead University	AG0170
Lamar University	TX1400
Lander University	SC0800
Lane College	TN0800
Lane Community College	OR0350
Laney College	CA2450
Langston University	OK0450
Lansing Community College	MI1200
Laramie County Community College	WY0115
Laredo Community College	TX1425
Laurel University	NC1025
Laurentian University	AG0150
Lawrence University	WI0350
Lebanon Valley College	PA1900
Lee College	TX1450
Lee University	TN0850
Lees-McRae College	NC1050
Leeward Community College	HI0160
Lehigh University	PA1950
Lenoir Community College	NC1075
Lenoir-Rhyne University	NC1100
Levine School of Music	DC0170
Lewis and Clark College	OR0400
Lewis and Clark Community College	IL1500
Lewis University	IL1520
Lewis-Clark State College	ID0130
Liberty University	VA0650
Limestone College	SC0850
Lincoln Christian College	IL1550
Lincoln College	IL1600
Lincoln Land Community College	IL1610
Lincoln Memorial University	TN0900
Lincoln Trail College	IL1612
Lincoln University	MO0600
Lincoln University	PA2000
Lindenwood University	MO0650
Lindsey Wilson College	KY0860
Linfield College	OR0450
Lipscomb University	TN0930
Livingstone College	NC1150
Lock Haven University	PA2050
Lon Morris College	TX1510
Long Beach City College	CA2550
Long Island Univ-Brooklyn Campus	NY2102
Long Island Univ-LIU Post Campus	NY2105
Longwood University	VA0700
Longy School of Music	MA1175
Lorain County Community College	OH1300
Loras College	IA0940
Los Angeles City College	CA2600
Los Angeles Harbor College	CA2650
Los Angeles Mission College	CA2660
Los Angeles Pierce College	CA2700
Los Angeles Southwest College	CA2710
Los Angeles Trade Tech College	CA2720
Los Angeles Valley College	CA2750
Los Medanos College	CA2775
Louisburg College	NC1200
Louisiana College	LA0150
Louisiana State University	LA0200
Louisiana Tech University	LA0250
Lourdes College	OH1330
Lower Columbia College	WA0480
Loyola Marymount University	CA2800
Loyola University	LA0300
Loyola University	IL1615
Lubbock Christian University	TX1550
Lurleen B Wallace Comm College	AL0620
Lurleen B Wallace Comm College	AL0630
Luther College	IA0950
Lycoming College	PA2100
Lynchburg College	VA0750
Lyndon State College	VT0300
Lynn University	FL1125
Lyon College	AR0425
Macalester College	MN0950
MacEwan University	AA0020
MacMurray College	IL1650
Macomb Comm College-Center Campus	MI1250
Macon State College	GA1260
Madonna University	MI1260
Malone University	OH1350
Manchester College	IN1050
Manhattan School of Music	NY2150
Manhattanville College	NY2200
Mannes College	NY2250
Mansfield University	PA2150
Marian University	IN1100
Marian University of Fond Du Lac	WI0400
Marietta College	OH1400
Maritime Conserv of Perform Arts	AF0120
Marquette Unversity	WI0425
Mars Hill College	NC1250
Marshall University	WV0400
Martin Luther College	MN1030
Martin Methodist College	TN0950
Mary Baldwin College	VA0800
Marygrove College	MI1300
Marylhurst University	OR0500
Marymount College	CA2801
Maryville College	TN1000
Maryville University	MO0700
Marywood University	PA2200
Massachusetts College of Lib Arts	MA1185
Massachusetts Inst of Technology	MA1200
Masters College, The	CA2810
McDaniel College	MD0520
McGill University	AI0100
McGill University	AI0150
McKendree University	IL1740
McLennan Community College	TX1600
McMaster University	AG0200
McMurry University	TX1650
McNeese State University	LA0350
McPherson College	KS0900
Medicine Hat College	AA0040
Memorial Univ of Newfoundland	AD0050
Mendocino College	CA2840
Merced College	CA2900
Mercer County Community College	NJ0750
Mercer University	GA1300
Mercy College	NY2400
Mercyhurst College	PA2250
Meredith College	NC1300
Meridian Community College	MS0370
Merritt College	CA2910
Mesa Community College	AZ0440
Messiah College	PA2300
Methodist University	NC1350
Metropolitan State Coll of Denver	CO0550
Miami University	OH1450
Miami-Dade College-Kendall	FL1300
Miami-Dade Comm College-North	FL1310
Michigan State University	MI1400
Michigan Technological University	MI1450
Middle Georgia State College	GA1400
Middle Tennessee State University	TN1100
Middlebury College	VT0350
Midland College	TX1660
Midland University	NE0400
Midwestern State University	TX1700
Miles College	AL0650
Millersville University	PA2350
Milligan College	TN1150
Millikin University	IL1750
Mills College	CA2950
Millsaps College	MS0385
Milwaukee Area Technical College	WI0450
Mineral Area College	MO0750
Minn West Comm and Tech College	MN1175
Minneapolis Comm & Tech College	MN1050
Minnesota State Univ Moorhead	MN1120
Minnesota State Univ-Mankato	MN1000
Minot State University	ND0250
MiraCosta College	CA2960
Mission College	CA2975
Mississippi College	MS0400
Mississippi Gulf Coast College	MS0420
Mississippi State University	MS0500
Mississippi University for Women	MS0550
Mississippi Valley State Univ	MS0560
Missouri Southern State Univ	MO0800
Missouri State University	MO0775
Missouri Univ of Science & Tech	MO0825
Missouri Western State University	MO0850
Mitchell College	CT0246
Mitchell Community College	NC1400

Alphabetical Listing of Institutions

Modesto Junior College	CA3000	Northern State University	SD0400	Pitzer College	CA3620
Molloy College	NY2450	Northern Virginia Comm College	VA0975	Plymouth State University	NH0250
Monmouth College	IL1800	Northland College	WI0600	Point Loma Nazarene University	CA3640
Monmouth University	NJ0760	Northland Comm & Tech College	MN1270	Point Park University	PA2900
Monroe Community College	NY2500	Northland Pioneer College	AZ0460	Polytechnic University	NY3100
Monroe County Community College	MI1500	Northwest College	WY0130	Pomona College	CA3650
Montana State University-Billings	MT0175	Northwest Florida State College	FL1430	Porterville College	CA3700
Montana State University-Bozeman	MT0200	Northwest Mississippi Comm College	MS0575	Portland Community College	OR0800
Montclair State University	NJ0800	Northwest Missouri State Univ	MO0950	Portland State University	OR0850
Monterey Peninsula College	CA3050	Northwest Nazarene College	ID0150	Potomac State College of WV Univ	WV0500
Montgomery College	MD0550	Northwest University	WA0550	Prairie View A&M University	TX2100
Montgomery County Comm College	PA2400	Northwestern College	MN1280	Presbyterian College	SC1000
Montreat College	NC1450	Northwestern College	IA1200	Prince Georges Community College	MD0700
Moody Bible Institute	IL1850	Northwestern Michigan College	MI1650	Princeton Theological Seminary	NJ0850
Moorpark College	CA3100	Northwestern Oklahoma State Univ	OK0600	Princeton University	NJ0900
Moraine Valley Community College	IL1890	Northwestern University	IL2250	Principia College	IL2400
Moravian College	PA2450	Notre Dame de Namur University	CA3270	Providence College	RI0150
Morehead State University	KY0900	Nyack College	NY2900	Puerto Rico Conservatory of Music	PR0115
Morehouse College	GA1450	Oakland City University	IN1250	Purdue University	IN1310
Morgan State University	MD0600	Oakland Comm Coll-Orchard Ridge	MI1700	Purdue University	IN1300
Morningside College	IA1100	Oakland University	MI1750	Queens University	AG0250
Morton College	IL1900	Oberlin College	OH1700	Queens University of Charlotte	NC2000
Mount Allison University	AE0050	Occidental College	CA3300	Queensborough Community College	NY3250
Mount Aloysius College	PA2500	Odessa College	TX1850	Quincy University	IL2450
Mount Holyoke College	MA1350	Oglethorpe University	GA1550	Quinnipiac College	CT0250
Mount Hood Community College	OR0550	Ohio Dominican College	OH1750	Radford University	VA1100
Mount Marty College	SD0300	Ohio Northern University	OH1800	Ramapo College of New Jersey	NJ0950
Mount Mary College	WI0500	Ohio State University-Columbus	OH1850	Randolph College	VA1125
Mount Mercy College	IA1140	Ohio State University-Lima Campus	OH1860	Randolph-Macon College	VA1150
Mount Olive College	NC1500	Ohio University	OH1900	Raritan Valley Community College	NJ0975
Mount Royal University	AA0050	Ohio University-Lancaster	OH1905	Red Deer College	AA0080
Mount San Antonio College	CA3200	Ohio University-Zanesville	OH1910	Red Rocks Community College	CO0625
Mount St Marys College	CA3150	Ohio Valley University	WV0440	Redlands Community College	OK1030
Mount St Marys University	MD0610	Ohio Wesleyan University	OH2000	Reed College	OR0900
Mount Vernon Nazarene Univ	OH1600	Ohlone College	CA3320	Reedley College	CA2400
Mountain View College	TX1725	Oklahoma Baptist University	OK0650	Regis College	MA1600
Muhlenberg College	PA2550	Oklahoma Christian University	OK0700	Regis University	CO0650
Multnomah University	OR0600	Oklahoma City University	OK0750	Reinhardt University	GA1700
Murray State University	KY0950	Oklahoma Panhandle State Univ	OK0770	Rend Lake College	IL2500
Muskegon Community College	MI1550	Oklahoma State University	OK0800	Rensselaer Polytechnic Institute	NY3300
Muskingum University	OH1650	Oklahoma Wesleyan Univ	OK0825	Rhode Island College	RI0200
Napa Valley College	CA3250	Old Dominion University	VA1000	Rhodes College	TN1200
Naropa University	CO0560	Olivet College	MI1800	Rice University	TX2150
Nassau Community College	NY2550	Olivet Nazarene University	IL2300	Richard Stockton College, The	NJ0990
National University	CA3258	Olney Central College	IL2310	Richland Community College	IL2510
National-Louis University	IL2000	Olympic College	WA0600	Rider University	NJ1000
Navarro College	TX1750	Onondaga Community College	NY2950	Ridgewater College	MN1285
Nazareth College	NY2650	Oral Roberts University	OK0850	Rio Hondo College	CA3750
Nebraska Wesleyan University	NE0450	Orange Coast College	CA3350	Ripon College	WI0700
Neosho County Community College	KS0950	Orange County Community College	NY3000	Riverland Community College	MN1290
New College of Florida	FL1360	Oregon State University	OR0700	Riverside Community College	CA3800
New England Conservatory	MA1400	Ottawa University	KS1000	Rivier College	NH0300
New Jersey City University	NJ0825	Otterbein University	OH2050	Roane State Community College	TN1250
New Mexico Highlands University	NM0150	Ouachita Baptist University	AR0500	Roanoke College	VA1250
New Mexico Junior College	NM0200	Our Lady of Holy Cross College	LA0560	Roberts Wesleyan College	NY3350
New Mexico Military Institute	NM0250	Our Lady of the Elms College	MA1550	Rochester College	MI1830
New Mexico State University	NM0300	Our Lady of the Lake University	TX1900	Rock Valley College	IL2560
New Mexico State University	NM0310	Oxnard College	CA3375	Rockhurst University	MO1010
New Mexico Tech	NM0350	Pacific Lutheran University	WA0650	Rockingham Community College	NC2050
New Orleans Baptist Theo Seminary	LA0400	Pacific Union College	CA3400	Rockland Community College	NY3400
New River Community College	VA0900	Pacific University Oregon	OR0750	Rocky Mountain College	MT0350
New School, The	NY2660	Paine College	GA1600	Rollins College	FL1550
New York City Technical College	NY2700	Palm Beach Atlantic University	FL1450	Rose State College	OK1050
New York University	NY2740	Palm Beach Community College	FL1470	Rowan University	NJ1050
New York University	NY2750	Palo Verde College	CA3450	Russell Sage College	NY3450
Newberry College	SC0900	Palomar College	CA3460	Rust College	MS0600
Newman University	KS0980	Panola College	TX2000	Rutgers the State Univ-Camden	NJ1100
Niagara County Community College	NY2800	Paris Junior College	TX2050	Rutgers the State Univ-New Brnswk	NJ1130
Nicholls State University	LA0450	Park University	MO1000	Rutgers the State Univ-Newark	NJ1140
Norco College	CA3265	Parkland College	IL2350	Sacramento City College	CA3850
Norfolk State University	VA0950	Pasadena City College	CA3500	Sacred Heart University	CT0300
Normandale Community College	MN1200	Patten University	CA3520	Saginaw Valley State University	MI1850
North Carolina A&T State Univ	NC1550	Peabody Conservatory of Music	MD0650	Saint Mary's College	IN1450
North Carolina Central University	NC1600	Peace College	NC1800	Salem College	NC2205
North Carolina State University	NC1700	Pearl River Community College	MS0580	Salem State College	MA1650
North Carolina Wesleyan College	NC1750	Peninsula College	WA0700	Salisbury University	MD0800
North Central College	IL2050	Penn College of Technology	PA2675	Salve Regina University	RI0250
North Central Texas College	TX1775	Penn State Univ-Abington	PA2700	Sam Houston State University	TX2250
North Central University	MN1250	Penn State Univ-Altoona	PA2710	Samford University	AL0800
North Dakota State University	ND0350	Penn State Univ-Beaver	PA2713	San Antonio College	TX2260
North Georgia Coll & State Univ	GA1500	Penn State Univ-Erie	PA2715	San Bernardino Valley College	CA3950
North Greenville University	SC0950	Penn State Univ-McKeesport	PA2720	San Diego Christian College	CA3975
North Hennepin Community College	MN1260	Penn State Univ-Schuylkill	PA2740	San Diego City College	CA4000
North Idaho College	ID0140	Penn State Univ-University Park	PA2750	San Diego Mesa College	CA4050
North Iowa Area Community College	IA1170	Penn State Univ-Worthington	PA2775	San Diego State University	CA4100
North Park University	IL2100	Pensacola State College	FL1500	San Francisco Conserv of Music	CA4150
Northeast Alabama Comm College	AL0750	Pepperdine University at Malibu	CA3600	San Francisco State University	CA4200
Northeast Community College	NE0460	Peru State College	NE0500	San Jacinto College Central	TX2295
Northeast Mississippi Comm Coll	MS0570	Pfeiffer University	NC1900	San Jacinto College North	TX2300
Northeastern Illinois University	IL2150	Philadelphia Biblical University	PA2800	San Jacinto College South	TX2310
Northeastern Junior College	CO0600	Philander Smith College	AR0550	San Joaquin Delta College	CA4300
Northeastern Oklahoma A&M College	OK0500	Phoenix College	AZ0470	San Jose City College	CA4350
Northeastern State University	OK0550	Piedmont College	GA1650	San Jose State University	CA4400
Northeastern University	MA1450	Piedmont International Univ	NC1950	San Juan College	NM0400
Northern Arizona University	AZ0450	Piedmont Virginia Comm College	VA1030	Sandhills Community College	NC2210
Northern Essex Community College	MA1500	Pierce College	WA0750	Santa Barbara City College	CA4410
Northern Illinois University	IL2200	Pikeville College	KY1100	Santa Clara University	CA4425
Northern Kentucky University	KY1000	Pima Community College	AZ0480	Santa Fe College	FL1675
Northern Michigan University	MI1600	Pine Manor College	MA1560	Santa Monica College	CA4450
Northern Montana College	MT0300	Pittsburg State University	KS1050	Santa Rosa Junior College	CA4460

Alphabetical Listing of Institutions

Sarah Lawrence College	NY3560
Sauk Valley Community College	IL2730
Savannah State University	GA1750
Schenectady County Comm College	NY3600
Schoolcraft College	MI1900
Scottsdale Community College	AZ0490
Scripps College	CA4500
Seattle Pacific University	WA0800
Seattle University	WA0850
Selkirk College	AB0070
Selma University	AL0830
Seminole State College of Florida	FL1700
Seton Hall University	NJ1160
Seton Hill University	PA3000
Seward County Community College	KS1110
Shasta College	CA4550
Shaw University	NC2300
Shawnee State University	OH2100
Shelton State Junior College	AL0831
Shenandoah Conservatory	VA1350
Shepherd University	WV0550
Sheridan College	WY0150
Sherwood Community Music School	IL2750
Shippensburg University	PA3050
Shoreline Community College	WA0860
Shorter University	GA1800
Siena College	NY3680
Siena Heights University	MI1950
Sierra College	CA4580
Silver Lake College of	WI0770
Simmons College	MA1700
Simon Fraser University	AB0080
Simpson College	IA1350
Simpson University	CA4600
Sinclair Community College	OH2120
Sioux Falls Seminary	SD0450
Skagit Valley College	WA0900
Skidmore College	NY3650
Skyline College	CA4625
Slippery Rock University	PA3100
Smith College	MA1750
Snead State Community College	AL0850
Snow College	UT0190
Solano College	CA4650
Sonoma State University	CA4700
South Carolina State University	SC1050
South Dakota Schl of Mines & Tech	SD0500
South Dakota State University	SD0550
South Florida Community College	FL1730
South Plains College	TX2350
South Suburban College	IL2775
Southeast Baptist Theo Seminary	NC2350
Southeast Comm College-Beatrice	NE0525
Southeast Missouri State Univ	MO1500
Southeastern Bible College	AL0890
Southeastern Community College	IA1390
Southeastern Illinois College	IL2800
Southeastern Louisiana University	LA0650
Southeastern Oklahoma State Univ	OK1150
Southeastern University	FL1740
Southern Adventist University	TN1350
Southern Arkansas University	AR0600
Southern Baptist Theo Seminary	KY1200
Southern Connecticut State Univ	CT0450
Southern Illinois Univ-Carbondale	IL2900
Southern Illinois Univ-Edwardsvle	IL2910
Southern Methodist University	TX2400
Southern Nazarene University	OK1200
Southern Oregon University	OR0950
Southern Union State Comm College	AL0900
Southern University and A & M	LA0700
Southern University-New Orleans	LA0720
Southern Utah University	UT0200
Southern Wesleyan University	SC1080
Southwest Baptist University	MO1550
Southwest Minnesota St Univ	MN1500
Southwest Tennessee Comm College	TN1380
Southwestern Adventist University	TX2550
Southwestern Assemblies of God Univ	TX2570
Southwestern Baptist Theo Sem	TX2600
Southwestern College	KS1200
Southwestern College	CA4850
Southwestern Community College	IA1400
Southwestern Illinois College	IL2970
Southwestern Michigan College	MI1985
Southwestern Oklahoma State Univ	OK1250
Southwestern Oregon Comm College	OR1000
Southwestern University	TX2650
Spelman College	GA1900
Spokane Community College	WA0940
Spokane Falls Community College	WA0950
Spring Arbor University	MI2000
Springfield College	MA1850
St Ambrose University	IA1300
St Anselm College	NH0310
St Augustines College	NC2150
St Bonaventure University	NY3475
St Catharine College	KY1150
St Catherine University	MN1295
St Cloud State University	MN1300
St Edwards University	TX2170
St Francis Xavier University	AF0150
St Gregorys University	OK1100
St Johns River State Coll	FL1570
St Johns University	NY3500
St Joseph Abbey Seminary College	LA0600
St Joseph College	CT0350
St Josephs College	IN1350
St Lawrence University	NY3550
St Leo University	FL1600
St Louis Comm Coll-Florissant	MO1100
St Louis Comm Coll-Forest Park	MO1110
St Louis Comm College-Meramec	MO1120
St Louis University	MO1250
St Mary of the Woods College	IN1400
St Marys College of California	CA3920
St Marys College of Maryland	MD0750
St Marys University	TX2200
St Marys University of Minnesota	MN1400
St Michaels College	VT0400
St Norbert College	WI0750
St Olaf College	MN1450
St Paul School of Theology	MO1350
St Pauls College	VA1300
St Petersburg College	FL1650
St Philips College	TX2220
St Vincent College	PA2950
St Xavier University	IL2650
Stanford University	CA4900
State College of Florida	FL1745
State Univ of New York	NY3717
State Univ of New York-Albany	NY3700
State Univ of New York-Binghamton	NY3705
State Univ of New York-Cortland	NY3720
State Univ of New York-Fredonia	NY3725
State Univ of New York-Geneseo	NY3730
State Univ of New York-New Paltz	NY3760
State Univ of New York-Oneonta	NY3765
State Univ of New York-Oswego	NY3770
State Univ of New York-Plattsburgh	NY3775
State Univ of New York-Potsdam	NY3780
State Univ of New York-Purchase	NY3785
State Univ of New York-Stony Brook	NY3790
Stephen F Austin State University	TX2700
Stephens College	MO1650
Sterling College	KS1250
Stetson University	FL1750
Stillman College	AL0950
Suffolk County Comm College	NY4050
Suffolk County Comm College	NY4060
Sul Ross State University	TX2710
Surry Community College	NC2370
Susquehanna University	PA3150
Swarthmore College	PA3200
Sweet Briar College	VA1400
Syracuse University	NY4100
Syracuse University	NY4150
Tabor College	KS1300
Tacoma Community College	WA0960
Taft College	CA4950
Talladega College	AL1000
Tallahassee Community College	FL1790
Tarleton State University	TX2750
Taylor University-Upland	IN1560
Teachers College/Columbia Univ	NY4200
Temple College	TX2800
Temple University	PA3250
Tennessee State University	TN1400
Tennessee Tech University	TN1450
Tennessee Temple University	TN1500
Tennessee Wesleyan College	TN1550
Terra State Comm College	OH2140
Texarkana College	TX2850
Texas A&M University-College Sta	TX2900
Texas A&M University-Commerce	TX2955
Texas A&M University-Corpus Chris	TX2930
Texas A&M University-Kingsville	TX2960
Texas Christian University	TX3000
Texas College	TX3050
Texas Lutheran University	TX3100
Texas Southern University	TX3150
Texas State University-San Marcos	TX3175
Texas Tech University	TX3200
Texas Wesleyan University	TX3250
Texas Woman's University	TX3300
Thiel College	PA3260
Thomas More College	KY1300
Thomas University	GA1990
Three Rivers Community College	MO1710
Toccoa Falls College	GA2000
Tompkins-Cortland Comm College	NY4250
Tougaloo College	MS0650
Towson University	MD0850
Transylvania University	KY1350
Treasure Valley Comm College	OR1010
Trevecca Nazarene University	TN1600
Trine University	IN1485
Trinity Christian College	IL3100
Trinity College	CT0500
Trinity International University	IL3150
Trinity Lutheran College	WA0980
Trinity University	DC0250
Trinity Valley Community College	TX3360
Trinity Western University	AB0090
Triton College	IL3200
Troy University	AL1050
Truckee Meadows Comm College	NV0125
Truett-McConnell College	GA2050
Truman State University	MO1780
Tufts University	MA1900
Tulane University	LA0750
Tulsa Comm College-Southeast Campus	OK1300
Tusculum College	TN1650
Tuskegee University	AL1100
Tyler Junior College	TX3370
Umpqua Community College	OR1020
Union College	NE0550
Union College	KY1400
Union College	NY4310
Union University	TN1660
United States Air Force Academy	CO0750
United States Naval Academy	MD0900
Univ Advent de Las Antillas	PR0125
Univ at Buffalo (SUNY)	NY4320
Univ de Moncton	AE0100
Univ de Puerto Rico	PR0150
Univ du Quebec-Montreal	AI0210
Univ du Quebec-Trois-Riviere	AI0220
Univ of Akron	OH2150
Univ of Alabama	AL1170
Univ of Alabama-Birmingham	AL1150
Univ of Alabama-Huntsville	AL1160
Univ of Alaska-Anchorage	AK0100
Univ of Alaska-Fairbanks	AK0150
Univ of Alberta	AA0100
Univ of Alberta-Augustana Campus	AA0110
Univ of Arizona	AZ0500
Univ of Arkansas-Fayetteville	AR0700
Univ of Arkansas-Fort Smith	AR0730
Univ of Arkansas-Little Rock	AR0750
Univ of Arkansas-Monticello	AR0800
Univ of Arkansas-Pine Bluff	AR0810
Univ of Bridgeport	CT0550
Univ of British Columbia	AB0100
Univ of Calgary	AA0150
Univ of California-Berkeley	CA5000
Univ of California-Davis	CA5010
Univ of California-Irvine	CA5020
Univ of California-Los Angeles	CA5032
Univ of California-Los Angeles	CA5031
Univ of California-Los Angeles	CA5030
Univ of California-Riverside	CA5040
Univ of California-San Diego	CA5050
Univ of California-Santa Barbara	CA5060
Univ of California-Santa Cruz	CA5070
Univ of Central Arkansas	AR0850
Univ of Central Florida	FL1800
Univ of Central Missouri	MO1790
Univ of Central Oklahoma	OK1330
Univ of Charleston	WV0560
Univ of Chicago	IL3250
Univ of Cincinnati	OH2200
Univ of Colorado Denver	CO0830
Univ of Colorado-Boulder	CO0800
Univ of Colorado-Colorado Springs	CO0810
Univ of Connecticut	CT0600
Univ of Dayton	OH2250
Univ of Delaware	DE0175
Univ of Delaware	DE0150
Univ of Denver	CO0900
Univ of Dubuque	IA1450
Univ of Evansville	IN1600
Univ of Findlay	OH2275
Univ of Florida	FL1850
Univ of Georgia	GA2100
Univ of Great Falls	MT0370
Univ of Guam	GU0500
Univ of Guelph	AG0350
Univ of Hartford	CT0650
Univ of Hawaii-Hilo	HI0200
Univ of Hawaii-Manoa	HI0210
Univ of Houston	TX3400
Univ of Idaho	ID0250
Univ of Illinois	IL3300
Univ of Illinois-Chicago	IL3310
Univ of Indianapolis	IN1650
Univ of Iowa	IA1550
Univ of Kansas	KS1350
Univ of Kentucky-Lexington	KY1450
Univ of Kentucky-Louisville	KY1460
Univ of La Verne	CA5100
Univ of Lethbridge	AA0200
Univ of Louisiana-Lafayette	LA0760
Univ of Louisiana-Monroe	LA0770
Univ of Louisville	KY1500
Univ of Maine-Augusta	ME0340
Univ of Maine-Farmington	ME0410
Univ of Maine-Fort Kent	ME0420
Univ of Maine-Machias	ME0430
Univ of Maine-Orono	ME0440

Alphabetical Listing of Institutions

Univ of Manitoba	AC0100
Univ of Mary	ND0400
Univ of Mary Hardin-Baylor	TX3415
Univ of Mary Washington	VA1475
Univ of Maryland	MD1010
Univ of Maryland-Baltimore Cnty	MD1000
Univ of Maryland-Eastern Shore	MD1020
Univ of Massachusetts Amherst	MA2000
Univ of Massachusetts Boston	MA2010
Univ of Massachusetts Dartmouth	MA2020
Univ of Massachusetts Lowell	MA2030
Univ of Memphis	TN1680
Univ of Miami	FL1900
Univ of Michigan-Ann Arbor	MI2100
Univ of Michigan-Dearborn	MI2110
Univ of Michigan-Flint	MI2120
Univ of Minnesota Duluth	MN1600
Univ of Minnesota-Crookston	MN1590
Univ of Minnesota-Morris	MN1620
Univ of Minnesota-Twin Cities	MN1623
Univ of Mississippi	MS0700
Univ of Missouri	MO1800
Univ of Missouri-Kansas City	MO1810
Univ of Missouri-St. Louis	MO1830
Univ of Mobile	AL1195
Univ of Montana	MT0400
Univ of Montana-Western	MT0450
Univ of Montevallo	AL1200
Univ of Mount Union	OH2290
Univ of Nebraska-Kearney	NE0590
Univ of Nebraska-Lincoln	NE0600
Univ of Nebraska-Omaha	NE0610
Univ of Nevada-Las Vegas	NV0050
Univ of Nevada-Reno	NV0100
Univ of New Brunswick (UNB)	AE0120
Univ of New Hampshire	NH0350
Univ of New Haven	CT0700
Univ of New Mexico	NM0450
Univ of New Orleans	LA0800
Univ of North Alabama	AL1250
Univ of North Carolina-Asheville	NC2400
Univ of North Carolina-Chapel Hill	NC2410
Univ of North Carolina-Charlotte	NC2420
Univ of North Carolina-Greensboro	NC2430
Univ of North Carolina-Pembroke	NC2435
Univ of North Carolina-Wilmington	NC2440
Univ of North Dakota-Grand Forks	ND0500
Univ of North Florida	FL1950
Univ of North Texas	TX3420
Univ of Northern Colorado	CO0950
Univ of Northern Iowa	IA1600
Univ of Notre Dame	IN1700
Univ of Oklahoma	OK1350
Univ of Oregon	OR1050
Univ of Ottawa	AG0400
Univ of Pennsylvania	PA3350
Univ of Pittsburgh	PA3420
Univ of Pittsburgh-Bradford	PA3400
Univ of Pittsburgh-Johnstown	PA3410
Univ of Portland	OR1100
Univ of Puget Sound	WA1000
Univ of Redlands	CA5150
Univ of Regina	AJ0100
Univ of Rhode Island	RI0300
Univ of Richmond	VA1500
Univ of Rochester	NY4350
Univ of Saint Mary	KS1375
Univ of San Diego	CA5200
Univ of San Francisco	CA5353
Univ of Saskatchewan	AJ0150
Univ of Science & Arts of Oklahoma	OK1400
Univ of Scranton	PA3500
Univ of Sioux Falls	SD0580
Univ of South Alabama	AL1300
Univ of South Carolina Aiken	SC1100
Univ of South Carolina-Columbia	SC1110
Univ of South Dakota	SD0600
Univ of South Florida	FL2000
Univ of Southern California	CA5300
Univ of Southern Maine	ME0500
Univ of Southern Mississippi, The	MS0750
Univ of St. Francis	IL3370
Univ of St. Mary of the Lake	IL3400
Univ of St. Thomas	MN1625
Univ of St. Thomas	TX3450
Univ of Tampa	FL2050
Univ of Tennessee at Martin	TN1720
Univ of Tennessee-Chattanooga	TN1700
Univ of Tennessee-Knoxville	TN1710
Univ of Texas at Tyler	TX3535
Univ of Texas-Arlington	TX3500
Univ of Texas-Austin	TX3510
Univ of Texas-Brownsville	TX3515
Univ of Texas-El Paso	TX3520
Univ of Texas-Pan American	TX3525
Univ of Texas-Permian Basin	TX3527
Univ of Texas-San Antonio	TX3530
Univ of the Arts	PA3330
Univ of the Cumberlands	KY1425
Univ of the District of Columbia	DC0350
Univ of the Incarnate Word	TX3410
Univ of the Ozarks	AR0900
Univ of the Pacific	CA5350
Univ of the South	TN1800
Univ of the Virgin Islands	VI0050
Univ of Toledo	OH2300
Univ of Toronto	AG0450
Univ of Tulsa	OK1450
Univ of Utah	UT0250
Univ of Vermont	VT0450
Univ of Victoria	AB0150
Univ of Virginia	VA1550
Univ of Virginia-College at Wise	VA1580
Univ of Washington	WA1050
Univ of Waterloo	AG0470
Univ of West Alabama	AL1350
Univ of West Florida	FL2100
Univ of West Georgia	GA2130
Univ of Western Ontario	AG0500
Univ of Windsor	AG0550
Univ of Wisconsin-Baraboo	WI0800
Univ of Wisconsin-Barron County	WI0801
Univ of Wisconsin-Eau Claire	WI0803
Univ of Wisconsin-Fond Du Lac	WI0804
Univ of Wisconsin-Fox Valley	WI0806
Univ of Wisconsin-Green Bay	WI0808
Univ of Wisconsin-La Crosse	WI0810
Univ of Wisconsin-Madison	WI0815
Univ of Wisconsin-Manitowoc	WI0817
Univ of Wisconsin-Marathon County	WI0925
Univ of Wisconsin-Marinette	WI0920
Univ of Wisconsin-Marshfield	WI0922
Univ of Wisconsin-Milwaukee	WI0825
Univ of Wisconsin-Oshkosh	WI0830
Univ of Wisconsin-Parkside	WI0835
Univ of Wisconsin-Platteville	WI0840
Univ of Wisconsin-Richland	WI0842
Univ of Wisconsin-River Falls	WI0845
Univ of Wisconsin-Rock County	WI0847
Univ of Wisconsin-Sheboygan	WI0848
Univ of Wisconsin-Stevens Point	WI0850
Univ of Wisconsin-Stout	WI0855
Univ of Wisconsin-Superior	WI0860
Univ of Wisconsin-Washington Ctny	WI0862
Univ of Wisconsin-Waukesha	WI0960
Univ of Wisconsin-Whitewater	WI0865
Univ of Wyoming	WY0200
Universite de Montreal	AI0200
Universite Laval	AI0190
Ursinus College	PA3550
Utah State University	UT0305
Utah State University	UT0300
Utah Valley University	UT0325
Utica College	NY4400
Valdosta State University	GA2150
Valencia Community College	FL2120
Valley City State University	ND0600
Valley Forge Christian College	PA3560
Valparaiso University	IN1750
Vancouver Academy of Music	AB0200
Vanderbilt University	TN1850
VanderCook College of Music	IL3450
Vanguard University	CA5355
Vassar College	NY4450
Ventura College	CA5360
Vermilion Community College	MN1630
Vernon College	TX3540
Victor Valley College	CA5400
Victoria College	TX3600
Victoria Conservatory of Music	AB0210
Villa Maria College of Buffalo	NY4460
Vincennes University	IN1800
Virginia Commonwealth Univ	VA1600
Virginia Intermont College	VA1650
Virginia Polytech Inst & St Univ	VA1700
Virginia State University	VA1750
Virginia Union University	VA1800
Virginia Wesleyan College	VA1830
Virginia Western Comm College	VA1840
Viterbo University	WI1100
Volunteer State Community College	TN1900
Wabash College	IN1850
Wagner College	NY4500
Wake Forest University	NC2500
Wake Tech Community College	NC2525
Waldorf College	IA1750
Walla Walla University	WA1100
Wallace State Community College	AL1450
Walsh University	OH2370
Warner Pacific College	OR1150
Warner Southern College	FL2130
Warren Wilson College	NC2550
Wartburg College	IA1800
Washburn University	KS1400
Washington & Jefferson College	PA3580
Washington & Lee University	VA1850
Washington Bible College	MD1050
Washington College	MD1100
Washington State University	WA1150
Washington University	MO1900
Waycross College	GA2175
Wayland Baptist University	TX3650
Wayne State College	NE0700
Wayne State University	MI2200
Weatherford College	TX3700
Weber State University	UT0350
Webster University	MO1950
Wellesley College	MA2050
Wenatchee Valley College	WA1200
Wesley College	DE0200
Wesleyan College	GA2200
Wesleyan University	CT0750
West Chester University	PA3600
West Kentucky Comm & Tech College	KY1540
West Liberty University	WV0600
West Los Angeles College	CA5500
West Texas A&M University	TX3750
West Valley College	CA5510
West Virginia Inst of Technology	WV0650
West Virginia State University	WV0700
West Virginia Univ-Parkersburg	WV0760
West Virginia University	WV0750
West Virginia Wesleyan College	WV0800
Westchester Conservatory of Music	NY5000
Western Carolina University	NC2600
Western Connecticut State Univ	CT0800
Western Conserv Baptist Seminary	OR1210
Western Illinois University	IL3500
Western Kentucky University	KY1550
Western Michigan University	MI2250
Western Nebraska Comm College	NE0710
Western Nevada Community College	NV0150
Western New Mexico University	NM0500
Western Oklahoma State College	OK1500
Western Oregon University	OR1250
Western State College	CO1050
Western Texas College	TX3800
Western Washington University	WA1250
Westfield State University	MA2100
Westminster Choir College	NJ1350
Westminster College	PA3650
Westminster College	UT0400
Westmont College	CA5550
Wharton County Junior College	TX3850
Wheaton College	IL3550
Wheaton College	MA2150
Wheelock College	MA2200
Whitman College	WA1300
Whittier College	CA6000
Whitworth University	WA1350
Wichita State University	KS1450
Widener University	PA3680
Wilberforce University	OH2400
Wilfrid Laurier University	AG0600
Wilkes Community College	NC2640
Wilkes University	PA3700
Willamette University	OR1300
William Carey University	MS0850
William Jewell College	MO2000
William Paterson University	NJ1400
William Penn College	IA1950
William Woods University	MO2050
Williams Baptist College	AR0950
Williams College	MA2250
Windward Community College	HI0300
Wingate University	NC2650
Winona State University	MN1700
Winston-Salem State University	NC2700
Winthrop University	SC1200
Wisconsin Conservatory of Music	WI1150
Wisconsin Lutheran College	WI1155
Wittenberg University	OH2450
Worcester State College	MA2300
Wright State University	OH2500
Xavier Univ of Louisiana	LA0900
Xavier University	OH2550
Yakima Valley College	WA1400
Yale University	CT0900
Yale University	CT0850
Yavapai College	AZ0510
York College	NE0720
York College of Pennsylvania	PA3710
York University	AG0650
Young Harris College	GA2300
Youngstown State University	OH2600
Yuba College	CA6050